KU-210-564

NUTTALL'S STANDARD DICTIONARY OF THE ENGLISH LANGUAGE

BASED ON THE LABOURS OF THE MOST EMINENT LEXICOGRAPHERS

Entirely Revised and Enlarged Edition

COMPRISING

MANY THOUSANDS OF NEW WORDS WHICH MODERN LITERATURE, SCIENCE, WAR, ART, AND SPORT HAVE CALLED INTO EXISTENCE WITH FULL DEFINITION, PRONUNCIATIONS, DERIVATIONS, AND APPENDIX OF USEFUL INFORMATION, ETC.

Edited and Revised by

LAWRENCE H. DAWSON

WITH AN ARTICLE ON THE PRONUNCIATION OF FOREIGN WORDS

under the direction of

DANIEL JONES, M.A., D.Phil.

Professor of Phonetics at University College
University of London

FREDERICK WARNE & CO., LTD.

LONDON AND NEW YORK

First Edition
1863
Revised Editions and Reprints 1867–1885

New Edition 1886
entirely revised and reset
Revised Editions and Reprints 1887–1928

New Edition 1929
entirely revised and reset
Reprinted with Supplement 1930
Reprinted with extended Supplement 1931
Reprinted with further extended Supplement 1932
Reprinted 1933–1950

New Edition
entirely revised and reset
1951
Reprinted 1954
Reprinted 1956

Printed in Great Britain

PREFACE

IN the first edition of the " Standard Pronouncing Dictionary of the English Language "—the original of the present work—published in 1863, the editor, P. Austin Nuttall, LL.D., already well known as the author or compiler of many educational and other works, laid down the principle that any dictionary intended for popular use should, as respects the words with which it is concerned, be at least a reliable guide to (*a*) their Spelling, (*b*) their Pronunciation, and (*c*) their Signification, and that this should be effected with the utmost brevity and conciseness " so that the greatest quantity of matter should be compressed in the smallest compass " ; and we think we can now claim, after nearly a century of testing by a public that has year by year been growing both numerically and in critical capacity, that the outstanding success and popularity of NUTTALL'S STANDARD DICTIONARY is chiefly due to the fact that all subsequent editors have rigorously adhered to the scheme so well and truly laid by its founder. The first of these was the Rev. James Wood, translator of Auguste Barth's " Religions of India," who was responsible for the first complete revision in 1886 ; this was later revised and much enlarged by W. J. Gordon, editor and author of works on Natural History, and, after the war of 1914–18, by Arthur L. Haydon, to whom it was indebted, *inter alia*, for a supplement of additional words, full use of which has gratefully been made in the preparation of this entirely revised and reset edition.

The present-day editor of an English Dictionary that is necessarily restricted to certain limits is faced at once with the question of *Vocabulary* ; for it is obvious that, especially with the great increase of recent years both of new words and new uses of old ones, due to scientific, technological, political, and artistic extensions—not to mention the impact of world-wide wars and vast movements of the peoples—it is quite impossible to include everything that is and has been English. New words are constantly being coined for new or newly discovered things, for new or newly examined branches of science, philosophy, psychology, politics, or the arts : such coinages, together with a large amount of current and obsolescent slang and half-naturalized Americanisms we have included liberally, but we have had to be selective when considering the claim to entry of new drugs (many of which are of an experimental nature), of technological processes and kindred matters that come into the province only of specialists, and of certain nonce-words coined for some definite purpose and used solely in connexion with it : *bipartisan*, for instance, we give ; but not *bizone, bizonal*, for these refer only to political arrangements arising from the 1945 partition of Germany and, in their context, are self-explanatory. Our aim, however, has always been to include rather than exclude ; and it is confidently believed that few if any of the neologisms brought into general literary use from such departments of modern scientific enquiry as psycho-analysis, biochemistry, genetics, astro-physics, radioactivity, nuclear energy, and atomic fission have been omitted. This policy has necessarily entailed certain sacrifices, but such as have been made have been made with the greatest care, and, in the faith that a dictionary is of greater use when acting as a guide to modern culture and civilization rather than as a mere repository of curiosities and bygones, to others appertaining only to some special trade (as farriery, glass-blowing, shipbuilding, etc.) which should properly be classed as jargon and relegated to the pages of a glossary, they have been confined to words long disused and not appearing in literature commonly read or written to-day, and to a sprinkling of unnaturalized terms—mainly of Asiatic origin—met with only in the works of travellers where their import is almost always defined.

Another large and growing class of words that has needed selective treatment is that of Trade-marks and "Proprietary" names, many of which now form part of the English language and therefore should be included. These are duly notified as "Trade name" or "Proprietary," and the publishers wish to make it quite clear that their inclusion and definition in the DICTIONARY is no justification for their public use in any way that might infringe the rights of their registered owners or give ground for legal action. Modern creations involving prefixes or suffixes such as *anti-*, *de-*, *dis-*, *-ization*, *mis-*, *un-*, etc., have, unless they have acquired some transferred or secondary meaning, been included only sparingly; but all steps have been taken to ensure that no word is used in a definition unless it is itself defined in our own columns.

We have treated of that disputable topic SPELLING elsewhere (*see* page xiii): but if it is dangerous to dogmatize about spelling it is recklessly foolhardy to do so in the matter of PRONUNCIATION. "Correct" pronunciation of English is the pedant's dream—and the phonetician's jest; for even if answers were to be found to the questions, "Correct for when?", "Correct for where?", we would be no nearer to a definite correctitude for all. One could never get a Yorkshireman, a Cornishman, a Mancunian, Oxonian, or Londoner to admit that his pronunciation was "incorrect," and were the inquiry extended to Scotland, Eire, or Australia, the result would be the same intensified; while the pronunciation, accent, and intonation of English words by English speakers in the times respectively of Queen Elizabeth (to go no further back), Queen Anne, Queen Victoria, and King George VI were by no means one and the same: as an instance, the present writer well remembers how, when pronouncing *blouse* as a rhyme to *vows*, he was severely corrected by an early Victorian aunt who insisted that it rhymed with *ooze*—as, indeed, it nearly did when introduced from France in her girlhood days.

So, in default of any standard of correctness all the lexicographer can do is to record as clearly as circumstances will allow that pronunciation most usual at the time among the educated classes of his countrymen, and, when two or more pronunciations of a given word seem to have an equal right to be heard, to give such variants as seem to him advisable, placing first that which, for phonological, etymological, historical, or customary reasons has his preference.

Our method of indicating pronunciation is, we believe, peculiar to NUTTALL'S, in that we use no diacritics or accent marks, and no modifications or distortions of the ordinary letters of the English alphabet; it aims at being simple and intelligible and has no pretensions to being "scientific"; but, especially as it has stood the test of time and well met the needs of countless thousands of students without obliging them to memorize some complicated scheme or to be constantly referring to a table of esoteric signs and symbols, it was thought unwise to introduce any change, except by way of making the method even more simple and, perhaps, a little more consistent with itself.

Each main word (except in the case of hyphenated compounds, the pronunciation of the component parts of which is given elsewhere in the DICTIONARY, and some few derivatives, e.g. *strivingly*, *suffraganship*, which can cause no difficulty as they are in immediate proximity to their base and are similarly pronounced) has been re-spelt according to the sound as accurately and simply as our alphabet will allow, and (monosyllables, of course, excepted) has been divided into syllables, the syllable or syllables bearing a stress being printed in *italics*. Accentuation of all but monosyllables is, more often than not, variable with the position of the word in a sentence or with the weight or emphasis it is intended to bear (as the trisyllable in, "We asked the Archbishop to tea" compared with "Archbishop Benson came to tea"); the accentuation we show, therefore, is that of the word itself taken apart from any context in which it temporarily may be.

It is admitted that in the case of a very few English words complete success is difficult to obtain by means of this highly simplified phonetic system, and that with a large number of words adopted from the French and not fully acclimatized (e.g. *embonpoint*, *feuilleton*, *masseuse*, *rencontre*) it was not to be expected; in the case of these latter, therefore, the direction "(App.)" is given in place of (and sometimes in addition to) the usual re-spelling, to indicate that the pronunciation, recorded by the International Phonetic Association's method (see pp. 1089–98), will be found in the list given in the Appendix at pp. 1109–16.

But, after all, the main purpose for which a dictionary is consulted is SIGNIFICATION, and this art of defining, always a difficult one, has become more and more difficult as more and more persons have been using and inventing more and more words. For concrete objects, such as a table, an article of dress, or a piece of mechanism, and for simple actions or conceptions a succinct but sufficient means of verbal identification can usually be found, and the same is true—though to a less extent—with the manifold ideas expressible by such words as *bar*, *board*, *close*, *humour*, *part*, *set*, *touch*, etc., that branch off into various significations and often into different parts of speech; but in many departments of learning—psychiatry, therapeutics, advanced mathematics, atomic research for instance—a complete definition that will be readily understandable by one who has not already mastered the groundwork of the subject it is impossible to give, and in many cases we have had to content ourselves with an indication that will, at least, put the student on the right track.

The subject is further highly complicated by the divergent development of nations, which has had the consequence of endowing so many etymologically identical terms with truly divergent connotations. Even in the last century Lord Acton complained that Liberty (his projected "History" of which remained unwritten) "resembles the camel, and enjoys more definitions than any other object in nature"[1] (he had found two hundred of them ![2]); and who to-day is to define in small compass and in such a way that it will meet with anything approaching universal approval such ideas as Democracy, Civilization, Justice, Progress, Communism, Capitalism, Fascism, and many more? When we remember that Karl Marx himself disclaimed being a "Marxist," that in our own day Viscount Cecil of Chelwood gave as a definition of *appeasement* "placating your enemies by sacrificing your friends,"[3] and that the combined wisdom of the United Nations had the greatest difficulty in drafting a definition of the newly coined term *genocide*, one realizes the extent of the problem. For ourselves, we can only say that in this new edition every former entry has been carefully scrutinized and, where necessary, has been brought up to date, that

[1] On Bright's "History of England": Eng. Hist. Rev., iii, 1888.
[2] Lecture on "The Study of History": Cambridge, 1895.
[3] "A Great Experiment: an Autobiography," p. 275, 1941.

definitions of new terms and new meanings of old ones have been framed only after consultation of the best and most representative authorities, and that we have endeavoured to follow the advice of the seventeenth-century philosopher, John Locke, to frame our definitions " as near as may be " according to " such ideas as common use has annexed " to the word defined.

As well as new words and new meanings we have taken this opportunity of making large additions to the phrases already given, and among minor innovations is the setting of all main words and phrases in black small letters instead of capitals for the main words, thus enabling us to show when capitalization is called for, and the marking of all the 850 " basic " words of BASIC ENGLISH with an asterisk. Further, largely for the sake of the space saved, we have discontinued the practice of giving in full the participles and present tense of verbs, except when their formation does not follow the general rule. Etymologies, revised where necessary, have been treated as before, the language from which the word originally came being indicated and further particulars added when it appeared that such would elucidate the meaning.

The contents of the APPENDIX, in spite of the transference of the Prefixes and Suffixes (with many additions) to their places in the DICTIONARY, and the omission of certain sections which seem to have outlived their usefulness, have also been entirely revised and much increased in scope. This is especially so in the case of the long article on the Pronunciation of Foreign Words (pp. 1089–1108), in which full use has necessarily been made of the International Phonetic Association's method of transcription. The article is based on that originally contributed to NUTTALL'S in 1929 by the late Arthur Lloyd James, M.A., a former Professor of Phonetics and Linguistic Adviser to the B.B.C., and now rewritten and augmented by Dr. Daniel Jones, Professor of Phonetics at University College, University of London, assisted by his colleagues Major A. C. Gimson, B.A., and (for the new section on the pronunciation of Russian) Mrs. Monica Partridge. This is followed by two entirely new features—the list giving, in phonetic script, the pronunciation of adopted and semi-anglicized foreign words appearing in the DICTIONARY, to which reference has been made above, and a page devoted to the non-Roman alphabets, Greek, Hebrew, and Russian. The pronouncing lists of Geographical, Personal, Classical, and Scriptural names have been brought into accordance with the best modern usage; in the two former we have, for the sake of clarity, made occasional use of the characters of the International Phonetic Association, and both have been greatly extended by the inclusion of names of obscure pronunciation publicized by the world-wide events of recent years.

The remaining sections of the Appendix have been similarly extended, and among the numerous entries now given for the first time may be mentioned a list of the Chemical Elements, giving their Symbols, Atomic Weights, and other particulars; a table of Meteorological Symbols; the letters, figures, and signs of the Morse Code; a comprehensive section on English Weights and Measures, with the comparison between them and those of the Metric System; paper sizes, degrees of Longitude, Altitudes, the Thermometric Scales, and a useful series of diagrams showing the divergence between Greenwich Mean Time and that of other places.

Finally, our list of Formal Addresses, which has been compiled from the most authoritative sources, will be found to cover practically every case that is likely to occur in writing to holders of title, rank, or office to whom the writer is not personally or socially known, or on all purely formal occasions. L. H. D.

CONTENTS

N.B. For complete list of Tables and other matter included in the Appendix see pp. 1087–8

THE ENGLISH LANGUAGE

THE English language, which is now the mother-tongue of over 200 million people and is used as a *lingua-franca* or as a chief alternative means of communication by many millions more, originated in a group of dialects brought into what is now known as Great Britain by various tribes from the north of Germany and Denmark which settled in much of its southern half during the fifth and sixth centuries of the Christian era.

Of these tribes the chief were those of the Angles, hailing from the district roughly corresponding with the modern Schleswig-Holstein; the Saxons, from the low-lying lands between the Zuyder Zee and the lower Elbe; and the Jutes, from what is now the Danish peninsula. The indigenous "Ancient Britons," mainly of Celtic stock, were gradually driven westward into the mountainous parts of Wales where, much hybridized but still speaking a modernized form of their ancient tongue, they are still to be found, and south-westward into Cornwall, where the language became extinct before the close of the eighteenth century, though the anthropologist can still discern the original Celtic strain in the bodily build and physiognomy of many of the descendants of its speakers still remaining in the locality.

The Angles, forming the strongest and most numerous body of invaders, settled in the east of the country with, as its probable outside limits, the Firth of Forth to the north, and to the south the river Stour which divides East Anglia (modern Norfolk and Suffolk) from Essex; "Essex" and "Wessex" formed the eastern and western portions of the settlements of the Saxons; while the Jutes, of whom there seem to have been few, were content with Kent and, perhaps, some adjacent parts. Angles, Saxons, and Jutes spoke slightly different dialects of a common language that formed part of the West Germanic group of the Teutonic branch of the Aryan or Indo-European family of languages (of which Celtic was another branch). Of these dialects that spoken by the Angles of Northumbria was the first to achieve any literary prominence; but, owing to the transference of political and military power to Wessex in the early ninth century, when practically all Britain south of the Forth came under the rule of Egbert, it was supplanted by West Saxon, which, however, retained the name "Englisc" ("belonging to the Angles") that had come to be applied to Angles, Saxons, and Jutes collectively.

The term "Anglo-Saxon" is of very much later coinage (seventeenth century), and is used in NUTTALL'S STANDARD DICTIONARY to denote the earliest of the three periods into which the history of the English language is usually divided, viz., that (i) from about A.D. 450 to 1150 (often referred to as "Old English"), the other periods being (ii) "Middle English," from about 1150 to 1500, marked by the disappearance of most of the remaining inflexional forms of the earlier language and the complete absorption of the Norman-French (Romance) that had been introduced first through the marriage of Ethelred "the Unready" (1002) to the daughter of the Norman Duke Richard the Fearless, and much extended after the accession of their son Edward the Confessor (1042) and especially by the Conquest in 1066; and (iii) "Modern English," the tongue to which the crowning touch was given by Shakespeare and the Authorized Version of the English Bible of 1611.

The Teutonic character of the original English language has undergone vast changes during the centuries. Even before the Anglo-Saxon invasion the vocabulary of the invaders had been affected by contact with Rome, and they acquired a few more Latin words from the partly Romanized Britons, though the Celtic of these latter—except for some few place-names—disappeared (as noted above) almost entirely into the wilds of Wales and Cornwall. The Latin element in English is, however, attributable to three later and distinct causes: (i) the introduction and spread of Christianity and the influence of the Church in the sixth and later centuries, (ii) the Norman-French influence referred to above, still further expanded by the accession of the Angevin Henry II in 1154, and (iii) the Revival of Learning in the fifteenth and sixteenth centuries, with large subsequent additions made (*a*) by the coinages of seventeenth- and eighteenth-century Latinists, large numbers of which served no useful purpose and therefore died an early death, and (*b*) especially in later times, mainly from Latin and direct from Greek (earlier Greek borrowings having for the most part come by way of Latin) to satisfy the demands of technical and scientific expansion. In the second of these periods the Norman-French, which, after the Conquest, had been imposed upon the common people by a victorious aristocracy, maintained its ascendancy in court circles and the higher ranks of society till roughly the middle of the twelfth century, about when " Old English " passed into " Middle English " ; while the second French inflow, coming as it did mainly from Paris and Central France, consisted largely of gallicized Latin. By the mid-fourteenth century (*temp.* Edward III) the foreign vocabulary had been nationalized, and English gradually took the place of French for all purposes—court, public, and personal ; it had been used *officially* for the first time since the Conquest in 1258, when the text of the Provision of Oxford was issued in English as well as in Latin and French ; but a Parliamentary session was not opened with an English speech until 1363, and it is not till the accession of Henry IV (1399) that it can be said that English had become the native language of the English kings.

The only other influence on the structure and vocabulary of Old English of any note was that of the Danes and Northmen, through their settlements and widespread conquests of the eighth to the eleventh centuries ; many of our words in common use to-day come direct from this source, and it has left its special mark on the place-names, and especially the dialects, of midland and northern England : but Modern English, from the time of the Renaissance, with its invention of printing and discovery of America, to the present day has been affected in its vocabulary by every country under the sun, and by every great movement whether political, social, military, industrial, or ideological. The great Continental and World Wars, the expansion of the British Empire, the French and Russian Revolutions, the even more recent racial upheavals have all contributed, as did the maritime activities of the Dutch and the artistic triumphs of the Italians. The welcome invasion of the pure and applied sciences of the realm of literature ; the application of the principles of psycho-analysis to the work of the novelist, poet, biographer, and historian ; the popularization of philosophy and of what passes as such both by the radio and the printed word have, no less than the lavish return we are now receiving from the great people of the United States of America in part-payment of the linguistic debt that they incurred to our forefathers, all contributed to make English, in the hands of the expert, an unsurpassable means of communicating alike the most subtle and delicate nuance to which thought can attach a meaning and the most direct or obvious statement.

A NOTE ON GRAMMAR

EACH of the many thousand words of which our language is composed belongs to one or more of the eight grammatical categories known as "Parts of Speech," viz., NOUN, ADJECTIVE, PRONOUN, VERB, ADVERB, PREPOSITION, CONJUNCTION, or INTERJECTION; in addition to which we have the so-called ARTICLES, *a*, *an*, and *the*, which, together with the numerals *one*, *two*, *three*, etc., in reality form subdivisions of other parts of speech.

A word is a NOUN when it names a person, place, or thing, an action, an idea, a quality, or, indeed, any abstraction. Note that any word of any part of speech may, for the nonce, be used as a noun, as in "Blessed are the *meek*"; "The *rich* have been soaked, but the *poor* are still with us"; "Never mind the *why* and *wherefore*." An ADJECTIVE is a word "added to" a noun to qualify it in some way or to differentiate it from something else, and in general to amplify its meaning and limit its application. A PRONOUN is a word used in place of a noun, to avoid its repetition, or in reference to some person or thing mentioned, asked for, or understood by reason of the context, as well as to indicate certain rhetorical relations or logical connexions. The VERB is the "word" (L. *verbum*) of a sentence, and that which affirms, predicates, or makes the assertion, as well as asks a question or expresses a command; in this Dictionary verbs are described as *transitive* when they are active, *intransitive* (i.e. neither active nor passive) when they are not; *reflexive* when they denote an action that is directed back upon the agent or subject; and *auxiliary* when used with other verbs to form their compound tenses, voices, or moods. An ADVERB is a word properly appended to a verb to express some modifying circumstance of place, time, manner, or cause regarding it, and of degree or number, opposition or affirmation, but is also used to qualify any other qualifying word (e.g., an adjective, or another adverb) or qualifying phrase. The PREPOSITION is a word placed before a noun or pronoun to show its relation (as in position, direction, time, etc.) to some other word in the sentence. The CONJUNCTION is a word used to join together sentences, clauses, phrases, or words, and to indicate the relation in which these stand to each other. The INTERJECTION is an abrupt ejaculatory exclamation "thrown between" the words of a sentence to express some related emotion on the part of the speaker; often it is somewhat of an exaggeration to call it a word at all—a cry, like "*whew!*", a sound that is little more than a grunt, like "*humph!*", or even a meaningful sigh, may all be classed as interjections.

Large numbers of the words here given are of more than one part of speech, and many of the verbs are both transitive and intransitive, according to the senses in which they are used; these are all clearly distinguished, and the separate definitions given separately.

SPELLING

ORTHOGRAPHY, to give it its learned title, may be defined as "the art of spelling," and it should always be remembered that spelling *is* an art and not a science. For a variety of reasons, some going back to the very diversified origins of the language, some to the personal preferences of scribes and the customs of the early printers, but all connected with the fact that although we employ some forty distinct sounds in the utterance of our syllables the English alphabet contains only twenty-six letters (and some of these redundant) with which to represent them. English spelling is, therefore, a mass of inconsistencies, and as a guide to pronunciation a never-ending source of confusion—a state of things that cannot be remedied until that distant and unexpected day when new letters are introduced or some such workable system as that of the International Phonetic Association (see p. 1094) is generally adopted.

To add to the difficulty of writers, editors, and compositors alike, there is no generally recognized authority on the "correct" spelling of English; it is still largely a matter of printing-house custom whether or not the *-e* of *judge* is dropped in *judgment*, whether the *-ct* of connect should or should not be changed to *-x-* in its derivative noun *connexion*, whether *alignment* or *alinement*, *felspar* or *feldspar*, *inquire* or *enquire*, *mackintosh* or *macintosh*, *thorp* or *thorpe* is "right"; in such matters the printers and publishers of books, newspapers, and periodicals are still at variance among themselves and, for the most part, make their own rules; and all the lexicographer can do is to record, in so far as he considers necessary, all the variants giving, as we have done in NUTTALL'S STANDARD DICTIONARY, the definitions and other particulars under that which, to-day, seems to be the more generally accepted form.

A few simple rules of a general nature may, however, be given.

Words ending with a mute *-e* on receiving an augment beginning with a vowel usually drop the *-e*, as in *give*, *giving*; *sense*, *sensible*, *sensitive*, *sensory*, *sensual*; *cure*, *curable*, *curative*, *curing*; *fame*, *famous*. There are exceptions, however. When the mute *-e* is preceded by *c* or *g* soft, it is usually retained before *-able* and *-ous* (*peaceable*, *replaceable*, *manageable*; *courageous*, *outrageous*, *umbrageous*); it is also retained, for the purpose of ready recognition, in *blameable*, *nameable*, *saleable*, *shapeable*, *liveable*, and *rateable*—though *ratable* is sometimes seen and *datable* is fully accepted. The *-e* is retained before *-ful*, *-less*, *-ly*, *-ment*, *-ness*, *-some*, as *careful*, *nameless*, *wisely*, *excitement*, *whiteness*, *wholesome*. It is also an established rule that words which end with the vowel *-e* with the effect of lengthening the sound of a preceding vowel (as in *file*, *intone*, *refuse*, *abide*), should drop the *-e* on receiving a termination and becoming a derivative, if that termination began with a vowel (as *-er*, *-ed*, *-ing*, *-ance*, etc.). Thus *file*, *filer*, *filing* (not *fileer*, *fileing*); *intone*, *intonation*, *intoning*; *refuse*, *refusal*, *refused*; *abide*, *abiding*, *abidance*; *cube*, *cubic*. Before *-fy* and *-ty* the *-e* usually becomes *-i-*, as in *pure*, *purity*, *purify*; *active*, *activity* (but note *nice*, *nicety*, *safe*, *safety*).

Elision of one of the *e*'s takes place when *-er*, *-ed*, or *-est* is appended to words ending in *-ee*; as *see*, *seer*, (thou) *seest*; *agree*, *agreed*; *free*, *freer*, *freest*. After *-nge* (*change*, *revenge*, *impinge*, *sponge*, *lounge*, etc.) and *-rge* (*charge*, *diverge*, *forge, surge,* etc.) the final *-e* is dropped before *-er, -est, -ed,* and *-ing,* the only exceptions being *singe, swinge,* and *tinge,* in each of which it is retained before *-ing* (*singeing, swingeing, tingeing*) to avoid confusion with *singing, swinging,* and *tinging.* Note, however, that the derived nouns *singer* (one who or an appliance which singes) and *swinger* (a "whopper," a forcible blow) are thus spelt though pronounced with the *g* soft, the actual signification of the printed or written words being ascertainable only through their context.

Monosyllabic words ending in a single consonant, not preceded by a long vowel, and words of more than one syllable, ending in a single accented consonant, and, of course, not preceded by a long vowel, *double the final consonant* in all the derivatives which are formed by a termination beginning with a vowel, as fit, fit*t*ed, fit*t*eth, fit*t*est, fit*t*ing ; bar, bar*r*ed, bar*r*ing ; abet, abet*t*ed ; compel, compel*l*ed. But for this doubling of the final consonant, the vowel in the accented syllable of the originating word (as the *-e-* in *abet*) would be wrongly pronounced in the derivative (abetted, etc.), namely, with its long sound—fited, bared, abeted. Hence words having the long vowel sound do not double the last consonant, as *feared, defiled, bloated.*

Words ending in a single consonant, but not having the accent on the last syllable, do not double the final consonant in derivatives, as limit, limi*t*ed ; rivet, rive*t*er ; civil, civi*l*ity ; enter, ente*r*ed ; yet there still remain a small number which do, such as leveller, traveller, rivalling, worshipper. A word ending in *ll* usually drops one *l* on becoming part of a compound word, as *all, always* ; *fill, fulfil* ; *full, fruitful* ; *till, until.* But there are some exceptions to this rule, as *recall, refill, uphill.* Words ending in *-y,* preceded by a consonant, change the *-y* into *-i-* on receiving certain augments, as *holy, holier, holiest, holiness, holiday* ; *pity, pitied, pitiful* ; *salary, salaried* ; *dandy, dandify* ; *cry, crier* ; but with others, especially *-ing, -ish, -ism, -dom, -like,* it is retained, as in *crying, babyish, dandyism, topsy-turvydom, ladylike* ; it is also retained when preceded by a vowel, as *gray, grayness* ; *clay, clayey* ; *convey, conveyance* ; *survey, surveyor* ; *cloy, cloyed* ; *joy, joyful* ; *buy, buyer* ; *flunkey, flunkeydom.*

ABBREVIATIONS

used in NUTTALL'S STANDARD DICTIONARY

(For extended list of CUSTOMARY ABBREVIATIONS *see* Appendix, pp. 1201–17)

A

a.	adjective
Abbrev.	Abbreviation
ad.	Adverb
Agric.	Agriculture
Alg.	Algebra
Algonq.	Algonquian
Amer.	American
Amerind.	American-Indian
Anat.	Anatomy
Anglo-Ind.	Anglo-Indian
Anthrop.	Anthropology
Antiq.	Antiquities
App.	Appendix (list at pp. 1109–16 to be consulted for pronunciation)
Ar.	Arabic
Arch.	Architecture
Archæol.	Archæology
Arith.	Arithmetic
A.S.	Anglo-Saxon
Assam.	Assamese
Astrol.	Astrology
Astron.	Astronomy
Austral.	Australian
aux.	auxiliary (verb)
Av.	Aviation

B

Biol.	Biology
Bot.	Botany
Braz.	Brazilian
Bret.	Breton
Build.	Building

C

cap.	capital (letter)
Carp.	Carpentry
Celt.	Celtic
cf.	compare (L., confer)
Chem.	Chemistry
Chin.	Chinese
Chron.	Chronology
Cine.	Cinematography
Coll.	Colloquial
Collect.	Collectively
comb. f.	combining form
Comm.	Commercial
Conch.	Conchology
conj.	conjunction
Corn.	Cornish
Cryst.	Crystallography

D

Dan.	Danish
Dial. Eng.	English dialect
Dim.	Diminutive
Dut.	Dutch

E

Eccles.	Ecclesiastical
Econ.	Economics
Elect.	Electricity
Eng.	Engineering
Engl.	England; English
Entom.	Entomology
esp.	especially
Ethn.	Ethnology
Etym.	Etymology

F

fem.	feminine
Fig.	Figuratively
Flem.	Flemish
Fort.	Fortification
Fr.	French

G

Gael.	Gaelic
Geneal.	Genealogy
Geog.	Geography
Geol.	Geology
Geom.	Geometry
Ger.	German
Gr.	Greek
Gram.	Grammar

H

Heb.	Hebrew
Her.	Heraldry
Hind.	Hindustani
Hist.	History
Hort.	Horticulture
Hung.	Hungarian

I

Ice.	Icelandic
Ichth.	Ichthyology
Imit.	Imitative
imp.	imprecation
int.	interjection
Ir.	Irish
It.	Italian

J

Jap. Japanese

L

L. Latin
Lapp. Lappic
l.c. lower case
Lith. Lithuanian
Log. Logic

M

Magnet. Magnetism
Malac. Malacology
Man. Manège (horsemanship)
Manu. Manufacturing
masc. masculine
Math. Mathematics
M.E. Middle English
Mech. Mechanics; mechanism
Med. Medicine
Met. Metaphysics
Metal. Metallurgy
Meteor. Meteorology
Mex. Mexican
Mil. Military
Min. Mineralogy
Mus. Music
Myth. Mythology

N

N. Norse
n. noun
Nat. Hist. Natural History
Naut. Nautical
Nav. Naval
Navig. Navigation
Norw. Norwegian
Numis. Numismatics

O

O.Fr. Old French
O.N. Old Norse
Opt. Optics
Ornith. Ornithology

P

p. past tense
Paint. Painting
Path. Pathology
Per. Persian
pers. personal
Persp. Perspective
Peruv. Peruvian
Pharm. Pharmacy
Phil. Philosophy
Philol. Philology
Phon. Phonetics
Phot. Photography
Phys. Physiology
pl. plural
Poet. Poetry
Pol. Polish
Polit. Politics
Port. Portuguese
poss. possessive
pp. past participle
ppr. present participle
pref. prefix
prep. preposition
Print. Printing; typography
prob. probably
pron. pronoun
Pros. Prosody
Psych. Psychology
Psychan. Psycho-analysis
Pyr. Pyrotechny

R

Rhet. Rhetoric
Rly. Railway
Rom. Cath. Roman Catholic
Russ. Russian

S

Sans. Sanskrit
Scand. Scandinavian
Scots. Scottish
Sculp. Sculpture
sing. singular
Slav. Slavonic
Sp. Spanish
superl. superlative
Surg. Surgery
Surv. Surveying
Swed. Swedish
Syr. Syrian

T

Teleg. Telegraphy
Teut. Teutonic
Theat. Theatre
Theol. Theology
Theos. Theosophy
Tib. Tibetan
Turk. Turkish

U

Univ. University
U.S.A. United States of America
usu. usually

V

v. (t., i., aux., reflex.) verb (transitive, intransitive, auxiliary, reflexive)
Vet. Veterinary
Vulg. Vulgarity

W

W. Welsh
Wire. Wireless; radio

Z

Zool. Zoology

DICTIONARY
OF THE
ENGLISH LANGUAGE

A

A, ay, is the first vowel, and the first letter, of the English alphabet, and represents seven principal sounds (as in *palm, pate, pare, pall, pat, was, many*) besides some weak or indeterminate sounds (*abhor, chaotic, beverage, collar*). In music it is the sixth note of the diatonic scale, corresponding to the *la* of Guido's scale and the tonic sol-fa notation.

★**a,** ay, or ★**an,** an, the indefinite article (from A.S. *ān,* one). **a** is used before words beginning with a consonant (including *h* aspirate, as in *horse, hospital*) and before those beginning with the sound of *w* (*one, once*), *wh* (*whip*), and *y* (eulogy, uniform). **an** takes the place of **a** before words beginning with a vowel (other than those mentioned above), silent *h* (*heir, hour*), and aspirated *h* if the accent is not on the first syllable (*harangue, hotel*); it is also used before those contractions, etc., which, though initialled with a consonant, are pronounced with a vowel, as *an LL.D., an M.P.* The article has distributive force in such phrases as *five hundred a year, twice a month, fourpence an ounce.*

a-, A.S. prefix signifying (1) *on,* as in *aboard, asleep, ajar, a-hunting,* or (2) *of, from,* as in *adown, akin, anew*; Latin prefix representing (1) *ab-,* as in *avert,* (2) *ad-,* as in *ascend,* or (3) *ex-,* as in *amend*; and Greek prefix (*a-, an-,* not), of negative force, as in *asymmetrical, atonic, anarchy.*

A1, ay-*wun,* in Lloyd's Register, the mark of a wooden ship of the first class, 'A' referring to quality of hull, and '1' to that of equipment; first-rate.

aam, *n. ahm,* a former Dutch and German wine measure of about 30–40 gallons. (Dut. *Aam.*)

aard-vark, *n. ard*-vark, the Cape ant-eater, an African edentate of the genus *Orycteropus.* (Dut., earth-pig.)

aard-wolf, *n. ard*-woolf, the African carnivore, *Proteles cristatus.* (Dut., earth-wolf.)

Aaronic, *a.* air-*ron*-ik. Aaronical.

Aaronical, *a.* pertaining to Aaron (Exod. iv) or his priesthood.

Aaronite, *n. air*-ro-nite, any descendant, or follower, of Aaron.

Aaron's-beard, *n. air*-ronz-*beerd,* the large-flowered St. John's wort, *Hypericum calycinum.*

Aaron's-rod, *n.* the great mullein [Bot.]; a decorative moulding entwined with scroll-work or the like [Arch.].

Ab, *n.* ab, the eleventh month of the civil, and fifth of the ecclesiastical, year in the Jewish calendar, corresponding to parts of July and August. (Chaldaic.)

ab-, Latin prefix signifying from; away from.

aba, *n. ah*-ba, a coarse goat- or camel-hair fabric; a sleeveless garment of this worn by Arabs. (Ar.)

abaca, *n. ab*-a-ka, Manilla hemp, the fibre of *Musa textilis.*

abacist, *n. ab*-a-sist, user of an abacus.

aback, *ad.* a-*bak,* towards the back; driven back by the wind against the mast [Naut.]. **taken aback,** surprised and put out. (A.S. *onbæc,* backwards.)

abactor, *n.* a-*bak*-tor, formerly one who stole herds of cattle. (L. *abactum,* driven away.)

abacus, *n. ab*-a-kus, a simple calculating device consisting of beads sliding on rods in a frame; a flat tablet forming the upper member of the capital of a column [Arch.]. (L. *abacus,* a board, a tablet for counting on.)

Abaddon, *n.* a-*bad*-don, the destroying angel; the bottomless pit. (Heb. *abad,* he was lost.)

abaft, *ad.* a-*bahft,* at or towards the stern of a ship. (A.S. *beæftan,* behind.)

abalienate, *v.t.* ab-*ay*-le-an-ate, to transfer the title of a property to another. (L.)

abalienation, *n.* act of abalienating [Law].

abalone, *n.* ab-a-*loh*-ni, the ear-shell, a source of mother-of-pearl.

abandon, *v.t.* a-*ban*-don, to desert; to give up: *n.* unrestrained impulsiveness; frankness or enthusiasm of manner. (Fr. *abandonner,* to desert.)

abandoned, *a.* a-*ban*-dond, deserted; given up, generally to ruin or vice; extremely profligate.

abandonedly, *ad.* in an abandoned fashion.

abandonee, *n.* a-ban-don-*ee,* person to whom anything is abandoned, esp. [Law] an underwriter to whom is given the salvage of a sunken vessel.

abandonment, *n.* a-*ban*-don-ment, act of abandoning or state of being abandoned.

abase, *v.t.* a-*base,* to humble; to degrade. (O.Fr. *abaissier,* to lower.)

abasement, *n.* a-*base*-ment, state of being abased.

abash, *v.t.* a-*bash,* to put to confusion through shame on being discovered in a guilty or unworthy action or condition. (O.Fr. *esbaiss-ant.*)

abashment, *n.* confusion through shame.

abasia, *n.* a-*bay*-ze-a, inability properly to control the muscles used in walking. (Gr. *a-,* not, *basis,* a step.)

abask, *a.* a-*bahsk,* basking.

abatable, *a.* a-*bate*-a-bl, that which may be abated.

abate, *v.t.* a-*bate,* to deduct; to lessen: *v.i.* to become less; to fail. (Fr. *abattre,* bring down.)

abatement, *n.* a-*bate*-ment, act of abating; sum deducted from an account; a mark of dishonour in a coat of arms [Her.].

abater, *n.* a-*bate*-er, person or thing that abates.

abat-jour, *n.* (App.), a skylight; something that throws light downwards. (Fr., skylight.)

abattis, *n.* a-*bat*-tis, an obstruction of felled trees, with branches pointing outwards [Fort.].

abattoir, *n.* (App.), a slaughterhouse. (Fr.)

abature, *n. ab*-a-tewr, trail of a hunted stag.

abat-voix, *n.* (App.), the sounding-board of a rostrum or pulpit. (Fr.)

abb, *n.* ab, weaver's warp-yarn. **abb-wool,** wool for this.

abba, *n. ab*-bah, father; a bishop or superior in certain Eastern Churches. (Aramaic.)

abbacy, *n.* *ab*-a-se, office, rank, or establishment of an abbot.
abbatial, *a.* a-*bay*-shal, pertaining to an abbey.
abbé, *n.* *ab*-bay, a French ecclesiastic; title often given in pre-Revolutionary France to secular holders of benefices employed as men of letters, tutors, or university professors.
abbess, *n.* *ab*-es, the lady superior of a nunnery or convent. (O.Fr. *abesse.*)
abbey, *n.* *ab*-e, originally a community of religious persons of either sex, secluded from the world, and professing celibacy; the church attached to an abbey; a mansion formerly in abbatial precincts. (O.Fr. *abeie.*)
abbot, *n.* *ab*-ot, the superior of an abbey. **abbot of misrule** or **unreason,** *see* **misrule.** (A.S. *abbod.*)
abbotship, *n.* the office of an abbot.
abbreviate, *v.t.* ab-*bre*-ve-ate, to shorten; to abridge. (L. *abbreviatum,* abbreviated.)
abbreviation, *n.* ab-*bre*-ve-*ay*-shon, a shortening; act of shortening; one or more letters used for a word, as *Lat.* for *Latin, A.D.* for *Anno Domini.*
abbreviator, *n.* ab-*bre*-ve-ate-or, one who abridges; title of an officer of the Papal chancery.
abbreviatory, *a.* tending to shorten.
abbreviature, *n.* an abbreviation; an abridgment or epitome.
ABC, *n.* ay-bee-see, the alphabet, hence the elements of any subject; a railway time-table arranged alphabetically; a child's book of the alphabet.
abdal, *n.* *ab*-dal, member of a sect of Moslem fanatics. (Ar. *abd,* servant, *Allah,* God.)
Abderian, *a.* ab-*deer*-e-an, characterized by foolish laughter.
Abderite, *n.* *ab*-der-ite, an inhabitant of Abdera, in Thrace; a stupid person. Democritus, a native much given to laughter, is so called.
abdest, *n.* *ab*-dest, Moslem rite of hand-washing before prayers. (Pers. *ab,* water, *dast,* hand.)
abdicant, *a.* *ab*-di-kant, abdicating; renouncing: *n.* the person abdicating.
abdicate, *v.t.* *ab*-de-kate, to give up or resign a right, post, or office; to disown and disinherit [Law]. (L. *abdicatum,* abdicated.)
abdication, *n.* ab-de-*ka*-shon, act of abdicating.
abditory, *n.* *ab*-dit-o-re, place or chest for secreting valuables. (L. *abditorium,* hiding-place.)
abdomen, *n.* ab-*doh*-men *or* *ab*-do-men, the belly; the posterior section of an insect. (L. *abdomen.*)
abdominal, *a.* ab-*dom*-in-al, situated in or pertaining to the abdomen.
abdominoscopy, *n.* ab-dom-e-*nos*-ko-pe, inspection and examination of the abdomen for disease [Med.].
abdominous, *a.* having a large belly.
abduce, *v.t.* ab-*dews,* to abduct.
abducent, *a.* having the property of drawing back or away or of separating; used of the abductor muscles, which act in opposition to the adducent muscles or adductors [Anat.].
abduct, *v.t.* ab-*dukt,* to take away by stealth or force; to draw away from its usual position [Anat.]. (L. *abducere,* lead away.)
abduction, *n.* ab-*duk*-shon, act of abducting; the illegal taking and carrying away of a child, ward, or wife [Law].
abductor, *n.* ab-*duk*-tor, one guilty of abduction; a muscle which serves to draw or pull back a certain part of the body [Anat.].
abeam, *ad.* a-*beem,* at right angles to a vessel's keel; abreast of [Naut.].
abear, *v.t.* a-*bare,* to endure; to tolerate.
abecedarian, *n.* a-be-see-*dare*-re-an, one who teaches or is learning the alphabet; a novice: *a.* alphabetical. **abecedarian psalms,** psalms the sections of which are arranged alphabetically. (From A-B-C.)
abecedary, *n.* *ab*-e-*see*-da-re, an abecedarian.
abed, *ad.* a-*bed,* in or gone to bed. (A.S. *a-,* on, *bed.*)
abele, *n.* a-*beel,* the white poplar, *Populus alba.*
Abelians, *n.pl.* a-*bel*-yanz, Abelites.
abelite, *n.* *ay*-bel-ite, an explosive containing ammonium nitrate and a hydro-carbon. (Named from Sir F. A. Abel, Eng. chemist.)
Abelites, *n.pl.* *ay*-bel-ites, a sect of the early church who married, but lived in continence, after the manner, as they surmised, of Abel.
abelmosk, *n.* *ay*-bel-mosk, a species of the Syrian mallow, so called from the musky odour of its seeds, *Abelmoschus moschatus.*
Abelonians, *n.pl.* ay-bel-*loh*-ne-anz, Abelites.
Aberdeen, *n.* ab-er-*deen,* a small, short-legged rough-haired Scotch terrier, named from the burgh.
aberdevine, *n.* *ab*-er-de-vine, a song bird resembling the goldfinch, allied to the siskin, *Carduelis spinus.*
Aberdonian, *a.* ab-er-*doh*-ne-an, of, from, or belonging to the Scottish burgh, Aberdeen: *n.* a native of Aberdeen.
aberrance, *n.* ab-*er*-rance, a deviation; error. (L. *aberrare,* go astray.)
aberrancy, *n.* aberrance.
aberrant, *a.* wandering from the right way; differing from normal type [Zool. and Bot.].
aberration, *n.* ab-er-*ray*-shon, deviation from the right or normal straight line or course; alienation of the mind; a small apparent displacement of heavenly bodies, occasioned by the passage of light and the earth's diurnal or annual motion in its orbit [Astron.]; a divergence of reflected or refracted rays of light preventing them from uniting in one point [Opt.]. **crown of abberration,** a luminous circle apparently surrounding the sun, due to the aberration of light.
aberrometer, *n.* ab-er-*rom*-e-ter, an instrument for measuring small observational errors due to optical aberration.
abet, *v.t.* a-*bet,* to incite by encouragement, countenance, or aid, generally from an interested motive and in a bad sense. (O.Fr. *abeter.*)
abetment, *n.* a-*bet*-ment, the act of abetting.
abeto, *n.* a-*bay*-toh, the Mexican tree, *Abies religiosa*; the medicinal gum exuded by this.
abetter, *n.* a-*bet*-ter (or **abettor,** a-*bet*-tor), an accessory to the committal of a crime [Law]; one who abets.
abeyance, *n.* a-*bay*-ans, expectation or contemplation; a state of suspension or temporary suppression. (O.Fr. *abeiance,* waiting.)
abeyant, *a.* a-*bay*-ant, in abeyance.
abhor, *v.t.* ab-*hawr,* to regard with loathing; to detest, hate, or loathe; to turn away in horror from a person. **abhorred. abhorring.** (L. *abhorrēre,* shrink back in dread.)
abhorrence, *n.* ab-*hor*-rens, abhorrency.
abhorrency, *n.* ab-*hor*-ren-se, detestation.
abhorrent, *a.* ab-*hor*-rent, detesting; repugnant to; inconsistent with.
abhorrently, *ad.* with abhorrence.
abhorrer, *n.* ab-*hawr*-rer, a person detesting anything; nickname of those Tories who, in 1679, expressed in petitions their abhorrence of those who would curtail Charles II's royal prerogative.
abhorring, *n.* abhorrence; an object of hatred.
Abib, *n.* *ay*-bib, ancient name of the Jewish month Nisan. (Heb.)
abide, *v.i.* a-*bide,* to stay in any place for a shorter or longer period; to remain; to continue; to be firm: *v.t.* to wait for; to be prepared for; to await; to endure. **abide by,** to remain beside; to stand by; to accept. **abiding. abode.** (A.S. *ābīdan,* wait, abide.)
abider, *n.* one who dwells or continues; a resident.
abiding, *a.* continuing; permanent: *n.* continuance; residence; an enduring.
abidingly, *ad.* in an abiding manner.
Abies, *n.* *ab*-i-eez, a genus of conifers including the silver fir and the Canada balsam tree. (L., the fir-tree.)
abietic, *a.* ab-i-*et*-ik, pertaining to the genus *Abies.*
abietin, *n.* *ab*-i-et-in, a resinous substance, the product of *Abies balsamea.*
Abigail, *n.* *ab*-e-gale, a female personal name; colloquially a lady's maid, from Abigail, 1 Sam. xxv, who entitled herself a handmaid. (Heb., joy of my father.)
abigeat, *n.* a-*bidj*-e-at, cattle-stealing [Old Law].
abilities, *n.pl.* a-*bil*-i-tiz, the mental powers.
ability, *n.* a-*bil*-i-ti, power, whether bodily or mental, natural or acquired; force of understanding; moral or legal power; wealth; means; solvency. (O.Fr. *ableté,* cleverness.)
abintestate, *a.* ab-in-*tes*-tate, inheriting the estate of one who died intestate [Law].
abiogenesis, *n.* a-by-o-*jen*-e-sis, the doctrine of spontaneous generation. (Gr. *abios,* lifeless, and *genesis,* bringing to birth.)
abiogenetic, *a.* a-by-o-je-*net*-ik, pertaining to spontaneous generation.

abiogenist, *n.* ay-by-*oj*-en-ist, one believing in the theory of abiogenesis.
abiogenous, *a.* ay-by-*oj*-e-nus, produced by abiogenesis.
abiogeny, *n.* ay-by-*oj*-e-ne, abiogenesis.
abiology, *n.* ay-by-*ol*-o-je, the study of inanimate objects.
abiosis, *n.* ay-by-*oh*-sis, absence of life [Biol.].
abject, *a.* *ab*-jekt, sunk to a low condition; low in estimation; worthless; mean: *n.* a person in the lowest condition, and despicable. (L. *abjectus*, downcast.)
abjectedness, *n.* ab-*jek*-ted-nes, a low or despicable condition.
abjection, *n.* ab-*jek*-shon, a state of being cast down; a depressed state; baseness; abjectedness.
abjectly, *ad.* *ab*-jekt-le, in an abject manner.
abjectness, *n.* *ab*-jekt-nes, state of being abject.
abjudicate, *v.t.* ab-*joo*-de-kate, to transfer by judgment from one to another. (L. *abjudicatus.*)
abjuration, *n.* ab-ju-*ray*-shon, the act of abjuring. **an abjuration of the realm,** a solemn oath made to quit the kingdom for ever; anciently in England, felons, other than those guilty of treason or sacrilege, who took sanctuary saved their lives thus.
abjure, *v.t.* ab-*jure*, to renounce upon oath or formally; to disclaim with solemnity; to recant. **abjuring.** (L. *abjurare*, to deny upon oath.)
abjurement, *n.* renunciation.
abjurer, *n.* person abjuring.
abkari, *n.* ahb-*kah*-re, the production and vending of intoxicants; distilling; in India an excise duty on spirits. (Per. *abkari*, distilling.)
ablactation, *n.* ab-lak-*tay*-shon, act of weaning from the breast; inarching [Hort.]. (L. *ablactatus*, weaned.)
ablaqueation, *n.* *ab*-lak-we-*ay*-shon, laying bare the roots of trees. (L. *ablaqueatum*, disentangled.)
ablation, *n.* ab-*lay*-shon, act of taking away what is hurtful or unnecessary; attrition of a glacier or rock [Geol.]. (L. *ablatum*, taken away.)
ablative, *a.* *ab*-la-tiv, taking away from: *n.* the sixth case in Latin. **ablative absolute,** a Latin construction in which the noun and its adjunct—both in the ablative—form an adverbial phrase.
ablaut, *n.* *ab*-lowt, substitution of vowel in a word, usually indicating tense-change, as in r*i*ng, r*a*ng, r*u*ng; known also as vowel graduation or permutation. (Ger.)
ablaze, *ad.* a-*blaze*, on fire; in a blaze; in a state of excitement (of a person).
⋆**able,** *a.* aybl, having sufficient power, physically or intellectually, to do a thing; possessed of competent wealth, knowledge, or skill, or of the requisite qualifications or legal power. (O.Fr. *hable*, easily managed.)
able-bodied, *a.* strong of body for work. **able-bodied seaman,** a trained sailor (A.B.) in the Royal Navy, one of higher rating than Ordinary Seaman.
ablegate, *n.* *ab*-leg-ate, a Papal envoy, especially the bearer of the Red Hat to a newly appointed Cardinal.
ablet, *n.* *ab*-let, a small freshwater fish, the bleak.
abloom, *ad.* a-*bloom*, in a thriving state.
abluent, *a.* *ab*-lu-ent, having the power of cleansing: *n.* that which purifies the blood; a detergent [Med.]. (L. *abluens*, washing away.)
ablush, *ad.* a-*blush*, blushing.
ablution, *n.* ab-*loo*-shon, the act of washing, esp. the ceremonial purification of the body preparatory to a religious rite; the water or other liquid so used. (Fr. *ablution*, washing.)
ablutionary, *a.* pertaining to ablution.
ably, *ad.* *ay*-ble, in an able manner.
abnegate, *v.t.* *ab*-ne-gate, to deny or renounce; to abjure. (L. *abnegatus*, refused.)
abnegation, *n.* ab-ne-*gay*-shon, renunciation.
abneural, *a.* ab-*new*-ral, situated in or pertaining to the side opposite the central nervous system [Anat.].
abnormal, *a.* ab-*nor*-mal, deviating from the rule or type. (Fr. *anormal*, out of the ordinary.)
abnormalism, *n.* ab-*nor*-ma-lizm, abnormality; devotion to or cultivation of abnormality; something abnormal.
abnormality, *n.* ab-nor-*mal*-e-te, the state of being abnormal; an irregularity.
abnormally, *ad.* ab-*nor*-ma-le, in an abnormal manner.
abnormity, *n.* ab-*norm*-e-te, the quality of being abnormal; abnormality.
aboard, *ad.* a-*bawrd*, on board; within a ship; *prep.* into a vessel. **to fall aboard of,** to strike a ship's side. **to get aboard,** get foul of. **to go aboard,** to embark. (*a-*, and A.S. *bord*, ship's side.)
abode, *n.* a-*bode*, stay; continuance in a place for a longer or shorter time; a dwelling-place. **to make abode,** to reside. (A.S. as **abide.**)
aboil, *ad.* a-*boyl*, boiling; raging (of a person).
abolish, *v.t.* a-*bol*-ish, to annul; to do away with (Fr. *abolir*, annul.)
abolishable, *a.* that may be abolished.
abolishment, *n.* the act of abolishing; the state of being abolished.
abolition, *n.* ab-o-*lish*-on, abolishment; putting an end to.
abolitionism, *n.* the principles of an abolitionist; advocacy of these.
abolitionist, *n.* one who works for the abolition of anything, especially slavery.
aboma, *n.* a-*boh*-ma, a large South American snake of the constrictor type.
abomasus, *n.* ab-o-*may*-sus, the fourth stomach of ruminants and their real organ of digestion.
abominable, *a.* a-*bom*-i-nabl, detestable; hateful.
abominableness, *n.* the quality or state of being abominable.
abominably, *ad.* in an abominable manner; excessively.
abominate, *v.t.* a-*bom*-in-ate, to detest; to abhor. **abominating.** (L. *abominatus*, detested.)
abomination, *n.* a-bom-in-*ay*-shon, extreme hatred; disgust; the object of detestation.
abondance, *n*, *see* **abundance.**
aboral, *n.* ab-*awr*-al, remote from the mouth.
aboriginal, *a.* ab-o-*rij*-i-nal, original; indigenous; autochthonous, when used of the native inhabitants, animals, or flora of a country: *n.* an original settler in a country; a primitive inhabitant.
aborigines, *n.pl.* ab-o-*rij*-i-neez, the first or primitive inhabitants of a country; its original flora and fauna. (L. *ab origine*, from the commencement.)
abort, *v.i.* a-*bawrt*, to be prematurely delivered (of a child); to miscarry; to be checked in growth; sterile [Biol.]. (L. *abortus*, miscarriage.)
aborted, *a.* born out of time, imperfectly developed.
aborticide, *n.* a-*bawr*-ti-side, the act of destroying an unborn fœtus; an abortifacient.
abortifacient, *a.* a-bawr-ti-*fay*-shent, causing abortion: *n.* anything that causes abortion [Med.].
abortion, *n.* a-*bawr*-shon, act of bringing forth young prematurely; a fœtus so produced; miscarriage; anything failing to come to maturity. (L. *abortitum*, miscarried.)
abortionist, *n.* one who illegally procures abortion.
abortive, *a.* a-*bawr*-tiv, brought forth in an immature state; imperfectly formed; coming to nought; procuring abortion: *n.* result of an abortion; a physic or anything inducing abortion.
abortively, *ad.* immaturely; untimely.
abortiveness, *n.* state of being abortive.
aboulia, *n.* a-*boo*-le-a, abulia [Psych.]. (Gr.)
abound, *v.i.* a-*bound*, to be or to have in abundance; to be plentifully supplied; to be very prevalent. (O.Fr. *abonder*, overflow.)
abounding, *a.* in abundance.
⋆**about,** *prep.* a-*bout*, round; near to; on the point of; concerned or engaged in; relating to; respecting: *ad.* around; circuitously; nearly; here and there. **to bring a ship about,** to place it on another tack [Naut.]. **about town,** frequenting fashionable places about town. **about turn!** turn from one direction to the opposite [Mil.]. (A.S. *ābūtan*, around.)
above, *prep.* a-*buv*, higher or superior in any respect; more in number, quantity, or degree; beyond; too proud for; too elevated in mind or rank: *ad.* overhead; in a higher place; before; on high; in heaven: *n.* heaven; the aforesaid. **above all,** before every other thing or consideration. **above-board,** openly. **above-ground,** not buried; alive. **above the rest,** in particular. **above the world,** above the judgment of the world or dependence on it. (A.S. *ābufan*, above.)
abracadabra, *n.* *ab*-ra-ka-*dab*-ra, anything meaningless; moonshine. A cabalistic word formerly used as a charm and worn as an amulet when written

on paper in the form of an equilateral triangle as many times as it has letters, omitting the last letter each time, thus :—

A B R A C A D A B R A
A B R A C A D A B R
A B R A C A D A B
A B R A C A D A
A B R A C A D
A B R A C A
A B R A C
A B R A
A B R
A B
A

abradant, *n.* ab-*rade*-ant, a substance for producing abrasion such as emery, quartz, pumice, etc.
abrade, *v.t.* ab-*rade*, to rub off or wear away by friction. (L. *abradere*, scratch off.)
abrading, *n.* the crumbling away, wearing down or wasting by friction.
Abrahamic, *a.* ay-bra-*ham*-ik, pertaining to Abraham or his system of rule.
Abraham-men, *n.pl.* *ay*-bra-ham-men, a class of lunatics who, in the 16th and 17th centuries, were occasionally allowed out to beg ; impostors who wandered about the country affecting lunacy. **to sham Abraham,** to feign sickness. (Perhaps from story of Lazarus, Luke xvi.)
Abranchians, *n.pl.* a-*brang*-ke-anz, an order of annelida, which have no gills, as the earthworms and leeches [Zool.]. (Gr. *a-*, without, *branchia*, gills.)
abranchiate, *a.* a-*brang*-ke-ate, having no gills.
abrasion, *n.* a-*bray*-zhon, the act of wearing or rubbing off ; substance worn off by attrition.
abrasive, *a.* a-*bray*-ziv, anything causing abrasion : *n.* an abradant.
abrastol, *n.* a-*bras*-tol, a white-red compound of calcium and naphthosulphonate used for preserving food and as an antipyretic and analgesic. (Gr. *a-*, not, *brastos*, boiling up.)
abraxas, *n.* a-*brak*-sas, a charm or amulet engraved with this word, the name of a god worshipped by certain Christian Gnostics in Egypt in the 2nd century, under whom were 365 dependent deities ; the gooseberry or magpie moth [Entom.]. (Gr., the letters in the word represent the number 365.)
abreast, *ad.* a-*brest*, side by side ; a line (marching *abreast*) ; up-to-date, as *abreast* of modern literature.
abreuvoir, *n.* (App.), the joint or mortar-space. between two stones [Masonry]. (Fr.)
abridge, *v.t.* a-*bridj*, to shorten ; to epitomize ; to contract ; to retrench ; to lessen ; to deprive. **abridging.** (O.Fr. *abregier*, cut short.)
abridgment, *n.* an epitome or a compend of a book ; diminution of any kind ; contraction ; synopsis.
abroach, *ad.* a-*broach*, broached ; in a position for letting out the liquor contained, as a cask.
abroad, *ad.* a-*brawd*, at large ; widely ; beyond the bounds of a house or country ; before the public at large. **all abroad,** at a loss ; far astray.
abrogable, *a.* *ab*-ro-ga-bl, that may be abrogated.
abrogate, *v.t.* *ab*-ro-gate, to repeal by authority ; to cancel. **abrogating.** [L. *abrogatum*, repealed (of a law.).]
abrogation, *n.* the act of abrogating ; repeal.
abrotanum, *n.* a-*brot*-a-num, southernwood. (Gr.)
abrupt, *a.* a-*brupt*, steep ; craggy ; sudden ; brusque ; unceremonious ; truncated ; terminating abruptly, as if the end were cut off [Bot.]. (L. *abruptus*, broken off.)
abruptedly, *ad.* suddenly ; abruptly.
abruption, *n.* a sudden or violent separation ; state of being truncated.
abruptly, *ad.* in an abrupt manner.
abruptness, *n.* state of being abrupt ; suddenness.
abscess, *n.* *ab*-ses, a collection of purulent matter in some part or organ of the body. (L. *abscessus.*)
abscind, *v.t.* ab-*sind*, to cut off ; to rend asunder. (L. *abscindo*, cut off.)
abscissa, *n.* ab-*sis*-a, a straight line from any point drawn parallel to one co-ordinate axis and meeting the other [Math.].
abscission, *n.* ab-*sish*-on, act of cutting off ; state of being cut off ; severance ; removal by cutting [Surg.] ; an abrupt breaking off of a sentence, thus : "He is a man of so much honour and of such generosity—but I need say no more." [Rhet.].
abscond, *v.i.* ab-*skond*, to make off suddenly and secretly from a place, especially in order to avoid a legal process. (L. *abscondo*, hide.)
abscondence, *n.* the act of hiding ; concealment.
absconder, *n.* a person who disappears for a felonious reason ; a fugitive.
absence, *n.* *ab*-sens, state of being absent ; inattention to things present, as in the expression **absence of mind** ; non-appearance, or not being in court to answer [Law]. (L. *absens*, absent.)
absent, *a.* *ab*-sent, not present ; away from home ; inattentive to what is going on.
absent, *v.t.* ab-*sent*, to keep purposely away.
absentee, *n.* ab-sen-*tee*, one who is absent from his country, estate, or work ; applied, by way of reproach, to a land-owner living away from his estates.
absenteeism, *n.* ab-sen-*tee*-izm, the practice, habit, or condition of an absentee.
absently, *ad.* *ab*-sent-le, absent-mindedly.
absent-minded, *a.* forgetful ; pre-occupied ; unobservant of surroundings.
absent-mindedly, *ad.* in an absent-minded manner.
absent-mindedness, *n.* the state of being absent-minded.
absinth, *n.* *ab*-sinth, wormwood ; a bitter plant, *Artemisia absinthium*, used as a tonic ; a green-coloured spirituous liqueur, containing wormwood oils, anise, and various aromatics. (Fr. *absinthe.*)
absinthian, *a.* ab-*sin*-thi-an, pertaining to wormwood, or to absinth.
absinthiated, *a.* impregnated with wormwood oils.
absinthic, *a.* ab-*sin*-thik, absinthian.
absinthin, *n.* ab-*sin*-thin, the bitter principle of wormwood.
absolute, *a.* *ab*-so-lewt, unconditional and unlimited ; unlimited in power ; arbitrary ; despotic ; complete in itself, perfect ; not relative ; self-dependent, self-existing ; pure, unmixed ; independent of arbitrary standards ; derived from some fundamental unit [Phys.]. **rule absolute,** a peremptory order following a rule nisi [Law]. **the absolute,** *n.* the independent and self-existent being or cause of things ; the infinite. (O.Fr. *absolut*, unlimited.)
absolutely, *ad.* in an absolute manner.
absoluteness, *n.* the quality or state of being absolute.
absolution, *n.* ab-so-*lew*-shon, among Catholics, the remission of sin to a penitent after confession ; among Protestants, declaration of remission on repentance ; an acquittal [Law].
absolutism, *n.* *ab*-so-lew-tizm, absoluteness ; the principles and doctrine of unconditional sovereignty as residing in a ruler, autocrat, dictator, etc. ; despotism ; the doctrine of predestination [Theol.].
absolutist, *a.* ab-so-*lew*-tist, despotic ; arbitrary : *n.* *ab*-so-lew-tist, one who is in favour of absolutism ; one identifying subject with object [Phil.].
absolutory, *a.* ab-*sol*-ew-to-re, absolving.
absolvatory, *a.* ab-*sol*-va-to-re, conferring absolution ; absolutory.
absolve, *v.t.* ab-*solv*, to set free from some engagement or obligation ; to pronounce absolution ; to acquit. **absolving.** (L. *absolvo*, set free.)
absolvitor, *n.* ab-*sol*-vi-tor, an acquittal [Scots law].
absonant, *a.* *ab*-so-nant, absurd ; contrary to reason ; discordant. (L. *absonus*, out of tune.)
absonous, *a.* *ab*-so-nus, absonant.
absorb, *v.t.* ab-*sawrb*, to imbibe ; to suck or swallow up ; to apprehend ; to engage wholly. (L. *absorbere*, to swallow up.)
absorbability, *n.* ab-sawr-ba-*bil*-e-te, the state or quality of being absorbable.
absorbable, *a.* ab-*sawr*-ba-bl, that may be absorbed.
absorbed, *a.* ab-*sawrbd*, deeply engaged in or on anything ; engrossed.
absorbedly, *adv.* ab-sawr-bed-le, in an absorbed manner.
absorbefacient, *a.* ab-sawr-be-*fay*-shent, likely to result in absorption : *n.* anything that produces absorption [Med.]. (L. *absorbere*, and *facere*, to make.)
absorbency, *n.* ab-*sawr*-ben-se, the quality of being absorbent.
absorbent, *a.* ab-*sawr*-bent, having absorbing power : *n.* anything which absorbs fluids ; a substance having the property of absorbing gases or liquids [Chem.] ; any substance that absorbs ; or neutralizes acidity in the stomach and bowels [Med.].

absorbing, *a.* that absorbs; engrossing, as an *absorbing* book.
absorptance, *n.* ab-*sawrp*-tance, the proportion of radiant energy absorbed [Physics].
absorptiometer, *n.* ab-*sawrp*-shi-*om*-e-ter, an instrument for measuring the absorption of gases by liquids.
absorption, *n.* ab-*sawrp*-shon, the act of absorbing; state of being absorbed; entire occupation of mind; taking up of matter by the absorbent vessels [Physiol.]; the incorporation of a gas into the mass of a liquid [Chem.]; the dissipation of energy in the dielectric of a condenser [Elect.].
absorptive, *a.* ab-*sawrp*-tiv, having the power to absorb; absorbent.
absorptiveness, *n.* the quality of being absorptive; tendency or capacity to absorb.
absquatulate, *v.i.* ab-*skwot*-yew-late, get off with you; decamp [U.S.A. slang].
abstain, *v.i.* ab-*stane*, to forbear; to refrain, especially voluntarily from what gratifies the appetite. (Fr. *abstenir*, forgo.)
abstainer, *n.* one who abstains, especially from intoxicants.
abstemious, *a.* ab-*stee*-me-us, sparing in food, strong drink, and indulgence of every kind; temperate; devoted to abstinence. (L. *abstemius*, abstaining from intoxicating drinks.)
abstemiously, *ad.* in an abstemious manner.
abstemiousness, *n.* the quality of being abstemious.
abstention, *n.* ab-*sten*-shon, the act of holding off or refraining; not voting at an election.
absterge, *v.t.* ab-*sterj*, to wipe clean; to purge. (L. *abstergeo*, wipe away.)
abstergent, *a.* ab-*ster*-jent, having a cleansing quality; wiping clean: *n.* whatever cleanses; a detergent.
abstersion, *n.* ab-*ster*-shon, the act of cleansing.
abstersive, *a.* ab-*ster*-siv, cleansing; abstergent.
abstinence, *n.* *ab*-sti-nens, a voluntary refraining from; total or partial forbearance from food and drink, as in fasting; abstaining from the use of strong liquors. (Fr. *abstinence*, sobriety.)
abstinency, *n.* *ab*-sti-nen-se, abstinence; the habit of abstaining.
abstinent, *a.* *ab*-sti-nent, refraining from indulgence, especially in food and strong drinks.
abstinently, *ad.* with abstinence.
abstract, *v.t.* ab-*strakt*, to draw away; to separate mentally and consider separately; to epitomize or reduce to a summary; to purloin; to separate the volatile parts of a substance [Chem.]. (L. *abstractus*, drawn away.)
abstract, *a.* *ab*-strakt, considered apart from its applications, as **abstract science;** considered apart from particulars, or in general, and hence abstruse. An **abstract idea,** an idea separated from a complex object, or from other ideas which naturally accompany it, as the solidity of marble contemplated apart from its other qualities [Met.]. **abstract terms,** those which express abstract ideas, as beauty, roundness, without regard to any subject in which they exist [Gram. and Logic]. **abstract of title,** a list of title-deeds with particulars. **abstract numbers,** numbers used without application to any particular object. **abstract** or **pure mathematics,** that which treats of the properties of magnitude, figure, or quantity, absolutely and generally considered, without restriction to any particular object; thus distinguished from **mixed mathematics,** which treats of the applied relations of quantity, as in astronomy, mechanics or optics [Math.].
abstract, *n.* *ab*-strakt, a summary containing the substance, or the principal heads, of a treatise or writing; an extract, in smaller quantity, containing the essence of a larger. **in the abstract,** in a state of separation; without reference to particular persons or things.
abstracted, *pp.* and *a.* ab-*strakt*-ed, separated; mentally separated; absent in mind.
abstractedly, *ad.* in an abstract or absent manner.
abstractedness, *n.* the state of being abstracted.
abstracter, *n.* one who abstracts; one who constructs abstracts.
abstraction, *n.* ab-*strak*-shon, the act of abstracting; the state of being abstracted; the operation of the mind by which qualities are considered apart from their substances, and abstract ideas are formed from concrete objects; a separation from worldly objects; absence of mind; purloining; the separation by distillation of the volatile parts of a compound [Chem.].
abstractionist, *n.* one who mistakes abstractions for realities; a visionary.
abstractive, *a.* having the power or quality of abstracting.
abstractively, *adv.* in an abstract, abstracting, or abstractive way.
abstractly, *ad.* *ab*-strakt-le, in an abstract manner.
abstractness, *n.* ab-*strakt*-ness, the state or quality of being abstract.
abstruse, *a.* ab-*stroos*, hidden from view; obscure; difficult to comprehend, as opposed to obvious. (L. *abstrusus*, thrust.)
abstrusely, *ad.* in an abstruse manner.
abstruseness, *n.* the state or quality of being abstruse.
abstrusity, *n.* abs-*troo*-se-te, abstruseness; that which is abstruse or recondite.
absurd, *a.* ab-*surd*, plainly inconsistent with or opposed to sense and reason. (L. *absurdus*, irrational.)
absurdity, *n.* absurdness; an absurd incident, notion, etc.
absurdly, *ad.* in an absurd manner.
absurdness, *n.* the quality of being absurd.
abulia, *n.* a-*boo*-le-a, loss of will power or capacity to act, esp. in the insane [Psych.]. (Gr. *a*-, not, *boule*, will.)
abundance, *n.* a-*bun*-dans, great plenty; affluence; (also **abondance**) a call at Solo Whist. **abondance declarée,** a call of thirteen tricks. (Fr. *abondance*, plenty.)
abundant, *a.* a-*bun*-dant, plentiful; fully sufficient.
abundantly, *ad.* in plenty.
abusable, *a.* a-*bew*-zabl, that can be abused.
abuse, *v.t.* a-*bewz*, to make a wrong or bad use of; to use ill; to impose on; to berate; to violate; to defile; to pervert the meaning of; to misapply, as words. (Fr. *abuser*, ill-treat.)
abuse, *n.* a-*bews*, the ill use, treatment, employment, or application of anything; rude reproach; violation of a female.
abuser, *n.* a-*bew*-zer, one who abuses.
abusive, *a.* a-*bew*-siv, containing or practising abuse; opprobrious.
abusively, *ad.* in an abusive manner.
abusiveness, *n.* abusive usage.
abut, *v.i.* a-*but*, to border upon or touch by point or line; to terminate: *v.t.* to cause to abut. **abutted. abutting.** (O.Fr. *abouter*, hit against.)
Abutilon, *n.* a-*bew*-ti-lon, a genus of plants of the mallow family, of which one yields a coarse jute-like fibre.
abutment, *n.* a-*but*-ment, a solid support for the extremity of a bridge or an arch, or of anything which presses outward; that which abuts.
abutter, *n.* the owner of land abutting upon a public road or another person's land.
abuzz, *a.* a-*buz*, full of buzzing sound.
abysm, *n.* a-*bizm*, an abyss; the void of the ancient cosmogonies. (O.Fr. *abisme*, gulf.)
abysmal, *a.* a-*biz*-mal, bottomless or fathomless; pertaining to an abyss.
abyss, *n.* a-*bis*, a depth or gulf immeasurable or bottomless; a fathomless mass of waters supposed to have encompassed the earth in its state of chaos; an immense cavern in which all the waters were supposed to have been collected on the third day of the creation; the ocean; hell; Erebus; that which is immeasurable; that in which anything is lost, as the abyss of time; also, metaphorically, the abyss of ignorance; in heraldry, the centre, or fesse-point, in an escutcheon. (L. *abyssus*, a bottomless pit.)
abyssal, *a.* relating or pertaining to the oceanic depths [Biol.]; anything unfathomable. **abyssal rocks,** Plutonic rocks [Geol.].
Abyssinian, *a.* ab-i-*sin*-i-an, pertaining to Abyssinia: *n.* a native of Abyssinia.
Acacia, *n.* a-*kay*-sha, a large and variable genus of tropical trees and shrubs with pinnated leaves; (*l.c.*) the popular name of a species of *Robinia*. (L.)
academe, *n.* *ak*-a-deem, academy.
academian, *n.* ak-a-*dee*-me-an, a member of or student at an academy; an academician.
academic, *a.* ak-a-*dem*-ik, academical: *n.* a student in a college or university; one who adheres to the

philosophy of Plato, the founder of the **Academic school**, in Greece.
academical, *a.* belonging or proper to an academy, college, or university; pertaining to the school or philosophy of Plato.
academically, *ad.* in an academical manner.
academicals, *n.pl.* official robes worn by professors, students, etc., at universities and colleges.
academician, *n.* a-*kad*-e-mish-an, a member of an academy or society for promoting arts and sciences, especially of the French Academy and the Royal Academy of Arts.
academism, *n.* a-*kad*-e-mizn, the doctrine of the academic philosophy.
academist, *n.* a-*kad*-e-mist, an academician.
academy, *n.* a-*kad*-e-me, originally the school of Plato, so called from the garden, grove, or villa, near Athens, where he taught; hence, a seminary in which the higher branches of learning are taught; a school for teaching some particular art or science; a society for the promotion of the arts and sciences, or of some particular science or art; a house for the use of an academy. **academy figure**, a drawing or painting after a nude model for the use of art students. **Royal Academy**, a British institution (estabd. 1768) for the encouragement of painting, sculpture, and architecture. **Royal Military Academy**, a college for Royal Artillery and Royal Engineers cadets. (Gr. *Academus*, said to be the name of an Attic hero who originally owned the site of Plato's Academy.)
Acadian, *a.* and *n.* a-*kay*-di-an, pertaining to, or a native of Nova Scotia. (Fr. *Acadie*, former name of Nova Scotia.)
acajou, *n.* *ak*-a-zhoo, the cashew nut, *Anacardium occidentale*. (Brazilian *acaju*.)
Acalephæ, *n.pl.* ak-a-*lee*-fee, an old name for certain classes of jelly-fish which cause, when touched, a sensation similar to the sting of a nettle. (Gr. *akalēphe*, a nettle.)
acalephan, *a.* ak-a-*lee*-fan, belonging to the Acalephæ.
acantha, *n.* a-*kan*-tha, the prickle of a plant [Bot.]; the spine or prickly fin of a fish, or one of the acute processes of the vertebræ [Zool.]. (Gr. *akantha*, a prickle.)
acanthaceous, *a.* ak-an-*thay*-shus, armed with sharp prickles.
acanthine, *a.* a-*kan*-thin, pertaining to or resembling the acanthus.
acanthoid, *a.* a-*kan*-thoid, spiny; like a spine.
acanthopod, *a.* a-*kan*-tho-pod, having spiny feet [Zool.].
Acanthopterygii, *n.pl.* a-*kan*-thop-te-*rij*-e-i, fishes having the rays of their fins, especially the dorsal, prickly at the extremities, as in the perch [Ichth.]. (Gr. *pterygion*, a fin.)
acanthous, *a.* a-*kan*-thus, spinous.
acanthus, *n.* a-*kan*-thus, the plant called bear's breech or brank-ursine; an ornament resembling the foliage of *Acanthus spinosus*, used in the capitals of the Corinthian and Composite orders [Arch.]. (L. *acanthus*, the bear's foot, *Helleborus fœtidus*.)
acapu, *n.* ah-kah-*poo*, the tropical American tree, *Andira americana*, and its timber.
acardia, *n.* a-*kahr*-de-a, absence of heart [Anat.].
acardiac, *a.* a-*kahr*-de-ak, without a heart. (Gr. *akardios*.)
Acarida, *n.* a-*ka*-re-da, an order of arachnids that includes mites and ticks; acarina. (Gr. *akari*, mite.)
acaridan, *a.* a-*ka*-re-dan, belonging or pertaining to the acarida: *n.* a member of the acarida.
Acarina, *n.* ak-a-*ry*-na, an order of arachnida, including the mites and ticks [Biol.]. (Gr. *a-*, not, *keiro*, to cut.)
acarpelous, *a.* ay-*kahr*-pe-lus, without any carpels.
acarpous, *a.* ay-*kahr*-pus, unfruitful; sterile. (Gr. *akarpos*, barren.)
acarus, *n.* *ak*-a-rus, a tick or mite.
acatalectic, *n.* ay-kat-a-*lek*-tik, a verse which has the complete number of syllables peculiar to the measure, without defect or excess: *a.* complete in syllables. (Gr. *akatalēktos*, unceasing.)
acatalepsia, *n.* ay-kat-a-*lep*-si-a, uncertainty in the diagnosis or prognosis of diseases [Med.].
acatalepsy, *n.* a-*kat*-a-lep-se, incomprehensibleness; the sceptical doctrine that there is no such thing as certainty.
acataleptic, *a.* incomprehensible; not to be known with certainty: *n.* one who believes that we know nothing certainly; a sceptic. (Gr. *akatalēptos*, what cannot be grasped.)
acatharsia, *n.* a-ka-*thar*-se-a, impure matter, esp. [Med.] that proceeding from a wound; suppuration. (Gr. *akatharsia*, foulness.)
acaulescent, *a.* ay-kaw-*les*-ent, nearly stemless.
acauline, *a.* a-*kaw*-lin, acaulose.
acaulose, *a.* a-*kaw*-lohs, having no true stem; with leaves springing directly from the root, and flowers resting on the ground [Bot.]. (Gr. *akaulos*, stalkless.)
acaulous, *a.* a-*kaw*-lus, acaulose; stemless.
accede, *v.i.* ak-*seed*, to agree or assent; to come to, as heir. (L. *accedo*, go near.)
accelerando, *ad.* ak-sel-e-*ran*-doh, gradually quicker [Mus.]. (It.)
accelerate, *v.t.* ak-*sel*-er-rate, to hasten; to quicken the speed of; to cause to happen earlier. (L. *acceleratum*, hastened.)
accelerated, *a.* quickened in motion; hastened in progress. **accelerated force**, the variation in force which a body exerts in consequence of the acceleration of its motion [Mech.]. **accelerated motion**, that which is continually receiving greater or lesser accessions of velocity [Mech.].
acceleration, *n.* ak-sel-er-*ray*-shon, the act of accelerating; state of being accelerated. **acceleration of the moon**, her increase of mean motion, compared with the diurnal motion of the earth, being about 11″ in a century. **acceleration of a planet**, the excess of its *real* above its *mean* diurnal motion. The **diurnal acceleration** of the fixed stars is the time by which they, in one revolution, anticipate the mean diurnal revolution of the sun, which is nearly 3′56″ of solar time sooner each day [Astron.].
accelerative, *a.* ak-*sel*-er-ray-tiv, causing, or relating to, acceleration.
accelerator, *n.* ak-*sel*-er-ray-tor, that which accelerates; a device to increase mechanical speed, as in motor-engines; a chemical that hastens a reaction, or that hastens the development of a sensitized and exposed photographic plate.
acceleratory, *a.* ak-sel-er-*ray*-to-re, accelerative.
accelerograph, *n.* ak-*sel*-ero-graf, an instrument recording acceleration, also one recording the pressure caused by an explosion within a confined space [Mil.].
accelerometer, *n.* *ak*-sel-e-*rom*-e-ter, an instrument recording acceleration; an apparatus for measuring gas-pressure in any part of a gun [Mil.].
accendibility, *n.* ak-sen-de-*bil*-e-te, inflammability.
accendible, *a.* ak-*sen*-de-bl, capable of being kindled; inflammable. (L. *accendere*, set on fire.)
accensor, *n.* ak-*sen*-sor, an acolyte.
accent, *n.* *ak*-sent, a particular stress of voice upon a syllable or word; a mark used in writing to direct the stress of the voice in pronunciation or to mark the length of a vowel sound; a modulation of the voice expressive of certain passions or sentiments; stress of voice or instrument regulating the time [Mus.]; words, language, or expressions in general. (Fr. *accent*, expression.)
accent, *v.t.* ak-*sent*, to express or note the accent; to lay stress upon (as individual views or opinions).
accentor, *n.* ak-*sent*-or, formerly, the leading performer in a choir or orchestra; the hedge-sparrow, *Accentor modularis*. (L. *ad-*, to, *cantor*, singer.)
accentual, *a.* ak-*sent*-yew-al, relating to or characterized by accent.
accentuate, *v.t.* ak-*sent*-yew-ate, to mark or pronounce with an accent, or accents; to emphasize. (Med. L. *accentuare*, lay emphasis upon.)
accentuation, *n.* ak-sent-yew-*ay*-shon, the act of placing or pronouncing accents.
accept, *v.t.* ak-*sept*, to take what is offered; to receive with favour, or acquiesce; to agree to; to grant; to receive as terms of a contract. To **accept a bill of exchange**, to subscribe it according to the legal form, and thereby agree to pay the amount when due [Comm.]. (Fr. *accepter*, receive.)
acceptability, *n.* ak-sep-ta-*bil*-e-te, acceptableness.
acceptable, *a.* ak-*sep*-ta-bl, deserving of acceptance; welcome, gratifying.
acceptableness, *n.* the quality of being agreeable to a receiver.

acceptably, *ad.* in an acceptable manner.
acceptance, *n.* ak-*sept*-ans, the taking or accepting; favourable reception; agreement to terms of proposals; admission to favour; the subscribing of, or subscription to, a bill of exchange; a bill of exchange accepted [Comm.].
acceptation, *n.* ak-sep-*tay*-shon, the act of accepting; state of being acceptable; favourable regard; acceptance; the meaning or sense in which a word or expression is generally received.
accepter, *n.* ak-*sep*-ter, one who accepts.
acceptor, *n.* ak-*sep*-tor, he who, being the drawee, has accepted a bill of exchange [Comm.].
access, *n.* *ak*-ses or ak-*ses*, admission to a place or person; approach; means of approach; increase; addition; return of a fit or paroxysm of disease. (L. *accessus*, coming towards.)
accessary, *a.* and *n.* ak-*ses*-a-re, accessory.
accessibility, *n.* ak-ses-e-*bil*-e-te, the quality of being accessible, of admitting approach.
accessible, *a.* ak-*ses*-ibl, that may be approached; easy of approach.
accessibly, *ad.* so as to be accessible.
accession, *n.* ak-*sesh*-on, a coming to; an acceding or assenting to; act of being joined to; increase by something added; that which is added; augmentation; act of arriving at a throne, office, or dignity; acquisition of property due to increase by natural or artificial growth [Law].
accessional, *a.* additional.
accessorial, *a.* ak-se-*saw*-re-al, pertaining to an accessory.
accessorily, *ad.* ak-*ses*-o-re-le, in the manner of an accessory.
accessoriness, *n.* the state of being accessory.
accessory, *a.* ak-*ses*-o-re, contributing; aiding to the principal agent, or in a subordinate way to the general effect: *n.* one guilty of a felony, not as principal, but by aiding, abetting, or concealing the offender; an accomplice; parts of a design added merely for ornament, also any secondary accompaniment [Paint. and Sculp.].
acciaccatura, *n.* aht-*chahk*-a-*too*-rah, a short discordant grace-note; the short appogiatura [Mus.]. (It., a crushing.)
accidence, *n.* *ak*-se-dens, that part of grammar which treats of inflections of words, declension of nouns, and conjugation of verbs [Gram.].
accident, *n.* *ak*-se-dent, anything which happens; generally, an unintended or unexpected untoward occurrence; a mishap; a non-essential; also what happens without intelligent design; a non-essential property or quality [Logic]; an inessential feature in a coat of arms [Her.]. (Fr. *accident*, a fortuitous occurrence.)
accidental, *n.* ak-se-*den*-tal, a property or quality non-essential; a sharp, flat, or natural implying change of key [Mus.]: *a.* happening by chance, or unexpectedly; non-essential; not necessarily belonging to. **accidental colours,** complementary colours seen after looking steadily for some time at a bright-coloured object.
accidentalism, *n.* ak-se-*den*-ta-lizm, effect produced by accidental rays of light.
accidentally, *ad.* in an accidental manner.
accidentalness, *n.* the quality of being accidental.
accidented, *a.* ak-se-*dent*-ed, of undulating surface; thus, an accidented plateau or field.
accidie, *n.* *ak*-se-de, acedia [Med.].
Accipiter, *n.* ak-*sip*-e-ter, the genus of birds of prey including the smaller hawks. (L., a hawk.)
accipitral, *a.* pertaining to the hawks; hawk-like.
accipitrine, *a.* ak-*sip*-e-trin, predatory; rapacious; sharp-sighted; pertaining to birds of prey.
accite, *v.t.* ak-*site*, to call; to summon. (L.)
acclaim, *n.* a-*klaym*, a shout of joy; applause; acclamation: *v.t.* to applaud vociferously; to welcome enthusiastically. (L. *acclāmāre*, shout out.)
acclamation, *n.* ak-la-*may*-shon, a shout of applause; the unanimous vote of an assembly, as at the election of a chairman, etc.; the response in antiphonal singing [Mus.].
acclamatory, *a.* a-*klam*-a-to-re, expressive of applause by shouts or clapping of hands.
acclimatation, *n.* a-kly-ma-*tay*-shon, acclimatization.
acclimate, *v.t.* a-*kly*-mat, or *ak*-li-mate, to acclimatize.
acclimation, *n.* ak-li-*may*-shon, spontaneous accommodation to strange climatic conditions.
acclimatization, *n.* a-*kly*-ma-ty-*zay*-shon, the process of becoming or state of being habituated to a foreign climate.
acclimatize, *v.t.* and *i.* a-*kly*-ma-tize, to habituate or inure a plant or animal to a climate not native to it. (Fr. *acclimater*, accustom to a climate.)
acclivitous, *a.* a-*kliv*-e-tus, rising with a slope; uphill.
acclivity, *n.* a-*kliv*-e-te, an ascending slope; the talus of a rampart. (L. *acclivitas*, an ascent.)
acclivous, *a.* a-*kly*-vus, sloping upward; acclivitous.
accolade, *n.* ak-oh-*layd*, the gentle blow of a sword upon the shoulder in the ceremony of conferring knighthood; so called because originally conferred by putting the hand on the neck; an upright line or brace joining two or more staves [Mus.]. (Fr. *accolade*, embrace.)
accolated, *a.* *ak*-o-lay-ted, accollé.
accollé, *a.* ak-o-*lay*, gorged [Her.]; side by side or overlapping (of profiles on a coin, etc.). (Fr. *accolé*, united.)
accommodate, *v.t.* a-*kom*-o-date, to adapt; to make to agree or harmonize; to adjust; to supply with conveniences of any kind. (L. *accommodatum*, fitted to a thing.)
accommodating, *a.* adapting one's self to; obliging.
accommodation, *n.* a-kom-o-*day*-shon, adaptation, especially of one thing to another, so as to make them agree or correspond; adjustment; reconciliation; provision of conveniences in supply of a want; a loan of money. **accommodation bill** or **note,** one drawn and accepted for the purpose of borrowing money, in contradistinction to one given for value received [Comm.]. **accommodation ladder,** a light ladder hung over the side of a ship at the gangway.
accommodative, *a.* a-*kom*-o-day-tiv, furnishing accommodation; accommodating.
accompanier, *n.* a-*kum*-pa-ne-er, one who accompanies.
accompaniment, *n.* a-*kum*-pa-ne-ment, something that attends as a circumstance, or which is added by way of ornament to the principal thing, or for the sake of symmetry; the music and also the instruments which accompany the voice.
accompanist, *n.* a-*kum*-pa-nist, one who plays the accompaniment.
accompany, *v.t.* a-*kum*-pa-ne, to go with; to attend as a companion; to escort; to be with as connected; to play an accompaniment [Mus.]. (Fr. *accompagner*, go with.)
accomplice, *n.* a-*kom*-plis, an associate in a crime. (Fr. *complice*, ally.)
accomplish, *v.t.* a-*kom*-plish, to complete; to execute; to fulfil; to equip. (Fr. *accomplissant*, finishing.)
accomplishable, *a.* capable of accomplishment.
accomplished, *a.* a-*kom*-plisht, complete; finished; possessed of the accomplishments and graces prized in good or fashionable society.
accomplishment, *n.* fulfilment; cultured attainment in either art or manners, according to the standard of good breeding.
accompt, *n.* a-*kownt*, account.
accomptant, *n.* a-*kown*-tant, an accountant.
accord, *n.* a-*kawrd*, agreement; harmony of minds; concurrence of opinion or will; harmony of sounds; just correspondence of things; will, or spontaneous impulse; adjustment of a difference: *v.t.* to grant or concede: *v.i.* to agree; to be in correspondence; to harmonize. (Fr. *accorder*, agree.)
accordance, *n.* a-*kawrd*-ans, the state or action of agreeing; accordancy.
accordancy, *n.* agreement with a person; conformity with a thing; harmony.
accordant, *a.* corresponding; consonant.
accordantly, *ad.* in an accordant manner.
according, *part. a.* and *ad.* agreeing; harmonious. **according as,** in proportion as. **according to,** in accordance with; agreeably to the statement or opinion of.
accordingly, *ad.* agreeably to something said or done; consequently.
accordion, *n.* a-*kawr*-de-on, a small keyed wind-instrument, whose tones are generated by a bellows-like action upon metallic reeds. **accordion pleating,** folds like those of an accordion bellows. (It. *accordare*, play in tune.)

accordionist, *n.* a player on the accordion.
accost, *v.t.* a-*kost*, to draw near to and address; to salute. (Fr. *accoster*, address anyone personally.)
accostable, *a.* easy of access; familiar.
accosted, *a.* back to back, or side by side, as of two beasts on a heraldic coat of arms.
accouchement, *n.* (App.), delivery in childbed; a lying-in. (Fr.)
accoucheur, *n.* (App.), a man-midwife; an obstetrician. (Fr.)
accoucheuse, *n.* (App.), a midwife. (Fr.)
★**account,** *n.* a-*kount*, computation or method of reckoning; a register of debits and credits; a written statement in detail of moneys due for goods purchased, or services of any kind rendered; the sum total; a narrative; a recital of particular transactions and events, verbal or written; a statement or explanation; reason or consideration, as a motive; importance; estimation; profit; advantage; behalf; sake: *v.t.* to deem or judge: *v.i.* to render an account or relation of particulars; to give reasons for. **current account,** a running, or open, account with a bank or another person. **to account of,** to hold in esteem; to value. (O.Fr. *aconter*, reckon up.)
accountability, *n.* a-koun-ta-*bil*-e-te, liability to give account; responsibility.
accountable, *a.* a-*kownt*-abl, liable to be called to account; responsible.
accountableness, *n.* the state of being accountable.
accountably, *ad.* in an accountable manner.
accountancy, *n.* a-*kount*-an-se, the profession of an accountant.
accountant, *n.* a-*koun*-tant, one skilled in keeping accounts; a person professionally employed in examining accounts; a book-keeper in a public office. **accountant-general,** a former high official of the Court of Chancery. **chartered accountant,** a member of an institute of accountants established by Royal Charter.
accountantship, *n.* the office or duties of an accountant.
account-book, *n.* a book in which accounts are kept.
accoutre, *v.t.* a-*koo*-ter, to dress in military array; to equip for military service. (O.Fr. *accoutrer*.)
accoutrements, *n.pl.* a-*koo*-ter-ments, military dress and array; military equipment other than arms.
accredit, *v.t.* a-*kred*-it, to give authority to; to procure credit for; to send as envoy or ambassador. (Fr. *accréditer*, sanction.)
accrementition, *n.* *ak*-re-men-*tish*-on, organic growth by fission or by development of similar material [Phys.]. (L. *accrementum*, an increase.)
accrescence, *n.* a-*kres*-ens, gradual growth; an accretion.
accrescent, *a.* a-*kres*-ent, increasing; continuing to grow. (L. *accrescens*, growing on.)
accrete, *v.i.* a-*kreet*, to grow together; to become combined: *a.* fastened to another body and growing with it [Bot.]. (L. *accretus*, increased.)
accretion, *n.* a-*kree*-shon, an increase in growth, particularly by external accessions; the growing together of parts naturally separate, as the fingers or toes [Med.]; the adhering of something to property by reason of which its owner becomes enriched, also the increase of a legacy through the death of a co-legatee [Law]. (L. *accretio*, an increment.)
accretive, *a.* a-*kree*-tiv, increasing by growth.
accrue, *v.i.* ak-*kroo*, to proceed or come; to be added to, as increase, profit, or damage. **accruing.** (O.Fr. *acrew*, increased.)
accrument, *n.* a-*kroo*-ment, addition; the act or process of increasing.
accubation, *n.* ak-ew-*bay*-shon, lying or reclining at table, as did the ancients. (L. *accubitus*, reclining at table.)
accumbent, *a.* a-*kum*-bent, leaning or reclining, as the ancients at their meals.
accumulate, *v.t.* a-*kew*-mew-late, to heap up; to collect or bring together; to amass: *v.i.* to increase by repeated addition. (L. *accumulatum*, heaped up.)
accumulation, *n.* a-kew-mew-*lay*-shon, the act of accumulating; the state of being accumulated; a mass; a heap. (L. *accumulatio*, a heaping up.)
accumulative, *a.* ak-*kew*-mew-la-tiv, that accumulates; that is accumulated.
accumulatively, *ad.* in an accumulative manner.
accumulator, *n.* ak-*kew*-mew-lay-tor, one that accumulates; an apparatus for storing hydraulic or electric energy; a storage battery. (L. *accumulator*, one who heaps up.)
accuracy, *n.* *ak*-kew-ra-se, correctness, resulting from care. (L. *accurātum*, bestowed care upon.)
accurate, *a.* *ak*-kew-rate, exact; correct; done with care.
accurately, *ad.* in an accurate manner.
accurateness, *n.* accuracy; exactness.
accursed, *a.* a-*kurst* or a-*kurs*-ed, under a curse; doomed to ruin; deserving to be cursed; execrable; detestable. (A.S. *a*-, and *cursian*, curse.)
accurst, *a.* a-*kurst*, accursed.
accusable, *a.* a-*kew*-za-bl, chargeable with a crime; blamable.
accusal, *n.* a-*kew*-zal, an accusation.
accusant, *n.* a-*kew*-zant, one who accuses another.
accusation, *n.* ak-ew-*zay*-shon, act of accusing; charge brought against one. (L. *accūsātio*, a complaint.)
accusative, *n.* a-*kew*-za-tiv, the objective case [Gram.]: *a.* of or pertaining to the objective case.
accusatively, *ad.* relating to the accusative case. (L. *accūsātivus*, the accusative case.)
accusatorial, *a.* a-kew-za-*taw*-re-al, accusatory.
accusatory, *a.* a-*kew*-za-to-re, containing or involving an accusation. (L. *accūsātōrius*.)
accuse, *v.t.* a-*kewz*, to charge with a crime or fault; to blame. (O.Fr. *acuser*, accuse.)
accusingly, *adv.* a-kew-zing-le, in accusing fashion.
accustom, *v.t.* a-*kus*-tom, to make familiar by habit; to habituate. (O.Fr. *acostumer*, render customary.)
accustomably, *ad.* according to custom; in a customary manner.
accustomed, *a.* ak-*kus*-tomd, usual; often practised; frequent; habitual.
accustomedness, *n.* state, fact, or quality of being accustomed.
ace, *n.* ace, a unit; the one of cards or dice; a particle; a trifle; a particularly successful fighting airman. (O.Fr. *as*, from L. *as*, a unit.)
acedia, *n.* ay-*see*-de-a, listlessness; torpor; a morbid mental condition characterized by melancholia; accidie [Med.]. (Gr. *akedia*.)
acedia, *n.* a-*see*-de-a, a flat fish found from the West Indies to Brazil. (Sp.)
Aceldama, *n.* a-*sel*-da-ma, a field near Jerusalem, purchased with the bribe which Judas took for betraying his Master (Acts i, 19); any place of murderous associations; a field of blood. (Syr. *okel*, *hakal*, field, *damo*, blood.)
acentric, *a.* ay-*sen*-trik, not centred; without centre; not aligned with the centre of gravity [Mech.]; not pertaining to a nerve centre [Med.]. (Gr. *ākentros*, centreless.)
acephalan, *n.* ay-*sef*-a-lan, one of a class of molluscs having no head, as the oyster [Zool.]. (Gr. *ăkephalos*, wanting a head.)
acephalism, *n.* ay-*sef*-a-lizm, the state of being headless.
acephalist, *n.* ay-*sef*-a-list, one who acknowledges no leader; (*with cap.*) a member of the Acephalites.
Acephalites, *n.pl.* ay-*sef*-a-lites, members of early Christian sects acknowledging no earthly leader [Eccl. Hist.]; members of a mythical headless race, mentioned by ancient writers.
acephalous, *a.* ay-*sef*-a-lus, without a head or superior; with the style attached to the base of the ovary [Bot.].
acephalus, *n.* ay-*sef*-a-lus, a headless monster [Med.].
Acer, *n.* *ay*-ser, a genus of over a hundred species of plants comprising the sycamore and the maples. (L. *acer*, maple-tree.)
aceraceous, *a.* as-er-*ay*-shus, of the maple order [Bot.].
acerb, *a.* a-*serb*, sour, with bitterness and astringency. (L. *acerbus*, harsh to the taste.)
acerbate, *v.t.* *as*-er-bate, to make sour and bitter; to exasperate: *a.* irritated, embittered.
acerbic, *a.* a-*serb*-ik, severe, sour.
acerbity, *n.* a-*serb*-e-te, a harsh sour taste; applied to persons or things, harshness; severity; bitterness. (Fr. *acerbité*, sharpness.)
acerose, *a.* *as*-er-ohs, chaffy; needle-shaped and stiff, like the fir-tree leaf [Bot.]. (L. *acerosus*, husky, full of chaff.)

acerous, *a.* *as*-er-us, acerose.
acervate, *a.* *as*-er-vate, growing in closely compacted clusters [Bot.]. (L. *acervatum*, heaped up.)
acescence, *n.* a-*ses*-ens, souring by acetous fermentation; the quality of turning sour.
acescent, *a.* a-*ses*-ent, turning sour; slightly sour or acid. (L. *ascescens*, turning sour.)
acetabulum, *n.* a-se-*tab*-yew-lum, a cavity in a bone for receiving the end of another bone; a sucker in cuttle-fishes and in leeches; a lobe in the placenta of ruminants [Anat.]. (L., a cup-shaped vessel for vinegar.)
acetanilide, *n.* as-e-*tan*-e-lide, a white crystalline powder with analgesic and antipyretic properties [Med.].
acetarious, *a.* as-e-*tair*-e-us, fit for or used in salads. (L. *acetaria*, salad, vegetables.)
acetate, *n.* *as*-e-tate, a salt of acetic acid.
acetated, *a.* *as*-e-tay-ted, mixed or treated with acetic acid.
acetic, *a.* a-*see*-tik, or a-*set*-ik, relating to vinegar; sour. **acetic acid,** the pure acid of vinegar. (L. *acetum*, vinegar.)
acetification, *n.* a-*set*-e-fi-*kay*-shon, the process or operation of acetifying.
acetifier, *n.* a-*set*-e-fy-er, an appliance to produce acetification.
acetify, *v.t.* or *v.i.* a-*set*-e-fy, to turn into acetic acid or vinegar.
acetimeter, *n.* as-e-*tim*-e-ter, an acetometer.
acetometer, *n.* as-e-*tom*-e-ter, an instrument for ascertaining the strength of vinegar or acids.
acetometry, *n.* the measurement of, or the process of ascertaining, the strength of acids, or of acid content.
acetone, *n.* *as*-e-tone, a light inflammable liquid; a ketone [Chem.].
acetose, *a.* *as*-e-tose, producing vinegar or acetic acid; sour: *n.* a form of cellulose acetate used in film making, etc.
acetous, *a.* a-*see*-tus, acetose.
acetylene, *n.* a-*set*-i-leen, a colourless hydro-carbon gas, evolved from calcium carbide and water, and giving a brilliant white light when burned. **acetylene welding,** welding by means of an oxy-acetylene flame.
Achæan, *a.* a-*kee*-an, pertaining to Achaia, a state of ancient Greece, or to ancient Greece.
acharnement, *n.* (App.), barbarous ferocity; bloodthirstiness. (Fr.)
Achates, *n.* a-*kay*-teez, a companion of Æneas, after the fall of Troy; hence, a faithful friend.
ache, *v.i.* ayk, to be in pain; to suffer distress: *n.* a continued pain. (A.S. *acan*, pain.)
achene, *n.* a-*keen*, a dry, single-seeded fruit with a separable pericarp. (Gr.)
Acheron, *n.* *ak*-er-on, a river of the underworld, hence Hades [Gr. Myth.].
Acheulian, *a.* a-*shoo*-li-an, pertaining to the third Palæolithic period, between the Chellean and Mousterian [Archæol.]. (Fr. *acheuléen*, of St. Acheul, a site near Amiens.)
acheweed, *n.* *aitch*-weed, a local name of *Ægopodium podagraria*; gout-weed.
achievable, *a.* a-*cheev*-abl, that may be achieved.
achieve, *v.t.* a-*cheev*, to perform; to finish. **achieving.** (O.Fr. *à chef venir*, come to a head.)
achievement, *n.* the act of achieving; exploit; a great or heroic deed; an escutcheon; the shield of a person deceased.
achiever, *n.* one who achieves.
Achillea, *n.* ak-il-*lee*-a, a large genus of plants of the thistle family; yarrow; sneezewort.
achilous, *a.* a-*ky*-lus, having only rudimentary or no lips [Bot.]. (Gr. *a*-, and *cheilos*, lip.)
achlamydeate, *a.* ak-la-*mid*-e-ate, without calyx and corolla [Bot.]. (Gr. *a*-, and *chlamys*, a cloak.)
acholia, *n.* a-*koh*-li-a, want of bile [Med.]. (Gr.)
achondroplasia, *n.* a-kon-droh-*play*-zi-a, arrest in the formation of cartilage leading to dwarfism [Med.]. (Gr. *a*-, and *chondros*, cartilage, *plassein*, to form.)
achor, *n.* *ay*-kawr, the scald-head, a disease of the skin, generally on infants. (Gr.)
achromatic, *a.* ak-ro-*mat*-ik, colourless; refracting or transmitting light pure and undecomposed [Opt.]. (Gr. *akhrōmatos*, wanting colour.)
achromatically, *ad.* in an achromatic manner.
achromatism, *n.* a-*kroh*-ma-tizm, the quality or state of being achromatic.
achromatize, *v.t.* a-*kroh*-ma-tize, to make achromatic; to deprive of colour.
achromatopsy, *n.* a-*kroh*-ma-top-se, colour-blindness.
acicula, *n.* a-*sik*-ew-la (*pl.* **aciculæ**), a prickly spike [Zool. and Bot.]. (L., a small pin for a headdress.)
acicular, *a.* of needle shape; sharp as a needle.
acicularly, *ad.* in the manner of needles or prickles.
aciculate, *a.* a-*sik*-yew-late, furnished with prickles or bristles; prickly; marked as with fine scratches.
aciculiform, *a.* a-*sik*-ew-le-form, needle-shaped.
★**acid,** *a.* *as*-id, sour and sharp to the taste: *n.* a sour substance; a substance capable of uniting with salifiable bases and forming salts [Chem.]. (L. *acidus*, sour.)
acidic, *a.* a-*sid*-ik, pertaining to or resembling acid; acid-forming.
acidiferous, *a.* as-e-*dif*-e-rus, containing or yielding an acid.
acidifiable, *a.* a-*sid*-e-*fy*-abl, capable of being acidified.
acidific, *a.* as-e-*dif*-ik, producing acid or acidity; converting into an acid.
acidification, *n.* a-*sid*-e-fe-*kay*-shon, the process of acidifying; state of being acidified.
acidifier, *n.* a principle whose presence is necessary for acidity.
acidify, *v.t.* and *i.* a-*sid*-e-fy, to make acid; to become or convert into an acid.
acidimeter, *n.* as-e-*dim*-e-ter, an acetometer.
acidimetry, *n.* as-e-*dim*-e-tre, acetometry.
acidity, *n.* a-*sid*-e-te, the quality of being acid; tartness.
acidness, *n.* acidity.
acidometer, *n.* as-e-*dom*-e-ter, an acidimeter; a hydrometer for measuring the specific gravity of accumulator acid [Wire.].
acidosis, *n.* as-e-*doh*-sis, superfluity of acid in the system resulting from defective metabolism [Med.].
acidulate, *v.t.* a-*sid*-yew-late, to make slightly acid; to give an acid flavour to.
acidulent, *a.* acidulous.
acidulous, *a.* a-*sid*-yew-lus, slightly sour; caustic; petulant; sub-acid. (L. *acidulus*, sourish.)
acierage, *n.* *ay*-se-a-raj, the process of electroplating metal with steel or iron. (Fr. *aciérage*.)
acinaceous, *a.* as-e-*nay*-shus, full of kernels; having berries in a cluster.
acinaciform, *a.* as-e-*nas*-e-form, scimitar-shaped [Bot.]. (L. *acīnaces*, short Persian sabre or scimitar.)
acinarious, *a.* as-e-*nair*-e-us, covered with small round stalked vesicles like grape seeds [Bot.].
acini, *n.pl.* *as*-e-ne, granulations [Anat.]; compound berries [Bot.]. (L. *acinus*, any juicy berry with seeds.)
aciniform, *a.* a-*sin*-e-form, of glands in clusters like grapes [Anat.].
acinose, *a.* *as*-e-nohs, acinous; aciniform.
acinous, *a.* *as*-e-nus, acinose; consisting of minute granular concretions [Min.].
Acipenser, *n.* as-e-*pen*-ser, the genus of fishes containing the sturgeons. (L.)
ack-ack, *n.* and *a.* ak-*ak*, anti-aircraft. (From the Morse name of the initials, AA). **ack-emma,** morning (A.M.) [Slang].
acknowledge, *v.t.* ak-*nol*-ej, to own; to admit; to confess; to recognize; to admit the receipt of. (A.S. *a*-, on, and *knowledge*.)
acknowledgeable, *a.* that may be acknowledged.
acknowledgeably, *ad.* in an acknowledgeable manner.
acknowledgment, *or* **acknowledgement,** *n.* the act of acknowledging; confession; recognition; receipt of a benefit or money, etc., received.
acknowledger, *n.* one who acknowledges.
acle, *n.* *ak*-le, the Asiatic tree, *Xylia xylocarpa*; its timber, known as ironwood of Pegu. (Tagalog.)
aclinic, *a.* ay-*klin*-ik, having no dip [Mag.]. **aclinic line,** the magnetic equator (on which the needle does not dip). (Gr. *aklines*, unswerving.)
acme, *n.* *ak*-me, the highest point attained; the prime; the crisis [Med.]. (Gr. *akme*, a point.)
acne, *n.* *ak*-ne, a hard, inflamed pimple; a skin disease. (Gr. *akme*, a point.)
acock, *a.* a-*kok*, alert: *ad.* in a cocked position.
a-cockbill, *ad.* a-*kok*-bil, said of an anchor hanging at the cathead ready to drop; and of the yards when tipped at an angle from the deck.

Acœmeti, *n.* a-*sem*-i-ti, an order of 5th-century Eastern monks and nuns who kept up service day and night. (Gr. *akoimetoi*, without sleep.)
acology, *n.* a-*kol*-o-je, the science treating of medical and surgical remedies. (Gr. *akos*, cure, *logos*, science.)
acolyte, *n.* *ak*-o-lite, an attendant; a subordinate official in the Roman Catholic Church, who trims the lamps and prepares the sacramental elements. (Fr. *acolyte*, companion or servitor.)
acondylose, *a.* a-*kon*-di-lohs, acondylous.
acondylous, *a.* a-*kon*-di-lus, having stalks without joints; jointless [Bot.]. (Gr. *akondulos*, knuckleless.)
aconite, *n.* *ak*-on-ite, *Aconitum napellus*, wolf's-bane; monk's hood [Bot.]; aconitine. (Fr. *aconit*.)
aconitic, *a.* a-kon-*it*-ik, pertaining to monk's-hood.
aconitine, *n.* a-*kon*-i-teen, the essential principle of aconite; a poisonous extract of it.
acopic, *a.* a-*kop*-ik, preventing or removing tiredness [Med.]. (Gr. *a*-, not, *kopos*, weariness.)
acoria, *n.* ay-*kaw*-re-a, insatiable hunger [Med.].
acorn, *n.* *ay*-korn, the fruit of the oak; a small conical piece of wood resembling this. (A.S. *æcern*, nut.)
acorn-cup, *n.* the capsule of the acorn.
acorned, *a.* *ay*-kornd, furnished or fed with acorns; an oak-tree bearing acorns [Her.].
acorn-shell, *n.* a species of *Balanus*, a cirriped allied to the barnacle.
acorus, *n.* a-*kaw*-rus, the plant sweet-flag. (Gr.)
acosmism, *n.* ay-*koz*-mizm, denial of the existence of an external world. (Gr. *akosmos*, confusion.)
acotyledon, *n.* ay-kot-i-*lee*-don, a plant which has no visible seed leaves.
acotyledonous, *a.* having no distinct seed-leaves.
acouchy, *n.* a-*koo*-she, a small rodent allied to the agouti. (Fr., from Tupi.)
acoumetry, *n.* a-*kou*-me-tre, the measurement of hearing power or acuteness.
acoustic, *a.* a-*kous*-tik, pertaining to the ear, to the sense of hearing, or to the science of sound. **acoustic duct,** external passage of the ear. **acoustic mine,** *see* **mine. acoustic nerve,** the auditory nerve. [Anat.]. (Gr. *akous-tikos*.)
acoustically, *ad.* in an acoustic manner.
acoustician, *n.* a-kous-*tish*-an, one skilled in acoustics.
acoustics, *n.* a-*kous*-tiks, the science of sound, its production, transmission, and effects; the sound qualities of a room, auditorium, etc.
acquaint, *v.t.* a-*kwaynt*, to make one know or familiar with; to inform. **acquaint oneself with,** to gain an intimate or particular knowledge of. (O.Fr. *acointer*, familiarize with.)
acquaintance, *n.* a-*kwayn*-tans, knowledge; familiar knowledge; one whom one knows casually, not intimately.
acquaintanceship, *n.* the state of being acquainted; familiar knowledge.
acquest, *n.* a-*kwest*, something acquired; an acquisition; possession acquired other than by inheritance [Law]. (L. *acquisitio*, act of acquiring).
acquiesce, *v.i.* ak-we-*es*, to rest in, or remain satisfied with, generally implying previous opposition; to assent to in a passive way. (L. *acquiescere*, repose.)
acquiescence, *n.* a silent submissive assent and compliance.
acquiescent, *a.* ak-we-*es*-ent, resting satisfied; acquiescing.
acquiescently, *ad.* in an acquiescent manner.
acquirability, *n.* a-*kwire*-ra-*bil*-e-te, the state of being acquirable.
acquirable, *a.* a-*kwire*-ra-bl, that may be acquired.
acquire, *v.t.* a-*kwire*, to become possessed of, esp. through one's own exertions or capabilities. (L. *acquirĕre*, obtain.)
acquired, *a.* gained by oneself, not originally bestowed by nature.
acquirement, *n.* the act of acquiring, or that which is acquired; attainment.
acquisition, *n.* ak-wi-*zish*-on, the act of acquiring; the thing acquired. (L. *acquisitio*, act of acquiring.)
acquisitive, *a.* a-*kwiz*-i-tiv, capable or desirous of making acquisitions; greedily disposed.
acquisitively, *ad.* in an acquisitive manner: **by way of gain.**
acquisitiveness, *n.* the quality of being acquisitive; an inordinate or morbid desire to acquire property.
acquit, *v.t.* a-*kwit*, to set free or release from an obligation, charge, or suspicion; to declare not guilty [Law]. (O.Fr. *aquiter*, satisfy a demand.)
acquittal, *n.* deliverance from a charge, debt, or obligation; a judicial discharge.
acquittance, *n.* a discharge from a debt; vindication; the act of releasing; receipt barring further demand. (O.Fr. *aquitance*, an acquittal.)
Acraniates, *n.pl.* ay-*kray*-ne-ayts, the lancelets, a group of skull-less vertebrates. [Zool.]. (Gr. *a*-, not, and *kranion*, skull.)
acre, *n.* *ay*-ker, a measure of land containing 160 square rods or perches, or 4,840 square yards. **God's acre,** the churchyard. (A.S. *æcer*, field.)
acreable, *a.* *ay*-ker-a-bl, of an acre; per acre.
acreage, *n.* *ay*-ker-aj, sum of acres in a piece of land.
acred, *a.* *ay*-kerd, possessing acres or land in comb., as a many-*acred* man.
acrid, *a.* *ak*-rid, sharp or biting to the taste; pungent; bitter; corrosive; extremely acrimonious. (L. *acer*, *acris*, sharp.)
acridly, *ad.* in an acrid manner.
acridian, *n.* a-*krid*-i-an, an insect of the locust family. (Gr. *akridion*, little locust.)
acridity, *n.* ak-*rid*-i-te, corrosive or inflammatory bitterness; acridness.
acridness, *n.* *ak*-rid-nes, the quality of being acrid.
acrimonious, *a.* ak-ri-*moh*-ne-us, characterized by acrimony.
acrimoniously, *ad.* in an acrimonious manner.
acrimoniousness, *n.* the state or quality of being acrimonious.
acrimony, *n.* *ak*-ri-mo-ne, sharpness or severity of manner or temper; bitterness of language. (O.Fr. *acrimoine*, keenness.)
Acrita, *n.pl.* *ak*-re-ta, former zoological group comprising animals (sponges, polyps, etc.) difficult to differentiate from plants. (Gr. *akritos*, confused.)
acritical, *a.* ay-*krit*-e-kal, not having, or not manifesting, a crisis [Med.]. (Gr.)
acritude, *n.* *ak*-re-tewd, acridity.
acro-, *ak*-ro, *pref.*, used in combination to signify position in regard to the culmination of anything. (Gr. *akros*, topmost point.)
acroamatic, *a.* ak-ro-a-*mat*-ik, esoteric, abstruse; applied in the school of Aristotle to instruction fit only for the ear of the initiated, and not committed to writing. (Gr. *akroamatikos*, intended solely for hearing.)
acroatic, *a.* and *n.* ak-ro-*at*-ik, acroamatic.
acrobat, *n.* *ak*-ro-bat, a gymnast; a tumbler; a contortionist; a rope-dancer. (Fr. *acrobate*.)
acrobatic, *a.* ak-ro-*bat*-ik, pertaining to the feats of an acrobat, or to acrobatics.
acrobatics, *n.* ak-ro-*bat*-iks, the art of an acrobat; aerobatics [Slang].
acrocarpous, *a.* *ak*-ro-*kahr*-pus, bearing fruit to the top of the main stem (esp. of mosses) [Bot.]. (Gr. *akros*, top, *karpus*, fruit.)
acrocephalic, *a.* *ak*-ro-se-*fal*-ik, pyramidal-skulled [Ethn.] (Gr. *akros*, and *kephale*, the head.)
acrogen, *n.* *ak*-ro-jen, a cryptogamic plant which grows mainly by increase in length [Bot.]. (Gr. *akros*, and *gennao*, produce.)
acrogenous, *a.* a-*kroj*-e-nus, of the nature of an acrogen; increasing at the top.
acrography, a-*krog*-ra-fe, the art or process of making designs in relief on metal or stone for reproduction.
acrolith, *n.* *ak*-ro-lith, a statue of which only the head and extremities are of stone [Sculp.]. (Gr. *akro*, and *lithos*, a stone.)
acrolithan, *a.* a-*krol*-e-than, formed in the manner of an acrolith.
acromegaly, *n.* ak-ro-*meg*-a-le, morbid enlargement or over-development of the extremities of the body. (Gr. *akros*, and *megale*, large.)
acronical, *a.* ay-*kron*-i-kal, of the rising of a star at sunset, or its setting at sunrise; opposed to cosmical [Astron.]. (Gr. *akronuchos*, nightfall.)
acronically, *ad.* in an acronical manner; at sunset.
acropetal, *a.* a-*krop*-e-tal, developing in an upward direction; in the direction of the apex. (Gk. *akron*, a height, and L. *petere*, to seek.)
acrophobia, *n.* ak-ro-*foh*-bi-a, fear of being at a height [Path.].

acropolis, *n.* a-*krop*-o-lis, a citadel, particularly that of Athens. (Gr. *akropolis*, upper-city.)
acroscopic, *a.* ak-ro-*skop*-ik, looking towards the apex [Bot.].
acrospire, *n. ak*-ro-spire, first sprout of a seed, especially of barley. (Gr. *akro*, and *speira*, a spiral.)
★**across,** *ad.* or *prep.* a-*kros*, from side to side; opposed to along; passing over at any angle; contrarily; in opposition. **to put it across,** to make one's point; to delude or impose on; to get even with (one).
acrostic, *n.* a-*kros*-tik, a verse composition in which the first letters of the lines, taken in order, form a word or words; a psalm, like the CXIX, in which the successive stanzas commence with successive letters of the Hebrew alphabet: *a.* relating to, or containing an acrostic. (Gr. *akrostichis*, acrostic.)
acrostically, *ad.* as an acrostic.
acroter, *n.* a-*kroh*-ter, an acroterium.
acroterial, *a.* ak-ro-*teer*-e-al, pertaining to an acroterium.
acroterium, *n.* ak-ro-*teer*-i-um (*pl.* **acroteria,** ak-ro-*teer*-i-a), a pedestal at the middle and extremities of a pediment to support a statue or another ornament; a figure so supported [Arch.]. (Gr. *akroterion*, the extreme point.)
acrotomous, *a.* a-*krot*-o-mus, having a cleavage parallel with the top of a crystal [Min.]. (Gr. *akrotomos*, sharply cut off.)
★**act,** *v.i.* akt, to be in action or motion; to exert power; to produce effects; to operate; to perform; to behave: *v.t.* to perform; to play the part of: *n.* action; performance; a deed; a state of reality, as opposed to possibility; a main division of a play; a law made by a legislative body; a decree; an edict; a document proving the truth of some transaction [Law]; a thesis maintained in public by a candidate for a degree. **act of God,** an uncontrollable natural occurrence such as an earthquake [Law]. **act of grace,** a special extension of clemency or pardon to an offender. **act of indemnity,** an act absolving one from penalties incurred through acting illegally in pursuance of his duties. **act up to,** to be equal to in action. (Fr. *acte*, act.)
acta, *n.pl. ak*-ta, acts; accounts of acts [Law]. **Acta Sanctorum,** accounts of the lives of Christian saints and martyrs begun by Bollandists in 1643; the acts of the saints.
acting, *a. ak*-ting, in actual discharge of the duties of an office: *n.* action; performance of an assumed or dramatic part.
Actinia, *n.* ak-*tin*-e-a, a genus of sea-anemones.
actinic, *a.* ak-*tin*-ik, pertaining to rays, esp. the chemical rays of the sun.
actiniform, *a.* ak-*tin*-i-fawrm, in radiated shape.
actinism, *n. ak*-ti-nizm, the chemical, as distinct from the illuminating and heating, property of the sun's rays. (Gr. *aktis*, *aktinos*, a ray.)
actinium, *n.* ak-*tin*-e-um, a rare radioactive element formed from protoactinium by loss of an alpha-particle.
actinograph, *n.* ak-*tin*-o-graf, an instrument for measuring and registering actinic effects. (Gr. *aktinos*, and *grapho*, to write.)
actinolite, *n.* ak-*tin*-o-lite, a greenish variety of amphibole. (Gr. *aktinos*, and *lithos*, stone.)
actinolitic, *a.* ak-tin-o-*lit*-ik, pertaining to actinolite.
actinology, *n.* ak-tin-*ol*-o-je, the science of actinism.
actinometer, *n.* ak-tin-*om*-e-ter, an instrument for measuring the heating power of the sun's rays; also one for measuring actinic radiations. (Gr. *aktinos*, and *metron*, a measure.)
actinomycosis, *n.* ak-tin-o-my-*koh*-sis, an infective disease of cattle and humans, due to certain parasitical fungi; potato scab.
actinon, *n. ak*-ti-non, a heavy, gaseous, radioactive element of the actinium group.
actino-therapy, *n.* the treatment of disease by light rays, usually ultra-violet.
Actinozoa, *n.* ak-tin-o-*zoh*-a, a group of animals including the sea-anemones and coral polypes.
action, *n. ak*-shon, the state of acting or being active; operation; a deed; conduct; behaviour; gesture in speaking; a battle; a suit or process [Law]; the normal or abnormal performance of the function of an organ [Physiol.]; the movements of a horse; the mechanism of a keyed musical instrument; the series of events in a piece, the subject or fable [Poet.]; the expressive attitude or position of the several parts of the body in a work of art. [Paint. and Sculp.]. (Fr. *action*.)
actionable, *a.* affording opportunity for an action at law.
actionably, *ad.* in a manner that subjects to legal process.
activate, *v.t. ak*-te-vate, to make active; to render radio-active.
activation, *n.* ak-te-*vay*-shon, the action of activating or state of being activated; the treatment of sewage by aeration and chemical ferment.
active, *a. ak*-tiv, having the power of acting; quick of movement; agile; busy, or constantly engaged in action; vigorous; assiduous; requiring action or exertion; practical, as opposed to speculative; quick in operating [Med.]; implying action [Gram.]. (Fr. *actif*.)
actively, *ad.* in an active manner or sense.
activeness, *n.* the quality or state of being active.
activism, *n. ak*-ti-vizm, the advocacy of action or of an active policy.
activity, *n.* ak-*tiv*-e-te, activeness; physical motion; energetic action; an instance of being active; rate of acting [Chem.].
acton, *n. ak*-ton, a padded jerkin, worn under a coat of mail; a steel-covered jacket. (O.Fr. *auqueton*, a stuffed jacket.)
actor, *n. ak*-tor, he who acts; a stage-player.
actress, *n. ak*-tress, a female actor.
actual, *a. ak*-tew-al, real; existing in act or fact; existing at present. (Fr. *actuel*.)
actualism, *n.* the doctrine that existence is active or spiritual, not inert or dead [Phil.].
actualist, *n.* one who deals only with the real, as opposed to the ideal; an adherent of actualism.
actuality, *n.* ak-tew-*al*-e-te, the state of being actual; reality; realism.
actualization, *n. ak*-tew-a-ly-*zay*-shon, making actual.
actualize, *v.t. ak*-tew-a-lyz, to make actual; to describe or depict realistically.
actually, *ad.* really; as a fact.
actuarial, *a.* ak-tew-*air*-re-al, pertaining to an actuary or his profession.
actuary, *n. ak*-tew-a-re, a registrar, or clerk of a court; one skilled in statistics, esp. those connected with insurance. (L. *actuarius*, book-keeper.)
actuate, *v.t. ak*-tew-ate, to move or incite to action; to influence. (L. *actuatus*, moved.)
actuation, *n.* ak-tew-*ay*-shon, state of being actuated; a putting in action; operation.
acuity, *n.* a-*kew*-e-te, acuteness, of wit; sharpness, of a needle. (Fr. *acuité*, keenness.)
Aculeata, *n.* a-*kew*-le-*ah*-ta, a sub-order of Hymenoptera, embracing the ants, bees, and wasps. (L. *acus*, a needle.)
aculeate, *a.* a-*kew*-le-ate, having prickles or a sting [Bot. and Zool.]; incisive.
aculeiform, *a.* a-*kew*-le-e-fawrm, prickle-shaped.
aculeus, *n.* a-*kew*-le-us, a prickle, as in the blackberry [Bot.]; a sting [Zool.]. (L. *aculeus*, a sting.)
acumen, *n.* a-*kew*-men, keenness and quickness of perception. (L. *acumen*, a sharpened point.)
acuminate, *a.* a-*kew*-me-nate, sharpened to a tapering point [Bot.].
acuminated, *a.* a-*kew*-me-nay-ted, acuminate.
acumination, *n.* a-kew-me-*nay*-shon, act of sharpening; a point produced by this. (L. *acuminatus*, sharpened.)
acuminous, *a.* a-*kew*-me-nus, possessing acumen; acuminate [Bot.].
acupressure, *n.* ak-ew-*presh*-ur, the checking of hæmorrhage in arteries during an operation by compressing instead of tying their orifices [Surg.]. (L. *acus*, a needle, and *pressum*, press.)
acupuncturation, *n. ak*-ew-*punk*-tew-*ray*-shon, acupuncture.
acupuncture, *n.* ak-ew-*punk*-tewr, the operation of pricking tissues with needles [Surg.]. (L. *acus*, and *punctūra*, a puncture.)
acushla, *n.* a-*koosh*-lah, darling, an Irish term of endearment.
acute, *a.* a-*kewt*, sharp-pointed; keen and penetrating; having nice or quick sensibility; sharp or high as opposed to grave [Mus.]; elevation of the voice [Rhet.]; an acute accent, marked thus (′); attended with symptoms of severity, opposed to

chronic [Med.]; less than a right angle [Math.]. (L. *acūtus*, sharpened.)
acutely, *ad.* in an acute manner.
acuteness, *n.* the quality of being acute.
acutifoliate, *a.* a-kew-ti-*foh*-li-ate, with sharp-pointed leaves [Bot.]. (L. *acus*, and *folium*, a leaf.)
acyclic, ay-*sik*-lik, having leaves arranged spirally on flower receptacles [Bot.]. (Gr. *a*-, and *kyklos*, circle.)
ad, *n.* ad, an advertisement [Slang].
ad-, a Latin prefix signifying to, at, or into.
adactylous, *a.* a-*dak*-ti-lus, having no fingers or toes [Zool.]. (Gr. *a*-, and *daktylos*, a finger.)
adage, *n. ad*-aj, an old saying. (Fr. *adage*, proverb.)
adagial, *a.* a-*day*-ji-al, full of adages; proverbial.
adagio, *n.* a-*dah*-ji-oh, a slow movement: *ad.* slowly, and with grace [Mus.]. (It. *adagio*, softly.)
Adam, *n. ad*-am, the name (in *Genesis*) of the first man. **Adam's ale,** water [Coll.]. **Adam's apple,** the projection in front of the throat formed by the thyroid cartilage. **Adam's needle,** the yucca. **the old Adam,** the unregenerate state of man; original sin. (Heb., man.)
adamant, *n. ad*-a-mant, a substance of extreme hardness; the diamond; the loadstone. (O.Fr.)
adamantean, *a.* ad-a-man-*tee*-an, adamantine; extremely hard.
adamantine, *a.* ad-a-*man*-tine, made of or hard as adamant; that cannot be broken or penetrated. (L. *adamantinus*, hard as steel.)
Adamic, *a.* a-*dam*-ik, pertaining to or resembling Adam.
Adamite, *n. ad*-a-mite, a descendant of Adam; one of an early sect members of which claimed innocence and went naked [Eccl. Hist.].
Adamitism, *n. ad*-a-my-tizm, the doctrines of the sect of Adamites.
adapt, *v.t.* a-*dapt*, to make to fit or suitable for; to accommodate. (Fr. *adapter*, fit.)
adaptability, *n.* a-*dap*-ta-*bil*-e-te, quality of being adaptable; capability of adaptation.
adaptable, *a.* a-*dap*-ta-bl, that may be adapted.
adaptation, *n.* ad-ap-*tay*-shon, act of making, or state of being suitable; that which is adapted; the process by which the eye accustoms itself to variable light; modification in animals or plants to fit them better for conditions of life [Biol.].
adaptedness, *n.* a-*dap*-ted-nes, the state of being adapted; suitability.
adapter, *n.* one adapting (in any way) anything; a connecting part in various scientific instruments and apparatus; a device enabling a camera to take plates or films of varying sizes.
adaptive, *a.* a-*dap*-tiv, characterized by or tending to adaptation.
adaptively, *adv.* in an adaptive manner.
adaptiveness, *n.* the quality of being adaptive; tendency to make adaptations.
Adar, *n. ay*-dar, the twelfth month of the Hebrew sacred year, covering parts of February and March.
add, *v.t.* ad, to join on; to sum up; to increase; to subjoin. (L. *addere*, lay on.)
adda, *n. ad*-dah, the common skink (*Scincus officinalis*) of North Africa and Syria.
addable, *a. ad*-abl, incorrect form of **addible.**
addax, *n. ad*-aks, a maned antelope of North Africa, Arabia, and Syria.
addeem, *v.t.* a-*deem*, to award or adjudge; to consider. (*ad-* and *deem*).
addendum, *n.* a-*den*-dum (*pl.* **addenda,** a-*den*-da), a thing to be added; an appendix. (L. *addendere.*)
adder, *n. ad*-er, a viper, the only venomous snake in Britain, *Vipera berus.* (A.S. *nædre*, a snake.)
adder, *n. ad*-er, one who adds; an adding-machine.
adder-fly, *n.* the dragon-fly.
adder-pike, *n.* a fish, the viper-weever.
adder's-grass, *n.* the early purple orchis, *Orchis mascula.*
adder-stone, *n.* any stone popularly believed to be efficacious against snake-bite.
adder's-tongue, *n.* any fern of the genus *Ophioglossum*, so called from the appearance of its fructification.
addibility, *n.* ad-e-*bil*-e-te, the possibility of being added.
addible, *a. ad*-e-bl, that may be added.
addict, *v.t.* a-*dikt*, reflectively, to give oneself up to, usually in a bad sense; to habituate. (L. *addictus*, assented to.)
addict, *n. ad*-dikt, one addicted to a habit, as drug addict.
addictedness, *n.* a-*dikt*-ed-nes, the state or quality of being addicted.
addiction, *n.* a-*dik*-shon, addictedness; propensity.
★**addition,** *n.* a-*dish*-on, the act or process of adding; anything added; an accession; the uniting of two or more numbers into one sum; the branch of arithmetic which treats of adding; a title annexed to a man's name, to show his rank, occupation, etc. [Law]; a dot at the right side of a note, to lengthen its sound one half [Mus.]; anything added as an indication of honour [Her.]. (Fr. *addition.*)
additional, *a.* that is added; supplementary: *n.* anything added.
additionally, *ad.* in addition to.
additive, *a. ad*-i-tiv, that may be added.
addle, *v.t.* adl, to make corrupt; to muddle.
addled, *a. ad*-dld, rotten, applied to eggs that can yield no chick; non-productive; barren. (A.S. *adela*, filth.)
addle-headed, *a.* muddled.
addlement, *n.* state or process of being addled or of addling.
addle-pated, *a.* having barren or weak brains.
addorsed, *a.* a-*dawrst*, having the backs turned to each other [Her.]. (L. *ad.* and *dorsum*, the back.)
address, *v.t.* a-*dres*, to direct; to speak or write to; to direct in writing, as a letter; to make suit as a lover; to consign; to get ready: *n.* a discourse; a written speech; a message of respect; formal application or communication in writing; direction of a letter; manners; adroitness: *pl.* attentions of a lover. (Fr. *adresser*, send or speak *direct* to.)
addressee, *n.* ad-dres-*ee*, one addressed in a letter.
addresser, *n.* a-*dres*-er, one who addresses.
addressograph, *n.* a-*dres*-o-graf, the trade-name of a machine for addressing letters, etc.
adduce, *v.t.* a-*dewce*, to bring forward by way of proof; to cite. (L. *adduco*, lead forth.)
adducent, *a.* a-*dew*-sent, applied to those muscles of the body which bring forward or draw together the parts to which they are attached [Anat.].
adducer, *n.* one who adduces.
adducible, *a.* a-*dew*-se-bl, that may be adduced.
adduction, *n.* a-*duk*-shon, the act of bringing forward, drawing together, or citing.
adductive, *a.* a-*duk*-tiv, tending to adduce.
adductor, *n.* a muscle which draws one part of the body towards another [Anat.].
adeem, *v.t.* a-*deem*, to cancel a bequest [Law]. (L. *ad-*, to, and *emere*, take.)
adelphous, *a.* a-*del*-fus, having the stamens collected into a bundle [Bot.]. (Gr. *adelphos*, a brother.)
ademption, *n.* a-*demp*-shon, the revocation of a grant or bequest [Law]. (L. *ademptio*, a taking away.)
adenalgia, *n.* ad-en-*al*-je-a, pain seated in a gland. (Gr. *adēn*, gland, *algos*, pain.)
adeniform, *a.* a-*den*-i-fawrm, gland-like, gland-shaped. (Gr. *adēn*, gland, and *form.*)
adenitis, *n.* ad-en-ny-tis, inflammation of a gland.
adenography, *n.* ad-en-*og*-ra-fe, the part of anatomy which treats of the glands.
adenoid, *a. ad*-en-oid, glandiform.
adenoids, *n.pl. ad*-en-oidz, enlargement of the adenoid tissue between the nose and throat.
adenology, *n.* ad-en-*ol*-o-je, the branch of physiology treating of the glands, their nature and uses. (Gr. *aden*, and *logos*, word.)
adenoma, *n.* ad-e-*noh*-ma, a non-malignant tumour in or resembling glandular tissue [Med.]. (Gr. *aden*, and *oma*, tissue.)
adenophore, *n. ad*-en-o-fohr, the stalk of a nectar gland [Bot.].
adenose, *a. ad*-en-ohs, glandulous; abounding in glands.
adenotomy, *n.* ad-e-*not*-o-me, a cutting or incision of a gland. (Gr. *adēn*, and *tomē*, cutting.)
adeps, *n. ad*-eps, animal fat. (L.)
adept, *n. ad*-ept, one fully skilled in any art: *a.* a-*dept*, well skilled. (L. *adeptus*, attained.)
adequacy, *n. ad*-e-kwa-se, adequateness; a sufficiency for a particular purpose.
adequate, *a. ad*-e-kwate, equal to; proportionate fully sufficient. (L. *adæquatus*, made equal to.)
adequately, *ad.* in an adequate manner.
adequateness, *n.* the state of being adequate; sufficiency.

adespota, *n.pl.* ad-*es*-po-ta, writings the authorship of which is unknown. (Gr. *a-*, *despotēs*, master.)
adfected, *a.* ad-*fekt*-ed, made up of different powers of an unknown quantity [Alg.]. (L. *affectus*, put to.)
adhere, *v.i.* ad-*heer*, to stick to; to remain firmly attached to. (L. *adhærere*, stick to.)
adherence, *n.* ad-*heer*-ens, the quality or state of adhering; steady attachment.
adherency, *n.* ad-*heer*-en-se, adherence.
adherent, *a.* sticking to; united with: *n.* a follower; a partisan.
adherently, *adv.* in an adherent manner.
adherer, *n.* an adherent.
adhesion, *n.* ad-*hee*-zhon, the act or state of adhering; adherence; steady attachment; the tendency of two surfaces to remain attached when in contact [Physics]; the union through inflammation of injured surfaces by formation of new tissue [Med.]. (L. *adhaesio*, a cleaving.)
adhesive, *a.* ad-*hee*-siv, sticking; tenacious: *n.* an adhesive substance; a postage-stamp with gummed back.
adhesively, *ad.* in an adhesive manner.
adhesiveness, *n.* power or state of being adhesive; stickiness; propensity to form attachments.
adhibit, *v.t.* ad-*hib*-it, to apply; to attach. (L. *adhibitus*, held to.)
adhibition, *n.* ad-hib-*ish*-on, act of applying; use.
adiabatic, *a.* ad-e-a-*bat*-ik, impervious, esp. in relation to changes in pressure or volume unaccompanied by gain or loss of heat [Phys.]; remaining at constant temperature. (Gr. *adiabatos*, impassable.)
adiactinic, *a.* a-de-ak-*tin*-ik, impervious to actinic rays [Opt.]. (Gr. *a-*, *dia-*, through, and *aktis*, a ray.)
adiantum, *n.* *ad*-e-*an*-tum, a maidenhair fern. (Gr. *adiantos*, dry—from its habitat.)
adiaphoresis, *n.* ay-dy-af-o-*ree*-sis, absence or deficiency of perspiration [Med.]. (Gr. *a-*, and *diaphorein*, to perspire.)
adiaphorism, *n.* ad-e-*af*-o-rizm, religious indifference; latitudinarianism.
adiaphorous, *a.* ay-dy-*af*-o-rus, immaterial; non-essential. (Gr. *adiaphoros*, not different.)
adiathermic, *a.* ay-dy-a-*ther*-mik, not transmitting radiant heat [Physics]. (Gr. *a-*, not, *dia-*, through, *therma*, heat.)
adieu, *ad.* a-*dew*, farewell; good-bye: *n.* a farewell. (Fr. *à Dieu*, I entrust you to God.)
adipescent, *a.* ad-e-*pes*-ent, becoming fatty. (L. *adeps*, fat.)
adipic, *a.* a-*dip*-ik, pertaining to or derived from fat. **adipic acid,** a compound formed by the action of nitric acid on fats. (L. *adeps*.)
adipocere, *n.* *ad*-e-po-*seer*, a fatty spermaceti-like substance, such as is produced from the decomposition of animal matter when buried in humid places; fatty mineral matter found in argillaceous iron ore [Min.]. (Fr. *adipocire*.)
adipocerous, *a.* ad-e-*pos*-er-us, containing or of the nature of adipocere.
adipose, *a.* *ad*-e-pohs, consisting of or containing fat: *n.* animal fat. (L. *adiposus*, fatty.)
adiposity, *n.* ad-e-*pos*-e-te, the state or quality of being fat; fatness.
adipsia, *n.* a-*dip*-se-a, absence of thirst [Med.].
adit, *n.* *ad*-it, a horizontal or inclined passage to or from a mine [Mining]. (L. *aditus*, access.)
adjacency, *n.* ad-*jay*-sen-se, state of being adjacent to; that which is adjacent.
adjacent, *a.* ad-*jay*-sent, lying near to or contiguous; bordering on. (L. *adjacens*, lying near.)
adjacently, *ad.* ad-*jay*-sent-le, so as to be adjacent.
adject, *v.t.* ad-*jekt*, to annex or join to. (L. *ad-*, to, *jectus*, thrown.)
adjectival, *a.* ad-jek-*ty*-val, like or pertaining to an adjective.
adjectivally, *ad.* adjectively.
adjective, *n.* *ad*-jek-tiv, a word which qualifies, defines, or particularizes a noun [Gram.]: *a.* pertaining to an adjective; fixable by some base or mordant so as to become permanent [Dyeing]. (Fr. *adjectif*.)
adjectively, *ad.* *ad*-jek-tiv-le, as an adjective; in an adjectival manner.
adjoin, *v.i.* ad-*joyn*, to lie next to; to be contiguous. (O.Fr. *adjoindre*, adjoin.)
adjoining, *a.* ad-*joyn*-ing, adjacent.
adjourn, *v.t.* ad-*jurn*, to put off to another time; to postpone. (O.Fr. *ajorner*, to dawn.)
adjournment, *n.* ad-*jurn*-ment, the putting off till another time; the interval which elapses in adjourning; postponement.
adjudge, *v.t.* ad-*judj*, to determine or award; to sentence judicially. (O.Fr. *ajuger*, to judge.)
adjudgment, *or* **adjudgement,** *n.* ad-*judj*-ment, the act of adjudging; the decision.
adjudicate, *v.t.* ad-*joo*-de-kate, to judge; to determine: *v.i.* to pronounce judgment; to determine judicially. (L. *adiudicatum*, adjudged.)
adjudication, *n.* ad-joo-de-*kay*-shon, the act of adjudging; judgment or decision of a court.
adjudicator, *n.* ad-*joo*-de-ka-tor, one who adjudicates.
adjunct, *a.* *ad*-junkt, conjoined or united with: *n.* something united to another, but not essentially part of it; an attribute of the body or mind, whether natural or acquired [Met.]; word added to illustrate or amplify the force of others [Gram.].
adjunction, *n.* ad-*junk*-shon, the act of joining; the thing joined.
adjunctive, *a.* ad-*junk*-tiv, joining; having the quality of joining: *n.* one who or that which is joined.
adjunctively, *ad.* ad-*junk*-tiv-le, as an adjunctive.
adjunctly, *ad.* *ad*-junkt-le, by way of adjunct; connected with.
adjuration, *n.* ad-joo-*ra*-shon, act of adjuring; form of oath proposed; a solemn entreaty. (L. *adiuratio*, adjuration.)
adjuratory, *a.* ad-*joo*-ra-tor-e, containing or pertaining to an adjuration; solemnly urging.
adjure, *v.t.* ad-*joor*, to charge on pain of God's wrath; to urge with solemnity. (L. *adiuro*, swear to.)
adjust, *v.t.* ad-*just*, to fit; to adapt; to put in order; to settle satisfactorily. (O.Fr. *adjuster*.)
adjustable, *a.* ad-*just*-a-bl, that may be adjusted.
adjuster, *n.* ad-*just*-er, one who adjusts.
adjustive, *a.* ad-*just*-iv, serving to adjust.
★**adjustment,** *n.* ad-*just*-ment, the act of adjusting; arrangement; settlement.
adjutage, *n.* *ad*-joo-taj, a tube fitted to the mouth of a vessel through which water is played. (Fr. *ajoutage*, tube.)
adjutancy, *n.* *ad*-joo-tan-se, the office or rank of an adjutant.
adjutant, *n.* *ad*-joo-tant, an assistant; a regimental officer who assists the commanding officer in details of duty and discipline, etc. (L. *adiutantem*, assisting.)
adjutant-bird, *n.* *ad*-joo-tant-berd, an Indian stork, *Leptoptilus dubius*, protected as a scavenger.
adjuvant, *a.* *ad*-joo-vant, helping: *n.* an assistant; an ingredient added to a prescription to aid its action [Med.]. (L. *adiuvans*, helping.)
adlegation, *n.* ad-le-*gay*-shon, the right formerly claimed by the several states of the Holy Roman Empire of participating in Imperial decisions. (L. *ad*, and *legatio*, an embassy.)
admeasure, *v.t.* ad-*mezh*-ur, to ascertain measurments; to apportion [Law]. (O.Fr. *amesurer*, to measure up.)
admeasurement, *n.* ad-*mezh*-ur-ment, the measuring of dimensions by a rule; the dimension ascertained; the apportionment of shares [Law].
adminicle, *n.* ad-*min*-i-kl, that which aids; additional or interpretative evidence [Law].
adminicular, *a.* ad-min-*ik*-yew-lar, helping; helpful. (L. *adminiculum*, a prop.)
adminiculate, *v.t.* and *v.i.* ad-min-*ik*-yew-late, to add corroborative testimony.
administer, *v.t.* ad-*min*-is-ter, to manage as minister or agent; to direct the execution or application of laws; to supply; to dispense; to tender, as an oath; to prescribe: *v.i.* to act as an administrator; to bring aid or supplies. (O.Fr. *aministrer*, serve.)
administrable, *a.* ad-*min*-is-tra-bl, capable of administration.
administrant, *n.* ad-*min*-ist-rant, one who administers.
administrate, *v.t.* ad-*min*-ist-rate, to administer.
administration, *n.* ad-min-is-*tray*-shon, the act of administering or conducting any office or employment; the executive or administrative power or body; dispensation; the power, office, or commission of an administrator. (L. *administratio*, aid.)

administrative, *a.* ad-*min*-is-tra-tiv, that administers, or by which one administers; executive. (L. *administrativus*, practical.)
administratively, *ad.* ad-*min*-is-tra-tiv-le, in an administrative manner.
administrator, *n.* ad-*min*-is-tray-tor, one who directs, manages, or dispenses; one who administers the estate of an intestate. (L. *administrator*, manager.)
administratorship, *n.* ad-min-is-*tray*-tor-ship, the office of an administrator.
administratrix, *n.* ad-min-is-*tray*-triks, a woman who administers.
admirable, *a.* *ad*-me-ra-bl, having qualities to excite admiration; excellent.
admirableness, *n.* *ad*-me-ra-bl-ness, the quality of being admirable.
admirably, *ad.* *ad*-me-rab-le, in an admirable manner.
admiral, *n.* *ad*-me-ral, the chief commander of a fleet or of one of its main divisions: formerly also the ship of the admiral; a gastropod mollusc of the genus *Conus* [Zool.]; a species of butterfly [Entom.]. **Lord High Admiral,** in Great Britain, an officer who formerly superintended all naval affairs, now replaced by the Lords Commissioners of the Admiralty. **Admiral of the Fleet,** the highest rank in the Royal Navy. **vice-admiral,** an officer next in rank below an admiral. **rear-admiral,** an officer next below a vice-admiral. (O.Fr. *amiral*, a naval commander, from the Arabic, *amīr-al-bahr*, prince or commander of the sea.)
admiralty, *n.* *ad*-me-ral-te, the office or jurisdiction of an admiral; the board administering British naval affairs (under the **Lords Commissioners of the Admiralty**); the building in which its business is transacted. **Admiralty Court,** the supreme court for the trial of maritime causes. (O.Fr. *amiralle*, office of admiral.)
admiration, *n.* ad-me-*ray*-shon, the act of admiring; wonder. (Fr. *admiration*.)
admirative, *a.* *ad*-me-ra-tiv, expressing admiration.
admire, *v.t.* ad-*mire*, to regard with pleasure; to have a high opinion of: *v.i.* to feel admiration; to wonder. (Fr. *admirer*, to admire.)
admired, *a.* ad-*mired*, highly regarded.
admirer, *n.* ad-*mire*-er, one who admires; a lover.
admiring, *a.* ad-*mire*-ing, thinking highly of.
admiringly, *ad.* ad-*mire*-ing-le, with admiration.
admissibility, *n.* ad-mis-se-*bil*-e-te, the quality of being admissible.
admissible, *a.* ad-*mis*-se-bl, that may be admitted.
admissibly, *ad.* ad-*mis*-se-ble, so as to be admitted.
admission, *n.* ad-*mish*-on, the act of admitting; the state of being admitted; permission to enter; concession in argument; acknowledgment.
admissive, *a.* ad-*mis*-siv, of the nature of or implying admission; tending to admit.
admissory, *a.* ad-*mis*-o-re, pertaining to admission.
admit, *v.t.* ad-*mit*, to suffer to enter; to grant entrance into a place, an office, or the mind; to allow as valid; to concede as true; to acknowledge. (L. *admittere*, admit.)
admittable, *a.* ad-*mit*-a-bl, that may be admitted.
admittably, *ad.* ad-*mit*-a-ble, admittedly.
admittance, *n.* ad-*mit*-tans, the act of admitting; leave to enter; admission.
admittedly, *ad.* ad-*mit*-ed-le, accepted as correct.
admix, *v.t.* ad-miks, to mingle with something else.
admixture, *n.* ad-*miks*-tewr, the act of mixing; compound formed by mixing; substance added in mixing. (L. *admixtus*, mixed.)
admonish, *v.t.* ad-*mon*-ish, to reprove with mildness; to warn; to exhort. (O.Fr. *amonester*, to warn.)
admonishment, *n.* ad-*mon*-ish-ment, act of admonishing; admonition.
admonition, *n.* ad-mo-*nish*-on, gentle reproof; friendly counsel; caution. (O.Fr.)
admonitive, *a.* ad-*mon*-e-tiv, containing or implying admonition.
admonitively, *ad.* ad-*mon*-e-tiv-le, by admonition.
admonitor, *n.* ad-*mon*-e-tor, one who admonishes.
admonitorial, *a.* ad-mon-e-*taw*-re-al, admonishing.
admonitory, *a.* ad-*mon*-e-to-re, that admonishes.
admortization, *n.* ad-mort-e-*zay*-shon, amortization.
adnascent, *a.* ad-*nass*-ent, growing on to. (L. *adnascens*, growing to.)
adnate, *a.* *ad*-nate, growing to by its whole length [Anat. and Bot.]. (L. *adnatus*, grown to.)
adnation, *n.* ad-*nay*-shon, the state of being adnate.
adnominal, *a.* ad-*nom*-in-al, adjectival; relating to a noun. (L. *agnomen*, surname.)
adnoun, *n.* *ad*-noun, an adjective, when used as a noun; an attribute of a noun.
ado, *n.* a-*doo*, to-do; fuss; bustle; difficulty. (Scand. *at*, meaning *to* with the infinitive, and *do*.)
adobe, *n.* a-*doh*-be, a brick dried by the sun: *a.* made or built of such bricks. (Sp. *adobe*, an unburnt brick.)
adolescence, *n.* ad-o-*less*-ens, the period between childhood and manhood or womanhood.
adolescency, *n.* ad-o-*less*-en-se, adolescence.
adolescent, *a.* ad-o-*less*-ent, advancing to maturity: *n.* a person in the adolescent stage. (L. *adolescens*, growing up.)
Adonean, *a.* a-*doh*-ne-an, pertaining to Adonis.
Adonic, *a.* a-*don*-ik, Adonean: *n.* a species of short verse, first used in a dirge for Adonis. (Fr. *adonique*.)
Adonis, *n.* a-*doh*-nis, a youth beloved by Venus, who, having received a mortal wound from a boar while hunting, was changed by her into the flower, *Adonis autumnalis*, the pheasant's eye, or bird's eye; hence, a beautiful or dandified youth. (Gr.)
adopt, *v.t.* a-*dopt*, to receive and regard as one's own, esp. of a child, heir, candidate, etc.; to embrace some principle or cause, etc. (L. *adopto* choose.)
adoptable, *a.* a-*dopt*-a-bl, fit to be adopted.
adoptedly, *ad.* a-*dopt*-ed-le, by adoption.
adoption, *n.* a-*dop*-shon, the act of adopting; admission to the rights and privileges of a family.
Adoptionism, *n.* a-*dop*-shon-izm, the early heretical doctrine that Jesus Christ, born a mere man, became the Son of God by divine adoption.
adoptive, *a.* a-*dop*-tiv, that adopts or is adopted; fitted to adopt; by reason of adoption.
adoptively, *ad.* in an adoptive manner.
adorable, *a.* a-*dore*-a-bl, that ought to be adored; worthy of highest honours.
adorableness, *n.* a-*dore*-a-bl-ness, the quality of being adorable.
adorably, *ad.* a-*dore*-a-ble, in a manner worthy of adoration. (L. *adorabilis*, worthy of adoration.)
adoral, *a.* ad-*aw*-ral, near the mouth [Anat. and Zool.].
adoration, *n.* ad-or-*ray*-shon, worship or homage; deep regard; homage to one in high station or esteem. (L. *adoratio*, worship.)
adore, *v.t.* a-*dore*, to worship with profound reverence; to love or regard in the highest degree. (L. *adoro*, worship.)
adorer, *n.* a-*dore*-er, an admirer; a worshipper.
adorn, *v.t.* a-*dorn*, to decorate; to embellish; to display the beauty of; to dress. (L. *adorno*, get ready.)
adorning, *n.* a-*dorn*-ing, decoration; adornment.
adornment, *n.* a-*dorn*-ment, ornament; embellishment.
adosculation, *n.* ad-*os*-kew-*lay*-shon, impregnation by external contact only [Bot. and Zool.]; the inserting of one part of a plant into another [Bot.]. (L. *adosculatum*, kiss at.)
adown, *prep.* and *ad.* a-*doun*, down; towards the ground. (A.S. *ofdūne*, down.)
adpressed, *a.* ad-*prest*, rising, as a leaf, parallel and close to the stem [Bot.].
adrenal, *a.* ad-*reen*-al, close to the kidneys. **adrenal glands,** two ductless glands over the kidneys.
adrenalin, *n.* ad-*ren*-al-in, a crystalline compound with stimulating properties prepared from the adrenal glands.
adrift, *a.* and *ad.* a-*drift*, floating at random; cast loose (*a-*, and *drift*, *q.v.*).
adroit, *a.* a-*droit*, expert with the hands; dexterous; skilful. (Fr. *adroit*, ingenious.)
adroitly, *ad.* a-*droit*-le, in an adroit manner.
adroitness, *n.* a-*droit*-ness, the quality of being adroit.
adrue, *n.* ad-*roo*-e, the root of the Guinea rush, used as a stomachic.
adry, *ad.* and *a.* a-*dry*, thirsty.
adscititious, *a.* ad-se-*tish*-us, adopted by way of supplement. (L. *ascitus*, assumed.)
adscript, *n.* *ad*-skript, one held to service, as attached to a place; a serf: *a.* attached to the soil (of serfs). (L. *ascriptum*, inserted in writing.)

adscriptive, *a.* ad-*skrip*-tiv, attached as an adscript.
adsorption, *n.* ad-*sorp*-shon, the adhesion of a gaseous or liquid substance to a solid surface. (L. *ad*, to, *sorbeo*, suck in.)
adularia, *n.* ad-yew-*lare*-e-a, moonstone, a semi-transparent variety of felspar. (*Adula*, Switzerland.)
adulate, *v.t.* *ad*-yew-late, to flatter for a purpose. (L. *adulatus*, fawned like a dog.)
adulation, *n.* ad-yew-*lay*-shon, excessive flattery; fawning. (Fr. *adulation*, flattery.)
adulator, *n.* *ad*-yew-late-or, a flatterer.
adulatory, *a.* *ad*-yew-late-or-e, flattering; servilely praising.
Adullamite, *n.* a-*dul*-am-ite, an obstructionist in a political party; esp. one of the Liberal seceders of 1866 (1 Sam. xxii).
adult, *a.* a-*dult*, grown up; arrived at the age of puberty: *n.* any full-grown person, animal, or plant. (L. *adultus*, full grown.)
adulterant, *n.* a-*dul*-ter-ant, the person or thing that adulterates.
adulterate, *v.t.* a-*dul*-ter-ate, to deteriorate by admixture of baser materials: *a.* debased by foreign mixture. (L. *adulteratus*, defiled.)
adulterately, *ad.* in an adulterate manner.
adulterateness, *n.* a-*dul*-ter-ate-ness, the quality or state of being adulterated.
adulteration, *n.* a-*dul*-ter-*ay*-shon, the act of adulterating; the state of being adulterated. (L. *adulteratio*, adulteration.)
adulterer, *n.* a-*dul*-ter-er, one guilty of adultery.
adulteress, *n.* a-*dul*-ter-ess, a woman guilty of adultery.
adulterine, *a.* a-*dul*-ter-in, proceeding from adulterous commerce; spurious; illegal; not officially licensed or authorized: *n.* child of adultery [Law]. (L. *adulterīnus*, adulterous.)
adulterous, *a.* a-*dul*-ter-us, pertaining to or guilty of adultery; illicit.
adulterously, *ad.* a-*dul*-ter-us-le, in an adulterous manner.
adultery, *n.* a-*dul*-ter-e, unchastity of the married. (O.Fr. *avouterie*, adultery.)
adultness, *n.* a-*dult*-nes, the state of being adult.
adumbrant, *a.* ad-*um*-brant, giving a faint shadow or resemblance of. (L. *adūmbrans*, shadowing.)
adumbrate, *v.t.* ad-*um*-brate, to shadow out; to indicate faintly. (L. *adūmbratus*, shadowed.)
adumbration, *n.* ad-um-*bray*-shon, the act of adumbrating; a faint or imperfect representation.
adumbrative, *a.* ad-*um*-bra-tiv, faintly representing; able only to shadow forth.
aduncous, *a.* a-*dung*-kus, bent in the form of a hook. (L. *aduncus*, hooked.)
adust, *a.* a-*dust*, burned and dried up with heat of any kind, or as if so. (L. *adustus*, sunburnt.)
advance, *a.* ad-*vahns*, before: *n.* the act of coming forward; gradual progression; promotion; first step; movement towards; rise in price; furnishing of money or goods to others, in expectation of reimbursement; the property so furnished [Comm.]: *v.i.* to go forward; to make progress; to rise: *v.t.* to bring forward; to promote; to raise; to enhance; to improve; to forward; to supply beforehand or on credit. **in advance,** in front; beforehand. **advance note,** a draft on the owner of a ship (usually for a month's pay) given to a crew when signing Articles of Agreement.
advanced, *a.* ad-*vahnst*, in the front rank as regards progress; imbued with new ideas; well up in years.
advancement, *n.* ad-*vahns*-ment, the act of advancing; the state of being advanced; promotion; the payment of money in advance; money or property advanced.
advancer, *n.* ad-*vahns*-er, a promoter; a money-lender; the second branch of a buck's horn.
advancive, *a.* ad-*vahn*-siv, tending to advance.
advantage, *n.* ad-*vahn*-taj, any favourable state, condition, or circumstance; gain; profit; superiority; (in tennis and lawn tennis) the next point won after deuce, vantage: *v.t.* to benefit; to promote the interest of. (Fr. *avantage*.)
advantageous, *a.* ad-van-*tay*-jus, being of advantage; profitable; serviceable.
advantageously, *ad.* in an advantageous manner.
advantageousness, *n.* the quality or state of being advantageous.
advene, *v.i.* ad-*veen*, to accede. (L. *advenio*, come.)
advent, *n.* *ad*-vent, coming, or approach; (*cap.*) the coming of Christ as Saviour of mankind; the four weeks before Christmas, being preparatory to the Nativity [Eccles.]. (L. *adventus*, an arrival.)
adventitious, *a.* ad-ven-*tish*-us, accidental; not essentially inherent; out of the ordinary course. (L. *adventicius*, strange.)
adventitiously, *ad.* ad-ven-*tish*-us-le, in an adventitious manner.
adventitiousness, *n.* ad-ven-*tish*-us-ness, the state of being adventitious.
adventure, *n.* ad-*vent*-yur, hazard; risk; an enterprise of hazard or risk; a speculation: *v.t.* to risk or hazard. **a bill of adventure,** a declaration that a shipment carried is the venture of another and that the shipper or carrier is responsible only for safe delivery. **the great adventure,** euphemism for death. (Fr. *aventure*.)
adventureful, *a.* ad-*vent*-yur-ful, given to adventure; daring.
adventurer, *n.* ad-*vent*-yur-er, one who hazards or attempts extraordinary enterprises; one who seeks to advance his position by pretence or imposture; a speculator. **merchant adventurers,** members of incorporated trading companies in Tudor times. (Fr. *aventurier*, adventurer.)
adventuresome, *a.* ad-*vent*-yur-sum, adventurous.
adventuresomeness, *n.* ad-*vent*-yur-sum-ness, the quality of being adventurous.
adventuress, *a.* ad-*vent*-yur-ess, a female adventurer; a woman seeking social position in questionable ways.
adventurous, *a.* ad-*vent*-yur-us, inclined to adventures; enterprising.
adventurously, *ad.* ad-*vent*-yur-us-le, in an adventurous manner.
adventurousness, *n.* ad-*vent*-yur-us-ness, the act or quality of being adventurous.
adverb, *n.* *ad*-verb, a word or phrase modifying a verb, participle, adjective, or another adverb [Gram.]. (Fr. *adverbe*, adverb.)
adverbial, *a.* ad-*ver*-be-al, pertaining to an adverb.
adverbially, *ad.* in the manner of an adverb.
adversaria, *n.* ad-ver-*sare*-e-a, a collection of notes and extracts; a commonplace book. (L. *adversaria*, notebook.)
adversary, *n.* *ad*-ver-sa-re, an opponent; an enemy: *a.* having an opposite party [Law]. (L. *adversarius*, opposite or opposed to.)
adversative, *a.* ad-*ver*-sa-tiv, denoting contrariety or contrast [Gram.]: *n.* a word denoting contrariety or contrast. (L. *adversativus*, adversative.)
adverse, *a.* *ad*-verse, acting in a contrary direction; opposing; thwarting; unpropitious. (O.Fr. *avers*, turned from.)
adversely, *ad.* *ad*-verse-le, in an adverse manner.
adverseness, *n.* *ad*-verse-ness, state of being adverse.
adversity, *n.* ad-*ver*-se-te, an adverse state of things; calamity; misfortune. (L. *adversitas*, antipathy.)
advert, *v.i.* ad-*vert*, to turn attention to; to regard or notice. (L. *adverto*, turn towards.)
advertence, *n.* ad-*vert*-ens, attention; regard.
advertency, *n.* ad-*vert*-en-se, advertence.
advertent, *a.* ad-*vert*-ent, attentive; heedful.
advertently, *ad.* ad-*vert*-ent-le, in an advertent manner.
advertise, *v.i.* and *t.* *ad*-ver-tize, to give notice generally to the public; to call attention to by display, etc.; to make conspicuous. (Fr. *avertissant*, informing.)
advertisement, *n.* ad-*ver*-tiz-ment, public announcement, esp. in a public print or by poster or other display; legal notification; notice.
advertiser, *n.* *ad*-ver-ty-zer, one who, or that which, advertises.
advice, *n.* ad-*vice*, counsel; deliberate consideration; in the *pl.*, intelligence; information in detail given by one merchant or banker to another, by letter, as to the bills or drafts drawn upon him [Comm.]. (O.Fr. *avis*, a judgment.)
advice-boat, *n.* ad-*vice*-boat, former term for a swift vessel carrying dispatches.
advisability, *n.* ad-vize-a-*bil*-e-te, advisableness.
advisable, *a.* ad-*vize*-a-bl, proper to be advised; expedient.
advisableness, *n.* ad-*vize*-a-bl-ness, the quality of being advisable.

advisably, *ad.* ad-*vize*-ab-le, with advice; advisedly.
advise, *v.t.* ad-*vize*, to counsel; to communicate notice to: *v.i.* to consult. (O.Fr. *aviser*, to be of opinion.)
advised, *a.* ad-*vized*, acted or done with advice or deliberation; intended.
advisedly, *ad.* ad-*vize*-ed-le, in an advised manner.
advisedness, *n.* ad-*vize*-ed-ness, deliberate consideration; prudent procedure.
adviser, *n.* ad-*vize*-er, one who gives advice, generally with the accessory idea of responsibility.
advisory, *a.* ad-*vize*-or-e, having power to advise; containing advice.
advocacy, *n.* *ad*-vo-ka-se, a pleading for; intercessional or judicial pleading; the function or office of an advocate. (O.Fr. *advocacie*, pleading.)
advocate, *n.* *ad*-vo-kate, one who pleads the cause of another before a judge in a court of law; a barrister; one who defends or promotes a cause: *v.t.* to plead in favour of; to vindicate. **Faculty of Advocates,** the body of members of the Scottish bar. **Lord Advocate,** the principal crown counsel and public prosecutor in Scotland, and a functionary of the government for the time being. **Judge Advocate,** in courts martial, an officer who conducts the prosecution. **devil's advocate,** a person appointed to show reason why a proposed canonization should not be made. (Fr. *avocat.*)
advocateship, *n.* *ad*-vo-kate-ship, the office or duty of an advocate; advocacy.
advowee, *n.* ad-vou-*ee*, one who has the right of advowson; the patron of a benefice.
advowson, *n.* ad-*vou*-zon, a right of presentation to a vacant benefice. (O.Fr. *avoeson*, patronage.)
adynamia, *n.* ad-e-*nay*-me-a, weakness occasioned by disease [Med.]; diminution of the vital powers. (Gr. *a*-, and *dunamis*, power.)
adynamic, *a.* ad-e-*nam*-ik, pertaining to adynamia; weak; destitute of strength.
adytum, *n.* *ad*-e-tum, the inner and most sacred part of a temple; a sanctum. (L. *adytum*, the sanctuary.)
adze, *n.* adz, a cutting or chipping instrument like an axe, with the blade at right angles to the handle; *v.t.* to chip with an adze. (A.S. *adesa.*)
ædile, *n.* *ee*-dile, a Roman magistrate and municipal officer whose chief business was the supervision of public and private building.
Ægean, *a.* ee-*jee*-an, pertaining to the prehistoric civilization (about 3000–1000 B.C.) of the shores and islands of the Ægean Sea, the arm of the Mediterranean east of Greece.
ægis, *n.* *ee*-jis, the shield of Minerva; hence, a protecting shield; any protecting influence. (L. *ægis*, a defence.)
ægrotat, *n.* e-*groh*-tat, a certificate of sickness given to university undergraduates. (L. *ægrotat*, he is sick.)
Æneid, *n.* *ee*-ne-id, a celebrated epic poem by Virgil, of which Æneas is the hero.
Æolian, *a.* ee-*oh*-le-an, pertaining to the ancient Greek colony Æolia, or to Æolus, god of the winds: *n.* the Æolic dialect. **Æolian attachment,** a contrivance attached to a pianoforte by which a stream of air can be thrown on the strings, greatly increasing the volume of sound. **Æolian harp,** a stringed instrument emitting sounds from the action of air currents. **Æolian mode,** the ninth of the church modes [Mus.].
Æolic, *a.* ee-*ol*-ik, pertaining to Æolia, ancient Greek colony of Asia Minor. **Æolic dialect,** one of the five dialects of the Greek tongue.
æolipile, *n.* ee-*ol*-e-pile, a simple apparatus consisting of a hollow metal ball with a small calibre outlet pipe for demonstrating the power of steam. (L. *Æolus*, god of the winds, and *pila*, a ball.)
æolotropic, *a.* ee-o-lo-*trop*-ik, possessing æolotropy [Physics].
æolotropy, *n.* ee-o-*lot*-ro-pe, the property of showing different capacities (of conductivity, compressibility, etc.) in different directions [Physics]. (Gr. *aiolos*, changeful, *tropia*, turning.)
æon, *n.* *ee*-on, a very long but indefinite period of time; an age; in the Platonic philosophy, a perfection existing from eternity; among the Gnostics, a power supposed to have emanated from the divine nature anterior to time, and to have presided over the successive creations and transformations of being. (Gr. *aion*, time.)
Æpyornis, *n.* *ee*-pe-*or*-nis, a genus of large extinct flightless birds of Madagascar. (Gr. *aipis*, high, *ornis*, bird.)
aerate, *v.t.* *ay*-er-ate, to combine with carbonic dioxide or other gas; to arterialize; to oxygenate the blood by respiration; to charge with carbonic acid gas. (L. *aër*, air.)
aeration, *n.* ay-er-*ay*-shon, the act of aerating.
aerator, *n.* *ay*-er-ate-or, an apparatus for aerating.
aerial, *a.* ay-*eer*-e-al, belonging to the air; consisting of air; produced by air; existing or moving in the air; graceful; high in the air; elevated: *n.* the elevated conductor through which wireless messages are radiated and received; an antenna. **aerial perspective,** the expression of space and distance by gradation in colour, clarity, etc. [Paint.]. **aerial plants,** those which derive their nourishment chiefly from the atmosphere. (L. *aërius*, airy.)
aeriality, *n.* ay-eer-e-*al*-e-te, airiness; unsubstantiality.
aerially, *ad.* ay-*eer*-e-a-le, in an aerial manner.
aerie, *n.* *ayr*-e, eyrie, the nest of a bird of prey; an isolated dwelling on a height. (O.Fr. *aire.*)
aeriferous, *a.* ayr-*if*-er-us, conveying air. (L. *aër*, and *fero*, carry.)
aerification, *n.* ayr-e-fe-*kay*-shon, act of aerifying, or of becoming gaseous; the state of being aerified, or aeriform.
aeriform, *a.* *ayr*-e-form, having the form or nature of air; gaseous. (L. *aër*, and *forma*, shape.)
aerify, *v.t.* *ayr*-e-fy, to change into a gaseous state; to fill or combine with air.
aero-, *pref.* *ayr*-oh *or* *ay*-e-roh, denoting air or pertaining to the air. (L. *aër*, air.)
aerobatics, *n.* ayr-o-*bat*-iks, trick-flying by airmen; stunting in the air.
aerobe, *n.* *ayr*-rohb, a bacterium or plant for the continued existence of which oxygen is necessary.
aerobic, *a.* ayr-*ob*-ik, living or active only in the presence of oxygen; pertaining to aerobes.
aerobiosis, *n.* ayr-o-by-*oh*-sis, existence in air or in oxygen.
aerocyst, *n.* *ayr*-o-sist, an air-bladder in seaweed.
aerodonetics, *n.* ayr-roh-do-*net*-iks, the science of gliding. (L. *aëro*-, *and* Gr. *donētos*, shaken.)
aerodrome, *n.* *ayr*-o-drome, a large level tract equipped as a starting- and landing-ground for aeroplanes. (L. *aëro*-, and Gr. *dromos*, a course.)
aerodynamics, *n.* ayr-o-dy-*nam*-iks, the science treating of the mechanical effects of gases in motion. (L. *aëro*-, and Gr. *dunamis*, power.)
aerofoil, *n.* *ayr*-o-foyl, the wing or plane of an aeroplane; any surface having similar functions.
aerogram, *n.* *ayr*-o-gram, a message sent by radio or by telegraph or telephone and aircraft.
aerograph, *n.* *ayr*-o-graf, the trade-name of a[n] atomizer for applying liquid coats of paint, etc.
aerography, *n.* ayr-*og*-ra-fe, description of th[e] atmosphere.
aerolite, *n.* *ayr*-o-lite, a meteoric stone. (L. *aëro*- and Gr. *lithos*, a stone.)
aerolith, *n.* *ayr*-o-lith, an aerolite.
aerolithology, *n.* ayr-o-lith-*ol*-o-je, the study [o]f meteoric stones.
aerolitic, *a.* ayr-o-*lit*-ik, relating to aerolites.
aerological, *a.* ayr-o-*loj*-e-kal, pertaining [t]o aerology.
aerologist, *n.* ayr-*ol*-o-jist, one versed in aerology.
aerology, *n.* ayr-*ol*-o-je, the science treating of th[e] atmosphere, its constituent parts, properties, a[nd] phenomena. (L. *aëro*-, and Gr. *logos*, science.)
aeromancy, *n.* *ayr*-o-man-se, divination by mea[ns] of the air and winds; forecasting the weathe[r]. (L. *aëro*-, and Gr. *manteia*, prophetic power.)
aeromantic, *a.* ayr-o-*man*-tik, pertaining to aer[o]mancy.
aerometer, *n.* ayr-*om*-e-ter, an instrument f[or] measuring the weight or the density of air an[d] gases. (L. *aëro*-, and Gr. *metron*, a measure.)
aerometric, *a.* *ayr*-o-*met*-rik, relating to the pro[]perties of the air.
aerometry, *n.* ayr-*om*-e-tre, the science of measurin[g] the properties of the air; pneumatics.
aero-motor, *n.* *ayr*-o-*moh*-tor, an aircraft engine.
aeronaut, *n.* *ayr*-o-nawt, one who travels or float[s] in the air; a balloonist. (Fr. *aéronaute.*)
aeronautical, *a.* ayr-o-*naw*-te-kal, pertaining to aerial navigation or machines.

aeronautics, *n.* ayr-o-*naw*-tiks, the science of navigating the air; ballooning.

aeronautism, *n.* ayr-o-*naw*-tizm, the theory and practice of aeronautics.

aerophobia, *n.* ayr-o-*foh*-be-a, morbid dread of a current of air [Med.]. (L. *aëro-*, and Gr. *phobos*, panic fear.)

aerophone, *n.* *ayr*-o-fohn, an amplifier of sound waves.

aerophore, *n.* *ayr*-o-for, a portable container of compressed air, used by divers, etc.

aerophyte, *n.* *ayr*-o-fite, an epiphyte.

aeroplane, *n.* *ayr*-o-plane, a mechanically driven, heavier-than-air flying machine, having its main supporting surfaces fixed. (L. *aëro-*, and Gr. *planēs*, a wanderer.)

aeroscepsy, *n.* ayr-o-*sep*-se, the faculty of perception by the medium of the air ascribed to the antennæ of insects. (L. *aëro-*, and *skopeo*, observe.)

aeroscopy, *n.* ayr-*os*-ko-pe, the observation of variations in the air; aeromancy.

ærose, *a.* *ee*-rohs, coppery, brassy. (L. *aërosus.*)

aerostat, *n.* *ayr*-o-stat, a lighter-than-air aircraft; a balloon or airship. (Fr. *aërostat.*)

aerostatic, *a.* ayr-o-*stat*-ik, pertaining to aerostatics or to aerostation.

aerostatics, *n.* ayr-o-*stat*-iks, the science of atmospheric pressure or equilibrium in gases, and so of managing aircraft. (L. *aëro-*, and Gr. *statikos*, bringing to a standstill.)

aerostation, *n.* ayr-os-*tay*-shon, aerial navigation, esp. (as opposed to *aviation*) by lighter-than-air aircraft.

aerotaxis, *n.* ayr-o-*tak*-sis, aerobic reaction to the presence of oxygen.

aerotherapeutics, *n.* *ayr*-o-*the*-ra-*pew*-tiks, treatment of disease by air or natural or artificial sunshine.

æruginous, *a.* ee-*roo*-je-nus, like or of the nature of verdigris. (L. *ærugo*, rust of copper, verdigris.)

aery, *a.* *ay*-er-e, ethereal; visionary.

Æsculapian, *a.* es-kew-*lape*-e-an, medical; pertaining to the healing art. (Æsculapius, son of Apollo and Greek god of medicine.)

Æsopian, *a.* e-*sope*-e-an, like the fables of Æsop, the Greek story-teller of the 6th century B.C.

æsthesia, *n.* es-*thee*-ze-a, state of being sensible; capacity for feeling or sensation. (Gr. *aisthesis*, sensation.)

æsthesiometer, *n.* ees-*thee*-ze-*om*-e-ter, an instrument for measuring the sensibility and discrimination of the nerves to touch.

æsthete, *n.* *ees*-theet, one affecting an extravagant sense of the beautiful.

æsthetic, *a.* ees-*thet*-ik, pertaining to the science and perception of the beautiful. (Gr. *aisthetikos*, perception through the senses.)

æsthetically, *ad.* ees-*thet*-e-ke-le, in an æsthetic manner.

æstheticism, *n.* ees-*thet*-e-sizm, devotion, real or affected, to the study of the beautiful.

æsthetics, *n.pl.* ees-*thet*-iks, the science of the beautiful in nature and the fine arts.

æstho-physiology, *n.* *ees*-tho-fiz-e-*ol*-o-je, the physiology of the organs of sensation.

æstival, *a.* *ees*-te-val, estival; pertaining to or produced in the summer.

æstivate, *v.i.* *ees*-te-vate, to summer, to remain in one place during the summer; to fall into summer torpor [Zool.].

æstivation, *n.* ees-te-*vay*-shon, remaining torpid during the summer [Zool.]; the arrangement of the petals within the bud [Bot.]. (L. *æstivatum*, passed the summer.)

æther, *n.* *ee*-ther, the ether.

æthrioscope, *n.* *eeth*-re-o-skope, an instrument for measuring changes in temperature due to varying conditions in the sky. (Gr. *aithrios*, clear, *skopeo*, see.)

ætiological, *a.* ee-te-o-*loj*-e-kal, pertaining to etiology.

ætiology, *n.* ee-te-*ol*-o-je, the science and philosophy of causation; assignment of a cause; the study of causes of disease [Med.].

afar, *ad.* a-*far*, at great distance.

afeard, *a.* a-*feerd*, frightened; afraid.

affability, *n.* af-fa-*bil*-e-te, affableness; courtesy of manners.

affable, *a.* *af*-fa-bl, of easy access and manners; courteous; complaisant; mild. (Fr. *affable.*)

affableness, *n.* *af*-fa-bl-ness, the quality of being affable.

affably, *ad.* *af*-fa-ble, in an affable manner.

affair, *n.* af-*fare*, business of any kind; that which is to be done; matter; an intrigue; a minor military action: *pl.* public concerns and their management; finances. (O.Fr. *afeire*, a transaction.)

affect, *v.t.* af-*fekt*, to act upon; to produce an effect or change upon; to move or touch; to aim at; to be fond of; to love; to attempt to imitate in a manner not natural; to make a show or pretence of; to tend to. (L. *affecto*, feign.)

affect, *n.* *af*-fekt, emotion, desire, etc. considered as a determining factor in thought and conduct [Psych.].

affectation, *n.* af-fek-*tay*-shon, assumption and pretence of what is not natural or real; artificial appearance or show. (L. *affectatio*, eager desire for.)

affected, *a.* af-*fekt*-ed, inclined or disposed; distressed; given to affectation; assumed; not natural; influenced (as by weather or illness).

affectedly, *ad.* af-*fekt*-ed-le, in an affected manner.

affectedness, *n.* af-*fekt*-ed-ness, the quality of being affected; affectation.

affectibility, *n.* af-fekt-e-*bil*-e-te, the state of being affectible.

affectible, *a.* a-*fekt*-e-bl, that may be affected.

affecting, *a.* af-*fekt*-ing, having power to excite or move the affections; pathetic; touching.

affectingly, *ad*, af-*fekt*-ing-le, in an affecting manner.

affection, *n.* af-*fek*-shon, the state of being affected, generally in one's emotions; feeling; disposition; inclination; attachment; kindness; fondness; love; an attribute, quality, or property; a disease, or morbid condition [Med.]. (Fr. *affection.*)

affectional, *a.* af-*fek*-shon-al, implying affection; pertaining to the affections.

affectionate, *a.* af-*fek*-shon-at, full of affection; fond.

affectionately, *ad.* af-*fek*-shon-at-le, with affection.

affectionateness, *n.* af-*fek*-shon-at-ness, fondness.

affectioned, *a.* af-*fek*-shond, disposed.

affective, *a.* af-*fekt*-iv, that affects. (Fr. *affectif.*)

affectively, *ad.* af-*fekt*-iv-le, in an affective or impressive manner.

affeer, *v.t.* af-*feer*, to settle a fine [Law]. (O.Fr.)

afferent, *a.* *af*-fer-ent, bringing inward; leading towards a centre, as in afferent nerves [Physiol.]. (L. *afferens*, conveying to.)

affettuoso, af-fet-too-*oh*-zo, with feeling [Mus.]. (It.)

affiance, *n.* af-*fy*-ans, promise of marriage; faith pledged; trust: *v.t.* to betroth; to bind by promise to marry. (O.Fr. *afiance*, faith.)

affianced, *n.* af-*fy*-anst, a betrothed; a person pledged to marry another.

affiche, *n.* af-*feesh*, a placard. (Fr.)

affidavit, *n.* af-fe-*day*-vit, a voluntary declaration in writing, sworn to before a magistrate or commissioner. (L. *affidavit*, he or she pledges.)

affiliable, *a.* af-*fil*-e-a-bl, that may be affiliated.

affiliate, *v.t.* af-*fil*-e-ate, to receive into a family, society, etc., or into some intimate relationship; to assign (a bastard) to its father; to refer to as origin. (L. *ad-*, and *filius*, a son.)

affiliation, *n.* af-fil-e-*ay*-shon, adoption; the act of affiliating; the assignment of a bastard to its father; connection with a society or institution.

affined, *a.* af-*fined*, united by affinity; leagued or allied. (O.Fr. *affiner*, to join.)

affinity, *n.* af-*fin*-e-te, relationship by marriage, in contradistinction to consanguinity or relationship by blood; agreement; connection; any natural inclination or attraction; the tendency of particles of dissimilar bodies to combine and form new compounds [Chem.]; structural resemblance [Zool.]. (Fr. *affinité.*)

affirm, *v.t.* af-*ferm*, to confirm or ratify; to declare positively or solemnly. (O.Fr. *afermer*, to determine.)

affirmable, *a.* af-*ferm*-a-bl, that may be affirmed.

affirmably, *ad.* af-*ferm*-a-ble, in a way capable of affirmation.

affirmance, *n.* af-*ferm*-ans, confirmation.

affirmant, *n.* af-*ferm*-ant, one who affirms.

affirmation, *n.* af-fer-*may*-shon, the act of affirming; that which is asserted; confirmation; a solemn declaration, made under penalties, in lieu of oath [Law].

affirmative, *a.* af-*ferm*-a-tiv, that affirms, as opposed to negative; confirmative; in approval: *n.* that which contains an affirmation. (Fr.)
affirmatively, *ad.* af-*ferm*-a-tiv-le, in an affirmative manner.
affirmatory, *a.* af-*ferm*-a-tor-e, confirmatory.
affirmer, *n.* af-*ferm*-er, a person who affirms.
affix, *v.t.* af-*fiks*, to fix to; to annex; to attach; to append. (L. *affixus*, fastened to.)
affix, *n.* *af*-fiks, a syllable or letter added to the beginning or end of a word.
afflation, *n.* af-*flay*-shon, the act of breathing upon.
afflatus, *n.* af-*flay*-tus, breathing on; inspiration from above. (L. *afflātus*, breathed upon.)
afflict, *v.t.* af-*flikt*, to visit with sore pain, grief, or distress. (L. *afflicto*, harass.)
afflicted, *a.* af-*flikt*-ed, stricken with heavy calamity.
afflicting, *a.* af-*flikt*-ing, distressing.
afflictingly, *ad.* af-*flikt*-ing-le, in an afflicting manner.
affliction, *n.* af-*flik*-shon, the state of being afflicted, or its cause; calamity. (Fr. *affliction*.)
afflictive, *a.* af-*flikt*-iv, causing affliction; distressing.
afflictively, *ad.* af-*flikt*-iv-le, in an afflictive manner.
affluence, *n.* *af*-flu-ens, a flowing to; concourse; abundance of wealth. (Fr. *affluence*.)
affluency, *n.* *af*-flu-en-se, affluence.
affluent, *a.* *af*-flu-ent, flowing to; wealthy: *n.* a river tributary to another.
affluently, *ad.* *af*-flu-ent-le, in an affluent manner.
afflux, *n.* *af*-fluks, a flowing to, or that which flows to. (L. *affluxum*, flowed to.)
affluxion, *n.* af-*fluk*-shon, afflux.
afforce, *v.t.* af-*fors*, to add technical experts to a jury, etc. [Law]. (O.Fr. *aforcier*, to force.)
afforcement, *n.* af-*fors*-ment, an adding weight to, or strengthening.
afford, *v.t.* af-*foard*, to yield; to be able to bear the cost of. (A.S. *forthian*, to further.)
afforest, *v.t.* af-*fo*-rest, to convert into forest; to plant with trees.
afforestable, *a.* af-*fo*-res-ta-bl, capable of being afforested.
afforestation, *n.* af-fo-res-*tay*-shon, the act of converting land into forest.
affranchise, *v.t.* af-*fran*-shize, to make free. (Fr. *affranchir*, to set free.)
affranchisement, *n.* af-*fran*-shiz-ment, the act of affranchising; emancipation.
affray, *n.* af-*fray*, a fight or riot in a public place, creating alarm; a brawl: *v.t.* to startle; to scare. (O.Fr. *effraier*, to frighten.)
affreightment, *n.* af-*frayt*-ment, the chartering of a ship for cargo. (Fr. *affréter*, to charter.)
affricate, *n.* *af*-re-kat, a consonant in sounding which a plosive is immediately followed by a fricative, as *ch* in *church*, *dg* in *badger*, *th* in *eighth*: *a.* uttered thus [Phonetics.].
affricative, *a.* a-*frik*-a-tiv, affricate [Phonetics].
affright, *n.* af-*frite*, sudden or great fear: *v.t.* to impress with fear; to terrify. (A.S. *āfyrhtan*, to frighten.)
affrightedly, *ad.* af-*frite*-ed-le, with fright.
affront, *v.t.* af-*frunt*, to insult openly; to abash; to confront hostilely: *n.* insult; contemptuous or rude treatment. (O.Fr. *afronter*, to face with.)
affronted, *a.* af-*frunt*-ed, offended; insulted.
affusion, *n.* af-*few*-zhon, the act of pouring on; baptism effected thus.
affy, *v.t.* and *i.* a-*fy*, to betroth; to espouse; to confide; to put one's trust in.
Afghan, *n.* *af*-gan, a native of, or the language of, Afghanistan: *a.* pertaining to Afghanistan, its inhabitants, or language.
afield, *ad.* a-*feeld*, to or in the field.
afire, *a.* and *ad.* a-*fire*, on fire.
aflame, *a.* and *ad.* a-*flame*, flaming.
aflat, *ad.* a-*flat*, level with the ground; flat.
afloat, *ad.* and *a.* a-*float*, floating; abroad; adrift.
afoot, *ad.* a-*foot*, on foot.
afore, *ad.* a-*fore*, in front; before; in or towards the front part of a ship. (A.S. *on foran*, in front of.)
aforegoing, *a.* a-*fore*-go-ing, going before: *n.* that which precedes or has preceded.
aforehand, *ad.* a-*fore*-hand, in time previous.
aforementioned, *a.* a-*fore*-men-shond, mentioned before: *n.* that just mentioned.
aforenamed, *a.* a-*fore*-naymd, named before.
aforesaid, *a.* a-*fore*-sed, said or mentioned before.
aforethought, *a.* a-*fore*-thawt, premeditated; prepense.
aforetime, *ad.* a-*fore*-time, in time past; in a former time.
afoul, *ad.* and *a.* a-*foul*, entangled; in collision.
afraid, *a.* a-*frayd*, struck with fear; terrified.
afreet, *n.* *af*-reet, a powerful demon of Mohammedan mythology. (Ar. *ifrit*, an evil djinn.)
afresh, *ad.* a-*fresh*, anew; again.
African, *a.* *af*-re-kan, pertaining to Africa: *n.* a native of Africa.
Afrikaans, *n.* af-re-*kahnz*, the language of the South African or Cape Dutch; Taal.
Afrikander, *n.* *af*-re-*kand*-er, a South African native-born white man, esp. of Dutch stock. (Dut. *Afrikaner*.)
afrit, *n.* *af*-reet, an afreet.
aft, *a.* and *ad.* ahft, near or towards the stern. **fore and aft,** the whole length of a ship; rigged without square sails [Naut.]. (A.S. *æftan*, behind.)
after, *a.* *ahft*-er, later in time; succeeding; further aft [Naut.]: *prep.* behind in place; later in time; in pursuit or search of; in imitation of; according to; next to; concerning: *ad.* posterior; later. **after all,** after taking everything into consideration.
afterbirth, *n.* *ahft*-er-berth, the placenta and membranes connected with the fœtus expelled directly after parturition [Obstet.].
after-body, *n.* *ahft*-er-bod-e, the part of a vessel behind the midship section [Naut.].
afterclap, *n.* *ahft*-er-klap, an unexpected subsequent event.
aftercost, *n.* *ahft*-er-kost, the expense after the execution of the original plan.
aftercrop, *n.* *ahft*-er-krop, the second crop in the same year.
afterdamp, *n.* *ahft*-er-damp, choke-damp.
aftergame, *n.* *ahft*-er-game, a game to reverse the result of a previous game.
afterglow, *n.* *ahft*-er-gloh, glow in the sky after sunset, or remaining in a metal cooling from white-heat.
after-grass, *n.* *ahft*-er-grahs, new grass springing up after the first mowing.
aftergrowth, *n.* *ahft*-er-groath, second and subsequent growth.
afterguard, *n.* *ahft*-er-gahrd, the seamen stationed aft to work the after-sails [Naut.].
after-hold, *n.* *ahft*-er-hohld, that part of a vessel's hold behind the mainmast.
after-image, *n.* the impression retained on the retina after the direct stimulus has been withdrawn.
afterings, *n.pl.* *ahft*-er-ingz, the last milk drawn from a cow.
afterlife, *n.* future life; life hereafter; condition after death.
aftermath, *n.* *ahft*-er-mahth, a second crop of grass in a season; hence, consequences. (A.S. *maeth*, measure.)
aftermost, *a.* *ahft*-er-mohst, furthest aft; nearest the stern [Naut.]. (A.S. *æfternest*, hindmost.)
afternoon, *n.* *ahft*-er-*noon*, time between noon and evening.
afterpains, *n.pl.* *ahft*-er-paynz, pains after childbirth.
afterpart, *n.* *ahft*-er-part, the latter part; towards the stern [Naut.].
afterpiece, *n.* *ahft*-er-peece, a short piece performed after a more important play.
afterproof, *n.* *ahft*-er-proof, proof only subsequently ascertained.
aftersails, *n.pl.* *ahft*-er-saylz, the sails on the mizenmast and stays, between the main and mizenmasts [Naut.].
afterswarm, *n.* *ahft*-er-swawrm, a cast, or second swarm of bees leaving a hive in the same season.
aftertaste, *n.* *ahft*-er-tayst, the taste which remains after eating or drinking.
afterthought, *n.* *ahft*-er-thawt, reflection after the act; a later thought or expedient.
afterward, *ad.* *ahft*-er-ward, afterwards.
afterwards, *ad.* *ahft*-er-wardz, in a later or subsequent time. (A.S. *æftanward*, following.)
afterwit, *n.* *ahft*-er-wit, wit that comes too late.
aftward, *a.* *ahft*-ward, towards the stern [Naut.].

Aga, *n.* *ah*-ga, a commander or chief officer in Turkey; a court official; also used as a title of respect. (Turk. *aghā*, lord.)
again, *ad.* a-*gayn* or a-*gen*, a second time; another time; once more; moreover; back; on the other hand. **again and again,** repeatedly. (A.S. *ongēan.*)
against, *prep.* a-*gaynst*, in opposition to; opposite to; bearing or leaning upon; in preparation or provision for. **up against it,** in serious difficulty; at the end of resources.
agalactia, *n.* ag-a-*lak*-te-a, agalaxy [Med.].
agalactous, *a.* ag-a-*lak*-tus, destitute of, or deficient in, milk [Med.].
agalaxy, *n.* *ag*-a-lak-se, the absence of or deficiency in milk after childbirth [Med.].
agalloch, *n.* a-*gal*-lok, a soft, resinous East Indian wood burnt as a perfume; lign-aloes, the aloes of the Bible. (Gr. *agallochon*, the bitter aloe.)
agalmatolite, *n.* ag-al-*mat*-o-lite, a soft, compact stone used in China for images; figure-stone. (Gr. *agalma*, an image, and *lithos*, a stone.)
Agama, *n.* *ag*-a-ma, a genus of 200 species of lizards, found chiefly in Australia, India, and Malaya [Zool.]. (Sp., from Carib.)
agami, *n.* *ag*-a-me, the trumpeter bird of tropical America, *Psophia crepitans*.
agamic, *a.* a-*gam*-ik, asexual; reproducing without impregnation.
agamogenesis, *n.* *ag*-a-mo-*jen*-e-sis, reproduction asexually.
agamous, *a.* *ag*-a-mus, cryptogamic.
Agapanthus, *n.* ag-a-*pan*-thus, a genus of ornamental plants including the African lily.
agape, *ad.* a-*gape*, staring with the mouth wide open.
agape, *n.* *ag*-a-pe, a primitive Christian love-feast, held in connection with the sacrament of communion. (Gr. *agape*, love, especially brotherly love.)
agar-agar, *n.* *ah*-gar-*ah*-gar, a gelatinous substance made from certain seaweed, used chiefly for the cultivation of bacteria, and in the East for soups and jellies.
agaric, *n.* a-*ga*-rik, a fungus of the genus *Agaricus* [Bot.]. **agaric mineral,** a light deposit of calcium carbonate formed in fissures of limestone [Min.]. (L. *agaricon*, larch fungus.)
agastric, *a.* a-*gas*-trik, destitute of a stomach or alimentary canal [Zool.]. (Gr. *a-*, and *gaster*, the belly.)
agate, *n.* *ag*-at, a variegated variety of chalcedonic quartz, the colours of which are arranged in clouds, spots or bands, used for seals, beads, small handles, etc. [Min.]; in Printing, the former American name for 5½-point type, formerly "ruby" in England; any appliance fitted with agate. (Fr., from Gr. *achates.*)
agatine, *a.* *ag*-a-tin, pertaining to or like agate.
agatized, *a.* *ag*-a-tyzd, coloured like agate [Min.].
agaty, *a.* *ag*-a-te, of the nature of, or containing, agate.
Agave, *n.* a-*gay*-ve, a large genus of tropical american plants of the amaryllis family, including (*l.c.*) the American aloe, known also as the century plant from a mistaken notion that it does not bloom until a hundred years old. (Gr. *agauos*, illustrious.)
agaze, *ad.* a-*gayz*, staring; struck with wonder.
agazed, *a.* a-*gayzd*, struck with amazement.
age, *n.* ayj, the period of time during which a person or thing exists or has existed; extreme verge of a long life; a lifetime; time of life; maturity; majority; an historical period, or epoch; a generation; a century; a long time; a division of time. **age of consent,** the age before which carnal connection with a girl—whether she consent or not—is rape, and a criminal offence [Law]: *v.i.* to grow, or seem to grow, old; to mellow; to suffer change through lapse of time: *v.t.* to cause to grow old; to give the characteristics of age to; to mellow. **of age,** 21 years old or more. (O.Fr. *aage.*)
aged, *a.* *ay*-jed, of a certain age; advanced in years: *n.pl.* old persons collectively.
ageless, *a.* *ayj*-less, without appearing to grow old.
agency, *n.* *ay*-jen-se, action; instrumentality; the office or business of an agent; a commercial organization or its place of business. (L. *ageno*, doing.)
agenda, *n.pl.* a-*jen*-da, things to be done; items of business; a record of business done; a programme of business to be done. (L., pl. of *agendum*, gerundive of *agĕre*, to do.)
agenesis, *n.* ay-*jen*-e-sis, imperfect development [Physiol.]. (Gr. *a-*, not, *genesis.*)
agennesis, *n.* ay-*jen*-e-sis, sterility in a male; impotence. (Gr. *a-*, not, *gennēsis*, an engendering.)
agent, *a.* *ay*-jent, acting: *n.* a person or thing that acts, or produces an effect; the means whereby anything is effected; a factor; one who acts for another. **Agent General,** a representative in London of certain parts of the British Dominions.
agential, *a.* a-*jen*-shal, pertaining to agency.
agglomerate, *v.t.* and *v.i.* ag-*glom*-er-ate, to gather into a ball or mass: *a.* gathered into a ball or mass: *n.* a rock composed of angular volcanic fragments [Geol.]. (L. *agglomerāre*, gather into a mass.)
agglomeration, *n.* ag-*glom*-er-*ay*-shon, the act of agglomerating; the state of being agglomerated; a confused mass or heap.
agglomerative, *a.* ag-*glom*-er-ra-tiv, apt to agglomerate.
agglutinant, *a.* ag-*gloo*-tin-ant, gluing; uniting closely: *n.* any viscous substance that causes or intensifies adhesion. (L. *agglutinans*, gluing to.)
agglutinate, *v.t.* ag-*gloo*-tin-ate, to unite by adhesion; to turn into glue; to form by agglutination: *a.* united as with glue; combined into a compound. (L. *agglutinatum*, glued to.)
agglutination, *n.* ag-*gloo*-tin-*ay*-shon, the act of agglutinating; the state of being agglutinated; imperfect union of the inflectional suffix with the root [Phil.].
agglutinative, *a.* ag-*gloo*-tin-a-tiv, that tends to cause adhesion or agglutination.
agglutinin, *n.* ag-*gloo*-tin-in, an organic substance causing agglutination of blood corpuscles, bacteria, etc.
aggrandization, *n.* ag-grand-e-*zay*-shon, the act of aggrandizing.
aggrandize, *v.t.* *ag*-grand-ize, to make great or greater in power, rank, or honour; to exalt; to enlarge. (Fr. *agrandir.*)
aggrandizement, *n.* ag-*grand*-iz-ment, the act of aggrandizing; the state of being aggrandized; advancement. (Fr. *agrandissement.*)
aggravate, *v.t.* *ag*-gra-vate, to make worse or less tolerable; to intensify; to exaggerate; to provoke. (L. *aggravatum*, made heavier.)
aggravating, *a.* *ag*-gra-vate-ing, provoking; making less excusable.
aggravatingly, *ad.* *ag*-gra-vate-ing-le, in an aggravating manner.
aggravation, *n.* ag-gra-*vay*-shon, the act of aggravating; accession of what aggravates; exaggeration; provocation.
aggravator, *n.* *ag*-gra-vate-or, a person causing aggravation.
aggregate, *a.* *ag*-gre-gat, formed by a collection of particulars into a whole mass; composed of several florets united at the base by the receptacle [Bot.]; composed of distinct minerals [Geol.]; composed of individuals united into one corporation [Law]: *n.* the sum or assemblage of particulars; an aggregate rock [Geol.]; a whole formed by the union of homogeneous particles [Phys.]: *v.t.* to collect together into a sum or mass. (L. *aggregatum*, collected into a flock.)
aggregately, *ad.* *ag*-gre-gat-le, collectively.
aggregation, *n.* ag-gre-*gay*-shon, the act of aggregating; the state of being aggregated; an aggregate.
aggregative, *a.* *ag*-gre-ga-tiv, taken together.
aggress, *v.t.* ag-*gress*, to be the first to attack; to begin the quarrel. (Fr. *aggresser*, to attack first.)
aggression, *n.* ag-*gresh*-on, an unprovoked act of injury or hostility.
aggressive, *a.* ag-*gress*-iv, making the first attack; involving aggression; quarrelsome.
aggressively, *ad.* ag-*gress*-iv-le, in an aggressive manner.
aggressiveness, *n.* ag-*gress*-iv-ness, quarrelsomeness.
aggressor, *n.* ag-*gress*-or, he who first commences hostility or gives offence.
aggrieve, *v.t.* ag-*greev*, to give pain or sorrow; to oppress. (O.Fr. *agrever*, to hurt.)
aggrieved, *a.* ag-*greevd*, suffering from injustice; having a grievance.

aghast, *a.* and *ad.* a-*gahst,* struck silent with horror. (A.S. *a-,* and *gæstan,* to terrify.)
agile, *a. aj*-jile, nimble ; active. (Fr. *agile.*)
agilely, *ad. aj*-jile-le, in an agile manner.
agileness, *n. aj*-jile-ness, the quality of being agile.
agility, *n.* a-*jil*-e-te, nimbleness ; activity.
agio, *n. aj*-je-o, the difference in value between coined and paper money, or between one sort of coined money and another ; money-changing ; the charge for changing money. (It. *aggio,* ease.)
agiotage, *n. aj*-je-o-taj, exchange business ; speculative dealing in stocks.
agist, *v.t.* a-*jist,* to pasture the cattle of others at a certain sum ; to levy a rate on land [Law]. (O.Fr. *a,* and *giste,* place to lie in.)
agistment, *n.* a-*jist*-ment, the action or practice of agisting, or the price paid for this ; the pasture or right of pasture in a forest.
agistor, *n.* a-*jist*-or, a person pasturing cattle in return for a rent ; in English history, an officer of the royal forests [Law].
agitate, *v.t. aj*-e-tate, to shake or move briskly ; to stir violently ; to disturb ; to excite ; to revolve in the mind ; to discuss : *v.i.* to arouse and stimulate public attention. (L. *agitatus,* excited.)
agitated, *a. aj*-e-tate-ed, excited ; expressing excitement kept open by public discussion.
agitation, *n.* aj-e-*tay*-shon, the act of agitating or of arousing attention ; the state of being agitated ; commotion ; discussion ; public excitement.
agitative, *a. aj*-e-tay-tiv, tending to agitate.
agitato, *n.* aj-e-*tah*-to, a broken, restless, spasmodic style of performance [Mus.].
agitator, *n. aj*-e-tay-tor, one who agitates or excites for party or private interest a commotion in the state ; a machine with a rotatory contrivance for shaking and mixing [Mech.].
aglet, *n. ag*-let, tag of a lace ; a pendant ; a spangle. (Fr. *aiguillette,* little needle.)
agley, *ad.* a-*glee* or a-*gly,* askew ; aside [Scots.].
aglimmer, *ad.* a-*glim*-er, in a glimmering way.
aglow, *a.* a-*gloh,* glowing.
agnail, *n. ag*-nayl, a whitlow ; a piece of dried skin hanging from the edge of a finger-nail. (A.S. *angnægl,* corn.)
agname, *n. ag*-name, a nickname ; a cognomen added to the name and surname.
agnate, *a. ag*-nate, related on the father's side : *n.* any relation on this side. (L. *agnātus,* related.)
agnatic, *a.* ag-*nat*-ik, pertaining to agnates or to descent in the male line.
agnation, *n.* ag-*nay*-shon, relationship through an agnate ; descent in a direct male line [Law].
agnomen, *n.* ag-*noh*-men, a nickname or epithet applied to a person on account of some exploit or distinguishing quality. (L. *agnōmen,* a surname.)
agnostic, *n.* ag-*nos*-tik, one who denies that we can know, prove, or disprove anything beyond material phenomena, though such may exist : *a.* pertaining to agnosticism or agnostics ; sceptical of the unknown. (Gr. *a-,* and *gnostikos,* able to know.)
agnosticism, *n.* ag-*nos*-tis-izm, the doctrine of the agnostics ; the state of being agnostic.
Agnus, *n. ag*-nus, the lamb as a Christian symbol. **Agnus bell,** the bell rung at the recital of the Agnus Dei in the Mass. **Agnus Dei,** an amulet or waxen cake stamped with the figure of a lamb bearing the cross ; a prayer beginning with these words. (L. *Agnus Dei,* Lamb of God.)
ago, *ad.* and *a,* a-*goh,* past ; gone. (A.S. *āgān.*)
agog, *ad,* a-*gog,* in eager excitement. (O.Fr. *en gogues,* in laughter.)
agoing, *ad.* a-*goh*-ing, in a state of motion.
agone, *ad.* a-*gon,* ago ; past ; since.
agonic, *a,* a-*gon*-ik, having no dip ; used esp. of an imaginary line on the earth's surface on which the magnetic needle points due north and south, and hence is without magnetic declination.
agonistic, *a.* ag-o-*nist*-ik, pertaining to athletic encounters. (Gr. *agonistes,* a combatant.)
agonistical, *a.* ag-o-*nist*-ik-al, agonistic.
agonistically, *ad.* ag-o-*nist*-ik-al-le, in an agonistic manner.
agonistics, *n.pl.* ag-o-*nist*-iks, the scientific study of athletics.
agonize, *v.i. ag*-o-nize, to be in extreme pain ; to suffer violent anguish : *v.t.* to distress with extreme pain ; to torture. (Fr. *agoniser.*)
agonizing, *a. ag*-o-ny-zing, giving extreme pain.
agonizingly, *ad. ag*-o-ny-zing-le, in an agonizing manner.
agonothete, *n.* a-*goh*-no-theet, the officer presiding over the public games in ancient Greece. (Gr.)
agony, *n. ag*-o-ne, extreme pain of body or mind ; violent struggle, as for life. (Fr. *agonie.*)
agora, *n. ag*-o-ra, the market-place of an ancient Greek town. (Gr. *agora,* an assembly.)
agoraphobia, *n. ag*-o-ra-*foh*-be-a, a morbid fear of large open spaces [Psych.]. (Gr. *agora,* and *phobia,* madness.)
agouti, *n.* a-*goo*-te, a South American rodent of the genus *Dasyprocta.* (Fr. *acuti,* native.)
agraffe, *n.* a-*graff,* an ornamented clasp affixed to armour ; a clamping-iron ; a cramp, hook, or other fastening device. (Fr. *agrafe.*)
agraphia, *n,* a-*graf*-e-a, a mental disorder causing inability to write [Path.]. (Gr. *a-,* and *grapho,* write.)
agrarian, *a.* a-*grare*-e-an, pertaining to landed property and cultivated land, and to its apportionment : *n.* an advocate of an equable distribution of landed property among the inhabitants of a country. **agrarian crime,** crime arising out of a dispute about land. **agrarian laws,** laws regulating the ownership and division of land. (L. *agrarius,* pertaining to land.)
agrarianism, *n.* a-*grare*-e-an-izm, an equable distribution of lands, or the principles of those who favour such distribution.
agrarianize, *v.t.* a-*grare*-e-an-ize, to apportion land equally ; to infect with ideas of agrarianism.
agree, *v.i.* a-*gree,* to be of one mind ; to live in concord ; to consent ; to settle by stipulation ; to come to one opinion or mind ; to be reconciled ; to harmonize ; to resemble ; to correspond ; to suit ; to correspond in gender or number [Gram.]. (O.Fr. *agreer,* to come to terms.)
agreeability, *n.* a-gree-a-*bil*-e-te, agreeableness ; conformity ; accordance.
agreeable, *a.* a-*gree*-a-bl, suitable ; conformable to ; in conformity with ; pleasing ; willing to agree.
agreeableness, *n.* a-*gree*-a-bl-ness, state of being agreeable ; a quality that affords pleasure.
agreeably, *ad.* a-*gree*-a-ble, in an agreeable manner.
★**agreement,** *n.* a-*gree*-ment, the state of being agreed ; harmony of sentiment ; correspondence ; bargain ; a contract ; concord [Gram.].
agrestic, *a.* a-*gres*-tik, rustic, rude. (L. *agrestis,* rustic.)
agricultural, *a.* ag-re-*kul*-tewr-al, pertaining to agriculture.
agriculturalist, *n.* ag-re-*kul*-tewr-al-ist, one skilled in agriculture.
agriculture, *n. ag*-re-*kul*-tewr, the science, art, or practice of cultivating the ground. (L. *agri,* of a field, and *cultura,* tilling.)
agriculturist, *n.* ag-re-*kul*-tewr-ist, an agriculturalist.
agrimony, *n. ag*-re-mo-ne, a plant of the genus *Agrimonia,* one species of which, *Agrimonia eupatoria,* was once valued as a tonic. (O.Fr. *aigrimoine,* liver-wort.)
agrimotor, *n. ag*-re-mo-tor, a tractor for use on farms.
agrin, *a.* a-*grin,* grinning.
agriologist, *n.* ag-re-*ol*-o-jist, a student of agriology.
agriology, *n.* ag-re-*ol*-o-je, the comparative study of man in his primitive state. (Gr. *agrios,* savage, *logos,* science.)
agrom, *n. ag*-rom, a disease of the East Indies in which the tongue chaps and cleaves. (Gujerati.)
agronomic, *a. ag*-ro-*nom*-ik, relating to agronomics or agronomy.
agronomics, *n.* ag-ro-*nom*-iks, the branch of political economy treating of the allotment and care of the land, especially as regarding its nationalization. (Fr. *agronome,* an agriculturalist.)
agronomist, *n.* ag-*ron*-o-mist, a student of agronomics, or a person practising agronomy.
agronomy, *n.* ag-*ron*-o-me, scientific agriculture.
agrostography, *n.* ag-ros-*tog*-ra-fe, a description of the grasses. (Gr. *agrostis,* grass.)
agrostology, *n.* ag-ros-*tol*-o-je, that part of botany which treats of the grasses.
aground, *ad.* a-*ground,* on the ground ; stranded [Naut.] ; brought to a stand.

agua, *n.* *ah*-gwa, a large toad, *Bufo agua,* of S. America and the W. Indies.
aguardiente, *n.* *ah*-gwawr-dee-*en*-ta, an inferior Spanish brandy. (Sp. *aguardiente,* brandy.)
ague, *n.* *ay*-gew, malaria; an intermittent fever, with cold shiverings; a chill, with shivering, though in health. **ague tree,** former name of the sassafras, reputed to have febrifugal properties. (O.Fr. *ague,* sharp.)
ague-cake, *n.* *ay*-gew-kake, a tumour caused by a hardening of the spleen, frequently due to ague.
agued, *a.* *ay*-gewd, having a fit of ague; shivering.
aguish, *a.* *ay*-gew-ish, malarial; somewhat cold or shivering; causing ague.
ah, *int.* ah, an exclamation expressive of surprise, pity, complaint or contempt, according to the manner of utterance. (O.Fr. *a !*)
aha, *int.* ah-*ha,* an exclamation expressing triumph, contempt, or surprise, according to look or utterance.
ahead, *ad.* a-*hed,* further in advance; headlong. **go ahead,** start at once; keep on.
aheap, *a.* or *ad.* a-*heep,* trembling with fear; crouching together from fear.
ahem, *int.* a-*hem,* exclamation indicating surprise or disbelief, or to attract notice or gain time.
ahoy, *int.* a-*hoy,* a sea term, used in hailing.
Ahriman, *n.* *ah*-re-man, the Zoroastrian impersonation of the dark or evil principle, in opposition to Ormuzd. (Per., from Zend *arira mainyu,* an unfriendly spirit.)
ahull, *ad.* a-*hull,* with all sails furled, and helm lashed on the lee-side [Naut.].
ai, *n.* *ah*-ee, the three-toed sloth, an edentate of the genus *Bradypus.* (Braz., from its plaintive cry.)
Aich's-metal, *n.* *ikes*-met-al, an alloy of copper, zinc, and iron. (Johann Aich.)
aid, *n.* ayd, help; succour; the person or thing that helps; an aide-de-camp; a tax for a special purpose; a tribute exacted by a lord from his vassal: *v.t.* to help; to succour; to relieve. **first aid,** help to the injured before the arrival of a doctor. (O.Fr. *aider,* help.)
aide-de-camp, *n.* (App.) (*pl.* **aides-de-camp**), an officer attendant on the sovereign or a general. (Fr.)
aide-mémoire, *n.* (App.), a document, etc., serving as anaid to memory; a memorandum: a mnemonic guide. (Fr.)
aidless, *a.* *ayd*-less, without aid; unsupported.
aigre, *n.* ay-*ger,* an eagre.
aigremore, *n.* *ay*-ger-mor, charcoal prepared for use in the manufacture of gunpowder. (Fr.)
aigrette, *n.* *ay*-gret, an egret's plume; a tuft of feathers; a spray of jewels.
aiguille, *n.* ay-*gweel,* a slender spire; a rock-drill; a peak; a needle-like point. (Fr. *aiguille,* a needle.)
aiguillesque, *a.* ay-gwe-*lesk,* like an aiguille in shape.
aiguillette, *n.* *ay*-gwe-*let,* an aglet.
ail, *v.t.* ayl, to affect with pain or uneasiness, either of body or mind: *v.i.* to be in pain or trouble; to be the matter with. (A.S. *eglan,* to suffer pain.)
Ailantus, *n.* ay-*lan*-tus, a genus of East Indian and Chinese trees, including the tree of heaven, *A. glandulosa.*
aileron, *n.* *ay*-ler-on, a side wall concealing a church aisle, or a half-gable [Architect.]; a hinged auxiliary tip to an aeroplane wing to assist in keeping its lateral balance [Av.]. (Fr. *aileron.*)
aillette, *n.* ayl-*let,* the steel shoulder-plate of a coat of mail. (Fr. *aile,* a wing.)
ailment, *n.* *ayl*-ment, indisposition; disease.
aim, *n.* aym, the act of aiming; the object aimed at; purpose; design: *v.i.* to point at with a missive weapon; to direct the intention or effort; to endeavour: *v.t.* to direct or point, as a weapon. (O.Fr. *aesmer,* to estimate.)
aimless, *a.* *aym*-less, without aim.
aimlessly, *ad.* *aym*-less-le, without aim.
aimlessness, *n.* *aym*-less-ness, the quality or state of being aimless.
ain't, aynt, vulgar for "are not" and "am not." [Colloq.].
★**air,** *n.* ayr, the atmosphere; an aeriform body or a gas; a light breeze; a tune; melody; peculiar look, appearance, or mien, as a ridiculous air; an affected manner; show of pride, haughtiness, as an air of triumph, airs and graces: *v.t.* to expose to the air; to ventilate; to dry or warm by a fire. **Air Chief Marshal, Marshal,** and **Vice-Marshal,** R.A.F. officers equivalent in rank respectively to Admiral, Vice-Admiral, and Rear-Admiral and General, Lieut.-General, and Major-General. **Air Commodore,** R.A.F. officer equivalent in rank to a naval Commodore and an army Brigadier. **Air Officer,** the R.A.F. equivalent of Flag Officer and General Officer. **hot air,** *see* **hot. take the air,** to walk in the open air. **castles in the air,** fanciful ideas. **up in the air,** highly excited. (Fr. *air,* from L. *āer,* from Gr. *aēr,* air.)
air-base, *n.* *ayr*-base, an aerodrome used as a base by military or naval aircraft [Mil.].
air-bath, *n.* an apparatus for regulating temperature of substances in chemical, etc. processes; exposure of the body to air for hygienic reasons.
air-bed, *n.* *ayr*-bed, a bed inflated with air.
air-bladder, *n.* *ayr*-blad-der, a vesicle containing air; the sound or swim-bladder of a fish.
air-bone, *n.* *ayr*-bone, a hollow bone containing air [Ornith.].
airborne, *a.* *ayr*-born, carried or disseminated by atmospheric agency [Bot. etc.]; transported by aircraft.
air-brake, *n.* *ayr*-brake, a brake worked by compression of air or through the action of air on a vacuum.
air-brick, *n.* *ayr*-brik, a ventilating brick.
air-built, *a.* *ayr*-bilt, chimerical.
air-bump, *n.* state of the air causing sudden change of direction or drop in altitude of aircraft; a change or drop so caused.
air-casing, *n.* *ayr*-kase-ing, iron casing filled with air, and enclosing, so as to isolate, a heated pipe.
air-cell, *n.* *ayr*-sel, a cavity containing air [Bot. and Anat.].
air-chamber, *n.* *ayr*-chaym-ber, a chamber enclosing air for buoyancy or shock-absorption; a a cavity in a hydraulic machine from which the air on the admission of water acts as an equalizing force upon its flow.
air-cock, *n.* an outlet from a pipe, etc. controlled by a tap, to allow escape of air.
air-condenser, *n.* an apparatus in which steam is cooled by contact with air-cooled surfaces [Mech.]; a condenser in which air forms the dielectric [Elec.].
air-conditioning, *n.* *ayr*-kon-*dish*-on-ing, the process of cleansing, humidifying, and dehumidifying air before it enters a building, hall, etc.
air-cooling, *a.* *ayr*-kool-ing, diminishing heat in the cylinders of internal-combustion engines by means of currents of air only.
air-course, *n.* a flue or passage for admitting air.
aircraft, *n.* *ayr*-krahft, collective name for machines designed to travel or float in the air, as aeroplanes, airships, gliders, helicopters, kite-balloons, etc. **aircraft-carrier,** a large naval vessel built as a floating seaplane base with deck suitable for taking off and alighting of aircraft.
aircraftman, *n.* *ayr*-krahft-man, one trained to manage aircraft; a member of the R.A.F. ranking with an army private.
air-cushion, *n.* *ayr*-koosh-on, a cushion that is inflated with air.
air-drain, *n.* *ayr*-drayn, a protection round the external walls of a building to prevent dampness.
Airedale, *n.* *ayr*-dale, a large variety of terrier, originally bred for otter-hunting in the river Aire.
air-engine, *n.* *ayr*-en-jin, engine moved by the expansion and compression of air.
airer, *n.* *ayr*-er, one who airs; a clothes-horse.
air-field, *n.* the open ground of an aerodrome; a flat space suitable for the landing and taking off of aircraft.
air-force, *n.* that branch of an armed service designed for hostilities in the air.
airframe, *n.* *ayr*-frame, the structure of an aeroplane without motor or internal fittings.
air-furnace, *n.* *ayr*-fur-nace, a furnace in which air is heated; a furnace other than a blast-furnace.
air-gap, *n.* *ayr*-gap, the space between the poles of a magnet, or between the stator and rotor of a motor or generator [Elect.].
air-gas, *n.* *ayr*-gas, air mingled with hydrocarbon vapour so that it becomes combustible and can be used for lighting and heating; also a producer gas consisting chiefly of carbon-monoxide and nitrogen.
airgraph, *n.* *ayr*-graf, a letter or document photographed in miniature for transmission in bulk by

air, the result being photographically enlarged before delivery.
air-gun, *n.* *ayr*-gun, a gun which propels bullets by compressed air.
air-hole, *n.* *ayr*-hole, an opening for air; a flaw in cast metal.
airily, *ad.* *ayr*-e-le, in an airy manner.
airiness, *n.* *ayr*-e-ness, state of being airy; lightness.
airing, *n.* *ayr*-ing, exposure to the air, or a fire, to warm or dry; exercise in the open air.
air-jacket, *n.* *ayr*-jak-et, a swimming jacket inflated with air.
airless, *a.* *ayr*-less, not freely communicating with the open air; not airy.
air-line, *n.* *ayr*-line, a straight line in the air between two points; a system of aircraft transportation, or the organization operating it.
air-liner, *n.* a large transport aeroplane [Colloq.].
air-lock, *n.* *ayr*-lok, the intervening chamber between the air and the interior of a pneumatic or submarine caisson.
air-log, *n.* *ayr*-log, an instrument for measuring and recording the speed of aircraft.
air-mail, *n.* the system of carrying mail by air; the mail so carried.
airman, *n.* *ayr*-man, one who navigates the air.
airmanship, *n.* *ayr*-man-ship, the art of handling and esp. piloting aircraft.
air-mechanic, *n.* *ayr*-me-*kan*-ik, a mechanic employed on the repair and adjustment of aircraft.
airplane, *n.* *ayr*-plane, an aeroplane.
air-plant, *n.* an epiphyte deriving its sustenance from the air [Bot.].
air-pocket, *n.* *ayr*-pok-et, a local atmospheric condition caused by currents or abrupt change in wind direction, making an aeroplane drop suddenly while flying.
air-port, *n.* *ayr*-port, an aperture admitting light and air [Naut.]; an air-line station at which passengers and freight are received and discharged.
air-pump, *n.* *ayr*-pump, a pump for exhausting air from a vessel or enclosed space.
air-raid, *n.* *ayr*-rade, an attack by aircraft.
air-sac, *n.* *ayr*-sak, one of the cavities in the bony structure of birds filled with air and communicating with the lungs [Ornith.].
airscrew, *n.* *ayr*-skroo, the propeller of an aircraft.
airship, *n.* *ayr*-ship, a dirigible balloon. **non-rigid airship,** one the shape of which is maintained by internal pressure.
air-sickness, *n.* *ayr-sik*-ness, a form of *mal de mer* to which persons in aircraft are liable.
air-space, *n.* *ayr*-space, space containing air, as a room; interval betwixt two walls; cavity holding air in a bird's body.
airspeed, *n.* *ayr*-speed, speed relative to stationary air as distinguished from that relative to the earth; speed through the air.
air-stove, *n.* *ayr*-stohv, a stove from which heated air is discharged into a room.
air-stream, *n.* a current of air surrounding a solid body either in motion or stationary; a cooling air current [Eng.].
air-strip, *n.* a makeshift temporary landing and taking-off place for planes.
airt, *n.* ayrt, direction; a point of the compass [Scots.]. (Gael. *aird*, a quarter of the compass.)
air-tight, *a.* *ayr*-tite, impermeable to air.
air-trap, *n.* *ayr*-trap, contrivance for escape of foul air from drains.
airway, *n.* *ayr*-way, passage for admitting air [Mining]; a set route for aerial navigation.
air-worthiness, *n.* fitness for flying.
air-worthy, *a.* ayr-*wur*-the, fit for flying; able to bear the strain of flight.
airy, *a.* *ayr*-e, consisting of air; belonging to the air; in air; open to a free current of air; light as, or like, air; unsubstantial; unreal; vain; gay; sprightly; light of heart.
aisle, *n.* ile, the wing or side passage of a church, separated from the nave by pillars. (Fr. *aile*, aisle.)
aisled, *a.* iled, furnished with aisles.
ait, *n.* ayt, a small island in a river or lake; an eyot. (A.S. *iggath*, small island.)
aitch-bone, *n.* *aych*-bone, the part of an ox cut from between the rump and the buttock. (For *natch-bone*, from O.Fr. *nache*, buttock, and *bone*.)
ajar, *ad.* a-*jahr*, partly open, as a door. (A.S. *oncirran*, to turn away.)
ajog, *ad.* a-jog, leisurely progression, as of a pony-trap *jogging* along.
Ajuga, *n.* a-*joo*-gah, a large genus of herbs of the mint family, 30 labiate plants which including the bugle, *Ajuga reptans*.
akee, *n.* a-*kee*, the tropical African fruit-tree, *Blighea sapida*.
akimbo, *ad.* a-*kim*-bo, hands on hips with elbows outwards.
akin, *a.* a-*kin*, allied by blood or by nature.
al-, a prefix of Arabic origin, equivalent to *the*.
ala, *n.* *ay*-la, a wing-shaped process, as one of the lateral cartilages of the nose [Anat.]. (L. *ala*, a wing.)
alabandite, *n.* al-a-*ban*-dite, a native black manganese sulphide originally found at Alabanda, Asia Minor.
alabaster, *n.* *al*-a-bas-ter, a compact granular variety of sulphate of calcium; gypsum: *a.* made of alabaster. (O.Fr. *alabastre*.)
alabastrine, *a.* al-a-*bas*-treen, pertaining to, or like, alabaster.
alabastrum, *n.* *al*-a-*bas*-trum, a vessel for perfumes, usu. made of alabaster; formerly, a flower-bud.
alack, *int.* a-*lak*, alas! an expression of sorrow. (Perhaps from int. *O!* and *lack*, denoting a want.)
alack-a-day, *int.* a-*lak*-a-*day*, alas the day! expressing sorrow.
alacrity, *n.* a-*lak*-re-te, cheerful or ardent promptitude. (L. *alacritātem*, briskness.)
alacritous, *a.* a-*lak*-re-tus, brisk; lively.
Aladinist, *n.* a-*lad*-in-ist, one of a Mohammedan sect of freethinkers founded by 'Ala'-al-din, a 15th-century divine.
alalia, *n.* a-*lay*-le-a, aphasia [Path.].
alameda, *n.* ah-la-*may*-da, an avenue of trees forming a public promenade. (Sp. *álamo*, poplar.)
alamode, *ad.* a-la-*mode*, in the fashion: *n.* a thin glossy silk for hoods and scarfs; small pieces of meat stewed with vegetables. (Fr. *à la mode*, according to the fashion.)
alamort, *ad.* *al*-a-mort, mortally: *a.* melancholy; depressed. (Fr. *à la mort*, to the death.)
alantin, *n.* a-*lan*-tin, a former name of inulin.
alar, *a.* *ay*-lar, pertaining to, or having wings.
alarm, *n.* a-*lahrm*, signal in warning of approaching danger; a summons to arms; sudden terror excited by apprehension of danger; contrivance for waking persons from sleep, or exciting attention; an appeal or challenge [Fencing]: *v.t.* to rouse to vigilance and exertion in imminency of danger; to disturb with terror. (Fr. *alarme*, warning.)
alarm-bell, *n.* a-*lahrm*-bel, a bell rung to give an alarm.
alarm-clock, *n.* a-*lahrm*-klok, a clock contrived so that it can be set to strike an alarm at any time.
alarm-gun, *n.* a-*lahrm*-gun, gun fired as a danger warning.
alarming, *a.* a-*lahrm*-ing, exciting alarm or apprehension.
alarmingly, *ad.* a-*lahrm*-ing-le, in an alarming manner.
alarmist, *n.* a-*lahrm*-ist, one needlessly exciting alarm.
alarm-post, *n.* a meeting-place appointed for use in the event of an alarm [Mil.].
alarm-watch, *n.* a-*lahrm*-wotch, a watch acting as an alarm-clock.
alarum, *n.* a-*lahr*-um, *or* a-*la*-rum, an alarm; an alarm-clock or -watch.
alary, *a.* *ayl*-a-re, wing-shaped [Bot. and Anat.].
alas, *int.* a-*lass*, *or* a-*lahss*, an exclamation expressive of sorrow, grief, pity, concern, or apprehension of evil. (O.Fr. *a*, ah! and *las*, miserable that I am!)
alate, *a.* *ay*-late, having wings or processes like wings [Bot. and Conch.]. (L. *ālātus*, winged.)
alb, *n.* alb, a full-length ecclesiastical vestment of white linen. (O.Fr. *albe*.)
albacore, *n.* *al*-ba-kore, a large species of tunny. (Port. from Ar. *albakr*, the young camel.)
Albanian, *a.* al-*bay*-ne-an, pertaining to Albania: *n.* a native of Albania; the language of modern Albania.
albata, *n.* al-*bah*-ta, a silver-like alloy of nickel, tin, zinc, and copper. (L. *albus*, white.)
albatross, *n.* *al*-ba-tross, a long-winged petrel of the genus *Diomedea*, the largest of living seafowl. (Port. *alcatraz*, a pelican.)

albeit, *conj.* awl-*be*-it, although; notwithstanding.
albert, *n.* *al*-bert, a watch-chain attached to a buttonhole by a cross-piece; a size of notepaper ($3\frac{7}{8}''$ by 6"). (After *Albert*, Prince Consort.)
albescence, *n.* al-*bess*-ens, the act of becoming or state of being white.
albescent, *a.* al-*bess*-ent, becoming white, or whitish. (L. *albescens*, becoming white.)
Albigenses, *n.pl.* al-be-*jen*-seez, a sect of Reformers who separated from the Church of Rome in the 12th century. (From *Albigeois*, inhabitants of Albi, a town in Languedoc, France.)
albinism, *n.* *al*-bin-izm, the state or condition of an albino; leucopathy.
albino, *n.* al-*bee*-no, a person, or animal, with an unusually pale skin and fair hair, often with weak pinkish eyes; a plant deficient in chlorophyll; a colourless impression from a die. (Port. *albino*, formerly whitish.)
albinotic, *a.* al-be-*not*-ik, pertaining to or affected with albinism.
Albion, *n.* *al*-be-on, an ancient, and still a poetic, name for England. (Celt. *alb*, cliff, and *ban*, white.)
albite, *n.* *al*-bite, one of the soda felspars. (L. *albus*.)
albugineous, *a.* al-bew-*jin*-e-us, resembling the white of an egg. (L. *albuginis*, whiteness.)
albugo, *n.* al-*bew*-go, a white opaque spot on the cornea obstructing vision, leucoma [Med.]; a parasitic fungus [Bot.].
album, *n.* *al*-bum, a white table containing a list of public officers and transactions [Rom. Antiq.]; a MS. book for autographs and written or drawn mementoes; a blank book for photographs, stamps, etc. (L. *album*, whiteness.)
albumen, *n.* al-*bew*-men, the white of an egg; the endosperm or perisperm of plants [Bot.]; albumin [Chem.]. (L. *albūmen*, white of an egg.)
albumenize, *v.t.* al-*bew*-min-ize, to convert into or impregnate with albumen.
albumin, *n.* al-*bew*-min, one of a group of simple proteins, soluble in water, existing in white of egg, in the blood, and in certain animal and vegetable solids and fluids.
albuminate, *n.* al-*bew*-min-ate, an alkali compound of an albumin.
albuminoid, *a.* al-*bew*-min-oyd, resembling albumen: *n.* one of a group of simple proteins which are insoluble and form part of the composition of supporting tissues.
albuminose, *a.* al-*bew*-min-ohs, albuminous: *n.* albumose.
albuminosis, *n.* al-bew-min-*oh*-sis, a morbid condition due to excess of albuminous matter in the blood [Path.].
albuminous, *a.* al-*bew*-min-us, resembling, consisting of, or having the properties of albumin.
albuminuria, *n.* al-*bew*-min-*yewr*-e-a, a disease in the kidneys involving presence of albumin in the urine. [Med.]. (L. *albūmen*, and Gr. *ouron*, urine.)
albumose, *n.* *al*-bew-mohs, a crystalloid product of the action of pepsin on albuminous matter.
alburnous, *a.* al-*bur*-nus, pertaining to or consisting of alburnum.
alburnum, *n.* al-*burn*-um, the wood between the inner bark and the hard wood, sap-wood [Bot.]. (L.).
Alca, *n.* *al*-ka, a genus of sea-birds which includes the razorbill. (Ice. *alka*, an auk.)
Alcaic, *a.* al-*kay*-ik, pertaining to the Greek poet Alcæus of Mitylene (about 600 B.C.), or the metre he first used: *n.pl.* verses in this metre.
alcayde, *n.* al-*kayd*, a judge, commander, governor, or gaoler in Spain and Spanish Africa. (Ar. *al-*, and *qādī*, a cadi or judge.)
alcazar, *n.* al-ka-*thar*, a Moorish fortress or palace, esp. that of Seville in Spain. (Sp.)
Alcedo, *n.* al-*see*-do, a genus of birds comprising the kingfishers. (L. *alcēdo*, kingfisher.)
alchemic, *a.* al-*kem*-ik, relating to alchemy.
alchemically, *ad.* al-*kem*-ik-al-le, in the manner of alchemy.
alchemist, *n.* *al*-kem-ist, a student of alchemy.
alchemistic, *a.* al-kem-*ist*-ik, practising or relating to alchemy.
alchemize, *v.t.* *al*-kem-ize, to transmute, as by alchemy.
alchemy, *n.* *al*-kem-e, the early form of chemistry, comprising the search for the philosophers' stone, etc.; the magic power of transmutation. (O.Fr. *alchemie*.)
alclad, *n.* *al*-klad, an alloy of aluminium used in sheets coated with pure aluminium in aeroplane construction. (*Al*uminium, and *clad*.)
alcohol, *n.* *al*-ko-hol, pure spirit, a liquid product of fomentation, esp. *ethyl alcohol*, the intoxicating agent of alcoholic beverages; hence, any intoxicating liquor. (Ar. *al-*, and *kohl*, fine powder of antimony.)
alcoholate, *n.* *al*-ko-hol-ate, a crystalline compound in which alcohol acts as water of crystallization.
alcoholic, *a.* al-ko-*hol*-ik, pertaining to, containing, or due to alcohol: *n.* one addicted to immoderate consumption of alcoholic beverages.
alcoholism, *n.* *al*-ko-hol-izm, an impaired condition due to the excessive use of alcoholic drinks.
alcoholization, *n.* *al*-ko-hol-e-*zay*-shon, the act of rectifying spirit.
alcoholize, *v.t.* *al*-ko-hol-ize, to convert into alcohol; to rectify spirit.
alcoholometer, *n.* *al*-ko-hol-*om*-e-ter, an instrument for determining the amount of alcohol in liquors.
alcoholometry, *n.* *al*-ko-hol-*om*-et-re, the determination of the amount of alcohol in spirituous liquids.
alcoometer, *n.* al-ko-*om*-e-ter, an alcoholometer.
Alcoran, *n.* *al*-ko-rahn, Alkoran.
alcove, *n.* *al*-kove, a vaulted recess in a room; an arbour; any sheltered retreat. (Fr. *alcôve*.)
Alcyonaria, *n.pl.* *al*-se-o-*nair*-re-a, a group of the Anthozoa including sea-pens and sea-fans [Zool.].
aldehyde, *n.* *al*-de-hide, a limpid volatile liquid, of a suffocating odour, produced by oxidation of alcohol. (*Alcohol*, *de*, from, and *hydrogen*.)
aldehydic, *a.* al-de-*hide*-ik, containing aldehyde.
alder, *n.* *awl*-der, a tree of the genus *Alnus*, usually growing in moist places. (A.S. *alor*, an alder.)
alderman, *n.* *awl*-der-man, one of a body of civic dignitaries of whom the mayor or lord mayor is chief; a similar official of a county. (A.S. *earldorman*, a head-man.)
aldermancy, *n.* *awl*-der-man-se, the office or term of office of an alderman.
aldermanic, *a.* awl-der-*man*-ik, pertaining or relating to an alderman.
aldermanly, *a.* *awl*-der-man-le, like or worthy of an alderman.
aldermanry, *n.* *awl*-der-man-re, the office or rank of an alderman; an alderman's ward or district.
aldern, *a.* *awl*-dern, made of alder.
Alderney, *n.* *awl*-der-ne, one of a breed of cattle originally raised in the Channel Islands. (Name of one of the islands.)
Aldine, *a.* *al*-dine, a style of type used by Aldus. **Aldine editions,** books, chiefly the classics, printed at Venice by the family of Aldus Manutius in the 16th century.
ale, *n.* ayl, a fermented intoxicating liquor brewed from malt and hops. (A.S. *ealu*, ale.)
aleatory, *a.* *ayl*-e-a-to-re, depending on dice or chance. (L. *alea*, dice.)
ale-bench, *n.* *ayl*-bench, a bench in or before an alehouse.
aleconner, *n.* *ayl*-kon-ner, an ale-taster; an inspector of ale or measures in licensed houses.
alecost, *n.* *ayl*-kost, costmary, a plant of the tansy family, formerly used to flavour ale.
alectryomachy, *n.* a-*lek*-tre-*om*-a-ke, cock-fighting. (Gr. *alektryon*, a cock, *machē*, fight.)
alectryomancy, *n.* a-*lek*-tre-o-*man*-se, an ancient practice of telling events by means of a cock pecking grains of corn. (Gr. *alektryon*, *manteia*, prediction.)
alee, *ad.* a-*lee*, on or to the lee side [Naut.].
alegar, *n.* *ayl*-e-gar, sour ale; vinegar made from ale. (*Ale*, and Fr. *aigre*, sour.)
ale-hoof, *n.* *ayl*-hoof, ground-ivy.
ale-house, *n.* *ayl*-house, a public house licensed to sell beer by retail but not spirits.
alembic, *n.* a-*lem*-bik, a vessel formerly used in distillation, made of glass, metal, or earthenware. (Ar. *al-anbīq*, the still.)
alembroth, *n.* a-*lem*-broth, the salt of wisdom of the alchemists, the double chloride of mercury and ammonium.
alength, *ad.* a-*length*, at full-length; length-wise.

alepidote, *a.* a-*lep*-e-dote, having no scales : *n.* any fish without scales. (Gr. *a-*, not, *lepis*, a scale.)
alert, *a.* a-*lert*, watchful ; brisk ; ready for action ; quick-witted : *n.* state of being ready ; an audible warning of an anticipated air-raid, gas-attack, etc. (Fr. *alerte.*)
alertly, *ad.* a-*lert*-le, briskly ; vigilantly.
alertness, *n.* a-*lert*-ness, the state of being alert.
ale-taster, *n.* *ayl*-tayst-er, an aleconner.
alethiology, *n.* a-*lee*-the-*ol*-o-je, a branch of logic, dealing with the nature of truth and falsehood. (Gr. *alēthia*, truth, *logos*, science.)
alette, *n.* a-*let*, a small pilaster or buttress [Arch.]. (Fr. *ailette*, a small wing.)
aleurometer, *n.* al-yew-*rom*-e-ter, an instrument for estimating the bread-making qualities of flour. (Gr. *aleuron*, wheaten flour, and *metron*, a measure.)
aleurone, *n.* a-*lew*-rohn, an albuminoid substance found in the endosperm of ripe seeds.
alevin, *n.* *al*-e-vin, fry of salmon or other fish. (Fr.)
alewife, *n.* *ayl*-wife, a woman who keeps an ale-house ; the allis shad, also *Pomolobus pseudo-harengus* of the N. American Atlantic coast [Ichth.].
alexanders, *n.* al-ek-*sahn*-derz, the umbelliferous plant, *Smyrnium olusatrum*, horse-parsley.
alexandrine, *n.* al-ek-*zan*-drin, verse of twelve syllables, used in O.Fr. poems on Alexander the Great.
alexandrite, *n.* al-ek-*zan*-drite, a green variety of chrysoberyl, used as a gem-stone.
alexia, *n.* a-*lek*-se-a, inability, through brain lesion, to comprehend the meaning of words read. (Gr. *a-*, and *lexis*, word.)
alexin, *n.* a-*lek*-sin, a defensive proteid in the body destructive of bacteria. (Gr. *alexo*, ward off.)
alexipharmic, *a.* a-lek-se-*fahrm*-ik, acting as an antidote : *n.* a counteractive. (Gr. *alexo*, to ward off, *pharmakon*, poison.)
alexipyretic, *n.* a-*lek*-se-py-*ret*-ik, a febrifuge. (Gr. *alexo*, to repel, *pyretos*, fever.)
alexiteric, *a.* a-lek-se-*te*-rik, counteracting poison : *n.* an antidote against poison ; a preservative from contagion. (Gr. *alexētērios*, able to ward off.)
alfa, *n.* *al*-fa, esparto grass, a species of *Stipa*.
alfalfa, *n.* al-*fal*-fa, a variety of lucerne.
alfresco, *a.* and *ad.* al-*fress*-ko, under the open sky. **alfresco meal,** a picnic meal. (It., in the fresh.)
algæ, *n.pl.* *al*-je, a large group of thallophytes nearly all aquatic, related to the fungi ; the sea-weeds [Bot.]. (L.)
algebra, *n.* *al*-je-bra, universal arithmetic, in which symbols are employed to denote operation, and letters to represent number and quantity. (Ar. *al-*, and *jabr*, reduction of fractions to whole numbers.)
algebraic, *a.* al-je-*bray*-ik, algebraical.
algebraical, *a.* al-je-*bray*-ik-al, pertaining to algebra.
algebraically, *ad.* al-je-*bray*-ik-al-le, by algebraic process.
algebraist, *n.* al-je-*bray*-ist, one who is versed in algebra.
algebraize, *v.t.* *al*-je-bra-ize, to reduce to algebraic form.
Algerine, *n.* al-je-*reen*, a native or inhabitant of Algiers ; hence, a pirate. (Algiers.)
algesia, *n.* al-*jee*-se-a, excessive sensitiveness to pain [Med.].
algid, *a.* *al*-jid, cold [Med.]. (Fr. *algide.*)
algidity, *n.* al-*jid*-e-te, chilliness.
algin, *n.* *al*-jin, a viscid substance found in seaweeds and used to stiffen textiles.
algist, *n.* *al*-jist, a specialist on seaweeds.
algoid, *a.* *al*-goyd, like algæ.
algology, *n.* al-*gol*-o-je, the study of seaweeds.
Algonquian, *a.* al-*gong*-ke-an, pertaining to and designating the largest group of N. American Indian tribes ; an individual of this group ; any of its languages.
algor, *n.* *al*-gor, an unusual coldness [Med.].
algorism, *n.* *al*-go-rizm, the decimal system of numeration ; arithmetic. (Ar. *Al-Khowārazmi*, a 9th-century Arab mathematician.)
algous, *a.* *al*-gus, pertaining to seaweed.
alguazil, *n.* al-gwah-*zeel*, a Spanish constable. (Sp.)
algum, *n.* *al*-gum, a tree, probably sandal-wood, mentioned in the Old Testament. (Heb.)
Alhambra, *n.* al-*ham*-bra, the 13th- to 14th-century fortress-palace at Granada, an outstanding example of Moorish architecture. (Ar. *al-hamra*, the red house.)
Alhambresque, *a.* al-ham-*bresk*, like the Alhambra in architectural style.
alias, *ad.* *ay*-le-as, otherwise ; at another time : *n.* an assumed name ; a second writ issued when the first has failed to enforce the judgment [Law]. (L.)
alibi, *ad.* *al*-e-by, elsewhere : *n.* a plea by accused that he was elsewhere when the crime was committed. (L.)
alicante, *n.* al-e-*kan*-te, *or* *al*-e-kant, a red, sweet wine from Alicante, Spain.
alidade, *n.* *al*-e-dade, the movable arm of a graduated instrument for taking altitudes and distances. (Ar. *al-*, the, *'adad*, upper arm.)
alien, *a.* *ayl*-yen *or* *ay*-le-en, foreign ; of a different nature ; adverse to : *n.* a foreigner ; one of another nationality ; one not having the privileges of a citizen. (O.Fr. *alien.*)
alienability, *n.* *ayl*-yen-a-*bil*-e-te, the capacity of being alienated.
alienable, *a.* *ayl*-yen-a-bl, that may be alienated.
alienage, *n.* *ayl*-yen-aj, the state of being an alien ; an alien's legal position.
alienate, *v.t.* *ayl*-yen-ate, to transfer property to another ; to estrange ; to misapply : *a.* estranged. (L. *alienatus*, alienated.)
alienation, *n.* ayl-yen-*ay*-shon, transference or conveyance of property to another [Law] ; the state of being alienated ; the action of estranging ; mental derangement.
alienator, *n.* *ayl*-yen-ay-tor, a person who alienates anything.
alienee, *n.* ayl-yen-*ee*, one to whom a right of ownership is transferred.
alienism, *n.* *ayl*-yen-izm, the state of being an alien ; the treatment or study of insanity.
alienist, *n.* *ayl*-yen-ist, a specialist in mental diseases.
aliform, *a.* *al*-e-form, having the shape of a wing.
alight, *v.t.* a-*lite*, to get down ; to descend and settle or lodge on ; to happen on. (A.S. *ālīhtan.*)
alight, *a.* or *ad.* a-*lite*, lighted ; into light ; on fire.
align, *v.t.* a-*line*, to form in a line ; to adjust or regulate by a line. (Fr. *aligner.*)
alignment, *n.* a-*line*-ment, the act of aligning ; the state of being adjusted to a line ; the line of adjustment ; a ground-plan.
alike, *a.* a-*like*, having resemblance ; similar : *ad.* in the same manner, form, or degree ; equally. (A.S. *onlīc*, alike.)
aliment, *n.* *al*-e-ment, nutriment ; food ; the sum paid to one who has a right to claim support [Scots. Law] : *v.t.* to maintain by legal obligation [Scots. Law]. (Fr. *aliment.*)
alimental, *a.* al-e-*ment*-al, pertaining to aliment ; supplying food ; nourishing.
alimentally, *ad.* al-e-*ment*-al-le, so as to serve for nourishment.
alimentary, *a.* al-e-*ment*-a-re, pertaining to aliment ; nourishing ; conveying nourishment. **alimentary canal,** the passage through which food passes during eating, digestion and excretion.
alimentation, *n.* al-e-ment-*ay*-shon, the act or power of affording nutriment ; the state of being nourished.
alimentative, *a.* al-e-*ment*-a-tiv, nutritive ; pertaining to the function of nutrition.
alimentiveness, *n.* al-e-*ment*-iv-ness, the instinct of appetite for food and drink.
alimony, *n.* *al*-e-mun-e, allowance, by decree of court, out of a husband's estate, for support of his wife on her legal separation. (L. *alimōnia*, sustenance.)
aline, *v.t.* a-*line*, to align.
alinement, *n.* a-*line*-ment, alignment.
aliped, *n.* *al*-e-ped, an animal, like the bat, having toes connected by a membrane serving as a wing ; *a.* wing-footed. (L. *ala*, a wing, *pes*, *pedis*, a foot.)
aliphatic, *a.* al-e-*fat*-ik, pertaining to or derived from fat [Chem.]. **aliphatic compounds,** fatty acids ; derivatives from methane and the paraffin hydrocarbons. (Gr. *aleiphar*, and *-phatos*, oil, fat.)
aliquant, *a.* *al*-e-kwant, of a number not contained an exact number of times in another ; thus, 6 is an aliquant part of twenty [Arith.]. (Fr. *aliquante.*)

aliquot, *a.* *al*-e-kwot, of a number contained an exact number of times in another; thus, 6 is an aliquot part of 18 [Arith.]. (Fr. *aliquote.*)
alish, *a.* *ayl*-ish, like ale; having the qualities of ale.
alisma, *n.* a-*liz*-ma, the water-plantain. (Gr.)
alitrunk, *n.* *al*-e-trunk, the segment of the body of an insect to which the wings are attached. (L. *ala*, and *truncus*, trunk.)
alive, *a.* a-*live*, living, or in life; in force, action, or operation; astir; lively; keenly attentive to; susceptible of. (A.S. *on līfe*, alive.)
alizarin, *n.* a-*liz*-a-rin, a colouring matter obtained from madder; a red synthetic dye. (Probably Ar. *al-acōrah*, sap.)
alkahest, *n.* *al*-ka-hest, the universal solvent of the alchemist. (Coined on Ar. model.)
alkalescence, *n.* *al*-ka-*les*-sens, state of becoming alkaline.
alkalescency, *n.* *al*-ka-*les*-sen-se, a tendency to become alkaline.
alkalescent, *a.* al-ka-*les*-sent, slightly alkaline; tending to become alkaline: *n.* an alkalescent substance.
alkali, *n.* *al*-ka-le, *or* -ly, a hydroxide of sodium or potassium, soluble in water, capable of neutralizing acids and changing red vegetable colours to blue. (Ar. *al-*, and *qalī*, ashes of saltwort.)
alkalifiable, *a.* *al*-ka-le-*fy*-a-bl, that may be made alkaline or converted into an alkali.
alkalify, *v.t.* *al*-ka-le-fy, to convert into an alkali: *v.i.* to become an alkali.
alkaligenous, *a.* al-ka-*lij*-e-nus, generating alkali.
alkalimeter, *n.* al-ka-*lim*-e-ter, an instrument for determining the amount of alkalinity or quantity of alkali in a substance.
alkalimetrical, *a.* al-ka-le-*met*-rik-al, relating to alkalimetry.
alkalimetry, *n.* al-ka-*lim*-e-tre, the art of ascertaining the strength of alkalies.
alkaline, *a.* *al*-ka-line, *or* -lin, having the properties of an alkali.
alkalinity, *n.* al-ka-*lin*-e-te, the quality of being alkaline; that which constitutes an alkali.
alkalization, *n.* al-ka-ly-*zay*-shon, the act of rendering alkaline.
alkalize, *v.t.* and *v.i.* *al*-ka-lize, to alkalify.
alkaloid, *n.* *al*-ka-loyd, the active principle of medicinal plants; a nitrogenized substance of vegetable origin possessing alkaline properties: *a.* like an alkali. (*alkali*, and Gr. *eidos*, form.)
alkaloidal, *a.* al-ka-*loy*-dal, of the nature of an alkaloid.
alkanet, *n.* *al*-ka-net, the plant *Alkanna tinctora*, whose root yields a red dye; the dye itself. (Ar. *al-kenna.*)
alkekengi, *n.* al-ke-*ken*-je, the winter-cherry, a species of *Physalis*. (Ar., *al-kākanj.*)
alkermes, *n.* al-*kerm*-eez, a cordial with a preparation from a species of kermes for base.
Alkoran, *n.* *al*-ko-rahn, the Koran, the sacred book of the Mohammedans.
Alkoranist, *n.* al-ko-*rahn*-ist, one who adheres strictly to the letter of the Koran, rejecting all traditions.
★**all,** *n.* awl, the whole; everything; the whole number of; the whole quantity, extent, duration, amount, quality, or degree: *ad.* wholly; completely; entirely. **all but,** almost. **all the better,** better by the whole difference. **all in,** without exception; exhausted [Slang]. **all in all,** everything to one; as a whole; altogether. **all in the wind,** too close to the wind, so that the sails shake in it only [Naut.]; wavering; uncertain. **all one,** quite the same. **all out,** to the fullest extent. **all over,** *see* **over. all there,** alert; ready-witted [Slang]. **after all,** *see* **after. at all,** in the least degree—used by way of enforcement or emphasis, usually in negative or interrogative sentences. (A.S. *eall*, all.)
all-, in *composition*, enlarges or adds force to the meaning; thus "all-absorbing," absorbing or engrossing to the exclusion of everything else.
alla, *a.* *ahl*-lah, in the manner of [Mus.]. **alla brevi** (*bray*-va), a direction that 4-time is to be treated as 2-time [Mus.]. (It.)
Allah, *n.* *al*-la, or al-*lah*, the Moslem word for the Deity. (Ar. *al-*, the, *ilah*, god.)
allanite, *n.* *al*-lan-ite, a silicate of cerium allied to epidote. (Named from T. *Allan*, who identified it.)

allantoic, *a.* *al*-lan-*toh*-ik, contained in the allantois.
allantoid, *a.* al-*lan*-toyd, pertaining to the allantois; sausage-shaped.
allantoin, *n.* a-*lan*-to-in, a crystalline substance found in urine and synthetically prepared from uric acid.
allantois, *n.* al-*lan*-to-iss, an important part of the alimentary canal in the embryo of the higher vertebrates [Zool.]. (Gr. *allas*, *allantos*, a sausage.)
allay, *v.t.* al-*lay*, to quiet; to still; to repress; to alleviate. (A.S. *ālecgan*, to lay down.)
allayment, *n.* a-*lay*-ment, alleviation; mitigation.
allegation, *n.* al-le-*gay*-shon, the act of alleging; assertion; that which is asserted or alleged; an excuse; statement of what a party in a case undertakes to prove [Law]. (Fr. *allégation.*)
allege, *v.t.* al-*lej*, to adduce and assert as a fact in proof or in plea. **alleging.** (O.Fr. *esligier*, to exculpate legally.)
allegeable, *a.* al-*lej*-a-bl, that may be alleged.
alleged, *a.* al-*lejd*, averred to be true; stated to be.
allegedly, *ad.* al-*lej*-ed-le, according to or by allegation.
allegiance, *n.* a-*lee*-jans, the fidelity of a subject to his sovereign; fealty; the duty owed by a subject to the state. (O.Fr. *ligeance*, liege.)
allegiant, *a.* a-*lee*-jant, loyal: *n.* one owing allegiance; a subject.
allegorical, *a.* al-le-*go*-re-kal, in the manner of allegory; figurative.
allegorically, *ad.* al-le-*go*-re-ka-le, by way of allegory.
allegorist, *n.* *al*-le-go-rist, one who treats a subject allegorically; a writer of allegories.
allegorization, *n.* *al*-le-go-ry-*zay*-shon, act of making an allegory.
allegorize, *v.t.* *al*-le-go-rize, to treat or interpret allegorically: *v.i.* to use allegory.
allegory, *n.* *al*-le-go-re, a figurative manner of speaking or writing, in which a subject of a higher order is described in terms of that of a lower; a representation in which something else is intended than what is actually exhibited [Paint and Sculp.]; an emblem. (Gr. *allēgoria*, a description of one thing under the image of another.)
allegretto, *a.* al-la-*gret*-to, not quite as quick as *allegro* [Mus.]. (It.)
allegro, *a.* al-*lay*-groh, briskly; gaily [Mus.]. (It. *allegro*, gay.)
allelomorph, *n.* al-*lel*-o-morf, one of a pair of contrasted characters alternative to each other which become segregated in reproduction [Biol.]. (Gk. *allelon*, of one another, *morphe*, form.)
allelomorphic, *a.* al-*lel*-o-morf-ik, pertaining to allelomorphs.
allelomorphism, *n.* al-*lel*-o-morf-izm, the presence of allelomorphic characters.
Allelujah, *int.* al-le-*loo*-yah, halleluiah.
allemande, *n.* al-le-*mahnd*, a German dance; the first movement after the prelude of a suite [Mus.]. (Fr. *allemand*, German.)
allergic, *a.* al-*ler*-jik, pertaining to or possessing allergy.
allergy, *n.* *al*-er-je, a physical condition of supersensitiveness to a substance, usually a protein, or an agent such as light or heat, normally harmless [Med.].
allerion, *n.* a-*leer*-e-on, an eagle without beak or feet [Her.]. (Fr. *alérion.*)
alleviate, *v.t.* a-*lee*-ve-ate, to lighten; to mitigate. **alleviating.** (L. *allēvo*, make smooth.)
alleviation, *n.* a-*lee*-ve-*ay*-shon, the act of alleviating; that which alleviates.
alleviative, *a.* a-*lee*-ve-a-tiv, alleviating.
alley, *n.* *al*-le, a way, walk, or passage, generally narrow; a court for skittles. (O.Fr. *alee*, a gallery.)
All-fools' Day, *n.* *awl*-foolz-day, the first of April.
all-fours, *n.* awl-*fawrz*, a card-game, so called from its four points (high, low, jack and game); a game at dominoes in which four or a multiple thereof counts towards score. **on all fours,** on legs and arms. **to be on all-fours,** to be on an equality.
all-hail, *int.* awl-*hayl*, a wish of all health.
All-Halloween, *n.* *awl*-hal-lo-*een*, the thirty-first of October, the eve of All Hallows.
All-Hallows, *n.* awl-*hal*-lohz, All Saints' Day, the first of November. (A.S. *eall*, all, *hālgan*, saint.)
All-Hallowtide, *n.* awl-*hal*-lo-tide, on or about the first of November.

all-heal, *n.* *awl*-heel, a popular name of several plants, such as valerian, mistletoe and self-heal.
alliaceous, *a.* al-le-*ay*-shus, pertaining to the onion family; having the properties of garlic. (L. *allium*, garlic.)
alliance, *n.* al-*ly*-ans, the state of being allied; relation or union by marriage; union by treaty or league; the treaty itself; any union or connection of interests; the parties allied. (O.Fr. *aliance.*)
allice, *n.* *al*-liss, the Severn shad, *Clupea alosa*.
alligate, *v.t.* *al*-le-gate, to tie together; to solve by alligation [Arith.].
alligation, *n.* al-le-*gay*-shon, act of binding together; a rule for finding the value of a mixture of ingredients of different values [Arith.]. (L. *alligātio*, a tying to.)
alligator, *n.* *al*-le-gay-tor, a large saurian of the genus *Alligator* found in America and China. (Sp. *el lagarto*, the lizard.)
alligator-pear, *n.* *al*-le-gay-tor-pare, the avocado.
allis, *n.* *al*-lis, the allice shad.
alliteral, *a.* al-*lit*-er-al, alliterative; characterized by alliteration.
alliterate, *v.t.* al-*lit*-er-ate, to render alliterative; to be alliterative.
alliteration, *n.* al-lit-er-*ay*-shon, the repetition of the same initial letter or sound in closely successive words. (L. *ad-*, and *litera*, a letter.)
alliterative, *a.* al-*lit*-er-a-tiv, pertaining to alliteration.
alliteratively, *ad.* al-*lit*-er-a-tiv-le, in the manner of, or by means of, alliteration.
alliterativeness, *n.* al-*lit*-er-a-tiv-ness, the quality of being alliterative.
Allium, *n.* *al*-e-um, a genus of bulbous plants of the lily family including the onion, chive, and garlic.
allocate, *v.t.* *al*-lo-kate, to allot; to assign to each his share. (L. *ad-*, and *locare*, to place.)
allocation, *n.* al-lo-*kay*-shon, the act of allocating; allowance made on an account.
allocatur, *n.* al-o-*kay*-tur, a certificate of allowance of costs [Law]. (Mediæval L., it is allowed.)
allochroite, *n.* al-*lok*-ro-ite, a variety of garnet.
allochroous, *a.* al-*lok*-ro-us, changing colour, esp. [Med.] as a symptom.
allocution, *n.* al-lo-*kew*-shon, a formal address, esp. by the Pope to the clergy. (L. *allocutio*, an address.)
allodial, *a.* al-*loh*-de-al, freehold; not feudal. (O.Fr. *alōd*, entire estate.)
allodium, *n.* al-*loh*-de-um, freehold estate; land which is the absolute property of the owner.
allogamous, *a.* al-*log*-a-mus, pertaining to cross-fertilization.
allogamy, *n.* al-*log*-a-me, cross-fertilization in plants.
allograph, *n.* *al*-lo-graf, a writing or signature made for a person by another. (Gr. *allos*, other, *grapho*, write.)
allomerism, *n.* a-*lom*-er-izm, the property of certain minerals of variation in chemical composition without change in crystalline form. (Gr. *allo*, other, *meros*, part.)
allomerous, *a.* a-*lom*-er-us, characterized by allomerism [Min.].
allomorph, *n.* al-o-*morf*, a mineral with two or more distinct crystalline forms; any one of such forms. (Gr. *allo*, other, *morphe*, form.)
allomorphism, *n.* al-o-*mor*-fizm, the characteristic property of allomorphs [Min.].
allomorphous, *a.* al-o-*mor*-fus, characterized by allomorphism [Min.].
allonge, *n.* (App.), an attachment to a bill of exchange for extra endorsements [Law and Comm.]; a lunge [Fencing]. (Fr. *allonge*, a lengthening.)
allopathic, *a.* al-lo-*path*-ik, pertaining to allopathy.
allopathist, *n.* al-*lop*-a-thist, one who practises allopathy.
allopathy, *n.* al-*lop*-a-the, ordinary medical practice as opposed to homœopathy. (Gr. *allos*, other, *pathos*, feeling or suffering.)
allophane, *n.* *al*-lo-fane, a hydrous aluminium silicate. (Gr. *allophanes*, seeming otherwise.)
Allophylian, *n.* al-lo-*fil*-e-an, one of a race other than Aryan or Semitic; *a.* of such a race; pertaining to the Allophylians. (L. *allophylus*, foreign.)
allot, *v.t.* al-*lot*, to distribute by lot; to give to each his share; to assign. **allotted. allotting.**
allotheism, *n.* *al*-lo-thee-izm, worship of strange gods, or the gods of a foreign people.
allotment, *n.* al-*lot*-ment, the act of allotting; the share assigned; a small plot of land for cultivation. (Fr. *allotement.*)
allotrope, *n.* *al*-o-trope, an allotropic form.
allotropic, *a.* al-lo-*trop*-ik, pertaining to allotropy; existing in diverse forms [Chem.].
allotropism, *n.* al-*lot*-ro-pizm, allotropy.
allotropy, *n.* al-*lot*-ro-pe, the existence of an element in two or more different forms [Chem.]. (Gr. *allotropos*, in another manner.)
allottable, *a.* a-*lot*-a-bl, capable of being allotted.
allottee, *n.* al-lot-*tee*, one to whom a share or allotment is assigned.
allow, *v.t.* al-*lou*, to grant; to admit; to permit; to approve; to deduct: *v.i.* to concede as an abatement. (O.Fr. *alouer*, to praise.)
allowable, *a.* al-*lou*-a-bl, that may be allowed; lawful.
allowableness, *n.* al-*lou*-a-bl-ness, the quality of being allowable.
allowably, *ad.* al-*lou*-a-ble, in an allowable manner.
allowance, *n.* al-*lou*-ans, the act of allowing; permission; admission; fixed quantity or sum allowed; approbation; abatement; deduction: *v.t.* to put upon allowance. (O.Fr. *alouance.*)
allowed, *a.* al-*loud*, permitted; admitted.
allowedly, *ad.* al-*lou*-ed-le, admittedly.
alloxan, *n.* al-*loks*-an, an oxidation product of uric acid.
alloxanic, *a.* al-lok-*san*-ik, pertaining to or derived from alloxan.
alloy, *n.* al-*loy*, a mixture of metals, esp. of an inferior with one of greater value; a base admixture: *v.t.* to mix metals; to impair, to debase [Fig.]. (O.Fr. *aleier*, to enter into combination.)
All-Saints' Day, *n.* awl-*saints*-day. All-Hallows.
allseed, *n.* *awl*-seed, name given to knotweed, goosefoot, and various many-seeded plants.
All-Souls' Day, *n.* awl-*sohlz*-day, the festival (Nov. 2) in commemoration of the faithful departed.
allspice, *n.* *awl*-spice, the berry of *Eugenia pimenta*, said to combine the flavour of many spices.
allude, *v.i.* al-*lewd*, to refer to something vaguely and indirectly; to hint at. (L. *allūdere*, allude to.)
allure, *v.t.* al-*lewr*, to attract or tempt by the offer of some good, real or apparent; to entice: *n.* allurement; charm; attractiveness. (O.Fr. *aleurrer*, to tempt with something.)
allurement, *n.* al-*lewr*-ment, that which allures.
alluringly, *ad.* al-*lewr*-ing-le, in an alluring manner.
allusion, *n.* al-*lew*-zhon, a reference to something not explicitly mentioned; a hint. (L. *allūsio*, a playing with.)
allusive, *a.* al-*lew*-siv, having allusion; hinting at.
allusively, *ad.* al-*lew*-siv-le, by way of allusion.
allusiveness, *n.* al-*lew*-siv-ness, the quality of being allusive.
alluvial, *a.* al-*lew*-ve-al, pertaining to alluvium; formed by deposit in water.
alluvion, *n.* al-*lew*-ve-on, the gradual increase of land by the action of sea or river; the land thus added [Law]; the mass of substances so collected. (L. *alluvio*, a washing against.)
alluvium, *n.* al-*lew*-ve-um, earth and other substances, washed down by rivers, floods, etc., from high grounds, and available as serviceable land [Geol.].
ally, *n.* *al*-le, a large or special marble used in the boys' game. (Perh. contraction of *alabaster.*)
ally, *n.* al-*ly*, one that is allied; a confederate: *pl.* **allies,** persons or things interdependent upon each other; states in league for mutual defence or offence: *v.t.* to unite by marriage or treaty; to connect, as by similitude or friendship. (O.Fr. *alier*, to join up.)
allyl, *n.* *al*-il, an unsaturated aliphatic radical present in garlic, etc. [Chem.].
alma, *n.* *al*-ma, an Egyptian singing and dancing girl. (Ar. *almah*, learned.)
almacantar, *n.* al-ma-*kan*-tar, a circle of the sphere parallel to the horizon; a circle of altitude; an instrument having an arc of 15°, formerly used to take observations of the sun. (Ar. *al-*, and *quantara*, to bend.)
almadie, *n.* *al*-ma-de, a long swift river boat used in India; a canoe of African rivers. (Ar.)
almagest, *n.* *al*-ma-jest, an astronomical treatise by Ptolemy (2nd century A.D.); any similar work. (Gr. *majistī*, greatest.)

almagra, *n.* al-*may*-gra, a fine deep-red ochre. (Sp.)

Alma Mater, *see* **mater.**

almanac, *n.* *awl*-ma-nak, a calendar for the year; a daily register noting astronomical data, church festivals, etc. **nautical almanac,** an official register of astronomical observations calculated in advance. (Late L. *almanach*, origin unknown.)

almandine, *n.* *al*-man-dine, a precious garnet of violet colour. (L. *Alabanda*, a town in Caria.)

almightily, *ad.* awl-*my*-te-le, in an almighty manner; omnipotently.

almightiness, *n.* awl-*my*-te-ness, omnipotence.

almighty, *a.* awl-*my*-te, possessing all power: irresistible; great [Slang].: *n.* (*cap.*) God, as all-powerful. (A.S. *ealmihtig*, almighty.)

almond, *n.* *ah*-mund, a small peach-like tree, *Amygdalus communis*; the stone of its fruit; an object of almond shape, as a tonsil. (O.Fr. *almande*.)

almond-cake, *n.* *ah*-mund-*kake*, what is left of the almond after the oil is expressed; a cake flavoured with or containing almonds.

almond-furnace, *n.* *ah*-mund-*fur*-nas, a furnace used to separate metals from dross. (Ger. *Allemand*, German.)

almond-oil, *n.* an oil obtained from almonds, used in pharmacy, perfumery, etc.

almond-paste, *n.* *ah*-mund-*payst*, a cosmetic composed largely of bitter almonds.

almond-willow, *n.* *ah*-mund-*wil*-loh, a British species of willow, *Salix amygdalina*.

almoner, *n.* *ahl*-mun-er, a distributor of alms; a hospital official who inquires into the social circumstances etc. of patients. **Lord High Almoner,** a prelate attached to the Royal Household responsible for the distribution of royal alms, esp. on Maundy Thursday. (O.Fr. *aumoner*.)

almonry, *n.* *awm*-re, the place of distribution of alms, or residence of an almoner. (O.Fr. *aumosnerie*.)

***almost,** *ad.* *awl*-mohst, nearly; all but. (A.S.)

alms, *n.pl.* ahmz, anything given out of charity to the poor. (A.S. *ælmæsse*, alms.)

almsdeed, *n.* *ahmz*-deed, an act or gift of charity.

alms-fee, *n.* *ahmz*-fee, an annual tribute formerly paid to the Pope; Peter's Pence.

alms-giving, *n.* *ahmz*-giv-ing, the bestowment of alms.

almshouse, *n.* *ahmz*-hous, a house where the poor are lodged and provided for by charitable endowment.

almsman, *n.* *ahmz*-man, a person supported by alms.

almucantar, *n.* al-mew-*kan*-tar, the almacantar.

alnage, *n.* *al*-naj, a measuring by the ell. (Fr. *aunage*, ell-measure.)

alnager, *n.* *al*-na-jer, former official inspecting woollen goods.

aloe, *n.* *al*-oh, a succulent plant of the liliaceous genus *Aloe*, all native of warm climates. (L. *aloë*, the aloe.)

aloes, *n.* *al*-ohz, the inspissated juice of aloes, used as a purgative [Med.].

aloes-wood, *n.* *al*-ohz-wood, agalloch.

aloetic, *a.* al-o-*et*-ik, pertaining to the aloe or aloes; containing aloes: *n.* a medicine consisting chiefly of aloes.

aloft, *ad.* a-*loft*, on high; above; at the mast-head; up the rigging [Naut.]. (Ice. *á lopt*, in the air.)

alogical, *a.* ay-*loj*-ik-al, not based on reason; not logical.

aloin, *n.* *al*-oh-in, the active principle of aloes.

alone, *a.* a-*lone*, single; solitary; only: *ad.* singly; by itself. **let alone,** disregarding; not to mention, much less [Coll.]. **to let alone,** to leave undisturbed. (*All*, and *one*.)

along, *ad.* a-*long*, lengthwise; in a line with the length; onward. (A.S. *gelang*, along). **all along,** the whole length. **along shore,** by the shore [Naut.]. **along with,** in company. **lying along,** pressed down by the weight of sail [Naut.]

alongside, *ad.* a-*long*-side, side by side.

aloof, *ad.* a-*loof*, at a distance, though within view; keeping away from. (Dut. *loef*, windward.)

aloofness, *n.* a-*loof*-ness, state of holding aloof.

alopecia, *n.* al-o-*pees*-yah, a skin-disease in which the hair falls off. (L. *alōpecia*, fox-mange.)

aloud, *ad.* a-*loud*, loudly; with a loud voice; audibly. (A.S. *on*, and *hlūd*, loud.)

alow, *ad.* a-*loh*, to or in a lower part.

alp, *n.* alp, a high mountain; a mountain pasture; a peak of the mountain-chain separating France and Italy. (L. *alpes*.)

alpaca, *n.* al-*pak*-a, a domesticated variety of the guanaco; cloth made from its long soft woolly hair; a mixture of silk and wool. (Sp. *alpaca*, the llama.)

alpenhorn, *n.* *al*-pen-hawrn, a long curved horn used by the Swiss herdsmen signalling. (Ger.)

alpenstock, *n.* *al*-pen-stok, a long, iron-shod stick used in mountaineering. (Ger.)

alpha, *n.* *al*-fa, the first letter in the Greek alphabet; the first or beginning; used in astronomy, chemistry, physics, etc., to designate the first in a group or series. **alpha-particle,** an atom of helium stripped of its two electrons [Phys.]. **alpha-ray** a stream of positively charged particles given off by certain radioactive substances during transformation. **alpha and omega,** the whole; from beginning to end. (L. *alpha*.)

alphabet, *n.* *al*-fa-bet, the letters of a language arranged in the usual order; first principles. (L. *alphabetum*, from Gr. *alpha*, *beta*, the first two letters.)

alphabetarian, *n.* *al*-fa-bet-*ayr*-e-an, one just learning his alphabet; a beginner.

alphabetical, *a.* al-fa-*bet*-ik-al, in the order of, or furnished with, an alphabet.

alphabetically, *ad.* al-fa-*bet*-ik-al-le, in an alphabetical order or manner.

alphabetize, *v.i.* *al*-fa-be-*tize*, to place in alphabetical order.

Alphonsine, *a.* al-*fon*-sin, compiled under Alphonso X of Castile (13th cent.).

alphos, *n.* *al*-fos, a non-contagious form of leprosy; psoriasis. (Gr.)

alpine, *a.* *al*-pine *or* *al*-pin, pertaining to the Alps, or any lofty mountain; very high; produced on high mountains.

Alpini, *n.pl.* al-*pee*-ne, Italian troops specially trained for mountain warfare. (It.)

alpinist, *n.* *al*-pin-ist, a climber in the Alps or other high mountains.

alpist, *n.* *al*-pist, the seed of canary grass used for feeding birds. (Fr. *alpiste*.)

alquifou, *n.* al-ke-*foo*, a native lead sulphide used to give earthenware a green glaze; galena; potter's ore. (Sp.)

already, *ad.* awl-*red*-e, by or before a specified time.

Alsatia, *n.* al-*say*-sha, formerly cant for the Whitefriars district in London, because, from being a sanctuary, it became a nest of bad characters; hence, any asylum for criminals. (Late L. *Alsatia*, Alsace.)

Alsatian, *a.* al-*say*-shan, pertaining to Alsace or Alsatia: *n.* an inhabitant of either of these; a breed of large German sheep-dog.

alsike, *n.* *al*-sik, Swedish clover, *Trifolium hybridum*.

Alsirat, *n.* al-se-*raht*, in Moslem mythology the bridge, no wider than a thread and sharper than a razor-edge, leading over the abyss into Paradise; hence, the strait way of righteousness. (Ar. *al-sirat*, the road.)

also, *ad.* and *conj.* *awl*-so, likewise; besides.

alt, *n.* *alt*, the high notes in the scale [Mus.].

altar, *n.* *awl*-ter, an elevated structure for offering sacrifices; the communion table; a place of worship.

altarage, *n.* *awl*-ter-aj, offerings upon the altar to the church or priest. (O.Fr. *auterage*.)

altar-bread, *n.* *awl*-ter-bred, the bread of the communion.

altar-cloth, *n.* *awl*-ter-kloth, the cloth which covers an altar.

altar-piece, *n.* *awl*-ter-pees, a painting or sculpture in a frame over the altar; a reredos.

altar-screen, *n.* *awl*-ter-skreen, a screen between the altar and the choir.

altar-tomb, *n.* *awl*-ter-toom, a tomb or monument resembling an altar.

altar-wise, *ad.* *awl*-ter-wize, placed north and south, like an altar.

altazimuth, *n.* al-*taz*-e-muth, an instrument for measuring both altitude and azimuth [Astrom.].

alter, *v.t.* *awl*-ter, to change or vary in some degree; to change entirely or materially: *v.i.* to change in some respects. (L. *alter*, other.)

alterability, *n.* awl-ter-a-*bil*-e-te, alterableness.

alterable, *a.* *awl*-ter-a-bl, that may be altered.
alterableness, *n.* *awl*-ter-a-bl-ness, susceptibility of alteration.
alterably, *ad.* *awl*-ter-a-ble, in a manner that may be altered.
alterant, *n.* *awl*-ter-ant, able to alter; a reagent serving to alter the colour of a dye [Dyeing]: *a.* producing alteration.
alteration, *n.* awl-ter-*ay*-shon, the act of altering; the change made. (Fr. *altération.*)
alterative, *a.* *awl*-ter-a-tiv, having the power to alter: *n.* a medicine which gradually restores the healthy functions [Med.]. (Fr. *altératif.*)
altercate, *v.i.* *awl*-ter-kate, to dispute hotly; to wrangle. (L. *altercatus,* wrangled.)
altercation, *n.* awl-ter-*kay*-shon, warm contention in words; wrangle.
altered, *a.* *awl*-terd, modified. **altered chord,** a chord whose tones have been chromatically modified [Mus.].
alter-ego, *n.* al-ter-*eg*-o, a second self; an intimate, a bosom friend. (L. *alter ego,* other I.)
altern, *a.* and *ad.* *alt*-ern, alternate; in turns.
alternant, *a.* awl-*ter*-nant, composed of alternating layers [Geol.]. (L. *alternans,* alternating.)
alternate, *a.* awl-*ter*-nate, one after the other in regular succession of time or place; succeeding regularly on opposite sides of a branch [Bot.], or of a line [Math.]; succeeding with regular breaks [Zool.]: *n.* *awl*-ter-nat, one who alternates with another, esp. in an office, the taking of duty, etc.; a deputy; a substitute.
alternate, *v.t.* *awl*-ter-nate, to perform by turns; to cause to succeed by turns, or reciprocally: *v.i.* to happen by turns. **alternating current,** an electric current of which the polarity or direction changes at a given rate, as opposed to direct current [Elect.]. (L. *alternātus,* done by turns.)
alternately, *ad.* awl-*ter*-nat-le, in reciprocal succession.
alternateness, *n.* awl-*ter*-nat-ness, the quality of being alternate.
alternation, *n.* awl-ter-*nay*-shon, act of alternating; state of being alternate; the regular succession of the one after the other; permutation [Math.]; response in church service [Eccles.]. **alternation of generations,** the alternate occurrence in a life-history of two or more forms produced in different ways. (L. *alternātio,* an alternation.)
alternative, *a.* awl-*ter*-na-tiv, offering a choice of two: *n.* choice of two; a proposal, course of action, etc. other than that in mind.
alternatively, *ad.* awl-*ter*-na-tiv-le, in the manner of an alternative.
alternativeness, *n.* awl-*ter*-na-tiv-ness, the quality or state of being alternative.
alternator, *n.* *awl*-ter-*nay*-tor, a dynamo or generator producing alternating electric currents.
alternipinnate, *a.* *awl*-ter-ne-*pin*-at, having leaves on either side of the stem [Bot.].
Althæa, *n.* al-*thee*-a, a genus of plants including the marsh-mallow and hollyhock. (L.)
although, *conj.* awl-*thoh,* granting all that; though.
altigraph, *n.* *awl*-te-graf, a recording altimeter.
altimeter, *n.* al-*tim*-e-ter, instrument for taking altitudes. (L. *altus,* high, Gr. *metron,* a measure.)
altimetry, *n.* al-*tim*-e-tre, the art of measuring altitudes.
altiscope, *n.* *al*-te-skope, a periscope.
altisonant, *a.* al-*tiss*-o-nant, high-sounding; pompous in language. (L. *altus,* and *sonus,* sound.)
altitude, *n.* *al*-te-tewd, height; height above the horizon; highest point or degree. (Fr. *altitude.*)
altitudinal, *a.* al-te-*tewd*-in-al, relating to altitude.
altitudinarian, *a.* *al*-te-tewd-in-*ayr*-e-an, doctrinaire; lofty or idealistic.
alto, *a.* *al*-toh, high: *n.* formerly the highest male voice, the counter-tenor, now the lowest female voice, the contralto; the tenor violin, or viola [Mus.]. (It. *alto,* high.)
altogether, *ad.* awl-too-*geth*-er, wholly; completely: *n.pl.* tights covering the whole body [Colloq.]. **the altogether,** the nude [Colloq.].
altometer, *n.* al-*tom*-e-ter, an altimeter; a theodolite.
alto-relievo, *n.* *al*-to-re-*lee*-vo, high relief; figures that project half or more from a flat surface [Sculp.]. (It. *alto-rilievo.*)
altruism, *n.* *al*-troo-izm, the doctrine which inculcates sacrifice of self for the interests of others. (It. *altrui,* of others.)
altruist, *n.* *al*-troo-ist, a practiser of altruism.
altruistic, *a.* al-troo-*ist*-ik, agreeable to altruism.
altruistically, *ad.* *al*-troo-*is*-tik-al-e, in an altruistic manner.
aludel, *n.* *al*-yew-del, a pear-shaped pot open at each end and capable of being fitted in series, formerly used by alchemists for sublimation. (Fr.)
alula, *n.* *al*-yew-la, a bastard-wing; a small scaly appendage at the base of the wing of certain *Diptera* and water-beetles. (L. *ala,* wing.)
alum, *n.* *al*-um, a double sulphate of alumina and potash, a salt of great use in medicine and the arts: *v.i.* to impregnate with alum. (O.Fr. *alum.*)
alumina, *n.* a-*lew*-min-a, the oxide of aluminium, the most abundant of the earths, and the characteristic ingredient of common clay. (L. *alumen,* alum.)
aluminated, *a.* a-*lew*-min-ay-ted, treated or impregnated with alum.
aluminic, *a.* al-yew-*min*-ik, containing alum.
aluminiferous, *a.* a-lew-min-*if*-er-us, containing alum or alumina.
aluminite, *n.* a-*lew*-min-ite, a sulphate of alumina.
aluminium, *n.* *al*-yew-*min*-e-um, a silvery, malleable, tractable metallic element extracted from bauxite; extensively used when lightness combined with strength is desired, as in aeroplanes. **aluminium gold,** a copper aluminium alloy used in cheap jewellery. (L. *alumen,* alum.)
aluminous, *a.* a-*lew*-min-us, pertaining to or containing alum.
aluminum, *n.* a-*lew*-min-um, aluminium.
alumish, *a.* *al*-um-ish, somewhat resembling alum.
alumnus, *n.* a-*lum*-nus, *fem.* **alumna,** a-*lum*-nah, a graduate, or former pupil. (L. *alumnus,* foster-son.)
alum-stone, *n.* *al*-um-stone, alunite.
alunite, *n.* *al*-yew-nite, a hydrated sulphate of potassium and aluminium. (Fr. *aluminilite.*)
alunogen, *n.* al-*yew*-no-jen, aluminium sulphate occurring in a white feather-like efflorescence.
aluta, *n.* a-*lew*-ta, a soft leather treated with alum (L.)
alveary, *n.* *al*-ve-a-re, a beehive, or something resembling one; hollow of the external ear [Anat.]. (L. *alveus,* a hollow.)
alveolar, *a.* al-*vee*-o-lar, containing or pertaining to sockets; socket-shaped; pronounced with the tip of the tongue (as *d, t, n*) [Phonetics.].
alveolate, *a.* *al*-ve-o-late, deeply pitted, so as to resemble a honeycomb.
alveolus, *n.* al-*vee*-o-lus, a cell in a honeycomb, or in a fossil; the socket in which a tooth is fixed.
alvine, *a.* *al*-vin, pertaining in the intestines or belly. (L. *alvus,* the belly.)
alway, *ad.* *awl*-way, always.
always, *ad.* *awl*-wayz, continually; regularly. (A.S. *eall,* every, all, *weg,* way.)
Alyssum, *n.* a-*lis*-um, a genus of dwarf herbs with white or yellow flowers.
am, am, the first person of the verb to be. (A.S. *eom.*)
amacratic, *a.* am-a-*krat*-ik, amasthenic.
amadavat, *n.* a-*mad*-a-vat, the small Indian songbird, *Sporœginthus amandava.*
amadou, *n.* *am*-a-doo, German tinder, prepared from a dried fungus, *Polyporus fomentarius,* steeped in saltpetre. (Fr. *amadou.*)
amah, *n.* *ah*-ma, a child's nurse or female servant in S. India. (Anglo-Ind., from Port. *ama.*)
amain, *ad.* a-*mayn,* with force; suddenly; at once.
amalgam, *n.* a-*mal*-gam, an alloy of mercury; a compound of different things. (Fr. *amalgame.*)
amalgamate, *v.t.* a-*mal*-ga-mate, to mix mercury with another metal; to compound: *v.i.* to combine in an amalgam; to blend; to unite with: *a.* united by amalgamation. (Mediæval L. *amalgamatus,* united.)
amalgamation, *n.* a-*mal*-ga-*may*-shon, the act of amalgamating; the blending of different things; the process of separating gold and silver from ores by means of mercury [Metal.]; a merger; the union of two or more companies of the same nature into one concern [Comm.].
amalgamative, *a.* a-*mal*-ga-may-tiv, having a tendency to amalgamation.

amalgamator, *n.* a-*mal*-ga-may-tor, a person amalgamating anything; a machine used in the extraction of free mercury.
amandin, *n.* a-*man*-din, the representative proteid of peach kernels and sweet almonds. (Fr. *amandine.*)
amandine, *n.* a-*man*-deen, an ointment prepared from sweet almonds.
amanuensis, *n.* a-man-yew-*en*-sis, one who writes to another's dictation; a secretary. (L. *amanuensis.*)
amaracus, *n.* a-*ma*-ra-kus, the plant marjoram.
amaranth, *n.* *am*-a-ranth, the plant called love-lies-bleeding; an imaginary flower that never fades; a colour inclining to purple. (L. *amarantus*, amaranth.)
amaranthine, *a.* am-a-*ranth*-in, relating to amaranth; unfading.
Amaryllis, *n.* am-a-*ril*-lis, the genus of the belladonna lily, an autumn-flowering plant.
amass, *v.t.* a-*mass*, to collect in large quantity or amount; to accumulate. (Fr. *amasser*, to gather up.)
amassment, *n.* a-*mass*-ment, a heap; an accumulation.
amasthenic, *a.* am-as-*then*-ik, perfectly uniting the rays of light into one focus (of photographic lenses).
amateur, *n.* *am*-a-tewr, one who cultivates any study or art from mere love of it without pursuing it professionally; a non-professional sportsman: *a.* done by an amateur. (Fr. *amateur.*)
amateurish, *a.* *am*-a-*tewr*-ish, unskilful; indicative of an untrained worker or an amateur.
amateurishly, *ad.* in an unskilful or unprofessional manner.
amateurishness, *n.* *am*-a-*tewr*-ish-ness, unskilfulness.
amateurism, *n.* *am*-a-*tewr*-rizm, the state of being an amateur, or unskilled; dilettantism.
amative, *a.* *am*-a-tiv, of, or relating to, sexual love; amorous. (L. *amatus*, loved.)
amativeness, *n.* *am*-a-tiv-ness, the faculty supposed to influence sexual love; the propensity itself.
amatol, *n.* *am*-a-tol, a powerful explosive consisting of trinitrotoluene and ammonium nitrate, used in hand-grenades.
amatorial, *a.* am-a-*taw*-re-al, amatory.
amatory, *a.* *am*-a-to-re, relating to or producing sexual love. (L. *amātōrius*, loving.)
amaurosis, *n.* am-aw-*roh*-sis, a decay or loss of sight from disease of the optic nerve. (Gr. *amaurōsis*, darkening.)
amaurotic, *a.* am-aw-*rot*-ik, affected with amaurosis.
amaze, *v.t.* a-*maze*, to confound with fear, surprise or wonder: *n.* the state of being amazed. (A.S. *amasian*, to amaze.)
amazedly, *ad.* a-*maze*-ed-le, in amazement.
amazedness, *n.* a-*maze*-ed-ness, amazement.
amazement, *n.* a-*maze*-ment, the state of being amazed; astonishment; perplexity.
amazing, *a.* a-*maze*-ing, exciting amazement, astonishment or surprise.
amazingly, *ad.* a-*maze*-ing-le, in an amazing manner.
amazon, *n.* *am*-a-zon, one of a fabled race of formidable female warriors; a masculine woman; a virago. (Gr.)
amazonian, *a.* am-a-*zoh*-ne-an, pertaining to or resembling an amazon; (*cap.*) pertaining to the river Amazon or its basin.
amazonite, *n.* *am*-a-zon-ite, a green variety of microline found in the valley of the Amazon.
amb-, amb, a Latin prefix signifying about; around.
ambages, *n.* am-*bay*-jeez, a winding; a roundabout way of expression; circumlocution; quibble; subterfuge. (O.Fr. *ambages.*)
ambagious, *a.* am-*bay*-jus, circumlocutory.
ambagiousness, *n.* circumlocution.
amban, *n.* *am*-ban, a Chinese resident official in Tibet or Mongolia. (Manchu, a minister.)
ambassador, *n.* am-*bas*-sa-dor, a minister who represents the sovereign power and dignity of his State at a foreign court, being ordinary when resident, and extraordinary when sent on a special mission. (Fr. *ambassadeur.*)
ambassadorial, *a.* am-bas-sa-*daw*-re-al, pertaining to an ambassador.
ambassadress, *h.* am-*bas*-sa-dress, the wife of an ambassador; a female ambassador.
amber, *n.* *am*-ber, a yellow semi-transparent fossil resin, which when rubbed is electrified: *a.* consisting of or resembling amber. (Fr. *ambre.*)
ambergris, *n.* *am*-ber-greece, an ash-coloured odorous wax-like substance used in perfumery, a morbid secretion from the alimentary canal of the sperm-whale found floating in the seas it frequents. (*Amber*, and Fr. *gris*, grey.)
amberite, *n.* *am*-ber-rite, a smokeless explosive.
amberoid, *n.* *am*-ber-royd, ambroid.
amber-seed, *n.* *am*-ber-seed, musk-seed; a seed resembling millet used in perfumery.
amber-tree, *n.* *am*-ber-tree, a shrub of the genus *Anthospermum*, whose leaves when bruised yield a fragrant odour.
ambidexter, *n.* am-be-*deks*-ter, one who uses both hands with equal facility; a double-dealer; one taking bribes from both parties [Law]: *a.* ambidextrous. (L. *ambi*, both, *dexter*, right hand.)
ambidexterity, *n.* *am*-be-deks-*te*-re-te, faculty of being ambidextrous.
ambidextrous, *a.* am-be-*deks*-trus, able to use both hands equally; double-dealing.
ambidextrously, *ad.* am-be-*deks*-trus-le, in an ambidextrous manner.
ambidextrousness, *n.* am-be-*deks*-trus-ness, ambidexterity.
ambient, *a.* *am*-be-ent, encompassing; surrounding. (L. *ambiens*, going about.)
ambiguity, *n.* am-be-*gew*-e-te, uncertainty of meaning. (L. *ambiguitas.*)
ambiguous, *a.* am-*big*-yew-us, of doubtful signification; equivocal; obscure. (L. *ambiguus*, uncertain.)
ambiguously, *ad.* am-*big*-yew-us-le, in an ambiguous manner.
ambiguousness, *n.* am-*big*-yew-us-ness, ambiguity.
ambit, *n.* *am*-bit, extent of place, action or words; precinct; compass; verge. (L. *ambitus*, a moving around.)
ambition, *n.* am-*bish*-on, the desire generally of superiority in honour and power; a generous impulse after excellence; the object of ambitious desire. (Fr. *ambition.*)
ambitious, *a.* am-*bish*-us, desirous of superiority in honour and power; aspiring; very desirous; indicating ambition.
ambitiously, *ad.* am-*bish*-us-le, in an ambitious manner.
ambitiousness, *n.* am-*bish*-us-ness, the quality of being ambitious.
ambitus, *n.* *am*-be-tus, an external edge, esp. of a leaf or shell. (L., as *ambit.*)
ambivalence, *n.* am-*biv*-a-lens, simultaneous attraction towards and repulsion from a person, thing, etc.; simultaneous attractiveness and repulsiveness. (L. *ambi*, both, *valēre*, to be worth.)
ambivalent, *a.* am-*biv*-a-lent, marked by ambivalence.
amble, *n.* *am*-bl, an easy rolling pace: *v.i.* to move at an amble; to move easily, without jolts; to move affectedly. (O.Fr. *ambler*, to go easily.)
ambling, *a.* *am*-bling, having an easy, rolling pace.
amblygonite, *n.* am-*blig*-on-ite, a pale green crystalline compound of fluorine, aluminium, lithium, and phosphorus.
amblyopia, *n.* am-ble-*oh*-pe-a, dim or defective vision. (Gr. *amblyopēs*, darkening of the sight.)
amblyopic, *a.* am-ble-*op*-ik, weak of sight.
amblyopsis, *n.* am-ble-*op*-sis, the blind fish of the Mammoth Cave of Kentucky.
Amblystoma, *n.* *am*-ble-*stoh*-ma, the genus of salamandroid amphibians found in Mexico of which the axolotl is the permanent larval form.
ambon, *n.* *am*-bon, an elevated reading-desk; a pulpit. (Gr. *ambōn*, crest of a hill.)
amboyna, *n.* am-*boy*-na, a variegated wood from the island of Amboyna.
ambreada, *n.* ahm-bray-*ah*-da, a kind of factitious amber.
ambrein, *n.* *am*-bray-in, a fatty substance from ambergris. (Fr. *ambréine.*)
ambroid, *n.* *am*-broyd, a synthetic amber formed from fragments of amber and often other resins.
ambrosia, *n.* am-*broh*-ze-a, the fabled food of the gods [Myth.]; anything very pleasing to taste or smell; a branch of the Compositæ comprising wormwood, ragweed, etc. [Bot.]. (Gr. *ambrosia*, food of the gods.)
ambrosial, *a.* am-*broh*-ze-al, possessing the qualities of ambrosia; fragrant; delicious.

ambrosially, *ad.* am-*broh*-ze-al-le, with an ambrosial odour.
ambrosian, *a.* am-*broh*-ze-an, ambrosial; (*cap.*) pertaining to St. Ambrose, a 4th-cent. Bishop of Milan. **Ambrosian chant**, plainsong used at Milan and ascribed to St. Ambrose. **Ambrosian ritual**, *or* **liturgy**, formula of worship still in use in the church of Milan, instituted by St. Ambrose.
ambry, *n.* *am*-bre, a place where alms are deposited for distribution; a niche with a door near the altar for the sacred vessels; a cupboard. (O.Fr. *aumaire*, a repository for alms, or anything else.)
ambs-ace, *n.* *aymz*-ace, a double ace; the worst throw at dice; hence, bad luck. (O.Fr. *ambesas.*)
ambulacral, *a.* am-bew-*lay*-kral, pertaining to the ambulacrum.
ambulacrum, *n.* am-bew-*lay*-krum, a row of pores on the exterior of an echinoderm.
ambulance, *n.* *am*-bew-lans, a movable hospital for the wounded in battle; a vehicle or wheeled stretcher, etc., for conveyance of wounded or sick. (Fr. *ambulance.*)
ambulant, *a.* *am*-bew-lant, moving about.
ambulate, *v.t.* *am*-bew-late, to move about; to walk backward and forward.
ambulation, *n.* am-bew-*lay*-shon, act of walking.
ambulator, *n.* *am*-bew-lay-tor, a pedometer, odometer, or surveyor's wheel.
ambulatory, *a.* *am*-bew-la-to-re, that has the power of walking; moving from place to place; formed for walking: *n.* a space, as a cloister or corridor, for walking in.
ambury, *n.* *am*-ber-e, an anbury.
ambuscade, *n.* *am*-bus-*kade*, an ambush: *v.t.* to place in ambush. (Sp. *emboscada*, an ambush.)
ambush, *n.* *am*-bush, a lying concealed in wait to attack an enemy by surprise; the place of ambuscade; the attack; the troops in waiting: *v.t.* to lie in wait for; to attack suddenly from a concealed position. (O.Fr. *embuscher*, to fix an ambush.)
ameer, *n.* a-*meer*, an oriental ruler; emir, title long borne by the Afghan kings.
ameliorable, *a.* a-*meel*-yo-ra-bl, that may be ameliorated.
ameliorate, *v.t.* a-*meel*-yo-rate, to make better; to improve: *v.i.* to grow better. (Fr. *améliorer*, to improve.)
amelioration, *n.* a-meel-yo-*ray*-shon, a making or becoming better; improvement.
ameliorative, *a.* a-*meel*-yo-ra-tiv, tending to make better.
amen, *ad.* and *int.* *ay-men*, or *ah-men*, so let it be; verily; used to ratify solemn expressions of faith: *v.t.* to ratify; to sanction. (L. from Heb. *āmēn*, be it so.)
amenability, *n.* a-*mee*-na-*bil*-e-te, amenableness.
amenable, *a.* a-*mee*-na-bl, liable to be called to account and answer. (Fr. *amener*, to bring to.)
amenableness, *n.* a-*mee*-na-bl-ness, state of being amenable.
amenably, *ad.* a-*mee*-na-ble, in an amenable manner.
amend, *v.t.* a-*mend*, to alter for the better; to improve: *v.i.* to grow or become better. (Fr. *amender*, to amend.)
amendatory, *a.* a-*mend*-a-to-re, tending to amend; corrective.
amende, *n.* (App.), a fine by way of reparation. **amende honorable**, a formal public apology with full acknowledgment of error. (Fr.)
amendment, *n.* a-*mend*-ment, an alteration for the better; reformation; recovery of health; a word, clause or paragraph added, or proposed to be added, to a bill or a motion; the correction of an error in a writ or process [Law].
amends, *n.pl.* a-*mendz*, compensation; reparation.
amenity, *n.* a-*meen*-e-te, quality of being pleasant; pleasantness, and that which conduces thereto. (Fr. *amenité.*)
amenorrhœa, *n.* a-men-or-*ree*-a, non-natural abscence of menstruation. (Gr. *a*-, *mēn*, month, and *rein*, flow.)
ament, *n.* *am*-ent, a catkin [Bot.]. (L. *amentum*, a thong.)
amentaceous, *a.* am-en-*tay*-shus, of the nature of, or bearing catkins.
amentia, *n.* a-*men*-she-a, imbecility. (L. *āmentia*, madness.)
amerce, *v.t.* a-*mers*, to punish with a fine; to punish. (O.Fr. *amercier*, to acquit.)
amercement, *n.* a-*mers*-ment, a fine inflicted at the discretion of the court.
amerciable, *a.* a-*mers*-ya-bl, liable to amercement.
American, *a.* a-*me*-re-kan, pertaining to America, especially the United States: *n.* a native of America or of the United States. (*Amerigo Vespucci*, Italian navigator who claimed to have landed on the American continent in 1497.)
Americanism, *n.* a-*me*-re-kan-izm, an American idiom; the peculiar meaning given to an English word or phrase in the U.S.A.
Americanization, *n.* a-*me*-re-ka-ny-*zay*-shun, the act or process of Americanizing.
Americanize, *v.t.* a-*me*-re-kan-ize, to render American in character; to naturalize in America.
Amerind, *n.* am-er-*rind*, a member of one of the aboriginal American races: *a.* pertaining to any of these races or their languages.
ametabolic, *a.* ay-met-a-*bol*-ik, not subject to metamorphosis [Entom.].
amethyst, *n.* *am*-e-thist, a violet-blue variety of crystalline quartz, supposed by the ancients to prevent inebriation when worn. (L. *amethystus*, from Gr. *amethustos*, a preventive of intoxication.)
amethystine, *a.* am-e-*thist*-in, pertaining to, resembling, or composed of amethyst.
Amharic, *n.* am-*ha*-rik, the official language of Abyssinia, a subdivision of Ethiopic. (*Amhara*, a former kingdom of Abyssinia.)
amiability, *n.* ay-me-a-*bil*-e-te, the quality of being amiable.
amiable, *a.* *ay*-me-a-bl, possessed of kindly qualities; lovable; worthy of affection. (O.Fr. *amable.*)
amiably, *ad.* *ay*-me-a-ble, in an amiable manner.
amianthiform, *a.* am-e-*an*-the-form, having the form of amianthus.
amianthoid, *n.* am-e-*an*-thoyd, a variety of asbestos: *a.* resembling amianthus.
amianthus, *n.* am-e-*an*-thus, fine fibrous asbestos, so called because it is uninjured by fire. (Gr. *a*-, not, *miantos*, stained.)
amic, *a.* *am*-ik, relating to or derived from ammonia.
amicable, *a.* *am*-e-ka-bl, friendly; implying a disposition to be friendly. (L. *amicabilis*, friendly.)
amicableness, *n.* *am*-e-ka-bl-ness, the quality of being amicable.
amicably, *ad.* *am*-e-ka-ble, in an amicable manner.
amice, *n.* *am*-is, a flowing cloak, with a hood, formerly worn by the clergy; a strip of white linen worn round the shoulders by a priest when officiating at mass. (O.Fr. *amis*, a covering or cloak.)
amid, *prep.* a-*mid*, in the midst or middle; among.
amide, *n.* *am*-ide, a derivative from ammonia, esp. one formed by substituting univalent acid radicals for hydrogen atoms.
amidin, *n.* *am*-e-din, the soluble principle of starch.
amidine, *n.* *am*-e-dine, a crystalline compound derived from an amide and, as a base, forming a stable salt.
amidol, *n.* *am*-e-dol, proprietary name of a salt of di-amido-phenol used as a developer [Phot.].
amidships, *ad.* a-*mid*-ships, midway in a line between stem and stern [Naut.].
amidst, *prep.* a-*midst*, amid.
amine, *n.* *am*-in, a derivative from ammonia obtained by substituting hydrocarbon radicals for hydrogen atoms.
amir, *n.* a-*meer*, an ameer.
amiss, *a.* a-*miss*, wrong: *ad.* in a faulty manner. **not amiss**, pretty fair.
amissing, *ad.* a-*miss*-ing, lost; wanting.
amity, *n.* *am*-e-te, friendly relationship. (Fr. *amitié.*)
ammeter, *n.* *am*-me-ter, an instrument for measuring strength in ampères of an electric current.
ammonal, *n.* *am*-mon-al, an explosive consisting of a mixture of nitrate of ammonia and powdered aluminium.
ammonia, *n.* a-*moh*-ne-a, a compound of nitrogen with three parts of hydrogen; spirits of hartshorn, a powerful alkali. (L. *ammoniacum*, a gum distilled from trees growing near the temple of Jupiter Ammon.)
ammoniac, *a.* a-*moh*-ne-ak, ammoniacal. **gum-ammoniac**, a gum resin used in medicine and as a cement.
ammoniacal, *a.* am-mo-*ny*-a-kal, pertaining to ammonia, or possessing its properties.

ammoniated, *a.* a-*moh*-ne-ay-ted, combined or saturated with ammonia.
ammonite, *n.* *am*-mon-ite, a fossil cephalopodous shell curved into a spiral form, like the ram's horn on the statues of Jupiter Ammon.
ammonite, *n.* *am*-mon-ite, an explosive of many types used in blasting, all containing ammonium nitrate and some form of nitro-naphthalene.
ammonium, *n.* am-*moh*-ne-um, the basic radical of ammonia.
ammunition, *n.* am-mew-*nish*-on, military stores in general; the projectiles and explosives discharged from firearms and ordnance: *a.* made by contract for the use of soldiers. (O.Fr. *amunition*, corruption for *munition*, military stores.)
amnesia, *n.* am-*nee*-se-a, loss of memory; a gap in one's memory. (Gr. *amnesia*, forgetfulness.)
amnesty, *n.* *am*-nes-te, a general pardon, esp. of political offenders. (Fr. *amnestie.*)
amnion, *n.* *am*-ne-on, the innermost membrane surrounding the fœtus in the womb. (Gr. *amnion.*)
amniotic, *a.* am-ne-*ot*-ik, pertaining to the amnion.
amœba, *n.* a-*mee*-ba, a simple microscopic organism consisting of an extensile and contractile mass of protoplasm that is constantly changing its shape; (*cap.*) a genus of the protozoa. (Gr. *amoibe* change.)
amœbean, *a.* am-e-*bee*-an, alternately answering.
amœbiform, *a.* a-*mee*-be-form, amœboid.
amœboid, *a.* a-*mee*-boyd, resembling the amœba.
amok, *n.* a-*muk*, a Malayan nervous disease marked by homicidal frenzy; amuck.
Amomum, *n.* a-*moh*-mum, a genus of tropical plants, including the cardamom and grains of paradise, whose seeds have pungent and aromatic properties. (L. *amōmum*, an aromatic shrub.)
★**among,** *prep.* a-*mung*, mingled with; in the midst or number of. (A.S. *onmang*, among.)
amongst, *prep.* a-*mungst*, among.
amontillado, *n.* a-*mon*-til-*yah*-doh, a variety of pale dry sherry. (Sp.)
amoral, *a.* a-*mo*-ral, non-moral; not connected with the department of morals.
amorist, *n.* *am*-o-rist, a gallant; a philanderer. (L. *amor*, love.)
amorous, *a.* *am*-o-rus, inclined to love; in love; inspired by or pertaining to love. (O.Fr. *amoros.*)
amorously, *ad* *am*-o-rus-le, in an amorous manner.
amorousness, *n.* *am*-o-rus-ness, the quality of being amorous.
Amorpha, *n.* a-*mor*-fa, a genus of North American plants including the bastard indigo.
amorphism, *n.* a-*mor*-fizm, state of being amorphous; absence of crystallization.
amorphous, *a.* a-*mor*-fus, having no determinate form; uncrystallized; not conforming to standard [Biol.]. (Gr. *amorphos*, misshapen.)
amorphousness, *n.* a-*mor*-fus-ness, the state or quality of being shapeless.
amort, *a.* a-*mort*, in a half-dead state; thoroughly dispirited. (Fr. *à la mort*, to the death.)
amortization, *n.* a-*mor*-ty-*zay*-shon, the provision for the paying off of a loan by a sinking fund; the act or right of amortizing.
amortize, *v.t.* a-*mor*-tize, to alienate in mortmain, that is, to transfer lands or tenements in perpetuity to a corporation or fraternity [Law]; to redeem by a sinking fund [Comm.]. (Fr. *amortir.*)
★**amount,** *v.i.* a-*mount*, to rise to, or reach, a certain sum by accumulation of particulars; to come to, in effect, or substance; to be equivalent: *n.* the sum total; the effect, substance or result. (O.Fr. *amonter*, to amount to.)
amour, *n.* a-*moor*, an affair of gallantry; a love intrigue. (Fr. *amour.*)
amourette, *n.* am-oor-*ret*, a minor love affair; a cupid; quaking-grass [Bot.]. (Fr. *amour.*)
amp, *n.* amp, an ampere [Colloq.].
ampelopsis, *n.* am-pel-*op*-sis, a climbing plant of the old genus *Ampelopsis* including the Virginia creeper, now united with *Vitis*. (Gr. *ampelos*, a vine.)
amperage, *n.* *am*-per-aj, the strength of a current in amperes [Elect.].
ampere, *n.* *am*-pare, the electrical unit of current; the current sent by one volt through one ohm. (From A. M. *Ampère*, French physicist.)
ampersand, *n.* *am*-per-sand, the character &. (*And*, *per se*, *and*, *i.e.* 'and by itself and'.)
amphi-, *am*-fe, Greek prefix signifying both, about, around.
amphiarthrosis, *n.* am-fe-ahr-*throh*-sis, a form of articulation permitting only a slight degree of motion. [Anat.]
amphibia, *n.pl.* am-*fib*-e-a, the class of vertebrates, intermediate between fishes and reptiles, which breathe by gills during immaturity and by lungs when adult [Zool.]. (Gr. *amphibios*, living a double life, *i.e.* on both land and water.)
amphibian, *a.* am-*fib*-e-an, amphibious: *n.* one of the amphibia; an aeroplane or other contrivance adapted for use both on land and water.
amphibiological, *a.* am-fib-e-o-*loj*-e-kal, pertaining to amphibiology.
amphibiology, *n.* am-fib-e-*ol*-o-je, the study of the amphibia. (Gr. *amphibios*, and *logos*, science.)
amphibious, *a.* am-*fib*-e-us, able to live in air and water; pertaining to or adapted to both land and water.
amphibiousness, *n.* am-*fib*-e-us-ness, the quality of being amphibious.
amphibole, *n.* *am*-fe-bole, hornblende and similar rock-forming silicates. (Gr. *amphibolos*, doubtful.)
amphibolic, *a.* am-fe-*bol*-ik, ambiguous; of the nature of amphiboly; pertaining to or resembling amphibole.
amphibolite, *n.* am-*fib*-o-lite, a metamorphic rock, the basis of which is amphibole.
amphibological, *a.* am-fib-o-*loj*-e-kal, doubtful; equivocal.
amphibologically, *ad.* am-fib-o-*loj*-e-ka-le, with a doubtful meaning.
amphibology, *n.* am-fe-*bol*-o-je, a sentence admitting of two different interpretations [Logic.]; equivocation. (Gr. *amphibolos*, and *logos*, science.)
amphibolous, *a.* am-*fib*-o-lus, not clear; uncertain; ambiguous. (L. *amphibolus*, ambiguous.)
amphiboly, *n.* am-*fib*-o-le, amphibology.
amphibrach, *n.* *am*-fe-brak, a foot of three syllables, the middle long, the first and last short [Pros.]. (Gr. *amphibrachus*, short at both ends.)
amphicarpic, *a.* *am*-fe-*kar*-pik, having two kinds of fruit or times of ripening [Bot.]. (Gr. *amphi*, and *karpos*, fruit.)
amphicarpous, *a.* am-fe-*kar*-pus, amphicarpic.
amphicœlus, *a.* am-fe-*see*-lus, doubly concave; hollow on both sides (as the vertebræ of fish). (Gr. *amphi-*, and *koilos*, hollow.)
amphictyonic, *a.* am-*fik*-te-*on*-ik, pertaining to the Amphictyons. **amphictyonic council,** a body of delegates, especially the council at Delphi.
amphictyons, *n.pl.* am-*fik*-te-onz, the deputies from twelve of the states of ancient Greece. (Gr.)
amphictyony, *n.* am-*fik*-te-*oh*-ne, an alliance of States in Ancient Greece for protection of common concerns. (Gr.)
amphigamous, *a.* am-*fig*-a-mus, with no recognizable trace of reproductive organs [Bot.].
amphigen, *n.* *am*-fe-jen, a plant, like a lichen, which grows in all directions. (Fr. *amphigène.*)
amphigory, *n.* am-*fig*-o-re, a meaningless but high-sounding verse-composition; rigmarole.
amphimacer, *n.* am-*fim*-a-ser, a foot of three syllables, the middle short, and the others long [Pros.]. (L. *amphimacrus.*)
amphimixis, *n.* *am*-fe-*mik*-zis, sexual reproduction [Biol.]. (Gr. *amphi-*, and *mixis*, a mingling.)
amphioxus, *n.* *am*-fe-*ok*-sus, the lancelet [Ichth.].
amphipoda, *n.pl.* am-*fip*-o-da, crustaceans, with sessile eyes and two sets of limbs, the anterior directed forward and the posterior backward. (Gr.)
amphipodous, *a.* am-*fip*-o-dus, pertaining to the amphipoda.
amphiprostyle, *n.* am-*fip*-ro-stile, an edifice having a columned portico at each end [Arch.]. (Gr. *amphiprostūlos*, having a double prostyle.)
amphisarca, *n.* am-fe-*sar*-ka, fruit having many cells and seeds, with a hard shell and pulpy interior. (Gr. *amphi*, both, *sarx*, flesh.)
amphisbæna, *n.* am-fis-*bee*-na, a fabulous snake with a head at either end and able to move in either direction; a genus of limbless lizards with a short blunt tail. (Gr. *amphisbaina*, a species of serpent.)
amphistomous, *a.* am-*fis*-to-mus, with a mouth-like organ at both ends. (Gr. *amphi-*, and *stoma*, mouth.)

amphitheatre, *n.* *am*-fe-*thee*-a-ter, the lower gallery of a theatre; an oval or circular theatre, with a central arena surrounded by rows of seats rising one above another; a place for public contests. (L. *amphitheātrum.*)
amphitheatrical, *a.* *am*-fe-the-*at*-re-kal, pertaining to, or exhibited in, an amphitheatre.
amphitropal, *a.* am-*fit*-ro-pal, so recurved that the ends point in the same direction (of ovules) [Bot.]. (Gr. *amphi-*, and *tropos*, turning.)
amphitropous, *a.* am-*fit*-ro-pus, amphitropal.
Amphitryon, *n.* am-*fit*-re-on, a host, esp. the giver of a feast. (From Molière's comedy of his name).
amphora, *n.* *am*-fo-ra, an ancient two-handled vessel for wine or oil; also a liquid measure—Roman about 6 gallons, Greek about 9. (Gr. *amphoreus.*)
amphoral, *a.* *am*-fo-ral, pertaining to or resembling an amphora.
amphoric, *a.* am-*fo*-rik, giving a sound similar to that yielded by blowing into an empty decanter [Med.].
amphoteric, *a.* *am*-fo-*te*-rik, exhibiting in itself opposing qualities, esp. [Chem.] reacting both as acid and base. (Gr. *amphoteros*, both.)
ample, *a.* *am*-pl, large; spacious; sufficient; liberal; full. (Fr. *ample.*)
ampleness, *n.* the state of being ample.
amplexicaul, *a.* am-*pleks*-e-kawl, almost surrounding the stem.
ampliative, *a.* *am*-ple-a-tiv, adding to the primary idea or attributes of a subject [Logic].
amplification, *n.* am-ple-fe-*kay*-shon, enlargement; the act of amplifying; diffusiveness of description or argument [Rhet.]; increase in strength of signals [Wire.]. (L. *amplificātio*, an enlarging.)
amplifier, *n.* *am*-ple-fy-er, anything that enlarges; a device for magnifying the electrical impulses in wireless telephony; an enlarging lens [Opt.].
amplify, *v.t.* *am*-ple-fy, to enlarge or dilate upon: *v.i.* to be diffuse in argument or description; to dilate. (L. *amplifico*, extend.)
amplitude, *n.* *am*-ple-tewd, largeness or extent; the arc of the horizon intercepted between the east or west point and the centre of the sun or a star at its rising or setting [Astron.]; the range of a projectile. **magnetic amplitude,** the arc of the horizon between the sun or a star at rising or setting, and the east or west point of the horizon by the compass. (L. *amplitudo*, width.)
amply, *ad.* *am*-ple, in an ample manner.
ampoule, *n.* am-*pool*, a small sealed glass container esp. for a hypodermic dose [Med.]. (L. *ampulla*.
ampulla, *n.* am-*pul*-la, a narrow-necked vessel used among the Romans in anointing the body; a vessel for the eucharistic wine [Eccles.]; the dilated end of any vessel [Anat.]; a small membranaceous attachment to the leaves of some aquatic plants [Bot.]. (L. *ampulla.*)
ampullaceous, *a.* am-pul-*lay*-shus, like a bottle or inflated bladder; swelling.
amputate, *v.t.* *am*-pew-tate, to cut off a limb or portion of an animal body. (L. *amputatus*, cut off.)
amputation, *n.* am-pew-*tay*-shon, the operation of amputating.
amputator, *n.* *am*-pew-tay-tor, one who amputates.
amputee, *n.* am-pew-*tee*, one who has lost a limb or limbs by amputation.
amuck, *a.* a-*muk*, possessed by homicidal frenzy: *ad.* in a murderous manner. **to run amuck,** to rush madly about and attack everyone encountered.
amulet, *n.* *am*-yew-let, something worn about the person as a charm against evil or disease; a charm; a talisman. (Fr. *amulette.*)
amuletic, *a.* am-yew-*let*-ik, of the nature of an amulet; pertaining to amulets.
amurca, *n.* am-*ur*-ka, lees of olive oil.
amusable, *a.* a-*mewz*-a-bl, capable of being amused.
amuse, *v.t.* a-*mewz*, to occupy attention agreeably with agreeable objects; to divert and to beguile with false promises or representations. (Fr. *amuser.*)
★**amusement,** *n.* a-*mewz*-ment, that which amuses; entertainment; recreation.
amusing, *a.* a-*mewz*-ing, that has the power of causing amusement; diverting; laughable.
amusingly, *ad.* in an amusing manner.
amusive, *a.* a-*mewz*-iv, affording or tending to amusement or entertainment.

amygdalate, *a.* a-*mig*-da-late, like or made of almonds: *n.* milk of almonds [Med.]; a salt of amygdalic acid [Chem.].
amygdalic, *a.* a-*mig*-da-lik, pertaining to or obtained from almonds. (Gr. *amygdalos*, an almond.)
amygdalin, *n.* a-*mig*-da-lin, a crystalline glucoside obtained from the kernel of the bitter almond and other stone fruit.
amygdaline, *a.* a-*mig*-da-line, pertaining to or resembling almonds.
amygdaloid, *a.* a-*mig*-da-loyd, almond-shaped: *n.* a rock embedding nodules of various minerals, and resembling almonds in a cake.
amygdaloidal, *a.* a-*mig*-da-*loy*-dal, of the nature of the rock amygdaloid.
amyl, *n.* *am*-il, a hydrocarbon radical whose compounds occur in fusel-oil, fruit essences, etc.
amylaceous, *a.* am-il-*ay*-shus, pertaining to starch, or the farinaceous part of grain. (L. *amylum*, starch.)
amylic, *a.* am-*il*-ik, derived from or pertaining to amyl, or starch. **amylic acid,** a volatile acid from starch.
amyloid, *a.* *am*-il-oyd, starchy, or like starch: *n.* an albuminous substance found in certain seeds.
amylopsin, *n.* am-e-*lop*-sin, the enzyme of the pancreatic juice that converts the starch into sugar.
an, an, the indefinite article (*see* **a**).
an, conj. an, obsolete form of "and," also of "and if."
an-, a form of the Greek *a-*, not, of the Greek prefix *ana-*, and (before *n*) of the Latin *ad-*.
ana, *n.pl.*, *ah*-na, literary gossip; a collection of memorable sayings.
ana-, *an*-na, Greek prefix, up, throughout, back, again, according to.
anabaptism, *n.* an-a-*bap*-tizm, the doctrine of the Anabaptists; second baptism.
anabaptist, *n.* an-a-*bap*-tist, one who holds that baptism should be by immersion and administered only to adults after professing their faith in Christ, and that those baptized in infancy should be baptized again; a member of a German sect founded in 1521. (Gr. *ana-*, again, *baptizo*, dip in water.)
anabaptistic, *a.* an-a-bap-*tist*-ik, relating to the Anabaptists, or anabaptism.
anabas, *n.* *an*-a-bas, an Indian perch, *A. scandens*, that can leave the water and is said to climb trees. (Gr. *anabaino*, walk up.)
anabasis, *n.* a-*nab*-a-sis, a military advance, particularly the famous expedition of Cyrus the Younger related by Xenophon; the course of a disease to its climax [Med.]. (Gr. *anabasis*, a going up.)
anabatic, *a.* an-a-*bat*-ik, increasing in intensity [Med.]; moving upward (of winds).
anabolism, *n.* a-*nab*-o-lizm, constructive metabolism [Biol.].
anabranch, *n.* *an*-a-brahnch, a stream that leaves a river and rejoins it lower down.
anacathartic, *a.* and *n.* *an*-a-ka-*thar*-tik, cleansing, or that which cleanses, by exciting vomiting or expectoration. (Gr. *ana-*, and *katharsis*, a cleansing.)
anachronism, *n.* a-*nak*-ro-nizm, an error in the dating of an historical event; anything too early or too late for the date given. (Gr.)
anachronistic, *a.* a-*nak*-ro-*nis*-tik, anachronous.
anachronous, *a.* a-*nak*-ro-nus, erroneous in date.
anaclastic, *a.* an-a-*klas*-tik, due or pertaining to refraction [Physics]. (Gr. *anaklasis*, a flexure.)
anacoluthic, *a.* *an*-a-ko-*lew*-thik, relating to anacoluthon.
anacoluthon, *n.* an-a-ko-*lew*-thon (*pl.* **anacolutha**), a break in the structure of a sentence [Gram.]. (Gr. *anakoluthon*, inconsequent.)
anaconda, *n.* an-a-*kon*-da, the huge tropical South American snake *Eunectes murinus.*
anacreontic, *a.* a-*nak*-re-*on*-tik, in the manner of Anacreon; in praise of love and wine; jovial; amatory: *n.* a poem in this manner. (Gr.)
anacrusis, *n.* an-a-*kroo*-sis, the unemphasized syllables occurring before the regular rhythm in verse. (Gr. *anakrousis*, a forcing back.)
anacrustic, *a.* an-a-*kruss*-tik, relating to anacrusis.
anadem, *n.* *an*-a-dem, a garland or chaplet. (L.)
anadromous, *a.* a-*nad*-ro-mus, passing from the sea into rivers [Ichth.]. (Gr. *anadromos*, running up.)

anæmia, *n.* a-*nee*-me-a, a deficiency in the constituents of the blood; lack of blood. (Gr. *anaimia*, want of blood.)
anæmic, *a.* a-*nee*-mik, pertaining to, or affected with, anæmia.
anærobia, *n.pl.* an-*ay*-er-*oh*-be-a (*sing.* **anærobe,** an-*ay*-er-ohb), bacteria able to exist without free oxygen [Biol.].
anærobic, *a.* an-*ay*-er-*oh*-bik, pertaining to the anærobia; living without free oxygen.
anæsthesia, *n.* an-es-*thee*-ze-a, loss of the sense of touch or feeling [Med.]. (Gr. want of feeling.)
anæsthetic, *a.* an-es-*thet*-ik, producing anæsthesia: *n.* an agent that deadens sensibility.
anæsthetist, *n.* an-*ees*-thet-ist, a specialist in the administration of anæsthetics.
anæsthetization, *n.* an-*ees*-the-ty-*zay*-shon, the act or process of administering anæsthetics.
anæsthetize, *v.t.* an-*ees*-the-tize, to administer an anæsthetic to.
anaglyph, *n.* *an*-a-glif, a figure embossed or cut in low relief; a stereoscopic picture viewed simultaneously through a red and a green glass. (L. *anaglyphus*, carved in bas-relief.)
anaglyphic, *a.* an-a-*glif*-ik, anaglyptic.
anaglyphy, *n.* a-*nag*-le-fe, the art of embossing, chasing, or working in low relief.
anaglyptic, *a.* an-a-*glip*-tik, pertaining to an anaglyph or to anaglyptics.
anaglyptics, *n.* an-a-*glip*-tiks, the art of carving in low relief.
anaglyptographic, *a.* *an*-a-glip-to-*graf*-ik, representing on paper the appearance of embossing.
anaglyptography, *n.* *an*-a-glip-*tog*-ra-fe, the anaglyptographic art. (Gr. *anaglyptos*, embossed, *grapho*, write.)
anagoge, *n.* an-a-*goh*-je, anagogy.
anagogical, *a.* an-a-*goj*-e-kal, allegorical; mystical.
anagogy, *n.* *an*-a-go-je, allegorical, spiritual, or mystical interpretation. (Gr. *anagōgē*, a leading-up.)
anagram, *n.* *an*-a-gram, a word or sentence, formed by transposing the letters of another. (Fr.)
anagrammatical, *a.* *an*-a-gram-*mat*-e-kal, pertaining to or resembling an anagram.
anagrammatically, *ad.* *an*-a-gram-*mat*-e-ka-le, in the manner of an anagram.
anagrammatism, *n.* an-a-*gram*-ma-tizm, the art or practice of making anagrams.
anagrammatist, *n.* an-a-*gram*-ma-tist, a maker of anagrams.
anagrammatize, *v.i.* an-a-*gram*-ma-tize, to make anagrams.
anal, *a.* *ay*-nal, pertaining to or near the anus; under the tail [Ichth.]. (L. *ānus*, ring.)
analect, *n.* *an*-a-lekt (*pl.* **analecta,** an-a-*lek*-ta), a collection of extracts from different authors. (Gr. *analektos*, choice.)
analectic, *a.* an-a-*lek*-tik, composed of things selected.
analemma, *n.* an-a-*lem*-ma, a projection of the sphere on the plane of the meridian [Geom.]; an instrument of wood or brass, on which such a projection is drawn; a scale on a terrestrial globe showing day by day the sun's declination and the equation of time. (Gr. *analēmma*, anything used for repairing or holding up anything.)
analepsis, *n.* an-a-*lep*-sis, recovery of strength after illness, or paroxysm [Med.]. (Gr. *analēpsis*, recovery.)
analeptic, *a.* an-a-*lep*-tik, restorative; adding to strength: *n.* a restorative medicine.
analgesia, *n.* an-al-*jee*-se-a, absence of, or insensibility to, pain. (Gr. *analgēsia*, loss of feeling.)
analgesic, *a.* an-al-*jee*-sik, pertaining to or producing analgesia: *n.* an anodyne.
analogic, *a.* an-a-*loj*-ik, analogical.
analogical, *a.* an-a-*loj*-e-kal, pertaining to or implying analogy.
analogically, *ad.* an-a-*loj*-e-ka-le, in an analogical manner.
analogism, *n.* a-*nal*-o-jizm, an argument from the cause to the effect; investigation of things by their analogies.
analogist, *n.* a-*nal*-o-jist, one who employs analogy.
analogize, *v.t.* a-*nal*-o-jize, to explain by analogy; to treat analogically: *v.i.* to reason from analogy.
analogous, *a.* a-*nal*-o-gus, presenting some analogy; similar.
analogously, *ad.* a-*nal*-o-gus-le, in an analogous manner.
analogousness, *n.* a-*nal*-o-gus-ness, similitude.
analogue, *n.* *an*-a-log, a word or thing bearing resemblance or analogy to another; something that acts similarly, or has the same function; a corresponding part.
analogy, *n.* a-*nal*-o-je, an agreement or likeness in certain respects between things; similitude of relations; conformity of words to the structure or general rules of a language [Gram.]; similitude of ratios [Math.]. (Fr. *analogie.*)
analysable, *a.* an-a-*lize*-a-bl, that can be analysed.
analyse, *v.t.* *an*-a-lize, to resolve into elements; to make an analysis; to subject to critical, or minute, examination. (Fr. *analyser.*)
analyser, *n.* *an*-a-lize-er, one who or that which analyses; the part of a polariscope that shows that the light has been polarized.
analysis, *n.* a-*nal*-e-sis (*pl.* **analyses**), the resolution of a compound into its constituent parts or elements; the resolving of problems by algebraical equations [Math.]; an orderly arrangement of the heads of a discourse; classification of the items of an account; a sort of synopsis. (Gr. *analusis*, a releasing.)
analyst, *n.* *an*-a-list, one versed in analysis, especially in chemical or pathological analysis.
analytic, *a.* an-a-*lit*-ik, analytical.
analytical, *a.* an-a-*lit*-e-kal, pertaining to analysis; resolving a compound into its constituents; obtained by analysis; reasoning from particulars to generals; inductive.
analytically, *ad.* an-a-*lit*-e-ka-le, in the manner of analysis.
analytics, *n.* an-a-*lit*-iks, the science of analysis.
anamnesis, *n.* an-am-*nee*-sis, the medical history of a case; the bringing into recollection of forgotten things. (Gr. *amnēsia*, forgetfulness.)
anamorphosis, *n.* an-a-*mor*-fo-sis, a distorted image or representation of an object, which, when viewed from a certain point, or reflected from a curved mirror, appears regular and in right proportion [Opt.]; an anomalous development in any part of a plant [Bot.]; an evolutionary form-alteration observable in higher animals and plants. (Gr. *anamorphōsis*, a re-forming.)
anamorphous, *a.* an-a-*mor*-fus, abnormally developed.
Ananias, *n.* an-a-*ny*-as, a liar [Colloq.]. (Acts v.)
ananas, *n.* a-*nah*-nas, the pineapple. (Brazilian.)
anandrous, *a.* an-*an*-drus, destitute of a stamen [Bot.]. (Gr. *anandros*, husbandless.)
anantherous, *a.* an-*an*-ther-us, without anthers [Bot.].
ananthous, *a.* an-*an*-thus, flowerless [Bot.].
anapæst, *n.* *an*-a-peest, a reversed dactyl; a metrical foot of two short syllables followed by a long. (L. *anapæstus.*)
anapæstic, *n.* an-a-*peest*-ik, the anapæstic measure: *a.* pertaining to or consisting of anapæsts.
anaphora, *n.* a-*naf*-o-ra, repetition of the same word or words at the beginning of succeeding clauses of a sentence [Rhet.]. (Gr. *anaphora*, rising.)
anaphrodisiac, *a.* an-*af*-ro-*diz*-e-ak, having power to allay sexual desire: *n.* a drug intended to produce this effect. (Gr.)
anaphylactic, *a.* *an*-a-fy-*lak*-tik, pertaining to or caused by anaphylaxis.
anaphylaxis, *n.* *an*-a-fy-*lak*-sis, hypersensitiveness to a biologically foreign protein following an initial sensitizing dose or injection [Med.]; allergy. (Gr. *ana-*, and *phylassein*, to guard.)
anaplasty, *n.* *an*-a-*plas*-te, the operation of repairing superficial lesions by the transfer of tissue [Surg.]. (Gr. *anaplastos*, that can be moulded.)
anaplerosis, *n.* *an*-a-ple-*roh*-sis, renewing of destroyed or lost tissue, as in healing of wounds [Med.]. (Gr. *anaplērōsis*, a means of filling up.)
anaplerotic, *a.* an-a-ple-*rot*-ik, supplying deficiencies of tissue: *n.* a remedy effecting this [Med.].
anaptotic, *a.* an-ap-*tot*-ik, used of languages that have lost their inflexions through phonetic decay. (Gr. *an-*, and *aptōtos*, indeclinable.)
anarch, *n.* *an*-ark, a revolutionary leader; an anarchist.
anarchic, *a.* *an*-*ark*-ik, anarchical.
anarchical, *a.* an-*ark*-e-kal, without civic rule; in a state of lawless confusion.

anarchically, *ad.* an-*ark*-e-ka-le, in an anarchical manner.
anarchism, *n.* *an*-ark-izm, the principles of anarchy.
anarchist, *n.* *an*-ark-ist, one who excites or promotes anarchy; one opposing every form of government.
anarchy, *n.* *an*-ark-e, a state of society in which there is either in fact or in effect no governing power; want of law or order generally. (Fr. *anarchie.*)
anarthrous, *a.* an-*arth*-rus, without the article [Gr. Gram.]; without distinct joints [Zool.]. (Gr. *anarthros*, jointless.)
anasarca, *n.* an-a-*sar*-ka, dropsy of the connective cellular tissue [Med.]. (Gr. *ana-*, and *sarx*, flesh.)
anasarcous, *a.* an-a-*sar*-kus, dropsical.
anastatic, *a.* an-a-*stat*-ik, with characters or illustrations in relief [Print.]. (Gr. *anastatos*, compelled to stand up.)
anastigmatic, *a.* *an*-as-tig-*mat*-ik, free from astigmatism (of photographic lenses).
anastomose, *v.i.* a-*nas*-to-mohz, to inosculate; to unite by anastomosis.
anastomosis, *n.* a-nas-to-*moh*-sis, inosculation, or the opening of one vessel into another, as of one artery or vein into another [Anat. and Bot.]; intercommunication of a network of veins, etc. (Gr. *anastomōsis*, an opening.)
anastomotic, *a.* a-nas-to-*mot*-ik, pertaining to anastomosis; tending to remove obstructions [Med.].
anastrophe, *n.* a-*nas*-tro-fe, an inversion of the natural order of words [Rhet.]. (Gr. *anastrophē*, a turning upside down.)
anatase, *n.* *an*-a-tays, native crystalline dioxide of titanium; octahedrite [Min.].
anathema, *n.* a-*nath*-e-ma, a curse solemnly pronounced by ecclesiastical authority; excommunication; the person or thing accursed; a curse or ban generally. (L. *anathema.*)
anathematic, *a.* *an*-ath-e-*mat*-ik, relating to anathema.
anathematization, *n.* a-*nath*-e-ma-ty-*zay*-shon, the action or process of pronouncing accursed [Eccl.].
anathematize, *v.t.* a-*nath*-e-ma-tize, to pronounce an anathema against. (L. *anathematizo*, anathematize.)
anatine, *a.* *an*-a-tine, pertaining to or characteristic of ducks: *n.* a bird of the duck family. (L. *anas*, a duck.)
anatomical, *a.* an-a-*tom*-e-kal, relating to anatomy.
anatomically, *ad.* an-a-*tom*-e-ka-le, in an anatomical manner.
anatomism, *n.* a-*nat*-o-mizm, a theory accounting for vitality by anatomical structure and thus opposed to animism; in art, the application of anatomical principles.
anatomist, *n.* a-*nat*-o-mist, one versed or skilled in anatomy.
anatomization, *n.* a-*nat*-o-my-*zay*-shon, the act or process of anatomizing; dissection.
anatomize, *v.t.* a-*nat*-o-mize, to dissect; to analyse; to discriminate minutely.
anatomy, *n.* a-*nat*-o-me, the art of dissecting an organized body so as to discover the structure, situation and economy of its parts; the science treating of the structure of organized bodies; the act of dissecting or minutely examining anything intellectual or corporeal; a skeleton. (Fr. *anatomie.*)
anatreptic, *a.* an-a-*trep*-tik, overturning. (Gr. *anatreptikos.*)
anatripsis, *n.* an-a-*trip*-sis, friction applied to the body as a remedy; massage [Med.]. (Gr. *anatripsis*, chafing.)
anatriptic, *n.* an-a-*trip*-tik, relating to anatripsis.
anatropous, *a.* a-*nat*-ro-pus, with an inverted ovule [Bot.]. (Gr. *anatropeus*, an over-turner.)
anbury, *n.* *an*-bew-re, a soft blood-filled tumour on a horse or ox; the infectious plant disease "fingers and toes," caused by the slime fungus *Plasmodiophora brassicæ*.
ancestor, *n.* *an*-ses-tor, one from whom a person has descended; a forefather; one from whom property has descended [Law]; a low-type organism as progenitor of those of higher type [Biol.]. (O.Fr. *ancestre.*)
ancestorial, *a.* an-ses-*taw*-re-al, ancestral.
ancestral, *a.* an-*ses*-tral, relating to or possessed by ancestors; descending from ancestors.
ancestress, *n.* *an*-ses-tress, a female ancestor.
ancestry, *n.* *an*-ses-tre, a line of ancestors; lineage; persons composing the line of natural descent.
anchithere, *n.* *ang*-ke-theer, an extinct three-toed ancestor of the horse. (Gr.)
anchor, *n.* *ang*-ker, a heavy hooked iron implement dropped from a ship to grapple the bottom and hold her fast; any contrivance serving this purpose; anything giving stability or security: *v.t.* to secure by or as by an anchor: *v.i.* to cast anchor; to stop or rest on. **cast anchor,** to drop it [Naut.]. **weigh anchor,** to raise it [Naut.]. (A.S. *ancor*, anchor.)
anchorage, *n.* *ang*-ker-aj, place for anchoring; act of anchoring; toll imposed for anchoring.
anchoress, *n.* *ang*-ko-ress, a female anchorite.
anchoret, *n.* *ang*-ko-ret, anchorite.
anchoretic, *a.* ang-ko-*ret*-ik, pertaining to an anchorite, or to his mode of life.
anchoretical, *a.* ang-ko-*ret*-e-kal, pertaining to hermits or to the hermit life.
anchoretism, *n.* *ang*-ko-re-tizm, the principles and practice of anchorets.
anchor-ice, *n.* *ang*-ker-ice, ice formed at the bottom of streams, etc.; ground ice.
anchorite, *n.* *ang*-ko-rite, a hermit; a religious recluse; a person living in solitude. (Fr. *anachorète.*)
anchovy, *n.* an-*choh*-ve, a small herring-like food-fish of the family *Engraulidæ*, esteemed for its flavour. (Sp. *anchova.*)
anchovy-pear, *n.* an-*choh*-ve-pare, the mango-like fruit of a West Indian tree of the genus *Grias*.
anchylose, *v.t.* *ang*-ke-lohz, to stiffen by anchylosis: *v.i.* to become stiff; to grow together.
anchylosis, *n.* ang-ke-*loh*-sis, an immovable stiffening of a joint; the coalescence of two bones or of parts of a bone [Med.]. (Gr. *angkūlōsis*, anchylosis.)
anchylotic, *a.* ang-ke-*lot*-ik, pertaining to or afflicted with anchylosis.
ancient, *a.* *ayn*-shent, old; that happened or existed in former times, or antiquity; past; former: *n.* an aged or patriarchal person; one of Greek or Roman antiquity. (Fr. *ancien.*)
ancient, *n.* *ayn*-shent, an ensign, both as flag and as flag-bearer. (O.Fr. *enseigne.*)
anciently, *ad.* *ayn*-shent-le, in ancient times.
ancientness, *n.* *ayn*-shent-ness, the state of being ancient; existence from old times.
ancientry, *n.* *ayn*-shent-re, ancient lineage; antiquity.
ancillary, *a.* an-*sil*-la-re, subservient; auxiliary. (L. *ancillāris*, relating to women-servants.)
ancipital, *a.* an-*sip*-e-tal, double-faced or double-formed; double-edged. (L. *ancipitis*, two-headed.)
ancon, *n.* *ang*-kon, the upper end of the elbow; a console [Arch.]. (Gr. *angkōn*, bend of the arm.)
anconeal, *a.* ang-*koh*-ne-al, relating to the elbow [Phys.].
ancress, *n.* *ang*-kress, an anchoress.
★**and,** *conj.* and, signifying addition, and connecting words and sentences. (A.S. *and.*)
Andalusian, *a.* an-da-*loo*-ze-an, pertaining to Andalusia: *n.* a native of Andalusia; (*l.c.*) a breed of domestic fowls. **Andalusian school,** the school of 16th-cent. Spanish painting represented by Murillo.
andalusite, *n.* an-da-*loo*-zite, an aluminium silicate first found in gem form in Andalusia.
andante, *a.* an-*dan*-tay, moderately slow: *n.* a movement in moderately slow time [Mus.]. (It.)
Andean, *a.* an-*dee*-an, pertaining to, or like, the Andes; hence, lofty, grand.
andesine, *n.* *an*-de-zin, a felspar found as a constituent of andesite.
andesite, *n.* *an*-de-zite, a crystalline igneous rock of varied composition but consisting mainly of plagioclase, found in the Andes and elsewhere.
andiron, *n.* *and*-*i*-urn, one of a pair of horizontal iron bars for supporting the logs in a wood fire; a fire-dog. (O.Fr. *andier*, andiron.)
andro-, *comb. f.* indicating the male sex or gender, masculine. (Gr. *anēr*, *andros*, man.)
andrœceum, *n.* an-*dree*-se-um, the stamens of a flower [Bot.]. (Gr. *andro-*, and *oikion*, a house.)
androgynal, *a.* an-*droj*-e-nal, androgynous.

androgynally, *ad.* an-*droj*-e-na-le, in the manner of a hermaphrodite [Bot.].
androgyne, *n.* *an*-dro-jin, an androgynous plant.
androgynous, *a.* an-*droj*-e-nus, partaking of the characteristics of both sexes; hermaphroditical; bearing stamens and pistils on the same plant or in the same flower [Bot.]. (L. *androgynus*, a hermaphrodite.)
androgyny, *n.* an-*droj*-e-ne, hermaphroditism [Bot. and Zool.].
andropetalous, *a.* *an*-dro-*pet*-al-us, having, as in double flowers, the stamens converted into petals [Bot.]. (Gr. *andros*, male, *petalon*, a leaf.)
androphagous, *a.* an-*drof*-a-gus, man-eating; cannibalistic. (Gr. *andro-*, and *phagein*, to eat.)
anear, *prep.* a-*neer*, near.
anecdotage, *n.* *an*-ek-*dote*-aj, anecdotes collectively; garrulous senility.
anecdotal, *a.* *an*-ek-*dote*-al, pertaining to, or full of, anecdotes.
anecdote, *n.* *an*-ek-dote, a short relation of an isolated fact or event, usually of a biographic or characteristic nature. (Gr. *anecdota*.)
anecdotic, *a.* *an*-ek-*dot*-ik, addicted to or pertaining to anecdotes.
anecdotist, *n.* *an*-ek-*dote*-ist, one who tells anecdotes.
anele, *v.t.* a-*neel*, to anoint; to give extreme unction to. (A.S. *an*, and *œl*, oil.)
anelectric, *n.* an-e-*lek*-trik, a substance not made electric by friction.
anelectrode, *n.* an-a-*lek*-trode, former term for anode [Elect.].
anemo-, *comb. f.* denoting wind, or a current of air. (Gr. *anemos*, wind.)
anemogram, *n.* a-*nem*-o-gram, the register made by an anemograph.
anemograph, *n.* a-*nem*-o-graf, an apparatus which registers the amount and variation of the force of the wind. (Gr. *anemos*, wind, *grapho*, write.)
anemometer, *n.* *an*-e-*mom*-e-ter, an instrument for measuring the course, force and velocity of the wind or of other air-currents. (Gr. *anemos*, and *metron*, a measure.)
anemometry, *n.* an-e-*mom*-et-re, the determination of the strength, velocity and direction of the winds.
anemone, *n.* a-*nem*-o-ne, the wind-flower: (*cap.*) a genus of plants distinguished by the bracts being some distance down the flower stem. **sea anemone,** a cœlenterate animal of the genus *Actinia*, and its allies. (Gr. *anemōnē*, wind-flower.)
anemophilous, *a.* an-e-*mof*-e-lus, fertilized by wind-borne pollen [Bot.]. (Gr. *anemos*, and *phileo*, love.)
anemoscope, *n.* a-*nem*-o-skohp, a device for indicating, and sometimes recording, the direction of the wind.
anent, *prep.* a-*nent*, concerning.
aneroid, *a.* *an*-er-oyd, denoting a barometer in which atmospheric pressure is measured by its action on the thin top of an air-exhausted metallic box: *n.* such a barometer. (Fr. *anéroïde*.)
aneurysm, *n.* *an*-yew-rizm, a morbid swelling in the diseased coat of an artery, esp. the aorta. (Gr. *aneurusma*, an aneurism.)
aneurysmal, *a.* an-yew-*riz*-mal, pertaining to an aneurysm.
anew, *ad.* a-*new*, over again; once more; in a new form.
anfractuose, *a.* an-*frak*-tew-ohs, anfractuous.
anfractuosity, *n.* an-frak-tew-*oss*-e-te, tortuousness; a winding channel, esp. one marking convolutions in the brain.
anfractuous, *a.* an-*frak*-tew-us, full of windings and turnings; sinuous. (Fr. *anfractueux*.)
angary, *n.* *ang*-ga-re, the right of a belligerent to seize and, if need be, destroy property belonging to neutral states. (Gr. *aggareia*, customs or port service.)
angekok, *n.* *ang*-ge-kok, a sorcerer or medicine-man among the Eskimos. (Eskimo.)
angel, *n.* *ayn*-jel, a messenger from God; a spiritual intermediary; an attendant spirit; an old English gold coin, an angel-noble, bearing the figure of the archangel Michael. (O.Fr. *angele*.)
angel-fish, *n.* *ayn*-jel-fish, a species of shark so named from its wing-like pectoral fins.
angelic, *a.* an-*jel*-ik, angelical.
angelica, *n.* an-*jel*-e-ka, an umbelliferous plant of the carrot family, esp. *Angelica archangelica*, the preserved leaf-stalks of which are used as a confection; a liqueur flavoured with this. (Fr. *angélique*.)
angelical, *a.* an-*jel*-e-kal, resembling, or of the nature of, an angel.
angelically, *ad.* like an angel.
angelology, *n.* ayn-jel-*ol*-o-je, the doctrine of angelic beings; a treatise on angels.
angelophany, *n.* ayn-jel-*of*-a-ne, the visible manifestation of angels to man.
angelot, *n.* *an*-je-lot, an ancient lute; a Louis XI French gold coin bearing the figure of the archangel Michael; a coin made by the English under Henry VI at Paris.
Angelus, *n.* *an*-jel-us, a devotional service in the Roman Catholic Church in commemoration of the incarnation, said in the morning, at noon, and in the evening, when the Angelus bell rings.
angel-water, *n.* *ayn*-jel-waw-ter, a liquid perfume and cosmetic based on angelica.
anger, *n.* *ang*-ger, passion of the mind, prompted by a sense of wrong and provoking resentment; indignation of mind: *v.t.* to excite to anger; to provoke. (Ice. *angr*, sorrow.)
Angevin, *a.* *an*-je-vin, pertaining to or characteristic of Anjou, or the Plantagenet kings of England, 1154–1485, descended from Geoffrey, Count of Anjou and Matilda, daughter of Henry I of England: *n.* any of these kings; a native of Anjou. (Fr.)
angina, *n.* an-*jy*-nah, tonsilitis, or quinsy, tending to spasmodic fits of suffocation. **angina-pectoris,** an acutely painful disease marked by constriction in the lower and left side of the chest and weakness of the heart. (L. *angina*, quinsy.)
angiocarpous, *a.* *an*-je-oh-*kar*-pus, with the fruit in an envelope distinct from the calyx [Bot.].
angiography, *n.* an-je-*og*-ra-fe, a description of the blood-vessels and lymphatics [Med.]. (Gr. *angeoin*, vessel, and *grapho*, write.)
angiology, *n.* an-je-*ol*-o-je, the science of the blood-vessels and lymphatics [Med.].
angioma, *n.* an-je-*oh*-ma (*pl.* **angiomata**), a vascular tumour consisting chiefly of dilated or connected blood vessels.
angiomatous, *a.* an-je-*oh*-ma-tus, of the nature of, or affected with, angioma.
angiosperm, *n.* *an*-je-o-sperm, a plant which has its seeds enclosed in a pericarp [Bot.]. (Gr. *angeion*, vessel, and *sperma*, seed.)
angiospermous, *a.* *an*-je-o-*sperm*-us, having the seeds enclosed in a pericarp.
***angle,** *n.* *ang*-gl, a corner; the inclination of two lines at a point; the space between such lines or between planes similarly inclined: *v.t.* to confine in or direct to an angle [Sport]. (Fr. *angle*.)
angle, *n.* *ang*-gl, a fish-hook; a fishing-rod with line and hook: *v.t.* to fish for with a rod and line: *v.i.* to fish with a rod and line; to entice; to seek something, as to angle for an invitation (Colloq.). (A.S. *angel*, fish-hook.)
Angle, *n.* *ang*-gl, a member of the Teutonic tribe that settled in England in the 5th cent. A.D. and ultimately gave the country its name.
angled, *a.* *ang*-gld, having angles or an angel.
angle-iron, *n.* a piece of iron of L-section used for strengthening framework, joining parts, etc.
anglemeter, *n.* *ang*-gl-mee-ter, an angle measurer.
angler, *n.* *ang*-gler, one who fishes with rod and line; *Lophius piscatorius*, the sea-devil, a large cartilaginous fish of the ray family in which the front spins of the dorsal fin are modified into tentacle-like organs.
anglesite, *n.* *ang*-gl-site, a sulphate of lead, a common lead ore first recorded from Anglesea.
Anglican, *a.* *ang*-glik-an, pertaining to England or, esp., the Church of England; English, *i.e.*, not Roman [Eccl.]: *n.* a member of the English High Church party.
anglicanism, *n.* *ang*-glik-an-izm, the principles and practices of the English High Church party.
anglice, *ad.* *ang*-glis-se, in English or in an English manner.
anglicism, *n.* *ang*-glis-izm, an English idiom.
anglicize, *v.t.* *ang*-glis-ize, to give an English form to; to make English.
anglify, *v.t.* *ang*-gle-fy, to anglicize.
angling, *n.* *ang*-gling, fishing with a rod and line.
Anglo-, *comb. f.* English; pertaining to or derived from the English.

Anglo-American, *n.* *ang*-glo-a-*me*-re-kan, an American of English descent; an Englishman whose home is in the U.S.A.: *a.* pertaining to Anglo-Americans.

Anglo-Catholic, *a.* *ang*-glo-*kath*-o-lik, pertaining, or belonging, to the Church of England but embracing Catholic rather than Protestant principles and ritual: *n.* a member of the High Church party.

Anglo-Catholicism, *n.* *ang*-glo-ka-*thol*-is-sizm, the doctrines of the High Church party, esp. that the English is a branch of the Catholic Church.

Anglo-French, *n.* *ang*-glo-*frensh*, the French language used in England after the Norman Conquest: *a.* pertaining to England and France.

Anglo-Indian, *n.* *ang*-glo-*ind*-yan, an Englishman born or living in India: *a.* pertaining to such, or to England and India.

Anglo-Irish, *n.pl.* *ang*-glo-*ire*-rish, the descendants of the original settlers within the Pale, or of Irish and English ancestors; English persons born or long resident in Eire: *a.* pertaining to England and Ireland or England and Eire.

anglomania, *n.* *ang*-glo-*may*-ne-a, excessive fondness for everything English.

Anglo-Norman, *n.* *ang*-glo-*nor*-man, a Norman living in England after the Conquest, also, his language: *a.* pertaining to French as spoken by the Normans and their descendants.

anglophile, *n.* *ang*-glo-fil, a warm admirer of England, English ways, things, etc.: *a.* well-affected towards England.

anglophobe, *n.* *ang*-glo-fohb, one affected with anglophobia.

anglophobia, *n.* *ang*-glo-*foh*-be-a, hatred or distrust of England and everything English. (*Anglo-* and *-phobia.*)

Anglo-Saxon, *a.* *ang*-glo-*sak*-son, Old English; English: *n.* an Englishman; one of English race.

Anglo-Saxonism, *n.* *ang*-glo-*sak*-so-nizm, an English peculiarity and idiom; belief in the Anglo-Saxon's superiority.

angola, *n.* an-*goh*-la, a corruption of **angora.**

angor, *n.* *ang*-gor, intense pain [Med.]. (L.)

Angora, *n.* an-*gaw*-a, name of an Anatolian city, now the capital of Turkey, applied to varieties of the domestic goat, cat, and rabbit, each having long silky fur; (*l.c.*) cloth made from angora wool. **angora wool,** the hair of the Angora goat; mohair.

angostura, *n.* an-gos-*tew*-ra, the bitter febrifugal bark of a species of *Cusparia*; an aperitif flavoured with this. (*Angostura*, now Ciudad Bolivar, in Venezuela, whence first imported.)

angrily, *ad.* *ang*-gre-le, in an angry manner.

angriness, *n.* *ang*-gre-ness, the state of being annoyed or angry.

★angry, *a.* *ang*-gre, provoked; expressing anger; inflamed [Med.].

angstrom, *n.* *ang*-strum, the "angstrom unit," a minute unit of length, equal to one ten-millionth part of a millimetre, used in wave-length measurement. (A. J. *Angström*, d. 1874, Swed. physicist.)

anguiform, *a.* *an*-gwe-form, snake-shaped. (L. *anguis*, a snake, *forma*, shape.)

anguilliform, *a.* an-*gwil*-le-form, eel-shaped; resembling an eel. (L. *anguilla*, an eel, *forma*, shape.)

anguine, *a.* *an*-gwin, pertaining to or resembling a snake. (L. *anguineus*, snaky.)

anguish, *n.* *ang*-gwish, intense pain of body or mind; any keen feeling: *v.t.* to distress with extreme pain or grief. (O.Fr. *anguisse.*)

angular, *a.* *ang*-gew-lar, having angles or corners; forming or in an angle; stiff; bony. **angular motion,** rotation about an axis. **angular velocity,** the speed of angular motion; the angle described in unit time.

angularity, *n.* ang-gew-*la*-re-te, the state or quality of being angular.

angularly, *ad.* *ang*-gew-lar-le, with angles.

angulate, *a.* *ang*-gew-lat, having angles; formed with angles; angular.

angulate, *v.t.* *ang*-gew-late, to make angular.

angustifoliate, *a.* ang-gus-te-*foh*-le-at, narrow-leaved. (L. *angustus*, narrow, *folium*, a leaf.)

anharmonic, *a.* an-har-*mon*-ik, not harmonic [Math.]. (Fr. *anharmonique.*)

anhelation, *n.* an-he-*lay*-shon, a panting: difficult respiration. (Fr. *anhélation.*)

anhima, *n.* a-*nyee*-ma, or *an*-he-ma, the horned screamer, *Anhima cornuta*, a S. American bird with a horn-like process on the head and two spurs on each wing. (Port., from Tupi.)

anhydride, *n.* an-*hy*-dride, a substance which when combined with water forms an acid, or that is formed from an acid by the abstraction of its water.

anhydrite, *n.* an-*hy*-drite, anhydrous calcium sulphate.

anhydrous, *a.* an-*hy*-drus, without water, esp. water of crystallization. (Gr. *an-*, and *hydros*, water.)

aniconic, *a.* an-eye-*kon*-ik, symbolic, but not in human or animal form (of primitive idols, fetishes, etc.). (Gr. *an-*, not, and *iconic.*)

aniconism, *n.* an-*eye*-ko-nizm, worship of, or by means of, aniconic images.

anicut, *n.* *an*-e-kut, a dam for irrigation purposes in India. (Tamil.)

anigh, *prep.* and *ad.* a-*ny*, near to.

anil, *n.* *an*-il, the indigo plant. (Ar.)

anile, *a.* *an*-ile, doting, like an old woman; feeble; infirm. (L. *anilis*, old womanish.)

aniline, *n.* *an*-il-in, an aromatic base used in dye-production, first obtained from indigo and now prepared by reduction of nitro-benzene with nascent hydrogen: *a.* pertaining to anil or aniline.

anility, *n.* a-*nil*-e-te, the state of being anile; dotage.

animadversion, *n.* *an*-e-mad-*ver*-shon, criticism or censure; reproof.

animadvert, *v.i.* an-e-mad-*vert*, to observe; to direct attention to; to remark upon by way of criticism or censure. (L. *animadverto*, turn.)

★animal, *n.* *an*-e-mal, an organized being endowed with life, sensation, and power of voluntary motion; a living being as distinct from a plant: *a.* pertaining to animals; belonging to the animal or sensual part only; consisting of the flesh of animals. **animal heat,** heat generated in the animal body by the processes of oxidization. **animal spirits,** cheerful exuberance of health and temper. (L. *animal*, a living being.)

animalcula, *n.pl.* an-e-*mal*-kew-la, *see* **animalcule.**

animalcular, *a.* an-e-*mal*-kew-lar, pertaining to animalcules.

animalcule, *n.* an-e-*mal*-kewl (*scientific pl.* **animalcula**), a very minute animal nearly or quite invisible to the naked eye. (L. *animal*, and *culum*, little.)

animalculism, *n.* an-e-*mal*-kew-lizm, an abandoned theory that made germs the originating factor of both life and disease.

animalculist, *n.* an-e-*mal*-kew-list, one versed in the knowledge of animalcules; one holding the theory of animalculism.

animalism, *n.* *an*-e-mal-izm, the state of being actuated by sensual appetites only; the doctrine that man is merely an animal.

animality, *n.* an-e-*mal*-e-te, the qualities distinctive of an animal; animal nature.

animalization, *n.* an-e-mal-eye-*zay*-shon, the act or process of animalizing.

animalize, *v.t.* *an*-e-mal-ize, to give animal life to; to convert into animal substance; to lower to a mere animal; to brutalize.

animate, *v.t.* *an*-e-mate, to give life or spirit to; to rouse; to enliven: *a.* endowed with life; pertaining to living things. (L. *animātus*, gifted with life.)

animated, *a.* *an*-e-mate-ed, possessing life; full of life; vigorous; full of spirit.

animatedly, *ad.* an-e-*mate*-ed-le, with animation.

animating, *a.* *an*-e-*mate*-ing, life-giving; inspiring.

animation, *n.* an-e-*may*-shon, the act of animating; the state of being animated; vivacity.

animatism, *n.* *an*-e-ma-tizm, the primitive belief that inanimate things possess personality and reason.

animative, *a.* *an*-e-mate-iv, capable of animating.

animator, *n.* *an*-e-mate-or, some one or thing that animates.

animé, *n.* *an*-e-may, a transparent amber-coloured resin, used as a varnish; any resin. (Sp.)

animism, *n.* *an*-e-mizm, the theory which refers organized life and its movements to a separately existing immaterial soul, and holds that all objects possess natural life; the related theory which refers derangement in the organism to derangement in the soul.

animist, *n.* *an*-e-mist, one who maintains one or other doctrine of animism.

animistic, *a.* an-e-*mis*-tik, founded on, pertaining to, animism.
animosity, *n.* an-e-*moss*-e-te, bitter hatred; active enmity. (Fr. *animosité.*)
animus, *n. an*-e-mus, mind; spirit; purpose; intention; hostile spirit. (L., soul, spirit.)
anion, *n.* an-*y*-on, the ion in an electrolyte that carries the negative charge.
anise, *n. an*-iss, an annual plant, *Pimpinella anisum*, the seeds of which are used against flatulence.
aniseed, *n. an*-e-seed, the seed of the anise plant.
anisette, *n.* an-e-*set*, a liqueur distilled from aniseed.
aniso-, a prefix denoting in botanical and zoological terms inequality or lack of symmetry. (Gr. *anisos*, unequal.)
anisodactylic, *n.pl.* an-e-so-dak-*til*-ik, having toes of unequal length [Ornith.]. (Gr. *aniso-*, and *daktylos*, toe.)
anisodynamous, *a.* an-e-so-*din*-a-mus, growing with more force on one side of the axis than on the other [Bot.]. (Gr. *aniso-*, and *dynamis*, power.)
anisomeric, *a.* an-eye-so-*me*-rik, not isomeric.
anisometric, *a. an*-eye-so-*met*-rik, having nonsymmetrical parts; not isometric [Cryst.]. (Gr. *a-*, not, and *isometric.*)
anker, *n. ang*-ker, an old Dutch or German liquid measure of about 8½ gallons; a cask of this capacity. (Dut.)
ankh, *n.* angk, a T-shaped cross with a loop at the head, a sacred symbol of the ancient Egyptians.
ankle, *n. ang*-kl, the joint uniting the foot to the leg. (A.S. *ancléow.*)
anklet, *n. ang*-klet, an ornament for the ankle in the shape of a bangle or ring; a support for the ankle.
ankylosis, *n.* ang-ke-*loh*-sis, anchylosis.
ankylostoma, *n.* ang-ke-*los*-to-ma, lock-jaw. (Gr. *ankylos*, crooked, *stoma*, mouth.)
ankylostomiasis, *n. ang*-ke-*los*-to-*my*-a-sis, infestation of the intestines by parasitic hook-worms; severe anæmia caused by this.
ankus, *n. ang*-kus, an elephant-goad with spike and hook used in India.
anlace, *n. an*-lace, a broad dagger.
anna, *n. an*-na, one-sixteenth of a rupee, about one penny. (Hind.)
annalist, *n. an*-nal-ist, a writer of annals.
annals, *n.pl. an*-nalz, a relation of events in order of time; in the Roman Catholic Church, masses said steadily throughout the year. (L. *annālēs*, chronicles.)
annat, *n. an*-nat, the right of the executors of a deceased clergyman to a half-year's revenue of his benefice [Scots Law].
annates, *n.pl. an*-nayts, firstfruits; the first year's revenue of benefice or see, paid to the Pope. (L. *annus*, a year.)
annatto, *n.* an-*nat*-to, the seed of *Bixa orellana*, yielding a dye used for colouring cheese.
anneal, *v.t.* an-*neel*, to temper glass or metals by subjection to intense heat followed by very slow cooling; to heat glass and earthenware so as to fix colours; to temper by heat; to bake, as tiles. (A.S. *onælan*, to burn, confused with M.E., *anelen*, to enamel, from Fr. *nieler.*)
annealing, *n.* an-*neel*-ing, the art or process of tempering glass or metals.
annectent, *a.* an-*nekt*-ent, connecting.
Annelida, *n.pl.* an-*nel*-e-da, a group of articulate invertebrates, including worms and leeches, whose elongated bodies are composed of annular segments. (L. *annulus*, a ring, and *eidos*, form.)
annex, *v.t. an*-neks, to unite; to add on at the end; to unite a smaller thing to a greater; to connect; to take as one's own [Slang]. (Fr. *annexer.*)
annex, *n. a*-neks, a building attached; an addition.
annexation, *n. an*-eks-*ay*-shon, the act of annexing; something (often unlawfully) annexed.
annexationist, *n.* an-eks-*ay*-shon-ist, one favourable to annexation.
annexe, *n.* an-*neks*, an annex. (Fr.)
annihilable, *a.* an-*ny*-hil-a-bl, that may be annihilated; capable of annihilation.
annihilate, *v.t.* an-*ny*-hil-ate, to reduce to nothing; to destroy a thing as such. (L. *annihilātus.*)
annihilation, *n.* an-*ny*-hil-*ay*-shon, the act of annihilating; the state of being annihilated; complete destruction.
annihilationism, *n.* an-*ny*-hil-*ay*-shon-ism, the belief that the wicked are annihilated after death.
annihilationist, *n.* an-*ny*-hil-*ay*-shon-ist, one who believes in annihilationism.
annihilator, *n.* an-*ny*-hil-ay-tor, some one who, or that which, annihilates.
anniversary, *a. an*-ne-*ver*-sa-re, recurring at a stated time, with the year; yearly: *n.* the return of the day of the year on which a remarkable event took place; a celebration taking place on an anniversary. (L. *anniversārius*, annual.)
Anno Domini, *ad. phr. an*-no *dom*-e-ny, in the (specified) year of the Christian era, *i.e.*, from the date assigned to the birth of Christ. (L., "in the year of our Lord.")
annomination, *n.* an-nom-e-*nay*-shon, the juxtaposition of words of similar sound but different meaning; punning; paranomasia.
annotate, *v.t. an*-no-tate, to explain by the addition of notes; to comment upon: *v.i.* to write notes. (L. *annotatum*, written down.)
annotation, *n.* an-no-*tay*-shon, the act of annotating; a note in explanation.
annotator, *n. an*-no-tay-tor, a writer of annotations; a commentator.
annotatory, *a.* an-*noh*-ta-to-re, containing annotations; pertaining to an annotator.
annotinous, *a.* an-*not*-e-nus, one year old [Bot. and Zool.]. (L. *annōtinus*, a year old.)
annotto, *n.* an-*not*-to, annatto.
announce, *v.t.* an-*nouns*, to make known or proclaim; to pronounce or declare judicially; to proclaim the approach or arrival of. (O.Fr. *anoncier.*)
announcement, *n.* an-*nouns*-ment, the act of announcing; the notice given.
announcer, *n.* an-*nouns*-er, one who announces, esp. news and information by radio.
annoy, *v.t.* an-*noy*, to plague by continued or repeated acts; to tease; to molest. (O.Fr. *anoi.*)
annoyance, *n.* an-*noy*-ans, the act of annoying; the state of being annoyed; that which annoys.
annoyer, *n.* an-*noy*-er, one who annoys.
annoying, *a.* an-*noy*-ing, causing trouble and vexation.
annoyingly, *ad.* an-*noy*-ing-le, provokingly.
annual, *a. an*-new-al, returning every year; lasting only one year or season; reckoned by the year; performed in a year: *n.* a plant that lives but one year or season; a book published yearly; an anniversary mass for the dead. (Fr. *annuel.*)
annually, *ad. an*-new-al-le, yearly; every year.
annuent, *a. an*-new-ent, causing to nod or bend forward, esp. of certain muscles in the head) [Anat.]. (L. *annuens*, nodding.)
annuitant, *n.* an-*new*-e-tant, one who receives an annuity.
annuity, *n.* an-*new*-e-te, a sum of money payable yearly. (Fr. *annuité.*)
annul, *v.t.* an-*nul*, to render void or null; to abolish; to reduce to nothing. (Fr. *annuler.*)
annular, *a. an*-new-lar, in the form of a ring. **annular eclipse** of the sun, when the moon so covers his disk that only a bright ring is seen round the border. (L. *annulāris*, ring-like.)
annularly, *ad. an*-new-lar-le, in an annular manner.
annulary, *n. an*-yew-la-re, the third finger ("ring-finger") of the left hand.
annulate, *a. an*-new-late, annulated.
annulated, *a. an*-new-lay-ted, formed or divided into rings; wearing or marked with rings.
annulation, *n.* an-new-*lay*-shon, a ring-like or annulate formation; state of being annulate.
annulet, *n. an*-new-let, a little ring; a fillet. [Arch.].
annuller, *n.* an-*nul*-er, one who annuls.
annulment, *n.* an-*nul*-ment, the act of annulling; nullification; repeal. (Fr. *annulement.*)
annulose, *a. an*-new-lohs, furnished with rings; having an external ringed skeleton [Zool.].
annulus, *n. an*-new-lus, a plane figure bounded by two concentric circles; a ring, or ring-like part. (L.)
annunciate, *v.t.* an-*nun*-se-ate, to bring tidings; to announce. (L. *annuntiatus*, make known.)
annunciation, *n.* an-nun-se-*ay*-shon, the act of announcing. **Annunciation Day,** a Church festival on the 25th of March, in commemoration of the angel's salutation of the Virgin Mary; Lady Day. **Annunciation lily,** the Madonna lily. (L. *annuntiatio*, annunciation.)

annunciator, *n.* an-*nun*-se-ay-tor, a mechanism connected with a bell to indicate the room where attendance is required; one who announces.
annunciatory, *a.* an-*nun*-se-*ay*-to-re, announcing.
anoa, *n.* a-*noh*-a, a small wild ox, *Bos depressicornis*, of Celebes, allied to the buffalo.
anode, *n.* *an*-ode, the positive electric pole, the electrode by which the electric current enters substances through which it passes on its way to the other pole. (Gr. *ana-*, and *hodos*, a way.)
anodyne, *n.* *an*-o-dine, any medicine which allays pain; anything that soothes ruffled feelings: *a.* assuaging pain. (L. *anodynos*, stilling pain.)
anoesis, *n.* an-oh-*ee*-sis, consciousness that is receptive but incapable of exercising the mental faculty [Psych.]. (Gr.)
anoint, *v.t.* a-*noynt*, to pour oil on; to rub over with oil; to consecrate with oil. (O.Fr. *enoint*, anointed.)
anointing, *n.* a-*noynt*-ing, anointment.
anointment, *n.* a-*noynt*-ment, the act of anointing, or state of being anointed.
Anolis, *n.* a-*noh*-lis, a genus of American lizards.
anomaliped, *a.* a-*nom*-a-le-ped, having the middle toe united to the outer by three phalanges, and to the inner by one only; syndactyl [Ornith.]: *n.* a syndactyl bird. (Gr. *anōmalia*, unevenness, *pod*, foot.)
anomalism, *n.* a-*nom*-a-lizm, an anomaly; an instance of irregularity.
anomalistic, *n.* a-*nom*-a-*list*-ik, irregular; departing from common or established rule. **anomalistic month,** the time taken by the moon between perigee and perigee. **anomalistic year,** the time in which the earth traverses her orbit, which is 25 minutes longer than the tropical year, on account of the precession of the equinoxes.
anomalous, *a.* a-*nom*-a-lus, irregular; deviating from rule. (Gr. *anōmalos*, uneven.)
anomalously, *ad.* a-*nom*-a-lus-le, irregularly.
anomalousness, *n.* a-*nom*-a-lus-ness, irregularity.
anomalure, *n.* a-*nom*-a-*lewr*, the scale-tailed flying squirrel, a rodent of West Africa.
anomaly, *n.* a-*nom*-a-le, irregularity; deviation from rule; the angular distance of a planet from its perihelion; an irregularity in a planet's motion [Astron.]; slight deviation from a perfect interval [Mus.]. (Gr. *anōmalia*.)
anon, *ad.* a-*non*, immediately thereupon; soon thereafter; then again; coming, sir! **ever and anon,** every now and then. (A.S. *on ān*, in one moment.)
Anona, *n.* a-*noh*-na, a genus of tropical American trees and plants including the custard-apple and soursop.
anonym, *n.* *an*-oh-nim, one whose name is not divulged; an assumed name. (Fr. *anonyme*.)
anonymity, *n.* a-non-*im*-et-e, the condition of being anonymous.
anonymous, *a.* a-*non*-e-mus, having no known name; without the name of the author being attached. (Gr. *anōnumos*, nameless.)
anonymously, *ad.* a-*non*-e-mus-le, without a name.
anonymousness, *n.* a-*non*-e-mus-ness, anonymity.
anopheles, *n.* a-*nof*-e-leez, a malarial mosquito.
anopsia, *n.* an-*op*-se-a, lack of sight; blindness. (Gr. *an-*, not, *opsis*, sight.)
anorexia, *n.* *an*-o-*reks*-e-a, want of appetite. (Gr.)
anorthic, *a.* an-*or*-thik, not regular in crystallization; without right angles [Min.]. (Gr. *anorthos*, not erect.)
anorthite, *n.* a-*nor*-thite, silicate of calcium and aluminium occurring in translucent or transparent crystals [Min.].
anosmia, *n.* an-*oz*-me-a, lack of the sense of smell. (Gr. *an-*, not, *osme*, a smell.)
another, *a.* an-*uth*-er, not the same; one more; any other.
anotto, *n.* a-*not*-to, annatto. (Sp. American.)
anourous, *a.* a-*nou*-rus, tailless. (Gr. *an-*, not, *oura*, tail.)
ansa, *n.* *an*-sa, decorated vase-handle [Arch.]. (L.)
ansated, *a.* *an*-say-ted, having a handle.
Anschluss, *n.* *ahn*-shloos, a union or joining, esp. the union of the Austrian Republic and the German Reich in 1938. (Ger.)
anserine, *a.* *an*-se-rine, belonging to, resembling, the goose or the skin of a goose; stupid. (L. *anserīnus*, relating to geese.)

★**answer,** *v.t.* *ahn*-ser, to reply to; to respond to; to refute; to atone for; to be sufficient for; to suit; to be opposite to; to solve: *v.i.* to reply; to respond; to be suitable: *n.* a reply; an account to be rendered to justice; a solution; a written defence [Law]. **answer for,** to be responsible or answerable for. **answer to,** to correspond; to accord. (A.S. *andswerian*, speak in answer.)
answerable, *a.* *ahn*-ser-ra-bl, that may be replied to; obliged or liable to give an account; responsible.
answerably, *ad.* *ahn*-ser-ra-ble, correspondingly.
★**ant,** *n.* ant, a social hymenopterous insect of the genus *Formica*. (A.S. *æmette*, ant.)
ant-, *pref.* ant-, anti-; ante-.
anta, *n.* *an*-ta (*pl.* **antæ,** *an*-tee), a pilaster, or square projection on the wall of a building. (L.)
antacid, *a.* ant-*ass*-id, counteractive of acidity: *n.* any medicine that counteracts acidity.
antagonism, *n.* an-*tag*-o-nizm, opposition in a struggle or strife. (Gr. *antagōnisma*, a fight with.)
antagonist, *n.* an-*tag*-o-nist, one who contends or strives with another; an opponent: *a.* counteracting (of muscles) [Anat.].
antagonistic, *an*-tag-o-*nis*-tik, contending against; antagonist; a muscle counteracting in action another.
antagonistically, *ad.* *an*-tag-o-*nis*-te-ka-le, in an antagonistic manner.
antagonize, *v.t.* an-*tag*-o-nize, to contend against; to make antagonistic.
antalgic, *a.* an-*tal*-jik, relieving or preventing pain: *n.* an anodyne.
antalkali, *n.* ant-*al*-ka-le, a substance that neutralizes the action of alkalies.
antalkaline, *a.* ant-*al*-ka-lin, capable of neutralizing alkalies: *n.* an antalkali [Med.].
antaphrodisiac, *a.* and *n.* *ant*-af-ro-*diz*-e-ak, anaphrodisiac.
antarctic, *a.* ant-*ark*-tik, belonging to the circle and zone round the south pole: *n.* (*cap.*) the regions adjacent to the south pole. (L. *antarcticus*, southern.)
antarthritic, *a.* and *n.* ant-ar-*thrit*-ik, alleviating or remedying gout.
antasthmatic, *a.* and *n.* ant-as-*mat*-ik, relieving or remedying asthma.
ant-bear, *n.* *ant*-bare, a S. American edentate, *Myrmecophaga jubata*, with long prehensile tongue, living largely on ants; the anteater.
ante, *n.* *an*-te, a stake at poker nominated after seeing one's cards but before drawing: *v.t.* to make such a stake.
ante-, *an*-te, a Latin prefix, signifying before.
ante-act, *n.* *an*-te-akt, an act preceding.
anteater, *n.* *ant*-eet-er, any mammal that feeds on ants, especially the ant-bear.
antecede, *v.t.* *an*-te-*seed*, to go before in place or time. (L. *antecēdo*, go before.)
antecedence, *n.* an-te-*seed*-ens, the act or state of going before in time; precedence; an apparent motion of a planet towards the west, or contrary to the order of the signs [Astron.].
antecedency, *n.* an-te-*seed*-en-se, antecedence; the quality or state of being antecedent.
antecedent, *a.* an-te-*seed*-ent, going before in time; prior: *n.* that which goes before in time or place; the noun to which a relative refers [Gram.]; the conditional clause of a hypothetical proposition [Logic.]; the first of two terms of a ratio [Math.]: *pl.* prior conduct; past circumstances.
antecedently, *ad.* an-te-*seed*-ent-le, previously.
antecessor, *n.* an-te-*ses*-sor, one who goes before; progenitor; previous possessor [Law].
antechamber, *n.* *an*-te-chaym-ber, an anteroom.
antechapel, *n.* *an*-te-chap-el, anteroom to a chapel, forming a transept north and south outside the choir-screen.
antechoir, *n.* *an*-te-kwire, a space reserved for clergy and choristers at the entrance to the choir.
antecians, *n.pl.* an-*tee*-shanz, those living under the same meridian, and at the same distance from the equator, but on opposite sides of it [Geog.]. (Gr. *antoikos*, living opposite.)
antedate, *v.t.* *an*-te-date, to date before the true time; to anticipate; to precede in time: *n.* a prior date.
antediluvian, *a.* an-te-de-*lew*-ve-an, existing or happening before the deluge; antiquated: *n.*

one who lived before the deluge; a very old-fashioned person. (L. *ante-*, and *diluvium*, the flood.)

ant-eggs, *n.pl.* *ant*-egz, the pupæ of ants.

antelope, *n.* *an*-te-lope, a hollow-horned ruminant of kin to the deer and goat. (O.Fr. *antelop.*)

antelucan, *a.* an-te-*lew*-kan, before daylight. (L. *ante-*, and *lux*, light.)

antemeridian, *a.* *an*-te-me-*rid*-e-an, before noon, A.M.

antemetic, *a.* ant-e-*met*-ik, allaying or checking vomiting: *n.* a remedy to allay vomiting.

antemundane, *a.* an-te-*mun*-dane, in being or happening before the world existed.

antenatal, *a.* an-te-*nay*-tal, existing or occurring before birth.

antenna, *n.* an-*ten*-na (*pl.* **antennæ**), a feeler attached to the heads of insects and crustaceans; an aerial; a wire or collection of elevated wires for the direct transmission and reception of electric waves into and from the ether [Wireless]. (L.)

antennal, *a.* an-*ten*-nal, belonging to the antennæ.

antenniferous, *a.* an-ten-*nif*-er-us bearing antennæ.

antenniform, *a.* an-*ten*-ne-form, shaped like antennæ.

antenuptial, *a.* an-te-*nup*-shal, preceding or happening before marriage.

antepast, *n.* *an*-te-pahst, a foretaste; anciently, an appetizing snack before a meal. (L. *ante-*, and *pastus*, fed.)

antependium, *n.* an-te-*pen*-de-um, the embroidered cloth hanging in front of the altar.

antepenult, *n.* *an*-te-pe-*nult*, antepenultimate, the last syllable of a word except two.

antepenultimate, *a.* *an*-te-pe-*nul*-te-mate, pertaining to the antepenult: *n.* the antepenult.

antepileptic, *a.* and *n.* ant-ep-e-*lep*-tik, remedying and a remedy for epilepsy.

anteposition, *n.* *an*-te-po-*zish*-on, placing of a word before another, which, by ordinary rules, ought to follow it [Gram.].

anteprandial, *a.* an-te-*pran*-de-al, before dinner.

anterior, *a.* an-*teer*-re-or, before in time or place; going before. (L. *anterior*, that is before.)

anteriority, *n.* an-*teer*-re-o-re-te, the state of being anterior.

anteriorly, *ad.* an-*teer*-re-or-le, previously.

anteroom, *n.* *an*-te-room, a room leading into the chief apartment; an entrance-room.

antetemple, *n.* an-te-*tem*-pl, the portico of an ancient church; a narthex.

anthæmorrhagic, *a.* and *n.* ant-*hem*-o-*ray*-jik, remedying or relieving hæmorrhage.

anthelion, *n.* ant-*hee*-le-on (*pl.* **anthelia**, ant-*hee*-le-a), a halo thrown on a fog bank or cloud opposite the sun, due to diffraction of light; a mock sun. (Gr. *antēlios*, opposite the sun.)

anthelmintic, *a.* and *n.* an-thel-*min*-tik, destroying or expelling intestinal worms. (Gr. *anti-*, and *helminthos*, a worm.)

anthem, *n.* *an*-them, a hymn sung in alternate parts; a biblical quotation set to music; a national hymn. (A.S. *antefne*, antiphon.)

Anthemis, *n.* *an*-the-mis, a large genus of composite plants, including camomile. (L. *anthemis*, camomile.)

anther, *n.* *an*-ther, the male organ in a flowering plant, the head of the stamen [Bot.]. (Gr. *anthēros*, blooming.)

antheral, *a.* *an*-ther-ral, pertaining to anthers.

anther-dust, *n.* *an*-ther-dust, pollen.

antheridium, *n.* *an*-ther-*rid*-e-um (*pl.* **antheridia**), the male organ in ferns and mosses.

antheriferous, *a.* an-ther-*rif*-er-us, producing or bearing anthers.

antherogenous, *a.* an-ther-*roj*-en-us, andropetalous [Bot.].

antheroid, *a.* *an*-ther-royd, resembling an anther.

anthesis, *n.* an-*thee*-sis, that state of inflorescence in which flowers arrive at full bloom. (Gr. *anthēsis*, the full bloom, of flower or plant.)

ant-hill, *n.* *ant*-hill, the mound thrown up by a community of ants in forming their nest.

anthobian, *n.* an-*thoh*-be-an, a beetle that lives on flowers. (Gr. *anthos*, flower, *bios*, life.)

anthocarp, *n.* *an*-tho-karp, a collective fruit formed by masses of flowers adhering together, as the fir-cone and pine-apple. (Gr. *anthos*, and *karpos*, fruit.)

anthocarpous, *a.* an-tho-*kar*-pus, bearing, or pertaining to, anthocarps [Bot.].

anthodium, *n.* an-*thoh*-de-um, the head of any flower of the order *Compositæ*; a compound flower [Bot.].

anthoid, *a.* *an*-thoyd, resembling a flower in form.

anthological, *a.* an-tho-*loj*-e-kal, relating to anthology.

anthologist, *n.* an-*thol*-o-jist, the compiler of an anthology.

anthologize, *v.i.* an-*thol*-o-jize, to compile an anthology or anthologies.

anthology, *n.* an-*thol*-o-je, a collection of poems, epigrams or choice passages from various authors; a collection of devotional pieces [Eccles.]. (Gr. *anthologia*, a gathering of flowers.)

antholysis, *n.* an-*thol*-e-sis, the backward change of the parts of a flower, as of stamens into petals. (Gr. *anthos*, and *lyo*, loose.)

anthomania, *n.* an-tho-*may*-ne-a, a passion for rare or exotic flowers.

anthophore, *n.* *an*-tho-fore, the stalk raising the receptacle of a flower above the calyx [Bot.]. (Gr. *anthos*, and *phero*, bear.)

anthophyllite, *n.* an-*thof*-il-lite, hornblende of a clove-brown colour [Min.].

Anthozoa, *n.pl.* an-tho-*zoh*-a, an order of the Cœlenterata comprising sea-anemones and corals [Zool.]. (Gr. *anthos*, flower, *zoon*, life.)

anthracene, *n.* *an*-thra-seen, a hydro-carbon dye-stuff; a crystalline hydro-carbon derived from coal tar.

anthraciferous, *a.* an-thra-*sif*-er-us, anthracite-yielding.

anthracite, *n.* *an*-thra-site, a hard, lustrous, non-bituminous coal burning without smoke, with intense heat and with almost no flame. (Gr. *anthrakitēs*, anthracite.)

anthracitic, *a.* an-thra-*sit*-ik, pertaining to or resembling anthracite.

anthracoid, *a.* *an*-thra-koyd, resembling anthrax.

anthraconite, *n.* an-*thrak*-on-ite, black Kilkenny marble; coal-black bituminous limestone.

anthracosaurus, *n.* *an*-thra-ko-*saw*-rus, a large fossil lizard found in the English coal-measures [Geol.].

anthracosis, *n.* an-thra-*koh*-sis, a respiratory disease to which coal-miners are subject; coal-miners' lung.

Anthracotherium, *n.* *an*-thra-ko-*theer*-re-um, an extinct genus of Tertiary pachyderms related to the swine [Geol.].

anthracotic, *a.* an-thra-*kot*-ik, pertaining to or affected with anthracosis.

anthrax, *n.* *an*-thraks, a malignant disease common to sheep and cattle, and occurring in man; wool-sorters' disease. (Gr., a carbuncle.)

anthropo-, *comb. f.* relating to man. (Gr. *anthropos*, a man.)

anthropic, *a.* an-*throp*-ik, belonging to man [Biol.].

anthropocentric, *a.* an-thro-po-*sen*-trik, taking man as the pivot of the universe.

anthropogeny, *n.* an-thro-*poj*-en-e, the science of the origin and evolution of man.

anthropography, *n.* an-thro-*pog*-ra-fe, a description of the characteristics of the different races of man distributed over the globe; ethnography.

anthropoid, *a.* *an*-thro-poyd, resembling man [Zool.]: *n.* a member of the highest sub-order of primates; one of the higher apes. (Gr. *anthrōpoeides.*)

anthropolatry, *n.* *an*-thro-*pol*-a-tre, man-worship; the according of divine honours to man. (Gr. *anthropo-*, *-latry.*)

anthropolite, *n.* an-*throp*-o-lite, a human fossil. (Gr. *anthrōpos*, and *lithos*, a stone.)

anthropological, *a.* an-thro-po-*loj*-e-kal, pertaining to anthropology.

anthropologist, *n.* an-thro-*pol*-o-jist, one versed in anthropology.

anthropology, *n.* an-thro-*pol*-o-je, the science of man and mankind as regards physical and mental constitution, condition, and environment. (Gr. *anthrōpologos*, speaking about man.)

anthropomancy, *n.* *an*-thro-po-*man*-se, divination by inspecting the entrails of a human being. (Gr. *anthrōpos*, and *manteia*, divination.)

anthropometry, *n.* *an*-thro-*pom*-e-tre, measurement of the human body.

anthropomorphic, *a.* an-thro-po-*mor*-fik, pertaining to anthropomorphism.
anthropomorphism, *n.* *an*-thro-po-*mor*-fizm, ascription of a human form or characteristics to deity, or of human faculties to the lower animals. (Gr. *anthrōpomorphos*, of human form.)
anthropomorphist, *n.* an-thro-po-*mor*-fist, one who ascribes to deity human form and passions.
anthropomorphite, *n.* *an*-thro-po-*mor*-fite, an anthropomorphist.
anthropomorphitic, *a.* *an*-thro-po-mor-*fit*-ik, of the nature of or pertaining to anthropomorphism.
anthropomorphitism, *n.* *an*-thro-po-*mor*-fit-izm, the doctrines of the anthropomorphists.
anthropomorphize, *v.t.* *an*-thro-po-*mor*-fize, to attribute human form to.
anthropomorphosis, *n.* *an*-thro-po-mor-*foh*-sis or *an*-thro-po-*morf*-o-sis, transformation into human form.
anthropomorphous, *a.* *an*-thro-po-*mor*-fus, having a form resembling that of man.
anthropopathically, *ad.* *an*-thro-po-*path*-e-kal-le, in the manner of anthropopathy.
anthropopathy, *n.* an-thro-*pop*-a-the, the ascription of human passions, etc., to God.
anthropophagi, *n.pl.* *an*-thro-*pof*-a-jy, men that eat human flesh. (Gr. *anthrōpophagos*, man-eating.)
anthropophagism, *n.* *an*-thro-*pof*-a-jizm, the practice of cannibalism.
anthropophagite, *n.* *an*-thro-*pof*-a-jite, one addicted to the eating of human flesh; a cannibal.
anthropophagous, *a.* *an*-thro-*pof*-a-gus, feeding on human flesh.
anthropophagy, *n.* *an*-thro-*pof*-a-je, cannibalism.
anthropophuism, *n.* *an*-thro-*pof*-yew-izm, the ascribing of a human nature to the gods.
anthropophyte, *n.* an-*throp*-o-fite, a plant fortuitously introduced during cultivation [Bot.].
Anthropopithecus, *n.* *an*-throp-o-*pith*-e-kus, the genus of simians most nearly resembling man: the chimpanzee. (Gr. *anthrops*, and *pithekos*, ape.)
anthroposophist, *n.* *an*-thro-*pos*-o-fist, one possessed of a knowledge, or the wisdom, of men.
anthroposophy, *n.* *an*-thro-*pos*-o-fe, human wisdom; the knowledge of men.
anthropotomy, *n.* *an*-thro-*pot*-o-me, human anatomy.
anthypnotic, *a.* and *n.* ant-hip-*not*-ik, antihypnotic.
anti-, *an*-te, Greek prefix signifying against, opposite, or in place of.
anti-abolitionist, *n.* *an*-te-ab-o-*lish*-on-ist, one opposed to the abolition of slavery.
antiacid, *a.* and *n.* *an*-te-*as*-id, antacid.
anti-aircraft, *a.* *an*-te-*ayr*-krahft, employed in defence against aircraft.
antiar, *n.* *ant*-yar, the upas tree, *Antiaris toxicaria*.
antiarine, *n.* *ant*-yar-reen, the active principle of upas poison.
antiarthritic, *n.* an-te-ar-*thrit*-ik, antarthritic.
antibacchius, *n.* *an*-te-ba-*ky*-us, a foot of three syllables, the first two long, the last short [Pros.].
antibilious, *a.* an-te-*bil*-yus, counteractive of bilious complaints.
antibiotic, *a.* an-te-by-*ot*-ik, inimical to or destructive of living matter.
antibody, *n.* *an*-te-bod-e, a counteractive substance in the blood; an antitoxin.
antic, *a.* *an*-tik, odd; ludicrous; whimsical; fantastic: *n.* a buffoon; a grotesque or playful trick. (It. *antico*, grotesque.)
anticachectic, *n.* *an*-te-ka-*kek*-tik, a corrective of malnutrition: *a.* remedying cachexy.
anticatarrhal, *n.* and *a.* *an*-te-ka-*tah*-ral, a remedy for, and remedying, catarrh.
antichlor, *n.* *an*-te-klor, a substance used to free paper pulp and goods bleached by chloride of lime, from the after-effects of chlorine.
Antichrist, *n.* *an*-te-kryst, the opposite and opponent of Christ. (O.Fr. *antecrist*.)
antichristian, *a.* *an*-te-*krist*-yan, opposite to, and opposing, Christ and the spirit of Christ: *n.* one opposed to Christ or Christianity; a supporter of Antichrist.
antichristianism, *n.* *an*-te-*krist*-yan-izm, what is contrary and opposed to christianity.
anticipant, *a.* an-*tiss*-e-pant, anticipating; operating in advance: *n.* one who anticipates.
anticipate, *v.t.* an-*tiss*-e-pate, to be beforehand in acting, seeing, or realizing; to forestall; to foresee; to foretaste; to be prepared for: *v.i.* to take up beforehand. (L. *anticipation*, having already taken.)
anticipation, *n.* an-tiss-e-*pay*-shun, act of anticipating; foretaste; preconception; expectation; occurrence of symptoms before the usual time [Med.].
anticipative, *a.* an-*tiss*-e-pay-tiv, containing an anticipation; anticipatory.
anticipator, *n.* an-*tiss*-e-pay-tor, a person that anticipates.
anticipatory, *a.* an-tiss-e-*pay*-to-re, in anticipation.
anticlastic, *a.* an-te-*klas*-tik, having a surface curved convexly in one direction and concavely in the other (in opposition to "synclastic.").
anticlerical, *a.* an-te-*kle*-re-kal, against the clergy, their influence, or their sacerdotal claims.
anticlericalism, *n.* an-te-*kle*-re-ka-lizm, a movement opposing some or all of the sacerdotal, political, or social claims of the clergy or their influence in general.
anticlimax, *n.* *an*-te-*kly*-maks, bathos.
anticlinal, *a.* *an*-te-*kly*-nal, dipping or sloping in opposite directions: *n.* an axis, crest, or fold from which strata dip in opposite directions [Geol.]. (Gr. *anti-*, and *klino*, bend.)
anticline, *n.* *an*-te-kline, an anticlinal.
anticor, *n.* *an*-te-kor, an inflammatory swelling in the chest of horses. (Gr. *anti-*, and L. *cor*, the heart.)
anticous, *a.* *an*-te-kus, having the line of dehiscence in an anther turned towards the pistil [Bot.]. (L. *anticus*, foremost.)
anticum, *n.* an-*ty*-kum, a front porch [Arch.].
anticyclone, *n.* *an*-te-*sy*-klone, an atmospheric condition, with regard to wind and pressure, opposite to that of a cyclone; the central area of this condition, where winds blow spirally outward.
anticyclonic, *a.* an-te-sy-*klon*-ik, pertaining to, or due to, an anticyclone.
antidemocratic, *a.* *an*-te-dem-o-*krat*-ik, opposed to democracy; totalitarian.
antidotal, *a.* *an*-te-*doh*-tal, having the quality of an antidote; acting as an antidote.
antidote, *n.* *an*-te-dote, a medicine given to counteract the effects of poison; a counteractive against any evil. (Fr. *antidote*.)
antiepiscopal, *a.* *an*-te-e-*pis*-ko-pal, adverse to episcopacy.
antievangelical, *a.* *an*-te-ee-van-*jel*-e-kal, opposed to evangelicalism.
antifanatic, *n.* *an*-te-fa-*nat*-ik, an enemy of fanaticism.
antifebrile, *a.* an-te-*fee*-bril, allaying fever: *n.* a medicine that cures or allays fever; a febrifuge.
antifouling, *n.* *an*-te-*foul*-ing, a preparation for checking the formation of seaweeds and barnacles on ships' hulls.
antigen, *n.* *an*-te-jen, any substance, such as an enzyme or toxin, which, when introduced into the body or present in the blood, gives rise to an antibody.
antihelix, *n.* an-te-*hee*-liks, the semicircular prominence within the helix of the ear.
antihypnotic, *a.* an-te-hip-*not*-ik, tending to prevent sleep: *n.* a medicine that prevents or tends to prevent sleep.
antihysteric, *n.* *an*-te-his-*te*-rik, a medicine to counteract hysterical affections.
anti-knock, *n.* *an*-te-*nok*, an internal-combustion engine fuel, or a substance added to this, which eliminates detonation during combustion.
antilegomena, *n.pl.* an-te-le-*gom*-en-a, the deuterocanonical books of the New Testament. (Gr. *antilegomena*, contradicted.)
antilibration, *n.* *an*-te-ly-*bray*-shon, a balancing.
antilog, *n.* *an*-te-log, antilogarithm.
antilogarithm, *n.* an-te-*log*-a-rithm, the number which a logarithm represents; also, the complement of the logarithm of any sine, tangent, or secant, to 90 degrees.
antilogous, *a.* an-*til*-o-gus, denoting that pole of a crystal which, when heating, is negative, and when cooling, positive [Elect.]. (Gr. *antilogia*.)
antilogy, *n.* an-*til*-o-je, a contradiction in terms or ideas. (Gr. *antilogia*, contradiction.)
antilopine, *a.* an-te-*loh*-pine, pertaining to the antelopes [Zool.].

antimacassar, *n.* *an*-te-ma-*kas*-sar, a covering on chair-backs and sofas to save them from being soiled by oiled hair. (*anti-*, and macassar oil.)
antimask, *n.* *an*-te-mahsk, a grotesque interlude introduced into a masque.
antimasonic, *a.* *an*-te-ma-*son*-ik, opposed to freemasonry.
antimeter, *n.* an-te-*mee*-ter, an obsolete optical instrument for measuring angles under 10°. (Gr. *anti-*, and *metron*, a measure.)
antiministerial, *a.* *an*-te-min-is-*teer*-re-al, opposed to the ministry [Politics].
antimonarchical, *a.* *an*-te-mon-*ar*-ke-kal, opposed to monarchy, or government by one person.
antimonarchist, *n.* an-te-*mon*-ar-kist, one opposing monarchy.
antimonial, *a.* an-te-*moh*-ne-al, pertaining to, or composed of, antimony: *n.* a medicine in which antimony is a principal ingredient. **antimonial wine,** wine with tartar emetic dissolved in it.
antimoniate, *n.* an-te-*moh*-ne-ate, a salt of antimonic acid and a base.
antimonic, *a.* an-te-*mon*-ik, pertaining to antimony. **antimonic acid,** an acid composed of two equivalents of antimony and five of oxygen.
antimonious, *a.* an-te-*moh*-ne-us, containing or consisting of antimony; denoting a compound in which antimony is a trivalent [Chem.].
antimonite, *n.* *an*-te-mon-*ite*, any salt of antimonious acid; stibnite.
antimony, *n.* *an*-te-mon-e, a brittle silvery-white unoxidizable metallic element, a constituent of many alloys and used in medicine. (Late L. *antimōnium.*)
antinational, *a.* an-te-*nash*-on-al, against, or hostile to, one's nation; opposed to a national party or policy, etc.
antinatural, *a.* an-te-*nat*-yew-ral, opposed to what is natural.
antinephritic, *n.* *an*-te-ne-*frit*-ik, a medicine efficacious in diseases of the kidneys: *a.* counter-acting nephritis.
antinomian, *a.* an-te-*noh*-me-an, against the moral law; pertaining to the Antinomians: *n.* (*cap.*) one of a sect maintaining that, for Christians, law is set aside by the gospel. (Gr. *anti-*, and *nomos*, law.)
antinomianism, *n.* an-te-*noh*-me-an-izm, the tenets of Antinomians; rejection of the moral law.
antinomy, *n.* *an*-te-noh-me *or* an-*tin*-o-me, a contradiction between two laws, or two parts of the same law; the contradiction which arises when we carry the categories of the understanding above experience, and apply them to the sphere of the absolute [Kant's metaphysics]; paradox. (L. *antinomia*, a contradiction between laws.)
antipapal, *a.* an-te-*pay*-pal, opposing the Pope, the Papacy, or popery.
antiparalytic, *a.* and *n.* *an*-te-pa-ra-*lit*-ik, preventing, and a preventive of, paralysis.
antipathetic, *a.* an-te-pa-*thet*-ik, having a natural contrariety or antipathy to.
antipathetical, *a.* an-te-pa-*thet*-e-kal, antipathetic.
antipathic, *a.* an-te-*path*-ik, opposite, and opposed; contrary in character; allopathic [Med.].
antipathist, *n.* an-*tip*-a-thist, one controlled by antipathy; an opposite.
antipathy, *n.* an-*tip*-a-the, a natural contrariety or opposition; aversion; dislike. (Gr.)
antipatriotic, *a.* *an*-te-pat-re-*ot*-ik, opposed or indifferent to the welfare of one's country.
antiperiodic, *a.* and *n.* an-te-peer-re-*od*-ik, effective against, and a preventive of, the periodic return of paroxysms [Med.].
antiperistaltic, *a.* *an*-te-pe-re-*stal*-tik, acting contrary to peristaltic motion, *i.e.*, upwards [Physiol.].
anti-personnel, *a.* *an*-te-per-so-*nel*, denoting an explosive for use against troops and population rather than buildings, defences, etc. [Mil.].
antiphlogistic, *a.* *an*-te-flo-*jis*-tik, counteracting inflammation [Med.]; opposed to the doctrine of phlogiston: *n.* a remedy allaying inflammation.
antiphon, *n.* *an*-te-fon, an anthem sung by two choirs in alternate sentences; a series of versicles sung alternately; an antiphony.
antiphonal, *a.* an-*tif*-on-al, pertaining to antiphony or alternate singing: *n.* a book of antiphons.
antiphonary, *n.* an-*tif*-o-na-re, an antiphonal.
antiphony, *n.* an-*tif*-o-ne, alternate singing; an anthem, etc., sung alternately, esp. by one choir divided into two parts; an antiphon; opposition of sound. (Gr. *antiphōnos*, sounding in answer.)
antiphrasis, *n.* an-*tif*-ra-sis, the use of words in a sense opposite to their true meaning [Rhet.]. (Gr.)
antiphrastic, *a.* an-te-*fras*-tik, pertaining to antiphrasis.
antipodal, *a.* an-*tip*-o-dal, antipodean.
antipode, *n.* *an*-te-pode, one of the antipodes.
antipodean, *a.* an-*tip*-o-*dee*-an, pertaining to the antipodes.
antipodes, *n.pl.* an-*tip*-o-deez, those parts of the globe that are diametrically opposite to each other; persons living on diametrically opposite sides of the globe; the exact opposite. (Gr. *antipous*, having the feet opposite.)
antipole, *n.* *an*-te-pole, an opposite; the opposite pole.
antipope, *n.* *an*-te-pope, one claiming to be Pope in opposition to him canonically chosen.
antipsoric, *a.* and *n.* an-tip-*sor*-ik, remedying, and a remedy for, the itch. (Gr. *psora*, the itch.)
antipyretic, *a.* an-te-py-*ret*-ik, effective against fever and pain: *n.* a febrifuge. (Gr. *anti-*, and *pyretos*, fever.)
antipyrin, *n.* an-te-*pire*-rin, a colourless, tasteless drug derived from coal-tar products, valuable in reducing pain and fever.
antiquarian, *a.* an-te-*kware*-re-an, pertaining to antiquaries, or to antiquity: *n.* an antiquary; a large size of drawing-paper (31″×53″).
antiquarianism, *n.* an-te-*kware*-re-an-izm, a fondness for antiquities; antiquarian pursuits.
antiquary, *n.* *an*-te-kwa-re, one devoted to the study of antiquity or antiquities; a collector of or dealer in antiques. (L. *antīquārius*, an antiquary.)
antiquate, *v.t.* *an*-te-kwate, to make obsolete; to put out of use through age.
antiquated, *a.* *an*-te-kway-ted, old-fashioned; fallen obsolete. (L. *antiquatus*, restored to its original state.)
antique, *a.* an-*teek*, ancient; old-fashioned: *n.* anything very old; a relic of antiquity. (Fr.)
antiqueness, *n.* an-*teek*-ness, the quality of being antique.
antiquity, *n.* an-*tik*-we-te, state of having existed in times long past; great age; ancient times; the people, manners, or events, etc., of ancient times; a relic of old times. (Fr. *antiquité*.)
antirabic, *a.* an-te-*rab*-ik, counteracting the virus of rabies; pertaining to the cure of rabies.
antirevolutionary, *a.* *an*-te-rev-o-*loo*-shon-a-re, adverse to revolutions in government.
antirevolutionist, *n.* *an*-te-rev-o-*loo*-shon-ist, anyone opposed to revolution.
antirheumatic, *a.* and *n.* *an*-te-roo-*mat*-ik, efficacious in cases of, and a remedy for, rheumatism.
antirrhinum, *n.* an-te-*ry*-num, any plant of the genus *Antirrhinum*, including the snapdragon. (Gr. *antirrinon*, snap-dragon.)
antiscorbutic, *n.* and *a.* an-te-skor-*bew*-tik, a remedy for, and counteracting, scurvy.
anti-semites, *n.pl.* *an*-te-*see*-mites, opponents of the Jews, on racial, political and economic grounds.
anti-semitic, *a.* *an*-te-se-*mit*-ik, opposed to the Jews; indoctrinated with anti-semitism.
anti-semitism, *n.* an-te-*see*-me-tizm, fanatic hatred of the Jews and all things Jewish; the theory (originating in Germany) that the Jews are a permanently inferior race.
antiseptic, *a.* an-te-*sep*-tik, resisting the growth of putrefaction causing bacteria: *n.* any substance used to destroy or counteract putrefaction and its causes. (Gr. *anti-*, and *sēptikos*, septic.)
antisocial, *a.* an-te-*soh*-shal, tending to interrupt or destroy social intercourse; acting in opposition to the best interests of the community.
antisocialist, *n.* an-te-*soh*-shal-ist, one opposed to socialism.
antispasmodic, *a.* *an*-te-spaz-*mod*-ik, counteractive of spasms; steadying the nerves: *n.* an antispasmodic agent.
antispast, *n.* *an*-te-spast, a foot of four syllables, in which the first and last are short, and the two middle ones long [Pros.]. (L.)
antispastic, *a.* an-te-*spas*-tik, antispasmodic [Med.]; containing or pertaining to antispasts [Pros.].
antistrophe, *n.* an-*tis*-tro-fe, the stanza of an ode alternating with the strophe, and originally sung

by the chorus in returning to the right, the strophe having been sung in moving to the left; the inversion of the same terms in different clauses [Rhet.]. (Gr. *antistrophē*, a turning about.)
antistrophic, *a.* an-te-*strof*-ik, pertaining or belonging to antistrophes.
antistrumous, *a.* an-te-*stroo*-mus, relieving scrofulous diseases.
antisyphilitic, *a.* *an*-te-sif-e-*lit*-ik, efficacious against syphilis: *n.* a remedy for syphilis.
antitheism, *n.* an-te-*thee*-izm, opposition to theism; denial of the existence of God.
antitheist, *n.* an-te-*thee*-ist, one who opposes theism; an atheist.
antitheistic, *a.* *an*-te-thee-*ist*-ik, pertaining to antitheism.
antithesis, *n.* an-*tith*-e-sis (*pl.* **antitheses,** an-*tith*-e-seez), opposition; contrast; expression by contrast [Rhet.]. (Gr.)
antithetical, *a.* an-te-*thet*-e-kal, pertaining to, abounding in, or prone to, antithesis.
antithetically, *ad.* an-te-*thet*-e-ka-le, by antithesis.
antitoxic, *a.* an-te-*tok*-sik, neutralizing the poison of disease.
antitoxin, *n.* an-te-*tok*-sin, one of several substances soluble in the blood that neutralize the action of toxins; an artificial preparation having this effect.
antitrades, *n.pl.* *an*-te-traydz, westerly winds of the middle latitudes blowing above the trade-winds.
antitragus, *n.* an-*tit*-ra-gus, the conical prominence on the lower part of the outer ear, opposite the tragus. (Gr. *antitragos.*)
antitrinitarian, *n.* *an*-te-trin-e-*tare*-re-an, one who denies the doctrine of the Trinity: *a.* opposing or rejecting this doctrine.
antitrinitarianism, *n.* *an*-te-trin-e-*tare*-re-a-nizm, the denial of the doctrine of the Trinity.
antitypal, *a.* *an*-te-*ty*-pal, pertaining to an antitype; explaining the type.
antitype, *n.* *an*-te-tipe, that of which the type is the example. (Gr. *antitypon.*)
antitypical, *a.* an-te-*tip*-e-kal, antitypal.
antivenene, *n.* *an*-ti-*ven*-een, an antidote to snake-poison. (L.)
antivivisection, *n.* *an*-te-viv-e-*sek*-shon, opposition to vivisection.
antivivisectionist, *n.* *an*-te-viv-e-*sek*-shon-ist, an opponent of vivisection.
antivenereal, *a.* *an*-te-ve-*neer*-re-al, relieving or curing venereal disease.
antizymic, *a.* an-te-*zim*-ik *or* -*zy*-mik, preventive of fermentation: *n.* a substance effecting this.
antizymotic, *a.* an-te-zy-*mot*-ik, preventing decomposition or fermentation.
antler, *n.* *ant*-ler, a branch of the horns of a deer; (*pl.*) the complete horns. (O.Fr. *antoillier.*)
antlered, *a.* *ant*-lerd, furnished with antlers.
antlia, *n.* *ant*-le-a, the suctorial organ of lepidoptera. (L.)
ant-lion, *n.* *ant*-ly-on, a neuropterous insect of the genus *Myrmeleon*, whose larvæ feed on insects caught in the pits they make to catch them.
antœcians, *n.pl.* an-*tee*-shanz, antecians.
antonomasia, *n.* an-to-no-*may*-ze-a, the substitution of a common noun for a proper, as *the philosopher* for *Aristotle*, or a proper noun for a common, as *a Cicero* for *an orator* [Rhet.]. (Gr.)
antonym, *n.* *an*-ton-im, a word absolutely opposed in meaning to another word. (Gr. *anti-*, and *onyma*, name.)
antre, *n.* *an*-ter, a cavern; a den. (L. *antrum.*)
antrorse, *a.* an-*trawse*, turning upward or forward [Bot.]. (Gr. *anti-*, and L. *versus*, turned.)
Anubis, *n.* an-*yew*-bis, an Egyptian deity, with the body of a man and the head of a jackal, the guardian and judge of the souls of the departed.
anura, *n.* an-*yew*-ra, a former group-name for the frogs and toads. (Gr. *an-*, without, *oura*, tail.)
anus, *n.* *ay*-nus, the lower orifice of the alimentary canal [Anat.]. (L.)
anvil, *n.* *an*-vil, an iron block on which smiths hammer and shape their work; anything on which blows are struck; a small bone in the ear. **on the anvil,** in a state of discussion, formation, or preparation. (A.S. *anfilti*, anvil.)
anvilled, *a.* *an*-vild, wrought on an anvil.
anxiety, *n.* ang-*zy*-e-te, the state of being anxious; intense solicitude; mental distress. (Fr. *anxiété.*)
anxious, *a.* *angk*-shus, greatly concerned respecting something future or unknown; full of solicitude; very desirous. (L. *anxius*, distressed.)
anxiously, *ad.* *angk*-shus-le, in an anxious manner.
anxiousness, *n.* *angk*-shus-ness, the state of being anxious.
★**any,** *a.* *en*-ne one indefinitely; some or an indefinite number. (A.S. *ænig*, any.)
anybody, *n.* *en*-ne-bod-de, one person out of many; nobody in particular.
anyhow, *ad.* and *conj.* *en*-ne-hou, in any kind of way; at least; in any case; in disorder.
anything, *n.* *en*-ne-thing, something of any kind; to any extent.
anywhere, *ad.* *en*-ne-whare, in any place.
anywise, *ad.* *en*-ne-wize, in any manner; anyhow.
Anzac, *n.* *an*-zak, the Australian-New Zealand Army Corps which fought in Gallipoli and elsewhere, 1915–18; any member of that Corps. (The initial letters.)
Aonian, *a.* ay-*oh*-ne-an, pertaining to the Muses, or to Aonia, in which part of Bœotia was the fountain, Aganippe, sacred to them.
aorist, *n.* *ay*-o-rist, an indeterminate past tense in the Greek verb. (Gr. *aoristos*, without limits.)
aoristic, *a.* ay-o-*rist*-ik, pertaining to the aorist; indefinite as regards time.
aorta, *n.* ay-*ort*-a, the great artery, or main trunk of the arterial system, proceeding immediately from the left ventricle of the heart [Anat.]. (Gr.)
aortic, *a.* ay-*ort*-ik, pertaining to the aorta.
aoudad, *n.* ah-*oo*-dad, the goat-like wild sheep, *Ovis lervia*, of N. Africa, the Barbary sheep.
apace, *ad.* a-*pace*, quickly; steadily; step by step.
apache, *n.* a-*pahsh*, a Parisian hooligan. (Name of a tribe of N. Amer. Indians.)
apagoge, *n.* *ap*-a-go-je, proof of a proposition by exposure of the absurdity that would follow from denying it [Logic]. (Gr., taking away.)
apagogical, *a.* ap-a-*goj*-e-kal, pertaining to apagoge; proving by demonstrating the absurdity or impossibility of the contrary.
apanage, *n.* *ap*-an-aj, lands or other provision made and assigned for the maintenance of younger sons of a royal house; a territorial dependency; a necessary attribute; any perquisite. (O.Fr. *apaner*, to nourish.)
apart, *ad.* a-*pahrt*, separately, as regards—(*a*) place, (*b*) purpose, (*c*) thought, (*d*) wholeness; aside; independently. (Fr. *à part*, alone.)
apartment, *n.* a-*pahrt*-ment, a room in a house: *pl.* a set of rooms; lodgings. (Fr. *appartement.*)
apathetic, *a.* ap-a-*thet*-ik, insensible; indifferent.
apathetical, *a.* ap-a-*thet*-e-kal, in a state of apathy.
apathy, *n.* *ap*-a-the, want of feeling; want of passion; indifference; mental indolence. (Gr. *apatheia*, absence of feeling.)
apatite, *n.* *ap*-a-tite, a widely occurring phosphate of calcium. (Gr. *apatē*, deceit.)
apay, *v.t.* a-*pay*, to satisfy; to please.
ape, *n.* ayp, an anthropoid; any monkey without a tail; any large monkey; a servile or silly imitator: *v.t.* to imitate servilely; to mimic. (A.S. *apa.*)
apeak, *ad.* a-*peek*, perpendicular, or nearly so [Naut.].
apepsia, *n.* a-*pep*-se-a, defective digestion; dyspepsia. (Gr. *apeptos*, not digested.)
apepsy, *n.* a-*pep*-se, apepsia.
aper, *n.* *ay*-per, one who apes another.
aperient, *a.* a-*peer*-e-ent, opening; laxative: *n.* laxative medicine. (L. *aperiens*, opening.)
aperiodic, *a.* ay-peer-e-*od*-ik, having no natural period; of irregular occurrence.
aperiodicity, *n.* *ay*-peer-e-oh-*dis*-e-te, the state or quality of being aperiodic.
aperitif, *n.* a-*pe*-re-tif, an alcoholic drink, taken before meals to stimulate the appetite; an appetizer.
aperitive, *a.* a-*pe*-re-tiv, having aperient qualities.
apert, *a.* a-*pert*, open; public.
aperture, *n.* *ap*-er-tewr, an opening; a gap or passage; the space in an optical instrument through which light passes. (L. *apertūra*, opening.)
apery, *n.* *ayp*-er-e, mimicry; a monkey-house.
apetalous, *a.* ay-*pet*-a-lus, having no petals [Bot.]. (Gr. *a-*, and *petalon*, a leaf.)
apex, *n.* *ay*-peks (*pl.* **apices,** *ap*-e-seez, or **apexes**), the tip, point or summit of anything. (L.)
aphæresis, *n.* a-*feer*-re-sis, the taking of a letter or syllable from the beginning of a word. (Gr. *aphaeresis*, taking away.)

aphaniptera, *n.pl.* af-a-*nip*-ter-a, insects with rudimentary scales instead of wings.
aphanite, *n.* *af*-a-nite, a dark mineral consisting of hornblende, quartz, and felspar [Min.]. (Gr. *aphanes*, invisible.)
aphasia, *n.* ay-*fay*-ze-a, impairment or loss of speech through brain lesion [Med.]. (Gr. *aphasia.*)
aphelion, *n.* a-*fee*-le-on (*pl.* **aphelia**), that point of a planet or comet's orbit most distant from the sun [Astron.]. (Gr. *apo-*, from, *helios*, the sun.)
apheliotropic, *a.* a-*fee*-le-o-*trop*-ik, turning away from the sun [Bot.]. (Gr. *apo-*, from, *helios*, the sun, *trepo*, turn.)
apheliotropism, *n.* a-*fee*-le-*ot*-ro-pizm, the characteristic of turning away from the sun [Bot.].
aphemia, *n.* a-*fee*-me-a, aphasia marked by difficulty in articulation [Med.]. (Gr. *a-*, and *phēmē*, speech.)
apheresis, *n.* a-*feer*-re-sis, aphæresis.
aphesis, *n.* *af*-e-sis, the gradual dropping of an unstressed vowel at the beginning of a word, *e.g.* squire, from esquire. (Gr. *aphesis*, dismissal.)
aphid, *n.* *ay*-fid, a plant-louse of the genus *Aphis.*
aphides, *n.* *af*-e-deez, *pl.* of aphis.
aphidian, *a.* a-*fid*-e-an, pertaining to the aphides: *n.* an aphid.
aphidivorous, *a.* *af*-e-*div*-o-rus, devouring aphides.
aphis, *n.* *ay*-fis (*pl.* **aphides,** *af*-e-deez), a plant-louse; green fly. (L.)
aphlogistic, *a.* af-lo-*jis*-tik, burning without flame. (Gr. *aphlogistos*, uninflammable.)
aphonia, *n.* a-*foh*-ne-a, loss of voice through defect in the vocal chords. (Gr. *aphonia*, speechlessness.)
aphonous, *a.* *af*-o-nus, destitute of voice.
aphony, *n.* *af*-on-e, aphonia.
aphorism, *n.* *af*-o-rizm, a principle or truth briefly and pithily expressed; a maxim. (Gr. *aphorismos*, a definition.)
aphorist, *n.* *af*-o-rist, a writer of aphorisms.
aphoristic, *a.* af-o-*ris*-tik, in the form of aphorisms.
aphoristically, *ad.* af-o-*ris*-te-ka-le, in the manner of aphorisms.
aphorize, *v.i.* *af*-o-rize, to make or use aphorisms.
aphrite, *n.* *af*-rite, an earthy variety of calcite, having a silvery lustre [Min.]. (Gr. *aphros*, foam.)
aphrizite, *n.* *af*-re-zite, a variety of black tourmaline.
aphrodisia, *n.* af-ro-*diz*-e-a, sexual passion. (Gr.)
aphrodisiac, *a.* af-ro-*diz*-e-ak, exciting sexual desire: *n.* a drug that excites sexual desire. (Gr.)
aphrodisiacal, *a.* af-ro-de-*zy*-a-kal, aphrodisiac.
aphrodisian, *a.* af-ro-*diz*-e-an, pertaining to Aphrodite, the goddess of beauty and love; given to sexual passion. (Gr.)
aphtha, *n.* *af*-tha, the infantile disease, thrush [Med.]. (Gr., ulceration of the mouth.)
aphthæ, *n.pl.* *af*-thee, small white ulcers upon the tongue and inside the mouth, seen in thrush [Med.].
aphthitalite, *n.* af-*thit*-a-lite, a potassium sodium sulphate occurring in crystalline form. (Gr. *aphthitos*, imperishable, *lithos*, stone.)
aphthous, *a.* *af*-thus, pertaining to, of the nature of, the thrush [Med.].
aphyllous, *a.* *af*-il-lus, destitute of leaves [Bot.]. (Gr. *aphyllos*, leafless.)
apian, *a.* *ay*-pe-an, pertaining to bees; apiarian.
apiarian, *a.* ay-pe-*ayr*-re-an, relating to bees or to bee-keeping: *n.* an apiarist.
apiarist, *n.* *ay*-pe-a-rist, one who rears bees.
apiary, *n.* *ay*-pe-a-re, a place where bees are kept. (L. *apiārium.*)
apical, *a.* *ay*-pe-kal, belonging to, at, or towards the apex.
apices, *n.* *ap*-e-seez, *pl.* of apex.
apiculated, *a.* a-*pik*-yew-lay-ted, terminated abruptly in a point [Bot.].
apiculture, *n.* *ay*-pe-*kult*-tewr, the rearing of bees.
apiece, *ad.* a-*pees*, to each; each by itself.
apiocrinite, *n.* ay-pe-*ok*-re-nite, a pear-shaped oolitic encrinite. (Gr. *apion*, a pear, *krinon*, a lily.)
apish, *a.* *ayp*-ish, like or befitting an ape; servilely imitative; foolish.
apishly, *ad.* *ayp*-ish-le, in an apish manner.
apishness, *n.* *ayp*-ish-ness, the quality of being apish.
aplacental, *a.* ap-la-*sen*-tal, without a placenta.
aplanatic, *a.* ap-la-*nat*-ik, entirely free from aberration of the rays of light; correcting aberration [Opt.]. (Gr. *aplanētos*, that cannot err.)
aplastic, *a.* ay-*plas*-tik, not plastic or easily moulded. (Gr. *aplastos*, incapable of being formed.)
aplomb, *n* a-*plom*, self-possession; assurance. (Fr.)
aplome, *n.* *ap*-lohm, a dark brown variety of garnet. (Gr. *haploos*, simple.)
aplustre, *n.* a-*plus*-ter, the ornamental end to the keel carried by ancient ships. (L.)
apnœa, *n.* ap-*nee*-a, suspension of breathing. (Gr. *apnoia*, loss of wind.)
apo-, *ap*-o, a Greek prefix signifying away from.
Apocalypse, *n.* a-*pok*-a-lips, the Revelation of St. John. (Gr. *apokalupsis*, a revelation.)
apocalyptic, *a.* a-pok-a-*lip*-tik, apocalytpical.
apocalyptical, *a.* a-pok-a-*lip*-te-kal, pertaining to revelation, or to the Apocalypse.
apocalyptically, *ad.* a-pok-a-*lip*-te-ka-le, in an, or the, apocalyptic manner.
apocarpous, *a.* ap-o-*karp*-us, having carpels either entirely or partially distinct [Bot.]. (Gr. *apo-*, and *karpos*, fruit.)
apocatastasis, *n.* *ap*-o-ka-*tass*-ta-sis, return to a previous condition; the eventual restitution of all things and return of lost souls to divine forgiveness [Theol.]. (Gr.)
apochromatic, *a.* *ap*-o-kro-*mat*-ik, highly achromatic (of lenses).
apocopate, *v.t.* a-*pok*-o-pate, to cut off or drop the last letter or syllable of a word [Gram.].
apocope, *n.* a-*pok*-o-pe, the cutting off or dropping of the last letter or syllable of a word. (Gr.)
apocrustic, *a.* ap-o-*krust*-ik, repelling; astringent [Med.]. (Gr. *apokroustikos*, capable of repelling.)
Apocrypha, *n.* a-*pok*-re-fa, writings or statements of doubtful authority, esp. certain books appended to the Old Testament which are not recognized by the Jews and are excluded from the Authorized Version of the Bible. (Gr. *apokruphos*, concealed.)
apocryphal, *a.* a-*pok*-re-fal, of uncertain authorship or intent; fictitious; not canonical.
apocryphally, *ad.* a-*pok*-re-fal-le, in an apocryphal manner; uncertainty.
apod, *n.* *ap*-od (*pl.* **apoda,** *ap*-o-da), any fish, reptile, or amphibian in which the limbs or corresponding members are absent or deficient. (Gr. *apous*, without feet.)
apodal, *a.* *ap*-o-dal, footless; destitute of ventral fins.
apodeictic, *a.* ap-o-*dike*-tik, clearly demonstrative; incontrovertibly established. (L. *apodicticus*, demonstrative.)
apodeictically, *ad.* ap-o-*dike*-tik-al-le, so as to be evident beyond contradiction.
apodictic, *a.* ap-o-*dik*-tik, apodeictic.
apodosis, *n.* a-*pod*-o-sis, the consequent clause in conditional and other propositions [Gram.]; the concluding clause of a sentence. (Gr. *apodosis.*)
apodyterium, *n.* a-*po*-de-*teer*-re-um, the apartment for undressing in a Roman bath.
apogean, *a.* *ap*-o-*jee*-an, belonging to the apogee.
apogee, *n.* *ap*-o-je, that point in the orbit of the moon or a planet which is at the greatest distance from the earth [Astron.]. (Fr. from Gr.)
apograph, *n.* *ap*-o-graf, a transcript; an exact copy. (Gr. *apographē*, a copying.)
apolaustic, *a.* ap-o-*lawst*-ik, devoted to enjoyment or self-indulgence. (Gr. *apolaustikos.*)
Apollyon, *n.* a-*pol*-yon, the destroying angel; Satan. (Gr. from *apollumi*, utterly destroy.)
apologetic, *a.* a-pol-o-*jet*-ik, excusing; defensive without admitting error; vindicatory; by way of apology.
apologetical, *a.* a-*pol*-o-*jet*-e-kal, apologetic.
apologetically, *ad.* a-pol-o-*jet*-e-ka-le, by way of apology. (Fr.)
apologetics, *n.* a-pol-o-*jet*-iks, that branch of theology which seeks to vindicate the claims of the Christian religion.
apologia, *n.* ap-o-*loh*-je-a, a formal defence or vindication. (L.)
apologist, *n.* a-*pol*-o-jist, one who pleads in apology or defence; a professed defender of Christianity.
apologize, *v.i.* a-*pol*-o-jize, to make an apology or excuse for.
apologizer, *n.* a-*pol*-o-jize-er, one who apologizes.
apologue, *n.* *ap*-o-log, a moral fable. (Fr. from Gr.)
apology, *n.* a-*pol*-o-je, something said or written in justification or extenuation; a defence, vindication,

or excuse; acknowledgment of error; a bad attempt or substitute, a makeshift [Slang]. (L. *apologia.*)

aponeurosis, *n.* ap-o-new-*roh*-sis (*pl.* **aponeuroses,** ap-o-new-*roh*-seez), a membrane of interlaced fibre in the form of an extension of a tendon or the envelope of a muscle [Anat.]. (Gr. *aponeurōsis.*)

aponeurotic, *a.* ap-o-new-*rot*-ik, relating to an aponeurosis.

apoop, *ad.* a-*poop,* towards or on the poop; astern [Naut.].

apophasis, *n.* a-*pof*-a-sis, the seeming waiving or omission by a speaker of what he would plainly insinuate [Rhet.]. (Gr. *apophasis,* denial.)

apophlegmatic, *a.* ap-o-fleg-*mat*-ik, exciting discharges of phlegm or mucus: *n.* a medicine effecting this. (Gr. *apophlegmatikos.*)

apophthegm, *n.* *ap*-o-them, a terse pithy saying; a sententious maxim. (Gr. *apophthegma.*)

apophthegmatic, *a.* *ap*-o-theg-*mat*-ik, of the nature of, or given to the use of apophthegms.

apophthegmatist, *n.* *ap*-o-*theg*-ma-tist, a maker or collector of apophthegms.

apophyge, *n.* a-*pof*-e-je, the part of a column where it springs out of its base [Arch.]. (Gr. *apophugē.*)

apophysis, *n.* a-*pof*-e-sis (*pl.* **apophyses,** a-*pof*-e-seez), a process or offshoot of a bone [Anat.]; in mosses, a swelling of the spore case. (Gr. *apophusis,* offshoot.)

apoplectic, *a.* ap-o-*plek*-tik, pertaining to or predisposed to apoplexy: *n.* a person effected with apoplexy.

apoplexy, *n.* *ap*-o-plek-se, a sudden loss of sense and voluntary motion, usually occasioned by hæmorrhage into the brain. (Gr. *apoplektos,* crippled by a blow.)

aport, *ad.* a-*port,* towards or on the left side or port; said especially of the helm [Naut.].

aposiopesis, *n.* *ap*-o-*sy*-o-*pee*-sis, a sudden stopping short in a discourse, generally for rhetorical effect [Rhet.]. (Gr. *aposiōpaō,* keep silence.)

apostacy, *n.* a-*pos*-ta-se, apostasy.

apostasy, *n.* a-*pos*-ta-se, the abandonment of a faith or of principles once professed; desertion of one's party. (Gr. *apostasia,* revolt.)

apostate, *n.* a-*pos*-tate, one who has apostatized; a pervert: *a.* false; traitorous.

apostatical, *a.* ap-os-*stat*-e-kal, after the manner of an apostate.

apostatize, *v.i.* a-*pos*-ta-tize, to forsake one's principles, faith, or party.

apostematous, *a.* ap-o-*stem*-a-tus, pertaining to, of the nature of, or characterized by abscesses.

aposteme, *n.* *ap*-o-steem, an abscess. (Gr. *apo-,* and *histemi,* to stand.)

apostil, *n.* a-*pos*-til, a marginal note; a gloss. (Fr.)

apostle, *n.* a-*pos*-sl, one of the Twelve commissioned by Christ to preach the Gospel; one sent on or dedicated to some high mission; an early or first missionary; a leader of reform. **Apostles' Creed,** the oldest confession of Christian faith. (A.S. *apostol.*)

apostleship, *n.* a-pos-*sl*-ship, the office or dignity of an apostle.

apostolate, *n.* a-*pos*-to-late, the office of an apostle, esp. that of the Pope.

apostolic, *a.* ap-os-*tol*-ik, pertaining or according to the Apostles; derived directly from them; papal (the Pope being regarded as the successor of St. Peter). **Apostolic Fathers,** Christian teachers in part contemporary with the Apostles. **Apostolic See,** the Holy See. **Apostolic succession,** the doctrine of the transmission from the Apostles, through the episcopal laying on of hands, of spiritual authority.

apostolical, *a.* ap-os-*tol*-e-kal, apostolic.

apostolically, *ad.* ap-os-*tol*-e-ka-le, in the manner of Apostles.

apostrophe, *n.* a-*pos*-tro-fe, a digression in the course of a speech, esp. one as though addressed to some one absent or dead [Rhet.]; the contraction of a word by the omission of a letter or letters, and the insertion of a punctuation sign [Gram.]; this sign ('), used also to denote the possessive case. (Gr.)

apostrophic, *a.* ap-o-*strof*-ik, pertaining to or resembling an apostrophe.

apostrophize, *v.t.* a-*pos*-tro-fize, to address by apostrophe; to make an omission and insert the apostrophe.

apothecary, *n.* a-*poth*-e-ka-re, one who prepares and sells medicines; a druggist. (Fr. *apothecaire.*)

apothecia, *n.pl.* ap-o-*thee*-se-ah, the peltate disks containing the spores on the surface of lichens. (Gr. *apothecium,* from *apotheke,* a storehouse.)

apothegm, *n.* *ap*-o-them, apophthegm.

apothegmatize, *v.i.* ap-o-*theg*-ma-tize, to compose or utter apophthegms.

apothem, *ap*-o-them, a line connecting the centre of a regular polygon with the centre of any one of its sides [Math.]. (Gr. *apo-,* and *thema,* that which is placed.)

apotheosis, *n.* a-poth-e-*oh*-sis or ap-oh-*thee*-o-sis, deification; enrolment among the gods. (L.)

apotheosize, *v.t.* a-*poth*-e-*oh*-size, to deify.

apotomy, *n.* a-*pot*-o-me, the difference between two quantities that are commensurate, or commensurable only in power [Math.]; in ancient Greek music, a major semitone. (Gr. *apotomē,* a cutting off.)

apozem, *n.* *ap*-o-zem, a decoction or infusion from plants. (Gr. *apo-,* and *ze-ein,* boil.)

appal, *v.t.* ap-*pawl,* to depress with fear; to terrify; to dismay. (O.Fr. *apalir,* to grow pale.)

appalling, *a.* ap-*pawl*-ing, calculated to inspire dismay or horror.

appallingly, *ad.* ap-*pawl*-ing-le, in a manner to appal.

appanage, *n.* *ap*-pan-aj, apanage.

★**apparatus,** *n.* (*sing.* and *pl.*) ap-a-*ray*-tus, a set of instruments or utensils for performing any operation or experiment, or for practising any art; a group of bodily organs subserving the same purpose [Physiol.]. (L. *apparatus,* prepared for.)

apparel, *n.* ap-*pa*-rel, clothes; dress; decorations to ecclesiastical vestments; the sails, rigging, etc., of a ship: *v.t.* to dress or clothe; to adorn, equip, or furnish. (O.Fr. *apareiller,* to clothe.)

apparent, *a.* ap-*pa*-rent, that may be easily seen; obvious; seeming, not real. **heir apparent,** one whose right to succession is indefeasible. (Fr.)

apparently, *ad.* ap-*pa*-rent-le, to outward appearance; seemingly.

apparentness, *n.* ap-*pa*-rent-ness, the state of being apparent.

apparition, *n.* ap-pa-*rish*-on, the act of appearing; appearance; the state of becoming visible; a ghost, or a spectre; the first appearance of a luminary after occultation [Astron.]. (Fr.)

apparitional, *a.* ap-pa-*rish*-on-al, pertaining to apparitions.

apparitor, *n.* ap-*pa*-re-tor, an officer who executed the orders of magistrates [Rom. Antiq.]; a process-server in a civil or spiritual court; a university beadle. (L., an attendant.)

appeach, *v.t.* ap-*peech,* to inform, or give evidence, against; to impeach; to censure.

appeal, *v.i.* ap-*peel,* to refer to a superior judge or court; to refer to another as witness; to invoke aid, pity, or mercy; to have recourse to: *n.* the act of appealing; the right of appeal; a summons to answer a charge; a reference to another; recourse. **Court of Appeal,** a higher court of law in which appeals are heard. (O.Fr. *apeler,* to summon.)

appealable, *a.* ap-*peel*-a-bl, that may be appealed to, or against; that may be accused.

appealer, *n.* ap-*peel*-er, one who appeals.

appealing, *a.* ap-*peel*-ing, of the nature of an appeal; imploring.

appealingly, *ad.* ap-*peel*-ing-le, in an appealing manner.

appear, *v.i.* ap-*peer,* to come into view; to become visible; to come before; to be manifest; to be evident; to seem. (O.Fr. *apareir.*)

appearance, *n.* ap-*peer*-rans, the act of appearing; the thing seen; a phenomenon; apparent likeness; semblance; introduction to the public in a particular character; a coming into court [Law]. **to all appearance,** as far as may be seen. **to keep up appearances,** to suppress evidence of impoverishment or failure, etc. **to put in an appearance,** to appear personally. (O.Fr.)

appeasable, *a.* ap-*peez*-a-bl, that may be appeased.

appeasableness, *n.* ap-*peez*-a-bl-ness, the quality of being appeasable.

appease, *v.t.* ap-*peez,* to quiet; to pacify; to

allay; to attempt to placate by making a sacrifice. (O.Fr. *apeser.*)
appeasement, *n.* ap-*peez*-ment, the act of appeasing; the state of being appeased.
appeaser, *n.* ap-*peez*-er, one who appeases.
appellant, *n.* ap-*pel*-lant, one who appeals to a higher tribunal; one who makes complaint before a judge: *a.* appealing; relating to appeals. (Fr.)
appellate, *a.* ap-*pel*-lat, pertaining to appeals; having cognizance of appeals. **party appellate,** the party appealed against. (L. *appellatus*, called upon.)
appellation, *n.* ap-pel-*lay*-shon, the name by which a person or thing is called; a specific name; nomenclature. (L. *appellatio*, a naming.)
appellative, *a.* ap-*pel*-la-tiv, serving to name; common [Gram.]: *n.* a common, as distinct from a proper, name; a specific designation.
appellatively, *ad.* ap-*pel*-la-tiv-le, in the manner of an appellative noun. (L. *appellativus.*)
appellatory, *a.* ap-*pel*-la-to-re, pertaining to an appeal or an appellant.
appellee, *n.* ap-pel-*lee*, the defendant in an appeal.
appellor, *n.* ap-*pel*-lor, a prosecutor.
append, *v.t.* ap-*pend*, to hang or attach; to subjoin. (L. *appendere*, to hang.)
appendage, *n.* ap-*pend*-aj, something appended or attendant; a subsidiary organ [Anat.].
appendant, *a.* ap-*pend*-ant, annexed; attached: *n.* that which is annexed or appended.
appendices, *n.* ap-*pend*-e-seez, *pl.* of appendix.
appendicitis, ap-*pen*-de-*sy*-tis, inflammation of the vermiform appendix.
appendicle, *n.* ap-*pen*-de-kl, a small appendage. (L.)
appendicular, *ad.* ap-pen-*dik*-yew-lar, of the nature of an appendicle or appendix.
appendiculate, *a.* ap-pen-*dik*-yew-lat, furnished with small appendages [Bot.].
appendix, *n.* ap-*pend*-iks (*pl.* **appendices** and **appendixes**), something appended; a supplement. **vermiform appendix,** a narrow short tube opening off the large intestine, in man a continuation of the cæcum. (L.)
apperceive, *v.t.* ap-per-*seev*, to attain comprehension of something by assimilation of one's knowledge of it with ideas already possessed; to adjust newly acquired ideas to old [Psych.].
apperception, *n.* ap-per-*sep*-shon, perception of one's own mental processes [Psych.]; consciousness of self. (Fr.)
appertain, *v.i.* ap-per-*tayn*, to belong to; to relate to; to be appropriate. (Fr. *appartenir.*)
appertinent, *a.* ap-*per*-te-nent, belonging to.
appetence, *n.* *ap*-pe-tens, desire or craving of any kind, especially bodily craving; natural inclination or propensity. (L. *appetens*, striving after.)
appetency, *n.* *ap*-pe-ten-se, appetence.
appetent, *a.* *ap*-pe-tent, desiring; very desirous.
appetite, *n.* *ap*-pe-tite, desire for what gratifies, generally the senses, especially that of hunger; craving; longing. (Fr.)
appetitive, *a.* ap-*pet*-e-tiv, that desires gratification; possessing appetite.
appetize, *v.t.* *ap*-pe-tize, to create or give appetite (of things).
appetizer, *n.* *ap*-pe-tize-er, something that creates or stimulates appetite; an aperitif.
applaud, *v.t.* ap-*plawd*, to praise in any way, esp. by clapping the hands, or by acclamation. (L. *applaudo.*)
applause, *n.* ap-*plawz*, praise; the act of applauding; praise loudly expressed. (L. *applausum.*)
applausive, *a.* ap-*plawz*-iv, applauding; approbative.
★**apple,** *n.* *ap*-pl, the fruit of the tree *Pyrus malus*, closely allied to the pear, also the tree itself; the fruit of the forbidden tree; an object resembling an apple. **apple of discord,** cause of contention. **apple of the eye,** the pupil; any precious object. **apple of sodom,** a fabulous fruit said to turn to ashes at a touch; any disappointment. **Adam's apple,** the projection in the front of the neck formed by the thyroid cartilage. (A.S. *æppel.*)
apple-brandy, *n.* *ap*-pl-*bran*-de, a liquor distilled from cider.
apple-butter, *n.* *ap*-pl-*but*-ter, a sauce or preserve of apples stewed in cider.
apple-jack, *n.* *ap*-pl-jak, apple-brandy.
apple-john, *n.* *ap*-pl-jon, an apple which is considered best when it becomes withered.
apple-mint, *n.* *ap*-pl-mint, the herb *Mentha rotundifolia.*
apple-pie, *n.* *ap*-pl-*py*, apples in a dish covered with paste, and baked; apple-tart. **apple-pie bed,** a bed made with the sheets so folded that it cannot be got into. **apple-pie order,** perfect order.
apple-sauce, *n.* *ap*-pl-*sawce*, sauce made of apples.
Appleton-layer, *n.* *ap*-pl-ton-*lay*-er, an ionized stratum of the upper atmosphere (altitude about 140 miles) reflecting short waves and facilitating long-distance transmission [Wire.]. (Named from discoverer.)
applewoman, *n.* *ap*-pl-*woom*-an, a woman who sells apples at a stall.
appliance, *n.* ap-*ply*-ans, the act of applying; the thing applied.
applicability, *n.* *ap*-ple-ka-*bil*-e-te, the quality of being applicable.
applicable, *a.* *ap*-ple-ka-bl, that may be applied; suitable.
applicant, *n.* *ap*-ple-kant, one who applies; a petitioner.
applicate, *n.* *ap*-ple-kat, a chord bisected by the diameter [Math.]: *a.* applied. **applicate ordinate,** a right line applied at right angles to the axis of any conic section, and bounded by the curve. (L. *applicatus.*)
application, *n.* ap-ple-*kay*-shon, the act of applying; thing applied; request or petition; the employment of means; close attention. (L. *applicatio.*)
applicative, *a.* ap-*plik*-a-tiv, practical; characterized by application.
applicatory, *a.* ap-*plik*-a-to-re, with the property of applying.
appliqué, *n.* ap-*plee*-kay, ornamental work of one material laid on and fastened to another. (Fr.)
apply, *v.t.* ap-*ply*, to lay or put on; to employ; to adapt; to devote; to address to: *v.i.* to suit; to refer to; to make application; to study. (L. *applico.*)
appoggiatura, *n.* ap-poj-a-*toor*-ra, a grace-note preceding the principal note [Mus.]. (It.)
appoint, *v.t.* ap-*poynt*, to fix; to designate; to set apart; to ordain; to assign; to furnish, or to equip: *v.i.* to determine. (O.Fr. *apointer.*)
appointee, *n.* ap-poyn-*tee*, a person appointed to a post.
appointer, *n.* ap-*poyn*-ter, a person having a power of appointment.
appointment, *n.* ap-*poynt*-ment, the act of appointing to an office; situation, or office assigned; fixing by mutual agreement; what is decreed or appointed; command or order; allowance; a devise or grant to a charitable use [Law]: *pl.* equipments of a house, ship, army, etc.; accoutrements.
apport, *n.* ap-*port*, among spiritualists, a material object that has been transported by immaterial agency.
apportion, *v.t.* ap-*por*-shon, to divide and assign in just shares; to distribute. (O.Fr. *apportioner.*)
apportionment, *n.* ap-*por*-shon-ment, the act of apportioning; a dividing into just shares.
apposite, *a.* *ap*-po-zit, suitable; appropriate; very applicable. (L. *appositus*, applied to.)
appositely, *ad.* *ap*-po-zit-le, in an apposite manner.
appositeness, *n.* *ap*-po-zit-ness, the quality of being apposite.
apposition, *n.* ap-po-*zish*-on, the act of adding to; addition; the placing of a noun in the same case with another which it attributively explains and defines [Gram.]. (L. *appositio*, apposition.)
appositional, *a.* ap-po-*zish*-on-al, relating to apposition.
appositive, *a.* ap-*poz*-e-tiv, placed in apposition; belonging to or construed in apposition [Gram.].
appraisal, *n.* ap-*pray*-zal, a valuation by authority; estimated value.
appraise, *v.t.* ap-*praze*, to value, particularly as an appraiser. (O.Fr. *a-*, and *preiser*, to set a price.)
appraisement, *n.* ap-*praze*-ment, the act of appraising; a valuation.
appraiser, *n.* ap-*pray*-zer, one who values; properly, one licensed and sworn to estimate and fix the value of goods and estates.
appreciable, *a.* ap-*pree*-she-a-bl, that may be estimated or determined.

appreciably, *ad.* ap-*pree*-she-a-ble, to a perceptible or appreciable extent.
appreciate, *v.t.* ap-*pree*-she-ate, to value; to estimate duly; to esteem highly: *v.i.* to rise in value. (L. *appretiatus*, valued.)
appreciation, *n.* ap-pre-she-*ay*-shon, the act of (*a*) valuing, (*b*) duly valuing, and (c) rising in value; an expression of approbation or of gratitude; a favourable criticism.
appreciative, *a.* ap-*pree*-she-a-tiv, appreciatory; esteeming favourably.
appreciator, *n.* ap-*pree*-she-a-tor, one who appreciates.
appreciatory, *a.* ap-*pree*-she-ay-to-re, capable of duly appreciating; expressing appreciation.
apprehend, *v.t.* ap-pre-*hend*, to take hold of; to seize; to arrest; to lay hold of with the mind; to understand; to think with fear; to anticipate: *v.i.* to form a conception; to understand. (Fr. *appréhender.*)
apprehensible, *a.* ap-pre-*hen*-se-bl, that may be apprehended.
apprehension, *n.* ap-pre-*hen*-shon, the act of apprehending, seizing, or arresting; the faculty of conception; opinion; fear or dread of future evil. (Fr.)
apprehensive, *a.* ap-pre-*hen*-siv, afraid; anxious; suspicious; distrustful.
apprehensively, *ad.* ap-pre-*hen*-siv-le, in an apprehensive manner.
apprehensiveness, *n.* ap-pre-*hen*-siv-ness, the quality of being apprehensive; fear.
apprentice, *n.* ap-*pren*-tiss, one bound for a term of years to serve some craft or trade under a master, who binds himself to instruct him; a novice; a learner: *v.t.* to bind under a master to craft or trade; a sum given to a master for receiving an apprentice. (O.Fr. *aprentis.*)
apprenticeship, *n.* ap-*pren*-tis-ship, the state of an apprentice; the term for which he is bound to serve.
apprise, *v.t.* ap-*prize*, to give notice of; to inform. (Fr. *appris*, learn.)
apprize, *v.t.* ap-*prize*, to appraise; to estimate the worth of. (O.Fr. *aprisier*, praise.)
appro, *n. ap*-proh, approval; esp. in phrase "on appro" [Commercial abbr.].
approach, *v.i.* ap-*proach*, to come or go near; to draw near; to approximate: *v.t.* to come near to; to resemble: *n.* the act of drawing or advancing near; access; an avenue; a stroke at golf intended to land the ball on the green: *n.pl.* works to protect besiegers in their advance [Mil.]. **to graft by approach,** to inarch. (O.Fr. *aprochier.*)
approachability, *n.* ap-*proach*-a-*bil*-e-te, the condition or quality of being approachable; accessibility.
approachable, *a.* ap-*proach*-a-bl, that may be approached; accessible.
approbate, *v.t. ap*-pro-bate, to approve authoritatively. (L. *approbatus*, assented.)
approbation, *n.* ap-pro-*bay*-shon, the act of approving: approval; commendation. (L. *approbatio.*)
approbative, *a.* ap-pro-*bay*-tiv, characterized by approbation; approbatory.
approbatory, *a.* ap-pro-*bay*-to-re, implying or expressing approbation; tending to sanction.
appropinquity, *n.* ap-pro-*ping*-kwe-te, contiguity; proximity. (L. *appropinquatus*, approached.)
appropriable, *a.* ap-*proh*-pre-a-bl, that may be appropriated.
appropriate, *v.t.* ap-*proh*-pre-ate, to take as one's own as by exclusive right; to set apart to one particular use; to alienate a benefice [Law]: *a.* set apart for a particular use or person; suitable; belonging peculiarly. (L. *appropriatus*, appropriated.)
appropriately, *ad.* ap-*proh*-pre-at-le, in an appropriate manner.
appropriateness, *n.* ap-*proh*-pre-at-ness, the quality of being appropriate; suitability.
appropriation, *n.* ap-proh-pre-*ay*-shon, the act of appropriating to one's own use or to some special purpose; a sum of money set aside for a specified object; the sequestering of a benefice to the perpetual use of a spiritual corporation [Law]. **appropriation clause,** a clause in a money bill by which Parliament assigns revenue for a special purpose. (L. *appropriatio.*)
appropriative, *a.* ap-*pro*-pre-a-tiv, that appropriates or tends to appropriate; involving appropriation.
appropriator, *n.* ap-*pro*-pre-*ay*-tor, one who appropriates; corporation or person possessed of an appropriated benefice [Law.]
approvable, *a.* ap-*proov*-a-bl, meriting approbation.
★**approval,** *n.* ap-*proov*-al, approbation; sanction.
approve, *v.t.* ap-*proov*, to be pleased with; to think favourably of; to commend; to ratify; to increase the value of (of land) [Law]. (O.Fr. *aprover.*)
approved, *a.* ap-*proovd*, tried; proved; worthy of or regarded with approbation.
approvement, *n.* ap-*proov*-ment; the improvement of common lands, by enclosing and converting them to the uses of husbandry [Law]; formerly also, the act of proving accomplices guilty by turning King's evidence.
approver, *n.* ap-*proov*-er, one who approves; one who makes approvement; formerly, one who turns King's evidence [Law].
approvingly, *ad.* ap-*proov*-ing-le, in an approving manner.
approximate, *a.* ap-*prok*-se-mate, approaching; nearly correct; set close together (of teeth) [Zool.]; close to the stem (of leaves) [Bot.]; nearly but not absolutely equal (of quantities) [Math.]: *v.t.* to draw or advance near; to cause to approach: *v.i.* to come near; to approach. (L. *approximatus*, approached.)
approximately, *ad.* ap-*prok*-se-mat-le, in an approximate manner.
approximation, *n.* ap-*prok*-se-*may*-shon, the act of approximating; approach; a continual approach nearer and nearer to a quantity sought, when there is no means of computing it exactly [Math. and Physics.].
approximative, *a.* ap-*prok*-se-ma-tiv, of an approximate nature; approaching.
appui, *n.* ah-*pwee*, a prop; a defensive support [Mil.]. **point d'appui,** a basis; the prearranged position on which troops form into line. (Fr.)
appulse, *n.* ap-*pulse*, the act of striking against; the approach of a planet or star to the meridian or to conjunction with the sun or moon [Astron.]. (L. *appulsus*, driven.)
appulsive, *a.* ap-*pul*-siv, striking against.
appurtenance, *n.* ap-*pur*-ten-ans, that which belongs to something else; an adjunct; an appendage. (O.Fr. *apurtenaunce.*)
appurtenant, *a.* ap-*pur*-te-nant, belonging or pertaining to of right; pertinent.
apricot, *n. ay*-pre-kot, the stone-fruit of the tree *Prunus armeniaca*, allied to the plum; the tree itself. (L. *præcox*, early ripe.) (Fr. *abricot.*)
April, *n. ay*-pril, the fourth month. (L. *Aprīlis.*)
apron, *n. ay*-prun, an outer garment worn on the fore part of the body to protect the clothes or (in freemasonry, Eccles., etc.) as a part of official robes; a piece of leather drawn before a person in a road-vehicle; the fat skin covering the belly of a goose; a flat piece of lead that covered the vent of a cannon; a piece of curved timber just above the foremost end of the keel of a ship; a platform or hard-surfaced area at the entrance of a dock, hangar, etc. **apron string,** the attachment of an apron; **tied to the apron strings** (of a woman), under the control of, or strongly influenced by, her). (O.Fr. *naperon.*)
aproned, *a. ay*-prund, wearing an apron.
apropos, *a.* ap-ro-*poh*, appropriate; pertinent to; opportune: *ad.* in regard or with reference to; appropriately; in the proper place, time and manner. (Fr. *à propos.*)
apse, *n.* aps, a domed semicircular or polygonal recess in a building; any vaulted recess. (L. *apsis.*)
apsidal, *a. ap*-se-dal, pertaining to an apse, apsis, or the apsides; resembling an apse.
apsidiole, *n.* ap-*sid*-e-ole, a minor or small apse.
apsis, *n. ap*-sis (*pl.* **apsides,** *ap*-se-deez), an apse; the point of greatest and the point of least distance from the sun; **line of the apsides,** the line connecting these [Astron.]. (L.)
apt, *a.* apt, fit; suitable; pertinent; liable; inclined to; prompt and ready; quick. (L. *aptus*, fitted.)

apteral, *a.* *ap*-ter-al, wingless; with columns in front or rear, but none at the sides [Arch.] (Gr. *apteros*, wingless.)
apterous, *a.* *ap*-ter-us, destitute of, or having only rudimentary, wings; without membranous expansions [Bot.].
apteryx, *n.* *ap*-ter-iks, the kiwi, a nearly extinct bird of New Zealand, with mere rudiments of wings, and no tail. (Gr. *a-*, and *pteryx*, wing.)
aptitude, *n.* *ap*-te-tewd, fitness; tendency; readiness in learning. (Fr.)
aptly, *ad.* *apt*-le, in an apt manner.
aptness, *n.* *apt*-ness, the quality of being apt.
aptote, *n.* *ap*-tote, an indeclinable noun [Gram.]. (L. *aptōta.*)
aptotic, *a.* ap-*tot*-ik, without grammatical inflexion [Gram.].
apyretic, *a.* ay-py-*ret*-ik, with absence or intermission of fever. (Gr. *apuretos*, feverless.)
apyrexy, *n.* *ap*-e-reks-e, abatement or intermission of fever.
apyrous, *a.* a-*pire*-rus, unchanged by heat; incombustible.
aqua, *n.* *ak*-wa, water. **aqua regia,** a mixture of nitric and hydrochloric acids used in dissolving gold and platinum. **aqua Tofana,** a poison, supposed to be a solution of arsenic, used for assassination by a Sicilian woman named Tofana in the 17th cent. **aqua vitæ,** brandy. (L.)
aquafortis, *n.* *ak*-wa-*for*-tis, nitric acid.
aquafortist, *n.* *ak*-wa-*for*-tist, one who engraves or etches with aquafortis.
aquamarine, *n.* ak-wa-ma-*reen*, a sea-blue or green beryl [Min.]: *a.* greenish-blue. (L., sea water.)
aquarelle, *n.* ak-wa-*rel*, a painting in water-colours and Indian ink. (Fr.)
aquarium, *n.* a-*kware*-re-um, a tank, a vessel, or a collection of such for aquatic plants and animals; a place for the exhibition of these. (L.)
Aquarius, *n.* a-*kware*-re-us, the Water-bearer, the 11th sign of the zodiac, which the sun enters about the 21st of January. (L.)
aquatic, *a.* a-*kwat*-ik *or* a-*kwot*-ik, inhabiting or growing in water; on the water: *n.* a plant which grows in water: *pl.* exercises in or on the water. (L. *aquāticus.*)
aquatint, *n.* *ak*-wa-tint, a variety of etching imitating water-colour. (L. *aqua*, and *tinto*, dye.)
aqueduct, *n.* *ak*-we-dukt, an artificial conduit or structure for conveying water from a distance; a small passage or canal in an organ [Phys.]. (L. *aquaeductus.*)
aqueous, *a.* *ay*-kwe us, consisting of, containing, or formed in, water. **aqueous humour,** a transparent limpid fluid filling the space between the cornea and crystalline lens of the eye. **aqueous rocks,** rocks formed by deposit in water. (L. *aqua.*)
aquiculture, *n.* *ak*-we-*kul*-tewr, cultivation of animals and plants, etc., inhabiting water.
aquiferous, *a.* a-*kwif*-e-rus, conducting or yielding water. (L. *aqua*, and *fero*, bear.)
aquiform, *a.* *ak*-we-form, in the state of water; liquid. (L. *aqua*, and *forma*, shape.)
Aquilegia, *n.* ak-we-*lee*-je-a, a genus of plants comprising the columbines.
aquiline, *a.* *ak*-we-lin, *or* *ak*-we-line, belonging to the eagle; eagle-like; curved like the beak of an eagle. (L. *aquilinus*, pertaining to an eagle.)
aquosity, *n.* a-*kwos*-e-te, wateriness.
Arab, *n.* *a*-rab, a native of Arabia; an Arabian horse; an outcast: *a.* belonging to Arabia; Arabian. **street arab,** a child without a home.
araba, *n.* ah-*rah*-bah, a springless, hooded, oriental vehicle drawn by oxen. (Ar.)
arabesque, *a.* a-ra-*besk*, in the artistic manner of the Arabians, which, excluding animal forms, consists mainly of intertwined foliage, plants, and geometrical figures: *n.* an ornament executed in the arabesque style; a posture in ballet-dancing.
arabesqued, *a.* a-ra-*beskt*, decorated with arabesques.
Arabian, *a.* a-*ray*-be-an, pertaining to Arabia: *n.* an Arab; an Arab horse. **Arabian Nights,** a famous collection of oriental tales.
Arabic, *a.* *a*-ra-bik, pertaining to Arabia or its language: *n.* the language of the Arabs.
arabin, *n.* *a*-ra-bin, gum-arabic; the pure soluble principle in this.
Arabis, *n.* *a*-ra-bis, a genus of brassiaceous herbs, with white or purple flowers; rock-cress. (L.)
arabist, *n.* *ar*-ra-bist, one well versed in the Arabic language or literature.
arable, *a.* *a*-ra-bl, fit for ploughing or tillage. (Fr.)
Araby, *n.* *a*-ra-be, a poetical name for Arabia.
Arachis, *n.* *ar*-ra-kiss, the genus of the plant known as the ground-nut, earth-nut, or pea-nut, *A. hypogæa.*
arachnid, *n.* a-*rak*-nid, a spider, mite or scorpion. (Gr. *arachnes*, a spider, and *eidos*, form.)
arachnoid, *a.* a-*rak*-noyd, resembling or pertaining to the arachnids; covered with filamentous hairs [Bot.]; cobweb-like: *n.* a thin membrane spread over the brain and spinal cord between the dura mater and the pia mater [Anat.].
arachnologist, *n.* a-rak-*nol*-o-jist, one versed in arachnology.
arachnology, *n.* a-rak-*nol*-o-je, the science treating of the arachnids. (Gr. *arachnes*, and *logos*, science.)
aræometer, *n.* arr-e-*om*-e-ter, areometer.
aræostyle, *n.* a-*re*-o-stile, an arrangement of columns at wide intervals [Arch.]. (Gr.)
aræosystyle, *n.* a-re-o-*sis*-tile, columns in pairs with an interval generally of half a diameter betwixt the coupled ones, and of three diameters and a half betwixt the pairs. (Gr.)
aragonite, *n.* *a*-ra-go-nite, a variety of calcite, from which it differs chiefly in its crystallization. (Aragon, where first found.)
Aramaic, *a.* a-ra-*may*-ik, pertaining to the Syrians and Chaldeans: *n.* Syriac; the language of Palestine at the time of Christ. (*Aram*, a son of Shem.)
Aramean, *a.* a-ra-*mee*-an, pertaining to Aram (Syria) or its language; Aramaic.
Araneidæ, *n.pl.* ar-ra-*nee*-e-de, the spider family. (L. *arānea*, spider, Gr. *eidos*, form.)
araneidan, *a.* a-ra-*nee*-e-dan, of the spider family: *n.* a spider.
araneiform, *a.* a-ra-*nee*-e-form, in the shape of a spider.
araneose, *a.* a-*ray*-ne-ohs, cobweb-like. (L.)
araneous, *a.* a-*ray*-ne-us, resembling a cobweb.
arango, *n.* a-*rang*-go, a bead of rough cornelian. (East Indian.)
arapaima, *n.* a-ra-*py*-ma, a very large bony-scaled food-fish of S. American rivers. (Tupi.)
arapunga, *n.* a-ra-*pung*-ga, the campanero. (Tupi.)
arar, *n.* *ah*-rar, the wood of the sandarac tree.
araucaria, *n.* a-raw-*kare*-re-a, any conifer of the genus *Araucaria*, including *A. imbricata*, the monkey-puzzle and *A. excelsa*, the Norfolk Island pine.
arbalist, *n.* *ar*-ba-list, a cross-bow. (O.Fr. *arbaleste.*)
arbalister, *n.* *ar*-ba-lis-ter, a crossbow-man.
arbiter, *n.* *ar*-be-ter, a person chosen by parties in a dispute to decide between them; an umpire.
arbitrage, *n.* *ar*-be-traj, the buying and selling in different markets simultaneously so as to profit by the differences in rates of exchange; chiefly traffic in bills of exchange and stocks of a financial nature. (Fr.)
arbitral, *a.* *ar*-be-tral, belonging to arbitration.
arbitrament, *n.* ar-*bit*-ra-ment, decision; award; power or liberty of deciding.
arbitrarily, *ad.* *ar*-be-tra-re-le, in an arbitrary manner.
arbitrariness, *n.* *ar*-be-tra-re-ness, the quality of being arbitrary.
arbitrary, *a.* *ar*-be-tra-re, determined solely by one's own judgment or good pleasure; exercised according to one's own discretion; subject to the will or control of no other; absolute; despotic; capricious. (L. *arbitrarius.*)
arbitrate, *v.i.* *ar*-be-trate, to hear and decide as an arbitrator; to determine: *v.t.* to decide; to judge of. (L. *arbitrātus*, decided.)
arbitration, *n.* ar-be-*tray*-shon, the hearing and determining of a dispute by an arbiter or by persons chosen by the parties.
arbitrator, *n.* *ar*-be-tray-ter, an umpire in arbitration; an arbiter.
arbitress, *n.* *ar*-be-tress, a female arbitrator; a despotic woman.
arbor, *n.* *ar*-bor, a tree, as distinguished from a shrub [Bot.]; an arbour; the axis of a wheel. **Arbor Day,** a public spring-time holiday in the U.S.A., for tree-planting. **arbor dianæ,** the tree of Diana, an arborescent precipitate made by

putting mercury into a solution of nitrate of silver. **arbor saturni**, the tree of Saturn, a similar precipitate, made by putting zinc into a solution of acetate of lead. **arbor vitæ**, a tree of the genus *Thuja*. (L.)

arboraceous, *a.* ar-bo-*ray*-shus, wooded; like a tree.

arboreal, *a.* ar-*baw*-re-al, abounding in trees; pertaining to, connected with, or living in trees; growing on trees. (L. *arboreus*, relating to a tree.)

arborescence, *n.* ar-bo-*ress*-ens, the state of being arborescent, or in the form of a tree.

arborescent, *a.* ar-bo-*ress*-ent, resembling a tree; growing like a tree; dendritic. (L. *arboresco*, grow to a tree.)

arboret, *n.* *ar*-bo-ret, a small tree; a shrub.

arboretum, *n.* ar-bo-*ree*-tum, a place in which rare trees are cultivated for exhibition or research purposes. (L.)

arboriculture, *n.* *ar*-bo-re-*kul*-tewr, the systematic cultivation of trees.

arboriculturist, *n.* *ar*-bo-re-*kul*-tew-rist, one who cultivates trees.

arborist, *n.* *ar*-bo-rist, one who makes trees his study.

arborization, *n.* ar-bo-ry-*zay*-shon, arborescence in minerals.

arborized, *a.* *ar*-bo-ryzd, having a tree- or plant-like appearance [Min.]; arborescent.

arborous, *a.* *ar*-bo-rus, pertaining to or consisting of trees.

arbour, *n.* *ar*-bur, a seat covered with branches of trees, or other plants, for shade; a bower. (O.Fr. *herbier*, herb.)

arbuscle, *n.* *ar*-bus-sl, a dwarf tree, or a tree-like shrub. (L. *arbuscula*, shrub.)

Arbutus, *n.* *ar*-bew-tus, a genus of trees and shrubs including *A. unedo*, the strawberry-tree.

arc, *n*, ark, a segment or part of a circle; a segment of the visible path of a heavenly body [Astron.]: *v.i.* to discharge with the formation of an arc [Elect.]. **arc-lamp**, an electric lamp in which the current is converted into light by the resistance of the heated air between two carbon poles. **electric arc**, the luminous path of an electric current between two terminals separated by air and other gas [Elect.]. **arc of fire**, the angular field that a gun can command. **arc welding**, a method of welding in which the material forms one electrode of an arc. (Fr.)

arcade, *n.* ar-*kayd*, a series of arches supported on columns; a walk arched above; a long arched building or passage, lined on each side with shops. (Fr.)

arcaded, *a.* ar-*kay*-ded, furnished with or built like an arcade.

Arcadian, *a.* ar-*kay*-de-an, pertaining to Arcadia, a district of Greece whose primitive inhabitants were said to live in rural bliss; ideally pastoral; rustic: *n.* an inhabitant of Arcadia.

arcanum, *n.* ar-*kay*-num (*pl.* **arcana**), a secret; a mystery. (L.)

arc-boutant, *n.* ark-*boo*-tong, a flying buttress. (Fr.)

★**arch**, *n.* artch, a curved structure so arranged that the parts by mutual pressure support each other; a curve or structure in this form; an archway; a vault; the vault of heaven; the sky. **arches court**, the supreme court of appeal in ecclesiastical causes for the province of Canterbury, anciently held at the church of St. Mary of the Arches, now called St. Mary-le-Bow: *v.t.* to cover with an arch; to form into a curve: *v.i.* to make an arch or arches. (Fr. *arche*.)

arch, *a.* artch, shrewd; waggish; roguish. (A.S.)

arch-, *pref.* artch, chief; of the first class; as in archbishop.

archæan, *a.* ar-*kee*-an, relating to the most ancient period or strata known to geology. (Gr.)

archæo-, *comb. f.* *ar*-ke-o, signifying ancient, of great antiquity. (Gr. *archaios*, primitive.)

archæological, *a.* ar-ke-o-*loj*-e-kal, pertaining to archæology.

archæologically, *ad.* ar-ke-o-*loj*-e-ka-le, in an archæological manner.

archæologist, *n.* ar-ke-*ol*-o-jist, one versed in archæology.

archæology, *n.* ar-ke-*ol*-o-je, the science which treats of human antiquities, and especially of prehistoric remains. (Gr. *archaiologia*, ancient lore.)

archæopteryx, *n.* ar-ke-*op*-ter-iks, a primitive extinct bird of Jurassic age, with teeth and having certain reptilian characteristics. (Gr. *archaios*, and *pteryx*, wing.)

archaic, *a.* ar-*kay*-ik, ancient; antiquated; obsolescent. (Gr. *archaios*, from the origin.)

archaism, *n.* *ar*-kay-izm, an old-fashioned or obsolete expression. (Gr. *archaismos*, an old phrase.)

archaistic, *a.* ar-kay-*is*-tik, relating to the archaic; affecting archaism.

archaize, *v.t.* and *i.* ar-kay-*ize*, to use archaisms; to speak in an old-fashioned way.

archangel, *n.* ark-*ayn*-jel, an angel of the highest order. (Gr. *archangelos*.)

archangelic, *a.* ark-an-*jel*-ik, pertaining to archangels.

archbishop, *n.* artch-*bish*-op, a chief bishop, or the bishop of a province, and also of his own diocese.

archbishopric, *n.* artch-*bish*-op-rik, the province of an archbishop.

arch-brick, *n.* *artch*-brik, a brick shaped for building arches.

archdeacon, *n.* artch-*dee*-kon, a church dignitary, next in rank below a bishop; the superintendent of rural deans.

archdeaconry, *n.* artch-*dee*-kon-re, the office, jurisdiction or residence of an archdeacon; the portion of the diocese in his charge.

archdeaconship, *n.* artch-*dee*-kon-ship, the office of an archdeacon.

archdiocese, *n.* artch-*dy*-o-ses, the diocese or the jurisdiction of an archbishop.

archdruid, *n.* artch-*droo*-id, chief pontiff of the Druids.

archducal, *a.* artch-*dew*-kal, pertaining to an archduke.

archduchess, *n.* artch-*dutch*-ess, wife of an archduke; a daughter of the house of Habsburg.

archduchy, *n.* artch-*dutch*-e, archdukedom; the territorial possessions giving title to an archduke.

archduke, *n.* artch-*dewk*, a prince of the House of Habsburg-Lorraine; the title formerly borne by male descendants of the Emperor Frederick III.

archdukedom, *n.* artch-*dewk*-dum, the rank of an archduke or archduchess; an archduchy.

archegonium, *n.* ar-ke-*goh*-ne-um, the female organ of ferns, horsetails, and most cryptogams [Bot.].

archelogy, *n.* ar-*kel*-o-je, the scientific study of first principles. (Gr. *arche*, beginning, and *-logy*.)

arch-enemy, *n.* artch-*en*-e-me, a principal enemy; Satan, as the arch-fiend.

archer, *n.* *artch*-er, a bowman; the ninth sign of the zodiac. **archer fish**, a species of *Toxotes*, that shoots drops of water for bringing down insects as food. (O.Fr. *archier*.)

archeress, *n.* *artch*-er-ess, a female archer.

archery, *n.* *artch*-er-e, the art or act of shooting with a bow and arrow.

archetypal, *a.* *ark*-e-*ty*-pal, pertaining to or constituting an archetype; primitive.

archetype, *n.* *ark*-e-tipe, the original model from which, or ideal after which, anything is made; the standard weight by which others are adjusted [Coining]. (Fr.)

arch-fiend, *n.* artch-*feend*, a chief fiend: Satan.

arch-flamen, *n.* artch-*flay*-men, a chief flamen or priest.

arch-heresy, *n.* artch-*he*-re-se, the chief or mother heresy; extreme heresy.

arch-hypocrite, *n.* artch-*hip*-o-krit, a great or notorious hypocrite.

archidiaconal, *a.* ark-e-dy-*ak*-on-al, pertaining to an archdeacon.

archiepiscopacy, *n.* ark-e-e-*pis*-ko-pa-se, the government of the church by archbishops. (L. *archiepiscopus*, archbishop.)

archiepiscopal, *a.* ark-e-e-*pis*-ko-pal, pertaining to an archbishop or archbishopric.

archiepiscopate, *n.* ark-e-e-*pis*-ko-pate, the office, dignity, or jurisdiction of an archbishop; his tenure of office; an archbishopric.

archil, *n.* *artch*-il, any lichen of the genus *Rocella*; orchil, a dye prepared from this. (O.Fr. *orchil*.)

archilochian, *a.* ark-e-*loh*-ke-an, denoting a verse of seven feet, the first four dactyls or spondees, the last three trochees, used by Archilochus, a Greek satiric poet.)

archimagus, *n.* ark-e-*may*-gus, the high priest of

the Persian worshippers of fire; a chief magician. (Gr. *magos*, sorcerer.)
archimandrite, *n.* ark-e-*man*-drite, the superior of a monastery in the Greek Church. (L. *archimandrita*, an abbot.)
Archimedean, *a.* ar-ke-me-*dee*-an, pertaining to Archimedes, the Greek mathematician. **archimedean screw,** a machine for raising water, invented by Archimedes, and consisting of a tube rolled in a spiral form round a cylinder.
arching, *a. artch*-ing, curving like an arch: *n.* an arched structure.
archipelagic, *a.* ark-e-pe-*laj*-ik, pertaining to an archipelago.
archipelago, *n.* ark-e-*pel*-a-go, a sea interspersed with many islands, esp. the Ægean; a group of islands. (It. *arcipelago*.)
architect, *n. ark*-e-tekt, one who plans and designs buildings, and superintends their erection; a contriver or maker. (L. *architectus*.)
architective, *a.* ark-e-*tekt*-iv, used in, proper for, or pertaining to architecture.
architectonic, *a.* ark-e-tekt-*on*-ik, having skill in designing and construction; pertaining to an architect or master-builder; of the nature of architectural work; relating to the systematization of knowledge. (L. *architectonicus*, relating to architecture.)
architectonics, *n.* ark-e-tekt-*on*-iks, the science of architecture; structural design; systematic construction in literary, musical, or other artistic production; the doctrine of the abstract systematization of knowledge.
architectural, *a.* ark-e-*tek*-tewr-ral, pertaining to or according to the rules of architecture.
architecturally, *ad.* ar-ke-*tek*-tew-ra-le, in the manner of, or as regards, architecture.
architecture, *n. ar*-ke-tek-tewr, the art or science of building, especially houses, bridges and other edifices and structures; construction; workmanship; style of building. **military architecture,** the art of fortification. **naval architecture,** the art of building ships. (L. *architectura*.)
architrave, *n. ark*-e-trave, that part of an entablature which rests immediately on the column; the ornamental moulding round a door or window. (Fr.)
archival, *ad.* ar-*ky*-val, pertaining to, or contained in, archives.
archives, *n.pl. ar*-kyvz, the place in which the public papers or records of a state or community are kept; the papers themselves. (Fr. *archif*.)
archivist, *n. ar*-ke-vist, a keeper of archives.
archivolt, *n. ark*-e-volt, the inner contour of an arch, or a band adorned with mouldings, running over the faces of the archstones [Arch.]. (It. *archivolto*.)
archly, *ad. artch*-le, in an arch manner.
archness, *n. artch*-ness, the quality of being arch; waggishness.
archon, *n. ark*-on, a chief magistrate of ancient Athens; an official of the Byzantine Empire; one who presides. (Gr.)
archonship, *n. ark*-on-ship, the office of an archon.
archpriest, *n.* artch-*preest*, a chief priest; a rural dean in the Lutheran Church.
archstone, *n. artch*-stone, the keystone.
archway, *n. artch*-way, a way or passage under an arch; an arched entrance.
archwise, *a. artch*-wize, in the form of an arch.
arc-lamp, *see* **lamp.**
arcograph, *n. ark*-o-graf, an instrument for drawing a circular arc without a central point. (L. *arcus*, a bow, Gr. *grapho*, write.)
arctation, *n.* ark-*tay*-shon, the constriction of a passage of the body, as the anus; constipation due to anal inflammation [Med.]. (L. *arctatus*, pressed together.)
arctic, *a. ark*-tik, northern; pertaining to the region round the north pole: *n.* (*cap.*) the North Polar region. **arctic circle,** a lesser circle, parallel to the equator, 23° 28′ from its centre, the north pole. **arctic fox,** a small species of fox with fine and beautiful fur. (Fr. *arctique*.)
Arcturus, *n.* ark-*tew*-rus, a fixed star of the first magnitude, in the constellation of Boötes. (Gr. *arktouros*, the bear-guard.)
arcuate, *a. ark*-yew-ate, bent, as a bow. (L.)
arcuation, *n.* ark-yew-*ay*-shon, the act of bending; the state of being bent; a method of propagating trees by bending the branches to the ground, and covering the small shoots with earth.
ardeb, *n. ar*-deb, a dry measure of Moslem countries varying, in different places, from 1 gall. to about 7½ bushels. (Ar.)
ardency, *n. ar*-den-se, quality or state of being ardent; ardour.
ardent, *a. ar*-dent, hot; burning; fierce; intense; eager; zealous. **ardent spirits,** alcoholic spirits. (O.Fr. *ardant*, burning.)
ardently, *ad. ar*-dent-le, in an ardent way.
ardour, *n. ar*-dor, heat; warmth of affection or emotion; fierce heat; zeal. (Fr. *ardeur*.)
arduous, *a. ard*-yew-us, difficult to attain or accomplish; laborious; energetic. (L. *arduus*, steep.)
arduously, *ad. ard*-yew-us-le, in an arduous manner.
arduousness, *n. ard*-yew-us-ness, state or quality of being arduous.
are, ahr, the plural of the present tense of the verb to be. (Northumbrian *aron*.)
are, *n.* ahr, the unit of French superficial measure, containing 100 square metres, or 1076·44 English square feet. (L. *area*.)
area, *n. ayr*-re-a, any plane surface included within limits; an enclosed space about the sunken basement of a building; a region of the earth; a tract of country; the superficial contents of any figure [Geom.]. (L.)
areal, *a. ayr*-re-al, pertaining to an area.
areca, *n.* a-*ree*-ka, the palm which yields the betel-nut. (Port.)
arefaction, *n.* a-re-*fak*-shon, the act or process of drying; making arid; state of being dried.
arefy, *v.t. a*-re-fy; to dry up; to make dry.
arena, *n.* a-*ree*-na, the open central space, strewed with sand, in an amphitheatre, for the exhibition of gladiatorial and other combats; any place or scene of public contest or exertion; an amphitheatre. (L. sand.)
arenaceous, *a.* a-re-*nay*-shus, sandy; composed of sand-grains. (L. *arena*.)
Arenaria, *n.* a-re-*nayr*-re-a, a genus of low-tufted plants with white flowers; (*l.c.*) the sandwort.
areng, *n.* a-*reng*, the sago-palm. (Malayan.)
arenicolites, *n.pl.* a-re-*nik*-o-lites, markings on sandstones, supposed to be worm burrows [Geol.]. (L. *arena*, and *colo*, dwell, Gr. *lithos*, a stone.)
arenose, *a. a*-re-nohs, sandy; full of sand.
areography, *n.* a-re-*og*-ra-fe, the physical geography of the planet Mars. (Gr. *Ares*, Mars, and *grapho*, write.)
areola, *n.* a-*ree*-o-la, a small area; the coloured circle round the nipple, or a pustule; an interstitial space or mesh in tissues. (L. *area*, a vacant space.)
areolar, *a.* a-*ree*-o-lar, containing areolæ. **areolar tissue,** cellular tissue.
areolate, *a.* a-*ree*-o-late, divided into small spaces by intersecting lines.
areolation, *n.* a-re-o-*lay*-shon, any small space bounded by some part differing in colour, texture, etc.; state of being aerolate.
areole, *n. a*-re-ole, an areola.
areology, *n.* a-re-*ol*-o-je, the scientific study of the planet Mars.
areometer, *n.* a-re-*om*-e-ter, any instrument for measuring the specific gravity of liquids; an hydrometer. (Gr. *araios*, thin, *metron*, a measure.)
areometrical, *a.* a-re-o-*met*-re-kal, pertaining to areometry.
areometry, *n.* a-re-*om*-e-tre, the art of measuring the specific gravity of fluids; hydrometry.
Areopagite, *n.* a-re-*op*-a-jite, a judge of the Areopagus.
Areopagitic, *a. a*-re-op-a-*jit*-ik, pertaining to the Areopagus.
Areopagus, *n.* a-re-*op*-a-gus, a celebrated tribunal that assembled on the hill of Mars in ancient Athens. (Gr. *Ares*, Mars, *pagos*, a hill.)
areostyle, *n. ayr*-re-o-stile, aræostyle.
areosystyle, *n.* ayr-re-o-*sis*-tile, aræosystile.
arête, *n.* a-*rate*, an acute and rugged ridge of a mountain. (Fr.)
argal, *n. ar*-gal, argol.
argal, *ad. ar*-gal, therefore. (L. *ergo*.)
argala, *n. ar*-ga-la, the adjutant bird. (Hind.)
argali, *n. ar*-ga-le, the horned wild sheep of Siberia and Central Asia, *Ovis ammon*. (Mongol.)

argand, *n.* *ar*-gand, a hollow and circular wick or burner admitting air and so increasing the current of air and intensifying the flame. (Name of inventor.)
argent, *n.* *ar*-jent, the white colour representing silver, the symbol of purity, justice, and gentleness [Her.] : *a.* silvery ; resembling silver. (Fr. *argent.*)
argental, *a.* ar-*jen*-tal, pertaining to, containing, or resembling, silver.
argentic, *a.* ar-*jen*-tik, containing silver in chemical composition.
argentiferous, *a.* ar-jen-*tif*-er-us, yielding or containing silver. (L. *argentum*, and *fero*, carry.)
argentine, *n.* *ar*-jen-tine, a deep-water, semi-transparent fish of the salmon family ; the silver weed, *Potentilla anserina* ; a variety of porcelain coated with metal ; a silvery white variety of carbonate of lime : *a.* like silver ; silvery.
Argentine, *n.* *ar*-jen-tine, a native of the Argentine Republic : *a.* pertaining to this or its people.
argentite, *n.* *ar*-jen-tite, sulphide of silver, silver glance, an important ore of silver.
argentous, *a.* ar-*jen*-tus, argentic ; containing silver in bivalent proportion.
arghool, *n.* ar-*gool*, a reed musical pipe used in Egypt consisting of two tubes and a mouthpiece. (Ar.)
argil, *n.* *ar*-jil, potters' earth ; alumina. (Fr. *argile.*)
argillaceous, *a.* ar-jil-*lay*-shus, of the nature of, or consisting of, clay. (L. *argillaceus*, clayey.)
argilliferous, *a.* ar-jil-*lif*-er-us, containing or producing clay.
argillite, *n.* *ar*-jil-lite, clay-slate, an argillaceous rock resembling slate but without its cleavage.
argillitic, *a.* ar-jil-*lit*-ik, pertaining to or containing argillite.
argillo-, *comb. f.* ar-*jil*-lo, denoting that the material contains clay.
argillous, *a.* ar-*jil*-lus, consisting of clay ; clayey.
Argive, *a.* *ar*-gyv, inhabiting or relating to Argos in Greece ; hence, *n.* a Greek.
argol, *n.* *ar*-gol, a hard crude tartar deposited by wine on the sides of casks, and used by dyers and as a source of tartaric acid.
argon, *n.* *ar*-gon, an inert gaseous element present in the atmosphere in minute quantities. (Gr. *aergos*, idle.)
Argonaut, *n.* *ar*-go-nawt, one of the mythic heroes who sailed in the Argo with Jason in quest of the golden fleece ; a paper-nautilus, or other member of the *Argonauta*, a genus of marine cephalopod molluscs. (L.)
argonautic, *a.* ar-go-*nawt*-ik, pertaining to the Argonauts, or to their expedition : *n.* a member of the expedition.
argosy, *n.* *ar*-go-se, a large richly laden merchantman, or a fleet of these. (Originally a ship from Ragusa on the Adriatic.)
argot, *n.* *ar*-got, *or* *ar*-go, a jargon among professional thieves ; words and expressions peculiar to a particular group ; any slang. (Fr.)
arguable, *a.* *ar*-gew-a-bl, capable of being argued ; reasonable but not proven.
argue, *v.i.* *ar*-gew, to show reason ; to dispute ; to debate ; to signify : *v.t.* to debate or discuss ; to prove or evince ; to persuade by reasons. (Fr. *arguer.*)
arguer, *n.* *ar*-gew-er, a person taking part in an argument ; one fond of arguing.
argufy, *v.t.* and *i.* *ar*-gew-fy, to carry on an argument without reason or till other persons are wearied ; to persist irritatingly in an argument ; to wrangle [Slang].
arguing, *n.* *ar*-gew-ing, reasoning ; argumentation.
***argument**, *n.* *ar*-gew-ment, a reason offered in proof ; a debate or discussion ; the subject of a discourse or writing ; an abstract or summary of a book. (L. *argumentum.*)
argumental, *a.* ar-gew-*ment*-al, belonging to argument ; consisting in argument.
argumentation, *n.* ar-gew-men-*tay*-shon, act or process of reasoning ; a systematic argument.
argumentative, *a.* ar-gew-*ment*-a-tiv, consisting of argument ; showing reasons for ; addicted to argument ; disputations.
argumentatively, *ad.* ar-gew-*ment*-a-tiv-le, in an argumentative manner.
argumentativeness, *n.* ar-gew-*ment*-a-tiv-ness, the quality of being argumentative.

Argus, *n.* *ar*-gus, a watchful person ; a large and beautiful species of Asiatic pheasant with spotted plumage ; a genus of butterflies with eye-like spots on the wings. **argus-eyed**, very observant. **argus shell**, a tropical marine gastropod shell beautifully variegated with spots. (*Argus*, a mythological being with a hundred eyes.)
argute, *a.* ar-*gewt*, subtle ; ingenious ; shrill. (L. *argutus*, made clear.)
argyria, *n.* ar-*ji*-re-a, a dark discoloration of the skin brought about by the continued medicinal use of silver nitrate. (Gr. *argyros*, silver.)
aria, *n.* *ah*-re-a, an air, song, or tune. (It.)
Arian, *a.* *ayr*-re-an, pertaining to Arius (4th cent.) or his heresy : *n.* a follower of Arius, who denied the consubstantiality of the Son with the Father in the Trinity.
Arianism, *n.* *ayr*-re-an-izm, the doctrines of the Arians.
Arianize, *v.t.* *ayr*-re-a-nyz, to imbue with Arianism : *v.i.* to propagate Arianism ; to become Arian.
aricine, *n.* *a*-re-seen, a crystalline alkaloid obtained from cinchona bark. (*Arica*, Chile, whence first brought.)
arid, *a.* *a*-rid, dry ; parched up with heat. (L. *aridus*, dry.)
aridity, *n.* a-*rid*-it-e, the state of being arid ; absence of moisture ; drought.
aridness, *n.* *a*-rid-ness, aridity.
ariel, *n.* *ayr*-e-el, a flying phalanger of Australia of the genus *Petaurus* ; (*with cap.*) the inner satellite of Uranus. (*Ariel*, an aerial spirit of mediæval myth.)
ariel, *n.* *ayr*-re-el, a gazelle of Arabia. (Ar. *aryal*, stag.)
Aries, *n.* *ayr*-re-eez, the Ram, a constellation, the first of the twelve signs of the zodiac, which the sun enters on or about the 21st of March. (L.)
arietta, *n.* a-re-*et*-ta, a short air or song [Mus.]. (It.)
aright, *ad.* a-*rite*, rightly ; without mistake.
aril, *n.* *a*-ril, the exterior coat or covering of a seed, fixed to it at the base only. (*Larillus.*)
arillated, *a.* *a*-re-lay-ted, arilled.
arilled, *a.* *a*-rild, furnished with an aril.
arioso, *n.* a-re-*oh*-zo, a short aria ; a brief melody in or concluding a recitative : *a.* in the manner of an air [Mus.]. (It.)
ariot, *a.* a-*ry*-ot, in riot ; in a riotous manner ; riotously.
aripple, *a.* a-*rip*-pl, rippling ; in a rippling manner.
arise, *v.i.* a-*rize*, to rise up ; to spring up ; to appear ; to originate ; to occur : *pp.* **arose, arisen.** (A.S. *àrisan.*)
arista, *n.* a-*ris*-ta (*pl.* **aristæ**), the awn or pointed beard of grasses. (L.)
aristarch, *n.* *ar*-ris-tark, a severe critic. (*Aristarchus* of Alexandria, 2nd cent. B.C.)
aristarchian, *a.* a-ris-*tar*-ke-an, severely critical.
aristate, *a.* a-*ris*-tate, furnished with awns ; bearded [Bot.].
aristocracy, *n.* a-ris-*tok*-ra-se, government by the best for the benefit of all ; government by the nobility ; a state under such government ; the upper class ; the best. (Gr. *aristokratia*, government by the best.)
aristocrat, *n.* *a*-ris-to-krat, or a-*ris*-to-krat, one of the nobility or good birth ; a member of an aristocracy. (Fr. *aristocrate.*)
aristocratic, *a.* a-ris-to-*krat*-ik, under or belonging to an aristocracy ; of noble bearing ; grand.
aristocratically, *ad.* a-ris-to-*krat*-e-ka-le, in an aristocratic manner.
aristocratism, *n.* a-ris-*tok*-ra-tizm, the spirit and manners of the aristocracy.
Aristophanic, *a.* a-ris-to-*fan*-ik, pertaining to Aristophanes, a celebrated comic poet of Athens (5th cent. B.C.) ; shrewd ; witty.
Aristotelian, *a.* a-ris-to-*tee*-le-an, pertaining to the philosophy of Aristotle (4th cent. B.C.) : *n.* a follower of Aristotle.
Aristotelianism, *n.* a-ris-to-*tee*-le-a-nizm, the philosophy of Aristotle.
arithmancy, *n.* *a*-rith-man-se, divination by the use or observation of numbers. (Gr. *arithmos*, number, *manteia*, divination.)
arithmetic, *n.* a-*rith*-me-tik, the science of numbers, or the art of computation ; a treatise on computation. (Fr. *arithmétique.*)

arithmetical, *a.* a-rith-*met*-ik-al, pertaining to arithmetic; according to the rules or methods of arithmetic. **arithmetical progression,** continued proportion in which the numbers in a series increase or decrease at equal intervals in numerical order.
arithmetically, *ad.* a-rith-*met*-e-ka-le, in the manner of arithmetic.
arithmetician, *n.* a-rith-me-*tish*-an, one skilled in arithmetic.
arithmocracy, *n.* a-rith-*mok*-ra-se, government by a numerical majority; majority rule. (Gr. *arithmos*, number, and *cracy*.)
arithmometer, *n.* a-rith-*mom*-e-ter, a computing machine. (Gr. *arithmos*, number, *metron*, measure.)
ark, *n.* ark, a chest or coffer; the sacred repository of the tables of the law among the Jews; the vessel in which Noah and his family were preserved during the deluge; the cradle which concealed the infant Moses; a large boat, used on American rivers to transport produce to market. (L. *arca*, a chest.)
arles, *n.pl.* arlz, money given in token of the conclusion of a bargain. **arles-penny,** *n.* earnest-money. (Scots.)
★**arm,** *n.* arm, the limb of the human body which extends from the shoulder to the hand; anything resembling this; a sleeve; the forelimb of an anthropoid or of a lower mammal; a tentacle, etc.; any branch, such as of a sea, a tree, a machine, or a service; power or might. (A.S. *earm*.)
arm, *n.* arm, a weapon; one of the branches of the military service (*see* **arms,** *n.pl.*): *v.t.* to furnish with arms, or means of defence, or anything requisite to fortify; to prepare for war: *v.i.* to take arms; to prepare for war. (Fr. *armer*.)
armada, *n.* ar-*may*-da *or* ar-*mah*-da, a fleet of warships and transports, especially that equipped by Spain for the invasion of England in 1588. (Sp.)
armadillo, *n.* ar-ma-*dil*-lo, a South American edentate armed with hard bony plates. (Sp.)
Armageddon, *n.* ar-ma-*ged*-don, the final battlefield between the powers of good and evil; hence, any momentous conflict. (Rev. xvi, 16.)
armament, *n.* *arm*-a-ment, a force equipped for war; equipment for war. (Fr. *armement*.)
armature, *n.* *arm*-a-tewr, armour; means of defence; a piece of iron which connects the two poles of a magnet, to keep the magnetic power undiminished; the rotating portion of a dynamo or an electric motor. **armature winding,** the coil of wire wound on an armature. (L. *armātūra*, armour.)
arm-chair, *n.* *arm*-chare, a chair with arms; an elbow-chair.
armed, *a.* armd, provided with arms, or with natural armour, as claws, etc.; fortified; provided with an armature [Magnet.]; of a different colour from the rest of the body [Her.].
Armenian, *a.* ar-*meen*-e-an, relating to Armenia; *n.* a native of Armenia; the language of the Armenians; a member of the Armenian Church. **Armenian Church,** the earliest of national Churches, founded in 301 A.D., presided over by the Catholics, and since the Council of Chalcedon (451) independent of the Orthodox Church, with which it is in doctrinal agreement. **bole armenian,** a red argillaceous earth from Armenia, used medicinally and for colouring.
armet, *n.* *ar*-met, a light helmet of the late Middle Ages, shaped to fit the wearer's head.
armful, *n.* *arm*-ful, as much as the arms can hold.
armhole, *n.* *arm*-hole, the cavity under the shoulder, or the armpit; a hole in a garment for the arm.
armiger, *n.* *arm*-e-jer, one entitled to bear arms; a squire or esquire. (L. *arma*, arms, and *gero*, bear.)
armilla, *n.* ar-*mil*-la (*pl.* **armillæ**), a bracelet; an iron ring, hoop or brace, in which the gudgeons of a wheel move; the circular ligament of the wrist, binding the tendons of the hand [Anat.]. (L.)
armillary, *a.* *arm*-il-la-re, resembling a bracelet; consisting of rings or circles. **armillary sphere,** a celestial globe with hoops representing the different astronomical circles as the equator, ecliptic, etc., in their relative positions.
Arminian, *a.* ar-*min*-e-an, pertaining to Arminius (Harmensen, Dut. theologian, 1560–1609) or his principles: *n.* a member of the protestant sect named from him, mainly characterized by their assertion of free-will in opposition to Calvin.
Arminianism, *n.* ar-*min*-e-a-nizm, the tenets of the Arminians.
armipotent, *a.* ar-*mip*-o-tent, mighty in arms. (L. *arma*, and *potens*, powerful.)
armistice, *n.* *ar*-mis-tis, a temporary suspension of hostilities by agreement of the parties; a truce. (Fr.)
armless, *a.* *arm*-less, without an arm; destitute of arms or branches.
armlet, *n.* *arm*-let, a small arm, as of the sea armour, or an ornament, for the arm; a brassard.
armoire, *n.* arm-*wahr*, a large press or cupboard in which arms were stored; an aumbry. (Fr.)
armorial, *a.* ar-*maw*-re-al, pertaining to heraldic arms: *n.* a book on armorial bearings. **armorial bearings,** the heraldic insignia borne on a coat of arms.
Armorican, *n.* ar-*mo*-re-kan, a Breton; a native of Armorica; the language: *a.* pertaining to Brittany; denoting the interval between the Carboniferous and Permian periods [Geol.]. (L. *Armorica*, the region now known as Brittany.)
armorist, *n.* *arm*-ur-ist, one skilled in heraldry.
armory, *n.* *arm*-ur-e, the science of heraldry. (O.Fr. *armoirie*.)
armour, *n.* *arm*-ur, defensive covering of a warrior or [Zool.] of an animal; any habit worn to protect the body in battle; defensive sheathing of a warship, armoured vehicle, tank, etc. (O.Fr. *armure*).
armour-bearer, *n.* *arm*-ur-bare-er, a squire who carried the armour of a knight.
armourclad, *a.* *arm*-ur-klad, heavily armoured: *n.* an ironclad, or warship so protected.
armoured, *a.* *ar*-murd, clad in or protected by armour.
armourer, *n.* *arm*-ur-er, a maker of armour or arms; one who has the care of the arms of another, and buckles on his armour; the petty officer or N.C.O. in charge of the small arms of a ship or battalion.
armour-plate, *n.* *arm*-ur-plate, the defensive steel-plating affixed to ships, forts, vehicles, etc.
armoury, *n.* *arm*-ur-e, a place where arms are deposited and kept in good order; the craft or skill of an armourer.
armozine, *n.* ar-mo-*zeen*, a strong silk, usually black, from which clerical robes are made. (Fr.)
armpit, *n.* *arm*-pit, the hollow under the shoulder; the axilla.
arms, *n.pl.* armz, weapons of war; armour for the body; war; armorial bearings. **to arms!** a summons to take up arms. **to be in arms,** to be in a state of hostility. **to be under arms,** to be armed and ready for action. **a stand of arms,** a complete set for one soldier. (O.Fr. *armes*.)
arm's-length, *n.* *armz*-length, the length of one's arm. **at arm's-length,** beyond striking distance.
★**army,** *n.* *ar*-me, an organized body of armed men for warfare on land; a great number; a vast multitude. **army corps,** the largest unit of an army, consisting of two or more divisions with headquarters staff and auxiliaries. **army council,** a committee of military and civil members of the War Office of which the Secretary of State for War is the chairman. **army list,** the official list of officers of the army. (Fr. *armée*.)
army-worm, *n.* *ar*-me-wurm, the larva of the fungus-midge, *Sciara militaris*.
Arnica, *n.* *ar*-nik-a, a genus of composite plants including *A. montana*, the perennial herb yielding the tincture (*l.c.*) used as a remedy for bruises.
arnot, *n.* *ar*-not, the pig-nut or earth-nut.
arnotto, *n.* ar-*not*-to, annatto, *Bixa orellana*; the dye obtained from this.
aroid, *a.* *ayr*-royd, belonging to the arum family: *n.* any plant of this family [Bot.].
aroint, *int.* a-*roynt*, Away with you! Be off!
aroma, *n.* a-*roh*-ma, the fragrance in plants, spices, and other substances; a pleasant odour; a pungent odour; pervasive quality. (Gr.)
aromal, *a.* *a-roh*-mal, pertaining to or connected with aroma or aromas.
aromatic, *a.* a-ro-*mat*-ik, fragrant; yielding aroma; produced by an aroma: *n.* a plant, spice, or drug with a fragrant smell.
aromatization, *n.* *a*-ro-mat-iz-*ay*-shon, the act of aromatizing; state of being aromatized.
aromatize, *v.t.* a-*roh*-ma-tize, to impregnate with aroma; to scent; to render fragrant.

arose, a-*roze*, the *p.* of arise.
around, *prep.* a-*round*, about; on all sides; encircling; from place to place: *ad.* in a circle; on every side; about; near.
arouse, *v.t.* a-*rouze*, to wake up; to stir up; to excite; to stimulate.
arow, *ad.* a-*roh*, in a row; successively.
arpeggio, *n.* ar-*pej*-e-o, sounding the notes in a chord in quick succession from below upwards instead of simultaneously, after the manner of playing on a harp; the distinct sound of the notes of an instrumental chord [Mus.]. (It.)
arquebus, *n.* *ar*-kwe-bus, a harquebus.
arquerite, *n.* *ar*-ker-ite, a native amalgam of silver, found at Arqueros in Chile.
arracacha, *n.* a-ra-*kah*-chah, an umbelliferous plant of tropical America with an edible root.
arrack, *n.* *a*-rak, a spirituous liquor, distilled from palms, molasses or rice. (Ar. *araq*, essence.)
arragonite, *n.* *a*-ra-go-nite, aragonite.
arrah, *int.* *a*-ra, an interjection denoting mild interest or amazement used in Southern Ireland.
arraign, *v.t.* a-*rayn*, to call or set a prisoner at the bar of a court to answer to an indictment; to impeach; to set in order, or fit for trial; to call to account at any bar; to accuse (O.Fr. *araisnier*.)
arraignment, *n.* a-*rayn*-ment, the act of arraigning; accusation.
arrange, *v.t.* a-*raynj*, to put in the proper order for any purpose; to adjust, or settle; to plan in advance; to adapt [Mus.]. (Fr. *arranger*.)
arrangement, *n.* a-*raynj*-ment, the act of arranging; the state or result of being arranged; settlement; adjustment; classification.
arrant, *a.* *a*-rant, notorious, in an ill sense; downright. (Fr. a variation of *errant*.)
arrantly, *ad.* *a*-rant-le, notoriously; infamously.
arras, *n.* *ar*-ras, tapestry used as wall hangings. (*Arras*, in France, noted for its manufacture.)
arrasene, *n.* a-ra-*seen*, a material of mixed wool and silk for embroidery work.
array, *n.* a-*ray*, order, esp. of battle; a body of men or force in military order; an orderly arrangement for show; dress, ornamentally disposed; the act of impannelling a jury; a jury impannelled; those summoned to serve [Law]: *v.t.* to dispose in order, as troops in battle; to deck, or dress; to set a jury in order for a trial. (O.Fr. *arraier*, to set in order.)
arrear, *n.* a-*reer*, what remains still to pay (generally in the plural); state of being behindhand. **in arrears,** behind in payment. (Fr. *arrière*, behind.)
arrearage, *n.* a-*reer*-raj, arrears.
arrect, *a.* ar-*rekt*, erect; attentive; pricked up (of an animal's ears). (L. *arrectus*, raised.)
arrest, *v.t.* a-*rest*, to stop; to check; to seize or apprehend by legal warrant; to seize and fix: *n.* stoppage by seizure; hindrance; interruption; a legal seizure of the person. **arrest of judgment,** the staying or stopping of a judgment after verdict, for causes assigned [Law]. (O.Fr. *arester*.)
arrestation, *n.* a-res-*tay*-shon, the act of arresting; arrest; detention. (Fr.)
arrester, *n.* a-*rest*-er, one who arrests; the person at whose suit an arrest is made [Scots Law]; a device for stopping an electric discharge.
arresting, *n.* a-*rest*-ing, the action of the verb "to arrest": *a.* outstanding, striking, very attractive.
arrestive, *a.* a-*rest*-iv, inclining to hold or detain (usually said of the mind or attention).
arrestment, *n.* a-*rest*-ment, the act of arresting; the detention of a criminal till he finds bail; a warrant which enables a creditor to attach money or movable property held by another belonging to his debtor [Scots Law].
arret, *n.* a-*ray* *or* a-*ret*, the decision of a court or council; a decree published; the edict of a sovereign prince. (Fr.)
arride, *v.t.* a-*ride*, to laugh scornfully at a person; also, to gratify. (L. *arridere*, laugh at.)
arrière, *n.* a-re-*ayr*, the rear of an army. **arrière ban,** a general proclamation of the French kings summoning by which not only their immediate feudatories but the vassals of the latter to war; the troops thus collected; a general levy. **arrière fee,** a fee or fief held of a feudatory. **arrière vassal,** the vassal of a vassal. (Fr.)
arris, *n.* *a*-ris, the line or edge at which two bodies forming an exterior angle meet each other [Carp.] (O.Fr. *areste*.)
arris-wise, *ad.* *a*-ris-wize, arranged in ridge formation; diagonally.
arrival, *n.* a-*rive*-al, the act of arriving from a distance; the attainment of any object; the person or thing that has arrived; a new-born child.
arrive, *v.i.* a-*rive*, to come to or reach a place; to gain or compass by effort. (Fr. *arriver*.)
arroba, *n.* a-*roh*-bah, a weight in use in parts of Spanish America varying from about 25 to 33 lb.; a liquid measure of about 3¼ to 4¼ gal. in Spain and Portugal, used for wine. (Sp.)
arrogance, *n.* *a*-ro-gans, the act or quality of being arrogant; undue assumption; overbearing conceit. (L. *arrogantia*.)
arrogant, *a.* *a*-ro-gant, given to claim or assume too much; full of assumption; proceeding from an undue claim or self-importance. (L. *arrogans*, arrogating.)
arrogantly, *ad.* *a*-ro-gant-le, in an arrogant manner.
arrogate, *v.t.* *a*-ro-gate, to make undue claims, from vanity, pride, or false pretensions. (L. *arrogātum*.)
arrogation, *n.* a-ro-*gay*-shon, the act of arrogating; undue pretension.
arrondissement, *n.* (App.), a district forming a sub-division of a French territorial department. (Fr. *arrondir*, to make round.)
arrow, *n.* *a*-ro, a straight, slender, pointed, and barbed weapon, made to be shot from a bow; a sign indicating direction. (A.S. *arwe*.)
arrow-head, *n.* *a*-ro-hed, the head of an arrow; aquatic plants of the genus *Sagittaria*, whose leaves resemble the head of an arrow [Bot.].
arrow-headed, *a.* *a*-ro-*hed*-ed, shaped like the head of an arrow; wedge-shaped; cuneiform.
arrowroot, *n.* *a*-ro-root, a nutritive farinaceous substance, manufactured from the roots of the several species of *Maranta*, and so called from the juice having been applied by Indians to cure wounds caused by poisoned arrows.
arrowy, *a.* *a*-ro-e, formed or moving like an arrow consisting of, or as of, arrows.
arse, *n.* arse, the buttocks, rump, or hind part. (A.S. *ærs*.)
arsenal, *n.* *ar*-sen-al, a state-owned establishment where arms, munitions, and other military equipment are manufactured, repaired, or stored. (It.)
arsenate, *n.* *ar*-sen-ate, a salt formed by arsenic acid combined with any base.
arsenic, *n.* *ar*-sen-ik, a brittle semi-metallic element of a steel-grey colour; also, popularly, white arsenic, an extremely poisonous substance. **arsenic** (ar-*sen*-ik) **acid,** a compound of four parts of arsenic and ten of oxygen. **white arsenic,** arsenious trioxide, a virulent poison. (L. *arsenicum*.)
arsenical, *a.* ar-*sen*-e-kal, belonging to, or containing arsenic.
arsenicate, *v.t.* ar-*sen*-e-kate, to combine or treat with arsenic.
arsenious, *a.* ar-*see*-ne-us, pertaining to or containing arsenic. **arsenious acid,** white arsenic; also an hitherto not isolated acid in which arsenic combines as a triod.
arsenite, *n.* *ar*-sen-ite, a salt of arsenious acid.
arsenopyrite, *n.* *ar*-sen-o-*pyr*-rite, mispickle [Min.].
arshin, *n.* ar-*sheen*, a measure of 28 in. in Russia and 1 metre in Turkey. (Turk. an ell.)
arsine, *n.* *ar*-sin, or *ar*-seen, colourless, very poisonous; smelling like garlic; formed by the action of hydrogen on an arsenic solution.
arsis, *n.* *ar*-sis (*pl.* **arses,** *ar*-seez), the rising inflection of the voice, as distinguished from the thesis, or falling; that part of a foot on which the stress of the voice falls [Pros.]; the accentuation of the voice; the upbeat in beating time [Mus.]. (Gr. *arsis*, lifting.)
arson, *n.* *ar*-son, the wilful burning of a house or other property [Law]. (O.Fr.)
art, art, the second person singular, indicative mood, present tense of the verb *to be*.
*__art,__ *n.* art, the employment of means to the accomplishment of some end, directed by knowledge and skill; a system of rules directive of the skill in the attainment of a certain end; the practice of a system directed to the production of a work of art, generally

of fine art; practical skill; dexterity; cunning; *pl.* pursuits requiring skill and ingenuity, including the *fine arts* (music, poetry, dancing, the drama, painting, sculpture, architecture), and the *useful*, or *mechanical arts* (manufactures and those relying mainly on manual labour); the humanities, constituting an academic education; the faculty for teaching such subjects. **art and part,** the contriving and participation in a criminal act. [Scots Law]. (O.Fr.)

artel, *n.* ar-*tel*, a guild of workmen, temporary or permanent, undertaking work and dividing the profits. (Russ.)

Artemisia, *n.* ar-te-*miz*-ya, a genus of composite plants including southernwood and wormwood. (Gr.)

arterial, *a.* ar-*teer*-re-al, pertaining to or contained in an artery. **arterial road,** a first-class main road connecting large centres. (Gr. *arteria.*)

arterialization, *n.* ar-*teer*-re-a-ly-*zay*-shon, the process of making arterial.

arterialize, *v.t.* ar-*teer*-re-a-lize, to convert venous blood into arterial.

arteriole, *n.* ar-*teer*-re-ohl, a minute artery. (Fr.)

arterio-sclerosis, *n.* ar-*teer*-re-o-skler-*roh*-sis, abnormal thickening and hardening of the arteries usually occurring in old age. (Gr. *arteria*, and *sklērōsis*, hardening.)

arteriotomy, *n.* ar-teer-re-*ot*-o-me, the opening of an artery; the dissection of the arteries. (Gr. *arteria*, and *tome*, cutting.)

arteritis, *n.* ar-ter-*ry*-tis, inflammation of the arteries or an artery.

artery, *n.* *ar*-ter-re, one of the vessels which convey the blood from the heart to all parts of the body; a main channel. (Gr. *artēria.*)

Artesian, *a.* ar-*tee*-zahn, pertaining to Artois, in France. **Artesian wells,** wells first made at Artois by boring for water to a stratum where it is lower than its source, so as to obtain a constant supply.

artful, *a.* *art*-ful, performed with art or skill; artificial; cunning; crafty.

artfully, *ad.* *art*-ful-le, in an artful manner.

artfulness, *n.* *art*-ful-ness, the quality of being artful.

arthritic, *a.* ar-*thrit*-ik, pertaining to or affecting the joints; gouty; good for the gout. (Gr. *arthron*, a joint.)

arthritis, *n.* ar-*thry*-tis, any inflammation of the joints; gout. (Gr.)

arthrodia, *n.* ar-*throh*-de-a, an articulation, in which the head of one bone is received into the socket of another. (Gr.)

arthrodic, *a.* ar-*throd*-ik, pertaining to arthrodia.

arthrology, *n.* ar-*throl*-o-je, the division of anatomy treating of the joints; a treatise on the joints. (Gr. *arthron*, and *logos*, science.)

Arthropoda, *n.pl.* ar-*throp*-o-da, animals with jointed limbs, a large sub-kingdom of invertebrates comprising insects, spiders, crustaceans, etc.

arthropodous, *a.* ar-*throp*-o-dus, belonging to the Arthropoda.

arthrosis, *n.* ar-*throh*-sis, an articulation uniting two bones [Anat.] (Gr.)

artichoke, *n.* *ar*-te-choke, a species of *Cynara* cultivated as a culinary vegetable, having large scaly heads like the cone of a pine (It. *articiocco*). **Jerusalem artichoke,** a species of sun-flower, *Helianthus tuberosus*, with edible tuberous roots. (It. *girasole*, turning to the sun.)

article, *n.* *ar*-te-kl, a single particular in a statement, treaty, contract, or account; a point of faith; a distinct part; a separate substance or commodity; a contribution to a periodical, cyclopædia, etc.; a word used before nouns, to limit or define their application [Gram.]. **Articles of Association,** a legal document detailing the duties, responsibilities and discretionary powers of the governing body of an association or public company [Law]. **Articles of War,** in Great Britain, and in the U.S.A., the regulations by which the military forces of the respective nations are governed. **Thirty-nine Articles,** the statements of religious belief to which the clergy of the Church of England must subscribe.

article, *v.t.* *ar*-te-kl, to draw up in distinct particulars; to bind, esp. an apprentice, by article of agreement; to indict. (Fr.)

articled, *a.* *ar*-te-kld, bound by indenture, esp. to learn a specified profession (as the law) or business.

articular, *a.* ar-*tik*-yew-lar, belonging or relating to the joints. (L. *articulata*, jointed.)

articularly, *ad.* ar-*tik*-yew-lar-le, in an articular or articulate manner.

Articulata, *n.pl.* ar-*tik*-yew-lay-ta, in Cuvier's classification, the sub-kingdom of invertebrates comprising segmented animals, the insects, crustaceans, centipedes, and worms.

articulate, *a.* ar-*tik*-yew-late, formed with joints; composed of segments [Biol.]; pertaining to or of the Articulata [Zool.]; distinctly syllabled by correct management of the organs of speech: *v.i.* to form a joint with; to speak distinctly: *v.t.* to unite by a joint; to join in correct order; to utter distinctly. (L. *articulatus*, spoken distinctly.)

articulately, *ad.* ar-*tik*-yew-lat-le, in an articulate manner.

articulateness, *n.* ar-*tik*-yew-lat-ness, the quality of being articulate.

articulation, *n.* ar-*tik*-yew-*lay*-shon, the act of articulating; the joining or juncture of the bones [Anat.]; the connection of the parts of a plant by joints [Bot.]; distinct utterance; a consonant, as representing the contact of two organs of speech [Gram.]. (L. *articulatio*, putting forth new joints.)

articulator, *n.* ar-*tik*-yew-lay-tor, a distinct speaker; a prosector; a dental instrument for ensuring proper connection between artificial teeth; an instrument used by telephonists.

artifact, *n.* *ar*-te-fakt, a product of primitive art, esp. a flint implement; a structure appearing in a tissue after death or through the use of reagents [Biol.].

artifice, *n.* *art*-e-fis, an artful or crafty device or contrivance; a trick; trickery; cunning. (Fr.)

artificer, *n.* ar-*tif*-e-ser, a skilled workman; a mechanic; an inventor.

artificial, *a.* art-e-*fish*-al, made by art; not natural; affected; fictitious; cultivated; not indigenous.

artificiality, *n.* *art*-e-fish-e-*al*-e-te, quality, state, or condition of being artificial; an artificial thing.

artificialized, *a.* *ar*-te-*fish*-a-lyzd, made artificial.

artificially, *ad.* art-e-*fish*-al-le, in an artificial manner.

artificialness, *n.* art-e-*fish*-al-ness, the quality of being artificial.

artillerist, *n.* ar-*til*-er-rist, one skilled in gunnery.

artillery, *n.* ar-*til*-le-re, weapons of war; ordnance, together with its equipment; the military force in charge of the guns; the science of gunnery. **train of artillery,** a number of mobile guns in marching order. **artillery plant,** a species of *Pilea*, so called from the puffs of pollen ejected by the exploding stamens. (Fr.)

artilleryman, *n.* ar-*til*-er-re-man, a soldier of the artillery.

artiness, *n.* *art*-e-ness, the quality of being arty.

Artiodactyla, *n.pl.* *ar*-te-o-*dak*-til-a, the sub-order of even-toed ungulates, ranging from the oxen, sheep, goats, and deer to the pig, camel, and hippopotamus: *sing.*, **artiodactyl.**

artisan, *n.* *art*-e-zan, one skilled in a mechanic art; a handicraftsman. (Fr.)

artist, *n.* *ar*-tist, one who professes and practises any of the fine arts, esp. painting; an artistic performer.

artiste, *n.* ar-*teest*, a stage performer; a specially proficient chef, coiffeur, etc. (Fr.)

artistic, *a.* ar-*tist*-ik, pertaining to an artist; conformable to art; manifesting skill or good taste.

artistically, *ad.* ar-*tist*-e-ka-le, in an artistic manner.

artistry, *n.* *ar*-tist-re, the vocation of an artist; the quality of art; artistic ability.

artless, *a.* *art*-less, without art; unskilful without guile, craft, or stratagem; sincere; simple.

artlessly, *ad.* *art*-less-le, in an artless manner.

artlessness, *n.* *art*-less-ness, the quality of being artless.

artocarpad, *n.* *ar*-to-*kar*-pad, any tree of the genus *Artocarpus*, esp. the breadfruit, *A. communis.* (Gr. *artos*, bread, *karpos*, fruit.)

arts, *n.pl.* arts, *see* **art.**

artsilk, *n.* *art*-silk, artificial silk.

arty, *a.* *ar*-te, aping the artistic; affectedly artistic.

arui, *n.* ah-*roo*-e, a wild sheep of North Africa, *Ammotragus lervia.*

arum, *n.* *ayr*-rum, any plant of the genus *Arum*,

including the wake robin. **arum lily,** the calla lily, *Richardia africana.* (L.)
arundinaceous, *a.* a-*run*-din-*ay*-shus, reedy; consisting of or like reeds.
arundineous, *a.* a-run-*din*-e-us, abounding with reeds.
aruspex, *n.* a-*rus*-peks, haruspex.
Aryan, *a.* *ayr*-re-an, or *ay*-re-an, linguistically descended from the primitive peoples presumed to have populated Europe from Central Asia and N. India and to have provided the source of most European languages; Indo-European: *n.* a person belonging to this linguistic group; a non-Semite.
arytenoid, *a.* a-rit-*ee*-noyd, funnel-shaped; relating to the cartilages at the uppermost rear part of the larynx. (Gr. *arytainocides,* funnel-like.)
★as, *ad,* az, like to; in the manner in which; when; for example; in the state of: *conj.* since: *pro.* that. **as if,** as it would be if; **as though,** as if. **as to, as for,** with respect to. **as well as,** equally with. **as yet,** till now. (A.S. *als.*)
as, *n.* ass, in ancient Rome, the pound of 12 ounces, and a bronze coin originally of this weight but gradually reduced to ½ oz.
asafœtida, *n.* ass-a-*fet*-id-a, the garlic-smelling milky juice of plants of the fennel family, used in cookery and medicine. (Pers. *aza,* gum, L. *fetidus,* fetid.)
asar, *n.pl.* *ass*-ar, ridges of gravel and sand of glacial age; eskar; kames. (Swed.)
asarabacca, *n.* ass-a-ra-*bak*-ka, a plant with bitter leaves, used as an emetic and in medicated snuffs. (L. *asarum,* wild spikenard, *bacca,* a berry.)
asarone, *n.* *ass*-a-rone, an inodorous crystalline compound obtained from the oil of plants of the asarabacca family.
asbestic, *a.* az-*bes*-tik, pertaining to, or consisting of, asbestos.
asbestiform, *a.* az-*bes*-te-form, having the structure of asbestos.
asbestine, *a.* az-*bes*-tin, pertaining to asbestos, or partaking of its nature and qualities; incombustible.
asbestinize, *v.t.* az-*bes*-te-nize, to render inflammable.
asbestoid, *a,* az-*bes*-toyd, resembling asbestos.
asbestos, *n.* az-*bes*-toss, an incombustible fibrous kind of hornblende, from which fireproof fabrics are made. (Gr. *asbestos,* inextinguishable.)
ascaris, *n.* ass-*ka*-ris (*pl.* **ascaridæ,** ass-*kar*-ri-dee), a parasitic intestinal worm, esp. the round worm or thread-worm. (Gr.)
ascend, *v.i.* and *t.* as-*send,* to rise; to mount up; to proceed from an inferior to a superior degree; to go backwards in the order of time; to rise to a more acute note [Mus.]; to move towards the zenith [Astron.]; to climb up anything. (L. *ascendo,* ascend.)
ascendable, *a.* as-*send*-a-bl, that may be ascended.
ascendancy, *n.* as-*send*-an-se, ascendency.
ascendant, *a.* as-*send*-ant, rising; superior; predominant; above the horizon, moving towards the zenith [Astron.]: *n.* superiority or commanding influence; one who precedes in genealogy; height; elevation; the ecliptic which rises in the eastern point of the horizon at the instant of one's birth [Astrol.]. **in the ascendant,** having commanding power or influence; predominant. (L. *ascendans,* ascending.)
ascendency, *n.* as-*send*-en-se, governing or controlling influence; governing power.
ascendent, *a.* as-*send*-ent, ascendant.
ascension, *n.* as-*sen*-shon, the act of ascending; a rising. **Ascension Day,** a festival in commemoration of Christ's ascension, kept on the fortieth day after Easter; Holy Thursday. **oblique ascension,** an arc of the equator, intercepted between the first point of Aries and that point of the equator which rises at the same time with a star [Astron.]. **right ascension,** celestial longitude, degree of the equator, reckoned from the first point of Aries, which comes to the meridian on the same instant with a star [Astron.]. (L. *ascensio,* ascent.)
ascensional, *a.* as-*sen*-shon-al, ascensive; inclining upwards; relating to ascension.
ascensive, *a.* as-*sen*-siv, rising; tending to rise.
ascent, *n.* as-*sent,* act or process of ascending; upward motion; way of ascending; an acclivity; degree of elevation.
ascertain, *v.t.* as-ser-*tane,* to make sure of; to determine; to find out accurately; to establish. (O.Fr. *ascertener.*)
ascertainable, *a.* as-er-*tane*-a-bl, that may be ascertained by examination.
ascertainment, *n.* as-ser-*tane*-ment, the act of ascertaining; finding out.
ascetic, *a.* a-*set*-ik, unduly self-denying and devoted: *n.* one who retires from the world and devotes himself to a life of severe self-denying discipline. (Gr. *askētēs,* hermit.)
ascetical, *a.* a-*set*-e-kal, pertaining to asceticism.
ascetically, *ad.* a-*set*-e-ka-le, in an ascetical manner.
asceticism, *n.* as-*set*-e-sizm, the state or practice of an ascetic austerity.
asci, *n.pl.* *ass*-ky, *see* **ascus.**
ascidians, *n.pl.* a-*sid*-e-anz, the sea-squirts, a group of semivertebrates belonging to the Tunicata. (Gr. *askidion,* a little bottle, or bottle-shaped.)
ascidium, *n.* a-*sid*-e-um (*pl.* **ascidia**), a hollow appendage, resembling a small pitcher or bottle [Bot.].
ascites, *n.* as-*sy*-teez, a dropsical swelling of the abdomen [Med.].
ascititious, *a.* as-se-*tish*-us, adscititious.
asclepiad, *n.* as-*klee*-pe-ad, a verse of four feet, a spondee, a choriambus, and two dactyls [Pros.]. (*Asklepiades,* its inventor.)
asclepiad, *n.* as-*klee*-pe-ad, any member of the swallowwort family [Bot.].
asclepiadean, *a.* as-*klee*-pe-a-*dee*-an, pertaining to or resembling an asclepiad [Pros.]: *n.* an asclepiad [Pros.].
Asclepias, *n.* as-*klee*-pe-as, the genus including the swallowwort. (Gr. *Asklepios,* the god of medicine.)
ascribable, *a.* as-*kribe*-a-bl, attributable.
ascribe, *v.t.* as-*kribe,* to attribute, impute, or assign; to allege; to belong. (L. *ascribo,* write down an account.)
ascription, *n.* as-*krip*-shon, the act of ascribing; that which is ascribed (esp. the "Glory be to the Father . . .", at the end of a sermon). (L. *ascriptio,* an addition in writing.)
ascus, *n.* *ass*-kus (*pl.* **asci,** *ass*-ky), the spore sac of certain fungi. (Gr. *askos,* bladder.)
aseity, *n.* a-*see*-e-te, causeless existence, especially of God as Self-Creator. (L. *a-,* by, *se,* oneself.)
asepsis, *n.* ay-*sep*-sis, condition of being aseptic; process or method of asepticizing. (Gr. *a-,* and *sepomai,* putrefy.)
aseptic, *a.* ay-*sep*-tik, not subject to putrefaction: *n.* an aseptic agent. (Gr. *a-,* and *sepomai,* putrefy.)
asepticize, *v.t.* ay-*sep*-te-size, to render aseptic; to sterilize [Med.].
asexual, *a.* ay-*seks*-yew-al, not having sex or sexual action; not pertaining to sex. (L. *a-,* not, and *sexual.*)
asexuality, *n.* *ay*-seks-yew-*al*-e-te, the condition of being asexual; absence of sex.
Asgard, *n.* *ass*-gard, the heaven of Scandinavian mythology; the place to which heroes slain in battle went. (*As,* god, *gard,* yard.)
ash, *n.* ash, the forest tree, *Fraxinus excelsior*; the wood of the ash-tree: *a.* pertaining to, like or made of ash. **mountain ash,** the rowan tree. (A.S. *æse.*)
ash, *n.* ash, *pl.* **ashes,** the residue of combustion. **Ash Wednesday,** the first day of Lent (from the ancient custom of sprinkling ashes on the head on that day).
ashamed, *a.* a-*shaymd,* affected with shame; abashed by conviction of wrong or impropriety, etc. (A.S. *āscamod,* put to shame.)
ashamedly, *ad.* a-*shay*-med-le, in an ashamed way.
ashen, *a.* *ash*-en, pertaining to, or made of ash; greyish; ash-coloured.
ashery, *n.* *ash*-er-re, a place or receptacle for ashes.
ashes, *n.pl.* *ash*-ez, the remains of anything burnt; the remains of a cremated body; a dead body; the dust of the dead; in cricket [Slang], the reputation of the losing side in any series of tests between England and Australia.
ashet, *n.* *ash*-et, a large meat-dish [Scot.]. (Fr. *assiette.*)
a-shiver, *ad.* a-*shiv*-er, shivering.
Ashkenazim, *n.pl.* ash-ke-*naz*-im, the Jews of Cent. and N. Europe as contrasted with the Sephardim of Spain and Portugal. (Heb.)
ashlar, *n.* *ash*-lar, hewn stones used for the facing of

walls, etc. ; a facing of wrought and squared stones [Arch.]. (O.Fr. *aiseler*, small board.)
ashore, *ad.* a-*shore*, on shore ; to the shore ; on land.
ash-pan, *n.* *ash*-pan, a pan beneath a grate for ashes.
ash-pit, *n.* *ash*-pit, receptacle or place for ashes.
ash-tray, *n.* *ash*-tray, a small receptacle for tobacco ash.
ashy, *a.* *ash*-e, belonging to, composed of, or like ashes ; ash-coloured ; whitish-grey ; pale.
Asian, *a.* *aysh*-yan, pertaining to Asia ; Asiatic.
Asiatic, *a.* ay-she-*at*-ik, belonging or relating to Asia : *n.* a native of Asia.
aside, *ad.* a-*side*, on or to one side ; apart ; away ; off ; off the right : *n.* a remark in an undertone.
asinine, *a.* *ass*-e-nine, of or pertaining to the ass, stupid ; obstinate. (L. *asinus*, an ass.)
asininity, *n.* ass-e-*nin*-e-te, the quality of being asinine ; obstinate stupidity.
asiphonate, *a.* ay-*sy*-fon-at, having no siphon [Conch.] : *n.* an asiphonate mollusc.
ask, *v.t.* ahsk, to request ; to seek to obtain by words ; to petition ; to require, expect, or claim ; to demand ; to question ; to inquire about ; to invite : *v.i.* to request or petition ; to make inquiry. **asked in church,** to have the banns published. (A.S. *āscian.*)
askance, *ad.* a-*skans*, sideways ; obliquely ; towards one corner of the eye.
askant, *ad.* a-*skant*, askance.
askari, *n.* *ass*-ka-ree, a native East African in European military service.
asker, *n.* *ahsk*-er, one who asks ; a suppliant.
asker, *n.* *ahsk*-er, a newt [local name].
askew, *ad.* a-*skew*, awry ; asquint.
aslant, *ad.* a-*slahnt*, on the slant ; obliquely. (Scand.)
asleep, *a.* and *ad.* a-*sleep*, sleeping ; in a state of sleep.
aslope, *ad.* a-*slope*, in a sloping or leaning attitude.
asmoulder, *ad.* a-*smohl*-der, smouldering.
asomatous, *a.* a-*soh*-ma-tus, unembodied ; immaterial. (Gr. *a-*, not, *soma*, body.)
asp, *n.* asp, a small venomous serpent of Egypt, the Egyptian cobra, *Naja Haje* ; the European viper, *Vipera aspis*. (L.)
asp, *n.* asp, the aspen.
asparagin, *n.* ass-*pa*-ra-jin, a nitrogenous crystallizable substance, first found in asparagus.
asparaginous, *a.* ass-pa-*raj*-e-nus, like, or allied to, asparagus.
asparagus, *n.* ass-*pa*-ra-gus, any perennial liliaceous herb of the large genus *Asparagus*, including *A. officinalis*, the culinary plant. (L.)
aspartate, *n.* ass-*par*-tate, a salt of aspartic acid.
aspartic, *a.* ass-*par*-tik, pertaining to or obtained from asparagin.
aspect, *n.* *ass*-pekt, look ; view ; appearance ; position as regards the points of the compass ; the situation of one planet with respect to another [Astron.]. (L. *aspectus*, glance.)
aspen, *n.* *ass*-pen, a poplar tree, *Populus tremula*, remarkable for the trembling of its leaves : *a.* pertaining to or like the aspen ; made of aspen wood. (A.S. *æspe.*)
asper, *n.* *ass*-per, the Greek aspirate or rough breathing ; the sign ['] for this. (L., rough.)
asperate, *v.t.* *ass*-per-ate, to make rough or uneven.
asperges, *n.* ass-*per*-jeez, the ceremony of sprinkling altar, clergy and congregation with holy water. (L. *asperges*, thou shalt sprinkle.)
aspergilliform, *a.* ass-per-*jil*-e-form, shaped like a brush or aspergillus [Bot.].
aspergillum, *n.* *ass*-per-*jil*-um, the brush used to sprinkle holy water ; a genus of boring bivalve molluscs in which the shell consists of a tube resembling the spout of a watering-pot ; the water-pot shell. (L. *aspergo*, sprinkling.)
Aspergillus, *n.* ass-per-*jil*-us, a genus of microscopic fungi [Bot.].
asperifoliate, *a.* *ass*-per-e-*foh*-le-ate, having rough leaves [Bot.]. (L. *asper*, and *folium*, a leaf.)
asperifolious, *a.* *ass*-per-e-*foh*-le-us, asperifoliate.
asperity, *n.* ass-*pe*-re-te, roughness of surface ; harshness of sound ; sharpness ; acrimony. (Fr.)
aspermous, *a.* ay-*sperm*-us, without seed [Bot.]. (Gr.)
asperse, *v.t.* ass-*perse*, to besprinkle ; to bespatter with evil reports, to slander ; to defame. (L. *aspersus*, scattered.)
aspersion, *n.* ass-*per*-shon, the act of aspersing ; calumny ; slander.
aspersive, *a.* ass-*per*-siv, tending to asperse.
aspersorium, *n.* ass-pur-*sore*-e-um, a vessel for holy water.
aspersory, *a.* as-*per*-so-re, aspersive.
asphalt, *n.* *ass*-falt, mineral pitch, a hard, bituminous substance used in paving flooring, and roofing, etc. : *v.t.* to pave with asphalt. (Gr. *asphaltos.*)
asphaltic, *a.* ass-*falt*-ik, pertaining to or containing asphalt ; bituminous.
asphodel, *n.* *ass*-fo-del, a plant of the genus *Asphodelus*, sacred to Proserpine ; the king's-spear. **bog asphodel,** the liliaceous plant *Narthecium ossifragum*, also known as **Lancashire asphodel. Scotch asphodel,** *Tofieldia palustris*, a liliaceous plant. (Gr., the plant, king's-spear.)
asphyxia, *n.* ass-*fiks*-e-a, suspended animation, particularly from suffocation, drowning, or inhaling irrespirable gases. (Gr. *asphixia*, cessation of the pulse.)
asphyxial, *a.* ass-*fiks*-se-al, pertaining to or indicating asphyxia.
asphyxiant, *n.* ass-*fiks*-e-ant, a substance causing asphyxia.
asphyxiate, *v.t.* ass-*fiks*-e-ate, to put into a condition of asphyxia ; to suffocate a person.
aspic, *n.* *ass*-pik, a savoury meat jelly ; a species of lavender [Bot.]. (Fr.)
aspidistra, *n.* ass-pe-*dis*-tra, any foliage plant of a small liliaceous genus *Aspidistra*, much used for house decoration. (Gr.)
aspirant, *n.* ass-*pire*-ant *or* *ass*-per-ant, one who aspires ; a candidate.
aspirate, *v.t.* *ass*-pe-rate, to pronounce with an audible breathing, or the sound of "h" ; to mark with an asper : *n.* an aspirated sound, or a letter marked with an asper ; a mark of aspiration : *a.* pronounced with a full breath. (L. *aspiratus*, breathed upon.)
aspiration, *n.* ass-pe-*ray*-shon, the act of aspiring ; the act of breathing ; an aspirated sound ; an eager desire after something high.
aspirator, *n.* *ass*-pe-*ray*-tor, one who or that which aspires ; an apparatus or instrument used to move gases or liquids by suction.
aspiratory, *a.* as-*pire*-a-to-re, pertaining to breathing ; suited to the inhaling of air.
aspire, *v.i.* as-*pire*, to desire and seek eagerly ; to aim high ; to rise or soar up. (L. *aspīro*, breathe.)
aspirin, *n.* *ass*-pe-rin, a white crystalline acetate of salicylic acid used for the alleviation of rheumatic and neuralgic pain. (Ger. trade-name.)
aspiring, *a.* as-*pire*-ing, ambitious ; animated with an eager desire of power or excellence.
aspiringly, *ad.* as-*pire*-ing-le, in an aspiring manner.
Asplenium, *n.* as-*plee*-ne-um, a large genus of polypodiaceous ferns ; the spleenworts. (Gr.)
asport, *v.t.* as-*port*, to remove forcibly or feloniously. (L. *asporto*, carry off.)
asportation, *n.* as-por-*tay*-shon, the felonious displacement or removal of goods [Law].
asprawl, *ad.* a-*sprawl*, sprawling.
asprout, *ad.* a-*sprout*, sprouting.
asquint, *ad.* a-*skwint*, to the corner of the eye ; obliquely ; with suspicion ; furtively.
ass, *n.* ass, one of several species of *Equus*, esp. *E. asinus*, the African, or *E. hemionus*, the Asiatic wild ass ; a domesticated variety of either species ; a donkey ; a dull, obstinate, stupid fellow. (A.S. *assa.*)
assafetida, *n.* as-sa-*fet*-e-da, asafœtida.
assagai, *n.* *as*-se-gy, a Kaffir javelin or spear made of a hard wood tipped with metal. (Ar.)
assai, *ad.* as-*sah*-e, enough ; very [Mus.]. (It.)
assail, *v.t.* a-*sayl*, to fall upon with violence ; to attack ; to assault. (Fr. *assailler.*)
assailable, *a.* a-*sayl*-a-bl, that may be assailed.
assailant, *n.* a-*sayl*-ant, one who assails : *a.* attacking ; assaulting.
Assamese, *n.*, *s.* and *pl.* ass-a-*meez*, a native or the natives of Assam : *a.* of or pertaining to Assam.
assapan, *n.* as-sa-*pan*, the flying squirrel of Maryland and Virginia. (Native name.)
assart, *n.* as-*sart*, the offence of grubbing up trees and destroying coverts ; land thus converted into arable, a forest clearing : *v.t.* to grub up trees [Law]. (O.Fr. *essarter.*)

assassin, *n.* as-*sas*-sin, one who kills, or attempts to kill, by surprise or secret assault. (*Hashashin*, a mediæval sect of Moslem fanatics who infested the Lebanon and fortified themselves for murder by drinking *hashish*, an intoxicant made from hemp.)
assassinate, *v.t.* as-*sas*-sin-ate, to kill or attempt to kill by surprise or secret assault, esp. for political or dynastic reasons.
assassination, *n.* as-sas-sin-*ay*-shon, the act of assassinating; secret and sudden murder for other than private ends.
assassinator, *n.* as-*sas*-in-ay-tor, an assassin.
assault, *n.* as-*sawlt*, a violent, often sudden, attack; an attack by storm; an attack by hostile words or proceedings; an attempt or threat to do bodily injury to another [Law]: *v.t.* to attack with hostile intention; to fall on with violence; to storm; to attack by words, arguments, or unfriendly measures. **assault-at-arms,** a public exhibition of military exercises. (O.Fr. *assaulter.*)
assaultable, *a.* as-*sawl*-ta-bl, that may be assaulted.
assaulter, *n.* as-*sawl*-ter, one who assaults: an assailant.
assay, *n.* as-*say*, examination; the determination of the quantity of any particular metal in an ore, alloy, or other metallic compound, and esp. in coin or bullion; the metal to be assayed [Metal.]: *v.t.* to test; to analyse metals: *v.i.* to attempt or endeavour. **assay ton,** a weight of 29·166 grammes used for convenience in assaying. (O.Fr. *assayer.*)
assayable, *a.* as-*say*-a-bl, that can be assayed.
assayer, *n.* as-*say*-er, a metallurgist; one who assays bullion.
assaying, *n.* as-*say*-ing, the determination of the amount of any particular metal in a compound.
assay-master, *n.* as-*say*-mah-ster, an official of the Mint who assays both the bullion and coin.
assegai, *n.* *as*-se-gy, an assagai.
assemblage, *n.* as-*sem*-blaj, the act of assembling; the state of being assembled; a concourse; a collection of individuals or of particular things.
assemble, *v.t.* as-*sem*-bl, to bring or call together a number of individuals or things into one place or body; to bring together the disconnected parts of a whole [Mech.]: *v.i.* to meet or come together; to congregate. (O.Fr. *assembler.*)
assembling, *n.* as-*sem*-bling, a meeting together; a fitting together [Mech.].
assembly, *n.* as-*sem*-ble, the act of assembling or state of being assembled; a company of individuals met for a common purpose; the putting together of a machine or structure from its components; the falling-in signal of a drum or bugle, etc. [Mil.]. **assembly room,** a room in which persons assemble, especially for dancing. **general assembly,** the supreme court, consisting of clerical and lay representatives from each of the presbyteries, of the Church of Scotland. (Fr. *assemblée.*)
assent, *n.* as-*sent*, the act of admitting, agreeing to or approving; acquiescence; agreement; approval. **royal assent,** the assent of the sovereign to Bills passed by Parliament: *v.i.* to admit as true; to concur; to sanction. (O.Fr. *assenter.*)
assentation, *n.* as-sent-*ay*-shon, compliance.
assentient, *a.* as-*sen*-she-ent, assenting: *n.* one who assents.
assentor, *n.* as-*sent*-er, one who assents, esp. to the nomination of a Parliamentary candidate.
assert, *v.t.* as-*sert*, to declare positively; to affirm; to maintain or defend; to vindicate a claim or title to. (L. *assertus*, asserted.)
assertable, as-*sert*-a-bl, capable of being asserted.
asserter, *n.* as-*sert*-er, one who declares, maintains, or asserts.
assertion, *n.* as-*ser*-shon, the act of asserting; positive declaration; affirmation.
assertive, *a.* as-*sert*-iv, positive; affirming confidently; dogmatical; pushing.
assertively, *ad.* as-*sert*-iv-le, in an assertive manner.
assertor, *n.* as-*sert*-or, one who asserts; a champion of a cause.
assertory, *a.* as-*sert*-o-re, affirming; maintaining.
assess, *v.t.* as-*sess*, to charge with a certain sum upon, as a tax; to value property for the purpose of taxation; to rate; to set or fix. (O.Fr. *assesser.*)
assessable, *a.* as-*sess*-a-bl, that may be assessed.
assessably, *ad.* as-*sess*-a-ble, by assessment.
assessment, *n.* as-*sess*-ment, official valuation; act of assessing; a valuation of property for taxation, or a specific sum charged on the person or property; act of determining the amount of damages by a jury.
assessor, *n.* as-*sess*-or, one appointed to assess property for taxation; one who sits by another as next in dignity and assistant in council; a technical adviser to a judge in court.
assessorial, *a.* as-ses-*saw*-re-al, pertaining to an assessor.
assets, *n.pl.* *as*-sets, the stock-in-trade and entire property of a merchant or of a trading association; goods or estate of a deceased person; the property of an insolvent debtor. (Fr. *assez*, enough.)
asseverate, *v.t.* as-*sev*-er-ate, to affirm or aver positively or with solemnity. (L. *asseverātus*, spoken seriously.)
asseveration, *n.* as-sev-er-*ay*-shon, act of asseverating; a solemn affirmation; an oath.
assibilate, *v.t.* as-*sib*-e-late, to make sibilant. (L. *assibilatus*, hissed.)
assibilation, *n.* as-*sib*-e-*lay*-shon, the changing of a mute into a sibilant consonant.
assiduity, *n.* as-se-*dew*-e-te, constant or close application; diligence; attentiveness to persons: *pl.* studied and constant attentions. (L. *assiduitas*, attendance.)
assiduous, *a.* as-*sid*-yew-us, diligent; persevering; attentive; performed with assiduity.
assiduously, *ad.* as-*sid*-yew-us-le, in an assiduous manner.
assiduousness, *n.* as-*sid*-yew-us-ness, assiduity; the quality of being assiduous.
assiento, *n.* as-se-*ent*-o, a contract formerly entered into between Spain and other powers for the importation of negro slaves into South America. (Sp.)
assiette, *n.* ass-*yet*, an ashet; a composition used as a gilding surface by bookbinders. (Fr.)
assign, *v.t.* as-*sine*, to allot; to apportion; to fix, specify or designate; to appoint; to transfer; to allege or show in particular; to point out: *n.* a person to whom property or an interest is, or may be, transferred; an assignee. (O.Fr. *assigner.*)
assignable, *a.* as-*sine*-a-bl, that may be assigned or transferred; capable of being designated as a source or reason.
assignat, *n.* *ass*-ig-nat, *or* ass-een-*yah*, a public note or bill issued 1789–96 by the revolutionary government of France. (Fr.)
assignation, *n.* as-sig-*nay*-shon, the act of assigning; an appointment to meet; a tryst; a making over by transfer of title, or the deed of transfer [Scots Law]; an attribution of origin. (L. *assignatio*, an assignment.)
assignee, *n.* as-se-*nee*, one to whom an assignment is made; one appointed by another to do some act or enjoy some right or privilege; a trustee; an agent. **assignees in bankruptcy,** persons appointed to manage the estate of a bankrupt for his creditors [Law].
assignment, *n.* as-*sine*-ment, an allotting or appointment to a particular person or use; a transfer of title or interest; the writing by which an interest is transferred; the thing or property transferred; a pointing out [Law]; a task assigned.
assignor, *n.* as-sine-*or*, a person who assigns or transfers an interest.
assimilable, *a.* as-*sim*-e-la-bl, that may be assimilated.
assimilate, *v.t.* as-*sim*-e-late, to bring to a likeness; to liken; to compare; to convert into a like organic substance; to incorporate: *v.i.* to become similar; to perform the act of converting food into the substance of the body; to be converted into the substance of the body. (L. *assimilatus.*)
assimilation, *n.* as-sim-e-*lay*-shon, the act or process of assimilating; the state of being assimilated; comparison; the process by which an organism absorbs and converts nutriment into its own substance [Physiol.].
assimilative, *a.* as-*sim*-e-lay-tiv, having power of converting to a likeness, or to a like substance.
assimilator, *n.* as-*sim*-e-lay-tor, one who or that which assimilates.
assimilatory, *a.* as-*sim*-e-lay-to-re, tending to assimilate; assimilative.
assist, *v.t.* as-*sist*, to aid, help or succour; to support; to promote: *v.i.* to lend aid; to be present; to take part in. (Fr. *assister.*)

assistance, *n.* as-*sist*-ance, help; aid; support.
assistant, *a.* as-*sist*-ant, helping; supporting; auxiliary: *n.* one who assists another; an auxiliary.
assize, *n.* as-*size*, a sitting of a court of law; a trial in which assessors decide on matters of fact; an ordinance regulating weight, measure, and price of certain articles of common consumption; the decision arrived at: *pl.* courts held periodically in every county of England by one or more judges for trying civil and criminal actions; the time or place of holding such court: *v.t.* to fix the weight, measure, or price of commodities; to assess.
assizer, *n.* as-*size*-er, an officer who has the care or inspection of weights and measures.
assizor, *n.* as-*size*-or, a juror [Scots Law].
associability, *n.* as-soh-sha-*bil*-e-te, the quality of being associable.
associable, *a.* as-*soh*-sha-bl, that may be joined to or associated; sociable; liable to be affected by sympathy [Med.].
associate, *v.t.* as-*soh*-she-ate, to join in company as friend, companion, or confederate; to unite; to combine: *v.i.* to unite in, or to keep, company, inplying intimacy; to join in association; to unite in action: *a.* joined in interest, purpose, or office: *n.* companion; partner; ally. (L. *associatus*, united with.)
associateship, *n.* as-*soh*-she-ate-ship, the state or office of an associate.
association, *n.* as-*soh*-se-*ay*-shon, the act of associating; a society formed for promoting some object; connexion. **association football,** the game played under the laws of the Football Association. **association of ideas,** that relation among ideas and feelings by which they tend to suggest and recall one another.
associational, *a.* as-soh-se-*ay*-shon-al, pertaining to an association.
associationism, *n.* as-soh-se-*ay*-shon-izm, the theory that association of ideas is the efficient cause of mental and moral phenomena [Psych.].
associationist, *n.* as-soh-se-*ay*-shon-ist, a believer in associationism.
associative, *a.* as-*soh*-she-a-tiv, having the quality of associating; tending to associate.
assoil, *v.t.* as-*soyl*, to free from guilt or sin; to forgive or pardon; to absolve. (O.Fr. *assoudre.*)
assoilzie, *v.t.* as-*soyl*-yee, to acquit [Scots Law].
assonance, *n.* *as*-so-nans, the quality of being assonant; resemblance of sounds.
assonant, *a.* *as*-so-nant, having a resemblance in sound; corresponding in the sounds of vowels but not of consonants [Pros.]. (L. *assonans*, sounding.)
assort, *v.t.* as-*sort*, to arrange into sorts or lots as required: *v.i.* to agree; to match; to be in accordance with. (Fr. *assortir.*)
assorted, *a.* as-*sort*-ed, of various sorts, qualities, or sizes.
assortment, *n.* as-*sort*-ment, the act of assorting; a quantity of things assorted; the class under which they are assorted.
assuage, *v.t.* as-*swaje*, to soften, mitigate, allay, or soothe: *v.i.* to abate or subside. (O.Fr. *assouagier.*)
assuagement, *n.* as-*swaje*-ment, the act of assuaging; mitigation; abatement.
assuasive, *a.* as-*sway*-ziv, softening; mitigating: *n.* a soothing medicine or agent.
assume, *v.t.* as-*sewm*, to take on; to take upon one's self; to arrogate; to take for granted; to appropriate; to admit; to affect: *v.i.* to be arrogant; to claim more than is due; to undertake [Law]. (L. *assūmo*, take up.)
assumed, *a.* as-*sewmd*, supposed; taken for granted; put on or usurped, as an assumed manner.
assuming, *a.* as-*sewm*-ing, arrogant; haughty: *n.* presumption; arrogance.
assumpsit, *n.* as-*sump*-sit, *or* as-*sum*-sit, an action to recover damages for a breach of contract, also an informal contract on which such an action may be brought [Law]. (L., literally, he undertook.)
assumption, *n.* as-*sump*-shon, the act of assuming; the thing assumed; a supposition, postulate, or proposition; the minor proposition in a categorical syllogism; the taking up a person into heaven; a festival in honour of the miraculous ascent of the Virgin Mary. (L. *assumptus*, adopted.)
assumptive, *a.* as-*sump*-tiv, that is or may be assumed; taken for granted; arrogant.
assumptively, *ad.* as-*sump*-tiv-le, in an assumptive manner.
assurable, *a.* a-*shoor*-a-bl, that may be assured or insured.
assurance, *n.* a-*shoor*-ance, the act of assuring; confidence; firmness of mind; intrepidity; impudence; legal evidence of the conveyance of property [Law]; insurance, or a contract to pay a given sum on a person's death. (Fr.)
assurant, *n.* a-*shoor*-ant, one who takes out an assurance policy.
assure, *v.t.* a-*shoor*, to make certain; to confirm; to give confidence to; to protest with assurance; to insure. (Fr. *assurer.*)
assured, *pp.* and *a.* a-*shoord*, certain; undoubting; confident; full of assurance.
assuredly, *ad.* a-*shoor*-ed-le, certainly.
assuredness, *n.* a-*shoord*-ness, the state of being assured; certainty.
assurer, *n.* a-*shoor*-er, an insurer or underwriter.
assurgent, *a.* as-*sur*-jent, rising in a curve or pointing upwards [Bot.]. (L. *assurgentis*, of rising up.)
assuringly, *ad.* a-*shoor*-ing-le, in a way to create confidence or assurance.
Assyrian, *a.* as-*si*-re-an, pertaining to Assyria: *n.* a native of Assyria.
Assyriologist, *n.* as-si-re-*ol*-o-jist, one versed in the antiquities and language of ancient Assyria.
Assyriology, *n.* as-si-re-*ol*-o-je, the study of the history, language, and religions of ancient Assyria.
astare, *ad.* a-*stayr*, staring.
astart, *ad.* a-*start*, suddenly.
astatic, *a.* ay-*stat*-ik, not remaining fixed; without polarity [Mag.]. (Gr. *astatos*, unstable.)
astay, *ad.* a-*stay*, said of the cable when in a line with the stays of the ship.
asteism, *n.* *ass*-te-izm, refined irony; polite and ingenious derision. (Gr. *asteïsmos*, witty talk.)
astel, *n.* *ass*-tel, an obstruction to hold up water or rubble in a mine. (O.Fr., splinter.)
aster, *n.* *ass*-ter, a composite plant of the large genus *Aster*. **China aster,** a species of *Callistephus*. (Gr., star.)
asteriated, *a.* ass-*teer*-re-ay-ted, radiated like a star.
asterisk, *n.* *ass*-ter-isk, the little star (*) used in printing to refer to a note, or to denote omission; *v.t.* to mark with this. (Gr. *asteriskos*, a small star.)
asterism, *n.* *ass*-ter-izm, a small cluster of stars; a constellation [Astron.]; in printing, a group of asterisks as ⁂ for drawing attention. (Gr. *asterismos*, marking with stars.)
astern, *ad.* a-*sturn*, in, at, or towards the hinder part of a ship; behind a ship.
asteroid, *n.* *ass*-ter-oyd, one of the minor planets between the orbits of Mars and Jupiter of which over 1,100 are known: *a.* starlike; resembling a starfish [Zool.] or a plant of the aster family [Bot.]. (Gr. *astero-eidēs*, starlike.)
asteroidal, *a.* ass-ter-*oyd*-al, asteroid.
asterolepis, *n.* *ass*-te-*rol*-e-pis, a fossil ganoid fish of the Old Red Sandstone [Geol.]. (Gr. *aster*, and *lepis*, a scale.)
asthenia, *n.* ass-the-*ny*-a *or* ass-*thee*-ne-a, lack of strength; loss of vitality; general debility [Med.]; in chickens, a disease characterized by emaciation. (Gr. *astheneia*, weakness.)
asthenic, *a.* ass-*then*-ik, feeble; without strength.
asthma, *n.* *ass*-ma *or* *asth*-ma, a chronic intermittent disorder of respiration, commonly attended with cough, wheezing, and constriction of the chest. (Gr., panting.)
asthmatic, *a.* ass-*mat*-ik, asthmatical.
asthmatical, *a.* ass-*mat*-e-kal, pertaining to asthma; affected by asthma.
astigmatic, *a.* as-tig-*mat*-ik, affected by, relating to, or characterized by, astigmatism.
astigmatism, *n.* a-*stig*-ma-tizm, a defect of vision due to the refracting surfaces of the eye not being spherical; a similar defect in optical apparatus. (Gr. *a*-, and *stigma*, a point.)
astir, *ad.* a-*stir*, in motion; stirring.
astomatous, *a.* a-*stom*-a-tus, without a mouth. (Gr. *astomos*, without a mouth.)
astomous, *a.* *ass*-to-mus, astomatous; denoting a moss in which the capsule is not dehiscent by an operculum [Bot.].
astonish, *v.t.* ass-*ton*-ish, to strike with sudden wonder or surprise; to amaze; to surprise. (O.Fr. *estoner*, to shock.)

astonishing, *a.* ass-*ton*-ish-ing, very wonderful; fitted to astonish.
astonishingly, *ad.* ass-*ton*-ish-ing-le, in an astonishing manner or degree.
astonishment, *n.* ass-*ton*-ish-ment, the state of being astonished; amazement; surprise; an object causing this.
astound, *v.t.* ass-*tound*, to astonish greatly; to strike dumb with amazement. (L.Lat. *extonare*, thunder out.)
astounding, *a.* ass-*tound*-ing, calculated to astound.
astraddle, *ad.* a-*strad*-dl, astride.
astragal, *n.* *ass*-tra-gal, a little moulding round the top or bottom of a column, in the form of a ring [Arch.]; a round moulding on cannon near the mouth. (Gr. *astragalos*, the ankle-bone.)
astragaloid, *a.* ass-*trag*-a-loyd, relating to the astragalus.
astragalus, *n.* ass-*trag*-a-lus, the ankle or sling-bone; the bone articulating with the tibia [Anat.]; a cosmopolitan genus of leguminous plants including the milk-vetches.
astrakhan, *n.* ass-tra-*kan*, lambskin with curled wool or an imitation of it, originally from Astrakhan.
astral, *a.* *ass*-tral, belonging to the stars; starry. **astral body,** a spirit; the immaterial counterpart of the physical body, which it normally survives [Theosophy]. **astral spirits,** an order of fallen beings conceived as infesting and controlling the stars; the inhabitants of the astral plane [Theosophy]. (L. *astrālis*, relating to stars.)
astray, *ad.* a-*stray*, out of the right way.
astrict, *v.t.* ass-*trikt*, to bind or confine; to constrict; to restrict [Scots Law].
astriction, *n.* ass-*trik*-shon, the act of binding close; a contraction of parts by applications; the stopping of hæmorrhages; constipation; binding a tenant of lands to grind at a particular mill [Scots Law]. (L. *astrictio*, astringency.)
astrictive, *a.* ass-*trikt*-iv, able to astrict; binding; styptic: *n.* an astringent.
astride, *ad.* a-*stride*, with the legs apart; astraddle.
astringe, *v.t.* ass-*trinj*, to press together; to constrict; to render costive. (L. *astringere*, draw tight.)
astringency, *n.* ass-*trinj*-en-se, the quality of being astringent; severity.
astringent, *a.* ass-*trinj*-ent, binding; contracting; strengthening, opposed to laxative; harsh; severe: *n.* a medicine that contracts the tissues and checks discharges [Med.]. (L. *astringens*, binding tight.)
astringently, *ad.* ass-*trinj*-ent-le, in an astringent manner.
astro-, *comb. f.* *ass*-tro-, pertaining to the stars. (Gr. *astron*, star.)
astrography, *n.* ass-*trog*-ra-fe, mapping the stars, or the art of describing them. (Gr. *astron*, a star, *grapho*, write).
astrolabe, *n.* *ass*-tro-labe, an instrument formerly used for taking the altitude of the sun or stars; a planisphere. (Gr. *astrolabon*, astrolabe.)
astrolatry, *n.* ass-*trol*-a-tre, the worship of the stars. (Gr. *astron*, and *latreia*, worship.)
astrologer, *n.* ass-*trol*-o-jer, one versed in astrology.
astrological, *a.* ass-tro-*loj*-e-kal, pertaining to, or practising astrology.
astrologically, *ad.* ass-tro-*loj*-e-ka-le, in the manner of astrology.
astrologize, *v.i.* and *t.* ass-*trol*-o-jize, to practise astrology; to apply astrology to.
astrology, *n.* ass-*trol*-o-je, a theory that the heavenly bodies have an occult influence on personal character, action, and destiny; the supposed art of foretelling future events by the situation and aspect of the stars; formerly, the science of astronomy. (Fr. *astrologie*.)
astrometer, *n.* ass-*trom*-e-ter, an instrument for testing the comparative brightness of the stars.
astrometry, *n.* ass-*trom*-et-re, the branch of astronomy which treats of the measurement of the ostensible magnitudes of the stars. (Gr. *astron*, and *metron*, measure.)
astronomer, *n.* ass-*tron*-o-mer, one versed in astronomy; a person engaged in observing the heavenly bodies. **Astronomer Royal,** the head of Greenwich Observatory. (L. *astronomia*, knowledge of the stars.)
astronomic, *a.* ass-tro-*nom*-ik, astronomical.
astronomical, *a.* ass-tro-*nom*-e-kal, pertaining to astronomy; enormously great (in number or extent) [Coll.]; **astronomical year,** *see* **year.**
astronomically, *ad.* ass-tro-*nom*-e-ka-le, in an astronomical manner; by the principles of astronomy.
astronomy, *n.* ass-*tron*-o-me, the science which treats of the celestial bodies, their positions, magnitudes, motions, and all relative phenomena. (Fr. *astronomie*.)
astro-photography, *n.* *ass*-tro-fo-*tog*-ra-fe, the science of taking photographs of stars and planets.
astro-physics, *n.* *ass*-tro-*fiz*-iks, the science treating of the physical composition and characteristics of the heavenly bodies.
astroscope, *n.* *ass*-tro-skope, an obsolete astronomical instrument on which the constellations were delineated. (Gr. *astroskopia*, study of the stars.)
astrut, *ad.* a-*strut*, in a strutting manner.
astute, *a.* ass-*tewt*, shrewd; penetrating; cunning; sagacious.
astutely, *ad.* ass-*tewt*-le, in an astute manner.
astuteness, *n.* ass-*tewt*-ness, the quality of being astute. (L. *astūtus*, clever.)
astylar, *a.* ay-*sty*-lar, columnless, without pilasters. (Gr. *astylos*, without prop.)
asunder, *ad.* a-*sun*-der, apart; into parts; separately. (A.S. *on-sundran*, apart.)
aswarm, *a.* and *ad.* a-*swawrm*, swarming.
asway, *a.* and *ad.* a-*sway*, swaying.
asylum, *n.* a-*sy*-lum, a sanctuary or place of refuge where a criminal or debtor might be free from arrest; any place of retreat and security; an institution for the care or relief of the dumb, blind, insane, or destitute. (L. *asylum*.)
asymmetrical, *a.* ay-sim-*met*-re-kal, without symmetry.
asymmetry, *n.* ay-*sim*-me-tre, the want of symmetry or proportion between the parts of anything. (Gr. *asymmetria*, inadequacy.)
asymptote, *n.* *as*-im-tote, a line approaching nearer and nearer to some curve, but not meeting it within a finite distance [Math.]. (Gr. *asumptōtos*, not close.)
asymptotical, *a.* as-simp-*tot*-e-kal, of the nature of an asymptote.
asynartete, *a.* a-*sin*-ar-teet, disconnected; used of sentences whose members are not united by connected particles, as, 'I came, I saw, I conquered' [Gram.], and of verses consisting of two members having different rhythms [Pros.]. (Gr. *asunartētos*, unconnected.)
asynchronism, *n.* ay-*sing*-kron-izm, a lack of concurrence in time; want of simultaneity. (Gr. *a-*, and *sunchronos*, contemporaneous.)
asynchronous, *a.* ay-*sing*-kro-nus, not synchronous; not coinciding in period.
asyndetic, *a.* *ass*-in-*det*-ik, relating to asyndeton.
asyndeton, *n.* a-*sin*-de-ton, a figure which omits the connective, as *veni, vidi, vici*, I came, I saw, I conquered [Rhet.]. (Gr. *asundētos*, unconnected.)
asyntactic, *a.* *ass*-in-*tak*-tik, or *ay*-sin-*tak*-tik, irregular; not grammatical. (Gr. *a-*, and *suntaktikos*, composing.)
asystole, *n.* a-*sis*-to-le, cessation of the contractile ability of the heart. (Gr. *a-*, and *systole*, contraction.)
★**at,** *prep.* at, denotes in general presence or nearness, but less definitely than in or on; also, towards, with, in, on, by, near by, in consequence of. (A.S. *æt*.)
atabal, *n.* *at*-a-bal, a Moorish kettledrum. (Sp.)
atacamite, *n.* a-*tak*-a-mite, a copper chloride occurring in greenish translucent crystals. (*Atacama*, Chile, where first found.)
ataghan, *n.* *at*-a-gan, a yataghan.
ataman, *n.* *at*-a-man, a Cossack chief or hetman [Rus.].
ataraxia, *n.* *at*-a-*rak*-se-ah, ataraxy.
ataraxy, *n.* *at*-a-*rak*-se, impassiveness; calmness of mind; stoicism. (Gr. *ataraxia*, coolness.)
ataunt, *ad.* a-*tawnt*, with all sails set [Naut.]. (Fr. *autant*, as much.)
atavism, *n.* *at*-a-vizm, tendency in offspring to return to ancestral type; resemblance in special features to remote ancestry; recurrence of an ancestral peculiarity in a remote descendant [Med.]. (L. *atavus*, an ancestor.)

atavistic, *a.* *at*-a-*vis*-tik, relating to atavism.
ataxia, *n.* a-*tak*-se-a, ataxy.
ataxic, *a.* a-*tak*-sik, irregular [Med.].
ataxy, *n.* a-*tak*-se, want of order; disorder; irregularity in the functions of the body or forms of a disease [Med.]. (Gr. *ataxia*, disorderliness.)
ate, et, the preterite of the verb *to eat.*
atelier, *n.* *at*-el-yay, a sculptor's or painter's studio or workshop. (Fr.)
athalamous, *a.* a-*thal*-a-mus, said of lichens whose thallus is without shields or beds for the spores [Bot.]. (Gr. *a*-, and *thalamos*, a marriage bed.)
athanasia, *n.* *ath*-an-*aysh*-e-a, immortality; without death. (Gr. immortality.)
Athanasian, *a.* ath-a-*nay*-shan, pertaining to St. Athanasius, bishop of Alexandria (4th cent.); *n.* one who espouses the doctrines of Athanasius. **Athanasian Creed,** a formulary of Christian faith, formerly ascribed to St. Athanasius.
athanasy, *n.* a-*than*-a-se, athanasia.
athanor, *n.* *ath*-an-or, a furnace employed by alchemists to keep up constant heat. (Sp.)
atheism, *n.* *ay*-the-izm, disbelief in the existence of a personal God; disbelief in any gods; godlessness.
atheist, *n.* *ay*-the-ist, a disbeliever in God or in the existence of gods; one who teaches or encourages atheism: *a.* atheistical. (Gr. *a-theos*, without God.)
atheistical, *a.* *ay*-the-*ist*-e-kal, pertaining to, implying, or containing atheism; impious.
atheistically, *ad.* *ay*-the-*ist*-e-ka-le, in an atheistical manner.
atheize, *v.t.* *ay*-the-ize, to render atheistic.
atheling, *n.* *ath*-el-ing, ætheling, an Anglo-Saxon nobleman; generally, the heir to an estate or to the Crown. (A.S., of noble birth.)
Athenæum, *n.* ath-en-*ee*-um, a temple in Athens, dedicated to Athene, frequented by scholars and poets for rehearsal of their works; an institution provided with library, lectureships, and appliances for the encouragement of literary and scientific culture. (*Athene*, the goddess of wisdom.)
Athenian, *a.* a-*thee*-ne-an, pertaining to Athens: *n.* a native or inhabitant of Athens.
atheology, *n.* ay-the-*ol*-o-je, opposition to theology.
atheous, *a.* *ay*-the-us, not recognizing, but not denying the possible existence of, a personal God.
Atherine, *n.* *ath*-e-rin, a genus of small fishes, *Atherirva*, allied to the mullet. (Gr. *atherinē*, smelt.)
athermancy, *n.* a-*ther*-man-se, non-conductivity.
athermanous, *a.* a-*ther*-man-us, not conducting heat. (Gr. *a*-, and *thermos*, heat.)
atheroma, *n.* ath-e-*roh*-ma, a disease of the arteries characterized by fatty degeneration of the inner coat. (Gr.)
atheromatous, *a.* ath-e-*roh*-ma-tus, pertaining to or of the nature of atheroma.
athirst, *a.* a-*thurst*, thirsty; wanting drink; eager. (A.S. *ofthyrsted*, having thirst.)
athlete, *n.* *ath*-leet. a competitior in physical sports; one having great strength of body, and trained to exercise it. (Gr. *athlētēs*, combatant.)
athletic, *a.* ath-*let*-ik, pertaining to contests in physical sports or to athletes; strong; robust; vigorous.
athletically, *ad.* ath-*let*-e-ka-le, in an athletic manner.
athleticism, *n.* ath-*let*-e-sizm, the practice of athletic exercises; devotion to athletics.
athletics, *n.pl.* ath-*let*-iks, physical exercises and outdoor sports and games that develop muscular strength; the practice of such.
at-home, *n.* at-*home*, a reception for guests.
athrob, *a.* a-*throb*, throbbing.
athwart, *prep.* a-*thwawrt*, across; transversely: *ad.* in a manner to cross and perplex.
atilt, *ad.* a-*tilt*, in the position or with the action of one thrusting; in the manner of a cask tilted.
Atlantean, *a.* at-lan-*tee*-an, pertaining to or resembling Atlas.
Atlantes, *n.pl.* at-*lan*-teez, figures of men, used instead of columns or pilasters, to support an entablature [Arch.]. (Gr.)
Atlantic, *a.* at-*lan*-tik, pertaining to the Atlantic Ocean: *n.* the ocean so called. (From Mt. *Atlas.*)
Atlantosaurus, *n.* at-*lan*-to-*saw*-rus, a genus of gigantic herbivorous lizards of the Upper Jurassic.
atlas, *n.* *at*-las, a collection of maps in a volume; a work in tabular form; a large-sized paper; the first vertebra of the neck, which supports the head atlas-wise [Anat.]. **atlas beetle,** the large olive-green beetle, *Chalcosoma atlas.* (*Atlas*, a Titan who was fabled to be gigantic and to bear the world on his shoulders.)
atmological, *a.* at-mo-*loj*-e-kal, belonging to atmology.
atmologist, *n.* at-*mol*-o-jist, an expert in atmology.
atmology, *n.* at-*mol*-o-je, the science which treats of vaporization and its phenomena. (Gr. *atmos*, vapour, *logos*, science.)
atmolysis, *n.* at-*mol*-e-sis, the separation of gases, or mixture of gases, into their constituents. (Gr. *atmos*, vapour, and *lysis*, unbinding.)
atmometer, *n.* at-*mom*-e-ter, an instrument to measure the quantity of exhalation from a humid surface in a given time; an evaporometer. (Gr. *atmos*, and *metron*, a measure.)
atmosphere, *n.* *at*-mos-feer, the air surrounding the earth; the air with which any body is surrounded; in painting, reproduction of atmospheric effect; a weight of 15 lb. to the square inch; a spiritual influence; moral environment. (Gr. *atmos*, and *sphaira*, a globe.)
atmospheric, *a.* at-mos-*fe*-rik, of or dependent on the atmosphere; existing in or of the nature of air: *n.pl.* noises due to electrical disturbances in the ether [Wire.]. **atmospheric engine,** an engine whose piston is driven up by steam, and down by pressure of the atmosphere.
atmospherically, *ad.* at-mos-*fe*-re-ka-le, by means of the air.
atoll, *n.* *at*-ol *or* a-*tol*, an island consisting of a ring-like reef of coral surrounding a central lagoon. (Malayan.)
atom, *n.* *at*-om, the smallest part of an element taking part in chemical action and preserving the properties of that element [Chem.]; a combination of a positively charged nucleus and a number of negatively charged electrons [Physics]; anything extremely small. (Gr. *atomos*, uncut.)
atomic, *a.* a-*tom*-ik, pertaining to or consisting of atoms; extremely minute. **atomic energy,** the force generated by the process of nuclear fission. **atomic number,** the number indicating individual position in a list of elements in order of their atomic weights [Chem.]. **atomic philosophy,** the ancient Epicurean doctrine that atoms are endued with gravity and motion, by which all things were formed. **atomic theory,** the doctrine that all chemical combinations take place between the ultimate particles of bodies, and that these unite, either atom with atom or in a proportion expressed by some simple multiple of the number of atoms [Chem.]. **atomic weight,** the relative weight of an atom of an element when an atom of oxygen equals 16.
atomicity, *n.* at-o-*miss*-e-te, the state of consisting of atoms; the number of atoms contained in a molecule; valency; the number of replaceable atoms in the molecule of a compound.
atomism, *n.* *at*-om-izm, the doctrine of atoms; the atomic philosophy.
atomist, *n.* *at*-om-ist, one who holds the atomic philosophy.
atomization, *n.* at-om-ize-*ay*-shon, the formation of a liquid into a spray [Med.].
atomize, *v.t.* *at*-om-ize, to reduce to atoms; to reduce a liquid to a very fine spray.
atomizer, *n.* *at*-om-ize-er, an apparatus that reduces liquids to a state of very fine subdivision; one who or that which atomizes.
atomy, *n.* *at*-o-me, a pigmy; midget; a skeleton.
atonable, *a.* a-*tone*-a-bl, fit for atonement; able to be expiated.
atone, *v.i.* a-*tone*, to make reparation, amends, or satisfaction for an offence or crime: *v.t.* to expiate or make amends for. (Mediæval Eng. *at*, and *one.*)
atonement, *n.* a-*tone*-ment, the act of atoning; reparation; expiation; the expiation of sin made by the sufferings of Christ [Theol.].
atonic, *a.* a-*ton*-ik, wanting tone [Med.]; unaccented [Gram.]: *n.* a soothing medicine [Med.]; an unaccented word [Gram.]. (Gr. *atonos*, feeble.)
atony, *n.* *at*-o-ne, debility; want of tone [Med.].
atop, *ad.* a-*top*, on or at the top.
atrabilarious, *a.* *at*-ra-bil-*ayr*-re-us, atrabiliar.
atrabiliar, *a.* at-tra-*bil*-yar, affected with melancholy, or a melancholic temperament; splenetic. (L. *ater*, black, *bilis*, bile.)

atrabiliary, *a.* at-ra-*bil*-ya-re, atrabiliar.
atrabilious, *a.* at-ra-*bil*-yus, pertaining to or affected by black bile; hypochondriacal; atrabiliar.
atramental, *a.* at-ra-*ment*-al, inky; black like ink. (L. *ātrāmentum*, any black fluid.)
atremble, *a.* a-*trem*-bl, trembling.
atrip, *ad.* a-*trip*, said of the anchor when it is just out of the ground, and of the sails when hoisted to the mast-head [Naut.].
atrium, *n.* *at*-re-um, the entrance hall and chief apartment in a Roman house; a fore-court; a cavity of the body, esp. the upper part of one of the auricles of the heart [Anat.]. (L.)
atrocious, *a.* a-*troh*-shus, extremely heinous, criminal, or cruel; horrible; outrageous; violent. (L. *atrox*, horribly cruel.)
atrociously, *ad.* a-*troh*-shus-le, in an atrocious manner.
atrociousness, *n.* a-*troh*-shus-ness, the quality of being atrocious.
atrocity, *n.* a-*tross*-e-te, horrible cruelty or wickedness; an atrocious act; barbarity.
atropal, *a.* *at*-ro-pal, atropous.
atrophic, *a.* a-*trof*-ik, pertaining to atrophy; atropous.
atrophied, *a.* *at*-ro-fid, caused by atrophy.
atrophy, *n.* *at*-ro-fe, wasting of a part through defective nutrition or disease [Med.]: *v.i.* to waste away. (Gr. *atrophis*, lack of food.)
atropine, *n.* *at*-ro-pin, a vegetable alkaloid extracted from deadly nightshade. *Atropa belladonna*. (Gr. *atropos*, intrepid, name of one of the three Fates.)
atropism, *n.* *at*-ro-pizm, a morbid state of the system due to misuse of atropine or belladonna.
atropous, *a.* *at*-ro-pus, unturned; remaining erect [Bot.]; characterized by atrophy. (Gr. *atropos*.)
attaboy, *int.* *at*-a-boy, an exclamation of encouragement, etc.; "Go to it!" [U.S.A., Slang.]
attach, *v.t.* at-*tatch*, to fasten on; to bind; to connect with; to lay hold on; to win or gain over; to arrest the person or lay hold of property by writ [Law]; to attribute. (O.Fr. *attacher*.)
attachable, *a.* at-*tatch*-a-bl, that may be attached.
attaché, *n.* at-*tash*-ay, one attached to an embassy, or in the suite of an ambassador. **attaché case**, a small travelling case for carrying papers and light articles.
attachment, *n.* at-*tatch*-ment, the act of attaching; that which attaches; the thing attached, or adjunct; adherence; fidelity; regard; affection; apprehension of person, goods, or estate by writ or precept in a civil action, to secure a debt or demand; a writ issued for this purpose [Law]. **foreign attachment**, seizure of the property of foreign or absent debtors for the satisfaction of creditors [Law].
★**attack,** *v.t.* at-*tak*, to fall upon with violence; to assault; to assail, so as to discredit and damage; to assail harmfully: *v.i.* to make an attack: *n.* the act of attacking; assault; falling on with violence; abuse, injury, or disease. (Fr. *attaquer*.)
attackable, *a.* at-*tak*-a-bl, that can be attacked.
attain, *v.i.* at-*tayn*, to reach; to arrive at: *v.t.* to reach, gain, or achieve by exertion an object, place, or position; to accomplish. (O.Fr. *ataindre*.)
attainability, *n.* at-*tayn*-a-*bil*-e-te, the quality of being attainable.
attainable, *a.* at-*tayn*-a-bl, that may be attained.
attainder, *n.* at-*tayn*-der, the act or process of attainting; the state of being attainted; deprivation of all civil rights and of the power to inherit or transmit property, consequent on a sentence of death or outlawry for treason or felony [Law].
attainment, *n.* at-*tayn*-ment, the act of attaining; that which is attained; an acquisition; an acquirement.
attaint, *v.t.* at-*taynt*, to subject to attainder; to taint; to disgrace; to stain or corrupt: *n.* attainder; formerly, the conviction, or process of conviction, of a jury for delivering a false verdict [Law]; a wound on a horse's leg [Vet.]. (O.Fr. *ateint*.)
attaintment, *n.* at-*taynt*-ment, attainture.
attainture, *n.* at-*taynt*-yur, attainder; the being attainted; dishonour.
attar, *n.* *at*-tar, perfume extracted from flowers; otto. (Ar. *'utūr*, scent.)
attemper, *v.t.* at-*tem*-per, to modify by mixture or heat; to soften or mollify; to mix in just proportion; to fit or make suitable. (O.Fr. *atempre*, to alter.)
attemperator, *n.* at-*tem*-pe-*ray*-tor, one who attempers; coiled piping through which hot and cold water may be run to regulate the temperature.
attemperment, *n.* at-*tem*-per-ment, tempering or due proportion; the state of being tempered.
★**attempt,** *v.t.* at-*tempt*, to try; to endeavour; to attack; to make trial of: *n.* an essay, trial, or endeavour; an effort to gain a point; an attack. (Fr. *attenter*.)
attemptability, *n.* at-tempt-a-*bil*-e-te, the quality of being attemptable.
attemptable, *a.* at-*tempt*-a-bl, that may be attempted, tried, or attacked; liable to an attempt.
attempter, *n.* at-*tempt*-er, one attempting; an attacker.
attend, *v.t.* at-*tend*, to accompany; to wait on; to be present at; to accompany as a consequence: *v.i.* to listen; to regard with attention; to be in attendance. (O.Fr. *atendre*, to wait upon.)
attendance, *n.* at-*tend*-ance, the act of attending; presence; service; the persons attending, a retinue.
attendant, *a.* at-*tend*-ant, accompanying as subordinate or consequential; depending on or owing service to [Law]: *n.* one who attends or accompanies; a personal servant; a paid companion.
attender, *n.* at-*tend*-er, an attendant; one paying attention to what is said.
★**attention,** *n.* at-*ten*-shon, the act of attending; heeding; regarding attentively; act of civility or courtesy: *pl.* acts of special regard. (L. *attentio*.)
attentive, *a.* at-*tent*-iv, heedful; intent; regardful.
attentively, *ad.* at-*tent*-iv-le, in an attentive manner.
attentiveness, *n.* at-*tent*-iv-ness, the state or quality of being attentive.
attenuant, *a.* at-*ten*-yew-ant, making thin; diluting: *n.* a medicine which thins the blood; a diluent.
attenuate, *v.t.* at-*ten*-yew-ate, to make thin; to dilute; to make slender; to refine away; *v.i.* to become thin or slender: *a.* thin or less viscid in consistency; made slender. (L. *attenuatus*, thinned.)
attenuated, *pp.* and *a.* at-*ten*-yew-ay-ted, made attenuate; growing slender towards the extremity.
attenuation, *n.* at-ten-yew-*ay*-shon, act of attenuating; state of being attenuated; diminution of thickness, density, force, etc.; weakening.
attenuator, *n.* at-*ten*-yew-ay-tor, a type of resistance control providing specified attenuation [Wire.].
attest, *v.t.* at-*test*, to bear witness to, especially officially; to certify; to call to witness; to invoke; to manifest; to enrol for military service: *v.i.* to bear witness. (L. *attesto*, witness.)
attestable, *a.* at-*test*-a-bl, capable of being borne witness to.
attestation, *n.* at-tes-*tay*-shon, the act of attesting or certifying as a witness or officially the administration of an oath; formal verification.
attestor, *n.* at-*test*-or, one who attests or bears testimony; a witness.
Attic, *a.* *at*-tik, pertaining to Attica, or to its principal city, Athens: *n.* a native of Attica; the Attic dialect of Greek; (*l.c.*) a low story erected over an entablature or cornice and having neither capital nor base [Arch.]; the top story of a house, or a room in it; a garret. **Attic base**, a base consisting of an upper torus, a scotia, and lower torus, with fillets between them, used in the Ionic order and sometimes in the Doric [Arch.]. **Attic dialect**, the Greek dialect spoken by the ancient Athenians. **Attic faith**, inviolable faith. **Attic order**, an order of small square pillars at the uppermost extremity of a building [Arch.]. **Attic style**, a pure, classical and elegant style. **Attic wit** or **salt**, poignant, delicate wit, such as the Athenians were famous for. (Gr. *Attikos*, Attic.)
Atticism, *n.* *at*-te-sizm, the peculiar style and idiom of the Greek language used by the Athenians; refined and elegant Greek; a concise and elegant expression; partiality for Athens or for the Athenians.
Atticize, *v.t.* *at*-te-size, to make conformable to the language or idiom of Attica: *v.i.* to use Atticisms, or the idiom of the Athenians; to side with the Athenians.

attire, *v.t.* at-*tire*, to dress; to array; to adorn with elegant or splendid apparel: *n.* dress; clothes; headdress; the horns of a stag, etc. [Her.]. (O.Fr. *atirer*, to dress up.)
attired, *a.* at-*tired*, provided with horns or antlers [Her.].
attitude, *n.* *at*-te-tewd, the posture, bodily or mental; bearing; gesture; posture of things as well as persons as possessing significance. (It. *attitudine*, skill.)
attitudinal, *a.* at-te-*tew*-din-al, pertaining to attitude.
attitudinarian, *n.* *at*-te-tew-din-*ayr*-re-an, one who affects attitudes; a poseur.
attitudinize, *v.i.* at-te-*tew*-din-ize, to assume affected attitudes or airs; to pose.
attollent, *a.* at-*tol*-lent, that raises or lifts up: *n.* a muscle which raises some part, as the upper eyelid [Anat.]. (L. *attollens*, lifting.)
attorn, *v.i.* at-*turn*, to assign; to transfer homage to a new possessor [Feud. Law]. (O.Fr. *atorner*, to turn.)
attorney, *n.* at-*turn*-e, one legally qualified to manage matters in law for others; a solicitor; an agent or factor. **Attorney-General,** in Britain, the official head of the Bar, a member of the Government, and chief Law Officer of the Crown, which he represents in the courts. **letter, power,** or **warrant of attorney,** a formal written authority by which one authorizes another to transact business for him.
attorneyship, *n.* at-*turn*-e-ship, the office of an attorney; agency for another.
attornment, *n.* at-*turn*-ment, the act of a feudatory vassal or tenant, by which he consents, on the alienation of an estate, to receive the new lord as superior.
attract, *v.t.* at-*trakt*, to draw to or cause to approach; to draw by influence of a moral kind; to allure; to entice: *v.i.* to have power to attract. (L. *attractus*, draw to.)
attractability, *n.* at-*trakt*-a-*bil*-e-te, the quality of being attractable.
attractable, *a.* at-*trakt*-a-bl, that may be attracted; subject to attraction.
attractile, *a.* at-*trakt*-ile, able to attract.
★**attraction,** *n.* at-*trak*-shon, the power or act of attracting; an attracting quality or attractive thing; the force inherent in particles of matter by which they are drawn towards each other and resist separation [Physics].
attractive, *a.* at-*trakt*-iv, having the quality or power of attracting; alluring.
attractively, *ad.* at-*trakt*-iv-le, in an attractive manner.
attractiveness, *n.* at-*trakt*-iv-ness, the quality of being attractive.
attractor, *n.* at-*trakt*-or, that which attracts.
attrahent, *a.* *at*-tra-hent, drawing to or attracting: *n.* that which draws to. (L. *attrahens*, attracting.)
attributable, *a.* at-*trib*-yew-ta-bl, that may be attributed.
attribute, *v.t.* at-*trib*-yewt, to ascribe, impute, or assign, as belonging or due. (L. *attributus*, assigned.)
attribute, *n.* *at*-tre-bewt, that which is attributed as a property or a characteristic; an adjective [Gram.]; a symbol of office or character, as the trident of Neptune, the club of Hercules [Paint. and Sculp.].
attribution, *n.* at-tre-*bew*-shon, the act of attributing; the quality ascribed; commendation.
attributive, *a.* at-*trib*-yew-tiv, pertaining to or expressing an attribute: *n.* the thing attributed; a word significant of an attribute, as an adjective, verb or participle [Gram.]
attributively, *ad.* at-*trib*-yew-tiv-le, as an adjective, and not as a predicate [Gram.].
attrite, *a.* at-*trite*, worn by friction; penitent only through fear of punishment [Theol.]. (L. *attrītus*, worn off.)
attrited, *a.* at-*try*-ted, worn down by attrition.
attriteness, *n.* at-*trite*-ness, the being much worn.
attrition, *n.* at-*trish*-on, abrasion; the act of rubbing down; the state of being rubbed down; penitence arising only from fear of punishment. (L.)
attritus, *n.* at-*try*-tus, material produced by erosion or abrasion.
attune, *v.t.* at-*tewn*, to tune; to adjust one sound to another; to make accordant.

atween, *ad.* a-*tween*, atwixt; between whiles.
atwixt, *ad.* a-*twikst*, between or betwixt.
atypic, *a.* ay-*tip*-ik, of no special type; irregular.
aubade, *n.* o-*bahd*, a daybreak serenade; a musical composition for performance in the morning; a concert before noon. (Fr.)
auberge, *n.* o-*bairzh*, an inn; a road-house. (Fr.)
aubergiste, *n.* o-bair-*zheest*, a keeper of an auberge.
aubergine, *n.* o-bair-*zheen*, the egg plant, *Solanum melongena*, or its fruit.
aubrietia, *n.* oh-*bree*-shya, a hardy evergreen trailer of the order *Cruciferæ*, with purplish flowers.
auburn, *a.* *aw*-burn, reddish or golden brown. (O.Fr. *auborne*.)
auction, *n.* *awk*-shon, a public sale of property to the highest bidder, by a person licensed for the purpose; a card game (also called **auction bridge**) in which the players bid for the privilege of naming trumps; the bidding for this privilege in bridge, auction, or contract. **candle auction,** one at which bids are accepted only as long as a lighted candle-end remains alight. **Dutch auction,** a sale at which property is offered above its value and the price is gradually lowered till someone takes it. (L. *auctio*, auction.)
auctionary, *a.* *awk*-shon-a-re, belonging to an auction.
auctioneer, *n.* awk-shon-*eer*, one licensed to sell property by public sale; the manager of an auction.
auctorial, *a.* awk-*taw*-re-al, relating to an author.
audacious, *a.* aw-*day*-shus, daring; impudent; implying effrontery. (L. *audax*, bold.)
audaciously, *ad.* aw-*day*-shus-le, in an audacious manner.
audaciousness, *n.* aw-*day*-shus-ness, the quality of being audacious.
audacity, *n.* aw-*dass*-e-te, boldness; daring; impudence; effrontery.
audibility, *n.* *awd*-e-bil-e-te, audibleness.
audible, *a.* *awd*-e-bl, that may be heard; loud enough to be heard. (Late L. *audibilis*.)
audibleness, *n.* *awd*-e-bl-ness, the quality of being audible.
audibly, *ad.* *awd*-e-ble, in an audible manner.
audience, *n.* *awd*-e-ence, the act of hearing; admittance to a hearing or a formal interview; an assembly of hearers; those addressed either by the spoken or the printed word.
audient, *a.* *awd*-e-ent, recognizing sound; listening.
audile, *a.* *awd*-ile, pertaining to the auditory nerves; received by way of hearing: *n.* one who relies chiefly on hearing for outside contacts.
audiometer, *n.* awd-e-*om*-e-ter, an instrument for testing the sense of hearing, or for measuring the intensity of sound. (L. *audio*, hear, Gr. *metron*, measure.)
audiphone, *n.* *awd*-e-fone, an instrument which, when pressed against the teeth, conveys sound waves to the auditory nerve and enables the deaf to hear. (L. *audio*, hear, Gr. *phone*, sound.)
audit, *n.* *awd*-it, an authorized examination of accounts; a statement of account; a final account: *v.t.* to examine and adjust accounts. **audit ale,** a special ale brewed for use at Oxford and Cambridge colleges. **Commissioner of Audit, a** commissioner having cognizance of the public accounts. (L. *auditus*, listening.)
audit-house, *n.* *awd*-it-house, an annex to a cathedral for the transaction of its business.
audition, *n.* awd-*ish*-on, the act or faculty of hearing; a performance (esp. for stage, broadcasting, etc.) as a test of competency. (L. *auditio*, a hearing.)
auditive, *a.* *awd*-it-iv, pertaining to hearing.
auditor, *n.* *awd*-it-or, a member of an audience; one appointed to audit accounts. (L. *audītor*.)
auditorial, *a.* *aw*-de-*taw*-re-al, auditory; pertaining to an audit.
auditorium, *n.* aw-de-*taw*-re-um, the part of a public building in which an audience assembles, as in a theatre; a hall or building used for public gatherings. (L.)
auditorship, *n.* *awd*-it-or-ship, the profession of an auditor.
auditory, *a.* *aw*-de-to-re, pertaining to the sense or organs of hearing: *n.* an audience or assembly of hearers; a place for hearing.
Augean, *a.* aw-*jee*-an, full of accumulated filth;

arduous and toilsome. (*Augeas*, mythic king of Elis, the cleansing of whose stables was effected when Hercules turned the river Alpheus into them.)

auger, *n.* *awg*-er, a tool used by carpenters for boring large holes; an instrument for boring rocks. (A.S. *nafu*, nave of a wheel, *gar*, borer.)

aught, *n.* awt, anything; a jot or tittle: *ad.* at all; in any way. (A.S. *āht*.)

augite, *n.* *aw*-jite, a greenish-black aluminous silicate of calcium, iron, and magnesium occurring in volcanic rocks; a variety of pyroxene [Min.]. (L. *augites*, a precious stone.)

augitic, *a.* aw-*jit*-ik, pertaining to, resembling or composed of augite.

augment, *v.t.* awg-*ment*, to make large; to increase; to prefix an argument [Gram.]; to make an augmentation to (a coat of arms) (Her.]: *v.i.* to grow larger; to increase. (Fr. *augmenter*.)

augment, *n.* *awg*-ment, increase; a syllable prefixed to a word or an increase of the quantity of the initial vowel [Gram.].

augmentable, *a.* awg-*ment*-a-bl, that may be augmented.

augmentation, *n.* awg-men-*tay*-shon, the act of augmenting; the state of being augmented; addition, or thing added; increasing the time-value of the notes of the subject of a fugue or canon [Mus.]; an honourable addition to a coat of arms [Her.]. **Augmentation Court,** a court erected by Henry VIII to deal with confiscated Church property on the suppression of the monasteries. **process of augmentation,** action at the instance of a parish clergyman for increase of stipend [Scots Law].

augmentative, *a.* awg-*ment*-a-tiv, having the quality or power of augmenting: *n.* an affix intensifying or enlarging the meaning, opposite of diminutive [Gram.].

augmented, *a.* awg-*ment*-ed, increased, added to; made wider by a semitone (of intervals) [Mus.].

augmenter, *n.* awg-*ment*-er, he who or that which augments.

augur, *n.* *aw*-gur, among the Romans a priest or official who foretold future events by observing the actions of birds and by other signs or omens; a soothsayer: *v.i.* to conjecture from signs or omens; to forebode: *v.t.* to foretell by signs. (L.)

augural, *a.* *aw*-gew-ral, pertaining to augury; presaging; betokening the future.

augurial, *a.* *aw*-gewr-re-al, augural.

augurship, *n.* *aw*-gur-ship, the office of augur.

augury, *n.* *aw*-gew-re, the art or practice of auguring an omen; divination; prognostication.

August, *n.* *aw*-gust, the eighth month of the year, named in honour of the Emperor Augustus.

august, *a.* aw-*gust*, grand; majestic; inspiring awe or reverence. (L. *augutus*, honoured.)

Augustan, *a.* aw-*gus*-tan, under the Emperor Augustus, as, the Augustan age; distinguished by refined and brilliant literary activity; pertaining to Augsburg (Augusta Vindelicorum), Bavaria. **Augustan confession,** a statement of Protestant doctrine drawn up at Augsburg (Augusta Vindelicorum) by Luther and Melancthon in 1530.

Augustinian, *a.* aw-gus-*tin*-e-an, pertaining to St. Augustine the Great, his order, or his teaching: *n.* a member of the black habited order of monks following his doctrines and rules, an Austin Canon or Austin Friar; one holding his doctrines.

augustly, *ad.* aw-*gust*-le, in a majestic way.

augustness, *n.* aw-*gust*-ness, the quality of being august.

auk, *n.* awk, a web-footed sea-bird (genus, *Alca*) with rudimentary wings, found in the northern hemisphere. (Scand.)

aularian, *n.* aw-*lare*-re-an, a member of a university hall as distinguished from a member of a college: *a.* appertaining to a hall. (L. *aula*, a court, a hall.)

auld, *a.* awld, old. **auld lang syne,** bygone days. (Scots.)

aulic, *a.* *aw*-lik, pertaining to a royal court. **Aulic council,** the privy council of the Holy Roman emperor.

aumbry, *n.* *awm*-bre, an ambry.

aunt, *n.* ahnt, the sister of one's father or mother, or the wife of an uncle. **Aunt Sally,** a game in which a bludgeon is thrown at the head of a figure to smash a pipe out of its mouth. (O.Fr. *aunte*.)

aura, *n.* *aw*-ra, the peculiar sensation premonitory to an attack of epilepsy, hysteria, etc. [Med.]; any subtle, invisible emanation from a body or substance; a saint's or angel's halo; an electrical influence proceeding from or surrounding an electrified body. (L. *aura*, a wafting breeze.)

aural, *a.* *aw*-ral, pertaining to an aura.

aural, *a.* *aw*-ral, pertaining to the ear or to hearing. (L. *auris*, the ear.)

aurate, *n.* *aw*-rate, a salt of auric acid [Chem.].

aurated, *a.* *aw*-ra-ted, resembling or containing gold; gilded. (L. *aureātus*, decorated with gold.)

aureate, *a.* *aw*-re-ate, aurate; glittering.

aurelia, *n.* aw-*ree*-le-a, a chrysalis. (It. *aurelio*, golden.)

aurelian, *a.* aw-*ree*-le-an, like or pertaining to an aurelia; golden: *n.* an entomologist.

aureola, *n.* aw-*ree*-o-la, the gold disk with which early painters surrounded the head of Christ, the Virgin, and the saints; a nimbus. (L. *aureolus*, golden.)

aureole, *n.* *aw*-re-ohl, a halo surrounding the sun or moon; an aureola.

aureoled, *a.* *aw*-re-ohld, furnished with an aureole.

auric, *a.* *aw*-rik, pertaining to gold; denoting a compound in which gold is trivalent [Chem.].

auricle, *n.* *aw*-re-kl, the external ear, or that part which is prominent from the head: *pl.* two muscular cavities of the heart situated above the ventricles. (L. *auricula*, the ear-lap.)

auricled, *a.* *aw*-re-kid, having auricles, or ear-like appendages.

auricula, *n.* aw-*rik*-yew-la, a species of *Primula*, called, from the shape of its leaves, bear's ear. (L.)

auricular, *a.* aw-*rik*-yew-lar, pertaining to the ear, or to the sense of hearing; confided to the ear; known by hearsay; pertaining to the auricles of the heart: *n.pl.* the feathers covering the ear-opening in birds.

auricularly, *ad.* aw-*rik*-yew-lar-le, in an auricular manner; by way of whisper; secretly.

auriculate, *a.* aw-*rik*-yew-lat, ear-shaped; having ear-like appendages; eared.

auriferous, *a.* aw-*rif*-er-us, gold-bearing. (L.)

auriform, *a.* *aw*-re-form, ear-shaped. (L.)

Aurignacian, *a.* aw-rig-*nay*-she-an, denoting the culture of the earlier Upper Palæolithic period, first studied at Aurignac in Southern France.

auriscope, *n.* *aw*-ris-kope, an instrument for examining the ear passages. (L. *auris*, and Gr. *skope*, view.)

aurist, *n.* *aw*-rist, one skilled in disorders of the ear.

aurited, *a.* *aw*-re-ted, having lobes or appendages like the ear [Zool. and Bot.].

aurochs, *n.* *aw*-roks, the extinct wild ox; the European bison. (Gr.)

Aurora, *n.* aw-*raw*-ra, dawn; the rising light of the morning. **Aurora borealis,** a luminous phenomenon in northern latitudes usually appearing in streams of light ascending towards the zenith from a dusky line a few degrees above the horizon; the northern lights or streamers. **Aurora australis,** a corresponding phenomenon in southern latitudes. (L., the goddess of the morning.)

auroral, *a.* aw-*raw*-ral, pertaining to the dawn or to the aurora or northern lights; roseate.

aurulent, *a.* *aw*-roo-lent, of a golden colour. (L. *aurulentus*, of gold-colour.)

aurous, *a.* *aw*-rus, pertaining to or containing gold.

aurum, *n.* *aw*-rum, gold (as the chemical element). **aurum fulminans,** fulminating gold, an explosive powder produced by the action of ammonia on gold oxide. (L.)

auscultate, *v.t.* *aws*-kul-tate, to test or examine by means of auscultation [Med.].

auscultation, *n.* aws-kul-*tay*-shon, the act of listening; a method of diagnosis, by observing the sounds made by internal organs, either directly or by means of a stethoscope [Med.]. (L. *auscultatus*, a hearing.)

auscultator, *n.* *aws*-kul-*tay*-tor, one who practises auscultation.

auscultatory, *a.* aws-*kul*-ta-to-re, pertaining to auscultation.

auspex, *n.* *aw*-speks, in ancient Rome one who took the auspices. (L., bird-observer.)

auspicate, *v.t.* *aw*-spe-kate, to inaugurate formally; to foreshow: *v.i.* to predict; to augur. (L. *auspicatus*, consecrated by auguries.)

auspice, *n.* *aw*-spis, an omen drawn from the movements of birds or otherwise; augury; protection; patronage; influence (generally in the plural). (L. *auspicium*, divination from birds.)

auspicious, *a.* aw-*spish*-us, having omens of success, or favourable appearances; fortunate; propitious.

auspiciously, *ad.* aw-*spish*-us-le, in an auspicious manner; with favourable omens.

auspiciousness, *n.* aw-*spish*-us-ness, state of being auspicious, or of fair promise.

Aussie, *n.* *aw*-se, an Australian, esp. an Australian soldier [Slang].

auster, *n.* *aws*-ter, the south wind. (L.)

austere, *a.* aw-*steer*, severe; harsh; rigid; stern; sour; rough to the taste; unadorned; strictly true to fact and nature. (L. *austērē*, rigidly.)

austerely, *ad.* aw-*steer*-le, in an austere manner.

austereness, *n.* aw-*steer*-ness, the quality of being austere.

austerity, *n.* aw-*ste*-re-te, severity of manner or life; rigour; strictness; harsh discipline; lack of adornment. (Fr. *austérité*.)

Austral, *a.* *aws*-tral, southern; pertaining to the south; lying or being in the south. **Austral signs,** the six signs of the zodiac south of the equator. (L. *austrālis*, southern.)

Australasian, *a.* *aws*-tra-*laysh*-an, pertaining to Australasia, *i.e.*, Australia, New Zealand, and the adjacent islands: *n.* an inhabitant of Australasia.

Australian, *a.* aws-*trale*-yan, pertaining to Australia: *n.* a native of Australia.

Austrian, *a.* *aws*-tre-an, pertaining to Austria: *n.* a native of Austria.

autarch, *n.* *aw*-tark, a tyrant or autocrat.

autarchy, *n.* *aw*-tar-ke, autocracy; absolute sovereignty. (Gr. *autarchia*.)

autarky, *n.* *aw*-tar-ke, self-sufficiency; government without external control. (Ger. *autarkie*, from Gk. *autarchia*.)

authentic, *a.* aw-*then*-tik, having a genuine origin or authority; being what it professes to be; genuine; true; of approved authority, and reliable; vested with all due formalities, and legally attested [Law]. **authentic melodies,** such as have their principal notes contained between the key-note and its octave [Mus.]. (O.Fr. *autentique*.)

authentically, *ad.* aw-*then*-te-ka-le, in an authentic manner.

authenticalness, *n.* aw-*then*-te-kal-ness, the quality of being authentic.

authenticate, *v.t.* aw-*then*-te-kate, to render authentic; to give authority to by the necessary formalities; to determine as genuine. (L. *authenticus*, genuine.)

authentication, *n.* *aw*-then-te-*kay*-shon, the act of authenticating.

authenticity, *n.* aw-then-*tiss*-e-te, the quality of being authentic; genuineness.

author, *n.* *aw*-thor, one who produces, creates or brings into being; the beginner, or first mover; the cause; the writer or composer of a literary work. (O.Fr. *autor*.)

authoress, *n.* *aw*-tho-ress, a female author.

authorial, *a.* aw-*thaw*-re-al, of or pertaining to an author.

authorism, *n.* *aw*-tho-rizm, the specific character or practice of authorship.

authoritarian, *a.* *aw*-tho-re-*tayr*-re-an, pertaining to or advocating the principle of obedience to authority as opposed to individual liberty: *n.* an adherent of this principle.

authoritarianism, *n.* *aw*-tho-re-*tayr*-re-a-nizm, authoritarian principles.

authoritative, *a.* aw-*tho*-re-tay-tiv, having due authority; having an air of authority; dictatorial.

authoritatively, *ad.* aw-*tho*-re-tay-tiv-le, in an authoritative manner.

authoritativeness, *n.* aw-*tho*-re-tay-tiv-ness, the quality of being authoritative.

★**authority,** *n.* aw-*tho*-re-te, legal power, or a right to command or to act; one or, in the plural, people, invested with this power; power, weight, or influence derived from rank, office, character, age, or experience; precedent, or official declaration; a recognized expert, or a standard work or reference. (Fr. *autorité*.)

authorizable, *a.* *aw*-tho-*rize*-a-bl, that can be authorized.

authorization, *n.* *aw*-tho-ry-*zay*-shon, the act of authorizing; establishment by authority.

authorize, *v.t.* *aw*-tho-rize, to give authority to; to empower; to make legal; to establish by authority; to justify. **Authorized Version** of the Bible, that published in 1611. (Fr. *autoriser*.)

authorless, *a.* *aw*-thor-less, anonymous.

authorship, *n.* *aw*-thor-ship, the quality or state of being an author; literary work.

auto, *n.* *aw*-toh, an automobile, motor-car [Amer.].

auto-, *pref.* signifying self, done from within, independently (Gr. *autos*, self.)

autobahn, *n.* *aw*-to-bahn, a highway in Germany designed for fast motor traffic; an arterial road. (Ger.).

autobiographer, *n.* *aw*-to-by-*og*-ra-fer, one who writes an account of his own life.

autobiographical, *a.* *aw*-to-by-o-*graf*-e-kal, pertaining to, or containing, autobiography.

autobiography, *n.* *aw*-to-by-*og*-ra-fe, the memoirs of one's life written by oneself. (Gr. *autos*, self, and *biography*.)

autocar, *n.* *aw*-to-kar, a motor-car.

autocarpous, *a.* aw-to-*karp*-us, consisting of pericarp only [Bot.]. (Gr. *autos*, and *karpos*, fruit.)

autocephalous, *a.* aw-to-*sef*-a-lus, self-governing or independent—used of the Eastern Churches having the same communion but no central common authority. (Gr., independent.)

autochthon, *n.* aw-*tok*-thon, one of the earliest known inhabitants; in ancient Greece a member of a race supposed to be indigenous; that which is original to a particular country. (Gr. *autochthōn*, raised from the soil itself.)

autochthonal, *a.* aw-*tok*-thon-al, autochthonous.

autochthonic, *a.* aw-tok-*thon*-ik, autochthonous.

autochthonous, *a.* aw-*tok*-thon-us, native to the soil; native where first discovered.

autoclave, *n.* *aw*-to-klave, a cooking-vessel with tight-fitting cover to prevent entrance of steam; a vessel for sterilizing or for heating liquids under pressure. (Gr. *auto-*, and L. *clavis*, key.)

autocracy, *n.* aw-*tok*-ra-se, independent power; supreme, uncontrolled authority, or right of governing, vested in a single person.

autocrat, *n.* *aw*-to-krat, an absolute ruler; a title of the Tsars as Autocrats of all the Russias. (Gr. *autokrateia*, absolute rule.)

autocratic, *a.* aw-to-*krat*-ik, autocratical.

autocratical, *a.* aw-to-*krat*-e-kal, pertaining to autocracy; absolute.

autocratically, *ad.* aw-to-*krat*-e-ka-le, in an autocratic manner.

autocratrix, *n.* aw-*tok*-ra-triks, a female absolute sovereign.

auto-cycle, *n.* *aw*-to-*sy*-kl, a motor-cycle.

auto-da-fé, *n.* *aw*-to-da-fay (*pl.* **autos-da-fé,** *aw*-tose-da-fay), a solemn ceremony of the mediæval Inquisition preliminary to the execution of a heretic; the sentence pronounced and read to the criminal; the burning of a heretic. (Port., action for the faith.)

autodyne, *n.* *aw*-to-dyn, a type of heterodyne in which the current is developed in the rectifier [Wire.].

autogamy, *n.* aw-*tog*-a-me, self-fertilization.

autogenous, *a.* aw-*toj*-e-nus, self-begotten; generating itself. (Gr. *autos*, self, *gennao*, beget.)

autogeny, *n.* aw-*toj*-e-ne, self-generation.

autogiro, *n.* aw-to-*jyr*-ro, proprietary name of an early form of rotaplane, the Cierva Autogiro.

autograph, *n.* *aw*-to-graf, a person's own handwriting: *v.t.* to write with one's own hand; to sign; to reproduce by autography. (Gr. *autos*, and *grapho*, write.)

autographic, *a.* aw-to-*graf*-ik, pertaining to an autograph; pertaining to, or used in, autography; self-recording.

autographical, *a.* aw-to-*graf*-e-kal, autographic.

autography, *n.* aw-*tog*-ra-fe, writing with one's own hands; a person's own handwriting; an autograph; a process by which a writing or drawing is lithographically reproduced.

autogravure, *n.* aw-to-gra-*voor*, a variety of photographic engraving, or photo-etching.

autogyro, *n.* aw-to-*jyr*-ro, autogiro.

autoharp, *n.* aw-to-harp, proprietary name of a zither-like instrument having mechanical compound dampers [Mus.].

auto-intoxication, *n.* *aw*-to-in-tok-se-*kay*-shon, poisoning by toxic matter produced within the body.

autolatry, *n.* aw-*tol*-a-tre, worship of oneself. (Gr. *autos*, and *latreia*, worship.)

autology, *n.* aw-*tol*-o-je, the scientific study of oneself. (Gr. *autos*, and *logos*, science.)
autolysis, *n.* aw-*tol*-e-sis, the destruction of cellular tissue by the action of self-generated ferments [Zool. and Bot.].
autolytic, *a.* aw-to-*lit*-ik, of, or of the nature of, autolysis.
automata, *n.pl.* aw-*tom*-a-ta, automatons.
★**automatic,** *a.* aw-to-*mat*-ik, self-acting; moving of itself from within; acting involuntarily (of physical functions); purely mechanical: *n.* a quick-firing pistol [Slang].
automatically, *ad.* aw-*to-mat*-e-ka-le, in a self-acting manner; spontaneously.
automatism, *n.* au-*tom*-a-tizm, the quality of being automatic; automatic or unconscious action; the theory that action does not depend on consciousness [Phil.].
automatist, *n.* aw-*tom*-a-tist, one who upholds the theory of automatism [Phil.]; one who does automatic writing [Spiritualism].
automaton, *n.* aw-*tom*-a-ton (*pl.* **automatons** *or* **automata**), a self-moving figure, esp. one that imitates the action of a living body; any machine mechanically self-acting, like a watch. (L. *automatus*, self-acting.)
automatous, *a.* aw-*tom*-a-tus, acting spontaneously; having the power of motion within itself.
autometry, *n.* aw-*tom*-e-tre, self-estimation.
automobile, *n.* aw-to-mo-*beel*, a motor-car.
automobilism, *n.* aw-to-*moh*-be-lizm, the art and practice of using motor-cars; the acts and methods of those who use motor-cars.
automobilist, *n.* aw-to-*moh*-be-list, a motorist.
automorphic, *a.* aw-to-*mor*-fik, characterized by automorphism; after one's own image.
automorphism, *n.* *aw*-to-*mor*-fizm, ascribing to another the personal characteristics of oneself. (Gr. *autos*, and *morphe*, shape.)
autonomic, *a.* aw-to-*nom*-ik, pertaining to or possessing autonomy.
autonomist, *n.* aw-*ton*-o-mist, a believer in or advocate of autonomy. (Fr.)
autonomous, *a.* aw-*ton*-o-mus, under self-government; independent; autonomic.
autonomy, *n.* aw-*ton*-o-me, the power or right of self-government; an independent community; freedom of will; the living according to one's own law, according to right of reason as sovereign [Meta.]. (Gr. *autonomia*, freedom.)
autonym, *n.* *aw*-to-nim, a surname as contrasted with a pseudonym; a work published under the author's true name. (Gr. *autos*, and *onoma*, name.)
autophagi, *n.pl.* aw-*tof*-a-jy, birds that can feed themselves as soon as hatched. (Gr. *autophagos*, self-feeding.)
autophoby, *n.* aw-*tof*-o-be, dislike of being mentioned or of referring to oneself. (Gr. *autos*, and *phobos*, fear.)
autoplastic, *a.* *aw*-to-*plas*-tik, relating to autoplasty.
autoplasty, *n.* *aw*-to-plas-te, reparation of a lesion from an adjoining healthy part [Surg.]. (Gr. *autoplastos*, self-formed.)
autoplate, *n.* *aw*-to-plate, a machine for producing curved stereotype plates for rotary presses; a plate so produced [Print.].
autopsy, *n.* aw-*top*-se, or *aw*-top-se, dissection of a corpse to learn the cause of death; a post-mortem. (Gr. *autopsia*, seeing with one's own eyes.)
autoptical, *a.* aw-*top*-te-kal, seen with one's own eyes.
autoptically, *ad.* aw-*top*-te-ka-le, by one's own observation.
autoschediasm, *n.* aw-to-*skee*-de-azm, an impromptu; anything done without previous thought or preparation. (Gr. *autoschediasma*, an impromptu.)
autosome, *n.* *aw*-to-sohm, a chromosome being one of a pair of the same sex [Biol.].
auto-suggestion, *n.* *aw*-to-suj-*jest*-yon, suggestion to one's self as compared with suggestion emanating from another, esp. in hypnotism.
autotheism, *n.* *aw*-to-*thee*-izm, the worship or deification of oneself.
autotomy, *n.* aw-*tot*-o-me, the act of deliberately parting with limbs; the protective shedding of a part or organ; cell-division [Biol.]. (Gk. *autos*, self, *tome*, a cutting.)
autotoxæmia, *n.* *aw*-to-tok-*see*-me-a, auto-intoxication.
autotoxik, *a.* aw-to-tok-sik, producing or caused by an autotoxin.
autotoxin, *n.* *aw*-to-*tok*-sin, toxin produced by alteration of the tissues in the body.
autotype, *n.* *aw*-to-type, a process in photography for producing pictures in monochrome; a facsimile: *v.t.* to reproduce by this process.
autotypography, *n.* *aw*-to-ty-*pog*-ra-fe, the process of drawing upon gelatine relief designs that are subsequently pressed on to plates of soft metal from which prints are made.
autumn, *n.* *aw*-tum, the third season of the year, astronomically beginning at the equinox, when the sun enters Libra, and ending at the winter solstice; but popularly comprising from about mid-August to mid-November; a period of decline. (Fr. *automne.*)
autumnal, *a.* aw-*tum*-nal, belonging or peculiar to autumn; produced or gathered in autumn; belonging to the decline of life: *n.* a plant that flowers in autumn. **autumnal equinox,** the time, about 22 September, when day and night are of equal length.
auxanometer, *n.* awks-a-*nom*-e-ter, an instrument by whose aid the rate of growth in plants can be ascertained. (Gr. *auxanein*, cause to grow.)
auxiliaries, *n.pl.* awg-*zil*-ya-riz, foreign troops, confederate and auxiliary in war.
auxiliary, *a.* awg-*zil*-ya-re, helping; aiding; subsidiary or additional to: *n.* a helper; an assistant; a confederate; a verb which helps to form the moods and tenses of other verbs [Gram.]. (L. *auxiliārius*, helping.)
ava, *n.* *ah*-va, the narcotic beverage kava.
avahi, *n.* a-*vah*-hee, a long-tailed lemur of Madagascar.
avail, *v.t.* *a-vayl*, to be of value or use; to profit or assist; to advise: *v.i.* to be of use or service; to have the effect : *n.* profit; advantage; benefit; utility. (L. *ad-*, and *valeo*, strong or of value.)
availability, *n.* a-*vayl*-a-*bil*-e-te, availableness.
available, *a.* a-*vayl*-a-bl, that may be made use of; that may be of use or efficacious.
availableness, *n.* a-*vayl*-a-bl-ness, the quality of being available.
availably, *ad.* a-*vayl*-a-ble, in an available manner.
avalanche, *n.* *av*-a-lahnsh, a large body of snow or ice sliding down a mountain and sweeping all before it; anything that comes on with sudden overwhelming force. (Fr.)
avant-courier, *n.* (App.), one dispatched before another to notify his approach; a scout. (Fr. *avant*, before, and *courir*, to run.)
avant-garde, *n.* (App.), vanguard. (F.)
avanturine, *n.* a-*van*-tew-rin, aventurine.
avarice, *n.* *av*-a-ris, an inordinate desire of gain; covetousness. (Fr.)
avaricious, *a.* av-a-*rish*-us, greedy of gain; covetous.
avariciously, *ad.* av-a-*rish*-us-le, in an avaricious manner.
avariciousness, *n.* av-a-*rish*-us-ness, the quality of being avaricious.
avast, *int.* a-*vahst*, cease; stop; stay [Naut.]. (Dut.)
avatar, *n.* av-a-*tahr*, embodiment; the incarnation or visible appearance on earth of a deity [Hindu Myth.]. (Sans., descent.)
avaunt, *int.* a-*vawn'*, begone; depart; a word of contempt or abhorrence. (Fr. *avant.*)
ave, *int.* *ah*-vay, hail: *n.* an Ave Maria. **ave-bell,** a bell rung when the Ave Maria should be said. **Ave Maria,** an invocation to the Virgin Mary. (L. *ave*, hail!)
avellan, *n.* a-*vel*-an *or* *av*-e-lan, a filbert. **avellan cross,** a cross composed of four filbert nuts meeting at right angles at their bases [Her.] (L.)
avenaceous, *a.* av-en-*ay*-shus, pertaining to, or partaking of the nature of, oats. (L. *avena*, oats.)
avenge, *v.t.* a-*venj*, to take satisfaction for an injury by inflicting suffering on the injuring party; to vindicate the just, or a just cause, by the defeat of the adversary (as distinct from revenge, the unjust retributory infliction of pain or evil): *v.i.* to have or receive just satisfaction, by the punishment of the offender; to execute vengeance. (O.Fr. *avengier.*)
avengement, *n.* a-*venj*-ment, the act of avenging vengeance; retributory punishment.
avenger, *n.* a-*venj*-er, one who avenges.
avens, *n.* *av*-enz, herb bennet, *Geum urbanum*, or

water avens, *G. rivale*; mountain avens, *Dryas octopetala*.

aventail, *n.* *av*-ent-ayl, the visor of a helmet; the opening in this. (O.Fr. *esventail*, an opening to let in air.)

Aventine, *a.* *av*-ent-ine, pertaining to Mount Aventinus, one of the seven hills of Rome: *n.* a secure position; an Italian political party formerly opposing the Fascists.

aventurine, *n.* a-*ven*-tew-rin, a manufactured glass in which are embedded coloured spangles; a glittering variety of translucent quartz [Min.]; a fine gold powder for sprinkling on the first layer of varnish in japanning. (Fr.)

avenue, *n.* *av*-en-ew, a means of approach; a broad passage or road bordered by trees; a fine wide street. (Fr.)

aver, *v.t.* a-*ver*, to declare to be true; to affirm positively; to offer to verify [Law]. (Fr. *avérer*.)

average, *n.* *av*-er-aj, the mean sum, quantity, or value of unequal sums, quantities, or values; the sum, quantity, value, rate, etc., usually prevailing; the mean; [in Marine Insurance] a partial loss, or apportionment of this, of ship, cargo, or freight (**general average,** the proportion of loss borne by all the insurers of ship and cargo due to acts intentionally done to save time; **particular average,** any loss due to partial damage from the common perils incident to the sea and navigation not involving the general safety of ship and cargo, this falling on the individual owner or insurer): *a.* containing a mean proportion; ordinary: *v.t.* to find the mean of unequal sums or quantities; to reduce to a mean; to divide proportionately: *v.i.* to form a mean sum or quantity. **on an average,** taking the mean of numbers or quantities. (O.Fr., from Late L. *averagium*, property.)

averagely, *ad.* *av*-er-aj-le, in an average manner.

averager, *n.* *av*-er-a-jer, one who adjusts liabilities arising from general averages [Marine Insurance].

averment, *n.* a-*ver*-ment, the act of averring; affirmation; positive assertion; an offer of either party to justify or prove what he alleges [Law].

avernian, *a.* a-*ver*-ne-an, pertaining to Lake Avernus, near Puzzuoli, fabled by the ancients to be the entrance to Hades; infernal.

averroism, *n.* *av*-er-*roh*-izm, the doctrines of Averroes the 12th-cent. Arabian philosopher, who taught a form of pantheism.

averruncate, *v.t.* *av*-er-*rung*-kate, to turn off or away. (L. *averruncātus*, turned from.)

averruncator, *n.* *av*-er-*rung*-ka-ter, an instrument for pruning trees, consisting of a pair of shears fixed on the end of a rod or pole.

averse, *a.* a-*verse*, averted; feeling a repugnance or dislike; unwilling; disinclined.

aversely, *ad.* a-*verse*-le, in an averse manner.

averseness, *n.* a-*verse*-ness, the state of being averse; disinclination. (L. *aversus*, turned away.)

aversion, *n.* a-*ver*-shon, repugnance of mind; hatred; dislike; disinclination; opposition; contrariety of nature; the cause or object of dislike.

avert, *v.t.* a-*vert*, to turn from or away; to ward off. (L. *averto*, turn away.)

avertedly, *ad.* a-*vert*-ed-le, in an averted manner.

avertible, *a.* a-*vert*-e-bl, that which can be avoided; preventable.

avian, *a.* *ay*-ve-an, pertaining to birds. (L. *avis*, a bird.)

aviarist, *n.* *ay*-ve-a-rist, the keeper of an aviary.

aviary, *n.* *ay*-ve-a-re, a place for keeping or breeding birds in captivity. (L.)

aviate, *v.i.* *ay*-ve-ate, to travel in the air; to navigate aircraft. (L. *avis*, a bird.)

aviation, *n.* ay-ve-*ay*-shon, the science of flying; the act of navigating an airship or aeroplane.

aviator, *n.* *ay*-ve-a-tor, the pilot of an aeroplane; one skilled in the management of aircraft.

aviculture, *n.* *ay*-ve-kult-yur, the breeding and rearing of birds; bird-fancying.

avid, *a.* *av*-id, greedy; desiring keenly; hungry. (L.)

avidity, *n.* a-*vid*-e-te, greediness; eagerness. (Fr.)

avidly, *ad.* *av*-id-le, in an avid manner.

avifauna, *n.* av-e-*faw*-na the bird fauna.

avigation, *n.* av-i-*gay*-shon, the science and art of navigation as applied to aircraft.

aviso, *n.* a-*vee*-zo, a dispatch boat. (Span.)

avital, *a.* *av*-it-al, ancestral; ancient. (L. *avitus*, relating to grandfather.)

avizandum, *n.* av-e-*zan*-dum, a hearing in chambers by a judge, followed by his private consideration of the case [Scots Law].

avocado, *n.* av-o-*kah*-do, the alligator pear of the West Indies, the fruit of a species of *Persea*.

avocation, *n.* av-o-*kay*-shon, originally the act of calling aside, or diverting from one's proper calling, or that which does so; now that calling, business, trade, or profession itself. (L. *āvocātio*, a calling off.)

avocet, *n.* *av*-o-set, a bird of the snipe family with the bill curving upwards, *Recurvirostra avocetta*.

avoid, *v.t.* a-*voyd*, to keep at a distance from; to shun; to eschew; to make void [Law]; to annul. (O.Fr. *esvuidier*, to empty out.)

avoidable, *a.* a-*voyd*-a-bl, that may be avoided.

avoidance, *n.* a-*voyd*-ance, the act of shunning, annulling or becoming vacant; the state of being vacant.

avoidless, *a.* a-*voyd*-less, unavoidable; inevitable.

avoirdupois, *n.* and *a.* *av*-er-du-*poyz*, a system of weights used for solid commodities other than the precious metals, gems, and drugs, of which the pound contains 16 ounces, each of 437½ grains. (Fr., to have weight.)

avouch, *v.t.* a-*vouch*, to affirm or own openly; to maintain; to vindicate: *n.* evidence. (O.Fr.)

avouchable, *a.* a-*vouch*-a-bl, that may be avouched.

avouchment, *n.* a-*vouch*-ment, declaration; the act of avouching.

avow, *v.t.* a-*vou*, to declare openly as prepared to justify; to own; to admit freely. (Fr. *avouer*.)

avowable, *a.* a-*vou*-a-bl, that may be avowed.

avowably, *ad.* a-*vou*-a-ble, in an avowable manner.

avowal, *n.* a-*vou*-al, frank acknowledgment; an open declaration.

avowant, *n.* a-*vou*-ant, the defendant in replevin, who admits the distress of the goods, and justifies the taking [Law].

avowedly, *ad.* a-*vou*-ed-le, in an open manner; with frank acknowledgment.

avowry, *n.* a-*vou*-re, the act of the distrainer of goods, who, in an action of replevin, avows and justifies the taking in his own right [Law]. (O.Fr.)

avulsion, *n.* a-*vul*-shon, the act of pulling or tearing from or asunder; a rending or forcible separation. (L. *āvulsio*, a shoot turn off from a plant.)

avuncular, *a.* a-*vung*-kew-lar, pertaining to or like an uncle. (L.)

await, *v.t.* a-*wayt*, to wait for; to look for or expect; to be in store for; to attend. (O.Fr. *agaitier*.)

★**awake,** *v.t.* a-*wake*, to rouse from sleep, or a state resembling it; to put into action or new life: *v.i.* to bestir; to rise; to waken or bestir out of sleep; to become alert: *a.* not sleeping; in a state of vigilance or action: *p.* **awoke**: *pp.* **awoke** and **awaken.** (A.S. *awacen*.)

awaken, *v.t.* a-*wake*-en, to wake up; to rouse: *v.i.* to become awake.

awakener, *n.* a-*wake*-en-er, he or that which awakens.

awakening, *n.* a-*wake*-en-ing, the act of awaking; a throwing off of lethargy: *a.* rising as from sleep; inspiring.

awantibo, *n.* a-*won*-te-bo, a tailless lemur, *Perodicticus calabarensis*, of W. Africa, allied to the polto. (Native.)

awanting, *a.* a-*wont*-ing, wanting; absent.

award, *v.t.* a-*wawrd*, to adjudge; to assign by sentence; to apportion: *v.i.* to judge; to determine; to make an award: *n.* judgment; sentence; the decision of arbitrators; the document containing such decision. (O.Fr. *esuarder*, to award.)

awardable, *a.* a-*wawrd*-a-bl, that can be awarded.

awardment, *n.* a-*wawrd*-ment, award.

aware, *a.* a-*ware*, apprised; conscious. (A.S.)

awareness, *n.* a-*ware*-ness, apprehension; the state or quality of being aware.

awash, *a.* and *ad.* a-*wosh*, washed by the waves (of a ship's deck); at the mercy of the sea.

awave, *a.* and *ad.* a-*wave*, waving, as of a flag.

away, *ad.* a-*way*, absent; at a distance; apart: *int.* begone. **away with,** cannot bear or endure. **make away with,** to destroy. (A.S. *onweg*.)

awe, *n.* aw, dread; reverential fear or veneration; wonder inspired by something sublime: *v.t.* to strike with fear and reverence; to influence or restrain by fear, terror, or respect. (Scand.)

aweary, *a.* a-*weer*-re, tired; weary.

aweather, *ad.* a-*weth*-er, on the weather side, or towards the wind; opposed to alee [Naut.].

aweigh, *ad.* a-*way*, atrip [Naut.].
aweless, *a. aw*-less, wanting reverence; void of respectful fear; wanting power to awe.
awesome, *a. aw*-sum, terrible; weird; causing horror in a person or thing.
awe-struck, *a. aw*-struk, impressed with dread.
awful, *a. aw*-ful, inspiring or expressing awe; dreadful; fearful; shocking; hence, very great, extreme, out of the ordinary [Slang].
awfully, *ad. aw*-ful-le, in an awful manner; very.
awfulness, *n. aw*-ful-ness, the quality of being awful.
awhile, *ad.* a-*while*, for a space of time; some time; for a short time. (A.S.)
awkward, *a. awk*-ward, wanting dexterity; bungling; ungraceful; inelegant. (Scand.)
awkwardly, *ad. awk*-ward-le, in an awkward manner.
awkwardness, *n. awk*-ward-ness, the quality of being awkward.
awl, *n.* awl, a sharp tool for piercing small holes, used by workers in leather. (A.S. *al.*)
awlwort, *n. awl*-wurt, a plant with awl-shaped leaves, *Subularia aquatica*.
awn, *n.* awn, the beard or slender sharp bristle in the flower of grasses: *v.t.* to separate the awn from grain. (Scand.)
awned, *a.* awnd, bearded; having awns [Bot.].
awner, *n. awn*-er, an implement or machine for awning grain.
awning, *n. awn*-ing, a light removable cover to protect from the sun's rays; that part of a poop deck which is continued forward beyond the bulkhead of the cabin [Naut.]. (Perhaps from Fr. *auvent*, a penthouse.)
awnless, *a. awn*-less, without awns; beardless.
awny, *a. awn*-e, having awns.
awoke, a-*woke*, *p.* and *pp.* of the verb to awake.
awrong, *ad.* a-*rong*, wrongly.
awry, *a.* and *ad.* a-*ry*, twisted towards one side or position; asquint; amiss; in a wry manner.
axe, *n.* aks, a tool for hewing timber and chopping wood; reduction of expenses [Slang]: *v.t.* to reduce expenses, esp. by dismissal of staff [Slang]. **an axe to grind,** an ulterior object. (A.S. *æx.*)
axestone, *n. aks*-stone, jade.
axial, *a. aks*-e-al, pertaining to or along an axis.
axially, *ad. aks*-e-al-le, along or in the direction of the axis.
axiferous, *a.* aks-*if*-er-us, having an axis only, as certain fungi, etc. [Bot.]. (L. *axis*, and *fero*, bear.)
axiform, *a. aks*-e-form, in the form of an axis.
axil, *n. aks*-il, the angle formed on the upper side by a branch with the stem, or by a leaf with the stem or branch [Bot.]. (L.)
axile, *a. aks*-il, pertaining to the axis.
axilla, *n.* aks-*il*-a, the armpit; an axil [Bot.]. (L.)
axillary, *a. aks*-il-la-re, pertaining to the armpit; growing from the axil [Bot.]. (L. *axilla*, armpit.)
axinite, *n. aks*-in-ite, the mineral yanolite.
axinomancy, *n.* aks-*in*-o-man-se, divining by the aid of an axe. (L. *axinomantia.*)
axiology, *n.* aks-e-*ol*-o-je, the science of values [Psych.].
axiom, *n. aks*-e-um, a self-evident truth; an established principle in an art or science. (Fr. *axiome.*)
axiomatic, *a.* aks-e-o-*mat*-ik, self-evident.
axiomatically, *ad.* aks-e-o-*mat*-e-ka-le, by the use of axioms.
axis, *n. ak*-sis (*pl.* **axes,** *ak*-seez), the straight line, real or imaginary, round which a body revolves; a straight line in a plain figure, about which it revolves to produce a solid [Geom.]; a right line dividing the section into two equal parts, and cutting all its ordinates at right angles [Conic Sections]; the second vertebra of the neck, with an upward process on which the atlas turns [Anat.]; the central part or column of a plant, around which the other parts are disposed [Bot.]; a particular ray of light from any object falling perpendicularly on the eye, called also the optic or visual axis [Opt.]; (*cap.*) the entente of 1936 between Germany and Italy which developed into a full political and military alliance in 1939 and in 1940 was joined by Japan, the three peoples collectively constituting the **Axis Powers. axis of a balance,** that line about which it turns [Mech.]. **axis of oscillation,** a right line parallel to the horizon, about which a pendulum vibrates [Physics.] **axis in peritrochio,** or wheel and axle, one of the mechanical powers, consisting of a wheel concentric with a cylindrical axis, with which it revolves [Mech.]. (L.)
axis, *n. aks*-is, the Indian spotted deer, *Cervus axis*.
axle, *n. aks*-el, the spindle or bar on which a wheel revolves or which revolves with it.
axle-box, *n. aks*-el-boks, the lining for the hub of a wheel; the journal-box of a rotating axle.
axle-pin, *n. aks*-el-pin, a linchpin.
axletree, *n. als*-el-tree, a piece of timber, or bar of iron, which passes through the centre of a wheel, and on which it revolves. (Scand.)
axoid, *a. aks*-oyd, pertaining to the axis vertebra.
axolotl, *n. aks*-o-lotl, any of the Mexican larval salamanders of the genus *Amblystoma*. (Aztec.)
axotomous, *a.* aks-*ot*-o-mus, having a cleavage with a single face perpendicular to the axis [Cryst.]. (Gr. *axōn*, axle, *tomos*, cut.)
axunge, *n. aks*-unj, hog's lard; grease used for wheels. (L. *axungia*, cart-grease.)
ay, *ad.* eye, always, ever; aye; yes.
ayah, *n. ah*-ya, a native Hindu nurse or waiting woman. (Anglo-Indian.)
aye, *ad.* eye, yea; yes; indeed; more than that: *n. pl.* **ayes,** ize, one of those voting for a motion.
aye, *ad.* ay, always; for ever; continually. (Ice. *ei*, for ever.)
aye-aye, *n. eye*-eye, *a.* Madagascan lemur of the genus *Cheiromys*, so named from its peculiar cry.
ayelp, *a.* and *ad.* a-*yelp*, yelping.
ayry, *n. ay*-re, eyrie.
azalea, *n.* a-*zay*-le-a, a shrubby plant of the evergreen showy-flowered genus *Azalea* of the heath family, allied to the rhododendrons.
azarole, *n. az*-a-role, a shrub, *Cratægus azarolus*, of S.E. Europe or its edible fruit. (Arab.)
azedarac, *n.* a-*zed*-a-rak, the bead-tree, a tall oriental evergreen grown in glasshouses; a drug obtained from its bark. (Pers.)
Azilian, *a.* az-*zil*-e-an, pertaining to the period between the palæolithic and neolithic ages [Archæol.]. (Le Mas d'*Azil*, S. France.)
azimuth, *n. az*-e-muth, an arc of the horizon intercepted between the meridian of a place and the vertical circle passing through the centre of a heavenly body [Astron.]. **azimuth-circle,** a great circle passing through the zenith and nadir, and cutting the horizon at right angles. **azimuth compass,** an instrument for finding either the magnetic azimuth or the amplitude of a heavenly object. **azimuth dial,** a dial whose gnomon is at right angles to the plane of the horizon. **magnetic azimuth,** an arc of the horizon, intercepted between the azimuth passing through the centre of any heavenly body, and the magnetic meridian. (Ar. *as-samūt*, the ways.)
azimuthal, *a. az*-e-mewth-al, pertaining to the azimuth; in azimuth.
azoic, *a.* a-*zoh*-ik, without vestige of life; having no organic remains [Geol.]. (Gr. *azōos*, lifeless.)
azonic, *a.* a-*zon*-ik, not native to any special district or zone. (Gr. *azōnikos.*)
azote, *n.* a-*zote*, a former name of nitrogen, because fatal to animal life [Chem.]. (Fr.)
azoth, *n. az*-oth, the first principle of metals; mercury; a universal medicine [Alchem.]. (Ar.)
azotic, *a.* a-*zot*-ik, pertaining to, or formed of, azote.
azotize, *v.t. az*-o-tize, to impregnate with, or to combine with, nitrogen.
aztec, *n. az*-tek, a member of the Indian tribe dominant in Mexico at the time of the Spanish conquest (1521); the language of this tribe: *a.* pertaining to the Aztecs.
azure, *a. az*-yeur, sky-blue; resembling the clear blue colour of the sky; blue [Her.]: *n.* a fine blue colour like that of the sky; the sky, or azure vault of heaven; a blue colour in coats of arms: *v.t.* to colour blue. (Fr. *azur.*)
azurine, *n. az*-yeur-reen, the blue roach, a species of *Leuciscus*; a bluish-black aniline dye.
azurite, *n. az*-yeur-rite, lazulite; blue malachite.
azygous, *a. az*-e-gus, occurring singly; not paired. [Anat.]. (Gr. *azygos*, yokeless.)
azyme, *n. az*-im, *or az*-eem, the unleavened Passover bread of the Jews. (Gr. *azymos*, unleavened.)
Azymite, *n. az*-e-mite, a user of unleavened bread in celebrating the Eucharist.
azymous, *a. az*-e-mus, unleavened; unfermented.

B

B, bee, the second letter and first consonant in the English and other related alphabets, is a flat labial mute formed by pressing the whole length of the lips together and forcing them open with a strong breath. It has a near affinity with P and V, and in some languages is interchanged with them. B, or *te* (Italian *si*), in music, is the designation of the seventh note in the natural diatonic scale of C.
baa, *n.* bah, the cry or bleating of sheep: *v.i.* to cry or bleat as sheep.
Baal, *n.* *bay*-al (*pl.* **Baalim**), a Phœnician god; a false god; an idol. (Heb. *baal*, a lord.)
baas, *n.* bahs, boss; master; Sir [S. Afr.]. (Dut.)
Baba, *n.* *bah*-ba, a title of respect in Western Asia, given especially to the Patriarch of Alexandria. (Turk.)
baba, *n.* *bah*-ba, a small finger-shaped cake. (Fr.)
babacoote, *n.* *bah*-ba-koot, the indri (Malagasy, *babakoto.*)
Babbit metal, *n.* *bab*-it, an anti-friction alloy of tin, antimony, and copper in varying proportions. (Isaac *Babbit*, *d.* 1862, inventor.)
babble, *v.i.* *bab*-bl, to utter words imperfectly or indistinctly, as children; to utter sounds incessantly and indistinctly, as a brook; to talk idly, irrationally, or much; to tell secrets: *v.t.* to prate; to utter: *n.* idle talk; senseless prattle. (Imitative.)
babblement, *n.* *bab*-bl-ment, idle talk; senseless prate; the "chatter" of brooks.
babbler, *n.* *bab*-bl-er, one who or that which babbles; an idle talker; a teller of secrets; a tropical bird of the thrush family.
babe, *n.* bayb, an infant; a young child of either sex. (Probably from "babble.")
babel, *n.* *bay*-bl, a confusion of sounds; tumult; disorder. (*Babel*, anc. capital of Babylonia.)
babelish, *a.* *bay*-bl-ish, thoroughly commingled. (*Babel.*)
Babiism, *n.* *bah*-be-izm, Babism.
babirusa, *n.* bab-e-*roos*-a, the wild swine of the East Indies, *Babirusa alfurus.* (Malay *babi*, hog, *rusa*, deer.)
babish, *a.* *bay*-bish, babyish; befitting a babe.
Babism, *n.* *bah*-bizm, a Persian religion founded in 1844 by Mirza Ali, whose disciple called himself the Bab or gate. (Pers. *Bābī*, a gate.)
baboo, *n.* ba-*boo*, babu.
baboon, *n.* ba-*boon*, a monkey with short tail, long face, large strong tusks and the nostrils placed at the extreme end of the snout; any species of the African genus *Cynocephalus.* (Fr. *babouin.*)
baboonery, *n.* ba-*boo*-ner-re, baboons collectively; baboon-like behaviour.
babu, *n.* bah-*boo*, a title of respect to a gentleman among the Hindus; a native clerk; a superficially Europeanized Hindu. (Hindu.)
babuina, *n.* bab-yew-*ee*-na, a female baboon.
babuism, *n.* bah-*boo*-izm, the superficial culture of babus.
★**baby,** *n.* *bay*-be, a young child of either sex; a doll; a babe: *a.* pertaining to an infant. (*Babe.*)
baby-farming, *n.* *bay*-be-farm-ing, the practice and business of housing and nursing newly born infants for payment.
babyhood, *n.* *bay*-be-hood, the state of infancy; infants collectively.
babyish, *a.* *bay*-be-ish, like a baby; childish.
babyishly, *ad.* *bay*-be-ish-le, childishly.
babyishness, *n.* *bay*-be-ish-ness, childishness.
babyism, *n.* *bay*-be-izm, the characteristics of a baby; babyishness.
Babylon, *n.* *bab*-e-lon, the great capital (*circa* 2300 B.C.) of Babylonia, notorious for the vice and luxury of its citizens; hence, any great and dissolute city; also, the mystical city of the Apocalypse, hence applied by some Protestants to Rome and to papacy. (Heb. *bab*-el, gate of the god.)
Babylonian, *a.* bab-e-*loh*-ne-an, pertaining to Babylon; confused, like the language of Babel; luxurious; dissolute; papistical.
Babylonic, *a.* bab-e-*lon*-ik, Babylonian.
Babylonish, *a.* bab-e-*loh*-nish, Babylonian.
baccalaureate, *n.* bak-ka-*law*-re-at, the university degree of bachelor.
baccarat, *n.* *bak*-ka-rah, a game at cards played between punters and a banker. (Fr. *baccara.*)
baccate, *a.* *bak*-kat, berried; berry-shaped; pulpy, like a berry [Bot.]. (L. *bacca*, a berry.)
bacchanal, *a.* *bak*-ka-nal, pertaining to Bacchus or his orgies; bacchanalian: *n.* a votary of Bacchus; one who indulges in drunken revels; an orgy.
Bacchanalia, *n.pl.* bak-ka-*nay*-le-a, feasts in honour of Bacchus; drunken feasts. (L. *Bacchănalia*, the orgies in honour of Bacchus.)
bacchanalian, *a.* bak-ka-*nay*-le-an, pertaining to bacchanals; revelling in drunkenness; riotous: *n.* a bacchanal; a sot.
bacchant, *n.* *bak*-kant, a priest of Bacchus; a drunken reveller: *a.* given to drunken revelry.
bacchante, *n.* ba-*kant*-e, a priestess of Bacchus; a woman bacchanal.
bacchantic, *a.* ba-*kan*-tik, pertaining to Bacchus, his worship, or his priests; mad, or as if mad, with intoxication.
bacchic, *a.* *bak*-kik, bacchantic.
bacchius, *n.* ba-*ky*-us, a foot of one short followed by two long syllables [Pros.]. (Gr.)
Bacchus, *n.* *bak*-us, the god of wine in Greek and Roman religion; intoxication personified.
bacciferous, *a.* bak-*sif*-er-us, berry-bearing. (L.)
bacciform, *a.* *bak*-se-form, berry-shaped [Bot.].
baccivorous, *a.* bak-*siv*-o-rus, subsisting on berries. (L. *bacca*, a berry, *voro*, devour.)
bachelor, *n.* *batch*-e-lor, an unmarried man; one who has taken the first degree at a university; formerly a knight in the military service of another. (O.Fr. *bacheler.*)
bachelordom, *n.* *batch*-e-lor-dum, bachelors collectively.
bachelorhood, *n.* *batch*-e-lor-hood, the condition of a bachelor; celibacy.
bachelor's-buttons, *n.pl.* *batch*-e-lorz-*but*-tonz, a popular name of several species of *Ranunculus* and other plants.
bachelorship, *n.* *batch*-e-lor-ship, the state or condition of a bachelor.
bacillary, *a.* ba-*sill*-a-re, pertaining to or caused by bacilli; composed of small rods.
bacilliform, *a.* ba-*sill*-e-form, rod-shaped.
bacillus, *n.* ba-*sill*-us, a rod-shaped bacterium of the genus *Bacillus* present in certain diseases or diseased tissues. (L. *bacillum*, a little staff.)
★**back,** *n.* bak, the hinder part of the trunk of the human body; the upper part of an animal; the part of anything opposed to front; the part most remote from that which fronts the speaker or actor; the part of a cutting tool opposed to the edge; the upper part; a ship's keel; the top of the lode in a metalliferous mine; a thick, well-tanned hide; a football player who plays nearest his own goal: *a.* that lies beyond, in the rear, or distant; returning backward: *ad.* to the place from which one came; to a former state, condition, or station; behind, not advancing, or not coming or bringing forward; towards times or things past; again; in return; away: *v.t.* to mount or get upon the back; to second or support; to sign or endorse, as a warrant or note of exchange; to put backward; to cause to retreat or recede; to furnish with a back; to bet in favour of: *v.i.* to move or go backward; to retreat, or recede. **back-blocks,** the interior parts of a district [Amer. and Austral.]. **back-chat,** saucy rejoinder, esp. from an inferior. **back the field,** to bet against a particular horse that some one of all the other runners will beat it. **back the oars,** to pull the oars backwards so as to stay the progress of a boat [Naut.]. **back out,** to retreat; to withdraw. **back up,** to second or

support. **behind one's back,** when one is absent; without one's knowledge. **see the back of,** to be rid of. **turn the back on,** to turn coldly away from. (A.S. *bæc*, back.)

back, *n.* bak, a large shallow vat used in brewing and distilling. (Dut. *bak*, a trough.)

back-bencher, *n.* a member of the House of Commons occupying a seat on the rear benches; a non-office-holder or non-ex-office-holder.

backbite, *v.t. bak*-bite, to speak evil of; to slander; to censure the absent malignantly.

backbiting, *n. bak*-bite-ing, slander; malignment of the absent.

backboard, *n. bak*-bord, a board for the back of anything; the thin board backing a picture frame; a board to correct stooping in the young.

backbone, *n. bak*-bone, the spinal column; what is like a backbone or serves as such; decision. **to the backbone,** through and through.

backdoor, *n.* bak-*dawr*, a door at the rear of a house, or one giving entrance to the kitchens: *a.* indirect; clandestine.

backed, *a. bakt*, having a back; on which a bet has been placed.

backer, *n. bak*-er, a supporter, an endorser; one who bets that a horse will win.

backfall, *n. bak*-fawl, a throw on the back in wrestling; a lever in the coupler of an organ.

backfire, *n. bak*-fire, an explosion reversing the stroke in an internal combustion engine; an ignited discharge from the breech of a gun: *v.i.* to have a backfire; to explode prematurely.

backfiring, *n.* bak-*fire*-ring, premature ignition or explosion in an internal combustion engine.

back-flow, *n. bak*-floh, a flowing back; a reversal of direction.

back-formation, *n.* bak-for-*may*-shon, a word, or the making of a word, derived from or providing a supposititious source of an existing word, as "gloam" from "gloaming," "commentate" from "commentator."

backgammon, *n. bak*-gam-on, a game of skill played by two persons upon a board with dice and draughtsmen; a win when opponent has removed no men: *v.i.* to win in this way. (*Back*, and *gammon*.)

background, *n. bak*-ground, ground in the rear; the space behind the principal group in a picture; the shade, where one is not noticed or seen; a situation little seen or noticed.

backhand, *n. bak*-hand, writing leaning to the left; the hand turned backward, as in taking a stroke to the left at tennis.

backhanded, *a.* bak-*han*-ded, with the hand turned backward; unfair; indirect; reverse: *ad.* with the hand directed backward.

backhander, *n.* bak-*han*-der, a stroke with the back of the hand; metaphorically, any unexpected intelligence usually of an unpleasant nature.

backing, *n. bak*-ing, mounting; supporting; endorsing; putting or going back; furnishing with a back; stuff used for making a back.

backing-up, *n. bak*-ing-up, supporting, helping; the advance of the non-striker towards the striker's wicket in readiness for the run [Cricket].

backlash, *n. bak*-lash, the friction between the teeth of geared wheels as they disengage.

backlog, *bak*-log, work, orders, etc. in arrear [Comm.].

back-marker, *n.* bak-*mar*-ker, a competitor starting at scratch in a race, etc. [Coll.].

back-number, *n.* bak-*num*-ber, an out-of-date issue of a periodical; an old fogy, a "has-been" [Coll.].

back-pedal, *v.i.* bak-*ped*-al, to slow down by pressure on the pedal as it rises [Cycling]; to exercise restraint, to withdraw [Coll.].

backpiece, *n. bak*-peece, the piece of armour which covers the back; a piece forming a back.

back-rest, *n. bak*-rest, a support for the back when reclining; a support at the rear of anything.

backsaw, *n. bak*-saw, a saw, as a tenon-saw, the back of which is specially stiffened.

back-scratcher, *n. bak*-skratch-er, a long-handled instrument for scratching the back; one given to sychophantic flattery, a boot-licker [Coll.].

back-settlement, *n.* bak-*set*-tl-ment, outlying land that is being settled and cultivated.

backsheesh, *n. bak*-sheesh, baksheesh.

backside, *n. bak*-side, the back part or rear of anything; vulgarly (bak-*side*), the buttocks.

backsight, *n. bak*-site, the sight towards the bench-mark with which the surveyor begins his levelling; the rear gun-sight.

back-slang, *n. bak*-slang, slang in which the intended word is pronounced as though spelled backward, as "ekorb" for "broke."

backslide, *v.i. bak*-slide, to relapse into sin; to abandon a faith once held.

backslider, *n. bak*-slide-er, one who backslides.

backsliding, *n. bak*-slide-ing, the act of apostatizing; lapsing into unbelief or sin.

backstaff, *n. bak*-stahf, an obsolete quadrant in using which the back of the observer was turned towards the sun.

backstairs, *n.pl. bak*-starez, back or private stairs: *a.* underhand; scandalous.

backstays, *n.pl. bak*-stayz, stays on both sides of a ship to assist the shrouds in supporting the mast when strained by a weight of sail [Naut.].

backster, *n. bak*-ster, a wooden sandal for walking on shingle.

backstitch, *n. bak*-stitch, a stitch which begins a little behind the front of another: *v.t.* and *i.* to sew with this stitch.

back-stroke, *n. bak*-stroke, a stroke in return; a backhander; a stroke in swimming when the swimmer is lying on his back.

backsword, *n. bak*-sawrd, a sword with one sharp edge; a fencing-stick with a basket handle.

backward, *a. bak*-ward, unwilling; hesitating; dilatory; dull of comprehension; behind in progress; behind in time: *ad.* backwards.

backwardation, *n. bak*-war-*day*-shon, allowance to purchasers of stock or shares for an extension of time in the delivery [Comm.].

backwardly, *ad. bak*-ward-le, in a backward manner.

backwardness, *n. bak*-ward-ness, the state of being backward.

backwards, *ad. bak*-wardz, with the back foremost; towards the back; on the back; towards past times; by way of reflection; from a better to a worse state; in time past; reversely; from the end to the beginning; in a contrary manner.

backwash, *n. bak*-wosh, water thrown back, as by oars or paddle-wheels; a wave caused by the passage of a sea- or air-craft; a result from some occurrence.

backwater, *n. bak*-waw-ter, a pool fed by the stream alongside it owing to some obstruction or rise in the tide below; water kept back at high tide to cleanse the channel; backwash.

backwoods, *n.pl. bak*-woodz, unreclaimed forest land in a new country.

backwoodsman, *n.* bak-*woodz*-man, a settler in the backwoods; a person estranged from civilized life [Coll.]; a peer on a rare appearance in the House of Lords (Slang].

bacon, *n. bay*-kon, the back and sides of a pig cured for eating. **save one's bacon,** to escape from loss or harm. (O.Fr. *bacon*.)

Baconian, *a.* ba-*koh*-ne-an, pertaining to Francis Bacon (*d.* 1621), to his inductive philosophy, or to the fantasy that he was the author of the works known as Shakespeare's: *n.* an upholder of this fantasy.

bacteria, *n.pl.* bak-*teer*-e-a (*sing.* **bacterium**), minute rod-shaped fungoid plants living in decomposing substances. (Gr. *bacterion*, a little stick.)

bacterial, *a.* bak-*teer*-e-al, pertaining to or caused by bacteria.

bactericidal, *a.* bak-*teer*-e-*sy*-dal, fatal to bacteria.

bactericide, *n.* bak-*teer*-re-syd, any agent that destroys bacteria.

bacteriology, *n.* bak-*teer*-e-*ol*-o-je, the study of bacteria and other minute fungoid plants.

bacteriolysis, *n. bak*-teer-e-*ol*-e-sis, the destruction of bacteria, esp. by a serum.

bacteriolytic, *a.* bak-*teer*-e-o-*lit*-ik, pertaining to bacteriolysis; bactericidal.

Bactrian, *a. bak*-tre-an, pertaining to Bactria, in ancient Persia: *n.* a native, or the language, of Bactria. **Bactrian camel,** the two-humped camel.

Bactris, *n. bak*-tris, a genus of tropical American palms of the family *Arecaceæ*. (Gr. *baktron*, a staff.)

baculite, *n.* *bak*-yoo-lite, any fossil cephalopod with straight tapering shell of the genus *Baculites.* (L. *baculus,* a staff, Gr. *lithos,* a stone.)
***bad,** *a.* bad, opposite of good; ill; evil; hurtful; wicked; immoral; unfortunate; unhappy; unsound: *n.* that which is bad. **to the bad,** to ruin; to evil ways; to the wrong side of the account (M.E. *badde.*)
baddish, *a. bad*-ish, rather bad.
bade, *v.t.* bad, *p.* of bid.
badge, *n.* badj, a mark or token by which a person or thing is distinguished; a cognizance: *v.t.* to mark with a badge.
badger, *n. badj*-er, a carnivore of the genus *Meles* with a thick body and short legs, about the size of a fox, dwelling in burrows, and living on carrion and fruit; an artist's brush of badger's hair: *v.t.* to pursue with eagerness; to pester; to annoy.
badger, *n. badj*-er, a corn-chandler; a huckster or licensed pedlar in any goods.
badian, *n. bad*-e-an, the seed of the Chinese anise, yielding an oil used for seasoning. (Fr. *badiane.*)
badigeon, *n.* ba-*dee*-jon, a cement used by sculptors to repair defects in their material; a similar cement used by woodworkers. (Fr.)
badinage, *n.* bad-e-*nahzh,* light, playful talk, or banter. (Fr. *badinage.*)
badly, *ad. bad*-le, in a bad manner; not well.
badminton, *n. bad*-min-ton, a game played with shuttlecocks over a net; a claret-cup. (Place-name.)
badness, *n. bad*-ness, the state of being bad.
baff, *v.t.* baf, to strike ball and ground simultaneously with a wooden club in golf and so send the ball up into the air. (From baffy.)
baffle, *v.t. baf*-fl, to elude by artifice; to frustrate; to defeat; to disconcert; to check: *n.* a plate or other device for deflecting or regulating flow of heat, wave-transmission, etc. (Origin uncertain.)
baffling, *a. baf*-fling, perplexing and defeating.
bafflingly, *ad. baf*-fling-le, in a baffling manner.
baffy, *n. baf*-e, a short wooden golf club with a much lofted face. (Scots.)
baft, *n.* baft, *or* **baftah,** *baf*-ta, a cheap cotton cloth manufactured for the African market. (Per.)
***bag,** *n.* bag, a sack; a pouch; a receptacle in animal bodies containing some secretion; the contents of a game-bag; a determinate quantity of a commodity [Comm.]; *pl.* trousers [Slang]: *v.t.* to put into a bag; to steal; to shoot: *v.i.* to swell like a full bag; to distend. **bag and baggage,** all one's belongings; completely. **bag o'bones,** an emaciated person. (Ice. *baggi,* a bundle.)
bagasse, *n.* ba-*gas,* the refuse stalks of the sugar-cane. (Fr. *bagasse.*)
bagatelle, *n. bag*-a-*tel,* a trifle; a thing of no importance; a game played on a nine-holed board with nine balls and a cue. (Fr. *bagatelle,* a trifle.)
bagful, *n. bag*-ful, as much as a bag will hold.
baggage, *n. bag*-aj, the tents, utensils, and other portable necessaries of an army; the clothing and other conveniences accompanying a traveller; a low worthless woman; a playful saucy female. (O.Fr. *bagage,* a number of packages.)
bagginess, *n. bag*-e-ness, baggy appearance.
bagging, *n. bag*-ing, cloth or material for bags: *a.* bulging, distended.
baggit, *n. bag*-it, a salmon just before or after spawning. (Scots., pregnant.)
baggy, *a. bag*-e, bulging like a bag; shapeless.
bagman, *n. bag*-man, a commercial traveller.
bagnio, *n. bahn*-yo, a bathing-house; a brothel; an Oriental gaol. (It. *bagno,* bath or prison.)
bagpipe, *n. bag*-pipe, an ancient musical wind instrument, still used in Scotland, consisting of a leather bag which receives the air by a tube, stopped by a valve, and of pipes into which the air is pressed by the performer.
bagpiper, *n. bag*-pipe-er, one who plays the bagpipes.
baguette, *n.* bag-*et,* a small rounded moulding [Arch.]. (Fr. *baguette,* a rod.)
bah, *int.* bah, an exclamation of contempt. (Fr.)
bahadur, *n.* ba-*hah*-door, a title of respect applied by Hindus to English officers. (Hind., brave.)
Bahamian, *a.* ba-*hah*-me-an, pertaining to the Bahamas or their inhabitants: *n.* an inhabitant of the Bahamas.
baignoire, *n.* bay-nwahr (or App.), a ground-floor box at the theatre. (Fr., bath-tub.)
bail, *n.* bayl, the temporary release of a prisoner upon security being given for his appearance in court when required; the person or persons who become surety, or the sum of money in which they are bound; the surety of a prisoner on bail: *v.t.* to give security for a prisoner on bail for his appearance at trial; to admit to bail; to release; to deliver goods in trust, upon a contract. **bail up,** to stick up, as a bushranger. **admit to bail,** to release on security. **find bail,** to procure security. (O.Fr. *bail,* safe-keeping.)
bail, *n.* bayl, a bar or division between stalls in a stable; a frame for holding the head of a cow when being milked: *pl.* the cross-pieces on the stumps completing the wicket [Cricket]. (L. *baculum,* a stick.)
bail, *n.* bayl, the handle of a kettle, the spreader beneath a canvas or tarpaulin tent or tilt. (M.E. *beyl,* from Ice. *beygla,* ring.)
bail, *n.* bayl, a baler: *v.t.* to bale water.
bailable, *a. bayl*-a-bl, that may be bailed.
bailage, *n. bayl*-aj, duty payable on the delivery of goods.
bail-bond, *n. bayl*-bond, a bond or obligation given by a prisoner and his surety upon being bailed.
bailee, *n.* bayl-*ee,* the person to whom goods are committed in trust [Law].
bailer, *n. bayl*-er, a bailor.
bailey, *n. bayl*-e, formerly, the external wall round a castle; any encircling castle-wall save the innermost; the space enclosed by such wall. **the Old Bailey,** the London Central Criminal Court.
bailie, *n. bayl*-e, a municipal officer in Scotland corresponding to an alderman; a bailiff.
bailiff, *n. bayl*-if, an officer of the sheriff who serves writs and executes arrests; a land steward. **water bailiff,** an officer to guard rivers from poachers. (O.Fr. *baillif,* a custodian.)
bailiwick, *n. bayl*-e-wik, the jurisdiction of a bailie or bailiff. (O.Fr. *baillif,* and A.S. *wic,* a territory.)
bailment, *n. bayl*-ment, a delivery of goods in trust [Law]; the bailing of a prisoner.
bailor, *n. bayl*-or, one who delivers goods to another in trust; one who stands bail for another.
bailsman, *n. baylz*-man, one who stands bail.
bain-marie, *n.* ban-ma-*ree,* a cooking vessel, half filled with hot water in which smaller saucepans are put. (Fr., bath of the Virgin.)
Bairam, *n. by*-rahm, the Spring festival of the Moslems; the lesser Bairam being held seventy days after it. (Turk.)
bairn, *n.* bayrn, a child. (A.S. *bearn.*)
bait, *n.* bayt, a lure or enticement, generally to deceive and catch fish or other animals; food or refreshment on a journey: *v.t.* to entice with actual or imitation food fish, fowls, and other animals into one's power; to allure; to give food and drink to a beast upon the road; to provoke and harass by dogs, or in any way; to worry: *v.i.* to take food and drink for refreshment on a journey. (Ice. *beita,* to cause to bite.)
baize, *n.* bayz, a coarse woollen cloth. (Fr. *baies.*)
bake, *v.t.* bake, to dry and harden by heat, either in an oven, kiln, or furnace, or by the solar rays; to prepare for food by drying and hardening in an oven; to harden: *v.i.* to do the work of baking; to dry and harden in heat. (A.S. *bacan,* to bake.)
bakehouse, *n. bake*-house, a house or building for the business of baking.
bakelite, *n. bayk*-e-lyt, a synthetic resinous material, used in insulation and for small moulded objects. (From L. H. *Baekeland,* Amer.-Belg. inventor, 1907.)
bakemeats, *n.pl. bake*-meets, meats cooked in an oven; pies.
baker, *n. bake*-er, one whose occupation is to bake bread or biscuits; a small oven. **baker's dozen,** thirteen.
bakery, *n. bake*-er-e, the trade of a baker; a bake-house.
bakestone, *n. bake*-stone, the stone or iron plate on which cakes are baked in an oven.
baking, *n. bake*-ing, the act of baking; the quantity baked at one time: *a.* very hot; fresh from the oven.
baking-powder, *n.,* a mixture containing carbonate of soda and an acid for leavening bread, cakes, etc.
baksheesh, *n. bak*-sheesh, a gratuity. (Pers.)
Balaclava-helmet, *n. bal*-a-*klah*-va-*hel*-met, a

woollen or warmly lined covering for head and neck leaving the face exposed. (Battle of *Balaclava*, 1854, where worn.)
balalaika, *n.* bal-a-*ly*-ka, a Russian guitar-like musical instrument with three strings.
★**balance,** *n.* *bal*-ans, a pair of scales; a weighing apparatus of any kind; poise; equipoise, or equality of weight or power; the weight or sum necessary to make two unequal weights or sums equal; the difference between the debtor and creditor side of an account; the part of a timepiece which regulates the beats; an impartial state of mind in deliberating; that which renders weight or authority equal; a sign in the zodiac, Libra [Astron.]: *v.t.* to bring to an equipoise; to compare by weighing or estimating as in a balance; to keep in equipoise; to counterpoise; to adjust an account; to make the two sides equal: *v.i.* to have equal weight, or be in equipoise; to hesitate. **balance of power,** that equality of power as between different states which appears to offer security for the general safety. **balance of trade,** the difference in value between exports and imports. (Fr. *balance.*)
balance-fish, *n.* *bal*-ans-fish, the hammerhead shark, *Zygaena malleus.*
balance-knife, *n.* *bal*-ans-nife, a table-knife which rests on the handle without the blade touching the tablecloth.
balancer, *n.* *bal*-an-ser, one who or that which balances; one of a pair of halteres [Entom.]; a device for balancing currents or circuits [Elect.]. **balancer meal,** a synthetic product providing a balanced diet for fowls in absence of grain.
balance-reef, *n.* *bal*-anse-reef, a reef-band that crosses a sail diagonally, used to contract it in a storm [Naut.].
balance-sheet, *n.* *bal*-anse-sheet, a statement of assets and liabilities.
balance-wheel, *n.* *bal*-anse-wheel, the contrivance in a watch which regulates the beat.
balanite, *n.* *bal*-a-nite, a fossil shell of the barnacle family. (L. *balanus*, an acorn.)
balanitis, *n.* bal-a-*ny*-tis, inflammation of the glans of the penis [Med.].
balas, *n.* ba-*lass*, a variety of spinel ruby. (Fr.)
balata, *n.* ba-*lah*-ta, a tree of the genus *Mimusops.* **balata gum,** chicle, the milky juice of this tree.
balaustine, *n.* ba-*laws*-tin, the flower of the wild pomegranate. (L. *balaustium.*)
balbriggan, *n.* bal-*brig*-an, a knitted cotton fabric used for underwear, etc. (Place-name, Eire.)
balbutient, *a.* bal-*byew*-she-ent, stammering. (L.)
balconied, *a.* *bal*-ko-nid, having balconies.
balcony, *n.* *bal*-ko-ne, a platform provided with a railing or parapet, projecting from the external wall of a house, usually in front of windows; the projecting gallery at the stern of an old man-o'-war; a gallery in theatres, usually that next above the dress-circle. (It. *balcone.*)
bald, *a.* bawld, without hair or feathers on the head; bare; unadorned; undisguised.
baldachin, *n.* *bawl*-da-kin, a rich embroidered silk fabric of mediæval times; a canopy of this supported by columns and placed over thrones and altars; a canopy of various kinds. (It. *baldacchino*, canopy.)
balderdash, *n.* *bawl*-der-dash, words jumbled together without sense or judgment; a worthless mixture. (Origin uncertain.)
baldhead, *n.* *bawld*-hed, a man bald on the head.
baldicoot, *n.* *bawl*-de-koot, popular name for a coot.
baldly, *ad.* *bawld*-le, in a bald manner.
baldmoney, *n.* *bawld*-mun-e, the yellow spignel, *Meum athamanticum* [Bot.].
baldness, *n.* *bawld*-ness, the state of being bald.
baldpate, *n.* *bawld*-pate, a bald-headed man; a variety of duck or pigeon.
baldric, *n.* *bawl*-drik, a richly ornamented shoulder belt. (O.Fr. *baldut*, girdle.)
baldwin, *n.* *bawld*-win, an eating apple.
bale, *n.* bayl, a bundle or package of goods: *v.t.* to make up into a bale. (O.Fr.)
bale, *n.* bayl, a baler: *v.t.* to scoop the water out of a boat. **to bale out,** to descend from aircraft by parachute.
bale, *n.* bayl, evil; calamity; destruction. (A.S. *bealo.*)
bale, *n.* bayl, a beacon fire; funeral pyre. (A.S. *bael.*)
baleen, *n.* ba-*leen*, whalebone. (L. *balæna*, a whale.)
bale-fire, *n.* *bayl*-fire, a signal fire; a bonfire; a funeral pyre.
baleful, *a.* *bayl*-ful, full of evil; bringing misery or sorrow; pernicious.
balefully, *ad.* *bayl*-ful-le, in a baleful manner.
balefulness, *n.* *bayl*-ful-ness, the quality of being baleful.
baler, *n.* *bayl*-er, the bucket or bowl used in baling out a boat.
baling-paper, *n.* *bayl*-ing-*pay*-per, paper for packing.
baling-press, *n.* *bayl*-ing-press, a press for compressing goods to be put up in bales.
balistraria, *n.* bal-is-*trayr*-re-a, a loophole in the wall of a fortress, through which cross-bowmen shot.
balk, *or* **baulk,** *n.* bawk, a ridge of land left unploughed; a rough beam; an obstacle; frustration; disappointment; at billiards, that part of the table behind a line across the bottom end: *v.t.* to disappoint; to frustrate; intentionally to leave untouched; to omit: *v.i.* to stop suddenly, to refuse a jump (of horses). (A.S. *balca*, a ridge.)
balker, *n.* *bawk*-er, among fishermen, a huer.
balky, *a.* *bawk*-e, apt to stop suddenly (of horses).
★**ball,** *n.* bawl, anything round to roundish; a bullet; the globe; a game with a ball; the pill used in veterinary practice: *v.t.* to form into a ball: *v.i.* to form into balls, as snow on horses' hoofs, in travelling. **ball and socket,** a form of universal joint in which a ball turns in any direction within a close-fitting socket partially enclosing it. **ball bearings,** a series of small hard steel balls placed in the **ball race** between a wheel and the shaft or axle for the purpose of reducing friction. (Fr. *balle*, a ball.)
ball, *n.* bawl, an assembly for dancing. (Fr. *bal.*)
ballad, *n.* *bal*-lad, a popular semi-epic or patriotic tale of adventure or daring in verse, originally sung to the harp; a short air of simple construction. (O.Fr. *ballade.*)
ballade, *n.* bal-*lahd*, a poem consisting of three stanzas and a refrain with a particular rhyme sequence.
balladmonger, *n.* *bal*-lad-mung-ger, a trader in ballads; a composer of ballads.
balladry, *n.* *bal*-lad-re, the subject or style of ballads; ballads collectively.
ballad-singer, *n.* *bal*-lad-sing-er, one who sings ballads in the streets.
ballast, *n.* *bal*-last, heavy matter laid in the hold of a ship to keep it steady when there is no cargo; that which is used to make anything steady; the earth or gravel used to fill up the spaces between the rails on a railway or as road foundation: *v.t.* to place ballast in; to keep steady.
ballastage, *n.* *bal*-las-taj, a duty paid for leave to take ballast.
ballasting, *n.* *bal*-las-ting, anything used for ballast.
ball-cartridge, *n.* *bawl*-*kar*-tridj, a cartridge charged with a bullet.
ball-cock, *n.* *bawl*-kok, a water-cock of a cistern that automatically regulates the supply.
ballerina, *n.* bal-ay-*ree*-nah, a ballet-girl. (It.)
ballet, *n.* *bal*-ay, a scenic representation of actions, characters, and passions, by means of dancing, gesture, and music; a company of ballet dancers; the art of the ballet. (Fr. *ballet.*)
balletomane,. *n* *bal*-a-to-mane, one affected with balletomania.
balletomania, *n.* *bal*-a-to-*may*-ne-a, excessive devotion to the ballet, its history, performance, and executants.
ball-flower, *n.* *bawl*-flou-er, an ornament like a ball enclosed by the petals of a flower [Arch.].
balling-gun, *n.* *bawl*-ing-gun, an instrument for forcing medicine in balls into a horse's gullet.
ballista, *n.* bal-*lis*-ta, a military engine used by the ancients for throwing darts and stones. (L. *ballista.*)
ballistic, *a.* bal-*lis*-tik, pertaining to the throwing of missiles or to ballistics. **ballistic curve,** the path of a projectile. **ballistic pendulum,** an instrument for measuring the velocity of projectiles.
ballistics, *n.pl.* bal-*lis*-tiks, the science of the motion of projectiles.
ballistite, *n.* ba-*lis*-tite, a smokeless form of dynamite used as a high explosive.

ballium, *n.* *bal*-le-um, the court within a fortified castle; an outer bulwark; a bailey.
ballonet, *n.* *bal*-lon-net, small balloon, or air-bag, within an airship; a small auxiliary gas-bag; a division of the air reservoir of an airship.
balloon, *n.* ba-*loon*, any spherical hollow body; a large spherical bag of silk or other light material, which, being filled with gas or heated air, rises and floats in the air; a glass receiver, of a spherical form, used in distilling [Chem.]; a kind of firework resembling a bomb [Pyr.]; a ball, or globe on the top of a pillar or cupola [Arch.]. **balloon barrage,** a system of tethered balloons used as a defence against aircraft attack. **balloon-tyre,** a low-pressure pneumatic tyre with large cross-section, for large motor vehicles and aeroplanes. **nurse-balloon,** a small balloon used as a portable gas-reservoir. **observation balloon,** *see* **observation.** (O.Fr. *balon*, a small ball.)
ballooning, *n.* bal-*loon*-ing, the construction and management of balloons; aeronautics.
balloonist, *n.* bal-*loon*-ist, one who makes balloon ascents.
ballot, *n.* *bal*-lot, a little ball, ticket, or anything used to give a secret vote; the act, practice, or method of voting by balls or tickets; the number of votes given: *v.i.* to vote by ballot. (It. *ballotta*, a small ball used in voting.)
ballotage, *n.* *bal*-lo-tahzh, in France, the second ballot between the two highest candidates. (Fr.)
ballot-box, *n.* *bal*-lot-boks, a box used for the balls or tickets in voting by ballot.
balloting, *n.* *bal*-lot-ing, the act of voting by ballot.
ballroom, *n.* *bawl*-room, a hall or large room suited for balls and dancing.
ball-valve, *n.* a valve closed by a ball-cock.
bally, *a.* *bal*-e, a vague intensive signifying " very " [Slang]. (Euphemistic for *bloody.*)
ballyhoo, *n.* bal-e-*hoo*, grandiloquence; boosting advance publicity; eye-wash; flummery [U.S.A. Slang.]
balm, *n.* bahm, the sap or juice of odoriferous trees or shrubs; any fragrant or valuable ointment; anything which soothes or mitigates pain; the name of several aromatic plants, particularly of the genus *Melissa* [Bot.]: *v.t.* to anoint with balm; to assuage; to soothe. **balm of Gilead,** a small evergreen tree of N. Africa and Arabia, the resin of *Commiphora meccanensis*; the resin of this, or of the N. American coniferous tree, *Abies balsamea*, also known as Canada balsam. (O.Fr. *basme*, resin of balsam.)
balm-cricket, *n.* bahm-*krik*-it, the field-cricket.
balmily, *ad.* *bahm*-e-le, in a balmy manner.
balmy, *a.* *bahm*-e, like balm; fragrant; soothing; mild; barmy, daft [Slang].
balneal, *a.* *bal*-ne-al, pertaining to bathing or to medicinal baths.
balneology, *n.* bal-ne-*ol*-o-je, the scientific study of bathing for therapeutic purposes [Med.]. (L. *balneum*, a bath.)
balsa, *n.* *bahl*-sa, the very light wood of the tropical American tree, *Ochroma lagopus*; a raft made of this.
balsam, *n.* *bawl*-sam, an oily, aromatic, resinous substance, flowing spontaneously, or by incision, from certain plants; balm; a soothing ointment containing resin; the balsamine. **balsam of Peru,** *see* **Peruvian balsam.** (L. *balsamum*, gum of balsam-tree.)
balsamic, *a.* bal-*sam*-ik, having the qualities of balsam; unctuous; soft; soothing: *n.* a warm, demulcent, oily medicine.
balsamically, *ad.* bal-*sam*-e-ka-le, in a balsamic manner.
balsamiferous, *a.* bal-sa-*mif*-er-us, yielding balsam.
balsamine, *n.* *bawl*-sa-mine, the plant touch-me-not, *Impatiens noli-me-tangere.*
Balsamodendron, *n.* *bawl*-sam-o-*den*-dron, a genus of oriental trees from which balm is obtained. (L. *balsamum*, and Gr. *dendron*, a tree.)
Baltimore-bird, *n.* *bawl*-te-more-burd, the Baltimore hangnest, *Icterus galbula*, an American singing bird, about the size of a linnet, with a body of bright gold colour.
Baluchi, *n.* ba-*loo*-chee, an inhabitant of Baluchistan; the language of that country.
baluster, *n.* *bal*-us-ter, a small column used for balustrades; a banister. (Fr. *baluster.*)
balustrade, *n.* *bal*-us-trade, a row of balusters joined by a rail or coping, serving as a fence or for ornament.
bam, *n.* bam, a hoax, a falsehood: *v.t.* to cheat in order to deceive; to bamboozle.
bambino, *n.* bam-*bee*-no, a figure of the infant Christ in swaddling-bands. (It., a child.)
bamboo, *n.* bam-*boo*, a plant of a species of *Bambusa*, a genus of tropical and sub-tropical giant grasses ranging up to 120 feet in height and a foot in diameter. (Malay, *bambu.*)
bamboozle, *v.t.* bam-*boo*-zl, to confound; to mystify.
bamboozlement, *n.* bam-*boo*-zl-ment, the act of bamboozling; mystification; a hoax.
ban, *n.* ban, proclamation; interdiction; proscription; curse; excommunication; a pecuniary mulct or penalty: *v.t.* and *v.i.* to curse; to interdict. (A.S. *gebann*, a proclamation.)
ban, *n.* ban, fine muslin made from banana fibre.
ban, *n.* ban, former title of the governor of certain parts of the Austro-Hungarian Empire.
banal, *a.* *bay*-nal *or* *ban*-al, trite; commonplace.
banality, *n.* ba-*nal*-e-te, triviality; a commonplace; commonplaceness. (Fr. *banalité.*)
banana, *n.* ba-*nah*-na, a tropical plant, *Musa sapientum*, closely allied to the plantain; its clustering and very nutritious fruit. (Sp.)
banbury, *n.* *ban*-be-re, a sweet cake containing mincemeat. (From the Oxfordshire town, *Banbury.*)
banco, *n.* *bang*-ko, a bench or a bank; bank money in contrast with local currency. **in banco,** said of a sitting when several judges are together on the bench [Law]. (It.)
***band,** *n.* band, anything which binds together; a narrow strip of cloth for binding or weaving round anything; a bandage; a fillet; a tie; a chain; something worn about the neck, as a clergyman's bands; any flat, low member or moulding, broad, but not deep [Arch.]; a belt for the transmission of power in a machine [Mech.]; a transverse stripe [Entom.]; a limited range of wave-lengths [Wire.]: *v.t.* to bind with a band; to unite in a troop, company, or confederacy: *v.i.* to associate; to unite. (Ice. *band.*)
band, *n.* band, a body of armed men; a company of musical performers; a company of persons united in any common design. (A.S.)
bandage, *n.* *ban*-daj, a strip of woven or flexible fabric used in dressing and binding up wounds and injuries; that which is bound over something else: *v.t.* to bind with a bandage.
bandalore, *n.* *ban*-da-lore, a toy consisting of a disk grooved on the edge to take a length of string along which it is made to move to and fro by jerks of the hand.
bandanna, *n.* ban-*dan*-nah, a silk handkerchief manufactured in India, having small white or brightly coloured spots on a dark-coloured ground; a cotton handkerchief of similar pattern. (Hind. *bāndhnū.*)
bandar, *n.* *bun*-dahr, the rhesus, *Macacus rhesus*, of northern India. (Hind.)
bandbox, *n.* *band*-boks a light box of thin material for hats, caps, bonnets, etc. (originally for "bands" or ruffs.)
bandeau, *n.* *ban*-doh (*pl.* **bandeaux**), a fillet for the hair; a woman's head-band. (Fr.)
banded, *a.* *band*-ed, joined in or as in a band; striated with coloured bands.
bandelet, *n.* *band*-e-let, a little band; a flat moulding [Arch.].
banderilla, *n.* *ban*-de-*ril*-la, a bull-fighter's barbed dart. (Sp.)
banderole, *n.* *band*-er-ole, a long narrow streamer; a pennant flown at the mast-head, or used to mark a military position; a flat decorative band with an inscription [Arch.]. (Fr.)
bandfish, *n.* *band*-fish, the ribbonfish, or other fish characterized by an elongated strap-like body.
bandicoot, *n.* *band*-e-koot, a huge Indian rat, *Nesocia bandicota*, whose flesh is used for food; an Australian marsupial insectivore of the genus *Perameles.* (Telugu, *pandi-kokku*, pig-like rat.)
bandiness, *n.* *band*-e-ness, the condition of being bandy-legged.
bandit, *n.* *ban*-dit (*pl.* **banditti,** ban-*dit*-te), an outlaw; a robber; a highwayman; a lawless or desperate fellow. (It. *bandito*, exiled or outlawed.)

bandlet, *n.* *band*-let, a small fillet; a bandelet.
bandmaster, *n.* *band*-mahs-ter, the conductor of a naval or military band.
bandog, *n.* *ban*-dog, a large dog kept chained; a watchdog. (*Bind* and *dog.*)
bandoleer, *n.* *ban*-do-*leer*, a leather belt formerly worn by musketeers over the right shoulder to sustain their firearms; small cases of wood or leather attached to a bandoleer, each containing a charge of powder; a shoulder-belt for holding cartridges. (Fr. *bandoulière.*)
bandolero, *n.* ban-do-*leer*-oh, a highway robber. (Sp.)
bandolier, *n.* *band*-o-leer, bandoleer.
bandoline, *n.* *ban*-do-leen, a substance applied to the hair to keep it flat and smooth. (Fr.)
bandore, *n.* *ban*-dore, an ancient kind of lute. (Sp. *bandurria.*)
bandsaw, *n.* *band*-saw, a thin saw stretched on a frame; an endless saw working over two pulleys.
bandsman, *n.* *bandz*-man, a member of a band.
bandstand, *n.* *band*-stand, a roofed platform for performers in open-air concerts, etc.
bandy, *n.* *band*-e, a club bent at the end for striking a ball; a game at ball with such a club; hockey, esp. on the ice: *a.* having an outward bend: *v.t.* to beat to and fro, as at bandy; to toss to and fro; to give and take; to toss about: *v.i.* to contend as at bandy. (Fr. *bandé*, bent.)
bandy, *n.* *band*-e, a cart, gig, or bullock-drawn vehicle used in parts of India. (Telugu.)
bandy-legged, *a.* *band*-e-legd, having bow legs.
bane, *n.* bane, poison; any fatal cause; ruin; destruction. (A.S. *bana*, destruction.)
baneberry, *n.* *bane*-be-re, the herb-christopher, the berries of which are poisonous, *Actæa spicata.*
baneful, *a.* *bane*-ful, destructive; deadly.
banefully, *ad.* *bane*-ful-le, in a baneful manner.
banefulness, *n.* *bane*-ful-ness, the quality of being baneful.
banewort, *n.* *bane*-wurt, the deadly-nightshade, lesser spearwort, or other poisonous plant.
bang, *v.t.* bang, to beat; to handle roughly; to force to with a loud noise; to surpass: *v.i.* to resound with a loud noise; to thump at: *n.* a sudden slamming sound; a thump; front hair cut straight across. (Ice. *banga*, to beat.)
bang, *n.* bang, bhang.
bangle, *n.* *bang*-gl, an ornament worn upon the arms or ankles. (Hind. *bangrī*, a glass bracelet.)
bangle-ears, *n.pl.* *bang*-gl-eerz, loose hanging ears, like those of a dog (an imperfection in a horse).
bang-tail, *n.* *bang*-tayl, a horse with the tail cut off square.
Banian, *n.* *ban*-yan, one of a strictly vegetarian caste of Hindu travelling merchants; (*l.c.*) a Bengali house servant in European employ; a man's loose morning gown as worn by the Banians; the banyan-tree. **banian day,** among seamen [Slang], a day on which no meat is served. (Port., from Gujarati.)
banish, *v.t.* *ban*-ish, to condemn to exile; to drive or force away. (O.Fr. *banis*, from *banir*, to exile.)
banishment, *n.* *ban*-ish-ment, the act of banishing; the state of being banished; exile; expulsion.
banister, *n.* *ban*-is-ter, a light column supporting the handrail at the side of a staircase; (*pl.*) the whole railing. (Corruption of *baluster.*)
banjo, *n.* *ban*-joh, a stringed musical instrument with a body like a tambourine and a head and neck like a guitar, and played with the fingers.
banjoist, *n.* *ban*-jo-ist, one who plays the banjo.
bank, *n.* bank, a mound or ridge of earth or of sand; an embankment; the margin of a river or lake; a rising gradient; the side of a railway cutting; a shoal; a rowing bench; the coal-face in a mine; the surface round the top of a mine shaft; a pile of clouds; a bed of shellfish; a row of keys in an organ; a row, as of cylinders or boilers [Eng.]; a particular assemblage of fixed contacts used in automatic telephony: *v.t.* to raise a mound about; to embank; to enclose, defend, or fortify with a bank; to tilt (an aircraft) in turning [Av.]: *v.i.* to roll or tilt in turning (of aircraft) [Av.]. **bank a fire,** to shut in a fire so that it may burn low. (M.E. *banke.*)
bank, *n.* bank, an establishment which trades in money, by investing, lending, or exchanging it; the banking office; a company associated in banking business; a fund; the pool at a gaming table: *v.t.* to deposit money in a bank: *v.i.* to do banking; to act as banker. **bank holiday,** a public holiday declared by Act of Parliament, such as Boxing Day, Easter Monday, Whit Monday, and the first Monday in August, in England, and Christmas Day, New Year's Day, Good Friday, and the first Mondays in May and August, in Scotland. **bank rate,** the rate at which the Bank of England discounts bills of exchange. (Fr. *banque*, bench.)
bankable, *a.* *bank*-a-bl, receivable at a bank.
bank-bill, *n.* *bank*-bill, a note, or a bill of exchange of a bank, payable at some future specified time.
bank-book, *n.* *bank*-book, a pass-book, or copy of a customer's account with a bank.
bank-credit, *n.* *bank*-kred-it, permission, on security given, to draw to a certain amount.
banker, *n.* *bank*-er, one who keeps a bank or traffics in money; a vessel in the cod-fishery on the banks of Newfoundland; a stone bench used by masons; a gambling card game, also, the player holding the pool.
banket, *n.* *bank*-et, the conglomerate rock forming the gold reef of the Transvaal. (Dut., name of a kind of almond-rock.)
banking, *n.* *bank*-ing, the act of casting up a bank; embankment; the business of a banker; the tilting of an aeroplane when rounding a curve: *a.* pertaining to or conducted by a bank.
bank-note, *n.* *bank*-note, a promissory note, payable on demand, issued by a bank.
bankrupt, *n.* *bank*-rupt, one who is unable to pay his debts; an insolvent debtor: *a.* unable to pay one's debts; insolvent: *v.t.* to break one in trade; to make insolvent; to discredit. (Fr. *banqueroute.*)
bankruptcy, *n.* *bank*-rupt-se, the state of being a bankrupt; the act of becoming a bankrupt. **act of bankruptcy,** an act by which a debtor renders himself liable to be declared a bankrupt.
Banksia, *n.* *bank*-se-a, a genus of Australasian evergreen flowering shrubs. (Sir Joseph *Banks.*)
banksman, *n.* *banks*-man, an overseer at a pit-head.
bank-stock, *n.* *bank*-stok, the capital stock of a bank, esp. the Bank of England.
banlieue, *n.* *bahn*-lew, the territory without the walls of a town but within its jurisdiction. (Fr. *banlieue.*)
banner, *n.* *ban*-ner, a rectangular flag, ensign, or standard bearing some device or emblem; a flag borne between two poles; the upper petal of a papilionaceous corolla [Bot.]. (O.Fr. *baniere.*)
bannered, *a.* *ban*-nerd, furnished with banners.
banneret, *n.* *ban*-ner-et, a knighthood conferred on the field of battle, in reward for valour; a knight so created; a Swiss officer who had charge of the banner of his canton. (O.Fr. *baneret.*)
bannerol, *n.* *ban*-ner-ole, a small banner carried at a funeral.
bannock, *n.* *ban*-nok, a flat oatmeal or barley-meal cake baked on an iron plate over the fire. (Gael. *bannach.*)
banns, *n.pl.* banz, notice of an intention of marriage, given in a church.
banquet, *n.* *bank*-wit, a sumptuous feast; a dinner with speeches, etc.: *v.t.* to treat with a feast or rich entertainment: *v.i.* to feast; to regale one's self with rich fare. (Fr. *banquet.*)
banqueter, *n.* *bank*-we-ter, a guest at a banquet.
banqueting, *n.* *bank*-we-ting, the act of feasting; luxurious living.
banquette, *n.* *ban*-ket, a firestep in a trench or fortification; the footway of a road or bridge.
banshee, *n.* *ban*-shee, female spirit supposed in Ireland to be attached to a house and to give evil omens. (Gael. *beanshith.*)
bant, *v.i.* bant, to practise banting.
bantam, *n.* *ban*-tam, a dwarf fowl, perhaps first brought from Bantam, in Java; a small pugnacious man; a boxer not exceeding 8 st. 6 lb. in weight: *a.* of bantam breed; small.
banter, *v.t.* *ban*-ter, to ridicule humorously; to make a joke of: *n.* chaff; pleasant raillery; ridicule.
banting, *n.* *bant*-ing, the reduction of corpulency by means of a diet excluding sugar, starch, etc. (Wm. *Banting*, its Eng. originator, *c.* 1850.)
bantling, *n.* *bant*-ling, a young child; a bastard infant. (Ger. *bänkling*, bastard.)

Bantu, *n.* *bahn*-too, a group of South African tribes of mixed negroid and Hamitic stock; their language: *a.* pertaining to this stock.

banxring, *n.* *banks*-ring, a small insectivorous squirrel-like mammal of Malaysia. (Javanese.)

banyan, *n.* *ban*-yan, the Indian fig, *Ficus benghalensis*, a tree whose branches, bending to the ground, take root and form new stocks, till they cover a prodigious extent of ground; banian.

banzai, *n.* bahn-*zah*-ee, the Japanese cheer ("Live for ever!").

baobab, *n.* *bay*-o-bab, the monkey bread or sour gourd, an African tree with a stem of great thickness, *Adansonia digitata*.

Baphometic, *a.* baf-o-*met*-ik, pertaining to Baphomet, an idol alleged to have been worshipped by the Templars, or to the rites connected with his worship.

baptism, *n.* *bap*-tizm, the initiatory rite or sacrament of the Christian Church by solemn immersion in or sprinkling with water; used also of the ceremonial naming of ships, etc. (O.Fr. *baptiser*.)

baptismal, *a.* bap-*tiz*-mal, pertaining to baptism.

baptismally, *ad.* bap-*tiz*-ma-le, by baptism.

Baptist, *n.* *bap*-tist, one who administers baptism; a member of a Church holding that baptism should be administered only to adults.

baptistery, *n.* *bap*-tis-ter-e or *bap*-tis-tre, the place where baptism is administered; the tank used in baptism by immersion.

baptistry, *n.* *bap*-tis-tre, baptistery.

baptizable, *a.* bap-*tize*-a-bl, that may be baptized.

baptize, *v.t.* bap-*tize*, to administer baptism; to christen; to consecrate or initiate.

bar, *n.* bar, a substantial solid rod used as a lever, axis, or obstruction; a cross beam or bolt; a barrier for defence; a bank of sand, gravel, etc., obstructing entrance at the mouth of a river or harbour; the railing that encloses the place which barristers occupy in courts of justice; the place in a court at which criminals stand during trial; the rail just within the door of either House of Parliament beyond which non-members are not admitted; those who plead at the bar; any tribunal, as, the bar of public opinion; the enclosed place or counter of a tavern, etc., where liquors are served out; the clasp on a medal ribbon denoting an additional distinction; anything laid across another, as stripes in colour, and the like; the highest part of the place in a horse's mouth between the grinders and tusks; the space included by two straight lines drawn across an escutcheon [Her.]; a peremptory exception, sufficient to destroy the plaintiff's action [Law]; a line drawn perpendicularly across the lines of the staff, including between each two a certain quantity of time, or number of beats [Mus.]; an ingot of precious metal run in a mould and unwrought [Comm.]: *v.t.* to fasten with a bar; to obstruct; to exclude; to except; to cross with stripes of a different colour. **trial at bar,** *see* **trial.** (Fr. *barre*.)

bar, *n.* bar, the unit of atmospheric pressure, equal to the pressure of one million dynes per square centimetre, or the weight of a column of mercury of one square centimetre 29·5306 inches high at a temperature of 32° F. [Meteor.]; a pressure of one dyne per square centimetre [Chem.]. (Gr. *baros*, weight.)

barathea, *n.* ba-ra-*thee*-a, a fine-textured fabric of mixed silk or cotton with wool.

barb, *n.* barb, a beard, or that which resembles it, or grows in the place of it; part of the armour of a mail-clad warhorse; the throat piece of a wimple as worn by nuns; a hooked hair [Bot.]; the points that stand backward in an arrow or fish-hook; a lateral filament of the shaft of a feather: *v.t.* to furnish with barbs, as a fishhook or spear. (L. *barba*, a beard.)

barb, *n.* barb, a horse of Barbary breed; a variety of pigeon originally from Barbary.

barbacan, *n.* *bar*-ba-kan, a barbican.

Barbados-cherry, *n.* bar-*bay*-doze-*che*-re, the West Indian tree, *Malpighia urens*, also its slightly acid fruit. **Barbados leg,** elephantiasis.

barbarian, *n.* bar-*bare*-re-an, a savage; one in a rude uncivilized state; one destitute of pity or humanity: *a.* rude; uncivilized; cruel; inhuman. (Gr. and L. *barbaros*, speaking a language foreign to that of either Greece or Rome.)

barbaric, *a.* ba-*ba*-rik, pertaining to barbarians; indicating barbarism.

barbarically, *ad.* bar-*ba*-re-ka-le, in a barbaric, uncivilized, or illiterate fashion.

barbarism, *n.* *bar*-ba-rizm, a form of speech contrary to the pure idioms of a language; a rude, ignorant, uncivilized state; brutality; cruelty; lack of culture.

barbarity, *n.* bar-*ba*-re-te, the state of being barbarous; an act of brutality; inhumanity.

barbarization, *n.* *bar*-ba-ry-*zay*-shon, the act of making, or state of being barbarous.

barbarize, *v.t.* *bar*-ba-rize, to make barbarous.

barbarous, *a.* *bar*-ba-rus, rude; uncivilized; barbaric; cruel; unidiomatic; uncultured.

barbarously, *ad.* *bar*-ba-rus-le, in a barbarous manner.

barbarousness, *n.* *bar*-ba-rus-ness, the quality or state of being barbarous.

Barbary-ape, *n.* *bar*-ba-re-*ayp*, the tailless ape of N. Africa and Gibraltar.

Barbary-sheep, *n.* *bar*-ba-re-*sheep*, the maned wild sheep of N. Africa, *Ovis tragelophus*.

barbastelle, *n.* bar-ba-*stel*, a European and Himalayan bat of the genus *Plecotus*. (Fr.)

barbate, *a.* *bar*-bat, bearded; awned [Bot.].

barbecue, *n.* *bar*-be-kew, a framework on which meat is smoked or dried; any large animal broiled or roasted whole; hence, an open-air picnic at which animals are roasted whole; a platform on which coffee beans are dried in the sun: *v.t.* to smoke or cure meat; to roast whole. (Sp. *barbacoa*.)

barbed, *a.* barbd, bearded; furnished with barbs; furnished with armour. **barbed wire,** strong fencing wire armed with sharp points.

barbel, *n.* *bar*-bel, a freshwater fish, allied to the carp, with beard-like appendages on its upper jaw, *Barbus vulgaris*; *pl.* small fleshy processes appended to the mouths of some fishes.

barbellate, *a.* *bar*-bel-ate, having short stiff hooked bristles [Bot.].

barber, *n.* *bar*-ber, one who shaves beards, and cuts and dresses hair: *v.t.* to shave or cut hair. **barber surgeon,** one who practised both shaving and surgery. **barber's itch,** sycosis. (L. *barba*, a beard.)

barberry, *n.* *bar*-be-re, a thorny shrub of the genus *Berberis*; its red acid berry.

barbet, *n.* *bar*-bet, a tropical climbing bird allied to the toucans; a variety of poodle.

barbette, *n.* bar-*bet*, a terrace inside a parapet from which cannon can be fired over the top [Fort.]; the armoured turret of a warship. (Fr.)

barbican, *n.* *bar*-be-kan, an outer fortification to a castle or town; a watchtower guarding a gate or drawbridge. (O.Fr. *barbacan*.)

barbital, *n.* *bar*-be-tal, a hypnotic chemically and pharmaceutically resembling veronal.

barbiton, *n.* *bar*-be-ton, an ancient musical stringed instrument allied to the lyre. (Gr. *barbitos*.)

barbitone, *n.* *bar*-be-tone, veronal.

barbituric, *a.* bar-be-*tewr*-rik, designating a crystalline acid obtained by heating a preparation of dilute nitric acid and uric acid used in the manufacture of medicinal hypnotics.

barbola, *n.* bar-*boh*-la, a form of decoration by modelling in prepared paste and colouring; a modern form of gesso.

barbule, *n.* *bar*-bewl, a minute barb or beard.

barcarole, *n.* *bar*-ka-role, a melody sung by Venetian gondoliers; any similar composition; a boat song. (It. *barcaruolo*, boat song.)

bard, *n.* bard, an armoured horse's breastplate.

bard, *n.* bard, a Celtic minstrel; a poet. (W. *bardd*.)

bard, *n.* bard, a thin slice of bacon for larding: *v.t.* to lard with such slices. (Fr.)

bardic, *a.* *bard*-ik, pertaining to bards, or their poetry; written by a bard.

bardish, *a.* *bard*-ish, bardic.

bardism, *n.* *bard*-izm, the learning and maxims of bards; the method of bards.

bardolater, *n.* bard-*ol*-a-ter, one addicted to bardolatry.

bardolatry, *n.* bard-*ol*-a-tre, excessive or indiscriminating reverence for Shakespeare or his works. (*Bard* of Avon, and *-olatry*.)

bare, obsolete *p.* of the verb to bear.

bare, *a.* bare, naked; unclothed; with head uncovered as a mark of respect; unadorned; poor; destitute; much worn; empty: *v.t.* to strip; to make bare. **bare poles,** the masts of a ship without sails set. (A.S. *bær*, naked.)
bareback, *a. bare*-bak, without a saddle.
barefaced, *a. bare*-fayst, with face uncovered; without concealment; shameless; beardless.
barefacedly, *ad. bare*-fayst-le, in a barefaced manner; impudently.
barefacedness, *n. bare*-fayst-ness, the quality of being barefaced.
barefoot, *a.* and *ad. bare*-foot, with the feet naked.
barège, *n.* ba-*rayzh*, a thin gauzy fabric of worsted and silk or cotton. (*Barèges*, S. France.)
bare-headed, *a.* bare-*hed*-ed, having the head uncovered.
barely, *ad. bare*-le, in a bare manner; poorly; scarcely.
bareness, *n. bare*-ness, the state or quality of being bare.
bare-ribbed, *a. bare*-ribd, very lean.
bargain, *n. barg*-en, a contract, generally concerning sale and purchase; the thing bought or sold; an advantageous purchase: *v.i.* to make a contract or agreement; to haggle: *v.t.* to transfer for a consideration. **strike a bargain,** to complete a bargain. **into the bargain,** over and above. (Fr. *barguigner*, to higgle.)
bargainee, *n. barg*-en-ee, he who accepts a bargain; a purchaser.
bargainer, *n. barg*-en-er, he who makes a bargain; a seller; a haggler.
barge, *n.* barj, a large boat, generally flat-bottomed, used for loading and unloading ships, or for freighting on rivers and canals; a boat of state; a houseboat; the boat of a superior officer of a ship of war: *v.i.* to move clumsily; to lurch; to butt in. (It. *barca*, a boat.)
bargeboard, *n. barj*-bord, the facing board at the gable of a building that conceals the barge-couples [Arch.]. (Of uncertain origin.)
barge-couples, *n.pl. barj*-kup-plz, two beams mortised the one into the other, to strengthen the building [Arch.].
barge-course, *n. barj*-koarse, tiling which projects beyond the external face of the gable; the coping of a wall formed by a course of bricks set on edge.
bargee, *n.* bar-*jee*, a bargeman.
bargeman, *n. barj*-man, the manager of a barge.
bargemaster, *n. barj*-mahs-ter, the owner of a barge or barges.
barghest, *n. bar*-gest, a legendary dog-like spectre whose appearance foretells death or disaster. (Ger.)
baric, *a. ba*-rik, barometric. (Gr. *baros*, weight.)
baric, *a. bare*-rik, pertaining to or containing barium.
barilla, *n.* ba-*ril*-la, an impure sodium carbonate obtained from the ashes of certain seaweeds or from those of Salsola Soda, a plant found on the coast of Spain; this plant itself. (Sp.)
barillet, *n.* ba-*ril*-let, the cylinder containing the mainspring of a watch. (Fr. *baril*, a barrel.)
baritone, *n. ba*-re-tone, a male voice between tenor and bass; a singer having this voice; a small bass sax-horn [Mus.]; a word unaccented on the last syllable [Gr. gram.]: *a.* of, pertaining to, or having a baritone voice or compass.
barium, *n. bare*-re-um, a malleable metallic chemical element allied to calcium and strontium; it occurs only in combination and is the base of baryta.
bark, *n.* bark, a small vessel; a barque. (Fr. *barque.*)
bark, *n.* bark, the outer coverings of a plant beyond the wood, and formed of tissue parallel with it; Peruvian bark; tanner's bark exhausted of tannic acid; an outer covering: *v.t.* to peel; to strip off the bark; to tan; to cover with bark; to graze the skin. (Dan. *bark.*)
bark, *n.* bark, the cry of a dog or wolf: *v.i.* to make the noise of dogs; to cough; to speak sharply. **bark up the wrong tree,** to misdirect one's endeavours; to pursue a mistaken object. (A.S. *beorcan*, to bark.)
bark-bed, *n. bark*-bed, a hotbed made of tanner's spent bark; any similar hotbed [Hort.].
bark-bound, *a. bark*-bound, having the bark so firm or close as to hinder growth.
barkentine, *n. bark*-en-teen, a barquentine.
barker, *n. bark*-er, one who strips trees of their bark; one who clamours unreasonably; one who stands at a shop door to invite customers; an automatic pistol [Slang].
barking-iron, *n. bark*-ing-i-urn, an implement for stripping tan-bark from trees; a pistol [Slang.]
bark-mill, *n. bark*-mill, a mill for crushing bark.
bark-pit, *n. bark*-pit, a tan-vat.
barky, *a. bark*-e, consisting of or containing bark; resembling or covered with bark.
barley, *n. bar*-le, a cereal of the genus *Hordeum*, used especially for making malt. **pearl barley,** dressed barley. **pot barley,** barley stripped of the husk. **barley wine,** an extra strong ale. (A.S. *bærlic*, barley-like.)
barley-brake, *n. bar*-le-brake, an ancient rustic game played round stacks of grain.
barley-bree, *n. bar*-le-bree, strong beer.
barley-broth, *n. bar*-le-broth, Scotch broth, a broth made by boiling barley and flesh along with certain vegetables; barley-bree.
barleycorn, *n. bar*-le-kawrn, a grain of barley; the third of an inch. **John Barleycorn,** the personification of malt liquors.
barley-meal, *n. bar*-le-meel, barley ground into flour.
barley-mow, *n. bar*-le-moh, a place for storing reaped barley; a stack of barley.
barley-sugar, *n. bar*-le-*shu*-gar, sugar boiled till it is brittle, formerly with a decoction of barley.
barley-water, *n. bar*-le-waw-ter, a cooling drink made by boiling pearl-barley in water.
barlow, *n. bar*-loh, a large single-bladed pocket-knife (U.S.A. Name of maker.)
barm, *n.* barm, yeast; the froth upon malt liquor when fermenting, and used as leaven. (A.S. *beorma*, yeast.)
barmaid, *n. bar*-made, a female attendant at a drinking bar.
barman, *n. bar*-man, a man who serves at the bar of an inn or other place of refreshment; a tapster.
barmbrack, *n. barm*-brak, a light currant cake or loaf baked in Ireland.
Barmecide, *a. bar*-me-side, unreal; imaginary. (From the imaginary feast provided for the beggar by the Barmecide prince in the Arabian Nights.)
barmkin, *n. barm*-kin, part of a castle's outer fortification; a barbican.
barmy, *a. barm*-e, containing barm; light-headed; crazy.
barn, *n.* barn, a covered building for storing grain, hay or straw; a similar building for cattle or other farm purpose. (A.S. *bere*, barley, *ærn*, house.)
barnacle, *n. barn*-a-kl, a cirriped found attached to the bottoms of ships, rocks, and timber, below the surface of the sea; a species of goose formerly supposed either to grow from trees or to be developed from the cirriped from which it is named: *pl.* an instrument put upon a horse's nose, to confine him for shoeing, bleeding, or dressing; a pair of spectacles [Slang]. (Fr. *barnaque.*)
barn-dance, *n.* a country-dance in which couples dance successively singly and together [Amer.].
barn-door, *n. barn*-dawr, door of a barn: *a.* reared in the farmyard (of fowls).
barney, *n. bar*-ne, jollification; a spree [Slang].
barn-owl, *n. barn*-oul, the screech owl, *Strix flammea.*
barnstormer, *n. barn*-storm-er, a strolling player; an uncultured or vociferous actor.
barogram, *n. ba*-ro-gram, the record obtained from a barograph.
barograph, *n. ba*-ro-graf, an aneroid barometer that records the variations in atmospheric pressure. (Gr. *baros*, weight, *grapho*, write.)
barology, *n.* ba-*rol*-o-je, the science of weight.
barometer, *n.* ba-*rom*-e-ter, an instrument for measuring the pressure of the atmosphere, and so indicating changes of weather, as well as determining altitudes. (Gr. *baros*, and *metron*, measure.)
barometric, *a.* ba-ro-*met*-rik, barometrical.
barometrical, *a.* ba-ro-*met*-re-kal, pertaining to, relating to, or indicated by, the barometer.
barometrically, *ad.* ba-ro-*met*-re-ka-le, by means of a barometer.
barometz, *n. ba*-ro-metz, a fern, *Cibotium barometz*, which, from its shaggy nature and habit, was formerly thought to be both animal and vegetable; Scythian lamb. (Russ. *baranets.*)

baron, *n. ba*-ron, a member of the lowest degree of nobility in the British peerage; originally, one who held by military service from the king; a judge of the old court of Exchequer; a husband, as, **baron and feme,** husband and wife [Law]. **baron of beef,** two sirloins not cut asunder. **Barons of the Cinque Ports,** members of the House of Commons formerly elected by the Cinque Ports. (Fr.)

baronage, *n. ba*-ron-aj, the body of the barons; the dignity of a baron; the land giving title to a baron; a record of barons and their families.

baroness, *n. ba*-ron-ess, a baron's wife or widow; a woman holding the baronial title in her own right.

baronet, *n. ba*-ron-et, an hereditary order of commoners, entitled "Sir" and taking precedence next below a baron and above a knight. (Diminutive of baron.)

baronetage, *n. ba*-ron-et-aj, the collective body of baronets; the rank of baronet; a record of baronets and their families.

baronetcy, *n. ba*-ron-et-se, the dignity or rank of a baronet.

baronial, *a.* ba-*roh*-ne-al, pertaining to or befitting a baron.

barony, *n. ba*-ron-e, the lordship of a baron; a subdivision of an Irish county; a mediæval land-tenure. (O.Fr. *baronie.*)

baroque, *n.* ba-*roke*, a lavish architectural style dating from mid-17th cent. and rococo in character: *a.* of a rococo or grotesque nature.

baroscope, *n. ba*-ro-skope, an early form of barometer. (Gr. *baros*, and *skopeo*, view.)

barouche, *n.* ba-*roosh*, a double-seated four-wheel carriage, with a folding roof. (Ger. *barutsche.*)

bar-posts, *n.pl. bar*-pohsts, posts sunk in the ground to form the sides of a field-gate.

barque, *n.* bark, a three-masted ship with no squaresails on the mizenmast. (Fr.)

barquentine, *n. bark*-en-*teen*, a three-masted vessel square-rigged on the foremast and fore-and-aft rigged on the main and mizen. (Fr. *barque.*)

barracan, *n. ba*-ra-kan, a coarse Levantine fabric, formerly of wool and goat's hair, resembling camlet. (Ar. *barrakan.*)

barrack, *n. ba*-rak, a large building to lodge soldiers in, generally plural; any large plain building for housing persons: *v.i.* to jeer noisily, esp. at sporting events, as a sign of displeasure. [Slang]. (Fr. *baraque.*)

barracking, *n. ba*-rak-ing, ironical cheering.

barracoon, *n.* ba-ra-*koon*, an African fortified slave depot. (Sp.)

barracuda, *n.* ba-ra-*koo*-dah, a large pike-like predatory marine fish of the family *Sphyrænidæ*, allied to the mullet. (Sp.)

barrage, *n. ba*-raj, the act of barring; the forming an artificial bar in a stream to increase the depth of water; a curtain of artillery fire rendering a sector, or given line, impassable. **barrage balloon,** one of a number of captive kite-balloons protecting with their wire cables a given area against low-flying attack by aircraft. (Fr.)

barras, *n, ba*-ras, a resin, obtained from fir-trees, the the basis of Burgundy pitch.

barrator, *n. ba*-ra-ter, an encourager of litigation; one who commits barratry [Comm.]. (O.Fr. *baratour*, a cheating knave.)

barratrous, *a. ba*-ra-trus, guilty of or addicted to barratry.

barratry, *n. ba*-ra-tre, the practice of exciting or encouraging lawsuits; fraud or negligence by a shipmaster by which the owners, freighters, or insurers are injured. (O.Fr. *baraterie.*)

barrel, *n. ba*-rel, a round oblong vessel, bulging in the middle, built of staves or bars, girt with loops and closed at both ends; a cask; the quantity which a barrel should contain; anything hollow and long, as the barrel of a gun; a cylinder about which anything is wound; a tube; a measure of 36 gallons: *v.t.* to draw off into or pack in a barrel. **barrel of the ear,** a cavity behind the tympanum. (Fr. *baril.*)

barrelage, *n. ba*-rel-aj, the amount in or drawn from barrels.

barrel-bulk, *n.* five cubic feet [Naut.].

barrelled, *a. ba*-reld, having a barrel or tube; packed in, or shaped like, a barrel.

barrel-organ, *n.* an instrument producing music by means of a revolving cylinder studded with pegs which open valves that let in air to pipes.

barrel-vault, *n.* a semi-cylindrical vault or roof.

barren, *a. ba*-ren, incapable of producing young or fruit; unproductive; unfruitful; uninventive: *n.* any unproductive tract of land; prairie land bearing only stunted trees. (O.Fr. *baraine.*)

barrenly, *ad. ba*-ren-le, in a barren manner.

barrenness, *n. ba*-ren-ness, the quality of being barren; sterility.

barret, *n. ba*-ret, a biretta; a beret. (Fr.)

barricade, *n. ba*-re-*kade*, a fortification, made in haste, of anything that will serve to obstruct an enemy or as shelter from attack; any bar or obstruction; that which defends: *v.t.* to stop up a passage; to fortify. (Fr. *barricade.*)

barricado, *n.* ba-re-*kay*-doh, a barricade.

barrico, *n.* ba-*ree*-koh, a small keg. (Sp. *barrica.*)

barrier, *n. ba*-re-er, anything which hinders approach or attack; an enclosing fence or material obstruction; any limit or boundary. **barrier reef,** a barrier of coral round islands and along shores with a lagoon between. (O.Fr. *barrière.*)

barring, *prep. bar*-ring, excepting.

barring-out, *n.* bar-ring-*out*, exclusion, especially of a schoolmaster by his pupils in sport at Christmas.

barrister, *n. ba*-ris-ter, one called to the bar as a qualified advocate in the higher courts. **revising barrister,** *see* **revise.** (*Bar.*)

barrow, *n. ba*-ro, a tumulus; a prehistoric grave-mound. (A.S. *beorg*, a hill.)

barrow, *n. ba*-ro, a light small carriage; a hand-cart; a frame covered in the middle with boards, and borne between two men; a frame with a box, supported by one wheel. **barrow-boy,** an intinerant street salesman, a costermonger [Coll.]. (A.S. *ber-an*, to carry.)

barrow, *n. ba*-ro, an infant's long sleeveless garment of flannel. (A.S. *beorgan*, to protect.)

barrow, *n. ba*-ro, a castrated boar. (A.S. *bearg*, boar.)

barrulet, *n. ba*-roo-let, a stripe, one-fourth the width of a bar, running horizontally [Her.].

barruly, *a. ba*-roo-le, divided horizontally by barrulets [Her.].

barry, *a. ba*-re, divided horizontally into a number of partitions by bars of two alternate colours (of heraldic shields). (O.Fr. *barré*, bent.)

bar-shears, *n. bar*-sheerz, a contrivance for cutting metal bars.

bar-shoe, *n. bar*-shoo, a kind of horseshoe to protect the frog of the foot from injury.

bar-shot, *n.* double-headed shot, consisting of a bar, with a half-ball or round head at each end.

bar-tender, *n. bar*-tend-er, a barman [U.S.A.].

barter, *n. bar*-ter, traffic by exchange of commodities: *v.t.* to traffic by exchange: *v.i.* to give one thing for another. (O.Fr. *bareter*, to cheat.)

bartizan, *n. bar*-te-zan, a small overhanging turret, projecting from the corners of ancient fortifications.

barton, *n. bar*-tn, the domain lands of a manor; the manor itself; the outhouses; a farmyard. (A.S. *bere*, barley, *tūn*, an enclosed space.)

barwood, *n. bar*-wood, a red dye-wood from Africa; camwood.

bary-, *pref. ba*-re, signifying "heavy." (Gr. *barys*, weighty.)

barycentric, *a. ba*-re-*sen*-trik, at or pertaining to the centre of gravity.

barysphere, *n. ba*-re-sfeer, the innermost portion of the earth, enclosed by the lithosphere.

baryta, *n.* ba-*ry*-ta, barium monoxide.

barytes, *n.* ba-*ry*-teez, heavy-spar; native barium sulphate. (Gr. *barytēs*, weight.)

barytic, *a.* ba-*rit*-ik, pertaining to, formed of, or containing barytes or baryta.

barytone, *n.* and *a. ba*-re-tone, baritone.

basal, *a. bay*-sal, pertaining to, or constituting, the base; fundamental.

basally, *ad. bay*-sal-le, fundamentally.

basalt, *n. bas*-awlt, an igneous rock, often columnar, of a dark colour, and consisting chiefly of augite and felspar, with grains of magnetic or titanic iron. (L. *basaltes*, a N. African syenite.)

basaltic, *a.* ba-*sawl*-tik, pertaining to basalt; formed of, or containing, basalt.

basaltiform, *a.* ba-*sawl*-te-form, having the columnar structure of basalt.
basan, *n. bas*-an, bookbinder's basil.
basanite, *n. baz*-a-nite, Lydian stone, or touchstone, a compact variety of flinty slate of a black colour. (L. *basanites lapis*, a touchstone.)
bascinet, *n. bas*-se-net, a spherical helmet of the 15th cent., usually without vizor. (O.Fr. *bacinet.*)
bascule, *n. bas*-kewl, a balanced lever. **bascule bridge,** a balanced drawbridge. (Fr.)
★**base,** *a.* base, low in value, worth, or origin, or in social scale, spirit, etc.; worthless; mean; despicable; counterfeit: *n.* the foundation on which a thing stands or rests; the starting line in certain sports and games; prisoners' base, an old game; a goal; one of four stations at baseball; the broad part of anything; the lowest side of a figure on which it is supposed to stand [Geom.]; the lower part of a column between the shaft and the plinth [Arch.]; the headquarters or central supply depot of an army in the field or of a naval or air force [Mil.]; that with which an acid unites to form a salt [Chem.]: *v.t.* to found; to lay the base or foundation of; to set or place. (Fr. *bas*, low.)
baseball, *n. base*-bawl, a ball-game derived from rounders, the national ball-game of the United States and Canada.
base-born, *a. base*-born, born out of wedlock; of low parentage; vile; mean.
base-court, *n. base*-koart, the back yard; an inferior court; the farmyard.
basel, *n. baz*-el, tanned sheepskin, basil.
baseless, *a. base*-less, without base or foundation.
base-line, *n. base*-line, the line from which surveying and military operations begin.
basely, *ad. base*-le, in a base manner.
basement, *n. base*-ment, the lowest part of anything, esp. a building; a floor next below the principal floor, esp. when below ground level.
baseness, *n. base*-ness, meanness, vileness.
basenji, *n.* ba-*sen*-je, a terrier-like dog from the Belgian Congo, remarkable for being mute.
bash, *n.* bash, a hard blow: *v.t.* to strike a smashing blow. (Scand. *baske*, to slap.)
bashaw, *n.* ba-*shaw*, a pasha; a proud, tyrannical man. (Turk.)
bashful, *a. bash*-ful, easily disconcerted or put out; shy; diffident; excessively modest.
bashfully, *ad. bash*-ful-le, in a bashful manner.
bashfulness, *n. bash*-ful-ness, the quality of being bashful.
bashi-bazouks, *n.pl. bash*-e-ba-*zooks*, former irregular Turkish soldiery notorious for the committal of atrocities. (Turk. *bashi-bozuq*, one of ill-balanced head.)
bashlyk, *n. bash*-lik, the Caucasian cowl, a cloth hood with ear-flaps. (Russ.)
basial, *a. bay*-ze-al, pertaining to kissing. (L. *basium*, a kiss.)
basic, *a. bay*-sik, relating to or constituting a base; performing the office of a base in a salt; having the base in excess [Chem.]; poor in silica (of rocks) [Min.]. **Basic English,** a simplified form of English using only 850 words (exclusive of certain international, technical, and scientific terms). **basic slag,** a by-product in the manufacture of steel used, when pulverized, as a fertilizer.
basicity, *n.* ba-*siss*-e-te, the ratio of the combination of an acid with a base; the combining power of an acid.
basil, *n. baz*-il, bezel.
basil, *n. baz*-il, an aromatic culinary herb, *Ocymum basilicum.* (O.Fr. *basile.*)
basil, *n. baz*-il, bark-tanned sheepskin leather used by bookbinders.
basilar, *a. bas*-e-lar, pertaining to or situated at the base, esp. [Anat.] of the skull.
Basilian, *a.* ba-*zil*-e-an, pertaining to St. Basil the Great or his order: *n.* a member of the monastic order founded *c.* 362 by St. Basil.
basilic, *a.* ba-*zil*-ik, basilican; kingly; royal. **basilic vein,** the middle vein of the arm [Anat.].
basilica, *n.* ba-*zil*-e-ka, an oblong public hall among the Romans for the transaction of business and the administration of justice, later with an apse at the end for the judges; a Christian church on the same plan; a structure over the grave of a royal person. (L. *basilica*, royal.)
basilican, *a.* ba-*zil*-e-kan, basilic; in the manner of a basilica; pertaining to the basilic vein.
basilicon, *n.* ba-*zil*-e-kon, a kind of salve or ointment.
basilisk, *n. baz*-e-lisk, a fabulous monster whose mere breath or look was alleged by the ancients to be fatal; the cockatrice; an early cannon of large size; a genus of creasted arboreal lizards, *Basiliscus*, living in tropical South America.
★**basin,** *n. bay*-sn, a shallow hollow vessel to hold water for washing and other uses; a pond, a dock, or any reservoir for water; the scale of a balance when hollow and round; a synclinal, forming a hollow [Geol.]; the entire tract of country drained by a river [Phys. Geog.]; an appliance used in grinding convex glasses [Opt.]. (O.Fr. *bacin.*)
basinet, *n. bas*-se-net, bascinet.
basipetal, *a.* ba-*sip*-et-al, developing at or proceeding towards the base [Bot.].
basis, *n. bay*-sis (*pl.* **bases**), *bay*-seez, the base or foundation; the lowest part of a column; the groundwork, or first principle. (Gr.)
bask, *v.i.* bahsk, to repose in the sunshine or in genial warmth or under fostering influence: *v.t.* to warm by continued exposure to heat: *n.* a spell of basking. (Ice. *batha-sk*, to bathe one's self.)
★**basket,** *n. bahs*-ket, a domestic vessel made of plaited twigs, rushes, or other flexible material; as much as a basket will contain: *v.t.* to put in a basket. (O.Fr. *basche.*)
basket-ball, *n. bahs*-ket-bawl, a game in which the two goals are baskets at the top of short poles.
basket-chair, *n. bahs*-ket-chare, a wickerwork chair.
basket-fish, *n. bahs*-ket-fish, a species of star-fish, *Astrophyton linckii.*
basketful, *n. bahs*-ket-ful, as much as fills a basket.
basket-hilt, *n. bahs*-ket-hilt, a sword-hilt, the pattern of which resembles basket-work.
basketry, *n. bahs*-ket-re, wickerwork.
basketwork, *n. bahs*-ket-wurk, wickerwork.
basking-shark, *n. bahs*-king-shark, a large but harmless shark, *Cetorhinus maximus.*
bason, *n. bay*-sn, a basin.
Basque, *n.* bahsk, a non-Aryan race inhabiting parts of the western Pyrenees; their language; (*l.c.*) a woman's jacket extending below the waist: *a.* pertaining to the Basque people or language.
bas-relief, *n. bah*-re-*leef* or *bass*-re-leef, low relief; a carving in low relief.
bass, *n.* bass, the sea perch, *Labrax lupus.* (A.S. *bærs*, a perch.)
bass, *n.* bass, the American linden-tree, called also bass-wood, *Tilia americana*; the bast or inner bark of this tree; matting made of it. **bass-broom,** a broom for rough work, made chiefly of piassava. (*Bast.*)
bass, *n.* bass, a bitter ale, so called from the brewer.
bass, *n.* base, the lowest part in the harmony of a musical composition; the lowest of male voices; a singer with this voice; the lowest tones of an instrument: *a.* low; deep; grave; pertaining to the bass: *v.t.* to utter in a deep tone. **bass horn,** the ophicleide. **bass viol,** *see* **viol.**
bass-bar, *n.* base-bar, a longitudinal wooden strut strengthening the belly of instruments of the violin family [Mus.].
basset, *n. bass*-et, an obsolete game at cards. (Fr.)
basset, *n. bass*-et, outcrop of strata [Geol.]: *a.* inclined upward: *v.i.* to incline upward, as strata.
basset, *n. bass*-et, a short-legged hound, the badger hound.
basset-horn, *n. bass*-et-hawrn, a tenor clarinet of great compass.
bassetto, *n.* ba-*set*-toh, a small 4-stringed bass viol formerly in use; a 4-ft. reed organ stop.
bassinet, *n. bass*-in-et, a cradle of wickerwork with a hood; a light perambulator. (Fr.)
basso, *n. bass*-oh, bass; a bass singer. (It.)
bassoon, *n.* ba-*soon*, a wood-wind instrument with a double reed, the bass oboe. (Fr. *basson.*)
bassoonist, *n.* ba-*soon*-ist, a performer on the bassoon.
basso-relievo, *n. bas*-soh-re-le-*ay*-vo, low relief.
bassorin, *n. bas*-o-rin, a superior yellowish-white gum obtained from tragacanth. (*Bassorah*, now *Basra*, Iraq.)

bass-wood, *n.* *bass*-wood, the wood of the bass or American linden.
bast, *n.* bast, the inner bark of the lime and other trees; rope or matting made of it. (A.S. *bæst.*)
bastard, *n.* *bas*-tard, a child born out of wedlock; anything spurious: *a.* begotten as a bastard; not genuine; non-standard; so impure as to be practically worthless [Geol.]. (O.Fr. *bastard.*)
bastardization, *n.* *bas*-tar-dy-*zay*-shon, declaration of illegitimacy.
bastardize, *v.t.* *bast*-ar-dize, to declare illegitimate; to prove to be bastard; to debase.
bastard-wing, *n.* the feathers attached to the representative of the thumb in a bird's wing.
bastardy, *n.* *bas*-tar-de, illegitimacy; the state of being a bastard.
baste, *v.t.* bayst, to beat with a stick; to drip fat upon meat while roasting. (Of uncertain origin.)
baste, *v.t.* bayst, to sew with long stitches; to sew slightly. (O.Fr. *bastir.*)
Bastille, *n.* bas-*teel*, an old fortress in Paris, long used as a state prison and demolished by the people in 1789; any fortress prison; anciently, a wheeled wooden tower used at sieges. (Fr.)
bastinado, *n.* bas-te-*nah*-do, a mode of punishment in the East by beating an offender on the soles of his feet; a blow or beating with a stick or cudgel; a cudgel: *v.t.* to inflict bastinado on. (Sp. *bastonado.*)
bastion, *n.* *bas*-te-on, an advanced work with two flanks and two faces standing out from the angles of a rampart; a salient angle [Fort.]. (Fr. *bastion.*)
bastioned, *a.* *bas*-te-ond, provided with bastions.
basto, *n.* *bas*-to, the ace of clubs at quadrille. (Sp.)
bat, *n.* bat, a heavy club; a thick broad blade of wood, with a cylindrical handle, used to strike the ball in cricket; a batsman; shale, or bituminous shale; a sheet of wadding for quilting; a piece of brick; pace, rate of speed [Slang]: *v.i.* to wield a bat at cricket. (A.S. *batt.*)
bat, *n.* bat, a nocturnal mammal with a body like a mouse and the forelimbs modified to form wings by means of which they fly with great rapidity. **bat fowling,** a mode of catching birds at night, by holding a light before a net and beating the roost. (Scand. *bakke.*)
batable, *a.* *bayt*-a-bl, debateable; disputable.
batata, *n.* bah-*tah*-ta, the sweet potato. *Batatas edulis*, of the West Indies. (Haytian.)
Batavian, *n.* ba-*tay*-ve-an, a native of ancient Batavia; a Dutchman: *a.* pertaining to ancient Batavia or to the Dutch.
batch, *n.* batch, the quantity of bread baked at one time; a quantity of similar things; a set.
bate, *v.t.* bate, to diminish; to deduct; to abate; to restrain; to remove: *v.i.* to dwindle; to fall away; to decrease in intensity or strength. (*abate*).
bate, *n.* bate, an alkaline lye used to clean and soften hides [Tanning]; the bath containing this: *v.t.* to steep in bate.
bateau, *n.* *bat*-oh (*pl.* **bateaux,** *bat*-ohz), a long narrow light boat. **bateau-bridge,** a pontoon-bridge. (Fr.)
bated, *a.* *bayt*-ed, artificially restrained.
★**bath,** *n.* bahth, a vessel, or the water in it, for bathing in; a bath-house; the act of bathing; a vessel holding a liquid to immerse any body in [the Arts]; a vessel holding a substance to regulate or modify the temperature of a body immersed in it [Chem.]: *v.t.* to wash or put in a bath (of children, invalids, dogs, etc.). **Order of the Bath,** a British order of knighthood initiation into which was originally preceded by ceremonial immersion in a bath. (A.S. *bæth*, bath.)
bath, *n.* bath, an ancient Hebrew liquid measure of about 8 gallons. (Heb.)
bath-brick, *n.* *bahth*-brik, a preparation of siliceous earth in the form of a brick for cleaning and polishing stone and metal.
bath-bun, *n.* *bahth*-bun, a rich spiced bun.
bath-chair, *n.* bahth-*chare*, a hooded wheeled-chair for the outdoor use of invalids.
bathe, *v.t.* baythe, to cleanse by immersion, as in a bath, or in the sea; to moisten or suffuse with a liquid: *v.i.* to be or lie in a bath: *n.* the act of bathing, especially in the sea. (A.S. *bathian*, to bathe.)
bather, *n.* *bayth*-er, one who bathes.
bathetic, *a.* ba-*thet*-ik, characterized by bathos.
bathing, *n.* *bayth*-ing, the act or practice of bathing. **bathing machine,** a covered vehicle from which to bathe in the sea.
bath-metal, *n.* *bahth*-met-al, a variety of brass.
bathometer, *n.* ba-*thom*-e-ter, an instrument for measuring depth by a spring balance. (Gr. *bathos*, depth, *metron*, a measure.)
bat-horse, *n.* *bat*-horse, a horse allowed a batman for carrying the utensils in his charge; a pack-horse.
bathos, *n.* *bayth*-os, a ludicrous descent from the elevated to the mean in writing or speech; anti-climax. (Gr. *bathos*, depth.)
bath-room, *n.* *bahth*-room, an apartment for containing a bath.
bath-stone, *n.* bahth-*stone*, an oolitic building stone quarried near Bath.
bathybius, *n.* ba-*thib*-e-us, a gelatinous non-organic substance found at the sea-bottom at great depths. (Gr. *bathys*, deep, *bios*, life.)
bathymetrical, *a.* bath-e-*met*-re-kal, pertaining to soundings; as regards depth in the sea.
bathymetry, *n.* ba-*thim*-e-tre, the art and method of taking soundings. (Gr. *bathos*, depth, *metron*, a measure.)
bathysphere, *n.* *bath*-e-sfeer, a spherical diving chamber for use in making deep-sea observations.
batik, *n.* *bat*-ik, a method of decorating textiles, parts to remain uncoloured being coated with wax which is removed after dyeing. (Javanese).
bating, *prep.* *bate*-ing, abating; deducting; except.
batiste, *n.* ba-*teest*, a kind of cambric. (Fr.)
batlet, *n.* *bat*-let, a small bat for beating linen.
batman, *n.* *bat*-man, an officer's servant; formerly, one in charge of the cooking utensils of a company in the field. (Fr. *bât*, a pack-saddle.)
baton, *n.* *bat*-on, a short staff or truncheon held in the hand as a badge of office; a marshal's staff; a conductor's wand [Mus.]; a mark of illegitimacy [Her.]: *v.t.* to strike or beat with a baton. (Fr.)
Batrachia, *n.pl.* ba-*trak*-ya, an order of amphibians, including frogs, toads, and newts. (Gr. *batrachos*, a frog.)
batrachian, *a.* ba-*trak*-yan, pertaining to the Batrachia.
batrachite, *n.* *bat*-ra-kite, a fossil batrachian; a frog-coloured gem-stone.
batrachoid, *a.* *bat*-ra-koyd, having the form of a frog.
Batrachomyomachy, *n.* *bat*-ra-kon-my-*om*-a-ke, The Battle between the Frogs and Mice, a burlesque poem ascribed to Homer. (Gr. *batrachos*, *mus*, a mouse, *mache*, a battle.)
batrachophagous, *a.* bat-ra-*kof*-a-gus, feeding on frogs.
batsman, *n.* *bats*-man, in cricket, and similar games, the one who wields the bat.
batswing, *n.* *bats*-wing, a gas-burner giving a flat flame.
batta, *n.* *bat*-ta, an allowance, in addition to their pay, made to troops in India when in the field. (Dravidian, "rice in the husk.")
batta, *n.* *bat*-ta, Anglo-Indian term for rate of exchange, also for a discount allowed on non-current or under-weight coin. (Urdu.)
battalia, *n.* ba-*tay*-le-a, an army in battle array.
battalion, *n.* ba-*tal*-yon, a division of an infantry regiment consisting of a small number of companies; the British unit of infantry.
battalioned, *a.* ba-*tal*-yond, formed into battalions.
battel, *v.i.* *bat*-tel, to stand indebted in the college books at Oxford for battels; to reside at a university. (Of uncertain origin.)
batteler, *n.* *bat*-tel-er, one who battels at Oxford, or who stands indebted on the college books.
battels, *n.* *bat*-telz, provisions from the buttery at Oxford; the charge for these; college accounts.
batten, *v.i.* *bat*-ten, to grow or become fat; to live in ease and luxury; to revel in. (Ice. *batna*, to become better.)
batten, *n.* *bat*-ten, a piece of board or scantling of a few inches in breadth; a bar in a silk loom: *v.t.* to form, secure, or strengthen with battens.
battening, *n.* *bat*-ten-ing, the act of attaching battens for nailing up laths or securing the hatches on hatchways; the battens thus attached.
batter, *n.* *bat*-ter, a mixture of flour and eggs

beaten together [Cookery]; the leaning back of a wall; paste; a blow; a piece of defaced printers' type: *v.t.* to beat with successive blows, so as to bruise, shake, or demolish; to attack with engines of war, as artillery; to wear or impair with beating, or by use; to paste together (Scots): *v.i.* to incline backwards from its base, as a wall. (Fr. *battre*, to beat.)

batter, *n.* *bat*-ter, one who bats; a mallet for flattening out potter's clay.

battering-ram, *n.* *bat*-ter-ing-ram, an ancient military engine used to batter down walls.

battering-train, *n.* *bat*-ter-ing-trayn, a siege train [Mil.].

battery, *n.* *bat*-ter-re, apparatus used in battering; a unit of artillery, its equipment and men; the men of a battery; a raised work on which guns are placed, with magazines below, and shelters to accommodate the men not on duty; a warship's guns, or a section of them; an assault by blows; the unlawful beating or even touching of another [Law]; a group of cells for the production of current [Elect.]; a combination of appliances or instruments, etc., used in various sciences and industries. **storage battery,** an accumulator [Elect.]. (Fr. *batterie.*)

batting, *n.* *bat*-ing, the management of a bat at a game; cotton fibre or wool prepared for quilts.

battle, *n.* *bat*-tl, a fight or an engagement between enemies or opposing armies: *v.i.* to contend in fight; to struggle. **battle array,** array or order of battle. **battle royal,** a fight among gamecocks in which more than two took part; a free fight, one in which all are engaged. (O.Fr. *bataille.*)

battle-axe, *n.* *bat*-tl-aks, an axe formerly used in war; a broad-axe; a halberd.

battle-cruiser, *n.* *bat*-tl-*krooz*-er, a warship of high speed, with heavy guns but lighter armour than a battleship.

battle-cry, *n.* *bat*-tl-kry, a war cry, a slogan.

battled, *pp.* *bat*-tld, battlemented.

battledore, *n.* *bat*-tl-dore, a light bat of parchment stretched over a frame with a handle to strike a ball or shuttlecock; the game in which this is used. (Prov. *batedor*, a beater.)

battle-dress, *n.* *bat*-tl-dress, the working uniform, as opposed to parade or ceremonial dress, of the British army.

battlefield, *n.* *bat*-tl-feeld, the site of a battle.

battleground, *n.* *bat*-tl-ground, a battlefield; the scene of any conflict.

battlement, *n.* *bat*-tl-ment, a crenellated parapet, the embrasures being the crenelles, divided from each other by the merlons. (O.Fr. *batailler*, to fortify.)

battlemented, *a.* *bat*-tl-ment-ed, having battlements.

battle-piece, *n.* *bat*-tl-peece, a picture representing a battle; a poetical description of a battle.

battle-plane, *n.* *bat*-tl-plane, a large fighting aeroplane.

battler, *n.* *bat*-tl-er, a fighter; a batteler.

battleship, *n.* *bat*-tl-ship, a warship of the highest class for service in the line of battle; a capital ship.

battology, *n.* bat-*tol*-o-je, a needless repetition of words. (Gr. *battos*, a stammer, *logos*, speech.)

battue, *n.* *bat*-too, the surrounding of a preserve by a number of men who drive the game towards the sportsmen; this method of sport; the game beaten up; wanton killing of anything. (Fr.)

batty, *a.* *bat*-te, crazy; mad; balmy [Slang].

baubee, *n.* *baw*-bee, a bawbee.

bauble, *n.* *baw*-bl, a piece of showy finery without real value; a childish gewgaw; a jester's wand. (O.Fr. *baubel*, a toy.)

baudekin, *n.* *baw*-de-kin, baldachin.

baulk, *n.* and *v.* bawk, balk.

bauxite, *n.* *boh*-zite *or* *bawk*-zite, a clay consisting chiefly of aluminium hydroxides and forming the principal source of aluminium. (Les *Baux*, France.)

Bavarian, *a.* ba-*vare*-re-an, pertaining to Bavaria: *n.* a native of Bavaria.

bavin, *n.* *bav*-in, a brushwood faggot.

bawbee, *n.* *baw*-bee, a halfpenny. (Scots.)

bawble, *n.* *baw*-bl, a bauble.

bawd, *n.* bawd, a procuress; a brothel-keeper. (O.Fr. *baud*, bold.)

bawdily, *ad.* *bawd*-e-le, obscenely; lewdly.

bawdiness, *n.* *bawd*-e-ness, obscenity; lewdness.

bawdrick, *n.* *bawd*-rik, a belt; a baldric.

bawdry, *n.* *bawd*-re, the practice of procuring women for the gratification of lust; obscenity; filthy, unchaste language.

bawdy, *a.* *bawd*-e, unchaste; lewd; obscene: *n.* bawdy talk, writing, or behaviour.

bawdy-house, *n.* *bawd*-e-house, a brothel.

bawl, *v.i.* bawl, to cry out, or aloud, with vehemence: *v.t.* to shout aloud; *n.* violent clamour. (Ice. *baula*, to make a noise like a cow's low.)

bawley, *n.* *baw*-le, borley, a Thames fishing-boat.

bawn, *n.* bawn, an enclosure for cattle; a courtyard of a fortification. (Origin unknown.)

bay, *a.* bay, inclining to a chestnut colour: *n.* a horse of that colour. (O.Fr. *bai*, bay-coloured.)

bay, *n.* bay, a recess of the sea, caused by a bend inward of the land; a roadstead; a dam for holding water, also a pond formed by a dam; a recess or opening in walls between columns; the forepart of a ship between decks; addition to room caused by protecting window beyond wall-line [Arch.]. (O.Fr. *baie*, an opening, as in a wall.)

bay, *n.* bay, the hardy evergreen shrub, *Laurus nobilis*, the bay-laurel. (L. *bacca*, a berry.)

bay, *n.* bay, the bark of a hound; barking, esp. when prolonged: *v.i.* to bark, as a dog at his game: *v.t.* to bark at; to follow with barking; so to chase as to bring to bay. **at bay,** the state of being compelled to turn upon pursuers from an inability to escape. **keep at bay,** to ward off an attack; to keep an enemy from closing in. (O.Fr. *bayer*, to bark.)

bayadère, *n.* *bay*-ya-deer, a dancing girl in India; a nautch girl. (Fr. *bayadère.*)

bayard, *n.* *bay*-ard, a bay horse; a horse. (*Bay.*)

bayberry, *n.* *bay*-be-re, the wax-myrtle, *Myrica cerifera*; also, in Jamaica, the bay-rum tree. **bayberry tallow,** a waxy substance obtained from the wax-myrtle, also called myrtle-wax.

bayed, *a.* bayd, having bays, as a building.

bayonet, *n.* *bay*-on-et, a stabbing or thrusting weapon for attachment to the rifle muzzle; a pin which plays in and out of a hole made to receive it, and thus serves to engage or disengage some part of a machine: *v.t.* to stab with a bayonet; to compel by the bayonet or by armed force. (*Bayonne*, where first made.)

bayou, *n.* *by*-oo, in America, the marshy outlet of a lake; a sluggish effluent branch of a main stream. (Fr. *boyau*, bowel.)

bay-rum, *n.* bay-*rum*, an aromatic liquid cosmetic prepared from distilled oil of bay or of bayberry, with alcohol, etc. **bay-rum tree,** a small W. Indian tree, *Pimenta acris*, of the myrtle family; local name of the bayberry.

bays, *n.pl.* bayz, honorary garland, usually of laurel, bestowed as a prize for any kind of victory; literary fame or distinction. (*Bay*, laurel.)

bay-salt, *n.* *bay*-sawlt, salt formed in pits or basins by exposure of sea-water to evaporation.

bay-tree, *n.* *bay*-tree, the laurel, *Laurus nobilis.*

bay-window, *n.* *bay*-win-doh, the angular window of a recess in a room.

bay-wood, *n.* *bay*-wood, a soft kind of mahogany from Campeachy Bay.

bazaar, *n.* ba-*zar*, an Oriental exchange, market place, or place where goods are exposed for sale; in Europe, a fancy fair or sale of articles for some benevolent object, also an establishment at which fancy articles and knick-knacks are sold. (Pers. *bāzār*, a market.)

bdellium, *n.* *del*-le-um, an aromatic gum-resin produced by certain trees in Africa and in the East Indies. (L. *bdellium.*)

★**be,** *v.i.* bee, to exist; to have a real state or existence; to be fixed; to be made to be; to become; to remain. **let be,** omit, let alone. **am. are. art. been. being. is. was. were. wert.** (A.S. *bēon*, to be.)

be-, be, an Anglo-Saxon prefix signifying to make, about, for, over, by, etc.

beach, *n.* beech, the shore of the sea, or of a lake, washed by the tide and waves; the strand; a former shore [Geol.]: *v.t.* to haul up a boat on a beach, to run on to a beach. (Origin unknown.)

beachcomber, *n.* *beech*-koh-mer, a long rolling wave; one who lies in wait for wrecks with a view to plunder; a loafing longshoreman.

beached, *a.* beecht, having a beach; drawn or driven on a beach.

beachmaster, *n.* *beech*-mahs-ter, an officer in charge of the disembarkation of an attacking force.

beachy, *a.* *beech*-e, having a beach or beaches; like a beach; shingly.

beacon, *n.* *bee*-kon, a fire lighted on an eminence as a signal, generally of danger; anything that warns of danger; a conspicuous hill: *v.t.* to afford light, as a beacon; to light up; to mark with beacons: *v.i.* to act as a beacon. (A.S. *bēacn.*)

beaconage, *n.* *bee*-kon-aj, money paid for the maintenance of beacons, buoys, and lighthouses; a system of marking with beacons.

bead, *n.* beed, a small perforated ball of glass, or other material, of which necklaces and rosaries are made; any small globular body; a ridge on a pneumatic tyre; a beading; a round moulding [Arch.]; a bubble due to effervescence. **be at one's beads,** or **tell one's beads,** to be at prayer. (A.S. *bed,* a prayer, hence applied to the stringed beads used in counting prayers.)

beaded, *a.* *beed*-ed, decked with or having beads; like beads.

beadframe, *n.* *beed*-frame, a form of abacus used in teaching children to count.

beadhouse, *n.* *beed*-house, a house of prayer; a bede-house.

beading, *n.* *beed*-ing, a narrow wooden moulding; bead-work.

beadle, *n.* *bee*-dl, a messenger or crier of a court; an officer of a college; a parish officer. (O.Fr. *bedel.*)

beadledom, *n.* *bee*-dl-dom, beadles collectively, or their ways and characteristics; pompous officiousness.

beadleship, *n.* *bee*-dl-ship, the office of a beadle.

bead-roll, *n.* *beed*-role, a list of persons for the repose of whose souls prayers are to be said; a list generally.

beadsman, *n.* *beedz*-man, one employed in praying for others; an almsman.

beadswoman, *n.* *beedz*-woom-an, the feminine of beadsman.

bead-tree, *n.* *beed*-tree, a species of *Melia,* the nuts of which are bored and manufactured into rosaries.

bead-work, *n.* *beed*-wurk, ornamental work in beads.

beady, *a.* *beed*-e, bead-like; foaming with bubbles.

beagle, *n.* *bee*-gl, a small hound used to hunt hares by scent; a cross-country runner.

beagling, *n.* *bee*-gl-ing, the sport of hunting with beagles; hunting, or following a hunt, with beagles.

beak, *n.* beek, the bill of a bird or turtle; anything ending in a point like a beak; a pointed piece of wood, fortified with brass, fastened to the end of ancient galleys, intended to pierce the vessels of an enemy; a spout; a magistrate [Slang]: *v.t.* among cock-fighters, to take hold with or fight with the beak. (Fr. *bec.*)

beaked, *a.* beekt, having a beak; sharp-pointed; having beak and legs of a colour different from that of the body [Her.].

beaker, *n.* *beek*-er, a drinking cup; a thin glass vessel, generally with a lip, used in the laboratory. **Beaker folk,** a European people of pre-Bronze Age period whose culture is characterized by bell-shaped drinking-cups. (Ice. *bikarr,* cup.)

beakiron, *n.* *beek*-i-urn, a bickern; the projecting end of a blacksmith's anvil.

beam, *n.* beem, a large piece of timber or metal laid across the walls to support the principal rafters in a building; a transverse piece of timber, the width of a ship, supporting the deck and staying the sides; the breadth of a ship; any large and long piece of timber; the part of a balance, from the ends of which the scales are suspended; the pole of a carriage; a cylinder, or part of a loom, on which weavers wind the warp; a cylinder on which the cloth is rolled, as it is woven; the piece of a plough by which it is drawn; the shank of an anchor; the horn or mainshaft on the head of a stag which bears the antlers; a collection of parallel rays of light emitted from the sun, or other luminous body; short waves transmitted undispersed by means of a special apparatus which includes a reflector [Wire.]; a ray; a smile or happy look: *v.t.* to send forth; to emit: *v.i.* to emit rays of light; to shine. **beam radio,** a method of transmission by means of short waves in a concentrated non-dispersing beam [Wire.]. **on the beam,** at right angles to the keel. **on her beam ends,** when a ship is thrown so much over on one side that the beams approach a vertical position. **to be on one's beam ends,** to be in extreme embarrassment. (A.S. *beam.*)

beam-compass, *n.* *beem*-kum-pas, an instrument for describing large circles, consisting of a rod on which slide small sockets, carrying steel or pencil points.

beamed, *a.* beemd, having a beam or beams; antlered.

beam-engine, *n.* *beem*-en-jin, a steam engine in which the crank is worked by a horizontal beam attached to the piston-rod.

beam-filling, *n.* *beem*-fil-ling, the filling in of mason-work between beams or joists; cargo between the beams [Naut.].

beaming, *a.* *beem*-ing, bright; radiant; manifestly pleased: *n.* the emission of rays.

beamless, *a.* *beem*-less, emitting no rays; having no beams.

beam-tree, *n.* *beem*-tree, the white-beam *Pyrus aria,* a tree yielding a hard tough wood.

beamy, *a.* *beem*-e, emitting rays of light; radiant; massive like a beam; antlered; broad (of ships).

bean, *n.* been, a seed of several leguminous plants, esp. *Faba vulgaris,* also the plant itself. (A.S. *bēan,* bean.)

bean-caper, *n.* *been*-kay-per, a plant of the genus *Zygophyllum,* yielding buds used as capers.

beanfeast, *n.* *been*-feest, an annual dinner or outing given by employers to their staff.

bean-goose, *n.* *been*-goos, the migratory wild goose, *Anser segetum.*

beano, *n.* *been*-o, a beanfeast; a spree.

bean-stalk, *n.* *been*-stawk, the stem of the bean.

bean-trefoil, *n.* *been*-tref-oyl, popular name for the laburnum, the coral tree, the buck bean, and shrubs of the leguminous genus *Anagyris.*

bear, *v.t.* bare, to support; to carry; to wear; to suffer; to endure; to cherish; to admit of; to bring forth or produce, to give birth to; to possess and use, as power: *v.i.* to suffer; to press or to weigh upon; to imply; to behave; to take effect; to relate; to be situated as to the point of compass with respect to something else. **bear against,** to be in contact with; to approach for attack or seizure. **bear a hand,** to help. **bear away,** to change the course of a ship, when close-hauled, or sailing with a side wind, and make her run before the wind [Naut.]. **bear down,** to drive or tend to [Naut.]; to overthrow or crush by force. **bear hard,** to press or urge. **bear off,** to carry off; to keep from approach; to remove to a distance [Naut.]. **bear on,** to press against; to incite or animate. **bear out,** to give countenance to; to support; to justify; to confirm. **bear up,** to have fortitude; to be firm; to bring the vessel before the wind [Naut.]. **bear with,** to endure what is unpleasing. **bare. bore. born. borne.** (A.S. *beran.*)

bear, *n.* bare, a plantigrade mammal of the genus *Ursus*; a rude unmannerly man; either of two northern constellations, the Great or the Lesser Bear [Astron.]; a speculator who sells securities in the expectation that before delivery is due the price will have fallen and he will make a profit by buying them back (cp. **bull**): *v.i.* to conduct this transaction; to depreciate the values of stocks and shares [Stock Exchange]. (A.S. *bera.*)

bear, *n.* beer, the six-rowed barley. (A.S. *bera.*)

bearable, *a.* *bare*-ra-bl, that can be borne; tolerable.

bearableness, *n.* *bare*-ra-bl-ness, the state of being bearable.

bearably, *ad.* *bare*-ra-ble, in a bearable manner.

bear-baiting, *n.* *bare*-bayt-ing, baiting chained bears with dogs.

bearberry, *n.* *bare*-be-re, the plant *Arctostaphylos uva-ursi,* whose leaves are used in medicine.

bearbind, *n.* *bare*-bynd, a species of bindweed *Convolvulus sepium.*

beard, *n.* beerd, the hair that grows on the chin and the adjacent parts; the awn of grasses; a barb, as of an arrow or fishhook; the part of a horse's lower jaw bearing the curb of the bridle; the feathers at the base of a bird's beak; the barbules of a fish, gills of the oyster, or hairs of the mussel and similar shell-fish; the space between the foot of a letter and the bottom edge of type; the rays of a comet: *v.t.* to take or pull by the beard; to oppose to the face; to set at defiance. **old man's beard,** traveller's joy, *Clematis vitalba.* (A.S. *beard.*)

bearded, *a. beerd*-ed, having a beard; awned; barbed.

beardless, *a. beerd*-less, without a beard; youthful.

beardlessness, *n. beerd*-les-ness, state of being beardless.

beardmoss, *n. beerd*-moss, the lichen *Usnea barbata.*

bearer, *n. bare*-rer, one who bears, sustains, or conveys; a carrier; an Indian house-servant; one of those who carry the coffin at a funeral; one who bears anything; a tree or plant that yields fruit; the presenter of a cheque or banknote; a support [Arch.].

bear-garden, *n. bare*-gar-den, a place where bears were kept for sport; a rude, turbulent assembly.

bearing, *n. bare*-ring, patient endurance; deportment; the situation of one object with respect to another; production; the part of a wheel or shaft that bears the friction; the points of support of a piece of timber [Arch.]; a charge [Her.]. **bearing-rein,** *n.* a strap from the bit to the harness to hold the horse's head up.

bearish, *a. bare*-rish, having the qualities of a bear; rude, churlish, uncouth.

bearleader, *n. bare*-leed-er, a travelling tutor; a guide; a keeper of a performing bear.

bear-pit, *n. bare*-pit, a shallow pit in which bears are kept, generally with a pole in the centre.

bear's-breech, *n. barez*-breech, brank-ursine.

bear's-ear, *n. barez*-eer, the plant *Primula auricula.* **bear's-ear sanicle,** *Cortusa matthioli.*

bear's-foot, *n. barez*-foot, stinking hellebore, *Helleborus fœtidus.*

bear's-grease, *n. barez*-greece, fat of bears made into a pomatum and used in ointments.

bearskin, *n. bare*-skin, the skin of a bear; a cap made of it; a shaggy woollen cloth for overcoats; the tall fur cap worn by the Guards Brigade.

bear-ward, *n. bare*-wawrd, a bear-keeper.

beast, *n. beest,* an animal, as distinguished from man; any animal with four legs; a bovine animal; a person rude, coarse, filthy, or acting in a manner unworthy of a human being. (O.Fr. *beste.*)

beastings, *n.pl. beest*-ingz, beest.

beastliness, *n. beest*-le-ness, the quality of being beastly; resemblance to a beast.

beastly, *a. beest*-le, like a beast in form or nature; brutal; filthy; coarse; annoying: *ad.* in the manner of a beast; exceedingly.

beat, *v.t.* beet, to strike repeatedly; to bruise or break, by beating or pounding; to shape metal by hammering; to extend by beating; to strike, at bushes to rouse game; to thrash; to mix or agitate by beating; to dash or strike, as water; to strike or brush, as wind; to tread, as a path; to vanquish or conquer; to harass; to overlabour; to baffle: *v.i.* to move with pulsation; to throb; to strike or dash with force, as a storm; to knock, as at a door; to make way against the wind [Naut.]. **beat about,** to try to find; to tack [Naut.]. **beat about the bush,** to address oneself to a question in an indirect way. **beat back,** to compel to retire. **beat down,** to break, or throw down; to lay flat down; to crush; to lower the price. **beat into,** to instil. **beat it,** run away, clear out [Slang]. **beat off,** to drive back. **beat out,** to hammer out. **beat the band,** to excel, to be remarkable [Slang]. **beat the bounds,** to follow the parish boundaries and strike the boundary marks, and sometimes to thrash a boy at each. **beat the general,** to give the signal to march [Mil.]. **beat the hoof,** to go on foot. **beat the tattoo,** to summon to quarters [Mil.]. **beat time,** to measure or regulate the time by the motion of the hand or foot [Mus.]. **beat up,** to attack suddenly and repeatedly; to make progress to windward or against the tide [Naut.]. **beat up and down,** to run first one way and then another [Hunting]. **beat up for,** to go about, in order to procure. (A.S. *bēatan,* to beat.)

beat, *n.* beet, a stroke or blow; a recurring stroke; pulsation or throb; a footfall; a round or course which is often trodden; a place of habitual resort; the rise and fall of the hand or foot in regulating the time [Mus.]; a grace-note [Mus.]: *a.* beaten; dead-beat; exhausted. **beat of drum,** a succession of beats on a drum variously arranged to give different orders. (A.S. *bēat,* a thrashing.)

beaten, *a. beet*-en, trodden into a path; defeated; fatigued; flattened by the wind.

beater, *n. beet*-er, one who beats or strikes; an instrument for pounding substances; one who beats up game for sportsmen. (A.S. *bēatere,* beater.)

beatific, *a.* bee-a-*tif*-ik, making supremely happy; conferring beatitude.

beatifically, *ad.* bee-a-*tif*-e-ka-le, in a beatific manner.

beatification, *n.* be-*at*-e-fe-*kay*-shon, the act of beatifying; the papal declaration that the departed is enjoying supreme felicity in heaven and is to be reverenced as blessed, the first step towards canonization.

beatify, *v.t.* be-*at*-e-fy, to make supremely happy; to bless with celestial enjoyment; in the Church of Rome, to make, *ex cathedra,* the declaration of beatification. (L. *beātus,* happy, *facere,* to make.) (Fr. *bēatifice.*)

beating, *n. beet*-ing, the act of striking or giving blows; punishment or chastisement by blows; pulsation or throbbing; knocking; overthrow; defeat; sailing against the wind [Naut.]; the keeping of time in music, with the hands or feet [Mus.].

beatitude, *n.* be-*at*-e-tewd, felicity of the highest kind; heavenly bliss; a saying ascribing blessedness to particular virtues. (Fr. *bēatitude.*)

beat-note, *n. beet*-note, a note, formed by two superaudible notes, the frequency of which, being at the difference between the two, becomes audible [Wire]; a note caused by the interaction of two audible notes of nearly the same frequency [Acoustics].

beau, *n.* boh (*pl.* **beaux,** bohz), a man studious of fashion in dress; a suitor to a lady: *v.t.* to escort; to play the beau to. (Fr. *beau.*)

Beaufort-scale, *n. boh*-fort-*skale,* a system of grading (from 0 to 12) the strength of winds, devised (1805) by Sir F. Beaufort, R.N.

beau-idéal, *n.* (App.) ideal excellence; the mental conception of complete perfection. (Fr.)

beauish, *a. boh*-ish, like a beau; foppish; fine.

beaujolais, *n. boh*-jo-lay, a red Burgundy wine from the town of that name in the Lyonnais.

beau-monde, *n.* (App.) the fashionable world. (Fr.)

beaune, *n.* bohn, a red Burgundy wine from the town of that name in the Cote d'Or.

beauteous, *a. bew*-te-us, endowed with beauty.

beauteously, *ad. bew*-te-us-le, in a beauteous or beautiful manner.

beauteousness, *n. bew*-te-us-ness, the state or quality of being beauteous.

beautifier, *n. bew*-te-fy-er, he or that which beautifies.

★beautiful, *a. bew*-te-ful, having the attributes of beauty; full of beauty; delicious. **the beautiful,** that which constitutes beauty.

beautifully, *ad. bew*-te-ful-le, in a beautiful manner.

beautifulness, *n. bew*-te-ful-ness, the quality of being beautiful.

beautify, *v.t. bew*-te-fy, to make or render beautiful; to adorn: *v.i.* to grow beautiful.

beautiless, *a. bew*-te-less, without beauty.

beauty, *n. bew*-te, an assemblage of properties in a person or object, which attracts and pleases the senses, especially the eye; a particular feature, grace, or ornament; any particular thing which is beautiful and pleasing; a beautiful woman; embellishment. (O.Fr. *beaute.*)

beauty-parlour, *bew*-te-*par*-lor, an establishment at which women's faces are beautified by massage, hair-waving, the application of cosmetics, etc.

beauty-sleep, *n. bew*-te-sleep, sleep before midnight.

beauty-spot, *n. bew*-te-spot, a patch or spot placed on the face by way of foil to heighten beauty; a beautiful place amid beautiful surroundings.

beaver, *n. bee*-ver, a rodent of the genus *Castor,* valuable for its fur; the fur of the beaver; a hat made of beaver; a felted woollen cloth used for overcoats. (A.S. *befer,* beaver.)

beaver, *n. bee*-ver, bever.

beaver, *n. bee*-ver, that part of a helmet which covers the face, and is movable up and down. (O.Fr. *bavière,* a child's bib.)

beavered, *a. bee*-verd, covered with or wearing a beaver.

beaver-rat, *n.* *bee*-ver-rat, the musquash of N. America; the web-footed aquatic rodent, *Hydromis chrysogaster*, of Australasia.
beaverteen, *n.* *bee*-ver-teen, a twilled cloth with a pile of uncut loops.
beaver-tree, *n.* *bee*-ver-tree, the white laurel or sweet-bay, *Magnolia glauca.*
bebeerin, *n.* be-*beer*-in, an alkaloid with quinine-like properties obtained from the bebeeru.
bebeeru, *n.* be-*beer*-roo, a tropical S. American tree, *Nectandra leucantha*, the greenheart.
beblubbered, *a.* be-*blub*-berd, swollen or red with weeping.
becall, *v.t.* be-*kawl*, to abuse by calling names; to miscall.
becalm, *v.t.* be-*kahm*, to calm or still; to soothe.
becalmed, *a.* be-*kahmd*, motionless for want of wind.
became, be-*kaym*, *p.* **become.**
★**because,** *conj.* be-*kawz* or be-*koz*, by cause, or by the cause; on this account; for this reason; inasmuch as.
beccafico, *n.* bek-a-*fee*-ko, the fig-pecker or garden warbler, *Sylvia hortensis.* (*Beak*, and It. *fico*, a fig.)
béchamel, *n.* *baysh*-a-mel, a white sauce of savoury herbs, so called from its inventor.
bechance, *v.t.* be-*chahnce*, to befall; to happen to: *ad.* by chance.
becharm, *v.t.* be-*charm*, to charm; to captivate.
bêche-de-mer, *n.* *baysh*-de-mare, sea-cucumber or trepang, a species of *Holothuria* much esteemed as a delicacy by the Chinese; also the polyglot trading language of Melanesia. (Fr., sea-spade.)
beck, *n.* bek, a nod, or a motion of the hand, especially as a sign of command: *v.i.* to nod or make a sign with the head or hand: *v.t.* to call by such a motion. (*beckon.*)
beck, *n.* bek, a brook. (Ice. *bekkr*, a little stream.)
becket, *n.* *bek*-et, a device in ships to confine loose ropes, tackles, or spars, as a large hook, a wooden bracket, or a rope with a knot and eye.
beckon, *v.i.* or *v.t.* *bek*-on, to make a sign by a nod, a motion of the hand, or other gesture. (A.S. *bēcnan*, a sign.)
becloud, *v.t.* be-*kloud*, to cover with or as with a cloud; to obscure; to dim.
become, *v.i.* be-*kum*, to pass from one state to another; to come to be: *v.t.* to suit; to befit; to accord with; to adorn. **to become of,** to be the fate or end of. (A.S. *becuman*, to occur.)
becoming, *ppr.* and *a.* be-*kum*-ing, suitable; befitting; graceful.
becomingly, *ad.* be-*kum*-ing-le, in a becoming manner.
becomingness, *n.* be-*kum*-ing-ness, the quality of being becoming.
becurled, *a.* be-*kurld*, covered with curls.
★**bed,** *n.* bed, something to sleep and rest on or in; marriage; a plot of ground for plants to grow in; an animal's resting-place; the channel of a river; the sea-bottom; that on which anything lies or is embedded; a layer or a stratum [Geol.]; the foundation of a street, railway, etc.; the horizontal surfaces of stones in position; a layer of oysters: *v.t.* to place in bed; to plant in beds; to lay in order, or flat: *v.i.* to cohabit; to use the same bed. **bed of justice,** a formal session of the French Parlement, under the presidency of the king, for the compulsory registration of royal edicts. **brought to bed,** delivered of a child. **from bed and board,** the separation of husband and wife [Law]. **keep,** or **take, to one's bed,** remain in, or be confined to, bed through sickness. (A.S. *bedd.*)
bedabble, *v.t.* be-*dab*-bl, to wet; to sprinkle.
bedad, *int.* be-*dad*, an asseveration or exclamation. (Ir.)
bedaggle, *v.t.* be-*dag*-gl, to soil by trailing in the dirt.
bedarkened, *pp.* and *a.* be-*dark*-nd, buried in darkness; wrapped in gloom.
bedash, *v.t.* be-*dash*, to bespatter with a liquid or mud; to dash with colour.
bedaub, *v.t.* be-*dawb*, to daub over; to besmear with anything viscous, or thick and dirty.
bedazzle, *v.t.* be-*daz*-zl, to confuse by dazzling; to confound with splendour.
bed-bug, *n.* *bed*-bug, the wingless blood-sucking insect *Cimex lectularius.*

bed-chair, *n.* *bed*-chare, a frame with a movable back, to support an invalid sitting in bed.
bedchamber, *n.* *bed*-chame-ber, a room to sleep in. **ladies of the bedchamber,** and **bedchamber women,** certain ladies appointed to wait in rotation upon a queen. **gentlemen** and **grooms of the bedchamber,** former officers of the royal household, whose duty was to wait upon the sovereign.
bed-clothes, *n.pl.* *bed*-kloathz, sheets, blankets, coverlets, etc., for beds.
bedder, *n.* *bed*-der, a plant for a flower-bed; the nether stone of an oil-mill; a bed-maker (Cambridge Univ.).
bedding, *n.* *bed*-ding, a bed and its furniture; bed-clothes; the materials of a bed, whether for man or beast; stratification, or the line or plane of stratification [Geol.].
bede, *n.* beed, a prayer.
bedeck, *v.t.* be-*dek*, to deck; to adorn; to dress up.
bedeguar, *n.* *bed*-e-gar, moss-like gall, produced by the gall-fly on rose-bushes. (Fr.)
bede-house, *n.* *beed*-house, a hospital or alms-house, where the poor prayed for their benefactors.
bedel, *n.* *bee*-dl, an official at Oxford and Cambridge; a beadle.
bede-roll, *n.* *beed*-role, bead-roll.
bedesman, *n.* *beedz*-man, a beadsman.
bedevil, *v.t.* be-*dev*-il, to throw into utter disorder and confusion; to destroy or render unfit for use; to bewitch.
bedevilment, *n.* be-*dev*-il-ment, state of exasperating confusion; demoniacal possession.
bedew, *v.t.* be-*dew*, to moisten gently, as with dew; to sprinkle.
bed-fast, *a.* *bed*-fahst, kept close to bed; bedridden.
bed-fellow, *n.* *bed*-fel-lo, a joint occupant of a bed.
bed-gown, *n.* *bed*-goun, a nightgown.
bed-hangings, *n.pl.* *bed*-hang-ingz, the drapery or curtains of a bed.
bedight, *a.* be-*dite*, adorned; decked with ornaments.
bedim, *v.t.* be-*dim*, to make dim; to obscure.
bedizen, *v.t.* be-*dy*-zen or be-*diz*-en, to adorn; to dress out gaudily.
bedizenment, *n.* be-*dy*-zen-ment or be-*diz*-en-ment, gaudy adornment.
bed-key, *n.* *bed*-kee, a wrench for securing the nut of the framework of a bedstead.
bedlam, *n.* *bed*-lam, a madhouse; a lunatics' asylum; a scene of wild uproar: *a.* pertaining to or fit for a madhouse. (*Bethlehem*, a priory in London, converted into a hospital for the insane in 1547.)
bedlamite, *n.* *bed*-lam-ite, a madman: *a.* mad.
bed-linen, *n.* *bed*-lin-en, linen for beds.
Bedlington, *n.* *bed*-ling-ton, a long-legged curly-coated terrier with rounded forehead and filbert ears. (Name of a village, Northumberland.)
bed-maker, *n.* *bed*-make-er, one who makes beds, sweeps rooms, etc., in a college.
bed-mate, *n.* *bed*-mate, a bed-fellow.
bed-moulding, *n.* *bed*-mohld-ing, the members of a cornice below the coronet [Arch.].
Bedouin, *n.* *bed*-a-win, an Arab of the desert: *a.* pertaining to the nomad Arabs; nomadic. (Ar.)
bed-pan, *n.* *bed*-pan, a utensil for the use of invalids in bed; a warming-pan.
bed-plate, *n.* *bed*-plate, the foundation plate of a machine.
bed-post, *n.* *bed*-pohst, a post supporting the top of a bedstead; an upright support of a bed.
bed-presser, *n.* *bed*-press-er, a lazy fellow.
bed-quilt, *n.* *bed*-kwilt, the thick outer covering of a bed.
bedrabbled, *a.* be-*drab*-ld, soiled with wet dirt.
bedraggle, *v.t.* be-*drag*-gl, to soil, as the garments, by allowing them to drag in the dirt.
bedrench, *v.t.* be-*drench*, to drench; to saturate.
bed-rest, *n.* *bed*-rest, a bed-chair; a contrivance for supporting the back when sitting up in bed.
bedrid, *a.* *bed*-rid, bedridden.
bedridden, *a.* *bed*-rid-dn, permanently confined to bed by age or infirmity. (A.S. *bedreda*, bed-rider, *i.e.*, one incapable of riding a horse.)
bed-rock, *n.* the solid underlying rock [Geol.]; a foundation; the lowest level.
bedroom, *n.* *bed*-room, an apartment for sleeping in.
bedrop, *v.t.* be-*drop*, to besprinkle; to speckle.
bedside, *n.* *bed*-side, the side of a bed; place by a

sick-bed: *a.* suited for a sick bed; professionally sympathetic, as a doctor's manner when visiting a patient.
bed-sore, *n. bed*-sore, sore caused by lying in bed.
bed-spread, *n. bed*-spred, a linen or other cover spread upon the top of a made bed.
bed-staff, *n. bed*-stahf, a pin formerly inserted on the sides of bedsteads, to keep the clothes from slipping.
bedstead, *n. bed*-sted, a frame for supporting a bed.
bed-stone, *n.* a foundation stone; the lower of a pair of millstones.
bedstraw, *n. bed*-straw, straw for filling a mattress; plants of the genus *Galium.*
bed-swerver, *n. bed*-swerv-er, one unfaithful to the marriage vow.
bed-table, *n.* bed-*tay*-bl, a table for the use of a patient in bed.
bedtick, *n. bed*-tik, a case of linen or cotton cloth, for enclosing feathers or other materials of a bed.
bedtime, *n. bed*-time, the usual hour of going to bed: *a.* pertaining to or suitable for, this time.
bedward, *ad. bed*-ward, towards bed or bedtime.
bedwarf, *v.t.* be-*dworf*, to make little; to stunt.
bedye, *v.i.* be-*dy*, to dye; to stain.
★**bee,** *n.* bee, any one of the numerous hymenopterous social insects of the genus *Apis*, esp. the honey-producing and partly domesticated *Apis mellifera*; a busy worker; an industrious frugal person; a social meeting in aid of a person in need; a meeting of ladies to sew for the poor. **a bee in the bonnet,** a crazy obsession; a delusion. (A.S. *bēo.*)
bee-bird, *n. bee*-berd, the spotted flycatcher.
bee-bread, *n. bee*-bred, the pollen of flowers collected by bees, as food for their larvæ; clover or other plant yielding nectar.
beech, *n.* beech, a forest tree of the genus *Fagus*, esp. the common beech, *Fagus sylvatica*; the wood of the beech. (A.S. *bēce.*)
beechen, *a. beech*-en, consisting of, made of, or derived from beech. (A.S. *bēcen*, beechen.)
beech-marten, *n. Mustela foina*, one of the martens; the stone-marten.
beechmast, *n. beech*-mahst, the fruit of the beech.
beech-oil, *n. beech*-oyl, oil expressed from beech-mast.
bee-eater, *n. bee*-eet-er, a bird of the genus *Merops.*
beef, *n.* beef, the flesh of ox, bull, or cow as food; snuff [Slang]. (O.Fr. *boef.*)
beefeater, *n. beef*-eet-er, one who eats beef; (*cap.*) a yeoman of the guard of the British sovereign, also a warder at the Tower of London; an African bird of the genus *Buphaga*, allied to the starling, that picks ticks from the backs of cattle.
beefiness, *n. beef*-e-ness, the state or quality of being beefy.
bee-flower, *n. bee*-flou-er, the bee-orchis.
beef-steak, *n.* beef-stake, a slice of hindquarters' beef for broiling.
beef-tea, *n.* beef-tee, broth made simply of gravy-beef, without bones or stock.
beef-witted, *a. beef*-wit-ted, dull in intellect; stupid.
beefwood, *n. beef*-wood, the very hard timber of certain Australasian trees of the genus *Casuarina*; she-oak.
beefy, *a. beef*-e, resembling beef; fleshy, brawny; stolid; well supplied with beef.
bee-garden, *n. bee*-gard-en, an enclosure for bee-hives.
bee-glue, *n. bee*-gloo, propolis.
bee-hawk, *n. bee*-hawk, the honey-buzzard.
beehive, *n. bee*-hive, an artificial dwelling for bees, esp. of wood as opposed to the skep of straw. **beehive-house,** a small prehistoric dwelling, common in west Scotland, with a conical roof and walls of long stones overlapping each other.
bee-line, *n. bee*-line, a straight course, as that of the bee making for its hive.
Beelzebub, *n.* be-*el*-ze-bub, the prince of demons or devils; Satan. (Heb. *Ba'al-zebūb*, ruler of flies.)
bee-master, *n. bee*-mahs-ter, one who keeps bees.
bee-moth, *n. bee*-moth, a moth of the genus *Macroglossa*, pernicious to bees.
been, *pp.* been *or* bin, *pp.* of the verb to be
bee-orchis, *n. bee*-awr-kis, the European orchid *Ophrys apifera*, whose flowers have some resemblance to insects.
beer, *n.* beer, a fermented liquor made from any farinaceous grain, but generally from malted barley, flavoured with hops, including ale-bitter, stout, porter, lager, etc.; an inferior beverage, as ginger beer or spruce beer. (A.S. *bēor.*)
beer-engine, *n. beer*-en-jin, a pump for drawing beer up from the cellar.
beer-money, *n. beer*-mun-e, allowance to servants in lieu of beer; money set aside for drink.
beerocracy, *n.* beer-*rok*-ra-se, brewers collectively, with their vested interests and political power [Slang].
beershop, *n. beer*-shop, a licensed house where malt liquors only are sold by retail; an alehouse.
beery, *a. beer*-re, like beer; maudlin; beer-stained.
beest, *n.* beest, or **beestings,** *beest*-ingz, the first milk drawn from a cow after calving. (A.S. *bȳsting.*)
beeswax, *n. beez*-waks, a substance secreted by bees, and employed by them in the construction of their combs: *v.t.* to rub or polish with this.
beeswing, *n. beez*-wing, a gauze-like film of tartar on old port wine or sherry.
beet, *n.* beet, a plant of the genus *Beta*, grown for its root which is used as a vegetable and also in the manufacture of sugar. (A.S. *bēte.*)
beetle, *n.* beetl, a heavy wooden mallet or rammer: *v.t.* to beat with a beetle. **beetle-headed,** dull, stupid. (A.S. *bytel*, hammer.)
beetle, *n.* beetl, an insect with horny wing-cases covering the active pair of wings; popularly, a cockroach. (A.S. *bitela*, beetle, lit., one that bites.)
beetle, *v.i.* beetl, to jut out; to hang over: *a.* projecting; scowling. **beetle-brow,** a prominent brow. **beetle-browed,** having projecting or overhanging brows.
beetling, *a. beet*-tl-ing, overhanging; prominent.
beet-radish, *n. beet*-rad-ish, beet-rave.
beet-rave, *n. beet*-rave, the red beet used for salad. (Fr. *betterave.*)
beeves, *n.pl.* of *beef*, beevz, animals of the ox kind.
befall, *v.t.* be-*fawl*, to happen to: *v.i.* to happen; to come to pass.
befit, *v.t.* be-*fit*, to suit; to be suitable to; to become.
befittingly, *ad.* be-*fit*-ting-le, suitably; in a befitting manner.
beflatter, *v.t.* be-*flat*-ter, to flatter; to cajole.
beflower, *v.t.* be-*flou*-er, to cover with or as with flowers; to sprinkle with eruptive spots.
befog, *v.t.* be-*fog*, to involve in a fog; to confuse.
befool, *v.t.* be-*fool*, to fool; to delude; to infatuate.
★**before,** *prep.* be-*fore*, preceding in space, time, or rank; in front of; in presence or sight of; under the cognizance of; in preference to: *ad.* farther onward in place, or progress in a place; preceding; previously; already; hitherto. **before the mast,** not berthed aft of the mainmast, as being only a common sailor. **before the wind,** moving in the direction of the wind and by its impulse.
before-cited, *a.* be-*fore*-sy-ted, cited in a preceding part.
before-going, *a.* be-*fore*-goh-ing, preceding.
beforehand, *ad.* be-*fore*-hand, in anticipation; by way of preparation; before the time.
before-mentioned, *a.* be-*fore*-men-shond, mentioned before.
befoul, *v.t.* be-*foul*, to soil; to make dirty; to pollute.
befriend, *v.t.* be-*frend*, to act as a friend to.
befringe, *v.t.* be-*frinj*, to furnish or decorate with or as with a fringe.
befur, *v.t.* be-*fur*, to cover with fur.
beg, *v.t.* beg, to ask or supplicate in charity; to ask earnestly; to entreat or beseech; to take for granted: *v.i.* to practise begging; to live by asking alms. **to beg the question,** to assume the thing that is to be proved. (M.E. *beggen.*)
beg, *n.* beg, bayg, *or* bay, bey.
begad, *int.* be-*gad*, a polite oath meaning By God!
began, be-*gan*, *p.* of begin.
begem, *v.t.* be-*jem*, to adorn, or to set, with or as with gems.
beget, *v.t.* be-*get*, to procreate; to generate; to produce; to cause.
begetter, *n.* be-*get*-ter, one who begets; a father.
beggable, *a. beg*-a-bl, that may be begged.
beggar, *n. beg*-ar, one who lives by begging; one reduced to complete poverty; colloquially, a chap

or fellow: *v.t.* to reduce to beggary; to exhaust. **beggar-my-neighbour,** a juvenile game with cards.
beggarliness, *n.* *beg*-ar-le-ness, the quality or state of being beggarly.
beggarly, *a.* *beg*-ar-le, very poor; mean: *ad.* in the manner of a beggar.
beggary, *n.* *beg*-a-re, extreme poverty; beggarly appearance; beggars collectively.
begging, *n.* *beg*-ing, the act or practice of soliciting alms. **to go begging,** to be acceptable by nobody.
Beghard, *n.* *beg*-hard, one of a Flemish religious order of laymen of the 13th cent. allied to the Béguines.
begilt, *a.* be-*gilt*, gilded.
begin, *v.i.* be-*gin*, to have an original or first existence; to take rise; to commence: *v.t.* to do the first act of; to enter on; to commence; to trace from anything as the first ground. (A.S. *beginnan*, to start.)
beginner, *n.* be-*gin*-ner, a learner; one with little experience; one who originates anything.
beginning, *n.* be-*gin*-ning, the first cause or origin; the first state or commencement; the rudiments.
begird, *v.t.* be-*gerd*, to bind with or as with a girdle; to surround; to enclose.
begirdle, *v.t.* be-*ger*-dl, to begird.
Beglerbeg, *n.* *beg*-ler-beg, the governor of a Turkish province under the Ottoman Empire. (Turk.)
begloom, *v.t.* be-*gloom*, to make gloomy.
begnaw, *v.t.* be-*naw*, to eat away; to corrode.
begone, *int.* be-*gon*, go away; depart; haste away.
begonia, *n.* be-*goh*-ne-a, a tropical ornamental plant with lopsided leaves of the large genus *Begonia*. (Michael *Begon*, Fr. botanist.)
begored, *a.* be-*goard*, besmeared with gore.
begot, be-*got*, **begotten,** be-*got*-tn, *p.* and *pp.* of **beget.**
begrime, *v.t.* be-*grime*, to soil deeply with dirt or soot; to blacken.
begrudge, *v.t.* be-*gruj*, to envy the possession of.
beguile, *v.t.* be-*gile*, to deceive or cheat; to elude by craft; to pass pleasingly (of time).
beguilement, *n.* be-*gile*-ment, act of beguiling; a temptation; deceit.
beguiler, *n.* be-*gile*-er, he or that which beguiles.
beguilingly, *ad.* be-*gile*-ing-le, in a manner to beguile.
Béguine, *n.* bay-*geen*, one of a sisterhood in the Netherlands, who, without taking monastic vows, devote themselves to religious exercises and charity. (The founder, Lambert le *Bègue*, a Liège priest of the 12th cent.)
begum, *n.* *bee*-gum, in the East Indies, a Mohammedan queen, princess, or lady of high rank. (Hind. *bigam*, princess.)
begun, be-*gun*, *p.* of begin.
behalf, *n.* be-*hahf*, favour; advantage; support; defence; side; stead.
behave, *v.t.* be-*hayv*, to conduct; to demean: *v.i.* to act; to conduct oneself; to conduct oneself well. (*be* and *have*.)
★**behaviour,** *n.* be-*hayv*-yur, manner of behaving, whether good or bad; conduct; manners; demeanour; the manner in which a thing acts.
behaviourism, *n.* be-*hayv*-yur-izm, the branch of psychology that, in its inquiry into human behaviour, excludes consideration of subjective phenomena (sensations, feelings, consciousness, etc.) and relies solely on objective observation and experiment.
behead, *v.t.* be-*hed*, to cut off the head; to decapitate.
beheading, *n.* be-*hed*-ing, the act of decapitating.
beheld, be-*held*, *p.* of **behold.**
behemoth, *n.* *bee*-he-moth, a large animal mentioned in Job, probably the hippopotamus. (Heb., beasts.)
behest, *n.* be-*hest*, command; mandate. (A.S. *behæs*, order.)
behind, *prep.* be-*hynd*, at the back of; after; inferior to: *ad.* at the back or in the rear; backwards; held back; out of sight; remaining; past in time: *n.* the rump. **behind one's back,** when not present. **behind the back,** out of notice or regard. (A.S. *behindan*.)
behindhand, *a.* be-*hynd*-hand, in a backward state; tardy; late; in arrears.
behold, *int.* be-*hohld*, see; lo; observe: *v.t.* to fix the eyes upon; to look at; to observe with care: *v.i.* to look. (A.S. *behealdan*.)
beholden, *a.* be-*hohld*-n, obliged; under obligation; bound in gratitude.
beholder, *n.* be-*hohld*-er, an observer.
behoof, *n.* be-*hoof*, advantage; profit; benefit. (A.S. *behōf*, profit.)
behoove, *v.t.* and *v.i.* be-*hoove*, to behove.
behove, *v.t.* and *v.i.* be-*hove*, to be necessary, fit, or proper for. (A.S. *behōfian*.)
behoveful, *a.* be-*hove*-ful, advantageous.
behung, *a.* be-*hung*, draped.
beige, *n.* bayzh, a fabric of undyed wool; undyed serge: *a.* yellowish-grey.
being, *n.* *bee*-ing, the state of existing; existence; thing or person existing; nature; essence.
beisa, *n.* *by*-sa, an African antelope, *Oryx beisa*, supposed to be the legendary unicorn; the oryx.
bejan, *n.* *bee*-jan, a freshman at Aberdeen or St. Andrews. (Fr. *béjaum*, ninny.)
bejewelled, *a.* be-*jew*-eld, wearing many jewels.
bekah, *n.* *bee*-ka, a weight of half a shekel. (Heb., half.)
bekiss, *v.t.* be-*kiss*, to give many kisses.
beknave, *v.i.* be-*nave*, to call a knave.
beknown, *a.* be-*nohn*, known.
bel, *n.* bel, the logarithmic unit for expressing intensity of sound and other power-level ratios [Physics.].
belabour, *v.t.* be-*lay*-bur, to labour at; to beat soundly; to thump.
belace, *v.t.* be-*lace*, to adorn with lace.
belated, *a.* be-*lay*-ted, detained till late; behind time; benighted.
belatedness, *n.* be-*lay*-ted-ness, the state of being belated.
belaud, *v.t.* be-*lawd*, to praise greatly.
belay, *v.t.* be-*lay*, to fasten a rope by winding, round a belaying-pin, cleat, or mast [Naut.]. (Dut. *beleggen*, to lay over.)
belaying-pin, *n.* be-*lay*-ing-pin, a strong pin in the side of a vessel to which a running rope may be hitched [Naut.].
belch, *n.* belch, the act of belching an eructation: *v.i.* to eject wind from the stomach; to issue out, as by eructation: *v.t.* to eject with force or with violence, as wind from the stomach. (A.S. *bealcian*.)
belcher, *n.* *belch*-er, a coloured neckerchief called after a famous boxer, Jem Belcher.
beldam, *n.* *bel*-dam, an old woman; a hag. (O.Fr. *beldame*, grandmother.)
beleaguer, *v.t.* be-*lee*-ger, to besiege; to blockade.
beleaguerment, *n.* be-*lee*-ger-ment, the act of beleaguering; siege; investment.
belemnite, *n.* *bel*-em-nite, a straight pointed fossil cephalopod, the thunder-bolt or thunder-stone. (Gr. *belemnon*, a dart.)
belfry, *n.* *bel*-fre, that part of a steeple or tower in which a bell is hung; a bell tower attached to or detached from a church or other building; a movable timber tower formerly used to overlook a besieged place; a watch-tower near a fortified place. (O.Fr. *berfrei*, an outlook tower.)
belga, *n.* *bel*-ga, the Belgian unit of currency for foreign exchange (in 1956 about 140 to the £ stg.).
Belgian, *a.* *bel*-jan, pertaining to Belgium or its people: *n.* a native of Belgium. **Belgian hare,** *see* **hare.**
Belgic, *a.* *bel*-jik, pertaining to the ancient Belgæ; Belgian.
Belgravian, *a.* bel-*gray*-ve-an, belonging to Belgravia, an aristocratic quarter of London, or to fashionable life: *n.* one of the upper class.
Belial, *n.* *bee*-le-al, Satan; the spirit of evil: *a.* worthless, wicked. **sons of Belial,** worthless, wicked men. (Heb. *beli*, without, *yaal*, use.)
belie, *v.t.* be-*ly*, to give the lie to; to speak falsely of; to calumniate; to counterfeit.
★**belief,** *n.* be-*leef*, a persuasion of the truth of anything; credence; opinion; faith or persuasion in regard to religious, esp. Christian, truth; the thing believed; creed. (A.S. *gelēafa*.)
believability, *n.* be-*leev*-a-*bil*-e-te, credibility.
believable, *a.* be-*leev*-a-bl, that may be believed.
believableness, *n.* be-*leev*-a-bl-ness, the quality of being believable; credibility.
believe, *v.t.* and *v.i.* be-*leev*, to accept as true; to confide in; to have reliance on; to think or suppose loosely; to have faith. (A.S. *geliefan*, to hold dear.)

believer, *n.* be-*leev*-er, one who believes; one who has faith, especially in Christianity.
believing, *a.* be-*leev*-ing, having all faith.
believingly, *ad.* be-*leev*-ing-le, in a believing manner; with faith.
belike, *ad.* be-*like*, probably; likely; perhaps.
Belisha-beacon, *n.* be-*lee*-sha-*bee*-kon, an English road-traffic sign indicating a pedestrian crossing-place. (L. Hore-*Belisha*, Minister of Transport, 1934–37, when introduced.)
belittle, *v.t.* be-*lit*-tl, to depreciate; to disparage.
belittlement, *n.* be-*lit*-tl-ment, disparagement.
★**bell**, *n.* bel, a hollow body of metal, expanded at the mouth and emitting a clear, ringing sound when struck; the cry of a rutting buck; a bell-shaped corolla [Bot.]; anything in the form of a bell; the stroke of the bell at each half-hour of a watch at sea: *v.t.* to put on a bell: *v.i.* to grow in the form of a bell [Bot.]; to bellow as deer in rutting-time. **bear away the bell**, to take the prize. **bear the bell**, to be leader, in allusion to the bellwether of a flock. **bell the cat**, to undertake a hazardous deed, esp. for the sake of others (from the fable of the mice resolving to put a bell on the cat.) **curse by bell, book, and candle**, an excommunication accompanied by the tolling of a bell. (A.S. *bellan*, bellow.)
belladonna, *n.* *bel*-la-*don*-na, deadly nightshade, *Atropa belladonna*, the source of the poisonous alkaloid atropine. **belladonna lily**, the South African plant *Amaryllis belladonna*. (It., a beautiful woman.)
bell-bird, *n.* *bel*-burd, a bird with bell-like notes, esp. the S. American campanero; a New Zealand bird of the genus *Anthornis*, and the Australian *Manorina melanophrys*.
bellbuoy, *n.* *bell*-boy, a buoy which rings a bell as it rolls in the water.
bellcote, *n.* *bell*-kot, a shelter for a bell.
belle, *n.* bel, a fashionable young lady; any young lady much admired. (Fr.)
belled, *a.* beld, hung with bells.
belles-lettres, *n.pl.* bel-*letr*, polite literature; pure literature; that branch of literature belonging to the domain of art. (Fr.)
belletrist, *n.* bel-*let*-rist, a writer of, or one devoted to, belles-lettres.
belletristic, *a.* bel-let-*ris*-tik, pertaining to belles-lettres.
bell-flower, *n.* *bel*-flou-er, a plant with bell-shaped flower, esp. of the genus *Campanula*; a variety of apple.
bellfounder, *n.* *bel*-found-er, a maker of bells.
bell-foundry, *n.* *bel*-found-re, a place for casting bells.
bell-gable, *n.* *bel*-gay-bl, a gable surmounted by a turret for one or more bells.
bell-glass, *n.* *bel*-glahs, a bell-shaped glass vessel with an open bottom; the receiver of an air-pump.
bellhanger, *n.* *bel*-hang-er, one who hangs or fixes bells.
bellhanging, *n.* *bel*-hang-ing, the act of hanging bells.
bellicose, *a.* *bel*-le-kose, inclined to war or to fighting; warlike; pugnacious. (L. *bellicosus*, warlike.)
bellied, *pp.* and *a.* *bel*-ed, having a belly; swelled out like the belly; swelled out in the middle [Bot.].
belligerence, *n.* bel-*lij*-er-ence, belligerency.
belligerency, *n.* bel-*lij*-er-en-se, a state of war; the status of a belligerent.
belligerent, *a.* bel-*lij*-er-ent, waging war; pertaining to warring peoples: *n.* a state, faction, or individual carrying on war. (L. *belligerans*, waging war.)
belling, *a.* *bel*-ing, growing full and ripe (esp. of hops) [Bot.]: *n.* the cry of a deer in rutting-time.
bellman, *n.* *bel*-man, a town-crier who rings a bell to summon attention.
bell-metal, *n.* *bel*-met-tl, an alloy of copper and tin, usually with a little zinc and lead, used for making bells.
Bellona, *n.* bel-*loh*-na, the Roman goddess of war.
bellow, *n.* *bell*-oh, a loud outcry; a roar: *v.i.* to make a loud resonant noise as a bull; to make a loud, hollow, continued sound, as the sea in a tempest, or as the wind when violent; in contempt, to vociferate or clamour. (A.S. *bellan*.)
bellowing, *n.* *bell*-oh-ing, a loud hollow sound, or roar, as of a bull; loud outcry.
bellows, *n.* sing. and *pl.* *bell*-oze, a contrivance for blowing a fire, or supplying wind to an organ. (A.S. *bælig*, a bag.)
bellows-fish, *n.* *bell*-oze-fish, the trumpet-fish.
bell-pepper, *n.* *bell*-pep-per, Guinea pepper, *Capricum anuum*, a source of Cayenne pepper.
bellpull, *n.* *bell*-pool, a bellrope; a handle to pull a bell-wire with.
bell-punch, *n.* *bell*-punch, a ticket perforator fitted with a bell.
bellringer, *n.* *bell*-ring-er, the ringer of a church or other bell.
bellrope, *n.* *bell*-rope, the rope by which a bell is rung.
bell-shaped, *a.* *bell*-shaypt, in the form of a bell; companulate [Bot.].
bell-tent, *n.* *bell*-tent, a conical army tent.
bell-turret, *n.* *bell*-tu-ret, a turret containing a bell or bells.
bell-wether, *n.* *bell*-weth-er, the sheep which leads the flock with a bell on her neck; a leader.
belly, *n.* *bell*-e, the part of the body from the chest to the thighs; the abdomen; the corresponding part of a beast; the womb; the part of anything which swells or bulges out; the front curved part of a violin; an interior; any hollow enclosed place: *v.t.* to fill; to swell out: *v.i.* to swell and become protuberant. (A.S. *bælig*, a bag.)
belly-ache, *n.* *bell*-e-ayk, pain in the stomach or intestines; colic [Vulg.].
bellyband, *n.* *bell*-e-band, a band that passes under the belly of a horse, ass, etc.; a girth.
bellyful, *n.* *bell*-e-ful, as much as satisfies the appetite; a sufficiency; more than enough.
belly-god, *n.* *bell*-e-god, a glutton.
bellying, *a.* *bell*-e-ing, protuberant; swelling out.
belly-slave, *n.* *bell*-e-slave, a slave to appetite.
belomancy, *n.* *bell*-o-man-se, divination by marked arrows. (Gr. *belos*, an arrow, *manteia*, divination.)
belone, *n.* *bell*-o-ne, the garfish, or mackerel guide.
belong, *v.i.* be-*long*, to be the property, attribute, or appendage of; to be the concern or business of; to appertain; to be a resident or native of; to be suitable for. (M.E. *bilongen*.)
belongings, *n.pl.* be-*long*-ingz, qualities; property; possessions; one's relatives [Slang].
beloved, *a.* be-*luvd* *or* be-*luv*-ed, greatly loved; very dear: *n.* one who is much loved.
below, *prep.* be-*loh*, beneath in place; inferior in rank or excellence; unworthy of: *ad.* in a lower place; on earth; in hell or in the regions of the dead; in an inferior law court [Law]; coming lower on the same page or on the next.
belt, *n.* belt, a girdle; a band or strap by which a weapon is hung; a broad strip; anything similar; a broad band passing over pulleys or round wheels, etc., for communicating motion, transmitting power, etc. [Mech.]; a strait [Geog.]; a zone of Jupiter [Astron.]: *v.t.* to encircle; to encompass as with a belt; to beat with a belt. **belt-conveyor**, an apparatus for carrying packages by means of an endless band working over rollers or terminal pulleys. (A.S.)
Beltane, *n.* *bel*-tane, an ancient May-day festival of the Scottish Highlands and islands, during which fires were kindled on the tops of the hills; a former Scottish quarter-day. (Gael. *bealltainn*.)
belted, *a.* *belt*-ed, wearing a belt; attached by means of a belt; surrounded by a belt.
belting, *n.* *belt*-ing, belts collectively, especially as connected with machinery; the material of which belts are made; a thrashing with a belt.
beluga, *n.* be-*loo*-ga, a species of dolphin, the white whale, *Delphinapterus leucas*; the white sturgeon, *Acipenser huso*. (Russ.)
belvedere, *n.* *bel*-ve-deer, a pavilion or turret on the top of a house, or a small summer-house, used as a prospect tower [Arch.]. (It., a beautiful view.)
bema, *n.* *bee*-ma, the platform of ancient Greek orators; the judge's seat in a basilica, afterwards the site of the altar; a chancel. (Gr. *bēma*, a raised place.)
bemean, *v.t.* be-meen, to lower in dignity; to debase.
bemire, *v.t.* be-*mire*, to soil or drag in the mire.
bemoan, *v.t.* be-*mone*, to lament; to bewail.

bemock, *v.t.* be-*mok*, to treat with mockery; to flout; to deride.
bemuddle, *v.t.* be-*mud*-dl, to confuse; to stupefy.
bemused, *a.* be-*mewzd*, overcome with musing; stupefied; dazed; fuddled with drink.
ben, *n.* ben, a mountain-peak. (Gael. *beinn.*)
ben, *ad.* and *prep.* ben, in, into, or within the inner part (of a house): *n.* the inner room of a small house. **but and ben,** the whole house—parlour, kitchen, and inner apartment; hence, **to live but and ben,** to live in close intimacy with.
ben, *n.* ben, the seed of the East African *Moringa oleifera*, the horse-radish tree. **oil of ben,** the oil expressed from this, used as a lubricant and in perfumery. (Ar. *bān.*)
bench, *n.* bench, a long seat or form; a carpenter's or mechanic's work-table; a strengthening ledge left in an earthwork, quarry, etc.; a seat in a boat; a thwart [Naut.]; the seat where judges sit in court; the persons who sit as judges in court: *v.t.* to furnish with benches: *v.i.* to sit on a bench, esp. on a seat of justice. **bench of bishops,** the English Episcopate collectively, esp. those bishops sitting in the House of Lords. **King's** or **Queen's Bench,** a division of the British Supreme Court originally presided over by the sovereign. (A.S. *benc*, akin to *bank.*)
bencher, *n.* *bench*-er, a senior member of an inn of court, with governing powers and other privileges.
benchmarks, *n.pl.* *bench*-marks, marks left on a line of survey for reference at a future time.
bench-warrant, *n.* *bench*-wo-rant, a warrant issued by a judge as distinct from a magistrate's warrant.
bend, *n.* bend, a curve; a turn in a road or a river; a particular kind of knot [Naut.]; half a butt of the stoutest leather; an honourable ordinary formed by lines drawn from the dexter corner to the sinister base, and containing a third part of the field when charged, and a fifth when plain [Her.]; a spree [Slang]: *v.t.* to make crooked, or to curve; to direct to a certain point, as one's course; to apply closely; to incline; to be determined; to subdue; to fasten a rope to anything; to tie into a knot; to fasten [Naut.]: *v.i.* to be crooked or incurvated; to incline; to lean or turn; to jut over; to be prone to; to bow; to be submissive. **bend sinister,** a bend drawn from the sinister corner to the dexter base, wrongly supposed to have indicated illegitimacy [Her.]. **bend the brow,** to knit the brow; to frown. **bends of a ship,** the thickest and strongest planks in her sides, the wales [Naut.]. (A.S. *bendan*, to bend.)
bendable, *a.* *bend*-a-bl, that may be bent.
bender, *n.* *bend*-er, an instrument for bending; a stretcher; a sixpence [Slang].
bend-leather, *n.* *bend*-leth-er, the stoutest leather, used chiefly for soles.
bendlet, *n.* *bend*-let, a narrow bend, one occupying a sixth part of the shield [Her.].
bendy, *a.* *bend*-e, having the field divided into an even number of alternately coloured bendlets [Her.].
beneaped, *a.* be-*neept*, left aground by a neap tide or by the ebb of the tide.
beneath, *prep.* be-*neeth*, under; lower in rank or excellence; unworthy of: *ad.* in a lower place; below; on earth. (A.S. *beneothan*, below.)
benedicite, *n.* ben-e-*dee*-se-te, a blessing; grace before a meal; the invocation to a blessing. (L., bless ye! from the apocryphal *Song of the Three Holy Children* used as a canticle in the English Prayer Book.)
Benedick, *n.* *ben*-e-dik, a confirmed bachelor who suddenly takes to matrimony; a newly married man. (*Benedick*, in "Much Ado about Nothing.")
Benedictine, *n.* ben-e-*dik*-tin, a monk of the order of St. Benedict; a Black Friar: *a.* pertaining to this order: (*l.c.*) *n.* a liqueur formerly distilled by these monks.
benediction, *n.* ben-e-*dik*-shon, the act of blessing or invoking a blessing; a giving praise or thanks to God for blessings; a blessing pronounced; thanks; the advantage conferred by blessing; the form of instituting an abbot, answering to the consecration of a bishop [Eccles.]. (Fr. *bénédiction.*)
benedictive, *a.* ben-e-*dik*-tiv, tending to bless; benedictory.
benedictory, *a.* ben-e-*dik*-to-re, expressing or pertaining to benediction.
benefaction, *n.* ben-e-*fak*-shon, the act of conferring a benefit; a benefit conferred, especially a charitable donation. (L. *benefactus*, benefited.)
benefactor, *n.* *ben*-e-fak-tor, a giver, a patron.
benefactory, *a.* ben-e-*fak*-to-re, conferring benefits.
benefactress, *n.* *ben*-e-fak-tress, a woman benefactor.
benefice, *n.* *ben*-e-fis, a church living; property held in virtue of an ecclesiastical office. (Fr. *bénéfice.*)
beneficed, *a.* *ben*-e-fist, possessed of a benefice.
beneficence, *n.* be-*nef*-e-sens, the practice of doing good; active goodness; charitableness. (L. *beneficentia*, kindness.)
beneficent, *a.* be-*nef*-e-sent, doing good; characterized by benevolence.
beneficently, *ad.* be-*nef*-e-sent-le, in a beneficent manner.
beneficial, *a.* ben-e-*fish*-al, profitable; useful; helpful; entitled to the benefit or usufruct [Law.]
beneficially, *ad.* ben-e-*fish*-a-le, in a beneficial manner.
beneficiary, *a.* ben-e-*fish*-a-re, holding as in the manner of a benefice: *n.* one who holds a benefice; one who receives a favour or a free gift.
benefit, *n.* *ben*-e-fit, an act of kindness; a favour conferred; advantage; profit; a performance, at a match, etc., the proceeds of which go to one of the actors or players or to some individual, institution, or charity; a pension or bonus due under an insurance scheme: *v.t.* to do good to; to profit: *v.i.* to gain advantage; to make improvement. **benefit of clergy,** the privilege granted to clergy, and later to others of some education, of exemption from sentence in secular courts in certain cases. **benefit society,** a friendly society for mutual benefit. (O.Fr. *bienfait.*)
benevolence, *n.* be-*nev*-o-lence, disposition to do good; goodwill; an act of kindness; a forced loan levied by the kings of England till abolished in 1689. (Fr. *bénévolence.*)
benevolent, *a.* be-*nev*-o-lent, wishing well to others, and doing them good; kind; charitable.
benevolently, *ad.* be-*nev*-o-lent-le, in a benevolent manner.
Bengal, *n.* ben-*gawl*, a thin fabric of silk and hair made in Bengal; an imitation of this.
Bengalese, *n. sing.* and *pl.* ben-ga-*leez*, a native or the natives of Bengal; Bengali.
Bengali, *n.* ben-*gaw*-le, the Aryan language or dialect spoken in Bengal; a native of Bengal.
Bengal-light, *n.* ben-gawl-*lite*, a species of firework producing a steady and vivid blue-coloured light.
Bengal-stripes, *n.* ben-*gawl*-stripes, a cotton cloth woven with coloured stripes; a gingham.
benighted, *a.* be-*ny*-ted, overtaken with night; involved in moral darkness or ignorance.
benign, *a.* be-*nine*, of, or proceeding from, a kindly nature or disposition; favourable; mild; non-malignant [Med.]. (O.Fr. *benigne.*)
benignant, *a.* be-*nig*-nant, kind; gracious; favourable.
benignantly, *ad.* be-*nig*-nant-le, in a benignant manner.
benignity, *n.* be-*nig*-ne-te, graciousness; mildness.
benignly, *ad.* be-*nine*-le, in a benign manner.
benignness, *n.* be-*nine*-ness, benignity.
benison, *n.* *ben*-e-zon, blessing; benediction. (O.Fr. *beneison.*)
benitier, *n.* bay-*nee*-te-ay, a holy-water stoup. (Fr.)
benjamin, *n.* *ben*-ja-min, benzoin. **benjamin-tree,** any tree or shrub yielding benzoin, as *Styrax benzoin*, *Ficus benjamina*, and others. (Corruption of *benzoin.*)
Benjamin, *n.* *ben*-ja-min, the youngest of the family (from Joseph's son, Gen. xiii, 4); an overcoat fashionable in the early 19th cent.
benne, *n.* *ben*-ne, the sesame or oil-plant.
bennet, *n.* *ben*-net, the wood avens, or herb bennet, *Geum urbanum*.
ben-oil, *n.* *ben*-oyl, oil of ben (*see* **ben**).
★**bent,** *a.* bent, curved; made crooked or not straight. (*pp.* of "bend.")
bent, *n.* bent, utmost exertion; inclination; leaning or bias of mind; fixed tendency; particular direction.

bent, *n.* bent, a wiry creeping grass; a withered stalk of grass; unenclosed grassland.
bent-grass, *n. bent*-grahs, a grass of the genus *Agrostis.* (A.S. *beonet.*)
benthal, *a. ben*-thal, pertaining to the benthos.
Benthamism, *n. ben*-tham-izm, the utilitarian philosophy of Jeremy Bentham.
Benthamite, *n. ben*-tham-ite, a disciple of Bentham; a Utilitarian.
benthos, *n. ben*-thos, the bottom of the sea; its flora and fauna. (Gr., depth.)
benty, *a. bent*-e, overgrown with bents; like bents.
benumb, *v.t.* be-*num*, to make torpid or numb.
benumbedness, *n.* be-*numd*-ness, the state of being benumbed; torpidity; absence of feeling.
benumbment, *n.* be-*num*-ment, the act of benumbing; benumbedness; torpor.
benzene, *n. ben*-zeen, an aromatic hydrocarbon, a colourless and very inflammable liquid used as a solvent of fats, as an illuminant, and in the manufacture of dyes, motor-fuel, etc. (*benzoic.*)
benzine, *n. ben*-zin or ben-*zeen*, a distilled, inflammable, solvent liquid from petroleum, used as a cleaning agent and in dyeing, etc.
benzoate, *n. ben*-zo-ate, a salt of benzoic acid.
benzoic, *a.* ben-*zoh*-ik, pertaining to or derived from benzoin. **benzoic acid,** a crystalline acid occurring in benzoin and other balsams and used in dyeing and perfumery and as an antiseptic and preservative.
benzoin, *n. ben*-zo-in, gum benjamin; a fragrant, concrete resinous juice, flowing from *Styrax benzoin*, a tree of the Malay Archipelago, used as a cosmetic, and as incense. (Fr. *benjoin*; Ar. *lubān jāwi.*)
benzol, *n. ben*-zol, benzene.
benzoline, *n. ben*-zo-lin, impure benzene; petrol.
bepaint, *v.t.* be-*paynt*, to cover with paint.
bepity, *v.t.* be-*pit*-e, to pity greatly.
bepommel, *v.t.* be-*pum*-el, to pommel well.
bepowder, *v.t.* be-*pou*-der, to besprinkle with powder.
bepraise, *v.t.* be-*prayz*, to praise extravagantly.
bequeath, *v.t.* be-*kweeth*, to leave by will; to transmit. (A.S. *be*, and *cwethan*, to say.)
bequeathable, *a.* be-*kweeth*-a-bl, that may be bequeathed.
bequeathal, *n.* be-*kweeth*-al, bequeathment.
bequeather, *n.* be-*kweeth*-er, one who bequeaths.
bequeathment, *n.* be-*kweeth*-ment, the act of bequeathing; a bequest.
bequest, *n.* be-*kwest*, something bequeathed; a legacy.
berate, *v.t.* be-*rate*, to chide vehemently; to scold.
Berber, *n. ber*-ber, a member of the leading native race of N.W. Africa; their Hamitic language: *a.* pertaining to this people or language.
berberin, *n. ber*-be-rin, a yellow bitter principle, contained in the root of the barberry plant.
berberry, *n. ber*-be-re, the barberry.
berceuse, *n. ber*-serz (or App.), a lullaby, cradle-song [Mus.]. (Fr.)
bere, *n.* beer, bigg; four-rowed barley.
bereave, *v.t.* be-*reev*, to deprive; to make destitute; to render desolate. (A.S. *berēafian*, to deprive of.)
bereavement, *n.* be-*reev*-ment, deprivation, particularly by the loss of a relative or friend by death.
bereft, *a.* be-*reft*, bereaved.
beret, *n. be*-ray, a round flat cap of soft cloth as worn by Basque peasants. (Fr.)
berg, *n.* berg, an iceberg.
bergamask, *n. ber*-ga-mahsk, a kind of rustic dance. (*Bergamo*, Italy, whose people were reputedly clownish.)
bergamot, *n. ber*-ga-mot, a variety of orange, *Citrus bergamia*, which yields an essential oil; a species of mint; snuff perfumed with bergamot. (*Bergamo*, in Italy.)
bergamot, *n. ber*-ga-mot, a highly-flavoured variety of pear. (Turk. *beg-armudi*, prince's pear.)
bergylt, *n. ber*-gilt, a bright orange-red sea-perch, *Sebastes norvegicus*; also the black goby.
berhyme, *v.t.* be-*rime*, to celebrate in verse; to ridicule in rhyme.
beri-beri, *n. be*-re-*be*-re, a tropical deficiency disease caused by lack of vitamin B in the diet. (Sinhalese.)
berlin, *n. ber*-lin *or* ber-*lin*, a four-wheeled carriage with a covered seat at the back. **Berlin blue,** Prussian blue. **Berlin iron,** iron capable of a high degree of fluidity. **Berlin warehouse,** a warehouse for fancy goods. **Berlin wool,** fine worsted for the fancy work called Berlin work. (*Berlin*, the German capital.)
berline, *n.* ber-*lin*, an enclosed motor-car body with a glass partition between the driver's and passengers' seats.
berm, *n.* berm, the narrow ledge or path between the rampart and the moat or fosse [Fort.]; the sloping bank on the side opposite the towing-path in canal. (O.Fr. *barme*, brim.)
Bermudian, *a.* ber-*mew*-de-an, pertaining to the Bermudas or their inhabitants: *n.* an inhabitant of the Bermudas.
bernacle, *n. ber*-na-kl, barnacle.
Bernardine, *a. ber*-nar-din, pertaining to the order of Cistercians founded in 1115, by St. Bernard, bishop of Clairvaux: *n.* a monk of this order.
berried, *a. be*-rid, furnished with berries.
★**berry,** *n. be*-re, a succulent or pulpy fruit, containing seeds; a single egg of a fish or crustacean: *v.i.* to bear or produce berries; to go and pick berries. (A.S. *berie.*)
bersaglieri, *n. pl.* ber-*sahl*-yayr-re, Italian light infantry. (It.)
berserk, *n.* and *a. ber*-serk, berserker: *ad.* in furious rage.
berserker, *n. ber*-ser-ker, one of the old Norse warriors, who were said to be inspired with such fury in battle as to be invulnerable and irresistible: *a.* inspired with similar fierce battle fury. (Ice. *bear*, and *sark*, shirt.)
berth, *n.* berth, a station in which a ship rides at anchor; sufficient sea room to manœuvre; a sleeping-place in a ship, or in a railway-carriage, caravan, etc.; a situation or appointment: *v.t.* to allot berths; to moor; to give a place to anchor. **give a wide berth to,** to keep well clear of. **berthed. berthing. berths.** (Connected with *bear.*)
bertha, *n. berth*-a, a wide lace collar to a low-necked dress.
berthage, *n. berth*-aj, money paid for accommodation in a dock; the accommodation itself.
Bertholletia, *n.* ber-tho-*lee*-she-a, a genus of tall S. American trees one of which bears the Brazil nut. (C. L. *Berthollet*, Fr. chemist, *d.* 1822.)
berthon, *n. ber*-thon, a type of collapsible boat. (From its inventor, E. L. *Berthon*, *d.* 1899.)
beryl, *n. be*-ril, a silicate of aluminium and glucinum, a gem nearly identical with the emerald, but less brilliant in colour. (O.Fr. *beril.*)
berylia, *n.* be-*ril*-e-a, glucina.
berylline, *a. be*-ril-lin, resembling beryl.
beryllium, *n.* be-*ril*-e-um, a silver-white malleable metalic element related to magnesium and aluminium.
beryx, *n. beer*-riks, a spiny-finned sea-fish of the order Berycidæ.
besainted, *a.* be-*sayn*-ted, canonized; treated as a saint; peopled by saints.
besant, *n. bez*-ant, a bezant.
bescrawl, *v.t.* be-*skrawl*, to scrawl; to scribble over.
bescreen, *v.t.* be-*skreen*, to screen; to shelter; to conceal.
bescribble, *v.t.* be-*skrib*-bl, to scribble over.
beseech, *v.t.* be-*seech*, to ask for with urgency; to entreat; to implore. *pp.* **besought.** (*be-*, and M.E. *secean*, to seek.)
beseecher, *n.* be-*seech*-er, a suppliant.
beseechingly, *ad.* be-*seech*-ing-le, in a beseeching manner.
beseem, *v.t.* be-*seem*, to become; to befit; to be worthy of.
beseeming, *ppr.* and *a.* be-*seem*-ing, becoming; meet.
beseemingly, *ad.* be-*seem*-ing-le, in a beseeming manner.
beseemingness, *n.* be-*seem*-ing-ness, quality of being beseeming.
beseemly, *a.* be-*seem*-le, becoming; fit; suitable.
beseen, *pp.* be-*seen*, looking; appearing; accomplished. **well-beseen,** of good appearance; well equipped.
beset, *v.t.* be-*set*, to surround; to press on all sides, so as to perplex; to fall upon. **besetting sin,** a failing to which one is prone. (A.S. *besettan*, to put.)
besetment, *n.* be-*set*-ment, the state of being beset.
beshadow, *v.t.* be-*shad*-o, to overshadow.

beshame, *v.t.* be-*shame*, to make ashamed.
beshrew, *imp.* be-*shroo*, used as an exclamation. **beshrew me!** curse me; confound it.
beside, *prep.* be-*side*, at the side of; near; over and above; distinct from; aside from; out of. **beside oneself,** out of one's wits through excitement.
besides, *prep.* be-*sidez*, over and above; distinct from; in addition: *ad.* moveover; more than that.
besiege, *v.t.* be-*seej*, to lay siege to, or surround with armed forces; to crowd round.
besiegement, *n.* be-*seej*-ment, act of besieging; state of being besieged.
besieger, *n.* be-*seej*-er, one who besieges.
besiegingly, *ad.* be-*seej*-ing-le, in a besieging manner; urgently.
besigh, *v.t.* be-*sy*, to sigh over.
besilver, *v.t.* be-*sil*-ver, to cover with silver.
besit, *v.t.* be-*sit*, to fit suitably; to sit well upon.
beslave, *v.t.* be-*slave*, to enslave.
beslaver, *v.t.* be-*slav*-er, to defile with or cover with slaver; to flatter fulsomely.
beslobber, *v.t.* be-*slob*-ber, to beslaver; to besmear; to kiss in a slobbering manner.
besmear, *v.t.* be-*smeer*, to bedaub with anything soft, viscous, or adhesive; to soil.
besmirch, *v.t.* be-*smurtsh*, to soil; to discolour.
besmoke, *v.t.* be-*smoke*, to foul with smoke; to fumigate.
besom, *n.* *bee*-zom, a broom made of birch twigs or heather. (A.S. *besma*.)
besort, *v.t.* be-*sort*, to suit; to fit; to become.
besot, *v.t.* be-*sot*, to make sottish; to fuddle with liquor.
besottedly, *ad.* be-*sot*-ted-le, after the manner of a sot; in an infatuated way.
besottedness, *n.* be-*sot*-ted-ness, the state of being besotted; infatuation.
besought, *pp.* be-*sawt*, beseeched.
besouled, *a.* be-*sohld*, endowed with a soul.
bespangle, *v.t.* be-*spang*-gl, to sprinkle or adorn with or as with spangles.
bespatter, *v.t.* be-*spat*-ter, to soil by spattering; to asperse.
bespeak, *v.t.* be-*speek*, to speak for or engage beforehand; to speak so as to gain favour; to speak to; to betoken. *p.* **bespoke.** *pp.* **bespoken.**
bespeckle, *v.t.* be-*spek*-kl, to mark with speckles or spots; to variegate.
bespectacled, *a.* be-*spek*-ta-kld, wearing spectacles.
bespeed, *v.t.* be-*speed*, to help onward; to hurry up.
bespice, *v.t.* be-*spice*, to season with spices or drugs.
bespoke, *a.* be-*spoke*, made to order.
bespot, *v.t.* be-*spot*, to mark or cover with spots.
bespread, *v.t.* be-*spred*, to spread or cover over.
besprent, *a.* be-*sprent*, besprinkled; sprinkled over; sprinkled about.
besprinkle, *v.t.* be-*spring*-kl, to sprinkle or scatter over.
Bessemer, *n.* *bess*-e-mer, a Bessemer converter. **bessemer converter,** a type of furnace used in the Bessemer process. **bessemer process,** a process for converting cast-iron into steel, so named from Sir Henry Bessemer, its inventor.
best, *a.* best, *superl.* of good; good or excellent in the highest degree; most desirable: *n.* utmost; highest endeavour, as to do one's best: *v.t.* to get the better of. **best man,** a groomsman. **at best,** in the utmost degree; as far as could be expected. **to the best of,** to the utmost extent of. **to have the best of,** to have the advantage. **to make the best of,** to realize the most that one can out of anything; to make the most of; to put up with. **the best part,** the greater part: *ad.* (*superl.* of well); in the highest degree; beyond all others; most easily or successfully.
bestain, *v.t.* be-*stayn*, to mark with spots or stains.
bestead, *a.* be-*sted*, circumstanced; treated.
bested, *a.* be-*sted*, bestead.
bestial, *a.* *bes*-te-al, pertaining to or like an inferior animal; resembling a beast; brutish; sensual. (Fr. *bestial*.)
bestiality, *n.* bes-te-*al*-e-te, the state or quality of being bestial; obscenity; lewdness; unnatural intercourse between a human and an animal.
bestialize, *v.t.* *bes*-te-a-lize, to make like a beast.
bestially, *ad.* *bes*-te-a-le, in a bestial manner.
bestiary, *n.* *bes*-te-a-re, a book of moral fables in which animals are the speakers and actors. (L. *bestia*, beast.)
bestick, *v.t.* be-*stik*, to stick over; to adorn; to transfix.
bestill, *v.t.* be-*stil*, to make quiet.
bestir, *v.t.* be-*stir*, to rouse into vigorous action.
bestow, *v.t.* be-*stoh*, to give; to confer; to give in marriage; to apply or make use of; to lay up or deposit for safe keeping.
bestowal, *n.* be-*stoh*-al, the act of bestowing; disposal.
bestower, *n.* be-*stoh*-er, one who bestows.
bestowment, *n.* be-*stoh*-ment, the act of bestowing; that which is bestowed; donation.
bestraught, *a.* be-*strawt*, distracted; frenzied.
bestreak, *v.t.* be-*streek*, to mark with streaks.
bestrew, *v.t.* be-*stroo*, to scatter over; to besprinkle.
bestrid, *a.* be-*strid*, beneath legs astride.
bestride, *v.t.* be-*stride*, to stand or sit over with the legs astraddle; to step across; to span.
bestuck, *a.* be-*stuk*, pierced in many places.
bestud, *v.t.* be-*stud*, to adorn with studs or bosses.
bet, *n.* bet, a wager; a stake: *v.t.* to wager on an uncertain contingency; to stake: *v.i.* to lay wagers. (Of unknown origin.)
beta, *n.* *bee*-ta, the second letter of the Greek alphabet; used to denote the second member in various series, the second star in a constellation, etc. **beta-particle,** an electron. **beta rays,** streams of electrons given off by radioactive substances.
betaine, *n.* *bee*-ta-een, a crystalline base occurring in beet-juice. (L. *beta*, beet.)
betake, *v.t.* be-*take*, to take, in the sense of to remove or repair to. *pp.* **betaken.** *p.* **betook.**
betel, *n.* *bee*-tl, a species of pepper, *Piper betle*, the leaves of which with the betel-nut and lime are used for chewing in the East Indies. **betel-nut,** *Areca catechu*, the nut of the areca-palm. (Port.)
bethankit, *n.* be-*thang*-kit, a grace after meat, "God be thanked." (Scots.)
Bethel, *n.* *beth*-el, a mission-room; a dissenting place of worship. (Heb. *bĕth'ēl*, God's house.)
bethink, *v.t.* be-*think*, to recall to mind: *v.r.*, to have in recollection; to consider.
bethrall, *v.t.* be-*thrawl*, to enslave.
bethumb, *v.t.* be-*thum*, to soil or crease with the thumb.
bethump, *v.t.* be-*thump*, to beat soundly.
bethwack, *v.t.* be-*thwak*, to thrash.
betide, *v.t.* be-*tide*, to happen to; to betoken: *v.i.* to happen; to come to pass.
betimes, *ad.* be-*tymz*, in good time; early; in a short time.
bêtise, *n.* *bay*-teez, stupidity; a foolish act. (Fr.)
betitle, *v.t.* be-*ty*-tl, to give a title to.
betoken, *v.t.* be-*toh*-kn, to be a sign of; to foreshow.
beton, *n.* *bet*-on, a kind of concrete. (Fr.)
betony, *n.* *bet*-on-e, a plant of the genus *Stachys*.
betook, *p.* be-*took*, betake.
betoss, *v.t.* be-*toss*, to toss; to agitate violently.
betray, *v.t.* be-*tray*, to deliver into hostile hands by treachery or breach of trust; to prove unfaithful to, as a trust; to disclose treacherously what has been intrusted for secrecy; to expose to injury by violation of confidence; to deceive; to seduce; to lead astray; to discover; to show. (*be-*, and O.Fr. *traïr*, to hand over.)
betrayal, *n.* be-*tray*-al, the act of betraying; violation or breach of trust.
betrayer, *n.* be-*tray*-er, a traitor; one who betrays.
betrim, *v.t.* be-*trim*, to array in order; to deck.
betroth, *v.t.* be-*trothe*, to affiance; to promise to marry; to become engaged.
betrothal, *n.* be-*trothe*-al, engagement to marry.
betrothed, *n.* be-*trothed*, one who is engaged to be married: *a.* affianced; engaged to be married.
betrothment, *n.* be-*trothe*-ment, a mutual contract between two persons with a view to marriage; betrothal.
better, *a.* *bet*-ter, *comp.* of good; good or excellent in a greater degree than another; more desirable; improved in health; greater in degree: *ad. comp.* of well, in a superior or more excellent manner; more correctly or fully; with more profit; in a higher degree; more: *n.pl.* social superiors: *v.t.* to make better; to improve on; to exceed; to give advantage to: *v.i.* to become better. **better half,** a wife. **to be better off,** to be in better

circumstances. **to get, or gain, the better,** to obtain the advantage, superiority, or victory. **for the better,** for the advantage, superiority, or victory; for the advantage or improvement. (A.S. *betera.*)
better, *n. bet*-ter, a bettor.
betterment, *n. bet*-ter-ment, improvement; enhancement of value due to local improvements.
bettermost, *a. bet*-ter-mohst, best.
betterness, *n. bet*-ter-ness, the quality of being better; superiority; improvement.
betting, *n. bet*-ting, the proposing or laying of a wager.
bettong, *n. bet*-tong, the kangaroo-rat. (Maori.)
bettor, *n. bet*-tor, one who bets or lays wagers.
betty, *n. bet*-te, a burglar's housebreaking tool; a jemmy; a Florence flask; a man who does the house-work.
betumbled, *a.* be-*tum*-bld, rolled about; disordered.
★**between,** *prep.* be-*tween,* in the intermediate space of; from one to another; belonging to two or more; having mutual relation to two or more; noting difference or discrimination of one from another: *n.* a needle between a sharp and a blunt. (A.S. *betwēonan.*)
between-decks, *n.* be-*tween*-deks, between any two decks; below the main deck [Naut.].
between-maid, *n.* be-*tween*-made, a maid-servant who helps other servants in their duties; a tweeny.
between-whiles, *prep. be-tween*-whilez, in the intervals; now and then.
betwixt, *prep.* be-*twikst,* between. (A.S. *betweox.*)
bevel, *n. bev*-el, a kind of square with a pivoted arm for taking angles; an edge slanting from a right line: *a.* slanting; oblique; having the form of a bevel: *v.t.* to cut to a bevel angle: *v.i.* to slant, or incline off to a bevel edge. **bevel angle,** either an obtuse or an acute angle. **bevel wheel,** a toothed wheel with teeth inclined at an angle to the shaft. (Fr. *biveau,* bevel.)
bevel-gear, *n. bev*-el-geer, a system of engaging bevel wheels.
bevelled, *a. bev*-eld, formed to a bevel angle.
bevelling, *a. bev*-el-ling, slanting towards a bevel angle; bending from a right line; *n.* a hewing of timber with a slant towards a bevel angle; the slant or bevel of timber.
bevelment, *n. bev*-el-ment, the process of bevelling; the replacement of an edge by two similar planes, or faces, equally inclined to the including faces or adjoining planes [Min.].
bever, *n. beev*-er, a quick repast; a snack. (O.Fr. *beivre,* drinking.)
beverage, *n. bev*-er-aj, liquor for drinking, esp. an agreeable liquor; a term for various drinks, as a mixture of cider and water. (O.Fr. *berrage,* drink.)
bevy, *n. bev*-e, a flock of birds, esp. larks or quails; an assembly of women. (Origin unknown.)
bewail, *v.t.* be-*wayl,* to lament: *v.i.* to express grief.
bewailing, *n.* be-*wayl*-ing, loud lamentation.
bewailingly, *ad.* be-*wayl*-ing-le, in a bewailing manner; dolefully.
bewailment, *n.* be-*wayl*-ment, the act of bewailing.
beware, *v.i.* be-*ware,* to regard with caution; to avoid; to take care: *v.t.* to be wary of.
beweep, *v.t.* be-*weep,* to weep over; to bedew with tears: *v.i.* to weep.
beweltered, *a.* be-*welt*-erd, heavily bloodstained.
bewet, *v.t.* be-*wet,* to wet thoroughly.
bewigged, *a.* be-*wigd,* wearing a wig; pompous; characterized by "red tape."
bewilder, *v.t.* be-*wil*-der, to perplex; to lead astray.
bewilderedness, *n.* be-*wil*-derd-ness, bewilderment.
bewilderingly, *ad.* be-*wil*-der-ing-le, so as to bewilder.
bewilderment, *n.* be-*wil*-der-ment, state of being bewildered; act of bewildering; perplexity.
bewitch, *v.t.* be-*witch,* to enchant, as by a spell of witchcraft; to fascinate to such a degree as to take away the power of resistance.
bewitchery, *n.* be-*witch*-er-re, resistless power of anything that fascinates; bewitchment.
bewitching, *a.* be-*witch*-ing, alluring; fascinating; that has power to bewitch.
bewitchingly, *ad.* be-*witch*-ing-le, in a bewitching manner; charmingly.
bewitchment, *n.* be-*witch*-ment, that which bewitches; fascination; bewitchery.
bewrap, *v.t.* be-*rap,* to wrap up; to enclose.
bewray, *v.t.* be-*ray,* to disclose; to betray unintentionally. (A.S. *be-,* and *wregan,* to disclose.)
bewrayer, *n.* be-*ray*-er, a divulger of secrets.
bewrayingly, *ad.* be-*ray*-ing-le, in a manner to bewray.
bewrought, *a.* be-*rawt,* worked.
bey, *n.* bay, a provincial governor under the Ottoman Empire; a former Turkish curtesy-title (abolished in 1935); title of the native hereditary ruler of Tunis since 1705. (Turk. *bey,* a lord.)
beylik, *n. bay*-lik, a province governed by a bey.
beyond, *prep.* be-*yond,* on the farther side of; farther onward than; farther than any given limit; before, or at a place not yet reached; past or out of reach of; above, or in a degree exceeding or surpassing: *ad.* at a distance; yonder: *n.* the hereafter; that which is distant, remote, or outside experience. **back of beyond,** anywhere out-of-the-way. **go beyond,** to exceed in ingenuity, in research, or in anything else; in a bad sense, to circumvent. (A.S. *begeondan,* beyond.)
bezant, *n. bez*-ant, a gold coin of the Byzantine Empire; a gold roundlet [Her.]. (O.Fr. *besant.*)
bez-antler, *n. bay-ant*-ler, the tine of a deer's horn next above the brow-antler. (L. *bis,* twice, and *antler.*)
bezel, *n. bez*-zl, the slope at the cutting edge of a chisel or plane; the upper part of the collet of a ring, which holds the stone; the groove into which the glass of a watch fits. (Fr.)
bezique, *n.* be-*zeek,* a game at cards in which the term is used when a hand contains the queen of spades and the knave of diamonds. (Fr.)
bezoar, *n.* be-*zoh*-er, a calculous concretion found in the intestines of certain ruminants, formerly supposed to possess antidotal qualities. **fossil bezoar,** a coprolite resembling bezoar. (O.Fr. *bezoar.*)
bezoardic, *a.* bez-o-*ar*-dik, composed of bezoar: *n.* a medicine containing bezoar; an antidote.
bezonian, *n.* be-*zoh*-ne-an, a beggar; a rascal. (It. *bisogno,* want.)
bhang, *n.* bang, Indian hemp, *Cannabis sativa*; a narcotic prepared from this; hashish.
bharal, *n. bu*-ral, a wild ruminant of the Himalayas, *Pseudois nahoor,* intermediate between sheep and goats. (Native.)
bheestie, *n. bees*-te, a Hindu water-carrier.
bi-, by, a Latin prefix signifying two, twice, or two-fold.
biacid, *a.* and *n.* by-*as*-id, diacid.
biangular, *a.* by-*ang*-gew-lar, having two angles or corners.
biarticulate, *a.* by-ar-*tik*-yoo-lat, having or consisting of two joints.
bias, *n. by*-as, the factor that causes a bowl when bowled to swerve from its direct course; the tendency of a bowl to swerve; a leaning of the mind; inclination; prepossession; partiality; obliquity: *a.* oblique; slanting: *adv.* obliquely; on the slant (Dressmaking): *v.t.* to cause to incline to one side; to prepossess; to prejudice. (Fr. *biais,* slant.)
biased, *a. by*-ast, partial; unfair.
biauriculate, *a.* by-aw-*rik*-yoo-lat, having two auricles [Anat.].
biaxial, *a.* by-*ak*-se-al, having two axes [Opt.].
bib, *n.* bib, a small piece of linen to put under the chin of an infant when feeding or teething; the whiting pout, *Gadus luscus*: *v.i.* and *t.* to sip; to tipple; to drink frequently. (L. *bibo,* drink.)
bibacious, *a.* be-*bay*-shus, addicted to drinking.
bibasic, *a.* by-*bay*-sik, dibasic.
bibb, *n.* bib, one of the brackets bolted to the mast to support the trestle-trees [Naut.].
bibber, *n. bib*-ber, a tippler.
bibble-babble, *n. bib*-bl-*bab*-bl, prating; idle talk.
bibelot, *n. bee*-bloh, a small article of virtu; a trinket or ornamental knick-knack. (Fr.)
Bible, *n. by*-bl, the book which contains the scriptures accepted as sacred by the Christian Church; hence (*l.c.*) sacred writings of any religion; any authoritative book. **Bible clerk,** one of a class of undergraduates at certain Oxford colleges who read the Lessons, etc. **Bible Society,** a society for the distribution of the Bible. (Fr. *bible.*)
biblical, *a. bib*-le-kal, pertaining to the Bible.
biblically, *ad. bib*-le-ka-le, according to the Bible.
biblicist, *n. bib*-le-sist, one skilled in biblical knowledge.

bibliographer, *n.* bib-le-*og*-ra-fer, one versed in bibliography; one who compiles a record of literary productions or who writes about books. (Gr. *bibliographos*, a writer of books.)
bibliographical, *a.* bib-le-o-*graf*-e-kal, relating to bibliography.
bibliography, *n.* bib-le-*og*-ra-fe, the systematic study of books; a record or description of books, as to authorship, subject, date, or edition. (Gr. *bibliographia*, the writing of books.)
bibliolater, *n.* bib-le-*ol*-a-ter, a Bible worshipper.
bibliolatry, *n.* bib-le-*ol*-a-tre, making an idol of a book, especially of the Bible.
bibliological, *a.* bib-le-o-*loj*-e-kal, relating to bibliology.
bibliology, *n.* bib-le-*ol*-o-je, the study of biblical literature or doctrine; bibliography. (Gr. *biblion*, and *logos*, science.)
bibliomancy, *n.* *bib*-le-o-man-se, divination from chance passages of Scripture. (Gr. *biblion*, and *manteia*, divination.)
bibliomania, *n.* bib-le-o-*may*-ne-a, a rage for possessing rare and curious books. (Gr. *biblion*, and *mania*, madness.)
bibliomaniac, *n.* bib-le-o-*may*-ne-ak, one who has bibliomania.
bibliopegy, *n.* bib-le-*op*-e-je, bookbinding. (Gr. *biblion*, and *pēgnunai*, make fast.)
bibliophile, *n.* *bib*-le-o-fil, a lover of books. (Gr. *biblion*, and *philos*, a friend.)
bibliophilism, *n.* bib-le-*off*-e-lizm, love of bibliography or of books.
bibliophilist, *n.* bib-le-*off*-e-list, a lover of bibliography or of books.
bibliophobia, *n.* bib-le-o-*foh*-be-a, a dread or loathing of books. (Gr. *biblion*, and *phobos*, fear.)
bibliopole, *n.* *bib*-le-o-pole, a bookseller. (L. *bibliopōla*, a bookseller.)
bibliopolical, *a.* bib-le-o-*pol*-e-kal, relating to bookselling or booksellers.
bibliopolist, *n.* bib-le-*op*-o-list, a bookseller.
bibliopoly, *n.* bib-le-*op*-o-le, bookselling.
bibliotheca, *n.* *bib*-le-o-*thee*-ka, a library. (L.)
bibliothecal, *a.* *bib*-le-o-*thee*-kal, of or pertaining to a library.
biblist, *n.* *bib*-list *or* *by*-blist, one who is conversant with the Bible; one who makes the Bible the sole rule of faith.
bibulous, *a.* *bib*-yoo-lus, imbibing; inclined to tippling; absorptive. (L. *bibulus*, freely drinking.)
bibulously, *ad.* *bib*-yoo-lus-le, in a bibulous manner.
bicalcarate, *a.* by-*kal*-ka-rat, furnished with two spurs [Bot. and Zool.].
bicameral, *a.* by-*kam*-e-ral, consisting of two chambers of legislative assemblies. (L. *bi-*, and *camera*, a chamber.)
bicapsular, *a.* by-*kap*-sew-lar, with two seed-capsules to a flower [Bot.]. (L. *bi-*, and *capsula*, a small box.)
bicarbonate, *n.* by-*kar*-bon-at, a carbonate containing two equivalents of carbonic acid to one of a base [Chem.].
bice, *n.* bice, a pale blue or a green pigment made from smalt. (Fr. *bis*, dusky.)
bicentenary, *n.* by-*sen*-ten-a-re *or* by-sen-*teen*-a-re, a two-hundredth anniversary; a celebration of this: *a.* occurring after or pertaining to two hundred years.
bicentennial, *a.* by-sen-*ten*-e-al, lasting two hundred years, or occurring every two hundred years.
bicephalous, *a.* by-*sef*-a-lus, two-headed. (L. *bi-*, and Gr. *kephale*, the head.)
biceps, *n.* *by*-seps, a muscle having two heads; fore-muscle of upper arm and the corresponding muscle of the leg [Anat.]. (L. *bi-*, and *caput*, the head.)
bichloride, *n.* by-*klaw*-ride, a compound having two equivalents of chlorine to one of a base.
bichromate, *n.* by-*kroh*-mat, a compound having two equivalents of chromic acid to one of a base.
bicipital, *a.* by-*sip*-e-tal, having two heads or origins, as a muscle; pertaining to the biceps.
bicker, *n.* *bik*-er, a confused brawl; contention; strife: *v.i.* to quarrel; to contend in petulant altercation; to move quickly; to ripple; to be tremulous. (O.Fr. *bequer*, to hit with the beak.)
bicker, *n.* *bik*-er, a wooden cup or beaker [Scot.].
bickering, *n.* *bik*-er-ing, quarrel; noisy altercation.
bickern, *n.* *bik*-ern, an anvil ending in a beak or point. (Fr. *bigorne*.)
bicoloured, *a.* *by*-kul-erd, of or having two colours.

biconjugate, *a.* by-*kon*-joo-gat, in pairs, side by side [Bot.].
bicorn, *a.* *by*-kawrn, having two horns or horn-like processes [Bot. and Zool.]: *n.* a two-horned animal.
bicorporal, *a.* by-*kor*-po-ral, having two bodies.
bicuspid, *a.* by-*kus*-pid, having two cusps: *n.* a tooth with two cusps.
bicuspidate, *a.* by-*kus*-pe-dat, with two points or fangs [Anat. and Bot.]. (L. *bi-*, and *cuspis*, a prong.)
bicycle, *n.* *by*-sikl, a light, metal-framed velocipede having a rider's seat between the two wheels in line and propelled by pedals: *v.t.* to ride a bicycle. (L. *bi-*, and Gr. *kyklos*, a circle.)
bicyclist, *n.* *by*-se-klist, one skilled in bicycle riding.
bid, *v.t.* bid, to pray. **to bid beads,** to pray with beads. (A.S. *biddan*, to pray.)
bid, *v.t.* bid, to command, to invite; to offer; to propose; to proclaim; to wish: *v.i.* and *t.* to make a call at a card game: *n.* an offer of a price as at an auction; a call at a card game. **bid fair,** to open or offer a good prospect; to appear likely. (A.S. *bēodan*, to order.)
bid-ale, *n.* *bid*-ayl, formerly, an entertainment at which the guests made contributions for the benefit of some necessitous person.
biddable, *a.* *bid*-a-bl, inclined to do what is required.
bidder, *n.* *bid*-er, one who bids.
biddery, *n.* *bid*-der-e, bidri; a kind of pewter metal ware usually inlaid with gold or silver.
bidding, *n.* *bid*-ding, command; offer at an auction. **bidding prayer,** one in which the congregation are invited to join; the prayer before the sermon in the English Church service.
biddy, *n.* *bid*-de, a fowl; a chicken. **red biddy,** methylated spirit dyed and treated for illicit use as a beverage.
bide, *v.i.* bide, to dwell; to remain: *v.t.* to endure; to suffer; to wait for. (A.S. *bīdan*, to stay.)
bident, *n.* *by*-dent, a two-pronged implement.
bidentate, *a.* by-*den*-tat, two-toothed; divided into two tooth-like processes.
bidentated, *a.* by-*den*-ta-ted, bidentate.
bidet, *n.* be-*det* *or* bee-*day*, a small horse; a pack-horse; a kind of sitz-bath. (Fr., a pony.)
bidigitate, *a.* by-*dij*-e-tate, with two fingers or two toes.
bidri, *n.* *bid*-re, biddery. (Made at *Bidar* in India.)
bield, *n.* beeld, shelter; a dwelling: *a.* cosy [Scot.]
biennial, *a.* by-*en*-e-al, lasting for only two years; happening once in two years: *n.* a plant which lasts but two years. (L. *biennālis*, continuing two years.)
biennially, *ad.* by-*en*-e-al-le, once in two years; at the return of two years.
bier, *n.* beer, a litter or frame of wood for conveying the dead to the grave. (A.S. *bēr*, a litter.)
biestings, *n.* *beest*-ingz, beest.
bifacial, *a.* by-*faysh*-al, having two faces; with the opposite surfaces alike.
bifarious, *a.* by-*fare*-re-us, disposed in two rows; pointing in opposite directions [Bot.].
biff, *n.* bif, a blow: *v.i.* and *t.* to hit [Slang].
biffin, *n.* *bif*-fin, a red-skinned apple; one of these dried and pressed. (Formerly *beefin*, from the colour of raw beef.)
bifid, *a.* *by*-fid, two-cleft; partly split in two [Bot.]. (L. *bi-*, and *findo*, cleave.)
bifidate, *a.* *bif*-e-dat, bifid.
bifilar, *a.* by-*fy*-lar, with two fine threads. (L. *bi-*, and *filum*, a thread.)
biflex, *a.* *by*-fleks, twice curved. (L. *bi-*, and *flecto*, bend.)
biflorate, *a.* by-*flaw*-rat, biflorous.
biflorous, *a.* by-*flaw*-rus, bearing two flowers.
bifocal, *a.* by-*foh*-kal, having two foci; used, esp. of a spectacle lens one part of which corrects near, and the other distant, vision: *n.* a bifocal glass.
bifold, *a.* *by*-fohld, twofold; double; of two kinds.
bifoliate, *a.* by-*foh*-le-ate, having two leaves.
biform, *a.* *by*-form, having two forms.
bifurcate, *a.* *by*-fur-kate, bifurcated: *v.t.* and *i.* to divide into two branches; to fork.
bifurcated, *a.* *by*-fur-kay-ted, divided into two branches or prongs. (L. *bi-*, and *furca*, a fork.)
bifurcation, *n.* by-fur-*kay*-shon, a forking into two branches; the point of division, or either of the two branches.

big, *a.* big, large or great in bulk; grown up; pregnant; full and ready to bring forth; haughty in air; proud; great in spirit; lofty; brave. **big game,** the larger mammals shot for sport. (M.E.)

big, *n.* big, bigg.

biga, *n.* *by*-ga, a chariot drawn by two horses abreast. (L.)

bigamist, *n.* *big*-a-mist, one who has committed bigamy.

bigamous, *a.* *big*-a-mus, involving bigamy.

bigamously, *ad.* *big*-a-mus-le, in a bigamous manner.

bigamy, *n.* *big*-a-me, the crime of having two wives or two husbands at a time. (Fr. *bigamie.*)

bigaroon, *n.* big-a-*roon*, the large white-heart cherry.

big-bellied, *a.* *big*-*bel*-led, having a protuberant belly; in advanced pregnancy.

big-boned, *a.* *big*-bohnd, having large bones; strong.

bigeminate, *a.* by-*jem*-e-nat, twin-forked [Bot.]. (L. *bi-*, and *geminus*, double.)

big-end, *n.* *big*-end, the crank end of a connecting-rod [Mech.].

bigener, *n.* *by*-jen-er, a cross between two species of different genera. (L. *bi-*, and *genus*, a kind.)

bigg, *n.* big, four-rowed barley; bere. (Scots.)

biggin, *n.* *big*-in, a child's cap; a night-cap. (Fr. *béguin*, head-covering.)

biggish, *a.* *big*-ish, rather large.

biggonet, *n.* *big*-on-et, a large cap with ear-like flaps.

bighorn, *n.* *big*-horn, the American wild sheep, the Rocky Mountain sheep, *Ovis canadensis.*

bight, *n.* bite, a small bay; the loop or coil of a rope; an angle or hollow, as of the knee or elbow. (A.S. *byht*, corner.)

bigly, *ad.* *big*-le, in a haughty, blustering manner.

bigness, *n.* *big*-ness, the quality of being big.

Bignonia, *n.* big-*noh*-ne-a, a genus of plants comprising the trumpet flowers. (The Abbé *Bignon.*)

bigot, *n.* *big*-ot, the obstinate holder of a particular opinion; an intolerant party-member or devotee of a creed, etc. (Fr. *bigot*, hypocrite.)

bigoted, *a.* *big*-ot-ed, affected with bigotry.

bigotry, *n.* *big*-o-tre, narrow-minded zeal in the interest of some creed, system, or party.

bigwig, *n.* *big*-wig, one of weight and authority (from the great wigs formerly worn by such). [Slang.]

bijou, *n.* *bee*-zhoo, a trinket: *a.* small; compact. (Fr.)

bijouterie, *n.* be-*zhoo*-te-re, jewellery; trinkets.

bijugate, *a.* by-*joo*-gat, showing two heads in profile, one superimposed on the other (of coins); having two pairs of leaflets [Bot.].

bike, *n.* byk, a nest of wasps, wild bees, or hornets; a swarm [Scots.].

bike, *n.* byk, a bicycle: *v.i.* to ride a bicycle [Coll.].

bilabial, *a.* by-*lay*-be-al, formed with the aid of both lips: *n.* a consonant so formed, as *b*, *p*, *m* [Phonetics].

bilabiate, *a.* by-*lay*-be-at, having two lips [Bot.]. (L. *bi-*, and *labium*, a lip.)

bilaminar, *a.* by-*lam*-e-nar, having two thin plates.

bilander, *n.* *bil*-an-der, a two-masted vessel with a cross-jack mainsail; kind of hoy. (Dut. *bijlander.*)

bilateral, *a.* by-*lat*-er-al, having two sides.

bilberry, *n.* *bil*-be-re, the fruit of the whortleberry; the plant itself. (Scand.)

bilbo, *n.* *bil*-bo, a rapier; a sword. (*Bilbao*, in Spain.)

bilboes, *n.pl.* *bil*-boze, long bars of iron with shackles, used at sea to confine the feet of prisoners or offenders.

bile, *n.* bile, a viscid greenish-orange fluid, secreted by the liver; ill humour; an inflamed tumour or boil. (L. *bilis.*)

bile-stone, *n.* *bile*-stone, a biliary calculus; gall-stone.

bilge, *n.* bilj, the bulging part of a cask; the broadest part of a ship's bottom: *v.i.* to spring a leak by a fracture in the bilge: *v.t.* to cause to leak [Naut.]. **bilge keel,** a projection along the bilge parallel to the true keel to minimize rolling, or act as a protection when aground. **bilge-pump,** a pump to draw off bilge-water. **bilge-water,** water which accumulates in the bilge of a ship.

bilgy, *a.* *bil*-je, smelling like bilge-water.

Bilharzia, *n.* bil-*hart*-se-a, a genus of trematode worms, of which *B. hæmatobius* is a dangerous human parasite, attacking also horses, sheep, cattle, camels, etc. (T. *Bilharz*, the discoverer, 1851.)

bilharziasis, *n.* bil-hart-*zy*-a-sis, a disease caused by the presence of blood flukes of the genus *Bilharzia* in the body; schistosomiasis.

biliary, *a.* *bil*-ya-re, pertaining to the bile; conveying the bile. **biliary calculus,** a gall-stone.

bilingual, *a.* by-*ling*-gwal, in two languages. (L. *bi-*, and *lingua*, tongue.)

bilinguist, *n.* by-*ling*-gwist, one knowing or speaking two languages.

bilious, *a.* *bil*-yus, biliary; affected or produced by excess of bile; melancholic; peevish.

biliousness, *n.* *bil*-yus-ness, the state of being bilious.

bilirubin, *n.* by-le-*roo*-bin, the reddish-yellow colouring matter of bile.

biliteral, *a.* by-*lit*-er-al, consisting of two letters.

bilk, *v.t.* bilk, to defraud by non-payment, or by non-fulfilment of an engagement; to escape from: *n.* a rogue; a swindler.

bilker, *n.* *bilk*-er, one who bilks.

bill, *n.* bil, the beak of a bird; a horny process resembling this, as in the octopus, platypus, etc.; a narrow promontory; the point of an anchor fluke: *v.i.* to caress, as doves, by joining bills; to fondle. (A.S. *bile.*)

bill, *n.* bil, a short axe or hatchet with a hooked point; a kind of halberd or battle-axe. (A.S. *bill.*)

bill, *n.* bil, written statement of particulars; an account; a promissory note; a proposed law; an advertisement or announcement posted up; a declaration in writing, expressing a wrong sustained or committed [Law]: *v.t.* to advertise or announce by publicly displayed posters; to cover with placards; to announce in a programme. **bill of credit,** a document empowering another to receive money or goods from a third party; a promissory note issued on the credit of the state and passed as money [Comm.]. **bill of divorce,** in the Jewish law, a writing given by the husband to the wife, by which the marriage relation was dissolved. **bill of entry,** a written account of goods entered at the custom-house. **bill of exceptions,** a written statement of errors in law. **bill of exchange,** an order drawn on a person requesting him to pay on a given date money to some person assigned by the drawer, in consideration of value received [Comm.]. **bill of fare,** a menu, a list of the fare provided. **bill of health,** a certificate from the proper authorities as to the state of health of a ship's company at the time of her leaving port [Comm.]. **bill of lading,** a shipowner's formal acknowledgment of the receipt of goods for shipment to a specified destination [Comm.]. **bill of mortality,** an account of the number of deaths in a place in a given time. **bill of rights,** a summary of rights and privileges claimed by a people, esp. the declaration of William and Mary on their accession to the English throne in 1689. **bill of sale,** a document authorizing a creditor to dispose of goods therein named if a debt is not repaid within a specified time and to reimburse himself out of the proceeds [Law]. **bill of sight,** a provisional entry, at the custom house, of goods respecting which the importer has not full information [Comm.]. **true bill,** a declaration by a grand jury that the evidence against a prisoner is sufficient to warrant a trial. (From Late L. *billa.*)

billabong, *n.* *bil*-a-bong, a backwater or blind channel leading from a river [Austral.].

bill-broker, *n.* *bil*-bro-ker, one who trades in or discounts money-bills.

bill-chamber, *n.* *bil*-chame-ber, a department of the Scottish Court of Session for the issue of edicts in urgent cases.

bill-discounter, *n.* bil-*dis*-kount-er, bill-broker.

billed, *a.* bild, furnished with a bill; advertised or announced on a bill.

billet, *n.* *bil*-let, a small note; a ticket directing soldiers at what house to lodge; a soldier's lodging; a situation, job [Slang]: *v.t.* to quarter or lodge, as soldiers: *v.i.* to be quartered. (Dim. of Late L. *billa.*)

billet, *n.* *bil*-let, a small log of wood; an ornament in Norman architecture; a bearing of an oblong square form [Her.]. (Fr. *billette*, a billet.)

billet, *n.* *bil*-et, the coalfish, *Gadus virens*.
billet-doux, *n.* *bil*-lay-doo, a short love-letter. (Fr.)
billetee, *n.* bil-let-*ee*, one who is billeted.
bill-head, *n.* *bil*-hed, the printed heading of a tradesman's account form; the form itself.
bill-hook, *n.* *bil*-hook, a tool used for cutting hedges.
billiard, *a.* *bil*-yerd, pertaining to the game of billiards.
billiards, *n.pl.* *bil*-yerdz, a game played on a rectangular table with balls of ivory or some substitute, which the players aim to send into pockets by driving one against another with a cue. (Fr. *billard*, billiards.)
billing, *a.* and *n.* *bil*-ing, caressing or fondling, like doves. **billing and cooing**, making love like birds.
billingsgate, *n.* *bil*-ingz-gate, foul language, like that for which the London fish-market of this name was reputedly notorious.
billion, *n.* *bil*-yun, a million millions (in England and Germany); a thousand millions (in France and U.S.A.). (Fr.)
billon, *n.* *bil*-lon, an alloy of silver with a greater weight of copper or tin; debased coin. (Fr. *bille*, a log.)
billot, *n.* *bil*-lot, gold or silver in the bar or mass.
billow, *n.* *bil*-lo, a large rolling wave: *v.i.* to swell; to rise and roll in waves or surges. (Ice, *bylgja*.)
billowed, *a.* *bil*-lode, swollen like a billow.
billowy, *a.* *bil*-lo-e, pertaining to or like billows.
bill-sticker, *n.* *bil*-stik-er, one who sticks up bills.
billy, *n.* *bil*-e, a comrade (Scot.); a tin can used for cooking (Austral.).
billy-boy, *n.* *bil*-le-boy, a bluff-bowed ketch.
billy-cock, *n.* *bil*-e-kok, a low-crowned hard felt hat.
billy-goat, *n.* *bil*-e-goat, a male goat; a goatee beard.
bilobate, *a.* by-*loh*-bat, bilobed.
bilobed, *a.* *by*-lohbd, divided into two lobes.
bilocation, *n.* by-lo-*kay*-shon, the power or faculty of being in two places at the same time.
bilocular, *a.* by-*lok*-yoo-lar, containing two cells [Bot.]. (L. *bi-*, and *loculus*, a little place.)
biltong, *n.* *bil*-tong, strips of meat dried in the sun. (S. Africa.)
bimanal, *a.* *by*-ma-nal, bimanous.
bimanous, *a.* *by*-ma-nus, having two hands.
bimbashi, *n.* bim-*bah*-she, an officer of the Turkish Imperial army; a British officer in the former Egyptian army.
bimensal, *a.* by-*men*-sal, occurring once in two months; continuing for two months. (L. *bi-*, and *mensis*, a month.)
bimestrial, *a.* by-*mes*-tre-al, bimensal.
bimetallic, *a.* by-me-*tal*-ik, consisting of two metals; pertaining to bimetallism.
bimetallism, *n.* by-*met*-al-izm, the use of two metals as standard currency at a fixed relative value to each other.
bimetallist, *n.* by-*met*-al-ist, a supporter of bimetallism.
bimonthly, *a.* by-*munth*-le, occurring every two months; lasting two months.
bin, *n.* bin, a receptacle for corn, flour, dust, coal, etc.; a partition in a cellar for wine-bottles: *v.t.* to store in a bin. (A.S. *binn*, manger.)
binary, *a.* *by*-na-re, composed of two. (L. *binārius*, that consists of two.)
binate, *a.* *by*-nat, growing in pairs [Bot.].
bind, *v.t.* bynd, to fasten together with a band; to wrap or gird with a cover or bandage; to confine or restrain with a bond or otherwise; to oblige; to engage; to compel; to confirm or ratify; to make costive; to make hard or firm; to form a border; to fasten with a band or anything that strengthens the edges; to sew together and cover as a book; to cover or secure by a band; to oblige or serve by contract: *v.i.* to contract; to grow hard or stiff; to become costive; to be obligatory: *n.* that which binds; a tie; a brace [Mus.]; a bine; a measure (250) of eels. *pp.* **bound**. (A.S. *bindan*.)
binder, *n.* *bynd*-er, a person who binds, especially books or sheaves; anything that binds; a bandage.
bindery, *n.* *bynd*-er-re, a place where books are bound.
binding, *a.* *bynd*-ing, that binds; that obliges; obligatory: *n.* the act of binding; anything that binds; a bandage; the cover of a book; something that secures the edges of cloth.
bindingly, *ad.* *bynd*-ing-le, in a binding manner.
bindingness, *n.* *bynd*-ing-ness, the quality of being binding.
bindweed, *n.* *bynd*-weed, the woodbine, *Convolvulus sepium*.
bine, *n.* byn, a slender stem, as of the hop plant.
binervate, *a.* by-*nerv*-ate, having two longitudinal ribs [Bot.].
bing, *n.* bing, a heap, especially of corn or alum. (Scand. cf. Ice, *bingr*, a heap.)
binge, *n.* binj, a drinking bout; a spree [Slang].
bingle, *n.* *bing*-gl, a shortened bob style of hair-dressing for women.
bingo, *n.* *bing*-goh, brandy, or other spirituous liquor [Slang].
binnacle, *n.* *bin*-a-kl, the compass-box of a ship. (Port. *bitacola*, a bittacle.)
binocle, *n.* *bin*-o-kl, a binocular telescope or field-glass.
binocular, *a.* by-*nok*-yoo-lar, suited for both eyes: *n.* a field-glass with two tubes, enabling one to see an object with both eyes. (L. *bi-*, and *oculus*, eye.)
binodal, *a.* by-*noh*-dal, having or consisting of two nodes [Bot.].
binomial, *a.* by-*noh*-me-al, pertaining to binomials; binominal: *n.* an expression consisting of two terms, connected by plus or minus [Alg.]. **binomial theorem**, Newton's formula for raising a binomial to any power without performing the multiplications. (L. *bi-*, and *nomen*, a name.)
binominal, *a.* by-*nom*-in-al, having two names.
binotonous, *a.* by-*not*-o-nus, consisting of two notes only.
binous, *a.* *by*-nus, binate [Bot.].
binoxide, *n.* by-*noks*-ide, a dioxide [Chem.].
binturong, *n.* *bint*-yoo-rong, a nocturnal mammal, *Arctitis binturong*, allied to the palm-civets, inhabiting the Malayan forests. (Native name.)
bio-, *comb. f.* *by*-o, signifying life. (Gr. *bios*, life.)
bioblast, *n.* *by*-o-blast, the hypothetical molecule of protoplasm. (Gr. *bios*, and *blastos*, a bud.)
biocellate, *a.* by-*os*-e-lat, having two ocelli [Zool.].
biochemistry, *n.* by-o-*kem*-is-tre, the chemistry of living things; physiological chemistry.
biodynamics, *n.* by-o-dy-*nam*-iks, the branch of physiology that treats of the action of living organisms.
biogenesis, *n.* by-o-*jen*-e-sis, the science of the origin of life; the doctine that life is derived from life only. (Gr. *bios*, and *genesis*, generation.)
biogenetic, *a.* by-o-je-*net*-ik, pertaining to biogenesis.
biogenetically, *ad.* *by*-o-je-*net*-e-ka-le, in a biogenetic sense.
biogeography, *n.* *by*-o-je-*og*-ra-fe, the study of the geographical distribution of animals and plants.
biograph, *n.* *by*-o-graf, an instrument for exhibiting life-movements by photography; an early form of cinematograph. (Gr. *bios*, and *grapho*, depict.)
biographer, *n.* by-*og*-ra-fer, a writer of biography.
biographic, *a.* by-o-*graf*-ik, biographical.
biographical, *a.* by-o-*graf*-e-kal, pertaining to, or containing, biography.
biographically, *ad.* by-o-*graf*-e-ka-le, in the manner of a biography.
biography, *n.* by-*og*-ra-fe, the history of the life and character of a particular person; biographic literature. (Gr. *bios*, and *grapho*, write.)
biological, *a.* by-o-*loj*-e-kal, relating to biology.
biologically, *ad.* by-o-*loj*-e-ka-le, with reference to, or in accordance with the laws of, biology.
biologist, *n.* by-*ol*-o-jist, one skilled in biology.
biology, *n.* by-*ol*-o-je, the science of life in its various forms. (Gr. *bios*, and *logos*, science.)
biolytic, *a.* by-o-*lit*-ik, destructive to life. (Gr. *bios*, and *lyo*, loosen.)
biomagnetism, *n.* by-o-*mag*-net-izm, animal magnetism; mesmerism.
biometrics, *n.* by-o-*met*-riks, the study of the statistics and valuation of biological facts.
biometry, *n.* by-*om*-e-tre, the science which calculates the probable duration of life. (Gr. *bios*, and *metron*, a measure.)
bionomics, *n.* by-o-*nom*-iks, the study of the life of plants and animals as affected by their environment.
biophysics, *n.* by-o-*fiz*-iks, the scientific study of the physics of organic life.

biophyte, *n.* *by*-o-fyt, a plant living on living organisms.
bioplasm, *n.* *by*-o-plazm, living protoplasm, as the germ of growth.
bioscope, *n.* *by*-o-skope, a biograph.
biostatics, *n.* by-o-*stat*-iks, the study of the structure of living organisms.
biotechnics, *n.* by-o-*tek*-niks, the science and study of the utilization of living natural resources.
biotic, *a.* by-*ot*-ik, pertaining to life.
biotics, *n.* by-*ot*-iks, the study of the functions of living organisms. (Gr. *biotikos*, lively.)
biotite, *n.* *by*-o-tite, a dark species of mica. (J. B. *Biot*, Fr. mineralogist.)
biparous, *a.* *bip*-a-rus, bringing forth two at a birth. (L. *bi-*, and *pario*, bring forth.)
bipartient, *a.* by-*par*-shent, dividing into two parts.
bipartisan, *a.* by-par-te-*zan*, composed of, represented by, or proceeding from two parties [Polit.].
bipartite, *a.* by-*par*-tite, having two corresponding parts; divided into two parts to the base, as a leaf [Bot.]. (L. *bipartīto*, in two ways.)
bipartition, *n.* *by*-par-*tish*-on, the act of dividing into two; division into two.
biped, *n.* *by*-ped, an animal having only two feet: *a.* having two feet. (L. *bi-*, and *pes*, foot.)
bipedal, *a.* *by*-pe-dal, pertaining to a biped; biped.
bipeltate, *a.* by-*pel*-tat, double-shielded [Zool.].
bipennate, *a.* by-*pen*-nat, having two wings or wing-like processes. (L. *bipennis*.)
bipennated, *a.* by-*pen*-na-ted, bipennate.
bipetalous, *a.* by-*pet*-a-lus, having two petals.
bipinnate, *a.* by-*pin*-nat, doubly pinnate.
bipinnatifid, *a.* by-pin-*nat*-e-fid, pinnatifid with the pinnæ similarly divided [Bot.].
biplane, *n.* *by*-plane, an aeroplane with two supporting planes, one above the other.
biplicate, *a.* *bip*-le-kat, doubly folded transversely [Bot.].
bipolar, *a.* by-*poh*-lar, having two poles.
bipontine, *a.* by-*pont*-ine, relating to editions of classic authors printed at Zweibrucken (L. *Bipontium*), Bavaria, during the 18th century.
bipp, *n.* bip, an antiseptic and deodorant dressing for wounds, named from the initials of its components—bismuth, iodoform, and paraffin paste.
biquadrate, *n.* by-*kwod*-rate, the square of a square, the biquadratic [Math.]: *v.t.* to raise to the fourth power.
biquadratic, *n.* by-kwod-*rat*-ik, the fourth power, arising from the multiplication of a square by itself [Math.]: *a.* pertaining to this power.
biquintile, *n.* by-*kwin*-tile, the aspect of planets when they are separated by 144 degrees (twice the fifth part) of a great circle [Astrol.]. (L. *bi-*, twice, *quintus*, a fifth.)
biramous, *a.* by-*ray*-mus, having two branches.
birch, *n.* berch, a tree of the genus *Betula*; a bundle of birch twigs formerly used in schools for correction: *v.t.* to flog with a rod of birch: *a.* made of or consisting of birch.
birchen, *a.* *berch*-en, birch.
birching, *n.* *berch*-ing, a flogging with a birch.
★**bird,** *n.* berd, any feathered vertebrate, biped and oviparous: *v.t.* to catch or snare birds. **arabian bird,** the phœnix. **bird of Jove,** the eagle. **bird of Juno,** the peacock. **bird of night,** the owl. **bird of peace,** the dove. **bird of paradise,** any one of the *Paradiseidæ* family of birds of New Guinea remarkable for their beautiful plumage. **bird of passage,** a migratory bird. **birds of a feather,** people of similar tastes. (A.S. *bridd*.)
bird-bolt, *n.* *berd*-boalt, a blunt arrow to shoot birds with.
bird-cage, *n.* *berd*-kaje, a fitted framework of wire or wicker for keeping birds.
bird-call, *n.* *berd*-kawl, a pipe constructed to imitate the notes of birds and decoy them.
bird-cherry, *n.* *berd*-che-re, a tree of the genus *Prunus*; the mazard, its small black cherry.
bird-eyed, *a.* *berd*-ide, quick-sighted or glancing.
bird-fancier, *n.* *berd*-fan-se-er, one who takes pleasure in rearing birds; one who keeps live birds for sale.
birdie, *n.* *berd*-e, a little bird; a term of endearment; in golf, a hole played in one stroke under bogey [Slang.]
birdlike, *a.* *berd*-like, resembling a bird.
birdlime, *n.* *berd*-lime, a viscous jelly used for catching birds: *v.t.* to smear with birdlime; to catch with, or as with, this.
birdman, *n.* *berd*-man, a fowler; a dealer in birds; an airman [Coll.].
bird-pepper, *n.* *berd*-pep-per, the plant *Capsicum baccatum*, a source of Cayenne pepper.
birdseed, *n.* *berd*-seed, grain suitable for feeding to small cage-birds.
bird's-eye, *a.* *berdz*-eye, seen from above, or at a glance, as by a flying bird; hence, general, not detailed; marked with small eye-like spots: *n.* a kind of tobacco; the popular name of several plants. **bird's-eye-maple,** a maple with spotted grain.
bird's-foot, *n.* *berdz*-foot, a popular name of various plants and small ferns.
bird's-foot trefoil, *n.* *berdz*-foot-*tref*-oyl, a leguminous plant of the genus *Lotus*.
bird's-mouth, *n.* *berdz*-mouth, a notch cut at the end of a piece of timber to receive the edge of another piece [Carp.].
bird's-nest, *n.* *berdz*-nest, the nest in which a bird lays eggs and hatches her young; the nest of a species of swift, esteemed a great delicacy in China; the wild-carrot, and other plants; a crow's-nest [Naut.]: *v.i.* to search for or take nests or birds' eggs. **bird's-nest fern,** *Asplenium nidus*. **bird's-nest orchis,** *Neottia nidus-avis*.
bird's-tongue, *n.* *berdz*-tung, a popular name for numerous plants and grasses.
bird-witted, *a.* *berd*-wit-ted, without the faculty of attention; flighty.
bireme, *n.* *by*-reem, a Roman galley with two tiers of oars. (L. *birēmis*, two-oared.)
biretta, *n.* be-*ret*-ta, a square cap worn by clergy (esp. Roman Catholic), and by doctors of divinity. (It. *berretta*.)
birk, *n.* berk, the birch-tree (Scot.).
birostrate, *a.* by-*ros*-trate, having a double beak, or beak-like process. (L. *bi-*, and *rostrum*, a beak.)
birr, *n.* bur, a whirring, rattling noise; an accent in speaking. (Scots.)
★**birth,** *n.* berth, the act of coming into life, or of being born; the act of bringing forth; the condition and environment in which a person is born; rank by birth, especially high rank; that which is born; that which is produced, whether animal or vegetable. **birth control,** the regulation or limitation of the number of children born, esp. by the use of contraceptives. (A.S. *beorth*.)
birthday, *n.* *berth*-day, the day of one's birth, or its recurrence: *a.* relating to the day of one's birth.
birthdom, *n.* *berth*-dum, birthright.
birthmark, *n.* *berth*-mark, a congenital mark on the body, peculiar to the individual.
birthplace, *n.* *berth*-place, the place of one's birth.
birthrate, *n.* *berth*-rate, the ratio of births to population.
birthright, *n.* *berth*-rite, right acquired by birth.
birthwort, *n.* *berth*-wurt, the plant *Aristolochia clematitis*, and others formerly reputed to assist parturition.
bis, *ad.* bis, encore; to be repeated [Mus.].
Biscayan, *n.* and *ad.* bis-*kay*-an, a native of or pertaining to the Spanish province Biscay.
biscuit, *n.* *bis*-kit, a thin, hard or crisp kind of bread; a kind of unglazed earthenware: *a.* of light-brown colour. (Fr. *biscuit*, from L. *bis coctus*, twice-baked.)
bise, *n.* beez, a cold north-west winter wind in Switzerland and on the Mediterranean. (Fr.)
bisect, *v.t.* by-*sekt*, to cut or divide into two equal parts: *v.i.* to fork. (L. *bis*, and *sectum*, cut.)
bisection, *n.* by-*sek*-shon, division into two equal parts or into two branches.
bisector, *n.* by-*sek*-tor, one who or that which divides anything into two equal parts; a bisecting line.
biseriate, *a.* by-*see*-re-at, arranged in two rows.
bisexual, *a.* by-*sek*-sew-al, of two sexes; having stamens and pistils in the same envelope [Bot.].
bishop, *n.* *bish*-op, a spiritual overseer in the early Church; or one invested with the cure of souls; a Church dignitary presiding over the clergy in a diocese ranking next below an archbishop; a drink composed of mulled wine, oranges, and sugar; a piece in the game of chess. (A.S. *bisceop*, bishop.)

bishop, *v.t.* *bish*-op, to camouflage the age or appearance of a horse; to murder by drowning; to burn or let burn (all Slang).
bishop-cap, *n.* *bish*-op-kap, the mitre-wort.
bishopric, *n.* *bish*-op-rik, the jurisdiction or the office of a bishop; a diocese.
bishop-sleeve, *n.* *bish*-op-sleev, a wide sleeve resembling that of a bishop's robe.
bishop's-weed, *n.* *bish*-ops-weed, an umbelliferous plant of the genus *Ammi*; also goutweed (*Ægopodium podagraria*, and others.
bishop's-wort, *n.* *bish*-ops-wurt, wood-betony, *Stachys betonica.*
bisk, *n.* bisk, bisque.
Bisley, *n.* *biz*-le, the National Rifle Association meeting held near the town of that name in Surrey.
bismar, *n.* *biz*-mahr, a rough weighing instrument or steelyard used in the north of Scotland. [Scan.]
bismillah, *int.* bis-*mil*-ah, "in the name of God," a common Mohammedan interjection. (Ar.)
bismite, *n.* *biz*-mite, bismuth ochre, the native trioxide of bismuth occurring in yellowish earthy masses.
bismuth, *n.* *biz*-muth, a brittle yellowish or reddish-white metallic element used in the arts and in medicine. **bismuth ochre,** bismite. (Ger.)
bismuthic, *a.* *biz*-muth-ik, pertaining to or containing bismuth.
bismuthine, *n.* *biz*-muth-in, native sulphide of bismuth.
bismuthite, *n.* *biz*-muth-ite, native carbonate of bismuth.
bison, *n.* *by*-son, the European wild ox; the American buffalo. (L.)
bisque, *n.* bisk, a rich gelatinous soup of shellfish, etc.; a kind of ice-cream. (Fr.)
bisque, *n.* bisk, an unglazed earthenware for statuettes, etc.; the colour reddish-yellow. (*Biscuit.*)
bisque, *n.* bisk, a term for the odds at tennis; a stroke granted to a weaker opponent at golf, croquet, etc. (Fr.)
bissextile, *n.* bis-*seks*-til, leap-year; *a.* pertaining to leap year. (L. *bis*, twice, *sextus*, sixth, because in that year the sixth day before the kalends of March [24 Feb.] was reckoned twice.)
bistort, *n.* *bis*-tort, snakeweed, *Polygonum bistorta*, a plant with twisted root. (L. *bis*, twice, *torta*, twisted.)
bistoury, *n.* *bis*-toor-re, a surgical knife. (O.Fr.)
bistre, *n.* *bis*-ter, a brown pigment from wood-soot: *a.* of this colour. (Fr.)
bisulcate, *a.* by-*sul*-kat, cloven-footed: *n.* an animal with cloven hoofs. (L. *bis*, and *sulcus*, a furrow.)
★**bit,** *n.* bit, a morsel; a small piece; a whit or jot; a tool for boring holes; the cutting part of a carpenter's plane; the part of a key in which are the wards; the steel part of the bridle put in a horse's mouth: *v.t.* to put the bit in the mouth; to restrain. (A.S. *bita*, a little piece.)
bitch, *n.* bitch, the female of the dog, wolf, or fox; a woman of loose character. (A.S. *bicce*, bitch.)
★**bite,** *n.* bite, the act of biting; a grip with the teeth; a wound made by the teeth; a mouthful; a cheat; a trick; the action of acid on metal in process engraving, etc.: *v.t.* to break, crush, or seize with the teeth; to pinch or pain, as with cold; to make the mouth smart; to pierce, cut, or wound; to wound with reproach or sarcasm: to cheat; to trick; to enter the ground and hold fast, as an anchor; to take hold, as a screw; to eat into, as an acid. *pp.* **bitten.** (A.S. *bitan.*)
biter, *n.* *bite*-er, one who or that which bites; a cheat.
biternate, *a.* by-*tern*-at, doubly ternate [Bot.].
biting, *a.* *bite*-ing, sharp; severe; sarcastic. **biting in,** corroding by means of acids [Etching].
bitingly, *ad.* *bite*-ing-le, in a biting manner.
bitmaker, *n.* *bit*-make-er, one who makes bits.
bitt, *v.t.* bit, to put the cable around the bitts [Naut.].
bitten, *bit*-tn, *pp.* of **bite.**
★**bitter,** *a.* *bit*-ter, sharp or biting to the taste; acrid; harsh; piercing; painful; distressing; mournful: *n.* anything bitter; bitter ale: *v.t.* to make bitter. **bitter almond,** a variety of the almond. **bitter cress,** various plants of the genus *Cardamine.* **bitter gourd,** the colocynth. (A.S. *biter.*)
bitterish, *a.* *bit*-ter-ish, somewhat bitter.
bitterling, *n.* *bit*-ter-ling, a small freshwater fish, *Rhodens amarus*, resembling the carp.
bitterly, *ad.* *bit*-ter-le, with a bitter taste; in a bitter manner.
bittern, *n.* *bit*-tern, a wading bird of the genus *Botaurus*, allied to the heron. (Fr. *butor.*)
bittern, *n.* *bit*-tern, the brine remaining after the salt is concreted in salt works.
bitterness, *n.* *bit*-ter-ness, the quality of being bitter.
bitter-root, *n.* *bit*-ter-root, the Rocky Mountain plant *Lewisia rediviva*, the State plant of Montana.
bitters, *n.pl.* *bit*-terz, a liquor, generally spirituous, in which bitter herbs or roots have been steeped.
bitter-spar, *n.* *bit*-ter-spahr, a kind of dolomite.
bitter-sweet, *a.* *bit*-ter-sweet, bitter and sweet commingled; giving pleasure attended by pain: *n.* woody nightshade, *Solanum dulcamara*; also the meadow-sweet, and a variety of the apple.
bitter-vetch, *n.* *bit*-ter-vetch, a popular name for some of the vetches used as forage.
bitterwood, *n.* *bit*-ter-wood, popular name of the West Indian tree yielding quassia.
bitterwort, *n.* *bit*-ter-wurt, one of the gentians.
bittock, *n.* *bit*-tok, a small piece or distance. (Dial.)
bittour, *n.* *bit*-toor, the bittern.
bitts, *n.pl.* bits, two strong pieces of timber fixed in the deck of a ship for fastening the cables.
bitumen, *n.* be-*tew*-men *or* *bit*-yoo-men, mineral pitch; asphalt; an inflammable mineral substance consisting chiefly of hydrocarbons.
bituminiferous, *a.* be-*tew*-min-*if*-er-us, producing bitumen.
bituminization, *n.* be-*tew*-me-ny-*zay*-shon, the transformation of organic matters into bitumen; the art or process of converting into bitumen.
bituminize, *v.t.* be-*tew*-min-ize, to convert into or impregnate with bitumen.
bituminous, *a.* be-*tew*-min-us, containing or having the qualities of bitumen.
bivalent, *a.* *biv*-al-ent, divalent.
bivalve, *n.* *by*-valv, a mollusc having a shell of two valves or parts, like the oyster [Zool.]; a pericarp whose seed-vessel opens into two valves [Bot.]: *a.* having two shells or valves.
bivalvous, *a.* by-*val*-vus, bivalve.
bivalvular, *a.* by-*valv*-yoo-lar, bivalve.
bivious, *a.* *biv*-e-us, offering two courses; leading in two directions.
bivouac, *n.* *biv*-oo-ak, an encampment of soldiers for the night, without tents, in readiness for action: *v.i.* to pass the night in bivouac. (Ger. *bei*, at, *wache*, watch.)
bi-weekly, *a.* by-*week*-le, occurring once fortnightly.
bixin, *n.* *bik*-zin, the colouring principle of annatto.
bizarre, *a.* be-*zahr*, odd; fantastic; whimsical. (Fr.)
bizarrerie, *n.* be-*zahr*-ra-re, grotesqueness; incongruousness; an example of eccentricity. (Fr.)
blab, *n.* blab, a blabber; a tell-tale; one who blabs: *v.t.* to divulge indiscreetly; to betray: *v.i.* to tattle; to tell tales. (Origin uncertain.)
blabber, *n.* *blab*-ber, a tell-tale: *v.i.* to blab.
★**black,** *a.* blak, of the darkest colour; destitute of light; dark; sullen; having a cloudy look; clad in black; atrociously wicked; horrible; dismal; mournful: *n.* the darkest of all colour; want of colour; a Negro; a black pigment or dye; a black dress; mourning; a particle of soot or dirt: *v.t.* to blacken; to blacklead; to soil. **black art,** magic; witchcraft; necromancy (on the supposition that "necromancy" came from *niger*, black). **black and blue,** livid. **black and white,** writing or print; drawn with pen and ink. **black book,** the name of various English historical compilations; a book which treats of necromancy; a book of misdemeanours kept at some universities; a list of law-breakers or habitual criminals. **in one's black books,** out of favour; in disgrace with one. **black bottom,** an American negro clog-dance. **black bourse,** a black market in securities. **black bread,** rye bread. **black buck,** the small Indian antelope, *Antilope cervicapra.* **black cap,** the velvet cap worn by a judge in full dress and donned when sentencing a prisoner to death. **black country,** a general name for those parts of the industrial English Midlands begrimed by factory-smoke, etc. **black death,** a specially

virulent plague that ravaged Europe in the 14th cent. and England in 1348–9 and some later years. **black draught,** an aperient of senna and salts. **black eye,** discoloration of the parts surrounding the eye through a blow. **black maria,** a prison-van [Slang]; **black market,** one lacking official recognition; an organization for conducting illicit deals in controlled commodities. **black mass,** a blasphemous or obscene travesty of the Mass. **black monks,** the Benedictines. **black rod,** the usher of the Order of the Garter, who is also gentleman usher to the Lord Chamberlain and of the House of Lords. **Black Watch,** the old 42nd of the line, now the Royal Highlanders, so called from their dark tartan kilts. (A.S. *blæc.*)

blackamoor, *n. blak*-a-moor, a Negro; a black man.

blackball, *n. blak*-bawl, heelball; a negative or rejecting vote in a ballot: *v.t.* to reject by vote; to vote against; to ostracize [Slang].

black-band, *n. blak*-band, carbonaceous ironstone.

black-beetle, *n. blak*-bee-tl, the cockroach.

blackberry, *n. blak*-be-re, the bramble, *Rubus fruticosus,* and its fruit; in N. England and Scotland sometimes applied to the black currant, bilberry, etc.

blackbird, *n. blak*-berd, a species of the merle, *Merula*; the American grackle, and other birds.

black-birding, *n. black*-berd-ing, the kidnapping of Negroes or Polynesians for slavery.

blackboard, *n. blak*-bord, a board painted black, used to write or draw on, for purposes of instruction.

blackbuck, *n. blak*-buk, the Indian antelope, the sasin.

blackcap, *n. blak*-kap, the warbler *Sylvia atricapilla*; an apple roasted till black.

black-chalk, *n. blak*-chawk, a mineral of a bluish-black colour; a variety of argillaceous slate.

black-coat, *n. blak*-koat, a clergyman: *a.* denoting a professional or clerical as distinguished from a manual worker.

black-cock, *n. blak*-kok, the heath-cock, or black grouse, *Tetrao tetrix.*

black-currant, *n.* blak-*ku*-rant, the fruit of *Ribes nigrum*; the shrub itself.

black-drop, *n. blak*-drop, an infusion of opium in vinegar; the drop-like appearance of Venus and Mercury at ingress and egress of solar transits [Astron.].

black-earth, *n. blak*-erth, rich dark mould.

blacken, *v.t. blak*-en, to make black; to darken; to sully; to defame: *v.i.* to grow black or dark.

blackey, *n. blak*-e, a blacky.

blackfellow, *n. blak*-fel-lo, an Australian aboriginal.

blackfish, *n. blak*-fish, the pilot whale; a salmon that has just spawned; the tautog; also a popular name for various fishes.

black-flux, *n. blak*-fluks, a mixture of carbonate of potash and charcoal, used as a reducing flux.

black-fly, *n. blak*-fly, the turnip-flea beetle, and other field and garden pests.

blackfriar, *n.* blak-*fry*-ar, a Dominican friar.

blackgame, *n. blak*-game, blackcock and grey hen.

blackguard, *n. blag*-gard, a low, worthless fellow; a tough or rough: *v.t.* to revile in scurrilous language: *a.* vile; worthless. (Originally a menial or scullion.)

blackguardism, *n. blag*-gard-izm, the conduct or language of a blackguard.

blackguardly, *ad. blag*-gard-le, in the manner of a blackguard: *a.* characteristic of a blackguard.

black-gum, *n. blak*-gum, a North American tree, *Nyssa sylvatica*; its timber.

blackhead, *n. blak*-hed, a black spot due to the stopping up of a sebaceous gland; a black-headed gull, or other bird, or sheep, etc.

blackheart, *n. blak*-hart, a kind of cherry so dark-red in colour as to be practically black.

black-hearted, *a. blak*-hart-ed, having a wicked heart.

black-hole, *n. blak*-hole, a place of confinement for refractory prisoners; a guard-room.

blacking, *n. blak*-ing, the action of making black; a preparation for giving polish to blackened leather.

blackish, *a. blak*-ish, somewhat black.

black-jack, *n. blak*-jak, a name given by miners to blende; a drinking-vessel of leather.

blacklead, *n. blak*-led, plumbago or graphite: *v.t.* to polish or cover with blacklead.

black-leg, *n. blak*-leg, a low gambler; a swindler; a disease among cattle and sheep; a non-trade-union worker; one who remains at work when his fellows are on strike; a strike-breaker: *v.i.* to act as a black-leg.

black-letter, *n. blak-let*-ter, old English or modern Gothic: *a.* written or printed in black-letter [Print.].

black-list, *n. blak*-list, an official or private list of fraudulent or insolvent people, or of law-breakers: *v.t.* to put on a black-list.

blackly, *ad, blak*-le, darkly; glumly; atrociously.

blackmail, *n. blak*-mayl, a tribute paid to robbers to secure freedom or protection from molestation; extortion by threat of exposure: *v.t.* to extort blackmail.

blackmailer, *n.* blak-*mayl*-er, one who blackmails.

black-martin, *n. blak*-mar-tin, the swift.

black-match, *n. blak*-match, a pyrotechnic match or sponge.

black-Monday, *n.* blak-*mun*-day, any inauspicious day; the first Monday after a vacation; originally Easter Monday 1360, a day of unusual gloom and cold.

blackness, *n. blak*-ness, the quality of being black.

black-out, *n. blak*-out, a sudden cessation of light; a temporary loss of consciousness; a period during which no artificial light, unless lawfully permitted, may be visible from any street or open space: *v.t.* to expunge; to render (a building, window, etc.) proof against any emergence of light: *a.* suitable for black-out purposes or for use in a black-out.

black-pudding, *n. blak*-pood-ing, a sausage of blood and meat.

black-rent, *n. blak*-rent, rent paid in corn, kind, or debased coin; money formerly paid to the Irish chiefs by the English to secure allegiance.

black-rot, *n. blak*-rot, any fungoid or bacterial plant-disease causing decay and dark discoloration [Bot.].

black-rust, *n. blak*-rust, a disease in wheat.

black-sheep, *n.* blak-sheep, a person of bad character; a scapegrace.

blackshirt, *n. blak*-shirt, a Fascist; a member of the former British Union of Fascists. (From a distinctive feature of their attire.)

black-silver, *n. blak*-sil-ver, stephanite.

blacksmith, *n. blak*-smith, a smith who works in iron.

blacksnake, *n. blak*-snake, any snake of dark colour, esp. the American *Zamenis constrictor* and the Australian *Pseudechis porphyriaceus.*

blackstart, *n. blak*-start, the black redstart, *Ruticilla titys.*

blackstrap, *n. blak*-strap, a mixture of rum and molasses; a cheap wine formerly drunk by seamen in the Mediterranean.

blacktail, *n. blak*-tayl, a kind of perch.

blackthorn, *n. blak*-thorn, the sloe, *Prunus spinosa.*

black-wash, *n. blak*-wosh, a lotion of calomel and lime-water: *v.t.* to treat or cover with this.

blackwater-fever, *n. blak*-waw-ter-*fee*-ver, a severe form of malaria occurring in the tropics.

black-work, *n. blak*-wurk, blacksmiths' work.

blackwort, *n. blak*-wurt, the comfrey.

blacky, *n. blak*-e, a black person; a Negro.

bladder, *n. blad*-der, a thin membranous bag in animals serving as the receptacle of some secreted fluid, esp. that containing the urine; any vesicle, blister, or pustule; anything inflated with air. (A.S. *blaedre,* a blister.)

bladdered, *a. blad*-derd, inflated like a bladder; packed or put up in bladders.

bladder-kelp, *n. blad*-der-kelp, the seaweed *Fucus vesiculosus,* with vesicles on its fronds.

bladderwort, *n. blad*-der-wurt, a plant of the genus *Utricularia.*

bladder-wrack, *n. blad*-der-rak, bladder-kelp.

bladdery, *a. blad*-der-re, like a bladder; containing bladders.

★**blade,** *n.* blade, a leaf of grass or of a plant; a spire of grass; the broad part of a leaf or of a petal; the cutting part of a tool or weapon; the flat part of an oar or paddle; an arm of a screw-propeller; a dashing rakish fellow: *v.t.* to furnish with a blade: *v.i.* to put forth blades. (A.S. *blæd.*)

blade-bone, *n. blade*-bone, the scapula, the upper bone of the shoulder.

bladed, *a. blade*-ed, having a blade or blades; with plates like a blade [Min.].

blade-fish, *n.* *blade*-fish, one of the ribbon-fishes; also the hairtail, *Trichiurus lepturus.*
bladesmith, *n.* *blade*-smith, a sword cutler.
blae, *a.* blay, blackish or bluish-black; livid; lead-coloured; bleak [Scot.].
blaeberry, *n.* *blay*-be-re, the whortleberry, *Vaccinium myrtillus.* (Ice. *blā*, livid, and *berry*.)
blague, *n.* blahg, boastful humbug; swagger. (Fr.).
blah, *n.* blah, inane or pretentious talk: *int.* expressive of contempt.
blain, *n.* blayn, an inflammatory swelling; a pustule; a blister; a disease in cattle. (A.S. *blegen*, a boil.)
blame, *v.t.* blame, to censure; to find fault with: *n.* the act of censuring; imputation of a fault; censure; a fault. **to blame,** blameable. (O.Fr. *blasmer*, to reproach.)
blameable, *a.* *blame*-a-bl, deserving of blame.
blameableness, *n.* *blame*-a-bl-ness, the state of being blameable.
blameably, *ad.* *blame*-a-ble, in a blameable manner.
blameful, *a.* *blame*-ful, deserving of blame; prone to blame; fault finding.
blamefully, *ad.* *blame*-ful-e, in a blameful manner.
blamefulness, *n.* *blame*-ful-ness, state of being blameful.
blameless, *a.* *blame*-less, innocent; faultless; not meriting censure.
blamelessly, *ad.* *blame*-les-le, in a blameless manner.
blamelessness, *n.* *blame*-les-ness, the state of being blameless.
blameworthiness, *n.* *blame*-wur-the-ness, the quality of deserving censure.
blameworthy, *a.* *blame*-wur-the, reprehensible; deserving censure.
blanch, *v.t.* blahnch, to whiten, by taking out the colour; to whiten by exclusion of the light [Hort.]: *v.i.* to grow white. (Fr. *blanchir*, to whiten.)
blanch-farm, *n.* *blahnch*-farm, rent paid in silver, not in labour or kind; also a quit-rent (Scot.).
blanch-holding, *n.* *blahnch*-hohld-ing, a tenure held by payment of quit-rent only (Scot. law).
blanching, *a.* *blahnch*-ing, whitening. **blanching liquor,** a bleaching solution of chloride of lime.
blanc-mange, *n.* bla-*monge*, a white jelly, made of gelatine or cornflour, milk and sugar, boiled to a thick consistence. (O.Fr. *blancmanger*, white food.)
blanco, *n.* *blank*-oh, a proprietary preparation for whitening straps and equipment: *v.t.* to whiten with this.
bland, *a.* bland, mild; gentle; kindly; affable. (L. *blandus*, smooth-tongued.)
blandiloquence, *n.* blan-*dil*-o-kwence, fair flattering speech; cajoling talk.
blandish, *v.t.* *bland*-ish, to flatter by kindness, to wheedle. (Fr. *blandir*, to flatter.)
blandishment, *n.* *bland*-ish-ment, soft, flattering, often enticing, speech or treatment; charm.
blandly, *ad.* *bland*-le, mildly.
blandness, *n.* *bland*-ness, state of being bland.
blank, *a.* blank, void; empty; not written upon or marked; confused; dispirited; dejected; pure: *n.* a paper unwritten upon or not filled in; a ticket in a lottery which draws no prize; a piece of metal before stamping or cutting (as for coin, keys, etc.); any void space; an uneventful period; the white point in the centre of a target; aim; range: *v.t.* to make or render blank; to dumbfound. **blank cartridge,** cartridge without ball. **blank cheque,** a signed cheque with the amount left to be filled in. **blank credit,** permission to draw on an individual or firm up to a certain amount. **blank door, window,** etc., a semblance of, or imitation, door, window, etc. **blank verse,** unrhymed verse, particularly the heroic verse of five feet. **blank wall,** a wall devoid of opening, an unbroken wall. (Fr. *blanc*, white.)
blanket, *n.* *blang*-ket, a soft loosely woven woollen cloth, used for bed-coverings and wrappers; the material covering the metal impression surface on a rotary press [Print.]: *v.t.* to cover with a blanket; to toss in a blanket; to take the wind out of a vessel's sails by drawing to windward alongside. **wet blanket,** a person with depressive tendencies; one who damps enthusiasm or joy.
blanketing, *n.* *blang*-ke-ting, cloth or materials for blankets; tossing in a blanket.
blankly, *ad.* *blank*-le, in a blank manner.
blankness, *n.* *blank*-ness, state of being blank.
blare, *v.i.* blayr, to emit a bellowing noise: *n.* a trumpet or bellowing noise. (Dut. *blaren*.)
blarney, *n.* *blar*-ne, smooth flattery; deceitful speech; gammon: *v.t.* and *i.* to wheedle. (Castle *Blarney*, Ireland, a certain stone in the wall of which was said to endow the person that kissed it with a fair-spoken tongue.)
blasé, *a.* *blah*-zay, used up; worn out; with all relish and energy exhausted. (Fr.)
blaspheme, *v.t.* blas-*feem*, to speak blasphemously of: *v.i.* to utter blasphemy. (Gr. *blasphēmia*.)
blasphemer, *n.* blas-*feem*-er, one who blasphemes.
blaspheming, *n.* blas-*feem*-ing, the act of blasphemy.
blasphemous, *a.* *blas*-fe-mus, uttering or containing blasphemy; impious.
blasphemously, *ad.* *blas*-fe-mus-le, in a blasphemous manner.
blasphemy, *n.* *blas*-fe-me, impious contemptuous speech or behaviour in reference to God and things sacred; profane speaking.
blast, *n.* blahst, a violent gust of wind; a forcible stream of air; the sound made by blowing a wind instrument, steam-whistle, etc.; explosion in splitting rocks, or of inflammable air; the sound of an explosion; the sudden increase in air-pressure, and the concussion, caused by an explosion; air introduced into a furnace artificially; any pernicious or destructive influence upon animals or plants; a blight; a flatulent disease in sheep: *v.t.* to strike with and make to wither under some pernicious influence; to blight; to ruin; to strike with terror or calamity; to split rocks with gunpowder; to cause damage or destruction with high explosives, or to clear by means of these: *int.* confound! damn it! [Vulg.]. (A.S. *blæst*.)
blasted, *a.* *blahs*-ted, confounded.
blastema, *n.* blas-*tee*-ma, the formative material of plants and animals; the basis of an organ or organism yet to be formed. (Gr. *blastēma*, an offshoot.)
blastemal, *a.* blas-*tee*-mal, relating to the blastema.
blaster, *n.* *blahst*-er, he who or that which blasts or destroys; a blast producer.
blast-furnace, *n.* *blahst*-*fur*-nace, a furnace for smelting by means of a steady blast of hot air.
blasting, *n.* *blahst*-ing, a blast; blight; the splitting of rocks by an explosive.
blastocarpous, *a.* *blas*-to-*kar*-pus, germinating inside the pericarp [Bot.]. (Gr. *blastos*, a germ, *karpos*, fruit.)
blastocolla, *n.* blas-to-*kol*-a, a sticky substance coating certain buds.
blastoderm, *n.* *blas*-to-derm, the germinal membrane lying immediately beneath the *membrana vitelli* of the ovum. (Gr. *blastos*, a germ, *derma*, skin.)
blastogenesis, *n.* *blas*-to-*jen*-e-sis, reproduction by budding. (Gr. *blastos*, a germ, *genēsis*, birth.)
blast-pipe, *n.* *blahst*-pipe, a pipe in locomotives to convey waste steam up the chimney, and urge the fire by creating a stronger current of air.
blatancy, *n.* *blay*-tan-se, obtrusive vulgarity.
blatant, *a.* *blay*-tant, bellowing like a beast; vulgarly loud.
blatantly, *ad.* *blay*-tant-le, in a blatant manner.
blate, *a.* blayt, bashful. (Scots.)
blather, *v.i.* *blath*-er, to talk foolishly or nonsensically: *n.* one who does this; foolish talk; rigmarole; blether.
blatherskite, *n.* *blath*-er-skite, a noisy talkative person; nonsense; blather.
blatta, *n.* *blat*-ta, the cockroach or black-beetle. (L.)
blatter, *v.i.* *blat*-ter, to make a senseless noise; to patter: *n.* a clatter.
blattnerphone, *n.* *blat*-ner-fone, an instrument for simultaneously recording and reproducing sounds or speech, etc. for broadcasting [Wire.].
blay, *n.* blay, a small river-fish, the bleak.
blaze, *n.* blaze, the stream of light from a body when burning; full streaming light; an outburst as of display or passion: *v.i.* to flame; to send forth a bright and expanded light; to be conspicuous. (A.S. *blæse*, torch.)
blaze, *v.t.* blaze, to make known far and wide; to proclaim abroad; to emblazon. (Ice. *blāsa*, to blow.)
blaze, *n.* blaze, a white spot on the forehead or face of a horse; a mark made on trees by notching the bark: *v.t.* to mark trees by paring the bark.

blazer, *n.* *blay*-zer, a coloured flannel sports-jacket.
blazing, *a.* *blay*-zing, emitting flame or light; flaming.
blazon, *n.* *blay*-zon, the act or art of drawing or explaining coats of arms; publication; pompous display: *v.t.* to describe or depict armorial bearings; to embellish; to trumpet; to make widely known. (Fr. *blason*, coat of arms.)
blazoner, *n.* *blay*-zon-er, one who blazons; a herald; a propagator of scandal.
blazonment, *n.* *blay*-zon-ment, the act of blazoning; publication.
blazonry, *n.* *blay*-zon-re, heraldic painting or description; armorial bearings; brilliant or ostentatious display.
bleach, *n.* bleech, chloride of lime: *v.t.* to make white, especially by bleaching: *v.i.* to grow white. (A.S. *blæcan*, grow pale.)
bleacher, *n.* *bleech*-er, one who or that which bleaches; a vessel used in bleaching.
bleachery, *n.* *bleech*-er-re, a bleaching establishment.
bleach-field, *n.* *bleech*-feeld, a field for bleaching in the sun.
bleaching, *n.* *bleech*-ing, the act or art of whitening, especially cloth, by means of decolorizing agents. **bleaching liquid,** a solution of **bleaching powder,** or chloride of lime.
bleak, *n.* bleek, a small cyprinoid river-fish, with silvery scales, *Alburnus lucidus*. (Scand. *bleikja*.)
bleak, *a.* bleek, unsheltered; cold; cheerless; devoid of vegetation. (A.S. *blac*.)
bleakish, *a.* *bleek*-ish, rather bleak.
bleakly, *ad.* *bleek*-le, in a bleak manner.
bleakness, *n.* *bleek*-ness, the state of being bleak.
blear, *a.* bleer, sore and dim, with watery humour.
blearedness, *n.* *bleerd*-ness, the state of being bleared; dimness.
blear-eyed, *a.* *bleer*-ide, having sore weak eyes.
bleat, *n.* bleet, a sheep's cry: *v.i.* to cry as a sheep: *v.t.* to utter in a bleating or sheepish way. (A.S. *blætan*.)
bleating, *n.* *bleet*-ing, the cry of a sheep.
bleb, *n.* bleb, a little vesicle or blister; a bubble.
blebby, *a.* *bleb*-e, abounding with blebs.
bled, bled, *p.* and *pp.* of the verb to bleed.
bleed, *v.i.* bleed, to lose blood; to die a violent death; to drop or issue, as blood: *v.t.* to let blood; to take blood from; to extort money from [Slang]. *p.* and *pp.* **bled.** (A.S. *blēdan*, to lose blood.)
bleeder, *n.* *blee*-der, one who or that which bleeds; one who bleeds excessively from slight wounds; a hæmophiliac.
bleeding, *n.* *blee*-ding, a running or issuing of blood; a hæmorrhage; the operation of letting blood, or of drawing sap: *a.* running with blood.
blemish, *n.* *blem*-ish, what stains, mars or impairs; a flaw; what tarnishes or impairs reputation; a moral defect: *v.t.* to mar; to impair; to tarnish. (O.Fr. *blesmir*, to spot.)
blench, *v.i.* blensh, to shrink from; to flinch; to blink. (A.S. *blencan*, to deceive.)
blend, *n.* blend, a mixture, esp. one of different qualities of the same commodity: *v.t.* to mingle together: *v.i.* to be indistinguishably mixed; to be united; to pass insensibly into each other. (A.S. *blandan*.)
blende, *n.* blend, native sulphide of zinc. (Ger. *blenden*, to deceive.)
blender, *n.* *blend*-er, one who or that which blends.
Blenheim, *n.* *blen*-em, a breed of spaniels; the Blenheim orange, a variety of apple.
blennorrhœa, *n.* *blen*-o-*ree*-a, inordinate discharge of mucus; gonorrhœa. (Gr. *blenna*, mucus, *rheo*, to flow.)
blenny, *n.* *blen*-ne, a small spiny-finned marine and freshwater fish of the genus *Blennius*.
blent, *a.* blent, blended, mixed.
blepharitis, *n.* blef-a-*ry*-tis, inflammation of the eyelids. (Gr. *blepharon*, eyelid, and *-itis*.)
blesbok, *n.* *bless*-bok, a white-faced South African antelope, *Bubalis albifrons*.
bless, *v.t.* bless, to invoke a blessing upon; to wish happiness to; to make happy or prosperous; to consecrate or pronounce holy; to praise; to esteem or count happy. (A.S. *bletsian*.)
blessed, *a.* blest *or* *bless*-ed, happy; prosperous; bestowing or connected with blessing: *n.* those (collectively) enjoying eternal blessedness; the saints.
blessedness, *n.* *bless*-ed-ness, the state of being blessed. **single blessedness,** the unmarried state.
blessing, *n.* *bless*-ing, an invocation of happiness or success; any means or cause of happiness; grace before or after meat; a gift, benefit, or advantage; divine favour.
blest, *a.* blest, blessed.
blether, *n.* *bleth*-er, noisy or frothy talk: *v.i.* to talk nonsense; to blather.
bletonism, *n.* *blet*-on-izm, a former term for dowsing or water-divining. (M. *Bleton*, Fr. dowser, *c.* 1815.)
blew, bloo, *p.* of blow.
blewit, *n.* *bloo*-it, an edible mushroom with pale bluish top.
blight, *n.* blite, a disease in plants variously caused, under which they wither; mildew; anything which blasts or destroys; a malignant influence: *v.t.* to affect with blight; to frustrate; to blast. (Origin uncertain.)
blighter, *n.* *bly*-ter, one who or that which blights; a chap, a fellow (formerly a contemptible person) [Slang].
blightingly, *ad.* *bly*-ting-le, in a blighting manner.
Blighty, *n.* *bly*-te, the soldier's name for England. (Hind. *belati*, *bilayati*, foreign, hence European.)
blimp, *n.* blimp, a small non-rigid airship [Coll.].
blind, *a.* blynd, destitute of sight, destitute of vision of any kind, such as understanding or judgment; unseeing; unseen; dark; obscure; heedless; reckless; inconsiderate; admitting no light; having no outlet; having insufficient address (of postal packets): *n.* a window-screen; a protecting screen or blindage [Mil.]; a blinker; something to mislead; (pl.) blind persons collectively: *v.t.* to deprive of sight; to darken; to deceive: *ad.* blindly; insensibly. **blind alley,** a cul-de-sac, that which leads nowhere; an occupation affording no hope for promotion. **blind drunk,** intoxicated to the stage of insensibility [Coll.]. **blind flying,** aerial navigation by means of instruments only. **blind gut,** the cæcum [Anat.]. **blind spot,** the point in the retina insensitive to light; an area in which radio reception, or mental discernment, is ineffective. (A.S. *blind*.)
blindage, *n.* *blynd*-aj, a screen protecting defenders from hostile fire [Fort.].
blind-coal, *n.* *blynd*-koal, a coal that does not flame or smoke; anthracite.
blinder, *n.* *blynd*-er, anything that blinds; a horse's blinker.
blindfold, *a.* *blynd*-fohld, having the eyes bandaged or covered, so as not to see: *v.t.* to cover the eyes. (A.S. *blind*, and *fellen*, to hit.)
blind-harry, *n.* blynd-*ha*-re, blindman's-buff.
blindly, *ad.* *blynd*-ly, in a manner as if blind.
blindman, *n.* *blynd*-man, one who is blind; a post office official dealing with ill-written addresses. **blindman's holiday,** dusk.
blindman's-buff, *n.* *blynd*-manz-*buf*, a game in which a blindfolded player tries to catch and name other players.
blindness, *n.* *blynd*-ness, the state of being blind; lack of discernment or of moral perception; ignorance.
blind-side, *n.* *blynd*-side, the side most easily assailed; the weak side; a foible.
blindworm, *n.* *blynd*-wurm, the slow-worm, a small burrowing legless lizard, *Anguis fragilis*.
blink, *n.* blink, a glimpse; a glimmer; a glance; an instant: *v.i.* to wink; to peer with the eyes half shut; to twinkle: *v.t.* to shut out of sight; to avoid or purposely evade. **blink ice,** iceblink. (A.S. *blencan*, to deceive.)
blinkard, *n.* *blink*-ard, one with bad eyes; an obtuse person.
blinkers, *n.pl.* *blink*-erz, leather screens attached to a headstall to prevent a horse from seeing sideways.
blinky, *a.* *blink*-e, blinking; inclined to blink.
blirt, *n.* blirt, a gust accompanied by rain [Naut.]; a burst of weeping (Scot.): *v.i.* to burst into tears.
bliss, *n.* bliss, the highest happiness or blessedness; the joy of heaven; heaven itself. (A.S.)
blissful, *a.* *bliss*-ful, full of or causing bliss.
blissfully, *ad.* *bliss*-ful-le, in a blissful manner.
blissfulness, *n.* *bliss*-ful-ness, the state of being blissful.
blister, *n.* *bliss*-ter, a pustule or thin vesicle raised

by some injury on the skin, containing watery matter or serum; a plaster to raise a blister; any similar rising on a surface; the protective outer hull of a warship [Slang]: *v.i.* to rise in blisters: *v.t.* to raise a blister; to apply a blistering plaster. **blister gas,** any of a group of vaporizing liquids bodily contact with which causes serious burning and blistering. (M.E.)

blister-fly, *n.* *bliss*-ter-fly, the Spanish fly, *Cantharis vesicatoria*, used in blistering.

blister-steel, *n.* *bliss*-ter-steel, crude steel covered with blisters.

blistery, *a.* *bliss*-ter-re, full of blisters.

blite, *n.* blyt, wild spinach, or other plant of the order *Chenopodiaceæ*. **sea blite,** *Suæda maritima*.

blithe, *a.* blythe, gay; merry; joyous; sprightly. (A.S.)

blithely, *ad.* *blythe*-le, in a blithe manner.

blitheness, *n.* *blythe*-ness, the quality of being blithe or blithesome.

blithering, *a.* *blith*-er-ring, blathering; used as an intensive, as in blithering fool, meaning consummate fool.

blithesome, *a.* *blythe*-sum, gay; merry; cheerful.

blithesomeness, *n.* *blythe*-sum-ness, blitheness.

blitz, *n.* blits, a sudden, heavy, and prolonged bombardment, esp. from the air; a series of such; a period of intensive air attack: *v.t.* to subject to a blitz [Coll.]. (Ger., lightning.)

blitzkrieg, *n.* *blits*-kreeg, sudden and intensive warfare. (Ger. *blitz*, lightning, *krieg*, war.)

blizzard, *n.* *bliz*-ard, a cold violent snowstorm accompanied by a gale. (Origin uncertain.)

bloat, *v.t.* bloat, to cause to swell; to puff up; to make vain; to dry by smoke: *v.i.* to grow turgid; to dilate. (M.E.)

bloated, *a.* *bloat*-ed, large and unwieldly from over self-indulgence; puffed up with pride.

bloatedness, *n.* *bloat*-ed-ness, the state or quality of being bloated.

bloater, *n.* *bloat*-er, a salted herring dried with smoke.

blob, *n.* blob, a blot, a round drop of liquid.

blobber-lipped, *a.* *blob*-ber-lipt, having thick or pouting lips.

bloc, *n.* blok, a combination, esp. in a legislative assembly, of members of political parties for some definite object; a political or racial union for taking common action or for furthering specified aims. **en bloc,** as a single unit; wholesale. (Fr.)

block, *n.* blok, a solid mass of wood or stone; the wood on which criminals are beheaded; a frame of wood, with one or more sheaves for ropes; a solid piece of hard wood, on which figures are cut or engraved, also a cliché taken from this; a wooden or other mould, on which a thing is shaped; a continuous row of buildings; an obstruction; a number of detachable sheets of writing-, drawing-, or blotting-paper on a stiff foundation; the block-hole at cricket; a stop, as a block section of a railway; an unsympathetic person; a block-head; the head [Slang]: *v.t.* to enclose or shut up; to stop up; to stop a train by a block signal; to shape roughly. **block machine,** a machine for making blocks for a ship's rigging. **block signal,** a signal to stop a train in consequence of the next section not being reported clear. **block system,** a system of traffic on railways which requires a section of the line to be reported clear before a train is allowed to enter it. **block tin,** impure tin run into ingots. (Probably from Fr. *bloc*.)

blockade, *n.* blok-*ade*, a siege, a cutting-off of supplies to compel surrender: *v.t.* to surround by or subject to a blockade; to deprive the enemy of supplies by blocking his communications by sea, land, or air. **blockade runner,** a ship for breaking through a blockade by sea. **paper blockade,** one that remains ineffective though proclaimed.

block-book, *n.* *blok*-book, a book printed from wooden blocks engraved in relief.

blockhead, *n.* *blok*-hed, a dull stupid person.

block-hole, *n.* a mark a yard in front of the wicket indicating the batsman's position at cricket.

block-house, *n.* *blok*-house, a small temporary detached fort, constructed chiefly of hewn timber.

blockish, *a.* *blok*-ish, stupid; dull; clumsy.

blockishly, *ad.* *blok*-ish-le, in a blockish manner.

blockishness, *n.* *blok*-ish-ness, the quality of being blockish.

block-plane, *n.* a plane having its blade set to cut across the grain.

block-printing, *n.* *blok*-print-ing, a mode of printing from engraved wooden blocks.

bloke, *n.* bloke, a fellow; a man [Slang].

blond, *n.* blond, a man with fair hair and blue eyes: *a.* light in colour or complexion.

blonde, *n.* blond, a woman of very fair complexion, with light hair and light blue eyes; a silk lace with hexagonal interstices. (Fr.)

★**blood,** *n.* blud, the vital fluid circulating through the vascular system of vertebrates, nourishing and oxygenating all parts of the body; an analogous fluid in invertebrates; offspring; connexion by descent; honourable or high birth; the royal family; of royal descent; slaughter; murder; carnal part opposed to spiritual; temper; passion; a man of a fiery spirit; a rake, or dissipated character; juice, especially if red: *a.* like blood; of good breed: *v.t.* to bleed by opening a vein; to stain with blood; to inure to blood, as a hound; to exasperate. **bad blood,** resentment; bitterness. **half** or **whole blood,** connexion through one parent, or through both. (A.S. *blōd*.)

blood-boltered, *a.* *blud*-boal-terd, blood-soiled.

blood-brother, *n.* *blud*-bruth-er, a brother of both parents.

blood-count, *n.* *blud*-kount, a count of the corpuscles contained in a given volume (usu. 1 cu. mm.) of blood.

blooded, *a.* *blud*-ed, of pure or nearly pure blood or breed; smeared with blood or given the first taste of it.

blood-feud, *n.* *blud*-fewd, a vendetta.

blood-group, *n.* any one of the four types in which human blood is classified according to its content.

blood-guiltiness, *n.* *blud*-gilt-e-ness, the guilt of shedding blood.

blood-guilty, *a.* *blud*-gilt-e, responsible for shedding blood or murder.

blood-heat, *n.* *blud*-heet, heat of the blood, about 98° Fahrenheit.

blood-horse, *n.* *blud*-horse, a thoroughbred horse.

bloodhound, *n.* *blud*-hound, a dog, remarkable for the acuteness of its scent, formerly used for man-hunting; a sleuth; a person relentless in pursuit.

bloodily, *ad.* *blud*-e-le, in a bloody manner.

bloodiness, *n.* *blud*-e-ness, the state of being bloody.

bloodless, *a.* *blud*-less, without blood; without bloodshed; effete; spiritless.

bloodlessly, *ad.* *blud*-less-le, without bloodshed.

blood-letting, *n.* *blud*-let-ting, the act or process of letting blood; phlebotomy.

blood-money, *n.* *blud*-mun-e, reward to informer for securing conviction for murder; compensation for the murder of a relative.

blood-orange, *n.* *blud*-o-ranj, a variety of sweet orange with reddish pulp and juice.

blood-poisoning, *n.* *blud*-*poyz*-on-ing, septicæmia.

blood-pressure, *n.* *blud*-presh-ur, the pressure of the blood on the walls of the arteries, etc., esp. as indicating physical condition.

blood-pudding, *n.* *blud*-pood-ding, black-pudding.

blood-red, *a.* *blud*-red, red as or red with blood.

blood-relation, *n.* *blud*-re-*lay*-shon, one related by descent or consanguinity.

bloodshed, *n.* *blud*-shed, the shedding of blood; murder; slaughter.

bloodshot, *a.* *blud*-shot, red and inflamed, as the eye, by a turgid state of the blood-vessels.

blood-spavin, *n.* *blud*-spav-in, a dilatation of the vein inside of the hock of a horse.

blood-sports, *n.pl.* hunting, and any sport involving the chase and slaughter of animals.

bloodstained, *a.* *blud*-staynd, stained with blood; guilty of bloodshed.

bloodstock, *n.* *blud*-stok, thoroughbred and pedigree horses.

blood-stone, *n.* *blud*-stone, a dark-green chalcedony, spotted with jasper, as if with blood; a heliotrope; an amulet thought to prevent bleeding at the nose; **red** hæmatite.

bloodsucker, *n.* *blud*-suk-er, an animal that sucks blood; a cruel man; an extortioner or usurer.

blood-tax, *n.* *blud*-taks, conscription for national defence [Coll.].

blood-test, *n.* *blud*-test, an analysis of the blood to ascertain the nature of an infection or as a means of determining parentage.

bloodthirstiness, *n.* *blud*-therst-e-ness, a bloodthirsty disposition.
bloodthirsty, *a.* *blud*-therst-e, eager for slaughter; delighting in deeds of bloodshed.
blood-vessel, *n.* *blud*-ves-sel, any vessel in which blood circulates in an animal; an artery; a vein.
bloodwood, *n.* *blud*-wood, logwood, and other trees having red sap or timber.
bloodworm, *n.* *blud*-wurm, the larva of a gnat used as fishing-bait; a parasite living in the blood.
bloodwort, *n.* *blud*-wurt, a popular name for *Rumex sanguineus* and other plants.
bloody, *a.* *blud*-e, blood-stained; cruel; murderous; attended with bloodshed; used also in slang as a vulgar intensive: *v.t.* to stain with blood; to render bloody.
bloody-faced, *a.* *blud*-e-fayst, having a bloody appearance; sanguinary.
bloody-flux, *n.* *blud*-e-fluks, a former term for dysentery.
bloody-minded, *a.* *blud*-e-*mine*-ded, of a cruel disposition.
bloody-sweat, *n.* *blud*-e-*swet*, a sweat accompanied by a discharge of blood; the sweating sickness.
bloom, *n.* bloom, a blossom or flower; the blue colour upon newly gathered plums, grapes, etc.; full maturity; the rosy flush of full life: *v.i.* to put forth blossoms; to flower; to be in a state of bloom; to flourish. (Ice. *blōm*, a flower.)
bloom, *n.* bloom, a mass of heated iron that has passed the bloomery and undergone the first hammering.
bloomer, *n.* *bloom*-er, a plant that blooms, as "early-bloomer"; a mistake [Slang].
bloomers, *n.pl.* *bloom*-erz, a loose knickerbocker costume for women (from its introducer, Mrs. Bloomer, in 1850); women's closed knickers.
bloomery, *n.* *bloom*-er-re, the first forge through which iron passes after it is smelted from the ore.
blooming, *a.* *bloom*-ing, in a state of bloom; flourishing; the process of converting cast into malleable iron [Metal.]; a clouded appearance which varnish sometimes assumes on the surface of a picture [Paint.]; a synonym for bloody [Slang].
bloomingly, *ad.* *bloom*-ing-le, in a blooming manner.
bloomy, *a.* *bloom*-e, full of bloom; blooming.
blore, *n.* blore, a heavy gust of wind. (Dial. Eng.)
blossom, *n.* *blos*-som, the flower, especially in anticipation of the fruit; an indication of future success: *v.i.* to put forth blossoms. (A.S. *blōstma*, flower or fruit.)
blossomy, *a.* *blos*-so-me, full of blossoms.
blot, *n.* blot, a spot or stain; an obliteration of something written; a spot in reputation; a disgrace: *v.t.* to spot or stain; to stain with infamy; to obliterate or efface; to dry with blotting-paper. (Origin uncertain.)
blot, *n.* blot, a man in backgammon in a position to be taken; hence, any weak spot.
blotch, *n.* blotch, a pustule or skin eruption; a blemish; a plant disease: *v.t.* to mark with blotches.
blotchy, *a.* *blotch*-e, having blotches; spotted.
blotter, *n.* *blot*-ter, a pad or book of blotting-paper; that which blots.
blotting, *n.* *blot*-ting, the drying of blots. **blotting-pad,** a block of blotting-paper. **blotting-paper,** a soft unsized paper for absorbing ink.
blotto, *a.* *blot*-o, drunk and incapable [Slang].
blouse, *n.* blouz, a light, loose, outer garment for the trunk; a bodice belted at the waist. (Fr.)
★**blow,** *n.* blo, a gale of wind; a breath of fresh air; an egg of the flesh-fly: *v.i.* to make a current of air; to pant; to sound as a horn by being blown; to flower; to blossom; to come to blossom: *v.t.* to drive a current of air upon; to drive by a current of air; to put out of breath; to inflate with air; to puff up; to sound a wind instrument; to spread by report; to taint by depositing eggs upon, as flies; to shatter by explosives. **to blow in,** to visit, or to arrive, unexpectedly; to squander. **blow hot and cold,** to vacillate. **to blow out,** to extinguish by blowing upon; to scatter, as by a pistol-shot. **a blow out,** a good meal [Slang]. **to blow over,** to pass away without effect; to subside. **to blow up,** to be broken and scattered or burst, by the explosion of gunpowder; to inflate; to kindle; to bring to nought suddenly; to scold. **to blow upon,** to make stale or common, as a passage in a writer; to speak ill of; to regard as worthless; to divulge. *p.* **blew.** *pp.* **blown.** (A.S. *blawan*, to blow.)
blow, *v.i.* blo, to blossom; to flourish: *n.* the state of blossoming; bloom. (A.S. *blowan*.)
blow, *n.* blo, a stroke; an act of hostility; a sudden calamity. (Origin uncertain.)
blow-ball, *n.* *blo*-bawl, the downy head of the dandelion.
blower, *n.* *blo*-er, one who or that which blows; a contrivance for producing a current of air or delivering air or gas at increased pressure [Eng.]; a whale; a race-course telephone or telegraph [Slang].
blow-fly, *n.* *blo*-fly, a fly which taints meat by deposition of its eggs; a species of the genus *Calliphora*.
blow-gun, *n.* *blo*-gun, a tube through which darts are blown by the breath.
blow-hole, *n.* *blo*-hole, the nostril of a whale; a hole in ice for seals to breathe through; a defect in a casting caused by escape of gas during solidification [Metal.].
blowlamp, *n.* *blo*-lamp, a portable lamp with pressurized fuel for applying intense local heat.
blow-milk, *n.* *blo*-milk, skimmed milk.
blowpipe, *n.* *blo*-pipe, a tube through which a current of air is driven into a flame to increase its power of combustion; a tube used for projecting poisoned arrows by the breath; a blow-gun.
blowy, *a.* *blo*-e, windy; blowing; exposed to the wind.
blowze, *n.* blouz, a ruddy, fat-faced woman.
blowzed, *a.* blouzd, blowzy; dishevelled.
blowzy, *a.* *blouz*-e, coarse, fat, slatternly.
blub, *v.i.* blub, to shed tears [Slang].
blubber, *v.i.* *blub*-ber, to weep noisily, so as to swell the cheeks: *v.t.* to swell the cheeks with weeping; to utter with sobs: *n.* the fat of whales and other cetaceans; the sea-nettle.
blubber-lip, *n.* *blub*-ber-lip, blobber-lip.
blucher, *n.* *bloo*-cher, a kind of stout leather half-boot, so called from Marshal von Blücher.
bludgeon, *n.* *bludj*-un, a short heavy stick: *v.t.* to strike down with this.
★**blue,** *n.* bloo, a primary colour of various shades; the colour of the cloudless azure sky; the sky itself; the sea; a blue pigment or dye; a representative in certain sports of Oxford or Cambridge; a bluecoat boy; a preparation used in washing linen: *a.* of a blue colour; sky-coloured; cast down or low in spirits; learned or pedantic (of women); obscene [Slang]: *v.t.* to make blue; to temper steel; to treat with washing-blue. **blue blood,** aristocratic lineage. **blue bonnet,** a Scottish trooper; the flat cap of a Scottish peasant; the cornflower. **blue devils,** lowness of spirits; delirium tremens. **blue funk,** abject fear [Slang]. **blue gum,** a tree of the genus *Eucalyptus*. **blue jay,** a North American bird, *Cyanocitta cristatus*. **blue john,** blue fluor-spar [Mining]. **blue peter,** a blue flag with a white square in the centre, flown as a signal for sailing. **blue ribbon,** the ribbon of the order of the garter; a badge of success; success itself; a ribbon worn by total abstainers. **blue rock,** the rock dove. **blue ruin,** a cant name for gin. **blue spar,** lazulite. **blue vitriol,** copper sulphate. **blue water,** the deep sea. **the Blues,** the Royal Horse Guards. **the blues,** a dance; blue devils. **true blue,** genuine and thorough. (O.Fr. *bleu*.)
Bluebeard, *n.* *bloo*-beerd, a husband of many wives, esp. a miscreant who murders them.
blue-bell, *n.* *bloo*-bel, the popular name of *Hyacinthus non-scriptus*, and, in Scotland, of the hair-bell, *Campanula rotundifolia*.
blue-berry, *n.* *bloo*-be-re, the bilberry.
bluebird, *n.* *bloo*-berd, a small singing bird of the genus *Sialia*, the U.S.A. harbinger of spring.
blue-black, *a.* *bloo*-blak, blue tinged with black.
blue-book, *n.* *bloo*-book, a book containing a Government account or report, printed by order of Parliament, usually in a blue cover; a list of Government officials in the U.S.A.
bluebottle, *n.* *bloo*-bot-tl, the cornflower, also other blue flowers; the blow-fly; a policeman [Slang].
blue-breast, *n.* *bloo*-brest, the bluethroat.
blue-cap, *n.* *bloo*-kap, the coal fish; a titmouse.
bluecoat, *n.* *bloo*-koat, a dress commonly worn by

children in charity schools, esp. in Christ's Hospital; a Christ's Hospital boy: *a.* belonging to Christ's Hospital.

blue-fish, *n.* *bloo*-fish, the widely distributed and voracious food-fish, *Pomatomus saltatrix,* and (as popular name) other fish.

bluegown, *n.* *bloo*-goun, in Scotland, a bedesman who held a royal licence to beg.

blueing, *n.* *bloo*-ing, the giving a bluish tint to clothes; the heating of metal until it assumes a blue colour.

bluejacket, *n.* *bloo*-jak-et, a seaman in the Royal Navy, also in the United States Navy.

bluely, *ad.* *bloo*-le, of a blue colour.

blueness, *n.* *bloo*-ness, the quality of being blue.

blue-nose, *n.* *bloo*-noze, the popular name for a native of Nova Scotia.

blue-ointment, *n.* bloo-*oynt*-ment, mercurial ointment.

blue-pill, *n.* *bloo*-pil, a mercurial pill.

blue-print, *n.* *bloo*-print, a plan or drawing made by printing on sensitized paper, the design showing in white lines on a blue ground; a final draft [Fig.].

blues, *n.pl.* blooz, *see* **blue.**

blue-stocking, *n.* *bloo*-stok-ing, a literary woman, originally one of the Blue Stocking Society, a club that met about 1750 to discuss literature. (Blue stockings, *i.e.* not full evening dress.)

bluethroat, *n* *bloo*-throat, the blue-breast, a singing-bird of the species *Cyanecula.*

bluey, *a.* *bloo*-e, bluish.

bluff, *a.* bluf, full-faced; frank and free; outspoken; gruff; steep and overhanging: *n.* a headland. **bluff-bowed,** having broad bows [Naut.]. **bluff-headed,** having an upright stem [Naut.]. (Dut. *blaf,* broad.)

bluff, *v.t.* bluf, to deceive; to hoodwink; to mislead (at cards, etc.) by feigning to be in a stronger position than one is: *n.* the action of bluffing; boasting with intent to mislead; an empty threat; a game like poker. (American; of uncertain origin.)

bluffer, *n.* *bluf*-er, one addicted to bluffing.

bluffness, *n.* *bluf*-ness, frankness; surliness.

bluffy *a.* *bluf*-e, having bluffs or bold points of coast.

bluish, *a.* *bloo*-ish, slightly blue.

bluishness, *n.* *bloo*-ish-ness, the quality of being bluish.

blunder, *n.* *blun*-der, a gross mistake: *v.i.* to mistake grossly; to err stupidly; to flounder: *v.t.* to mismanage. (Origin uncertain.)

blunderbuss, *n.* *blun*-der-bus, a short gun with a conical muzzle. (Dut. *donderbus,* thunder gun.)

blunderer, *n.* *blun*-der-er, one given to committing blunders.

blunderhead, *n.* *blun*-der-hed, a stupid fellow.

blunderingly, *ad.* *blun*-der-ing-le, in a blundering manner.

blunge, *v.t.* blunj, to mix clay with water [Pottery].

blunger, *n.* *blun*-jer, an implement or machine for mixing clay.

blunt, *n.* blunt, a thick needle; money (Slang): *a.* having an edge or point that is not sharp; dull in understanding; abrupt in address; unceremonius: *v.t.* to dull the edge or point; to repress or weaken: *v.i.* to become blunt. (Origin unknown.)

bluntish, *a.* *blunt*-ish, somewhat blunt.

bluntly, *ad.* *blunt*-le, in a blunt manner.

bluntness, *n.* *blunt*-ness, the quality of being blunt.

blur, *n.* blur, a blot; a stain; a blemish: *v.t.* to soil; to obscure; to dim. (Origin unknown.)

blurb, *n.* blurb, publisher's eulogistic description of book [U.S.A. slang].

blurt, *v.t.* blurt, to utter hastily and unadvisedly, or inadvertently. (Probably imitative.)

blush, *n.* blush, redness in the cheeks from modesty, etc.; a red or reddish colour; a glance: *v.i.* to grow red in the face from modesty, shame or confusion; to feel ashamed; to bloom. (Perhaps connected with **blaze.**)

blushful, *a.* *blush*-ful, full of blushes.

blushfully, *ad.* *blush*-ful-le, in a blushful manner.

blushing, *n.* *blush*-ing, the act of turning red; colour, as of blushing: *a.* with blushes; blooming.

blushingly, *ad.* *blush*-ing-le, in a blushing manner.

blushless, *a.* *blush*-less, without a blush; unblushing.

bluster, *n.* *blus*-ter, a loud confused noise, as of wind in impotent gusts; boasting; boisterousness: *v.i.* to make a loud boisterous noise; to bully; to swagger; to boast.

blusterer, *n.* *blus*-ter-er, a noisy swaggerer.

blustering, *a.* *blus*-ter-ing, windy; noisy; tumultuous; boastful.

blusteringly, *ad.* *blus*-ter-ing-le, in a blustering manner.

blusterous, *a.* *blus*-trus, noisy; tumultuous.

bo, *int.* bo, a word used by children to frighten.

boa, *n.* *boh*-a, any of non-venomous snakes of the genus *Boa,* crushing their prey in their coils; a boa-shaped wrap of fur worn by women round the neck. **boa-constrictor,** *see* **constrictor.** (L. *boa.*)

boanerges, *n.* boh-a-*ner*-jeez, a vehement preacher. (Gr. from Heb. *pl.* sons of thunder.)

boar, *n.* bore, the uncastrated male of wild or domesticated swine. (A.S. *bār.*)

★**board,** *n.* bord, a piece of timber sawn thin, of considerable length and breadth; a table for food; food served at table; a charge for meals; a table at which a council or court sits; a number of persons who have the management of a public company; a table or frame for a game, as a chess-board; a notice-board; pasteboard; cover of a book; the deck of a ship; the interior part of a ship or boat; the line over which a ship runs between tack and tack [Naut.]; a passage at right angles to the coal-face (Mining): *pl.* the stage; playing-cards [Amer. slang]: *v.t.* to cover with boards; to enter a ship by force; to accost; to furnish with board; to place as a boarder: *v.i.* to be furnished with board. **by the board,** close to the deck; completely [Naut.]. (A.S. *bord,* a table.)

boardable, *a.* *bord*-a-bl, that may be boarded.

boarder, *n.* *bord*-er, one who lives in another's house at an agreed charge; a pupil who lives in the school during term; one who boards a ship in action.

boarding-clerk, *n.* *bord*-ing-klark, a clerk in the custom house, or a shipping firm, whose duty it is to communicate with ships on their arrival in port.

boarding-house, *n.* *bord*-ing-house, a house where board may be had and boarders accommodated.

boarding-school, *n.* *bord*-ing-skool, a school at which most of, or all, the scholars board.

board-room, *n.* *bord*-room, the room in which the meetings of the board of a company, etc., are held.

board-school, *n.* *bord*-skool, a school managed by a board set up under the Education Act of 1870.

board-wages, *n.pl.* *bord*-way-jez, money allowed to servants to keep themselves in victuals.

boarfish, *n.* *bore*-fish, the red and silver sea-fish, *Capros aper,* and other fishes.

boarhound, *n.* *bore*-hound, a large hound used in hunting the wild boar.

boarish, *a.* *bore*-rish, swinish; brutal; cruel.

boar-spear, *n.* *bore*-speer, a spear used in boar-hunting.

boast, *n.* boast, an expression of ostentation or pride; a brag; cause of boasting; laudable exultation: *v.i.* to brag; to glory in: *v.t.* to brag of; to magnify or exalt; to vaunt; to own and display; to have. (Origin uncertain.)

boaster, *n.* *boast*-er, one who boasts, a braggart; a stonemasons' broad-faced chisel.

boastful, *a.* *boast*-ful, given to boasting.

boastfully, *ad.* *boast*-ful-le, in a boastful manner.

boastfulness, *n.* *boast*-ful-ness, state of being boastful.

boasting, *n.* *boast*-ing, act of boasting; vaunting.

boastingly, *ad.* *boast*-ing-le, in a boasting manner.

★**boat,** *n.* boat, a small open vessel, moved by oars or rowing; a vessel moved by steam or sails; a small boat-shaped table-vessel, a tureen: *v.t.* to convey in a boat: *v.i.* to go in a boat; to practise boating as a sport. **in the same boat,** in the same predicament, category, etc. (A.S. *bát.*)

boatable, *a.* *boat*-a-bl, navigable for small boats.

boatage, *n.* *boat*-aj, carriage, or charge for carriage, by boat.

boat-bill, *n.* *boat*-bil, a S. American heron with boat-like beak, *Canchroma cochlearia.*

boat-car, *n.* *boat*-kar, a trolley for carrying canal boats on inclined planes; a wheeled frame used in launching or beaching boats.

boat-deck, *n.* *boat*-dek, a deck on a liner, etc., for accommodating life-boats.

boater, *n.* *boat*-er, one who boats; a hard straw hat with flat top and brim.

boat-fly, *n.* *boat*-fly, the water-boatman, an insect of the genus *Notonecta*.
boatful, *n.* *boat*-ful, as much as the boat will hold.
boat-hook, *n.* *boat*-hook, a large hook with a point on the back, fixed to a staff, to push or pull a boat.
boat-house, *n.* *boat*-house, a shed to shelter boats.
boating, *n.* *boat*-ing, the act or practice of rowing, or sailing in boats; boats collectively.
boatman, *n.* *boat*-man, a man who manages a boat, or who lets boats on hire.
boat-race, *n.* *boat*-race, a rowing match.
boatswain, *n.* *boh*-sn, a warrant officer in the Royal Navy (the chief of the crew in the merchant service), who has charge of the boats, sails, rigging, etc., and calls the men to duty. (A.S. *bát*, and *swegen*, boy.)
boatswain-bird, *n.* the tropic-bird, *Phaëthon lepturus*.
boat-train, *n.* a railway train so timed that it connects with the arrival or sailing of a liner.
bob, *n.* bob, a short jerking motion or action; a slight blow; anything which swings with a bob; a pendant; an ear-ring; the ball of a pendulum, or plumb-line; a curtsy; a woman's hair when cut short; a curl like a tassel; a knot of worms, at the end of a line, used in catching eels; a bob-wig; a shilling; a peal of several courses, or sets of changes in bell-ringing: *v.t.* to move with a short jerking motion; to move jerkily up and down; to cut short; to cheat: *v.i.* to play backward and forward; to angle with a bob. **dry-bob,** an Etonian who practises land games as distinguished from the **wet-bob,** who devotes himself to rowing.
bobac, *n.* *boh*-bak, a marmot of N.E. Europe and Asia. (Polish.)
Bobadil, *n.* *bob*-a-dil, a boastful swaggerer. (Captain *Bobadil* in "Every Man in His Humour," by Ben Jonson, 1598.)
bobbery, *n.* *bob*-er-re, a rumpus: *a.* of all sorts and kinds [Slang]. (Hind. *bap re!* Oh, father!)
bobbin, *n.* *bob*-bin, a spool on which thread, or wire, etc., is wound; a reel; round tape. (Fr. *bobine.*)
bobbinet, *n.* *bob*-bin-et, a machine-made lace.
bobbin-lace, *n.* *bob*-bin-lace, lace made with bobbins by hand.
bobbin-work, *n.* *bob*-bin-wurk, work woven with bobbins.
bobbish, *a.* *bob*-bish, hearty; in good spirits.
bobbie, *n.* *bob*-bl, the up and down motion of disturbed water; a small pompon used on women's dresses. (Dial. Eng.)
bobby, *n.* *bob*-e, a policeman [Slang].
bob-cherry, *n.* *bob*-che-re, a child's game of catching a suspended or bobbing cherry in the mouth.
bobolink, *n.* *bob*-o-link, the rice-bird or reed-bird of America, *Dolichonyx oryzivorus*.
bob-sled, *n.* *bob*-sled, a bob-sleigh.
bob-sleigh, *n.* *bob*-slay, a short sleigh used for tobogganing.
bobstay, *n.* *bob*-stay, the rope or chain that steadies the bowsprit.
bobtail, *n.* *bob*-tayl, a tail cut short; the rabble. **bobtail wig,** a bob-wig.
bobtailed, *a.* *bob*-tayld, having the tail cut short.
bob-white, *n.* *bob*-white, the American partridge, or quail, *Colinus virginianus*.
bob-wig, *n.* *bob*-wig, a short, as opposed to a full-bottomed, wig.
bocal, *n.* *boh*-kal, a wide-mouthed glass jar with short neck; the mouthpiece of a trumpet, trombone, etc. (Fr.)
Boche, *n.* boash, a German; name given to German soldiers in the War of 1914–18 [Fr. slang].
bock-beer, *n.* *bok*-beer, a strong lager beer. (Ger.)
bocking, *n.* *bok*-ing, a coarse woollen cloth; rough baize. (*Bocking*, village in Essex.)
bocland, *n.* *bok*-land, freehold land; bookland.
bode, *v.t.* and *i.* bode, to foretell; to portend; to be an omen of. (A.S. *bodian*, to tell.)
bodeful, *a.* *bode*-ful, ominous of evil.
bodega, *n.* bo-*dee*-ga, a wine shop. (Sp.)
bodement, *n.* *bode*-ment, a presentiment; omen.
bodge, *n.* and *v.* bodj, botch.
bodhi-tree, *n.* *boh*-de-tree, the bo-tree. (Sans. *bodha*, enlightenment.)
bodice, *n.* *bod*-is, the part of a woman's gown above the waist, as fitting the body.
bodied, *a.* *bod*-id, having a body; embodied.
bodiless, *a.* *bod*-e-less, having no body; incorporeal.
bodily, *a.* *bod*-e-le, relating to the body; in the form of a body: *ad.* corporeally; united with a body or matter; in a body; entirely.
boding, *n.* *bode*-ing, a prognostication or premonition; an omen: *a.* foreshowing.
bodkin, *n.* *bod*-kin, a large blunt needle with a long eye for threading tape, etc., usually through a hem; an instrument for piercing holes; a hatpin or long hairpin; a small dagger. **to ride bodkin,** to be wedged between two others on a carriage-seat.
bodle, *n.* *boh*-dl, an old Scottish coin, worth the sixth of a penny; anything valueless.
Bodleian, *a.* *bod*-le-an, pertaining to Sir Thomas Bodley, or the library which he founded at Oxford in 1597: *n.* the Bodleian Library.
★**body,** *n.* *bod*-e, the material structure of an animal; the main part of any structure; the trunk as distinct from the head and limbs; the part of a motor-car, aircraft, etc., in which are the seats; a corpse; a bodice; solidity; substance; matter, as opposed to spirit; a person; a collective mass or collection; a number of individuals united for a purpose; a corporation; a military force; the main part; strength or substance; a solid [Geom.]: *v.t.* to give shape to; to produce in some form; to embody. (A.S. *bodig.*)
body-colour, *n.* *bod*-e-kul-ur, a pigment possessing consistence, body, and colouring power; pigment mixed with white laid on thickly.
bodyguard, *n.* *bod*-e-gard, a life-guard, especially of a sovereign; a guardian escort; a retinue.
body-line, *a.* fast and short-pitched on the leg side (of bowling) [Cricket].
body-politic, *n.* *bod*-e-*pol*-e-tik, a nation viewed as a body; the State.
body-servant, *n.* *bod*-e-ser-vant, a valet or other personal attendant.
body-snatcher, *n.* *bod*-e-*snatch*-er, one who disinters bodies for dissection.
body-whorl, *n.* *bod*-e-whorl, the last turn of the spiral in the shell of a gastropod.
Bœotian, *a.* be-*oh*-she-an, pertaining to, or like the people of, Bœotia, a district of ancient Greece; dull; stupid.
Boer, *n.* boor, a South African of Dutch descent; an early Dutch colonist in South Africa. (Dut.)
bog, *n.* bog, a marsh; a quagmire; a bog-house [Slang]: *v.t.* to whelm or plunge, as in mud and mire. (Ir. *bogach*, from *bog*, soft.)
bog-bean, *n.* *bog*-been, the buckbean.
bog-berry, *n.* *bog*-be-re, a name of the cranberry.
bog-butter, *n.* *bog*-but-ter, a fatty substance found in peat bogs.
bog-earth, *n.* *bog*-erth, an earth or soil composed of sand and decomposed vegetable fibre.
bogey, *n.* *boh*-ge, the number of strokes in which a supposititious "scratch" player would hole out at each hole on a golf-course, the bogey for the course being the sum total of these strokes; a bogy.
bogey-man, *n.* *boh*-ge-man, a bogy.
boggard, *n.* *bog*-ard, a bogy, spectre, or apparition; a bugbear.
boggle, *v.i.* *bog*-gl, to stop, as if afraid to proceed; to waver; to equivocate.
boggler, *n.* *bog*-gl-er, a waverer; a timorous person.
boggy, *a.* *bog*-ge, full of bogs; marshy; swampy.
bog-house, *n.* *bog*-house, a privy.
bogie, *n.* *boh*-ge, a low four-wheeled truck. **bogie carriage,** one mounted on two bogies connected with it by swivel joints, adapted to take a curve readily.
bog-land, *n.* *bog*-land, a boggy country; marshy land.
bogle, *n.* *boh*-gl, a goblin; bugbear; scarecrow.
bogmoss, *n.* *bog*-moss, a peat moss of the genus *Sphagnum*.
bog-myrtle, *n.* *bog*-mer-tl, the sweet-gale.
bog-oak, *n.* *bog*-oke, oak found preserved in bogs.
bog-ore, *n.* *bog*-awr, an iron ore found in boggy land.
bog-rush, *n.* *bog*-rush, any sedge growing in bogs, esp. of the genus *Schœnus*.
bog-spavin, *n.* *bog*-spav-in, an encysted tumour on the inside of a horse's hock.
bog-trotter, *n.* *bog*-trot-ter, one accustomed to traverse bogs; a Scottish moss-trooper or (humorously) an Irishman.

bogus, *a.* *boh*-gus, spurious; counterfeit [Slang].
bogy, *n.* *boh*-ge, a phantom; a spectre; a bugbear; a special dislike. (*Bogle.*)
bohea, *n.* bo-*hee*, one of the kinds of black tea. (From *Bohea* hills in China.)
Bohemian, *a.* bo-*hee*-me-an, pertaining to or characteristic of Bohemia, its people, or its language; Czech: *n.* a native or the language of Bohemia.
bohemian, *n.* bo-*hee*-me-an, a gipsy (Bohemia being formerly accounted their ancient home); a person, generally affecting art of some kind, who despises conventionality: *a.* unconventional; gipsy-like.
bohemianism, *n.* bo-*hee*-me-an-izm, the life, habits, or conduct of a bohemian.
boiar, *n.* *boy*-ar, a boyar.
boil, *v.i.* boyl, to be agitated by the action of heat, as liquids; to bubble or heave like boiling water; to reach boiling-point; to be cooked by boiling; to be agitated with passion: *v.t.* to bring a liquid to boiling-point; to cook by boiling; to subject to heat in a boiling liquid. **boil away,** to evaporate by boiling. **boil down,** to reduce by boiling; to abridge. **boiled shirt,** a dress-shirt, or one with a starched front. (O.Fr. *boillir.*)
boil, *n.* boyl, a hard inflamed suppurating tumour; a furuncle. (A.S. *byl.*)
boiler, *n.* *boyl*-er, one who boils; a vessel in which anything is boiled; a vessel in which steam is generated; a tank for supplying hot water; a copper for boiling clothes. **boiler-suit,** a strong combination garment worn over the clothes to keep them unsoiled when doing rough work.
★**boiling,** *a.* *boyl*-ing, in a state of ebullition by heat. **boiling spring,** a spring emitting hot water and steam; a geyser. **keep the pot boiling,** continue without flagging; to ward off starvation. **the whole boiling,** all; the lot [Slang].
boiling-point, *n.* *boyl*-ing-poynt, the temperature at which a fluid is converted into vapour with ebullition, that of water being 212° F. or 100° C.
bois-de-rose, *n.* bwah-de-*rose* (or App.), the tropical American tree *Aniba panurensis*, also its yellow timber; a yellowish-red or dull pink colour. (Fr.)
boisterous, *a.* *boyce*-ter-us, noisy; turbulent; violent; stormy. (M.E. *boistous.*)
boisterously, *ad.* *boyce*-ter-us-le, in a boisterous manner.
boisterousness, *n.* *boyce*-ter-us-ness, the state or quality of being boisterous.
boko, *n.* *boh*-ko, the nose [Slang].
bolar, *a.* *boh*-lar, partaking of the nature of clay.
bolas, *n.* *boh*-las, two or three balls on a leather thong used by S. American natives for throwing round the legs of animals in hunting.
bold, *a.* boald, courageous; daring; exhibiting courage; planned or executed with courage and spirit; audacious; impudent; standing out to view; striking; steep; abrupt. **to make bold,** or **to be so bold,** to venture. (A.S. *bald.*)
bold-face, *n.* *boald*-face, impudence; an impudent person; a heavy, black type [Print.].
bold-faced, *a.* *boald*-fayst, impudent; shameless; having a heavy face (of type) [Print.].
boldly, *ad.* *boald*-le, in a bold manner.
boldness, *n.* *boald*-ness, the quality of being bold.
bole, *n.* bole, the trunk of a tree. (Scand.)
bole, *n.* bole, a friable clayey earth tinged with peroxide of iron. (Gr. *bolos*, a clod.)
bole, *n.* bole, a small rectangular niche in a wall; also a windowless opening [Scots.]. (Gr. *bolos*, a clod.)
bolection, *n.* bo-*lek*-shon, a raised moulding.
bolero, *n.* bo-*lare*-ro, a popular Spanish dance; a jacket that does not reach to the waist. (Sp.)
boletic, *a.* bo-*let*-ik, pertaining to or obtained from a fungus of the genus *Boletus*.
bolide, *n.* *boh*-lyd, a meteor that explodes and scatters its fragments. (Gr. *bolis*, missile.)
bolivar, *n.* *bol*-e-var, the currency unit in Venezuela (approx. 2*s.* 0*d.*) and Bolivia (approx. 2*d.*).
Bolivian, *a.* bo-*liv*-e-an, pertaining to Bolivia: *n.* a native of Bolivia.
boll, *n.* bole, a globular seed vessel. (Bot.). **boll weevil,** an insect preying on American cotton crops, *Anthonomous grandis*. **boll worm,** a caterpillar that destroys cotton pods, *Heliothis armigera*.
boll, *n.* bole, an old grain-measure of from two to six bushels; a weight of 10 stone of flour. (Scots.)
bollard, *n.* *bol*-lard, a strong post for holding a hawser; a post in a whaleboat round which the harpoon line is worked [Naut.].
bolling, *n.* *boh*-ling, a pollarded tree.
bolo, *n.* *boh*-lo, the long knife or cutlass of the Filipinos. (Native name.)
Bologna-flask, *n.* bo-*lone*-ya-flahsk, a flask of glass suddenly cooled, which flies in pieces when scratched.
Bologna-sausage, *n.* bo-*lone*-ya-*sos*-aj, a large sausage; a polony.
Bolognese, *a.* bo-*lone*-yeez, pertaining to Bologna. **Bolognese stone,** radiated sulphate of barium, first discovered near Bologna.
bolograph, *n.* *boh*-lo-graf, the photographic record of variations in temperature furnished by the bolometer.
bolometer, *n.* bo-*lom*-e-ter, an electrical instrument for measuring radiant heat. (Gr. *bolē*, ray, *metron*, measure.)
Bolshevik, *n.* *bol*-she-vik, an adherent of Bolshevism; a Communist; a revolutionary, esp. one advocating the destruction of capitalism by force: *a.* Bolshevist.
Bolshevism, *n.* *bol*-she-vizm, the political system of the Communists of Tsarist and Soviet Russia, based on the teaching of Marx and Engels, and having among its objects the public ownership of the means of production and the forcible abolition of capitalism; the doctrine and practices of the Bolshevists; communism. (Russ. *bolshe*, the larger—members of the pre-Soviet Russian Social Democratic Party favouring this having been in the majority.)
Bolshevist, *n.* *bol*-she-vist, a Bolshevik: *a.* pertaining to or favouring Bolshevism or the Bolshevists.
Bolshy, *n.* and *a.* *bol*-she, Bolshevik; Bolshevist [Slang].
bolster, *n.* *boal*-ster, a long round pillow; a pad for various purposes: *v.t.* to support with a bolster, or any soft pad; to support or hold up. (A.S.)
bolstering, *n.* *boal*-ster-ing, a prop; a support.
bolt, *n.* boalt, the short blunted arrow, or quarrel, used with a cross-bow; a stout pin of iron or other metal; a sliding bar; a metal pin secured by a nut; the portion of a lock that slides and makes fast; the sliding part by which the breech of a rifle, etc., is opened and closed; a stroke of lightning; a sudden start; a hasty swallow of unchewed food: *v.t.* to fasten with a bolt; to secure; to swallow hastily: *v.i.* to dart forth, or off; to run away; to desert one's party suddenly. (A.S.)
bolt, *v.t.* boalt, to sift; to separate bran from flour; to examine by sifting; to discuss. (O.Fr. *buleter.*)
bolt-auger, *n.* *boalt*-awg-er, a large boring instrument.
bolter, *n.* *boalt*-er, a machine for separating bran from flour; a sieve; a cloth for sieves; a person, or a horse, that bolts.
bolt-head, *n.* *boalt*-hed, the head of a bolt; a matrass or receiver used in distilling [Chem.].
bolt-hole, *n.* *boalt*-hole, a place or means of escape.
bolting, *n.* *boalt*-ing, the act of bolting; fastening with a bolt; sudden flight.
bolting-cloth, *n.* *boalt*-ing-kloth, linen or hair cloth for bolters.
bolting-hutch, *n.* *boalt*-ing-hutch, a tub for bolted flour.
bolting-mill, *n.* *boalt*-ing-mil, a machine for sifting meal.
boltonite, *n.* *boal*-tun-ite, a greenish granular variety of olivine. (*Bolton*, U.S.A.)
bolt-rope, *n.* *boalt*-rope, a rope to which the edges of sails are sewn to strengthen them.
bolt-sprit, *n.* *boalt*-sprit, the old word for bowsprit.
bolt-upright, *a.* *boalt*-up-rite, perfectly upright.
bolus, *n.* *boh*-lus, a large pill; a round lump; a mouthful of masticated food. (Gr. *bōlos*, a lump.)
bom, *n.* bom, the American tree-boa aboma.
bomb, *n.* bom, a hollow case or ball filled with high explosives, and thrown from a mortar or by hand, or dropped from the air: *v.t.* to bombard; to attack with bombs, esp. from the air. **gas-** or **stink-bomb,** a bomb that on exploding releases noxious gases. **volcanic bomb,** a porous mass of igneous rock ejected from a volcano. (Gr. *bombos*, a deep dull sound.)
bombard, *v.t.* bom-*bard*, to attack with bombs or artillery; to storm; to assail persistently, as with questions. (Fr. *bombarde*, a big gun.)

bombardier, *n.* bom-ba-*deer*, a non-commissioned officer of artillery ranking as corporal; a beetle of the genus *Brachinus*.
bombardment, *n.* bom-*bard*-ment, an artillery attack; an attack with bombs.
bombardon, *n.* bom-*bar*-don, a musical wind instrument, much like a bassoon; a brass bass instrument of the saxhorn group. (It.)
bombast, *n.* *bom*-bast, a loose stuff used to swell garments; language inflated with senseless high-sounding words; fustian. (O.Fr. *bombace.*)
bombastic, *a.* bom-*bas*-tik, characterized by inflated diction; turgid; grandiloquent.
bombastically, *ad.* bom-*bas*-te-ka-le, in a bombastic manner.
bombax, *n.* *bom*-baks, the silk-cotton tree. (L.)
Bombay-duck, *n.* *bom*-bay-*duk*, the bummalo, a small East Indian fish of the genus *Harpodon*, which is salted, fermented and dried.
bombazette, *n.* bom-ba-*zet*, a sort of thin worsted cloth with a smooth surface.
bombazine, *n.* bom-ba-*zeen*, a twilled fabric of silk and worsted; the material of which a barrister's gown is made. (Fr.)
bomber, *n.* *bom*-er, one trained in bombing [Mil.]; an aeroplane used for bombing.
bomb-ketch, *n.* *bom*-ketch, an obsolete naval vessel armed with mortars.
bomb-proof, *a.* *bom*-proof, impenetrable by bombs.
bombshell, *n.* *bom*-shel, a bomb; a great or an alarming surprise.
bomb-sight, *n.* *bom*-site, an apparatus for directing the flight of a bomb from aircraft.
bomb-vessel, *n.* *bom*-ves-sel, a strongly built ship for throwing bombs; a bomb-ketch.
bombycid, *a.* *bom*-be-sid, pertaining to the *Bombycidæ*, the genus of moths containing the silkworm.
bombyx, *n.* *bom*-biks, the silkworm. (L.)
bona fide, *ad.* and *a.* (*hyphenated*) boh-na-*fy*-de, with good faith; without fraud or deception. (L.)
bona fides, *n.* boh-na-*fy*-deez, good faith; freedom from fraud.
bonanza, *n.* bo-*nan*-za, a very paying mine; an exceptional run of luck; a windfall. (Sp., a fair wind.)
Bonapartism, *n.* *boh*-na-par-tizm, the policy of Napoleon or of the Bonapartes; attachment to the French dynasty founded by Napoleon Bonaparte.
Bonapartist, *n.* an adherent of the family, or supporter of the policy, of the Bonapartes.
bonbon, *n.* *bon*-bon, sugar confectionery; a sugar-plum; a Christmas cracker. (Fr.)
bonbonnière, *n.* bon-*bon*-e-ayr, a small fancy box or dish for sweets. (Fr.)
bond, *n.* bond, anything that binds, as a cord or band; the disposition of stones or bricks in a wall so that the vertical joints are separated from each other; link of connection; an obligation or promise in writing to do or pay something on or before a given day; a security issued by a government or company; any written promise; a government store for dutiable goods till the duty is paid; chains; imprisonment; captivity: *a.* in a state of servitude or slavery: *v.t.* to put imported goods in a bonded warehouse till the duties chargeable thereon are paid; to lay bricks in bond. (A.S. *bōnda.*)
bondage, *n.* *bond*-aj, slavery; captivity.
bondager, *n.* *bond*-aj-er, a tenant on a farm bound at stated seasons to assist the farmer.
bond-debt, *n.* *bond*-det, a debt contracted under the obligation of a bond.
bonded, *a.* *bond*-ed, under a bond. **bonded goods,** those for the duties on which bonds are given at the custom house. **bonded warehouse,** the place in which such goods are stored pending payment of the duty leviable.
bondholder, *n.* *bond*-hohld-er, a creditor secured by a bond.
bondmaid, *n.* *bond*-mayd, a female slave.
bondman, *n.* *bond*-man, a man slave.
bondservant, *n.* *bond*-ser-vant, a slave.
bondslave, *n.* *bond*-slave, a person in a state of slavery.
bondsman, *n.* *bondz*-man, a surety; a slave.
bondwoman, *n.* *bond*-woom-an, a woman slave.
★**bone,** *n.* bone, a firm hard substance, composing the skeleton of an animal body; a separate and distinct piece of the skeleton; *pl.* castanets; bobbins of bone for making lace; dice, or dominoes [Slang]: *a.* made of bone: *v.t.* to take out the bones; to put bones in; to steal [Slang]. **body and bones,** altogether. **bone of contention,** a cause of dispute. **to have a bone to pick,** to have something disagreeable to settle. **to make no bones,** to make no scruple. (A.S. *bān.*)
bone-ace, *n.* *bone*-ace, an old game at cards.
bone-ache, *n.* *bone*-ake, pain in the bones.
bone-ash, *n.* *bone*-ash, the residue of burnt bones.
bone-bed, *n.* *bone*-bed, a layer of rock containing fossil bones [Geol.].
bone-black, *n.* *bone*-blak, charcoal from burnt bones; animal charcoal.
bone-breaker, *n.* *bone*-brake-er, a name for the osprey and other large fish-hawks.
bone-cave, *n.* *bone*-kave, a cave containing bones of prehistoric animals [Geol.].
boned, *a.* bohnd, deprived of bones; having bones.
bone-dust, *n.* *bone*-dust, bones ground for manure.
bone-earth, *n.* *bone*-erth, the earthly residuum of bones; bone-ash.
bone-lace, *n.* *bone*-lace, a lace made with bobbins by hand, bobbin-lace.
boneless, *a.* *bone*-less, without bones; wanting bones; lacking stamina or backbone.
bonemeal, *n.* *bone*-meel, a fertilizer and animal-feed made from pulverized bones.
bonesetter, *n.* *bone*-set-ter, a surgeon, esp. one not officially qualified as such, who sets dislocated or broken bones; an osteopath.
bonesetting, *n.* *bone*-set-ting, the art of setting bones; osteopathy.
boneshaker, *n.* *bone*-shake-er, a wooden bicycle, a bicycle without rubber tyres.
bone-spavin, *n.* *bone*-spav-in, a bony excrescence on the inside of the hock of a horse's leg.
bonfire, *n.* *bon*-fire, a fire in the open for burning rubbish or serving as a beacon or sign of rejoicing. (Originally for burning bones.)
bongo, *n.* *bong*-go, a large, massive-horned antelope of Equatorial African forests. (Native.)
bongrace, *n.* *bon*-grace, a protection against the sun worn on the front of a woman's bonnet; a woman's broad-brimmed hat. (Fr.).
bonhomie, *n.* *bon*-no-meh (or App)., good-nature; geniality. (Fr.)
boniface, *n.* *bon*-e-face, an innkeeper. (From "The Beaux' Stratagem," by Farquhar, 1707.)
boning, *n.* *boh*-ning, the act of judging of a plane surface, or of setting objects in the same plane or line by the eye. **boning rods,** poles used in boning by being set up at certain distances.
bonito, *n.* bo-*nee*-to, a small species of tunny. (Sp.)
bonmot, *n.* bon-*moh*, a witticism, or a witty repartee. (Fr., a good saying.)
bonne, *n.* bon, a French or Swiss nursemaid. (Fr.)
bonnet, *n.* *bon*-net, a brimless head-covering, esp. one worn out of doors by women; a Scotch cap; a covering for other purposes; the hood over the engine of a motor-car; a safety cap over machinery; a chimney cowl; a small sail attached to a larger; a kind of little ravelin; an accomplice acting as a decoy [Slang] [Fort.]: *v.i.* to pull off the bonnet: *v.t.* to crush hat over eyes. (Fr.)
bonneted, *a.* *bon*-net-ed, wearing a bonnet.
bonnet-rouge, *n.* *bon*-ne-*roozh*, an extreme Republican; so called because of the red caps worn by the sansculottes in 1793. (Fr., red cap.)
bonnily, *ad.* *bon*-ne-le, in a bonny manner.
bonniness, *n.* *bon*-ne-ness, quality of being bonny.
bonny, *a.* *bon*-ne, handsome; pretty; pleasant; considerable. (Fr. *bonne*, fem. of *bon*, good.)
bonny-clabber, *n.* *bon*-ne-*klab*-ber, milk thickened and sour. (Ir. *baine*, milk, *clabar*, mud.)
bonspiel, *n.* *bon*-speel, a curling match. (Scots.)
bontebok, *n.* *bon*-te-bok, the South African antelope *Bubalis pygargus*.
bon-ton, *n.* (App.), good fashion; the height of fashion. (Fr.)
bonus, *n.* *boh*-nus; a consideration for a service; a premium given for a privilege, or, in addition to interest, for a loan; an extra dividend to shareholders out of accumulated profits. (L.)
bon-vivant, *n.* (App.), a luxurious liver; a jovial companion. (Fr., living well.)
bonxie, *n.* *bonk*-se, the great skua.
bony, *a.* *boh*-ne, consisting of, or pertaining to, bones; having large or prominent bones; stout; strong.

bonze, *n.* bonz, a Buddhist priest in China, Japan, etc. (Jap. *bonzo*, priest.)
boo, *n.* boo, a noisy indication of disapproval; the lowing of a cow: *v.i.* to make this noise: *v.t.* to hoot in disapproval.
boob, *n.* boob, a silly conceited dandy; a general butt; a booby.
booby, *n.* *boob*-e, a stupid fellow; one of various birds of the gannet family (from their apparent stupidity). **booby prize**, a prize given, esp. in ridicule, to the lowest scorer. (Sp. *bobo*, fool.)
booby-hatch, *n.* *boob*-e-hatch, the covering of the hatchway to the forepeak [Naut.].
booby-hutch, *n.* *boob*-e-hutch, a clumsy, ill-contrived covered carriage.
booby-trap, *n.* *boob*-e-trap, anything placed on the top of a door so as to fall when the door is opened wider.
boodle, *n.* boodl, money made by bribery or fraud; the whole lot, a crowd [Slang]; the corn-marigold, *Chrysanthemum segetum.*
boohoo, *v.i.* boo-*hoo*, to weep loudly: *n.* the sound made by this; a cry of contempt.
***book,** *n.* book, a collection of sheets printed on, written on, or blank, and bound in a volume; a literary composition, or one of its larger divisions; a libretto; a number of printed forms, cheques, or stamps, etc., bound together; a writing: *v.t.* to enter, write, or register in a book; to get booked. **in good books,** in kind remembrance; in favour. **to bring to book,** to require to give an exact reckoning. **to make a book,** to take bets. **to speak by book,** to speak on accurate knowledge. **without book,** by memory; without authority. (A.S. *boc.*)
book-account, *n.* *book*-a-kount, an account or register of debt or credit in a book.
bookbinder, *n.* *book*-byn-der, one who binds books.
bookbindery, *n.* *book*-byn-de-re, a place for binding books.
bookbinding, *n.* *book*-byn-ding, the art or act of binding books.
bookcase, *n.* *book*-kace, a case with shelves for books; a cover for a book.
book-debt, *n.* *book*-det, a debt charged in an account book.
booked, *a.* bookt, registered; provided with a ticket; engaged [Slang].
book-end, *n.* *book*-end, a support for the end of a row of standing books.
book-holder, *n.* *book*-hohld-er, a prompter.
book-hunter, *n.* *book*-hunt-er, an eager collector of old and rare books.
bookie, *n.* *book*-e, a bookmaker; one who takes bets.
booking, *n.* *book*-ing, registry in a book; selling numbered tickets. **booking clerk,** the clerk who issues the tickets for a railway or other journey. **booking office,** the office where the tickets are obtained.
bookish, *a.* *book*-ish, given to reading; acquainted only with what is written in books.
bookishly, *ad.* *book*-ish-ly, in the manner of one who is bookish.
bookishness, *n.* *book*-ish-ness, bookish disposition.
book-keeper, *n.* *book*-keep-er, a keeper of accounts.
book-keeping, *n.* *book*-keep-ing, the art of keeping accounts.
book-knowledge, *n.* *book*-nol-lej, book-learning.
bookland, *n.* *book*-land, charter-land, or land held by a simple deed, land taken from folkland and given to a private owner; freehold land [O.E. Law].
book-learned, *a.* *book*-lern-ed, versed in books; well-read.
book-learning, *n.* *book*-lern-ing, learning acquired by reading, often as opposed to that by experience and observation.
booklet, *n.* *book*-let, a small book.
bookmaker, *n.* *book*-make-er, one who writes or compiles books; one who takes bets systematically on sporting events and enters the bets in a book.
bookmaking, *n.* *book*-make-ing, the practice of compiling books; the practice of betting systematically.
bookman, *n.* *book*-man, a literary man; a scholar; a lover of reading.
bookmark, *n.* *book*-mark, a card, paper, ribbon, etc., for marking a page in a book.
book-muslin, *n.* *book*-muz-lin, a coarse muslin.
book-name, *n.* *book*-name, a name of a plant or animal given in books but not in popular use.
book-oath, *n.* *book*-oath, an oath made on the Bible.
book-plate, *n.* *book*-plate, the owner's label inside a book-cover.
book-post, *n.* *book*-pohst, the transmission by the post office of printed matter at a lower charge than by letter-post.
book-rest, *n.* *book*-rest, an adjustable support for holding an open book.
bookseller, *n.* *book*-sel-ler, one who trades in books.
bookselling, *n.* *book*-sel-ling, the business of a bookseller.
book-slide, *n.* *book*-slide, an expanding shelf for holding books.
bookstall, *n.* *book*-stawl, an open stall for retailing books.
bookstand, *n.* *book*-stand, a stand or a case for books.
bookstore, *n.* *book*-store, a bookseller's shop; a place of storage in a library for rarely wanted books.
bookworm, *n.* *book*-wurm, the larva of a beetle, *Anobium paniceum*, that eats holes in books; an indiscriminate reader of books.
boom, *n.* boom, a long pole or spar to extend a sail; a strong iron chain, line of spars, or other bar, extended across a river, or harbour mouth, to obstruct the passage. (D. *boom*, a tree.)
boom, *n.* boom, a hollow sound, as of waves, distant gun-fire, etc.; the cry of the bittern; a sudden and increasing demand for a thing; a sudden outburst of popular favour: *v.i.* to rush, as a ship under a press of sail; to sound with a boom; to increase rapidly in value [Stock Exchange]: *v.t.* to utter in a booming manner; to force into great activity, etc.; to boost.
boomer, *n.* *boom*-er, a boomster; the great grey kangaroo *Macropus giganteus.*
boomerang, *n.* *boom*-er-rang, a curved wooden missile that returns to the thrower, peculiar to the aborigines of Australia.
boomslang, *n.* *boom*-slang, a large venomous S. African tree-snake, *Dispholidus typus.*
boomster, *n.* *boom*-ster, one who booms or boosts anything [Slang].
boon, *n.* boon, a gift; a favour; a privilege. (Ice. *bon*, a prayer.)
boon, *n.* boon, the refuse from dressed flax.
boon, *a.* boon, genial; jovial. (L. *bonus*, good.)
boor, *n.* boor, a countryman; a coarse uneducated man. (Dut. *boer*, a peasant.)
boorish, *a.* *boor*-ish, clownish; rude in manners; illiterate.
boorishly, *ad.* *boor*-ish-le, in a boorish manner.
boorishness, *n.* *boor*-ish-ness, the quality of being boorish.
boose, *n.* booz, strong drink; a drinking bout: *v.i.* to drink to excess; to tipple. (Dut. *buyzen*, to drink.)
boost, *v.t.* boost, to lift or raise by pushing; to push by advertising [Slang]; to increase pressure, force [Eng.], or voltage [Elect.]. (Dial. Eng.)
booster, *n.* *boost*-er, one who boosts; a machine for raising voltage [Elect.] or intake pressure [Eng.]; an auxiliary engine.
boosy, *a.* *boo*-ze, a little intoxicated; merry with liquor; given to tippling.
***boot,** *n.* boot, a covering for the foot and lower part of the leg, generally of leather; a kind of rack for the leg, formerly used to torture criminals; a compartment for parcels on a vehicle; a leather apron for the driving seat of a chaise or gig; protective covering, as a leather case for a bottle: *v.t.* to put boots on; to torture with the boot. (O.Fr. *bote.*)
boot, *n.* boot, profit; gain; advantage; that which is given to make the exchange equal: *v.t.* to profit; to advantage: *v.i.* to avail. **to boot,** in addition to; over and above. (A.S. *bôt*, compensation.)
bootblack, *n.* *boot*-blak, one who cleans boots and shoes, esp. of passers-by.
booted, *a.* *boot*-ed, having boots on.
bootee, *n.* boo-*tee*, a kind of half or short boot; an infant's knitted boot.
booth, *n.* booth, a stall at a market or fair; a temporary shelter or structure, as a **polling booth** for use at elections; the sound-proof enclosure used by cinematograph operators. (Ice. *buth.*)

boot-hook, *n.* *boot*-hook, a hook to pull on long boots.
bootikin, *n.* *boot*-e-kin, a little boot; a soft glove or boot worn by sufferers from gout; a form of the boot (instrument of torture).
bootjack, *n.* *boot*-jak, an appliance to assist the drawing off of long boots.
bootlace, *n.* *boot*-lace, a lace or narrow leather strip for fastening a boot.
boot-last, *n.* *boot*-lahst, a metal boot-tree used in making boots.
bootleg, *v.i.* *boot*-leg, to engage in bootlegging; to smuggle: *n.* bootlegged liquor: *a.* illegally imported; smuggled [Slang].
bootlegger, *n.* *boot*-leg-ger, one engaged in the wholesale smuggling of alcoholic liquor (originally concealed in the leg of the smuggler's boot); hence a smuggler [Slang].
bootlegging, *n.* *boot*-leg-ging, the act or practice of a bootlegger; smuggling [Slang].
bootless, *a.* *boot*-less, unavailing; useless.
bootlessly, *ad.* *boot*-less-le, so as to be unavailing.
bootlessness, *n.* *boot*-less-ness, state of being bootless or unavailing.
boot-licker, *n.* *boot*-lik-er, a toady, a sycophant [Slang].
boots, *n.* boots, the servant at an inn who cleans the boots and attends to the luggage; the youngest officer in a mess [Slang].
boot-topping, *n.* *boot*-top-ping, the cleansing of a ship's bottom near the surface of the water, and rubbing it with tallow, etc.
boot-tree, *n.* *boot*-tree, an appliance for stretching boots, or keeping them in shape.
booty, *n.* *boo*-te, spoil taken in war, or by force; plunder. **to play booty,** to play dishonestly with intent to lose. (Ice. *byta*, to divide.)
booze, *n.* and *v.i.* booz, boose.
boozy, *a.* *boo*-ze, boosy.
bopeep, *n.* boh-*peep*, a game to amuse children by peeping from behind something and crying *bo!*
bora, *n.* *baw*-ra, a cold north-easterly wind of the northern Adriatic. (L. *Boreas*, the north wind.)
borachio, *n.* bo-*rahtch*-yo, a bottle or cask; a drunkard. (Sp. *borracha*, a leather wine bag.)
boracic, *a.* bo-*rass*-ik, pertaining to, or produced from, borax. **boracic acid,** an antiseptic and preservative derived from boron trioxide.
boracite, *n.* *bo*-ra-site, native borate and chloride of magnesium.
borage, *n.* *bu*-raj, a plant, *Borago officinalis*, sprigs of which were believed to be cordial, and were infused in drinks. (Fr. *bourrache.*)
boraginaceous, *a.* bora-je-*nay*-shus, belonging to or resembling the borage family. (Bot.)
borate, *n.* *baw*-rate, a salt of boracic acid.
borax, *n.* *baw*-raks, borate of sodium, a crystalline white or colourless salt, known commercially as tincal and used as an antiseptic, a flux, and in soldering. (Ar. *bōraq.*)
bord, *n.* bord, the face of the coal parallel to the cleavage [Min.].
bordage, *n.* *bord*-aj, tenure by which a bordar held from a feudal lord.
bordar, *n.* *bord*-ar, a cottager; a villein or cotter of feudal days. (L. *bordarius*, a cottager.)
Bordeaux, *n.* bor-*doh*, claret produced in the neighbourhood of Bordeaux in the Gironde. **Bordeaux mixture,** a preparation of copper sulphate, lime, and water for destroying fungi injurious to plants.
bordel, *n.* *bord*-el, a brothel. (Fr., a hut.)
border, *n.* *bord*-er, the edge of anything; margin; boundary; frontier; a flower-bed bordering a lawn or path, etc.: *v.i.* to be adjacent; to approach: *v.t.* to make or adorn with a border; to reach or be contiguous to. (O.Fr. *bordure.*)
borderer, *n.* *bord*-er-er, one who dwells on the borders of a country; a frontiersman.
borderland, *n.* *bord*-er-land, land on the border, usually debatable; the fringe of a subject.
bordure, *n.* *bor*-dewr, a border forming a charge or difference on an escutcheon [Her.].
bore, *n.* bor, the hole made by boring; the diameter of a tube or calibre of a gun: *v.t.* to pierce or drill a hole in or through; to hamper by moving along too closely to: *v.i.* to be pierced; to push forward toward a certain point; to act so as to force a competitor (in a race, etc.) out of place or a boxing opponent to the ropes; ; to lean heavily on the bit, as a horse. (A.S. *borian.*)
bore, *n.* bor, one who wearies those he talks to: *v.t.* to weary with repetition or twaddle.
bore, bor, *p.* of the verb to bear.
bore, *n.* bor, a sudden influx in certain estuaries of a tidal wave rushing up with great violence and a loud noise. (Perhaps from Ice. *bara*, a billow.)
boreal, *a.* *baw*-re-al, northerly, pertaining to the north wind; living in or pertaining to the north. (*Boreas.*)
Boreas, *n.* *baw*-re-as, the god of the north wind; the wind itself. (L. and Gr.)
borecole, *n.* *bor*-koal, a winter cabbage, the leaves of which are curled. (Dut.)
boredom, *n.* *bor*-dum, the state of being bored; the behaviour, or the society, of bores.
borer, *n.* *bor*-rer, an awl, piercer, or other boring instrument; one who, or a horse that, bores; a boring or burrowing animal; the shipworm.
boric, *n.* *bo*-rik, boracic.
boring, *n.* *bor*-ring, the act of, or a hole made by, boring: *n.pl.* the chips produced in boring.
borish, *a.* *bor*-rish, tending to bore or weary; tedious.
borley, *n.* *bor*-le, a single-masted fishing boat used in the Thames estuary. (Dial. Eng.)
born, born, *pp.* of bear, brought forth as an animal. **born again,** imbued through conversion, with a new and nobler principle of life. **born with a silver spoon in one's mouth,** born to a fortune. **to be born,** to be brought into life. (A.S.)
borne, born, *pp.* of bear; carried; supported; defrayed.
borné, *a.* bor-nay, of narrow outlook; narrow-minded. (Fr., limited.)
bornite, *n.* *bor*-nite, a purplish-red sulphide of copper and iron, a valuable copper ore. (von *Born*, Austrian mineralogist.)
boron, *n.* *bor*-ron, the gray and very hard non-metallic element occurring in borax.
borough, *n.* *bu*-ru, a corporate town. **county borough,** one whose local government is independent of the county and which ranks as an administrative county. **metropolitan borough,** any one of the 27 major local government units, each having its own mayor, into which the administrative county of London is divided. **municipal borough,** a corporate town, part of the local government of which is the responsibility of its county council. **parliamentary borough,** one sending its own representative or representatives to parliament. **pocket,** or **rotten, borough,** a borough in which, before the Reform Act, 1832, parliamentary representation was in the gift of some person or corporation. (A.S. *burg*, *burh*, port, town, or burrow.)
borough-english, *n.* a former customary descent, in certain English counties, of lands to the youngest son or brother (abolished in 1925).
boroughmonger, *n.* *bu*-ru-*mung*-ger, one who bought or sold the parliamentary representation of pocket boroughs.
borrel, *n.* *bo*-rel, rustic, unlearned. (O.Fr., coarse cloth.)
borrow, *v.t.* *bo*-roh, to obtain a loan; to appropriate and employ; to copy; to assume. (A.S. *borgian.*)
borsch, *n.* *borsh*, a Russian soup or stew, highly flavoured and reddened with beet-root.
Borstal, *n.* *bors*-tal, a system which, while punishing, aims at the reformation of juvenile delinquents. (From *Borstal*, Kent, where it was begun in 1902.)
bort, *n.* bort, coarse or broken diamonds pounded into dust, and used in grinding and polishing.
borzoi, *n.* *bor*-zoy, the Russian wolfhound, a large, handsome, silky-coated hunting-dog. (Russ., swift.)
boscage, *n.* *bosk*-aj, woodland; underwood growing in a leafy mass; thick foliage; a wooded landscape [Painting]. (O.Fr., a grove.)
bosh, *n.* bosh, empty talk; nonsense; a mixture of butter and margarine [Slang]. (Turk.)
Bosjesmans, *n.pl.* *boosh*-manz, the bushmen, the aboriginal race of South Central Africa.
bosk, *n.* bosk, a thicket; a bosket.
bosket, *n.* *bosk*-et, a grove; a small wood; an arbour formed by branches of trees. (Fr. *bosquet.*)
bosky, *a.* *bosk*-e, thickly wooded; shady; fuddled with drink [Slang].
bos'n, *n.* *boh*-sn, a corruption of boatswain.
bosom, *n.* *booz*-um, the human breast; the folds of

the dress that cover the breast; the breast as the seat of the affections and passions, or as containing the secrets of the heart; the surface of the sea, etc.; a hollow, cavity, or interior; embrace: *a.* intimate; confidential; dear: *v.t.* to conceal or enclose in or as in the bosom; to keep with care; to embosom; to cherish. **bosom friend,** a friend who knows your thoughts. (A.S. *bōsm.*)

boss, *n.* bos, a protuberant part; a stud or nob; a raised ornament. (Fr. *bosse,* a swelling.)

boss, *n.* bos, a master mechanic; a foreman or superintendent; a leader; a wirepuller [U.S.A.]: *v.t.* to oversee; command [Slang]. (Dut. *baas,* a master.)

boss, *n.* bos, a miss or bungle; a bad shot: *v.t.* to miss or bungle: *v.i.* to make a bad shot. **boss-eyed,** having only one eye, or a squint; squinting [Slang].

bossage, *n. bos*-aj, a stone boss left projecting in the rough to be carved; rustic stone work; bosses collectively [Arch.].

bossy, *a. bos*-e, containing or ornamented with bosses; inclined to be masterly [Colloq.].

bostangi, *n.* bos-*tan*-je, a royal servant in the Turkish Empire; a guard of the Sultan's seraglio. (Turk.)

boston, *n. bos*-ton, a variety of whist; a kind of waltz. (From *Boston,* U.S.A.)

bot, *n.* bot, the larva of the bot-fly.

botanic, *a.* bo-*tan*-ik, botanical. **botanic garden,** a garden for the culture of plants collected to illustrate the science of botany.

botanical, *a.* bo-*tan*-e-kal, pertaining to botany.

botanically, *ad.* bo-*tan*-e-ka-le, in a botanical reference.

botanist, *n. bot*-a-nist, one skilled in botany.

botanize, *v.i. bot*-a-nize, to seek for plants for the purpose of botanical investigation; to study plants: *v.i.* to explore or describe botanically.

botanomancy, *n. bot*-an-o-*man*-se, divination by means of plants, esp. the fig.

botany, *n. bot*-a-ne, the science of plants; fine Australian wool, originally shipped from Botany Bay (Sydney, N.S.W.).

botargo, *n.* bo-*tar*-go, a relish made of salted mullet or tunny roes. (It.)

botch, *n.* botch, an eruptive discoloured swelling on the skin; a clumsy patch; ill-finished work: *v.t.* to mend or patch clumsily; to put together unsuitably or unskilfully. (O.Fr. *boce.*)

botcher, *n. botch*-er, one who botches or patches; a bungler; a young salmon.

botchery, *n. botch*-er-re, botched work; patchwork.

botchily, *ad. botch*-e-le, in an unskilful, clumsy, or bungling manner.

botchy, *a. botch*-e, characterized by clumsy work or bungling; marked with or full of botches.

bot-fly, *n. bot*-fly, parasitic horse-fly; the gadfly.

both, *ad.* and *pron.* boath, the one and the other; as well. (Ice. *bāthir.*)

bother, *n. both*-er, annoyance; a nuisance; a fuss: *int.* expressing vexation or impatience: *v.t.* to tease or pester; to vex: *v.i.* to trouble one's self; to make a fuss. (Of uncertain origin.)

botheration, *n. both*-er-*ray*-shon, trouble; worry: *int.* bother it.

bothersome, *a. both*-er-sum, causing trouble.

bothie *or* **bothy,** *n. boh*-the, a hut; in Scotland a cottage in which unmarried farm servants are housed.

botoné, *a. bot*-o-ne, bottony.

bo-tree, *n. boh*-tree, the sacred pipal tree, *Ficus religiosa,* under which Buddha attained enlightenment.

botryoid, *a. bot*-re-oyd, botryoidal.

botryoidal, *a. bot*-re-*oyd*-al, having the form of a bunch of grapes. (Gr. *botrys,* a bunch of grapes, *eidos,* likeness.)

bott, *n. bot,* the gadfly or bot.

bottine, *n. bot*-teen, a half-boot; a boot for weak ankles, etc., in children; a lady's boot. (Fr.)

★bottle, *n. bot*-tl, a vessel with a narrow mouth, for holding liquors; an infant's feeding flask; the contents of a bottle: *v.t.* to put into bottles. **the bottle,** strong drink; drinking. (O.Fr. *botteile.*)

bottle, *n. bot*-tl, a bundle of hay. (O.Fr. *botte,* a bundle.)

bottlebrush, *n. bot*-tl-brush, a brush for cleaning an infant's or other bottle; a popular name of various plants, as the mare's-tail and an Australian plant of the genus *Callistemon.*

bottled, *a. bot*-tld, tipsy; drunk [Slang].

bottlefish, *n. bot*-tl-fish, a deep-sea fish that is able to distend its body to a bottle shape. *Saccopharynx ampullaceous.*

bottle-flower, *n. bot*-tl-flou-er, the cornflower.

bottle-glass, *n. bot*-tl-glahs, a coarse green glass used for making bottles.

bottle-gourd, *n. bot*-tl-goord, the common pumpkin, whose husk is used as a bottle.

bottle-green, *a. bot*-tl-green, of the colour of bottle-glass.

bottlehead, *n. bot*-tl-hed, the bottlenose whale.

bottle-holder, *n. bot*-tl-*hohl*-der, one who waits on a combatant in a prize-fight with refreshment, and to assist; a second; an abettor.

bottleneck, *n. bot*-tl-nek, the neck of a bottle; a narrow or congested entrance or exit; a place or stage at which progress is retarded by congestion.

bottlenose, *n. bot*-tl-noze, the beaked whale, *Hyperoōdon rostratus.*

bottle-party, *n.* a convivial gathering, esp. at a night-club, the participators in which supply the alcoholic refreshment.

bottler, *n. bot*-tl-er, one who bottles liquors.

bottle-tit, *n. bot*-tl-tit, the long-tailed tit, *Parus longicaudatus,* so called from its nest.

bottle-washer, *n. bot*-tl-wosh-er, one who washes the bottles; a general help; an underling.

bottom, *n. bot*-tum, the lowest, deepest, or remotest part of anything; an abyss; the ground under any body of water; the foundation or base; the part on which a thing rests or sits; the posterior; the seat of a chair; a valley; a ship; a ship's keel; cause; stamina; strength: *n.pl.* dregs, sediment: *v.t.* to found or build upon; to furnish with a bottom; to fathom: *a.* pertaining to or at the bottom; in a low situation. **bottom heat,** underground heat supplied by decomposing substances or by a hot-water system [Hort.]. **to touch bottom,** to reach the worst. **bottomed,** having a bottom. (A.S. *botm.*)

bottomless, *a. bot*-tum-less, without a bottom or seat; fathomless.

bottommost, *a. bot*-tum-mohst, lowest down.

bottomry, *n. bot*-tum-re, borrowing of money on the security of a ship: *v.t.* to pledge a ship thus. [Maritime Law].

bottony, *a. bot*-ton-e, having trefoil-shaped ends (of a certain form of heraldic cross). (O.Fr. *bottoné.*)

botts, *n.* bots, a disease of horses and other livestock caused by the bot or gadfly.

botuliform, *a. bot*-yoo-le-form, sausage-shaped.

botulism, *n. bot*-yoo-lizm, poisoning due to the bacillus (*B. botulinus*) which infects imperfectly preserved canned foods, sausage-meat, etc. (L. *botulus,* sausage.)

boudoir, *n. boo*-dwahr, a lady's own room; a private sitting-room. (Fr. *bouder,* to sulk.)

Bougainvillea, *n. boo*-gayn-*vil*-e-a, a group of tropical American climbing plants, cultivated for their showy flowers.

bough, *n.* bou, an arm or large branch of a tree. (A.S. *bōg.*)

bought, bawt, *pp.* buy: *a.* purchased, not home-made.

bougie, *n. boo*-zhee, a contrivance for insertion into passages of the body for dilatation, examination, or the removal of obstructions [Surg.]. (Fr., a wax taper.)

bouillabaisse, *n.* boo-yah-*bayce,* a chowder or highly seasoned stew made of fish. (Fr.)

bouilli, *n.* boo-*yee,* stewed or simmered meat. (Fr.)

bouillon, *n. boo*-yong, broth; soup. (Fr.)

boulder, *n. bohl*-der, a large stone worn roundish by water; a rounded mass of rock transported to a distance from its native bed [Geol.] (Swedish *bullersten.*)

boulder-clay, *n.* the clay deposited by glaciers.

boule, *n.* bool, buhl. (Fr.)

boulevard, *n.* boo-*yong,* a street or promenade occupying the line of demolished fortifications; a promenade planted with trees around or in a town. (Fr.)

bouleversement, *n.* bool-*vers*-mahn, overthrow; turning upside down; ruin. (Fr.)

boulter, *n. bohlt*-er, a fishing line furnished with a number of hooks.

bounce, *n.* bounce, a heavy blow, thrust, or thump; a rebound, as of a dropped rubber ball; impudence; bluster; a boast; the nurse-hound; a species of dogfish: *v.i.* to leap, spring, or rush out suddenly; to rebound; to boast or brag: *v.t.* to drive against; to cause to rebound. (Dut. *bonzen*, to strike.)

bouncer, *n. boun*-ser, one who or that which bounces; anything large and bouncing; a boaster; a bold lie.

bouncing, *a. boun*-sing, large and heavy; stout; strong. **bouncing bet,** the soapwort.

bouncingly, *ad. boun*-sing-le, with a bounce; boastful.

bound, *n.* bound, boundary; limit; territory: *v.t.* to set limits to; to form the boundary of; to restrain; to confine. (O.Fr. *bonde.*)

bound, *n.* bound, a leap; a spring; a jump; a rebound: *v.i.* to leap; to move forward by leaps; to bounce. (Fr. *bondir.*)

bound, *pp.* of the verb to bind: *a.* destined; going, or intending to go.

boundary, *n. bound*-a-re, a mark indicating a limit; limit.

bounden, *a. bound*-en, enslaved; obligatory; morally binding.

bounder, *n. bound*-er, a vulgar, ill-bred, or pushful man [Slang].

boundless, *a. bound*-less, without bound or limit.

boundlessly, *ad. bound*-less-le, in a boundless manner.

boundlessness, *n. bound*-less-ness, the quality of being boundless.

bounds, *n.* boundz, a boundary; an area including the boundary line.

bounteous, *a. boun*-te-us, liberal; bountiful.

bounteously, *ad. boun*-te-us-le, in a bounteous manner; largely.

bounteousness, *n. boun*-te-us-ness, the quality of being bounteous.

bountiful, *a. boun*-te-ful, full of bounty; liberal; generous; munificent.

bountifully, *ad. boun*-te-ful-le, in a bountiful manner.

bountifulness, *n. boun*-te-ful-ness, the quality of being bountiful.

bounty, *n. boun*-te, liberality; generosity in giving; a gift freely bestowed; a premium given to induce men to enlist into the public service, or to encourage a branch of industry. **Queen Anne's Bounty,** a provision made in that queen's reign for augmenting poor church livings. (O.Fr. *bonte.*)

bouquet, *n.* boo-*kay*, a nosegay; a bunch of flowers; the aromatic odour of wine. (Fr.)

bouquet-garni, *n. boo*-kay-*gar*-nee, a bunch of mixed herbs used in cooking. (Fr.)

bouquetin, *n. boo*-ke-tin, the ibex. (Fr.)

Bourbonism, *n. boor*-bon-izm, adherence to the Bourbon dynasty in France, and hence to any dynastically legitimate royal line.

Bourbonist, *n. boor*-bon-ist, a supporter of the Bourbons; a legitimist.

bourdon, *n. boor*-don, the bass stop in an organ or reed in an harmonium; the drone of a bagpipe. (Fr.)

bourg, *n.* boorg, a fortified town; a burg.

bourgeois, *n.* bur-*joyce*, printing type larger than brevier and smaller than long primer; 9-point.

bourgeois, *n. boor*-zhwah, a member of the middle-class; a trader; a rentier or small property-owner: *a.* middle-class; hidebound; conventional; capitalistic. (Fr. from *bourg*, a town.)

bourgeoisie, *n. boor*-zwah-zee, the middle or shop-keeping classes.

bourgeon, *n.* and *v.i. bur*-jun, burgeon.

bourn, *n.* boorn, a stream; a burn. (A.S. *burna.*)

bourne *or* **bourn,** *n.* boorn *or* borne, a bound; a limit; a destination. (Fr. *borne.*)

bournonite, *n. boor*-nun-ite, a crystalline antimonial sulphide of lead and copper.

bourrée, *n.* bu-*ray*, a lively dance in 2/4 time beginning on an up-beat. (Fr.)

bourse, *n.* boorce, an exchange where merchants meet to transact business; the money market. (Fr.)

bour-tree, *n. boor*-tree, the elder. (Scots.)

bouse, *n.* and *v.i.* booz, boose.

boustrophedon, *n.* bou-stro-*fee*-don, an ancient mode of writing from right to left, and left to right alternately, as in ploughing. (Gr. *bous*, an ox, *strepho*, to turn.)

bout, *n.* bout, a turn, or round; as much as can be done at one time; a spell of, as of illness, intemperance, etc. (Dan. *bugt*, a bend.)

boutade, *n.* boo-*tahd*, a whim or fancy; a caprice; a sudden outburst. (Fr.).

bouts-rimés, *n.* boo-*ree*-may, a game in which verses are written to fit given rhymes. (Fr.)

bovate, *n. boh*-vate, an oxgang.

bovine, *a. boh*-vine, pertaining to cattle; dull, stupid. (L. *bos, bovis*, an ox or cow.)

bovril, *n. bov*-ril, trade name of an extract of beef.

bow, *n.* bou, a respectful inclination of the head, or bending of the body: *v.t.* to cause to bend; to bend, as the head or body, in token of respect or condescension; to depress; to crush; to subdue: *v.i.* to bend or incline the body out of respect or in assent, etc.; to stoop; to sink under pressure. (A.S. *bugan*, to bend.)

bow, *n.* bou, the fore-end of a ship, boat, or aircraft; the oarsman nearest the bow: *pl.* the meeting of the port and starboard sides towards the prow. (As *bough.*)

bow, *n.* boh, a weapon or instrument to shoot arrows with; anything bent or in form of a curve, as the rainbow; the doubling of a string or ribbon in a slip knot; a ribbon, etc., tied thus, as a necktie; the instrument with which the strings of a violin are sounded; an appliance for turning a drill; an arch: *v.t.* to use a violin-bow. **saddle bow,** the arched part of a saddle tree. (A.S. *boga.*)

bow-brace, *n. boh*-brace, a guard on the left arm against the springing back of the bow-string.

bow-compasses, *n.pl.* boh-*kum*-pas-sez, a pair of compasses in which the distance between the points is controlled by a screw.

bowdlerism, *n. boud*-ler-rizm, expurgation of what is deemed indelicate.

bowdlerize, *v.i.* and *v.t. boud*-ler-rize, to expurgate or modify literary works for the sake of propriety, as in Bowdler's edition of Shakespeare (1818).

bow-drill, *n. boh*-dril, a drill worked by a bow.

bowed, *a.* bohd, bent like a bow; crooked; played with a bow [Mus.].

bowel, *v.t. bou*-el, to take out the bowels.

bowels, *n.pl. bou*-elz, the intestines of an animal, especially of man; the interior part of anything; tenderness; pity. (O.Fr. *boël.*)

bower, *n. bou*-er, a shelter made with boughs of trees; a shady recess. (A.S. *bur*, a chamber.)

bower, *n. bou*-er, an anchor at the bow of a ship.

bower, *n. bou*-er, one of two knaves in euchre.

bower-bird, *n. bou*-er-berd, the name of several species of Australian birds allied to the starling that build a bower to play in near their nest.

bowery, *a. bou*-er-re, shady; containing bowers. **the Bowery,** a notorious district of New York.

bowfin, *n. boh*-fin, the voracious North American freshwater ganoid fish *Amia calva*; the mudfish of the Great Lakes.

bow-grace, *n. bou*-grace, a fender of junk, to guard the sides or bows of ships from injury by ice [Naut.].

bow-hand, *n. boh*-hand, the hand that draws a bow.

bowie-knife, *n. boh*-e-nife, a long knife formerly notorious as a weapon in the Western States of America, invented by a Col. Bowie.

bowing, *n. boh*-ing, the art of using a violin-bow.

bowl, *n.* bohl, a round hollow; a basin; a drinking-cup; the hollow part of anything. (A.S. *bolla.*)

bowl, *n.* bohl, a ball of wood with a bias for rolling along the ground: *v.i.* to play bowls; to move smoothly and rapidly like a ball; to deliver a ball at a wicket: *v.t.* to roll as a bowl or ball; to strike the wicket with a bowled ball and put the batsman out at cricket. **bowl out,** at cricket, to hit the wicket by bowling; to defeat or convict [Slang]. (Fr. *boule.*)

bow-legged, *a. boh*-legd, having crooked legs, esp. bent outward at the knee.

bowler, *n. bohl*-er, one who plays at bowls, or who bowls the ball at cricket.

bowler, *n. bohl*-er, a low-crowned hard felt hat.

bowline, *n. boh*-lin, a rope used to steady the weather-edge of a sail forward when the ship is sailing close to the wind. **bowline knot,** a safe knot that does not slip or jam, originally used for fastening the bowline bridles to the cringles.

bowling, *n. bohl*-ing, playing bowls; delivering the ball at the wicket in cricket. **bowling-alley,** a covered place for playing skittles or American

bowls. **bowling-crease,** the line from behind which the ball is delivered at cricket. **bowling-green,** a level piece of turf kept smooth for playing bowls.
bowls, *n.* bohlz, an open-air game in which bowls are rolled on a bowling-green towards a jack.
bowman, *n. boh*-man, an archer; the rower nearest the bow.
bow-net, *n. boh*-net, a kind of wicker basket used for catching lobsters and crayfish.
bow-oar, *n. bou*-awr, the oarsman nearest the bow; No. 1 of a racing crew.
bow-pen, *n. boh*-pen, **bow-pencil,** *n.* boh-*pen*-sil, bow compasses fitted with pen or pencil.
bow-saw, *n. boh*-saw, a flexible saw in a frame used for cutting curves.
bowser, *n. bou*-zer, a mechanized petrol-carrier.
bowshot, *n. boh*-shot, the distance to which space an arrow can be shot.
bowsprit, *n. boh*-sprit, the large spar which projects over the stem of a ship to carry sail forward.
bow-string, *n. boh*-string, the string of a bow: *v.t.* to furnish with a bow-string; to strangle with the string of a bow, as was done in Turkey.
bow-window, *n. boh*-win-do, a rounded bay-window.
bow-wow, *n. bou*-wou, the bark of a dog; a dog.
bowyer, *n. boh*-yer, a maker of bows.
box, *n.* boks, a case of any size and material for containing anything solid; the contents of the case; a money-chest; the case that contains the compass; an enclosed space, such as for seats in a theatre or eating-house, etc.; a separate apartment; a cylindrical hollow iron in which the axletree of a wheel runs; a hollow tube in a pump, closed with a valve; the driver's seat on a coach; a small lodge; a present, as at Christmas: *v.t.* to enclose in a box; to furnish with a box; to make a hole or cut in a tree, to procure the sap. **to box the compass,** to go round the points of the compass in order; hence, to make a complete round. (A.S.)
★**box,** *n.* boks, a blow with the open hand: *v.t.* to give a box to: *v.i.* to fight or spar with gloved fists. (Origin uncertain.)
box, *n.* boks, a shrub, *Buxus sempervirens*; its wood.
box-calf, *n. boks*-kahf, trade term for calfskin tanned with chrome salts.
box-cloth, *n. boks*-kloth, a heavy closely woven cloth used for box-coats.
box-coat, *n. boks*-koat, a heavy overcoat for driving.
box-day, *n. boks*-day, day for lodging papers [Law].
box-drain, *n. boks*-drayn, a square underground drain, boxed up on the sides and on the top.
box-elder, *n. boks*-eld-er, the ash-leaved maple.
boxen, *a. boks*-n, made of box-wood; resembling box.
boxer, *n. boks*-er, one who fights with his fists, usually with gloves; a pugilist; a member of a late 19th-cent. Chinese anti-foreigner secret society.
boxhaul, *v.t. boks*-hawl, to veer a ship round on her keel [Naut.].
boxing, *n. boks*-ing, the art or act of fighting with the fists.
Boxing-day, *n. boks*-ing-day, the day after Christmas, when Christmas boxes are given.
boxing-glove, *n.* one of a pair of padded gloves, having a thumb but no fingers, used in boxing.
box-iron, *n. boks*-i-urn, a box-shaped smoothing-iron containing a heater.
box-kite, *n. boks*-kite, a kite like a long box with four rectangular planes.
box-office, *n. boks*-of-fis, an office at which seats at a theatre, concert, etc., may be booked.
box-pleat, *n. boks*-pleet, a pleating first to the right and then to the left continuing so alternately.
box-spanner, *n. boks*-span-ner, a strong metal tube, one or both ends of which fit a nut, turned by a bar inserted in a transverse hole.
box-thorn, *n. boks*-thorn, a rambling plant of the genus *Lycium*.
box-wood, *n. boks*-wood, the wood of the box.
★**boy,** *n.* boy, a male child; a lad; a male servant; a native workman. **Boy Scouts,** an organization, founded in England (1908) and afterwards world-wide, aiming at the promotion among boys of the ideals of honour, good citizenship, and useful service. (Origin doubtful.) (M.E. *boi.*)
boyar, *n. boy*-ar, one of a class of aristocrats in Russia whose privileges were withdrawn by Peter the Great; one of a former class of landed proprietors in Rumania. (Russ.)
boycott, *v.t. boy*-kot, to ostracize; to combine together to have no dealings with one on account of his political opinions: *n.* an act, or the system, of boycotting. (From Captain *Boycott*, its first victim in Ireland, 1880.)
boyhood, *n. boy*-hood, the state of being a boy; the duration or period of this state.
boyish, *a. boy*-ish, like a boy; puerile; suitable for boys.
boyishly, *ad. boy*-ish-le, in a boyish manner.
boyishness, *n. boy*-ish-ness, the quality of being boyish.
boy's-love, *n. boyz*-luv, southernwood.
brabble, *n. brab*-bl, a quarrel; a broil: *v.i.* to squabble; to dispute captiously. (Origin unknown.)
braccate, *a. brak*-at, having the tarsus and foot well feathered [Ornith.]. (L. *bracatus*, wearing breeches.)
brace, *n.* brace, that which holds anything tight; a cincture or bandage; a thick strap supporting the body of a coach; a pair or a couple; tension; tightness; a crooked line connecting two or more words or lines, thus: ⏞ [Print.]; a timber or scantling to strengthen a wall or building [Arch.]; a rope to work a ship's yards with; a crank or curved handle for holding a bit; the core that tightens a drum: *pl.* two straps to support the trousers from the shoulders: *v.t.* brace, to fasten together; to tighten; to bind or tie close; to make tense; to strain up; to furnish with braces; to strengthen. (O.Fr. *bracer.*)
bracelet, *n. brace*-let, an ornament for the wrist; a handcuff [Slang]. (Fr.)
bracer, *n. bray*-ser, that which braces; a band or bandage; a defence for the arm; a tonic medicine.
brach, *n.* bratch, a female hound. (O.Fr. *brache.*)
brachelytrous, *a.* brak-e-*lit*-rus, pertaining to the group of beetles characterized by short wing-cases.
brachial, *a. brak*-e-al, pertaining to or resembling the arm.
brachiate, *a. brak*-e-at, having branches in pairs, decussated, all nearly horizontal, and each pair at right angles with the next [Bot.].
brachio-, *comb. f. brak*-e-o, the arm [Anat.]. (Gr.)
brachiocephalic, *a. brak*-e-o-se-*fal*-ik, designating the blood-vessels common to arms and head [Anat.].
brachiopod, *n. brak*-e-o-pod, a bivalve mollusc with bilaterally symmetrical valves, one of a class of invertebrates of which fossil forms are numerous and a few species are still in existence. (Gr. *brachion*, the arm, and *pous*, foot.)
brachiopodous, *a. brak*-e-*op*-o-dus, belonging to the brachiopod group.
brachy-, *comb. f. brak*-e, short. (Gr. *brachys.*)
brachycephalic, *a. brak*-e-se-*fal*-ik, short-headed; having a skull whose breadth with a head is in the ratio of 4 to 5 to the length. (Gr. *brachys*, and *kephale*, head.)
brachygraphy, *n.* bra-*kig*-ra-fe, shorthand writing. (Gr. *brachys*, and *grapho*, to write.)
brachyural, *a.* brak-e-*yewr*-ral, short-tailed, descriptive of a group of crustaceans, comprehending the crabs [Zool.]. (Gr. *brachys*, and *oura*, a tail.)
bracing, *a. brace*-ing, giving strength or tone: *n.* that which braces.
bracken, *n. brak*-n, the brake fern, *Pteris aquilina.* (A.S. *braccan.*)
bracket, *n. brak*-et, an angular stay to support anything to a wall; a short isolated shelf fastened on to a wall; a gas pipe projecting from a wall; a mark used in printing thus [ ]: *v.t.* to furnish with brackets; to enclose in brackets: *v.i.* to ascertain the range of a target by placing a shell on either side of it and calculating the mean. (Sp. *bragueta*, a corbel.)
brackish, *a. brak*-ish, saltish; saline. (Dut. *brak.*)
brackishness, *n. brak*-ish-ness, the quality of being brackish.
bract, *n. brakt*, a leaf growing out beneath the calyx from the peduncle of a flower [Bot.]. (L., a thin plate of metal.)
bracteate, *a. brak*-te-at, having bracts; formed of thinly beaten metal: *n.* a bracteate plate, coin, etc.
bracteated, *a. brak*-te-ay-ted, plated over with a richer metal [Numis.].
bracteolate, *a. brak*-te-o-lat, having bracteoles [Bot.].

bracteole, *n.* *brak*-te-ole, a little bract [Bot.].
brad, *n.* brad, a nail without a head, but with a projection from one side; a thin flat nail. (Scand.)
bradawl, *n.* *brad*-awl, a small boring tool for making holes for brads.
Bradshaw, *n.* *brad*-shaw, a British railway guide called after the compiler's name.
bradypod, *n.* *brad*-e-pod, one of the sloth tribe. (Gr. *bradys*, slow, *pous*, foot.)
brae, *n.* bray, the side of a hill, a steep bank. (Scots.)
brag, *n.* brag, a boast; a game at cards: *v.i.* to boast.
braggadocio, *n.* *brag*-ga-*doh*-she-o, a boasting fellow; a boast. (Spenser's name in "The Faërie Queen" for the personification of Vainglory.)
braggart, *n.* *brag*-gart, a boaster; a vain fellow: *a.* boastful. (O.Fr. *bragard.*)
bragging, *n.* *brag*-ging, boastful language.
Brahma, *n.* *brah*-mah, a breed of domestic fowl first imported from the river Brahmaputra.
Brahman, *n.* *brah*-man, Brahmin.
Brahmanas, *n.* *brah*-ma-naz, treatises on the ceremonial system of Brahminism.
Brahmin, *n.* *brah*-min, one of the sacred caste among the Hindus that boasts of direct descent from Brahma, the Creator of Hindu theology, and is therefore of high priestly rank. (Sans. lit., prayer.)
Brahminee, *n.* *brahm*-in-ee, a female Brahmin.
Brahminical, *a.* brah-*min*-e-kal, pertaining or relating to the Brahmins.
Brahminism, *n.* *brah*-min-izm, the creed and ritual of the Brahmins.
Brahmoism, *n.* *brah*-mo-izm, the rationalized form of Hinduism practised by the Brahmo-Samaj.
Brahmo-Samaj, *n.* *brah*-mo-sa-*mahzh*, a revival of Hinduism on deistic principles and the rational ideas and philosophy of Europe, led by the society of this name. (Sans. *brahmā*, and Hind. *samāj*, meeting.)
braid, *n.* braid, a narrow band formed by plaitings; a plait of hair: *v.t.* to intertwine; to plait; to use braid on; to dress the hair with plaits or ribbons. (A.S. *brēdan.*)
brail, *n.* brail, a piece of leather to bind a hawk's wing; a rope passing through a block on a hoop of the mizen-mast or gaff to the leech of a fore-and-aft sail, to truss the sail up with: *v.i.* to truss up a fore-and-aft sail. (O.Fr. *braiel.*)
braille, *n.* brail, printing in relief for the blind, by an alphabet of dots. (*Braille*, its inventor.)
★**brain,** *n.* brain, the convoluted mass of grey and white matter enclosed in the skull and forming the centre of the nervous system and the seat of sensation, perception, consciousness, and will in vertebrates; the cephalic ganglion in invertebrates: *pl.* the substance of which the brain is composed; intelligence; understanding: *v.t.* to dash out the brains. **brains trust,** a selected body of consultants; a group of intellectuals who engage (usually unrehearsed) in debate in public [Coll.]. (A.S. *brægen.*)
brain-coral, *n.* brain-*ko*-ral, a massive reef-building coral of the genus *Meandrina.*
brain-fag, *n.* *brain*-fag, nervous exhaustion.
brain-fever, *n.* *brain*-fee-ver, inflammation of the brain; meningitis.
brainish, *a.* *brain*-ish, headstrong; brainsick.
brainless, *a.* *brain*-less, silly; thoughtless; witless.
brainpan, *n.* *brain*-pan, the skull.
brainsick, *a.* *brain*-sik, disordered in the understanding; produced by a deranged mind.
brainsickness, *n.* *brain*-sik-ness, the state of being brainsick; mental derangement.
brainstorm, *n.* *brain*-storm, sudden mental derangement; strong mental agitation.
brainwave, *n.* *brain*-wave, a good idea.
brainy, *a.* *brain*-e, clever; quick of thought.
braird, *n.* braird, the first springing up of the seed of a grain crop: *v.i.* to sprout. (Scots.)
braise, *v.t.* braze, to cook meat in a covered pan, properly with heat above as well as below. (Fr. *braiser*, to bake in an oven.)
braising-pan, *n.* *braze*-ing-pan, a covered pan for braising meat in.
brake, *n.* brake, bracken; a place overgrown with brake, brambles, etc.; a thicket. (M.E. *brāke.*)
★**brake,** *n.* brake, a tool for breaking flax or hemp; the handle of a pump; a baker's kneading implement; a heavy harrow for breaking clods; a frame for fettering refractory horses while shoeing them; a carriage for breaking in horses; a large wagonette; an appliance to a wheel to check motion; anything that retards progress: *v.t.* to use a brake; to retard with or as with a brake. **Westinghouse brake,** a continuous brake used on railway-trains and worked by compressed air (named from inventor). *pp.* **braked.** (Late Ger. *brake*, a flax-brake.)
brake, brake, *p.* of break.
brakeless, *a.* *brake*-less, having no brake.
brake-man, *n.* *brake*-man, a brakesman [U.S.A.].
brakesman, *n.* *brakes*-man, a man who has charge of the brake; the man in charge of a winding engine.
brake-van, *n.* *brake*-van, the compartment in a train in which the brakes are worked; the guard's van.
braky, *a.* *brake*-e, full of bracken; rough; thorny.
bramble, *n.* *bram*-bl, the blackberry; any rough, prickly, wild shrub. (A.S. *bremel.*)
brambled, *a.* *bram*-bld, overgrown with brambles.
bramble-net, *n.* *bram*-bl-net, a kind of net to catch birds.
brambling, *n.* *bram*-bling, the mountain finch, *Fringilla montifringilla.*
brambly, *a.* *bram*-ble, full of brambles.
bran, *n.* bran, the husks of ground corn, separated from the flour by bolting. (O.Fr.)
brancard, *n.* *brank*-ard, a litter borne by horses. (Fr.)
★**branch,** *n.* brahnch, the shoot or limb of a tree; any offshoot, or any member, part, or subdivision of a body, system, business organization, mountain-range, etc.; any individual of a family descending in a collateral line: *v.i.* to ramify: to shoot out in branches or into subdivisions; a licence authorizing a pilot to act as such in certain waters: *v.t.* to divide into branches, or subordinate divisions; to embroider with representations of flowers and sprigs. **branched work,** the sculptured leaves and branches in monuments and friezes. **branches of a bridle,** two pieces of bent iron which bear the bit, the cross-chains, and the curb. **branch out,** to extend one's activities; to speak diffusively. (Fr.)
brancher, *n.* *brahnch*-er, that which branches forth; a young bird when it begins to take to the branches.
branchery, *n.* *brahnch*-er-re, a mass of branches; branches collectively.
branchiæ, *n.pl.* *brank*-e-ee, the gills of fishes and certain amphibians. (Gr. *branchia*, gills.)
branchial, *a.* *brank*-e-al, pertaining to gills.
branchiate, *a.* *brank*-e-at, having gills.
branchiferous, *a.* bran-*kif*-e-rus, having gills.
branchiness, *n.* *brahnch*-e-ness, fulness of branches.
branching, *a.* *brahnch*-ing, shooting out branches; dividing into branches.
branchiopod, *n.* *brank*-e-o-pod, a crustacean in which the gills are on the feet. (Gr. *branchia*, and *pous*, foot.)
branchiopodous, *a.* brank-e-*op*-o-dus, pertaining to the branchiopods; having gills on the feet.
branchiostegan, *n.* brank-e-*os*-te-gan, a fish which has its gills covered with a membrane. (Gr. *branchia*, and *stegos*, covering.)
branchiostegous, *a.* brank-e-*os*-te-gus, having the gills covered; pertaining to the branchiostegans.
Branchiostoma, *n.* brank-e-*os*-to-ma, a genus of semivertebrates comprising the lancelets and the amphioxus. (Gr. *branchia*, and *stoma*, a mouth.)
branchlet, *n.* *brahnch*-let, a little branch; a twig.
branchy, *a.* *brahnch*-e, full of branches; spreading.
brand, *n.* brand, a burning piece of wood; a piece partly burnt; a sword; a mark burnt in, or instrument for making such mark; a trade-mark; quality; a mark of infamy; a blight in plants: *v.t.* to mark with a brand; to stigmatize. (A.S.)
branded, *a.* *bran*-ded, marked with a brand; bearing a trade-mark. **branded goods,** merchandise sold under a trade-mark and usually in a distinctive packing or container [Comm.].
brander, *n.* bran-der, a branding-iron; a gridiron [Scots.]; *v.t.* to cook on this.
brandied, *a.* *bran*-ded, mixed or strengthened with brandy.
branding-iron, *n.* *bran*-ding-i-urn, an iron to brand with; a trivet to set a pot on.
brandish, *n.* *bran*-dish, a flourish: *v.t.* to wave a wand, or flourish a weapon. (Fr.)

brandling, *n.* *brand*-ling, a dunghill worm banded or striped with red and yellow; a young salmon.
brand-new, *a.* brand-new, quite new, as though fresh from fire.
brandreth, *n.* *bran*-dreth, a rail round a well-mouth; an iron support for pans placed before or over the fire; a brazier; a framework to support a rick, a barrel, etc. **brandreth stone,** a boundary stone at the meeting of three counties. (Dial. Eng.)
brandy, *n.* *bran*-de, spirit distilled from wine. **brandy-ball,** a small ball of toffee with ginger flavouring. **brandy-pawnee,** brandy and water [Anglo-Indian]. (Dut. *brande-wijn.*)
brangle, *v.i.* *brang*-gl, to wrangle; to squabble: *n.* a quarrel.
brank, *n.* brank, buckwheat. (Dial. Eng.)
branks, *n.* branks, a kind of bridle to gag scolding women [Scots.].
brank-ursine, *n.* *brank*-ur-sin, the plant bear's-breech, a species of *Acanthus.* (Fr.)
bran-mash, *n.* bran-*mash,* a mixture of bran and hot water for feeding livestock and poultry.
bran-new, *a.* bran-new, error for brand-new.
branny, *a.* *bran*-ne, like or containing bran.
brant, *n.* brant, the brent goose.
brantail, *n.* *bran*-tale, the redstart.
brant-fox, *n.* *brant*-foks, a dark-furred fox.
brash, *a.* brash, hasty; impetuous; brittle.
brash, *n.* brash, rock disintegrated into small fragments [Geol.]. (Fr. *brèche,* breach.)
brash, *n.* brash, slight indigestion; a belch of acid fluid.
★**brass,** *n.* brahss, an alloy of copper and zinc, or anything made of it; a plate of it engraved with effigies, etc., inlaid on a tombstone; money [Slang]; impudence [Slang]: *pl.* brass musical instruments in a band. **to get down to brass tacks,** to come to realities. (A.S. *bræs.*)
brassage, *n.* *bras*-saj, sum levied for expenses of coinage. (Fr.)
brassard, *n.* *bras*-sard, an armlet. (Fr.)
brassart, *n.* *bras*-sart, armour protecting the upper arm. (Fr. *bras,* arm.)
brass-band, *n.* *brahss*-band, a band with wind instruments of brass.
brass-bounder, *n.* *brahss*-boun-der, a midshipman; an apprentice in the mercantile marine [Slang]
brasserie, *n.* *bras*-er-re, a saloon in which beer and light refreshments are served. (Fr., brewery.)
brass-founder, *n.* *brahss*-found-er, a workman in a brass foundry; a maker of brass castings.
brass-hat, *n.* *brahss*-hat, a staff officer or officer of high rank [Mil. slang].
Brassica, *n.* *bras*-se-ka, the cabbage family of plants. (L.)
brassie, *n.* *bras*-se, a golf-club with a brass sole.
brassière, *n.* *bras*-e-ayr, a woman's light under-bodice to support the breasts. (Fr.)
brassiness, *n.* *brahss*-e-ness, the quality of being brassy.
brassy, *a.* *brahss*-e, like or made of brass; hard as brass: *n.* a brassie (golf-club).
brat, *n.* brat, a child, an infant, so called in contempt. (Origin uncertain.)
bratling, *n.* *brat*-ling, a little brat.
brattice, *n.* *brat*-is, a partition; a timber lining to a shaft or headway [Mining].
bratticing, *n.* *brat*-tis-ing, a temporary parapet; a ridge to a parapet; a boarded partition; a breastwork. (O.Fr. *bretiche.*)
braunite, *n.* *brou*-nite, native manganese silicate. (From M. *Braun,* of Gotha.)
bravado, *n.* bra-*vah*-do, a boast; an arrogant menace; ostentatious bravery. (Sp.)
brave, *a.* brave, courageous; fearless; valiant; of noble mien; showy; excellent: *n.* a Red Indian warrior; a bravo: *v.t.* to defy; to dare; to encounter with courage and fortitude. (Fr.)
bravely, *ad.* *brave*-ly, in a brave manner.
bravery, *n.* *brave*-er-re, the quality of being brave; courage; finery.
bravissimo, *int.* brah-*viss*-e-mo, very well done! (It.)
bravo, *n.* *brah*-vo, a bandit; a hired assassin. (It.)
bravo, *n.* brah-*voh,* *int.* well done! (It.)
bravura, *n.* bra-*voor*-ra, a florid, showy piece of music: *a.* spirited, difficult, and brilliant. (It.)
brawl, *n.* brawl, noisy quarrel; a disturbance in a church or churchyard; a kind of dance; the sound of shallow water flowing over gravel: *v.i.* to quarrel noisily; to make a noise; to create a disturbance. (Dan. *bralle.*)
brawling, *a.* *brawl*-ing, noisy; quarrelsome.
brawlingly, *ad.* *brawl*-ing-le, in a brawling manner.
brawn, *n.* brawn, muscle; muscular strength; the fleshy parts; pig's head boiled, boned, seasoned and pressed. (O.Fr. *braon,* a piece of meat.)
brawniness, *n.* *brawn*-e-ness, the quality of being brawny.
brawny, *a.* *brawn*-e, muscular; strong.
braxy, *n.* *brak*-se, an inflammatory disease in sheep; mutton of a sheep affected with it.
bray, *v.t.* bray, to pound or beat small. (Fr.)
bray, *n.* bray, the cry of an ass; a harsh grating sound: *v.i.* to utter a harsh sound, as an ass; the sound of a trumpet: *v.t.* to utter with a bray. (O.Fr. *braier.*)
brayer, *n.* *bray*-er, a hand ink-roller; formerly a wooden instrument used to temper ink [Print.].
braying, *n.* *bray*-ing, loud but senseless clamour.
braze, *v.t.* braze, to solder with an alloy of brass and zinc. (A.S. *brasian.*)
brazen, *a.* *bray*-zn, made of brass; impudent: *v.i.* to behave brazenly; to face impudently; to make shameless. **brazen age,** the age of violence. **brazen it out,** carry a matter off impudently. (A.S. *bræsen,* of brass.)
brazen-faced, *a.* *bray*-zn-fayst, impudent; shameless.
brazenly, *ad.* *bray*-zn-le, in a brazen manner.
brazenness, *n.* *bray*-zn-ness, the quality of being brazen or insolent.
brazier, *n.* *braze*-yer, a pan for burning charcoal; a worker in brass.
braziery, *n.* *bray*-ze-e-re, brass-work.
braziletto, *n.* *braz*-e-*let*-to, an inferior kind of Brazil-wood.
Brazilian, *a.* bra-*zil*-e-an, of or pertaining to Brazil: *n.* a native of Brazil.
brazilin, *n.* *braz*-il-in, the colouring matter of Brazil-wood.
Brazil-nut, *n.* bra-*zil*-nut, the fruit of *Bertholletia excelsa,* a myrtaceous tree of Brazil.
Brazil-tea, *n.* bra-*zil*-tee, maté, *Ilex paraguayensis.*
Brazil-wood, *n.* bra-*zil*-wood, a wood for dyeing red, mainly certain species of *Cæsalpinia.*
breach, *n.* breech, a breaking; a break; a gap or broken opening; violation of a law, contract, or engagement; infringement; quarrel; injury; a whale's leap out of water: *v.t.* to make an opening, as in a wall. **breach of promise,** such non-fulfilment of a matrimonial engagement as renders the party liable to damages at law. (A.S. *brecan,* break.)
★**bread,** *n.* bred, food made of flour and baked; food; livelihood. **bread-and-butter,** means of living; school-girlish, soppy [Slang]. (A.S.)
bread-basket, *n.* *bred*-bahs-ket, a basket for bread; the stomach [Slang].
bread-corn, *n.* *bred*-korn, corn for making bread.
bread-crumb, *n.* *bred*-krum, the soft part of bread; crumbled bread: *v.t.* to sprinkle or cover with bread-crumbs.
bread-fruit, *n.* *bred*-froot, the fruit of *Artocarpus incisa* which, when roasted, has some resemblance to bread.
breadless, *a.* *bred*-less, without bread; destitute of food.
bread-nut, *n.* *bred*-nut, the fruit of *Brosimum alicastrum,* used in Jamaica and Mexico as a flour substitute.
bread-room, *n.* *bred*-room, an apartment in a ship's hold where the bread and biscuits are kept.
breadroot, *n.* *bred*-root, prairie-turnip, *Psoralea esculenta.*
breadstuff, *n.* *bred*-stuff, cereals; flour; meal.
breadth, *n.* bredth, measure from side to side; width; broadness. (A.S. *brædu.*)
breadthways, *ad.* and *a.* *bredth*-ways, broad, across the width.
breadthwise, *ad.* and *a.* *bredth*-wize, breadth ways
bread-winner, *n.* *bred*-win-ner, the member of a family whose earnings support it.
break, *n.* brake, the act of breaking; the state of being broken; an opening or breach; an interruption; a line in writing or printing, noting suspension of the sense; a twist imparted by the bowler to the ball in cricket, and the resulting change in its

direction after striking the ground; a single turn of a player at billiards, also the score made in this; the point where one voice register changes to another [Mus.]: *v.t.* to part by force; to rend apart; to rupture; to shatter; to disperse; to weaken or impair; to subdue; to tame or make tractable; to make bankrupt; to dismiss or cashier; to violate, as a law; to interrupt; to intercept; to lessen the force of; to make a first disclosure of, as a scheme or tidings: *v.i.* to part in pieces; to burst; to show the first light or dawn; to burst forth; to utter or exclaim; to become bankrupt; to decline in health and strength; to force a way; to interrupt friendship; to fall out; to change; to change direction after striking the ground (of a ball); to make the first stroke at billiards; to change register, as a boy's voice at puberty; to become public news [Slang]. **break a deer,** to cut it up at table. **break a lance,** to have trial of skill. **break bulk,** to begin to unload. **break cover,** to come forth from a lurking-place. **break down,** to destroy; to dilute spirits; to overcome; to give away. **break ground,** to plough; to dig; to open trenches; to commence an undertaking. **break in,** to tame; to train to something; to enter by force; to intrude. **break into,** to enter unlawfully, to interrupt. **break loose,** to escape from captivity; to shake off restraint. **break of day,** dawn. **break off,** to part by breaking; to abandon; to desist suddenly. **break out,** to issue forth; to discover itself by its effects; to arise or spring up; to appear in eruptions; to throw off restraint. **break the back,** to ruin; to break the keel [Naut.]; to get through with the most part. **break the heart,** to afflict grievously; to destroy with grief. **break the ice,** to overcome the first difficulties. **break up,** to dissolve, or put an end to; to open, or lay open; to separate; to disband. **break upon the wheel,** to stretch and break the bones by torture upon the wheel. **break wind,** to give vent to wind from the anus. **break with,** to part in enmity; to cease to be friends. *p.* **broke.** *pp.* **broken.** (A.S. *brecan.*)

breakable, *a. brake*-a-bl, capable of being broken.

breakage, *n. brake*-aj, the act of breaking; state of being broken; an interruption; an allowance for things accidentally broken.

breakaway, *n. brake*-a-way, a sudden and voluntary parting; a stampede of cattle, sheep, etc.; a premature start of competitors in a race, etc.

breakdown, *n. brake*-doun, downfall; failure; collapse, esp. in health or nerve; a negro dance. **breakdown gang,** party of men sent to repair damage after an accident on a railway, etc.

breaker, *n. brake*-er, a small water-cask. (Sp. *bareca.*)

breaker, *n. brake*-er, one who or that which breaks; a wave broken over rocks.

breakfast, *n. brek*-fast, the first meal in the day: *v.i.* to take breakfast: *v.t.* to furnish a breakfast. **wedding-breakfast,** the entertainment immediately following the marriage ceremony. (*Break* and *fast.*)

break-joint, *n. brake*-joynt, the disposition of the stones or bricks, so that the joints shall not fall immediately over one another.

breakneck, *a. brake*-nek, endangering the neck; blundering; hazardous.

breakwater, *n. brake*-waw-ter, a mole to break the force of the waves, and protect shipping.

bream, *n.* breem, a broad, thin fresh-water fish of the carp tribe, of the genus *Abramis*; a sea-fish of the order Sparidæ. (O.Fr. *bresme.*)

bream, *v.t.* breem, to burn off the seaweed, ooze, etc., from a ship's bottom [Naut.].

breast, *n.* brest, the fore part of the body, between the neck and the abdomen; the soft protuberance on the thorax, terminating in a nipple; the bosom; the heart; the seat of the affections and passions; the front or fore part of a coat, etc.; the working face of a mine or tunnel: *v.t.* to meet in front; to face; to oppose. **make a clean breast,** to reveal all one knows. **breast up a hedge,** to cut the face of it. (A.S. *brēost.*)

breastband, *n. brest*-band, a band across a horse's breast which answers the purpose of a collar.

breastbone, *n. brest*-bone, the flat bone of the breast, the sternum.

breast-deep, *a. brest*-deep, up to the breast.

breast-drill, *n. brest*-dril, a drill worked against the breast.

breasted, *a. brest*-ed, having a breast; (*obsolete*) with a fine voice.

breastfast, *n. brest*-fahst, a large rope to confine a ship sidewise to a wharf or quay, or to another ship.

breast-high, *a. brest*-hy, high as the breast.

breast-hooks, *n.pl. brest*-hooks, the timbers placed across the stem of a ship, to strengthen the fore part.

breast-knot, *n. brest*-not, a knot of ribbons worn on the breast.

breast-pin, *n. brest*-pin, a pin worn in a tie or scarf, or on the breast; a brooch.

breast-plate, *n. brest*-plate, armour for the breast; a strap across a horse's breast; part of the vestment of the Jewish high-priest; the plastron of a turtle or tortoise; the inscription plate on a coffin.

breastplough, *n. brest*-plou, a kind of small plough propelled by the hands, used to cut or pare turf.

breastsummer, *n. brest*-sum-mer, a bressummer.

breast-wall, *n. brest*-wawl, a retaining wall.

breastwheel, *n. brest*-wheel, a water-wheel which receives the water at the level of its axis.

breastwise, *ad. brest*-wize, abreast.

breastwork, *n. brest*-wurk, a work thrown up breast-high for defence [Fort.]; a parapet.

***breath,** *n.* breth, the air inhaled and expelled in respiration; life; power of breathing freely; a single respiration, or the time of this; respite, or time to breathe; an instant; breeze; air in gentle motion; an exhalation; a rumour or whisper. (A.S.)

breathable, *a. breethe*-a-bl, that may be breathed.

breathableness, *n. breethe*-a-bl-ness, state of being breathable.

breathe, *v.i.* breethe, to inhale and exhale air; to live; take a breath or pause; to pass as air: *v.t.* to inhale, as air, into the lungs, and expel it; to respire; to exercise or keep in breath; to inspire or blow into; to utter softly; to give vent to; to express; to manifest.

breather, *n. breethe*-er, a spell of exercise; a breathing-space [Slang].

breathing, *a. breethe*-ing, as if living: *n.* respiration; aspiration; a gentle breeze; inspiration; exercise; a pause to take a breath; an aspirate.

breathing-place, *n. breethe*-ing-place, a place to pause at.

breathing-pore, *n. breethe*-ing-pawr, a microscopic aperture in the cuticle of plants.

breathing-space, *n. breethe*-ing-space, time for a breath; a pause; a short interval of rest.

breathless, *a. breth*-less, out of breath; panting; unable to breathe; without breath; dead.

breathlessly, *ad. breth*-less-le, in a breathless manner; in a tearing hurry.

breathlessness, *n. breth*-less-ness, the state of being breathless.

breccia, *n. bretch*-e-a, a rock composed of conglomerated angular fragments. (It.)

brecciated, *a. bretch*-e-ay-ted, in the form of breccia.

bred, bred, *p.* of breed.

bree, *n.* bree, broth; liquor in which something has been cooked [Scots.]. (A.S. *briw.*)

breech, *n.* britch *or* breech, the lower part of the body behind; the hinder part of a gun or anything: *v.t.* to put into breeches; to whip on the breech.

breech-band, *n. britch*-band, a horse's breeching.

breech-block, *n. britch*-blok, the block that closes the breech of a gun.

breeches, *n.pl. britch*-ez, a garment worn by men, covering the lower part of the body to the knees. **wear the breeches,** said of a wife who usurps the authority of her husband. (A.S. *brēc.*)

breeching, *n. britch*-ing, a whipping; the strong leather band round the haunches of a shaft-horse; ropes with which a cannon was lashed to the sides of a ship to prevent its recoil.

breech-loader, *n. breech*-lode-er, a firearm loaded at the breech.

breed, *n.* breed, race or progeny from the same parents or stock; kind: *v.t.* to generate; to cause; to occasion; to produce; to form by education; to bring up; to rear: *v.i.* to bring forth young; to be pregnant; to have birth; to be produced; to raise a breed. **breed in and in,** to breed from nearly related animals. *p.* **bred.** (A.S. *brēdan.*)

breeder, *n.* *breed*-er, one who breeds animals, as a cattle-breeder.

breeding, *n.* *breed*-ing, the act of generating or producing; the raising of a breed; descent; nurture; manners. **good breeding,** politeness.

breeks, *n.* breeks, breeches; trousers. (Scots.)

breeze, *n.* breez, a stinging fly; the gad-fly. (A.S.)

breeze, *n.* breez, a light wind; a gentle gale; a slight quarrel or disturbance; a rumour. **land breeze,** breeze blowing from the land. **sea breeze,** breeze blowing from the sea. (Sp. *brisa*, the N.E. wind.)

breeze, *n.* breez, small cinders; siftings of coke; sweepings. (O.Fr. *brese.*)

breezily, *ad.* *breez*-e-le, in a breezy manner; vivaciously.

breezy, *a.* *breez*-e, fanned by, or subject to, breezes; hearty; jovial; bluff in manner.

bregma, *n.* *breg*-ma, the anterior fontanel of the skull.

brehon, *n.* *bre*-hon, an ancient Irish judge, one to each tribe, and usually hereditary. **Brehon law,** the unwritten common law of Ireland till the early 17th century. (Ir., meaning judge.)

Bren gun, *n.* bren gun, a light machine-gun with detachable barrels, used by infantry. (*Brno*, or Brunn, Czechoslovakia, where first made.)

brent, *n.* brent, the brent goose, *Bernicla brenta.*

bressummer, *n.* *bres*-sum-mer, a beam placed horizontally to support an upper wall or partition [Arch.]. (*Breast*, and Fr. *sommier*, a rafter.)

brethren, *breth*-ren, *n.pl.* of brother; members of the same profession, society, or persuasion.

Breton, *a.* *bret*-on, pertaining to Brittany or the Bretons: *n.* a native of Brittany; the language of ancient Brittany, Armorican. (Fr.)

brettice, *n.* *bret*-is, brattice.

Bretwalda, *n.* bret-*wawl*-da, the title of the chief, for the time being, of the Anglo-Saxon kings. (A.S.)

breve, *n.* breev, a note equal to two semibreves [Mus.]; a mark (˘) over a short syllable. (L. *brevis*, short.)

brevet, *n.* bre-*vet* *or* *brev*-et, a rise in army rank without rise in regimental seniority or pay; nominal rank above real rank; a patent: *a.* taking rank by brevet; nominal. (Fr.)

brevetcy, *n.* *brev*-et-se, rank taken or held by virtue of a brevet.

breviary, *n.* *breev*-ya-re *or* *brev*-ya-re, a book containing the daily service of the Roman Catholic Church. (Fr. *bréviaire.*)

brevier, *n.* bre-*veer*, a type-size between bourgeois and minion, 8-point; so called as used in printing breviaries.

breviped, *a.* *brev*-e-ped, having short legs or feet. (L. *brevis*, and *pes*, foot.)

brevipennate, *a.* *brev*-e-*pen*-nat, short-winged.

brevirostrate, *a.* *brev*-e-*ros*-trat, having a short beak [Zool.].

brevity, *n.* *brev*-e-te, briefness; shortness; conciseness. (L. *brevitas.*)

brew, *v.t.* broo, to make liquor by boiling and fermentation, as from malt and hops; to concoct; to contrive; to plot: *v.i.* to perform the business of brewing; to be forming or collecting. (A.S. *breôwan.*)

brewage, *n.* *broo*-aj, something brewed; a mixture; the process of brewing.

brewer, *n.* *broo*-er, one whose trade is brewing.

brewery, *n.* *broo*-er-re, a building used for brewing.

brewhouse, *n.* *broo*-house, a brewery.

brewing, *n.* *broo*-ing, the process of preparing liquors from malt and hops; quantity brewed at once; a gathering of storm-clouds.

brewis, *n.* *broo*-is, broth, soup. (Fr. *brouet.*)

brewster, *n.* *broo*-ster, a brewer. **Brewster Sessions,** the sessions for granting licences to sell alcoholic drinks.

briar, *n.* *bry*-er, a brier; a plant with a thorny stem; a plant of the genus *Rosa*; the white heath, *Erica arborea*; a tobacco-pipe made from the root of this. (A.S. *brēr.*)

briarean, *a.* bry-*ayr*-re-an, many-handed. (*Briareus*, a hundred-handed giant.)

briared, *a.* bry-erd, set with briars.

briar-root, *n.* *bry*-er-root, root of the tree heath, *Erica arborea.*

briary, *a.* *bry*-er-re, full of briars; rough; thorny.

bribable, *a.* *bribe*-a-bl, open to bribery.

bribe, *n.* bribe, something given or promised, with a view to pervert justice and judgment; anything that seduces: *v.t.* to influence by a bribe. (O.Fr. a lump of bread given as alms.)

bribeless, *a.* *bribe*-less, unbribable.

briber, *n.* *bribe*-er, one who gives or attempts to give a bribe.

bribery, *n.* *bribe*-er-re, the crime of giving or taking bribes.

bric-a-brac, *n.* *brik*-a-brak, curiosities; knick-knacks. (Fr.)

***brick,** *n.* brik, a block of clay and sand burnt hard for building; anything like a brick; a loaf of bread so shaped; a dependable fellow, a good chap [Slang]: *a.* made of, or like, brick: *v.t.* to lay or pave with brick; to imitate brick in plaster. **brick up,** block or enclose with brickwork. (Fr. *brique.*)

brickbat, *n.* *brik*-bat, half a brick; a piece or fragment of a brick.

brick-clay, *n.* *brik*-klay, clay suitable for making bricks.

brickdust, *n.* *brik*-dust, finely ground sandstone.

brick-earth, *n.* *brik*-erth, earth used for brick-making.

brickfield, *n.* *brik*-feeld, a brickyard.

brick-kiln, *n.* *brik*-kiln, a kiln for burning bricks.

bricklayer, *n.* *brik*-lay-er, an artisan who lays or sets bricks.

brickle, *a.* *brik*-kl, brittle; fragile; uncertain.

brick-nogging, *n.* *brik*-nog-ging, brickwork carried up and fitted in between timber framing [Arch.].

brick-red, *a.* *brik*-red, greyish red.

brick-tea, *n.* *brik*-tee, tea compressed into blocks, esp. for camel transport.

brickwork, *n.* *brik*-wurk, builders' work in brick; the laying of bricks.

bricky, *a.* *brik*-e, full of, formed of, or like bricks.

brickyard, *n.* *brik*-yard, a place where bricks are made.

bricole, *n.* *brik*-ole, the bounce of a tennis ball from the wall of the court; a shot off the cushion in billiards; a form of ballista; an apparatus to enable guns to be dragged over ground impassable to horses. (Fr.)

bridal, *a.* *bride*-al, pertaining to a bride or a wedding: *n.* the nuptial ceremony; a nuptial feast. (A.S. *bryd*, and *ealo*, ale, hence a bride-feast.)

bride, *n.* bride, a woman on her wedding-day and during her honeymoon. (A.S. *bryd.*)

bridecake, *n.* *bride*-kake, a rich cake for distribution among the guests at a wedding.

bridechamber, *n.* *bride*-chame-ber, the nuptial apartment.

bridegroom, *n.* *bride*-groom, a man on his wedding-day and during his honeymoon.

bridesmaid, *n.* *bridez*-mayd, an unmarried girl-friend who attends on the bride at a wedding.

bridesman, *n.* *bridez*-man, a man attendant on a bridegroom and bride.

bridewell, *n.* *bride*-wel, a house of correction; so called from the palace (*cap.*) near St. Bride's or Bridget's Well off Fleet Street, London, which was turned into a penitentiary.

bridewort, *n.* *bride*-wurt, the meadowsweet.

***bridge,** *n.* bridj, a structure thrown over a river, etc., as a roadway across; anything like a bridge, as the supporter of the strings of a violin; a rest for a billiard cue; the bony part of the nose; the part connecting the lens frames in a pair of spectacles; a gangway; a raised platform across a ship's deck: *v.t.* to build a bridge over. **Wheatstone bridge,** a device for measuring electrical resistance (named from its inventor and the bridge of wire forming a connection). (A.S. *bricg.*)

bridge, *n.* bridj, a variety of whist of Russian origin, introduced as bridge-whist and later developed into auction-bridge and contract.

bridgeboard, *n.* *bridj*-bord, a board supporting stair-ends.

bridge-head, *n.* *bridj*-hed, a fortification defending that end of a bridge nearest the enemy [Mil.].

bridge-train, *n.* *bridj*-trane, a company of engineers with their apparatus for bridge-making [Mil.].

bridle, *n.* *bry*-dl, the head-stall, bit and reins of a horse; a curb; a check: *v.t.* to put a bridle upon; to guide by a bridle; to check; to control: *v.i.* to hold up the head and draw in the chin in real or affected pride or scorn. (A.S.)

bridle-hand, *n.* *bry*-dl-hand, the hand that holds the reins; the left hand.
bridlepath, *n.* *bry*-dl-pahth, a bridle-way.
bridle-rein, *n.* *bry*-dl-rayn, the thong of a bridle.
bridle-way, *n.* *bry*-dl-way, a road too narrow for carts; a horse-track.
bridoon, *n.* brid-*oon*, the snaffle of a military bridle and its rein. (Fr.)
brief, *a.* breef, short; concise: *n.* a short statement, esp. [Law] of a client's case for the instruction of counsel, or [Mil.] of a plan of operations for any offensive action; [Law.] a writ or summons; a letter patent, authorizing a collection of money in churches for a charitable purpose; a papal letter: *v.t.* to give a brief to a barrister, or to an air-crew, commando, etc. **in brief,** in a few words. **watching brief,** the brief of counsel attending a hearing on behalf of a client indirectly concerned. (Fr. *bref.*)
briefless, *a.* *breef*-less, without a brief or client.
briefly, *ad.* *breef*-le, in a brief manner.
briefness, *n.* *breef*-ness, the quality of being brief.
brier, *n.* *bry*-er, briar.
brig, *n.* brig, a vessel with two masts, both square-rigged. (Short for *brigantine.*)
brigade, *n.* bre-*gade*, an army subdivision, of varying composition at different dates and in different armies, commanded by a general officer; a group of batteries of artillery; an organized body, usually with a uniform: *v.t.* to form into a brigade. (Fr.)
brigade-major, *n.* bre-*gade-may*-jor, an officer who assists the brigadier in the management of his brigade.
brigadier, *n.* brig-a-*deer*, the officer commanding a brigade, ranking above colonel and below major-general.
brigand, *n.* *brig*-and, a robber; an outlaw; one of a gang of bandits. (Fr.)
brigandage, *n.* *brig*-an-daj, highway robbery; the occupation or practices of a brigand.
brigandine, *n.* *brig*-an-deen, a tunic armoured with rings or plates. (Fr.)
brigantine, *n.* *brig*-an-teen, a two-masted vessel, square-rigged on the foremast and fore-and-aft rigged on the mainmast; a swift-sailing vessel, formerly used by pirates. (Fr.)
★**bright,** *a.* brite, shining; full of light; brilliant; clear; glorious; cheerful; happy; quick in intellect; witty; lively. (A.S. *beorht.*)
brighten, *v.t.* *bry*-tn, to make bright or brighter; to make gay or cheerful, acute or witty: *v.i.* to grow bright; to clear up (of the weather).
brightly, *ad.* *brite*-le, in a bright manner.
brightness, *n.* *brite*-ness, the state of being bright.
Bright's disease, *n.* *bryts*-de-*zeez*, acute and chronic nephritis. (Dr. Richard *Bright*, *d.* 1858.)
brightsome, *a.* *brite*-sum, bright; cheery.
brigue, *n.* breeg, a cabal; intrigue; strife.
brill, *n.* bril, a smooth flat fish of the turbot family.
brillante, *a.* bril-*lan*-tay, gay: *ad.* in lively manner [Mus.]. (It.)
brilliance, *n.* *bril*-yance, brilliancy.
brilliancy, *n.* *bril*-yan-se, the quality of being brilliant.
brilliant, *a.* *bril*-yant, shining; sparkling; splendid: *n.* a diamond of the finest cut, formed into facets, so as to display great brilliancy. (Fr. *brilliant*, glittering.)
brilliantine, *n.* *bril*-yan-teen, an oily preparation for imparting gloss to the hair.
brilliantly, *ad.* *bril*-yant-le, in a brilliant manner.
brilliantness, *n.* *bril*-yant-ness, the state of being brilliant; brilliancy.
brim, *n.* brim, the upper edge of a vessel; the brink of a fountain or river; margin; the edging of a hat: *v.t.* to fill to the top: *v.i.* to be full to the top. **brim over,** flow over. (M.E. *brymme*, edge of the sea.)
brimful, *a.* *brim*-ful, full to the top; completely full.
brimless, *a.* *brim*-less, having no brim.
brimmed, *a.* brimd, with a brim; up to the brim.
brimmer, *n.* *brim*-mer, a bowl full to the top.
brimming, *a.* *brim*-ming, full to the top or brim.
brimstone, *n.* *brim*-ston, sulphur. **brimstone butterfly, moth,** a sulphur coloured butterfly (*Gonepteryx rhamni*) or moth (*Rumia cratægata*). (M.E. *bren*, burn, and *stone.*)
brin, *n.* brin, a rib of a fan. (Fr.)
brindle, *n.* *brin*-dl, the state of being brindled: *a.* tawny.
brindled, *a.* *brin*-dld, brown marked with dull coloured streaks. (*brand.*)
brine, *n.* brine, water saturated with salt; the sea; tears: *v.t.* to steep in brine; to pickle. (A.S.)
brine-pan, *n.* *brine*-pan, a pit of salt water, where salt is formed by evaporation.
brine-pit, *n.* *brine*-pit, a pit or well of salt water.
bring, *v.t.* bring, to fetch; to carry; to conduct; to lead; to cause to come; to induce; to prevail upon. **bring about,** bring to pass; effect. **bring back,** recall. **bring down,** humble or abase. **bring forth,** give birth to; produce; bring to light. **bring forward,** produce; adduce; show off (a child); continue from a preceding page. **bring in,** import; introduce; place in a particular condition; yield. **bring off,** convey from; procure to be acquitted; carry to a successful conclusion; cause to escape. **bring on,** cause to begin; originate or cause to exist; aid in advancing. **bring out,** introduce; exhibit, or cause to exhibit; publish; expose. **bring over,** convert; cause to change sides. **bring to,** restore to consciousness; check the course of a ship by trimming the sails. **bring under,** subdue; restrain; reduce to obedience. **bring up,** nurse; educate; feed and clothe; cause to advance near; cast anchor [Naut.]. *p.* and *pp.* **brought.** (A.S. *bringan.*)
brinish, *a.* *brine*-ish, like brine; briny; saltish.
brinishness, *n.* *brine*-ish-ness, quality of being saltish.
brinjal, *n.* *brin*-jawl, the fruit of the egg-plant.
brink, *n.* bringk, the edge or margin of a steep place or of a body of water; verge. (Scand.)
briny, *a.* *brine*-e, partaking of the nature of brine; salt. **the briny,** the sea.
brio, *n.* *bree*-o, vivacity; spirit [Mus.]. (It.)
brioche, *n.* *bree*-ohsh, a cake of light flaky pastry; a sponge-cake. (Fr.)
briony, *n.* *bry*-o-ne, bryony.
briquette, *n.* bre-*ket*, a block of small coal or compressed coal-dust. (Fr.)
brisance, *n.* (App.), the shattering quality or effect of certain explosives. (Fr.)
brisk, *a.* brisk, lively; active; full of spirit; effervescing; burning freely: *v.t.* to make brisk; to freshen. **to brisk up,** to come up with life and speed; to dress smartly. (Origin doubtful.)
brisket, *n.* *bris*-ket, the breast of an animal, or the part of the breast next the ribs. (O.Fr. *bruschet.*)
briskly, *ad.* *brisk*-le, in a brisk manner.
briskness, *n.* *brisk*-ness, the quality of being brisk.
brisling, *n.* *bris*-ling, a sardine-like food-fish of Norwegian waters.
brisque, *n.* *breesk*, a card of enhanced value in certain games, esp. bèzique.
bristle, *n.* *bris*-sl, the stiff hair of swine; a short stiff hair on an unshaven face; a hairy pubescence on plants: *v.t.* to cause to bristle up; to fix a bristle: *v.i.* to stand erect as bristles; to show anger or defiance. (M.E. *bristel.*)
bristle-tail, *n.* *bris*-sl-tale, wingless insect belonging to the order Thysanura.
bristliness, *n.* *bris*-le-ness, quality of being bristly.
bristling, *n.* *bris*-tling, brisling.
bristly, *a.* *bris*-le, thick set with bristles; rough.
Bristol-board, *n.* *bris*-tl-board, a fine smooth cardboard.
Bristol-brick, *n.* *bris*-tl-*brik*, a brick for cleaning cutlery; bath-brick.
Bristol-diamond, *n.* *bris*-tl-*dy*-a-mond, rock crystal found near Bristol.
Bristol-fashion, *n.* *bris*-tl-*fash*-on, *ad.* in good order; shipshape [Naut.].
Bristol-stone, *n.* *bris*-tl-stone, Bristol-diamond.
brit, *n.* brit, the fry of herring, sprats, and other fish, often sold as whitebait.
Britannia-metal, *n.* bre-*tan*-ya-*met*-tl, a white alloy of tin, antimony, and copper, sometimes with zinc and bismuth.
Britannic, *a.* bre-*tan*-nik, British. (L. *Britannicus.*)
Briticism, *n.* *brit*-e-sizm, an idiom or usage current in Great Britain but not in the United States.
British, *a.* *brit*-ish, pertaining to ancient Britain or to Great Britain, the British Empire, or their inhabitants. **the British,** British people. **British Thermal Unit,** *see* **thermal.** (A.S. *Bryttisc* British.)

Britisher, *n.* *brit*-e-sher, an American term for a native of Great Britain.
Britishness, *n.* *brit*-ish-ness, the quality or character peculiar to the British.
Briton, *n.* *brit*-on, a native of Britain; one of the race living in South Britain before the Anglo-Saxon conquest; a native of the British Empire.
brittle, *a.* *brit*-tl, apt to break; fragile; not tough. (A.S. *breotan*, to break.)
brittleness, *n.* *brit*-tl-ness, the state of being brittle.
brittle-star, *n.* *brit*-tl-star, a long-armed starfish.
britzka, *n.* *britch*-ka, an open carriage with a folding hood and space to recline in. (Polish.)
broach, *n.* broach, an awl; a bodkin; a drill bit; a tool for reaming and countersinking; a young stag's first horn; a broach-spire; a roasting spit: *v.t.* to pierce, as a cask, in order to draw off the liquor; to open up; to start; to mention as a subject for conversation. **broach to,** to incline suddenly to windward [Naut.]. (Fr. *brocher*, to pierce.)
broacher, *n.* *broach*-er, a first enunciator or publisher of a new idea.
broach-spire, *n.* *broach*-spire, a spire rising directly and not from within a parapet.
broad, *a.* brawd, wide; large; extensive; vast; not narrow; liberal; full; open; unconfined; bold; gross; indelicate: *n.* the broad part of a thing; a freshwater lake or expansion of a river's course. **as broad as it is long,** the same, whichever way. **broad church,** that section of the Church of England which inclines to liberal opinions, and is opposed to those who would narrow either spirit or form. (A.S. *brad.*)
broad-arrow, *n.* brawd-*a*-ro, the arrow-head mark of British Government property.
broad-awake, *a.* brawd-a-*wake*, fully awake.
broad-axe, *n.* *brawd*-aks, an ancient military weapon; an axe for hewing timber.
broadbean, *n.* *brawd*-been, the fruit of *Vicia faba.*
broadbill, *n.* *brawd*-bill, the shoveller duck; the spoonbill, a species of *Platalea*; and other birds.
broadbrim, *n.* *brawd*-brim, a broad-brimmed Quaker hat; a Quaker.
broadcast, *n.* *brawd*-kahst, the sowing of seed at large by hand [Agr.]; radio transmission; a radio programme: *a.* sown by the hand at large; wide-scattered; disseminated by wireless: *ad.* by scattering at large or widely: *v.t.* to transmit by radio or by wireless telephony, etc., to an unlimited number of receiving stations: *v.i.* to disseminate (announcements, news, entertainment, etc.) by wireless.
broadcaster, *n.* *brawd*-kahs-ter, one who broadcasts; a wireless announcer; a broadcasting company or instrument.
broadcloth, *n.* *brawd*-kloth, a fine napped and calendered woollen cloth.
broaden, *v.i.* *braw*-dn, to grow broad or broader; to spread: *v.t.* to make broad.
broad-gauge, *n.* *brawd*-gaje, distance more than 4 ft. 8½ in. between the rails of a railway.
broadish, *a.* *brawd*-ish, rather broad.
broadly, *ad.* *brawd*-le, in a broad manner.
broadness, *n.* *brawd*-ness, the quality of being broad; coarseness; vulgarity.
broad-seal, *n.* *brawd*-seel, the great or official seal of any Government; the national seal.
broadsheet, *n.* *brawd*-sheet, a large sheet of printed paper; a broadside blank on the back.
broadside, *n.* *brawd*-side, the side of a ship; discharge of all the guns on one side at once; a sheet printed on one side.
broad-spoken, *a.* brawd-*spoh*-ken, speaking plainly or coarsely or rudely.
broadsword, *n.* *brawd*-sawrd, a broad-bladed sword; a claymore; a soldier armed with this.
broadways, *ad.* *brawd*-wayz, broadwise.
broadwise, *ad.* *brawd*-wize, along the breadth.
brobdingnagian, *a.* brob-ding-*nay*-je-an, gigantic: *n.* a gigantic person; properly a native of Brobdingnag in "Gulliver's Travels," by Swift.
brocade, *n.* bro-*kade*, silk stuff woven with raised patterns and gold and silver threads: *v.t.* to make, or to embellish with, brocade. (Sp. *brocado.*)
brocard, *n.* *brok*-ard, or *broh*-kard, an accepted maxim or principle. (*Burchard*, an 11th-cent. compiler of ecclesiastical canons.)

broccoli, *n.* *brok*-o-le, a hardy variety of the cauliflower. (It., sprouts.)
broch, *n.* brokh, one of the prehistoric circular stone towers built as habitations by the Picts of Northern Scotland.
brochantite, *n.* *brok*-an-tite, a basic copper sulphate. (From *Brochan* de Villiers, Fr. mineralogist, *d.* 1840.)
brochure, *n.* bro-*shoor*, a stitched pamphlet. (Fr.)
brock, *n.* brok, a badger; a brocket. (Celt.)
brocked, *a.* brokt, coloured black and white. (Scots.)
brocket, *n.* *brok*-et, a red deer two years old; a small S. American deer. (Fr. *brocart.*)
brodekin, *n.* *brode*-kin, a buskin, or half-boot. (Fr.)
brog, *n.* brog, an awl: *v.t.* to pierce. (Dial. Eng.)
brogue, *n.* brohg, a low, leather shoe; a dialect pronunciation, esp. that of the Irish when speaking English. (Ir. *brog*, a shoe.)
broider, *v.t.* *broyd*-er, to embroider. (O.Fr. *broder.*)
broil, *n.* broyl, a tumult; a noisy quarrel; discord.
broil, *v.t.* broyl, to cook over, or in front of, the fire, generally upon a gridiron: *v.i.* to be greatly heated; to sweat with heat. (Origin uncertain.)
broiler, *n.* *broyl*-er, one who or that which broils; a gridiron; food for broiling.
broiling, *a.* *broyl*-ing, extremely hot; sweating.
brokage, *n.* *broh*-kaj, brokerage.
broke, broke, *pp.* of break: *a.* penniless; ruined; dismissed from the army.
broke, *v.i.* broke, to transact business for others; to act as broker.
★**broken,** *pp.* *broke*-en, in fragments; not whole; infirm; crushed; violated; intermittent.
broken-backed, *a.* *broke*-en-bakt, having the back broken.
broken-down, *a.* *broke*-en-doun, ruined; decrepit; useless.
broken-hearted, *a.* *broke*-en-*har*-ted, crushed in spirit with grief.
brokenly, *ad.* *broke*-en-le, in a broken manner.
broken-meat, *n.* *broke*-en-meet, the remains of a repast.
brokenness, *n.* *broke*-en-ness, the state of being broken.
broken-winded, *a.* *broke*-en-*win*-ded, having diseased or defective respiratory organs; habitually short of breath.
broker, *n.* *broke*-er, one who buys and sells, especially stocks or shares, for others; a dealer in secondhand household goods, clothes, etc.; a go-between; a pimp. (M.E. *brocor.*)
brokerage, *n.* *broke*-er-raj, the business of a broker; the commission charged by him on a transaction.
broking, *n.* *broke*-ing, the trade of a broker.
brolly, *n.* *brol*-le, an umbrella [Slang].
bromal, *n.* *brome*-al, a colourless oily fluid obtained by the action of bromine on alcohol.
bromate, *n.* *brome*-ate, a salt of bromic acid.
brome-grass, *n.* *brome*-grahs, a coarse oat-like grass of which one kind is used for forage.
Bromelia, *n.* broh-*mee*-le-a, a genus of tropical American plants allied to the pineapple.
bromic, *a.* *brome*-ik, pertaining to or containing bromine.
bromide, *n.* *brome*-ide, one of the compounds of bromine with a base, some of which are powerful sedatives; hence, a sedative; a tiresome person, a trite saying [Slang]. **bromide paper,** sensitized paper for producing prints by artificial light [Phot.].
bromine, *n.* *brome*-in, a deep red, malodorous, poisonous, fluid, non-metallic element extracted from sea-water. (Gr. *bromos*, a stench.)
bromism, *n.* *brome*-izm, a diseased condition due to excessive use of bromine or its compounds.
bromize, *v.t.* *brome*-ize, to treat with bromine or with a bromide [Phot., Med.].
bronchi, *n.pl.* *brong*-ky, the ramifications of the windpipe, which carry air into the lungs. (Gr. and L.)
bronchial, *a.* *brong*-ke-al, pertaining to the windpipe.
bronchitis, *n.* brong-*ky*-tis, inflammation of the bronchial tubes. (Gr. *bronchos*, windpipe.)
bronchocele, *n.* *brong*-ko-seel, goitre. (Gr. *bronchos*, and *kele*, a swelling.)
bronchoscope, *n.* *brong*-ko-skope, an instrument for visual inspection of the bronchi [Med.].
bronchotomy, *n.* brong-*kot*-om-e, tracheotomy.

bronco, *n.* *brong*-ko, an unbroken horse. (Sp., rough.)
brontosaurus, *n.* *bront*-o-*saw*-rus, a gigantic herbivorous dinosaur of the Jurassic period.
bronze, *n.* bronz, a brownish alloy of copper with tin and usually a little zinc or lead; a colour to imitate bronze; a work of art cast in bronze: *v.t.* to make like bronze in appearance of colour: *v.i.* to become tanned or brown. **Bronze Age,** the period following the Stone and preceding the Iron Age, when bronze implements were in use [Archæol.] (Fr., from Lat. *aes Brundisinum*, brass from Brindisi.)
bronze-powder, *n.* *bronz*-poud-er, a metallic powder for imitating bronze.
bronzewing, *n.* *bron*-zwing, the Australian pigeon, *Phaps chalcoptera.*
bronzite, *n.* *bron*-zite, a variety of diallage [Min.].
bronzy, *a.* *bron*-ze, having a bronze-like appearance or character.
brooch, *n.* broach, an ornamental clasp with a pin and catch. (Fr. *broche.*)
brood, *n.* brood, the number of birds hatched at once; offspring; that which is bred: *v.t.* to sit over and cover; to hatch; to cherish or foster with care; *v.i.* to sit on in order to hatch; to cover with the wings; to continue anxiously pondering. (A.S. *brōd.*)
brooding, *a.* *brood*-ing, deeply pondering.
brood-mare, *n.* *brood*-mare, a mare kept for breeding.
broody, *a.* *brood*-e, wanting to hatch eggs; inclined to brood; sullen.
brook, *n.* brook, a small stream. (A.S. *brôc*, a spring.)
brook, *v.t.* brook, to bear; to put up with; to endure. (A.S. *brūcan*, to use.)
brooklet, *n.* *brook*-let, a small brook.
brooklime, *n.* *brook*-lime, a species of speedwell found in ditches. (*brook*, and A.S. *hleomoc*, hemlock.)
brooky, *a.* *brook*-e, abounding with brooks.
broom, *n.* broom, a yellow-flowered shrub of either of the genera *Cytisus* or *Genista*; a long-handled besom, originally made of broom twigs: *v.t.* to sweep with a broom. (A.S. *brom.*)
broom-corn, *n.* *broom*-kawrn, a species of *Sorghum*, of which brooms and brushes are made.
broom-rape, *n.* *broom*-rape, strangleweed, a plant of the genus *Orobanche.*
broomstick, *n.* *broom*-stik, the staff or handle of a broom.
broomy, *a.* *broom*-e, abounding in broom; consisting of broom.
brose, *n.* broze, a Scottish dish made by pouring boiling water on oatmeal. **Athole brose,** a mixture of honey and whisky. (Scots.)
broth, *n.* broth, liquor in which flesh has been boiled. **a broth of a boy** [Irish], a reckless fellow. (A.S.)
brothel, *n.* *broth*-el, a house appropriated to the purposes of prostitution. (A.S.)
★**brother,** *n.* *bruth*-er (*pl.* **brothers** *or* **brethren**), a son of the same father and mother; any one closely connected; an associate; one of the same profession or society; one who resembles another; a fellow-creature. **half brother,** a son of the same parent, either father or mother. (A.S.)
brother-german, *n.* *bruth*-er-*jer*-man, a full brother.
brotherhood, *n.* *bruth*-er-hood, the relationship of brother; brotherly affection; a fraternity; an association.
brother-in-law, *n.* *bruth*-er-in-law, the brother of a husband or wife, or a sister's husband.
brotherless, *a.* *broth*-er-less, without a brother.
brotherlike, *a.* *bruth*-er-like, as a brother; affectionate.
brotherliness, *n.* *bruth*-er-le-ness, state of being brotherly.
brotherly, *a.* *bruth*-er-le, suitable to a brother; fraternal: *ad.* as a brother; fraternally.
brother-uterine, *n.* *bruth*-er-*yoo*-ter-ine, a brother on the mother's side only.
brougham, *n.* broom, a one-horse, four-wheeled, closed carriage named after Lord Brougham.
brought, brawt, *p.* and *pp.* of bring.
brow, *n.* brou, the ridge over the eyes; the arch of hair that covers it; the forehead; the general air of the countenance; the edge of a slope or top of a hill. **knit the brows,** to frown. (A.S. *brū.*)
brow, *n.* brou, a movable gangway from the ship to the wharf.
brow-antler, *n.* *brou*-ant-ler, the branch of an antler nearest the head.
browbeat, *v.t.* *brou*-beet, to overbear by word or look; to bully.
★**brown,** *a.* broun, of a dusky colour, inclining to red: *n.* a colour of various shades, resulting from a mixture of red, black, and yellow: *v.t.* to make brown: *v.i.* to become brown; to get tanned in the sun. **brown bear,** *Ursus arctos*, a large bear, widely distributed in N. Europe and Asia. **brown bess,** a flint-lock musket. **brown bread,** bread of unbolted flour; bread with Indian meal mixed in it. **brown study,** absent-minded reverie. **browned off,** thoroughly tired of or fed up with; disgruntled [Slang]. (A.S. *brūn.*)
brownbill, *n.* *broun*-bil, a halberd in military use in the 16th and 17th centuries.
brown-coal, *n.* *broun*-koal, wood coal or lignite.
Brownian, *a.* *brou*-ne-an; **Brownian motion,** the vibratory movement of minute particles when suspended in a fluid. (Dr. Robert *Brown*, Scots. botanist, *d.* 1858.)
brownie, *n.* *broun*-e, a good-natured domestic elf; (*cap.*) a junior member of the Girl Guides.
browning, *n.* *broun*-ing, the process by which a brown colour is imparted to various articles of iron; a brown liquid, largely prepared from burnt sugar, used as colouring in cookery.
Browning, *n.* *broun*-ing, a type of automatic pistol or rifle. (Named from Amer. inventor.)
brownish, *a.* *broun*-ish, somewhat brown.
Brownist, *n.* *broun*-ist, an Independent or Congregationalist, so called from Robert Brown, an early 17th-cent. leader of the denomination.
brownness, *n.* *broun*-ness, the shade of brown colour.
brown-rust, *n.* *broun*-rust, a disease in wheat due to the fungus *Puccinia graminis.*
brown-spar, *n.* *broun*-spahr, a variety of dolomite.
browse, *n.* brouz, the tender branches of trees and shrubs, fit for cattle to eat; the act of browsing: *v.t.* to nibble and eat: *v.i.* to feed on the shoots and leaves of shrubs and trees; to read haphazard or desultorily. (O.Fr. *broust*, a sprout.)
brucine, *n.* *broo*-sin, a bitter poisonous vegetable alkaloid, present in nux vomica. (After James *Bruce*, *d.* 1794, African explorer.)
brucite, *n.* *broo*-site, a hydrate of magnesia; a compound silicate and fluoride of magnesia. (A. *Bruce*, Amer. mineralogist.)
bruckle, *a.* brukl, fragile, brittle [Scots.].
Bruin, *n.* *broo*-in, a name for a bear. (Dut., brown.)
bruise, *n.* brooz, discoloration of the skin caused by a blow: *v.t.* to crush by beating, pounding, or squeezing; to injure so as to discolour; to contuse; a hurt with a blunt or heavy instrument; a contusion. (A.S. *brysan.*)
bruiser, *n.* *brooze*-er, one that bruises; a boxer.
bruit, *n.* broot, report; rumour: *v.t.* to report; to noise abroad. (Fr. *bruit*, noise.)
brumal, *a.* *broo*-mal, wintry; pertaining to the winter. (L. *bruma*, winter.)
brumby, *n.* *brum*-be, a wild horse [Australian].
brume, *n.* broom, fog. (L. *bruma.*)
Brummagem, *a.* *brum*-a-jem, sham; cheap. (*Birmingham*, celebrated for its plated and cheap ware.)
brumous, *a.* *broo*-mus, wintry; foggy.
brunch, *n.* brunch, a meal combining breakfast and lunch [Slang].
brunette, *n.* broo-*net*, a woman with dark hair and brownish complexion: *a.* with dark eyes and hair. (Fr.)
Brunonian, *a.* broo-*noh*-ne-an, according to John Brown, an 18th-cent. Edinburgh physician. **Brunonian theory,** a doctrine which regards and treats diseases as due either to defective or excessive excitation.
Brunswick-black, *n.* *brunz*-wik-blak, a compound of asphaltum, linseed oil, and oil of turpentine, used as a black varnish for ironwork.
Brunswick-green, *n.* *brunz*-wik-green, a pigment of copper carbonate or copper chloride.
brunt, *n.* brunt, the fiercest attack: the shock.

★**brush,** *n.* brush, an implement for sweeping, dusting, etc., generally made of bristles, twigs, or feathers; a tool for painting, colouring, whitewashing, etc., made of hair; brushwood; a thicket; a skirmish, or slight encounter; a bushy tail, particularly of a fox; the brush-like discharge of electric sparks; an appliance for conducting current to or from the armature of a dynamo [Elect.]: *v.t.* to sweep or scrub with a brush; to touch slightly in passing; to remove by brushing: *v.i.* to move with haste; to skim over. (O.Fr. *brosse.*)

brushiness, *n.* *brush*-e-ness, the quality of being brushy.

brush-turkey, *n.* *brush*-tur-ke, an Australasian mound-building bird of the megapode family.

brush-wheel, *n.* *brush*-wheel, a wheel turning a similar wheel by means of cloth, buff leather, or other material affixed to the circumference of each.

brushwood, *n.* *brush*-wood, underwood; close thicket; branches of trees cut off.

brushy, *a.* *brush*-e, rough or shaggy, like a brush; covered with brushwood.

brusque, *a.* brusk *or* broosk, rude; blunt; abrupt in manner. (Fr.)

brusquely, *ad.* *brusk*-le *or* *broosk*-le, in a brusque manner.

brusqueness, *n.* brusk-ness *or* *broosk*-ness, the quality of being brusque.

Brussels-sprouts, *n.pl.* *brus*-selz-sprouts, miniature cabbages, which sprout from an upright stem or stalk.

brutal, *a.* *broo*-tal, pertaining to or like a brute; savage; cruel; inhuman; blunt; sensual.

brutalism, *n.* *broo*-tal-izm, brutality.

brutalitarian, *a.* broo-tal-e-*tare*-re-an, advocating systematic brutality or practising this: *n.* one who does this.

brutality, *n.* bru-*tal*-e-te, quality of being brutal; a brutal act.

brutalize, *v.t.* *broo*-tal-ize, to make like a brute: *v.i.* to become brutal.

brutally, *ad.* *broo*-tal-le, in a brutal manner.

brute, *a.* broot, senseless; unconscious; irrational; brute-like; sensual; unintelligent: *n.* a mammal other than a man; a brutal person; a savage; a low-bred, unfeeling man. (L. *brutus,* irrational.)

brutify, *v.t.* *broo*-te-fy, to render brutal; to brutalize; to make unfeeling.

brutish, *a.* *broot*-ish, like a brute; stupid; unfeeling; gross; bestial.

brutishly, *ad.* *broot*-ish-le, in a brutish manner.

brutishness, *n.* *broot*-ish-ness, the quality of being brutal; brutish character.

brutism, *n.* *broot*-izm, brutishness.

bryologist, *n.* bry-*ol*-o-jist, a student of mosses.

bryology, *n.* bry-*ol*-oj-e, the science or the study of mosses. (Gr. *bruon,* moss, *logos,* science.)

bryony, *n.* *bry*-o-ne, a genus of climbing plants, including **black bryony,** *Tamus communis,* and **white bryony,** *Bryonia dioica.* (L. *bryōnia.*)

bryophyte, *n.* *bry*-o-fyt, any of the *Bryophyta,* the group comprising the mosses and liverworts [Bot.]. (Gr. *bruon,* moss, *phyton,* plant.)

bryozoa, *n.* bry-o-*zoh*-a, the polyzoa. (Gr. *bruon,* moss, *zōon,* animal.)

Brythonic, *a.* bry-*thon*-ik, pertaining to the Celtic races of ancient Britain, or to the ancient Cornish, Welsh, or Breton languages. (W., Briton.)

bub, *n.* bub, drink, esp. strong malt liquor. (Slang.)

bubalis, *n.* *bew*-ba-lis, a large antelope of North Africa and the Near East.

bubble, *n.* *bub*-bl, a sphere or blob of water or other fluid, filled with air or gas; a cavity in a solid that has been liquid, as ice, cast metal, glass, etc.; anything that wants firmness or solidity; a fraudulent scheme: *v.i.* to rise in bubbles; to run with a gurgling noise: *v.t.* to cause to bubble; to cheat. **bubble and squeak,** a réchauffé of fried cabbage and potato. (From the sound.)

bubbling, *n.* *bub*-bl-ing, the sound of boiling or flowing water.

bubbly, *a.* *bub*-bl-e, full of bubbles: *n.* champagne [Slang].

bubbly-jock, *n.* *bub*-ble-jok, a turkey-cock. (Scots.)

bubo, *n.* *bew*-bo, an inflammatory swelling in the groin or armpit [Med.]. (Gr. *bubon,* the groin.)

bubonic, *n.* bew-*bon*-ik, characterized by buboes. **bubonic plague,** a malignant contagious disease transmitted by rats, fleas, etc.

bubonocele, *n.* bew-*bon*-o-seel, a rupture in the groin. (Gr. *bubon,* and *kele,* a tumour.)

buccal, *a.* *buk*-kal, pertaining to the cheek. (L. *bucca,* the cheek.)

buccaneer, *n.* buk-ka-*neer,* one of the English and French pirates who, in the 17th and 18th cents., made depredations on the Spaniards in America; a freebooter: *v.t.* to play the pirate. (Fr. *boucanier,* from Brazilian *boucan,* a frame on which meat was smoked and roasted.)

buccinator, *n.* buk-se-*nay*-tor, a muscle of the cheek, used in blowing [Anat.]. (L. *buccina,* a trumpet.)

bucentaur, *n.* bew-*sen*-tawr, the state barge of the doges of Venice. (It.; etymology doubtful.)

bucephalus, *n.* bew-*sef*-al-us, a riding-horse. (From the celebrated horse of Alexander the Great.)

Buchmanite, *n.* *buk*-ma-nite, a follower of Frank Buchman (*b.* 1878), the American founder of the quasi-religious movement propagated in England by the Oxford Group.

buck, *n.* buk, lye, in which clothes are soaked in bleaching, or in which they are washed: *v.t.* to soak or wash in lye. **buck-basket,** a clothes basket. (M.E. *bouken.*)

buck, *n.* buk, the male of the fallow deer, antelope, rabbit, etc.; a fop or dashing young man; a male Negro; boastful talk [Slang]; swagger [Slang]; an object which, when possessed by the dealer, entails the declaration of a jack-pot; a dollar [U.S.A. slang]: *v.i.* to jump up and down. **to buck up,** to exert oneself; to cheer up. **to pass the buck,** to shift the responsibility to someone else [Slang]. (A.S. *buc.*)

buck, *n.* buk, a wickerwork eel trap. (Dial. Eng.)

buckbean, *n.* *buk*-been, a water plant of the genus *Menyanthes.*

buckboard, *n.* *buk*-bord, a four-wheeled vehicle in which the seats rest on a spring-board stretching from axle to axle.

★**bucket,** *n.* *buk*-et, a pail; a vessel for drawing or holding water, and other purposes; a bucketful; the scoop of a dredger, mechanical navvy, etc.; the holder of a carbine slung from a saddle; a whip-socket: *v.t.* to draw in buckets; to ride a horse furiously; to row hurriedly. (Origin uncertain.)

bucketful, *n.* *buk*-et-ful, as much as a bucket will hold.

bucket-shop, *n.* *buk*-et-shop, an office for speculating in stocks and shares.

buckeye, *n.* *buk*-eye, a horse-chestnut of the United States, *Æsculus ohioensis.*

buckhound, *n.* *buk*-hound, a variety of deerhound.

buckie, *n.* *buk*-e, the shell of the whelk. (Scots.)

buckish, *a.* *buk*-ish, pertaining to a buck; foppish.

buckism, *n.* *buk*-izm, the quality of a buck or fop; foppery; swagger.

buck-jump, *n.* *buk*-jump, a leap from the ground like that of a buck made by a vicious or untrained horse: *v.i.* to leap thus.

buck-jumper, *n.* *buk*-jump-er, a horse or mule given to buck-jumping.

buckle, *n.* *buk*-kl, a metal clasp having a tongue for fastening straps, etc.; a curl of hair, or the state of the hair crisped and curled: *v.t.* to fasten with a buckle; to prepare for action; to join in battle; to confine; to curl: *v.i.* to bend; to wrinkle. **buckle to,** apply oneself to with vigour. **buckle with,** engage with in close combat. (O.Fr. *bocle.*)

buckler, *n.* *buk*-ler, a small round shield with a boss in the centre; any protection. (O.Fr. *bucler.*)

buckler-thorn, *n.* *buk*-ler-thorn, Christ's thorn, a species of *Paliurus,* the seeds buckler-shaped.

buckra, *n.* *buk*-ra, a negro name for the white man, signifying master.

buckram, *n.* *buk*-ram, a coarse cloth of linen, jute, or cotton stiffened with gum: *a.* stiff; formal. (O. Fr. *boucaran.*)

bucksaw, *n.* *buk*-saw, a frame-saw.

buckshee, *a.* *buk*-shee, given away, obtained without payment, extra; *n.* anything obtained without payment [Slang]; a military paymaster [E. India]. (Persian *bakhshi.*)

buckshot, *n.* *buk*-shot, a large-size shot for sporting guns.

buckskin, *n.* *buk*-skin, the skin of a buck; a soft yellow leather, originally of buckskin: *pl.* breeches of this leather: *a.* made of buckskin.

buckthorn, *n. buk*-thorn, a shrub of the genus *Rhamnus*, used as a cathartic, and in dyeing. **sea buckthorn,** a plant of the genus *Hippophae*.
buck-tooth, *n. buk*-tooth, a large projecting tooth.
buckwheat, *n. buk*-wheet, a species of *Polygonum*, with three-cornered edible seeds like beech-nuts. (A.S. *bôc*, beech.)
bucolic, *a.* bew-*kol*-ik, pastoral : *n.* a pastoral poem. (L. *bucolicus*, pastoral.)
bud, *n.* bud, the first shoot from a stem or branch ; an unexplained leaf or flower ; a bud-like part of an organism that develops into a new individual [Zool.] : *v.i.* to put forth buds ; to begin to grow : *v.t.* to graft by inserting a bud under the bark of another tree. (M.E. *budde*.)
Buddhism, *n. boo*-dizm, the religion founded by Sakyamuni (who was entitled "Buddha" or "the Enlightened") in the 5th cent. B.C., which, eschewing theological speculation, taught that the merging of the individual in the unity of being, "nirvana," through the mortification of private passion and desire was the highest attainable good.
Buddhist, *n. boo*-dist, a follower of Buddha ; a believer in Buddhism : *a.* Buddhistic.
Buddhistic, *a. boo*-dist-ik, relating to or connected with Buddhism.
budding, *a. bud*-ding, opening out as a bud : *n.* the putting forth of buds ; propagation by grafting with a bud [Hort.] ; reproduction by buds [Zool.].
buddle, *n. bud*-dl, a large oblong vat used in washing ore : *v.i.* to wash ore. (Origin unknown.)
Buddleia, *n.* bud-*lee*-a, a large genus of subtropical trees or shrubs, with opposite leaves and clusters of showy flowers of various colours. (Adam *Buddle*, Eng. botanist ; *d.* 1715.)
buddy, *n. bud*-e, a pal, mate ; a raw recruit [Amer. slang]. (Form of *brother*.)
bude-light, *n.* bewd-lite, a brilliant light, produced by introducing oxygen into an Argand burner. (*Bude*, residence of the inventor.)
budge, *v.i.* budj, to give way ; to move slightly : *v.t.* to move (some heavy object) from its place. (Fr. *bouger*.)
budge, *n.* budj, the dressed fur of lambs : *a.* formal ; pedantic. **budge bachelors,** men dressed in gowns of budge who accompanied the Lord Mayor of London at his inauguration. **budge-barrel,** a barrel for carrying gunpowder. (O.Fr. *bouge*, a bag.)
budgeree, *a. budj*-er-ree, good ; fine [Austral. slang].
budgerigar, *n. budj*-e-re-gar, the small Australasian parakeet, *Melopsittacus undulatus*. (Austral.)
budget, *n. bud*-jet, a little leather bag, with its contents ; a stock ; a supply of news ; the financial statement annually made in the House of Commons by the Chancellor of the Exchequer : *v.i.* to provide for the expenditure required by the estimates ; to estimate for. (Fr. *bougette*, a tiny bag.)
budgetary, *a. budj*-e-ta-re, pertaining to, or exercised through, a financial budget.
budlet, *n. bud*-let, a little bud.
buff, *n.* buf, a leather prepared from the skin of the buffalo ; the skins of other animals similarly dressed ; a military coat of buff ; the colour of buff, pale yellow ; buffy-coat [Med.] ; the naked skin [Coll.] : *a.* of buff leather ; pale flesh colour : *v.t.* to polish with buff ; to give (leather) a velvety surface. (Fr. *buffle*, a buffalo.)
buff, *n.* buf, a blow. **to stand buff,** to face boldly.
buffalo, *n. buf*-fa-lo, a wild ox ; the American bison. **buffalo bird,** any small bird that feeds on the parasites of the buffalo. **buffalo chips,** dry dung of the bison used as fuel. **buffalo grass,** prairie grass. **buffalo robe,** the skin of the bison, prepared with the hair on. (Port., *bufalo*.)
buffer, *n. buf*-fer, anything that lessens shock, as the contrivance attached to railway carriages to deaden the effect of a concussion, the recoil-absorber of a gun, etc. ; an oldish man ; a blockhead [Slang]. **buffer state,** a small independent state between two large ones. (Fr.)
buffet, *n. boof*-fay, a sideboard ; a refreshment bar. (Fr.)
buffet, *n. buf*-fet, a blow with the hand or fist, particularly in the face ; a slap ; a cuff : *v.t.* to strike with the hand or fist ; to beat back ; to contend against : *v.i.* to struggle, as with the arms in boxing ; to contend. (O.Fr. *bufet*.)
buffing-spring, *n. buf*-fing-spring, a spring in a buffer.
buffle, *n. buf*-l, a buffle-head. (*Buff*.)
buffle-head, *n. buf*-l-hed, a N. American duck with dense plumage on the head ; a stupid fool, a dull lout [Slang].
buffleheaded, *a.* having a large head ; stupid.
buffo, *n. boof*-fo, a comic actor ; a clown. (It.)
buffoon, *n.* bu-*foon*, one who makes low jests, grimaces and contortions, etc., as a business or otherwise ; a merry-andrew ; a jester ; a mimic. (Fr. *bouffon*.)
buffoonery, *n.* bu-*foon*-er-re, the jests and pranks of a buffoon.
buffoonish, *a.* bu-*foon*-ish, like a buffoon.
Buffs, *n.pl.* buffs, the name of the East Kent Regiment. (From the buff facings of their uniform.)
buffy, *a. buf*-fe, of the colour of buff ; pertaining to buffy-coat or its colour. **buffy-coat,** a yellow substance forming on coagulated blood [Med.].
bug, *n.* bug, an insect infesting houses and plants, esp. the blood-sucking fetid house-bug or bed-bug, of the genus *Cimex* ; in the U.S.A. any insect, esp. a beetle ; a spook, bugbear, or any spectre causing terror. (M.E. *bugge*, scarecrow ; of doubtful origin.)
bugaboo, *n. bug*-a-*boo*, a bugbear.
bugbear, *n. bug*-bare, an object of dread, generally either spectral or imaginary.
bugger, *n. bug*-ger, a sodomite [Law] ; a chap, a fellow [Low slang]. (Fr. *bougre*, L. *Bulgarus*, one of a sect of 11th-cent. Bulgarian heretics to whom many vices were attributed.)
buggery, *n. bug*-ger-re, unnatural vice between males ; the practice of sodomy ; used also as a vulgar expletive.
bugginess, *n. bug*-ge-ness, the state of being buggy.
buggy, *a. bug*-ge, infested with bugs.
buggy, *n. bug*-ge, a four-wheeled one-horse light carriage ; a gig.
bughouse, *n. bug*-house, a lunatic asylum : *a.* crazy ; daft [Amer. slang].
bugle, *n. bew*-gl, a huntsman's horn ; a signal horn for military commands, having a shorter and more conical tube than the trumpet and a narrower bell. **key bugle,** a bugle provided with keys. (Formerly **bugle-horn,** from O.Fr. *bugle*, wild ox.)
bugle, *n. bew*-gl, a long glass bead, usually black.
bugle, *n. bew*-gl, a plant of the genus *Ajuga*. (Fr.)
bugler, *n. bew*-gler, the man who sounds the bugle.
buglet, *n. bew*-glet, a small bugle.
bugle-weed, *n. bew*-gl-weed, the American plant, *Lycopus virginiacus*.
bugloss, *n. bew*-glos, the name of various plants of the borage family, as *Echium vulgare* (viper's bugloss) and *Lycopsis arvensis* (the wild bugloss). (Gr. *bous*, ox, *glossa*, tongue.)
buhl, *n.* bool, unburnished gold, brass, or mother-of-pearl, or tortoise-shell, used for inlaying. **buhl-work,** work or furniture with such inlay. (*Boule*, a French cabinet-maker.)
buhr-stone, *n. bur*-stone, burrstone.
build, *n.* bild, make ; form or figure ; construction : *v.i.* to practise building ; to construct a nest : *v.t.* to construct and raise ; to pile together by art ; to raise or rear ; to establish. *pp.* **built.** (A.S. *bold*, a house.)
builder, *n. bild*-er, one who builds ; a contractor working under an architect.
★**building,** *n. bild*-ing, the trade of a builder ; the act of erecting ; an edifice. **building society,** a co-operative loan society, using the subscriptions as capital to be lent to the subscribers for building or purchasing their own houses.
built, *a.* bilt, formed ; fashioned ; composed of parts.
★**bulb,** *n.* bulb, a subterranean plant bud yielding stem and roots, like that of an onion ; a similar expansion, as that of a thermometer ; an electric lamp : *v.i.* to become bulb-shaped ; to be protuberant. **bulb-tuber,** a corm. (L. *bulbus*.)
bulbaceous, *a.* bul-*bay*-shus, bulbous.
bulbed, *a.* bulbd, with a bulb ; bulb-shaped.
bulbiferous, *a.* bul-*bif*-er-us, producing bulbs.
bulbiform, *a. bul*-be-form, bulb-shaped.
bulbil, *n. bul*-bil, a secondary bulb, esp. one that, when separated, is capable of propagating the plant. (Bot.)

bulbous, *a.* *bul*-bus, possessing or producing bulbs; bulb-shaped.
bulbul, *n.* *bull*-bull, the Persian nightingale, a bird of the genus *Pycnonotus*, allied to the thrushes. (Pers.)
Bulgar, *n.* *bul*-gar, one of Bulgarian race or nationality; the Bulgarian language.
Bulgarian, *a.* bul-*gare*-re-an, pertaining to Bulgaria or its language: *n.* a native or the language of Bulgaria.
Bulgaric, *n.* bul-*ga*-rik, the language of the ancient Bulgars.
bulge, *n.* bulj, the protuberant part of a cask; an irregular protuberance: *v.i.* to swell out unequally; to be protuberant. (O.Fr. *boulge.*)
bulginess, *n.* *bul*-je-ness, protuberance.
bulgy, *a.* *bul*-je, clumsily swollen; protuberant.
bulimea, *n.* bew-*lim*-e-a, a morbidly insatiable appetite; voracity. (Gr.)
bulk, *n.* bulk, magnitude or size; the major portion; the main mass or body; the whole contents of a ship's hold: *v.i.* to assume size or importance: *v.t.* to ascertain the bulk of. **laden in bulk,** having the cargo loose in the hold. **to break bulk,** to begin to unload. **bulked. bulking. bulks.** (M.E. *bulke*, from Scand.)
bulkhead, *n.* *bulk*-hed, a partition in a ship; a partition of masonry, timber, etc., to retain earth as in an embankment, tunnel, etc.
bulkiness, *n.* *bulk*-e-ness, the quality of being bulky; greatness in bulk.
bulky, *a.* *bulk*-e, large; of great size.
bull, *n.* bull, the male of cattle; a bull's-eye, or a hit in this; Taurus, one of the twelve signs of the zodiac; a speculator who buys securities in the expectation that an increase in their value will enable him to sell them at a profit before settlement is due [Stock Exchange]: *a.* of a large size; male: *v.i.* and *v.t.* to speculate for, or to produce, a rise in, the value of securities [Stock Exchange]. (A.S. *bule.*)
bull, *n.* bull, an edict of the Pope. (L. *bulla*, a boss, a leaden seal attached to the edict.)
bull, *n.* bull, a ludicrous inconsistency or blunder in speech. (Perhaps from O.Fr. *boule*, deceit.)
bulla, *n.* *bull*-a, a bleb; (*cap.*) a genus of mollusca. (L.)
bullace, *n.* *bull*-as, a kind of wild plum. (Fr.)
bullate, *a.* *bull*-at, having blisters; puckered [Bot. and Phys.]. (L. *bulla*, a bubble.)
bull-baiting, *n.* *bull*-bate-ing, exciting bulls with dogs.
bull-beef, *n.* *bull*-beef, flesh of a bull; coarse beef.
bull-calf, *n.* *bull*-kahf, a male calf; a stupid fellow.
bulldog, *n.* *bull*-dog, an English dog of remarkable courage, formerly used in baiting bulls; a University proctor's attendant [Slang].
bulldoze, *v.t.* *bull*-dohz, to flog severely; to intimidate; to coerce: *n.* a severe thrashing [Amer. slang].
bulldozer, *n.* *bull*-doh-zer, one who uses violent coercion [Amer. slang]; a large mobile mechanical excavator or steam-shovel used in road-making, fortification, etc.
bullet, *n.* *bull*-et, the projectile used with small-arms. (Fr.)
bulletin, *n.* *bull*-e-tin, an official report of something of public interest: *v.t.* to report by bulletin. (Fr.)
bullet-proof, *a.* *bull*-et-proof, capable of resisting a bullet.
bull-fight, *n.* *bull*-fite, a Spanish sport, in which men fight with baited bull.
bullfinch, *n.* *bull*-finsh, a bird of the genus *Pyrrhula.*
bullfinch, *n.* *bull*-finsh, a high quickset hedge with a ditch alongside. (Perhaps *bull* and *fence.*)
bull-frog, *n.* *bull*-frog, a large species of frog of N. America, with a bellowing note.
bullhead, *n.* *bull*-hed, a stupid fellow; a small, black water insect; the small fresh-water fish, *Cottus gobio*, or miller's thumb, and other fish.
bullion, *n.* *bull*-yon, uncoined gold or silver; fringe of gold or silver thread. (O.Fr. *bouillon.*)
bullionist, *n.* *bull*-yon-ist, an opponent of paper currency.
bullock, *n.* *bull*-ok, a gelded bull. (A.S.)
bullring, *n.* *bull*-ring, the arena of a bullfight.
bull-roarer, *n.* *bull*-*raw*-rer, a piece of wood so cut that when whirled rapidly by a string it booms.
bull's-eye, *n.* *bullz*-eye, a small circular window or opening; a thick round glass let into a ship's ports or deck to admit light [Naut.]; the centre of a target; a small ball of peppermint toffee.
bull-terrier, *n.* bull-*te*-re-er, a cross-breed between the bull-dog and the terrier.
bull-trout, *n.* *bull*-trout, a large species of sea-trout, *Salmo eriox.*
bullweed, *n.* *bull*-weed, knapweed.
bullwort, *n.* *bull*-wurt, bishop's-weed.
bully, *n.* *bull*-e, a noisy, blustering, overbearing fellow: *v.t.* to overbear with blustering menaces: *v.i.* to be noisy and quarrelsome: *a.* fine, jolly [Slang, obsolete] (Origin uncertain.)
bully, *n.* *bull*-e, a miner's hammer; a scrimmage in Eton football; the crossing of the sticks with which a hockey match begins or is resumed.
bully-beef, *n.* *bull*-e-beef, tinned, cooked, or pickled beef. (Fr. *bouilli*, boiled.)
bullyrag, *v.t.* *bull*-e-rag, to abuse grossly; to badger.
bulrush, *n.* *bull*-rush, a large strong water-rush of the genus *Scirpus*; also the reed mace, *Typha latifolia.*
bulrushy, *a.* *bull*-rush-e, full of bulrushes.
bulse, *n.* bulse, a bag or package of diamonds or gold-dust. (Port. *bolsa*, purse.)
bulwark, *n.* *bull*-wurk, a rampart; a fortification; any means of defence or security; a ship's side above the deck: *v.t.* to fortify with a bulwark. (Scand.)
bum, *n.* bum, the buttocks; a bailiff or bumbailiff: a tramp or hobo [U.S.A. slang]: *v.i.* to tramp around begging,to cadge [U.S.A. slang]. (Origin uncertain.)
bumbailiff, *n.* bum-*bay*-lif, an under-bailiff.
bumbaze, *v.t.* bum-*bayz*, to bamboozle [Scots.].
bumble-bee, *n.* *bum*-bl-bee, a large wild bee, the humble bee, a species of *Bombus.*
bumbledom, *n.* *bum*-bl-dum, petty incapable officialism in general. (Mr. *Bumble*, in "Oliver Twist.")
bumblepuppy, *n.* *bum*-bl-pup-e, a name for various children's games, also for unscientific play at whist.
bumboat, *n.* *bum*-boat, a boat carrying provisions, etc., to vessels.
bumkin, *n.* *bum*-kin, a short boom standing from each bow; a small outrigger over the stern of a boat to extend the mizen [Naut.]. (Dut. *boom*, a log.)
bummalo, *n.* *bum*-a-lo, the small Asiatic fish, *Harpodon nehereus*, known as Bombay duck when salted and dried.
bummaree, *n.* *bum*-a-ree, a factor or middleman at Billingsgate fish-market.
bummer, *n.* *bum*-mer, a camp-follower of the American Civil War; a tramp or hobo [U.S.A.].
bummock, *n.* *bum*-muk, a large brewing of ale [Scots.].
bump, *n.* bump, a thump; a collision; a dull heavy blow; a swelling caused by a blow or collision; the sound of the collision; a protuberance on the cranium supposed by phrenologists to indicate mental or moral qualities; the touching of a boat by the one following (in rowing); an air-pocket [Av. slang]: *v.t.* to strike heavily against anything large or solid; to make the ball bounce high (in cricket); to touch the boat in front with one's prow (in rowing): *v.i.* to strike, to move along with bumbs. **bump off,** do away with by murder [Slang]. **bump out,** spread type to fill a certain space [Print.]. (From the sound.)
bump, *n.* bump, the boom of the bittern: *v.i.* to make a loud or hollow noise like the bittern.
bumper, *n.* *bump*-er, one who or that which bumps; a glass filled to the brim; a buffer on a motor-car; a crowded house at a theatre; anything very large, generous, or wonderful.
bumpiness, *n.* *bump*-e-ness, irregularity of surface or [Av.] in atmospheric density.
bumpkin, *n.* *bump*-kin, an awkward heavy rustic.
bumptious, *a.* *bump*-shus, noisily self-assertive.
bumptiously, *ad.* *bump*-shus-le, in a bumptious manner.
bumpy, *a.* *bump*-e, abounding in bumps; jolty; affected by thermal or eddy currents [Av.].
bun, *n.* bun, a small rounded soft cake; a compactly twisted coil of hair at the back of the head. (O.Fr. *bugne*, a swelling.)
buna, *n.* *boo*-nah, a synthetic rubber manufactured, and much used, in Germany.

bunce, *n.* bunce, money; perquisites [Slang].
bunch, *n.* bunsh, a cluster, or a number of the same things growing or tied together; a knot; a tuft; a group of persons: *v.i.* to swell out in or grow into a bunch: *v.t.* to form or tie in a bunch or bunches. (Origin unknown.)
bunchiness, *n.* *bunsh*-e-ness, the state of being bunchy.
bunchy, *a.* *bunsh*-e, growing in bunches; having tufts; resembling a bunch.
buncombe, *n.* *bung*-kum, bunkum.
bund, *n.* bund, a raised embankment, causeway, or promenade in India and the Far East. (Hind.)
Bundesrat, *n.* *boon*-des-raht, the upper house of the legislature in the former German and Austrian Empires; the 7-member Swiss Federal Council.
bundle, *n.* *bun*-dl, a number of things bound together loosely; anything wrapped in a convenient form for conveyance; a package: *v.t.* to tie in a bundle; to pack off unceremoniously: *v.i.* to depart hurriedly or confusedly; to sleep together without undressing [U.S.A.]. (As *bind.*)
bung, *n.* bung, a stopper for a bung-hole; a shive; a publican [Slang]: *v.t.* to stop the hole of a cask with a bung; to close up. (Dut. *bonde.*)
bungaloid, *a.* *bung*-ga-loyd, in bungalow style; infested with bungalows [Coll.].
bungalow, *n.* *bung*-ga-lo, a lightly built house with ground floor only. (Hind. *bangala.*)
bunghole, *n.* *bung*-hole, the hole in the bulge of a cask to fill it by.
bungle, *v.t.* *bung*-gl, to perform clumsily: *v.i.* to make or mend clumsily; to botch; to manage awkwardly: *n.* a botching; a clumsy performance. (Origin uncertain.)
bungler, *n.* *bung*-gler, a clumsy awkward person.
bungling, *a.* *bung*-gling, clumsy; awkward; ill done.
bunglingly, *ad.* *bung*-gling-le, in a bungling manner; unskilfully.
bung-vent, *n.* *bung*-vent, the spile-hole in a bung.
bunion, *n.* *bun*-yon, a painful enlargement of the joint of the big toe. (O.Fr. *buigne*, a swelling.)
bunk, *n.* bungk, a board or metal frame for a bed; a shelf for sleeping on; a sleeping-berth. (Origin unknown.)
bunk, *v.t.* bungk, to get away; to clear off [Slang].
bunk, *n.* bungk, frothy verbiage; nonsensical talk; hot air [Slang]. (*bunkum*).
bunker, *n.* *bung*-ker, a large bin for coals; a stowage place for coals in steamships; a bench; a sandy hollow or other obstruction on a golf course.
bunkered, *a.* *bungk*-erd, stopped by a bunker [Golf]; in a difficult place.
bunko, *n.* *bung*-ko, swindling at cards, gaming, or by the confidence trick, etc. **bunko-steerer,** a confidence-man's or gamester's confederate [Amer. slang].
bunkum, *n.* *bung*-kum, speech spoken merely to please one's supporters or constituents and secure their votes: mere talk; nonsense. (*Buncombe*, in N. Carolina, the representative of which once insisted on delivering an irrelevant speech in Congress solely to flatter his constituents.)
bunny, *n.* *bun*-ne, a rabbit. (Origin unknown.)
bunny-hug, *n.* *bun*-ne-hug, a ragtime dance of negro origin.
bunsen, *n.* *bun*-sen *or* *boon*-sen, a gas burner for heating purposes in which gas and air are burnt together. (Named after *Bunsen*, the inventor.)
bunt, *n.* bunt, the stinking-smut of wheat, a destructive fungoid disease.
bunt, *n.* bunt, the middle part or cavity of a sail [Naut]; the bag of a fishing net.
bunt, *v.t.* and *i.* bunt, to push; to butt with horns: *n.* such a push; an aeroplane manœuvre in which the loop and roll are combined [Av.].
Bunter, *a.* *boon*-ter, pertaining to or denoting rocks in the lowest of the three divisions of the Triassic period [Geol.]. (Ger., mottled.)
bunting, *n.* *bunt*-ing, a general name for birds of the genus *Emberizidæ*, closely allied to the finches.
bunting, *n.* *bunt*-ing, a thin woollen fabric of which the flags are made; a ship's flags; flags collectively.
buntline, *n.* *bunt*-lin, a rope attached to the foot-rope of a sail to turn it up forward.
bunya, *n.* *bun*-ya, an Australian conifer, *Araucaria bidwillii*, the seeds of which are eaten by the aborigines.
bunyip, *n.* *bun*-yip, a mythical monster of the swamp. (Australian native word.)
buoy, *n.* boy, a moored and floating sea-mark indicating a fairway, shoal, rock, or other danger-spot: *v.t.* to keep afloat; to sustain; to keep from sinking; to fix buoys as a direction to mariners. **buoy-rope,** the rope which fastens a buoy to an anchor. (O.Fr. *boie*, from Teut.)
buoyage, *n.* *boy*-aj, the provision of buoys.
buoyancy, *n.* *boy*-an-se, capacity for floating; specific lightness; elasticity of spirit; power of recovery from depression.
buoyant, *a.* *boy*-ant, floating; light; that will not sink; cheerful.
buoyantly, *ad.* *boy*-ant-le, in a buoyant manner.
buphaga, *n.* *bew*-fa-ga, the beef-eater, a bird preying upon ticks infesting cattle. (Gr. *bous*, ox, *phago*, eat.)
buprestidans, *n.pl.* bew-*pres*-tid-anz, a group of beetles with brilliant metallic colouring. (Gr.)
bur, *n.* bur, a prickly fruit or flower-head; a woody excrescence on a tree; any rough knob; burr.
burble, *v.i.* burbl, to gurgle; to simmer (with joy, or rage, etc.); to bubble.
burbot, *n.* *bur*-bot, a freshwater fish of the genus *Lota*, allied to the cod.
burdash, *n.* *burd*-ash, a sash with a fringe.
burden, *n.* *bur*-dn, something borne or carried; a load; anything that is grievous, wearisome, or oppressive to bear; quantity that a ship will carry; cargo; a refrain or chorus; that which is often repeated; the main topic: *v.t.* to load; to encumber; to oppress. (A.S. *byrthen.*)
burdensome, *a.* *bur*-dn-sum, heavy to be borne; cumbersome; wearisome; oppressive.
burdensomely, *ad.* *bur*-dn-sum-le, in a burdensome manner.
burdensomeness, *n.* *bur*-dn-sum-ness, the quality of being burdensome.
burdock, *n.* *bur*-dok, a plant of the genus *Arctium*. (*Bur* and *dock.*)
bureau, *n.* bew-*roh* (*pl.* **bureaux,** bew-*rohz*), a writing-table with drawers for papers; a chest of drawers; an office for public business; a government department. (Fr.)
bureaucracy, *n.* bew-*rok*-ra-se, government administration in departments, each under a chief; centralization of government; government by officials; officialism. (Fr. *bureaucratie.*)
bureaucrat, *n.* *bew*-roh-krat, a bureaucratist; a government official.
bureaucratic, *a.* bew-ro-*krat*-ik, characterized by or relating to bureaucracy; relying on precedent and formality in government.
bureaucratically, *ad.* bew-ro-*krat*-e-ka-le, in a bureaucratic manner.
bureaucratist, *n.* bew-*rok*-ra-tist, an advocate or upholder of bureaucracy.
burette, *n.* bew-*ret*, a graduated vessel for measuring small quantities of liquid. (Fr.)
burg, *n.* burg, a fortified place; a borough. (Ger.)
burgage, *n.* *burg*-aj, a feudal tenure obtaining in towns, whereby lands or tenements were held for a yearly rent.
burganet, *n.* *bur*-gan-et, a burgonet.
burgee, *n.* bur-*jee*, a triangular or swallow-tailed pennant, esp. of a yacht club [Naut.]; a kind of small coal.
burgeois, *n.* bur-*joyce*, bourgeois (the type).
burgeon, *v.i.* *bur*-jun, to sprout: *n.* a bud. (Fr.)
burgess, *n.* *bur*-jes, a borough freeman; a borough voter; formerly a borough or University parliamentary representative. (O.Fr. *burgeis.*)
burgess-ship, *n.* *bur*-jes-ship, the condition or status of a burgess.
burggrave, *n.* *burg*-grave, a burgrave.
burgh, *n.* *bu*-ru, a Scottish incorporated town; a borough. **Royal burgh,** a corporate body erected by a charter from the crown. **burgh of barony,** a Scottish burgh chartered by the sovereign but holding its lands from a feudal superior.
burghal, *a.* *burg*-al, pertaining to a burgh.
burgher, *n.* *burg*-er, an inhabitant or freeman of a borough. (Dut. *burger.*)
burghership, *n.* *burg*-er-ship, the privileges or status of a burgher.
burglar, *n.* *burg*-lar, one who commits burglary.
burglarious, *a.* burg-*lare*-re-us, pertaining to burglary.

burglariously, *ad.* burg-*lare*-re-us-le, in the manner of a burglar.
burglary, *n.* *burg*-la-re, the act or crime of breaking into a house by night, with intent to commit felony. (Low L. *burglaria.*)
burgle, *v.t.* *bur*-gl, to break into a house at night as a burglar: *v.i.* to commit burglary.
burgomaster, *n.* *burg*-o-mahs-ter, the chief magistrate of a Dutch or Flemish municipal town; the glaucous gull. (Dut. *burgemeester.*)
burgonet, *n.* *burg*-o-net, a steel cap; a helmet with a visor. (Fr. *bourguignotte,* of Burgundy.)
burgoo, *n.* bur-*goo,* oatmeal porridge [Naut. and Mil. slang]. (Turk. *burghul.*)
burgrave, *n.* *bur*-grave, in Germany, a governor of a town or castle; later, an hereditary title of nobility. (Ger. *burggraf,* lord of a castle.)
Burgundian, *a.* bur-*gun*-de-an, of or pertaining to Burgundy.
Burgundy, *n.* *bur*-gun-de, a kind of red or white wine made in Burgundy, France. **Burgundy-mixture,** a fungicide composed of sodium carbonate and copper sulphate used for spraying potatoes, etc. **Burgundy-pitch,** the resinous juice of the silver fir.
burial, *n.* *be*-re-al, the act of burying, especially a dead person; a funeral. **burial ground** or **place,** a cemetery or place set apart for burial. **burial service,** the Church service for burials. (A.S. *byrgels,* a grave.)
burin, *n.* *bew*-rin, a graver; a tool for engraving. (Fr.)
burke, *v.t.* burk, to murder, particularly by suffocation; to smother quietly, and get rid of; to avoid discussion; to hush up. (*Burke,* an Irishman who, in 1828, smothered many persons and sold the bodies for dissection.)
burl, *n.* burl, a small knot or end of thread in cloth: *v.t.* to pick burls from. (O.Fr. *bourle.*)
burlap, *n.* *bur*-lap, a coarse canvas for packages.
burler, *n.* *burl*-er, one who burls; a cloth-dresser.
burlesque, *n.* bur-*lesk,* grotesque representation; a composition in which the contrast between the subject and the manner of treating it renders it ludicrous: *v.t.* to travesty; to turn to ridicule: *a.* mock-serious; tending to excite laughter by burlesque. (Fr., from It.)
burletta, *n.* bur-*let*-ta, a comic opera; a musical farce. (It.)
burliness, *n.* *bur*-le-ness, the state of being burly.
burly, *a.* *bur*-le, bulky; robust; portly; bluff. (A.S. *bŭrlic,* suitable [in appearance] for a lady's bower.)
Burman, *a.* and *n.,* *bur*-man, Burmese.
Burmese, *a.* bur-*meez,* pertaining to Burma: *n.* a native or the language of Burma; Burman.
burn, *n.* burn, a brook; a bourn.
***burn,** *n.* burn, the effect of burning; a bodily hurt caused by fire; the operation of burning or baking, as in brick-making: *v.i.* to be on fire; to glow; to be inflamed with passion or desire; to feel excess of heat: *v.t.* to consume, injure, or destroy by fire; to subject to the action of fire; to affect, as by the action of fire; to consume chemically; to cauterize. **burn one's fingers,** to suffer from speculating or meddling. (A.S. *beornan.*)
burner, *n.* *burn*-er, the device by which a flame is controlled.
burnet, *n.* *burn*-et, plants of the genera *Poterium* and *Sanguisorba.* **burnet moth,** a moth of the genus *Zygæna.* (Fr.)
burning, *a.* *burn*-ing, much heated; scorching; powerful; vehement; exciting. **burning glass,** a convex lens that will concentrate the sun's rays and produce intense heat. **burning mirror,** a concave mirror acting with similar effect.
burnish, *n.* *burn*-ish, polish; brightness; lustre: *v.i.* to grow bright: *v.t.* to polish by friction; to make bright. (Fr. *brunir,* to make brown.)
burnisher, *n.* *burn*-ish-er, a person who burnishes; an instrument or material used in polishing.
burnous, *n.* *burn*-oos *or* burn-*ooz,* a hooded cloak worn by Arabs. (Ar., a high cap.)
burnt, *pp.* and *a.* burnt, treated with fire, as burnt wine.
burnt-ear, *n.* *burnt*-eer, a fungoid disease in corn in which the ear seems black as if burnt.
burnt-offering, *n.* *burnt*-of-er-ring, a burnt sacrifice.
burnt-sacrifice, *n.* burnt-*sak*-re-fyce, an offering by fire on an altar.
burnt-sienna, *n.* *burnt*-se-*en*-na, an orange-red pigment produced by calcining and grinding sienna.
burr, *n.* bur, a bur; a rough edge; a roughness; the round knob of a horn next a deer's head; a clinker, or badly burnt brick; a triangular chisel; a round iron ring used with a cannon, lance, etc.; the full sound of the letter R; a whirring noise; siliceous rock occurring in softer formations; a whetstone; a hanger-on, one difficult to shake off [Coll.]. (Origin uncertain.)
burrel, *n.* *bu*-rel, the wild sheep of the Himalayas, the bharal, *Ovis nahura.*
burrel-fly, *n.* *bu*-rel-fly, the gadfly or bot-fly.
burro, *n.* *bu*-ro, a donkey. (U.S.A. from Sp.)
burrow, *n.* *bu*-ro, a hole in the ground excavated by rabbits, etc., for shelter and habitation: *v.t.* to excavate a burrow; to work a way underground; to delve deeply into (a book, etc.). (*Borough.*)
burrow-duck, *n.* *bu*-ro-duk, the sheldrake.
burrowing-owl, *n.* *bu*-ro-ing-owl, a small diurnal owl of N. America living in burrows.
burrstone, *n.* *bur*-stohn, a rough-surfaced siliceous rock used for making mill-stones.
burry, *a.* *bur*-re, covered with burrs or spiny hooks.
bursar, *n.* *bur*-sar, a treasurer or purser; a student who holds a bursary. (Mediæval L. *bursa,* a purse.)
bursarship, *n.* *bur*-sar-ship, the office of a bursar.
bursary, *n.* *bur*-sa-re, the treasury of a college or monastery; in Scotland a scholarship granted to a student to aid him in the prosecution of his studies.
burse, *n.* burse, in Scotland a scholarship or a fund for maintaining one; the silk-covered case in which the Communion cloth is kept when not in use. (L. *bursa,* purse.)
bursiform, *a.* *bur*-se-form, shaped like a purse.
***burst,** *n.* burst, a sudden breaking forth; a sudden explosion or shooting forth; a rent; a sprint; a spree [Slang]: *v.i.* to break or fly open suddenly and with violence; to disrupt violently; to explode; to rush forth or fall upon suddenly or with violence: *v.t.* to break or rend open violently. (A.S. *berstan.*)
burthen, *n.* and *v.t.* *bur*-then, burden.
burton, *n.* *bur*-ton, a small tackle formed by two or three blocks [Naut.].
Burton, *n.* *bur*-ton, the thwart-ways method of stowing casks, etc. afloat [Naut.]; a strong ale brewed at Burton-on-Trent. (Place-name.)
bury, *v.t.* *be*-re, to inter with funeral rites in a grave; to cover with earth, etc.; to hide; to withdraw into seclusion; to forget and forgive. **bury the hatchet,** to make peace (from the old American-Indian custom). (A.S. *byrgan.*)
burying, *n.* *be*-re-ing, interment; burial.
burying-ground, *n.* *be*-re-ing-ground, a cemetery.
burying-place, *n.* *be*-re-ing-place, a sepulchre.
bus, *n.* bus, an omnibus; a motor-cycle, motor-car, or aeroplane [Slang]: *v.i.* to go by bus. **to miss the bus,** to lose an opportunity.
bus-bar, *n.* *bus*-bar, one of the main terminals, usually a copper bar, of a switch-board in a power station [Elect.]. **bus-bar voltage,** the voltage between bus-bars.
busby, *n.* *buz*-be, the tall black cap of bearskin, Persian lamb, or other material worn with full dress by certain British regiments.
bush, *n.* bush, a thick shrub; a cluster of shrubs; a branch of ivy as a tavern sign; a wild uncultivated woodland; anything like a bush; a luxuriant growth of hair: *v.i.* to grow thick or bushy: *v.t.* to set about with bushes. **beat about the bush,** to go to work in a roundabout way. (Scand.)
bush, *n.* bush, a circle of metal let into round holes or orifices, or into the sheaves of such blocks as have iron pins, to reduce wear by friction: *v.t.* to furnish a block with a bush. (Dut. *bus,* a box.)
bush-baby, *n.* *bush*-bay-be, any of the small African nocturnal lemurs of the genus *Galago.*
bushbuck, *n.* *bush*-buk, a S. African antelope.
bushcat, *n.* *bush*-kat, the serval; the civet cat.
bush-cow, *n.* *bush*-kou, the zamouse.
bushed, *pp.* busht, lost in the bush [Austral.].
bushel, *n.* *bush*-el, a dry measure of eight gallons. (O.Fr. *boissel.*)
bushel, *n.* *bush*-el, the bush in the nave of a wheel.
bushfighting, *n.* *bush*-fite-ing, firing here and there from behind bushes; guerilla warfare.

bush-harrow, *n.* *bush*-ha-ro, a harrow of three or more bars, in which bushes are interwoven.

Bushido, *n.* *boo*-she-doh, the so-called code of chivalry evolved by the Samurai in the Japanese feudal period. (Jap.)

bushiness, *n.* *bush*-e-ness, the quality of being bushy.

bushman, *n.* *bush*-man, one living in the bush, esp. in Australia; a country-dweller.

Bushman, *n.* bush-man, one of a primitive race of yellow-skinned short-statured aboriginals of South Africa. (Dut. *boschman.*)

bushmaster, *n.* *bush*-mas-ter, a large venomous snake, *Lachesis mutis* of Central and South America.

bushranger, *n.* *bush*-rayn-jer, in Australia, one who has taken to the bush and lives by robbery.

bushy, *a.* *bush*-e, full of branches; thick and spreading; overgrown with shrubs.

busily, *ad.* *biz*-e-le, actively; officiously.

★**business,** *n.* *biz*-ness, employment; occupation; trade; bargaining; profession; concerns or affairs; duty; a matter; action on the stage as distinct from speech: *a.* relating to business. **to do the business for a man,** to kill, destroy, or ruin him. **to make it one's business,** to see to it.

business-like, *a.* *biz*-ness-like, befitting business; accurate and punctual; methodical.

busk, *n.* busk, a piece of steel, whalebone, etc., to strengthen corsets in front.

busk, *v.t.* busk, to prepare; to dress. (Scand.)

busked, *a.* buskt, wearing a busk.

buskin, *n.* *busk*-in, a kind of half-boot, anciently worn by actors in tragedy, and furnished with high soles; the tragic drama; the tragic vein. (O.Fr.)

buskined, *a.* *busk*-ind, wearing the buskin; pertaining to tragedy; sublime.

busman, *n.* *bus*-man, the driver of a bus. **busman's holiday,** one spent in watching others at one's own accustomed work.

buss, *n.* bus, a loud kiss: *v.t.* to kiss. (Fr. *baisir,* to kiss.)

buss, *n.* bus, a two-masted herring lugger with the mizen smaller than the mainsail. (O.Fr. *busse.*)

bust, *n.* bust, the human figure, or a sculptured representation of it, comprising the head, neck, shoulders, and breast; the chest. (Fr.)

bustard, *n.* *bust*-ard, a game-bird of the genus *Otis* allied to the cranes and plovers, including the great bustard, the largest land bird of Europe. (O.Fr. *bistarde.*)

bustle, *n.* *bus*-sl, hurry; great stir; tumult: *v.i.* to stir about fussily; to be actively and confusedly busy; to hustle. (Scand.)

bustle, *n.* *bus*-sl, a frame or stuffed pad to pouch a woman's skirt behind.

bustler, *n.* *bus*-sl-er, an active, stirring person.

busy, *a.* *biz*-e, very closely engaged; actively employed; diligent; marked by activity; officious; meddling: *v.t.* to occupy (oneself): *n.* a detective [Slang]. (A.S. *bysig.*)

busybody, *n.* *biz*-e-*bod*-e, a meddling officious person; a mischief-maker.

busyness, *n.* *biz*-e-ness, the state of being busy.

★**but,** *conj.* but, except; unless; except that; which not; yet; nevertheless; than: *prep.* except: *ad.* only; outside [Scot.]: *n.* the room of entry in a cottage (in Scotland and the North). **but and ben,** *see* **ben.** (A.S. *būtan.*)

butcher, *n.* *bootsh*-er, one whose business is to slaughter animals for food; a dealer in meat; one who delights in deeds of blood or who kills men needlessly: *v.t.* to slaughter animals for food; to murder with cruelty; to slaughter wantonly; to spoil (music, acting, etc.) by bad performance. (O.Fr. *bochier,* a slayer of goats.)

butcher-bird, *n.* *bootsh*-er-burd, the shrike.

butcher's-broom, *n.* *bootsh*-erz-broom, the knee-holly, an evergreen shrub.

butchery, *n.* *bootsh*-er-re, the business of a butcher; the place where animals are killed; murder of unusual barbarity; great slaughter, carnage.

butler, *n.* *but*-ler, the principal manservant, who has charge of the wines, plate, etc. (M.E. *boteler.*)

butlerage, *n.* *but*-ler-raj, a duty formerly paid to the king's butler on imported wine.

butlery, *n.* *but*-ler-re, a butler's pantry; a buttery.

butment, *n.* *but*-ment, an abutment.

butt, *n.* but, the end of a thing; the thick and heavy end; the part by which a tool or weapon is wielded; a hide from the back and sides; the bole of a tree; certain flat-fish. **butt weld,** a welded butt-joint. (O.Fr. *bot,* end.)

butt, *n.* but, a target or mark to shoot at; an object to aim at; the mound behind a target; a screened stand for a grouse-shooter; an object of ridicule; goal; *pl.,* a shooting-range. (F. *but,* goal.)

butt, *v.i.* but, to push or thrust with the head (esp. of animals) or horns; to meet end to end; to abut: *v.t.* to strike or drive off by or as by butting; *n.* a push with the head or horns.

butt, *n.* but, a large cask; a liquid measure of 120 gallons of wine, or 108 gallons of beer. (Fr. *botte,* a cask.)

butte, *n.* but, a ridge; hill with flat top [Amer.]. (Fr.)

butt-end, *n.* *but*-end, the thick and heavy end.

★**butter,** *n.* *but*-ter, the fatty substance obtained from cream by churning; applied to other substances of the consistence of butter; fulsome flattery [Slang]: *v.t.* to spread with butter; to flatter. **butter and eggs,** the name of several plants with two shades of yellow in the flower. (A.S. *butere.*)

butter-bird, *n.* *but*-ter-berd, the rice-bunting; the name in Jamaica for the bobolink.

butterboat, *n.* *but*-ter-boat, a small sauce tureen.

butterbump, *n.* *but*-ter-bump, the bittern.

butterbur, *n.* *but*-ter-bur, sweet colt's-foot.

buttercup, *n.* *but*-ter-kup, a ranunculus, with a cup-like yellow flower.

butter-fingered, *a.* *but*-ter-*fing*-gerd, unable to hold things, esp. catches at cricket.

butterfingers, *n.* *but*-ter-*fing*-gerz, one who cannot hold catches; one who is clumsy with the hands.

butterfish, *n.* *but*-ter-fish, the gunnel, and other fish with a slimy coating on the scales.

butterfly, *n.* *but*-ter-fly, any specimen of the diurnal Lepidoptera with clubbed antennæ; a flighty, thoughtless, or showily dressed person. **butterfly flower,** schizanthus. **butterfly nut,** a thumb-screw with two wings.

butterine, *n.* *but*-ter-rin, an imitation butter.

butteriness, *n.* *but*-ter-re-ness, the quality of butter; state of being buttery.

butteris, *n.* *but*-ter-ris, a knife for paring a horse's hoof for shoeing.

butter-knife, *n.* *but*-ter-nife, a knife for cutting butter.

butterman, *n.* *but*-ter-man, a retailer of butter.

buttermilk, *n.* *but*-ter-milk, the acid-flavoured milk that remains after the butter is extracted.

butter-muslin, *n.* *but*-ter-*muz*-lin, loosely woven unsized cotton cloth with a small mesh; cheese-cloth.

butternut, *n.* *but*-ter-nut, the American white walnut, *Juglans cinerea,* and its fruit; also a S. American tree of the genus *Caryocar* and its nut, the souari.

butter-scotch, *n.* *but*-ter-skotch, a toffee made with brown sugar and butter.

butter-stamp, *n.* *but*-ter-stamp, a carved piece of wood to stamp butter.

butter-tree, *n.* *but*-ter-tree, the shea, and other tropical trees yielding a butter-like substance.

butter-wife, *n.* *but*-ter-wife, a butterwoman.

butter-woman, *n.* *but*-ter-woom-an, a woman who sells butter.

butterwort, *n.* *but*-ter-wurt, a marsh plant with oil-secreting prickles, *Pinguicula vulgaris.*

buttery, *a.* *but*-ter-re, having the qualities or appearance of butter; not grasping firmly; nauseatingly flattering, wheedling [Fig.].

buttery, *n.* *but*-ter-re, a storeroom for provisions and liquors; in some colleges, a refreshment-room for the students. **buttery-hatch,** a half-door between buttery and hall, through which provisions are served. (O.Fr. *boterie,* a wine-store.)

butt-joint, *n.* *but*-joynt, a joint in which the ends of the two parts come together but do not overlap [Eng.].

buttock, *n.* *but*-tok, the rump or protuberant part behind; a certain hold and throw in wrestling: *v.t.* to throw a wrestler by using this. (*Butt.*)

★**button,** *n.* *but*-tn, a knob; a small ball; a disk of metal, or other substance, to fasten the dress: *v.t.* to fasten, or furnish, with buttons. (Fr. *bouton.*)

button-bush, *n.* *but*-tn-bush, the North American shrub, *Cephalanthus occidentalis.*

buttonhole, *n.* *but*-tn-hole, a hole or loop to admit a button; a flower or nosegay for wearing: *v.t.* to make buttonholes; to detain in conversation.

buttonhook, *n.* *but*-tn-hook, a hook for drawing a button through the buttonhole.
button-mould, *n.* *but*-tn-mohld, a blank to be covered with material to form a button.
buttons, *n.* *but*-onz, a page in livery; the plant tansy.
button-stick, *n.* a slotted metal strip for shielding cloth while buttons sewn thereto are polished.
buttonwood, *n.* *but*-tn-wood, the plane-tree of North America.
buttony, *a.* *but*-tn-e, having many buttons; button-like.
buttress, *n.* *but*-tress, an abutment of masonry, to strengthen and support a wall; any prop or support: *v.t.* to support by a buttress; to prop. (O.Fr. *bouterez.*)
butty, *n.* *but*-te, a mate; a foreman; a term applied to an equal dividend system among labourers. **butty gang,** a body of navvies who contract to do a given piece of work on that system. (Dial. Eng.)
butyraceous, *a.* bew-te-*ray*-shus, having the qualities of butter; buttery. (L. *butyrum*, butter.)
butyrate, *n.* *bew*-te-rate, a salt of butyric acid.
butyric, *a.* bew-*ti*-rik, relating to or derived from butter. **butyric acid,** a colourless rancid acid found in butter.
butyrine, *n.* *bew*-te-rin, an oily liquid existing in butter, associated with oleine and stearine.
butyrous, *a.* *bew*-te-rus, butyraceous.
buxine, *n.* *buks*-in, an alkaloid obtained from the box-tree. (L. *buxus*, the box-tree.)
buxom, *a.* *buks*-um, plump and comely; healthy; jolly. (A.S. *būgan*, to bend.)
buxomly, *ad.* *buks*-um-le, in a buxom manner.
buxomness, *n.* *buks*-um-ness, the quality of being buxom.
buy, *v.t.* by, to purchase or acquire by paying a price, or some equivalent; to bribe. **buy in,** to buy for oneself what one has set up for sale. **buy off,** to pay a price for release or non-opposition. **buy out,** to buy off; to purchase the share or shares of a person; to obtain release from the army by a money payment. *p.* and *pp.* **bought.** (A.S. *bycgan.*)
buyable, *a.* *by*-a-bl, capable of being bought; bribable [Slang].
buyer, *n.* *by*-er, one who buys; a customer; a retailer's agent for the selection and purchase of stock from wholesalers. **buyers' market,** the condition in which consumers' goods are plentiful and, hence, prices are low [Econ.].
buzz, *n.* buz, the hum of a bee or fly; a confused hum; a report secretly spread about: *v.i.* to hum; to whisper or speak with a low hissing sound: *v.t.* to whisper; to spread abroad secretly. **buzz bomb,** a flying-bomb [Coll.]. **buzz off!** get away out of it! [Slang]. **buzz saw,** a circular saw.
buzzard, *n.* *buz*-zard, a rapacious hawk of the genus *Buteo*; a blockhead; a dunce. (O.Fr. *busard.*)
buzzard, *n.* *buz*-zard, any nocturnal flying insect that buzzes. **buzzard-clock,** the cockchafer. (*Buzz.*)
buzzer, *n.* *buz*-zer, a scandal-monger or tattler; a steam whistle; a hooter; an electric device for producing a buzzing sound.
buzzing, *a.* *buz*-zing, resembling or making a buzz.
buzzingly, *ad.* *buz*-zing-le, in a buzzing manner.
★**by,** *prep.* by, in the presence of; at a short distance; retired; obscure; out of the way; incidental; with; through, as author, maker, cause, means; according to; in the measure or quantity of; during; not later than: *ad.* near; aside; away: *a.* as prefix, signifies side, secondary, private. **by and by,** in a short time after; presently. **by and large,** on the whole. **by oneself,** alone. **by-the-bye,** by the way, as a passing remark aside from the main subject, incidentally. (A.S. *bi.*)
by, *n.* by, bye.
by-bidder, *n.* *by*-bid-der, one who bids at an auction to tempt others to bid high.
by-blow, *n.* *by*-bloh, a side blow; a bastard.
by-business, *n.* by-*biz*-ness, a secondary business.
by-drinking, *n.* *by*-dring-king, drinking between times or on the sly.
bye, *n.* by, something subsidiary or incidental; in cricket, a ball from which runs are obtained which passes the striker without touching his bat or his person and is neither a " wide " nor a " no ball "; **leg bye,** a similar ball which touches the striker's person; the unplayed holes after the termination of a match [Golf]; one for whom there is no opponent when the competition is played in pairs.
bye-bye, *n.* *by-by*, good-night; bed-time; good-bye.
by-election, *n.* *by*-e-*lek*-shon, an election held to fill a vacancy occurring between general elections.
by-end, *n.* *by*-end, private selfish end.
bygone, *a.* *by*-gon, past; gone by: *n.* something gone by; an antique; *pl.* the past; past affronts. **let bygones be bygones,** let the past be forgotten.
by-lane, *n.* *by*-lane, a side lane.
by-law, *n.* *by*-law, an authoritative private regulation of a corporation or society. (Scand. *byr*, village, *lag*, law.)
by-matter, *n.* *by*-mat-ter, something incidental.
by-name, *n.* *by*-name, a nickname; a name of reproach.
by-pass, *n.* *by*-pahss, a channel through which a small portion of a main supply of liquid or gas is led; a road constructed to relieve traffic at congested centres: *v.t.* to conduct through or go by way of a by-pass.
by-passage, *n.* *by*-pas-saj, a private or retired passage.
bypath, *n.* *by*-pahth, a private or unfrequented path.
by-play, *n.* *by*-play, acting carried on aside or in dumb show, while the main action proceeds.
by-plot, *n.* *by*-plot, a subsidiary plot.
by-product, *n.* *by*-prod-ukt, an incidental product of a main process.
by-purpose, *n.* *by*-pur-pus, indirect or concealed design; an incidental purpose.
byre, *n.* bire, a cow-house. (A.S. *byre*, a shed.)
by-road, *n.* *by*-road, a subsidiary or unfrequented road.
Byronic, *a.* by-*ron*-ik, in the manner, or poetical style, of Lord Byron; cynical; misanthropic.
byssine, *a.* *bis*-sin, made of fine linen; like byssus.
byssoid, *a.* *bis*-soyd, fringed, with the threads unequal in length.
byssolite, *n.* *bis*-so-lite, a fine fibrous tremolite; asbestos.
byssus, *n.* *bis*-sus, among the ancients, a cloth of exceedingly fine texture, either of linen, cotton, or silk; a tuft of filaments, by which certain shell-fish are attached to rocks; a tuft. (L., fine cloth, usually linen.)
bystander, *n.* *by*-stand-er, a looker-on; one standing by.
by-street, *n.* *by*-street, a side street.
by-walk, *n.* *by*-wawk, a secluded or private walk.
by-way, *n.* *by*-way, a private or obscure way.
byword, *n.* *by*-wurd, a common saying: a proverb; an object of derision. (A.S. *biword*, proverb.)
byzant, *n.* *biz*-ant, bezant (the gold coin).
Byzantian, *a.* be-*zan*-shan, Byzantine.
Byzantine, *a.* be-*zan*-tin, belonging or relating to Byzantium or Constantinople; of the architectural style characteristic of the Eastern, Greek, or **Byzantine Empire** (395–1453): *n.* an inhabitant of Byzantium.

C

C, see, is the third letter and second consonant of the English alphabet. It has a hard or close sound, like *k* before *a*, *o*, *u*, *l*, and *r*, as also when it is a final, as in *tunic*; before *e*, *i*, and *y* it has a soft or sibilant sound like *s*. When combined with *h* as *ch* it has three different sounds: (1) that of *tsh*, as in *chair*, *church*; (2) that of *k*, as in *chaos*, *chemistry*; and (3), in a few words derived from the French, that of *sh*, as in *chaise*, *chemise*.

C, in music, when placed after the clef, is the mark of common time; and when a bar is perpendicularly drawn through it, *alla-breve* time, or a quicker movement, is indicated. C is also the first note of the diatonic scale, answering to the tonic sol-fa *doh*, the Italian *do*, and the French *ut*.

Caaba, *n.* *ka*-ah-ba, the Kaabah.

caaing-whale, *n.* *kah-* or *kaw*-ing-whale, the black-fish, a small toothed whale of the N. Atlantic.

cab, *n.* kab, a small one-horse passenger conveyance licensed for hire; a taxi; the covered part of a locomotive in which the driver and stoker stand: *v.i.* to travel by cab. (Shortened from *cabriolet*.)

cab, *n.* kab, a Hebrew measure, equal to nearly three pints. (Heb. *qabab*, to hollow.)

cabal, *n.* ka-*bal*, a small party united in some secret state intrigue; secret artifices of such a party; a clique: *v.i.* to plot for a secret purpose. (*Cabbala*.)

Cabala, *n.* *kab*-a-la, Cabbala.

caballer, *n.* ka-*bal*-ler, one who cabals; an intriguer.

caballine, *a.* *kab*-a-line, fit for, or pertaining to, a horse. (L. *caballinus*, of horses.)

cabana, *n.* ka-*bah*-nya, a brand of cigars made in Havana and so named after the exporter.

cabane, *n.* kah-*bahn*, the tripod of struts supporting the wings of an aeroplane [Av.]. (F.)

cabaret, *n.* *kab*-a-ray or *kab*-a-ret, a French tavern; a restaurant at which entertainment is provided; a cabaret show. **cabaret show**, an entertainment of song and dancing given in restaurants and imitating those of the Parisian cabarets. (Fr.)

cabbage, *n.* *kab*-aj, the culinary plant *Brassica oleracea*. **cabbage butterfly** (*Pieris*), **fly** (*Anthomyia*), **moth** (*Mamestra*), species of insects the larvæ (**cabbage worms**) of which feed on cabbages. (Fr. *caboche*, large head.)

cabbage, *n.* *kab*-aj, shreds of cloth filched by tailors: *v.i.* to purloin, as small pieces of cloth after cutting out a garment; to pilfer.

cabbage-tree, *n.* *kab*-aj-tree, any tropical palm-tree, the terminal bud of which is eaten like a cabbage.

Cabbala, *n.* *kab*-a-la, the secret science traditionally preserved, by which the rabbis affect to interpret the mystic sense of the words, letters, and very accents of Scripture; oral tradition; any mystic science. (Heb. *qabal*, to receive.)

cabbalism, *n.* *kab*-al-izm, occultism; the mystical interpretation of the Bible.

cabbalist, *n.* *kab*-a-list, a person skilled in the cabbala.

cabbalistic, *a.* kab-a-*lis*-tik, pertaining to the cabbala; containing an occult meaning.

cabbalistically, *ad.* kab-a-*lis*-te-ka-le, in a cabbalistic manner.

cabby, *n.* *kab*-be, the driver of a cab [Coll.].

caber, *n.* *kay*-ber, a stout pole with the bark on, tossed in Highland games; a pole. (Gael., rafter.)

cabin, *n.* *kab*-in, a small room; a cottage or hut; an apartment in a ship: *v.i.* to live in a cabin: *v.t.* to confine in a cabin. **cabin boy**, one who waits on the officers of a ship. (Fr. *cabane*.)

cabinet, *n.* *kab*-in-et, a closet or small room; a private room; the secret council of a monarch; the collective body of ministers who direct the government of a state; a piece of furniture, consisting of a chest or box, with drawers and doors, esp. one in which things of value are deposited. **cabinet council**, a council of cabinet ministers: *a.* suitable for a cabinet; of small size (of photographs, pictures, note-paper, etc.). **cabinet minister**, a member of a cabinet. **shadow cabinet**, that that would replace the existing cabinet on the opposition's accession to office. (Fr.)

cabinetmaker, *n.* *kab*-in-et-make-er, one who makes the finer kinds of household furniture.

Cabir, *n.* *kay*-ber (*pl.* **Cabiri**, ka-*byr*-re), certain divinities to whom mystic honours were paid in Lemnos and other islands in connection with nature worship, fire, corn, and the vine. (L.)

Cabirian, *a.* ka-*bi*-re-an, Cabiric.

Cabiric, *a.* ka-*bi*-rik, pertaining to the Cabiri.

cable, *n.* *kay*-bl, a long strong rope or chain, such as is used to hold a vessel at anchor; a measure of 100 fathoms (600 ft.), or the tenth of a nautical mile (608 ft.); a number of insulated wires protected in a sheath for submarine or underground telegraphy; a cablegram; a moulding resembling a rope [Arch.]: *v.t.* to fasten with a cable; to send a message by cable. **cable tier**, the place where the cables are kept coiled up [Naut.]. **cable tramway**, a tram road on which the cars were moved by means of an endless cable. (Fr.)

cablegram, *n.* *kay*-bl-gram, a message by cable.

cable-laid, *a.* *kay*-bl-lade, twisted like a cable, with three ropes twisted to the left, each rope of three strands twisted to the right.

cablet, *n.* *kay*-blet, a small cable; a tow-rope.

cableway, *n.* *kay*-bl-way, a rope railway or ropeway.

cabman, *n.* *kab*-man, the driver of a cab.

cabob, *n.* ka-*bob*, an oriental dish of meat roasted with spices: *v.t.* to cook such a dish. (Per. *kab*, ox.)

caboched, *a.* ka-*boshd*, showing an animal's head full-faced, without any of the neck [Her.]. (O.Fr.)

cabochon, *n.* (App.), any jewel shaped like a carbuncle and polished, but without facets. (Fr.)

caboodle, *n.* ka-*boo*-dl, all; the whole crowd of people [Slang].

caboose, *n.* ka-*booce*, the galley or kitchen of a ship; a car for staff or passengers on a goods train [U.S.A.]. (Dut.)

cabotage, *n.* *kab*-o-taj or -tahzh, the coasting-trade; shore-navigation; the reservation to a nation of all traffic within its territories [Av.]. (Fr.)

cab-rank, *n.* *kab*-rank, a place for waiting cabs.

cabriole, *n.* *kab*-re-ohl, the curved leg typical of Queen Anne style of furniture.

cabriolet, *n.* kab-re-o-*lay*, a one-horsed covered carriage; a cab; a type of motor-car body. (Fr. *cabriole*, the leap of a goat.)

cab-stand, *n.* *kab*-stand, a cab-rank.

ca'canny, *n.* kah-*kan*-ne, the practice or policy of going slow adopted by dissatisfied workers: *v.i.* to slacken off; to take it easy: *int.* go easy!

cacao, *n.* ka-*kay*-o, the chocolate-tree. **cacao butter**, a fixed oil from the seeds of this. (Sp.)

cachæmia, *n.* ka-*kee*-me-a, bad or poisoned state of the blood. (Gr. *kakos*, bad, *haima*, blood.)

cachalot, *n.* *kash*-a-lot, the sperm whale. (Fr.)

cache, *n.* kash, a place, esp. in the ground, for concealing provisions, ammunition, etc.; the goods so hidden: *v.t.* to put or store in a cache. (Fr. *cacher*, to hide.)

cachectic, *a.* ka-*kek*-tik, pertaining to cachexia.

cachet, *n.* *kash*-ay, a seal; a distinctive mark; a sign of authenticity; a soluble capsule [Med.]. **lettre de cachet**, in France, before the revolution, a royal warrant for the imprisonment of a person without being brought to trial. (Fr.)

cachexia, *n.* ka-*kek*-se-a, a chronic condition of ill-health due to some constitutional disorder; a debased mental state. (Gr. *kakos*, bad, *hexis*, condition.)

cachinnate, *v.i.* *kak*-e-nayt, to laugh immoderately or loudly. (L. *cachinnare*.)

cachinnation, *n.* kak-e-*nay*-shon, loud or hysterical laughter.

cacholong, *n.* *katch*-o-long, a white opaque variety of opal. (Fr.)

cachou, *n.* ka-*shoo*, a small aromatic sweetmeat sucked to sweeten the breath. (Fr.)

cachucha, *n.* ka-*choo*-chah, a Spanish dance like the bolero. (Sp.)
cacique, *n.* ka-*seek*, a native chief of Mexico and Central America; a political boss in Spain or Spanish America; a tropical American oriole.
caciquism, *n.* ka-*see*-kizm, the rule or system of political caciques.
cackle, *n.* *kak*-kl, the noise of a goose or of a hen when it has laid; idle talk: *v.i.* to make a cackling noise; to talk idly; to tattle; to giggle. (From the sound.)
cacodemon, *n.* kak-o-*dee*-mon, a nightmare; a wicked sprite. (Gr. *kakodaimon.*)
cacodyl, *n.* *kak*-o-dil, an oily, highly inflammable arsenical radical, the salts of which have a most offensive smell. (Gr. *kakōdēs*, bad-smelling.)
cacoepy, *n.* kak-o-*ee*-pe *or* ka-*koh*-e-pe, false pronunciation of words. (Gr. *kakos*, and *epos*, word.)
cacoethes, *n.* kak-o-*ee*-theez, a bad or irresistible habit. **cacoethes scribendi,** a diseased propensity or itch for writing. (Gr. *kakoēthēs*, malicious.)
cacogastric, *a.* kak-o-*gas*-trik, dyspeptic.
cacography, *n.* ka-*kog*-ra-fe, bad writing or spelling. (Gr. *kakos*, and *grapho*, write.)
cacolet, *n.* *kak*-o-lay *or* -let, a litter used for transport of wounded on mules. (Fr.)
cacology, *n.* ka-*kol*-o-je, incorrect pronunciation; using wrong words. (Gr. *kakologos*, evil-saying.)
cacomistle, *n.* *kak*-o-misl, a carnivore, *Bassariscus astutus*, of California and Mexico, related to the civet cats.
cacophonous, *a.* ka-*kof*-o-nus, harsh-sounding.
cacophony, *n.* ka-*kof*-o-ne, harsh or discordant sound; a discord [Mus.]. (Gr. *kakophōnia*, ill-sounding.)
cactaceous, *a.* kak-*tay*-shus, pertaining to the cactus family.
cactus, *n.* *kak*-tus (*pl.* **cacti,** *kak*-ty), a plant with fleshy spiny stem, adapted for the storage of water in dry regions. (Gr.)
cad, *n.* kad, a vulgar or ill-mannered fellow. (Fr.)
cadastral, *a.* ka-*das*-tral, pertaining to a detailed and accurate survey of the lands of a country. (Fr. *cadastre.*)
cadaver, *n.* ka-*day*-ver, a human corpse, esp. one for dissection. (L.)
cadaveric, *a.* kad-a-*ve*-rik, relating to corpses; corpse-like, as in an appearance of rigidity. (L. *cadaver*, a dead body.)
cadaverous, *a.* ka-*dav*-er-rus, having the appearance of a corpse; with the pallor of death.
cadaverously, *ad.* in a cadaverous form.
cadaverousness, *n.* ka-*dav*-er-rus-ness, the quality of being cadaverous.
caddice, *n.* *kad*-dis, caddis.
caddie, *n.* *kad*-de, one who carries a golfer's clubs.
caddis, *n.* *kad*-dis, the larva of a caddis-fly; a kind of tape or ribbon lint for dressing wounds.
caddis-fly, *n.* *kad*-dis-fly, a species of the *Trichoptera*, the larvæ of which are aquatic.
caddish, *a.* *kad*-ish, behaving like a cad; badly bred.
caddishly, *ad.* *kad*-ish-le, in a caddish manner.
caddy, *n.* *kad*-de, a small box for keeping tea. (Malay.)
cade, *a.* kade, tame; bred by hand; domesticated: *v.t.* to bring up by hand: *n.* a pet lamb, foal, etc.
cade, *n.* kade, a cask of 500 herrings or 1,000 sprats. (Fr.)
cadelle, *n.* ka-*del*, a small voracious beetle infesting granaries.
cadenas, *n.* *kad*-en-as, a casket for holding salts and spices for table use in the Middle Ages. (Fr.)
cadence, *n.* *kay*-dence, a fall of the voice at the end of a sentence, or in modulation; the general modulation in reading, especially verse; sound or tone; the modulation of the bars or clauses in music; a cadenza [Mus.]: *v.t.* to regulate by musical measure. (Fr.)
cadency, *n.* *kay*-den-se, descent from a younger branch. **marks of cadency,** symbols distinguishing the arms of the younger members of a family from those of the head of the house, and of each other [Her.].
cadent, *n.* *kay*-dent, having cadence. (L. *cadens*, falling.)
cadenza, *n.* ka-*den*-za, a flourish introduced at the close of a vocal or instrumental piece [Mus.]. (It.)
cadet, *n.* ka-*det*, a younger son; the youngest branch of a family; one who served in the army as a private, to acquire skill and obtain a commission; a pupil in a naval or military academy; a Constitutional Democrat in Tsarist Russia. (Fr.)
cadetship, *n.* ka-*det*-ship, the position of a cadet; the state of being a cadet.
cadge, *v.t.* and *i.* kadj, to hawk or peddle; to sponge; to beg. (Perhaps from *catch.*)
cadger, *n.* *kad*-jer, one who carries produce to market; a huckster; one who cadges.
cadi, *n.* *kah*-de *or* *kay*-de, an Oriental judge or magistrate. (Ar. *qadi*, a judge.)
Cadmean, *a.* kad-*mee*-an, relating to Cadmus, the legendary Greek inventor of the sixteen simple letters of the alphabet. **Cadmean victory,** a victory having fatal consequences for the victor.
cadmium, *n.* *kad*-me-um, a malleable and ductile metallic element resembling tin. **cadmium yellow,** a pigment made from a sulphide of cadmium.
cadrans, *n.* *kad*-ranz, a graduated instrument used by jewellers in cutting facets. (Fr.)
cadre, *n.* kahdr, an outline or scheme; the nucleus or permanent headquarters personnel of a battalion or regiment. (Fr. *cadre*, a frame.)
caducean, *a.* ka-*dew*-se-an, pertaining to Mercury's wand. (L. *caduceus*, a winged rod entwisted with two serpents, carried by Mercury.)
caducibranchiate, *a.* ka-*dew*-se-*brang*-ke-at, losing the gills before full maturity, as in the frogs.
caducity, *n.* ka-*dew*-se-te, transitoriness.
caducous, *a.* ka-*dew*-kus, falling off early, as leaves [Bot.]. (L. *caducus*, easily falling.)
cæcal, *a.* *see*-kal, of or like the cæcum; having a blind end.
cæcum, *n.* *see*-kum, a cavity open at one end, esp. the blind pouch forming the beginning of the colon [Anat.]. (L. *cæcus*, blind.)
Cæsar, *n.* *see*-zar, title of the Roman emperors till A.D. 138; hence, any great autocrat. (L., of uncertain origin.)
Cæsarian, *a.* se-*zare*-re-an, pertaining to Cæsar or the Cæsars. **Cæsarian section,** the operation of taking a child from the womb by cutting the abdominal walls. (Said to have been performed at the birth of Julius Cæsar.)
Cæsarism, *n.* *see*-za-rizm, the theory or practice of imperial rule on the model of the Roman Cæsars; autocratic government; imperialism.
cæsious, *a.* *see*-zhe-us, of a greyish-blue colour. (L. *cæsius*, blue-grey.)
cæsium, *n.* *see*-ze-um, a silver-like metallic element, one of the alkali metals.
cæspitose, *a.* *ses*-pe-tose, growing in tufts [Bot.].
cæsura, *n.* se-*zew*-ra *or* se-*sew*-ra, a metrical pause in verse; in Latin verse, the separation of the last syllable of a word from that which precedes it, and the carrying of it forward into another foot. (L.)
cæsural, *a.* se-*zew*-ral *or* se-*sew*-ral, pertaining to the cæsura.
café, *n.* *kaf*-ay, a coffee-house, tea-shop, or place in which light refreshments can be procured. (Fr.)
cafeteria, *n.* *kaf*-e-*teer*-re-a, a restaurant in which the customers wait on themselves.
caffeic, *a.* kaf-*fee*-ik, obtained from coffee.
caffeine, *n.* *kaf*-e-in *or* ka-*feen*, the vegetable alkaloid of coffee and tea.
caffeism, *n.* *kaf*-e-izm, a morbid state due to prolonged or excessive absorption of caffeine.
Caffre, *n.* *kaf*-fer, Kaffir.
caftan, *n.* *kaf*-tan *or* kaf-*tahn*, a long girdled gown with long sleeves worn in the East. (Turk.)
cage, *n.* kaje, an enclosure made of wire and wood, or of wicker, for confining birds or small animals, or of iron bars for wild beasts; a prison for petty criminals; a lift working in a mine-shaft; an outer work of timber, enclosing another [Carp.]: *v.t.* to confine in a cage. (Fr.)
cage-bird, *n.* a bird commonly kept in a cage; a cageling.
cageling, *n.* *kaje*-ling, a bird confined in a cage.
cagmag, *n.* *kag*-mag, a tough old goose; meat unfit for food; idle talk. (Dial. Eng.)
Cagot, *n.* ka-*goh*, a member of a nearly extinct pariah race found in the Pyrenees. (Fr.)
Cagoulard, *n.* (App.), one of a French pro-Nazi and Royalist secret society (*Comité Secret d'Action Revolutionnaire*) of the late 1930's, the uniform of whose members included a hood. (Fr. *cagoule*, cowl.)

cahier, *n.* kah-*yay*, a book formed of sheets of paper loosely stitched together; specially, a number of a work published in parts; a report. (Fr.)
cahoot, *n.* ka-*hoot*, copartnership [U.S.A. Slang].
caiman, *n. kay*-man, the cayman.
Cainozoic, *a.* and *n.* ky-no-*zoh*-ik, tertiary [Geol.].
caique, *n.* ka-*eek*, a light rowing-boat used on the Bosphorus; a small sailing-vessel of Greek and Levantine waters. (Fr.)
cairn, *n.* kayrn, a conical heap of stones anciently erected as a memorial, esp. over a grave or as a boundary mark; a small shaggy and compactly built terrier originally bred in Scotland. (Gael. *carn.*)
cairngorm, *n. kayrn*-gorm, a yellow or smoky brown variety of rock crystal found on Cairngorm mountain. (Gael. *carn*, cairn, *gorm*, blue.)
caisson, *n. kay*-son, an ammunition-chest or wagon; a wooden chest, with bombs, for use as a land-mine; a wooden framework or casing; a water-tight case for working in under water [Eng.]. **caisson disease,** a form of paralysis to which persons subjected to increased atmospheric pressure are liable. (Fr.)
caitiff, *n. kay*-tif, a mean despicable knave: *a.* base; vile. (O.Fr.)
cajole, *v.t.* ka-*jole*, to deceive by flattery or fair promises; to wheedle; to coax. (Fr. *cajoler.*)
cajolement, *n.* ka-*jole*-ment, blandishment or flattery; cajolery.
cajoler, *n.* ka-*jole*-er, a flatterer.
cajolery, *n.* ka-*jole*-er-re, the act of cajoling; wheedling.
cajolingly, *ad.* ka-*jole*-ing-le, in a flattering way.
cajuput, *n. kaj*-e-poot, an oil-yielding tree of the Moluccas, a species of *Melaleuca*. (Malay.)
★**cake,** *n.* kake, a small mass of dough baked; a composition of flour, butter, sugar, or other ingredients, baked usually in a small mass; anything in the form of a cake; any mass of matter concreted: *v.t.* to form into a cake: *v.i.* to concrete into a hard mass. **cake-walk,** a negro entertainment in which a cake is the reward of a graceful performer. (Scand. *kaka.*)
Calabar-bean, *n. kal*-a-bahr-*been*, the extremely poisonous seed of a West African tree, used in medicine and, by the natives, in witchcraft trials. (*Calabar*, W. Africa.)
calabash, *n. kal*-a-bash, a tall tree of tropical America, *Crescentia cujete*; also the hard-shelled gourd it bears or a utensil made from this shell. (Fr. *calebasse.*)
calaber, *n. kal*-a-ber, the fur of the Siberian grey squirrel.
calaboose, *n.* kal-a-*booce*, a prison [U.S.A. Coll.].
Caladium, *n.* ka-*lay*-de-um, a genus of plants of the Arum family, with ornamental leaves.
calamanco, *n.* kal-a-*mang*-ko, woollen stuff, of a fine gloss, and checkered in the warp.
calamary, *n. kal*-a-ma-re, a cuttle-fish. (L.)
calamiferous, *a.* kal-a-mif-er-rus, producing reeds; reeds. (Lat. *calamus*, reed, *fero*, to bear.)
calamine, *n. kal*-a-min, an ore of zinc. (Fr.)
calamint, *n. kal*-a-mint, an aromatic plant of the genus *Calamintha*. (Fr. *calament.*)
calamite, *n. kal*-a-mite, a variety of tremolite; a fossil plant resembling a horsetail.
calamitous, *a.* ka-*lam*-e-tus, producing or arising out of calamity, distress, or wretchedness.
calamitously, *ad.* ka-*lam*-e-tus-le, in a calamitous manner.
calamitousness, *n.* ka-*lam*-e-tus-ness, a calamitous state of things.
calamity, *n.* ka-*lam*-e-te, a misfortune that causes either wide-spread or great distress; cause of misery; adversity; affliction; disaster. (Fr. *calamité.*)
calamus, *n. kal*-a-mus, the sweet-flag, *Acorus calamus*, or its aromatic medicinal root; a reed pen; the barrel of a feather; (*cap.*) a large genus of tropical Asiatic palms, species of which yield dragon's blood, rattan and Malacca canes, etc. (L. a reed.)
calando, *a.* and *ad.* ka-*lan*-do, gradually diminishing time and sound [Mus.]. (It.)
calash, *n.* ka-*lash*, a light low-wheeled carriage; the folding hood of a carriage; a covered framework formerly worn by women to protect their headdress. (Fr. *calèche.*)
calcaneal, *a.* kal-*kay*-ne-al, relating to or forming the calcaneum [Anat.].
calcaneum, *n.* kal-*kay*-ne-um, a bone forming part of the tarsus [Anat.]; the hypotarsus in birds. (L. *calx*, heel.)
calcar, *n. kal*-kar, a calcinating furnace used in glass-works. (L. *calcāria*, a lime-kiln.)
calcar, *n. kal*-kar, a spur-like process in flowers [Bot.]. (L. *calx*, heel.)
calcarate, *a. kal*-ka-rat, having a spur [Bot.].
calcareo-, kal-*kare*-re-o, prefix denoting the presence of lime in a compound; as **calcareo-argillaceous,** consisting of clay with a mixture of lime.
calcareous, *a.* kal-*kare*-re-us, partaking of the nature of lime; containing lime. **calcareous spar,** calc-spar. **calcareous tufa,** calc-tuff. (L. *calcārius*, pertaining to lime.)
calced, *a.* kalst, shod (of monks who wear shoes or sandals).
calceolaria, *n.* kal-se-o-*lare*-re-a, any plant of the genus *Calceolaria* comprising the slipperworts. (L. *calceolus*, slipper.)
calceolate, *a. kal*-se-o-lat, slipper-shaped [Bot.].
calcic, *a. kal*-sik, containing or pertaining to lime.
calcification, *n.* kal-se-fe-*kay*-shon, the process of calcifying; impregnation with lime.
calcify, *v.i. kal*-se-fy, to become stony by secretion of lime: *v.t.* to make stony in this way. (L. *calx*, lime, *facio*, make.)
calcimine, *n. kal*-se-myn, a wash for ceilings, etc., made from clear glue and whiting, often tinted: *v.t.* to distemper with this.
calcinable, *a.* kal-*sine*-a-bl *or kal*-se-na-bl, that may be calcined.
calcination, *n.* kal-se-*nay*-shon, the process of calcining; the condition of being calcined.
calcine, *v.t. kal*-sine *or kal*-sin, to reduce to powder or a friable state by expelling the volatile matter with heat; to desiccate: *v.i.* to become calcined. (L. *calcināre.*)
calcite, *n. kal*-site, calc-spar, native crystallized carbonate of lime.
calcitration, *n.* kal-se-*tray*-shon, a kicking; vigorous opposition. (L. *calcitrare*, to kick.)
calcium, *n. kal*-se-um, the silvery-white metallic element forming the base of lime. (L. *calx*, lime.)
calcography, *n.* kal-*kog*-ra-fe, chalcography.
calc-sinter, *n. kalk*-sin-ter, stalactitic carbonate of lime; calc-tuff.
calc-spar, *n. kalk*-spar, crystallized carbonate of lime; calcite.
calc-tuff, *n. kalk*-tuf, carbonate of lime in alluvial deposit.
calculable, *a. kal*-kew-la-bl, that may be calculated.
calculate, *v.t. kal*-kew-late, to compute; to reckon; to adjust; to adapt: *v.i.* to conclude or estimate by calculation; believe or suppose [U.S.A.]. (L. *calculātus*, reckoned.)
calculating, *a. kal*-kew-lay-ting, reckoning carefully beforehand; scheming.
calculation, *n.* kal-kew-*lay*-shon, the act or process of calculating; the estimate come to by this; computation; reckoning; reasoned deduction; inference; opinion. (L. *calculatio*, a reckoning.)
calculative, *a. kal*-kew-lay-tiv, pertaining to calculation; involving or given to calculation.
calculator, *n. kal*-kew-lay-tor, one who calculates; a machine for performing calculations; a schemer.
calculatory, *a. kal*-kew-*lay*-to-re, calculative.
calculous, *a. kal*-kew-lus, gritty; of the nature of calculus [Med.]; affected with or arising from the stone [Med.]. (L. *calculōsus*, stony.)
calculus, *n. kal*-kew-lus (*pl.* **calculi**), a morbid concretion of a hard or stony consistence formed in different organs of the body [Med.]; a method of calculating. **differential calculus,** the method of differencing quantities, or of finding an infinitely small quantity which, being taken an infinite number of times, shall be equal to a given quantity. **exponential calculus,** a method of finding and summing up the differentials of exponential quantities. **integral calculus,** a method of integrating or summing up differential quantities. (L. *calculus*, a pebble.)
caldarium, *n.* kal-*dare*-re-um, the hot-bath room in a Roman villa. (L.)
caldera, *n. kahl*-day-rah, a crater-like depression due to volcanic action [Geol.]. (Sp., cauldron.)
caldron, *n. kawl*-dron, a cauldron.

calecannon, *n.* kale-*kan*-on, colcannon.
calèche, *n.* ka-*laysh*, a calash.
Caledonian, *a.* and *n.* kal-e-*don*-ne-an, pertaining to or a native of Scotland. (L. *Caledonia*, N. Britain.)
calefacient, *n.* kal-e-*fay*-she-ent, a heat-exciting substance: *a.* warming; heating [Med.]. (L. *calefaciens*, warming.)
calefaction, *n.* kal-e-*fak*-shon, the production of heat; state of being heated. (L. *calefactio.*)
calefactory, *a.* kal-e-*fak*-to-re, imparting warmth; fit to make hot.
calembour, *n.* *kal*-em-boor (or App.), a pun. (Fr.)
calendar, *n.* *kal*-en-der, a register of the year; an almanac; a list or roll; a register of persons or things, esp. a list of criminal causes which stand for trial; a catalogue of documents arranged chronologically: *v.t.* to enter in a calendar; to register; to catalogue and make a précis of documents. **calendar line,** the date-line. **calendar month,** a solar month as it stand in almanacs. (L. *calendārium*, an account-book.)
calender, *n.* *kal*-en-der, a machine consisting of two hot rollers for pressing cloth smooth and glossy; a person who calenders: *v.t.* to press in a calender. (Fr. *calandre.*)
calender, *n.* *kal*-en-der, a mendicant dervish in the East. (Pers. *qualandar.*)
calends, *n.pl.* *kal*-endz, the first day of each month in the ancient Roman calendar. **Greek calends,** never, as the Greeks had no calends. (L. *calendæ.*)
calendula, *n.* ka-*len*-dew-la, the common marigold.
calenture, *n.* *kal*-en-tewr, sunstroke; a delirium attacking seamen in the tropics. (Fr.)
calescence, *n.* ka-*les*-ence, increasing heat. (L. *calescens*, growing hot.)
calf, *n.* kahf (*pl.* **calves,** kahvz), the young of the cow and other bovine animals, also of certain large animals, as the elephant, moose, and whale; calf-skin leather; a stupid cowardly fellow. **calf love,** a silly boyish or girlish love. (A.S.)
calf, *n.* kahf, the muscles behind the shin.
calfish, *a.* *kahf*-ish, like a calf; loutish; inexperienced.
calfskin, *n.* *kahf*-skin, a calf's skin; the leather it is made into.
Caliban, *n.* *kal*-e-ban, the monster so named in "The Tempest"; hence, a boor; a monstrosity.
calibrate, *v.t.* *kal*-e-brate, to find out the calibre of; to ensure that all the projectiles from a battery will strike at uniform distance and direction by sighting and charging in accordance with the results obtained from experimental shots.
calibration, *n.* kal-e-*bray*-shon, the act of taking the calibre or of calibrating.
calibre, *n.* *kal*-e-ber, diameter of the bore of a gun; capacity of mind; character. (Fr.)
caliche, *n.* ka-*leesh*, the sodium nitrate deposits of Chile and Peru. (Sp.)
calicle, *n.* *kal*-e-kl, a small cup-like organ, as in the corals [Biol.]. (L. *caliculus*, a little cup.)
calico, *n.* *kal*-e-ko, cotton cloth, so called as originally from Calicut; a printed calico. **calico printing,** the art of printing figured patterns on calico.
calicular, *a.* ka-*lik*-yoo-lar, cup-shaped [Bot.].
calid, *a.* *kal*-id, hot; burning. (L. *calidus*, warm.)
calidity, *n.* ka-*lid*-e-te, warmth, heat.
calif, *n.* *kay*-lif, caliph.
caliginous, *a.* ka-*lij*-en-us, misty; dark; obscure. (L. *calīgineus.*)
caligo, *n.* ka-*ly*-go, a disease of the eye, causing dimness of sight. (L., darkness.)
caligraphy, *n.* ka-*lig*-ra-fe, calligraphy.
caliology, *n.* kal-e-*ol*-o-je, the scientific study of birds' nests. (Gr. *kalia*, nest, *-ology.*)
calipash, *n.* kal-e-*pash*, the green fat next to a turtle's upper shell [Cookery]. (Fr. *carapace.*)
calipee, *n.* kal-e-*pee*, the yellow fat on a turtle's lower shell [Cookery].
calipers, *n.pl.* *kal*-e-perz, callipers.
caliph, *n.* *kay*-lif, a title given to the successors of Mohammed regarded as supreme in both civil and religious matters. (Ar. *khatifah*, successor.)
caliphate, *n.* *kal*-e-fate, the office, dignity, or government of a caliph.
caliver, *n.* *kal*-e-ver *or* ka-*lee*-ver, a light musket used in the 16th century. (Fr.)
calix, *n.* *kay*-liks, a cup-like organ [Phys.]. (L., a cup.)
calk, *v.t.* kawk, caulk.
calk, *n.* kawk, a calkin; a pointed piece of iron on the shoes to prevent slipping on the ice [U.S.A.]: *v.t.* to caulk; to furnish with a calk or a calkin [U.S.A.] (L. *calx*, heel.)
calk, *v.t.* kalk, to copy a drawing by chalking its back and tracing its outline with a style so that a copy appears on paper beneath it. (Fr. *calquer.*)
calker, *n.* *kawk*-er, a caulker; a calkin.
calkin, *n.* *kal*-kin, a prominent part at the extremity of a horseshoe to prevent the animal from slipping.
calking, *n.* *kaw*-king, caulking.
calking, *n.* *kal*-king, the act or art of copying a drawing by treating the back with chalk, crayon, or other colouring matter and tracing the lines of the design with a style on a surface, placed beneath it.
call, *n.* kawl, a vocal address, summons, command or citation; demand; the act of signalling a person to listen at the telephone; a telephone conversation; an invitation, esp. one to become the minister to some particular congregation; a short visit; the cry of an animal, esp. a bird, to its young or its mate; a note on the horn by a huntsman to cheer on the hounds; the whistle of the boatswain; a requirement of duty; a demand for payment of instalments due on shares, also the option of claiming delivery of stock at a certain date and price: *v.i.* to speak loudly; to cry aloud; to make a short visit: *v.t.* to name; to describe as; to summon; to convoke; to proclaim; to appoint; to invoke; to signal; to arouse from sleep; to attract (bird or animal) by imitating its cry. **call back,** to revoke or retract; to recall. **call for,** to demand; to visit so as to bring someone or something away. **call forth,** to bring or summon to action. **call in,** to collect; to withdraw from circulation; to summon together; to invite together. **call in question,** to dispute. **call of the house,** in parliamentary language, an authoritative summons to members to be present at a stated time. **call off,** to summon away; to divert. **call on,** to make a short visit to; to invoke; to demand the performance of a duty, or the payment of a debt. **call out,** to challenge to fight; to summon into service; to utter in a loud voice; to bawl. **call over,** to read aloud a list, name by name. **call over the coals,** to scold. **call to mind,** to recollect. **call to the bar,** admission as a barrister. **call up,** to bring into view or recollection; to bring into action or discussion; to require payment; to enrol as an active member of one of the fighting services. **call upon,** to implore. (Ice. *kalla.*)
calla, *n.* *kal*-la, a floating water plant, the bog arum. **calla lily,** a species of *Richardia.*
call-bird, *n.* *kawl*-berd, a bird trained to allure others.
call-boy, *n.* *kawl*-boy, one who calls the actors on the stage; a hotel or ship's messenger boy.
caller, *n.* *kawl*-er, one who calls; one who pays a call, a visitor; one making a telephone-call.
caller, *a.* *kal*-ler, fresh. (Scots.)
callet, *n.* *kal*-let, a low, scolding woman. (Fr.)
calligraphic, *a.* kal-le-*graf*-ik, pertaining to calligraphy.
calligraphical, *a.* kal-le-*graf*-e-kal, calligraphic.
calligraphist, *n.* kal-*lig*-ra-fist, an elegant penman.
calligraphy, *n.* kal-*lig*-ra-fe, the art of beautiful writing; elegant penmanship; handwriting. (Gr. *kalligraphia*, beautiful writing.)
calling, *n.* *kawl*-ing, vocation; profession; trade; class of persons engaged in a profession; a solemn or divine summons.
Calliope, *n.* kal-*ly*-o-pe, the muse of eloquence and heroic poetry [Myth.]; (*l.c.*) a series of steam whistles on which tunes can be played. (Gr. *Kalliopē*, the beautiful-voiced Muse.)
callipers, *n.pl.* *kal*-le-perz, compasses with curved legs for measuring convex or round bodies, or with points turned outwards for measuring calibres.
callisthenic, *a.* kal-is-*then*-ik, promoting strength and beauty; relating to callisthenics.
callisthenics, *n.pl.* kal-lis-*then*-iks, exercises for promoting gracefulness of carriage and physical beauty. (Gr. *kalos*, beautiful, *sthenos*, strength.)
call-money, *n.* *kawl*-mun-e, money borrowed which is returnable on demand.
call-note, *n.* *kawl*-note, call of a bird to its mate.
callosity, *n.* ka-*los*-e-te, callousness; skin thickened and hardened as by constant pressure or friction; a callus.

callous, *a.* *kal*-lus, hard; indurated; insensible; unfeeling. (L. *callōsus*, with a hard skin.)
callously, *ad.* *kal*-lus-le, in a callous manner.
callousness, *n.* *kal*-lus-ness, the state of being callous.
callow, *a.* *kal*-lo, unfledged; immature; inexperienced; (of land) liable to flooding. (A.S. *calu*, bald.)
callowness, *n.* *kal*-lo-ness, the state of being callow.
calluna, *n.* kal-*yoo*-na, the heather or ling. (Late Lat.)
callus, *n.* *kal*-lus, a callosity; a bony formation uniting fractured bones; tissue forming over the wounded surface of a stem [Bot.]. (L.)
calm, *a.* kahm, still; undisturbed; tranquil: *n.* the state of being calm; complete absence of wind [Naut.]: *v.t.* to still; to quiet: *v.i.* to become still. (Fr. *calme.*)
calmative, *a.* *kahm*-a-tive *or* *kal*-ma-tiv, possessing a soothing or sedative effect: *n.* a sedative [Med.].
calmly, *ad.* *kahm*-le, in a calm manner.
calmness, *n.* *kahm*-ness, the state of being calm.
calmy, *a.* *kahm*-e, calm; quiet.
calomel, *n.* *kal*-o-mel, a sub-chloride of mercury used as a cathartic. (Gr. *kalos*, fair, *melas*, black.)
calorescence, *n.* kal-o-*res*-ence, the transmutation of calorific rays into luminous ones [Physics]. (L. *calescens*, growing hot.)
caloric, *n.* ka-*lo*-rik, heat: *a.* pertaining to heat. (L. *calor*, heat.)
caloricity, *n.* kal-o-*ris*-e-te, power of developing heat, esp. in living beings.
calorie, *n.* *kal*-o-re, a unit of heat; the **small calorie**, raises the temperature of 1 gram of water 1° C., the **large** or **great calorie** that of 1 kilo of water 1° C., and the **centuple** or **rational calorie** raises the temperature of 1 gram of water from 0° to 100° C. (Fr.)
calorifacient, *a.* ka-*lo*-re-*faysh*-ent, heat-producing; supplying animal heat [Physiol.].
calorific, *a.* kal-o-*rif*-ik, heating; causing heat. **calorific rays**, the invisible heating rays of the sun. (L. *calor*, and *facio*, make.)
calorimeter, *n.* kal-o-*rim*-e-ter, an apparatus for measuring quantities of heat, or the specific heat of bodies, or the heat given out by a body in cooling. (L. *calor*, and Gr. *metron*, a measure.)
calotte, *n.* ka-*lot*, a skull-cap or coif worn by ecclesiastics, and formerly by serjeants-at-law; anything of the shape of a cap; a round cavity or cupola, like a cap [Arch.]. (Fr.)
calotype, *n.* *kal*-o-tipe, an obsolete photographic process employing paper treated with silver idoide, known also as talbotype from the inventor, W. H. F. Talbot. (Gr. *kalos*, beautiful, *typos*, form.)
caloyer, *n.* ka-*loy*-er, a monk of the Greek Church. (Fr.)
calpac, *n.* *kal*-pak, a high black hat of felt or sheepskin worn in the Near East. (Turk.)
caltrop, *n.* *kal*-trop, a spiked instrument formerly thrown on the ground to impede the progress of an enemy's cavalry [Mil.]; various trailing plants that may entangle the feet, also a kind of thistle [Bot.]. (A.S. *calcatrippe*, from *colletrappe*, a thistle.)
calumba, *n.* ka-*lum*-ba, the plant *Jateorhiza calumba*, of East Africa, the root of which is a bitter tonic.
calumet, *n.* *kal*-yoo-met, the North American Indian ceremonial tobacco-pipe used at the ratification of treaties and as a symbol of peace. (Fr.)
calumniate, *v.t.* ka-*lum*-ne-ate, to charge falsely and maliciously with something criminal, immoral, or disgraceful; to slander: *v.i.* to utter calumnies; to propagate evil reports, with evil intent. (L. *calumniatus*, censured.)
calumniation, *n.* ka-*lum*-ne-*ay*-shon, the act of calumniating.
calumniator, *n.* ka-*lum*-ne-ay-tor, one who calumniates.
calumniatory, *a.* ka-*lum*-ne-a-to-re, calumnious.
calumnious, *a.* ka-*lum*-ne-us, slanderous; defamatory.
calumniously, *ad.* ka-*lum*-ne-us-le, in a calumnious manner.
calumniousness, *n.* ka-*lum*-ne-us-ness, the quality of being calumnious.
calumny, *n.* *kal*-um-ne, false accusation of a crime or offence, maliciously made or reported; a false charge; slander. (Fr. *calomnie.*)
Calvary, *n.* *kal*-va-re, a place of skulls, the mount where Christ was crucified; in Roman Catholic countries, an elevation on which crosses representing the crucifixion are erected for the purpose of devotion; a cross set upon three steps [Her.]. (L. *calvāria*, skull.)
calve, *v.i.* kahv, to bring forth a calf; to bring forth young. (A.S. *cealfian*, calve.)
Calvinism, *n.* *kal*-vin-izm, the system of Calvin and his followers, the chief characteristics of which are the doctrines of predestination and of the sovereign action and persistent operation of divine grace.
Calvinist, *n.* *kal*-vin-ist, one who accepts the doctrines of Calvin.
Calvinistic, *a.* kal-ve-*nis*-tik, pertaining to Calvinism.
Calvinistically, *ad.* kal-ve-*nis*-te-ka-le, in a Calvinistic manner.
calvities, *n.* kal-*vish*-e-eez, baldness. (L. *calvus*, bald.)
calx, *n.* kalks, the residue of a metal or mineral remaining after calcination. (L.)
Calycanthus, *n.* kal-e-*kan*-thus, a genus of N. American shrubs including the Carolina allspice. (Gr. *kalyx*, a cup, *anthos*, a flower.)
calyciform, *a.* ka-*lis*-e-form, shaped like a calyx.
calycinal, *a.* ka-*liss*-e-nal, pertaining to a calyx; situated on a calyx.
calycine, *a.* *kal*-e-sine, calycinal.
calycle, *n.* *kal*-ikl, a row of leaflets at the base of the calyx on the outside [Bot.]; a small cup-like prominence on a coral, containing a polype-cell [Zool.]. (L. *calyculus*, diminutive for *calyx.*)
calyptra, *n.* ka-*lip*-tra, a hood-like covering [Bot.]; the capsule cap of mosses.
calyptrate, *a.* ka-*lip*-trat, having a calyptra or hood [Bot.]. (Gr. *kalyptra*, a covering or hood.)
calyptriform, *a.* ka-*lip*-tre-form, in the form of a calyptra.
calyx, *n.* *kay*-liks, the whorl or cup of sepals of a flower [Bot.]. (Gr. *kalyx*, a cup.)
cam, *a.* kam, curved; crooked. (Gael.)
cam, *n.* kam, a projection for changing rotary to reciprocal motion. (A.S., a comb.)
camaieu, *n.* kah-may-*yoo* (or App.), a cameo; a method of painting in monochrome. (Fr.)
camaraderie, *n.* kam-a-*rah*-de-re, good-fellowship; friendship and fealty between comrades. (Fr.)
camarilla, *n.* kam-a-*ril*-la, a clique of secret counsellors who come between a monarch and his regular ministry. (Sp.)
camber, *n.* *kam*-ber, a slight arching or convexity upwards; the convexity of a road-surface; a camber-beam; a small tidal basin: *v.t.* or *v.i.* to bend; to arch. **camber-beam**, a piece of timber cut archwise, or with an obtuse angle in the middle. **cambered-deck**, an arched deck, sloping towards the stem and stern. (Fr. *cambrer*, to bend.)
cambism, *n.* *kam*-bizm, the art, business, or profession of a cambist.
cambist, *n.* *kam*-bist, a banker; one who deals in bills and notes of exchange; one skilled in the science of exchange. (Fr. *cambiste.*)
cambium, *n.* *kam*-be-um, the mucilaginous layer of cellular tissue between the wood and bark of exogenous plants in the spring. (Late L. *cambium*, exchange.)
cambrel, *n.* *kam*-brel, a crooked piece of wood or iron to hang meat on; a gambrel.
Cambrian, *a.* *kam*-bre-an, pertaining to Wales or to the palæozoic strata next below the Silurian [Geol.]. (L. *Cambria*, Wales.)
cambric, *n.* *kame*-brik, a species of fine white linen, originally manufactured at Cambray.
came, kame, *p.* of the verb to come.
came, *n.* kame, a grooved strip of lead holding panes in latticed windows. (Scots.)
camel, *n.* *kam*-el, a large ungulate of the genus *Camelus* used in Asia and Africa as a beast of burden, the Bactrian (*C. bactrianus*) having two humps on the back, and the Arabian (*C. dromedarius*) one; a large floating machine for bearing ships over bars into a harbour. **camel's hair**, in the so-called camel-hair brushes, hair from the tail of the squirrel. (L. *camelus.*)

camel-backed, *a.* *kam*-el-bakt, humpbacked.
camellia, *n.* ka-*mel*-le-a, a species of evergreen shrub, native of India, China, and Japan. (G. J. *Kamel*, who introduced it from China about 1740.)
camelopard, *n.* ka-*mel*- or *kam*-el-o-parhd, the giraffe. (Gr.)
camelot, *n.* *kam*-e-lot, camlet.
camelry, *n.* *kam*-el-re, troops mounted on camels.
camembert, *n.* kam-em-*bair* (or App.), a soft cheese made in Normandy. (Fr., name of village where made.)
cameo, *n.* *kam*-e-o, a precious stone cut in relief, esp. one composed of different coloured layers, the under layer forming the background; a shell so carved. (It. *cammeo.*)
★**camera,** *n.* *kam*-er-ra, a Judge's chamber [Law]; a council chamber; the adaptation of the camera obscura used in photography. **in camera,** not in open court. **camera lucida,** an apparatus by means of which the image of any object may be made to appear on the wall of a light room, or on paper, canvas, etc. [Optics]. **camera obscura,** an apparatus by means of which the images of external objects are exhibited distinctly, and in their native colours, on a white surface placed in the focus of the lens [Optics]. (L., a chamber.)
cameralistics, *n.* *kam*-er-ra-*lis*-tiks, the management of public finance or state property (esp. in imperial Germany). (Ger., from Lat.)
camera-man, *n.* *kam*-er-ra-man, one who takes photographs for the press; a cinematographer.
camerated, *a.* *kam*-er-ray-ted, arched; vaulted [Arch.]; divided into chambers [Zool.].
camerlingo, *n.* kam-er-*ling*-go, the papal chamberlain (invariably a Cardinal, and head of the Church during a vacancy of the Holy See through death). (It.)
Cameronian, *n.* kam-er-*roh*-ne-an, a follower of Richard Cameron, a Scottish Covenanter of the 17th cent., or of his doctrines; a member of the Reformed Presbyterian Church; *pl.* the old 26th and 90th Foot, now the Scottish Rifles.
cami-knickers, *n.* *kam*-e-nik-erz, a woman's undergarment serving as camisole and knickers combined.
camion, *n.* *kam*-e-on, a low-built truck or dray, formerly one for transport of cannon.
camisade, *n.* kam-is-*ahd*, camisado.
camisado, *n.* kam-e-*sah*-doh, a night-attack by soldiers, originally with shirts worn over the armour as a means of recognition. (Fr.)
camisole, *n.* *kam*-e-sole, a light under-bodice, or corset-cover, worn by women. (Fr.)
camlet, *n.* *kam*-let, a thin stuff, originally of camel's hair, but now usually of wool or goat's hair mixed with silk. (Fr. *camelot.*)
cammock, *n.* *kam*-ok, the plant restharrow. (A.S.)
camomile, *n.* *kam*-o-mile, any of the aromatic creeping plants of the allied genera *Anthemis*, *Matricaria*, and *Chamomilla*, some of which yield a bitter tonic and stomachic. (Gr. *chamaimēlon*, earth-apple.)
Camorra, *n.* ka-*mor*-ra, a secret terrorist society in Italy in the 19th century. (It.)
camouflage, *n.* *kam*-oo-flahzh, the disguising of weapons, ships, buildings, sites, etc., for the purpose of concealing them from an enemy; the disguise so used; any means of masking or concealing one's intentions: *v.t.* to disguise or hide by or as by camouflage. (Fr. *camoufler*, to disguise.)
camp, *n.* kamp, the ground on which an army or travelling party pitches its tents; the collection of the tents; an army or body of troops camping; a station for military training; a body of followers: *v.t.* or *v.i.* to encamp. **camp meeting,** a religious meeting held in a marquee or in the open air. (L. *campus*, a plain.)
campagnol, *n.* *kam*-pan-yol, the short-tailed field-vole. (Fr.)
campaign, *n.* kam-*pane*, an extensive tract of open plain; the time that an army keeps the field during a season; a series of military (or other, as political, commercial, etc.) operations: *v.i.* to serve in a campaign. (Fr. *campagne*, the open country.)
campaigner, *n.* kam-*pane*-er, one who has served in many campaigns; an old experienced soldier.
campanero, *n.* kam-pan-*ay*-ro, the white-plumaged bell-bird of South America. (Sp., a bell-ringer.)
campaniform, *a.* kam-*pan*-e-form, bell-shaped [Bot.].
campanile, *n.* kam-pan-*ee*-le, a detached bell-tower; a clock-tower; a steeple. (It.)
campanologist, *n.* kam-pan-*ol*-o-jist, a student of, or expert in, campanology.
campanology, *n.* kam-pan-*ol*-oj-e, the art and principles of bell-ringing.
Campanula, *n.* kam-*pan*-yoo-la, a large genus of plants with campanulate flowers, including the harebell, Canterbury bell, etc.
campanulate, *a.* kam-*pan*-yoo-lat, bell-shaped.
camp-bedstead, *n.* kamp-*bed*-sted, a bedstead made to fold up.
camp-craft, *n.* *kamp*-krahft, the art of camping in the open, esp. for health or holiday purposes.
campeachy-wood, *n.* kam-*peech*-e-wood, logwood. (*Campeche*, a town in Mexico.)
camper, *n.* *kamp*-er, one who camps out, or who takes part in a camp or a camp-meeting; one addicted to camp-craft.
campestral, *a.* kam-*pes*-tral, pertaining to or growing in fields. (L. *campester*, field.)
camp-fire, *n.* *kamp*-fire, the main fire in a camp; a social gathering or singsong round this.
camp-follower, *n.* *kamp*-fol-lo-er, a civilian who accompanies an army in the field, as a sutler.
camphine, *n.* *kam*-feen, an illuminant consisting of rectified oil of turpentine.
camphor, *n.* *kam*-for, a whitish solid semi-translucent substance, procured chiefly from *Laurus camphora* and other trees of Eastern Asia, with a bitterish taste and a fragrant odour. (Fr. *camphre.*)
camphoraceous, *a.* kam-fo-*ray*-shus, of the nature of camphor.
camphorate, *n.* *kam*-fo-rat, a salt of camphoric acid: *v.t.* to treat or impregnate with camphor.
camphoric, *a.* kam-*fo*-rik, pertaining to or containing camphor. **camphoric acid,** any of several acids obtained by the oxidation of camphor [Chem.].
camphor-tree, *n.* *kam*-for-tree, any tree yielding camphor, esp. *Cinnamomum camphora*.
campion, *n.* *kam*-pe-on, any one of the plants included in *Lychnis* and *Silene*.
camp-meeting, *n.* *kamp*-mee-ting, an open-air gathering for religious services held over two or more days [U.S.A.].
campstool, *n.* *kamp*-stool, a folding stool.
campus, *n.* *kam*-pus, the grounds of a college or school, esp. those enclosed by the buildings [U.S.A.]. (L., a field.)
campylospermous, *a.* kam-pil-o-*sper*-mus, with the seed curved at the margin [Bot.].
campylotropous, *a.* kam-pil-*ot*-ro-pus, bent so that the apex of the ovule is close to the base. [Bot.]. (G. *kampulos*, bent, *tropein*, to turn).
camshaft, *n.* *kam*-shahft, the shaft for controlling the cams which operate the valves of an engine.
cam-wheel, *n.* *kam*-wheel, a wheel so designed that it acts as a cam.
camwood, *n.* *kam*-wood, a red dye-wood, a species of *Baphia* of tropical Africa.
can, *n.* kan, a canister; a metal cup or vessel for liquors; an hermetically sealed metal container in which foods, fruit, etc., are preserved: *v.t.* to put into a tin for preserving. (A.S. *canne.*)
can, *v.i.* kan (*p.* **could**), to be able; to have sufficient power. **can but,** can merely. **cannot away with,** cannot brook. **cannot but,** cannot help. (A.S. *cunnan*, to know.)
Canadian, *a.* ka-*nay*-de-an, pertaining to Canada. **Canada balsam,** a kind of turpentine obtained from the balsam fir, used in medicine and the arts. **Canada pitch,** the resin of the hemlock spruce. **Canadian pondweed,** a species of *Anacharis*.
canaille, *n.* ka-*nile*, the mob; the rabble. (Fr.)
canal, *n.* ka-*nal*, an artificial waterway, specially for the passage of ships or boats; a duct in the body for any of its fluids, etc. [Anat.]; a fluting or groove [Arch.]. (L. *canalis*, a channel.)
canaliculate, *a.* kan-a-*lik*-yoo-lat, channelled; striated; minutely furrowed.
canalization, *n.* *kan*-a-ly-*zay*-shon, the construction of canals.
canalize, *v.t.* *kan*-a-lize, to convert into a canal or navigable waterway.
canapé, *n.* *kan*-a-pay, any appetizer on toast. (Fr.)
canard, *n.* ka-*nahr*, a hoax; a fabricated story palmed off as a fact. (Fr., a duck.)
canariensis, *n.* ka-nare-re-*en*-sis, canary creeper.

canary, *n.* ka-*nare*-re, wine made in the Canary Islands; an old dance; a singing bird, *Serinus canarius*, originally brought from the Canary Islands. **canary creeper**, a yellow species of *Tropæolum*. **canary grass**, the canary seed plant, a species of *Phalaris*.

canasta, *n.* ka-*nas*-ta, a double-pack gambling card-game, elaborated from rummy, in which jokers are used and all deuces rank as jokers. (Sp., a basket.)

canaster, *n.* ka-*nas*-ter, a rush basket in which tobacco was packed; a kind of tobacco. (Sp. *canasta*.)

can-buoy, *n.* *kan*-boy, a large buoy in the form of a cone.

cancan, *n.* (App.), a lascivious dance. (Fr.)

cancel, *n.* *kan*-sel, the deletion and reprinting of part of a book; the part so deleted [Print.]: *v.t.* to blot out by drawing lines across; to annul; to strike out; to suppress. (Fr. *canceller*.)

cancellated, *a.* *kan*-sel-lay-ted, cross-barred; having cross lines; reticulated [Bot.].

cancellation, *n.* kan-sel-*lay*-shon, the act of cancelling; state of being cancelled.

cancellous, *a.* *kan*-sel-us, resembling lattice-work (of the spongy part of bone).

cancer, *n.* *kan*-ser, the crab; one of the signs of the zodiac, the sign of the summer solstice [Astron.]; carcinoma, a malignant tumour whose appearance suggested to the ancients the claws of a crab [Med.]. (L., a crab.)

cancerate, *v.i.* *kan*-ser-rate, to become cancerous.

canceration, *n.* kan-ser-*ray*-shon, a growing cancerous.

cancerous, *a.* *kan*-ser-rus, of or like a cancer; affected with cancer.

cancriform, *a.* *kang*-kre-form, of the form of a cancer or crab.

cancrine, *a.* *kang*-krin, having the qualities of a crab, or of a palindrome.

cancrisocial, *a.* kang-kre-*soh*-shal, living commensally with a crab [Zool.].

cancroid, *a.* *kang*-kroyd, crab-like; like cancer, but not really so [Med.]: *n.* any member of the crab family; a cancer-like disease. (L. *cancer*, and Gr. *eidos*, form.)

candelabrum, *n.* kan-de-*lay*-brum (*pl.* **candelabra**), a tall lamp-stand; a high ornamental candlestick, usually with branches.

candent, *a.* *kand*-ent, glowing with white-heat.

candescence, *n.* kan-*des*-ens, white heat.

candescent, *a.* kan-*des*-ent, glowing with or as with white heat; dazzling.

candid, *a.* *kan*-did, frank; sincere; ingenuous; free from prejudice. (L. *candidus*, white.)

candidacy, *n.* *kan*-de-da-se, the state or term of being a candidate.

candidate, *n.* *kan*-de-dat, one who seeks, or is brought forward, to fill some office or post of honour, so called because it was the custom in Rome for such to dress in white.

candidateship, *n.* *kan*-de-dat-ship, candidacy.

candidature, *n.* *kan*-de-da-tewr, candidacy.

candidly, *ad.* *kan*-did-le, in a candid manner.

candidness, *n.* *kan*-did-ness, quality of being candid.

candied, *pp.* and *a.* *kan*-did, preserved or encrusted with sugar; glistening; flattering.

candle, *n.* *kan*-dl, a roll of tallow, wax, or similar substance, with a wick in the centre, to give light; a light; candle-power. **candle-power**, the unit for measuring light, nearly equal to the amount given by a standard candle burning at a rate of 120 grains per hour. **not fit to hold the candle to**, not fit to be the lowest menial of. **not worth the candle**, not worth the seeking. (L. *candela*.)

candleberry, *n.* *kan*-dl-be-re, the fruit of the wax-myrtle.

candle-coal, *n.* *kan*-dl-kohl, cannel.

candle-light, *n.* the light of a candle; evening.

candlemas, *n.* *kan*-dl-mass, the feast (Feb. 2nd) in commemoration of the Purification of the Virgin, when candles are blessed.

candlestick, *n.* *kan*-dl-stik, a utensil to hold a candle.

candle-tree, *n.* *kan*-dl-tree, a tree from which some illuminant is obtained, as *Parmentiera cerifera*, of Panama, *Aleurites triloba*, of the Moluccas, etc.

candock, *n.* *kan*-dok, the yellow water-lily.

candour, *n.* *kan*-dur, frankness; sincerity; freedom from prejudice. (L. *candor*, whiteness.)

candy, *n.* *kan*-de, sugar crystallized; a sweetmeat; sweetstuff of any kind [Amer.]: *v.i.* to become candied: *v.t.* to conserve with sugar; to crystallize; to encrust with crystals. (Fr. *candi*.)

candytuft, *n.* *kan*-de-tuft, a plant of the genus *Iberis*. (*Candia*, in Crete, and *tuft*.)

cane, *n.* kane, a reed-stem; sugar-cane; the stem of the raspberry; the bamboo; the rattan; a walking-stick: *v.t.* to beat with a cane; to work with split cane. **cane sugar**, sugar made from the sugar-cane as distinguished from other sugars. (L. *canna*.)

cane-brake, *n.* *kane*-brake, a thicket of canes.

cane-chair, *n.* *kane*-chare, one with a seat of plaited cane.

canella, *n.* ka-*nel*-la, a West Indian tree with an aromatic bark. (L. *canna*, a reed.)

cane-mill, *n.* *kane*-mil, a mill for grinding sugar canes.

canephor, *n.* *kan*-e-for, a figure of a woman bearing a basket on her head used as an architectural ornament. (Gr. *kānephoros*, a bearer at a festival.)

canescent, *a.* ka-*nes*-ent, growing white or hoary. (L. *canescens*, growing white.)

cane-trash, *n.* *kane*-trash, refuse of sugar-cane after grinding.

cangue, *n.* kang, a Chinese pillory consisting of a large board placed round the criminal's neck so that he cannot lie down or eat. (Fr.)

can-hook, *n.* *kan*-hook, a tackle for slinging a cask.

canicular, *a.* kan-*ik*-yoo-lar, pertaining to the dog-star; excessively hot, as in the dog-days. (L. *canicularis*, the dog-star.)

canine, *a.* *kane*-ine *or* kan-*ine*, pertaining to or like the dog. **canine appetite**, insatiable appetite. **canine laugh**, a sardonic laugh. **canine teeth**, two sharp-pointed teeth in each jaw, one on each side, between the incisors and molars. (L. *caninus*.)

caning, *n.* *kane*-ing, a beating with a cane or stick.

canister, *n.* *kan*-is-ter, a box or case, originally of reed, now generally of thin metal; the case in which case-shot is put for discharge; case-shot. (L. *canistrum*.)

canker, *n.* *kang*-ker, a fungus causing the bark of trees to rot and fall; a corroding ulceration in the mouth, esp. of children; anything that corrodes, corrupts, or destroys; a gangrenous disease in a horse's foot; the dog-rose: *v.i.* to grow corrupt; to decay: *v.t.* to corrode; to infect; to pollute. (L. *cancer*, a crab.)

cankered, *a.* *kang*-kerd, affected with canker; ill-natured; crabbed.

cankerous, *a.* *kang*-ker-rus, corroding like a canker.

canker-worm, *n.* *kang*-ker-wurm, any caterpillar destructive to plants, esp. to fruit-trees.

cankery, *a.* *kang*-ker-re, cankered; rusty; surly.

canna, *n.* *kan*-na, an ornamental plant of the genus *Canna* including *C. indica*, the Indian shot and *C. edulis* which yields a kind of arrowroot. (Gr. *kanna*, reed.)

cannabin, *n.* *kan*-na-bin, a narcotic resin extracted from hemp. (L. *cannabis*, the hemp plant.)

canned, *a.* kand, packed and sold in cans, tinned; drunk, tight [Slang].

cannel, *n.* *kan*-nel, a hard, compact, bituminous coal, which burns with a bright flame like a candle.

cannelure, *n.* *kan*-ne-lewr, a groove such as the fluting on a column or round a bullet. (Fr.)

canner, *n.* *kan*-ner, an owner of a canning business; one engaged in, or a machine for, canning; a beast fit only for canning.

cannery, *n.* *kan*-ner-re, a factory for the canning of meat, fruit, or other food-stuff.

cannibal, *n.* *kan*-ne-bal, a human being that eats human flesh; an animal that feeds on the flesh of its own kind; *a.* pertaining to cannibalism; blood-thirsty. (Sp.; corruption of Carib, a native of the Caribees.)

cannibalism, *n.* *kan*-ne-bal-izm, the act or practice of eating human flesh by mankind; murderous cruelty.

cannibalistic, *a.* *kan*-ne-ba-*lis*-tik, of or pertaining to cannibals or cannibalism.

cannikin, *n.* *kan*-e-kin, pannikin; a small can or cup.

cannily, *ad.* *kan*-e-le, in canny fashion.

canniness, *n.* kan-e-ness, the quality of being canny.

canning, *n.* *kan*-ing, the process or occupation of preserving comestibles in sealed tins.

cannon, *n.* *kan*-non, a large mounted gun; a stroke in billiards by which the player strikes both his opponent's and the red ball with his own; a rebound off one object on to another; a hollow shaft containing another, both revolving independently [Mech.]; the cannon-bone: *v.t.* to make a cannon at billiards; to knock or come up against.
cannonade, *n.* kan-non-*ade*, an attack with artillery, generally a fast, sustained attack; a bombardment: *v.t.* to attack or batter with artillery: *v.i.* to discharge cannon.
cannon-ball, *n.* *kan*-non-bawl, a ball, usually of cast iron, to be thrown from cannon; a projectile.
cannon-bit, *n.* *kan*-non-bit, a round smooth horse bit.
cannon-bone, *n.* *kan*-non-bone, the long bone between the knee and fetlock of a horse.
cannoneer, *n.* kan-non-*eer*, an artilleryman.
cannon-proof, *a.* *kan*-non-proof, proof against artillery.
cannon-shot, *n.* *kan*-non-shot, the range of a cannon.
cannot, *kan*-not, unable (the words *can* and *not* are thus united in common usage).
cannula, *n.* *kan*-new-la, a small tube used to drain fluid from a body-cavity [Surg.]. (*Canna*, a reed.)
cannular, *a.* *kan*-new-lar, tubular.
canny, *a.* *kan*-ne, knowing; cautious; prudent; easy-going. **ca' canny,** be cautious or go slowly (of the policy of limiting output). (Scots.)
canoe, *n.* ka-*noo*, a light boat worked with paddles: *v.i.* to go by canoe. (Sp. *canoa*.)
canoeist, *n.* ka-*noo*-ist, one skilled in managing a canoe.
canon, *n.* *kan*-on, a law or rule, specially in Church matters; a standard or criterion; the Book of Holy Scriptures received as genuine by the Church; a dignitary of the Church, who possesses a prebend or revenue allotted for the performance of divine service in a cathedral or collegiate church; the catalogue of canonized saints; the rules, or the book of rules, of a monastic order; a kind of continual fugue [Mus.]; a large type, approximately 48-point [Print.] **canon law,** ecclesiastical law. (A.S.)
cañon, *n.* *kan*-yon, a canyon.
canoness, *n.* *kan*-on-ess, a woman living as a member of a religious community but not under perpetual vows.
canonical, *a.* ka-*non*-e-kal, included in the canon, specially of Scripture; prescribed by canon law, or the canons. **canonical hours,** hours appointed by the canons for the offices of prayer and devotion (matins, prime, tierce, sext, nones, vespers, and compline); the hours between which it is lawful to celebrate marriages.
canonically, *ad.* ka-*non*-e-ka-le, in a manner conformable to the canon.
canonicalness, *n.* ka-*non*-e-kal-ness, the quality of being canonical; canonicity.
canonicals, *n.pl.* ka-*non*-e-kalz, the dress of a clergyman when officiating, prescribed by canon.
canonicate, *n.* ka-*non*-e-kate, the office of a canon.
canonicity, *n.* kan-o-*nis*-e-te, the quality of belonging to the canon, or the genuine books of Scripture. (Late L. *canonicus*.)
canonist, *n.* *kan*-on-ist, one skilled in canon law.
canonistic, *a.* kan-o-*nis*-tik, pertaining to a canonist.
canonization, *n.* kan-o-ny-*zay*-shon, the act or process of canonizing.
canonize, *v.t.* *kan*-on-ize, to declare a man or woman a saint, and rank him or her in the catalogue called the canon; to sanction authoritatively.
canonry, *n.* *kan*-on-re, the benefice of a canon.
canoodle, *v.i.* and *v.t.* ka-*noo*-dl, to caress or fondle; to bill and coo. [Prob. S.E. Eng. Dial.]
Canopic, *a.* ka-*noh*-pik, of Canopus, a city of ancient Egypt named from the bright star in the constellation *Argo*. **Canopic jar,** or **vase,** an urn for preserving the viscera of an embalmed body.
canopied, *a.* *kan*-o-pid, covered with a canopy.
canopy, *n.* *kan*-o-pe, a rich covering over an altar, throne, bed, etc.; a covering of state borne over the Host or a distinguished person; a projecting moulding round the head of a Gothic arch [Arch.]: *v.t.* to cover with a canopy. (Fr. *canapé*.)
canorous, *a.* ka-*naw*-rus, tuneful. (L. *canto*, sing.)
cant, *n.* kant, slang; a mode of speaking peculiar to a certain sect or party, esp. the jargon of vagrants; hypocritical affectation of sincerity; sanctimoniousness: *a.* of the nature of cant: *v.i.* to speak whiningly, peculiarly, or insincerely. (L. *canto*, sing.)
cant, *n.* kant, an external angle; an inclination from a horizontal line; a thrust; a jerk: *v.t.* to tilt over; to incline. (Late L. *cantus*, a turning.)
cantab, *n.* *kan*-tab, a graduate, or undergraduate, of Cambridge University. (L. *Cantabrigia*, Cambridge.)
cantabile, *a.* kan-*tah*-be-lay, in a graceful singing style: *n.* a piece in this style [Mus.] (It.)
cantaloup, *n.* *kan*-ta-loop, a small round variety of musk-melon. (*Cantalupo*, a castle near Rome.)
cantankerous, *a.* kan-*tang*-ker-rus, cross-grained; quarrelsome. (Origin doubtful.)
cantankerously, *ad.* kan-*tang*-ker-rus-le, in a cantankerous manner.
cantar, *n.* kan-*tahr*, a weight of the Near East, of from about 100 to 125 lb.
cantata, *n.* kan-*tah*-ta, a narrative poem, set to melody and recitative; a dramatic choral composition.
cantatrice, *n.* *kan*-ta-treece, a songstress.
canteen, *n.* kan-*teen*, a covered bottle or other liquor-container forming part of a soldier's equipment; the place in a camp, barracks, etc., where drink, provisions, and small goods are obtained; the meals-room of a factory, works, community-centre, etc.; a case fitted with articles for use in campaigning or travelling; a chest of or for cutlery. (It. *cantina*, wine-cellar.)
canter, *n.* *kant*-er, a horse's gait between a trot and a gallop: *v.i.* to move as a horse at a moderate gallop: *v.t.* to make to canter. **in a canter,** easily. (From the easy pace at which pilgrims rode to Canterbury.)
canterbury, *n.* *kant*-er-be-re, a stand with divisions to hold music, portfolios, or papers. **Canterbury bell,** the plant *Campanula medium*.
cantharides, *n.pl.* kan-*tha*-re-deez, Spanish flies, which are dried for use in medicine. (Gr., blistering flies.)
cantharidin, *n.* kan-*tha*-re-din, the active principle of cantharides, causing vesication.
cantharus, *n.* *kan*-tha-rus, a deep, long-stemmed drinking-cup with two loop-shaped handles. (Gr.)
canthus, *n.* *kanth*-us, the corner of the eye. (Gr.)
canticle, *n.* *kan*-te-kl, a song; a chant. **canticles,** the Song of Solomon. (L. *canticulum*, a little song.)
cantilever, *n.* *kant*-e-*lee*-ver, a truss in a bridge; a beam or structure carrying a load and supported at one end only [Eng.]: *a.* constructed on the cantilever principle. (*Cant* and *lever*.)
cantillate, *v.t.* *kant*-e-late, to chant; to intone, esp. as in synagogues.
canting, *a.* *kant*-ing, whining; hypocritical.
cantingly, *ad.* *kant*-ing-le, in a canting manner.
cantle, *n.* *kan*-tl, the projection at the rear of a saddle; any piece cut away. (O.Fr. *cantel*.)
canto, *n.* *kan*-to, a division of a poem; the highest vocal part, or the leading melody [Mus.]. **canto-fermo,** the tenor part [Mus.]; the part which is the subject of counterpoint [Mus.]. (It.)
canton, *n.* kan-*ton*, a small division of territory; in Switzerland, a distinct state; the quarter of a flag; the corner of a heraldic shield: *v.t.* to divide into cantons; (pron. kan-*toon*), to billet the different divisions of a body of troops. (Fr., corner.)
cantonal, *a.* *kan*-ton-al, pertaining to a canton.
cantonment, *n.* kan-*toon*-ment *or* kan-*ton*-ment, quarters for troops.
cantor, *n.* *kan*-tor, a precentor. (L.)
cantorial, *a.* kan-*taw*-re-al, pertaining to the northern side, the precentor's side, of a choir.
canty, *a.* *kan*-te, cheerful; talkative. (Scots.)
Canuck, *n.* ka-*nuk*, a French-Canadian. (U.S.A.)
★**canvas,** *n.* *kan*-vas, a coarse cloth made of hemp or flax, used for tents, sails, painting on, etc.; a clear unbleached cloth, woven regularly in little squares, used for tapestry; sails in general. **under canvas,** living in a tent [Coll.]; with all sails set [Naut.]: *a.* made of canvas. (O.Fr. *canevas*.)
canvas-back, *n.* *kan*-vas-bak, the American sea-duck *Nyroca valisneria*.
canvass, *n.* *kan*-vas, close examination; discussion; solicitation of votes: *v.i.* to go about to solicit votes, interest, or orders: *v.t.* to examine; to discuss; to solicit votes. (From *canvas*, as a material for use in sifting.)

canvasser, *n.* *kan*-vas-er, one who solicits votes or orders.
cany, *a.* *kane*-e, full of canes; made of cane.
canyon, *n.* *kan*-yon, a deep ravine; a precipitous gorge. (Sp. *cañon.*)
canzone, *n.* kan-*tzoh*-nay, a popular part-song. (It.)
canzonet, *n.* kan-tzon-*et*, a short air or song.
caoutchouc, *n.* *kou*-chuk, raw rubber; an elastic impermeable substance found in the milky juices of certain plants. (Carib. *cahuchu.*)
cap, *n.* kap, a covering for the head; a cover; the top; anything in form of a cap; the proceeds of a collection, esp. for a huntsman: *v.t.* to cover the top or end; to put a cap on; to complete; to top and beat; to confer a degree; to award a player (esp. at football) his cap. **cap and bells,** the traditional insignia of a Court Fool. **cap of liberty,** the conical cap worn by manumitted slaves in ancient Rome, adopted by the French Revolutionists and hence the emblem of republicanism. **cap of maintenance,** a ceremonial cap borne before English sovereigns at their coronation and before some mayors. **cap-paper,** a coarse paper. **to set one's cap at,** to try to attract. (A.S. *cæppe.*)
capa, *n.* *kah*-pa, the tobacco leaf used for the outer covering of Havana cigars; a Spanish cloak. (Sp.)
capability, *n.* kay-pa-*bil*-e-te, the quality of being capable, especially intellectually.
capable, *a.* *kay*-pa-bl, susceptible; able; competent; qualified; skilful. (Fr.)
capableness, *n.* *kay*-pa-bl-ness, the state or quality of being capable.
capably, *ad.* *kay*-pa-ble, in a capable manner.
capacious, *a.* ka-*pay*-shus, able to hold much; roomy; spacious; comprehensive. (L. *capio*, take.)
capaciously, *ad.* ka-*pay*-shus-le, in a capacious manner.
capaciousness, *n.* ka-*pay*-shus-ness, the quality of being capacious.
capacitate, *v.t.* ka-*pas*-e-tate, to qualify; to render competent.
capacity, *n.* ka-*pas*-e-te, the power of containing or holding; room; capability; intellectual ability; position; cubic contents; legal qualification. **to capacity,** with the house crowded [Theatre]. (Fr. *capacité.*)
cap-à-pie, *ad.* kap-a-*pee*, from head to foot. (Fr.)
caparison, *n.* ka-*pa*-re-son, state trappings; rich clothing of a horse; equipment: *v.t.* to cover with state trappings; to adorn with rich dress. (O.Fr. *caparasson.*)
cape, *n.* kape, a point of land extending into the sea; a headland. **the Cape,** Cape Colony. **Cape boy,** a South African half-breed. **Cape cart,** a two-wheeled vehicle with a hood and pole. **Cape diamond,** one that is slightly yellowish or off colour. **Cape gooseberry,** the tropical shrub *Physalis peruviana*, or its acid fruit. **Cape hunting dog,** the African hyæna-like wild dog, *Lycaon pictus.* **Cape pigeon,** a species of petrel, *Daption capensis.* **Cape smoke,** a raw kind of brandy made in Cape Colony. (L. *caput*, head.)
cape, *n.* kape, the shoulder-piece of a coat or cloak; a loose covering for the shoulders. (L. *cappa*, cap.)
capelin, *n.* *kap*-e-lin, a small smelt, *Mallotus villosus*, used as bait in the Canadian and Newfoundland fisheries. (Fr. *capelan.*)
capeline, *n.* *kap*-e-lin, a surgical hood-shaped bandage; a lady's evening hood. (Fr.)
caper, *n.* *kay*-per, the flower-bud of a species of *Capparis* used in sauces. (Fr. *capre.*)
caper, *n.* *kay*-per, a frolicsome leap, spring, or jump; a prank: *v.i.* to skip or jump; to frisk about. (It. *capriola.*)
capercailzie, *n.* kap-er-*kale*-zee, the wood-grouse, *Tetrao urogallus*, or cock of the wood. (Gael. *capull*, horse, *coille*, wood.)
capful, *n.* *kap*-ful, a small quantity.
capias, *n.* *kap*-e-as *or* *kay*-pe-as, a writ authorizing seizure of person or goods. (L., take hold.)
capibara, *n.* kap-e-*bah*-ra, capybara.
capillaceous, *a.* kap-e-*lay*-shus, hair-like.
capillaire, *n.* kap-e-*lare*, the maidenhair fern; a syrup flavoured with maidenhair or with orange flowers, or with both. (Fr.)
capillarity, *n.* kap-e-*la*-re-te, the state of being capillary; the rising of a liquid within a capillary tube above the level it reaches outside.
capillary, *a.* *kap*-il-a-re *or* ka-*pil*-a-re, resembling a hair in bore; pertaining to capillary vessels: *n.* a tube with a hair-like bore; a minute blood-vessel. **capillary attraction** or **repulsion,** the cause which determines the ascent or the descent of a fluid in capillary vessels. (L. *capillaris*, hair-like.)
capillose, *a.* *kap*-e-lose, hairy.
capital, *a.* *kap*-e-tal, pertaining to the head; first in importance; chief; principal; punishable by loss of the head or life; excellent; first-rate; belonging to capital: *n.* the head part of a column or pillar; the principal thing; the chief city in a state; a large letter; money; invested wealth; the entire property of a person or corporation at a given time, or that portion of it available for the promotion of business; an aggregate of money, machinery, goods, etc., used in the production of wealth or of other goods, as distinct from the labour without which these could not be used. **capital levy,** a tax on capital. **capital punishment,** the death penalty. (Fr.)
capitalism, *n.* *kap*-e-ta-lizm, the ownership of capital; the economic organization of society in which the chief power lies in the hands of the moneyed or landed classes; the control of the means of production by private and competing individuals or trusts, etc., instead of (as under Socialism) by the State.
capitalist, *n.* *kap*-e-ta-list, one who possesses capital; a man of large means.
capitalistic, *a.* kap-e-ta-*lis*-tik, pertaining to or achieved by means of capitalism or capitalists.
capitalistically, *ad.* kap-e-ta-*lis*-te-ka-le, in a capitalistic manner.
capitalization, *n.* *kap*-e-ta-ly-zay-shon, the act of capitalizing or converting into capital.
capitalize, *v.t.* *kap*-e-ta-lize, to convert into capital; to calculate the present value of payments made periodically; to provide capital for; to write or print with a capital or in capitals.
capitally, *ad.* *kap*-e-ta-le, in a first-rate manner.
capitan, *n.* kah-pe-*tahn*, a Turkish naval officer. **Capitan Pasha,** the admiral commanding-in-chief the former Imperial Turkish Navy. (Sp., captain.)
capitate, *a.* *kap*-e-tate, having a head; growing in a head [Bot.]. (L. *capitatus*, possessing a head.)
capitation, *n.* kap-e-*tay*-shon, a tax upon each head or person; a poll-tax. (L. *capitatio.*)
capite, *n.* *kap*-e-te, a tenant who held land "in capite," *i.e.* immediately of the king [Law].
Capitol, *n.* *kap*-e-tol, a temple and citadel in Rome, on the Capitoline rock, dedicated to Jupiter; in the U.S.A. the edifice in which Congress meets; the senate-house of an American state.
Capitolian, *a.* kap-e-*toh*-le-an, capitoline.
Capitoline, *a.* *kap*-e-to-line, pertaining to the Capitol in Rome. **Capitoline games,** games in honour of Jupiter and commemorating the preservation of the Capitol from the Gauls.
capitular, *a.* ka-*pit*-yoo-lar, growing in small heads [Bot.]; pertaining to the knobbed end of a bone [Anat.], or to a chapter [Eccles.]: *n.* a capitulary.
capitularly, *ad.* ka-*pit*-yoo-lar-le, in the form of an ecclesiastical chapter.
capitulary, *n.* ka-*pit*-yoo-la-re, a statute passed in a chapter, either of knights or canons; a body of laws, esp. those of the Frankish kings; a member of a chapter. (L. *capitulum*, a chapter.)
capitulate, *v.i.* ka-*pit*-yoo-late, to surrender on conditions.
capitulation, *n.* ka-pit-yoo-*lay*-shon, the act of capitulating; the conditions of surrender; *pl.* the articles under which European foreigners in Turkey and some other states were formerly granted certain extraterritorial rights. (Fr.)
capitulator, *n.* ka-*pit*-yoo-lay-tor, one who surrenders or capitulates.
capitulum, *n.* ka-*pit*-yoo-lum, a close cluster of flowers as in composite plants; a protuberance on a bone fitting into a hollow in another bone.
capnomancy, *n.* *kap*-no-man-se, divination from smoke. (Gr. *kapnos*, smoke, *manteia*, divination.)
capon, *n.* *kay*-pon, a castrated male fowl: *v.t.* to castrate. (A.S. *capun.*)
caponiere, *n.* kap-o-*neer*, a covered lodgment; a passage from one part of a work to another, protected by a parapet [Fort.]. (Fr.)
caporal, *n.* *kap*-o-rahl, a coarse tobacco. (Fr.)

capot, *n.* ka-*poh* or ka-*pot*, a winning of all the tricks at piquet: *v.t.* to win at piquet. (Fr.)
capote, *n.* ka-*pote*, a kind of long cloak. (Fr.)
cappagh-brown, *n.* *kap*-pa-*broun*, a colouring matter extracted from earth-deposits at Cappagh, Co. Cork.
caprate, *n.* *kap*-rate, a salt of capric acid.
capreolate, *a.* *kap*-re-o-lat, having tendrils [Bot.]. (L. *capreolus*, a tendril.)
capric, *a.* *kap*-rik, pertaining to or smelling of the goat. **capric acid,** a fatty acid with a goat-like smell contained in butter. (L. *caper*, a goat.)
capriccio, *n.* ka-*prit*-cho, a free fanciful composition [Mus.]. (It.)
capriccioso, *a.* ka-prit-*choh*-so, in a free fantastic style [Mus.]. (It.)
caprice, *n.* ka-*preece*, a change without reason of opinion or humour; a whim; a freak. (Fr.)
capricious, *a.* ka-*prish*-us, led by caprice; whimsical; prone to sudden and unexpected change.
capriciously, *ad.* ka-*prish*-us-le, in a capricious manner.
capriciousness, *n.* ka-*prish*-us-ness, the quality of being capricious.
Capricorn, *n.* *kap*-re-kawrn, the Goat, the tenth sign of the zodiac, the winter solstice. (L. *capricornus*, goat-horned.)
caprification, *n.* *kap*-re-fe-*kay*-shon, the process of maturing the cultivated fig by fertilizing the fruit by means of an insect produced on the wild fig. (L. *caprificus*, the wild fig.)
caprifoil, *n.* *kap*-re-foyl, a former name of the honeysuckle.
capriform, *a.* *kap*-re-form, having the form of a goat.
caprin, *n.* *kap*-rin, one of the glycerine fats giving butter its peculiar taste.
caprine, *a.* *kap*-rin or *kay*-prine, like a goat.
capriole, *n.* *kap*-re-ole, a leap made by a horse without advancing; a caper in dancing: *v.i.* to leap or caper thus. (Fr.)
caproic, *a.* ka-*proh*-ik, pertaining to the goat. **caproic acid,** a fatty acid from butter, coconut oil, etc., which smells like a goat.
capsicine, *n.* *kap*-se-sin, an alkaloid in capsicums.
Capsicum, *n.* *kap*-se-kum, an American genus of tropical plants from one species of which chillies and cayenne are obtained. **bastard capsicum,** *see* **winter-cherry.** (L. *capsa*, a box.)
capsize, *v.t.* kap-*size*, to upset or overturn: *v.i.* to be upset: *n.* an overturn.
capstan, *n.* *kap*-stan, a vertical windlass. (Fr. *cabestan.*)
capstone, *n.* *kap*-stone, a coping; the top bed in a quarry [Geol.]; the horizontal stone of a trilith [Archæol.]; fossil echinite.
capsular, *a.* *kap*-sewl-ar, pertaining to or resembling a capsule.
capsulated, *a.* *kap*-sew-lay-ted, enclosed in a capsule.
capsule, *n.* *kap*-sewl, the seed-vessel of a plant; a shallow saucer [Chem.]; a membranous production enclosing a part like a bag [Anat.]; a soluble envelope in which a nauseous dose is swallowed [Med.]. (L. *capsula*, a little box.)
captain, *n.* *kap*-tn, a leader or chief commander; the commander of a company, a troop, or a ship; an overseer; the leader of a side at cricket or other games; a great warrior: *v.t.* to act as captain. **Captain of the Fleet,** the chief staff-officer of a fleet. (O.Fr. *capitain.*)
captaincy, *n.* *kap*-tn-se, the rank, commission, or office of a captain; leadership.
Captain-General, *n.* *kap*-tn-*jen*-e-ral, a supreme commander; a Spanish provincial or colonial governor.
captainship, *n.* *kap*-tn-ship, the post of captain or chief commander; military skill.
captation, *n.* kap-*tay*-shon, use of clever appeals to popular feeling to obtain applause. (L. *captatio.*)
caption, *n.* *kap*-shon, the act of taking a person by a judicial process; a certificate of authority appended to a legal instrument [Law]; arrestment for debt [Scots. Law]; a chapter, page, or paragraph heading, or the titling of a picture. (L. *captum*, take.)
captious, *a.* *kap*-shus, fault-finding; apt to cavil; proceeding from a cavilling disposition. (Fr. *captieux.*)
captiously, *ad.* *kap*-shus-le, in a captious manner.
captiousness, *n.* *kap*-shus-ness, disposition to be captious.
captivate, *v.t.* *kap*-te-vate, to charm; to fascinate. (L. *captivatus*, charmed.)
captivating, *a.* *kap*-te-vay-ting, fascinating.
captivation, *n.* kap-te-*vay*-shon, the act of fascinating or charming; a charm.
captive, *n.* *kap*-tiv, one taken prisoner, especially in war; one fascinated or ensnared: *a.* made prisoner; kept in bondage; captivated. **captive balloon,** a tethered balloon. (L. *captivus*, a captive.)
captivity, *n.* kap-*tiv*-e-te, the state of being captive. **the Captivity,** the 50 years' exile of the Jews in Babylon during the 6th cent. B.C.
captor, *n.* *cap*-tor, one who takes a prisoner or a prize. (L., one who takes.)
capture, *n.* *kap*-tyur, the act of taking or seizing; the thing taken; a prize: *v.t.* to take or seize by force; to take as a prize. (Fr.)
capuche, *n.* ka-*poosh*, a long pointed cowl or hood, esp. that worn by the Capuchins. (It. *capuccio.*)
capuchin, *n.* kap-yoo-*sheen* or *kap*-oo-chin, a Franciscan friar, so called from his capuche; a hooded cloak worn by women; a pigeon with a hood-like tuft of feathers. **capuchin monkey,** the American hooded monkey, a species of *Cebus*. (Fr. *capucin.*)
capulin, *n.* *kap*-yoo-lin, the Mexican tree *Prunus capuli*, or its edible cherry; other tropical American timber-trees.
caput, *n.* *kay*-put or *kap*-ut, the head. **caput mortuum,** literally a dead head; the alchemists' name for the inert residuum after sublimation or distillation; what remains after life and worth are gone. (L.)
capybara, *n.* kap-e-*bah*-ra, the largest living rodent, *Hydrochœrus capibara*, of South America.
car, *n.* kahr, a light vehicle; a chariot of war or triumph; a railway carriage; a motor car, tram, or other passenger carriage mechanically propelled; a low two-wheeled truck; the part of an aircraft accommodating personnel, passengers, or power-plant. (O.Fr. *carre.*)
carabine, *n.* *ka*-ra-bin, a carbine.
carabinier, *n.* *kahr*-be-*neer*, a cavalryman armed with a carbine. **The Carabiniers,** the 6th Dragoon Guards.
caracal, *n.* *ka*-ra-kal, the Persian lynx. (Turk.)
caracara, *n.* *kah*-ra-*kah*-ra or *ka*-ra-*kah*-ra, the Brazilian carrion-hawk, a species of *Polyborus*.
carack, *n.* *ka*-rak, a carrack.
caracole, *n.* *ka*-ra-kole, the movement of a horse in making a half-turn; a winding staircase [Arch.]: *v.i.* to wheel in a caracole. (Fr.)
caracul, *n.* *ka*-ra-kul, a broad-tailed sheep of Uzbekistan; its astrakhan-like fur.
carafe, *n.* ka-*rahf*, a glass water-bottle. (Fr.)
carambola, *n.* ka-ram-*boh*-lah, the Coromandel gooseberry, an East Indian species of *Averrhoa.*
carambole, *n.* ka-ram-*bole*, the stroke in billiards usually known as the cannon. (Fr.)
caramel, *n.* *ka*-ra-mel, burnt sugar, used to colour spirits and soups; a sweetmeat; a light brown colour. (Fr.)
carapace, *n.* *ka*-ra-pace, the upper shell of the chelonians; applied also to that of the reptiles, crustaceans and to the shell of the armadillo, etc. (Fr.)
carap-oil, *n.* *ka*-rap-oyl, oil of the crab-wood tree, *Carapa guianensis*. (South American native word).
carat, *n.* *ka*-rat, a weight of 200 milligrams (3.086 grains troy); a 24th part of a gold alloy, gold of 22 carats containing 22 parts pure gold. (Fr.)
carauna, *n.* kah-*raw*-na, a resinous substance formerly used in medicine, and obtained from certain South American trees. (Native name).
caravan, *n.* *ka*-ra-van or ka-ra-*van*, a company of merchants or pilgrims, associated together for mutual security in traversing a desert; a house on wheels, esp. one used by showmen; a large light covered wagon. (Fr. *caravane*, from Per. *karwan.*)
caravaneer, *n.* ka-ra-va-*neer*, one in charge of the camels of a caravan.
caravansary, *n.* ka-ra-*van*-sa-re, in the East a large unfurnished inn, with a spacious court for the accommodation of caravans at night; a large hotel [Coll.]. (Per. *karwan*, and *sarai*, an inn.)
caravel, *n.* *ka*-ra-vel, a lateen-rigged four-masted ship. (It *caravella.*)

caraway, *n.* *ka*-ra-way, the umbelliferous plant, *Carum carui*, or its small dried fruit. (Sp. *alcarahueya.*)
carbide, *n.* *kahr*-bide, a combination of carbon with another element, generally a metal; popular name for calcium carbide, used for generating acetylene.
carbine, *n.* *kahr*-bine, a short rifle for use by mounted soldiers. (Fr. *carabine*, a rifle.)
carbineer, *n.* kahr-be-*neer*, a carabineer.
carbo-hydrate, *n.* *kahr*-bo-*hy*-drate, any one of the organic compounds (starches, sugars, cellulose, etc.) consisting of carbon, hydrogen, and oxygen, the later two in the proportion of two to one as in water [Chem.].
carbolic, *a.* kahr-*bol*-ik, derived from coal-tar: *n.* carbolic acid, or phenol.
carbolize, *v.t.* *kahr*-bo-lize, to impregnate, or to disinfect, with carbolic acid.
carbon, *n.* *kahr*-bon, a non-metallic element occurring in most organic compounds, and as diamond, graphite, and charcoal; the carbon rod used in an arc-lamp; a piece of carbon paper, also a copy made with it. **carbon dioxide,** carbonic acid gas. **carbon monoxide,** carbonic oxide. **carbon paper,** manifold paper for copying purposes. (L. *carbo*, coal.)
carbonaceous, *a.* kahr-bon-*ay*-shus, pertaining to, containing, or composed of, carbon; like coal; abounding in coal [Geol.].
carbonado, *n.* kahr-bon-*ah*-do, a black uncrystallized diamond; meat slish-slashed across with a sharp knife and grilled on an open fire. (Sp.)
Carbonari, *n.pl.* kahr-bo-*nah*-ree, a secret republican society existing in the early 19th cent. in Italy and France. (Literally, charcoal-burners.)
carbonate, *n.* *kahr*-bon-ate, a salt of carbonic acid: *v.t.* to form into a carbonate; to combine or impregnate with carbonic acid; to aerate (liquids).
carbonic, *a.* kahr-*bon*-ik, pertaining to carbon. **carbonic acid,** a very weak acid consisting of carbon, hydrogen, and oxygen, obtained by passing carbon dioxide through water, with which it combines. **carbonic acid gas,** carbon dioxide.
carboniferous, *a.* kahr-bon-*if*-er-us, producing or containing coal; (cap.) the geological formation between the Devonian and the Permian. (L. *carbo*, and *fero*, bear.)
carbonization, *n.* kahr-bo-ny-*zay*-shon *or* kahr-bon-ize-*ay*-shon, the process of carbonizing.
carbonize, *v.t.* *kahr*-bo-nize, to convert into carbon by combustion or the action of fire.
carborundum, *n.* kahr-bo-run-dum, trade-name of an abrasive consisting of a fused mixture of silicon and carbon.
carboy, *n.* *kahr*-boy, a large globular glass bottle, usually protected by basket-work. (Per. *qarabah.*)
carbuncle, *n.* *kahr*-bung-kl, a gem of a deep red colour, esp. a garnet cut cabochon; a painful, highly inflamed coreless boil with gangrene of the subcutaneous tissues; a charge consisting of eight decorated rays [Her.]. (L., a little coal.)
carbuncled, *a.* *kahr*-bung-kld, set with carbuncles; afflicted with carbuncles.
carbuncular, *a.* kahr-*bung*-kew-lar, pertaining to or resembling a carbuncle; red; inflamed.
carburet, *n.* *kahr*-bew-ret, a carbide: *v.t.* to combine with carbon. **carburetted hydrogen,** a gaseous compound of carbon and hydrogen.
carburetion, *n.* kahr-bew-*resh*-on, the process of atomizing and mixing liquid fuel with air in the correct proportions for explosion in internal combustion engines.
carburetter, *n.* *kahr*-bew-ret-ter, the part of an internal combustion engine in which the fuel is atomized and mixed with air.
carburize, *v.t.* *kahr*-bew-rize, to carburet.
carcajou, *n.* *kahr*-ka-zhoo, the wolverine or glutton.
carcanet, *n.* *kahr*-kan-et, a chain or collar of jewels. (Fr., a little collar.)
carcase, *n.* *kahr*-kas, the body, usually when dead; the trunk of a slaughtered beast with hide and offals removed; the mere framework of anything, as of a house or ship; a perforated bombshell filled with combustibles, formerly used to set fire to buildings [Mil.]. (Fr. *carcasse*, a skeleton.)
carcass, *n.* *kahr*-kas, a carcase.
carcinology, *n.* kahr-sin-*ol*-o-je, the study of crustaceans. (Gr. *karkinos*, a crab, *logos*, science.)
carcinoma, *n.* kahr-se-*noh*-ma, a form of cancer. (Gr.)
carcinomatous, *a.* kahr-se-*noh*-ma-tus, cancerous.
★**card,** *n.* kahrd, a piece of pasteboard, with painted figures or points on it, for playing with, or with a person's name on it, or with an invitation a programme, or a business advertisement; a post-card; a paper on which the points of the compass are marked; a knowing fellow [Slang]; (*pl.*) a game with cards; card-playing. **card game,** any game played with the whole, or a specified part, of one or more packs of 52 cards in four suits. **card vote,** a vote taken at a meeting of delegates, each of whose votes is of a value proportionate to the number of members he represents. (Fr. *carte.*)
card, *n.* kahrd, an instrument for combing wool or flax: *v.t.* to comb wool, flax, hemp, etc. (L. *carduus*, a thistle.)
cardamine, *n.* *kahrd*-a-mine, bitter cress. (Gr.)
cardamom, *n.* *kahrd*-a-mum, the aromatic, pungent, capsule of *Elettaria cardamomum* or the seed of *Amomum*, used as a condiment and in medicine. (Fr. *cardamone.*)
cardan, *a.* *kahr*-dan, applied in engineering to the **cardan joint,** a universal joint, and the **cardan shaft,** a shaft having a cardan joint at one or both ends. (Name of It. mathematician, *d.* 1576.)
cardboard, *n.* *kahrd*-bord, pasteboard.
card-case, *n.* *kahrd*-kace, a case for holding visiting cards.
cardiac, *a.* *kahr*-de-ak, pertaining to the heart; exciting action in the heart through the medium of the stomach; strengthening; heart-shaped: *n.* a cordial which excites action in the stomach, and animates the spirits. **cardiac passion,** heart-burn.
cardialgia, *n.* *kahr*-de-*al*-je-a, heartburn.
cardigan, *n.* *kahr*-de-gan, a jacket of knitted wool. (From the 7th Earl of *Cardigan*, of Crimean fame.)
cardinal, *a.* *kahr*-din-al, chief; principal; pre-eminent, or fundamental; a deep red colour (that of a cardinal's cassock): *n.* one of the seventy dignitaries of the Roman Church ranking next to the Pope, whom they elect from among themselves; a woman's short cloak; mulled red wine [Slang]. **cardinal numbers,** the numbers one, two, three, etc., in distinction from the ordinals first, second, third, etc. **cardinal points,** the four original points of the compass. **cardinal signs,** Aries, Libra, Cancer, and Capricorn, or the two equinoxes and two solstices [Astron.]. **cardinal virtues,** with the ancients, Prudence, Temperance, Justice, and Fortitude; in theological parlance, Faith, Hope, and Charity. (L. *cardinalis*, chief.)
cardinalate, *n.* *kahr*-din-al-ate, the office, rank, or dignity of a cardinal.
cardinal-bird, *n.* *kahr*-din-al-berd, a North American singing bird with a crest and red plumage, *Cardinalis virginianus*, and others.
cardinal-flower, *n.* *kahr*-din-al-flou-er, a plant, *Lobelia cardinalis*, bearing brilliant red flowers.
cardinalship, *n.* *kahr*-din-al-ship, cardinalate.
card-index, *n.* kahrd-*in*-deks, an index having each entry on a separate card: *v.t.* to make a card-index of.
carding-machine, *n.* *kahrd*-ing-ma-sheen, a machine for combing, breaking, and cleansing wool or fibres.
cardiogram, *n.* *kahr*-de-o-gram, a graphic delineation of the movements of the heart effected by the cardiograph.
cardiograph, *n.* *kahr*-de-o-graf, an instrument for registering the beats of the heart.
cardiography, *n.* *kahr*-de-*og*-ra-fe, anatomical description of the heart; the use of the cardiograph. (Gr. *kardia*, and *grapho*, write.)
cardioid, *n.* *kahr*-de-oyd, a geometrical heart-shaped curve. (Gr. *kardia*, heart, *eidos*, like.)
cardiology, *n.* kahr-de-*ol*-o-je, the study of, or a treatise on, the heart. (Gr. *kardia*, and *logos*, science.)
cardiometer, *n.* kahr-de-*om*-e-ter, an instrument for measuring the action of the heart.
carditis, *n.* kahr-*dy*-tis, inflammation of the heart.
cardoon, *n.* kahr-*doon*, a culinary vegetable, *Cynara cardunculus*, allied to the artichoke. (Fr. *cardon.*)
cardsharper, *n.* *kahrd*-sharp-er, one who cheats at cards.
card-table, *n.* *kahrd*-tay-bl, a table for playing cards on.

Carduus, *n.* *kahr*-dew-us, the large genus of thistles. **carduus benedictus,** the blessed thistle.

★**care,** *n.* kare, solicitude; anxiety; caution; regard; attention; heed; charge or oversight; the object of care: *v.i.* to be anxious or solicitous; to be concerned about; to be inclined; to like. (A.S. *caru.*)

careen, *v.t.* ka-*reen*, to lay a ship on her side, for the purpose of caulking or repairing; *v.i.* to incline to one side under press of sail. (L. *carina*, keel.)

careenage, *n.* ka-*reen*-aj, a place for, or the cost of, careening.

career, *n.* ka-*reer*, course of action; course through life; progressive development in professional, business, or artistic activity; a race: *v.i.* to move or run rapidly. (Fr. *carrière*, race-course.)

careerist, *n.* ka-*reer*-ist, one absorbed in his own success or personal advancement.

carefree, *a.* *kare*-free, free from care or anxiety.

careful, *a.* *kare*-ful, full of care; anxious; solicitous; provident; heedful; watchful; with care.

carefully, *ad.* *kare*-ful-le, in a careful manner.

carefulness, *n.* *kare*-ful-ness, the quality of being careful.

careless, *a.* *kare*-less, having no care; heedless; free from care; unconcerned; thoughtless; without care.

carelessly, *ad.* *kare*-less-le, in a careless manner.

carelessness, *n.* *kare*-less-ness, the quality of being careless.

caress, *n.* ka-*ress*, an act of endearment; a tender embrace: *v.t.* to treat with affection; to fondle; to embrace. (Fr. *caresse.*)

caressingly, *ad.* ka-*res*-sing-le, in a caressing manner.

caret, *n.* *ka*-ret, a mark thus, ∧, used in writing to indicate that something has been there omitted, which is interlined above, or inserted in the margin. (L. *careo*, be wanting.)

caretake, *v.i.* and *t.* *kare*-take, to take charge of, esp. a house in the absence of the occupier.

caretaker, *n.* *kare*-tay-ker, one put in charge of an unoccupied house or other building. **caretaker government,** a government acting as a stopgap between the announcement of a dissolution and the general election.

careworn, *a.* *kare*-worn, wearied by worry or trouble; showing the effects of anxiety.

carex, *n.* *kare*-reks, a sedge.

carfax, *n.* *kahr*-faks, the meeting of four roads, as at Oxford. (Fr.)

cargo, *n.* *kahr*-go, the freight of a ship; the goods. (Sp.)

cargoose, *n.* *kahr*-goos, the crested grebe.

Carib, *n.* *ka*-rib, one of an aboriginal race of Central and the northern parts of South America.

caribe, *n.* ka-*ree*-bay, a small voracious S. American freshwater fish. (Sp., cannibal.)

caribou, *n.* *ka*-re-boo, the reindeer, *Rangifer caribou*, of N. America and Greenland. (Native.)

caricature, *n.* *ka*-rik-a-tewr, a representation or description, which, though resembling the original, is so exaggerated as to be ridiculous: *v.t.* to make or draw such a grotesque; to ridicule. (It. *caricatura.*)

caricaturist, *n.* ka-rik-a-*tewr*-rist, one who caricatures.

caries, *n.* *kare*-re-eez, rottenness or ulceration of a bone. (L.)

carillon, *n.* *ka*-ril-yon, a ring of bells worked either by hand or by machinery; a chime of bells; an air for performance on small bells. (Fr.)

carina, *n.* ka-*ry*-na, the keel-like part of a flower, bone, shell, etc. [Zool. and Bot.]. (L., the keel of a ship.)

carinate, *a.* *ka*-re-nate, having a keel-shaped ridge [Bot. and Zool.].

carinated, *a.* *ka*-re-nay-ted, carinate.

cariosity, *n.* kare-re-*os*-e-te, a carious state or formation.

carious, *a.* *kare*-re-us, rotten or ulcerated, as a bone.

cark, *n.* kahrk, care; anxiety: *v.i.* to be anxious or concerned; to worry. (O.Fr. *karkier.*)

carking, *a.* *kahrk*-ing, distressing; perplexing; giving anxiety.

carle, *n.* kahrl, a rustic; a strong man, or an old or rude-mannered one. (A.S., a man.)

carline, *n.* *kahr*-lin, an old woman; a witch [Scots.]

carline, *a.* *kahr*-line, pertaining to Charles. **carline thistle,** *Carlina vulgaris*, so called from Charlemagne.

Carlism, *n.* *kahr*-lizm, support of the claims to the Spanish throne of Don Carlos (*d.* 1855) and his heirs.

Carlist, *a.* *kahr*-list, pertaining to Carlism: *n.* an adherent of Carlism.

carlock, *n.* *kahr*-lok, a kind of isinglass obtained from Russia. (Russ.)

Carlovingian, *a.* kahr-lo-*vin*-je-an, Carolingian.

carmagnole, *n.* kahr-man-*yole*, a French Republican song or dance; a violent Jacobin, or the dress he wore; a boastful bulletin. (Fr.)

carman, *n.* *kahr*-man, a man who drives a car or van, or conveys goods, etc., by this means.

Carmelite, *a.* *kahr*-mel-ite, belonging to the order of Carmelites, or White Friars: *n.* a member of this order; a sort of pear.

carminative, *n.* kahr-*min*-a-tiv, curative of flatulence and colic: *a.* acting as a carminative. (L. *carminatus*, cleansed.)

carmine, *n.* *kahr*-mine, a crimson pigment obtained from cochineal. (Sp. *carmin.*)

carnage, *n.* *kahr*-naj, slaughter; butchery of men.

carnal, *a.* *kahr*-nal, fleshly; sensual; temporal, not spiritual; not after the spirit. **carnal knowledge,** sexual intercourse. (L. *carnalis*, fleshly.)

carnalist, *n.* *kahr*-nal-ist, one given to carnality.

carnality, *n.* kahr-*nal*-e-te, carnal state of mind.

carnallite, *n.* *kahr*-na-lyt, a hydrated potassium-magnesium chloride found as a reddish mass in saline deposits, a source of potassium and a fertilizer.

carnally, *ad.* *kahr*-na-le, in a carnal manner.

carnal-minded, *a.* kahr-nal-*mine*-ded, not spiritually-minded.

carnassial, *a.* kahr-*nas*-se-al, adapted to eat flesh [Anat.]. **carnassials,** the flesh teeth of the carnivora. (Fr. *carnassier*, flesh-eating.)

carnation, *n.* kahr-*nay*-shon, flesh-colour; a flesh-coloured flower; a variety of the pink, *Dianthus caryophyllus*. (Fr.)

carnauba, *n.* kahr-*nou*-ba, the Brazilian wax-bearing palm, *Corypha cerifera*. (Native name.)

carnelian, *n.* kahr-*neel*-yan, cornelian.

carneous, *a.* *kahr*-ne-us, flesh-coloured [Bot.]. (L.)

carney, *v.t.* and *i.* *kahr*-ne, to wheedle; to act in a coaxing manner.

carnification, *n.* kahr-ne-fe-*kay*-shon, the act of carnifying; a morbid alteration in a tissue; the act of transubstantiation of consecrated elements.

carnify, *v.i.* *kahr*-ne-fy, to turn abnormally into flesh. (L. *caro*, flesh, *facio*, make.)

carnival, *n.* *kahr*-ne-val, a season of festivity and revelry ending on Shrove Tuesday; revelry. (It. *carne vale!* flesh, farewell!)

Carnivora, *n.pl.* kahr-*niv*-o-ra, the large order of mammals that subsist on flesh. (L.)

carnivore, *n.* *kahr*-ne-vor, one of the Carnivora; a carnivorous plant.

carnivorous, *a.* kahr-*niv*-o-rus, feeding on flesh.

carnose, *a.* *kahr*-nose, fleshy; flesh-like.

carnosity, *n.* kahr-*nos*-e-te, a fleshy excrescence.

carnotite, *n.* *kahr*-no-tite, a radium-containing vanadate of potassium and uranium found in Colorado, Utah, the Belgian Congo, etc.

carob, *n.* *ka*-rob, the locust or algaroba tree, *Ceratonia siliqua*, of Mediterranean lands. (Fr. *caroube.*)

carol, *n.* *ka*-rol, a song of joy or praise, esp. in honour of the Nativity and originally with dancing; a warble: *v.i.* to sing carols; to warble: *v.t.* to celebrate in song. (O.Fr. *carole*, a dance with singing.)

Carolingian, *a.* ka-ro-*linj*-e-an, pertaining to Charlemagne or to the second dynasty of Frankish kings (751–987) founded by his father, Pepin: *n.* any one of these sovereigns, or of the Emperors (800–911) of this dynasty.

carolus, *n.* *ka*-ro-lus, a gold coin of Charles I. equal to 20s. afterwards, 23s. (L., Charles.)

carom, *n.* *ka*-rom, the cannon in billiards, curling, etc.

carosse, *n.* ka-*ross*, a kaross.

carotid, *a.* ka-*rot*-id, relating to the two arteries in the neck which convey the blood from the aorta to the head: *n.* either of these arteries. (Gr. *karōtides.*)

carousal, *n.* ka-*rou*-zal, a feast; a drinking bout.

carouse, *n.* ka-*rouz*, a carousal; a merry or noisy revel: *v.i.* to drink freely and heartily; to revel. (O.Fr. *carousser.*)

carouser, *n.* ka-*rouz*-er, a reveller.
carousingly, *ad.* ka-*rouz*-ing-le, in a carousing manner.
carp, *v.i.* kahrp, to catch at small faults; to bicker querulously; to cavil. (Ice. *karpa*, to boast.)
carp, *n.* kahrp, a freshwater fish of the genus *Cyprinus*, esp. *C. carpio*. (O.Fr. *carpe*.)
carpal, *a.* *kahrp*-al, pertaining to the wrist.
carpel, *n.* *kahrp*-el, a modified leaf of one, or several, of which the pistil of a flower is formed [Bot.]. (Gr. *karpos*, fruit.)
carpellary, *a.* *kahr*-pel-la-re, pertaining to a carpel.
carpenter, *n.* *kahr*-pen-ter, a worker in timber, esp. for house- or ship-building: *v.i.* to do work as a carpenter: *v.t.* to make by carpentry. (O.Fr. *carpentier*.)
carpentering, *n.* *khar*-pen-ter-ing, a carpenter's employment; carpentry.
carpentry, *n.* *kahr*-pen-tre, working in wood.
carper, *n.* *kahr*-per, a person who speaks or acts in a carping manner.
carpet, *n.* *kahr*-pet, a fabric for covering floors or stairs: *v.t.* to cover with a carpet; to reprimand [Coll.]. **on the carpet,** under consideration; under reproof. **carpet bag,** a travelling-bag made of carpet. **carpet bagger,** a parliamentary candidate who is a stranger to the constituency. **carpet bombing,** attack by bomber-planes to clear a way for ground-troops. **carpet knight,** one who has received his honour by favour, not for service. (O.Fr. *carpite*, from L. *carpo*, pluck.)
carpeting, *n.* *kahr*-pet-ing, material for carpets; the action of laying carpets; a reprimand [Coll.].
carpet-snake, *n.* *kar*-pet-snake, a python found in Australia.
carpet-sweeper, *n.* *kar*-pet-*sweep*-er, one who sweeps carpets; an apparatus for sweeping carpets in which the brush revolves.
carphology, *n.* kahr-*fol*-o-je, a plucking at the bedclothes in delirium (a symptom of acute illness). (Gr. *karphos*, tiny, *legō*, pull.)
carping, *a.* *kahrp*-ing, cavilling; captious.
carpingly, *ad.* *karp*-ing-le, in a carping manner.
carpolite, *n.* *kahr*-po-lite, a fossil fruit.
carpology, *n.* kahr-*pol*-o-je, that part of botany which treats of fruit and seeds. (Gr. *karpos*, fruit, *logos*, science.)
carpophagous, *a.* kahr-*pof*-a-gus, living on fruits.
carpus, *n.* *kahr*-pus, the wrist [Anat.]. (L.)
carr, *n.* kahr, boggy ground; marshland reclaimed or in process of reclamation. (Scand.)
carrack, *n.* *ka*-rak, a large merchantman, deep in draught and armed for attack and defence.
carrageen, *n.* *ka*-ra-geen, Irish moss, the sea-weed *Chondrus crispus*. (*Carragheen*, near Waterford.)
carraway, *n.* *ka*-ra-way, caraway.
carriable, *a.* *ka*-re-a-bl, that may be carried.
★**carriage,** *n.* *ka*-raj, a wheeled vehicle; the act of, means of, or price of, carrying or conveying; transportation or conveyance of merchandise, etc.; the manner of carrying oneself; behaviour; mien; the wheeled framework of a vehicle, cannon, etc.; a sliding part of a machine carrying another part [Mech.]; that part of a printing press on which the types are placed to be printed [Print.]. (O.Fr. *cariage*.)
carrick-bend, *n.* *ka*-rik-bend, a particular kind of knot [Naut.].
carrier, *n.* *ka*-re-er, one who conveys goods; anything that carries; a cycle adapted for carrying goods; a bag or other container in which light goods are carried; an indirect transmitter of disease. **carrier-pigeon,** a breed of pigeon trained to convey letters.
carriole, *n.* *ka*-re-ole, a light carriage with a special form of harness; a light covered cart; a Canadian sleigh. (Fr.)
carrion, *n.* *ka*-re-on, dead and putrifying flesh: *a.* relating to or feeding upon carrion; putrid. **carrion crow,** the crow, *Corvus corone*, with whitish bases to its body feathers. (O.Fr. *caroigne*.)
carronade, *n.* ka-ron-*ade*, a short ship's cannon originally made at Carron, in Scotland.
carron-oil, *n.* *ka*-ron-*oyl*, a mixture of linseed oil and lime-water, used (originally at Carron ironworks) for burns and scalds.
carrot, *n.* *ka*-rot, the red or yellow-coloured esculent root of *Daucus carota*. (Fr. *carote*.)
carroty, *a.* *ka*-rot-e, like a carrot in colour; sandy reddish yellow.
carry, *v.t.* *ka*-re, to bear, to convey, or transport; to transfer; to take away; to effect; to accomplish; to gain an object; to lead or draw; to have; to imply or import; to show or display; to contain or comprise; to extend; to obtain possession of by force: *v.i.* to act as bearer; to propel, as a gun, etc.; to run on ground which sticks to the feet, as a hare; to bear the head in a particular manner, as a horse; to propel the ball over a distance or an obstacle [Golf]. **carry away,** to lose [Naut.]. **carry coals to Newcastle,** to bring things to a place where they already abound; to lose one's labour. **carry off,** to remove. **carry on,** to manage; to prosecute; to continue; to help forward; to behave unrestrainedly or reprehensibly. **carry oneself,** to behave or demean. **carry the bat,** to go in first at cricket and bat all through the innings. **carry through,** to sustain; to accomplish. (O.Fr. *carier*.)
carrying, *n.* *ka*-re-ing, a bearing, conveying, removing, or transporting. **carrying trade,** transport of goods, specially by water. **carryings on,** outrageous or indecorous behaviour [Coll.].
carse, *n.* kahrse, low, fertile, alluvial land, adjacent to a river. (Scand. *kers*, a marsh.)
★**cart,** *n.* kahrt, a two-wheeled carriage for heavy goods: *v.t.* to convey on a cart; to expose in a cart: *v.i.* to use carts for carriage. **in the cart,** at a disadvantage; in the wrong box [Slang]. (Ice. *kartr*.)
cartage, *n.* *kahrt*-aj, the act of carting, or the price paid for it.
carte, *n.* kahrt, a card; a bill of fare. (Fr., card.)
carte, *n.* kahrt, a thrust at the inside of the upper part of the body in fencing. (Fr. *quarte*, fourth.)
carte-blanche, *n.* kahrt-*blahnsh*, a blank paper with a signature given to another person to fill up as he pleases; unlimited power to act. (Fr.)
carte-de-visite, *n.* kahrt-de-ve-*zeet*, a person's photograph on a small card. (Fr.)
cartel, *n.* kahr-*tel* or *kahr*-tel, a challenge; an agreement between belligerents relating to the exchange of prisoners; a vessel used for exchanging prisoners of war; an association of political interests; a combination of firms to ensure maintenance of price. (Fr.)
carter, *n.* *kahrt*-er, one who carts goods or who drives a cart.
Cartesian, *a.* kahr-*tee*-ze-an, pertaining to the French philosopher Descartes, or his philosophy.
carthamine, *n.* *kahr*-tha-min, a red crystalline dyestuff obtained from the saffron or safflower, *Carthamus tinctoris*.
cart-horse, *n.* *kahrt*-horse, a heavy draught horse.
Carthusian, *n.* kahr-*thew*-ze-an, one of an order of monks so called from Chartreuse, Dauphiné, where founded by St. Bruno in 1086; a past or present pupil of Charterhouse School; a pensioner of the Charterhouse, London.
cartilage, *n.* *kahr*-te-laj, gristle; the elastic substance in which bone is formed. (Fr.)
cartilaginous, *a.* kahr-te-*laj*-e-nus, pertaining to or consisting of cartilage. **cartilaginous fishes,** fishes with cartilage for bones; the elasmobranchs.
cart-load, *n.* *kahrt*-lode, as much as will load a cart.
cartographer, *n.* kahr-*tog*-ra-fer, a maker of maps.
cartography, *n.* kahr-*tog*-ra-fe, the science of map-drawing. (Fr. *carte*, and Gr. *grapho*, write.)
cartomancy, *n.* *kahr*-to-man-se, divination or fortune-telling by means of playing-cards.
carton, *n.* *kahr*-ton, a small pasteboard box; a small disc within the bull's-eye of a target; a shot hitting this.
carton-pierre, *n.* *kahr*-ton-pe-*air*, papier-mâche for imitating statuary. (Fr.)
cartoon, *n.* kahr-*toon*, a drawing on strong paper for fresco subjects, or as a pattern for tapestry; a large-sized sketch, esp. one of a satirical or political nature in a periodical. (Fr. *carton*.)
cartophilist, *n.* kar-*tof*-e-list, a collector of cigarette-cards.
cartouche, *n.* kahr-*toosh*, a cartridge; a cartridge-box; the device round the titles and names on ancient monuments in Egypt; a scroll intended for an inscription [Arch.]. (Fr. *cartouche*.)
cartridge, *n.* *kahr*-trij, a case with the exact charge of explosive for a fire-arm. **ball cartridge,** one

containing explosive and projectile. **blank cartridge,** one containing only the explosive. (Fr. *cartouche.*)
cartridge-paper, *n.* continuous rough-surfaced drawing paper; Manilla paper.
cartulary, *n. kahr*-tew-la-re, a register of ecclesiastical or monastic charters, deeds, and documents; the officer in charge of it. (Late L. *cartulanium,* register.)
cart-wheel, *n. kahrt*-wheel, the wheel of a dray or cart; a somersault, also a crown-piece [Slang].
cartwright, *n. kahrt*-rite, an artificer who makes carts.
carucage, *n. ka*-roo-kaj, a tax on a carucate.
carucate, *n. ka*-roo-kat, as much land as a team can plough in a year. (Late L. *caruca,* a plough-team.)
caruncle, *n.* ka-*rung*-kl, a soft fleshy excrescence, either natural, as a cock's comb, or morbid. (L.)
caruncular, *a.* ka-*rung*-kew-lar, in the form of, or resembling, a caruncle.
carus, *n. kare*-rus, entire loss of consciousness [Med.]. (Gr. *karos,* deep sleep.)
carvacrol, *n. kahr*-va-krohl, an oil obtained from plants of the mint family, used as an anodyne and antiseptic.
carve, *v.t.* kahrv, to cut; to hew; to cut or hew into some particular form or design; to cut into slices; to apportion: *v.i.* to practise the art of a sculptor; to cut up meat. (A.S. *ceorfan.*)
carvel, *n. kahr*-vel, a caravel. **carvel-built,** in ship-building, having the planks meeting along their edges instead of over-lapping as in clinker-built.
carver, *n. kahrv*-er, one who cuts meat at table; a sculptor; a large knife used at table for carving.
carving, *n. kahrv*-ing, the act or art of cutting meat, or figures in wood or stone, a carved figure.
caryatic, *a.* ka-re-*at*-ik, pertaining to caryatides. **caryatic order,** an order in which the entablature is supported by female figures [Arch.].
caryatid, *n.* ka-re-*at*-id (*pl.* **caryatides,** ka-re-*at*-e-deez), a figure of a woman dressed in long robes, serving to support an entablature, etc. [Arch.]. (Gr. *karyatid,* a priestess of Caryæ.)
caryophyllic, *a. ka*-re-o-*fil*-ik, derived from oil of cloves. (Gr. *karyon,* a nut, *phyllon,* a leaf.)
caryopsis, *n.* ka-re-*op*-sis, a fruit in which, as in the grasses, seed and pericarp are as one [Bot.]. (Gr.)
casal, *a. kace*-al, pertaining to a case [Gram.].
cascabel, *n. kas*-ka-bel, the knob or loop at the end of a cannon. (Sp., a small bell.)
cascade, *n.* kas-*kade,* a small waterfall; a lace collar: *v.i.* to fall like a cascade. (Fr. *cascade.*)
cascara, *n.* kas-*kah*-rah, a laxative made from the bark of the Californian buckthorn, *Rhamnus purshiana* [Med.]; a birch-bark canoe. (Sp., bark.)
cascarilla, *n.* kas-ka-*ril*-la, the bitter aromatic bark of *Croton eleuteria.* (Sp., little bark.)
case, *n.* kace, a covering, box, or sheath; a receptacle for types; a quantity: *v.t.* to cover with or put in a case. **upper, lower case** [Print.], *see* these words. (O.Fr. *casse.*)
case, *n.* kace, that which befalls or happens; an event, particular state, condition, or predicament of a person; an instance; question at issue; a cause or suit in court; change in the termination of a noun, etc., to express relation [Gram.]. **case law,** law as determined by previous judicial decisions. **in case,** in the event. **in good case,** fit, in good condition of body. (Fr. *cas.*)
caseate, *n. kace*-e-at, a salt of caseic acid.
case-harden, *v.t. kace*-hahrd-en, to harden the outer face, esp. of iron by converting it into steel.
caseic, *a. kay*-se-ik, obtained from or pertaining to cheese. (L. *caseus,* cheese.)
casein, *n. kay*-se-in, the main protein of clotted milk and cheese.
case-knife, *n. kace*-nife, a knife carried in a sheath; a hunting-knife.
caseman, *n. kace*-man, a compositor [Print.].
casemate, *n. kace*-mate, a vault in any work of defence, with embrasures for cannon [Fort]; a bomb-proof chamber; an armoured covering round naval guns. (Fr.)
casement, *n. kace*-ment *or kaze*-ment, a window made to open on hinges; a hollow moulding. **casement cloth,** cotton cloth used chiefly for curtains. (Fr.)
casemented, *a. kace*-ment-ed, having casements.
caseous, *a. kay*-se-us, having the qualities of cheese.
casern, *n. kay*-zern *or* kah-*zern,* a barrack, esp. one near the ramparts of a town. (Fr. *caserne.*)
case-shot, *n. kace*-shot, musket-balls, stones, old iron, etc., put in cases, to be discharged from cannon.
case-worm, *n. kace*-wurm, the caddis.
cash, *n.* kash, money; ready money: *v.t.* to turn into or exchange for money. **cash on delivery,** or **C.O.D.,** the payment on delivery for goods received by rail, post, or hand. **petty cash,** *see* **petty. to cash in,** to settle accounts; to clear matters; to take advantage and so make a success (of) [Slang]. (O.Fr. *casse,* money-box.)
cashew, *n.* ka-*shoo or kash*-ew, a tropical American tree, *Anacardium occidentale,* or its fruit, the **cashew-nut.** (Fr. *acajou.*)
cashier, *n.* kash-*eer,* one who has charge and keeps accounts of cash or monetary transactions. (Fr.)
cashier, *v.t.* kash-*eer,* to dismiss from an office; to discharge, esp. from service under the Crown with permanent exclusion therefrom. (Fr. *casser,* to break.)
cashmere, *n. kash*-meer, the long fine silky hair of the Cashmere goat; a cashmere shawl; a fine woollen material for dresses. (*Kashmir.*)
cash-register, *n.* a money-box fitted with a device that automatically records the amounts of money placed in it.
casing, *n. kace*-ing, a covering; a case.
casino, *n.* ka-*see*-no, a public building containing rooms for social meetings, music, dancing, etc., and (on the Continent) gambling; cassino. (It., a little cottage.)
cask, *n.* kahsk, a close wooden vessel for containing liquors, or butter, etc.; the quantity contained. (Sp. *casca,* husk.)
casket, *n. kahsk*-et, a small case for jewels, etc.; a coffin (U.S.A.): *v.t.* to put into a casket. (Fr. *cassette,* small chest.)
Caslon, *n. kaz*-lon, an old-face printing-type modelled on that of the Elzevirs. (Name of 18th-cent. family of type-founders.)
casque, *n.* kahsk, a helmet. (Sp. *casco,* a skull.)
cassareep, *n. kas*-sa-reep, a condiment made from the juice of the bitter cassava. (Carib.)
cassation, *n.* kas-*say*-shon, the reversal of a judicial sentence. **Court of Cassation,** in France and Belgium the highest court of appeal. (Fr.)
cassava, *n.* kas-*sah*-va, the manioc, or the flour prepared from its roots; a food-stuff made from this. (Haytian.)
casserole, *n. kas*-ser-role, an earthenware or glass cooking utensil fitted with a lid. (Fr., a little bowl.)
Cassia, *n. kash*-ya *or kass*-ya, a genus of leguminous plants including the senna; (*l.c.*) a spice-bearing plant mentioned in the Bible. (L.)
cassideous, *a.* ka-*sid*-e-us, helmet-shaped [Bot.]. (L. *cassidus,* a helmet.)
cassimere, *n. kas*-se-meer, a twilled woollen cloth. (*Cashmere.*)
cassino, *n.* ka-*see*-no, the name of a game at cards.
Cassiopeia, *n. kas*-se-o-*pee*-ya, the constellation like a W in the Northern hemisphere.
cassiopeium, *n.* kas-se-o-*pee*-yum, an early name of lutecium.
cassis, *n. kas*-sis, a cordial made from black-currants. (Fr.)
cassiterite, *n.* ka-*sit*-er-rite, tinstone, the chief ore of tin. (Gr. *kassietros,* tin.)
cassock, *n. kas*-sok, a vestment worn by clergymen, choristers, etc., under the surplice. (Fr. *casaque.*)
cassolette, *n. kas*-so-let, a little box containing perfume; a vinaigrette. (Fr.)
cassone, *n.* ka-*soh*-na, a large decorated coffer with hinged lid for the outfit of an Italian bride. (It.)
cassowary, *n. kas*-so-ware-re, a large East Indian bird of the genus *Casuarius,* allied to the emu. (Malay, *kasuārī.*)
cast, *n.* kahst, the act of casting; a throw; the thing thrown; the distance thrown; the part of a fishing-line carrying the hook or hooks; motion or turn of the eye; direction, look, or glance; a squint; a throw of dice; chance; the form into which a thing is cast; a thing so formed; an impression; shape; mould; a tinge; manner or mien; allotment of parts in a play; the body of actors allotted; an afterswarm, or second swarm of bees in a season: *a.* thrown; made by casting; condemned [Law]: *v.t.* to throw, fling, drive, or

thrust; to shed; to direct; to discharge; to throw up, or down; to condemn [Law]; to compute; to contrive; to assign, as the parts in a play to the actors; to mould; to throw off, as a proof [Print.]: *v.i.* to throw, as a fishing-line; to reckon accounts; to consider; to receive form or shape; to warp. **cast aside,** to dismiss or reject as useless or inconvenient. **cast away,** to reject; to waste; to wreck. **cast down,** to throw down; to depress. **cast forth,** to throw out; to emit. **cast in the teeth,** to upbraid; to charge; to twit. **cast off,** to discard. **cast off copy,** to ascertain how many printed pages must be allotted to a MS. **cast oneself on,** to resign oneself to the disposal of, without reserve. **cast out,** to turn out. **cast up,** to reckon up; to upbraid; to vomit. (Ice, *kasta,* throw.)
Castalian, *a.* kass-*tay*-le-an, pertaining to Castallia, a spring on Mount Parnassus, sacred to the Muses.
castanets, *n.pl.* *kass*-tan-ets, small, spoon-shaped, concave clappers of ivory or hard wood, fastened to the fingers in pairs, and rattled to a dance or tune. (Fr. *castăgnettes.*)
castaway, *n.* *kahst*-a-way, one wrecked on an unfrequented coast; one abandoned: *a.* rejected; useless; of no value.
caste, *n.* kahst, among the Hindus, rank in society of an exclusive nature, due to birth; an hereditary and exclusive social class. (Port, *casta,* breed.)
castellan, *n.* *kass*-tel-lan, the governor of a castle. (O.Fr. *castelain.*)
castellany, *n.* *kass*-tel-la-ne, the lordship or jurisdiction of a castellan.
castellated, *a.* *kass*-tel-ay-ted, with turrets, parapet, and battlements. (Late L. *castellatus,* fortified.)
caster, *n.* *kahst*-er, one who or that which casts; a glass or other container with a perforated top; a table-cruet or its stand; a small wheel on a swivel, attached to the legs of furniture.
caster-sugar, *n.* *kahst*-er-*shoo*-gar, sugar in a powdered form for use at table.
castigate, *v.t.* *kass*-te-gate, to chastise; to criticize for correction; to correct. (L. *castigatus,* made pure.)
castigation, *n.* kass-te-*gay*-shon, the act of castigating; chastisement.
castigator, *n.* kas-te-*gay*-tor, a chastiser.
castigatory, *a.* *kass*-te-ga-to-re, corrective; punitive.
castile-soap, *n.* *kass*-teel-*sope,* a hard soap, first made in Castile, Spain, from olive-oil and soda.
Castilian, *n.* kass-*til*-e-an, a native of Castile; the standard dialect of Spanish there spoken.
casting, *n.* *kahst*-ing, the act of throwing, founding, moulding, or warping; anything formed by casting or taking of casts.
casting-net, *n.* *kahst*-ing-net, a net which is cast and drawn.
casting-vote, *n.* *kahst*-ing-vote, the deciding vote of a president when the votes are equal.
cast-iron, *a.* kahst-*i*-urn, made of **cast iron** (iron melted and cast in moulds); strong; unyielding.
castle, *n.* *kah*-sl, a fortified house or fortress; the mansion of a nobleman or prince; the rook in the game of chess: *v.i.* to move king and castle simultaneously under a certain law at chess. **castle in the air,** a visionary project. (O. Fr. *castel.*)
castle-builder, *n.* *kah*-sl-*bild*-er, a visionary schemer.
castled, *a.* *kah*-sld, furnished with castles.
cast-off, *a.* *kahst*-off, laid aside as of no further use.
castor, *n.* *kahst*-or, a horny knob on the inside of a horse's leg, also known as a chestnut.
Castor, *n.* *kahst*-or, the beaver genus of rodents; (*l.c.*) a hat, properly a beaver hat; castoreum. (Gr.)
castor, *n.* *kahst*-or, caster (of the cruet, etc., and also of furniture).
castoreum, *n.* kass-*taw*-re-um, an oily secretion of the beaver used in perfumery and medicine.
castor-oil, *n.* *kahst*-or-oyl, the oil of *Ricinus communis,* an Indian plant, used as a cathartic.
castral, *a.* *kass*-tral, pertaining to a camp. (L.)
castrametation, *n.* *kas*-tra-met-*ay*-shon, the art or act of encamping. (L. *castra,* a camp, *metari,* measure.)
castrate, *v.t.* *kass*-trate, to deprive of generative power by removing the testicles; to remove the anthers; to emasculate or weaken; to expurgate. (L. *castratus,* emasculated.)
castration, *n.* kass-*tray*-shon, the act of castrating.
castrato, *n.* kass-*trah*-to, a person emasculated for the purpose of improving his voice for singing. (It.)
cast-steel, *a.* made of **cast steel** (steel fused and run into moulds).
casual, *a.* *kaz*-yoo-al, happening by chance; accidental; occasional: *n.* one admitted for a night into the workhouse of a district to which he does not belong. **casual labourer,** a man living by doing odd jobs. **casual ward,** a workhouse ward for casuals. (Fr. *casuel.*)
casualism, *n.* *kaz*-yoo-a-lizm, the doctrine that all things are brought about by mere chance.
casually, *ad.* *kaz*-yoo-a-le, in a casual manner.
casualness, *n.* *kaz*-yoo-al-ness, the quality of being casual.
casualty, *n.* *kaz*-yoo-al-te, that which chances; an accident, resulting in injury or loss of life. **casualty ward,** the ward in a hospital for the treatment of persons accidentally injured.
Casuarina, *n.* *kaz*-yoo-a-*ry*-na, a large genus of Australasian trees, including the beefwood. (From resemblance of its twigs to cassowary-feathers.)
casuist, *n.* *kaz*-yoo-ist, one who is versed in casuistry; a quibbler. (Fr. *casuiste.*)
casuistic, *a.* kaz-yoo-*is*-tik, relating to casuistry.
casuistically, *ad.* kaz-yoo-*is*-te-ka-le, in a casuistic manner.
casuistry, *n.* *kaz*-yoo-is-tre, the doctrine which professes to determine the lawfulness or unlawfulness of particular acts by rules derived from some accepted standard of right; sophistical reasoning. (L. *casus,* a case, as of conscience.)
★**cat,** *n.* kat, any one of many species of the genus *Felis* (including the lions and tigers), esp. *F. domesticus* the domestic cat and *F. catus* the wild cat; a spiteful woman [Coll.]; a scourge, or cat-o'-nine-tails; an old rig of ship with a narrow stern, projecting quarters, and deep waist; a strong tackle or combination of pulleys, to draw an anchor to the cathead [Naut.]; a double, six-footed tripod; a short stick pointed at both ends; tipcat: *v.t.* to raise to the cathead and stow there; to scourge with the cat: *v.i.* to retch or vomit [Slang]. **cat beam,** the broadest beam in a ship (Naut.]. (A.S. *cat.*)
cata-, *kat*-a, a prefix signifying down, back, against, away, wrongly, thoroughly. (Gr. prep. *kata.*)
catabolism, *n.* ka-*tab*-o-lizm, katabolism.
catacaustic, *a.* kat-a-*kaws*-tik, formed by reflected rays, as catacaustic curves: *n.* a curve formed by reflection [Opt.].
catachresis, *n.* kat-a-*kree*-sis, an abuse of a trope or metaphor, as when a term is used apart from its natural sense [Rhet.]. (Gr. *kata,* against, *kresis,* use.)
catachrestic, *a.* kat-a-*kres*-tik, wrested from its natural sense.
cataclysm, *n.* *kat*-a-klizm, a great flood; a sudden physical, political, or social change. (Gr. *kataklysmos.*)
cataclysmal, *a.* kat-a-*kliz*-mal, pertaining to a cataclysm.
cataclysmist, *n.* kat-a-*kliz*-mist, one who ascribes geological changes to cataclysms, esp. to the Deluge.
catacomb, *n.* *kat*-a-kome, a subterranean place for the burial of the dead. (Fr. *catacombe.*)
catacoustics, *n.* kat-a-*kous*-tiks, that part of acoustics which treats of echoes or reflected sounds.
catadioptric, *a.* kat-a-dy-*op*-trik, refracting and reflecting light [Opt.].
catadromous, *a.* ka-*tad*-ro-mus, descending a river to spawn in the sea. (Gr.)
catafalque, *n.* *kat*-a-falk, a temporary platform representing a tomb on which was placed the coffin of a distinguished person at his funeral. (It.)
catagenesis, *n.* *kat*-a-*jen*-e-sis, retrogressive evolution.
Catalan, *a.* and *n.* *kat*-al-an, pertaining to, or a native of, Catalonia, Spain; the language there spoken.
catalectic, *a.* kat-a-*lek*-tik, wanting a syllable [Pros.]. (Gr. *kata* and *lego,* cease.)
catalepsy, *n.* *kat*-a-lep-se, a condition, often hysterical, in which the limbs are apparently powerless and remain for a short time in any position in which they are placed. (Gr. *katalepsis,* seizing.)
catalexis, *n.* *kat*-a-*lek*-sis, absence of a half-foot or syllable from a line [Pros.].

catallactics, *n.* kat-al-*lakt*-iks, the science of exchange. (Gr. *katallasso*, exchange.)
catalogue, *n.* *kat*-a-log, an arranged list: *v.t.* to make a list of. **catalogue raisonné** (ray-*zon*-ay), a descriptive catalogue of books, pictures, etc. (Fr.).
Catalpa, *n.* ka-*tal*-pa, a genus of ornamental American and Asiatic trees, including the catawba. (Native Indian.)
catalyse, *v.t.* and *i.* *kat*-a-lyz, to break down by dissolving; to decompose.
catalysis, *n.* ka-*tal*-e-sis, a change in composition effected on a body by the mere presence of another which remains unchanged; dissolution and re-composition [Chem.]. (Gr.)
catalyst, *n.* *kat*-a-list, a body which produces chemical changes in another, itself remaining unchanged; the agent in catalysis. [Chem.]
catalytic, *a.* kat-a-*lit*-ik, relating to catalysis: *n.* a medicine which is thought to act by the destruction or counteraction of morbid agencies in the blood.
catamaran, *n.* *kat*-a-ma-*ran*, a raft or flat-bottomed surf-boat; a double boat. (Tamil, *katta*, tie, *maram*, wood.)
catamenia, *n.pl.* kat-a-*mee*-ne-a, the menses. (Gr., monthly.)
catamenial, *a.* kat-a-*mee*-ne-al, pertaining to the catamenia.
catamite, *n.* *kat*-a-mite, one submitting to sodomy for hire; a youth kept for unnatural purposes. (Gr. *Ganymede*, name of the cupbearer to Zeus.)
catamount, *n.* *kat*-a-mount, the puma.
catapan, *n.* *kat*-a-pan, a provincial governor of the Byzantine Empire.
cataphonics, *n.* kat-a-*fon*-iks, the science of reflected sounds. (Gr. *kata*, again, *phone*, sound.)
cataphoresis, *n.* *kat*-a-fo-*ree*-sis, the propulsion of solid particles through a fluid by electric force, esp. the introduction of drugs into the system by this means [Med.]. (Gr. *kata*, down, *phoresis*, a bearing.)
cataphract, *n.* *kat*-a-frakt, a piece of scaly armour [Zool.]. (L. *cataphracto.*)
cataphracted, *a.* kat-a-*frakt*-ed, completely armed, covered with a thick hard skin, or horny plates [Zool.].
cataphyllary, *a.* kat-a-*fil*-la-re, pertaining to a rudimentary leaf. (Gr.)
cataplasm, *n.* *kat*-a-plazm, a poultice [Med.].
cataplexy, *n.* *kat*-a-pleks-e, hypnotic sleep in animals induced by great fear; the condition of feigning death. (Gr. *kataplessein*, hit down.)
catapult, *n.* *kat*-a-pult, an ancient military engine for hurling missiles; a toy with a rubber loop for throwing small stones; an apparatus for projecting aircraft from the deck of a ship or aircraft-carrier. (L. *catapulta.*)
cataract, *n.* *kat*-a-rakt, a great waterfall; opacity in the crystalline lens of the eye [Med.]. (L. *cataracta.*)
cataractous, *a.* kat-a-*rakt*-us, relating to or affected with cataract [Med.].
catarrh, *n.* ka-*tahr*, inflammation of mucous membrane associated with abnormal secretion of mucus [Med.]; a cold. (Gr. *katarrhine*, to flow down.)
catarrhal, *a.* ka-*tahr*-ral, connected with catarrh.
catarrhine, *a.* *kat*-a-rine, narrow-nosed as compared with platyrrhine (applied specially to monkeys of the Old World). (Gr. *kata*, down, *rhin*, the nose.)
catarrhous, *a.* ka-*tahr*-rus, catarrhal.
catasta, *n.* ka-*tas*-ta, the block upon which slaves were placed to be sold. (L.)
catastasis, *n.* ka-*tas*-ta-sis, the part of an oration in which the matter in question is unfolded [Rhet.]; the part of a Greek drama leading to the catastrophe. (Gr., laying.)
catastrophe, *n.* ka-*tas*-tro-fe, the wind-up, or final issue; an unfortunate conclusion; a great calamity; supposed violent convulsion of the globe, causing the elevation or subsidence of its solid parts [Geol.]. (Gr.)
catastrophic, *a.* kat-a-*strof*-ik, violently changing; of the nature of a catastrophe.
catastrophism, *n.* ka-*tas*-tro-fizm, the theory which accounts for geologic changes by the hypothesis of the action of violent convulsive forces.
catastrophist, *n.* ka-*tas*-tro-fist, one who holds the catastrophic theory of the earth's formation.
catawba, *n.* ka-*taw*-ba, an Ohio grape; its wine. (From the river *Catawba.*)
cat-bird, *n.* *kat*-berd, the American song-bird, *Dumetella carolinensis*; a bower-bird of Australia, *Ailuroedus crassirostris.*
catboat, *n.* *kat*-bote, a boat with a mast in the bow.
cat-block, *n.* *kat*-blok, a block used to cat the anchor.
cat-burglar, *n.* *kat*-burg-lar, a thief who enters a house at night by climbing.
catcall, *n.* *kat*-kawl, a squeaking instrument used in theatres to condemn plays; a sound in imitation.
catch, *n.* katch, the act of seizing; seizure; anything that seizes, takes hold, or checks; a seizure and holding of the ball at cricket; amount (esp. of fish) caught; an acquisition; a watching an opportunity to seize; advantage; a song, the parts of which are caught up in succession by different singers; a play upon words: *v.i.* to get entangled; to communicate; to be contagious; to take hold; to spread epidemically: *v.t.* to seize; to intercept from falling; to seize in pursuit; to ensnare; to captivate; to get entangled with; to get possession of; to receive; to receive by sympathy, contagion, or infection; to engage and attach to; to come upon suddenly. **catch at,** to endeavour to seize suddenly. **catch a Tartar,** *see* **Tartar**. **catch it,** to receive a scolding. *p.* and *pp.* **caught**. (O.Fr. *cachier*, take.)
catchable, *a.* *katch*-a-bl, that may be caught.
catch-drain, *n.* *katch*-drane, a drain across a declivity or by a canal to catch the surplus water.
catchfly, *n.* *katch*-fly, the name of certain plants in which insects are caught.
catchiness, *n.* *katch*-e-nes, the quality of being catchy.
catching, *a.* *katch*-ing, infectious; charming.
catchment, *n.* *katch*-ment, an area which may be drained of its water.
catchpenny, *a.* *katch*-pen-ne, worthless; trumped up or made merely to catch money.
catchpoll, or **-pole,** *n.* *katch*-pole, a constable.
catchup, *n.* *katch*-up, ketchup.
catchweed, *n.* *katch*-weed, the madwort, goosegrass, or cleavers.
catch-weight, *n.* *katch*-wate, a boxer or wrestler competing in a tournament without restriction of weight as to what class of contest he enters.
catchword, *n.* *katch*-wurd, a word under the last line of a page, as being the first of the next page; the word that heads the page or column in works of reference; the word explained or defined in an encyclopædia or dictionary entry; an actor's cue.
catchy, *a.* *katch*-e, catching; attractive; deceptive.
catechetic, *a.* kat-e-*ket*-ik, consisting of questions and answers; pertaining to catechism.
catechetically, *ad.* kat-e-*ket*-e-ka-le, in a catechetical manner. (L. *catecheticus.*)
catechism, *n.* *kat*-e-kizm, a form or a book of instruction by means of question and answer.
catechist, *n.* *kat*-e-kist, one who teaches by catechizing, or imparts elementary instruction, esp. in the principles of religion.
catechistic, *a.* kat-e-*kis*-tik, in the form of a catechism.
catechistically, *ad.* kat-e-*kis*-te-ka-le, in a catechistical manner.
catechization, *n.* *kat*-e-ky-*zay*-shon, the process or act of catechizing.
catechize, *v.t.* *kat*-e-kize, to instruct by asking questions and receiving answers; to question closely. (Late L. *catechizo.*)
catechu, *n.* *kat*-e-choo, a brown astringent gum, obtained chiefly from *Acacia catechu.* (Malay *kāchu.*)
catechuic, *a.* kat-e-*choo*-ik, pertaining to catechu.
catechumen, *n.* kat-e-*kew*-men, one who is under Christian instruction preparatory to admission into the Church; a beginner in any art or science. (Late L. *catechumenus.*)
categorematic, *a.* *kat*-e-go-re-*mat*-ik, applied to a word capable of being employed by itself as a term [Logic]. (Gr. *katēgorēma.*)
categorical, *a.* kat-e-*go*-re-kal, pertaining to a category or the categories; absolute; positive; not conditional. **categorical imperative,** the absolute command of the moral law [Kant]. (Gr. *katēgorikos.*)
categorically, *ad.* kat-e-*go*-re-ka-le, in a categorical manner

categorize, *v.t.* *kat*-e-go-rize, to place in a category; to classify.
category, *n.* *kat*-e-go-re, an order or a class; a summum genus, or highest class, that is, a class which comes under no higher, of which classes Aristotle recognized ten [Logic]; in the philosophy of Kant, one of the twelve primitive forms of thought contributed by the understanding independently of experience. (Gr. *katēgoria*, a statement.)
catelectrode, *n.* *kat*-e-*lek*-trode, the negative pole or electrode of a battery.
catena, *n.* ka-*tee*-na, a series chronologically or otherwise connected. (L., a chain.)
catenarian, *a.* kat-e-*nare*-re-an, catenary.
catenary, *n.* *kat*-en-a-re, the curve formed by a chain of uniform density and thickness, when hanging freely between two points of suspension [Geom.]: *a.* like, or having the properties of, a chain. (L. *catena*, a chain.)
catenulate, *a.* ka-*tee*-new-late, having chain-like characteristics [Bot. and Zool.].
cater, *v.i.* *kay*-ter, to provide food or amusement. (Fr. *achat*, purchase.)
cateran, *n.* *kat*-er-ran, a Highland or Irish predatory irregular soldier; a Highland freebooter. (Gael.)
cater-cousin, *n.* *kay*-ter-kuz-n, an intimate friend (not necessarily a relation). (Probably from *cater*, not from L. *quatuor*, four.)
caterer, *n.* *kay*-ter-rer, one who caters.
caterpillar, *n.* *kat*-er-pil-lar, the larva of a moth or butterfly. **caterpillar wheel**, a series of two or more wheels in line over which runs an endless metal belt to provide a better wheel-base for crossing rough ground. (O.Fr. *chatepelose*.)
caterwaul, *v.i.* *kat*-er-wawl, to make a noise like a rutting cat. (M.E. *caterwawen*.)
cates, *n.pl.* kayts, viands; dainties. (Fr.)
cat-eyed, *a.* *kat*-ide, able to see in the dark.
catfish, *n.* *kat*-fish, the wolf-fish, *Anarrichas lupus*; the nurse-hound, *Scyllium catulus*; and others.
catgut, *n.* *kat*-gut, a thin tough cord made from sheep's intestines and used for the strings of musical instruments, and in surgery, angling, etc.
catharism, *n.* *kath*-a-rizm, the beliefs of a catharist.
catharist, *n.* *kath*-a-rist, one who pretends to greater purity than others. (Gr. *katharos*, pure.)
catharsis, *n.* ka-*thar*-sis, purgation of the body [Med.]; an intellectual and moral purgation [Aristotle]. (Gr.)
cathartic, *a.* ka-*thar*-tik, purgative: *n.* a purgative medicine.
cathartical, *a.* ka-*thar*-te-kal, cathartic.
cathartin, *n.* ka-*thar*-tin, the active principle of senna. (Gr. *kathartikos*, purgative.)
cathead, *n.* *kat*-hed, a horizontal beam over a ship's bows to raise the anchor and secure it to; *v.t.* to make fast to the cathead [Naut.].
cathedra, *n.* ka-*thee*-dra *or* *kath*-e-dra, a bishop's throne; a professor's official chair. **ex cathedra**, with full authority. (Gr. *kathedra*, a seat.)
cathedral, *n.* ka-*thee*-dral, the principal church in a diocese, in which is the throne of the bishop: *a.* pertaining to a cathedral or cathedra.
catheretic, *n.* kath-er-*ret*-ik, a slightly caustic substance [Med.]. (Gr. *kathairetikos*, destructive.)
catherine-pear, *n.* *kath*-er-rin-pare, a variety of small pear.
catherine-wheel, *n.* *kath*-er-rin-wheel, an ornamental circular window, with radiating divisions [Arch.]; a firework which, as it goes off, rotates like a wheel; a cart-wheel somersault. (With reference to the wheel upon which St. Catherine was martyred.)
catheter, *n.* *kath*-e-ter, a tubular instrument for drawing fluid from body-cavities, esp. urine from the bladder [Surg.]. (Gr. *kath*, down, *ienai*, to send.)
cathetometer, *n.* kath-e-*tom*-et-er, a device for measuring minute differences in levels of various liquids contained in tubes.
cathode, *n.* *kath*-ode, the negative electrode from which the current flows towards the anode. **cathode ray**, a stream of electrons in a highly evacuated glass tube. (Gr. *kathodos*, descending.)
catholic, *a.* *kath*-o-lik, universal; embracing or embraced by the whole Church; liberal; pertaining to or affecting Roman Catholics: *n.* a member of the Church Catholic; a Roman Catholic. **Catholic Church**, the whole Christian Church; the Roman Catholic Church. **the Catholic Epistles**, the general Epistles (James, Peter, Jude, I John). **the Catholic Faith**, the common faith of Christendom. (Gr. *katholikos*, from *kata*, entirely, *holos*, whole.)
catholicism, *n.* ka-*thol*-e-sizm, what is catholic, esp. what is distinctively Roman Catholic.
catholicity, *n.* kath-o-*lis*-e-te, universality; the quality of being catholic.
catholicize, *v.t.* ka-*thol*-e-size, to convert to Catholicism; *v.i.* to become catholic or Catholic.
catholicon, *n.* ka-*thol*-e-kon, a universal remedy.
Catholicos, *n.* ka-*thol*-e-kos, the primate of the Armenian and certain other Eastern Churches.
Catilinarian, *n.* kat-e-le-*nare*-re-an, one who conspires against his country. (*Catiline*, Roman conspirator.)
cat-ice, *n.* *kat*-ice, thin surface-ice from under which the water has receded.
cation, *n.* *kat*-eye-on, the element which, in electrolysis, passes to the negative electrode. (Gr., descending.)
catkin, *n.* *kat*-kin, a pendulous inflorescence, like that of the hazel. **catkin valve**, a thermionic valve having a metal instead of a glass container [Wire.]. (O.Dut. *katteken*, kitten.)
catling, *n.* *kat*-ling, a kitten; catgut.
catmint, *n.* *kat*-mint, a plant of the order Nepeta.
catnip, *n.* *kat*-nip, catmint (U.S.A.).
catodont, *a.* *kat*-o-dont, having teeth in the lower jaw only [Zool.].
Catonian, *a.* ka-*toh*-ne-an, resembling Cato; severe.
cat-o'-nine-tails, *n.* *kat*-o-*nine*-taylz, a whip or scourge having a number of lashes or cords.
catoptric, *a.* ka-*top*-trik, relating to catoptrics.
catoptrics, *n.* kat-*op*-triks, that part of optics which treats of reflected light. (Gr. *katoptron*, a mirror.)
catoptromancy, *n.* ka-*top*-tro-man-se, divination by looking into a mirror under water. (Gr. *katoptron*, and *manteia*, divination.)
cat's-cradle, *n.* kats-*kray*-dl, a child's game for two players with a piece of string intertwined and transferred by the fingers.
cat's-eye, *n.* *kats*-eye, an opalescent quartz, a chrysoberyl, known also as cymophane.
cat-silver, *n.* *kat*-sil-ver, a variety of mica.
cat's-paw, *n.* *kats*-paw, one who is duped into acting as the tool of another; a rippling of the surface of the water [Naut.]; a turn in the bight of a rope to hook a tackle on [Naut.].
cat's-tail, *n.* *kats*-tale, the reed mace *Typha latifolia*; the grass, timothy; a catkin.
cat's-whisker, *n.* *kats*-whis-ker, a thin wire brought in contact with the crystal in a receiving-set to rectify the current and produce audibility [Wire.].
cattalo, *n.* *kat*-a-lo, a hybrid bred from the buffalo and the domestic cow. (From *cattle* and *buffalo*.)
cattish, *a.* *kat*-tish, feline; spiteful.
cattle, *n.pl.* *kat*-tl, beasts of pasture, especially oxen, bulls, and cows; live-stock. (O.Fr. *catel*.)
catty, *a.* *kat*-te, cat-like; spiteful; cattish.
catty, *n.* *kat*-te, a weight of China and the Far East equal to from about 1·3 to 1·4 lbs. avoirdupois.
Caucasian, *a.* kaw-*kaze*-yan, pertaining to the Caucasus, or to the Indo-European division of the human race: *n.* a member of this race.
caucus, *n.* *kaw*-kus, a political organization for electoral purposes.
caudal, *a.* *kaw*-dal, pertaining to the tail. (L. *cauda*, tail.)
caudate, *a.* *kaw*-dat, having a tail, or a termination like a tail [Zool. and Bot.].
caudex, *n.* *kaw*-deks, the stem or axis of a plant. (L.)
caudle, *n.* *kawd*-l, a warm drink; spiced wine thickened with eggs or gruel. (O.Fr. *caudel*.)
caught, *kawt*, *p.* and *pp.* of **catch**.
caul, *n.* kawl, a membrane covering the lower intestines; a thin membrane covering the head of some children at birth; a kind of net for the hair. (O.Fr. *cale*, veil.)
cauldron, *n.* *kawl*-dron, a large kettle or boiler shaped like a bowl. (Norman Fr. *cauderon*.)
caulescent, *a.* kawl-*es*-sent, with a true stem [Bot.]. (L. *caulis*, a stalk.)
caulicle, *n.* *kawl*-e-kl, a short stem [Bot.].
caulicule, *n.* *kawl*-e-kewl, a little stalk, especially one rising from the neck of the root [Bot.].
cauliferous, *a.* kawl-*if*-er-us, having a stalk [Bot.].

cauliflower, *n.* *kol*-le-flou-er, a variety of cabbage, the inflorescence of which is edible. **cauliflower ear,** a deformation of the ear produced by repeated blows, as in pugilism.
cauliform, *a.* *kawl*-e-form, having the form of a stalk.
cauline, *a.* *kawl*-in, of or belonging to the stem [Bot.].
caulk, *v.t.* kawk, to make a vessel watertight by driving oakum into the seams of its planking or deck, and treating them with pitch.
caulker, *n.* *kawk*-er, one who caulks ships; a final drink [Slang]; a corker [Slang].
caulking, *n.* *kawk*-ing, the oakum used in this operation. (O.Fr. *cauquer.*)
caulking-iron, *n.* *kawk*-ing-eye-urn, the chisel-like tool used in stopping seams with oakum; the oakum employed.
causal, *a.* *kawz*-al, relating to or expressing cause; of the nature of a cause; due to a cause.
causality, *n.* kaw-*zal*-e-te, action as a cause; the faculty of tracing effects to causes; the theory of causation.
causally, *ad.* *kaw*-za-le, in a casual manner or order.
causation, *n.* kaw-*zay*-shon, the act of causing; the connection between cause and effect; the theory that everything has its cause [Phil.].
causationist, *n.* kaw-*zay*-shon-ist, one who believes in the theory of causation [Phil.].
causative, *a.* *kaw*-za-tiv, causing; expressing cause.
causatively, *ad.* *kaw*-za-tiv-le, in a causative manner.
★**cause,** *n.* kawz, that which produces an effect, or contributes to it; that which always precedes an effect; reason; motive; the object sought; sake; subject in debate; case; ground of action; a law suit; a party or a party object: *v.t.* to effect; to produce; to bring about. (Fr. *cause.*)
causeless, *a.* *kawz*-less, having no cause; self-caused; without just reason.
causelessly, *ad.* *kawz*-less-le, without cause or reason.
causelessness, *n.* *kawz*-less-ness, the state of being causeless.
causerie, *n.* *koh*-ze-ree, brief informal essay. (Fr.)
causeuse, *n.* (App.), a small sofa for two. (Fr.)
causeway, *n.* *kawz*-way, a raised roadway over wet ground; a pavement. (O.Fr. *caucié.*)
causey, *n.* *kaw*-ze, a causeway.
causidical, *a.* kaw-*zid*-e-kal, pertaining to an advocate, or legal advocacy. (L. *causidicus*, a pleader.)
caustic, *n.* *kaws*-tik, a substance which burns or corrodes organic matter, esp. silver nitrate: *a.* burning; corroding; searing; bitter; cutting; sarcastic. **caustic curve,** a curve to which the rays of light reflected or refracted by another curve are tangents [Geom.]. (L. *causticus.*)
caustically, *ad.* *kaws*-tik-a-le, in a caustic manner.
causticity, *n.* kaws-*tis*-e-te, the quality of being caustic.
cautelous, *a.* *kaw*-te-lus, deceitful; wary.
cauter, *n.* *kaw*-ter, a searing or branding iron. (Gr.)
cauterant, *n.* *kaw*-te-rant, a cauterizing substance.
cauterization, *n.* kaw-ter-ry-*zay*-shon, the act or process of cauterizing.
cauterize, *v.t.* *kaw*-ter-rize, to burn some morbid part with a caustic, a hot iron, or electricity; to sear.
cautery, *n.* *kaw*-ter-re, burning with a hot iron or with electricity or caustic; an instrument for cauterizing; for burning; a caustic or cauterant. (L. *cauterium.*)
caution, *n.* *kaw*-shon, prudence; provident care against contingent evil; wariness; a warning; something, or a person, queer or extraordinary [Slang]: *v.t.* to warn. **caution money,** money lodged as security for good behaviour. (Fr. *caution.*)
cautionary, *a.* *kaw*-shon-a-re, cautioning; cautious; given as a pledge.
cautioner, *n.* *kay*-shon-er *or* *kaw*-shon-er, one who becomes security for another [Scots. Law].
cautious, *a.* *kaw*-shus, exercising caution; wary.
cautiously, *ad.* *kaw*-shus-le, in a cautious manner.
cautiousness, *n.* *kaw*-shus-ness, the quality of being cautious; prudence.
cavalcade, *n.* kav-al-*kade*, a procession on horseback; a train of mounted persons. (Fr.)
cavalier, *n.* kav-a-*leer*, a horseman; a knight or gentleman soldier; a gay military man; a lady's man; an adherent of Charles I; a Royalist; an elevation for cannon within a bastion [Fort.]: *a.* gay, easy and off-hand, like a cavalier; haughty; disdainful; connected with the cavaliers: *v.t.* to escort a lady; to act superciliously. (Fr.)
cavalierly, *ad.* kav-a-*leer*-le, in a disdainful way.
cavally, *n.* ka-*val*-le, the horse-mackerel, a food-fish of the genus *Caranx*, of tropical American coasts. (Sp.)
cavalry, *n.* *kav*-al-re, mounted troops; a branch of the British army mainly mechanized by 1939. (O.Fr. *cavallerie.*)
cavalryman, *n.* *kav*-al-re-man, a member of a cavalry regiment.
cavatina, *n.* kav-a-*tee*-na, a short simple song or air [Mus.]. (It.)
cave, *n.* kave, a hollow place in the earth; a den; a group of adullamites or seceders from a political party. **cave bear,** the extinct *Ursus spelæus*. **cave in,** to fall in and leave a hollow; to give in. **cave men** or **dwellers,** members of any prehistoric or primitive race inhabiting caves. (L. *cavus*, hollow.)
cave, *int.* *kay*-ve, look out; beware. (L.)
caveat, *n.* *kave*-e-at, a warning; a process to stop procedure [Law]; a notice of intention to apply for a patent (U.S.A.): *v.t.* to enter a caveat. (L., let him beware.)
caveator, *n.* *kave*-e-ate-or, one who enters a caveat.
cavendish, *n.* *kav*-en-dish, sweetened tobacco pressed into cakes; negro-head. (Maker's name.)
cavern, *n.* *kav*-ern, a deep hollow place in the earth: *v.t.* to hollow out; to keep in a cavern. (L. *caverna.*)
caverned, *a.* *kav*-ernd, with caverns; hollowed out.
cavernous, *a.* *kav*-ern-us, hollow; full of caverns.
cavernulous, *a.* ka-*vern*-yew-lus, full of little cavities; porous.
cavesson, *n.* *kav*-es-son, a nose-band for a horse.
caviar *or* **caviare,** *n.* kav-e-*ahr*, the roes of certain fish, esp. the sturgeon, prepared and salted; anything requiring a highly cultivated taste for its true appreciation. (Fr.)
cavicorn, *a.* *kav*-e-kawn, hollow-horned: *n.* a hollow-horned ruminant. (L. *cavus*, hollow, *cornu*, horn.)
cavie, *n.* *kay*-ve, a hen-coop. (Scots.)
cavil, *n.* *kav*-il, an objection; a sophism: *v.i.* to raise captious and frivolous objections. (O.Fr. *caviller*, pick holes in.)
caviller, *n.* *kav*-il-ler, one who cavils.
cavilling, *a.* *kav*-il-ing, raising frivolous objections.
cavillingly, *ad.* *kav*-il-ing-le, in a cavilling manner.
cavity, *n.* *kav*-e-te, a hollow place or part. (Fr. *cavité.*)
cavort, *v.i.* *ka*-vort, to prance like a horse. (Slang.)
cavy, *n.* *kay*-ve, any rodent of the genus *Cavia*, esp. the domesticated guinea pig. (Carib.)
caw, *n.* kaw, a cry: *v.i.* to cry like a rook. (Imit.)
cawk, *n.* kawk, a compact variety of barytes.
cawker, *n.* *kaw*-ker, a caulker.
cawky, *a.* *kawk*-e, containing or like cawk.
caxon, *n.* *kaks*-on, an old-fashioned wig.
Caxton, *n.* *kaks*-ton, a book in black-letter printed by Caxton (*d.* 1491), who introduced printing into England; a black-letter type.
cay, *n.* kay, a reef; a shoal. (Sp. *cayo*, shoal.)
cayenne-pepper, *n.* *kay*-en-*pep*-per, pungent red pepper, obtained from several varieties of capsicum. (*Cayenne*, French Guiana.)
cayman, *n.* *kay*-man, the name of several alligators of the genus *Caiman* found in tropical America. (Sp. *caiman.*)
cayuse, *n.* *ky*-yoos, a small Indian pony; any horse in bad condition [U.S.A.].
cazique, *n.* ka-*zeek*, a cacique or Central American chief.
cease, *v.i.* seece, to stop; to desist; to come to an end: *v.t.* to put a stop or an end to. (Fr. *cesser.*)
ceaseless, *a.* *seece*-less, unceasing; unending.
ceaselessly, *ad.* *seece*-less-le, unceasingly.
ceasing, *n.* *seece*-ing, cessation; pause.
cecils, *n.pl.* *ses*-sils, fried balls of seasoned mince.
cecity, *n.* *see*-se-te, loss of sight; physical or mental blindness. (L. *caecitas*, blindness.)
cedar, *n.* *see*-dar, the popular name of many evergreen coniferous trees, esp. the cedar of Lebanon, *Cedrus libani*, the Atlantic cedar, *C. atlantica*, and the

deodar, *C. deodara*: *a.* made of cedar. (O.Fr. *cedre.*)
cedared, *a. see*-derd, covered with cedars.
cedarn, *a. see*-dern, consisting of, or made of cedar.
cede, *v.t.* seed, to yield; to give up: *v.i.* to submit; to give way. (L. *cedo,* give place to.)
cedilla, *n.* se-*dil*-la, a mark used under the *c* (thus, ç), to show that it is to be sounded like *s.* (Fr.)
cedrat, *n. see*-drat, a species of citron. (Fr.)
cedrine, *a. see*-drin *or see*-drine, pertaining to cedar.
cee-spring, *n. see*-spring, C-spring, a C-shaped spring upholding a carriage-frame.
ceil, *v.t.* seel, to cover with a ceiling. (Fr. *ceil,* the sky.)
ceiling, *n. seel*-ing, the inner roof of an apartment; the upper interior surface; the lining or planks on the inside of a ship's frame [Naut.]; the height to which an aircraft can fly [Av.]. **service ceiling,** the height at which the rate of ascent of an aeroplane has decreased to 100 ft. per. minute [Av.].
ceilinged, *a. seel*-ingd, furnished with a ceiling.
celadon, *n. sel*-a-don, a pale green colour; a greenish Chinese porcelain. (Fr.)
celandine, *n. sel*-an-dine, the swallow-wort, a species of *Chelidonium* believed to flower with the coming and die with the going of the swallow. **lesser celandine,** the pilewort, a species of *Ranunculus.* (Gr. *chelidon,* a swallow.)
celanese, *n.* sel-a-*neez,* a registered trade mark denoting the products of British Celanese Ltd., including artificial textiles, plastics and chemicals.
celebrant, *n. sel*-e-brant, the officiating priest at Mass or Holy Communion. (Fr. *célébrant.*)
celebrate, *v.t. sel*-e-brate, to praise; to commemorate by ceremonies and marks of joy and respect; to perform with the appropriate rites and ceremonies. (L. *celebratus,* renowned.)
celebrated, *a. sel*-e-bray-ted, having celebrity; famous.
celebration, *n.* sel-e-*bray*-shon, the act of celebrating.
celebrity, *n.* se-*leb*-re-te, fame; renown; a renowned or distinguished person. (L. *celeber,* famous.)
celeriac, *n.* se-*le*-re-ak, turnip-rooted celery.
celerity, *n.* se-*le*-re-te, rapidity; swiftness. (Fr. *célérité,* swiftness.)
celery, *n. sel*-le-re, a salad vegetable, *Apium graveolens.* (L. *celeri.*)
celesta, *n.* sel-*less*-ta, a keyboard instrument the hammers of which strike steel plates [Mus.].
celestial, *a.* se-*lest*-yal, heavenly; belonging to, relating to, or dwelling in heaven; excellent in a supreme degree: *n.* an inhabitant of heaven; a native of China. **Celestial Empire,** China. (O.Fr. *celestiel.*)
celestially, *ad.* se-*lest*-yal-le in a heavenly manner.
celestina, *n.* sel-es-*tee*-na, a form of harpsichord; a 4-ft. organ-stop of delicate tone.
celestine, *n. sel*-es-tin, native sulphate of strontium [Min.].
Celestines, *n.pl. sel*-es-tinz, a strict order of Benedictines founded by Pietro da Murrone, who later (1294) became Pope as Celestine V.
celiac, *a. see*-le-ak, cœliac.
celibacy, *n. sel*-e-ba-se, the unmarried state. (L.)
celibatarian, *n.* sel-e-ba-tare-re-an, one favouring celibacy; a bachelor: *a.* favouring celibacy.
celibate, *n. sel*-e-bate, a person who is unmarried: *a.* unmarried. (L. *cælibatus,* unmarried.)
cell, *n.* sel, enclosed space in a prison or a convent; the retreat of a hermit; a small cavity; the unit of organic structure; a single division of a bee's comb; a mass of protoplasm containing a nucleus; an appliance consisting of two metal electrodes immersed in solid or liquid chemicals, used for generating electricity; a unit group of communists; a ballonet of an airship. (L. *cella,* a little room, from *celo,* hide.)
cellar, *n. sel*-lar, underground accommodation for stores, especially for wines; a stock of wine; a small receptacle, as a salt-cellar. (Fr. *cellier.*)
cellarage, *n. sel*-la-raj, cellars; space for cellars; charge for storage in a cellar.
cellarer, *n. sel*-la-rer, an official (in monasteries a monk) having the care of the cellar and provisions; a wine-merchant.
cellaret, *n.* sel-la-*ret,* a case, or a cupboard in a sideboard, for holding wine, etc.
cellaring, *n. sel*-la-ring, cellarage; storing in cellars.
cellarman, *n. sel*-lar-man, one employed to look after the liquor in a cellar.
celled, *a.* seld, having cells.
celliferous, *a.* sel-*lif*-er-us, bearing or producing cells.
cellist, *n. chel*-list, a violoncellist.
cello, *n. chel*-lo, a violoncello.
cellophane, *n.* sel-lo-*fayn,* trade-name of a transparent waterproof material made from solidified viscose and used for wrapping.
cellular, *a. sel*-lew-lar, consisting of, or containing cells; pertaining to or resembling a cell or cells: *n.* a plant without distinct stem or leaves; a cryptogam. **cellular tissue,** tissue composed of numerous minute cells communicating with one another.
cellulated, *a. sel*-lew-lay-ted, formed of cells.
cellule, *n. sel*-lewl, a little cell.
celluliferous, *a.* sel-lew-*lif*-er-us, bearing little cells. (*Cell,* and L. *fero,* bear.)
cellulitis, *n.* sel-yew-*ly*-tis, inflammation of the cellular tissues.
celluloid, *n. sel*-lew-loyd, an inflammable nitrocellulose plastic used as a substitute for ivory, bone, horn, tortoise-shell, etc.: *a.* resembling a cell or cells.
cellulose, *a. sel*-lew-lose, containing cells: *n.* the basic substance of the cellular tissue of plants.
celotex, *n. sel*-o-teks, trade-name of an artificial building- and insulating-board made from compressed bagasse.
celsius, *n. sel*-se-us, the name of the Swedish inventor, Anders Celsius (1701–1744), applied to the centigrade thermometer.
Celt, *n.* selt *or* kelt, a member of or descendant from the branch of Indo-Europeans which included the ancient inhabitants of Gaul, Britain, and Ireland. (Fr. *Celte.*)
celt, *n.* selt, a prehistoric cutting implement of stone or bronze. (Perh. late L. *celtis,* chisel.)
Celtic, *a. selt*-ik *or kelt*-ik, pertaining to the Celts: *n.* their language.
Celtologist, *n.* sel-*tol*-o-jist, a student of Celtic antiquities, etc., or language.
cembalist, *n. sem*-ba-list, a player of a cembalo; the pianoforte-player in an orchestra.
cembalo, *n. sem*-ba-lo, a harpsichord or similar instrument in which the strings are struck with hammers [Mus.]. (It. *clavicembalo.*)
cement, *n.* se-*ment,* an adhesive substance for making bodies, especially stones, cohere; bond of union; that which unites firmly; a material for stopping teeth: *v.t.* to unite with cement; to unite firmly or closely: *v.i.* to unite and cohere. (O.Fr. *ciment.*)
cementation, *n.* sem-en-*tay*-shon, the act of cementing; the process of surrounding a solid body with the powder of other substances, and heating the whole in a close vessel so that the one combines with the other without fusing, as in the conversion of iron into steel through the medium of charcoal powder.
cemetery, *n. sem*-et-er-re, a public burying-place other than a churchyard. (L. *cemeterium.*)
cenacle, *n. sen*-a-kl, a supper-room, especially that which was the scene of the Last Supper. (Fr. *cénacle.*)
cenobite, *n. sen*-o-bite, a member of a religious order living in a community, as opposed to an anchorite. (Gr. *koinos,* common, *bios,* life.)
cenobitic, *a.* sen-o-*bit*-ik, living in community.
cenotaph, *n. sen*-o-taf, a monument erected in memory of one buried elsewhere. **the Cenotaph,** the monument in Whitehall, London (orig. erected 1919) commemorating the dead of the British armed forces during the wars of 1914–18 and 1939–45. (Gr. *kenos,* empty, *taphos,* tomb.)
cense, *v.t.* sense, to burn incense; to worship with incense; to perfume with incense.
censer, *n. sen*-ser, a thurible; a vessel for burning incense or other perfume. (O.Fr. *censier.*)
censor, *n. sen*-sor, an officer in ancient Rome who took the census, imposed taxes, and watched over the manners and morals of the citizens; an official who examines plays before their public performance is licensed, to ensure that they contain nothing of a seditious, immoral, or offensive nature; an officer who in time of war examines correspondence, press and broadcast communications, etc., deleting

anything harmful to the state or of which an enemy might make use; one addicted to censure: *v.t.* to examine anything written in order to expunge objectionable matter; to expurgate; to do work as a censor. (L.)

censorial, *a.* sen-*saw*-re-al, pertaining to a censor; full of censure; censorious.

censorious, *a.* sen-*saw*-re-us, addicted to criticizing; severe in judging; expressing censure.

censoriously, *ad.* sen-*saw*-re-us-le, in a censorious manner.

censoriousness, *n.* sen-*saw*-re-us-ness, the quality of being censorious.

censorship, *n.* *sen*-sor-ship, the office of censor; the time during which he holds office; the power or the action of a censor.

censual, *a.* *sen*-sew-al, pertaining to a census.

censurable, *a.* *sen*-shoor-a-bl, worthy of censure; blameable.

censurableness, *n.* *sen*-shoor-a-bl-ness, the quality of being censurable.

censurably, *ad.* *sen*-shoor-a-ble, in a censurable manner.

censure, *n.* *sen*-shoor, blame; imputation of wrong; reproof; judgment or sentence of condemnation: *v.t.* to blame; to find fault with. (Fr. *censurer.*)

census, *n.* *sen*-sus, an official enumeration and classification of the inhabitants of a country; the statistical result of this. (L.)

cent, *n.* sent, a hundred; a coin, whose value is the hundredth part of the standard unit, as (U.S.A.) a dollar; a halfpenny. **per cent,** a rate by the hundred. (L. *centum*, a hundred.)

centage, *n.* sen-taj, rate by the hundred; percentage.

cental, *n.* *sen*-tal, a hundred pounds weight.

centaur, *n.* *sen*-tawr, a Greek mythological figure, half man and half horse. (Gr. *kentauros.*)

centaury, *n.* *sen*-taw-re, the annual plant *Erythræa centaurium* with red flowers; any one of the large genus *Centaurea*, which includes the cornflowers, the **great centaury,** *C. centaurium*, and the **yellow centaury,** or yellow-wort.

centavo, *n.* sen-*tah*-voh, a small coin of Portugal and Spanish S. America, $\frac{1}{100}$ escudo, peso, etc.

centenarian, *n.* sen-te-*nare*-re-an, one a hundred years old or more. (L. *centenarius.*)

centenary, *n.* sen-*teen*-a-ree *or* *sent*-en-ar-re, a hundred years; commemoration after a hundred years: *a.* relating to a hundred or a centenary.

centennial, *a.* sen-*ten*-e-al, pertaining to a centenary; lasting or having lived a hundred years; happening every hundred years: *n.* a centenary. (L. *centum*, and *annus*, a year.)

center, *n.*, *v.t.* and *v.i.* *sen*-ter, centre.

centering, *n.* *sen*-ter-ing, the frame on which an arch is supported during its construction [Arch.].

centesimal, *n.* sen-tes-e-mal, a hundredth part; *a.* hundredth. (L. *centesimus.*)

centiare, *n.* *song*-te-ar (or App.), a square metre, 1,550 square inches. (Fr.)

centibar, *n.* *sen*-te-bar, the hundredth part of a bar [Meteor.]. (Fr.)

centigrade, *a.* *sen*-te-grade, divided into a hundred degrees. **centigrade thermometer,** that of Celsius, in which the interval between the freezing- and the boiling-points of water is divided into 100 degrees. (L. *centum*, and *gradus*, step.)

centigram, *n.* *sen*-te-gram, centigramme.

centigramme, *n.* *sen*-te-gram, the hundredth part of a gramme, or 0·15432 grain. (Fr.)

centilitre, *n.* sen-te-*lee*-ter, the hundredth part of a litre. (Fr.)

centillion, *n.* sen-*til*-yon, the one-hundredth power of one million or, in U.S.A., of a thousand.

centime, *n.* song-*teem* (or App.), the hundredth part of a franc. (Fr.)

centimetre, *n.* *sen*-te-mee-ter, the hundredth part of a metre, 0·3937 of an inch. (Fr.)

centipede, *n.* *sen*-te-peed, a many-legged arthropod. (L. *centum*, and *pes*, the foot.)

centner, *n.* *sent*-ner, a Continental weight of 50 kilograms (110·23 lb.); an assayer's weight of one dram.

cento, *n.* *sen*-to, a composition formed of selections from various authors. (L., patchwork.)

central, *a.* *sen*-tral, relating to, placed in, containing, or from, the centre. **central forces,** the antagonistic forces (centrifugal and centripetal) under whose action bodies revolve round a central point [Physics and Mech.]. **central heating,** warming by radiators heated from a central boiler.

centralism, *n.* *sent*-ral-izm, the quality of being collected in a centre; centralization of government.

centralist, *n.* *sen*-tra-list, one who advocates centralization in government.

centrality, *n.* sen-*tral*-e-te, the state or quality of being central.

centralization, *n.* sent-ra-ly-*zay*-shon, the act of centralizing, or of bringing, especially the government of a country or an administrative organization, to one centre.

centralize, *v.t.* *sent*-ra-lize, to draw to a centre.

centrally, *ad.* *sent*-ral-le, in a central manner.

centre, *n.* *sen*-ter, the point round which a circle is described; a nucleus; the middle point of anything; the middle or central object; the head of an organization; a political party holding a position midway between two extremes; the troops in the line between the wings [Mil.]; a centering: *v.t.* to place on a centre; to collect to a point: *v.i.* to be collected to a point; to be placed in the centre. **centre forward,** a player occupying the middle of the front line in Association football and hockey. **centre of buoyancy,** the point in an airship or ship at which the resultant force due to air or water buoyancy acts [Eng.]. **centre of gravity,** the point about which the parts of a body, when left free, exactly balance each other [Physics]. **centre of pressure,** the point at which the resultant pressure or force on a body acts [Eng.]. (Gr. *kentron*, a point.)

centre-bit, *n.* *sen*-ter-bit, a boring tool worked with a brace.

centre-board, *n.* *sen*-ter-bord, a movable keel which can be lowered from a boat to vary the draught.

centre-piece, *n.* *sen*-ter-peece, an ornament placed in the centre of a table or ceiling, etc.

centric, *a.* *sen*-trik, central. (Gr. *kentrikos.*)

centrically, *ad.* *sen*-tre-ka-le, in a central position.

centricity, *n.* sen-*tris*-e-te, the state or quality of being centric.

centrifuge, *n.* *sen*-tre-fewj, a rotatory machine separating by centrifugal force cream from milk, or other light and heavy bodies. (*Centre*, and L. *fugere*, to flee.)

centrifugal, *a.* sen-*trif*-yew-gal, from the centre; expanding first at the summit, and later at the base [Bot.]. **centrifugal force,** the force by which a body moving round another body in a curve tends to fly off from the axis of its motion. (*Centre*, and L. *fugio*, flee.)

centring, *n.* *sen*-tring, centering.

centripetal, *a.* sen-*trip*-e-tal, tending towards the centre; expanding first at the base, and afterwards at the summit [Bot.]. **centripetal force,** the force which draws a revolving body towards a centre. (*Centre*, and L. *peto*, seek.)

centrist, *n.* *sen*-trist, a member of a political Centre Party.

centrobaric, *a.* *sen*-tro-*ba*-rik, pertaining to the centre of gravity. (*Centre*, and Gr. *baros*, weight.)

centroid, *n.* *sen*-royd, a centre of mass or of gravity; a central position.

centrolineal, *a.* *sen*-tro-*lin*-e-al, converging towards a centre.

centrum, *n.* *sen*-trum, a central part, esp. [Anat.] of a vertebra; the site at which an earthquake originated.

centumvir, *n.* sen-*tum*-ver, a Roman judge in civil suits.

centuple, *n.* *sen*-tew-pl, a hundredfold: *v.t.* to multiply a hundredfold. (L. *centum*, and *plica*, a fold.)

centuplicate, *v.t.* sen-*tew*-ple-kate, to make a hundredfold: *n.* a centuple: *a.* hundredfold.

centurion, *n.* sen-*tewr*-re-on, among the Romans, a military officer who commanded a hundred men; the captain of a century in a legion. (L. *centuria.*)

century, *n.* *sen*-tew-re, a hundred; a period of a hundred years; a division of the Roman people or army. **century plant,** the maguey or American aloe, from the mistaken notion that it flowers but once in a hundred years.

ceorl, *n.* cherl, a freeman in Anglo-Saxon times; one ranking between a noble and a serf. (A.S.)

cephalalgic, *a.* sef-al-*al*-jik, relating to headache: *n.* a medicine for headache [Med.]. (Gr. *kephale*, the head, *algos*, pain.)

Cephalaspis, *n.* sef-a-*las*-pis, a genus of fossil ganoids. (Gr. *kephale*, and *aspis*, a shield.)
cephalic, *a.* se-*fal*-ik, pertaining to the head: *n.* a medicine for disorders in the head. **cephalic index,** the expression of the ratio of the greatest breadth to the greatest length of the skull when the greatest length is taken as 100.
cephalitis, *n.* sef-a-*ly*-tis, inflammation of the brain.
cephaloid, *a. sef*-a-loyd, headshaped [Bot.].
cephalopod, *n. sef*-a-lo-pod, a mollusc with the organs of motion and prehension attached to the head; the cuttle-fish. (Gr. *kephale*, and *pous*, foot.)
cephalothorax, *n. sef*-a-lo-*thaw*-raks, the union of head and chest as in the arthropods.
cephalotomy, *n.* sef-a-*lot*-o-me, dissection of the head [Anat.]. (Gr. *kephale*, and *tome*, cutting.)
cephalous, *a. sef*-a-lus, having a head.
Cepheid, *a. sef*-e-id, pertaining to or like the variable star δ Cephei: *n.* any variable star; any of the shower of meteors appearing to radiate from the constellation Cepheus [Astron.].
ceraceous, *a.* se-*ray*-shus, like wax. (L. *cera*, wax.)
ceramic, *a.* se-*ram*-ik, pertaining to pottery: *n.pl.* pottery; objects made by process of moulding, modelling, or otherwise treating clay. (Gr. *keramos*, potter's earth.)
cerargyrite, *n.* se-*rahr*-je-rite, kerargyrite.
cerasin, *n. se*-ra-sin, the insoluble part of the gum of the cherry and plum trees. (L. *cerasus*, the cherry-tree.)
cerastes, *n.* se-*ras*-teez, the horned viper, *Cerastes cornutus*, a venomous snake of the Near East. (Gr. *keras*, a horn.)
cerate, *n. seer*-rate, an ointment of wax, oil, etc.
cerated, *a. seer*-*ray*-ted, covered with wax; waxy.
ceratitis, *n.* se-ra-*ty*-tis, keratitis.
ceratoid, *a. se*-ra-toyd, horny. (Gr. *keras*, horn, *eidos*, like.)
ceraunics, *n.* se-*raw*-niks, the study of thunderstorms. (Gr. *keraunos*, thunder.)
ceraunoscope, *n.* se-*raw*-no-skohp, the device with which the ancients produced stage-thunder.
cerberean, *a.* ser-*beer*-re-an, pertaining to Cerberus, the monster that guarded the entrance to the nether world of Pluto, or to a vigilant guardian.
cere, *n.* seer, the naked wax-like skin that covers the base of the bill of many birds: *v.t.* to cover with wax. (Fr. *cire*.)
cereal, *a. seer*-re-al, pertaining to corn or edible grain: *n.* any edible grain; a food, esp. breakfast food, made from a cereal. (L. *Ceres*, the goddess of corn.)
cerealin, *n. seer*-re-a-lin, a nitrogenous substance extracted from the inner layer of bran [Chem.].
cerebellar, *a.* se-re-*bel*-lar, relating to the cerebellum.
cerebellum, *n.* se-re-*bel*-lum, the hinder and lower part of the brain. (L., the little brain.)
cerebral, *a. se*-re-bral, pertaining to the brain. **cerebral hemispheres,** the two main divisions of the brain.
cerebralism, *n. se*-re-bra-lizm, the theory which resolves mind into a function of the brain.
cerebration, *n.* se-re-*bray*-shon, the conscious or unconscious action of the brain.
cerebric, *a. se*-re-brik, cerebral.
cerebriform, *a.* se-*reb*-re-form, resembling the brain; encephaloid.
cerebrine, *n. se*-re-brin, any of several nitrogenous substances present in the brain and nerve tissue [Chem.].
cerebro-spinal, *a. se*-re-bro-*spy*-nal, pertaining to both brain and spinal chord [Anat.]. **cerebro-spinal meningitis,** inflammation of the membranes of the cerebrum and spinal cord; spotted fever.
cerebrum, *n. se*-re-brum, the part of the brain filling the upper cavity of the skull. (L.)
cerecloth, *n. seer*-kloth, a cloth smeared with wax for embalming. (*L. cera*, wax.)
cerement, *n. seer*-ment, a cerecloth; grave-clothes.
ceremonial, *a.* se-re-*moh*-ne-al, relating to ceremony; performed with ceremonies: *n.* the prescribed order for a ceremony; a book of rules for the conduct of rites or ceremonies.
ceremonialism, *n.* se-re-*moh*-ne-a-lizm, adherence to ceremony; ritualism.
ceremonially, *ad.* se-re-*moh*-ne-a-le, in a ceremonial manner.
ceremonious, *a.* se-re-*moh*-ne-us, punctiliously observant of form; according to prescribed form.
ceremoniously, *ad.* se-re-*moh*-ne-us-le, in a ceremonious manner.
ceremoniousness, *n.* se-re-*moh*-ne-us-ness, the quality of being ceremonious.
ceremony, *n. se*-re-mo-ne, a prescribed form of observance of a more or less religious and solemn nature; the celebration of it; prescribed formality. **Master of Ceremonies,** one who sees that the due forms are observed. (Fr. *cérémonie*.)
cereous, *a. seer*-re-us, waxen; like wax.
Ceres, *n. seer*-reez, the Roman goddess of growth; the Earth-Mother. (L.)
cerge, *n.* serj, a cierge.
ceriferous, *a.* se-*rif*-er-us, wax-producing.
cerin, *n.* se-rin, a waxy crystalline compound present in cork.
ceriph, *n. se*-rif, a serif.
cerise, *n.* se-*reez*, cherry-colour. (L. *cerasus*.)
cerite, *n. seer*-rite, the silicate of cerium.
cerium, *n. seer*-re-um, a grey metallic element, one of the rare earths.
cernuous, *a. ser*-new-us, drooping [Bot.]. (L.)
cerographical, *a.* se-ro-*graf*-e-kal, pertaining to cerography.
cerographist, *n.* se-*rog*-ra-fist, one skilled in cerography.
cerography, *n.* se-*rog*-ra-fe, engraving on wax; painting in wax-colours; encaustic painting. (Gr. *keros*, wax, *grapho*, write.)
ceromancy, *n. se*-ro-man-se, divination by dropping melted wax into water. (Gr. *keros*, wax, *manteia*, divination.)
ceroplastics, *n.* se-ro-*plast*-iks, the art of modelling in wax. (Gr. *keroplastikos*.)
cerotic, *a.* se-*rot*-ik, pertaining to or designating a fatty acid constituent of beeswax.
cert, *n.* sert, a certainty [Slang].
★**certain,** *a. ser*-ten, sure; assured; regular; fixed; one; some. (L. *certus*, determined.)
certainly, *ad. ser*-ten-le, without doubt or without fail.
certainty, *n. ser*-ten-te, that which is certain; complete assurance.
certes, *ad. ser*-tez, certainly; verily. (Fr.)
certifiable, *a.* ser-te-*fy*-a-bl, open to certification; liable to be certified, esp. as insane; hence, insane.
certificate, *n.* ser-*tif*-ik-ate, a written testimony or voucher; a testimonial of character or qualification; *v.t.* and *v.i.* to give a certificate of qualification to; to attest by certificate; to license by certificate. (L. *certificatus*, certified.)
certification, *n.* ser-te-fe-*kay*-shon, notification; the act of certifying.
certifier, *n. ser*-te-fy-er, a person who certifies.
certify, *v.t. ser*-te-fy, to testify in writing; to give certain information; to assure. (Fr. *certifier*.)
certiorari, *n.* ser-she-o-*rare*-re, a writ issuing out of a superior court to call up the records of an inferior court, or remove a cause there depending, that it may be tried in the superior court. (Late L., to be certified.)
certitude, *n. ser*-te-tewd, certainty; assurance. (Fr.)
cerulean, *a.* se-*roo*-le-an, sky blue. (L. *cæruleus*.)
cerulin, *n. se*-roo-lin, a mordant dye-stuff prepared from coal-tar and from indigo dissolved in sulphuric acid.
cerumen, *n.* se-*roo*-men, wax secreted by the ear.
ceruse, *n. seer*-rooz, white-lead, a carbonate of lead used as a cosmetic. (Fr.)
cerussite, *n. se*-rus-ite, native carbonate of lead.
cervical, *a. ser*-ve-kal *or* ser-*vy*-kal, pertaining to the neck. (L. *cervix*, the neck.)
cervine, *a. ser*-vine, pertaining to a stag or deer.
Cesarevitch, *n.* se-*zah*-re-vitch, Tsesarevich.
cespitose, *a. ses*-pit-ose, growing in tufts; matted [Bot.]. (L. *cespes*, turf.)
cespitous, *a. ses*-pit-us, pertaining to turf; turfy.
cess, *v.t.* ses, to lay a tax on; to assess.
cessation, *n.* ses-*say*-shon, a ceasing; pause; rest.
cessio, *n. sesh*-e-o *or* sesh-o, the act of surrendering or assigning anything in Civil Law. **cessio bonorum,** a surrender by an insolvent debtor of his property to his creditors [Law]. (L., a surrender of goods.)
cession, *n. sesh*-un, relinquishment; a yielding up or surrender, as of property; the required surrender

of a benefice by an incumbent on his acceptance of another [Eccles. Law]. (Fr.)
cessionary, *n.* *sesh*-un-a-re, an assign or assignee. **cessionary bankrupt,** one who has surrendered all his effects for division among his creditors [Law].
cesspit, *n.* *ses*-pit, a cesspool or midden.
cesspool, *n.* *ses*-pool, a pit for drainage; any receptacle for filth. (Origin uncertain.)
cestoid, *a.* *ses*-toyd, pertaining to the *Cestoidea* or tape-worms; ribbon-like [Zool.]: *n.* a tape-worm. (L. *cestus.*)
cestus, *n.* *ses*-tus, the embroidered girdle of Venus; a marriage-girdle. (Gr. *kestos.*)
cestus, *n.* *ses*-tus, the Roman boxing-glove, made with thongs and loaded. (L. *cæstus.*)
Cetacea, *n.pl.* se-*tay*-se-a, the group of marine mammals containing the whales, dolphins, etc. [Zool.]. (Gr. *ketos*, a sea-monster.)
cetacean, *n.* se-*tay*-se-an, one of the Cetacea: *a.* cetaceous.
cetaceous, *a.* se-*tay*-se-us, pertaining to the cetacea.
cetic, *a.* *see*-tik, pertaining to the whales.
cetine, *n.* *see*-tin, a crystalline fat forming the basis of spermaceti.
cetology, *n.* se-*tol*-o-je, the branch of zoology treating of the cetacea. (Gr. *ketos*, and *logos*, science.)
cetyl, *n.* *see*-til, a radical present in spermaceti, beeswax, etc. (L. *cetus*, whale.)
Ceylonese, *a.* see-lo-*neez*, of or pertaining to Ceylon: *n.* a native of Ceylon.
ceylonite, *n.* *see*-lon-ite, pleonaste, a dark-coloured spinel found in Ceylon [Min.].
Chablis, *n.* shah-*blee*, a white Burgundy wine from Chablis, in central France. (Fr.)
chabouk, *n.* *shah*-book, a whip with a long lash used in the East for flogging criminals. (Hind.)
chacma, *n.* *chak*-ma, a S. African baboon. (Hottentot.)
chaco, *n.* *shak*-o, a shako.
chaconne, *n.* shah-*kone*, a slow dance in triple time, and the music for it. (Sp.)
chætodon, *n.* *kee*-to-don, one of the Chætodontidæ, a large family of spiny finned and brilliantly coloured fish. (Gr. *chaitē*, hair, *odous*, tooth.)
chætopod, *n.* *kee*-to-pod, one of the *Chætopoda*, a class of marine and other worms provided with bristles on foot-like organs. (Gr. *chaitē*, hair, *pous*, foot.)
chafe, *v.t.* chafe, to excite heat by friction; to wear by rubbing; to fret; to make angry: *v.i.* to fret; to be worn by rubbing: *n.* fret; passion; an abrasion. (Fr. *chauffer*, to warm.)
chafer, *n.* *chay*-fer, one who chafes; a chafing-dish.
chafer, *n.* *chay*-fer, a beetle that, when adult, feeds on leaves; a cockchafer. (A.S. *ceafor.*)
chafery, *n.* *chafe*-er-re, a forge in which metal is subjected to a welding heat. (Fr. *chaufferie.*)
chaff, *n.* chahf, the husk of grain; fodder of straw finely cut; worthless matter. (A.S. *ceaf.*)
chaff, *n.* chahf, banter: *v.t.* and *i.* to banter.
chaffer, *n.* *chah*-fer, one who chaffs.
chaffer, *v.i.* *chaf*-fer, to treat about a purchase; to haggle about the price; to talk much and idly. (A.S. *ceap*, a bargain.)
chaffinch, *n.* *chaf*-finsh, the small finch, *Fringilla cœlebs*, of which the sexes migrate in separate flocks.
chaffingly, *ad.* *chah*-fing-le, in a chaffing or bantering manner.
chaffy, *a.* *chah*-fe, like chaff; full of chaff; light; worthless; full of joke and banter.
chafing-board, *n.* *chafe*-ing-board, a batten to prevent the ropes chafing [Naut.].
chafing-dish, *n.* *chafe*-ing-dish, a portable charcoal stove; a dish heated at table.
chagrin, *n.* sha-*grin*, *shag*-rin *or* sha-*green*, vexation; ill-humour; mortification: *v.t.* to vex. (Fr.)
***chain,** *n.* chane, a series of links or rings, connected or fitted into each other; a bond, or anything which binds; bondage; a series linked together; a series of atoms linked together, esp. in an organic molecule [Chem.]; a surveyor's measure of 100 links, or 66 feet: *v.t.* to fasten with a chain; to restrain; to connect; to enslave; to obstruct. **chain reaction,** a reaction that is self-sustaining and self-propagating, esp. that occurring in radioactive substances and is capable of yielding enormous amounts of energy. (Fr. *chaine.*)
chain-belt, *n.* *chane*-belt, a chain used as a belt in power-transmission.
chain-bridge, *n.* *chane*-bridj, suspension-bridge.
chain-gang, *n.* *chane*-gang, a working-party of slaves or convicts chained together.
chainless, *a.* *chane*-less, having no chain or chains; free.
chainlet, *n.* *chane*-let, a small chain.
chain-letter, *n.* *chane*-let-ter, a letter of which a certain number of copies is to be sent by the recipient to others, each of whom is to send a similar number of copies to others.
chain-mail, *n.* *chane*-male, armour of interwoven iron links.
chain-pump, *n.* *chane*-pump, a machine for raising water, consisting principally of a long chain equipped with a number of buckets, and actuated by means of wheels.
chain-shot, *n.* *chane*-shot, two cannon-balls, or half-balls, connected by a chain for damaging rigging.
chain-smoker, *n.* *chane*-smoh-ker, one who smokes cigarettes without intermission.
chain-stitch, *n.* *chane*-stitch, an ornamental stitch; a loop-stitch; a stitch made with two threads.
chain-store, *n.* *chane*-store, a multiple shop [U.S.A.].
chainwork, *n.* *chane*-wurk, needlework with looped or linked stitches; chain-stitch.
chair, *n.* chare, a movable seat with a back, for one person; a seat of authority or office; an office; a professorship; a chairman; a sedan; a Bath-chair; an iron socket which supports and secures the rails of a railroad: *v.t.* to carry publicly in a chair in triumph; to install a chairman or president. (Fr. *chaire*, from L. *cathedra.*)
chairman, *n.* *chare*-man, the president of a meeting or of a committee; the porter of a sedan chair; one who wheels a Bath-chair.
chairmanship, *n.* *chare*-man-ship, the office of a chairman.
chaise, *n.* shaze, a light one-horsed carriage. **chaise longue,** a sofa or couch. (Fr.)
chalaza, *n.* ka-*lay*-za, either of the filaments connecting the yolk-bag of an egg with the lining membrane of the shell [Zool.]; the point on a seed at which the integument and nucleus are united [Bot.].
chalcedonic, *a.* kal-se-*don*-ik, pertaining to chalcedony.
chalcedony, *n.* kal-*sed*-o-ne, translucent quartz of several varieties and various colours. (Perhaps named from *Chalcedon*, Asia Minor.)
chalcedonyx, *n.* kal-*sed*-o-niks *or* kal-se-*don*-iks, a variety of agate.
chalcocite, *n.* *kal*-ko-site, native metallic sulphide of copper, occurring in beds and veins; copper-glance.
chalcography, *n.* kal-*kog*-ra-fe, the art or process of engraving on copper or brass. (Gr. *chalkos*, copper, brass, *grapho*, write.)
Chaldaic, *a.* kal-*day*-ik, relating to the Chaldeans or Chaldea: *n.* the language of Chaldea.
Chaldean, *a.* kal-*dee*-an, *or* **Chaldee,** kal-*dee*, Chaldaic: *n.* a native of ancient Chaldea, in Mesopotamia; Chaldaic.
chaldron, *n.* *chawl*-dron *or* *chahl*-dron, a measure of coals of 36 bushels. (Fr. *chaudron*, kettle.)
chalet, *n.* *shal*-ay, a Swiss cottage. (Fr.-Swiss.)
chalice, *n.* *chal*-is, a cup, esp. a communion cup. (L. *calix*, a cup.)
chaliced, *a.* *chal*-ist, with a cup-like part (of flowers).
chalicosis, *n.* *kal*-e-*koh*-sis, an affection of the lungs caused by the inhalation of stone dust; silicosis [Path.]. (Gr. *chalix*, gravel.)
***chalk,** *n.* chawk, a fine-grained limestone, generally white, consisting of fossil foraminifera; the uppermost formation of the Secondary rocks; a piece of chalk for use as a crayon, for marking cloth, or for chalking a billiard-cue, etc.: *v.t.* to rub or mark with chalk; to manure with chalk. **chalk out,** to lay out; to plan. **chalk up,** to give or take credit. **black chalk,** a slaty clay mixed with carbon. **brown chalk,** umber. **French chalk,** soapstone. **by a long chalk,** by a wide margin [Slang]. (A.S. *cealc.*)
chalkiness, *n.* *chawk*-e-ness, the state or quality of being chalky.
chalk-pit, *n.* *chawk*-pit, a pit from which chalk is dug.
chalk-stone, *n.* *chawk*-stone, a chalky concretion in the joints of persons affected with gout.
chalky, *a.* *chawk*-e, containing or like chalk.

challenge, *n.* *chal*-lenj, a defiance or summons to fight a duel; an invitation to a contest of any kind; the call of a sentinel; the calling in question of a person's right; exception taken to a juror; the crying of hounds at finding the scent: *v.t.* to defy a person by calling on him to make good his point in single combat; to call to a contest of any kind; to summon to answer; to demand a right; to object to. (O.Fr. *chalenge.*)
challengeable, *a.* *chal*-lenj-a-bl, that may be challenged.
challenger, *n.* *chal*-lenj-er, one who challenges or opposes.
challis, *n.* *shal*-le, a fine silk and woollen fabric.
chalone, *n.* *kal*-ohn, an internal secretion restraining growth, as a hormone stimulates it. (Gr., relaxing.)
chalumeau, *n.* shal-loo-*moh*, a shepherd's flute or pipe. (Fr.)
chalybeate, *a.* ka-*lib*-e-at, impregnated with iron; steel-like: *n.* a mineral water impregnated with iron. (Gr. *chalyps*, steel.)
chalybite, *n.* *kal*-e-bite, spathic iron ore; siderite.
cham, *n.* kam, the khan of Tartary; any autocrat.
chamade, *n.* sha-*mahd*, beat of drum or sound of trumpet inviting an enemy to a parley. (Fr.)
chamber, *n.* *chame*-ber, an apartment; a bed-room; a judge's room; a place where a legislative assembly meets; the assembly itself; a hall of justice; a body of persons for the promotion of some common interest; a hollow or cavity; that part of the bore of a gun where the powder lay; a magazine; *pl.* hired lodgings; a suite of apartments; the office of a barrister; rooms in the law courts for the settlement of matters of routine and of minor importance. **chamber of commerce,** a local or other society for the promotion of business interests. **chambers of a lock,** the space between the gates of a lock in a canal. (Fr. *chambre.*)
chamber-council, *n.* *chame*-ber-*koun*-sil, a secret council.
chamber-counsel, *n.* *chame*-ber-*koun*-sel, a counsellor who gives his opinion at his chambers, but does not plead.
chambered, *a.* *chame*-berd, divided into compartments [Malac.].
chamberer, *n.* *chame*-ber-er, a wanton; a gallant.
chamber-fellow, *n.* *chame*-ber-*fel*-lo, one who sleeps in the same apartment.
chamber-hanging, *n.* *chame*-ber-*hang*-ing, tapestry for a chamber.
chambering, *n.* *chame*-ber-ing, licentious indulgence.
chamberlain, *n.* *chame*-ber-lin, an officer charged with the management of the household and private apartments of a monarch or noble; a male servant who has the care of suites of chambers in a hotel, etc.; the treasurer of a city or corporation. **Lord Chamberlain,** the head of the British Royal Household and licenser of London theatres and of plays. **Lord Great Chamberlain,** an hereditary British state official with mainly ceremonial duties. (Fr. *chamberlain.*)
chamberlainship, *n.* *chame*-ber-lin-ship, the office of a chamberlain.
chambermaid, *n.* *chame*-ber-mayd, a female servant who has the care of the bedrooms of a hotel.
chamber-music, *n.* *chame*-ber-*mew*-zik, orchestral music written to be played in a room as distinct from a hall, church, or large building.
chamber-pot, *n.* *chame*-ber-pot, a bedroom utensil for holding urine.
chamber-practice, *n.* *chame*-ber-*prak*-tis, the practice of a chamber-counsel.
Chambertin, *n.* shahm-bare-*tan(g)*, a red Burgundy wine of the Côte-d'Or. (Name of the vineyard.)
chamæleon, *n.* ka-*mee*-le-on, any one of a family (*Rhiptoglossa*) of slow-moving Old World lizards, with a long extensile tongue, laterally compressed body, and the power of changing their colour to suit their mood or surroundings; a changeable person. (Gr. *chamai*, on the ground, *leon*, lion.)
chamfer, *n.* *cham*-fer, a small furrow; a bevel: *v.t.* to groove or bevel, esp. in stone. (Fr.)
chamfron, *n.* *cham*-fron, a horse's head armour. (Fr.)
chamois, *n.* *sham*-wah, the goat-like antelope of Europe, *Rupicapra tragus*; (pron. *sham*-me), a soft leather first made from its skin. (Fr.)
chamomile, *n.* *kam*-o-mile, camomile.
champ, *v.t.* and *v.i.* champ, to keep biting with the teeth; to chew; to crunch. (From the sound.)
champagne, *n.* sham-*payn*, a light, brisk, sparkling wine from Champagne, in France. **champagne brandy,** brandy made from wine produced at Cognac, in France. **champagne cider,** cider aerated with carbonic acid gas. **fine champagne** (Fr.), liqueur brandy.
champaign, *n.* sham-*payn*, a flat, open country: *a.* open; level. (O.Fr.)
champak, *n.* *cham*-pak *or* *cham*-puk, an Indian magnolia, *Michelia champaca*, cultivated for its fragrant flowers.
champertor, *n.* *cham*-per-tor, a party to champerty.
champertous, *a.* *cham*-per-tus, of the nature of champerty.
champerty, *n.* *cham*-per-te, maintenance of a party in a lawsuit upon condition of sharing with him the thing at issue if recovered [Law]. (Fr. *champart*, a field-rent paid to a feudal lord.)
champignon, *n.* sham-*pin*-yon, the fairy-ring agaric, a small mushroom. (Fr.)
champion, *n.* *cham*-pe-on, one who comes forward to defend a cause single-handed; a defender; the first in some athletic sport or trial of skill; an exhibit first in its class at a show: *a.* top-hole; first-rate [Coll.]. **Seven Champions of Christendom,** *see* **seven.** (Fr.)
championship, *n.* *cham*-pe-on-ship, the rank of champion; a contest for this; the act of championing; advocacy.
champlevé, *a.* shawm-*lev*-ay, ornamental work in which spaces cut in a metal ground are filled in with enamel. (Fr.)
★**chance,** *n.* chahnce, the result of unknown causes; the course of events; luck; accident; risk; possibility; opportunity: *a.* happening by chance; fortuitous: *v.i.* to happen: *v.t.* to risk [Coll.]. **off chance,** *see* **off.** (O.Fr.)
chance-comer, *n.* *chahnce*-kum-er, one who comes by chance.
chanceful, *a.* *chahnce*-ful, fortuitous; eventful.
chancel, *n.* *chahn*-sel, the eastern part of a church; that part of a church where the altar is. (O.Fr.)
chancellery, *n.* *chahn*-sel-e-re, the department of a chancellor; a chancellor's court or official establishment; the office of an embassy or consulate.
chancellor, *n.* *chahn*-sel-or, a president or chief officer of a court, public department, or university; the secretary to a cathedral chapter; a diocesan bishop's adviser in matters of canon and civil law; an officer who seals the commissions and mandates of an order of knighthood. **Chancellor of the Duchy of Lancaster,** the representative of the King as Duke of Lancaster, usually a Cabinet Minister. **Chancellor of the Exchequer,** the chief finance minister of the British government, always a Cabinet Minister. **Lord High Chancellor,** or **Lord Chancellor,** the highest judicial officer of the British Crown, a Cabinet Minister, the Keeper of the Great Seal, chief law adviser of the government, and prolocutor of the House of Lords. (O.Fr. *chancelier.*)
chancellorship, *n.* *chahn*-sel-or-ship, the office of a chancellor; the period of his holding office.
chancellory, *n.* *chahn*-sel-o-re, a chancellery.
chancel-screen, *n.* *chahn*-sel-skreen, the screen, dividing the chancel from the body of a church.
chance-medley, *n.* *chahnce*-med-le, the unintentional killing of another, esp. by misadventure or in self-defence [Law]; haphazard action; pure chance. (Fr. *chance-medlée*, mingled chance.)
chancery, *n.* *chahn*-se-re, in England, formerly the highest court of justice next to the parliament, now a division of the High Court of Justice; a court of equity [U.S.A.]. **get into chancery,** to get involved in an interminable lawsuit, hence, into a hopeless predicament. (Fr. *chancellerie.*)
chancre, *n.* *shank*-er, a venereal ulcer. (Fr.)
chancrous, *a.* *shank*-rus, ulcerous; like a chancre.
chancy, *a.* *chahn*-se, risky; dubious; uncertain; untrustworthy [Slang].
chandelier, *n.* shan-de-*leer*, a hanging fitting for a number of lights, usually with branches. (Fr.)
chandler, *n.* *chahnd*-ler, a maker or a seller of candles; a retailer of groceries, oil, etc. (O.Fr. *chandelier.*)
chandlery, *n.* *chahnd*-le-re, goods sold by a chandler.
★**change,** *v.t.* chaynj, to make different or alter; to

put one thing in the place of another; to give or take an equivalent in other coin; to exchange: *v.i.* to suffer a change; to become new or different; to become worse; to put on fresh clothes: *n.* any alteration or variation; shifting; transition; alteration in the order, specially of ringing bells; small coin; the amount returnable when the money tendered is in excess of that required; spare clothes, or the act of changing them; a Stock Exchange. (L. *cambio*, to barter.) (O.Fr. *changer.*)

changeability, *n.* chaynj-a-*bil*-e-te, changeableness.

changeable, *a.* *chaynj*-a-bl, liable to change; variable; fickle; inconstant; unstable.

changeableness, *n.* *chaynj*-a-bl-ness, the quality of being changeable.

changeably, *ad.* *chaynj*-a-ble, in a changeable manner.

changeful, *a.* *chaynj*-ful, full of change; inconstant; fickle.

changefully, *ad.* *chaynj*-ful-le, in a changeful manner.

changefulness, *n.* *chaynj*-ful-ness, the quality of being changeful.

changeless, *a.* *chaynj*-less, not subject to change.

changeling, *n.* *chaynj*-ling, a child substituted for another; anything substituted; one apt to change.

changer, *n.* *chaynj*-er, one who changes; or who changes something; a money-changer.

changing, *a.* *chaynj*-ing, changeful; altering.

chank, *n.* chank, a species of conch-shell, *Turbinella pyrum.* (Sans. *chanka*, conch-shell.)

channel, *n.* *chan*-nel, a river-bed; a watercourse; the deeper part of a strait, bay, or harbour; a narrow sea between two continents, or between a continent and an island; means of conveying or transmitting; a groove or furrow, as in a column; a gutter: *v.t.* to groove. **channel-iron,** a structural member shaped as a three-sided channel with adjacent sides at right angles [Eng.]. (O.Fr. *chanel.*)

channelled, *pp.* and *a.* *chan*-neld, grooved lengthwise.

chanson, *n.* *shahn*-song (or App.), a song. **chanson de geste,** an epic ballad composed in the Middle Ages in France. (Fr.)

chansonette, *n.* *shahn*-son-*net*, a ditty. (Fr.)

chant, *n.* chahnt, song; melody; a psalm or other words in church service recited to musical tones: *v.i.* and *v.t.* to sing solemnly; to celebrate in song; to intone. **chant a horse,** to advertise it falsely. (Fr. *chanter*, to sing.)

chantage, *n.* (App.), extortion by threat of exposure; blackmail [Law]. (Fr.)

chanter, *n.* *chahnt*-er, one who chants; a precentor; the tenor or treble pipe in a bagpipe.

chanterelle, *n.* shan-ter-*rel*, a species of edible mushroom, *Cantharellus cibarius.* (L. *cantharellus.*)

chanticleer, *n.* shahnt-e-*kleer*, a crowing cock. (Fr. *chanteclair.*)

chantry, *n.* *chant*-re, a chapel endowed to support a priest or priests to chant mass daily for one deceased; a body of such priests; the part of a church used as a chantry. (O.Fr. *chanterie.*)

chanty, *n.* *shahn*-te, a shanty (sailors' song).

chaos, *n.* *kay*-os, that confusion in which matter was supposed to have existed before it was reduced to order; confusion; disorder. (Gr.)

chaotic, *a.* kay-*ot*-ik, resembling chaos; confused.

chaotically, *ad.* kay-*ot*-e-ka-le, in a chaotic manner.

chap, *n.* chap, a crack in the skin; a longitudinal cleft, gap, or chink: *v.i.* to crack; to open in cracks: *v.t.* to cause to cleave, crack, or open in long slits. (Dut. *kappen*, to cut.)

chap, *n.* chap, a boy or man, originally a chapman.

chap, *n.* chap *or* chop, the lower part of the cheek; *pl.* the jaws. **chap-fallen,** with the lower jaw depressed; dejected; low-spirited.

chaparral, *n.* chap-a-*ral*, a low oak groove; a dense thicket [U.S.A.]. (Sp.)

chap-book, *n.* *chap*-book, a small book of ballads or wonderful tales, once hawked about by chapmen.

chape, *n.* chape; the catch of anything, as of a buckle; a metal plate at the end of a scabbard; the frog of a sword-belt. (Fr.)

chapeau, *n.* shap-*poh*, a hat; a cap of dignity or maintenance. (Fr.)

chapel, *n.* *chap*-el, a place of worship connected with but subordinate to a church; a place of worship in a palace or private dwelling; a dissenters' place of worship; an association of journeymen printers in a printing establishment; a meeting of such a body. **chapel of ease,** an extra church in a parish. **chapel royal,** the chapel of a royal palace; the clergy and musical staff, under the supervision of a dean conducting the religious services of the Royal Family. (O.Fr. *chapelle.*)

chapelry, *n.* *chap*-el-re, the district of a chapel.

chaperon, *n.* *shap*-er-ohn, an escort, usually an elderly lady, escorting a young unmarried lady: *v.t.* to act as chaperon. (Fr.)

chaperonage, *n.* *shap*-er-ohn-aj, the part or duties of a chaperon.

chapiter, *n.* *chap*-e-ter, the upper part of the capital of a column. (O.Fr. *chapitre.*)

chaplain, *n.* *chap*-lin, a clergyman who officiates at court, conducts in a ship, a regiment, a public establishment, or a family. (Fr. *chapelain.*)

chaplaincy, *n.* *chap*-lin-se, the post or rank of a chaplain.

chaplainship, *n.* *chap*-lin-ship, the office of a chaplain.

chaplet, *n.* *chap*-let, a garland or wreath for the head; a rosary consisting of one-third of the usual number of beads; a little moulding, carved into round beads, pearls, etc. [Arch.]; a tuft of feathers on the head of a peacock or other bird. (O.Fr. *chapelet.*)

chapleted, *a.* *chap*-let-ed, crowned with a chaplet.

chapman, *n.* *chap*-man, a hawker or pedlar, originally a buyer or seller. (A.S. *ceapman*, merchant.)

chapped, *a.* chapt, seamed with chaps.

chappie, *n.* *chap*-pe, a good fellow; a little chap; a buck or fop [Coll.].

chappy, *a.* *chap*-pe, full of chaps; cleft.

chapter, *n.* *chap*-ter, a division of a book; a division of the Acts of Parliament of a single session; the clergy attached to a cathedral or collegiate church, presided over by the dean; a chapter-house; a meeting of the members of a religious order and of certain other societies; an organized branch of some society or fraternity: *v.t.* to divide into chapters; to put headings to chapters. **chapter and verse,** exact authority for any statement made. (Fr. *chapitre.*)

chapter-house, *n.* *chap*-ter-house, a building or room in which a chapter meets.

chaptrel, *n.* *chap*-trel, a capital supporting an arch.

char, *n.* chahr, a genus of fish allied to the salmon, some species being lacustrine and others migratory, living in glacial lakes. (Gael. *ceara*, red.)

char, *n.* chahr, a spell of work; a single job; a charwoman [Coll.]: *v.i.* to work at others' houses by the day; to do small jobs; to chore. (A.S. *cierr*, a turn.)

char, *v.t.* chahr, to reduce to charcoal; to burn partially: *v.i.* to become blackened by fire.

char-à-banc, *n.* *sha*-ra-bang (or App.), a pleasure-van; a long open motor car with seats facing forwards; a motor coach. (Fr., car with benches.)

character, *n.* *ka*-rak-ter, a mark made by cutting, engraving, or writing; a letter or sign; a peculiar form of letter; peculiar distinctive qualities; the qualities which distinguish an individual or an office; good moral qualities; moral strength; decided qualities; a description exhibiting qualities; a certificate of qualities; a person or personage (esp. in a literary work): one of the dramatis personæ (of a play); an odd individual. **generic characters,** those which constitute a genus. **specific characters,** those which distinguish a species. (Fr. *caractère.*)

characteristic, *a.* *ka*-rak-ter-*ris*-tik, constituting or exhibiting peculiar qualities: *n.* that which constitutes the character; that which distinguishes one person or thing from another. **characteristic of a logarithm,** its index or exponent.

characteristically, *ad.* *ka*-rak-ter-*ris*-te-ka-le, in a characteristic manner.

characterization, *n.* *ka*-rak-ter-ry-*zay*-shon, act of characterizing; a piece descriptive of character.

characterize, *v.t.* *ka*-rak-ter-ize, to give character to; to stamp or distinguish; to describe by peculiar qualities. (Gr. *charakterizo*, to describe distinctly.)

characterless, *a.* *ka*-rak-ter-less, having no character; commonplace.

charade, *n.* sha-*rahd*, a species of riddle, the subject of which is a word that has to be deduced from an acted representation of each syllable and the whole word. (Fr.)

charcoal, *n.* *chahr*-kole, impure carbon obtained by partially burning wood, either in covered piles or externally heated cylinders.

charcutier, *n.* shahr-*koo*-te-yay, a dresser or retailer of pork and other pig-meat, sausages and the like, collectively known as **charcuterie.** (Fr., cooked flesh.)

chardonnet, *n.* *shahr*-do-nay, trade-name of an artificial silk fabric of a nitro-cellulose basis. (Name of Fr. inventor, *d.* 1924.)

chare, *n.* chare, work done by the day; char.

charge, *n.* chahrj, care; custody; the object of care; order or command; injunction; duty; attack or onset; a load; burden; the quantity with which a gun is loaded; the instructions given by a judge to a jury, or by a bishop to his clergy; accusation; price; an entry on the debit side of an account; a quantity of electricity; any figure represented on an escutcheon [Her.]: *v.i.* to make an onset: *v.t.* to rush on and attack; to load or fill; to saturate a liquid with gas; to accumulate electricity in a battery; to lay on or impose; to enjoin; to fix a price; to place on the debit side of an account; to impute; to accuse; to entrust; to give directions to. (Fr. *charger.*)

chargeable, *a.* *chahrj*-a-bl, liable to be charged; imposable; ratable; imputable; accusable.

chargeableness, *n.* *chahrj*-a-bl-ness, state of being chargeable.

chargé d'affaires, *n.* (App.), a temporary or secondary member of the staff of an embassy or legation.

chargeless, *a.* *chahrj*-less, free from charge.

charger, *n.* *chahrj*-er, a military officer's horse; a large strong dish for the principal joint.

charge-sheet, *n.* *chahrj*-sheet, a list of offenders taken into custody by the police, and their offences.

charily, *ad.* *chare*-e-le, frugally; stingily; with care.

chariness, *n.* *chare*-e-ness, the quality of being chary.

chariot, *n.* *cha*-re-ot, a four-wheeled carriage of pleasure or state; a two-wheeled car formerly used in war and racing, and in public triumphs. (Fr.)

charioteer, *n.* cha-re-ot-*eer*, a chariot-driver.

charioteering, *n.* cha-re-ot-*eer*-ing, the act, art, or practice of driving a chariot.

charism, *n.* *ka*-rizm, a gift; a power to perform miracles conferred on the early Christians [Eccles.]. (Gr. *charisma.*)

charitable, *a.* *cha*-re-ta-bl, benevolent; liberal to the poor; liberal in judging others; pertaining to or supported by charity; springing from or intended for charity. (Fr.)

charitableness, *n.* *cha*-re-ta-bl-ness, disposition to be charitable.

charitably, *ad.* *cha*-re-ta-ble, in a charitable manner.

charity, *n.* *cha*-re-te, a disposition to think kindly of others, and to do them good; an act prompted by this; liberality to the poor, or alms-giving; alms; liberality in judging of men and their actions; a charitable gift or institution. **charity school,** an endowed school for poor children. **sisters of charity,** a religious society devoted to relieving poverty and sickness. (Fr. *charité.*)

charivari, *n.* shahr-e-*vahr*-e, a mock serenade of discordant music, designed to insult and annoy; a hullabaloo. (Fr.)

charlady, *n.* chahr-lay-de, a charwoman [Coll.].

charlatan, *n.* *shahr*-la-tan, a prating boaster; an impostor; a quack. (Fr.)

charlatanic, *a.* shahr-la-*tan*-ik, quackish.

charlatanically, *ad.* shahr-la-*tan*-e-ka-le, after the manner of a charlatan.

charlatanism, *n.* *shahr*-la-ta-nizm, charlatanry.

charlatanry, *n.* *shahr*-la-tan-re, imposture: quackery.

Charles's-wain, *n.* chahrls-ez-*wane*, the Plough, seven stars in the constellation of the Great Bear [Astron.]. (A.S. *carles wægn.*)

charleston, *n.* *chahrl*-ston, a modern dance involving peculiar action of the knees. (From *Charleston,* U.S.A.)

charley, *n.* *chahr*-le, a night-watchman [Slang].

charlock, *n.* *chahr*-lok, the wild mustard, *Sinapis arvensis.* (A.S. *cerlic.*)

charlotte, *n.* *shahr*-lot, an apple-charlotte, or baked pudding of apples with sugar and bread-and-butter or breadcrumbs. **charlotte russe,** cream enclosed in sponge-cakes. (Personal name.)

charm, *n.* chahrm, words, philters, or characters acting as a spell; any magic spell or enchantment; an amulet or trinket; a power of pleasing; attractiveness: *v.i.* to act as a charm; to use charms: *v.t.* to bewitch; to fascinate; to delight. (O.Fr. *charme.*)

charmer, *n.* *chahr*-mer, one who uses charms, or who fascinates.

charmeuse, *n.* *shahr*-murz (or App.), a light-weight silk dress fabric with a satiny surface. (Fr.)

charming, *a.* *chahr*-ming, pleasing in the highest degree; delightful.

charmingly, *ad.* *chahr*-ming-le, in a manner to charm.

charmingness, *n.* *chahr*-ming-ness, the quality of being charming.

charnel, *a.* *chahr*-nel, pertaining to burial or to carcases: *n.* a charnel-house. **charnel-house,** a place where the bones of the dead are deposited; a mortuary. (O.Fr.)

Charon, *n.* *kare*-ron, the ferryman of the ghosts of men into Hades [Gr. Myth.].

charpie, *n.* *shahr*-pe, lint for dressing wounds. (Fr.)

charpoy, *n.* *chahr*-poy, an Indian bedstead of interlaced tape in a bamboo frame. (Hind.)

charqui, *n.* *chahr*-ke, beef strips dried in the sun. (Peruv.)

charry, *a.* *chahr*-re, pertaining to or like charcoal.

chart, *n.* chahrt, a map of some part of the sea, with the coasts, rocks, banks, channels, etc., for the use of sailors; a tabulated account or statement; a graph: *v.t.* to delineate on a chart. (O.Fr. *charte.*)

chartaceous, *a.* kahr-*tay*-shus, resembling paper.

charter, *n.* *chahr*-ter, a state document conferring or confirming certain powers, rights, privileges, and immunities; a patent; a grant; a charter-party; a claim of rights: *v.t.* to establish or to license by charter; to hire or let by charter-party. **Charterhouse,** a London Carthusian monastery which in Tudor times became a hospital for destitute gentlemen and a school, the latter being removed to Godalming in 1872. (O.Fr. *chartre.*)

chartered, *a.* *chahr*-terd, invested with privileges by charter; granted by charter; hired or let as a ship. **chartered accountant,** a qualified member of the British Institute of Chartered Accountants. **chartered company,** an organization trading, and frequently governing, under a royal charter.

charter-land, *n.* *chahr*-ter-land, land held by charter.

charter-party, *n.* *chahr*-ter-*pahr*-te, an agreement respecting the hire of a vessel and the freight [Comm.]. (Fr. *charte-partie,* literally, a divided charter, each contractor holding a half.)

Chartism, *n.* *chahr*-tizm, the principles of a democratic body in the early 19th century called Chartists, the chief of which were universal suffrage, annual parliaments, vote by ballot, electoral districts, and payment of members of parliament.

Chartist, *n.* *chahr*-tist, a supporter of Chartism.

chartless, *a.* *chahrt*-less, of which there is no chart.

chartography, *n.* kar-*tog*-ra-fe, cartography.

Chartreuse, *n.* shahr-*trooz*, a celebrated monastery of Carthusians, near Grenoble, France; (*l.c.*) an aromatic liqueur, so called from its having been originally made at that monastery. (Fr.)

chartulary, *n.* *chahrt*-yoo-la-re, a cartulary.

charwoman, *n.* *chahr*-woom-an, a woman who does odd jobs for others by the day.

chary, *a.* *chare*-re, careful; wary; frugal. (A.S. *cearig,* full of concern.)

chase, *n.* chase, earnest pursuit; hunting; that which is chased; open land with deer and other game: *v.t.* to pursue; to hunt; to drive away. (O.Fr. *chace.*)

chase, *n.* chase, a frame in which type is set in columns or pages for printing; a wide groove; the length of a gun in front of the trunnions; a term in the game of tennis. (O.Fr. *chacier,* to chase.)

chase, *v.t.* chase, to engrave; to emboss; to cut into the form of a screw.

chaseable, *a.* *chase*-a-bl, that may be hunted.

chaser, *n.* *chase*-er, a pursuer; an enchaser; a tool in screw-cutting; a small and speedy military aeroplane; a steeple-chaser; a drink taken immediately after another [Slang].

chasing, *n.* *chase*-ing, the art of engraving or embossing on metals.

chasm, *n. kaz*-m, a yawning or wide and deep cleft in the earth. (L. *chasma*, gulf.)
chassé, *n. shas*-ay, a gliding dance-step: *v.i.* to move with this step. (Fr.)
chassepot, *n. shas*-po, a breech-loading rifle used by the French in the war of 1871. (Inventor's name.)
chasseur, *n.* shas-*ser*, a light-armed French foot soldier or cavalryman. (Fr., a hunter.)
chassis, *n. shas*-se, the frame and machinery of a motor vehicle or aeroplane; the movable carriage of a gun. (Fr.)
chaste, *a.* chayst, pure in heart and conduct, or morally pure; pure in thought and speech; pure in taste; pure in style; virtuous; modest; unadulterated. (O.Fr. *chaste.*)
chastely, *ad. chayst*-le, in a chaste manner.
chasten, *v.t. chase*-en, to afflict or punish, in order to correct and purify, or make chaste; to purify.
chasteness, *n. chayst*-ness, the quality or state of being chaste.
chastening, *a. chase*-en-ing, punishing with a view to correction; *n.* chastisement, correction.
chastisable, *a.* chass-*ty*-za-bl, able or liable to be chastised.
chastise, *v.t.* chass-*tize*, to punish with a view to correction; to chasten; to punish; to reduce to order or obedience. (O.Fr. *chastier.*)
chastisement, *n. chass*-tiz-ment, punishment; correction.
chastity, *n. chass*-te-te, the state of being chaste; sexual purity; celibacy; purity of conduct. (Fr. *chasteté.*)
chasuble, *n. chass*-yoo-bl, an outward vestment, nearly circular in form, worn by a priest over the alb when officiating at Mass. (Fr.)
chat, *n.* chat, familiar conversation; idle talk: *v.i.* to talk in a familiar manner, or idly.
chat, *n.* chat, the name of certain small birds (mainly warblers), as the stonechat, whinchat, etc.
château, *n.* shat-*toh*, a castle; a country seat. (Fr.)
chatelaine, *n. shat*-tel-lane, the lady governor of a castle; a bunch of short chains worn by ladies for attaching keys and small articles. (Fr., a castellan's lady.)
chatoyant, *a.* shat-*wa*-yant (or App.), changing lustre or colour, like a cat's eye in the dark: *n.* a hard stone with a changing lustre. (Fr. *chat*, cat, *œil*, eye.)
chattel, *n. chat*-tl, movable property; any article of property, except such as is freehold [Law]. (O.Fr. *catel.*)
chatter, *n. chat*-ter, sounds like those of a magpie or monkey; idle talk: *v.i.* to utter sounds rapidly and indistinctly, as a magpie; to clatter the teeth, as in shivering with cold; to talk idly or rapidly; to jabber. (M.E. *chatteren*, from the sound.)
chatteration, *n.* chat-ter-*ray*-shon, talkativeness; persistent chattering [Coll.].
chatterbox, *n. chat*-ter-boks, an incessant talker.
chatterer, *n. chat*-ter-er, one who chatters; a bird of the waxwing family.
chatty, *a. chat*-te, familiarly talkative.
Chaucerian, *a.* chaw-*seer*-re-an, relating to Chaucer, or his works: *n.* a student of Chaucer's works.
chaud-mellé, *n. shode*-mel-le, slaying another person in the heat of passion [Scots. law]. (Fr., a heated affray.)
chauffer, *n. shoh*-fer, a small portable furnace; a metal basket for live coals. (Fr. *chauffer*, to heat.)
chauffeur, *n.* shoh-*fur*, one who drives a motor-car as a business. (Fr., a stoker.)
chauffeuse, *n.* shoh-furz, a woman chauffeur. (Fr.)
chaulmoogra, *n.* chaw-*moo*-gra, a tall evergreen jungle tree of Burma and Malaya. **chaulmoogra oil,** oil expressed from the seeds of this used in the treatment of leprosy.
chaumontelle, *n.* shoh-mon-*tel*, a sort of pear. (Fr.)
chaunter, *n. chahn*-ter, chanter.
chausses, *n.* shohs, a kind of trunk-hose; leg-armour. (Fr.)
chaussure, *n.* sho-*soor*, boots and shoes; foot-wear. (Fr.)
chautauquan, *a.* sha-*taw*-kwan, pertaining to the system of home-study instituted by the educational organization having (since 1874) headquarters at Chautauqua, New York State.
chauvinism, *n. sho*-vin-izm, political fanaticism; undue glorification of one's own country. (N. *Chauvin*, an idolator of Napoleon.)
chaw, *v.t.* chaw, to chew: *n.* a quid of tobacco [Slang].
chawdron, *n. chaw*-dron, entrails. (O.Fr.)
chaya-root, *n. chay*-ya-root, the root of a species of *Oldenlandia*, used in India to give the red to the Madras cottons. (Tamil word.)
chay-root, *n. chay*-root, chaya-root.
***cheap,** *a.* cheep, purchasable at a low price or a trifling cost; of small value or esteem. **cheap-jack,** a travelling hawker. (A.S. *ceap*, price, bargain.)
cheapen, *v.t. cheep*-en, to beat down or lessen the price or value of: *v.i.* to become cheap.
cheaply, *ad. cheep*-le, at a small price.
cheapness, *n. cheep*-ness, the quality of being cheap.
cheat, *n.* cheet, a fraud committed by deception; a person who cheats; a swindler: *v.t.* to deceive and defraud; to impose on: *v.i.* to act as a cheat.
cheatable, *a. cheet*-a-bl, easily cheated.
cheater, *n. cheet*-er, one who cheats; a sharper.
cheatery, *n. cheet*-er-re, the practice of swindling; trickery.
check, *n.* chek, a sudden stoppage or restraint; one who or that which checks; a reverse; reproof or reprimand; a mark put against entries in going over a list; something corresponding to compare with; a check-roll; a ticket; a token serving for identification; a cheque; a checkered fabric or pattern; the situation of the king in chess when it must be either moved or guarded; a term used when a hawk forsakes her quarry to follow other birds: *v.i.* to stop; to pause: *v.t.* to cause to stop; to restrain; to chide or reprove; to test accuracy by comparison with a standard or duplicate; to mark as having been examined; to put in check [Chess]; to ease off a little (of a rope) [Naut.]; to stopper the cable [Naut.]. **clerk of the check,** an officer of the British royal household and adjutant of the Yeoman of the Guard. (Fr. *échec.*)
check, *a.* chek, chequered. (Short for *checker.*)
checker, *v.t. chek*-er, to chequer: *n.* one who checks; a ticker-collector; chequer; *pl.* draughts [U.S.A.]. (O.Fr. *eschekier.*)
checkmate, *n.* chek-*mate*, the winning move in chess, when the adversary's king is in check and can neither move out of it nor interpose a piece; defeat; overthrow: *v.t.* to put the king in checkmate; to defeat; to place in a position from which there is no escape. (Fr. *échec mat*, from Per. *shāh mat*, the king is dead.)
check-rail, *n*, guard-rail [Railway].
check-rein, *n. chek*-rane, a bearing-rein.
check-roll, *n. chek*-role, a roll of employees in a business or factory.
checkweigher, *n. chek*-way-er, the miners' representative in a colliery who checks the amount of coal mined.
checky, *a. chek*-e, chequered like a chess-board [Her.].
cheddar, *n. ched*-dar, a kind of cheese, so called from a village in Somersetshire where originally made.
cheddar-pink, *n. ched*-dar-pink, the wild flower *Dianthus cæsius.*
cheddite, *n. ched*-ite, a high explosive used principally for blasting. (*Chedde*, town in France.)
cheek, *n.* cheek, the side of the face; one of two sides which correspond, or which are double and alike; insolence: *v.t.* to be impertinent. **cheek by jowl,** *i.e.*, jaw, side by side, closeness. (A.S. *ceace.*)
cheek-bone, *n. cheek*-bone, the bone of the cheek.
cheek-tooth, *n. cheek*-tooth, a molar tooth.
cheeky, *a. cheek*-e, saucy; impertinent [Coll.].
cheep, *n.* cheep, the cry of a young bird: *v.i.* to pipe or chirp thus. (From the sound.)
cheeper, *n. cheep*-er, a young game-bird.
cheer, *n.* cheer, an expression of cheerfulness; a state of gladness or joy; that which makes cheerful; entertainment; good fare; a shout of joy or applause: *v.i.* to grow cheerful; to raise a cheer; to utter cheers: *v.t.* to gladden; to cause to rejoice; to applaud; to encourage. **cheer up,** to make cheerful; to enliven. (O.Fr. *chère*, the face.)
cheerful, *a. cheer*-ful, having good spirits; lively; animated; gladsome; joyful.
cheerfully, *ad. cheer*-ful-le, in a cheerful manner.
cheerfulness, *n. cheer*-ful-ness, the state of being cheerful.
cheerily, *ad. cheer*-re-le, in a cheery manner.
cheeriness, *n. cheer*-re-ness, the state of being cheery.

cheering, *a.* *cheer*-ing, gladdening ; encouraging : *n.* applause ; cheers.
cheeringly, *ad.* *cheer*-ing-le, in a cheering manner.
cheerio, *int.* cheer-re-*oh*, good cheer ! good-bye ! [Coll.].
cheer-leader, *n.* *cheer*-leed-er, a director of organized applause [U.S.A.].
cheerless, *a.* *cheer*-less, joyless ; sad ; gloomy.
cheerlessness, *n.* *cheer*-less-ness, the state of being cheerless.
cheery, *a.* *cheer*-re, cheerful ; making cheerful ; merry ; slightly tipsy [Coll.].
★**cheese,** *n.* cheez, the curd of milk pressed in a mould into a solid mass ; anything in the form of cheese ; the appearance of a lady's skirt when curtseying ; the correct thing [Slang]. **cheese it !** shut up ! don't talk rot ! [Slang]. (A.S. *cēse.*)
cheese-cake, *n.* *cheez*-kake, a cake made of soft curds, sugar, and butter.
cheese-cloth, *n.* *cheez*-kloth, butter-muslin as used in pressing cheese curds.
cheese-fly, *n.* *cheez*-fly, the small black fly bred in cheese.
cheese-hopper, *n.* *cheez*-hop-er, the maggot of the cheese-fly, *Piophila casei.*
cheese-mite, *n.* *cheez*-mite, the arachnid found in cheese, *Tyroglyphus siro.*
cheesemonger, *n.* *cheez*-mung-ger, a dealer in cheese.
cheese-paring, *a.* *chez*-pare-ing, parsimonious ; mean : *n.pl.* useless or worthless scraps.
cheese-press, *n.* *cheez*-press, a press for pressing curd into cheese.
cheese-rennet, *n.* *cheez*-ren-net, the yellow lady's bedstraw, *Galium verum*, used in coagulating milk.
cheese-vat, *n.* *cheez*-vat, the vat in which curds are pressed.
cheesy, *a.* *cheez*-e, resembling cheese ; chic [Slang].
cheetah, *n.* *chee*-ta, the hunting leopard of India. (Hind. *chita.*)
chef, *n.* shef, a chief cook ; a male cook. (Fr.)
chef-d'œuvre, *n.* shay-*doovr* (or App.), a masterpiece. (Fr.)
cheiroptera, *n.pl.* ky-*rop*-te-ra, the group of mammals comprising the bats. (Gr. *cheir*, hand, *pteron*, a wing.)
Cheka, *n.* *chay*-ka, the secret political police of Soviet Russia from 1918 till succeeded by the Ogpu, 1922. (Initials of Russian name.)
chela, *n.* *kee*-la, the prehensile claw of a crab, lobster, etc. (Gr. a claw.)
chela, *n.* *chay*-lah, a Buddhist disciple or novice. (Hind. *celā.*)
cheliferous, *a.* kel-*if*-er-us, furnished with claws.
cheliform, *a.* *kel*-e-form, having the form of a claw.
Chellean, *a.* *shel*-le-an, pertaining to the most primitive type of the Lower Palæolithic culture [Anthrop.]. (*Chelles*, France, where first studied.)
chelonia, *n.pl.* ke-*loh*-ne-a, the sub-class of the reptiles whcih includes the tortoises and turtles. (Gr. *chelone*, a tortoise.)
chelonian, *a.* ke-*loh*-ne-an, pertaining to the chelonia : *n.* an individual of the chelonia.
★**chemical,** *a.* *kem*-e-kal, pertaining to chemistry, or its phenomena : *n.* a substance produced by or used in chemical process.
chemically, *ad.* *kem*-e-ka-le, according to the principles of chemistry ; by chemical process.
chemico-electric, *a.* *kem*-e-ko-e-*lek*-trik, electrical from chemical action ; also chemical from electrical action.
chemin de fer, *n.* (App.), a variety of baccarat. (Fr., railway.)
chemise, *n.* she-*meez*, an under-garment for the body worn by women. (Fr.)
chemisette, *n.* shem-e-*zet*, a light under-garment for the neck, shoulders, and breast, worn by women.
chemist, *n.* *kem*-ist, one versed in chemistry ; a dealer in drugs and medical preparations. **analytical chemist,** one trained in chemical analysis. **chemist and druggist,** one who has passed the minor examination of the Pharmaceutical Society. **pharmaceutical chemist,** one who has passed the major examination of the Pharmaceutical Society. (*Alchemist.*)
chemistry, *n.* *kem*-is-tre, the science which treats of the elements and their combinations, with the properties that distinguish and the laws that govern them. **inorganic chemistry,** the analysis of mineral compounds. **organic chemistry,** the analysis of vegetable and animal compounds.
chemitype, *n.* *kem*-e-tipe, the process of producing by chemical means an engraving in relief on a metal plate.
chemolysis, *n.* ke-*mol*-e-sis, decomposition by chemical agency.
chemosmosis, *n.* kem-oz-*moh*-sis, chemical action taking effect through an intervening membrane. (Gr. *chemeia*, chemistry, and *osmos*, pushing.)
chemosmotic, *a.* kem-oz-*mot*-ik, pertaining to chemosmosis.
chemotactic, *a.* *kem*-o-*tak*-tik, pertaining to chemotaxis.
chemotaxis, *n.* *kem*-o-*tak*-sis, the property which certain living cells have of moving towards or away from chemical substances. (*Chemo* and Gk. *taxis*, order.)
chemotherapeutics, *n.* *kem*-o-the-ra-*pew*-tiks, chemotherapy.
chemotherapy, *n.* *kem*-o-*the*-ra-pe, the treatment of microbic diseases by direct chemical attack on the micro-organism responsible. (*Chemo* and Gk. *therapeuo*, heal.)
chenille, *n.* she-*neel*, a loose, soft, fluffy cord of silk or cotton used in embroidery. (Fr., a woolly caterpillar.)
Chenopodium, *n.* kee-no-*poh*-de-um, the goosefoot genus of plants. (Gr.)
cheque, *n.* chek, a draft or order for money, drawn on a banker or merchant.
cheque-book, *n.* *chek*-book, a book of blank cheques issued by a bank.
chequer, *v.t.* *chek*-er, to form into small squares, like a chess-board, by lines or stripes of different colours ; to diversify ; to variegate : *n.* a single square in a pattern made of squares in alternating colours : *pl.* checkers. **chequer-work,** work consisting of chequers of varied colours and materials.
cherimoya, *n.* che-re-*moy*-a, the fruit of *Anona cherimolia*, a tree of Peru and Ecuador.
cherish, *v.t.* *che*-rish, to hold as dear ; to treat with fostering affection ; to foster ; to nourish ; to encourage, to harbour. (Fr. *chérissant.*)
cherishingly, *ad.* *che*-rish-ing-le, in a cherishing manner.
cheroot, *n.* sher-*root*, a cigar made in India, Burma, or Manila, and cut at both ends. (Tamil, *shuruttu*, a roll.)
cherry, *n.* *che*-re, a stone fruit of the genus *Cerasus* ; the tree of the plum family bearing this : *a.* of the colour of a cherry ; ruddy. **winter cherry,** the alkekengi. (O.Fr. *cherise.*)
cherry-brandy, *n.* *che*-re-*bran*-de, brandy in which cherries have been steeped.
cherry-pie, *n.* che-re-*py*, the garden heliotrope.
cherry-pit, *n.* *che*-re-pit, a child's game of throwing cherry-stones into a hole.
chersonese, *n.* *ker*-so-neez, a peninsula. (Gr.)
chert, *n.* chert, an impure kind of flint ; hornstone. (Origin doubtful.)
cherty, *a.* *chert*-te, like or containing chert.
cherub, *n.* *che*-rub (*pl.* **cherubs** *or* **cherubim**), an angel next in order to a seraph ; a winged head of a child ; a beautiful child. (Heb.)
cherubic, *a.* che-*roo*-bik, pertaining to cherubs ; angelic.
chervil, *n.* *cher*-vil, a culinary herb of the genus *Chærophyllum.*
chervonets, *n.* *cher*-vo-nets, the gold monetary unit of the Soviet Union till 1936, equal to 10 roubles or 7·74234 grms. of fine gold (then valued 21*s.* 1¾*d.*). (Russ., ducat.).
Cheshire, *n.* *chesh*-er, a cheese made in England in that county. **Cheshire cat,** a cat of folk-legend with a fixed stare or grin, whence the phrase, to grin like a Cheshire cat.
chesil, *n.* *ches*-sil, gravel or shingle. (A.S. *cesil.*)
chess, *n.* chess, a game played by two persons, each with sixteen pieces, on a board divided into sixty-four squares. **chess-board,** the board. **chessman,** any one of the pieces used in playing chess. (Fr. *échecs*, from Per. *shah*, king.)
chessel, *n.* *ches*-sel, a cheese mould.
★**chest,** *n.* chest, a large box ; the quantity contained in it ; a coffer for money, hence the funds of a corporation, etc. ; the trunk of the body from the neck to the abdomen ; the thorax. **chest of drawers,** a case of drawers. (A.S. *cist.*)

chested, *a.* *ches*-ted, having a chest as particularized, such as broad-chested.
Chesterfield, *n.* *ches*-ter-feeld, a long sofa with upright ends; an overcoat. (Earl of *Chesterfield.*)
chestnut, *n.* *chess*-nut, the edible nut of the chestnut-tree, *Castanea vesca*; the inedible horse-chestnut; a reddish-brown colour; a horse of this colour; an old, well-worn joke or yarn [Slang]: *a.* of a chestnut colour; reddish-brown. (O.Fr. *chastaigne*, chestnut.)
cheval, *n.* she-*val*, a support or frame. (Fr., a horse.) **cheval glass,** a large swing-glass mounted on a frame. **cheval-de-frise** (*pl.* **chevaux-de-frise**), a military fence composed of a piece of timber armed with long spikes [Fort.]. (Fr., Friesland horse.)
chevalier, *n.* shev-a-*leer*, a cavalier; a knight; a gallant young man; a member of certain Continental knightly orders, or of the French Legion of Honour; the greenshank. (Fr.)
chevelure, *n.* *shev*-el-oor, the arrangement of the hair; the nebulous envelope round the nucleus of a comet. (Fr.)
cheveril, *n.* *chev*-er-il, kid-leather: *a.* yielding; pliable, as cheveril. (O.Fr. *chevrele.*)
chevet, *n.* she-*vay*, a variety of apse [Arch.]. (Fr.)
cheville, *n.* she-*veel*, the peg of a violin or other stringed instrument. (Fr.)
chevin, *n.* *chev*-in, the chub, *Leuciscus cephalus*.
cheviot, *n.* *chev*-e-ot, a sheep bred on the Cheviots; rough cloth made from its wool.
chevisance, *n.* *shev*-e-zance, achievement; an illegal transaction [Law].
chevrette, *n.* shev-*ret*, a thin glove-leather of goat-skin. (L. *capra*, a goat.)
chevron, *n.* *shev*-ron, an honourable ordinary representing two rafters meeting at the top [Her.]; an ornament of zigzag work [Arch.]; a sleeve-badge worn by soldiers, airmen, and police denoting non-commissioned rank or length of service. (Fr., a rafter, from L. *capra*, a goat.)
chevronel, *n.* *shev*-ro-nel, a chevron of half-width [Her.].
chevrotain, *n.* shev-ro-*tane*, a very small deer-like ruminant of the genus *Tragulus*; the mouse-deer. (Fr.)
chevy, *v.t.* *chiv*-ve, to chase; to hustle about; to pester: *n.* a playground game. (From place-name, or ballad, *Chevy* Chase.)
chew, *v.t.* choo, to bruise and grind with the teeth; to masticate; to ruminate or meditate on: *v.i.* to champ; to ruminate: *n.* a mouthful; that which is chewed; a quid of tobacco. (A.S. *ceowan.*)
chewer, *n.* *choo*-er, one who chews tobacco or gum.
chewing-gum, *n.* *choo*-ing-gum, a rubber-like gum composed mainly of chicle, sweetened and flavoured for mastication.
Chian, *a.* *ky*-an, relating to the island of Chios: *n.* a native of Chios. **Chian turpentine,** the oleoresin exuded by the terebinth; common turpentine.
Chianti, *n.* ke-*ahn*-te, a red wine grown in Tuscany.
chiaroscuro, *n.* *ky*-ah-ro-*skoo*-ro, the treatment of light and shade in art; the effects of light and shade; contrast; a black-and-white sketch. (It., literally, clear-obscure.)
chiasm, *n.* *ky*-azm, a crossing of two portions of the optic nerve [Anat.]. (Gr. *chiasma*, a cross.)
chibol, *n.* *chib*-ol, the Welsh onion or stone-leek; a shallot. (N.Fr. *chiboule.*)
chibouk, *n.* che-*book*, a Turkish tobacco-pipe. (Turk.)
chic, *n.* sheek, style; taste; the best or latest fashion: *a.* stylish; just right. (Fr.)
chica, *n.* *chee*-kah, chicha; also, a fermented liquor made of Indian corn; a red colouring substance from a species of Brazilian *Bignonia*. (Native name.)
chicane, *n.* she-*kane*, quibbling captious artifice and manœuvring; a hand at bridge without a trump: *v.i.* to prolong a contest by chicane; to trick; to cheat. (Fr. *chicaner.*)
chicanery, *n.* she-*kay*-ner-re, the employment of chicane; pettifogging action.
chich, *n.* chitch, the chick-pea. (Fr.)
chicha, *n.* *chee*-cha, a fermented liquor made from Indian corn. (Haytian.)
chick, *n.* chik, a chicken.
chick, *n.* chik, a bamboo sunblind; a door-screen. (Hind. *chik.*)
chickadee, *n.* *chik*-a-dee, an American crestless titmouse. (From its song.)
chickaree, *n.* *chik*-a-ree, the American red squirrel. (From its cry.)
chicken, *n.* *chik*-en, the young of a fowl, particularly the domestic hen; a person of tender years; a child. **Mother Carey's chicken,** the stormy petrel, *Hydrobates pelagica*. (A.S. *cicen.*)
chicken-hearted, *a.* *chik*-en-*har*-ted, timid; also cowardly.
chickenpox, *n.* *chik*-en-poks, a pustulous contagious disease, generally occurring in childhood; varicella.
chickling, *n.* *chik*-ling, the common vetch, cultivated as a fodder-plant.
chick-pea, *n.* *chik*-pee, a dwarf pea with one- or two-seeded puffy pods, used as food, *Cicer arietinum*.
chickweed, *n.* *chik*-weed, a small weed, *Cerastium arvense*, or any species of *Stellaria*.
chicle, *n.* cheekl, a gum, used for the basis of chewing-gum, obtained from various trees, esp. the sapodilla of tropical America.
chicory, *n.* *chik*-o-re, a composite blue-flowered plant of the genus *Cichorium*, with a carrot-like root, which, when roasted and ground, is employed to mix with coffee. (Fr. *chicorée.*)
chide, *n.* chide, a reproof; bickering; murmur; gentle noise: *v.t.* and *i.* to scold; to reprove; to blame; to fret. (A.S. *cidan.*)
chiding, *n.* *chide*-ing, a scolding; a reproof.
chidingly, *ad.* *chide*-ing-le, in a chiding manner.
★**chief,** *a.* cheef, principal; highest in office or rank; most eminent; most important; leading; main: *n.* a head or principal person; a leader or commander; a departmental manager; the principal thing; the largest part; the upper part of an escutcheon [Her.]. **to hold land in chief,** to hold it directly from the sovereign by honourable personal services. **The Lord Chief Justice of England,** the president of the King's Bench Division. **Chief Justice of the United States,** the president of the Supreme Court. (Fr. *chef.*)
chiefless, *a.* *cheef*-less, without a chief or leader.
chiefly, *ad.* *cheef*-le, principally; especially; above all.
chieftain, *n.* *cheef*-tan, a commander; the head of a tribe; the head of a Highland clan. (O.Fr. *chevetaine.*)
chieftaincy, *n.* *cheef*-tan-se, the office or rank of chieftain.
chieftainess, *n.* *cheef*-ta-ness, a female chieftain.
chieftainship, *n.* *cheef*-tan-ship, chieftaincy.
chiel, *n.* cheel, a young fellow [Scots].
chiff-chaff, *n.* *chif*-chaf, the small British warbler, *Phylloscopus collybita*.
chiffon, *n.* *shif*-fong, a gauze material; trimmings for women's dresses. (Fr. *chiffe*, a rag.)
chiffonier, *n.* *shif*-fo-*neer*, a sideboard or ornamental cupboard. (Fr. *chiffon*, a rag-gatherer.)
chignon, *n.* she-*nyong*, a large roll of natural or artificial hair formerly worn by women on the back of the head. (Fr., the nape of the neck.)
chigoe, *n.* *chig*-o, a flea of the W. Indies and S. America, the female of which burrows under the skin of the feet causing serious, and sometimes fatal, disorder; the jigger, a species of *Sarcopsylla*. (West Indian and U.S.A. term.)
chilblain, *n.* *chil*-blane, an inflamed state of the skin of hand or foot caused by cold. (*Chill* and *blain.*)
child, *n.* chyld (*pl.* **children,** *chil*-dren), a son or a daughter; offspring; a very young person; an infant; one young in knowledge, experience, judgment, or attainments: *pl.* spiritual offspring; descendants, however remote; the inhabitants of a country. **with child,** pregnant. (A.S. *cild.*)
child-bearing, *a.* *chyld*-bare-ing, bearing children: *n.* the act of bearing children.
childbed, *n.* *chyld*-bed, the state of a woman lying in.
child-birth, *n.* *chyld*-berth, parturition; the time or act of bringing forth a child.
childe, *n.* chyld, the eldest son of a nobleman who has not yet attained to knighthood. (*Child.*)
Childermas, *n.* *chil*-der-mas, the Feast of Holy Innocents on the 28th of December, in commemoration of the innocents slain by Herod. (A.S. *cyldamæsse*, the children's mass.)
childhood, *n.* *chyld*-hood, the state of being a child; the time from infancy to near puberty.
childish, *a.* *chyld*-ish, of or like a child; puerile; silly. (A.S. *cildisc.*)
childishly, *ad.* *chyld*-ish-le, in a childish manner.

childishness, *n.* *chyld*-ish-ness, the state or quality of being childish.
childless, *a.* *chyld*-less, having no child or offspring.
childlessness, *n.* *chyld*-les-ness, state of being childless.
childlike, *a.* *chyld*-like, like a child; beseeming a child; docile; simple; artless.
children, *chil*-dren, *n.pl.* of child.
childrenite, *n.* *chil*-dren-ite, hydrated phosphate of aluminium and iron. (The Eng. mineralogist, J. G. *Children, d.* 1852.)
Chilean, *a.* *chil*-le-an, pertaining to Chile: *n.* a native or the language of Chile.
chiliad, *n.* *kil*-e-ad, a thousand; a thousand years. (Gr. *chilioi*, a thousand.)
chiliagon, *n.* *kil*-e-a-gon, a plane geometrical figure of a thousand angles. (Gr.)
chiliahedron, *n.* *kil*-e-a-*hee*-dron, a figure of a thousand sides. (Gr. *chilioi*, and *hedra*, a seat.)
chiliarchy, *n.* *kil*-e-ar-ke, a corps of a thousand men.
chiliasm, *n.* *kil*-e-azm, the millennial doctrine that Christ in person will reign on earth for a thousand years. (Gr. *chiliasmos.*)
chiliast, *n.* *kil*-e-ast, a millenarian.
chiliastic, *a.* kil-e-*as*-tik, relating to chiliasm.
chill, *n.* chil, chilliness; coldness; a sensation of cold, esp. as a symptom of feverishness; anything that depresses or discourages: *a.* cold, so as to cause shivering; shivering with cold; coldly formal; chilling or depressing: *v.t.* to make cold; to depress; to discourage; to cool suddenly [Metal.]. (A.S. *ciele*, coldness.)
chilled, *a.* child, hardened by chilling (of steel, etc.); refrigerated, kept in cold storage (of meat, etc.).
chiller, *n.* *chil*-ler, a machine, or a person, that chills.
chilli, *n.* *chil*-le, the pod of cayenne pepper, a species of *Capsicum*. (Mexican.)
chilliness, *n.* *chil*-e-ness, the state of being or making chilly.
chillingly, *ad.* *chil*-ing-le, in a chilling manner.
chillness, *n.* *chil*-ness, the state of being chill.
chilly, *a.* *chil*-le, cold; feeling cold; susceptible of cold; distant, stand-offish.
chiloma, *n.* ky-*loh*-ma, the upper lip of the camel and other ungulates [Zool.]. (Gr. *cheiloma*, lip.)
Chiltern, *a.* *chil*-tern, pertaining to the Chilterns. **Chiltern Hundreds,** a nominal stewardship in Buckinghamshire and Oxfordshire under the crown, which a member of parliament, as he cannot resign, may accept, if he wishes to vacate his seat.
Chimæra, *n.* ky-*meer*-ra, a widely distributed genus of marine cartilaginous fishes including the king-of-the-herrings, or rabbit-fish, *Chimæra monstrosa*; the chimera.
chimb, *n.* chime, the chime of a cask.
chime, *n.* chime, the consonant or harmonious sound of musical instruments; a set of bells tuned to the musical scale and struck with hammers; the sound of the bells of a clock at the quarters of the hour; correspondence of sounds; harmony; correspondence of relation: *v.i.* to sound in consonance or harmony; to sound at the quarters of an hour; to accord; to agree: *v.t.* to move, strike, or cause to sound in harmony. (O.Fr. *chimble.*)
chime, *n.* chime, the edge or brim of a cask or tub, formed by the ends of the staves. (A.S. *cimb*, a box.)
chimera, *n.* ky-*meer*-ra, a monster with the head of a lion, the body of a goat, and the tail of a dragon, vomiting flames [Myth.]; an incongruous and impossible conception of the fancy. (L. from Gr.)
chimere, *n.* she-*meer*, the upper robe of a bishop. (O.Fr. *chamarre.*)
chimerical, *a.* ky-*me*-re-kal, purely imaginary.
chimerically, *ad.* ky-*me*-re-ka-le, in a chimerical manner.
chimney, *n.* *chim*-ne, a passage for the escape of smoke from a fire; a flue; a funnel; a glass funnel to intensify the combustion of a lamp; a vent in a volcano; a nearly vertical fissure in rock. (Fr. *cheminée.*)
chimney-board, *n.* *chim*-ne-bord, a fire-board.
chimney-breast, *n.* *chim*-ne-brest, the projection in a room in which the fireplace is put.
chimney-cap, *n.* *chim*-ne-kap, a cowl to improve the draught of a chimney.
chimney-corner, *n.* *chim*-ne-*kor*-ner, a nook or place near the fire.
chimney-hook, *n.* *chim*-ne-hook, a hook for holding pots and kettles over a fire.
chimney-money, *n.* *chim*-ne-mun-e, a tax on each chimney.
chimney-piece, *n.* *chim*-ne-peece, an ornamental framing of wood, marble, etc., round a fireplace.
chimney-pot, *n.* *chim*-ne-pot, an extension of the chimney-shaft; a tall silk hat [Slang].
chimney-shaft, *n.* *chim*-ne-shahft, the portion of a chimney which rises above the rest of the building.
chimney-sweeper, *n.* *chim*-ne-sweep-er, one whose occupation is to sweep chimneys.
chimpanzee, *n.* chim-pan-*zee*, a large anthropoid ape, *Anthropopithecus troglodytes*, of equatorial African forests. (Native name.)
★**chin,** *n.* chin, the front part of the under jaw. (A.S. *cin.*)
china, *n.* *chy*-na, porcelain, first brought from China in the 16th century; translucent earthenware: *a.* made of porcelain; (*cap*) pertaining to China.
China-aster, *n.* *chy*-na-*ass*-ter, a species of *Callistephus*.
china-clay, *n.* *chy*-na-klay, the finest kind of potter's clay; kaolin.
china-grass, fibre obtained from the inner bark of *Bœhmeria nivea*; ramie.
Chinaman, *n.* *chy*-na-man, a native of China.
China-orange, *n.* *chy*-na-*o*-ranj, the sweet orange, said to have been introduced from China.
china-root, *n.* *chy*-na-root, the root of a species of *Smilax*, used as sarsaparilla.
China-rose, *n.* *chy*-na-roze, any one of a number of beautiful garden roses; erroneously applied to the Chinese rose.
china-shop, *n.* *chy*-na-shop, a shop for the sale of china-ware.
Chinatown, *n.* *chy*-na-toun, the Chinese quarter in any city.
china-ware, *n.* *chy*-na-ware, articles made of china.
chincapin, *n.* *ching*-ka-pin, the chinkapin.
chinch, *n.* chinch, the bed-bug, a species of *Cimex*; a species of *Blissus*, destructive to grain. (Sp. *chinche.*)
chinchilla, *n.* chin-*chil*-la, the small South American rodent, *Chinchilla laniger*; its fur of a grey-pearl colour, used for making wraps, coats, etc.; a variety of domestic rabbit with a silky fur. (Sp.)
chin-chin, *int.* *chin-chin*, a toasting phrase, meaning "Good luck," or as a salutation [Slang].
chincough, *n.* *chin*-kof, the whooping-cough.
chine, *n.* chine, the backbone or spine of an animal; a piece of the back of an animal, properly of a pig, cut for cooking: *v.t.* to cut through the backbone of. (O.Fr. *eschine.*)
chine, *n.* chine, a ravine running down to the sea. (A.S. *cinu.*)
chined, *a.* chynd, having a backbone.
Chinee, *n.* chy-*nee*, a Chinese [Slang].
Chinese, *a.* chy-*neze*, of or relating to the country, people, or state of China: *n.* a native or the natives of China. **Chinese lantern,** a collapsible paper lantern. **Chinese lantern plant,** the alkekengi. **Chinese puzzle,** any intricate problem. **Chinese rose,** the beautiful red-flowered mallow, *Hibiscus rosa-sinensis*. **Chinese white,** oxide of zinc.
chink, *n.* chink, a narrow aperture; a cleft or rent: *v.t.* to form into or close up a chink. (A.S. *cinu.*)
Chink, *n.* chink, a Chinaman [Slang].
chink, *n.* chink, the clink, as of a coin; ready money [Slang]: *v.t.* to cause to jingle, as money: *v.i.* to clink. (From the sound.)
chinkapin, *n.* *ching*-ka-pin, the dwarf chestnut of North America, *Castanea pumila*. (Indian.)
chinky, *a.* *ching*-ke, full of chinks; gaping.
chinned, *a.* chind, having a chin, as particularized.
chinoiserie, *n.* she-*nwah*-ze-ree, Chinese conduct or mannerism; a specimen of Chinese art, decoration, etc. (Fr.)
Chinook, *n.* chin-*ook*, a patois of French, English, Indian and other terms formerly used by traders and Indians; the warm SW. wind of the eastern slope of the Rocky Mountains. (Name of Indian tribe.)
chinquapin, *n.* *ching*-ka-pin, the chinkapin.
chin-strap, *n.* *chin*-strap, a strap for holding head-gear in place when worn.
chintz, *n.* chints, cotton cloth or calico, printed with flowers and other devices, in different colours. (Hind.)

chip, *n.* chip, a small piece chopped off; a thin slip of wood; a fragment; a counter; a piece of money [Slang]; *pl.* fried chipped potatoes; a carpenter [Coll.]: *v.t.* to cut into chips; to banter; to tease [Slang]: *v.i.* to break or fly off in chips. **chip-hat,** a hat made from strips of dried palm leaves. **chip of the old block,** his father's son. **to chip in,** to join in; to interpose in a conversation.

chipmuck, *n. chip*-muk (*or* **chipmunk,** *chip*-munk), a N. American ground squirrel of the genus *Tamias.*

Chippendale, *n. chip*-pen-dale, a style of furniture made in the 18th century by Thomas Chippendale.

chipper, *a. chip*-per, lively; cheerful; chirpy: *n.* light talk: *v.i.* to twitter, as a bird [U.S.A.].

chipping, *n. chip*-ping, the act of cutting off in chips; a chip; the flying or breaking off, in chips, from the edges of earthenware; banter.

chippy, *a. chip*-pe, abounding in chips; seedy, off colour, irritable [Slang].

chiragra, *n.* ky-*rag*-ra, gout in the joints of the fingers. (Gr. *cheir,* the hand, *agra,* seizure.)

chirk, *a.* cherk, lively; cheerful [U.S.A. Slang].

chirm, *n.* cherm, din or hum of voices: *v.i.* to chirp as a bird; to hum. (Dial. Eng.)

chirognomy, *n.* ky-*rog*-no-me, judgment of character from the hand. (Gr. *cheir,* and *gnome,* judgment.)

chirograph, *n. ky*-ro-graf, a formal written document, as a bond, indenture, charter, etc. (Gr. *cheir,* and *grapho,* write.)

chirographer, *n.* ky-*rog*-ra-fer, a former law official who engrossed chirographs.

chirography, *n.* ky-*rog*-ra-fe, penmanship; style or character of handwriting.

chirogymnast, *n.* ky-ro-*jim*-nast, an instrument for strengthening the fingers in pianoforte playing [Mus.]. (Gr. *cheir,* and *gymnast.*)

chirological, *a.* ky-ro-*loj*-e-kal, pertaining to chirology.

chirologist, *n.* ky-*rol*-o-jist, one versed in chirology.

chirology, *n.* ky-*rol*-o-je, the art or practice of conversing by signs made by the hands and fingers. (Gr. *cheir,* and *logos,* discourse.)

chiromancer, *n. ky*-ro-man-ser, one skilled in chiromancy.

chiromancy, *n. ky*-ro-man-se, the reading of one's character or fortune by the lines of the hand; palmistry. (Gr. *cheir,* and *manteia,* divination.)

chiromantic, *a.* ky-ro-*man*-tik, pertaining to chiromancy.

chironomy, *n.* ky-*ron*-o-me, the science of expression by means of gesture. (Gr. *cheir,* and *nomos,* law.)

chiropodist, *n.* ky-*rop*-o-dist, one skilled in chiropody; a foot-doctor. (Gr. *cheir,* and *pes,* the foot.)

chiropody, *n.* ky-*rop*-o-de, the treatment of superficial and minor ailments of the feet.

chiropractic, *n.* ky-ro-*prak*-tik, a method of treating nervous disease by manipulation of the spinal column. (Gk. *cheiro,* hand, *prattein,* do.)

chiropractor, *n.* ky-ro-*prak*-tor, one who practises chiropractic.

chiroptera, *n.* ky-*rop*-ter-a, cheiroptera.

chirp, *n.* cherp, a bird note: *v.i.* to utter short sharp cheerful notes, as certain birds and insects. (Imit.)

chirper, *n. cherp*-er, a chirping bird or insect.

chirpingly, *ad. cherp*-ing-le, in a chirping manner.

chirpy, *a. cher*-pe, cheerful; chatty.

chirr, *v.i.* cher, to imitate a bird's note; to trill; to coo: *n.* the sound so made.

chirrup, *v.i. chi*-rup, to chirp.

chirurgeon, *n.* ky-*rur*-jon, a surgeon. (Fr.)

chisel, *n. chiz*-el, an edged tool operated direct by hand or struck with a mallet or hammer: *v.t.* to cut, pare, or engrave with a chisel; to take advantage of, to cheat [Slang]. (O.Fr. *cisel.*)

chiselled, *a. chiz*-ld, cut with or as with a chisel; clear cut.

chiselly, *a. chiz*-l-e, gritty; gravelly.

Chisleu, *n. kis*-lew, the ninth month of the Jewish ecclesiastical year, answering to a part of November and December. (Hebrew.)

chit, *n.* chit, a child; a pert young girl. (Perhaps from *kitten.*)

chit, *n.* chit, a memorandum; a note or voucher; a recommendation. (Hind. *chitti.*)

chital, *n. chit*-al, the axis deer; a venomous sea-snake of the genus *Hydrophis.* (Hind.)

chit-chat, *n. chit*-chat, small talk; gossip.

chitin, *n. ky*-tin, the horny substance giving strength to the exoskeleton of many invertebrate animals. (Fr.)

chitinous, *a. ky*-tin-us, like or consisting of chitin.

chiton, *n. ky*-ton, inner robe worn in ancient Greece by both sexes; (*cap*) a genus of molluscs with shells formed of overlapping portions. (Gr., a tunic.)

chittagong, *n.* chit-ta-*gong,* the wood of Indian trees of several species, used for cabinet-making; a breed of domestic fowl from India.

chitter, *v.i. chit*-ter, to shiver with cold (*chatter*).

chitterlings, *n.pl. chit*-ter-lingz, the small intestines, esp. of swine, used for food. (Ger. *kutteln,* intestines.)

chitty, *n. chit*-te, a chit or memorandum.

chivalric, *a. shiv*-al-rik *or chiv*-al-rik, pertaining to or in the spirit of chivalry; worthy of a knight: brave; gallant; nobly daring.

chivalrous, *a. shiv*-al-russ *or chiv*-al-russ, characterized by knightly qualities; chivalric.

chivalrously, *ad. shiv*-al-russ-le *or chiv*-al-russ-le, in a chivalrous spirit.

chivalry, *n. shiv*-al-re *or chiv*-al-re, the mediæval system of knighthood with its usages and privileges; the body or order of knights, or any such body; the qualifications of a knight, such as dignity, courtesy, bravery, respect for the right, respect for womanly dignity and purity, and military address; gallantry; a former tenure by knight's service [Law]. (O.Fr. *chevalerie,* horsemanship.)

chive, *n.* chive, the small onion, *Allium schœnoprasum,* allied to the garlic.

chivy, *v.t.* and *n. chiv*-e, chevy.

chlamyphorus, *n.* klam-e-*faw*-rus, the pichiciago, so named from its cloak-like covering. (Gr. *chlamys,* cloak, *phero,* bear.)

chlamys, *n. klam*-is, a tunic or scarf worn by the ancients; a floral envelope [Bot.]. (Gr., cloak.)

chloanthite, *n. kloh*-an-thite, arsenide of nickel.

chloasma, *n.* klo-*az*-ma, a skin disease in which yellow patches appear on face and neck. (Gr. *chloazo,* turn green.)

chloral, *n. klaw*-ral, a narcotic liquid first obtained by the action of chlorine upon alcohol.

chloralism, *n. klaw*-ra-lizm, morbid state of body induced by the habitual use of chloral.

chlorate, *n. klaw*-rat, a salt of chloric acid.

chloric, *a. klo*-rik, of or from chlorine. **chloric acid,** an acid of chlorine and oxygen.

chloridate, *v.t. klo*-re-date, to chloridize.

chloride, *n. klaw*-ride, a compound of chlorine with another element or radical.

chloridize, *v.t. klo*-re-dyz, to treat with chlorine or a chloride; to convert into a chloride.

chlorinate, *v.t. klo*-re-nate, to combine or otherwise treat with chlorine; to sterilize with chlorine.

chlorination, *n.* klo-re-*nay*-shon, the act or process of chlorinating.

chlorine, *n. klaw*-rin, one of the chemical elements, a greenish-yellow gas; a powerful disinfectant and bleaching agent, and used also in gas-warfare. (Gr. *chloros,* green.)

chlorite, *n. klaw*-rite, a soft olive-green mineral, soapy to the touch; a salt of chlorous acid [Chem.].

chloritic, *a.* klo-*rit*-ik, containing chlorite.

chloroform, *n. klo*-ro-form, a colourless volatile liquid prepared from alcohol and calcium hypochlorite and used in surgery to induce insensibility and as an antiseptic: *v.t.* to administer chloroform to; to anæsthetize with this. (Gr. *chloros,* and *formyl.*)

chlorometer, *n.* klo-*rom*-e-ter, an instrument for testing the bleaching powers of chloride of lime. (Gr. *chloros,* and *metron,* a measure.)

chlorometry, *n.* klo-*rom*-e-tre, the measurement of chlorine content, esp. in bleaching powder.

chlorophyll, *n. klo*-ro-fil, the green colouring matter of plants, especially in leaves [Bot.]. (Gr. *chloros,* and *phyllon,* a leaf.)

chlorosis, *n.* klo-*roh*-sis, the green sickness, a form of anæmia giving girls a pale greenish hue; any plant disease resulting in etiolation [Bot.]

chlorotic, *a.* klo-*rot*-ik, pertaining to, or affected by, chlorosis.

chlorous, *a. klaw*-rus, pertaining to or containing chlorine. **chlorous acid,** an acid composed of chlorine and oxygen, the salts of which are chlorites.

chobdar, *n.* *chob*-dar, an attendant upon an Indian potentate. (Pers.)

chock, *n.* chok, a block or wedge to prevent movement or (esp. in aeroplanes) to strengthen a connexion. (From *choke.*)

chock-a-block, *a.* chok-a-*blok*, packed tightly together; absolutely full (former nautical term implying " hoisted to the limit ").

chocker, *v.t.* *chok*-er, to block a sequence, etc., in the game of patience.

chock-full, *a.* *chok*-ful, quite full; as full as possible.

chocolate, *n.* *chok*-o-lat, the nut of the chocolate-tree; cocoa in the form of paste; a beverage made by infusing the nut or dissolving chocolate in boiling water or milk: *a.* of the brown colour of chocolate. (Sp.)

chocolate-tree, *n.* *chok*-o-lat-tree, the S. American tree, *Theobroma cacao*, from the nut of which chocolate and cocoa are prepared.

choctaw, *n.* *chok*-taw, a step in figure-skating executed on the right foot outside forward. (From the name of a North American Indian tribe.)

choice, *n.* choyce, the act or the power of choosing; discrimination; selection; the thing chosen; care in selecting; the best or preferable part: *a.* selected with care; select; of great value. **Hobson's choice,** a choice in which there is no alternative. (*Hobson*, a Cambridge jobmaster, whose customers were allowed to take only the horse nearest the door.) (O.Fr. *chois.*)

choicely, *ad.* *choyce*-le, with care in choosing; eminently; carefully.

choiceness, *n.* *choyce*-ness, the quality of being choice; discriminativeness; superior worth.

choir, *n.* kwire, a band of singers, especially in a church service; the part of a church for the singers; the chancel; a large hall adjoining the body of a church, separated by a grating, where the nuns sing the office: *v.i.* and *t.* to sing in or as in choir; to sing together. (O.Fr. *cuer.*)

choir-organ, *n.* *kwire*-awr-gan, the softest of the three organs that make up a great multiple organ.

choir-screen, *n.* *kwire*-skreen, a partition of carved lattice work dividing off the choir from the body of a church.

choir-service, *n.* *kwire*-ser-vis, the part of the service performed by the choir.

choke, *v.t.* choke, to block or compress the windpipe so as to stop the passage of the breath; to stop by filling; to stifle; to obstruct; to reduce the bore of a tube at one end: *v.i.* to have the windpipe stopped; to be suffocated or nearly so; to be obstructed: *n.* the act of choking; anything that causes choking; an obstructing device to check an outflow [Mech.]; a device to check the electrical current [Wire.]. **choke coupling,** intervalve coupling by one or more chokes [Wire.]. **choke filter,** a device used to isolate the loud-speaker from the direct high-tension current [Wire.]. **choking coil,** a coil of wire used to limit the supply of current in electric lighting [Elect.]. (A.S. *ceocian.*)

choke-bore, *n.* *choke*-bore, the bore of a gun when narrowed at the extremity.

choke-cherry, *n.* *choke*-che-re, the N. American wild cherry, *Prunus virginiana*, or its astringent fruit.

choke-damp, *n.* *choke*-damp, carbonic acid gas generated in wells, coal-mines, and other pits.

choke-pear, *n.* *choke*-pare, an astringent variety of pear; an aspersion which puts to silence.

choker, *n.* *choke*-er, that which cannot be answered; a high collar or cravat.

chokey, *n.* *choke*-e, gaol; prison [Slang]. (Hind. *chauki.*)

choky, *a.* *choke*-e, causing or having a feeling of choking.

cholæmia, *n.* ko-*lee*-me-a, a diseased condition due to the presence of bile in the blood.

cholagogue, *n.* *kol*-a-gog, a medicine to promote the flow of bile. (Gr. *chole*, bile, *ago*, lead.)

cholangitis, *n.* kol-an-*jy*-tis, acute infection and inflammation of the bile-ducts [Med.].

choler, *n.* *kol*-er, bile; anger; irascibility. (Fr. *colère.*)

cholera, *n.* *kol*-er-ra, a bilious disease characterized by vomiting and purging, with great pain and debility; called **English cholera,** to distinguish it from **cholera morbus,** an epidemic disease of Asiatic origin characterized by most of the symptoms of cholera in a very aggravated form. (Gr.)

choleraic, *a.* kol-er-*ray*-ik, pertaining to cholera.

choleric, *a.* *kol*-e-rik, full of choler; irascible; angry. (Fr. *cholérique.*)

cholerine, *n.* *kol*-er-rin, the first stage of epidemic cholera, or its reputed cause; a mild form of cholera morbus, " summer cholera."

cholesteric, *a.* ko-*les*-te-rik, pertaining to or obtained from cholesterol.

cholesterin, *n.* ko-*les*-te-rin, cholesterol.

cholesterol, *n.* ko-*les*-te-rol, a white, fatty, crystalline substance found in nerve-tissue and the bile and forming the chief part of gall-stones. (Gr. *chole*, and *stereos*, solid.)

choliamb, *n.* *koh*-le-amb, a verse having an iambic foot in the fifth place and a spondee in the sixth or last [Pros.]. (L. *choliambus.*)

choliambic, *n.* koh-le-*am*-bik, a choliamb: *a.* having the quality of a choliamb.

cholic, *a.* *kol*-ik, pertaining to or obtained from bile, as cholic acid.

cholochrome, *n.* *kol*-o-krome, a colouring matter in the bile. (Gr. *chole*, and *khroma*, colour.)

choltry, *n.* *chole*-tre, a choultry.

chondral, *a.* *kon*-dral, pertaining to cartilage; cartilaginous.

chondrine, *n.* *kon*-drin, a gelatinous liquid obtained from the tissue of cartilage in the ribs, trachea, nose, etc. (Gr. *chondros*, cartilage.)

chondritis, *n.* kon-*dry*-tis, inflammation of cartilage.

chondrodite, *n.* *kon*-dro-dite, any one of the granular forms of humite [Min.].

chondrography, *n.* kon-*drog*-ra-fe, the descriptive study of cartilages. (Gr. *chondros*, and *grapho*, write.)

chondrology, *n.* kon-*drol*-o-je, the science treating of cartilage. (Gr. *chondros*, and *logos*, science.)

chondroma, *n.* kon-*droh*-ma, a cartilaginous tumour [Med.].

chondropterygian, *n.* *kon*-drop-te-*rij*-e-an, one of the two great sections of fishes, the bones and fin-spines of which are formed of gristle, as in the sturgeons and sharks: *a.* pertaining to this section. (Gr. *chondros*, and *pteryx*, a wing, a fin.)

chondrotomy, *n.* kon-*drot*-o-me, the cutting or dissection of cartilage. (Gr. *chondros*, and *tome*, cutting.)

choose, *v.t.* chooz, to make choice of; to select; to feel inclined; to prefer: *v.i.* to make selection; to determine. *p.* **chose**; *pp.* **chosen.** (A.S. *ceosan.*)

chooser, *n.* *chooz*-er, one who chooses.

choosey, *a.* *chooz*-e, over-fastidious; fussy; given to picking and choosing [Coll.].

chop, *n.* chop, a piece chopped off; the act of chopping; a stroke that cuts; a small slice of meat with a rib, as a mutton-chop; a cleft: *pl.* broken waves: *v.i.* to do anything with a quick motion, like that of a blow; to chap: *v.t.* to cut off suddenly with a sharp instrument; to cut into parts or small pieces, to mince. **chop logic,** to wrangle.

chop, *v.i.* chop, to shift suddenly, as the wind: *v.t.* to exchange; to barter. **chop and change,** to be variable; to change one's mind frequently.

chop, *n.* chop, the chap or jaw; the mouth: *pl.* an animal's mouth.

chop, *n.* chop, a seal, brand, or trade-mark in the Far East. (Hind. *chaāp.*)

chopfallen, *a.* *chop*-fawl-en, low-spirited; dejected.

chop-house, *n.* *chop*-house, an eating-house.

chopin, *n.* *chop*-pin, a former liquid measure, in France about a pint, in Scotland about a quart. (Fr. *chopine.*)

chopine, *n.* chop-*peen*, a high patten formerly worn by women. (Sp. *chapin*, clog.)

chopper, *n.* *chop*-per, one who chops; an axe; a butcher's cleaver.

chopping, *a.* *chop*-ping, choppy (of waves).

chopping-block, *n.* *chop*-ping-blok, a wooden block on which anything is laid to be chopped.

chopping-knife, *n.* *chop*-ping-nife, a mincing-knife.

choppy, *a.* *chop*-pe, full of clefts or cracks; roughish with short broken waves (of the sea).

chopsticks, *n.pl.* *chop*-stiks, two small sticks of wood or ivory, held between the fingers of one hand, used in China to eat with.

chop-suey, *n.* chop-*soo*-e, a Chinese dish of meat or fowl stewed with onions, mushrooms, etc., and flavoured with sesame-oil.

choragic, *a.* ko-*raj*-ik *or* ko-*ray*-jik, pertaining to a choragus. **choragic monument,** a monument in

honour of the choragus who produced the best musical or theatrical entertainment at the festival of Bacchus [Antiq.].
choragus, *n.* ko-*ray*-gus, the leader or organizer of a chorus among the ancient Greeks; a musical conductor. (L.)
choral, *a.* *kaw*-ral, pertaining to or sung by a choir or chorus; chanted or sung. (Late L. *choralis.*)
chorale, *n.* ko-*rahl,* a metrical composition to a plain tune sung in unison.
choralist, *n.* *kaw*-ra-list, one who sings in a chorus.
chorally, *ad.* *kaw*-ra-le, in the manner of a chorus.
chord, *n.* kawrd, the string of a musical instrument; a harmonious combination of musical tones; harmony of colour; a right line joining the extremities of the arc of a circle [Geom.]: *v.t.* to furnish with musical strings. **vocal chords,** *see* **vocal.** (Gr. *chordē,* an intestine.)
chore, *n.* chore, a small job; charwork. (U.S.A.)
chorea, *n.* ko-*ree*-a, St. Vitus's dance, a disease occasioning convulsive movements. (Gr. *choreia,* a dance.)
choree, *n.* ko-*ree or koh*-re, a trochee. (Gr.)
choreographer, *n.* kor-re-*og*-ra-fer, an arranger or composer of ballets.
choreography, *n.* kor-re-*og*-ra-fe, the art of representing a dance by signs, as a tune by notes; ballet-dancing. (Gr. *choreia,* dance, *graphein,* write.)
chorepiscopal, *a.* kor-re-*pis*-ko-pal, pertaining to a local, suffragan, or country bishop. (Gr. *chora,* place, *episcopos,* bishop.)
choriamb, *n.* ko-re-*amb,* a foot of four syllables, of which the first and last are long, and the others short [Pros.]. (Gr.)
choriambic, *n.* ko-re-*am*-bik, a choriamb: *a.* pertaining to or like a choriamb.
choriambus, *n.* ko-re-*am*-bus, a choriamb.
choric, *a.* *kaw*-rik, pertaining to or like a chorus.
chorion, *n.* *kaw*-re-on, the exterior membrane investing the fœtus in utero [Anat.]; the exterior membrane of a seed [Bot.]. (Gr.)
choripetalous, *a.* *kaw*-re-*pet*-a-lus, polypetalous; having separate petals. (Gr. *choris,* apart, and *petalous.*)
chorister, *n.* *ko*-ris-ter, a singer, esp. in a choir; a choir-boy.
chorographer, *n.* ko-*rog*-ra-fer, one skilled in chorography.
chorographical, *a.* ko-ro-*graf*-e-kal, pertaining to the description of a country.
chorography, *n.* ko-*rog*-ra-fe, the description of a particular district or country; regional geography. (Gr. *choros,* region, *graphein,* to write.)
choroid, *n.* *koh*-royd, a vascular membrane in the eye: *a.* resembling or pertaining to the chorion [Anat.].
chorology, *n.* ko-*rol*-o-je, the science of the geographical distribution of plants and animals. (Gr. *chora,* a place, *logos,* science.)
chortle, *v.i.* and *t.* *chore*-tl, to chuckle aloud; to sing with a chortle: *n.* the act of chortling; a chortling sound. (Invented by Lewis Carroll, in "Through the Looking-glass.")
chorus, *n.* *kaw*-rus, a band of singers and dancers employed at feasts in honour of the gods, hence a company of persons singing in concert; a piece performed by a company in concert; part of a song in which the company join the singer; a musical composition of two or more parts; in the ancient drama, persons introduced as beholding what passes in the acts of a piece, and who sing or recite their sentiments between the acts; the speaker of prologue or epilogue in Elizabethan drama: *v.t.* and *i.* to sing or speak in concert. (Gr. *choros.*)
chose, chohz, *p.* of **choose.**
chose, *n.* shoze, a thing. **chose in action,** property which a person has a right to sue for, as a debt [Law]. **chose jugée,** an issue already decided. (Fr.)
chosen, *choh*-zn, *pp.* of **choose**: *a.* distinguished by preference.
chou, *n.* shoo, an ornamental ribbon or rosette, etc., worn on a woman's dress or hat. (Fr.)
chouette, *n.* *shoo*-et, a game, esp. at backgammon, in which one player opposes two or more partners. (Fr.)
chough, *n.* chuff, a bird of the crow family, *Pyrrhocorax graculus,* with red legs, and a red beak, which lives in community and nests in cliffs. (A.S. *cēo.*)
choultry, *n.* *chole*-tre, a road-house or caravanserai in India. (Hind.)
chouse, *n.* chouz, a trick; an imposition; one easily cheated: *v.t.* to cheat. (Turk. *chiaus,* an interpreter; one such sent to England in 1609 having distinguished himself by his swindling.)
chow, *n.* chou, a Chinese dog with a black tongue and a thick furry coat. (Chinese.)
chow-chow, *n.* chou-chou, a preserve made of ginger; a mixture of pickles. (Chinese.)
chowder, *n.* *chou*-der, a dish of fish or clams boiled with biscuit, salt pork, vegetables, etc.: *v.t.* to make a chowder of [U.S.A.]. (Fr. *chaudière,* a pot.)
chowry, *n.* *chou*-re, in India, a whisk to keep off flies. (Hind. *chaunrī.*)
choy-root, *n.* *choy*-root, chaya-root.
chrematistics, *n.* krem-a-*tis*-tiks, the science of wealth; political economy. (Gr. *chrematistikos,* relating to money-making.)
chrestomathy, *n.* kres-*tom*-a-the, a book of extracts for learning a language. (Gr. *chrestomatheia.*)
chrism, *n.* krizm, consecrated oil used in the Roman Catholic and Greek Churches in baptism, confirmation, ordination, and sacramental unction generally. (A.S. *crisma.*)
chrismal, *a.* *kriz*-mal, pertaining to chrism.
chrismatory, *n.* *kriz*-ma-to-re, a vessel to hold chrism.
chrisom, *n.* *kriz*-om, a linen cloth anointed with chrism laid over a child's face at baptism; a christening robe. **chrisom child,** a child just baptized, or one that died within a month after.
Christ, *n.* kryst, an appellation given to Jesus, the Saviour, synonymous with the Hebrew Messiah, and signifying The Anointed One. (L. *cristus,* anointed.)
Christadelphian, *n.* kris-ta-*del*-fe-an, a member of a Unitarian religious sect, founded in the U.S.A. by John Thomas about 1848. (Gr. *christadelphos,* brotherhood with Christ.)
Christ-cross-row, *n.* *kris*-kros-*roh,* criss-cross-row, an old term for the alphabet.
christen, *v.t.* *kris*-n, to baptize in the name of Christ; to name. (A.S. *cristnian.*)
christendom, *n.* *kris*-sen-dom, the whole body of Christians; the countries where they form the majority. (A.S. *cristendom.*)
christening, *n.* *kris*-sen-ing, the ceremony of baptism.
Christian, *n.* *kris*-tyan, one who professes faith in Christ or his teaching; vaguely, one born in a Christian country or of Christian parents; a civilized person as opposed to a savage: *a.* pertaining to Christ or Christianity. **Christian name,** name given at christening, distinct from the surname. **Christian Science,** a religious organization founded in the U.S.A. by Mrs. Mary Baker Eddy in 1866, based on its own interpretation of Scripture, and teaching that sin and disease are due to mental errors. (L. *Christianus.*)
Christianity, *n.* kris-te-*an*-e-te, the Christian religion; faith in Christ; the state of being a Christian; Christian conduct.
Christianize, *v.t.* *kris*-tya-nize, to make Christian; to convert to Christianity: *v.i.* to be converted to Christianity.
Christianlike, *a.* *kris*-tyan-like, befitting a Christian.
Christianly, *a.* *kris*-tyan-le, befitting a Christian: *ad.* in a Christian manner.
Christless, *a.* *kryst*-less, without the grace of Christ; unchristian.
Christmas, *n.* *kris*-mas, the festival on the 25th of December, in memory of the birth of Christ; Christmastide: *a.* belonging to or appropriate to the period of Christmas or its festivities. **Christmas card,** a decorated greeting-card sent between friends at Christmastide. **Christmas carol,** a hymn or joyful song for Christmastide. **Christmas daisy,** the plant *Aster grandiflorus.* **Christmas day,** the 25th of December. **Christmas eve,** the 24th of December. **Christmas number,** the special issue for that season of a periodical. **Christmas pride,** the plant *Ruellia paniculata.* **Christmas rose,** a species of the genus *Helleborus.* **Christmas tree,** a fir, or other evergreen tree, which is decorated and hung with small gifts illuminated for Christmas day. (*Christ* and *Mass.*)
Christmas-box, *n.* *kris*-mas-*boks,* a Christmas present.
Christmassy, *a.* *kris*-mas-se, like or befitting Christmas.

Christmastide, *n. kris*-mas-tide, Christmas-time.

Christmas-time, *n, kris*-mas-time, the season of Christmas, which extends formally from 24th December (Christmas eve) to 6th January (Epiphany).

Christology, *n.* kris-*tol*-o-je, that branch of theology which treats of the person and attributes of Christ. (Gr. *christos*, and *logos*, science.)

Christophany, *n.* kris-*tof*-an-e, appearance of Christ to mankind after his resurrection.

Christ's-thorn, *n. krysts*-thorn, the prickly shrub, *Paliurus aculeata*, or other plant supposed to have furnished the crown of thorns.

chromate, *n. kroh*-mate, a salt of chromic acid.

chromatic, *a.* kro-*mat*-ik, relating to colour; coloured; proceeding by semitones [Mus.]: *n.* a kind of music that proceeds by semitones or accidental semitones. **chromatic scale,** a scale rising by semitones. (L. *chromaticus*.)

chromatically, *ad.* kro-*mat*-e-ka-le, in a chromatic manner.

chromatics, *n.* kro-*mat*-iks, that branch of optics which treats of colours.

chromatin, *n. kroh*-ma-tin, the network structure of the nucleus of a cell [Biol.].

chromatism, *n. kroh*-ma-tizm, chromatic aberration in optics; chromism [Bot.].

chromatography, *n. kroh*-ma-*tog*-ra-fe, a treatise on colours. (Gr. *chroma*, and *grapho*, write.)

chromatology, *n. kroh*-ma-*tol*-o-je, the science of colours.

chromatometer, *n. kroh*-ma-*tom*-e-ter, a scale for measuring the intensity of colours. (Gr.)

chromatophore, *n. kroh*-ma-to-for, a pigment-carrying cell which effects change of colour in certain animals. (Gr. *chroma*, and *phero*, bear.)

chromatosphere, *n. kroh*-ma-to-sfeer, chromosphere.

chromatrope, *n. kroh*-ma-trope, a revolving lantern-slide by which a kaleidoscopic effect can be produced. (Gr. *chroma*, and *trepo*, turn.)

chromatype, *n. kroh*-ma-tipe, a photograph on paper sensitized by a chromium salt; the process of producing such.

chrome, *n.* krome, chromium; a yellow pigment from chromate of lead, remarkable for the beauty and variety of the colours of its compounds, esp. **chrome-green,** prepared from the oxide of chromium, **-orange,** and **-red,** from chromate of lead, and **-yellow** from the neutral chromate. (Fr.)

chromic, *a. kroh*-mik, pertaining to or obtained from chromium.

chromism, *n. kroh*-mizm, abnormal coloration in plants.

chromite, *n. kroh*-mite, the double oxide of chromium and iron, the chief source of the chromic dyes and pigments.

chromium, *n. kroh*-me-um, chrome, the steel-grey metallic element which forms a valuable alloy with steel.

chromogen, *n. kroh*-mo-jen, organic colouring-matter containing a chromophore; a mordant dye derived from naphthaline.

chromograph, *n. kroh*-mo-graf, a transfer copying process from a gelatine pad; the apparatus for this. (Gr. *chroma*, and *grapho*, write.)

chromo-lithograph, *n. kroh*-mo-*lith*-o-graf, a picture done by chromo-lithography: *v.t.* and *i.* to print by chromolithography.

chromo-lithography, *n. kroh*-mo-lith-*og*-ra-fe, the art of colour-printing from a succession of stones.

chromophore, *n. kroh*-mo-fore, a chemical combination whose presence in a given class of organic compounds is necessary to produce colours.

chromoplasm, *n. kroh*-mo-plazm, the part of a cell readily taking up colouring matter; chromatin.

chromosome, *n. kroh*-mo-sohm, one of the minute gene-bearing bodies into which the chromatin is resolved before cell-division [Biol.].

chromosphere, *n. kroh*-mo-sfeer, the gaseous envelope of the sun, through which the light of the photosphere passes. (Gr. *chroma*, and *sphere*.)

chromotype, *n. kroh*-mo-tipe, a process for procuring a coloured photograph. (Gr. *chroma*, and *type*.)

chromotypography, *n. kroh*-mo-ty-*pog*-ra-fe, picture printing in different colours.

chromoxylography, *n. kroh*-mo-zy-*log*-ra-fe, colour-printing with wooden blocks.

chromule, *n. kroh*-mewl, the colouring matter in plants, green excepted.

chronic, *a. kron*-ik, relating to time; recurring or of long continuance [Med.]; bad, objectionable, rotten [Slang]. **a chronic disease,** one which is of long continuance as distinct from an acute disease. (Gr. *chronos*, time.)

chronicity, *n.* kro-*nis*-e-te, the quality of being chronic [Med.].

chronicle, *n. kron*-e-kl, a record of events in the order of time; a history; annals; a record: *v.t.* to record in history; to register. (Fr. *chronique*.)

chronicler, *n. kron*-e-kler, the writer of a chronicle; an annalist.

Chronicles, *n.pl. kron*-e-klz, two canonical records of the kingdom of Judah contained in the Old Testament.

chronogram, *n. kron*-o-gram, an inscription which contains the date of an action mentioned, as in the motto of a medal struck by Gustavus Adolphus in 1632:—

ChrIstVs DVX; ergo trIVMphVs.

chronogrammatic, *a. kron*-o-gra-*mat*-ik, pertaining to or containing a chronogram. (Gr. *chronos*, and *gramma*, a letter.)

chronograph, *n. kron*-o-graf, a chronometer that measures and registers minute divisions of time; a stop-watch. (Gr. *chronos*, and *grapho*, write.)

chronographer, *n.* kro-*nog*-ra-fer, a chronologer.

chronography, *n.* kro-*nog*-ra-fe, a chronological description of past events; use of the graphic method in measuring intervals of time in rapid successive motions.

chronologer, *n.* kro-*nol*-o-jer, one versed in chronology; an annalist.

chronological, *a.* kron-o-*loj*-e-kal, relating to chronology; containing an account of events in the order of time; according to the order of time.

chronologically, *ad.* kron-o-*loj*-e-ka-le, in a chronological manner.

chronologist, *n.* kro-*nol*-o-jist, a chronologer.

chronologize, *v.t.* kro-*nol*-o-jyz, to arrange in order of time; to make chronological.

chronology, *n.* kro-*nol*-o-je, a method or the science of computing time; the arrangement of dates in history; a register or tabular view of dates. (Gr. *chronos*, and *logos*, account.)

chronometer, *n.* kro-*nom*-e-ter, any instrument that measures time, such as a clock, watch, or dial; specially one registering with the greatest possible exactness, such as is used by mariners for determining longitude at sea. **chronometer tables,** calculations for use in any latitude which aid in effecting chronometric correction by an observation of the altitude of the sun. (Gr. *chronos*, and *metron*, a measure.)

chronometric, *a.* kron-o-*met*-rik, pertaining to a chronometer; measured by a chronometer.

chronometrical, *a.* kron-o-*met*-re-kal, chronometric.

chronometry, *n.* kron-*om*-et-re, the art of measuring time; the measuring of time by periods or divisions.

chronopher, *n. kron*-o-fer, an instrument by which time-indications are borne to distant places by electricity. (Gr. *chronos*, and *phero*, bear.)

chronoscope, *n. kron*-o-skope, an instrument for measuring time velocities or minute intervals of time. (Gr. *chronos*, and *skopeo*, view.)

chronoscopy, *n.* kro-*nos*-ko-pe, the study of, or the measurement of, minute intervals of time.

chrysalid, *n. kris*-a-lid, a chrysalis.

chrysalis, *n. kris*-a-lis (*pl.* **chrysalides,** kris-*al*-id-eez, or **chrysalises**), the pupa, or apparently torpid state, of a lepidopterous insect before it assumes its wings; a transitional or immature state. (Gr. *chrysos*, gold.)

chrysanthemum, *n.* kre-*san*-the-mum, any composite plant of a genus including *Pyrethrum*, of which the ox-eye daisy and corn marigold are the common British representatives, and *C. indicum*, and *C. sinense*, are cultivated garden varieties. (L.)

chryselephantine, *a. kris*-el-e-*fan*-tine, partly made of gold and ivory or overlaid with them. (Gr. *chryselephantinos*, made of ivory and gold.)

chrysoberyl, *n. kris*-o-be-ril, aluminate of beryllium, a gem-stone of a yellowish-green colour.

Chrysochloris, *n. kris*-o-klaw-ris, a genus of S. African moles, whose fur reflects metallic hues; the golden mole.

chrysocolla, *n.* kris-o-*kol*-la, a greenish opaline hydrous silicate of copper.
chrysocracy, *n.* kre-*sok*-ra-se, plutocracy. (Gr. *chrysos*, gold, *kratein*, rule.)
chrysolite, *n.* *kris*-o-lite, a yellow transparent variety of olivine. (Gr. *chrysos*, and *lithos*, a stone.)
chrysology, *n.* kre-*sol*-o-je, the science of the production of wealth. (Gr. *chrysos*, and *logos*, science.)
chrysophan, *n.* *kris*-o-fan, a bitter glucoside obtained from rhubarb.
chrysoprase, *n.* *kris*-o-praze, a pale green variety of chalcedony. (Gr. *chryos*, and *prason*, a leek.)
chthonian, *a.* *kthoh*-ne-an *or* *thoh*-ne-an, relating to the underworld, esp. of the Greeks, or its deities. (Gr. *chthonos*, earth.)
chthonic, *a.* *kthon*-ik *or* *thon*-ik, chthonian; Tartarean.
chub, *n.* chub, a coarse freshwater-fish, *Leuciscus cephalus*, of the carp family. (Dan. *kobbe*, seal.)
chubbiness, *n.* *chub*-be-ness, the state of being chubby.
chubby, *a.* *chub*-be, plump; short and thick.
chub-faced, *a.* *chub*-fayst, having a plump round face.
chuck, *n.* chuk, the call of a hen; a sudden small noise; a word of endearment: *v.i.* to call as a hen: *v.t.* to call, as a hen her chickens. (Imit.)
chuck, *n.* chuk, a pat under the chin; a toss or throw to a short distance; a jerk: *v.t.* to touch or give a gentle blow; to throw, with a quick motion; to jerk to a short distance; to pitch. **chuck it,** stop, cease [Slang]. (Perhaps Fr. *choquer*.)
chuck, *n.* chuk, a device for holding work, or a tool, in a lathe.
chucker-out, *n.* *chuk*-er-*out*, an attendant at a place of public assembly who ejects disorderly persons.
chuck-farthing, *n.* *chuk*-far-thing, a game in which a farthing or other piece of money is pitched into a hole.
chuckle, *n.* *chuk*-kl, the call of a hen; a short suppressed laugh in amusement, triumph or derision: *v.i.* to cackle; to laugh in a suppressed or broken manner; to feel inward triumph or exultation: *v.t.* to call, as a hen her chickens. (Imit.)
chucklehead, *n.* *chuk*-kl-hed, one with a large head; a booby.
chuckle-headed, *a.* *chuk*-kl-hed-ed, thick-headed.
chuckling, *n.* *chuk*-kl-ling, suppressed, amused, self-satisfied, self-exultant laughter.
chuddar, *n.* *chud*-ar, a wool shawl worn by women of N. India; a cloth laid on a Mohammedan tomb; a sheet to sleep on [Anglo-Indian]. (Hind. *chadar*, a square of cloth.)
chuff, *n.* chuf, a clown; a coarse, heavy, surly fellow. (Dial. Eng.)
chuffy, *a.* *chuf*-e, bloated; swollen out, especially in the cheeks; clownish; surly; angry.
chug, *v.i.* chug, to emit a series of dull explosive sounds. **to chug along,** to proceed to this accompaniment [Coll.].
chukker, *n.* *chuk*-ker, a period of play at polo.
chum, *n.* chum, one who occupies the same room or rooms; an intimate familiar friend: *v.i.* to occupy a room or rooms with another; to mess with another. (Origin unknown.)
chummery, *n.* *chum*-er-re, intimacy; friendship; the rooms of chums.
chummy, *a.* *chum*-e, cordially fraternal; matey; intimate.
chump, *n.* chump, a short, thick, heavy piece of wood; the thick end; a stupid fellow. **off his chump,** out of his right mind. (Origin unknown.)
chump-end, *n.* chump-end, the thick end, esp. of a loin of mutton or veal.
chunk, *n.* chunk, a thick lump of anything.
chupatty, *n.* chu-*pat*-te, unleavened bread in a thin cake. (Hind. *chapati*.)
★**church,** *n.* church, a building consecrated to Christian worship and ordinances; the collective body of Christians; a particular body of Christians; the followers of Christ in a particular city or province; the clergy, in distinction from the laity; the communicants of a congregation [U.S.A.]; divine service; ecclesiastical authority: *v.t.* to assist, as a priest, a woman after childbirth in the office of returning thanks in the church; in Scotland, to escort to church, as a bride after her marriage: *a.* ecclesiastical; pertaining to church. **Church Army,** a Church of England organization for social and evangelistic work among the poor. **Church catholic,** the collective body of Christians in their unity from the commencement. **Church invisible,** the collective body of Christians in heaven and on earth. **Church militant,** the body of Christians regarded as warring against spiritual evil of all kinds. **Church triumphant,** Christians in heaven. (A.S. *circe*.)
church-ale, *n.* *church*-ale, a wake or feast connected with a church, esp. a dedication festival.
church-burial, *n.* church-*be*-re-al, burial according to the rites of a church.
church-court, *n.* church-*koart*, a court trying ecclesiastical suits.
churched, *a.* churchd, presented at church, esp. in the office of churching.
church-goer, *n.* *church*-go-er, one who habitually attends church.
church-going, *a.* *church*-go-ing, usually attending church; calling to church.
churching, *n.* *church*-ing, the act of returning thanks in church on the part of a woman after her confinement; presentation in church.
churchism, *n.* *church*-izm, ecclesiasticism; rigid adherence to church-forms.
churchite, *n.* *church*-ite, a hydrous cerium calcium phosphate. (Sir A. H. *Church*, Eng. chemist, *d.* 1915.)
church-land, *n.* *church*-land, land belonging to the church.
churchman, *n.* *church*-man, an ecclesiastic; a member of a state or national church, as the Church of England; in the U.S.A., an episcopalian.
churchmanly, *a.* *church*-man-le, like a churchman.
churchmanship, *n.* *church*-man-ship, state of being a churchman, or of belonging to the church.
church-music, *n.* *church*-mew-zik, a musical service in a church; music suited to church service.
church-owl, *n.* *church*-owl, the common barn-owl.
church-service, *n.* *church*-ser-vis, religious service in a church; a book containing Common Prayer and the scriptural lessons.
church-text, *n.* *church*-tekst, a decorative black-letter type [Print.].
churchwarden, *n.* church-*wawr*-den, one of two officials elected in every Anglican parish to take care of the church property, enforce decorum in church, and act as the legal representatives of the parish; a long-stemmed clay pipe [Coll.].
church-way, *n.* *church*-way, a road or pathway that leads to or round a church.
church-work, *n.* *church*-wurk, work for or on a church; work in connection with the church.
churchy, *a.* *church*-e, relating to or characteristic of the church; fanatically devoted to ecclesiasticism.
churchyard, *n.* *church*-yard, the consecrated ground adjoining a church in which the dead are buried.
churinga, *n.* chu-*ring*-ga, a totemistic amulet of the Australian aborigines. (Native name.)
churl, *n.* churl, a rude, surly, ill-bred man; a rustic; a miser; a niggard. (A.S. *ceorl*, a countryman.)
churlish, *a.* *churl*-ish, rude; surly; sullen; uncivil; ill-natured; selfish; untractable.
churlishly, *ad.* *churl*-ish-le, in a churlish manner.
churlishness, *n.* *churl*-ish-ness, the quality of being churlish.
churly, *a.* *churl*-e, churlish.
churn, *n.* churn, a vessel in which milk or cream is agitated for the production of butter; a large can for the transportation of milk: *v.t.* to agitate in a churn for the production of butter; to agitate with violence or continued motion: *v.i.* to make butter by churning; to swirl about and foam (of waves). (A.S. *cyrin*.)
churning, *n.* *churn*-ing, the operation of churning; as much butter as is made at one operation.
churn-staff, *n.* *churn*-stahf, a staff used in churning.
churr, *v.i.* and *n.* chur, chirr.
churrworm, *n.* *chur*-wurm, the mole-cricket.
chut, *int.* chut, expressing impatience or annoyance.
chute, *n.* shoot, a fall, as in a rapid, for floating timber down; an inclined trough for conveying parcels, grain, etc., to a lower level. **water chute,** a shallow stream on a sloping wooden floor used for tobogganing into water. (Fr.)
chutney, *n.* *chut*-ne, an E. Indian condiment used

with curry, generally made from spices, fruits, and vinegar.
chylaceous, *a.* ky-*lay*-shus, chylous; like chyle.
chyle, *n.* kile, a milky fluid, separated in the small intestines from the chyme by its action on the pancreatic juice and the bile, which when absorbed by the lacteal vessels is gradually assimilated into blood [Phys.]. (Gr. *chylos*, juice, from *cheo*, flow.)
chylifactive, *a.* kile-if-*ak*-tiv, forming or changing into chyle; having the power to make chyle.
chyliferous, *a.* kile-*if*-er-us, transmitting chyle. (Gr. *chylos*, and L. *fero*, bear.)
chylific, *a.* kile-*if*-ik, chylifactive.
chylification, *n.* kile-if-ik-*ay*-shon, the process of making chyle. (Gr. *chylos*, and L. *facio*, make.)
chylificatory, *a.* *kile*-if-ik-*ay*-tor-e, chylifactive.
chylify, *v.t.* *kile*-i-fy, to convert into chyle.
chylopoietic, *a.* kile-o-poy-*et*-ik, relating to the production of chyle.
chylous, *a.* *kile*-us, pertaining to or consisting of chyle.
chyluria, *n.* kile-*yew*-re-a, a condition of having chyle in the urine. (Gr. *chylos*, and *ouron*, urine.)
chyme, *n.* kime, the pulpy mass into which the food is converted in the stomach prior to the separation of the chyle. (Gr. *chymos*, juice.)
chymic, *a.* *kim*-ik, chemical.
chymification, *n.* *ky*-mif-ik-*ay*-shon, the process of becoming or being formed into chyme.
chymify, *v.t.* and *v.i.* *ky*-mif-y, to form into or to become chyme.
chymist, *n.* *kim*-ist, chemist.
chymous, *a.* *kime*-us, relating to or consisting of chyme.
cibol, *n.* *sib*-ol, a chibol, or Welsh onion.
ciborium, *n.* se-*baw*-re-um, a baldachin [Arch.]; the vessel in which the eucharist is kept, or a shrine for this [Eccles.]. (L., a drinking cup.)
cicada, *n.* se-*kay*-da, a group of homopterous insects remarkable for the loud sounds they emit from a complicated apparatus of membranes and fibres situated under the abdomen. (L.)
cicala, *n.* se-*kah*-la, a cicada.
cicatrice, *n.* *sik*-a-tris, a scar remaining after a wound or ulcer is healed. (L. *cicatrix*, scar.)
cicatricial, *a.* sik-a-*trish*-al, pertaining to a cicatrice.
cicatricose, *a.* sik-*at*-re-kohs, marked with scars [Bot.].
cicatricle, *n.* sik-*at*-re-kl, a cicatricula.
cicatricula, *n.* sik-a-*trik*-yew-la, the germinating or fœtal point in the embryo of a seed or the yolk of an egg. (L. diminutive of *cicatrix*.)
cicatrisive, *a.* sik-a-*try*-siv, inducing a cicatrice.
cicatrix, *n.* *sik*-a-triks, a cicatrice. (L.)
cicatrizant, *n.* sik-a-*try*-zant, a cicatrisive application.
cicatrization, *n.* sik-a-try-*zay*-shon, the process of forming a cicatrice; the state of being cicatrized.
cicatrize, *v.t.* *sik*-a-trize, to heal a wound or ulcer by inducing the formation of a skin or cicatrix: *v.i.* to be healed or skin over.
cicatrose, *a.* *sik*-a-troze, cicatricose.
cicely, *n.* *sis*-e-le, the plant *Myrrhis odorata*, of the parsley family. (L. *seselis*.)
cicerone, *n.* che-chay-*roh*-nay *or* sis-er-*oh*-ne (*pl.* **ciceroni**), a guide; one who shows strangers the curiosities of a place. (It., from L. *Cicero*.)
Ciceronian, *a.* sis-er-*roh*-ne-an, resembling Cicero in style; classical or eloquent.
Ciceronianism, *n.* sis-er-*oh*-ne-an-izm, Ciceronian style or mode of expression.
cichlid, *n.* *sik*-lid, any one of a large family of spiny-finned fishes found in the fresh and brackish waters of the tropics.
cichoraceous, *a.* sik-o-*ray*-shus, pertaining to or resembling the chicory family of plants.
cicisbeism, *n.* che-chiz-*bee*-izm *or* se-*siz*-be-izm, the practice of a cicisbeo.
cicisbeo, *n.* che-chiz-*bee*-o *or* se-siz-*bee*-o, one who dangles about a married woman with the devotion of a lover; a *cavaliere servente*. (It.)
cicuta, *n.* se-*kew*-ta, any plant of the genus comprising cow-bane or water-hemlock, *C. virosa*. (L.)
cid, *n.* sid, a chief; a commander; esp. (*cap.*) the Spanish hero, Rodrigo Diaz, who fought the Moors in the 11th cent., or an epic about him. (Sp.)
cider, *n.* *sy*-der, the fermented juice of the apple (formerly applied to strong liquor). **cider brandy,** a distillation from cider. (Fr. *cidre*.)
ciderkin, *n.* *sy*-der-kin, a liquor from apples after the juice has been expressed for cider.
ci-devant, *a.* (App.), late; former. (Fr., formerly.)
cierge, *n.* seerj, a wax candle used in religious processions. (Fr. from L. *cera*, wax.)
cigar, *n.* se-*gar*, a small roll of tobacco-leaves, rounded off at the end to be inserted in the mouth for smoking. (Sp. *cigarro*.)
cigarette, *n.* sig-a-*ret*, finely cut tobacco rolled in paper for smoking.
cigar-holder, *n.* se-*gar*-hold-er, a mouthpiece for a cigar.
cigar-shaped, *a.* se-*gar*-shaypt, of cylindrical form with tapering extremities.
cilery, *n.* *sil*-er-e, carved ornamental foliage, etc. at the head of columns [Arch.]. (Perhaps L. *celare*, to conceal.)
cilia, *n.pl.* *sil*-e-a, the eyelashes; long hairs on leaves [Bot.]; minute vibratile filaments on the lower invertebrates [Zool.]. (L.)
ciliary, *a.* *sil*-ya-re, pertaining to the eyelids or to cilia.
ciliate, *a.* *sil*-e-at, furnished with cilia.
cilice, *n.* *sil*-is, hair-cloth, or a penitential garment made of this. (Gr. *kilikion*, of Cilician goat's hair.)
cilicious, *a.* sil-*ish*-us, made of goat's hair.
ciliform, *a.* *sil*-e-form, like cilia for fineness and number.
ciliograde, *a.* *sil*-e-o-grade, moving by means of cilia [Zool.].
Cimbric, *a.* *sim*-brik, pertaining to the Cimbri, a former people of N. Germany: *n.* the language of the Cimbri.
cimeter, *n.* *sim*-e-ter, a scimitar.
cimex, *n.* *sy*-meks, an insect of the genus containing the bed-bug, *C. lectularius*. (L.)
Cimmerian, *a.* sim-*meer*-re-an, pertaining to the Cimmerii, or their country—a district, variously localized, and fabled to have been unvisited by a single ray of the light of the sun; extremely dark.
cimolite, *n.* *sim*-o-lite, a clay-like hydrous aluminium silicate. (L. *cimolia*.)
cinch, *n.* sinch, an American game of cards; a saddle-girth; a certainty, or sure thing [Slang]. (Sp. *cincha*, cincture.)
Cinchona, *n.* sin-*koh*-na, a genus of Andesian trees, several of which yield Peruvian bark, or Jesuit's bark, the source of quinine. (Countess of *Chinchon*, vicereine of Peru in 1638.)
cinchonaceous, *a.* sin-ko-*nay*-shus, pertaining to or resembling cinchona.
cinchonate, *n.* *sin*-ko-nate, a salt of cinchonic acid.
cinchonic, *a.* sin-*kon*-ik, obtained from cinchona bark: *n.* a medicinal preparation containing cinchona.
cinchonine, *n.* *sin*-ko-nyn, an alkaloid obtained from several species of *Cinchona*.
cinchonism, *n.* *sin*-ko-nizm, a disordered state of the body due to overdoses of quinine.
Cincinnatus, *n.* sin-se-*nay*-tus, in popular use, a great statesman called from retirement to aid his nation in a crisis. (From the Roman dictator, *Cincinnatus*.)
cincture, *n.* *sink*-tewr, a belt, girdle, or band; an enclosure; a ring or fillet at the top and bottom of the shaft of a column [Arch.]: *v.t.* to encircle; to encompass. (L. *cinctura*.)
cinder, *n.* *sin*-der, anything burnt but not reduced to ashes; a partly burnt piece of coal; the refuse of burnt coal or wood. (A.S. *sinder*.)
Cinderella, *n.* *sin*-der-*rel*-la, any person whose beauty or goodness of character escapes general notice. **Cinderella-dance,** a dance ceasing at midnight. (From the fairy-story.)
cinder-path, *n.* *sin*-der-pahth, a running track made of or surfaced with cinders.
cinder-sifter, *n.* *sin*-der-sift-er, a household utensil for sifting cinders from ashes.
cindery, *a.* *sin*-der-re, like or composed of cinders.
cine-camera, *n.* sin-e-*kam*-er-ra, a photographic camera for taking motion pictures.
cinema, *n.* *sin*-e-ma, a public building in which cinematographic films are shown; a motion-picture theatre; the pictures or movies [Coll.].
cinematize, *v.t.* *sin*-e-ma-tyz, to adapt (a novel, play, etc.) for exhibition as a film.
cinematograph, *n.* sin-e-*mat*-o-graf, a projector

for showing photographs of moving objects; a camera for taking such photographs; a cinema: *v.t.* and *i.* to photograph with a cinematograph. (Gr. *kinema*, motion, *grapho*, depict.)

cinematographer, *n.* *sin*-e-ma-*tog*-ra-fer, one who takes, or directs the taking of, motion-pictures.

cinematographic, *a.* *sin*-e-mat-o-*graf*-ik, pertaining to or displayed by cinematography.

cinematography, *n.* *sin*-e-ma-*tog*-ra-fe, the science and art of taking and reproducing motion-pictures.

cinemize, *v.t.* *sin*-e-myz, to cinematize.

cinenchyma, *n.* sin-en-*ky*-ma, laticiferous tissue of plants.

Cineraria, *n.* sin-er-*rare*-re-a, a South African genus of composite plants. (L. *cinerarius*, of ashes.)

cinerarium, *n.* sin-er-*rare*-re-um, a building in which the ashes of the cremated dead are kept.

cinerary, *a.* *sin*-er-a-re, pertaining to ashes. **cinerary urn,** a vase used to hold the ashes of the dead, esp. when cremated. (L. *cinerarius*.)

cineration, *n.* sin-er-*ray*-shon, reduction to ashes.

cinerator, *n.* *sin*-er-ray-tor, an incinerator, esp. at a crematorium.

cinereous, *a.* se-*neer*-re-us, ash-coloured; like ashes.

cineritious, *a.* sin-er-*rish*-us, ash-coloured; pertaining to the grey matter of the brain. [Anat.].

cine-theodolite, *n.* sin-e-the-*od*-o-lyt, an instrument that records on a photographic film the position of bursts of projectiles fired from anti-aircraft guns.

Cingalese, *n.* sing-ga-*leez*, a native or the natives of Ceylon: *a.* pertaining to Ceylon, or its people.

cingle, *n.* *sing*-gl, a girth for a horse. (O.Fr. *cingle*.)

cingulum, *n.* *sing*-gew-lum, the band round the waist of a priest's alb; any band or zone, such as the carapace of an armadillo. (L.)

cinnabar, *n.* *sin*-na-bar, native mercuric sulphide, the principal ore of mercury; vermilion. (L. *cinnabaris*, vermilion.)

cinnabarine, *a.* *sin*-na-ba-rin, pertaining to, consisting of, or containing cinnabar.

cinnamic, *a.* sin-*nam*-ik, cinnamonic.

cinnamon, *n.* *sin*-na-mon, the aromatic inner bark of *Cinnamomum zeylanicum*, an East Indian tree. (L. *cinnamōmum*.)

cinnamonic, *a.* sin-na-*mon*-ik, obtained from cinnamon.

cinnamon-stone, *n.* *sin*-na-mon-stone, essonite, a yellowish red garnet.

cinque, *n.* sink, five; a five at cards or dice. **Cinque Ports,** the five English ports of Dover, Sandwich, Hastings, Romney, and Hythe, to which Winchelsea, Rye, and others were added, that enjoyed special privileges in return for providing a navy. (Fr. *cinq*.)

cinquecentist, *n.* ching-kwe-*chen*-tist, an artist or writer of the Italian 16th-century school, or one who models his style upon that school. (It.)

cinquecento, *n.* ching-kwe-*chen*-to, the 16th century (A.D. 1501–1600) in Italian art and literature. (It., 500—*mil.* 1000, being understood.)

cinquefoil, *n.* *sink*-foyl, the creeping potentilla, *Potentilla reptans*, and other plants of this genus; an ornamental foliation, in five compartments, with five points or cusps, used in windows, etc. [Arch.]. (Fr. *cinque*, L. *folium*, a leaf.)

cinquepace, *n.* *sink*-pace, a slow-movement dance.

cinque-spotted, *a.* *sink*-spot-ted, having five spots.

cintre, *n.* *sin*-ter, a centering [Arch.].

cipher, *n.* *sy*-fer, the arithmetical character 0; any arithmetical figure; a character in general; an intertexture of letters, as the initials of a name; a device; a secret way of writing, consisting of an agreed code that is unintelligible without the key; something written in this; a thing of no consequence or importance; a nonentity: *v.i.* to compute by figures: *v.t.* to write in occult characters; to write in code or cipher. (O.Fr. *cifre*.)

ciphering, *n.* *sy*-fer-ing, the art of writing in code: *a.* for ciphering in or on.

cipher-key, *n.* *sy*-fer-kee, a key for deciphering coded writings.

cipolin, *n.* *sip*-o-lin, a green marble with white zones, like the section of an onion. (It. *cipolla*, an onion.)

cippus, *n.* *sip*-pus, a small monumental column, bearing an inscription or epitaph. (L.)

circ, *n.* serk, a prehistoric stone circle.

circar, *n.* *ser*-kar, in Hindustan, a district or province under Mogul domination. (Hind.)

Circassian, *a.* ser-*kas*-se-an, pertaining to Circassia: *n.* a native of Circassia; a kind of woollen cloth.

Circe, *n.* *ser*-se, an enchantress; any fascinating woman. (A sorceress of Greek myth.)

Circean, *a.* ser-*see*-an, magically and fatally infatuating. (From *Circe*.)

circensian, *a.* ser-*sen*-she-an, pertaining to the circus in ancient Rome. (L. *circensis*.)

circinate, *a.* *ser*-sin-ate, rolled in spirally downwards, as in ferns [Bot.]. (L. *circinus* compasses.)

★**circle,** *n.* *ser*-kl, a plane figure comprehended by a line, every part of which is equally distant from a point within it, called the centre [Geom.]; a circular line or anything in that form; a round body; a circular enclosure; a ring; compass; circuit; a series ending where it begins, and perpetually repeated; a number of persons, or things, or ideas considered as connected by some central tie or bond or a common interest; a complete system; a territorial division; a gallery in a theatre; an inconclusive form of argument, in which a proposition is disguisedly employed to prove itself [Logic]: *v.t.* to move round; to encircle: *v.i.* to move round in a circle; to revolve. **vicious circle,** *see* **vicious.** (A.S. *circul*.)

circled, *a.* *ser*-kld, having the form of a circle; marked with a circle; encircled.

circlet, *n.* *ser*-klet, a small circle; a finger-ring.

circlewise, *ad.* *ser*-kl-wize, in a circle.

circuit, *n.* *ser*-kit, the act of moving or passing round; way round about; the space enclosed in a circle, or within certain limits; the path of electric action; that which encircles, or the boundary; the periodical visitation of a judge or judges for holding assizes; the district in which they administer justice; an associated group of nonconformist chapels; a chain of theatres, etc., under one management: *v.t.* and *i.* to move in a circle; to go round. **open circuit,** an electric current not closed upon itself so that a current cannot flow all round it [Elect.]. **reflex circuit,** a circuit arranged so that a single valve gives both high-frequency and low-frequency amplification [Wire.]. (Fr.)

circuiteer, *n.* *ser*-ke-*teer*, one, esp. a judge or lawyer, who travels on a circuit.

circuitous, *a.* ser-*kew*-e-tus, roundabout; indirect.

circuitously, *ad.* ser-*kew*-e-tus-le, in a circuitous manner.

circuity, *n.* ser-*kew*-e-te, indirect proceeding.

circulable, *a.* *ser*-kew-la-bl, that may be circulated.

circular, *a.* *ser*-kew-lar, pertaining to or in the shape of a circle; round; forming part of a circle; performed in a circle, so as to return back; ending in itself; addressed to a number of persons, as a circular letter: *n.* a letter, or printed notice, of which a copy is sent to many persons. **circular instrument,** one graduated for the whole circle. **circular lines,** lines of sines, tangents, and secants, on the plane scale and sector. **circular note,** an order for payment on demand in connection with a letter of credit, issued by bankers for customers travelling abroad. **circular numbers,** those whose powers terminate in the same digits as the roots. (L. *circulus*.)

circularity, *n.* ser-kew-*la*-re-te, the state of being circular.

circularize, *v.t.* *ser*-kew-la-rize, to appeal to by means of circulars; to send circulars to.

circularly, *ad.* *ser*-kew-lar-le, in a circular manner.

circulate, *v.i.* *ser*-kew-late, to move round, as blood in the body; to traverse certain channels, as sap in plants; to pass from point to point, or hand to hand, as money; to be spread or diffused about: *v.t.* to cause to pass from place to place, or from person to person; to spread. (L. *circulatus*, make round.)

circulating, *a.* *ser*-kew-lay-ting, moving in a circle, or in prescribed channels; passing from one to another; passing current; recurring [Math.]. **circulating decimal,** a decimal in which one or more figures are constantly repeated in the same order. **circulating library,** a library from which books are lent to subscribers. **circulating medium,** the currency of a country, whether money, bank notes, or any other articles.

circulation, *n.* ser-kew-*lay*-shon, the act of circulating; the state of being circulated; a currency

or circulating medium; diffusion; extent of diffusion; the average number of copies of a newspaper or other publication sold during a given period. **circulation of the blood,** the natural motion of the blood in the living animal. (Fr.)
circulative, *a.* *ser*-kew-la-tiv, circulating, promoting, or producing circulation.
circulator, *n.* *ser*-kew-lay-tor, that which circulates; a recurring decimal [Math.].
circulatory, *a.* *ser*-kew-lay-to-re, circular; circulating.
circum-, *ser*-kum, a Latin prefix signifying around, about, on all sides, in a circle.
circumambages, *n.pl.* *ser*-kum-*am*-ba-jez, circumlocutory methods or style of speech.
circumambiency, *n.* ser-kum-*am*-be-an-se, the state or act of going round; environment.
circumambient, *a.* ser-kum-*am*-be-ent, going round about; surrounding.
circumambulate, *v.i.* ser-kum-*am*-bew-late, to walk around. (L. *ambulatus*, walked.)
circumambulation, *n.* *ser*-kum-am-bew-*lay*-shon, the act of walking around.
circumambulatory, *a.* *ser*-kum-am-bew-*lay*-to-re, marked by circumambulation; indirect.
circumbendibus, *n.* ser-kum-*ben*-de-bus, circuity; circumlocution. (Humorous formation.)
circumcise, *v.t.* *ser*-kum-size, to cut off the foreskin, as among the Jews; to mortify the flesh; to purify. (L. *circumcisus*, cut round.)
circumciser, *n.* *ser*-kum-size-er, one who circumcises.
circumcision, *n.* ser-kum-*sizh*-on, the act of circumcising, esp. as a religious rite among the Jews, Moslems, and certain Eastern nations.
circumclusion, *n.* ser-kum-*kloo*-zhon, the act of enclosing by surrounding; a method of compressing an artery [Surg.].
circumduct, *v.t.* *ser*-kum-dukt, to nullify [Law]; to declare elapsed [Scots Law]. (L. *ductum*, lead.)
circumduction, *n.* ser-kum-*duk*-shon, a leading about; the act of circumducting [Law].
circumference, *n.* ser-*kum*-fe-rence, the line that bounds a circle, or that encompasses any figure; the periphery; circuit. (L. *circumferentia*.)
circumferential, *a.* ser-kum-fe-*ren*-shal, pertaining to the circumference.
circumferentor, *n.* ser-kum-fe-*ren*-tor, a surveyor's horizontal compass.
circumflex, *n.* *ser*-kum-fleks, a mark thus (^) to indicate accent, quantity, contraction, etc. [Gram.]: *v.t.* to mark or pronounce with a circumflex: *a.* bent; curving round. (L. *flecto*, bend.)
circumflexion, *n.* ser-kum-*flek*-shon, circular or winding course; marking or pronouncing with a circumflex.
circumfluence, *n.* ser-*kum*-floo-ence, a flowing round on all sides; an enclosure of waters.
circumfluent, *a.* ser-*kum*-floo-ent, flowing around; encompassing, as a fluid. (L. *fluens*, flowing.)
circumfluous, *a.* ser-*kum*-floo-us, circumfluent.
circumfuse, *v.t.* *ser*-kum-fewz, to pour around, as a fluid; to spread around. (L. *fusum*, poured.)
circumfusion, *n.* ser-kum-*few*-zhon, the act of circumfusing; the state of being circumfused.
circumgyrate, *v.t.* ser-kum-*jire*-rate, to whirl; to roll or turn round. (L. *gyrus*, a circle.)
circumgyration, *n.* ser-kum-jire-*ray*-shon, the act of circumgyrating; the turning on an axis.
circumincession, *n.* ser-kum-in-*sesh*-on, the existence of each person of the Trinity in the others. (L., going round, rotating.)
circumjacent, *a.* ser-kum-*jay*-sent, lying round anything; bordering. (L. *jacens*, lying.)
circumlittoral, *a.* ser-kum-*lit*-to-ral, adjacent to or along the sea-shore. (L. *littoralis*, pertaining to the shore.)
circumlocution, *n.* *ser*-kum-lo-*kew*-shon, the use of evasive or indirect language, or of too many words to express an idea. (L. *locutio*, speaking.)
circumlocutory, *a.* ser-kum-*lok*-yew-to-re, involving circumlocution; periphrastic.
circum-meridian, *a.* ser-kum-me-*rid*-e-an, situated or occurring near the meridian [Astron.].
circummured, *a.* ser-kum-*mewrd*, walled round.
circumnavigable, *a.* ser-kum-*nav*-e-ga-bl, that may be sailed round.
circumnavigate, *v.t.* ser-kum-*nav*-e-gate, to sail completely round. (L. *circumnavigatus*.)
circumnavigation, *n.* ser-kum-nav-e-*gay*-shon, the act of sailing round, especially round the globe.
circumnavigator, *n.* ser-kum-*nav*-e-gay-tor, one who sails round; one who has sailed round the globe.
circumnutation, *n.* ser-kum-new-*tay*-shon, the tendency in growing plants to incline successively to all points of the compass.
circumoral, *a.* ser-kum-*aw*-ral, surrounding or put round the mouth.
circumpolar, *a.* ser-kum-*poh*-lar, round or near either the celestial or terrestrial north or south pole: *n.* a star situated within a few degrees of either pole; one which, at a given locality, never rises or sets.
circumpose, *v.t.* ser-kum-*poze*, to place round.
circumposition, *n.* ser-kum-po-*zish*-on, the act of placing around, or state of being so placed.
circumrotation, *n.* ser-kum-ro-*tay*-shon, the act of revolving or rotating; the state of being whirled round. (L. *rota*, a wheel.)
circumrotatory, *a.* ser-kum-*roh*-ta-to-re, pertaining to circumrotation; whirling round.
circumscissile, *a.* ser-kum-*sis*-sile, opening by a transverse circular separation of the sides of the ovary [Bot.]. (L. *scissum*, cut.)
circumscribable, *a.* ser-kum-*skribe*-a-bl, capable of being circumscribed.
circumscribe, *v.t.* *ser*-kum-skribe, to draw round; to limit; to enclose; to define [Logic]. (L. *scribo*, write.)
circumscriber, *n.* ser-kum-*skribe*-er, one who circumscribes.
circumscriptible, *a.* ser-kum-*skrip*-te-bl, circumscribable.
circumscription, *n.* ser-kum-*skrip*-shon, the act of circumscribing; limitation; bounding line; a circular inscription; a definition.
circumscriptive, *a.* ser-kum-*skrip*-tiv, limiting; limited.
circumscriptively, *ad.* ser-kum-*skrip*-tiv-le, in a limited manner.
circumsolar, *a.* ser-kum-*soh*-lar, near or around the sun.
circumspect, *a.* *ser*-kum-spekt, watchful on all sides; wary; prudent. (L. *circumspectus*, cautious.)
circumspection, *n.* ser-kum-*spek*-shon, careful consideration beforehand; thoughtfulness.
circumspective, *a.* ser-kum-*spek*-tiv, employing circumspection.
circumspectly, *ad.* *ser*-kum-spekt-le, in a circumspect manner.
circumspectness, *n.* *ser*-kum-spekt-ness, the quality of being circumspect.
circumstance, *n.* *ser*-kum-stans, something attending, appendant, or relative to a fact or case; incident; event; pomp or fuss; *pl.* condition in regard to worldly estate; situation, state of things: *v.t.* to place in a particular situation. (O.Fr. *circonstance*.)
circumstanced, *a.* *ser*-kum-stanst, situated.
circumstantial, *a.* ser-kum-*stan*-shal, not direct; incidental; depending on circumstances; detailed; minute; particular: *n.* a thing incidental but not essential. **circumstantial evidence,** inferential, as distinct from direct and positive, evidence; that which is obtained from circumstances which are necessarily or usually relative to similar cases.
circumstantiality, *n.* ser-kum-*stan*-she-*al*-e-te, the state of being circumstantial.
circumstantially, *ad.* ser-kum-*stan*-sha-le, in a circumstantial manner.
circumstantiate, *v.t.* ser-kum-*stan*-she-ate, to set forth, prove, or confirm by circumstances; to verify.
circumvallate, *v.t.* ser-kum-*val*-late, to surround with a rampart. (L. *vallum*, a rampart.)
circumvallation, *n.* ser-kum-va-*lay*-shon, the throwing up of fortifications around a place; such a fortification.
circumvent, *v.t.* ser-kum-*vent*, to overreach; to outwit; to deceive; to cheat. (L. *circumventus*.)
circumvention, *n.* ser-kum-*ven*-shon, the act of circumventing; outwitting.
circumvolation, *n.* *ser*-kum-vo-*lay*-shon, flying round.
circumvolution, *n.* ser-kum-vo-*lew*-shon, the act of rolling round; the state of being rolled round; a winding; anything winding or tortuous; a coil.

circumvolve, *v.t.* and *v.i.* ser-kum-*volv*, to roll or move round; to revolve. (L. *volvo*, roll.)
circus, *n. ser*-kus, a large oblong edifice, with an open space in the centre, surrounded by tiers of seats, in which public games, sports, and combats were exhibited [Rom. Antiq.]; a place for the exhibition of horsemanship, acrobatics, etc.; a troupe of performers at such; a noisy group of persons, or one at a common task [Slang]; a raiding-party, an aeroplane squadron [Mil. slang]; a circular space, esp. at an intersection of streets. (L.)
cirl-bunting, *n. serl*-bunt-ing, the small migratory bird, *Emberiza cirlus*. (It. *zarlare*, to twitter, *bunting*.)
cirque, *n.* serk *or* seerk, an amphitheatre; a circular space; a natural arena at the head of a valley. (Fr.)
cirrhosis, *n.* se-*roh*-sis, a yellow morbid secretion of the liver; a disease of the liver involving increase of fibrous tissue. (Gr. *kirrhos*, yellowish.)
cirrhotic, *a.* se-*rot*-ik, like, or affected with, cirrhosis.
cirri, *n.pl. se*-ry, *pl.* of **cirrus.**
cirriferous, *a.* se-*rif*-er-rus, bearing or producing tendrils. (L. *cirrus*, and *fero*, bear.)
cirriform, *a. se*-re-form, formed like a tendril.
cirrigrade, *a. se*-re-grade, moving by means of cirri [Zool.].
cirripede, *n. se*-re-pede, one of the *Cirripedia*, a subclass of marine crustacea including the barnacles and acorn-shells. (L. *cirrus*, and *pes*, the foot.)
cirro-cumulus, *n. se*-ro-*kew*-mew-lus, a formation of cloud broken up into small fleecy masses. (L. *cumulus*, a heap.)
cirrose, *a. se*-rohs, terminating or coiled in a tendril [Bot.].; furnished with cirri [Zool.]; like cirrus clouds [Meteor.].
cirro-stratus, *n. se*-ro-*stray*-tus, a formation of cloud in fleecy sheets. (L. *stratus*, laid flat.)
cirrous, *a. se*-rus, cirrose.
cirrus, *n. se*-rus (*pl.* **cirri**), a tendril [Bot.]; a curled filament [Zool.]; a cloud like a distended lock of hair. (L., a curl of hair.)
cis-, sis, a Latin prefix, signifying on this side.
cisalpine, *a.* sis-*al*-pine, on the Roman or south side of the Alps (opposed to transalpine).
cisatlantic, *a.* sis-at-*lan*-tik, on this side of the Atlantic (opposed to transatlantic).
cisco, *n. sis*-ko, the lake-herring, *Leucichthys artedi* and related food-fishes of the Great Lakes of N. America.
ciselure, *n. seez*-loor, chasing; chased metal work. (Fr. *ciseler*, to carve.)
cis-Leithan, *a.* sis-*lite*-an, Austrian, not Hungarian; lying west of the R. Leitha, the former dividing line.
cismontane, *a.* sis-*mon*-tane, on the north side of the Alps (contrasted with ultramontane).
cispadane, *a.* sis-*pay*-dane, on the south side of the R. Po. (L. *Padanus*, the Po.)
cissoid, *n. sis*-soyd, a curve, invented by Diocles, to trisect a plane angle and to construct two geometric means between two given straight lines [Geom.]. (Gr. *kissos*, ivy, *eidos*, form.)
cissy, *n. sis*-e, an effeminate youth or man [Slang]. (*Sister*.)
cist, *n.* sist, prehistoric tomb consisting of rows of stones on edge covered with rough slabs [Archæol.]; a chest for the sacred utensils used in the ancient Greek mysteries. (L., a chest.)
Cistercian, *n.* sis-*ter*-shan, a monk or member of a reformed order of Benedictines founded by St. Bernard of Clairvaux, also known as Bernardines. (*Cistercium*, now Citeaux, France.)
cistern, *n. sis*-tern, a receptacle for water or other liquids; a reservoir; a place containing water. (Fr. *cisterne*.)
cistus, *n. sis*-tus, a plant of the genus *Cistus* including the rock-rose. (Gr. *kistos*, rock-rose.)
cistvaen, *n. kist*-vay-en, a kistvaen.
cit, *n.* sit, a citizen (in contempt).
citable, *a. sy*-ta-bl, that may be cited or quoted.
citadel, *n. sit*-a-del, a fortress in or near a city; the keep; the strongest fortified position. (Fr. *citadelle*.)
citation, *n.* sy-*tay*-shon, a summons to appear in court; quotation; mention; reference; mention (for meritorious service, etc.) in orders or dispatches [Mil., U.S.A.]. (L. *citatus*, cited.)
citatory, *a. sy*-ta-to-re, citing; in the form of a citation.
cite, *v.t.* site, to summon to answer in a court: to quote; to refer to, esp. as an authority. (L. *cito*, call.)
cithara, *n. sith*-a-ra, a stringed instrument; the ancient Greek lyre. (Gr.)
citharist, *a. sith*-a-rist, a player on the cithara.
cither, *n. sith*-er, a zither, or cithern.
cithern, *n. sith*-ern, a form of lute used in the Middle Ages. (O.Fr. *guiterne*, guitar.)
citied, *a. sit*-ed, containing cities.
citified, *a. sit*-e-fyd, rendered city-like; having the habits or peculiarities of a city-dweller.
citigrade, *a. sit*-e-grade, moving swiftly (esp. of certain spiders) [Zool.]. (L. *citus*, quick, *gradus*, step.)
citizen, *n. sit*-e-zn, an inhabitant of a city; a freeman of a city; a townsman; a member of a sovereign state in the enjoyment of full political rights: *a.* having the character of a citizen. **citizen soldier,** a part-time or non-professional soldier; a volunteer. (Fr. *citoyen*.)
citizenize, *v.t. sit*-e-zn-ize, to make a citizen of.
citizenship, *n. sit*-e-zn-ship, the rank of a citizen; the state of being a citizen.
citole, *n. sit*-ohl, a mediæval stringed instrument of the lute family; a cithern.
citrate, *n. sit*-rate, a salt of citric acid [Chem.].
citric, *a. sit*-rik, obtained from lemons or citrons. **citric acid,** the acid from which lemons and other acid fruits derive their sourness.
citril, *n. sit*-ril, a beautiful song finch of Italy, *Chrysomitris citrinella*. (It. *citrinella*.)
citrine, *a. sit*-rin, like a citron; greenish-yellow: *n.* a yellow pellucid variety of quartz. (Fr. *citrin*.)
citron, *n. sit*-ron, the fruit of *Citrus medica*, resembling the lemon but larger in size. **citron water,** a liquor distilled from citron-rind. (Fr.)
citronella, *n.* sit-ro-*nel*-la, a fragrant grass of tropical Asia. **citronella oil,** an essential oil yielded by this, used in perfumery and for mosquito-bites.
Citrus, *n. sit*-rus, a genus of trees including the orange, grape-fruit, citron, lemon, lime and others. (L.)
cittern, *n. sit*-tern the cithern.
city, *n. sit*-e, a large important corporate town; one which is or has been the seat of a bishop; a town; any English town having a Lord Mayor; the collective body of citizens: *a.* pertaining to a city. **the City,** the small, earliest part of London, separately governed by the Lord Mayor and Corporation; the financial and commercial centre of the British Empire. **City Company,** a corporation representing one of the ancient trading guilds of London. **city editor,** the financial editor of a periodical. **the Eternal City,** Rome. (Fr. *cité*.)
citywards, *ad. sit*-e-wardz, towards the city.
civet, *n. siv*-et, the civet-cat; a musky substance got from a gland under the tail of the African civet-cat, and used as a perfume: *v.t.* to scent with civet. (Fr. *civette*.)
civet-cat, *n. siv*-et-kat, a small nocturnal carnivore of the genus *Viverra*, of which most species are Asiatic and one, *V. civetta*, is confined to Africa.
civic, *a. siv*-ik, pertaining to a city or citizen; municipal. **civic crown,** a garland of oak-leaves given to a Roman soldier, who had saved the life of a citizen in battle. (L. *civicus*.)
civics, *n. siv*-iks, the science and art of municipal administration; the science of the rights and duties of citizenship.
civies, *n.pl. siv*-iz, civvies.
civil, *a. siv*-il, relating to a community or people, as citizens and subjects of a state; political or private, as opposed to criminal [Law]; lay, as opposed to ecclesiastical; intestine, as opposed to foreign; municipal, commercial, legislative, etc., as opposed to military; well regulated, opposed to rude and barbarous; civilized; polite; courteous. **civil architecture** the art of constructing buildings for the purposes of civil life. **civil death,** that which cuts off a man from civil society, or its privileges, as banishment, outlawry, entering into a monastery, etc. [Law]. **civil engineer,** one employed in civil engineering. **civil engineering,** the science or art of constructing canals, railroads, docks, etc., as distinguished from electrical, military,

or mechanical engineering, etc. **civil law,** Roman law; the law peculiar to any state; law relating to property and private matters as distinguished from criminal law. **civil list,** the sum granted annually for the support of the British sovereign's household and the dignity of the crown. **civil list pension,** a pension granted by royal favour generally for work done in literature, science, or art. **civil lord,** any civilian commissioner of the British Board of Admiralty other than the First Lord. **civil servant,** a member of the Civil Service who receives his appointment direct from the Crown or by certificate from the Civil Service Commissioners. **Civil Service,** the public administrative service of a state other than that supplied by its armed forces; the body of civil servants. **civil suit,** an action between citizen and citizen, as opposed to a criminal process, which is between the sovereign or state and a citizen. **civil war,** a war between people of the same state. **civil year,** the legal year as distinguished from the astronomical year. (Fr.)

civilian, *a.* se-*vil*-yan, pertaining to civil matters: *n.* one skilled in or a student of civil law; one engaged in civil, not military pursuits. (O.Fr. *civilien.*)

civility, *n.* se-*vil*-e-te, the quality of being civil; politeness; courtesy: *pl.* acts or expressions of politeness. (Fr. *civilité.*)

civilizable, *a.* siv-e-*ly*-za-bl, that may be civilized.

civilization, *n.* siv-e-ly-*zay*-shon, the act of civilizing, or the state of being civilized; a national or tribal culture.

civilize, *v.t.* *siv*-e-lize, to reclaim from barbarism; to instruct in the arts and refinements of civil life; to make cultured; to tame. (Fr. *civiliser.*)

civilly, *ad.* *siv*-e-le, in a civil manner.

civism, *n.* *siv*-izm, citizenship; the principles of citizenship. (Fr. *civisme.*)

civvies, *n.* *siv*-iz, mufti; plain clothes [Slang].

civvy, *a.* and *n.*, *siv*-i, civilian [Slang].

clabber, *n.* *klab*-ber, milk thickened and sour.

clachan, *n.* *klakh*-an, a Highland hamlet. (Celt.)

clack, *n.* klak, a loud click; a sharp abrupt sound, frequently repeated; anything that clacks; a continual talking; incessant tattle; the tongue, in contempt; a ball-valve in some pumps; a contrivance giving aural notice of some stage in a mechanical operation: *v.i.* to make a sudden sharp noise, as by striking or cracking; to go on talking with short, sharp, abrupt sounds: *v.t.* to cause to clack. **clack valve,** a hinged pump-valve.

clack dish, *n.* *klak*-dish, a dish used by mendicants, with a cover which they kept clacking.

clacker, *n.* *klak*-er, one who or that which clacks; a clack-valve.

clad, *a.* klad, clothed.

cladode, *n.* *klad*-ode, a leaf-like branch as in *Ruscus aculeatus*, the butcher's-broom. (Gr. *klados*, twig.)

Cladonia, *n.* kla-*doh*-ne-a, a genus of lichens including *Cladonia rangiferina*, the reindeer moss.

claes, *n.pl.* klayz, clothes [Scots.].

claik, *n.* klake, the barnacle goose [Scots.].

claim, *n.* klame, a demand of a right or supposed right; a right to claim; the thing claimed; a piece of land which a settler claims a right to purchase when it is put up for sale; a portion of land marked out for mining: *v.t.* to demand as a right or as due. (O.Fr. *claimer.*)

claimable, *a.* *klame*-a-bl, that may be claimed.

claimant, *n.* *klame*-ant, one who makes a claim.

clair-audience, *n.* klare-*aw*-de-ence, a state in which the hearing is preternaturally acute. (Fr. *clair*, clear, and *audience.*)

clairschach, *n.* *klare*-shakh, the ancient Celtic harp. (Ir. *clairseach.*)

clairvoyance, *n.* klare-*voy*-ans, a power attributed to certain persons, or to persons in a trance-like state, of discerning objects not present to the senses. (Fr., literally, clear-seeing.)

clairvoyant, *n.* klare-*voy*-ant, one who professes the power of clairvoyance: *a.* having the power of clairvoyance.

clam, *n.* klam, a clamp, clutch, or vice; the lining, or a jaw, of a vice. (A.S. *clamm.*)

clam, *n.* klam, the popular name for certain species of edible bivalve molluscs; a reticent or close-fisted person [Slang]. (A.S. *clamm.*)

clam, *n.* klam, clamminess: *v.t.* to clog with viscous matter. (A.S. *clæman.*)

clamant, *a.* *klam*-ant *or* *klame*-ant, clamorous; crying; insistent.

clamatory, *a.* *klam*-a-to-re, clamorous.

clamber, *v.i.* *klam*-ber, to climb with difficulty, as by hands and feet; to grow by clinging [Bot.]: *n.* a climb. (Scand.)

clammily, *ad.* *klam*-me-le, in a clammy manner.

clamminess, *n.* *klam*-me-ness, the state of being clammy; viscosity; sliminess.

clammy, *a.* *klam*-me, viscous; glutinous; adhesive.

clamorous, *a.* *klam*-mo-rus, full of clamour; vociferous; noisy.

clamorously, *ad.* *klam*-mo-rus-le, in a clamorous manner.

clamorousness, *n.* *klam*-mo-rus-ness, the state or quality of being clamorous.

clamour, *n.* *klam*-mor, a great outcry; continued vociferation or loud noise; uproar; importunate demand; complaint: *v.t.* to cry aloud; to stun or overpower with noise: *v.i.* to utter loud sounds or outcries; to vociferate; to make importunate demands; to complain. (O.Fr. *clamour.*)

clamp, *n.* klamp, a piece of timber or iron used to fasten work together; a vice used to hold pieces of wood together [Carp.]; a batten to prevent boards warping; a thick plank on the inner part of a ship's side sustaining the ends of the beams [Naut.]; a pile, as of bricks laid up for burning; a stack or heap, as of potatoes, turves, etc.: *v.t.* to fasten or strengthen with clamps; to fit a piece of board to the end of another piece across the grain to prevent warping [Carp.]; to pile in a mound; to store in a clamp. (Perhaps Dut. *klampen*, to make fast.)

clamp, *n.* klamp, a heavy footstep or tread, particularly of many persons: *v.i.* to tread heavily.

clamper, *n.* *klamp*-er, an iron attachment to the sole for walking on ice; an iron patch on a ship's hull: *v.t.* to botch.

clan, *n.* klan, a tribe or collection of families united under a chieftain, usually having the same surname, and supposed to be descended from a common ancestor; a clique, sect, or body of persons closely united. (Gael. *clann*, a tribe.)

clandestine, *a.* klan-*des*-tin, hidden; kept secret; concealed; underhand; surreptitious; implying evil intent. (L. *clandestinus.*)

clandestinely, *ad.* klan-*des*-tin-le, in a clandestine manner.

clang, *n.* klang, a sharp ringing sound, as of the striking together of pieces of metal: *v.t.* and *i.* to make or emit a sharp ringing sound, as by striking metallic substances; to strike with a sharp sound. (L. *clango*, resound.)

clangorous, *a.* *klang*-o-rus, sounding with clangour.

clangour, *n.* *klang*-or, a sharp, harsh sound. (L.)

clank, *n.* klank, the loud, sharp sound as of heavy chains, made by a collision of metallic or other sonorous bodies: *v.t.* and *i.* to make this sound. (Imit., or from Dut. *klank.*)

clannish, *a.* *klan*-nish, disposed to draw closely together and stand by one another, as the members of a clan; pertaining to a clan.

clannishly, *ad.* *klan*-nish-le, in a clannish manner.

clannishness, *n.* *klan*-nish-ness, a clannish disposition.

clanship, *n.* *klan*-ship, a state of union, as in a clan; the clan system.

clansman, *n.* *klanz*-man, one of a clan.

clap, *n.* klap, a noise made by the collision of flat surfaces; a sudden act or motion; a burst of sound, particularly of thunder; an act of applause; a heavy slap: *v.i.* to move or drive together suddenly with noise; to strike the hands together in applause: *v.t.* to strike with a quick motion lightly or heavily, esp. with something flat; to thrust or drive together suddenly; to shut hastily; to put or place suddenly or hastily; to applaud by striking the hands together. **clap up,** to make hastily; to imprison hastily or with informality. (Scand.)

clap, *n.* klap, gonorrhea [Slang.]. (O.Fr. *clapoir.*)

clap-board, *n.* *klap*-bord, a stave for a cask; a thin narrow board for covering houses: *v.t.* to cover with clap-boards. (U.S.A.)

clap-dish, *n.* *klap*-dish, a clack-dish.

clap-net, *n.* *klap*-net, a folding net for taking birds.

clapper, *n.* *klap*-per, one who claps, or applauds by

clapping; the tongue of a bell; anything that claps or clacks.
clapperclaw, *v.t.* *klap*-per-klaw, to fight and scratch; to scold; to revile. (*Clap* and *claw.*)
claptrap, *a.* *klap*-trap, aiming at applause: *n.* a contrivance to imitate clapping formerly used in theatres; bunkum to gain applause or public favour.
claque, *n.* klak, a body of claqueurs; the system of hiring applauders. (Fr.)
claqueur, *n.* *klak*-er, one hired to applaud in a theatre. (Fr.)
clarabella, *n.* klah-rah-*bel*-la, the organ-stop with a flute-like note. (L. *clarus*, clear, *bellus*, lovely.)
clare, *n.* klare, a nun of the order of St. Clare.
clarence, *n.* *kla*-rence, a closed four-wheeled cab to seat four. (Duke of *Clarence*, afterwards King William IV.)
Clarenceux, *n.* *kla*-ren-sew, the king-of-arms, whose jurisdiction ranges south of the Trent, and who comes next in rank to Garter King-of-arms. From the first holder, the Duke of Clarence, son of Edward III.)
clarendon, *n.* *kla*-ren-don, a heavy-faced printing type as used for the first word of these entries.
clare-obscure, *n.* *klare*-ob-skewr, chiaroscuro.
claret, *n.* *kla*-ret, a clear red wine; the red wine of Médoc; blood [Slang]: *a.* claret-coloured. (O.Fr.)
claret-cup, *n.* *kla*-ret-kup, an iced drink of claret, brandy, lemon, etc.
clarification, *n.* *kla*-re-fe-*kay*-shon, the act of clarifying. (Fr.)
clarifier, *n.* *kla*-re-fy-er, one who or that which clarifies or purifies; a vessel in which liquor or sugar, etc., is clarified.
clarify, *v.t.* *kla*-re-fy, to make clear or pure; to purify, especially liquors, from feculent matter; to make lucid: *v.i.* to become clarified. (O.Fr. *clarifier.*)
clarinet, *n.* *kla*-rin-et, an important wood-wind instrument of the oboe class, with a reed in the mouthpiece. (Fr. *clarinette.*)
clarinettist, *n.* kla-re-*net*-ist, a player of the clarinet.
clarion, *n.* *kla*-re-on, a kind of trumpet having a narrow tube and a very shrill clear tone; an organ-stop reproducing this tone; the sound of a clarion: *a.* loud and clear. (O.Fr.)
clarionet, *n.* *kla*-re-o-net, a clarinet.
clarity, *n.* *kla*-re-te, distinctness. (O.Fr. *clarté.*)
clarkia *n.* *klahr*-ke-a, any hardy annual of a small genus *Clarkia* (nat. ord. *Onagraceæ*) with large red or purple flowers. (Wm. *Clark*, Amer. explorer, *d.* 1838.)
claro-obscuro, *n.* *klah*-ro-ob-*skoo*-ro, chiaroscuro.
clarty, *a.* *klart*-e, wet and dirty; miry. (Scots.)
clary, *n.* *klare*-re, the sweet herb *Salvia selarea*, whose dried leaves are used as a seasoning. (Fr. *sclarée.*)
clary-water, *n.* *klare*-re-waw-ter, a cordial of brandy, sugar, clary-flowers, and cinnamon, with a little ambergris.
clash, *v.i.* klash, to strike or drive against with force; to make a noise by mutual collision; to act or meet in opposition or conflict; to interfere with: *v.t.* to strike one thing against another, so as to produce a noise: *n.* a noise from the violent collision of bodies; opposition; contradiction. (From the sound.)
clashing, *n.* *klash*-ing, noisy concussion; conflict: *a.* opposing; conflicting.
clasp, *n.* klahsp, a catch or hook for fastening; a fastening; a brooch or buckle; a bar for a war medal; an embrace, by throwing the arms round: *v.t.* to fasten or provide with a clasp; to catch and hold to by twining; to embrace; to grasp. (A.S. *clyppan*, embrace.)
clasper, *n.* *klahsp*-er, that which clasps; a tendril; a clasping organ, generally a modified limb.
clasp-knife, *n.* *klahsp*-nife, a knife which shuts up or folds into the handle.
clasp-nail, *n.* *klahsp*-nale, a nail with a head to clasp into the wood.
class, *n.* klahs, a rank or order of persons or things; grade; quality; the system of social rank or caste; a number of students of the same standing and taught together; a scientific division, esp. one subordinate to a kingdom and including orders under it: *v.t.* to arrange in a class or classes; to arrange according to some method; to classify. **class conscious,** actuated by attachment to the supposed interests of one's social class. **class struggle,** conflict between different classes, esp. between the capitalist and the proletarian. (Fr. *classe.*)
classable, *a.* *klahs*-abl, that may be classed.
classic, *a.* *klas*-sik, belonging to ancient Greek and Latin authors of the first rank; resembling the pure and elegant literature of ancient Greece and Rome; of the first rank, especially in literature and the fine arts; academic; versed in the classics; pure; correct; refined; well proportioned; pertaining to a class or classes: *n.* an author of the first rank, originally a Greek or Latin author of this class; a book written by a classic, especially of Greece or Rome; one versed in the classics. **classic races,** the five chief horse-races in England, the Two Thousand and One Thousand Guineas, the Derby, the Oaks, and the St. Leger. (L. *classicus*, a citizen of the first class.)
classical, *a.* *klas*-sik-al, classic; pertaining to the classics.
classicalism, *n.* *klas*-sik-al-izm, a classic style or idiom; devotion to Greek or Roman art.
classicalist, *n.* *klas*-sik-al-ist, a classicist.
classicality, *n.* klas-sik-*al*-e-te, the quality of being classical.
classically, *ad.* *klas*-sik-al-le, in a classic manner.
classicalness, *n.* *klas*-sik-al-ness, classicality.
classicism, *n.* *klas*-sis-izm, a classic idiom or style.
classicist, *n.* *klas*-se-sist, one devoted to the classics or to classic style; a classical scholar; an advocate of the study of the classics.
classicize, *v.t.* and *v.i.* *klas*-se-size, to copy a classic style; to make classic.
classifiable, *a.* *klas*-se-*fy*-a-bl, capable of being classed or classified.
classification, *n.* *klas*-se-fe-*kay*-shon, the act of classifying; arrangement; system; class.
classificatory, *a.* *klas*-se-fe-*kay*-to-re, relating to classification; classifying.
classifier, *n.* *klas*-se-fy-er, one who classifies.
classify, *v.t.* *klas*-se-fy, to arrange in classes or divisions; to class. (L. *classis*, and *facio*, make.)
classless, *a.* *klahs*-les, having or admitting of no class or classes, esp. of the Communist form of government.
classman, *n.* *klahs*-man, one who has, after examination, gained a certain rank towards graduation in arts at an English university.
classy, *a.* *klahs*-se, high-toned, superior [Slang].
clastic, *a.* *klas*-tik, fragmentary [Geol.]. (Gr. *klastikos.*)
clatter, *n.* *klat*-ter, a repetition of abrupt sharp sounds; a confused repetition of rattling sounds: *v.i.* to make rattling sounds; to rattle; to talk fast and idly: *v.t.* to strike so as to make a thing rattle. (A.S. *clatrung*, clattering.)
clatterer, *n.* *klat*-ter-er, one who clatters; a babbler.
clatteringly, *ad.* *klat*-ter-ing-le, with clattering.
Claude Lorraine glass, *klawd*-lo-*rayn*-glahs, a convex mirror of black or tinted glass for obtaining a concentrated view of a reflected landscape. (The Fr. 17th-cent. painter.)
Claudian, *a.* *klaw*-de-an, pertaining to or of the period (A.D. 14–68) of one of the Roman Emperors of the Claudius gens (Tiberius, Caligula, Claudius, and Nero).
clause, *n.* klawz, part of a complex or a compound sentence [Gram.]; an article, or a distinct part, of a contract, will, agreement, charter, commission, or other writing; stipulation. (Fr.)
claustral, *a.* *klaws*-tral, relating to or like a cloister; monastic; secluded.
claustration, *n.* klaw-*stray*-shon, the act of confining to a cloister or monastery, etc.
claustrophobia, *n.* klaw-stro-*foh*-be-a, morbid fear of being in a narrow or confined space.
claustrum, *n.* *klaw*-strum, grey matter lying in the hemispheres of the cerebellum. (L.)
clausular, *a.* *klaw*-zew-lar, consisting of, or of the nature of, clauses.
clavate, *a.* *klay*-vate, club-shaped; knobbed [Bot. and Zool.]; jointed like a nail into its hole [Anat.]. (L. *clava*, a club.)
clavation, *n.* kla-*vay*-shon, articulation like that of a nail in its hole [Anat.].
clavecin, *n.* *klav*-e-sin, an early form of harpsichord; the keyboard of a carillon. (Fr.)
claver, *v.i.* *klay*-ver, to gossip; to palaver [Scots.]

clavicembalo, *n.* klah-ve-*chem*-bah-lo, the harpsichord.
clavichord, *n.* *klav*-e-kord, a precursor of the pianoforte; a stringed musical instrument in which the strings were struck by brass tangents or wedges.
clavicle, *n.* *klav*-e-kl, the collar-bone. (Fr. *clavicule.*)
clavicorn, *n.* *klav*-e-korn, one of a family of beetles having club-shaped antennæ. (L. *clava*, club, *cornu*, horn.)
clavicular, *a.* kla-*vik*-yew-lar, pertaining to the clavicle.
clavier, *n.* *klay*-ve-er *or* kla-*veer*, the keyboard of an organ or pianoforte. (Fr.)
claviform, *a.* *klav*-e-form, club-shaped; clavate.
clavis, *n.* *klay*-vis, a key; a translation. (L.)
claw, *n.* klaw, the sharp hooked nail of an animal; the whole foot of a bird or beast armed with hooked nails; the limb of a crustacean; the hand, in contempt; anything like a claw; a clutch: *v.t.* to pull, scratch, or tear with or as with claws. **claw off** or **away,** to turn and beat to windward to prevent falling on a lee shore [Naut.]; to get off or escape. (A.S. *clawu.*)
clawback, *n.* *klaw*-bak, one who flatters; a sycophant.
clawed, *a.* klawd, furnished or armed with claws; damaged by clawing.
claw-hammer, *n.* *klaw*-ham-mer, a hammer with a split peen for extracting nails.
clawless, *a.* *klaw*-less, destitute of claws.
clay, *n.* klay, hydrated silicate of alumina derived from the waste of rocks, mixed with impurities; soft tenacious plastic earth; the grosser part of human nature or the material part of the body; a corpse: *a.* formed or consisting of clay: *v.t.* to cover or manure with clay; to purify and whiten with clay, as sugar; to puddle with clay. (A.S. *clæg.*)
clay-cold, *a.* *klay*-koald, cold as clay; lifeless.
claye, *n.* klay, a hurdle of stakes interwoven with osiers [Fort.] (Fr. *claie*, hurdle.)
clayey, *a.* *klay*-e, consisting of clay; like clay; soiled with clay.
clayish, *a.* *klay*-ish, of the nature of clay.
clay-marl, *n.* *klay*-mahrl, a whitish, smooth, chalky clay.
claymore, *n.* *klay*-more, the large two-edged sword, formerly used by the Scottish Highlanders; a basket-hilted sword. (Gael., great sword.)
clay-pit, *n.* *klay*-pit, a pit where clay is dug.
clay-slate, *n.* *klay*-slate, argillaceous schist; roofing-slate.
clay-stone, *n.* *klay*-stone, an earthy stone resembling compact or calcareous marl.
clayweed, *n.* *klay*-weed, the coltsfoot.
★**clean,** *a.* kleen, free from stain, or alloy, blemish, imperfection, disease, awkwardness, or any defect; pure; guiltless; holy; having no fish (of fishing-vessels); needing no correction (of printers' proofs): *ad.* quite; entirely; leaving no trace; dexterously: *v.t.* to make clean; to purify; to cleanse. **clean bill,** a bill declaring a ship free from infection. **to clean out,** to deprive of all money [Slang]. **clean slate,** a new beginning. **clean sweep,** an entire removal of rubbish, etc. (A.S. *clæne.*)
cleaner, *n.* *kleen*-er, he who or that which cleans.
clean-handed, *a.* *kleen*-hand-ed, absolved from all blame in a matter.
cleanish, *a.* *kleen*-ish, rather clean.
cleanlily, *ad.* *klen*-le-le, in a cleanly manner.
clean-limbed, *a.* *kleen*-limd, having well-proportioned limbs.
cleanliness, *n.* *klen*-le-ness, freedom from dirt.
cleanly, *a.* *klen*-le, clean; clean in person and habits.
cleanness, *n.* *kleen*-ness, the state of being clean.
cleansable, *a.* *klen*-za-bl, that may be cleansed.
cleanse, *v.t.* klenz, to make clean; to purge away. (A.S. *clænsian.*)
cleanser, *n.* *klen*-zer, he who or that which cleanses; a detergent.
★**clear,** *a.* kleer, free from what darkens, obscures, or dims; bright; luminous; translucent: transparent; sharply intelligent; lucid; evident; indisputable; serene; irreproachable; free; unembarrassed; unentangled; unshackled; unobstructed; distinctly audible; unmistaken; free from deduction, net: *ad.* plainly; quite; completely: *n.* a clear space; open sky; the space between parts with nothing intervening, clearance: *v.t.* to make clear; to free from obscurity or ambiguity; to free from obstruction, encumbrance, or nuisance; to remove; to pass untouched; to liberate or disengage; to exonerate; to acquit; to profit beyond all expenses and charges; to pass or leap over without touching: *v.i.* to become clear, fair, bright, or fine; to be disengaged from encumbrances, distress, or entanglements; to become free or disengaged. **clear a ship,** to perform the required conditions at the custom-house, and procure permission to sail [Naut.]. **clear a ship for action,** to remove every encumbrance from the decks and prepare to fight. **clear off,** to depart; to exchange, as in clearing-houses [Comm.]. **clear the land,** to have open sea-room, without danger of going on shore [Naut.]. (Fr. *clair.*)
clearage, *n.* *kleer*-raj, the removing of anything; a clearance.
clearance, *n.* *kleer*-rance, the act or result of clearing or removing; clear profit; a certificate that a ship has been cleared at the custom house; the space between two adjacent parts [Mech.].
clearcole, *n.* *kleer*-koal, size and whiting, the first coat in house-painting: *v.t.* to paint with clearcole. (Fr. *claire colle*, clear glue.)
clear-cut, *a.* *kleer*-kut, clearly and finely outlined, as if cut.
clearer, *n.* *kleer*-rer, one who or that which clears.
clear-headed, *a.* *kleer*-hed-ed, acute; intelligent.
clearing, *n.* *kleer*-ing, the act of freeing; the act of justifying; a place or tract of land cleared of wood for cultivation; among bankers, the exchanging of the drafts on each other's houses, and settling of the differences [Comm.]. **clearing hospital,** a field hospital for the early treatment of wounded and sick.
clearing-house, *n.* *kleer*-ing-house, the institution effecting the exchange between banking-houses of bills and cheques and the settlement of balances; the office of this.
clearing-nut, *n.* *kleer*-ing-nut, the seed of the tree *Strychnos potatorum*, used in India for clearing muddy water.
clearing-station, *n.* *kleer*-ing-stay-shon, a temporary front-line hospital [Mil.].
clearly, *ad.* *kleer*-le, in a clear manner; evidently; plainly.
clearness, *n.* *kleer*-ness, transparency; brightness.
clear-sighted, *a.* *kleer*-*sy*-ted, keen-sighted; acute; discerning.
clear-sightedness, *n.* *kleer*-*sy*-ted-ness, discernment.
clear-starch, *n.* *kleer*-stahrch, colourless starch: *v.t.* to stiffen and dress with this.
clear-starcher, *n.* *kleer*-stahrch-er, one who clear-starches; a laundress.
clearstory, *n.* *kleer*-staw-re, a clerestory.
clearwing, *n.* *kleer*-wing, any one of the hawk-moths, *Ægeridæ*, which have translucent wings.
cleat, *n.* kleet, a fixing to belay ropes to [Naut.]; a narrow strengthening strip of wood, nailed on, in joinery; a thin metallic plate. (Early Eng. *clete.*)
cleavable, *a.* *kleev*-a-bl, that may be split or divided.
cleavage, *n.* *kleev*-aj, the act of cleaving or splitting; the fracture, or particular manner, in which any rock or mineral, having a regular structure, may be cleaved [Min.].
cleave, *v.i.* kleev, to adhere or cling to; to be faithful to. (A.S. *clifian.*)
cleave, *v.t.* kleev, to part or divide by force; to rive; to part or open naturally: *v.i.* to part asunder; to crack. *p.* **cleft** and **clove**; *pp.* **cloven.** (A.S. *cleofan.*)
cleaver, *n.* *kleev*-er, one who or that which cleaves; a butcher's chopper.
cleavers, *n.* *kleev*-erz, a plant of the genus *Galium*; goose-grass.
cledge, *n.* kledj, clayey soil; the upper stratum of beds of fuller's earth.
cleek, *n.* *kleek*, a golf-club with an iron head and narrow upright face; a large hook or crook: *v.t.* to seize or clutch; to pluck. [Scots.]
clef, *n.* klef, a character at the beginning of a staff to determine the degree of elevation occupied by that staff in the system, and to point out the names of the notes contained in the line of that clef [Mus.]. (Fr., a key.)

cleft, *n.* kleft, an opening made by splitting; a crack; a fissure; a piece made by splitting; a morbid crack on the bend of the pastern of a horse.
cleft-footed, *a.* kleft-*foot*-ed, cloven-hoofed.
cleft-graft, *v.t.* *kleft*-grahft, to engraft by cleaving the stock and inserting a scion [Hort.].
cleft-palate, *n.* kleft-*pal*-at, a defect of the palate by which the halves are left apart from each other, commonly accompanied by hare-lip.
cleg, *n.* kleg, a gadfly or breeze-fly. (Dial. Eng.)
cleistogamic, *a.* *kly*-sto-*gam*-ik, having flowers that do not open and are therefore self-pollinated. (Gr. *kleistos*, closed, *gamos*, marriage.)
clem, *v.t.* and *v.i.* klem, to starve; to be pinched with hunger. (Ger. *klemmen*, to pinch.)
Clematis, *n.* *klem*-a-tis, a genus of ranunculaceous plants, mostly climbers, including the virgin's bower or traveller's joy. (Gr. *klēmatis.*)
clemency, *n.* *klem*-en-se, the quality of being clement; leniency; mercy. (L. *clementia.*)
clement, *a.* *klem*-ent, mild; gentle; kind; tender; compassionate. (L.)
Clementine, *a.* *klem*-en-tin, pertaining to St. Clement, or the constitutions of Pope Clement V.
clementine, *n.* *klem*-en-tin, a fruiterers' name for a variety of tangerine orange.
clemently, *ad.* *klem*-ent-le, in a clement manner.
clench, *v.t.* klench, to grip; to make fast or firm; to clinch.
clepe, *v.t.* and *i.* kleep, to call or name. (A.S. *clepan.*)
clepsydra, *n.* *klep*-sid-ra, an instrument used by the ancients to measure time, by the dropping of water through a hole from one vessel into another. (Gr. *klepto*, steal, *hydor*, water.)
clerestory, *n.* *kleer*-staw-re, the upper part of the nave, choir, etc., of a Gothic church or other building, with windows above the aisle roofs [Arch.]. (*Clear, story.*)
clergiable, *a.* *kler*-je-a-bl, entitled to benefit of clergy.
clergy, *n.pl.* *kler*-je, the body of men set apart by ordination for the service of religion in the Christian Church; the body of ecclesiastics in distinction from the laity. **benefit of clergy,** the former exemption of clerics from criminal process before a secular judge, an immunity granted in certain cases to those who could read. (O.Fr. *clergie.*)
clergyman, *n.* *kler*-je-man, a man in holy orders; one of the clergy; an ordained Christian minister, esp. of the Church of England. **clergyman's throat,** a chronic form of pharyngitis brought on by constant overstrain of the voice.
cleric, *n.* *kle*-rik, a clerk or clergyman: *a.* clerical.
clerical, *a.* *kle*-re-kal, pertaining to the clergy; pertaining to a writer, clerk, or transcriber. **clerical error,** error made by a copyist; a venial error.
clericalism, *n.* *kle*-re-ka-lizm, clerical domination.
clerisy, *n.* *kle*-ris-e, the literati or intelligentsia.
clerk, *n.* klahrk, a clergyman or ecclesiastic; a scholar; a layman who reads the responses in the church service, to direct the congregation; an assistant with the correspondence, accounts, etc., in an office or bank, etc.; one who records the proceedings of a public or associated body; an assistant shopman [U.S.A.]. **Bible clerk,** a scholar whose duty it is to read the lessons in a college chapel. **clerk of the weather,** an imaginary controller of the weather; the Meteorological Office [Coll.]. **clerk of the works,** one who superintends a building in progress. (A.S. *clerc*, a priest.)
clerkess, *n.* *klahrk*-ess, a female clerk.
clerk-like, *a.* *klahrk*-like, like a clerk; learned.
clerkly, *a.* *klahrk*-le, pertaining to a clerk; scholarly; learned: *ad.* in a learned manner.
clerkship, *n.* *klahrk*-ship, scholarship; the office or situation of a clerk.
cleromancy, *n.* *kle*-ro-man-se, divination by casting lots with dice. (Gr. *kleros*, lot, *manteia*, divination.)
cleve, *n.* kleev, a cliff; a valley, esp. in Devonshire. (*Cliff.*)
clever, *a.* *klev*-er, dexterous; skilful; ingenious; quick or ready-witted; intelligent. (Perhaps from M.E. *cliver*, claw, hence " quick at grasping.")
cleverish, *a.* *klev*-er-ish, moderately clever.
cleverly, *ad.* *klev*-er-le, in a clever manner; well.
cleverness, *n.* *klev*-er-ness, the quality of being clever; dexterity; skill.
clevis, *n.* *klev*-is, the draught-iron of a plough; a sharply curved iron at the end of a beam to which harness or tackle is attached. (*Cleave.*)
clew, *n.* kloo, a ball of thread; the thread that forms a ball; a thread to guide a person in a labyrinth, like that given by Ariadne to guide Theseus through the labyrinth at Crete; anything that guides or directs one in an intricate case; a key or a hint to the solution of a mystery; the lower corner of a squaresail, and the aftermost corner of a staysail [Naut.]; the lines suspending a hammock: *v.t.* to truss up sails to the yard [Naut.]. **clew garnets,** tackles fastened to the clews of the sails on the mainmast and foremast, to truss them up to the yard [Naut.]. **clew lines,** a similar tackle applied to the smaller squaresails [Naut.]. (A.S. *cliwen.*)
cliché, *n.* *klee*-shay, a proof impression of a die; a stereotype, or electrotype [Phot.]; a trite phrase; an overworked literary expression. (Fr. stereotyped.)
click, *n.* klik, a short sharp sound; the latch of a door; a small piece of iron that falls into a notched or ratchet wheel; a peculiar articulation occurring in certain S. African languages: *v.i.* to make a small sharp sound, or a succession of such sounds, as by a gentle striking; to tick; to have a bit of luck, to be successful [Slang]: *v.t.* to cause to click. (Imit.)
click-beetle, *n.* *klik*-bee-tl, the skipjack, or any beetle of the family *Elateridæ*.
click-clack, *n.* *klik*-klak, a clicking noise, as the click-clack of a typewriter.
clicker, *n.* *klik*-er, a shop-assistant who stands at the door touting for customers; one who cuts out the leather and apportions it to the workmen [Shoemaking]; a maker-up; a responsible foreman compositor [Print.].
clicket, *n.* *klik*-et, the knocker, the latch of a door; anything shutting to with a click.
client, *n.* *kly*-ent, a Roman plebeian who put himself under the protection of a noble or man of influence, termed his patron; one who entrusts any business, esp. legal, to a professional in such matters; a customer; a dependent. (Fr. *client.*)
clientage, *n.* *kly*-en-taj, the system of patron and client; one's clients or dependents as a body; the condition of a client.
cliental, *a.* kly-en-tal, pertaining to a client.
clientelage, *n.* *kly*-en-*tee*-laj, the relation of a client to his patron; a clientele.
clientele, *n.* kly-en-*tel*, clients collectively; one's customers, patients, or adherents. (Fr.)
clientship, *n.* *kly*-ent-ship, the condition of a client.
cliff, *n.* klif, a high and steep rock; a precipice; the steep face of the high ground on a coast. (A.S. *clif*, a rock.)
cliffy, *a.* *klif*-e, having cliffs; broken; craggy.
clift, *n.* klift, a cleft; a cliff.
climacteric, *n.* kly-mak-*te*-rik *or* kly-*mak*-te-rik, a critical period in human life, or a period in which some great change is supposed to take place in the human constitution or in a person's fortunes; generally taken to be those years obtained by multiplying 7 by 3, 5, 7, and 9, to which a few add the 81st year; the menopause: *a.* pertaining to a climacteric; critical; observed in persons advanced in life [Path.]. **grand climacteric,** the 63rd year. (O.Fr. *climactere.*)
climacterical, *a.* kly-mak-*te*-re-kal, climacteric.
climactic, *a.* kly-*mak*-tik, relating to a climax.
climatarchic, *a.* kly-ma-*tar*-kik, presiding over a clime or region. (*Climate*, and Gr. *archo*, rule.)
climate, *n.* *kly*-mat, the condition of a region of the earth's surface as regards temperature and atmospheric changes in their relation to or effects upon plants and animals; the weather, temperature, and general meteorological conditions prevailing in a place or country; formerly, a region. (Fr. *climat.*)
climatic, *a.* kly-*mat*-ik, pertaining to climate; limited by climate.
climatically, *ad.* kly-*mat*-e-ka-le, as regards climate.
climation, *n.* kly-*may*-shon, act of inuring or of becoming inured to a new climate; acclimation.
climatize, *v.t.* and *i.* *kly*-ma-tize, to acclimatize.

climatographical, *a.* *kly*-ma-to-*graf*-e-kal, relating to climatography.
climatography, *n.* kly-ma-*tog*-ra-fe, a description of climates. (*Climate,* and *grapho,* write.)
climatological, *a.* *kly*-ma-to-*loj*-e-kal, pertaining to climatology.
climatology, *n.* kly-ma-*tol*-o-je, the branch of meteorology treating of climate; the investigation of the causes which form a climate. (*Climate,* and *logos,* science.)
climature, *n.* *kly*-ma-tewr, a climate.
climax, *n.* *kly*-maks, a series of sentences so arranged as to rise in force, importance, or dignity to the close of the series [Rhet.]; the highest point; culmination: *v.t.* and *i.* to bring to or rise to a climax or culmination. (Gr., a ladder.)
climb, *v.i.* and *v.t.* klime, to ascend with labour and difficulty, esp. by clutching with the hands and feet; to ascend with a slow motion; to fly upward [Av.]; to creep up by means of tendrils, etc., as a plant: *n.* the act or process of climbing; an ascent by climbing; the ascent of aircraft; rate of ascent [Av.]. **climb-down,** an ignominious surrender. (A.S. *climban.*)
climbable, *a.* *klime*-a-bl, that can be climbed.
climber, *n.* *klime*-er, one who climbs; a plant that climbs on some support; a bird that climbs.
climbing, *a.* *klime*-ing, creeping or ascending. **climbing boy,** one who swept chimneys by climbing them. **climbing irons,** grips of iron affixed to a climber's legs to give him a better hold. **climbing perch,** an Indian fish, *Anabas scandens,* which is said to climb trees by means of its strong spines. **climbing shaft,** a shaft leading up through the interior of an airship.
clime, *n.* klime, a climate; a tract or region; a country. (L. *clima.*)
clinamen, *n.* kly-*nay*-men, a bias or inclination. (L. *clinare,* slope.)
clinanthium, *n.* kly-*nan*-the-um, the receptacle of a composite plant on which are the small flowers [Bot.]. (Gr. *kline,* a bed, *anthos,* a flower.)
clinch, *n.* klinch, the act of clinching; a grip; a holdfast; a word with a double meaning; a pun; a special kind of knot for large ropes [Naut.]: *v.t.* to rivet by bending the point of a nail that has been driven through anything; to fix or confirm; to grasp tightly; to close firmly; to join or make fast with a clinch [Naut.]. (*Clench.*)
clincher, *n.* *klinch*-er, he who or that which clinches; a holdfast; a decisive reply or argument.
clincher-built, *a.* *klinch*-er-bilt, clinker-built.
cling, *v.i.* kling, to adhere closely, especially by winding round or embracing; to adhere closely in interest or affection. *p.* and *pp.* **clung.** (A.S. *clingan,* to wither up, to adhere.)
clingstone, *n.* *kling*-stone, a variety of peach in which the pulp adheres closely to the stone.
clingy, *a.* *kling*-e, apt to cling; adhesive.
clinic, *n.* *klin*-ik, medical and surgical instruction at the bedside in a hospital; a hospital outpatients' department; a centre at which advice and assistance in matters of health, hygiene, maternity, etc., are given; a dispensary. (Fr. *clinique.*)
clinical, *a.* *klin*-ik-al, pertaining to the sick-bed, to a patient, or to medical instruction given in a hospital ward. **clinical baptism,** baptism administered to one sick or dying. **clinical convert,** a deathbed convert. **clinical thermometer,** a thermometer for taking the body temperature.
clinically, *ad.* *klin*-ik-al-le, by the bedside.
clinique, *n.* klin-*eek*, a lecture at the bedside; a clinic. (Fr.)
clink, *n.* klink, a small ringing sound caused by striking two sounding bodies together: *v.i.* to sound with a clink; to ring or jingle: *v.t.* to cause to clink. (Imit.)
clink, *n.* klink, a gaol; a lock-up; a detention-cell [Slang]. (Name of a former prison in Southwark, London.)
clinkant, *a.* *kling*-kant, clinquant.
clinker, *n.* *kling*-ker, a vitreous cinder or slag formed in furnaces; a vitrified mass of bricks; a kind of hard-baked brick or tile.
clinker, *a.* *kling*-ker, having overlapping strakes. **clinker-built,** built of planks with overlapping edges, fastened together with clinched nails (of boats).
clinkstone, *n.* *klink*-stone, a felspathic rock which rings or clinks when struck; phonolite.
clinochlore, *kly*-no-klor, ripidolite.
clinograph, *n.* *kly*-no-graf, a right-angled set-square having hinged to one end a movable arm that can be set at any angle.
clinoid, *a.* *kly*-noyd, like a bed (applied to certain processes of the sphenoid bone) [Anat.]. (Gr. *kline,* a bed, *eidos,* like.)
clinometer, *n.* kly-*nom*-e-ter, an instrument for measuring angles of slope, esp. the dip of rock strata. (Gr. *klino,* bend, *metron,* a measure.)
clinometric, *a.* kly-no-*met*-rik, ascertained by a clinometer; according to clinometry.
clinometrical, *a.* *kly*-no-*met*-re-kal, clinometric.
clinquant, *n.* *kling*-kant, Dutch gold; false glitter: *a.* glittering; dressed in tinsel finery. (Fr.)
clint, *n.* klint, a hard rock, esp. one projecting from a hill-side or river-bed.
Clio, *n.* *kly*-o, the muse of history and epic poetry [Myth.]; a genus of minute marine molluscs, forming the chief food of the whalebone whales [Zool.]. (Gr.)
clip, *n.* klip, that which clips or holds; a small fastener; the wool of a season's sheep-shearing; a blow or stroke with the hand [Slang]: *v.i.* to move with rapidity; to go or run with speed: *v.t.* to cut off with shears or scissors; to shear sheep; to diminish coin by paring the edges; to cut short. **to clip one's wings,** to put a check on one's ambitious designs. (Scand.)
clipper, *n.* *klip*-per, one who clips; an instrument for cutting or clipping (*often in pl.*); a fast-goer, as a trotting horse; a sharp-built, fast-sailing vessel, with aft-raking masts and forward-raking bow; a full-sized, full-rigged ship; a smart or first-rate chap [Slang].
clipping, *n.* *klip*-ping, a piece separated by clipping; a cutting from a newspaper.
clique, *n.* kleek, a number of persons united in a design, usually of a selfish character; a small social coterie; an exclusive party. (Fr.)
cliquish, *a.* *kleek*-ish, disposed to join in cliques; socially exclusive.
cliquism, *n.* *kleek*-izm, the methods or principles of cliques; tendency to form cliques.
cliquy, *a.* *kleek*-e, characteristic of, or tending to form, cliques.
clish-clash, *n.* *klish*-klash, gossip: *v.i.* to sound like the clashing of swords [Scots.]. (Imit.)
clitellum, *n.* kle-*tel*-lum, the thickened glandular central part of the earthworm.
clitoris, *n.* *klit*-o-ris, a rudimentary part of the female genital organs homologous to the penis in males. (Gr.)
clitter-clatter, *n.* *klit*-ter-*klat*-ter, gossiping talk; empty chatter.
clivers, *n.* *kly*-verz, cleavers; goose-grass.
cloaca, *n.* klo-*ay*-ka, the receptacle in birds, reptiles and monotremes into which the alimentary canal opens and which receives the products of the reproductive organs and kidneys; a sewer. (L.)
cloacal, *a.* klo-*ay*-kal, relating to a cloaca.
cloak, *n.* kloke, a loose outer garment worn both by men and women; that which conceals; a disguise or pretext: *v.t.* to cover with a cloak; to conceal (O.Fr. *cloque,* a bell-shaped cape.)
cloaking, *n.* *kloke*-ing, material for cloaks; concealment; disguise.
cloak-room, *n.* *kloke*-room, a room at a place of public resort where hats and coats, etc., may be left; a place at a railway-station for leaving luggage until called for; a public lavatory.
cloam, *n.* klome, earthenware. (Dial. Eng.)
clobber, *n.* *klob*-ber, a paste formerly used by cobblers to conceal cracks in leather; clothes or equipment [Slang]: *v.t.* to patch up; to botch.
cloche, *n.* klohsh, a glass shaped like a bell for forcing plants. **cloche hat,** a tight-fitting bell-shaped hat for women. (Fr.)
★**clock,** *n.* klok, an instrument for measuring and indicating time, consisting of wheels moved by weights or springs, and regulated by a pendulum, esp. one that tells the hours by the stroke of a hammer upon a bell or spring: *v.t.* and *i.* to check the time of arrival for work; to time with a stop-watch. **what's o'clock?** or **what o'clock is it?** What hour of the clock is it? (Low L. *cloca,* a bell.)

clock, *n.* klok, an ornamental design worked on the leg of a stocking. (Origin unknown.)
clock, *n.* klok, a beetle, esp. the dung-beetle. (Origin unknown.)
clock-golf, *n.* klok-golf, a game played with a golf putter and ball on a green numbered like the face of a clock.
clockwise, *ad.* and *a.* *klok*-wize, moving in the same direction as the hands of a clock, from left to right.
clockwork, *n.* *klok*-wurk, machinery of, or as of, a clock; a train of wheels.
clod, *n.* klod, a lump of earth or clay; a mass of earth and turf; the ground; any mass concreted; that which is earthy, base, and vile; a gross stupid fellow; a dolt: *v.i.* to clot. (A.S., as *clot.*)
cloddish, *a.* *klod*-dish, boorish; stupid.
cloddy, *a.* *klod*-de, abounding in clods; earthy; gross.
clodhopper, *n.* *klod*-hop-per, a farm labourer; a rustic.
clodpate, *n.* *klod*-pate, a stupid fellow; a dolt; a blockhead.
clodpated, *a.* *klod*-pate-ed, stupid; dull; doltish.
clodpoll, *n.* *klod*-pole, a clodpate.
cloff, *n.* kloff, an allowance in weight given by wholesaler to retailer.
clog, *n.* klog, anything that hinders motion or renders it difficult; a shoe with a wooden sole; a wooden shoe; a patten: *v.t.* to encumber with something that retards or hinders motion; to impede; to obstruct; to choke up: *v.i.* to coalesce; to be encumbered with extraneous matter. (M.E.)
clog-almanac, *n.* *klog*-awl-ma-nak, a square block of wood or bone, variously notched all round with notches equal to the days in the year.
clog-dance, *n.* *klog*-dahnce, a dance in which the dancers wear clogs.
clogginess, *n.* *klog*-ge-ness, the state of being cloggy.
clogging, *n.* *klog*-ging, an obstruction.
cloggy, *a.* *klog*-ge, that clogs; adhesive.
cloisonné, *n.* kloy-*zon*-nay, oriental enamel-work in which the coloured parts are separated by metallic partitions. (Fr.)
cloister, *n.* *kloys*-ter, an arched or roofed walk for recreation surrounding monastic or collegiate quadrangles, etc.; an ambulatory; a place of religious retirement; a monastery or nunnery; a piazza: *v.t.* to confine in a cloister; to immure. (O.Fr. *cloistre.*)
cloistered, *a.* *kloys*-terd, living in a cloister; provided with cloisters; retired from the world; secluded; enclosed.
cloister-garth, *n.* *kloys*-ter-gahrth, a court or grass-plot surrounded by a cloister [Arch.].
cloistral, *a.* *kloys*-tral, pertaining to a cloister.
cloistress, *n.* *kloys*-tress, a nun.
clonic, *a.* *klon*-ik, convulsive; alternately contracting and relaxing [Path.]. (Gr. *klonos,* violent movement.)
clonus, *n.* *kloh*-nus, a spasm with violent contraction and relaxation of the muscles. (Gr.)
cloop, *n.* kloop, sound in drawing a cork. (Imit.)
cloot, *n.* kloot, a cloven hoof. **Cloots** (or **Clootie**), the Devil [Scots.].
close, *n.* kloze, the act of closing; conclusion; a grapple in wrestling: *v.t.* to shut to; to make fast; to end; to conclude; to fill up; to unite together; to bring nearer together; to confine; to enclose: *v.i.* to shut; to unite; to coalesce; to cease; to come to terms; to grapple. **close on,** or **upon,** to come to a mutual agreement. **close with,** to accede to; to consent or agree to; to come to an agreement with; to unite with. **close with,** or **close in with,** to join closely; to grapple, as persons in a contest. (O.Fr. *clos.*)
close, *n.* klose, an enclosure or place fenced in; the confines of a cathedral or abbey; an entry from a street; a blind alley; a cadence; *a.* shut fast, so as to have no opening; compact; well guarded; without ventilation; warm and damp, relaxing (of the weather); confined; narrow; near in place or time; very nearly equal; secret; having the quality of secrecy; reserved; intent; attentive; concise; strictly adhering to the original; compressed, as thoughts or words; intimate; accurate; penurious; not liberal; pronounced with the lips partly closed [Phonetics]; characterized by cramped development (of the opening at chess): *ad.* close to; near; closely; nearly; densely; secretly; pressingly. **close by,** within a little distance; very near. **close communion,** among certain Baptists, communion in the Lord's Supper with only those of their own sect. **close corporation,** a corporation which fills up its own vacancies. **close scholarship,** one not open to general competition. **close shave,** narrow escape from an accident. **close to the wind,** *see* **wind.**
close-banded, *a.* *klose*-band-ed, being in close order; closely united.
close-barred, *a.* *klose*-bahrd, with little spaces between the bars, hence, well shut-up.
close-fisted, *a.* *klose*-fist-ed, close-handed.
close-grained, *a.* *klose*-graynd, compact.
close-handed, *a.* *klose*-hand-ed, penurious; niggardly.
close-handedness, *n.* *klose*-hand-ed-ness, penuriousness.
close-hauled, *a.* *klose*-hawld, sailing as close to the wind as possible [Naut.].
closely, *ad.* *klose*-le, in a close manner.
closeness, *n.* *klose*-ness, the state of being close.
close-quarters, *n.pl.* klose-*kwaw*-terz, strong bulkheads formerly used in a ship for defence when boarded. **to come to close quarters,** to come into direct conflict with an enemy.
closer, *n.* *kloze*-er, that which, or one who, closes or concludes, esp. a debate; a stone or brick terminating the horizontal course of a wall [Arch.].
close-reefed, *a.* *klose*-reefd, with every reef taken in [Naut.].
close-season, *n.* *klose*-see-zon, close-time.
close-stool, *n.* *klose*-stool, a chamber utensil enclosed in a box; a night-stool.
closet, *n.* *kloz*-et, a small room for privacy or retirement, or a small room or recess used as a cupboard; a water-closet or privy: *v.t.* to take into a private apartment for consultation or deliberation.
close-time, *n.* *klose*-time, a season when it is illegal to catch certain fish and shoot certain game; the breeding season.
close-tongued, *a.* *klose*-tungd, reticent.
close-up, *n.* *klose*-up, a motion picture taken at a close range, usually a small part of the main picture giving greater detail.
closing, *n.* *kloh*-zing, conclusion. **closing time,** the hour at which any shop, office, place of public resort, etc., ceases business for the day.
closure, *n.* *kloh*-zhur, the act of shutting; that which closes; enclosure; conclusion; the means by which an end is made to a debate in a legislative or deliberative assembly; the completing of a circuit [Elec.]; the breech-block in a breech-loading gun; the right of the batting side in a cricket match to declare their innings closed. (L. *clausura,* closing.)
clot, *n.* klot, a soft or fluid mass coagulated, as blood; a dull heavy fellow: *v.i.* to form into clots; to coagulate: *v.t.* to cause to clot; to cover with clots. (A.S.)
★**cloth,** *n.* kloth, a woven or felted fabric, esp. of wool but also of hemp, flax, silk, cotton, or bark, used for garments or other covering; a tablecloth; the dress of a profession, esp. the clerical. **the cloth,** the clergy, from their usual black cloth garb. **cloth of gold,** a weave of gold threads with silk. **cloth of state,** the canopy held over a king's head. (A.S. *clath.*)
clothe, *v.t.* kloathe, to invest or cover as with a garment; to furnish with clothes. (A.S. *clathian.*)
clothes, *n.pl.* kloathz, wearing apparel; dress; bed-clothes. (A.S. *clathas.*)
clothes-basket, *n.* *kloathz*-bahs-ket, a receptacle for clothes and linen for the wash.
clothes-brush, *n.* *kloathz*-brush, a brush for cleaning clothes.
clothes-horse, *n.* *kloathz*-horse, a frame to dry clothes on.
clothes-line, *n.* *kloathz*-line, a line for drying clothes on.
clothes-man, *n.* *kloathz*-man, a dealer in clothes.
clothes-moth, *n.* *kloathz*-moth, any moth of the genus *Tinea,* whose larvæ feed on cloth, fur, etc.
clothes-peg, *n.* *kloathz*-peg, a forked peg for fastening clothes on a line.
clothes-press, *n.* *kloathz*-press, a device for pressing clothes; a wardrobe.

cloth-hall, *n.* *kloth*-hawl, a building used in mediæval times as a Cloth Exchange.
clothier, *n.* *kloh*-the-er, a seller of cloth or clothing; a maker of cloth.
clothing, *n.* *kloh*-thing, garments; clothes; dress.
cloth-shearer, *n.* *kloth*-sheer-er, one who shears cloth and frees it from superfluous nap.
clothworker, *n.* *kloth*-wurk-er, a maker of cloth.
clothyard, *n.* *kloth*-yard, a measure for cloth, since about 1550 the standard yard (36 ins.), earlier of varying lengths.
clotpoll, *n.* *klot*-pole, a clodpoll.
clotted, *a.* *klot*-ted, concreted into a mass; coagulated. **clotted cream,** cream that forms in clots when new milk is warmed.
clotter, *v.t.* *klot*-ter, to clot; to coagulate.
clotty, *a.* *klot*-te, full of clots.
clou, *n.* *kloo,* the chief attraction; the point of greatest interest. (Fr., a nail.)
★**cloud,** *n.* kloud, a collection of visible vapour, or watery particles, suspended in the atmosphere; a volume of smoke or dust floating or drifting in the air; a dark or varied colour in a vein or spot on a stone or other body; a great multitude; obscurity; a veil which obscures or darkens; suspicion: *v.t.* to overspread with clouds; to darken; to variegate with dark-coloured spots; to make gloomy or sullen; to sully: *v.i.* to become clouded. **in the clouds,** out of sight from confusion of idea; mystical; away from reality; absent in mind. **under a cloud,** under suspicion; suffering temporary misfortune. (A.S. *clūd,* a round mass.)
cloudberry, *n.* *kloud*-be-re, the mountain bramble, *Rubus chamæmorus,* or its strawberry-like fruit.
cloud-built, *a.* *kloud*-bilt, built of clouds or idle fancies; visionary.
cloudburst, *n.* *kloud*-burst, a sudden torrential and destructive rainfall within a small area.
cloud-capped, *a.* *kloud*-kapt, topped with clouds; very lofty.
cloud-castle, *n.* *kloud*-kah-sl, an imaginary thing; a day-dream.
cloud-chamber, *n.* *kloud*-chame-ber, a laboratory apparatus facilitating the study of gaseous ions.
cloud-compeller, *n.* *kloud*-kom-*pel*-ler, he that makes or directs clouds; Jupiter; a smoker [Coll.].
cloud-compelling, *a.* *kloud*-kom-*pel*-ling, collecting clouds or driving clouds.
clouded, *a.* *kloud*-ed, overcast (of weather); mottled; with colours unequally blended. **clouded leopard,** a carnivore of SE. Asia, "the tiger of the trees," *Felis nebulosa.*
cloudily, *ad.* *kloud*-e-le, in a cloudy manner.
cloudiness, *n.* *kloud*-e-ness, the state of being cloudy.
cloud-kissing, *a.* *kloud*-kis-sing, touching the clouds.
cloudless, *a.* *kloud*-less, without a cloud; clear; bright.
cloudlessly, *ad.* *kloud*-less-le, in a cloudless manner.
cloudlet, *n.* *kloud*-let, a little cloud.
cloudwards, *ad.* *kloud*-wardz, in the direction of the clouds.
cloud-wrack, *n.* *kloud*-rak, torn fragments of cloud in the sky after a storm.
cloud-wrapped, *a.* *kloud*-rapt, enveloped in clouds; involved in mist or obscurity.
cloudy, *a.* *kloud*-e, overcast with clouds; consisting of a cloud or clouds; obscure; sullen; marked with veins or spots; wanting in clearness.
clough, *n.* kluf, a cleft or ravine in a rock or a hillside.
clout, *n.* klout, a piece of cloth, leather, or metal, used to mend or patch something; a patch; a rag; a mark for archers to shoot at; an iron plate on an axletree, to keep it from wearing; a blow with the hand: *v.t.* to mend by sewing on a clout; to patch; to cover with a piece of cloth; to join clumsily; to make fast with nails; to strike heavily with the hand. (A.S. *clut,* a patch.)
clouted, *a.* *klout*-ed, patched; mended clumsily; studded with nails. **clouted cream,** clotted cream.
clouterly, *a.* *klout*-er-le, clumsy; awkward. (Dial. Eng.)
clout-nail, *n.* *klout*-nale, a short large-headed nail for the soles of stout shoes.
clove, *n.* klohv, a very pungent aromatic spice, the dried unexpanded flower-bud of the East Indian tree *Eugenia aromatica.* (L. *clavus,* a nail.)
clove, *n.* klohv, a small bulb formed in the axils of the scales of another bulb. (A.S. *cluf.*)
clove, *n.* klohv, a weight of 7 to 8 lb. formerly used for wool and cheese.
clove-gillyflower, *n.* klohv-*jil*-le-flou-er, a species of *Dianthus,* the flower of which smells like cloves.
clove-hitch, *n.* klohv-hich, two half-hitches round a spar or rope.
cloven, *a.* *kloh*-vn, cleft; divided into two parts, as a hoof.
cloven-footed, *a.* *kloh*-vn-foot-ed, cloven-hoofed.
cloven-hoofed, *a.* *kloh*-vn-hooft, having the hoof divided into two parts, as the ox; bisulcate.
clove-pink, *n.* *klohv*-pink, the clove-gilliflower.
clover, *n.* *kloh*-ver, a plant of the genus *Trifolium,* used for fodder. **to live in clover,** to live luxuriously or in abundance. (A.S. *clāfre.*)
clown, *n.* kloun, a rustic; one who has the manners of a rustic; a buffoon in pantomime or at a circus: *v.i.* to play the clown. (Scand.)
clownery, *n.* *kloun*-er-e, behaviour like a clown's.
clownish, *a.* *kloun*-ish, pertaining to or like a clown; clumsy; ungainly; rude.
clownishly, *ad.* *kloun*-ish-le, in a clownish manner.
clownishness, *n.* *kloun*-ish-ness, the state of being clownish.
cloy, *v.t.* and *v.i.* kloy, to satiate; to glut; to surfeit; to fill to loathing. (Fr. *clou,* a nail.)
cloyless, *a.* *kloy*-less, that cannot cloy or satiate.
club, *n.* klub, a stick or piece of wood, with one end thicker and heavier than the other; a thick heavy stick; a stick bent and weighted at the end for driving a ball; any of the sticks used in golf; a club-shaped knot or tail to a wig; the suit of playing-cards now bearing the trefoil but formerly (esp. in Spain) the club: *v.t.* to beat with a club. **to club the musket,** to wield it so as to beat with the butt-end. (Scand.)
club, *n.* klub, a number of persons associated for the promotion of some common purpose, as of social intercourse, literature, science or politics, and who are usually governed by certain self-imposed regulations or by-laws; the collective body of members composing a club, or who support a club-house; a share or proportion paid to form a common stock, or the fund thus raised; joint charge or effort: *v.i.* to join as in a club; to pay an equal proportion of a common reckoning or charge: *v.t.* to combine means for a purpose, each contributor paying an equal share. (Scand.)
clubbable, *a.* *klub*-a-bl, disposed to club life; suitable for club membership.
clubbed, *a.* klubd, thickened at the end.
clubber, *n.* *klub*-er, a clubbist.
clubbish, *a.* *klub*-ish, rustic; clubbable.
clubbism, *n.* *klub*-izm, the club system.
clubbist, *n.* *klub*-ist, a club-member.
club-foot, *n.* *klub*-foot, a short deformed foot; talipes.
club-footed, *a.* *klub*-foot-ed, having a club foot.
club-grass, *n.* *klub*-grahs, popular name of various jointed grasses.
club-haul, *v.t.* *klub*-hawl, to make a ship tack about, by letting go the lee anchor, and slipping the cable, as soon as she pays off.
club-headed, *a.* *klub*-hed-ed, having a thick head.
club-house, *n.* *klub*-house, a house occupied by a club; the home of a club, in which members meet, dine, etc., and often can be temporarily accommodated.
club-land, *n.* *klub*-land, the district round St. James's and Pall Mall in London, within which the most noted clubs are situated.
club-law, *n.* *klub*-law, government by violence.
club-man, *n.* *klub*-man, a club-member; a man passing the greater part of his time in his clubs.
club-moss, *n.* *klub*-moss, a plant of the genus *Lycopodium.*
club-room, *n.* *klub*-room, a room in which a club meets.
club-root, *n.* *klub*-root, a plant disease due to *Plasmodiophora brassicæ,* one of the slime fungi and characterized by protuberances on the roots.
club-rush, *n.* *klub*-rush, a plant of the genus *Scripus.*
cluck, *n.* kluk, the call of a hen; a similar sound; the click of South African tribes: *v.i.* to call chickens, as a hen: *v.t.* to call by clucking. (*Clack.*)
clue, *n.* kloo, a clew, particularly as a key or hint serving as a guide in an investigation.

clumber, *n.* *klum*-ber, a species of spaniel so called from having been bred at Clumber, the Duke of Newcastle's seat in Nottinghamshire.
clump, *n.* klump, a thick, short, shapeless piece of wood or other solid substance; a cluster of trees or shrubs; an additional sole nailed to a shoe; a heavy footfall; a hard blow with the hand: *v.t.* to nail an extra sole on to a shoe or boot; to give a hard blow with the hand. (Dan. *klump.*)
clumpy, *a.* *klum*-pe, consisting of clumps; massive; shapeless.
clumsily, *ad.* *klum*-ze-le, in a clumsy manner.
clumsiness, *n.* *klum*-ze-ness, the quality of being clumsy.
clumsy, *a.* *klum*-ze, awkward; ungainly; ill made; badly constructed. (M.E. *clumsen*, to benumb.)
clunch, *n.* klunch, the lower and harder beds of the Upper Chalk [Geol.]; indurated clay or chalk marl, found in coal-pits next to the coal; stiff coarse clay. (Dial. Eng.)
clung, klung, *pp.* of the verb to cling.
Cluniac, *n.* *kloo*-ne-ak, one of a reformed order of Benedictine monks founded in the 10th cent. at Cluny, Burgundy.
clupeoid, *n.* *kloo*-pe-oyd, a fish of the genus *Clupeoidæ*, which includes the herring, sprat, pilchard, and shads: *a.* resembling a herring. (L. *clupea*, a small freshwater fish.)
cluster, *n.* *klus*-ter, a bunch; a number of things of the same kind growing or joined together; a number of individuals or things collected or gathered into a close body; a collection; a group; a crowd: *v.i.* to grow or collect in clusters: *v.t.* to collect into a bunch or group. (A.S., a bunch.)
clustered, *a.* *klus*-terd, grouped together. **clustered column,** a column apparently made up of several columns bound together [Arch.]. **clustered saxifrage,** the plant *Saxifraga nivalis.*
clustery, *a.* *klus*-te-re, in clusters; like, or abounding in, clusters.
clutch, *a.* klutch, to double in the fingers, and compress them together; to seize; to grasp: *n.* a gripping or pinching with the fingers; grasp; seizure; a projecting tooth, or other piece of machinery, for connecting moving parts; the control by which an engine is put into and out of gear; the batch of eggs laid by one bird; a set of eggs for hatching: *pl.* paws or talons; hands; tyrannous power. (A.S. *clyccan*, to catch.)
clutter, *n.* *klut*-ter, a confused mass; a confused noise; bustle: *v.t.* to encumber with litter: *v.i.* to make a noise or bustle.
cly, *v.t.* kly, to seize; to steal: *n.* money; anything that may be stolen; a pocket [Slang].
Clydesdale, *n.* *klydz*-dale, one of a breed of heavy draught horses. (Originally from the *Clyde* district, Scotland.)
Clypeaster, *n.* klip-e-*as*-ter, a genus of sea-urchins. (L. *clypeus*, a shield, Gr. *aster*, a star.)
clypeate, *a.* *klip*-e-at, shaped like a shield; scutate (of heads of certain insects).
clypeiform, *a.* *klip*-e-e-fawrm, clypeate.
clypeus, *n.* *klip*-e-us, a shield-like plate on the fore part of an insect's head. (L., a shield.)
clyster, *n.* *klis*-ter, an injection; an enema; a liquid substance injected into the lower intestines to promote alvine discharges or for other purposes.
clyster pipe, a tube of an enema syringe. (L.)
cnemis, *n.* nee-mis, the shin or tibia [Zool.]. (Gr. *knēmē*, tibia.)
co-, ko, a prefix of Latin origin with the meaning of together, mutually, joint, or with.
coacervate, *a.* ko-*as*-ser-vat, heaped together; collected into a crowd; clustered [Bot.].
coach, *n.* koach, a close four-wheeled double-seated vehicle or carriage; a railway carriage; a tutor to prepare for an examination; a trainer for athletic sports: *v.i.* to ride in a coach; to study under a tutor: *v.t.* to travel or to carry in a coach; to prepare for an examination; to train. (Hung. *kocsi*, pertaining to the village of Kocs, Hungary.)
coach-box, *n.* *koach*-boks, the driver's seat on a coach.
coach-built, *a.* *koach*-bilt, built by craftsmanship, not by mass-production (of motor-car bodies).
coachee, *n.* *koach*-e, a coachman [Slang].
coachful, *n.* *koach*-ful, as many as a coach will hold.
coach-hire, *n.* *koach*-hire, price for the use of a coach.
coach-horse, *n.* *koach*-horse, a horse for drawing a coach.
coach-house, *n.* *koach*-house, an outhouse for accommodating a coach or carriage.
coaching, *n.* *koach*-ing, the driving of a coach, esp. as a sport or for pleasure; the tutoring of a person for an examination, or athletic contest.
coachmaker, *n.* *koach*-make-er, one who makes coaches.
coachman, *n.* *koach*-man, the driver of a coach.
coachmanship, *n.* *koach*-man-ship, skill in driving.
coachmaster, *n.* *koach*-mahs-ter, the proprietor of a coach, or of a livery stable.
coach-office, *n.* *koach*-of-fis, a booking office of a stage coach.
coach-whip, *n.* *koach*-whip, the long-lashed whip used by the driver of a coach; a harmless tree-snake of the southern U.S.A. **coach-whip bird,** an Australian passerine bird with a call like the crack of a whip.
coact, *v.i.* ko-*akt*, to act together or in concert: *v.t.* to exercise control over. (*Co-* and *act.*)
coaction, *n.* ko-*ak*-shon, joint action; compulsion.
coactive, *a.* ko-*ak*-tiv, compulsory; acting in concurrence.
coadapted, *a.* ko-ad-*ap*-ted, mutually adapted.
coadjustment, *n.* ko-ad-*just*-ment, mutual adjustment.
coadjutant, *n.* ko-ad-*joo*-tant *or* ko-*aj*-oo-tant, an assistant: *a.* mutually assisting or operating.
coadjutor, *n.* ko-ad-*joo*-tor, an assistant; a fellow-helper; an associate; a colleague; one appointed to perform the duties of another [Canon Law]. (L. *co-adjutor*, a helper.)
coadjutorship, *n.* ko-ad-*joo*-tor-ship, joint assistance.
coadjutrix, *n.* ko-ad-*joo*-triks, a female assistant.
coadunate, *a.* ko-*ad*-yew-nat, united, esp. of leaves united at the base [Bot.]. (Low L. *coadjunatus.*)
coagency, *n.* ko-*ay*-jen-se, joint agency.
coagent, *n.* ko-*ay*-jent, an assistant; an associate.
coagulability, *n.* ko-*ag*-yew-la-*bil*-e-te, capability of being coagulated.
coagulable, *a.* ko-*ag*-yew-la-bl, capable of coagulating.
coagulant, *n.* ko-*ag*-yew-lant, a substance causing coagulation.
coagulate, *v.t.* ko-*ag*-yew-late, to curdle; to change from a fluid to an inspissated or curd-like state; to clot: *v.i.* to curdle. (L. *coagulatus*, curdled.)
coagulation, *n.* ko-ag-yew-*lay*-shon, the act of coagulating; the state of being coagulated; that which is coagulated. (L. *coagulatio.*)
coagulative, *a.* ko-*ag*-yew-la-tiv, productive of coagulation; tending to coagulate.
coagulator, *n.* ko-*ag*-yew-lay-tor, a coagulant.
coagulum, *n.* ko-*ag*-yew-lum, a coagulated mass; a clot of blood; a coagulant, as rennet. (L.)
coaita, *n.* ko-*ite*-a, one of various spider-monkeys (*Ateles*) of S. America.
coak, *n.* koak, a small cylinder of hard wood, let into the ends of the pieces to be joined, to render the joining more secure; a dowel [Carp.].
***coal,** *n.* koal, a black carbonaceous substance of vegetable origin, usually found beneath overlying strata, used as fuel; a piece of wood or other combustible substance, ignited, burning, or charred; a cinder: *v.t.* to supply a ship with coals: *v.i.* to take in coal. **blow the coals,** to stir up strife. **carry coals to Newcastle,** to waste one's labour. **haul over the coals,** to take to task; to reprimand. (A.S. *col.*)
coal-backer, *n.* *koal*-bak-er, a coal-porter.
coal-bed, *n.* *koal*-bed, a coal-stratum, or one containing coal.
coal-black, *a.* *koal*-blak, black as coal; very black.
coal-box, *n.* *koal*-boks, a coal-scuttle; a bin for coals.
coalbrand, *n.* *koal*-brand, a disease in wheat in which the ear fills with a coal-black powder.
coal-brass, *n.* *koal*-brahss, iron pyrites found in coal.
coal-bunker, *n.* *koal*-bung-ker, a bin or receptacle for coals, esp. on a ship.
coal-cellar, *n.* *koal*-sel-lar, a storeroom for coals.
coalesce, *v.i.* koh-a-*less*, to grow together; to unite.
coalescence, *n.* koh-a-*less*-ence, union; fusion.

coalescent, *a.* koh-a-*les*-sent, growing together, uniting. (L. *coalescens.*)
coal-factor, *n.* *koal*-fak-tor, the middleman between the colliery owner and the coal-merchant.
coal-field, *n.* *koal*-feeld, a bed of coal; land containing coal strata.
coalfish, *n.* *koal*-fish, a fish of the cod family with a greenish black back.
coal-gas, *n.* *koal*-gas, impure carburetted hydrogen got from coal, used for lighting and heating.
coal-heaver, *n.* *koal*-hee-ver, one employed in carrying or loading coals.
coal-hole, *n.* *koal*-hole, a small coal-cellar.
coaling, *n.* *koal*-ing, the operation of filling a ship's bunkers with coal. **coaling station,** a fortified port where ships of war can take in coal.
coalite, *n.* *koal*-ite, a registered trade name for a smokeless fuel.
coalition, *n.* *koh*-a-*lish*-on, union; a temporary union of different political or other parties. (L. *coalitus.*)
coalitionist, *n.* koh-a-*lish*-on-ist, a supporter of a political or other coalition.
coal-master, *n.* *koal*-mahs-ter, one who works a coal-mine.
coal-measures, *n.pl.* *koal*-mezh-erz, a group of coal-seams with the associated rocks.
coal-mine, *n.* *koal*-mine, a mine from which coal is obtained.
coal-miner, *n.* *koal*-mine-er, a worker in a coal-mine.
coal-mouse, *n.* *koal*-mous, the coal-tit.
coal-pit, *n.* *koal*-pit, a pit where coal is dug; a place where charcoal is made.
coal-plant, *n.* *koal*-plahnt, a plant of the Carboniferous Period, the fossilized remains of which form coal [Geol.].
coal-screen, *n.* *koal*-skreen, a mechanical sieve for sorting coal.
coal-scuttle, *n.* *koal*-skut-tl, a carrier in which to put coals for immediate use; a poke-bonnet.
coal-seam, *n.* *koal*-seem, a stratum of coal.
coal-ship, *n.* *koal*-ship, a ship that transports coal; a collier.
coal-tar, *n.* *koal*-tahr, tar obtained by the distillation of bituminous coal.
coal-tit, *n.* *koal*-tit, a small passerine bird, either *Parus britannicus*, the British coal-tit, or *Parus ater*, the Continental species.
coal-whipper, *n.* *koal*-whip-per, one who unloads coal from ships, or a machine for this purpose.
coaly, *a.* *koal*-e, like or containing coal: *n.* a coal-heaver.
coaming, *n.* *koam*-ing, the raised border of a hatchway [Naut.]. (*Comb.*)
coaptation, *n.* koh-ap-*tay*-shon, the adaptation or adjustment of parts to each other. (L. *coaptatus*, fitted together.)
coarb, *n.* *koh*-arb, a bishop or abbot of the early Irish or Scottish Churches as successor to the patron saint or founder. (Ir. *comharba.*)
coarctate, *a.* ko-*ark*-tate, pressed together [Bot. and Entom.]. (L. *coarctatus*, pressed together.)
coarctation, *n.* koh-ark-*tay*-shon, pressure; contraction.
coarse, *a.* korse, of average or inferior quality; common; large in texture; rough; uncivil; gross; indelicate.
coarse-grained, *a.* *korse*-graynd, of large grains; unrefined.
coarsely, *ad.* *korse*-le, in a coarse manner.
coarsen, *v.t.* and *i.* *korse*-n, to make or become coarse.
coarseness, *n.* *korse*-ness, the quality of being coarse.
coarsish, *a.* *korse*-ish, inclining towards coarseness.
co-assessor, *n.* koh-a-*ses*-sor, a joint assessor.
co-assume, *v.t.* koh-a-*sewm*, to assume with another.
coast, *n.* koast, the margin of the land next the sea; the sea-shore; formerly any frontier-line of a country or district; a toboggan slide; a run down a declivity on a cycle or other vehicle: *v.i.* to sail near the shore, or in sight of land; to sail from port to port in the same country; to free-wheel on a bicycle, etc., down-hill; to toboggan or slide on a sledge down-hill: *v.t.* to sail by or near to; to keep close to. **the coast is clear,** the danger is over; the enemy has departed. (O.Fr. *coste.*)
coastal, *a.* *koas*-tal, relating to the coast; bordering on a coast line.
coaster, *n.* *koas*-ter, a vessel employed in trading from port to port in the same country; a tray on which decanters are passed round; a free-wheel bicycle; one who coasts.
coastguard, *n.* *koast*-gahrd, one of a trained and disciplined body of men guarding the coast.
coasting, *a.* *koast*-ing, pertaining to the coast; sailing along the coast. **coasting trade,** the trade carried on between the ports of the same country. **coasting vessel,** a vessel employed in the coasting trade; a coaster.
coastline, *n.* *koast*-line, the shore line; the coastal outline of a country.
coast-waiter, *n.* *koast*-way-ter, a customs official superintending the examination of the cargoes of coasters.
coastwards, *ad.* *koast*-wardz, towards the coast.
coastwise, *ad.* *koast*-wize, along the coast.
★**coat,** *n.* koat, a sleeved outer garment; external covering, as the hair or fur of a beast; any membrane that serves as a cover; a layer of any substance covering another; a coat of arms: *v.t.* to cover; to spread over with a layer of any substance. **coat of arms,** heraldic bearings of an esquire or one of higher rank; the tabard of a herald. **coat of mail,** a shirt-like piece of armour consisting of a network of iron rings, plates, or scales fastened on leather. **red coat,** the traditional British army uniform; hence, **red-coat,** a soldier. **trail one's coat,** *see* **trail.** (O.Fr. *cote.*)
coat-armour, *n.* *koat*-ar-mor, a coat of arms; a loose vestment worked with armorial ensigns worn by knights over their armour.
coat-card, *n.* *koat*-kahrd, a playing-card bearing a coated figure, now called a court-card.
coatee, *n.* koh-*tee*, a tight-fitting coat with short tails.
coati, *n.* ko-*ah*-te, one of two species of *Nasua*, a long-nosed South American plantigrade carnivore of the racoon family, known also as the **coatimundi.** (Native name.)
coating, *n.* *koat*-ing, a covering, or the act of covering; a substance spread over for cover or defence; cloth for coats.
coat-link, *n.* *koat*-link, two buttons held loosely together by a link.
coax, *v.t.* koaks, to persuade by fondling or flattery; to wheedle; to soothe. (M.E. *cokes*, a fool.)
coaxer, *n.* *koaks*-er, a wheedler; a flatterer.
co-axial, *a.* ko-*ak*-se-al, having a common axis.
coaxingly, *ad.* *koaks*-ing-le, in a coaxing manner.
cob, *n.* kob, a lumpy or rounded piece; a horse rather larger than a pony; the spike of maize; a ball or pellet for cramming fowls; a spider; a male swan; a species of gull; a composition of clay mixed with straw; a kind of wicker basket, used in husbandry; a Spanish dollar: *v.t.* to punish by striking the breech with a belt or flat piece of wood; to pull by the hair or ears. (Origin uncertain.)
cobalt, *n.* *koh*-bawlt, a brittle metallic element of a reddish-grey or greyish-white colour, and weak lustre. **cobalt bloom,** acicular arsenate of cobalt. **cobalt blue,** a pigment of alumina and cobalt. **cobalt crust,** earthy arsenate of cobalt. **cobalt glance,** cobaltite. **cobalt green,** a lasting green colouring matter. (Ger. *Kobold*, a goblin, for the trouble it gave the miners.)
cobaltic, *a.* ko-*bawl*-tik, pertaining to cobalt.
cobaltine, *n.* *ko*-bawl-tin, cobaltite.
cobaltite, *n.* *ko*-bawl-tite, a crystalline compound of cobalt with arsenic and sulphur.
cobber, *n.* *kob*-ber, a good fellow; a chum or pal [Austral. slang].
cobble, *v.t.* *kob*-bl, to make or mend coarsely, as shoes; to make or do clumsily: *v.i.* to work clumsily. (Origin unknown.)
cobble, *n.* *kob*-bl, a rounded stone or boulder; a pebble; a roundish lump of coal; a coble: *v.t.* to pave with cobbles. (*Cob*, a lump.)
cobbler, *n.* *kob*-bler, a mender of shoes; a clumsy workman; a cooling beverage sucked through a straw [U.S.A.]. **cobbler's punch,** beer mixed with spirits, sugar, and spice, and served hot. **cobbler's wax,** resinous wax used for waxing threads.
cobble-stone, *n.* *kob*-bl-stone, a large pebble; a rounded paving-stone.
cobbly, *a.* *kob*-bl-e, paved with cobbles; uneven.
cobby, *a.* *kob*-be, stout; brisk.

cob-coals, *n.pl.* *kob*-koalz, large round coals; cobbles.

Cobdenism, *n.* *kob*-den-izm, the Free Trade policy advocated by Richard Cobden (*d.* 1865).

Cobdenite, *n.* *kob*-den-ite, an adherent of Cobdenism.

cobego, *n.* ko-*bee*-go, the flying-lemur of Malaya.

co-belligerent, *a.* koh-bel-*lij*-er-ent, carrying on war conjointly: *n.* a nation carrying on war conjointly with another.

coble, *n.* *koh*-bl, a short flat-bottomed fishing-boat, usually with a deep rudder. (Welsh *ceubal.*)

cob-loaf, *n.* *kob*-loaf, a loaf that is rough and crusty.

cobnut, *n.* *kob*-nut, a large hazel-nut, *Corylus tubulosa*.

cob-pipe, *n.* *kob*-pipe, a tobacco-pipe made from a corn-cob.

cobra, *n.* *koh*-bra, a venomous serpent, *Naja tripudians*, of S. Asia, which when excited dilates the skin about its neck into a hood. **Egyptian cobra,** the aspis, *N. haje.* **king cobra,** a large variety, *N. hannah*, ranging from India to the Philippines. **spitting cobra,** the ringhals. (Port. *cobra de capello*, the snake of the hood.)

coburg, *n.* *koh*-burg, a worsted and cotton or silk fabric, having one side twilled. (*Coburg*, in Germany.)

cob-wall, *n.* *kob*-wawl, a wall made of mud or unburned clay, mixed with straw.

cobweb, *n.* *kob*-web, the fine-spun network spread by a spider to catch its prey; a flimsy snare to entrap the simple or unwary; a weak and flimsy entanglement: *a.* thin, flimsy, slender, feeble. (M.E. *coppe*, a spider, and *web.*)

cobwebbed, *a.* *kob*-webd, covered with cobwebs; covered with a thick interwoven pubescence [Bot.].

cobwebbery, *n.* *kob*-web-er-re, a mass of cobweb.

cobwebby, *a.* *kob*-web-e, covered with or resembling cobwebs.

coca, *n.* *koh*-ka, a highly stimulating narcotic, the dried leaf of *Erythroxylon coca*, found wild in Peru, and chewed. (Sp.)

Cocaigne, *n.* ko-*kane*, Cockaigne.

cocaine, *n.* ko-*kane*, an alkaloid of coca forming the base of many drugs used as local anæsthetics.

cocainism, *n.* ko-*kane*-izm, cocaine poisoning; a morbid state brought about by excessive use of cocaine.

cocainist, *n.* ko-*kay*-nist, one addicted to cocaine.

cocainization, *n.* ko-*kay*-ny-*zay*-shon, the state of being under the influence of cocaine.

cocainize, *v.t.* ko-*kay*-nize, to treat with, or to stupefy with, cocaine.

coccagee, *n.* kok-a-*jee*, a cider apple, and the cider itself. (Ir., goose-dung, because so coloured.)

cocciferous, *a.* kok-*sif*-er-us, bearing berries. (L. *coccum*, a berry, *fero*, bear.)

Coccinella, *n.* kok-se-*nel*-la, genus of small beetles including the ladybirds. (Gr. *kokkinos*, scarlet).

coccolite, *n.* *kok*-ko-lite, a variety of pyroxene. (Gr. *kokkos*, a berry, *lithos*, a stone.)

coccoliths, *n.pl.* *kok*-ko-liths, minute algal remains found in deep-sea ooze and in chalk.

coccosphere, *n.* *kok*-ko-sfeer, a minute rounded body composed of coccoliths.

Cocculus, *n.* *kok*-kew-lus, a genus of Indian menispermaceous plants. **cocculus indicus,** the achene of *Anamirta cocculus*, employed in medicine as a narcotic, and sometimes to adulterate beer. (Gr. *kokkos.*)

Coccus, *n.* *kok*-kus, (*pl.* **cocci,** *kok*-sy) a genus of hemipterous insects, some of which are destructive to grain; (*l.c.*) an order of spheroidal bacteria; a spore mother-cell in certain cryptogams [Bot.]. (Gr. *kokkos.*)

coccygeal, *a.* kok-*sij*-e-al, relating to the coccyx.

coccyx, *n.* *kok*-siks, the bone at the base of the spine [Anat.]. (Gr., a cuckoo.)

cochin, *n.* *koch*-in, a variety of domestic fowl with feathered legs, originally from Cochin-China.

cochineal, *n.* *koch*-e-neel, a small insect, *Coccus cacti*, found chiefly in Mexico, the dried bodies of the females of which are used in the preparation of crimson and scarlet dyes and in the manufacture of carmine pigment. (Sp. *cochinilla.*)

cochineal-fig, *n.* *koch*-e-neel-fig, the cactaceous plant, *Nopalea coccinellifera*, on which the cochineal insect is found and extensively cultivated.

cochlea, *n.* *kok*-le-a, spiral-shaped cavity of the internal ear. (L., a snail or a spiral shell.)

cochlean, *a.* *kok*-le-an, cochleate.

cochleariform, *a.* kok-le-*ayr*-re-form, having the form of a snail-shell.

cochleate, *a.* *kok*-le-ate, twisted like a snail-shell; spiral.

cock, *n.* kok, the male of birds, particularly of domestic fowls; a male; a weathervane in shape of a cock; a tap, faucet, etc., for drawing off or regulating the flow of liquid; a small conical pile of hay; the style or gnomon of a dial; the piece which covers the balance in a clock or watch; the hammer in the lock of a firearm, and its position; the mark aimed at in curling; a familiar form of address: *a.* turning up: *v.t.* to set erect; to place, as the hat, on one side of the head; to turn or set up with an air of pertness; to set a firearm's cock or trigger in the firing position: *v.i.* to hold up the head; to strut; to look big, pert, or menacing. **cock-a-hoop,** triumphant; exulting. **cock-a-doodle-doo,** a nursery name for a cock and for its crow. **cock-and-bull story,** a tedious absurd story, or a ridiculous exaggerated story. **cock-a-leekie,** a soup of boiled fowl with leeks. **cock-of-the-north,** the brambling. **cock-of-the-rock,** the handsome South American passerine bird, *Rupicola crocea.* **cock-of-the-wood,** the capercailzie. (A.S. *coc.*)

cockabondy, *n.* kok-a-*bon*-de, an angler's artificial fly. (W. *coch a bon ddu*, red with black body.)

cockade, *n.* ko-*kade*, a knot or ribbon stuck in the hat as a badge; a leather badge or rosette worn on the hat. (Fr. *cocarde*, from *coq*, a cock.)

cockaded, *a.* ko-*kay*-ded, wearing a cockade.

cock-ahoop, *a.* kok-a-*hoop*, exultant; jubilant [Coll.].

Cockaigne, *n.* ko-*kane*, an imaginary country of idleness and luxury; used also of London as the home of cockneys.

cockal, *n.* *kok*-al, a game, former name of the game of knuckle-bones.

cockalorum, *n.* kok-a-*law*-rum, a perky, self-satisfied little man; a game of progressive leap-frog.

cockateel, *n.* kok-a-*teel*, an Australian crested parrot allied to the grass parrakeets.

cockatoo, *n.* kok-a-*too*, a crested parrot; a small farmer in Australia [Coll.]. (Malay, *kākātuā.*)

cockatrice, *n.* *kok*-a-triss, a fabulous serpent hatched from a cock's egg; the basilisk; an imaginary bird with a serpent's tail. (O.Fr. *cocatrice*, a crocodile.)

cock-bill, *n.* *kok*-bil, said of the anchor when it is suspended perpendicularly from the cathead ready to be let go [Naut.].

cock-boat, *n.* *kok*-boat, a small ship's boat.

cock-brained, *a.* *kok*-braynd, giddy; rash.

cock-broth, *n.* *kok*-broth, broth made by boiling a cock.

cockchafer, *n.* *kok*-chay-fer, a beetle of the genus *Melolontha.* (*Cock* and *chafer.*)

cock-crow, *n.* *kok*-kroh, the crow of a cock; the early dawn.

cock-crowing, *n.* *kok*-kroh-ing, cock-crow.

cocked, *a.* kokt, erect; set upon one side, as a cocked hat.

cocker, *v.t.* *kok*-er, to fondle; to indulge; to pamper. (Probably Scand.)

cocker, *n.* *kok*-er, a breeder of fighting-cocks; a patron of cock-fighting; a variety of spaniel.

cockerel, *n.* *kok*-e-rel, a young cock.

cocket, *n.* *kok*-et, a seal of the custom-house; a certificate from the custom-house that duty has been paid. (Anglo-Fr. *cokette.*)

cockeye, *n.* *kok*-eye, a squinting eye.

cockeyed, *a.* *kok*-ide, having squinting eyes; inaccurate; not quite right [Slang].

cockfight, *n.* *kok*-fite, a fight between gamecocks.

cockfighting, *n.* *kok*-fite-ing, the sport or practice of making gamecocks fight; a cock-fight.

cockhorse, *a.* *kok*-horse, on horseback.

cockily, *ad.* *kok*-e-le, in a cocky manner.

cockiness, *n.* *kok*-e-ness, the state of being cocky or impudent; impudence.

cock-laird, *n.* *kok*-layrd, a yeoman [Scot. coll.].

cockle, *n.* *kok*-kl, darnel, a weed that grows among corn. (A.S. *coccel.*)

cockle, *n.* *kok*-kl, a bivalve mollusc of the genus *Cardium*; the shell of this; a small shallow boat. (Fr. *coquille*, a shell.)

cockle, *v.i.* and *t.* *kok*-kl, to contract into wrinkles; to pucker, crease, or wrinkle, as cloth. **cockles of the heart,** innermost feelings; the depths of the heart. (Fr. *coquiller.*)

cockle-oast, *n.* *kok*-kl-oast, that part of a hop-kiln or oast where the fire is made.

cockler, *n.* *kok*-kl-er, one who collects and sells cockles.

cockle-stair, *n.* *kok*-kl-stare, a spiral or winding stair.

cockle-stove, *n.* kok-kl-*stohv*, a cockle-oast.

cockloft, *n.* *kok*-loft, the top loft next the roof.

cockney, *n.* *kok*-ne, a native of London, esp. one born within sound of Bow bells (Cheapside): *a.* pertaining to a cockney. (M.E. *coken ey*, cock's egg.)

cockneydom, *n.* *kok*-ne-dum, cockneys collectively.

cockneyfied, *a.* *kok*-ne-fide, like a cockney.

cockneyish, *a.* *kok*-ne-ish, relating to or like a cockney.

cockneyism, *n.* *kok*-ne-izm, the peculiar dialect or manners of a cockney.

cock-paddle, *n.* *kok*-pad-dl, the lump-fish [Scot.].

cockpit, *n.* *kok*-pit, a pit or area where gamecocks fight; a place on the lower deck in a ship of war for the wounded in an action [Naut.]; an open-air space in the fuselage with a seat or seats [Av.]. **the cockpit of Europe,** Belgium.

cockroach, *n.* *kok*-roach, the so-called black beetle (which is not a beetle, but belongs to the orthoptera) *Periplaneta orientalis* or its allies. (Sp. *cucaracha.*)

cockscomb, *n.* *koks*-kome, the comb of a cock; a plant of the genus *Celosia*; the yellow rattle, *Rhinanthus crista-galli*; a fop or coxcomb.

cock's-foot, *n.* *koks*-foot, the pasture grass, *Dactylis glomerata.*

cock's-head, *n.* *koks*-hed, sainfoin, from the shape of the pod.

cock-shot, *n.* *kok*-shot, a shot or throw at an object for amusement; a mark or target for this.

cockshut, *n.* *kok*-shut, the close of the day, when fowls go to roost; twilight.

cock-shy, *n.* *kok*-shy, a cock-shot.

cock-sparrow, *n.* kok-*spa*-roh, male of the sparrow; a little, pert, presuming fellow.

cockspur, *n.* *kok*-spur, the spur of a cock; the Virginian hawthorn, and other plants.

cock-sure, *a.* *kok*-shoor, confidently certain.

cocksy, *a.* *kok*-se, conceited; cocky.

cocktail, *n.* *kok*-tale, a rove-beetle; a horse with its tail docked; a drink of bitters and spirits, usually iced.

cock-up, *a.* *kok*-up, applied to an initial letter extending above the first line of text and aligning with it [Print.].

cocky, *a.* *kok*-e, aggressively impudent; conceited.

cockyleekie, *n.* kok-e-*leek*-e, leek and chicken broth [Scot.].

cockyolly, *n.* kok-*yol*-le, a nursery name for any bird.

cocoa, *n.* *koh*-ko, the tropical palm that bears the coconut; a preparation or beverage made of the cocoa-bean.

cocoa-bean, *n.* *koh*-ko-been, the dried and partly fermented seed of *Theobroma cacao*, an evergreen tree of Central and South America.

cocoa-nibs, *n.pl.* *koh*-ko-nibz, crushed cocoa-beans.

cocoa-nut, *n.* *koh*-ko-nut, the coconut.

cocoa-plum, *n.* *koh*-ko-plum, the fruit of *Chrysobalanus icaco.*

coco-de-mer, *n.* koh-ko-de-*mare*, the double coconut, *Lodoicea sechellarum.*

coconut, *n.* *koh*-ko-nut, the fruit of the tropical palm, *Cocos nucifera*, spelt in commerce cokernut. (Sp. *coco*, bugbear, on account of the ugly marking on the nut.)

cocoon, *n.* ko-*koon*, the silky covering which the larvæ of certain insects spin for their protection in their pupal state. (Fr. *cocon.*)

cocoonery, *n.* ko-*koon*-er-re, a place or apartment for silkworms, when feeding and forming cocoons.

cocotte, *n.* ko-*kot*, a woman of easy virtue. (Fr.)

coco-wood, *n.* *koh*-ko-wood, kokra-wood.

coctile, *a.* *kok*-tile, made by baking, or exposing to heat, as a brick. (L. *coctilis.*)

coction, *n.* *kok*-shon, the act of boiling; cooking; digestion. (L. *coctio*, from *coquo*, cook.)

cocus-wood, *n.* *koh*-kus-wood, green or Jamaica ebony, a hard wood furnished by the West Indian tree *Brya ebenus.*

cod, *n.* kod, a husk or pod; the scrotum; a pillow: *v.i.* to enclose in a pod: *v.t.* to mislead, to hoax or humbug [Slang]. (A.S.)

cod, *n.* kod, a cod-fish. **cod-liver oil,** a medicinal oil obtained from the liver of the cod and allied fishes.

coda, *n.* *koh*-da, the winding-up of a composition by an extra melodic phrase [Mus.]. (L. *cauda*, a tail.)

coddam, *n.* *kod*-d'm, a simple guessing- or tossing-game played in public-houses.

codder, *n.* *kod*-der, a ship or person engaged in the cod-fishery; a gatherer of cods or peas; a leather-worker or saddler; a hoaxer.

coddle, *v.t.* kodl, to pamper or cocker; to treat as an invalid: *n.* a pampered person; a molly-coddle.

code, *n.* kode, any orderly collection or digest of laws; a body of laws or regulations; the accepted principles of any class or group of persons, or of an art, etc.; a telegraphic cipher; a selection of words or groups of letters having a special meaning, known only to its possessors: *v.t.* to codify; to transpose into code.

co-declination, *n.* *koh*-dek-le-*nay*-shon, complement of declination [Astron.].

codeine, *n.* *koh*-de-een, a narcotic alkaloid obtained from opium. (Gr. *kodeia*, poppy-head.)

codetta, *n.* koh-*det*-ta, a small coda [Mus.].

codex, *n.* *koh*-deks (*pl.* **codices**), an ancient manuscript; a body of prescriptions [Med.]. **Codex Sinaiticus,** a 4th-cent. Greek MS. of the Scriptures, formerly in a convent on Mount Sinai and acquired by the British Museum in 1933. **Codex Vaticanus,** a 4th-cent. Greek MS. of the New Testament in the Vatican library. (L., a tree-trunk, a tablet, a book.)

cod-fish, *n.* *kod*-fish, the large deep-sea food-fish *Gadus morrhua.*

cod-fishery, *n.* *kod*-fish-er-re, the organized occupation of fishing for cod: *pl.* the area, esp. off Newfoundland, in which this is carried on.

codger, *n.* *koj*-er, any old man, esp. an oddity or a miser. (*Cadger.*)

codicil, *n.* *kod*-e-sil, a supplement to a will; an appendix. (L. *cōdicillus.*)

codicillary, *a.* kod-e-sil-a-re, of the nature of a codicil.

codification, *n.* *koh*-de-fe-*kay*-shon, the process or result of codifying.

codifier, *n.* *koh*-de-fy-er, one who codifies.

codify, *v.t.* *koh*-de-fy, to reduce to a code or digest; to systematize.

codilla, *n.* ko-*dil*-la, the coarsest part of hemp or flax. (L. *cauda*, tail.)

codille, *n.* ko-*deel*, a term at ombre, when the game is won by the person challenged. (Fr.)

co-director, *n.* koh-dy-*rek*-tor, a joint director.

codlin, *n.* *kod*-lin, a cooking-apple; a baked apple. (Ir. *cueirt*, apple-tree.)

codling, *n.* *kod*-ling, a young cod.

coeducation, *n.* *koh*-ed-yew-*kay*-shon, the teaching of the two sexes in the same class or school.

coefficient, *n.* koh-e-*fish*-ent, that which unites in action with something else to produce the same effect; a number put before a quantity, into which it is supposed to be multiplied [Alg.]; the coefficient of any generating term is the quantity which arises from the division of that term by the generated quantity [Fluxions].

cœlenterate, *a.* see-*len*-te-rat, of or belonging to the *Cœlenterata*, a phylum of the invertebrates which includes the jelly-fishes, corals, and sea-anemones.

cœliac, *a.* *see*-le-ak, pertaining to the abdominal cavity. **cœliac artery,** the artery which issues from the aorta just below the diaphragm. (Gr. *koilia*, a hollow.)

cœliotomy, *n.* see-le-*ot*-o-me, laparotomy. (Gr. *koilia*, belly, *tome*, cutting.)

cœlomate, *a.* see-*loh*-mat, having a cœlome [Anat.].

cœlome, *n.* *see*-lome, the body-cavity [Anat.]. (Gr. *koilos*, hollow.)

cœlostat, *n.* *see*-lo-stat, a clockwork-driven mirror by the use of which the moving of a telescope in examining a star is rendered unnecessary [Astron.]. (L. *cælum*, *cœlum*, the heavens.)

coemption, *n.* koh-*emp*-shon, the act of purchasing the whole quantity of any commodity for the purpose of forestalling. (L. *coemptio.*)

cœnæsthesis, *n.* see-nes-*thee*-sis, the general bodily consciousness. (Gr. *koinos*, general, *aisthēsis*, consciousness.)

cœnobite, *n. see*-no-bite, a cenobite.
cœnogamy, *n.* se-*nog*-a-me, community of wives or of husbands. (Gr. *koinos*, common, *gamos*, marriage.)
cœnure, *n. see*-newr, the larval form of a tapeworm of a dog which, when eaten by sheep, produces staggers.
coequal, *a.* ko-*ee*-kwal, equal to another; of the same rank, dignity, or power; *n.* one equal to another.
coequality, *n.* ko-e-*kwol*-e-te, the state of being coequal.
coequally, *ad.* ko-*ee*-kwal-le, with joint equality.
coerce, *v.t.* ko-*erse*, to restrain by force; to compel. (L. *coerceo*, press together.)
coercible, *a.* ko-*er*-se-bl, that may be coerced.
coercibleness, *n.* ko-*er*-se-bl-ness, the state of being coercible.
coercion, *n.* ko-*er*-shon, restraint; check, particularly by law or authority; government by force; compulsion.
coercionary, *a.* ko-*er*-shon-a-re, of the nature of coercion.
coercionist, *n.* ko-*er*-shon-ist, one who uses coercion; one who advocates government by force.
coercive, *a.* ko-*er*-siv, that has power or authority to restrain; compulsory; constraining.
coercively, *ad.* ko-*er*-siv-le, by constraint.
coessential, *a.* ko-es-*sen*-shal, having the same essence.
coessentiality, *n.* ko-es-*sen*-she-*al*-e-te, participation of the same essence.
coessentially, *ad.* ko-es-*sen*-shal-le, in a coessential manner.
coestablishment, *n.* ko-es-*tab*-lish-ment, joint establishment.
coetaneous, *a.* ko-e-*tay*-ne-us, of the same age with another; beginning to exist at the same time; coeval. (L. *coaetaneus*.)
coeternal, *a.* ko-e-*ter*-nal, equally eternal with another.
coeternally, *ad.* ko-e-*ter*-nal-le, with equal eternity.
coeternity, *n.* ko-e-*ter*-ne-te, equal eternity.
coeval, *a.* ko-*ee*-val, of the same age: *n.* a contemporary; one of the same age. (L. *co-*, and *aevum*, age.)
co-executor, *n.* ko-ek-*sek*-yew-tor, an executor with another.
coexist, *v.i.* ko-eg-*zist*, to exist at the same time.
coexistence, *n.* ko-eg-*zist*-ence, existence at the same time.
coexistent, *a.* ko-eg-*zist*-ent, existing at the same time.
coextend, *v.t.* and *i.* ko-eks-*tend*, to extend through the same space; to be or to make coextensive.
coextension, *n.* ko-eks-*ten*-shon, the act of extending equally, or the state of being equally extended.
coextensive, *a.* ko-eks-*ten*-siv, equally extensive.
coextensively, *ad.* ko-eks-*ten*-siv-le, in a coextensive manner.
coextensiveness, *n.* ko-eks-*ten*-siv-ness, equal extensiveness.
coffee, *n. kof*-fe, a beverage made from the seeds or berries of one of the tropical shrubs of the genus *Coffea*, esp. *C. arabica*, after they have been roasted and ground; the seed itself, also the powder into which it is ground; the brown colour of coffee. (Ar. *qahweh*.)
coffee-bean, *n. kof*-fe-been, a coffee-berry.
coffee-cup, *n. kof*-fe-kup, a cup for drinking coffee; the largest size of tea-cup.
coffee-house, *n. kof*-fe-house, a house where coffee and other refreshments are sold.
coffee-mill, *n. kof*-fe-mil, a mill for grinding coffee.
coffee-pot, *n. kof*-fe-pot, a pot in which coffee is made, or brought upon the table for drinking.
coffee-room, *n. kof*-fe-room, the public dining-room in a commercial hotel.
coffee-tavern, *n. kof*-fe-tav-ern, a temperance house of refreshment; a working-class tea-shop.
coffer, *n. kof*-fer, a chest for holding money or valuables; a treasury; a square depression in each interval between the modillions of a cornice [Arch.]; a sunk panel in vaults and domes [Arch.]; a caisson or cofferdam: *v.t.* to lay up in a coffer. (O.Fr. *cofre*.)
cofferdam, *n. kof*-fer-dam, an enclosure for excluding water during bridge-building and dock-work.
coffered, *a. kof*-ferd, enclosed in a coffer; ornamented or furnished with coffers.
cofferer, *n. kof*-fer-er, a former officer of the Royal Household, next under the Controller.
coffer-fish, *n. kof*-fer-fish, the trunk-fish, a species of *Ostracion* in which the body is protected by a mosaic of hexangular plates.
coffin, *n. kof*-fin, a chest in which a corpse is buried; a mould of paste for a pie; a conical twist of paper used by grocers; the hoof of a horse below the coronet, including, the **coffin-bone,** the last phalangeal bone [Farriery]: *v.t.* to enclose in a coffin: to shut from sight. (O.Fr. *cofin*.)
coffin-ship, *n. kof*-fin-ship, an unseaworthy vessel still sent to sea.
coffle, *n. kof*-fl, a band of chained slaves on the march; a train of animals. (Ar. *qufala*, caravan.)
cog, *v.t.* and *i*, kog, to wheedle; to seduce or draw from by adulation or artifice; to cheat; to deceive. **cog a die,** to load it. (Scand.)
cog, *n.* kog, the tooth of a wheel, by which it drives another wheel or ratchet; a broad-beamed mediæval vessel used in trade and war; a cock-boat; a cogue: *v.t.* to furnish with cogs, as a wheel. **hunting cog,** an extra cog on one wheel so as to vary the contacts at each revolution.
cogency, *n. koh*-jen-se, state or quality of being cogent; convincing power.
cogent, *a. koh*-jent, forcible; convincing; conclusive; powerful. (L. *cogentis*, of driving together.)
cogently, *ad. koh*-jent-le, in a cogent manner.
coggie, *n. kog*-ge, a small cogue [Scots.].
cogging, *n. kog*-ging, deceiving; cheating; using a crib at examinations.
cogitable, *a. koj*-e-ta-bl, conceivable; thinkable.
cogitate, *v.i. koj*-e-tate, to think; to meditate: *v.t.* to think over; to meditate about. (L. *cogitatus*.)
cogitation, *n.* koj-e-*tay*-shon, deep thought; meditation; a reflection; a conception.
cogitative, *a. koj*-e-ta-tiv, given to contemplation; meditative.
cognac, *n. kone*-yak, the best kind of French brandy, so named from a town in France.
cognate, *a. kog*-nate, of common origin; allied by blood; akin by the mother's side [Law]; of the same kind or nature: *n.* any male relation through the mother [Scots. Law]. (L. *cognatus*, joined by birth.)
cognateness, *n. kog*-nate-ness, the state of being cognate.
cognation, *n.* kog-*nay*-shon, cognate relationship; affinity of origin or of nature.
cognition, *n.* kog-*nish*-on, the faculty of knowing, perceiving, or conceiving as from personal view or experience; a perception; the process of knowing; cognizance [Law]. (L. *cognitio*.)
cognitive, *a. kog*-ne-tiv, pertaining to cognition; having the power of knowing or apprehending by the understanding.
cognizable, *a. kog*-niz-a-bl *or kon*-iz-a-bl, that may be known or apprehended; that falls under judicial notice [Law].
cognizably, *ad. kog*-niz-a-ble *or kon*-iz-ab-le, in a cognizable manner.
cognizance, *n. kog*-niz-ance *or kon*-iz-ance, knowledge; notice; distinguishing mark or badge; judicial notice or knowledge by trial in court; jurisdiction or right to try a cause; an acknowledgment or confession with plea of justification [Law]. (O.Fr. *connoissance*.)
cognizant, *a. kog*-niz-ant *or kon*-iz-ant, having cognizance of; having right to judge of [Law].
cognize, *v.t.* kog-*nize*, to have conscious knowledge or perception of; to recognize.
cognizee, *n. kon*-niz-ee, one to whom a fine in land or tenements is acknowledged [Law].
cognizor, *n. kon*-niz-or, one who acknowledges the right of the plaintiff or cognizee in a fine [Law].
cognomen, *n.* kog-*noh*-men, a family name or surname; the last of the three names of an ancient Roman citizen; a nickname. (L., a surname.)
cognominal, *a.* kog-*nom*-in-al, pertaining to a cognomen; having the same name.
cognosce, *v.t.* kog-*noss*, to inquire into judicially [Scots. Law]. (L. *cognosco*, know.)
cognoscente, *n.* kon-yo-*shen*-tay (*pl.* **cognoscenti**), a connoisseur. (It.)
cognoscible, *a.* kog-*nos*-se-bl, that may be known; that may be judicially inquired into [Scots. Law].
cognovit, *n.* kog-*noh*-vit, an acknowledgment by a defendant that the plaintiff's claim is just, and his

consent that judgment be entered accordingly [Law]. (L., he has acknowledged.)
cogue, *n.* kohg, a small wooden milking-vessel; a small wooden bowl or cup; a dram [Scots.]
cog-wheel, *n. kog*-wheel, a toothed wheel.
cog-wood, *n. kog*-wood, the hard wood of the Jamaican tree *Zizyphus chloroxylon*, used for cogs in machinery.
cohabit, *v.i.* ko-*hab*-it, to live together, esp. as husband and wife (usually applied to persons not legally married). (L. *cohabito*, live together.)
cohabitant, *n.* ko-*hab*-e-tant, one who dwells with another, or in the same place.
cohabitation, *n.* ko-hab-e-*tay*-shon, the act or state of dwelling together, or of cohabiting.
coheir, *n.* ko-*ayr*, a joint heir.
coheiress, *n.* ko-*ayr*-ess, a joint heiress.
cohere, *v.i.* ko-*heer*, to stick together; to adhere; to be logically connected or consistent. (L. *cohaereo*, stick.)
coherence, *n.* ko-*heer*-ence, sticking together; consistency; electrical conductivity.
coherency, *n.* ko-*heer*-en-se, coherence.
coherent, *a.* ko-*heer*-ent, sticking together; logically connected; consistent.
coherently, *ad.* ko-*heer*-ent-le, in a coherent manner.
coherer, *n.* ko-*heer*-er, the part of a receiving set in wireless telegraphy or telephony which becomes conducting when electric waves or currents reach it; an electrical resistance made of particles which cohere.
coheritor, *n.* ko-*he*-re-tor, a coheir.
cohesion, *n.* ko-*hee*-zhon, the act of cohering; the state of being united by natural attraction; the power by which the particles of bodies of the same nature are held together; connection; dependence; coherence; consistency. (L. *cohaesus*.)
cohesive, *a.* ko-*hee*-siv, producing cohesion; causing to cohere; cohering.
cohesively, *ad.* ko-*hee*-siv-le, in a cohesive manner.
cohesiveness, *n.* ko-*hee*-siv-ness, the quality of being cohesive.
cohibit, *v.t.* ko-*hib*-it, to restrain. (L. *cohibere*.)
cohort, *n. koh*-hort, the tenth part of a Roman legion, a body of about 600 men; a band or body of warriors; a group of families constituting a division of a class in botany. (L., a company.)
cohune-oil, *n. koh*-hoon-oyl, oil obtained from the fruit of the Honduras palm, *Attalea cohune*. (Native.)
coif, *n.* koyf, a close-fitting cap; the distinctive badge of the serjeants-at-law represented by a black-centred white patch on the wig, which black centre is worn by judges when in full dress and is known as the black cap: *v.t.* to cover with a coif. (Fr.)
coiffeur, *n.* kwof-*fer*, a hairdresser. (Fr.)
coiffure, *n.* kwof-*foor*, a headdress; a manner of dressing the hair. (Fr.)
coign, *n.* koyn, a corner; a quoin. **coign of vantage,** an advantageous standpoint or viewpoint. (O.Fr., a wedge.)
coil, *v.t.* and *i.* koyl, to gather or wind round into a ring or spiral, as a rope or a serpent; to twist: *n.* the formation of anything coiled; a single ring of this; a rope laid in a circle or spiral; a coiled lock of hair; an electrical apparatus with wire coiled round a bobbin for strengthening by induction. **induction coil,** *see* **induction. coil ignition,** the firing of the mixture in a motor by the spark from an electric coil. **coil up,** to gather up into a small space like a serpent. (O.Fr. *coillir*, gather.)
coil, *n.* koyl, trouble; turmoil. **mortal coil,** the troubles of this life. (Origin unknown.)
coin, *n.* koyn, a piece of metal stamped and current as money; metallic money as distinct from paper money; a die used in coining; that which serves for payment; formerly a wedge or quoin: *v.t.* to convert metal into money; to mint; to forge; to fabricate; to invent. (O.Fr., a wedge.)
coinage, *n. koyn*-aj, the act or art of coining money; coin; the pieces coined; the expense of coining; invention; fabrication.
coincide, *v.i.* ko-in-*side*, to occupy the same position in space; to occur at the same time; to concur; to correspond. (L. *co-*, with, *in-*, in, *cado*, fall.)
coincidence, *n.* ko-*in*-se-dence, the act, fact, or condition of coinciding; a remarkable instance of concurrence with no ascertainable cause.
coincident, *a.* ko-*in*-se-dent, coinciding.
coincidental, *a.* ko-in-se-*den*-tal, coincident; of the nature of coincidence.
coincidently, *ad.* ko-*in*-se-dent-le, with coincidence.
coindication, *n.* ko-in-de-*kay*-shon, concurrent indication; an additional symptom [Med.].
coiner, *n. koyn*-er, one who stamps coin; a maker of base or counterfeit money; an inventor.
co-inhere, *v.i.* ko-in-*heer*, to inhere together.
co-inheritance, *n.* ko-in-*he*-re-tance, joint inheritance.
co-inheritor, *n.* ko-in-*he*-re-tor, a joint heir; a co-heir.
coinstantaneous, *a.* ko-in-stan-*tay*-ne-us, occurring at the same moment.
Cointreau, *n.* (App.), proprietary name of a sweet orange-flavoured liqueur made at Angers, France.
coir, *n.* koyr, coconut fibre; cordage made of this material. (Malay, *kayar*, cord.)
coistril ,*n. koys*-tril, an under-groom; a knave. (O.Fr.)
coition, *n.* ko-*ish*-on, sexual intercourse. (L. *coitio*.)
cojuror, *n.* ko-*jew*-ror, a witness to another's credibility. (L. *con-*, and *juror*.)
coke, *n.* koke, coal deprived of its volatile constituents by heating in closed furnaces; the charcoal of pit-coal: *v.t.* to convert into coke. (Prob. M.E.)
cokernut, *n. koh*-ker-nut, the coconut (Comm. spelling).
cokery, *n. koh*-ke-re, a coke-making plant.
col-, kol. form of con- or cum- as a prefix before l. (L.)
col, *n.* kol, an elevated pass in a mountain range; a region of low pressure between two anticyclones [Meteor.]. (Fr., neck.)
colander, *n. kul*-lan-der, a perforated bowl for culinary purposes. (L. *colare*, to strain.)
cola, *n. koh*-la, the kola, or kola-nut.
colatitude, *n.* ko-*lat*-e-tewd, 90° minus the latitude.
colcannon, *n.* kol-*kan*-non, a stew made with potatoes and green vegetables—an Irish recipe; calecannon. (*Cole*, cabbage, and *cannon*.)
colchicine, *n. kol*-ke-sin, a poisonous alkaloid prepared from colchicum.
colchicum, *n. kol*-ke-kum, a bulbous plant of a genus including the meadow saffron, *C. autumnale*. (*Colchis*, Medea's country.)
colcothar, *n. kol*-ko-thar, red peroxide of iron, used for polishing, the "rouge" of jewellers. (Ar.)
★**cold,** *a.* koald, wanting in warmth; causing coldness or the sensation of cold; shivering; wanting passion, zeal, or ardour; unaffected; spiritless; not affectionate, cordial, or friendly; unconcerned; indifferent; reserved; chaste; not hasty; not violent; (in hunting) not affecting the scent strongly: *n.* the sensation produced in animal bodies by the abstraction of heat; the cause of that sensation; privation of heat; indisposition occasioned by cold; catarrh; a chill. **cold chisel,** a chisel for use on cold metal. **cold comfort,** not consoling; depressing. **cold cream,** a mild and cooling ointment for the skin. **cold drawn** (of tubing, oils, etc.), drawn without the application of heat. **cold feet,** fear. **cold hammer,** to work cold metal. **cold steel,** hand-to-hand without fire-arms or other missile weapons. **cold storage,** the preservation of perishable provisions by refrigeration. **cold water,** discouragement. (A.S. *cald*.)
cold-blast, *n. koald*-blahst, a blast of cold air; cold air forced into a furnace.
cold-blooded, *a. koald*-blud-ed, having cold blood; without sensibility or feeling; hard-hearted.
cold-hearted, *a. koald*-har-ted, wanting feeling; indifferent.
cold-heartedly, *ad.* in a cold-hearted manner.
cold-heartedness, *n.* the quality of being cold-hearted.
coldish, *a. koald*-ish, somewhat cold; cool.
coldly, *ad. koald*-le, in a cold manner.
coldness, *n. koald*-ness, the state of being cold.
cold-short, *a. koald*-short, brittle when cold, as a metal.
cold-shoulder, *n.* koald-*shole*-der, cool neglect; rebuff: *v.t.* to treat with neglect or off-handedly.
cole, *n.* koal, cabbage that does not grow a head; sea-kale. (A.S. *caul*.)
colectomy, *n.* ko-*lek*-to-me, surgical excision of part of the colon. (Gr. *kolon*, and *tomē*, cutting.)

colemanite, *n.* *koal*-ma-nite, a hydrous calcium borate occurring in monoclinic crystals, formerly the chief source of borax.
cole-mouse, *koal*-mous, the coal-tit.
coleoptera, *n.pl.* kol-e-*op*-ter-a, the beetles; an order of insects having wing-cases, or outside wings, which serve as a covering and protection for the true wings. (Gr. *koleos*, a sheath, and *pteron*, a wing.)
coleopterist, *n.* kol-e-*op*-ter-ist, one versed in coleopterous insects; a collector of beetles.
coleopterous, *a.* kol-e-*op*-te-rus, belonging to the coleoptera.
coleorhiza, *n.* kol-e-o-*ry*-za, the sheath of the root in the embryos of some grasses and flowering plants.
cole-rape, *n.* *koal*-rape, the common turnip.
coleseed, *n.* *koal*-seed, cabbage-seed; rape-seed as a source of colza oil.
cole-tit, *n.* *koal*-tit, the coal-tit.
colewort, *n.* *koal*-wurt, cabbage cut young; any cabbage that does not heart.
colic, *n.* *kol*-ik, spasmodic pain in the abdomen: *a.* pertaining to or affecting the colon. (Fr. *colique.*)
colicky, *a.* *kol*-ik-e, pertaining to colic.
colin, *n.* *kol*-in, a quail of the genus *Ortyx.* (Mex.)
Coliseum, *n.* kol-e-*see*-um, Colosseum.
colitis, *n.* ko-*ly*-tis, inflammation of the lining of the colon.
coll, *v.t.* kol, to embrace. (L. *collum*, the neck.)
collaborate, *v.i.* kol-*lab*-o-rate, to work conjointly. (L. *collaboratus.*)
collaborateur, *n.* kol-*lab*-o-ray-*toor*, a collaborator. (Fr.)
collaboration, *n.* kol-lab-o-*ray*-shon, a working with; joint labour.
collaborationist, *n.* kol-*lab*-o-*ray*-shon-ist, one co-operating with the enemy; an active traitor: *a.* traitorous.
collaborator, *n.* kol-*lab*-o-ray-tor, an associate in labour, particularly literary or scientific.
collagen, *n.* *kol*-a-jen, a protein occurring in cartilage and bone which is converted into gelatine when boiled in water (Gr. *kolla*, glue, *gen*, from *gignesthai*, become.)
collapse, *n.* ko-*laps*, a falling in, as of the sides of a hollow vessel; a sudden and utter prostration of strength; a breakdown: *v.i.* to fall in or together; to give way; to break down. (L. *collapsus*, slid.)
collapsible, *a.* co-*lap*-se-bl, liable to collapse; constructed so as to be easy to be packed.
***collar,** *n.* *kol*-lar, anything worn round the neck; the part of a garment round the neck; the special neck decoration belonging to each order of knighthood; a part of a harness for the neck of a draught animal; anything like a collar or a ring; a collar-beam; the upper part of a stay or a rope wreath to which a stay is confined [Naut.]; a ring, cincture, or astragal [Arch.]: *v.t.* to seize by the collar; to put a collar on; to pickle, roll, and compress (beef, brawn, etc.); to seize upon an opponent who is carrying the ball [Rugby football]; to steal or appropriate, to master [Slang]. **collar work,** drudgery. **slip the collar,** to get free; to escape. (O.Fr. *colier.*)
collar-beam, *n.* *kol*-lar-beem, horizontal piece of timber connecting and bracing two opposite rafters.
collar-bone, *n.* *kol*-lar-bone, the clavicle.
collar-day, *n.* *kol*-lar-day, a day on which members of the different orders of knighthood appear at court wearing their decorations.
collared, *a.* *kol*-lard, with a collar on the neck; caught; pressed (of meat).
collarette, *n.* kol-la-*ret*, a lace collar; a small collar worn by ladies.
collar-maker, *n.* one who makes horse-collars.
collate, *v.t.* kol-*late*, to bring (esp. books, MSS., etc.) together, in order to ascertain by comparison the points in which they agree and differ; to gather and place in order, as the leaves of a book for binding; to compare; to present and institute to a benefice. (L. *collatus*, brought together.)
collateral, *a.* ko-*lat*-er-ral, being by the side, or side by side; parallel; not direct or immediate; subsidiary; concurrent; descending from the same ancestor, though not lineally related, as the children of brothers: *n.* an indirect ancestor; a collateral relation or kinsman; collateral security. **collateral security,** security for the performance of covenants or the payment of money, besides the principal security. (L. *collateralis*, side by side.)
collaterally, *ad.* ko-*lat*-er-ra-le, in a collateral manner; side by side; indirectly; not lineally.
collation, *n.* kol-*lay*-shon, the act of collating; critical textual comparison, or the result of this; a light repast; the presentation of a clergyman to a benefice by a bishop having it in his own gift or patronage; in Scots. law, the equivalent of the English hotchpot. **collation of seals,** one seal set on the same label, on the reverse of another [Law]. (Fr.)
collative, *a.* kol-*lay*-tiv, passing by collation, the bishop and patron being one and the same.
collator, *n.* kol-*lay*-tor, one who collates books or MSS.; one who collates to a benefice.
colleague, *n.* *kol*-leeg, a co-worker; an associate in employment: *v.t.* and *i.* kol-*leeg*, to join in league. (Fr. *collègue.*)
colleagueship, *n.* partnership in office.
collect, *v.t.* ko-*lekt*, to gather together into one body or mass; to assemble; to gain by observation or information; to infer: *v.i.* to accumulate. **to collect oneself,** to recover one's self-command or composure after some agitation. (O.Fr. *collecter.*)
collect, *n.* *kol*-lekt, a short comprehensive prayer; a prayer adapted to a particular day or occasion. (L. *collecta.*)
collectable, *a.* ko-*lek*-ta-bl, able to be collected.
collectanea, *n.pl.* kol-lek-*tane*-e-a, a selection of passages from various authors, usually for instruction. (L.)
collected, *a.* kol-*lek*-ted, cool; self-possessed; presented in one volume or set of volumes (of an author's works).
collectedly, *ad.* in a collected manner.
collection, *n.* ko-*lek*-shon, the act of collecting; that which is collected; an assemblage; a mass; a heap; a sum collected for a religious or charitable purpose. (L. *collectio.*)
collective, *a.* ko-*lek*-tiv, formed by collecting or gathering; gathered into one mass, sum, or body; aggregated; characteristic of or relating to a group: *n.* a collective noun; a collective farm or other collectivized body. **collective bargaining,** the arrangement of terms of employment by agreement between authorized representatives of employers and employees. **collective farm,** a form of rural economy, esp. in the U.S.S.R., under which peasants are united in common effort on the basis of communal ownership of stock, implements, and means of production. **collective note,** a note subscribed by all the Powers represented [Political]. **collective noun,** a noun in the singular denoting a number conceived as one body, as a company, an army [Gram.]. **collective security,** a system of mutual guarantee of the political and territorial integrity of each of its members, esp. as given after the War of 1914–18 by the League of Nations.
collectively, *ad.* in a collective manner.
collectivism, *n.* the doctrine that all the means of production should be collectively controlled by the state; non-revolutionary socialism.
collectivist, *n.* an advocate of collectivism.
collectivity, *n.* kol-lek-*tiv*-e-te, quality or state of being collective; a community as a whole; collective ownership.
collectivization, *n.* kol-*lek*-te-vy-*zay*-shon, the act, process, or results of collectivizing.
collectivize, *v.t.* kol-*lek*-te-vize, to organize or establish on a collective basis; to amalgamate; to transfer from private to public or semi-public ownership.
collector, *n.* ko-*lek*-tor, one who or that which collects; one specializing in the collection of certain objects; one authorized to collect and receive customs, taxes, etc.; the chief administrative official of a district in British India; one of the hairs on the styles of certain plants serving to collect and retain the pollen [Bot.]. (L. *collectus.*)
collectorate, *n.* ko-*lek*-to-rate, a collector's district in India; the staff, or residence, of a collector.
collectorship, *n.* ko-*lek*-tor-ship, the office of a collector of customs or taxes.
colleen, *n.* *kol*-leen, a girl; a lass. (Ir. *cailin.*)
college, *n.* *kol*-lej, an organized collection or body of men, invested with certain powers and rights, performing certain duties, or engaged in some

common pursuit; a corporation; a seminary of learning incorporated by authority, esp. one forming a constituent part of a University; an institution for instruction in any particular study; a scholastic establishment; a house or edifice appropriated to such use; the incorporated legal faculty (Scots.); a political or electoral body. **College of Arms**, or **Heralds' College**, a British collegiate body consisting of kings-of-arms, heralds, and pursuivants presided over by the Earl Marshal. **College of Cardinals**, or **Sacred College**, the Papal Council of 70 Cardinals. **college cap**, a tasselled academic cap with a square projecting top; a "mortar-board." **college pudding**, a small pudding for one person. (Fr.)

colleger, *n.* *kol*-le-jer, a foundation scholar at Eton College, as distinct from an oppidan.

collegial, *a.* kol-*lee*-je-al, constituted as a college.

collegian, *n.* kol-*leej*-e-an, a member of a college; a student at a university.

collegiate, *a.* kol-*lee*-je-at, pertaining to a college; containing a college; instituted like a college; said of a church under a joint pastorate (Scots. and U.S.A.): *v.t.* to make collegiate; to constitute as a college. **collegiate church**, one that has no bishop's see, but has its college of dean, canons, and prebends, and is regulated, in matters of divine service, as a cathedral. (Low L. *collegiatus*, a member of a society.)

collenchyma, *n.* kol-*leng*-ke-ma, elastic cell tissue of the higher plants [Bot.].

collet, *n.* *kol*-let, a ring or band; a ferrule; the horizontal face or plane at the bottom of brilliants, or the part of a ring in which the stone is set.

collide, *v.i.* kol-*lide*, to strike or dash against each other; to come into conflict. (L. *collido*, strike together.)

collie, *n.* *kol*-le, a Scottish sheep-dog. (Dial. Eng.)

collier, *n.* *kol*-yer, a worker in a coal-mine; a dealer in coals; a vessel employed in the coal trade. (M.E. *colier.*)

colliery, *n.* *kol*-ye-re, a coal-mine.

colligate, *v.t.* *kol*-lig-ate, to bring into connexion; to unite by common interest. (L. *colligatus*, bound.)

colligation, *n.* kol-le-*gay*-shon, alliance; the summing of a number of details into a single expression [Logic].

collimate, *v.t.* *kol*-lim-ate, to bring into line, or render parallel, as of rays coming through a lens; to correct error of sight [Opt.]. (L. *collimatus*, from *collineatus*, lined together.)

collimation, *n.* kol-lim-*ay*-shon, adjustment to the line of sight. In a telescope, the **line of collimation**, the line of sight, or that which passes through the centre of the object-glass and intersects at right angles the wires placed in the focus [Opt.]. The **error of collimation**, the amount of deviation from the line [Opt.].

collimator, *n.* *kol*-lim-*ay*-tor, an auxiliary telescope for determining the error of collimation; a slotted tube with a convex lens for throwing parallel rays on the prism of a spectroscope [Opt.].

collinear, *a.* kol-*lin*-e-ar, lying in the same straight line.

collineation, *n.* kol-lin-e-*ay*-shon, the act of aiming at, or directing in a line to, a fixed object. (L. *collineatus.*)

collingual, *a.* ko-*ling*-gwal, having the same language. (L. *col-*, and *lingua*, speech.)

Collins, *n.* *kol*-inz, the letter of thanks sent to a host by a guest after his departure [Coll.]. (Name of a character in Jane Austen's "Pride and Prejudice.")

colliquative, *a.* kol-*lik*-wa-tiv, causing a wasting away, esp. by excessive excretions of liquid [Med.].

collision, *n.* kol-*lizh*-on, act of colliding; conflict; opposition; antagonism. (L. *collisus*, struck.)

collocate, *v.t.* *kol*-lo-kate, to place in order; to station in a given place. (L. *collocatus.*)

collocation, *n.* kol-lo-*kay*-shop, act of disposing or arranging; position; connexion; arrangement.

collocution, *n.* kol-lo-*kew*-shon, conference.

collocutor, *n.* ko-*lok*-yew-tor, a speaker in a dialogue or conference. (L. *collocutus*, spoken.)

collodion, *n.* kol-*loh*-de-on, a gummy solution of nitro-cellulose or pyroxylin in ether and alcohol, formerly much employed in surgery and photography. (Gr. *kōllodeō*, gluelike.)

collodionize, *v.t.* kol-*loh*-de-on-ize, to treat with collodion.

collograph, *n.* *kol*-lo-graf, a duplicating apparatus in which a film of gelatine is used; a form of collotype.

collography, *n.* kol-*log*-ra-fe, the art or process of reproducing copies with the collograph.

collogue, *v.i.* kol-*loag*, to scheme or plot together. (L. *colloquor*, speak together.)

colloid, *a.* *kol*-loyd, like jelly or glue: *n.* any gelatinous or semi-solid substance which, when apparently dissolved, will pass through bladder or similar membranes either not at all or only with great slowness. (Gr. *kollōdēs.*)

colloidal, *a.* kol-*loy*-dal, pertaining to or like a colloid; in colloid form.

colloidality, *n.* kol-loy-dal-e-te, colloidal nature.

collop, *n.* *kol*-lop, a slice of meat; a thick piece of flesh: *pl.* minced and seasoned meat. **Collop Monday**, the day preceding Shrove Tuesday. (Origin unknown.)

colloquial, *a.* kol-*loh*-kwe-al, relating to or used in common conversation. (L. *colloquium.*)

colloquialism, *n.* kol-*loh*-kwe-a-lizm, a colloquial or not formally correct form of expression.

colloquially, *ad.* in a colloquial manner.

colloquist, *n.* *kol*-lo-kwist, a speaker in conversation.

colloquize, *v.i.* *kol*-lo-kwize, to hold colloquy.

colloquy, *n.* *kol*-lo-kwe, mutual discourse; conversation; conference; dialogue. (L. *colloquium.*)

collotype, *n.* *kol*-lo-tipe, a process of reproducing photographic prints by means of sensitized gelatine and actinic rays; a print obtained by this method. (G. *kolla*, and *typos*, type.)

collude, *v.i.* kol-*lewd*, to play into each other's hands; to conspire in a fraud; to act in concert. (L. *colludo*, play together.)

collusion, *n.* kol-*lew*-zhon, a secret compact for a fraudulent purpose. (L. *collusio.*)

collusive, *a.* kol-*lew*-siv, fraudulently concerted.

collusively, *ad.* in a collusive manner.

collusiveness, *n.* the quality of being collusive.

colluvies, *n.pl.* kol-*lew*-ve-eez, a collection of filth, off-scouring, or refuse. (L. *colluo*, wash.)

colly, *n.* *kol*-le, the smut or soot of coal: *v.t.* to grime with this; to make foul. (*Coal.*)

collyrite, *n.* *kol*-le-rite, a white variety of clay. (Gr. *kollyrion*, a fine clay.)

collyrium, *n.* kol-*li*-re-um, an eye salve. (Gr.)

collywobbles, *n.* *kol*-e-woblz, stomach-ache [Slang].

colmey, *n.* *kol*-me, the coal-fish, *Gadus virens.*

Colocasia, *n.* *kol*-o-*kay*-sha, a small genus of plants of the arum family; (*l.c.*) taro, the edible root of *Colocasia esculenta.*

colocolo, *n.* kol-o-*koh*-lo, a black and white South American cat with dark grey legs, *Felis colocolo.*

colocynth, *n.* *kol*-o-sinth, the bitter cucumber, *Citrullus colocynthis*, common in Asia and North Africa; the violent purgative medicine obtained from this, also its fruit, the coloquintida. (Gr. *kolokynthos.*)

colocynthin, *n.* kol-o-*sinth*-in, the active medicinal principle of the colocynth.

Cologne-earth, *n.* ko-*lone-erth*, a native pigment of a violet-brown colour.

Cologne-water, *n.* eau-de-Cologne.

colon, *n.* *koh*-lon, the large intestine [Anat.]; the punctuation mark thus (:), used to mark a pause greater than that of a semicolon but less than that of a period [Gram.]. (Gr., the intestine.)

colonel, *n.* *kur*-nel, an army officer holding the highest regimental rank. (L. *columna*, a column.)

colonelcy, *n.* *kur*-nel-se, the office, rank, or commission of a colonel.

colonelship, *n.* *kur*-nel-ship, colonelcy.

colonial, *a.* ko-*loh*-ne-al, pertaining to a colony: *n.* a resident in a colony. **Colonial Office**, the department of State concerned with the business of the overseas British Empire, excluding the self-governing Dominions and certain other territories. **colonial system**, the 18th-cent. theory that colonies existed solely for the benefit of the mother country. (L. *colonialis.*)

colonialism, *n.* ko-*loh*-ne-a-lizm, a colonial peculiarity; the colonial system.

colonist, *n.* *kol*-on-ist, one who colonizes; a settler in or member of a colony.

colonization, *n.* kol-o-ny-*zay*-shon, the act or practice of colonizing; the state of being colonized.

colonizationist, *n.* kol-o-ny-*zay*-shon-ist, an advocate for colonization, esp. state-assisted.
colonize, *v.t.* *kol*-o-nize, to plant or establish a colony in; to migrate and settle in: *v.i.* to found a colony; to settle in a distant country.
colonnade, *n.* kol-o-*nade*, any series or range of columns placed at certain intervals. (Fr.)
colony, *n.* *kol*-o-ne, a section of the community settled in a distant land owned by the mother country; the settlement so formed; those of one nationality, trade, etc., living as a body in an alien community; an isolated group of persons of one occupation or class, etc.; a body of organisms (as corals, etc.) living and growing together. (Fr. *colonie.*)
colophon, *n.* *kol*-o-fone, a device, with the place and date of publication, etc., formerly at the end of a book; an imprint. (Gr., the summit.)
colophonic, *a.* kol-o-*fon*-ik, obtained from colophony.
colophonite, *n.* ko-*lof*-on-ite, an inferior variety of garnet.
colophony, *n.* ko-*lof*-o-ne, rosin; a dark-coloured resin obtained from turpentine. (*Colophon*, in Asia Minor, where it was first obtained.)
coloquintida, *n.* kol-o-*kwin*-te-da, the bitter apple or cucumber, the fruit the colocynth.
color, *n.* *kul*-ur, colour [American spelling].
Colorado-beetle, *n.* kol-oh-*rahd*-doh-beetl, a small black-and-yellow striped leaf-beetle, *Leptinotarsa decemlineata*, native to western N. America, but introduced into Europe, and very destructive to the potato.
coloration, *n.* kul-o-*ray*-shon, the art or practice of colouring; the state of being coloured; particular arrangement of colouring. (L. *coloratus*, coloured.)
coloratura, *n.* *kul*-or-a-*tewr*-ah, incidental trills, etc., introduced to make a song or other piece of music more agreeable [Mus.]. (It. *coloratura.*)
colorific, *a.* kul-o-*rif*-ik, that has the quality of tinging; able to give colour or tint to other bodies. (L. *color*, and *facio*, make.)
colorimeter, *n.* kul-o-*rim*-e-ter, an instrument for testing the intensity of colours and dyes.
colossal, *a.* ko-*los*-sal, like a colossus; very large; gigantic.
Colosseum, *n.* kol-os-*see*-um, the Flavian amphitheatre (built by Vespasian and Titus) at Rome, which was the largest in the world.
Colossus, *n.* ko-*los*-sus (*pl.* **Colossi**), the gigantic statue of Apollo, which stood at the harbour of Rhodes, one of the Seven Wonders of the World; hence, any statue of more than life size, or any great person or genius. (Gr.)
colostrum, *n.* ko-*los*-trum, the first milk after parturition; beestings. (L.)
colotomy, *n.* ko-*lot*-o-me, the operation of opening the colon [Surg.]. (Gr. *kolon*, and *tome*, cutting.)
***colour,** *n.* *kul*-or, any of the decomposed constituents of light or their combinations; the hue or appearance of a body to the eye; paint; pigment; appearance of blood in the face; appearance; false show; pretence; kind; species; character; timbre [Mus.]: *pl.* a flag, ensign, or standard; a badge: *v.t.* to paint; to dye; to tinge; to stain; to palliate; to give a specious appearance to; to make plausible; to exaggerate: *v.i.* to turn red; to blush. **complementary colours,** those that are wanting to make up white. **man of colour,** one not of white race, esp. a Negro. **off colour,** not very well; past one's prime. **primary colours,** loosely, the prismatic colours, strictly, red, green, and violet. **prismatic colours,** those into which pure light is resolved when transmitted through a triangular glass prism, viz. red, orange, yellow, green, blue, indigo, and violet. **water-colours,** such as are used in painting without being mixed with oil. (O.Fr.)
colourable, *a.* *kul*-u-ra-bl, specious; plausible.
colourableness, *n.* speciousness.
colourably, *ad.* plausibly; apparently, not really.
colouration (error for **coloration**).
colour-blind, *a.* *kul*-ur-blynd, with an imperfect sense of colour.
colour-blindness, *n.* being more or less colour-blind.
colour-box, *n.* box for paints and paint-brushes.
colour-company, *n.* the company, usually the first, having the battalion's colours in its keeping.
coloured, *a.* *kul*-urd, having a colour, esp. other than white or black; dark-complexioned; Negro; of some race other than white; having a specious appearance.
colourful, *a.* *kul*-ur-ful, full of colour; [Fig.] very picturesque or ornate; full of animation; vivid.
colouring, *n* act or art of giving a colour; manner of applying colours; a specious appearance.
colourist, *n.* *kul*-u-rist, one who colours; a painter who excels in the use of colours.
colourless, *a.* *kul*-ur-less, not distinguished by any hue; transparent; without character.
colourman, *n.* a preparer and seller of colours.
colour-process, *n.* a process by which prints may be reproduced in the natural colours.
colour-sergeant, *n.* former title and rank, of the highest non-commissioned officer in a company.
coloury, *a.* *kul*-u-re, abounding in or characterized by colour [Coll.]; having a colour denoting good quality [Comm.].
colportage, *n.* *kol*-pawr-taj, the system of distributing books and tracts by hawkers. (Gr.)
colporteur, *n.* kol-pawr-*toor*, one who travels about vending religious books, pamphlets, etc. (Fr., a hawker from *col*, neck, *porter*, to carry.)
colstaff, *n.* *kol*-stahf, a cowlstaff.
colt, *n.* koalt, a young horse, properly of the male kind; a young, foolish, inexperienced person; a professional cricketer in his first season as such: *v.i.* to frisk, riot, or frolic like a colt. (A.S.)
colt, *n.* koalt, proprietary name of a certain pistol or automatic gun. (Inventor, Samuel *Colt.*)
colter, *n.* *koalt*-er, coulter.
coltish, *a.* *koalt*-ish, like a colt; frisky; wanton.
colt's-foot, *n.* *koalts*-foot, a species of *Tussilago*, whose leaves were once much employed in medicine.
Coluber, *n.* *kol*-yew-ber, a genus of non-venomous snakes of S. Europe, Asia Minor, and N. Africa.
colubrine, *a.* *kol*-yew-brine, relating to or resembling the colubers; serpentine.
columbarium, *n.* kol-um-*bare*-re-um, a pigeon-house; a chamber fitted with niches like pigeon-holes for cinerary urns. (L.)
columbate, *n.* ko-*lum*-bate, a salt of columbic acid.
Columbian, *a.* ko-*lum*-be-an, pertaining to the United States of America or to Christopher Columbus.
columbic, *a.* ko-*lum*-bik, produced from niobium.
columbier, *n.* ko-*lum*-beer, a size of writing and drawing paper of approximately $23\frac{1}{2} \times 34\frac{1}{2}$ in. (Fr.)
Columbine, *n.* *kol*-um-bine, the wife of Harlequin and chief female dancer in pantomine.
columbine, *a.* *kol*-um-bine, of or like a dove; of a dove-colour: *n.* a plant of the genus *Aquilegia*. (O.Fr. *columbin.*)
columbite, *n.* ko-*lum*-bite, a mineral containing niobium, iron, and (usually) manganese, with tantalum, of which it is a principal source.
columbium, *n.* ko-*lum*-be-um, niobium.
columella, *n.* kol-yew-*mel*-la, the axis of fruit [Bot.]; the central upright pillar of most of the univalve shells [Malac.]. (L. dim. of *columen*, column.)
column, *n.* *kol*-lum, a long round pillar of wood or stone used to support or adorn a building, composed of a base, a shaft, and a capital; anything resembling a column pressing perpendicularly on its base, and of the same diameter as its base, as a column of mercury; a large body of troops drawn up in deep files; a number of ships in line ahead; a row; a perpendicular section of a page in printing, or a line of figures in arithmetic; the stamen of a plant, when the filaments are united into a tube around the styles [Bot.]. **dodging the column,** shirking one's duty [Mil. slang]. **fifth column,** any organized body of traitors within an attacked country or town, etc. (L. *columna.*)
columnar, *a.* ko-*lum*-nar, formed in columns; having the form of columns; like the shaft of a column.
columnated, *a.* *kol*-um-nay-ted, furnished with columns [Arch.].
columned, *a.* *kol*-lumd, having columns [Arch.].
columniation, *n.* ko-*lum*-ne-*ay*-shon, the regular arrangement of columns or pillars in building.
columnist, *n.* *kol*-um-ist *or* *kol*-um-nist, a gossip-writer; originally, one in editorial charge of a newspaper column. **fifth columnist,** a traitor, esp. a member of a fifth column.

colure, *n.* ko-*lewr,* either of the two great circles intersecting at right angles at the celestial poles, one passing through the solstitial and the other through the equinoctial points of the ecliptic [Astron., Geog.]. (Gr. *kolouros,* dock-tailed, from *kolos,* docked, *oura,* a tail.)

colza, *n. kol*-za, rape oil from cole-seed, *Brassica campestris oleifera.* (Fr., a wild cabbage.)

com-, kom, a Latin prefix, meaning with or completely.

coma, *n. koh*-ma, a state of deep insensibility [Med.]; lethargy. (Gr.)

coma, *n. koh*-ma, a small fascicle of leaves or hairs on the top of a stem; a tuft of hair on certain seeds; the branches forming the head of a forest tree [Bot.]; the nebulous covering surrounding the nucleus of a comet [Astron.]. (L., a head of hair.)

co-mate, *n.* koh-mate, a fellow-mate or companion.

comatose, *a. koh*-ma-tohz, in a state of coma; lethargic.

★**comb,** *n.* koam, a toothed instrument for separating, cleansing, and adjusting hair, wool, or flax, also for fastening the hair; a wire-toothed implement used by house-painters for graining; a conductor with a row of points for collecting a charge [Elect.]; the crest or red fleshy tuft on a cock's head; a crest; the cellular substance in which bees lodge their honey: *v.t.* to separate, cleanse, and adjust with a comb; *v.i.* to roll over, as the crest of a wave, and break in foam [Naut.]. **comb out,** to tidy or disentangle with a comb; to sort or separate, esp. to take (selected persons) for military or other service [Fig.]. (A.S. *camb.*)

combat, *n. kom*-bat, a fight; battle; contest: *v.i.* to fight; to struggle or contend with; *v.t.* to oppose; to contend against. *p.* and *pp.* **combated.** *ppr.* **combating.** (Fr. *combattre,* beat.)

combatable, *a.* kom-*bat*-a-bl, that may be combated, disputed, or opposed.

combatant, *n. kom*-ba-tant, one who combats or contends with another: *a.* contending; disposed to contend. **combatant officer,** a fighting officer as opposed to a non-combatant such as a chaplain or doctor. (Fr. *combattant.*)

combative, *a. kom*-ba-tiv, pugnacious.

combativeness, *n.* state of being combative; pugnacity.

comb-brush, *n.* a brush to clean combs.

combe, *n.* koom, the head of a valley; a coomb.

comber, *n. koam*-er, one who or that which combs; a machine for combing wool, etc.; a long foam-crested billow.

comber, *n. kom*-ber, a variety of (1) the sea-perch, *Serranus cabrilla,* and (2) the wrasse, *Labrus maculata.*

combinable, *a.* kom-*bine*-a-bl, that may be combined.

combinableness, *n.* state of being combinable.

combination, *n.* kom-be-*nay*-shon, the act of combining; state of being combined; union; association for some object; union of bodies or qualities in a mass or compound; chemical union; a unit consisting of motor-cycle and sidecar; the union or grouping of certain numbers or quantities in every possible manner [Math.]: *pl.* an undergarment consisting of bodice, or vest, and drawers. **combination-room,** the common room of the Cambridge colleges, to which the fellows withdraw after dinner.

combinative, *a. kom*-be-na-tiv, tending to combine.

combinatorial, *a.* kom-bi-na-*taw*-re-al, relating to mathematical combinations.

combinatory, *a.* kom-be-*nay*-to-re, combinative.

combine, *n. kom*-bine, an industrial combination for the purpose of stabilizing prices or dealing with wages; a ring for the control of a market or commodity; a threshing and harvesting machine.

combine, *v.t.* kom-*bine,* to unite; to unite closely; to cause to unite: *v.i.* to unite, agree, or coalesce; to unite in friendship or league; to unite by affinity. **combined operations,** military action undertaken by two or all of the three services conjointly; the department responsible for the commandos [Mil.]. (L. *com-,* and *binus,* two by two.)

combing, *n. koam*-ing, a cleaning with a comb: *pl.* refuse removed by a comb.

combust, *a.* kom-*bust,* said of a planet situated so near the sun as to be obscured by it [Astron.].

combustibility, *n.* kom-*bust*-e-*bil*-e-te, the state of being combustible.

combustible, *a.* kom-*bust*-e-bl, that will take fire and burn; excitable: *n.* an inflammable substance.

combustibleness, *n.* combustibility.

combustion, *n.* kom-*bust*-yon, the production of flame or heat; the act or process of burning. (L. *com-,* and *ustum,* burn.)

★**come,** *v.i.* kum, to move to this place, draw near, or approach; to arrive; to advance or move into view; to appear; to arrive at some state or condition; to happen, or fall out; to issue; to become: *int.* a call arousing attention or inviting to motion or joint action; when repeated, expressing remonstrance or impatience. **that is to come,** that is in the future. **the world to come,** the future life. **to come about,** to change or come round; to come to pass. **to come at,** to reach; to attain. **to come away,** to leave; to become parted. **to come back,** to return. **to come by,** to pass near; to obtain or acquire. **to come down,** to descend; to be humbled. **to come down upon,** to punish; to demand payment from. **to come home,** to affect deeply. **to come in,** to enter; to become fashionable; to become a partner or accomplice; to enter as an ingredient; to accrue. **to come in for,** to arrive in time to participate in. **to come into,** to join with; to comply with; to acquire; to inherit. **to come into the world,** to be born. **to come near,** to approach. **to come off,** to escape; to get free; to take place. **to come on,** to advance; to thrive. **to come over,** to pass above or across; to pass from one side, etc., to another; to occur to; to have a feeling of. **to come out,** to depart or proceed from; to become public; to be introduced into society; to appear after being clouded; to turn out; to go on strike. **to come out of,** to issue forth, as from confinement; to proceed or depart from. **to come out with,** to give publicity to; to disclose. **to come round,** to change; to recover; to circumvent. **to come short,** to fail. **to come to,** to consent or yield; to amount to; to recover, as from a swoon. **to come to grief,** to meet with a disaster or accident. **to come to himself,** to recover his senses. **to come together,** to meet or assemble. **to come to pass,** to happen. **to come up,** to ascend; to spring; to come into use; to slacken, as a rope, etc. [Naut.]; to come into residence in a university. **to come up to,** to approach near. **to come up with,** to overtake. **to come upon,** to fall on; to attack. **to come it strong,** to over-emphasize [Slang]. *p.* **came.** *pp.* **come.** (A.S. *cuman.*)

come-at-able, *a.* kum-*at*-a-bl, easy of access.

come-back, *n. kum*-bak, a return to, or reinstatement in, a former position.

comedian, *n.* ko-*mee*-de-an, an actor or writer of comedy; a player in general.

comedienne, *n.* ko-mee-de-*enn,* an actress specializing in comedy; a singing and dancing actress.

comedietta, *n.* kom-*ee*-de-*et*-ta, a slight comedy.

comedo, *n.* ko-*mee*-do, a blackhead due to the inaction or obstruction of a sebaceous gland.

comedy, *n. kom*-e-de, a dramatic representation of the characters and incidents of ordinary life, generally with a happy ending; a funny, entertaining or amusing situation or spectacle. (Gr. *komos,* a revel, *ode,* a song.)

comeliness, *n. kum*-le-ness, attractiveness.

comely, *a. kum*-le, nice-looking; pleasing in person; becoming.

comer, *n. kum*-er, one who comes. **all comers,** all indifferently. **first comer,** the first to arrive.

comestible, *n.* ko-*mes*-te-bl, an eatable. (L. *com-,* and *esum,* eat.)

comet, *n. kom*-et, a nebulous body revolving round the sun in a very eccentric orbit, and, when perfect, consisting of three parts—nucleus, coma, and tail; an obsolete game of cards. (Gr. *koma,* hair.)

cometary, *a. kom*-e-ta-re, pertaining to or resembling a comet.

comet-finder, *n.* a low-powered telescope used to locate comets.

cometic, *a.* ko-*met*-ik, relating to comets.

cometography, *n.* kom-e-*tog*-ra-fe, a description or treatise of comets.

cometology, *n.* kom-e-tol-o-je, the branch of astronomy treating of comets.

comfit, *n.* *kum*-fit, a sugar-plum; a small dry sweetmeat. (O.Fr. *confit.*)
★**comfort,** *n.* *kum*-fort, consolation; satisfaction; content; that which comforts; assistance; encouragement: *v.t.* to relieve from distress; to cheer; to console. (L. *com-*, and *fortis*, strong.)
comfortable, *a.* *kum*-for-ta-bl, enjoying or affording comfort; free from pain, hardship, etc.; sufficiently provided for; contented.
comfortably, *ad.* in a comfortable manner.
comforter, *n.* *kum*-for-ter, one who comforts; a long knitted woollen wrapper for the neck; a baby's coral or dummy; (*cap.*) the Holy Ghost.
comfortless, *a.* *kum*-fort-less, without comfort; cheerless; inconsolable.
comfrey, *n.* *kum*-fre, the wild plant *Symphytum officinale*, formerly much prized as a vulnerary.
comfy, *a.* *kum*-fe, snug, comfortable [Coll.].
comic, *a.* *kom*-ik, relating to comedy; comical: *n.* a music-hall comedian; a comic paper. **comic strip,** *see* **strip.**
comical, *a.* exciting mirth; droll; ludicrous.
comicality, *n.* kom-i-*kal*-e-te, ludicrousness.
comically, *ad.* in a manner befitting comedy; in a comical manner.
comicalness, *n.* the quality of being comical.
Cominform, *n.* kom-in-*form*, an international organization set up in 1947 to co-ordinate the activities of communist states and parties. (Abbr. of *Com*munist *Inform*ation Bureau.)
coming, *n.* *kum*-ing, act of approaching; approach; arrival: *a.* future; expected to come.
coming-in, *n.* *kum*-ing-*in*, entrance; income.
Comintern, *n.* kom-in-*tern*, the Third (Communist) International, 1919-43, headquarters of which were in Moscow.
comitadji, *n.* kom-e-*tah*-jee, one of a band of irregular Balkan soldiers; the band itself. (Turk. *qomitaji*, guerilla.)
comitatus, *n.* kom-e-*tay*-tus, in feudal days, a county or shire; a great noble's escort. (L.)
comitia, *n.pl.* ko-*mish*-e-a, an assembly of the people [Rom. Antiq.]. (L. *com-*, and *eo*, to go.)
comitial, *a.* ko-*mish*-e-al, relating to the comitia; relating to assemblies.
comity, *n.* *kom*-e-te, courtesy; civility. **comity of nations,** the courtesy by which one nation permits another to execute certain acts or laws within its territory. (L. *comis*, courteous.)
comma, *n.* *kom*-ma, the point (,), denoting the shortest pause in reading; an enharmonic interval, or the difference between the major and the minor semitone [Mus.]; the butterfly *Polygonia c.-album*, named from the mark on its wings. **inverted commas,** quotation marks thus "....." **comma bacillus,** a comma-like bacillus found in cases of cholera.
command, *n.* kom-*mahnd*, the right, power, or act of commanding; supreme power or authority; mandate or order given; the power of overlooking; a body of troops, or any armed force or station, under the command of a particular officer: *v.i.* to have or exercise supreme authority or influence; to give orders: *v.t.* to order; to control; to have in power; to dominate or overlook; to enforce. (L. *com-*, and *mando*, to commit.)
commandant, *n.* kom-man-*dant*, the commanding officer of a fortress, camp, or garrison town.
commandeer, *v.t.* kom-man-*deer*, to seize or make use of for military purposes.
commander, *n.* kom-*mahnd*-er, one who is in command; the commanding officer of an army, or of any division of it; an officer in the navy, next in rank below the captain; one on whom is bestowed a commandry; a rank in certain orders of knighthood; a heavy beetle or wooden mallet, used in paving. **commander-in-chief,** a supreme commander, esp. of the military forces of a state or of a large and self-contained portion of them. **commander of the faithful,** a title of the Caliph.
commandership, *n.* the office of a commander.
commandery, *n.* kom-*mahnd*-er-e, a district containing estate with a revenue annexed, belonging to a military order, and governed by a knight; the body of knights of any one order.
commanding, *a.* kom-*mahnd*-ing, having command; influencing authoritatively; dignified; dominating; domineering; with a sweeping view.
commandingly, *ad.* in a commanding manner.
commandment, *n.* kom-*mahnd*-ment, command; precept; a law, especially of the decalogue.
command-night, *n.* a special theatrical performance given at the Royal command.
commando, *n.* kom-*mahn*-do, a body of men specially selected and trained for hazardous combined operations of naval, land, and air forces; a body of irregulars; an expedition on which such a body is engaged. (Dut.)
commandry, *n.* kom-*mahn*-dre, a commandery.
commatic, *a.* kom-*mat*-ik, with short clauses or sentences.
commeasurable, *a.* kom-*mezh*-ew-ra-bl, commensurable.
commemorable, *a.* kom-*mem*-o-ra-bl, memorable; worthy to be remembered, or noticed with honour.
commemorate, *v.t.* kom-*mem*-o-rate, to call to remembrance by a solemn act; to celebrate with honour. (L. *commemoratus.*)
commemoration, *n.* kom-mem-o-*ray*-shon, the act of commemorating; an annual celebration in honour of founders and benefactors.
commemorative, *a.* kom-*mem*-o-rat-iv, tending or serving to commemorate.
commemoratory, *a.* kom-*mem*-o-ra-to-re, commemorative.
commence, *v.i.* kom-*mence*, to begin; to originate; to begin to be; to take an academic degree: *v.t.* to begin; to enter upon. (O.Fr. *comencer.*)
commencement, *n.* kom-*mence*-ment, beginning; rise; origin; first existence; a day on which certain degrees are conferred at Cambridge and Dublin and in American Universities.
commend, *v.t.* kom-*mend*, to recommend as worthy of notice, regard, or kindness; to praise; to approve; to commit to the charge of. **commend me to,** remember me to. (L. *commendare*, commit.)
commendable, *a.* that may be commended.
commendableness, *n.* state of being commendable.
commendably, *ad.* in a commendable manner.
commendam, *n.* kom-*mend*-am, the temporary holding of an ecclesiastical benefice or living until a regular incumbent is provided; formerly also, the temporary trust of the revenues of a vacant benefice to a layman. (L.)
commendatary, *a.* kom-*men*-da-ta-re, holding *in commendam*: *n.* a commendator.
commendation, *n.* kom-men-*day*-shon, the act of commending; praise; declaration of esteem; ground of esteem or praise; service; respects.
commendator, *n.* kom-*men*-da-tor, one who holds a living *in commendam.*
commendatory, *a.* kom-*men*-da-to-re, that serves to commend; holding a benefice *in commendam*: *n.* a commendation; eulogy.
commensal, *n.* kom-*men*-sal, a plant or animal living with or off another without being parasitic: *a.* living on the food of another [Zool.]; dining at the same table. (L. *com-*, and *mensa*, a table.)
commensalism, *n.* the being commensal.
commensurability, *n.* kom-*men*-sew-ra-*bil*-e-te, the state of being commensurable.
commensurable, *a.* kom-*men*-sew-ra-bl, having a common measure.
commensurableness, *n.* commensurability.
commensurably, *ad.* in a commensurable manner.
commensurate, *a.* kom-*men*-sew-rat, of equal measure or extent; proportionate to. (L. *commensuratus.*)
commensurately, *ad.* so as to be commensurate.
commensurateness, *n.* quality or state of being commensurate.
commensuration, *n.* kom-*men*-sew-*ray*-shon, a state of having a common measure; proportion.
comment, *v.i.* kom-*ment*, to make explanatory or critical remarks, esp. on a book, etc.; to criticize adversely.
comment, *n.* *kom*-ment, a note in explanation; remark; criticism. (L. *commentari.*)
commentary, *n.* *kom*-men-ta-re, a comment; a book of comments; a historical narrative of particular transactions; a broadcast description of an event in progress. (L. *commentarius.*)
commentate, *v.t.* *kom*-men-tate, to annotate; to act as wireless commentator.
commentation, *n.* *kom*-men-*tay*-shon, the making of comments; commenting.
commentator, *n.* *kom*-men-tay-tor, an expositor;

a writer of a commentary; one broadcasting a description of a sporting or other event in progress.
commentatorial, *a.* kom-*men*-ta-*taw*-re-al, relating to comments or commentaries.
commerce, *n.* *kom*-merce, an interchange in commodities between nations or individuals; foreign trade; traffic; intercourse, esp. sexual; a game of cards. (Fr.)
commercial, *a.* kom-*mer*-shal, pertaining to commerce; mercantile; trading; proceeding from trade: *n.* a commercial traveller [Coll.]. **commercial room,** a room in an hotel reserved for use of commercial travellers. **commercial traveller,** a representative of a business house visiting retailers to solicit orders.
commercialism, *n.* commercial practices.
commercialist, *n.* kom-*mer*-shal-ist, one engaged in commerce; one believing in commercialism.
commercialize, *v.t.* kom-*mer*-shal-ize, to make commercial or in accordance with trading methods; to subject to the power of trade.
commercially, *ad.* in a commercial view.
commère, *n.* *kom*-mare, a godmother; a gossip; a woman acting as compère. (Fr. *mère*, mother.)
commerge, *v.i.* kom-*merj*, to merge; to agree.
commination, *n.* kom-me-*nay*-shon, threatening; denunciation; a Church of England service, "denouncing God's anger and judgments against sinners," used on the first day of Lent. (Fr.)
comminatory, *a.* kom-*min*-a-to-re, denunciatory. (L. *comminatorius.*)
commingle, *v.t.* and *i.* kom-*ming*-gl, to mix or mingle together.
comminute, *v.t.* *kom*-min-yewt, to reduce to minute particles; to pulverize. **comminuted fracture,** the state of a bone broken in more than one place or into small pieces. (L. *comminutus*, broken into minute pieces.)
comminution, *n.* kom-min-*yew*-shon, the act of comminuting; fracture into small pieces [Surg.].
commiserate, *v.t.* kom-*miz*-er-rate, to feel or express pity for; to compassionate. (L. *commiseratus.*)
commiseration, *n.* kom-miz-er-*ray*-shon, compassion; sympathy. (O.Fr.)
commiserative, *a.* kom-*miz*-er-ra-tiv, compassionate.
commiserator, *n.* kom-*miz*-er-ray-tor, one who pities.
commissar, *n.* kom-me-*sahr*, the head of a State department in the U.S.S.R.
commissarial, *a.* kom-mis-*sare*-re-al, pertaining to a commissary.
commissariat, *n.* kom-mis-*sare*-re-at, the provisioning branch of an army; the body of officers belonging to it; a department of State of the Soviet Union; the rank or office of a commissar.
commissary, *n.* *kom*-mis-a-re, one to whom some charge, duty, or office is committed; a commissioner; an officer formerly charged with furnishing provisions, etc. [Mil.]; a bishop's deputy acting in remote parts of the diocese or during the bishop's temporary absence; a judge in a commissary court [Scots. Law]. **commissary court,** the court of a bishop's commissary; a former Scottish court dealing with probate and divorce; a county court presided over by the sheriff [Scots.]. **commissary general,** a chief commissary; the chief officer of a commissariat department. (Low L. *commissarius.*)
commissaryship, *n.* the office of a commissary.
commission, *n.* kom-*mish*-on, the act of committing; the act of perpetrating; the act of entrusting; the thing entrusted or committed; power and authority given; a writing from proper authority, given to a person as his warrant for exercising certain powers or the performance of any duty; a number of persons joined in an office or trust; a committee of enquiry or management; the state of acting under authority in the purchase and sale of goods for another; allowance made to a factor, commission merchant, or other agent, for transacting business; the period of active service of a naval vessel: *v.t.* to authorize; to give a commission to; to put a ship into commission. **Commission Day,** the opening day of assizes, when the judge's commission is read aloud. **Commission of the Peace,** a commission under the Great Seal of England for appointing Justices of the Peace. **in commission** (of offices), placed under the control of a commission. **to put a ship into commission,** to equip it for immediate service. (Fr.)
commission-agent, *n.* a merchant buying or selling goods on a commission basis.
commissionaire, *n.* kom-mish-o-*nayr*, a member of the Corps of Commissionaires, a body of ex-service men acting as door-keepers, caretakers, etc. (Fr.)
commissional, *a.* kom-*mish*-o-nal, pertaining to a commission appointing or appointed by warrant.
commissioned, *a.* kom-*mish*-ond, holding a commission, esp. from the crown. **commissioned officer,** an officer who is appointed by a commission.
commissioner, *n.* kom-*mish*-o-ner, a person who has a commission to perform some office, or business; a member of a commission; the title of the heads of certain branches of the public service. **Lord High Commissioner,** the sovereign's representative at the annual General Assembly of the Church of Scotland.
commissural, *a.* kom-mis-*yewr*-ral, relating to a commissure.
commissure, *n.* *kom*-mis-yewr, a joint, seam, or closure; a cleft or interstice; the place where two bodies or their parts meet and unite; a suture of the cranium or skull; the corners of the lips, eyelids, etc.; also, certain parts in the ventricles of the brain, uniting the two hemispheres [Anat.]; the face by which the carpels cohere in umbelliferous plants. (L. *commissura.*)
commit, *v.t.* kom-*mit*, to entrust; to consign; to send for trial; to send to prison; to compromise; to engage or pledge; to refer to a committee; to do; to perpetrate; to memorize. (L. *committo* send.)
commitment, *n.* kom-*mit*-ment, the act of committing; the state of being committed; the act of entrusting, pledging, or referring; that which is entrusted, etc.; liability; perpetration; imprisonment; an order for confining in prison.
committable, *a.* liable to be committed.
committal, *n.* kom-*mit*-tal, the act of committing; commitment. **committal service,** the service read at the committal of a body to the grave.
***committee,** *n.* kom-*mit*-tee, two or more persons appointed by a collective body acting together, to whom some particular matter or business is referred.
committee, *n.* kom-mit-*tee*, the person to whom the care of an idiot or lunatic is committed, the Lord Chancellor being the committor.
committer, *n.* kom-*mit*-ter, perpetrator; one who commits.
committor, *n.* kom-*mit*-tor, one who commits (a minor, or insane person) to the care of an individual or institution.
commix, *v.t.* and *v.i.* kom-*miks*, to mix; to blend.
commixture, *n.* kom-*miks*-tewr, the act of mixing; the state of being mingled; the mass formed by mingling. (L. *commixtura.*)
commode, *n.* kom-*mode*, a head-dress formerly worn by women; a chest of drawers, often with shelves above; a close-stool. (Fr.)
commodious, *a.* kom-*moh*-de-us, convenient or suitable; roomy. (L. *commodiosus.*)
commodiously, *ad.* in a commodious manner.
commodiousness, *n.* the state of being commodious.
commodity, *n.* kom-*mod*-e-te, convenience, or that which affords it; an article of commerce: *pl.* goods; wares. (Fr. *commodité.*)
commodore, *n.* *kom*-mo-dor, a naval officer next below rear-admiral and above captain; the commander of a squadron or detachment of ships; the senior captain when three or more ships of war are cruising in company; the senior captain of a shipping-line; the leading ship in a fleet of merchant-men or fishing boats; the chief official of a yacht club. **Air Commodore,** *see* **air.** (Sp. *comendador.*)
***common,** *a.* *kom*-mon, belonging equally to more than one, or to many indefinitely; belonging to all; public; general; frequent; usual; of little value; of low or no rank; vulgar; of verbs, both active and passive; of nouns, both masculine and feminine, also applicable to a whole class [Gram.]: *n.* a tract of open ground, the common property of all the members of a community; conjoint possession [Law]: *v.i.* to have a joint right in some common ground; to board together. **common council,** the governing body of a city or corporate town. **common crier,** one who makes

public proclamations. **common divisor** or **measure,** a quantity which divides two or more quantities without leaving a remainder [Math.]. **common law,** the unwritten law, or law which receives its binding force from immemorial usage and universal reception, in distinction from the written or statute law. **common prayer,** the liturgical formulary of the Church of England. **common room,** in Oxford and London Universities and Trinity College, Dublin, a room to which the Fellows retire after dinner. **common seal,** a seal used by a corporation. **common sense,** sound practical judgment; that judgment in regard to first principles in which all men in general agree: *a.* marked by common sense. **common serjeant,** a judge of the City of London, ranking next to the Recorder. **common time,** those varieties of time in which each measure is divided into two or four equal parts [Mus.]. (O.Fr. *comun.*)

commonable, *a. kom*-mon-a-bl, held in common; that may be pastured on common land.

commonage, *n. kom*-mon-aj, the right of pasturing on a common; right of using anything in common; common land; commonalty.

commonalty, *n. kom*-mon-al-te, the common people; all below the rank of a peer of the realm; the commonwealth; a corporation. (O.Fr. *comunalte.*)

commoner, *n. kom*-mon-er, one of the commonalty; a member of the House of Commons; one who has a joint right in common ground; a student of the second rank in the university of Oxford, corresponding to the pensioner at Cambridge; a partaker; a prostitute. **the First Commoner,** Mr. Speaker. **the Great Commoner,** William Pitt, afterwards Earl of Chatham.

commoney, *n. kom*-mon-e, a playing-marble made of clay [schoolboy slang].

commonly, *ad. kom*-mon-le, usually; in an ordinary manner; cheaply.

commonness, *n. kom*-mon-ness, the quality or state of being common or usual; meanness.

commonplace, *a. kom*-mon-place, common; ordinary; trite; not new or striking: *n.* an ordinary or common topic; a trite remark; anything ordinary.

commonplace-book, *n.* a book in which extracts or things to be remembered are recorded.

commonplaceness, *n.* the state of being commonplace.

Common-Pleas, *n. kom*-mon-*pleez,* a division of the English High Court of Justice abolished in 1875.

commons, *n.pl. kom*-monz, the mass of the people, or those not in possession of hereditary titles; (*cap.*) the lower house of the British Parliament, consisting of elected representatives and commonly called the **House of Commons**; (*l.c.*) food provided at a common table, as in colleges; food. **short commons,** restricted supply; stinted fare.

commonty, *n. kom*-mon-te, land held in common; a common [Scots.]. (O.Fr. *communite.*)

commonweal, *n. kom*-mon-weel, the welfare of the community; the public good.

commonwealth, *n. kom*-mun-welth, the body politic; the whole body of people in a state; an established form of government; the state; the official title of the federation of the six states of Australia. **the British Commonwealth,** the entire British Empire. **the Commonwealth,** in English history, the form of government which existed from 1649 to 1659 under the Lord Protectorship of Oliver, and later Richard, Cromwell.

commonwealthsman, *n. kom*-mun-welths-man, one who favoured the English Commonwealth.

commorancy, *n. kom*-mo-ran-se, residence; abode [Law.]. (L. *commorans,* staying.)

commotion, *n.* kom-*moh*-shon, agitation; excitement; perturbation; disturbance; tumult; disorder. (L. *commotus.*)

commove, *v.t.* kom-*moov,* to agitate; to disturb; to excite. (L. *commoveo.*)

communal, *a. kom*-ew-nal *or* ko-*mew*-nal, pertaining to a commune or to the people at large; in India, pertaining to the various racial and religious communities in a district; characteristic of or derived from a simple form of social life; public.

communalism, *n.* kom-*mew*-na-lizm, the system of government through local communes or small political units; communism; the association of ants, bees, etc., in permanent colonies [Zool.].

communalist, *n.* kom-*mew*-na-list, a believer or participator in communalism.

communalistic, *a.* kom-mew-na-*lis*-tik, relating to or characteristic of communalism.

communard, *n. kom*-mew-nard, a supporter of the Paris Commune of 1871. (Fr.)

commune, *v.i.* kom-*mewn,* to interchange thoughts and feelings in private or familiar converse; to hold intimate converse; to partake of the Lord's Supper: *n.* intimate converse. (O.Fr. *communer.*)

commune, *n. kom*-moon, a committee for local government; a small territorial district in France under a mayor roughly equivalent to a parish; the inhabitants of a commune. **The Commune,** a revolt in Paris in 1871 in favour of communistic government. (Fr.)

communicability, *n.* kom-*mew*-ne-ka-*bil*-e-te, the quality or capability of being communicable.

communicable, *a.* kom-*mew*-ne-ka-bl, capable of being communicated; communicative. (L.)

communicableness, *n.* state of being communicable.

communicably, *ad.* with communication; in a communicable manner.

communicant, *a.* kom-*mew*-ne-kant, communicating; imparting: *n.* one who partakes of Holy Communion. (L. *communicans.*)

communicate, *v.t.* kom-*mew*-ne-kate, to impart; to bestow; to reveal: *v.i.* to have intercourse; to have a communication or passage from one to another; to participate; to partake of Holy Communion. (L. *communicatus,* partaken.)

communication, *n.* kom-*mew*-ne-*kay*-shon, the act of communicating; interchange of thoughts or opinions; intercourse; correspondence; connecting passage, or means of passing from place to place; that which is communicated or imparted. **line of communication,** the protected route by means of which an army in the field keeps touch with its base.

communicative, *a.* kom-*mew*-ne-ka-tiv, inclined to communicate, or impart to others; not reserved.

communicativeness, *n.* the quality of being communicative.

communicator, *n.* kom-*mewn*-e-kay-tor, one who or that which communicates; part of a telegraphic transmitter; a device by which the guard or driver of a train can be communicated with by a passenger.

communicatory, *a.* imparting knowledge.

communion, *n.* kom-*mew*-nyon, the act of communing or communicating; mutual intercourse; fellowship; union in religious worship or in doctrine and discipline; the eucharist or Lord's Supper; the act of partaking of the eucharist; a religious body, esp. of Christians having a common faith and discipline. **Communion service,** the office used in the celebration of the eucharist or Holy Sacrament. **communion table,** the altar or table on which the Lord's Supper is laid, and at which it is administered. (L. *communio,* from *communis,* common.)

communionist, *n.* kom-*mew*-nyo-nist, one who is of the same communion.

communiqué, *n.* kom-moon-e-*kay,* a communication or statement issued officially. (Fr.)

communism, *n. kom*-mew-nizm, community of property among all the inhabitants; a state of things in which there are no individual or separate rights in property; an advanced form of socialism in which, theoretically, all means of production are in the hands of the community, the products of industry are equitably distributed, and the private ownership of property and capital is non-existent. (Fr. *communisme.*)

communist, *n. kom*-mew-nist, one who holds the principles of communistic socialism.

communistic, *a. kom*-ew-*nis*-tik, relating to communism; adhering, or inclined, to communism.

communitarian, *n. kom*-mew-ne-*tare*-re-an, a (pre-Marxist) communist.

community, *n.* kom-*mew*-ne-te, the public or people in general; a society of people having common rights and privileges, or common interests, or living under the same laws and regulations; an association, especially of persons maintaining the same religious tenets and discipline; common possession; common character. **community singing,** singing in chorus by a gathering under a leader.

communization, *n. kom*-mewn-ny-*zay*-shon, the act

of making private property the property of the community.
communize, *v.t.* *kom*-mew-nize, to make communistic; to convert to a belief in communism.
commutability, *n.* kom-*mew*-ta-*bil*-e-te, the quality of being commutable. (L. *commutabilis.*)
commutable, *a.* kom-*mew*-ta-bl, that may be commuted, exchanged, or mutually changed.
commutate, *v.t.* *kom*-mew-tate, to direct or regulate (a current) so that its direction is made continuous [Elect.].
commutation, *n.* kom-mew-*tay*-shon, act of commuting; change; exchange; the change of a penalty or punishment from a greater to a less; substitution of one kind of payment for another [Law.].
commutative, *a.* kom-*mew*-ta-tiv, relating to exchange; interchangeable.
commutatively, *ad.* by way of exchange.
commutator, *n.* *com*-mew-tay-tor, an instrument for reversing the current through an electric coil or circuit.
commute, *v.t.* kom-*mewt*, to exchange; to substitute one penalty or punishment for another of less severity; to substitute one kind of payment for another [Law]; to commutate [Elect.]: *v.i.* to pay in one kind of way for another. (L. *commuto*, change.)
comose, *a.* *koh*-mose, hairy; downy [Bot.].
compact, *a.* kom-*pakt*, firm; close; firmly and closely united; dense; brief; pithy; not diffuse or verbose; held together; compacted; composed: *v.t.* to unite or connect firmly; to press close together; to consolidate. (Fr. *compacte.*)
compact, *n.* *kom*-pakt, a mutual agreement or contract; a treaty; a league; a confederacy; a small vanity-case for powder, etc.; a compress [Med.]. (L. *compactum.*)
compacted, *a.* kom-*pak*-ted, joined together; closely united.
compactedly, *ad.* in a compact manner.
compactedness, *n.* state of being compact.
compactible, *a.* kom-*pak*-te-bl, that may be joined.
compactly, *ad.* kom-*pakt*-le, in a compact manner.
compactness, *n.* the state of being compact.
compactum, *n.* kom-*pak*-tum, a lady's fancy pocket-case containing powder, puff, and mirror.
compages, *n.* kom-*pay*-jeez, a system or structure of many parts united. (L.)
compaginate, *v.t.* kom-*paj*-e-nate, to unite strongly. (L. *compaginatus*, firmly joined.)
compagination, *n.* kom-paj-e-*nay*-shon, union of parts; structure; connection.
companion, *n.* kom-*pan*-yon, one who keeps company or frequently associates with another; a comrade; a person, esp. a woman, paid to live with another; one who accompanies another; anything that matches another; an associate; the lowest rank in an order of knighthood: *a.* attendant; matching: *v.t.* to accompany. **companion-in-arms,** a fellow-soldier. **Companion of Honour** (C.H.), a member of a British Order, instituted in 1917 and ranking next below the 1st Class of the Order of the British Empire. **lady companion,** a lady paid to live with another. (O.Fr. *compainon.*)
companion, *n.* kom-*pan*-yon, the shelter over a staircase on a ship; the low framework with windows on deck through which light passes to the saloon and cabins below. **companion hatch,** an opening leading from the deck to cabins below. **companion ladder,** the ladder by which officers ascend to and descend from the quarter-deck. **companion way,** the staircase, porch or berthing of the ladder-way to the cabins. (Ital. *camera della campagna*, store-room.)
companionable, *a.* kom-*pan*-yon-a-bl, fit for good fellowship; sociable.
companionably, *ad.* in a companionable manner.
companionate, *a.* kom-*pan*-yon-ate, shared by companions. **companionate marriage,** a proposed form of "marriage" in which neither "spouse" would have marital responsibilities, and "divorce" would be by mutual consent.
companionship, *n.* kom-*pan*-yon-ship, fellowship; condition of being a companion; a number of compositors working together.
★**company,** *n.* *kum*-pa-ne, any assemblage of persons; persons collected by invitation or otherwise, for entertainment or festivity; a number of persons associated together in one common interest, or joint concern; a society; fellowship; a body of actors who perform together; a sub-division of a battalion under the command of a captain; the officers and crew of a ship. **company officer,** the commander of a company. **City Company,** a livery company. **limited company,** one of which the liability of the shareholders is limited to the amount unpaid on their shares. **Livery Company,** a guild of the City of London. **to bear company,** to accompany. **to keep company,** to accompany; to associate with frequently or habitually; to court. (O.Fr. *compainie.*)
comparable, *a.* *kom*-pa-ra-bl, capable of being compared; worthy of comparison.
comparably, *ad.* in a manner comparable.
comparative, *a.* kom-*pa*-ra-tiv, estimated by comparison; expressing comparison; not positive; not absolute; grounded on comparison [Gram.]: *n.* the comparative degree of a word [Gram.]. **comparative anatomy,** the anatomy of all organized bodies, by which the general phenomena of organic structure are demonstrated. **comparative religion,** the science and study of the world's religious systems and esp. of their interrelationships.
comparatively, *ad.* by comparison; not positively or in itself.
comparator, *n.* *kom*-pa-ray-tor, an instrument for the comparison of standards of various kinds, as of length, colour, temperature, etc.
compare, *v.i.* kom-*pare*, to hold comparison; to be like or equal: *v.t.* to set things together and examine their relations as regards likeness or unlikeness; to liken; to represent as similar, for the purpose of illustration; to inflect an adjective in the degrees of comparison [Gram.]: *n.* comparison; similitude. **to compare notes,** to interchange opinions. (L. *comparo*, adjust.)
★**comparison,** *n.* kom-*pa*-ris-on, act of comparing; state of being compared; comparative estimate; a simile, or illustration by similitude; the act of inflecting an adjective in its several degrees [Gram.]. (Fr. *comparaison.*)
compart, *v.t.* kom-*part*, to divide; to mark out into parts or subdivisions. (Late L. *compartio.*)
compartment, *n.* kom-*part*-ment, a division or separate part of a general design; a division partitioned off; a railway carriage forming part of a coach.
compass, *n.* *kum*-pas, circuit; space; limit; reach; range; moderate bounds or due limits; an instrument indicating the magnetic meridian and used to ascertain direction, esp. of the course of a ship at sea; a mathematical instrument with two movable legs for measuring distances or describing arcs or circles, or with three legs for measuring triangles: *v.t.* to stretch round; to encircle; to surround; to invest; to go or walk round; to obtain; to accomplish; to contrive or plot. **to fetch a compass,** to make a circuit. (Fr. *compas.*)
compassable, *a.* that may be compassed.
compass-box, *n.* a box for holding the mariner's compass.
compass-card, *n.* the suspended card on which the points of the compass are drawn.
compass-dial, *n.* a pocket dial fitted into a box, to show the hour by the direction of the needle.
compasses, *n.pl.* a mathematical compass.
compassion, *n.* kom-*pash*-on, sympathy with the sufferings and sorrows of others; pity. (Fr.)
compassionate, *a.* kom-*pash*-on-ate, inclined to feel and show compassion; full of pity: *v.t.* to pity; to commiserate; to have compassion for.
compassionately, *ad.* in a compassionate manner.
compassionateness, *n.* the quality of being compassionate.
compass-needle, *n.* the magnetized needle of a compass.
compass-plant, *n.* the prickly lettuce, *Lactuca scariola*, and other plants, which regularly present the edges of their leaves north and south.
compass-saw, *n.* a narrow saw that cuts curves; a large keyhole saw.
compass-timber, *n.* curved timber [Shipbuilding].
compass-window, *n.* a bow-window.
compaternity, *n.* kom-pa-*ter*-ne-te, the relationship of godparents among themselves and with the parents of the godchild.

compatibility, *n.* kom-*pat*-e-*bil*-e-te, the quality of being compatible, or co-existible with; suitableness.
compatible, *a.* kom-*pat*-e-bl, that may co-exist with; consistent; suitable; congruous. (Fr.)
compatibleness, *n.* state of being compatible.
compatibly, *ad.* in a compatible manner.
compatriot, *n.* kom-*pay*-tre-ot, one of the same country; a fellow-countryman: *a.* of the same country.
compear, *v.i.* kom-*peer*, to appear in court [Scots. Law]. (L. *comparo*, appear together.)
compeer, *n.* kom-*peer*, an equal; an associate: *v.t.* to equal or be equal with. (O.Fr. *comper.*)
compel, *v.t.* kom-*pel*, to drive or urge with force irresistibly; to force; to oblige; to constrain; to overpower. (L. *compello*, drive.)
compellable, *a.* that may be compelled.
compellably, *ad.* by compulsion.
compellation, *n.* kom-pel-*lay*-shon, style of address, as Sire, Sir, Madam. (L., accosting.)
compellative, *n.* kom-*pel*-a-tiv, the style or name by which a person is addressed.
compellingly, *ad.* by compulsion.
compend, *n.* *kom*-pend, a compendium.
compendious, *a.* kom-*pend*-e-us, containing the substance of a subject or work in a narrow compass; short; concise; comprehensive. (Fr. *compendieux.*)
compendiously, *ad.* in a compendious manner.
compendiousness, *n.* the quality of being compendious.
compendium, *n.* kom-*pend*-e-um, an abridgment; a summary. (L., what is weighed together or saved.)
compensate, *v.t.* *kom*-pen-sate, to give equal value for; to recompense; to make up or make amends for: *v.i.* to make amends; to supply an equivalent. (L. *compensatus*, weighed against another.)
compensation, *n.* kom-pen-*say*-shon, the act of compensating; an equivalent for services, debt, want, loss, or suffering; recompense; amends. **compensation balance** or **pendulum,** one so constructed as to beat equally under all changes of temperature.
compensative, *a.* kom-*pen*-sa-tiv, compensatory: *n.* an equivalent.
compensator, *n.* *kom*-pen-say-tor, one who compensates; a device or agent used to compensate.
compensatory, *a.* kom-*pen*-sa-to-re, that makes amends or compensation.
compère, *n.* kom-*pare*, one who introduces the entertainers and comments on the turns at broadcast and cabaret entertainments, etc.: *v.t.* to direct such a show; to act as compère.
compesce, *v.t.* kom-*pes*, to hold in check. (L. *compesco.*)
compete, *v.t.* kom-*peet*, to seek or strive for the same thing as another; to rival. (L. *competo*, seek.)
competence, *n.* *kom*-pe-tence, state of being competent; fitness; suitableness; ability; sufficiency; means sufficient to furnish the necessaries and conveniences of life, without superfluity; legal capacity; legal right or authority. (Fr. *compétence.*)
competent, *a.* *kom*-pe-tent, suitable; fit; adequate; able; having legal capacity or power; properly belonging. (Fr.)
competently, *ad.* in a competent manner.
***competition,** *n.* kom-pe-*tish*-on, the act of competing; strife in common for the same object; contention for superiority; the struggle for gain or existence [Econ. and Comm.]; rivalry.
competitive, *a.* kom-*pet*-e-tiv, relating to competition.
competitively, *ad.* in a competitive manner.
competitor, *n.* kom-*pet*-e-tor, one who competes; a rival.
competitory, *a.* kom-*pet*-e-to-re, acting in competition.
compilation, *n.* kom-pe-*lay*-shon, the act of compiling; that which is compiled, esp. a literary work composed of materials from various sources.
compile, *v.t.* kom-*pile*, to compose a literary work by collecting passages or material from various authors; to compose; to amass, as a score at cricket, etc. (L. *compilo*, plunder.)
compiler, *n.* kom-*pile*-er, one who compiles.
complacence, *n.* kom-*play*-sence, pleasure; inward satisfaction; the cause of the pleasure; pleasantness of manners; deportment and address; civility (L. *complacentis*, of pleasing.)
complacency, *n.* kom-*play*-sen-se, complacence.
complacent, *a.* kom-*play*-sent, gratified; self-satisfied; expressing complacency.
complacently, *ad.* in a complacent manner.
complain, *v.i.* kom-*playn*, to express grief, pain, censure, or resentment; to lament; to murmur; to bring a charge against. (Fr. *complaindre.*)
complainant, *n.* kom-*play*-nant, a complainer; a sufferer; a prosecutor; a plaintiff [Law].
complaining, *a.* querulous: *n.* complaint.
complainingly, *ad.* in a complaining manner.
complaint, *n.* kom-*playnt*, expression of grief, regret, pain, censure, or resentment; cause or subject of complaint; pain and uneasiness in the body; disease; a formal allegation [Law]; accusation. (Fr. *complainte.*)
complaisance, *n.* kom-*play*-zance *or* *kom*-pla-zance, pleasing deportment; civility; courtesy; desire of pleasing; disposition to oblige. (Fr.)
complaisant, *a.* kom-*play*-zant *or* *kom*-pla-zant, desirous of pleasing; courteous; obliging; expressing complaisance.
complaisantly, *ad.* in a complacent manner.
complanate, *a.* *kom*-pla-nate, flattened [Bot.].
complect, *v.t.* kom-*plekt*, to interweave; to knit together. (L. *complecto*, embrace.)
complement, *n.* *kom*-ple-ment, that which completes or makes up the full number or quantity; the full number or quantity; fulness; that which is added, not as necessary, but as ornamental; something adventitious to the main thing: *v.t.* to supplement. **complement of an arc** or **angle,** the difference between the arc or angle and 90° [Math.]. **complement of a number,** the difference between the number and 10, 100, 1,000, etc., used chiefly in working propositions by logarithms [Arith.]. **complements of a parallelogram,** the two spaces which, with the parallelograms about the diagonal, make up or complete the whole parallelogram [Math.]. **complement of a ship,** her full crew. (L. *complementum.*)
complemental, *a.* kom-ple-*men*-tal, partaking of the nature of a complement.
complementary, *a.* kom-ple-*men*-ta-re, completing; supplying a deficiency. **complementary angles,** angles whose sum equals a right angle. **complementary colours,** colours which together make up white.
***complete,** *a.* kom-*pleet*, perfect; entire; absolute; finished: *v.t.* to finish; to perfect; to accomplish; to make good deficiencies. (L. *completus*, filled.)
completely, *ad.* in a complete manner.
completeness, *n.* the state of being complete.
completion, *n.* kom-*plee*-shon, act of completing; state of being complete; fulfilment; accomplishment.
completive, *a.* kom-*plee*-tiv, making complete.
completory, *a.* kom-*plee*-to-re, fulfilling; accomplishing: *n.* compline.
***complex,** *n.* *kom*-pleks, a collection of things complex; an exceptional mental state caused by partial or complete repression of sexual, or other, primitive instincts; an obsession [Coll.]: *a.* (*or* kom-*pleks*), composed of many parts; not simple; complicated; intricate. (L. *complexus.*)
complexedness, *n.* kom-*plek*-sed-ness, state of being complex.
complexion, *n.* kom-*plek*-shon, the colour of the skin, particularly of the face; the external aspect; the temperament, habitude, or natural disposition of the body. (Fr.)
complexional, *a.* kom-*plek*-sho-nal, depending on or pertaining to the complexion.
complexioned, *a.* kom-*plek*-shond, having a certain complexion.
complexity, *n.* kom-*plek*-se-te, the state of being complex; intricacy; complication.
complexly, *ad.* kom-*pleks*-le, in a complex manner.
complexness, *n.* kom-*pleks*-ness, complexity.
complexus, *n.* kom-*plek*-sus, a complicated system or structure; a complex; the large muscle at the back and side of the neck serving to bend the head back.
compliable, *a.* kom-*ply*-a-bl, compliant.
compliance, *n.* kom-*ply*-ance, act of complying; yielding; consent; submission.

compliant, *a.* kom-*ply*-ant, yielding; obliging.
compliantly, *ad.* in a compliant manner.
complicacy, *n. kom*-ple-ka-se, state of being complicated.
complicant, *a. kom*-ple-kant, overlapping (of the wings of certain insects).
complicate, *a. kom*-ple-kate, complex; folded together [Bot.]: *v.t.* to intertangle; to make complex or intricate; to involve. (L. *complicatus*, folded.)
complicated, *a. kom*-ple-kay-ted, intricate. **complicated fracture,** a fracture accompanied by other important injuries.
complicatedly, *ad. kom*-ple-*kay*-ted-le, in a complicated manner.
complication, *n.* kom-ple-*kay*-shon, the act of complicating; the state of being complicated; something complicated.
complicity, *n.* kom-*plis*-e-te, participation; state of being an accomplice, esp. in evil-doing. (Fr. *complicité*.)
complier, *n.* kom-*ply*-er, one who complies; one of an easy yielding temper.
compliment, *n. kom*-ple-ment, an expression of regard; praise; delicate flattery; a favour: *v.t.* to address with approbation or respect; to congratulate; to praise; to flatter; *v.t.* to pass compliments; to use ceremony or ceremonious language. (Fr.)
complimental, *a.* kom-ple-*men*-tal, of the nature of a compliment; complimentary.
complimentary, *a.* kom-ple-*men*-ta-re, expressive of regard or praise; conveying compliments.
complimenter, *n. kom*-ple-men-ter, one who compliments; a flatterer.
complin, *n. kom*-plin, compline.
compline, *n. kom*-plin, the last prayer or service in the Roman Catholic breviary, so called as completing the service of the day.
complot, *n. kom*-plot, a joint plot; a conspiracy: *v.i.* kom-*plot*, to plot together; to conspire.
compluvium, *n.* kom-*ploo*-ve-um (*pl.* **compluvia**), an opening in the roof of a Roman atrium to allow the entrance of light and air. (L.)
comply, *v.i.* kom-*ply*, to yield and conform to the wishes of another; to consent. (It. *complire*, fulfil.)
compo, *n. kom*-poh, trade term for various compositions, as mortar, concrete, ivory-substitute for billiard-balls, etc. (Short for *composition*.)
component, *a.* kom-*pone*-ent, constitutive: *n.* a constituent part. (L. *componentis*, of placing.)
comport, *v.i.* kom-*port*, to agree; to accord; to suit: *v.t.* to behave; to conduct. (Fr. *comporter*.)
comportment, *n.* kom-*port*-ment, behaviour; deportment.
compose, *v.t.* kom-*poze*, to form, by putting two or more things or parts together; to form by combination; to think out; to arrange and put together a piece of literature or music; to calm; to quiet; to settle; to adjust; to settle into a quiet state; to set types in order for printing: *v.i.* to practise composition. (Fr. *composer*.)
composed, *a.* kom-*pozed*, settled; calm; sedate.
composedly, *ad.* kom-*poze*-ed-le, in a composed manner.
composedness, *n.* kom-*poze*-ed-ness, a state of being composed.
composer, *n.* kom-*poze*-er, one who composes, especially a piece of music; an author; a tranquillizer; one who adjusts a difference.
composing, *n.* kom-*poze*-ing, a placing together. **composing frame,** a printer's elevated working frame, on which the cases of type rest obliquely. **composing machine,** a machine for setting and arranging types, worked by keys like a typewriter. **composing stick,** a slide in which types are set from the cases, and adjusted to the length of the lines.
Compositæ, *n.pl.* kom-*poz*-e-tee, the largest natural order of plants, containing over 12,000 species in over 800 genera, and comprising the mostly highly evolved of the diocotyledons. (L.)
composite, *a. kom*-po-zit, compounded, made up of distinct parts or elements; belonging to the Compositæ. **composite candle,** a candle made of stearic acid and cocoa-nut oil. **composite carriage,** a railway coach with compartments of different classes. **composite flower,** one in which the flowers are in the form of heads, consisting of a number of florets densely packed together, each head being surrounded by an involucre of bracts though each floret is a flower by itself whether it is situated in the ray or in the disc. **composite number,** one which can be measured exactly by a number exceeding unity as 6 by 2 or 3 [Arith.]. **composite portrait,** a portrait formed from the superimposition of a number of negatives. **Composite order,** the last of the five architectural orders, so called because its capital is composed of Ionic and Corinthian features. (L. *compositus*, placed together.)
composition, *n.* kom-po-*zish*-on, the act of composing; the thing composed, such as a piece of literature or art; a mixture or combination of several ingredients; an artificially compounded substance used in various trades for various purposes; orderly disposition; mutual agreement to terms or conditions; compensation given in lieu of that stipulated or required; settlement of a debt by an accepted reduction; amount accepted; the forming of compound words [Gram.]; putting words together in sentences [Gram.]; that combination of the several parts in which each is presented in its due proportion [Fine Arts]; the art of setting types [Printing]. **composition of a felony,** abstention from prosecuting in return for some benefit, and itself a crime. **composition of forces,** a determination of the amount and direction of a force as the resultant of others acting at different angles [Mech.]. (L. *compositio*.)
compositive, *a.* kom-*poz*-e-tiv, having the power of compounding; combining; synthetic.
compositor, *n.* kom-*poz*-e-tor, one who sets type [Print.].
compossibility, *n.* kom-*pos*-e-*bil*-e-te, possibility of existing together.
compossible, *a.* kom-*pos*-e-bl, able to live together; compatible.
compost, *n. kom*-post, a fertilizing mixture of mould and various manures; a mixture for plastering the exterior of houses; stucco: *v.t.* to convert to or to treat with compost; to plaster. (O.Fr.)
composure, *n.* kom-*poze*-yewr, a settled state of mind; calmness; tranquillity; agreement.
compotation, *n.* kom-po-*tay*-shon, the act of drinking or tippling together.
compote, *n. kom*-pote, fruit stewed or preserved in syrup. (Fr.)
compound, *v.t.* kom-*pound*, to mingle or unite two or more ingredients in one mass; to combine; to settle amicably; to adjust by agreement. **to compound felony,** to abstain from prosecuting a felony in return for some valuable consideration: *v.i.* to come to terms of agreement by abating something of the first demand; to settle with a creditor by agreement. (O.Fr. *compondre*.)
compound, *a. kom*-pound, composed of two or more ingredients, or of different elementary bodies; combined; composite; composed of two or more words [Gram.]: *n.* a body formed by the union of two or more elementary substances, the result of composition; a mixture. **compound addition, subtraction, multiplication,** and **division,** calculation of quantities of different denominations [Arith.]. **compound flower,** a composite flower [Bot.]. **compound fracture,** a breakage of a limb or bone with consequent production of an open wound. **compound fructification,** fructification consisting of several confluent florets [Bot.]. **compound householder,** a tenant whose rates are included in his rent. **compound interest,** interest added to the principal, and bearing interest [Comm.]. **compound leaf,** a leaf with several leaflets on one petiole [Bot.]. **compound lens,** a lens composed of two or more simple lenses on a common axis. **compound quantity,** a quantity composed of two or more simple quantities or terms, connected by the sign + (plus), or − (minus) [Alg.]. **compound raceme,** a raceme composed of several small ones [Bot.]. **compound ratio,** the ratio which the product of the antecedents of two or more ratios has to the product of their consequents [Arith.].
compound, *n. kom*-pound, the fenced-in ground round a bungalow or factory, etc., in India and the Far East; the fenced area round a mine to which indentured labourers are confined [S. Africa]. (Malay, *kampong*, native village.)

compoundable, *a.* kom-*pound*-a-bl, capable of being compounded.
compounder, *n.* kom-*pound*-er, one who mixes different things; one who effects a compromise; one who compounds with a debtor or a felon.
comprador, *n.* kom-pra-*dor*, a native agent employed by European merchants, etc., in the Far East. (Port.)
comprecation, *n.* kom-pre-*kay*-shon, a praying together.
comprehend, *v.t.* kom-pre-*hend*, to comprise; to include; to grasp mentally; to understand. (L. *comprehendo*, hold.)
comprehensible, *a.* kom-pre-*hen*-se-bl, that may be comprehended or included; intelligible.
comprehensibleness, *n.* capability of being comprehended.
comprehensibly, *ad.* in a comprehensible manner.
comprehension, *n.* kom-pre-*hen*-shon, the act of comprehending or comprising; inclusion; capacity of the mind to understand; the sum of the attributes which a term implies [Logic.]. (L. *comprehensio.*)
comprehensive, *a.* kom-pre-*hen*-siv, having the quality of comprising much; having the power to comprehend many things at once; extensive; full.
comprehensively, *ad.* in a comprehensive manner.
comprehensiveness, *n.* the quality of being comprehensive.
compress, *v.t.* kom-*pres*, to press together; to force into a narrower compass; to condense. (L. *compressus*, pressed.)
compress, *n.* *kom*-pres, a pad to press on any part by means of a bandage [Surg.]; a wet application to reduce inflammation.
compressibility, *n.* kom-pres-e-*bil*-e-te, the quality of being compressible.
compressible, *a.* kom-*pres*-e-bl, capable of being compressed into a narrower compass; squeezable.
compressibleness, *n.* compressibility.
compression, *n.* kom-*presh*-on, the act of pressing into a narrower compass; the state of being compressed; condensation. **compression tap,** a tap in a motor-engine by which the charge can be allowed to escape from the cylinder-head with a consequent loss of compression. (L. *compressio.*)
compressive, *a.* kom-*pres*-siv, having power to compress.
compressor, *n.* kom-*pres*-sor, he who or that which compresses. (L.)
compressure, *n.* kom-*presh*-ur, pressure.
comprisal, *n.* kom-*pry*-zal, inclusion, the act of comprising.
comprise, *v.t.* kom-*prize*, to include; to embrace or contain. (O.Fr. *compris.*)
compromise, *n.* *kom*-pro-mize, a settlement of a difference by mutual concessions; the result of such a settlement: *v.t.* to settle by compromise; to agree; to endanger reputation by indiscretion: *v.i.* to agree; to accord. (Fr. *compromis.*)
compromission, *n.* kom-pro-*mish*-on, the submission of a dispute to arbitration; compromise.
comprovincial, *n.* kom-pro-*vin*-shal, one belonging to the same province or archiepiscopal jurisdiction.
comptoir, *n.* *komp*-twahr, a commercial agency in a foreign country. (Fr., a counter.)
comptometer, *n.* kom-*tom*-e-ter, trade name of a type of automatic calculating machine.
comptroller, *n.* kon-*trole*-er, controller.
compulsative, *a.* kom-*pul*-sa-tiv, compelling; constraining; operating by force.
compulsatory, *a.* kom-*pul*-sa-to-re, exercising compulsion; compulsory; necessitated.
compulsion, *n.* kom-*pul*-shon, the act of driving or urging by force, physical or moral; constraint of the will. (L. *compulsio*, from *compulsus*, forced.)
compulsive, *a.* kom-*pul*-siv, compulsory.
compulsively, *ad.* in a compulsive manner.
compulsiveness, *n.* compulsion.
compulsorily, *ad.* in a compulsory manner.
compulsory, *a.* kom-*pul*-so-re, having power to compel; employing compulsion; enforced by compulsion.
compunction, *n.* kom-*punk*-shon, contrition; regret; restraint by conscience. (O.Fr.)
compunctious, *a.* kom-*punk*-shus, causing compunction; remorseful.
compunctiously, *ad.* with compunction.
compurgation, *n.* kom-pur-*gay*-shon, exculpation of a man on the oath of others that his protestation of innocence may be accepted [Old Law]; vindication. (Late L. *compurgatio.*)
compurgator, *n.* *kom*-pur-ga-tor, a witness to the good character of an accused person, esp. one of a number brought forward to testify on oath, the practice prevailing before trial by jury.
computable, *a.* kom-*pew*-ta-bl, capable of being computed, numbered, or reckoned.
computation, *n.* kom-pew-*tay*-shon, computing; the quantity or amount computed; estimate.
compute, *v.t.* kom-*pewt*, to number, reckon, or calculate. (L. *computo*, reckon.)
computer, *n.* kom-*pew*-ter, one who computes; a reckoner; a calculator, esp. in an observatory; a calculating machine.
computist, *n.* *kom*-pew-tist, one who computes.
comrade, *n.* *kom*-rad, a companion; an associate; a fellow-member; among Communists, a form of address equivalent to "Mr.," "Mrs.," or "Miss." (Fr. *camarade.*)
comradely, *a.* *kom*-rad-le, like a comrade.
comradery, *n.* *kom*-rad-re, comradeship; camaraderie.
comradeship, *n.* *kom*-rad-ship, state of being comrades; friendship.
Comtism, *n.* *kont*-izm, the Positivism of Comte.
Comtist, *n.* *kont*-ist, a disciple of Comte.
con, *prep.* kon, against, as in the phrase "pro and con," for and against. (L. *contra.*)
con, *v.t.* kon, to go over carefully; to study; to direct how to steer [Naut.]. (A.S. *cunnan*, to know.)
con-, kon, a Latin prefix, denoting with. (L. *cum.*)
conarium, *n.* kon-*nayr*-re-um, the pineal gland [Anat.].
conation, *n.* ko-*nay*-shon, the effort of volition; the faculty of voluntary agency. (L. *conatus*, attempted.)
conative, *a.* *koh*-na-tiv, pertaining to conation; expressing endeavour [Gram.].
concamerate, *v.t.* kon-*kam*-er-rate, to arch over; to divide into chambers [Conch.] (L. *concameratus*, arched together.)
concameration, *n.* kon-kam-er-*ray*-shon, a vaulting; division into cells or chambers.
concatenate, *v.t.* kon-*kat*-e-nate, to link together; to unite in a successive series. (L. *concatenatus*, linked together.)
concatenation, *n.* kon-kat-e-*nay*-shon, a series of links united; a series of things, circumstances, terms, etc., depending on each other.
concave, *a.* *kon*-kave, with a curved hollow, as that of a basin; opposed to convex: *n.* a curved hollow; an arch or vault: *v.t.* to make hollow. (Fr.)
concavely, *ad.* kon-*kave*-le, in a concave manner.
concaveness, *n.* *kon*-kave-ness, concavity.
concavity, *n.* kon-*kav*-e-te, state of being concave; hollowness; a depression; the internal surface of a hollow spherical body.
concavo-concave, *a.* kon-*kay*-vo-*kon*-kave, concave on both surfaces.
concavo-convex, *a.* kon-*kay*-vo-*kon*-veks, concave on one side and convex on the other.
conceal, *v.t.* kon-*seel*, to hide; to keep secret; to forbear to disclose or keep from sight; to disguise. (O.Fr. *conceler.*)
concealable, *a.* that may be concealed.
concealment, *n.* kon-*seel*-ment, the act of concealing or keeping secret; the condition of being concealed; privacy; the place of hiding; secrecy; disguise; the suppression of material facts [Law]. (O.Fr. *concelement*)
concede, *v.i.* kon-*seed*, to admit as true or proper; to grant; to give or yield up: *v.t.* to admit; to grant. (L. *concedere*, yield.)
conceit, *n.* kon-*seet*, conception; apprehension; opinion; a whim; a baseless fancy; an over-estimate of self; a pleasant and ingenious, generally whimsical, notion. **out of conceit with,** having lost all favour for. (O.Fr. *concept.*)
conceited, *a.* kon-*seet*-ed, vain; having a high opinion of oneself; egotistical.
conceitedly, *ad.* in a conceited manner.
conceitedness, *n.* state of being conceited; vanity.
conceivability, *n.* kon-*seev*-a-*bil*-e-te, conceivableness.
conceivable, *a.* kon-*seev*-a-bl, imaginable.
conceivableness, *n.* quality of being conceivable.

conceivably, *ad.* in a conceivable or intelligible manner.
conceive, *v.t.* kon-*seev*, to receive into and form in the womb; to form in the mind; to frame a notion of; to imagine; to think; to express: *v.i.* to become pregnant; to form a conception of. (O.Fr. *concever.*)
concelebrate, *v.t.* kon-*sel*-e-brate, to celebrate Mass with the ordaining bishop (of a newly ordained priest).
concent, *n.* kon-*sent*, concert of voices; harmony. (L. *concentus*, sung together.)
concentrate, *v.t.* *kon*-sen-trate, to bring to a common centre, point, or focus; to bring to bear on; to rectify: *v.i.* to think intensely; to meet at one point: *n.* that which is produced by concentration [Metal.]. (L. *con-*, and *centrum*, centre.)
concentration, *n.* kon-sen-*tray*-shon, the act of concentrating; state of being concentrated. **concentration camp,** a camp for the accommodation of non-combatants in a militarily occupied area; in authoritarian states, a large location for the confinement and punishment of those for whom the authorities, for any reason, deem it advisable.
concentrative, *a.* kon-*sen*-tra-tiv, tending to concentrate.
concentrativeness, *n.* kon-*sen*-tra-tiv-ness, the faculty of concentrating.
concentrator, *n.* *kon*-sen-tray-tor, an apparatus for concentrating solutions [Chem.]; a pneumatic machine used in mining to separate particles of ore [Min.].
concentre, *v.i.* kon-*sen*-ter, to meet in a common centre or combine for a common object; to coincide: *v.t.* to draw or direct to a common centre. (Fr. *concentrer.*)
concentric, *a.* kon-*sen*-trik, having a common centre.
concentrically, *ad.* kon-*sen*-tre-ka-le, in a concentric manner.
concentricity, *n.* kon-sen-*tris*-e-te, state of being concentric.
concept, *n.* *kon*-sept, a conception of the mind; a notion; a mental image; an idea embracing the essential attributes of its class. (L. *conceptus*, conceived.)
conceptacle, *n.* kon-*sep*-ta-kl, that in which anything is contained; a receptacle; a follicle [Bot.]; part of the reproductive equipment of fungi and certain low organisms [Zool.]. (L. *conceptaculum.*)
conception, *n.* kon-*sep*-shon, act of conceiving; the first formation of the fœtus of an animal; idea, thought, or image conceived; a notion. (Fr.)
conceptional, *a.* kon-*sep*-shon-al, of the nature of a conception.
Conceptionist, *n.* kon-*sep*-shon-ist, a member of any one of the Roman Catholic orders dedicated to the Immaculate Conception.
conceptive, *a.* kon-*sept*-iv, capable of conceiving.
conceptual, *a.* kon-*sept*-yew-al, belonging to or relating to conception.
conceptualism, *n.* kon-*sept*-yew-al-izm, the theory of the conceptualists.
conceptualist, *n.* kon-*sept*-yew-al-ist, one who maintains, in logic, that a general term represents an abstract conception, and is less than a thing, but more than a name [Logic].
conceptualize, *v.t.* kon-*sept*-yew-a-lize, to form a concept of.
concern, *n.* kon-*sern*, that which belongs to or concerns one; business; interest; solicitude; anxiety; an object; a business, firm, or commercial undertaking in which a number are interested: *v.t.* to relate or belong to; to interest or affect; to disturb; to make uneasy. (Fr. *concerner.*)
concerned, *a.* kon-*sernd*, engaged; interested; solicitous; anxious.
concernedly, *ad.* kon-*ser*-ned-le, in a concerned manner.
concerning, *prep.* relating to; about; anent.
concernment, *n.* kon-*sern*-ment, the thing in which one is concerned or interested; concern; interposition; importance.
concert, *v.t.* kon-*sert*, to contrive, arrange, or adjust. (Fr. *concerter.*)
concert, *n.* *kon*-sert, agreement in a design or plan; harmony; musical harmony; a musical entertainment. (Fr.)
concerted, *a.* kon-*ser*-ted, mutually planned; arranged in parts [Mus.].
concert-grand, *n.* *kon*-sert-grand, a grand piano of very brilliant tone for use at concerts.
concertina, *n.* kon-ser-*tee*-nah, a musical instrument, held in the hands, with an expansible bellows causing air pressure on metal reeds, and having keys by the action of which the air is used to produce the notes. (It. *concerto.*)
concerto, *n.* kon-*chare*-to, a piece of music composed for particular instruments, with orchestral accompaniment [Mus.]. **concerto grosso,** a concerted suite for orchestra and soloists. (It.)
concert-pitch, *n.* *kon*-sert-pitch, a pitch slightly higher than that usually given to a musical note.
concession, *n.* kon-*sesh*-on, the act of conceding; that which is conceded; a grant, as of land or of special facilities, for a special purpose.
concessionaire, *n.* kon-*sesh*-on-*ayr*, the person or company, etc., holding a concession. (Fr. *concessionnaire.*)
concessionary, *a.* kon-*sesh*-on-a-re, yielding by indulgence or allowance: *n.* a concessionaire.
concessionist, *n.* kon-*sesh*-on-ist, one who is in favour of making concessions.
concessive, *a.* kon-*ses*-siv, of the nature of concession; tending to or implying concession.
concessively, *ad.* by way of concession.
concettism, *n.* kon-*chet*-tizm, addiction to fanciful turns in writing.
concetto, *n.* kon-*chet*-to, affected wit or conceit. (It.)
conch, *n.* kongk, the shell of *Strombus gigas*, a large marine univalve mollusc; any large spirally turned marine shell, esp. one used as a trumpet; the dome of a semicircular apse; the larger cavity of the external ear. (L. *concha*, a shell.)
conchifer, *n.* *kong*-ke-fer, a bivalve mollusc.
conchiferous, *a.* kong-*kif*-er-rus, shell-bearing.
conchitic, *a.* kongk-*it*-ik, abounding in fossil shells [Geol.].
conchoid, *n.* *kong*-koyd, a shell-like curve: *a.* conchoidal. (L. *concha*, and *eidos*, like.)
conchoidal, *a.* kong-*koy*-dal, fracturing with shell-like surfaces [Min.].
conchological, *a.* kong-ko-*loj*-e-kl, pertaining to conchology.
conchologist, *n.* kong-*kol*-o-jist, one versed in the natural history of shells; a collector of shells.
conchology, *n.* kong-*kol*-o-je, the science of shells and the animals that inhabit them; the collecting of shells. (L. *concha*, and Gr. *logos*, science.)
conchospiral, *n.* *kong*-ko-*spire*-ral, the kind of spiral curve commonly seen in shells.
conchy, *n.* *kon*-she, a conscientious objector to military service [Slang abbrev.].
conchylaceous, *a.* *kong*-ke-*lay*-shus, pertaining to, or of the nature of, the shells of molluscs.
concierge, *n.* (App.), a hall-porter, lodge-keeper, or door-keeper; a caretaker of flats. (Fr.)
conciliable, *a.* kon-*sil*-e-a-bl, that may be conciliated.
conciliar, *a.* kon-*sil*-yar, pertaining to a council.
conciliate, *v.t.* kon-*sil*-e-ate, to reconcile, or bring to a state of friendship; to gain or win over. (L. *conciliatus*, brought together.)
conciliation, *n.* kon-*sil*-e-*ay*-shon, the act of conciliating; reconciliation; reconcilement.
conciliative, *a.* kon-*sil*-e-a-tiv, tending to conciliate; reconciling; conciliatory.
conciliator, *n.* one who conciliates.
conciliatoriness, *n.* kon-*sil*-e-a-to-re-ness, the quality of being conciliatory.
conciliatory, *a.* kon-*sil*-e-a-to-re, tending or endeavouring to conciliate.
concinnity, *n.* kon-*sin*-e-te, elegance in oratory or literary style; neatness. (L. *concinnitas.*)
concinnous, *a.* kon-*sin*-nus, suitable; becoming; harmonizing. (L. *concinnus*, well ordered.)
concipient, *a.* kon-*sip*-e-ent, conceiving.
concise, *a.* kon-*sise*, comprehending much in few words; brief; terse. (L. *concisus*, cut.)
concisely, *ad.* kon-*sise*-le, in a concise manner.
conciseness, *n.* the quality of being concise.
concision, *n.* kon-*sizh*-on, a faction; circumcision of Gentiles. (Late L. *concisio.*)
conclamation, *n.* kon-kla-*may*-shon, an outcry or shout of many together. (L. *con-*, and *clamo*, cry.)

conclave, *n.* *kon*-klave, the assembly of cardinals shut up for the election of a Pope; the body of cardinals; the apartment where they are locked up; a private meeting or close assembly. (L., a room that may be locked; *con-*, and *clavis*, key.)
conclavist, *n.* *kon*-kla-vist, an ecclesiastic attending upon a cardinal in conclave.
conclude, *v.t.* kon-*klood*, to infer, as from premises; to determine; to bring to a conclusion or end; to arrange finally, as a treaty: *v.i.* to infer; to determine; to form a final judgment; to end. (L. *concludo*, shut.)
concludingly, *ad.* kon-*klood*-ing-le, conclusively.
conclusion, *n.* kon-*kloo*-zhon, the close or end; the sum; logical inference; final decision; experiment. (Fr.)
conclusive, *a.* kon-*kloo*-siv, decisive; convincing.
conclusively, *ad.* in a conclusive manner.
conclusiveness, *n.* quality of being conclusive.
conclusory, *a.* kon-*kloo*-so-re, conclusive.
concoct, *v.t.* kon-*kokt*, to boil together; to digest; to purify; to ripen; to form and prepare in the mind; to devise; to plot. (L. *concoctus*, boiled together.)
concocter, *n.* kon-*kok*-ter, one who concocts.
concoction, *n.* kon-*kok*-shon, the act of concocting; the thing concocted; devising.
concoctive, *a.* kon-*kok*-tiv, pertaining to any concoction.
concolorous, *a.* kon-*kul*-o-rus, of one colour only; uniform in colour [Nat. Hist.].
concomitance, *n.* kon-*kom*-e-tance, the state of being concomitant. (Fr.)
concomitancy, *n.* kon-*kom*-e-tan-se, concomitance.
concomitant, *a.* kon-*kom*-e-tant, accompanying; conjoined with: *n.* a thing that accompanies another; accompaniment. (Low L. *concomitans*, going with.)
concomitantly, *ad.* in a concomitant way.
concord, *n.* *kon*-kawrd, agreement between persons; union in opinions, sentiments or interests; harmony; agreement of words in construction [Gram.]. (Fr. *concorde.*)
concordance, *n.* kon-*kawrd*-ance, the state of being concordant; agreement; accordance; an index; an alphabetical list of the words in a book with references to the passages where they occur, as in the Bible or Shakespeare. (Fr.)
concordancy, *n.* kon-*kawrd*-an-se, agreement.
concordant, *a.* kon-*kawrd*-ant, agreeing; correspondent; harmonious: *n.* that which is accordant.
concordantly, *ad.* in a concordant manner.
concordat, *n.* kon-*kawrd*-at, an agreement or compact made by the head of a state with the Pope; a compact, covenant, or agreement concerning some beneficiary matter [Canon Law]. (Fr. from L. *concordatus*, agreed.)
concorporate, *v.t.* kon-*korp*-o-rate, to unite different things in one mass or body; to incorporate; *a.* united in one body.
concourse, *n.* *kon*-koarse, a flocking or crowding together; confluence; a crowd; an assembly; an assemblage; the general platform at a railway terminus with which the train platforms communicate. (Fr. *concours.*)
concreate, *v.t.* *kon*-kre-ate, to create at the same time.
concremation, *n.* kon-kre-*may*-shon, the act of burning or cremating together.
concrement, *n.* *kon*-kre-ment, growth by concretion; concretion.
concrescence, *n.* kon-*kres*-sense, growing together; union of parts or organs [Biol.]. (L. *concrescentia.*)
concrescible, *a.* kon-*kres*-se-bl, capable of solidifying or concreting.
concrete, *n.* *kon*-kreet, a mass formed by concretion; an artificial stone formed of cement with stones or other hard materials. **reinforced concrete,** concrete strengthened by the setting within it of steel rods, bars, or network.
concrete, *a.* *kon*-kreet, formed by concretion into one mass; made of concrete; as existing in nature [Logic]; denoting a real thing, opposed to abstract [Logic]. (L. *concretus*, grown.)
concrete, *v.i.* kon-*kreet*, to unite or coalesce into a mass or solid body; to apply concrete: *v.t.* to form into a mass by the coalescence of separate particles; to treat with or pave with concrete.

concretely, *ad.* kon-*kreet*-le, in a concrete manner; in a manner not abstract.
concreteness, *n.* kon-*kreet*-ness, a state of being concrete.
concretion, *n.* kon-*kree*-shon, the act of concreting; an aggregated mass; a calculus or stone [Med.]; a ball-like aggregation of mineral matter [Geol.].
concretionary, *a.* kon-*kree*-shon-a-re, pertaining to, made up of, or forming concretions.
concubinage, *n.* kon-*kew*-be-naj, cohabiting as man and wife without being married; the practice or state of being or having a concubine.
concubinary, *a.* kon-*kew*-be-na-re, pertaining to or living in concubinage.
concubine, *n.* *kong*-kew-bine, a woman who cohabits with a man without a legal marriage; among polygamous peoples, a legal but secondary or inferior wife. (L. *concubina.*)
concupiscence, *n.* kon-*kew*-pe-sens, lust; inordinate or sinful sexual desire. (Fr.)
concupiscent, *a.* kon-*kew*-pe-sent, lustful.
concupiscible, *a.* kon-*kew*-pe-se-bl, characterized by concupiscence.
concur, *v.i.* kong-*ker*, to meet in one point; to agree; to unite or meet together; to unite to produce a result. (L. *concurro.*)
concurrence, *n.* kon-*ku*-rens, the act of concurring; union; conjunction; agreement; consent; approbation. (L. *concurrentia.*)
concurrent, *a.* kon-*ku*-rent, concurring; acting in conjunction; contributing to the same effect; conjoined: *n.* one who or that which concurs or accompanies.
concurrently, *ad.* with concurrence.
concurrentness, *n.* state of being concurrent.
concuss, *v.t.* kon-*kus*, to agitate; to coerce or overawe by threats. (L. *concussus*, shaken.)
concussion, *n.* kon-*kush*-on, the act of shaking by sudden contact; the state of being so shaken; a shock; undue pressure; extortion by threats; effect on the brain, etc., of a shock [Med.]. **concussion fuse,** a fuse igniting upon impact. (L. *concussio.*)
concussive, *a.* kon-*kus*-siv, pertaining to or like concussion.
concutient, *a.* kon-*kew*-shent, colliding suddenly and violently.
concyclic, *a.* kon-*sik*-lik, lying upon the circumference of a circle, as of a series of points [Geom.].
cond, *v.t.* kond, to direct the helmsman in what direction to steer [Naut.].
condemn, *v.t.* kon-*dem*, to blame or censure; to pronounce or judge guilty; to doom to punishment; to judge or pronounce unfit for use or service; to judge or pronounce to be forfeited. **condemned cell,** the cell in a prison in which one sentenced to death is confined pending execution. (O.Fr. *condemner.*)
condemnable, *a.* kon-*dem*-na-bl, blamable; culpable.
condemnation, *n.* *kon*-dem-*nay*-shon, the act of condemning; the state of being condemned; the reason for condemning. (L. *condemnatus*, condemned.)
condemnatory, *a.* kon-*dem*-na-to-re, bearing or involving condemnation or censure.
condensability, *n.* kon-*den*-sa-*bil*-e-te, the quality of being condensable.
condensable, *a.* kon-*den*-sa-bl, that may be compressed into a smaller compass.
condensation, *n.* kon-den-*say*-shon, the act of condensing; the state of being condensed; a condensed mass; compression of meaning; conciseness. (L. *condensatius*, condensed.)
condense, *v.t.* kon-*dense*, to make more dense or compact; to compress; to reduce into a denser form, as from gaseous into liquid or solid; to subject to condensation: *v.i.* to become dense or more compact; to grow thick. (Fr. *condenser.*)
condensed, *a.* kon-*denst*, made denser by pressure or lowering of temperature; terse, as a condensed style of writing; close or compressed.
condenser, *n.* kon-*den*-ser, anything that condenses; a pneumatic engine or syringe in which air may be compressed; a vessel in which aqueous or spirituous vapours are reduced to a liquid form; an apparatus for storing electricity or increasing the strength of an electric charge; a concentrating lens.
condensity, *n.* kon-*den*-se-te, condensed quality.

conder, *n.* *kond*-er, one who signals to the fishermen the course of the shoals of fish; a huer.
condescend, *v.i.* kon-de-*send*, to descend or stoop voluntarily from a superior to an inferior position; to lower oneself; to be kind to inferiors; to deign. (Fr. *condescendre* from L. *condescensus*, descended.)
condescendence, *n.* kon-de-*send*-ence, condescension.
condescending, *a.* marked by condescension; patronizing.
condescendingly, *ad.* in a condescending manner.
condescension, *n.* kon-de-*sen*-shon, the act of condescending; stooping to equality with, or courtesy to, inferiors; patronizing behaviour.
condign, *a.* kon-*dine*, deserved; merited. (O.Fr. *condigne*.)
condignly, *ad.* kon-*dine*-le, according to deserts.
condignness, *n.* agreeableness to deserts.
condiment, *n.* *kon*-de-ment, seasoning; sauce. (L. *condimentum*.)
condimental, *a.* kon-de-*men*-tal, of or resembling a condiment; spicy.
condisciple, *n.* kon-de-*sy*-pl, a schoolfellow.
★**condition,** *n.* kon-*dish*-on, state; environment; rank; attribute; state of mind; a preliminary requirement; term of a contract; stipulation: *v.i.* to make terms; to stipulate; to test; to bring or put into condition; to make fit. (Fr.)
conditional, *a.* kon-*dish*-on-al, containing or depending on a condition or conditions; not absolute: *n.* what expresses a condition; a limitation; the conditional mood, a conditional conjunction [Gram.]. (L. *conditionalis*.)
conditionalism, *n.* kon-*dish*-on-a-lizm, the doctrine that any future life is conditional on the virtue and righteousness of the individual; annihilationism [Theol.].
conditionality, *n.* kon-dish-o-*nal*-e-te, the quality of being conditional or limited.
conditionally, *ad.* kon-*dish*-on-a-le, with certain limitations.
conditionate, *a.* kon-*dish*-on-ate, conditional; subject to or established on certain terms: *v.t.* to qualify; to regulate; to put under conditions. (L. *conditionatus*, mentioned together.)
conditioned, *a.* kon-*dish*-ond, having conditions or qualities; limited by or depending upon certain conditions. **conditioned reflex, stimulus,** etc., one extraneously and artificially imposed [Psychan.].
condolatory, *a.* kon-*doh*-la-to-re, expressing condolence.
condole, *v.i.* kon-*dole*, to grieve with; to sympathize with one in sorrow. (L. *condoleo*.)
condolement, *n.* kon-*dole*-ment, condolence.
condolence, *n.* kon-*dole*-ence, the expression of grief excited by the suffering or distress of another.
condom, *n.* *kun*-dum, a sheath used by practisers of birth-control to ensure non-conception.
condominium, *n.* kon-do-*min*-e-um, the joint sovereignty of two or more powers; the territory or state over which this is exercised. (L. *con* -, and *dominium*, lordship.)
condonation, *n.* kon-doh-*nay*-shon, the act of condoning; the forgiveness by one spouse of an act of adultery by the other [Law]. (L. *condonatus*, remitted.)
condone, *v.t.* kon-*done*, to pardon; to forgive (esp. a marital offence). (L. *condono*, remit.)
condor, *n.* *kon*-dor, the large vulture of the Andes, *Sarcorhamphus gryphus*; a gold coin of certain S. American countries. (Sp.)
condottiere, *n.* kon-do-*tyare*-re, an Italian soldier of fortune; a mercenary. (It.)
conduce, *v.i.* kon-*dewce*, to tend to some end or object; to contribute (to a result). (L. *conduco*, lead.)
conducive, *a.* kon-dew-siv, that may conduce or contribute.
conduciveness, *n.* the quality of conducing.
conduct, *n.* *kon*-dukt, guidance; the act of guiding or leading; management; mode or manner of action; deportment; behaviour; control. **safe conduct,** a promise of a safe passage. (L. *conductus*, guidance.)
conduct, *v.t.* kon-*dukt*, to lead; to guide; to escort; to direct [Mus.]; to govern; to manage; to comport; to transmit. **conduct money,** expenses refunded to a witness in a legal case. (L. *conductus*, led.)
conductance, *n.* kon-*duk*-tance, the act of conducting; conducting power (Elect.); the reciprocal of electrical resistance.
conductibility, *n.* kon-*duk*-te-*bil*-e-te, capability of being conducted.
conductible, *a.* kon-*duk*-te-bl, that may be conducted.
conduction, *n.* kon-*duk*-shon, transmission by a conductor; conductivity. (L. *conductio*.)
conductive, *a.* kon-*duk*-tiv, having transmissive power.
conductivity, *n.* kon-duk-*tiv*-e-te, the quality of being conductive.
conductor, *n.* kon-*duk*-tor, a leader; a guide; a commander; a director of an orchestra; a guard, as of a railway train; an attendant who takes the fares in a public conveyance; a medium for the transmission of heat or electricity [Physics]; a lightning-rod. (L.)
conductress, *n.* kon-*duk*-tres, a female conductor.
conduit, *n.* *kon*-dit *or* *kun*-dit, a pipe, channel, or underground passage for water, sewage, electric cables, etc.; a narrow passage, often under ground, between the apartments of a building. (O.Fr.)
conduplicate, *a.* kon-*dew*-plik-at, doubled or folded over or together [Bot.].
condurrite, *n.* kon-*du*-rite, an arsenical oxide of copper. (*Condurrow*, in Cornwall, where mined.)
condylar, *a.* *kon*-de-ler, pertaining to a condyle.
condyle, *n.* *kon*-dile, a rounded protuberance on the end of a bone. (Gr. *kondylos*, a knuckle.)
condyloid, *a.* *kon*-de-loyd, resembling a condyle. **condyloid process,** the posterior protuberance at the extremities of the under jaw. (Gr. *kondylos*, and *eidos*, like.)
condyloma, *n.* kon-de-*loh*-ma, a wart-like growth on the skin or mucous membrane.
cone, *n.* kone, a solid body or figure tapering to a point from a circular base, like a sugar-loaf; fruit shaped like a cone, as that of the pine; anything cone-shaped: *v.i.* to bear cones. (Fr. *cône*.)
cone, *n.* kone, any species of *Conus*, a genus of univalve molluscs with inversely conical shells.
coneine, *n.* *koh*-ne-in, conine.
cones, *n.* kohnz, very fine flour with which troughs for kneading bread are sprinkled.
coney, *n.* *koh*-ne, a cony. **coney fur,** trade name for dressed and dyed rabbit-skins.
confab, *n.* *kon*-fab, familiar talk or conversation; confabulation [Coll.].
confabulate, *v.i.* kon-*fab*-yew-late, to talk familiarly. (L. *confabulatus*, talked together.)
confabulation, *n.* kon-*fab*-yew-*lay*-shon, familiar talk.
confect, *n.* *kon*-fekt, a sweetmeat; a comfit. (L. *confectus*, made up.)
confection, *n.* kon-*fek*-shon, the act of mixing ingredients; a thing compounded; anything prepared with sugar; a sweetmeat; a soft electuary; an article of woman's apparel, as a mantle. (Fr.)
confectionary, *a.* kon-*fek*-shon-a-re, pertaining to confections or confectionery; like a sweetmeat.
confectioner, *n.* kon-*fek*-shon-er, one whose occupation is to make or sell pastries, tarts, sweetmeats, etc.
confectionery, *n.* kon-*fek*-shon-er-re, the wares of a confectioner; sweetmeats in general.
confederacy, *n.* kon-*fed*-er-ra-se, a contract between two or more persons, bodies, or states, combined in support of each other in some act or enterprise; a league; federal compact; the confederate bodies; a coalition; a conspiracy.
confederate, *a.* kon-*fed*-er-rat, united in a league; allied by treaty: *n.* one who is united with others in a league; an ally; a Southerner in the Civil War of 1861-65 [U.S.A. history]: *v.t.* and *i.* to unite in a league; to ally. (L. *confœderatus*, joined by treaty.)
confederation, *n.* kon-*fed*-er-*ray*-shon, the act of confederating; a league; a compact for mutual support; the bodies in league.
confederatism, *n.* kon-*fed*-er-ra-tizm, the principles, system, organization, etc., of a confederacy or confederates.
confederative, *a.* kon-*fed*-er-ra-tiv, relating to a confederacy or to confederates.
confer, *v.i.* kon-*fer*, to consult together; to counsel or advise with; to converse: *v.t.* to give or bestow. (L. *confero*, bring together.)

conferee, *n.* kon-fe-*ree*, one who is conferred with; one on whom something is conferred.
conference, *n.* *kon*-fe-rence, the act of conferring; a meeting for consultation or deliberation; a meeting of the two branches of a legislature to adjust differences; a meeting for international deliberation. (Fr. *conference.*)
conferential, *a.* kon-fe-*ren*-shal, relating to conference or to a conference.
conferment, *n.* kon-*fer*-ment, a conferring; the action of bestowing.
conferrable, *a.* kon-*fer*-a-bl, capable of being conferred.
conferrer, *n.* kon-*fer*-er, one who confers.
conferruminated, *a.* kon-fe-*roo*-me-nay-ted, as if soldered together [Bot.]. (L. *conferruminatus*, cemented together.)
confervaceous, *a.* kon-fer-*vay*-shus, pertaining to the *Confervæ*, a genus of fresh-water algæ. (L.)
confervite, *n.* kon-*fer*-vite, a confervaceous fossil.
confervoid, *a.* kon-*fer*-voyd, articulated like the *Confervæ*; consisting of delicate filaments [Bot.].
confess, *v.t.* kon-*fess*, to acknowledge or own, esp. a crime, failing, etc.; to acknowledge sins; to hear the confession of; to admit: *v.i.* to make confession; to disclose faults. (O.Fr. *confesser.*)
confessant, *n.* kon-*fes*-sant, one who confesses to a priest.
confessedly, *ad.* kon-*fes*-sed-le, by confession or admittedly; avowedly.
confession, *n.* kon-*fesh*-on, the acknowledgment of a crime or fault; avowal; profession; the formal disclosure of sins or faults to a priest for the purpose of receiving absolution. **confession of faith,** a formulary comprising the articles of the creed of a church. (Fr.)
confessional, *n.* kon-*fesh*-on-al, the place where a priest or confessor sits to hear confessions: *a.* pertaining to a confession of faith, or to auricular confession. **Confessional Church,** that part of the Lutheran Church in Germany that withstood nazification.
confessionary, *n.* kon-*fesh*-on-a-re, the tomb of a martyr or confessor: *a.* pertaining to auricular confession.
confessionist, *n.* kon-*fesh*-on-ist, one who makes a profession of faith; one who adopts a certain creed or confession.
confessor, *n.* kon-*fes*-sor, a priest who hears confession; one who makes profession of his faith in Christ, especially in the face of persecution; any male saint other than an apostle or martyr. (O.Fr.)
confetti, *n.pl.* kon-*fet*-te, small roundlets of thin coloured paper thrown at a bridal couple, or in a carnival, etc. (It.)
confidant, *n.* kon-fe-*dant* (*fem.* **confidante**), one entrusted with secrets; a bosom friend.
confide, *v.i.* kon-*fide*, to trust or have all faith in: *v.t.* to entrust; to commit to the charge of. (L. *confido.*)
confidence, *n.* *kon*-fe-dens, a firm trust; trust in self, or self-reliance; object of trust; assurance of safety; boldness. **confidence man,** a cheat or thief employing the confidence trick. **confidence trick,** any deception played by gaining first the victim's confidence. (L. *confidentia.*)
confident, *a.* *kon*-fe-dent, firmly trusting; bold; fully assured.
confidential, *a.* kon-fe-*den*-shal, enjoying the confidence of another; intended to be treated as private; told or done in confidence. (Fr.)
confidentially, *ad.* in confidence.
confidently, *ad.* in a confident manner.
confider, *n.* kon-*fy*-der, one who confides.
confiding, *a.* kon-*fy*-ding, trustful; credulous.
confidingly, *ad.* in a confiding manner.
configuration, *n.* kon-*fig*-yew-*ray*-shon, external form or figure due to adjustment of parts; contour; outline; relative position or aspects of the planets at any given time. (Fr.)
configure, *v.t.* kon-*fig*-ur, to dispose in a certain form, figure, or shape; to give form to.
confinable, *a.* kon-*fy*-na-bl, that may be confined.
confine, *n.* *kon*-fine (usu. in *pl.*), border; boundary; limit; a borderland [Lit. and Fig.].
confine, *v.t.* kon-*fine*, to restrain within limits; to shut up; to limit in application. (Fr. *confiner.*)
confined, *a.* kon-*fynd*, narrowly limited; bound; in childbed; delivered of a child.
confinement, *n.* kon-*fine*-ment, the act of confining; the state of being confined, esp. by childbirth; seclusion; restraint.
confinity, *n.* kon-*fin*-e-te, nearness; neighbourhood.
confirm, *v.t.* kon-*ferm*, to make firm or firmer; to strengthen; to establish; to corroborate; to ratify; to admit into full church privilege [Eccles.]. (O.Fr. *confermir.*)
confirmable, *a.* that may be confirmed.
confirmation, *n.* kon-fer-*may*-shon, the act of confirming; additional corroborative evidence; the ceremony of admitting the baptized into full church privileges by a bishop. (Fr.)
confirmative, *a.* kon-*fer*-ma-tiv, confirmatory.
confirmatively, *ad.* in a confirmative manner.
confirmatory, *a.* serving to confirm.
confirmed, *a.* kon-*fermd*, established; fixed; irreclaimable; having received confirmation.
confirmedly, *ad.* kon-*fer*-med-le, in a confirmed manner.
confirmedness, *n.* kon-*fer*-med-ness, a fixedness of state.
confirmee, *n.* kon-fer-*mee*, one who has been confirmed [Eccles.].
confirmer, *n.* kon-*fer*-mer, he who or that which confirms.
confiscable, *a.* kon-*fis*-ka-bl, liable to forfeiture.
confiscate, *a.* *kon*-fis-kate, forfeited and adjudged to the public treasury, as the goods of a criminal; seized as forfeited: *v.t.* to adjudge to be forfeited, as a penalty, to the public treasury for public use; to seize as forfeited. (L. *confiscatus*, laid up in a coffer.)
confiscation, *n.* kon-fis-*kay*-shon, the act of confiscating; the appropriation of private property to the public use.
confiscator, *n.* *kon*-fis-kay-tor, one who confiscates.
confiscatory, *a.* kon-*fis*-ka-to-re, consigning to forfeiture.
confiteor, *n.* kon-*fit*-e-or, the general confession repeated at the beginning of a mass in the Roman Catholic church. (L., I confess.)
confix, *v.t.* kon-*fiks*, to fix down; to fasten firmly.
conflagrant, *a.* kon-*flay*-grant, blazing; burning.
conflagration, *n.* kon-fla-*gray*-shon, a great and destructive fire; a general burning. (*con*-, and L. *flagare*, to burn.)
conflate, *v.t.* kon-*flate*, to blend variant readings into a composite text: *a.* combined (of variant texts) [Lit.].
conflation, *n.* kon-*flay*-shon, intermingling or uniting, as of turning two variant versions of a text into one. (L. *conflatio.*)
conflict, *n.* *kon*-flikt, collision; contest; opposition of opinion, etc.; mental struggle. (L. *conflictus*, dashed together.)
conflict, *v.i.* kon-*flikt*, to strike or dash against; to strive or struggle to resist and overcome; to be in opposition or contradictory.
conflicting, *a.* kon-*flik*-ting, contending together; contradictory; inconsistent.
conflictive, *a.* kon-*flik*-tiv, conflicting; tending to conflict.
conflictory, *a.* kon-*flik*-te-re, conflictive.
confluence, *n.* *kon*-floo-ence, a flowing together; the point of junction of two or more streams; a concourse. (L. *confluens*, flowing together.)
confluent, *a.* *kon*-floo-ent, flowing together; meeting in their course; running together [Med.]; united at some part [Bot.]: *n.* a stream that unites with another; a tributary.
conflux, *n.* *kon*-fluks, a flowing together; a meeting of currents; a confluence. (L. *confluxus*, flowed together.)
confocal, *a.* kon-*foh*-kal, having the same foci [Geom.].
conform, *a.* kon-*fawrm*, conformable: *v.t.* to make like in shape or character; to adapt: *v.i.* to comply with. (Fr. *conformer.*)
conformability, *n.* kon-*fawr*-ma-*bil*-e-te, the condition of being conformable.
conformable, *a.* kon-*fawr*-ma-bl, having the same form; resembling; agreeable; suitable; compliant; in parallel arrangement [Geol.].
conformably, *ad.* in a conformable manner.
conformance, *n.* kon-*fawr*-mance, conformity.
conformation, *n.* kon-fawr-*may*-shon, the manner in which a body is formed; form; structure; the

act of conforming. (L. *conformatio*, from *conformatus*, conformed.)
conformer, *n.* kon-*fawr*-mer, one who complies with established forms or doctrines.
conformist, *n.* kon-*fawr*-mist, a conformer, esp. to the doctrines of the Church of England.
conformity, *n.* kon-*fawr*-me-te, likeness; congruity; consistency; compliance.
confound, *v.t.* kon-*found*, to mingle indistinguishably; to throw into disorder; to perplex; to astonish; to destroy; to overthrow. (Fr. *confondre.*)
confounded, *pp.* and *a.* kon-*found*-ed, confused; astonished; mistaken for something else; enormous; detestable.
confoundedly, *ad.* excessively; abominably.
confraternity, *n.* kon-fra-*ter*-ne-te, brotherhood; a brotherhood having some lay or religious object. (Late L. *confraternitas.*)
confrère, *n.* (App.), a colleague or associate; a fellow-member. (Fr.)
confront, *v.t.* kon-*frunt*, to stand facing; to face with defiance; to meet as an enemy; to oppose; to bring face to face. (Fr. *confronter.*)
confrontation, *n.* kon-frun-*tay*-shon, the act of bringing face to face or confronting.
Confucian, *a.* kon-*few*-shan, pertaining to Confucius: *n.* a disciple of Confucius, a Chinese sage.
Confucianism, *n.* kon-*few*-shan-izm, the philosophical system of Confucius, which, as grounded on sovereign respect for filial piety and the eternal verities, has become the basis of the religion, education, and statecraft of China. (Chinese, *K'ung-fû-tsze*, K'ung the Master.)
confuse, *v.t.* kon-*fewz*, to mix, so as to be undistinguishable; to throw into disorder; to perplex; to disconcert. (L. *confusus*, confused.)
confusable, *a.* kon-*few*-za-bl, capable of being confused.
confusedly, *ad.* kon-*few*-zed-le, in a confused manner.
confusedness, *n.* a state of being confused.
confusion, *n.* kon-*few*-zhon, act of confusing; state of being confused; disorder; tumult; perturbation; shame; overthrow. (Fr.)
confutable, *a.* kon-*few*-ta-bl, that may be confuted.
confutant, *n.* kon-*few*-tant, one who confutes or undertakes to disprove.
confutation, *n.* kon-few-*tay*-shon, the act of confuting; refutation. (L. *confutatus*, confuted.)
confutative, *a.* kon-*few*-ta-tiv, fitted to confute.
confute, *v.t.* kon-*fewt*, to prove to be false; to disprove. (L. *confutare*, to check the boiling of a liquid.)
conga, *n.* *kong*-ga, a rhumba-like group dance of Cuban origin.
congé, *n.* (App.), leave; farewell; parting ceremony; a bow in reverence or as a courtesy: *v.i.* to congee. **congé d'élire** (Fr., leave to elect), the king's licence to a dean and chapter to choose a bishop.
congeal, *v.t.* kon-*jeel*, to change from a fluid to a solid state by cold; to cause to freeze or coagulate: *v.i.* to pass by loss of heat from fluid to solid; to coagulate. (Fr. *congeler.*)
congealable, *a.* that may be congealed.
congealment, *n.* a clot or concretion; congelation.
congee, *v.i.* *kon*-jee, to take leave with the customary civilities; to bow or curtsy. (O.Fr. *congeer.*)
congee, *n.* kon-*jee*, water in which rice has been boiled; rice gruel. (Hind.)
congelation, *n.* kon-je-*lay*-shon, act or process of congealing; state of being congealed; a concretion. (L. *congelatio*, from *congelatus*, congealed.)
congener, *n.* *kon*-je-ner, a thing or organism of the same genus or nature. (L.)
congeneric, *a.* kon-je-*ne*-rik, of the same kind, genus, or nature.
congenial, *a.* kon-*jee*-ne-al, of kindred spirit and tastes; pleasant and sympathetic. (L.)
congeniality, *n.* kon-*jee*-ne-*al*-e-te, the state or quality of being congenial.
congenially, *ad.* in a congenial manner.
congenital, *a.* kon-*jen*-e-tal, existing from birth; constitutional. (L. *congenitus*, born with.)
conger, *n.* *kong*-ger, the sea-eel, *Conger vulgaris*. (L.)
congeries, *n.* kon-*jeer*-e-eez, a collection of several particles or bodies in one mass; an aggregation. (L.)
congest, *v.t.* kon-*jest*, to cause to accumulate, esp. [Med.] as blood in an organ. **congested area,** a district too over-crowded to support its population. (L. *congestus*, borne.)
congestion, *n.* kon-*jes*-tyon, an excessive accumulation, esp. of blood in an organ, deranging its action [Med.], or of traffic, inhabitants, etc.
congestive, *a.* kon-*jes*-tiv, inducing or due to congestion.
conglobate, *a.* *kon*-globe-ate, formed or gathered into a ball: *v.t.* to collect or form into a ball. (L. *conglobatus*, formed into a globe.)
conglobation, *n.* kon-glo-*bay*-shon, the act of forming into a ball; a round body.
conglobe, *v.t.* and *i.* kon-*globe*, to conglobate.
conglomerate, *a.* kon-*glom*-er-rat, gathered into a ball or round body: *n.* a rock composed of pebbles cemented together; pudding-stone [Geol.]: *v.t.* and *i.* to gather into a ball or round body; to collect into a round mass. (L. *conglomeratus*, heaped together.)
conglomeration, *n.* kon-*glom*-er-*ray*-shon, a gathering into a ball; collection; accumulation.
conglutinate, *v.t.* kon-*gloo*-te-nate, to glue together; to unite the parts of a wound by a glutinous substance: *v.i.* to adhere; to coalesce. (L. *conglutinatus*, glued together.)
conglutination, *n.* kon-*gloo*-te-*nay*-shon, the act of gluing together; union by adhesion.
conglutinative, *a.* kon-*gloo*-te-na-tiv, able to coalesce; enabling to adhere.
congou, *n.* *kong*-goo, a species of black tea from China. (Chin.)
congratulant, *a.* kon-*grat*-yew-lant, congratulating: *n.* one who congratulates.
congratulate, *v.t.* kon-*grat*-yew-late, to express pleasure or joy to one on account of some fortunate event; to wish joy to: *v.i.* to express congratulations. (L. *congratulatus*, wished joy.)
congratulation, *n.* kon-*grat*-yew-*lay*-shon, the act of congratulating; felicitation.
congratulatory, *a.* kon-*grat*-yew-la-to-re, expressing congratulation.
congregant, *n.* *kong*-gre-gant, a member of the congregation of a Jewish synagogue.
congregate, *v.t.* *kong*-gre-gate, to gather or collect together: *v.i.* to come together; to assemble. (L. *congregatus*, gathered together.)
congregation, *n.* *kong*-gre-*gay*-shon, an assemblage, esp. one for religious worship, habitually meeting in the same place; an assembly of rulers; an assembly of ecclesiastics or cardinals; the deliberative assembly of certain English Universities.
congregational, *a.* *kong*-gre-*gay*-shon-al, pertaining to a congregation or to congregationalism.
Congregationalism, *n.* *kong*-gre-*gay*-shon-al-izm, that system of church government which vests all authority in the congregation of each local church.
Congregationalist, *n.* *kong*-gre-*gay*-shon-al-ist, one who belongs to a congregational church or society.
congress, *n.* *kong*-gress, a meeting as of envoys, commissioners, or deputies, esp. for the settlement of international questions; (*cap.*) the federal legislative body of the United States; the legislative body of Mexico, Cuba, and certain S. American republics; in India, the elected body of mainly Hindu representatives (founded 1884), advocating, during British rule, many democratic reforms and complete independence and self-government for India. (L. *congressus*, met together.)
congressional, *a.* kong-*gresh*-on-al, pertaining to a congress, or to the United States Congress.
Congressman, *n.* *kong*-gres-man, a member of Congress.
congreve, *n.* *kong*-greve, an early kind of lucifer match. **congreve rocket,** a former military rocket filled with inflammable matter. (Inventor's name.)
congruence, *n.* *kong*-groo-ence, suitableness; agreement; consistency. (L. *congruentia.*)
congruency, *n.* *kong*-groo-en-se, congruence.
congruent, *a.* *kong*-groo-ent, suitable; agreeing.
congruity, *n.* kon-*groo*-e-te, agreement between things; fitness; consistency. (Fr. *congruité.*)
congruous, *a.* *kong*-groo-us, accordant; suitable; consistent. (L. *congruus.*)
congruously, *ad.* in a congruous manner.
congruousness, *n.* congruity; consistency.
conic, *a.* *kon*-ik, conical; pertaining to a cone;

n. a conic section. **conic sections,** curved lines formed by the intersection of a cone and plane, *viz.*, the parabola, hyperbola, and ellipse.
conical, *a. kon*-e-kal, having the form of a cone.
conically, *ad.* in the form of a cone.
conicalness, *n.* state or quality of being conical.
conico-cylindrical, *a. kon*-e-ko-se-*lin*-dre-kal, in the form of a cylinder, but tapering to a point.
conics, *n. kon*-iks, that part of geometry which treats of the cone, and the curves which arise from its sections.
conifer, *n. koh*-ne-fer, a plant bearing cones; any tree or shrub of the order *Coniferæ*.
Coniferæ, *n.pl.* ko-*nif*-e-ree, an order of plants, including the fir, pine, and cedar, bearing cones in which the seeds are contained. (L. *conus*, cone, *fero*, bear.)
coniferous, *a.* ko-*nif*-er-us, bearing cones.
coniform, *a. koh*-ne-form, in form of a cone; conical.
coniin, *n. koh*-ne-in, conine.
conima, *n. kon*-im-a, a fragrant gum-resin akin to elemi, obtained from *Brusera icicariba* and other S. American trees.
conine, *n.* ko-*neen*, a yellow, oily, poisonous alkaloid obtained from hemlock. (Gr. *conia*, hemlock.)
conirostral, *a.* koh-ne-*rost*-ral, having a cone-shaped beak [Ornith.]. (L. *conus*, and *rostrum*, a beak.)
conium, *n. koh*-ne-um, hemlock; the narcotic drug prepared from this. (Gr.)
conjecturable, *a.* kon-*jek*-tewr-ra-bl, that may be guessed or conjectured.
conjectural, *a.* kon-*jekt*-tewr-ral, without proof; depending on conjecture.
conjecturally, *ad.* in a conjectural manner.
conjecture, *n.* kon-*jek*-tewr, a guess; a surmise: *v.t.* and *i.* to judge by guess; to guess. (L. *conjectura.*)
conjee, *n. kon*-jee, congee.
conjoin, *v.t.* kon-*joyn*, to join together: *v.i.* to unite; to join; to league. (O.Fr. *conjoindre.*)
conjoint, *a.* kon-*joynt*, united; connected; associated; co-operating.
conjointly, *ad.* in a conjoint manner.
conjugal, *a. kon*-joo-gal, pertaining to marriage. (Fr.)
conjugally, *ad.* matrimonially; connubially.
conjugate, *a. kon*-joo-gate, united in pairs; paired [Bot.]; interchangeably related [Math.]; agreeing in grammatical derivation [Gram.]: *n.* a word agreeing in derivation with another word; a conjugate axis, etc.: *v.t.* to give the inflections of a verb in expressing mood, tense, etc.; to combine or unite in conjugation [Biol.]. (L. *conjugatus*, yoked.)
conjugation, *n.* kon-joo-*gay*-shon, the act of or process of conjugating or uniting; the union of two or more cells of different origin [Biol.]; inflection of a verb; the manner of inflecting; a class of verbs conjugated alike [Gram.]. (L. *conjugatio.*)
conjugational, *a.* relating to conjugation.
conjunct, *a.* kon-*junkt*, conjoined; united; closely connected: *n.* one who or that which is conjunct: a conjuncture. (L. *conjunctus*, joined.)
conjunction, *n.* kon-*junk*-shon, union; connection; the apparent meeting or passing of two heavenly bodies [Astron.]; a connecting word [Gram.]. **in conjunction,** in the same longitude or right ascension [Astron.]. (L. *conjunctio.*)
conjunctional, *a.* relating to a conjunction.
conjunctiva, *n. kon*-junk-*ty*-va, the lining of mucous membrane on the inner surface of the eyelids and extending to the front portion of the eyeball.
conjunctive, *a.* kon-*junk*-tiv, closely united; serving to unite. **conjunctive mood,** that expressing condition or contingency [Gram.].
conjunctively, *ad.* in a conjunctive manner.
conjunctivitis, *n.* kon-*junk*-te-*vy*-tis, inflammation of the conjunctiva.
conjunctly, *ad.* kon-*junkt*-le, in a conjunct manner.
conjuncture, *n.* kon-*junk*-tewr, a combination of circumstances; an occasion; a crisis. (L. *conjunctura.*)
conjuration, *n.* kon-joor-*ray*-shon, the act of conjuring or solemnly invoking; a magic spell; a form of incantation; earnest entreaty. (Fr.)
conjurator, *n. kon*-joor-*ray*-tor, one bound by oath with others [Old Law]; a conjuror.
conjure, *v.t.* kon-*joor*, to call on or summon by a sacred name or with solemnity; to bind by an oath. (Fr. *conjurer.*)
conjure, *v.t. kun*-jur, to act upon by supernatural or magical influence; to raise up or frame without reason: *v.i.* to practise the arts of a conjurer.
conjurement, *n.* kon-*joor*-ment, a solemn demand or adjuration; serious injunction.
conjurer, *n. kun*-jur-er, a juggler; one who does tricks by sleight of hand or feigned magic.
conjuror, *n.* kon-*joor*-or, one sworn with others.
conjury, *n. kun*-jur-e, magic; the art of conjuring.
conk, *n.* kongk, nose; big-nose [Slang].
conk, *v.i.* kongk, to break down, to fail (esp. of machinery); to die [Coll.].
conker, *n. kong*-ker, a horse-chestnut, esp. for threading on a string and use in a boys' game.
connate, *a. kon*-nate, born with one: inborn; congenitally or firmly united [Biol.]; united at the base [Bot.]; congenital [Med.]. (L. *connatus*, born together.)
connatural, *a.* ko-*nat*-yewr-al, inherent; connected by nature; of the same nature. (L. *connaturalis.*)
connaturalize, *v.t.* ko-*nat*-yewr-al-ize, to make connatural.
connaturally, *ad.* by the act of nature.
connect, *v.t.* ko-*nekt*, to knit or link together; to conjoin; to unite; to associate: *v.i.* to join; to cohere; to make contact. (L. *connecto*, tie.)
connectedly, *ad.* in a connected manner.
connecting, *a.* ko-*nek*-ting, serving to connect. **connecting-rod,** a rod jointed to two or more moving parts, esp. (in a steam-engine) one connecting the piston-rod with the crank-pin.
connection, *n.* ko-*nek*-shon, connexion.
connective, *a.* ko-*nek*-tiv, having the power of connecting: *n.* that which joins; a conjunction [Gram.].
connectively, *ad.* in a connective manner.
connector, *n.* he who or that which connects.
conner, *n. kon*-ner, an inspector; one who cons.
***connexion,** *n.* ko-*nek*-shon, the act of connecting, or state of being connected; relationship by blood, but esp. by marriage; one so connected; any relationship, esp. association ecclesiastically; customers collectively; coition; the joining up of current by contact, or a device for effecting this [Elect.]. (Fr. *connexion.*)
connexional, *a.* ko-*nek*-shon-al, having connexion; pertaining to a connexion.
conning-tower, *n. kon*-ning-tou-er, the armoured observation chamber in a man-o'-war or submarine, from which her movements are directed and which has direct communication with all parts of the vessel.
connivance, *n.* ko-*ny*-vance, act of conniving; collusion; tacit consent.
connive, *v.i.* ko-*nive*, to wink at intentionally, or overlook; voluntarily to neglect to see a fault; to allow by collusion or inaction. (Fr. *conniver.*)
connivent, *a.* ko-*ny*-vent, convergent [Biol.].
connoisseur, *n.* kon-ne-*sur*, a critical judge of the fine arts; a man of taste. (Fr.)
connoisseurship, *n.* kon-ne-*sur*-ship, the skill or quality of a connoisseur.
connotation, *n.* kon-no-*tay*-shon, inference; that which is connoted by a term; comprehension [Logic].
connotative, *a.* kon-*noh*-ta-tiv, tending to connote; having or pertaining to connotation.
connote, *v.t.* kon-*note*, to imply; to include in the meaning, esp. [Logic] of a term denoting a subject and implying attributes. (L. *con-*, and *nota*, a mark.)
connubial, *a.* ko-*new*-be-al, pertaining to the married state. (L. *connubialis*, of marriage.)
connubially, *ad.*, in a connubial manner.
conodont, *n. koh*-no-dont, a minute fossil denticle from the Ordovician and later strata, once thought to be a tooth of one of the Cyclostomata.
conoid, *a. koh*-noyd, cone-like: *n.* a solid formed by the revolution of a conic section about its axis [Geom.]; a conoidal object. (Gr. *konos*, and *eidos*-form.)
conoidal, *a.* koh-*noy*-dal, like a conoid; nearly, but not exactly, conical.

co-nominee, *n.* *koh*-nom-e-*nee*, one nominated with another.
conquer, *v.t.* *kong*-ker, to subdue, esp. in war and after a struggle; to gain dominion or sovereignty over; to overcome: *v.i.* to overcome; to gain the victory. (Fr. *conquérir.*)
conquerable, *a.* that may be overcome.
conqueringly, *ad.* in a victorious manner.
conqueror, *n.* *kong*-ker-or, one who has conquered. **the Conqueror,** in English history, William, Duke of Normandy, who became king after the Battle of Hastings in 1066. (O.Fr.)
conquest, *n.* *kong*-kwest, the act of conquering; that which is conquered; acquisition of sovereignty by force of arms; victory; subjugation. **the Conquest** the conquest of England by William, Duke of Normandy, in 1066. (O.Fr.)
conquistador, *n.* kon-*kwiss*-ta-dor, one of the Spanish conquerors of South America. (Sp.)
consanguineous, *a.* kon-sang-*gwin*-e-us, of the same blood; related by birth. (L. *consanguineus.*)
consanguinity, *n.* kon-sang-*gwin*-e-te, relationship by blood; the relationship between igneous rocks derived from a common magma [Geol.].
conscience, *n.* *kon*-shence, the moral faculty; the sense of right and wrong; private thoughts; consciousness. **conscience clause,** a clause in an Act to relieve those who have religious scruples from certain requirements in it. **conscience money,** money paid to relieve one's conscience, esp. to the Treasury as restitution for an unduly withheld tax-payment. (Fr.)
conscienceless, *a.* *kon*-shence-less, without conscience.
conscientious, *a.* kon-she-*en*-shus, actuated by a strict regard to the dictates of conscience. **conscientious objector,** one who, professedly on the dictate of his conscience, refuses to comply with public regulations, esp. in relation to military service.
conscientiously, *ad.* according to the direction of conscience.
conscientiousness, *n.* a scrupulous regard to the decisions of conscience.
conscionable, *a.* *kon*-shon-a-bl, according to conscience; reasonable; just.
conscionably, *ad.* in a conscionable manner.
★**conscious,** *a.* *kon*-shus, possessed of self-consciousness; having immediate knowledge; sensible; aware. (L. *conscius,* knowing.)
consciously, *ad.* in a conscious manner.
consciousness, *n.* *kon*-shus-ness, the fact, faculty, or state of being conscious; the power which the mind has of knowing itself, its acts and affections [Psych.]; immediate knowledge; sense; perception; cognition.
conscribe, *v.t.* kon-*skribe*, to enrol compulsorily; to place on the military strength as a conscript.
conscript, *a.* *kon*-skript, enrolled; enlisted: *n.* one compelled to serve as a soldier; one taken by compulsion. **conscript fathers,** the senators of Rome.
conscript, *v.t.* kon-*skript*, to conscribe [Coll.].
conscription, *n.* kon-*skrip*-shon, a compulsory enrolment of persons for service in an armed force.
consecrate, *v.t.* *kon*-se-krate, to set apart or devote to some sacred service or purpose; to declare one sacred or a saint; to dedicate; to render venerable; to sanctify: *a.* consecrated. (L. *consecratus,* sacred.)
consecration, *n.* kon-se-*kray*-shon, the act or ceremony of separating from a common to a sacred use; the state of being consecrated; the act of publicly enrolling among the saints; the benediction of the elements in the eucharist.
consecrator, *n.* *kon*-se-kray-tor, one who consecrates.
consecratory, *a.* *kon*-se-kray-to-re, making sacred.
consectary, *n.* kon-*sek*-ta-re, consequence; corollary.
consecution, *n.* kon-se-*kew*-shon, state of being consecutive; a train of consequences; succession in series. (L. *consecutus,* followed.)
consecutive, *a.* kon-*sek*-yew-tiv, succeeding in a regular order; following without a break; expressing consequence or result [Gram.]. (O.Fr. *consecutif.*)
consecutively, *ad.* in a consecutive manner.
consecutiveness, *n.* state of being consecutive.
consenescence, *n.* kon-se-*nes*-sense, a growing old; decay from age; senility. (L. *con-,* and *senex,* old.)
consension, *n.* kon-*sen*-shon, agreement; accord.
consensual, *a.* kon-*sen*-sew-al, formed or existing by the mere consent of the parties; due to sympathetic action [Phys.].
consensus, *n.* kon-*sen*-sus, agreement; unanimity. (L.)
consent, *n.* kon-*sent*, agreement to what is done, proposed, or stated by another; acquiescence; concurrence; accord of minds; agreement of opinion; correspondence in parts, qualities, or operation: *v.i.* to agree or assent; to yield. **age of consent,** *see* **age.** (Fr. *consentir.*)
consentaneity, *n.* kon-*sen*-ta-*nee*-e-te, mutual agreement.
consentaneous, *a.* kon-sen-*tane*-e-us, agreeable; accordant; consistent with. (L. *consentaneus.*)
consentaneously, *ad.* in a consentaneous manner.
consentaneousness, *n.* agreement; accordance; consistency.
consenter, *n.* kon-*sent*-er, one who consents.
consentient, *a.* kon-*sen*-she-ent, agreeing in mind; accordant in opinion; unanimous. (L. *consentiens.*)
consentingly, *ad.* kon-*sent*-ing-le, with consent.
consequence, *n.* *kon*-se-kwence, that which follows; effect; inference; importance. (L. *consequentia.*)
consequent, *a.* *kon*-se-kwent, following as an effect; following by necessary inference: *n.* the correlative to an antecedent; effect; conclusion by inference; the second term of a ratio [Math.]. (O.Fr.)
consequential, *a.* kon-se-*kwen*-shal, following as the effect; self-important; pompous.
consequentiality, *n.* *kon*-se-kwen-she-*al*-e-te, logical sequence; quality or state of being consequential; self-importance.
consequentially, *ad.* kon-se-*kwen*-shal-le, in a consequential manner; logically.
consequently, *ad.* *kon*-se-kwent-le, in consequence of something; accordingly.
conservable, *a.* kon-*ser*-va-bl, that may be preserved.
conservancy, *n.* kon-*ser*-van-se, conservation; preservation; a board or commission controlling the navigation, fisheries, etc., of a river. (L. *conservans.*)
conservant, *a.* kon-*ser*-vant, having the power of preserving from decay or destruction.
conservation, *n.* kon-ser-*vay*-shon, the act of conserving; preservation in a safe or entire state. **conservation of energy,** the doctrine that, however it may change in form or character, no smallest quantity of force in the universe is ever lost. (L. *conservatio.*)
conservatism, *n.* kon-*ser*-va-tizm, the practice and principles of the Conservatives; conservative doctrine in general.
conservative, *a.* kon-*ser*-va-tiv, tending to conserve; inclined to conserve, especially what is established; disposed to uphold all established institutions; preservative; moderate; cautious: *n.* (*cap.*) a member of a political party which is suspicious of change and seeks to maintain the existing form of government; one who dislikes change.
conservatoire, *n.* kon-*ser*-va-*twahr*, a school of music, and sometimes of elocution and dramatic art. (Fr.)
conservator, *n.* kon-*ser*-va-tor, one who preserves from injury or violation; a curator; a member of a conservancy; an officer who has the charge of the public peace or the rights and privileges of a community. (L.)
conservatory, *a.* kon-*ser*-va-to-re, having the quality of preserving from decay, etc.: *n.* a greenhouse attached to a dwelling-house; a glass house for displaying plants; a conservatoire [U.S.A.]. (L. *conservatorium.*)
conserve, *v.t.* kon-*serv*, to keep entire or in a sound state; to preserve: *n.* a sweetmeat made of fresh fruits; a preserve of fruit; jam. (Fr. *conserver.*)
conserver, *n.* kon-*ser*-ver, one who keeps from loss or injury; a preparer of conserves.
consider, *v.t.* kon-*sid*-er, to fix the mind on; to contemplate; to view attentively; to observe and examine; to attend to; to relieve; to have regard to; to respect; to regard: *v.i.* to think seriously or carefully; to deliberate. (O.Fr. *considerer.*)

considerable, *a.* kon-*sid*-er-a-bl, worthy of consideration or regard; moderately large; of some importance or value. (Fr.)
considerableness, *n.* quality of being considerable; some degree of importance, dignity, etc.
considerably, *ad.* in a degree deserving notice.
considerate, *a.* kon-*sid*-er-ate, given to sober reflection; circumspect; thoughtful of others; careful. (L. *consideratus*, considered.)
considerately, *ad.* in a considerate manner.
considerateness, *n.* quality of being considerate.
consideration, *n.* kon-*sid*-er-*ray*-shon, the act of considering; regard for others; serious deliberation; meditation; motive of action; influence; important reason; compensation; the price or motive of a stipulation [Law].
considering, *a.* taking into account.
consideringly, *ad.* with consideration or deliberation.
consign, *v.t.* kon-*sine*, to transfer into the possession, the keeping, or the trust of another; to commit; to entrust; to send goods. (Fr. *consigner.*)
consignable, *a.* kon-*sine*-a-bl, capable of being consigned.
consignation, *n.* kon-sig-*nay*-shon, the act of consigning; the act of blessing with the sign of the cross. (Fr.)
consigned, *a.* kon-*sined*, sent; deposited in trust.
consignee, *n.* *kon*-se-*nee*, the person to whom goods are consigned.
consigner, *n.* kon-*sine*-er, the person who consigns or commits goods to another.
consignment, *n.* kon-*sine*-ment, the act of consigning; the thing consigned; the writing by which a thing is consigned.
consignor, *n.* kon-*sine*-or, consigner.
consilience, *n.* kon-*sil*-e-ence, coincidence; concurrence. (L. *con-*, and *saliens*, leaping.)
consilient, *a.* kon-*sil*-e-ent, accordant; concurring.
consist, *v.i.* kon-*sist*, to be and keep in a fixed state; to be composed of; to continue to exist; to subsist; to be compatible with; to agree. (Fr. *consister.*)
consistence, *n.* kon-*sis*-tence, consistency.
consistency, *n.* kon-*sis*-ten-se, a standing together, as the parts of a body; state of a body with respect to material existence; degree of density; substance; cohesion; firmness of constitution; harmony of all parts of a complex thing among themselves; congruity; uniformity; state of rest. (L. *consistens*, standing together.)
consistent, *a.* kon-*sis*-tent, compatible; not self-contradictory; congruous; uniform.
consistently, *ad.* in a consistent manner.
consistorial, *a.* kon-sis-*taw*-re-al, pertaining to a consistory.
consistorian, *n.* kon-sis-*taw*-re-an, a Presbyterian.
consistory, *n.* kon-*sis*-to-re, an assembly or council; the court of a bishop, held in the cathedral church, for the trial of ecclesiastical causes; the college of cardinals at Rome; in Presbyterian churches, a deliberative and judicial assembly of ministers and elders. (L. *consistorium.*)
consociate, *n.* kon-*soh*-she-ate, a confederate; an accomplice: *a.* associated: united in fellowship: *v.t.* to unite; to unite in convention [U.S.A.]: *v.i.* to unite; to meet in convention [U.S.A.]. (L. *consociatus*, companioned.)
consociation, *n.* kon-so-she-*ay*-shon, fellowship; companionship; association; a federation of churches or religious societies [U.S.A.].
consolable, *a.* kon-*sole*-a-bl, that may be comforted.
consolation, *n.* kon-so-*lay*-shon, alleviation of misery or mental distress; that which comforts or refreshes the spirits. **consolation prize,** a reward given to an unsuccessful but deserving competitor.
consolatory, *a.* kon-*sol*-a-to-re, tending to comfort.
console, *v.t.* kon-*sole*, to comfort; to soothe and cheer in distress or depression. (Fr. *consoler.*)
console, *n.* *kon*-sole, a bracket to support a cornice or for ornamentation [Arch.]; a bracket table supported by consoles, or pier table having legs similar to consoles; the section of an organ containing the principal mechanism controlling the instrument. [Fr.]
consoler, *n.* kon-*sole*-er, one consoling; a comforter.
consolidate, *v.t.* kon-*sol*-e-date, to form into a compact and solid body; to unite into one; to combine: *v.i.* to grow firm and hard; to become solid. **consolidated annuities,** consols. **consolidated fund,** a fund formed from certain portions of the revenue appropriated to the payment of certain specified public charges. (L. *consolidatus*, made solid.)
consolidation, *n.* kon-*sol*-e-*day*-shon, the act or process of consolidating; state of being consolidated; the uniting of several things into one body; solidification [Med.].
consols, *n.pl.* kon-*solz*, British national debt annuities granted at different times, and consolidated in 1751 into a single stock. (Abbr. for "consolidated annuities.")
consommé, *n.* kon-som-*may*, a clear soup. (Fr.)
consonance, *n.* *kon*-so-nance, accord or agreement of sounds; agreement; congruity; agreeableness; assonance [Mus.]. (L. *consonantia.*)
consonancy, *n.* *kon*-so-nan-se, consonance.
consonant, *a.* *kon*-so-nant, in accordance; agreeing in sound; producing harmony: *n.* a letter of the alphabet, as *d* or *g*, which cannot be sounded without the aid of a vowel. (Fr.)
consonantal, *a.* kon-so-*nan*-tal, relating to or of the nature of a consonant.
consonantly, *ad.* *kon*-so-nant-le, in consonance; in a consonant manner.
consonous, *a.* *kon*-so-nus, agreeing in sound.
consort, *n.* *kon*-sawrt, a companion; a partner; an intimate associate; a wife or husband; concurrence; a vessel accompanying another. **Prince Consort,** the title of the husband of Queen Victoria. **Queen consort,** the wife of a king, as distinguished from a queen regnant. (L. *consors.*)
consort, *v.i.* kon-*sawrt*, to associate; to keep company: *v.t.* to join or keep company; to associate; to harmonize.
consortism, *n.* *kon*-sawr-tizm, symbiosis [Biol.].
consortium, *n.* kon-*sawr*-te-um, partnership [Law]; an association; an international agreement, usually on financial or commercial matters.
consortship, *n.* *kon*-sawrt-ship, the state of a consort; fellowship; partnership.
conspecific, *a.* kon-spe-*sif*-ik, of the same species.
conspectus, *n.* kon-*spek*-tus, a general view; a draught or sketch. (L.)
conspicuity, *n.* kon-spe-*kew*-e-te, conspicuousness.
conspicuous, *a.* kon-*spik*-yew-us, obvious to the sight; manifest; eminent; prominent. (L. *conspicuus*, visible.)
conspicuously, *ad.* in a conspicuous manner.
conspicuousness, *n.* state of being conspicuous.
conspiracy, *n.* kon-*spi*-ra-se, combination for an evil purpose or to commit a crime, particularly some act of treason in concert; a plot of two or more; concurrence. (O.Fr. *conspiracie.*)
conspiration, *n.* kon-spire-*ray*-shon, concurrence of things to one and the same end.
conspirator, *n.* kon-*spi*-ra-tor, one who conspires.
conspire, *v.i.* kon-*spire*, to agree, by oath or otherwise, to commit a crime, specially treason; to concur; to agree falsely and maliciously to charge an innocent person with felony [Law]: *v.t.* to devise and seek to compass. (Fr. *conspirer.*)
conspirer, *n.* kon-*spire*-rer, a conspirator.
conspue, *v.t.* kon-*spew*, to make an outcry against; to decry; to express hatred. (Fr. *conspuer.*)
constable, *n.* *kun*-sta-bl, a policeman; an officer charged with the preservation of the peace; a high state functionary of certain countries in mediæval times. **Chief Constable,** the head of a separate police force. **police constable,** a policeman. **special constable,** *see* **special.** (O.Fr. *conestable*, from L. *comes stabuli*, count of the stable.)
constableship, *n.* the office of a constable.
constabulary, *a.* kun-*stab*-yew-la-re, relating to or consisting of constables: *n.* the police generally; an individual police force.
constancy, *n.* *kon*-stan-se, fixedness; immutability; firmness of mind; unshaken determination; steadfastness; fidelity in love or friendship.
constant, *a.* *kon*-stant, fixed; firm; unchangeable; firm in mind or principle; resolute; faithful in affection; without intermission: *n.* that which remains unchanged, as the revolution of the earth [Physics]; a quantity which remains the same under the same conditions [Math.]. (Fr.)
Constantia, *n.* kon-*stan*-she-a, a sweet South African wine. (*Constantia*, near Capetown.)

constantly, *ad.* in a constant manner; steadily; frequently.
constellate, *v.i.* *kon*-stel-late, to shine with united radiance: *v.t.* to unite in one splendour; to adorn with stars; to form into a constellation.
constellation, *n.* kon-stel-*lay*-shon, a group of fixed stars conceived generally as being within some mythological figure; an assemblage of splendours or excellences. (*con-*, and L. *stella*, a star.)
consternate, *v.t.* *kon*-ster-nate, to dismay; to affect with terror or alarm. (L. *consternatus*, terrified.)
consternation, *n.* kon-ster-*nay*-shon, a state of terror that confounds and incapacitates; dismay.
constipate, *v.t.* *kon*-stip-ate, to stop up (the bowels); to make costive. (L. *constipatus*, crammed together.)
constipation, *n.* kon-ste-*pay*-shon, costiveness.
constituency, *n.* kon-*stit*-yew-en-se, a body of constituents or of electors; the district or the electorate of a parliamentary division.
constituent, *a.* kon-*stit*-yew-ent, constituting or forming an essential or elementary part; having the power of constituting or appointing: *n.* he who or that which constitutes; that which constitutes an essential part; one of those who elect a person to office as their representative; a voter. **constituent assembly,** the name given to elected bodies that have formed new constitutions, esp. those in France in 1789, 1848, 1871, and 1945–46, and in Germany in 1848 and 1919. (L. *constituens*, establishing.)
constitute, *v.t.* *kon*-stit-yewt, to establish; to form or compose; to frame; to make a thing what it is; to give legal form to; to enact; to appoint to an office or employment. (L. *constitutus*, established.)
constitution, *n.* kon-stit-*yew*-shon, the act of constituting or appointing; that form of being or structure of parts which constitutes a system or body; frame or temper of mind; natural strength of the body; affections or passions; an established form of government; a system of fundamental rules or principles of government; a law or ordinance made by the authority of some superior body, either ecclesiastical or civil. **apostolic constitutions,** a code regulative of faith and church discipline ascribed by some to the apostles [Eccles.]. **Constitutions of Clarendon,** certain statutes defining the jurisdiction of church and state drawn up at Clarendon in 1164. (Fr.)
constitutional, *a.* kon-stit-*yew*-shon-al, inherent in the constitution or natural frame; consistent with or authorized by the constitution or fundamental rules of a government: *n.* a walk for health's sake. **constitutional government,** one in which the chief of the state is in his sovereign capacity subject to a constitution.
constitutionalism, *n.* respect for or adherence to constitutional principles.
constitutionalist, *n.* an upholder of a particular constitution or of constitutional government in general.
constitutionality, *n.* *kon*-stit-yew-sho-*nal*-e-te, the state of being constitutional, either physically or politically.
constitutionalize, *v.t.* kon-stit-*yew*-sho-na-lize, to make constitutional: *v.i.* to take a constitutional.
constitutionally, *ad.* according to a constitution.
constitutionist, *n.* kon-stit-*yew*-shon-ist, a constitutionalist.
constitutive, *a.* *kon*-stit-yew-tiv, tending to constitute; elemental; having power to enact or establish; determinative.
constitutively, *ad.* in a constitutive manner.
constrain, *v.t.* kon-*strane*, to urge by force, either by impelling or restraining; to urge with irresistible power; to necessitate; to confine or restrain by force. (O.Fr. *constreindre.*)
constrainable, *a.* kon-*stray*-na-bl, that may be constrained; liable to constraint.
constrained, *a.* kon-*straynd*, restrained; forced.
constrainedly, *ad.* kon-*stray*-ned-le, by constraint.
constraint, *n.* kon-*straynt*, irresistible force, restraint, compulsion, or confinement.
constrict, *v.t.* kon-*strikt*, to bind or draw together; to cramp; to cause to contract. (L. *constrictus*, drawn tight).
constriction, *n.* kon-*strik*-shon, contraction by means of some inherent power, or by spasm, as of a muscle or fibre.
constrictive, *a.* kon-*strik*-tiv, tending to constrict.
constrictor, *n.* kon-*strik*-tor, that which contracts or draws together; a muscle which draws together [Anat.]; a boa-constrictor or similar snake.
constringe, *v.t.* kon-*strinj*, to constrict. (L. *constringo*, draw tight.)
constringent, *a.* kon-*strinj*-ent, contractive.
construct, *v.t.* kon-*strukt*, to build; to form; to put together the parts of a thing in their proper place and order; to compose; to interpret. (L. *constructus*, piled up.)
construction, *n.* kon-*struk*-shon, the act of constructing; fabrication; the thing constructed; structure; the form of construction; conformation; interpretation; the arrangement and connexion of words in a sentence; the syntax [Gram.]; the drawing of such lines and figures as are necessary to the solution of a problem [Math.]. (Fr.)
constructional, *a.* kon-*struk*-shon-al, agreeable to construction or interpretation or meaning.
constructive, *a.* kon-*struk*-tiv, relating to construction; not directly expressed, but inferred.
constructively, *ad.* in a constructive manner.
constructiveness, *n.* the constructive faculty.
constructor, *n.* kon-*struk*-tor, one who constructs; a supervisor of naval shipwrights.
construe, *v.t.* *kon*-stroo *or* kon-*stroo*, to arrange words in their natural order, or to translate them so as to discover the sense; to translate closely; to interpret; to explain: *n.* an act of construing; a literal translation. (L. *construo*, build.)
consubstantial, *a.* kon-sub-*stan*-she-al, having the same substance, essence, or nature. (Low L. *consubstantialis.*)
consubstantialist, *n.* kon-sub-*stan*-she-a-list, an adherent of the doctrine of consubstantiation.
consubstantiality, *n.* kon-sub-*stan*-she-*al*-e-te, the quality of being consubstantial or co-essential; participation of the same nature.
consubstantiate, *v.t.* kon-sub-*stan*-she-ate, to unite in one common substance: *v.i.* to hold the doctrine of consubstantiation. (L. *con-*, and *substantia.*)
consubstantiation, *n.* kon-sub-*stan*-she-*ay*-shon, the doctrine that the body and blood of Christ are present and united with the sacramental elements after their consecration.
consuetude, *n.* *kon*-swe-tewd, custom or usage, esp. when having the force of law; human intercourse. (L. *consuetus*, accustomed.)
consuetudinary, *a.* kon-swe-*tew*-de-na-re, customary; established by custom: *n.* a manual containing the ritual and customs of a monastic foundation.
consul, *n.* *kon*-sul, the supreme magistrate of ancient Rome, invested with regal authority for one year; one of the three chief magistrates of the First Republic in France (1799–1804); an agent commissioned by a state to reside in a foreign country to protect its rights and subjects and report on commercial matters. **consul general,** a consul having jurisdiction over other consuls. (L.)
consulage, *n.* *kon*-sew-laj, a duty paid for protection by a consul.
consular, *a.* *kon*-sew-lar, relating to consuls.
consulate, *n.* *kon*-sew-late, the office, residence, or jurisdiction of a consul, or the term of his office. **the Consulate,** the consular government in France, or the period of its duration (Nov. 1799–May 1804). **consulate of the sea,** a 14th-cent. Catalan collection of maritime customs and observances, printed at Barcelona in 1494. (L. *consulatus.*)
consulship, *n.* *kon*-sul-ship, the status, office, or period of office of a consul.
consult, *v.i.* kon-*sult*, to take counsel together; to seek the opinion or advice of another: *v.t.* to ask advice of; to seek the opinion of another, as a guide to one's own judgment; to have regard to, as to consult one's case. **consulting physician,** a specialist called in in consultation. **consulting room,** the room in which a doctor interviews his patients. (Fr. *consulter.*)
consultant, *n.* kon-*sul*-tant, a consulting physician or surgeon; one who consults.
consultation, *n.* kon-sul-*tay*-shon, the act of consulting; deliberation of two or more persons with a view to some decision; a meeting to consult together. (L. *consultatio.*)

consultative, *a.* kon-*sul*-ta-tiv, deliberative.
consultee, *n.* kon-sul-*tee*, one who is consulted.
consulter, *n.* kon-*sul*-ter, one who asks counsel or information.
consumable, *a.* kon-*sume*-a-bl, capable of being consumed : *n.* that which may be consumed.
consume, *v.t.* kon-*sume*, to use up ; to destroy ; to waste ; to squander ; to spend ; to exterminate : *v.i.* to waste away slowly ; to be exhausted. (Fr. *consumer.*)
consumedly, *ad.* kon-*sume*-ed-le, greatly ; completely.
consumer, *n.* kon-*sume*-er, one who or that which consumes ; one who buys for use and not for sale ; the actual user of commodities (opposed to the producer) [Econ.].
consummate, *v.t.* *kon*-sum-mate, to finish by completing what was projected ; to perfect, as of marriage by sexual intercourse. (L. *consummatus*, perfected.)
consummate, *a.* kon-*sum*-mat, complete ; perfect ; to the utmost extent.
consummately, *ad.* kon-*sum*-at-le, completely ; perfectly.
consummation, *n.* kon-sum-*may*-shon, completion ; perfection of any work, process, or scheme ; end.
consummative, *a.* kon-*sum*-a-tiv, consummating.
consumption, *n.* kon-*sump*-shon, the act of consuming or wasting away ; the state of being wasted ; a wasting of flesh ; a gradual decay of the body ; a disease of the lungs, attended with hectic fever, cough, etc. ; pulmonary tuberculosis ; phthisis [Med.] ; the use and expenditure of the industrial productions of a state [Econ.]. (L. *consumptus*, consumed.)
consumptive, *a.* kon-*sump*-tiv, destructive ; wasting ; disposed to or affected with pulmonic disease.
consumptiveness, *n.* tendency to consumption.
contabescence, *n.* kon-ta-*bes*-ense, a wasting away ; consumption [Med.] ; abortion of stamens and pollen [Bot.]. (L. *contabescens.*)
contact, *n.* *kon*-takt, a touch ; close union or juncture ; a person who may spread illness through being with a sufferer having an infectious disease ; the point where the electric conductors meet and through which the circuit passes ; the act of the ignition of an aircraft or motor-car engine becoming operative, or the state of being operative ; the apparent touching of the edges of two heavenly bodies, or of the disk of one with the shadow of another [Astron.] : *v.t.* and *i.* to come or bring into contact ; to establish a connexion with [Comm.]. **angle of contact,** the angle formed by the meeting of a curvilinear and a straight line [Math.]. **point of contact,** the point where a curvilinear touches a straight line [Math.]. (L. *contactus*, a touching.)
contact-breaker, *n.* an instrument for interrupting an electric circuit.
contact-maker, *n.* a device for joining two conductors through which a current passes, or for making or breaking such contact at will. [Elect.].
contactor, *n.* kon-*tak*-tor, a power-operated device for repeatedly making or breaking a circuit [Elect.].
contactual, *a.* kon-*tak*-tew-al, pertaining to or implying contact.
contadino, *n.* kon-ta-*dee*-no (*pl.* **contadini**), *fem.* **contadina** (*pl.* **contadine**), an Italian peasant. (It.)
contagion, *n.* kon-*tay*-jon, the communication of a disease by contact, or by the matter communicated ; that which communicates evil from one to another, or propagates mischief ; a pestilential influence ; poisonous exhalation. (Fr.)
contagionist, *n.* kon-*tay*-jon-ist, one who believes in the contagious character of certain diseases.
contagious, *a.* kon-*tay*-jus, communicable by contact or by excreted matter ; pestilential ; containing evil that may be transmitted ; affecting others.
contagiousness, *n.* quality of being contagious.
contagium, *n.* kon-*tay*-je-um, the substance, organism, or other agent transmitting disease from one to another.
contain, *v.t.* kon-*tane*, to hold, as a vessel ; to comprehend, comprise, or include ; to hold or restrain ; to restrict the movement of (the enemy) [Mil.]. (Fr. *contenir.*)
containable, *a.* that may be contained.
containant, *n.* kon-*tane*-ant, a container.
container, *n.* one who or that which contains.
contaminate, *v.t.* kon-*tam*-e-nate, to pollute, defile, or taint : *a.* contaminated. (L. *contaminatus*, defiled.)
contamination, *n.* kon-*tam*-e-*nay*-shon, act or process of contaminating ; state of being contaminated ; pollution ; deflement.
contaminative, *a.* kon-*tam*-e-na-tiv, calculated to contaminate ; polluting ; infective.
contango, *n.* kon-*tang*-go, percentage paid for accommodating either a buyer or a seller, by carrying the engagement to pay money or deliver shares over to the next account day. **contango day,** the first day of the Account, when contangos are made up [Stock Exchange]. (Sp. *contengo*, I check.)
conte, *n.* (App.), a short story, as a method of essay-form in literature. (Fr.)
contemn, *v.t.* kon-*tem*, to despise ; to disregard. (L. *contemno*, slight.)
contemner, *n.* kon-*tem*-er *or* kon-*tem*-ner, a despiser ; a scorner.
contemper, *v.t.* kon-*tem*-per, to blend together ; to moderate ; to adapt by tempering.
contemplate, *v.t.* *kon*-tem-plate, to regard with continued attention ; to meditate on ; to regard as likely ; to intend : *v.i.* to think studiously ; to meditate. (L. *contemplatus*, considered.)
contemplation, *n.* kon-tem-*play*-shon, the act of contemplating ; meditation ; continued attention to a particular subject ; intention ; an object for contemplation. (Fr.)
contemplative, *a.* kon-*tem*-pla-tiv, given to contemplation or study ; studious ; thoughtful.
contemplatively, *ad.* in a contemplative manner.
contemplativeness, *n.* disposition to contemplate.
contemplator, *n.* *kon*-tem-play-tor, one employed in study or meditation.
contemporaneity, *n.* kon-*tem*-po-ra-*nee*-e-te, contemporaneousness.
contemporaneous, *a.* kon-*tem*-po-*ray*-ne-us, being, living, or happening at the same time. (L.)
contemporaneously, *ad.* at the same time with some other event.
contemporaneousness, *n.* the state or fact of being contemporaneous.
contemporariness, *n.* kon-*tem*-po-ra-re-ness, existence at the same time.
contemporary, *a.* kon-*tem*-po-ra-re, living at the same time ; existing at the same period ; *n.* one who lives at the same time as another. (L. *con-*, and *temporārius*, temporary.)
contemporize, *v.t.* kon-*tem*-po-rize, to synchronize.
contempt, *n.* kon-*tempt*, the act of contemning or treating as mean, vile, and worthless ; disdain ; scorn ; the state of being contemned ; disgrace ; disobedience of the rules and orders of a court, legislative body, etc. [Law]. (O.Fr.)
contemptible, *a.* kon-*temp*-te-bl, worthy of contempt ; despicable. **the Old Contemptibles,** the original British force in France in August, 1914 (from the German Emperor's alleged reference to them—later denied—as " French's contemptible little army.")
contemptibleness, *n.* the state of being contemptible.
contemptibly, *ad.* in a contemptible manner.
contemptuous, *a.* kon-*temp*-tew-us, expressing contempt or disdain ; scornful.
contemptuously, *ad.* in a contemptuous manner.
contemptuousness, *n.* disposition to contempt ; scornfulness.
contend, *v.i.* and *t.* kon-*tend*, to strive (with) ; to struggle in opposition (against) ; to strive to obtain or to keep ; to dispute (with) ; to strive to convince ; to assert. (L. *contendo*, stretch.)
contendent, *n.* kon-*tend*-ent, an antagonist.
contender, *n.* kon-*tend*-er, one who contends ; a combatant ; one given to contention.
content, *a.* kon-*tent*, satisfied ; contented : *n.* satisfaction of mind ; acquiescence : *v.t.* to satisfy the mind ; to appease ; to make easy in any situation ; to please or gratify. (Fr. *contenter.*)
content, *n.* *kon*-tent *or* kon-*tent*, capacity ; that which is contained in anything ; the quantity of matter or space included in certain limits ; length ; area ; volume [Geom.]. (Fr.)

contentation, *n.* kon-ten-*tay*-shon, contentment; satisfaction.
contented, *a.* kon-*ten*-ted, satisfied; easy in mind.
contentedly, *ad.* in a contented manner.
contentedness, *n.* satisfaction.
contention, *n.* kon-*ten*-shon, strife; a violent effort to obtain something; controversy; quarrel; conflict; competition; point contended for. (Fr.)
contentious, *a.* kon-*ten*-shus, given to contention or strife; quarrelsome; involving contention; litigious. (L. *contentiosus.*)
contentiously, *ad.* in a contentious manner.
contentiousness, *n.* quarrelsomeness.
contentless, *a.* kon-*tent*-less, void of content or meaning; discontented.
contentment, *n.* kon-*tent*-ment, satisfaction of mind; content; acquiescence; gratification.
contents, *n.pl.* *kon*-tents *or* kon-*tents*, that which is contained; that which is comprised in any writing or book; the list of chapter headings.
conterminal, *a.* kon-*ter*-me-nal, having the same bounds. (L. *con-*, and *terminus*, a boundary.)
conterminate, *a.* kon-*ter*-me-nate, conterminous.
conterminous, *a.* kon-*ter*-me-nus, of the same extent (in time, etc.); with two ends meeting; having the same bounds.
contest, *v.t.* kon-*test*, to contend for; to struggle to maintain; to controvert; to dispute: *v.i.* to strive; to contend; to vie; to emulate. (Fr. *contester.*)
contest, *n.* *kon*-test, a struggle for victory or superiority; dispute; strife in argument.
contestable, *a.* kon-*tes*-ta-bl, that may be disputed.
contestant, *n.* kon-*tes*-tant, a person who contests.
contestation, *n.* kon-tes-*tay*-shon, the act of contesting; controversy; that which is contended for.
context, *n.* *kon*-tekst, the full statement from which a quotation is made; the passages which precede or follow the text. (L. *contextus*, woven.)
contextual, *a.* kohn-*teks*-tew-al, relating to the context.
contexture, *n.* kon-*teks*-tewr, the interweaving of several parts into one body; the disposition and union of the constituent parts of an object or a literary work with respect to each other; composition of parts; structure.
conticent, *a.* *kon*-tis-ent, hushed into silence. (L. *con-*, and *taceo*, be silent.)
contignation, *n.* kon-tig-*nay*-shon, a framework of beams; a story; act of framing together into a fabric. (L. *con-*, and *tignum*, a beam.)
contiguity, *n.* kon-te-*gew*-e-te, state of being in contact, or very near, or continuous; proximity in time or space; a continuous mass.
contiguous, *a.* kon-*tig*-yew-us, meeting in contact; adjoining; near. (L. *contiguus*, near.)
contiguously, *ad.* in a manner so as to touch.
contiguousness, *n.* a state of contact.
continence, *n.* *kon*-tin-ence, self-restraint, esp. in regard to sexual desire; chastity. (Fr.)
continency, *n.* *kon*-tin-ence-e, continence.
continent, *a.* *kon*-tin-ent, chaste; refraining from undue or unlawful indulgence in sexual intercourse; moderate in the indulgence of lawful pleasure; temperate; capable of containing.
continent, *n.* *kon*-tin-ent, the largest geographical division of the surface of the earth; that which contains anything; (*cap.*) the mainland of Europe. (Fr.)
continental, *a.* kon-te-*nen*-tal, pertaining or relating to a continent, esp. that of Europe; worthless [U.S. slang]: *n.* an inhabitant of the European continent.
continentalize, *v.t.* kon-te-*nen*-ta-lize, to give continental (or European) characteristics to.
continently, *ad.* *kon*-tin-ent-le, in a continent manner; chastely.
contingence, *n.* kon-*tin*-jence, contingency.
contingency, *n.* kon-*tin*-jen-se, state of being contingent; the possibility of coming to pass; a fortuitous event; an accident: *pl.*, incidental expenses.
contingent, *a.* kon-*tin*-jent, conditional; that may or may not happen; dependent on a contingency; that may or may not be true [Logic]: *n.* a fortuitous event; that which falls to one in a division or apportionment among a number; a self-contained body of troops; the force supplied by each state confederate in a war. **contingent liability,** a liability arising only in a certain event. (L. *contingens*, touching.)
contingently, *ad.* in a contingent manner.
continuable, *a.* that may be continued.
continual, *a.* kon-*tin*-yew-al, without interruption; incessant; often repeated. (Fr. *continuel.*)
continually, *ad.* without cessation; very often.
continuance, *n.* kon-*tin*-yew-ance, persistence; perseverance; duration; uninterrupted succession; continuation; continuity. (O.Fr.)
continuant, *n.* kon-*tin*-yew-ant, a consonant, the sound of which can be prolonged, as *f, v, s, th.*
continuate, *a.* kon-*tin*-yew-ate, long-continued; closely united; uninterrupted; unbroken.
continuation, *n.* kon-*tin*-yew-*ay*-shon, act of continuing; an extension; extension in a series or line; extension or carrying on to a farther point; extension in space; a carrying on in length; the carrying over of stocks to next account by payment of contango [Stock Exchange]. **continuation day,** contango day. **continuation school,** a school for young persons in employment. (L. *continuatis*, continued.)
continuative, *a.* kon-*tin*-yew-a-tiv, tending or serving to continue.
continuator, *n.* kon-*tin*-yew-ay-tor, one who continues, esp. a literary work begun by another.
continue, *v.i.* kon-*tin*-yew, to remain; to last; to endure; to persevere: *v.t.* to protract; to extend; to produce or draw out in length; to persevere in; to let remain. (Fr. *continuer.*)
continued, *a.* kon-*tin*-yewd, drawn out; protracted; extended in length; extended without intermission; proceeding without cessation; unceasing.
continuedly, *ad.* in a continued manner.
continuer, *n.* kon-*tin*-yew-er, one who continues.
continuing, *a.* kon-*tin*-yew-ing, permanent.
continuity, *n.* *kon*-te-*new*-e-te, uninterrupted connexion; cohesion; close union of parts; unbroken texture. **law of continuity,** the principle that nothing passes from one state into another without passing through all the intermediate states [Physics]. **solution of continuity,** rupture in what is continuous. (Fr. *continuité.*)
continuous, *a.* kon-*tin*-yew-us, conjoined without intervening space or time; uninterrupted. (L. *continuus.*)
continuously, *ad.* in a continuous manner.
continuum, *n.* kon-*tin*-yew-um, a continuous series; something that is absolutely continuous and of identical substance throughout.
cont-line, *n.* *kont*-line, casks in their stowage; the empty space left between such casks; the external interval betwixt strands in a rope.
conto, *n.* *kon*-toh, a money of account equalling a million reis, or, in Portugal 1,000 escudos, and in Brazil 1,000 milreis. (Port., a million.)
contorniate, *a.* kon-*tawr*-ne-at, having a deep furrow round the inside of the edge: *n.* a coin or medallion with such a furrow. (It.)
contort, *v.t.* kon-*tawrt*, to twist together; to writhe. (L. *con-*, and *torqueo, tortum*, twist.)
contorted, *a.* kon-*tawr*-ted, twisted over each other in oblique directions [Geol.].
contortion, *n.* kon-*tawr*-shon, the act of twisting; a writhing; a wresting; a twisting or wresting of a limb or member of the body out of its natural situation; partial dislocation. [Med.].
contortionist, *n.* an acrobat who performs contortions.
contour, *n.* *kon*-toor, the outline; the line that bounds or defines a figure: *v.t.* to form a contour; to mark with contour lines. **contour lines,** lines on survey maps indicating altitude.
contra-, *kon*-tra, a Latin prefix, signifying against or in opposition.
contra, *prep.* *kon*-tra, on the other side: *n.* an opposite; anything set against another; an offset in an account; the opposite, or lower, applied to alto and tenor, when they form the lowest part in the harmony [Mus.].
contraband, *a.* *kon*-tra-band, prohibited; smuggled contrary to ban or edict: *n.* traffic prohibited by law; the goods prohibited. **contraband goods,** goods prohibited to be imported or exported, either by the laws of a particular state or by the law of nations. **contraband of war,** any goods passing from a neutral to a belligerent in time of war that, under international law, are liable to seizure. (L. *contra-*, and *ban.*)

contrabandist, *n.* *kon*-tra-band-ist, one who traffics illegally; a dealer in contraband; a smuggler.
contrabass, *n.* *kon*-tra-base, the largest kind of bass-viol, usually called the double-bass. (It.)
contraception, *n.* kon-tra-*sep*-shon, the artificial prevention of conception.
contraceptive, *n.* kon-tra-*sep*-tiv, any agent or appliance for preventing conception: *a.* hindering conception.
contract, *n.* *kon*-trakt, an agreement; a bargain; the act by which a man and woman are betrothed to each other; the writing which contains an agreement, with the terms and conditions; any promise enforceable at law; contract-bridge, also the winning declaration or the number of tricks named by the highest bidder. **contract note,** the particulars of the business done, esp. one sent by stockbroker to client. **social contract,** *see* **social** (L. *con-*, and *traho, tractum*, draw.)
contract, *v.t.* kon-*trakt*, to draw together; to draw into less compass; to abridge; to shorten; to betroth; to bring on; to acquire; to incur: *v.i.* to shrink; to become shorter or narrower; to bargain; to form a contract.
contract-bridge, *n.* *kon*-trakt-, a card game for four, a variety of bridge and differing from auction esp. in the method of scoring.
contracted, *a.* kon-*trak*-ted, drawn together; narrow; betrothed; mean; selfish.
contractedly, *ad.* in a contracted manner.
contractedness, *n.* the state of being contracted; narrowness; meanness.
contractibility, *n.* kon-*trak*-te-*bil*-e-te, quality of suffering contraction.
contractible, *a.* kon-*trak*-te-bl, capable of contraction.
contractile, *a.* kon-*trak*-tile, tending to contract; having the power to contract.
contractility, *n.* kon-trak-*til*-e-te, the inherent quality or force by which bodies shrink or contract.
contraction, *n.* kon-*trak*-shon, the act of contracting; the state of being contracted; abbreviation; the shortening of a word by the omission of a letter or letters [Gram.].
contractive, *a.* kon-*trak*-tiv, able or tending to contract; of the nature of contraction.
contractor, *n.* kon-*trak*-tor, one who contracts, esp. to perform any work or service at a certain price or rate; that which contracts, esp. a muscle.
contractual, *a.* kon-*trak*-tew-al, pertaining to or implying a contract; of the nature of a contract.
contra-dance, *n.* *kon*-tra-dahnce, a contredanse.
contradict, *v.t.* kon-tra-*dikt*, to oppose by words; to affirm the contrary; to deny; to be directly contrary to: *v.i.* to deny the truth of. (L. *contra-*, and *dico*, say.)
contradictable, *a.* kon-tra-*dik*-ta-bl, deniable.
contradiction, *n.* kon-tra-*dik*-shon, the act of asserting to the contrary; contrary statement; denial; opposition; repugnancy; inconsistency with itself.
contradictious, *a.* kon-tra-*dik*-shus, inconsistent; inclined to contradict; disputatious.
contradictive, *a.* kon-tra-*dik*-tiv, contradictory.
contradictively, *ad.* by contradiction.
contradictorily, *ad.* in a contradictory manner.
contradictoriness, *n.* being contradictory.
contradictory, *a.* kon-tra-*dik*-to-re, affirming the contrary; inconsistent; opposite; of propositions having the same terms, but differing in quantity and quality [Logic]: *n.* a proposition which denies or opposes another in all its terms; contrariety.
contradistinction, *n.* kon-tra-dis-*tink*-shon, distinction by opposite qualities.
contradistinctive, *a.* kon-tra-dis-*tink*-tiv, distinguishing or distinguished by opposite qualities.
contradistinguish, *v.t.* kon-tra-dis-*ting*-gwish, to distinguish by contrasting opposite qualities.
contrahent, *a.* *kon*-tra-hent, contracting; entering into a covenant.
contra-indicant, *n.* kon-tra-*in*-de-kant, a symptom that forbids the usual treatment [Path.].
contra-indicate, *v.t.* kon-tra-*in*-de-kate, to indicate a different or contrary treatment [Path.].
contra-indication, *n.* a contra-indicant.
contralateral, *a.* kon-tra-*lat*-er-al, situated or occurring on the opposite side [Med.].
contralto, *n.* kon-*tral*-to, the part immediately below the treble; the counter-tenor; a contralto singer: *a.* singing contralto [Mus.]. **contralto voice,** the deepest-toned female singing-voice. (It.)
contraplex, *a.* *kon*-tra-pleks, pertaining to the simultaneous transmission on one line of two telegraphic messages in opposite directions.
contraposition, *n.* *kon*-tra-po-*zish*-on, a placing over against; opposite position; a species of conversion by means of negation [Logic].
contraption, *n.* kon-*trap*-shon, a makeshift; a contrivance; a gadget [Slang].
contrapuntal, *a.* kon-tra-*pun*-tal, pertaining to counterpoint. (It. *contrappunto*, counterpoint.)
contrapuntist, *n.* kon-tra-*pun*-tist, one skilled in counterpoint.
contrariant, *a.* kon-*trare*-e-ent, opposed; mutually antagonistic. (Fr.)
contrariety, *n.* kon-tra-*ry*-e-te, opposition in fact, essence, or principle; inconsistency. (Fr. *contrariété.*)
contrarily, *ad.* *kon*-tra-re-le, in a contrary manner.
contrariness, *n.* kon-*trare*-re-ness, contrariety; opposition.
contrarious, *a.* kon-*trare*-re-us, perverse; inclined to oppose.
contrariwise, *ad.* *kon*-tra-re-wize, on the contrary; on the other hand; perversely.
contrary, *a.* *kon*-tra-re, opposite; adverse; contradictory; repugnant or inconsistent; given to opposition; captious; antagonistic: *n.* a thing of opposite qualities; a proposition contrary to another: *pl.*, universal propositions which differ in quality [Logic]. (Fr. *contraire.*)
contrast, *n.* *kon*-trast, opposition or dissimilitude of things or qualities; the presentation of opposite things with a view to comparison; notable difference. (Fr. *contraste.*)
contrast, *v.t.* kon-*trast*, to set in opposition different things or qualities, to show more strikingly the superior excellence of one to another: *v.i.* to stand in contrast or opposition. (Fr. *contraster.*)
contrastive, *a.* kon-*tras*-tiv, that may be contrasted; forming a contrast.
contra-tenor, *n.* *kon*-tra-*ten*-or, a middle part between tenor and treble; contralto [Mus.]. (It.)
contrate, *a.* *kon*-trate, having cogs or teeth which project at right angles to the plane of the wheel.
contravallation, *n.* *kon*-tra-val-*lay*-shon, ramparts thrown up by besiegers as protection against sallies by the garrison [Fort.]. (Fr. *contrevallation.*)
contravene, *v.t.* kon-tra-*veen*, to oppose; to obstruct; to transgress. (Fr. *contrevenir.*)
contravention, *n.* kon-tra-*ven*-shon, opposition; violation.
contrayerva, *n.* kon-tra-*yer*-va, the root of several species of the tropical American herb *Dortsenia* and of the Jamaican plant *Aristolochia odoratissima*, both used in medicine. (Sp., an antidote.)
contredanse, *n.* (App.) a quadrille or other dance in which partners take position opposite each other. (Fr., *contre*, opposite, and *dance*).
contretemps, *n.* (App.), an unexpected accident, which throws everything into confusion. (Fr.)
contributable, *a.* that can be contributed.
contribute, *v.t.* kon-*trib*-yewt, to give for a common purpose; to pay a share: *v.i.* to give a part; to have a share in any act or effect; to supply for publication. (L. *contributus*, contributed.)
contribution, *n.* kon-tre-*bew*-shon, the act of contributing; that which is contributed; a levy; a tax paid by a country or town to a hostile force to secure itself against spoliation; an article for publication in a periodical, encyclopædia, etc. (Fr.)
contributive, *a.* kon-*trib*-yew-tiv, contributing, helping.
contributor, *n.* one who contributes.
contributory, *a.* kon-*trib*-yew-to-re, contributing to the same stock or purpose; promoting the same end: *n.* a contributor, esp. one who is liable, in part, for the debts of a company on its winding-up [Law].
contrite, *a.* *kon*-trite, broken-hearted or deeply grieved; penitent. (Fr. *contrit.*)
contritely, *ad.* in a contrite manner.
contrition, *n.* kon-*trish*-on, deep sorrow; penitence.
contriturate, *v.t.* kon-*trit*-yew-rate, to pulverize.
contrivable, *a.* kôn-*trive*-a-bl, that may be contrived.

contrivance, *n.* kon-*trive*-ance, the act of contriving; the thing contrived; a device; an invention.
contrive, *v.t.* kon-*trive*, to devise; to plan: *v.i.* to scheme or devise. (Fr. *controuver*, to find.)
contriver, *n.* kon-*trive*-er, an inventor; a schemer.
★**control,** *n.* kon-*trole*, restraint; authority; command; means of controlling; mechanism that controls, esp. motor vehicles and aeroplanes; a place or area where traffic is controlled; a station where control is exercised or tests are made; a standard of comparison to check results of experiments; a spirit directing a spiritualistic medium: *v.t.* to restrain, govern, or direct; to check by a counter-register or double account. **control column,** the lever by which the pilot of an aeroplane moves the elevators and ailerons [Av.]; the pillar supporting a hand wheel by which an aeroplane or motor-car is steered. **control desk,** a switchboard [Elec.]. **control room,** a room from which controls [Mech.] are worked, or [Mil.] operations are directed. (Fr. *controle.*)
controllable, *a.* subject to control; that may be controlled.
controller, *n.* kon-*trole*-er, one who controls or has authority to control; specially an officer appointed to control or verify the accounts of other officers; one who adjusts and keeps the public accounts [U.S.A.]; a controlling mechanism.
controllership, *n.* the office of a controller.
controlment, *n.* kon-*trole*-ment, the power or act of controlling; control; restraint.
controversial, *a.* kon-tro-*ver*-shal, pertaining to or given to controversy; relating to points in dispute. (L. *controversia.*)
controversialist, *n.* kon-tro-*ver*-shal-list, one who carries on a controversy; a disputant.
controversially, *ad.* kon-tro-*ver*-shal-le, in a controversial manner.
controversion, *n.* *kon*-tro-*ver*-shon, the act of controverting; turning to the other side.
controversy, *n.* *kon*-tro-ver-se, the act of disputing; a cause of dispute; disputation; a debate between parties, particularly in writing; contest. (L. *controversia.*)
controvert, *v.t.* *kon*-tro-vert, to dispute; to oppose by reasoning; to argue against. (L. *contra-*, and *verto*, turn.)
controverter, *n.* one who controverts.
controvertible, *a.* *kon*-tro-*vert*-e-bl, disputable.
controvertibly, *ad.* in a controvertible manner.
controvertist, *n.* *kon*-tro-vert-ist *or* kon-tro-*vert*-ist, one skilled in debate; a controversialist.
contumacious, *a.* kon-tew-*may*-shus, stubborn; persistently obstinate; opposing rightful authority with pride and stubbornness; wilfully disobedient to the orders of a court [Law].
contumaciously, *ad.* in a contumacious manner.
contumaciousness, *n.* a contumacious temper.
contumacy, *n.* *kon*-tew-ma-se, wilful, perverse, unyielding obstinacy or stubbornness; a wilful contempt of and disobedience to a judicial order [Law]. (L. *contumacia.*)
contumelious, *a.* kon-tew-*mee*-le-us, haughtily and scornfully abusive and reproachful; insolent.
contumeliously, *ad.* in a contumelious manner.
contumeliousness, *n.* quality of being contumelious.
contumely, *n.* *kon*-tew-me-le, rude, haughty, and scornful abuse or reproach; insolence; contemptuous rudeness or treatment. (O.Fr. *contumelie.*)
contuse, *v.t.* kon-*tewz*, to bruise; to injure the flesh without breaking the skin. (L. *contusus*, beaten.)
contusion, *n.* kon-*tew*-zhon, the act of beating and bruising; the state of being contused; a bruise.
conundrum, *n.* ko-*nun*-drum, a verbal puzzle; a riddle dependent on a play of words or founded on a fanciful resemblance between things unlike.
conurbation, *n.* kon-ur-*bay*-shon, a population group comprised within two or more administrative areas; a city with its suburbs.
conure, *n.* *kon*-newr, a Central and South American parakeet of the genus *Conurus*.
convalesce, *v.t.* kon-va-*les*, to recover health after sickness. (L. *convalesco*, grow strong.)
convalescence, *n.* kon-va-*les*-ense, gradual recovery of health and strength.
convalescent, *a.* kon-va-*les*-ent, recovering health: *n.* one who is convalescent. **convalescent home,** an establishment, usually connected with a hospital, for convalescents.
convallaria, *n.* kon-va-*lare*-re-a, the lily of the valley, *C. majalis*. (L. *convallis*, a deep valley.)
convection, *n.* kon-*vek*-shon, the act of conveying, esp. heat by the ascent of the heated particles in a gas or liquid. (L. *convectus*, carried.)
convective, *a.* kon-*vek*-tiv, able to transmit; conveying.
convenable, *a.* kon-*veen*-a-bl, that may be convened.
convenance, *n.* *kon*-ve-nonce (or App.), conventional behaviour; the proprieties. (Fr.)
convene, *v.i.* kon-*veen*, to come together; to assemble: *v.t.* to call together; to convoke. (L. *convenio*, come.)
convener, *n.* kon-*veen*-er, one who calls others together; the caller of a meeting; the chairman of a meeting [Scots.].
convenience, *n.* kon-*veen*-e-ence, fitness; suitableness; comfort; ease; accommodation; that which is suited to wants or necessity; opportunity; a (public) urinal or w.c. (L. *convenientia*).
conveniency, *n.* kon-*veen*-e-ence-e, convenience.
convenient, *a.* kon-*veen*-e-ent, fit; suitable; close by; properly adapted; commodious.
conveniently, *ad.* in a convenient manner.
convent, *n.* *kon*-vent, a community of religious recluses of either sex (but more usually of women); the buildings of such a community. (L. *conventus.*)
conventicle, *n.* kon-*vent*-e-kl, a clandestine assembly or meeting; (in contempt) a meeting or meeting-house of dissenters; a secret meeting of the Scottish Covenanters for worship. (L. *conventiculum*, a little assembly.)
conventicler, *n.* one frequenting conventicles.
convention, *n.* kon-*ven*-shon, the act of coming together; an assembly; union; coalition, specially of representatives for some definite purpose; a contract; an agreement between military commanders previous to a definitive treaty; a custom; one of certain recognized modes of play in contract-bridge and other card-games. (Fr.)
conventional, *a.* kon-*ven*-shon-al, settled by stipulation or by tacit consent; as sanctioned and currently accepted by tacit agreement; agreeable to accepted standards; slavishly adhering to tradition; stereotyped.
conventionalism, *n.* observance of conventionality; a conventional practice.
conventionality, *n.* kon-*ven*-shon-*al*-e-te, the state or quality of being conventional; a conventional mode of living and acting.
conventionalize, *v.t.* kon-*ven*-shon-al-lize, to form, fashion, or represent agreeably to conventional rules; to make conventional.
conventionally, *ad.* in a conventional manner; by following traditional method.
conventionary, *a.* kon-*ven*-shon-a-re, acting or holding according to convention as distinct from custom [Law.]: *n.* a conventionary tenant.
conventionist, *n.* kon-*ven*-shon-ist, one who enters into a convention; a member of a convention.
conventual, *a.* kon-*ven*-tew-al, belonging to a convent: *n.* a member of a convent.
converge, *v.i.* kon-*verj*, to tend to the same point: *v.t.* to cause to converge. **converging rays,** those rays of light which proceed from different points of an object and tend toward a single point [Opt.]. **converging series,** that in which the magnitude of the several terms gradually diminishes [Math.]. (L. *convergo*, incline.)
convergence, *n.* kon-*verj*-ence, state of being convergent; tendency to one point; the development of similar characters in animals of different groups [Biol.]. (Fr.)
convergency, *n.* kon-*verj*-en-se, convergence.
convergent, *a.* kon-*verj*-ent, tending to one point; having or acquiring similar characteristics [Biol.].
conversable, *a.* kon-*verse*-a-bl, disposed to converse; sociable.
conversably, *ad.* in a conversable manner.
conversance, *n.* *kon*-ver-sance, the quality of being conversant.
conversant, *a.* *kon*-ver-sant, well acquainted with, through study or use; versed; proficient; having intercourse or associating with.
conversation, *n.* kon-ver-*say*-shon, the act of conversing; familiar talk or intercourse; familiarity. **criminal conversation,** adultery; crim-con. (Fr.)

conversational, *a.* kon-ver-*say*-shon-al, pertaining to conversation; in mutual discourse or talk.
conversationalist, *n.* one given to conversation; a good talker.
conversationist, *n.* kon-ver-*say*-shon-ist, a conversationalist.
conversative, *a.* kon-*ver*-sa-tiv, inclined to converse; talkative.
conversazione, *n.* *kon*-ver-sat-ze-*oh*-ne, a meeting for conversation, generally on literary, artistic, or scientific topics. (It.)
converse, *v.i.* kon-*verse*, to hold intercourse with; to interchange thoughts or talk familiarly with.
converse, *n.* *kon*-verse, conversation; acquaintance by frequent or customary intercourse; familiarity; the proposition resulting from transposing the terms [Logic]; an inverted proposition [Math.]: *a.* opposite or reciprocal. (Fr. *converser.*)
conversely, *ad.* kon-*verse*-le, with change of order; in a contrary order; reciprocally.
conversion, *n.* kon-*ver*-shon, the act of changing from one state to another; transmutation; a regenerative change of heart or disposition; an abrupt change of religion or from one party, school of thought, etc., to another; the act of appropriating to private use; the change of one or more security issues into a new issue or of one kind of security for another; the reconstruction of a monetary system; the inference of one proposition from another by transposing the terms [Logic]. **conversion of equations,** the reduction of a fractional equation into an integral one [Alg.]. (L. *conversus*, lived with.)
convert, *v.t.* kon-*vert*, to change from one state to another; to change or turn from one religion or party, etc., to another; to change the heart and moral character; to bring about conversion of any kind; to appropriate to one's own use; to change one proposition into another by transposing the terms: *v.i.* to turn or be changed; to undergo a change; in Rugby football, to score a goal from a place-kick after a try. (O.Fr. *convertir.*)
convert, *n.* *kon*-vert, a person converted, generally from one creed or religious system to another, or from an irreligious to a religious state of mind.
convertend, *n.* *kon*-ver-*tend*, the proposition to be converted [Logic]. (L. *convertendus.*)
converter, *n.* kon-*ver*-ter, one who makes converts: the vessel in which molten iron is converted into bessemer steel; a machine for changing alternating current to direct, or *vice versa* [Elect.].
convertibility, *n.* kon-*ver*-te-*bil*-e-te, the capability of being converted. (L. *convertibilis.*)
convertible, *a.* kon-*ver*-te-bl, that may be converted; susceptible of change; transmutable; transformable; exchangeable for coin.
convertibly, *ad.* reciprocally; with interchange of terms.
convertite, *n.* *kon*-ver-tite, a convert; a magdalen.
convex, *a.* *kon*-veks, protuberant; swelling on the exterior surface into a rounded form, opposed to concave: *n.* a convex body. (Fr. *convexe.*)
convexed, *a.* *kon*-vekst, made convex.
convexity, *n.* kon-*vek*-se-te, quality or state of being convex; roundness.
convexly, *ad.* *kon*-veks-le, in a convex form.
convexness, *n.* kon-*veks*-ness, convexity.
convexo-concave, *a.* kon-*veks*-o-*kon*-kave, convex on one side and concave on the other.
convexo-convex, *a.* convex on both sides.
convexo-plane, *a.* convex on one side and flat on the other.
convey, *v.t.* kon-*vay*, to carry or transport; to transmit; to transfer; to impart; to steal [Slang]: *v.i.* to play the thief. (O.Fr. *convoyer.*)
conveyable, *a.* that may be conveyed or transferred.
conveyance, *n.* kon-*vay*-ance, the act, means, or instrument of conveying; a vehicle; the transferring of property from one person to another; the writing by which it is transferred [Law].
conveyancer, *n.* kon-*vay*-ance-er, a lawyer who investigates title-deeds and draws up conveyances of property.
conveyancing, *n.* kon-*vay*-ance-ing, preparing deeds, leases, or other writings for transferring the title to property from one to another.
conveyer, *n.* kon-*vay*-er, he who or that which conveys; a conveyor.
conveyor, *n.* kon-*vay*-or, the mechanism for carrying grain or goods along endless bands working over rollers.
convict, *v.t.* kon-*vikt*, to prove guilty; to find guilty; to convince of sin; to show by proof or evidence; to prove false. (L. *convictus*, conquered with.)
convict, *n.* *kon*-vikt, a condemned criminal undergoing a sentence of penal servitude.
conviction, *n.* kon-*vik*-shon, the act of convicting; the state of being convicted; the state of being convinced; assured belief.
convictism, *n.* *kon*-vik-tizm, the convict system; the convict class.
convictive, *a.* kon-*vik*-tiv, convincing; having the power to convince or convict.
convince, *v.t.* kon-*vince*, to satisfy the mind, or compel belief by evidence. (L. *convinco*, conquer with.)
convincement, *n.* kon-*vince*-ment, conviction.
convincible, *a.* kon-*vince*-e-bl, capable of persuasion.
convincingly, *ad.* in a convincing manner.
convincingness, *n.* the capacity to convince.
convive, *n.* *kon*-veev, a boon companion; a fellow-guest at a banquet. (L. *conviva.*)
convivial, *a.* kon-*viv*-e-al, feasting in company; drinking with others; jovial; social. (L. *convivialis*, of feasting.)
convivialist, *n.* one of convivial habits.
conviviality, *n.* kon-*viv*-e-*al*-e-te, the good humour or mirth indulged in at an entertainment; good fellowship.
convivially, *ad.* in a convivial manner.
convocation, *n.* kon-vo-*kay*-shon, the act of calling or assembling by summons; the synod of the clergy of either Canterbury or York which together form in their upper and lower houses the first two houses of the Church Assembly, the third house being that of the laity; an academical assembly at Oxford and Durham in which the business of the university is transacted. (L. *convocatio.*)
convocational, *a.* relating to a convocation.
convocator, *n.* *kon*-vo-*kay*-tor, one who summons or convokes an assembly.
convoke, *v.t.* kon-*voke*, to call together; to assemble by summons; to convene. (L. *convoco*, call together.)
convolute, *a.* *kon*-vo-lewt, rolled together, or upon itself. (L. *convolutus*, rolled together.)
convoluted, *a.* coiled or rolled up.
convolution, *n.* kon-vo-*lew*-shon, the act of convolving; the state of being convolved; a winding; a fold; a winding motion.
convolve, *v.t.* kon-*volv*, to roll or wind together; to roll one part on another. (L. *convolvo*, roll together.)
convolvulus, *n.* kon-*vol*-vew-lus, a trailing and twining plant of the genus *Convolvulus*, including *C. arvensis*, the bindweed. (L., bindweed.)
convoy, *n.* *kon*-voy, a protecting force accompanying ships or land transport on their way from place to place, either by sea or land; the act of convoying; the ship or fleet which is convoyed. (Fr. *convoyer.*)
convoy, *v.t.* kon-*voy*, to accompany on the way, for protection, either by sea or land; to escort.
convulse, *v.t.* kon-*vulse*, to agitate violently; to draw or contract, as the muscular parts of an animal body; to affect by irregular spasms; to move to extravagant laughter. (L. *convulsus*, plucked.)
convulsion, *n.* kon-*vul*-shon, a violent and involuntary spasmodic contraction of the muscular parts of an animal body; any violent and irregular motion, commotion, or agitation.
convulsionary, *a.* relating to convulsion; caused by or affected with convulsions.
convulsionist, *n.* a catastrophist [Geol.].
convulsive, *a.* kon-*vul*-siv, producing or attended with convulsions or spasms.
convulsively, *ad.* in a convulsive manner.
cony, *n.* *koh*-ne, the common rabbit, or its fur when dyed and dressed; the pika, also (esp. in the Bible), the daman, one of the small hyraxes. (O.Fr. *conin* or *connil.*)
cony-catcher, *n.* *koh*-ne-katch-er, a sharper; a cheat.
coo, *v.i.* koo, to call as a dove or pigeon; to make love: *v.t.* to express in a cooing manner: *int.* indicating surprise, incredulity, or admiration [Slang]. (Imit.)

cooee, *n.* *koo*-ee, a native signal call used in Australia, as audible over great distances : *v.t.* to make such a call or signal.
***cook,** *n.* kook, one whose occupation is to cook ; a cooking process ; a chess problem to which there is an alternative and inadvertent solution : *v.t.* to prepare food for eating ; to concoct ; to fake or garble ; to falsify, as a financial statement. **cook his goose,** finish him ; do for him [Slang]. (A.S. *coc*, from L. *coquo*, boil.)
cooker, *n.* *kook*-er, a cooking-stove or apparatus ; one who cooks or garbles.
cookery, *n.* *kook*-er-re, the art or practice of cooking ; the practice of falsifying.
cook-house, *n.* *kook*-house, a room or building for cooking ; a ship's galley ; a caboose.
cookie, *n.* *kook*-e, a small round sweet bun ; in Scotland, a long oblong sweet sugar-covered bun.
cook-shop, *n.* *kook*-shop, an eating-house.
cool, *a.* kool, moderately cold ; not retaining heat ; not ardent or zealous ; calm ; dispassionate ; indifferent ; impudent ; not hasty ; deliberate : *n.* a moderate state of cold ; a cool place : *v.t.* to make cool or cold ; to allay heat or passion : *v.i.* to become less hot ; to become less ardent, angry, zealous, or affectionate. (A.S. *col.*)
cooler, *n.* *kool*-er, that which abates heat or excitement ; a vessel in which liquors are cooled ; a detention cell or prison [Slang].
coolie, *n.* *koo*-le, an East Indian porter or carrier ; a native labourer in India or China. (Hind.)
coolish, *a.* *kool*-ish, somewhat cool.
coolly, *ad.* *kool*-le, in a cool or indifferent manner.
coolness, *n.* *kool*-ness, the state of being cool or apathetic ; indifference.
coom, *n.* koom, soot that gathers over an oven's mouth ; refuse axle-grease, etc., exuding from the naves of wheels. (Dial. Eng.)
coomb, *n.* koom, a corn measure of four bushels, or half a quarter. (A.S. *cumb.*)
coomb, *n.* koom, a combe ; a deep valley in downland in the south of England ; a short, deep valley, leading down to the sea-coast. (A.S. *cumb.*)
coon, *n.* koon, a Negro ; a nigger minstrel ; a sly, shrewd fellow [Slang]. (Abbrev. of *raccoon.*)
coon-can, *n.* *koon*-kan, a card game in which the aim of the players is to make sequences.
coop, *n.* koop, a box of boards, grated or barred on one side, for keeping fowls ; an enclosed place for small animals ; a kipe ; *v.t.* to confine in a coop or a narrow compass. (M.E. *cupe*, basket.)
cooper, *n.* *koop*-er, one who makes barrels, tubs, and casks of various kinds ; a mixture of stout and porter (originally supplied by brewers to their coopers) : *v.t.* to do the work of a cooper ; to repair. (L. *cupa*, cask.)
cooperage, *n.* *koop*-er-aj, a cooper's work ; the price paid for it ; a cooper's workshop.
co-operant, *a.* ko-*op*-er-ant, co-operating : *n.* one who or that which co-operates.
co-operate, *v.i.* ko-*op*-er-ate, to work or act conjointly for the same end : *v.i.* to act as a co-operator [Econ.]. (L. *co-operatus*, worked with.)
co-operation, *n.* ko-*op*-er-*ray*-shon, the act of co-operating, specially the system of co-operating in the production, provision, or distribution of goods for the common benefit ; mutual profiting from mutual working or trading.
co-operative, *a.* ko-*op*-er-ra-tiv, working or acting conjointly for the same end or a common interest. **Co-operative Society,** a wholesale and retail organization selling to its members at **Co-operative Stores,** eliminating (as far as possible) the middleman's profits and dividing these among its members.
co-operator, *n.* ko-*op*-er-ray-tor, one who co-operates ; an official or member of a Co-operative Society [Econ.].
co-opt, *v.t.* ko-*opt*, to elect into a society or public body by the votes of the existing members.
co-optation, *n.* ko-op-*tay*-shon, the act of co-opting or electing ; election by members.
co-optative, *a.* ko-*op*-ta-tiv, pertaining to, elected by, or eligible for, co-optation.
co-ordinate, *a.* ko-*awr*-de-nate, of the same order, rank, or authority : *n.pl.* the system of lines to which points under consideration are referred, and by means of which their position is determined [Geom.] : *v.t.* to make co-ordinate ; to correlate. (L. *co-ordinatus*, ordered with.)
co-ordinately, *ad.* in the same order or rank.
co-ordinateness, *n.* state of being co-ordinate.
co-ordination, *n.* ko-*awr*-de-*nay*-shon, the act of co-ordinating or arranging in co-ordinate ranks ; state of being co-ordinate or able to work together punctually and harmoniously.
co-ordinative, *a.* ko-*awr*-de-na-tiv, able, or tending, to co-ordinate.
coot, *n.* koot, the water-fowl, *Fulica atra*, having a white shield on the forehead and frequenting lakes and still waters ; a bit of an ass [Slang].
cop, *n.* kop, the head or top of a thing ; a tuft ; in spinning, a ball of thread wound round a spindle ; (A.S.)
cop, *v.t.* kop, to catch ; *n.* a catch ; a policeman [Slang].
copaiba, *n.* ko-*pay*-ba, an oleo-resin obtained from incisions made in the stem of the copaiba or copaiva, a species of *Copaifera* of the West Indies and Brazil. (Sp.)
copal, *n.* *koh*-pal, the resin of several tropical trees, used for varnishing. (Sp.)
copalite, *n.* *koh*-pa-lite, a fossil resin found in the London Clay at Highgate.
coparcenary, *n.* ko-*par*-se-na-re, joint heirship or ownership : *a.* pertaining to coparceners. (L. *con-*, and *pars*, a part.)
coparcener, *n.* ko-*par*-se-ner, a co-heir.
copartner, *n.* ko-*part*-ner, a joint partner or sharer.
copartnership, *n.* ko-*part*-ner-ship, joint concern in business ; the persons who have a joint concern ; partnership between employers and employed.
copartnery, *n.* ko-*part*-ner-re, copartnership.
copatain, *a.* *kop*-a-tane, high-crowned ; pointed.
cope, *n.* kope, a hood ; a sleeveless vestment worn by priests on solemn occasions ; anything extended over the head, as the arch or concave of the sky, the roof or covering of a house, the arch over a door ; a coping : *v.t.* to cover as with a cope ; to form a cope. (L. *capa.*)
cope, *v.i.* kope, to contend with in equal combat ; to match ; to encounter ; to contend. (O.Fr. *coper*, to strike.)
copec, *n.* *koh*-pek, a kopeck. (Russ.)
Copepoda, *n.* ko-*pep*-o-da, a sub-class of the crustacea including the fish-lice, water-fleas, etc., and forming an important part of the plankton. (Gr. *kope*, oar, *pous*, foot.)
coper, *n.* *koh*-per, a horse-faker ; a dishonest dealer ; formerly also a floating tavern for North Sea fishermen.
Copernican, *a.* ko-*per*-nik-an, relating to the astronomical system of Copernicus, in which the sun was the centre of the universe.
copestone, *n.* *kope*-stone, a coping-stone.
cophosis, *n.* ko-*foh*-sis, total deafness. (Gr. *kophosis*, from *kophos*, deaf.)
copier, *n.* *kop*-e-er, one who copies.
coping, *n.* *koh*-ping, the top course of a wall. **coping-stone,** a stone used to form a coping ; the topmost stone of a building.
copious, *a.* *koh*-pe-us, abundant ; plentiful ; prolific ; profuse. (L. *copiosus*, plentiful.)
copiously, *ad.* in a copious manner ; diffusely.
copiousness, *n.* abundance ; diffusiveness of style or manner of treating a subject.
***copper,** *n.* *kop*-per, a malleable, ductile, and tenacious metallic element of a pale red colour, tinged with yellow ; a vessel made of copper, particularly a large boiler ; a copper or bronze coin ; a policeman [Slang] : *a.* made of or like copper : *v.t.* to sheath with sheets of copper ; to electroplate with copper. (A.S. *copor*, from Gr. *kypros*, Cyprus, an ancient source of the metal.)
copperas, *n.* *kop*-per-as, sulphate of iron, or green vitriol. (Fr. *couperose.*)
copper-bottomed, *a.* sheathed with copper below the waterline [Naut.].
copper-captain, *n.* a sham or quack captain.
copper-glance, *n.* *kop*-per-glahnce, chalcocite, or redruthite, a native sulphide of copper, occurring as a greyish-black mineral with a metallic lustre.
copperhead, *n.* *kop*-per-hed, the moccasin snake, *Agkistrodon contortrix* ; a foe professing peace ; a former term of contempt for a Northern sympathizer with the South during the American Civil War.
copper-nickel, *n.* *kop*-per-*nik*-el, niccolite.
copperplate, *n.* *kop*-per-plate, a plate of polished

copper on which something is engraved ; impression from a copperplate : beautiful handwriting : *a.* relating to the process or impression of engraving on copper ; neat and clear (of writing).
copper-pyrites, *n.* *kop*-per-py-*ry*-teez, chalcopyrite, the most important copper ore.
coppersmith, *n.* *kop*-per-smith, one whose occupation is to manufacture copper utensils.
copper-work, *n.* *kop*-per-wurk, articles in copper.
coppery, *a.* *kop*-per-e, mixed with or made of copper ; like copper in taste or smell.
coppice, *n.* *kop*-pis, a thicket of brushwood ; a wood cut for fuel. (O.Fr. *copeiz.*)
coppin, *n.* *kop*-in, a cop of thread.
copra, *n.* *koh*-prah, dried coconut kernels, the source of coconut oil. (Hind.)
coprolite, *n.* *kop*-ro-lite, petrified dung, chiefly of extinct saurians ; any phosphatic nodule. (Gr. *kopros*, dung, *lithos*, a stone.)
coprolitic, *a.* kop-ro-*lit*-ik, containing or resembling coprolites.
coprology, *n.* kop-*rol*-o-je, obscenity ; moral impurity in literature or art.
coprophagan, *n.* kop-*rof*-a-gan, a beetle which lives on or in dung. (Gr. *kopros*, and *phago*, eat.)
coprophagous, *a.* ko-*prof*-a-gus, feeding on dung.
copse, *n.* kops, a coppice.
copse-wood, *n.* *kops*-wood, brushwood ; underwood.
copsy, *a.* *kop*-se, having copses.
Coptic, *a.* *kop*-tik, pertaining to the Copts, the natives of upper Egypt, esp. those adhering to Monophysitism : *n.* their language. (Ar. *Quft.*)
copula, *n.* *kop*-yew-la, that which couples ; the word which unites the subject and predicate of a proposition [Logic]. (L., a bond, from *con-*, and *apto*, fit or fasten.)
copulate, *a.* *kop*-yew-late, joined : *v.i.* to unite in sexual embrace. (L. *copulatus*, joined.)
copulation, *n.* kop-yew-*lay*-shon, the act of coupling ; the embrace of the sexes in coition ; connexion [Gram. and logic].
copulative, *a.* *kop*-yew-la-tiv, that unites or couples ; copulatory : *n.* a copulative conjunction which connects two or more subjects or predicates [Gram.].
copulatory, *a.* *kop*-yew-la-to-re, relating to or serving for copulation.
★**copy,** *n.* *kop*-pe, a transcript or an impression from an original ; a thing made in imitation of another ; the original, specially the matter given to a printer to set up in type ; one reproduction of a particular work, book, etc. : *v.t.* to make a copy of ; to write, print, paint, engrave, etc., according to an original ; to transcribe ; to imitate ; to follow as a pattern in manners or life : *v.i.* to imitate or endeavour to be like. (L. *copia*, plenty.)
copy-book, *n.* a book in which copies are written or printed for learners of writing to imitate.
copyhold, *n.* *kop*-pe-hohld, a tenure of by copy of court roll, or a tenure for which the tenant has nothing to show, except the rolls made by the steward of the lord's court ; property held by this tenure [Law].
copyholder, *n.* one who is possessed of land in copyhold ; a proof-reader's assistant [Print.].
copying-ink, *n.* ink thickened with glycerine or the like, making it suitable for writings of which copies can be taken by pressure.
copying-press, *n.* a machine for taking an exact copy of a MS. recently written in copying-ink.
copyist, *n.* *kop*-e-ist, a transcriber ; an imitator ; a plagiarist.
copyright, *n.* *kop*-pe-rite, the exclusive right of an author or his heirs to publish copies of his work : *a.* protected by copyright : *v.t.* to protect by copyright ; to secure a copyright on.
coque, *n.* kohk *or* kok, a small loop of ribbon, etc., for decorating hats, boas, etc. (Fr.)
coquelicot, *n.* *kohk*-le-ko, the wild poppy ; its colour. (Fr.)
coquet, *v.i.* ko-*ket*, to flirt ; to trifle with in love ; to attract with a view to deceive ; to toy with. (Fr.)
coquetry, *n.* *kok*-et-re, flirting ; trifling in love ; attempts to attract admiration or love from vanity ; affectation of amorous advances.
coquette, *n.* ko-*ket*, a minx or female flirt ; a jilt. (Fr.)
coquettish, *a.* ko-*ket*-ish, practising coquetry.
coquettishly, *ad.* in a coquettish manner.
coquilla-nut, *n.* ko-*kil*-la-nut, the fruit of *Attalea funifera*, a Brazilian pissava palm, used in turnery.
coquito, *n.* ko-*kee*-toh, the honey-yielding palm, *Jubæa spectabilis*, of Chile. (Sp.)
cor, *n.* kawr, a horn [Mus.]. **cor anglais,** the tenor oboe. (Fr.)
cor, *n.* kawr, a homer, a Hebrew measure. (Heb.)
coracle, *n.* *ko*-ra-kl, an ancient British boat still used in Wales and Ireland, made by covering a wicker frame with skins, leather, or canvas.
coracoid, *a.* *ko*-ra-koyd, shaped like a crow's beak, hook-shaped [Anat.] : *n.* a small sharp process of the scapula. (Gr. *korax*, a crow, *eidos*, like.)
co-radicate, *a.* koh-*rad*-e-kat, derived from the same root [Philology]. (L. *co-*, and *radix*, root.)
coral, *n.* *ko*-ral, a calcareous substance secreted by marine polyps, and forming their skeletons, which grow up in various forms and masses from the bottom of the sea ; a piece of coral used by children as a plaything ; the ovaries or roe of a lobster : *a.* made of or resembling coral. **coral island,** an island formed of one or more ridges of coral, or **coral reef.** (Fr.)
Corallian, *n.* ko-*ral*-yan, a series of Jurassic rocks formed between the Oxford and Kimeridge clays.
coralliferous, *a.* ko-ra-*lif*-er-rus, containing coral. (*Coral*, and L. *fero*, bear.)
coralliform, *a.* ko-*ral*-e-fawrm, resembling coral ; forked and crooked. (*Coral*, and L. *forma*, shape.)
coralligenous, *a.* ko-ra-*lij*-e-nus, producing coral. (*Coral*, and Gr. *gennao*, produce.)
coralline, *a.* *ko*-ra-line, containing or consisting of coral ; like coral : *n.* a semi-calcareous moss-like seaweed ; applied to any of the polyzoa ; an orange-red dye.
corallite, *n.* *ko*-ra-lite, a mineral petrifaction in the form of coral ; the skeleton of a single zoophyte ; coralline marble.
coralloid, *a.* *ko*-ra-loyd, having the form of coral ; branching like coral : *n.* a coral-like organism. (*Coral*, and Gr. *eidos*, like.)
corallum, *n.* ko-*ral*-um, the hard calcareous skeleton of a compound coral.
coral-rag, *n.* a coralliferous limestone found in the Corallian [Geol.].
coral-snake, *n.* any of the several species of the genus *Elaps.*
coral-tree, *n.* *ko*-ral-tree, any of the shrubby tropical scarlet-flowered plants of the genus *Erythrina.*
coral-wort, *n.* toothwort, *Dentaria bulbifera.*
coranto, *n.* ko-*rant*-oh, the old dance, courant.
corb, *n.* kawrb, an iron basket used in collieries ; a basket. (L. *corbis*, a basket.)
corban, *n.* *kawr*-ban, among the ancient Jews, a thing consecrated to God ; the poor-box in the Temple at Jerusalem. (Heb. *qorban*, an offering.)
corbeil, *n.* *kawr*-bel, a sculptured basket [Arch.] ; formerly, an earth-filled basket as protection against beseigers' fire [Fort.]. (Fr.)
corbel, *n.* *kawr*-bel, a bracket of timber, stone, or iron projecting from a wall to support a weight : *v.t.* to support on corbels. (O.Fr.)
corbicula, *n.* kawr-*bik*-yew-la, the hairy surface of the hind tibia of a bee whereon the pollen is carried.
corbie, *n.* *kawr*-be, a raven ; a carrion crow. **corbie steps,** a series of steps crowning a gable wall ; crowsteps. (Scots.)
corcass, *n.* kawr-kass, a salt marsh (in parts of Eire). (Ir. *corcach*, a marsh.)
Corchorus, *n.* *kawr*-ko-rus, a genus of tropical plants of the lime-tree family, some of which yield jute.
★**cord,** *n.* kawrd, a string or thin rope, composed of several strands twisted together ; anything like a cord ; a ribbed cloth, corduroy ; a measure of fuel-wood (128 cu. ft. or 4 ft. × 4 ft. × 8 ft.), originally measured with a cord ; anything which binds or draws : *v.t.* to bind with or furnish with a cord ; to form into a cord. (Fr. *corde.*)
cordage, *n.* *kawr*-daj, ropes or cords, esp. of the rigging of a ship, collectively ; a store of ropes. (Fr.)
cordate, *a.* *kawr*-dat, heart-shaped [Bot.].
corded, *a.* *kawr*-ded, bound with cords ; made of cords ; furrowed ; ribbed.

cordelier, *n.* kawr-de-*leer*, a member of the strictest sect of Franciscan friars, so called from his girdle of knotted cord; a member of a French revolutionary club which met (1790–95) in the church of the Cordeliers, Paris. (Fr.)
cordial, *a.* *kawr*-de-al, proceeding from the heart; hearty, sincere, warm, or affectionate: *n.* an aromatic spirituous beverage; anything that comforts or that raises the spirits when weak and depressed. (Fr.)
cordiality, *n.* kawr-de-*al*-e-te, the quality of being cordial; hearty goodwill. (Fr. *cordialité.*)
cordialize, *v.t.* and *i.* *kawr*-de-a-lize, to render or to become cordial.
cordially, *ad.* in a cordial manner.
cordierite, *n.* *kawr*-dye-*rite*, iolite.
cordiform, *a.* *kawr*-de-fawrm, heart-shaped; in the form of the human heart. (L. *cor*, the heart, and *form.*)
cordillera, *n.* kawr-*dil*-le-ra *or* kawr-dil-*yay*-ra, any one of a number of parallel mountain ranges, esp. of the Andes and their northern extension in Central America and Mexico. (Sp., little rope.)
cordite, *n.* *kawr*-dite, a smokeless propellant with a nitroglycerine basis, prepared in the form of short lengths of cord.
cordon, *n.* *kawr*-don, a ribbon or ornamental cord, esp. as a badge of honour; a row of stones jutting from a wall; a line or series of military posts, blockading ships, etc. **cordon sanitaire** (App.), a line of posts preventing communication with a district infected with disease. (Fr.)
cordovan, *n.* *kawr*-do-van, Spanish leather. (Cordova.)
corduroy, *n.* *kawr*-doo-roy, a thick cotton stuff, corded or ribbed; *pl.* corduroy trousers: *a.* made of corduroy. **corduroy road,** a causeway of logs laid over a swamp [U.S.A.]. (Probably Fr. *corde du roi*, king's cord.)
cordwain, *n.* *kawrd*-wane, Spanish leather; goatskin tanned and dressed. (O.Fr. *cordovan.*)
cordwainer, *n.* *kawrd*-wane-er, a worker in cordwain; a shoemaker.
cord-wood, *n.* fuel-wood to be sold by the cord.
core, *n.* kawr, the heart or inner part of anything; the central radical part; the essence; the portion of a mould shaping the interior of, or forming a hole in, a casting [Eng.]. (L. *cor.*)
Corean, *n.* and *a.* ko-*ree*-an, Korean.
co-regent, *n.* koh-*ree*-jent, a joint regent or ruler.
co-relative, *n.* ko-*rel*-at-iv, correlative.
co-religionist, *n.* koh-re-*lij*-on-ist, a person of the same religious belief or sect as another.
Coreopsis, *n.* *ko*-re-*op*-sis *or* *koh*-re-*op*-sis, a large genus of plants of the thistle family, some of which are garden plants known as tick seeds. (Gr. *koris*, a bug, and *opsis*, appearance.)
co-respondent, *n.* koh-re-*spon*-dent, a joint-respondent in any suit, but especially one, as an associate of another in adultery, in a divorce suit [Law].
corf, *n.* kawrf, a basket for minerals in mines; a basket-like cage for keeping lobsters or fish alive in water.
corgi, *n.* *kawr*-ge, a small rough-haired terrier originally bred in Wales. (W. *corr*, dwarf, *ci*, dog.)
coriaceous, *a.* ko-re-*ay*-shus, consisting of or resembling leather; leathery; tough. (L. *corium*, leather.)
coriander, *n.* ko-re-*an*-der, the *Coriandrum sativum*, whose fruits known as seeds are highly aromatic and carminative. (Fr. *coriandre.*)
Corinthian, *a.* ko-*rin*-the-an, pertaining to Corinth, a city of Greece: *n.* a profligate: a rake (early 19th cent.); a wealthy sporting-man [U.S.A.]. **Corinthian order,** the most delicate and ornate of the orders, the capital being enriched with a graceful assemblage of foliated forms added to the volutes of the Ionic capital [Arch.].
corium, *n.* *koh*-re-um, the deeper and sensitive layer of the skin. (L., leather.)
co-rival, *n.* ko-*ry*-val, a fellow-rival.
co-rivalry, *n.* ko-*ry*-val-re, joint rivalry.
★**cork,** *n.* kawrk, the outer layer of bark of the cork-tree; a stopper or bung made of this: *a.* made of cork: *v.t.* to stop with a cork; to blacken with burnt cork: *v.i.* to become corked. (Sp. *corcho.*)
corkage, *n.* *kawrk*-aj, a hotel charge for serving a guest's own wine; the corking, or uncorking, of bottles.
corked, *a.* kawrkt, stopped or filled with cork; tasting of the cork, as of wine.
corker, *n.* *kawrk*-er, anything that clinches an argument; a poser; a thumping lie [Slang].
corking-pin, *n.* *kawrk*-ing-pin, a pin of a large size.
cork-jacket, *n.* kawrk-*jak*-et, a kind of waistcoat lined with cork to aid in swimming or as a life-preserver at sea.
corkscrew, *n.* *kawrk*-skroo, a screw to draw corks: *v.t.* to move or twist spirally.
cork-tree, *n.* *kawrk*-tree, a species of oak, *Quercus suber*, cultivated in southern Europe, etc., for its bark which is manufactured into corks. **Indian cork-tree,** *Millingtonia hortensis.*
corkwood, *n.* *kawrk*-wood, name given to various American trees, the wood of which is very light.
corky, *a.* *kawrk*-e, resembling cork in taste or appearance; lively or skittish [Slang].
corm, *n.* kawrm, a solid bulbous underground stem [Bot.]. (Gr. *kormos*, a trunk.)
cormorant, *n.* *kawr*-mo-rant, a sea-bird of the genus *Phalacrocorax*, distinguished for its voracity; a glutton; a very avaricious person. (Fr. *cormoran.*)
corn, *n.* kawrn, a grain; the grain of cereals, wheat, or [U.S.A.] maize; the plants which yield grain; a small hard particle: *v.t.* to preserve and season with salt, as corned beef; to granulate. (A S.)
corn, *n.* kawrn, a hard excrescence or induration of the skin on a toe or some part of the feet. (L. *cornu*, a horn.)
corn-brake, *n.* a maize plantation [U.S.A.].
cornbrash, *n.* *kawrn*-brash, a coarse shelly limestone of the Lower Oolite, forming a good soil for corn.
corn-bread, *n.* bread from Indian corn.
cornchandler, *n.* *kawrn*-chahnd-ler, a dealer in corn and forage.
corn-cob, *n.* the centre-part of the stalk, or spike, on which the ears of Indian corn grow, used for the bowls of corn-cob tobacco-pipes.
corncockle, *n.* *kawrn*-kok-kl, a purple-flowered plant, *Lychnis githago*, growing among corn.
corncrake, *n.* *kawrn*-krake, the land-rail.
cornea, *n.* *kawr*-ne-a, the strong horny transparent membrane in the fore part of the eye. (L.)
cornel, *n.* *kawr*-nel, the cornelian cherry-tree, or other tree of the genus *Cornus.*
cornelian, *n.* kawr-*nee*-le-an, carnelian; a precious stone, a variety of chalcedony. (Fr. *cornaline.*)
cornelian, *n.* kawr-*nee*-le-an, the wild cherry or dogwood, *Cornus mascula*; its small edible fruit resembling cherries. (L. *cornus.*)
cornel-tree, *n.* *kawr*-nel-tree, cornelian-tree.
cornemuse, *n.* *kawr*-ne-moose, the French bagpipe.
corneous, *a.* *kawr*-ne-us, horny; like horn; hard.
corner, *n.* *kawr*-ner, the point where two converging lines meet; an angle; an enclosed place; a secret or retired place; a nook; a kick [Soccer] or hit [Hockey] from a corner, awarded in certain circumstances; the position obtaining when a clique buys up stock or the supply of an article in order to raise the price: *v.t.* to create an apparent scarcity by securing the control of the supply; to force into a corner or an untenable position [U.S.A.]: *v.i.* to make a corner (in commodities). (O.Fr. *cornière.*)
cornered, *a.* *kawr*-nerd, having corners or angles; placed in an awkward situation; brought to bay.
corner-stone, *n.* the stone which unites two walls of a building at the corner; the principal stone; that on which a thing rests.
corner-wise, *ad.* diagonally; with the corner in front.
cornet, *n.* *kawr*-net, a brass wind instrument of the nature of a trumpet; formerly, the lowest commissioned officer of cavalry; a conical paper bag or receptacle; a conical wafer containing ice-cream. (Fr.)
cornet-à-piston, *n.* *kawr*-net-ah-*pis*-ton, a cornet furnished with valves and stoppers.
cornetcy, *n.* *kawr*-net-se, the rank of a cornet.
cornflag, *n.* *kawrn*-flag, the wild gladiolus.
cornflour, *n.* *kawrn*-flour, finely ground maize.
corn-flower, *n.* *kawrn*-flou-er, the corn bluebottle, *Centaurea cyanus.*
cornice, *n.* *kawr*-nis, the moulding which projects from the top of a wall, column, or entablature; a picture-rail. (O.Fr.)

corniculate, *a.* kawr-*nik*-yew-lat, horned; having horns; bearing a little spur or horn [Bot.].
cornific, *a.* kawr-*nif*-ik, producing horns or horny matter. (L. *cornu*, and *facio*, make.)
corniform, *a. kawr*-ne-fawrm, horn-shaped.
cornigerous, *a.* kawr-*nij*-er-us, having horns; horned. (L. *cornu*, and *gero*, bear.)
cornin, *n. kawr*-nin, a principle in the bark of *Cornus florida*, with properties like those of quinine.
corning-house, *n.* a house or place where gunpowder is granulated.
Cornish, *a. kawr*-nish, relating to Cornwall: *n.* the ancient Celtic language of Cornwall. **Cornish boiler,** a steam-engine boiler with one short, horizontal, cylindrical flue.
cornland, *n. kawrn*-land, land appropriated or suitable to the production of corn.
corn-loft, *n.* a granary for corn.
corn-marigold, *n.* the composite plant, *Chrysanthemum segetum*.
corn-mill, *n.* a mill for grinding corn.
corn-moth, *n.* the grain-moth, *Tinea granella*, whose larvæ are destructive to corn in granaries.
cornopean, *n.* kor-*noh*-pe-an, the cornet-à-piston.
corn-parsley, *n.* the umbelliferous plant, *Petroselinum segetum*.
corn-rent, *n.* a rent paid in corn, or the amount of which depends on the current price of corn.
corn-salad, *n. kawrn*-sal-ad, any species of *Valerianella*, used as salad.
cornstalk, *n. kawrn*-stawk, an Australian of European descent, esp. one born in New South Wales [Slang].
corn-stone, *n. kawrn*-stone, a mottled kind of limestone of the Old Red Sandstone.
cornubianite, *n.* kawr-*new*-be-a-nite, a slaty rock abundant in Cornwall, found in contact with granite. (*Cornubia*, coined Latin for Cornwall.)
cornucopia, *n.* kawr-new-*koh*-pe-a, the horn of plenty, an emblem of abundance of fruits; the figure of a horn, from which fruits and flowers are represented as proceeding [Arch. and Sculp.]; an abundance. (L. *cornu*, and *copia*, plenty.)
cornute, *a.* kawr-*newt*, with horns; horn-shaped: *v.t.* to bestow horns; to cuckold. (L. *cornutus*, horned.)
corn-violet, *n.* the purple bell-flower, *Campanula hybrida*.
corn-weevil, *n.* the granary weevil, *Calandra granaria*.
corny, *a. kawrn*-e, horny; resembling horn; producing, containing, or produced from corn.
corody, *n. ko*-ro-de, an obsolete allowance in kind to retainers, etc. for maintenance. (O.Fr. *conrei*, provision.)
corolla, *n.* ko-*rol*-la, the inner whorl of the flower, composed of the petals [Bot.]. (L., a little garland.)
corollaceous, *a.* ko-rol-*ay*-shus pertaining, to a corolla; enclosing and protecting like a wreath.
corollary, *n.* ko-*rol*-la-re, an inference from a preceding proposition. (L. *corollarium*, the amount paid for a garland.)
corollate, *a. ko*-rol-lat, like or having a corolla.
coroline, *a. ko*-rol-line, pertaining to a corolla.
corona, *n.* ko-*roh*-na, a large flat member of a cornice, usually of considerable projection, to carry off rain [Arch.]; a crowning part, esp. of a tooth [Anat.]; the circumference or margin of a radiated compound flower [Bot.]; a halo or luminous circle around the sun or moon; the sun's envelope outside the chromosphere [Astron.]; a form of luminous electrical discharge; a suspended circular chandelier for tapers, which are lighted on solemn occasions [Eccles.]. (L., a crown.)
coronach, *n. ko*-ro-nahkh, a lament for the dead, esp. for a chief; a dirge. (Ir.)
coronal, *a.* ko-*roh*-nal, belonging to the crown of the head: *n.* a circlet; a wreath; a garland. **coronal suture,** the first suture of the skull. (Fr.)
coronamen, *n.* ko-ro-*nay*-men, the coronet of a hoof.
coronary, *a. ko*-ron-a-re, resembling or pertaining to a crown; placed as a crown. **coronary arteries,** two arteries which spring from the aorta [Anat.]. **coronary vessels** and **ligaments,** those which spread round certain viscera and bones [Anat.]. (L. *coronarius.*)
coronated, *a. ko*-ro-*nay*-ted, having a crown or arranged crown-wise [Zool. and Bot.]; surmounted with a row of eminences like a crown [Malac.]. (L. *coronatus*, crowned.)
coronation, *n.* ko-ro-*nay*-shon, the solemnity of crowning a sovereign; the pomp or assembly attending a coronation. **coronation oath,** the oath taken by a sovereign at his coronation.
coroner, *n. ko*-ro-ner, an officer of the crown whose chief duty is to inquire, in the presence of a jury, into the cause of any death suspected to be due to some non-natural cause. (O.Fr. *coruner*, from L. *corona*, crown.)
coronet, *n. ko*-ro-net, a small or inferior crown worn, in less or more simple designs according to rank, by princes and peers on state occasions; an ornamental head-dress or part thereof; the hairy upper part of a horse's hoof. (Fr.)
coroneted, *a.* wearing or entitled to wear a coronet.
coronis, *n.* ko-*roh*-nis, the Greek sign (') of contraction or of crasis. (Gr.)
coronium, *n.* ko-*roh*-ne-um, a hypothetical element or form of an element in the solar atmosphere or corona. (L. *corona*, crown.)
coronoid, *a. ko*-ro-noyd, shaped like the beak of a crow [Anat.]. (Gr. *korone*, a crow, *eidos*, like.)
corozo-nut, *n.* ko-*roh*-zoh-nut, the nut of an American palm, *Phytelephas macrocarpa*, used by turners as vegetable ivory. (S. American name.)
corporal, *n. kawr*-po-ral, an army non-commissioned officer of a company, next below a sergeant. **ship's corporal,** a naval petty officer under the master-at-arms. (O.Fr.)
corporal, *a. kawr*-po-ral, relating to the body; material; not spiritual. **corporal punishment,** flogging, or any other chastisement of the body. (L. *corporalis*, of the body.)
corporal, *n. kawr*-po-ral, a fine linen cloth, used to cover the elements in the eucharist [Eccles.]. **corporal oath,** a solemn protestation, as with the hand on the corporal(e).
corporale, *n.* kawr-po-*ray*-le, a corporal [Eccles.].
corporality, *n.* kawr-po-*ral*-e-te, materiality.
corporally, *ad. kawr*-po-ra-le, bodily.
corporalship, *n.* a corporal's office.
corporas, *n. kawr*-po-ras, the corporale.
corporate, *a. kawr*-po-rat, united into a body, with the rights of an individual; collectively one; united. **corporate town,** a town possessing a corporation and full municipal rights. (L. *corporatus*, shaped into a body.)
corporately, *ad.* in a corporate capacity.
corporation, *n.* kawr-po-*ray*-shon, a body politic or corporate, authorized by law to act as an individual; an incorporated trading or financial company; a prominent stomach [Slang].
corporative, *a. kawr*-po-ra-tiv, pertaining to or consisting of a corporation. **Corporative State,** a dictatorship in which parliamentary representation is confined to its adherents, and is based on functional groups, not individual voters.
corporator, *n. kawr*-po-ra-tor, a member of a corporation.
corporeal, *a.* kor-*paw*-re-al, pertaining to the body; having a body; material; tangible. (L. *corporeus.*)
corporeality, *n.* kor-paw-re-*al*-e-te, the state of being corporeal; materiality.
corporealize, *v.t.* kor-*paw*-re-a-lize, to make corporeal.
corporeally, *ad.* in a corporeal manner.
corporeity, *n.* kor-po-*ree*-e-te, material existence; materiality of being.
corposant, *n. kor*-po-zant, seamen's name for a luminous electric phenomenon about the rigging and mastheads of a ship; St. Elmo's fire. (Sp. *cuerpo santo*, holy body.)
corps, *n.* kawr (*pl.* **corps,** kawrz), a body of troops; any division of an army; any trained group; **army corps,** one of the complete grand divisions of an army. **corps de ballet,** a company of ballet-dancers. **corps diplomatique,** the body of ambassadors, ministers, chargés d'affaires, etc., accredited to a court. (Fr.)
corpse, *n.* kawrps, a dead body, esp. of a human being. **corpse-candle,** a will-o-the-wisp; a tall candle placed beside a bier. **corpse-gate,** a lych-gate. (Fr. *corps.*)
corpulence, *n. kawr*-pew-lence, state of being corpulent; obesity.
corpulency, *n. kawr*-pew-len-se, corpulence.

corpulent, *a. kawr*-pew-lent, having a superfluity of flesh or fat.
corpulently, *ad.* in a corpulent manner.
corpus, *n. kawr*-pus, a body; a collection; a word of extensive use in anatomy, as *corpus callosum* (a callous body), *corpus cavernosum,* etc. **Corpus Christi,** a festival held on the first Thursday after Trinity Sunday in honour of the eucharist. (L.)
corpuscle, *n. kawr*-pusl, a minute physical body; a minute cell existing free in the blood. (L. *corpusculum,* a little body.)
corpuscular, *a.* kawr-*pus*-kew-lar, pertaining to, consisting of, or of the nature of corpuscles. **corpuscular forces,** forces which act on corpuscles, and determine the forms and relations of matter. **corpuscular philosophy,** the philosophy which resolves the universe into adjustments produced by the action of corpuscular forces; the atomic theory.
corpuscularian, *n.* kawr-*pus*-kew-*lare*-re-an, an adherent of the corpuscular philosophy: *a.* relating to corpuscles; atomic.
corral, *n.* ko-*rahl,* an enclosure to pen up cattle, or for defence: *v.t.* to arrange so as to form a corral; to drive into a corral. (Sp.)
correct, *a.* ko-*rekt,* conformable to truth or some standard; free from error; accurate: *v.t.* to make right; to remove faults or errors; to punish for faults or deviations from moral rectitude; to obviate by counteracting. (L. *correctus,* put right.)
correction, *n.* ko-*rek*-shon, the act of correcting; amendment; punishment; discipline; counteraction; critical notice; animadversion. **house of correction,** a house where disorderly persons are confined; a penitentiary or gaol. (Fr.)
correctional, *a.* intended to correct.
correctitude, *n.* ko-*rek*-te-tewd, correctness of behaviour; propriety.
corrective, *a.* ko-*rek*-tiv, having the power to correct; tending to rectify; *n.* that which is corrective; an antidote; restriction.
correctly, *ad.* ko-*rekt*-le, in a correct manner.
correctness, *n.* the state of being correct.
corrector, *n.* one who or that which corrects.
corregidor, *n.* ko-*rej*-e-dawr, a Spanish chief magistrate. (Sp.)
correlatable, *a.* ko-re-*late*-a-bl, capable of being correlated.
correlate, *n. ko*-re-late, he who or that which is mutually related, as father and son: *v.t.* to bring into mutual relation. (L. *con-,* and *relatus,* related.)
correlation, *n.* ko-re-*lay*-shon, reciprocal relation; mutual relationship of parts, functions, etc., of an organism [Biol.].
correlative, *a.* ko-*rel*-a-tiv, having a reciprocal relation: *n.* that which stands in a reciprocal relation to something else.
correlatively, *ad.* in a correlative relation.
correlativeness, *n.* state of being correlative.
correption, *n.* ko-*rep*-shon, a shortening in pronunciation. (L.)
correspond, *v.i.* ko-re-*spond,* to be congruous; to suit or agree; to hold intercourse by sending and receiving letters. (Fr. *correspondre.*)
correspondence, *n.* ko-re-*spon*-dence, relation; congruity; mutual adaptation of one thing to another; intercourse by means of letters; the letters which pass between correspondents. **correspondence school,** a school that coaches its students by means of written instructions, and corrections to their answers, sent through the post. (Fr. *correspondance.*)
correspondency, *n.* correspondence.
correspondent, *a.* ko-re-*spon*-dent, suitable; agreeing or congruous with: *n.* one with whom intercourse is kept up by letters or messages.
correspondently, *ad.* in a corresponding manner.
corresponding, *a.* suiting; communicating by correspondence.
corridor, *n. ko*-re-dawr, a passage way; a gallery giving access to the apartments of a building; a narrow strip of land connecting two countries or two parts of a country; the covered way encircling a place [Fort.]; the passage leading from one railway coach to another, giving access to the various compartments. (Fr.)
corrie, *n. ko*-re, a deep hollow in a hill enclosed by steep sides. (Gael. *coire.*)
corrigenda, *n.pl.* ko-re-*jen*-da (*sing.* **corrigendum**), corrections to be made, esp. in a book. (L.)
corrigent, *a. ko*-re-jent, corrective: *n.* a corrective [Med.]. (L. *corrigens,* correcting.)
corrigible, *a. ko*-re-je-bl, that may be corrected; reformable.
corrival, *n.* ko-*ry*-val, a co-rival.
corroborant, *a.* ko-*rob*-o-rant, giving or adding strength: *n.* a medicine that strengthens; a tonic.
corroborate, *v.t.* ko-*rob*-o-rate, to strengthen; to confirm; to make more certain. (L. *corroboratus,* strengthened.)
corroboration, *n.* ko-*rob*-o-*ray*-shon, the act of strengthening or confirming; confirmation.
corroborative, *a.* ko-*rob*-o-ra-tiv, tending to confirm: *n.* a corroborant.
corroborator, *n.* ko-*rob*-o-ray-tor, one who corroborates.
corroboratory, *a.* ko-*rob*-o-ra-to-re, tending to corroborate; confirmatory.
corroboree, *n.* ko-*rob*-o-ree, a nocturnal convention and dance of the aboriginal Australians. (Native name.)
corrode, *v.t.* ko-*rode,* to wear away or destroy by degrees; to consume gradually: *v.i.* to become corroded; to rot. (L. *corrodo,* gnaw away.)
corrodent, *a.* ko-*roh*-dent, causing corrosion: *n.* any substance or medicine that corrodes.
corrodible, *a.* ko-*roh*-de-bl, corrosible.
corrody, *n. ko*-ro-de, corody.
corrosibility, *n.* ko-*roh*-ze-*bil*-e-te, the quality of being corrodible.
corrosible, *a.* ko-*roh*-ze-bl, that may be corroded.
corrosion, *n.* ko-*roh*-zhon, the action of eating or wearing away by slow degrees; a corroded state. (L. *corrosus,* gnawed away.)
corrosive, *a.* ko-*roh*-siv, having the power of corroding: *n.* that which has the quality of corroding. **corrosive sublimate,** bichloride of mercury, a virulent poison and powerful antiseptic.
corrosively, *ad.* in a corrosive manner.
corrosiveness, *n.* the quality of corroding.
corrugate, *a. ko*-ru-gate, wrinkled: *v.t.* to bend or contract into folds or wrinkles: *v.i.* to become wrinkled. (L. *corrugatus,* wrinkled.)
corrugated, *a. ko*-ru-gay-ted, formed into folds; furrowed; wrinkled. **corrugated iron,** sheet-iron, usually galvanized, which has been bent into parallel grooves and ridges.
corrugation, *n.* ko-ru-*gay*-shon, the act of corrugating; corrugated state; a fold or wrinkle.
corrugator, *n. ko*-ru-gay-tor, a muscle which contracts the skin (esp. of the brow) into wrinkles.
corrupt, *a.* ko-*rupt,* changed from a sound to a putrid state; vitiated; depraved; debased; rendered impure; open to or perverted by bribery; not genuine; infected with errors or mistakes: *v.i.* to become corrupt: *v.t.* to change from a sound to an unsound or putrescent state; to vitiate or deprave; to defile; to pervert or vitiate integrity; to bribe; to debase or render impure. (L. *corruptus,* corrupted.)
corrupter, *n.* one who or that which corrupts.
corruptibility, *n.* ko-*rup*-te-*bil*-e-te, the possibility of being corrupted.
corruptible, *a.* ko-*rup*-te-bl, susceptible of or liable to corruption; mortal.
corruptibleness, *n.* corruptibility.
corruptibly, *ad.* in a manner to be corrupted.
corruption, *n.* ko-*rup*-shon, the act of corrupting or state of being corrupt; the dissolution or disintegration of bodies in the process of putrefaction; putrid matter; deterioration; a debased or impure state; bribery; a taint in the blood as a consequence of an act of attainder [Law].
corruptive, *a.* ko-*rup*-tiv, having the quality of corrupting, tainting, or vitiating.
corruptless, *a.* not susceptible of corruption or decay.
corruptly, *ad.* in a corrupt manner.
corruptness, *n.* the state of being corrupt.
corsac, *n. kawr*-sak, a small fox, *Vulpes corsac,* of Far Eastern Russia.
corsage, *n. kawr*-saj, a body of a dress. (Fr.)
corsair, *n. kawr*-sare, a pirate; one who ranges about for plunder; the vessel of a pirate. (Fr. *corsaire.*)
corse, *n.* kawrse, a corpse. (O.Fr. *cors.*)
corset, *n. kawr*-set, a close-fitting stiffened garment

worn to give shape to the body ; a bodice : *v.t.* to enclose in corsets. (Fr.)
orsetry, *n. kawr*-set-re, the craft of making or fitting corsets ; corsets and similar garments collectively.
Corsican, *a. kawr*-se-kan, pertaining to Corsica : *n.* a native of Corsica ; the Italian dialect spoken in Corsica. **the Corsican,** a sobriquet for Napoleon.
orsite, *n. kawr*-site, an orbicular variety of diorite found in Corsica ; napoleonite.
orslet, *n. kawrs*-let, light sleeveless armour to protect the body [Antiq.] ; the thorax [Entom.]. (Fr.)
orsned, *n. kawrse*-ned, an ordeal in early English times which consisted in the swallowing of consecrated bread by the accused ; if it stuck in his throat, he was deemed guilty. (A.S.)
ortège, *n.* kawr-*tayzh*, a train of attendants ; a procession. (Fr. from It. *corte*, court.)
ortes, *n.pl. kawr*-tez, the assembly of the states of the kingdom of Spain or Portugal. (Sp. courts.)
ortex, *n. kawr*-teks (*pl.* **cortices**), the outer bark of a tree ; a covering having some resemblance to bark [Anat. and Zool.] (L.)
cortical, *a. kawr*-te-kal, pertaining to, consisting of, or resembling bark ; pertaining to the exterior [Bot. and Zool.]. **cortical substance,** the exterior of the brain and kidneys.
corticate, *a. kawr*-te-kat, resembling the bark of a tree ; covered with bark. (L. *corticatus.*)
orticiferous, *a. kawr*-te-*sif*-er-us, producing bark or that which resembles it. (L. *cortex*, and *fero*, bear.)
orticiform, *a.* kawr-*tis*-se-fawrm, resembling bark.
orticin, *n. kor*-te-sin, a yellowish alkaloid obtained from the bark of the aspen.
orticolous, *a.* kor-te-*koh*-lus, growing on the surface of bark.
corticose, *a. kawr*-te-kose, corticate ; full of bark.
corticous, *a. kawr*-te-kus, corticate.
cortile, *n.* kor-*teel*-ay, the open internal court of a building. (It.)
corundum, *n.* ko-*run*-dum, native oxide of aluminium, a mineral of extreme hardness, which when opaque and impure is **emery** ; when colourless, **lux sapphire** ; when red, **ruby** ; when blue, **sapphire** ; when yellow, **oriental topaz** ; when green, **oriental emerald** ; when purple, **oriental amethyst.** (Hind.)
coruscant, *a.* ko-*rus*-kant, flashing. (L. *coruscans.*)
coruscate, *v.i. ko*-rus-kate, to throw off flashes of light ; to sparkle.
coruscation, *n.* ko-rus-*kay*-shon, a sudden flash of light ; intellectual brilliancy.
orvée, *n.* kor-*vay*, obligation to render certain services, as the repairing of roads, to a lord superior ; forced labour [Feudal Law]. (Fr.)
orvette, *n.* kor-*vet*, a flush-decked full-rigged warship of less than 21 guns ; an auxiliary armed vessel of modern navies. (Fr.)
corvine, *a. kor*-vine, pertaining to the crow family.
corvus, *n. kor*-vus, the crow ; a genus of birds, including the raven, the carrion-crow, the jackdaw, and the rook ; a military engine used by the Romans for grappling and boarding ships, etc. [Antiq.]. (L.)
corybantic, *a.* ko-re-*ban*-tik, wildly agitated ; inflamed like the Corybantes, the frenzied priests of Cybele.
Corydon, *n. ko*-re-don, the typical rustic of pastoral poetry. (L.)
Corylus, *n. ko*-re-lus, a genus of shrubs including the hazel. (L.)
corymb, *n. ko*-rimb, a raceme or panicle, in which the stalks of the lower flowers are longer than those of the upper so that they rise to the same level [Bot.]. (Gr. *korymbos*, the top, from *korys*, a helmet.)
corymbiated, *a.* ko-*rim*-be-ay-ted, garnished with berries or blossoms in the form of corymbs.
corymbiferous, *a.* ko-rim-*bif*-er-us, bearing flowers, fruit, or berries in corymbs.
corymbose, *a.* ko-*rim*-bose, like, or pertaining to, a corymb ; borne in a corymb.
corymbous, *a.* ko-*rim*-bus, corymbose.
coryphæus, *n.* ko-re-*fee*-us, the chief of a chorus ; a chief or leader. (Gr. *koruphaios.*)
coryphee, *n.* koh-re-*fay*, a principal female ballet dancer. (Fr., from Gr. *koruphaios*, leader.)
coryphene, *n. ko*-re-feen, a swift-darting, metallic lustrous fish, with the dorsal fin extending along the whole back, *Coryphæna hippuris*, the dolphin. (Gr. *korys*, a helmet, and *phaino*, show.)
coryza, *n.* ko-*ry*-za, inflammation of the mucous membrane of the nose ; a cold in the head. **allergic coryza,** hay-fever. (Gr.)
cos, *n.* koss, a curly variety of lettuce originally grown in Cos (now Stauko) in the Ægean. (Gr.)
cosaque, *n.* kos-*sahk*, a bonbon ; a small sweet placed in crackers. (Fr.)
cose, *v.i.* koze, to make oneself cosy [Coll.].
cosecant, *n.* ko-*see*-kant, the secant of the complement of an arc or angle [Geom.].
coseismal, *n.* ko-*size*-mal, the line along which an earthquake is simultaneously felt : *a.* pertaining to such line, or to points upon it. (*Co-* and Gr. *seismos.*)
coseismic, *a.* ko-*size*-mik, coseismal.
cosh, *n.* kosh, a short, loaded bludgeon ; a life-preserver : *v.t.* to strike with this. [Slang].
cosher, *v.t. kosh*-er, to levy coshering ; to cosset ; to pamper or treat indulgently.
coshering, *n. kosh*-er-ing, a right to bed and board for himself and retainers formerly claimed by Irish chiefs from their tenants.
co-signatory, *n.* koh-*sig*-na-to-re, one who signs jointly with others : *a.* signing jointly.
cosily, *ad. koh*-ze-le, snugly ; comfortably.
cosine, *n. koh*-sine, the sine of the complement of an arc or angle [Geom.].
cosiness, *n. koh*-ze-ness, the condition of being comfortable or cosy.
cosmetic, *a.* koz-*met*-ik, beautifying ; improving the beauty of the skin or hair : *n.* any external application that renders the skin soft, pure, and white, or helps to improve the complexion. (Gr. *kosmetikos*, clever in beautifying.)
cosmic, *a. koz*-mik, relating to or holding of the order of the universe, or the world as a part of it ; co-extensive with a period in the history of the world ; vast in extent or duration ; pertaining to cosmism. (Gr. *kosmikos*, from *kosmos*, world.)
cosmical, *a. koz*-me-kal, cosmic ; rising or setting with the sun [Astron.] ; occurring near sunrise.
cosmically, *ad.* with the sun at rising or setting.
cosmism, *n. koz*-mizm, a philosophy of things which is based on the doctrine of evolution.
cosmogonic, *a.* koz-mo-*gon*-ik, relating to cosmogony.
cosmogonist, *n.* koz-*mog*-on-ist, one versed in cosmogony.
cosmogony, *n.* kos-*mog*-on-e, a theory respecting the origin of the universe ; a treatise or dissertation on such. (Gr. *kosmogonia.*)
cosmographer, *n.* koz-*mog*-ra-fer, one versed in cosmography.
cosmographical, *a.* koz-mo-*graf*-e-kal, pertaining to cosmography.
cosmography, *n.* koz-*mog*-ra-fe, a description of the world or universe. (Gr. *kosmographos*, writing about the world.)
cosmological, *a.* koz-mo-*loj*-e-kal, pertaining to cosmology.
cosmologist, *n.* one versed in cosmology.
cosmology, *n.* koz-*mol*-o-je, the science treating of the laws of the universe ; a treatise relating to the structure, motion, and constituent parts of the universe ; the branch of metaphysics dealing with this [Phil.]. (Gr. *kosmos*, and *logos*, science.)
cosmopolis, *n.* koz-*mop*-o-lis, any great cosmopolitan centre.
cosmopolitan, *a.* koz-mo-*pol*-e-tan, without national or local prejudices ; common to the whole world : *n.* a cosmopolite.
cosmopolitanism, *n.* koz-mo-*pol*-e-ta-nizm, citizenship of the world ; cosmopolitism.
cosmopolite, *n.* koz-*mop*-o-lite, a citizen of the world ; one who is at home everywhere. (Gr. *kosmos*, and *polis*, a city.)
cosmopolitism, *n.* koz-*mop*-ol-e-tizm, superiority to mere local or national prejudice.
cosmorama, *n.* koz-mo-*rah*-ma, an exhibition of a series of views of different parts of the world, so arranged as to produce the effects of actual vision. (Gr. *kosmos*, and *horama*, a view.)
cosmoramic, *a.* koz-mo-*ram*-ik, pertaining to a cosmorama.
cosmos, *n. koz*-mos, the universe ; an ordered system ; order (as opposed to chaos). (Gr.)

Cosmos, *n. koz*-mos, a genus of tropical American plants with ornamental flowers. (Gr., beautiful.)
cosmosphere, *n. koz*-mo-sfeer, an apparatus for showing the relative position of the earth and fixed stars at any given time. (Gr. *kosmos*, and *sphere*.)
cosmotheism, *n.* koz-mo-*thee*-izm, identification of the Deity with the whole of creation; pantheism. (Gr. *kosmos*, and *theos*, god.)
coss, *n.* koss, a Hindu measure of length, varying in different parts from about 2,200 to 4,400 yds.
cossack, *n. kos*-sak, one of a warlike race of mixed Russo-Turkish origin, skilful as horsemen, inhabiting the south-eastern steppes of Russia. **cossack post,** a small military outpost of mounted men. (Russ.)
cosset, *n. kos*-set, a pet lamb; a pet: *v.t.* to pet; to fondle; to pamper. (A.S. *cot-sæta*, a cottager.)
cost, *n.* kost, the price charged or paid for a thing; expense; loss; detriment; pain; suffering: *pl.* the sums allowed by the court for charges of a suit awarded against the party losing: *v.t.* to be bought for; to require to be expended. **cost of living,** *see* **living. cost price,** the price paid by the seller, or by the retailer to the wholesaler; prime cost. **prime cost,** the cost of production. (O.Fr. *coster*.)
costal, *a. kos*-tal, pertaining to the side of the body or the ribs of mammals, to a wing-margin of insects, or to the midrib of a leaf. (L. *costa*, a rib.)
costard, *n. kos*-tard, an apple, round and bulky like the head; the head [Slang]. (L. *costatus*, ribbed.)
costate, *a. kos*-tate, ribbed [Bot. and Zool.].
costean, *v.i.* kos-*teen*, to dig shafts to expose and show the course of a tin outcrop (Cornish).
coster, *n. kos*-ter, a costermonger.
costermonger, *n. kos*-ter-*mung*-ger, a street hawker, esp. of green-grocery, fish, etc., from a barrow. (*Costard* and *monger*.)
costing, *n. kos*-ting, the costs of producing articles; estimation of the cost of making a thing, of a process used in industry, etc.
costive, *a. kos*-tiv, having the excrements obstructed or the motion of the bowels too slow; constipated. (O.Fr. *costeve*, constipated.)
costiveness, *n. kos*-tiv-ness, state of being costive.
costliness, *n. kost*-le-ness, quality of being costly.
costly, *a. kost*-le, of a high price; expensive; sumptuous.
costmary, *n. kost*-ma-re, an aromatic plant of the aster family; tansy.
costrel, *n. kost*-rel, a large flask of wood, leather, or earthenware slung from the waist.
costume, *n. kos*-tewm, dress; accustomed mode of dress; a complete dress suitable in all details to character, time, and place [Art]; stage clothes; fancy dress. (Fr.)
costumer, *n.* kos-*tew*-mer, one who deals in costumes for fancy dress balls; a costumier.
costumier, *n.* kos-*tew*-me-er, one who makes, sells, or hires out costumes; a dressmaker.
cosy, *a. koh*-ze, snug or comfortable: *n.* a teapot cover; a seat or nook for two.
cot, *n.* kot, a small bed or crib; a child's bed; a bed in a military hospital; a hammock. (Hind. *khăt*, couch.)
cot, *n.* kot, a cottage or small house; a hut; a sheepfold. (A.S. *cote*, den.)
cotangent, *n.* koh-*tan*-jent, the tangent of the complement of an arc or angle [Geom.].
cote, *n.* kote, a cot; a sheepfold. (A.S.)
coteline, *n.* kot-e-*leen*, a white muslin fabric, usually corded. (Fr. *côte*, a rib.)
co-tenant, *n.* koh-*ten*-ant, a tenant in common.
coterie, *n. koh*-te-re, a circle of people on a familiar footing for social or other intercourse; a clique; a social circle. (Fr., joint tenancy in land.)
coterminous, *a.* koh-*ter*-min-us, conterminous; with a similar distribution [Zool.].
cothurnate, *a.* ko-*thur*-nate, buskined; relating to tragedy. (L. *cothurnus*, a buskin.)
cothurnus, *n.* ko-*thur*-nus, the buskin worn by Greek and Roman actors in tragic parts; tragedy; the tragic vein. (L., a buskin.)
cotidal, *a.* koh-*tide*-al, indicating an equal tide-level in different places at the same time.
cotillion, *n.* ko-*til*-yon, a round dance by eight persons; music for this. (Fr. *cotillon*, a petticoat.)
Cotinga, *n.* ko-*ting*-ga, a genus of South American birds known as chatterers.
cotise, *n. kot*-is, a bendlet reduced one-half, and borne on each side of the bend [Her.]. (Fr.)
cotland, *n. kot*-land, land appendant to a cottage.
Cotoneaster, *n.* ko-*toh*-ne-*as*-ter, a widely distributed genus of hardy ornamental trees and shrubs of the apple family.
cotquean, *n. kot*-kween, a man who busies himself with women's affairs. (*Cot*, hut, and *quean*.)
co-trustee, *n. koh*-trus-*tee*, a joint trustee.
cotswold, *n. kots*-wohld, a breed of long-wooled sheep bred on the Cotswold Hills, Gloucestershire.
cotta, *n. kot*-ta, a short surplice. (Late L.)
cottage, *n. kot*-taj, a cot; a hut; a small but neat and tasteful dwelling. **cottage hospital,** a small hospital for local service, usually with no resident doctor. **cottage loaf,** a loaf of bread in two rounded portions, the smaller above the larger. **cottage piano,** an upright piano for use in a small room.
cottager, *n. kot*-ta-jer, one who lives in a hut or cottage; a cottar.
cottar, *n. kot*-tar, one who lives on a common without paying any rent or having land of his own [Law]; a peasant, esp. in Scotland, paying his rent by his labour; a cottier. (L. *cottarius*.)
cotter, *n. kot*-ter, a cottager; a cottar.
cotter, *n. kot*-ter, a pin or thin wedge driven through a slot in the end of a bar to prevent its withdrawal.
cottier, *n. kot*-te-er, a peasant holding cot and land on a special tenancy arrangement.
cottoid, *a. kot*-oyd, pertaining to the fishes of the genus *Cottus*.
★**cotton,** *n. kot*-ton, a soft downy substance resembling fine wool, growing in the capsules of the cotton-plant; cloth made of cotton: *a.* made or consisting of cotton: *v.i.* to rise with a nap; to harmonize. **to cotton on to,** to take to; to be attracted by [Slang]. (Fr. *coton*.)
cotton-cake, *n.* the residue of cotton-seed after extraction of the oil, used as a cattle-food and fertilizer.
cotton-gin, *n. kot*-ton-jin, a machine for separating the seeds from cotton.
cotton-grass, *n.* a species of sedge of the genus *Eriophorum*, with long downy tufts.
cottonocracy, *n. kot*-to-*nok*-ra-se, the economic and political power of the cotton industry and its proprietors.
cotton-press, *n.* a press in which cotton is compressed into bales.
cotton-seed, *n.* the seed of the cotton-plant yielding a valuable oil and cotton-cake.
cottontail, *n. kot*-ton-tale, the common name in America for various species of rabbit.
cotton-waste, *n.* refuse from cotton-mills used by engineers, etc., for wiping.
cotton-weed, *n.* the cudweed.
cotton-wood, *n.* a name for various American species of poplar.
cotton-wool, *n. kot*-ton-*wool*, raw cotton used as wadding and for surgical and medical purposes.
cotton-worm, *n. kot*-ton-wurm, the larva of the owlet moth, *Aletia xylina*.
cottony, *a. kot*-to-ne, downy; nappy; soft like cotton.
cotyle, *n. kot*-e-lee, the cavity of a bone which receives the end of another in articulation [Anat.]; a cup-like organ or cavity. (Gr. *kotule*, a drinking vessel.)
Cotyledon, *n.* kot-e-*lee*-don, a genus of plants of several species including navel-wort; (*l.c.*) a lobe within the embryo of a seed, containing nourishment for the young plant during germination; a cup-shaped vascular body, adhering to the chorion of some animals [Anat.]. (Gr. *kotuledon*, a cup-shaped hollow.)
cotyledonal, *a.* in the form of a seed-leaf.
cotyledonous, *a.* pertaining to cotyledons; having a seed-leaf.
cotyliform, *a.* ko-*til*-e-fawrm, like a cotyle.
cotyloid, *a. kot*-e-loyd, cup-shaped, esp. of the socket of the hip-bone [Anat.]. (Gr. *kotule*, and *eiodos*, like.)
coucal, *n. koo*-kal, a ground-cuckoo of Africa and S. Asia of the genus *Centropus*.
couch, *n.* kouch, a sofa; a bed; a place for rest or sleep; a layer or stratum; a preliminary coat

of colour, size, etc., on the surface to be painted [Painting]; to spread (barley) on the floor to germinate [Malting]: *v.i.* to lie down, as on a bed or place of repose; to stoop and recline on the knees, as a beast; to lie in secret or in ambush; to lie in a stratum; to stoop; to bend in reverence: *v.t.* to lay down on a bed or place of rest; to spread on a bed or floor; to lay close; to hide; to express in obscure terms; to fix, as a spear in rest; to remove cataract in the eye. (Fr. *coucher.*)

couchant, *a. kouch*-ant, lying down with the head raised [Her.]. (Fr.)

couchee, *n. koosh*-ay, an evening reception. (Fr.)

couch-grass, *n. kouch*-grahs, the creeping, rapidly spreading, weed grass, *Agropyrum repens*; quitch.

couching, *n. kouch*-ing, the act of stooping; the removing of cataract; the spreading of malt to dry; in needlework, the laying down of one or more threads held by single stitches placed at intervals across them.

cougar, *n. koo*-gar, the puma. (Native name.)

***cough,** *n.* kof *or* kawf, a noisy convulsive effort of the throat due to irritation of the breathing organs or the presence of foreign matter: *v.i.* to make such an effort: *v.t.* to expectorate by coughing. (Imit.)

cough-drop, *n.* a medicated lozenge sucked to ease a cough.

cough-mixture, *n.* a medicinal liquid preparation for the alleviation of coughing.

could, kood, *p.* of can.

coulée, *n.* koo-*lay*, a ravine with sloping sides; a stream or sheet of lava [Geol.]. (Fr.)

couleur-de-rose, *n.* koo-*ler*-de-*roze*, a rose colour; an aspect of beauty and attractiveness. (Fr.)

coulisse, *n.* koo-*lees*, a grooved timber forming a slide, as for a sluice-gate or side-scene [Theatre]; a side-scene: *pl.* the space between the side-scenes. (Fr., a groove.)

couloir, *n.* kool-*wahr*, a mud-dredge; a deep gorge or cleft in a mountain. (Fr.)

coulomb, *n.* koo-*lom*, the unit of electrical quantity; the quantity of electricity developed by a current of one ampere in one second. (C. A. de *Coulomb*, Fr. physicist, *d.* 1806.)

coulter, *n. kole*-ter, the fore iron of a plough which cuts the sod in advance of the share. (A.S. *culter*, knife.)

coumara-nut, *n.* koo-*mah*-ra-nut, the tonka-bean. (Brazilian *cumaru.*)

coumarin, *n. koo*-ma-rin, a substance with the perfume of new-mown hay obtained from the tonka-bean, the woodruff, and other plants.

coumarone, *n.* koo-*ma*-rohn, a heavy oil obtained indirectly from coumarin and forming a chief constituent of certain synthetic resins.

council, *n. koun*-sil, an assembly convened for consulation, deliberation, and advice; a body of advisers to a sovereign or chief magistrate in the administration of the government; an assembly of prelates and doctors, convened for regulating matters of doctrine and discipline in the Church; the administrative body of a local government unit; the governing or deliberative body of some Universities. **council school,** a school under the management of a county, borough, or urban district council. **Common Council** of a city, the body of representatives of the citizens. **Œcumenical Council,** an assembly of prelates and doctors, representing the whole Church. **Privy Council,** a select council for advising a sovereign in the administration of the government. (Fr. *concile*, from L. *concilium*, an assembly, from *con-*, and *calo*, call.)

council-board, *n.* the table round which a council sits; the council itself.

council-chamber, *n.* the room in which the members of a council meet to transact business.

councillor, *n. koun*-si-lor, the member of a council.

councilman, *n. koun*-sil-man, a member of a Common Council.

counsel, *n. koun*-sel, advice; consultation; deliberation, or opinion given following this; design; purpose; a barrister; an advocate or body of advocates: *v.t.* to give advice to; to advise. **King's** (or **Queen's**) **Counsel,** a barrister called within the bar by letters patent giving him preference in all the courts and the right to wear silk. (Fr. *conseiller.*)

counsellor, *n. koun*-se-lor, one who gives counsel one whose profession is to give advice in law and manage causes for clients; the law-officer of an embassy or legation.

counsellorship, *n.* the office of a counsellor.

count, *n.* kount, the act of numbering; the number counted; a particular charge in an indictment, or narration in pleading, setting forth the cause of complaint [Law]: *v.i.* to be reckoned in and added on; to found an account or scheme on; to rely: *v.t.* to number or sum up; to reckon; to place to an account; to esteem; to consider. **to count out,** to adjourn a meeting after finding that there is not a quorum. (Fr. *compter*, from L. *con-*, and *puto*, reckon.)

count, *n.* kount, a continental title of nobility equivalent to the English earl. **count palatine,** a former high judicial officer of the Holy Roman Empire: in England, the proprietor of a county palatine. (O.Fr. *conte*, from L. *comes*, a companion.)

countable, *a. kount*-ab-l, that may be numbered.

countenance, *n. koun*-ten-ance, the face, visage, look, aspect, or expression of the face; favour; patronage; encouragement: *v.t.* to favour; to encourage. **in countenance,** in favour; assured; confident. **out of countenance,** confounded; abashed. **to keep countenance,** to preserve composure; to appear unruffled. **to put out of countenance,** to shame; to abash. (Fr. *contenance.*)

counter, *n. kount*-er, an article used as means of reckoning; a substitute for a coin used in games; a table or board on which money is counted or goods laid; one who or that which counts, esp. [Eng.] an instrument for recording the number of revolutions or operations performed. (O.Fr. *conteour.*)

counter, *n. kount*-er, an opposite or contrary; the curved part of the stern of a ship; an under part serving as contrast to the principal parts; that part of a horse between the shoulder and under the neck; a parry in fencing; a blow given to an opponent who is about to strike [Boxing]; the part of a boot or shoe round the heel: *a.* opposite; contrary; in opposition; contrariwise. (Fr. *contre*, from L. *contra-*, against.)

counter-, *kount*-er, prefix, expressing opposition.

counter, *v.t. kount*-er, to oppose: *v.i.* to meet in opposition; to engage; to return a blow while guarding one [Boxing].

counteract, *v.t.* kount-er-*akt*, to act in opposition to; to hinder; to defeat; to neutralize.

counteraction, *n.* contrary action; hindrance.

counteractive, *a.* opposing; tending to counteract; *n.* one who or that which counteracts.

counter-agent, *n.* that which counteracts.

counter-approach, *n.* a series of defences thrown up in front of a besieged place [Fort.].

counter-attack, *n.* an attack made in opposition to an attack.

counterbalance, *n. kount*-er-*bal*-ance, equal weight, power or agency acting in opposition to anything: *v.t.* to weigh against with an equal weight or power.

counterblast, *n. kount*-er-blahst, anything done or written in opposition to anything else.

counter-brace, *n.* the lee brace of the fore-topsail yard: *v.t.* to brace in contrary directions [Naut.].

counterchange, *n.* exchange; reciprocation: *v.t.* to give and receive, or to cause to change places.

countercharge, *n.* a charge in opposition; a set-off: *v.t.* to make a countercharge; to charge (charging troops) in opposition.

countercheck, *n.* a second check; a censure to check a reprover: *v.t.* to check against.

counterclaim, *n.* a set-off; a claim made by a defendant against a plaintiff [Law]: *v.t.* to submit such a claim.

counter-clockwise, *ad.* and *a.* in the reverse direction to the movement of the hands of a clock.

counter-current, *n.* a current running in a contrary direction to another current.

counter-die, *n.* the upper stamp of a die.

counterdrain, *n. kount*-er-drane, a drain parallel to a watercourse for collecting the leakage water.

counter-ermine, *n.* like ermine, but with black with white counterchanged [Her.].

counter-espionage, *n.* the employment, or the acts, of spies against the spies of the enemy.

counter-evidence, *n.* evidence opposing other evidence.
counterfeit, *a.* *kount*-er-feet, forged; made in imitation, with a view to being passed as genuine; not genuine; having the resemblance of: *n.* one who pretends to be what he is not; an imitation: *v.i.* to feign; to dissemble; to carry on a deception: *v.t.* to forge; to copy or imitate without authority or right, and palm off as genuine; to imitate. (O.Fr. *contrefait.*)
counterfeiter, *n.* a forger; one who imitates.
counterflory, *a.* *kount*-er-*flaw*-re, flory on opposite sides [Her.].
counterfoil, *n.* *kount*-er-foyl, a counter-tally, esp. in the former court of exchequer; the counterpart of a document given, retained in the hands of the giver; the stub or counterpart of a cheque retained by its drawer.
counterforce, *n.* a counteracting force.
counterfort, *n.* a buttress built at right angles to a wall or terrace, to prevent it bulging.
counter-gauge, *n.* an adjustable gauge for transferring measurements from one timber to another [Carp.].
counter-glow, *n.* gegenschein [Astron.].
counter-irritant, *n.* a medicament employed to produce counter-irritation [Med.].
counter-irritation, *n.* production of an irritation in order to relieve one elsewhere.
counter-jumper, *n.* a shop-assistant [Coll.].
countermand, *n.* kount-er-*mahnd*, revocation of a former command: *v.t.* to revoke or to give an order contrary to one before given; to reverse; to annul. (Fr. *contremander.*)
countermarch, *n.* *kount*-er-march, a marching back; a change of the wings or face of a battalion, so as to bring the right to the left, or the front into the rear [Mil.]; a change of measures or conduct: *v.i.* to march back again.
countermark, *n.* *kount*-er-mark, an additional identification mark, esp. on goods belonging to several owners; the mark of the Goldsmiths' Company to show the quality of the metal; a mark added to a metal long after it has been struck, by which the change in its value may be known: *v.t.* to add a countermark.
countermine, *n.* *kount*-er-mine, a gallery running underground in search of the enemy's mine, or till it meets it, to defeat its effect [Mil.]; a stratagem or project to frustrate any contrivance: *v.t.* to mine a mine; to oppose by a countermine: *v.i.* to make or place countermines.
countermove, *n.* a move in reply.
countermure, *n.* *kount*-er-mewr, a wall raised behind another to supply its place when a breach is made; a reserve defence. (L. *murus*, a wall.)
counter-offensive, *n.* an offensive undertaken by a force that has hitherto been acting on the defensive [Mil.].
counterpane, *n.* *kount*-er-pane, a coverlet for a bed; a quilt. (O.Fr. *contrepoincte.*)
counterpart, *n.* the correspondent part; a counterfoil; a copy; a duplicate; the part which fits another, as the key to a cipher; the complementary part; a part to accompany another [Mus.].
counterplea, *n.* a reply to a plea or request [Law].
counterplot, *n.* a plot opposed to another: *v.t.* and *i.* to oppose plot to plot in order to frustrate.
counterpoint, *n.* *kount*-er-poynt, the art of harmonious composition; the setting of a harmony of one or more parts to a melody, originally by point opposite point [Mus.]. (Fr. *contrepoint.*)
counterpoise, *n.* *kount*-er-poyz, a weight or force sufficient to balance another; equilibrium; a position of the rider in which his body is duly balanced in his seat [Man.]: *v.t.* to weigh against with equal weight; to act against with equal power or effect.
counter-proof, *n.* *kount*-er-proof, a reversed impression taken from a proof newly printed for comparison with the plate [Engraving].
counter-prove, *v.t.* to take a counter-proof of.
Counter-Reformation, *n.* a reformation produced in opposition to another; the Roman Catholic movement which came after, and was the result of, the Protestant Reformation.
counter-revolution, *n.* a revolution having the object of reversing another and restoring things as they were.
counterscarp, *n.* the outer slope of a ditch opposite the scarp [Fort.]. (Fr. *contrescarpe.*)
counter-security, *n.* a security given to one who has become security for another.
counter-shaft, *n.* *kount*-er-shaft, an intermediate shaft propelled by the chief shaft of a machine.
countersign, *n.* *kount*-er-sine, a private sign given to soldiers on guard, members of a secret society, etc.; a pass-word: *v.t.* to attest by counter-signature; to sanction.
counter-signature, *n.* *kount*-er-*sig*-na-tewr, an additional or corroborating signature, esp. that of a secretary or subordinate officer.
countersink, *n.* kount-er-*sink*, a drill for countersinking; the depression so made: *v.t.* to drill a conical depression in wood or metal, as at the top of a hole for the head of the screw.
counter-tally, *n.* a tally corresponding to another.
counter-tenor, *n.* one of the middle parts between the tenor and the treble; high tenor; alto [Mus.]. (It. *contratenore*).
countervail, *v.t.* kount-er-*vayl*, to act against with equal effect; to equal; to compensate: *v.i.* to counterbalance. (O.Fr. *contrevaloir.*)
countervailing, *a.* equalizing; counterbalancing. **countervailing duty,** *n.* a duty placed on imports to equalize the price of home goods.
countervallation, *n.* *koun*-ter-val-*lay*-shon, a chain of redoubts; a contravallation.
counter-vote, *v.t.* to vote against; to outvote.
counterweight, *n.* *kount*-er-wate, a counterbalancing weight.
countess, *n.* *kount*-ess, the wife or widow of an earl or count; a woman holding this rank in her own right; a slate measuring 20 inches by 10 inches. (Fr. *comtesse.*)
counting-house, *n.* the department appropriated to the keeping of business books, accounts, letters, and papers; the office.
countless, *a.* that cannot be counted.
count-out, *n.* *kount*-out, the end of a debate when it is found by counting that there are not enough members present to form a quorum.
countrified, *a.* *kun*-tre-fide, of rustic or rural appearance; with rustic manners; uncouth.
★**country,** *n.* *kun*-tre, a territory; its inhabitants; one's own land; the rural part as distinct from the city; a dwelling-place; the outfield at cricket [Slang]: *a.* pertaining to the country; rural; rustic; peculiar to one's own country. (O.Fr. *contree.*)
country-dance, *n.* *kun*-tre-danhce, a dance in which the partners are arranged opposite to each other in lines; a contra-dance.
countryman, *n.* *kun*-tre-man, one born in the same country with another; one who dwells in the country; a rustic; a husbandman; an inhabitant or native of a region.
country-seat, *n.* *kun*-tre-*seet*, the mansion in the country of a family having one in town.
countryside, *n.* *kun*-tre-side, a rural district with its inhabitants, fauna, and flora.
countrywoman, *n.* a female countryman.
count-wheel, *n.* *kount*-wheel, the wheel in a clock which causes it to strike the hours correctly.
county, *n.* *kount*-e, formerly the district ruled by a count; now a large territorial unit for administrative and certain other purposes; a shire. **county borough,** a borough that, under the Local Government Act, 1888, has the status of an administrative county. **county college,** an institution for further education maintained by a local education authority. **county corporate,** a city and borough enjoying most or all of the privileges of a county borough, but by favour of a royal charter or immemorial custom. **county council,** a body elected by the ratepayers of a county for the administration of county affairs. **county court,** a court whose jurisdiction was limited to a county; a local tribunal for the recovery of small debts and other legal business. **county palatine,** a county formerly invested with regal privileges, as those of Durham, Chester, and Lancaster. **county school** a school under the control of a county council. **county town,** the administrative centre of the county. (Fr. *comté*, the district administered by a *comte.*)
county-court, *v.t.* to sue in a county court [Coll.].
coup, *n.* koo, a stroke or sudden blow; a successfu

stroke. **coup d'état,** a sudden change effected in the body politic by unconstitutional or extraneous means. **coup de grace,** the finishing blow. **coup de main,** a sudden blow or assault. **coup d'œil,** a general appreciation of a situation or scene taken at a glance. **coup-de-poing,** a flint hand-axe of early palæolithic times. (Fr.)

oupé, *n.* koo-pay, the front part of a French diligence; a front compartment in a first-class railway coach; a closed carriage or motor-car, usually for two persons only. (Fr.)

oupee, *n.* koo-*pee*, a motion in dancing, where one leg is a little bent and suspended from the ground, while with the other a motion is made forward. (Fr.)

ouple, *n. kup*-pl, two of a kind connected together; a pair; a man and wife; a betrothed pair; a coupling; two opposite parallel forces, the moments of which are equal [Mech.]: *v.t.* to connect together; to marry; to unite: *v.i.* to copulate. (Fr.)

ouplement, *n. kup*-pl-ment, the act of coupling or state of being coupled; union.

oupler, *n. kupl*-ler, a ring, link, etc., forming a coupling; a device for connecting two manuals or two keys in an organ; a contrivance coupling two electric circuits [Wire.].

ouplet, *n. kup*-let, two lines of verse which rhyme together; a strophe; a pair.

oupling, *n. kupl*-ling, that which couples or connects; the apparatus for coupling vehicles together.

oupling-box, *n.* a contrivance for permanently connecting two shafts [Mech.].

oupling-pin, *n.* a bolt used for coupling together railway carriages and other machinery.

oupon, *n. koo*-pon, a piece cut off; a detachable ticket entitling the legal holder to some payment, service, right to purchase a rationed article, etc.; an interest certificate attached to transferable bonds, which is cut off on receipt of payment; any similar promise to pay; one of a stated number of vouchers entitling the holder to a bonus; official recognition by a party leader of a parliamentary candidate. (Fr.)

ourage, *n. ku*-raj, that quality of character which enables men, by overcoming fear, to encounter danger and difficulties; bravery. **Dutch courage,** bravery inspired by drink. (Fr.)

ourageous, *a.* ku-*ray*-jus, imbued with a daring spirit; brave. (Fr. *courageux.*)

ourageously, *ad.* with courage.

ourageousness, *n.* the quality of being courageous.

ourant, *n.* koo-*rant or koo*-rant, an old quick-step Italian dance; music for this; formerly, a newspaper: *a.* running [Her.]. (Fr.)

ourbaril, *n. koor*-ba-ril, the West Indian locust-tree, *Hymenæa courbaril*: the resin, animé, from this. (Fr.)

ourier, *n. koo*-re-ur, a messenger sent express with letters or dispatches; a travelling attendant who makes arrangements beforehand. (O.Fr.)

ourlan, *n. koor*-lahn, a tropical South American bird allied to the cranes, *Aramus scolopaceus.*

ourse, *n.* koarse, the act of running; a race; a career; a current; the line or direction of motion; the route; voyage; ground on which a race is run; a greyhound chase after a hare; the progress of anything; method of procedure; succession; a methodical series; conduct; act of running in the lists; any regular series; a dish, with its accompaniments, forming part of a meal; a continued range of stones or bricks, level or of the same height, throughout the whole length of the building: *pl.* the main staysails of brigs and schooners; the sails set on the lower yards [Naut.]; the menstrual discharge: *v.t.* to hunt; to pursue; to cause to run; to run through or over: *v.i.* to run; to circulate, as the blood; to chase hares with greyhounds. **in due course,** at the appointed time; in proper order. **matter of course,** a natural event. **matter-of-course,** *a.* such as might be expected. **of course,** by consequence; naturally; without special direction. **true course,** the angle between the longitudinal axis of a ship or aircraft and the true meridian. (Fr.)

ourser, *n. koarse*-er, a swift horse; a war-horse; one who pursues the sport of coursing; a dog for coursing; a stone or brick forming part of a course; a bird of the genus *Cursorius*, allied to the plovers. (Fr. *coursier.*)

coursing, *n. koarse*-ing, hunting hares with greyhounds.

court, *n.* koart, a space enclosed by houses; a quadrangle; a narrow street or entry; a marked or enclosed area for certain games; the residence of a monarch; his courtiers, or those who compose his retinue or council; a royal reception; place where justice is administered; the judges assembled for hearing and deciding causes; any jurisdiction, civil, military, or ecclesiastical; address to gain favour: *v.t.* to endeavour to please by civilities and address; to solicit a woman in marriage; to flatter or woo; to county-court [Coll.]: *v.i.* to woo. **Court of Session,** the supreme civil court in Scotland. **Court of St. James's,** the court of the British monarch. **General Court,** the state legislature of Massachusetts and New Hampshire. **High Court,** the supreme court of justice. (O.Fr. *cort.*)

court-baron, *n.* a former manorial court exercising certain limited jurisdiction.

court-card, *n.* the king, queen, or knave in cards; originally a coat-card.

court-day, *n.* a day in which a court sits to administer justice.

court-dress, *n.* special dress for appearance at court or levée.

courteous, *a. kurt*-e-us, of court-like or polished manners; well-bred; polite. (O.Fr. *corteous.*)

courteously, *ad.* in a courteous manner.

courteousness, *n.* civility of manners.

courter, *n. koart*-er, one who courts; a wooer.

courtesan, *n. koart*-e-zan, a woman of loose virtue; a prostitute. (Fr.)

courtesy, *n. kur*-te-se, politeness of manners, especially accompanied with kindness and some degree of dignity; an act of civility or respect; an act of kindness done with politeness; a favour; a curtsy. **Courtesy of England,** or **tenure by courtesy,** a tenure by which the widower of a woman owning land, who has left living issue, holds the estate for life. **courtesy title,** a title accorded officially and by custom to the issue of peers, which does not raise the bearers above the status of commoners. (O.Fr. *courtesie.*)

court-guide, *n.* a directory of persons of social standing, esp. of those who have been presented at the Court of St. James's.

court-hand, *n. koart*-hand, a manner of writing used in records and judicial proceedings.

court-house, *n. koart*-house, a house appropriated to judicial courts.

courtier, *n.* koart-yer, one who attends or frequents the courts of princes; one of courtly manners; one who courts or flatters. (O.Fr.)

courting, *n. koart*-ing, the act of paying court or wooing.

court-leet, *n. koart*-leet, a former manorial court of record having local jurisdiction in minor criminal and civil cases.

courtlike, *a. koart*-like, polite; elegant.

courtliness, *n.* the quality of being courtly.

courtly, *a. koart*-le, relating to a court; elegant; polite with dignity; flattering: *ad.* in the manner of courts.

court-martial, *n.* koart-*mar*-shal (*pl.* **courts-martial**), a court consisting of military, naval, or air officers for the trial of offences within its jurisdiction: *v.t.* to try by court-martial.

court-plaster, *n.* koart-*plahs*-ter, sticking-plaster on silk, so called because employed by ladies in the patches on the face once fashionable at court.

courtship, *n. koart*-ship, the act of wooing in love.

court-yard, *n. koart*-yard, enclosure or open area from which a house is entered.

couscous, *n. kooss*-kooss, an African dish of millet flour, flesh, and the leaves of the baobab, *Adansonia digitata.* (Native name.)

cousin, *n. kuz*-n, the son or daughter of an uncle or aunt; a title given by a king to certain noblemen. **cousins german,** the children of brothers and sisters; first cousins. (Fr.)

cousinhood, *n. kuz*-n-hood, cousins collectively; relationship, esp. of cousins.

cousinly, *a. kuz*-n-le, like or becoming a cousin.

cousinry, *n. kuz*-n-re, relatives.

cousinship, *n. kuz*-n-ship, relationship.

couteau, *n. koo*-toh, a large knife for use as a weapon. (Fr.. knife.)

coutille, *n.* koo-*teel*, a strong cotton fabric used for corsets, mattresses, etc. (Fr. *coutil*, twill.)
couvade, *n.* koo-*vahd*, among primitive peoples, a custom whereby the father goes to bed at the birth of a child thereby claiming his paternity. (Fr.)
cove, *n.* kove, a small inlet, creek, or bay; any kind of concave moulding or vault [Arch.]: *v.t.* to arch over; to cause to slope in. (A.S. *cofa*, a chamber.)
cove, *n.* kove, a man; a bloke or chap [Slang].
coven, *n.* *kuv*-n, a gathering of witches. (*Convent.*)
covenant, *n.* *kuv*-en-ant, a mutual agreement; the document containing its terms; a bond name given to certain agreements in Scottish history recognizing the Reformation and approving Presbyterianism; the first twenty-six articles of the Treaty of Versailles, 1919, by which the League of Nations was authorized and constituted: *v.i.* to bind oneself by contract: *v.t.* to grant or promise. (O.Fr.)
covenanted, *a.* pledged by covenant; held under covenant and bound to be fulfilled.
covenanter, *n.* one who covenants; a subscriber to the Scottish National Covenant of 1638.
Coventry, *n.* *kov*-en-tre, banishment from gentlemanly society. (A town in Warwickshire.)
★**cover,** *n.* *kuv*-er, anything that covers; a screen; shelter; the binding or case of a book; an envelope; protection; underbrush concealing or sheltering game: *pl.* dining apparatus for each person at table: *v.t.* to spread over with something; to conceal by something overspread or interposed; to clothe; to overwhelm; to conceal from notice or punishment; to refrain from disclosing or confessing; to wrap or envelop; to shelter; to incubate; to copulate with (of animals); to be of equal extent; to be equivalent to; to include or embrace; to fulfil an engagement [Journalism]; to protect by insurance; to aim at with a fire-arm; in cricket, to stand behind a player to stop the balls he misses. (O.Fr. *covrir.*)
coverage, *n.* *kuv*-er-aj, the state of being covered; the total of items, space, liabilities, or risks, etc., covered.
coverchief, *n.* *kuv*-er-chif, a kerchief.
covering, *n.* *kuv*-er-ing, that which covers; a cover. **covering letter,** a letter explanatory of documents, etc., enclosed with it.
coverlet, *n.* *kuv*-er-let, the outer cover of a bed; a quilt. (O.Fr. *covrelit.*)
cover-point, *n.* *kuv*-er-poynt, a position in the cricket-field to the right of point.
co-versed sine, *n.* *koh-verst*-sine, the sine of an arc or angle subtracted from unity.
covert, *a.* *kuv*-ert, covered; concealed; sheltered; under protection: *n.* a place which covers and shelters (esp. game); one of the special feathers on the wing and tail quills of birds [Ornith.]. **femme covert,** a married woman [Law]. (O.Fr.)
covert-coat, *n.* *kuv*-ert-*koat*, a light showerproof overcoat made of a wool or wool and cotton twilled fabric.
covertly, *ad.* *kuv*-ert-le, in a covert manner.
covertness, *n.* the state of being covert.
coverture, *n.* *kuv*-er-tewr, covering; shelter; defence; the state of a married woman, who is considered as under the protection of her husband [Law]. (O.Fr.)
covert-way, *n.* *kuv*-ert-way, a sunken space round the outside of the ditch, between the counterscarp and glacis [Fort.].
covet, *v.t.* *kuv*-et, to desire earnestly to obtain anything; to desire what is unlawful; to long for or hanker after: *v.i.* to have a desire for. (O.Fr. *coveiter.*)
covetable, *a.* *kuv*-et-a-bl, that may be coveted.
covetingly, *ad.* *kuv*-et-ing-le, with eager desire.
covetiveness, *n.* *kuv*-e-tiv-ness, cupidity; avarice.
covetous, *a.* *kuv*-e-tus, very desirous; excessively eager to obtain and possess; avaricious.
covetously, *ad.* with a strong or an inordinate desire to obtain and possess.
covetousness, *n.* a strong or an inordinate desire of possessing; avarice.
covey, *n.* *kuv*-e, a small flock of certain birds, esp. partridges; a company; a set. (O.Fr. *covee.*)
covin, *n.* *kuv*-in, a collusive or fraudulent compact to another's prejudice [Law]. (O.Fr. *covine.*)
coving, *n.* *koh*-ving, the projection of the upper storeys of houses over the lower; (*pl.*) the curved incline sides of a fireplace.
★**cow,** *n.* kou (*pl.* **cows,** kouz, or **kine**), the female of the bull, buffalo, or any bovine animal, also of the moose, cetaceans, seals, etc. **sea cow,** the dugong or other sirenian. (A.S. *cu.*)
cow, *v.t.* kou: to impress with fear; to oppress with habitual timidity. (Scand.)
cowage, *n.* *kou*-aj, cowhage.
coward, *n.* *kou*-ard, one destitute of courage: *a.* destitute of courage; base; proceeding from fear or timidity; represented with its tail between its legs [Her.]. (O.Fr. *couard*, from L. *cauda*, a tail.)
cowardice, *n.* *kou*-ar-dis, want of courage; faintheartedness. (Fr. *couardise.*)
cowardliness, *n.* the state of being cowardly.
cowardly, *a.* wanting courage; timid; mean; base *ad.* in a cowardly manner.
cow-bane, *n.* water-hemlock, *Cicuta virosa.*
cowberry, *n.* *kou*-be-re, the red whortleberry.
cow-bird, *n.* an American starling of the genus *Molothrus*, which, like the cuckoo, builds no nest.
cowboy, *n.* *kou*-boy, a man herding cattle [U.S.A.].
cow-catcher, *n.* a grating on the front of a locomotive to prevent obstacles passing under the wheels.
cowed, *a.* koud, dispirited; crushed.
cower, *v.i.* *kou*-er, to crouch or shrink through fear (Scand.)
cow-fish, *n.* the sea-cow; an Indian and American fish, *Ostracion quadricorne.*
cow-grass, *n.* the meadow trefoil; red clover.
cowhage, *n.* *kou*-aj, a leguminous plant of the genus *Mucuna*; its sharp stinging hairs. (Hind.)
cowherd, *n.* *kou*-herd, one who tends cows.
cowhide, *n.* *kou*-hide, the hide of a cow; a coarse riding-whip: *v.t.* to whip with a cow-hide.
cowish, *a.* *kou*-ish, like a cow; stolid; obtuse.
cow-itch, *n.* *kou*-itch, cowhage.
cowl, *n.* koul, a monk's hood; a rotatory part of a chimney-top; wire cap of a locomotive funnel; a cowling; a water-vessel carried on a cowlstaff (A.S. *cūle.*)
cowled, *a.* kould, wearing a cowl; hooded.
cowlick, *n.* *kou*-lik, a tuft of hair disordered or turned back over the forehead, as if licked by a cow.
cowling, *n.* *koul*-ing, the metal covering of the engine of an aircraft or motor-car.
cowlstaff, *n.* *koul*-staff, a staff or pole on which a pail or other vessel is supported between two persons (O.Fr. *curel*, and *staff.*)
cowman, *n.* *kou*-man, a man who attends to cows.
co-worker, *n.* koh-*wurk*-er, one who works with another.
cow-parsley, *n.* the umbelliferous plant, wild chervil, *Anthriscus sylvestris.*
cow-parsnip, *n.* a plant of the genus *Heracleum.*
cow-pock, *n.* *kou*-pok, a pustule of cow-pox.
cow-pox, *n.* *kou*-poks, a pustular affection on the udders of cows which, when transferred to human by vaccination, protects from smallpox.
cowpuncher, *n.* *kou*-punch-er, a cowboy.
cowry, *n.* *kour*-re, a small marine gastropod shell of the genus *Cypræa*, formerly used as money in India and some regions of Africa. (Hind.)
cowslip, *n.* *kou*-slip, a wild plant of the primrose family, *Primula veris.* (A.S. *cūslyppe*, cow-dung.)
cow-tree, *n.* *kou*-tree, various trees yielding a milky juice, including *Brosimum galactodendron*, of S. America.
cow-wheat, *n.* *kou*-wheet, a plant with wheat-like seeds, of the genus *Melampyrum.*
cox, *n.* koks, a coxswain, esp. of a racing rowing-boat: *v.t.* and *i.*, to act as cox [Coll.].
coxa, *n.* *kok*-sa (*pl.* **coxæ,** *kok*-see), the hip or hip joint [Anat.]; the nearest joint to the body on the leg of an insect [Entom.]. (L.)
coxal, *a.* *kok*-sal, pertaining to the coxa.
coxalgia, *n.* kok-*sal*-je-a, pain in the hip [Med.].
coxcomb, *n.* *koks*-kome, the comb, resembling that of a cock, worn by a jester; a fop; a vain showy fellow (*Cock's-comb.*)
coxcombry, *n.* *koks*-kum-re, manners of a coxcomb.
coxcomical, *a.* koks-*kom*-e-kal, foppish; vain.
coxitis, *n.* kok-*sy*-tis, inflammation of the hip or hip-joint.
coxswain, *n.* *kok*-sn, a steersman of a rowing-boat; the petty officer in charge of a boat's crew [Nav.].
coy, *a.* koy, shrinking from familiarity; reserved, modest, or bashful; arch: *v.i.* to behave coyly. (O.Fr. *coi*, from L. *quietus*, quiet.)
coyish, *a.* *koy*-ish, somewhat coy or reserved.

coyly, *ad.* *koy*-le, in a coy manner.
coyness, *n.* *koy*-ness, a coy disposition or habit.
coyote, *n.* koy-*oh*-te, the prairie wolf *Canis latrans* of western N. America (Mex.).
coypu, *n.* *koy*-poo, a S. American aquatic rodent, *Myopotamus coypu*, the fur of which is marketed as nutria.
coz, *n.* kuz, a cousin (familiarly used).
cozen, *v.t.* *kuz*-en, to cheat; to deceive. (Fr. *cousiner*, to claim kinship for advantage, to sponge.)
cozenage, *n.* *kuz*-en-aj, deceit; practice of cheating.
cozener, *n.* *kuz*-en-er, a cheat.
crab, *n.* krab, a crustacean with ten articulated limbs and a short tail; a sign in the zodiac; the travelling lifting-gear of a gantry crane, or other large lifting apparatus with claws; a pillar used sometimes as a capstan; the drum of a winch: *pl.* the throw of two aces (the lowest) at hazard: *v.i.* to move sideways as a crab does. **catch a crab**, to miss one's stroke in rowing. (A.S. *crabba.*)
crab, *n.* krab, the fruit of a wild apple-tree, and so named from its sour taste (also called the **crab-apple**) [Bot.]; a peevish, morose person: *a.* sour; rough; austere: *v.t.* to scratch or claw [Falconry]; to find fault with unfairly; to injure.
crabbed, *a.* *krab*-bed *or* krabd, sour, peevish, or morose; rough or harsh; difficult; perplexing.
crabbedly, *ad.* *krab*-bed-le, in a crabbed manner.
crabbedness, *n.* the state of being crabbed.
crabby, *a.* *krab*-e, peevish; sullen; fault-finding.
crab-louse, *n.* *krab*-louse, a species of body louse, *Phthirius inguinalis.*
crab's-eyes, *n.pl.* *krabz*-ize, concretions formed in the stomachs of crayfish.
crabwood, *n.* *krab*-wood, a tropical American tree of the genus *Carapa.*
crab-yaws, *n.* *krab*-yawz, a West Indian type of framboesia affecting the palms and soles.
★**crack**, *n.* krak, a disruption; a chink or fissure; a sharp or loud sound uttered suddenly or with vehemence; change of voice in puberty; a boast; a good story; a smart retort; craziness of intellect; an instant of time; a cracksman, a burglary [Coll.]: *a.* having qualities to be boasted of; excellent; first-rate: *v.i.* to open in chinks; to fall to ruin; to be impaired; to utter a loud or sharp sudden sound; to boast; to chat; to change (of the voice at puberty): *v.t.* to break into chinks; to break partially or wholly; to produce a sharp abrupt sound, like that of rending; to snap; to utter with smartness; to affect deeply; to open (a bottle) and drink or share; to make crazy. (A.S. *cracian.*)
crack-brained, *a.* *krak*-braynd, crazy.
cracked, *a.* krakt, split; broken; crazy; deranged.
cracker, *n.* *krak*-er, one who or that which cracks; a small noisy firework; a paper bonbon containing an explosive which discharges when it is correctly torn open; a hard biscuit; a lie: *n.pl.* a tool for cracking nuts.
crackers, *a.* *krak*-erz, daft; crazy [Slang].
crack-jaw, *a.* *krak*-jaw, difficult to pronounce [Coll.].
crackle, *v.i.* *krak*-kl, to make slight frequent cracking sounds; to crepitate: *n.* china ornamented with a net-work of cracks.
crackling, *n.* *krak*-kling, the making slight frequent cracking sounds; the rind of roast pork.
cracknel, *n.* *krak*-nel, a brittle variety of biscuit. (Fr. *craquelin.*)
cracksman, *n.* *kraks*-man, a house-breaker; a burglar [Slang].
Cracovienne, *n.* kra-*koh*-ve-*en*, a Polish peasant dance. (Cracow.)
cradle, *n.* *kray*-dl, a crib for rocking children to sleep; birthplace or nursery; infancy; a frame in which a thing is embedded; a case or frame to protect the body or a broken or damaged limb in bed [Surg.]; a frame placed under the bottom of a ship for launching; a steel instrument resembling a chisel used by mezzotint engravers; a frame with long teeth fastened to a scythe, for cutting and laying corn in a swathe; a contrivance to prevent horses from biting; a gold-washing machine; cradling: *v.t.* to lay or rock in a cradle; to nurse in infancy; to cut and lay corn with a cradle: *v.i.* to lie or lodge, as in a cradle. (A.S. *cradol.*)
cradle-scythe, *n.* a broad scythe used with a cradle for cutting grain.
cradle-walk, *n.* a walk under an avenue of trees.
cradling, *n.* *kray*-dling, a framework of wood; the timber for sustaining the lathing and plastering of vaulted ceilings [Arch.].
craft, *n.* krahft, art; dexterity; cunning; an occupation or handicraft; the body of members of a particular trade; a vessel. **small craft**, small vessels of all kinds, as sloops, schooners, cutters, etc. **the craft**, freemasonry. (A.S. *cræft*, Ger. *kraft*, power.)
craftily, *ad.* in a crafty manner.
craftiness, *n.* the quality of being crafty.
craftsman, *n.* *krahfts*-man, one who practises a craft; a skilled artificer or mechanic.
craftsmanship, *n.* the finished art of a craftsman.
crafty, *a.* *krahft*-te, artful; cunning.
crag, *n.* krag, a rough, broken, steep rock, or point of a rock; certain highly fossiliferous beds of the Pliocene [Geol.]. **crag and tail**, a ridge sloping up, generally westward, and terminating in a crag [Geol.]. (Gael, *creag.*)
cragged, *a.* *krag*-ged, full of crags or broken rocks; rugged; rough.
craggedness, *n.* the state of being cragged.
cragginess, *n.* the state of being craggy.
craggy, *a.* *krag*-ge, cragged.
cragsman, *n.* *kragz*-man, a skilled rock-climber.
crake, *n.* krake, the corncrake or other species of the genus *Crex*; the harsh cry of these birds: *v.i.* to cry like the corncrake. (Imit.).
crakeberry, *n.* *krake*-be-re, the black crowberry.
cram, *n.* kram, the cramming system (for examinations); information acquired by cramming; a lie: *v.i.* to eat greedily or beyond satiety; to undergo cramming for an examination: *v.t.* to stuff; to fill to superfluity; to fill beyond satiety; to thrust in by force; to prepare for an examination by storing the mind with formulæ and answers. (A.S. *crammian.*)
crambo, *n.* *kram*-bo, a game in which one person gives a word, to which another finds a rhyme; a rhyming word. (L. *crambe repetita*, cabbage boiled again; something frequently repeated.)
crammable, *a.* *kram*-a-bl, able to be crammed.
crammer, *n.* *kram*-mer, one who or that which crams; a machine for fattening poultry, etc., by forcible feeding; one who coaches pupils to enable them to pass an examination; a lie [Slang].
cramoisy, *a.* *kram*-oy-ze *or* *kram*-e-ze, crimson: *n.* a crimson textile material.
cramp, *n.* kramp, a painful spasmodic and involuntary contraction of a muscle; restraint; a piece of iron bent at the ends, serving to hold together pieces of timber, stones, etc.; a cramp-iron: *v.t.* to affect with spasms; to restrain; to hinder; to fasten with a cramp-iron: *a.* cramped; difficult; knotty. (Fr. *crampe.*)
cramp-bark, *n.* the cranberry-tree; its dried bark, used medicinally as an antispasmodic.
cramp-bone, *n.* a sheep's patella, formerly used as a charm against cramp.
cramp-fish, *n.* the electric ray or torpedo.
cramp-iron, *n.* *kramp*-i-urn, a piece of metal, bent at right angles at each end, for fastening stonework together; crampon.
crampon, *n.* *kram*-pon, a grappling iron; a pair of chained iron hooks, or a scissor-like appliance, for gripping heavy objects to be hoisted by a crane; one of a number of sharp spikes fixed to mountaineering boots; an aerial root, as of ivy [Bot.]. (Fr.)
cran, *n.* kran, a measure for fresh herrings containing 37½ gallons, or 750–800 fish [Scots.].
cranage, *n.* *kray*-naj, the right of using a crane at a wharf; the price paid for the use.
cranberry, *n.* *kran*-be-re, a shrubby plant of the genus *Oxycoccus*, the red berry of which is used for tarts, sauces, etc.; the marsh whortleberry. (Ger. *kranbeere.*)
crane, *n.* krane, a migratory wading bird with long legs, neck, and bill, of the genus *Grus*; a machine for raising and removing great weights; a pivoted iron arm as fireplace support for a kettle, etc.; a bent pipe for drawing liquors out of a cask: *v.t.* and *i.* to move with a crane; to draw out the neck like a crane. (A.S. *cran.*)
crane-fly, *n.* an insect of the genus *Tipula*, the daddy-longlegs.
crane's-bill, *n.* any plant of the species *Geranium*; a pair of pincers used by surgeons.

cranial, *a.* *kray*-ne-al, pertaining to the cranium.
craniofacial, *a.* *kray*-ne-o-*fay*-shal, relating to the relative breadth of cranium and face.
craniological, *a.* pertaining to craniology.
craniologist, *n.* one versed in craniology.
craniology, *n.* *kray*-ne-*ol*-o-je, the science which treats of skulls. (Gr. *kranion*, and *logos*, science.)
craniometer, *n.* kray-ne-*om*-e-ter, an instrument for measuring the cubic capacity of skulls.
craniometrical, *a.* kray-ne-o-*met*-re-kal, pertaining to craniometry.
craniometry, *n.* *kray*-ne-*om*-e-tre, the art of measuring the cranium for the purpose of discovering its capacity and distinguishing characteristics.
cranioscopy, *n.* kray-ne-*os*-ko-pe, the examination of the skull with a view especially to determine the relative size of the brain organs. (Gr. *kranion*, and *skopeo*, view.)
craniotomy, *n.* kray-ne-*ot*-o-me, the operation of cutting into the head of the fœtus to effect delivery. (Gr. *kranion*, and *tome*, cutting.)
cranium, *n.* *kray*-ne-um, the skull, esp. that part enclosing the brain. (Gr. *kranion*.)
crank, *n.* krank, a bent axle for the conversion of lineal into rotary motion or the reverse ; any bend, turn, or winding ; an iron brace for various purposes : *v.t.* to use a crank ; to bend in the form of a crank ; to fasten with or furnish with a crank. **crank bird,** the lesser spotted woodpecker, *Picus minor*. **single-crank,** a handle at the end of an axis. **to crank up,** to start a motor engine. (M.E. *cranke*.)
crank, *a.* krank, liable to upset [Naut.] ; crazy : *n.* a caprice ; a sportive twisting or turning in speech ; a faddist ; an eccentric individual. (A.S. *cranc*, weak.)
crankcase, *n.* *krank*-kase, the case containing a moving crank or crankshaft.
crankily, *ad.* in a cranky manner.
crankle, *n.* *krang*-kl, a twist, a crinkle : *v.t.* to crinkle : *v.i.* to bend in and out.
crankshaft, *n.* *krank*-shahft, the shaft connecting the cranks on a multi-cylinder engine.
cranky, *a.* *krang*-ke, slightly deranged ; crotchety ; unreliable ; liable to upset [Naut.].
crannied, *a.* *kran*-ed, full of chinks.
crannog, *n.* *kran*-og, in Scotland and Ireland, a prehistoric lake-dwelling, usually fortified with a palisade. (Ir.)
cranny, *n.* *kran*-ne, a rent, chink, or fissure ; a secret retired place ; an iron instrument for forming the necks of glasses [Glass-making]. (Fr. *cran*, notch.)
crants, *n.* krants, a garland ; a wreath. (Ger. *kranz*.)
crape, *n.* krape, a thin, transparent gauze made of gummed raw silk, usually dyed black, and worn in mourning. (Fr. *crêpe*, from L. *crispus*, curled.)
craps, *n.* kraps, an American gambling game played with two dice.
crapulence, *n.* *krap*-yew-lence, sickness due to drink ; gross intemperance. (L. *crapula*, intoxication.)
crapulent, *a.* *krap*-yew-lent, given to or suffering from over-indulgence in liquor ; habitually fuddled.
crapulous, *a.* *krap*-yew-lus, crapulent.
crapy, *a.* *krape*-e, similar to crape.
crash, *n.* krash, the loud mingled sound of many things falling and breaking at once ; a break-up in bankruptcy ; the wreck of an aeroplane : *v.t.* to break with violence : *v.i.* to make a crash ; to fall to the ground in flight. **crash-dive,** a sudden dive made by a submarine to avoid danger. **crash-helmet,** tight-fitting head-dress of padded leather worn by airmen, motor-cycle dispatch-riders, etc. (Imit.)
crash, *n.* krash, a coarse linen cloth, mostly used for towels. (L. *crassus*, coarse.)
crasis, *n.* *kray*-sis, the contraction of two vowels into a long one or a diphthong [Gr. Gram.]. (Gr., mixing.)
crass, *a.* kras, gross ; thick ; coarse ; stupid. (L. *crassus*, thick.)
crassamentum, *n.* kras-a-*men*-tum, the clot formed in coagulated blood. (L., sediment.)
crassitude, *n.* *kras*-e-tewd, crassness.
crassness, *n.* *kras*-ness, the quality of being crass.
Cratægus, *n.* kra-*tee*-gus, a genus of thorny shrubs including the hawthorn, *C. oxyacantha*. (Gr.)
cratch, *n.* kratch, a grated crib for hay ; a manger. (O.Fr. *creche*.)
crate, *n.* krate, a framework packing case. (L. *cratis*, wickerwork.)
crater, *n.* *kray*-ter, the mouth of a volcano ; the hole in the ground made by an explosion, esp. of a bomb, mine, etc. (Gr., a large bowl.)
crateriform, *a.* kra-*te*-re-fawrm, in the form of a crater ; cup- or bowl-shaped.
craunch, *v.t.* krawnch, to crunch.
cravat, *n.* kra-*vat*, a necktie, adopted from the Croats. (Fr. *cravate*, a Croat.)
crave, *v.t.* krave, to beg earnestly ; to entreat humbly ; to require or demand ; to long for. (A.S. *crafian*.)
craven, *n.* *krave*-en, a coward ; a recreant ; a weak-hearted spiritless fellow ; originally the cry of the vanquished in the ancient trial by battle : *a.* cowardly : *v.t.* to make recreant, weak, or cowardly. **to cry craven,** to acknowledge defeat. (M.E. *cravant*, one who craves his life.)
craver, *n.* *krave*-er, one who craves.
craving, *n.* *krave*-ing, strong desire ; a longing.
cravingly, *ad.* *krave*-ing-le, in a craving manner.
craw, *n.* kraw, the crop or first stomach of birds or insects. (M.E. *crawe*.)
craw-craw, *n.* *kraw*-kraw, a contagious parasitic skin disease among W. African Negroes. (Native.)
crawfish, *n.* *kraw*-fish, the crayfish.
crawl, *v.i.* krawl, to creep ; to move slowly, weakly or timorously ; to wrinkle (of paint-work) ; to swarm with crawling things ; to feel as though insects were crawling over the skin : *n.* the act of crawling ; slow motion ; a certain fast stroke in swimming. **pub crawl,** a progress from tavern to tavern [Slang]. (Ice. *krafla*, crawl.)
crawl, *n.* krawl, a staked enclosure in shallow water for containing fish. (Dut. *kraal*, a pen.)
crawler, *n.* *krawl*-er, one that crawls ; a reptile ; a cringing sycophant [Coll.] ; a cab plying for hire by loitering [Slang] : *pl.* an infant's overalls.
crawling, *a.* *krawl*-ing, moving slowly or timorously ; insinuating ; abounding in crawling things.
crawlingly, *ad.* in a crawling manner.
crayfish, *n.* *kray*-fish, the freshwater crustacean, *Astacus fluviatilis* ; the marine rock or spiny lobster, of the genus *Palinurus*. (O.Fr. *crevisse*.)
crayon, *n.* *kray*-on, a pencil of white or coloured chalk for drawing ; a drawing made with crayons ; the carbon point of an electric arc-light : *v.t.* to sketch with a crayon ; to sketch. (Fr. *craie*, L. *creta*, chalk.)
craze, *n.* kraze, an inordinate or insane passion ; a mania : *v.t.* to derange, shatter, or impair the intellect. **in the craze,** in the fashion. [Scand.]
crazed, *a.* krayzd, deranged in intellect ; decrepit.
crazily, *ad.* *kraze*-e-le, in a crazy manner.
craziness, *n.* *kraze*-e-ness, a crazy state.
crazing-mill, *n.* a mill for grinding tin.
crazy, *a.* *kraze*-e, broken down ; decrepit ; feeble ; weakened or deranged in intellect. **crazy about,** very keen on. **crazy paving,** a pavement of flat stones of irregular shapes.
creak, *n.* kreek, a sharp, grating sound : *v.i.* to make a sharp, harsh, grating sound. (Imit.).
creaky, *a.* *kreek*-e, apt to creak ; squeaky ; frail.
cream, *n.* kreem, the oily part of milk from which butter is made ; a preparation of cream ; the choicest part of anything ; what rises to the surface, and is skimmed off : *v.t.* to take off cream ; to add cream to : *v.i.* to gather cream ; to mantle. **cream of tartar,** a white crystalline tartrate or bitartrate of potassium obtained from grape juice. (Fr. *crême*.)
cream-cake, *n.* a cake containing cream or custard.
cream-cheese, *n.* a soft cheese made of unskimmed milk and cream.
creamer, *n.* *kreem*-er, a machine or appliance for separating cream from milk ; a milk-jug.
creamery, *n.* *kreem*-er-ee, an establishment for the preparation and distribution of milk products ; a shop for the sale of dairy produce.
cream-faced, *a.* pale ; having a cowardly look.
cream-laid, *a.* of laid paper of a cream colour.
cream-nut, *n.* the Brazil nut.
cream-wove, *a.* of woven paper of a cream colour.
creamy, *a.* *kreem*-e, full of cream ; like cream.
creance, *n.* *kree*-ance, a fine small line fastened to a hawk's leash when it is first lured [Falconry]. (Fr.)

crease, *n.* kreece, a mark made by folding or doubling anything: *v.t.* to make a crease: *v.i.* to become creased; to wrinkle. **bowling crease,** the white line at a cricket wicket. **popping crease,** the line four feet in front of this. (Origin uncertain.) (Bret. *kriz*, a wrinkle.)
creasy, *a. kreece*-e, marked by creases.
creatable, *a.* kre-*ay*-ta-bl, that may be created.
create, *v.t.* kre-*ate*, to bring into being out of nothing; to beget; to bring forth; to bring about or cause; to make. (L. *creatus*, made.)
creatine, *n. kree*-a-tin, a nitrogenous substance found in striped muscle, blood, etc. (Gr. *kreas*, flesh.)
creation, *n.* kre-*ay*-shon, formation; the act of creating, especially the world; the things created; the universe; the act of investing with a new character; a thing produced by the intellect or by skill; a fashionable dress. (Fr.)
creational, *a.* kre-*ay*-shon-al, pertaining to creation.
creationism, *n.* kre-*ay*-shon-izm, the doctrine that the existence of each individual soul is due to a separate act of creation; the theory that the universe was made by the Creator out of nothing, and that all species were individually created.
creative, *a.* kre-*ay*-tiv, having the power to create.
creatively, *ad.* in a creative manner.
creativeness, *n.* state of being creative.
Creator, *n.* kre-*ay*-tor, the being that creates; the thing that creates; the Maker of all things. (L.)
creature, *n. kree*-tewr, that which is created; a created living being; a human being in contempt or endearment; one who owes his rise or fortune to another; a mere tool: *a.* pertaining to the body. **the creature,** spirituous liquor [Coll.]. (O.Fr.)
creaturely, *a.* pertaining to the creature; having the qualities of a creature.
crèche, *n.* kraysh, a day nursery for infants and children while their parents are at work. (Fr.)
credence, *n. kree*-dence, belief; credit; that which gives a claim to credit or belief; a credence-table. **credence-table,** a small table or shelf at the side of the altar for the bread and wine before consecration [Eccles.]. (F.)
credenda, *n.pl.* kre-*den*-da, things to be believed. (L.)
credential, *a.* kre-*den*-shal, giving a title to credit: *n.* a certificate as to confidence: *pl.* documents which certify to one's claims or pretensions.
credibility, *n.* kred-e-*bil*-e-te, the quality or state of being credible.
credible, *a. kred*-e-bl, worthy of credit; having a claim to credit. (O.Fr.)
credibly, *ad.* in a manner deserving of belief.
***credit,** *n. kred*-it, belief or faith; reliance on the truth of something said or done; reputation; estimation; that which procures or is entitled to belief; authority or power derived from one's character, or the confidence of others or other cause; influence; a pass-with-credit award in certain examinations; confidence in one's solvency and probity, which entitles him to trust; sale on trust; the time given for payment of goods sold on trust [Comm.]; the right side of an account, as opposed to the left, or debit, side [Book-keeping]: *v.t.* to confide in the truth of; to trust; to do credit; to set to the credit of. **letter of credit,** an order to receive money from an agent. **public credit,** confidence in the ability and disposition of a borrowing nation to make good its engagements with its creditors. (Fr. *crédit*.)
creditable, *a. kred*-it-a-bl, reputable; honourable.
creditableness, *n.* quality of being creditable.
creditably, *ad.* in a creditable manner.
creditor, *n. kred*-it-or, one to whom a debt is due; one who has a just claim for money. (L.)
Credo, *n. kree*-do, a creed, esp. the Apostles' or the Nicene, of which this is the first word. (L., I believe.)
credulity, *n.* kre-*dew*-le-te, easiness of belief.
credulous, *a. kred*-yew-lus, apt to believe without sufficient evidence; unsuspecting; easily imposed upon. (L. *credulus*.)
credulously, *ad.* in a credulous manner.
credulousness, *n.* credulity.
creed, *n.* kreed, a brief summary of the articles of religious faith; that which is believed; any system of principles believed or professed. (A.S. *crēda*.)
creek, *n.* kreek, a narrow inlet, bay, or cove; a backwater; a piece of land between mountains; a small river [U.S.A. and Australia]. (A.S. *crecca*, turn.)
creeky, *a.* having creeks; full of creeks; winding.
creel, *n.* kreel, an osier basket for carrying fish. (Scots.)
creep, *v.i.* kreep, to move, as a worm; to crawl; to grow along, as a creeping plant; to move slowly and insensibly; to move secretly; to steal in; to behave with servility; to fawn; to have a sensation as of something creeping; to drag with a creeper or grapnel; to crawl (of paint or varnish); to shift slowly or become slightly displaced: *n.* a movement of or like creeping; gradual or imperceptible movement, as of that through expansion [Eng.] or climatic changes [Geol.]. **creep-hole,** a hole into which an animal may creep to escape danger; a subterfuge; an excuse. **creeping-jenny,** the trailing hedge-plant, *Lysimachia nummularia*. (A.S. *creopan*.)
creepage, *n. kreep*-aj, a gradual creeping movement; electrical leakage.
creeper, *n. kreep*-er, a person or thing that creeps; a reptile; a plant that clings by rootlets; an iron used to slide along the grate in kitchens; a kind of patten worn by women; a shoe spiked against slipping; a grapnel for drawing up things from the bottom of a well, river, or harbour; a name given to several genera of small birds, such as the tree-creepers.
creepingly, *ad.* by creeping; slowly; sneakingly.
creepy, *a. kreep*-e, unpleasantly exciting; eerie.
creese, *n.* kreece, the kris, a Malay dagger.
cremaster, *n.* kre-*mas*-ter, a muscle of the spermatic cord upholding a testicle [Anat.].
cremate, *v.t.* kre-*mate*, to consume by fire; to reduce, esp. a corpse, to ashes.
cremation, *n.* kre-*may*-shon, the disposal of the dead by burning. (L. *crematio*.)
cremationist, *n.* kre-*may*-shon-ist, a supporter of the practice of cremation.
cremator, *n.* kre-*may*-tor, a furnace for burning corpses or refuse; one who cremates a dead body.
crematorium, *n.* krem-a-*taw*-re-um, an establishment at which the funeral rites and cremation of the dead are carried out.
crematory, *a. krem*-a-to-re, pertaining to or employed in cremation; *n.* a crematorium.
crême-de-menthe, *n.* (App.), a clear green liqueur of peppermint flavour. (Fr.)
Cremona, *n.* kre-*moh*-na, a violin made at Cremona.
crenate, *a. kree*-nate, notched; indented; scalloped [Bot.]. (L. *crena*, a notch.)
crenature, *n. kren*-a-tewr, a scallop like a notch; a rounded projection on a leaf-edge. [Bot.].
crenel, *n. kren*-el, a loophole for shooting from; a crenature [Bot.].
crenellate, *v.t. kren*-el-late, to furnish with loopholes or battlements.
crenulate, *a. kren*-yew-lat, indented; having the edge cut into very small scallops [Bot.].
Creole, *n. kree*-ole, one of European descent born in Spanish America or the West Indies; a pure-bred descendant of the early French and Spanish settlers in the southern U.S.A.; a Creole and negro half-breed; the French patois of certain Creoles: *a.* pertaining to the Creoles. **Creole Negro,** a Negro born in America. (Fr. *créole*.)
creophagous, *a.* kree-*off*-a-gus, eating flesh; carnivorous. (Gr. *kreas*, flesh, *phago*, eat.)
creosol, *n. kree*-o-sol, a liquid resembling phenol.
creosotal, *n. kree*-oh-*soh*-tal, creosote carbonate, a yellow viscous liquid used in bronchial affections [Med.].
creosote, *n. kree*-oh-sote, an antiseptic liquid, the product of wood, oily and colourless, with the smell of smoke; a liquid containing hydrocarbons and phenols, derived from coal-tar. **creosote-plant,** a Mexican shrub, *Larrea mexicana*, that binds drifting sand and smells like wood creosote. (Gr. *kreas*, flesh, *soter*, preserver.)
crêpe, *n.* krape, crape. **crêpe-rubber,** a prepared rubber used for the soles of shoes, etc.
crêpe-de-Chine, *n. krape*-de-sheen, a silk material used for ladies' dresses. (Fr.)
crepitant, *a. krep*-e-tant, crackling.
crepitate, *v.i. krep*-e-tate, to crackle; to burst with a crackling noise, like salt in the fire. (L. *crepitatus*, creaked.)

crepitation, *n.* krep-e-*tay*-shon, the act of crackling; the noise of fractured bones when moved by a surgeon to ascertain a fracture; the rattling sound heard in pneumonia [Med.].
crepoline, *n.* *krep*-o-leen, a material like crape used for women's dresses. (Fr.)
crepon, *n.* *krep*-on, a stuff made of wool or silk resembling crape. (Fr. *crépon.*)
crept, krept, *pp.* of creep.
crepuscular, *a.* kre-*pus*-kew-lar, pertaining to, or [Zool.] active at, twilight; glimmering. (L.)
crescendo, *ad.* kre-*shend*-oh, with an increasing volume of sound [Mus.]. (It.)
crescent, *n.* *kres*-sent, the increasing or new moon; a figure of the moon as in the first or last quarter; the Turkish standard, the Turkish power; Islamism; a hollow curve of buildings; a bearing in the form of a half-moon [Her.]: *a.* increasing; having the form of a half-moon. (L. *crescentis*, of growing.)
crescive, *a.* *kres*-siv, increasing; growing.
cress, *n.* kres, the name of several species of plants having a warm aromatic taste, and used as a salad, esp. *Lepidium sativum* (*see* **mustard and cress**), and **water cress,** *Nasturtium officinale.* (A.S.)
cresset, *n.* *kres*-set, a large beacon light; the grating or vessel to hold it; a torch, esp. one in a vessel carried on a pole. (O.Fr.)
crest, *n.* krest, a tuft or a swelling growing on the top of the head; a plume or device at the apex of a helmet; the figure placed over a coat of arms [Her.]; the foam on the top of a wave; the top of a ridge; pride or courage: *v.t.* to furnish with a crest; to reach the crest (of a ridge, etc.). (O.Fr. *creste.*)
crested, *pp.* and *a.* *kres*-ted, bearing a crest or tuft.
crestfallen, *a.* *krest*-fawl-en, dejected; dispirited.
crestless, *a.* *krest*-less, without a crest; not dignified with coat-armour; of low birth.
cretaceous, *a.* kre-*tay*-shus, composed of or like chalk. **cretaceous formation,** the uppermost formation of the secondary rocks. (L., chalky.)
Cretan, *a.* *kree*-tan, pertaining to the Mediterranean island of Crete, or its inhabitants: *n.* a native or inhabitant of Crete.
cretic, *n.* *kree*-tik, the amphimacer [Pros.]. (*Crete.*)
cretin, *n.* *kree*-tin, one afflicted by cretinism; one mentally deficient. (Fr. *crétin.*)
cretinism, *n.* *kret*-in- *or* *kree*-tin-izm, a congenital condition of physical non-development and, usually, idiocy due to absence of, or deficient secretion from, the thyroid gland. (Fr.)
cretinous, *a.* *kret*-in-us, of the nature of, or affected with, cretinism; idiotic.
cretonne, *n.* *kret-on*, a patterned cotton cloth for upholstery purposes. (Fr.)
crevasse, *n.* kre-*vass*, a crevice; a breach; a deep crack in a glacier. (O.Fr.)
crevice, *n.* *krev*-iss, a crack; a rent or fissure. (O.Fr. *crevasse.*)
crew, *n.* kroo, a ship's company; a company of people associated (usually in a bad sense); a band or gang. (Dim. of *accrue.*)
crewel, *n.* *kroo*-el, a kind of embroidery, or the yarn it is wrought with.
crib, *n.* krib, a rack or manger; a stall for oxen; a small cottage; a child's bed; a situation; a box for salt; a literary theft or thing cribbed; a literal translation of a classic, to crib from; a set of cards at cribbage made up of cards discarded by each player and scored by the dealer; a basket salmon-trap; heavy timbers crossed and secured to form a dam, or foundation under water, or in loose soil; the timber lining of a mine shaft: *v.t.* to confine; to coop up; to pilfer; to plagiarize; to use a crib: *v.i.* to bite the crib (of horses). **crib-biting,** a bad habit peculiar to some horses, which is occasioned by uneasiness during teething, or from bad feeding. (A.S. *crib.*)
cribbage, *n.* *krib*-aj, a game of cards in which the dealer makes up a third hand for himself, partly from the hand of his opponent or opponents. **cribbage-board,** a board on which the progress of the game is marked.
cribbing, *n.* *krib*-ing, appropriating; plagiarizing; the plank lining of a mine shaft.
cribriform, *a.* *krib*-re-fawrm, like a sieve; perforated like a sieve. (L. *cribrum*, sieve, *forma*, shape.)
cribrose, *a.* *krib*-rohs, cribriform [Bot.].
crick, *n.* krik, a painful stiffness of the muscles; spasmodic affection from stiffness in the neck or the back: *v.t.* to produce a crick. (*Creek.*)
cricket, *n.* *krik*-et, the English summer outdoor game played with bat, ball, and wickets, between opposing sides of, generally, eleven each: *v.i.* to engage in cricket. **not cricket,** not playing the game; unfair; dishonourable. (O.Fr. *criquet*, staff.)
cricket, *n.* *krik*-et, a straight-winged insect, of which there are several species, esp. the house-cricket, *Gryllus domesticus*, and the field cricket, *G. campestris.* (Fr. *criquet*, from *creak.*)
cricket, *n.* *krik*-et, a low wooden stool. (Origin unknown.)
cricketer, *n.* *krik*-et-er, one who plays cricket.
cricoid, *a.* *krik*-oyd, ring-shaped. **cricoid cartilage,** the cartilage of the larynx [Anat.]. (Gr. *krikos*, a ring, *eidos*, like.)
crier, *n.* *kry*-er, one who makes proclamation; an official who shouts public announcements. (Fr. *crieur.*)
crim-con, *n.* krim-kon, criminal converse; adultery.
★**crime,** *n.* krime, an act in violation of law; a gross violation; any great wickedness or wrong: *v.t.* to accuse; to charge [Mil.]. **capital crime,** a crime punishable with death. **crime sheet,** roster of those crimed, with their offences [Mil.]. (Fr.)
crimeless, *a.* *krime*-less, free from crime; innocent.
criminal, *a.* *krim*-e-nal, guilty of a crime; involving a crime; relating to crime: *n.* one guilty of a crime; a culprit; a convict. (Fr. *criminel.*)
criminality, *n.* krim-e-*nal*-e-te, criminalness.
criminally, *ad.* in violation of a law; wickedly.
criminate, *v.t.* *krim*-e-nate, to charge with or to prove guilty of a crime; to blame severely. (L. *criminatus*, charged with a fault.)
crimination, *n.* krim-e-*nay*-shon, the act of criminating; charge; strong censure.
criminatory, *a.* *krim*-e-na-to-re, criminating.
criminology, *n.* krim-e-*nol*-o-je, the science or study of crime and the criminal.
criminous, *a.* *krim*-e-nus, very wicked; heinous; guilty of, or involving, great crime.
crimp, *n.* krimp, one who decoys another into going to sea: *v.t.* to decoy for service, esp. on board ship.
crimp, *v.t.* krimp, to crisp or crimple; to plait, bend, or fold into ridges; to crimple or cause to contract, as the flesh of a live fish, by gashing it with a knife to give it greater hardness [Cookery]; to compress so as to shape. **crimping-iron,** an iron for curling hair. **crimping-machine,** a machine for crimping ruffles or frills; a machine for corrugating metal sheets. (A.S. *crempan.*)
crimpage, *n.* *krim*-paj, payment made to a crimp for his services.
crimple, *v.t.* and *i.* *krim*-pl, to wrinkle; to make or become frizzy (of hair): *n.* a fuzzy or wavy look (in hair).
crimpy, *a.* *krim*-pe, wrinkled; fuzzy; crimped.
crimson, *n.* *krim*-zon, a deep red colour; a red in general: *a.* of a deep red: *v.t.* and *i.* to dye or to become crimson; to blush. (O.Fr. *cramoisin.*)
crinal, *a.* *kry*-nal, pertaining to hair. (L. *crinalis*, hair-like.)
cringe, *n.* krinj, a fawning civility: *v.i.* to bend with servility; to fawn; to make court by mean compliances. (A.S. *cringan.*)
cringeling, *n.* *krinj*-ling, a mean cringer; an abjectly obsequious person.
cringer, *n.* *krinj*-er, one who cringes.
cringingly, *ad.* in a cringing manner.
cringle, *n.* *kring*-gl, a hole in the bolt-rope of a sail, with a ring or thimble in it [Naut.]. (Ice. *krihngla*, circle.)
crinite, *a.* *kry*-nite, resembling a tuft of hair; hairy, tufted [Bot. and Zool.].
crinkle, *n.* *kring*-kl, a wrinkle; a winding or turn; a twist: *v.i.* to wrinkle; to run in and out in little bends: *v.t.* to form with short turns or twists; to mould into inequalities. (A.S. *crincian.*)
crinkly, *a.* *kring*-kle, full of crinkles; crackling.
crinoid, *a.* *krin*-oyd, shaped like a lily [Zool.]: *n.* any one of the *Crinoidea*; an encrinite. (Gr. *krinon*, a lily, *eidos*, like.)
crinoidal, *a.* kri-*noy*-dal, pertaining to or containing crinoids.
Crinoidea, *n.pl.* kri-*noy*-de-a, of a large order of

extinct and living echinoderms growing on long jointed stalks, including the sea-lilies.

crinoline, *n.* *krin*-o-leen, a stiffened petticoat formerly worn by women for extending the skirt; a netting to keep off torpedoes from warships. (Fr.)

criosphinx, *n.* *kry*-o-sfinks, a ram-headed sphinx. (Gr. *krios*, a ram.)

cripple, *n.* *krip*-pl, a lame person: *a.* lame: *v.t.* to lame; to deprive of power. (A.S. *crypel.*)

crippling, *n.* *krip*-pling, shoring for the support of a building.

crisis, *n.* *kry*-sis (*pl.* **crises,** *kry*-seez), the change in a disease which indicates recovery or death, the sudden fall of temperature; the point when an affair must soon undergo a change for better or worse; a period when momentous changes are effected. (Gr.)

crisp, *a.* krisp, with short stiff curls; indented; winding; brittle; brisk; fresh and firm: *v.t.* to curl; to twist; to wreathe or interweave; to cause to wave slightly or ripple: *v.i.* to ripple: *n.pl.* thin fried slices of potato, dried, and sold in packets. **crisping-iron,** an iron for crimping. **crisping-pin,** a simple form of crimping-iron. (L. *crispus.*)

crispate, *a.* *kris*-pat, having a crisped appearance; curled at the edges [Bot.]. (L. *crispatus*, curled.)

crispation, *n.* kris-*pay*-shon, the state of being curled or crisped; a minute undulation.

crisper, *n.* *kris*-per, one who or that which crisps; a tool for friezing or crisping cloth; a crisping-iron.

Crispin, *n.* *kris*-pin, a shoemaker. (St. *Crispin*, the patron saint of shoemakers.)

crisply, *ad.* *krisp*-le, in a crisp manner.

crispness, *n.* *krisp*-ness, state of being crisp.

crispy, *a.* *kris*-pe, curled; brittle.

criss-cross, *n.* *kris*-kros, a pattern of intersecting lines; a child's game played on slates [U.S.A.]; *ad.* in opposite directions; at cross purposes: *a.* in cross lines; awry. (Christ's cross, as in *Christ-cross-row.*)

cristate, *a.* *kris*-tate, crested; having tufts of hairs [Bot. and Zool.]. (L. *cristatus*, crested.)

criterion, *n.* kry-*teer*-re-on (*pl.* **criteria,** kry-*teer*-e-a), a standard of quality. (Gr.)

crith, *n.* krith, an obsolete unit of volume-weight for gases. (Gr. *krithē*, barley-corn.)

critic, *n.* *krit*-ik, one who criticizes; a reviewer; one who censures. (Gr. *krites*, a judge.) (Fr. *critique.*)

critical, *a.* *krit*-e-kal, pertaining to a crisis; relating to or skilled in criticism; discriminating; nicely judicious; inclined to find fault; cavilling; decisive; involving risk.

critically, *ad.* in a critical manner; at the crisis or exact time; in a critical situation.

criticizable, *a.* capable of being criticized.

criticize, *v.t.* and *i.* *krit*-e-size, to examine critically and pass criticism; to censure; to play the critic.

criticism, *n.* *krit*-e-sizm, the art or act of judging of a work of literature or art; a judicious examination; a critical opinion.

critique, *n.* kri-*teek*, a critical estimate, esp. of a literary or artistic work; a critical examination. (Fr.)

croak, *n.* kroke, the low harsh sound uttered by a frog or a raven: *v.t.* to make such a noise in the throat; to grumble; to forebode evil; to kill [Slang]: *v.i.* to die [Slang]. (Imit.)

croaker, *n.* *kroke*-er, one who croaks; a grumbler; popular name of certain marine and freshwater fish which croak when caught.

croaky, *a.* *kroke*-e, croaking; hoarse and guttural.

Croat, *n.* *kroh*-at, a Slavic native of Croatia; one of the light irregular cavalry of the former Austro-Hungarian Empire in which many Croats served.

Croatian, *a.* kroh-*ay*-shan, pertaining to the Croats: *n.* a Croat; the language of the Croats.

croceate, *a.* *kroh*-se-at, croceous [Bot.].

croceous, *a.* *kroh*-she-us, of or like saffron; yellow; consisting of saffron. (L. *croceus.*)

crochet, *n.* *kroh*-shay, a fancy knitting-work made by means of a small hook: *v.t.* and *i.* to work in crochet. (Fr., a little hook.)

crocidolite, *n.* kro-*sid*-o-lite, a light blue or green fibrous silicate of iron and sodium. (Gr. *krokis*, nap, *lithos*, stone.)

crock, *n.* krok, an earthen vessel or pitcher; a shard of earthenware; a broken-down horse; a useless or disabled person: *v.i.* to become a crock (of persons); to break down. (A.S. *crocca.*)

crock, *n.* krok, soot, or the black matter collected from combustion on pots and kettles, or in a chimney: *v.t.* and *i.* to blacken or become black with soot.

crockery, *n.* *krok*-er-re, the coarser kind of earthenware; earthenware vessels.

crocket, *n.* *krok*-et, an ornamentation of curved and bent foliage, running up on the edge of a gable, spire, pinnacle, etc. [Arch.]. (O.Fr. *croket.*)

crocodile, *n.* *krok*-o-dile, a large amphibious reptile having the back and tail covered with large, hard, horny scales; a group of school-children walking out in double file; a captious sophism to ensnare an adversary [Rhet.]: *a.* false or affected, the crocodile being fabled to weep over its victim [Fig.]. **crocodile-bird,** a plover, *Pluvianus ægyptus*, which picks parasites from the skin and teeth of the crocodile. (Fr.)

crocodilian, *a.* krok-o-*dil*-e-an, of or like the crocodile.

crocoite, *n.* *kroh*-ko-ite, red lead ore, a native chromate of lead.

crocus, *n.* *kroh*-kus (*pl.* **crocuses**), a large genus of cormous plants of the iris family, including the saffron and many ornamental garden varieties; any metal calcined to a red or deep yellow colour for use as a polishing powder. (L.)

Croesus, *n.* *kree*-sus, a very wealthy person. (From *Croesus*, King of Lydia, famed for his wealth.)

croft, *n.* kroft, a small field adjoining or near a dwelling-house; a small Highland farm. (A.S., a field.)

crofter, *n.* *krof*-ter, a peasant who farms a croft, usually jointly with others [Scots.].

Cro-Magnon, *a.* kroh-*man*-yon, denoting a West European race (originating in Africa) of later palæolithic age, remarkable for their height and large and very long heads. (From place of discovery, 1868, in Dordogne, France.)

cromfordite, *n.* *krom*-for-dite, phosgenite. (Village in Derbyshire.)

cromlech, *n.* *krom*-lekh, a prehistoric structure consisting of a huge flat stone resting as a table on two others. (W. *crom*, bent, *llech*, a stone.)

cromorna, *n.* kro-*mor*-na, one of the reed stops of an organ. (*Cromorne.*)

cromorne, *n.* kro-*morn*, an obsolete wood-wind instrument with double reed [Mus.]. (Fr., from Ger. *Krummhorn*, crooked horn.)

crone, *n.* krone, an old ewe; an old woman. (O.Fr. *carogne.*)

crony, *n.* *kroh*-ne, an intimate companion.

croodle, *v.i.* *kroo*-dl, to cower; to lie close and snug.

crook, *n.* krook, a bend; anything bent; a shepherd's staff, curving at the end; the staff of a bishop; a pothook; a short curved tube for altering the key of a trumpet, etc. [Mus.]; an artifice or trick; a scoundrel; a criminal or deceitful person [Slang]: *v.t.* to bend; to make a curve or hook; to pervert: *v.i.* to bend or be bent. **by hook or by crook,** by right means or by wrong. (Scand.)

crookback, *n.* *krook*-bak, one who has a crooked back or round shoulders; a humpback.

crooked, *a.* *krook*-ed, bent; winding; not straight; slippery; fraudulent; dishonest.

crookedly, *ad.* in a crooked manner.

crookedness, *n.* the state of being crooked.

crookesite, *n.* *krook*-site, selenide of copper, thallium, and silver. (Sir Wm. *Crookes*, *d.* 1919, discoverer.)

croon, *n.* kroon, a continued moan; a soft, plaintive song: *v.i.* to hum to oneself; to intone or moan in the sentimental manner affected by certain dance-band vocalists. (Scots.)

crooner, *n.* *kroon*-er, one who moans, or sings, songs with exaggerated sentimentality.

crooning, *n.* *kroon*-ing, a low humming; the moaning, or singing, of crooners.

crop, *n.* krop, the first stomach of a fowl; the craw; corn or fruit as growing, or as gathered in harvest; anything cut off or gathered; hair cut close or short; the stick of a hunting whip; an outcrop [Mining]; an entire hide [Comm.]: *v.t.* to cut off the ends of anything; to mow; to reap; to pluck; to gather before it falls; to raise crops on: *v.i.* to yield harvest; to bear fruit. **neck and crop,**

altogether. **to crop out,** to appear as an outcrop [Geol.]. **to crop up,** to come to light; to arise unexpectedly. (A.S. *cropp*, the craw, a swelling.)
crop-ear, *n. krop*-eer, a horse with ears cropped.
crop-eared, *a. krop*-eerd, having the ears cropped.
cropful, *a. krop*-ful, having a full crop; satiated.
cropper, *n. krop*-per, one who or that which crops; a cloth-facing machine; a plant which yields a crop; a heavy fall. **to come a cropper,** to experience a disappointment, or to fall.
croppy, *n. krop*-pe, one with ears or with hair cropped.
crop-sick, *a. krop*-sik, sick from repletion.
croquet, *n. kroh*-kay, an open-air game played with hoops, balls, and mallets: *v.t.* to send off another's ball by striking one's own in contact with it: *v.i.* to play croquet. (Fr.)
croquette, *n.* kro-*ket*, a fried force-meat ball of minced meat or fowl with other ingredients; a rissole. (Fr.)
crore, *n.* krore, ten million rupees (£750,000), or 100 lakhs; the number 10,000,000. (Hind.)
crosier, *n. kroh*-ze-er *or kroh*-zher, the pastoral staff, or crook, of a bishop or abbot, his symbol of authority. (Fr. *croc*, hook.)
cross, *n.* kros, an upright with a transverse bar; the intersection of two bars; a gibbet consisting of two pieces of timber placed across each other, either in form of a †, +, T, or ×; the cross on which Christ suffered; Christ's sufferings or passion; the symbol of the Christian religion; the Christian religion itself; an ornament, monument, or mark, like a cross; a line drawn across another; anything that crosses, thwarts, obstructs, perplexes, or distresses; an affliction; a mixing of breeds in producing animals; the offspring of such crossing; a mixture; the chance contact of two circuits [Elect.]; a pre-arranged swindle, any piece of dishonesty (Slang]. **Cross of Calvary,** a cross on three steps. **fiery cross,** a wooden cross with its ends charred and dipped in blood formerly used as a call to arms. **Latin cross,** one with cross-beam two-thirds up, †. **St. Andrew's cross,** one like ×. **St. George's cross,** the Greek cross, +. **Tau cross,** St. Anthony's cross, T. **on the cross,** dishonestly, fraudulently [Slang]. **to take up the cross,** to be resolved to sacrifice self for some sacred interest in the spirit of Christ. **Victoria Cross,** the highest British award for bravery in action, open to all members of the armed forces and to certain other services and civilians attached thereto. (L. *crux*.)
cross, *a.* kros, transverse; falling athwart; opposite; adverse; perverse; untractable; peevish; interchanged; of a cross breed; not fair and square, dishonest [Slang]: *ad.* athwart; across; contrariwise.
cross, *v.t.* kros, to draw a line or lay one thing, as a sword, across another; to erase by cross lines; to cancel; to make the sign of the cross; to pass or move over from side to side; to thwart; to obstruct; to be inconsistent with; to debar; to cause to interbreed; to fertilize one variety from another; (of a cheque) to mark in such a way that it becomes payable only through a bank: *v.i.* to lie or be athwart; to pass from side to side directly or obliquely; to meet and pass (of letters, etc.): to hybridize.
cross-action, *n.* kros-*ak*-shon, a case in which the defendant brings an action against the plaintiff in respect of matters arising out of the original action [Law].
cross-arrow, *n.* a crossbow arrow.
cross-banded, *a.* with the grain of the veneer transverse to that of the veneered surface.
crossbar, *n. kros*-bar, a transverse bar. **cross-barred,** secured by transverse bars. **crossbar-shot,** a shot with an iron bar passing through it.
cross-beam, *n.* a large beam running from wall to wall.
cross-bearer, *n.* one who bears or wears a cross; the chaplain of an archbishop who bears a cross before him.
cross-belt, *n.* a belt crossing the body obliquely from over one shoulder.
cross-bench, *n.* a bench in either House of Parliament occupied by independent members; hence, **cross-bench mind,** an impartial outlook.
cross-bill, *n.* a bill filed by a defendant against the plaintiff; a bill of exchange given in view of another bill [Law.].
crossbill, *n. kros*-bil, a bird of the genus *Loxia*.
cross-birth, *n.* a labour in which the fœtus lies transversely in the uterus.
cross-bones, *n.pl.* a representation of two human thigh bones crossed, usually beneath a skull, used as a symbol of death and piracy.
cross-bow, *n. kros*-boh, a weapon for shooting, formed by placing a bow athwart a stock. **cross-bowman,** one who shoots with a crossbow.
cross-bred, *a.* produced from different strains or varieties; hybrid.
cross-breed, *n.* a breed produced from different breeds; a hybrid: *v.t.* to produce from different varieties; to cross-fertilize.
cross-buttock, *n.* a throw in wrestling in which one opponent pulls the other over his hip; an unanticipated defeat.
cross-channel, *a.* crossing the English Channel.
cross-country, *a. kros*-kun-tre, across fields and woodlands as in hunting and hare-and-hounds.
cross-current, *n.* a current running counter to another; a conflicting tendency.
crosscut, *n. kros*-kut, a short traverse; a dancing step; a figure in skating: *v.t.* to cut across. **cross-cut saw,** a saw adapted for cutting across the grain.
crosse, *n.* kros, the long racket-like stick used in lacrosse.
crossed, *pp.* krost, having a line drawn over; cancelled; thwarted. **crossed cheque,** a cheque which, being crossed, can be paid only through a bank, or through the bank specified in the crossing.
cross-examination, *n.* a close and rigid examination of a witness by the opposing counsel.
cross-examine, *v.t. kros*-eg-*zam*-in, to examine a witness by the opposite counsel, esp. with intent to clarify evidence previously given.
cross-eyed, *a. kros*-ide, squinting inwards; affected by strabismus.
cross-fertilization, *n.* the fertilization of a plant by pollen from one of another species.
cross-fertilize, *v.t.* and *i.* to accomplish or to undergo cross-fertilization.
cross-fire, *n.* firing in crossing directions [Mil.].
cross-frog, *n.* a device enabling flanged wheels to cross from one set of rails to another [Rly. Eng.].
cross-garnet, *n.* a T-shaped door-hinge, the cross-piece being screwed to the jamb, the long arm to the door.
cross-grained, *a. kros*-graynd, with grain or fibres across or irregular; perverse; intractable.
cross-hatching, *n.* crossing regularly to produce effects of shade, said of lines in engraving.
crosshead, *n. kros*-hed, the block at the end of the piston rod where the connecting rod joins on [Eng.]; a heading across a page or column [Print.].
crossing, *n. kros*-sing, the act of crossing; place of crossing; the intersection of roads, railways, etc., also of the transepts and nave of a church; opposition; contradiction.
crossjack, *n. kros*-jak, the lowest yard on the mizen-mast.
cross-legged, *a. kros*-legd, with one leg resting on the other.
crosslet, *n. kros*-let, a small cross on the arms of another cross; a cross crossed at a small distance from the ends [Her.].
crossly, *ad. kros*-le, in a cross manner.
cross-moline, *n.* kros-*moh*-line, *see* **moline.**
crossness, *n. kros*-ness, the state of being cross, especially in temper.
cross-over, *n.* that which crosses over; a place for crossing over; a wrap covering the shoulders and crossing over the breast; a fabric with a design extending from selvage to selvage.
crosspatch, *n. kros*-patch, a disagreeable person.
cross-piece, *n.* a piece crossing at any angle; a rail extending over the windlass [Naut.].
cross-pollination, *n.* cross-fertilization.
cross-purpose, *n.* a contrary purpose; contradiction. **at cross-purposes,** misunderstanding, or intentionally acting contrary to, each other.
cross-question, *v.t.* to cross-examine: *n.* a question put in cross-examination.
cross-reference, *n.* a reference from one subject to another, or from one part of a book to another, where additional information may be found: *v.t.* to provide with a cross-reference or cross-references

crossroad, *n.* the intersection of two or more roads (generally in *pl.*) ; a by-road leading from one main road to another. **at the crossroads,** at a critical juncture or turning-point.
cross-ruff, *v.i.* to trump one's opponents' cards alternately (of partners at bridge, contract, etc.).
cross-section, *n.* a cutting at right angles to the axis of anything ; the surface so exposed.
cross-springer, *n.* in groined vaulting, the rib extending from one pier to another.
cross-staff, *n.* an instrument formerly used at sea to take altitudes ; one to take off-sets in surveying.
cross-stitch, *n.* needlework in which the stitches cross each other.
cross-stone, *n.* the mineral harmotome.
cross-talk, *n. kros*-tawk, back-chat ; mutual interference of two or more telephonic or other conversations.
cross-tie, *n.* a railway sleeper ; a connecting band in building [Arch.].
cross-trees, *n.pl.* horizontal pieces of timber across the mast-head to spread the upper shrouds [Naut.].
cross-vaulting, *n.* the intersection of two or more simple vaults of arch-work [Arch.].
crossway, *n. kros*-way, a crossroad ; an intersection of roads.
crossways, *a.* and *ad. kros*-wayz, intersecting like a cross ; placed or done in a thwart direction ; transversely.
cross-wind, *n.* a side wind ; an unfavourable wind.
crosswise, *ad. kros*-wize, across ; in the form of a cross.
crossword, *n. kros*-wurd, a puzzle consisting of a diagram divided into squares for containing letters which, according to the clues provided, make words across and downwards.
crosswort, *n. kros*-wurt, popular name of various plants, including *Galium cruciatum*, with leaves arranged crosswise.
crotaline, *a. kroh*-ta-line, pertaining to the rattlesnakes. (L. *crotalum*, a rattle.)
crotch, *n.* krotch, a forking ; the parting of two legs or branches ; a crooked timber placed on the keel in the fore and aft parts of a ship [Naut.]. (*Crook.*)
crotched, *a.* krotcht, having a crotch ; forked.
crotchet, *n. krotch*-et, a bracket including words, a sentence, or a passage distinguished from the rest, thus [ ] [Print.] ; a note or character (♩) equal in time to half a minim, and the double of a quaver [Mus.] ; a peculiar turn or twist of mind ; a whim, fancy, or conceit. (Fr. *crochet*, a hook.)
crotchetiness, *n.* quality of being crotchety.
crotchety, *a. krotch*-e-te, having crotchets ; faddy.
Croton, *n. kroh*-ton, a large genus of plants of the spurge family, of which *C. tiglium* yields croton-oil and *C. cascarilla*, cascarilla bark. (Gr., a tick or mite, which the seeds resemble.)
crotonate, *n. kroh*-to-nate, a salt of crotonic acid.
crotonic, *a.* kro-*ton*-ik, produced by the croton-plant. **crotonic acid,** an acid derived from the croton-plant.
crottle, *n. krot*-tl, any of several lichens used in dyeing. (Gael. *crotal.*)
crouch, *v.i.* krouch, to bend or stoop low ; to lie close to the ground ; to fawn ; to cringe : *n.* the act or posture of crouching. (O.Fr. *crochir*, to become crooked.)
crouchware, *n. krouch*-ware, a salt-glazed ware formerly made in Staffordshire.
croup, *n.* kroop, an inflammation of the larynx and trachea, accompanied with a hoarse cough and difficult respiration. (Imit.)
croup, *n.* kroop, the rump of a fowl ; the buttocks of a horse ; the part behind the saddle. (Fr. *croupe.*)
croupade, *n.* kroo-*pade*, a leap in which a horse pulls up his hind legs, as though to draw them up to his belly. (Fr.)
croupier, *n. kroo*-pe-er, the president of a gaming-table ; a vice-chairman. (Fr.)
croupy, *a. kroo*-pe, with the symptoms of croup.
croûton, *n. kroo*-ton, a small piece of fried bread served with soups and as a garnish to dishes. (Fr.)
crow, *n.* kroh, a bird of the genus *Corvus* ; a crowbar ; the cry of the cock ; the joyful cry of an infant : *v.i.* to make a noise like a cock, in joy, gaiety, or defiance ; to boast in triumph ; to exult. **carrion crow,** *C. corone.* **hooded crow,** *C. cornix.* a **crow to pluck,** a charge to make which requires explanation. (A.S. *crāwan.*)
crowbar, *n. kroh*-bar, a bar of iron bent at one end, and used as a lever.
crowberry, *n. kroh*-be-re, a heath-like plant, *Empetrum nigrum*, so called from its black berry.
crowd, *n.* kroud, a number of things or persons collected closely and promiscuously together ; any group, large or small, of supers photographed in a film [Cine.] ; the lower orders ; the rabble : *v.t.* to press ; to drive together ; to fill to excess ; to urge [U.S.A.] *v.i.* to press in numbers or urge forward ; to swarm. **to crowd sail,** to carry an extraordinary spread of sail [Naut.]. (A.S. *crūdan.*)
crowd, *n.* kroud, an obsolete six-stringed instrument resembling the violin. (Welsh, *crwth.*)
crowder, *n. kroud*-er, a performer on the crowd ; a fiddler.
crowdie *or* **crowdy,** *n. kroud*-e, a mixture of meal and cold water, sometimes with milk. (Scots.)
crowfoot, *n. kroh*-foot, a complication of small cords spreading out from a long block [Naut.] ; any plant of the genus *Ranunculus* [Bot.].
crow-garlic, *n.* wild garlic, *Allium vineale.*
crowkeeper, *n. kroh*-keep-er, a boy employed to scare crows from new-sown land ; a bird scarer.
crown, *n.* kroun, a garland of honour ; a headband of gold surmounted by a diadem, esp. that worn by a ruling sovereign ; regal power ; royalty ; splendour ; the top of the head, of a mountain, or hat ; completion ; a five-shilling piece ; the English name of certain foreign coins ; a size of paper, 20 by 15 in. ; the uppermost member of the cornice, including the corona [Arch.] ; the vertex of an arch ; the highest part of a road, bridge, etc. ; the part of a tooth above the gum ; the end of an anchor shank : (*cap.*) the sovereign as head of the state : *v.t.* to invest with a crown or with regal power ; to honour, dignify, or adorn ; to reward ; to complete ; to provide (a defective tooth) with an artificial crown : *a.* belonging to the sovereign or the state. **crown agent,** an official acting as the commercial and financial agent in the United Kingdom for the government of a crown colony, or protectorate, etc. ; in Scotland, the solicitor in charge, under the Lord Advocate, of criminal prosecutions. **crown colony,** a colony governed direct by the Crown, as distinct from the self-governing dominions ; a colony directly administered by the Colonial Office. **Crown Derby,** a special porcelain made in Derby. **crown glass,** a leadless alkali-lime-silica glass used for electric-lamp bulbs, etc. ; a bull's-eye window of similar glass. **crown imperial,** the beautiful flowering plant, *Fritillaria imperialis.* **crown jewels,** the jewels adorning the crowns, or belonging to the state regalia of a monarch. **crown land,** land or other real property belonging to the state. **crown law,** part of the common law of England applicable to criminal matters. **crown lawyer,** a lawyer in the service of the Crown. **Crown living,** a living or benefice of which the Crown is patron. **crown octavo,** a book-page size, 7×5 in. **crown office,** a branch of the High Court which conducts the administrative business of the Crown in issuing writs and other ways. **crown prince,** the male heir apparent to certain thrones. (Fr. *couronne.*)
crown-antler, *n.* the topmost tine of a stag's horns.
crowner, *n. kroun*-er, an obsolete form of " coroner."
crowning, *a. kroun*-ing, that crowns or completes : *n.* the completion of a member or any ornamental work [Arch.] ; the finishing part of a knot or interweaving of the strands [Naut.].
crownless, *a.* without, or deprived of, a crown.
crownpost, *n. kroun*-pohst, a kingpost [Arch.].
crown-wheel, *n.* a wheel with cogs at right angles to its plane ; the wheel which drives the balance in a watch.
crowquill, *n. kroh*-kwil, a slender steel pen for fine sketching, originally made from the quill of a crow.
crow's-bill, *n.* a kind of forceps for extracting bullets and other things from wounds [Surg.].
crow's-foot, *n. krohz*-foot, a wrinkle about the outer corners of the eyes ; a caltrop [Mil.] ; an arrangement of ropes to carry an awning [Naut.] ; an arrangement in which the strands of a rope are opened out for sticking to a fabric surface.

crow's-nest, *n.* a look-out station on a mast.
crowsteps, *n.pl.* *kroh*-steps, the series of steps crowning a gable wall.
crow-stone, *n.* *kroh*-stone, a gable topstone.
croy, *n.* kroy, an enclosure for catching fish; a barrier built out into a river to prevent erosion.
croze, *n.* kroze, a tool used by coopers; the groove that holds the cask-head.
crozier, *n.* *kroh*-ze-er *or* *kroh*-zher, a crosier.
crucial, *a.* *kroo*-shal, transverse; intersecting [Surg.]; in form of a cross [Anat.]; severe; decisive. (Fr.)
crucian, *n.* *kroo*-shan, a fish of the same genus *Carassius*, as the goldfish. (Low Ger. *karusse.*)
cruciate, *a.* *kroo*-she-at, cruciform [Bot. and Zool.]. (L. *cruciatus*, tortured.)
crucible, *n.* *kroo*-se-bl, a small pot of some refractory material used by chemists, founders, etc., for melting purposes; a sump at the bottom of a furnace to receive the melted metal; a severe test or trial. **crucible steel**, fine hard steel used in making tools. (L. *crucibulum.*)
Cruciferæ, *n.pl.* kroo-*sif*-e-ree, a natural order of plants, the petals of whose flowers are disposed crosswise [Bot.]. (L. *crux*, and *fero*, bear.)
cruciferous, *a.* kroo-*sif*-e-rus, bearing the cross; with four petals in the form of a cross [Bot.].
crucifix, *n.* *kroo*-se-fiks, a representation or effigy of Christ on the cross. (Fr.)
crucifixion, *n.* kroo-se-*fik*-shon, the act of crucifying; punishment by death on the cross; (*cap.*) the death of Christ on the cross; a picture of this.
cruciform, *a.* *kroo*-se-fawrm, cross-shaped; disposed in the form of a cross [Bot.]. (L. *crux*, and *forma*, shape.)
crucify, *v.t.* *kroo*-se-fy, to put to death by nailing hands and feet to a cross; to mortify the power of.
crude, *a.* krood, raw; in the natural state; unripe; not digested; immature; imperfectly considered and developed; ill arranged. (L. *crudus.*)
crudely, *ad.* in a crude manner.
crudeness, *n.* the state of being crude.
crudity, *n.* *krood*-e-te, crudeness; something in a crude or undigested state.
★**cruel**, *a.* *kroo*-el, disposed to give pain or sorrow to others; unfeeling; hard-hearted; proceeding from cruelty; causing pain. (Fr.)
cruelly, *ad.* *kroo*-el-le, in a cruel manner.
cruelty, *n.* *kroo*-el-te, the quality of being cruel; cruel disposition; a cruel act; inhumanity. (O.Fr. *cruelte.*)
cruet, *n.* *kroo*-et, a small container of glass, porcelain, etc., or set of these, for holding table-condiments; a eucharistic flagon. **cruet-stand**, *n.* a stand for holding cruets. (Dim. of O.Fr. *cruie.*)
cruise, *v.t.* krooz, to go to sea for naval purposes, or for pleasure: *n.* a voyage for such purpose. (Dut. *kruisen.*)
cruiser, *n.* *kroo*-zer, a person or a ship that cruises; a ship of war less heavily armoured than a battleship; a member of a cruising party. **cruiser-weight**, [Boxing] not exceeding 174 lb.
cruive, *n.* kroov, a wattle enclosure on a tidal flat for trapping fish.
crumb, *n.* krum, a small fragment of bread; the soft part of a loaf; a small piece of anything: *v.t.* to break into or spread with crumbs. **crumb-brush**, *n.* a curved brush for sweeping crumbs from a table-cloth. (A.S. *cruma.*)
crumble, *v.t.* *krum*-bl, to break into crumbs: *v.i.* to fall into small pieces; to fall to decay. (*Crumb.*)
crumbly, *a.* *krum*-ble, easily crumbled.
crumby, *a.* *krum*-e, not crusty.
crummy, *a.* *krum*-me, plump; buxom; lousy [Slang].
crump, *n.* krump, a hard hit; a bursting shell, or the sound it makes.
crumpet, *n.* *krum*-pet, a soft spongy cake, buttered and eaten when hot; the head [Slang]. (M.E. *crompit.*)
crumple, *v.t.* *krum*-pl, to draw or press into wrinkles; to rumple: *v.i.* to become creased. **to crumple up**, to collapse; to surrender. (A.S. *cromp.*)
crunch, *v.t.* and *i.* krunch, to crush something hard with the teeth.
cruor, *n.* *kroo*-or, clotted blood; gore. (L.)
crupper, *n.* *krup*-er, a strap extending from the saddle to and under a horse's tail, to keep the saddle from slipping forward; hind-quarters, esp of a horse: *v.t.* to put a crupper on. (Fr. *croupière.*)
crural, *a.* *kroor*-ral, pertaining to the leg or thighs. (L. *cruralis*, of the leg.)
crusade, *n.* kroo-*sade*, one of those military expeditions undertaken during the Middle Ages under the banner of the cross for the recovery of the Holy Land from the power of the Saracens; any joint enterprise conducted in an enthusiastic or fanatical spirit of opposition: *v.i.* to join in a crusade. (Fr. *croisade*, and Sp. *cruzada.*)
crusader, *n.* kroo-*say*-der, one engaged in a crusade.
crusado, *n.* kroo-*say*-doh, a former Portuguese silver coin, stamped with a cross. (Port. *cruzado.*)
cruse, *n.* krooz, a small pot or bottle. (M.E., perhaps from O.Scand. *krūs*, a little vessel.)
★**crush**, *n.* krush, a violent collision which bruises; a crowd; pressure by a crowd; a large social gathering: *v.t.* to press or squeeze into a mass; to bruise or break by pressure; to overwhelm by power; to subdue; to bruise small: *v.i.* to be pressed into a smaller compass by external weight or force. **crush room**, a saloon with refreshment bar at a theatre, etc., for use between the acts. (O.Fr. *cruisir*, break.)
crusher, *n.* *krush*-er, one who or that which crushes.
crust, *n.* krust, a hard outside rind, coating, or covering, as of a loaf; a piece of hard bread; the top pastry of a pie; a deposit from wine as it ripens, collected on the interior of bottles: *v.t.* to cover with a crust: *v.i.* to gather into a crust. **crust of the earth**, its solid exterior. (L. *crusta*, the hard surface of a body.)
crustacea, *n.pl.* krus-*tay*-she-a, one of the classes of the arthropoda, including lobsters, shrimps, and crabs, so called from their crust-like shell.
crustacean, *a.* krus-*tay*-she-an, belonging to the crustacea: *n.* one of the crustacea.
crustaceological, *a.* krus-*tay*-she-o-*loj*-e-kal, pertaining to crustaceology.
crustaceologist, *n.* krus-*tay*-she-*ol*-o-jist, one versed in crustaceology.
crustaceology, *n.* krus-*tay*-she-*ol*-o-je, the science of the crustacea. (L. *crusta*, and Gr. *logos*, science.)
crustaceous, *a.* krus-*tay*-she-us, pertaining to crust; of the nature of crust or shell; thin, hard, and brittle [Bot.]; crustacean.
crustate, *a.* *krus*-tat, crusted; crustaceous.
crustation, *n.* krus-*tay*-shon, an incrustation.
crustily, *ad.* *krus*-te-le, in a crusty manner.
crustiness, *n.* the quality of being crusty.
crusty, *a.* *krus*-te, like crust; hard; outwardly harsh; surly; snappish; peevish; morose.
crutch, *n.* krutch, a staff with a cross piece for the armpit, as a support to a lame person; a support like a crutch; the leg-rest of a side-saddle; the fork or crotch of the body; various devices used for spars, etc. [Naut.]; *v.i.* to go on crutches: *v.t.* to support on crutches. (A.S. *cryce.*)
crutched, *pp.* and *a.* krutcht, bearing or wearing a cross. **crutched friars**, name of a former minor order of friars.
crux, *n.* kruks, (*pl.* **cruxes**, *kruk*-sez, *or* **cruces**, *kroo*-seez), anything that puzzles much. (L.)
cruzeiro, *n.* kroo-*zay*-roh, the Brazilian currency unit that in 1942 superseded the milreis, equal to 100 centavos, or then about 3⅛*d*.
crwth, *n.* krooth, a crowd; the old Welsh violin. (W.)
★**cry**, *v.i.* kry, to call loudly or vehemently or importunately; to weep; to utter a loud voice in weeping; to proclaim; to bawl; to squall; to yelp: *v.t.* to proclaim loudly and publicly in giving notice. **cry against**, to exclaim with a loud voice, by way of reproof, threatening, or censure. **cry down**, to decry; to depreciate. **cry off**, to withdraw. **cry out**, to exclaim; to vociferate; to clamour. **cry out against**, to complain loudly, with a view to censure; to blame. **cry quits**, to declare matters equal. **cry stinking fish**, to decry that in which one has a personal interest. **cry to**, to implore. **cry up**, to praise; to applaud. **much cry, little wool**, *see* **wool**. (Fr. *crier.*)
cry, *n.* kry (*pl.* **cries**, kryz), a loud or vehement sound especially of weeping or lamentation; call; exclamation of triumph, wonder, or other passion; shout; proclamation; public notice, as by a hawker of his wares; bitter complaint of oppression and injustice; rumour; party call; the sound or voice of certain animals; expression of joy,

fright, alarm, or want; a pack of hounds; a pack. **a far cry,** a long way off; a progression through a long sequence. **in full cry,** in eager pursuit.
crying, *a. kry*-ing, specially calling for punishment; notorious: *n.* importunate call; clamour; outcry.
cryogen, *n. kry*-o-jen, any freezing mixture [Chem.].
cryolite, *n. kry*-o-lite, Greenland spar, a fluoride of aluminium and sodium transparent when immersed in water [Min.]. (Gr. *kryos,* icy cold, *lithos,* a stone.)
cryometer, *n.* kry-*om*-e-ter, an alcohol or other thermometer for measuring low temperatures.
cryophorus, *n.* kry-*of*-er-us, an instrument for freezing water by its own evaporation. (Gr. *kryos,* and *phero,* produce.)
crypt, *n.* kript, a subterranean cell or cave for purposes of interment; a vaulted basement under a church, used for religious service and burial. (L. *crypta,* vault.)
crypt-, crypto-, *comb. f.* signifying hidden, secret, or clandestine, as in **crypto-communist, crypto-Jew,** etc.
cryptæsthesia, *n. krip*-tee-*thee*-ze-a, clairvoyant or telepathic power of perception [Psych.]. (*crypt-,* and *æsthesia.*)
cryptarchy, *n. krip*-tar-ke, secret government. (*crypt-,* and *archein,* rule.)
cryptic, *a. krip*-tik, hidden; secret; occult.
cryptically, *ad. krip*-te-ka-le, secretly.
cryptobranchiate, *a.* krip-to-*brang*-ke-at, having inconspicuous gills.
cryptogam, *n. krip*-to-gam, a flowerless plant.
Cryptogamia, *n.* krip-to-*gay*-me-a, that division of plants whose organs of fructification are concealed or not distinctly visible, such as ferns mosses, and lichens. (Gr. *krypto,* hide, *gamos,* marriage.)
cryptogamic, *a.* krip-to-*gam*-ik, pertaining to plants of the cryptogamia.
cryptogamist, *n.* krip-*tog*-a-mist, one skilled in cryptogamic botany.
cryptogamous, *a.* krip-*tog*-a-mus, cryptogamic.
cryptogamy, *n.* krip-*tog*-a-me, concealed fructification.
cryptogram, *n. krip*-to-gram, a writing in cipher.
cryptograph, *n. krip*-to-graf, a writing or system of writing in secret characters. (Gr. *krypto,* and *grapho,* write.)
cryptographer, *n.* krip-*tog*-ra-fer, one skilled in cryptography.
cryptographical, *a.* krip-to-*graf*-e-kal, written in cryptograph.
cryptography, *n.* krip-*tog*-ra-fe, the act or art of writing in secret characters.
crypto-Jew, *n. krip*-to-*joo,* a Jew who while professing some other religion is a secret practiser of his own.
cryptology, *n.* krip-*tol*-o-je, secret or enigimatic language.
Cryptomeria, *n.* krip-to-*meer*-re-a, a genus of evergreen conifers comprising only the Japanese cedar, *C. japonica.*
cryptonym, *n. krip*-to-nim, a name one bears in a secret society. (Gr. *krypto,* and *onoma,* a name.)
crystal, *n. kris*-tal, an inorganic body which has assumed the form of a regular solid, terminated by a certain number of plane and smooth surfaces; glass of a superior composition and manufacture; anything clear as crystal: *a.* consisting of crystal; clear and transparent like crystal. **crystal set,** a simple wireless receiving apparatus in which the valves are replaced by a small piece of galena, molybdenite, or other crystal and a " cat's whisker " [Wire.]. (Fr. *cristal,* from Gr. *krystallos,* ice, from *kryos,* icy cold.)
crystal-gazing, *n.* the practice of divination or fortune-telling by means of peering into a crystal; scrying.
crystalline, *a. kris*-ta-lin, of or like crystal; clear; transparent. **crystalline lens,** a white, transparent firm substance, situated behind the iris of the eye [Anat.]. (L. *crystallinus.*)
crystallite, *n. kris*-ta-lite, a whinstone that has cooled slowly after fusion; a minute and imperfect crystal.
crystallizable, *a. kris*-ta-*lize*-a-bl, that may form or be formed into crystals.
crystallization, *n. kris*-ta-ly-*zay*-shon, the act or process by which the parts of a solid body, after separation by solution in a fluid or by fusion, coalesce into regular crystalline form.
crystallize, *v.t. kris*-ta-lize, to cause to form crystals; to coat with crystals: *v.i.* to be or become converted into crystalline form.
crystallogenic, *a. kris*-ta-lo-*jen*-ik, forming crystals; producing crystallization.
crystallogeny, *n.* kris-ta-*loj*-en-e, the branch of science dealing with the formation of crystals. (Gr. *krystallos,* and *gennoa,* produce.)
crystallographer, *n. kris*-ta-*log*-ra-fer, one who describes crystals, or the manner of their formation.
crystallographic, *a. kris*-ta-lo-*graf*-ik, pertaining to crystallography.
crystallography, *n.* kris-ta-*log*-ra-fe, the science of the forms, properties, and structure of crystals. (Gr. *krystallos,* and *grapho,* write.)
crystalloid, *a. kris*-ta-loyd, like a crystal: *n.* a crystalloid substance, esp. a minute crystalline particle of protein present in certain vegetable oils; a substance which will pass through membrane in dialysis. (Gr. *krystallos,* and *eidos,* like.)
crystallomancy, *n. kris*-tal-o-*man*-se, divination by crystals or translucent stones; scrying. (Gr. *krystallos,* and *manteia,* divination.)
crystoleum, *n.* kris-*toh*-le-um, an obsolete process of transferring photographs to glass. (Gr. *krystallos,* and L. *oleum,* oil.)
csardas, *n. char*-dahsh, czardas. (Hung.)
ctene, *n.* teen, one of the swimming-organs or comb-plates of a ctenophore.
ctenoid, *a. tee*-noyd, pectinate; comb-shaped. (Gr. *kteis, ktenos,* a comb, *eidos,* like.)
Ctenoidei, *n.pl.* te-*noy*-de-e, Agassiz's, the third order of fishes (now grouped with the Teleostei), having scales with pectinate edges, as the perch.
ctenophore, *n. tee*-no-fore, a cœlenterate animal swimming with fringed or comb-like organs.
cub, *n.* kub, the young of certain animals, as the bear and fox; a puppy; a junior Boy Scout; a boy, in contempt: *v.i.* to bring forth cubs. (Perhaps from Ir. *cuib,* whelp.)
cubage, *n. kew*-baj, the contents of a solid; cubature.
Cuban, *n. kew*-ban, a native of Cuba: *a.* pertaining to Cuba.
cubature, *n. kew*-ba-tewr, the finding exactly the solid or cubic contents.
cubbing, *n. kub*-bing, hunting fox-cubs.
cubbish, *a. kub*-bish, ill-mannered; boorish.
cubby-hole, *n. kub*-be-hole, a snuggery; a small storage place.
cube, *n.* kewb, a regular solid body, with six equal square sides, and containing equal angles; the product of a number multiplied into itself, and that product multiplied into the same number [Arith.]; *v.t.* to raise to the third power or cube; to calculate the cubic content of. **cube root,** the number or quantity which, raised to the third power, produces the cube. (Fr.)
cubeb, *n. kew*-beb, the small spicy medicinal berry of *Piper cubeba,* akin to pepper. (Sp. *cubeba.*)
cubebine, *n. kew*-be-bine, a vegetable principle, neutral and tasteless, found in cubeb seeds.
cubic, *a. kew*-bik, having the form of a cube; contained within a cube; isometric (of crystals). **cubic equation,** an equation in which the highest power of the unknown quantity is a cube [Alg.].
cubical, *a. kew*-be-kal, cubic.
cubically, *ad. kew*-be-ka-le, in a cubical way.
cubicle, *n. kew*-be-kl, a small bedroom; a division of a dormitory. (L. *cubiculum,* a little bedroom.)
cubiform, *a. kew*-be-fawrm, in the form of a cube.
cubism, *n. kew*-bizm, a style dating from the early 20th cent. in art in which the subject is presented in a way which gives the effect of an arrangement of geometrical figures.
cubist, *n. kew*-bist, an artist who works in the style of cubism: *a.* pertaining to cubism.
cubit, *n. kew*-bit, a former measure of length, based on a man's fore-arm and varying from 18 to 22 inches. (L. *cubitus,* the elbow.)
cubital, *a. kew*-be-tal, of the length of a cubit; pertaining to the fore-arm or corresponding part in animals. (L. *cubitalis.*)
cubitus, *n. kew*-be-tus, the forearm [Anat.]; the part of an insect's foreleg corresponding to the tibia [Ent.]. (L.)

cuboid, *a.* *kew*-boyd, having nearly the form of a cube: *n.* a cube-like solid but having unequal sides. (Gr. *kybos*, and *eidos*, like.)
cuboidal, *a.* kew-*boy*-dal, cuboid
cucking-stool, *n.* *kuk*-ing-stool, a chair of an undignified construction in which scolds and minor offenders were exposed or ducked. (O. Scand. *kuka*, to void excrement, and **stool.**)
cuckold, *n.* *kuk*-kold, a man whose wife is unfaithful; the husband of an adulteress: *v.t.* to make a man a cuckold by adultery with his wife, or a husband such by adultery with another man. (M.E., perhaps from **cuckoo.**)
cuckoldom, *n.* *kuk*-kol-dum, the state of being a cuckold.
cuckoldry, *n.* *kuk*-ol-dre, the practice of cuckolds.
cuckoo, *n.* *kook*-oo, a family of birds including *Cuculus canorus*, the common cuckoo, which deposits its eggs in other birds' nests. **cuckoo ray,** a species of skate, *Raia circularis*. **cuckoo's mate,** the wryneck. **cuckoo's-meat,** the wood sorrel, and other plants. (L. *cuculus.*)
cuckoo-clock, *n.* a clock in which the hours are marked by the appearance and call of a cuckoo.
cuckoo-flower, *n.* the name of several plants, esp. lady's smock, *Cardamine pratensis*.
cuckoo-pint, *n.* the plant *Arum maculatum*.
cuckoo-spit *or* **-spittle,** *n.* a frothy secretion exuded by the frog-hopper to hide its larvæ.
cucullate, *a.* *kew*-kul-lat, hooded; having the shape of a hood. (L. *cucullatus*, hooded.)
cucumber, *n.* *kew*-kum-ber, the trailing plant, *Cucumis sativus*, and its fruit, extensively used as a pickle and salad. (L. *cucumis*, cucumber.)
cucumiform, *a.* kew-*kew*-me-form, having the elongated shape of a cucumber.
cucurbit, *n.* kew-*kur*-bit, a gourd; a chemical vessel in the shape of a gourd. (L., a gourd.)
cucurbitaceous, *a.* kew-*kur*-be-*tay*-shus, like a gourd; belonging to the cucumber family.
cud, *n.* kud, food which ruminating animals return to the mouth, and chew at leisure. **to chew the cud,** to ruminate; [Fig.] to ponder. (A.S. *ceowan*, to chew.)
cudbear, *n.* *kud*-bare, the lichen, *Lecanora tartarea*, used in dyeing purple; the dye obtained from this. (After Dr. *Cuthbert* Gordon.)
cuddle, *v.i.* *kud*-dl, to embrace closely; to lie close or snug together: *v.t.* to hug; to fondle. (Origin unknown.)
cuddlesome, *a.* *kud*-dl-sum, fit for cuddling; inviting to be cuddled.
cuddy, *n.* *kud*-de, a small cabin in the fore part of a boat; a cupboard; the coal-fish.
cuddy, *n.* *kud*-de, an ass; a donkey.
cudgel, *n.* *kud*-jel, a short thick stick: *v.t.* to beat with a cudgel; to beat. **to cudgel one's brains,** to strive to recollect something or to get a notion of. **to take up the cudgels,** to strike in and fight. (A.S. *cycgel.*)
cudweed, *n.* *kud*-weed, a species of *Gnaphalium*. **cudweed moth,** *Cucullia gnaphalii*. **mountain cudweed,** *Antennaria dioica*.
cue, *n.* kew, the tail or end of a thing, especially of a wig; the last words of a speech which give the next speaker or player an intimation to begin; the part one is to take up; a hint; turn or temper of mind; the tapering rod used in playing billiards. **cue ball,** the ball struck by the cue. (Fr. *queue.*)
cueist, *n.* *kew*-ist, a billiard-player [Slang].
cuff, *n.* kuf, a blow with the hand; a stroke; a box: *v.t.* to strike with the hand. (Scand.)
cuff, *n.* kuf, the fold at the end of a sleeve: a detached linen band for the wrist. (Etym. unknown.)
Cufic, *n.* *kew*-fik, Kufic.
cuirass, *n.* kwe-*ras*, a leather or metal breastplate and backplate strapped together as body-armour; an analagous covering of animals; a woman's close-fitting bodice. (Fr. *cuirasse.*)
cuirassier, *n.* kwe-ra-*seer*, a cavalryman wearing a cuirass. (Fr.)
cuir-bouilli, *n.* (App.), leather boiled and prepared with certain gums. (Fr.)
cuish, *n.* kwish, cuisse.
cuisine, *n.* kwe-*zeen*, the kitchen department; cookery; style of cooking. (Fr.)
cuisse, *n.* kwis, defensive armour for the thighs. (Fr.)

culch, *n.* kulch, cultch.
Culdee, *n.* *kul*-dee, one of a monastic order having settlements in Scotland and Ireland in the 8th cent. and later. (Ir. *célé dé*, servant of God.)
cul-de-sac, *n.* *kool*-de-*sak*, a street open only at one end; a situation with no retreat in flank or rear [Mil.]. (Fr. literally, bottom of the bag.)
culet, *n.* *kew*-let, the collet, the flat surface forming the base of a diamond cut as a brilliant.
Culex, *n.* *kew*-leks, the genus of dipterous insects comprising the gnats and mosquitoes. (L.)
culiciform, *a.* kew-*lis*-e-fawrm, in the form of a gnat.
culinary, *a.* *kul*-e-na-re, relating to the kitchen, or to the art of cookery. (L. *culina*, the kitchen.)
cull, *n.* kul, an animal selected as unsuitable for breeding purposes and so fattened for killing.
cull, *v.t.* kul, to select; to pick out. (O.Fr. *cuillir.*)
cullender, *n.* *kul*-len-der, a colander.
cullet, *n.* *kul*-let, broken glass intended for remelting.
cullion, *n.* *kul*-yon, a base wretch; a bulbous root. (Fr. *couille*, a testicle.)
cullionly, *a.* *kul*-yon-le, mean; base.
cullis, *n.* *kul*-lis, broth of meat; a strained jelly. (Fr.)
cully, *n.* *kul*-le, a pal or mate; one easily imposed on; a silly dupe [Slang].
culm, *n.* kulm, the stalk or stem of grasses, jointed and hollow [Bot.]. (L. *culmus*, stalk.)
culm, *n.* kulm, anthracitic shale, an impure shaly kind of coal; small coal; slack. (M.E.)
culmiferous, *a.* kul-*mif*-er-us, abounding in culm or anthracite; having a jointed stalk [Bot.].
culminant, *a.* *kul*-me-nant, having reached its greatest altitude [Astron.]; at the summit; topmost.
culminate, *v.i.* *kul*-me-nate, to be vertical; to reach the highest point: *v.t.* to bring to a head, or to a conclusion. (L. *culminatus*, culminated.)
culmination, *n.* kul-me-*nay*-shon, the transit of a heavenly body across the meridian; its highest or lowest altitude or point attained.
culpability, *n.* kul-pa-*bil*-e-te, culpableness.
culpable, *a.* *kul*-pa-bl, deserving or involving blame. (O.Fr., from L. *culpa*, a fault.)
culpableness, *n.* the quality of being culpable; liability to blame.
culpably, *ad.* *kul*-pa-ble, in a culpable manner.
culprit, *n.* *kul*-prit, one in fault; an offender a person arraigned in court for a crime [Law]. (O.Fr. *culpable*, with *prest*, meaning prepared to prove it).
cult, *n.* kult, a particular system of worship; a code of rites and ceremonies; excessive devotion to some person, theory, etc. (Fr. *culte.*)
cultch, *n.* kulch, the material (broken shells, tiles, etc.) of which an oyster-bed is made; rubbish.
cultivable, *a.* *kul*-te-va-bl, capable of being cultivated.
cultivate, *v.t.* *kul*-te-vate, to till; to raise by tillage; to improve by labour or study; to study; to cherish, to foster, to labour to improve; to civilize; to seek the friendship of. (L. *cultivatus*, tilled.)
cultivation, *n.* kul-te-*vay*-shon, the art or practice of cultivating; the state of being cultivated; culture; refinement; study.
cultivator, *n.* *kul*-te-vay-tor, one who tills land; one who improves or studies to improve; a harrow for use on land with growing crops.
cultrate, *a.* *kul*-trate, shaped like a knife-edge [Zool.]. (L. *cultratus*, knife-like.)
cultriform, *a.* *kul*-tre-form, cultrate [Zool.].
cultural, *a.* *kul*-tewr-ral, pertaining to culture, or to a culture.
culture, *n.* *kul*-tewr, the act of tilling; cultivation; the application of labour, with a view to production or improvement; intellectual or moral discipline and training; the result of cultivation; a type or stage of civilization; artificial production of microscopic organisms; organisms developed in this way: *v.t.* to cultivate; to grow in or inoculate with a culture [Bacteriol.]. (Fr.)
cultureless, *a.* *kul*-tewr-less, having no culture.
cultus, *n.* *kul*-tus, cult. (L.)
culver, *n.* *kul*-ver, a wood-pigeon. (A.S. *culfre*, dove.)
culverin, *n.* *kul*-ver-in, an early form of musket, also a long gun, usually an 18-pounder, with snake handles—both obsolete. (Fr. *coulevrine.*)

culver-key, *n.* *kul*-ver-kee, the columbine.
culvert, *n.* *kul*-vert, an arched drain for passage of water under a road, canal, etc. (Origin unknown.)
cumbent, *a.* *kum*-bent, lying down. (L. *cumbens.*)
cumber, *n.* *kum*-ber, that which cumbers: *v.t.* to be a burden merely; to overload and hamper; to hamper and hinder; to perplex; to encumber. (O.Fr. *combrer.*)
cumberless, *a.* without anything to cumber.
cumbersome, *a.* *kum*-ber-sum, burdensome; troublesome; unwieldy; unmanageable.
cumbersomely, *ad.* in a manner to encumber.
cumbersomeness, *n.* the quality of being cumbersome.
Cumbrian, *a.* *kum*-bre-an, pertaining to the ancient British kingdom, Cumbria, or to Cumberland.
cumbrous, *a.* *kum*-brus, cumbersome; vexatious; obstructive.
cumbrously, *ad.* in a cumbrous manner.
cumbrousness, *n.* state of being cumbrous.
cumin, *n.* *kum*-in, an umbelliferous plant, *Cuminum cyminum,* with aromatic and carminative seeds. (A.S.)
cummer, *n.* *kum*-mer, a godmother; a gossip. (Fr. *commère.*)
cummerbund, *n.* *kum*-mer-bund, a waist-sash worn in India. (Pers. *kammerbund.*)
cummin, *n.* *kum*-in, cumin.
cumquat, *n.* *kum*-kwot, the kumquat.
cumshaw, *n.* *kum*-shaw, a present; baksheesh, in the East (Pidgin-Eng.)
cumulate, *v.t.* and *i.* *kew*-mew-late, to accumulate: *a.* accumulated; heaped up.
cumulative, *a.* *kew*-mew-la-tiv, increased by additions; at compound interest; increasing in cogency by accumulation of proof [Logic].
cumulus, *n.* *kew*-mew-lus, a cloud in convex masses piled one upon another. **cumulo-nimbus,** large cumulus clouds with a rain-cloud base resembling a nimbus. **cumulo-stratus,** cumulus clouds having a stratified appearance. (L., a heap.)
Cunarder, *n.* kew-*nar*-der, a vessel belonging to the Cunard, or Cunard-White Star, Line.
cunctative, *a.* *kunk*-ta-tiv, dilatory; given to delaying.
cuneate, *a.* *kew*-ne-at, wedge-shaped [Bot.]. (L. *cuneatus,* wedged.)
cuneiform, *a.* kew-*nee*-e-fawrm, wedge-shaped; *n.* cuneiform characters or writing. **cuneiform letters,** those in which inscriptions of ancient Persia, Babylonia, etc., are written, so termed from their wedge-like appearance. (L. *cuneus,* and *forma,* shape.)
cunning, *a.* *kun*-ning, knowing; skilful; artful; crafty; wrought with skill: *n.* knowledge acquired by experience; skill; art; craft; deceit. (A.S. *cunnan,* to know; connected with *ken* and *can.*)
cunningly, *ad.* *kun*-ning-le, in a cunning manner.
cunningness, *n.* craftiness; quality of being cunning.
***cup,** *n.* kup, a vessel to drink out of; the liquor contained in it; a cupful; the lot one is called on to endure; a sporting prize or trophy; the Eucharistic chalice; anything hollow like a cup; a cupping-glass; a cooling drink made with wine or cider, etc., flavoured with herbs: *v.t.* to apply a cupping-glass to draw blood from a scarified part of the body [Surg.]. (A.S. *cuppe.*)
cup-bearer, *n.* *kup*-bare-er, an officer of the king's household who tasted the wine before giving it to drink; an attendant to give wine at a feast.
cupboard, *n.* *kub*-ord, a closet or enclosed space with shelves; a sideboard. **cupboard love,** self-interested love.
cupel, *n.* *kew*-pel, a shallow vessel for refining precious metals: *v.t.* to assay or refine in a cupel. (Fr. *coupelle.*)
cupellation, *n.* kew-pel-*lay*-shon, refining or assaying by cupel.
cupful, *n.* *kup*-ful, the full contents of a cup.
Cupid, *n.* *kew*-pid, the Roman god of love [Myth.]. (L. *cupido,* passion.)
cupidity, *n.* kew-*pid*-e-te, an eager inordinate desire to possess; avarice; covetousness. (Fr. *cupidité.*)
cupola, *n.* *kew*-po-la, a cup-shaped vault on the top of an edifice; a small dome; a revolving armoured turret for a gun; a kind of furnace for melting metals. (It.)
cupper, *n.* *kup*-per, one who applies a cupping-glass.
cupping, *n.* *kup*-ping, the process of drawing blood with a cupping-glass. **cupping-glass,** a glass vessel like a cup applied to the skin in cupping.
cupreous, *a.* *kew*-pre-us, of, like, or composed of copper. (L. *cupreus,* coppery.)
cupric, *a.* *kew*-prik, containing divalent copper.
cupriferous, *a.* kew-*prif*-er-us, yielding copper.
cuprite, *n.* *kew*-prite, ruby copper; the red oxide of copper. (L. *coprum,* copper.)
cuproid, *n.* *kew*-proyd, a solid or a crystal having twelve equal triangular faces.
cupro-nickel, *n.* *kew*-pro-nikl, an alloy of 75 per cent copper and 25 per cent nickel replacing silver in the British coinage, 1946; also one of about four parts copper to one of nickel for the jackets of rifle bullets.
cuprous, *a.* *kew*-prus, containing univalent copper.
cup-tie, *n.* *kup*-ty, a game in a sporting contest in which the ultimate winner is awarded a cup; the final game in such a contest.
cupule, *n.* *kew*-pewl, the cup of the acorn, husk of the filbert, etc. [Bot.]; a cup-like organ [Zool.]. (L., a little cup.)
cur, *n.* kur, a worthless mongrel dog; a surly, unpleasant fellow. (Imit. of snarling.)
curable, *a.* *kewr*-a-bl, that may be cured or remedied.
curableness, *n.* a curable state. (Late L. *curabilis.*)
curacoa, *n.* *kew*-ra-*soh,* a liqueur flavoured with orange peel, cinnamon, and mace, deriving its name from the island of Curaçao.
curacy, *n.* *kewr*-a-se, the post of a curate; the benefice of a perpetual curate.
curare, *n.* kew-*rah*-re, the exudation of the South American tree *Strychnos toxifera,* used by the Indians as an arrow poison; the tree itself. (Tupi or Carib.)
curarine, *n.* kew-*rah*-rin, an alkaloid from curare.
curassow, *n.* kew-*ras*-so, a large-crested gallinaceous bird of the genus *Crax.* (The island, *Curaçao.*)
curate, *n.* *kewr*-rat, a clergyman in the Church of England appointed to assist the incumbent. **perpetual curate,** the incumbent of the church of an ecclesiastical district constituting part of an ancient parish (commonly known as a vicar). (L. *curatus.*)
curative, *a.* *kewr*-ra-tiv, curing; tending to cure.
curator, *n.* kew-*ray*-tor, one who has the superintendence of anything, esp. of a museum; a member of a governing body in certain Universities; the guardian appointed to manage for a minor or lunatic [Scots. Law]. (L.)
curatorship, *n.* the office of a curator.
curb, *n.* kurb, a chain attached to the branches of the bridle and running under the lower jaw, which it presses on when the rein is tightened [Men.]; restraint; check; anything that retains; a kerb or kerbstone; a swelling on a horse's leg due to strain or rupture of the ligament: *v.t.* to restrain; to guide and manage; to furnish with a curb. **curb roof,** a mansard roof. (Fr. *courber,* to bend, from L. *curvus,* curved.)
curbless, *a.* *kurb*-less, having no curb or restraint.
curculio, *n.* kur-*kew*-le-o, the corn-weevil. (L.)
Curcuma, *n.* *kur*-kew-ma, the genus of plants of the ginger family, of which *C. angustifolia* yields East Indian arrowroot, *C. longa* turmeric, and *C. zedoaria* zedoary. **curcuma paper,** a paper stained with turmeric, and used to test the presence of an alkali. (Ar. *kurkum,* saffron.)
curcumine, *n.* *kur*-kew-mine, the colouring matter obtained from the roots of the turmeric plant.
curd, *n.* kurd, the thickened part of milk; coagulated milk or matter of any kind. (A.S. *crūdan,* to press.)
curdle, *v.i.* *kur*-dl, to coagulate; to thicken into curd; to congeal: *v.t.* to change into curd; to coagulate or congeal.
curdy, *a.* *kur*-de, like curd; full of curd; coagulated.
cure, *n.* kewr, the act of healing; restoration to health or soundness; that which cures or heals; the care or spiritual charge of souls; the office of a curate; a parish: *v.t.* to heal; to restore to health or soundness; to preserve by salting and drying. **cure of souls,** ecclesiastical jurisdiction in a parish. (O.Fr.)
cure, *n.* kewr, an odd, whimsical, or eccentric person; a curious fellow [Slang].
curé, *n.* *kewr*-ray, a French parish priest. (Fr.)
cureless, *a.* *kewr*-less, that cannot be cured.

curer, *n. kewr*-rer, one who cures; one who prepares preserved food; a fish-drier.
curettage, *n.* kew-*ret*-aj, the act of scraping or cleaning with a curette.
curette, *n.* kew-*ret*, a scoop-like surgical instrument: *v.t.* to operate with this. (Fr.)
curfew, *n. kur*-few, the ringing of a bell at night as a signal to extinguish fires; the time of this, also the bell used for this. (Fr. *couvre-feu*, cover fire.)
curia, *n. kew*-re-a, a subdivision of a Roman tribe; the place of its assembly; a senate-house; a court of justice in the Middle Ages; the great council of the Anglo-Norman kings, the Curia Regis. **the Curia,** the Papal Court. (L.)
curialist, *n. kew*-re-a-list, a member, supporter, or student of the Papal Court.
curie, *n. kew*-re, the standard unit of radium emanation, the quantity in equilibrium with one gram of radium. (M. and Mme. *Curie*.)
curing-house, *n. kewr*-ing-hous, a building in which food is cured, sugar drained and dried, etc.
curio, *n. kew*-re-o, a curiosity; an objet d'art or article of virtu. (Abbr. for *curiosity*.)
curiosity, *n.* kew-re-*os*-e-te, a desire to know; inquisitiveness; an object of curiosity; a rarity.
curioso, *n.* kew-re-*oh*-soh, a collector of, or specialist in, curiosities. (It.)
curious, *a. kew*-re-us, desirous to know; inquisitive; careful about; nice; artful; wrought with care and art; singular; strange. (O.Fr. *curios*.)
curiously, *ad. kew*-re-us-le, in a curious manner.
curiousness, *n.* the quality of being curious.
curium, *n. kew*-re-um, the trans-uranic element No. 96. (*See* **curie**)
curl, *n.* kurl, a ringlet of hair or anything like it undulation; sinuosity; a scornful curving of the lip; a disease in potatoes, in which the leaves seem curled and shrunk up: *v.i.* to shrink into ringlets; to rise in undulations; to ripple; to writhe; to shrink back; to play curling: *v.t.* to twist into ringlets; to bend; to coil; to dress with curls; to raise in undulations or ripples. (M.E. *crul*, curl.)
curlew, *n. kur*-lew, one of a number of migratory wading birds with long curved bill, partly naked legs, and short tail, esp. the whaup and the whimbrel. (O.Fr. *corlieu*.)
curlicue, *n. kur*-le-kew, a quaintly twisted lock of hair; a flourish in writing.
curliness, *n.* a state of being curly; sinuosity.
curling, *n. kur*-ling, a Scottish winter game, played on ice, in which contending sides launch from the hand a heavy cheese-shaped stone having a handle on one flattened side, with the object of approaching nearest to the mark or tee. **curling stone,** the stone used, limited to: weight, 44 lb.; circumference, 36 in.; depth, not less than $\frac{1}{8}$th circumference.
curlingly, *ad.* in a waving manner; in curls.
curling-tongs, *n.* an instrument for curling the hair.
curl-paper, *n.* a strip of paper used in twisting hair into curls.
curly, *a. kur*-le, having curls; tending to curl; full of ripples; having wavy margins [Bot.].
curmudgeon, *n.* kur-*mudj*-on, an avaricious churlish fellow; a miser. (Unknown origin.)
curmudgeonly, *a.* avaricious; churlish.
curr, *v.i.* kur, to murmur like a dove or barn owl; to purr: *n.* this sound. (Imit.)
curragh, *n. ku*-rah, a coracle; marshy ground. **the Curragh,** military camp and racecourse near Kildare, Eire. (Ir.)
currant, *n. ku*-rant, a small kind of dried seedless grape, a species of *Vitis*, imported from the Levant; a similar-sized red, black, or white fruit of a species of *Ribes*. (*Corinth*, from which the former was first brought.)
currency, *n. ku*-ren-se, constant flow; state of being current; prevalence; a continual passing from hand to hand or circulation, as coin or bills of credit; the circulating medium of a state, issued by authority, either as coin or in the form of paper, commonly called money; that which is current or in circulation; the period during which anything is current. **currency note,** a British Treasury note for £1 or 10*s*., replaced by Bank of England notes in 1928. (L. *currentia*.)
★**current,** *a. ku*-rent, now passing; pertaining to the present week, month, etc., as specified; general popular; generally received; that will pass a genuine; in circulation: *n.* a running stream a flow of water or air in a definite direction; progressive motion or movement; general drift; the passage of electricity from one pole of an apparatu to the other [Elect.]. (L. *currentis*, of running.)
currently, *ad.* with continued progression; generally
curricle, *n. ku*-re-kl, a two-wheeled carriage draw by two horses abreast. (L. *curriculum*, race.)
curriculum, *n.* ku-*rik*-yew-lum (*pl.* **curricula**), fixed or regular course of study. (L., race-course.
currier, *n. ku*-re-er, one who dresses and colour leather after it is tanned.
curriery, *n. ku*-re-er-re, the trade or establishmen of a currier.
currish, *a. kur*-ish, like a cur; snarling; spiteful quarrelsome.
currishly, *ad.* in a currish manner.
currishness, *n.* a currish disposition.
curry, *n. ku*-re, a condiment much used in Indi containing turmeric, the leaves of the curry-lea tree, *Murraya koenigii*, pepper, ginger, and othe ingredients; a hash or stew flavoured with this *v.t.* to season with curry. (Tamil, *kari*, sauce.)
curry, *v.t. ku*-re, to dress leather after it is tanned to rub and clean (a horse) with a curry-comb; t thrash. **curry-comb,** *n.* an iron instrument o comb for grooming horses. **to curry favour** (o **favel,** *i.e.* a chestnut horse), to seek favour b flattery. (O.Fr. *courroier*, dress leather.)
curse, *n.* kurse, imprecation of evil; the evil im precated; the cause of evil; sentence of divin vengeance on sinners; a profane oath: *v.i.* to utte imprecations; to affirm or deny with imprecation of divine vengeance: *v.t.* to imprecate evil upon to bring evil upon by a curse; to vex, harass or torment with great calamities. **curse o Scotland,** the nine of diamonds. (A.S. *cursian*.)
cursed, *a.* kurst *or kur*-sed, execrated; blasted by curse; deserving a curse; detestable.
cursedly, *ad. kur*-sed-le, in a cursed manner miserably.
cursedness, *n.* state of being under a curse.
cursing, *n. kur*-sing, execration; the uttering of curse; a dooming to vexation or misery.
cursitor, *n. kur*-se-tor, holder of an office (abolishe 1835) in the Court of Chancery, whose busines was to make out original writs. (L.)
cursive, *a. kur*-siv, written in a running hand: *n* handwriting, or type, of this character.
cursor, *n. kur*-sor, a part of a mathematical instru ment moving upon another part, esp. the transparen runner of a slide-rule carrying a hair line.
cursorial, *a.* kur-*saw*-re-al, fitted for running o walking.
cursorily, *ad. kur*-so-re-le, in a cursory manner.
cursory, *a. kur*-so-re, hasty; superficial. (L *cursorius*, hasty.)
curst, *a.* kurst, cursed; ill-tempered; crusty.
curt, *a.* kurt, short; abrupt; rudely terse. (L *curtus*, short.)
curtail, *v.t.* kur-*tale*, to shorten; to cut off th end or a part; to abridge. **curtail-step,** *n.* th lowest step in a flight of stairs, ending at its oute extremity in a scroll. (O.Fr. *cortald*, L. *curtus*.)
curtailment, *n.* kur-*tale*-ment, the act of curtail ing; state of being curtailed.
★**curtain,** *n. kur*-tan, a piece of fabric hung as screen; a cloth hanging round a bed, or at a window which may be drawn together or aside at pleasure a cloth hanging used in theatres to conceal th stage from the spectators or to prevent the sprea of fire; a protective barrier; a division within th envelope of an airship; that part of the rampar which is between the flanks of two bastions [Fort.] a barrier of gun-fire; *v.t.* to enclose with curtains to furnish with curtains. **curtain-lecture,** *n* reproof administered in bed or in private by a wif to her husband. **curtain-raiser,** *n.* a shor dramatic piece played before the curtain rises o the play of the evening. **iron curtain,** *see* **iron** (Fr. *courtine*.)
curtal, *n. kur*-tal, a horse, dog, etc., with a docke tail: *a.* having a cropped tail; curt; brief.
curtana, *n.* kur-*tah*-na, the pointless Sword o Mercy carried before the kings of England at thei coronation. (L. *curtus*.)

curtate, *a.* *kur*-tat, reduced. **curtate distance,** the distance of a planet or comet from the sun or earth reduced to the plane of the ecliptic [Astron.]. (L. *curtatus*, shortened.)
curtation, *n.* kur-*tay*-shon, the interval between the distance of a planet or comet from the sun and the curtate distance.
curtilage, *n.* *kur*-te-laj, a yard or enclosure belonging to a dwelling-house and within the same fence. [Law]. (O.Fr.)
curtly, *ad.* *kurt*-le, briefly.
curtness, *n.* *kurt*-ness, shortness.
curtsy, *n.* *kurt*-se, the act of salutation or respect on the part of a woman by slightly bending the body and knees : *v.i.* to make a curtsy. (*Courtesy.*)
curule, *a.* *kew*-rool, entitled to occupy a curule chair ; magisterial. **curule chair,** among the Romans, a large portable folding stool without a back which only the chief magistrates were permitted to sit upon. (L. *currus*, a chariot.)
curvate, *a.* *kur*-vat, curved ; bent in a regular form. (L. *curvatus*, curved.)
curvation, *n.* kur-*vay*-shon, a **curve** ; the act of curving or state of being curved.
curvative, *a.* *kur*-va-tiv, with the margins slightly curved [Bot.].
curvature, *n.* *kur*-va-tewr, the continual flexure or bending of a line from a rectilinear direction ; the amount of curve ; a curved shape.
*__curve,__ *n.* kurv, a bending without angles ; that which is bent ; a flexure ; a line of which no three consecutive points are in the same straight line [Geom.] : *v.t.* to bend ; to inflect regularly. (L. *curvus*, bent.)
curvet, *n.* kur-*vet*, a leap ; a frolic ; a particular leap of a horse in which all his legs are simultaneously off the ground [Men.] : *v.i.* to leap ; to spring and make a curvet ; to leap and frisk. (It. *corvetta*, leap.)
curvicaudate, *a.* kurv-e-*kawd*-at, having a curved tail. (L. *curvus*, and *cauda*, a tail.)
curvicostate, *a.* kurv-e-*kost*-at, marked with small bent ribs. (L. *curvus*, and *costa*, a rib.)
curvifoliate, *a.* kurve-e-*foh*-le-at, having reflexed leaves. (L. *curvus*, and *folium*, a leaf.)
curviform, *a.* *kurv*-e-fawrm, of a curved form.
curvilinear, *a.* kurv-e-*lin*-e-ar, bounded by curved lines. (L. *curvus*, and *linea*, a line.)
curvirostral, *a.* kurv-e-*ros*-tral, having a curved beak. (L. *curvus*, and *rostrum*, a beak.)
curvometer, *n.* kur-*vom*-e-ter, a device for measuring curved lines ; an opisometer ; a rotameter. (L. *curvo*, bend, Gr. *metron*, measure.)
cusco-bark, *n.* *kus*-ko-bark, a variety of cinchona bark, *Cinchona pubescens*.
cuscus, *n.* *kus*-kus, a phalanger of the genus *Cuscus*, native to the East Indian Archipelago ; couscous ; khus-khus.
cushat, *n.* *kush*-at, the ringdove or wood-pigeon, also the stockdove. (A.S. *cūscote*, pigeon.)
*__cushion,__ *n.* *koosh*-on, a pad for sitting, leaning, or resting on, stuffed with wool, hair, or other soft material ; anything padded ; an elastic stuffing ; the spring side of a billiard-table ; a flat sand-filled leather bag used by engravers to support the plate ; a pad used by gilders for receiving the leaves of gold from the paper ; any device for checking shock ; a cushion-like organ or part [Bot. and Zool.] : *v.t.* to seat on a cushion ; to furnish or protect with cushions. **lady's cushion,** a species of *Saxifraga*. **sea cushion,** thrift, the sea pink. (O.Fr. *coussin.*)
cushy, *a.* *koosh*-e, easy and well paid ; abounding in comfort [Slang]. (Hind. *khush*, pleasant.)
cusp, *n.* kusp, a point or apex ; one of the horns of the crescent moon ; the point in a curve at which its two branches have a common tangent [Math.] ; a projecting point forming a pendant, or in the foliation of tracery, panels, etc. [Arch.] ; a projection on a molar tooth. (L. *cuspis*, a point.)
cuspate, *a.* *kus*-pat, cusp-shaped ; having cusps.
cuspid, *n.* *kus*-pid, a canine tooth.
cuspidal, *n.* *kus*-pe-dal, pointed ; ending in a point.
cuspidate, *a.* *kus*-pe-dat, tapering to a sharp end [Bot.].
cuspidor, *n.* *kus*-pe-dor, a spittoon. (Port. *cuspideira*, *escuspidor.*)
cuss, *n.* kus, a fellow (in contempt) ; a curse [Slang].
cussedness, *n.* *kus*-sed-ness, obstinacy ; deliberate wrongheadedness. (*See* **curse.**)
custard, *n.* *kus*-tard, a composition of milk and eggs, sweetened and baked or boiled. **custard coffin,** the raised crust of a custard pie. (M.E. *crustade*, a pie with crust.)
custard-apple, *n.* *kus*-tard-*ap*-pl, the West Indian tree, *Anona reticulata* ; its soft pulpy fruit.
custodial, *a.* kus-*toh*-de-al, relating to guardianship.
custodian, *n.* kus-*toh*-de-an, one who has the care or custody of a building, etc. ; a guardian ; a keeper. (L. *custodia*, guard.)
custody, *n.* *kus*-to-de, guardianship ; imprisonment. (L. *custodia.*)
custom, *n.* *kus*-tum, frequent repetition of the same act ; habitual practice ; established mode ; usage ; a buying of goods ; a frequenting a shop to purchase ; long-established practice, as constituting the unwritten law, long consent to which gives it authority [Law] ; *pl.* duties imposed by law on merchandise imported or exported : *v.t.* to make familiar ; to give custom to : *v.i.* to be accustomed. (O.Fr. *costume.*)
customable, *a.* *kus*-tum-a-bl, liable to the payment of customs duties.
customably, *ad.* according to custom.
customarily, *ad.* habitually ; commonly.
customariness, *n.* frequency ; commonness ; habitual use or practice.
customary, *a.* *kus*-tum-a-re, according to custom ; in common practice ; holding by custom ; held by custom : *n.* a book containing laws and usages, or customs. (O.Fr. *costumier.*)
customed, *a.* *kus*-tumd, usual ; accustomed ; furnished with customers.
customer, *n.* *kus*-tum-er, a regular purchaser at a particular place of business ; a fellow one has to deal with. (O.Fr. *costumier.*)
custom-house, *n.* the establishment by means of which the customs revenue is collected, and its regulations enforced ; the place where ships are entered or cleared and duties paid.
custos, *n.* *kus*-tos, a custodian ; a keeper. **custos rotulorum,** the principal justice of a county, and keeper of its records, whose deputy is the clerk of the peace. (L., a keeper.)
*__cut,__ *v.t.* kut, to separate or cleave as with a knife ; to make an incision ; to sever ; to divide ; to hew ; to mow ; to carve ; to wound or affect deeply ; purposely to ignore ; to absent oneself from ; to intersect or cross ; to reduce (length, price, etc.) by cutting ; to castrate : *v.i.* to sever, as a knife ; to be divided by a knife ; to divide by passing through ; to perform a surgical operation by cutting ; to undersell ; to make an oblique stroke [Cricket, etc.] ; to divide a pack of cards. **to cut a caper,** to frisk about. **to cut across,** to pass by a shorter course, so as to cut off an angle. **to cut a dash,** to make a show. **to cut down,** to fell by severing. **to cut in,** to intervene in anything ; to take the road quickly in front of an overtaken car [Motoring] ; to start playing towards a green ahead of the rightful players [Golf]. **to cut off,** to separate one part from another ; to extirpate ; to put to untimely death ; to interrupt ; to intercept ; to end ; to finish. **to cut out,** to remove by cutting or carving ; to contrive to take the precedence of. **to cut out a ship,** to enter a harbour, and seize and carry off a ship by a sudden attack. **to cut short,** to stop by interruption ; to shorten ; to abridge. **to cut up,** to cut in pieces ; to eradicate ; to criticize severely ; to affect deeply. **to cut up rough,** to become insulting or quarrelsome. (Origin unknown.)
cut, *a.* kut, gashed ; divided, shortened, reduced in price, etc. **cut and dry,** prepared for use ; lacking freshness ; not spontaneous. **cut grass,** spear-grass.
cut, *n.* kut, the opening, cleft, gash, or wound, made by an edged instrument ; a stroke or blow, as with a whip ; a wound to one's feelings ; direct ignoring of an acquaintance ; a channel made by cutting or digging ; a canal ; a piece cut off ; a near passage shortening a route ; the omission of part of a dramatic or literary work ; a picture cut or carved on wood or metal ; the stamp on which a picture is carved, and by which it is impressed ; the impression ; the act of dividing a pack of cards;

shape in which a thing is cut; in cricket, etc., an oblique stroke. **a cut above,** a class above someone else; superior to.

cut-and-cover, *n.* tunnelling by arching or cutting and then covering in.

cutaneous, *a.* kew-*tay*-ne-us, pertaining to or affecting the skin. (L. *cutis*, a skin.)

cut-away, *a.* *kut*-a-way, having a part cut off: *n.* a coat with skirts rounded from the front to the tails.

cutch, *n.* kutch, catechu [Comm.]; tannin from mangrove bark; couch grass.

cutchery, *n.* *kutch*-e-re, a court of justice in India; also a business office. (Anglo-Indian term.)

cute, *a.* kewt, acute; keen-witted; adroit; attractive [U.S.A., Coll.].

cuticle, *n.* *kewt*-e-kl, the scarf-skin; the thin external covering of bark [Bot.]. (L. *cuticula*, little skin.)

cuticular, *a.* kew-*tik*-yew-lar, pertaining to the cuticle.

cutis, *n.* *kew*-tis, the true skin under the cuticle. (L).

cutlass, *n.* *kut*-las, a broad slightly curving one-edged sword, esp. for naval use. (Fr. *coutelas.*)

cutler, *n.* *kut*-ler, one who makes or sells cutting instruments.

cutlery, *n.* *kut*-ler-e, sharp-edged instruments in general; the business of a cutler. (Fr. *coutelier.*)

cutlet, *n.* *kut*-let, a small piece of meat, esp. off the loin or neck, for cooking; a small chop. (Fr. *côtelette.*)

cut-off, *n.* *kut*-off, a device that shortens, or that divides one part from another; a device on a steam engine by which the steam can be cut off from the cylinder; the point in the stroke at which steam is cut off.

cut-out, *n.* *kut*-out, a circuit-breaker which breaks the circuit of electricity when the current exceeds a determined strength.

cutpurse, *n.* *kut*-purse, one who steals from the person; a thief.

cutter, *n.* *kut*-ter, one who cuts or hews; one who cuts out cloth to measure; an instrument that cuts; a softish brick that can be rubbed to shape; a small boat used by ships of war; a single-masted vessel fore-and-aft rigged; a light sledge [U.S.A.]. **cutter-bar,** *n.* the bar of a boring machine, in which the cutters or cutting tools are fixed; the bar along which the knife of a mowing-machine runs.

cut-throat, *n.* *kut*-throte, a murderer; an assassin: *a.* murderous; barbarous; intensive (of competition); three-handed (of bridge, etc.).

cutting, *ppr.* and *a.* *kut*-ting, dividing by an edged instrument; piercing the heart; wounding the feelings; satirical: *n.* a separation or division; a slip from a plant; a printed extract; a press-cutting; the operation of removing the stone; an excavation through a hill for a railway, canal, etc.

cuttingly, *ad.* in a cutting manner; sarcastically.

cuttle, *n.* *kut*-tl, the cuttle-fish. **cuttle-bone,** *n.* the internal shell of the cuttle-fish, used in polishing powders. **cuttle-fish,** *n.* any cephalopod of the genus *Sepia*, esp. the octopus, *S. officinalis.* (A.S. *cudele.*)

cutty, *a.* *kut*-te, short; shortened; hasty: *n.* a short tobacco-pipe. (Scots.)

cutty-stool, *n.* a bench in old Scottish churches on which female offenders against chastity sat, and were publicly rebuked.

cutwater, *n.* *kut*-waw-ter, the fore-part of a ship's prow which cuts the water.

cut-worm, *n.* *kut*-wurm, any caterpillar destructive to young plants.

cuvette, *n.* kew-*vet*, a clay crucible. [Glass-making].

cyanate, *n.* *sy*-an-ate, a salt of cyanic acid.

cyanic, *a.* sy-*an*-ik, containing cyanogen.

cyanide, *n.* *sy*-an-ide, a compound of cyanogen with a metal: *v.t.* to treat with a cyanide; to fumigate with hydrogen-cyanide gas.

cyanine, *n.* *sy*-an-in, a blue colouring matter.

cyanite, *n.* *sy*-an-ite, a silicate of aluminium, a hard, infusible mineral occurring in bluish blade-like crystals. (Gr. *kyanos*, blue.)

cyanogen, *n.* sy-*an*-o-jen, an extremely poisonous gas composed of one equivalent of nitrogen and one of carbon, having an odour like that of crushed peach-leaves, and burning with a pink flame, edged with green; a univalent carbon and nitrogen radical some compounds of which are intensely blue. (Gr. *kyanos*, blue, and *gennao*, produce.)

cyanometer, *n.* sy-a-*nom*-e-ter, an instrument to ascertain the degree of blueness of the sky.

cyanosis, *n.* sy-a-*noh*-sis, a disease rendering the skin blue, due to defective aeration of the blood.

cyanotype, *n.* sy-*an*-o-tipe, a process of taking sunlight prints in Prussian blue; a blue-print.

cyathiform, *a.* sy-*ath*-e-fawrm, in the form of a deep cup [Bot.]. (Gr. *kyathos*, a cup, and *form.*)

cycad, *n.* *sy*-kad, a palm-like plant of the order *Cycadaceæ*, a large family of ancient tropical gymnosperms.

cycadaceous, *a.* sik-a-*day*-shus, pertaining to the cycads.

cyclamen, *n.* *sik*-la-men, sow-bread: (*cap.*) a genus of bulbous plants of the primrose family with beautiful flowers [Bot.]. (Gr. *kyklaminos*, from *kyklos*, a circle.)

cycle, *n.* *sy*-kl, a series of years, events, or phenomena which recur in the same order; a long period; an imaginary circle in the heavens; a body of legend connected with some mythical subject; a bicycle or tricycle; a single period of an alternating current [Elect.]: *v.i.* to revolve in a circle; to ride a cycle. **cycle of indiction,** a period of fifteen years. **cycle of the moon,** the Metonic cycle. **cycle of the sun** or **solar cycle,** a recurrent period of twenty-eight years, at the end of which the days of the month return to the same days of the week. (Fr.)

cycle-car, *n.* *sy*-kl-kar, a cycle with a small car combined with it; a motor-cycle combination.

cyclic, *a.* *sik*-lik, pertaining to or contained in a cycle; with the parts arranged in whorls, not in spirals [Bot.]. **cyclic chorus,** at Athens, one which sang and danced in a circle round the altar of Bacchus in performing the dithyrambic odes. **cyclic poets,** certain epic poets who followed Homer, and kept within the cycle of the Trojan war; a group of poets specially connected with any cycle of legends. (L. *cyclicus.*)

cyclical, *a.* *sik*-le-kal, cyclic; rolled up in a circle [Bot.].

cycling, *n.* *sy*-kling, riding on a bicycle or tricycle.

cyclist, *n.* *sy*-klist, one who rides a cycle.

cyclograph, *n.* *sik*-lo-graf, one of various instruments for describing arcs without the use of compasses; a form of panoramic camera.

cycloid, *n.* *sy*-kloyd, a geometrical curve described by a point in the circumference of a circle as it rolls along a straight line till it has completed a revolution: *a.* circular; resembling a circle; cycloidal; having cycloid scales [Ichth.].

cycloidal, *a.* sy-*kloy*-dal, pertaining to a cycloid.

cycloidean, *n.* sy-*kloy*-de-an, any fish of the group *Cycloidei*, which includes those with cycloid scales.

cyclometer, *n.* sy-*klom*-e-ter, a device recording the revolutions of a wheel, esp. in registering distance travelled.

cyclometry, *n.* sy-*klom*-e-tre, the art or process of measuring circles. (Gr. *kyklos* and *meter.*)

cyclone, *n.* *sy*-klone, an intertropical rotatory hurricane; a group of winds rotating round a centre of low barometric pressure. **cyclone centre,** the place of lowest barometric pressure in a cyclonic system. (Gr. *kyklōn*, whirled round.)

cyclonic, *a.* sy-*klon*-ik, relating to a cyclone.

cyclonology, *n.* sy-klo-*nol*-o-je, the study of cyclones.

cyclopædia, *n.* sy-klo-*pee*-de-a, an encyclopædia.

Cyclopean, *a.* sy-klo-*pee*-an, pertaining to the Cyclops; vast; denoting prehistoric masonry of a rude and very massive kind, erected at an enormous expenditure of physical energy. (Gr. *Cyclops*, one of a race of one-eyed giants in Greek mythology.)

cyclorama, *n.* sy-klo-*rah*-ma, a form of panorama giving the spectator the illusion of motion; a stage or film setting on which light or cloud effects are projected. (Gr. *kyklos*, and *horama*, a view.)

cyclosis, *n.* sy-*kloh*-sis, a movement in the contents of cells [Bot.]; the occurrence of cycles [Geom.]. (Gr. *kyklosis*, an encircling.)

Cyclostomata, *n.pl.* *sy*-klo-*stom*-a-ta *or* -*stoh*-ma-ta, the lowest class of vertebrate animals, consisting of the lampreys and the hagfishes. (Gr. *kyklos*, and *stoma*, a mouth.)

cyclostomous, *a.* sy-*klos*-to-mus, having a circular mouth, as the lamprey.
cyclostyle, *n.* *sy*-klo-stile, an apparatus for manifolding documents or drawings by means of a stencil made with a small toothed wheel used as a pen: *v.t.* to manifold with this. (Gr. *kyklos*, and *stylos*, pen.)
cyclotron, *n.* *sy*-klo-tron, an electro-magnetic apparatus imparting extremely high velocities to electrified particles without employing excessive voltages, and used, in a vacuum, for splitting the atom.
cyesiology, *n.* *sy*-ee-se-*ol*-o-je, the branch of medical science treating of pregnancy. (Gr. *kyesis*, pregnancy, and *-logy*.)
cygnet, *n.* *sig*-net, a young swan. (Fr. *cygne*.)
cylinder, *n.* *sil*-in-der, a long roller-like body, solid or hollow, of uniform circumference; the chamber in which steam acts upon the piston in a steam-engine; the explosion chamber in an internal combustion engine; a roller-like stone or clay object bearing cuneiform inscriptions, etc., used as a seal by the ancient Babylonians, etc. (Fr. *cylindre*.)
cylindric, *a.* se-*lin*-drik, having the form of a cylinder. (Gr. *kylindrikos*.)
cylindrical, *a.* se-*lin*-dre-kal, cylindric.
cylindrically, *ad.* in the manner of a cylinder.
cylindriform, *a.* having the form of a cylinder.
cylindrite, *n.* *sil*-in-drite, a dark grey sulphide of lead, tin, and antimony with a metallic lustre.
cylindroid, *n.* *sil*-in-droyd, a solid body like a cylinder, with the bases elliptical, but parallel and equal. (Gr. *kylindros*, and *eidos*, like.)
cyma, *n.* *sy*-ma, a moulding of a cornice with a wave-like profile [Arch.]; a cyme [Bot.].
cymar, *n.* *sy*-mar, a woman's loose robe or under-garment.
cymatium, *n.* sy-*may*-she-um, a cyma. (L.)
cymbal, *n.* *sim*-bal, a hollow basin-like musical instrument of brass, one of a pair beaten together and producing a sharp clashing sound. (Fr. *cymbale*.)
cymbiform, *a.* *sim*-be-fawrm, shaped like a boat; navicular (of certain bones). (L. *cymba*, a boat.)
cymbocephalic, *a.* *sim*-bo-se-*fal*-ik, having a long narrow skull with receding forehead. (Gr. *kymba*, boat, and *kephale*, head.)
cyme, *n.* sime, a flat or convex inflorescence like that of the elder [Bot.]. (Gr. *kyma*, a wave.)
cymoid, *a.* *sy*-moyd, like a cyme or cyma.
cymometer, *n.* sy-*mom*-e-ter, an obsolete instrument for determining wave-frequencies [Wire.]. (Gr. *kyma*, wave *metron*, measure.)
cymophane, *n.* *sim*-o-fane, a chatoyant variety of chrysoberyl. (Fr.)
cymophanous, *a.* sy-*mof*-a-nus, chatoyant; opalescent.
cymoscope, *n.* *sy*-mo-skope, any apparatus for detecting electric waves [Elect.].
cymose, *a.* *sy*-mohs, pertaining to, like, or derived from a cyme.
Cymric, *a.* *kim*-rik, Welsh; pertaining to the Welsh: *n.* the Welsh language. (W. *cymraeg*.)
Cymry, *n.* *kim*-re, the ancient Brythonic and modern Welsh peoples. (W.)
cynanche, *n.* sy-*nang*-ke, quinsy, or other inflammatory disease of the throat. (Gr. *kyon*, a dog, *ancho*, throttle.)
cynanthropy, *n.* se-*nan*-thro-pe, a madness in which one fancies himself a dog. (Gr. *kyon*, and *anthropos*, a man.)
cynic, *n.* *sin*-ik, one of a sect of austere philosophers of ancient Athens who openly scorned the current wisdom and ways of the world, a school of which Diogenes was the most celebrated member; a sarcastic fault-finding person; a sneerer; a misanthrope: *a.* cynical.
cynical, *a.* *sin*-e-kal, snarling; fault-finding; morose; sarcastic; contemptuous of others; pertaining to the cynics. (L. *cynicus*, dog-like.)
cynically, *ad.* in a cynical manner.
cynicalness, *n.* the quality of being cynical.
cynicism, *n.* *sin*-e-sizm, the temper and practice of a cynic, especially as a scorner of others.
cynocephalous, *a.* *sy*-no- *or* *sin*-o-*sef*-a-lus, dog-headed.
cynosure, *n.* *sy*-no- *or* *sin*-o-shoor, a centre of attraction; a constellation which, as containing the pole star, is a centre of interest to all sailors. (L. *cynosura*, the Little Bear constellation, in which is the pole star.)
cypher, *n.* *sy*-fer, cipher.
cyphonism, *n.* *sy*-fo-nizm, a punishment among the ancients which consisted in applying a heavy collar which bent the neck. (Gr. *kyphon*, pillory.)
cy-pres, *a.* and *ad.* see-*pray*, near; used of the application of a bequest that is not practicable to an object as near as possible to the testator's intention [Law]. (O.Fr.)
cypress, *n.* *sy*-pres, a tree of the genus *Cupressus*; a branch of this as an emblem of mourning; cyprus. (O.Fr.)
Cyprian, *a.* *sip*-re-an, of or pertaining to Cyprus: *n.* a Cypriot; a prostitute.
cyprine, *a.* *sip*-rin, pertaining to the cypress-tree; cyprinoid: *n.* a blue variety of vesuvianite.
cyprinoid, *a.* *sip*-re-noyd, pertaining or belonging to the *Cyprinidæ*, a large genus of freshwater fish including the carps and goldfish; resembling a member of this genus: *n.* a member of this genus.
Cypriot, *n.* *sip*-re-ot, an inhabitant of Cyprus; the Greek dialect of the Cypriots.
cyprus, *n.* *sy*-prus, any textile formerly imported from Cyprus, esp. a thin transparent lawn used, in black, for mourning.
Cyrenaic, *a.* sy-re-*nay*-ik, pertaining to Cyrene, or to the hedonistic school of philosophy there founded by Aristippus.
Cyrillic, *a.* si-*ril*-lik, relating to the Slavic alphabet, said to have been invented by St. Cyril in the 9th century A.D.
cyst, *n.* sist, a bladder; a tumour containing fluid or semi-solid matter. (Gr. *kystis*, a bladder.)
cystic, *a.* *sist*-ik, pertaining to, resembling, or containing a cyst; encysted.
cystiform, *a.* *sist*-e-form, in the shape of a cyst.
cystine, *n.* *sist*-in, a kind of calculus rarely formed in the human bladder.
cystitis, *n.* sis-*ty*-tis, inflammation of the bladder.
cystocele, *n.* *sist*-o-seel, hernia of a bladder, esp. the urinary bladder. (Gr. *kistis*, and *kele*, a tumour.)
cystoid, *a.* *sis*-toyd, of the nature of a cyst.
cystoma, *n.* sis-*toh*-ma, a tumour containing cysts.
cystoscope, *n.* *sist*-o-skope, an instrument for viewing the interior of the bladder.
cystose, *a.* *sist*-ose, containing cysts.
cystotomy, *n.* sis-*tot*-o-me, the act or practice of opening cysts, particularly the operation of cutting into the bladder to remove a stone or other matter. (Gr. *kystis*, and *tome*, cutting.)
Cytherean, *a.* sith-er-*ree*-an, belonging or pertaining to Venus, the goddess of love. (L. *Cythere*, Aphrodite.)
cytisine, *n.* *sit*-e-sin, a bitter, very poisonous alkaloid obtained from the laburnum. (L. *cytisus*, clover.)
cytitis, *n.* sy-*ty*-tis, inflammation of the skin; dermatitis. (Gk. *kytos*, skin, and *-itis*.)
cytoblast, *n.* *sy*-to-blahst, the nucleus of a cell. (Gr. *kytos*, a hollow vessel, *blastos*, a sprout.)
cytogenesis, *n.* sy-to-*jen*-e-sis, the formation and development of cells.
cytogenous, *a.* sy-*toj*-e-nus, producing cells.
cytology, *n.* sy-*tol*-o-je, the study of the structure, functions, etc., of cells [Biol.].
cytoplasm, *n.* *sy*-to-plazm, the protoplasm in a cell which is not the nucleus.
Czar, Czarevich, czarism, etc., *see* **Tsar,** etc.
czardas, *n.* *char*-dahsh, a Hungarian dance (Hung.).
Czech, *n.* chek, a Slav of Moravia and Bohemia; the Czech language.
Czechish, *a.* *chek*-ish, relating to the Czechs, their language or country.
Czechoslovak, *a.* and *n.* *chek*-o-slo-*vak*, Czechoslovakian.
Czechoslovakian, *a.* *chek*-o-slo-*vak*-e-an, relating to the race comprising the Czechs and Slovaks, or to the republic of Czechoslovakia; *n.* an inhabitant of this state.

D

D is the fourth letter of the English alphabet, and the third consonant. It is a dental articulation, formed by placing the tip of the tongue against the fore part of the palate, and nearly approaches in sound to the letter T. In English words it has but the one phonetic value, except in *soldier* (*-dzh-*) and *handkerchief*, *handsome* (mute), and in certain past tenses and participles (*e.g. packed, kissed, stopped*), when the *-ed* has the effect of *-t*. In music it is the second note of the scale of C, corresponding to *ray* (Italian *re*); in the Roman numeration it represents 500; it is the symbol—as in **D-day**—for the future data on which a planned operation is to commence; and it has been used euphemistically for the expletive *damn*.

dab, *n.* dab, a gentle blow; a light stroke with something soft; a small lump or mass of anything soft or moist: *v.t.* to strike gently with some soft or moist substance. (From the sound.)

dab, *n.* dab, one expert at anything, a dabster.

dab, *n.* dab, a small marine flatfish found in sandy places, esp. *Pleuronectes limanda.*

dabber, *n.* *dab*-ber, one who or that which dabs; an inking ball [Print.].

dabble, *v.t.* *dab*-bl, to dip a little and often; to wet by little dips; to spatter lightly: *v.i.* to play about in water, splashing a little and often; to dip into or meddle slightly and superficially with anything. (*Dip, dab.*)

dabbler, *n.* *dab*-bler, one who dabbles in a thing.

dabblingly, *ad.* *dab*-bling-le, in a dabbling manner.

dabchick, *n.* *dab*-chik, a small species of grebe, *Podiceps fluviatilis*; also, the moorhen. (Literally, Dipchick.)

dabster, *n.* *dab*-ster, an expert at anything.

da capo, dah-*kah*-poh, a direction that the first part of a tune is to be repeated from the beginning [Mus.]. (It., from the beginning.)

dace, *n.* dace, a small silvery cyprinoid river fish, *Leuciscus vulgaris.* (O.Fr. *dars.*)

dachshund, *n.* *dahks*-hoont, a short-legged hound formerly used in badger-hunting. (Ger., badger-dog.)

dacoit, *n.* da-*koyt*, one of a murderous gang of Burmese or Indian brigands. (Hind.)

dacoity, *n.* da-*koy*-te, marauding or robbery by a gang of dacoits.

dacryoma, *n.* dak-re-*oh*-ma, a diseased state of the lachrymal ducts, preventing the passage of tears. (Gr. *dakryon*, a tear.)

dactyl, *n.* *dak*-til, a metrical foot of three syllables, one long and two short, like the finger-joints [Pros.]. (Gr. *daktylos*, a finger.)

dactylic, *a.* dak-*til*-lik, pertaining to or consisting of dactyls: *n.* a dactylic line or verse.

dactylioglyph, *n.* dak-*til*-e-o-glif, the inscription of the name of the artist on a finger-ring or gem; a gem engraver. (Gr. *daktylos*, and *glypho*, carve.)

dactylioglyphy, *n.* dak-til-e-*og*-le-fe, the art of gem-engraving.

dactyliomancy, *n.* dak-*til*-e-o-man-se, divination by finger-rings. (Gr. *daktylos*, and *manteia*, divination.)

dactylogram, *n.* dak-*til*-o-gram, a finger-print.

dactylology, *n.* dak-til-*ol*-o-je, the study of the dumb alphabet; the art of conversing with the fingers. (Gr. *daktylos*, and *logos*, speech.)

dactylopterus, *n.* dak-te-*lop*-te-rus, the flying gurnard. (Literally, finger-finned).

dactylorhiza, *n.* dak-til-lo-*ry*-za, finger-and-toe disease in turnips. (Gr. *daktylos*, and *rhiza*, root.)

dad, *n.* dad, **dadda,** *dad*-dah, a child's name for father.

dadaism, *n.* *dah*-da-izm, a short-lived movement in Continental art-circles about 1920, having no definite technique and ending in Surrealism.

daddle, *v.i.* *dad*-dl, to walk totteringly.

daddy, *n.* *dad*-de, an affectionate form of dad. **daddy-longlegs,** *n.* a species of cranefly of the genus *Tipula*, with very long legs.

dado, *n.* *day*-do, the square part of a pedestal, between base and cornice; wainscotting round a wall; the lower part of a wall when treated decoratively. (It., a die.)

dædal, *a.* *dee*-dal, formed with art; intricate; maze-like. (L. *Dædalus*, an artificer of Greek myth.)

dædalian, *a.* de-*day*-le-an, dædal.

dædaloid, *a.* *dee*-da-loyd, labyrinthiform [Bot.].

dæmon, *n.* *dee*-mon (*pl.* **dæmones,** dee-*moh*-neez), an impersonal deity, or supernatural power, of Greek religion; an indwelling guide, mentor, or spirit. (*See* **demon.**)

daffodil, *n.* *daf*-fo-dil, a plant of the genus *Narcissus*; the Lent lily. (L. *asphodelus*, a lily-like plant.)

daft, *a.* dahft, foolish; frolicsome; crazy.

dag, *n.* dag, an obsolete large-bore pistol. (Fr.)

dag, *v.i.* dag, to trail in the wet or dirt. (Dial. Eng.)

dagger, *n.* *dag*-ger, a short two-edged weapon for stabbing; a blunt blade of iron with a basket hilt, used for defence [Fencing]; a mark of reference, thus (†), or a double dagger (‡) [Printing]. **at daggers drawn,** on the point of quarrelling; in a state of fierce enmity. **to look daggers,** to look with ferocity or threateningly. (Fr. *dague.*)

daggle, *v.t.* *dag*-gl, to trail in mud or wet grass; to dirty, as the lower end of a garment: *v.i.* to run through mud and water. **daggle-tail,** *a.* having the lower ends of garments defiled with mud: *n.* a slut.

dag-lock, *n.* *dag*-lok, a lock of wool on sheep that hangs and drags in the wet.

dago, *n.* *day*-go, a seaman's name for a native of the south of Europe [Slang]. (The Spanish name *Diego*, James.)

dagoba, *n.* da-*goh*-ba, a Buddhist relic temple in India, Burma, or Ceylon. (Cingalese.)

daguerreotype, *n.* da-*ge*-ro-tipe, the process of photographing on silver plates sensitized by iodine and developed by mercuric vapour; a photograph so produced: *v.t.* to photograph thus; to picture exactly. (French inventor, L. J. M. *Daguerre.*)

dah, *n.* dah, the short knife-like sword of the Burmese.

dahabiya, *n.* *dah*-hah-*bee*-yah, a large light-draught passenger- or house-boat used on the Nile, lateen-rigged and (usually) power-propelled. (Ar.)

dahlia, *n.* *dale*-ya, a Mexican plant with a beautiful compound flower, of almost every variety of hue. (*Dahl*, a Swedish botanist.)

Dail Eireann, *n.* doyl-ay-*rahn*, the Chamber of Deputies, or Lower House of the Parliament of Eire. (Ir.)

daily, *a.* *day*-le, happening, appearing, bestowed, or enjoyed every day; done day by day: *n.* a daily newspaper; a non-resident domestic servant [Coll.]: *ad.* every day; day by day. (A.S. *dæglic.*)

daimio, *n.* *dy*-me-o, one of the former feudal barons of Japan. (Jap., great title.)

daintily, *ad.* *dane*-te-le, fastidiously; delicately.

daintiness, *n.* *dane*-te-ness, delicacy; elegance.

dainty, *a.* *dane*-te, of a nice taste to the palate; nice in one's tastes; over nice; fastidious; ceremonious; delicately elegant; affectedly fine: *n.* something nice and delicate to the taste; a delicacy. (O.Fr.)

dairy, *n.* *dare*-re, the department of a farm or the place where milk is produced and kept, or converted into cream, butter, or cheese; a shop for the sale of dairy produce; a dairy-farm: *a.* belonging to a dairy or its business. (Scand.) **dairy-farm,** *n.* a farm for dairy produce only.

dairying, *n.* *dare*-re-ing, dairy-farming.

dairymaid, *n.* *dare*-re-made, a female servant employed in the dairy.

dairyman, *n.* *dare*-re-man, one who keeps a dairy.

daïs, *n.* *day*-iss, a raised floor at the upper end of a hall; a raised seat, formerly the chief seat at the principal table; a canopy. (O.Fr. *deis*, table.)

daisied, *a.* *day*-zid, full of, or adorned with, daisies.

daisy, *n.* *day*-ze, a small composite weed of the genus *Bellis*; other plants with similar flowers; a first-rate person or object [Slang]. **daisy-chain,** *n.* a string of daisies tied to each other by their stems. **daisy-cutter,** *n.* a ball bowled swiftly along the ground [Cricket]; a horse that barely lifts its feet. (A.S. *dæges-eage,* "eye of day.")

dak, *n.* dahk *or* dawk, a relay method of transmitting letters and dispatches by post in the East. **dak bungalow,** a travellers' rest house in India. (Hind.)

daker, *n. day*-ker, a set of ten. (*Dicker.*)

dal, *n.* dal, dholl.

Dalai-lama, *n. dah*-ly-*lah*-ma, the spiritual head of the Tibetans, who is believed, when he dies, to transmit his soul to his successor. (Tibetan.)

dale, *n.* dale, a low vale or valley. (A.S. *dæl.*)

dalesman, *n. daylz*-man, a native of a dale, esp. in northern England.

dalliance, *n. dal*-le-ance, dallying.

dallier, *n. dal*-le-er, one who fritters away time; a dawdler; a trifler.

dally, *v.i. dal*-le, to waste or put off time in idling, trifling, toying, or fondling; to delay; to idle; to trifle; to toy; to fondle. (O.Fr. *dalier,* to chat.)

Dalmatian, *a.* dal-*may*-shan, of or pertaining to Dalmatia: *n.* a native of Dalmatia; a Dalmatian dog, a spotted dog, formerly trained to run behind carriages, bred in Dalmatia.

dalmatic, *n.* dal-*mat*-ik, a long white gown with sleeves worn by deacons and bishops of the Roman and Greek Churches; a similar robe worn by monarchs at their coronation. (Introduced from Dalmatia.)

Daltonian, *a.* dawl-*toh*-ne-an, pertaining to John Dalton (Eng. chemist, *d.* 1844) or to his atomic theory: *n.* one affected with Daltonism.

Daltonism, *n. dawl*-ton-izm, colour-blindness. (*Dalton* the chemist, who was afflicted with it.)

dam, *n.* dam, a female parent (of quadrupeds; applied to women only in contempt). (*Dame.*)

dam, *n.* dam, a bank or mound of earth raised to obstruct a current of water, and collect it; an embankment: *v.t.* to obstruct and collect by a dam; to confine or restrain. (O.Ger. *tam.*)

dam, *n.* dam, a former Indian copper coin, the fortieth part of a rupee. (Hind.)

★**damage,** *n. dam*-aj, injury, hurt, or detriment; the value of what is lost; cost [Slang]: *pl.* the estimated reparation in money for damage sustained [Law]: *v.t.* to hurt, injure, or impair; to lessen the soundness, goodness, or value of: *v.i.* to receive damage. **damage feasant,** the injury, recoverable in law, sustained by the beasts of another coming upon a man's land and damaging his crops. (L. *damnum,* loss.)

damageable, *a. dam*-aj-a-bl, susceptible of damage.

daman, *n. dam*-an, the Syrian rock-badger, *Hyrax Syriacus,* an herbivorous ungulate, the cony of Scripture. (Ar.)

damar, *n. dam*-ar, dammar.

damascene, *a. dam*-a-seen, belonging to Damascus or its manufacture: *n.* a native of Damascus; the damson plum: *v.t.* to ornament by incrusting or inlaying, usually with gold or silver.

damask, *n. dam*-ask, a textile fabric, originally made at Damascus of silk, now of linen and other stuffs, inwoven with figures of flowers, fruits, etc.; the colour of the damask rose: *a.* of a red colour, like the damask rose: *v.t.* to form flowers, etc., on stuffs; to variegate; to damascene. **damask plum,** the damson. **damask rose,** a beautiful old-fashioned variety of rose. **damask steel,** a fine steel from the Levant, used for the best sword-blades. **damask stitch,** a satin stitch worked on a linen foundation. (*Damascus.*)

damaskeen, *v.t.* dam-as-*keen,* to damascene.

damassin, *n. dam*-as-sin, silk damask interwoven with flowers or patterns in gold and silver.

dame, *n.* dame, the wife of a knight or baronet; the title of a lady member of the highest and of the second class of the Order of The British Empire, Dames Grand Cross (G.B.E.) and Dames Commanders (D.B.E.); a matron of rank and dignity; the mistress of a house; a woman of mature years; the mistress of an elementary school; at Eton, a matron keeping a boarding-house, also a house-master not teaching classics; any woman or girl (U.S.A., Coll.]. **dame school,** an infant school kept by a woman. (Fr.)

dammar, *n. dam*-mar, a resin obtained from certain conifers of the genus *Agathis* in Australasia and the East Indies, esp. **white dammar** (from *Vateria Indica*), **black dammar** (*Dammara officinalis*), and kauri gum (*Dammara Australis*).

damn, *n.* dam, an oath damning profanely; type of worthlessness (as in "not care a damn"): *v.t.* to sentence to eternal perdition; to condemn as guilty, or as bad; to condemn to punishment. (Fr. *damner.*)

damnability, *n.* dam-na-*bil*-e-te, state or quality of deserving damnation.

damnable, *a. dam*-na-bl, deserving damnation; detestable; pernicious.

damnably, *ad.* in a manner to incur damnation; odiously.

damnation, *n.* dam-*nay*-shon, condemnation to everlasting perdition; that perdition itself; a crime that merits it; condemnation: int. damn!

damnatory, *a. dam*-na-to-re, containing a sentence of condemnation; condemnatory.

damnification, *n. dam*-ne-fe-*kay*-shon, the infliction of damage or loss [Law].

damnify, *v.t. dam*-ne-fy, to cause damage, injury, or loss to; to wrong [Law]. (O.Fr. *damnefier.*)

damning, *a. dam*-ing *or dam*-ning, involving, or exposing to, damnation.

Damoclean, *a.* dam-o-*klee*-an, pertaining to a position of constant peril, like that of Damocles who was seated at a banquet with a sword hanging over his head by a single hair, at the orders of Dionysios of Syracuse.

damosel, *n. dam*-o-zel, a damsel.

damp, *a.* damp, moist; humid; depressed; chilled: *n.* moist air; humidity; fog; choke-damp or fire-damp; depression of spirits: *v.t.* to moisten; to chill; to weaken; to deaden; to check; to discourage. **damp-course,** *n.* a course impervious to damp built into a wall. **damping off,** the killing of plants, due to excess of moisture [Hort.]. (Ger. *dampf,* vapour.)

dampen, *v.t. dam*-pn, to make damp. (M.E.)

damper, *n. dam*-per, that which damps; a valve or sliding plate in a flue to regulate the draught of air; a contrivance in a pianoforte by which the sound is deadened; a cake of flour and water baked in hot ashes [Austral.].

damping, *n. dam*-ping, the progressive diminution of oscillations or vibrations; the suppression of these [Wire.].

dampish, *a. dam*-pish, moderately damp.

damply, *ad. damp*-le, in a damp manner.

dampness, *n. damp*-ness, the state of being damp.

dampy, *a. dam*-pe, somewhat damp; containing foul gases through defective ventilation (of mines).

damsel, *n. dam*-zel, a young unmarried woman; a maiden, originally of gentle birth; a female servant. (O.Fr. *damoisel.*)

damson, *n. dam*-zn, a small plum of dark purple colour; a damson plum. (*Damascene.*)

dan, *n.* dan, an old complimentary title of honour equivalent to don, as "Dan Chaucer."

dance, *n.* dahnce, a stepping with motions of the body adjusted to the measure of a tune, particularly of two or more in concert; a tune for dancing to; a particular form or pattern of dancing; a turn of dancing; a ball or dancing-party: *v.i.* to leap or move with rhythmic steps to music; to leap and frisk about; to move nimbly or up and down: *v.t.* to perform (a specified dance); to make to dance; to dandle. **dance of death,** a mediæval allegorical representation of the universal power of death. **to dance attendance,** to wait upon so as to gain favour by obsequious attentions. (O.Fr. *danser.*)

dancer, *n. dahnce*-er, one who dances; a male or female professional performer of dances.

dancette, *n.* dan-*set,* a fesse with large indentations [Her.]; in the Norman architecture, a moulding bearing zigzag patterns. (Fr.)

dancing, *n. dahnce*-ing, the art of the dance. **dancing-master,** one who teaches the art of dancing.

dandelion, *n. dan*-de-ly-on, a composite plant of the genus *Taraxacum,* with a bright yellow flower and a denticulate leaf. (Fr. *dent de lion,* lion's tooth.)

dander, *n. dan*-der, scurf; dandruff; anger; ruffled temper: *v.i.* to saunter about idly; to talk incoherently.

dandiacal, *a.* dan-*dy*-a-kal, pertaining to a dandy.

Dandie Dinmont, *n. dan*-de-*din*-mont, a breed of rough Scottish terriers named after a character in Scott's "Guy Mannering."
dandified, *a. dan*-de-fide, with the dress or manners of a dandy.
dandify, *v.t. dan*-de-fy, to make like a dandy.
dandiprat, *n. dan*-de-prat, an urchin; a term of fondness or contempt; an English coin (value 1½*d.*) of the 16th century. (Of unknown origin.)
dandle, *v.t. dan*-dl, to move up and down or toss playfully, as dancing a child on the knee; to fondle; to toy or trifle with, as with a child.
dandruff, *n. dan*-druff, a scurf which forms on the scalp among the hair. (Origin unknown.)
dandy, *n. dan*-de, a fop; a man of fashion; the wire gauze cylinder which, in paper-making, impresses the watermark; a cutter or sloop with a jigger-mast aft, on which is placed a lugsail: *a.* in the style of a fop; handy, as **dandy line, dandy roller,** etc.; fine, first-rate [U.S.A. Slang].
dandy-brush, *n. dan*-de-brush, a whalebone brush.
dandy-cart, *n. dan*-de-kahrt, a spring-cart.
dandy-cock, *n. dan*-de-kok, a bantam fowl.
dandy-horse, *n. dan*-de-horse, a velocipede, the earliest form of bicycle.
dandyish, *a. dan*-de-ish, like a dandy.
dandyism, *n. dan*-de-izm, the manners and dress of a dandy.
dandy-note, *n.* a Customs' document directing goods to be moved from bond for shipment. (*Addenda note.*)
dane, *n.* dane, a native of Denmark; one of Danish descent. **Great Dane,** a breed of large smooth-coated dogs formerly used for deer- and boar-hunting.
danegelt, *n. dane*-gelt, an annual tax levied from 10th to 12th cents. on the English to maintain forces to oppose the Danes, or to furnish tribute to procure peace. (A.S. *Dene*, Dane, *geld*, money-payment.)
Danelagh, *n. dane*-law, the part of England occupied by the Danes, allotted to them in 878 by the treaty of Wedmore; the Danish law enforced in that part of England. (A.S. *Dena lagu.*)
dane-wort, *n.* dane-wurt, the dwarf elder, *Sambucus ebulus.*
★**danger,** *n. dane*-jer, exposure to any harm; peril; hazard; anything causing this. **danger-signal,** *n.* a signal warning against danger ahead. (O.Fr.)
dangerous, *a. dane*-jer-us, fraught with danger; threatening danger; unsafe.
dangerously, *ad.* so as to involve or threaten danger.
dangerousness, *n.* the quality of being dangerous; a state of being exposed to evil or harm.
dangle, *v.i. dang*-gl, to hang loose and swing; to keep hovering about to win some favour; *v.t.* to cause to dangle; to offer (as a bait, etc.). (Scand. *dingla*, to swing.)
dangler, *n. dang*-gler, one who dangles, especially about women.
Danish, *a. dane*-ish, belonging to the Danes: *n.* the language of the Danes.
dank, *a.* dank, moist; humid: *n.* humidity. (Scand.)
dankish, *a. dank*-ish, somewhat damp.
Dannebrog, *n. dan*-ne-brog, the national flag of Denmark, a white cross on a red ground. (Dan.)
Dantean, *a.* dan-*tee*-an, relating to, or in the manner of, Dante: *n.* a student of Dante.
Dantesque, *a.* dan-*tesk*, in the style of Dante, especially in his "Inferno"; sombre, incisive, and sublime.
Danubian, *a.* da-*new*-be-an, pertaining to the river Danube, or to the lands or peoples of its basin.
dap, *v.t.* and *i.* dap, to drop the bait gently into the water; to fish in this way. (Imit.)
Daphne, *n. daf*-ne, a genus of shrubs, partly evergreen; the laurel. (*Daphne*, who was changed into a laurel.)
daphnin, *n. daf*-nin, the bitter principle in different species of *Daphne.* (Gr. *daphne*, bay-tree.)
dapifer, *n. dap*-e-fer, the steward of a mediæval king or noble. (L. *daps*, a feast, and *fero*, bring.)
dapper, *a. dap*-per, nimble; active; sprightly, small and neat. (Dut.)
dapperling, *n. dap*-per-ling, a dandified little fellow.
dapple, *a. dap*-pl, marked with spots, blotches, or streaks of different colours or shades: *v.t.* to variegate with such. (Scand.)
darbies, *n.pl. dar*-biz, handcuffs [Slang].
Darby, *n. dar*-be, the husband of an old happily married couple. (From *Darby* and Joan.)
darby, *n. dar*-be, the long tool used by plasterers for ceiling work. (Dial. Eng.)
Darbyites, *n.pl. dar*-be-ites, a branch of the Plymouth Brethren, so called from their chief evangelist (1830), John Darby.
dare, *v.i.* dare, to have courage for any purpose; to be bold or adventurous; *v.t.* to challenge; to defy; to venture. (A.S.)
dare, *v.t.* dare, to scare so as to paralyse (of birds): *n.* a contrivance for dazing and trapping larks. (A.S. *darian.*)
dare, *n.* dare, the dace. (O.Fr. *dars.*)
daredevil, *n. dare*-dev-il, a reckless fellow without fear: *a.* characteristic of such.
darg, *n.* darg, the work that can be done in one day; a day's work. (Scots.)
darger, *n. darg*-er, a day-labourer. (Scots.)
dari, *n. du*-ree, durra, Indian millet.
daric, *n. da*-rik, an ancient Persian gold coin of Darius I stamped with an archer. (Gr. *dareikos.*)
daring, *a. dare*-ing, courageous; intrepid; fearless; audacious: *n.* venturesome courage.
daring, *n. dare*-ing, the taking of larks by means of a daring-net, and a looking-glass.
daringly, *ad. dare*-ing-le, in a daring manner.
daringness, *n. dare*-ing-ness, a daring spirit.
daring-net, *n.* a net thrown over birds that have been dared.
★**dark,** *a.* dark, destitute of light; wholly or partially black; gloomy; disheartening; obscure; not easily understood; mysterious; unenlightened; without spiritual light; wicked; blind; uncertain; not fair in complexion: *n.* the absence of light; secrecy; obscurity; a state of ignorance: *v.t.* to darken; to obscure. **dark ages,** the period in European history approximately between the fifth and eleventh centuries. **dark blues,** the representatives of Oxford in sporting contests. **dark horse,** a competitor whose chances are unknown. **dark room,** an apartment in which photographs are developed. **dark slide,** the flat box in which a plate is carried and exposed in the camera [Phot.]. (A.S. *deorc.*)
dark-browed, *a.* stern of aspect.
darken, *v.t. dar*-kn, to make dark; to obscure; to deprive of vision; to render gloomy; to render ignorant or stupid; to render less clear or intelligible; to make foul: *v.i.* to grow dark or darker.
dark-house, *n.* former term for a madhouse.
darkish, *a. dark*-ish, dusky; somewhat dark.
dark-lantern, *n.* a portable lantern capable of being obscured by the bearer.
darkling, *a.* and *ad. dark*-ling, in the dark; gloomy: *n.* the dusk; nightfall.
darkly, *ad. dark*-le, in the dark; not clearly.
darkness, *n. dark*-ness, absence of light; the state or condition, physical, intellectual, or spiritual, in which things are dark, invisible or obscure; obscurity.
darksome, *a. dark*-sum, dark; gloomy.
darky, *n. dark*-e, a man of colour; a Negro.
darling, *a. dar*-ling, dearly beloved; *n.* one dearly beloved; a favourite. (A.S. *dēorling*, favourite.)
darn, *n.* darn, a place mended by darning: *v.t.* to mend a hole by imitating the texture of the stuff. (W. *darn*, a patch.)
darn, *v.t.*, *n.*, and *int.* darn, a euphemistic form of the expletive "damn." [U.S.A.]
darnel, *n. dar*-nel, a grass, *Lolium temulentum.* (Fr.)
darner, *n. dar*-ner, one who darns; a darning-machine or -needle.
daroo, *n.* da-*roo*, the sycamore tree of Palestine, and Egypt, *Ficus sycomorus.* (Egyptian.)
dart, *n.* dart, a pointed missile to be thrown or blown as a weapon or thrown in the game of darts; a short lance; anything that pierces and wounds; a tapering seam to allow of fit [Dressmaking]: *n.pl.* a popular indoor game in which light feathered darts are aimed at a dart-board: *v.t.* to throw a pointed weapon with a sudden thrust; to shoot: *v.i.* to fly rapidly; to start suddenly and run; to play darts [Coll.]. (O.Fr.)
dart, *n.* dart, the dace, a freshwater fish.

dartars, *n.* *dar*-tars, an ulcer under the skin of lambs. (Fr. *dartre.*)
dart-board, *n.* the board on which is marked the target (13½ in. diam.) used in the game of darts; the target itself.
darter, *n.* *dar*-ter, one who or that which darts; a warrior armed with a dart; the snakebird; one of several small American freshwater fish of the perch family.
dartingly, *ad.* *dart*-ing-le, rapidly, like a dart.
dartre, *n.* *dar*-ter, herpes, or any herpetic skin-disease.
dartsman, *n.* *darts*-man, a player at darts.
Darwinian, *n.* dar-*win*-e-an, an evolutionist; a believer in the Darwinian theory: *a.* pertaining to evolution as described by Charles Darwin (*d.* 1882).
Darwinism, *n.* *dar*-win-izm, the doctrine of Darwin: evolution, esp. Darwin's theory (1859) of the origin of species by natural selection.
dash, *n.* dash, a violent striking of two bodies; a slight admixture; a rushing or onset with violence; a sudden stroke; a blow; a sudden check; swift action; a mark noting a break in the sentence, thus —; a small mark, thus ('), denoting that the note over which it is placed is to be performed in a short distinct manner [Mus.]; vivacity; display; brilliancy: *v.i.* to strike against and break; to rush with violence; to behave showily: *v.t.* to strike suddenly or violently; to break by collision; to throw suddenly; to bespatter; to sprinkle; to mix by throwing in another substance; to erase at a stroke; to destroy; to frustrate; to confound; to abash (Etym. uncertain; perhaps imit.)
dash-board, *n.* *dash*-bord, a mudguard; a float of a paddle-wheel; a splash-board, esp. on the front of a vehicle; the board facing the driver of a motor-car, aeroplane, etc., bearing certain controls, indicators, etc.
dasher, *n.* *dash*-er, a dash-board; a plunger; the device used in a churn which acts as the plunger; a dashing person; one who makes a dash.
dashing, *a.* *dash*-ing, bold; showy; spirited.
dashpot, *n.* *dash*-pot, a device for avoiding shock or damping out oscillation by means of a cushion of very slowly escaping air or liquid at the end of the piston stroke [Eng.].
dastard, *n.* *das*-tard, a contemptible coward; one who injures another without risking danger: *a.* cowardly; meanly shrinking from danger. (Perhaps from *daze.*)
dastardliness, *n.* *das*-tard-le-ness, cowardliness; base timidity.
dastardly, *a.* *das*-tard-le, cowardly.
dasymeter, *n.* da-*sim*-e-ter, an instrument for ascertaining the density of gases. (Gr. *dasūs*, thick, *metron*, measure.)
dasyure, *n.* *day*-se-yewr, a small carnivorous marsupial of Australia and Tasmania, known as the native cat. (Gr. *dasys*, and *oura*, a tail.)
data, *n.pl.* *day*-ta. *See* **datum.**
datable, *a.* *day*-ta-bl, that can be dated.
datal, *a.* *day*-tal, pertaining to or containing a date; chronological.
dataria, *n.* da-*tare*-re-a, the papal chancery at Rome from which all bulls are issued.
datary, *n.* *day*-ta-re, the officer who affixes *datum Romæ* (given at Rome) to the Pope's bulls.
date, *n.* date, the time when an event happened or anything was done; the specification of this in a document or letter; duration; period; an engagement [Coll.]: *v.t.* to affix the date to; to note or fix the time of an event or transaction: *v.i.* to reckon; to begin; to be dated; to afford evidence of its period [Coll.]. **out of date,** antiquated; obsolete. **up to date,** in the fashion; according to present knowledge. (L. *datum*, given.)
date, *n.* date, the fruit of the date-palm; the tree itself. (Fr. *datte*, from Gr. *dactylos*, a finger.)
dateless, *a.* *date*-less, having no date; immemorial.
date-line, *n.* *date*-line, the imaginary line in the Pacific where the date changes, *i.e.* (with local deviations) 180° from Greenwich.
date-palm, *n.* *date*-pahm, the palm-tree of Scripture, *Phœnix dactylifera*, common in N. Africa and S.W. Asia and cultivated elsewhere.
date-plum, *n.* *date*-plum, the cherry-sized fruit of a tree of S. Europe, *Diospyros lotus*; a Chinese species, *Diospyros kaki*, the persimmon; a North American species, *Diospyros virginiana*, cultivated for its wood and fruit, also known as the persimmon.
Datisca, *n.* da-*tis*-ka, a genus of tall herbs including the bastard hemp, *D. cannabina.*
datival, *a.* da-*ty*-val, belonging to the dative case.
dative, *n.* *day*-tiv, the case of nouns when they follow verbs that express giving, taking, or some act directed to an object; given; free to be given [Gram.]. (L. *dativus*, relating to giving.)
datolite, *n.* *dat*-o-lite, a hydrated borosilicate of calcium. (Gr. *dateomai*, divide, *lithos*, stone.)
datum, *n.* *day*-tum (*pl.* **data**), something given or admitted; a quantity or fact given, known, or admitted, by which things or results unknown may be found. **ordnance datum,** the mean level of the tide at Newlyn, Cornwall [Surveying]. (L.)
datum-line, *n.* the line along a fixed plane from which are reckoned all the heights along a section.
datura, *n.* da-*tew*-rah, the thorn-apple. (Hind.)
daturine, *n.* da-*tew*-rin, a poisonous alkaloid obtained from the thorn-apple.
daub, *n.* dawb, any material with which to daub; a smear; a badly painted picture: *v.i.* to paint in a crude style: *v.t.* to smear with a soft adhesive substance; to paint coarsely; to disguise; to lay on without taste; to flatter grossly. (O.Fr.)
dauber, *n.* *dawb*-er, one who daubs; a plasterer; an implement used in daubing; a coarse painter.
daubing, *n.* *dawb*-ing, coarse painting; gross flattery.
daubster, *n.* *dawb*-ster, a bad painter; a dauber.
dauby, *a.* *dawb*-e, viscous; glutinous; sticky; badly painted.
★**daughter,** *n.* *daw*-ter, a female child (in relation to her parents); a daughter-in-law; a female descendant; a female member of a community, race, etc.; a female in a child-like relation, as a penitent to her father confessor. (A.S. *dohtor.*)
daughter-in-law, *n.* *daw*-ter-in-law, a son's wife.
daughterlike, *a.* *daw*-ter-like, like a daughter.
daughterliness, *n.* *daw*-ter-le-ness, the state of being a daughter; the conduct becoming a daughter.
daughterly, *a.* *daw*-ter-le, daughterlike; pertaining to a daughter: *ad.* in a daughterlike way.
daunt, *v.t.* dawnt, to intimidate; to dishearten; to crush the spirit of. (O.Fr. *danter.*)
dauntless, *a.* *dawnt*-less, fearless; intrepid.
dauntlessly, *ad.* in a dauntless manner.
dauntlessness, *n.* fearlessness; intrepidity.
dauphin, *n.* *daw*-fin, the eldest son of the king of France from 1349 to the Revolution of 1830, so called from the principality of Dauphiné, the Counts of which had a blue dolphin as badge, having been the appanage of the heir-apparent to the crown. (Fr. *dauphin*, dolphin.)
dauphiness, *n.* *daw*-fin-ess, the wife of the dauphin.
davenport, *n.* *dav*-en-port, a writing table fitted with drawers at the side, named from the maker.
davit, *n.* *dav*-it, one of a pair of curved iron bars, or straight pieces of timber projecting over a ship's side, with tackles to hoist up a boat [Naut.]. **fish davit,** a spar over the bows, to hoist up the anchor clear of the ship [Naut.]. (Through Fr. from a personal name.)
davy, *n.* *day*-ve, an affidavit [Slang].
Davy Jones, *n.* *day*-ve-johnz, an imaginary malign being that presides over the evil spirits of the deep. **Davy Jones's locker,** a sailor's name for the sea as the lockfast of its victims.
Davy-lamp, *n.* *day*-ve-lamp, a safety-lamp for miners invented by Sir H. Davy.
davyne, *n.* *day*-vin, a variety of nepheline of a hexahedral form, found on Vesuvius, and named after Sir H. Davy.
daw, *n.* daw, the jackdaw, *Corvus monedula.*
dawdle, *v.i.* *daw*-dl, to waste time; to hang about.
dawdler, *n.* *daw*-dler, a trifler at doing anything.
dawk, *n.* dawk, dak (the Indian post).
dawn, *n.* *dawn*, daybreak; beginning or first appearance: *v.i.* to begin to grow light; to begin to open, expand, or appear. (Scand.)
dawning, *n.* *dawn*-ing, dawn; the time of dawn; a first unfolding.
★**day,** *n.* day, the time of light from sunrise to sunset, or from dawn to dark; the space of twenty-four hours, commencing at midnight, called the civil or astronomical day; the period of twenty-four hours, less four minutes, in which the earth makes

one complete revolution on its axis, called the sidereal day; the interval between the sun being in the meridian, and his return to it, called the solar day; among the Jews, the period from sunset to sunset; the daylight; a battle or victory of a day; any period of time distinguished from other time; an appointed or fixed time; time of commemorating an event. **call it a day,** decide to do no more; pack up, work being over for the day [Coll.]. **day about,** on alternate days. **day by day,** daily; each day in succession. **day nursery,** a crèche. **day of doom,** the day of judgment. **day of grace,** the time when mercy is offered to sinners [Theol.]. **day of judgment,** the end of the world. **day off,** day away from work. **day's journey,** in the East the distance that can be accomplished in twenty-four hours. **days of grace,** days granted by the court for delay, at the prayer of the plaintiff or defendant; a customary number of days allowed for the payment of a note or bill of exchange, after it becomes due [Comm.]. **day's work,** the work of one day; the account or reckoning of a ship's course for twenty-four hours, from noon to noon [Naut.]. **day ticket,** a ticket available for an outward and return journey on the same day only. **to-day,** this day; at present. **win the day,** to gain the victory. (A.S. *dæg*.)

day-bed, *n.* a bed where one rests or idles by day.

day-blindness, *n.* indistinct vision only by day.

day-boarder, *n.* a pupil having a daily meal at school, but not residing there.

day-book, *n.* a book in which are recorded the accounts of the day, generally so far as the sales are concerned.

day-boy, *n.* a non-boarding pupil at a boarding-school; a home-boarder.

daybreak, *n. day*-brake, first appearance of daylight.

daydream, *n. day*-dream, a vain fancy; a reverie; a visionary scheme: *v.i.* to indulge in daydreams.

daydreamer, *n. day*-dreem-er, a visionary schemer.

day-fly, *n.* a May-fly, any species of *Ephemera*, whose life in the winged state lasts from only a few hours to several days.

day-girl, *n.* a maid coming in by the day.

day-labour, *n.* labour by the day.

day-labourer, *n.* a labourer by the day.

daylight, *n. day*-lite, the light of the sun, as opposed to that of the moon or an artificial light. **daylight lamp,** a lamp the artificial light of which is as nearly as possible that of daylight. **daylight reflector,** a reflector placed at or over a window to throw in more light. **daylight saving,** putting the clock forward (usually 1 or 2 hours) for the working day to begin and end earlier, thereby bringing summer-time into effect.

day-lily, *n. day*-lil-le, a lily which blooms but a day, *Hemerocallis fulva.*

day-school, *n.* a school at which pupils are taught, but not boarded.

daysman, *n. dayz*-man, an umpire, so called as appointing a day for arbitration.

dayspring, *n. day*-spring, the dawn.

day-star, *n. day*-star, the morning star; the sun [Poet.].

daytime, *n. day*-time, the period of daylight.

day-woman, *n.* a woman working by the day.

day-work, *n.* work by the day; work by day.

daze, *n.* daze, the state of being dazed; mica [Min.]: *v.t.* to overpower with light; to stupefy. (Scand.)

dazzle, *n. daz*-zl, that which merely dazzles; bewilderment; a method of distorting the apparent outline of ships, etc., by lines and splashes of colour: *v.i.* to be too bright: *v.t.* to bewilder by a glare of light; to mislead by unusual coloration; to camouflage (esp. ships). (From *daze*.)

dazzlement, *n. daz*-zl-ment, the state of being dazzled; the cause or the power of dazzling.

dazzling, *a. daz*-zl-ing, excessive in brilliancy.

dazzlingly, *ad. daz*-zl-ling-le, in a dazzling manner.

de-, Latin prefix signifying down or away from, used in English with the force of (1) down, as in *descend, depose*; (2) intensification or wholly (*denigrate, denude*); (3) doubly or twice over, esp. in scientific terms, as *decompound*); and (4) reversal, negation, or separating from (*decompression, defrost, dehair, detrain, devulcanize,* etc. This group of words is so large that, in this Dictionary, many, whose meaning is obvious from the root, have not been separately entered.

deacon, *n. deek*-on, one who had charge of collecting and distributing the alms or of ministering to the poor and sick; in the Church of England and other episcopal Churches, a cleric who has not taken priest's orders; in the Presbyterian Church, one who superintends the financial and secular affairs of a congregation; in the Congregational Church, one who admits to membership and assists at the communion; in Scotland, the master of an incorporated company of craftsmen; an officer in freemasonry. (Gr. *diakonos*, a servant.)

deaconess, *n. deek*-on-ess, a female deacon; a member of an order of women church-workers.

deaconry, *n. deek*-on-re, the whole body of deacons; the diaconate; deaconship.

deaconship, *n. deek*-on-ship, the office or ministry of a deacon.

★**dead,** *a.* ded, having ceased to live; without life; deathlike; still or motionless as death; blank; sure as death; useless; unprofitable; obsolete; unreal; dull; tasteless; vapid; deep; not acting; spiritless; without spiritual life, or the principle of Christian life; cut off from the rights of a citizen [Law]; not glossy; not gay or bright [Painting]: *ad.* thoroughly; exactly; directly. **dead as a doornail,** undoubtedly dead. **dead ball,** a ball out of play. **dead certainty,** something sure to occur. **dead drunk,** helpless with drink. **dead end,** a cul-de-sac; a pipe, etc., with one end stopped; an impasse. **dead hand,** mortmain. **dead language,** a language which is no longer spoken, and known only in writings. **dead level,** flat country which offers no obstruction to railway or road making [Surveying]. **dead lift,** a heavy weight; an extreme exigency. **dead-man's handle,** a controlling handle on an electric vehicle so constructed that if the driver releases his grip the current is cut off and the brakes applied. **dead march,** a piece of solemn music played in honour of the dead. **dead of night,** the stillest part of the night. **dead ropes,** those which do not run in any block [Naut.]. **dead set,** the act of a setter in pointing at game; a deadlock; a steady and determined effort. **dead shot,** a good marksman. **dead stand,** a determined opposition; a resolute purpose. **dead stop,** the cessation, or sudden cessation, of motion. **dead wall,** a wall with no windows or openings. **dead water,** the eddy water which closes in with a ship's stern as she passes through the water; water where there is no current [Naut.]. **dead wire,** a wire cut off from the electric current [Elect.]. **flogging a dead horse,** working to no purpose. **the dead,** those who are dead. (A.S.)

deadalive, *ded*-a-lyve, or **dead-and-alive,** *a.* dreary; monotonous.

dead-beat, *a.* exhausted; tired out; making a beat devoid of recoil (of watches, galvanometers, etc.): *n.* a worthless idler. [U.S.A.]

dead-centre, *n.* a point in a revolution when the crank is in line with the connecting-rod.

dead-colouring, *n.* the first layer of colours in a picture, bringing out its parts, usually in some shade of grey.

deaden, *v.t. ded*-en, to diminish the force of; to render less susceptible of feeling; to retard; to blunt; to make vapid or spiritless; to take off gloss or brilliancy: *v.i.* to lose spirit or strength.

deadeye, *n. ded*-eye, a round, flattish wooden block encircled by a rope or an iron band, and pierced with three holes to receive the lanyards [Naut.].

dead-freight, *n. ded*-frate, payment for space taken but not occupied; such unoccupied space.

deadhead, *n. ded*-hed, one who has a free pass to an entertainment, for a journey, etc.

dead-heat, *n.* a race in which two or more competitors are level at the winning post.

dead-house, *n.* a mortuary.

deadish, *a. ded*-ish, dull; practically obsolete, etc.

dead-letter, *n.* a letter which cannot be delivered to the addressee; a law that has fallen into disuse.

deadlights, *n.pl. ded*-lites, strong ports made exactly to fit the cabin windows, for use during stormy weather [Naut.].

dead-line, *n.* a fixed boundary or limit in space or time.

deadliness, *n.* *ded*-le-ness, power of being deadly.
deadlock, *n.* *ded*-lok, a stoppage of progress, generally through the refusal of two or more opposing parties to compromise.
deadly, *a.* *ded*-le, that may occasion death ; mortal ; appeasable only with death : *ad.* in a manner resembling death ; mortally ; implacably ; destructively.
deadly-nightshade, *n.* the poisonous plant, *Atropa belladonna*, a purple-berried shrub.
deadness, *n.* *ded*-ness, the state of being dead ; inertness ; indifference.
dead-nettle, *n.* any species of *Lamium*.
dead-point, *n.* the dead-centre.
dead-reckoning, *n.* the calculation made of the present position of a ship or aircraft without observation of the heavenly bodies.
dead-weight, *n.* *ded*-wate, the unrelieved weight of a motionless body ; an oppressive or weighty burden.
deadwood, *n.* *ded*-wood, useless materials, methods, persons, etc. ; certain solid timbers built into the keel of a ship, particularly at the extremities [Naut.].
deaf, *a.* def, incapable or dull of hearing ; inattentive to what is said ; spiritually dull of hearing ; muffled, deadened (of sounds). (A.S.)
deafen, *v.t.* *def*-n, to render incapable or dull of hearing ; to make a sound inaudible by a louder one ; to stun ; to render impervious to sound by filling with mortar or other substances [Arch.].
deafish, *a.* *def*-ish, slightly deaf.
deafly, *ad.* *def*-le, in a deaf manner ; obscurely.
deaf-mute, *n.* *def*-mewt, one deaf and dumb.
deafness, *n.* *def*-ness, the state of being deaf.
deal, *n* deel, firwood or pinewood ; a plank of 7 inches or more in breadth, 3 inches or less in thickness, and 6 feet or over in length. (Dut. *deel.*)
deal, *n.* deel, a part or portion ; an indefinite quantity ; the distribution of cards ; a trade bargain ; a clandestine arrangement ; an international or inter-party agreement : *v.i.* to trade or negotiate ; to act between man and man ; to behave well or ill ; to act ; to distribute cards ; *v.t.* to distribute ; to scatter ; to throw about ; to throw out in succession. **deal by,** to treat either well or ill. **deal in,** to have to do with ; to be engaged in ; to trade in. **deal with,** to use well or ill ; to treat with by way of discipline [Eccles.] ; to contend with. *p.* and *pp.* **dealt,** delt. (A.S. *dælan.*)
dealer, *n.* *deel*-er, a trader ; a merchant ; a Stock Exchange jobber ; one who distributes cards to the players.
dealfish, *n.* *deel*-fish, a deep-sea fish with elongated body allied to the ribbonfish.
dealing, *n.* *deel*-ing, conduct in relation to others ; intercourse in buying and selling ; behaviour ; traffic ; trade.
dean, *n.* deen, an ecclesiastical dignitary in cathedral and collegiate churches ; the head of the chapter of a cathedral ; the head of a faculty in a university. **dean and chapter,** a bishop's council to aid him with their advice in the spiritual and temporal concerns of his see. **dean of faculty,** the head of the faculty of advocates in Scotland. **dean of guild,** in Scotland, originally the head of a guildry and, as such, a member of the municipality of a royal burgh, now a magistrate whose duty it is to see to the security of buildings, etc. **rural dean,** *see* **rural.** (O.Fr. *deien.*)
deanery, *n.* *deen*-er-re, the office, residence, or jurisdiction of a dean.
deanship, *n.* *deen*-ship, the office of a dean.
★dear, *a.* deer, high in price ; scarce ; greatly valued ; beloved : *n.* a darling. (A.S. *dēore.*)
dearly, *ad.* *deer*-le, at a high price ; with great fondness.
dearness, *n.* *deer*-ness, the quality of being dear ; tender affectionateness.
dearth, *n.* derth, scarcity ; that which makes food dear ; famine ; barrenness. (Scand.)
deary, *n.* *deer*-re, a word of familiar endearment ; a dear. (Dim. of *dear.*)
deasil, *ad.* *dee*-sil, righthandwise ; as the hands of a clock or course of the sun : *n.* motion towards the right.
★death, *n.* deth, the extinction of life ; the state of being dead or extinct ; the state of the dead ; the manner of dying ; a skeleton, as a symbol of death; destroyer or agent of death ; the instrument of death ; the penalty of death ; state of temporary or final extinction of spiritual life. **civil death,** the separation of a man from civil society by banishment, etc. **death duties,** estate duties, taxes payable on the value of all property of one who has died, before it can be distributed. (A.S.)
death-adder, *n.* the deadliest of Australian snakes, *Acanthophis antarcticus*.
deathbed, *n.* *deth*-bed, the bed on which one dies : *a.* made or done when dying.
death-blow, *n.* a blow extinguishing life or hope.
deathful, *a.* *deth*-ful, fraught with or suggestive of death.
deathless, *a.* *deth*-less, not subject to death ; immortal ; imperishable.
deathlessly, *ad.* everlastingly.
deathlessness, *n.* the quality of being immortal.
deathlike, *a.* *deth*-like, resembling death.
deathly, *a.* *deth*-le, deadly ; *ad.* as death.
death-mask, *n.* *deth*-mahsk, the plaster cast of the face of one newly dead.
death-rate, *n.* *deth*-rate, the proportion of deaths in a given district within a given period.
death-rattle, *n.* *deth*-rat-tl, a rattle in the throat of a dying person.
death-roll, *n.* *deth*-role, a list of those slain in a battle or killed in an accident, etc.
death's-door, *n.* a near approach to death.
death's-head, *n.* *deths*-hed, a human skull, or a representation of it ; the emblem of mortality ; the pirate flag ; the hawk-moth, *Acherontia atropos*, so called from markings on its thorax roughly resembling the human skull.
death-stroke, *n.* a fatal stroke ; a death-blow.
death-struggle, *n.* the struggle preceding death.
death-throe, *n.* *deth*-throh, the pangs of death.
death-trap, *n.* a place, building, ship, etc., apparently safe but dangerous to life.
death-warrant, *n.* an order for the execution of a criminal ; that which puts an end to something.
death-watch, *n.* any small beetle, esp. *Anobium tessellatum*, inhabiting old woodwork and making a ticking sound (the call of the male for its mate), which was formerly supposed to prognosticate death.
deb, *n.* deb, a débutante [Coll.].
debacle, *n.* de-*bah*-kl, a violent rush of water, as at the breaking up of ice, hurling rocks and all opposing objects before it [Geol.] ; any such rush ; a rout, an overthrow. (Fr. *débâcle.*)
debag, *v.t.* dee-*bag*, forcibly to remove the trousers (of another) [Slang].
debar, *v.t.* de-*bar*, to hinder from approach, entry, or enjoyment. (O.Fr. *débarrer.*)
debark, *v.t.* and *i.* de-*bark*, to disembark.
debarkation, *n.* dee-bar-*kay*-shon, disembarkation.
debase, *v.t.* de-*base*, to lower in quality, purity, or value ; to adulterate ; to degrade.
debasement, *n.* de-*base*-ment, the act of debasing ; degradation ; adulteration.
debaser, *n.* de-*base*-er, one who debases.
debasing, *a.* de-*base*-ing, tending to debase.
debasingly, *ad.* so as to debase.
debatable, *a.* de-*bate*-a-bl, that may be disputed. **debatable land,** a borderland ; the tract formerly claimed by both England and Scotland, west of the Esk.
debate, *n.* de-*bate*, contention or discussion in words or argument ; contention ; contest : *v.t.* to contend for or discuss in words or arguments ; to contend for : *v.i.* to deliberate ; to dispute. **debating society,** a society for the purpose of debate and improvement in extemporaneous speaking. (Fr. *débattre.*)
debater, *n.* de-*bate*-er, one skilled in argument ; a disputant.
debauch, *n.* de-*bawtch*, a fit or act of debauchery ; excessive intemperance : *v.i.* to revel : *v.t.* to corrupt or vitiate ; to seduce from duty or from virtue. (Fr. *débaucher.*)
debauchedly, *ad.* de-*bawtch*-ed-le, in a profligate manner.
debauchedness, *n.* de-*bawtch*-ed-ness, the quality of being debauched ; intemperance.
debauchee, *n.* deb-o-*shee*, a sensual person ; a libertine.
debaucher, *n.* de-*bawtch*-er, one who debauches another ; a seducer.

debauchery, *n.* de-*bawtch*-er-re, excessive intemperance; habitual lewdness; seduction from duty or allegiance.
debauchment, *n.* de-*bawtch*-ment, act of debauching.
debenture, *n.* de-*bent*-yewr, a note acknowledging a debt; a deed of mortgage for repayment with interest of money lent; a bond; one of an issue of bonds; a certificate of drawback [Comm.]. **debenture issue,** a loan raised by a company, etc., as opposed to capital subscribed by shareholders. (L. *debentur*, these are owing.)
debentured, *a.* de-*bent*-yewrd, entitled to drawback; secured by debenture.
debilitant, *a.* de-*bil*-e-tant, having a debilitating action; allaying excitement: *n.* a medicine for this purpose; a depressant [Med.].
debilitate, *v.t.* de-*bil*-e-tate, to impair the strength; to weaken; to enervate. (L. *debilitatus*, weakened.)
debilitating, *a.* de-*bil*-e-*tay*-ting, weakening.
debilitation, *n.* de-*bil*-e-*tay*-shon, the act of weakening.
debility, *n.* de-*bil*-e-te, functional weakness; feebleness of purpose. (Fr. *débilité.*)
debit, *n.* *deb*-it, that which is entered in an account as a debt; the left-hand side of the ledger, where all articles charged to an account are entered: *v.t.* to charge with debt; to enter on the debtor side of an account. (L. *debitum*, a debt.)
debituminize, *v.t.* dee-be-*tew*-me-nize, to deprive of bitumen.
debonair, *a.* deb-o-*nare*, of gentle, complaisant manners; genial; well-bred; jaunty. (Fr. *de bon air*, of good manner.)
debonairness, *n.* deb-o-*nare*-ness, gentleness; complaisance. (Fr. *débonnaire.*)
debouch, *v.i.* de-*boosh*, to march out of a confined place, or from defiles [Mil.]; to flow out from a ravine. (Fr. *déboucher.*)
debouchment, *n.* de-*boosh*-ment, the act of debouching; the mouth of a river, or of a mountain pass, etc.
debouchure, *n.* day-boo-*shoor*, the mouth of a river or a strait; an outward opening. (Fr.)
debris, *n.* *deb*-ree *or* *day*-bree, ruins or fragments of rock and other substances, piled up in confusion, as the wreck of some wasteful force or disaster; the wreck of an army [Mil.]; broken leavings; rubbish. (Fr.)
★**debt,** *n.* det, that which is due from one person to another; that which any one is obliged to do or to suffer; a failure in duty. **action of debt,** an action to recover a sum of money by legal process [Law]. **debt of honour,** one (*e.g.* incurred by gambling) not recoverable at law. **debt of nature,** death. **national debt,** the debt owing by the state to lenders or to investors in its securities, of which the **funded debt** is that part represented by bonds, annuities, etc., and the **floating debt** that part that is repayable at a stated time or on demand. (Fr. *dette.*)
debtee, *n.* *det*-tee, one to whom a debt is due [Law].
debtless, *a.* *det*-less, free from debt.
debtor, *n.* *det*-tor, one who owes another anything; the debit side of an account. (O.Fr. *detor.*)
debunk, *v.t.* dee-*bunk*, to degrade the reputation of by revision of a former over-estimate; to divest of flattery [U.S.A. slang].
debus, *v.i.* dee-*bus*, to alight from a bus or other motor transport. (Originally Mil. slang.)
début, *n.* de-*boo*, the first appearance before the public; beginning or start. (Fr.)
débutant, *n.masc.* *day*-boo-tan (*fem.* **débutante,** App.), one who makes a début, esp. a lady who makes her début in society. (Fr.)
deca-, *pref.* *dek*-a, ten. (Gr., ten.)
decachord, *n.* *dek*-a-kawrd, an ancient musical instrument of ten strings. (Gr. *deka*, ten, and *chord.*)
decadal, *a.* *dek*-a-dal, pertaining to, consisting of, tens; pertaining to a decade.
decade, *n.* *dek*-ade, a group or aggregate of ten; a period of years. (Fr.)
decadence, *n.* de-*kay*-dence, decay, degeneration, deterioration. (Fr.)
decadency, *n.* de-*kay*-den-se, decadence; decaying condition.
decadent, *a.* de-*kay*-dent, in a state of decadence: *n.* a degenerate; a writer or artist having or affecting weaknesses and obscurities in style.
decagon, *n.* *dek*-a-gon, a plane figure of ten sides and angles [Geom.]. (Gr. *deka*, and *gonia*, an angle.)
decagonal, *a.* de-*kag*-o-nal, having ten angles.
decagramme, *n.* *dek*-a-gram, a metric weight of ten grammes, equal to ·35 oz. avoirdupois.
decagynian, *a.* *dek*-a-*jin*-e-an, belonging to the Linnæan order of plants comprising those with ten pistils [Bot.]. (Gr. *deka*, and *gyne*, a female.)
decahedral, *a.* *dek*-a-*hee*-dral, having ten sides.
decahedron, *n.* *dek*-a-*hee*-dron, a solid figure having ten sides [Geom.]. (Gr. *deka*, and *hedra*, a seat.)
decalcification, *n.* dee-*kal*-se-fe-*kay*-shon, extraction of calcareous matter from bones.
decalcify, *v.t.* dee-*kal*-se-fy, to deprive of lime or calcareous matter. (L. *de-*, and *calx*, lime.)
decalcomania, *n.* de-*kal*-ko-*may*-ne-a, the transfer of a coloured picture from paper to glass or china. (Fr. *decalquer*, to transfer a design, and *mania.*)
decalitre, *n.* *dek*-a-lee-ter, a metric measure of capacity, containing 10 litres, or 2·2 gallons.
decalogist, *n.* de-*kal*-o-jist, a commentator on the decalogue.
decalogue, *n.* *dek*-a-log, the ten commandments. (Gr. *deka*, and *logos*, a word.)
Decameron, *n.* de-*kam*-er-on, a collection of a hundred tales by Boccaccio, represented as related in ten days. (It. *decamerone.*)
decametre, *n.* *dek*-a-mee-ter, a metric measure of length, of ten metres, equal to 10·936 yards.
decamp, *v.i.* de-*kamp*, to strike camp; to march off; to take oneself off, esp. clandestinely. (Fr. *décamper.*)
decampment, *n.* de-*kamp*-ment, a marching off; a furtive stealing away.
decanal, *a.* de-*kay*-nal, pertaining to a dean or a deanery, or to the dean's (*i.e.*, the south) side of the choir. (L. *decanus*, dean.)
Decandria, *n.pl.* de-*kan*-dre-a, a Linnæan group of plants having ten stamens [Bot.]. (Gr. *deka*, and *aner*, a male.)
decandrian, *a.* de-*kan*-dre-an, decandrous.
decandrous, *a.* de-*kan*-drus, having ten stamens.
decangular, *a.* de-*kang*-gew-lar, having ten angles.
decani, *a.* de-*kay*-ny, pertaining to the dean's, or south, side of the choir in antiphonal singing.
decant, *v.t.* de-*kant*, to pour off gently; to pour from one vessel into another. (Fr. *décanter.*)
decantation, *n.* dee-kan-*tay*-shon, the act of decanting.
decanter, *n.* de-*kan*-ter, a vessel for holding and pouring out decanted liquor; one who decants liquors.
decaphyllous, *a.* de-*kaf*-il-us, having ten leaves [Bot.]. (Gr. *deka*, and *phyllon*, a leaf.)
decapitate, *v.t.* de-*kap*-e-tate, to behead; to cashier [U.S.A.]. (L. *decapitatus*, beheaded.)
decapitation, *n.* de-*kap*-e-*tay*-shon, the act of beheading.
decapod, *a.* *dek*-a-pod, having ten limbs, as a crab, lobster, etc.: *n.* a crustacean with ten feet; a heavy freight locomotive engine having ten driving-wheels. (Gr. *deka*, and *pous*, a foot.)
decapodal, *a.* de-*kap*-o-dal, having ten feet; belonging to the order decapoda.
decapodous, *a.* de-*kap*-o-dus, having ten feet.
decarbonate, *v.t.* de-*kar*-bo-nate, to deprive of carbon dioxide or carbonic acid.
decarbonization, *n.* de-*kar*-bo-ny-*zay*-shon, the process of decarbonizing.
decarbonize, *v.t.* de-*kar*-bo-nize, to deprive of carbon; to remove carbon deposit from the combustion chamber, etc., of an internal combustion engine.
decarburize, *v.t.* de-*kar*-bew-rize, to deprive of carbon or carbonic acid.
decarburization, *n.* de-*kar*-bew-ry-*zay*-shon, the process of decarburizing.
decare, *n.* *dek*-air, an obsolete French measure of area, a thousand square metres, ·247 acres. (Fr.)
decastere, *n.* *dek*-a-steer, a French measure of volume containing 10 cu. metres, or 13·08 cu. yards.
decastich, *n.* *dek*-a-stik, a poem consisting of ten lines. (Gr. *deka*, and *stichos*, a verse.)
decastyle, *n.* *dek*-a-stile, a portico with ten columns in front. (Gr. *deka*, and *stylos*, a column.)
decasualize, *v.t.* dee-*kaz*-yew-a-lize, to replace casual by the regular employment of labour.
decasyllabic, *a.* *dek*-a-sil-*lab*-ik, with ten syllables. (Gr. *deka*, and *syllabē*, syllable.)

decasyllable, *n.* *dek*-a-*sil*-la-bl, a word of ten syllables.
decathlon, *n.* de-*kath*-lon, a contest involving ten specified events in the Olympic Games. (Gr. *deka*, ten, *athlon*, contest.)
decatholicize, *v.t.* dee-ka-*thol*-e-size, to deprive of Catholicizm, or of catholicity.
decay, *n.* de-*kay*, gradual failure or decline towards dissolution or extinction; a wasting away; decayed matter: *v.i.* to decline, waste, or wither away; to deteriorate. (O.Fr. *decair.*)
decayed, *a.* de-*kayd*, fallen off in quality; ruined; broken in fortune.
decayer, *n.* de-*kay*-er, that which causes decay.
decease, *n.* de-*seece*, departure from life; death: *v.i.* to die. (Fr. *décès.*)
deceased, *a.* de-*seest*, dead: *n.* one recently dead.
deceit, *n.* de-*seet*, deception; a propensity to deceive; that which purposely deceives or misleads; fraud; any underhand practice to defraud another [Law]. (O.Fr. *deceite.*)
deceitful, *a.* de-*seet*-ful, full of deceit; tending to mislead or ensnare.
deceitfully, *ad.* de-*seet*-ful-le, in a deceitful manner.
deceitfulness, *n.* de-*seet*-ful-ness, tendency or disposition to deceive.
deceivable, *a.* de-*seev*-a-bl, apt to be deceived.
deceive, *v.t.* de-*seev*, to mislead; to impose on; to beguile; to disappoint: *v.i.* to act in a deceitful manner. (Fr. *décevoir.*)
deceiver, *n.* de-*seev*-er, one who deceives; an impostor.
decelerate, *v.t.* and *i.* dee-*sel*-er-rate, to cause to go slower; to reduce speed.
deceleration, *n.* dee-sel-er-*ray*-shon, the act of decelerating, state of being decelerated, or rate of diminution in the speed of anything in motion.
decem-, *pref.* Latin prefix signifying ten. (L.)
December, *n.* de-*sem*-ber, the last month in the year, so called by the Romans as being their tenth, owing to their year beginning in March.
Decemberly, *a.* de-*sem*-ber-le, cold and dreary.
decemfid, *a.* de-*sem*-fid, ten-cleft; divided into ten parts, having ten divisions [Bot.]. (L. *decem-*, and *fidi*, have divided.)
decempedal, *a.* de-*sem*-pe-dal, with ten feet. (L. *decem-*, and *pes*, a foot.)
decemvir, *n.* de-*sem*-vir, one of the decemviri.
decemviral, *a.* de-*sem*-ve-ral, pertaining to the decemviri.
decemvirate, *n.* de-*sem*-ve-rat, the office or term of office of the decemviri; a similar body.
decemviri, *n.pl.* de-*sem*-ve-re, a body of ten magistrates which, at various times, had absolute authority in ancient Rome. (L. *decem-*, and *vir*, a man.)
decency, *n.* *dee*-sen-se, that which is becoming in words or behaviour; modesty; respectability; avoidance of obscenity. (L. *decentia.*)
decennary, *n.* de-*sen*-na-re, a period of ten years: *a.* pertaining to such period.
decenniad, *n.* de-*sen*-e-ad, a decennium.
decennial, *a.* de-*sen*-ne-al, consisting of ten years, or happening every ten years (L. *decennālis*, of ten years.)
decennium, *n.* de-*sen*-ne-um, a decade, or period of ten years. (L.)
decent, *a.* *dee*-sent, becoming; proper; modest; moderate; tolerable; nice; free from obscenity. (O.Fr. *décent.*)
decentish, *a.* *dee*-sent-ish, rather decent.
decently, *ad.* *dee*-sent-le, in a decent manner.
decentness, *n.* *dee*-sent-ness, decency.
decentralist, *n.* dee-*sen*-tra-list, one in favour of decentralization.
decentralization, *n.* de-*sen*-tra-ly-*zay*-shon, the breaking up of a centralized administrative power into a number of centres; the distribution among many of powers centralized in one.
decentralize, *v.i.* de-*sen*-tra-lize, to break up (esp. a centralized administration) and redistribute power and functions; to place under local management.
deceptibility, *n.* de-sep-te-*bil*-e-te, the condition of being easily deceived; gullibility.
deception, *n.* de-*sep*-shon, the act of deceiving; the state of being deceived; a deceptive thing or action; a hoax; a fraud. (Fr. *déception.*)
deceptious, *a.* de-*sep*-shus, deceptive; deceiving.
deceptive, *a.* de-*sep*-tiv, tending or apt to deceive. (Fr. *déceptif.*)
deceptively, *ad.* in a manner to deceive.
deceptiveness, *n.* the quality of being deceptive.
deceptivity, *n.* dee-sep-*tiv*-e-te, that which deceives; a deceit; a sham.
decern, *v.t.* de-*sern*, to judge; to decree [Scots. Law]. (L. *decernere*, distinguish.)
dechristianize, *v.t.* dee-*krist*-yan-ize, to turn or pervert from Christianity. (L. *de-*, and *christianize.*)
deciare, *n.* *des*-e-air, the tenth of an are, a French measure equal to 11·96 sq. yards. (Fr.)
decibar, *n.* *des*-e-bar, one-tenth of a bar [Meteor.].
decibel, *n.* *des*-e-bel, one-tenth of a bel.
decidable, *a.* de-*side*-a-bl, that may be decided.
decide, *v.t.* de-*side*, to determine; to settle; to end: *v.i.* to determine. (L. *decidere*, cut off.)
decided, *a.* de-*side*-ed, resolute; determined; unmistakable; indusputable.
decidedly, *ad.* de-*side*-ed-le, in a decided manner.
decider, *n.* de-*side*-er, one who or that which decides; a contest to decide a tie; a final heat.
decidua, *n.* de-*sid*-yew-a, the membranous structure that develops in the gravid uterus and is expelled after parturition.
deciduate, *a.* de-*sid*-yew-at, having a decidua; formed in part from a decidua [Anat.].
deciduous, *a.* de-*sid*-yew-us, falling in winter; shed or falling off after a time or season, as certain kinds of hair, horns, and teeth in animals, and leaves in plants [Zool. and Bot.]. **deciduous cypress,** the bald cypress, *Taxodium distichum.* (L. *dēciduus*, ready to fall.)
deciduousness, *n.* de-*sid*-yew-us-ness, the quality of being deciduous.
decigramme, *n.* *des*-e-gram, a weight of one-tenth of a gramme, equal to 1·5432 grains troy.
decile, *n.* *des*-sil, aspect or position of two planets when they are a tenth part of the zodiac from each other [Astrol.]. (Fr.)
decilitre, *n.* *des*-se-lee-ter, a French measure of capacity equal to one-tenth of a litre, 0·176 pint.
decillion, *n.* des-*sil*-yon, in English usage, the tenth power of a million (represented by 1 followed by 60 ciphers); in American, a million multiplied by 1,000 nine times (1 followed by 33 ciphers). (L. *decem-*, and *illion*, as in million.)
decima, *n.* *des*-e-mah, the interval of a tenth; an organ stop $\frac{1}{10}$th higher than the open stops [Mus.]. (L., the tenth part.)
decimal, *a.* *des*-se-mal, pertaining to ten or tenths; numbered by tens; increasing or diminishing by ten times: *n.* a tenth; a fraction having some power of ten for its denominator. **decimal arithmetic,** that in which we count by tens, or that in which quantities are expressed by tens or tenths. **decimal fraction,** a fraction having some power of ten as its denominator. **decimal notation,** the Arabic system of numeration. **decimal point,** the dot between the whole number and the decimal. **decimal system,** the metric system of money, weights, and measures, in which the standard unit is multiplied and divided by ten. (Fr. *décimal.*)
decimalism, *n.* *des*-se-ma-lizm, the decimal system; the theory of decimal notation.
decimalist, *n.* *des*-e-ma-list, one advocating the use of the decimal system for coinage, weights, and measures.
decimalization, *n.* *des*-se-ma-ly-*zay*-shon, conversion into decimals.
decimalize, *v.t.* *des*-se-ma-lize, to reduce to terms of the decimal system.
decimally, *ad.* *des*-se-ma-le, by tens; by means of decimals.
decimate, *v.t.* *des*-se-mate, to take the tenth part; to put to death every tenth man; to destroy in great numbers. (L. *decimāre*, to decimate.)
decimation, *n.* *des*-se-*may*-shon, the act of decimating; the state of being decimated; the destruction of a tenth or of a large proportion. (L. *decimatio.*)
decimator, *n.* *des*-se-may-tor, one who or that which decimates.
decime, *n.* *des*-seem, the tenth part of a franc; a ten-centime piece. (Fr.)
decimetre, *n.* *des*-se-mee-ter, the metric measure of a tenth of a metre, equal to 3·937 inches.
decipher, *v.t.* de-*sy*-fer, to discover the meaning of

what is written in cipher; to decode; to make out what is obscurely written or obscurely expressed. (Fr. *déchiffrer.*)

decipherable, *a.* that may be deciphered.

decipherment, *n.* the act of deciphering; interpretation of cipher or of unknown or illegible writing.

★**decision,** *n.* de-*sizh*-on, final judgment; settlement; end; firmness and stability of purpose.

decisive, *a.* de-*sy*-siv, having the power or quality of deciding; final; conclusive; firm and resolute of purpose.

decisively, *ad.* de-*sy*-siv-le, in a decisive manner.

decisiveness, *n.* the state of being decisive.

decistere, *n. des*-e-stare *or des*-e-steer, the metric measure of a tenth of a stere, 3·53 cu. feet. (Fr.)

decivilize, *v.i.* dee-*siv*-e-lize, to make less civilized; to reduce to a savage state.

deck, *v.t.* dek, to cover; to clothe; to adorn; to cover or fit with a deck. (Dut. *dekken*, to cover.)

deck, *n.* dek, a floor or platform in a ship; a pack of cards piled regularly on each other. **deck cargo,** that part of the cargo which is stowed on the ship's deck, above the water-line. (Dut. *dek.*)

deck-chair, *n.* a light folding reclining chair with canvas seat.

decker, *n. dek*-er, a vessel having the specified number of decks, as **two-decker** or **three-decker,** a ship that has two or three gun decks [Naut.]; a deck-passenger.

deck-hand, *n.* a man employed on deck duties.

deck-house, *n.* a cabin on deck.

decking, *n. dek*-ing, ornament; embellishment; the material of which a deck is made.

deckle, *n.* dekl, the border in a paper-making machine that fixes the width of the paper. **deckle-edged,** of paper with rough untrimmed edges as left by the deckle. (Ger. *dekkel*, cover.)

deck-load, *n.* a deck cargo.

deck-passenger, *n.* a steerage passenger; a passenger not having cabin accommodation.

declaim, *v.i.* de-*klame*, to deliver a set speech or oration rhetorically; to speak by rhetorical rule and for mere rhetorical effect; to recite: *v.t.* to speak rhetorically. (L. *declamāre*, declaim.)

declaimer, *n.* de-*klame*-er, one who declaims; one who speaks clamorously.

declamation, *n.* dek-la-*may*-shon, the act or art of declaiming, according to rules, so as accurately to express the sentiment; an harangue; a display of empty impassioned rhetorical oratory. (L. *declamatio*, speaking-out.)

declamatory, *a.* de-*klam*-a-to-re, relating to the practice of declaiming; treated in the manner of a rhetorician; appealing to the passions; rhetorical without solid sense or argument; noisy in style.

declarable, *a.* de-*klare*-ra-bl, able to be declared; subject to declaration; customable.

declarant, *n.* de-*klare*-rant, one who makes a declaration [Law.].

declaration, *n.* dek-la-*ray*-shon, the act of declaring or openly proclaiming; that which is declared or proclaimed; the document containing this; a statement made verbally or reduced to writing [Law]; the naming of trumps (or "no trumps") at bridge, etc. (Fr. *déclaration.*)

declarative, *a.* de-*kla*-ra-tiv, making declaration; explanatory.

declaratively, *ad.* in a declarative manner.

declaratory, *a.* de-*kla*-ra-to-re, making declaration or exhibition; expressive.

declare, *v.t.* de-*klare*, to make known; to proclaim formally; to tell explicitly and plainly; to assert or affirm: *v.i.* to state fully; to make a declaration; to close an innings before the fall of ten wickets [Cricket]; to name a suit as trumps at bridge, etc.; to announce oneself or itself; to recite the causes of complaint against the defendant [Law]. **declare off,** to announce cancellation (as of a bet); to quit. **declare oneself,** to avow oneself. (Fr. *déclarer.*)

declared, *a.* de-*klayrd*, openly avowed; publicly announced.

declaredly, *ad.* de-*klare*-red-le, avowedly; explicitly.

declarer, *n.* the player making the declaration at bridge, etc.

declassed, *a.* dee-*klahsd*, degraded in social position.

declension, *n.* de-*klen*-shon, a declining; descent; a falling off; a tendency towards a less degree of excellence or perfection; inflection of nouns, adjectives, and pronouns, or a change in their termination to form the oblique cases [Gram.]. (O.Fr. *déclinaison.*)

declinable, *a.* de-*kly*-na-bl, capable of being declined [Gram.].

declinate, *a. dek*-le-nat, bending or bent downward, in a curve; declining [Bot.]. (L. *declinatus*, declined.)

declination, *n.* dek-le-*nay*-shon, the act of bending down; a declining or falling into a worse state; decay; deterioration; gradual appeasement or calming down; oblique motion; deviation from rectitude; refusal; the distance north or south of any heavenly body from the celestial equator, hence the latitude of a star [Astron.]. **declination of the compass** or **needle,** the variation of the needle from the true meridian of a place [Elect.]. The **declination of a wall** or **plane,** an arc of the horizon, contained between the plane and the prime vertical circle, if reckoned from the east or west or between the meridian and the plane, if reckoned from the north or south [Dialling]. (L. *declinatio*, a turning away.)

declinator, *n.* de-*kly*-na-tor, an instrument for measuring the angle of sloping planes; a clinometer.

declinatory, *a.* de-*kly*-na-to-re, intimating a refusal; involving a declination. **declinatory plea,** a former plea before trial or conviction, claiming exemption from jurisdiction or penalty [Law].

declinature, *n.* de-*kly*-na-tewr, a declining; courteous refusal; refusal of jurisdiction in a case [Scots. Law].

decline, *n.* de-*kline*, a falling off; a tendency to a worse state; decay; abatement; a gradual decay of strength; consumption [Med.]: *v.i.* to bend from a right line; to bend downward; to droop; to stoop; to deviate; to deviate from rectitude; to refuse; to draw to an end; to decay; to sink: *v.t.* to bend to one side or downward; to shun; to refuse; not to engage in; to inflect [Gram.]. (Fr. *décliner.*)

decliner, *n.* de-*kly*-ner, a dial which cuts either the plane of the prime vertical circle or the plane of the horizon obliquely [Dialling].

declinograph, *n.* de-*kly*-no-graf, an instrument that automatically records declinations.

declinometer, *n.* dek-le-*nom*-e-ter, an instrument for measuring the declination of the magnetic needle; an instrument that registers declinations [Astron.]. (L. *declino*, and Gr. *metron*, measure.)

declivitous, *a.* de-*kliv*-e-tus, having a well-marked downward slope.

declivity, *n.* de-*kliv*-e-te, inclination downward; land or a surface that slopes downward; a gradual but considerable incline. (L. *declivitas*, a sloping place.)

declivous, *a.* de-*kly*-vus, sloping downwards [Zool.].

declutch, *v.i.* dee-klutch, to put a clutch out of action [Eng.].

decoct, *v.t.* de-*kokt*, to prepare by boiling; to digest in boiling water; to digest in the stomach; to extract the virtues of a substance by boiling; to heat or inflame. (L. *decoctus*, cooked.)

decoctible, *a.* de-*kok*-te-bl, that may be decocted.

decoction, *n.* de-*kok*-shon, the act of boiling a substance in water to extract its virtues; the extract obtained by the boiling. (L. *decoctio*, boiling down.)

decode, *v.t.* dee-*kode*, to convert from code into plain language; to decipher.

decohere, *v.t.* and *i.* dee-ko-*heer*, to restore (a coherer) to normal condition [Wire.].

decoherer, *n.* dee-ko-*heer*-er, an appliance for restoring to a normal condition a coherer that has been electrically affected [Wire.].

decoke, *v.t.* dee-*koke*, to decarbonize [Coll.].

decollate, *v.t.* de-*kol*-late, to behead. (L. *decollatus*, taken off from the neck.)

decollation, *n.* dee-kol-*lay*-shon, a beheading, especially that of John the Baptist as represented in art; the shedding of the apex of gastropod shells [Couch.] (L. *decollatio*, beheading.)

décolletage, *n.* day-kol-*tahzh*, the upper border of a low-necked garment. (F.)

décolleté, *a.* day-kol-*tay*, low-necked; wearing a low-necked gown leaving arms and shoulders bare. (Fr. *décolleté*, bared.)

decolorant, *n.* dee-*kul*-ler-ant, a substance which removes colour: *a.* decolorizing.
decolorate, *v.t.* dee-*kul*-ler-ate, to decolorize.
decoloration, *n.* dee-*kul*-ler-*ray*-shon, the removal or absence of colour. (L. *decoloratio*, a discolouring.)
decolorize, *v.t.* dee-*kul*-ler-ize, to deprive of colour; to bleach.
decolour, *v.t.* dee-*kul*-ler, to decolorize.
decommission, *v.t.* dee-kom-*mish*-un, to put out of commission [Nav.].
decomplex, *a.* *dee*-kom-pleks, decompound; composed of complex parts or ideas.
decomposable, *a.* *dee*-kom-*poh*-za-bl, that may be decomposed.
decompose, *v.t.* dee-kom-*poze*, to separate the constituent parts of a body or substance; to resolve into original elements: *v.i.* to become decomposed. (Fr. *décomposer*.)
decomposite, *a.* dee-*kom*-poz-it, compounded of compounds; compounded more than once: *n.* a decomposite thing or substance.
decomposition, *n.* *dee*-kom-po-*zish*-on, the act of decomposing; the state of becoming or being decomposed; disintegration; dissolution. (Fr.)
decompound, *v.t.* dee-kom-*pound*, to compound a second time, or what is already compound: *a.* composed of things or words already compounded: *n.* a word or substance, etc. that is decompound. **decompound leaf,** one which is twice pinnated [Bot.].
decompoundable, *a.* dee-kom-*pound*-a-bl, that may be compounded.
decompress, *v.t.* dee-kom-*press*, to reduce a high pressure (esp. that of compressed air) to normal.
decompression, *n.* dee-kom-*presh*-un, the act or process of relaxing pressure, esp. that of compressed air [Eng.]; an operation to relieve pressure [Surg.]. **decompression chamber,** an enclosure from which compressed air can be gradually released until normal atmospheric pressure is attained.
deconsecrate, *v.t.* dee-*kon*-se-krate, to secularize.
decontaminate, *v.t.* dee-kon-*tam*-e-nate, to free from contamination, esp. of poison-gas.
decontamination, *n.* dee-kon-tam-e-*nay*-shon, the act or process of decontaminating.
decontrol, *v.t.* dee-kon-*trole*, to release from state control: *n.* the removal of control.
décor, *n.* de-*kawr*, the general lay-out or decorative scheme of interior decoration or a stage setting. (Fr.)
decorate, *v.t.* *dek*-o-rate, to deck with ornament; to beautify; to embellish. (L. *decoratus*, adorned.)
decoration, *n.* dek-o-*ray*-shon, the act of decorating; ornamentation; ornament; a badge of honour.
decorative, *a.* *dek*-o-ra-tiv, adorning; suited to embellish.
decoratively, *ad.* in a decorative manner.
decorativeness, *n.* quality of being decorative.
decorator, *n.* *dek*-o-ray-tor, one who adorns or embellishes; a house-painter.
decorous, *a.* de-*kaw*-rus, suitable; becoming; proper; befitting. (L. *decorus*, fitting.)
decorously, *ad.* de-*kaw*-rus-le, in a decorous manner.
decorousness, *n.* de-*kaw*-rus-ness, decorum or correctness of deportment.
decorticate, *v.t.* de-*kor*-te-kate, to strip off bark; to peel; to husk: *a.* devoid of a cortical layer [Bot.]. (L. *decorticatus*, barked.)
decortication, *n.* de-*kor*-te-*kay*-shon, the act of stripping off bark or husk. (L. *decorticatio*, barking.)
decorticator, *n.* de-*kor*-te-kay-tor, a machine or tool for decorticating.
decorum, *n.* de-*kaw*-rum, propriety of speech or behaviour; seemliness; decency. (L.)
decoy, *n.* de-*koy*, any lure that deceives and entraps; a place for catching wild fowls into which they are decoyed; a bird or the likeness of one used as a decoy: *v.t.* to lure into a snare; to entrap, esp. by deceit; to allure or entice. (L. *de-*, and Dut. *kooi*, cage.)
decoy-duck, *n.* a duck employed to draw others into a snare; one who decoys others.
decoyment, *n.* de-*koy*-ment, the act of decoying.
decrease, *n.* *dee*-krees, gradual diminution or decay; wane of the moon: *v.i.* de-*kreese*, to become less; to diminish gradually: *v.t.* to lessen; to diminish gradually. (O.Fr. *descreistre*.)
decreasingly, *ad.* dee-*krees*-ing-le, in a decreasing manner.

decree, *n.* de-*kree*, judicial determination of a case; a judgment; a decree nisi; an order or law made by a superior authority for the direction of others; established law or rule: *v.t.* to determine judicially; to fix or appoint: *v.i.* to make an edict; to resolve or determine. **decree nisi,** an order for divorce subject to evidence being produced against it within a certain time, not less than six months. (O.Fr. *decret*.)
decreeable, *a.* de-*kree*-a-bl, that may be decreed.
decrement, *n.* *dek*-re-ment, decrease; waste; the quantity lost by decrease; the ratio of the amplitudes of two successive half-waves in a train of damped vibrations [Wire.]; the wane of the moon [Her.]. **equal decrement of life,** the equal annual decrease among a given number of lives within a given period of years. (L. *decrementum*, diminution.)
decremeter, *n.* de-*krem*-e-ter, an instrument for measuring decrement [Wire.].
decrepit, *a.* de-*krep*-it, broken down and weakened by the infirmities of age; crippled by infirmities; feeble; delapidated. (L. *decrepitus*, noiseless.)
decrepitate, *v.t.* de-*krep*-e-tate, to roast or calcine in a strong heat, with a continual crackling: *v.i.* to crackle, as salt, when roasting. (L. *de-*, and *crepitatus*, rustled.)
decrepitation, *n.* de-*krep*-e-*tay*-shon, the act, or the noise, of decrepitating; the separation of parts with a crackling noise, occasioned by heat. (Fr.)
decrepitude, *n.* de-*krep*-e-tewd, physical infirmity due to old age; senility. (Fr.)
decrescendo, *n.* dee-kre-*shen*-doh, a gradual diminishing of sound; diminuendo [Mus.]. (It.)
decrescent, *a.* de-*kres*-sent, decreasing; waning. (L. *decrescens*, decreasing.)
decretal, *a.* de-*kree*-tal, appertaining to a decree; *n.* a decree, especially of the Popes: *pl.* a collection of these decrees, accepted as part of the canon law.
decretist, *n.* de-*kree*-tist, one versed in the decretals; a student of canon law.
decretive, *a.* de-*kree*-tiv, having the force of a decree.
decretory, *a.* *dee*-kre-to-re, pertaining to a decree; established by a decree; determining; decretive. (L. *decretorius*, decisive.)
decrial, *n.* dee-*kry*-al, a crying down; disparagement; a clamorous censure.
decrier, *n.* de-*kry*-er, a disparager.
decrown, *v.t.* dee-*kroun*, to deprive of a crown.
decry, *v.t.* de-*kry*, to cry down; to disparage, depreciate, or traduce. (O.Fr. *descrier*.)
decubitus, *n.* de-*kew*-be-tus, a patient's posture in bed [Med.].
decuman, *n.* *dek*-yew-man, the main gate of a Roman camp, where the tenth cohort was quartered: *a.* very large (of waves, the tenth being supposed to be the largest in a series). (L. *decumanus*, tenth.)
decumbence, *n.* de-*kum*-bence, decumbency.
decumbency, *n.* de-*kum*-ben-se, lying down; the posture of lying down.
decumbent, *a.* de-*kum*-bent, lying down; recumbent; prostrate; lying flat (through its own weight) with tip raised [Bot.]. (L. *decumbens*, lying down.)
decumbently, *ad.* in a decumbent posture.
decuple, *a.* *dek*-yew-pl, tenfold: *n.* a number ten times repeated: *v.t.* to increase tenfold. (Fr.)
decuplet, *n.* *dek*-yew-plet, a group of ten notes to be played in the time usually taken by the playing of eight [Mus.].
decurion, *n.* dee-*kewr*-re-on, a Roman officer over ten soldiers; an overseer of ten families. (L.)
decurrency, *n.* de-*ku*-ren-se, the state of being decurrent [Bot.].
decurrent, *a.* dee-*ku*-rent, extending downwards by a wing on the stem, as in thistles [Bot.]. (L. *decurrens*, running away.)
decurrently, *ad.* in a decurrent manner.
decursive, *a.* dee-*kur*-siv, decurrent [Bot.].
decurvation, *n.* dee-kur-*vay*-shon, the action of decurving; state of being decurved.
decurve, *v.t.* and *i.* de-*kurve*, to curve or bend downwards.
decurved, *a.* de-*kurvd*, bent downwards [Bot.].
decussate, *a.* dee-*kus*-at, decussated: *v.t.* and *i.* to cross, as lines, rays, or nerves [Zool. and Bot.]; to intersect at acute angles or diagonally. **decussate phyllotaxis,** opposite leaves with the pairs crossing

at right angles to each other. (L. *decussatus*, divided cross-wise.)
decussated, *a.* dee-*kus*-a-ted, crossed; intersected; arranged in pairs, which alternately and regularly cross each other, as the leaves of many plants [Bot.].
decussately, *ad.* dee-*kus*-at-le, in a decussate manner.
decussation, *n.* dee-kus-*say*-shon, the act of decussating; the state of being decussated. (L. *decussatio*, intersection of two lines.)
dedans, *n.* (App.), the spectators' gallery at the service end of a tennis court. (Fr.)
dedentition, *n.* dee-den-*tish*-on, the shedding of teeth. (L. *de-*, and *dens*, a tooth.)
dedicant, *n. ded*-e-kant, a dedicator.
dedicate, *v.t. ded*-e-kate, to set apart and consecrate solemnly to a special purpose; to devote; to inscribe to any one as an expression of obligation and esteem. (L. *dedicatus*, consecrated.)
dedicatee, *n.* ded-e-kay-*tee*, the person to whom a dedication is made.
dedication, *n.* ded-e-*kay*-shon, the act of dedicating; inscription or words used in dedicating a book, building, etc. (L. *dedicatio*, consecration.)
dedicator, *n. ded*-e-kay-tor, a person who dedicates.
dedicatory, *a. ded*-e-*kay*-to-re, serving as a dedication.
dedifferentiation, *n. dee*-dif-er-ren-she-*ay*-shon, loss of differentiation; simplification or disintegration of structure [Biol.].
dedimus, *n. dee*-de-mus, a commission to a private person to do some act in place of a judge [Law]. (L., we have given.)
deduce, *v.t.* de-*dewce*, to draw as a conclusion; to infer from reasoning or from what precedes; to trace, as a pedigree. (L. *deduco*, lead away.)
deducibility, *n.* de-*dew*-se-*bil*-e-te, deducibleness.
deducible, *a.* de-*dew*-se-bl, that may be inferred.
deducibleness, *n.* de-*dew*-se-bl-ness, quality of being deducible.
deduct, *v.t.* de-*dukt*, to take away; to subtract. (L. *deductus*, brought away.)
deductible, *a.* de-*duk*-te-bl, capable of being deducted.
deduction, *n.* de-*duk*-shon, the act of deducting; that which is deducted; abatement; the act of deducing; that which is deduced. (L. *deductio*, taking away.)
deductive, *a.* de-*duk*-tiv, that is or may be deduced; deducible. **deductive reasoning,** the process by which we explicate or deduce what is necessarily involved in given premises [Logic].
deductively, *ad.* by way of necessary inference.
deductory, *a.* de-*duk*-to-re, deductive.
dee, *n.* dee, the letter *d*; anything (esp. a metal loop) of the shape of a capital D.
deed, *n.* deed, a thing done deliberately; an act; a fact; exploit; action; actuality (as in **indeed**); a writing containing some contract; a sealed document; an instrument on paper or parchment conveying real estate to a purchaser or donee [Law]: *v.t.* to convey by deed [U.S.A.]. **deed-poll,** a deed made by one party only and so not indented, but polled, or cut straight [Law]. (A.S.)
deedful, *a. deed*-ful, full of exploits; marked by signal deeds.
deedless, *a. deed*-less, not performing any deeds.
deedy, *a. dee*-de, deedful; active; industrious.
deem, *v.t.* deem, to judge; to suppose or believe: *v.i.* to come to a decision. (A.S. *deman.*)
de-emanate, *v.t.* dee-*em*-a-nate, to render incapable of giving off radioactive emanations.
deemster, *n. deem*-ster, one of two judges in the Isle of Man.
★**deep,** *a.* deep, extending far down; profound; low in situation; far in; back from the front line [Mil.]; swallowed up in; hidden; secret; difficult to fathom or comprehend; penetrating; darkly designing; low in the musical scale; intense; strongly coloured: *n.* anything deep, especially the sea; that which is not easily fathomed, or not fathomable; the most still and solemn part: *ad.* to a great depth. **in deep water,** in great difficulties. (A.S. *deop.*)
deepen, *v.t. deep*-n, to make deeper: *v.i.* to become deeper.
deeping, *n. deep*-ing, a section of a drift-net, one fathom deep, with its lacings.
deep-laid, *a.* laid deeply; formed with care or cunning.
deeply, *ad. deep*-le, to a great depth; profoundly; with great emotion; gravely; with profound skill.
deepness, *n. deep*-ness, the state or quality of being deep; profundity.
deep-mouthed, *a.* with a loud hollow voice.
deep-read, *a. deep*-red, deeply versed.
deep-sea, *a. deep*-see, belonging to the sea at its greater depths: *n.* the ocean.
deer, *n.* deer, a solid-horned ruminant ungulate, the male of which is usually antlered, such as the stag, the fallow-deer, etc. (A.S. *deor*, a wild animal.)
deer-forest, *n.* an extensive and unenclosed tract of wild land on which red-deer breed and are stalked.
deerhound, *n. deer*-hound, a large rough-coated dog of greyhound type, formerly much used in deer-hunting.
deer-neck, *n.* a thin ill-formed neck in a horse.
deerskin, *n. deer*-skin, the skin of a deer; the supple leather made of it.
deerstalker, *n. deer*-stawk-er, one stealthily approaching deer to shoot them; a soft close-fitting low-crowned hat.
deerstalking, *n. deer*-stawk-ing, the hunting of red deer, by stealing upon them unawares.
deface, *v.t.* de-*face*, to destroy or injure the face of anything; to disfigure; to erase or obliterate. (O.Fr. *desfacier.*)
defaceable, *a.* de-*face*-a-bl, that may be defaced.
defacement, *n.* de-*face*-ment, the act of defacing; that which defaces; the injury done.
defacer, *n.* de-*face*-er, he who, or that which, defaces.
defæcate, *v.i. def*-e-kate, to defecate.
defalcate, *v.t. dee*-fal-kate, fraudulently to take away or deduct a part (chiefly of money, accounts, etc.); to embezzle: *v.i.* to commit embezzlement. (L. *defalcatus*, deduced.)
defalcation, *n.* dee-fal-*kay*-shon, a deficit of funds entrusted to one's care; embezzlement.
defalcator, *n. dee*-fal-kay-tor, one who defalcates; an embezzler.
defamable, *a.* de-*fame*-a-bl, that may be defamed.
defamation, *n.* def-a-*may*-shon, the act of defaming another with a view to injure him; calumny; slander; detraction or aspersion. (Fr. *diffamation.*)
defamatory, *a.* de-*fam*-a-to-re, calumnious; slanderous; libellous.
defame, *v.t.* de-*fame*, to speak evil of falsely; to speak evil with a view to injure; to calumniate; to blacken the character of. (Fr. *diffamer.*)
defamer, *n.* de-*fame*-er, a slanderer; a detractor.
defamingly, *ad.* in a defaming manner.
default, *n.* de-*fawlt*, failure; neglect of duty; defect; want; a fault; non-appearance in court when called upon: *v.i.* to fail in performing a contract; to fail to appear in court: *v.t.* to call a defendant officially to appear and answer in court, and, on his failing to answer, to declare him in default, and enter judgment against him [Law]; to fail in performance. **to suffer a default,** to permit an action to be called without appearing [Law]. **judgment by default,** decree against a defendant for non-appearance or failure to plead [Law]. (O.Fr. *defaute.*)
defaultant, *a.* de-*fawl*-tant, guilty of default.
defaulter, *n.* de-*fawl*-ter, one who fails to appear in court when called; one who fails to account for public money entrusted to him; one who fails in payment; a soldier undergoing a minor punishment, such as confinement to barracks.
defeasance, *n.* de-*fee*-zance, the act of rendering null; an instrument which defeats the force or operation of some other deed [Law]; the writing containing a defeasance. (O.Fr.)
defeasanced, *a.* de-*fee*-zansd, liable to be forfeited.
defeasible, *a.* de-*fee*-ze-bl, that may be annulled.
defeasibleness, *n.* the quality of being defeasible.
defeat, *n.* de-*feet*, overthrow, as of an army; frustration; a rendering null and void: *v.t.* to overthrow; to discomfit; to frustrate; to render null and void. (O.Fr. *defait.*)
defeatism, *n.* de-*feet*-izm, conduct or policy that tends to the defeat of one's own side, usually in the belief that this is for its ultimate benefit.
defeatist, *n.* one advocating defeatism: *a.* advocating defeatism.

defeature, *n.* de-*feet*-yewr, disfigurement.
defecate, *v.t.* *def*-e-kate, to clear from lees, dregs, or impurities; to purify; to purge: *v.i.* to become clear by depositing, or clean by purging, impurities; to void excrement. (L. *defæcatum*, refined.)
defecation, *n.* def-e-*kay*-shon, the act of separating from impurities, as lees, or dregs; discharge of the fæces; purification. (L. *defæcatio*, cleansing.)
defecator, *n.* one who or that which defecates; a filtering tank in which sugar-cane juice is clarified.
defect, *n.* de-*fekt*, deficiency; want; imperfection; fault; blemish; error: *v.i.* to desert; to abandon (a cause, policy, etc.). (L. *dēfectus*, weakened.)
defectible, *a.* de-*fek*-te-bl, liable to fail; defective.
defection, *n.* de-*fek*-shon, abandonment of allegiance or duty; revolt; apostasy. (L. *defectio*, failure.)
defectionist, *n.* de-*fek*-shon-ist, an abettor of defection.
defective, *a.* de-*fek*-tiv, wanting in something, physical or moral; imperfect; incomplete: *n.* one having a noticeable defect, esp. mental. (L. *defectivus*.)
defectively, *ad.* de-*fek*-tiv-le, in a defective manner.
defectiveness, *n.* the state of being defective.
defeminize, *v.t.* dee-*fem*-in-ize, to divest of femininity.
defence, *n.* de-*fence*, the act or the art of defending; that which defends; fortification; protection; vindication; the defendant's reply to the plaintiff's declaration, demands, or charges [Law]; a work that flanks another [Fort.]. **line of defence,** a series of fortified points so disposed as to form a continuous defence. (O.Fr. *defense*.)
defenceless, *a.* de-*fence*-less, without defence.
defencelessly, *ad.* in a defenceless manner.
defencelessness, *n.* the state of being defenceless.
defend, *v.t.* de-*fend*, to ward off; to maintain against an attack or a charge; to resist; to prohibit; to drive back a foe; to protect; to vindicate: *v.i.* to justify; to enter defence. (Fr. *défendre*.)
defendable, *a.* that may be defended.
defendant, *n.* de-*fend*-ant, one who defends; he who is summoned into court to defend or oppose a demand or charge [Law]: *a.* in the position of a defendant [Law].
defender, *n.* de-*fend*-er, one who defends; an advocate or champion; the defendant or person sued [Scots. Law]. **defender of the faith,** a title of the sovereign of England, first conferred by the Pope on Henry VIII in consideration of his writings in defence of the Church against the heresy of Luther.
defensible, *a.* de-*fence*-e-bl, defendable; capable of being vindicated; justifiable.
defensibly, *ad.* de-*fence*-e-ble, justifiably.
defensive, *a.* de-*fence*-iv, that serves to defend; carried on in defence; protective: *n.* an attitude of defence; that which defends. **on the defensive,** to be or stand in a state or posture of resistance in opposition to aggression or attack. (Fr. *défensif*.)
defensively, *ad.* in a defensive manner.
defer, *v.t.* and *i.* de-*fer*, to put off; to delay; to postpone; to procrastinate. (Fr. *differer*.)
defer, *v.t.* de-*fer*, to refer; to submit: *v.i.* to yield to another's opinion; to comply out of respect. (Fr. *déferer*.)
deference, *n.* *def*-e-rence, submission to the opinion or judgment of another; regard; respect. (Fr.)
deferent, *n.* *def*-e-rent, that which carries or conveys; a vessel or duct for the conveyance of fluids [Phys.]: *a.* conveying fluids [Phys.]. (L. *deferens*, carrying down.)
deferent, *a.* *def*-e-rent, deferential.
deferential, *a.* def-e-*ren*-shal, given to deference; expressing respect.
deferentially, *ad.* def-e-*ren*-sha-le, with deference.
deferment, *n.* de-*fer*-ment, postponement; delay.
deferrable, *a.* de-*fer*-ra-bl, capable of being deferred.
deferred, *a.* de-*ferd*, postponed; ranking for dividend after prior charges. **deferred annuity,** an annuity becoming payable at a date later than the end of the first year, or on the occurrence of some specified event. **deferred pay,** pay, esp. of a soldier, held over to be paid at a later date.
deferrer, *n.* de-*fer*-rer, one who delays or puts off.
defervescence, *n.* dee-fer-*ves*-ense, a loss of heat; a cooling down of zeal or fever. (L. *defervescens*, cooling down.)
defeudalize, *v.t.* de-*few*-da-lize, to deprive of feudal forms.
defiance, *n.* de-*fy*-ance, a challenge to fight; a challenge to meet in any contest; contempt of opposition or danger; provocation. (O.Fr.)
defiant, *a.* de-*fy*-ant, expressive of defiance; hostile in attitude; insolent; defying.
defiantly, *ad.* de-*fy*-ant-le, in a defiant manner.
defibrinated, *a.* de-*fy*-bre-nay-ted, deprived of fibrin (esp. of blood or lymph).
deficiency, *n.* de-*fish*-en-se, a falling short; want; defect; insufficiency; the amount of shortage. **deficiency bills,** advances made to Government by the Bank of England to meet a temporary deficiency. **deficiency disease,** any disease caused by a diet lacking in certain necessary vitamins.
deficient, *a.* de-*fish*-ent, wanting; not sufficient or adequate; not having an adequate supply; mentally defective: *n.* a mental defective. (L. *deficiens*, failing.)
deficiently, *ad.* de-*fish*-ent-le, in a defective manner.
deficit, *n.* *def*-e-sit, deficiency; the amount short; the excess of liabilities over assets. (L., it is wanting.)
defier, *n.* de-*fy*-er, one who dares to combat; one who acts in contempt of law or authority.
defilade, *v.t.* dee-fe-*lade*, to place a line of ramparts round a fortress so as to shelter the interior works when they are in danger of being commanded from some higher point [Fort.].
defile, *v.t.* de-*file*, to make foul or dirty; to soil or stain; to pollute; to corrupt; to violate; to desecrate. (L. *de-*, and A.S. *fylan*, foul.)
defile, *n.* de-*file*, a long narrow pass, as between hills, in which troops can march only in a file or with a narrow front; *v.i.* to march off in a line, or file by file; to file off. (Fr. *défiler*.)
defilement, *n.* de-*file*-ment, the act of defiling; the state of being defiled; foulness; corruption; impurity; pollution; the act of defilading.
defiler, *n.* de-*file*-er, one who or that which defiles.
definable, *a.* de-*fine*-a-bl, that may be defined.
definably, *ad.* de-*fine*-a-ble, in a defining manner.
define, *v.t.* de-*fine*, to lay down and fix the limit; to determine the limit; to explain accurately what a word or an expression means; to describe what a thing is. (Fr. *définir*.)
definer, *n.* de-*fine*-er, one who defines.
definite, *a.* *def*-e-nit, having fixed limits; determinate; fixed; precise; exact; limiting the application [Gram.].
definitely, *ad.* *def*-e-nit-le, in a definite manner; yes! certainly! [Slang].
definiteness, *n.* *def*-e-nit-ness, certainty of extent or signification; precision. (L. *dēfīnītus*, precise.)
definition, *n.* def-e-*nish*-on, the act of defining; a brief description of a thing by its properties; brief explanation of the meaning of a word or phrase; the making clear in outline; distinctness; the explication of the essence of a thing by its kind and difference, technically called its genus and differentia [Logic]. (L. *dēfīnītio*, a boundary.)
definitive, *a.* de-*fin*-e-tiv, determinate; positive; final; *n.* an adjective or pronoun as defining the application of a noun [Gram.]. (L., plainly.)
definitively, *ad.* de-*fin*-e-tiv-le, in a definitive way.
definitiveness, *n.* de-*fin*-e-tiv-ness, the quality of being definitive.
definitude, *n.* de-*fin*-e-tewd, the quality of being definite; exactitude.
deflagrate, *v.t.* *def*-la-grate, to burn with rapid or sparkling combustion: *v.i.* to be burnt or consumed thus. (L. *deflagratus*, burnt down.)
deflagration, *n.* def-la-*gray*-shon, sudden rapid combustion, accompanied with flame or sparkling [Chem.]. (L. *dēflagrātio*, a conflagration.)
deflagrator, *n.* *def*-la-*gray*-tor, an electric or other apparatus for effecting deflagration.
deflatable, *a.* de-*flay*-ta-bl, that may be deflated.
deflate, *v.t.* de-*flate*, to release air that has been used for distention; to bring about a fall in prices by reducing the volume of purchasing power [Econ.] (L. *deflatus*, blown away.)
deflation, *n.* de-*flay*-shon, the act of deflating the withdrawal or employment elsewhere of such currency as is redundant for present commercial requirements, occasioning a rise in money value and a fall in prices [Econ.]; the exposure of rock surface by the action of the winds [Geol.].

deflationist, *n.* one who advocates a policy of deflation [Econ.].
deflect, *v.i.* de-*flekt*, to turn aside from a straight or direct line or course: *v.t.* to cause to do this. (L. *deflecto*, bend downwards.)
deflected, *a.* de-*flek*-ted, deflexed [Bot.].
deflection, *n.* de-*flek*-shon, deflexion.
deflective, *a.* de-*flek*-tiv, able to deflect.
deflectometer, *n.* dee-flek-*tom*-e-ter, an instrument for measuring the extent of slight deflections due to strain, etc. [Eng.].
deflector, *n.* dee-*flek*-tor, a baffle in a furnace for improving combustion, by bringing the flame in closer contact with the gases; any deflecting agent.
deflexed, *a.* de-*flekst*, bent sharply down [Bot.].
deflexion, *n.* de-*flek*-shon, the act of deflecting; the calculation of the movement of a target in motion, as applied to the sights of a gun [Mil.]. (L. *deflexio*, a turning aside.)
deflexure, *n.* de-*flek*-sewr, bending down; deviation; turning aside. (L. *deflexum*, turned downwards.)
deflocculate, *v.t.* de-*flok*-yew-late, to convert into very fine particles; to subject to deflocculation.
deflocculation, *n.* de-*flok*-yew-*lay*-shon, reduction of a substance to the finest particles in which it can exist; deprivation of flocculence.
deflorate, *a.* de-*flaw*-rayt, having shed its pollen; with the flowers fallen [Bot.]. (L. *defloreo*, shed blossoms.)
defloration, *n.* dee-flo-*ray*-shon, the act of deflowering.
deflower, *v.t.* de-*flou*-er, to deprive a woman of her virginity, or (Fig.) anything of its original beauty and grace. (O.Fr. *defleurer*.)
defluent, *a.* *dee*-floo-ent, flowing down: *n.* the part of a main body (as an iceberg) that flows away.
defluxion, *n.* de-*fluk*-shon, a discharge of matter, esp. from the inflamed mucous membrane of the air-passages in catarrh [Med.]. (L. *defluxio*, a discharge.)
defoliate, *v.t.* dee-*foh*-le-ate, to strip of leaves.
defoliation, *n.* de-foh-le-*ay*-shon, the shedding, or the time of the shedding, of leaves. (L. *defoliatus*, stripped of leaves.)
deforce, *v.t.* de-*forse*, to keep out of lawful possession, esp. of an estate; to resist an officer of the law in the execution of his duty. (O.Fr. *deforcer*.)
deforcement, *n.* de-*forse*-ment, the holding of property to which another person has a right [Law]; resistance to an officer in the execution of law [Scots. Law].
deforciant, *n.* de-*forse*-e-ant, one who unlawfully deprives an owner of his lands or tenements [Law].
deforest, *v.t.* dee-*fo*-rest, to clear of trees; to disafforest.
deforestation, *n.* dee-fo-res-*tay*-shun, the clearance of an area of trees.
deform, *a.* de-*fawrm*, disfigured; displeasing to the eye: *v.t.* to mar or injure the form of; to disfigure; to make ugly. (L. *deformo*, shape.)
deformation, *n.* def-awr-*may*-shon, the act or process of deforming; a disfigurement; alteration of shape; change in the form of the earth's surface through the action of internal forces [Geol.]. (L. *deformatio*, defacing.)
deformed, *a.* de-*fawrmd*, disfigured; misshapen; ugly.
deformedness, *n.* de-*fawrm*-ed-ness, the state of being deformed; ugliness.
deformer, *n.* de-*fawrm*-er, one who deforms.
deformity, *n.* de-*fawrm*-e-te, the state of being deformed; a malformation, disfigurement; ugliness; anything that destroys beauty, grace, order, or propriety. (O.Fr. *déformité*.)
defraud, *v.t.* de-*frawd*, to deprive by deception or stealth; to withhold wrongfully; to defeat or frustrate wrongfully. (L. *defraudo*, cheat.)
defrauder, *n.* de-*frawd*-er, one who defrauds; a cheat, embezzler, or peculator.
defray, *v.t.* de-*fray*, to pay or meet the cost of, as expenses or charges. (Fr. *défrayer*.)
defrayal, *n.* de-*fray*-al, the act of defraying; defrayment.
defrayer, *n.* de-*fray*-er, one who defrays.
defrayment, *n.* de-*fray*-ment, payment of dues.
defrock, *v.t.* dee-*frok*, to unfrock.
defrost, *v.t.* dee-*frost*, to remove frost from; to unfreeze, esp. refrigerated foodstuffs.
deft, *a.* deft, dexterous; neat; fitting; handy. (A.S. *dæfte*, fitting.)
deftly, *ad.* *deft*-le, in a deft manner.
deftness, *n.* the quality of being deft.
defunct, *a.* de-*funkt*, done with life; dead: *n.* one lately deceased. (L. *defunctus*, finished.)
defy, *v.t.* de-*fy*, to challenge to a contest; to challenge to say or do anything; to dare or brave; to treat with contempt; to resist. (O.Fr. *desfier*.)
degasify, *v.t.* dee-*gas*-e-fy, to free from gas; to clear gas away from.
degauss, *v.t.* dee-*gouse*, to neutralize the magnetic quality of (esp. a ship's hull) by encircling the field with a current-carrying conductor [Elec.]. (*de-* and *gauss*.)
degeneracy, *n.* de-*jen*-er-ra-se, deterioration; a degenerate state or condition.
degenerate, *a.* de-*jen*-er-rat, reverted to a lower type; fallen from a good condition into one less excellent or worse; declined in natural or moral worth; base, mean, or corrupt: *n.* one of debased or deficient qualities; a pervert: *v.i.* to fall from a higher and better physical or moral type; to decay in good qualities; to pass from a good to a bad state; to become wild [Bot.]. (L. *degeneratus*, degenerated.)
degenerately, *ad.* in a degenerate manner.
degenerateness, *n.* a degenerate state.
degeneration, *n.* de-*jen*-er-*ray*-shon, degeneracy; deterioration.
degenerative, *a.* de-*jen*-er-ra-tiv, of the nature of or tending to degeneracy.
degerm, *v.t.* dee-*jerm*, to remove the germs from.
deglaze, *v.t.* dee-*glaze*, to remove the glaze from [Pottery, etc.]; to clear thick gravy, etc., with wine or water [Cookery].
deglutition, *n.* dee-gloo-*tish*-on, the act or power of swallowing. (Fr.)
degradation, *n.* deg-ra-*day*-shon, the act of degrading; the state of being degraded; a state of wretchedness or moral debasement; diminution or reduction of strength, excellence, or value; degeneration; a lessening and obscuring of the appearance of distant objects in a landscape [Painting]; the wearing away of rocks and beaches, due to the action of water, wind, etc. [Geol.].
degrade, *v.t.* de-*grade*, to reduce from a higher to a lower civil rank; to strip of office or honours, and so of civil rank; to disgrace; to lower in character and natural rank; to lessen in value; to disintegrate or wear down [Geol.]. (O.Fr. *degrader*.)
degraded, *pp.* de-*grade*-ed, reduced; mean; debased in character or morals; placed on steps [Her.].
degradement, *n.* de-*grade*-ment, deprivation of rank.
degrading, *ppr.* and *a.* de-*grade*-ing, lowering the level; lowering in character.
degradingly, *ad.* de-*grade*-ing-le, so as to degrade.
degrease, *v.t.* dee-*greece*, to remove the grease from.
★**degree**, *n.* de-*gree*, a step or grade of ascent or descent, in elevation, quality, dignity, or rank; relative position or rank; a certain distance or remove in the line of descent determining the proximity of blood; measure; extent; a line or space in the staff [Mus.]; the interval of one tone in the scale [Mus.]; a term applied to equations to denote the highest power of the unknown quantity [Alg.]; an academic grade or rank conferred by universities after examination, or in honour; the three hundred and sixtieth of a circle [Geom.], or of the circumference of the earth, *i.e.* 60 geographical miles [Geog.]; the unit of measurement of temperature; a division, space, or interval marked on a mathematical or other instrument. **by degrees**, step by step; gradually. **honorary degrees**, those conferred without residence or examination. **third degree**, severe examination of an accused person by the police to obtain a confession or some information (U.S.A.). **to a degree**, exceedingly. (Fr. *degré*.)
degression, *n.* de-*gresh*-on, progress in descension; a degressive decrease in a rate of taxation [Econ.].
degressive, *a.* de-*gres*-iv, tending to decrease, or [Bot.] to degenerate; pertaining to a graduated system of taxation decrease [Econ.].

dégringolade, *n.* (App.) deterioration; collapse; a going from bad to worse. (Fr., tumble.)
degum, *v.t.* dee-*gum*, to free from gum or gummy matter.
degust, *v.t.* de-*gust*, to taste; to relish. (L.)
dehisce, *v.i.* de-*hiss*, to gape; to split into regular parts, as the capsules of plants [Bot.]. (L. *dehisco*, gape.)
dehiscence, *n.* de-*his*-sense, the quality of being dehiscent.
dehiscent, *a.* de-*his*-sent, opening, as a capsule of a plant or the cell of an anther [Bot.]. (L. *dehiscens.*)
dehort, *v.t.* de-*hawrt*, to advise to the contrary. (L. *dehortari.*)
dehortation, *n.* dee-haw-*tay*-shon, the act of dehorting; dissuasion. (L. *dehortatio.*)
dehortative, *a.* de-*haw*-ta-tiv, tending to dissuade.
dehortatory, *a.* de-*haw*-ta-to-re, dissuading; belonging to dissuasion: *n.* dissuasive argument.
dehumanize, *v.t.* dee-*hew*-ma-nize, to deprive of human qualities; to brutalize.
dehumidify, *v.t.* dee-hew-*mid*-e-fy, to render (esp. a metal) proof against deterioration through damp.
dehydrate, *v.t.* de-*hy*-drate, to extract water or its component elements from; to desiccate.
dehydration, *n.* de-hy-*dray*-shon, abstraction of the water or its elements from a compound [Chem.]; desiccation. (L. *de-*, and Gr. *hydor*, water.)
dehydrogenize, *v.t.* de-*hy*-dro-je-nize, to extract the hydrogen from a chemical compound.
dehypnotize, *v.t.* de-*hip*-no-tize, to arouse from hypnotic sleep.
de-ice, *v.t.* dee-*ice*, to remove ice from, esp. parts of an aircraft in flight; to prevent ice forming on.
de-icer, *n.* dee-*ice*-er, an apparatus or agent for preventing the formation of ice, or removing it, esp. from parts of aircraft in flight.
deicide, *n.* *dee*-e-side the putting, of Christ to death; one concerned in the crime. (L. *deus*, God, and *cædo*, kill.)
deictic, *a.* *dike*-tik, proving directly [Logic]. (Gr. *deiktikos*, capable of showing.)
deific, *a.* dee-*if*-ik, making divine.
deification, *n.* dee-e-fe-*kay*-shon, the act of deifying, or of exalting to the rank of a deity.
deified, *a.* *dee*-e-fide, ranked among the gods; treated as a god.
deiform, *a.* *dee*-e-fawrm, like a god; of godlike form. (L. *deus*, god, *forma*, shape.)
deify, *v.t.* *dee*-e-fy, to exalt to the rank of a god; to worship supremely as a god. (Fr. *déifier*, from L.)
deign, *v.i.* dane, to condescend: *v.t.* to condescend to grant. (O.Fr. *deigner.*)
deil, *n.* deel, devil [Scots.].
deiparous, *a.* dee-*ip*-a-rus, bringing forth a god. (L. *deus*, and *pario*, produce.)
deipnosophist, *n.* dipe-*nos*-o-fist, title of a work by Athenæus in which a group of Greek philosophers discourse at meals; hence, a good table-talker, also, an adept in the art of dining. (Gr. *deipnos*, dinner, *sophizein*, to instruct.)
deiseal, *ad.* and *n.* *dee*-sel, deasil.
deism, *n.* *dee*-izm, the belief, on purely rational or natural grounds, in the existence of a god apart from and above the world, to the rejection, for most part, of a divine or special revelation. (Fr. *déisme.*)
deist, *n.* *dee*-ist, one who professes deism.
deistic, *a.* dee-*is*-tik, pertaining to deism or to deists; embracing deism.
deistical, *a.* dee-*is*-te-kal, deistic.
deistically, *ad.* after the manner of deists.
deity, *n.* *dee*-e-te, the divine nature; (*cap.*) the Supreme Being; a fabulous god or goddess; the divinity ascribed to a god or goddess. (O. Fr. *deite.*)
deject, *a.* de-*jekt*, cast down; low-spirited: *v.t.* to cast down; to depress the spirits of; to discourage or dishearten. (L. *dejectus*, dejected.)
dejecta, *n.pl.* de-*jek*-ta, fæces [Med.]. (L.)
dejectedly, *ad.* de-*jek*-ted-le, in a dejected manner.
dejectedness, *n.* the state of being dejected.
dejection, *n.* de-*jek*-shon, the state of being dejected; depression or lowness of spirits [Med.]; the act of voiding; excrement. (L. *dejectio*, a casting down.)
déjeuner, *n.* *day*-zhu-nay, breakfast; a fashionable luncheon. (Fr.)
deka-, *pref.* *dek*-a, a variant of **deca-.**
dekko, *n.* *dek*-oh, a peep; a look at [Mil. slang]. (Hind.)
delacrimation, *n.* dee-lak-re-*may*-shon, a profuse wateriness of the eyes. (L. *dēlacrimāre*, to weep.)
delaine, *n.* de-*lane*, a light dress material, usually of mixed cotton and wool or Botany worsted yarn. (Fr. *mousseline de laine*, woollen muslin.
delate, *v.t.* de-*late*, to inform against. (L. *delatus*, carried away.)
delation, *n.* de-*lay*-shon, accusation by an informer; denouncement. (L. *délatio*, an accusation.)
delator, *n.* de-*lay*-tor, an accuser or informer. (L.)
delay, *n.* de-*lay*, putting off, or deferring; lingering; procrastination; waste of time: *v.i.* to linger; to stop for a time: *v.t.* to put off; to defer; to retard; to detain. **delay action,** designating an apparatus, fuse, etc., timed to operate after a prearranged interval. (O.Fr. *delayer.*)
del-credere, *n.* del-*kree*-de-re, a guarantee on the part of a commission agent of the solvency of a purchaser [Comm.]. (It., literally, of trust.)
dele, *v.t.* *dee*-le, erase; omit; delete [written]. (L., erase.)
delectable, *a.* de-*lek*-ta-bl, delightful. (L. *delectabilis*, delightful.)
delectableness, *n.* delightfulness.
delectably, *ad.* de-*lek*-ta-ble, delightfully
delectation, *n.* dee-lek-*tay*-shon, delight; enjoyment; great pleasure.
delectus, *n.* de-*lek*-tus, a schoolbook of selected passages from classical authors for translation and parsing. (L., a selection.)
delegable, *a.* *del*-e-ga-bl, that can be delegated.
delegacy, *n.* *del*-e-ga-se, the system of delegation; the body of delegates.
delegate, *a.* *del*-e-gate, sent to act for or represent another: *n.* a person appointed and sent by another with power to act in his stead; a representative; a deputy; the representative of a Territory in the House of Representatives [U.S.A.]: *v.t.* to send with power to act as a representative; to entrust; to commit. (L. *delegatus.*)
delegation, *n.* del-e-*gay*-shon, the act of delegating; the person or body of persons deputed to act for others; a deputation; the assignment of a debt to another [Law]. (L. *delegatio.*)
delenda, *n.pl.* de-*len*-da, things to be deleted. (L.)
delete, *v.t.* de-*leet*, to blot out; to erase. (L. *deletus*, erased.)
deleterious, *a.* del-e-*teer*-re-us, inimical to health; injurious to mind or body; destructive; pernicious. (Gr. *dēlētērios*, noxious.)
deletion, *n.* de-*lee*-shon, act of deleting; erasure; that which is deleted. (L. *deletio.*)
deletory, *a.* de-*lee*-to-re effacing; that which destroys or blots out.
delf, *n.* delf, a kind of pottery glazed over, originally manufactured at Delft, in Holland.
delf, *n.* delf, an artificial watercourse, esp. one cut for drainage. (A.S. *delf*, a trench.)
Delian, *a.* *dee*-le-an, pertaining to the island of Delos, birthplace of Apollo and Artemis: *n.* an inhabitant of Delos. **Delian problem,** the problem of doubling the volume of a cube.
deliberate, *a.* de-*lib*-e-rat, determining with deliberation; slow in determining; formed with deliberation; done with deliberation; intentional: *v.t.* de-*lib*-e-rate, to weigh in the mind and consider well before determining or acting. (L. *deliberatus*, resolved upon.)
deliberately, *ad.* in a deliberate manner.
deliberateness, *n.* de-*lib*-e-rat-ness, the quality of being deliberate.
deliberation, *n.* de-*lib*-e-*ray*-shon, careful weighing and considering or pondering before determining or acting. (L. *deliberatio.*)
deliberative, *a.* de-*lib*-e-ra-tiv, proceeding or acting by deliberation. (L. *deliberativus.*)
deliberatively, *ad.* by deliberation.
delible, *a.* *del*-e-bl, that can be erased or blotted out. (L. *delebilis.*)
delicacy, *n.* *del*-e-ka-se, the state or quality of being delicate; anything delicate to the taste or to the susceptibilities, etc.; a luxury; fragility; niceness in perception, feeling, conduct, etc.; sensitiveness; gentleness.
★**delicate,** *a.* *del*-e-kate, pleasing to a nicely discriminating sense; dainty; requiring fineness of sense to distinguish; nice; fine; soft; effeminate;

slender; of a fine texture; nice in perception; fastidious; implying nice sensibility; refined; not constitutionally strong; highly susceptible of injury; tender; to be handled with caution: *n.* a delicacy; a dainty. (L. *dēlicātus*, charming.)
delicately, *ad.* in a delicate manner; daintily; luxuriously; with soft elegance; tenderly.
delicateness, *n.* the state of being delicate.
delicatessen, *n. del*-e-ka-*tes*-en, delicacies or relishes for the table; a shop where these are sold. (Ger.)
delicious, *a.* de-*lish*-us, highly pleasing to the taste or the senses; affording exquisite pleasure. (L. *dēliciōsus*, voluptuous.)
deliciously, *ad.* de-*lish*-us-le, in a delicious manner.
deliciousness, *n.* the quality of being delicious.
delict, *n.* de-*likt*, a legal offence; a crime; the commission of an offence. (L. *delictum*, a crime.)
deligation, *n.* del-e-*gay*-shon, bandaging; binding up with a ligature [Surg.]. (L. *deligatus*, tied up.)
delight, *n.* de-*lite*, a high degree of pleasure or satisfaction; that which gives great pleasure: *v.t.* to please highly: *v.i.* to be greatly pleased or rejoiced. (O.Fr. *deliter*.)
delighted, *a.* de-*lite*-ed, full of delight.
delightedly, *ad.* in a delighted manner.
delightful, *a.* de-*lite*-ful, highly pleasing; affording great pleasure and satisfaction.
delightfully, *ad.* de-*lite*-ful-le, in a manner to receive or afford great pleasure.
delightfulness, *n.* de-*lite*-ful-ness, the quality of being delightful.
delightsome, *a.* de-*lite*-sum, very pleasing.
delightsomely, *ad.* very pleasantly.
delightsomeness, *n.* pleasantness in a high degree.
delime, *v.t.* dee-*lime*, to free from lime.
delimit, *v.t.* de-*lim*-it, to fix the boundaries of. (Fr. *délimiter*.)
delimitate, *v.t.* de-*lim*-e-tate, to delimit.
delimitation, *n.* de-lim-e-*tay*-shon, the fixing of boundaries.
delineate, *v.t.* de-*lin*-e-ate, to mark or sketch out with lines; to sketch; to depict; to portray; to describe. (L. *delineatus*, sketched out.)
delineation, *n.* de-*lin*-e-*ay*-shon, the act of delineating; a draught, sketch, or representation; description. (L. *delineatio*.)
delineator, *n.* de-*lin*-e-a-tor, one who or that which delineates; an odometer.
delinquency, *n.* de-*ling*-kwen-se, failure or omission of duty; fault; a misdeed. (L. *delinquentia*, a crime.)
delinquent, *n.* de-*ling*-kwent, a culprit; a minor offender: *a.* neglecting or failing in duty. (L. *delinquens*, abandoning.)
deliquesce, *v.i.* del-e-*kwess*, to melt gradually by absorbing moisture from the atmosphere; to ramify (esp. of the veins of leaves) [Bot.]. (L. *deliquesco*, dissolve.)
deliquescence, *n.* del-e-*kwes*-sence, the process of deliquescing; the state of being deliquescent. (L. *deliquescens*.)
deliquescent, *a.* del-e-*kwes*-sent, absorbing moisture from the air; readily melting away; dividing into many branches [Bot.].
deliquium, *n.* de-*lik*-we-um, a swooning or fainting; a failure of vital powers. (L.)
deliration, *n.* del-e-*ray*-shon, alienation of mind; delirium. (L. *dēlīrātio*, a going astray.)
deliriant, *n.* de-*li*-re-ant, a drug causing delirium: *a.* causing or tending to cause delirium [Med.].
delirifacient, *a.* de-*li*-re-*fay*-she-ent, inducing delirium: *n.* a deliriant [Med.]. (L. *deliro*, rave, and *faciens*, making.)
delirious, *a.* de-*li*-re-us, affected with delirium; wandering in mind; wildly excited; mad with delight.
deliriously, *ad.* de-*li*-re-us-le, in a delirious manner.
deliriousness, *n.* the state of being delirious.
delirium, *n.* de-*li*-re-um, disorder of the brain causing hallucinations, delusions, non-co-ordination, etc.; mental aberration; a state in which the ideas of a person are wild, irregular, and unconnected; a state of rapt enthusiasm. **delirium tremens,** a disease of the brain produced by excessive and prolonged use of spirituous liquors. (L. *delirium*.)
delitescence, *n.* del-e-*tes*-sense, latent state; sudden subsidence of a tumour, inflammation, etc. [Med.]; the period during which the germs of a disease remain latent in the body [Med.]. (L. *delitescens*, lying hid.)
delitescent, *a.* del-e-*tes*-sent, latent; concealed.
deliver, *v.t.* de-*liv*-er, to free from danger or restraint; to rescue; to give; to transfer; to hand over; to give up; to effect the birth of a child; to communicate; to pronounce; to send; to discharge; to aim; to bowl. **deliver over,** to give or pass from one to another; to surrender or resign. **deliver up,** to surrender. (O.Fr. *delivrer*.)
deliverable, *a.* de-*liv*-er-a-bl, that is to be delivered; that can be delivered.
deliverance, *n.* de-*liv*-er-ance, the act of delivering; the state of being delivered; judgment or decision; rescue; state of release; acquittal. (Fr. *délivrance*.)
deliverer, *n.* de-*liv*-er-er, one who delivers; one who releases or rescues; a preserver.
delivery, *n.* de-*liv*-er-e, the act of delivering; release; rescue; surrender; a giving or passing from one to another; distribution (as of letters); that which is delivered; pronunciation; manner of speaking; manner of sending forth (as in bowling); childbirth.
dell, *n.* del, a small narrow valley; a dale. (A.S.)
Della-Robbia, *a. del*-la-*rob*-be-a, denoting a variety of earthenware founded on terra cotta, so called after the 15th-cent. Italian sculptor who revived the art.
delocalize, *v.t.* de-*loh*-ka-lize, to remove from its place; to centralize.
delouse, *v.t.* and *i.* dee-*louze*, to rid of lice.
Delphian, *a. del*-fe-an, Delphic.
Delphic, *a. del*-fik, pertaining to Delphi, or the oracle of Apollo there; as if inspired by Apollo.
Delphin, *a. del*-fin, pertaining to the Dauphin of France, and applied particularly to the edition of the Latin classics prepared under Louis XIV for the dauphin.
delphine, *n. del*-fine, pertaining to the dolphins [Zool.].
delphinic, *a.* del-*fin*-ik, obtained from dolphin oil. (L. *delphinus*, a dolphin.)
delphinine, *a. del*-fe-neen, pertaining to or of the nature of the dolphins: *n.* the poisonous alkaloid of a larkspur.
delphinium, *n.* del-*fin*-e-um, the genus of the larkspurs. (Gr. *delphinion*.)
delta, *n. del*-ta, the Greek letter D; a tract of alluvial land at the mouth of the Nile shaped like a capital delta (Δ); any alluvial deposit formed between the mouths of a river.
deltaic, *a.* del-*tay*-ik, relating to or like a delta.
deltoid, *a. del*-toyd, triangular, like the delta [esp. Bot. and Zool.]: *n.* the large triangular muscle of the shoulder [Anat.]. (Gr. *delta*, and *eidos*, like.)
deludable, *a.* de-*lew*-da-bl, liable to be deluded.
delude, *v.t.* de-*lewd*, to impose on; to deceive; to mislead by false representation. (L. *deludo*.)
deluder, *n.* de-*lew*-der, one who deludes.
deluge, *n. del*-yewj, a great flood or overflow of water; an inundation; a flood of words; a sweeping or overwhelming calamity: *v.t.* to inundate; to drench; to overrun, overwhelm, and sweep away. (O.Fr. *deluge*.)
delusion, *n.* de-*lew*-zhon, the act of deluding; the state of being deluded; a false belief; a fallacy; deception; an illusion. (L. *dēlūsio*, deluding.)
delusional, *a.* de-*lew*-zho-nal, pertaining to or characterized by delusions.
delusionist, *n.* one who habitually deludes; one given to delusions.
delusive, *a.* de-*lew*-siv, apt to deceive; deceptive; misleading. (L. *delusus*, mocked.)
delusively, *ad.* de-*lew*-siv-le, in a delusive manner.
delusiveness, *n.* the quality of being delusive.
delusory, *a.* de-*lew*-so-re, apt to deceive; deceptive.
delve, *v.t.* delv, to dig with a spade. (A.S. *delfan*.)
delver, *n. del*-ver, one who digs, as with a spade.
demagnetize, *v.t.* dee-*mag*-ne-tize, to deprive of magnetic properties.
demagogic, *a.* dem-a-*gog*-ik, like a demagogue; characteristic of a demagogue.
demagogism, *n. dem*-a-gog-izm, the acts or principles of a demagogue.
demagogue, *n. dem*-a-gog, a leader of the people, especially by means of oratory; one who from factious motives seeks to stir up and influence

the people against their rulers; an unprincipled political leader. (Gr. *dēmagōgos*, a leader of the people.)

emagogy, *n. dem*-a-gog-e, the arts of a demagogue.

emand, *n.* de-*mahnd*, a claim by right; an asking with authority; a desire to possess; the price demanded; question asked; the asking or seeking for what is due, or claimed as due, either expressly, by words, or by implication, as by seizure of goods or entry into lands [Law]: *v.t.* to claim or seek as due by right; to ask by authority; to require; to ask; to need; to sue for. **demand and supply,** express the relations between consumption and production, or the desire for commodities and the supply of them, so that when the former is in excess prices rise, and when the latter prices fall [Politcal Econ.]. **in demand,** much desired; in fashion. (Fr. *demander*.)

emandable, *a.* de-*mahn*-da-bl, that may be demanded.

emandant, *n.* de-*mahn*-dant, one who demands; the plaintiff in a real action; any plaintiff.

emander, *n.* de-*mahn*-der, one who demands.

emarcate, *v.t. dee*-mar-kate, to fix a boundary.

emarcation, *n.* dee-mar-*kay*-shon, the fixing or defining of a boundary line; the boundary or dividing line so fixed or defined. (Sp. *demarcacion.*)

émarche, *n.* de-*marsh*, a new departure; an ultimatum; in diplomacy, an announcement of a change of policy or new plan of action. (Fr.)

ematerialize, *v.t.* dee-ma-*teer*-re-a-lize, to deprive of materiality; to spiritualize; to lose, or cause to lose, material form [Spiritualism].

eme, *n.* deem, a township of Greece; one of the ten tribal divisions of ancient Attica; a commune in modern Greece. (Gr. *dēmos*, people.)

emean, *v.t.* de-*meen*, to behave; to conduct; to lower, to degrade; to debase. (O.Fr. *demener*; to conduct.)

emeanour, *n.* de-*mee*-nur, behaviour; deportment.

emembration, *n.* dee-mem-*bray*-shon, the malicious deprivation of a limb or member [Scots. Law].

ement, *v.t.* de-*ment*, to drive out of mind; to render insane. (L. *demento*, to make mad.)

ementate, *v.t.* de-*men*-tate, to make mad.

ementation, *n.* dee-men-*tay*-shon, madness; the act of making or the condition of being demented.

emented, *a.* de-*men*-ted, insane; crazy. (L. *demens*, raving.)

ementedness, *n.* de-*men*-ted-ness, insanity.

émenti, *n.* day-*mon*-te, an official contradiction, as when a government denies a rumour. (Fr.)

ementia, *n.* de-*men*-she-a, a weakening of intellect; insanity characterized by the degeneration or loss of mental faculties. **dementia præcox** (L., precocious), a form of schizophrenia. (L.)

emerara, *n.* dem-er-*rare*-ra, the yellowish brown variety of sugar grown principally in Demerara, British Guiana.

emerit, *n.* dee-*me*-rit, an undesirable trait; conduct deserving blame. (Fr. *démérite.*)

emeritorious, *a.* dee-me-re-*taw*-re-us, blameworthy; deserving censure.

emersal, *a.* de-*mer*-sal, living near to bottom (of fishes); hence, caught by a trawl, not by line.

emersed, *a.* de-*merst*, sub-aqueous; situate or growing under water [Bot.]. (L. *demersus*, plunged into.)

emesmerize, *v.t.* de-*mez*-mer-rize, to bring out of the mesmeric state.

emesne, *n.* de-*mane or* de-*meen*, the manor house and adjoining lands which the lord kept in his own hands for his own purposes; an estate in land. (O.Fr. *demeine.*)

emesnial, *a.* de-*may*-nyal, pertaining to a demesne.

emi-, *dem*-e, a prefix signifying half. (Fr.)

emibastion, *n. dem*-e-*bas*-tyon, part of a crown-work with one face and one flank cut off by the capital [Fort.].

emicadence, *n. dem*-e-*kay*-dence, a dominant cadence; a cadence that falls on any other than the key-note [Music.]

emi-cannon, *n. dem*-e-*kan*-non, an old piece of ordinance throwing a ball of from 30 to 36 lb.

emi-culverin, *n. dem*-e-*kul*-ver-in, a 16th-cent. piece of ordnance throwing a ball of 9 or 10 lb.

emigod, *n. dem*-e-god, an inferior deity; one who is the offspring of a god and mortal; a deified man.

demijohn, *n. dem*-e-jon, a glass or earthenware vessel with a large body and small neck, enclosed in wicker-work.

demilance, *n. dem*-e-lahnce, a light lance; a half pike.

demilitarization, *n. dee*-mil-e-ta-ry-*zay*-shun, the act, process, or result of demilitarizing.

demilitarize, *v.t.* dee-*mil*-e-ta-rize, to divest of military organization, fortifications, etc.; to free from militarism.

demilune, *n. dem*-e-loon, a crescent; a ravelin or work constructed for the defence of the curtain and shoulders of the bastion [Fort.].

demi-mondaine, *n.* (App.), one of the demi-monde.

demi-monde, *n.* (App.) women on the fringe of fashionable society; the upper class among courtesans. (Fr. *demi-*, and *monde*, society.)

demi-relief, *n.* dem-e-re-*leef*, carving in which the figure projects half the natural distance from the background; half relief [Sculp.].

demirep, *n. dem*-e-rep, a demi-mondaine; a woman of doubtful chastity. (*Demi-reputation.*)

demisable, *a.* de-*mize*-a-bl, that may be demised.

demise, *n.* de-*mize*, a death, especially of a royal person; a conveyance or transfer of an estate by lease or will [Law]: *v.t.* to transmit by succession or inheritance; to transfer or convey; to lease; to bequeath. **demise and redemise,** a conveyance where there are mutual leases made from one to another of the same land [Law]. **demise of the Crown,** the devolution of sovereignty by the death, deposition, or abdication of the sovereign. (Fr. *démettre*, to lay down.)

demisemiquaver, *n. dem*-e-*sem*-e-*kway*-ver, a note of the value of the fourth of a quaver [Mus.].

demission, *n.* de-*mish*-on, a laying down of an office; resignation; degradation; a lowering. (L. *dēmissio*, a laying down.)

demit, *v.t.* de-*mit*, to cause to descend; to resign office; to abdicate; to lay down formally. (L. *demitto*, drop.)

demi-tint, *n. dem*-e-tint, a graduation of colour between positive light and positive shade [Painting].

demitone, *n. dem*-e-tone, a semitone.

demiurge, *n. dem*-e-urj, the creator of the world in Platonic philosophy; the world-builder and maker. (L. *demiurgus*, the chief magistrate in certain Greek States.)

demiurgic, *a. dem*-e-*ur*-jik, pertaining to the demiurge; creative.

demi-volte, *n. dem*-e-volt, an artificial motion of a horse, in which he raises his fore legs in a particular manner [Man.]. (Fr.)

demob, *v.t.* dee-*mob*, to demobilize [Coll.].

demobilization, *n.* dee-*moh*-be-ly-*zay*-shon, the act of demobilizing.

demobilize, *v.t.* dee-*moh*-be-lize, to disband; to discharge from service in a mobilized body. (Fr. *démobiliser.*)

democracy, *n.* de-*mok*-ra-se, government by all classes for the benefit of all classes; a form of representative government characterized by equality of rights, absence of the hereditary principle, and in which the supreme power is directly or indirectly lodged in the hands of the people; a democratic state; the multitude. (Fr. *démocratie.*)

democrat, *n. dem*-o-krat, a supporter of the democratic principle; one of the democratic party [U.S.A.].

democratic, *a.* dem-o-*krat*-ik, pertaining to democracy. **Democratic Party,** the party in the United States opposing the Republicans and upholding the rights of the individual States as against centralized Federal power. (Gr. *demokratikos*, of a democracy.)

democratically, *ad.* dem-o-*krat*-e-ka-le, in a democratic manner.

democratism, *n.* de-*mok*-ra-tizm, the theory, principles, or practices of democracy.

democratize, *v.t.* and *i.* de-*mok*-ra-tize, to render or to become democratic.

démodé, *a.* (App.), out of fashion [Fr.].

demodulation, *n.* dee-mod-yew-*lay*-shon, the complete process of converting a modulated current or wave into the current or wave of the original signal [Wire.].

demogorgon, *n. dee*-mo-*gor*-gon, a mysterious infernal deity of mediæval legend. (Gr. *daimon*, demon, *gorgos*, horrible.)

demographer, *n.* de-*mog*-ra-fer, a student of demography.

demographic, *a.* dem-o-*graf*-ik, pertaining to demography.

demography, *n.* de-*mog*-ra-fe, that department of science which treats of statistics as regards health and disease in connection with births, marriages, and deaths. (Gr. *demos*, and *grapho*, write.)

demoiselle, *n. dem*-wa-zel, a young unmarried lady.

demoiselle crane, *Anthropoides virgo*, the Numidian crane, so called from its graceful form and bearing.(Fr.)

demolish, *v.t.* de-*mol*-ish, to raze; to pull down (esp. an unsafe building, etc.); to destroy; to ruin. (Fr. *demolir.*)

demolisher, *n.* de-*mol*-ish-er, one who demolishes.

demolishment, *n.* de-*mol*-ish-ment, demolition.

demolition, *n.* dem-o-*lish*-on, the act of demolishing; ruin; destruction. (Fr.)

demon, *n. dee*-mon, a guardian spirit; a spirit having a mystic influence and guardianship over the character and destiny of individuals, some good as connected with the upper, some bad as connected with the nether, world; one's oversoul or guiding genius; an evil spirit; an imp; a ferocious or inexorable person. (Gr. *daimon.*)

demoness, *n. dee*-mon-ess, a female demon.

demonetization, *n.* dee-*mun*- *or* dee-*mon*-e-ty-*zay*-shon, the act or process of demonetizing; the state of being demonetized.

demonetize, *v.t.* dee-*mun*- *or* dee-*mon*-e-tize, to divest of standard value, as money; to withdraw from use as currency. (L. *de-*, and *moneta*, money.)

demoniac, *a.* de-*moh*-ne-ak, pertaining to demons or evil spirits; influenced or produced by demons: *n.* a human being possessed by a demon. (L. *daemoniacus*, demoniac.)

demoniacal, *a.* dee-mo-*ny*-a-kal, devilish.

demoniacally, *ad.* in a demoniacal manner.

demonian, *a.* de-*moh*-ne-an, pertaining to or of the nature of a demon.

demonic, *a.* de-*mon*-ik, inspired by a demon.

demonism, *n. dee*-mon-izm, the belief in demons; the doctrine of demons.

demonist, *n. dee*-mon-ist, a believer in demons.

demonize, *v.t. dee*-mon-ize, to turn into a demon; to place under the power of a demon. (Gr. *daimonizomai*, possessed by a devil.)

demonolatry, *n.* dee-mon-*ol*-a-tre, the worship of demons. (Gr. *daimon*, and *latreia*, worship.)

demonological, *a.* dee-mon-o-*loj*-e-kal, pertaining to demonology.

demonologist, *n.* dee-mon-*ol*-o-jist, one versed in demonology.

demonology, *n.* dee-mon-*ol*-o-je, the branch of learning concerned with evil spirits; a treatise on demons. (Gr. *daimon*, and *logos*, discourse.)

demonomania, *n.* dee-mon-o-*may*-ne-a, a mania in which the person supposes himself to be the prey of devils.

demonry, *n. dee*-mon-re, demoniacal influence.

demonship, *n. dee*-mon-ship, the state of a demon.

demonstrable, *a.* de-*mon*-stra-bl, capable of demonstration. (L. *dēmonstrabilis.*)

demonstrableness, *n.* de-*mon*-stra-bl-ness, the quality of being demonstrable.

demonstrably, *ad.* de-*mon*-stra-ble, so as to preclude doubt.

demonstrate, *v.t. dem*-on-strate, to point out; to show, esp. by logical reasoning; to teach by examples; to prove beyond doubt; to indicate. (L. *dēmonstratum*, pointed out.)

demonstration, *n. dem*-on-*stray*-shon, the act of demonstrating; indubitable evidence or proof; exhibition with description; a series of syllogisms. all whose premises are either definitions, self-evident truths, or propositions already established [Logic]; display; the exhibition of objects for teaching purposes, as of parts dissected [Anat.]; a movement of troops with a view to deceive [Mil.]; a public exhibition of sympathy, esp. a march and mass meeting; a display of force ready to act if necessary. (L. *demonstratio.*)

demonstrational, *a.* dem-on-*stray*-shon-al, pertaining to demonstration.

demonstrative, *a.* de-*mon*-stra-tiv, logically conclusive; clearly exhibiting; pointing out the person or thing referred to [Gram.]; that expresses itself with emphasis; forcibly frank; effusive. (L. *dēmonstrātīvus.*)

demonstratively, *ad.* de-*mon*-stra-tiv-le, in a demonstrative manner.

demonstrativeness, *n.* de-*mon*-stra-tiv-ness, quality of being demonstrative.

demonstrator, *n. dem*-on-stray-tor, one who demonstrates; a professor's assistant; a practica teacher of science; a member of a public demon stration. (L.)

demonstratory, *a.* de-*mon*-stra-to-re, tending to demonstrate.

demoralization, *n.* de-*mo*-ra-ly-*zay*-shon, the act of demoralizing; the state of being demoralized.

demoralize, *v.t.* de-*mo*-ra-lize, to undermine o corrupt the morals or spirit of, and, in an army, th discipline. (Fr. *démoraliser.*)

Demos, *n. dee*-moss, democracy personified; th mob.

Demosthenic, *a.* dee-mos-*then*-ik, pertaining to o resembling the oratory of Demosthenes.

demote, *v.t.* de-*mote*, to reduce to a lower rank o status; to degrade [U.S.A.]. (Coined from *de-* an pro*mote.*)

demotic, *a.* de-*mot*-ik, in use among the people or la class, as distinct from hieroglyphic; popular vulgar. (Gr. *dēmotikos*, common.)

demotion, *n.* dee-*moh*-shun, reduction in grad [U.S.A.]. (*Demote.*)

dempster, *n. dem*-ster, a deemster.

demulcent, *a.* de-*mul*-sent, softening: *n.* a medicin which soothes irritation. (L. *demulcens*, soothing.)

demulsification, *n.* dee-mul-si-fi-*kay*-shon, the ac or process of breaking an emulsion into its com ponents.

demur, *n.* de-*mer*, the action of demurring; hesita tion; objection: *v.i.* hesitate from uncertainty; t delay proceeding till better advised; to object to o ground of scruple; to raise an objection in th course of pleadings and so to stay proceeding till it is decided [Law]. (L. *demoror*, linger.)

demure, *a.* de-*mewr*, serious in mien; staid; grave modest or affectedly modest in appearance. (O.Fr *de meurs*, of manners.)

demurely, *ad.* de-*mewr*-le, in a demure manner with an appearance of gravity.

demureness, *n.* de-*mewr*-ness, the state or qualit of being demure.

demurrable, *a.* de-*mer*-ra-bl, that may be demurre to.

demurrage, *n.* de-*mu*-raj, an allowance made b the freighters of a ship to its owners for delay in po beyond the appointed time of departure; th period of such delay [Comm.]; a fixed tariff for th detention of railway rolling stock belonging to othe companies; the charge of $1\frac{1}{2}d.$ per oz. formerl made by the Bank of England for the exchange c bullion into coin. (O.Fr. *demourage.*)

demurrant, *n.* de-*mu*-rant, one who demu [Law].

demurrer, *n.* de-*mur*-rer, one who demurs; a issue joined at a point in the pleadings to be dete mined by the judges [Law]; an objection.

demy, *n.* de-*my*, a size of paper, 22 by $17\frac{1}{2}$ in. fc printing, and 20 by $15\frac{1}{2}$ in. for writing or drawing a foundation scholar at Magdalen College, Oxfor formerly with half the allowance of a fellow.

demyship, *n.* de-*my*-ship, a scholarship at Magdale College, Oxford; the position held by a demy.

den, *n.* den, a cave for shelter; a wild beast's lai an animal's home; a private room or snugger a miserable hovel. (A.S. *denn*, a cave, a dell.)

denarius, *n.* de-*nare*-re-us, an ancient Roman silv coin worth 10 asses, or $7\frac{3}{4}d.$, and a gold coin wort 25 of these; the English penny (whence the d i L. s. d.). (L. *dēnārius*, containing ten.)

denary, *a. den*-a-re, containing ten; based on tl number ten; decimal: *n.* the number ten.

denationalization, *n.* de-*nash*-on-a-ly-*zay*-shon, tl act of denationalizing.

denationalize, *v.t.* de-*nash*-o-na-lize, to divest national character or rights; to deprive of stat hood.

denaturalization, *n.* de-*nat*-yew-ra-ly-*zay*-shon, tl act of denaturalizing; the state of being denatura ized.

denaturalize, *v.t.* de-*nat*-yew-ra-lize, to deprive natural qualities: to deprive of naturalization in state.

enaturant, *n.* de-*nay*-tewr-rant, a denaturing agent.
enaturation, *n.* *dee*-nay-tewr-*ray*-shon, the process of denaturing.
enature, *v.t.* de-*nay*-tewr, to adulterate so as to change the nature of; to render (alcohol) unfit for human consumption.
enazification, *n.* dee-*nat*-se-fe-*kay*-shon, the act or process of eradicating the authoritarian nationalistic principles of Hitlerism and German National Socialism.
enazify, *v.t.* dee-*nat*-se-fy, to subject to denazification.
endrachate, *n.* *den*-dra-kat, a variety of agate with markings resembling branches [Min.]. (Gr. *dendron*, a tree, *achates*, agate.)
endriform, *a.* *den*-dre-fawrm, of tree-like structure. (Gr. *dendron*, tree, L. *forma*, shape.)
endrite, *n.* *den*-drite, a mineral on or in which are figures resembling branches; a branching protoplasmic nerve-cell process [Biol.].
endritic, *a.* den-*drit*-ik, resembling dendrite; having tree-like markings; branched like a tree.
endrodentine, *n.* *den*-dro-*den*-tin, a blending of the substance of several teeth massed together, presenting a dendritic appearance. (Gr. *dendron*, and *dens*, a tooth.)
endrograph, *n.* *den*-dro-graf, an instrument that automatically records the diametrical growth of trees.
endrography, *n.* den-*drog*-ra-fe, the scientific description of trees; the use of the dendrograph.
endroid, *a.* *den*-droyd, tree-like.
endrolatry, *n.* den-*drol*-a-tre, the worship of trees. (Gr. *dendron*, and *latreia*, worship.)
endrolite, *n.* *den*-dro-lite, a petrified or fossil plant, or part of a plant; fossilized wood. (Gr. *dendron*, and *lithos*, a stone.)
endrologist, *n.* den-*drol*-o-jist, one versed in dendrology.
endrology, *n.* den-*drol*-o-je, a treatise on trees; the study of the natural history of trees. (Gr. *dendron*, and *logos*, science.)
endrometer, *n.* den-*drom*-e-ter, an instrument to measure the height and diameter of trees. (Gr. *dendron*, and *metron*, measure.)
ene, *n.* deen, a sandhill; a stretch of sandy ground.
enegation, *n.* de-ne-*gay*-shon, denial; contradiction. (L. *dēnegatus*, denied.)
ene-hole, *n.* *deen*-hole, an ancient excavation, generally in chalk, extending downwards for 25 feet or more and then widening into horizontal passages.
engue, *n.* *deng*-gay, a severe tropical fever transmitted by the mosquito and accompanied by rash and rheumatic pains. (Swahili, through W. Ind. Sp.)
eniable, *a.* de-*ny*-a-bl, that may be denied.
enial, *n.* de-*ny*-al, the act of denying, or of refusing, or of disowning; in bridge, etc., the change of a partner's bid to indicate lack of support. **self-denial,** *see* **self.**
enier, *n.* de-*ny*-er, one who denies or disowns.
enier, *n.* den-*eer*, a former French coin worth the twelfth of a sou; a measure of weight (one-twentieth gramme) used in the silk trade. (Fr.)
enigrate, *v.t.* *den*-e-grate, to blacken; to defame.
enigration, *n.* den-e-*gray*-shon, the act of blackening; defamation.
enim, *n.* *den*-im, coarse cotton drill used for aprons and overalls; also called Nîmes serge, because originally obtained from Nîmes in France.
nitrate, *v.t.* de-*ny*-trate, to clear from nitre, nitrate, or nitric acid.
nitration, *n.* dee-ny-*tray*-shon, a disengaging of compounds of nitre.
nization, *n.* den-e-*zay*-shon, the act of admission to citizenship; naturalization; condition of being a denizen.
nizen, *n.* *den*-e-zen, an inhabitant not native to the place; in England, an alien admitted to citizenship but ineligible for public office; a stranger admitted to certain rights in a foreign country; a plant or animal subsisting as native in a locality but originally introduced by man: *v.t.* to enfranchise; to make a denizen of; to supply with denizens. (O.Fr. *deinzein.*)
nizenship, *n.* *den*-e-zen-ship, state of being a denizen.

dennet, *n.* *den*-et, a light two-wheeled open carriage of the early 19th century.
denominable, *a.* de-*nom*-e-na-bl, that may be nominated or named.
denominate, *v.t.* de-*nom*-e-nate, to give a name or epithet to; to designate. (L. *denominatus*, named.)
denomination, *n.* de-*nom*-e-*nay*-shon, the act of naming; a name, title, or appellation; a group or collection of units of the same class; a religious sect. (L. *dēnōminatio.*)
denominational, *a.* de-*nom*-e-*nay*-shon-al, pertaining to a denomination; sectarian.
denominationalism, *n.* de-*nom*-e-*nay*-shon-a-lizm, a spirit of exclusive devotion to the interests of a sect or party.
denominationalize, *v.t.* de-*nom*-e-*nay*-shon-a-lize, to convert to a denominational condition.
denominationally, *ad.* by denominations.
denominative, *a.* de-*nom*-e-na-tiv, that gives a name; that has a distinctive name; derived from a noun: *n.* a verb formed from a noun.
denominatively, *ad.* by way of denomination.
denominator, *n.* de-*nom*-e-nay-tor, he who or that which gives a name; that number placed below the line which shows into how many parts an integer is divided and names the fraction [Arith.].
denotable, *a.* de-*noh*-ta-bl, that may be denoted.
denotation, *n.* dee-no-*tay*-shon, the act of denoting; a designation; signification; distinction by means of a name. **denotation of a term,** the extent of its application [Logic]. (L. *dēnotātio*, a pointing out.)
denotative, *a.* de-*noh*-ta-tiv, signifying; having power to denote; bearing a logical denotation [Logic].
denote, *v.t.* de-*note*, to indicate or show; to signify by a mark; to distinguish. (O.Fr. *dénoter.*)
denotement, *n.* de-*note*-ment, a sign or indication.
denouement, *n.* (App.), the final unravelling of a plot; the issue; the result; the explanation. (Fr. *dénouement.*)
denounce, *v.t.* de-*nounce*, to threaten solemnly or by some outward sign; to censure openly and threateningly; to accuse publicly; to proclaim as impending; formally to declare the termination of (a treaty, etc.) (O.Fr. *denoncer.*)
denouncement, *n.* de-*nounce*-ment, denunciation.
denouncer, *n.* de-*noun*-ser, one who denounces.
dense, *a.* dence, having its particles closely packed; opague; dull of comprehension. (L. *densus.*)
densely, *ad.* *dence*-le, in a dense manner.
denseness, *n.* the state of being dense.
densify, *v.t.* and *i.* *den*-se-fy, to make or become dense.
densimeter, *n.* den-*sim*-e-ter, an apparatus for ascertaining density or porosity [Phys.].
density, *n.* *den*-se-te, denseness; a crowded state; the ratio of mass to bulk; darkness of colour; obtuseness. (L. *densitas*, thickness.)
dent, *n.* dent, a dint; depression made by the pressure or blow of a harder body on a softer; indentation: *v.t.* to make a dent; to dint. (*dint.*)
dent, *n.* dent, a cog, the tooth of a wheel; the tooth of a comb, metallic brush, or weaver's card; a wire of the reed-frame of a weaver's loom. (Fr., tooth.)
dental, *a.* *den*-tal, pertaining to the teeth; formed by the teeth; pertaining to dentistry: *n.* an articulation or letter formed by placing the end of the tongue against the upper teeth. **dental formula,** the zoological notation used in denoting the number and kind of teeth in a mammal. **dental mechanic,** a craftsman who makes and repairs artificial teeth and their plates, etc. **dental surgeon,** a dentist. (L. *dens*, a tooth.)
dentalize, *v.t.* den-ta-*lize* to make dental; to change into a dental [Phonetics].
dentary, *n.* *den*-ta-re, a bone carrying the lower teeth in fishes and reptiles: *a.* relating to the teeth: on the teeth.
dentate, *a.* *den*-tat, toothed; notched [Bot. and Zool.] (L. *dentātus*, toothed.)
dentated, *a.* *den*-tat-ed, dentate.
dentately, *ad.* *den*-tat-le, in a dentate manner.
dentation, *n.* den-*tay*-shon, the formation of teeth; the state of being dentate.
dentato-, *pref.* den-*tay*-to, a Latin combining form signifying *dentate*, or *dentate as well as*, as in

dentato-sinuate, *a.* of a form intermediate between dentate and sinuate [Bot.].
dented, *a. dent*-ed, having dents or hollows.
dentel, *n. den*-tel, a dentil.
dentelle, *n.* den-*tel*, a lace- or tooth-like style of decoration. (F.)
denticle, *n. den*-te-kl, a small tooth or projecting point; a dentil. (L. *denticulus*, a little tooth.)
denticular, *a.* den-*tik*-yew-lar, slightly notched.
denticulate, *a.* den-*tik*-yew-lat, notched into projections [Bot.]; cut into dentils [Arch.]. (L. *denticulatus*, furnished with teeth.)
denticulation, *n.* den-tik-yew-*lay*-shon, the state of being set with small teeth; a diminutive tooth.
dentiform, *a. den*-te-fawrm, having the form or structure of a tooth. (L. *dens*, and *forma*, shape.)
dentifrice, *n. den*-te-fris, a powder, paste, or liquid preparation used in cleaning the teeth. (L. *dentifricium*, tooth-powder.)
dentigerous, *a.* den-*tij*-er-us, bearing teeth.
dentil, *n. den*-til, an ornament in cornices bearing some resemblance to teeth [Arch.].
dentilabial, *a.* and *n.* den-te-*lay*-be-al, labiodental.
dentilation, *n.* den-te-*lay*-shon, formation of teeth; denticulation; the perforated edge of postage-stamps.
dentilingual, *a.* den-te-*ling*-gwal, formed by applying the tongue to the gum above the teeth: *n.* a consonant so formed, as *d* [Phon.]. (L. *dens* and *lingual.*)
dentinasal, *a.* den-te-*nay*-zal, formed by placing the tongue against the teeth the nasal passage being open (as the *n* in *congé*): *n.* a consonant so formed [Phon.].
dentine, *n. den*-tin, a dense ivory tissue forming the body of a tooth.
dentiphone, *n. den*-te-fohn, an audiphone.
dentirostral, *n.pl.* den-*te*-*ros*-tral, having notches or tooth-like processes on the bill [Ornith.]. (L. *dens*, and *rostrum*, a beak.)
dentist, *n. den*-tist, a specialist in the diseases of the teeth and gums; one qualified to extract teeth and fit artificial teeth.
dentistry, *n. den*-tis-tre, the art or practice of a dentist; work done by a dentist.
dentition, *n.* den-*tish*-on, the cutting of teeth; the time of teething; arrangement of the teeth [Zool.]. (L. *dentitio*, a teething.)
dentoid, *a. den*-toyd, resembling a tooth. (L. *dens*, and Gr. *eidos*, like.)
denture, *n. dent*-yewr, a set of artificial teeth. (Fr.)
denudant, *n.* de-*new*-dant, a denuding agent [Geol.].
denudate, *v.t. den*-yew-date, to denude; to lay bare by erosion. (L. *denudus*, naked.)
denudation, *n.* den-yew-*day*-shon, laying bare; the laying of rocks bare by the washing away of overlying deposits [Geol.].
denude, *v.t.* de-*newd*, to strip,; to make naked or bare.
denunciate, *v.t.* de-*nun*-se-ate, to denounce.
denunciation, *n.* de-nun-se-*ay*-shon, the act of denouncing; a solemn threat. (L. *denunciatio.*)
denunciator, *n.* de-*nun*-se-*ay*-tor, one who denounces; an accuser. (L.)
denunciatory, *a.* de-*nun*-se-*ay*-to-re, characterized by denunciation.
denutrition, *n.* dee-new-*trish*-un, deprivation or failure of normal nutrition [Med.].
deny, *v.t.* de-*ny*, to gainsay; to refuse to admit; to assert to be untrue; to abjure; to withhold; to disown. **to deny oneself,** to practise self-denial; to abstain from. (Fr. *dénier.*)
deobstruct, *v.t.* dee-ob-*strukt*, to remove obstructions.
deobstruent, *a.* de-*ob*-stroo-ent, removing obstructions; resolving viscidities; aperient: *n.* a medicine which removes obstructions, and opens the natural passages of the body [Med.].
deodand, *n. dee*-o-dand, any personal chattel which is the immediate occasion of the death of a rational creature, and, for that reason, given to God, *i.e.*, forfeited to be applied to pious or charitable use [Law]. (L. *deo dandum*, to be given to God.)
deodar, *n. dee*-o-dar, a coniferous evergreen tree, *Cedrus deodara*, of the Western Himalayas, closely allied to the cedars; a Hindu sacred tree.
deodorant, *a.* de-*oh*-der-rant, overpowering or destroying offensive odours: *n.* a deodorizer.
deodorization, *n.* de-*oh*-do-ry-*zay*-shon, the art o[r] process of deodorizing.
deodorize, *v.t.* de-*oh*-do-rize, to deprive of odour to overpower an offensive smell by a pleasing one to disinfect.
deodorizer, *n.* de-*oh*-do-ry-zer, any substance use[d] to counteract or mask offensive odours.
deontology, *n.* de-on-*tol*-o-je, the Benthamit[e] doctrine of moral obligation. (Gr. *deon*, that whic[h] is fitting, and *logos*, science.)
deoxidate, *v.t.* de-*ok*-se-date, to deprive of oxyge[n] or reduce from the state of an oxide.
deoxidation, *n.* de-*ok*-se-*day*-shon, the act or proce[ss] of deoxidating.
deoxidization, *n.* de-*ok*-se-dy-*zay*-shon, deoxidatio[n]
deoxidize, *v.t.* de-*ok*-se-dize, to deoxidate.
deoxygenate, *v.t.* de-*ok*-se-je-nate, to deoxidate.
deoxygenation, *n.* de-*ok*-se-je-*nay*-shon, deoxida-tion.
depaint, *v.t.* de-*paynt*, to picture; to describe i[n] words.
depart, *v.t.* de-*part*, to go away; to leave; t[o] desist; to forsake; to deviate from; to di[e] (O.Fr. *departir.*)
departed, *a.* de-*par*-ted, gone; bygone; vanished dead. **the departed,** the deceased.
department, *n.* de-*part*-ment, a separate part [or] division or branch, especially of duty, busines[s] study, or inquiry; an administrative division [of] territory in a country, as in France. **departmen[t] store,** a large shop selling various classes of good[s] in different departments [U.S.A.]. (Fr. *départ[e]ment.*)
departmental, *a.* de-part-*men*-tal, pertaining t[o] a department of business or territory.
departmentalize, *v.t.* dee-part-*men*-ta-lize, t[o] form into departments.
departmentally, *ad.* in a manner typical of government or other bureaucratic office.
departure, *n.* de-*part*-yewr, the act of departing quitting; death; abandonment of defence i[n] pleading [Law]; the distance a ship has gone t[o] the east or west of the meridian from which sh[e] departed [Naut.]; the position of the point fro[m] which a vessels starts her dead reckoning [Naut.].
depasturage, *n.* de-*pahs*-tewr-raj, turning ou[t] cattle to graze; right of pasture.
depasture, *v.t.* de-*pahs*-tewr, to turn out to graz[e]
depauperate, *v.t.* de-*paw*-per-ate, to impoverish to deprive of vigour or fertility: *a.* ill-develope[d] [Bot.].
depauperize, *v.t.* de-*paw*-per-rize, to raise fro[m] pauperism; to free from paupers.
depend, *v.i.* de-*pend*, to hang down; to hang from to be connected with, as an effect on a cause or condition; to rely; to trust; to be pendin[g] (L. *dependeo*, hang.)
dependable, *a.* de-*pen*-da-bl, that may be depende[d] on; trustworthy.
dependableness, *n.* trustworthiness.
dependant, *n.* de-*pen*-dant, a retainer; one wh[o] depends on another for support or maintenance.
dependence, *n.* de-*pen*-dence, the state of bein[g] dependent; that on which one depends; reliance trust; connexion state of pending [Law].
dependency, *n.* de-*pen*-den-se, that which is attache[d] but subordinate to something; a territory remo[te] from the kingdom or state to which it belongs, b[ut] subject to its dominion.
★**dependent,** *a.* de-*pen*-dent, hanging down; connec[t]ed with as effect; subsisting or supported by subject to; relying on for support, favour, [or] benefit: *n.* that which depends on something else a dependant. (L. *dependens*, hanging down.)
dependently, *ad.* in a dependent manner.
depending, *a.* de-*pen*-ding, undetermined [Law].
depersonalize, *v.t.* de-*per*-son-a-lize, to withdra[w] the attribute of personalization; to treat divested of individuality.
dephase, *v.t.* dee-*fayz*, to cause to differ in pha[se] [Elect.].
dephosphorize, *v.t.* de-*foss*-fo-rize, to deprive [of] phosphorus.
depict, *v.t.* de-*pikt*, to make a likeness, as in colours to delineate; to portray; to picture or represent [in] words. (L. *depictus*, painted.)
depicter, *n.* de-*pik*-ter, a painter; a describer.
depiction, *n.* de-*pik*-shun, the act of depicting; description or representation.

depicture, *v.t.* de-*pikt*-yur, to paint; to picture; to represent in colours.
depilate, *v.t.* *dee*-pe-late, to strip off or remove hair. (L. *depilātus*, plucked out, of hair.)
depilation, *n.* dee-pe-*lay*-shon, removal of the hair; natural loss of hairy covering [Bot.].
depilatory, *a.* de-*pil*-a-to-re, having the power to remove hair: *n.* an application having this effect without causing injury to the skin.
deplane, *v.t.* and *i.* dee-*plane*, to alight from or take out of an aeroplane.
deplenish, *v.t.* de-*plen*-ish, to empty of contents, esp. a tenement of furniture or farm-stock.
deplete, *v.t.* de-*pleet*, to reduce anything, especially any fulness, by drawing off from some feeding source; to empty; to exhaust: *a.* depleted. (L. *dēplētus*, emptied out.)
depletion, *n.* de-*plee*-shon, the act of depleting; the act of diminishing the quantity of blood in the vessels by venesection; blood-letting [Med.].
depletive, *a.* de-*plee*-tiv, inducing depletion: *n.* a depleting agent.
depletory, *a.* de-*plee*-to-re, calculated to deplete; such as to obviate fulness of habit.
deplorable, *a.* de-*plaw*-ra-bl, to be deplored; pitiable; wretched; contemptible.
deplorableness, *n.* state of being deplorable.
deplorably, *ad.* in a manner to be deplored; miserably.
deploration, *n.* dep-lo-*ray*-shon, the act of lamenting. (L. *dēplōrātio*, a bewailing.)
deplore, *v.t.* de-*plore*, to feel deep grief or sorrow over; to grieve over; to bewail. (L. *deploro*, weep over.)
deploringly, *ad.* in a deploring manner.
deploy, *v.t.* de-*ploy*, to open out and extend from column into line, as for action: *v.i.* to form a more extended front. (Fr. *déployer*.)
deployment, *n.* de-*ploy*-ment, the act of deploying.
deplumation, *n.* dee-ploo-*may*-shon, the falling off of feathers; loss of plumes or honours.
deplume, *v.t.* de-*ploom*, to strip or pluck off feathers; to deprive of honours, etc. (L. *de-*, and *pluma*, a feather.)
depolarization, *n.* de-*poh*-la-ry-*zay*-shon, the act of depriving of polarity, as the rays of light.
depolarize, *v.t.* de-*po*-la-rize, to deprive of polarity; to change polarity.
depone, *v.t.* and *i.* de-*pone*, to testify under oath or under written declaration; to give evidence under oath. (L. *depono*, place.)
deponent, *a.* de-*poh*-nent, laying down: *n.* a witness.
deponent verb, one having a passive termination with an active signification [Latin Gram.]. (L. *deponens*, a deponent verb.)
depopulate, *v.t.* de-*pop*-yew-late, to deprive of inhabitants. (L. *depopulatus*, laid waste.)
depopulation, *n.* de-*pop*-yew-*lay*-shon, the act of dispeopling.
deport, *v.t.* de-*port*, to carry, demean, or behave (oneself, himself, etc.); to carry or send into exile; to expel. (L. *portare*.)
deportation, *n.* dee-por-*tay*-shon, a carrying away into exile; banishment; expulsion from a country.
deportee, *n.* dee-por-*tee*, a deported person; one under sentence of deportation.
deportment, *n.* de-*port*-ment, bearing; carriage; demeanour; behaviour. (Fr. *déportement*.)
deposable, *a.* de-*poze*-a-bl, that may be deposed.
deposal, *n.* de-*poze*-al, the act of deposing; divestment of office.
depose, *v.t.* de-*poze*, to remove from a throne or other high station; to divest of office; to bear witness: *v.i.* to bear witness. (O.Fr. *deposer*.)
deposit, *n.* de-*poz*-it, that which is deposited, as detritus in water, sediment in an accumulator cell, etc.; that which is entrusted for safe keeping or as a security, as money in a bank; money paid on account to make a contract binding; earnest money: *v.t.* to lay or drop down; to lay; to lay up; to lodge for safe keeping or as a pledge; to entrust. **on deposit,** in a state of pledge or safe keeping. (O.Fr. *depositer*.)
depositary, *n.* de-*poz*-e-ta-re, one with whom anything is lodged as a trust; a trustee.
deposition, *n.* dee-po-*zish*-on, the act of depositing; the laying down of sediment; that which is deposited; the act of deponing or testifying; testimony in writing under oath; an affidavit; the act of deposing or depriving of office. (Fr. *deposition*.)
depositional, *a.* dee-po-*zish*-o-nal, pertaining to or made by a deposition.
depositor, *n.* de-*poz*-e-tor, one who makes a deposit; a machine for depositing. (L.)
depository, *n.* de-*poz*-e-to-re, a place where anything is lodged for safe keeping; a storehouse for furniture, etc.; a depositary.
depot, *n.* *dep*-oh, a place of deposit for goods or stores of any kind, especially for military stores; the headquarters of a regiment, or its recruiting centre when the main body is abroad [Mil.]; a railway station; a place in the trenches, out of reach of the guns of a besieged place [Fort.]. **depot ship,** a vessel carrying provisions, spares, repair facilities, etc., for a flotilla of destroyers or submarines, etc. (Fr. *dépôt*.)
depravation, *n.* dee-pra-*vay*-shon, the act of depraving; a state of being depraved; degeneracy; debasement.
deprave, *v.t.* de-*prave*, to make bad or worse; to vitiate; to corrupt. (O.Fr. *depraver*.)
depraved, *a.* de-*prayvd*, morally debased; hopelessly corrupt; abandoned.
depravedly, *ad.* de-*pray*-ved-le, in a depraved manner.
depravedness, *n.* a depraved state.
depravement, *n.* de-*prave*-ment, depravation; a vitiated state.
depraver, *n.* de-*prave*-er, a corrupter; a vilifier.
depravingly, *ad.* de-*pray*-ving-le, in a depraving manner.
depravity, *n.* de-*prav*-e-te, a depraved state of heart or of morals; extreme wickedness; profligacy. (*Deprave*.)
deprecable, *a.* *dep*-re-ka-bl, to be deprecated.
deprecate, *v.t.* *dep*-re-kate, to desire earnestly that a present evil may be removed, or a threatened one averted; to protest strongly against; to regret deeply; to pray against. (L. *deprecatus*, beseeched.)
deprecatingly, *ad.* *dep*-re-*kay*-ting-le, by deprecation.
deprecation, *n.* *dep*-re-*kay*-shon, the act of deprecating; petitioning; a begging pardon for. (L. *dēprecātio*, a begging off.)
deprecative, *a.* *dep*-re-ka-tiv, expressing strong disapproval; deprecatory. (L. *dēprecātivus*.)
deprecator, *n.* *dep*-re-*kay*-tor, one who deprecates.
deprecatory, *a.* *dep*-re-*kay*-to-re, serving to deprecate; in the form of deprecation.
depreciant, *a.* de-*pree*-she-ant, depreciating.
depreciate, *v.t.* de-*pree*-she-ate, to bring down the value of; to undervalue; to disparage; *v.i.* to fall in value. (L. *dēpretiātus*, depreciated.)
depreciation, *n.* de-pree-she-*ay*-shon, the act of bringing down the value, or undervaluing; fall in value; state of being undervalued; allowance for loss in value owing to use and wear.
depreciative, *a.* de-*pree*-she-a-tiv, depreciatory.
depreciator, *n.* de-*pree*-she-ay-tor, one who depreciates. (L.)
depreciatory, *a.* de-*pree*-she-*ay*-to-re, tending to depreciate; undervaluing.
depredate, *v.t.* *dep*-re-date, to plunder or pillage, especially the country of an enemy; to prey upon; to lay waste: *v.i.* to make depredations. (L. *deprædatus*, ravaged.)
depredation, *n.* *dep*-re-*day*-shon, the act of plundering; pillage; robbery. (L. *deprædatio*.)
depredator, *n.* *dep*-re-day-tor, a plunderer; a robber. (L.)
depredatory, *a.* *dep*-re-*day*-to-re, characterized by depredation; plundering.
depress, *v.t.* de-*press*, to press down; to lower; to render gloomy or languid; to sink in altitude; to impoverish; to lower in value; to humble; to cast down or dispirit. **depressed area,** a distressed area. (L. *depressus*, depressed.)
depressant, *a.* de-*press*-ant, lowering vital activity: *n.* a sedative [Med.].
depressible, *a.* de-*press*-e-bl, that may be depressed.
depressingly, *ad.* de-*pres*-sing-le, in a depressing manner.
depression, *n.* de-*presh*-on, the act of depressing; state of being depressed; a hollow; a low state; the act of humbling; a sinking of the spirits; a low state of strength, or of business; the angular

distance of a celestial object below the horizon; the atmospheric condition in which a region of low barometric pressure is at the centre of higher pressures—usually a forerunner of unsettled weather [Meteor.]; couching [Surg.]. **depression of a gun,** the angle at which its axis is inclined below the horizontal. **depression of an equation,** the reduction of the equation to one of lower dimensions [Alg.]. **depression of the pole,** its approach to the horizon, as the spectator recedes from it toward the equator [Astron.]. (L. *depressio.*)

depressive, *a.* de-*pres*-siv, tending to depress.

depressor, *n.* de-*pres*-sor, one who or an appliance that depresses; a muscle that draws down the part to which it is attached; a nerve that when stimulated decreases activity [Anat.].

deprivable, *a.* de-*pry*-va-bl, that may be deprived.

deprivation, *n.* dep-re-*vay*-shon, the act of taking from; a state of being deprived; loss; bereavement; deposition from the clerical order or a benefice in the Church [Law].

deprivative, *a.* de-*pry*-va-tiv, characterized by deprivation; depriving.

deprive, *v.t.* de-*prive*, to take from; to dispossess; to debar from; to bereave; to divest of a dignity or office. (O.Fr. *depriver.*)

depriver, *n.* de-*pry*-ver, he who or that which deprives.

depth, *n.* depth, deepness; the measure of anything downward or inward; limitation of capacity; an abyss; a deep place; the sea or ocean; the middle, as the depth of winter or of a wood; abstruseness; that which is not easily explored, as the depths of metaphysics; immensity; profoundness; extent of penetration; the space from front to rear occupied by a body of troops [Mil.]. **depth of a sail,** the extent of the square sails from the head-rope to the foot-rope [Naut.]. **out of depth,** too deep for the bottom to be reached without diving. (A.S. *dēop*, deep.)

depth-charge, *n.* *depth*-charj, an explosive dropped on a submarine or other object in the sea to destroy it.

depth-gauge, *n.* *depth*-gaje, an instrument for measuring depth, esp. of holes, grooves, etc. [Mech.].

depthless, *a.* *depth*-less, having no depth.

depurate, *v.t.* and *i.* *dee*-pew-rate, to free, or become free, from impurities. (L. *depuratus*, cleansed.)

depuration, *n.* dep-yew-*ray*-shon, the freeing of fluids from impurities; the cleansing of the ducts, etc., or a wound from impure matter [Med.].

depurative, *a.* dee-*pew*-ra-tiv, depurating: *n.* that which depurates.

depuratory, *a.* dep-yew-*ray*-to-re, purifying.

deputation, *n.* dep-yew-*tay*-shon, the act of deputing; a special commission or authority to act; the person or persons deputed to transact business for another; a body of representatives. (Fr. *députation.*)

depute, *v.t.* de-*pewt*, to appoint as a substitute or agent to act for another; to appoint as representative: *n.* a deputy [Scots. Law]. (Fr. *députer.*)

deputize, *v.t.* *dep*-yew-tize, to act in place of another.

deputy, *n.* *dep*-yew-te, a person appointed or deputed to act for another; a representative or delegate; one who exercises an office in another's right [Law]; a member of certain national legislative chambers. (Fr. *député.*)

deracinate, *v.t.* de-*rass*-e-nate, to pluck up by the roots; to extirpate. (Fr. *de-*, and *racine*, a root.)

derail, *v.i.* de-*rale*, to run off the rails: *v.t.* to cause to run off the rails (of railway trains).

derailment, *n.* de-*rale*-ment, the act of derailing or state of being derailed.

derange, *v.t.* de-*raynj*, to put or throw out of order; to disorder, specially in mind. (Fr. *déranger.*)

deranged, *a.* de-*raynjd*, mentally unbalanced; slightly insane.

derangement, *n.* de-*raynj*-ment, a putting out of order; disturbance; disorder of the intellect.

derate, *v.t.* de-*rate*, to free from or reduce liability to rating.

deratization, *n.* dee-rat-eye-*zay*-shun, the systematic clearance of rats from infested places.

Derby, *n.* *dar*-be, a celebrated horse-race founded by the twelfth Earl of Derby in 1780, and run at the Epsom Summer Meeting every year; (*l.c.*) a narrow-rimmed bowler hat [Slang]. **Derbyshire neck,** a variety of goitre. **Derbyshire spa[r]** fluor-spar.

derelict, *a.* *de*-re-likt, left; abandoned: *n.* wreck adrift on the open sea; anything throw[n] away, relinquished, or abandoned by the own[er] [Law]; a tract of land left dry by the sea, and for cultivation or use [Law]: *n.pl.* goods abandon[ed] by the owner found at sea. (L. *derelictus*, aba[n]doned.)

dereliction, *n.* de-re-*lik*-shon, the state of bei[ng] abandoned; neglect (of duty); abandonme[nt] with an intention not to reclaim. (L. *derelictio.*)

derequisition, *v.t.* dee-rek-we-*zish*-on, to cancel t[he] requisition, or the temporary government control, [of]

dereserve, *v.t.* dee-re-*zerv*, to remove from reserved class or status.

deride, *v.t.* de-*ride*, to laugh at scornfully; mock. (L. *derideo*, laugh.)

derider, *n.* de-*ry*-der, a mocker; a scoffer.

deridingly, *ad.* de-*ry*-ding-le, by way of derision.

derision, *n.* de-*rizh*-on, contempt manifested [by] laughter; the act of deriding; ridicule. ([L.] *derisio*, mockery.)

derisive, *a.* de-*ry*-siv, mocking, expressing derisi[on]

derisively, *ad.* de-*ry*-siv-le, with mockery.

derisiveness, *n.* the state of being derisive.

derisory, *a.* de-*ry*-so-re, mocking; ridiculin[g] laughably insufficient.

derivable, *a.* de-*ry*-va-bl, that may be derive[d] deducible.

derivably *ad.* de-*ry*-va-ble, by derivation.

derivate, *n.* *de*-re-vate, a derivative.

derivation, *n.* de-re-*vay*-shon, the act of derivin[g] origin; the process of tracing a word to its roo[t] the old or foreign word from which its past present form was obtained; the process of deduci[ng] one function from another [Math.]; a drawi[ng] of humours from one part of the body to anoth[er] [Med.]; the thing derived or deduced. ([L.] *dērivātio*, a turning off into another course.)

derivational, *a.* relating to derivation.

derivationist, *n.* an evolutionist.

derivative, *a.* de-*riv*-a-tiv, derived; proceedi[ng] from another or something preceding; secondar[y] *n.* that which is derived; a word which takes origin in another word or is formed from it; differential coefficient [Math.]; an invert[ed] chord [Mus.]. **derivative chord,** one deriv[ed] from a fundamental combination [Mus.]. **der[i]vative conveyances,** secondary deeds, such releases, surrenders, or consignments [Law]. ([L.] *dērivātīvus*, derivative.)

derivatively, *ad.* in a derivative manner.

derivativeness, *n.* the state of being derivative.

derive, *v.t.* de-*rive*, to receive by regular tra[ns]mission or conveyance; to receive as from a sourc[e] to trace from; to deduce from a cause or origi[n] to deduce or draw: *v.i.* to come or proceed fro[m] (Fr. *deriver.*)

derm, *n.* derm, the true skin under the cuticle; t[he] skin. (Gr. *derma*, the skin.)

dermal, *a.* *der*-mal, pertaining to or consisting [of] skin; cutaneous.

dermatic, *a.* der-*mat*-ik, dermal.

dermatitis, *n.* der-ma-*ty*-tis, inflammation of t[he] skin; cytitis. (Gk. *derma*, skin.)

dermato-, *comb.f.* *der*-ma-to, pertaining to the sk[in] (Gr. *derma*, the skin.)

dermatogen, *n.* der-*mat*-o-jen, the layer of ce[lls] from which the epidermis of plants is develop[ed] [Bot.].

dermatographia, *n.* der-mat-o-*graf*-e-a, a sensiti[ve] condition in which slight pressure, as by a penc[il] point, gives rise to a reddish weal.

dermatography, *n.* der-ma-*tog*-ra-fe, the anatomic[al] description of the skin.

dermatoid, *a.* *der*-ma-toyd, like skin. (Gr. *derm[a]* and *eidos*, like.)

dermatologist, *n.* a student of dermatology.

dermatology, *n.* der-ma-*tol*-o-je, that departme[nt] of physiological and medical study which trea[ts] of the skin and its diseases. (Gr. *derma*, and *log[os]* science.)

dermatomycosis, *n.* der-mat-o-my-*koh*-sis, a[n] skin disease, as ring-worm, produced by a fungo[id] parasite.

dermatophyte, *n.* der-*mat*-o-fite, fungoid grow[th] under the cuticle causing certain skin diseas[es] [Med.]. (Gr. *derma*, and *phyton*, a plant.)

rmatopsy, *n.* der-ma-*top*-se, the condition of aving a skin that is sensitive to light [Zool.].
rmatorrhœa, *n.* der-ma-to-*ree*-a, a morbid xcess of secretion from the skin. (Gr. *derma*, and *reo*, flow.)
rmic, *a.* *der*-mik, relating to the skin.
rmography, *n.* der-*mog*-ra-fe, dermatography.
rmoskeleton, *n.* der-mo-*skel*-e-ton, the exoxeleton of crustaceans, etc.
rmoid, *a.* *der*-moyd, resembling skin.
rogate, *v.t.* *de*-ro-gate, to take away part; to etract from; to disparage; to invalidate some art of a law or established rule: *v.i.* to detract; lessen by taking away a part. (L. *dērogatus*, etracted from.)
rogately, *ad.* *de*-ro-gate-le, derogatorily.
rogation, *n.* de-ro-*gay*-shon, the act of derogating; the act of taking something from merit, putation, or honour; detraction; disparagement. (L. *dērogātio.*)
rogatorily, *ad.* de-*rog*-a-to-re-le, in a detracting anner.
rogatoriness, *n.* de-*rog*-a-to-re-ness, the quality being derogatory.
rogatory, *a.* de-*rog*-a-to-re, detracting from orth, honour, or validity; degrading. (L. *dērogōrius*, derogatory.)
rrick, *n.* *de*-rik, a crane or similar contrivance r raising heavy weights. (Named from *Derrick*, Tyburn hangman of about 1600, it having some semblance to a gallows.)
rring-do, *n.* *de*-ring-*doo*, heroic intrepidity; ravery; audaciousness. (From "daring to do.")
rringer, *n.* *de*-rin-jer, a short, rifled pistol of rge bore, so called from the inventor [U.S.A.].
rvish, *n.* *der*-vish, a Mohammedan friar, who prosses extreme poverty and leads an austere life; a natical warrior of the Mahdi's Sudanese army. **ancing dervish,** a member of one of the orders of ervishes who dance for the purpose of collecting ms. (Per., poor.)
scant, *n.* *des*-kant, a song composed in parts; a rt song; the soprano in a part-song; the variaon of an air; a discourse or discussion branching to parts; a series of comments; the art of mposing music in several parts, which may be ain, figurative, or double. (L. *discantus*, a song.)
scant, *v.i.* de-*skant*, to discourse at large; to coment freely; to run a division or musical variation th the voice or instrument in true measure lus.].
scanter, *n.* de-*skan*-ter, one who descants.
scend, *v.i.* de-*send*, to come or go down; to enter ; to fall upon or to invade; to proceed from a urce or be derived; to pass from a preceding ssessor according to law of succession; to pass m generals to particulars; to come down from higher to a lower level morally or socially; to ndescend; to pass from sharp to flat [Mus.]; to ove to the southward [Astron.]: *v.t.* to walk, ve, or pass downwards. (L. *dēscendo*, sink **down.**)
scendant, *n.* de-*sen*-dant, one who descends as spring from an ancestor: *a.* descending or king; proceeding from an original or ancestor. *descendens.*)
scender, *n.* de-*sen*-der, that portion of a letter s in "j", "p", etc.) that extends beneath the e; any letter with such portion [Print.].
scendible, *a.* de-*sen*-de-bl, transmissible from an cestor to an heir; capable of being descended.
scension, *n.* de-*sen*-shon, the act of going or ming down; a falling or sinking.
scensional, *a.* de-*sen*-shon-al, pertaining to scent; pertaining to or produced by disintegran [Geol.].
scensive, *a.* de-*sen*-siv, tending to descend.
scent, *n.* de-*sent*, the act of descending; downrd slope; progress downward; fall from a her to a lower state or station; a sudden asion of troops, esp. from the sea; transmission succession or inheritance; origin; birth; a gle degree in the scale of genealogy; descennts; the motion of a body caused by the attracn of gravity [Mech.]; a passing to a lower pitch us.]. (Fr. *descente.*)
scribable, *a.* de-*skribe*-a-bl, that may be described.
scribe, *v.t.* de-*skribe*, to delineate in words; to e an idea of a thing by specifying its nature, form, properties; to mark out or draw, esp. with compasses: *v.i.* to give a description. (L. *describo*, write down.)
descried, *a.* de-*skride*, observed; discovered. (*Descry.*)
description, *n.* de-*skrip*-shon, the delineation of a thing; the figure delineated; the representation or account of a thing by words or images; a class as described; an enumeration of properties or of accidental attributes [Logic]. (L. *dēscriptio*, a description.)
descriptive, *a.* de-*skrip*-tiv, containing description; serving to describe. **descriptive geometry,** that part of mathematical science which consists in the application of geometrical rules to the representation of the figures and the various relations of the forms of bodies.
descriptively, *ad.* de-*skrip*-tiv-le, by description.
descriptiveness, *n.* de-*skrip*-tiv-ness, state of being descriptive.
descry, *v.t.* de-*skry*, to discover by sight something hidden, obscure, or remote; to espy.
desecrate, *v.t.* *des*-se-krate, to divert from a sacred purpose, esp. to a profane purpose; to profane; to deprive of its sacred character. (L. *de-*, and *sacrāre*, to make sacred.)
desecration, *n.* *des*-se-*kray*-shon, the act of desecrating or profaning; profanation.
desensitize, *v.t.* dee-*sen*-se-tize, to render insensitive or less sensitive; to make insensitive to light [Phot.].
desert, *a.* *dez*-ert, uninhabited; waste; desolate: *n.* a barren tract of land; a waste solitude. (O.Fr.)
desert, *v.t.* de-*zert*, to forsake; to leave without permission, in violation of duty; to part from; to withdraw from: *v.i.* to run away from one's post. (Fr. *déserter*, to abandon.)
desert, *n.* de-*zert*, what one deserves either as reward or punishment. (O.Fr. from *deservir*, to merit.)
deserter, *n.* de-*zer*-ter, one who deserts or forsakes a cause, post, party, or friend; a wilful and illegal absentee from one of the armed forces. (L. *desertio*, deserting.)
deserticolous, *a.* *dez*-er-*tik*-o-lus, inhabiting deserts [Zool.].
desertion, *n.* de-*zer*-shon, the act of deserting; the state of being deserted or forsaken; abandonment.
desertless, *a.* de-*zert*-less, without merit; undeserving.
desertless, *a.* *dez*-ert-less, having no desert land.
deserve, *v.t.* de-*zerv*, to merit; to be worthy of; to earn: *v.i.* to be deserving. (O.Fr. *deservir.*)
deservedly, *ad.* de-*zerv*-ed-le, according to desert, whether of good or evil.
deserver, *n.* de-*zerv*-er, one who deserves or merits; one who is worthy of.
deserving, *a.* de-*zerv*-ing, worthy of reward; meritorious.
deservingly, *ad.* de-*zerv*-ing-le, with just desert.
desexualize, *v.t.* de-*seks*-yew-a-lize, to deprive of sexual capacity or characteristics.
deshabille, *a.* dez-a-*beel*, not fully dressed; untidily dressed: *n.* a dressing gown; a loose morning dress. **in deshabille,** not fully dressed. (Fr. *déshabillé*, undressed.)
desiccant, *a.* de-*sik*-ant, drying or tending to dry: *n.* *dess*-e-kant, a substance capable of absorbing moisture; a drying agent. (L. *desiccans*, drying up.)
desiccate, *v.t.* *des*-e-kate, to dry; to exhaust of moisture: *v.i.* to become dry. (L. *dēsiccātus*, dried up.)
desiccation, *n.* *des*-e-*kay*-shon, the process of making dry; the state of being dried.
desiccative, *a.* de-*sik*-a-tiv, tending to dry: *n.* an application which dries up morbid or ulcerous secretions.
desiccator, *n.* *des*-e-kay-tor, a machine or apparatus for absorbing the moisture from substances.
desiderate, *v.t.* de-*sid*-er-rate, to want; to miss; to feel the want of. (L. *dēsiderātus*, desired.)
desideration, *n.* de-sid-er-*ray*-shon, act of desiderating; a desideratum. (L. *dēsiderātio*, a desire for.)
desiderative, *a.* de-*sid*-er-ra-tiv, denoting desire: *n.* an object of desire. (L. *dēsiderātivus*, desideration.)
desideratum, *n.* de-*sid*-er-*ray*-tum (*pl.* **desiderata**), a real or felt want. (L.)
★design, *n.* de-*zine*, an original sketch for proposed

work; plan; a preliminary draft; scheme; project; intention; a pattern, copied from paintings or drawings [Manu.]; the disposition of every part and the general order of the whole [Mus.]: *v.t.* to sketch out; to plan; to formulate; to propose; to contrive; to purpose or intend; to designate. (Fr. *désigner.*)
designable, *a.* de-*zine*-a-bl, capable of being designed.
designate, *a.* *dez*-ig-nate, appointed: *v.t.* to point out; to indicate by lines, marks, or a description; to appoint; to assign; to nominate; to name. (L. *dēsignātus*, appointed.)
designation, *n.* *dez*-ig-*nay*-shon, the act of pointing or marking out; appellation; indication; appointment; assignment; application; description; title.
designative, *a.* *dez*-ig-nay-tiv, serving to indicate.
designator, *n.* *dez*-ig-nay-tor, one who designates; the ancient Roman officer who assigned to each person his place in public shows. (L.)
designatory, *a.* *dez*-ig-nay-to-re, pertaining to a designation or designator; designative.
designed, *pp.* de-*zined*, marked out; delineated.
designedly, *ad.* de-*zine*-ed-le, by design; purposely.
designee, *n.* dez-eye-*nee*, one who is designated.
designer, *n.* de-*zine*-er, one who designs, or plans, or plots; specially one who designs patterns for textiles, wall-papers, dress, furniture, etc.
designful, *a.* de-*zine*-ful, designing; purposeful.
designing, *a.* de-*zine*-ing, given to crafty scheming; insidious; intriguing: *n.* the art of drawing designs or patterns.
designless, *a.* de-*zine*-less, unintentional.
designlessly, *ad.* unintentionally; inadvertently.
desilverization, *n.* dee-*sil*-ver-ry-*zay*-shon, the act or process of desilverizing.
desilverize, *v.t.* dee-*sil*-ver-rize, to extract the silver from, esp. from lead ore.
desinence, *n.* *des*-e-nens, a termination or suffix [Gram.]. (L. *desinens*, ceasing.)
desipience, *n.* de-*sip*-e-ence, childishness; silliness; weakening of intellect.
desipient, *a.* de-*sip*-e-ent, trifling, foolish, or playful. (L. *desipiens*, acting foolishly.)
desirability, *n.* de-*zire*-ra-*bil*-e-te, desirableness.
desirable, *a.* de-*zire*-ra-bl, worthy of desire; that is to be earnestly wished; agreeable: *n.* one who or that which is desirable.
desirableness, *n.* de-*zire*-ra-bl-ness, the quality of being desirable.
desirably, *ad.* de-*zire*-ra-ble, in a desirable manner.
★**desire,** *n.* de-*zire*, an affection of the mind, directed to the obtaining or enjoying of an object; a prayer or request to obtain; the object of desire; love or lust: *v.t.* to crave; to long for the possession or enjoyment of anything; to express a wish to obtain; to long for. (O.Fr. *desirer.*)
desired, *a.* de-*zired*, wished for; coveted.
desireless, *a.* de-*zire*-less, free from desire.
desirer, *n.* de-*zire*-er, one who desires, or who wishes.
desirous, *a.* de-*zire*-us, wishing to obtain; full of desire; solicitous.
desirously, *ad.* with earnest desire.
desirousness, *n.* the state of being desirous.
desist, *v.i.* de-*zist*, to leave off; to stop, forbear, or discontinue. (L. *desisto*, stand.)
desistance, *n.* de-*zis*-tance, the action of leaving off; cessation; desisting.
desition, *n.* de-*sizh*-on, ceasing to exist; conclusion; an ending.
desk, *n.* desk, a table, board, or box, usually sloping, for writing on or for reading from; the place from which prayers are read; the pulpit in a church [U.S.A.]. (Late L. *desca*, from L. *discus*, a disk.)
desman, *n.* *des*-man, the Russian musk-rat, *Desmana moschata*; an aquatic insectivore allied to the shrews and moles. (Swed., musk.)
desmid, *n.* *des*-mid, one of the single-celled freshwater algæ. (Gr. *desmos*, band.)
desmine, *n.* *des*-min, a mineral that crystallizes in little silken tufts, found in the lavas of extinct volcanoes; stilbite. (Gr. *desmos*, a ligament.)
desmography, *n.* des-*mog*-ra-fe, a description of the ligaments of the body. (Gr. *desmos*, a ligament, and *grapho*, write.)
desmoid, *a.* *des*-moyd, arranged in tufts; like a ligament [Anat.].
desmology, *n.* des-*mol*-o-je, the scientific anatomy of ligaments and sinews. (Gr. *desmos*, and *logo*[s,] science.)
desmotomy, *n.* des-*mot*-o-me, the practical anatom[y] of ligaments and sinews; the cutting or dissecti[on] of a ligament. (Gr. *desmos*, and *tome*, cutting.)
desolate, *a.* *dess*-o-lat, destitute of inhabitant[s;] laid waste; solitary; deserted; miserable: *v*[.t.] *des*-o-late, to deprive of inhabitants; to lay wast[e;] to render forlorn or miserable. (L. *dēsōlātu*[s,] deserted.)
desolately, *ad.* *dess*-o-lat-le, in a desolate manner.
desolateness, *n.* a state of being desolate.
desolation, *n.* *dess*-o-*lay*-shon, the act of desola[t]ing; the state of being desolated; a desolate ruinous state. (L. *dēsōlātio*, desolation.)
desorption, *n.* dee-*sorp*-shon, the removal of substance from a state of absorption [Chem.].
despair, *n.* de-*spare*, hopelessness; despondenc[e;] that which causes despair: *v.i.* to be witho[ut] hope; to give up all hope. (L. *dēspēro*, give [up] hope.)
despairer, *n.* de-spare-rer, one who despairs.
despairing, *a.* de-*spare*-ring, giving way to despa[ir;] expressing despair; hopeless.
despairingly, *ad.* in a despairing manner.
despatch, *n.* de-*spatch*. *See* **dispatch.**
desperado, *n.* des-per-*ray*-do, a desperate ruff[ian] ready for crime; one urged on by some furi[ous] passion reckless of consequences. (Sp.)
desperate, *a.* *des*-per-rat, fearless of dang[er;] furious; headlong; without hope; hopele[ss;] lost or almost lost; beyond hope of recover[y;] done in despair; great in the extreme: *ad.* [ex]tremely, awfully [Coll.]. (L. *desperātus*, given u[p.])
desperately, *ad.* in a desperate manner; recklessl[y;] irretrievably.
desperateness, *n.* the state of being beyond ho[pe;] desperation.
desperation, *n.* des-per-*ray*-shon, a state of despa[ir;] fury or disregard of danger; recklessness due [to] despair. (L. *dēspērātio*, despair.)
despicable, *a.* *des*-pe-ka-bl, that deserves to [be] despised; contemptible, mean, vile, or worthle[ss.] (L. *dēspicābilis*, despicable.)
despicableness, *n.* *des*-pe-ka-bl-ness, the qual[ity] or state of being despicable.
despicably, *ad.* *des*-pe-ka-ble, meanly; c[on]temptibly.
despisable, *a.* de-*spy*-za-bl, to be treated w[ith] contempt; despicable; contemptible.
despisal, *n.* de-*spy*-zal, the act of despising; c[on]tempt.
despise, *v.i.* de-*spize*, to look down upon; to h[old] in contempt; to disdain; to scorn. (O.[Fr.] *despiser.*)
despisedness, *n.* de-*spy*-zed-ness, the state of be[ing] despised.
despiser, *n.* de-*spy*-zer, a contemner; a scorner.
despisingly, *ad.* de-*spy*-zing-le, with contempt.
despite, *n.* de-*spite*, extreme malice; defia[nce] with contempt; an act of malice or contem[pt:] *v.t.* to vex, offend, or tease: *prep.* in spite [of:] **despite of,** notwithstanding. (O.Fr. *despit.*)
despiteful, *a.* de-*spite*-ful, full of spite; ma[lig]nant.
despitefully, *ad.* de-*spite*-ful-le, with despite.
despitefulness, *n.* de-*spite*-ful-ness, the state [of] being despiteful.
despiteous, *a* de-*spit*-e-us. *See* **dispiteous.**
despoil, *v.t.* de-*spoyl*, to strip by force; to r[ob;] to deprive or bereave by any means. (O[.Fr.] *despoiller.*)
despoiler, *n.* de-*spoyl*-er, a plunderer.
despoilment, *n.* de-*spoyl*-ment, despoliation.
despoliation, *n.* de-spoh-le-*ay*-shon, the act [of] despoiling; a stripping or plundering.
despond, *v.i.* de-*spond*, to become dispirited f[rom] loss of hope or in presence of difficulty seemin[g] insuperable; to lose hope. (L. *despondeo.*)
despondence, *n.* de-*spon*-dence, the act of despo[nd]ing; despondency.
despondency, *n.* de-*spon*-den-se, a despond[ent] state of mind; dejection of spirit.
despondent, *a.* de-*spon*-dent, desponding; [de]jected in spirit.
despondently, *ad.* in a despondent manner.
despondingly, *ad.* de-*spon*-ding-le, in a despond[ent] manner.
despot, *n.* *des*-pot, a ruler or ruling body exerci[s]

or invested with absolute power in a state, irrespective of the wishes of the governed; a dictator; a tyrant. (Gr. *despotes*, a master.)

despotic, *a.* de-*spot*-ik, absolute; independent of control; arbitrary; dictatorial; tyrannical.

despotically, *ad.* de-*spot*-e-ka-le, in a despotic manner.

despotism, *n.* *des*-po-tizm, the power or principles of a despot; the government of a despot; absolute power; absolute or arbitrary government; tyranny.

despumate, *v.i.* de-*spew*-mate, to throw off impurities in froth or scum: *v.t.* to skim the scum from; to clarify by taking off the scum. (L. *despumatus*, skimmed.)

despumation, *n.* des-pew-*may*-shon, the act of throwing off froth or scum on the surface; the separation of impurities from a fluid. (L. *despumatio*, a skimming off.)

desquamate, *v.i.* *des*-kwa-mate, to peel off in scales: *v.t.* to scale [Surg.]. (L. *desquamatus*, scaled.)

desquamation, *n.* des-kwa-*may*-shon, a scaling or exfoliation of bone; the separation of the cuticle in small scales.

desquamatory, *a.* des-*kwam*-a-to-re, marked by desquamation.

dessert, *n.* de-*zert*, a service of fruit and confections, when the substantial part of a meal is removed. **dessert service,** the dishes and plates used for dessert. **dessert spoon,** a spoon intermediate in size between a tablespoon and a teaspoon. **dessert spoonful,** the quarter of a fluid ounce. (Fr., from *desservir*, to remove the cloth.)

destemper, *n.* des-*tem*-per, distemper (the disease in dogs).

destinate, *a.* *des*-te-nat, appointed; destined; determined: *v.t.* *des*-te-nate, to design or appoint.

destination, *n.* des-te-*nay*-shon, the act of destining or appointing; the purpose for which a thing is intended or appointed; the place to which a thing is appointed; the place assigned as the end of a journey. (L. *destinatio*.)

destine, *v.t.* *des*-tin, to ordain or appoint to a use, purpose, state, or place; to fix or appoint unalterably; to devote or doom. (O.Fr. *destiner*.)

destinism, *n.* des-te-nizm, fatalism.

destinist, *n.* *des*-te-nist, a fatalist; a believer in destiny.

destiny, *n.* *des*-te-ne, that to which a person or thing is preappointed; fate, fortune, or doom; the immutable power by which events are so ordered that they cannot possibly happen otherwise; invincible necessity. **Destinies,** the Fates, or the supposed powers which apportion, spin out, and bring to a close our lives. (Fr. *destinée*.)

destitute, *a.* *des*-te-tewt, not having or possessing; wanting; left in want; in great poverty. (L. *dēstitūtus*, abandoned.)

destitution, *n.* des-te-*tew*-shon, the state of being destitute; want of necessaries; poverty; deprivation. (L. *dēstitūtio*.)

destrier, *n.* *des*-tre-er, a charger; originally a spare war-horse, led on the knight's right hand. (O.Fr. from L. *dextra*, right hand.)

destroy, *v.t.* de-*stroy*, to pull down or demolish, so that as a structure it no longer exists; to ruin or annihilate by demolishing or burning; to overthrow and put an end to; to lay waste; to slay; to extirpate; to disprove. (O.Fr. *destruire*.)

destroyable, *a.* de-*stroy*-a-bl, that may be destroyed.

destroyer, *n.* de-*stroy*-er, one who or that which destroys; a small warship of great speed armed with light guns and torpedo tubes. (Originally a torpedo-boat-destroyer.)

destructibility, *n.* de-*struk*-te-*bil*-e-te, the being capable of destruction; liability to destruction.

destructible, *a.* de-*struk*-te-bl, liable to destruction; capable of being destroyed. (L. *dēstructibilis*, destructible.)

destruction, *n.* de-*struk*-shon, the act of destroying; state of being destroyed; that which destroys; ruin, by whatever means; death; slaughter. (L. *dēstructio*.)

destructional, *a.* de-*struk*-shon-al, pertaining to, or resulting from, destruction.

destructionist, *n.* de-*struk*-shon-ist, a destructive; one who believes that the final punishment of the wicked will be their annihilation [Theol.].

destructive, *a.* de-*struk*-tiv, causing destruction; given to destroy; mischievous; ruinous; negative, as opposed to constructive: *n.* one in favour of destruction, esp. of existing constitutions or institutions; a radical reformer. **destructive distillation,** the process of decomposing organic substances in retorts at a high temperature, and obtaining from them useful products having different properties, as gas from coal so treated. (L. *dēstructivus*.)

destructively, *ad.* de-*struk*-tiv-le, with destruction.

destructiveness, *n.* de-*struk*-tiv-ness, the quality of destroying or ruining.

destructivity, *n.* dee-struk-*tiv*-e-te, destructiveness.

destructor, *n.* de-*struk*-tor, a furnace for destroying refuse.

desudation, *n.* dee-sew-*day*-shon, a profuse or morbid sweating. (L. *dēsūdātio*, a violent sweating.)

desuetude, *n.* *des*-we-tewd, disuse; discontinuance of practice, custom, or fashion. (L. *dēsuētūdo*, disuse.)

desulphurate, *v.t.* dee-*sul*-fu-rate, to desulphurize.

desulphurization, *n.* dee-*sul*-fu-ry-*zay*-shon, the operation of depriving of sulphur.

desulphurize, *v.t.* dee-*sul*-fu-rize, to deprive of sulphur.

desultorily, *ad.* *dess*-ul-to-re-le, in a desultory manner.

desultoriness, *n.* *dess*-ul-to-re-ness, a desultory manner; unconnectedness.

desultory, *a.* *dess*-ul-to-re, rambling from one thing to another without order or connection; disjointed; unconnected; coming or occurring abruptly and suddenly. (L. *dēsultōrius*, relating to a *desultor*, a rider in the circus.)

desynonymize, *v.t.* dee-se-*non*-e-mize, to impart to synonyms, by a specific use made of them, a shade of difference in the meaning, as between wave and billow, originally synonyms.

detach, *v.t.* de-*tatch*, to separate or disengage; to remove anything attached; to separate men from their regiments, ships from a fleet, or aeroplanes from a squadron, and send them on a separate service. (Fr. *détacher*.)

detachable, *a.* de-*tatch*-a-bl, that may be detached.

detached, *pp.* de-*tatcht*, isolated; unattached; said of houses standing by themselves, and of figures so standing out from the background and each other as to show a space or atmosphere between them [Painting].

detachedness, *n.* de-*tatch*-ed-ness, the state of being detached.

detachment, *n.* de-*tatch*-ment, the act of detaching; a body of troops or a number of ships or aeroplanes detached from the main body and sent on a special expedition or separate service; aloofness; independence. (Fr. *détachement*.)

detail, *v.t.* de-*tale*, to relate or go over minutely; to select for a particular service [Mil., etc.].

★**detail,** *n.* *dee*-tale, an item; a minute account or report of particulars; one or a body selected for a particular service [Mil.]: *pl.* the minor parts of a composition to give verisimilitude and finish to it [Fine Arts]. **in detail,** part by part. (Fr. *détail*.)

detailed, *a.* de-*taled*, minutely related; exact.

detailer, *n.* de-*tale*-er, one who details.

detain, *v.t.* de-*tane*, to keep back or from; to withhold; to delay; to hold in custody. (O.Fr. *detinir*.)

detainee, *n.* dee-tay-*nee*, one lawfully detained, esp. for preventive purposes; an internee.

detainer, *n.* de-*tane*-er, one who withholds what belongs to another; a holding or keeping possession of what belongs to another [Law]; the holding of a person in custody; a writ of detainer, *i.e.* a writ lying against prisoners in custody in order that they may be detained till discharged [Law].

detainment, *n.* de-*tane*-ment, the act of detaining; detention [Law].

detect, *v.t.* de-*tekt*, to discover or find out; to bring to light; to rectify by means of a detector [Wire.]. (L. *dētectus*, exposed.)

detectable, *a.* de-*tek*-ta-bl, that may be detected.

detecter, *n.* de-*tek*-ter, a discoverer; one who finds out what another attempts to conceal; an indicator.

detection, *n.* de-*tek*-shon, the act of detecting; discovery of a purposely hidden person or something before unknown; the work of a detective;

rectification by a detector [Wire.]; demodulation [Wire.]. (L. *dētectio.*)
detective, *a.* de-*tek*-tiv, employed in detecting, esp. against those suspected of crime: *n.* one employed in the detection of crime, esp. a police officer; one who deduces theories from police cases. **detective story,** a story built up from an imaginary crime. **private detective,** a professional unattached to a police force who makes special inquiries.
detectophone, *n.* de-*tek*-to-fone, an instrument for attachment to a telephone system to enable private conversations to be overheard.
detector, *n.* de-*tek*-tor, a detecter; an electrical instrument for detecting wireless waves; a device for rectifying high-frequency oscillations.
detent, *n.* de-*tent*, a catch in a machine; a stop in a clock, which, by being lifted up or let down, locks or unlocks the clock in striking. (L. *dētentus*, held back.)
détente, *n.* (App.), the relaxation of strained international relations.
detention, *n.* de-*ten*-shon, the act of detaining; the state of being detained; confinement; restraint; delay. (L. *dētentio.*)
détenu, *n.* (App.), one who is detained, esp. a political prisoner.
deter, *v.t.* de-*ter*, to frighten from acting or proceeding; to prevent; to hinder. (L. *deterrere*, frighten.)
deterge, *v.t.* de-*terj*, to wipe or cleanse away, esp. foul matter from a wound. (L. *dētergēre*, wipe.)
detergency, *n.* de-*ter*-jen-se, purging or cleansing quality.
detergent, *a.* de-*ter*-jent, cleansing; purging: *n.* a cleansing agent or medicine; a solvent; a soap.
deteriorate, *v.i.* de-*teer*-re-o-rate, to grow worse; to degenerate: *v.t.* to make worse. (L. *dēteriōrātus*, made worse.)
deterioration, *n.* de-*teer*-re-o-*ray*-shon, a growing or making worse; the state of growing worse.
deteriorative, *a.* de-*teer*-re-o-ra-tiv, causing deterioration; tending to deteriorate.
deteriorationist, *n.* de-teer-re-o-*ray*-shon-ist, one holding the doctrine of deteriorism.
deteriorism, *n.* de-*teer*-re-o-rizm, the doctrine that the gradual deterioration of the human race is inevitable (opposed to meliorism).
determent, *n.* de-*ter*-ment, the act of deterring; that which deters.
determinability, *n.* de-*ter*-me-na-*bil*-e-te, quality of being determinable. (L. *dēterminābilis*, finite.)
determinable, *a.* de-*ter*-me-na-bl, that may be decided with certainty; clearly definable; terminable. **determinable freehold,** an estate for life which may determine upon future contingencies before the life for which it is created expires [Law].
determinant, *a.* de-*ter*-me-nant, determinative; decisive; pertaining to a determinant [Math.]: *n.* one who or that which serves to determine; a special kind of algebraic expression involving a square number of elements or quantities used as an instrument of classification, esp. in dealing with equations, etc. [Math.]; a qualifying phrase or adjective [Logic]. (L. *dēterminans*, limiting.)
determinantal, *a.* de-ter-me-*nan*-tal, pertaining to determinants [Math.].
determinate, *a.* de-*ter*-me-nat, limited or definite; settled or positive; determined; resolute. **determinate problem,** a problem which admits of one solution only, or of a limited number of solutions [Math.]. (L. *dēterminātus*, limited.)
determinately, *ad.* de-*ter*-me-nat-le, with certainty; resolutely.
determinateness, *n.* de-*ter*-me-nat-ness, the state of being determinate, certain, or precise.
determination, *n.* de-*ter*-me-*nay*-shon, the act of determining or deciding; that which is determined or resolved on; firm resolution; settlement by a judicial decision; direction to a certain end; a putting an end to; decision of character; ascertainment of amount [Chem.]; definition [Logic]; the reference of a specimen to its species. (L. *dēterminatio*, an end.)
determinative, *a.* de-*ter*-me-na-tiv, that directs to a certain end; that limits or bounds; that is employed in determining: *n.* one who or that which serves to determine, define, or decide; a demonstrative pronoun [Gram.].
determinator, *n.* de-*ter*-me-nay-tor, one who or that which determines. (L.)
determine, *v.t.* de-*ter*-min, to fix; to settle by mental or judicial decision; to fix on; to limit or bound; to give a direction to or influence the choice; to resolve; to put an end to; to settle or ascertain; to define: *v.i.* to decide; to end. (O.Fr. *determiner.*)
determined, *a.* de-*ter*-mind, having a firm purpose; manifesting a firm resolution; definite; resolute.
determinedly, *ad.* in a determined manner.
determinism, *n.* de-*ter*-me-nizm, the doctrine that human action is determined by motives which are the result of external forces influencing the will, which is therefore not a free agent.
determinist, *a.* de-*ter*-me-nist, relating to determinism: *n.* one who maintains the determinist doctrine.
deterministic, *a.* de-*ter*-me-*nis*-tik, pertaining to determinism.
deterrence, *n.* de-*te*-rence, determent; a deterrent; the act of deterring.
deterrent, *a.* de-*te*-rent, deterring: *n.* that which deters. (L. *deterrens*, frightening.)
detersion, *n.* de-*ter*-shon, the act of cleansing, as a sore. (L. *detersus*, cleansed.)
detersive, *a.* de-*ter*-siv, having power to cleanse away, esp. foul matter from a sore: *n.* a cleansing agent; a detersive or purging medicine.
detersiveness, *n.* the quality of being detersive.
detest, *v.t.* de-*test*, to hate intensely; to abhor. (Fr. *détester.*)
detestability, *n.* de-*tes* ta-*bil*-e-te, detestableness.
detestable, *a.* de-*tes*-ta-bl, extremely hateful; abominable.
detestableness, *n.* de-*tes*-ta-bl-ness, the quality of being detestable; extreme hatefulness.
detestably, *ad.* de-*tes*-ta-ble, very hatefully; abominably. (L. *dētestābilis*, execrable.)
detestation, *n.* dee-tes-*tay*-shon, extreme hatred; abhorrence; loathing. (L. *dētestātio*, cursing.)
detested, *pp.* and *a.* de-*tes*-ted, hated extremely; abhorred.
detester, *n.* de-*tes*-ter, one who hates.
dethrone, *v.t.* de-*throne*, to remove from a throne; to depose; to divest of royal authority or of rule.
dethronement, *n.* de-*throne*-ment, the act of dethroning; removal from a throne; deposition of a king or ruler.
dethroner, *n.* de-*throne*-er, one who dethrones.
detinue, *n.* *det*-e-new, unlawful detention [Law]. **writ of detinue,** a writ against one who wrongfully detains goods or chattels delivered to him or in his possession [Law]. (Fr. *détenu*, detained.)
detonable, *a.* *det*-on-abl, capable of detonation.
detonate, *v.t.* *det*-o-nate, to cause to explode; to cause to burst with a sudden report: *v.i.* to explode; to burst with a sudden report. (L. *dētonātus*, thundered.)
detonating, *a.* *det*-o-nay-ting, exploding; inflaming with a sudden report. **detonating powder** a compound which detonates when struck or heated owing to the expansion into a gaseous form of substance in it [Chem.]. **detonating tube,** a graduated glass tube for the detonation of gaseous bodies by means of electricity; a sudiometer.
detonation, *n.* *det*-o-*nay*-shon, the act of detonating; an explosion caused by instantaneous combustion; the noise caused by an explosion.
detonative, *a.* *det*-o-na-tiv, able to detonate; explosive; causing detonation.
detonator, *n.* *det*-o-nay-tor, any contrivance that explodes an explosive, as a percussion cap; a railway fog-signal; a primer.
detorsion, *n.* de-*tawr*-shon, detortion.
detortion, *n.* de-*tawr*-shon, the act of wresting perversion. (L. *dētorsus*, turned aside.)
detour, *n.* day-*toor*, a circuitous or roundabout way; deviation. (Fr. *détour.*)
detoxicate, *v.t.* dee-*tok*-se-kate, to deprive of poison or of poisonous effect.
detract, *v.t.* de-*trakt*, to take away from reputation or merit; to derogate from; to take away; to depreciate: *v.i.* to take away; to lessen reputation (L. *dētractus*, taken down.)
detractingly, *ad.* de-*trak*-ting-le, in a detracting manner.
detraction, *n.* de-*trak*-shon, the act of taking something from the merit or worth of another

from envy or malice, with a view to injure his reputation; depreciation; calumny. (L. *dētractio.*)

detractious, *a.* de-*trak*-shus, containing detraction; lessening reputation.

detractive, *a.* de-*trak*-tiv, having the quality or tendency to lessen the worth or estimation.

detractiveness, *n.* de-*trak*-tiv-ness, the quality of being detractive.

detractor, *n.* de-*trak*-tor, a slanderer.

detractory, *a.* de-*trak*-to-re, depreciatory; defamatory.

detrain, *v.t.* de-*trane*, to remove from a railway train: *v.i.* to alight from a train.

detriment, *n.* *det*-re-ment, loss, damage, hurt, or mischief. (O.Fr. *detriment.*)

detrimental, *a.* det-re-*men*-tal, causing loss or damage; injurious: *n.* one who or that which is detrimental; an undesirable suitor [Slang].

detrimentally, *ad.* in a detrimental manner.

detrimentalness, *n.* det-re-*ment*-al-ness, the quality of being detrimental.

detrital, *a.* de-*try*-tal, pertaining to or consisting of detritus.

detrited, *pp.* de-*try*-ted, worn down; disintegrated [Geol.].

detrition, *n.* de-*trish*-on, a wearing off or away by rubbing.

detritus, *n.* de-*try*-tus, waste rubbed off; accumulations formed by the disintegrated material of rocks [Geol.]; any matter produced by disintegration. (L.)

detrude, *v.t.* de-*trood*, to thrust or force down; to expel forcibly. (L. *dētrūdere*, thrust.)

detruncate, *v.t.* de-*trung*-kate, to cut off; to lop; to shorten by cutting. (L. *detruncatus*, lopped off.)

detruncation, *n.* dee-trung-*kay*-shon, the act of cutting off; the state of being cut short.

detrusion, *n.* de-*troo*-zhon, the act of detruding. (L. *detrusio*, a thrusting down.)

detrusor, *n.* de-*troo*-zor, a muscle (esp. of the bladder) causing expulsion by contraction [Anat.].

detumescence, *n.* dee-tew-*mes*-sence, the diminution of a swelling. (L. *dētumesco*, subside.)

detune, *v.t.* dee-*tewn*, to put out of tune or resonance by slightly changing the wave-length [Wire.].

deuce, *n.* dewce, two; a card or a die with two spots; the score at tennis (forty all) when two winning strokes in succession are required to decide the game. (Fr. *deux*, two.)

deuce, *n.* dewce, the evil one; mischief.

deuce-ace, *n.* *dewce*-ace, the two and one thrown simultaneously at dice; hence, bad luck.

deuced, *a.* *dewce*-ed, devilish; confounded.

deucedly, *ad.* confoundedly; excessively.

deut-, deuter-, *pref.* forms of *deutero-*.

deuteragonist, *n.* *dew*-ter-*rag*-o-nist, the second character in importance in a stage-play; the second to the protagonist in Greek drama.

deuterium, *n.* dew-*teer*-re-um, heavy hydrogen, the second isotope of hydrogen, discovered 1932. **deuterium oxide,** heavy water; water from which all hydrogen of the first isotope has been extracted.

deutero-, *pref.* *dew*-ter-ro, signifying second, secondary, or subsidiary. (Gr. *deuteros*, second.)

deuterocanonical, *a.* *dew*-ter-ro-ka-*non*-e-kal, applied to the books of Scripture received into the canon after the rest. (Gr. *deuteros*, second, and *canonical.*)

deuterogamist, *n.* dew-ter-*rog*-a-mist, one who marries a second time after the death of the spouse.

deuterogamy, *n.* dew-ter-*rog*-a-me, the marriage of a widow or widower after the death of the first husband or wife; digamy. (Gr. *deuteros*, and *gamos*, marriage.)

deuterogenous, *a.* dew-ter-*roj*-e-nus, of secondary origin.

deuteron, *n.* *dew*-ter-ron, the nucleus of the deuterium atom.

Deuteronomist, *n.* *dew*-ter-*ron*-o-mist, the author, or one of the authors, of Deuteronomy.

Deuteronomy, *n.* dew-ter-*ron*-o-me, the fifth book of the Pentateuch, so called as the second giving of the law. (Gr. *deuteronomion*, the repeated or second enunciation of the law.)

deuteropathic, *a.* dew-ter-ro-*path*-ik, pertaining to deuteropathy.

deuteropathy, *n.* dew-ter-*rop*-a-the, a sympathetic affection of one part of the body with another, as headache from an overloaded stomach. (Gr. *deuteros*, and *pathos*, disease.)

deuteroscopy, *n.* dew-ter-*ros*-ko-pe, the second intention; the meaning beyond the literal sense; second sight. (Gr. *deuteros*, and *skopeo*, view.)

deuto-, *pref.* *dew*-to, a form of *deutero-*.

deutoplasm, *n.* *dew*-to-plazm, the food of protoplasm; the part of the yolk that nourishes the protoplasmic embryo.

deutoplasmic, *a.* dew-to-*plaz*-mik, pertaining to deutoplasm.

deutoxide, *n.* dew-*tok*-side, a compound of two atoms or equivalents of oxygen with one of some base [Chem.].

Deutsch, *n.* doytch, the German language.

Deutzia, *n.* *doyt*-ze-a, a genus of ornamental shrubs of the hydrangea family, native to the Himalayas, the Far East, and Central America. (Jan *Deutz*, Dutch botanist.)

devacuee, *n.* *dee*-vak-yew-*ee*, a returned evacuee.

devalorize, *v.t.* de-*val*-o-rize, to devalue.

devaluate, *v.t.* de-*val*-yew-ate, to lower or extinguish the value of.

devaluation, *n.* de-*val*-yew-*ay*-shon, the act of devaluing; intentional depreciation of the accepted value.

devalue, *v.t.* dee-*val*-yew, to reduce the value of; to stabilize a currency at a rate lower than that previously in force [Econ.].

Devanagari, *n.* day-va-*nah*-ga-re, the Sanskrit alphabet, also called Nagari. (Sans.)

devaporation, *n.* de-vap-o-*ray*-shon, the change of vapour into water, as in the formation of rain.

devastate, *v.t.* *dev*-as-tate, to lay waste; to ravage. (L. *devastatus*, laid waste.)

devastation, *n.* dev-as-*tay*-shon, the act of devastating; the state of being devastated; waste, desolation, or ruin; waste of the goods of the deceased by an executor or administrator [Law].

devastavit, *n.* de-vas-*tay*-vit, waste of property by an executor; a writ issued against an executor for this offence [Law]. (L., he has wasted.)

develop, *v.t.* de-*vel*-op, to unfold and open up by degrees; to bring out into distinctness; to make a photographic negative visible; to enable to evolve what is latent or in embryo: *v.i.* to evolve by natural stages; to be evolved; to come distinctly out; to advance in structure. (Fr. *développer.*)

developable, *a.* capable of development.

developer, *n.* de-*vel*-op-er, he who or that which develops the chemical used in developing photographic negatives; an appliance for developing one's physical fitness.

★**development,** *n.* de-*vel*-op-ment, a gradual unfolding and exhibition of something previously hidden or involved; gradual growth; the series of changes in the growth from first to last of an organized being; the process of bringing the features of a picture into distinctness [Phot.]. **doctrine of development,** Lamarck's theory ascribing an innate expansive power to the organized universe, and tracing the most complex forms by intermediate links from the simplest, without the intervention of special acts of creation [Biol.].

developmental, *a.* de-*vel*-op-*men*-tal, pertaining to development.

developmentally, *ad.* in course of development.

devest, *v.t.* de-*vest*, to divest; to strip; to alienate [Law]: *v.i.* to be lost or alienated, as a title or an estate [Law]. (L. *devestio*, undress.)

deviate, *v.i.* *dee*-ve-ate, to turn aside from the way; to stray or swerve from the path of duty; to err: *v.t.* to cause to turn aside. (L. *deviatus*, turned away.)

deviation, *n.* dee-ve-*ay*-shon, a turning aside from the way, or direction, or the path of duty; error; deflection; the voluntary departure of a ship without necessity from the regular and usual course of the specific voyage insured [Comm.]. **deviation of the compass,** the deflection of the needle from the magnetic meridian due to external causes, such as iron in the ship's structure or cargo, or in rocks within the range of influence. **deviation of a falling body,** the deviation from the perpendicular of a falling body due to the rotation of the earth.

deviationist, *n.* *dee*-ve-*ay*-shon-ist, one (esp. a Communist) who diverges from orthodox principles, etc.

deviative, *a.* *dee*-ve-ay-tiv, causing deviation; tending to deviate.
device, *n.* de-*vice*, a plan, scheme, or stratagem devised or contrived, sometimes with good, usually with evil, intent; an emblem intended to represent a family, person, action, or quality, with a suitable motto, used in painting, sculpture, and heraldry; a motto used as an emblem; anything fancifully and cunningly contrived; invention; genius; faculty of devising. (O.Fr. *devise.*)
deviceful, *a.* de-*vice*-ful, full of devices; inventive.
devil, *n.* *dev*-il, Satan, the evil one; the personification of evil; one animated and possessed by the devil; great dash or energy, or a person possessing this; any great evil considered humorously; a night-watchman's fire-basket; a kind of firework; a multiple fishing-tackle; ruin; a false god; a barrister who prepares cases for another; an author who writes for another; a printer's errand-boy; a grilled dish highly seasoned; a rag-tearing machine; the Tasmanian devil: *v.t.* to cut up rags or cloth in a machine called the devil; to grill with hot seasoning: *v.i.* to do anonymous legal or literary work for another. **devil's advocate,** the official objector to a claim for canonization. **devil's bedpost,** the four of clubs. **devil's bit,** a blue scabious, *S. succisa.* **devil's bones,** dice. **devil's books,** playing cards. **devil's coach-horse,** the large rove-beetle, *Ocypus olens.* **devil's dirt,** asafœtida. **devil's dust,** old woollen materials made into shoddy. **devil's tattoo,** drumming with the fingers. **give the devil his due,** to credit him or his servant with the good he does. **play the devil with,** to harm and worry; to fritter away. (A.S. *deōful.*)
devil-devil, *n.* *dev*-il-*dev*-il, *Sarcophilus ursinus,* the Tasmanian devil.
devildom, *n.* *dev*-il-dom, the realm or power of Satan; diabolic influence.
devilet, *n.* *dev*-e-let, a little devil.
devil-fish, *n.* *dev*-il-fish, a gigantic ray of the family *Mobulidæ.*
deviling, *n.* *dev*-il-ing, a little devil; an imp.
devilish, *a.* *dev*-il-ish, partaking of the qualities of the devil; very evil and mischievous; excessive; enormous.
devilishly, *ad.* *dev*-il-ish-le, in a manner that is devilish; excessively.
devilishness, *n.* devilish qualities.
devilism, *n.* *dev*-il-izm, devil-worship; devilish practice; great wickedness.
devilkin, *n.* *dev*-il-kin, a little devil.
devilled, *a.* *dev*-ild, grilled and highly seasoned [Cookery].
devil-may-care, *a.* *dev*-il-may-*kare*, reckless, rollicking [Slang].
devilment, *n.* *dev*-il-ment, mischief; love of mischief.
devilry, *n.* *dev*-il-re, devilment; cruel mischief.
deviltry, *n.* dev-il-tre, devilry; diabolical conduct.
devil-worship, *n.* *dev*-il-wur-ship, homage paid by primitive tribes to the spirit of evil, in the belief this would save them from mischief.
devious, *a.* *dee*-ve-us, off the common way or track; rambling; erring. (L., turning aside.)
deviously, *ad.* *dee*-ve-us-le, in a devious manner.
deviousness, *n.* *dee*-ve-us-ness, departure from a regular course.
devisable, *a.* de-*vize*-a-bl, that may be devised or bequeathed; that may be contrived.
devisal, *n.* de-*vy*-zal, a devising.
devise, *n.* de-*vize*, the act of giving or distributing real estate by a testator; a will; a share of estate bequeathed: *v.i.* to consider: *v.t.* to contrive; to form in the mind; to scheme; to bequeath real estate by will. (O.Fr. *deviser.*)
devisee, *n.* dev-eye-*zee*, the person to whom a devise is made; one to whom real estate is bequeathed.
deviser, *n.* de-*vy*-zer, one who contrives or invents.
devisor, *n.* de-*vy*-zor, a testator.
devitalize, *v.t.* de-*vy*-ta-lize, to deprive of vitality.
devitaminize, *v.t.* dee-*vy*-ta-me-nize, to deprive of vitamins.
devitrification, *n.* de-*vit*-re-fe-*kay*-shon, the act or process of devitrifying; the conversion of glass, esp. during manufacture, into an opaque crystalline mass; deferred crystallization [Geol.].
devitrify, *v.t.* de-*vit*-re-fy, to render glass opaque.
devocalize, *v.t.* dee-*voh*-ka-lize, to deprive of vocal quality [Phon.].
devoice, *v.t.* dee-*voyce*, to devocalize [Phon.].
devoid, *a.* de-*voyd*, vacant; destitute. (O.Fr. *desvuidier*, to empty.)
devoir, *n.* *dev*-wahr, duty; best endeavour; an act of civility or respect due to another. (Fr.)
devolute, *v.t.* *dev*-o-lewt, to transfer (esp. authority); to depute; to devolve.
devolution, *n.* dev-o-*lew*-shon, delegation of authority, esp. the transference of legislative power from parliament to other bodies; a passing by inheritance or in natural succession; decentralization; degeneration of species [Biol.].
devolutionary, *a.* dev-o-*lew*-shon-a-re, pertaining to devolution.
devolve, *v.t.* de-*volv*, to transfer; to deliver over; to hand down: *v.i.* to be transferred or passed from one to another; to fall by succession. (L. *devolvo*, roll down.)
Devonian, *a.* de-*voh*-ne-an, pertaining to Devonshire: *n.* a native of Devon; the Old Red Sandstone, the geological formation lying above the Silurian and below the Carboniferous system as found in Devonshire [Geol.].
devonport, *n.* *dev*-on-port, a davenport.
devote, *v.t.* de-*vote*, to set apart and dedicate by vow; to give up wholly; to give up to doom; to give special care. (L. *devotus*, vowed.)
devoted, *a.* de-*voh*-ted, dedicated or consecrated; ardent; zealous; strongly attached.
devotedly, *ad.* in a devoted manner.
devotedness, *n.* the state of being devoted.
devotee, *n.* dev-o-*tee*, one who is zealously devoted; a votary; a bigot.
devotement, *n.* de-*vote*-ment, devotedness; vowed dedication.
devotion, *n.* de-*voh*-shon, the state of being consecrated, or solemnly set apart for a particular purpose; a devout yielding of the heart and affections to God; religious worship; an act of respect; ardent love or affection, shown in constant attention; ardour. (L. *dēvōtio*, a consecrating.)
devotional, *a.* de-*voh*-shon-al, pertaining or suited to devotion.
devotionalism, *n.* de-*voh*-shon-al-izm, devotional principles or character.
devotionalist, *n.* de-*voh*-shon-al-ist, one given to devotionalism; a devotionist.
devotionally, *ad.* in a devotional manner.
devotionist, *n.* de-*voh*-shon-ist, a devotee; a person formally devout.
devour, *v.t.* de-*vour*, to eat up; to eat with greediness or ravenously; to consume with rapidity and violence, as fire, etc.; to consume; to waste; to destroy; to ruin; to enjoy with avidity. (Fr. *dévorer*, to eat up.)
devourable, *a.* de-*vour*-a-bl, that may be devoured.
devourer, *n.* de-*vour*-er, one who or that which devours or preys upon.
devouring, *a.* de-*vour*-ing, consuming; wasting.
devouringly, *ad.* in a devouring manner.
devout, *a.* de-*vout*, God-fearing; reverential; religious; expressing devotion; prayerful; earnest. (O.Fr. *devot*, from L. *devotus*, devoted.)
devoutly, *ad.* de-*vout*-le, in a devout manner.
devoutness, *n.* the quality of being devout.
devulgarize, *v.t.* dee-*vul*-ga-rize, to free from vulgarity; to refine.
dew, *n.* dew, aqueous vapour condensed on the cool surfaces of plants and other bodies during the night; dewy moisture; freshness: *v.t.* to wet with dew; to moisten. **mountain-dew,** Scotch whisky [Slang]. (A.S. *deaw.*)
dewan, *n.* de-*wawn*, an officer of finance in the Mohammedan States of India; a major-domo or steward in Bengal. (Ar.)
dewberry, *n.* *dew*-be-re, the bramble, *Rubus cæsius.*
dewclaw, *n.* *dew*-klaw, a rudimentary claw in the feet of dogs and certain ungulates.
dewdrop, *n.* *dew*-drop, a drop of dew.
dew-fall, *n.* *dew*-fawl, the falling of dew; the time when dew begins to form.
dewiness, *n.* *dew*-e-ness, the quality of being dewy.
dewlap, *n.* *dew*-lap, the flesh that hangs from the throat of some dogs and oxen; the wattle of a turkey. (Probably because it laps or licks the dew in grazing.)

dewless, *a.* *dew*-les, having no dew.
dew-point, *n.* *dew*-poynt, the temperature at which dew begins to form.
dew-pond, *n.* *dew*-pond, an artificial pool, usually on chalk downs, kept supplied by the condensation of dews, mists, etc.
dew-retting, *n.* *dew-ret*-ting, the exposure of flax to the action of dew or rain to effect the decomposition of the gum which coats the fibre.
dew-worm, *n.* *dew*-wurm, the earth-worm.
dewy, *a.* *dew*-e, like dew ; moist with dew ; accompanied by dew ; resembling dew.
dexter, *a.* *deks*-ter, on the right-hand side ; on the right side of a shield or coat of arms, that is, the left-hand side of the drawing [Her.]. (L., on the right side.)
dexterity, *n.* deks-*te*-re-*te*, ready expertness, due to practice, in the employment of mechanical or mental resources ; expertness in using the right hand ; adroitness ; skill. (L. *dexteritas*, skilfulness.)
dexterous, *a.* *deks*-ter-us, ready and expert in the use of either a bodily or mental faculty ; adroit ; skilful ; right-handed ; done with dexterity.
dexterously, *ad.* *deks*-ter-us-le, with dexterity.
dexterousness, *n.* dexterity ; adroitness.
dextral, *a.* *deks*-tral, situated on the right, as opposed to left ; proceeding from left to right.
dextrality, *n.* deks-*tral*-e-te, the state of being on the right side.
dextrally, *ad.* *deks*-tra-le, towards the right ; in clockwise direction.
dextrin, *n.* *deks*-trin, starch gum ; the soluble matter into which the interior substance of starch globules is convertible by acids or diastase, so called because its action on polarized light is dextrorotatory [Chem.].
dextrinate, *v.t.* *deks*-tre-nate, to convert into or impregnate with dextrin.
dextrinous, *a.* *deks*-tre-nus, pertaining to or of the nature of dextrin.
dextro-, *pref.* *deks*-tro-, the combining form of **dexter,** indicating that it causes the polarized light ray to turn to the right.
dextro-glucose, *n.* *deks*-tro-*gloo*-kose, granular sugar, so called as having a dextrorotatory property.
dextro-gyrate, *a.* *deks*-tro-jire-rat, dextrorotatory.
dextrorotatory, *a.* *deks*-tro-ro-*tay*-to-re, turning in a clockwise direction ; turning polarized luminous rays to the right.
dextrorsal, *a.* deks-*tror*-sal, dextrorse.
dextrorse, *a.* *deks*-trorse, turning in a spiral from left to right [Bot.]. (L. *dextrorsum*, to the right.)
dextrose, *n.* *deks*-trose, grape-sugar so called from its dextrorotatory property [Chem.].
dextrous, *a.* *deks*-trus, dexterous.
dey, *n.* day, a title of dignity, formerly given to the Governors of Algiers and Tripoli. (Turk., a maternal uncle.)
dezinc, *v.t.* dee-*zink*, to dezincify.
dezincify, *v.t.* dee-*zing*-ke-fy, to remove the zinc from an alloy or solution of which it forms part.
dhak, *n.* dawk, an East Indian tree, *Butea frondosa*, having brilliant flowers. (Hind.)
dharma, *n.* *dar*-ma, the law of Buddha ; the holiness that underlies the law. (Sans.)
dhobie, *n.* *doh*-be, a Hindu laundryman. (Hind.)
dhole, *n.* dole, the so-called wild dog of the Deccan, *Cyon dukhunensis*.
dholl, *n.* dol, pigeon-pea, an edible pea cultivated in the East and West Indies, Seychelles, etc.
dhoolie, *n.* *dool*-e, a doolie.
dhoti, *n.* *doh*-te, the Hindu loin cloth. (Hind.)
dhow, *n.* dou, an Arab vessel with a lateen sail on one or two masts ; an Arab vessel used in the slave-trade.
dhurrie, *n.* *du*-re, a coarse cotton fabric, used for curtains, carpets, etc. (Hind.)
di-, a prefix signifying double, two, or twice, as in *diacid*, *didactylous*, etc. (Gr. *dis*, twice.)
di-, a prefix taking the place of *dis-* before certain consonants, as in *digest*, *dilute*, *diminish*, etc.
dia-, *dy*-a, a Greek prefix signifying through.
diabase, *n.* *dy*-a-base, greenstone, a crystalline granular rock, an altered form of basalt. (Gr. *diabasis*, a going through.)
diabasic, *a.* dy-a-*base*-ik, pertaining to, composed of, or containing diabase.
diabetes, *n.* dy-a-*bee*-teez, a disease characterized by great thirst, emaciation, and an excessive proportion of sugar in the urine. (Gr. *dia-*, and *baino*, go.)
diabetic, *a.* dy-a-*bet*-ik, pertaining to diabetes ; *n.* one suffering from diabetes.
diabetogenic, *a.* dy-a-bee-to-*jen*-ik, producing diabetes.
diablerie, *n.* de-*ah*-ble-re, dealings with the devil ; devilry ; sorcery. (Fr.)
diabolic, *a.* dy-a-*bol*-ik, diabolical. (Fr. *diabolique*.)
diabolical, *a.* dy-a-*bol*-e-kal, devilish ; extremely malicious ; outrageously wicked.
diabolically, *ad.* in a diabolical manner.
diabolicalness, *n.* devilishness ; the quality of being diabolical.
diabolify, *v.t.* dy-a-*bol*-e-fy, to ascribe diabolical qualities to.
diabolism, *n.* dy-*ab*-o-lizm, devil worship ; conduct worthy of the devil ; possession by the devil ; black magic ; witchcraft.
diabolize, *v.t.* dy-*ab*-o-lize, to make a devil of ; to make diabolical ; to represent as a devil.
diabolo, *n.* de-*ab*-o-loh, a game played with a top shaped like an hour-glass and a string held on two sticks ; the devil on two sticks. (It.)
diacaustic, *a.* dy-a-*kaws*-tik, formed by the intersection of refracted rays of light (used esp. of curves so formed) [Math.] : *n.* a diacaustic curve. (Gr. *dia-*, and *caustic*.)
diachylon, *n.* dy-*ak*-e-lon, sticking-plaster made by boiling litharge with olive oil and water, originally from expressed juices. (Gr. *diachylos*, exceedingly juicy.)
diachylum, *n.* dy-*ak*-e-lum, diachylon.
diacid, *n.* dy-*as*-id, an acid containing two atoms of hydrogen : *a.* having two atoms of hydrogen replaceable by radicals.
diacodium, *n.* dy-a-*koh*-de-um, a narcotic preparation made from the syrup of poppies. (Gr. *dia-*, and *kodis*, a poppyhead.)
diaconal, *a.* dy-*ak*-o-nal, pertaining to a deacon.
diaconate, *n.* dy-*ak*-o-nat, the office of a deacon ; deacons collectively.
diacope, *n.* dy-*ak*-o-pe, a tmesis. (Gr. *dia-*, and *kope*, cutting.)
diacoustic, *a.* dy-a-*kous*-tik, pertaining to diacoustics.
diacoustics, *n.* dy-a-*kous*-tiks, the science of sounds refracted by passing through media possessed of different densities. (Gr. *dia-*, and *acoustic*.)
diacritic, *a.* dy-a-*krit*-ik, diacritical : *n.* a diacritical mark.
diacritical, *a.* dy-a-*krit*-e-kal, that distinguishes. **diacritical marks,** a mark or sign distinguishing letters of the alphabet as printed or written, or to indicate pronunciation. (Gr. *diakritos*, excellent.)
diactinic, *a.* dy-ak-*tin*-ik, capable of transmitting actinic rays.
diadelphia, *n.pl.* dy-a-*del*-fe-a, plants whose stamens are united into two bodies or bundles by their filaments [Bot.]. (Gr. *di-*, twice, *adelphos*, a brother.)
diadelphous, *a.* dy-a-*del*-fus, having stamens united into two bodies by their filaments [Bot.].
diadem, *n.* *dy*-a-dem, the arch on a crown ; anciently a head-band or fillet worn as a badge of royalty ; anything worn on the head as a badge of royalty or sovereign dominion ; a crown ; sovereign power. **diadem spider,** the garden spider, the cross spider, *Araneus diadema*. (Fr. *diadème*.)
diademed, *a.* *dy*-a-demd, wearing a diadem.
Diadochi, *n.pl.* dy-*ad*-o-ky, the generals of Alexander the Great, who divided his empire among themselves on his death. (Gr., succeeding.)
diadromous, *a.* dy-a-*droh*-mus, with the veins of the leaves radiating fanwise [Bot.]. (Gr. *diadromos*, wandering about.)
diæresis, *n.* dy-*eer*-re-sis, the resolution of a diphthong or syllable into two ; the mark (¨) placed over the second of two vowels, denoting tha they are to be separately pronounced, as *coöpt*. (Gr. *diairesis*, divisibility.)
diaglyph, *n.* *dy*-a-glif, an intaglio.
diaglyphic, *a.* dy-a-*glif*-ik, sunk into the general surface [Sculp., Engraving. etc.]. (Gr. *diaglypho*, carve.)
diagnose, *v.t.* *dy*-ag-noze, to identify a disease from its symptoms ; to distinguish.
diagnosis, *n.* dy-ag-*noh*-sis, the identification of a

disease by its distinctive symptoms [Path.]; a brief discriminating description of a plant or animal distinguishing the species, etc. (Gr. *diagnosis*, a distinguishing.)

diagnostic, *a.* dy-ag-*nos*-tik, distinguishing; indicating the nature of a disease: *n.* the symptom by which a disease is known or distinguished from others; a characteristic: *pl.* the study of symptoms.

diagnostically, *ad.* *dy*-ag-*nos*-te-ka-le, by means of diagnosis.

diagnostician, *n.* *dy*-ag-nos-*tish*-an, an expert in diagnosing.

diagometer, *n.* dy-a-*gom*-e-ter, an instrument for measuring electro-conductive power. (Gr. *diago* convey, and *metron*, measure.)

diagonal, *a.* dy-*ag*-o-nal, extending from one angle to an opposite of a quadrilateral or multilateral figure, and dividing it into two; crossing a surface obliquely; having oblique ridges: *n.* an oblique line, beam, etc.; an oblique direction; any line of squares running obliquely across a chessboard; a cloth marked with diagonal twills; the line [/] dividing shillings and pence [Print.]. **diagonal scale,** a system of oblique-crossing lines by which minute fractions may be measured. (L. *diagōnālis*, diagonal.)

diagonally, *ad.* in a diagonal direction.

diagram, *n.* *dy*-a-gram, a drawing for the purpose of demonstrating the properties of any figure, as a square, triangle, circle, etc.; an illustrative drawing or figure: *v.t.* to represent in a diagram. (L. *diagramma*, a figure marked out by lines.)

diagrammatic, *a.* *dy*-a-gra-*mat*-ik, represented by diagram; of the nature of a diagram.

diagrammatically, *ad.* *dy*-a-gra-*mat*-e-ka-le, by means of a diagram.

diagrammatize, *v.t.* *dy*-a-*gram*-a-tize, to put as a diagram; to make a diagram of.

diagraph, *n.* *dy*-a-graf, a drawing instrument used for constructing outline sketches, perspectives, enlargements, etc. (Gr. *diagrapho*, write across.)

diagraphics, *n.* *dy*-a-*graf*-iks, the art of design or drawing.

diaheliotropic, *a.* *dy*-a-*hee*-le-o-*trop*-ik, turning sideways to the light [Bot.].

diaheliotropism, *n.* *dy*-a-*hee*-le-*ot*-ro-pizm, tendency of leaves to turn their upper surface to the sunlight [Bot.]. (Gr. *helios*, the sun, *trepo*, turn.)

dial, *n.* *dy*-al, an instrument for showing the time by the sun's shadow; the graduated face of a timepiece; anything similar with a movable index; a compass used in surveying; the face [Slang]: *v.t.* and *i.* to survey with a dial; to operate a dial (esp. of an automatic telephone). (L. *dialis*, daily.)

dialect, *n.* *dy*-a-lekt, the form or idiom of a language peculiar to a district; manner of speaking; speech; language. (Fr. *dialecte*.)

dialectal, *a.* dy-a-*lek*-tal, pertaining to or characteristic of a dialect or dialects.

dialectally, *ad.* dy-a-*lek*-ta-le, from a dialectal view.

dialectic, *n.* dy-a-*lek*-tik, dialectics; logical debate.

dialectical, *a.* dy-a-*lek*-te-kal, pertaining to dialectics; logical.

dialectically, *ad.* in a dialectic manner.

dialectician, *n.* *dy*-a-lek-*tish*-an, a logician; one versed in dialectics.

dialectics, *n.* dy-a-*lek*-tiks, the art of reasoning, arguing, or discussing; the investigation of truth by discussion or critical examination; that branch of logic which teaches the rules and modes of reasoning; the logic of the phenomenal; the logic of thought; the science of ideas.

dialectologist, *n.* *dy*-a-lek-*tol*-o-jist, a student of dialect.

dialectology, *n.* *dy*-a-lek-*tol*-o-je, the study of dialect. (Gr. *dialektos*, dialect, *logos*, science.)

dialist, *n.* *dy*-al-ist, a constructor of dials; one skilled in dialling.

diallage, *n.* dy-*al*-a-je, a rhetorical figure by which arguments are placed in various points of view, and then turned to one point [Rhet.]. (Gr., interchange.)

diallage, *n.* *dy*-a-laj, a dark green or bronze-coloured laminate pyroxene, similar in composition to augite [Min.].

diallagic, *a.* dy-a-*laj*-ik, pertaining to or formed of diallage [Min.].

diallagoid, *a.* dy-*al*-a-goyd, containing or of the nature of diallage [Min.].

dialling, *n.* *dy*-al-ing, the science of measuring time by dials; the art of constructing dials; the act of using a dial, esp. in telephony.

dialogical, *a.* dy-a-*loj*-e-kal, dialogistic.

dialogism, *n.* dy-*al*-o-jizm, a dialogue reported in the third person [Rhet.]. (Gr. *dialogismos*, debate.)

dialogist, *n.* dy-*al*-o-jist, a speaker in a dialogue; a writer of dialogues.

dialogistic, *a.* dy-al-o-*jis*-tik, in the form of a dialogue; argumentative.

dialogistically, *ad.* dy-al-o-*jis*-te-ka-le, in the manner of a dialogue.

dialogite, *n.* dy-*al*-o-jite, a carbonate of manganese of a rose-red colour.

dialogize, *v.t.* dy-*al*-o-jize, to discourse in dialogue.

dialogue, *n.* *dy*-a-log, a conversation between two persons; a literary composition in which two or more persons carry on a discourse: *v.i.* to discourse together; to confer. (Fr., from Gr. *dia-*, through *legomai*, to converse.)

dial-plate, *n.* the plate of a dial, esp. of a clock or watch.

dial-sight, *n.* a gun-sight for the measurement of lateral angles, used when firing at an unseen target.

dialysis, *n.* dy-*al*-e-sis, a diæresis mark; a solution of continuity; the separation of crystalloid from colloid substances in a solution by passage through a porous membrane [Chem.]. (Gr., a parting.)

dialytic, *a.* dy-a-*lit*-ik, pertaining to dialysis.

dialyze, *v.t.* *dy*-a-lize, to separate a colloid from a substance in solution by passing the latter through a membrane [Chem.]. (Gr. *dialyo*, loosen.)

dialyzer, *n.* *dy*-a-lize-er, the apparatus or the parchment membrane used in dialysis.

diamagnetic, *n.* *dy*-a-mag-*net*-ik, possessed of the property of being repelled by a magnetic pole: *n.* any substance having this property.

diamagnetism, *n.* *dy*-a-*mag*-ne-tizm, the branch of magnetism that treats of diamagnetic phenomena.

diamenté, *a.* (App.), having a sparkling effect: *n.* material of this nature. (Fr.)

diamantiferous, *a.* *dy*-a-man-*tif*-er-us, diamond bearing. (Fr. *diamantifère*.)

diameter, *n.* dy-*am*-e-ter, a straight line passing through the centre of a figure, dividing it into two equal parts; a straight line passing through the centre of a circle and terminating on each side at the circumference [Geom.]; the length of such a line. (Fr. *diamètre*.)

diametral, *a.* dy-*am*-e-tral, diametrical.

diametrical, *a.* dy-a-*met*-re-kal, pertaining to a diameter; in the direction of a diameter; direct.

diametrically, *ad.* dy-a-*met*-re-ka-le, in a diametrical direction; in direct opposition.

diamond, *n.* *dy*-a-mond, the hardest, and most valuable of all the precious stones, a crystal of pure carbon, transparent, brilliant, and usually colourless; a glazier's tool for cutting glass; the smallest type in general use, equal to 4½ pt. [Print.]; a rhomb; a playing card bearing a rhomboidal figure or figures; a small rhomboidal window pane; a lozenge [Her.]: *a.* like a diamond; made or set with diamonds. **diamond drill,** a rock-boring tool in which the cutters are bort diamonds. **diamond-field,** a region in which diamonds are found. **diamond jubilee,** the sixtieth anniversary. **diamond-shaped,** having the figure of an oblique-angled parallelogram or rhombus. **diamond snake,** a snake of Australia with diamond markings. **diamond wedding,** the sixtieth anniversary of the wedding day. **rough diamond,** a person of good qualities but uncouth manner or exterior. (O.Fr. *diamant*.)

diamondiferous, *a.* *dy*-a-mon-*dif*-er-us, bearing diamonds.

Diana, *n.* dy-*an*-a, the virgin goddess of hunting [Myth.]; the moon; a good horsewoman; a lady who hunts.

diandrous, *a.* dy-*an*-drus, having only two stamens or antheridia [Bot.]. (Gr. *di-*, twice, and *aner* a male.)

dianodal, *a.* dy-a-*noh*-dal, passing through a node or nodes [Math.].

dianoetic, *a.* *dy*-a-no-*et*-ik, pertaining to the rational faculty; capable of thought. (Gr. *diānoētikos*, of thinking.)

Dianthus, *n.* dy-*an*-thus, the large genus of flowering plants including the carnations, pinks, and sweet williams. (Gr. *dios*, divine, *anthos*, flower.

diapason, *n.* dy-a-*pay*-zon, the octave or interval which includes all the tones; concord of sound; the entire compass of tones; range; pitch; among musical instrument makers, a rule or scale by which they adjust the pipes of organs, the holes of flutes, etc., in due proportion for expressing the several tones and semi-tones. (L.)

diapedesis, *n.* *dy*-a-ped-*ee*-sis, the passage of white corpuscles through the walls of blood-vessels into the surrounding tissue. (Gr., an oozing through.)

diaper, *n.* *dy*-a-per, a cloth woven in a geometric pattern, much used for towels or napkins; a baby's napkin: *v.t.* to variegate with figures or flowers: *v.i.* to draw flowers or figures, as upon cloth. (Fr. *diaprer*, to variegate.)

diapering, *n.* *dy*-a-per-ing, work in diaper; a diaper pattern; a style of ornamentation similar to that of diaper [Her.].

diaphane, *n.* *dy*-a-fane, a silk stuff woven with transparent and coloured figures; a transparency. (Gr. *diaphanēs*, transparent.)

diaphaneity, *n.* *dy*-a-fa-*nee*-e-te, transparency; pellucidness.

diaphanie, *n.* dy-*af*-a-ne, the art of affixing coloured transparencies on glass with the effect as of staining; this process.

diaphanometer, *n.* *dy*-a-fa-*nom*-e-ter, an instrument for determining the comparative transparency of the air. (Gr. *diaphanes*, and *metron*, a measure.)

diaphanoscope, *n.* dy-a-*fan*-o-skope, an illuminating apparatus used in the examination from without of internal organs [Surg.].

diaphanous, *a.* dy-*af*-a-nus, pellucid; transparent.

diaphone, *n.* *dy*-a-fone, a specially constructed organ-stop of powerful tone. (Gr. *dia*-, through, phone, sound.)

diaphonic, *a.* dy-a-*fon*-ik, pertaining to diaphony.

diaphony, *n.* dy-*af*-o-ne, dissonance (as opposed to *symphony*) [Gr. Mus.]; a primitive form of counterpoint [Mus.].

diaphoresis, *n.* *dy*-a-fo-*ree*-sis, abnormal or artificially induced perspiration. (Gr., perspiration.)

diaphoretic, *a.* *dy*-a-fo-*ret*-ik, increasing perspiration: *n.* a medicine which promotes perspiration. (Gr. *diaphorētikos*, tending to produce perspiration.)

diaphototropism, *n.* dy-a-fo-*tot*-ro-pizm, diaheliotropism.

diaphragm, *n.* *dy*-a-fram, the large circular muscle forming a movable partition between the thorax and abdomen, its most important office being connected with the function of respiration; the midriff [Anat.]; a dividing membrane [Bot.]; any partition, commonly with an opening through it, especially in optical instruments, to cut off superfluous rays [Opt.]. (Fr.)

diaphragmal, *a.* dy-a-*frag*-mal, diaphragmatic.

diaphragmatic, *a.* *dy*-a-frag-*mat*-ik, pertaining to or resembling the diaphragm.

diaphysis, *n.* dy-*af*-e-sis, the shaft of a long bone [Anat.]; the abnormal prolongation of an inflorescence [Bot.]. (Gr., a bursting open of a bud.)

diapyetic, *a.* *dy*-a-py-*et*-ik, producing suppuration [Med.]. (Gr. *diapyētikos*, causing suppuration.)

diarchy, *n.* *dy*-ar-ke, government by two supreme rulers; a dual form of government, as that established in the provinces of British India in 1919. (Gr. *di*-, and *archo*, rule.)

diarian, *n.* dy-*ayr*-re-an, the writer of a diary: *a.* pertaining to a diary.

diarist, *n.* *dy*-a-rist, one who keeps a diary.

diarize, *v.t.* and *i.* *dy*-ar-ize, to enter in, or to keep, a diary.

diarrhœa, *n.* dy-a-*ree*-a, a morbidly frequent evacuation of the intestines. (Gr. *diarrhoia*, a flowing through.)

diarrhœtic, *a.* dy-a-*ret*-ik, producing diarrhœa.

diarthrosis, *n.* *dy*-ar-*throh*-sis, articulation of a bone that is movable in every direction [Anat.]. (Gr. *dia*-, and *arthron*, a joint.)

diary, *n.* *dy*-a-re, a register of daily occurrences; a book in which this is kept. (L. *diarium*, a diary.)

diaspora, *n.* dy-*as*-po-ra, the dispersion of the Jews, esp. that following the Babylonian captivity. (Gr., as next.)

diaspore, *n.* *dy*-a-spore, native hydrate of aluminium; a group of related minerals of which this is the type. (Gr. *diaspora*, a dispersion.)

diastase, *n.* *dy*-a-staze, an enzyme produced in barley during malting and capable of converting starch into sugar. (Fr.)

diastasis, *n.* dy-*as*-ta-sis, a forcible separation of bones without fracture [Surg.]. (Gr. separation.)

diastatic, *a.* dy-a-*stat*-ik, pertaining to diastase or the conversion of starch into sugar.

diastema, *n.* dy-a-*steem*-a, the space between two adjacent teeth, present in most mammals other than man. (L., interval.)

diastole, *n.* dy-*as*-to-le, the relaxation period of the cardiac cycle, as opposed to systole, or contraction period [Phys.]; the lengthening of a naturally short syllable [Gram.]. (Gr., expansion.)

diastolic, *a.* dy-a-*stol*-ik, pertaining to diastole.

diastyle, *n.* *dy*-a-stile, an arrangement of columns with spaces of three diameters of columns between. (L. *diastylos*, diastyle.)

diatessaron, *n.* dy-a-*tes*-sa-ron, a concord or harmonic interval, composed of a greater tone, a lesser tone, and one great semitone [Mus.]; a harmony of the four gospels [Theol.]. (L., a fourth.)

diathermal, *a.* dy-a-*ther*-mal, diathermanous.

diathermancy, *n.* dy-a-*ther*-man-se, the property of being diathermanous.

diathermanous, *a.* dy-a-*ther*-ma-nus, capable of transmitting radiant heat. (Gr. *diathermaino*, heat through.)

diathermic, *a.* dy-a-*ther*-mik, diathermanous.

diathermotherapy, *n.* *dy*-a-ther-mo-*the*-ra-pe, the treatment of disease by diathermy.

diathermy, *n.* *dy*-a-ther-me, the therapeutic generation of heat in body tissues by means of high-frequency electrical oscillations [Med.]. (Gr. *dia*-, through, *thermē*, heat.)

diathesis, *n.* dy-*ath*-e-sis, particular habit of body predisposing to certain diseases. (Gr., arrangement.)

diathetic, *a.* dy-a-*thet*-ik, pertaining to diathesis.

diatom, *n.* *dy*-a-tom, any of a large class of minute single-celled algæ with flinty skeletons.

diatomaceous, *a.* *dy*-a-to-*may*-se-us, pertaining to consisting of, or abounding in diatoms.

diatomic, *a.* dy-a-*tom*-ik, of two atoms; having two replaceable atoms or radicals [Chem.].

diatomite, *n.* dy-*at*-o-mite, kieselguhr.

diatomous, *a.* dy-*at*-o-mus, having crystals in one distinct diagonal cleavage [Min.]. (Gr., cutting in two.)

diatonic, *a.* dy-a-*ton*-ik, applied to the natural scale, which, proceeding by degrees, includes both tones and semi-tones; the notes belonging to the key in which a piece of music is written [Mus.]. (Gr. *diatonikon*, diatonic scale.)

diatonically, *ad.* dy-a-*ton*-e-ka-le, in a diatonic manner.

diatribe, *n.* *dy*-a-tribe, a disputation; a stream of invective; an abusive harangue. (Fr.)

diatropism, *n.* dy-*at*-ro-pizm, the tendency of some plant organs to place themselves with their main axis at right angles to the line of action of a stimulus.

dib, *v.i.* dib, to dip; to dibble. (Dial. Eng.)

dibasic, *a.* dy-*bay*-sik, having in the molecule two atoms of hydrogen replaceable by a base (of acids).

dibber, *n.* *dib*-ber, an agricultural implement with teeth or dibbles for making holes in the ground.

dibble, *n.* *dib*-bl, a pointed tool used in gardening, for making holes for planting seeds: *v.t.* to plant with a dibble: *v.i.* to dip [Angling].

dibbler, *n.* *dib*-bler, one who dibbles; a dibbling machine or tool.

dibranchiate, *a.* dy-*brang*-ke-at, having two gills. (Gr. *di*-, and *branchia*, gills.)

dibs, *n.pl.* dibz, the bones used in the game of knuckle-bones; the game itself; money [Slang].

dibstone, *n.* *dib*-stone, a stone thrown up from the palm and caught on the back of the hand as in knucklebones; *pl.* the game in which these are used.

dicacity, *n.* de-*kas*-e-te, pertness of speech; talkativeness. (L. *dicacitas*, raillery.)

dicast, *n.* *dy*-kast, a member of the jury courts of Athens. (Gr. *dikastēs* a judge.)

dice, *n.pl.* dice (*pl.* of **die**), numbered cubes for games of chance; a game with dice: *v.t.* to gamble (away) at dice; to cut into small cubes; to make or ornament with a pattern of small squares, to

checker : *v.i.* to play with dice. **dice-box,** the box from which dice are thrown in gaming.
diced, *a.* dyst, ornamented with diamond-shaped figures ; checkered.
dicephalous, *a.* dy-*sef*-a-lus, having two heads on one body. (Gr. *dikephalos*, having two heads.)
dicer, *n.* *dyce*-er, a dice-player.
dichastic, *a.* dy-*kas*-tik, capable of dividing spontaneously [Biol.].
dichlamydeous, *a.* *dy*-kla-*mid*-e-us, provided with both calyx and corolla [Bot.]. (Gr. *di-*, and *chlamys*, a covering.)
dichogamous, *a.* dy-*kog*-a-mus, with stamens and pistils ripening at different times [Bot.].
dichogamy, *n.* dy-*kog*-a-me, the state of being dichogamous [Bot.] ; the production of sexual glands of different sexes by the same individual at different times [Zool.]. (Gr. *dicha*, asunder, and *gamos*, marriage.)
dichord, *n.* *dy*-kawrd, the two-stringed lyre.
dichotomic, *a.* dy-*kot*-o-mik, dichotomous.
dichotomize, *v.t.* and *i.* dy-*kot*-om-ize, to cut or become cut into two parts. (Gr. *dichotomeo*, cut in two.)
dichotomous, *a.* dy-*kot*-o-mus, pertaining to or characterized by dichotomy ; regularly dividing by pairs from top to bottom [Bot.]. (Gr. *dichotomos*, cutting in two.)
dichotomy, *n.* dy-*kot*-o-me, repeated bifircation of branches into branches of equal size [Bot.] ; the aspect of the moon, or planet, when half illuminated [Astron.] ; continuous division by pairs, specially of a class in a descending series into pairs of groups distinguished by contradictory qualities [Logic]. (Gr. *dichotomia*, a cutting in two.)
dichroic, *a.* dy-*kroh*-ik, showing dichroism. (Gr. *dichroos*, two-coloured.)
dichroism, *n.* *dik*-ro-izm, the property some doubly refracting crystals have of presenting different colours when viewed in different directions
dichromatic, *a.* *dik*-ro-*mat*-ik, having or showing two colours ; based on two primary colours.
dichromatism, *n.* dy-*kroh*-ma-tizm, state or quality of being dichromatic ; colour-blindness in which red and green are indistinguishable.
dichromic, *a.* dy-*kroh*-mik, yielding two colours.
dicing, *n.* *dice*-ing, gaming with dice. **dicing-house,** a gaming house.
dick, *n.* dik, a leather apron ; a dike ; a side of a ditch.
dickens, *int.* *dik*-enz, the deuce ; the devil. (Perhaps from *devilkin*, or *Dickon*, a form of *Richard*.)
Dickensian, *a.* de-*ken*-ze-an, pertaining to Charles Dickens, or anything written in his style : *n.* a student or ardent admirer of Dickens's works.
dicker, *n.* *dik*-er, ten in number (esp. hides) [Comm.]; *v.t.* to barter [U.S.A.]. (L. *decuria*, a set of ten.)
dickey, *n.* *dik*-e, a separate shirt-front ; a bib ; a seat in a carriage behind or in front ; a fold-up outside rear seat in a motor car.
dicky, *n.* *dik*-e, a dickey ; a familiar name for a bird : *a.* precarious ; seedy, off colour [Slang].
diclinate, *a.* *dy*-kle-nat, having two of the axes obliquely inclined (of crystals). (Gr. *di-*, and *klino*, bend.)
diclinic, *a.* dy-*klin*-ik, diclinate.
diclinism, *n.* *dy*-kle-nizm, the state of having the sexes separate in different flowers [Bot.].
diclinous, *a.* *dy*-kle-nus, having the stamens and the pistils in different flowers, each flower being unisexual [Bot.]. (Gr. *di-*, and *kline*, a bed.)
dicoccous, *a.* dy-*kok*-us, dividing into two cocci [Bot.].
dicotyledon, *n.* *dy*-kot-e-*lee*-don, a plant with two cotyledons or seed-leaves.
dicotyledonous, *a.* *dy*-kot-e-*lee*-don-us, having two cotyledons.
dicrotic, *a.* dy-*krot*-ik, conveying the sensation of a double pulsation [Path.]. (Gr. *dikrotos*, beating time.)
dicta, *n.pl.* *dik*-tah, sayings. (L.)
dictaphone, *n.* *dik*-ta-fone, proprietary name of an instrument giving a record of speech which can be used in a phonograph.
dictate, *n.* *dik*-tate, authoritative prescription or direction ; a command ; impulse : *v.t.* dik-*tate*, to tell another what to do, or say, or write; to speak or read aloud for the words to be taken down ; to order or prescribe authoritatively. (L. *dictatu* said.)
dictation, *n.* dik-*tay*-shon, the act of dictating ; tha which is dictated. (L. *dictatio*.)
dictator, *n.* dik-*tay*-tor, one whose dictates a followed ; one invested for a time with absolu authority, especially in ancient Rome, in times exigence and danger ; one exercising absolu power ; one who dictates to a stenographer.
dictatorial, *a.* dik-ta-*taw*-re-al, relating to a dict tor ; absolute ; authoritative ; overbearing. (*dictatorius*.)
dictatorially, *ad.* in a dictatorial manner.
dictatorship, *n.* dik-*tay*-tor-ship, the office of dictator ; the term of his office ; authority imperiousness.
dictatory, *a.* *dik*-ta-to-re, overbearing ; dogmatica
dictatress, *n.* dik-*tay*-tress, a female dictator.
diction, *n.* *dik*-shon, expression of ideas by words manner of expression ; style of speech. (Fr.)
dictionary, *n.* *dik*-shon-a-re, a book containing th words of a language (or some specialized part of i arranged in alphabetical order, with their meaning etc. ; a lexicon ; a vocabulary ; any book information with the topics alphabetically arrange (L. *dictionarium*.)
dictograph, *n.* *dik*-to-graf, proprietary name an instrument recording speech.
dictum, *n.* *dik*-tum (*pl.* **dicta**), an authoritati saying or assertion ; an expression of opinion award [Law]. (L.)
dictyogen, *n.* *dik*-te-o-jen, one of a sub-class plants with net-veined leaves, intermediate betwee those of an endogenous and those of an exogenou structure [Bot.]. (Gr. *diktyon*, a net, *genna* produce.)
dicynodon, *n.* dy-*sin*-o-don, a large extinct repti of S. Africa with a beak like a turtle and two larg tusks in the upper jaw [Geol.]. (Gr. *di-*, and *kyō* dog, *odous*, a tusk.)
did, did, *p.* of the verb to do.
didactic, *a.* dy-*dak*-tik, didactical.
didactical, *a.* dy-*dak*-te-kal, adapted or intended t teach ; instructive ; preceptive. (Gr. *didaktiko* skilled in teaching.)
didactically, *ad.* in a didactic manner.
didacticism, *n.* dy-*dak*-te-sizm, the quality of bein didactic ; didactic method or practice.
didactics, *n.* dy-*dak*-tiks, the science or art communicating instruction.
didactyl, *a.* dy-*dak*-til, having only two fingers or tw toes on each limb : *n.* an animal with this chara teristic. (Gr. *di-*, and *daktylos*, a finger.)
didactylous, *a.* dy-*dak*-te-lus, having only tw digits on each limb [Zool.].
didapper, *n.* *did*-ap-per, the little grebe or dabchicl (*Dive* and *dapper*.)
didascalic, *a.* dy-das-*kal*-ik, didactic ; pertainin to a teacher. (Gr. *didaskaleia*, teaching or lectu ing.)
didder, *v.i.* *did*-der, to shiver with cold ; to dither
diddle, *v.t.* *did*-dl, to cheat or over-reach ; to mis lead : *v.i.* to totter, as a child in walking.
diddler, *n.* *did*-dler, one who diddles ; a cheat.
didelphia, *n.pl.* dy-*del*-fe-a, the marsupials, group of mammals possessing a double uteru (Gr. *di-*, and *delphys*, uterus.)
didelphoid, *a.* dy-*del*-foyd, pertaining to or resemb ling the didelphia or the opossums.
didst, didst, *p.* of the verb to do.
didunculus, *n.* de-*dung*-kew-lus, the tooth-bille pigeon of Samoa, *D. strigirostris*.
didymium, *n.* de-*dim*-e-um, a rare metal like an associated with lanthanum, formerly supposed t be an element but later identified as a mixture praseodymium and neodymium. (Gr. *didymo* twin.)
didymous, *a.* *did*-e-mus, twin ; growing in pair [Bot.].
didynamia, *n.pl.* dy-din-*ay*-me-a, a class of plant with four stamens, disposed in two pairs, one pa being shorter than the other [Bot.]. (Gr. *di-*, an *dynamis*, power.)
didynamous, *a.* dy-*din*-a-mus, containing four sta mens as in the didynamia [Bot.].
die, *v.i.* dy, to cease to live ; to expire ; to forfeit o give up life ; to perish ; to sink or faint ; t languish with affection, pleasure, or longing to become more and more faint ; to wither ; t

become vapid; to become indifferent, and as good as dead; to **perish** eternally. (Ice. *deyja.*)

die, *n.* dy (*pl.* **dice,** dice), a small cube, marked on its faces with numbers from one to six, used in gaming, by being thrown from a box; any cubic body; a flat tablet; hazard or chance. (L. *datus*, cast.)

die, *n.* dy (*pl.* **dies,** dize), a stamp used for coining money, or impressing a device; the cubical part of a pedestal, between its base and cornice [Arch.].

die-away, *a.* fainting or languishing away.

dieb, *n.* deeb, the wild dog or jackal of North Africa, *Canis anthus.*

die-hard, *n.* one who resists to the end. **the Die-Hards,** the Middlesex Regiment, the old 57th Foot.

dielectric, *a.* dy-e-*lek*-trik, insulating; non-conductive: *n.* a non-conducting substance through which the lines of force of an electrostatic field can pass; an insulating medium [Elect.]. (Gr. *dia-*, and *electric.*)

Diesel, *a. dee*-zel, pertaining to the inventions of Rudolph Diesel (Ger., 1858-1913). **Diesel-electric,** *a.* pertaining to a system of propulsion or drive in which power generated by a Diesel-engine is used to produce an electric current which then actuates the driving motors. **Diesel-engine,** *n.* an internal combustion engine burning heavy oil introduced by a blast of air and fired by the heat of compression.

die-sinker, *n.* an engraver of dies for embossing or stamping.

die-sinking, *n.* the process of engraving dies.

diesis, *n. dy*-e-sis, the double dagger reference mark (‡); the difference between the minor and major semitone [Mus.]; **enharmonic diesis,** the difference between three major thirds and an octave [Mus.]. (Gr., division.)

die-stock, *n.* the contrivance by which the dies used in screw-cutting are held in the lathe.

diet, *n. dy*-et, food; food prescribed by a physician; allowance of provisions: *v.t.* to board; to take food by rules prescribed; to furnish aliment to: *v.i.* and *t.* to eat or cause to eat according to rules prescribed. (Gr. *diaita*, mode of life, diet.)

diet, *n. dy*-et, a national assembly for legislative or administrative purposes of princes, dignitaries, delegates, etc. (used formerly of the Holy Roman Empire and of several Continental states). (As prec., but confused with L. *dies*, a day.)

dietarian, *n.* dy-et-*ayr*-re-an, one who diets; one who strictly conforms to his dietary.

dietary, *a. dy*-et-a-re, pertaining to diet or the rules of diet: *n.* rule or course of diet; allowance of food; a treatise on diet.

dieter, *n. dy*-et-er, one medically restricted to a diet; one who prescribes or advocates diets.

dietetic, *a.* dy-e-*tet*-ik, pertaining to diet, or to the rules for regulating it.

dietetics, *n.* dy-e-*tet*-iks, the science of food in its nutritive aspect; rules for diet.

dietetist, *n.* dy-e-*tet*-ist, a dietitian; an advocate of dieting.

dietine, *n. dy*-et-een, a subordinate or local diet; a cantonal convention. (Fr. *diétine.*)

dietist, *n. dy*-et-ist, a dietitian.

dietitian, *n.* dy-e-*tish*-an, one versed in dietetics.

dif-, a form of the prefix *dis-*.

differ, *v.i. dif*-fer, to be unlike, dissimilar, distinct, or various; to disagree; to be at variance; to strive: *v.t.* to cause to be different; to set at variance. (L. *differo*, bear.)

difference, *n. dif*-fer-ence *or dif*-rence, the state of being unlike or distinct; quality which distinguishes one thing from another; a contention; the point in dispute; distinction; mark of distinction; the balance; the remainder of a sum or quantity after a lesser sum or quantity is subtracted [Math.]; the alteration of the price of stock, etc., between different dates; the differentia [Logic]; a differential mark, esp. a figure added to a coat-of-arms to distinguish the branches of a family [Her.]: *v.i.* to distinguish; to make different; to assign a difference to [Her.]. (L. *differentia.*)

⋆**different,** *a. dif*-fer-ent *or dif*-rent, distinct; separate; various; unlike; out of the ordinary [Coll.].

differentia, *n.* dif-fer-*ren*-she-a, an essential attribute by which one species is distinguished from another of the same genus, and which, when added on to the generic name, defines the species

differential, *a.* dif-fer-*ren*-she-al, differing; tending to distinguish; causing or consisting of a difference; designed for changing gear speeds; special; creating a difference, as differential duties [Comm.]; pertaining to an infinitely small quantity, so small as to be less than any assignable quantity; pertaining to differentials [Math.]: *n.* an infinitely small difference between two states of a variable quantity [Math.]; a differential gear. **differential calculus,** *see* **calculus. differential coefficient,** a measure of the rate of change of one variable quantity with respect to another independent variable, of which it is a function; the ratio of an infinitesimal change of the function to an infinitesimal and casual change of the independent variable [Math.]. **differential gear,** a train of toothed wheels connecting two shafts or axles in the same line and allowing them to revolve at different speeds while that of the main driving member is unchanged [Mech.]. **differential screw,** a compound screw by which a differential motion is produced [Mech.]. **differential thermometer,** a thermometer for measuring minute differences of temperature [Physics].

differentially, *ad.* dif-fer-*ren*-she-a-le, by way of, or in relation to, difference; in two opposite directions.

differentiate, *v.t.* dif-fer-*ren*-she-ate, to make different; to distinguish between; to assign a separate part to; to specialize; to distinguish by the differentia; to find the differential of. (L. *differentia.*)

differentiation, *n.* dif-fer-*ren*-she-*ay*-shon, the act, process, or result of differentiating; modification of different parts.

differently, *ad.* in a different manner; variously.

difficile, *a. dif*-e-seel, difficult to get on with; hard to persuade. (Fr.)

difficult, *a. dif*-e-kult, hard to be done, or to accomplish; not easy; attended with labour and pains; hard to be pleased; hard to understand; not easily managed or persuaded; difficile. (L. *dis-*, and *facilis*, easy to do, from *facio*, do.)

difficultly, *ad. dif*-e-kult-le, with difficulty.

difficulty, *n. dif*-e-kul-te, something to be overcome; anything difficult; an obstacle; an objection. (Fr. *difficulté.*)

diffidence, *n. dif*-e-dence, distrust of one's own ability; a modest reserve or bashfulness. (L. *diffidens*, distrusting.)

diffident, *a. dif*-e-dent, distrustful; shy; bashful; wanting confidence; hesitating; reserved.

diffidently, *ad.* in a diffident manner.

diffluence, *n. dif*-floo-ence, the state of being diffluent; deliquescence.

diffluent, *a.* dif-*floo*-ent, flowing away on all sides; fluid; readily becoming fluid. (L. *diffluens*, flowing in varying directions.)

diffract, *v.t.* dif-*frakt*, to break into parts; to bend from a straight line [Opt.]. (L. *diffractus*, broken.)

diffraction, *n.* dif-*frak*-shon, a change which light undergoes, when, by passing very near the borders of an opaque body, it forms parallel bands or fringes [Opt.]; an analogous change in the direction of propagation of a sound- or electric-wave [Physics].

diffractive, *a.* dif-*frak*-tiv, causing diffraction.

diffractometer, *n.* dif-frak-*tom*-e-ter, an instrument for measuring diffraction [Opt.].

diffrangible, *a.* dif-*fran*-je-bl, capable of being diffracted.

diffuse, *v.t.* dif-*fewz*, to pour out and spread as a fluid; to spread or send out in all directions. (L. *diffusus*, poured.)

diffuse, *a.* dif-*fewce*, widely spread; dispersed; wordy; prolix; not concise in statement; not circumscribed [Path.]; loosely spreading [Bot.].

diffusedly, *ad.* dif-*few*-zed-le, in a diffused or disconnected manner.

diffusedness, *n.* the state of being diffused.

diffusely, *ad.* dif-*fewce*-le, in a diffuse or wide-spread manner.

diffuseness, *n.* dif-*fewce*-ness, the state of being diffuse.

diffuser, *n.* dif-*few*-zer, one who diffuses; an instrument or apparatus for diffusing air, heat, etc.

diffusibility, *n.* dif-*few*-ze-*bil*-e-te, diffusibleness.

diffusible, *a.* dif-*few*-ze-bl, that may be spread in all directions; that may be dispersed.
diffusibleness, *n.* dif-*fuze*-e-bl-ness, the quality of being diffusible.
diffusion, *n.* dif-*few*-zhon, a spreading abroad; dispersion; copiousness; exuberance of style; a spreading of a fluid in every direction; the mixing of a gas or gases whether in the same or different containers separated by permeable partitions. **diffusion-tube,** an instrument for ascertaining the rate of diffusion for different gases. (L. *diffusio.*)
diffusionism, *n.* dif-*few*-zho-nizm, the diffusionist theory.
diffusionist, *a.* dif-*few*-zho-nist, pertaining to the anthropological theory that all the higher types of civilization arose in and spread from Egypt: *n.* one holding this theory.
diffusive, *a.* dif-*few*-siv, having the quality of diffusing, as fluids, or of dispersing, as minute particles; extending in all directions.
diffusively, *ad.* in a diffusive manner.
diffusiveness, *n.* the power of diffusing, or state of being diffused; extensiveness; the quality of being diffuse.
diffusivity, *n.* dif-ew-*siv*-e-te, tendency to diffuse; rate or capacity of diffusion.
dig, *v.t.* dig, to break and turn up the earth with a spade, etc.; to hollow out by digging; to thrust into; to obtain by digging: *v.i.* to work with a spade or a similar piercing instrument; to do servile work; to work in search of; to lodge [Slang]: *n.* an act or spell of digging; a poke; (pl.) lodgings [Slang]. **dig down,** to undermine and cause to fall by digging. **dig out** or **from,** to obtain by digging. **dig through,** to open a passage through. *p.* **digged**; *pp.* **dug.** (A.S. *dic,* a ditch.)
digametic, *a.* dy-ga-*met*-ik, forming gametes of two different kinds [Biol.].
digamist, *n. dig*-a-mist, one who lawfully marries a second time.
digamma, *n.* dy-*gam*-ma, a letter in the ancient Greek alphabet which gradually fell into disuse, except among the Æolians, and had approximately the sound of *w*, so called from its resemblance to two gammas, one placed above the other.
digamous, *a. dig*-a-mus, lawfully married twice; of the nature of digamy.
digamy, *n. dig*-a-me, state of being twice legally married. (Gr. *di-*, and *gamos,* marriage.)
digastric, *a.* dy-*gas*-trik, having a double protuberance. **digastric muscle,** a muscle of the lower jaw [Anat.]. (Gr. *di-*, and *gaster,* the belly.)
digest, *n. dy*-jest, originally a collection of Roman laws, digested or arranged under their proper heads or titles, such as the Pandects of Justinian; any similar collection, compilation or summary. (L. *digestus,* borne.)
digest, *v.t.* de-*jest,* to arrange under suitable heads or titles; to classify; to arrange in the mind; to separate the nutritive from the non-nutritive elements of the food in the stomach; to convert (food) into chyme; to prepare in the mind; to brook; to soften and prepare by heat; to expose to a gentle heat as a preparation for chemical operations [Chem.]: *v.i.* to be digested; to be prepared by heat; to endure or put up with; to dissolve and be prepared for manure, as substances in compost.
digester, *n.* de-*jes*-ter, one who digests or disposes in order; one who digests his food; that which aids digestion or strengthens digestive power; a stock-pot; a strong metal vessel, with a safety-valve, in which substances may be boiled or heated under pressure [Chem.].
digestibility, *n.* de-*jes*-te-*bil*-e-te, digestibleness.
digestible, *a.* de-*jes*-te-bl, capable of being digested.
digestibleness, *n.* de-*jes*-te-bl-ness, the quality of being digestible.
digestibly, *ad.* de-*jes*-te-ble, in a digestive sense.
★digestion, *n.* de-*jest*-yon, the process of dissolving aliment in the stomach and preparing it for nourishment; the act of methodizing and reducing to order or maturing a design; the operation of exposing bodies to a gentle heat to prepare them for some action on each other, or the slow action of a solvent on any substance; the process of dissolution and preparation of substances for manure, as in compost [Chem.]. (Fr.)
digestive, *a.* de-*jes*-tiv, promoting digestion; reducing to order; dissolving; *n.* any preparation which increases the tone of the stomach and aids digestion [Med.]. (L. *digestivus.*)
digestively, *ad.* de-*jes*-tiv-le, by way of digestion.
diggable, *a. dig*-a-bl, that may be digged.
digger, *n. dig*-ger, one who or that which digs up; a gold-digger; an Australian or New Zealander [Slang].
digging, *n. dig*-ging, the operation of loosening earth by hand labour with a spade, fork, or pike; *pl.* an alluvial gold-field; lodgings [Slang].
dight, *a.* dite, arrayed; adorned; dressed. (A.S. *dihtan,* adorn.)
digit, *n. dij*-it, a finger or toe; a finger's breadth, or three-fourths of an inch; the twelfth part of the diameter of the sun or moon, a term to express the quantity of an eclipse [Astron.]; any integer under 10, so called from counting on the fingers. (L. *digitus,* a finger or toe.)
digital, *a. dij*-e-tal, pertaining to or resembling a digit: *n.* a key of an organ or piano; the terminal joint of a spider's pedipalp.
digitaliform, *a.* dij-e-*tay*-le-fawrm, finger-shaped [Bot.].
digitalin, *n.* dij-e-*tay*-lin *or dij*-it-a-lin, a crystalline glucoside present in digitalis seeds.
digitalis, *n.* dij-e-*tay*-lis, the foxglove, *D. purpurea*; a preparation from the dried leaf of this used as a cardiac stimulant [Med.].
digitate, *a. dij*-e-tat, digitated.
digitated, *a. dij*-e-tay-ted, branching into several distinct leaflets or lobes like fingers [Bot.]; having processes resembling fingers [Zool.]. (L. *digitatus,* possessing terminal members like fingers.)
digitately, *ad.* in a digitate manner.
digitation, *n.* dij-e-*tay*-shon, the state of being digitate; division into finger-like processes [Anat.].
digitiform, *a. dij*-e-te-fawrm, finger-shaped.
digitigrade, *a. dij*-e-te-grade, walking on the toes with the heel raised from the ground: *n.* a digitigrade animal, as the dog, cat, etc. [Zool.]. (L. *digitus,* and *gradior,* walk.)
digitorium, *n. dij*-e-*taw*-re-um, a contrivance for training the fingers for piano-playing.
digitoxin, *n. dij*-e-*toks*-in, an intensely poisonous crystallizable principle obtained from the foxglove. (L. *digitus,* and *toxicum,* poison.)
diglot, *a. dy*-glot, using or in two languages; bilingual. (Gr. *diglōttos,* two-tongued.)
diglyph, *n. dy*-glif, a projecting face having two grooves or channels [Arch.]. (Gr. *diglyphos,* indented twice.)
dignified, *a. dig*-ne-fide, invested with dignity; marked with dignity; stately.
dignify, *v.t. dig*-ne-fy, to invest with honour; to confer honour, dignity, or distinction on; to distinguish by some excellence, or that which gives celebrity; to make illustrious. (O.Fr. *dignifier.*)
dignitary, *n. dig*-ne-ta-re, one of high rank, esp. an ecclesiastic. (L. *dignitas,* worthy.)
dignity, *n. dig*-ne-te, nobleness or elevation of mind based on moral rectitude; degree of rank, either in estimation or in the order of nature; grandeur of mien; elevation of deportment; office giving high rank in society, or the rank attached to it; the rank or title of a nobleman; an advantage attaching to a planet on account of its position in the zodiac or in respect to other planets [Astrol.]. (Fr. *dignité.*)
digoneutic, *a.* dy-go-*new*-tik, producing two broods in one year [Zool.].
digonous, *a. dig*-on-us, having two angles, as a stem [Bot.]. (Gr. *di-*, and *gonia,* an angle.)
digraph, *n. dy*-graf, a union of two letters representing only one sound, as *ea* in head, and *ph* in phial. (Gr. *di-*, and *grapho,* write.)
digraphic, *a.* dy-*graf*-ik, pertaining to a digraph; written in two different characters, as script and shorthand.
digress, *v.i.* de-*gress,* to turn aside; to deviate; to ramble. (L. *digressus,* step aside.)
digression, *n.* de-*gresh*-on, departure from the direct course, esp. from the logical train of a narration or discourse; the passage in which the deviation occurs.
digressional, *a.* de-*gresh*-on-al, digressive.
digressive, *a.* de-*gres*-siv, digressing; partaking of the nature of digression; expatiating.
digressively, *ad.* by way of digression.

digue, *n.* deeg, a dyke; a sea-wall. (Fr.)
digynia, *n.pl.* dy-*jin*-e-a, a group of plants having two pistils [Bot.]. (Gr. *di-*, and *gyne*, a female.)
digynian, *a.* dy-*jin*-e-an, digynous.
digynous, *a.* *dij*-in-us, having two pistils.
dihedral, *a.* dy-*heed*-ral, having two sides or faces (of crystals); resembling a dihedron [Geom.]: *n.* a dihedron. **dihedral angle,** the angle between two planes [Geol.]; the angle between the right and left wings of an aeroplane [Av.].
dihedron, *n.* dy-*heed*-ron, a figure with two sides or surfaces [Geom.]. (Gr. *di-*, and *hedra*, a seat, a side.)
dihexagonal, *a.* *dy*-heks-*ag*-o-nal, having twelve angles of which the odd six and even six are not equal to each other though equal among themselves.
dihexahedral, *a.* *dy*-heks-a-*heed*-ral, in the form of a hexahedral prism with trihedral summits [Min.]. (Gr. *di-*, and *hexahedral.*)
di-iamb, *n.* dy-*eye*-am, a double iamb [Pros.].
dika, *n.* *dee*-kah, either of two oil-bearing trees of West Africa, *Irvingia barteri*, or *Irvingia gabonensis.* (Native name.)
dikamali, *n.* dik-a-*mal*-e, the gum of *Gardenia lucida*, used in India for dressing wounds. (Native name.)
dikast, *n.* *dy*-kast, a dicast.
dik-dik, *n.* *dik*-dik, native name of several small antelopes of East Africa.
dike, *n.* dike, a ditch; the bank of earth thrown up in ditching; a mound of earth, stones, or other materials, to prevent low lands from being inundated; a rough wall of turf or stone without cement [Scots.]; a wall-like mass of igneous rock formed in the rents or fissures of stratified rocks: *v.t.* to surround with a dike; to secure by a bank; to ditch. (A.S. *dic*, ditch.)
dilacerate, *v.t.* de-*lass*-er-rate, to tear or rend asunder; to separate by force.
dilaceration, *n.* de-*lass*-er-*ray*-shon, a tearing or rending. (L. *dilaceratio.*)
dilapidate, *v.i.* de-*lap*-e-date, to fall into ruin; to become ruinous by neglect: *v.t.* to pull down; to waste; to squander. (L. *dilapidatus*, ruined.)
dilapidated, *a.* de-*lap*-e-*day*-ted, in a state of ruinous decay; suffered to go to ruin.
dilapidation, *n.* de-lap-e-*day*-shon, disrepair; a state of decay or ruin; the wasting or suffering to go to decay of church property in possession of an incumbent [Eccles.]; (*pl.*) damage sustained by premises during a tenancy.
dilapidator, *n.* de-*lap*-e-day-tor, one who causes or permits dilapidation.
dilatability, *n.* dy-*lay*-ta-*bil*-e-te, the quality of being dilatable.
dilatable, *a.* dy-*lay*-ta-bl, capable of expansion; possessing elasticity; elastic.
dilatancy, *n.* dy-*lay*-tan-se, range of dilatation.
dilatation, *n.* dil-a-*tay*-shon, the act of dilating; distention; expansion; the state of being dilated. (Fr.)
dilate, *v.i.* dy-*late*, to widen; to expand in all directions; to speak at length or expatiate: *v.t.* to expand, enlarge, or extend in all directions; to relate at large. (L. *dilatus*, wide.)
dilater, *n.* dy-*lay*-ter, one who enlarges.
dilation, *n.* dy-*lay*-shon, dilatation.
dilator, *n.* dy-*lay*-tor, a muscle that dilates by its contraction [Anat.]; an instrument for dilating a part [Surg.]. (L.)
dilatorily, *ad.* *dil*-a-to-re-le, with delay.
dilatoriness, *n.* the quality of being dilatory.
dilatory, *a.* *dil*-a-to-re, slow; tardy; given to procrastination; not proceeding with diligence; tending to delay. (L. *dilatorius.*)
dilemma, *n.* dy- or de-*lem*-ma, perplexing situation in which from obstacles that present themselves it is difficult to determine what course to pursue; an argument which consists of two alternatives in which an adversary is caught, and the acceptance of either of which tells against him [Logic]. **horns of a dilemma,** alternatives, on one or other of which an adversary in a logical dilemma is caught. (Gr. *dilemma*, something taken or assumed.)
dilemmatic, *a.* *dy*-le- or *dil*-e-*mat*-ik, pertaining to dilemmas.
dilettante, *n.* dil-e-*tan*-te (*pl.* **dilettanti**), an amateur of the fine arts; a would-be critic of art; one given to dilettantism: *a.* pertaining to or characteristic of a dilettante. (It. *dilettante*, delighting.)
dilettantish, *a.* dil-e-*tan*-tish, amateurish.
dilettantism, *n.* dil-e-*tan*-tizm, the quality or method of dilettantes; an idle, often affected, always barren, admiration and study of the fine arts.
diligence, *n.* *dil*-e-jence, active steady application in business of any kind; assiduity; heedfulness. (Fr.)
diligence, *n.* de-le-*zhahnce*, a heavy public four-wheeled stage-coach, formerly used in western Europe. (Fr.)
diligent, *a.* *dil*-e-jent, industrious; applying oneself steadily and actively to business; painstaking; careful. (Fr.)
diligently, *ad.* in a diligent manner.
dill, *n.* dil, a herb of S. Europe and Africa, *Anethum graveolens*, resembling fennel, the seeds of which yield a carminative oil. (A.S. *dile.*)
dill-water, *n.* a preparation from the seeds of the dill, used for flatulence in children; gripe-water.
dilly, *n.* *dil*-le, a stage-coach (short for *diligence*); the daffodil (short for *daffodil*); a bag made by the Australian aborigines (native name).
dilly-dally, *v.i.* *dil*-le-*dal*-le, to delay, trifle, or loiter; to hesitate [Slang.]
dilogy, *n.* *dil*-o-je *or* *dy*-lo-je, ambiguity in speech· the use of, or an example of, this.
diluent, *a.* *dil*-yew-ent, diluting; liquefying: *n.* that which dilutes, esp. that which dilutes the blood, thus increasing the excretions [Med.]. (L. *diluens*, washing away.)
dilute, *v.t.* dy- *or* di-*lewt*, to weaken, as a spirit, or an acid, or a colour, by admixture; to make more fluid and thinner; to water down: *a.* diluted; weakened; colourless. (L. *dilutus*, washed away.)
dilutee, *n.* dil-yew-*tee*, an unskilled worker who, in an emergency, is put in the place of a skilled worker.
diluter, *n.* dy-*lew*-ter, that which dilutes.
dilution, *n.* dy-*lew*-shon, the act of diluting; a diluted liquid; substitution by the inferior; the employment of dilutees, the replacement of the skilled by the unskilled.
diluvial, *a.* dy-*lew*-ve-al, diluvian; pertaining to the drift formation [Geol.]. (L. *diluvialis.*)
diluvialist, *n.* dy-*lew*-ve-a-list, one who held that most geological phenomena were directly attributable to the Deluge.
diluvian, *a.* dy-*lew*-ve-an, pertaining to a flood; effected or produced by a flood.
diluvianism, *n.* dy-*lew*-ve-a-nizm, the obsolete theory held by the diluvialists.
diluvium, *n.* dy-*lew*-ve-um, a deposit of superficial loam, sand, gravel, etc., caused by large-scale water-action; drift [Geol.]. (L., a deluge.)
dim, *a.* dim, not seeing clearly; not clearly seen; obscure; somewhat dark; dull of apprehension; having its lustre obscured; tarnished: *v.t.* to cloud; to obscure; to render dull; to make less bright; to tarnish or sully. (A.S.)
dime, *n.* dime, a nickel coin of the value of ten cents, the tenth of a dollar [U.S.A.]. (Fr. from L. *decem-*, ten.)
dimension, *n.* de-*mensh*-on, generally, in *pl.*, linear measurement; measure in every form; magnitude; degree, as indicated by the number of literal factors that enter into a term [Alg.]. **the three dimensions,** length, breadth, and thickness; **the fourth dimension,** a hypothetical multiplier which is to volume what volume is to area and, in the theory of relativity, assumed to be time. (Fr.)
dimensional, *a.* de-*mensh*-on-al, concerning dimensions; having dimensions.
dimensioned, *a.* de-*mensh*-ond, having dimensions.
dimerous, *a.* *dim*-er-us, in two parts; in parts arranged in pairs [Biol.].
dimetallic, *a.* *dy*-me-*tal*-ik, containing two atoms or equivalents of a metal.
dimeter, *n.* *dim*-e-ter, a verse of two measures [Pros.]. (Gr. *dimetros*, two-metred.)
dimetric, *a.* dy-*met*-rik, having two measures [Pros.]; tetragonal (of crystals whose vertical axis is unequal to the lateral, as the square prism and square octahedron).
dimidiate, *v.t.* de-*mid*-e-ate, to divide into two equal parts: *a.* lop-sided; halved, with only one half developed [Bot.]; halved in function [Zool.]. (L. *dimidiatus*, divided in half.)

dimidiation, *n.* de-mid-e-*ay*-shon, the act of halving; impaling [Her.].
diminish, *v.t.* de-*min*-ish, to lessen; to decrease; to abate; to degrade; to take from; to take from a note by a sharp, flat, or natural [Mus.]: *v.i.* to become less; to taper. (Fr. *diminuer*, grow less.)
diminishable, *a.* de-*min*-ish-a-bl, capable of being diminished.
diminished, *a.* de-*min*-isht, reduced in size; lessened by a semitone, or (of intervals) made less than minor [Mus.].
diminisher, *n.* de-*min*-ish-er, that which or one who diminishes.
diminuendo, *n.* de-*min*-yew-*en*-doh, a direction gradually to lessen the volume of sound from loud to soft, noted thus, >; a passage treated in this way [Mus.]. (It., literally, diminishing.)
diminution, *n.* *dim*-in-*yew*-shon, the act of lessening; the state of becoming less; degradation; a lessening in estimation; the contraction of the diameter of a column as it ascends from its base to its capital [Arch.]; the division of a long note into shorter ones, as a semibreve into two minims [Mus.]. (Fr.)
diminutival, *a.* dim-e-new-*ty*-val, pertaining to a diminutive: *n.* a diminutive suffix.
diminutive, *a.* de-*min*-yew-tiv, small; narrow; contracted; diminishing: *n.* a word formed from another word to express a little thing of the kind [Gram.]. (L. *diminutivus.*)
diminutively, *ad.* de-*min*-yew-tiv-le, in a diminutive manner; in a manner to lessen.
diminutiveness, *n.* de-*min*-yew-tiv-ness, littleness.
dimissory, *a.* de-*mis*-o-re, dismissing; sending away or granting leave to depart to another jurisdiction [Eccles.]. (L. *dimissus*, sent away.)
dimity, *n.* *dim*-it-e, a stout cotton cloth, ribbed and figured, used chiefly for hangings and window-curtains. (Gr. *dimitos*, of double thread.)
dimly, *ad.* *dim*-le, in a dim manner.
dimmer, *n.* *dim*-er, an electric or other device for causing a light to shine less brightly.
dimmish, *a.* *dim*-ish, somewhat dim or obscure.
dimness, *n.* *dim*-ness, quality or state of being dim.
dimorphic, *a.* dy-*morf*-ik, having or occurring under two separate forms.
dimorphism, *n.* dy-*morf*-izm, the property of assuming crystallizing in two distinct forms, as sulphur when crystallizing at a high and at ordinary temperatures [Min.]; difference of form in corresponding parts of the same species [Bot.]; difference of individual form in the same species [Zool.]. (Gr. *dimorphos*, two-shaped.)
dimorphous, *a.* dy-*morf*-us, having the property of dimorphism.
dimple, *n.* *dimp*-l, a small natural depression in the cheek or other part of the face: *v.i.* to form dimples; to sink into dimples. (Perhaps connected with Ger. *tümpel*, a pool.)
dimpled, *a.* *dimp*-ld, set with dimples.
dimply, *a.* *dimp*-le, full of dimples.
dimyarian, *a.* dim-*yare*-re-an, having two muscular layers: *n.* a bivalve mollusc, the shells of which are worked with two muscles. (Gr. *di-*, and *mys*, muscle.)
din, *n.* din, a loud continued sound; a rattling, clattering, or rumbling sound, long continued; persistent repetition: *v.t.* to strike with continued or confused sound; to impress with noise; to harass with clamour: *v.i.* to make a din. (A.S. *dyn*, noise.)
dinanderie, *n.* (App.), coppersmith's work; brass or copper ecclesiastical and kitchen utensils. (Fr., from *Dinant*, Belgium, a mediæval centre for such work.)
dinar, *n.* *di*-nar, a former Byzantine gold coin, adopted in various Moslem countries; the Serbian (later Yugoslavian) franc; the gold monetary unit of Iraq, equal to £1 sterling; a Persian money of account worth 0·03 of a penny. (Ar., from L. *denarius.*)
dinarchy, *n.* *dy*-nar-ke, a diarchy.
dine, *v.i.* dine, to eat dinner: *v.t.* to provide with dinner. (Fr. *diner.*)
diner, *n.* *dine*-er, one who dines; a railway dining-car. **diner-out,** *n.* one who is fond of going out to dine in company.
ding, *v.t.* ding, to dash with violence; to enforce or urge: *v.i.* to thump; to fall heavily. (Imit.)
ding-dong, *n.* *ding*-dong, the sound of two bells rung alternately; any sound of like monotonous or steady movement: *a.* closely contested with many changes: *v.t.* and *i.* to ring in ding-dong; to jingle; to speak in ding-dong fashion; to repeat insistently.
dinghy, *n.* *ding*-ge, a small ship's boat; a light clinker-built skiff. (Hind. *dingi*, a row-boat.)
dingily, *ad.* *din*-je-le, in a dingy manner.
dinginess, *n.* *din*-je-ness, the quality of being dingy.
dingle, *n.* *ding*-gl, a small narrow wooded dale or glen. (*Dimple.*)
dingle-dangle, *ad.* *ding*-gl-*dang*-gl, hanging loosely or dangling.
dingo, *n.* *ding*-go, the native wild dog of Australia, *Canis dingo.*
dingy, *a.* *din*-je, soiled; of a dark colour; brown; dusky; dun; drab. (Perhaps from *dung.*)
dining-car, *n.* *dine*-ing-kar, a car in which meals are served on long-distance trains.
dining-hall, *n.* a hall to dine in.
dining-room, *n.* a room to dine in.
dining-table, *n.* a table for dining at.
dinkle, *n.* *ding*-kl, one-grained wheat. (Gr., *spelt.*)
dinkum, *n.* *ding*-kum, toil: *a.* honest; genuine; thorough. **fair dinkum,** fair play [Austral. slang].
dinky, *a.* *ding*-ke, neat, smart, trim [Slang].
dinner, *n.* *din*-ner, the principal meal of the day; an entertainment; a feast. **dinner bell,** the bell rung when dinner is ready. **dinner hour,** dinner-time. **dinner jacket,** a dress-coat without tails. **dinner party,** the company of diners. **dinner set,** the china, etc., used at dinner. **dinner-table,** a dining-table. **dinner-time,** the usual time for dining. **dinner-wagon,** a set of shelves on castors for use in the dining-room. (Fr. *diner.*)
dinnerless, *a.* *din*-ner-less, having no dinner.
Dinornis, *n.* dy-nawr-nis, a recently extinct genus of birds of a gigantic size, comprising the moas and allied to the kiwis, formerly inhabiting New Zealand. (Gr. *deinos*, terrible, extraordinary, *ornis*, a bird.)
dinosaur, *n.* *dy*-no-*sawr*, any one of the *Dinosauria*, an extinct group of reptiles of wide distribution. (Gr. *deinos*, and *sauros*, a lizard.)
dinothere, *n.* *dy*-no-theer, a large proboscidean of the extinct order *Dinotherium*, having a massive pair of downward-curving tusks in the lower jaw. (Gr. *deinos*, and *theiron*, beast.)
dint, *n.* dint, a blow; a stroke; the mark made by a blow; effort; power: *v.t.* to dent. (A.S. *dynt*, a blow.)
diocesan, *a.* dy-*os*-e-san, relating to a diocese: *n.* a bishop; one in possession of a diocese, and having ecclesiastical jurisdiction over it.
diocese, *n.* *dy*-o-sis *or* -seece, the circuit of country subject ecclesiastically to a bishop's jurisdiction. (Fr. *diocèse.*)
diode, *n.* *dy*-ode, a form of vacuum tube which rectifies alternating currents [Elect.].
Diodon, *n.* *dy*-o-don, a genus of telostean fishes, including the globe-fish and porcupine-fish, with two continuous bones, one in the upper and the other in the under jaw, for teeth. (Gr. *di-*, and *odous*, a tooth.)
diœcia, *n.pl.* dy-*ee*-she-a, a class of plants having the stamens on one individual and the pistils on another [Bot.]. (Gr. *di-*, and *oikos*, a house.)
diœcious, *a.* dy-*ee*-she-us, belonging to the diœcia [Bot.]; having the male organs on one individual and the female on another [Zool.].
Dionæa, *n.pl.* dy-o-*nee*-a, a genus of plants, allied to the sundew, of which the sole species is Venus's fly-trap. (*Dione*, mother of Venus.)
Dionysiac, *a.* dy-o-*nis*-e-ak, pertaining to Dionysius, the Greek god of wine, to his worship or festivals; Bacchic.
diophantine, *a.* dy-o-*fan*-tine, relating to the analysis of Diophantus, the Greek mathematician.
diopside, *n.* dy-*op*-side, a greyish-green transparent foliated variety of augite [Min.]. (Gr. *diopsis*, a seeing through.)
dioptase, *n.* dy-*op*-tase, a rare silicate of copper occurring in emerald green crystals. (Fr.)
diopter, *n.* dy-*op*-ter, a unit of measurement for lenses; a surgical speculum; the index arm of a graduated circle; an ancient form of theodolite. (Gr.)
dioptric, *a.* dy-*op*-trik, dioptrical: *n.* a diopter.

dioptrical, *a.* dy-*op*-tre-kal, assisting the sight in the view of distant objects; refracting light through lenses; pertaining to dioptrics. (Gr. *dioptrikos*, relating to the diopter, or theodolite, used by Hipparchus.)

dioptrics, *n.* dy-*op*-triks, that part of optics which treats of the refraction of light, or its transmission from one medium into another differing in kind.

diorama, *n.* dy-o-*rah*-ma, a pictorial representation lit up partly by a strong reflected light hidden from the spectators, partly by transmitted light, and seen through openings in a partition; a dissolving view; a building for a dioramic exhibition. (Gr. *diorao*, look through.)

dioramic, *a.* dy-o-*ram*-ik, pertaining to a diorama.

diorite, *n.* *dy*-o-rite, a very hard and close-grained igneous rock consisting chiefly of plagioclase feldspar with hornblende.

dioritic, *a.* dy-o-*rit*-ik, pertaining to diorite.

diorthosis, *n.* dy-or-*thoh*-sis, the setting right of crooked or distorted limbs [Surg.]. (Gr. *dia-*, and *orthos*, straight.)

diosmosis, *n.* dy-os-*moh*-sis, the passage of liquid through a membrane. (Gr. *di-*, and *ösmos*, pushing.)

diota, *n.* dy-*oh*-ta, a vessel for liquids with a narrow neck and two handles. (Gr. *diote*, two-eared.)

dioxide, *n.* dy-*oks*-ide, an oxide with two equivalents of oxygen [Chem.]. (Gr. *di-*, and *oxide*.)

dip, *n.* dip, the act of dipping; inclination downward; depression; bathing, esp. outdoor; a candle made by dipping; a sauce, custard, etc. [U.S.A.]; inclination downward from a horizontal line [Magnet.]; the downward inclination of strata [Geol.]: *v.i.* to sink; to pierce; to take a slight interest in; to look cursorily; to choose at random; to incline downward: *v.t.* to immerse for a short time; to lower and raise quickly; to take out, as with a ladle; to baptize by immersion; to moisten; to plunge. (A.S. *dyppan.*)

dipchick, *n.* *dip*-chik, the dabchick.

dipetalous, *a.* dy-*pet*-al-us, having two petals [Bot.]. (Gr. *di-*, and *petalon*, a leaf.)

diphase, *a.* *dy*-faze, two-phase [Elect.].

diphosgene, *n.* dy-*fos*-jeen, a poison-gas of the same composition as phosgene but with twice the molecular weight.

diphtheria, *n.* dif-*theer*-re-a, an acute infectious disease characterized by the formation in the back of the throat of false membranes on the mucous membranes. (Gr. *diphthera*, a skin stripped off.)

diphtherial, *a.* dif-*theer*-re-al, pertaining to diphtheria.

diphtheric, *a.* dif-*the*-rik, diphtheritic.

diphtheritic, *a.* dif-the-*rit*-ik, connected with or caused by diphtheria.

diphtheritis, *n.* dif-the-*ry*-tis, diphtheria.

diphtheroid, *a.* *dif*-the-royd, resembling diphtheria or its bacterium: *n.* any harmless bacterium similar morphologically to that causing diphtheria.

diphthong, *n.* *dif*-thong, a union of two vowels in one sound; a digraph; (loosely) a vowel-ligature, as æ. (Gr.)

diphthongal, *a.* dif-*thong*-gal, pertaining to a diphthong; consisting of two vowels sounded as one.

diphthongize, *v.t.* *dif*-thong-ize, to form into a diphthong.

diphyllous, *a.* dy-*fil*-us, two-leaved [Bot.]. (Gr. *di-*, and *phyllon*, a leaf.)

diphyodont, *a.* *dif*-fe-o-dont, having two successive sets of teeth—deciduous and permanent: *n.* a diphyodont animal. (Gr. *diphyes*, and *odous*, a tooth.)

dipl-, Greek prefix signifying " double."

diplegia, *n.* dy-*plee*-je-a, paralysis of corresponding parts on both sides of the body. (Gr. *di-*, and *plēgē*, blow or stroke.)

dipleidoscope, *n.* di-*ply*-do-skope, an instrument for observing the transit of the sun or other heavenly body over the meridian. (Gr. *diploos*, double, *eidos*, form, and *skopeo*, view.)

diplodocus, *n.* di-*plod*-o-kus, a member of a genus of gigantic herbivorous lizards of the Upper Jurassic of Colorado and Wyoming. (Gr. *diploos*, and *dokos*, a beam.)

diploe, *n.* *dip*-lo-e, the cancellous tissue between the layers of certain bones of the skull [Anat.]. (Gr. *diploos.*)

diplogenic, *a.* dip-lo-*jen*-ik, producing two substances; partaking of the nature of two bodies. (Gr. *diploos*, and *gennao*, produce.)

diploma, *n.* de-*ploh*-ma, a certificate conferring honour or authority; a document certifying graduation from an educational institution: *v.t.* to furnish with a diploma. (Gr., a writing folded double.)

diplomac *n.* de-*ploh*-ma-se, the art of negotiating relations between states, in accordance with the principles and usage of international law; forms of international negotiation; a diplomatic body at a foreign court; skill or dexterity in managing bodies of men; tact. (Fr. *diplomatie.*)

diplomat, *n.* *dip*-lo-mat, a diplomatist.

diplomate, *n.* *dip*-lo-mate, a holder of a diploma.

diplomatic, *a.* dip-lo-*mat*-ik, pertaining to diplomacy or to ambassadors; skilled in or characteristic of diplomacy; tactful. **diplomatic body** or **corps,** the whole number of diplomatic representatives accredited to any single government.

diplomatically, *ad.* dip-lo-*mat*-e-ka-le, according to the rules of diplomacy; tactfully.

diplomatics, *n.* dip-lo-*mat*-iks, the science of deciphering ancient writings, as diplomas and charters, and of ascertaining their authenticity and date.

diplomatist, *n* de-*ploh*-ma-tist, one engaged in diplomacy; a diplomat.

diplomatology, *n.* de-*ploh*-ma-*tol*-o-je, the science of diplomatics.

diploneural, *a.* de-ploh-*newr*-ral, supplied by two different nerves [Anat.].

diplopia, *n.* di-*ploh*-pe-a, double vision [Med.]. (Gr. *diploos*, and *ops*, the eye.)

diplostemonous, *a.* *dip*-lo-*steem*-on-us, with the stamens in two whorls, the outer alternating with the corolla [Bot.]. (Gr. *diploos*, and *stēmon*, warp.)

Dipnoi, *n.pl.* *dip*-no-e, the order comprising the lungfish. (Gr. *di-*, and *pneō*, breathe.)

dipnous, *a.* *dip*-no-us, provided with both lungs and gills [Zool.].

dipody, *n.* *dip*-o-de, a series of two feet; a double foot [Pros.]. (Gr. *di-*, and *pous*, foot.)

dipolar, *a.* dy-*poh*-lar, having, or pertaining to, two poles [Magnet.].

Dippels-oil, *n.* *dip*-pelz-oyl, an animal oil obtained by the dry distillation of bones. (J. C. *Dippel*, who first prepared it about 1710.)

dipper, *n.* *dip*-per, one who dips; a ladle or other dipping implement; the seven stars of the Great Bear [U.S.A.]; the water-ouzel, *Cinclus aquaticus.*

dipping-needle, *n.* *dip*-ping-*nee*-dl, a simple form of inclinometer showing the inclination of the magnetic needle to the horizon at any given place [Magnet.].

diprismatic, *a.* dy-priz-*mat*-ik, doubly prismatic; having cleavages parallel to the sides of a four-sided vertical prism and also to a horizontal prism [Min.].

diprotodon, *n.* de-*prot*-o-don, a gigantic extinct marsupial of Australia, allied to the kangaroo. (Gr. *di-*, and *protos*, first.)

dipsas, *n.* *dip*-sas, a fabulous serpent, whose bite was said to produce a mortal thirst. (Gr. *dipsa*, thirst.)

dip-sector, *n.* an instrument for measuring the true dip of the horizon.

dipsomania, *n.* *dip*-so-*may*-ne-a, morbid and recurrent uncontrollable craving for alcoholic drink. (Gr. *dipsa*, thirst, and *mania.*)

dipsomaniac, *n.* *dip*-so-*may*-ne-ak, one affected with dipsomania; a confirmed drunkard.

dipsosis, *n.* dip-*soh*-sis, morbid thirst accompanying disease [Med.].

dipstick, *n.* *dip*-stik, a rod for ascertaining the liquid content of a metal container.

diptera, *n.pl.* *dip*-ter-ra, a large order of two-winged insects comprising the true flies, mosquitoes, gnats, and many insect pests. (Gr. *dipteros*, two-winged.)

dipteral, *a.* *dip*-ter-ral, having a double peristyle [Arch.]. **dipteral temple,** a temple flanked or surrounded by two rows of columns.

dipteran, *a.* *dip*-ter-ran, pertaining to the diptera: *n.* one of the diptera.

dipterology, *n.* dip-ter-*rol*-o-je, the branch of entomology that treats of the diptera.

dipterous, *a.* *dip*-ter-rus, having two wings only; belonging to the diptera.

diptych, *n.* *dip*-tik, a writing tablet, folded in two, of ivory, metal, or wood, and waxed inside; a picture on two leaves opening like a screen, generally

serving as an altar-piece, externally often beautifully carved; a register of the names of Roman consuls and other magistrates and of early Christian bishops, martyrs, etc. (Gr. *diptycha*, two tablets forming a pair.)
dipus, *n.* *dy*-pus, any member of the Old World family of rodents, *Dipodidæ*, including the jerboas.
dipyre, *n.* de-*pire*, mizzonite [Min.]. (Gr. *dipyros*, twice fired.)
diradiation, *n.* dy-ray-de-*ay*-shon, the diffusion or emission of rays of light from a luminous body.
dire, *a.* dire, evil in a great degree; dreadful, dismal, horrible, or terrible. (L. *dirus*, terrible.)
direct, *a.* dy-*rekt*, straight; onward, opposed to retrograde; in line, as of father and son, opposed to collateral; going in a straight line or course; not circuitous; straightforward; plain; express: *n.* in plain-song notation, a character placed at the end of a staff to direct the performer to the first note of the next staff [Mus.]. **direct action,** action directed towards an immediate end, esp. [Econ.] pressure by means of strikes, sabotage, revolution, etc. **direct interval,** that which forms any kind of harmony on the fundamental sound which produces it, as the fifth, major, third, and octave [Mus.]. **direct tax,** a tax assessed directly on incomes, property, etc., as distinct from excise, customs, and other taxation on articles of consumption. (L. *directus*, straight.)
direct, *v.t.* dy-*rekt*, to aim in a straight line toward a place or object; to show the right road or course; to guide, conduct, or manage; to prescribe a course, sometimes with authority; to address, as a letter; to manage or act as director of. **direct current,** an electric current constant in direction as opposed to alternating current [Elect.].
★**direction,** *n.* dy-*rek*-shon, the act of directing; end aimed at; the line in which a body moves; course; the act of governing; management; guidance; instruction in what manner to proceed; the address on a letter; a body or board of directors. **direction finder** an instrument for finding the direction from which wireless signals are coming. (L. *directio.*)
directional, *a.* dy-*rek*-shon-al, pertaining to direction; pertaining to wireless equipment designed to act only in a given direction or to identify the direction of incoming signals. **directional aerial,** an aerial which will send out or receive wireless waves in a greater degree from one direction than from others.
directive, *a.* dy-*rek*-tiv, directing; regulative: *n.* a general instruction.
directly, *ad.* dy-*rekt*-le, immediately; straight to the point; expressly; *conj.* as soon as; immediately after [Coll.].
directness, *n.* dy-*rekt*-ness, the quality of being direct; straightness; nearness of way.
directoire, *a.* de-*rek*-twar, in the fashion or manner in vogue under the Directory of 1795–99 in France (used of furniture and women's wear).
director, *n.* dy-*rek*-tor, one who directs; one who superintends or manages; a counsellor, instructor, or guide; that which directs, controls, or regulates; one appointed to direct the affairs of a company; a theatrical producer; that which directs or controls by influence.
directorate, *n.* dy-*rek*-to-rat, the office or status of a director; a board of directors.
directorial, *a.* dy-*rek*-*taw*-re-al, pertaining to directors; containing direction.
directorship, *n.* dy-*rek*-tor-ship, the office of director.
directory, *a.* dy-*rek*-to-re, directing; containing directions: *n.* a book containing the names, residences, and occupations of the inhabitants of a place; a board of directors; a book of directions, especially for public worship or religious services; the executive council of the French Republic constituted in 1795, and governing until 1799.
directress, *n.* dy-*rek*-tress, a female director.
directrix, *n.* dy-*rek*-triks, a directress; a straight line perpendicular to the axis of a conic section in relation to which its nature may be defined [Math.].
direful, *a.* *dire*-ful, dire.
direfully, *ad.* *dire*-ful-le, in a direful manner.
direfulness, *n.* the quality of being direful.
diremption, *n.* dy-*remp*-shon, a forcible separation. (L.)
direness, *n.* *dire*-ness, the quality of being dire.
dirge, *n.* dirj, a hymn or melody expressive of grief and mourning; a lugubrious song. (L. *dirige*, direct, first word of some such hymn.)
dirhem, *n.* der-*hem*, a weight of Egypt and the Near East, of approximately 48½ grs. troy.
dirigibility, *n.* *di*-re-je-*bil*-e-te, the quality of being steerable.
dirigible, *a.* *di*-re-je-bl, guidable; steerable: *n.* an aircraft lighter than air.
diriment, *a.* *di*-re-ment, rendering void. **diriment impediment,** an impediment that nullifies a marriage from its start. (L. *dirimens*, taking apart.)
dirk, *n.* derk, a kind of dagger or poniard; a short sword: *v.t.* to stab with a dirk. (Perhaps from Dut. *dolk*, a dagger.)
dirt, *n.* dert, anything that is foul or renders foul; mud; mire; dust; dirtiness; land or soil [Coll.]; refuse; foul talk; trash: *v.t.* to make foul; to soil. **dirt cheap,** extremely cheap. **to eat dirt,** to put up with contempt or insult.
dirtily, *ad.* *der*-te-le, in a dirty manner.
dirtiness, *n.* the state of being dirty.
dirt-track, *n.* *dert*-trak, a specially constructed track for racing, esp. for motor-cycle racing.
★**dirty,** *a.* *der*-te, soiled with dirt; foul; filthy; soiled, or as if so; nasty; gusty, stormy (of weather); contemptible; obscene, lewd: *v.t.* to soil; to tarnish: *v.i.* to become dirty. **dirty work,** drudgery; questionable proceedings. (Ice. *drit*, excrement.)
dis-, dis, Latin prefix denoting separation, a parting from, and having therefore the force of a privative and negative, as in *disarm*, *disoblige*, *disagree*. For words with this prefix not included in this vocabulary reference should be made to the word so prefixed.
disability, *n.* dis-a-*bil*-e-te, the state of being disabled; want of competent bodily or mental ability; incapacity; unfitness; legal incapacity; inability.
disable, *v.t.* dis-*ay*-bl, to render unfit; to deprive of competent power; to deprive of adequate means or resources; to deprive of legal qualifications; to render incapable; to disqualify.
disablement, *n.* dis-*ay*-bl-ment, the fact or state of being injured or disabled; disability.
disabuse, *v.t.* dis-a-*bewz*, to free from mistake; to undeceive.
disaccord, *v.i.* dis-a-*kord*, to disagree; to be out of accord with: *n.* disagreement; discordancy.
disaccordant, *a.* dis-a-*kord*-ant, disagreeing; not accordant.
disaccustom, *v.t.* dis-a-*kust*-om, to destroy or free from the force of habit.
disacknowledge, *v.t.* dis-ak-*nol*-lej, to disown.
disadvantage, *n.* dis-ad-*vahn*-taj, that which prevents or is unfavourable to success; unfavourableness; prejudice to one's advantage; detriment; loss; injury: *v.t.* to act to the prejudice of.
disadvantageous, *a.* dis-ad-vahn-*tay*-jus, unfavourable to success or prosperity; not calculated to advantage one; depreciative.
disadvantageously, *ad.* in a manner to disadvantage.
disadvantageousness, *n.* the quality of being disadvantageous.
disadventurous, *a.* dis-ad-*ven*-tewr-us, unprosperous.
disaffect, *v.t.* dis-af-*fekt*, to alienate the affection or loyalty of.
disaffected, *a.* alienated in affection or loyalty.
disaffectedly, *ad.* in a disaffected manner.
disaffectedness, *n.* the quality of being disaffected.
disaffection, *n.* dis-af-*fek*-shon, alienation of affection, attachment, or good-will; want of affection; dislike, disloyalty. (Fr. *désaffection.*)
disaffiliate, *v.t.* dis-a-*fil*-e-ate, to annul the affiliation of; to disassociate.
disaffirm, *v.t.* dis-a-*ferm*, to show to be untrue; to deny; to contradict; to reverse; to overthrow or annul [Law].
disaffirmation, *n.* dis-af-er-*may*-shon, the act of disaffirming; refutation; annulment [Law].
disafforest, *v.t.* dis-a-*fo*-rest, to free from forest laws; to denude of forest growth.
disafforestation, *n.* *dis*-a-*fo*-res-*tay*-shon, disafforesting.
disaggregate, *v.t.* dis-*ag*-gre-gate, to separate an aggregate mass into its component parts.

disaggregation, *n.* dis-ag-gre-*gay*-shon, the act or result of disaggregating.

disagree, *v.t.* dis-a-*gree*, to differ; not to be exactly alike; to differ in opinion; to be unsuitable; to be in opposition; to be out of harmony; to fall out; to upset. (Fr. *désagréer.*)

disagreeable, *a.* dis-a-*gree*-a-bl, not agreeable; unpleasant; offensive: *n.* (*usually pl.*) annoyances; vexations.

disagreeableness, *n.* dis-a-*gree*-a-bl-ness, the state of being disagreeable.

disagreeably, *ad.* dis-a-*gree*-a-ble, in a disagreeable manner.

disagreement, *n.* dis-a-*gree*-ment, want of agreement; difference of opinion or sentiment; dissension; discord; unsuitableness.

disallow, *v.t.* dis-al-*lou*, not to permit; to refuse to sanction; not to approve; not to receive; not to allow or admit as just: *v.i.* to refuse permission; not to grant. (O.Fr. *desalouer.*)

disallowable, *a.* not allowable.

disallowance, *n.* dis-al-*lou*-ance, refusal to admit or permit; prohibition; rejection.

disally, *v.t.* and *i.* dis-a-*ly*, to free from, or to break, an alliance.

disanchor, *v.t.* and *i.* dis-*ang*-kor, to force or free a vessel from its anchor; to weigh anchor.

disanimate, *v.t.* dis-*an*-e-mate, to dishearten; to deprive of vitality.

disannul, *v.t.* dis-an-*nul*, to annul; to make void.

disannulment, *n.* rescinded annulment.

disanoint, *v.t.* dis-a-*noynt*, to annul consecration.

disapparel, *v.t.* dis-ap-*pa*-rel, to disrobe; to strip of raiment.

disappear, *v.i.* dis-a-*peer*, to vanish from sight; to cease to appear or show itself; to be lost; to cease to exist.

disappearance, *n.* dis-a-*peer*-rance, the act or fact of disappearing; ceasing to appear; removal from sight.

disappoint, *v.t.* dis-a-*poynt*, to defeat what is expected or intended; to fail to gratify another's wish; to frustrate; to balk. (Fr. *désappointer.*)

disappointed, *pp.* and *a.* dis-a-*poyn*-ted, having suffered disappointment; frustrated; unequipped.

disappointingly, *ad.* in a disappointing manner.

disappointment, *n.* dis-a-*poynt*-ment, defeat or failure of expectation, hope, wish, or intention; failure of design or plan.

disappreciate, *v.t.* dis-a-*pree*-she-ate, to undervalue.

disapprobation, *n.* dis-*ap*-pro-*bay*-shon, disapproval; condemnation.

disapprobatory, *a.* dis-*ap*-pro-*bay*-to-re, tending to disapprove.

disappropriate, *a.* dis-a-*proh*-pre-at, not appropriated, or not having appropriated church property. **disappropriated church,** a church from which the appropriated parsonage, glebe, and tithes are severed.

disappropriate, *v.t.* dis-a-*proh*-pre-ate, to remove from individual possession; to withdraw from an appropriate use; to deprive of appropriated property, as a church.

disapproval, *n.* dis-a-*proo*-val, disapprobation; dislike.

disapprove, *v.t.* dis-a-*proov*, not to approve of; to censure; to reject, as not approved of.

disapprovingly, *ad.* dis-a-*proo*-ving-le, by disapprobation.

disarm, *v.t.* dis-*arm*, to deprive of arms or of the means of harming; to render harmless; to subdue: *v.i.* to put aside arms; to reduce considerably, or to do away with, a military establishment. (Fr. *désarmer.*)

disarmament, *n.* dis-*arm*-a-ment, the act of disarming; the reduction of a military establishment to a minimum; the state of being disarmed.

disarrange, *v.t.* dis-a-*raynj*, to put out of order; to unsettle.

disarrangement, *n.* dis-a-*raynj*-ment, disturbance of order; confusion.

disarray, *n.* dis-a-*ray*, disorder; undress: *v.t.* to undress; to throw (esp. an army) into disorder; to rout. (Fr. *désarroi.*)

disarticulate, *v.t.* dis-ar-*tik*-yew-late, to take to pieces at the joints.

disarticulation, *n.* dis-ar-tik-yew-*lay*-shon, the act of disarticulating; amputation at a joint [Surg.].

disassemble, *v.t.* dis-a-*sem*-bl, to take (a piece of mechanism) to pieces.

disassimilation, *n.* *dis*-as-sim-e-*lay*-shon, the act of converting assimilated substances into other forms; such conversion.

disassociate, *v.t.* dis-as-*soh*-she-ate, to disunite; to disconnect things associated.

disaster, *n.* di-*zahs*-ter, any especially sudden misfortune; calamity; an omen of evil [Astrol.]: *v.t.* to blast by the stroke of an unlucky planet [Astrol.]. (Fr. *désastre.*)

disastrous, *a.* di-*zahs*-trus, calamitous; occasioning disaster; gloomy; threatening disaster.

disastrously, *ad.* in a disastrous manner.

disastrousness, *n.* misfortune or calamity.

disattach, *v.t.* dis-at-*tatch*, to separate from.

disavow, *v.t.* dis-a-*vou*, to deny; to disown; to disclaim.

disavowal, *n.* dis-a-*vou*-al, the act of disavowing; disowning; repudiation.

disband, *v.t.* dis-*band*, to break up and dismiss a band or body of men, as a regiment or an army; to demobilize; to disperse: *v.i.* to break up. (O.Fr. *desbander.*)

disbandment, *n.* dis-*band*-ment, the act of disbanding.

disbar, *v.t.* dis-*bar*, to expel a barrister from the bar.

disbark, *v.t.* dis-*bark*, to strip of bark.

disbarment, *n.* dis-*bar*-ment, the act of disbarring; state of being disbarred.

disbelief, *n.* dis-be-*leef*, act of disbelieving; refusal to believe; want of belief.

disbelieve, *v.t.* dis-be-*leev*, not to believe; to refuse to credit.

disbeliever, *n.* dis-be-*leev*-er, one who refuses belief; an infidel.

disbench, *v.t.* dis-*bench*, to deprive of his status as a bencher.

disbodied, *a.* dis-*bod*-id, disembodied.

disbowel, *v.t.* dis-*bou*-el, to take out the intestines.

disbranch, *v.t.* dis-*brahnch*, to deprive of branches.

disbud, *v.t.* dis-*bud*, to deprive of buds or shoots.

disburden, *v.t.* dis-*bur*-dn, to ease or rid of a burden, or anything troublesome or cumbersome; to get rid of: *v.i.* to ease the mind.

disburse, *v.t.* dis-*burse*, to pay out, as money; to spend or lay out. (O.Fr. *desbourser.*)

disbursement, *n.* dis-*burse*-ment, the act of disbursing from a public or private chest; the sum paid out.

disburser, *n.* dis-*burse*-er, he who disburses money.

disc, *n.* disk, a disk.

discal, *a.* *dis*-kal, pertaining to or resembling a disk; discoid.

discalceate, *a.* dis-*kal*-se-at, barefooted; sandalled: *n.* a barefoot friar or nun. (L. *discalceatus*, without shoes.)

discalced, *a.* dis-*kalst*, barefoot; unshod.

discandy, *v.i.* dis-*kan*-de, to melt; to dissolve.

discapacitate, *v.t.* dis-ka-*pas*-e-tate, to incapacitate.

discard, *n.* *dis*-kahrd, the throwing out of the unnecessary cards; the cards thrown out: *v.i.* dis-*kahrd*, to throw out of the hand such cards as are not needed: *v.t.* to dismiss; to cast off; to give up and be done with.

discase, *v.t.* dis-*kace*, to strip; to undress.

discern, *v.t.* di-*zern*, to distinguish clearly by the eye or the understanding; to judge; to discriminate; to know: *v.i.* to see or understand the difference. (Fr. *discerner.*)

discerner, *n.* di-*zern*-er, one who discerns.

discernible, *a.* di-*zern*-e-bl, perceptible.

discernibleness, *n.* the quality of being discernible.

discernibly, *ad.* in a manner to be discernible.

discerning, *a.* di-*zern*-ing, able to discern; sharp-sighted, penetrating, or acute: *n.* the act of discerning; discernment.

discerningly, *ad.* with discernment.

discernment, *n.* di-*zern*-ment, the act or faculty of discerning; power of perceiving differences; discrimination; acuteness. (Fr. *discernement.*)

discerp, *v.t.* di-*serp*, to tear off or pluck asunder. (L. *discerpo*, tear off.)

discerptibility, *n.* di-*serp*-te-*bil*-e-te, capability or liability to be torn asunder or disunited.

discerptible, *a.* di-*serp*-te-bl, that may be torn asunder; separable. (*dis-*, and L. *carpo*, pluck.)

discerption, *n.* di-*serp*-shon, the act of pulling to pieces, or of separating the parts.
discharge, *v.t.* dis-*chahrj*, to unload; to free from any load, burden, task, or charge; to explode; to shoot; to pay; to send away by paying; to free from claim or demand by giving a receipt in full; to free from an obligation; to clear from an accusation; to absolve; to give vent to; to perform or execute; to dismiss; to release; to cause to emit electricity; to remove colour from by bleaching; *v.i.* to empty itself; to unload; to go off (of a gun). (O.Fr. *descharger.*)
discharge, *n.* dis-*chahrj*, the act of discharging; unloading; emission; that which is discharged; dismissal; release; acquittal; payment; execution; exemption; a document certifying acquittal, exemption, etc.
discharger, *n.* dis-*chahr*-jer, one who or that which discharges; an instrument for discharging anything electrical [Elect.].
discharge-tube, *n.* a sealed tube or bulb of glass or quartz in which a luminous electric charge takes place [Elect.].
discharge-valve, *n.* a valve which covers the top of the barrel of the air-pump, and opens upwards; a discharge-tube [Elect.].
discharging-arch, *n.* an arch over a door, window, etc., to distribute or relieve the pressure [Arch.].
discharging-rod, *n.* a discharger [Elect.].
disciferous, *a.* dis-*sif*-er-rus, disk-bearing. (L. *discus*, and *fero*, bear.)
disciform, *a. dis*-e-fawrm, in the form of a disk. (L. *discus*, disk, and *forma*, shape.)
discinct, *a.* dis-*sinkt*, ungirded. (L. *dis-*, and *cinctus*, girt.)
disciple, *n.* de-*sy*-pl, one who receives or professes to receive instruction from another; an adherent to the doctrine of another; a learner; a follower. (Fr.)
discipleship, *n.* de-*sy*-pl-ship, the state of being a disciple.
disciplinable, *a. dis*-e-plin-a-bl, capable of being taught or trained; that may be made matter of discipline; subject to discipline.
disciplinal, *a. dis*-e-plin-al, pertaining to, or of the nature of discipline.
disciplinant, *n.* dis-e-plin-ant, one who subjects himself to discipline, esp. a member of a religious order given to acts of self-mortification.
disciplinarian, *a.* dis-e-ple-nare-re-an, pertaining to discipline: *n.* an expert in the art of discipline; one rigorous in enforcing discipline.
disciplinary, *a. dis*-e-plin-a-re, bearing on discipline; tending to discipline.
discipline, *n. dis*-e-plin, training generally; training according to rule or drill; rules of training, or method of regulating; subjection to rules; a course of instruction in a special branch of knowledge or art; punishment intended to correct crimes or errors; the rules and their enforcement binding upon the members of the Church [Eccles.]; chastisement, or the instrument of it: *v.t.* to train; to drill; to teach obedience. (Fr.)
discipliner, *n. dis*-e-plin-er, one who disciplines.
discipular, *a.* dis-*sip*-yew-lar, pertaining to a disciple.
disclaim, *v.t.* dis-*klame*, to deny and repudiate the possession of, connection with, or subjection to; to disown or disavow; to reject: *v.i.* to disavow all part or share. (O.Fr. *disclaimer.*)
disclaimant, *n.* dis-*klame*-ant, one who makes a disclaimer.
disclaimer, *n.* dis-*klame*-er, the act of disclaiming; disavowal; repudiation; renunciation; one who disclaims.
disclamation, *n.* dis-kla-*may*-shon, the act of disclaiming (esp. in Scots. law, by a tenant); repudiation.
disclose, *v.t.* dis-*kloze*, to uncover; to reveal; to lay open. (O.Fr. *desclose.*)
discloser, *n.* dis-*kloze*-er, one who discloses or reveals.
disclosure, *n.* dis-*kloze*-yewr, the act of disclosing or revealing; that which is disclosed or revealed.
discobolus, *n.* dis-*kob*-o-lus, a quoit-thrower of ancient Greece; a statue of such. (L. *discobolus*, quoit or discus.)
discodactylous, *a. dis*-ko-*dak*-te-lus, with the digits terminating in sucking disks (esp. of tree-frogs) [Zool.].
discoid, *a. dis*-koyd, having the form of a disk; round and flat; vertically convoluted on the same plane [Bot.]. **discoid flowers,** compound flowers, not radiated, with florets all tubular [Bot.]. (Gr. *diskoeides*, discus-like.)
discoloration, *n.* dis-kul-ur-*ray*-shon, the act of discolouring; the state of being discoloured.
discolour, *v.t.* dis-*kul*-ur, to alter the colour of, by staining or tarnishing; to alter the colour or give a false colour to: *a.* of two or more colours [Bot. and Zool.].
discoloured, *a.* dis-*kul*-urd, changed; variegated.
discolourment, *n.* dis-*kul*-ur-ment, change in colour; discoloration.
discomfit, *v.t.* dis-*kum*-fit, to disconcert; to frustrate; to defeat; to scatter in fight; *n.* discomfiture. (O.Fr. *desconfire*, literally, to undo completely.)
discomfiture, *n.* dis-*kum*-fe-tewr, defeat; overthrow; frustration; disappointment.
discomfort, *n.* dis-*kum*-fort, the want of comfort; uneasiness; pain; distress; grief; *v.t.* to cause discomfort; to make uncomfortable.
discomfortable, *a.* dis-*kum*-for-ta-bl, uncomfortable; comfortless; causing discomfort.
discommend, *v.t.* dis-kom-*mend*, to blame; to censure.
discommendable, *a.* dis-kom-*men*-da-bl, blameable; censurable; deserving disapprobation.
discommendation, *n. dis*-kom-men-*day*-shon, censure.
discommode, *v.t.* dis-kom-*mode*, to inconvenience; to incommode; to annoy. (Fr. *discommoder.*)
discommodity, *n.* dis-ko-*mod*-e-te, the quality of being unsuitable; a disadvantage.
discommon, *v.t.* dis-*kom*-mon, to appropriate common land by enclosing it [Law]; to deprive of the right to a common; to deprive of a privilege; to forbid a trader to serve undergraduates.
discommunity, *n.* dis-ko-*mew*-ne-te, want of community.
discompose, *v.t.* dis-kom-*poze*, to disorder; to disarrange; to disturb; to disquiet; to ruffle.
discomposedness, *n.* dis-kom-*poh-zed*-ness, the state of being discomposed.
discomposingly, *ad.* dis-kom-*poh*-zing-le, in a composing manner.
discomposure, *n.* dis-kom-*poh*-zhur, discomposedness; agitation; perturbation.
disconcert, *v.t.* dis-kon-*sert*, to throw into disorder and frustrate; to discompose; to confound the self-possession of. (O.Fr. *disconcerter.*)
disconcertion, *n.* dis-kon-*ser*-shon, the act of disconcerting; discomposure.
disconcertment, *n.* dis-kon-*sert*-ment, discomposure.
disconformable, *a.* dis-kon-*fawrm*-a-bl, unconformable; inconsistent.
disconformity, *n.* dis-kon-*fawrm*-e-te, want of agreement or conformity; inconsistency.
discongruity, *n.* dis-kon-*groo*-e-te, incongruity; disagreement; inconsistency.
disconnect, *v.t.* dis-kon-*nekt*, to separate; to disunite.
disconnected, *a.* dis-kon-*nek*-ted, separated; incoherent.
disconnectedly, *ad.* in a disconnected way.
disconnectedness, *n.* incoherence.
disconnection, *n.* disconnexion.
disconnective, *a.* dis-kon-*nek*-tiv, able to disconnect; disjunctive.
disconnexion, *n.* dis-kon-*nek*-shon, the act of disuniting; state of being disunited; want of union.
disconsolate, *a.* dis-*kon*-so-lat, without comfort or consolation, and expecting none; not affording comfort; cheerless; dejected. (L. *dis-*, and *consolatus*, consoled.)
disconsolately, *ad.* in a disconsolate manner.
disconsolateness, *n.* state of being disconsolate.
disconsolation, *n.* dis-kon-so-*lay*-shon, want of comfort.
discontent, *n.* dis-kon-*tent*, want of content; dissatisfaction; uneasiness; a malcontent: *a.* not content; dissatisfied; uneasy: *v.t.* to make uneasy at the present state; to dissatisfy.
discontented, *a.* dis-kon-*ten*-ted, uneasy in mind; dissatisfied.
discontentedly, *ad.* in a discontented manner.
discontentedness, *n.* dis-kon-*ten*-ted-ness, the state of being discontented.

discontentful, *a.* dis-kon-*tent*-ful, full of discontent.
discontentment, *n.* dis-kon-*tent*-ment, the state of being discontented.
discontiguous, *a.* *dis*-kon-*tig*-yew-us, not in contact.
discontinuable, *a.* dis-kon-*tin*-yew-a-bl, that may be discontinued.
discontinuance, *n.* dis-kon-*tin*-yew-ance, interruption of continuance; ceasing to continue; want of continuity; a breaking off or interruption of possession [Law]. **discontinuance of a suit,** interruption in the proceedings in his case by the plaintiff, as by not continuing the process regularly from day to day [Law].
discontinuation, *n.* dis-kon-*tin*-yew-*ay*-shon, interruption of continuity.
discontinue, *v.t.* dis-kon-*tin*-yew, to leave off; to break off; to cease to take: *v.i.* to cease; to lose continuity.
discontinuity, *n.* dis-*kon*-te-*new*-e-te, want of continuity.
discontinuous, *a.* dis-kon-*tin*-yew-us, broken off; interrupted; separated; wide or gaping.
discontinuously, *ad.* interruptedly.
discophoran, *n.* dis-*kof*-o-ran, a member of the sub-class *Discophora* of the Hydrozoa, comprising the jelly-fishes: *a.* pertaining to this group. (Gr., bearing a disk.)
discopodous, *a.* dis-*kop*-o-dus, having disk-shaped feet [Zool.].
discord, *n.* *dis*-kord, disagreement among persons or things; want of harmony; variance; strife; disagreement of sounds; a combination of sounds which is inharmonious, grating, and disagreeable to the ear [Mus.]. (Fr. *discorder.*)
discord, *v.i.* dis-*kord*, to disagree; to jar; to clash.
discordance, *n.* dis-*kor*-dance, discordancy; lack of concord.
discordancy, *n.* dis-*kor*-dan-se, the fact or state of being discordant. (Fr.)
discordant, *a.* dis-*kor*-dant, disagreeing; incongruous; being at variance; opposite; not coincident; not in unison; harsh; jarring; inharmonious.
discordantly, *ad.* dis-*kor*-dant-le, in a discordant manner; in a manner to jar or clash.
discordantness, *n.* dis-*kor*-dant-ness, the quality of being discordant; discordancy.
discorporate, *a.* dis-*kor*-por-at, deprived of corporate rights; disembodied.
discount, *n.* *dis*-kount, allowance; a sum deducted for prompt payment; an allowance or deduction from a sum due, or from a credit; a certain rate per cent deducted from the credit price of goods sold on account of prompt payment; a sum returned in payment; the deduction of a sum for advanced payment; the sum deducted; the act of discounting [Banking]. (O.Fr. *disconter.*)
discount, *v.t.* dis-*kount*, to deduct a certain sum or rate per cent from the principal sum; to lend or advance the amount of, deducting the interest or other rate per cent from the principal at the time of the advance; to deduct; to forestall; to take account of beforehand: *v.i.* to lend or make a practice of lending money, deducting interest at the time of loan.
discountable, *a.* dis-*koun*-ta-bl, that may be discounted.
discount-broker, *n.* one who cashes bills of exchange, and makes advances on securities.
discount-day, *n.* the day of the week on which a bank discounts notes and bills.
discountenance, *v.t.* dis-*koun*-ten-ance, to put out of countenance; to refuse approval; to discourage, as by frowns, censure, arguments, opposition, or cold treatment. (O.Fr. *descontenancer.*)
discounter, *n.* dis-*koun*-ter, one who discounts.
discounting, *n.* *dis*-koun-ting, the act or practice of lending money on discounts.
discourage, *v.t.* dis-*ku*-raj, to repress the courage of; to dishearten or depress; to discountenance, and try to repress or prevent. (O.Fr. *descourager.*)
discourageable, *a.* open to discouragement.
discouragement, *n.* dis-*ku*-raj-ment, the act of discouraging; that which discourages; the state of being discouraged; dissuasion.
discourager, *n.* dis-*ku*-ra-jer, one who or that which discourages.
discouraging, *a.* dis-*ku*-ra-jing, tending to dishearten, or to depress the courage.
discouragingly, *ad.* in a discouraging manner.
discourse, *n.* *dis*-korse, the power or the act of reasoning; a communication of thoughts by words; conversation; a formal treatise or dissertation; a sermon uttered or written. (Fr. *discours.*)
discourse, *v.i.* dis-*korse*, to converse; to communicate thoughts or ideas in a formal manner; to reason; to pass from premises to consequences: *v.t.* to treat of; to utter or give forth.
discourser, *n.* dis-*korse*-er, one who discourses; an orator; the writer of a treatise.
discourteous, *a.* dis-*kur*-te-us, uncivil; rude.
discourteously, *ad.* in a discourteous manner.
discourteousness, *n.* dis-*kur*-te-us-ness, the quality of being discourteous.
discourtesy, *n.* dis-*kur*-te-se, want of courtesy; incivility; rudeness.
discous, *a.* *dis*-kus, discoid; disk-shaped.
discover, *v.t.* dis-*kuv*-er, to disclose; to reveal; to descry, esp. first; to find out, esp. first; to detect. (O.Fr. *descouvrir.*)
discoverability, *n.* dis-*kuv*-er-ra-*bil*-e-te, the possibility of being discovered.
discoverable, *a.* dis-*kuv*-er-ra-bl, that may be discovered or seen, or made known: visible.
discoverer, *n.* dis-*kuv*-er-rer, one who discovers; an explorer.
discovert, *a.* dis-*kuv*-ert, not covert; unmarried or widowed. (O.Fr. *descovert.*)
discoverture, *n.* dis-*kuv*-er-tewr, the state of freedom of a woman, as unmarried or a widow, from the coverture of a husband. [Law].
★**discovery,** *n.* dis-*kuv*-er-re, the action of discovering; disclosure; that which is discovered, found out, or revealed; the unravelling or manner of unfolding the story of a comedy or tragedy [Drama].
discredit, *n.* dis-*kred*-it, want or loss of credit; ill repute; disgrace; state of being disbelieved: *v.t.* not to credit or believe; to deprive of credit, or bring into discredit or disrepute; to deprive of credibility.
discreditable, *a.* dis-*kred*-it-a-bl, tending to injure credit; not creditable; disgraceful.
discreditably, *ad.* in a discreditable manner.
discreet, *a.* dis-*kreet*, circumspect; wary; prudent; judicious, especially in selecting the best means to accomplish a purpose. (Fr. *discret.*)
discreetly, *ad.* dis-*kreet*-le, with discretion.
discreetness, *n.* dis-*kreet*-ness, the quality of being discreet; discretion. (Fr. *discret.*)
discrepance, *n.* dis-*krep*-ance, the fact of being discrepant; discrepancy.
discrepancy, *n.* dis-*krep*-an-se, difference; disagreement; inconsistency. (O.Fr. *descrepance.*)
discrepant, *a.* dis-*krep*-ant, different; disagreeing. (L. *discrepans*, differing in sound.)
discrete, *a.* *dis*-kreet, separate; distinct; disjunct; disjunctive [Gram.]. **discrete proportion,** a proportion in which the ratio of two or more pairs of numbers or quantities is the same, but there is not the same proportion between all the numbers, as 3 : 6 : : 8 : 16. **discrete quantity,** a quantity conceived of as made up of units, and distinct from a continued or continuous quantity. (L. *discretus.*)
discreteness, *n.* dis-*kreet*-ness, the quality of being discrete; disjunctiveness.
discretion, *n.* dis-*kresh*-on, management; that discernment which enables a person to judge critically of what is correct and proper to do, united with caution; nice discernment and judgment; liberty or power of acting without other control than one's own judgment. **at discretion** as may be chosen. **surrender at discretion,** to surrender without stipulation or terms at the mercy of the conqueror. **years of discretion,** of full age; grown up. (L. *discretio.*)
discretional, *a.* dis-*kresh*-on-al, pertaining to discretion; discretionary.
discretionally, *ad.* dis-*kresh*-on-al-le, at discretion; in a discretional manner.
discretionary, *a.* dis-*kresh*-on-a-re, left to discretion; unrestricted.
discretive, *a.* dis-*kree*-tiv, disjunctive. **discretive distinction,** one implying opposition or difference, as "not a man, but a beast" [Gram.]. **discretive proposition,** one that expresses some distinction, opposition, or variety by means of but, though, yet

etc., as, " travellers change their climates, but not their temper " [Logic].
discretively, *ad.* in a discretive manner.
discriminate, *a.* dis-*krim*-in-ate, having the difference marked; characterized by discrimination: *v.i.* to make a difference or distinction; to distinguish; *v.t.* to make a distinction between; to distinguish; to select from others; to distinguish by some note or mark. (L. *discriminare.*)
discriminately, *ad.* dis-*krim*-e-nat-le, distinctly; with minute distinction; particularly.
discriminateness, *n.* dis-*krim*-e-nat-ness, distinctness; marked difference.
discriminating, *a.* dis-*krim*-e-nay-ting, distinguishing; peculiar; distinctive; able to make nice distinctions.
discriminatingly, *ad.* in a discriminating way.
discrimination, *n.* dis-*krim* e-*nay*-shon, the act of discriminating; judgment; discernment; acuteness; distinction; the state of being distinguished; mark of distinction.
discriminative, *a.* dis-*krim*-e-na-tiv, that constitutes a mark of difference; characteristic; that observes distinctions.
discriminatively, *ad.* with discrimination.
discriminator, *n.* dis-*krim*-e-nay-tor, one who discriminates.
discriminatory, *a.* dis-*krim*-e-na-to-re, discriminative.
discrown, *v.t.* dis-*kroun*, to deprive of a crown.
disculpate, *v.t.* dis-*kul*-pate, to exculpate.
disculpation, *n.* dis-kul-*pay*-shon, a clearing from blame; exculpation.
discumber, *v.t.* dis-*kum*-ber, to disencumber.
discursion, *n.* dis-*kur*-shon, the act of digressing; digression; discursive reasoning.
discursive, *a.* dis-*kur*-siv, rambling from one thing to another; desultory; argumentative; reasoning regularly from premises to consequences. (L. *discursus.*)
discursively, *ad.* in a discursive manner.
discursiveness, *n.* dis-*kur*-siv-ness, the state or quality of being discursive.
discursory, *a.* dis-*kur*-so-re, rambling; digressive.
discursus, *n.* dis-*kur*-sus, discursive reasoning [Log.]; a reasoned argument. (L.)
discus, *n. dis*-kus, a quoit; a piece of iron, copper, or stone, usually flat and circular in shape, to be thrown. (L.)
discuss, *v.t.* dis-*kuss*, to examine a topic in disputation with another with a view to arrive at the truth about it; to debate; to break up, disperse, or dissolve, as a tumour [Med.]; to consume together, as a fowl or a bottle of wine; to exhaust the means of a principal debtor before taking action against the surety [Scots. Law]. (L. *discussus*, shaken asunder.)
discussible, *a.* dis-*kus*-se-bl, that may be discussed.
★**discussion,** *n.* dis-*kush*-on, the act of discussing; debate; dispersion [Med.]; the act of proceeding against a principal debtor by discussing [Scots. Law]. (Fr.)
discussive, *a.* dis-*kus*-siv, pertaining to discussion or to debate.
discutable, *a.* dis-*kew*-ta-bl, discussible.
discutient, *a.* dis-*kew*-she-ent, having the power of dispersing morbid matter [Med.]: *n.* a medicine or application which disperses a tumour or any coagulated fluid in the body. (L. *discutiens*, shaking asunder.)
disdain, *n.* dis-*dane*, scorn of a person or a thing, as regarded beneath one or beneath what one honours; contempt; haughtiness; arrogance: *v.t.* to consider to be unworthy of one either to do or to regard; to scorn. (O.Fr. *desdegnier*, to scorn haughtily.)
disdainful, *a.* dis-*dane*-ful, full of disdain; expressing disdain; contemptuous.
disdainfully, *ad.* in a disdainful manner.
disdainfulness, *n.* haughty scorn.
disdiapason, *n. dis*-dy-a-*pay*-zon, an interval of two octaves [Mus.]. (Gr.)
★**disease,** *n.* de-*zeez*, deviation from health; derangement in the structure or the function of any organ belonging to an organism, or to any organized body, such as a state; any malady. (O.Fr. *desaise.*)
diseased, *a.* de-*zeezd*, affected with disease.
diseaseful, *a.* de-*zeez*-ful, occasioning disease; affected with disease.
disedge, *v.t.* dis-*edj*, to blunt; to dull.
disedification, *n.* dis-*ed*-e-fe-*kay*-shon, the reverse of edification.
disedify, *v.t.* dis-*ed*-e-fy, to shock or injure the religious feelings; to weaken the faith of.
disembark, *v.t.* dis-em-*bark*, to land or remove from a ship: *v.i.* to land; to quit a ship. (Fr. *desembarquer.*)
disembarkation, *n. dis*-em-bar-*kay*-shon, the act of disembarking.
disembarkment, *n. dis*-em-*bark*-ment, disembarkation.
disembarrass, *v.t.* dis-em-*ba*-ras, to free from embarrassment or perplexity; to clear.
disembarrassment, *n.* dis-*em-ba*-ras-ment, the act of extricating from perplexity.
disembed, *v.t.* dis-em-*bed*, to free something that is embedded.
disembellish, *v.t.* dis-em-*bel*-lish, to deprive of embellishment.
disembodiment, *n.* dis-em-*bod*-e-ment, the act of disembodying or disbanding.
disembody, *v.t.* dis-em-*bod*-e, to divest or free from a body; to disband, as a military body.
disembogue, *v.t.* dis-em-*bohg*, to discharge, as a river, by its mouth into the ocean or a lake: *v.i.* to flow out at the mouth, as a river; to pass out of a gulf or bay [Naut.]. (Sp. *desembocar.*)
disemboguement, *n.* dis-em-*bohg*-ment, the discharge, or the place of discharge, of waters into the ocean or a lake.
disembosom, *v.t.* dis-em-*booz*-um, to reveal confidentially; to unburden oneself.
disembowel, *v.t.* dis-em-*bou*-el, to eviscerate; to wound so as to show the entrails.
disembowelment, *n.* dis-em-*bou*-el-ment, evisceration.
disembroil, *v.t.* dis-em-*broyl*, to free from trouble or confusion.
disemplane, *v.i.* dis-em-*plane*, to alight from an aeroplane.
disemploy, *v.t.* dis-em-*ploy*, to cease from employing to dismiss from employment.
disenable, *v.t.* dis-en-*ay*-bl, to deprive of power; to incapacitate.
disenamoured, *a.* dis-e-*nam*-erd, freed from being enamoured.
disenchant, *v.t.* dis-en-*chahnt*, to free from enchantment; to destroy the power of a charm or spell; to disillusionize.
disenchanter, *n.* dis-en-*chahnt*-er, one who or that which frees from the power of enchantment.
disenchantment, *n.* dis-en-*chahnt*-ment, act of disenchanting; state of being disenchanted.
disencumber, *v.t.* dis-en-*kum*-ber, to free from what encumbers, clogs, or hampers.
disendow, *v.t.* dis-en-*dou*, to divest of endowment.
disendowment, *n.* dis-en-*dou*-ment, the act of disendowing.
disenfranchise, *v.t.* dis-en-*fran*-chize, to disfranchise.
disengage, *v.t.* dis-en-*gaje*, to set a thing free from that with which it is in union; to detach; to disentangle or extricate; to free from what engages the mind; to free from any engagement; to release; to set free the wings of a battalion or regiment that have been overlapped [Mil.]; to quit that side of an adversary's blade on which one is opposed by his guard [Fencing].
disengaged, *a.* dis-en-*gayjd*, free from engagement; with the attention not particularly occupied; unoccupied in mind.
disengagedness, *n.* dis-en-*gay*-jed-ness, the quality or state of being disengaged.
disengagement, *n.* dis-en-*gayj*-ment, the act of disengaging; state of being disengaged; freedom from mental engagement or occupation.
disennoble, *v.t.* dis-en-*noh*-bl, to deprive of a peerage; to make ignoble; to degrade.
disenslave, *v.t.* dis-en-*slave*, to free from bondage.
disentail, *v.t.* dis-en-*tale*, to break the entail of.
disentangle, *v.t.* dis-en-*tang*-gl, to unravel; to free from entanglement; to disengage; to set free from impediments or difficulties.
disentanglement, *n.* dis-en-*tang*-gl-ment, the act of disentangling; freedom from entanglement.

disenthral, *v.t.* dis-en-*thrawl*, to liberate from bondage or oppression.
disenthralment, *n.* dis-en-*thrawl*-ment, liberation from bondage.
disenthrone, *v.t.* dis-en-*throne*, to dethrone.
disentitle, *v.t.* dis-en-*ty*-tl, to deprive of a title or of a right or claim.
disentomb, *v.t.* dis-en-*toom*, to take out of a tomb; to disinter.
disentrain, *v.t.* dis-en-*trane*, to alight from a train; to detrain [Mil.].
disentrance, *v.t.* dis-en-*trahnce*, to awaken from a trance or from deep sleep; to arouse from a reverie.
disentwine, *v.t.* dis-en-*twine*, to untwine; to untwist.
disenvelop, *v.t.* dis-en-*vel*-op, to unwrap.
disenviron, *v.t.* dis-en-*vire*-ron, to free from environment.
disepalous, *a.* dy-*sep*-a-lus, having or composed of two sepals [Bot.].
disequilibrium, *n.* *dis*-ee-kwe-*lib*-re-um, absence or loss of equilibrium; instability.
disestablish, *v.t.* dis-es-*tab*-lish, to remove from being established, esp. to sever a connexion subsisting between a Church and a State.
disestablisher, *n.* dis-es-*tab*-lish-er, an advocate of Church disestablishment.
disestablishment, *n.* dis-es-*tab*-lish-ment, the act or process of disestablishing, esp. a Church; the state of being disestablished.
disestablishmentarian, *n.* dis-es-*tab*-lish-men-*tare*-re-an, a disestablisher: *a.* pertaining to disestablishment.
disesteem, *n.* dis-es-*teem*, want of esteem; disregard: *v.t.* to dislike in a moderate degree; to slight.
disestimation, *n.* dis-es-te-*may*-shon, disesteem.
diseur, *n.masc.* (*fem.* **diseuse**) (App.), a raconteur; a professional reciter.
disfavour, *n.* dis-*fay*-vur, unfavourable regard; disesteem; a state in which one is not favoured, patronized, or befriended; an unkind or disobliging act: *v.t.* to discountenance; to withdraw support. (O.Fr. *desfaveur*.)
disfeature, *v.t.* dis-*feet*-yewr, to disfigure; to deface.
disfiguration, *n.* dis-fig-yew-*ray*-shon, the act of disfiguring or marring; disfigurement.
disfigure, *v.t.* dis-*fig*-ur, to mar or impair the figure or the appearance of; to deface; to deform. (O.Fr. *desfigurer*.)
disfigurement, *n.* dis-*fig*-ur-ment, the state of being disfigured; unsightly change of external form; defacement of beauty.
disforest, *v.t.* dis-*fo*-rest, to clear of forest; to turn into common land.
disform, *v.t.* dis-*fawrm*, to alter in shape or form.
disfranchise, *v.t.* dis-*fran*-chize, to deprive of granted rights and privileges, especially electoral ones.
disfranchisement, *n.* dis-*fran*-chiz-ment, the act of disfranchising; disfranchised state.
disfrock, *v.t.* dis-*frok*, to expel from holy orders; to unfrock.
disfurnish, *v.t.* dis-*fur*-nish, to deprive of furniture; to strip of apparatus, habiliments, or equipage.
disgavel, *v.t.* dis-*gav*-el, to take away the tenure of gavelkind [Law].
disgeneric, *a.* dis-je-*ne*-rik, belonging to different genera [Bot. and Zool.].
disgorge, *v.t.* and *i.* dis-*gorj*, to eject from the stomach; to vomit; to throw out or discharge violently; to give up what had been unjustly seized and appropriated. (O.Fr. *desgorger*.)
disgorgement, *n.* dis-*gorj*-ment, the act of disgorging.
disgorger, *n.* dis-*gorj*-er, an instrument for removing a hook from a fish's mouth.
disgrace, *n.* dis-*grace*, state of being out of favour; disesteem; state of ignominy; cause of shame; *v.t.* to dismiss out of favour; to dishonour; to bring shame upon. (Fr. *disgracier*.)
disgraceful, *a.* dis-*grace*-ful, entailing disgrace or ignominy; shameful.
disgracefully, *ad.* dis-*grace*-ful-le, with disgrace: in a disgraceful manner.
disgracefulness, *n.* dis *grace*-ful-ness, ignominy or shamefulness.
disgracer, *n.* dis-*grace*-er, one who or that which exposes to or brings into disgrace.
disgrade, *v.t.* dis-*grade*, to degrade, esp. formally; to unfrock
disgregation, *n.* dis-gre-*gay*-shon, separation; disintegration. (L. *disgregatus*, separated.)
disgruntle, *v.t.* dis-*grun*-tl, to annoy; to give offence to; to dissatisfy.
disguisal, *n.* dis-*gy*-zal, disguisement.
disguise, *n.* dis-*gyze*, a dress, mask, or manner intended to conceal the person who wears or adopts it; a false or assumed appearance, intended to deceive; a changed appearance: *v.t.* to conceal, as with a mask, or by a feigned appearance; to cloak by false show; to dissemble; to alter in form or manner. (O.Fr. *desguiser*.)
disguisedly, *ad.* dis-*gy*-zed-le, so as to be concealed.
disguisement, *n.* dis-*gyze*-ment, dress or appearance that disguises.
disguiser, *n.* dis-*gy*-zer, one who or that which disguises; a mummer.
disguising, *n.* dis-*gy*-zing, the act of giving a false appearance; theatrical mummery or masking.
★**disgust,** *n.* dis-*gust*, strong dislike of what is offensive to the taste, or offensive in any respect: *v.t.* to excite aversion; to offend the taste. (Fr. *desgouster*.)
disgustedly, *ad.* dis-*gus*-ted-le, in a manner expressing disgust.
disgustful, *a.* dis-*gust*-ful, offensive to the taste; nauseous; exciting disgust.
disgustfulness, *n.* state of being disgustful.
disgusting, *a.* dis-*gus*-ting, nauseating; exciting disgust; very distasteful.
disgustingly, *ad.* in a manner to give disgust.
dish, *n.* dish, a flat shallow vessel for serving up food at the table; the food served on a dish; a particular kind of food; a dish-like utensil or concavity; a trough in which ore is measured [Mining]: *v.t.* to put in a dish, as meat for table; to make concave like a dish [Mech.]; to disappoint or frustrate; to cheat: *v.i.* to assume concavity of form. **to dish out,** to distribute [Coll.] (A.S. *disc*.)
dishabilitate, *v.t.* dis-ha-*bil*-e-tate, to incapacitate or disqualify [Scots. Law].
dishabilitation, *n.* *dis*-ha-*bil*-e-*tay*-shon, disqualification [Scots. Law].
dishabille, *n.* *dis*-a-bil, deshabille.
dishabituate, *v.t.* *dis*-ha-*bit*-yew-ate, to render unaccustomed.
dishallowed, *a.* dis-*hal*-ode, desecrated.
dishallucination, *n.* *dis*-ha-lew-se-*nay*-shon, disillusion.
disharmonic, *a.* dis-har-*mon*-ik, not harmonic; having non-concordant features.
disharmonious, *a.* dis-har-*moh*-ne-us, inharmonious.
disharmoniously, *ad.* *dis*-har-*moh*-ne-us-le, in a disharmonious manner.
disharmonize, *v.t.* and *i.* dis-*har*-mo-nize, to be, or cause to be, out of harmony; to upset.
disharmony, *n.* dis-*har*-mo-ne, discord.
dish-cloth, *n.* a cloth used for washing and wiping dishes.
dish-clout, *n.* a dish-cloth.
dish-cover, *n.* a metal or earthenware cover for retaining the heat in a dish.
dishearten, *v.t.* dis-*hahr*-tn, to discourage.
disheartening, *a.* dis-*hahrt*-ning, discouraging.
dished, *a.* disht, concave; (of wheels in pairs) being nearer together at the top than the bottom.
dished wheel, a dish-wheel.
dishelmed, *a.* dis-*helmd*, with helmet removed.
disherison, *n.* dis-*he*-re-son, the act of disinheriting; disinheritance. (O.Fr. *disheritison*.)
dishevel, *v.t.* de-*shev*-el, to leave the hair in disorder and let it hang loosely and negligently: *v.t.* to spread or throw about in disorder (esp. of the hair). (Fr. *décheveler*.)
dishevelled, *pp.* and *a.* de-*shev*-eld, with hair in disorder; rumpled; hanging loosely and negligently.
dishevelment, *n.* de-*shev*-el-ment, the state of being dishevelled.
dishful, *n.* *dish*-ful, as much as a dish will hold.
dishonest, *a.* dis-*on*-est, wanting in honesty; destitute of probity; having or exercising a disposition to cheat and defraud; fraudulent; disgraceful; unchaste. (O.Fr. *deshoneste*.)
dishonestly, *ad.* in a dishonest manner.
dishonesty, *n.* dis-*on*-es-te, want of honesty or probity; a disposition to cheat or defraud;

violation of honesty or trust; fraud; treachery; deceit.
dishonour, *n.* dis-*on*-or, want of honour; disgrace: *v.t.* to bring disgrace or shame on; to treat with indignity; to violate the chastity of; to refuse or decline to accept or pay, as a draft [Comm.].
dishonourable, *a.* dis-*on*-o-ra-bl, showing want of honour; bringing dishonour, disgrace, or shame; destitute of honour. (Fr. *déshonorable.*)
dishonourableness, *n.* dis-*on*-o-ra-bl-ness, quality of being dishonourable.
dishonourably, *ad.* in a dishonourable manner.
dishonoured, *pp.* and *a.* dis-*on*-ord, disgraced; brought into disrepute.
dishonourer, *n.* dis-*on*-o-rer, one who dishonours; one who treats another with indignity; a debaucher.
dishorn, *v.t.* dis-*horn*, to deprive of horns.
dishorse, *v.t.* dis-*horse*, to unhorse: *v.i.* to dismount.
dishumour, *n.* dis-*hew*-mur, peevishness; ill-humour.
dish-washer, *n.* one who washes dishes; a kitchen-maid; the pied wagtail, *Motacilla alba.*
dish-water, *n.* water in which dishes are washed.
dish-wheel, *n.* a wheel which is concave on one side and convex on the other.
disilicide, *n.* dy-*sil*-e-side, a compound of two atoms of silicon with an element or radical [Chem.].
disillude, *v.t. dis*-il-*lewd*, to disillusionize.
disilluminate, *v.t. dis*-il-*lew*-min-ate, to turn off the lights; to darken.
disillusion, *n.* dis-il-*lew*-zhon, the dispelling of an illusion; freedom from illusion: *v.t.* disillusionize.
disillusionize, *v.t.* dis-il-*lew*-zhon-ize, to free from illusion; to disenchant.
disillusionment, *n.* dis il-*lew*-zhon-ment, the fact of being freed from illusion.
disimmure, *v.t. dis*-im-mewr, to disimprison.
disimprison, *v.t.* dis-im-*priz*-on, to set free; to release from confinement.
disimprove, *v.t.* dis-im-*proov*, to render worse: *v.i.* to grow worse.
disimprovement, *n.* dis-im-*proov*-ment, reduction from a better to a worse state.
disincarcerate, *v.t.* dis-in-*kar*-ser-rate, to liberate from prison.
disincarnate, *v.t.* dis-in-*kar*-nate, to divest of a material body; to disembody.
disincentive, *n.* dis-in-*sen*-tiv, any condition serving as a deterrent; a restraining influence.
disinclination, *n.* dis-in-kle-*nay*-shon, want of inclination, desire, or affection; unwillingness; dislike.
disincline, *v.t.* dis-in-*kline*, to cause dislike; to make unwilling: *v.i.* to be unwilling.
disincorporate, *v.t.* dis-in-*kor*-po-rate, to deprive of corporate powers; to dissolve a corporate body.
disincorporation, *n.* dis-in-*kor*-po-*ray*-shon, deprivation of the rights and privileges of a corporation.
disindividualize, *v.t.* dis-in-de-*vid*-yew-a-lize, to destroy the individual features of.
disinfect, *v.t. dis*-in-fekt, to purify from infection; to fumigate.
disinfectant, *a.* dis-in-*fek*-tant, preventing infection: *n.* any chemical compound that destroys disease germs and microbes.
disinfection, *n.* dis-in-*fek*-shon, purification from infecting matter.
disinfector, *n.* dis-in-*fek*-tor, an apparatus for disinfecting.
disinfest, *v.t.* dis-in-*fest*, to rid of infesting insects, etc.
disinfestation, *n.* dis-in-fes-*tay*-shon, the riddance of infesting insects or other pests.
disinfeudation, *n.* dis-in-few-*day*-shon, release from feudal tenure [Law].
disinflation, *n.* dis-in-*flay*-shon, the relief of pressure on prices (of consumer goods) otherwise than by increase in supply [Econ.].
disingenuity, *n. dis*-in-je-*new*-e-te, disingenuousness.
disingenuous, *a.* dis-in-*jen*-yew-us, not open, frank, and candid; insincere; meanly crafty; unbecoming true honour and dignity.
disingenuously, *ad.* in a disingenuous manner.
disingenuousness, *n.* dis-in-*jen*-yew-us-ness, the quality of being disingenuous; want of candour.
disinherison, *n.* dis-in-*he*-re-son, the act of disinheriting; the state of being disinherited.
disinherit, *v.t.* dis-in-*he*-rit, to cut off from hereditary right; to deprive of inheritance.
disinheritance, *n.* dis-in-*he*-re-tance, the fact or act of disinheriting or of being disinherited.
disinhume, *v.t.* dis-in-*hewm*, to disinter.
disintegrable, *a.* dis-*in*-te-gra-bl, capable of disintegration.
disintegrant, *n.* dis-*in*-te-grant, a disintegrating agent [Chem.]; *a.* disintegrating.
disintegrate, *v.t.* dis-*in*-te-grate, to separate into the component parts of; to reduce to fragments: *v.i.* to become separated; to crumble; to fall to pieces. (L. *dis-*, and *integer*, entire.)
disintegration, *n.* dis-*in*-te-*gray*-shon, the separation of the integrant parts of a substance; the wearing away of rocks by weathering [Geol.].
disintegrator, *n.* dis-*in*-te-gray-tor, a machine for grinding, crushing, or tearing apart.
disinter, *v.t.* dis-in-*ter*, to take out of a grave or out of the earth; to bring from obscurity into view.
disinterest, *n.* dis-*in*-ter-rest, that which is contrary to interest; detriment; disadvantage.
disinterested, *a.* dis-*in*-ter-res-ted, unbiased by considerations of self-interest; not dictated by considerations of private advantage; impartial.
disinterestedly, *ad.* dis-*in*-ter-res-ted-le, in a disinterested manner.
disinterestedness, *n.* dis-*in*-ter-res-ted-ness, the state or quality of being disinterested; impartiality.
disinterment, *n.* dis-in-*ter*-ment, the act of disinterring; that which has been disinterred.
disintricate, *v.t.* dis-*in*-tre-kate, to disentangle; to free from complication.
disinvest, *v.t.* dis-in-*vest*, to divest of that with which one is invested.
disinvestiture, *n.* dis-in-*ves*-te-tewr, disinvesting; the state of being disinvested.
disinvolve, *v.t.* dis-in-*volv*, to disentangle.
disjaskit, *a.* dis-*jas*-kit, cast down, dilapidated, worn out. (*Dejected.*)
disject, *v.t.* dis-*jekt*, to break asunder; to disperse.
disjection, *n.* dis-*jek*-shon, the act of scattering; state of being dispersed.
disjoin, *v.t.* dis-*joyn*, to part asunder; to disunite.
disjoint, *v.t.* dis-*joynt*, to put out of joint; to dislocate; to separate at a joining; to break the natural order or connection of; to make incoherent: *a.* disjointed.
disjointed, *a.* dis-*joyn*-ted, out of joint; not coherent.
disjointedly, *ad.* dis-*joyn*-ted-le, in a disjointed manner.
disjointedness, *n.* dis-*joyn*-ted-ness, state of being disjointed.
disjointly, *ad.* dis-*joynt*-le, disjointedly.
disjointure, *n.* dis-*joyn*-tewr, disjointedness; lack of connexion.
disjunct, *a.* dis-*jungkt*, having deep constrictions between head, thorax, and abdomen [Entom.]. (L. *disjunctus.*)
disjunction, *n.* dis-*junk*-shon, the act of disjoining; separation; disunion. (L. *disjunctio.*)
disjunctive, *a.* dis-*jungk*-tiv, separating; disjoining: *n.* a word that disjoins; a disjunctive proposition [Logic]. **disjunctive conjunction,** a word which unites sentences in construction, but disjoins the sense [Gram.]. **disjunctive proposition,** a proposition which, instead of a single predicate, has several alternatives united by the disjunctive conjunction "or." **disjunctive syllogism,** a syllogism with a disjunctive major premise and a categorical minor [Logic]. (L. *disjunctivus.*)
disjunctively, *ad.* dis-*jungkt*-iv-le, in a disjunctive manner.
disjuncture, *n.* dis-*junk*-tewr, disjunction.
disk, *n.* disk, a flat circular surface; the destination indicator on locomotives; the face of a celestial body; a quoit; the whole surface of a leaf; the central part of a radiate compound flower; a discoid mark [Bot.]; a flat rounded part of certain invertebrates [Zool.]; a gramophone record. **disk-clutch,** a friction-clutch. (L. *discus.*)
dislikable, *a.* dis-*like*-a-bl, such as to arouse dislike.
dislike, *n.* dis-*like*, disapprobation; distaste; aversion: *v.t.* to disapprove of; to regard with aversion; to disrelish.
disliker, *n.* dis-*like*-er, one who dislikes.

dislimb, *v.t.* dis-*lim,* to tear the limbs from; to dismember.
dislimn, *v.t.* dis-*lim,* to obliterate.
dislink, *v.t.* dis-*link,* to disunite; to uncouple.
dislocate, *v.t. dis*-lo-kate, to displace; to put out of joint; to derange; to break the continuity of strata [Geol.]. (Late L. *dislocatus,* put out of place.)
dislocation, *n.* dis-lo-*kay*-shon, the act of displacing, esp. of putting out of joint; a dislocated joint; the displacement of portions of a stratified rock from its original position; a fault [Geol.]. (Fr.)
dislocatory, *a. dis*-lo-*kay*-to-re, producing or arising from dislocation.
dislodge, *v.t.* dis-*lodj,* to drive from a place of lodgment, retirement, or defence; to drive an enemy from a position: *v.i.* to go from a place of rest; to remove. (O.Fr. *desloger.*)
dislodgment, *n.* dis-*lodj*-ment, act of dislodging or removing to another place; the state of being dislodged.
disloyal, *a.* dis-*loy*-al, not true to allegiance; false to a sovereign or to one's duty; unfaithful; not true to the marriage-bed; false in love.
disloyalist, *n.* dis-*loy*-al-ist, one who is disloyal.
disloyally, *ad.* dis-*loy*-a-le, in a disloyal manner.
disloyalty, *n.* dis-*loy*-al-te, want of fidelity; faithlessness; state of being disloyal.
dismal, *a. diz*-mal, gloomy; dreary; sorrowful; melancholy; depressing. **the dismal science,** political economy. **the dismals,** low spirits, the "blues" [Coll.]. (L. *dies mali,* unpropitious days.)
dismality, *n.* diz-*mal*-e-te, dismalness; anything dismal; cheerlessness.
dismally, *ad. diz*-mal-le, in a dismal manner.
dismalness, *n. diz*-mal-ness, the state of being dismal.
disman, *v.t.* dis-*man,* to unman; to deprive a country of its men.
dismantle, *v.t.* dis-*man*-tl, to strip of dress, furniture, apparatus, equipment, or fortifications; to divest; to unrig; to break or take down. (O.Fr. *desmanteller.*)
dismantlement, *n.* dis-*man*-tl-ment, dismantling.
dismarket, *v.t.* dis-*mark*-et, to deprive of the rights and privileges of a market.
dismast, *v.t.* dis-*mahst,* to deprive of a mast or masts.
dismastment, *n.* dis-*mahst*-ment, the act of dismasting; the state of being dismasted.
dismay, *n.* dis-*may,* loss of courage; loss or paralysis of ability or power caused by fear: *v.t.* to daunt; to dispirit by fear; to deprive of that strength or firmness of mind which constitutes courage; to depress. (O.Fr. *desmayer.*)
dismayedness, *n.* dis-*may*-ed-ness, a state of being dismayed; dejection of courage.
dismember, *v.t.* dis-*mem*-ber, to divide limb from limb; to cut or tear in pieces; to separate a member or part from the main body; to deprive of membership. (O.Fr. *desmembrer.*)
dismemberment, *n.* dis-*mem*-ber-ment, the act of dismembering; a dismembered or mutilated state; expulsion from membership.
dismiss, *v.t.* dis-*miss,* to send away; to permit to depart; to discard; to remove from office, service, or employment; to reject; to discontinue [Law]; to terminate an innings, etc. [Sport]: *v.i.* to disperse; to break away. (L. *dis-,* and *missus,* sent.)
dismissal, *n.* dis-*mis*-sal, discharge; removal from office.
dismissible, *a.* dis-*mis*-se-bl, liable to dismissal.
dismission, *n.* dis-*mish*-on, the act of dismissing; discharge from office or employment.
dismissive, *a.* dis-*mis*-siv, pertaining to or of the nature of dismissal.
dismissory, *a.* dis-*mis*-so-re, dismissive; sending away.
dismount, *v.i.* dis-*mount,* to alight from a horse; to descend from an elevation: *v.t.* to unhorse; to change a mounted regiment into a foot or a mechanized regiment; to throw or bring down from an elevation; to disassemble (machinery, etc.); to throw artillery from their carriages, or to break the carriages or wheels, and render the guns useless; to shatter, as fortifications; to remove from a mount (as a picture) or a setting (as a gem). (O.Fr. *desmonter.*)
disnaturalize, *v.t.* dis-*nat*-yew-ra-lize, to make alien; to denaturalize.
disnatured, *a.* dis-*nay*-tewrd, deprived or destitute of natural feelings; unnatural.
disobedience, *n.* dis-o-*bee*-de-ence, neglect or refusal to obey; violation of a command or prohibition; breach of a duty prescribed by authority; non-compliance. (O.Fr. *desobedience.*)
disobedient, *a.* dis-o-*bee*-de-ent, neglecting or refusing to obey; not observant of duty or rules prescribed by authority; refractory.
disobediently, *ad.* dis-o-*bee*-de-ent-le, in a disobedient manner.
disobey, *v.t.* dis-o-*bay,* to neglect or refuse to obey: *v.i.* to be disobedient. (Fr. *désobéir.*)
disoblige, *v.t.* dis-o-*blyj,* not to do what would, or to do what would not, oblige or gratify another; to be uncivil or unaccommodating to. (Fr. *désobliger.*)
disobligement, *n.* dis-o-*blyj*-ment, the act of disobliging.
disobliging, *a.* dis-o-*bly*-jing, not obliging; not disposed to gratify the wishes of another; unaccommodating.
disobligingly, *ad.* in a disobliging manner.
disobligingness, *n.* indisposition to oblige.
disomatous, *a.* dy-*soh*-ma-tus, having two bodies united. (Gr. *disomatos,* two-bodied.)
disorbed, *a.* dis-*orbd,* thrown out of the proper orbit; deprived of the orb of sovereignty.
disorder, *n.* dis-*awr*-der, want of order; confusion; turbulence or disturbance of social order; neglect of rule; breach of laws; disturbance of the functions of the animal economy; disease; discomposure or derangement of the mind; turbulence of passions: *v.t.* to throw into confusion; to disturb the functions of; to disturb the mind; to derange. (O.Fr. *desordre.*)
disordered, *a.* dis-*aw*-derd, deranged; disorderly; out of order.
disorderedness, *n.* dis-*aw*-derd-ness, a state of disorder or irregularity; confusion.
disorderliness, *n.* dis-*aw*-der-le-ness, state of being disorderly.
disorderly, *a.* dis-*aw*-der-le, confused; without proper order; acting without regularity; contrary to law: disposed to violate law and good order; inclined to break loose from restraint: *ad.* without order; confusedly; in a manner violating law and good order. **disorderly house,** a brothel, gaming-house, or other house used for improper purposes.
disordinate, *a.* dis-*awr*-de-nat, disorderly; living irregularly.
disordinately, *ad.* inordinately; irregularly.
disorganization, *n.* dis-*awr*-ga-ny-*zay*-shon, the act of disorganizing; the act of destroying order; the state of being disorganized.
disorganize, *v.t.* dis-*aw*-ga-nize, to break or destroy the organic structure or functions of; to disturb the regulated arrangement and harmony of; to reduce into disorder.
disorganizer, *n.* dis-*aw*-ga-ny-zer, one who disorganizes, or introduces disorder or confusion.
disorientate, *v.t.* dis-*aw*-re-en-tate, to turn from an easterly direction; to throw out of one's bearings; to site (a church) with the chancel pointing other than due east. (L. *dis-,* and *orient.*)
disorientation, *n.* dis-aw-re-en-*tay*-shon, the psychological state in which one is oblivious of one's own identity, etc., and is unable to co-ordinate oneself with one's surroundings.
disown, *v.t.* dis-*ohn,* to refuse to own; to renounce; to repudiate.
disownment, *n.* dis-*ohn*-ment, act of disowning; repudiation.
disoxidate, *v.t.* dis-*ok*-se-date, to deoxidate.
disoxidation, *n.* dis-oks-se-*day*-shon, deoxidation.
disoxygenate, *v.t.* dis-*oks*-e-je-nate, to deoxidate.
disoxygenation, *n.* dis-*oks*-e-je-*nay*-shon, deoxidation.
disparage, *v.t.* dis-*pa*-raj, to depreciate; to injure or dishonour; to lower in rank or estimation; to undervalue; to vilify. (O.Fr. *desparager.*)
disparageable, *a.* dis-*pa*-ra-ja-bl, that may be disparaged.
disparagement, *n.* dis-*pa*-raj-ment, depreciation; diminution of value or excellence; indignity; that which causes discredit or disgrace. (O.Fr. *desparagement.*)
disparager, *n.* dis-*pa*-ra-jer, one who disparages; one who habitually depreciates.

disparagingly, *ad.* dis-*pa*-ra-jing-le, in a manner to disparage.
disparate, *a.* *dis*-pa-rat, unequal; unlike; having nothing in common: *pl.* things so unequal or unlike that they cannot be compared with each other. (L. *disparatus*, separated.)
disparity, *n.* dis-*pa*-re-te, difference in degree, age, rank, condition, or excellence; dissimilitude. (Fr. *disparité*.)
dispark, *v.t.* dis-*park*, to divest park-land of its park character; to throw open a park for other purposes.
dispart, *v.i.* dis-*part*, to separate; to open; to cleave: *v.t.* to part asunder; to divide; to separate. (L. *dispartio*, cleave asunder.)
dispart, *n.* *dis*-part, the difference between the thickness of the metal of a piece of ordnance at the mouth and at the breech. **dispart-sight,** the sight about the middle of the gun for point-blank or horizontal firing to eliminate the difference of the diameters between the breech and the mouth [Gunnery].
dispassion, *n.* dis-*pash*-on, freedom from passion; an undisturbed or unmoved state of mind.
dispassionate, *a.* dis-*pash*-on-at, cool; calm; impartial; unmoved by feelings; not dictated by passion or bias of mind.
dispassionately, *ad.* dis-*pash*-on-at-le, in a dispassionate manner.
dispatch, *n.* dis-*patch*, the act of dispatching or being dispatched; speedy performance; speed; a message dispatched; an official report, or the paper containing such; dismissal: *v.i.* to conclude an affair with another; to hasten: *v.t.* to send away, especially messengers, agents, and letters on some special business, and often implying haste; to send with speed; to perform; to finish; to dispose of; to put to death. **dispatch-boat,** a small swift naval vessel for carrying dispatches. **dispatch-case,** a flat leather handbag for conveying papers or dispatches, etc. (Sp. *despachar*, to dispatch.)
dispatchful, *a.* dis-*patch*-ful, bent on haste; intent on speedy execution of business.
dispatriated, *a.* dis-*pay*-tre-ay-ted, expatriated.
dispauper, *v.t.* dis-*paw*-per, to deprive of public support as a pauper; to put it out of one's power to sue *in forma pauperis* [Law].
dispauperize, *v.t.* dis-*paw*-per-rize, to depauperize.
dispeace, *n.* dis-*peece*, want of peace; disquiet.
dispel, *v.t.* dis-*pel*, to dissipate; to disperse, drive away, or banish; to scatter by driving or force: *v.i.* to become dispersed. (L. *dis*-, and *pello*, drive.)
dispeller, *n.* dis-*pel*-er, he who or that which dispels.
dispend, *v.t.* dis-*pend*, to expend; to squander; to dispense.
dispensability, *n.* dis-pen-sa-*bil*-e-te, dispensableness.
dispensable, *a.* dis-*pen*-sa-bl, that may be dispensed with; unnecessary. (L. *dispenso*, give out.)
dispensableness, *n.* dis-*pen*-sa-bl-ness, the capability of being dispensed with.
dispensary, *n.* dis-*pen*-sa-re, a place from which medicines are issued; one from which medicines are dispensed to the poor and medical advice given free; a laboratory where medicines are compounded; a pharmacopœia.
dispensation, *n.* dis-pen-*say*-shon, the act of dispensing; administration; a system of religion during a particular era; the granting of a licence by the Pope, or the licence itself, to free one from an obligation, generally a prohibition, prescribed by the canons of the Church; permission granted to a clergyman by a bishop to do something, *e.g.* the holding of two or more benefices, that would otherwise be unlawful [Eccles.]. (Fr.)
dispensative, *a.* dis-*pen*-sa-tiv, granting dispensation.
dispensatively, *ad.* by dispensation.
dispensatory, *a.* dis-*pen*-sa-to-re, having power to grant dispensations: *n.* a book containing or prescribing the methods of preparing the various kinds of medicines; a pharmacopœia.
dispense, *v.t.* dis-*pense*, to deal out in parts or portions; to distribute; to prepare (drugs) for administration; to administer. **dispense with,** to permit the want of; to do without; to disregard; to excuse from; to let pass.
dispenser, *n.* dis-*pen*-ser, one who dispenses; a compounder of medicines.
dispensing, *a.* dis-*pen*-sing, granting dispensation; making up medicines.
dispeople, *v.t.* dis-*pee*-pl, to depopulate.
dispermatous, *a.* dy-*sper*-ma-tus, dispermous.
dispermous, *a.* dy-*sper*-mus, having only two seeds [Bot.]. (Gr. *di*-, and *sperma*, seed.)
dispersal, *n.* dis-*per*-sal, dispersion; the result of dispersion.
disperse, *v.t.* dis-*perse*, to scatter; to drive in different directions; to diffuse or spread; to dissipate: *v.i.* to separate; to be scattered; to vanish. (Fr. *disperser*.)
dispersedly, *ad.* dis-*per*-sed-le, in a dispersed manner; separately.
dispersedness, *n.* dis-*per*-sed-ness, the state of being dispersed or scattered; scatteredness.
disperser, *n.* dis-*per*-ser, one who or that which disperses.
dispersible, *a.* dis-*per*-sibl, capable of being dispersed.
dispersion, *n.* dis-*per*-shon, the act of scattering; the state of being scattered; the separation of light into its different coloured rays [Opt.]; the removing of inflammation from an affected part [Med. and Surg.]. **the Dispersion,** the Diaspora. (L. *dispersus*, scattered abroad.)
dispersive, *a.* dis-*per*-siv, scattering or dissipating.
dispersively, *ad.* in a dispersive manner.
dispirit, *v.t.* dis-*pi*-rit, to depress; to discourage; to deprive of spirit or vigour.
dispirited, *pp.* and *a.* dis-*pi*-re-ted, depressed in spirits; without spirit.
dispiritedly, *ad.* in a dispirited temper.
dispiritedness, *n.* depression of spirits.
dispiritment, *n.* dis-*pi*-rit-ment, the condition of being dispirited; that which dispirits.
dispiteous, *a.* dis-*pit*-e-us, having no pity.
dispiteously, *ad.* dis-*pit*-e-us-le, pitilessly.
dispiteousness, *n.* heartlessness.
displace, *v.t.* dis-*place*, to put out of the usual or proper place; to remove from any office or dignity; to dismiss; to supersede. **displaced person,** one uprooted or expatriated by reason of war, forced labour, or racial, religious or political persecution.
displaceable, *a.* dis-*play*-sa-bl, removable.
displacement, *n.* dis-*place*-ment, the act of displacing; the weight of water displaced by a floating body, as a ship at rest, the weight of which is equal to that of the floating body; the volume of air displaced by the volume of gas of a lighter-than-air aircraft; the process of extracting the active principles from organic bodies by solution in a liquid which, when charged, is displaced by another [Chem.]; the motion of electric charges due to the application of an electric force in a dielectric [Elect.].
displacency, *n.* dis-*play*-sen-se, the condition of being displeased; dislike.
displant, *v.t.* dis-*plahnt*, to remove a plant from where it has been planted; to drive away, as a nation, from the country where it was settled; to strip of inhabitants.
displantation, *n.* dis-plahn-*tay*-shon, the removal of a plant; the removal of inhabitants.
display, *n.* dis-*play*, unfolding; an exhibition of anything to the view; show with ostentation; the arrangement of a printed page: *v.i.* to make a display: *v.t.* to unfold or spread out; to spread before the view; to exhibit; to make an ostentatious exhibition of; to parade. (O.Fr. *desplaier*.)
displayed, *a.* dis-*playd*, printed in conspicuous letters; erect with wings expanded [Her.].
displayer, *n.* dis-*play*-er, he who or that which displays; an exhibitor.
displease, *v.t.* dis-*pleez*, to offend; to make angry, sometimes in a slight degree; to be disagreeable to: *v.i.* to raise aversion. (L. *displiceo*.)
displeasedness, *n.* dis-*plee*-zed-ness, displeasure.
displeasing, *a.* dis-*plee*-zing, distasteful.
displeasingness, *n.* dis-*plee*-zing-ness, the quality of being displeasing.
displeasure, *n.* dis-*plez*-zhur, irritation accompanied with a measure of anger, caused by conduct which gives offence or displeases; that which displeases or the cause of irritation; state of disfavour: *v.t.* to displease.

displicency, *n.* *dis*-plis-en-se, state of dissatisfaction; discontent.
displume, *v.t.* dis-*ploom*, to strip of plumes or feathers, or of badges of honour.
dispondee, *n.* dy-*spon*-dee, a double spondee, consisting of four long syllables [Pros.]. (L. *dispondeus.*)
dispone, *v.t.* dis-*pone*, to convey property from oneself to another in legal form [Scots. Law]. (O.Fr. *desponer.*)
disponee, *n.* dis-poh-*nee*, the person to whom a disposition is granted [Scots. Law].
disponer, *n.* dis-*poh*-ner, he who dispones [Scots. Law].
disponed, *a.* dis-*poped*, deprived of the popedom.
disporous, *a.* dy-*spaw*-rus, having two spores [Bot.].
disport, *n.* dis-*port*, play; sport; amusement; merriment: *v.i.* to play about; to wanton; to move lightly and without restraint; to move in gaiety: *v.t.* to divert or amuse. (O.Fr. *desporter.*)
disportment, *n.* dis-*port*-ment, amusement; diversion.
disposable, *a.* dis-*poze*-a-bl, at disposal; not previously engaged or employed; free to be used.
disposal, *n.* dis-*poze*-al, the act of disposing or arranging; regulation, order, or arrangement; power of ordering or arranging; power, right, or act of bestowing or giving away.
dispose, *v.t.* dis-*poze*, to set in order; to arrange; to distribute; to devote to a particular purpose; to turn to a particular end or consequence; to adapt; to incline: *v.i.* to bargain; to make terms: *n.* disposal; cast of mind or of behaviour. **dispose of,** to part with, sell or alienate; to put into another's hand or power, or bestow; to give away or transfer by authority; to direct the course of; to place in any condition; to direct what to do or what course to pursue; to use or employ; to put away. (Fr. *disposer.*)
disposed, *a.* dis-*pozed*, inclined.
disposedness, *n.* dis-*poh*-zed-ness, disposition; inclination.
disposer, *n.* dis-*poh*-zer, one who disposes; a bestower; a director; a regulator; that which disposes.
disposition, *n.* dis-po-*zish*-on, the act of disposing or state of being disposed; manner in which things or the parts of a complex body are arranged; arrangement; natural fitness or tendency; aptitude of mind; character; temper; a giving away or giving over to another [Scots. Law]; any unilateral writing, by which a person makes over to another a piece of heritable or movable property [Scots. Law]; the arrangement of the parts of a picture [Painting] or of the whole design of a building [Arch.]. (Fr.)
dispositional, *a.* pertaining to disposition.
dispositioned, *a.* dis-po-*zish*-ond, temperamentally inclined.
dispositive, *a.* dis-*poz*-e-tiv, determining or relating to disposal.
dispossess, *v.t.* dis-po-*zes*, to put out of possession; to deprive of occupancy, particularly of real estate; to eject. (O.Fr. *despossesser.*)
dispossession, *n.* dis-po-*zesh*-on, the act of dispossessing; the state of being dispossessed.
dispossessor, *n.* dis-po-*zes*-or, one who dispossesses.
dispossessory, *a.* dis-po-*zes*-o-re, pertaining or relating to dispossession.
dispost, *v.t.* dis-*pohst*, to remove from a post or position.
disposure, *n.* dis-*poh*-zewr, disposal; distribution.
dispraise, *n.* dis-*praze*, blame or censure; disparagement; dishonour or reproach: *v.t.* to blame; to censure; to mention with disapprobation or some degree of reproach.
dispraiser, *n.* dis-*praze*-er, one who dispraises.
dispraisingly, *ad.* dis-*praze*-ing-le, by way of dispraise.
dispread, *v.t.* dis-*pred*, to spread in different ways or directions: *v.i.* to expand or be spread out.
disprejudiced, *a.* dis-*prej*-yew-dist, freed from prejudice.
disprison, *v.t.* dis-*prizn*, to set free.
disprivilege, *v.t.* dis-*priv*-e-lej, to deprive of a privilege.
disprize, *v.t.* dis-*prize*, to undervalue.
disprofit, *n.* dis-*prof*-it, loss; detriment; disadvantage.
disproof, *n.* dis-*proof*, refutation; a proving to be false or erroneous.
dispropertied, *a.* dis-*prop*-er-ted, dispossessed.
disproportion, *n.* dis-pro-*por*-shon, want of proportion of one thing or part to another; want of symmetry; want of proper quantity, according to rules prescribed; want of suitableness or adequacy; inequality: *v.t.* to make unsuitable in form, size, length or quantity; to violate symmetry, harmony, or fitness in. (Fr.)
disproportionable, *a.* dis-pro-*por*-shon-a-bl, disproportional.
disproportionableness, *n.* dis-pro-*por*-shon-a-bl-ness, want of proportion; unsuitableness.
disproportionably, *ad.* dis-pro-*por*-shon-a-ble, with want of proportion; unsuitably.
disproportional, *a.* dis-pro-*por*-shon-al, wanting due proportion to something else; unsuitable; inadequate.
disproportionality, *n.* dis-pro-*por*-sho-*nal*-e-te, the state of being disproportional.
disproportionally, *ad.* dis-pro-*por*-shon-a-le, with want of proportion; unsuitably.
disproportionalness, *n.* dis-pro-*por*-shon-al-ness, the state of being disproportional.
disproportionate, *a.* dis-pro-*por*-shon-at, not proportioned; unsymmetrical; inadequate; unsuitable.
disproportionately, *ad.* dis-pro-*por*-shon-at-le, in a disproportionate degree.
disproportionateness, *n.* dis-pro-*por*-shon-at-ness, the state of being disproportionate.
disproportioned, *pp.* and *a.* dis-pro-*por*-shond, not proportioned; out of proportion.
disprovable, *a.* dis-*proov*-a-bl, capable of disproof.
disproval, *n.* dis-*proov*-al, disproof; the act of disproving. (O.Fr. *desprover.*)
disprove, *v.t.* dis-*proov*, to prove to be false, erroneous or unfounded; to refute; to confute.
disprover, *n.* dis-*proov*-er, one who disproves.
disprovided, *a.* dis-pro-*vy*-ded, unprovided.
dispunge, *v.t.* dis-*punj*, to discharge from or as from a sponge; to erase.
disputable, *a.* *dis*-pew-ta-bl, that may be disputed; controvertible; fond of disputation; disputatious.
disputableness, *n.* *dis*-pew-ta-bl-ness, the state of being disputable.
disputably, *ad.* *dis*-pew-ta-ble, in a disputable manner.
disputant, *n.* *dis*-pew-tant, one who disputes; one who is given to or experienced in disputation: *a.* disputing; engaged in controversy. (Fr.)
disputation, *n.* dis-pew-*tay*-shon, the act of disputing; a contest in argument on opposite sides of a question; an exercise in argumentation on opposite sides for the sake of practice. (Fr.)
disputatious, *a.* dis-pew-*tay*-shus, inclined to dispute; apt to cavil or controvert.
disputatiously, *ad.* dis-pew-*tay*-shus-le, in a disputatious manner.
disputatiousness, *n.* inclination to dispute.
disputative, *a.* dis-*pew*-ta-tiv, disposed to dispute; inclined to cavil or to reason in opposition.
dispute, *n.* dis-*pewt*, a contest in words or by arguments in opposition to another; a debate; a quarrel; an altercation; the possibility of being controverted: *v.i.* to contend in argument; to debate; to contend in opposition to a competitor: *v.t.* to argue; to attempt to disprove by arguments or statements; to contend for; to call in question the propriety of: to strive to maintain; to withstand. (Fr. *disputer.*)
disputed, *pp.* and *a.* dis-*pew*-ted, contested.
disputeless, *a.* dis-*pewt*-less, admitting no dispute.
disputer, *n.* dis-*pew*-ter, one who disputes or is given to disputation.
disqualification, *n.* dis-*kwol*-e-fe-*kay*-shon, the act of disqualifying; that which disqualifies.
disqualify, *v.t.* dis-*kwol*-e-fy, to deprive of the qualifications necessary for any purpose; to deprive of legal capacity, power, or right; to declare unfit; to disable.
disquiet, *a.* dis-*kwy*-et, restless; uneasy: *n.* want of quiet or quietude; uneasiness; restlessness; anxiety: *v.t.* to disturb the quiet or peace of; to render uneasy; to harass or vex.
disquieter, *n.* dis-*kwy*-et-er, one who disquiets, or that which makes uneasy.

disquietingly, *ad.* dis-*kwy*-et-ing-le, in a manner to cause uneasiness; alarmingly.
disquietly, *ad.* dis-*kwy*-et-le, in an uneasy state; in a manner to disquiet.
disquietness, *n.* dis-*kwy*-et-ness, state of disquiet.
disquietous, *a.* dis-*kwy*-et-us, causing uneasiness.
disquietude, *n.* dis-*kwy*-e-tewd, want of quietude; state of disquiet; uneasiness; anxiety.
disquisition, *n.* dis-kwe-*zish*-on, a treatise in formal and systematic examination of a subject; argumentative inquiry; an harangue [Coll.]. (L. *disquisitio.*)
disquisitional, *a.* pertaining to disquisition.
disquisitive, *a.* dis-*kwiz*-e-tiv, relating to disquisition; given to disquisition; closely examining.
disquisitor, *n.* dis-kwiz-e-tor, the author of a disquisition; an investigator.
disrank, *v.t.* dis-*rank,* to reduce in rank; to degrade.
disrate, *v.t.* dis-*rate,* to reduce in rating or rank; to remove from its rating (of ships).
disregard, *n.* dis-re-*gard,* want or omission of regard; neglect; slight; that which is disregarded: *v.t.* not to take notice of; to pay no attention to; to slight as unworthy of regard.
disregardful, *a.* *dis*-re-*gard*-ful, neglectful.
disregardfully, *ad.* heedlessly.
disrelish, *n.* dis-*rel*-ish, distaste or dislike with some degree of disgust; a bad taste; dislike: *v.t.* to dislike the taste of; to make nauseous or disgusting; to feel some disgust at.
disremember, *v.t.* *dis*-re-*mem*-ber, to fail to remember, to forget [Coll.].
disrepair, *n.* *dis*-re-*pare,* want of repair; the state of being in bad condition.
disreputable, *a.* dis-*rep*-yew-ta-bl, not reputable; in bad repute; disgraceful; dishonourable; mean: tending to bring into disrepute.
disreputably, *ad.* dis-*rep*-yew-ta-ble, in a disreputable manner.
disreputation, *n.* dis-rep-yew-*tay*-shon, disrepute; discredit.
disrepute, *n.* dis-re-*pewt,* loss or want of reputation or good name; discredit; dishonour; disgrace.
disrespect, *n.* dis-re-*spekt,* want of respect or reverence; disesteem; an incivility; rudeness: *v.t.* to have no respect for; to treat with disrespect.
disrespectable, *a.* dis-re-*spek*-ta-bl, not respectable; disregardful of respectability.
disrespectful, *a.* dis-re-*spekt*-ful, wanting in respect; showing disrespect; uncivil; rude.
disrespectfully, *ad.* dis-re-*spekt*-ful-le, in a disrespectful manner.
disrespectfulness, *n.* want of respect.
disrobe, *v.t.* dis-*robe,* to divest of a robe, covering, or investiture; to undress.
disrober, *n.* dis-*robe*-er, the attendant who takes off the robes.
disroof, *v.t.* dis-*roof,* to unroof.
disroot, *v.t.* dis-*root,* to tear up by the roots; to tear from a foundation; to loosen or undermine.
disrupt, *v.t.* dis-*rupt,* to separate; to break asunder; to rend. (L. *disruptus,* broken in pieces.)
disruption, *n.* dis-*rup*-shon, the act of rending asunder or rupturing; breach; rent. **the Disruption,** the split in the Church of Scotland, in 1843, resulting in the formation of the Free Church.
disruptive, *a.* dis-*rupt*-iv, tending to disrupt; causing disruption.
disrupture, *n.* dis-*rup*-tewr, disruption.
diss, *n.* diss, the Algerian name for *Arundo tenax,* a fibre used in making cordage.
dissatisfaction, *n.* *dis*-sat-is-*fak*-shon, the state of being dissatisfied; discontent.
dissatisfactoriness, *n.* *dis*-sat-is-*fak*-to-re-ness, the quality of being dissatisfactory.
dissatisfactory, *a.* *dis*-sat-is-*fak*-to-re, causing dissatisfaction or discontent.
dissatisfied, *a.* dis-*sat*-is-fide, discontented; not satisfied; not pleased; offended.
dissatisfy, *v.t.* dis-*sat*-is-fy, to fail to satisfy or gratify; to cause discontent; to fail to please.
disseat, *v.t.* dis-*seet,* to remove from a seat.
dissect, *v.t.* dis-*sekt,* to cut in pieces for examination; to anatomize; to analyse minutely and critically; to analyse accounts for the transfer of their items. (L. *dissectus,* cut.)
dissectible, *a.* dis-*sek*-te-bl, that may be dissected.
dissecting, *a.* dis-*sek*-ting, used in dissection, as a dissecting knife; in colour-printing, the imposing in separate chases of the parts of a composition to be printed in different colours.
dissection, *n.* dis-*sek*-shon, the act of dissecting; anything dissected; an anatomical specimen; critical analysis and examination.
dissectional, *a.* dis-*sek*-shon-al, pertaining to dissection.
dissective, *a.* dis-*sek*-tiv, pertaining to dissection; serving to dissect.
dissector, *n.* dis-*sek*-tor, one who dissects; an anatomist.
disseize, *v.t.* dis-*seez,* to dispossess wrongfully; to deprive of possession [Law]. (O.Fr. *dissaisir.*)
disseizee, *n.* dis-seez-*ee,* a person put out of possession of an estate unlawfully [Law].
disseizin, *n.* dis-*seez*-in, the act of disseizing; unlawful dispossession of lands, tenements, or incorporeal hereditaments [Law].
disseizor, *n.* dis-*seez*-or, one who disseizes.
dissel-boom, *n.* *dis*-sel-boom, the pole of an ox-wagon. (Dut.)
dissemblance, *n.* dis-*sem*-blance, want of resemblance; act of dissembling; dissimulation.
dissemble, *v.t.* dis-*sem*-bl, to hide under a false appearance; to pretend that not to be which really is; to pretend that to be which is not; to make a false appearance of; to dissimulate: *v.i.* to be hypocritical; to assume a false appearance. (Fr. *dissembler.*)
dissembler, *n.* dis-*sem*-bler, one who dissembles or conceals what he is, feels, or thinks; a hypocrite.
dissembling, *a.* dis-*sem*-bling, hiding under a false appearance: *n.* the act of dissembling; dissimulation.
dissemblingly, *ad.* with dissimulation.
disseminate, *v.t.* dis-*sem*-e-nate, to scatter with a view to propagation; to spread abroad; to diffuse; to disperse. (L. *disseminatus,* spread abroad.)
dissemination, *n.* dis-sem-e-*nay*-shon, the act of disseminating; diffusion.
disseminative, *a.* dis-*sem*-e-na-tiv, tending to disseminate or to become disseminated.
disseminator, *n.* dis-*sem*-e-nay-tor, one who or that which disseminates.
dissension, *n.* dis-*sen*-shon, disagreement in opinion, leading to contention and strife; discord; strife; breach of friendship and union. (Fr.)
dissent, *n.* dis-*sent,* difference of opinion; declaration of disagreement in opinion; separation from an established church, especially that of England; nonconformity: *v.i.* to disagree in opinion; to differ from the doctrines, rites, or government of an established church. (Fr. *dissentir.*)
dissentaneous, *a.* dis-sen-*tay*-ne-us, disagreeing; not in harmony with; contrary.
dissenter, *n.* dis-*sent*-er, one who dissents; one who declares or records his dissent; one who separates from the service and worship of an established church, particularly the Church of England; a nonconformist; a free churchman.
dissenterism, *n.* dis-*sent*-er-izm, the spirit or principles of dissent or dissenters.
dissentient, *a.* dis-*sen*-shent, disagreeing; holding contrary opinions; dissenting: *n.* one who disagrees and declares his dissent.
dissenting, *a.* dis-*sent*-ing, disagreeing in opinion; separating from the communion of an established church; belonging to a body so separated.
dissentious, *a.* dis-*sen*-shus, characterized by dissension; quarrelsome.
dissepiment, *n.* dis-*sep*-e-ment, a partition in an organ, esp. [Bot.] one formed in an ovary by the united sides of cohering carpels, which separate the inside into cells.(L., a partition, from *dis-*, and *sepes,* a hedge.)
dissepimental, *a.* *dis*-sep-e-men-tal, of the nature of a dissepiment.
dissert, *v.i.* dis-*sert,* to discourse; to make a dissertation.
dissertate, *v.i.* *dis*-ser-tate, to make a dissertation.
dissertation, *n.* dis-sert-*ay*-shon, a formal discourse intended to illustrate a subject; an argumentative treatise. (L. *dissertatus.*)
dissertational, *a.* dis-ser-*tay*-shon-al, in the form of a dissertation.
dissertative, *a.* *dis*-ser-tay-tiv, pertaining to or given to dissertation.

dissertator, *n.* *dis*-ser-tay-tor, one who writes a dissertation.
disserve, *v.t.* dis-*serv*, to do injury or the reverse of service to. (Fr. *desservir.*)
disservice, *n.* dis-*ser*-vis, ill service ; injury ; harm ; mischief.
disserviceable, *a.* dis-*ser*-vis-a-bl, injurious ; hurtful ; not serviceable.
disserviceably, *ad.* dis-*ser*-vis-a-ble, so as to be disserviceable.
dissever, *v.t.* dis-*sev*-er, to part in two ; to divide asunder.
disseverance, *n.* dis-*sev*-er-ance, the act or process of dissevering ; separation.
disseveration, *n.* *dis*-sev-er-*ray*-shon, act of dissevering.
disseverment, *n.* dis-*sev*-er-ment, disseverance.
dissidence, *n.* *dis*-se-dence, disagreement ; dissent.
dissident, *a.* *dis*-se-dent, not agreeing ; dissenting : *n.* a dissenter from the established religion ; one who votes or gives his opinion about any point in opposition to others. (L. *dissidens*, sitting aside from.)
dissight, *n.* *dis*-site, an eyesore.
dissilient, *a.* dis-*sil*-e-ent, starting asunder ; bursting and opening with violence [Bot.]. (L. *dissiliens*, flying aside.)
dissimilar, *a.* dis-*sim*-e-lar, unlike, either in nature, properties, or external form ; heterogeneous : *n.pl.* dissimilar or unlike things.
dissimilarity, *n.* *dis*-sim-e-la-re-te, the quality of unlikeness ; want of resemblance ; a point of difference.
dissimilarly, *ad.* in a dissimilar manner.
dissimilate, *v.t.* and *i.* dis-*sim*-e-late, to make or become unlike.
dissimilation, *n.* *dis*-sim-e-*lay*-shon, the changing of one of two similar sounds when they come together into another, as opposed to assimilation. (L. *dissimilis*, unlike.)
dissimilative, *a.* dis-*sim*-e-la-tiv, tending to cause dissimilation.
dissimile, *n.* dis-*sim*-e-le, comparison or illustration by contraries or things unlike (the opposite of simile) [Rhet.].
dissimilitude, *n.* *dis*-se-mil-e-tewd, unlikeness ; want of resemblance ; a dissimile. (L. *dissimilitudo.*)
dissimulate, *v.i.* dis-*sim*-yew-late, to dissemble ; to feign ; to pretend hypocritically. (L. *dissimulatus*, feigned.)
dissimulation, *n.* *dis*-sim-yew-*lay*-shon, the act of dissimulating ; a hiding under a false appearance.
dissimulator, *n.* dis-*sim*-yew-lay-tor, one who dissimulates.
dissipate, *v.t.* *dis*-e-pate, to scatter or disperse : to destroy by extravagance ; to squander ; to waste : *v.i.* to be dispersed and disappear ; to vanish ; to indulge in dissipation. (L. *dissipatus*, thrown away.)
dissipated, *a.* *dis*-e-pay-ted, squandered ; given to dissipation ; wasted by dissipation ; loose ; vicious.
dissipater, *n.* *dis*-e-pay-ter, one who or that which dissipates.
dissipation, *n.* dis-e-*pay*-shon, the act of dispersing ; the state of being dispersed ; that which diverts and takes the mind off any subject ; a distraction of energy and the resultant debility ; extravagant expenditure of life and property in the pursuit of pleasure ; excessive self-indulgence ; the insensible loss or waste of the minute parts of a body ; disintegration. (Fr.)
dissipative, *a.* *dis*-e-pa-tiv, tending to dissipate.
dissipator, *n.* *dis*-e-pay-tor, a dissipater ; part of a glacier in which gains by snow are more than off-set by loss through melting.
dissociable, *a.* dis-*soh*-she-a-bl, not sociable ; not well associated ; incongruous ; not reconcilable with. (L. *dissociabilis*, unsociable.)
dissocial, *a.* dis-*soh*-shall, unsocial.
dissociant, *n.* dis-*so*-she-ant, a substance employed to produce dissociation [Chem.].
dissociate, *v.t.* dis-*soh*-she-ate, to separate ; to disunite ; to disclaim complicity ; to separate the constituent elements of a compound, esp. by the action of heat [Chem.]. (L. *dissociatus*, separated.)
dissociation, *n.* dis-*soh*-she-*ay*-shon, the act of disuniting ; a state of separation or disunion ; disintegration into simpler constituents, esp. by heat or mechanical means [Chem.].
dissociative, *a.* dis-*soh*-she-a-tiv, tending to produce dissociation or antisocial effects.
dissolubility, *n.* *dis*-sol-yew-*bil*-e-te, dissolubleness.
dissoluble, *a.* *dis*-sol-yew-bl, capable of being dissolved ; disintegrable ; capable of being undone.
dissolubleness, *n.* *dis*-sol-yew-bl-ness, the quality of being dissoluble.
dissolute, *a.* *dis*-so-lewt, loose in behaviour and morals ; given to vice and dissipation ; licentious. (L. *dissolutus.*)
dissolutely, *ad.* in a dissolute manner.
dissoluteness, *n.* *dis*-so-lewt-ness, the habit of being dissolute ; dissipation.
dissolution, *n.* dis-so-*lew*-shon, the act or process of dissolving, disintegrating, or separating ; liquefaction ; the reduction of a body into very minute parts by a solvent, as of salts in water ; decomposition or solution ; the separation of the soul and body, death ; destruction or the separation of the parts which compose a connected system or body ; the termination of a partnership, company or society ; the breaking up of an assembly, or the putting an end to its existence.
dissolvable, *a.* di-*zol*-va-bl, that may be dissolved.
dissolvableness, *n.* di-*zol*-va-bl-ness, state of being dissolvable.
dissolve, *v.t.* di-*zolv*, to loosen ; to melt or liquefy by means of heat or moisture ; to separate ; to put an end to ; to break up ; to destroy ; to relax ; to rescind : *v.i.* to become liquefied ; to melt ; to sink away ; to melt away ; to break up ; to be decomposed ; to waste away ; to go into dissolution : *n.* a dissolving view [Cine.]. (L. *dissolvo*, loose.)
dissolvent, *a.* di-*zol*-vent, able to melt or dissolve : *n.* anything which has the power of dissolving or melting ; a solvent ; a menstruum [Med.].
dissolver, *n.* di-*zol*-ver, that which dissolves or has the power of dissolving.
dissolving, *a.* di-*zol*-ving, melting ; vanishing. **dissolving views,** magic lantern pictures that fade as the next one becomes distinct on the screen ; similar effects produced by cinematography.
dissonance, *n.* *dis*-son-ance, a mixture of harsh, inharmonious sounds ; a combination of sounds so out of harmony as to produce beats ; discord ; disagreement. (Fr.)
dissonancy, *n.* *dis*-son-an-se, dissonance.
dissonant, *a.* *dis*-son-ant, discordant ; jarring on the ear ; disagreeing ; incongruous. (Fr.)
dissonantly, *ad.* *dis*-son-ant-le, in a dissonant manner.
dissuade, *v.t.* dis-*swade*, to advise against doing or to seek to persuade not to do ; to persuade to refrain ; to represent as not advisable. (Fr. *dissuader.*)
dissuasion, *n.* dis-*sway*-zhon, the act of dissuading ; advice against a thing.
dissuasive, *a.* dis-*sway*-siv, tending to dissuade ; dehortatory : *n.* argument or counsel intended to dissuade.
dissuasively, *ad.* dis-*sway*-siv-le, in a way to dissuade.
dissuasory, *a.* dis-*sway*-so-re, dissuasive.
dissunder, *v.t.* dis-*sund*-er, to separate ; to rend.
dissyllable, *n.* dis-*sil*-la-bl, disyllable.
dissymmetrical, *a.* dis-sim-*met*-re-kal, non-symmetrical ; having two corresponding forms but placed in opposite directions (esp. of crystals).
dissymmetry, *n* dis-*sim*-e-tre, absence of symmetry though of similar shape.
distaff, *n.* *dis*-tahf, the staff to which the flax, tow, or wool was fastened, and from which the thread was drawn in spinning with the hand or the spinning-wheel ; used symbolically of a woman or woman's work. **distaff side,** the female ancestors in a pedigree. **distaff thistle,** the thistle, *Carthamus alatus*, so called from its woolly flowers. (A.S. *distaef.*)
distain, *v.t.* dis-*tane*, to stain ; to sully. (O.Fr. *destaindre.*)
distal, *a.* *dis*-tal, away from the point of growth ; furthest from the centre or axis ; terminal [Anat. and Bot.].
distally, *ad.* *dis*-ta-le, near or in the direction of a distal part [Anat. and Bot.].
★**distance,** *n.* *dis*-tance, space between two objects ; remoteness of space ; space of time ; ideal space

or separation; contrariety; the remoteness which respect requires; respect; reserve; coldness; remoteness in succession or relation; the interval between two notes [Mus.]; space left between bodies of men standing under arms in rank; a certain distance from the winning-post, varying with the length of the particular race, and marked by the **distance-post** [Horse-racing]; the boundary of view in a picture [Persp.]: *v.t.* to place remote; to leave behind in a race, especially by the interval between the distance-post and the winning-post; to leave at a great distance behind; to cause to seem distant. **angular distance,** space included between the lines drawn from two objects to the eye [Geom.]. **middle distance,** part of a picture midway between the foregound and the extreme distance [Perspect.]. **point of distance,** that part of a picture where the visual rays meet [Persp.]. **to keep one's distance,** to behave with coldness; to be reserved. (Fr.)

distanced, *a.* *dis*-tanst, outstripped; left behind; beaten by a distance or more [Horse-racing].

distant, *a.* *dis*-tant, far removed; remote in place, in time, in the line of succession, or in natural connection or consanguinity, etc.; remote in nature, and so not allied, or in view, and not very likely to be realized; remote in connexion, and so not easily seen or understood; reserved; cold. **distant signal,** a railway signal indicating, in the block system, whether or not the home signal is at danger. (Fr.)

distantly, *ad.* *dis*-tant-le, remotely; at a distance; with reserve.

distaste, *n.* dis-*taste*, aversion of the taste; disrelish; dislike: *v.t.* to disrelish or dislike; to offend or disgust; to spoil the relish or taste of.

distasteful, *a.* dis-*taste*-ful, unpleasant or disgusting to the taste; proceeding from distaste; offensive; displeasing.

distastefully, *ad.* in a distasteful manner.

distastefulness, *n.* disagreeableness.

distemper, *n.* dis-*tem*-per, a disordered state of health; a contagious infection affecting the mucous membranes of young dogs and certain other animals; a disordered state of mind; undue predominance of a passion or appetite; disorder; uneasiness; ill-humour: *v.t.* to derange the functions of the body or mind; to deprive of temper or moderation; to make disaffected, ill-humoured, or malignant. (L. *dis-*, and *temper.*)

distemper, *n.* dis-*tem*-per, a mixture of dry pigment with size or gluey solution and water, used chiefly in scene-painting and interior decoration; work done with this: *v.t.* to colour with distemper.

distemperate, *a.* dis-*tem*-per-rat, intemperate; immoderate.

distemperature, *n.* dis-*tem*-per-ra-tewr, intemperateness; excess of heat or cold, or of other qualities; perturbation of mind; slight illness, or indisposition.

distempered, *pp.* and *a.* dis-*tem*-perd, diseased in body; disordered in mind; disturbed or ruffled; immoderate; disordered; disaffected.

distemperedness, *n.* dis-*tem*-perd-ness, the state of being distempered.

distemperer, *n.* dis-*tem*-per-er, a workman who applies distemper to walls, etc.

distend, *v.t.* dis-tend, to swell out or expand in all directions; to extend; to spread apart. (Fr. *distendre.*)

distensibility, *n.* dis-ten-se-*bil*-e-te, the quality or capacity of being distensible. (Late L. *distensus*, stretched.)

distensible, *a.* dis-*ten*-se-bl, capable of being distended.

distensile, *a.* dis-*ten*-sile, distensible; capable of causing distention.

distensive, *a.* dis-*ten*-siv, distensible; distending.

distent, *a.* dis-*tent*, fully extended; swollen out.

distention, *n.* dis-*ten*-shon, the act of distending; the state of being distended.

disthene, *n.* *dis*-theen, cyanite, so called from its unequal hardness, and because its crystals can be electrified both positively and negatively. (Gr. *dis-*, twice, *sthenos*, force.)

disthrone, *v.t.* dis-*throne*, to dethrone.

distich, *n.* *dis*-tik, a couplet; a couple of poetic lines making complete sense; an epigram of two lines. (Gr. *distichos*, two-rowed.)

distichous, *a.* *dis*-tik-us, having two rows; disposed in two opposite vertical rows [Bot.].

distil, *v.i.* dis-*til*, to fall in drops; to flow gently; to use a still or to practise distillation: *v.t.* to let fall or cause to fall in drops; to obtain in a separate state or in a purified state by distillation. (Fr. *distiller.*)

distillable, *a.* dis-*til*-a-bl, that may be distilled; fit for distillation.

distillate, *n.* *dis*-te-late, the fluid left in the receiver of a distilling apparatus after distillation [Chem.].

distillation, *n.* dis-te-*lay*-shon, the act of distilling; the substance obtained by distilling; a distillate; the process of extracting spirit from a substance by means of evaporation and subsequent condensation into drops; the process of obtaining a substance pure, or of refining by that means; rectification. **destructive distillation,** the distillation of substances at very high temperatures, so that the ultimate elements are separated or evolved in new combinations. **dry distillation,** the distillation of substances by themselves, or without the addition of water. **fractional distillation,** the separating of the volatile elements of a compound by so moderating the heat that the more volatile shall be distilled off in succession from the less volatile. (Fr.)

distillatory, *a.* dis-*til*-la-to-re, pertaining to distillation; used for distilling: *n.* a still.

distiller, *n.* dis-*til*-ler, one whose occupation is the distillation of spirits.

distillery, *n.* dis-*til*-er-re, the building and works where distilling is carried on. (Fr. *distillerie.*)

distilling, *n.* dis-*til*-ing, the act or process of extracting spirit by distillation.

distilment, *n.* dis-*til*-ment, the process or the product of distilling; a distillate.

distinct, *a.* dis-*tinkt*, definitely separated; separate; clearly defined; definite; quite evident. (Fr.)

distinction, *n.* dis-*tink*-shon, the act of separating or distinguishing; a note or mark of difference; the distinguishing quality; discrimination; judgment; division; elevation of rank or of character; that which confers eminence or superiority; an honour as an award of merit, office, rank, or public favour. (Fr.)

distinctive, *a.* dis-*tink*-tiv, serving to mark a distinction; having the power to distinguish and discern; characteristic.

distinctively, *ad.* dis-*tink*-tiv-le, with distinction; plainly.

distinctiveness, *n.* dis-*tink*-tiv-ness, the state of being distinctive.

distinctly, *ad.* dis-*tinkt*-le, with distinctness; clearly; separately.

distinctness, *n.* dis-*tinkt*-ness, the quality or state of being distinct; clearness; precision.

distingué, *a.* dis-*tang*-gay, with an air of distinction; of superior bearing or manner. (Fr.)

distinguish, *v.t.* dis-*ting*-gwish, to indicate difference by some external mark; to recognize by characteristic marks; to discriminate between; to separate by any mark or quality which constitutes difference; to discern critically; to separate from others by some mark of honour or preference; to make eminent or known: *v.i.* to make a distinction; to differentiate. (O.Fr. *destinguer.*)

distinguishable, *a.* dis-*ting*-gwish-a-bl, capable of being distinguished; worthy of note.

distinguishableness, *n.* dis-*ting*-gwish-a-bl-ness, the state of being distinguishable.

distinguishably, *ad.* so as to be distinguished.

distinguished, *a.* dis-*ting*-gwisht, separated from others by being superior or extraordinary in some respect. **Distinguished Conduct Medal** (**D.C.M.**), awarded to warrant officers, non-commissioned officers and men of the Army. **Distinguished Flying Cross** (**D.F.C.**), for officers and warrant officers of the Royal Air Force and Fleet Air Arm. **Distinguished Flying Medal** (**D.F.M.**), for warrant officers, non-commissioned officers and men of the Royal Air Force and Fleet Air Arm. **Distinguished Service Cross** (**D.S.C.**), for officers in the Royal Navy below the rank of captain, and for warrant officers. **Distinguished Service Medal** (**D.S.M.**), for chief petty officers, petty officers, men, and boys of the Navy, similar ranks in the Marines, and others of corresponding position in the Service afloat. **Distinguished**

Service Order (D.S.O.), for commissioned officers in the Navy, Army, and Air Force.

distinguishedly, *ad.* dis-*ting*-gwisht-le, in a distinguished manner; eminently.

distinguisher, *n.* dis-*ting*-gwish-er, one who or that which distinguishes; a nice or judicious observer.

distinguishingly, *ad.* dis-*ting*-gwish-ing-le, with distinction; with some mark of preference.

distinguishment, *n.* dis-*ting*-gwish-ment, distinction; observation of difference.

distitle, *v.t.* dis-*ty*-tl, to disentitle; to deprive of right.

distomatous, *a.* dy-*stoh*-ma-tus, having two mouths or suckers [Zool.]. (Gr. *distomos*, double-mouthed.)

distort, *v.t.* dis-*tort*, to twist or force out of natural or regular shape, attitude, or direction; to wrest or pervert from the true meaning. (L. *distortus*, twisted.)

distortion, *n.* dis-*tor*-shon, the act of distorting; a twisting or writhing motion; deviation from natural shape or position; crookedness; a perversion of the true meaning of words; change in wave-form during transmission, or defect in electrical apparatus, resulting in faulty reception [Wire.].

distortionist, *n.* dis-*tor*-shon-ist, an acrobat who assumes distorted attitudes; a contortionist.

distortive, *a.* dis-*tort*-iv, causing distortion; distorted.

distract, *v.t.* dis-*trakt*, to draw in different directions; to draw off, as the attention, from an object; to draw the mind towards different objects, and so perplex, confuse, or harass; to disorder and derange the reason: *a.* distracted; deranged in mind. (L. *distractus*, drawn.)

distracted, *a.* dis-*trak*-ted, perplexed; harassed; driven mad or deranged.

distractedly, *ad.* in a distracted manner.

distractedness, *n.* a state of being distracted.

distracter, *n.* dis-*trak*-ter, one who or that which distracts.

distractible, *a.* dis-*trak*-te-bl, capable of being drawn aside.

distractingly, *ad.* dis-*trak*-ting-le, in a distracting manner.

distraction, *n.* dis-*trak*-shon, confusion of mind, from a multiplicity of objects crowding on it, and calling the attention different ways; perturbation of mind; dividedness of mind or heart; confusion of affairs; a state of disordered reason of a violent type; folly in the extreme, or amounting to insanity; mental aberration; extreme agitation, due to bodily or mental distress; relaxation; change of occupation. (Fr.)

distractive, *a.* dis-*trak*-tiv, causing distraction; perplexing.

distrain, *v.t.* dis-*trane*, to seize for debt; to transfer a personal chattel from the possession of a wrongdoer into the possession of the injured party, to satisfy a demand, or compel the performance of a duty [Law]: *v.i.* to make seizure of goods. (O.Fr. *destraindre*, to force.)

distrainable, *a.* dis-*tray*-na-bl, liable to be taken for distress; capable of being distrained for, or of being recovered by distraint.

distrainee, *n.* dis-tray-*nee*, one on whom an order of distress is levied.

distrainor, *n.* dis-*tray*-nor, he who seizes goods by distraint.

distraint, *n.* dis-*traynt*, levy of distress.

distrait, *a.* dis-*tray*, with the attention distracted; thinking of something else. (Fr.)

distraught, *pp.* and *a.* dis-*trawt*, distracted; agitated; perplexed.

distress, *n.* dis-*tress*, severe pain; anguish of body or mind; general affliction; want of necessaries; exhaustion; fatigue; a state of danger; the act of distraining goods [Law]; the thing taken by distraining [Law]: *v.t.* to afflict with pain or anguish; to harass; to make miserable; to compel by pain or suffering; to distrain [Law]. **distress signal, S.O.S.** (O.Fr. *destresser*.)

distressed, *pp.* and *a.* dis-*trest*, troubled; grieving; suffering great pain; afflicted; harassed; oppressed with calamity. **distressed area,** an industrial district having a continuous and high level of unemployment with helpless poverty.

distressedly, *ad.* dis-*tres*-sed-le, in a distressed manner.

distressful, *a.* dis-*tress*-ful, causing distress; indicating distress; worn with pain and labour.

distressfully, *ad.* in a painful manner.

distressing, *a.* dis-*tress*-ing, greatly troubling; affecting with severe pain.

distributable, *a.* dis-*trib*-yew-ta-bl, that may be distributed or assigned in portions.

distributary, *a.* dis-*trib*-yew-ta-re, that distributes or is distributed: *n.* a branch of a river or canal diverging from the main stream and not rejoining it [Geog.].

distribute, *v.t.* dis-*trib*-yewt, to divide among a number; to deal out and bestow in portions; to administer; to divide or separate, as into classes, orders, general, or species; to give in charity; to separate types and replace them in their proper boxes [Print.]. **distributed term,** a term employed in its full extent of meaning as denoting everything to which it is applicable [Logic]. (L. *distributus*, assigned.)

distributee, *n.* dis-trib-yew-*tee*, the receiver of a share in the distribution of the estate of an intestate [Law].

★**distribution,** *n.* dis-tre-*bew*-shon, the act of distributing; allotment; the act of giving in charity; administration separately to individuals; the act of distributing into distinct classes; the division and disposition of the parts of anything; the dispersal of commodities among consumers; the degree in which classes and persons share in the products of the community; the dividing and disposing of the several parts of a building according to some plan or to the rules of art [Arch.]; the division and apportionment of the estate of an intestate [Law]; a division and enumeration of the several qualities of a subject [Rhet.]; the separating of the type in a forme and placing each letter in its proper box [Print.]; the spreading of animals and plants into local fauna and flora. (L. *distributio*.)

distributional, *a.* dis-tre-*bew*-sho-nal, pertaining to distribution.

distributism, *n.* dis-*trib*-yew-tizm, an economic theory advocating the more equal distribution of actual and potential wealth.

distributive, *a.* dis-*trib*-yew-tiv, tending to distribute; tending to division and assignment; dealing to each his proper share; assigning the various species of a general term [Logic]; separating or dividing: *n.* a word implying division or distribution, as each, either, etc. [Gram.].

distributively, *ad.* dis-*trib*-yew-tiv-le, by distribution; singly; not collectively.

distributiveness, *n.* dis-*trib*-yew-tiv-ness, the quality of being distributive.

distributor, *n.* dis-*trib*-yew-tor, one who or that which distributes; a marketing agent or agency; a distributing part of a machine, etc.

district, *n.* *dis*-trikt, a limited extent of country; a circuit of territory or a town within which power, right, or authority may be exercised, and to which it is restrained; a definite region; a portion of territory without very definite limits: *v.t.* to divide into limited districts [U.S.A.]. **district commissioner,** a magistrate or government official exercising quasi-judicial authority in certain parts of the British Empire. **district court,** a court which has cognizance of certain causes within a district defined by law [U.S.A.]. **district judge,** the judge of a district court [U.S.A.]. **district school,** a school within a certain district of a town [U.S.A.]. **district visitor,** a churchworker in a section of a parish.

distringas, *n.* dis-*tring*-gas, a writ commanding the sheriff to distrain a person for debt or for his appearance at a certain time. **distringas in detinue,** one to compel delivery of goods [Law].

distrust, *n.* dis-*trust*, doubt or suspicion of reality or sincerity; want of confidence; discredit; suspicion: *v.t.* not to have confidence in; to doubt; to question the reality or sincerity of; to suspect of hostility.

distrustful, *a.* dis-*trust*-ful, apt to distrust; suspicious; not confident; doubting.

distrustfully, *ad.* in a distrustful manner.

distrustfulness, *n.* dis-*trust*-ful-ness, the state of being distrustful; want of confidence.

distrustingly, *ad.* in a distrustful manner.

distune, *v.t.* dis-*tewn*, to put out of tune.

disturb, *v.t.* dis-*turb*, to stir from a state of rest or tranquillity; to move or agitate; to trouble or render uneasy; to move from any regular course; to cause to deviate; to be a hindrance to. (O.Fr. *disturber.*)
disturbance, *n.* dis-*turb*-ance, any disquiet or interruption of peace; interruption of a settled state of things; tumult; emotion or agitation of the mind; disorder of thoughts; confusion; unwanted reception, as atmospherics, jamming, an intervening station, etc. [Wire.]; the hindering or disquieting of a person in the lawful and peaceable enjoyment of his right; the interruption of a right [Law]. (O.Fr.)
disturbant, *a.* dis-*turb*-ant, disturbing: *n.* one who makes or takes part in a disturbance.
disturber, *n.* dis-*turb*-er, a violator of peace; he who or that which excites passion or agitation, or causes perturbation; one that interrupts or incommodes another in the peaceable enjoyment of his right [Law].
disturbing, *pp.* and *a.* dis-*turb*-ing, tending to disturb or cause disturbance.
distyle, *n.* *dy*-style, a portico with two columns. (Gr. *dis-*, and *stylos*, column.)
disulphate, *n.* dy-*sul*-fate, a salt of sulphuric acid containing two equivalents of the acid with one of the base [Chem.].
disulphide, *n.* dy-*sul*-fide, a compound in which two atoms of sulphur are combined with another element or radical.
disulphuret, *n.* dy-*sul*-fer-ret, disulphide.
disuniform, *a.* dis-*yew*-ne-form, not uniform.
disuniformity, *n.* *dis*-yew-ne-*form*-e-te, want of uniformity.
disunion, *n.* dis-*yew*-nyon, want of union; breach of concord; contention; separation from the union.
disunionism, *n.* dis-*yew*-nyon-ism, the political principles of the disunionists [U.S.A.].
disunionist, *n.* dis-*yew*-nyon-ist, a person opposed to union, esp. [U.S.A.] a member of a former American party advocating the disunion of the United States.
disunite, *v.t.* dis-yew-*nite*, to separate, disjoin, or part: *v.i.* to fall asunder or become separate. (L. *disunitus*, separated.)
disunity, *n.* dis-*yew*-ne-te, a state of separation; want of concord.
disusage, *n.* dis-*yew*-zaj, gradual cessation of use or custom; neglect of use, exercise, or practice.
disuse, *n.* dis-*yewce*, cessation of use, practice, or exercise; cessation of custom; desuetude.
disuse, *v.t.* dis-*yewz*, to cease to use; to disaccustom. (O.Fr. *disuser.*)
disused, *a.* dis-*yewzd*, no longer used; obsolete.
disutility, *n.* dis-yew-*til*-e-te, the quality of being injurious; detriment.
disvalue, *v.t.* dis-*val*-yew, to undervalue; to disparage.
disvulnerability, *n.* *dis*-vul-ner-a-*bil*-e-te, the power of making a quick recovery from an injury, etc.
diswarrened, *pp.* dis-*wo*-rend, deprived of the character, or of the rights, of warren [Law].
disyllabic, *a.* *dy-* or *dis*-se-*lab*-ik, consisting of two syllables.
disyllabification, *n.* *dy-* or *dis*-se-*lab*-e-fe-*kay*-shon, the act of forming into two syllables.
disyllabify, *v.t.* *dy-* or *dis*-se-*lab*-e-fy, to form into two syllables.
disyllabism, *n.* dy- *or* dis-*sil*-a-bizm, having two syllables.
disyllabize, *v.t.* dy- *or* dis-*sil*-a-bize, to form into two syllables.
disyllable, *n.* dy- *or* dis-*sil*-a-bl, a word consisting of two syllables. (Fr. *dissyllabe.*)
disyoke, *v.t.* dis-*yoke*, to unyoke; to free from trammels.
dital, *n.* *dy*-tal, a key actuated by the thumb on a guitar, harp, etc., for raising the pitch a semitone. (It. *ditale*, thimble.)
ditch, *n.* ditch, a trench in the earth made by digging; an artificial watercourse; an open drain; an excavation round the works from which the earth of the rampart has been dug [Fort.]: *v.i.* to dig or make a ditch or ditches: *v.t.* to drain by a ditch; to surround with a ditch. **ditch-water,** stagnant or foul water in a ditch; stale or worthless matter. (A.S. *dic*, ditch.)
ditcher, *n.* *ditch*-er, one who digs ditches.
ditetrahedral, *a.* dy-tet-ra-*heed*-ral, having the form of a tetrahedral prism with dihedral summits [Min.]. (Gr. *di-*, and *tetrahedral.*)
dithecal, *a.* dy-*thee*-kal, dithecous.
dithecous, *a.* dy-*thee*-kus, having two thecæ; bilocular [Bot.].
ditheism, *n.* *dy*-the-izm, belief in the co-existence of two creative principles, the one good and the other evil, as in Manicheism. (Gr. *di-*, and *theos*, god.)
ditheist, *n.* *dy*-the-ist, a believer in ditheism.
ditheistic, *a.* dy-the-*is*-tik, pertaining to ditheism.
ditheistical, *a.* dy-the-*is*-te-kal, ditheistic.
dither, *v.i.* *dith*-er, to shiver with cold: *n.* excitement; apprehension, esp. in **all of a dither.**
dithery, *a.* *dith*-er-re, nervously apprehensive; in a trembling state.
dithyramb, *n.* *dith*-e-ram, a hymn conceived in a lofty and vehement style, originally in honour of Bacchus; an ode of a similarly wild enthusiastic character. (L.)
dithyrambic, *n.* dith-e-*ram*-bik, a dithyramb: *a.* boisterous; enthusiastic.
ditone, *n.* *dy*-tone, an interval comprehending two tones, the Pythagorean third [Mus.]. (Gr. *di-*, and *tone.*)
ditriglyph, *n.* dy-*try*-glif, an arrangement of two triglyphs in the frieze between the triglyphs that stand over the columns [Arch.]. (Gr. *di-*, and *triglyph.*)
ditrochee, *n.* dy-*troh*-kee, a double trochee; a foot of two trochees. (Gr. *ditrochaios.*)
dittander, *n.* dit-*tan*-der, pepperwort. (Dial.)
dittany, *n.* *dit*-ta-ne, an aromatic herb, *Origanum dictamnus*, formerly used in medicine as a vulnerary; fraxinella. (Fr. *dictame*, from Mount *Dikte*, in Crete, where it abounded.)
ditto, *n.* *dit*-to, (contracted into *do.*), that which has been said before; the same thing. **dittos,** a suit all of the same colour and material. **to say ditto,** to express agreement with what has been said. (Gr. *dittos*, double, or twice over.)
dittography, *n.* di-*tog*-ra-fe, unintentional repetition of a word or letter. (Gr. *dittos*, and *grapho*, write.)
dittology, *n.* di-*tol*-o-je, a twofold interpretation of a text.
ditty, *n.* *dit*-te, a song; a little poem to be sung; a refrain. (O.Fr. *dittie.*)
ditty-box, *n.* *dit*-te-boks, the caddy or small box in which a sailor keeps his valuables.
diuresis, *n.* dy-yew-*ree*-sis, excessive flow of urine [Med.]. (Gr. *dioureo*, urinate.)
diuretic, *a.* dy-yew-*ret*-ik, stimulating the discharge of urine: *n.* a medicine that increases the flow of urine.
diurnal, *a.* dy-*ur*-nal, relating to a day or to the daytime; daily; during daytime; performed in twenty-four hours; pertaining to the daytime only (as opposed to nocturnal) [Zool.]: *n.* a journal. (L. *diurnalis.*)
diurnally, *ad.* dy-*ur*-na-le, daily; every day.
diurnation, *n.* dy-ur-*nay*-shon, habitual dormancy by day [Zool.].
diuturnal, *a.* dy-yew-*tur*-nal, lasting for long. (L. *diu*, a long while.)
diuturnity, *n.* dy-yew-*tur*-ne-te, long duration.
div, *n.* deev, a demon or evil spirit of Persian mythology [Pers.].
diva, *n.* *dee*-vah, a prima donna. (It.)
divagate, *v.t.* *dy*-va-gate, to wander about; to digress. (L. *divagor*, wander.)
divagation, *n.* dy-va-*gay*-shon, digression.
divalent, *a.* *dy*-va- *or* *div*-a-lent, capable of replacing two atoms of hydrogen; combining with two univalents.
divan, *n.* de-*van*, the highest council of state in certain oriental communities; the great council, audience-chamber, or judicial tribunal of the former Turkish Empire; hence any council, hall, or saloon; a kind of sofa; a smoking room; a collection of poems by a single oriental author. (Per., literally, council.)
divaricate, *a.* dy-*va*-re-kate, branching off so as to form an obtuse angle above and an acute angle below [Bot.]: *v.i.* to fork or part into two branches; to branch off at an obtuse angle: *v.t.* to divide into two branches. (L. *divaricatus*, straddled.)
divarication, *n.* dy-va-re-*kay*-shon, a forking; a separation into two branches; a crossing or intersection of fibres at different angles.

dive, *v.i.* dyve, to plunge into water, as an animal, head first; to descend steeply with nose down (of aircraft); to go deep into any subject; to plunge into any matter, so as to be thoroughly engaged in it; to sink; to penetrate; to put one's hand into: *v.t.* to dip; to explore by diving: *n.* a sudden plunge, head foremost, into water; a sudden dart; a basement drinking-bar; a descent of aircraft with nose down [Av.]. (A.S. *dyfan.*)

divellent, *a.* dy- or de-*vel*-ent, drawing asunder; separating.

divellicate, *v.t.* dy-*vel*-e-kate, to pull in pieces.

diver, *n.* *dy*-ver, one who dives; one who works under water having air supplied from above; a pearl-fisher; a bird of the genus *Columbus.*

diverge, *v.i.* de-*verj*, to tend from a point in lines which recede farther and farther from each other; to vary from the type; to deviate. (Fr. *diverger.*)

divergement, *n.* de-*verj*-ment, act of diverging.

divergence, *n.* de-*ver*-jence, a receding farther from each other.

divergency, *n.* de-*ver*-jen-se, the quality or condition of being divergent; divergence.

divergent, *a.* de-*ver*-jent, receding farther from each other, as lines which proceed from the same point. (Fr.)

divergingly, *ad.* de-*ver*-jing-le, in a diverging manner.

divers, *a.* *dy*-verz, various; several; sundry. (Fr.)

diverse, *a.* *dy*-verse, different; unlike; various: *ad.* in different directions. (L. *diversus*, altered.)

diversely, *ad.* *dy*-verse-le, in different ways or directions; variously.

diversifiable, *a.* de-*ver*-se-*fy*-a-bl, that may be diversified.

diversification, *n.* de-*ver*-se-fe-*kay*-shon, the act of diversifying; the state of being diversified; modification; change; alteration.

diversiform, *a.* de-*ver*-se-form, of various forms.

diversify, *v.t.* de-*ver*-se-fy, to make different or various in form or qualities; to give variety or diversity to. (Fr. *diversifier.*)

diversiloquent, *a.* dy-ver-*sil*-o-kwent, speaking in different ways. (L. *diverse*, and *loquor*, speak.)

diversion, *n.* de-*ver*-shon, the act of turning aside from any course; that which diverts; that which turns the mind from care, business, or study, and thus relaxes and amuses; amusement; drawing the attention and force of an enemy from the point where the principal attack is to be made by attacking another point; a feint to divert attention [Mil.]. (Fr.)

diversity, *n.* de-*ver*-se-te, the state of being diverse or different; dissimilitude; variety; distinctness of being, as opposed to identity. (Fr. *diversité.*)

divert, *v.t.* de-*vert*, to turn off from any course, direction, or intended application; to turn aside; to turn the mind from business or study; to amuse; to draw the forces of an enemy to a different point [Mil.]. (Fr. *divertir.*)

diverter, *n.* de-*vert*-er, he who or that which diverts.

diverticulum, *n.* dy-ver-*tik*-yew-lum, a blind appendage branching from a canal, a cæcum; an abnormal protrusion of mucous membrane of the bladder, colon, or other hollow organ [Anat.].

divertimento, *n.* de-*ver*-te-*men*-to (*pl.* **-menti**), a short pleasant composition, vocal or instrumental, written in a light and familiar style [Mus.]. (It.)

divertingly, *ad.* de-*ver*-ting-le, in a diverting or entertaining manner.

divertisement, *n.* de-*ver*-tiz-ment, diversion; a divertissement. (Fr. *divertissement.*)

divertissement, *n.* de-ver-*teece*-mong, the act of diverting; entertainment; a short ballet or other turn introduced between the acts of a principal piece. (Fr.)

divertive, *a.* de-*ver*-tiv, tending to divert; amusing.

divest, *v.* de-*vest*, to strip off, as clothes, arms, or equipment; to deprive. (O.Fr. *devestir.*)

divestible, *a.* de-*ves*-te-bl, that can be divested.

divestiture, *n.* de-*ves*-te-tewr, the act of stripping, putting off, or depriving; alienation of property [Law]. (L. *devestitus*, divested.)

divestment, *n.* de-*vest*-ment, the act of divesting.

divesture, *n.* de-*ves*-tewr, devestiture.

divi, *n.* *div*-e, divvy.

dividable, *a.* de-*vide*-a-bl, divisible.

divide, *v.i.* de-*vide*, to part; to open; to cleave; to branch; to vote by the division of a legislative house into two parts: *v.t.* to part a thing into two or more pieces; to separate by a partition, or by an imaginary line or limit; to make partition of among a number; to distribute; to share; to cleave; to disunite in opinion or interest, or make discordant; to embarrass; to separate into two, for ascertaining opinions for and against a measure: *n.* a watershed [U.S.A.]. (L. *divido*, separate.)

divided, *pp.* and *a.* de-*vide*-ed, parted; disunited; said of leaves cut into divisions as far as the midrib [Bot.].

dividedly, *ad.* de-*vide*-ed-le, separately.

dividend, *n.* *div*-id-end, the number to be divided [Arith.]; a share; the share of the interest or profit of stock-in-trade, or other employment, which belongs to each proprietor according to his proportion of the stock or capital; a part or share assigned to creditors out of the estate of a bankrupt [Law]. **dividend warrant,** an order or authority upon which shareholders or stockholders receive their dividends [Law]. (L. *dividendus.*)

divider, *n.* de-*vide*-er, he who or that which divides; a distributor; a ladle; he who or that which disunites: *pl.* a pair of sharp-pointed compasses for measuring small intervals.

dividing, *a.* de-*vide*-ing, that indicates separation or difference: *n.* division. **dividing-engine,** a machine for marking graduations on scientific instruments.

dividingly, *ad.* de-*vide*-ing-le, by division.

divi-divi, *n.pl.* *div*-e-*div*-e, the tropical American tree *Cæsalpinia coriaria*; the wrinkled pods of this, used in tanning and dyeing [Comm.].

dividual, *a.* de-*vid*-yew-al, separated; shared or divided in common with others; divisible.

dividually, *ad.* de-*vid*-yew-a-le, separately; by dividing.

dividuous, *a.* de-*vid*-yew-us, dividual; divided; characterized by division. (L. *dividuus*, separable.)

divination, *n.* *div*-e-*nay*-shon, the act of divining; the foretelling of future events, or the discovery of things secret or obscure by alleged converse with supernatural powers or skill in the interpretation of omens; seeking for water, metal, etc., by means of a divining rod; conjectural presage; prediction. (Fr.)

divinatory, *a.* de-*vin*-a-to-re, professing divination; pertaining to divination.

divine, *a.* de-*vine*, pertaining to the deity; pertaining to a heathen god; godlike; heavenly; excellent in the highest degree; extraordinary; apparently superhuman; devoted to the service of the deity; pertaining to theology: *n.* a minister of the gospel; a man skilled in divinity; a theologian: *v.t.* to know beforehand; to foretell; to conjecture: *v.i.* to use or practise divination; to utter presages; to have presages; to guess or conjecture. **divine right,** the theory that a ruler holds his right to rule direct from God, and is not responsible for his actions as such to any lower tribunal or authority. **divine service,** the worship of God according to established forms. (Fr. *deviner.*)

divinely, *ad.* de-*vine*-le, in a divine manner; by God; in the highest degree; excellently.

divineness, *n.* de-*vine*-ness, the quality of being divine.

diviner, *n.* de-*vine*-er, one who professes and practises divination; a dowser; one who guesses.

divinified, *a.* de-*vin*-e-fide, treated as divine.

diving, *n.* *dive*-ing, the act or art of plunging under water to a greater or less depth, and remaining under it for a longer or shorter time.

diving-bell, *n.* *dive*-ing-bel, a hollow vessel, originally in the form of a bell, with the upper part closed and the lower open, in which a person may descend into and work under deep water, being supplied with air from above by means of an air-pump and tube.

diving-dress, *n.* *dive*-ing-dress, waterproof clothing to which is attached a helmet for under-water operations, and in which the wearer is supplied with air as in the diving-bell.

diving-pigeon, *n.* the black guillemot or dovekie, *Uria grylle.*

diving-spider, *n.* the water-spider, *Argyroneta aquatica.*

divinify, *v.t.* de-*vin*-e-fy, to regard as divine; to divinize.

divining-rod, *n.* the hazel or other forked rod used by dowsers.
divinity, *n.* de-*vin*-e-te, the state of being divine; the deity; a being regarded as a god; something supernatural; theology, or the science of divine things. (Fr. *divinité.*)
divinize, *v.t. div*-in-ize, to deify.
divisibility, *n.* de-viz-e-*bil*-e-te, the quality of being divisible.
divisible, *a.* de-*viz*-e-bl, capable of division into parts, classes, etc.; capable of being divided without remainder [Arith.]. (L. *divisibilis*, capable of division.)
divisibleness, *n.* de-*viz*-e-bl-ness, divisibility; capacity of being divided.
divisibly, *ad.* de-*viz*-e-ble, in a divisible manner.
★**division,** *n.* de-*vizh*-on, the act of dividing; the state of being divided; that which divides or separates; a partition; the part separated from the rest by a partition or line; a part or distinct portion; a separate body of men; one of the principal parts, including infantry, cavalry, artillery, and armour, into which an army is divided; a part of an army or militia; a part of a fleet under a commander, and distinguished by a particular flag; dissension; an elaborate solo variation, also a series of brilliant passages or vocal runs [Mus.]; the separation of voters in a legislative house; the dividing of a number or quantity into any part assigned, or the rule by which it is found how many times one number or quantity is contained in another [Arith.]; the separation of a genus into its several species. **division of labour,** specialization in industry. (Fr.)
divisional, *a.* de-*vizh*-o-nal, pertaining to division; noting or making divisions; belonging to a division.
divisionary, *a.* de-*vizh*-o-na-re, divisional.
divisionism, *n.* de-*vizh*-o-nizm, a neo-impressionist method of painting in which the pure spectral colours are placed in alternating dabs on the canvas.
divisionist, *n.* de-*vizh*-o-nist, an advocate of disunion; a practitioner or admirer of divisionism.
divisive, *a.* de-*vy*-siv, forming division or distribution; tending to make dissension or discord.
divisiveness, *n.* de-*vy*-siv-ness, the quality of being devisive; tendency to disunion.
divisor, *n.* de-*vy*-zer, the number by which the dividend is divided [Arith.]. (Fr. *diviseur.*)
divorce, *n.* de-*vorce*, a legal dissolution of marriage; the separation of husband and wife by judicial sentence; separation or disunion of things closely united; the sentence or writing by which marriage is dissolved: *v.t.* to dissolve the marriage contract between; to disunite things closely connected; to force asunder; to put away. (Fr.)
divorceable, *a.* de-*vorce*-a-bl, that can be divorced.
divorcee, *n.* div-or-*see*, a person divorced.
divorcement, *n.* de-*vorce*-ment, divorce; dissolution of the marriage tie.
divorcer, *n.* de-*vorce*-er, the person or cause that produces divorce.
divorcive, *a.* de-*vorce*-iv, having power to divorce.
divot, *n. div*-ot, a roofing turf (in Scotland and N. England); a fragment of turf dislodged by a golfer in playing a stroke.
divulgate, *v.t.* de- or dy-*vul*-gate, to make publicly known; to divulge.
divulgation, *n.* dy-vul-*gay*-shon, the divulging of something secret; a disclosure so made.
divulge, *v.t.* de-*vulj*, to reveal; to tell or make known something before private or secret; to disclose; to proclaim. (L. *divulgo*, publish.)
divulgement, *n.* de-*vulj*-ment, the act of divulging.
divulgence, *n.* de-*vul*-jence, divulgement.
divulger, *n.* de-*vul*-jer, one who divulges or reveals.
divulsion, *n.* de-*vul*-shon, the act of pulling or plucking away; a rending asunder. (L. *divulsio.*)
divulsive, *a.* de-*vul*-siv, that pulls asunder or rends.
divvy, *n. div*-e, a dividend; a bonus, esp. one paid out by a Co-operative Society [Slang].
dixie, *n. dik*-se, a camp kettle, esp. one of 12 gallons capacity.
dizain, *n.* de-*zane*, a poem or stanza of ten lines.
dizen, *v.t. dy*-zen, to dress gaudily; to deck.
dizzard, *n. diz*-zard, a blockhead.
dizzily, *ad. diz*-ze-le, in a dizzy way.
dizziness, *n. diz*-ze-ness, giddiness; vertigo.
dizzy, *a. diz*-ze, giddy; causing giddiness; dazed; vertiginous: *v.t.* to whirl round; to make giddy; to confuse. (A.S. *dysig*, foolish.)
dizzying, *a. diz*-ze-ing, whirling round; making dizzy.
djerid, *n.* je-*reed*, a blunt Turkish javelin, used in various ways for sport. (Ar. *jarid*, a palm-branch.)
djiggetai, *n. jig*-e-ty, dziggetai.
djinn, *n.* jin, a jinn; a demon.
★**do,** *v.t.* and *aux.* doo, to perform; to execute; to practise; to perform for the benefit or injury of another; to observe; to exert; to transact; to finish; to execute and bring to a conclusion; to take a step or measure; to answer the purpose; to make or cause; to work on; to prepare; to exhaust; to tour or visit [Coll.]; to cheat or swindle [Coll.]; to undergo (punishment). **do away,** to remove; to destroy. **do down,** get the better of [Slang]. **do in,** kill [Slang]. **do with,** to dispose of; to make use of; to employ; to gain; to effect by influence; to have business to deal: *v.i.* to act or behave in any manner; to fare or to be in a state with regard to sickness or health; to succeed or accomplish a purpose; to fit, be adapted, or answer the design in view. *p.* **did**; *pp.*, **done,** dun; *2nd sing.*, **doest,** *doo*-est *aux.*, **dost,** dust; *3rd sing.*, **does,** duz; *negative* **don't,** dohnt, **didn't, doesn't,** duznt. **do or die** determined to be deterred by nothing. **have to do with,** to have business with; to deal with; to have carnal commerce with. Do is used for a verb to save its repetition; in the imperative, to express an urgent request or command; as an auxiliary in asking questions; and also to express emphasis.
do, *n.* doo, a swindle; a fraud; a deed or performance; an entertainment; a feed; an assault [Mil.] (all Slang or Coll.).
do, doh, the first or C note in the scale [Mus.].
do., *n.* ditto, abbreviation of ditto.
doab, *n. doh*-ab, a tract of land lying between two rivers at their confluence, esp. in India. (Pers.)
doable, *a. doo*-a-bl, possible to be done.
do-all, *n. doo*-awl, a factotum.
Dobbin, *n. dob*-bin, an old draught-horse. (Personal name; a form of Robin, for Robert.)
dobby, *n. dob*-be, a childish old man; an imbecile; a sprite of wraith; an attachment to a loom for weaving small patterns. (as *Dobbin*)
docent, *a. doh*-sent, teaching: *n.* a lecturer, esp. one not on the regular staff [U.S.A. Universities].
Docetæ, *n.pl.* doh-*see*-tee, a sect in the early church who maintained that Christ's humanity was only seeming and not real. (Gr. *dokeo*, seem.)
docetic, *a.* doh-*set*-ik, pertaining to docetism.
Docetism, *n.* doh-*set*-izm, the doctrine of the Docetæ.
Docetist, *a.* doh-*set*-ist, Docetic: *n.* an adherent of Docetism.
doch-an-doris, *n. dokh*-an-*daw*-ris, a final drink; a stirrup-cup. (Gael. *deoch-an-doruis*, drink of the door.)
dochmiac, *n. dok*-me-ak, a metrical foot consisting of five syllables, a short, two longs, a short, and a long. (Gr. *dochme*, a Greek measure.)
docile, *a. doh*-sile, easily instructed; ready to learn; easily managed; tractable. (L. *docilis*, teachable.)
docility, *n.* doh-*sil*-e-te, the quality of being docile.
docimastic, *a.* dos-e-*mas*-tik, assaying by tests, especially ores or metals.
docimasy, *n. dos*-e-ma-se, the art or practice of assaying ores or metals; metallurgy; the art of testing in materia medica and jurisprudence. (Gr. *dokimasia*, examination.)
docimology, *n.* dos-e-*mol*-o-je, a treatise on the art of assaying or examining in metallurgy.
dock, *n.* dok, the popular name of several species of plants of the genera *Rumex*, *Arctia*, etc. (A.S. *docce.*)
dock, *n.* dok, the tail of a beast cut short; the stump; a case of leather to cover the stump; the amount (esp. of wages) docked: *v.t.* to cut short; to cut tail; to cut off; to deduct from.
dock, *n.* dok, an artificial enclosure or basin for the building, repair, or reception of ships; a wharf; a dockyard; a platform enclosure in which a railway line terminates; the place where a prisoner stands in court. **dock charges or dues,** certain dues payable on vessels and goods entering or leaving docks. **dry dock,** a dock from which the water can be pumped for building and repairing vessels. **floating dock,** a large structure of caissons by means of which ships can be lifted up out of the water for repairs. **graving dock,** a

dry dock, or one into which ships can be admitted at high-tide and left high and dry at low-tide. **naval dock,** a place provided with all necessary stores and materials for the royal navy. **wet dock,** a dock for the purpose of loading and unloading vessels. (Old Dut. *docke.*)

dockage, *n. dok*-aj, dock dues; dock accommodation.

dock-cress, *n. dok*-kress, the nipplewort.

docker, *n. dok*-er, a dock labourer.

docket, *n. dok*-et, a summary of a larger writing; a paper containing the heads of a writing [Law]; an abstract appended to letters patent by the clerk of the dockets [Law]; a bill tied to goods containing some direction, as the owner's name or their destination; a label [Comm.]; a list of cases in a court [Law]: *v.t.* to make an abstract or summary of the heads of a writing; to abstract and enter in a book; to enter in a docket; to mark the contents of papers on the back. **to strike a docket,** formerly, to enter a declaration of bankruptcy against a debtor [Law]. (Origin unknown.)

dockization, *n.* dok-ize-*ay*-shon, the act of dockizing.

dockize, *v.t. dok*-ize, to line a river with docks.

dockyard, *n. dok*-yard, a government establishment in which ships of war are built and repaired; a yard or magazine, near a harbour, for containing all kinds of naval stores and timber.

doctor, *n. dok*-tor, a qualified teacher, specially one so skilled in a profession as to be pronounced able to teach it; one who has passed at a university all the degrees in the faculty; the highest degree in a faculty; an honorary degree for literary or other distinction conferred by a university or the Archbishop of Canterbury; a learned man; a physician; a medical practitioner; a brightly coloured artificial fly (Angling]; a mechanical contrivance used as a makeshift or for adjusting or regulating: *v.t.* to treat with medicines; to mend; to confer the degree of doctor upon; to adulterate; to falsify; to tamper with; to geld (esp. a cat) [Coll.]. **Doctor of the Church,** one of several great teachers and theologians of the early Christian Church. **Doctors' Commons,** the former college of the doctors of civil law in London which became the seat of a number of the courts of law. (Fr. *docteur.*)

doctoral, *a. dok*-to-ral, relating to a doctor.

doctorally, *ad.* in the manner of a doctor.

doctorate, *n. dok*-to-rat, the degree of a doctor.

doctorial, *a.* dok-*taw*-re-al, doctoral.

doctoring, *n. dok*-to-ring, medical treatment; the adulteration of liquors and other articles of consumption; the doping or drugging of a race-horse.

doctorly, *a. dok*-tor-le, like a learned man.

doctorship, *n. dok*-tor-ship, the degree of a doctor.

doctrinaire, *n.* dok-tre-*nayr*, an unpractical theorizer, especially on social and political questions; (*cap.*) originally one of a set of politicians in France who, about 1816, sought to reform the constitution on the English model: *a.* pertaining to a doctrinaire; doctrinarian. (Fr.)

doctrinal, *a.* dok-*try*-nal *or dok*-tre-nal, pertaining to doctrine; containing or inculcating a doctrine; pertaining to the act or means of teaching: *n.* something that is a part of doctrine.

doctrinally, *ad.* dok-*try*-na-le *or dok*-tre-na-le, in the form of doctrine or instruction.

doctrinarian, *a.* dok-tre-*nayr*-re-an, pertaining to doctrinaires; impractical: *n.* a doctrinaire.

doctrinarianism, *n.* dok-tre-*nayr*-re-a-nizm, the principles of the Doctrinaires; political theorizing.

doctrine, *n. dok*-trin, a thing taught; a principle laid down as true by an instructor or master; dogma; the truth taught; teaching; learning; knowledge. (Fr.)

document, *n. dok*-yew-ment, an official paper; a record; a paper for information or proof, containing instructions for the establishment of facts; precept, or authoritative dogma: *v.t.* to furnish with documents or papers necessary to establish facts; to prove by means of documents. (Fr.)

documental, *a.* dok-yew-*men*-tal, pertaining to, consisting in, or derived from documents.

documentary, *a.* dok-yew-*men*-ta-re, pertaining to written evidence; consisting in documents.

documentation, *n. dok*-yew-men-*tay*-shon, documenting; the use of documents; the supplying (esp. a ship) with the necessary documents.

dodded, *a. dod*-ded, polled: hornless (esp. of sheep).

dodder, *v.i. dod*-der, to totter; to quake; to be feeble. (Dial. Eng.)

dodder, *n. dod*-der, the leafless parasitic plant of the genus *Cuscuta*, that, germinating in the ground, attaches itself to other plants, such as flax, clover, and vetches, and lives on them. (A.S. *dodder.*)

doddered, *a. dod*-derd decayed with age; overgrown with dodder.

dodder-grass, *n.* quaking grass, *Briza media.*

doddering, *a. dod*-der-ing, quivering; senile.

doddery, *a. dod*-der-re, given to doddering; tottering; infirm; senile.

dodecagon, *n.* do-*dek*-a-gon, a polygon of twelve equal sides and angles. (Gr. *dodeka*, twelve, and *gonia*, an angle.)

dodecagynia, *n.pl.* doh-dek-a-*jin*-e-a, a group of plants having either eleven or twelve pistils [Bot.]. (Gr. *dodeka*, and *gyne*, a female.)

dodecahedral, *a.* doh-dek-a-*heed*-ral, pertaining to a dodecahedron; having twelve sides.

dodecahedron, *n.* doh-dek-a-*heed*-ron, a regular solid having twelve equal pentagonal bases. (Gr. *dodeka*, and *hedra*, a base.)

dodecandria, *n.pl.* doh-de-*kan*-dre-a, a group of plants having from twelve to nineteen stamens [Bot.]. (Gr. *dodeka*, and *aner*, a male.)

dodecandrian, *a.* doh-de-*kan*-dre-an, pertaining to the dodecandria.

dodecandrous, *a.* doh-de-*kan*-drus, dodecandrian.

dodecane, *n. doh*-de-kane, a hydrocarbon of the paraffin group containing twelve atoms of carbon.

dodecapetalous, *a.* doh-dek-a-*pet*-a-lus, having twelve petals [Bot.]. (Gr. *dodeka*, and *petalon*, a leaf.)

dodecarchy, *n. doh*-de-kar-ke, government by twelve.

dodecastyle, *n.* do-*dek*-a-stile, a portico that has twelve columns in front [Arch.]. (Gr. *dodeka*, and *stylos*, a column.)

dodecasyllable, *n. doh*-dek-a-*sil*-a-bl, a word of twelve syllables.

dodge, *n.* dodj, a trick; an evasion; a device; a quibble: *v.i.* to start aside and evade; to evade and disappoint by mean shuffling tricks; to shuffle; to quibble: *v.t.* to evade by suddenly shifting one's position. (Origin unknown.)

dodger, *n. dodj*-er, one who dodges or evades; a trickster.

dodgery, *dodj*-er-re, trickery; the employment of artifice.

dodgy, *a. dodj*-e, artful; ingenious; evasive.

dodman, *n. dod*-man, a snail. (Dial. Eng.)

dodo, *n. doh*-doh, the large flightless pigeon of Mauritius, *Didus ineptus*, last recorded alive in 1681; an old-fashioned, narrow-minded person [Slang]. (Port. *doudo*, silly.)

dodonian, *a.* doh-*doh*-ne-au, applied to Jupiter, worshipped in the temple of Dodona, where he had a famous oracle.

doe, *n.* doh, the female of fallow-deer, and of hare or rabbit and the buck; applied also to some other animals, as the rat and goat. (A.S. *da.*)

doer, *n. doo*-er, a performer; one who performs what is required.

does, duz, *third per. sing. pres. ind.* of *do.*

doeskin, *n. doh*-skin, the skin of a doe; leather made from this; a compact twilled woollen cloth.

doff, *v.t.* doff, to put off, as dress; to divest; to get rid of; to put or shift off: *v.i.* to take the hat off in respect. (*Do off.*)

doffer, *n. dof*-fer, a revolving cylinder in a carding-machine, which strips the cotton from the cards; a worker who removes the full bobbins or spindles.

★dog, *n.* dog, a wild or domesticated carnivore of the genus *Canis*; a male dog; a fellow; a term of contempt given to a man; one of two constellations in the southern hemisphere; an andiron; an iron hook or bar with a sharp fang; a grappling iron; a pawl or other catching or gripping appliance: *v.t.* to follow as a dog; to follow close and constantly; to track; to worry with importunity: *a.* in composition, male; degenerate (as in **dog-fox, dog-Latin,** etc.): *ad.*, extremely; completely (as in **dog-cheap, dog-tired,** etc.). **dog's chance,** a bare chance in one's favour. **give or throw to the dogs,** to throw away. **go to the dogs,** to go to ruin. **the dogs,** greyhound racing, a meet for greyhound racing [Coll.] (A.S. *docga.*)

dogaressa, *n.* *doh*-gah-*res*-sah, the wife of a doge.
dogate, *n.* *doh*-gate, the office or dignity of doge.
dogbane, *n.* *dog*-bane, a plant of the genus *Apocynum.*
dogberry, *n.* *dog*-be-re, an ignorant parish official (after a character in "Much Ado About Nothing"); the berry of the dogwood, *Cornus sanguinea.*
dog-biscuit, *n.* biscuit sold for feeding dogs.
dogcart, *n.* *dog*-kahrt, a light double-seated two-wheeled one-horse vehicle, with a box, or boot, originally for carrying sporting dogs; a cart drawn by a dog or dogs.
dog-cheap, *a.* very cheap; of very small repute.
dog-collar, *n.*, a collar, with attachment for a chain, worn by a dog; a high, closely fitting shirt-collar.
dog-days, *n.pl.* *dog*-dayz, days in July and August preceding and succeeding that on which the dog-star rises and sets with the sun, a conjunction which was formerly supposed to account for the heat prevailing at that season.
dogdom, *n.* *dog*-dom, the world of dogs; dogs collectively.
doge, *n.* dohdzh, the name of the former chief magistrates of Venice and Genoa. (It. from L. *dux,* a leader.)
dog-eared, *a.* *dog*-eerd, with the corners of the leaves turned down. (*Dog's-ear.*)
dog-fight, *n.* a fight between dogs; a confused combat, esp. between opposing groups of armed aircraft.
dogfish, *n.* *dog*-fish, several species of small sharks, so called from following their prey in packs like dogs; applied also to the burbot, bowfin, tope, and other fish.
dog-fox, *n.* the male of the fox.
dogged, *a.* *dog*-ed, sullen; obstinate; determined.
doggedly *ad.* *dog*-ed-le, in a dogged manner.
doggedness, *n.* *dog*-ed-ness, the quality of being dogged; tenacity; obstinacy.
dogger, *n.* *dog*-er, a coarse ironstone; a two-masted Dutch fishing-smack used in the North Sea, particularly in the cod and herring fishery; (*cap.*) a shoal in the North Sea which is a famous fishing ground.
doggerel, *a.* *dog*-ger-rel, an epithet originally given to a kind of loose irregular measure in burlesque poetry, like that of Hudibras; poor in sense as well as versification: *n.* irregular measure in burlesque poetry; worthless verse.
doggery, *n.* *dog*-er-re, behaviour befitting a dog; dogs collectively.
dogginess, *n.* *dog*-e-ness, doggishness; interest in dogs.
doggish, *a.* *dog*-ish, like a dog; snappish; cynical; showily dressed [Coll.].
doggishness, *n.* the quality of being doggish.
doggo, *ad.* *dog*-go, silent and still; hidden.
dog-gone, *int.*, hang! drat! damn! [U.S.A.]. (Euphemistic for *God-damned.*)
dog-grass, *n.* couch grass, *Agropyrum repens.*
doggy, *a.* *dog*-e, fond of dogs; doggish: *n.* a little dog [Childish].
doghead, *n.* *dog*-hed, a gunlock hammer.
dog-hole, *n.* a place fit only for dogs.
dog-Latin, *n.* dog-*lat*-in, barbarous Latin.
dog-lead, *n.* *dog*-leed, a strap or chain for leading or restraining a dog.
dog-legged, *a.* *dog*-legd, crooked or bent like a dog's hind leg.
dog-lichen, *n.*, the common lichen *Peltigera canina,* formerly used as a cure for hydrophobia.
dogma, *n.* *dog*-ma, a settled opinion positively expressed; a doctrine settled and promulgated by authority and to be received as such; a principle, maxim, or tenet; a doctrinal notion, particularly in matters of faith and philosophy. (Gr., that which seems right, fitting, or true.)
dogmatic, *a.* dog-*mat*-ik, dogmatical.
dogmatical, *a.* dog-*mat*-e-kal, pertaining to a dogma or to established opinion; asserting or disposed to assert with authority, often with overbearingness and arrogance; dictatorial; overbearing in assertion: asserted with authority; authoritative.
dogmatically, *ad.* dog-*mat*-e-ka-le, positively; in a magisterial manner; arrogantly.
dogmaticalness, *n.* dog-*mat*-e-kal-ness, the quality of being dogmatical; positiveness.
dogmatics, *n.* dog-*mat*-iks, doctrinal theology.
dogmatism, *n.* *dog*-ma-tizm, positive dogmatic assertion of opinion; positiveness in opinion (Gr. *dogmatizo.*)
dogmatist, *n.* *dog*-ma-tist, a positive, often arrogant advancer of principles; one who dogmatizes; a member of a dogmatic school, esp. of philosophy.
dogmatize, *v.i.* *dog*-ma-tize, to assert positively; to teach with bold and undue confidence; to advance with arrogance.
dogmatizer, *n.* *dog*-ma-*tize*-er one who dogmatizes
dog-nail, *n.* a large nail with head on one side only; a nail with head slightly countersunk.
dog-rose, *n.* the wild rose, *Rosa canina.*
dog's-bane, *n.* a plant with a bitter root that possesses medicinal properties; dogbane.
dog's-ear, *n.* *dogz*-eer, the corner of a leaf in a book turned down like the ear of a dog: *v.t.* to make a dog's-ear in.
dog's-fennel, *n.* stinking mayweed, *Anthemis cotula.*
dogship, *n.* *dog*-ship, the quality or the personality of a dog.
dogshores, *n.pl.* *dog*-shorz, pieces of wood fitted to the upper end of the bilgeways on a building slip and knocked away at the launching of a vessel
dog-skin, *n.* *dog*-skin, the skin of a dog, esp. when tanned, or a textile imitation of this: *a.* made of the skin of a dog.
dog-sleep, *n.* *dog*-sleep, light, fitful sleep.
dog's-mercury, *n.* the common hedge plant *Mercurialis perennis.*
dog's-nose, *n.* a drink of mixed beer and gin [Slang].
dog's-rue, *n.* a plant, a species of *Scrophularia.*
dog's-tail-grass, *n.* pasture grass, *Cynosurus cristatus.*
dog-star, *n.* Sirius, the brightest of the stars, whose rising and setting with the sun gave name to the dog-days.
dog's-tongue, *n.* the weed, hound's-tongue.
dog-thistle, *n.* dog-*this*-l, the plant *Carduus arvensis.*
dog-tired, *a.* overtired; much fatigued.
dog-tooth, *n.* *dog*-tooth, a canine tooth; a sharp-pointed human tooth between the incisors and premolars; the eye-tooth; tooth ornament, a toothed moulding [Arch.]. **dog-tooth violet,** the bulbous purple-flowered plant, *Erythronium dens canis.*
dog-track, *n.* a greyhound-racing track.
dog-trot, *n.* and *a.* a gentle trot, like that of a dog; jog-trot.
dog-vane, *n.* a small vane composed of thread, cork, and feathers, placed on the weather gunwale [Naut.]
dog-violet, *n.* the blue-flowered, almost scentless violet, *Viola canina.*
dog-watch, *n.* *dog*-wotch, one of two watches of two hours each, between 4 and 8 p.m. [Naut.].
dog-whelk, *n.* a univalve shell of the genus *Nassa* very common on the British coast.
dogwood, *n.* *dog*-wood, wild cornel, the plant *Cornus sanguinea.*
doh, *n.* doh, the tonic note in any scale of the Tonic Sol-fa notation; do [Mus.].
doily, *n.* *doy*-le, a small ornamental napkin for use under a plate, bottle, etc. (The name of its original maker).
doings, *n.pl.* *doo*-ingz, things done; transactions; actions, good or bad; behaviour; stir; anything wanted or apposite at the moment [Slang].
doit, *n.* *doyt,* a small piece of money; a small Dutch copper coin, worth about half a farthing; a similar coin once current in Scotland; a trifle. (Dut. *duit.*)
dolabriform, *a.* do-*lab*-re-fawrm, having the form of the head of a pickaxe [Bot.]. (L. *dolabra,* a hatchet, and *form.*)
dolce, *ad.* *dol*-che, softly and tenderly [Mus.]. (It, from L. *dulcis,* sweet.)
doldrums, *n.* *dol*-drumz, a zone in the tropics between the regions of the trade-winds, where calms and variable winds prevail, with occasional squalls [Naut.]; depression; the dumps.
dole, *n.* dole, a portion dealt out or distributed; something given in charity; incorrectly applied to the weekly benefit paid to the unemployed under the British National Insurance Acts and to out-relief granted by the National Assistance Board: *v.t.* to deal out in small portions

to distribute. **on the dole**, in receipt of unemployment benefit. (A.S. *dal*, piece.)

dole, *n.* dole, grief; sorrow. (O.Fr.)

doleful, *a.* *dole*-ful, expressing grief; impressing sadness; sad; melancholy.

dolefully, *ad.* *dole*-ful-le, in a doleful manner.

dolefulness, *n.* the quality of being doleful.

dolent, *a.* *doh*-lent, sorrowful; grieving.

dolerite, *n.* *dol*-er-rite, a group of basic igneous rocks connecting the gabbros with the basalts and including many of the rocks once called greenstones. (Gr. *doleros*, deceit.)

dolesome, *a.* *dole*-sum, gloomy; dismal; doleful.

dolichocephalic, *a.* *doh*-lik-o-se-*fal*-ik, long-headed; having a skull measuring at least one-fourth more from front to back than from side to side [Ethn.]. (Gr. *dolichos*, long, *kephale*, the head.)

dolichurus, *n.* dol-e-*kewr*-rus, a verse with a foot or a syllable too many [Pros.]. (Gr. *dolichouros*, long-tailed.)

dolium, *n.* *doh*-le-um, a large earthenware wine-jar of the ancient Romans; (*cap.*) a genus of marine univalve molluscs, so called from their shape. (L., a cask or large jar.)

doll, *n.* dol, a puppet or image as a toy; a silly young woman with a pretty face. **to doll up**, to dress oneself smartly and attractively [Slang]. (From *Doll*, for *Dorothy*.)

dollar, *n.* *dol*-lar, a gold coin of 25·8 grains in weight, ·900 in fineness, the monetary unit of the U.S.A. (since 1873, but not coined since 1890) and of Canada, Liberia, and certain Latin-American countries; a silver coin of different values in different countries and periods; five shillings [Slang]. **Chinese dollar**, the yuan. (Ger. *thaler*, from *thal*, a dale, because first coined at Joachimsthal silver-mines in Bohemia.)

dollish, *a.* *dol*-ish, pretty, but as useless as a doll.

dollop, *n.* *dol*-lop, a shapeless lump. (Dial. Eng.)

dolly, *n.* *dol*-le, a doll; an appliance for washing clothes with; a contrivance for stirring ore in process of washing; the operating part of a tumbler switch [Elect.]: *v.t.* to treat in or with a dolly (of clothes or ore). **dolly shop**, a marine store.

dolman, *n.* *dol*-man, a long robe open in front worn by Turks; a woman's loose mantle; a hussar's jacket with hanging sleeves. (Turk. *dolaman*.)

dolmen, *n.* *dol*-men, a cromlech; a prehistoric monument consisting of a large unhewn stone resting on others. (Celt. *dol*, a table, *men*, a stone.)

dolomite, *n.* *dol*-o-mite, magnesian limestone; a mineral consisting of carbonate of lime and carbonate of magnesia, with carbonate of iron or carbonate of manganese, or both together, generally present. (So called from the Fr. geologist Deodat *Dolomieu*, d. 1801.)

dolomitic, *a.* dol-o-*mit*-ik, containing, resembling, or formed of dolomite.

dolomitization, *n.* dol-o-mit-e-*zay*-shon, the geological process of conversion into dolomite.

dolorific, *a.* dol-o-*rif*-ik, that causes or expresses pain or grief. (L. *dolor*, pain, *facio*, make.)

doloroso, *ad.* do-lo-*roh*-zo, tenderly and pathetically [Mus.]. (It.)

dolorous, *a.* *dol*-o-rus, doleful; impressing sorrow or grief; painful; distressing. (O.Fr. *doloreux*.)

dolorously, *ad.* in a manner to express pain.

dolorousness, *n.* sorrowfulness.

dolose, *a.* do-*lohz*, with criminal intent; deceitful. (L. *dolosus*, fraud.)

dolour, *n.* *dol*-er *or* *doh*-lor, grief; anguish. **the Seven Dolours**, seven sorrowful experiences in the life of the Virgin Mary. (O.Fr.)

dolphin, *n.* *dol*-fin, one of a group of toothed cetaceans of the genus *Delphinus*; the great mackerel or dorado, *Coryphæna hippuris*, which makes surprising changes of colour just before death; a conventional heraldic figure confusing these and combining their peculiarities; a heavy mass suspended from the yard-arm, to be dropped on an enemy's vessel [Grec. Antiq.]; a spar or buoy fastened to an anchor, to which an iron ring is usually attached, to enable vessels to ride by it [Naut.]; a mooring-post at a dock or wharf [Naut.]; the Dauphin. **dolphin striker**, the vertical spar or bar beneath the bowsprit [Naut.]. (Fr. *dauphin*.)

dolphinet, *n.* *dol*-fin-et, a former name for a female dolphin.

dolphin-fly, *n.* a black aphid destructive to beans.

dolt, *n.* dohlt, a dull, stupid fellow. (A.S. *dol*, dull.)

doltish, *a.* *dohlt*-ish, dull in intellect; stupid.

doltishly, *ad.* *dohlt*-ish-le, in a doltish manner.

doltishness, *n.* *dohlt*-ish-ness, stupidity.

-dom, dum, a termination denoting jurisdiction, condition, or quality, as dukedom, wisdom, freedom; also denoting a collective total of similars, as Christendom, heathendom. (A.S. *dôm*, doom.)

dom, *n.* dom, a title borne by dignitaries of the Benedictine and Carthusian orders. (Port.)

domain, *n.* do-*mane*, landed estate; a home park; dominion; sphere of influence; field of work; scope. (Fr. *domaine*.)

domal, *a.* *doh*-mal, pertaining to a house [Astrol.] or to a dome.

domanial, *a.* do-*may*-ne-al, relating to landed estates.

dom-boc, *n.* *dom*-bok, a book of statutes of the ancient English kings, esp. that compiled under Alfred the Great. (*Doom* and *book*.)

Domdaniel, *n.* dom-*dan*-e-el, a fabled hall under the ocean where the magicians paid annual homage to their master [Oriental Myth.].

dome, *n.* dome, a round or polygonal roof; a cupola; a noble fabric, as a temple, cathedral, etc.; the upper part of a furnace, resembling a hollow hemisphere or small dome [Chem.]; a crystal form in which two similar inclined faces meet in a horizontal edge like a roof-top; anything dome-shaped. (O.Fr.)

domed, *a.* dohmd, furnished with a dome.

domelike, *a.* *dome*-lyke, dome-shaped.

domesday, *n.* *dohmz-* *or* *doomz*-day, doomsday. **Domesday Book**, a famous record compiled by order of William the Conqueror in 1085-1086, and containing a survey of the estates with their owners and stock in the greater part of England.

domestic, *a.* do-*mes*-tik, belonging to the house or the home; remaining much at home and devoted to home life; tame, not wild; pertaining to the internal affairs of a nation; intestine, not foreign; made in one's own house, nation, or country: *n.* a servant employed on household duties and usually residing with a family. **domestic economy**, household management. (Fr. *domestique*.)

domesticable, *a.* do-*mes*-te-ka-bl, capable of being domesticated.

domestically, *ad.* do-*mes*-te-ka-le, in a domestic manner; privately; in relation to domestic affairs.

domesticate, *v.t.* do-*mes*-te-kate, to make domestic or familiar; to accustom to home life; to tame; to cultivate that which naturally is wild; to civilize. (L. *domesticus*.)

domestication, *n.* do-mes-te-*kay*-shon, the act of domesticating; the condition of being domesticated.

domesticity, *n.* do-mes-*tis*-e-te, state of being domestic; homeliness; a domestic interest.

domett, *n.* *dom*-et *or* doh-*met*, a loose flannel of which the warp is cotton and the weft woollen.

domical, *a.* *doh*-me-kal, appertaining to or shaped like a dome.

domicile, *n.* *dom*-e-sile, a place of abode or permanent residence; the length of residence required by the law of some countries for the purpose of founding jurisdiction in civil actions [Law]; the place at which a bill of exchange is payable; *v.t.* to establish a fixed residence or a residence that constitutes habitancy: *v.i.* to dwell. (Fr. *domicilier*.)

domiciliar, *n.* dom-e-*sil*-e-ar, a member of a minor order of canons having no vote in the chapter.

domiciliary, *a.* *dom*-e-*sil*-e-a-re, pertaining to a domicile. **domiciliary visit**, a visit to a private dwelling, particularly for the purpose of searching it under authority of law.

domiciliate, *v.t.* *dom*-e-*sil*-e-ate, to domicile; to establish in or as in a home.

domiciliation, *n.* *dom*-e-sil-e-*ay*-shon, permanent residence; inhabitancy.

dominance, *n.* *dom*-e-nance, the state of being dominant; ascendancy; predominance. (Fr.)

dominancy, *n.* *dom*-e-nan-se, dominant quality; dominance.
dominant, *a.* *dom*-e-nant, having rule or ascendancy; ruling; prevailing: *n.* that which is dominant; a dominant characteristic [Biol.] or term [Math.]; of the three notes essential to the tone, that which is fifth from the tonic [Mus.]. **dominant chord,** that which is practised on the dominant of the tone, and introduces a perfect cadence, thus—if the key be C, the dominant is G [Mus.]. (Fr.)
dominate, *v.t.* *dom*-e-nate, to rule; to predominate over; to tower above. (L. *dominatus*, governed.)
domination, *n.* dom-e-*nay*-shon, the act of dominating; power in ruling; government; arbitrary authority; tyranny; the fourth order of angelic beings. (Fr.)
dominative, *a.* *dom*-e-na-tiv, governing; imperious.
dominator, *n.* *dom*-e-nay-tor, a ruler or ruling power.
domineer, *v.t.* dom-e-*neer*, to rule over in an insolent, haughty, overbearing way: *v.i.* to use authority arrogantly and arbitrarily; to bluster; to hector; to tower over (of mountains, etc.). (Fr. *dominer*.)
domineeringly, *ad.* dom-e-*neer*-ing-le, in an overbearing way.
dominical, *a.* do-*min*-e-kal, relating to the Lord; indicating Sundays: *n.* the Lord's day; the dominical letter. **dominical letter,** the letter which, in almanacs, denotes the Sabbath, or Dies Domini, the Lord's day. (Late L. *dominicalis*, relating to the Sabbath.)
Dominican, *n.* do-*min*-e-kan, one of an order of preaching friars founded in 1216 by Domingo de Guzman, a Spaniard, born in 1170; a Black Friar (England) or Jacobins (France): *a.* pertaining to the Dominicans.
dominie, *n.* *dom*-e-nee, a schoolmaster. (L. *domine*, vocative of *dominus*, lord, master.)
dominion, *n.* do-*min*-yon, supreme power or authority; government; the power of controlling; territory under the authority of a prince or state; a self-governing colony: *pl.* the official name of the self-governing communities of the British Empire other than Great Britain and Northern Ireland. **Dominion day,** the National day and legal holiday in Canada (1st July) and New Zealand (4th Mon. in Sept.). (Fr.)
domino, *n.* *dom*-e-noh (*pl.* **dominoes**), a cape with a hood, worn by a master, or by a priest while officiating in a cold edifice; a long loose cloak of black silk, with a hood removable at pleasure, used as a general disguise at masquerades; one of twenty-eight oblong tablets bearing dots and blanks used in the game of dominoes. (L. *dominus*.)
dominoed, *a.* *dom*-e-nohd, wearing a domino.
dominus, *n.* *dom*-e-nus, a title equivalent to Master or Sir, formerly given to a clergyman, a gentleman, or the lord of a manor. (L.)
domite, *n.* *doh*-mite, a light grey mica-bearing variety of trachyte. (Puy-de-*Dôme* in Auvergne, in France, where it is found.)
don, *n.* don, a Spanish title equivalent to Sir, formerly given only to noblemen and gentlemen; a Spaniard; an important personage; a person of self-importance; the head, or a fellow or tutor of a college; an expert [Slang]. (Sp.)
don, *v.t.* don, to put on; to invest with. (*Do on.*)
donah, *n.* *doh*-nah, donna; a sweetheart; a woman [Coster slang].
donary, *n.* *doh*-na-re, a thing given, esp. as a votive offering or to a sacred use.
donate, *v.t.* doh-*nate*, to give for a special object; to bestow. (L. *donatus*, given.)
donation, *n.* doh-*nay*-shon, the act of giving; that which is given gratuitously; a gift or grant; benefaction; the contract by which a thing or the use of it is transferred to a person, or corporation, as a free gift [Law]. (L. *donatio*.)
donatism, *n.* *doh*-na-tizm, the doctrines of the Donatists.
Donatist, *n.* *doh*-na-tist, a member of an Arian sect founded in Carthage (early 4th cent.) by a certain Donatus, who insisted upon individual purity or holiness as one of the constitutive principles of Christianity and an indispensable qualification for church membership.
donative, *n.* *doh*-na-tiv, a gift; a largess; a benefice given and collated to a person, by the founder or patron, without either presentation, institution, or introduction by the ordinary [Canon Law]: *a.* vested or vesting by donation. (Fr. *donatif*.)
donator, *n.* doh-*nay*-tor, a donor.
done, dun, *pp.* of the verb *to do*; performed; executed; finished; exhausted; outwitted. **done for,** ruined. **have done with,** to cease to have concern or business with. **well done,** in cooking, done through; not at all uncooked.
done, *int.* dun, agreed; an exclamation by which a wager or bargain is concluded.
donee, *n.* doh-*nee*, the person to whom a gift is made, or to whom lands or tenements are granted. (O.Fr. *doné*.)
donga, *n.* *dong*-gah, a ravine; a gully. (Zulu.)
donjon, *n.* *dun*-jun, the massive central keep or tower of a mediæval castle, usually having below a dungeon for prisoners. (Fr.)
donkey, *n.* *dong*-ke, an ass; a stupid person. **donkey's years,** an indefinitely long time [Slang]. (Perhaps from *dun*, the colour.)
donkey-engine, *n.* a small auxiliary steam-engine, esp. one for hoisting, hauling, and pumping on board a ship.
donkey-man, *n.* a man in charge of riding donkeys, or of a donkey-engine.
donkey-pump, *n.* an auxiliary pump; a pump worked by a donkey-engine.
donna, *n.* *don*-na, the feminine of don; a lady; madam.
donnish, *a.* *don*-nish, with the air of a don.
donor, *n.* *doh*-nor, one who gives or bestows gratuitously; one who grants an estate [Law]; one who gives his blood for transfusion [Med.]. (O.Fr.)
do-nothing, *a.* *doo*-nuth-ing, with nothing to do: *n.* a loafer; a wastrel; one with nothing to do.
donship, *n.* *don*-ship, the quality, rank, or personality of a don.
don't, dohnt, colloquial abbreviation for "do not": *n.* a prohibition [Coll.]. **don't care,** indifferent; heedless; regardless.
donzel, *n.* *don*-zel, a prospective knight; a page.
doob-grass, *n.* *doob*-grahs, a perennial creeping grass, *Cynodon dactylon*, highly prized in India and the United States for lawns and pasture; Bermuda grass [U.S.A.]. (Hind.)
doodle, *n.* *doo*-dl, a trifler; a noodle; a simple fellow; a doodle-bug [U.S.A.]: *v.i.* to draw or scribble aimlessly and without meaning.
doodle-bug, *n.* the larva of various insects [U.S.A.]; the high-explosive projectile of a V1 weapon [Coll.].
doolie, *n.* *doo*-le, a covered litter made of bamboo; a palanquin; an ambulance litter [Anglo-Indian].
doom, *n.* doom, judgment or judicial sentence; condemnation; determination affecting the fate or future state of another; the state to which one is doomed or destined; ruin; destruction: *v.t.* to condemn to any punishment; to pronounce judgment on; to destine. **doom-book,** dom-boc. **crack of doom,** the dissolution of all things at the judgment. (A.S. *dom*, judgment.)
doomful, *a.* *doom*-ful, pregnant with destruction.
doom-palm, *n.* *doom*-pahm, the doum-palm.
doomsday, *n.* *doomz*-day, the Day of Judgment; the Last Day; domesday.
doomsman, *n.* *doomz*-man, a judge; a deemster.
★**door,** *n.* dawr, an opening into a house or a room by which persons enter; the frame of boards (usually turning on hinges) that shuts the opening of a house or closes the entrance into an apartment; a house-entrance; avenue, or means of approach. **indoors,** within the house; at home. **next door to,** near to; bordering on. **lie at one's door,** to be chargeable to one. **to open the door to,** to make possible. **to shut the door on,** to make impossible. **to show one the door,** to usher him out; to expel him. (A.S. *dor*.)
door-bell, *n.* a bell ringing inside but worked from outside the house.
door-case, *n.* the frame which encloses a door.
doorkeeper, *n.* *dawr*-kee-per, one who guards the entrance of a house or apartment; a concierge.
door-knocker, *n.* the knocker fixed on a door by which one signals for admittance or attention.
doormat, *n.* *dawr*-mat, the first mat within a house; a mat at a door; a poor-spirited person [Slang].

door-nail, *n.* a strong large-headed nail formerly used for studding doors.
door-plate, *n.* a metal plate bearing the name of the occupant on the door or door-post of a house.
door-post, *n.* *dawr*-pohst, one of the jambs or uprights on which a door swings or shuts.
doorway, *n.* *dawr*-way, the opening closed by a door.
dooryard, *n.* *dawr*-yard, the yard adjacent to a house-door.
dop, *n.* dop, an inferior brandy distilled in South Africa. (S. Afr. Dut.)
dope, *n.* dope, a drug to excite or stimulate; a varnish or similar form of protection against moisture, etc.; a substance added to the fuel of an internal combustion engine to prevent detonation: *v.t.* to administer drugs, esp. for a sinister purpose; to add dope to fuel; to varnish; to adulterate: *v.i.* to take drugs. (Dut. *doop*, dip.)
dopper, *n.* *dop*-per, a member of a very strict Calvinistic sect of South African Dutch. (Dut., a dipper.)
dopy, *a.* *doh*-pe, affected, or as though affected, by dope; drugged; sluggish; of a narcotic nature.
dor, *n.* dor, the cockchafer, the earth-boring beetle *Geotrupes stercorarius*, or other insect that makes a humming in flight. (A.S. *dorr*, drone.)
dora, *n.* *daw*-ra, the popular name of the Defence of the Realm Act, 1914; hence, irritating or petty restriction. (From the initials of the Act.)
dorado, *n.* do-*rah*-do, a large brilliantly coloured fish of the genus *Coryphæna*, often called the dolphin; a reddish-yellow colour. (Sp., gilded.)
dorcas, *n.* *dor*-kas, a society of ladies who meet to make garments for the poor (*see* Acts ix, 39).
dor-hawk, *n.* *dor*-hawk, the nightjar.
Dorian, *n.* *daw*-re-an, a member of an Hellenic race that settled in Doris (southern Greece) and other coasts and islands of the Mediterranean in the 12th cent. B.C.: *a.* pertaining to Doris or to the Dorians; Doric. **Dorian mode,** the first of the four principal Greek modes; the Gregorian mode commencing on D [Mus.].
Doric, *a.* *do*-rik, relating to Doris, in Greece; rustic; uncouth: *n.* one of the five dialects used among the ancient Greeks; any rustic or unrefined dialect; a sans serif type-face [Print.]. **Doric order,** the oldest, the strongest, and the simplest of the Greek orders of architecture.
Doricism, *n.* *do*-re-sizm, a phrase or idiom of Doric.
Dorism, *n.* *daw*-rizm, a Dorian characteristic; a Doricism.
dorking, *n.* *dawr*-king, a breed of domestic fowl, with five claws on each foot, originally reared at Dorking in Surrey.
dorlach, *n.* *dawr*-lakh, a bundle; a pack [Scots.].
dormancy, *n.* *dawr*-man-se, the quality or state of being dormant; abeyance. (Fr. *dormance.*)
dormant, *a.* *dawr*-mant, sleeping; hibernating; at rest or not in action; in a sleeping posture [Her.]; not used; in abeyance. **dormant partner,** a sleeping partner, one taking no active share in the business but entitled to a share of the profits and subject to a share in losses [Comm.]. (Fr.)
dormer, *n.* *dawr*-mer, a bedroom (*obsolete*). **dormer window,** a vertical window in a sloping roof, originally belonging to a sleeping room. (O.Fr. *dormeor*, sleeping-chamber.)
dormitive, *a.* *dawr*-me-tiv, of a nature to promote sleep: *n.* a soporific [Med.]. (L. *dormitus*, slept.)
dormitory, *n.* *dawr*-me-to-re, a place to sleep in, with several beds; a range of cubicles, esp. in a school, convent, etc.; any suburb of which many residents are daytime absentees [Coll.]. (L. *dormitorium.*)
dormouse, *n.* *dawr*-mouse (*pl.* **dormice**), a small hibernating nocturnal rodent, *Muscardinus avellanarius*, of squirrel-like appearance, allied to the mouse.
dormy, *a.* *dawr*-me, in golf, said of a player when he is as many holes up on his opponent as there remain holes to be played. (Possibly Fr. *dormir*, to be dormant.)
dornick, *n.* *dawr*-nik, a species of figured linen. (Flemish name of Tournay, Belgium, where originally made.)
dorp, *n.* dawrp, a small township; a village [mainly S. African].

dorsal, *a.* *dawr*-sal, pertaining to or situated on the back; shaped like a ridge: *n.* a dorsal fin. (Fr.)
dorsi-, *dawr*-se, a combining form of dorsal.
dorsibranchiate, *a.* *dor*-se-*brang*-ke-at, having the branchiæ distributed along the back [Zool.]. (L. *dorsum*, and *branchiæ*, gills.)
dorsiferous, *a.* dawr-*sif*-er-rus, bearing seeds on the back of their leaves [Bot.]; carrying the young on the back (as opossums) [Zool.]. (L. *dorsum*, and *fero*, bear.)
dorsifixed, *a.* dawr-se-*fikst*, fixed by the back along its whole length (esp. of anthers) [Bot.].
dorsispinal, *a.* dawr-se-*spy*-nal, pertaining to the spine and back [Anat.]. (L. *dorsum* and *spinal.*)
dorsiventral, *a.* dawr-se-*ven*-tral, differing in structure on the upper and lower surfaces [Bot. and Zool.].
dorsiventrality, *n.* *dawr*-se-ven-*tral*-e-te, the characteristic of being dorsiventral.
dorso-, *dawr*-so, a combining form of dorsal.
dorsum, *n.* *dawr*-sum, the back; the ridge of a hill; the upper side of an appendage, as the tongue [Anat.], or of the body of a shell [Malac.]. (L., the back.)
dortour, *n.* *dawr*-ter, a dormitory, esp. of a monastery.
dory, *n.* *daw*-re, the John Dory, *Zeus faber*, a yellowish grey sea-fish distinguished by a large circular black spot edged with yellow. (Fr. *dorée*, gilded.)
dory, *n.* *daw*-re, a small flat-bottomed boat (Amerind., *dóri*, dugout.)
dosage, *n.* *doh*-saj, the amount in a dose; method of dosing.
dose, *n.* dohs, the quantity of medicine prescribed to be taken at one time; anything disagreeable or nauseous that one is required to take or swallow; a quantity: *v.t.* to form into suitable doses; to give in doses; to give anything nauseous to; to adulterate. (Gr. *dosis*, a giving.)
dosimeter, *n.* do-*sim*-e-ter, a measure for small portions of liquids. (Gr. *dosis*, and *metron*, measure.)
doss, *n.* doss, a bed in a registered lodging-house; a spell of rest or sleeping: *v.i.* to sleep, esp. in a doss-house [Slang]. **doss-house,** a registered lodging-house.
dossal, *n.* *dos*-al, a hanging of rich drapery behind the daïs or chair of state; an altar hanging. (O.Fr. *dorsel.*)
dosser, *n.* *dos*-er, one who sleeps at a doss-house; a pannier or basket carried by a beast of burden or on one's shoulders; the bull's-eye or innermost circle of a dart-board [Slang]. (Fr. *dossier.*)
dossier, *n.* *dos*-e-a, a file of papers referring to the same subject; a brief. (Fr.)
dossil, *n.* *dos*-il, a plug or pledget for a wound; a roll for wiping an inked surface. (O.Fr., a stopple.)
dost, dust, *second pers. sing. pres. ind.* of *do.*
dot, *n.* dot, a small point or spot, as made with a pen or a sharp point; a speck; a decimal point; a unit in the Morse code; a point inserted immediately after a note to indicate that its length is to be increased by one half [Mus.]; a toddler: *v.t.* to mark with dots; to mark or diversify with small detached objects, like dots: *v.i.* to make dots or spots. (A.S. *dott.*)
dot, *n.* dot, a dowry; a marriage portion. (Fr.)
dotage, *n.* *doh*-taj, senility; weak excessive fondness. (*Dote.*)
dotal, *a.* *doh*-tal, pertaining to a dowry or marriage portion; comprised in a dower.
dotard, *n.* *doh*-tard, one in his dotage; one weakly and foolishly fond; a tree fallen into decay.
dotardly, *a.* *doh*-tard-le, like a dotard; foolish.
dotation, *n.* doh-*tay*-shon, the act of bestowing a marriage portion on a woman; endowment. (L. *doto*, endow.)
dote, *v.i.* dote, to wander in mind or drivel from the weakness of age; to be infatuated. **to dote on,** to regard with a silly and excessive fondness. (Dut. *doten*, to be silly.)
doter, *n.* *dote*-er, one who dotes; a dotard.
doth, duth, *third pers. sing. pres. ind.* of *do.*
doting, *a.* *dote*-ing, regarding with excessive fondness.
dotingly, *ad.* *dote*-ing-le, in a doting manner.
dotish, *a.* *dote*-ish, childishly fond; imbecile.
dotted, *pp.* and *a.* *dot*-ted, marked with dots.
dotterel, *n.* *dot*-ter-el, a migratory plover, *Eudromias*

morinellus, so called from its seeming stupidity in allowing itself to be easily taken. (*Dote.*)
dottle, *n.* dotl, the small plug of tobacco left unburnt in a pipe. (Scots.)
dotty, *a.* *dot*-te, dotted; silly, daft, deranged [Slang].
douane, *n.* doo-*ahn*, a French custom house. (Fr.)
douanier, *n.* doo-*ah*-ne-ay, a custom-house officer. (Fr.)
Douay, *n.* doo-ay, the Douay Bible, an English translation of the Vulgate, made at the Roman Catholic college at Douay, France, 1580–1609.
double, *a.* *dub*-bl, twofold; two of a sort together; in pairs; twice as much; acting two parts, one openly, the other in secret: *n.* twice as much; a double quantity (esp. of a tot of spirits); one whose resemblance to another is remarkable; a fold; a pace of 180 steps to the minute [Mil.]; a substitute or understudy; two faults in succession, lawn tennis; a game played by two a side; in racing, a bet any winnings from which are transferred as a wager to some later event; a Guernsey copper coin worth ⅛*d.*; a turn in running to escape pursuers; a duplicate; matter set up twice [Print.]; at whist, a score of five to one or two, or of ten to nothing; at dominoes, a piece having the same denomination on each half: *ad.* twice: *v.i.* to be increased by twice the number, amount, etc.; to turn upon one's tracks in running, as a hare; to play tricks; to run rapidly; to march at double time (180 steps a minute); to play a part as a double or to take two parts in the same play; to elude by doubling; to set up the same matter twice [Printing]: *v.t.* to fold; to multiply by two; to contain twice as much or as many; to add one to another in the same order; to sail round, as a cape, so that the cape shall be between a ship and her former situation [Naut.]; to unite two ranks or files in one [Mil.]. **double and twist,** to add one thread to another and twist them together. **double chin,** a fleshy fold under the chin. **double crown,** a size of printing paper, 20 by 30 in. **double dummy,** whist played by two players, each having a dummy. **double Dutch,** any language not understandable. **double entry,** a mode of book-keeping in which every transaction is entered twice, once on the *Dr.* side of the account that receives, and once on the *Cr.* side of the account that gives. **double first,** first in both classics and mathematics. **double flower,** one with more than the normal number of petals. **double octave,** an interval composed of fifteen notes in diatonic progression, which for that reason is also called a fifteenth. **double pneumonia,** pneumonia in which both lungs are affected. **double shuffle,** a type of clog dance or its characteristic step. **double six,** a 12-cylinder internal combustion engine of the V type; a domino with six spots on each half. **double star,** a binary; two stars optically very close to each other and distinguishable only with the telescope. **double upon,** to enclose between two fires. (Fr. *doubler.*)
double-acting, *a.* acting in two directions, as up and down; working on both strokes of the piston [Mech.].
double-banked, *a.* having two opposite oars managed by rowers on the same bench, or having two men to the same oar [Naut.].
double-barrelled, *a.* having two barrels, as a gun; having a twofold effect.
double-bass, *n.* *dub*-bl-*base*, the lowest-toned instrument of the violin group.
double-breasted, *a.* lapping over and buttoning on either side.
double-cross, *v.t.* to act treacherously; to betray; to swindle: *n.* an act or instance of such proceeding.
double-dealer, *n.* one who acts with duplicity, professing one thing and intending another.
double-dealing, *n.* duplicity.
double-decker, *n.* a ship with two decks; a warship with two gun decks; an omnibus, etc., with two floors of seats; a biplane [Coll.].
double-dyed, *a.* *dub*-bl-*dide*, dyed twice; deeply stained, thoroughgoing [Fig.].
double-eagle, *n.* a gold coin of the U.S.A., equal to twenty dollars.
double-edged, *a.* having two edges; cutting or telling both ways.
double-entendre, *n.* *doo*-bl-ang-*tang*-dr (or App.), an expression or phrase of more than one meaning, one of which is indelicate. (Fr.)
double-entry, *n.* a system of book-keeping in which each transaction is entered as a debit in one account and a credit in another.
double-faced, *a.* *dub*-bl-fayst, acting with duplicity; showing two faces; having two faces in different planes [Carp.].
double-first, *n.* the university distinction of first-class honours in two examination subjects or sections; a person awarded this.
double-flowered, *a.* having the stamens and pistils transformed into petals [Hort.].
double-ganger, *n.* an apparition of a living person.
double-handed, *a.* having two hands; adapted for use with two hands; deceitful.
double-hearted, *a.* having a false heart; deceitful; treacherous.
double-jointed, *a.* having abnormal joints that allow of the limbs being bent at unusual angles.
double-lock, *v.t.* to lock twice; to fasten with double security.
double-minded, *a.* of a different mind at different times; wavering; undecided.
doubleness, *n.* *dub*-bl-ness, the state of being doubled; duplicity; disingenuousness.
double-quick, *n.* a marching step at the rate of 180 steps a minute: *a.* at the rate of the double-quick; very quick [Mil.].
double-stopping, *n.* the playing on a stringed instrument of two (or more) notes simultaneously by stopping two (or more) strings at once [Mus.].
doublet, *n.* *dub*-let, one of a pair; a word radically the same as another but differing in meaning; the same number on two dice; a garment fitting close to the body with skirts extending a little below the girdle; a jerkin; a sleeved waistcoat; a counterfeit stone composed of two pieces of crystal with a colour between them; a lens formed by two glasses; a double [Print.]: *pl.* a game played with two dice. (Fr.)
doubleton, *n.* *dub*-bl-ton, two cards only of any particular suit held in a hand [Card-playing].
double-tongued, *a.* making contrary declarations on the same subject at different times; deceitful.
double-tonguing, *n.* *dub*-bl-*tung*-ing, an action of the tongue against the roof of the mouth in flute-playing, by which the most brilliant notes are produced of which the flute is capable.
doubling, *n.* *dubl*-ling, the act of making double; a fold or plait; a lining; the act of sailing round a cape or promontory; the winding about of a hare or fox to deceive the hounds; an artifice.
doubloon, *n.* dub-*loon*, a Spanish and S. American gold coin, of about the value of a guinea, so called as originally double of a pistole. (Fr. *doublon.*)
doublure, *n.* doo-bloor, a lining, esp. a rich or ornate lining to a book-cover. (Fr.)
doubly, *ad.* *dub*-le, in two ways or in a twofold manner; twice as much; deceitfully.
***doubt,** *n.* dout, uncertainty or hesitation of mind respecting truth or propriety, arising from defect of knowledge or evidence; matter of doubt; suspense; suspicion; fear: *v.i.* to waver in opinion; to hesitate; to be in suspense or uncertainty respecting the truth; to be apprehensive or suspect: *v.t.* to regard as questionable; to hesitate to believe; to suspect; to expect [Coll.]; to distrust. (Fr. *douter.*)
doubtable, *a.* *dout*-a-bl, that may be doubted.
doubter, *n.* *dout*-er, one who doubts, or is unsettled in opinion.
doubtful, *a.* *dout*-ful, not settled in opinion; uncertain; ambiguous, or not clear in meaning; admitting of doubt; of uncertain issue; suspicious; not confident; not clearly defined.
doubtfully, *ad.* in a doubtful manner; dubiously.
doubtfulness, *n.* the state of being doubtful.
doubtingly, *ad.* *dout*-ing-le, in a doubting manner.
doubtless, *a.* *dout*-less, confident; indubitable: *ad.* without doubt; unquestionably; no doubt.
doubtlessly, *ad.* with certainty; unquestionably.
douc, *n.* dook, a species of monkey, *Semnopithecus nemæus*, found in Cochin China, remarkable for the variety and brightness of its colours. (Fr.)
douceur, *n.* (App.), a present or tip; a bribe; a sop. (Fr. from L. *dulcis*, sweet.)

douche, *n.* doosh, a jet of water or vapour directed on some part of the body with a view to strengthen it; a syringe or other instrument for applying this; a shower-bath: *v.t.* to jet water or vapour; to drench: *v.i.* to take a douche. (Fr. from It. *doccia*, a water pipe, from L. *duco*, lead.)
dough, *n.* doh, a mass of flour or meal and yeast, moistened and kneaded, but not baked; anything of a doughy consistence; money [Slang]. **my cake is dough,** my affair has miscarried, or not come to maturity. (A.S. *dah.*)
doughboy, *n. doh*-boy, a dumpling; an American infantryman [Coll.].
dough-faced, *a. doh*-fayst, pasty-faced; cowardly; easily pliable [U.S.A.].
doughnut, *n. doh*-nut, a small roundish cake, cooked by frying, made of flour, eggs, yeast, and sugar, moistened with milk.
doughtily, *ad. dou*-te-le, with doughtiness.
doughtiness, *n. dou*-te-ness, the quality of being doughty, or capable and valiant to do.
doughty, *a. dou*-te, brave; valiant; strong; redoubtable. (A.S. *dyhtig.*)
doughy, *a. doh*-e, like dough; soft.
Doukhobors, *n.pl. doo*-ko-borz, a fanatical pacifist sect of Tsarist Russia many members of which migrated to Canada. (Russ.)
doum, *n.* doom, the large fan-palm, *Hyphæne thebaica*, of Upper Egypt, remarkable for its products and its many branchings.
dour, *a.* dooer, stern; grim; pertinacious. (Scots.)
doura, *n. door*-ra, durra; guinea corn or millet.
dourly, *ad. dooer*-le, in a dour manner.
dourness, *n. dooer*-ness, grimness; obstinacy.
douse, *v.t.* douse, to plunge suddenly into water; to slacken suddenly, as a sail [Naut.]; to extinguish: *v.i.* to fall suddenly into water. (Swed. *dunsa*, drop down.)
dout, *v.t.* dout, to put out; to extinguish. (*Do out.*)
douter, *n. dout*-er, an extinguisher for candles.
douzaine, *n.* (App.), the Parish Council of any Channel Islands parish, originally of twelve men. (Fr., dozen.)
dove, *n.* duv, a species of pigeon; the symbol of the Holy Ghost; a word of endearment, or an emblem of innocence. **dove-colour,** bluish grey. (A.S. *dûfan*, to dive.)
dovecot *or* **dovecote,** *n. duv*-kot, a small building or box in which domestic pigeons breed.
dovekie, *n. duv*-ke, the black guillemot [Eng.]; the little auk [U.S.A.].
dovelike, *a. duv*-like, gentle; innocent.
dove's-foot, *n. duvz*-foot, a plant with downy foliage, *Geranium molle.*
dovetail, *n. duv*-tale, the fastening of boards and timbers together by letting one piece into another in the form of a dove's tail spread, or a wedge reversed [Carp.]; a similar joining: *v.t.* to unite by a tenon of this shape let into a board or timber; to fit one thing into another firmly and exactly: *v.i.* to fit into exactly.
dovetailing, *n. duv*-tale-ing, the act of joining by dovetails; the junction thus made.
dowable, *a. dou*-a-bl, that may be endowed; entitled to dower [Law].
dowager, *n. dou*-a-jer, a widow with a jointure; the title of a widow, particularly of a prince or noble; an old lady [Slang]. (O.Fr. *douagiere.*)
dowd, *n.* doud, a dowdy.
dowdily, *ad. dou*-de-le, in a dowdy manner.
dowdy, *n. dou*-de, a slovenly, shabby, or badly dressed woman: *a.* poorly, shabbily, or unfashionably dressed. (Mid. Eng. *doude*, a slut.)
dowdyish, *a. dou*-de-ish, like a dowdy.
dowee, *n.* dou-*ee*, one having an endowment, or a dower.
dowel, *n. dou*-el, a pin of metal, stone, or wood serving as a bond between two pieces of stone or timber: *v.t.* to fasten together by dowels. (Fr. *douille*, a socket.)
dowelling, *n. dou*-el-ing, a method of joining two pieces together by dowels.
dower, *n. dou*-er, that portion of a husband's estate which falls to his widow for life, reverting to his heirs at her death; the property which a woman brings to her husband in marriage; endowment; gift: *v.t.* to provide with a dower; to endow.
dower house, the house reserved for the widow. (Fr. *douaire.*)
dowered, *a. dou*-erd, furnished with a dower or a portion.
dowerless, *a. dou*-er-less, destitute of dower.
dowlas, *n. dou*-las, a kind of coarse linen cloth. (*Daoulas*, in Brittany, where first made.)
down, *n.* doun, the fine under-feathers of birds, esp. of ducks; the first plumage of a bird; fine hair; a fine hairy substance, the pubescence of flowers; a fine feathery substance, by which seeds are wafted to a distance; anything soft and fluffy. (Ice. *dun.*)
down, *n.* doun, a bank of sand thrown up by the sea; a tract of treeless upland country mostly used as pasture. **the Downs,** a roadstead for shipping in the English Channel near Deal. (A.S. *dun*, a hill.)
down, *prep.* doun, along a descent; in a descending direction; from a higher to a lower place; toward the mouth of a river from the capital of a country; from the head terminus of a railway.
***down,** *ad.* doun, from a higher to a lower place; from the capital or the centre; on the ground; below the horizon; from a higher to a lower condition; into disrepute or disgrace; into smaller bulk; from earlier to later times; from north to south; away from a capital or university; extended or prostrate on the ground or on any flat surface: *a.* downcast; lower in spirit; dejected; paid at once; alee Naut.]: *n.* a descent; the act of putting down; a depressed state; the lead (esp. in dominoes and cribbage); a grudge, or ill-feeling: *v.t.* to knock down; to put down.
down-and-out, *a.* destitute; penniless and "out at elbows"; having neither possessions nor prospects (hence, **down-and-outer,** *n.* one in this predicament). **down in the mouth,** dispirited. **down on,** apt to find fault with. **down tools,** to cease work; to go out on strike. **down under,** in the Antipodes; Australia or New Zealand. **down with!** throw down! away with! **to go down,** to leave (temporarily or permanently) a University. **to go down well,** to be well received. **to let down,** *see* **let. to send down,** to expel from a University; to rusticate. **to shout down,** to overpower with noise. **up and down,** here and there. **ups and downs,** the vicissitudes of fortune. (A.S. *dun*, a hill.)
downcast, *a. doun*-kahst, cast downward; dejected; having a downward draught: *n.* a shaft for admitting air into a mine.
downcome, *n. doun*-kum, a sudden fall.
down-draught, *n.* a current of air downward.
down-easter, *n.* a native of New England [U.S.A.].
downfall, *n. doun*-fawl, a falling down as of a flood; what falls down with sudden violence; a sudden fall from eminence; ruin.
downfallen, *a. doun*-fawl-en, fallen; ruined.
downgrade, *n. doun*-grade, the downward path: *v.t.* to transfer to a lower grade.
downhaul, *n. doun*-hawl, a rope made fast to the upper corner of a sail to haul it down by [Naut.].
down-hearted, *a.* dejected in spirits.
downhill, *a.* and *ad.* doun-hill, sloping; descending: *n.* declivity; descent; slope downward.
downiness, *n. doun*-e-ness, the state of being downy.
Downing Street, *n. doun*-ing-street, the British cabinet or government. (Name of street in Westminster, where are the official residences of the Prime Minister—No. 10, the Foreign Office, etc.)
downland, *n. doun*-land, an area of downs; hilly pasture land.
down-line, *n.* the railway line used by outward-bound trains from the main terminus.
down-lying, *n.* the time of retiring to rest; time of repose: *a.* about to lie down, or to be in travail of childbirth [Scots.].
downmost, *a.* and *ad. doun*-mohst, farthest down.
downpour, *n. doun*-pawr, a heavy continuous pour of rain.
downright, *ad. doun*-rite, straight down; in plain terms; completely; at once; *a.* directly to the point; plain; open; artless; undisguised; unceremonious.
downrightness, *n.* doun-*rite*-ness, the quality of being downright; plain dealing.

downrush, *n.* *doun*-rush, a rushing down.

downsman, *n.* *dounz*-man, one who dwells on the downs.

downstage, *ad.* *doun*-staje, toward the front of the stage [Theat.]: *a.* pertaining to the front of the stage; affable, friendly [Coll.].

downstairs, *a.* doun-*stayrz*, on a lower floor; the lower part of a building.

downstream, *a.* doun-*streem*, with or in the direction of the stream.

downtake, *n.* *down*-take, a flue, pipe, etc., leading downward [Eng.].

downthrow, *n.* *doun*-throh, downfall; overthrow; the sinking in the strata where a fault occurs, or the distance sunk [Geol.].

down-train, *n.* an outward-bound train from the main terminus.

downtrodden, *a.* *doun*-trod-en, trodden down; trampled down; domineered over.

downward, *ad.* *doun*-ward, downwards: *a.* moving or tending down as regards place, or inclination, or condition; depressed; dejected.

downwards, *ad.* *doun*-wardz, in a direction from a higher place; from a source; from an ancestor; from an earlier time or a higher position; at the lower extremities.

downy, *a.* *doun*-e, resembling downland.

downy, *a.* *doun*-e, covered with down; made of or resembling down; soft; calm; soothing; smooth-dealing, knowing [Slang].

dowry, *n.* *dou*-e-re, the property which a woman brings to her husband in marriage; an endowment; a gift; a fortune given.

dowse, *v.i.* dous, to seek to find subterranean water, metals, etc., by means of the dowsing-rod.

dowse, *n.* douz, a blow on the face: *v.t.* to douse; to strike on the face.

dowser, *n.* *dous*-er, one who dowses, esp. with a dowsing-rod.

dowsing, *n.* *dous*-ing, discovering water or a mineral lode by the divining-rod. **dowsing-rod,** the forked hazel twig used by dowsers.

doxological, *a.* *dok*-so-*loj*-e-kal, pertaining to doxology; giving praise to God.

doxology, *n.* dok-*sol*-o-je, an ascription of praise to the deity. (Gr. *doxologia.*)

doxy, *n.* *dok*-se, a loose woman; a sweetheart or paramour; a little girl [Slang].

doxy, *n.* *dok*-se, religious opinion or doctrine. (Humorous formation from "orthodoxy" and "heterodoxy.")

doyen, *n.* (App.), the senior member of a society or assembly, esp. of a diplomatic corps. (Fr.)

doyley, *n.* *doy*-le, a doily.

doze, *n.* doze, a short sleep; a nap: *v.i.* to slumber or sleep lightly; to spend time drowsily; to be dull or half asleep: *v.t.* to pass or spend in drowsiness; to make dull; to stupefy. (Ice. *dusa*, doze.)

dozen, *a.* *duz*-en, twelve in number: *n.* the number twelve of things of a like kind; a great number. **baker's dozen,** thirteen. (O.Fr. *dozaine.*)

dozer, *n.* *doze*-er, one who dozes or slumbers.

doziness, *n.* *doze*-e-ness, inclination to sleep; the state of being dozy.

dozy, *a.* *doze*-e, drowsy; heavy; inclined to sleep.

drab, *n.* drab, a strumpet; a low sluttish woman: *v.i.* to associate with drabs.

drab, *n.* drab, a kind of wooden box used in saltworks for holding the salt when taken out of the boiling pans.

drab, *n.* drab, a kind of thick woollen cloth of a dun colour; a brownish grey: *a.* of a dun colour, like the cloth so called; drear; dismal; monotonous. (Fr. *drap*, cloth.)

drabbet, *n.* *drab*-et, a drab twilled linen principally used for smock-frocks. (Dial. Eng.)

drabbish, *a.* *drab*-ish, of the character of a drab or slut; of a colour like drab.

drabble, *v.t.* *drab*-bl, to draggle; to befoul by dragging or splashing through the mud: *v.i.* to fish, esp. for barbel, with a rod and a long line trailed on the bottom. (Ger. *drabbeln*, dribble.)

drabble-tail, *n.* a draggle-tail.

drabby, *a.* *drab*-e, drabbish; abounding in drabs.

drabler, *n.* *drab*-bl-er, a small additional sail laced to the bottom of a bonnet on a square sail [Naut.].

drachm, *n.* dram, a measure of weight equal to the eighth of an ounce, or 60 grains, in apothecaries' weight, and the sixteenth of an ounce, or 27⅓ grains, in avoirdupois; a drachma. **fluid drachm,** a teaspoonful, the eighth of a fluid ounce.

drachma, *n.* *drak*-ma, a silver coin among the Greeks, anciently differing in value in different states at different periods; the monetary unit of modern Greece; an ancient Greek weight of about 2 dwt. 7 grains troy. (Gr. *drachme.*)

draconian, *a.* dra-*koh*-ne-an, pertaining to Draco, the Athenian lawgiver, or to his laws, which were so severe that the slightest offence was punished with death; of great severity.

draconic, *a.* dra-*kon*-ik, Draconian.

draff, *n.* draf, refuse; lees; dregs, specially of malt after the liquor has been drawn off; pig-wash; any waste or worthless stuff.

draffish, *a.* *draf*-ish, dreggy; waste; worthless.

draffy, *a.* *draf*-e, like draff; draffish.

draft, *n.* drahft, the act of drawing; anything drawn off; a body of men or ships drawn off or detached for a special service; a written order for the payment of money; a bill of exchange; a cheque; a plan; outline; sketch; original notes for fair copying; draught: *v.t.* to draw an outline of; to compose and write; to draw off; to select; to select for and put into an armed force; to detach. (A.S. *dragan.*)

draftee, *n.* *drahf*-tee, one of a draft; a man drafted into an army, etc.

draftsman, *n.* *drahfts*-man, one who drafts documents; a draughtsman.

drag, *v.t.* drag, to draw along the ground by main force; to break land by drawing a drag or harrow over it [U.S.A.]; to draw slowly, as if heavy and tiresome; to draw along in contempt as unworthy to be carried; to haul about roughly and forcibly; to explore with a drag or grapnel; to put a drag on (a wheel): *v.i.* to hang so low as to trail on the ground; to fish with a drag; to be drawn along; to proceed slowly and heavily; to lag behind, esp. in singing. **drag an anchor,** to trail it along the bottom when loosened or when it will not hold the ship [Naut.]. (A.S. *dragan*, to draw.)

drag, *n.* drag, a contrivance for dragging and dredging under water; a heavy kind of harrow; a contrivance for retarding the speed of a vehicle by operating on one or more of the wheels; anything that retards movement; slow movement; the force resisting the forward motion of any body, such as aircraft, through the air; in billiards, the check imparted to the cue-ball by striking it below the centre; a lure for hounds instead of a fox; a heavy sled [U.S.A.]; a low cart or car; a private four-horse coach.

drag-anchor, *n.* a sea-anchor.

dragée, *n.* drah-zhay, a sweetmeat containing a nut, a small fruit, or a dose of medicine. (Fr.)

dragger, *n.* *drag*-ger, one who or that which drags.

draggle, *v.t.* *drag*-gl, to wet and dirty by drawing on the ground; to drabble: *v.i.* to be drawn on the ground; to become wet and dirty by being drawn on the ground. (*Draw.*)

draggle-tail, *n.* *drag*-gl-tale, a slut.

draggle-tailed, *a.* *drag*-gl-tayld, untidy; draggling on the ground.

drag-hound, *n.* *drag*-hound, a hound employed in following an artificial scent instead of a fox.

drag-hunt, *n.* *drag*-hunt, a hunt with hounds for whom the scent of some strong-smelling substance, as aniseed and fox litter, has been dragged along the chosen course for the hounds to follow instead of chasing a fox.

dragman, *n.* *drag*-man, a fisherman that uses a dragnet; the man trailing the drag in a drag-hunt.

drag-net, *n.* *drag*-net, a net drawn on the bottom of a river or pond for taking fish; a net drawn along the ground to take small game.

dragoman, *n.* *drag*-o-man (*pl.* **dragomans**), an interpreter attached to European embassies and consulates in countries using the Arabic, Turkish, or Persian languages; a guide or interpreter to foreigners in the Near or Middle East. (Ar. *tarjama*, to interpret.)

dragon, *n.* *drag*-on, a mythical and legendary impersonation of the evil principle, conceived of as a monstrous winged saurian endued with deadly powers, and the slaying of which is the crowning triumph in the lives of gods and heroes; a fiery shooting meteor; a fierce violent person, esp. a spiteful woman; a short carbine with a dragon's head, formerly hung to the belt of a dragoon; Draco, a constellation of the northern hemisphere; a variety of pigeon; any arboreal lizard of the genus *Draco*; various plants of the arum family, including the Mediterranean *Dracunculus vulgaris* and the North American green dragon, *Arisaema dracontia.* **dragon tree,** a tree of the lily order, *Dracæna draco,* a native of West Africa and the Canary Islands. (Fr.)

dragoness, *n.* drag-o-*ness,* a female dragon; a malevolent or implacable woman.

dragonet, *n.* *drag*-on-et, a little dragon; the sculpin, a brightly coloured fish of the genus *Callionymus.*

dragon-fish, *n.* the dragonet; also, a fish of the genus *Pegasus.*

dragon-fly, *n.* an insect of the family Odonata of the order Neuroptera, which have long bodies, narrow gauze-like wings, large heads and eyes, and strong mandibles.

dragonish, *a.* *drag*-on-ish, in the form of a dragon; dragon-like.

dragon-like, *a.* like a dragon; fiery; furious; fierce and implacable.

dragonnade, *n.* *drag*-on-nade, a persecution of the Protestants in France under Louis XIV, in which dragoons played a leading part; the abandoning of a place to the violence of soldiers: *v.t.* to persecute in this way. (Fr.)

dragon's-blood, *n.* the inspissated juice of certain tropical plants, of a red colour, used for staining marble, colouring varnishes, etc.

dragon's-head, *n.* the name of certain plants of the genus *Dracocephalum*; the ascending node of the moon or a planet [Astron.].

dragon's-mouth, *n.* the snapdragon [Bot.].

dragon's-tail, *n.* the descending node of the moon or a planet [Astron.].

dragonwort, *n.* *drag*-on-wurt, tarragon, *Artemisia dracunculus,* the bistort, *Polygonum bistorta,* or the North American green dragon.

dragoon, *n.* dra-*goon,* formerly a mounted infantry-man; a trooper of certain British cavalry or mechanized regiments as the Dragoon Guards and the Royal Dragoons; a variety of pigeon: *v.t.* to keep in subjection by military force; to harass; to persecute; to compel to submit by violent measures. (Fr. *dragon,* dragoon.)

dragoon-bird, *n.* the umbrella-bird.

drag-rope, *n.* *drag*-rope, a rope dragged by a balloon over the ground to check its speed and to regulate the height of ascent [Av.]; a rope with chain and hook attached, used as a brake on a gun-carriage [Mil.]; a trail-rope.

dragsman, *n.* *dragz*-man, one who drives a drag; one who hangs on to a carriage to steal the luggage.

drail, *n.* drale, a weighted fishing-line for dragging through the water: *v.i.* to fish with this. (*Trail.*)

★**drain,** *n.* drane, the act of draining; gradual withdrawal; a channel through which liquid flows off; a watercourse; a sewer; a small remainder; a persistent cause of expense: *v.i.* to flow off gradually; to be emptied of liquor by flowing or dropping: *v.t.* to draw off gradually; to filter; to empty of liquor; to draw water off; to make dry; to empty or exhaust. (A.S. *drēhnian.*)

drainable, *a.* *drane*-a-bl, capable of being drained.

drainage, *n.* *drane*-aj, the act or science of draining; system of sewerage; the mode in which the waters of a country pass off by its streams and rivers; that which is carried off by drains; the surface drained; the removal of morbid liquid matter from the body [Surg.]. **drainage-tube,** *n.* a tube introduced into an abscess, suppurating wound, etc., to allow of the discharge of its morbid content [Surg.].

drainer, *n.* *drane*-er, one who or that which drains; an appliance on which articles are placed to drain; a colander.

draining-plough, *n.* a plough for cutting drains.

draining-tile, *n.* a tile employed in draining.

drain-pipe, *n.* a pipe for drainage purposes.

drain-trap, *n.* a contrivance which, while it allows the outward flow of sewage, etc., prevents the return of foul gases.

drake, *n.* drake, the male of the duck; a pattern of artificial fly made from drake's feathers. **ducks and drakes,** *see* **duck.** (Of uncertain origin.)

drake, *n.* drake, the May-fly; esp. *Ephemera danica,* the green drake, or *E. vulgata,* the green drake. (L. *draco,* dragon.)

drake-stone, *n.* a flat stone so thrown as to skim over water.

dram, *n.* dram, the sixteenth part of an ounce or 27⅓ grains in avoirdupois, and in apothecaries' weight ⅛ ounce, or 60 grains; a drachm; a small quantity; as much spirituous liquor as is drunk at once. (O.Fr. *drame.*)

drama, *n.* *drah*-ma, a poem or composition representing persons speaking and acting in given situations, each agreeably to a given character; a stage play; dramatic art; dramatic representation; dramatic literature; a series of events developing in the manner and with the interest of a drama. (Gr., an action, from *drao,* perform.)

dramalogue, *n.* *dram*-a-log, a public reading of a play.

dramatic, *a.* dra-*mat*-ik, pertaining to the drama; in the form of drama; with the effect of a drama.

dramatically, *ad.* dra-*mat*-e-ka-le, by representation; in the manner of the drama.

dramatics, *n.* dra-*mat*-iks, dramatic compositions or performances (esp. in the phrase **amateur dramatics**).

dramatis personæ, *n.pl.* dra-*mat*-is-per-*soh*-nee, the characters in a play. (L.)

dramatist, *n.* *dram*-a-tist, a writer of stage plays; a playwright. (Fr. *dramatiste.*)

dramatizable, *a.* *dram*-a-*ty*-za-bl, that may be dramatized.

dramatization, *n.* *dram*-a-ty-*zay*-shon, the act of dramatizing; a dramatized version.

dramatize, *v.t.* *dram*-a-tize, to compose in the form of a stage play; to convert into a play; to represent or describe in a dramatic way. (Fr. *dramatiser.*)

dramaturge, *n.* *dram*-a-turj, a dramaturgist.

dramaturgic, *a.* dram-a-*tur*-jik, pertaining to dramatic representation; theatrical; histrionic.

dramaturgist, *n.* *dram*-a-tur-jist, the author of a drama; a playwright. (Gr. *dramatourgos.*)

dramaturgy, *n.* *dram*-a-tur-je, the art of dramatic composition and representation. (Gr. *drama,* and *ergon,* work.)

dramshop, *n.* *dram*-shop, a low-class public house.

drank, drank, *p.* of the verb to drink.

drape, *v.t.* drape, to cover; to dress; to arrange or to decorate with drapery. (Fr. *draper.*)

draped, *a.* draypt, clothed in drapery.

draper, *n.* *dray*-per, a dealer in drapery. **Drapers Company,** the third of the twelve great London Livery Companies, whose charter was granted in the time of Edward III. (Fr. *drapier.*)

drapery, *n.* *dray*-pe-re, the trade of dealing in cloth and similar textiles; cloth fabrics or goods; that with which anything is draped; the representation of the clothing or dress of human figures, etc. [Sculp. and Paint.]. (Fr. *draperie.*)

drastic, *a.* *dras*-tik, severe; promptly and effectively active, specially in purging: *n.* a purgative which acts promptly and effectively. (Gr. *drastikos.*)

drastically, *ad.* in a drastic manner.

drat, *in.* drat, a mild expletive, a euphemistic form of "damn" [Slang].

draught, *n.* drahft, draft; the act of drawing; the capacity of being drawn; the act of drinking; the quantity of liquor drunk at once; a current of air; the current of air which supplies oxygen for the combustion of fuel; the act of delineating; that which is delineated or sketched; a rough sketch in writing; the act of drawing a net for fish; that which is taken in a net by drawing; the drawing or bending of a bow; allowance for waste on goods sold by weight; the allowance on a pattern permitting of its being withdrawn from the casting mould; a military drafting or draft; a commercial draft; the depth of water necessary to float a ship freely: *v.t.* to draw off; to make a rough sketch of; to draft: *a.* for drawing, as a horse; drawn off, as liquor. (*Draw.*)

draught-board, *n.* the board on which the game of draughts is played.

draught-horse, *n.* a horse used in drawing a plough, cart, or other carriage.

draughtiness, *n.* *drahf*-te-ness, the condition of being draughty; prevalence of draughts.

draught-ox, *n.* an ox employed in drawing implements or vehicles.
draughts, *n.pl.* drahfts, a game played on the same patterned board as that used for chess, between two, each with twelve round pieces.
draught-screen, *n.* a screen protecting from draughts.
draughtsman, *n.* *drahfts*-man, a man who draws designs or plans; one skilled in drawing; a piece used in the game of draughts.
draughtsmanship, *n.* *drahfts*-man-ship, the work or art of draughtsman; skill in drawing.
draughty, *a.* *drahf*-te, allowing of currents of air; abounding in draughts of air.
Dravidian, *a.* dra-*vid*-e-an, pertaining to the presumed primitive race of India, driven south by the Aryan race, and now inhabiting the south of Hindustan, or to their language: *n.* a member of this race; its language. (*Dravida*, Southern India.)
draw, *v.t.* draw, to pull along after one; to pull out; to drag; to pull up from; to suck; to attract; to inhale; to take from; to cause to run out; to extract; to elicit; to bring on; to move gradually or slowly; to lengthen; to utter drawlingly, as a sigh; to extend, by marking or forming; to represent by lines; to represent by words; to represent in fancy; to derive; to deduce; to lead by persuasion or moral influence; to induce; to persuade; to attract toward; to leave a game undecided; to receive or take, as from a fund; to produce, as interest; to extort; to wrest; to write in due form; to receive or gain by drawing; to stretch; to require a certain depth of water for floating; to search (a covert, etc.) for game; to unsheathe (a sword); to bend (a bow); to eviscerate. **draw back,** to receive back, as duties on goods for exportation. **draw in,** to collect; to contract; to pull back; to entice or inveigle. **draw off,** to draw from or away; to withdraw; to abstract; to draw or cause to flow from; to extract by distillation. **draw on,** to allure; to persuade or cause to follow; to occasion; to invite; to bring on. **draw out,** to lengthen; to beat or hammer out; to lengthen in time; to extract, as the spirit of a substance; to bring forth; to pump out by questioning or address; to induce by motive; to detach; to arrange in battle. **draw over,** to raise, or cause to come over, as in a still; to persuade to leave an opposing party and join one's own. **draw together,** to collect or be collected. **draw up,** to raise; to lift; to form in order of battle; to compose in due form, as a writing. *pp.*, **drawn,** *p.*, **drew.** (A.S. *dragan*.)
draw, *v.i.* draw, to pull; to act as a weight; to shrink; to move or advance; to allow a free current, as a pipe; to unsheathe, as a sword; to use or practise the art of delineating figures; to contract (together); to draw lots; to cause to suppurate; to excite to inflammation, maturation, and discharge, as a blister draws well. **draw back,** to retire; to withdraw; to apostatize. **draw near** or **nigh,** to approach. **draw off,** to retire; to retreat. **draw on,** to advance; to approach; to gain on in pursuit; to demand payment by an order or draft. **draw up,** to form in regular order. *pp.*, **drawn.** *p.*, **drew.**
draw, *n.* draw, the act of drawing; the lot or chance drawn; an attraction; the moveable part of a drawbridge; a drawn game; the card or cards drawn in certain card-games.
drawable, *a.* *draw*-a-bl, that may be drawn.
drawback, *n.* *draw*-bak, money paid back by the customs to an importer on the exportation of imported goods, or paid back by the excise on the exportation of excisable goods of home manufacture; any loss of advantage; disadvantage; inconvenience.
draw-bar, *n.* an iron rod used to connect a locomotive with a tender or train.
drawbolt, *n.* *draw*-bolt, a coupling pin.
draw-boy, *n.* a boy assistant in weaving.
drawbridge, *n.* *draw*-bridj, a bridge the whole or part of which may be raised up, let down, or drawn aside at pleasure; a two-handed variation of the game of bridge.
Drawcansir, *n.* *draw*-kan-ser, a bullying swaggering braggart. (Name of a bully in Villiers' "The Rehearsal," 1671.)
drawee, *n.* draw-*ee*, the person on whom an order or bill of exchange is drawn, and who is responsible for the payment.
★**drawer,** *n.* *draw*-er, one who draws, as water from a well or liquors from a cask; one who or that which has the power of attraction, etc.; one who draws a bill of exchange or an order for the payment of money; a sliding box in a case or table: *pl.* (drawrz), an under-garment worn on the lower limbs. **chest of drawers,** a tier or series of drawers contained in a frame or case.
drawgate, *n.* *draw*-gate, a sluice gate or valve.
draw-gear, *n.* *draw*-geer, harness suitable for draught-horses; railway couplings.
drawing, *n.* *draw*-ing, the act of pulling, hauling, or attracting; delineation; a representation of objects on a plane surface by means of lines and shades, as with a pencil, crayon, etc.; a picture drawn; the distribution of prizes in a lottery: *pl.* money drawn; takings. **drawing-board,** a board on which paper is laid to make drawings on. **drawing-paper,** stout paper for drawing on.
drawing-room, *n.* *draw*-ing-room, a withdrawing-room, or room for the reception of company; the formal reception of evening company at a court or by persons in high station.
draw-knife, *n.* *draw*-nife, a spokeshave.
drawl, *n.* drawl, a lengthened and monotonous utterance of the voice: *v.i.* to speak with slow prolonged utterance.
drawlingly, *ad.* *drawl*-ing-le, in a drawling manner.
draw-link, *n.* a link for connecting railway carriages together.
drawn, *a.* drawn, equal on both sides, neither winning, as a drawn game or a drawn battle; with sword drawn; subjected to tension; eviscerated, as a drawn fowl.
draw-net, *n.* a net made with wide meshes for catching the larger sorts of birds.
drawn-work, *n.* a method of producing a pattern on linen by drawing out selected threads.
draw-plate, *n.* a steel plate having a graduated series of conical holes, through which wires are drawn in order to be reduced and elongated.
draw-well, *n.* a well from which water is drawn by a bucket with a long rope attached.
dray, *n.* dray, a low-built four-wheeled cart for heavy loads; a drey. (A.S. *dragan*, to drag.)
drayage, *n.* *dray*-aj, use of a dray or the charge for its use.
dray-horse, *n.* a strong heavy horse for drawing a dray.
drayman, *n.* *dray*-man, the man who drives a dray.
dread, *n.* dred, great fear in the apprehension of evil or danger; terror; awe; the cause of fear; the person or thing dreaded: *a.* exciting great fear; terrible; inspiring awe: *v.t.* to fear in a great degree; to fear with awe: *v.i.* to be in great fear. (A.S. *drædan*.)
dreadful, *a.* *dred*-ful, impressing great fear; frightful; inspiring awe; horrid, annoying [Coll.]. **penny dreadful,** a cheap sensational story, generally of criminal life.
dreadfully, *ad.* in a manner to be dreaded; very [Coll.].
dreadfulness, *n.* the quality of being dreadful.
dreadless, *a.* *dred*-less, fearless; intrepid.
dreadnought, *n.* *dred*-nawt, a fearless man; a garment made of a thick cloth with a long pile, used to keep off rain; a type of heavily armoured high-speed battle-ship of large displacement, its main armament being of guns of the same large calibre, first built in Great Britain in 1906; a capital ship.
dream, *n.* dreem, an involuntary train of seemingly real fancies passing through the mind in sleep; a mere vision; a vain fancy: a wild conceit: an unfounded suspicion: *v.i.* to have fancies or images in the mind in the state of sleep; to imagine; to think idly: *v.t.* to see in a dream. **dream away,** to spend idly or vainly. **dream-book,** *n.* a book purporting to interpret dreams. *p.* **dreamed,** dreemd, or **dreamt,** dremt. (A.S. *dream*, rejoicing, song.)
dreamer, *n.* *dreem*-er, one who has dreams; a visionary; one who forms or entertains vain schemes.
dreamery, *n.* *dreem*-e-re, dreaminess.
dreamful, *a.* *dreem*-ful, full of dreams.

dream-hole, *n.* *dreem*-hole, a small opening in a tower or steeple for admitting light and air.
dreaminess, *n.* *dreem*-e-ness, state of being dreamy.
dreamingly, *ad.* sluggishly; negligently.
dreamland, *n.* *dreem*-land, the imaginary region of dreams or mere fancies; fairyland.
dreamless, *a.* *dreem*-less, free from dreams.
dreamlessly, *ad.* in a dreamless manner.
dreamlessness, *n.* *dreem*-less-ness, the condition of being free from dreams.
dreamlike, *a.* resembling a dream; dreamy.
dreamy, *a.* *dreem*-e, full of dreams; given to dreaming; akin to dreams; dreamlike.
drear, *a.* dreer, dismal; gloomy with solitude.
drearily, *ad.* *dreer*-e-le, in a dreary manner.
dreariness, *n.* *dreer*-e-ness, the state of being dreary.
dreary, *a.* *dreer*-e, dismal; gloomy; sorrowful; distressing; uninteresting. (A.S. *dreorig*, sad.)
dredge, *n.* dredj, an apparatus for dragging under water and fetching up things at the bottom; a dredging-machine; a drag-net for taking oysters, etc.: *v.t.* to gather with a dredge; to deepen with a dredging-machine. (A.S. *dragan*, to drag.)
dredge, *v.t.* dredj, to sprinkle flour or any ground or powdered ingredient in cookery. (O.Fr. *dragee*, a sweetmeat.)
dredger, *n.* *dredj*-er, one who works on or with a dredge; a ship employed in dredging; a dredging-machine; a box with a perforated lid used as a sprinkler [Cookery].
dredging-machine, *n.* a machine used to dredge up mud or gravel from the bottom of harbours, canals, etc.
dree, *a.* dree, tedious; dreary: *v.t.* to suffer; to endure. **dree one's weird,** to suffer one's fate. (Scots.)
dregginess, *n.* *dreg*-e-ness, the state of being dreggy.
dreggy, *a.* *dreg*-e, containing dregs; muddy.
dregs, *n.pl.* dregz, the sediment of liquor; grounds; waste or worthless matter; refuse; the lowest class, viewed as worthless. (Ice. *dreggjar*.)
drench, *n.* drench, a draught of medicine for a horse; a soaking; a downpour: *v.t.* to wet thoroughly; to soak; to force a mixture down an animal's throat; to bate [Tanning]. (A.S. *drencan*, to give to drink.)
drencher, *n.* *drench*-er, one who drenches; a horn for drenching with; a heavy rainstorm.
Dresden, *n.* *drez*-den, Dresden china, a superior porcelain first made in 1709 at Meissen, near Dresden, Saxony.
***dress,** *v.t.* dress, to put straight or adjust to a right line; to put in good order; to trim; to put clothes on; to deck; to cook; to cleanse a wound and apply remedies; to make suitable or fit for use; to curry, rub, and comb: *v.i.* to put on clothes; to pay particular regard to dress; to arrange in due order, esp. troops so as to preserve an exact continuity of line in the whole front. **dress circle,** the principal gallery in a theatre. **dress coat,** a coat worn by gentlemen when in full dress. **dress goods,** fabrics for dresses. **dress-preserver,** a dress-shield. **dress rehearsal,** a full rehearsal of a stage play with scenery and costumes. **dress-shield,** a piece of rubberized material placed in the armpits of women's dresses to protect them from perspiration. **dress ship,** to array with flags on masts and rigging. **dress up,** to deck elaborately. (O.Fr. *dresser*.)
dress, *n.* dress, the covering or ornament of the body; apparel; habiliments; a lady's gown; full dress; style in dress; fastidiousness in dress.
dresser, *n.* *dress*-er, one who dresses, esp. another; an attendant in a stage dressing-room; a surgeon's assistant in a hospital [Med.].
dresser, *n.* *dress*-er, a table or bench on which meat and other things are dressed or prepared for use; a sideboard; an open cupboard for dishes, etc. (O.Fr. *dresseur*.)
dressily, *ad.* dress-e-le, in a dressy manner.
dressing, *n.* *dress*-ing, the action of the verb to dress; that which is used in dressing a wound, etc.; manure spread over land in preparing for a crop; a flogging or beating; salad dressing; stuffing or sauce in cookery; gum, starch, etc., used in stiffening or preparing silk, linen, and other fabrics; a process of cleaning metals after casting [Founding]; cleaning prior to smelting: *pl.* mouldings round doors, windows, etc. [Arch.]. **dressing-case,** a box fitted with toilet requisites. **dressing-gown,** a loose robe used while dressing or as a deshabille. **dressing-room,** a room for dressing in. **dressing-station,** a mobile medical post for the early treatment of the wounded [Mil.]. **dressing-table,** a table with conveniences for dressing at.
dressmaker, *n.* *dress*-make-er, one who makes ladies' gowns and (usually) other garments.
dressmaking, *n.* *dress*-make-ing, the art, process, or occupation of making dresses.
dressy, *a.* *dress*-e, showy in dress; stylish.
drew, droo, *p.* of the verb to draw.
drey, *n.* dray, a squirrel's nest. (Perhaps as *dray*.)
dribble, *v.i.* *drib*-bl, to fall in small drops, or in a quick succession of drops; to slaver, as a child or an idiot; to fall weakly and slowly; to be of a trifling nature; to want energy or vigour; to control the ball by slight kicks from alternate sides [Football]: *v.t.* to let drop; to urge on a ball by small kicks [Football]. (*Drip*.)
dribbler, *n.* *drib*-bler, one who slavers; a football player who dribbles.
driblet, *n.* *drib*-let, a small sum; a petty quantity.
dried, dride, *p.* and *pp.* of the verb *to dry*.
drier, *n.* *dry*-er, one who or that which dries; has the quality of that which may expel or absorb moisture; a desiccative; a material added to oil-paints to make them dry quickly; an apparatus, building, etc., used for drying purposes.
drift, *n.* drift, that which is driven by wind, water, or any force; a heap of any matter driven together, as snow; a driving or impelling force; course, aim, or object; meaning; intention; a drove, shower, or number of things driven at once; an underground passage, esp. one between shaft and shaft [Mining]; a ford [S. Africa]; deviation in the course of a ship, aircraft, or projectile, etc., due to cross-currents; the horizontal force which an arch exerts on its abutments [Arch.]; accumulations of earth and rocks which have been deposited on the surface by the action of ice or water, boulder-clay [Geol.]. **drift of a current,** its velocity.
drift, *a.* drift, drifted by a current: *v.i.* to be driven into heaps; to float or be carried along by a current; to move passively awaiting events; to make a drift in a mine: *v.t.* to drive into heaps. (A.S. *drifan*, drive.)
driftage, *n.* *drift*-aj, anything that drifts; deviation, or the amount of deviation, from the course of a ship, aircraft, or projectile due to cross-currents.
drift-bolt, *n.* *drift*-bohlt, a bolt or steel rod used for driving out bolts.
drifter, *n.* *drift*-er, a boat for use in fishing or in mine-sweeping with drift-nets; one who or that which drifts.
drift-net, *n.* *drift*-net, a large net used in herring and other fishery which, by means of weights and floats, drifts with the tide.
drift-sail, *n.* *drift*-sale, a sail immersed to lessen the drift of a ship during a storm.
drift-way, *n.* *drift*-way, a road across a common for driving cattle; course of a ship or aircraft drifting; a drift in mines.
drift-wood, *n.* *drift*-wood, wood drifted or floated by water.
drifty, *a.* *drift*-e, causing snow-drifts.
drill, *n.* dril, an edged or pointed instrument used for boring holes in metals, rock, or other hard substances by means of either rotatory or percussive action; the act of drilling; the act or exercise of training soldiers, sailors, etc., also the exercises performed in such training; diligent or rigorous instruction in any art or sport; manner of drilling: *v.i.* to engage in drill: *v.t.* to pierce or bore with a drill; to teach and train recruits, etc., in their duty by frequent exercise; to teach by repeated exercise or repetition of acts in the same order. (Dut. *drillen*, to bore, to drill.)
drill, *n.* dril, a furrow or shallow trench for seeds; a row of plants in a drill; a machine for sowing such: *v.t.* to sow grain in drills: *v.i.* to sow in drills.
drill, *n.* dril, coarse twilled linen or cotton (Ger.)
drill, *n.* dril, the West African baboon, *Papio leucophæus*, allied to and smaller than the mandrill and with a black face. (Native name.)

drill-barrow, *n.* a hand machine for drilling and sowing.
drill-bow, *n.* *dril*-boh, a small bow whose string is used for the purpose of rotating a drill.
drill-grubber, *n.* an agricultural implement for grubbing up the land.
drill-harrow, *n.* a small harrow used for pulverizing earth between the drills and extirpating weeds.
drill-husbandry, *n.* the practice of sowing land in drills by a machine.
drill-plough, *n.* a plough for sowing grain in drills.
drill-press, *n.* a machine for drilling holes in metals.
drill-sergeant, *n.* a military non-commissioned officer who trains recruits or drills schoolboys.
drill-stock, *n.* the holdfast for a metal drill.
drily, *ad.* *dry*-le, dryly.
★**drink,** *n.* drink, a beverage; something to be drunk; a draught; liquor that intoxicates, or excessive indulgence in it: *v.i.* to swallow a liquid; to be intemperate in the use of spirituous liquors: *v.t.* to swallow, as liquids; to imbibe; to take in by the senses; to inhale. **drink deep,** to drink to excess. **drink down,** to act on by drinking; to reduce or subdue. **drink health** or **to the health,** a customary civility, in which a person expresses his respect or kind wishes for another. **drink in,** to absorb; to take or receive into any inlet. **drink off,** to drink the whole at a draught. **drink to,** to salute in drinking; to invite to drink by drinking first; to wish well to in the act of taking the cup. **drink up,** to drink the whole. *p.*, **drank.** *pp.*, **drunk.** (A.S. *drincan.*)
drinkable, *a.* *dring*-ka-bl, that may be drunk; suitable for drink: *n.pl.* potable liquors; beverages provided.
drinkableness, *n.* *dring*-ka-bl-ness, state of being drinkable.
drinker, *n.* *dring*-ker, one who drinks; a drunkard; a tippler; the drinker moth, *Odonestis potatoria.*
drinking, *a.* *dring*-king, pertaining to or connected with the use of intoxicating drink: *n.* the practice of drinking, specially alcoholic liquors. **drinking-bout,** *n.* a convivial revelry, or a drunken spree. **drinking-fountain,** *n.* a public fountain at which to quench thirst. **drinking-horn,** *n.* an ancient drinking-cup made of horn. **drinking-song,** *n.* a song in praise of drinking.
drinkless, *a.* *drink*-less, destitute of drink.
drink-money, *n.* money given to buy liquor, originally to drink the health of the giver.
drink-offering, *n.* a Jewish offering of wine, etc., in religious worship; a libation.
drip, *n.* drip, a falling in drops or the sound it makes; that which falls in drops; the edge of a roof; the eaves; the drip-stone: *v.i.* to fall in drops; to shed moisture in drops: *v.t.* to let fall in drops. (A.S. *dryppan.*)
dripping, *n.* *drip*-ping, the fat which falls from meat in roasting; that which falls in drops.
dripping-eaves, *n.pl.* the lower edges of the roof of a building from which the rain drops [Arch.].
dripping-pan, *n.* a pan for receiving the fat which drips from meat in roasting.
drippy, *a.* *drip*-pe, characterized by dripping; drizzly.
drip-stone, *n.* *drip*-stone, a projecting tablet or moulding over the heads of doorways, windows, etc., to throw off rain [Arch.].
drivable, *a.* *drive*-a-bl, that may be driven.
drive, *n.* drive, a ride in a vehicle; a road for driving on, esp. the private road leading to a house; the means of imparting motion to a machine; the mechanism by which the propulsion of a mechanized vehicle is controlled and directed; a forward stroke in games, such as cricket, etc.; energy; the driving together of animals for some special object, as branding; a concerted effort to achieve some purpose, as the raising of funds; a whist drive; a blow [Slang]: *v.t.* to impel or urge forward by force; to force; to bore (a tunnel); to propel (machinery); to mean; to effect; to play the ball from the tee, esp. with a driver [Golf]; to strike the ball with a bat freely swung [Cricket]; to chase or frighten game; to hunt; to cause to move forward and to direct course of; to guide a vehicle; to convey in a carriage; to distress; to straiten; to urge; to press, as an argument; to prosecute; to carry on, as a trade; to overwork: *v.i.* to ride in a carriage; to be forced along; to rush and press with violence; to drift; to intend to aim at; to aim a blow. **drive a bargain,** to haggle about terms. **drive away,** to force to a distance; to scatter. **drive off,** to compel to remove; to drive to a distance. **drive out,** to expel. Drive, in all its senses, is opposed to lead and in all cases implies forcible or violent action. *p.*, **driven,** drivn. *pp.*, **drove,** drohv. (A.S. *drifan.*)
drivel, *n.* *driv*-el, saliva flowing from the mouth; slaver; silly senseless talk: *v.i.* to slaver; to let spittle flow from the mouth, like a child, idiot, or dotard; to talk childishly, to utter rubbish; to dote. (*Dribble.*)
driveller, *n.* *driv*-el-er, one who drivels; a person of weak intellect; a trifler; a fool or idiot.
drivelling, *n.* *driv*-el-ing, silly speech or conduct: *a.* slavering; [Fig.] footling, insensate, idiotic.
driver, *n.* *drive*-er, one who drives; he who drives a carriage; one who conducts a team of horses; a tool for driving; a small spanker, used esp. in bad weather [Naut.]; that which communicates motion to something else, as a wheel [Mech.]; a horse for driving; a bat or racket, etc., specially suitable for driving; a club with a wooden head used for driving the ball off the tee [Golf].
★**driving,** *n.* *drive*-ing, the action of the verb to drive: *a.* adapted for, or used for driving; impelling; of great force or impetus, as a driving storm; communicating driving power.
drizzle, *n.* *driz*-zl, rain; falling mist: *v.i.* to rain in small drops; to fall as water from the clouds in very fine particles: *v.t.* to shed in small drops or particles. (A.S. *dreosan,* to fall.)
drizzly, *a.* *driz*-zl-e, shed in very small drops; characterized by small drops of drizzle.
drogher, *n.* *droh*-ger, a small two-masted coasting vessel with lateen sails trading in the West Indies. (Native name.)
drogue, *n.* drohg, the drag attached to the end of a harpoon line [Naut.]; an open fabric bag used to show the direction of the wind at an aerodrome, or as an anchor at sea [Av.] (Perhaps from *drag.*)
droguet, *n.* dro-*gay,* a woollen fabric formerly used for dresses. (Fr., drugget.)
droil, *n.* droyl, a drudge; drudgery: *v.i.* to work sluggishly or slowly.
droit, *n.* droyt, a right; a legal perquisite. **droits of Admiralty,** those of the Crown as to wrecks, prizes of war, etc. (Fr.)
droitural, *a.* *droy*-tewr-ral, pertaining to the title to property as apart from its actual possession [Law].
droll, *a.* drole, odd; merry; facetious; comical; laughable; ludicrous: *n.* one who excites mirth; a jester; a farce: *v.i.* to jest; to play the buffoon. (Fr. *drôle.*)
drollery, *n.* *drole*-e-re, buffoonery; fun; what is done or said to provoke laughter.
drollish, *a.* *drole*-ish, somewhat droll.
drolly, *ad.* *drole*-ly, in a droll manner.
drome, *n.* drome, an aerodrome. (Abbrev., Slang.)
dromedarian, *n.* drum- *or* drom-e-*dare*-re-an, the rider of a dromedary: *a.* pertaining to the dromedary.
dromedary, *n.* *drum-* *or* *drom*-e-da-re, a camel bred and used for riding, esp. the Arabian or one-humped camel, *Camelus dromedarius,* as distinct from the two-humped Bactrian camel, *Camelus bactrianus.* (Fr. *dromadaire.*)
dromond, *n.* *drom-* *or* *drum*-ond, a large and swift mediæval sailing vessel.
drone, *n.* drone, the male of the honey-bee; an idler; a parasite who does nothing to support himself or others; a humming or low sound, or the instrument of humming; the largest pipe of the bagpipe, emitting a continuous bass note; any one of the large pipes of a bagpipe; an aircraft navigated by remote control [Av.]: *v.i.* to emit a low, heavy, dull sound; to speak monotonously; to live in idleness: *v.t.* to read or utter in a droning manner. (A.S. *dran.*)
drone-fly, *n.* a two-winged insect of the genus *Eristalis,* resembling the drone-bee.
drongo, *n.* *drong*-go, any one of the king-crows, an Old World group of birds of the family *Dicruridæ,* of South-Eastern Asia and Africa, distinguishable by their deeply forked tails. (Malagasy.)
dronish, *a.* *drone*-ish, like a drone; idle; lazy.

drony, *a. drone*-e, dronish ; sluggish.
drool, *v.t.* drool, to slaver. (*Drivel.*)
droop, *n.* droop, the act of drooping ; downward deflexion : *v.i.* to curve downwards ; to hang down limply ; to languish ; to flag ; to decline. (Ice. *drūpa*, bend down.)
drooping, *a. droop*-ing, hanging ; declining, wilting, languishing. **drooping tulip,** the fritillary, *Fritillaria meleagris.*
droopingly, *ad.* in a drooping manner.
★**drop,** *n.* drop, a small globule of a fluid, which falls at once ; something hanging in the form of a drop, as in an ear-ring ; a very small quantity of liquor, or of anything ; the act of dropping ; a fall ; anything arranged to drop ; the part of a gallows which sustains a criminal before execution, and which is suddenly dropped ; the distance a criminal is allowed to fall in hanging ; a machine for lowering anything heavy, into the holds of ships ; the curtain in front of the stage : *pl.* medicine in a liquid form, the dose of which is regulated by a certain number of drops [Med.] ; sweetmeats of various kinds : *v.t.* to pour or let fall in small drops ; to let fall ; to let go ; to dismiss ; to lay aside ; to leave ; to utter casually ; to insert incidentally ; to set down and leave ; to suffer to cease ; to give up ; to bedrop ; to speckle ; to lower ; to give birth to : *v.i.* to fall in small drops ; to let drops fall ; to fall ; to fall spontaneously ; to faint ; to die, or to die suddenly ; to come to an end ; to come unexpectedly ; to fall lower. **drop anchor,** to anchor. **drop astern,** to pass or move toward the stern ; to move back ; to slacken the velocity of a vessel, so as to let another pass beyond her. **drop down,** to sail, row, or move down a river, or toward the sea. **drop goal,** a goal scored from a **drop kick,** *i.e.*, a kick of the ball as it rises after falling from the hands of the kicker [Rugby Football]. **drop in,** to arrive unexpectedly. (A.S. *dropian.*)
drop-curtain, *n.* the curtain preventing view of stage from the front between the acts [Theat.].
drop-drill, *n.* a contrivance for simultaneously manuring and sowing in drills [Agric.].
drop-forging, *n.* the process of making articles in metal by means of a falling weight forcing the heated metal into a die ; an article so made.
drop-hammer, *n.* a heavy power hammer in which the strike is effected by a weight raised and then released to drop on the metal to be forged.
droplet, *n. drop*-let, a little drop.
drop-letter, *n.* a letter sent by post for delivery in the same district [U.S.A.].
dropper, *n. drop*-per, one who or that which drops ; a tube for passing liquids in drops ; a downward shoot from a bulb [Hort.] ; a dog that crouches when it sights game ; an instrument used in lace-making ; an offshoot of a main lode of ore [Min.].
dropping, *a. drop*-ping, falling in drops : *n.* the act of dropping ; that which drops ; a distilling ; a falling : *pl.* the dung of birds or beasts. **dropping bottle** and **dropping tube,** contrivances for supplying a liquid in drops. **dropping fire,** a constant irregular discharge of small arms [Mil.]. (A.S. *dropung.*)
drop-scene, *n.* a curtain suspended by pulleys, which descends or drops along the front or part of the stage ; the drop-curtain.
dropsical, *a. drop*-se-kal, affected with or tending to dropsy ; of the nature of dropsy.
dropsically, *ad.* in a dropsical way.
dropsied, *a. drop*-sid, diseased with dropsy ; swollen, as in dropsy.
dropsy, *n. drop*-se, a morbid collection of watery fluid in the tissues or cavities of the body ; œdema [Med.] ; distension of parts through excess of water [Bot.]. (Gr. *hydrops*, from *hydor*, water.)
dropwort, *n. drop*-wurt, a plant allied to the meadow-sweet, *Spiræa filipendula.* **water dropwort,** the umbelliferous plant, *Œnanthe crocata.*
Drosera, *n.pl. dros*-er-ra, the genus of plants which comprises the sundews. (Gr. *droseros*, dewy.)
drosky, *n. dros*-ke, a low four-wheeled open carriage, formerly common in Russia, esp. one with a bench on which passengers rode as on a saddle. (Russ.)
drosometer, *n.* dro-*som*-e-ter, an instrument for measuring the quantity of dew collected on the surface of a body during the night. (Gr. *drosos*, dew, and *meter.*)
dross, *n.* dross, the scum or extraneous matter of metals, thrown off in the process of melting ; slag ; waste or worthless matter ; refuse. (A.S. *dros.*)
drossiness, *n.* the condition of being drossy.
drossy, *a. dros*-se, like dross ; full of dross ; worthless ; foul ; impure.
drought, *n.* drout, dryness ; a protracted period in which there is no measurable rain ; aridity ; thirst. (A.S. *drugath.*)
droughtiness, *n.* the condition of being droughty.
droughty, *a. drout*-e, in a state of drought ; thirsty.
drouth, *n.* drouth, drought ; dry weather ; thirst.
drove, drove, *p.* of the verb to drive.
drove, *n.* drove, a number of animals, as oxen, sheep, etc., driven in a body ; a collection of animals driving or moving forward ; a road for driving cattle ; a crowd of people in motion ; a drain or narrow channel used in the irrigation of land [Agric.] ; a stone-cutter's broad chisel : *v.i.* to work as a drover : *v.t.* to cut or finish with a drove [Masonry]. (A.S. *draf.*)
drover, *n. drove*-er, one who drives cattle or sheep to market ; a dealer in cattle for market.
drown, *v.t.* droun, to overwhelm in water ; to deprive of life by submersion in water ; to overflow ; to overwhelm ; to overpower ; to extinguish : *v.i.* to be suffocated in water or other fluid ; to perish by drowning. (A.S. *druncnian*, from *drincan*, to drink.)
drowse, *n.* drouz, a nap ; a doze ; a drowsy state : *v.i.* to doze ; to be heavy with sleepiness ; to be heavy and dull : *v.t.* to make heavy with sleep ; to spend (time) idly. (A.S. *dreosan*, to fall.)
drowsily, *ad.* in a dull drowsy manner.
drowsiness, *n.* the condition of being drowsy.
drowsy, *a. drou*-ze, inclined to sleep ; sleepy ; dull ; sluggish ; heavy with sleepiness.
drub, *n.* drub, a blow with a stick or cudgel : *v.t.* to beat with a stick or cudgel ; to thrash. (Origin uncertain.)
drubber, *n. drub*-ber, one who drubs.
drubbing, *n.* a cudgelling ; a sound beating.
drudge, *n.* drudj, one who toils at servile work ; a slave ; a menial : *v.i.* to labour toilsomely at some mean work ; to slave : *v.t.* to spend laboriously. (M.E. *druggen.*)
drudger, *n. drudj*-er, one who drudges ; a drudging-box.
drudgery, *n. drudj*-e-re, toilsome, wearisome, or monotonous work ; ignoble toil ; hard work in servile occupations.
drudging-box, *n.* a dredger [Cookery].
drug, *n.* drug, any substance, vegetable, animal, or mineral used in the composition of medicines or chemical preparations ; a narcotic poison ; any commodity of slow sale for which there is little or no demand in the market : *v.t.* to prescribe drugs ; to season or mix with drugs ; to administer drugs to ; to dose to excess with drugs ; to stupefy or render insensible with drugs : *v.i.* to take drugs habitually. **drug-fiend,** *n.* one addicted to the taking of harmful drugs [Coll.]. **drug-store,** a pharmacy or chemist's shop [U.S.A]. (Fr. *drogue*, drug.).
druggery, *n. drug*-er-re, drugs collectively ; a place for the sale or manufacture of drugs.
drugget, *n. drug*-get, a coarse woollen cloth used as a covering or a substitute for carpets ; a former mixed fabric for clothing. (Fr. *droguet.*)
druggist, *n. drug*-gist, a dealer in drugs ; a pharmaceutical chemist.
Druid, *n. droo*-id, a priest and teacher among the ancient Gauls and British who held sacred the oak and the mistletoe that grew on it ; an officer of the Welsh Gorsedd. **Order of Druids,** a friendly society founded in London in 1781. (Fr. *druide.*)
Druidess, *n. droo*-id-ess, a female Druid.
Druidical, *a.* droo-*id*-e-kal, pertaining to or like Druids. **Druidical circles,** ancient circles of upright stones, as at Stonehenge, at one time presumed to be connected with the worship of the Druids.
Druidism, *n. droo*-id-izm, the system of religion and instruction taught by the Druids, or their doctrines, rites, and ceremonies.
drum, *n.* drum, a narrow hill ; a long narrow ridge of drift or alluvial formation [Geol.]. (*Drumlin.*)
drum, *n.* drum, a percussion musical instrument, in form a hollow cylinder, covered at the ends with

parchment or skin; a drum-shaped container, or the quantity (as of fruit or fish) that this will hold; a metal barrel for oil storage; sheet-iron in the shape of a drum to receive heat from a stove-pipe; a stretched membrane, the tympanum or barrel of the ear; the hollow part of the ear behind the membrane of the tympanum; the resonant organ in certain animals; the booming note of the bittern, etc.; a short revolving cylinder, esp. for turning several small wheels by means of straps passing round it [Mech.]; the rotor of a reaction turbine; the upright part of a cupola, either above or below a dome [Arch.]; the vase of a Corinthian or composite capital [Arch.]; formerly a large evening party or festivity: *v.i.* to beat or play a tune on a drum; to beat with the fingers, as on a table; to beat up for customers; to seek to attract and gather, as by going round with a drum: *v.t.* to play on a drum; to expel with beat of drum; to din something into a person repeatedly. **bass drum,** the large drum beaten on both ends. **side drum,** the small drum beaten only on one head. (Dut. *trom.*)

drumble, *v.i. drum*-bl, to dawdle; to be sluggish.

drum-fire, *n.* rapid artillery fire from a group of many batteries or machine guns, so called because the noise resembles the rolling of drums.

drum-fish, *n drum*-fish, any of several North American sea-fish so-called from the noise they make, esp. *Pogonias chromis*; a freshwater variety, *Aplodinatus grunniens*, of the Great Lakes.

drumhead, *n. drum*-hed, the skin stretched at the top of a drum; the top of a capstan; a variety of cabbage. **drumhead court-martial,** a summary court-martial held on the field.

drumlin, *n. drum*-lin, a small hog-backed hill formed by the accumulation of glacial drift. (Gael. *druim*, the ridge of a hill.)

drumly, *a. drum*-le, turbid; muddy [Scots.].

drum-major, *n.* drum-*may*-jor, the non-commissioned officer in charge of the drummers and preceding the band when on the march.

drummer, *n. drum*-mer, a player of a drum in a band or orchestra; a commercial traveller [Coll.].

Drummond-light, *n. drum*-mond-*lite*, the limelight, so called from Captain Drummond, who invented it.

drumstick, *n. drum*-stik, the stick with which a drum is beaten, or anything resembling it, esp. the leg of a cooked fowl.

drunk, *a.* drunk, intoxicated or affected in brain by alcoholic liquor; drenched or saturated: *n.* a drunken person [Coll.].

drunkard, *n. drung*-kard, one addicted to excess in drinking; one who is habitually or frequently drunk.

drunken, *a. drung*-ken, intoxicated; given to drunkenness; saturated; proceeding from intoxication or drunken people.

drunkenly, *ad.* in a drunken manner.

drunkenness, *n.* the practice or habit of drinking to excess; the state of being drunk; a frenzied state of mind resembling that induced by drink.

drupaceous, *a.* dru-*pay*-shus, belonging to the *Drupaceæ*, a sub-order including the plum, olive, and other trees bearing stone-fruit; producing drupes; having the form, or consisting, of drupes [Bot.].

drupe, *n.* droop, a succulent fruit containing a stone with a kernel, as the plum, peach, etc.; a stone fruit. (L. *drupa*, an over-ripe olive.)

drupel, *n. droop*-el, a small drupe containing a great many stony seeds in its pulp, like the raspberry.

druse, *n.* droos, a geode, or cavity in a rock having its interior surface studded with crystals; a globose cluster of crystals occurring in some plant cells [Bot.] (Gr., a gland.)

Druse, *n.* droos, one of a Syrian tribe of mixed race inhabiting part of Mount Lebanon, whose religion comprises elements from Islam, Judaism, and Christianity. (Turk.)

drusy, *a. droos*-e, abounding with very minute crystals.

★**dry,** *a.* dry, destitute of moisture; arid; free from rain or mist; free from juice, sap, or aqueous matter; without tears; not giving milk; thirsty; jejune; without interest; severe; sarcastic; formally cold or precise; sharply or frigidly precise in execution, or wanting a delicate contour in form [Paint. and Sculp.]; non-alcoholic; in favour of prohibiting sale of intoxicants: *v.t.* to free from or deprive of water or moisture; to deprive of natural juice, sap, or greenness; to scorch or parch with thirst; to drain; to exhaust: *v.i.* to grow dry; to evaporate wholly; to be exhaled. **dry battery,** an electric battery without liquid. **dry blow,** a blow which does not wound. **dry bob,** a schoolboy who takes no part in water sports. **dry canteen,** a canteen in which no alcoholic liquor is sold. **dry cell,** a primary cell without liquid. **dry cleaning,** the cleansing of textiles with agents other than water, esp. petrol or benzine. **dry cupping,** cupping without scarification. **dry dock,** *see* **dock. dry farming,** the special system of cultivation applicable to arid or semi-arid districts. **dry fly,** an artificial fly so constructed as to float on the surface of the water: *v.t.* and *i.* to fish with this. **dry goods,** cloths, stuffs, silks, laces, etc., in distinction from groceries [Comm.]. **dry measure,** a measure for goods that are dry, as a bushel. **dry plate,** a photographic plate ready for exposure without treating it with liquid. **dry steam,** superheated steam. **dry toast,** toast not buttered when hot. **dry up,** to deprive wholly of water; to wither; to suspend talking for want of matter. **dry wines,** those in which the saccharine matter and the ferment are so exactly balanced that they have decomposed each other by their mutual action (opposed to sweet). *p.* and *pp.* **dried,** dride. (A.S. *dryge.*)

dryad, *n. dry*-ad, a nymph of the woods and groves [Myth.]. (L. *dryas*, a dryad.)

dryasdust, *n. dry*-az-dust, one who writes dully if learnedly, and without any appreciation of the human interest in his subject: *a.* dull; prosy. (An imaginary character to whom Sir Walter Scott addressed prefaces to certain of his novels.)

dry-clean, *v.t.* to clean (textiles, etc.) with some solvent other than water.

dryer, *n. dry*-er, a drier.

dry-eyed, *a.* dry-ide, not having tears in the eyes.

dryfoot, *n. dry*-foot, dryshod.

drying, *a. dry*-ing, adapted to exhaust moisture; drying quickly and becoming hard: *n.* the act or process of depriving of moisture or greenness. **drying-oil,** linseed or other oil that has been heated with oxide of lead, and can thus form the basis of many paints and varnishes.

dryish, *a. dry*-ish, rather dry.

dryly, *ad. dry*-le, without moisture; coldly; uninterestingly; in a dry or sarcastic manner.

dryness, *n. dry*-ness, the state of being dry.

dry-nurse, *n.* a nurse who brings up a child without the breast; a subordinate who gives instruction to his superior: *v.t.* to rear without the breast; to act as a dry-nurse.

dry-point, *n. dry*-poynt, a needle for engraving on a copper plate without the use of acid; an engraving so produced: *v.i.* to engrave by this process.

dry-rot, *n. dry*-rot, a rapid decay of timber due to the presence of fungi, which convert it into a dry powder.

drysalter, *n. dry*-sawl-ter, a dealer in drugs, dye-stuffs, colours, and chemical substances generally; formerly a dealer in salted or dried meats, etc.

drysaltery, *n.* dry-*sawl*-ter-re, the articles kept by a drysalter; the business of a drysalter.

dryshod, *a.* and *ad. dry*-shod, without wetting the feet.

dry-stove, *n. dry*-stove, a hothouse for the cultivation of plants of dry and hot climates.

duad, *n. dew*-ad, dyad; union of two.

dual, *n. dew*-al, consisting of two; twofold; double; expressing two: *n.* the number expressing two only, as distinct from "plural" expressing two or more [Gram.]. (L. *duo*, two.)

dualin, *n.* dew-*a*-lin, a form of dynamite in which the explosive is impregnated with nitro-glycerine.

dualism, *n. dew*-a-lizm, twofoldness in the unity of being, or the doctrine that there are two opposite and independently existing principles which go to form everything, such as good and evil, spirit and matter, male and female, or yea and nay; any twofold union.

dualist, *n. dew*-a-list, one who holds a doctrine of dualism.

dualistic, *a.* dew-a-*lis*-tik, implying or expressing duality.

duality, *n.* dew-*al*-e-te, the state of being dual or double. (L. *dualis.*)

dualize, *v.t. dew*-a-lize, to divide into two; to regard as two.

duan, *n.* *dew*-an, a canto or division of a poem. (Celt.)
dub, *v.t.* dub, to confer knighthood by striking a blow or by a tap with a sword ; to confer any dignity, new character, title, or nickname ; to trim ; to smooth or dress : *v.i.* to make a quick noise. **dub a cock,** to prepare it for fighting. **dub a fly,** to prepare an artificial fly for fishing. **dub cloth,** to dress it with teazles. **dub up,** to pay up [Slang].
dubber, *n.* *dub*-ber, a large vessel of skin or leather used in India to hold ghee, oil, etc. (Anglo-Ind.)
dubbing, *n.* *dub*-bing, a thick oily composition, used for softening stiff and hard leather.
dubiety, *n.* dew-*by*-e-te, doubtfulness ; a matter of doubt. (L. *dubieta.*)
dubiosity, *n.* dew-be-*os*-e-te, dubiousness ; a dubious statement.
dubious, *a.* *dew*-be-us, wavering or fluctuating in opinion ; doubtful ; questionable ; uncertain ; not clear or plain ; of uncertain event or issue. (L. *dubiosus.*)
dubiously, *ad.* *dew*-be-us-le, in a dubious manner.
dubiousness, *n.* *dew*-be-us-ness, a state of wavering and indecision of mind ; uncertainty.
dubitable, *a.* *dew*-be-ta-bl, doubtful ; uncertain.
dubitably, *ad.* *dew*-be-ta-ble, in a dubitable manner.
dubitant, *a.* *dew*-be-tant, doubting : *n.* a doubter.
dubitate, *v.i.* *dewb*-it-ate, to doubt ; to hesitate. (L. *dubitatus,* doubted.)
dubitation, *n.* dew-be-*tay*-shon, the act of doubting ; doubt. (L. *dubitatus,* doubted.)
dubitative, *a.* *dew*-be-ta-tiv, inclined to doubt.
dubitatively, *ad.* in a dubitative manner.
ducal, *a.* *dew*-kal, pertaining to a duke or dukedom. (L. *dux,* a leader.)
ducat, *n.* *duk*-at, an obsolete coin of several European countries, first coined in silver in 1140 by the Duke of Apulia, and in 1252 issued in gold at Florence, and subsequently current over central and northern Europe ; in gold worth about 9*s.* 4*d.*, in silver from 3*s.* to 4*s.* ; a gold coin of modern Austria, Czechoslovakia, and Hungary (worth about 9*s.* 5*d.*), and of Poland (11*s.* 6*d.*).
ducatoon, *n.* duk-a-*toon,* an obsolete silver coin worth about 4*s.* 8*d.* at Venice, and 4*s.* 6*d.* in Holland.
Duce, *n.* *doo*-chay, the title, 1922–1943, of the head of the Italian Fascist State, who was nominally responsible to the King. (It., leader, chief, from L. *dux,* a leader.)
duchess, *n.* *dutch*-ess, the wife or widow of a duke ; a woman holding a duchy in her own right. (Fr. *duchesse.*)
duchesse, *n.* du-*shess,* a soft kind of satin. **duchesse table,** a dressing-table fitted with a swinging mirror. (Fr.)
duchy, *n.* *dutch*-e, the territory or jurisdiction of a duke ; a dukedom. **the Duchy,** either of the royal dukedoms of Cornwall and Lancaster. **Duchy-court,** *n.* the court of a duchy, esp. that of Lancaster. (Fr. *duché.*)
duck, *n.* duk, linen or cotton cloth, used for small sails and jackets, aprons, etc. : *pl.* trousers of this material. (Dut. *doek.*)
duck, *n.* duk, a web-footed water-fowl of the genus *Anas,* esp. the female as distinct from the drake ; an inclination of the head, resembling the motion of a duck in water ; a darling ; a pet ; a score of nothing, a duck's-egg [Cricket slang] : *v.t.* to dip or plunge into water, and suddenly withdraw ; to bow, stoop, or nod : *v.i.* to dip in water and immediately withdraw ; to drop the head suddenly ; to bow ; to cringe. **ducks and drakes,** the sport of throwing a flat stone, etc., obliquely, so as to make it rebound repeatedly from the surface of the water. **to play ducks and drakes with,** to squander recklessly. **lame duck,** a defaulter [Stock Exchange slang]. (Dut. *duiken,* to stoop.)
duck-ant, *n.* *duk*-ant, a Jamaican termite which builds its nest in trees.
duckbill, *n.* *duk*-bil, the platypus, *Ornithorhynchus anatinus,* a small aquatic egg-laying mammal peculiar to Australia.
duck-billed, *a.* *duk*-bild, having a bill like a duck.
duckboard, *n.* *duk*-bord, a boarded track or footpath laid on muddy ground ; a trench-board [Mil.].
ducker, *n.* *duk*-er, one who ducks ; a diving-bird ; a breeder, or a hunter, of ducks ; a gun for duck-shooting.
duck-hawk, *n.* *duk*-hawk, the marsh-harrier.
ducking, *n.* *duk*-ing, a thorough wetting ; the act of plunging into water.
ducking-stool, *n.* *duk*-ing-stool, a stool or chair attached to the end of a long lever, in which common scolds were formerly tied and ducked in water.
duckling, *n.* *duk*-ling, a young duck.
duck-mole, *n.* *duk*-mole, the duckbill.
duck's-egg, *n.* a score of nil, esp. at cricket [Slang]. (From the shape of the zero symbol, '0'.)
duck's-foot, *n.* *duks*-foot, a popular name of the plants lady's mantle and May-apple.
duck-shot, *n.* *duk*-shot, shot of the size for shooting wild duck.
duck-weed, *n.* *duk*-weed, a plant of the genus *Lemna,* covering the surface of still water.
duct, *n.* dukt, any tube or canal by which a fluid is conducted or conveyed, especially in the internal structures of animals and plants. (L. *ductum,* lead.)
ductile, *a.* *duk*-tile, that may be easily led ; yielding ; flexible ; that may be drawn out into wire or threads, as a metal. (L. *ductilis.*)
ductilimeter, *n.* duk-te-*lim*-e-ter, an instrument for measuring the ductility of metals.
ductility, *n.* duk-*til*-e-te, the capacity, particularly in metals, of being extended by drawing without breaking ; flexibility ; ready compliance.
ductless, *a.* *dukt*-less, devoid of ducts. **ductless glands,** masses of glandular tissue which, having no efferent ducts, discharge their secretions directly into the blood [Anat.]
dud, *n.* dud, a shell that does not explode ; a sham ; a failure : *a.* worthless ; useless ; counterfeit.
dude, *n.* dewd, a dandy ; an affected person [Slang].
dudeen, *n.* doo-*deen,* a short clay tobacco pipe. (Ir.)
dudelsack, *n.* *doo*-dl-zak, the German bagpipes. (Ger.)
dudgeon, *n.* *dud*-jun, a small dagger ; a handle to a dagger. (Origin uncertain.)
dudgeon, *n.* *dud*-jun, resentment ; sullenness ; indignant ire. (Origin unknown.)
duds, *n.pl.* dudz, old clothes ; tattered garments ; clothes. (Origin doubtful.)
due, *a.* dew, owed ; that ought to be paid or done to another ; proper ; becoming ; required by the circumstances ; exact ; owing ; that ought to have arrived before a time specified : *ad.* directly, as due east or west : *n.* that which is owed, or that which one contracts to pay or perform ; that which law, justice, office, station, social relation, or established rule, requires to be paid or done ; that which law or custom requires, as toll, tribute, fees of office, or other legal perquisites ; right. (Fr. *dû.*)
due-bill, *n.* a written acknowledgment of debt that is non-transferable and not a promise to pay ; an I.O.U. [Amer.].
duel, *n.* *dew*-el, a combat with deadly weapons between two at a pre-arranged time and place, for the purpose of deciding some private quarrel ; any contention between two : *v.i.* to fight in single combat. (Fr.)
dueller, *n.* *dew*-el-er, a duellist.
duelling, *n.* *dew*-el-ling, the act or practice of fighting in single combat.
duellist, *n.* *dew*-el-ist, one who engages in duelling.
duello, *n.* dew-*el*-lo, a duel ; the rules of duelling. (It.)
dueness, *n.* *dew*-ness, fitness ; propriety ; the quality of being due.
duenna, *n.* dew-*en*-na, an elderly woman having charge of the younger female members of a family ; a chaperon, the chief lady in waiting upon the former Queens of Spain. (Sp. *donna.*)
duet, *n.* dew-*et,* a piece of music composed for two performers, whether vocal or instrumental ; a performance by two persons. (It. *duetto.*)
duettino, *n.* dew-et-*tee*-no, a short duet. (It.)
duetto, *n.* dew-*et*-to, a duet.
duff, *n.* duff, a boiled pudding containing dried fruit, such as raisins and currants. (*Dough.*)
duff, *v.t.* duf, to steal cattle by altering brands [Austral. Slang] ; to fake : *a.* counterfeit ; inferior [Slang].
duffel, *n.* *duf*-fel, a thick coarse kind of woollen cloth, having a thick nap or frieze. (*Duffel,* in Belgium.)
duffer, *n.* *duf*-fer, a hawker, esp. one selling paste as genuine jewels professing to have smuggled them ; one who duffs cattle [Austral.] ; a dull brainless fellow ; a muff ; a counterfeit coin or other article [Slang]. (Ice. *daufr,* stupid.)

duffing, *n. duff*-ing, the practice of selling counterfeit articles as genuine ; the thieving of cattle [Austral.] : *a.* sham but tendered as genuine ; silly ; not good enough.
dug, dug, *pp.* of *dig.*
dug, *n.* dug, a nipple ; a teat. (Perhaps Scand. *dægga,* to suckle.)
dugong, *n. doo*-gong, the sea-cow, a large herbivorous aquatic mammal of the order *Sirenia,* allied to the manatee. (Malay.)
dugout, *n. dug*-out, a canoe hollowed out ; a subterranean shelter ; a retired officer or official recalled to service in an emergency [Coll.].
duiker, *n. dy*-ker, any small S. African antelope of the order *Cephalophus.*
duke, *n.* dewk, the highest hereditary title in the British peerage ; a holder of this ; on the Continent, the sovereign prince of a duchy. (L. *dux,* a leader.)
dukedom, *n. dewk*-dom, the territory, rank, or title of a duke.
Dukeries, *n.pl. dew*-ker-riz, a district in the English Midlands so called because of the numerous ducal seats there situated [Humorous Slang].
Dukhobors, *n. doo*-ko-bawrz, the Doukhobors.
dulcamara, *n.* dul-ka-*mah*-ra, the woody nightshade, or bittersweet, *Solanum dulcamara.* (L. *dulcis,* sweet, *amarus,* bitter.)
dulcet, *a, dul*-set, sweet to the taste ; sweet to the ear ; melodious ; pleasing. (O.Fr. *doucet,* sweet.)
dulcification, *n. dul*-se-fe-*kay*-shon, the act of sweetening or dulcifying.
dulcified, *a. dul-se*-fide, sweetened. **dulcified spirit,** a compound of alcohol with mineral acids.
dulcify, *v.t. dul*-se-fy, to sweeten ; to free from acidity, saltness, or acrimony ; to mollify. (Fr. *dulcifier.*)
dulcimer, *n. dul*-se-mer, a musical instrument strung with wires, which are struck with two little hammers. (O.Fr. *doulcemer.*)
dulcitol, *n. dul*-se-tol, a white crystalline compound of the nature of manna-sugar imported from Madagascar. (L. *dulcis,* sweet.)
dulcitone, *n. dul*-se-tone, a keyboard instrument in which tuning-forks are struck by the hammers [Mus.]. (L. *dulcis,* sweet, and *tone.*)
dulia, *n. dew*-le-a, the reverence paid to angels and saints as contrasted with latria, the supreme adoration due to God. (Gr. *douleia,* slavery.)
dull, *a.* dul, stupid ; doltish ; slow of hearing, seeing, understanding, or learning ; without life or spirit ; slow of motion ; sleepy ; drowsy ; sad ; depressing ; dreary ; insensible ; cheerless ; not clear ; tarnished ; not briskly burning ; dim ; obscure ; blunt ; obtuse ; cloudy ; being without wind [Naut.] : *v.t.* to make dull or stupid ; to blunt ; to depress ; to make insensible or slow to perceive ; to make heavy or slow of motion ; to sully ; to tarnish or cloud : *v.i.* to become dull. (A.S. *dol.*)
dullard, *a. dul*-ard, stupid : *n.* a stupid person.
dull-brained, *a.* stupid ; of dull intellect.
dull-eyed, *a.* having a saddened or listless look.
dullish, *a. dul*-ish, somewhat dull.
dullness, *n. dul*-ness, stupidity ; quality of being dull.
dull-sighted, *a.* having imperfect sight.
dull-witted, *a.* heavy or dull in intellect.
dully, *ad. dul*-le, in a dull manner.
dulocracy, *n.* dew-*lok*-ra-se, the domination of slaves or the lower orders in a state. (Gr. *doulos,* a slave, *krateo,* rule.)
dulse, *n.* dulse, the red seaweed *Rhodymenia palmata,* often eaten raw. (Gael. *duileasg,* water-leaf.)
duly, *ad. dew*-le, properly ; exactly.
Duma, *n. doo*-mah, the former Imperial Russian parliament, which met first in 1906.
dumb, *a.* dum, mute ; silent ; not speaking ; destitute of the power of speech ; not accompanied with speech : *v.t.* to silence ; to make dumb. **strike dumb,** to confound ; to astonish ; to render speechless by astonishment. (A.S.)
dumb-barge, *n. dum*-barj, a barge without sails ; a lighter.
dumb-bells, *n.pl.* pairs of weights connected by a short bar, swung in the hands for exercise.
dumb-cane, *n. dum*-kane, a W. Indian plant, *Dieffenbachia seguine,* which, when chewed, causes the tongue to swell.
dumbfound, *v.t.* dum-*found,* to strike dumb ; to confuse ; to astound.
dumb-iron, *n. dum*-i-urn, a carriage-spring of double semi-eliptical design ; an extension forward of each side of the chassis of a motor-vehicle to which is attached one end of the front spring.
dumbledor, *n. dum*-bl-dor, the humble-bee ; the common cockchafer.
dumbly, *ad. dum*-le, silently ; without words or speech.
dumbness, *n. dum*-ness, the state of being dumb.
dumb-show, *n.* gesture without words ; pantomime.
dumb-waiter, *n.* dum-*way*-ter, a mobile framework with shelves for conveying food, etc., between kitchen and dining-room ; a dining-room sideboard with revolving shelves serving as trays for food.
dum-dum, *n. dum*-dum, a soft-nosed expanding bullet formerly made at Dum-Dum arsenal, Bengal.
dumfoundered, *a.* dum-*foun*-derd, dumbfounded.
dummy, *n. dum*-me, one who is dumb ; an infant's comforter for sucking ; a sham package or figure in a shop ; the fourth hand, exposed at whist, etc., when there are three players ; the exposed hand at bridge, contract, etc. ; an actor in a piece who does not speak ; a lay figure ; a ventriloquist's puppet ; a hatter's pressing-iron : *a.* mute ; sham. **dummy cartridge,** a blank cartridge. **dummy whist,** whist for three players, one hand being exposed and played by dealer.
dump, *v.t.* dump, to unload, as a cart, by tilting up ; to deposit rubbish ; to export goods for sale at a lower price than they can be profitably sold at when produced locally : *n.* a mound of mining refuse, pile of rubbish, etc. ; a place for depositing such, or for the storing of war-material. (Scand.)
dump, *n.* dump, a clumsy leaden counter ; a rope quoit ; a kind of nail ; a thump or thud ; a dumpy person. (Probably Scand.)
dumpcart, *n. dump*-kart, a cart the body of which can be tilted for emptying.
dumpiness, *n. dump*-e-ness, state of being dumpy.
dumpish, *a. dump*-ish, dull ; moping ; depressed.
dumpishly, *ad.* in a moping manner.
dumpishness, *n.* a state of being dull, heavy, and moping.
dumpling, *n. dump*-ling, a small pudding, with or without fruit, and either boiled or baked ; a dumpy person [Coll.].
dumps, *n.pl.* dumps, a dull, gloomy, sulky state of the mind ; ill-humour ; low spirits. (Origin uncertain.)
dumpty, *n. dump*-te, a pouffe.
dumpy, *a. dump*-e, short and thick ; short and plump : *n.* a high hassock ; a short-handled umbrella. (*Dump.*)
dun, *a,* dun, greyish or yellowish brown ; dark ; gloomy : *n.* a dun-coloured horse : *v.t.* to cure fish so as to impart to them a dun colour [U.S.A.]. (A.S.)
dun, *v.t.* dun, to solicit or press repeatedly and with importunity, esp. for payment of a debt : *n.* an importunate creditor who urges for payment ; an urgent request or demand of payment ; a debt-collector.
dun, *n.* dun, a mound ; a hill-fortress or earthwork of the ancient Britons. (Ir. and Gael.)
dun-bird, *n. dun*-berd, the pochard ; the scaup.
dunce, *n.* dunce, a dullard ; one slow in learning. (*Duns* Scotus, a schoolman of the 13th cent. who opposed the study of the classics.)
duncery, *n. dun*-ser-re, the practice or condition of a dunce ; stupidity.
duncish, *a. dun*-sish, like a dunce ; sottish.
dunderhead, *n. dun*-der-hed, a dunce ; a blockhead.
dun-diver, *n. dun*-dy-ver, the goosander.
Dundrearys, *n.pl.* dun-*dreer*-riz, long side-whiskers, worn without a beard. (Lord *Dundreary,* in Taylor's "Our American Cousin," 1858.)
dune, *n.* dewn, a low hill of sand on the coast, generally due to the action of the wind. (A.S.)
dun-fish, *n. dun*-fish, cod-fish cured by dunning.
dung, *n.* dung, the excrement of animals : *v.t.* to manure with dung : *v.i.* to void excrement. (A.S.)
dungaree, *n. dung*-ga-ree, a stout cotton cloth used for overalls : *pl.* trousers or overalls made of this. (Anglo-Indian.)
dung-beetle, *n. dung*-bee-tl, any of several beetles the larvæ of which develop in dung.
dungeon, *n. dun*-jun, a close dark prison, usually underground ; a mediæval keep or donjon : *v.t.* to confine in a dungeon. (Fr. *donjon.*)

dunghill, *n. dung*-hil, a heap of dung; a mean or vile abode; any mean situation or condition: *a.* sprung from the dunghill; low; base; vile.
dungy, *a. dung*-e, full of dung; filthy; vile.
Dunker, *n. dung*-ker, a member in the U.S.A. of the sect of German Baptist Brethren. (Ger. *tunker.*)
dunlin, *n. dun*-lin, the red-backed sandpiper, *Tringa alpina.* (*Dun.*)
dunlop, *n. dun*-lop, a Scottish cheese, originally made in Dunlop, Ayrshire; a pneumatic tyre invented by Dr. Dunlop.
dunnage, *n. dun*-naj, brushwood, etc., stowed below cargo to raise it above the bilge-water [Naut.].
dunner, *n. dun*-ner, one who duns; a debt-collector.
dunning, *n. dun*-ning, the operation of curing cod-fish so as to give them a dun colour.
dunnish, *a. dun*-nish, somewhat dun.
dunnock, *n. dun*-nok, the hedge-sparrow.
dunny, *a. dun*-ne, deaf; dull of apprehension.
Dunstable, *a. dun*-sta-bl, straightforward; outright; plain-spoken. (The main road through Dunstable, Beds., which for long stretches runs in a straight line.)
dunt, *n.* dunt, the gid, a staggering affection peculiar to yearling lambs. (Dial. Engl.)
dunt, *n.* dunt, a heavy, dull blow. (Scots.)
duo, *n. dew*-oh, a song in two parts; a duet; a pair of artistes who perform together. (L., two.)
duodecennial, *a. dew*-o-de-*sen*-e-al, recurring every twelve years; consisting of twelve years. (L. *duodecim,* twelve, *annus,* a year.)
duodecimal, *a.* dew-o-*des*-e-mal, computed by or proceeding by twelves: *pl.* a rule in arithmetic in which the denominations rise by twelves, chiefly applied to the calculation of square feet and inches.
duodecimally, *ad.* by duodecimals.
duodecimo, *a.* dew-o-*des*-e-mo, having twelve leaves to a sheet; twelvemo: *n.* a book in which a sheet is folded into twelve leaves. (L. *duodecimus,* twelfth.)
duodenal, *n. dew*-o-*dee*-nal, pertaining to the duodenum.
duodenary, *a. dew*-o-*den*-a-re, relating to the number twelve; increasing twelvefold, said of arithmetic in which each figure increases twelvefold from right to left.
duodenitis, *n. dew*-o-de-*ny*-tis, inflammation of the duodenum.
duodenum, *n. dew*-o-*dee*-num, the first portion of the small intestine, immediately following the pylorus (approx. 12 in. long in man).
duologue, *n. dew*-o-log, conversation between two. (L. *duo,* two, Gr. *logos,* speech.)
duomo, *n. dwoh*-moh, a cathedral (in Italy). (It.)
dup, *v.t.* dup, to open, as the door. (*Do up.*)
dupability, *n.* dew-pa-*bil*-e-te, susceptibility of being duped.
dupable, *a. dew*-pa-bl, that can be duped.
dupe, *n.* dewp, one who is deceived, or easily deceived: *v.t.* to deceive; to impose upon; to gull. (Fr.)
duper, *n. dew*-per, one who dupes.
dupery, *n. dew*-pe-re, the act or practice of duping.
dupion, *n. dew*-pe-on, a double cocoon, formed by two or more silk-worms. (Fr. *doupion.*)
duple, *a. dew*-pl, double; duplicate; with two beats in a bar [Mus.]. **duple ratio,** that in which the antecedent is double the consequent, as 2 to 1, subduple being the reverse. (L. *duplus.*)
duplet, *n. dew*-plet, two notes played in the time of three [Mus.]; a doublet at dice.
duplex, *a. dew*-pleks, compound [Bot.]; double; a term applied to the retarding movement of a watch, as a duplex escapement. **duplex process,** the manufacture of steel in two furnaces, transference from the first to the second being made without interrupting the operation. (L. *duo,* two, *plico,* fold.)
duplexity, *n.* dew-*plek*-se-te, duplex quality or state.
duplicate, *a. dew*-ple-kat, double; twofold. **duplicate proportion** or **ratio,** the proportion or ratio of squares: *n.* another corresponding to the first, or a second thing of the same kind; a copy; a transcript; a method of playing bridge, etc., in which each deal is played by a number of players so as to make comparison between the play of pairs, teams, etc., possible: *v.t.* (*dew*-ple-kate), to double; to fold; to make a facsimile of; to make in duplicate; to part into two [Biol.]. (L. *duo,* two, *plico,* fold.)
duplication, *n. dew*-ple-*kay*-shon, the act of doubling; a folding over, or doubling. **duplication of the cube,** the celebrated Delian problem, in which the side of a cube whose contents shall be twice that of a given cube is to be ascertained [Geom.]. (L. *duplicatio.*)
duplicative, *a. dew*-ple-ka-tiv, having the quality of doubling, esp. by division; tending to duplicate.
duplicator, *n. dew*-ple-kay-tor, a duplicating machine.
duplicature, *n. dew*-ple-ka-tewr, a doubling; a fold; the fold of a membrane or vessel [Anat.].
duplicity, *n.* dew-*plis*-e-te, doubleness; double-facedness; the act of dissembling one's real opinions, with a design to mislead; in legal pleading, the pleading of two or more distinct matters [Law]. (Fr. *duplicité.*)
duplo-, *dew*-plo-, a prefix denoting doubling [Chem.].
duppy, *n. dup*-pe, a ghost or haunting spirit [West Indian]. (Negro word.)
durability, *n.* dewr-ra-*bil*-e-te, durableness. (Fr. *durabilité.*)
durable, *a. dewr*-ra-bl, capable of lasting long. (L. *duro,* last, from *durus,* hard.)
durableness, *n.* the quality of being durable.
durably, *ad.* in a lasting manner; with long continuance.
duralumin, *n.* dewr-*ral*-yew-min, proprietary name of a light aluminium alloy of great tensile strength. (L. *durus,* hard, and *aluminium.*)
duraluminium, *n.* dewr-*ral*-yew-*min*-e-um, duralumin.
dura mater, *dewr*-ra-*may*-ter, *see* **mater.**
duramen, *n.* dew-*ray*-men, the central layers of wood in the stem of an exogenous tree; the heart-wood. (L.)
durance, *n. dewr*-rance, imprisonment; durability.
duration, *n.* dew-*ray*-shon, continuance in time; length of time, indefinitely; power of continuance. (L. *duratio.*)
durbar, *n. dur*-bar *or* dur-*bar,* an audience-chamber; the court of an Indian prince; a state reception in India. (Per. and Hind. *darbar.*)
durdum, *n. dur*-dum, a great noise or uproar [Scots.].
dure, *v.i.* dewr, to last; to endure.
duress, *n. dew*-ress, imprisonment; restraint of liberty, or threat of violence, to compel one to do some act, or the plea of exculpation by one who has been so forced [Law]: *v.t.* to subject to duress. (O.Fr. *duresce.*)
durian, *n. dewr*-re-an, the edible but evil-smelling fruit of the East Indian tree durio, *Durio zibethinus.*
during, *ppr. dewr*-ring, continuing; throughout; while it lasts, as during life.
durio, *n. dewr*-re-o, the tree which yields the durian. (Malay *durī,* prickle.)
durmast, *n. dur*-mast, a variety of *Quercus sessiliflora,* an oak with very downy leaves.
durra, *n. door*-ra, Indian millet, *Sorghum vulgare,* cultivated as a cereal. (Ar.)
durst, durst, *pret.* of dare.
dusk, *n.* dusk, tending to darkness; darkish: *n.* a tending to darkness; twilight; tendency to a black colour; darkness of colour. (A.S.)
duskily, *ad. dusk*-e-le, with a tendency to blackness or darkness.
duskiness, *n.* the quality of being dusky.
duskish, *a. dusk*-ish, somewhat dusky; slightly dark or black.
dusky, *a. dusk*-e, partially dark or obscure; dark-coloured; gloomy; sad; intellectually clouded.
★**dust,** *n.* dust, fine dry particles of earth or other matter that may be easily raised and wafted by the wind; a stirring as of dust with like effects; a disturbance; earth; household refuse; the grave; the decomposed remains of the dead; a low condition; pollen [Bot.]; money [Slang]: *v.t.* to brush, wipe, or sweep away dust; to sprinkle with dust; to beat: *v.i.* to become dusty or reduced to dust. **bite the dust,** to be thrown in a contest. **eat dust,** to be humbled. **throw dust in one's eyes,** to confuse and mislead. (A.S.)
dustbin, *n.* a receptacle for household refuse; a dust-hole.
dust-brand, *n. dust*-brand, smut, a plant disease caused by *Ustilago segetum.*
dust-cart, *n.* a scavenger's cart.
dust-coat, *n.* a light overcoat.
dust-cover, *n.* the jacket, or detachable paper cover of a bound book.

duster, *n.* *dust*-er, a cloth or brush to clear off dust; a sieve; one who dusts; an appliance to remove dust from flower. **the old Red Duster,** the Red Ensign, since 1864 the flag of the British Mercantile Marine [Coll.].

dusthole, *n.* *dust*-hole, a place for refuse.

dustiness, *n.* *dust*-e-ness, the state of being dusty.

dustman, *n.* one who removes household refuse.

dustpan, *n.* a broad flat shovel for conveying dust brushed from the floor.

dust-shot, *n.* the smallest kind of shot.

dust-storm, *n.* a dust-laden whirlwind; a sandstorm.

dusty, *a.* *dust*-e, filled, covered, or sprinkled with dust; like dust. **dusty miller,** an artificial salmon-fly. **not so dusty,** good, or pretty good [Slang]. (A.S. *dystig.*)

Dutch, *n.* dutch, the people of Holland; the Low Germans; their language: *a.* pertaining to Holland, its inhabitants, or its language and, formerly, to the German or Teutonic peoples. **Dutch auction,** a sale started by the auctioneer bidding lower and lower until he reaches a price that suits a buyer. **Dutch cheese,** a small round cheese made from skim-milk. **Dutch clinker,** a long narrow brick, yellowish, very hard, and apparently vitrified by heat, made in Holland. **Dutch clover,** white clover, *Trifolium repens.* **Dutch courage,** false courage, or courage inspired by stimulants. **Dutch metal, leaf,** or **gold,** an alloy of copper and bronze made into leaves, and largely used for ornamenting toys, etc. **Dutch myrtle,** the sweet gale, *Myrica gale.* **Dutch oven,** a utensil for cooking, hung before the fire. **Dutch pink,** a pigment obtained from the dyer's rocket, *Reseda luteola.* **Dutch rush,** the rough horsetail, *Equisetum hyemale.* **Dutch tiles,** ornamental tiles glazed and painted. (Ger. *deutsch,* the people.)

dutch, *n.* dutch, a wife [*Duchess,* Coster Slang].

Dutchman, *n.* *dutch*-man, a native of Holland; a Hollander.

duteous, *a.* *dew*-te-us, devoted to duty; obedient; obsequious.

duteously, *ad.* in a duteous manner.

duteousness, *n.* obedience to duty.

dutiable, *a.* *dew*-te-a-bl, subject to the imposition of duty or customs.

dutied, *a.* *dew*-ted, subject to government duties or customs [U.S.A.].

dutiful, *n.* *dew*-te-ful, performing the duties or obligations required by law, justice, or propriety; obedient; submissive; expressive of respect or a sense of duty; required by duty.

dutifully, *ad.* *dew*-te-ful-le, in a dutiful manner; obediently, submissively, or respectfully.

dutifulness, *n.* reverence; respect.

duty, *n.* *dew*-te, that which a person is bound, by any natural, moral, or legal obligation, to pay, do, or perform; forbearance of that which is forbidden by morality, law, justice, or propriety; obedience; submission; act of reverence or respect; tax, toll, impost, customs, or excise; any sum of money required by government to be paid on the importation, exportation, manufacture, or sale of goods; any service or business. (*Due.*)

duumvir, *n.* dew-*um*-ver (*pl.* **duumviri**), one of two ancient Roman officers or magistrates united in the same public functions. (L. *duo,* two, *vir,* a man.)

duumviral, *a.* dew-*um*-ver-al, pertaining to the duumviri or duumvirate of Rome.

duumvirate, *n.* dew-*um*-ver-at, government by two; the office, dignity, or government of two men.

duvet, *n.* (App.), a down quilt. (Fr., down.)

dux, *n.* duks, the head of a class in a school [Scots.]; the chief melody, or subject, of a fugue [Mus.]. (L.)

dwale, *n.* dwale, the deadly nightshade, *Atropa belladonna.* (Scand.)

dwarf, *n.* dworf (*pl.* **dwarfs**), anything, esp. a human being, which is much below the ordinary size of its species or kind; an attendant on a lady or knight in romances; a diminutive sprite; one of a class of relatively small stars having high density and low luminosity [Astron.]: *a.* dwarfish; stunted; puny: *v.t.* to hinder from growing to the natural size; to make or keep small: *v.i.* to grow stunted. **dwarf tree,** a fruit tree whose branches are made to shoot from near the root; a tree artificially dwarfed

dwarfed wall, a low wall on which railings are usually fixed. (A.S. *dweorg.*)

dwarfish, *a.* *dworf*-ish, like a dwarf; of less than the normal size; very small; low; petty; despicable.

dwarfishly, *ad.* *dworf*-ish-le, like a dwarf.

dwarfishness, *n.* smallness of stature or size.

dwarfism, *n.* *dworf*-izm, nanism.

dwell, *v.i.* dwel, to abide as a permanent resident or an inhabitant for a time; to be in any state or condition; to continue fixed in attention; to hang upon with fondness. *p.* and *pp.* **dwelt.** (A.S. *dwelan,* to hinder.)

dweller, *n.* *dwel*-er, an inhabitant; a resident.

dwelling, *n.* *dwel*-ing, place of residence; abode. **dwelling house,** a house or flat for residential purposes as distinct from a place of business, a warehouse, or public building, etc. **dwelling place,** a residence.

dwindle, *v.i.* *dwin*-dl, to grow less; to shrink; to waste away; to degenerate; to fall away; to decline. (A.S. *dwinan,* to pine away; to fade.)

dyad, *n.* *dy*-ad, that which consists of two; a couple; a bivalent; an element, atom, or radical: *a.* bivalent [Chem.]. (Gr.)

dyadic, *a.* dy-*ad*-ik, pertaining to the number two; of two parts; pertaining to a dyad.

Dyak, *n.* *dy*-ak, one of the aborigines of Borneo; the language of this race.

dyarchy, *n.* *dy*-ar-ke, government by two elements; diarchy.

dye, *v.t.* dy, to give a new and permanent colour, chiefly to textile materials or fabrics: *n.* colour produced by dyeing; tinge; a colouring liquid. *p.* and *pp.* **dyed** (dide). *ppr.* **dyeing.** (A.S. *deagian.*)

dyeing, *n.* *dy*-ing, the art of the dyer; the process of permanently colouring textile fabrics, etc., with dyes.

dyer, *n.* *dy*-er, one whose occupation is dyeing. **dyer's weed,** *Reseda luteola,* a plant allied to mignonette, from which is obtained a yellow dye. **dyer's greenweed,** the dyer's broom, the woad-waxen, *Genista tinctoria.*

dyestuffs, *n.pl.* *dy*-stuffs, stuffs of mineral or vegetable origin used for dyeing purposes.

dying, *dy*-ing, *pp.* of to die: *a.* about to die; pertaining to death; mortal; given, uttered, or manifested just before death; supporting a dying person: *n.* death.

dyke, *n.* dike, a dike.

dynam, *n.* *dy*-nam, an obsolete term for the foot-pound as a unit of power. (Gr. *dynamis.*)

dynameter, *n.* dy-*nam*-e-ter, an instrument for determining the magnifying power of telescopes [Opt.]. (Gr. *dynamis,* and *meter.*)

dynametrical, *a.* dy-na-*met*-re-kal, pertaining to a dynameter.

dynamic, *a.* dy-*nam*-ik, pertaining to the action or the effect of the action of forces not in equilibrium; pertaining to dynamics; mobile as opposed to static; active; energetic; functional (of diseases).

dynamical, *n.* dy-*nam*-e-kal, dynamical; pertaining to dynamism.

dynamically, *ad.* in a dynamic manner.

dynamics, *n.* dy-*nam*-iks, that branch of mechanics which treats of the action of force, both as producing rest and producing motion; popularly, the division of kinetics which treats of force in relation to motion; force of any kind, as a motive power and its action; the science which treats of the relative force and intensity of notes [Mus.]. (Gr. *dynamis.*)

dynamism, *n.* *dy*-na-mizm, the philosophical doctrine of the universal latency of force; the physical theory that energy is the ultimate physical reality.

dynamitard, *n.* *dy*-na-me-tard, one guilty of the criminal use of dynamite.

dynamite, *n.* *dy*-na-mite, a powerful explosive substance, intensely local in its action, formed by impregnating an absorbent medium, such as siliceous earth, with nitro-glycerine: *v.t.* to use dynamite. (Gr. *dynamis.*)

dynamiter, *n.* *dy*-na-my-ter, one who uses dynamite, esp. illegally as a revolutionist, etc.

dynamitism, *n.* *dy*-na-my-tizm, the proceedings of dynamiters.

dynamo, *n.* *dy*-na-moh, a machine converting mechanical into electrical energy by the inductive action of magnets in rapid motion.

dynamoelectric, *a.* *dy*-na-mo-e-*lek*-trik, pertaining to the conversion of mechanical into electric (or electric into mechanical) energy by induction.
dynamoelectric generator, a dynamo.
dynamograph, *n.* dy-*nam*-o-graf, a recording dynamometer; the record given by this.
dynamometer, *n.* dy-na-*mom*-e-ter, an instrument for measuring force or power, esp. of men, animals, machines, etc. (Gr. *dynamis*, and *meter*.)
dynamometric, *a.* dy-na-mo-*met*-rik, pertaining to dynamometry or the dynamometer.
dynamometry, *n.* dy-na-*mom*-e-tre, the measurement of forces at work.
dynamotor, *n.* *dy*-na-mo-tor, a special form of motor generator that has two armature windings with a single field magnet and that acts both as generator and motor [Elect.].
dynast, *n.* *dy*-nast, a member of a dynasty; a ruler.
dynastic, *a.* dy-*nas*-tik, relating to a dynasty or line of kings.
dynasty, *n.* *din*-a-ste, a race or succession of kings of the same line or family. (Gr. *dynastes.*)
dyne, *n.* dine, the unit for measuring force, *i.e.*, the force which, acting on one gramme, will give it an acceleration of one centimetre per second.
dys-, dis, a Greek prefix, signifying ill, bad, difficult.
dysæsthesia, *n.* dis-es-*thee*-ze-a, impaired sensation; a tendency to insensibility [Med.]. (Gr. *dys-*, and *aisthanomai*, perceive.)
dyschroa, *n.* *dis*-kro-a, a discoloured state of the skin; bad complexion. (Gr. *dys-*, and *chroa*, skin.)
dyschronous, *a.* *dis*-kro-nus, separate in time; not synchronous.
dyscrasia, *n.* dis-*kray*-ze-a, an ill habit or state of the constitution. (Gr. *dys-*, and *krasis*, mixture.)
dysenteric, *a.* dis-en-*te*-rik, pertaining to dysentery; accompanied with, proceeding from, or afflicted with dysentery.
dysentery, *n.* *dis*-en-te-re, a disease attended by fever with discharges from the bowels, chiefly of blood and mucus, or other morbid matter, accompanied with griping and tenesmus. (Gr. *dys-*, *enteron*, intestine.)
dysgenic, *a.* dis-*jen*-ik, tending to cause racial degeneration; injurious to hereditary qualities [Biol.].
dyslogistic, *a.* dis-lo-*jis*-tik, implying condemnation; disparaging; censorious; the reverse of eulogistic. (Gr. *dys-*, and *lego*, say.)
dyslogistically, *ad.* in a disapproving manner.
dysluite, *n.* *dis*-lew-ite, a brown spinel consisting of zinc, manganese, and iron.
dysmenorrhœa, *n.* *dis*-men-o-*ree*-a, difficult or painful menstruation. (Gr. *dys-*, *men*, a month, *rheo*, flow.)
dysodile, *n.* *dis*-o-dile, a species of lignite burning with an exceedingly fetid odour. (Gr. *dysodēs*, ill-smelling.)
dyspepsia, *n.* dis-*pep*-se-a, indigestion, due to functional derangement of the stomach, of a painful and usually chronic nature. (L. *dyspepsia.*)
dyspeptic, *a.* dis-*pep*-tik, afflicted with dyspepsia; pertaining to or consisting of dyspepsia: *n.* a person afflicted with dyspepsia.
dysphagia, *n.* dis-*fay*-je-a, difficulty in swallowing.
dysphony, *n.* *dis*-fo-ne, a difficulty in speaking due to disease or malformation of the vocal organs. (Gr. *dys-*, and *phone*, the voice.)
dysphoria, *n.* dis-*for*-re-a, nervous restlessness; the fidgets. (Gr. *dys-*, and *phero*, bear.)
dyspnœa, *n.* disp-*nee*-a, difficulty in breathing. (Gr. *dys-*, and *pneo*, breathe.)
dyspnoic, *n.* disp-*noh*-ik, affected or connected with dyspnœa.
dysprosia, *n.* dis-*proh*-ze-a, oxide of dysprosium.
dysprosium, *n.* dis-*proh*-ze-um, a metallic element of the rare earth group discovered in holmium in 1886.
dystomous, *a.* *dis*-to-mus, having an imperfect fracture [Min.]. (Gr. *dys-*, and *tome*, cutting.)
dysury, *n.* *dis*-yewr-re, difficulty of voiding the urine; a morbid condition of that fluid. (Gr. *dys-*, and *ouron* urine.)
Dytiscus, *n.* dy-*tis*-kus, a genus of water-beetles. (Gr. *dytikos*, liking to dive.)
dyvour, *n.* *div*-oor, a debtor who makes cession or assignment of all his effects to escape imprisonment [Scots. Law]. (Origin unknown.)
dzeron, *n.* *dze*-ron, a goat-like antelope of Mongolia *Procapra gutturosa.* (Native name.)
dziggetai, *n.* *dzig*-ge-ty, the wild ass of Central Asia *Equus hemionus.* (Mongol, long-eared.)

E

E is the second vowel, and the fifth letter, of the English alphabet, and in more frequent use than any other letter. Its long and natural sound in English, as in *here, me,* coincides with the sound of *i* in the Italian and French languages. It also has a short sound, as in *met, men*; the sound of open *a*, as in *prey, vein,* that of the long *a* of *bare*, as in *there*, and the indeterminate sound heard in the final syllable of *banner, feather.* As a final letter, it is generally silent and serves to lengthen the sound of the preceding vowel, as in *mane, cone, plume.* After *c* and *g*, the final *e* serves to indicate that *c* is to be pronounced as *s*, and *g* as *j*. In music it is the third note of the diatonic scale, corresponding to *me* (Italian *mi*).

e-, *pref.* a form of ex-, as in *elicit, evict.*

each, *a.* eech, every one of any number separately considered. (A.S. *ælc.*)

eadish, *n. ee*-dish, eddish.

eager, *a. ee*-ger, excited by ardent desire to possess or to do; ardent; vehement; earnest; keen, bitter (of cold). (Fr. *aigre*, from L. *acer*, sharp.)

eagerly, *ad.* with ardent desire; in an eager manner.

eagerness, *n.* ardent desire; zeal; avidity.

eagle, *n. ee*-gl, any diurnal bird of prey of the genus *Aquila*, of which there are several species including *Aquila chrysaëtus*, the golden eagle, *A. heliaca*, the imperial eagle, *A. maculata* and *A. clanga*, the spotted eagles, and *A. rapax* and *A. vindhiana*, the tawny eagles; other genera include the sea eagles, one of which, *Haliaëtus leucocephalus*, is the emblem of U.S.A., the buzzard, harrier, and crested eagles, with others, most being of large size with great strength, powers of flight, and keenness of vision; a military standard surmounted by an eagle; in heraldry an emblem of magnanimity and fortitude; a gold coin of U.S.A., of the value of ten dollars; a lectern or church reading-desk in the form of an eagle; a hole played in two strokes under bogey [Golf]; the constellation Aquila, in the northern hemisphere [Astron.]. (Fr. *aigle*, from L. *aquila.*)

eagle-eyed, *a. ee*-gl-ide, sharp-sighted as an eagle; acutely discerning.

eagle-owl, *n.* the great horned owl, *Bubo ignavus.*

eagle-ray, *n.* a large sting-ray of the family *Myliobatis*, also called the devil-fish.

eagle-stone, *n.* a variety of argillaceous iron-ore in the form of nodules, which often contain loose kernels that rattle within.

eaglet, *n. ee*-glet, a young or diminutive eagle.

eagle-wood, *n. ee*-gl-wood, agalloch, a fragrant wood used for burning as incense.

eagre, *n. ee*-ger, a tide rising high in an estuary; a bore, as in the Severn and Solway. (Origin unknown.)

ean, *v.t.* or *v.i.* een, to bring forth (esp. of sheep); to lamb. (A.S. *eanian*, bring forth.)

eanling, *n. een*-ling, a lamb just brought forth.

★**ear**, *n.* eer, the organ of hearing, including the external, the middle, and the internal ear; the sense of hearing; the power of distinguishing sounds and judging of harmony; a favourable hearing; attention; manner of judging; an appendage like an external ear. **all ears**, eagerly attentive. **over head and ears, up to the ears**, deeply. **to be by the ears, to fall** or **go together by the ears**, to fight or scuffle; to quarrel. **to set by the ears**, to make strife; to cause to quarrel. (A.S. *ēare*, L. *auris*, ear.)

ear, *n.* eer, a spike or head of corn. (A.S. *ēar*, L. *acus, aceris*, a corn-husk.)

ear, *v.i.* eer, to form ears, as corn. (A.S. *erian*, to plough.)

earache, *n. eer*-ake, pain in drum of the ear.

ear-cap, *n.* a cover for the ears against cold.

ear-drop, *n.* a jewel hanging from the ear.

ear-drum, *n.* the tympanic membrane of the middle ear.

eared, *a.* eerd, having ears.

ear-hole, *n.* the opening of the external ear.

earing, *n. eer*-ring, a rope attached to the cringle of a sail, by which it is bent or reefed; a rope at the upper corner of a sail [Naut.].

earl, *n.* erl, a British nobleman, the third in rank, being next below a marquis, and next above a viscount; the oldest title in the peerage. **Earl Marshal**, one of the great officers of state, the head of the College of Arms, an office hereditary (since 1672) in the family of Howard, Dukes of Norfolk. (A.S. *eorl*; Ice. *jarl*, a strong man, a hero.)

earlap, *n. eer*-lap, the lobe of the ear.

earldom, *n. erl*-dum, the rank, title, or dignity of an earl, and formerly his seignory and jurisdiction.

earless, *a. eer*-less, having no ears.

earliness, *n. erl*-e-ness, a state of advance or forwardness.

★**early**, *a. erl*-e, in advance of something else; prior in time; forward; at or near the beginning; in good season: *ad.* soon; in good season; betimes. (A.S. *ærlice*, before.)

earmark, *n. eer*-mark, a mark on the ear, by which a sheep is known; any mark to identify: *v.t.* to mark, as a sheep, by cropping or slitting the ear; to mark or to set aside for a special purpose.

earn, *v.t.* ern, to merit or deserve by labour, service, or performance; to acquire by such means. (A.S. *earnian.*)

earnest, *a. ern*-est, ardent in the pursuit of an object; eager; urgent; intent; zealous; serious; real: *n.* seriousness; reality; a serious object. (A.S. *eornost*, earnestness.)

earnest, *n. ern*-est, a pledge or assurance of something more to come; a foretaste; earnest-money. (O.Fr. *erres*, L. *arrha.*)

earnestly, *ad. ern*-est-le, in an earnest manner.

earnest-money, *n. ern*-est-*mun*-ne, money paid as a pledge, or to close a bargain.

earnestness, *n. ern*-est-ness, the state of being earnest or in earnest.

earnings, *n.pl. ern*-ingz, that which is earned; wages; reward.

earphone, *n. eer*-fone, a headphone.

earpick, *n. eer*-pik, a small scoop for clearing wax from the ear.

ear-piercing, *a.* piercing the ear, as a shrill or sharp sound.

ear-plug, *n.* a small plug for insertion in the ear-hole to protect the aural organs from damage by impulse noises such as bomb explosions; an ornament worn by some primitive peoples in the lobe of the ear.

ear-ring, *n. eer*-ring, a pendant, sometimes jewelled, worn at the ear by means of a ring passing through, or screwed on to, the lobe.

ear-shell, *n.* the shell of the sea-ear.

earshot, *n. eer*-shot, hearing distance.

★**earth**, *n.* erth, the planet we inhabit; the soil we cultivate; any indefinite mass or portion of that soil; dry land opposed to the sea; the ground; a circuit connexion with the earth [Elect. and Wire.]; a fox's hole; a low condition: *v.t.* to cover with earth; to drive (a fox) to earth; to connect with the earth [Elect.]: *v.i.* to retire underground; to burrow. (A.S. *eorthe.*)

earth-board, *n.* the board of a plough that turns over the soil; the mould-board.

earth-born, *a.* born on the earth; terrigenous; mortal; earthly.

earth-bound, *a.* firmly fastened in the earth; given over to mundane interests; restrained from leaving this world (of disembodied spirits).

earth-bred, *a.* low; abject; grovelling.

earthen, *a. erth*-en, made of earth or of clay; frail.

earthenware, *n. erth*-en-ware, domestic vessels made of earth; crockery; pottery of the coarser kinds.

earth-fall, *n. erth*-fawl, a landslide

earth-flax, *n. erth*-flaks, amianthus, a fine variety of asbestos.

earth-hog, *n.* the aard-vark.
earth-house, *n. erth*-house, a prehistoric earth-covered structure built of unhewn stones.
earthiness, *n. erth*-e-ness, the quality of being earthy; grossness.
earth-light, *n.* earth-shine.
earthliness, *n.* the quality of being earthly.
earthling, *n. erth*-ling, an inhabitant of the earth; a mortal; a worldly person.
earthly, *a. erth*-le, pertaining to or connected with the earth or this world; belonging to our present state; carnal, as opposed to spiritual or heavenly; mean; corporeal, not mental; possible [Coll.].
earthly-minded, *a. erth*-le-*myn*-ded, having a mind devoted to earthly things or interests.
earth-nut, *n.* the tuber of a plant of the genus *Conopodium*; the pig-nut (a species of *Bunium*), ground-nut (*Apios*), peanut (*Arachis* or similar leguminous plant); the truffle.
earth-pea, *n.* the peanut.
earth-plate, *n.* a plate attached to electric apparatus to connect it with the earth.
earthquake, *n. erth*-kwake, a shaking, trembling, or convulsion of the earth's crust due to subterranean agency.
earth-shine, *n.* the light reflected from the earth by which that part of the new moon not illuminated by the sun is rendered faintly visible.
earth-smoke, *n. erth*-smoke, the plant fumitory.
earthward, *ad. erth*-ward, towards the earth.
earthwork, *n. erth*-wurk, a cutting or embankment of earth [Eng.]; a fortification of earth [Mil.].
earthworm, *n. erth*-wurm, a worm that lives in the ground, esp. one of the genus *Lumbricus*; a mean sordid wretch [Coll.].
earthy, *a, erth*-e, consisting of, resembling, or relating to earth; lifeless as earth; gross; not refined or spiritual; without lustre [Min.].
ear-trumpet, *n.* a trumpet-shaped tube applied to the ear to aid defective hearing.
ear-wax, *n.* the waxy substance secreted by the glands of the ear into the outer passage; cerumen.
earwig, *n. eer*-wig, an orthopterous insect of the genus *Forficula*; one who gains the confidence of a person by whispering insinuations; a prying informer: *v.t.* to gain by whispering insinuations about others. (A.S. *ēarwicga.*)
ease, *n.* eez, an undisturbed state; a quiet state or state of comfort; freedom from pain or disturbance; rest; facility; naturalness; unconstraint. **at ease,** in an undisturbed state; free from pain or anxiety.
ease, *v.t.* eez, to relieve, calm, or tranquillize; to free from pain or any disquiet or annoyance of body or mind; to assuage; to facilitate; to slacken: *v.i.* to relax one's efforts. **ease a ship,** to put the helm hard a-lee to prevent her pitching when close-hauled [Naut.]. **ease off,** or **away,** to slacken a rope gradually [Naut.]. **ill at ease,** in a state of disquiet, esp. mentally. **stand at ease,** a command to relax from the position of attention by placing the feet apart and the hands behind the back [Mil.]. (Fr. *aise.*)
easeful, *a. eez*-ful, quiet; peaceful; fit for rest.
easefully, *ad. eez*-ful-le, with ease or quiet.
easefulness, *n. eez*-ful-ness, state of being easeful.
easel, *n. ee*-zel, the frame on which painters place their pictures while painting them; the frame used for supporting a blackboard, a book, etc. **easel pieces,** pictures of such size as to have been painted on an easel. (Dut. *ezel,* a donkey.)
easeless, *a. eez*-less, wanting ease.
easement, *n. eez*-ment, that which gives ease, relief, or assistance; any privilege or convenience which one man has of another without profit, either by prescription or charter, as a way through his land, etc. [Law]. (O.Fr. *aisement.*)
easily, *ad. ee*-ze-le, in an easy manner.
easiness, *n. ee*-ze-ness, the state of being easy.
★**east,** *n.* eest, the compass-point at right angles to a line drawn from north to south; the point in the heavens where the sun rises only at the equinox; the quarter which ranges from the north-east to the south-east; the eastern parts of the earth, specially the countries which lie east of Europe; the east wind: *ad.* towards the rising sun or the east: *a.* situated in or proceeding from this direction. **Far East,** China and Japan. **Middle East,** the Levant to Persia, inclusive (and, for some purposes, Egypt). **Near East,** Turkey and the Balkan States (with sometimes the western parts of the Middle East). (A.S. *ēast, ad.* in the east.)
East-End, *n. eest*-end, the slum portions of a town, esp. the districts of London lying east of the city: *a.* pertaining to the above.
Easter, *n. eest*-er, a festival in commemoration of the resurrection of Christ, corresponding to the Passover and festivals of greater antiquity as marking the end of winter and beginning of spring. **Easter Day,** the first Sunday after the full moon happening on or next after 21 March, the vernal equinox. **Easter egg,** a painted or an artificial egg containing a present, given at Easter. **Easter lily,** any of several pure white and fragrant lilies, esp. the Madonna (*Lilium candidum*) or the Bermuda (*L. longiflorum eximium*) lily. **Easter offerings,** voluntary gifts to the clergy at Easter. **Easter term,** one of the four terms during which the superior courts are open, in April and May; a university term extending to some six weeks after Easter. **Easter week,** the week beginning on Easter Day. (A.S. *eastre,* from *Eostre,* goddess of spring.)
Easter-eve, *n.* the day before Easter Day.
Easterling, *n. eest*-er-ling, a native of a country lying east; mediæval trader from the House towns or from the Baltic shore.
easterly, *a. eest*-er-le, coming from the eastward; towards the eastward: *ad.* on the east; in an easterly direction.
eastern, *a. eest*-ern, oriental; being or dwelling in the East; towards the east: *n.* an Oriental; a member of the Orthodox Church. **Eastern Church,** the Orthodox Church. **Eastern Empire,** the Byzantine Empire (A.S. *ēasterne.*)
Easterner, *n. east*-er-ner, a dweller in the East, esp. [U.S.A.] in the Eastern or New England States.
easternmost, *a. eest*-ern-most, most easterly.
Eastertide, *n. eest*-er-tide, the week after Easter Sunday.
easting, *n. eest*-ing, the course east of any meridian; distance traversed on such a course; movement eastward.
eastward, *ad. eest*-ward, towards the east quarter.
easy, *a. ee*-ze, at ease; free from pain, disturbance, or annoyance; free from anxiety, care, solicitude, or embarrassment; causing no pain or discomfort; not difficult or arduous; moderate; yielding with little or no resistance; ready; comfortable; freeing from care or fatigue; affluent; unconstrained; flowing; not jolting; not heavy or burdensome.
easy-chair, *n.* a comfortable arm-chair.
easy-going, *a.* taking things easily; lax; careless; moving easily.
eat, *v.t.* eet, to bite or chew and swallow, as food; to corrode or gnaw away; to consume; to oppress; to enjoy; to feast: *v.i.* to take food; to gnaw; to taste. **eat in,** or **into,** to wear away by gnawing or corrosion. **eat one's terms,** to study for the English bar, so said as the student has to eat so many dinners each term in the public hall of the legal body to which he attaches himself. **eat one's words,** to take back or retract what has been uttered. *p.* **ate.** *pp.* **eaten.** (A.S. *etan.*)
eatable, *a. eet*-a-bl, fit to be eaten: *n.* anything that is fit for food; *pl.* the solid portions of a meal.
eatage, *n. eet*-aj, green fodder, esp. that from the aftermath.
eater, *n. eet*-er, one who or that which eats or corrodes.
eating-house, *n.* a cook-shop; a cheap restaurant.
eats, *n.pl.* eets, food, grub [Slang].
eau, *n.* oh, water. **Eau de Cologne,** a perfume prepared (originally at Cologne) by distillation from certain essential oils with rectified spirit. **Eau de Javelle,** an aqueous solution made by passing chlorine through a solution of a caustic alkali, used for bleaching and as an antiseptic and disinfectant. **eau de Nil,** a yellowish-green colour. **eau de vie,** aqua vitæ, brandy. **eau sucrée,** sweetened water. (Fr. *eau,* water.)
eaves, *n.pl.* eevz, the lower border of the roof of a building, which overhangs the walls and casts off the water that falls on the roof. (A.S. *efes.*)
eaves-board, *n.* the board placed along the lower ends of the rafters to keep the slates flat.
eavesdrop, *n. eevz*-drop, the water which drops from the eaves of a house: *v.i.* to listen under the eaves or near the windows of a house to what is said within; to watch for opportunities of overhearing private conversations.

eavesdropper, *n.* *eevz*-drop-per, one who surreptitiously listens to private conversations.
ebb, *n.* eb, the return of the tide to the sea; decline; decay: *v.i.* to flow back; to recede; to decay; to decline. (A.S. *ebba.*)
ebb-tide, *n.* *eb*-tide, the ebbing tide.
Ebionite, *n.* *ee*-be-on-ite, a member of a Judaizing sect of the Christian Church of the first two centuries A.D., consisting of Jewish converts: *a.* pertaining to this sect or its heresy. (Heb. *ebionim*, the poor, a Jewish designation of the Christians.)
Eblis, *n.* *eb*-lis, the chief of the fallen angels; the Mohammedan Satan. (Ar. *Iblis.*)
ebon, *a.* *eb*-on, consisting of or like ebony; black.
ebonite, *n.* *eb*-on-ite, a variety of vulcanite.
ebonize, *v.t.* *eb*-on-ize, to make black in imitation of ebony.
ebony, *n.* *eb*-on-e, the popular name of various trees of the genus *Diospryos*, and esp. of their wood, most of which are hard, heavy, durable, and susceptible of a fine polish, the most highly prized being of a black colour. **American ebony**, the granadilla tree: *a.* very black; made of ebony. (Fr. *ebène.*)
éboulement, *n.* (App.) the crumbling or falling of a wall [Fort.]; a sudden fall of rock in mountainous country [Geol.]. (Fr.)
ebracteate, *a.* ee-*brak*-te-at, without a bract [Bot.]. (L. *e-*, and *bractea*, a thin plate.)
ebriety, *n.* e-*bry*-e-te, drunkenness. (L. *ebrius*, drunk.)
ebriosity, *n.* ee-bre-*os*-e-te, habitual drunkenness.
ebrious, *a.* *ee*-bre-us, drunk; addicted to, or characteristic of, drunkenness.
ebullience, *n.* e-*bul*-yens, a boiling over; exuberancy; enthusiasm. (L. *ebulliens*, boiling up.)
ebulliency, *n.* e-*bul*-yen-se, ebullience.
ebullient, *a.* e-*bul*-yent, boiling over, as a liquor; exuberant.
ebullioscope, *n.* e-*bul*-e-o-skope, an instrument for determining the boiling-point and atmospheric pressure of distilled liquors.
ebullition, *n.* *eb*-oo-*lish*-on, the action of boiling; the bubbling agitation of a liquor by heat; effervescence occasioned by fermentation; a sudden outburst or display of feeling. (Late L. *ebullitio.*)
eburnation, *n.* ee-bur-*nay*-shon, in an abnormal deposition of osseous matter, chiefly in the joints [Med.]. (L. *ebur*, ivory.)
eburnean, *n.* e-*bur*-ne-an, relating to, of the nature of, or made of, ivory.
eburnification, *n.* ee-*bur*-ne-fe-*kay*-shon, the imparting to substances the appearance of ivory; a diseased condition in which the bones become hard and dense like ivory. (L. *ebur*, ivory, *facio*, make.)
eburnine, *a.* *eb*-ur-nin, eburnean.
ec-, the prefix *ex-* before words in *c-*.
écarté, *n.* ay-*kahr*-tay, a game at cards played by two with the 32 cards comprising 7 to King. (Fr.)
ecaudate, *a.* e-*kaw*-dat, without a tail [Zool.]; spikeless, without a stem [Bot.]. (L. *e-*, and *cauda*, a tail.)
ecbasis, *n.* *ek*-ba-sis, treatment of things according to their events or consequences [Rhet.]. (Gr. *ekbasis*, going out.)
ecbatic, *a.* ek-*bat*-ik, stating a consequence or result as distinct from an intention [Gram.].
ecbole, *n.* *ek*-bo-le, a digression [Rhet.]. (Gr. *ekbōle*, a casting out.)
ecbolic, *a.* ek-*bol*-ik, stimulating parturition by causing uterine contractions: *n.* a medicine with this effect [Med.].
Ecce Homo, *ek*-se-*hoh*-mo, a representation of Christ as he appeared before Pilate crowned with thorns. (L., Behold the Man.)
eccentric, *a.* ek-*sen*-trik, deviating or departing from the centre; said of not having, or revolving round, the centre, esp. of circles or spheres which are contained in some measure within each other; not terminating in the same point, nor directed by the same principle; deviating from established forms or rules; odd; anomalous; whimsical: *n.* a circle or wheel with its axis not in its centre; one who or that which is irregular or anomalous; eccentric gear. **eccentric gear**, the mechanism by which circular motion is converted into reciprocating rectilinear motion. (Gr. *ekkentros.*)
eccentrically, *ad.* ek-*sen*-tre-ka-le, with eccentricity; in an eccentric manner.
eccentricity, *n.* *ek*-sen-*tris*-e-te, deviation from a centre; the state of having a centre different from that of another circle; the distance of the centre of a planet's orbit from the centre of the sun [Astron.]; departure or deviation from that which is stated, regular, or usual; singularity of conduct.
eccentric-rod, *n.*, the rod transmitting the motion of an eccentric wheel.
eccentric-strap, *n.* the steel band grasping the circumference of an eccentric wheel within which it revolves.
eccentric-wheel, *n.* a wheel the axis of whose revolution is not in the centre.
ecchymosis, *n.* ek-e-*moh*-sis, an appearance of livid spots or areas on the skin, occasioned by the effusion of extravasated blood [Med.]. (Gr.)
ecclesia, *n.* ek-*klee*-ze-a, an assembly of free citizens in Athens; a church. (L., an assembly.)
ecclesiarch, *n.* ek-*klee*-ze-ark, a ruler of the Church. (L. *ecclesia*, and Gr. *arche*, rule.)
ecclesiastic, *n.* e-*klee*-ze-*as*-tik, one in orders or consecrated to the service of the Church and ministry of religion; a clergyman: *a.* ecclesiastical.
ecclesiastical, *a.* e-*klee*-ze-*ast*-ik-al, relating or pertaining to the Church or the body of the clergy. **Ecclesiastical Commissioners**, members of the Ecclesiastical and Church Estates Commission, a permanent body incorporated in 1836 and having the management of all property vested in the Church of England. **ecclesiastical courts**, the courts in which the canon law is administered, and spiritual causes determined; courts in Presbyterian churches that determine doctrine and discipline. **ecclesiastical music**, compositions written for the Church, esp. anthems, services, masses, and other cathedral music. **Ecclesiastical States**, the territories once subject to the Pope. **ecclesiastical year**, the year beginning with the season of Advent. (Late L. *ecclesiasticus.*)
ecclesiastically, *ad.* in an ecclesiastical manner.
ecclesiolatry, *n.* e-*klee*-ze-*ol*-a-tre, excessive veneration for church forms. (Gr. *ekklesia*, and *latreia*, worship.)
ecclesiological, *a.* e-*klee*-ze-o-*loj*-e-kal, pertaining ecclesiology.
ecclesiologist, *n.* e-*klee*-ze-*ol*-o-jist, one versed in ecclesiology.
ecclesiology, *n.* e-*klee*-ze-*ol*-o-je, the science of ecclesiastical art, and antiquities (Gr. *ekklesia*, and *logos*, science.)
ecdemic, *a.* ek-*dem*-ik, due to an outside source; not endemic [Med.]. (Gr. *ek-*, out, *demos*, people.)
ecdysis, *n.* ek-*dy*-sis, the act of casting off of the skin; moulting [Zool.]. (Gr.)
echelon, *n.* *esh*-e-lon, the arrangement of troops like a flight of steps in plan, each of the parallel lines of units overlapping that to the rear [Mil.]; such an arrangement generally, as of ships, etc. (Fr.)
echidna, *n.* e-*kid*-na, the spiny anteater, *Echidna aculeata*, an egg-laying mammal peculiar to Australia, resembling the hedgehog. (Gr., a viper.)
echinate, *a.* *ek*-in-at, set with prickles, like a hedgehog; prickly. (Gr. *echinos*, a hedgehog.)
echinidan, *n.* e-*kin*-e-dan, a sea-urchin. (Gr. *echinos*, and *eidos*, like.)
echinite, *n.* *ek*-e-nite, a fossil sea-urchin.
Echinocactus, *n.* e-*ky*-no-*kak*-tus, an American genus of plants of the cactus order, so called on account of the arrangement of their spines. (Gr.)
echinococcus, *n.* e-*ky*-no-*kok*-us, the larva of the small tapeworm.
echinoderm, *n.* e-*kin*- *or* e-*ky*-no-derm, one of the Echinodermata, a group of marine animals including the starfish and sea-urchins. (Gr. *echinos*, and *derma*, skin.)
echinoid, *a.* e-*ky*-noyd *or* *ek*-e-noyd, like or pertaining to the sea-urchins: *n.* a sea-urchin.
echinus, *n.* e-*ky*-nus, the sea-urchin [Zool.]; a prickly head or top of a plant [Bot.]; an ornament, called "the egg and tongue," or "the egg and anchor" ornament, carved on the ovolo, esp. in classical architecture [Arch.].
echo, *n.* *ek*-ko, a sound reflected or reverberated from a solid body; repetition of sound or of what is said; reflection of sound or radar waves; a vault or arch for redoubling sounds [Arch.]; the repetition of a melodic phrase [Mus.]; an echo-stop on the organ: *v.i.* to resound; to reflect sound; to be sounded back: *v.t.* to send back the sound of; to repeat what has been uttered. (Gr., sound.)

echoic, *a.* e-*koh*-ik, of the nature of an echo; onomatopœic.
echoism, *n.* *ek*-ko-ism, formation of words from sounds associated with the object indicated.
echoless, *n.* *ek*-ko-less, destitute of an echo.
echometer, *n.* e-*kom*-e-ter, an instrument for measuring the duration of sounds with the intervals and ratios [Mus.]. (Gr. *echo*, and *metron*, measure.)
éclair, *n.* ay-klare, a finger-shaped kind of sweet cake and cream, coated with chocolate. (Fr.)
éclaircissement, *n.* (App.), explanation; the clearing up of anything not before understood. (Fr.)
eclampsia, *n.* ek-*lamp*-se-a, a sudden attack of convulsions, esp. during pregnancy. (Gr. *eklampsis*, a shining forth.)
éclat, *n.* ay-*klah*, striking success; a burst of applause; acclamation; splendour; renown. (Fr.)
eclectic, *a.* e-*klek*-tik, selecting; choosing and adopting from the views of others what seems good: *n.* a philosopher who adopts from various systems such doctrines as he deems sound and rational (originally one who, having no system of his own, selected from Plato and Aristotle); one who, recognizing an element of truth in all systems, collects a new one out of the whole; an artist who seeks to combine in his work the various excellencies of the Old Masters. (Gr. *eklektikos*.)
eclectically, *ad.* ek-*lek*-te-ka-le, in the manner of the eclectic philosophers.
eclecticism, *n.* ek-*lek*-te-sizm, the practice of selecting from different sources.
eclipse, *n.* e-*klips*, an interception of the light of the sun, moon, or other luminary by the intervention of some opaque body, as of that of the sun by the intervention of the moon, or that of the moon by the shadow of the earth; occultation; obscuration; darkness: *v.t.* to hide a luminous body in whole or in part; to obscure; to darken; to disgrace; to extinguish: *v.i.* to suffer an eclipse. **annular eclipse,** one of the sun by the moon in which a ring of light is left round the shadow. **eclipse of the moon,** one in which the earth passes between the sun and the moon. **eclipse of the sun,** one in which the moon passes between the sun and the earth. **eclipse year,** the sun's time between its departure from a node and its return to it, 346·62 days. (O.Fr. from Gr.)
ecliptic, *n.* e-*klip*-tik, a great circle of the sphere, supposed to be drawn through the middle of the zodiac, making an angle with the equinoctial of about 23° 27′ 8″, which is the sun's greatest declination; the apparent path of the sun round the earth, from west to east, but in reality the path which the earth, as viewed from the sun, appears to describe among the fixed stars [Astron.]; a great circle on the terrestrial globe, answering to and falling within the plane of the celestial ecliptic [Geog.]: *a.* pertaining to or described by the ecliptic; pertaining to an eclipse. **ecliptic limits,** the greatest distances at which the moon can be from her nodes, in order that an eclipse of the sun or moon may happen. (Late L. *eclipticus*.)
eclogue, *n.* *ek*-log, a pastoral poem, esp. one in which shepherds converse. (L. *ecloga*.)
ecmnesia, *n.* ek-*mnee*-ze-a, loss of memory in relation to certain periods, circumstances, or events [Path.]. (Gr. *ek*-, out, *mnesis*, memory.)
ecological, *a.* ee-ko-*loj*-e-kal, pertaining to the natural surroundings of an organism [Biol.].
ecology, *n.* ee-*kol*-o-je, the study of the reciprocal relationship between organisms and their surroundings. (Gr. *oikos*, home, *logos*, science.)
economic, *a.* ee-ko-*nom*-ik, relating to economics; pertaining to commerce or industry; utilitarian; economical.
economical, *a.* ee-ko-*nom*-e-kal, pertaining to, managing with, or regulated by, economy; thrifty; frugal; relating to economics.
economically, *ad.* ee-ko-*nom*-e-ka-le, with economy.
economics, *n.* ee-ko-*nom*-iks, political economy; the study of the laws of production, distribution, and exchange of wealth; the science of wealth, its distribution, etc., in its relationship with social conditions. (L. *œconomicus*.)
economist, *n.* e-*kon*-o-mist, one skilled in or conversant with economics; one who manages with economy.
economization, *n.* e-*kon*-o-my-*zay*-shon, the act or practice of economizing.
economize, *v.i.* e-*kon*-o-mize, to manage pecuniary concerns with frugality; to reduce expenditure; to save: *v.t.* to use with prudence; to expend with frugality.
economizer, *n.* e-*kon*-o-*my*-zer, any apparatus that utilizes power, heat, etc., that would otherwise run to waste [Mech.]
economy, *n.* e-*kon*-o-me, the management of the concerns of a household, especially in money matters; a frugal and judicious use of money; distribution or due order of things; judicious and frugal management of public affairs; the regulation and disposition of the affairs of a state or nation, or of any department of government; the disposition or arrangement of any work; a system of rules and ceremonies; the regular operations of nature in the generation, nutrition, and preservation of animals or plants. (L. *œconomia*.)
écorché, *n.* ay-*kawr*-shay, an anatomical figure with the muscles, etc., exposed for the purpose of study by art students. (Fr., flayed.)
écossaise, *n.* ay-kos-*sayz*, a country dance of Scottish origin; music for this. (Fr.)
ecostate, *a.* e-*kos*-tat, having no central rib, said of leaves [Bot.], (L. *e*-, and *costa*, a rib.)
écraseur, *n.* ay-*kray*-zoor, a surgical instrument for removing diseased parts with only slight risk of hæmorrhage. (Fr. *écraser*, to crush.)
écru, *a.* ek-*roo*, beige or pale yellowish brown; of the colour of unbleached linen: *n.* this colour; cloth, etc., of this colour. (Fr.)
ecstasy, *n.* *ek*-sta-se, a state of mind in which the functions of the senses are suspended by the contemplation of some extraordinary or supernatural object; rapture or a degree of delight that arrests the whole mind; enthusiasm or excessive elevation and absorption of mind; exaltation; trance; a species of catalepsy, when the person remembers, after the paroxysm is over, the ideas he had during the fit [Med.]. (Gr. *ek*-, out, *histemi*, make to stand.)
ecstasize, *v.t.* and *i.* *ek*-sta-size, to go into, or cause to go into, ecstasies.
ecstatic, *a.* ek-*stat*-ik, causing ecstasy; proceeding from ecstasy; amounting to ecstasy; rapturous; delightful beyond measure.
ecstatically, *ad.* ek-*stat*-e-ka-le, in an ecstatic manner.
ecthyma, *n.* ek-*thy*-ma, an eruption of pimples on the skin [Med.]. (Gr.)
ecto-, *pref.* *ek*-to-, outside. (Gr.)
ectoblast, *n.* *ek*-to-blast, the epiblast [Zool.].
ectoderm, *n.* *ek*-to-derm, an outer layer of the embryo; the outer integumentary layer and tissues derived from it. (Gr. *ektos*, and *derma*, skin.)
ectophyte, *n.* *ek*-to-fyt, a vegetable ectozoon [Bot.].
ectopia, *n.* ek-*toh*-pe-a, the displacement of an organ from its normal position [Med.]. (Gr. *ek*-, and *topos*, a place.)
ectoplasm, *n.* *ek*-to-plazm, the outer layer of protoplasm in a cell; the emanation said by spiritualists to proceed from the body of a medium and to form to material basis of spirit faces, etc.
ectozoon, *n.* ek-to-*zoh*-on (*pl.* **ectozoa**), a parasite that lives on the external parts of other animals. (Gr. *ektos*, and *zoon*, an animal.)
ectropion, *n.* ek-*troh*-pe-on, an everted condition of the eyelid [Med.]. (Gr.)
ectypal, *a.* ek-*tipe*-al, of the nature of an ectype; taken from the original.
ectype, *n.* *ek*-tipe, a copy as distinct from an original; a cast [Sculp.]. (L. *ectypus*.)
ectypography, *n.* ek-te-*pog*-ra-fe, etching with the lines in relief. (Gr. *ectype*, and *grapho*, write.)
ecumenical, *a.* ee-kew-*men*-e-kal, general; universal; catholic (applied esp. to twenty councils that represented the whole of the Catholic Church). (Gr. *oikoumenikos*, from *oikoumene*, the inhabited globe.)
ecumenicity, *n.* *ee*-kew-me-*nis*-e-te, the state or quality of being ecumenical; catholicity.
eczema, *n.* *ek*-ze-ma, a skin disease characterized by an eruption of small vesicles with a watery discharge [Med.]. (Gr.)
eczematous, *a.* ek-*zee*-ma-tus, pertaining to or having the characteristics of eczema.
edacious, *a.* e-*day*-shus, given to eating; greedy; voracious. (L. *edo*, eat.)
edacity, *n.* e-*das*-e-te, greediness; voracity.

Edam, *n.* *ee*-dam, a spherical Dutch cheese. (From *Edam*, Holland.)
Edda, *n.* *ed*-da, a collection made in Iceland of primitive songs or chants consisting chiefly of tales of the gods and heroes of Scandinavian mythology (the Elder Edda); also a synopsis in prose of later date (the Younger Edda). (Ice.)
eddish, *n.* *ed*-dish, the latter pasture of grass that comes after mowing or reaping; a stubble field.
eddo, *n.* *ed*-do, a species of taro, or its edible tuber. (Probably W. African.)
eddy, *n.* *ed*-de, a current of water or air circling back, or in the direction contrary to the main stream; a slight whirlpool or whirlwind: *v.t.* and *i.* to move circularly or as an eddy. (Ice. *itha*, a whirlpool.)
eddy-water, *n.* *ed*-de-*waw*-ter, the water which falls back on the rudder of a ship under sail; dead-water [Naut.].
edelweiss, *n.* *ay*-del-vice, the Swiss plant, *Leontopodium alpinum*; any of the species of *Gnaphalium*. (Ger.)
edematous, *n.* e-*dem*-a-tus, œdematous.
Eden, *n.* *ee*-den, the Paradise of Adam and Eve; a delightful region; a state of perfect bliss. (Heb., delight.)
edenic, *a.* e-*den*-ik, pertaining to Eden; paradisaic.
edental, *a.* and *n.* ee-*den*-tal, edentate.
edentata, *n.pl.* ee-den-*tay*-ta, an order of animals having no, or only rudimentary, teeth, comprising the sloths, ant-eaters, armadillos, etc. (L. *e-*, and *dens*, a tooth.)
edentate, *a.* ee-*den*-tat, destitute of incisor teeth; belonging to the order Edentata: *n.* an animal of this order.
edentulous, *a.* ee-*den*-tew-lus, toothless.
edge, *n.* edj, the extreme border of anything; the margin; the cutting side of an instrument; that which cuts or wounds; a narrow part rising from a broader; sharpness of mind or appetite; keenness: *v.t.* to sharpen; to furnish with an edge; to border; to exasperate; to incite; to move sideways or by little and little: *v.i.* to move sideways or gradually; to sidle. **edge away,** to increase the distance gradually from. **set the teeth on edge,** to cause a tingling or grating sensation in the teeth. (A.S. *ecg*.)
edge-bone, *n.* *edj*-bone, the aitch bone.
edged, *pp.* and *a.* edjd, furnished with an edge or border; sharp; keen; having a border of different colour [Bot.].
edgeless, *n.* *edj*-less, not sharp; blunt; obtuse.
edge-tool, *n.* an instrument with a sharp edge.
edgeways, *ad.* *edj*-wayz, edgewise.
edgewise, *ad.* *edj*-wize, with the edge turned upward or forward or toward a particular point; in the direction of the edge; with the side foremost; sideways.
edging, *n.* *edj*-ing, that which is put on the edge of a garment for ornament, as lace; a row of small plants set along the border of a bed [Hort.].
edgy, *a.* *edj*-e, with an edge; with too hard an outline; irritable, easily provoked [Coll.].
edibility, *n.* ed-e-*bil*-e-te, the quality of being edible.
edible, *a.* *ed*-e-bl, fit to be eaten. (Late L. *edibilis*.)
edict, *n.* *ee*-dikt, command proclaimed by authority; an order issued by a prince to his subjects, as a rule or law requiring obedience. (L. *edictum*.)
edictal, *a.* e-*dik*-tal, belonging to or of the nature of an edict.
edification, *n.* *ed*-e-fe-*kay*-shon, the act of edifying or state of being edified; instruction or improvement of the mind in knowledge or moral character. (Fr.)
edificatory, *a.* *ad*-e-fe-*kay*-to-re, tending to edification.
edifice, *n.* *ed*-e-fis, a building, a structure, especially of some style and dimensions. (Fr.)
edificial, *a.* ed-e-*fish*-al, relating to a building; architectural.
edify, *v.t.* *ed*-e-fy, to improve the mind and character by instruction; to benefit spiritually. (O.Fr. *edifier*.)
edifying, *a.* *ed*-e-fy-ing, adapted to instruct.
edile, *n.* *ee*-dile, an ædile.
edit, *v.t.* *ed*-it, to select for publication; to prepare as a book for publication, by compiling, annotating, correcting, or selecting the matter; to pass through the press; to manage, as editor. (L. *editus*, given out.)
edition, *n.* e-*dish*-on, the publication of a book; republication, usually with revision and correction or in a different format, size, or binding, etc.; incorrectly used of any reprint, also of the number of copies printed at each order. (O.Fr. *edicion*.)
editor, *n.* *ed*-e-tor, one who edits; one who superintends the preparation or publication of a magazine or journal; one in charge of a single department of a newspaper, as news, sport, finance, drama, etc.; also one in charge during certain hours, as Day-editor, Night-editor. (L.)
editorial, *n.* ed-e-*taw*-re-al, pertaining to editing or to an editor: *n.* an article by the editor, or written under his instructions.
editorially, *ad.* as editor.
editorship, *n.* *ed*-e-tor-ship, the business of an editor; the period of an editor's control.
editress, *n.* *ed*-e-tress, a female editor.
educability, *n.* *ed*-yew-ka-*bil*-e-te, the quality of being capable of profiting by education.
educable, *a.* *ed*-yew-ka-bl, that may be educated.
educand, *n.* *ed*-yew-kand, one who is being, or is to be, educated.
educate, *v.t.* *ed*-yew-kate, to bring up; to train the faculties; to instruct. (L. *ēducātus*, brought up.)
★**education,** *n.* ed-yew-*kay*-shon, the bringing up, as of a child; the training that goes to cultivate the powers and form of character; instruction.
educational, *a.* ed-yew-*kay*-shon-al, pertaining to education; derived from education.
educationalist, *n.* ed-yew-*kay*-shon-al-ist, one skilled in educational methods.
educationally, *ad.* as regards education.
educationist, *n.* ed-yew-*kay*-shon-ist, an advocate of education; an educationalist.
educative, *a.* *ed*-yew-ka-tiv, tending to educate.
educator, *n.* *ed*-yew-kay-tor, one who or that which educates. (L.)
educe, *v.t.* e-*dewce*, to bring or draw out; to extract; to elicit; to infer. (L. *educere*, bring out.)
educible, *a.* e-*dewce*-e-bl, that may be educed.
educt, *n.* *e*-dukt, that which is educed; deduction; a substance separated from that of which it formed a part [Chem.].
eduction, *n.* e-*duk*-shon, the act of educing; an educt. **eduction-pipe,** *n.* an exhaust-pipe.
eductive, *a.* e-*duk*-tiv, tending to draw out.
edulcorate, *v.t.* e-*dul*-ko-rate, to purify or sweeten; to free from acids and salts, or other soluble impurities, by washing [Chem.]. (L. *e-*, and *dulcoratus*, sweetened.)
edulcoration, *n.* e-*dul*-ko-*ray*-shon, the act of edulcorating.
edulcorative, *a.* e-*dul*-ko-ra-tiv, having the quality of sweetening or purifying by washing.
edulcorator, *n.* e-*dul*-ko-ray-tor, one who or that which edulcorates; a kind of dropping bottle for supplying small quantities of water to test-tubes, etc.
Edwardian, *a.* ed-*wawr*-de-an, characteristic of the reign of any of the English kings Edward, esp. in modern times, of that of Edward VII (1901-1910): *n.* one who flourished in the reign of Edward VII.
eel, *n.* eel, a slender soft-finned fish of a serpent-like shape, covered with a thick slimy skin, which extends over the gill-covers, *Anguilla vulgaris*. (A.S. *æl*.)
eelbuck, *n.* *eel*-buk, a basket-net for catching eels.
eel-fare, *n.* *eel*-fare, a brood of young eels; a passage of eels upstream.
eel-grass, *n.* *eel*-grahs, grass-wrack.
eel-pot, *n.* *eel*-pot, a basket-trap for eels.
eel-pout, *n.* *eel*-pout, the burbot, *Lota vulgaris*; the viviparous blenny, a species of *Zoarces*.
eel-spear, *n.* *eel*-speer, a barbed fork-like implement for catching eels.
e'en, een, a contraction of *even*.
e'er, ayr, a contraction of *ever*.
eerie, *a.* *eer*-re, causing or feeling fear; weird. (A.S *earh*, timid.) **eerily: eeriness.**
ef-, *pref.*, a form of *ex-*, as in *efface*.
effable, *a.* *ef*-a-bl, capable of being verbally expressed; utterable.
efface, *v.t.* ef-*face*, to rub out; to expunge or erase, so as to render invisible; to destroy any impression on the mind. (Fr. *effacer*.)
effaceable, *a.* ef-*face*-a-bl, that may be effaced.
effacement, *n.* ef-*face*-ment, the act of effacing.
★**effect,** *n.* ef-*fekt*, that which is produced by an agent or cause; consequence; intent; advantage; force or validity; completion; reality; fact; general

impression; truthful imitation, heightened and made more impressive chiefly by the artifices of light, shade, and colour [Paint.]; that impression which a composition makes on the ear and mind, in performance [Mus.]: *pl.* goods; movables; personal estate: *v.t.* to produce; to cause to be; to accomplish or achieve. **for effect,** for the purpose of heightening or exaggerating. (O.Fr.)
effective, *a.* ef-*fek*-tiv, capable of effecting; operative, or having the quality of producing effects; causing to be; efficient; fit for action: *n.* one who is efficient; a soldier equipped and ready for duty [Mil.]. **effective range,** the range within which the gun is effective.
effectively, *ad.* ef-*fek*-tiv-le, with effect.
effectiveness, *n.* the quality of being effective.
effectivity, *n.* ef-fek-*tiv*-e-te, effectiveness.
effectless, *a.* ef-*fekt*-less, without effect; useless.
effectual, *a.* ef-*fek*-tew-al, producing an effect; having adequate power or force to produce the effect.
effectuality, *n.* ef-*fek*-tew-*al*-e-te, the quality of being effectual; efficacy.
effectually, *ad.* with effect; thoroughly.
effectualness, *n.* effectuality.
effectuate, *v.t.* ef-*fek*-tew-ate, to bring to pass; to achieve; to accomplish. (L. *effectus,* brought about.)
effectuation, *n.* ef-*fek*-tew-*ay*-shon, act of effectuating; accomplishment.
effeminacy, *n.* ef-*fem*-e-na-se, womanish characteristics, as softness, delicacy, and weakness, unsuited to men; unmanliness; indulgence in unmanly pleasures.
effeminate, *a.* ef-*fem*-e-nat, unmanly; womanish; voluptuous; bespeaking effeminacy: *n.* a delicate effeminate person. (L. *effeminatus,* weakened.)
effeminately, *ad.* in an effeminate manner.
effeminateness, *n.* state of being effeminate.
effeminize, *v.t.* ef-*fem*-e-nize, to make womanish; to unman; to weaken: *v.i.* to grow womanish or weak; to melt into weakness.
Effendi, *n.* ef-*fen*-de, a Turkish title of respect bestowed on officials and learned men; sir; monsieur; master. (Turk.)
efferent, *a.* *ef*-fer-ent, conveying outwards; discharging: *n.* an efferent duct, nerve, etc. [Phys.]; a stream running from a lake, etc. [Geog.]. (L. *efferens,* bringing out.)
effervesce, *v.t.* ef-fer-*vess,* to bubble up and hiss from the escape of gas, like liquor when gently boiling or fermenting; to froth up; to break forth irrepressibly. (L. *effervescere,* boil.)
effervescence, *n.* ef-fer-*vess*-ence, the rising of gas bubbles in and from a liquid; the state of being effervescent.
effervescent, *n.* ef-fer-*vess*-ent, gently boiling or bubbling, from the disengagement of gas.
effervescible, *a.* ef-fer-*vess*-e-bl, having the quality of effervescing; ready to effervesce.
effete, *a.* ef-*feet,* exhausted of vigour or effective power; incapable; barren; worn out. (L. *effetus,* worn out by bearing, from *ex-,* and *fœtus,* pregnant.)
effeteness, *n.* ef-*feet*-ness, effete or worn out condition.
efficacious, *a.* ef-e-*kay*-shus, adequate to produce the effect intended.
efficaciously, *ad.* in an efficacious manner.
efficaciousness, *n.* ef-e-*kay*-shus-ness, the quality of being efficacious.
efficacity, *n.* ef-e-*kas*-e-te, efficaciousness; efficacy.
efficacy, *n.* *ef*-e-ka-se, power to produce a given effect. (L. *efficacia.*)
efficiency, *n.* ef-*fish*-en-se, fitness; effectual agency; power of producing the effect intended; amount of the really effective force [Mech.]. (L. *efficientia.*)
efficient, *a.* ef-*fish*-ent, causing effects; effective; competent; fit: *n.* one who is fit for his duties; an effective; the agent or cause. (L. *efficiens,* making.)
efficiently, *ad.,* with effect; effectively.
effigial, *a.* ef-*fij*-e-al, pertaining to or of the nature of an effigy.
effigurate, *a.* ef-*fig*-yew-rat, having a distinct shape [Bot.].
effigy, *n.* *ef*-e-je, the image or likeness of a person, esp. as in a figure or model; the impression on a coin of the head of the monarch in whose reign it was issued. **to burn** or **hang in effigy,** to burn or hang the image or picture of a person. (L. *effigus.*)
effloresce, *v.t.* ef-flo-*ress,* to flower; to blossom; to become covered with whitish dust due to efflorescence [Chem.]. (L. *effloresco,* begin to flower, from *flos, floris,* a flower.)
efflorescence, *n.* ef-flo-*ress*-ence, the production of flowers; the time or the state of flowering [Bot.]; a redness of the skin or eruption, as in rash, measles, etc. [Med.]; the formation of a white incrustation on the surface of bodies, or the white powdery appearance on the surface of a salt when it loses its water of crystallization [Chem.]. (Fr.)
efflorescent, *a.* ef-flo-*ress*-ent, efflorescing; like an efflorescence; liable to effloresce [Chem.].
effluence, *n.* *ef*-floo-ence, the act or state of flowing out; an emanation. (L. *effluens,* flowing out.)
effluent, *a.* *ef*-floo-ent, flowing or issuing out: *n.* a stream that flows out of another or a lake; that which flows or issues from any body or substance.
effluvial, *a.* ef-*floo*-ve-al, pertaining to or consisting of effluvia.
effluvium, *n.* ef-*floo*-ve-um (*pl.* **effluvia**), the minute and generally invisible particles which exhale from bodies as odour; the noxious exhalations from putrefying animal or vegetable substances. (L.)
efflux, *n.* *ef*-fluks, the act of flowing out; effusion; that which flows out; emanation; expiry. (L. *effluxus,* flowed out.)
effluxion, *n.* ef-*fluk*-shon, efflux. **effluxion of time,** the passage of time.
effort, *n.* *ef*-fort, an exertion of strength; strenuous endeavour; struggle; an achievement. (Fr.)
effortless, *a.* *ef*-fort-less, making no effort; easy.
effrontery, *n.* ef-*frun*-ter-re, shameless or insolent boldness; impudence; audacity. (Fr. *effronterie.*)
effulge, *v.i.* ef-*fulj,* to shed effulgence. (L. *effulgeo,* shine forth.)
effulgence, *n.* ef-*ful*-jence, a flood of light; great lustre or brightness.
effulgent, *a.* ef-*ful*-jent, brightly shining; shedding effulgence. (L. *effulgens,* shining out.)
effulgently, *ad.* ef-*ful*-jent-le, with effulgence.
effuse, *v.t.* ef-*fewz,* to pour out, as a fluid; to shed: *v.i.* to emanate. (L. *effūsus,* poured out.)
effuse, *a.* ef-*fewce,* spreading loosely, applied to an inflorescence [Bot.]; with lips separated by a groove [Malac.].
effusion, *n.* ef-*few*-zhon, the act of pouring out, as a liquid, or words, or divine influence; that which is poured out; effusiveness; the escape of a fluid out of the vessel containing it into another part [Med.].
effusive, *a.* ef-*few*-siv, pouring out abundantly; spreading widely; demonstrative; gushing.
effusively, *ad.* in an effusive manner.
effusiveness, *n,* state of being effusive; a demonstrative manner.
eft, *n.* eft, the common newt. (A.S. *efete.*)
eftsoons, *ad.* eft-*soonz,* soon afterwards; in a short time; presently. (A.S. *eft,* after, and *soon.*)
egad, *int.* e-*gad,* a euphemistic (contraction of *by God,* used as a mild expletive).
egalitarian, *a.* e-gal-e-*tare*-re-an, equalitarian.
egality, *n.* e-*gal*-e-te, equality. (Fr. *égalité,* equality.)
egest, *v.t.* e-*jest,* to cast or throw out; to void, as excrement. (L. *egestus,* borne out.)
egesta, *n.pl.* e-*jes*-ta, excrements.
★**egg,** *n.* eg, an ovum, or body formed in the females of birds, reptiles, fishes, and many invertebrates, containing an embryo of the same species or the substance from which a like animal is produced; the ovum of domestic poultry, largely used as food; spawn; germ; anything like an egg; the early stage of anything. **bad egg,** a ne-er-do-well; a failure [Coll.]. (A.S. *æg.*)
egg, *v.t.* eg, to incite. (Ice. *eggja,* to edge.)
eggar, *n.* *eg*-gar, the egger moth.
egg-bird, *n.* the West Indian tern, *Hydrochelidon fuliginosum,* much prized for its eggs.
egg-cup, *n.* a cup used to hold an egg at table.
egger, *n.* *eg*-ger, a gatherer of eggs; any moth of the family *Lasiocampidæ,* esp. the oak-egger and grass-egger.
eggery, *n.* *eg*-ger-re, a place where eggs are laid.
egg-flip, *n.* a drink of warmed beer, flavoured with sugar, spirits, spices, and eggs beaten with it.
eggler, *n.* *eg*-ler, a dealer in eggs; a poulterer.
egg-nog, *n.* a drink composed of wine or spirits mixed with sugar and eggs.
egg-plant, *n.* the aubergine, *Solanum melongena,* a tropical plant which bears a fruit, shaped like an egg, used in cookery.

egg-shell, *n.* the shell of an egg. **egg-shell china,** a thin kind of porcelain.
egg-slice, *n.* a kitchen utensil for removing omelets or fried eggs from a pan.
egg-spoon, *n.* a small spoon for eating eggs with.
egg-tooth, *n.* the knob on the sheath of the bill with which the young bird breaks the shell from the inside.
egg-whisk, *n.* a wire bunch or brush for beating up eggs.
eggy, *a. eg*-ge, marked with egg-stains; pertaining to eggs.
egis, *n. ee*-jis, ægis.
eglandulose, *a.* e-*glan*-dew-lohs, destitute of glands.
eglantine, *n. eg*-lan-tine, the sweetbriar, *Rosa rubiginosa.* (Fr., from L. *aculeus,* a prickle.)
ego, *n. eg*-o, the self-conscious subject, as contrasted with the non-ego, or object; the entire man; personality. (L., the pronoun I.)
egocentric, *a.* eg-oh-*sen*-trik, centred on oneself and one's own interests; considering things only in relation to self.
egocentricity, *n.* eg-oh-sen-*tris*-e-te, the quality of being egocentric; self-centredness.
egoism, *n. eg*-o-izm, the philosophy of those who, uncertain of everything but the existence of the ego, resolve all existences into forms or modifications of its self-consciousness; the principle of private happiness; self-assertiveness; an inordinate regard to self in one's judgments and passions; a passionate love of self.
egoist, *n. eg*-o-ist, one who holds the philosophy of egoism; one who is self-assertive; one who is egocentric.
egoistic, *a. eg*-o-*is*-tik, egoistical.
egoistical, *a. eg*-o-*ist*-ik-al, pertaining to egoism; derived from the ego; self-centred.
egoistically, *ad.* in an egoistic manner.
egoity, *n.* e-*goh*-e-te, personality; identity.
egomania, *n.* eg-oh-*may*-ne-a, morbid or abnormal egoism.
egomaniac, *n.* eg-oh-*may*-ne-ak, one afflicted with egomania.
egotism, *n. eg*-o-tizm, the habit of speaking much of oneself, or the self-conceit which induces it; overweening self-sufficiency and self-assertiveness; self-praise; vanity.
egotist, *n. eg*-o-tist, one who is full of egotism; one who speaks much of himself and his own achievements.
egotistic, *a.* eg-o-*tis*-tik, egotistical.
egotistical, *a.* eg-o-*tist*-ik-al, addicted to egotism; displaying egotism; self-conceited; self-important.
egotistically, *ad.* in a self-conceited or egotistical manner.
egotize, *v.i. eg*-o-tize, to talk or write much of oneself; to make pretensions to self-importance.
egregious, *a.* e-*gree*-je-us, extraordinary; enormous; uncommon in a depreciatory sense. (L. *e-,* from, and *grex, gregis,* a flock.)
egregiously, *ad.* in an egregious manner.
egregiousness, *n.* the state of being egregious.
egress, *n. ee*-gress, the act of going or issuing out, or the power of departing from any enclosed or confined place; an exit; the way out; the end of an eclipse, occultation, or transit [Astron.]: *v.i.* to go out; to leave. (L. *egressus,* gone out.)
egression, *n.* e-*gresh*-on, the act of going out from any place.
egret, *n. ee*-gret, the name of several white species of heron, particularly those that, during the breeding season, show a lengthened soft feathery plumage on back and breast, as the little egret, *Egretta garzetta*; the flying feathery or hairy crown of seeds of composite plants [Bot.]; an aigrette. (Fr.)
Egyptian, *n.* e-*jip*-shan, a native or inhabitant of Egypt; the language of ancient Egypt; formerly, a gipsy; a kind of thick-faced type; a large-sized drawing-paper: *a.* pertaining to Egypt; gipsy (from Little Egypt, the imaginary locality whence the gipsies who spread over Europe in the 15th cent. said they came). **Egyptian kale,** a variety of the turnip-stemmed cabbage. **Egyptian lotus,** the water-lily, *Nymphæa lotus,* a sacred emblem of ancient Egypt. **Egyptian vulture,** a small species of vulture, *Neophron percnopterus,* of service in the East as cleansing away carrion.
Egyptological, *a.* e-jip-to-*loj*-e-kal, pertaining to Egyptology.
Egyptologist, *n.* e-jip-*tol*-o-jist, one versed in Egyptology.
Egyptology, *n.* e-jip-*tol*-o-je, the science and study of Egyptian antiquities, inscriptions, language, etc.
eh, *int.* ay, denoting inquiry or slight surprise.
eidam, *n. eye*-dam, a sort of Dutch cheese.
eident, *a. eye*-dent, diligent; busy [Scots.]. (O. Scand. *ithinn.*)
eider, *n. eye*-der, a large Arctic sea-duck of the genus *Somateria,* noted for its fine down. (Swed. *ejder.*)
eider-down, *n.* the fine, soft, light, elastic down of the eider.
eidetic, *a.* eye-*det*-ik, pertaining to the faculty visually and sub-conciously to recreate past visual impressions: *n.* one having this faculty. (Ger. *eidetisch,* from Gr. *eidetikos,* forming.)
eidograph, *n. eye*-do-graf, an instrument for copying plans or drawings, reduced or enlarged. (Gr. *eidos,* form, *grapho,* write.)
eidolon, *n. eye*-do-lon, a phantom; a visible representation or apparition. (Gr., an image.)
eight, *a.* ayt, twice four: *n.* the number eight; the figure 8; the shape of an 8; an eight-oared boat; its eight oarsmen. (A.S. *eahta.*)
eighteen, *a.* and *n.* ay-*teen,* twice nine.
eighteenmo, *n.* ay-*teen*-mo, denoting the size of a book in which a sheet is doubled into eighteen leaves.
eighteenth, *a.* ay-*teenth,* the next in order after the seventeenth: *n.* one of eighteen equal parts.
eightfold, *a. ayt*-fohld, eight times the quantity.
eighth, *a.* aytth, next after seventh: *n.* one of eight equal parts; the interval of an octave [Mus.].
eighthly, *ad. aytth*-le, in the eighth place.
eightieth, *a. ay*-te-eth, the next in order to the seventy-ninth; the eighth tenth: *n.* one of eighty equal parts.
eightsome, *n. ayt*-sum, a party of eight; a Scottish reel with eight dancers.
eighty, *a.* and *n. ay*-te, eight times ten; four-score.
eigne, *a.* ayn, first-born. **eigne title,** superior title [Law]. (Fr. *aîné.*)
eikon, *n. eye*-kon, an ikon. (Gr.)
Einsteinian, *a.* ine-*sty*-ne-an, pertaining to or derived from the theory of relativity developed by Albert Einstein (*b.* 1879), Ger.-Swiss physicist.
Eireann, *a. ire*-re-an or *ire*-ran, pertaining to the republic of Eire or its people; southern Irish.
eirenical, *a.* ire-*ren*-e-kal, irenical.
eirenicon, *n.* ire-*ren*-e-kon, a plea for peace. (Gr. *eirene,* peace.)
eisel, *n. ee*-zel, vinegar. (O.Fr. *aisil.*)
eisteddfod, *n.* ay-*steth*-vod, an assembly or congress held annually in Wales for the encouragement of native poetry and music; an assembly of Welsh bards. (W.)
either, *a., ad.,* and *pron. eye*-ther or *ee*-ther, one or other of any number; one of two; each; every one, separately considered: *conj.* correlative to or, and preceding it. (A.S. *ægther.*)
ejaculate, *v.t.* e-*jak*-yew-late, to utter earnestly, as a short prayer or cry for mercy: *v.i.* to exclaim. (L. *ejaculatus,* thrown out.)
ejaculation, *n.* e-*jak*-yew-*lay*-shon, the uttering of a short prayer or cry; the exclamation or prayer uttered; the act of ejecting a fluid [Phys.].
ejaculative, *a.* e-*jak*-yew-la-tiv, ejaculatory.
ejaculatory, *a.* e-*jak*-yew-*lay*-to-re, uttered in short sentences or exclamations.
eject, *v.t.* e-*jekt,* to throw or thrust out; to discharge; to dismiss; to dispossess; to expel; to reject: *n. ee*-jekt, something which is neither object nor subject, but is inferred [Psych.]. (L. *ejectus,* hurled out.)
ejecta, *n.pl.* e-*jek*-ta, matter ejected, as in vomiting or from a volcano.
ejection, *n.* e-*jek*-shon, the act of ejecting; expulsion; dismissal; dispossession; discharge; evacuation.
ejective, *a.* e-*jek*-tiv, tending to eject; pertaining to an eject.
ejectment, *n.* e-*jekt*-ment, a casting out; a dispossession; a writ or action for the recovery of possession of land [Law].
ejector, *n.* e-*jek*-tor, one who ejects or dispossesses another of his land; that which ejects, as a jet-pump, or a contrivance for automatically ejecting from a fire-arm the case of a spent projectile.
eke, *v.t.* eek, to add to; to supply what is wanted; to enlarge by addition; to lengthen. **eke out,** to make serve with difficulty: *ad.* also; likewise; in

addition. *pp.* **eking** or **ekeing**. (A.S. *eacian*, to add, akin to L. *auctum*, increase.)

elaborate, *a.* e-*lab*-o-rat, wrought with labour; executed with thoroughness and exactness; highly wrought: *v.t.* e-*lab*-o-rate, to produce with labour; to work on and finish with great pains; to improve or refine by successive operations. (L. *elaboratus*, worked out.)

elaborately, *ad.* with great labour or care.

elaborateness, *n.* the quality of being elaborate.

elaboration, *n.* e-*lab*-o-*ray*-shon, the act or process of elaborating; the process according to which substances, as tissue or sap, are elaborated or produced by the organs of plants or animals.

elaborative, *a.* e-*lab*-o-ra-tiv, contributing to elaborate, mature, and perfect.

elaborator, *n.* e-*lab*-o-ray-tor, one who or that which elaborates.

elæometer, *n.* el-e-*om*-e-ter, an oleometer.

elæoptene, *n.* el-e-*op*-teen, the liquid portion of a vegetable oil. (Gr. *elaion*, and *ptenos*, winged.)

elan, *n.* ay-*lahn*, dash; impetuosity; vivacity. (Fr.)

elance, *v.t.* e-*lance*, to throw or shoot; to dart.

eland, *n. ee*-land, either of the two ox-like antelopes, *Taurotragus oryx*, of S. Africa, or *T. derbianus*, of Senegambia, the largest known of the antelopes. (Dut., the elk.)

elanet, *n. ee*-lan-et, the black-winged kite, *Elanus cæruleus*, of Africa; the swallow-tailed kite, *Elanoides furcatus*, of America. (Gr. *elanos*, a kite.)

elapse, *v.i.* e-*laps*, to slip or glide away; to pass away silently. (L. *elapsus*, glided away.)

elasmobranchs, *n.pl.* e-*laz*-mo-branks, the group of fishes which includes the sharks, rays, and chimæras. (Gr. *elasmo*, a metal plate, *branchia*, gills.)

elasmotherium, *n.* e-*laz*-mo-*theer*-re-um, an extinct rhinoceros of the Lower Pleistocene of N. Europe and Siberia. (Gr. *elasmo*, and *therion*, beast.)

★**elastic,** *a.* e-*las*-tik, springing back; having the power of returning to the form from which it is bent, extended, depressed, or distorted; readily recovering oneself after a shock: *n.* a strip or piece of elastic material or of fabric rendered elastic. **elastic pitch,** elaterite. **elastic tissue,** a flexible tissue composed of yellowish fibres present in the ligaments of the vertebræ, jaw, etc. [Anat.]. (Gr. *elastikos.*)

elastically, *ad.* e-*las*-te-ka-le, in an elastic manner; by an elastic power; with a spring.

elasticity, *n.* ee-las-*tis*-e-te, the inherent property in bodies by which they recover their former figure or state after external pressure, tension, or distortion; a similar mental or moral quality.

elastin, *n.* e-*las*-tin, the albuminoid of which elastic fibres are chiefly composed.

elate, *n.* e-*late*, raised; elevated in spirits; flushed with success; exultant; lofty; haughty: *v.t.* to raise or swell, as the mind or spirits; to elevate with success; to puff up. (L. *elatus*, raised.)

elatedly, *ad.* e-*lay*-ted-le, with elation; conceitedly.

elater, *n. el*-a-ter, an elastic spiral filament attached to a spore [Bot.]; the skip-jacks or click-beetles; (*cap.*) a genus of coleopterous insects which, when they fall on their backs, right themselves with a jerk [Entom.]. (Gr., a driver.)

elaterin, *n.* e-*lat*-er-in, the active principle of elaterium.

elaterite, *n.* e-*lat*-er-ite, an elastic mineral pitch; elastic bitumen.

elaterium, *n.* el-a-*teer*-re-um, a strong purgative extracted from the juice of the squirting cucumber, *Ecballium elaterium*. (Gr. *elaterios*, purgative.)

elation, *n.* e-*lay*-shon, the state of being elated; pride, or haughtiness of spirit, resulting from success. (*Elate.*)

elbow, *n. el*-boh, the outer angle made by the bend of the arm; any flexure or angle; the obtuse angle of a wall, building, or road; any sharp turn or bend; a crossette [Arch.]: *v.t.* to push with the elbow; to push aside and take the place of: *v.i.* to jostle; to put oneself forward, thrusting others aside. **at the elbow,** at hand. **jog the elbow,** to remind. **out at elbows,** reduced in circumstances; ill off. **up to the elbows,** extremely busy. (A.S. *elboga.*)

elbow-chair, *n.* a chair with arms to support the elbows; an arm-chair.

elbow-grease, *n.* hard, continuous rubbing.

elbow-room, *n.* room for motion or action.

elchee, *n. el*-chee, an ambassador. (Turk. *ilchi.*)

eld, *n.* eld, old age; discrepitude; antiquity; old times. (A.S. *ield.*)

elder, *a. el*-der, older; having lived a longer time; prior in origin; preceding in the date: *n.* one who is older; one who, on account of his age and experience, is selected for office; one who held office in the early Christian Church; a member of the kirk session, the supervisory and administrative body of a Presbyterian congregation. **elder hand,** the player who leads at a game of cards. (A.S. *yldra.*)

elder, *n. el*-der, a small tree, *Sambucus nigra*, with a spongy pith, bearing white flowers and dark purple berries. (A.S. *ellen.*)

elderberry, *n. el*-der-*be*-re, the fruit of the elder.

elder-gun, *n.* a popgun of elder-wood.

elderliness, *n.* the state of being elderly.

elderly, *a. el*-der-le, somewhat old; advanced beyond middle age; bordering on old age.

eldership, *n. el*-der-ship, the state of being older; seniority; the office of an elder.

elder-wine, *n.* wine made from elderberries.

eldest, *a. el*-dest, oldest; most advanced in age.

Eldorado, *n.* el-do-*rah*-do, a region of fabulous riches; so called from the name given by the Spanish Conquistadores to an enormously wealthy being whose territory was supposed to lie in the hinterland of Guiana or thereabouts. (Sp. *el*, the, *dorado*, golden.)

eldritch, *a. el*-drich, ghastly; weird; inspiring fright. (Scots.)

Eleatic, *n.* el-e-*at*-ik, pertaining to or belonging to Elea, a town of ancient Italy, or to the school of Greek philosophers established there, to which Zeno belonged: *n.* a member of this school.

elecampane, *n.* el-e-kam-*pane*, a composite plant, *Inula helenium*, of a pungent taste and formerly of much repute in medicine; a sweetmeat made from the root. (O.Fr. *enule-campane.*)

elect, *a.* e-*lekt*, chosen; taken by preference from among two or more; chosen for an office, but not yet installed; chosen to salvation [Theol.]: *n.* one chosen or set apart; one chosen for salvation [Theol.]: *v.t.* to pick out; to select for an office or employment; to select by vote; to choose; to designate, choose, or select as an object of mercy or favour [Theol.]. (L. *electus*, chosen.)

election, *n.* e-*lek*-shon, the act of electing, esp. for office by vote; choice, option, or free will; discrimination; predestination to salvation [Theol.]; those predestined [Theol.]. **by-election,** an election for filling a single vacancy during the life of a parliament. **general election,** an election for the whole House of Commons. (O.Fr.)

electioneer, *v.i.* e-*lek*-sho-*neer*, to help in obtaining votes for a particular candidate or party at an election.

elective, *a.* e-*lek*-tiv, dependent on choice; pertaining to the right of election; exerting the power of choice; tending to combine with one thing rather than with another.

electively, *ad.* e-*lek*-tiv-le, by choice.

elector, *n.* e-*lek*-tor, one who elects; one who has a vote in election; one of seven German princes who had the right of electing the emperor, up to the dissolution of the Holy Roman Empire in 1806; in the U.S.A., a member of the Electoral College, chosen by popular vote, whose duty it is to elect the President and Vice-President.

electoral, *a.* e-*lek*-to-ral, pertaining to election or electors; consisting of electors.

electorate, *n.* e-*lek*-to-rat, the dignity or territory of an elector in the German Empire; the body of electors.

electorship, *n.* e-*lek*-tor-ship, the office of an elector.

electress, *n.* e-*lek*-tress, the wife or widow of a German Elector; a female elector.

★**electric,** *a.* e-*lek*-trik, containing electricity or capable of exhibiting it when excited by friction; pertaining to electricity; derived from or produced by electricity; conveying electricity; communicating a shock like electricity; acting like electricity. **electric battery,** a number of cells united so as to give a powerful discharge. **electric bell,** a bell worked by electricity. **electric blue,** a greenish-blue colour. **electric chair,** the chair in which a condemned criminal is fastened for electrocution [U.S.A.]. **electric circuit,** the path of electric action; the transmission of electricity from a body overcharged to one that is undercharged. **electric** column, a voltaic pile composed of thin plates of different metals, with paper interposed between them. **electric eel,** an eel of the genus *Gymnotus*, found in S. American rivers. **electric eye,** a photo-electric cell. **electric hare,** the artificial hare coursed by greyhounds in greyhound-racing. **electric light,** a brilliant white light due to the intense heat in a solid body caused by the passage of an electric current through it. **electric machine,** an apparatus for producing frictional electricity. **electric railway,** a railway in which the trains are moved by electric motors driving direct or obtaining their power from a cable or live rail. **electric ray,** a flat-fish of the genus *Torpedo*. **electric spark,** one of the forms in which an accumulation of electricity is discharged. **electric telegraph,** an apparatus for transmitting messages and intelligence by wire, either for long or short distances.

electric, *n.* e-*lek*-trik, a non-conductor; any substance in which electricity can be generated by friction.

electrical, *a.* e-*lek*-tre-kal, pertaining to electricity; electric.

electrically, *ad.* in the manner of electricity or by means of it.

electrician, *n.* ee-lek-*trish*-an, one versed in electricity; an electrical engineer or mechanic.

electricity, *n.* e-lek-*tris*-e-te, a natural force producing physical phenomena comprising chiefly attraction and repulsion, chemical decomposition, and the production of light and heat; the science treating of this force and its manifestations. **atmospheric electricity,** electrical effects such as lightning, aurora borealis, etc., due to natural electricity in the atmosphere [Elect.]. (Gr. *electron*, amber, which, when rubbed, has the power of attracting light bodies.)

electrics, *n.* e-*lek*-triks, the science treating of the laws and phenomena of electricity.

electrifiable, *a.* e-*lek*-tre-*fy*-a-bl, capable of being charged with electricity; capable of receiving and conducting electricity.

electrification, *n.* e-*lek*-tre-fe-*kay*-shon, the act of charging or state of being charged with electricity; making electric.

electrify, *v.t.* e-*lek*-tre-fy, to make electric; to charge with electricity; to give an electric shock to; to excite, surprise, or amaze, as by an electric shock: *v.i.* to become electric. (Gr. *electron*, L. *facio*, make.)

electrize, *v.t.* e-*lek*-trize, to electrify.

electro-, *pref.* e-*lek*-troh, appertaining to or resulting from electricity: **electro,** *n.* a printing plate produced by electrotype.

electro-biologist, *n.* one versed in electro-biology.

electro-biology, *n.* e-*lek*-tro-by-*ol*-o-je, the study of electric phenomena in living organisms.

electro-chemical, *a.* pertaining to electro-chemistry.

electro-chemistry, *n.* e-*lek*-tro-*kem*-is-tre, the science or study of the action of electricity in effecting chemical changes.

electrocute, *v.t.* e-*lek*-tro-kewt, to kill (esp. to execute a criminal) by electric shock.

electrocution, *n.* e-*lek*-tro-*kew*-shon, execution by electricity; killing by electricity.

electrode, *n.* e-*lek*-trode, either terminal (anode or cathode) of an electric circuit. (Gr. *electron*, and *hodos*, a way.)

electro-dynamic, *a.* pertaining to electro-dynamics.

electro-dynamics, *n.* e-*lek*-tro-dy-*nam*-iks, the dynamics of electricity.

electro-dynamometer, *n.* e-*lek*-tro-*dy*-na-*mom*-e-ter, an instrument for measuring the strength of an electric current.

electro-engraving, *n.* e-*lek*-tro-en-*gray*-ving, engraving by means of electricity.

electrograph, *n.* e-*lek*-tro-graf, an instrument for recording electrical conditions; the linear record of an electrometer. (Gk. *electron*, and *graphe*, writing.)

electro-kinetics, e-*lek*-tro-ky-*net*-iks, the branch of electricity treating of its distribution in currents, its heating effect, etc.

electrolier, *n.* e-*lek*-tro-*leer*, a pendant for an electric light or lights; a chandelier carrying electric lights in place of candles.

electrology, *n.* ee-lek-*trol*-o-je, the science of electricity. (Gr. *electron*, and *logos*, science.)

electrolysis, *n.* ee-lek-*trol*-e-sis, chemical change by electrical means; the science dealing with the decomposition of chemical substances by the passage through them of an electric current. (Gr. *electron*, and *lysis*, solution.)

electrolyte, *n.* e-*lek*-tro-lite, a compound which may be decomposed by an electric current.

electrolytic, *a.* e-lek-tro-*lit*-ik, pertaining to or deposited by electrolysis.

electrolyze, *v.t.* e-*lek*-tro-lize, to decompose by the direct action of electricity. (Gr. *elektron*, and *lyo*, loosen.)

electro-magnet, *n.* e-*lek*-tro-*mag*-net, a soft iron bar rendered magnetic by passing an electric current through wire coiled round it.

electro-magnetic, *a.* e-*lek*-tro-mag-*net*-ik, pertaining to electro-magnetism.

electro-magnetism, *n.* e-*lek*-tro-*mag*-ne-tizm, the science which treats of the relationship of magnetism and electricity and of the agency of electricity in producing magnetism; magnetism produced by electric current.

electro-metallurgy, *n.* e-*lek*-tro-me-*tal*-ur-je *or* -*met*-a-ler-je, that branch of metallurgy which achieves its results by means of electricity.

electrometer, *n.* ee-lek-*trom*-e-ter, an instrument for indicating the presence of electricity or for measuring the amount of its force.

electro-motive, *a.* e-*lek*-tro-*moh*-tiv, producing motion by means of electricity; causing electrical action. **electro-motive force,** the force which causes a current to flow in an electric circuit.

electromotor, *n.* e-*lek*-tro-*moh*-tor, a machine in which an electric current is generated; also one in which the motive power is electricity.

electron, *n.* e-*lek*-tron, the negative particle of an atom, the natural unit of negative electricity and electrical opposite of the proton; electrum.

electronarcosis, *n.* e-*lek*-tro-nar-*koh*-sis, a method of treating mental disorder by direct application of a mild electric current to the brain [Path.].

electronic, *a.* ee-lek-*tron*-ik, pertaining to electrons.

electronics, *n.* ee-lek-*tron*-iks, the branch of physics treating of electrons.

electropathy, *n.* ee-lek-*trop*-a-the, the treatment of disease by electricity; electrotherapeutics.

electrophone, *n.* e-*lek*-tro-fone, an instrument for producing or transmitting sound by means of electricity. (Gr. *elektron*, and *phone*, sound.)

electrophorus, *n.* ee-lek-*trof*-o-rus, a generator of static electricity; an instrument for exciting electricity in small quantities, consisting of a flat smooth cake of resin, acted upon by a circular plate of brass with an insulated handle. (Gr. *elecktron*, and *phero*, bear.)

electrophysiology, *n.* e-*lek*-tro-fiz-e-*ol*-o-je, the science of electric effects due to physiological causes.

electroplate, *n.* e-*lek*-tro-plate, articles of metal coated with another metal by electroplating: *v.t.* to coat with metal by means of electrolysis.

electro-polar, *a.* e-*lek*-tro-*poh*-lar, positively electrified at one end and surface, and negatively at the other.

electroscope, *n.* e-*lek*-tro-skope, an instrument for testing the presence, nature, and intensity of electricity. (Gr. *electron*, and *skopeo*, view.)

electrostatic, *a.* e-*lek*-tro-*stat*-ik, pertaining to electrostatics.

electrostatics, *n.* e-*lek*-tro-*stat*-iks, the science of the laws and phenomena of electricity that is stationary in space and constant in quantity.

electrotherapeutics, *n.* e-*lek*-tro-the-ra-*pew*-tiks treatment of disease by electricity; the laws and principles of such treatment.

electrotherapy, *n.* e-*lek*-tro-*the*-ra-pe, treatment of disease by electricity.

electro-thermic, *n.* e-*lek*-tro-*ther*-mik, relating to the generation of heat by electricity; combining electricity and heat.

electrotype, *n.* e-*lek*-tro-tipe, the process of producing a facsimile by the electric deposition of a film of copper on a prepared surface, or the facsimile so produced: *v.t.* to copy by electrotype.

electrotypist, *n.* e-*lek*-tro-*ty*-pist, a worker in electrotype.

electrum, *n.* e-*lek*-trum, German silver; nickel silver; among the ancients an alloy of gold and silver. (Gr. and L.)

electuary, *n.* e-*lek*-tew-a-re, a purgative compounded with sweets. (L. *electuarium*, a medicine that melts in the mouth, from Gr. *ekleicho*, lick up.)

eleemosynary, *a.* el-e-ee-*mos*-e-na-re, relating to alms; supported by or founded by charity; for th

distribution of charitable donations. (Late L. *eleemosynarius*, a charitable person.)
elegance, *n. el*-e-gance, the beauty of propriety ; the quality of being elegant ; neatness ; that which pleases by its nicety, symmetry, purity, or beauty. (L. *elegantia.*)
elegancy, *n. el*-e-gan-se, elegance.
elegant, *a. el*-e-gant, refined ; pleasing to good taste ; graceful ; expressing oneself with propriety and grace ; expressing fastidious taste ; beautiful in form and colour ; first-rate [Coll.].
elegantly, *ad.* with elegance.
elegiac, *a.* el-e-*jy*-ak, belonging to elegy ; expressing sorrow or lamentation ; used in elegies ; plaintive ; mournful : *n.pl.* verse consisting of alternate hexameters and pentameters, as in Greek or Latin elegies. (Gr. *elegeïakos.*)
elegist, *n. el*-e-jist, a writer of elegies.
elegit, *n.* e-*lee*-jit, a writ of execution putting a creditor in possession of the debtor's property until satisfaction of the claim [Law]. (L., "he has chosen.")
elegize, *v.t.* and *i. el*-e-jize, to compose an elegy on : to write an elegy.
elegy, *n. el*-e-je, a poem or musical composition expressive of sorrow or lamentation ; a dirge ; a poem pervaded by a tone of pensive sadness. (O.Fr. *elegie.*)
element, *n. el*-e-ment, first principle ; one of the simple constituent parts of anything ; an ingredient ; proper state or sphere ; outline or sketch ; one of the forms of matter that has not hitherto been decomposed by chemical analysis [Chem.] ; the active part of an electrical device ; the natural surroundings or proper sphere of any creature : *pl.* rudiments ; data ; the bread and wine used at the Eucharist ; fire, air, earth, and water, the four elements which were supposed to constitute the world. (L. *elementa*, first principles.)
elemental, *a.* el-e-*men*-tal, pertaining to elements ; arising from first principles : *n.* an elemental spirit ; a sub-human force perceptible, in certain conditions, to humans [Spiritualism and Theosophy]. **elemental spirits,** those of fire, air, earth and water, respectively salamanders, sylphs, gnomes, and undines.
elementalism, *n.* el-e-*men*-ta-lizm, the theory which raises to the rank of gods the elements and aspects of physical nature ; worship of the elemental spirits.
elementally, *ad.* el-e-*men*-ta-le, according to elements ; literally.
elementariness, *n.* el-e-*men*-ta-re-ness, the state of being elementary.
elementary, *a.* el-e-*men*-ta-re, simple ; uncompounded ; rudimentary ; containing, teaching, or discussing first principles ; treating of elements. **elementary school,** a school intermediate between the infants' and secondary schools, teaching elementary subjects.
elemi, *n. el*-e-me, a resinous exudation from several tropical trees, used medicinally in ointments and for toughening varnish. (Ar.)
elemin, *n. el*-e-min, the crystallizable resin obtained from elemi.
elenchus, *n.* e-*leng*-kus, a sophism ; a syllogism which confutes an adversary by making him contradict himself [Logic]. (Gr.)
elephant, *n. el*-e-fant, either of the two species of *Elephas*, the largest of existing mammals, having a thick skin, a long flexible trunk, and two ivory tusks, the two species being the Indian and the African. **elephant beetle,** the large lamellicorn Central American beetle, *Megasoma elephas.* **elephant grass,** the reed-mace ; also the sub-tropical forage grass, *Pennisetum purpureum*, resembling sugar-cane. **elephant leg,** elephantiasis, or a leg affected with this. **elephant paper,** a large-sized drawing paper, measuring 28 in. by 23 in. **white elephant,** a burdensome gift of more trouble than it is worth. (Fr. *éléphant.*)
elephantiasis, *n. el*-e-fan-*ty*-a-sis, a disease, usually caused by filarial worms, in which the limbs from their enlargement and the thick, wrinkled, tuberculate state of the skin, resemble those of the elephant [Med.]. (L.)
elephantine, *a.* el-e-*fan*-tine, pertaining to or resembling the elephant ; huge ; clumsy.
elephantoid, *a.* el-e-*fan*-toyd, resembling the form of an elephant ; pertaining to or resembling elephantiasis.

Eleusinian, *a.* el-yew-*sin*-e-an, relating to Eleusis in Greece, or to the mystic rites in honour of Ceres which were there annually celebrated.
eleutheromania, *n. el*-yew-theer-ro-*may*-ne-a, a frenzied passion for freedom. (Gr. *eleutheros*, free, and *mania.*)
elevate, *v.t. el*-e-vate, to raise from a lower place to a higher ; to raise to a higher rank or status ; to improve or raise in refinement or character ; to elate with pride ; to cheer ; to raise from any tone to one more acute ; to augment or swell. (L. *elevatus*, raised.)
elevated, *a. el*-e-vay-ted, exalted ; dignified ; elated ; slightly intoxicated ; high-pitched.
elevation, *n.* el-e-*vay*-shon, the act of elevating ; an elevated state ; exaltation ; dignity ; exaltation of mind, style, character, or manners ; height ; elevated ground ; a raising of voice ; altitude of a celestial object above the horizon [Astron.] ; the angle which the line of direction makes with the plane of the horizon [Gunnery] ; the angle which the style makes with the substylar line [Dialling] ; the progression of the tones from grave to acute, also the raising of the hand or foot in beating time [Mus.] ; a façade, also the height of a building above ground ; the side or end view of a building or other object drawn to scale without regard to perspective [Arch.]. **elevation of the host,** that part of the Mass in which the priest raises the Host above his head for the people to adore.
elevator, *n. el*-e-vay-tor, one who or that which raises, lifts, or exalts ; a lift [U.S.A.] ; a muscle which serves to raise a part of the body, as the lip or the eye [Anat.] ; an endless belt with scoops or other containers for raising grain, etc., from a lower to a higher floor ; a building in which grain is elevated, stored, and discharged ; a movable control in the tail of an aeroplane.
elevatory, *a. el*-e-vay-to-re, tending to elevate.
eleven, *a.* e-*lev*-en, ten and one added : *n.* the sum of this ; a symbol (11, xi) representing it ; a side at cricket or association football. (A.S. *endleofan.*)
elevenses, *n.* e-*lev*-en-zez, a drink, or a drink and snack, taken in the forenoon [Coll.].
eleventh, *a.* e-*lev*-enth, next in order to tenth ; forming one of eleven equal parts : *n.* of eleven equal parts ; the interval of the octave above the fourth [Mus.]. (A.S. *endlyfta.*)
eleventhly, *ad.* e-*lev*-enth-le, in the eleventh place.
elf, *n.* elf (*pl.* **elves**, elvz), one of a class of imaginary supernatural beings of capricious temper, represented as of diminutive size and as taking pleasure in playing sundry mischievous tricks on mortals, and imagined to haunt sequestered places ; a fairy ; a mischievous or diminutive person ; a child ; *v.t.* to entangle hair in an intricate manner. (A.S. *ælf.*)
elf-arrow, *n.* a flint arrow-head of the Stone Age, vulgarly supposed to be shot by fairies.
elf-bolt, *n.* an elf-arrow.
elf-child, *n.* a child left by the fairies in lieu of one carried off by them ; a changeling.
elfin, *a. el*-fin, elfish ; *n.* a little elf or urchin.
elfish, *a. el*-fish, relating to or resembling elves ; as if done by elves ; mischievous.
elf-lock, *n.* hair twisted in a lock, so denominated as if the work of fairies.
elf-struck, *a.* bewitched by elves.
elicit, *v.t.* e-*lis*-it, to draw out ; to bring to light ; to deduce ; to extract. (L. *elicitus*, enticed.)
elicitation, *n.* e-*lis*-e-*tay*-shon, evocation ; the act of eliciting.
elidable, *a.* e-*ly*-da-bl, elidible.
elide, *v.t.* e-*lide*, to omit, to annul [Law] ; to cut off a syllable [Gram.]. (L. *elido*, strike out.)
elidible, *a.* e-*ly*-di-bl, that may be elided.
eligibility, *n. el*-e-je-*bil*-e-te, fitness to be chosen ; the state of being suitable or desirable ; capability of being chosen to an office.
eligible, *a. el*-e-je-bl, worthy or fit to be chosen ; preferable ; desirable ; legally suitable or qualified to be chosen : *n.* one who is eligible, esp. as a suitor. (O.Fr.)
eligibly, *ad.* in a manner to be worthy of choice.
eliminable, *a.* e-*lim*-e-na-bl, that may be eliminated.
eliminant, *n.* e-*lim*-e-nant, a medicine to effect the elimination of morbid matter from the body.
eliminate, *v.t.* e-*lim*-e-nate, to expel ; to throw out or off ; to exclude ; to leave out in considering a

matter; to cause a quantity to disappear from an equation [Alg.]. (L. *eliminatus*, turned out of doors.)

elimination, *n.* e-lim-e-*nay*-shon, the act of leaving out; cancelling; ejection; the act of discharging or secreting by the pores [Physiol.]; the act of throwing out of account; removal of a quantity from an equation [Alg.].

eliminative, *a.* e-*lim*-e-na-tiv, relating to or carrying on elimination [Physiol.].

eliquation, *n.* el-e-*kway*-shon, the process of separating by means of heat a more fusible from a less fusible substance [Chem.]. (L. *eliquatus*, melted.)

elision, *n.* e-*lizh*-on, the eliding of a vowel at the end of a word for the sake of euphony or scansion. (L. *elisio*, striking out.)

elisor, *n.* e-*ly*-zor, one deputizing for a sheriff when disqualified for duty [Law].

elite, *n.* ay-*leet*, a select body; the best of anything selected from the rest. (Fr.)

elixir, *n.* e-*lik*-ser, a tincture composed of two or more ingredients in solution in alcohol [Pharmacy]; the alchemist's liquor for transmuting metals into gold or for prolonging life; a cure-all or panacea. (Ar. *al-iksir*.)

Elizabethan, *a.* e-liz-a-*bee*-than, pertaining to or characteristic of the reign of Queen Elizabeth (1558-1603): *n.* a person active in this period.

elk, *n.* elk, the largest of the deer family, *Alces alces*, a native of the north of Europe, Asia, and America; the moose (*A. Americana*) of North America, also the wapiti (*Cervus canadensis*). **Irish elk,** a large, extinct deer, *Cervus megaceros*, of Ireland and other parts of Europe. (O.Ger. *elch*.)

elkhound, *n.* *elk*-hound, a large and powerful dog first bred in Norway and used to herd reindeer.

elk-nut, *n.* *elk*-nut, the shrub *Pyrularia pubera*, also its oily nut.

elk-wood, *n.* *elk*-wood, the soft spongy wood of the umbrella-tree, a species of *Sciadopitys*.

ell, *n.* el, a measure of different lengths in different countries, used chiefly for measuring cloth (English, 45, Flemish, 27, Scottish, 37 inches). (A.S. *eln*.)

ellagic, *a.* el-*laj*-ik, pertaining to gall-nuts or to gallic acid. (Fr. *ellagique*, from *galle*, gall, spelt backwards.)

ellipse, *n.* el-*lips*, a figure formed by the intersection of a plane and cone, the plane passing obliquely through the opposite sides of the cone; a regular oval figure having two foci [Geom.]. (L. *ellipsis*.)

ellipsis, *n.* el-*lip*-sis (*pl.* **ellipses**), omission of one or more words, which are to be supplied by the reader or those addressed [Gram.].

ellipsograph, *n.* el-*lip*-so-graf, an instrument for describing ellipses. (L. *ellipsis*, and Gr. *grapho*, write.)

ellipsoid, *n.* el-*lip*-soyd, an elliptical spheroid: *a.* ellipsoidal [Geom.]. (Gr. *ellipse*, and *eidos*, form.)

ellipsoidal, *a.* el-lip-*soy*-dal, pertaining to an ellipsoid; having the form of an ellipsoid.

elliptic, *a.* el-*lip*-tik, pertaining to an ellipse [Geom.], or to an ellipsis [Gram.]. **elliptic compasses,** an ellipsograph.

elliptical, *a.* el-*lip*-te-kal, having the form of an ellipse; elliptic.

elliptically, *ad.* el-*lip*-te-kal-e, in the form of an ellipse; with a part omitted.

ellipticity, *n.* el-lip-*tis*-e-te, the quality of being elliptical; deviation from the form of a circle or sphere, specially in the case of the earth.

ell-wand, *n.* *el*-wond, a measuring rod an ell long.

elm, *n.* elm, a forest tree of the genus *Ulmus*, yielding valuable timber. (A.S. *elm*, L. *ulmus*.)

elmen, *a.* *elm*-en, of or pertaining to the elm.

elmy, *a.* *elm*-e, abounding with elms.

elocution, *n.* el-o-*kew*-shon, diction or power of expression; manner of speaking or oral delivery; the art of speaking; oratory. (L. *elocutio*.)

elocutionary, *a.* el-o-*kew*-shon-a-re, pertaining to elocution.

elocutionist, *n.* el-o-*kew*-shon-ist, one who is versed in or who treats of or teaches the art of elocution or voice production.

éloge, *n.* el-*ohj*, a funeral oration; a panegyric on one recently dead. (Fr. from L., *elogium*, an inscription on a tomb.)

Elohim, *n.pl.* el-*loh*-him, one of the names of the Creator in the Hebrew Bible. (Heb.)

Elohist, *n.* el-*loh*-hist, the name given to the author of certain parts of the Hexateuch in which the word Elohim is used.

Elohistic, *a.* el-o-*his*-tik, pertaining to, or characteristic of the writings, of the Elohist.

eloin, *v.t.* e-*loyn*, to remove, esp. out of the jurisdiction of a court [Law]. (Fr. *e*-, and *loin*, far.)

elongate, *a.* *ee*-long-gate, remarkable for length as contrasted with breadth [Bot.]: *v.t.* to lengthen; to extend: *v.i.* to grow longer, to taper [Bot.]. (Late L. *elongatus*, removed.)

elongation, *n.* ee-long-*gay*-shon, the act of growing longer; the state of being elongated; an extension; the angular distance of a planet from the sun or of a satellite from its primary [Astron.].

elope, *v.i.* e-*lope*, to run away with a lover (esp. of a married woman from her husband, or of an unmarried woman from her parents or guardians). (O.Fr. *alouper*, from Teut.)

elopement, *n.* e-*lope*-ment, the act of eloping; secret departure.

eloquence, *n.* *el*-o-kwence, speech conceived under and expressive of deep emotion or passion, and calculated to affect and sway the thoughts and feelings of others in like manner; rhetoric. (L. *eloquentia*.)

eloquent, *a.* *el*-o-kwent, speaking with fluency and effect; having the power of expressing strong emotions in vivid and impressive speech; vividly and impressively expressive of fervent or strong emotion; expressive. (O.Fr.)

eloquently, *ad.* with eloquence; in an eloquent manner.

else, *a.* and *pron.* else, other; one or something besides: *ad.* otherwise; in the other case; if the fact were different; besides; except that mentioned. (A.S. *elles*, other.)

elsewhere, *ad.* *else*-whare, in another place; in other places.

eltchi, *n.* *el*-che, elchee; an ambassador.

elucidate, *v.t.* e-*lew*-se-date, to make clear or throw light upon; to explain; to illustrate. (Late L. *elucidatus*, made clear.)

elucidation, *n.* e-lew-se-*day*-shon, the act of throwing light on any obscure subject; explanation.

elucidative, *a.* e-*lew*-se-da-tiv, making clear; explanatory.

elucidator, *n.* e-*lew*-se-day-tor, a person who elucidates.

elucidatory, *a.* e-*lew*-se-*day*-to-re, elucidative.

elude, *v.t.* e-*lewd*, to evade or escape; to avoid by artifice, deceit, or dexterity; to baffle; to escape being seen. (L *eludo*, deceive.)

Elul, *n.* e-lool, the 12th month of the civil Jewish year and the 6th of the ecclesiastical, corresponding nearly to August. (Heb.)

elusion, *n.* e-*lew*-zhon, the act of eluding; escape by artifice or deception; evasion. (L.)

elusive, *a.* e-*lew*-siv, evasive; difficult to catch; not easily understood.

elusiveness, *n.* e-*lew*-siv-ness, the state of being elusive; habit of elusion.

elusoriness, *n.* e-*lew*-so-re-ness, the state of being elusory.

elusory, *a.* e-*lew*-so-re, tending or endeavouring to elude or deceive.

elutriate, *v.t.* e-lew-*tre*-ate, to purify by straining to remove the lighter from the heavier components of pulverulent substances by washing [Chem.].

elutriation, *n.* e-*lew*-tre-*ay*-shon, the act or process of elutriating.

elutriator, *n.* e-*lew*-tre-*ay*-tor, an apparatus for effecting elutriation.

eluvial, *a.* e-*lew*-ve-al, pertaining to or composed of eluvium.

eluvium, *n.* e-*lew*-ve-um, gravel produced by the disintegration of rocks on the spot, as opposed to alluvium.

elvan, *n.* *el*-van, a porphyritic granite occurring in Cornwall; a vein or dyke of this.

elver, *n.* *el*-ver, a young eel. (*Eel-fare*.)

elves, elvz, *pl.* of *elf*.

elvish, *a.* *el*-vish, elfish.

Elysian, *a.* e-*liz*-e-an, pertaining to Elysium; yielding the highest pleasures; exceedingly delightful.

Elysium, *n.* e-*liz*-e-um, the fabled abode of the soul of the Greek heroes after death; hence, a place or state of perfect bliss and delight. (Gr.)

elytral, *a.* *el*-e-tral, pertaining to elytra.

elytriform, *a.* e-*lit*-re-form, in the form of a wing sheath. (Gr. *elytron*, and *form*.)

elytrine, *n.* *el*-e-trin, the chitin in the horny coverings of insects [Chem.]
elytroid, *a.* *el*-e-troyd, resembling an elytron.
elytron, *n.* *el*-e-tron (*pl.* **elytra**), one of the wing-sheaths of beetles, into which the fore-wings have been converted; the outer hard case, beneath which are the true wings. (Gr. *elytron.*)
Elzevir, *n.* *el*-ze-vir, a book (esp. an edition of the classics) published by the Elzevir family at Amsterdam, Leyden, etc., during the 16th and 17th centuries: *a.* printed by, or resembling type used by, the Elzevirs.
em-, a form of the English prefix *en-*. [Many words with the prefix (as *embrown, embrute,* etc.) are now more usually given the prefix *im-*, and in NUTTALL'S STANDARD DICTIONARY will be found with that spelling.]
em, *n.* em, the letter *m*; the square of the body of any size of type, used by printers as a unit of measurement.
'em, a contraction of *them.*
emaciate, *v.t.* e-*may*-she-ate, to cause to lose flesh gradually; to reduce to leanness. (L. *emaciatus.*)
emaciation, *n.* e-*may*-she-*ay*-shon, the act of making or becoming lean; the state of being reduced to leanness; emaciated condition.
emanate, *v.i.* *em*-an-ate, to issue, proceed, or spring from, as from a source. (L. *emanatus,* proceeded from.)
emanation, *n.* em-a-*nay*-shon, the act of emanating or that which emanates from any source, substance, or body; efflux; effluence; the radioactive gas emitted by actinium, the thorium compounds, and other radioactive substances. **theory of emanation,** the doctrine which derives all existence from the divine nature by process of emanation, as light from the sun.
emanative, *a.* *em*-a-na-tiv, issuing from another.
emancipate, *v.t.* e-*man*-se-pate, to set free from servitude by the voluntary act of the proprietor; to set free from bondage, restraint, restriction, or subjection of any kind; to set free from parental control [Rom. Law]. (L. *emancipatus,* set free.)
emancipation, *n.* e-*man*-se-*pay*-shon, the act of emancipating, or the state of being emancipated from any bondage or restriction.
emancipationist, *n.* e-*man*-se-*pay*-shon-ist, an advocate for the emancipation of slaves.
emancipator, *n.* e-*man*-se-pay-tor, one who emancipates.
emancipist, *n.* e-*man*-se-pist, a convict, esp. in Australia, who has served his sentence or received a pardon.
emarginate, *a.* e-*mar*-je-nate, emarginated: *v.t.* to take away the margin or edge; to notch. (L. *emarginatus,* deprived of the margin.)
emarginated, *a.* e-*mar*-je-*nay*-ted, having the margin notched; notched at the apex [Bot.]; having all the edges of the primitive form truncated, each by one face [Min.].
emargination, *n.* e-*mar*-je-*nay*-shon, the act of emarginating, or the state of being emarginated.
emasculate, *a.* e-*mas*-kew-late, castrated; deprived of vigour; enfeebled; bowdlerized: *v.t.* to castrate; to deprive of virility; to weaken or render effeminate; to remove, as from a book, what seems coarse. (Late L. *emasculatus,* castrated.)
emasculation, *n.* e-*mas*-kew-*lay*-shon, the act of emasculating; the state of being emasculated; effeminacy; unmanly weakness.
emasculatory, *a.* e-*mas*-kew-*lay*-to-re, tending to emasculate.
embalm, *v.t.* em-*bahm,* to preserve a dead body from decay by treating it with salts and spices, etc., after withdrawing the entrails, lungs, and brain; to fill with sweet scent; to preserve with care and affection, from loss or decay. (Fr. *embaumer.*)
embalmer, *n.* em-*bahm*-er, one who embalms bodies.
embalmment, *n.* em-*bahm*-ment, act of embalming.
embank, *v.t.* em-*bank,* to enclose or defend with a bank, mounds, or dykes.
embankment, *n.* em-*bank*-ment, the act of embanking; a long artificial mound or structure for confining a river or carrying a railway, road, etc.
embar, *v.t.* em-*bar,* to shut or fasten with a bar; to bar; to hinder; to put under embargo.
embargo, *n.* em-*bar*-go (*pl.* **embargoes**), a prohibition of ships to leave or enter a port, issued authoritatively; a prohibition of departure; imposition of any restraint: *v.t.* to lay an embargo on and stop; to requisition or seize goods for government service. (Sp. *embargar,* to impede.)
embark, *v.t.* em-*bark,* to put on board a ship or other vessel; to engage or invest in any affair: *v.t.* to go on board ship; to venture. (Fr. *embarquer.*)
embarkation, *n.* em-bar-*kay*-shon, the act of embarking; that which is embarked.
embarrass, *v.t.* em-*ba*-ras, to put a bar or difficulty in the way of; to perplex; to render intricate; to throw into perplexity; to subject to pecuniary pressure; to disconcert or put out. (Fr. *embarrasser.*)
embarrassing, *a.* em-*ba*-ras-ing, causing embarrassment; perplexing.
embarrassingly, *ad.* in a way to embarrass.
embarrassment, *n.* em-*ba*-ras-ment, state of being embarrassed; perplexity; pecuniary difficulty; insolvency.
embassy, *n.* *em*-ba-se, the charge, employment, or mission of an ambassador or envoy; the persons sent on an embassy; the official residence of an ambassador; a solemn weighty message. (Fr. *ambassade.*)
embattle, *v.t.* em-*bat*-tl, to arrange in order of battle; to furnish with battlements. (O.Fr. *em-,* and *bastiller,* fortify.)
embattled, *a.* em-*bat*-tld, in battle array; indented like a battlement [Her. and Arch.].
embay, *v.t.* em-*bay,* to enclose in a bay; to land-lock; to surround.
embayment, *n.* em-*bay*-ment, a bay.
embed, *v.t.* em-*bed,* to lay, as in a bed; to set firmly into other material.
embedment, *n.* em-*bed*-ment, the act of embedding or state of being embedded; that in which a thing is embedded.
embellish, *v.t.* em-*bel*-lish, to adorn, decorate, or beautify; to make graceful or elegant; to furnish with illustrations. (Fr. *embellir,* to beautify.)
embellisher, *n.* em-*bel*-lish-er, one who embellishes.
embellishment, *n.* em-*bel*-lish-ment, the act of embellishing or the state of being embellished; anything that adds beauty or elegance.
ember, *n.* *em*-ber, a live cinder: *pl.* the smouldering remains of a fire. (A.S. *æmyrgean,* embers.)
Ember days, *n.* *em*-ber-dayz, any one of a succession of three days appointed in the English Church for fasting and prayer, these falling on Wednesdays, Fridays, and Saturdays in the first week in Lent and the next after Whitsuntide, 14 Sept., and 13 Dec. **Ember week,** a week in which any of these periods falls. (A.S. *ymbryne,* a period.)
ember-goose, *n.* *em*-ber-goos, the great northern diver, *Colymbus glacialis,* or loon, a large bird of the northern seas. (Norw. *imbre.*)
embertide, *n.* *em*-ber-tide, an ember season.
embezzle, *v.t.* em-*bez*-zl, to appropriate fraudulently what is entrusted to one's care. (O.Fr. *enbesillier,* to ill-treat.)
embezzlement, *n.* em-*bez*-zl-ment, the fraudulent appropriation of money or goods received on behalf of one's employer.
embezzler, *n.* em-*bez*-zl-er, one who embezzles.
embitter, *v.t.* em-*bit*-ter, to make bitter; to render distressing or more distressing; to exasperate.
emblaze, *v.t.* em-*blaze,* to adorn with glittering embellishment; to emblazon; to set ablaze.
emblazon, *v.t.* em-*blaze*-on, to paint heraldically; to deck in glaring colours; to decorate; to celebrate.
emblazoner, *n.* em-*blaze*-on-er, one who emblazons; one who proclaims with pomp.
emblazoning, *n.* em-*blaze*-on-ing, the act or art of adorning with ensigns armorial.
emblazonment, *n.* em-*blaze*-on-ment, blazonry; an emblazoning.
emblazonry, *n.* em-*blaze*-on-re, blazonry.
emblem, *n.* *em*-blem, a device or picture conceived in order to embody and represent to the eye some spiritual idea or reality; a symbol; an heraldic device; a short poem developing the idea suggested by a symbol. (L. *emblēma,* inlaid work.)
emblemata, *n.pl.* em-ble-*mah*-ta, small removable figures with which the ancients used to decorate their vessels of gold, silver, etc. (Gr. *emblēma.*)
emblematic, *a.* em-b[illegible]-*mat*-ik, emblematical.
emblematical, *a.* e[illegible]-ble-*mat*-e-kal, emplo[illegible] serving as an emblem[illegible] pertaining to an emb[illegible]
emblematically, *ad.* [illegible] an emblematic man[illegible]

emblematist, *n.* em-*blem*-a-tist, a writer or inventor of emblems.
emblements, *n.pl.* *em*-ble-ments, the produce or fruits of land sown or planted by a tenant, which belong to him, though his lease may terminate before harvest, and are, in the event of the tenant's death, the property of his executors [Law]. (O.Fr. *emblaement*, harvest.)
emblemize, *v.t.* *emb*-lem-ize, to represent by an emblem.
emblossom, *v.t.* em-*blos*-som, to cover with blossom.
embodier, *n.* em-*bod*-e-er, he that embodies.
embodiment, *n.* em-*bod*-e-ment, the act of embodying; the state of being embodied; that in which a thing or idea, etc., is embodied.
embody, *v.t.* em-*bod*-e, to form or collect into a body; to invest with a body or a material form; to incorporate; to include.
embog, *v.t.* em-*bog*, to sink or plunge into a bog.
embolden, *v.t.* em-*bole*-den, to give boldness or courage to; to encourage.
embolic, *a.* em-*bol*-ik, pertaining to an embolus or to embolism [Med.].
embolism, *n.* *em*-bo-lizm, intercalation; the insertion of days, months, or years in an account of time, to produce regularity; intercalated time; total or partial blocking up of a bloodvessel by a clot of coagulated blood-fibrine, occasioning gangrene or paralysis and often death [Med.]. (O.Fr. *embolisme*.)
embolismic, *a.* em-bo-*liz*-mik, pertaining to intercalation; intercalated; inserted.
embolite, *n.* *em*-bo-lite, chloride and bromide of silver, an important silver ore.
embolus, *n.* *em*-bo-lus, something inserted or acting in another, as a wedge or a piston; the clot which causes embolism [Med.]. (Gr.)
emboly, *n.* *em*-bo-le, invagination [Zool.].
embonpoint, *a.* (App.), plump; fattish (esp. of women): *n.* fulness of figure; stoutness; rotundity.
emborder, *v.t.* em-*bor*-der, to adorn with a border.
embosom, *v.t.* to clasp to the bosom; to shelter; to surround with an embrace.
emboss, *v.t.* em-*boss*, to form bosses or protuberances on; to ornament in relief by hammering behind or from pressure with a die. (*en-* and *boss*.)
emboss, *v.t.* em-*boss*, to encase, esp. in armour; to cover; to conceal in a thicket. (Origin uncertain.)
embosser, *n.* em-*bos*-ser, one who embosses; a punch used in repoussé work.
embossment, *n.* em-*boss*-ment, a prominence like a boss; raised work; the formation of ornamental figures in relief.
embouchure, *n.* om-boo-*shoor* (or App.), the mouth of a river; the mouthpiece of a wind instrument; the shaping of the lips to this. (Fr.)
embound, *v.t.* em-*bound*, to shut in; to set bounds to.
embow, *v.t.* em-*boh*, to arch; to shape like a bow.
embowel, *v.t.* em-*bou*-el, to disembowel.
embowelment, *n.* em-*bou*-el-ment, the act of taking out the entrails; evisceration.
embower, *v.i.* em-*bou*-er, to lodge or rest in a bower: *v.t.* to cover with a bower; to shelter with plants.
emboxed, *a.* em-*bokst*, enclosed or seated in a box.
embrace, *n.* em-*brace*, pressure to the bosom with the arms; reception of one thing into another; conjugal endearment; sexual intercourse: *v.i.* to join in an embrace: *v.t.* to take and clasp in the arms; to press to the bosom in token of affection; to seize eagerly; to take with willingness that which offers or is offered; to twice round (as a plant); to comprehend; to comprise; to encompass; to accept. (O.Fr. *embracer*.)
embraceable, *a.* em-*brace*-a-bl, that may be embraced.
embracement, *n.* em-*brace*-ment; embrace; an embracing; state of being contained; a grapple.
embracer, *n.* em-*brace*-er, one who attempts to influence a jury corruptly [Law].
embracery, *n.* em-*brace*-er-re, an attempt to influence a jury corruptly by bribery [Law].
embracive, *a.* em-*brace*-iv, demonstratively caressing; comprehensive.
embranchment, *n.* em-*brahnch*-ment, branching; branching point; a ramification.
embrangle, *v.t.* em-*brang*-gl, to entangle; to perplex.
embrasure, *n.* em-*bray*-zewr, an opening in a wall or parapet, through which guns may be fired [Fort.]; the inward splaying of a door or window [Arch.]. (Fr.)
embrocate, *v.t.* *em*-bro-kate, to moisten and rub an injured part of the body with a liquid [Med.]. (Late L. *embrocatus*, fomented.)
embrocation, *n.* em-bro-*kay*-shon, the act of embrocating; a liniment; a lotion to be rubbed in.
embroider, *v.t.* em-*broy*-der, to border with ornamental needlework; to ornament with needlework; to fill out with picturesque details. (O.Fr. *embroder*.)
embroiderer, *n.* em-*broy*-der-rer, one who embroiders.
embroidery, *n.* em-*broy*-der-re, the art of embroidering; figured work in gold, silver, silk, or other thread, formed by the needle on textiles; variegation or diversity of figures and colours; artificial ornaments.
embroil, *v.t.* em-*broyl*, to involve in trouble; to throw into confusion. (Fr. *embrouiller*.)
embroilment, *n.* em-*broyl*-ment, a state of entanglement, confusion, disturbance, or contention; the act of embroiling.
embrown, *v.t.* em-*broun*, to make brown; to obscure.
embrute, *v.t.* em-*broot*, to imbrute.
embryectomy, *n.* em-bre-*ek*-to-me, removal of an embryo through an incision in the abdomen [Surg.].
embryo, *n.* *em*-bre-o, the germ of an organism, either plant or animal; a fœtus; the immature creature before emerging from the egg or uterus; the beginning or first state of anything while yet in a rude and undeveloped condition; *a.* rudimentary; undeveloped. **embryo-buds,** spheroidal solid bodies resembling woody nodules, formed in the bark of trees and capable of throwing out branches [Bot.]. **embryo sac,** the female spore in seed plants in which the fertilized egg is developed [Bot.]. (Fr. *embryon*.)
embryoctony, *n.* em-bre-*ok*-to-ne, destruction of the fœtus in the uterus [Surg.]. (Gr. *embryon*, and *kteino*, kill.)
embryogeny, *n.* em-bre-*oj*-en-e, the process of the formation and development of embryos (Gr. *embryon*, and *gennao*, produce.)
embryoid, *a.* *em*-bre-oyd, resembling an embryo.
embryology, *n.* em-bre-*ol*-o-je, that part of biology relating to embryogeny. (Gr. *embryon*, and *logos*, science.)
embryonated, *a.* *em*-bre-o-nay-ted, pertaining to or containing an embryo.
embryonic, *a.* em-bre-*on*-ik, resembling or relating to anything in an embryo state; undeveloped.
embryotomy, *n.* em-bre-*ot*-o-me, a cutting or forcible separation of the fœtus from the uterus [Surg.]. (Gr. *embryon*, and *tome*, cutting.)
embus, *v.t.* em-*buss*, to board, or put on board, a bus, van, or lorry, etc.
embusqué, *n.* (App.), one who takes a civil, esp. government, appointment with intent to avoid military service; a shirker. (Fr., in ambush.)
emend, *v.t.* e-*mend*, to amend; to correct or improve.
emendable, *a.* e-*men*-da-bl, capable of being amended.
emendation, *n.* ee-men-*day*-shon, the act of altering for the better, or correcting an error or fault; an alteration; a correction, esp. in the text of a book. (L. *emendātus*, freed from guilt.)
emendator, *n.* *ee*-men-day-tor, a corrector of errors or faults in writings; one who corrects or improves.
emendatory, *a.* e-*men*-da-to-re, contributing to emendation; corrective.
emerald, *n.* *em*-er-rald, a precious stone of a beautiful green colour, identical, except in colour, with beryl green [Her.]; former name of a small printing type of about 6½ point. **oriental emerald,** a green variety of corundum. **the Emerald Isle,** Ireland. (Fr. *émeraude*.)
emerald-copper, *n.* dioptase.
emerald-green, *n.* a light green pigment, produced from aceto-arsenite of copper.
emerge, *v.i.* e-*merj*, to rise out of a fluid or other covering; to issue or proceed from; to reappear after being eclipsed; to rise out of a state of depression or obscurity; to rise or come into view. (L. *emergo*, rise out of water.)
emergence, *n.* e-*mer*-jence, the act of emerging; the appearance of an imago from the cocoon, etc. [Entom.]; an outgrowth from a plant, esp. a thorn [Bot.].

emergency, *n.* e-*mer*-jen-se, a sudden or unexpected event; a crisis; exigence; pressing necessity. **emergency measures,** special legislation passed in time of war or of actual or anticipated civil disturbance. **emergency ration,** a small supply of concentrated food in a sealed container for use only in an emergency [Mil.].

emergent, *a.* e-*mer*-jent, issuing; occurring suddenly or unexpectedly; calling for immediate action; urgent; pressing. **emergent year,** the first year of any era used in dating.

emeritus, *n.* e-*me*-re-tus (*pl.* **emeriti**), one who has retired with honour, esp. a professor who is retired from office with a pension after long service. (L., worn out.)

emerods, *n.pl.* *em*-er-odz, hæmorrhoids.

emersion, *n.* e-*mer*-shon, emergence; the reappearance of a heavenly body after an eclipse or occultation, or of a star which has been screened by the sun's light [Astron.]. (L. *emersus*, risen.)

emery, *n.* *em*-er-re, an extremely hard variety of corundum, usually occurring in black or bluish-grey masses, the powder of which is used for polishing hard substances. (O.Fr. *emeril.*)

emery-cloth, *n.* cloth covered with emery for smoothing and polishing purposes.

emery-paper, *n.* paper treated and used as emery-cloth.

emery-wheel, *n.* a wheel faced with emery, used for smoothing and polishing.

emesis, *n.* *em*-e-sis, a vomiting. (Gr.)

emetic, *a.* e-*met*-ik, inducing vomiting: *n.* a medicine that causes vomiting [Med.]. (L. *emeticus.*)

emetically, *ad.* e-*met*-e-ka-le, in such a manner as to excite vomiting.

emetin, *n.* *em*-et-in, a bitter alkaloid present in the root of the ipecacuanha and forming its chief active principle.

emeto-cathartic, *a.* e-*met*-o-kath-*ar*-tik, producing vomiting and purging at the same time [Med.].

emeu, *n.* *ee*-mew, the emu.

émeute, *n.* (App.), the insurrectionary rising of a mob; a riot. (Fr.)

emiction, *n.* e-*mik*-shon, the discharging of urine; the urine discharged (*e-*, and L. *mictum*, make water.)

emictory, *a.* and *n.* e-*mik*-to-re, diuretic.

emigrant, *a.* *em*-e-grant, emigrating; pertaining to emigration: *n.* one who is emigrating or has emigrated.

emigrate, *v.i.* *em*-e-grate, to quit a native country to settle in another; to leave one's home for a new one. (L. *emigratus*, gone forth.)

emigration, *n.* em-e-*gray*-shon, the act of emigrating; a body of emigrants.

emigrational, *a.* em-e-*gray*-shon-al, pertaining to emigration.

emigrationist, *n.* em-e-*gray*-shon-ist, a promoter of or advocate for emigration.

emigratory, *a.* em-e-*gray*-to-re, pertaining to emigration; migratory.

émigré, *n.* (App.), an emigrant; a fugitive, esp. one of a suppressed party as at the French and Russian Revolutions (Fr.).

eminence, *n.* *em*-e-nence, height; a rising ground; highest part; a part rising or projecting beyond the rest or above the surface; an elevated station, either in rank, office, or celebrity; distinction; a title of honour given to cardinals. (Fr. *éminence.*)

eminency, *n.* *em*-e-nen-se, eminence.

eminent, *a.* *em*-e-nent, rising above others; exalted in rank; high in public estimation; distinguished above others. (O.Fr.)

eminently, *ad.* *em*-e-nent-le, in a high degree; in a degree to attract observation.

emir, *n.* e-*meer*, amir; ameer; a Mohammedan title of independent chiefs, viziers, pashas, and the descendants of Mohammed through Fatima, etc. (Ar., ruler.)

emissary, *n.* *em*-e-sa-re, a person sent on a mission to influence as well as watch the movements of some opposing party; a spy; an outlet or duct; an excretory vessel [Anat.]: *a.* pertaining to an emissary; spying. (L. *emissarius*).

emission, *n.* e-*mish*-on, the act of emitting or issuing; that which is emitted; the act of issuing or sending into circulation; the amount issued at one time; the stream of electrons flowing from the filament of a thermionic valve [Wire.]. (L. *emissio.*)

emissive, *a.* e-*mis*-siv, emitting.

emissivity, *n.* em-is-*siv*-e-te, tendency to emit; facility or rate of emission; radiating power [Wire.].

emissory, *a.* *em*-is-o-re, emissive; pertaining to emission.

emit, *v.t.* e-*mit*, to send forth; to throw or give out; to issue, as notes and bills of credit; to print and send into circulation. (L. *emitto.*)

emmenagogue, *n.* e-*men*-a-gog, a medicine that promotes the menstrual discharge. (Gr. *emmēna*, menses, *agōgos*, drawing forth.)

emmenology, *n.* em-en-*ol*-o-je, the branch of physiology, or a treatise, dealing with menstruation. (Gr. *emmēna*, and *logos*, science.)

emmet, *n.* *em*-met, an ant or pismire. (A.S. *æmet.*)

emmetropia, *n.* em-e-*troh*-pe-a, the normal condition of the lenses of the eye. (Gr. *emmetros*, proportioned, *ops*, eye.)

emollient, *a.* e-*mol*-e-ent, softening; making supple; acting as an emollient: *n.* a substance that softens that to which it is applied; an external application that allays irritation and alleviates inflammatory soreness, etc. [Med.]. (O.Fr.).

emolument, *n.* e-*mol*-yew-ment, remuneration arising from office or employment in compensation for services; gain; profit. (O.Fr.)

emotion, *n.* e-*moh*-shon, inherent feeling; mental agitation; excitement pleasurable or otherwise; a state under which the mind is moved with sensibility or passion, etc. (L. *emotus*, moved.)

emotional, *a.* e-*moh*-shon-al, pertaining to emotion; exciting or excited by emotion.

emotionalism, *n.* e-*moh*-sho-na-lizm, a tendency to yield to emotion or to lay an undue stress on the emotional.

emotionally, *ad.* e-*moh*-sho-na-le, in an emotional way; with respect to the emotions.

emotive, *a.* e-*moh*-tiv, emotional; attended or characterized by emotion.

emotivity, *n.* ee-moh-*tiv*-e-te, the capacity for emotion.

empale, *v.t.* em-*pale*, impale.

empalement, *n.* em-*pale*-ment, impalement.

empanel, *v.t.* em-*pan*-el, to form or to enter on a list of jurors or doctors; to enrol.

empanoply, *v.t.* em-*pan*-o-ple, to invest in full armour.

empark, *v.t.* em-*park*, impark.

empathy, *n.* *em*-pa-the, the faculty of entering into, or identifying oneself with, the experiences of others; sympathetic understanding. (Gr. *en*, in, *pathos*, suffering.)

empennage, *n.* em-*pen*-aj, the stabilizing planes after-end of an aeroplane or airship. (Fr., the feathering of an arrow.)

emperor, *n.* *emp*-er-ror, the sovereign or supreme monarch of an empire; the sovereign of the Holy Roman Empire; a title of dignity superior to that of king; a very large size of drawing-paper, 48 in. by 72 in., English usage, 40 by 60 in U.S.A. **emperor butterfly,** the purple emperor, *Apatura iris.* **emperor moth,** *Saturnia carpini.* **emperor penguin,** the largest known penguin, *Aptenodytes fosteri*, of the Antarctic.

empery, *n.* *em*-per-re, empire; absolute dominion.

emphasis, *n.* *em*-fa-sis, a particular stress laid on certain words or parts of a discourse to express the speaker's sense of their importance; a peculiar impressiveness of expression, or weight of thought; stress; accent. (L.)

emphasize, *v.t.* *em*-fa-size, to lay stress on; to make emphatic; to make more distinct.

emphatic, *a.* em-*fat*-ik, requiring emphasis; expressed with emphasis; forcible, earnest, or impressive.

emphatical, *a.* em-*fat*-e-kal, emphatic.

emphatically, *ad.* em-*fat*-e-ka-le, with emphasis.

emphractic, *a.* em-*frak*-tik, having the quality of closing the pores of the skin: *n.* a medicine affecting this. (Gr. *emphractikos.*)

emphraxis, *n.* em-*frak*-sis, stoppage; obstruction, esp. of the pores of the skin [Med.]. (Gr.)

emphysema, *n.* em-fe-*see*-ma, distension of a tissue due to a collection of air in the cellular membranes [Med.]. (Gr.)

emphysematous, *a.* em-fe-*see*-ma-tus, pertaining to emphysema [Med.]; resembling a bladder [Bot.].

empire, *n.* *em*-pire, supreme control or sway; the territory, region, or countries under the sway of a supreme monarch, usually of greater extent than a kingdom; the people of an empire; any region, land or water, under sway: *a.* denoting a style in furniture or dress of the first French Empire (1804–15). **the Empire,** the Holy Roman Empire. **Empire Day,** the 24th May, Queen Victoria's birthday, held as a patriotic festival throughout the British Empire. **Empire State,** the state of New York. (O.Fr., from L. *imperium.*)

empiric, *n.* em-*pi*-rik, one whose practice of an art, esp. medicine, is founded on mere empiricism, not scientific knowledge; a charlatan: *a.* empirical. (Fr. *empirique,* a quack.)

empirical, *a.* em-*pi*-re-kal, characteristic of empiries or quacks; resting on experience or observation alone; based on experiment without regard to science or theory.

empirically, *ad.* in an empirical manner.

empiricism, *n.* em-*pi*-re-sizm, dependence on mere observation and experience, to the exclusion of scientific knowledge, or the knowledge of the connexion between cause and consequence in any particular case; unscientific practice; quackery.

empiricist, *n.* em-*pi*-re-sist, an empiric.

emplace, *v.t.* em-*place,* to put into position (esp. of guns on an emplacement).

emplacement, *n.* em-*place*-ment, location; a placing in position; a gun site or platform. (Fr.)

emplane, *v.t.* and *i.* em-*plane,* to embark in or take on board an aeroplane.

emplead, *v.t.* em-*pleed,* to implead.

employ, *n.* em-*ploy,* employment; occupation; profession; office: *v.t.* to use as an agent, instrument, means, or material; to give occupation to. **employ oneself,** to busy oneself. (Fr. *employer.*)

employability, *n.* em-*ploy*-a-*bil*-e-te, the quality of being employable.

employable, *a.* em-*ploy*-a-bl, that may be employed; capable of being used; fit for use.

employee, *n.* em-*ploy*-ee, one employed to do any work for salary or wages. (Fr.)

employer, *n.* em-*ploy*-er, one who employs labour; one who engages or keeps in service.

employment, *n.* em-*ploy*-ment, the act of employing; the state of being employed; occupation. **Employment Exchange,** a governmental organization carrying out the duties that, since 1917, have been performed by the Labour Exchanges.

emplume, *v.t.* em-*ploom,* to adorn with plumes.

empoison, *v.t.* em-*poy*-zon, to poison; to taint or corrupt; to embitter; to render hostile.

empoisoner, *n.* em-*poy*-zon-er, who who poisons or administers poison; he who or that which embitters.

empoisonment, *n.* em-*poy*-zon-ment, the act of poisoning or of empoisoning.

emporium, *n.* em-*paw*-re-um, a commercial centre; a depot; a large general shop or store. (L., mart.)

empower, *v.t.* em-*pou*-er, to give power or authority to; to authorize.

empress, *n.* *emp*-res, the consort of an emperor; a woman who governs an empire; a woman invested with imperial power; a size in building slates, 26 by 16 inches. (O.Fr. *emperesse.*)

empressement, *n.* (App.), warm cordiality; eagerness. (Fr.)

emprise, *n.* em-*prize,* an adventurous enterprise; an undertaking of danger. (O.Fr.)

emptier, *n.* *emp*-te-er, one who or that which empties or exhausts.

emptiness, *n.* *emp*-te-ness, a state of being empty; vacuity; want of substance; want of intellect.

emption, *n.* *emp*-shon, the act of buying.

emptor, *n.* *emp*-tor, a purchaser [Rom. Law].

empty, *a.* *emp*-te, containing nothing, or nothing but air; not filled; unfurnished; containing no inhabitants, or no persons; void; devoid; destitute of force or effect; unsubstantial; without supply; hungry; unfurnished with intelligence or knowledge; ignorant; unfruitful; desolate; without effect: *n.* anything which has been emptied of its contents: *v.t.* to exhaust; to deprive of the contents; to pour out the contents; to make desolate: *v.i.* to pour out or discharge its contents, as a river; to become empty. (A.S. *æmtig,* from *æmta,* leisure.)

empty-handed, *a.* having nothing of any value in the hands.

empty-headed, *a.* having few ideas.

emptying, *n.* *emp*-te-ing, the act of making empty: *pl.* the lees of beer, cider, etc.; yeast [U.S.A.].

empurple, *v.t.* em-*pur*-pl, to tinge or dye of a purple colour; to discolour with purple; to redden.

empyema, *n.* em-py-*ee*-ma, a collection of purulent matter in the pleural cavity, causing pressure on the lungs and accompanied with hectic fever. (Gr.)

empyreal, *a.* em-py-*ree*-al *or* em-pi-*ree*-al, formed of pure fire or light; refined beyond aerial substance; ethereal; pertaining to the empyrean.

empyrean, *a.* em-pi-*ree*-an, empyreal: *n.* the highest heaven or region of pure elemental fire; the region whence the spiritual fire from time to time issues and inspires the souls of the elect. (L. *empyræus.*)

empyreuma, *n.* em-pi-*roo*-ma, the disagreeable odour and acridity of animal or vegetable substances when burned in close vessels or in process of destructive distillation. (Gr. *empyreuma,* a covered-in burning substance.)

empyreumatic, *a.* *em*-pi-roo-*mat*-ik, pertaining to or resembling empyreuma.

emu, *n.* *ee*-mew, a large Australian bird of the genus *Dromæus,* allied to the cassowary and ostrich, with wings which, though useless for flight, serve to balance the body when running. (Port.)

emulant, *n.* *em*-yew-lant, a rival; an emulator.

emulate, *v.t.* *em*-yew-late, to strive to equal or excel; to imitate, with a view to equal or excel; to vie with. (L. *æmulatus,* tried to equal.)

emulation, *n.* em-yew-*lay*-shon, the act of emulating; ambition to equal or excel the example of others; rivalry, with desire to outstrip and defeat.

emulative, *a.* *em*-yew-la-tiv, inclined to emulate or rival.

emulatively, *ad.* in an emulative manner.

emulator, *n.* one who emulates; a rival. (L.)

emulgent, *a.* e-*mul*-jent, draining out (of the renal arteries and veins) [Anat.]: *n.* an emulgent vessel [Anat.]; a medicine promoting the flow of bile [Med.]. (L. *emulgens,* milking.)

emulous, *a.* *em*-yew-lus, eager to imitate or excel another; rivalling; engaged in competition; factious; contentious. (L. *æmulus.*)

emulously, *ad.* with desire of equalling or excelling another.

emulousness, *n.* quality of being emulous.

emulsification, *n.* e-*mul*-se-fe-*kay*-shon, the action or the result of emulsifying.

emulsifier, *n.* e-*mul*-se-fy-er, any agent that effects emulsification; a rotatory apparatus used in making emulsions.

emulsify, *v.t.* e-*mul*-se-fy, to convert into an emulsion.

emulsin, *n.* e-*mul*-sin, an enzyme present in almonds and certain other plants. (L. *emulsus* milked.)

emulsion, *n.* e-*mul*-shon, a milky composition produced by uniting oil and water, through the intervention of some alkaline or mucilaginous substance; a suspension of sensitive silver salt used for coating plates and films [Phot.]. (O.Fr.)

emulsive, *a.* e-*mul*-siv, softening; milk-like; producing or yielding oil, or a milk-like substance.

emunctory, *n.* e-*munk*-to-re, any duct or organ serving to carry off excrementitious matter; an excretory duct [Anat.]: *a.* able, or serving, to excrete. (L. *emunctum,* wiped from the nose.)

emu-wren, *n.* *ee*-mew-*ren,* a small Australian bird of the genus *Stipiturus* whose tail-feathers somewhat resemble those of the emu.

Emys, *n.* *ee*-mis, a genus of marsh-tortoises including the terrapins. (Gr. *emys,* tortoise.)

en-, en, a prefix representing the Latin *in-* (Gr. and Fr. *en-*), signifying in or into, and sometimes intensifying the meaning. (Fr. *en.*)

-en, en, a suffix from Teutonic forming diminutives (as *chicken*), plurals (*brethren, oxen*), adjectives (*golden, wooden*), and verbs (*darken, lengthen*).

en, *n.* en, a printer's measure of half an em.

enable, *v.t.* e-*nay*-bl, to make able; to supply with power, physical or moral; to supply with means; to authorize. **enabling Act,** a statute legalizing the doing of something that would otherwise be unlawful.

enact, *v.t.* en-*akt,* to make, as a law; to pass, as a bill into a law; to decree; to establish as the will of the supreme power; to act; to perform.

enactive, *a.* en-*ak*-tiv, having power to enact.

enactment, *n.* en-*akt*-ment, the passing of a bill into a law; that which is enacted; a law.
enactory, *a.* en-*ak*-to-re, pertaining to enactment; enacting [Law].
enacture, *n.* en-*ak*-tewr, purpose; fulfilment.
enaliosaur, *n.* en-*al*-e-o-sawr, an extinct gigantic marine reptile allied to the crocodile. (Gr. *en-*, *hals*, the sea, *auros*, a lizard.)
enallage, *n.* en-*al*-a-je, a change of words, or a substitution of one gender, number, case, person, tense, mood, or voice of the same word for another [Gram.]. (Gr.)
enamel, *n.* e-*nam*-el, a substance of the nature of opaque glass applied by fusion to metal, porcelain, or other surfaces for their preservation or decoration; that which is enamelled; any smooth glossy surface of any colour, resembling enamel; the smooth ivory-like substance forming the surface of the visible part of a tooth: *v.t.* to lay enamel on a metal, etc.; to paint in enamel; to form a glossy surface like enamel; to variegate with diverse colours: *v.i.* to practise the art of enamelling. (Fr. *émail*, originally *esmail*, from root of *smelt*.)
enameller, *n.* e-*nam*-el-er, one whose occupation is to lay on enamels or inlay colours.
enamelling, *n.* e-*nam*-el-ing, the act or art of laying on enamels.
enamelware, *n.* e-*nam*-el-ware, kitchen or other utensils coated with enamel.
enamour, *v.t.* e-*nam*-ur, to inflame with love; to charm; to captivate. (O.Fr. *enamorer*.)
enanthema, *n.* en-an-*thee*-ma, an eruption of the mucous membrane [Med.].
enanthesis, *n.* en-an-*thee*-sis, an eruption of the skin proceeding from an internal affection, as in measles (Gr. *en-*, in, *antheo*, blossom.)
enantiomorphous, e-*nan*-te-o-*mawr*-fus, having a relationship as that of an object to its reflection (of crystals).
enantiopathy, *n.* e-*nan*-te-*op*-a-the, allopathy. (Gr. *enantios*, opposite, *pathos*, feeling.)
enantiosis, *n.* e-*nan*-te-*oh*-sis, an ironical figure of speech in which the negative is used for affirmative, or affirmative for negative [Rhet.]. (Gr. *enantios*, opposite.)
enarched, *a.* en-*archt*, in the shape of an arch; arched [Her.]; inarched [Bot.].
enarthrodial, *a.* en-ar-*throh*-de-al, in the ball-and-socket manner.
enarthrosis, *n.* en-ar-*throh*-sis, a ball-and-socket joint; the articulation in which the round end of a bone fits into the cup-like cavity of another, forming a joint movable in every direction [Anat.]. (Gr., a jointing.)
enation, *n.* e-*nay*-shon, an outgrowth, esp. a morbid outgrowth from the underside of a leaf [Bot.].
encænia, *n.pl.* en-*see*-ne-a, an annual commemorative festival, esp. of the foundation, of a city or consecration of a church; at Oxford University, the festival commemorating founders and benefactors. (L.)
encage, *v.t.* en-*kaje*, to shut up in a cage; to coop.
encamp, *v.i.* en-*kamp*, to pitch tents, as an army; to form an encampment: *v.t.* to form into a camp; to lodge in tents (of troops, etc.). (Fr. *en-*, in, and *camp*.)
encampment, *n.* en-*kamp*-ment, the act of encamping; the camp or the place where an army or company is encamped.
encapsule, *v.t.* en-*kap*-sewl, to enclose in or as in a capsule.
encarnalize, *v.t.* en-*kar*-na-lize, to embody in the flesh; to sensualize.
encarpus, *n.* en-*kar*-pus, a carved festoon of fruit, leaves, etc. [Arch.]. (Gr. *en-*, and *karpos*, fruit.)
encase, *v.t.* en-*kace*, to enclose or confine in a case; to protect with a case.
encasement, *n.* en-*kace*-ment, the act of encasing; the state of being encased; that which encases.
encash, *v.t.* en-*kash*, to pay in cash; to realize.
encashment, *n.* en-*kash*-ment, the payment in cash of a note, draft, etc.
encaustic, *a.* en-*kaws*-tik, produced by being burnt in; pertaining to the art of painting in heated or burned wax, by which colours were rendered permanent: *n.* this method of painting in heated or burned wax. **encaustic tile,** a tile inlaid with coloured clays, fired, and glazed. (L. *encausticus*.)
encave, *v.t.* en-*kave*, to hide in a cave or recess.
enceinte, *n.* (App.), a fortified enclosure; a surrounding wall or rampant [Fort.]: *a.* **pregnant:** with child. (Fr., encircled.)
encephal-, *comb. f.* en-*sef*-al-, denoting the brain. (Gr. *enkephalos*, brain.)
encephalic, *a.* en-se-*fal*-ik, of or pertaining to the head or brain.
encephalitis, *n.* en-*sef*-a-*ly*-tis, inflammation of the brain. **encephalitis lethargica,** sleepy sickness.
encephalocele, *n.* en-*sef*-a-lo-seel, hernia of the brain. (Gr. *enkephalos*, and *kele*, a tumour.)
encephalography, *n.* en-sef-a-*log*-ra-fe, radiography of the brain.
encephaloid, *a.* en-*sef*-a-loyd, resembling the matter of the brain; cerebriform (esp. of a form of cancer in which the diseased part resembles the brain-matter): *n.* an encephaloid cancer. (Gr. *enkephalos*, and *eidos*, like.)
encephalon, *n.* en-*sef*-a-lon, the brain; the whole contents of the cranium. (Gr.)
encephalotomy, *n.* en-*sef*-a-*lot*-o-me, dissection of the brain. (Gr. *enkephalon*, and *tome*, cutting.)
encephalous, *a.* en-*sef*-a-lus, having a distinct head or brain [Zool.].
enchain, *v.t.* en-*chane*, to bind or hold in chains; to hold fast; to link together.
enchainment, *n.* en-*chane*-ment, the act of enchaining or state of being enchained; concatenation.
enchant, *v.t.* en-*chahnt*, to affect, hold, or sway with a spell or charm; to bewitch; to fascinate; to charm; to delight in the highest degree. (Fr. *enchanter*.)
enchanter, *n.* en-*chahn*-ter, one who enchants; a sorcerer or magician; one who charms or delights. **enchanter's nightshade,** the plant *Circæa lutetiana*, found in damp shady places.
enchanting, *a.* en-*chahn*-ting, delightful; charming or ravishing.
enchantingly, *ad.* in a manner to delight or charm.
enchantment, *n.* en-*chahnt*-ment, the act of enchanting, esp. of producing magical effects by the help of spells; the use of magic arts, spells, or charms; that which enchants or charms. (Fr. *enchantement*.)
enchantress, *n.* en-*chahn*-tress, a sorceress or dealer in enchantments; a woman who charms.
encharge, *v.t.* en-*charj*, to enjoin; to entrust.
enchase, *v.t.* en-*chace*, to incase or enclose in another body, as a precious stone in gold; to adorn with embossed work; to chase; to adorn by fixing on or embedding in the surface. (Fr. *enchâsser*.)
enchiridion, *n.* en-ky-*rid*-e-on, a manual; a book to be carried in the hand; a book of selections. (Gr. *en-*, and *cheir*, the hand.)
enchondroma, *n.* en-*kon*-dro-ma, a cartilaginous tumour. (Gr. *en-*, and *chondros*, cartilage.)
enchorial, *a.* en-*kaw*-re-al, in common use among the natives of a country (esp. of the Egyptian demotic characters); demotic. (Gr. *enchorios*, a region or country.)
enchoric, *a.* en-*kaw*-rik, enchorial.
encincture, *v.t.* en-*sink*-tewr, to surround with or as with a girdle: *n.* encirclement.
encircle, *v.t.* en-*ser*-kl, to enclose or surround with a circle or ring, or with anything circular; to encompass; to embrace. (Gr. *en-*, and *circle*.)
encirclement, *n.* en-*ser*-kl-ment, the act of encircling; the state of being encircled.
enclasp, *v.t.* en-*klahsp*, to clasp; to embrace.
enclave, *n.* *en*-klave, a detached piece of territory surrounded by foreign dominions: *a.* shaped like a dovetail joint [Her.]. (Fr.)
enclavement, *n.* en-*klave*-ment, the condition of being an enclave.
enclitic, *n.* en-*klit*-ik, a particle or word, so closely united to another as to seem to be a part of it, throwing back the accent upon the foregoing syllable, as *que*, in *virumque*: *a.* subjoined [Gram.]; having the force of an enclitic. (Gr. *enklitikos*, dependent.)
enclitically, *ad.* in an enclitic manner, by throwing the accent back.
enclose, *v.t.* en-*kloze*, to surround; to fence off; to shut in; to include with a letter in an envelope.
encloser, *n.* en-*kloze*-er, one who or that which encloses; one who fences off ground from common land.
enclosure, *n.* en-*kloh*-zhur, the act of enclosing or state of being enclosed; that which is enclosed; that which encloses; the separation of land from a common by a fence for private use.

enclothe, *v.t.* en-*klothe,* to clothe.
encloud, *v.t.* en-*kloud,* to overcloud ; to obscure ; to darken.
encode, *v.t.* en-*kohd,* to convert (plain language) into code.
encomiast, *n.* en-*koh*-me-ast, a panegyrist ; one who composes encomiums ; a flatterer. (Gr. *enkomiastēs.*)
ecomiastic, *a.* en-ko-me-*as*-tik, laudatory.
encomiastically, *ad.* en-ko-me-*as*-te-ka-le, in an encomiastic manner.
encomium, *n.* en-*koh*-me-um (*pl.* **encomiums**), a high commendation, panegyric or eulogy. (L.)
encompass, *v.t.* en-*kum*-pas, to go round in a circle ; to encircle ; to surround.
encompassment, *n.* en-*kum*-pas-ment, a surrounding or being surrounded.
encore, *int.* and *ad.* *on*-kore, again ; once more : *n.* a call for a repetition of a particular item at a concert or theatre ; the item given : *v.t.* to call for a repetition. (Fr.)
encounter, *n.* en-*koun*-ter, a sudden or accidental meeting of two or more persons ; a conflict ; a fight ; an interview ; a sudden or unexpected address or accosting : *v.t.* to meet face to face, esp. suddenly or unexpectedly ; to engage with in battle ; to meet and strive to remove or surmount ; to attack and attempt to confute ; to meet with, as an obstacle : *v.i.* to meet face to face ; to fight. (O.Fr. *encontrer.*)
encourage, *v.t.* en-*ku*-raj, to give courage to or increase confidence of success ; to inspire with courage, spirit, or strength of mind ; to incite or stimulate. (Fr. *encourager.*)
encouragement, *n.* en-*ku*-raj-ment, the act of giving courage or confidence ; incitement to action or to practice ; that which serves to incite, support, promote, or advance. (Fr.)
encourager, *n.* en-*ku*-ra-jer, one who encourages, either by counsel, reward, or means of execution.
encouraging, *a.* en-*ku*-ra-jing, inspiring confidence ; furnishing ground to hope for success.
encouragingly, *ad.* in a manner to give courage or hope of success.
Encratism, *n.* *en*-kra-tizm, the principles and practices of the Encratites.
Encratite, *n.* *en*-kra-tite, a member of an early Christian sect who abstained from meat, wine, and marriage.
encrimson, *v.t.* en-*krim*-zn, to cover with a crimson colour ; to redden.
encrinital, *a.* en-kre-*ny*-tal, relating to or containing encrinites.
encrinite, *n.* *en*-kre-nite, a fossil crinoid or sea-lily. (Gr. *en-*, and *krinon,* a lily.)
encroach, *v.t.* en-*kroach,* to intrude, trench upon, or invade ; to take possession of by gradual advances ; to creep on stealthily and gradually. (O.Fr. *encrocher.*)
encroacher, *n.* en-*kroach*-er, one who encroaches.
encroachment, *n.* en-*kroach*-ment, silent gradual advance and invasion or intrusion ; that which is taken by encroaching ; unlawful interference with another's rights, etc. or taking more than one's due [Law]. (O.Fr. *encrochment.*)
encrust, *v.t.* en-*krust,* to cover with a crust.
encrustment, *n.* en-*krust*-ment, the act of encrusting ; incrustation.
encumber, *v.t.* en-*kum*-ber, to impede motion with a load, burden, or anything inconvenient ; to hamper and embarrass ; to load with pecuniary burdens. (O.Fr. *encombrer.*)
encumbrance, *n.* en-*kum*-brance, anything that encumbers ; anything impeding freedom of action ; a legal liability on an estate [Law].
encumbrancer, *n.* en-*kum*-bran-ser, one who has an encumbrance or a legal claim on an estate.
encyclical, *a.* en-*sike*-le-kal, sent about to many persons or places (esp. of a letter) : *n.* a papal letter addressed to the bishops or the Church generally on some ecclesiastical or doctrinal subject. (L. *encyclicus,* circular.)
encyclopædia (*or* **-pedia**), *n.* en-*sike*-lo-*pee*-de-a, a book or series of books containing a collection of articles on all or many branches of knowledge, or on a particular branch of knowledge, arranged in alphabetical order ; a general system of instruction or knowledge. (Fr. *encyclopédie.*)
encyclopedian, *a.* en-*sike*-lo-*pee*-de-an, comprising the whole range of knowledge ; of the nature of an encyclopædia.
encyclopedic, *a.* en-*sike*-lo-*pee*-dik, pertaining to or of the nature of encyclopædias ; containing information on every subject ; having very comprehensive knowledge.
encyclopedism, *n.* en-*sike*-lo-*pee*-dizm, the compilation of encyclopædias ; the doctrines of the writers of the French *Encyclopédie* ; possession of knowledge of all kinds.
encyclopedist, *n.* en-*sike*-lo-*pee*-dist, the compiler, or one assisting in the compilation, of an encyclopædia, esp. of the French *Encyclopédie* (1751–80) ; one possessed of wide learning.
encysted, *a.* en-*sis*-ted, enclosed in a bag, bladder, or vesicle [Anat.]. (Gr. *en-*, and *kystis,* cyst.)
★**end,** *n.* end, the extreme point of a line or of anything that has more length than breadth ; the last part ; the conclusion ; ultimate state ; the utmost point ; death ; cessation ; close of a particular state of things ; limit ; destruction ; cause of death ; final issue ; a fragment ; the point aimed at : *v.t.* to bring to an end ; to finish ; to put to death : *v.i.* to be finished ; to terminate ; to cease ; to come to a close. **end for end,** with the position of the ends reversed. **end to end,** from one end to the other ; the whole distance. **ends of the earth,** the remotest parts of the earth. **make an end of,** put a stop to. **make both ends meet,** to balance expenses with income. **off the deep end,** in a passionate or highly excited state. **on end,** upright ; erect. **rope's end,** a short piece of rope used for flogging. **shoemaker's end,** a length of waxed thread with a bristle at the end. **to keep one's end up,** to maintain one's position, reputation, etc. (A.S. *ende.*)
endamage, *v.t.* en-*dam*-aj, to bring loss or damage to ; to injure.
endanger, *v.t.* en-*dane*-jer, to expose to danger ; to expose to loss or injury.
endangerment, *n.* en-*dane*-jer-ment, the state of being in danger ; danger.
endear, *v.t.* en-*deer,* to make dear ; to make more beloved ; to bind by ties of affection.
endearing, *a.* en-*deer*-ing, winning the affections.
endearment, *n.* en-*deer*-ment, the act of endearing ; that which excites or increases affection ; the state of being endeared ; tender affection.
endeavour, *n.* en-*dev*-ur, exertion toward the attainment of an object ; effort ; exertion ; aim : *v.i.* to make endeavour or exertion for the accomplishment of an object : *v.t.* to make an attempt to gain. (*en-*, Fr. *devoir,* duty.)
endecagon, *n.* en-*dek*-a-gon, hendecagon.
endeictic, *a.* en-*dike*-tik, showing ; exhibiting. (Gr. *endeiktikos.*)
endeixis, *n.* en-*dike*-sis, a symptom indicating the remedial measures to be adopted [Med.]. (Gr.)
endemic, *a.* en-*dem*-ik, local ; indigenous ; peculiar to a district or special locality : *n.* an endemic disease. **endemic disease,** one to which the inhabitants of a particular district are peculiarly subject [Med.]. (Gr. *endemios,* native.)
endemically, *ad.* en-*dem*-e-ka-le, in an endemic manner.
endemicity, *n.* en-dem-*is*-e-te, the state or quality being endemic.
endemiology, *n.* en-*dem*-e-*ol*-o-je, that department of medical science which treats of endemic diseases. (Gr. *endemios,* and *logos,* science.)
endemism, *n.* *en*-dem-izm, endemicity.
endenizen, *v.t.* en-*den*-e-zen, to naturalize ; to admit to the privileges of a denizen.
ender, *n.* *end*-er, the last one ; the one that ends.
endermic, *a.* en-*der*-mik, acting through the skin ; applied to the skin after a blister [Med.]. (Gr. *en-*, and *derma,* skin.)
enderon, *n.* *en*-de-ron, the true skin ; the inner layer of the ectoderm [Zool.]. (Gr. *en-*, and *deros,* skin.)
ending, *n.* *en*-ding, termination ; latter part ; conclusion ; result ; the terminating syllable or letter of a word [Gram.].
endirons, *n.pl.* *end*-i-urnz, iron plates on each side of the fire in a kitchen grate, movable at pleasure.
endive, *n.* *en*-div, a species of chicory, *Cichorium endivia,* cultivated for used in salads. (Fr.)
endless, *a.* *end*-less, without end (of length, space, duration, or time) ; everlasting, infinite ; unlimited ; never ending or ceasing ; never leading to

any result. **endless chain** or **belt,** a chain or belt the ends of which are united [Mech.]. **endless saw,** a ribbon saw working over two wheels. **endless screw,** a screw combined with a wheel and axle, so that the threads of the screw work into the teeth fixed on the periphery of the wheel [Mech.].
endlessly, *ad. end*-les-le, so as to be endless.
endlessness, *n.* the quality of being endless.
endlong, *ad. end*-long, with the end forward.
endmost, *a.* farthest; at the extreme end.
endo-, *en*-do, a Greek prefix used in scientific terms, signifying within. (Gr. *endon,* within.)
endocardiac, *a,* en-do-*kar*-de-ak, pertaining to the endocardium.
endocarditis, *n.* en-do-kar-*dy*-tis, inflammation of the endocardium.
endocardium, *n.* en-do-*kar*-de-um, a membrane which lines the interior of the heart. (Gr. *kardia,* the heart.)
endocarp, *n. en*-do-karp, the inner coat of the pericarp of a fruit [Bot.]. (Gr. *karpos,* fruit.)
endochrome, *n. en*-do-krome, colouring matter in plants other than chlorophyll [Bot.]. (Gr. *chroma,* colour.)
endocrane, *n. en*-do-krane, the inner surface of the skull (*endo-*, and L. *cranium,* skull.)
endocrine, *a. en*-do-krin, secreting internally; pertaining to secretion: *n.* an endocrine gland.
endocrinology, *n. en*-do-kry-*nol*-o-je, the branch of biological science dealing with internal secretions and the endocrine glands.
endocrinous, *a.* en-do-*kry*-nus, pertaining to an endocrine gland or its secretions.
endocyst, *n. en*-do-sist, the inner membrane of a polyzoon [Zool.]. (*endo-* and *cyst.*)
endoderm, *n. en*-do-derm, the inner body, wall, or skin of certain invertebrate animals; the inner layer of the blastoderm [Zool.]. (Gr. *derma,* skin.)
endodermic, *a.* en-do-*der*-mik, pertaining to or derived from the endoderm.
endogamous, *a.* en-*dog*-a-mus, marrying only within the tribe.
endogamy, *n.* en-*dog*-a-me, the custom of marrying only within the tribe. (Gr. *gamos,* marriage.)
endogastric, *a. en*-do-*gas*-trik, pertaining to, or situated within, the inside of the abdomen.
endogen, *n. en*-do-jen, a monocotyledon; a plant, such as a palm, which grows from within and in which the stem has no cambium, and cannot increase in thickness when the outer edge becomes hard [Bot.]. (Gr. *gennao,* produce.)
endogenous, *a.* en-*doj*-e-nus, belonging to the endogens [Bot.]; developed internally [Biol.]; growing from within.
endolymph, *n. en*-do-limf, the fluid in the membranous labyrinth of the ear. (*endo-* and *lymph.*)
endomorph, *n. en*-do-morf, a mineral enclosed in a crystal or some other mineral. (Gr. *endon,* and *morphē,* shape.)
endoparasite, *n. en*-do-*pa*-ra-site, an internal parasite.
endophagy, *n.* en-*dof*-a-je, cannibalism among members of the same tribe.
endophyllous, *a.* en-*dof*-e-lus, within or evolved from a sheath (of leaves) [Bot.]. (Gr. *phyllon,* a leaf.)
endophyte, *n. en*-do-fyt, a plant growing within another.
endoplasm, *n. en*-do-plazm, the inner layer of protoplasm; endosarc.
endoplast, *n. en*-do-plast, a nucleated cell embedded in the protoplasm of certain protozoa [Zool.]. (Gr. *plasso,* form.)
endopleura, *n.* en-do-*ploor*-ra, the inner integument of a seed [Bot.]. (Gr. *pleura,* the side.)
endorhiza, *n.* en-do-*ry*-za, the radicle of the embryo in monocotyledons [Bot.]. (Gr. *rhiza,* a root.)
endorhizal, *a.* pertaining to the endorhiza.
endorsable, *a.* en-*dorse*-a-bl, that may be endorsed.
endorse, *v.t.* en-*dorse,* to write on the back of; to assign by endorsement; to confirm.
endorsee, *n.* en-dorse-*ee,* the person to whom a bill is endorsed.
endorsement, *n.* en-*dorse*-ment, the act of writing on the back (of a bill, etc.); that which is there written; approval.
endorser, *n.* en-*dorse*-er, the person who endorses.
endosarc, *n. en*-do-sark, endoplasm.
endoscope, *n. en*-do-skope, an optical instrument for examining internal organs.
endoscopy, *n.* en-*dos*-ko-pe, examination with the endoscope [Med.].
endoskeleton, *n.* en-do-*skel*-e-ton, the internal skeleton of vertebrates [Zool.]. (*endo-* and *skeleton.*)
endosmometer, *n.* en-dos-*mom*-e-ter, an instrument for measuring endosmosis.
endosmosis, *n.* en-dos-*moh*-sis, the transmission of liquids or gases through a membrane or porous substance from without inward. (*endo-*, and *osmos,* pushing.)
endosmotic, *a.* en-dos-*mot*-ik, pertaining to or in the manner of endosmosis.
endosperm, *n. en*-do-sperm, the albumen of seeds [Bot.]. (Gr. *sperma,* seed.)
endospermic, *a.* en-do-*sper*-mik, pertaining to or containing endosperm.
endospore, *n. en*-do-spore, the inner coat of a spore.
endosteitis, *n.* en-dos-te-*eye*-tis, inflammation of the osteum.
endosteum, *n.* en-*dos*-te-um, the periosteum lining the cavities of certain bones. (Gr. *osteon,* bone.)
endostome, *n. en*-dos-tome, the passage through the inner integument of a seed, immediately below the foramen [Bot.]. (Gr. *stoma,* a mouth.)
endothelium, *n. en*-do-*thee*-le-um, the lining membrane of blood-vessels, lymph-vessels, and serous cavities. (Gr. *thelē,* nipple.)
endow, *v.t.* en-*dou,* to settle a dower on; to provide a permanent income by endowment; to furnish with any gift, quality, or faculty. (O.Fr. *endouer.*)
endower, *n.* en-*dou*-er, one who endows.
endowment, *n.* en-*dou*-ment, the act of endowing or of settling a fund for the support of a person, official, or institution; property or revenue permanently appropriated to some such purpose; natural capacity or faculty bestowed on any one.
endue, *v.t.* en-*dew,* to invest with; to endow; to bestow.
endurable, *a.* en-*dewr*-ra-bl, that can be endured.
endurableness, *n.* the quality of being endurable.
endurably, *ad.* in an endurable manner.
endurance, *n.* en-*dewr*-rance, continuance; duration; state of enduring; bearing or suffering; a continuing under pain or distress without impatience or without sinking; patience; fortitude.
endure, *v.i.* en-*dewr,* to last; to continue; to suffer without resistance or without yielding; to bear or brook: *v.t.* to support without breaking or yielding to force or pressure; to bear without impatience or sinking under pressure; to undergo. (Fr. *endurer.*)
endurer, *n.* en-*dewr*-rer, one who endures; he who or that which continues long or continues firm.
enduring, *a.* en-*dewr*-ring, lasting long; permanent.
enduringly, *ad.* so as to endure.
enduringness, *n.* the quality of enduring.
endways, *ad. end*-wayz, on the end; in an upright position; with the end forward.
endwise, *ad. end*-wize, endways.
enema, *n.* e-*nee*-ma *or en*-e-ma, a medicinal injection, esp. one by the rectum; an appliance with which this is injected [Med.]. (Gr.)
enemy, *a. en*-e-me, belonging to the enemy; hostile: *n.* one who is hostile to another; a foe; one who hates or dislikes; the opposing force in war [Mil.]. **enemy No. 1,** the arch-enemy or chief offender [U.S.A.]. **public enemy,** one who belongs to a nation or party at war with another. **the enemy,** the devil [Theol.]; time [Slang]. (O.Fr. *enemi.*)
energetic, *a.* en-er-*jet*-ik, operating with force, vigour and effect; forcible, vigorous, or effective; exerting energy. (Gr. *energetikos.*)
energetically, *ad.* en-er-*jet*-e-ka-le, with energy.
energeticist, *n.* en-er-*jet*-e-sist, one who specializes in energetics.
energetics, *n.pl.* en-er-*jet*-iks, the science of physical as distinct from vital dynamics.
energic, *a.* en-*er*-jik, active in producing an effect; exerting great energy; in active operation.
energism, *n. en*-er-jizm, the theory that the highest good consists not in happiness but in devotion to some definite activity or work [Ethics].
energize, *v.i. en*-er-jize, to act with force or operate with vigour; to act in producing an effect: *v.t.* to impart energy to.
energizer, *n. en*-er-jize-er, he who or that which gives energy, or acts in producing an effect.
energumen, *n.* en-er-*gew*-men, one under some

powerful demoniac influence; a fanatic. (L. *energumenus.*)

energy, *n.* *en*-er-je, internal or inherent power; the power of operating; power exerted; vigorous operation; efficacy; strength or force of expression; power to effect work [Mech.]. **conservation of energy,** the doctrine that, however it may change in form and character, no force in the universe is ever destroyed [Physics]. (Fr. *énergie.*)

enervate, *v.t.* *en*-er-vate, to deprive of nerve, force, or strength; to weaken. (L. *enervatus,* weakened.)

enervate, *a.* e-*ner*-vat, weakened; weak; wanting in vigour.

enervation, *n.* en-er-*vay*-shon, the act of enervating; the state of being enervated.

enface, *v.t.* en-*face,* to write on the front of a bill, as opposed to endorsing.

enfacement, *n.* en-*face*-ment, the act of enfacing; the writing with which a bill, etc., is enfaced.

enfeeble, *v.t.* en-*fee*-bl, to deprive of strength; to weaken, debilitate, or enervate. (O.Fr. *enfeblir.*)

enfeeblement, *n.* en-*fee*-bl-ment, the act of enfeebling; enervation; state of weakness.

enfeebler, *n.* en-*fee*-bler, one who or that which enfeebles.

enfeoff, *v.t.* en-*feef,* to invest with a fief or fee; to give to another any corporeal hereditament, in fee simple or fee tail, by livery of seizin; to give freehold property; to invest legally with a right of property in an estate [Law]. (O.Fr. *enfeofer.*)

enfeoffment, *n.* en-*feef*-ment, the act of enfeoffing, the instrument or deed by which one is invested with the fee of an estate [Law].

enfilade, *n.* en-fe-*lade,* a position in a straight line; a fire of musketry or artillery raking a line from end to end [Mil.]: *v.t.* to rake with shot in the direction or through the whole length of a line [Mil.]. (Fr.)

enfold, *v.t.* en-*fohld,* to embrace; to fold; to clasp.

enforce, *v.t.* en-*force,* to give force to; to add force; to make or gain by force; to put in force; to press or urge; to compel. (O.Fr. *enforcer.*)

enforceability, *n.* en-force-a-*bil*-e-te, the quality of being enforceable.

enforceable, *a.* en-*force*-a-bl, that may be enforced.

enforcedly, *ad.* en-*force*-ed-le, by violence; not by choice.

enforcement, *n.* en-*force*-ment, the act of enforcing; compulsion; that which gives force or effect; sanction; that which urges or constrains; a putting in execution, as law.

enframe, *v.t.* en-*frame,* to put into a frame; to be a frame for.

enfranchise, *v.t.* en-*fran*-chize, to set free; to admit to the privileges of a freeman; to accord full parliamentary or municipal rights and privileges to; to give a vote to. (O.Fr. *enfranchir.*)

enfranchisement, *n.* en-*fran*-chiz-ment, the act of enfranchising; the state of being enfranchised, or admitted to civic privilege or freedom, specially the right of franchise. **enfranchisement of copyhold lands,** the legal conveyance of copyhold lands by the lord of a manor to his tenants, by which such tenements are converted into freeholds [Law].

enfranchiser, *n.* en-*fran*-chiz-er, one who enfranchises.

engage, *v.t.* en-*gaje,* to bind by compact or promise; to bind as surety; to pawn or stake as a pledge; to enlist; to hire; to bespeak; to embark; to win and attach; to attract and fix; to occupy; to encounter; *v.i.* to encounter; to meet in conflict; to embark in any business; to undertake; to promise or pledge one's word; to bind oneself; to be in gear [Mech.]; to cross blades [Fencing]. (O.Fr. *engager.*)

engaged, *a.* en-*gayjd,* betrothed; pledged; promised; enlisted; embarked; employed. **engaged column,** a column half sunk in a wall [Arch.].

engagement, *n.* en-*gaje*-ment, the act of engaging; obligation by agreement or contract; betrothment; occupation; an appointment; employment of the attention; a battle; obligation or motive.

engager, *n.* en-*gaje*-er, one who enters into an engagement or agreement; one who engages or employs another.

engaging, *a.* en-*gaje*-ing, winning; attractive; tending to draw the attention or the affections; pleasing.

engagingly, *ad.* in a manner to win the affections.

engarland, *v.t* en-*gahr*-land, to garland.

engender, *v.t.* en-*jen*-der, to beget; to breed; to bring forth; to bring about or stir up: *v.i.* to come into being. (Fr. *engendrer.*)

engenderer, *n.* en-*jen*-der-rer, he who or that which engenders.

engild, *v.t.* en-*gild,* to gild; to brighten.

★**engine,** *n.* *en*-jin, a machine intended to produce some effect by help of the mechanical powers, esp. a steam-engine [Mech.]; a prime mover; anything used to effect a purpose; a means; instrument; tool: *v.t.* to provide (a ship, chassis, etc.) with an engine. (O.Fr. *engin.*)

engine-driver, *n.* one who manages the running of a locomotive.

engineer, *n.* en-je-*neer,* one versed in and who practises the calling of any branch of engineering; one employed in delineating plans, and superintending the construction of public works; one employed in the construction and the working of mines, coal-pits, etc.; one who designs and constructs engines; the manager of an engine, esp. a locomotive; a member of a military body trained in military engineering: *v.t.* to superintend the engineering of; to try engineering measures with; to manage by ingenuity to carry through.

engineering, *n.* en-je-*neer*-ring, the business of an engineer of any branch, of which the chief are:—civil, mechanical, electrical, military, structural, railway, mining, sanitary, hydraulic; the art of making and using machinery; the art of utilizing natural forces and materials for the services of man. **civil engineering** connotes the formation of bridges, roads, embankments, canals, harbours, aqueducts, etc. **military engineering** relates to the construction of fortifications, throwing up earthworks, and surveying a country for the various operations of war.

enginery, *n.* *en*-jin-er-re, engines in general; implements of war; machination.

engine-turning, *n.* a complex kind of machine-turning on watch-cases, etc.

engirdle, *v.t.* en-*gerd*-dl, to encompass or surround with or as with a girdle.

englacial, *a.* en-*glay*-shal, embedded in, or flowing beneath, a glacier.

Englander, *n.* *ing*-glan-der, an Englishman [chiefly U.S.A.]. **Little Englander,** a British opponent of British imperialism.

English, *a.* *ing*-glish, pertaining to England or to its inhabitants: *n.* the people of England; the language of the English; a former size of type of about 14 point: *v.t.* to translate into English; to express in plain English. **the King's (Queen's) English,** standard or plain English. (A.S. *Englisc,* from the Angles, a Low-German tribe of Schleswig which settled in Britain in the 5th century A.D.)

Englishman, *n.* *ing*-glish-man, one of English descent; an inhabitant of England, native or naturalized; an English ship.

Englishry, *n.* *ing*-glish-re, the state of being an Englishman; those of English descent, esp. in Ireland or a foreign country.

englut, *v.t.* en-*glut,* to swallow; to satiate; to glut.

engorge, *v.t.* en-*gorj,* to swallow with greediness or in large quantities: *v.i.* to feed with voracity; to be congested (of blood-vessels, etc.) [Phys.]. (Fr. *engorger.*)

engorgement, *n.* en-*gorj*-ment, the act of gorging; state of being gorged, as a blood-vessel.

engraft, *v.t.* en-*grahft,* to insert a scion of one tree into another for propagation; to fix deep and firm.

engrafter, *n.* en-*grahf*-ter, one who engrafts.

engraftment, *n.* en-*grahft*-ment, the act of engrafting; a graft.

engrail, *v.t.* en-*grale,* to dot or indent round the edge; to indent in semicircular curves [Her.]; to ornament with such a design: *v.i.* to form an engrailed border [Her.]. (Fr. *engrêler.*)

engrailment, *n.* en-*grale*-ment, the state of being engrailed, the ring of dots round the edges of a medal; an engrailing [Her.].

engrain, *v.t.* en-*grane,* to dye deeply; to dye in the grain or before manufacture; to implant ineradicably.

engrave, *v.t.* en-*grave,* to cut on stone, metal, or wood with a graver; to scribe; to incise; to impress deeply. (*en-,* and A.S. *grafan,* to carve.)

engraver, *n.* en-*grave*-er, one who practises the art of engraving.

engraving, *n.* en-*grave*-ing, the act or art of producing decoration on a surface by cutting on it letters, figures, or devices, etc.; the art of cutting designs on metal plates or blocks of wood for the purpose of being printed from; an engraved plate, or an impression from this.

engross, *v.t.* en-*grohs*, to take up or occupy the whole of; to monopolize; to purchase in large quantities for the purpose of making a private profit on re-sale; to copy in a large hand or distinct legible characters for preservation as a record; to monopolize: *v.i.* to be occupied in engrossing as a clerk. (O.Fr. *engrossir.*)

engrosser, *n.* en-*groh*-ser, one who engrosses.

engrossing, *n.* en-*groh*-sing, the copying of a writing in fair and legible characters; the buying up of large quantities of a commodity in order to raise the price; absorbing.

engrossment, *n.* en-*grohs*-ment, the act of engrossing; that which has been engrossed or copied distinctly; the state of being engrossed or wholly occupied.

engulf, *v.t.* en-*gulf*, to swallow up. (O.Fr. *engolfer.*)

engulfment, *n.* en-*gulf*-ment, a swallowing up.

enhance, *v.t.* en-*hahnce*, to raise; to advance; to increase; to exaggerate: *v.i.* to grow larger. (O.Fr. *enhauncer.*)

enhancement, *n.* en-*hahnce*-ment, act of enhancing; state of being enhanced; rise; increase; aggravation.

enhancer, *n.* en-*hahn*-ser, one who enhances.

enhancive, *a.* en-*hahn*-siv, tending to enhance.

enharmonic, *a.* en-har-*mon*-ik, having intervals less than a semitone. **enharmonic equivalent,** any pair of double-named notes, as C-sharp and D-flat, D-sharp and E-flat, etc., in which there is a theoretical difference of pitch [Mus.]. (Gr. *enarmonikos*, in unison.)

enharmonically, *ad.* in an enharmonic way.

enhearten, *v.t.* en-*har*-ten, to encourage.

enhydrous, *a.* en-*hy*-drus, containing drops of water (of certain crystals). (Gr. *en-*, and *hydor*, water.)

enigma, *n.* e-*nig*-ma, a purposely obscure saying or question propounded for solution; a riddle; any puzzling or unaccountable phenomenon or proceeding. (Gr. *ainigma*, from *ainos*, a tale.)

enigmatic, *a.* en-ig-*mat*-ik, relating to, containing, or of the nature of, an enigma; obscurely expressed; puzzling to interpret.

enigmatical, *a.* en-ig-*mat*-e-kal, enigmatic.

enigmatically, *ad.* in a purposely obscure manner.

enigmatist, *n.* e-*nig*-ma-tist, a maker or dealer in enigmas and riddles.

enigmatize, *v.i.* e-*nig*-ma-tize, to conceive or utter enigmas; to deal in riddles.

enisle, *v.t.* en-*ile*, to place in isolation.

enjambment, *n.* en-*jamb*-ment, the continuation of a phrase or sentence from one couplet or stanza into the next [Pros.].

enjoin, *v.t.* en-*joyn*, to order or direct with urgency or authority; to command; to forbid judicially; to restrain by an injunction [Law]. (Fr. *enjoindre.*)

enjoiner, *n.* en-*joyn*-er, one who enjoins.

enjoinment, *n.* en-*joyn*-ment, an authoritative command or prohibition.

njoy, *v.t.* en-*joy*, to feel or perceive with joy, pleasure, or satisfaction in; to have the use and benefit of. **to enjoy oneself,** to be pleased and happy. (O.Fr. *enjoier.*)

njoyable, *a.* en-*joy*-a-bl, capable of being enjoyed.

njoyableness, *n.* quality of being enjoyable.

njoyably, *ad.* in an enjoyable manner.

njoyment, *n.* en-*joy*-ment, state of enjoying; source of joy; gratification.

nkindle, *v.t.* en-*kin*-dl to kindle; to set on fire; to excite; to rouse into action.

nlace, *v.t.* en-*lace*, to enfold; to entwine.

nlacement, *n.* en-*lace*-ment, act of enlacing; state of being enlaced.

nlarge, *v.t.* en-*larj*, to make larger; to dilate; to expand; to magnify to the eye; to make a larger photographic print from a smaller one; to release from restraint; to extend in a discourse: *v.i.* to grow larger; to dilate; to expand; to expatiate; to exaggerate. (O.Fr. *enlarger.*)

nlargement, *n.* en-*larj*-ment, increase of size or bulk, real or apparent; an enlarged copy; dilatation; expansion; expansion of view or sentiment; release from restraint; diffusiveness of speech or writing; an expatiation; the process of enlarging.

enlarger, *n.* en-*larj*-er, he who or that which enlarges or amplifies; a camera for making enlargements of photographs, etc.

enlighten, *v.t.* en-*lite*-en, to lighten or shed light on; to give intellectual light or knowledge to; to give spiritual light or guidance to.

enlightened, *a.* en-*lite*-end, advanced in knowledge or in spiritual understanding; freed from a state of ignorance or superstition.

enlightener, *n.* en-*lite*-en-er, he who or that which enlightens.

enlightenment, *n.* en-*lite*-en-ment, the act of enlightening or state of being enlightened.

enlink, *v.t.* en-*link*, to chain to; to connect.

enlist, *v.t.* en-*list*, to enter a name on a list; to engage in public service; to attach to a cause and engage the services of; to enrol the name as a soldier for military service: *v.i.* to engage in public service, esp. military service; to enter heartily into cause. (*en-* and *list.*)

enlistment, *n.* en-*list*-ment, the act of enlisting, esp. enrolling and binding a recruit for military service.

enliven, *v.t.* en-*live*-en, to put life into; to quicken into lively action; to give spirit or vivacity to; to make cheerful, gay, or joyous.

enlivener, *n.* en-*live*-en-er, he who or that which enlivens.

enmesh, *v.t.* en-*mesh*, to entangle in, or as in, the meshes of a net; to entrap.

enmeshment, *n.* en-*mesh*-ment, entanglement.

enmity, *n.* *en*-mit-e, the quality or state of being an enemy; unfriendly disposition; ill-will; a state of opposition or antagonism; hostility. (O.Fr. *enemistié.*)

ennead, *n.* *en*-ne-ad, a set or series of nine. (Gr. *ennea*, nine.)

enneagon, *n.* *en*-ne-a-gon, a polygon or plane figure with nine sides or nine angles [Geom.]. (Gr. *ennea*, nine, *gonia*, an angle.)

enneagonal, *a.* en-ne-*ag*-on-al, with nine angles [Geom.].

enneagynous, *a.* en-ne-*aj*-e-nus, with nine pistils [Bot.]. (Gr. *ennea*, and *gyne*, a female.)

enneahedral, *a.* *en*-ne-a-*heed*-ral, with nine sides [Geom.]. (Gr. *ennea*, and *hedra*, a side.)

enneandrian, *a.* *en*-ne-*an*-dre-an, enneandrous; *n.* a plant having nine stamens.

enneandrous, *a.* *en*-ne-*an*-drus, having nine stamens [Bot.]. (Gr. *ennea*, and *aner*, a male.)

enneapetalous, *a.* *en*-ne-a-*pet*-a-lus, having nine petals or flower-leaves [Bot.]. (Gr.)

enneaphyllous, *a.* *en*-ne-a-*fil*-lus, having nine leaflets composing a compound leaf [Bot.]. (Gr. *ennea*, and *phyllon*, a leaf.)

enneasepalous, *a.* *en*-ne-a-*sep*-a-lus, having nine sepals [Bot.]. (Gr.)

enneaspermous, *a.* *en*-ne-a-*sper*-mus, having nine seeds in a fruit [Bot.]. (Gr.)

enneasyllabic, *a.* en-ne-a-se-*lab*-ik, having nine syllables [Pros.].

enneatical, *a.* *en*-ne-*at*-e-kal, ninth; occurring once in nine times. (Gr. *ennea*, nine.)

ennoble, *v.t.* en-*noh*-bl, to make noble; to raise to the peerage; to elevate in degree, qualities, or excellence; to make illustrious. (Fr. *ennoblir.*)

ennoblement, *n.* en-*noh*-bl-ment, the act of ennobling; state of being ennobled, or advanced in nobility; elevation in degree or excellence.

ennui, *n.* (App.), a languid state of mind which nothing can interest or stir up, often a result of satiety; the listless weariness of one to whom what interests others has become a bore. (Fr.)

ennuied, *a.* affected with ennui.

ennuyé, *n. masc.* (App.), *fem.* **ennuyée,** a victim of ennui. (Fr.)

enomotarch, *n.* e-*nom*-o-tark, the commander of an enomoty. (Gr. *enomatia*, and *archo*, rule.)

enomoty, *n.* e-*nom*-o-te, in ancient Lacedæmon, a band of chosen warriors; the smallest unit of the Spartan army [Greek Antiq.]. (Gr. *enomotia.*)

enophthalmus, *n.* en-of-*thal*-mus, an abnormal sinking of the eyeball into the orbital cavity [Med.].

enoptromancy, *n.* en-*op*-tro-man-se, divination by help of a mirror. (Gr. *enoptron*, a mirror, *manteia*, divination.)

enormity, *n.* e-*nor*-me-te, any wrong, irregular, vicious, or sinful act; an atrocious crime; atrociousness; an excessive degree of crime or guilt. (Fr. *énormité*.)

enormous, *a.* e-*nor*-mus, going beyond the usual measure or rule; excessive; huge; atrocious. (L. *e-*, *ex-*, out of, and *norma*, rule.)

enormously, *ad.* excessively; beyond measure.

enormousness, *n.* the state of being enormous.

★**enough,** *a.* e-*nuf*, that suffices or gives content, or answers a purpose, or is adequate to a want; sufficient: *n.* a sufficiency; a quantity of a thing which satisfies desire or want: *ad.* in a satisfying quantity; in such quantity or degree as to command acquiescence: *int.* an exclamation denoting sufficiency. (A.S. *genog*.)

enounce, *v.t.* e-*nounce*, to enunciate; to pronounce; to proclaim.

enouncement, *n.* e-*nounce*-ment, the act of enouncing; a statement.

enow, *a.* and *ad.* e-*nou*, an obsolete form of *enough*.

enplane, *v.i.* and *t.* en-*plane*, to emplane.

enquire, *v.t.* en-*kwire*, to inquire.

enquiry, *n.* en-*kwire*-re, inquiry.

enrage, *v.t.* en-*raje*, to excite rage in; to exasperate; to provoke to fury; to make angry. (Fr. *enrager*.)

enrank, *v.t.* en-*rank*, to place in rank or order.

enrapt, *a.* en-*rapt*, enraptured; in an ecstasy.

enrapture, *v.t.* en-*rap*-tewr, to transport with rapture; to delight beyond measure.

enravish, *v.t.* en-*rav*-ish, to throw into ecstasy; to transport with delight; to enrapture.

enravishingly, *ad.* in a manner to enravish.

enregiment, *v.t.* en-*rej*-e-ment, to form into a regiment; to make orderly; to discipline.

enregister, *v.t.* en-*rej*-is-ter, to register; to enrol.

enrich, *v.t.* en-*rich*, to make rich or wealthy; to fertilize or supply with nutriment, as land; to store or to supply with an abundance of anything desirable, as the mind with information, foodstuffs with vitamins, etc.; to adorn. (Fr. *enrichir*.)

enrichment, *n.* en-*rich*-ment, the act of enriching; that which enriches; increase of wealth, fertility, knowledge, or ornament.

enring, *v.t.* en-*ring*, to encircle; to surround in a ring; to furnish with a ring.

enrobe, *v.t.* en-*robe*, to clothe with a robe; to invest.

enrol, *v.t.* en-*role*, to insert or enter a name in a list or catalogue; to record; to register. (Fr. *enrôler*.)

enroller, *n.* en-*role*-er, one who enrols or registers.

enrolment, *n.* en-*role*-ment, the act of enrolling or registering; an official entry or record.

enroot, *v.t.* en-*root*, to fix by the root; to fix fast.

ens, *n.* ens, entity; being; the absolute being; the essence or virtue of anything. (L. *being*.)

ensample, *n.* en-*sam*-pl, an example; a pattern or model: *v.i.* to show by example.

ensanguine, *v.t.* en-*sang*-gwin, to stain or cover with blood; to make the colour of blood.

ensate, *a.* *en*-sate, sword-shaped; ensiform [Bot.]. (L. *ensis*, a sword.)

ensconce, *v.t.* en-*skonce*, to place in cover or shelter; to protect; to hide.

enseam, *v.t.* en-*seem*, to sew up; to enclose by a seam.

ensear, *v.t.* en-*seer*, to sear; to cauterize.

ensemble, *n.* (App.), all in relation to the whole; effect of the whole; general effect; grouping of the parts or figures; a woman's costume, esp. one of two or more pieces: *ad.* all at once; together. (Fr.)

enshield, *v.t.* en-*sheeld*, to shield; to protect.

enshrine, *v.t.* en-*shrine*, to enclose or preserve in, or as in, a shrine; to cherish with sacred affection.

enshrinement, *n.* the act of enshrining.

enshroud, *v.t.* en-*shroud*, to cover entirely; to shroud; to veil; to conceal.

ensiform, *a.* *en*-se-form, having the shape of a straight sword-blade [Bot.]. (L. *ensis*, and *form*.)

ensign, *n.* *en*-sine, a national flag, esp. as used at sea; a distinguishing banner or emblem; till 1871 a second lieutenant of infantry in the British Army; a sub-lieutenant in the U.S. Navy: *v.t.* to distinguish by some ornament or symbol [Her.] **naval ensign,** in Great Britain, a blue, red, or white flag with the union in the upper corner next the staff, the blue being borne by the Royal Naval Reserve, the red by the merchant service, and the white by the Royal Navy and the Royal Yacht Squadron.

ensigncy, *n.* *en*-sine-se, the rank, office, or commission of an ensign.

ensilage, *n.* *en*-sil-aj, a process of preserving fodder and vegetable products green by packing them in a silo and subjecting them to pressure. (Fr. from L. *sirus*, an underground granary, through Sp.)

ensile, *v.t.* en-*sile*, to store in a silo; to convert into ensilage.

enskied, *a.* en-*skide*, placed in the heavens, or in heaven; made immortal.

enslave, *v.t.* en-*slave*, to reduce to slavery or make a slave of; to master or obtain the mastery over.

enslavement, *n.* en-*slave*-ment, the act of enslaving; the state of being enslaved; slavery; bondage.

enslaver, *n.* en-*slave*-er, one who enslaves.

ensnare, *v.t.* en-*snare*, to entrap.

ensoul, *v.t.* en-*sole*, to give a soul to; to become spiritually fused with.

ensphere, *v.t.* en-*sfeer*, to place in or as in a sphere; to make into a sphere.

enstamp, *v.t.* en-*stamp*, to impress, as with a stamp; to impress deeply.

enstatite, *n.* *en*-sta-tite, a silicate of magnesium occurring as a rock-forming mineral. (Gr. *enstatēs*, opponent.)

ensuant, *a.* en-*sew*-ant, ensuing; following on as a consequence.

ensue, *v.t.* en-*sew*, to follow; to pursue: *v.i.* to follow as a consequence; to follow as an event; to result; to succeed or come after. (Fr. *ensuivre*.)

ensuing, *a.* en-*sew*-ing, coming next after.

ensure, *v.t.* en-*shure*, to make safe or certain; to guarantee; to insure.

enswathe, *v.t.* en-*swaythe*, to wrap as with a bandage.

enswathement, *n.* en-*swathe*-ment, the act of enswathing; the enswathing material.

entablature, *n.* en-*tab*-la-tewr, that part of the order of a column which is over the capital, including, in upward succession, the architrave, frieze, and cornice. (Fr. from L. *in-*, and *tabula*, a board.)

entablement, *n.* en-*tay*-bl-ment, the platform above the dado and base on which a statue stands.

entail, *n.* *en*-tale, an estate entailed, or limited in descent to a particular heir or heirs; rule of descent for an estate: *v.t.* en-*tale*, to settle inalienably the descent of lands and tenements, by gift or bequest to a named person and to certain heirs specified or to a particular class of heirs [Law]; to involve and so lead to; to necessitate. (Fr. *entailler*, to cut into.)

entailment, *n.* en-*tale*-ment, the act of entailing; state of being entailed; something entailed.

entame, *v.t.* en-*tame*, to tame; to subdue.

entangle, *v.t.* en-*tang*-gl, to twist or interweave so as not to be easily separable; to involve, esp. in anything from which extrication is difficult; to embarrass; to ensnare; to perplex. (*en-* and *tangle*.)

entanglement, *n.* en-*tang*-gl-ment, state of being entangled; involution; a confused state; perplexity.

entangler, *n.* en-*tang*-gler, one who entangles.

entasis, *n.* *en*-ta-sis, the slight swelling outline given to the shaft of a column to correct apparent concavity [Arch.]. (Gr.)

entelechy, *n.* en-*tel*-e-ke, the complete actualization or perfection of a thing; that which realizes a final cause [Phil.]. (L. *entelechia*.)

entellus, *n.* en-*tel*-lus, the sacred monkey of the Hindus, the hanuman or true langur, *Semnopithecus entellus*.

entente, *n.* (App.), intention; friendly understanding. **entente cordiale,** international friendliness or goodwill, esp. that inaugurated between Great Britain and France in 1904. **Little Entente** the defensive and economic alliance entered into by Czechoslovakia, Yugoslavia, and Rumania in 1921 (Fr.)

enter, *v.t.* *en*-ter, to move or pass into a place; to come or go in; to penetrate; to advance into; to enlist or engage in; to become a member of; to admit; to set down in writing; to enrol; to lodge a manifest of goods at the custom-house and gain admittance or permission to land; to insert; to take possession of; to register formally: *v.i.* to go or come in; to penetrate; to engage in; to be initiated in; to be an ingredient. **enter into,** to engage in. **enter on,** to start on. (Fr., from L. *intra*, within.)

enterable, *a.* *en*-te-ra-bl, that may be entered.

enterate, *a.* *en*-te-rate, having an alimentary canal or enteron [Zool.]. (*enteron*.)

enteric, *a.* en-*te*-rik, relating to the intestines. **enteric fever,** typhoid fever. (Gr. *enterikos,* from *enteron,* intestine.)

enteritis, *n.* en-ter-*ry*-tis, inflammation of the small intestines.

entero-, *comb.f.* *en*-ter-o-, connoting the intestines. (Gr. *enteron,* intestine.)

enterocele, *n.* en-*ter*-o-seel, a hernia or hernial tumour containing some portion of the intestines [Surg.]. (Gr. *enteron,* and *kele,* a tumour.)

enterolite *n.* *en*-ter-o-lite, an intestinal concretion or calculus. (Gr. *enteron,* and *lithos,* a stone.)

enterology, *n.* *en*-ter-*rol*-o-je, the branch of physiology dealing with the bowels, abdomen, and internal parts of the body. (Gr. *enteron,* and *logos,* science).

enteron, *n.* *en*-ter-on, the digestive tract of vertebrates; the single body-cavity of cœlenterates. (Gr., an intestine.)

enteropathy, *n.* *en*-ter-*rop*-a-the, disease of the intestines. (Gr. *enteron,* and *pathos,* disease.)

enterotomy, *n.* *en*-ter-*rot*-o-me, dissection or incision of the bowels or intestines [Surg.]. (Gr. *enteron,* and *tome,* cutting.)

enterprise, *n.* *en*-ter-prize, something undertaken or attempted, esp. a bold, arduous, or hazardous undertaking, either physical or moral; a spirit of bold adventure; energy: *v.t.* to undertake; to venture on. (Fr. from *entre,* into, and *prendre,* to seize.)

enterpriser, *n.* *en*-ter-prize-er, one who undertakes an enterprise; a venturer or adventurer.

enterprising, *a.* *en*-ter-prize-ing, bold or forward in undertaking; resolute; active or prompt to attempt great or untried schemes; adventurous.

enterprisingly, *ad.* in an enterprising manner.

entertain, *v.t.* en-ter-*tane*, to receive and treat with hospitality; to engage the attention and occupy it agreeably; to maintain; to harbour; to cherish; to take into consideration with a view to decide; to amuse; to purvey to: *v.i.* to exercise hospitality. (Fr. *entretenir.*)

entertainer, *n.* en-ter-*tane*-er, one who entertains, esp. as a paid performer.

entertaining, *a.* en-ter-*tane*-ing, pleasing; amusing; diverting.

entertainingly, *ad.* in an entertaining manner.

entertainment, *n.* en-ter-*tane*-ment, the act of entertaining; the receiving and entertaining of guests; the hospitality provided; a banquet; an amusement; a performance for the amusement of an audience; that which entertains; the pleasure which the mind receives from such; reception by the mind.

enthral, *v.t.* en-*thrawl*, to enslave; to enchant; to interest intently.

enthralment, *n.* en-*thrawl*-ment, slavery; bondage.

enthrone, *v.t.* en-*throne*, to place on a throne; to exalt to the seat of royalty or to an elevated place or seat; to invest with sovereign authority; to induct or instal, as a bishop.

enthronement, *n.* en-*throne*-ment, the act of enthroning or of being enthroned.

enthronization, *n.* en-*throh*-ny-*zay*-shon, enthronement, esp. of a bishop or archbishop.

enthuse, *v.i.* en-*thewz*, to gush; to become enthusiastic: *v.t.* to make enthusiastic. (U.S.A., Coll.)

nthusiasm, *n.* en-*thew*-ze-azm, overflowing, irrepressible zeal or ardour; strong feeling in favour of some cause or object; fervid or overfervid zeal. (Fr. *enthousiasme.*)

nthusiast, *n.* en-*thew*-ze-ast, one inspired by enthusiasm; one whose imagination is warmed, or whose mind is highly excited with the love, or in the pursuit, of an object; a person of ardent zeal; one of elevated fancy or exalted ideas.

nthusiastic, *a.* en-*thew*-ze-*as*-tik, filled with or characterized by enthusiasm; ardent in the pursuit of an object; heated to animation; elevated; ardent, zealous, or visionary.

nthusiastically, *ad.* with enthusiasm.

nthymematical, *a.* *en*-the-me-*mat*-e-kal, pertaining to an enthymeme; including an enthymeme.

nthymeme, *n.* *en*-the-meem, a syllogism in which one of the propositions is suppressed [Logic]. (Gr. *enthymema.*)

ntice, *v.t.* en-*tice*, to tempt, esp. to evil; to allure; to attract. (O.Fr. *enticer.*)

nticement, *n.* en-*tice*-ment, the act or practice of enticing; allurement; that which allures or seduces; the state of being enticed.

enticer, *n.* en-*tice*-er, one who or that which entices.

enticing, *a.* en-*tice*-ing, having qualities that entice.

enticingly, *ad.* in an enticing manner.

entire, *a.* en-*tire*, whole; complete; full; sincere; undisputed; unmingled; wholly devoted; in full strength: *n.* porter as sent direct from the brewery; an entire horse. **entire horse,** a stallion. **entire leaves,** leaves which are not notched. **entire stem,** one without branches [Bot.]. (Fr. *entier.*)

entirely, *ad.* en-*tire*-le, wholly; completely; fully.

entireness, *n.* en-*tire*-ness, the state of being entire.

entirety, *n.* en-*tire*-te, wholeness; completeness; that which is entire; the whole.

entitative, *a.* *en*-te-ta-tiv, considered as, or of the nature of, an entity.

entitle, *v.t.* en-*ty*-tl, to give a title or name to; to give a claim to or give a right to demand or receive; to assign or appropriate by giving a title; to qualify; to dignify by a title. (Fr. *intituler.*)

entity, *n.* *en*-te-te, essence; essential nature; a reality; an existing thing. (L. *ens, entis,* being.)

ento-, pref. *en*-to-, connoting within, or inside. (Gr.)

entoblast, *n.* *en*-to-blast, the endoderm or its constituent matter; formerly, the nucleolus of a cell. (Gr. *entos,* within, *blastos,* a bud.)

entoderm, *n.* *en*-to-derm, endoderm.

entoil, *v.t.* en-*toyl*, to take with toils; to ensnare.

entomb, *v.t.* en-*toom*, to deposit in a tomb; to inter.

entombment, *n.* en-*toom*-ment, the act of entombing; state of being entombed.

entomic, *a.* en-*tom*-ik, relating to insects.

entomoid, *a.* *en*-to-moyd, like an insect.

entomojenous, *a.* en-to-*moj*-e-nus, growing in or upon the bodies of insects (of certain fungi) [Bot.].

entomological, *a.* *en*-to-mo-*loj*-e-kal, pertaining to entomology.

entomologically, *ad.* in an entomological manner.

entomologist, *n.* en-to-*mol*-o-jist, one versed in the study of insects.

entomologize, *v.t.* *en*-to-*mol*-o-jize, to collect and make a scientific study of insects.

entomology, *n.* en-to-*mol*-o-je, that part of zoology treating of insects. (Gr. *entomon,* and *logos,* science.)

entomophagous, *a.* *en*-to-*mof*-a-gus, feeding on insects.

entomophilous, *a.* *en*-to-*mof*-e-lus, attractive to insects (of flowers which are fertilized by insects) [Bot.]. (Gr. *entomon,* and *phileo,* love.)

entomophily, *n.* en-to-*mof*-e-le, insect pollination.

entomostracan, *n.* *en*-to-*mos*-tra-kan, a member of the lowest division of the crustacea. (Gr., insect-shelled, *entomon,* and *ostrakon,* a shell.)

entomostracous, *a.* *en*-to-*mos*-tra-kus, belonging to the entomostracans.

entomotomist, *n.* *en*-to-*mot*-o-mist, one versed in entomotomy.

entomotomy, *n.* *en*-to-*mot*-o-me, the scientific dissection of insects. (Gr. *entomon,* and *tome,* cutting.)

entophyte, *n.* *en*-to-fite, a parasitic plant growing inside other living plants or animals. (Gr. *entos,* within, *phyton,* a plant.)

entophytic, *a.* *en*-to-*fit*-ik, pertaining to entophytes.

entotic, *a.* *en*-*to*-tik, pertaining to the interior of the ear. (*en*-, and Gr. *ous, ōtos,* ear.)

entourage, *n.* (App.), attendants; associates; environment. (Fr.)

en-tout-cas, *n.* (App.), a light umbrella which can be used as a sunshade. (Fr., in any case.)

entozoa, *n.pl.* en-to-*zoh*-a (*sing.* **entozoon,** en-to-*zoh*-on), internal parasites, esp. worms, that live in the cavities or tissues of other animals. (Gr. *ento,* and *zoon,* an animal.)

entozoic, *a.* en-to-*zoh*-ik, pertaining to the entozoa; living within an animal or plant [Bot.].

entozoologist, *n.* *en*-to-zo-*ol*-o-jist, one versed in entozoology.

entozoology, *n.* *en*-to-zo-*ol*-o-je, the department of zoology which treats of internal parasites or entozoa. (Gr. *ento-, zoon,* and *logos,* science.)

entozoon, *n.* en-to-*zoh*-on, one of the entozoa.

entr'acte, *n.* (App.), the interval between the acts of a play; a performance during the interval. (Fr.)

entrails, *n.pl.* *en*-traylz, the internal parts of animal bodies; the bowels; the interior, as of the earth (Fr. *entrailles,* from L. *intra,* within.)

entrain, *v.t.* en-*trane,* to send by train, as goods or troops: *v.i.* to board a train.
entrammel, *v.t.* en-*tram*-mel, to entangle; to hamper; to trammel.
entrance, *n.* *en*-trance, the act of entering; the power or right to enter; the passage by which a place may be entered; beginning; initiation; the act of taking possession, as of land or of office; the act of entering a ship or goods at the custom-house; entry; entrance-fee; the fore-body of a ship below the waterline. **entrance-fee,** amount paid on admission, esp. to membership of a club, society, etc. (O.Fr.)
entrance, *v.t.* en-*trahnce,* to put into a trance; to put in an ecstasy; to ravish with delight or wonder.
entrancement, *n.* en-*trahnce*-ment, a state of trance or ecstasy.
entrancing, *a.* en-*trahnce*-ing, delightful; charming.
entrant, *n.* *ent*-rant, one who enters, esp. as a new member; a candidate or competitor. (Fr.)
entrap, *v.t.* en-*trap,* to catch, as in a trap; to ensnare; to catch by artifices; to involve in difficulties or contradictions.
entreat, *v.t.* en-*treet,* to ask earnestly; to petition or pray with urgency; to prevail on by prayer or solicitation; to treat; to use or manage; to deal with: *v.i.* to make an earnest petition or request. (O.Fr. *entraiter.*)
entreatingly, *ad.* en-*treet*-ing-le, in an entreating manner.
entreatment, *n.* en-*treet*-ment, the act of entreating; treatment; an interview.
entreaty, *n.* en-*treet*-e, urgent prayer; earnest request; importunity.
entrechat, *n.* (App.), a dancing step in which heels are clicked or feet crossed in the air. (Fr.)
entrée, *n.* (App.), entry; freedom of access; a dish or light course between the fish and meat courses at dinner. (Fr.)
entremets, *n.pl.* (App.), lighter dishes between the principal ones at dinner; side dishes. (Fr. *entre,* between, and *mets,* dishes.)
entrench, *v.t.* en-*trench,* to dig a trench; to defend by or shelter in a trench.
entrenchment, *n.* en-*trench*-ment, a trench with the excavated soil thrown up as a parapet.
entrepôt, *n.* (App.), a warehouse or magazine for the deposit of goods; a place where goods on which dues are charged are kept in bond against their exportation; a commercial centre from which goods are distributed. (Fr.)
entrepreneur, *n.* (App.), one who undertakes some particular business; an organizer, esp. of public musical or other entertainments; an impresario. (Fr., a contractor.)
entresol, *n.* (App.), a set of rooms between the first and ground floors; a mezzanine. (Fr.)
entrochal, *a.* *en*-tro-kal, pertaining to or containing entrochites.
entrochite, *n.* *en*-tro-kite, a fossil joint of the stem of a sea-lily, like a wheel in form [Geol.]. (Gr. *en-,* and *trochos,* a wheel.)
entropium, *n.* en-*troh*-pe-um, an inversion of the eyelashes towards the eyes. (Gr. *entropia,* turning toward.)
entropy, *n.* *en*-tro-pe, one of the variable factors determining the thermodynamic condition of a body; a static condition. (*en-,* and Gr. *tropē,* a turning or transformation.)
entrust, *v.t.* en-*trust,* to confide; to give in trust.
entrustment, *n.* en-*trust*-ment, the act of entrusting.
entry, *n.* *ent*-re, the passage into a building, etc.; a short alley-way; the act of entering; the act of committing to writing; the thing so entered; the exhibition or depositing of a ship's papers at the custom-house, to procure licence to land goods; the act of entering and taking possession of lands or tenements, when a person has title of entry [Law]. **card of entry,** a card with which the holder can secure the lead by playing it [Card-games]. **double entry,** a method of bookkeeping in which two entries are made for each transaction. (Fr. *entrée.*)
entwine, *v.t.* en-*twine,* to twine; to twist together; to interlace: *v.i.* to become twisted together.
entwinement, *n.* en-*twine*-ment, the state of being entwined; a twisting round.
entwist, *v.t.* en-*twist,* to twist or wreathe round; to form into a twist.
enucleate, *v.t.* e-*new*-kle-ate, to extricate and make clear what was before involved or obscure; to elucidate; to remove a tumour, etc., whole [Surg.]; to deprive of the nucleus [Biol.]: *a.* without a nucleus [Biol.]. (L. *enucleatus,* extricated.)
enucleation, *n.* e-*new*-kle-*ay*-shon, the act of enucleating; full exposition; the removal of tumours, etc., by a special method [Surg.].
enumerate, *v.t.* e-*new*-me-rate, to count; to reckon up or name over one by one; to go over in detail. (L. *enumeratus,* numbered.)
enumeration, *n.* e-*new*-me-*ray*-shon, the act of enumerating; a reckoning up; a detailed account.
enumerative, *a.* e-*new*-me-ra-tiv, having to do with enumeration; reckoning up.
enumerator, *n.* e-*new*-me-ray-tor, one who enumerates; a minor official employed in taking a census.
enunciable, *a.* e-*nun*-se-a-bl, capable of being enunciated or stated.
enunciate, *v.t.* e-*nun*-se-ate, to utter; to pronounce; to announce; to state formally or in terms. (L. *enuntiatus,* told.)
enunciation, *n.* e-*nun*-se-*ay*-shon, the act of enunciating or of declaring; manner of pronouncing or uttering; that which is enunciated; statement; expression in words of a proposition [Geom.].
enunciative, *a.* e-*nun*-se-a-tiv, pertaining to enunciation; declarative.
enunciatively, *ad.* declaratively.
enunciator, *n.* e-*nun*-se-ay-tor, one who enunciates; one who proclaims.
enure, *v.t.* and *i.* en-*newr,* inure.
enuresis, *n.* en-yew-*ree*-sis, incontinence of urine [Med.]. (Gr. *en-,* and *ouron,* urine.)
envelop, *v.t.* en-*vel*-op, to enwrap; to surround entirely; to cover on all sides; to hide. (Fr. *envelopper.*)
envelope, *n.* *en*-vel-ope (or as Fr., *see* App.), that which envelops or covers; the cover of a letter on which the address is written; one of the parts of fructification surrounding the stamens and pistils [Bot.]; the gas-container of a balloon or airship; the coma of a comet [Astron.].
envelopment, *n.* en-*vel*-op-ment, the act of enveloping or state of being enveloped; a wrapping; an enclosing on all sides.
envenom, *v.t.* en-*ven*-om, to taint or impregnate with any substance noxious to life; to make poisonous; to embitter; to exasperate. (Fr. *envenimer.*)
enviable, *a.* *en*-ve-a-bl, that may excite envy; capable of inspiring with envy; very desirable.
enviably, *ad.* *en*-ve-a-ble, in an enviable manner.
envied, *n.* *en*-vid, subjected to envy.
envier, *n.* *en*-ve-er, one who envies another.
envious, *a.* *en*-ve-us, feeling or harbouring envy; tinctured with envy; excited or directed by envy.
enviously, *ad.* *en*-ve-us-le, with envy.
environ, *v.t.* en-*vy*-ron, to surround; to encompass; to envelop; to invest. (Fr. *environ,* around.)
environal, *a.* en-*vy*-ro-nal, pertaining to or conditioned by environment.
environment, *n.* en-*vy*-ron-ment, the act of surrounding; the state of being environed; natural surroundings.
environmental, *a.* en-*vy*-ron-*men*-tal, pertaining to environment, esp. natural environment.
environs, *n.pl.* *en*-ve-ronz *or* en-*vire*-ronz, suburbs, places around. (Fr.)
envisage, *v.t.* en-*viz*-aj, to perceive intuitionally, to face directly; to view or consider attentively. (Fr. *envisager.*)
envisagement, *n.* en-*viz*-aj-ment, the act of envisaging.
envoy, *n.* *en*-voy, the concluding part of a literary, esp. poetical, composition; the final stanza of a ballade, etc. (O.Fr.)
envoy, *n.* *en*-voy, a diplomatic agent, next in rank below an ambassador, deputed by one sovereign state to another to transact some special business; a messenger. (O.Fr.)
envoyship, *n.* *en*-voy-ship, the office or the function of an envoy.
envy, *n.* *en*-ve, ill-will excited by the sight of another's superiority or success; the object of such feeling; malignity; rivalry: *v.t.* to regard with malevolent covetousness; to grudge; to wish for. (O.Fr. *envie.*)

enwind, *v.t.* en-*wynd*, to wind or coil itself around something else. *p.* and *pp.* **enwound,** en-*wound*.
enwomb, *v.t.* en-*woom*, to contain in or as in the womb; to enclose securely and in secret.
enwrap, *v.t.* en-*rap*, to envelop; to engross mentally.
enwreathe, *v.t.* en-*reethe*, to encompass with or as with a wreath.
enzootic, *a.* en-zo-*ot*-ik, endemic to the animals of a district (of diseases): *n.* an enzootic disease [Vet.]. (Gr. *en-*, and *zoon*, an animal.)
enzymatic, *a.* en-zy-*mat*-ik, pertaining to enzymes or their reactions.
enzyme, *n.* *en*-zyme, a colloidal organic catalyst produced by a living organism that conditions some chemical action (*e.g.*, fermentation) within the body, itself undergoing no permanent change [Chem.]. (Gr. *enzymos*, fermented.)
eo-, *pref.* *ee*-o-, pertaining to the dawn, or (esp. Geol., Archæol., etc.) to the earliest known period of. (Gr. *eos*, dawn.)
eoan, *a.* e-*oh*-an, pertaining to the dawn or to the east. (Gk. *eos*, dawn.)
Eoanthropus, *n.* ee-o-an-*throh*-pus, primitive man as deduced from the skull found at Piltdown, Sussex, in 1912. (Gk. *eos*, dawn, *anthropos*, man.)
Eocene, *a.* *ee*-o-seen, pertaining to the earliest tertiary rocks: *n.* a series of beds belonging to this period [Geol.]. (Gr. *ēos*, dawn, *kainos*, recent.)
Eolian, *a.* e-*oh*-le-an, Æolian.
Eolic, *a.* e-*oh*-lik, Æolic.
eolipile, *n.* e-*ol*-e-pile, æolipile.
eolith, *n.* *ee*-o-lith, the most rudimentary type of stone flint implement. (Gr. *ēos*, dawn, *lithos*, stone.)
eolithic, *a.* ee-o-*lith*-ik, pertaining to or designating the dawn of the Stone Age, preceding the palæolithic.
eon, *n.* *ee*-on, æon.
eonism, *n.* *ee*-o-nizm, the adoption of the habits, characteristics, and clothes, etc., of the opposite sex [Psychan.]. (From the Chevalier d'*Éon*, *d.* 1810, who for many years lived as a woman.)
eosin, *n.* *ee*-o-sin, a red dyestuff used as a stain in microscopy and in red ink manufacture: *a.* rose-red. (Gr. *ēos*, dawn.)
eosinophil, *a.* ee-o-*sin*-o-fil, readily taking the stain of eosin (esp. of leucocytes) [Biol.].
eozoic, *a.* *ee*-o-*zoh*-ik, pertaining to or denoting the pre-Cambrian rocks; pre-Cambrian [Geol.].
eozoon, *n.* *ee*-o-*zoh*-on, an intergrowth of calcite and serpentine, first found in the Laurentian rocks and erroneously supposed to consist of foraminiferous remains representing the earliest trace of organic life [Geol.]. (Gr. *ēos*, dawn, *zoon*, an animal.)
ep-, epi-, ep-, ep-e-, a Greek prefix signifying on or upon.
epact, *n.* *ee*-pakt, the age of the calendar moon on the first of January; the excess of the solar month above the lunar, or of the solar year above the lunar year of twelve synodical months [Chron.]. (O.Fr. *epacte*.)
epagoge, *n.* ep-a-*goh*-je, a figure of speech in which universal propositions are demonstrated by particulars; argument by induction [Rhet.]. (Gr.)
epagogic, *a.* ep-a-*goj*-ik, inductive.
epalpate, *a.* e-*pal*-pate, destitute of palpi or feelers [Entom.].
epanadiplosis, *n.* e-*pan*-a-de-*ploh*-sis, repetition; a figure of speech, when a sentence ends with the same word with which it begins [Rhet.]. (Gr.)
epanalepsis, *n.* e-*pan*-a-*lep*-sis, a figure by which the same word or clause is repeated in resuming the subject after a parenthesis [Rhet.]. (Gr.)
epanodos, *n.* e-*pan*-o-dos, a figure, when the second member of a sentence is an inversion of the first [Rhet.]; a recapitulation after a digression [Rhet.].
epanorthosis, *n.* *ep*-an-or-*thoh*-sis, a figure in which a speaker recalls what he has said for the sake of making it stronger [Rhet.]. (Gr.)
epanthous, *a.* e-*pan*-thus, growing upon flowers, as do some fungi [Bot.]. (Gr. *epi-*, and *anthos*, a flower.)
eparch, *n.* *ep*-ark, the governor, prefect, or bishop of an eparchy. (Gr. *eparchos*.)
eparchy, *n.* *ep*-ar-ke, a province, prefecture, or territorial subdivision of modern Greece; a diocese of the Orthodox Russian Church.
epaulement, *n.* e-*pawl*-ment, a sidework, or work to cover sidewise, made of gabions, fascines, or bags of earth, to protect the guns and gunners from an enfilading fire [Fort.].
epaulet *or* **epaulette,** *n.* *ep*-o-let, an ornamental badge worn on the shoulder of certain uniforms; a protection for the shoulder; a shoulder piece. (Fr.)
epauletted, *a.* *ep*-o-let-ted, furnished with epaulets.
épée, *n.* ay-*pay*, a light thrusting sword, sharp-pointed for duelling, blunt for fencing. (Fr., rapier)
epeiric *a.* e-*pyr*-rik, pertaining to continents; epeirogenic.
epeirogenic, *e.* e-pyr-ro-*jen*-ik, pertaining to the formation of continents [Geol.]. (Gr. *epeiros*, mainland, *gennao*, produce.)
epencephalic, *a.* *ep*-en-se-*fal*-ik, pertaining to the epencephalon.
epencephalon, *n.* ep-en-*sef*-a-lon, the cerebellar or anterior division of the brain [Anat.]. (Gr. *epi-*, *en-*, and *kephale*, the head.)
epenthesis, *n.* ep-*en*-the-sis, the insertion of a letter or syllable in the body of a word, as the "d" in "thunder" (from A.S. *thunor*) [Gram.]. (Gr.)
epenthetic, *a.* ep-en-*thet*-ik, pertaining to or effected by epenthesis [Gram.].
epergne, *n.* ay-*pern*, a tall ornamental stand for flowers or fruit in the centre of a table. (Fr. *épargne*, thrift.)
epexegesis, *n.* *ep*-ek-se-*jee*-sis, an explanation of the preceding context; further elucidation. (Gr.)
epexegetical, *a.* *ep*-ek-se-*jet*-e-kal, explanatory of that which immediately precedes; elucidatory.
ephah, *n.* *ee*-fah, a Hebrew dry measure equal to rather more than a bushel. (Heb.)
ephebe, *n.* e-*feeb* (*pl.* **ephebi,** e-*fee*-by), among the ancient Greeks a freeborn male citizen of from 18 to 20 years. (Gr. *ephēbos*, boy.)
ephebic, *a.* e-*fee*-bik, pertaining to the ephebi; adult [Biol.].
ephemera, *n.* e-*fem*-er-ra, a fever of one day's continuance only; the genus of neuropterous insects comprising the May-flies; a May-fly, or any short-lived insect. (Gr. *epi-*, and *hēmera*, a day.)
ephemeral, *a.* e-*fem*-er-ral, beginning and ending in a day: existing one day only; continuing for a short time only: *n.* anything that is ephemeral.
ephemeris, *n.* e-*fem*-er-ris (*pl.* **ephemerides,** ef-e-*me*-re-deez), a journal or account of daily transactions; a diary; an astronomical almanac; a collection of tables exhibiting the places of the planets every day at noon throughout the year [Astron.].
ephemeron, *n.* e-*fem*-er-ron, any short-lived winged insect; anything of merely fleeting duration. (Gr. *ephemeros*, lasting a day only.)
Ephesian, *a.* e-*fee*-zhan, pertaining to Ephesus: *n.* a native of Ephesus; one of dissolute life.
ephod, *n.* *ef*-od, a liturgical apron-like vestment worn by Jewish priests. (Heb. *aphad*, to put on.)
ephor, *n.* *ef*-or, one of the ephori; an overseer.
ephoralty, *n.* *ef*-o-ral-te, the office or term of office of an ephor.
ephori, *n.pl.* *ef*-o-ry, in ancient Sparta, five magistrates chosen by the people to control the kings and see to the proper administration of law and order in the state. (Gr., overseers, from *epi-*, and *horao*, see.)
epi-, ep-e-, Greek prefix signifying upon, to, at, or in addition.
epiblast, *n.* *ep*-e-blast, the outer layer of the blastoderm [Biol.]. (Gr. *epi-*, and *blastos*, a bud.)
epic, *a.* *ep*-ik, narrating in an elevated style some great event: *n.* an epic poem. **epic poem,** a poem embodying the story, real or fictitious, of some heroic action or series of actions and events of deep and lasting significance in the history of a people. (Gr. *epos*, a word.)
epical, *a.* *ep*-e-kal, characteristic of or resembling epic poetry.
epically, *ad.* in an epic manner.
epicalyx, *n.* ep-e-*kay*-liks, a whorl of leaves resembling an additional exterior calyx [Bot.].
epicarp, *n.* *ep*-e-karp, the outer skin of fruits; the rind [Bot.]. (Gr. *epi-*, and *karpos*, fruit.)
epicede, *n.* *ep*-e-seed, a funeral song or lament. (Gr. *epi-*, and *kedos*, concern, affliction.)
epicedial, *a.* ep-e-*see*-de-al, elegiac; mournful.
epicedium, *n.* ep-e-*see*-de-um, an epicede.
epicene, *a.* *ep*-e-seen, common to both sexes: *n.* a noun common to both genders, as parent [Gram.]; an effeminate male or masculine female. (Gr. *epi-*, and *koinos*, common.)

epicentre, *n.* *ep*-e-*sen*-ter, the point above the focus of an earthquake. (Gr. *epikentros.*)
epicheirema, *n.* *ep*-e-ky-*ree*-ma, a syllogism to either or both of the premises of which a reason is annexed in proof [Logic]. (Gr., an undertaking, from *epi-*, and *cheir*, the hand.)
epicolic, *a.* ep-e-*kol*-ik, relating to the region of the abdomen over the colon. (Gr. *epi-*, and *kolon.*)
epicranial, *a.* ep-e-*kray*-ne-al, pertaining to the epicranium; situated on the cranium [Anat.].
epicranium, *n.* ep-e-*kray*-ne-um, the skin and soft parts forming the scalp [Anat.]; the dorsal wall of the head [Entom.]. (Gr. *epi-*, and *kraniom*, the skull.)
epicure, *n.* *ep*-e-kewr, one with a refined taste in food and drink; an Epicurean.
Epicurean, *a.* *ep*-e-kew-*ree*-an, pertaining to Epicurus or to Epicureanism: *n.* a follower of Epicurus, a Greek philosopher who taught that a happy state of mind and body was the chief good; one addicted to the luxuries of the table.
Epicureanism, *n.* *ep*-e-kew-*ree*-a-nizm, attachment to the doctrines of Epicurus; those doctrines themselves; luxuriousness in living.
epicurism, *n.* *ep*-e-kew-rizm, the tastes and ways of epicures: (*cap.*) formerly Epicureanism.
epicycle, *n.* *ep*-e-sy-kl, a small circle whose centre moves round on the circumference of a larger circle [Ptolemaic Astron]. (Gr. *epikyklos.*)
epicyclic, *a.* ep-e-*sy*-klik, pertaining to an epicycle. **epicyclic gear,** a train of wheels meshed within the circumference of another wheel, used esp. in change-speed gears [Mech.].
epicycloid, *n.* ep-e-*sy*-kloyd, a curve generated by the revolution of a point on the circumference of a rolling epicycle [Geom.]. (Gr. *epikyklos*, and *eidos*, like.)
epicycloidal, *a.* ep-e-sy-*kloy*-dal, pertaining to or like an epicycloid.
epideictic, *a.* ep-e-*dike*-tik, done for effect or display of skill or power [Rhet.]; showing off. (Gr. *epi-*, and *deiknunai*, to show.)
epidemic, *a.* ep-e-*dem*-ik, generally prevalent for a time; affecting great numbers: *n.* a disease which attacks a great number of people at the same time and place. (Gr. *epi-*, and *dēmos*, people.)
epidemically, *ad.* in an epidemic manner.
epidemicity, *n.* ep-e-de-*mis*-e-te, the quality of being epidemic.
epidemiology, *n.* *ep*-e-dem-e-*ol*-o-je, the scientific study of, a treatise on, epidemic diseases.
epidermal, *a.* ep-e-*der*-mal, epidermic.
epidermic, *a.* ep-e-*der*-mik, pertaining to or of the nature of an epidermis.
epidermis, *n.* ep-e-*der*-mis, the semi-transparent cuticle or scarf-skin enveloping the true skin, and containing only flattened cells in layers [Anat.]; a similar covering to the leaves and stems of plants [Bot.]. (Gr. *epi-*, and *derma*, skin.)
epidermoid, *a.* ep-e-*der*-moyd, bearing some resemblance to the epidermis.
epidermolysis, *n.* ep-e-der-*mol*-e-sis, a loosening of the epidermis [Med.].
epidiascope, *n.* ep-e-*dy*-a-skope, an optical lantern for projecting on a screen naturally coloured images of opaque and transparent objects.
epidote, *n.* *ep*-e-dote, a green or greyish crystalline mineral found in igneous rocks and composed chiefly of silicate of alumina and lime. (Gr. *epidosis*, given in addition.)
epidotic, *a.* ep-e-*dot*-ik, pertaining to or containing epidote.
epigamic, *a.* ep-e-*gam*-ik, attractive to the opposite sex, esp. in the breeding season [Zool.].
epigastric, *a.* ep-e-*gas*-trik, pertaining to the upper and anterior part of the abdomen. (Gr. *epigastrion.*)
epigastrium, *n.* ep-e-*gas*-tre-um, the upper part of the abdomen, between the hypochondriac and umbilical regions. (Gr.)
epigene, *a.* *ep*-e-jeen, formed or originating on the surface of the earth [Geol.]; in a crystalline form not natural to a substance, pseudomorphous [Min.]. (Gr. *epi-*, and *ginomai*, cause to be.)
epigenesis, *n.* ep-e-*jen*-e-sis, the theory that the future organism (animal or plant) is not present in the germ but is gradually produced and co-ordinated in the embryonic stage [Biol.]. (Gr. *epi-*, and *genesis.*)
epigenesist, *n.* ep-e-*jen*-e-sist, one who holds the doctrine of epigenesis.
epigenetic, *a.* ep-e-je-*net*-ik, pertaining to epigenesis.
epigenous, *a.* e-*pij*-e-nus, growing on the surface of (a leaf, etc.) [Bot.].
epigeous, *a.* ep-e-*jee*-us, growing close to the ground [Bot.].
epiglottic, *a.* ep-e-*glot*-tik, pertaining to, or formed with the aid of, the epiglottis. (Gr. *epiglottis.*)
epiglottis, *n.* ep-e-*glot*-tis, a cartilage at the root of the tongue protecting the glottis during the passage of aliment. [Anat.]. (Gr.)
epignathous, *a.* e-*pig*-na-thus, having the upper jaw longer than the lower [Zool.].
epigone, *n.* *ep*-e-gohn, a descendant, esp. an undistinguished descendant of illustrious predecessors, *pl.* **epigoni,** e-*pig*-o-ny. (Gr. *epigonos.*)
epigonium, *n.* ep-e-*goh*-ne-um, the sac enclosing the spore-case of liverworts. (Gr. *epi-* and *gonē*, seed.)
epigram, *n.* *ep*-e-gram, a short poem treating with wit and antithesis as a single thought; a concise or pointed saying. (Gr. *epi-*, and *gramma*, a writing.)
epigrammatic, *a.* *ep*-e-gra-*mat*-ik, dealing in epigrams; suitable to, pertaining to, or like an epigram; short and to the point. (Gr. *epigrammatikos.*)
epigrammatically, *ad.* *ep*-e-gram-*mat*-e-ka-le, in an epigrammatic manner.
epigrammatist, *n.* ep-e-*gram*-a-tist, one who composes epigrams.
epigrammatize, *v.t.* ep-e-*gram*-a-tize, to turn into an epigram; to express epigrammatically: *v.i.* to compose epigrams.
epigraph, *n.* *ep*-e-graf, an inscription; a quotation, genuine or fictitious, placed at the commencement of a chapter, etc.; a motto. (Gr. *epigraphē.*)
epigraphic, *a.* ep-e-*graf*-ik, pertaining to or in the nature of an epigraph.
epigraphist, *n.* e-*pig*-ra-fist, a student of epigraphs.
epigraphy, *n.* e-*pig*-ra-fe, the study of inscriptions; the art of deciphering them.
epigynous, *a.* e-*pij*-e-nus, growing, as stamens, on the surface of the ovary [Bot.]. (Gr. *epi-*, and *gyne*, a female.)
epilepsy, *n.* *ep*-e-lep-se, a nervous disease characterized by convulsions and loss of sense and consciousness; the falling sickness. (Gr. *epilepsis.*)
epileptic, *a.* ep-e-*lep*-tik, pertaining to, affected with, or consisting of epilepsy: *n.* one afflicted with epilepsy. (Gr. *epileptikos.*)
epileptoid, *a.* ep-e-*lep*-toyd, of an epileptic nature.
epilogist, *n.* e-*pil*-o-jist, one who writes or recites an epilogue.
epilogistic, *a.* ep-e-lo-*jis*-tik, pertaining to or of the nature of an epilogue.
epilogue, *n.* *ep*-e-lohg, the closing part of a discourse, in which the principal matters are recapitulated [Rhet.]; a speech or short poem addressed to the audience by one of the actors after the conclusion of the play; a conclusion. (Fr., from Gr. *epi-*, and *logos*, speech.)
epinasty, *n.* *ep*-e-*nas*-te, curvature due to more rapid growth on the upper side. (Gr. *epi-*, and *nastos*, closely pressed.)
epiornis, *n.* ep-e-*or*-nis, the æpyornis.
epiperipheral, *a.* *ep*-e-per-*rif*-er-al, originating on the periphery or external surface [Phys.].
epipetalous, *a.* *ep*-e-*pet*-a-lus, growing on a petal.
Epiphany, *n.* e-*pif*-a-ne, a Church festival held annually on the 6th Jan., the twelfth day after Christmas, in commemoration of the manifestation of Christ to the Magi; a divine or superhuman manifestation. (Gr. *epi-*, and *phainein*, to show. Fr. *épiphanie.*)
epiphenomenon, *n.* ep-e-fe-*nom*-e-non (*pl.* **epiphenomena**), a phenomenon secondary to or a by-product of other phenomena; an additional or secondary phenomenon in a disease [Path.].
epiphonema, *n.* *ep*-e-fo-*nee*-ma, an abrupt exclamatory ejaculation in the course or at the close of a discourse [Rhet.]. (Gr. *epi-*, and *phone*, voice.)
epiphragm, *n.* *ep*-e-fram, the operculum in univalve shells; a membrane covering certain parts of some mosses and fungi. (Gr. *epiphragma*, a covering.)
epiphyllous, *a.* ep-e-*fil*-us, inserted upon the leaf [Bot.] (Gr. *epi-*, and *phyllon*, a leaf.)
epiphyseal, *a.* ep-e-*fy*-ze-al, pertaining to or of the nature of an epiphysis.

epiphysis, *n.* e-*pif*-e-sis, ossification in which the end of a bone is separate from the main bone until maturity; a bone that ossifies thus; the pineal gland. [Anat.] (Gr.)
epiphytal, *a.* e-*pif*-e-tal, pertaining to an epiphyte.
epiphyte, *n.* *ep*-e-fite, a plant growing upon another but not necessarily parasitic; a fungus parasitic on an animal. (Gr. *epi-*, and *phyton*, a plant.)
epiphytic, *a.* ep-e-*fit*-ik, epiphytal; having the nature of an epiphyte.
epiploic, *a.* ep-e-*ploh*-ik, pertaining to the epiploon.
epiploon, *n.* e-*pip*-loh-on, the caul or great omentum, a fatty membrane overspreading the small intestines [Anat.]. (Gr.)
epirhizous, *a.* ep-e-*ry*-zus, growing on a root. (Gr. *epi-*, and *rhiza*, root.)
episcopacy, *n.* e-*pis*-ko-pa-se, government of the church by bishops or prelates, or that form of church government in which there are superior and inferior orders of clergy; prelacy; the body of bishops. (Gr. *episcopos*, an overseer.)
episcopal, *a.* e-*pis*-ko-pal, belonging to or vested in bishops or prelates; governed by bishops.
episcopalia, *n.pl.* e-*pis*-ko-*pay*-le-a, the appurtenances of a bishop or diocese.
episcopalian, *a.* e-*pis*-ko-*pay*-le-an, pertaining to bishops or government by bishops; episcopal: *n.* one who belongs to an episcopal church, or adheres to the episcopal form of church government.
episcopalianism, *n.* e-*pis*-ko-*pay*-le-a-nizm, the doctrine and methods of episcopalians.
episcopally, *ad.* e-*pis*-ko-pa-le, by episcopal authority; in an episcopal manner.
episcopate, *n.* e-*pis*-ko-pat, the office, see, or dignity of a bishop; the bishops as a body: *v.t.* to act as a bishop; to fill the office of a prelate. (Late L. *episcopatus*.)
episcope, *n.* *ep*-e-skope, an optical lantern used for throwing on a screen an enlarged image of opaque objects; an epidiascope.
episode, *n.* *ep*-e-sode, a separate incident, story, or action interpolated in a literary work; an incidental narrative or digression separate from the main theme, yet arising out of it; a portion of a fugue deviating from the subject-matter and supplying the embodying harmony [Mus.]. (Gr. *epeisodion*, coming in.)
episodic, *a.* ep-e-*sod*-ik, pertaining to an episode or poetical digression.
episodically, *ad.* by way of episode.
epispastic, *a.* ep-e-*spas*-tik, drawing; attracting the humours to the skin; blistering: *n.* a counter-irritant; a blister [Med.]. (Gr. *epispastikos*, attracting to.)
episperm, *n.* *ep*-e-sperm, the outer integument of a seed [Bot.]. (Gr. *epi-*, and *sperma*, seed.)
epispermic, *a.* ep-e-*sper*-mik, pertaining to the episperm.
epistaxis, *n.* ep-e-*stak*-sis, bleeding from the nose [Med.]. (Gr.)
epistemological, *a.* e-*pis*-te-mo-*loj*-e-kal, pertaining to the theory of knowledge.
epistemology, *n.* e-*pis*-te-*mol*-o-je, the study of the source, nature, and limitations of knowledge. (Gr. *episteme*, learning, *logos*, science.)
episternum, *n.* *ep*-e-*ster*-num, the interclavicle; the upper part of the sternum [Anat.]. (Gr. *epi-*, and *sternum*, the breast-bone.)
epistilbite, *n.* ep-e-*stil*-bite, a colourless hydrated silicate of calcium and aluminium.
epistle, *n.* e-*pisl*, a writing communicating intelligence to a distant person; a letter; a lesson in the Church service, so called as generally taken from the Apostolic Epistles: *pl.* the letters forming part of the New Testament originally addressed by the Apostles to their followers. **epistle side,** the left side of the altar, looking from it, where the epistle is read. (L. *epistola*)
epistler, *n.* e-*pis*-ler, a writer of epistles; the reader of the epistles in a Church service.
epistolary, *a.* e-*pis*-to-la-re, pertaining to epistles or letters; suitable to letters and correspondence; familiar; contained in letters. (Late L. *epistolarius*.)
epistolize, *v.t.* e-*pis*-to-lize, to write epistles or letters to.
epistolography, *n.* e-*pis*-to-*log*-ra-fe, the art or practice of writing letters.
epistrophe, *n.* e-*pis*-tro-fe, a figure in which several successive sentences end with the same word or affirmation [Rhet.]; a refrain [Mus.]. (Gr., turning around.)
epistyle, *n.* *ep*-e-stile, an architrave.
epitaph, *n.* *ep*-e-taf, an inscription on a tomb in honour or commemoration of the dead; a eulogy in prose or verse, such as might be inscribed on a monument. (Gr. *epi-*, and *taphos*, tomb.)
epitasis, *n.* e-*pit*-a-sis, that part which embraces the main action of a play and leads on to the catastrophe; the paroxysm of a fever [Med.]. (Gr.)
epithalamial, *a.* *ep*-e-tha-*lay*-me-al, epithalamic.
epithalamic, *a.* ep-e-tha-*lam*-ik, pertaining to or in the style of an epithalamium.
epithalamium, *n.* ep-e-tha-*lay*-me-um, a nuptial song or poem in praise of the bride and bridegroom, and praying for their prosperity. (L. from Gr. *epi-*, and *thalamos*, bridal chamber.)
epithelial, *a.* *ep*-e-*thee*-le-al, pertaining to epithelium.
epithelium, *n.* ep-e-*thee*-le-um, a superficial cell-tissue of sometimes a single, sometimes several layers investing various parts of the body [Anat.]; a thin covering of the inner surface of cavities, etc. [Bot.]. (Gr. *epi-*, and *thele*, nipple.)
epithem, *n.* *ep*-e-*them*, any external application, such as a lotion or poultice [Med.]. (Gr. *epithēma*, cover.)
epithet, *n.* *ep*-e-thet, an adjective or phrase expressing some real quality, attribute, or characteristic: *v.t.* to entitle; to describe by epithets. (Gr. *epitheton*.)
epithetic, *a.* ep-e-*thet*-ik, pertaining to an epithet; consisting of or abounding in epithets.
epithymetic, *a.* ep-e-thy-*met*-ik, inclined to lust; pertaining to animal passion. (Gr. *epi-*, and *thumos*, the mind as the seat of passion.)
epitome, *n.* e-*pit*-o-me, a brief summary or abstract of a book, etc.; a summary representation. (Gr.)
epitomist, *n.* e-*pit*-o-mist, one who abridges; a writer of an epitome.
epitomize, *v.t.* e-*pit*-o-mize, to abridge, curtail, or condense, as a writing: *v.i.* to compose abstracts.
epitonic, *a.* ep-e-*ton*-ik, overstrained. (Gr. *epi-*, and *teino*, stretch.)
epitrite, *n.* *ep*-e-trite, a foot consisting of three long syllables and one short, in any order [Pros.]. (Gr. *epitritos*, having three and a third.)
epixylous, *a.* ep-e-*zy*-lus, growing on wood (esp. of fungi) [Bot.]. (Gr. *epi-*, and *xylon*, wood.)
epizoic, *a.* ep-e-*zoh*-ik, pertaining to or existing as any of the epizoa.
epizoon, *n.* ep-e-*zoh*-on (*pl.* **epizoa**, ep-e-*zoh*-a), an animal living parasitically on the exterior of others, as the fish-lice. (Gr. *epi-*, and *zoon*, an animal.)
epizootic, *a.* *ep*-e-zoh-*ot*-ik, prevalent as a disease among animals: *n.* a pestilence prevalent among animals corresponding to an epidemic among men.
epoch, *n.* *ee*-pok *or* *ep*-ok, a fixed point or period of time remarkable for some great event or series of events from which succeeding years are numbered; any remarkable period of time; date; the longitude of a planet at any given time [Astron.]. (Gr. *epochē*, a stop.)
epochal, *a.* *ee*-pok-al *or* *ep*-ok-al, marking an epoch or new starting point in history.
epode, *n.* *ep*-ode, the third or last part of the ode; that which follows the strophe and antistrophe; lyric poetry in which shorter lines follow one or more long lines; a chorus. (O.Fr.)
epodic, *a.* ep-*oh*-dik, pertaining to or resembling an epode.
eponym, *n.* *ep*-o-nim, a name given to a people or a country from that of a person; the name of a person to whom the origin of a people or country is mythically ascribed. (Gr. *eponymos*, having a surname.)
eponymic, *a.* ep-o-*nim*-ik, eponymous.
eponymous, *a.* e-*pon*-e-mus, giving an eponym to a people, etc.; known by the adoption of the name.
eponymy, *n.* e-*pon*-e-me, derivation of tribal or place-names from an eponym.
epopee, *n.* ep-o-*pee*, an epic poem; the subject-matter of an epic poem. (Fr. *épopée*.)
epos, *n.* *ee*-pos, an epic or epopee; primitive poetry of epic character. (Gr.)
eprouvette, *n.* ay-proo-*vet*, an apparatus for testing the strength of explosives [Gunnery]; a spoon or bar used in assaying; a probe [Surg.]. (Fr.)
epsilon, *n.* ep-*sy*-lon, the fifth letter of the Greek alphabet (Ε,ε), corresponding to the short " e " of *pen*.

epsomite, *n.* *ep*-som-ite, native hydrated sulphate of magnesia, commercially known as **Epsom salts,** because first extracted from a mineral spring at Epsom, Surrey.
epulary, *a.* *ep*-yew-la-re, pertaining to a banquet, or to feasting. (*L. epulum,* a feast.)
epuration, *n.* *ep*-yew-*ray*-shon, the act or process of cleansing; purification; a purge [Polit.]. (Fr.)
equability, *n.* *ee*-kwa-*bil*-e-te, state or quality of being equable; continued uniformity.
equable, *a.* *ee*-kwa-bl, equal and uniform at all times; not variable; tranquil. (L. *æquabilis.*)
equableness, *n.* *ee*-kwa-bl-ness, equability.
equably, *ad.* *ee*-kwa-ble, with continued uniformity.
★**equal,** *a.* *ee*-kwal, of the same size, value, qualities, condition, or degree, etc.; uniform; not variable; in just proportion; impartial; indifferent; of the same interest or concern; equitable; on the same terms; adequate; having competent ability or means: *n.* one not inferior or superior to another, having the same or a similar age, rank, station, talents, or strength, etc.: *v.t.* to make equal in size, quantity, rank, etc., with another; to be or become equal to; to make equivalent to; to match. (L. *æqualis.*)
equalitarian, *a.* *ee*-kwol-e-*tare*-re-an, pertaining to or asserting the doctrine that all men are equal; to do with a state of social equality: *n.* one holding such doctrine.
equalitarianism, *n.* *ee*-kwol-e-*tare*-re-a-nizm, belief in the equalitarian doctrine; the doctrine itself.
equality, *n.* e-*kwol*-e-te, the condition of being equal; evenness; uniformity. (O.Fr. *equalité.*)
equalization, *n.* *ee*-kwa-ly-*zay*-shon, the act of equalizing; the state of being equalized.
equalize, *v.t.* *ee*-kwa-lize, to make equal or uniform; to cause to correspond.
equalizer, *n.* one who or a device which equalizes.
equally, *ad.* in equal measure or proportion.
equanimity, *n.* e-kwa-*nim*-e-te, evenness of mind; that calm temper or mental firmness which is not easily elated or depressed. (L. *æquanimitas.*)
equanimous, *a.* e-*kwan*-e-mus, of an even, composed frame of mind; of a steady temper.
equate, *v.t.* e-*kwate*, to reduce to an average or to a common standard, as in questions of time to some common and convenient epoch; to adjust by making allowance for; to put in the form of an equation [Math.]. (L. *æquatus,* made equal.)
equation, *n.* e-*kway*-shon, the act of making equal; reduction to equality; a proposition asserting the equality of two quantities, and expressed by the sign = between them [Math.]; a representation by symbols of changes occurring during a chemical reaction [Chem.]; an expression of the same quantity in two dissimilar terms, as 3*s.* = 36*d.*, allowance for inaccuracy [Astron.]. **equation of light,** allowance made in determining the position of a heavenly body for the time occupied in the transmission of its light to the eye of an observer [Astron.] **equation of payments,** the process of determining the date at which a single payment should be made in lieu of several different payments due at various dates [Comm.]. **equation of time,** the interval by which apparent time differs from mean time [Astron.]. **personal equation,** *see* **personal.**
equational, *a.* e-*kway*-shon-al, pertaining to or involving equations.
equationally, *ad.* in the form of an equation.
equator, *n.* e-*kway*-tor, a great circle at right angles to the axis of the terrestrial globe, equally distant from the two poles, and dividing the earth into two hemispheres, the north and the south [Geog.]; a great circle in the heavens marked out by the extension to them of the plane of the earth's equator [Astron.]. (Late L. *æquator.*)
equatorial, *a.* ee-kwa-*taw*-re-al, pertaining to, or situated on or near, the equator: *n.* an astronomical instrument with a telescope furnished with a clockwork motion and so mounted that any star to which it is directed is kept stationary within the field of vision.
equatorially, *ad.* so as to have the motions of an equatorial.
equerry, *n.* *ek*-wer-re, an officer of a royal household, originally one in charge of the horses. (Fr. *écurie,* a stable.)
equestrian, *a.* e-*kwes*-tre-an, pertaining to horses or horsemanship; practised or skilled in horsemanship; on, or representing a person on, horseback; pertaining to knights, as the equestrian order: *n.* one skilled in horsemanship; a performer on horseback. (L. *equus,* a horse.)
equestrianism, *n.* e-*kwes*-tre-a-nizm, horsemanship.
equestrienne, *n.* e-*kwes*-tre-*en*, a good horsewoman; a woman circus-rider. (Fr.)
equi-, *pref.* *ee*-kwe *or* *ek*-we, a combining form implying having equally or in equal degree, as in **equibalanced,** of equal weight, etc. (L. *æquus,* equal.)
equiangular, *a.* ee-kwe-*ang*-gewl-ar, consisting of or having equal angles [Geom.]. (L. *æquus,* equal, and *angular.*)
equidifferent, *a.* ee-kwe-*dif*-fer-ent, having equal differences; arithmetically proportional.
equidistant, *a.* ee-kwe-*dis*-tant, equally distant; separated from each other by equal distances.
equilateral, *a.* ee-kwe-*lat*-er-al, having all the sides equal: *n.* a side exactly corresponding to others; any figure with its sides equal. (L. *æquus,* and *latus, lateris,* a side.)
equilibrate, *v.t.* ee-kwe-*ly*-brate, to balance equally; to keep in equipoise. (*equi-,* and L. *libra,* a balance.)
equilibration, *n.* *ee*-kwe-ly-*bray*-shon, equipoise; the act of keeping the balance even; the state of being equally balanced.
equilibrator, *n.* ee-kwe-*ly*-bray-tor, a device for maintaining equilibrium, esp. in an aeroplane.
equilibrist, *n.* ee-*kwil*-e-brist, a rope-walker or other performer who keeps his balance in unnatural positions.
equilibrity, *n.* *ee*-kwe-*lib*-re-te, the state of being equally balanced.
equilibrium, *n.* e-kwe-*lib*-re-um, equipoise; equality of weight or force; a state of rest produced by the mutual counteraction of two or more forces; a condition of just poise or balance so as to stand firmly; equal balancing or hesitation of the mind between motives or reasons. (L. *æquilibrium.*)
equimultiple, *a.* ek-we-*mul*-te-pl, multiplied by the same number: *n.* a quantity multiplied by the same number as another quantity [Math. and Arith.]. (L. *æquus,* and *multiple.*)
equine, *a.* *ee*-kwine *or* *ek*-wine, pertaining to a horse; pertaining to the genus *Equus.* (L. *equus.*)
equinia, *n.* e-*kwin*-e-a, glanders, farcy [Vet.].
equinoctial, *a.* *ek*-we-*nok*-shal, pertaining to the equinoxes, or to the regions or climate in or near the equator, or to the time when the sun passes the equinoctial points: *n.* the equinoctial circle; an equinoctial storm. **equinoctial circle,** the celestial equator, which is traversed by the sun at the time of an equinox; opening and closing at a definite time (of flowers) [Bot.]. **equinoctial line,** the terrestrial equator. **equinoctial points,** the two points where the ecliptic and the equator intersect each other. **equinoctial time,** time reckoned from moment when the mean sun is at the mean vernal equinox. (L. *æquinoctialis.*)
equinoctially, *ad.* ek-we-*nok*-shal-le, in the direction of, or towards, the equinox.
equinox, *n.* *ek*-we-noks, the precise time when the sun enters one of the equinoctial points, making the day and night of equal length, the first point of Aries about the 21st of March, and the first point of Libra about the 23rd of September, which are severally called the vernal and the autumnal equinoxes. (L. *æquinoctium*).
equip, *v.t.* e-*kwip*, to dress; to accoutre; to furnish with what is necessary for any service; to furnish with arms or with men, artillery, and munitions of war; to fit out. (Fr. *équiper.*)
equipage, *n.* *ek*-we-paj, that with which one is equipped; equipment; outfit; requisites for naval, military, or other service; carriage and horses with attendants. **camp equipage,** furniture of a camp, as tents and utensils. **field equipage,** vehicles and other equipment for mobile troops. (O.Fr.)
equipedal, *a.* ek-we-*pee*-dal, with the pairs of feet equal [Zool.]. (L. *æquus,* and *pes, pedis,* a foot.)
equipment, *n.* e-*kwip*-ment, the act of equipping; the state of being equipped; anything that is used in equipping; necessaries for an expedition, etc.; outfit; necessary adjuncts; mental qualifications. (Fr. *équipement.*)
equipoise, *n.* *eek*-we-poyz, equality of weight or

force ; equilibrium ; a state in which the two ends or sides of a thing are balanced : *v.t.* to counterbalance ; mentally to hold in suspense. (L. *æquus*, and *poise*.)
equipollence, *n.* ek-we-*pol*-lence, equality of power or force ; an equivalence between two or more propositions [Logic].
equipollent, *a.* ek-we-*pol*-lent, having equal power, force, or significance ; equivalent : *n.* an equivalent. (Fr.)
equipollently, *ad.* with equal power, etc.
equiponderant, *a.* ek-we-*pon*-der-ant, in a state of equipoise ; of equal force or weight.
equiponderate, *v.t.* ek-we-*pon*-der-ate, to equal in weight ; to counterpoise. (L. *æquus*, and *pondus*, weight.)
equipotential, *a.* *ek*-we-po-*ten*-shal, having the potential the same or constant at all points.
equirotal, *a.* ek-we-*roh*-tal, having front and rear wheels of the same diameter.
equisetaceous, *a.* *ek*-we-se-*tay*-shus, belonging to the family of the horsetails [Bot.]. (L. *equisætum*.)
equisetic, *a.* ek-we-*see*-tik, pertaining to or derived from any plants of the genus *Equisetum*. **equisetic acid,** aconitic acid obtained from some species of *Equisetum*.
Equisetum, *n.* ek-we-*see*-tum, a genus of plants comprising the horsetails. (L. *equus*, a horse, *seta*, a bristle.)
equisonance, *n.* ek-we-*soh*-nance, the consonance between octaves. (L. *æquus*, and *sonus*, sound.)
equitable, *a.* *ek*-we-ta-bl, impartial ; fair ; upright ; done with equity ; pertaining to the rules of or to a court of equity. **equitable charge,** a form of mortgage in the case of a temporary loan on securities. (Fr. *équitable*.)
equitableness, *n.* the quality of being equitable.
equitably, *ad.* in an equitable way.
equitant, *a.* *ek*-we-tant, riding on a horse ; overlapping (of leaves that overlap the bases of others) ; embracing at the base [Bot.]. (L. *equitans*, being on a horse.)
equitation, *n.* *ek*-we-*tay*-shon, horsemanship.
Equites, *n.pl.* *ek*-we-teez, the equestrian or second order of nobility in ancient Rome, the senators being the first ; the Knights. (L.)
equity, *n.* *ek*-we-te, the impartial distribution of justice ; the correction of law, when too severe or defective by considerations of justice ; the extension of the words of the law to cases not expressed, yet coming within the reason of the law ; the difference between the value of a mortgaged property and the amount of the debt incurred in mortgaging it ; the profit remaining after fixed charges or preference dividends, etc., have been paid [Comm.]. **equity of redemption,** the allowance, to a mortgager, of a reasonable time to redeem an estate that has been mortgaged for a sum less than its value [Law].
equivalence, *n.* e-*kwiv*-a-lence, the state of being equivalent.
equivalency, *n.* e-*kwiv*-a-len-se, equivalence.
equivalent, *a.* e-*kwiv*-a-lent, equal in value, effect, cogency, meaning, or moral worth, etc. ; commensurate ; equal in combining power ; equal in area or size [Geom.] : *n.* that which is equal in value or effect, etc. ; the proportion expressing the weight, or quantity by weight, of any substance which combines with another substance to make a definite compound [Chem.]. (L. *æquivalentia*.)
equivalently, *ad.* in an equivalent manner.
equivalve, *a.* *ek*-we-valv, having the valves equal in size and form (of bivalves) [Zool.].
equivocal, *a.* e-*kwiv*-o-kal, having two meanings ; of doubtful signification ; ambiguous ; susceptible of different constructions ; questionable ; uncertain ; proceeding from some unknown or unusual cause. (Late L. *æquivocus*.)
equivocality, *n.* e-kwiv-o-*kal*-e-te, equivocal character ; an equivoque.
equivocally, *ad.* ambiguously.
equivocalness, *n.* ambiguity ; double meaning ; equivocality.
equivocate, *v.i.* e-*kwiv*-o-kate, to use words of a doubtful signification ; to use ambiguous expressions with a view to mislead ; to prevaricate ; to quibble. (Late L. *æquivocatus*.)
equivocation, *n.* e-*kwiv*-o-*kay*-shon, prevarication ; the act of equivocating.
equivocator, *n.* e-*kwiv*-o-kay-tor, one who equivocates.
equivocatory, *a.* e-*kwiv*-o-ka-to-re, of a prevaricating or evasive character.
equivoque, *n.* *ek*-we-voke, an ambiguous term ; an equivocation. (Fr. *équivoque*.)
Equus, *n.* *ee*-kwus, the genus of ungulates that comprises the horses, asses, and zebras. (L.)
era, *n.* *eer*-a, a period of time reckoned from some remarkable event, as the Christian era ; the date from which this is reckoned. (L. *æra*, originally "counters," from *æs*, *æris*, money.)
eradiate, *v.i.* e-*ray*-de-ate, to shoot forth, as rays of light. (L. *e*-, and *radiatus*, radiated.)
eradicable, *a.* e-*rad*-e-ka-bl, that may be eradicated.
eradicate, *v.t.* e-*rad*-e-kate, to pull up by the roots ; to destroy ; to extirpate. (L. *eradicatus*, destroyed.)
eradication, *n.* e-*rad*-e-*kay*-shon, the act of eradicating ; the state of being eradicated ; extirpation.
eradicative, *a.* e-*rad*-e-ka-tiv, that extirpates ; serving or tending to eradicate : *n.* a medicine that effects a radical cure.
erasable, *a.* e-*raze*-a-bl, that may or can be erased.
erase, *v.t.* e-*raze*, to rub or scrape out ; to efface ; to obliterate ; to destroy to the foundation. (L. *erasus*, scratched out.)
erased, *a.* e-*rayzd*, forcibly torn off so as to leave jagged and uneven edges [Her.].
eraser, *n.* e-*raze*-er, one who or that which erases.
erasion, *n.* e-*ray*-zhon, the act of erasing ; erasure.
Erasmian, *a.* e-*raz*-me-an, pertaining to or following the teaching of Erasmus, a Dutch scholar who died in 1536 : *n.* a follower of Erasmus, esp. of his mode of pronouncing Greek.
Erastian, *n.* e-*ras*-te-an, one who would subject the Church to the State ; originally one who denied to the Church all authority in matters affecting civil rights : *a.* pertaining to the doctrines of Erastus, a Swiss theologian who died in 1583.
Erastianism, *n.* e-*ras*-te-a-nizm, the subjection of Church to State.
erasure, *n.* e-*rayz*-yewr, the act of erasing ; obliteration ; the place where something has been erased.
Erato, *n.* *e*-ra-toh, the muse of lyric and amorous poetry [Myth.]. (Gr. *eros*, love.)
erbium, *n.* *er*-be-um, a metallic element belonging to the yttrium sub-group of the rare-earths. (*Ytterby*, in Sweden.)
ere, *ad.* ayr, before ; sooner than : *prep.* before. (A.S. *ær*.)
Erebus, *n.* *e*-re-bus, one of the infernal deities of Greek myth ; the primal darkness ; the dark underworld. (Gr.)
erect, *a.* e-*rekt*, upright ; directed upwards ; upright and firm ; intent ; straight ; forming a very acute angle with the stem of the plant (of leaves) [Bot.] : *v.t.* to raise and set upright or perpendicularly ; to raise, as a building ; to found ; to set up or establish anew ; to elevate ; to exalt. **to erect a perpendicular,** to draw a line at right angles [Geom.]. (L. *erectus*, upright.)
erectable, *a.* e-*rek*-ta-bl, that can be erected.
erectile, *a.* e-*rek*-tile, erectable ; capable of becoming tense or rigid.
erection, *n.* e-*rek*-shon, the act of erecting, building, setting up, or establishing ; the state of being erected ; a building or structure ; the distended state of an organ due to accumulation of blood in the erectile tissue [Anat.].
erectly, *ad.* e-*rekt*-le, in an erect posture.
erectness, *n.* uprightness of posture or form.
erector, *n.* e-*rek*-tor, a workman engaged in erecting machinery or structures, etc. ; a muscle that erects [Anat.] ; a reversing lens [Opt.].
erelong, *ad.* ayr-*long*, before long.
eremite, *n.* *e*-re-mite, a hermit ; a solitary. (Gr. *eremitēs*.)
eremitic, *a.* e-re-*mit*-ik, living alone in seclusion from the world, like a hermit.
ereption, *n.* e-*rep*-shon, the act of taking away or snatching by force. (L. *ereptio*, taking forcibly.)
erethism, *n.* e-re-thizm, abnormal excitation or irritation in any part [Med.]. (Gr. *erithismos*.)
erethismic, *a.* e-re-*thiz*-mik, relating to or of the nature of erethism.
erewhile, *ad.* ayr-*while*, some time ago ; formerly.
erg, *n.* erg, the unit of work : the unit of energy ; the amount of work done when the point of application of a force of one dyne is moved a distance

of one centimetre along the line of action of that force [Mech.]. (Gr. *ergon*, work.)
ergo, *ad.* *er*-go, therefore. (L.)
ergometer, *n.* er-*gom*-e-ter, an instrument for measuring work or energy ; a dynamometer. (Gr. *ergon*, and *metron*, measure.)
ergophobia, *n.* er-go-*foh*-be-a, a morbid hatred or fear of work.
ergosterol, *n.* er-*gos*-te-rol, a sterol occurring in ergot, yeast, etc., from which vitamin D can be produced by its irradiation with ultra-violet light.
ergot, *n.* *er*-got, a fungus growing on rye and other grain ; a medical preparation made from this. (Fr., a cock's spur.)
ergotic, *a.* er-*got*-ik, pertaining to or derived from ergot.
ergotine, *n.* *er*-go-tin, a narcotic and pungent substance constituting the active principle of ergot [Chem.].
ergotism, *n.* *er*-go-tizm, the effect of the action of the ergot on the human system ; an epidemic disease due to consumption of grain affected by ergot ; the disease of ergot in cereals.
erica, *n.* e-*ry*-ka, any plant of the genus *Erica* comprising the heaths. (L. *erīca*.)
ericaceous, *a.* e-re-*kay*-shus, belonging to the heath family of plants.
erigeron, *n.* e-*rij*-er-on, any plant of the genus *Erigeron*, including fleabane, so called from their hoary appearance. (Gr. *eri*, early, *geron*, an old man.)
erinaceous, *a.* e-re-*nay*-shus, pertaining to or resembling the hedgehogs. (L. *erinaceus*, hedgehog.)
erineum, *n.* e-*rin*-e-um, a wool-like growth on leaves, etc., caused by mites [Bot.]. (Gr. *erineos*, woolly.)
eringo, *n.* e-*ring*-go, eryngo.
erinite, *n.* *e*-rin-ite, a native arsenate of copper, of an emerald-green colour. (*Erin*, Ireland.)
Erinnys, *n.* e-*rin*-is (*pl.* **Erinnyes,** e-*rin*-e-eez), one of the Furies or avenging goddesses [Myth]. (Gr.)
eriometer, *n.* e-re-*om*-e-ter, an optical instrument for measuring the diameters of minute fibres. (Gr. *erion*, wool, and *metron*.)
eristic, *a.* e-*ris*-tik, pertaining to disputation ; controversial : *n.* the art of controversy ; a controversialist. (Gr. *eristikos*, from *eris*, strife.)
erl-king, *n.* *erl*-king, the impersonation of the spirit of superstitious fear in Teutonic folklore. (Ger. *Erl-kōnig*, from Dan. *ellerkonge*, king of the elves.)
ermelin, *n.* *er*-me-lin, ermine.
ermine, *n.* *er*-min, any of the weasels that assume a snowy white coat in winter, esp. *Mustela erminea* ; the winter fur of the ermine, usually studded with its black tail-tips ; the dignity of a judge, whose robe was lined with ermine ; a fur represented by a white field with distinctive black spots [Her.]. (O.Fr.)
ermined, *a.* *er*-mind, clothed or adorned with ermine.
erminois, *n.* *er*-min-wah, a fur represented by distinctive black spots on a gold field [Her.]. (Fr.)
erne, *n.* ern, any eagle, but esp. the sea-eagle or the golden eagle. (A.S. *earn*.)
erode, *v.t.* e-*rode*, to gnaw away ; to eat away ; to corrode. (L. *erodo*, consume.)
eroded, *a.* e-*roh*-ded, eaten away or as if gnawed or eaten ; erose [Bot.].
erodent, *a.* e-*roh*-dent, caustic : *n.* a substance which eats away growths [Med.]. (L. *erodens*, consuming.)
erogenic, *a.* e-ro-*jen*-ik, productive of sexual desire. (Gr. *eros*, love.)
erose, *a.* e-*rohs*, eroded ; having small sinuses in the margin of a leaf [Bot.]. (L. *erosus*, consumed.)
erosion, *n.* e-*roh*-zhon, the act of wearing away ; the state of being eaten away ; the action of water or weather in wearing away rocks.
erosive, *a.* e-*roh*-siv, tending to erode.
erotetic, *a.* e-ro-*tet*-ik, interrogatory ; pertaining to questioning. (Gr. *erotesis*, a question.)
erotic, *a.* e-*rot*-ik, amatory ; pertaining to sexual love : *n.* an amorous composition or poem. (Gr. *erotikos*, pertaining to love, from *Eros*, love, the god of love.)
eroticism, *n.* e-*rot*-e-sizm, erotic character.
erotomania, *n.* e-ro-to-*may*-ne-a, insanity proceeding from sexual causes ; melancholy madness ; uncontrollable sexual desire. (Gr. *eros*, and *mania*.)
erotomaniac, *n.* e-rot-o-*may*-ne-ak, one afflicted with erotomania.
err, *v.i.* er, to wander from or miss the right way ; to deviate from the path of duty ; to mistake ; to commit error ; to sin. (O.Fr. *errer*.)
errand, *n.* *e*-rand, a verbal message ; a commission to say or do something ; the purpose of a journey. (A.S. *ærende*, connected with L. *aro*, plough.)
errant, *a.* *e*-rant, wandering ; roving ; rambling ; deviating from a certain course ; behaving as a knight-errant. (O.Fr.)
errantry, *n.* *e*-rant-re, a wandering, roving, or rambling about ; the way of life of a knight-errant.
errata, *n.pl.* e-*rah*-ta, *see* **erratum.**
erratic, *a.* e-*rat*-ik, wandering ; having no certain course ; eccentric ; not fixed or stationary ; having been transported from the original location (of boulders, etc.) [Geol.] : *n.* one who is erratic ; an erratic rock or boulder [Geol.]. (Fr. *erratique*.)
erratically, *ad.* without rule ; irregularly.
erratum, *n.* e-*rah*-tum (*pl.* **errata**), an error or mistake in writing or printing. (L.)
erroneous, *a.* e-*roh*-ne-us, deviating by mistake from the truth or from the right path ; wrong ; mistaken. (L. *erroneus*, straying.)
erroneously, *ad.* by mistake ; not rightly.
erroneousness, *n.* the state of being erroneous ; deviation from right.
★**error,** *n.* *e*-ror, a wandering or deviation from the truth ; a mistake made in writing or judgment, conduct, etc. ; deviation from law, justice, or right ; sin, iniquity, or transgression ; a mistake in pleading or in judgment [Law] ; a difference or divergence to be allowed for [Astron.]. **writ of error,** a writ founded on an alleged error in judgment, which carries the suit to another tribunal for redress [Law] (O.Fr. *errour*.)
errorist, *n.* *e*-ro-rist, one who errs or encourages and propagates error.
ersatz, *n.* er-*zatz*, a substitute ; makeshift for the genuine article : *a.* counterfeit ; substitutional. (Ger.)
Erse, *n.* erss, Gaelic spoken in the Scottish Highlands (incorrectly applied to Irish) : *a.* pertaining to the Scots Gaels or their language. (A variant of *Irish*, the name formerly given to the West Highland Scots.)
erst, *ad.* erst, formerly ; hitherto. (A.S. *ærest*.)
erstwhile, *ad.* *erst*-while, some time ago ; formerly : *a.* former.
erubescence, *n.* e-roo-*bes*-ence, a becoming red ; redness of the surface ; blushing.
erubescent, *a.* e-roo-*bes*-ent, red or reddish ; blushing. (L. *erubescens*, reddening.)
erubescite, *n.* e-roo-*bes*-ite, bornite.
eruciform, *a.* e-roo-se-form, resembling a caterpillar. (L. *eruca*, a caterpillar.)
eructate, *v.t.* e-*ruk*-tate, to belch. (L. *eructare*, to belch.)
eructation, *n.* e-ruk-*tay*-shon, the act of belching wind from the stomach ; a violent ejection of matter from a crater or geyser, etc.
erudite, *a.* *e*-roo-dite, learned ; characterized by erudition. (L. *eruditus*, instructed.)
eruditely, *ad.* with erudition or learning.
eruditeness, *n.* quality of being erudite.
erudition, *n.* e-roo-*dish*-on, learning ; scholarship ; knowledge gained by study of books.
erupt, *v.i.* e-*rupt*, to burst forth ; to break through : *v.t.* to cast out, as lava from a volcano. *L. eruptus*, broken out.)
eruption, *n.* e-*rup*-shon, the act of bursting forth from enclosure ; a violent emission of anything, particularly of flames and lava from a volcano ; a sudden or violent sally ; a breaking out ; a rash on the skin or its breaking out [Med.].
eruptive, *a.* e-*rup*-tiv, bursting forth ; produced by eruption ; attended with eruptions or efflorescence [Med.].
eruptivity, *n.* e-rup-*tiv*-e-te, the quality of being eruptive.
eryngo, *n.* e-*ring*-go, the sea-holly ; a sweetmeat made of its candied root. (Gr. *eryngion*.)
erysipelas, *n.* e-re-*sip*-e-las, a diffusive inflammatory affection of the skin, commonly of the subcutaneous aerolar tissue, accompanied with fever ; St. Anthony's fire or the rose. (L.)
erysipelatous, *a.* e-re-se-*pel*-a-tus, resembling erysipelas, or partaking of its nature.
erythema, *n.* e-re-*thee*-ma, an affection of the skin showing irregularly defined red patches. (Gr.)

erythematic, *a.* e-re-the-*mat*-ik, erythematous.
erythematous, *a.* e-re-*thee*-ma-tus, pertaining to erythema or any red affection of the skin.
erythrin, *n.* e-*rith*-rin, a colourless crystalline compound obtained from certain lichens from which a red dye-stuff is prepared.
erythrism, *n.* *e*-re-thrizm, abnormal redness of hair, plumage, etc.
erythrite, *n.* *e*-rith-rite, a hydrous arsenate of cobalt, occurring usually in rose-red crystals [Min.].
erythro-, *e*-re-throh, Greek combining form implying "red," as **erythrogenic,** producing a red colour or [Physiol.] a sensation of red. (Gr. *eruthros*, red.)
escalade, *n.* es-ka-*lade*, an assault made by troops on a fortified place, in which they use ladders: *v.t.* to storm by means of ladders. (Fr., from L. *scala*, ladder.)
escalator, *n.* *es*-ka-lay-tor, a stairway, the treads of which are so arranged on an endless belt that, when the latter is in motion, the former ascend or descend continuously. (As *escalade*.)
Escallonia, *n.* es-ka-*loh*-ne-a, a genus of evergreen shrubs, mostly natives of the Andes. (From name of Span. traveller, *Escallon*, their discoverer.)
escallop, *n.* es-*kal*-lop, the scallop, or its shell.
escapade, *n.* es-ka-*pade*, the fling of a horse; kicking with the hind legs; a mischievous freak; an insane proceeding. (Fr.)
escape, *n.* es-*kape*, the act of fleeing from danger, etc.; a being passed without receiving injury; the means of escaping; a leakage (as of gas, etc.); a cultivated plant growing wild [Bot.]; an evasion of legal restraint or the custody of the sheriff, without due course of law [Law]: *v.i.* to flee and be secure from danger; to be passed without harm: *v.t.* to free from and avoid without harm or unobserved; to avoid the danger of. **escape-warrant,** a process addressed to all sheriffs, etc., to capture a runaway prisoner. (Fr. *échapper*, from L. *ex-*, and *cappa*, a cape.)
escapee, *n.* es-kay-*pee*, one who has escaped; an escaped convict, prisoner, etc.
escapement, *n.* es-*kape*-ment, the mechanism by which the irregular action produced by the mainspring of a watch or the weights of a clock is checked and rendered regular; the balance wheel.
escaper, *n.* es-*kay*-per, one who or that which escapes.
escapism, *n.* es-*kay*-pizm, the tendency to avoid unpleasantnesses, responsibilities, etc., esp. by retreat into some congenial occupation or realm of fantasy [Psych.].
escapist, *n.* es-*kay*-pist, one who practises escapism.
escargot, *n.* es-kar-goh, on edible snail. (Fr.)
escarp, *n.* es-*karp*, a steep slope; the side or slope of the ditch next the rampart [Fort.]: *v.t.* to form into a scarp or sudden slope. **escarped. escarping. escarps.** (Fr. *escarpe*.)
escarpment, *n.* es-*karp*-ment, a steep artificial declivity for defence; the precipitous side of a hill or rock; a line of inland declivities due to denudation [Geol.].
eschalot, *n.* esh-a-*lot*, the shallot.
eschar, *n.* *es*-kar, a scab; a crust; the slough occasioned by burns or caustic applications [Surg.]. (Gr. *eschara*, scar.)
eschatological, *a.* *es*-ka-to-*loj*-e-kal, pertaining to eschatology.
eschatology, *n.* es-ka-*tol*-o-je, the study or doctrine of the four last things, viz., death, judgment, heaven, and hell [Theol.]. (Gr. *eschatos*, last, *logos*, doctrine.)
escheat, *n.* es-*cheet*, the reversion of any land or tenements to the lord within his manor, or to the state, through failure of heirs; the lands, etc., which so revert [Law]: *v.i.* to revert, as land, to the lord of a manor or to the state by means of the extinction of the blood of the tenant or otherwise: *v.t.* to forfeit. (O.Fr. from L. *ex-*, and *cado*, fall.)
escheatage, *n.* es-*chee*-taj, the right of succeeding to an escheat [Law].
escheator, *n.* es-*chee*-tor, an official who took note of escheats to the king in a county.
eschew, *v.t.* es-*choo*, to flee from; to abstain from; to shun. (O.Fr. *escherer*.)
eschewer, *n.* es-*choo*-er, one who eschews.
eschscholtzia, *n.* es-*kol*-sha, the Californian poppy, with large yellow flowers. (J. F. v. *Eschscholtz*, Ger. naturalist, *d.* 1831.)
escort, *n.* *ess*-kort, a guard; a body of troops attending an officer, or protecting baggage, provisions, or munitions, etc., in transit; a warship or number of warships protecting a convoy of merchant vessels; an accompanying attendant: *v.t.* es-*kort*, to attend and guard on a journey or excursion; to accompany as escort. (Fr. *escorter*.)
escot, *v.t.* es-*kot*, to pay the reckoning for; to support.
escribed, *a.* ee-*skrybd*, (of a circle) touching, exteriorly, one side of a triangle while touching, interiorly, each of the projected remaining sides [Geom.].
escritoire, *n.* es-krit-wahr, an enclosed writing table; a writing-desk. (Fr.; now *écritoire*.)
escrow, *n.* es-*kroh*, a deed or other bond delivered to third person to hold till some condition is performed by the grantee [Law].
escuage, *n.* *es*-kew-aj, the military service rendered, as rent, by certain feudal tenants.
escudo, *n.* ess-*kew*-doh, a Portuguese silver coin and monetary unit, value at par about 2½*d.*; a former gold or silver coin of Spanish America.
Esculapian, *a.* es-kew-*lay*-pe-an, Æsculapian.
esculent, *a.* *es*-kew-lent, edible; that may be used by man for food: *n.* something that is eatable. (L. *esculentus*, capable of being eaten.)
esculin, *n.* *es*-kew-lin, an antipyretic prepared from the inner bark of the horse-chestnut, *Æsculus hippocastanum* [Med.].
escutcheon, *n.* es-*kutch*-on, the shield or lozenge on which a coat of arms is represented; a name-plate on a coffin, etc.; a keyhole plate; the part of a ship's stern where her name is painted. **escutcheon of pretence,** an inescutcheon bearing the coat of arms of a wife who is an heiress [Her.]. (Fr.)
esemplastic, *a.* es-em-*plas*-tik, fashioning into one; unifying. (Gr. *eis*, into, *hen*, one, and *plasso*, fashion.)
eserine, *n.* *ee*-ser-in, the alkaloid of the Calabar bean. (*Esere*, the native name.)
esker, *n.* *es*-ker, a narrow ridge or flattened mound of gravel or sand deposited by a sub-glacial stream. (Ir. *eiscir*.)
Eskimo, *n.* *es*-ke-moh (*pl.* **Eskimos**), a member of a North American race, also known as Esquimaux, inhabiting Greenland and Arctic America. **Eskimo curlew,** the bird *Phaeopus borealis*. **Eskimo dog,** a powerful wolf-like dog used by the Eskimos for drawing sledges and hunting. (Indian word meaning "eaters of raw meat.")
esoenteritis, *n.* es-o-*en*-ter-*ry*-tis, inflammation of the mucous membrane of the intestines. (Gr. *eso*, within, *enteron*, an intestine.)
esogastritis, *n.* es-o-gas-*try*-tis, inflammation of the mucous membrane of the stomach. (Gr. *eso*, within, *gaster*, the belly.)
esophagus, *n.* es-*of*-a-gus, the œsophagus.
Esopian, *a.* e-*soh*-pe-an, Æsopian.
esoteric, *a.* es-o-*te*-rik, secret; for the initiated only, and intelligible only to them; arising from internal causes [Med.]. (Gr. *esoterikos*.)
esoterism, *n.* es-*sot*-e-rizm, esoteric doctrine.
espadon, *n.* *es*-pa-don, a long two-handed sword. (It.)
espagnolette, *n.* es-*pan*-yo-let, the fastening of a casement window. (Fr.)
espalier, *n.* es-*pal*-yer, a row of trees having the branches spread out like a fan against trellis work; a lattice-work on which to train fruit trees, etc. (Fr., from It. *spalliera*, a support for the shoulders.)
esparto, *n.* es-*pahr*-to, grasses of the genera *Lygeum* and *Stipa*, growing in Spain and Algeria and used in the manufacture of cordage, coarse cloth, paper, etc. (Sp.)
especial, *a.* es-*pesh*-al, special; distinguished above or from others of the same kind. (O.Fr.)
especially, *ad.* es-*pesh*-al-le, in an especial degree.
esperance, *n.* *es*-per-ance, hope. (Sp. *esperanza*.)
Esperantist, *n.* es-per-*ran*-tist, one proficient in Esperanto.
Esperanto, *n.* es-per-*ran*-to, an artificial language intended to be universal for commercial purposes.
espial, *n.* es-*py*-al, the act of spying or espying.
espièglerie, *n.* (App.), archness; roguishness. (Fr.)
espier, *n.* es-*py*-er, one who watches like a spy.
espionage, *n.* *es*-pe-o-nahj, spying; the practice or employment of spies; the secret systematic work of spies. (Fr.)
esplanade, *n.* es-pla-*nade*, a broad level roadway,

esp. one between the houses on the front and the beach at a seaside watering-place; originally the void space between the glacis of a citadel and the first houses of the town. (Fr.)

espousal, *n.* es-*pouz*-al, the act of espousing or betrothing; adoption: *pl.* the ceremony of matrimony; a mutual promise of marriage. (O.Fr. *espousailles*.)

espouse, *v.t.* es-*pouz*, to marry; to promise or engage in marriage; to adopt or defend (a cause, etc.). (Fr. *épouser*.)

esprit, *n.* es-*pree*, spirit; wit; sprightliness. **esprit de corps,** loyalty to one's comrades or to those of the same occupation, class, etc. (Fr.)

espy, *v.t.* es-*py*, to see at a distance; to detect something intended to be hid: *v.i.* to look narrowly. (O.Fr. *espier*.)

Esquimau, *n.* *es*-ke-moh (*pl.* **Esquimaux**), Eskimo. (Fr.)

esquire, *n.* es-*kwire*, the armour-bearer, squire, or attendant of a knight; a title of dignity next in degree below a knight; a title used by professional men and as an expression of respect in addressing a letter: *v.t.* to attend on. (Fr.)

ess, *n.* ess, the letter S; anything S-shaped.

essay, *v.t.* es-*say*, to try; to attempt; to make experiment of: *n.* *es*-say, an effort made for the performance of anything; trial; a test; a short informal literary composition. (O.Fr. *essai*.)

essayist, *n.* *es*-say-ist, a writer of essays.

essence, *n.* *es*-sence, that which constitutes the distinctive nature of a thing; that which makes a thing to be what it is; existence; being; an elemental or immaterial being; the extracted virtues of a plant or drug; the proper substance of anything; the solution of an essential oil in alcohol; a perfume, or the volatile matter constituting perfume: *v.t.* to perfume; to scent. (Fr.)

Essene, *n.* es-*seen*, a member of a cenobitic communistic Jewish fraternity of about the 2nd cent. B.C. to the 2nd cent. A.D., which is presumed to have represented Judaism in its purity and to have exercised some influence on Christianity. (Late L. *Esseni*.)

Essenism, *n.* *es*-en-izm, the doctrine and practice of the Essenes.

essential, *a.* es-*sen*-shal, relating to the essence of a thing; necessary to the existence of a thing; important in the highest degree; real, not accidental; highly rectified; pure: *n.* that which is constitutive or necessary to the being or existence of a thing. **essential character,** that single quality which serves to distinguish one genus, species, etc., from another; the differentia. **essential oils,** volatile odoriferous oils obtained from plants, usually by distillation with water. (Late L. *essentialis*.)

essentiality, *n.* ĕs-*sen*-she-*al*-e-te, the quality of being essential.

essentially, *ad.* es-*sen*-shal-le, by the constitution of nature; in an important degree.

essoign *or* **essoin,** *n.* es-*soyn*, an excuse offered for the non-appearance of one summoned to appear in court [Law]; an excuse: *v.t.* to allow an excuse for non-appearance in court; to excuse for absence [Law]. (O.Fr., from L. *ex-*, and *sunnis*, lawful excuse.)

essonite, *n.* *es*-son-ite, cinnamon-stone, yellow garnet. (Gr. *hesson*, inferior.)

establish, *v.t.* es-*tab*-lish, to set and fix firmly or unalterably; to found; to ordain; to appoint; to confirm; to substantiate; to set up and confirm; to set up; to set up by authority and endow. **the established Church,** the Church set up and supported by the State; the State Church. (O.Fr. *establissant*, established.)

establishment, *n.* es-*tab*-lish-ment, the act of establishing; settlement; confirmation; settled regulation, system, or constitution; fixed or stated allowance; that which is established; permanent civil or military force; a place of residence or of business; household equipment; an institution; the Church of England or the Church of Scotland established by law.

establishmentarian, *a.* es-*tab*-lish-men-*tare*-re-an, in favour of religious establishment or of the maintenance of an establishment, esp. the Church of England.

estafette, *n.* es-ta-*fet*, a military courier; a mounted orderly; an express messenger. (Fr.)

estaminet, *n.* es-*tam*-e-nay, an unpretentious wayside café; originally a restaurant where smoking was allowed. (Fr.)

estancia, *n.* es-*tan*-se-a, a cattle ranch in South America. (Sp.)

estate, *n.* es-*tate*, a fixed condition or state; condition; rank; the interest, or quantity of interest, that a man has in lands, tenements, or other effects [Law]; property, esp. landed property; the state or body politic; an order or class of men in the body politic: *pl.* dominions; possessions of a prince. **estate agent,** a manager of landed estates; a house agent. **estate duties,** death duties. **estates of the realm,** the bishops, peers, and commons, officially known as the lords spiritual, the lords temporal, and the commons. **fourth estate,** the newspaper press. **personal** and **real estate,** *see* these words. (O.Fr. *estat*.)

esteem, *n.* es-*teem*, estimation; high value or estimation; great regard: *v.i.* to consider as to value: *v.t.* to set a value on; to set a high value on; to regard with respect or friendship; to hold in opinion; to think highly of. (Fr. *estimer*.)

ester, *n.* *es*-ter, a chemical compound, originally known as an ethereal salt, analogous in structure to salts and occupying a similar place in organic chemistry to that which a salt does in inorganic chemistry. (Gr. *æther*, ether, *säure*, acid.)

esthesiometer, *n.* an æsthesiometer.

esthetic, *a.* es-*thet*-ik, æsthetic.

estimable, *a.* *es*-te-ma-bl, capable of being estimated or valued; worthy of esteem or respect; deserving good opinion. (Fr.)

estimableness, *n.* *es*-te-ma-bl-ness, the quality of deserving esteem.

estimably, *ad.* *es*-te-ma-ble, in an estimable manner.

estimate, *n.* *es*-te-mate, a valuing or rating in the mind; a judgment or opinion of the value, degree, extent or quantity of anything: *v.t.* to judge or form an estimate of; to rate by judgment; to appraise; to calculate. (L. *æstimatus*, valued.)

estimation, *n.* es-te-*may*-shon, the act of estimating; an opinion or judgment of anything formed without precise data; esteem; honour. (Fr.)

estimative, *a.* *es*-te-ma-tiv, having the power of comparing and adjusting the worth.

estimator, *n.* *es*-te-may-tor, one who estimates or values; contrivance for estimating.

estivage, *n.* *es*-te-vaj, a method of stowing much cargo into little space [Naut.]. (Fr., from L. *stipare*, to stuff full.)

estivation, *n.* es-te-*vay*-shon, æstivation.

estoile, *n.* *es*-twahl, a star, usually one having six waved points [Her.]. (Fr. *étoile*, a star.)

Estonian, *a.* es-*toh*-ne-an, pertaining to Estonia: *n.* a native, or the language, of Estonia.

estop, *v.t.* es-*top*, to impede or bar, esp. by one's own act [Law]. (O.Fr. *estoper*.)

estoppel, *n.* es-*top*-pl, an impediment, grounded on a man's own act, which estops or precludes him from averring anything to the contrary [Law].

estovers, *n.pl.* es-*toh*-verz, necessaries or supplies; a reasonable allowance out of lands or goods for the use of a tenant; alimony. (Fr.)

estrade, *n.* es-*trahd*, a level and slightly raised place in a room; a dais. (Fr.)

estrange, *v.t.* es-*traynj*, to keep at a distance; to withdraw; to withhold; to alienate. (O.Fr. *estranger*.)

estrangement, *n.* es-*traynj*-ment, the act of estranging; the state of being estranged; alienation.

estray, *n.* es-*tray*, a domestic animal found wandering or without an owner: *v.i.* to stray. (Fr. *estraié*.)

estreat, *n.* es-*treet*, a true copy of an original writing, esp. of fines entered in the rolls of a court: *v.i.* to copy from the records; to levy under estreat. (O.Fr. *estrait*.)

estridge, *n.* *es*-trij, the ostrich; the down of the ostrich [Comm.].

estuarine, *a.* *es*-tew-a-rine, pertaining to or formed in an estuary.

estuary, *n.* *es*-tew-a-re, the expanded mouth of a river extending inwards as far as the flow by the tide; a frith. (L. *æstuarium*, tidal.)

esurience, *n.* ee-*sewr*-re-ens, the state of being hungry; appetite.

esurient, *a.* e-*sewr*-re-ent, hungry; greedy; grasping. (L. *esuriens*, being hungry.)

etacism, *n.* *ay*-ta-sizm, the Erasmian method of pronouncing the Greek *eta* as the *a* in *bay*.
etcetera, *n.* et-*set*-ter-a, contracted into etc. and &c., the rest, or others of the kind; and so on; and so forth: *n.pl.* the trimmings; sundries as usual. (L., and the rest.)
etch, *v.t.* etch, to produce figures or designs on copper or other metallic plates by eating out or biting with an acid the lines previously drawn with a needle on a coated surface: *v.i.* to practise etching. (Dut. *etsen*, etch.)
etch, *n.* etch, ground from which a crop has been taken. (*eddish.*)
etcher, *n.* *etch*-er, one who makes etchings; an acid or other etching agent.
etching, *n.* *etch*-ing, the act of etching; an impression from an etched plate. **etching-ground,** *n.* the coating of the etching plate. **etching-needle,** *n.* a stylus or instrument of steel, with a fine point, used for tracing outlines on the etching-ground.
etern, *a.* e-*tern*, eternal; perpetual; endless.
eternal, *a.* e-*tern*-al, without beginning or end; everlasting; perpetual; ceaseless; unchangeable. **the Eternal,** the everlasting God. **the Eternal City,** Rome. (O.Fr. *eternel.*)
eternalist, *n.* e-*tern*-a-list, one who holds the past and future existence of the world to be infinite.
eternalize, *v.t.* e-*tern*-a-lize, to make eternal; to give endless duration to.
eternally, *ad.* e-*tern*-a-le, without beginning or end of duration; for ever; unchangeably.
eternity, *n.* e-*tern*-e-te, infinite duration; the forever of the past with the forever of the future; fixedness or unchangeableness of being; immortality; the state of being after death. (Fr. *éternité.*)
eternize, *v.t.* e-*tern*-ize, to make endless; to continue existence or duration indefinitely; to immortalize. (Fr. *éterniser.*)
etesian, *a.* e-*tee*-ze-an, periodic; at stated times. **etesian wind,** a north-westerly wind prevailing during the dog-days in the Levant. (L. *etesius*, etesian.)
ethane, *n.* *eth*-ayn, a colourless, odourless, gaseous hydrocarbon present in coal-gas, from which is derived acetic acid, ether, and alcohol.
ether, *n.* *ee*-ther, an hypothetical fluid pervading space and presumed to form the medium of transmission of light and heat; the upper regions of space, the clear sky; a very light, volatile, and inflammable fluid, produced by the distillation of alcohol with an acid and used as a general anæsthetic by inhalation [Chem.]. (Gr. *aither*, upper air.)
ethereal, *a.* e-*theer*-re-al, formed of upper ether, or filled with ether; celestial; of a spiritual or airy nature; pertaining to ether [Chem.]. **ethereal oil,** an essential oil containing ether and produced by distillation. (L. *ætherius.*)
etherealism, *n.* e-*theer*-re-a-lizm, the state or condition of being ethereal.
ethereality, *n.* e-*theer*-re-*al*-e-te, etherealism.
etherealize, *v.t.* e-*theer*-re-al-ize, to convert into ether, or into a very subtle fluid; to render ethereal.
ethereally, *ad.* e-*theer*-re-a-le, in an ethereal manner.
etheric, *a.* ee-*ther*-rik, ethereal.
etherification, *n.* e-*theer*-re-fe-*kay*-shon, the process of converting alcohol into ether. (Gr. *ether*, and L. *facio*, make.)
etheriform, *a.* *ee*-ther-re-form, having the appearance of ether.
etherism, *n.* *ee*-ther-rizm, the effects produced on the system by the administration of ether; etheromania.
etherist, *n.* *ee*-ther-rist, one who administers ether; a victim of etheromania.
etherization, *n.* *ee*-ther-ry-*zay*-shon, the process of converting into or subjecting to ether; the effect of its action.
etherize, *v.t.* *ee*-ther-rize, to convert into ether; to put under the influence of ether.
etheromania, *n.* *ee*-ther-ro-*may*-ne-a, a morbid addiction to the taking of ether as a drug or an intoxicant.
ethic, *n.* *eth*-ik, ethics; an ethical system; ethos.
ethical, *a.* *eth*-e-kal, relating to morals; treating of morality; moral.
ethically, *ad.* *eth*-e-kal-le, according to the doctrines of morality. (L. *ethicus*, moral.)
ethics, *n.* *eth*-iks, the science of morals, or of conduct as right or wrong; system of moral principles.
Ethiop, *n.* *ee*-the-ope, an Ethiopian.
Ethiopian, *a.* *ee*-the-*oh*-pe-an, belonging to Ethiopia, originally in the wide sense of the country of the black races: *n.* a native of Ethiopia; an Abyssinian.
Ethiopic, *a.* ee-the-*op*-ik, Ethiopian: *n.* the language of Ethiopia.
ethmoid, *a.* *eth*-moyd, resembling a sieve. **ethmoid bone,** the perforate bone between the two orbits of the eye, forming the root of the nose [Anat.]. (Gr. *ethmos*, a sieve, *eidos*, like.)
ethmoidal, *a.* eth-*moy*-dal, ethmoid.
ethnarch, *n.* *eth*-nark, the governor of a province. (Gr. *ethnarches*, ruler.)
ethnarchy, *n.* *eth*-nar-ke, the dominion, office, or rank of an ethnarch.
ethnic, *a.* *eth*-nik, ethnological; pertaining to race; pertaining to heathenism or to any religion other than Jewish and Christian. (Fr. *ethnique.*)
ethnical, *a.* *eth*-ne-kal, ethnic.
ethnographer, *n.* eth-*nog*-ra-fer, one versed in ethnography.
ethnographic, *a.* eth-no-*graf*-ik, ethnographical.
ethnographical, *a.* pertaining to ethnography.
ethnography, *n.* eth-*nog*-ra-fe, the scientific description of the different races of men. (Gr. *ethnos*, a nation, *grapho*, write.)
ethnological, *a.* eth-no-*loj*-e-kal, pertaining to ethnology.
ethnologist, *n.* eth-*nol*-o-jist, one versed in ethnology.
ethnology, *n.* eth-*nol*-o-je, the science which treats of the races of man, their varieties, peculiarities, and origins. (Gr. *ethnos*, and *logos*, science.)
ethological, *a.* eth-o-*loj*-e-kal, pertaining to ethology.
ethologist, *n.* e-*thol*-o-jist, one versed in ethology.
ethology, *n.* e-*thol*-o-je, the science which treats of character formation in individuals or races; behaviour study; bionomics [Zool.]. (Gr. *ethos*, manners, *logos*, science.)
ethos, *n.* *ee*-thoss, general disposition; characteristic spirit of a race, tribe, etc.
ethyl, *n.* *eth*-il, the hydrocarbon radical forming the base of ethane, ether, acetic acid, and the alcohols [Chem.]. (Gr. *ether*, and *hyle*, the material of anything.)
ethylene, *n.* *eth*-e-leen, *see* **olefiant gas.**
etiolate, *v.i.* *ee*-te-o-late, to become white or pale: *v.t.* to blanch by excluding the light or by disease [Bot. and Med.]. (Fr. *étioler*, to blanch.)
etiolation, *n.* *ee*-te-o-*lay*-shon, the act or operation of becoming etiolated.
etiology, *n.* *ee*-te-*ol*-o-je, ætiology.
etiquette, *n.* *et*-e-ket, the art of behaviour; conventional rules of ceremonial, procedure, etc., in a court or in society generally; a code of customary conduct, esp. for members of the professions. (Fr., a ticket.)
etna, *n.* *et*-na, a small spirit stove with a reversed cone for the boiler. (From *Etna*, a volcano in Sicily.)
Etnean, *a.* et-*nee*-an, pertaining to Mt. Etna.
Eton, *n.* *ee*-ton, town on the R. Thames, in Bucks, site of Eton College, type of the best class of English public school. **Eton collar,** a large starched white collar worn over the collar of the **Eton jacket,** a schoolboy's short black coat of special cut. **Eton crop,** a very close-cut and masculine style of women's hairdressing.
Etonian, *n.* ee-*toh*-ne-an, one educated at Eton College: *a.* pertaining to Eton or Etonians.
Etruscan, *a.* e-*trus*-kan, belonging to Etruria, an ancient district of Italy: *n.* a native of Etruria. **Etruscan vases,** vases mainly of Grecian design and workmanship found in Etruscan tombs. (L. *Etruscus.*)
etui, *n.* et-*wee*, a small case for light articles of personal use; a needle-case. (Fr. *étui*, a sheath.)
etymological, *a.* *et*-e-mo-*loj*-e-kal, pertaining to or in accord with etymology.
etymologically, *ad.* according to etymology.
etymologicon, *n.* *et*-e-mo-*loj*-e-kon, an etymological dictionary.
etymologist, *n.* et-e-*mol*-o-jist, one versed in etymology.
etymologize, *v.i.* et-e-*mol*-o-jize, to study etymology; to search into the origin of words; to deduce words from their roots.
etymology, *n.* et-e-*mol*-o-je, the science treating of the origin and history of words; the deduction of words from their originals; that part of grammar

which treats of the inflections, modifications, etc., of words. (Fr. *étymologie.*)

etymon, *n.* *et*-e-mon, the original root and primitive form of a word. (Gr. *etymos*, true.)

etypic, *a.* ee-*tip*-ik, not conforming to a type [Biol.].

eu-, yew, a Greek prefix signifying well, easy, true, etc.

eucaine, *n.* yew-*kane*, a synthetic alkaloid used as a local anæsthetic and similar in effect to cocaine.

eucalyptus, *n.* *yew*-ka-*lip*-tus, any Australian timber tree of the genus *Eucalyptus* of the myrtle order, some of which grow to great size and some of which (the gum trees) yield a resinous gum and an oil used in pharmacy, perfumery, etc. (Gr. *eu-*, and *kalypto*, cover.)

Eucharis, *n.* *yew*-ka-ris, the genus of South American plants comprising the Amazon lilies.

eucharist, *n.* *yew*-ka-rist, the sacrament of the Lord's Supper; the consecrated elements. (Gr., gratitude, thanksgiving, from *eu-*, and *charis*, grace, thanks.)

eucharistic, *a.* *yew*-ka-*ris*-tik, pertaining to the eucharist.

euchlorine, *n.* yew-*klaw*-rin, a highly explosive gas with bleaching properties, composed of chlorine and chlorine peroxide [Chem.].

euchology, *n.* yew-*kol*-o-je, a formulary of prayers; the liturgy of the Greek Church. (Gr. *euche*, prayer, *legos*, word.)

euchre, *n.* *yew*-ker, a game at cards, all below the sevens, eights, or nines being left out: *v.t.* to circumvent, to out-general [Slang]. (Fr.)

euclase, *n.* *yew*-klase, a monoclinic hydrated silicate of aluminium and beryllium, occurring in light green or colourless transparent crystals [Min.]. (Gr. *eu-*, easily, *klasis*, breaking.)

Euclid, *n.* *yew*-klid, the principles of Euclidean geometry.

Euclidean, *a.* yew-*klid*-e-an, pertaining to the mathematician Euclid of Alexandria (*c.* 350–300 B.C.), or his system of geometry.

eudemonics, *n.* yew-dee-*mon*-iks, the art or means of attaining happiness; the practice of eudemonism.

eudemonism, *n.* yew-*dee*-mo-nizm, the philosophy which maintains that the production of happiness or well-being is the aim and measure of virtue; the moral obligation to make happiness. (Gr. *eudaimon*, happy, from *eu-*, and *daimon*, presiding genius.)

eudiometer, *n.* *yew*-de-*om*-e-ter, an instrument originally for ascertaining the purity of the air, now for determining the composition of a gaseous mixture. (Gr. *eudios*, serene *metron*, measure.)

eudiometrical, *a.* *yew*-de-o-*met*-re-kal, pertaining to a eudiometer or to eudiometry.

eudiometry, *n.* *yew*-de-*om*-e-tre, the art or practice of ascertaining the composition of a gaseous mixture by the eudiometer.

eugenic, *a.* yew-*jen*-ik, pertaining or adapted to the production and development of healthy offspring.

eugenics, *n.* yew-*jen*-iks, the science of race-culture and human improvement and development. (Gr. *eugenēs*, well-born.)

eugenin, *n.* *yew*-je-nin, clove camphor, a substance obtained in laminal crystals from the water of cloves. (From *Eugenia caryophyllata*, the clove tree.)

eugenist, *n.* yew-*jen*-ist, a student of eugenics.

euhemerism, *n.* yew-*hee*-mer-rizm, the theory that myths are based on historic events, that the gods of antiquity are deified men and their feats exaggerated traditions of exploits of national heroes. (Gr., *Euhemeros*, a Greek who propounded the theory c. 316 B.C.)

euhemerist, *n.* yew-*hee*-mer-rist, a believer in euhemerism.

euhemeristic, *a.* yew-hee-mer-*ris*-tik, pertaining to euhemerism.

euhemerize, *v.t.* yew-*hee*-mer-rize, to assign historic origin to a myth.

eulalia, *n.* yew-*lay*-le-a, any ornamental grass belonging to the genus *Xiphagrostis.*

eulogist, *n.* *yew*-lo-jist, one who praises and commends another.

eulogistic, *a.* yew-lo-*jis*-tik, laudatory; full of praise.

eulogistically, *ad.* with commendation.

eulogium, *n.* yew-*loh*-je-um, a laudatory speech.

eulogize, *v.t.* *yew*-lo-jize, to praise; to speak or write in commendation of another; to extol.

eulogy, *n.* *yew*-lo-je, a speech or writing in commendation of a person; a panegyric. (Gr. *eulogia*, praise.)

Eumenides, *n.pl.* yew-*men*-e-deez, the euphuistic title of the Furies [Myth.]. (Gr. *eumenes*, well-disposed.)

eumerism, *n.* *yew*-mer-rizm, an aggregation of similar parts in an organism [Biol.].

eunomy, *n.* *yew*-no-me, a well-adjusted constitution of government. (Gr. *eu-*, and *nomos*, law.)

eunuch, *n.* *yew*-nuk, a castrated man; a harem attendant. (L. *eunuchus.*)

eunuchism, *n.* *yew*-nuk-izm, the state of being a eunuch.

eunuchize, *v.t.* *yew*-nuk-ize, to make a eunuch of.

eunuchoidism, *n.* *yew*-nu-koy-dizm, an abnormal absence of sexual characteristics in males.

euonymin, *n.* yew-*on*-e-min, an extract from the bark of the wahoo, *Euonymus atropurpureus.*

euonymous, *a.* yew-*on*-e-mus, suitably named. (Gr. *eu-*, and *onuma*, name.)

euonymus, *n.* yew-*on*-e-mus, any evergreen shrub of the genus *Euonymus*, including the spindle tree. (L. *euonymus.*)

eupatorium, *n.* yew-pa-*taw*-re-um, any of a genus of composite plants, including the hemp agrimony, *E. cannabinum.* (Gr., Mithridates the Great, surnamed *Eupator*, who used it medicinally.)

eupepsia, *n.* yew-*pep*-se-a, a healthy condition of the digestive organs. (Gr. *eu-*, and *pepto*, digest.)

eupeptic, *a.* yew-*pep*-tik, having good digestion.

euphemism, *n.* *yew*-fe-mizm, a mild or pleasant expression for one that is offensive, or the use of such [Rhet.]. (Gr. *euphēmismos.*)

euphemistic, *a.* yew-fe-*mis*-tik, containing or pertaining to euphemism.

euphemistically, *ad.* yew-fe-*mis*-te-ka-le, in euphemistic manner.

euphemize, *v.t.* *yew*-fe-mize, to speak of euphemistically; to express in euphemism.

euphonic, *a.* yew-*fon*-ik, euphonious.

euphonious, *a.* yew-*foh*-ne-us, agreeable in sound; pleasing to the ear.

euphoniously, *ad.* with euphony.

euphonism, *n.* *yew*-fon-izm, an agreeable combination of sounds.

euphonium, *n.* yew-*foh*-ne-um, the bass saxhorn.

euphonize, *v.t.* *yew*-fo-nize, to make agreeable in sound.

euphony, *n.* *yew*-fo-ne, an agreeable sound; an easy smooth enunciation of sounds. (Gr. *euphōnos*, pleasant-voiced.)

euphorbia, *n.* yew-*fore*-be-a, any plant of a large genus *Euphorbia*, including the spurges. (Gr., good nourishment, from *eu-*, and *pherbo*, feed.)

euphorbium, *n.* yew-*fore*-be-um, an acrid, poisonous, inspissated sap exuding from *Euphorbia resinifera.*

euphrasy, *n.* *yew*-fra-se, the eyebright. (Gr., delight.)

euphroe, *n.* *yew*-froh, uphroe.

euphuism, *n.* *yew*-few-izm, an affected, refined, bombastic, or high-flown diction. (*Euphues*, title of work by Lyly (1578–80), written in this style, from Gr. *eu-*, and *phuein*, to produce.)

euphuist, *n.* *yew*-few-ist, one who affects excessive refinement and elegance of language.

euphuistic, *a.* yew-few-*is*-tik, assuming excessive refinement of speech.

euphuize, *v.t.* *yew*-few-ize, to express in euphuism.

eupnœa, *n.* yewp-*nee*-a, normal respiration (opposed to dyspnœa) [Med.]. (Gr. *eu-*, and *pnoiē*, breath.)

Eurafrican, *n.* yewr-*af*-re-kan, one born of a European on the one side and an African on the other: *a.* pertaining to, characteristic of, or produced by both continents. (From *Europe* and *Africa.*)

Eurasian, *n.* yewr-*ay*-ze-an, one born of a European on the one side and an Asiatic on the other; in India the offspring of a male European and a native woman: *a.* pertaining to, characteristic of, or produced by both continents. (From *Europe* and *Asia.*)

eureka, *n.* yew-*ree*-kah, a discovery achieved; exultation over it. (Gr., "I have found it," the exclamation of Archimedes, on discovering how to test the purity of the gold in Hiero's crown.)

eurhythmics, *n.pl.* yew-*rith*-miks, the study or art of rhythmical movement; physical exercises consisting of rhythmic movements.

eurhythmist, *n.* yew-*rith*-mist, a teacher or exponent of eurhythmics.

eurhythmy, *n.* yew-*rith*-me, rhythmic movement, as in dancing; symmetry, harmonious proportion, (etc., in the arts; regularity of pulsation [Med.]. Gr. *eurythmia*, harmony.)

Euro-American, *a.* *yewr*-ro-a-*me*-re-kan, characteristic of or pertaining to both Europe and America.
Euroclydon, *n.* yew-*rok*-le-don, a tempestuous wind in the Mediterranean ; a levanter. (Gr. *euros*, the east wind, *klydon*, a wave.)
European, *a.* yewr-ro-*pee*-an, pertaining to Europe ; native to Europe : *n.* a native of Europe.
Europeanize, *v.t.* yewr-ro-*pee*-a-nize, to make European ; to naturalize in Europe.
europium, *n.* yew-*roh*-pe-um, a metallic element of the rare-earth group, obtained from monazite and samarskite, discovered in 1896 by Dumarcay.
Eurus, *n.* *yew*-rus, the east wind. (Gr. *euros*.)
Eusebian, *a.* yew-*see*-be-an, pertaining to Eusebius, bishop of Cæsarea, father of ecclesiastical history, or to Eusebius, bishop of Nicomedia, or to the Arian heresy favoured by him (both 4th cent.).
Euskarian, *n.* yew-*skare*-re-an, a Basque ; the language of the Basques : *a.* Basque ; denoting also any pre-Aryan racial group in Europe. (Basque.)
eusol, *n.* *yew*-sol, a strong antiseptic used chiefly for wounds. (*E*dinburgh *U*niversity *sol*ution.)
Eustachian, *n.* yew-*stay*-ke-an, pertaining to or named after Eustachius, a 16th-cent. Italian anatomist. **Eustachian tube,** a small duct running from cavity of the ear into the back part of the mouth. **Eustachian valve,** a membranous valve of the heart where the vena cava enters the right auricle.
eutectic, *a.* yew-*tek*-tik, melting readily or at a low temperature : *n.* a eutectic substance. (Gk. *eutektos*.)
eutectoid, *a.* yew-*tek*-toyd, like a eutectic.
Euterpean, *a.* yew-*ter*-pe-an, pertaining to Euterpe, the muse who presided over lyric song. (Gk. *Euterpe*.)
eutexia, *n.* yew-*tek*-se-a, the quality of melting readily at a low temperature.
euthanasia, *n.* yew-tha-*nay*-ze-a, painless death ; the act or practice of voluntary and intentional abandonment of life by incurables. (Gr. *eu-*, and *thanatos*, death.)
Eutychian, *n.* yew-*tik*-e-an, one of a 5th-cent. Christian sect which held that the divine and human natures of Christ, after their union, became so blended as to form but one nature. (*Eutychius*, the founder.)
evacuant, *a.* e-*vak*-yew-ant, emptying ; freeing from ; purgative : *n.* a purgative medicine.
evacuate, *v.t.* e-*vak*-yew-ate, to make empty ; to void ; to discharge ; to withdraw from : *v.i.* to withdraw. (L. *evacuatus*, emptied.)
evacuation, *n.* e-*vak*-yew-*ay*-shon, the act of evacuating ; withdrawing from ; discharges by stool or otherwise.
evacuative, *a.* and *n.* e-*vak*-yew-a-tiv, evacuant.
evacuee, *n.* e-vak-yew-*ee*, one withdrawn from his home or district by civil or military order.
evadable, *a.* e-*vade*-a-bl, that may be evaded.
evade, *v.t.* e-*vade*, to avoid or elude by dexterity, artifice, sophistry, or ingenuity ; to escape, so as not to be seized : *v.i.* to escape ; to attempt to escape ; to prevaricate. (L. *evado*, go.)
evagation, *n.* *ee*-va-*gay*-shon, the action of roving ; departure from a prescribed course. (L. *e-*, and *vagare*, to wander.)
evaginate, *v.t.* e-*vaj*-e-nate, to turn inside out : *a.* not having a sheath [Bot. and Zool.]. (Late L. *evaginatus*, unsheathed.)
evagination, *n.* e-vaj-e-*nay*-shon, turning inside out.
evaluate, *v.t.* e-*val*-yew-ate, to determine the exact value of. (L. *e-*, and *value*.)
evaluation, *n.* e-*val*-yew-*ay*-shon, the act, process, or result of evaluating.
evanesce, *v.i.* ev-a-*ness*, to disappear ; to dissipate in or as in. (L. *evanesco*.)
evanescence, *n.* ev-a-*nes*-sence, a vanishing from sight or possession ; the state of being evanescent.
evanescent, *a.* ev-a-*nes*-sent, liable to vanish ; fleeting ; liable to dissipation ; infinitesimal. (L. *evanescens*, vanishing away.)
evanescently, *ad.* in an evanescent manner.
evangel, *n.* e-*van*-jel, the message of the Christian dispensation ; any of the Four Gospels ; an announcement of good news. (Fr. *évangile*.)
evangelic, *a.* ee-van-*jel*-ik, evangelical.
evangelical, *a.* ee-van-*jel*-e-kal, pertaining to the gospel ; contained in the gospels ; according to the doctrine and spirit of the gospel ; Low Church ; Protestant : *n.* one who professes or maintains evangelical principles, esp. the doctrine that salvation is by faith in the atonement of Christ.
evangelicalism, *n.* ee-van-*jel*-e-ka-lizm, adherence to evangelical doctrines or those of the evangelicals.
evangelically, *ad.* ee-van-*jel*-e-ka-le, in a manner agreeable to the gospel or to evangelicals. (Late L. *evangelicus*.)
evangelism, *n.* e-*van*-jel-izm, the promulgation of the gospel ; evangelicalism. (Late L. *evangelismus*.)
evangelist, *n.* e-*van*-jel-ist, a writer of one of the gospels ; an evangelizing preacher of the gospel ; one authorized to preach. (O.Fr. *evangeliste*.)
evangelistary, *n.* e-van-jel-*is*-ta-re, a selection of passages from the gospels as lessons in divine service.
evangelistic, *a.* e-van-jel-*is*-tik, evangelizing ; evangelical.
evangelization, *n.* e-*van*-je-ly-*zay*-shon, the act of evangelizing.
evangelize, *v.t.* e-*van*-je-lize, to preach or teach the gospel to ; to convert to or instruct in the gospel : *v.i.* to go about preaching or teaching the gospel.
evanish, *v.i.* e-*van*-ish, to vanish ; to disappear [Poetry].
evanishment, *n.* e-*van*-ish-ment, a vanishing ; disappearance.
evaporable, *a.* e-*vap*-o-ra-bl, that may be converted into vapour ; that may be dissipated by evaporation.
evaporate, *v.i.* e-*vap*-o-rate, to pass off in vapour or be dissipated ; to disappear [Coll.] : *v.t.* to convert into or to dissipate in vapour ; to vaporize. (Late L. *evaporatus*, vanished in vapour.)
evaporation, *n.* e-*vap*-o-*ray*-shon, the act of evaporating ; the state of being evaporated ; that which is evaporated : discharge ; the draining of the vaporable portion of a substance in a liquid form in order to obtain it in a dry or concentrated state.
evaporative, *a.* e-*vap*-o-ra-tiv, pertaining to or producing evaporation.
evaporator, *n.* e-*vap*-o-ray-tor, an apparatus for eliminating moisture, preparing milk-powder, or condensing juice in sugar-manufacture, fruit-drying, etc. ; one in charge of an evaporator.
evaporometer, *n.* e-*vap*-o-*rom*-e-ter, an atmometer.
evasion, *n.* e-*vay*-zhon, the act of evading or eluding ; subterfuge, shuffling, or prevarication. (L. *evasus*.)
evasive, *a.* e-*vay*-ziv, using evasion ; shuffling ; characterized by evasion.
evasively, *ad.* e-*vay*-ziv-le, by evasion.
evasiveness, *n.* quality or state of being evasive.
eve, *n.* eev, the latter part or close of the day ; the evening before a holiday ; the day before a saint's day ; the period immediately preceding some important event. (A.S. *æfen*.)
evection, *n.* e-*vek*-shon, a change of form in the lunar orbit, by which its eccentricity is either increased or diminished [Astron.]. (Late L. *evectio*.)
even, *n.* *ee*-ven, evening.
★even, *a.* *ee*-ven, level ; smooth ; equal ; uniform ; parallel to ; equally favourable ; mutually at quits ; balanced ; in equilibrium ; capable of being divided into two equal parts without a remainder ; opposed to odd : *ad.* not only ; exactly ; actually ; moreover ; so much as : *v.t.* to make level ; to lay smooth ; to balance accounts. **even keel,** said of a vessel when drawing the same water abaft as aft, and listing neither to port nor starboard. **make even,** to space out matter so as to make the successive portions set up read straight on [Print.]. (A.S. *efen*.)
evener, *n.* *ee*-ven-er, one who, or that which, makes even.
even-handed, *a.* impartial ; equitable.
even-handedly, *ad.* in an even-handed manner.
even-handedness, *n.* the quality or state of being even-handed.
evening, *n.* *ee*-ven-ing, the close or decline of the day ; the decline of life ; the latter part of any period : *a.* being at the close of the day. **evening primrose,** a species of *Œnothera*, particularly *Œnothera biennis*. **evening star,** any planet seen in the west soon after-sunset. (A.S. *æfnung*.)
evenly, *ad.* *ee*-ven-le, in an even manner.
even-minded, *a.* having equanimity.
evenness, *n.* *ee*-ven-ness, the state of being even.
evens, *ad.* *ee*-venz, on even terms : quits [Coll.].
evensong, *n.* *ee*-ven-song, a form of worship for the evening ; the evening. (A.S. *æfensang*.)
★event, *n.* e-*vent*, anything that happens or falls out,

good or bad; the consequence of anything; anything of importance; the issue. (L. *eventus*, happened.)
even-tempered, *a.* having an equable mind or placid temper.
eventful, *a.* e-*vent*-ful, full of incidents; fraught with important issues.
eventide, *n. ee*-ven-tide, evening.
eventration, *n.* ee-ven-*tray*-shon, disembowelment; protrusion of the intestines from the abdomen [Med.].
eventual, *a.* e-*vent*-yew-al, happening as a consequence or result; ultimate; contingent; final. (Fr. *éventuel.*)
eventuality, *n.* e-*vent*-yew-*al*-e-te, possible event; a contingency.
eventualize, *v.i.* ee-*vent*-yew-a-lize, to occur as a result or contingently.
eventually, *ad.* in the event; in the final issue.
eventuate, *v.i.* e-*vent*-yew-ate, to turn out; to happen. (L. *eventus.*)
★**ever,** *ad. ev*-er, at any time; always; in any degree; without intermission. **ever and anon,** at one time and another; now and then. **ever so,** very; in a great degree. (A.S. *eofor.*)
everglade, *n. ev*-er-glade, a marshy tract of land, with patches of high grass here and there.
evergreen, *n. ev*-er-green, a plant that retains its verdure throughout the year: *a.* always green, fresh, and vigorous.
everlasting, *a. ev*-er-*lahs*-ting, eternal; lasting for ever; having lasted all through the past; perpetual; constantly recurring; endless: *n.* eternity; eternal duration, past and future; any plant the flower of which retains its colour when dried.
everlastingly, *ad.* eternally; perpetually.
everlastingness, *n.* the state of being everlasting; eternity.
evermore, *ad. ev*-er-*more*, always; for ever.
eversible, *a.* e-*ver*-se-bl, capable of turning outwards.
eversion, *n.* e-*ver*-shon, turning inside out; a turning outwards. (L. *eversio.*)
evert, *v.t.* e-*vert*, to turn inside out; to turn outwards. (L. *everto*, turn.)
everted, *a.* e-*ver*-ted, turned abruptly outward [Bot.].
★**every,** *a. ev*-er-re, each one of a number; all. (A.S. *æfre.*)
everybody, *n. ev*-er-re-bod-e, every person.
everyday, *a. ev*-er-re-day, met with or happening every day; common; routine.
Everyman, *n. ev*-er-re-man, mankind at large; the ordinary or "average" man.
everyone, *n. ev*-er-re-wun, everybody.
everything, *n. ev*-er-re-thing, the whole lot; all.
everyway, *ad. ev*-er-re-way, in all ways; in every respect.
everywhere, *ad. ev*-er-re-whare, in every place.
evict, *v.t.* e-*vikt*, to dispossess or remove from by authority of law. (L. *evictus*, overcome.)
eviction, *n.* e-*vik*-shon, dispossession from lands, etc., as declared by law to be the property of another.
evidence, *n. ev*-e-dence, testimony; that which makes evident; proof on the authority of sense or reason, or the witness of others; a witness: *v.t.* to make evident or clear; to attest; to adduce. **King's evidence,** evidence of a prisoner against his accomplices. (O.Fr.)
evident, *a. ev*-e-dent, clear and certain, as if seen; obvious: *n.* a proof [Scots. Law]. (O.Fr.)
evidential, *a.* ev-e-*den*-shal, affording evidence; clearly proving. (L. *evidentia.*)
evidentially, *ad.* in an evidential manner.
evidentiary, *a.* ev-e-*den*-sha-re, suitable as evidence; pertaining to or of the nature of evidence.
evidently, *ad. ev*-e-dent-le, clearly; obviously.
evidentness, *n.* state of being evident.
evil, *a. ee*-vil, having physical or moral qualities that are bad in themselves and are productive of mischief; fraught with evil; wicked; perverse; depraved: *n.* moral depravity; that which is both bad in itself and mischievous in its consequences; a malady: *ad.* in an evil manner; ill; injurious. **evil eye,** a supposed power of fascinating, bewitching, or otherwise injuring by the look. **King's evil,** scrofula. **the Evil One,** the devil. (A.S. *yfel.*)
evildoer, *n. ee*-vil-*doo*-er, one who does evil; one who commits sin, crime, or any moral wrong.
evilly, *ad. ee*-vil-e, wickedly; maliciously.
evil-minded, *a.* malicious or disposed to mischief.
evil-speaking, *n.* slander; defamation.
evil-starred, *a.* unfortunate.
evince, *v.t.* e-*vince*, to manifest; to make evident; to prove beyond doubt. (L. *evinco*, conquer.)
evincible, *a.* e-*vince*-e-bl, demonstrable.
evincive, *a.* e-*vince*-iv, tending to demonstrate.
eviration, *n.* ev-e-*ray*-shon, emasculation; condition of non-virility or effeminancy.
eviscerate, *v.t.* e-*vis*-ser-rate, to disembowel. (L.)
evisceration, *n.* e-*vis*-er-*ray*-shon, disembowelment; operative removal of internal contents [Surg.].
evitable, *a. ev*-it-a-bl, avoidable; that may be shunned. (L. *evitabilis.*)
evitate, *v.t. ev*-e-tate, to avoid; to shun.
evocation, *n.* ev-o-*kay*-shon, a calling forth; a summoning of a cause from an inferior by a superior court [Law]. (L. *evocatus*, called forth.)
evocatory, *a.* e-*vok*-a-to-re, able to evoke; pertaining to evocation.
evoke, *v.t.* e-*voke*, to call forth; to summon from one tribunal to another [Law]. (Fr. *évoquer.*)
evolute, *n. ev*-o-lewt, a curve from which another curve is described; the origin of the evolvent or involute [Geom.]: *a.* with the margins turned outward [Biol.]: *v.t.* to develop by or as by evolution [Coll.]. (L. *evolutus*, unrolled.)
evolution, *n.* ev-o-*lew*-shon, the act or process of unfolding or developing; a series of things unfolded or developed; the development of the forms of life from lower to higher organisms; the theory that all forms of life are derived earlier and simpler forms or from a single rudimentary form [Biol.]; the unfolding or opening of a curve, and making it describe an evolvent or involute [Geom.]; the extraction of roots, the reverse of involution [Alg. and Arith.]; the series of movements by which the disposition of troops, ships, or aircraft is changed [Mil.]; changes of position, as in dancing, skating, etc.
evolutional, *a.* ev-o-*lew*-shon-al, evolutionary.
evolutionary, *a.* ev-o-*lew*-shon-a-re, pertaining to evolution.
evolutionism, *n.* ev-o-*lew*-shon-izm, the theory or doctrine of evolution.
evolutionist, *n.* ev-o-*lew*-shon-ist, one who accepts the principle of evolution [Biol.]; one skilled in evolutions [Mil.].
evolutive, *a. ev*-o-*lew*-tiv, pertaining to or promoting evolution; evolutionary.
evolve, *v.t.* e-*volv*, to unfold; to open and expand; to throw out; to emit; to develop: *v.i.* to open or disclose itself. (L. *evolvo*, unroll or disclose.)
evolvement, *n.* e-*volv*-ment, the act of evolving; the state of being evolved.
evolvent, *n.* e-*vol*-vent, the involute; the curve resulting from the evolution of another curve, called the evolute [Geom.]. (L. *evolvens.*)
evulgation, *n. ee*-vul-*gay*-shon, the action of making public; divulgation.
evulsion, *n.* e-*vul*-shon, the act of plucking or pulling out by force; a rooting out. (L. *evulsio.*)
Evzone, *n.* evd-*zoh*-ne, a select corps of mountaineers in the Greek army; a member of this. (Gr.)
ewe, *n.* yew, a female sheep. **ewe lamb,** a poor man's only possession; an only child. **ewe necked,** having a thin arched neck (esp. of horses). (A.S. *eowu.*)
ewer, *n. yew*-er, a pitcher with a broad lip; a kind of jug with a handle, used for water on a washstand. (O.Fr. *ewere.*)
ewigkeit, *n. ay*-vig-kite, eternity. **into the ewigkeit** into the unknown. (Ger.)
ex-, eks, a Latin prefix, signifying out, out of, without, proceeding from, and beyond. Prefixed to names of office, it denotes that a person has ceased to hold it, as Ex-chancellor, Ex-president.
exacerbate, *v.t.* eks-*as*-ser-bate, to irritate; to exasperate; to embitter; to increase the virulence of, as a disease. (L. *exacerbatus*, irritated.)
exacerbation, *n.* eks-as-ser-*bay*-shon, the act of exacerbating; aggravation; increase of malignity; a periodical increase of virulence in the course of a disease [Med.]; increased severity.
exacerbescent, *a.* eks-as-er-*bes*-ent, liable to become exacerbated; irritable.
exact, *a.* egs-*akt*, accurate; precise; correct; observing strict method, rule, or order; punctual; strict. (L. *exactus*, determined.)
exact, *v.t.* egs-*akt*, to force from; to demand or

extort by means of authority; to demand of right; to enforce: *v.i.* to practise extortion. (O.Fr. *exacter*, to compel.)
exactable, *a.* egs-*akt*-a-bl, that may be exacted.
exacter, *n.* egs-*akt*-er, an exactor.
exacting, *a.* egs-*akt*-ing, severe or excessive in demanding.
exaction, *n.* egs-*ak*-shon, the act of exacting; an oppressive authoritative demand; extortion; that which is exacted; compulsory or excessive service. (Fr.)
exactitude, *n.* egs-*akt*-e-tewd, precision; exactness.
exactly, *ad.* egs-*akt*-le, in an exact manner; just so.
exactness, *n.* egs-*akt*-ness, the quality of being exact.
exactor, *n.* egs-*akt*-or, one who exacts or is unreasonably severe in his demands; an extortioner; a tax-collector. (O.Fr.)
exaggerate, *v.t.* egs-*aj*-jer-rate, to overstate; to represent as greater than truth will warrant; to be extravagant in delineating [Paint. and Sculp.]. (L. *exaggeratus.*)
exaggeratedly, *ad.* in an exaggerated way.
exaggeration, *n.* egs-*aj*-jer-*ray*-shon, overstatement; a representation of things beyond the truth; a representation of a thing with over-emphasized features [Paint. and Sculp.].
exaggerative, *a.* egs-*aj*-jer-ra-tiv, having a tendency to exaggerate.
exaggerator, *n.* egs-*aj*-jer-ray-tor, one who exaggerates.
exaggeratory, *a.* egs-*aj*-jer-ra-to-re, containing exaggeration.
exagitate, *v.t.* egs-*aj*-e-tate, to agitate; to reproach. (L. *exagitatus*, stirred up.)
exalbuminous, *a.* egs-al-*bew*-min-us, having no albumen (of seeds) [Bot.]. (L. *ex-*, and *albumen.*)
exalt, *v.t.* egs-*awlt*, to raise high; to elevate; to elevate in power, wealth, rank, or dignity; to elate; to raise above others; to extol; to elevate in diction or sentiment; to intensify. (Fr. *exalter.*)
exaltation, *n.* egs-awl-*tay*-shon, the act of exalting; elevation to power, office, rank, dignity, or excellence; extreme emotion; state of greatness or dignity; intensification [Med. and Chem.]; the influence acquired by a planet when in certain parts of the zodiac [Astrol.].
exaltedness, *n.* the state of being exalted.
exam, *n.* egs-*am*, an examination [Coll. abbrev.].
examen, *n.* egs-*ay*-men, investigation; a formal examination. (L., the tongue of a balance.)
examinability, *n.* egs-*am*-e-na-*bil*-e-te, the quality of being examinable.
examinable, *a.* egs-*am*-in-a-bl, that may be examined; proper for judicial examination or inquiry.
examinant, *n.* egs-*am*-in-ant, one who examines.
examinate, *n.* egs-*am*-in-ate, the person examined.
examination, *n.* egs-*am*-in-*nay*-shon, the act of examining; careful and accurate inspection; investigation or inquiry; test of qualification; a careful inquiry into facts by taking evidence [Law]. **examination in chief,** the examination of a witness by the party calling him [Law].
examinational, *a.* egs-*am*-in-*nay*-shon-al, pertaining to or based on examinations.
examinator, *n.* egs-*am*-in-nay-tor, an examiner.
examinatorial, *a.* egs-*am*-in-nay-*taw*-re-al, pertaining to examiners or examinations.
examine, *v.t.* egs-*am*-in, to inspect carefully, with a view to discover truth or the real state of a thing; to inquire into, as the facts of a case, by interrogating; to view in all aspects, with a view to a judgment; to test qualifications by propounding questions and problems; to try by a test; to try by rule or law. (Fr. *examiner*, from L.)
examinee, *n.* egs-am-in-*ee*, one who is examined.
examiner, *n.* egs-*am*-in-er, one who examines, tries, or inspects; one who interrogates a witness or an offender; an officer of the High Court of Justice (formerly of the Chancery Court) who examines, on oath, the witnesses for the parties.
★**example,** *n.* egs-*ahm*-pl, a sample; a pattern, copy, or model; a precedent, to be copied or avoided; an instance serving for illustration of a rule or precept; an induction of what may happen again from what has happened once before; a caution (O.Fr.)
exanimate, *a.* egs-*an*-im-ate, lifeless; spiritless; disheartened; depressed. (L. *exanimatus*, devoid of life.)
exanthema, *n.* eks-an-*thee*-ma (*pl.* **exanthemata**), any febrile disease such as measles, attended with a distinctive eruption; such eruption. [Med.]. (Gr.)
exanthematic, *a.* *eks*-an-the-*mat*-ik, exanthematous.
exanthematology, *n.* *eks*-an-the-ma-*tol*-o-je, the study of, or a treatise on, eruptive fevers. (Gr. *exanthema*, and *logos*, a word.)
exanthematous, *a.* *eks*-an-*thee*-ma-tus, belonging to exanthema; eruptive; efflorescent.
exarch, *n.* *eks*-ark, a provincial viceroy of the Byzantine emperors; the title of certain superior bishops of the Greek Church; a legate appointed by the eastern patriarchs. (*ex-*, and Gr. *archos*, ruler.)
exarchate, *n.* eks-*ark*-ate, the office, dignity, or administration of an exarch.
exarticulate, *a.* eks-ar-*tik*-yew-late, not jointed [Entom.].
exasperate, *v.t.* egs-*ahs*-per-rate, to rouse to anger; to irritate to a high degree; to aggravate; to embitter; to exacerbate. (L. *exasperatus*, annoyed.)
exasperation, *n.* egs-*ahs*-per-*ray*-shon, the act of exasperating or irritating; the state of being exasperated; provocation; rage; aggravation.
exasperative, *a.* egs-*ahs*-per-ra-tiv, irritative.
Excalibur, *n.* eks-*kal*-e-bur, the magic sword of King Arthur, which only he could wield.
excandescence, *n.* eks-kan-*des*-ence, the state of being white with heat; extreme heat of passion. (L. *excandescens*, kindling.)
excarnate, *a.* eks-*kar*-nate, deprived of flesh; not possessing corporeal existence.
excavate, *v.t.* *eks*-ka-vate, to hollow out; to cut, scoop, dig, or wear out the inner part of anything and make it hollow. (L. *excavatus*, hollowed out.)
excavation, *n.* eks-ka-*vay*-shon, the act or process of excavating; a hollow or a cavity formed by excavating; a cutting.
excavator, *n.* *eks*-ka-vay-tor, one who excavates; a machine for excavating; a steam navvy; a bulldozer; a dredger.
exceed, *v.t.* ek-*seed*, to pass or go beyond; to surpass; to excel: *v.i.* to go too far; to go beyond any given limit, number, or measure; to be more or larger; to drink intemperately. (Fr. *excéder.*)
exceeder, *n.* ek-*seed*-er, one who exceeds.
exceeding, *a.* ek-*seed*-ing, great in extent, quantity, or duration: *ad.* in a very great degree; unusually.
exceedingly, *ad.* to a very great degree; surpassingly.
excel, *v.t.* ek-*sel*, to exceed; to surpass: *v.i.* to have good qualities or to perform meritorious actions in an unusual degree; to be surpassingly eminent. (Fr. *exceller.*)
excellence, *n.* *ek*-se-lence, superiority; greatness; any meritorious or valuable quality; dignity; high rank in the scale of beings. (Fr.)
Excellency, *n.* *ek*-se-len-se, a title of honour formerly given to kings, now to ambassadors, governors, and certain other high officials.
excellent, *a.* *ek*-se-lent, excelling; of great virtue or worth; eminent for what is amiable, valuable, or laudable; of great value or use; remarkable for good properties; distinguished for superior attainments; consummate.
excellently, *ad.* in an excellent manner; well in a high degree.
excelsior, *a.* ek-*sel*-se-or, still higher. **Excelsior State,** New York (this beiug its motto). (L.)
except, *v.t.* ek-*sept*, to take or leave out; to exclude: *v.i.* to make objections: *prep.* exclusive of: *conj.* unless; omitting. (Fr. *excepter.*)
excepting, *prep.* and *conj.* ek-*sep*-ting, except; excluding.
exception, *n.* ek-*sep*-shon, the act of excluding from a specified number; exclusion; that which a rule does not include; objection; objection with dislike; offence; the denial of what is alleged and considered as valid by the other party, either in point of law or in pleading [Law]. **bill of exceptions,** a statement of exceptions or objections to the decision or instructions of a judge formerly (and in Scotland still) submissible to a higher court [Law]. (L. *exceptionis*, of restriction.)
exceptionable, *a.* ek-*sep*-shon-a-bl, liable to objection; objectionable.
exceptionableness, *n.* the quality of being exceptionable.
exceptional, *a.* ek-*sep*-shon-al, forming an exception; unusual; peculiar.

exceptionally, *ad.* in an exceptional way; by way of exception; unusually.
exceptionary, *a.* ek-*sep*-shon-a-re, indicating an exception.
exceptious, *a.* ek-*sep*-shus, peevish; disposed or apt to cavil.
exceptive, *a.* ek-*sep*-tiv, including an exception; forming an exception.
excerpt, *n.* *ek*-serpt, a passage extracted from a work; a separate reprint of an article: *v.t.* ek-*serpt*, to extract, or make an extract from; to select. (L. *excerptus*, picked out.)
excerptible, *a.* ek-*serp*-te-bl, that may be excepted; that from which excerpts may be made.
excerption, *n.* ek-*serp*-shon, selection; that which is selected.
excess, *n.* ek-*sess*, that which is beyond what is needed; superfluity; that which is beyond the common measure, proportion, or due quantity; superabundance; any transgression of due limits; undue indulgence; intemperance; that by which one number or quantity exceeds another [Arith. and Geom.]: *v.t.* to cause to pay an excess fare or for excess luggage. **excess fare,** the amount by which the fare of a journey taken exceeds the amount of the fare actually paid. **excess luggage,** luggage in excess of the weight allowed to a passenger by his ticket. **excess profits,** business profits exceeding the average annual profit over a stated period or number of years. (Fr. *excès*.)
excessive, *a.* ek-*ses*-siv, beyond any given limit, or the common measure, or proportion; beyond the bounds of justice, fitness, propriety, expedience, or utility; unreasonable; vehement. (Late L. *excessivus*.)
excessively, *ad.* in an extreme degree.
excessiveness, *n.* the state or quality of being excessive.
*__exchange,__ *n.* eks-*chaynj*, the act of giving or receiving something in return for its equivalent, or of giving and receiving reciprocally; the act of giving up or resigning one thing or state for another without contract; the contract of exchange; the thing given or received in exchange; the form of exchanging one debt or credit for another, or settling by order, draft, or bill of exchange; the system by which international accounts are kept and debts settled without the transfer of actual money; the place where the home and foreign financial business of a commercial centre is carried on; a Stock Exchange; a Labour Exchange [Coll.]: *v.t.* to barter or give one thing or commodity for another [Comm.]; to lay aside, quit, or resign one thing, state, or condition for another; to give and receive reciprocally; to interchange; to deal in money: *v.i.* to pass by exchange. **arbitration of exchange,** the calculation of the profits of exchanges at different places. **bill of exchange,** *see* **bill.** **par of exchange,** the fixed intrinsic value of the monetary unit of one country expressed in the terms of the currency of another that uses the same metal as a standard **rate of exchange,** that variable amount in the currency of one country which, at any given date, is offered for a fixed sum in the currency of another. (Fr. *échanger*.)
exchangeability, *n.* eks-*chaynj*-a-*bil*-e-te, the quality or state of being exchangeable.
exchangeable, *a.* eks-*chaynj*-a-bl, that may be exchanged; estimable by what could be got in exchange.
exchequer, *n.* eks-*chek*-er, a court of record, originally intended principally to collect and superintend the royal revenues, consisting afterwards of two divisions, the one with jurisdiction in revenue matters, and the other a court of common law for the administration of justice; the Treasury; a treasury; financial resources. **Chancellor of the Exchequer,** the Finance Minister of Great Britain. **exchequer bills,** bills for money or promissory bills, issued by the Exchequer as a floating debt. (O.Fr. *eschequier*, a chess-board; hence, the chequered cloth on which, by means of counters, accounts were reckoned in mediæval times.)
excipient, *n.* ek-*sip*-e-ent, an inert substance used as a vehicle in administering a medicine, as bread-crumb, jelly, etc. (L. *excipiens*, drawing out.)
excisable, *a.* ek-*size*-a-bl, liable or subject to excise.
excise, *n.* ek-*size*, a tax on articles produced and consumed in a country, and also on licences to deal in certain commodities, enjoy certain privileges, etc.; the Civil Service department dealing with this. (O.Fr. *acceis*, a tax.)
excise, *v.t.* ek-*size*, to cut out; to cut off and remove. (L. *excisus*, cut out.)
exciseman, *n.* ek-*size*-man, a collector of excise dues.
excision, *n.* ek-*sizh*-on, a cutting out or off of any part of the body; the cutting off of a person, etc., as a judgment; extirpation; excommunication. (Fr.)
excitability, *n.* ek-*site*-a-*bil*-e-te, the quality of being excitable.
excitable, *a.* ek-*site*-a-bl, susceptible to excitement, agitation, or irritation.
excitant, *n.* *ek*-se-tant *or* ek-*site*-ant, that which produces or may produce increased action in a living body or organ; a stimulant: *a.* tending to excite or stimulate. (L. *excitans*, waking up.)
excitation, *n.* ek-se-*tay*-shon, the act of exciting; the energizing of an electrical circuit [Elect.]; the magnetic force producing a given magnetic field [Elect.]. (L. *excitatio*, inciting.)
excitative, *a.* ek-*site*-a-tiv, having power to excite.
excitatory, *a.* ek-*site*-a-to-re, tending to excite.
excite, *v.t.* ek-*site*, to rouse; to stir up to action that which is dormant, stupid, or inactive; to give new or increased action to; to stir up and set a-going. (L. *excito*, wake, or stir, up.)
excitement, *n.* ek-*site*-ment, the act of exciting; stimulation, specially to increased action; the state of being excited; that which excites or induces agitation.
exciter, *n.* ek-*site*-er, he who or that which excites or puts in motion; an excitant; a stimulant [Med.]; an apparatus to produce excitation [Elect.].
exciting, *a.* ek-*site*-ing, thrilling; of absorbing interest.
excitingly, *ad.* ek-*site*-ing-le, in an exciting manner.
excitive, *a.* ek-*site*-iv, tending to excite.
excito-motory, *a.* ek-*sy*-to-*moh*-to-re, causing muscular contraction or movement independently of volition [Anat.].
exclaim, *v.i.* eks-*klame*, to cry out; to utter abruptly; to declare with loud vociferation. (Fr. *exclamer*.)
exclamation, *n.* eks-kla-*may*-shon, outcry; clamour; vehement or emphatic utterance; an interjection expressing some passion, as wonder [Gram.]. **note of exclamation,** the mark (!) used in printing and writing after an interjection or after an expression of strong feeling or an emphatic utterance. (Fr.)
exclamatory, *a.* eks-*klam*-a-to-re, using or expressing exclamation. (L. *exclamatus*, called out.)
exclave, *n.* *eks*-klave, an enclave in its relationship with the country of which it politically forms a part.
exclude, *v.t.* eks-*klood*, to hinder from entering or from participation or enjoyment; to shut out; to debar; to except; not to comprehend or include. (L. *excludo*, exclude.)
exclusion, *n.* eks-*kloo*-zhon, the act of excluding or shutting out; debarring or ejecting; exception. (L.)
exclusionary, *n.* eks-*kloo*-zhon-a-re, tending to exclude.
exclusionism, *n.* eks-*kloo*-zhon-izm, the system, or character, of exclusion; exclusivism.
exclusionist, *n.* eks-*kloo*-zhon-ist, one who would exclude another from some privilege.
exclusive, *a.* eks-*kloo*-siv, having the power or tendency to exclude; debarring from participation; to the exclusion of others; not taking into account; not including: *n.* one of a coterie who exclude others; an exclusive proposition [Logic]; a report, article, etc., appearing in or supplied only to a single periodical [Journalism].
exclusively, *ad.* with the exclusion of all others.
exclusiveness, *n.* the quality or state of being exclusive.
exclusivism, *n.* eks-*kloo*-siv-izm, the act or practice of excluding or being exclusive.
exclusory, *a.* eks-*kloo*-so-re, exclusionary; excluding.
excogitate, *v.t.* eks-*koj*-e-tate, to devise by thinking; to think out carefully. (L. *excogitatus*, sought out.)
excogitation, *n.* eks-koj-e-*tay*-shon, the act of thinking out or scheming, carefully; invention; contrivance. (L. *excogitatio*.)
excommunicable, *a.* eks-kom-*mew*-ne-ka-bl, liable or deserving to be excommunicated.
excommunicate, *v.t.* eks-kom-*mew*-ne-kate, to exclude from the rites and sacraments of the Church; to expel from any fellowship. (L. *excommunicatus*.)

excommunication, *n.* eks-kom-*mew*-ne-*kay*-shon, exclusion from participation in the rites of the Church; the greater excommunication disqualifies from the administration or reception of any Church ministrations, and the lesser excludes only from the eucharist.
excommunicative, *a.* eks-ko-*mew*-ne-ka-tiv, pertaining to, decreeing, or in favour of excommunication.
excommunicator, *n.* eks-ko-*mew*-ne-kay-tor, one who excommunicates.
excommunicatory, *a.* *eks*-ko-mew-ne-*kat*-to-re, affecting or causing excommunication.
excoriate, *v.t.* eks-*kaw*-re-ate, to strip, wear, or abrade the skin from. (L. *excoriatus*, stripped of its skin.)
excoriation, *n.* eks-kaw-re-*ay*-shon, the act or result of excoriating; a sore.
excorticate, *v.t.* eks-*kawr*-te-kate, to strip off the bark or rind. (L. *ex-*, and *cortex, corticis*, bark.)
excrement, *n.* *eks*-kre-ment, waste matter excreted and ejected from the body; ordure. (Fr. *excrément.*)
excremental, *a.* eks-kre-*men*-tal, excreted or ejected by the natural passages of the body.
excrementitious, *a.* *eks*-kre-men-*tish*-us, pertaining to, consisting of, or containing excrement.
excrescence, *n.* eks-*kres*-ence, anything that grows unnaturally or uselessly out of something else, as a wart; an outgrowth; a superfluity. (L.)
excrescent, *a.* eks-*kres*-ent, growing out of something else, esp. abnormally; superfluous. (L. *excrescentis*, of a morbid excrescence.)
excrescential, *a.* eks-kre-*sen*-shal, resembling an excrescence; redundant.
excreta, *n.pl.* eks-*kree*-ta, the waste products discharged from an animal body. (L.)
excrete, *v.t.* eks-*kreet*, to separate and throw off; to discharge. (L. *excretus*, separated.)
excretion, *n.* eks-*kree*-shon, the act of excreting matter from the body; that which is excreted.
excretive, *a.* eks-*kree*-tiv, able to excrete; for the purpose of excretion.
excretory, *a.* *eks*-kree-to-re, pertaining to excretion; able to excrete; conveying excretions: *n.* an excretory duct.
excruciate, *v.t.* eks-*kroo*-she-ate, to torture; to inflict severe pain. (L. *excruciatus*, tortured.)
excruciating, *a.* eks-*kroo*-she-ay-ting, extremely painful; distressing.
excruciatingly, *ad.* in an excruciating manner.
excruciation, *n.* eks-*kroo*-she-*ay*-shon, torture; vexation.
exculpable, *a.* eks-*kul*-pa-bl, that may be exculpated.
exculpate, *v.t.* *eks*-kul-pate, to exonerate; to clear from a charge. (L. *ex-*, and *culpa*, a fault.)
exculpation, *n.* eks-kul-*pay*-shon, the act of freeing from the imputation of a fault or crime.
exculpatory, *a.* eks-*kul*-pa-to-re, excusing; tending or contributing to exculpate.
excurrent, *a.* eks-*ku*-rent, accommodating an outgoing current [Zool.]; forming an undivided main stem, as the pine [Bot.]. (L. *excurrens*, running forth.)
excurse, *v.t.* eks-*kurse*, to digress; to wander; to make an excursion. (L. *excursus*, run forth.)
excursion, *n.* eks-*kur*-shon, a brief tour; a trip for health or pleasure; deviation from the fixed course [Astron.]; a digression. **excursion train,** a train for excursionists at a reduced fare. (L. *excursio.*)
excursionist, *n.* eks-*kur*-shon-ist, one who goes on an excursion for pleasure.
excursive, *a.* eks-*kur*-siv, ambling; deviating.
excursively, *ad.* in an excursive manner.
excursiveness, *n.* tendency to be excursive.
excursus, *n.* eks-*kur*-sus, (*pl.* **excursus** *or* **excursuses**), a supplemental treatise on some important point referred to in the main work. (L.)
excurved, *a.* eks-*kurvd*, curving outwards [Zool.].
excusable, *a.* eks-*kew*-za-bl, that may be excused; admitting of excuse. (Fr.)
excusably, *ad.* eks-*kew*-za-ble, in an excusable manner.
excusal, *n.* eks-*kew*-zal, act or fact of excusing (esp. a payment due, as of rates).
excusatory, *a.* eks-*kew*-za-to-re, making or containing excuse or apology; apologetical.
excuse, *v.t.* eks-*kewz*, to free from the imputation of blame or guilt; to pardon; to free from an obligation; to obtain an exemption for; to remit or not to exact; to accept an apology for; to apologize for. (Fr.)
excuse, *n.* eks-*kewce*, the act of excusing; a plea offered in extenuation of a fault, etc., or for release from an obligation, etc. (Fr.)
excuseless, *a.* eks-*kewce*-less, having or admiting of no excuse.
excusive, *a.* eks-*kew*-siv, excusing.
exeat, *n.* *eks*-e-at, leave of absence granted to students at universities; permission granted by a bishop to a priest to go out of his diocese. (L., let him depart.)
execrable, *a.* *eks*-e-kra-bl, meriting execration; abominable; hateful. (L. *execrabilis.*)
execrably, *ad.* *eks*-e-kra-ble, detestably.
execrate, *v.t.* *eks*-e-krate, to curse; to denounce evil against; to detest utterly: *v.i.* to utter curses. (L. *execratus*, cursed.)
execration, *n.* *eks*-e-*kray*-shon, the act of execrating; a pronounced malediction; intense loathing; the object execrated.
execrative, *a.* *eks*-e-kray-tiv, pertaining to or containing an execration; imprecatory.
execratory, *a.* *eks*-e-*kray*-to-re, denouncing evil; cursing.
executable, *a.* *eks*-e-*kew*-ta-bl, that may be executed.
executant, *n.* eks-*ek*-yew-tant, one who puts into execution; a performer, esp. on a musical instrument.
execute, *v.t.* *eks*-e-kewt, to perform; to carry into effect; to complete, as a legal instrument, or perform what is required to give validity to a writing; to inflict capital punishment on: *v.i.* to perform any act. (Fr. *executer.*)
execution, *n.* eks-e-*kew*-shon, the act of executing; performance; the carrying into effect a judgment of court [Law]; the warrant empowering an officer to carry a judgment into effect [Law]; the act of signing and sealing a legal instrument to render it valid [Law]; the infliction of punishment by death; effective result; destructive effort; the performance of music; the production of any work of art or skill [Paint. and Sculp.]. (O.Fr.)
executioner, *n.* eks-e-*kew*-shon-er, one who executes the sentence of capital punishment; a hangman.
executive, *a.* eks-*ek*-yew-tiv, executing; carrying into execution, or seeing effect given specially to a law or a decree: *n.* the administrative branch of government; any person or body of persons charged with administrative work; a responsible official. (L. *executus*, executed.)
executor, *n.* eks-*ek*-yew-tor, one appointed by a testator to carry out the provisions of his will.
executorial, *a.* eks-ek-yew-*taw*-re-al, pertaining to an executor or his duties; executive.
executorship, *n.* eks-*ek*-yew-tor-ship, the office or duties of an executor.
executory, *a.* eks-*ek*-yew-to-re, pertaining to the carrying out of decrees, etc.; executive; operative; to be carried into effect: *n.* an executive body.
executrix, *n.* eks-*ek*-yew-triks, a female executor.
exedra, *n.* ek-*see*-dra, a hall for conversation [Antiq.]; a recess; a vestibule; a bishop's throne. (L.)
exegesis, *n.* eks-e-*jee*-sis, exposition or interpretation esp. of the Scriptures. (Gr. *exēgētēs.*)
exegete, *n.* *eks*-e-jeet, one skilled in exegesis.
exegetic, *a.* eks-e-*jet*-ik, pertaining to exegesis; explanatory; expository.
exegetically, *ad.* eks-e-*jet*-e-ka-le, by way of explanation. (Gr. *exēgētikos.*)
exegetics, *n.pl.* eks-e-*jet*-iks, the science of biblical interpretation; exegesis.
exegetist, *n.* eks-e-*jee*-tist, an exegete.
exemplar, *n.* egs-*em*-plar, a model to be copied or imitated; an ideal or a typical model. (Fr. *exemplaire.*)
exemplarily, *ad.* egs-*em*-pla-re-le, in an exemplary manner.
exemplariness, *n.* egs-*em*-pla-re-ness, the state or quality of being exemplary or suitable for imitation; exemplary behaviour.
exemplarity, *n.* egs-em-*pla*-re-te, exemplariness; exemplary nature.
exemplary, *a.* egs-*em*-pla-re, worthy as a pattern for imitation; such as may serve for a warning; such as may attract notice and imitation. **exemplary damages,** damages on such a scale as to serve as a deterrent [Law]. (L. *exemplaris*, exemplary.)

exemplifiable. *n.* egs-*em*-ple-*fy*-a-bl, that may be exemplified or illustrated by example.
exemplification, *n.* egs-*em*-ple-fe-*kay*-shon, the act of exemplifying ; a copy ; an attested copy.
exemplify, *v.t.* egs-*em*-ple-fy, to show by example ; to copy ; to take an attested copy ; to prove by an attested copy. (Late L. *exemplifico.*)
exempt, *a.* eg-*zemt*, exempted ; not liable to ; released ; not included : *n.* one who is exempt ; one not subject ; an exon : *v.t.* to free, permit to be free, or grant immunity from. (O.Fr.)
exemption, *n.* eg-*zemp*-shon, the act of exempting ; the state of being exempt ; immunity.
exenterate, *v.t.* eks-*en*-ter-rate, to disembowel. (L. *exenteratus*, eviscerated.)
exequatur, *n.* eks-e-*kway*-tur, the certificate recognizing a consul or commercial agent issued by the government to which he comes accredited, and authorizing him to exercise his powers in the country ; official authorization, esp. for the exercise of episcopal functions under papal authority. (L., let him execute.)
exequial, *a.* eks-*ee*-kwe-al, pertaining to funerals.
exequies, *n.pl.* *eks*-e-kwiz, funeral rites ; the ceremonies of burial. (O.Fr. *exeques*, burials.)
exercisable, *a.* eks-er-*size*-a-bl, that may be exercised.
exercise, *n.* *eks*-er-size, a putting in use or practice ; exertion of the body for health, strength, or dexterity ; performance ; discipline ; drill ; a task appointed one to perform ; act of divine worship ; a lesson for practice ; any composition calculated to improve the voice or fingers of the young practitioner [Mus.] : *v.t.* to exert ; to cause to act in any manner ; to use ; to use for improvement in skill ; to perform the duties of ; to discipline ; to task ; to employ ; to busy ; to afflict ; to give anxiety to : *v.i.* to use action or exertion. (Fr. *exerciser.*)
exerciser, *n.* *eks*-er-sy-zer, an appliance for use in physical exercises ; a groom who exercises horses.
exercitation, *n.* eks-*er*-se-*tay*-shon, exercise ; practice ; a dissertation. (Fr.)
exergue, *n.* *eks*-erg *or* eg-*zerg*, the space below the design on a medal or coin intended for the date or other inscription ; the date or inscription. (Fr.)
exert, *v.t.* eg-*zert*, to put forth, as strength, force, or ability ; to bring into active operation ; to do or perform. **to exert oneself,** to use effort ; to strive. (L. *exertus*, stretched out.)
exertion, *n.* eg-*zer*-shon, the act of exerting or exercising with effort ; an effort.
exertive, *a.* eg-*zer*-tiv, tending to rouse into activity.
exes, *n.pl.* *ek*-siz, expenses [Slang ; abbrev.].
exeunt, *ek*-se-unt, *pl.* of **exit,** they quit the stage. (L.)
exfoliate, *v.i.* eks-*foh*-le-ate, to split into or break off in scales ; to flake off [Surg. and Min.]. (L. *exfoliatus*, stripped of leaves.)
exfoliation, *n.* eks-foh-le-*ay*-shon, the scaling off of dead tissues [Med.] ; separation in scales [Min.].
exhalable, *a.* eks-*hale*-a-bl, that may be exhaled.
exhalant, *a.* eks-*hale*-ant, having the quality of exhaling or evaporating.
exhalation, *n.* eks-ha-*lay*-shon, the act or process of exhaling or passing into vapour ; that which is exhaled ; vapour ; effluvia ; emanation. (Fr.)
exhale, *v.t.* eks-*hale*, to emit, as vapour or effluvia ; to draw out, or cause to be emitted, in vapour : *v.i.* to pass off in vapour ; to make an expiration. (Fr. *exhaler.*)
exhaust, *n.* egs-*awst*, the spent steam, gas, etc., that escapes from a cylinder or engine ; the escape of this ; an exhaust pipe : *v.t.* to draw out or drain off the whole of ; to empty by drawing off ; to use or expend the whole of by exertion, as one's strength ; to tire out ; to treat of, as a subject, so completely as to leave nothing unsaid. **exhausted receiver,** the receiver of an air-pump when the air has been pumped out. (L. *exhaustus*, drunk up.)
exhauster, *n.* egs-*aws*-ter, a fan, pump, or other device that exhausts.
exhaustibility, *n.* egs-*aws*-te-*bil*-e-te, capacity for exhaustion.
exhaustible, *a.* egs-*aws*-te-bl, that may be exhausted.
exhausting, *a.* egs-*aws*-ting, producing exhaustion.
exhaustion, *n.* egs-*aws*-shon, the act of exhausting ; the state of being exhausted ; prostration ; a method of proving the equality of two magnitudes by a *reductio ad absurdum* [Math.] ; a method of proving a point by demonstration of the absurdity of every other possible hypothesis [Logic].
exhaustive, *a.* egs-*aws*-tiv, that exhausts ; considering all possibilities, thorough.
exhaustively, *ad.* egs-*aws*-tiv-le, thoroughly.
exhaustiveness, *n.* quality of being exhaustive.
exhaustless, *a.* egs-*awst*-less, not to be exhausted.
exhaust-pipe, *n.* egs-*awst*-pipe, a pipe conveying the spent steam or gases of an internal combustion or other engine into the condenser or the atmosphere.
exheredation, *n.* *eks*-he-re-*day*-shon, the act of disinheriting ; disinheritance.
exhibit, *n.* eg-*zib*-it, anything exhibited ; a document or voucher produced as a proof of facts ; a deed or writing produced in court, sworn to by a witness [Law] : *v.t.* to present to public view ; to show ; to display ; to manifest publicly ; to present formally ; to administer [Med.]. (L. *exhibitus*, held forth.)
exhibiter, *n.* eg-*zib*-e-ter, one who exhibits (qualities, etc.) ; an exhibitor.
exhibition, *n.* eks-e-*bish*-on, the act of exhibiting ; display ; that which is exhibited ; a public show, esp. of works of art or manufacture, natural products, etc. ; representation of feats ; the producing of papers before a tribunal in proof of facts ; allowance of meat and drink ; a bursary to a student in a university ; a scholarship. **to make an exhibition of oneself,** to show oneself in a contemptible or unfavourable light. (L. *exhibitio*, giving up.)
exhibitioner, *n.* eks-e-*bish*-on-er, one who has been granted an exhibition at a college or school.
exhibitionism, *n.* eks-e-*bish*-on-izm, a perverted state of the mind in which the sufferer indecently exposes his person [Psychan.].
exhibitionist, *n.* one addicted to exhibitionism.
exhibitor, *n.* eg-*zib*-e-tor, the proprietor of an exhibit at an exhibition.
exhibitory, *a.* eg-*zib*-e-to-re, exhibiting ; displaying ; pertaining to exhibition.
exhilarant, *a.* eg-*zil*-a-rant, exciting joy, mirth, or pleasure : *n.* that which exhilarates.
exhilarate, *v.t.* eg-*zil*-a-rate, to make cheerful ; to gladden ; to cheer. (L. *exhilaratus*, delighted.)
exhilarating, *a.* gladdening ; cheering ; enlivening.
exhilaration, *n.* eg-*zil*-a-*ray*-shon, act of exhilarating ; state of being enlivened or cheerful.
exhilarative, *a.* eg-*zil*-a-ra-tiv, tending to exhilarate.
exhort, *v.t.* eg-*zort*, to urge by words or advice to good deeds ; to advise, warn, or caution ; to stimulate to exertion : *v.i.* to use words or arguments to incite to good deeds. (L. *exhortor*, strongly urge.)
exhortation, *n.* *eks*-or-*tay*-shon, the art or practice of exhorting to laudable deeds ; a form of words intended to incite and encourage ; a formal address ; an admonition.
exhortative, *a.* eg-*zor*-ta-tiv, pertaining to or containing exhortation. (L. *exhortativus.*)
exhortatory, *n.* eg-*zor*-ta-to-re, tending to exhort.
exhorter, *n.* eg-*zort*-er, one who exhorts.
exhumation, *n.* *eks*-hew-*may*-shon, the act of exhuming. (Late L. *exhumatus*, disinterred.)
exhume, *v.t.* eks-*hewm*, to dig up ; to disinter.
exigeant, *a.* (App.), exacting. (Fr.)
exigence, *n.* *ek*-se-jence, exigency. (Fr.)
exigency, *n.* *ek*-se-jen-se, urgency ; pressing necessity ; a case which demands immediate action.
exigent, *a.* *ek*-se-jent, urgent ; pressing ; requiring immediate attention or action. (L. *exigens*, driving forth.)
exigible, *n.* *ek*-se-je-bl, that may be exacted.
exiguity, *n.* ek-se-*gew*-e-te, scantiness.
exiguous, *a.* ek-*zig*-yew-us, diminutive ; scanty ; sparing. (L. *exiguus*, small.)
exile, *n.* *eks*-ile, banishment, whether voluntary or enforced ; one banished from his country : *v.t.* to banish from one's country. (Fr. *exil.*)
exilement, *n.* *eks*-ile-ment, banishment.
exilian, *a.* eg-*zil*-e-an, exilic.
exilic, *a.* eg-*zil*-ik, pertaining to exile, esp. to that of the Jews in Babylon.
exility, *n.* eg-*zil*-e-te, tenuity ; slenderness.
eximious, *a.* ek-*sim*-e-us, famous ; eminent.
exist, *v.i.* eg-*zist*, to be ; to have an actual being ; to live ; to endure. (L. *exsisto*, stand.)
★**existence,** *n.* eg-*zist*-ence, state of being or existing ; life ; continued being ; duration ; anything that exists ; all that exists. (Fr.)
existent, *a.* eg-*zist*-ent, existing.

existential, *a.* eg-zis-*ten*-shal, pertaining to or possessing existence.
existentialism, *n.* eg-zis-*ten*-sha-lizm, a pessimistic theory (French, 1945) depreciating the value and significance of human existence [Phil.].
existlessness, *n.* eg-*zist*-less-ness, non-existence.
exit, *n.* ek-*sit*, a direction for a player to quit the stage; the departure of a player from the stage; any departure; the act of quitting the stage of life; a way out. (L., he goes out, from *exeo*, go out.)
ex-libris, *n.* eks-*ly*-bris, a bookplate. (L., from the library of, customary on bookplates preceding the owner's name.)
ex-librist, *n.* eks-*ly*-brist, one who collects bookplates.
exo-, *ek*-zo, a Greek prefix signifying on the outside, without.
exocrine, *a.* eks-o-krine, secreting into a cavity or on to the surface of the body (of certain glands).
exode, *n.* *ek*-zode, the denouement of an ancient Greek drama; in the Roman theatre a kind of farce or satire staged after the main performance. (Fr., from Gr., as *exodus*.)
exoderm, *n.* ek-so-derm, the ectoderm; the epidermis. (Fr.)
exodus, *n.* *ek*-so-dus, a departure, esp. of a body of people in quest of a settlement elsewhere; the departure of the Israelites from Egypt under Moses, as recorded in the Book of this name, the second of the Old Testament. (L.)
ex-official, *a.* *eks*-o-*fish*-al, proceeding from office or authority.
ex-officio, *a.* and *ad.* *eks*-o-*fis*-se-o, by virtue of office, as the Archbishop of Canterbury is *ex officio* a Trustee of the British Museum.
exogamous, *a.* eks-*og*-a-mus, pertaining to exogamy.
exogamy, *n.* eks-*og*-a-me, marriage outside the tribe [Anthrop.]; union between gametes not closely related [Zool. and Bot.]. (Gr. *exo-*, and *gamos*, marriage.)
exogastritis, *n.* eks-o-gas-*try*-tis, inflammation of the external membrane of the stomach [Med.]. (Gr. *exo-*, and *gaster*, the belly.)
exogen, *n.* *eks*-o-jen, a plant whose stem is formed by successive additions to the outside of the wood; a dicotyledon [Bot.]. (Gr. *exo-*, and *gennao*, produce.)
exogenetic, *a.* eks-o-je-*net*-ik, exopathic.
exogenous, *a.* eks-*oj*-e-nus, having the wood augmented by annual external accretions [Bot.].
exomphalos, *n.* eks-*om*-fa-los, umbilical hernia; a navel rupture [Med.]. (Gr. *omphalos*, the navel.)
exon, *n.* *eks*-on, one of four junior officers of the Yeomen of the Guard. (Fr. *exempt*, an officer of the watch.)
exonerate, *v.t.* eg-*zon*-er-ate, to free or clear from blame or obligation. (L. *ex-*, and *onus, oneris*, burden.)
exoneration, *n.* eg-*zon*-er-*ray*-shon, the act of exonerating or freeing from an imputation.
exonerative, *a.* eks-*on*-er-ra-tiv, tending to exonerate.
exopathic, *a.* eks-o-*path*-ik, originating externally to the organism (of diseases).
exophagy, *n.* eks-*of*-a-je, cannibalism confined to eating those of a different tribe. (Gr. *exo-*, and *phagein*, eat.)
exophthalmia, *n.* eks-of-*thal*-me-a, abnormal protrusion of the eyeball [Med.]. (Gr. *ex-*, and *ophthalmos*, the eye.)
exorbitance, *n.* egs-*awr*-be-tance, the quality of being exorbitant, excessive, or exceeding due bounds; extravagance, esp. in charging.
exorbitancy, *n.* eg-*zawr*-be-tan-se, exorbitance.
exorbitant, *a.* eg-*zawr*-bit-ant, exceeding due bounds; grossly excessive; enormous. (L. *exorbitans*, deviating.)
exorbitantly, *ad.* eg-*zawr*-be-tant-le, excessively.
exorcism, *n.* *eks*-aw-sizm, the act or art of exorcising; a spell used in this.
exorcist, *n.* *eks*-aw-sist, an exorcizer; one of a minor order which exercised this function in the early Church [Eccles.].
exorcize, *v.t.* *eks*-awr-size, to adjure by some holy name an evil spirit to depart from a person; to expel evil spirits by conjurations, etc.; to deliver from the influence of evil spirits. (Gr. *exorkizo*, expel by adjuration.)
exorcizer, *n.* *eks*-awr-size-er, one who adjures or exorcises evil spirits.
exordial, *a.* eg-*zawr*-de-al, introductory; pertaining to or resembling an exordium.
exordium, *n.* eg-*zawr*-de-um, the introductory part of a discourse, etc.; the opening. (L., the beginning.)
exoskeleton, *n.* *eks*-o-*skel*-e-ton, an external skeleton, as the shell of a crustacean.
exosmosis, *n.* *eks*-oz-*moh*-sis, the transfusion of a gas or fluid in a living body through a porous membrane outwards. (Gr. *exo-*, and *osmos*, impulsion.)
exosmotic, *a.* eks-oz-*mot*-ik, pertaining to exosmosis.
exostome, *n.* *eks*-os-tome, the outermost of the perforations which make up the foramen of the ovule of a plant [Bot.]. (Gr. *exo-*, and *stoma*, a mouth.)
exostosis, *n.* eks-os-*toh*-sis, an abnormal protuberance on a bone; an osseous tumour [Anat.]; a disease in which knots form in the wood [Bot.]. (Gr. *exo-*, and *osteon*, bone.)
exoteric, *a.* eks-o-*te*-rik, such as is taught to the uninitiated (opposed to esoteric); public; ordinary. (L. *exotericus*, external.)
exotericism, *n.* eks-o-*te*-re-sizm, exoteric teaching; an exoteric doctrine.
exotherm, *n.* *eks*-o-therm, a compound which liberates heat when being formed and absorbs heat when being decomposed [Chem.]. (Gk. *exo-*, and *thermos*, hot.)
exothermic, *a.* eks-o-*ther*-mik, having the qualities of an exotherm [Chem.].
exothermous, *a.* eks-o-*ther*-mus, exothermic.
exotic, *a.* ek-*sot*-ik, introduced from a foreign country; not native; extraneous: *n.* anything introduced from abroad, esp. a plant. (L. *exoticus*.)
exoticism, *n.* ek-*sot*-e-sizm, exotic character; tendency to adopt foreign ways, etc.; an exotic.
expand, *v.t.* eks-*pand*, to open or spread out; to enlarge in length, surface, or bulk: *v.i.* to open out; to dilate; to become enlarged in bulk. (L. *expando*, spread.)
expanse, *n.* eks-*panse*, a widely extended surface; a wide extent of space; expansion. (L. *expansus*.)
expansibility, *n.* eks-*pan*-se-*bil*-e-te, the quality of being expansible.
expansible, *a.* eks-*pan*-se-bl, capable of being expanded.
expansile, *a.* eks-*pan*-sile, capable of being expanded.
★**expansion,** *n.* eks-*pan*-shon, the act of expanding; state of being expanded; enlargement; distention; extent; extension; increase in trade, currency, etc.; an increase of the bulk of any body from within; increase of volume, as of steam or gas in a cylinder. **expansion curb,** a contrivance to counteract expansion and contraction by heat, as in chronometers. **expansion engine,** a steam-engine in which the supply of steam is cut off previous to the stroke being complete, the rest of the power being supplied by the expansion of the steam already admitted. (L. *expansio*.)
expansionism, *n.* eks-*pan*-shon-izm, advocacy of expansion, esp. of national territory or of a currency.
expansionist, *n.* eks-*pan*-shon-ist, one in favour of expansionism.
expansive, *a.* eks-*pan*-siv, having the power to expand; having the capacity of being expanded; widely extending; comprehensive; effusive.
expansively, *ad.* in an expansive manner.
expansiveness, *n.* quality of being expansive.
expansivity, *n.* eks-pan-*siv*-e-te, expansiveness.
expatiate, *v.i.* eks-*pay*-she-ate, to speak or write copiously; to dilate upon; to range at large. (L. *expatiatus*, wandered.)
expatiation, *n.* eks-pay-she-*ay*-shon, the act of expatiating; a rambling discourse, etc.
expatiative, *a.* eks-*pay*-she-a-tiv, expansive.
expatiatory, *a.* eks-*pay*-she-a-to-re, given to expatiating; expatiating.
expatriate, *n.* eks-*pay*-tre-ate, one who is expatriated; an exile: *a.* expatriated: *v.t.* to banish from one's native land. **to expatriate oneself,** to quit one's country, renouncing allegiance to it. (Late L. *expatriatus*, expatriated.)
expatriation, *n.* eks-*pay*-tre-*ay*-shon, banishment; the forsaking of one's own country for another.
expect, *v.t.* eks-*pekt*, to wait for; to look for as likely to happen; to calculate on being done; to anticipate; to suppose [Coll.]: *v.i.* to wait; to look forward with expectation. (L. *expecto*, look for.)
expectance, *n.* eks-*pek*-tance, expectancy.

expectancy, *n.* eks-*pek*-tan-se, the act or state of expecting ; that which is expected ; hope ; abeyance, dependence on something future [Law].

expectant, *a.* eks-*pek*-tant, waiting ; looking for ; administered or treated in anticipation [Med.] : *n.* one who waits in expectation. **expectant estate,** an estate in expectancy, a reversionary estate [Law]. **expectant mother,** a pregnant woman. (L. *expectans*, looking for.)

expectation, *n.* eks-pek-*tay*-shon, the act of expecting ; the state of being expected ; that which is expected ; prospect of good to come ; the object of expectation ; promise ; the treatment of disease by leaving it to the course of nature. **expectation of life,** the mean or average duration of human life after a specified age. (L. *expectatio.*)

expectative, *a.* eks-*pek*-ta-tiv, pertaining to expectation ; reversionary.

expectingly, *ad.* eks-*pek*-ting-le, with expectation.

expectorant, *a.* eks-*pek*-tor-ant, having the quality of promoting expectoration : *n.* a medicine which promotes expectoration. (L.)

expectorate, *v.t.* and *i.* eks-*pek*-to-rate, to eject from the lungs or air-passages ; to spit. (L. *expectoratus*, driven from the throat.)

expectoration, *n.* eks-*pek*-to-*ray*-shon, the act of expectorating ; the matter discharged.

expectorative, *a.* eks-*pek*-to-ra-tiv, expectorant.

expedience, *n.* eks-*pee*-de-ence, expediency.

expediency, *n.* eks-*pee*-de-en-se, suitableness for effecting a purpose ; propriety under the particular circumstances of a case ; conduciveness to mere private advantage. (Fr. *expedience.*)

expedient, *a.* eks-*pee*-de-ent, tending to promote an object proposed ; serviceable for a purpose ; proper in the circumstances ; conducive to one's own ends ; *n.* that which serves to promote or accomplish a purpose ; means devised or employed in an exigency ; a makeshift. (O.Fr.)

expediential, *a.* eks-*pee*-de-*en*-shal, dictated by considerations of expediency or advantage.

expediently, *ad.* eks-*pee*-de-ent-le, fitly ; suitably.

expedite, *v.t.* *eks*-pe-dite, to hasten ; to accelerate ; to dispatch. (L. *expeditus*, set free.)

expedition, *n.* eks-pe-*dish*-on, haste ; quick dispatch ; a march, voyage, or flight of troops to a distance for hostile purposes ; any undertaking by a number that involves travel and probable hardship ; the collective body on an expedition. (L. *expeditio.*)

expeditionary, *a.* eks-pe-*dish*-o-na-re, suitable for or constituting an expedition.

expeditious, *a.* eks-pe-*dish*-us, done with expedition or promptitude ; characterized by efficiency.

expeditiously, *ad.* with celerity or dispatch.

expeditiousness, *n.* celerity ; quickness.

expel, *v.t.* eks-*pel*, to drive or force out ; to force to leave ; to eject ; to banish ; to sever from connexion with a society. (L. *expello*, to thrust out.)

expellable, *a.* eks-*pel*-a-bl, that may be expelled.

expellent, *a.* eks-*pel*-ent, expelling ; tending to expel.

expend, *v.t.* eks-*pend*, to lay out ; to spend ; to employ ; to consume. (L. *expendo*, weigh, pay.)

expendable, *a.* ex-*pen*-da-bl, that may be expended ; not entirely indispensable.

expenditure, *n.* eks-*pen*-de-tewr, the act of expending ; the amount expended ; expense.

expense, *n.* eks-*pense*, outlay ; cost ; disbursement ; price paid : *pl.* outlay for some special purpose ; reimbursement for such. (O.Fr.)

expensive, *a.* eks-*pen*-siv, costly ; involving great expense ; free in expending ; lavish in expending ; wealthy, ultra-fashionable [Coll.].

expensively, *ad.* with great expense.

expensiveness, *n.* quality of being expensive.

★**experience,** *n.* eks-*peer*-re-ence, ascertained result of a series of trials or experiments ; observation of a fact or of the same facts or events happening in like circumstances ; what one has felt and learned by enjoying or suffering ; knowledge derived from trials, use, practice, or a series of observations : *v.t.* to try by use, suffering, or enjoyment ; to know by practice or trial ; to suffer. (L. *experientia.*)

experienced, *a.* eks-*peer*-re-enst, taught by experience ; skilful or wise by means of experience.

experiential, *a.* eks-*peer*-re-*en*-shal, pertaining to or derived from experience or observation.

experientialism, *n.* eks-*peer*-re-*en*-shal-izm, the theory which derives all ideas from experience, or would refer all knowledge to the test of experience.

experientialist, *n.* eks-*peer*-re-*en*-sha-list, one who accepts the doctrine of experientialism.

experiment, *n.* eks-*pe*-re-ment, an act or operation designed to discover some unknown truth, principle, or effect, or to establish it when discovered, specifically by varying at will the combination of things and circumstances and then observing the result : *v.i.* to make an experiment ; to search by trial : *v.t.* to put to the proof ; to experience. (O.Fr.)

experimental, *a.* eks-pe-re-*men*-tal, pertaining to, derived from, or founded on experiment ; taught by or derived from experience. **experimental philosophy,** inductive philosophy, making of experiment and observation a *sine qua non* for the attainment of reasoned conclusions.

experimentalism, *n.* exs-pe-re-*men*-ta-lizm, the theory or habit of relying on experiment.

experimentalist, *n.* eks-pe-re-*men*-ta-list, one who makes or relies on experiments.

experimentalize, *v.i.* eks-*pe*-re-*men*-ta-lize, to make experiments.

experimentally, *ad.* by experiment ; by experience.

experimentation, *n.* eks-*pe*-re-men-*tay*-shon, the act or practice of experimenting.

experimentative, *a.* eks-*pe*-re-*men*-ta-tiv, experimental.

experimenter, *n.* eks-*pe*-re-men-ter, one who makes experiments ; one skilled in experiments.

experimentist, *n.* eks-*pe*-re-men-tist, an experimenter.

expert, *a.* eks-*pert*, experienced ; having familiar knowledge ; having a facility of operation or performance from practice ; skilful ; dexterous. (O.Fr.)

★**expert,** *n.* *eks*-pert, one specially qualified by study and practice in any department of science or art ; a scientific or specialist witness [Law].

expertise, *n.* eks-per-*teez*, expert opinion, skill, or knowledge ; quality of being expert. (Fr.)

expertly, *ad.* eks-*pert*-le, in a skilful or dexterous manner.

expertness, *n.* eks-*pert*-ness, quality of being expert.

expiable, *a.* *eks*-pe-a-bl, that may be expiated.

expiate, *v.t.* *eks*-pe-ate, to atone for ; to make satisfaction or reparation for ; to avert by some ritual observance. (L. *expiatus*, atoned for.)

expiation, *n.* eks-pe-*ay*-shon, the act of expiating a crime ; the means by which this is made.

expiator, *n.* *eks*-pe-ay-tor, one who expiates.

expiatory, *a.* *eks*-pe-*ay*-to-re, having power to expiate ; atoning.

expiration, *n.* eks-py-*ray*-shon, the act of breathing out ; the emission of volatile matter from any substance ; the matter expired ; cessation ; the end. (L. *expiratio.*)

expiratory, *a.* eks-*pire*-ra-to-re, pertaining to the expiration of breath from the lungs.

expire, *v.t.* eks-*pire*, to breathe out from the lungs ; to emit in minute particles ; to exhale : *v.i.* to breathe out ; to emit the last breath ; to die ; to come to an end. (O.Fr. *expirer.*)

expiry, *n.* eks-*pire*-re, termination ; expiration.

expiscate, *v.t.* eks-*pis*-kate, to fish out ; to search out by artful or careful means. (L. *expiscatus* found out.)

expiscation, *n.* eks-pis-*kay*-shon, the act of expiscating ; investigation.

explain, *v.t.* eks-*plane*, to make plain or intelligible ; to clear up and illustrate the meaning of : *v.i.* to give explanations. **explain away,** to modify by explaining ; to clear oneself by showing that one was misunderstood. (O.Fr. *explaner.*)

explainable, *n.* eks-*plane*-a-bl, that may be explained.

explanate, *a.* *eks*-pla-nate, spread out on the surface [Bot.].

explanation, *n.* eks-pla-*nay*-shon, the act of explaining ; the sense given by an expounder or interpreter that which explains or clears up ; the act or process of coming to a mutual understanding. (L. *explanatio.*)

explanative, *a.* eks-*plan*-a-tiv, explanatory.

explanatory, *a.* eks-*plan*-a-to-re, serving to explain containing explanation.

expletive, *a.* *eks*-ple-tiv *or* eks-*plee*-tiv, filling up inserted merely to fill up : *n.* a word or syllable added merely for ornament, emphasis, or to fill up an interjection ; a swear-word. (L. *expletivus.*)

expletory, *a.* *eks*-ple-to-re, serving to fill up.

explicable, *a.* *eks*-ple-ka-bl, admitting of explanation or explication. (L.)
explicate, *v.t.* *eks*-ple-kate, to unfold the meaning of; to explain at length; to interpret. (L. *explicatus*, spread out.)
explication, *n.* eks-ple-*kay*-shon, the act of explicating; a detailed description.
explicative, *a.* *eks*-ple-kay-tiv, explicatory.
explicatory, *a.* *eks*-plik-a-to-re, serving to unfold, interpret, or explain.
explicit, *a.* eks-*plis*-it, distinctly stated, not merely implied; definite; in plain language; open and distinct in statement. (L. *explicitus*, easy.)
explicit, *n.* eks-*plis*-it, the end or finis, formerly at the end of books. (L., it is unfolded.)
explicitly, *ad.* eks-*plis*-it-le, in an explicit manner.
explicitness, *n.* the quality of being explicit.
explode, *v.i.* eks-*plode*, to burst with violence and a loud report; to give a burst of laughter; to collapse: *v.t.* to cause to burst; to prove the fallacy of; to show to be absurd. (L. *explodo*, drive off by clapping.)
explodent, *n.* eks-*ploh*-dent, an explosive consonant [Phonetics].
exploder, *n.* eks-*ploh*-der, one who explodes or discredits; material or an appliance for firing a charge.
exploit, *n.* *eks*-ployt, a feat, deed, or achievement, esp. one heroic or distinguished. (O.Fr. *exploit.*)
exploit, *v.t.* eks-*ployt*, to use for profit; to make use of, esp. unfairly, illegitimately, or for purely selfish purposes.
exploitable, *a.* eks-*ploy*-ta-bl, capable of being exploited.
exploitation, *n.* eks-ploy-*tay*-shon, the act of exploiting, esp. of turning to one's own account for private benefit; unfair utilization; use for private ends. (Fr.)
exploiter, *n.* eks-*ploy*-ter, one who exploits, esp. for base or selfish ends.
exploration, *n.* eks-plor-*ray*-shon, act or process of exploring; geographical research; physical examination [Med.]; close and thorough search. (L. *exploratio.*)
explorational, *n.* eks-plor-*ray*-shon-al, pertaining to exploration.
explorative, *a.* eks-*plaw*-ra-tiv, exploratory.
exploratory, *a.* eks-*plaw*-ra-to-re, serving to explore; intended for exploration; searching.
explore, *v.t.* eks-*plore*, to search and examine with care; to examine closely with a view to discovery. (L. *ex-*, and *plorare*, to cause to flow; to elicit.)
explorer, *n.* eks-*plaw*-rer, one who explores, esp. unknown regions; an instrument used to explore a cavity in a tooth [Dentistry] or for probing a wound [Surg.]; any device or instrument used for exploratory purposes.
explosion, *n.* eks-*ploh*-zhon, a bursting with violence and a loud report; any violent outburst. (L. *explosus.*)
explosive, *a.* eks-*ploh*-siv, bursting with a loud report and disruptive force; liable to explode; causing explosion: *n.* an explosive substance; anything liable to explode; a consonant (*b*, *d*, *k*, etc.) produced by a sudden expulsion of breath.
explosively, *ad.* in an explosive manner.
exponent, *n.* eks-*poh*-nent, one who or that which represents or expounds and explains; an executant a number or letter placed at the right and above a; quantity to indicate how often that quantity is to be multiplied by itself, as 8^2, a^5; an index [Alg.]. **exponent of a ratio,** the quotient arising when the antecedent is divided by the consequent. (L. *exponens*, indicating.)
exponential, *a.* eks-po-*nen*-shal, pertaining to or involving exponents. **exponential calculus,** *see* **calculus. exponential curve,** one whose nature is defined by means of an exponential equation. **exponential equation,** one which contains an exponential quantity. **exponential quantity,** one whose exponent is variable.
export, *v.t.* eks-*port*, to carry or send out of a country in the way of commerce. (L. *exporto*, carry.)
export, *n.* *eks*-port, the act of exporting; a commodity conveyed from one country to another: *pl.* amount or value of commodities exported.
exportable, *a.* eks-*por*-ta-bl, that may be exported.
exportation, *n.* eks-por-*tay*-shon, the act of exporting. (L. *exportatio.*)
exporter, *n.* eks-*por*-ter, one engaged in exporting.

exposal, *n.* eks-*poh*-zal, exposure; an exposé.
expose, *v.t.* eks-*poze*, to lay open to view; to lay bare or uncover from what protects or shelters; to make liable or to subject; to put in the power of; to lay open to attack, censure, contempt, etc.; to put in danger; to cast out unprotected; to exhibit; to expound; to subject to the action of light [Phot.]. (O.Fr. *exposer.*)
exposé, *n.* eks-*poh*-zay, a formal explanatory statement; [Coll.] an exposure or revelation of something discreditable. (Fr.)
exposed, *pp.* and *a.* eks-*pohzd*, unprotected; open to attack; offered for sale.
exposition, *n.* eks-po-*zish*-on, the act of exposing, laying open or exhibiting; explanation or interpretation; a work containing such; a public exhibition. (Fr.)
expositive, *a.* eks-*poz*-e-tiv, expository; explanatory.
expositor, *n.* eks-*poz*-e-tor, one who expounds; an interpreter; a book which expounds. (L.)
expository, *a.* eks-*poz*-e-to-re, serving to explain or illustrate.
expostulant, *a.* eks-*pos*-tew-lant, expostulating.
expostulate, *v.i.* eks-*pos*-tew-late, to reason earnestly with a person; to remonstrate; to protect. (L. *expostulatus*, demanded.)
expostulation, *n.* eks-*pos*-tew-*lay*-shon, the act of expostulating; remonstrance. (L. *expostulatio.*)
expostulatory, *a.* eks-*pos*-tew-la-to-re, containing remonstrance.
exposure, *n.* eks-*poh*-zhur, the action of exposing; the state of being exposed; the act of submitting to the action of light [Phot.]; the time during which a plate or film is exposed [Phot.]; the situation of a place in regard to the points of the compass, or to a free access of air and light.
expound, *v.t.* eks-*pound*, to lay open the meaning of in detail; to explain or interpret. (O.Fr. *espondre.*)
express, *a.* eks-*press*, plain; clear; given in direct terms; explicit; exact; exactly resembling; intended for a particular purpose: *ad.* expressly: *n.* a special messenger or conveyance; the message sent; an express train: *v.t.* to press or squeeze out; to utter or set forth in words; to make manifest; to exhibit; to designate; to represent by symbols, etc. [Math.]; to dispatch by express. **express delivery,** delivery, or conveyance and delivery, of an article by special messenger [Post Office]. **express train,** a fast train stopping only, if at all, at important intermediate stations. (O.Fr. *expres.*)
expressible, *a.* eks-*pres*-se-bl, that may be uttered, declared, shown, or otherwise expressed.
expression, *n.* eks-*presh*-on, the act of expressing or forcing out by pressure; the art or power of uttering, declaring, or representing; utterance; declaration; representation; a phrase or mode of speech; diction; the peculiar manner of utterance suited to the occasion or any particular subject; representation, as suggestive of an idea, mood, etc., also the character or feeling as expressed in a representation [Art]; that manner which gives life and reality to ideas and sentiments; the representation of any quantity by its appropriate character or signs [Alg.]. (L. *expressus.*)
expressional, *a.* eks-*presh*-o-nal, pertaining to or having the power of expression; purposely expressive of an idea, emotion, etc.
expressionism, *n.* eks-*presh*-o-nizm, an anti-realistic movement in art, literature, and the drama expressing ideas by the exaggeration of essentials and suppression of non-essentials; the practice or advocacy of the free expression of individuality.
expressionist, *n.* eks-*presh*-o-nist, an expressionistic artist or writer; an advocate of expressionism: *a.* expressionistic.
expressionistic, *a.* eks-presh-o-*nis*-tik, pertaining to or characterized by expressionism; produced by expressionists.
expressionless, *a.* destitute of expression.
expressive, *a.* eks-*pres*-siv, serving to express; significant; expressing fully, vividly, or forcibly.
expressively, *ad.* in an expressive manner.
expressiveness, *n.* quality of being expressive.
expressly, *ad.* in direct terms; plainly; specially.
exprobation, *n.* eks-pro-*bay*-shon, reproof; censure; upbraiding.
expropriate, *v.t.* eks-*proh*-pre-ate, to take the property of, esp. for public use; to dispossess of property. (L. *ex-*, and *proprius*, one's own.)

expropriation, *n.* eks-*proh*-pre-*ay*-shon, the act of expropriating; depriving of property.
expropriator, *n.* eks-*proh*-pre-ay-tor, one who expropriates.
expulsion, *n.* eks-*pul*-shon, the act of expelling; the state of being expelled; ejection; eviction; banishment. (L. *expulsio.*)
expulsive, *a.* eks-*pul*-siv, able or serving to expel.
expunction, *n.* eks-*punk*-shon, the act of expunging; erasure.
expunge, *v.t.* eks-*punj*, to blot out; to rub or wipe out; to erase. (L. *expungo*, prick.)
expurgate, *v.t.* *eks*-pur-gate, to purge away; to remove (esp. from books) anything noxious, offensive, or erroneous. (L. *expurgatus.*)
expurgation, *n.* eks-pur-*gay*-shon, the act of expurgating; purification from noxious matter.
expurgator, *n.* *eks*-pur-gay-tor, one who expurgates; a censor, esp. of books, etc.
expurgatorial, *a.* eks-pur-ga-*taw*-re-al, that expurgates; serving to expurgate.
expurgatory, *n.* eks-*pur*-ga-to-re, expurgatorial. **expurgatory index,** a catalogue of books or passages from books forbidden to be read by the Church of Rome until they shall have been expurgated.
exquisite, *a.* *eks*-kwe-zit, choice; select; delicate; highly finished or perfected; very excellent or complete; of keen delicacy of perception or discrimination; acutely pleasurable or painful; very sensibly felt: *n.* one who dresses finically; a dandy. (L. *exquisitus*, literally, sought out with care.)
exquisitely, *ad.* in an exquisite manner.
exquisiteness, *n.* the quality of being exquisite.
exsanguinate, *v.t.* ek-*sang*-gwe-nate, to draw away or deprive completely of blood.
exsanguine, *a.* eks-*sang*-gwin, bloodless; destitute of red blood. (L. *exsanguinis.*)
exsanguinity, *n.* ek-sang-*gwin*-e-te, a state of bloodlessness; anæmia.
exscind, *v.t.* eks-*sind*, to cut out or off; to sever.
exserted, *a.* ek-*ser*-ted, projecting beyond something else; protruding. (L. *exsertus*, thrust out.)
exsertile, *a.* ek-*ser*-tile, that may be thrust out.
ex-service, *a.* eks-*ser*-vis, denoting former membership of one of the armed forces.
exsiccate, *v.t.* *ek*-sik-kate, to dry; to exhaust or evaporate moisture. (L. *exsiccatus*, quite dried.)
exsiccation, *n.* ek-sik-*kay*-shon, the act or operation of drying; evaporation of moisture; dryness.
exsiccative, *a.* ek-*sik*-a-tiv, tending to make dry; *n.* an exsiccative substance.
exstipulate, *a.* ek-*stip*-yew-late, having no stipules [Bot.]. (L. *ex*-, and *stipula.*)
exsuccous, *a.* ek-*suk*-kus, destitute of juice; dry. (L. *ex*-, and *succus*, juice.)
extant, *a.* *eks*-tant *or* eks-*tant*, still existing; surviving; in vogue. (L. *exstans*, standing forth.)
extemporal, *a.* eks-*tem*-po-ral, extemporaneous.
extemporally, *ad.* without premeditation.
extemporaneous, *a.* eks-*tem*-po-*ray*-ne-us, composed, performed, or uttered extempore.
extemporaneously, *ad.* without previous study.
extemporaneousness, *n.* the quality of being extemporaneous.
extemporarily, *ad.* without previous study.
extemporary, *a.* eks-*tem*-po-ra-re, composed, done, or uttered extempore.
extempore, *a.* and *ad.* eks-*tem*-po-re, without previous study or meditation; on the spur of the moment. (L. *ex*-, and *tempus, tempore*, time.)
extemporization, *n.* eks-*tem*-po-ry-*zay*-shon, the act of extemporizing; improvization.
extemporize, *v.i.* eks-*tem*-po-rize, to speak, etc., extempore; to produce without preparation; to discourse or play without notes or written composition [Mus.].
extend, *v.t.* eks-*tend*, to stretch in any direction; to stretch to the extreme; to reach out; to straighten out; to enlarge, expand, or dilate; to continue; to prolong; to bestow; to impart; to value lands taken by a writ of extent [Law]: *v.i.* to stretch; to reach; to be continued in length or breadth. **to extend oneself,** to exert all one's strength, to go "all out" [Coll.]. (O.Fr. *extendre.*)
extendedly, *ad.* in an extended manner.
extender, *n.* eks-*tend*-er, he who or that which extends.
extensibility, *n.* eks-*ten*-se-*bil*-e-te, the capacity of extension.
extensible, *a.* eks-*ten*-se-bl, that may be extended.
extensile, *a.* eks-*ten*-sile, extensible; capable of being protruded.
extension, *n.* eks-*ten*-shon, the act of extending; the state of being extended; the amount extended; a branch or addition; enlargement in breadth or continuation in length; that property of a body by which it occupies a portion of space in each of its three dimensions—length, breadth, and thickness [Physics]; a written engagement on the part of creditors, allowing a debtor further time for the payment of his debts [Comm.]; straightening out; the operation of straightening a bent or dislocated limb [Surg.]; the range of the application of a term, in contrast to its comprehension [Logic]. (L. *extensio.*)
extensity, *n.* eks-*ten*-se-te, the quality of extension; the faculty by which extent is rendered perceptible.
extensive, *a.* eks-*ten*-siv, of great extent; comprehensive. (L. *extensivus.*)
extensively, *ad.* widely; to a great extent.
extensiveness, *n.* the quality of being extensive.
extensometer, *n.* eks-ten-*som*-e-ter, an instrument for measuring minute strains in metals under test.
extensor, *n.* eks-*ten*-sor, a muscle serving to extend or straighten a limb or part [Anat.]. (Late L.)
extent, *n.* eks-*tent*, space or degree to which a thing is extended; length, range, or compass; bulk; size; distribution; a writ of execution against the body, lands, and goods, or the lands only, of a debtor [Law]. **extent in aid,** a writ issued against a debtor of the Crown [Law]. (O.Fr. *extente.*)
extenuate, *v.t.* eks-*ten*-yew-ate, to lessen; to palliate; to diminish the seriousness of; to make excuse for. (L. *extenuatus*, thinned.)
extenuating, *a.* eks-*ten*-yew-ay-ting, palliating.
extenuation, *n.* eks-*ten*-yew-*ay*-shon, the act or the process of underrating, or of representing anything as being less wrong, faulty, or criminal than it is. (L. *extenuatio.*)
extenuative, *a.* and *n.* eks-*ten*-yew-a-tiv, serving to, or that which serves to, extenuate.
extenuator, *n.* eks-*ten*-yew-*ay*-tor, one who extenuates; an apologist.
extenuatory, *a.* *eks*-ten-yew-*ay*-to-re, palliative.
exterior, *a.* eks-*teer*-re-or, external; outward; on the outside; extrinsic; foreign; relating to foreign nations: *n.* the outward surface; that which is external. (L. comparative of *exter*, outer.)
exteriority, *n.* eks-*teer*-re-*o*-re-te, externality; undue regard for the external form.
exteriorize, *v.t.* eks-*teer*-re-o-rize, to make exterior; to externalize.
exteriorly, *ad.* eks-*teer*-re-or-le, outwardly; superficially.
exterminate, *v.t.* eks-*ter*-min-ate, to destroy utterly; to root out; to extirpate. (L. *exterminatus*, expelled.)
extermination, *n.* *eks*-ter-min-*ay*-shon, the act of exterminating; total destruction; extirpation.
exterminator, *n.* eks-*ter*-min-*ay*-tor, he who or that which exterminates.
exterminatory, *a.* eks-*ter*-min-a-to-re, serving to exterminate.
extern, *a.* eks-*tern*, external; not inherent: *n.* outward form; a non-resident student. (Fr. *externe.*)
external, *a.* eks-*ter*-nal, pertaining to or situated on the outside; outward; exterior; from without; not being within; objective; relating to or connected with foreign nations; not essential: *n.* an external part: *pl.* non-essentials. (L. *externus*, external.)
externalism, *n.* eks-*ter*-na-lizm, excessive devotion to externals, esp. in religion.
externality, *n.* eks-ter-*nal*-e-te, the state of being external, esp. as regards the perceiving mind or the idea at bottom.
externalization, *n.* eks-*ter*-na-ly-*zay*-shon, embodiment in outward form.
externalize, *v.t.* eks-*ter*-na-lize, to make external or endue with external form; to treat as consisting of externals.
externally, *ad.* outwardly; in appearance.
exterritorial, *a.* eks-te-re-*taw*-re-al, outside the jurisdiction of the country; extraterritorial.
extinct, *a.* eks-*tinkt*, extinguished; no longer active (of volcanoes); having died out or ceased to exist [Zool. and Bot.]. (L. *extinctus*, extinguished.)
extincteur, *n.* (App.), a fire-extinguisher. (Fr.)

extinction, *n.* eks-*tink*-shon, the act of extinguishing; the state of being extinguished; suppression.
extine, *n. eks*-tin, outer coat of pollen-grain [Bot.].
extinguish, *v.t.* eks-*ting*-gwish, to put out; to end; to quench; to destroy; to suppress; to obscure by superior splendour. (L. *exstinguo*, quench.)
extinguishable, *a.* eks-*ting*-gwish-a-bl, that may be quenched, destroyed, or suppressed.
extinguisher, *n.* eks-*ting*-gwish-er, a conical cap with which to extinguish a candle, etc.
extinguishment, *n.* eks-*ting*-gwish-ment, extinction, esp. of an existing right by means of its being merged in or consolidated with another [Law].
extirpate, *v.t. eks*-ter-pate, to root out; to destroy totally, as weeds; to cut out or remove completely [Surg.]. (L. *exstirpatus*, rooted out.)
extirpation, *n.* eks-ter-*pay*-shon, the act of rooting out; eradication; excision.
extirpator, *n. eks*-ter-pay-tor, one who roots out; an agricultural machine for extirpating weeds.
extol, *v.t.* eks-*tol or* eks-*tole*, to praise highly, to magnify or glorify. (O.Fr. *extoller*.)
extoller, *n.* eks-*tole*-er, one who praises or magnifies.
extort, *v.t.* eks-*tawrt*, to force, wrest, or obtain from unjustly or illegally; to exact. (L. *extortus*, twisted.)
extortion, *n.* eks-*tawr*-shon, the act of extorting; oppressive or illegal exaction; that which is unduly exacted.
extortionary, *a.* eks-*tawr*-shon-a-re, pertaining to, or addicted to, extortion.
extortionate, *a.* eks-*tawr*-shon-ate, marked by extortion; exorbitant.
extortioner, *n.* eks-*tawr*-shon-er, one who practises extortion.
extortionist, *n.* eks-*tawr*-shon-ist, an extortioner.
extra, *a. eks*-tra, beyond what is agreed upon or what is usual; additional: *n.* something in addition to what is agreed upon or looked for as customary; an addition to the fixed charge: *pl.* byes, wides, and no-balls at cricket.
extra-, *eks*-tra, Latin prefix denoting outside of, beyond usual, or in excess.
extra-cosmical, *a.* outside the universe.
extract, *v.t.* eks-*trakt*, to draw out by force; to draw out, as the spirit or essence of a thing, by heat, distillation, or otherwise; to take out or select a part from, as a passage from a book or writing. **extract the root,** to find the root of a number or quantity [Math.]. (L. *extractus*, dragged out.)
extract, *n. eks*-trakt, that which is extracted; a passage taken from a book or writing; anything drawn from a substance; a solution containing one or more substances removed from a mixture by means of a solvent; a substance forming the essence of anything, or a preparation containing this.
extractable, *a.* eks-*trak*-ta-bl, that may be extracted; suitable for quotation.
extraction, *n.* eks-*trak*-shon, the act of extracting; derivation from a stock or family; lineage; birth; the operation of extracting. (L. *extractus*.)
extractive, *a.* eks-*trak*-tiv, serving to extract; that is or may be extracted: *n.* an extractive substance; the principle forming the basis in extracts [Chem.].
extractor, *n.* eks-*trak*-tor, he who or that which extracts; a forceps or instrument for extracting, used in midwifery, dentistry, etc. [Surg.].
extraditable, *a. eks*-tra-*dite*-a-bl, subject to extradition; rendering liable to extradition.
extradite, *v.t. eks*-tra-dite, to deliver up under a treaty of extradition; to secure the extradition of. (L. *ex-*, and *traditus*, delivered up.)
extradition, *n. eks*-tra-*dish*-on, delivery by one government to another of fugitives from justice. (Fr.)
extrados, *n.* eks-*tray*-dos, the upper or exterior curve of an arch [Arch.]. (Fr.)
extra-foraneous, *a. eks*-tra-fo-*ray*-ne-us, out-of-door. (L. *extra-*, and *foris*, out of doors.)
extragalactic, *a.* eks-tra-ga-*lak*-tik, outside the Milky Way [Astron.].
extra-illustrate, *v.t.* to grangerize.
extrajudicial, *a. eks*-tra-joo-*dish*-al, out of the proper court or the ordinary course of legal procedure.
extrality, *n.* eks-*tral*-e-te, extraterritoriality.
extramundane, *a. eks*-tra-*mun*-dane, beyond the limits of the material world. (L. *extramundanus*.)
extramural, *a. eks*-tra-*mewr*-ral, outside the walls, esp. of a city or university. (L. *extra-*, and *murus*, wall.)
extraneity, *n.* eks-tra-*nee*-e-te, the state or quality of being extraneous.
extraneous, *a.* eks-*tray*-ne-us, foreign; not belonging to a thing; not intrinsic; not essential; not properly belonging to the subject (L. *extraneus*.)
extraneously, *ad.* in an extraneous manner.
extra-official, *a.* not within the limits of official duty.
extraordinarily, *ad. eks*-tra-*or*-din-a-re-le, in a manner or degree beyond ordinary.
extraordinariness, *n. eks*-tra-*or*-din-a-re-ness, uncommonness; remarkableness.
extraordinary, *a. eks*-tra-*or*-din-a-re, unusual; exceeding the common degree or measure; remarkable; rare; wonderful; special; sent for a special purpose or on a particular occasion [Diplomacy]. (L. *extraordinarius*.)
extra-parochial, *a.* not within the limits of any parish; outside the parish.
extra-physical, *a.* outside the province or methods of physics.
extrapolate, *v.t.* and *i. eks*-tra-po-late *or* eks-*trap*-o-late, to obtain by, or to practise, extrapolation.
extrapolation, *n. eks*-tra-po-*lay*-shon *or* eks-*trap*-o-lay-shon, the calculation of unknown statistics, values, etc., from evidence derived from a known and correlated series [Math.].
extra-professional, *a.* foreign to a profession; not within the ordinary limits of professional duty.
extra-special, *n.* the latest edition of an evening paper; *a.* exceptionally good.
extra-spectral, *a.* beyond the visible spectrum.
extra-terrestrial, *a.* beyond the earth or its atmosphere.
extraterritorial, *a. eks*-tra-te-re-*taw*-re-al, beyond the limits of the local jurisdiction.
extraterritoriality, *n. eks*-tra-te-re-*taw*-re-*al*-e-te, the state of being not subject to the ordinary laws of the country to which they are accredited enjoyed by ambassadors and certain diplomatic agents.
extra-tropical, *a.* beyond the tropics; outside the tropics, north or south.
extravagance, *n.* eks-*trav*-a-gance, the state or quality of being extravagant; an extravagant act; irregularity; excess; excess in the expenditure of money or one's means. (Fr.)
extravagancy, *n.* eks-*trav*-a-gan-se, extravagance.
extravagant, *a.* eks-*trav*-a-gant, excessive; exceeding due bounds; profuse in expenses; unreasonable; irregular; wasteful; fantastic. (Fr.)
extravagantly, *ad.* in an extravagant manner.
extravagantness, *n.* extravagance.
extravaganza, *n.* eks-*trav*-a-*gan*-za, a musical composition distinguished by its absurdity and irregularity; any wild, wayward flight of fancy. (It.)
extravagate, *v.t.* eks-*trav*-a-gate, to wander beyond due limits.
extravasate, *v.t.* eks-*trav*-a-sate, to let or force out of the proper vessels [Med.]. (L. *vas*, vessel.)
extravasation, *n.* eks-trav-a-*say*-shon, the act of forcing or letting out of its proper vessels any body-fluids, esp. blood, through their rupture or injury; the escape of such fluid from its vessel; effusion; the state of being extravasated [Med.].
extravascular, *a.* eks-tra-*vas*-kew-lar, outside the vascular system [Anat.].
extravert, *n. eks*-tra-vert, an extrovert.
extreme, *a.* eks-*treem*, outermost; furthest off; most pressing; worst or best that can exist or be supposed; last; beyond which there is none; going extreme lengths: *n.* the utmost limit; end; furthest degree; extremity; the extreme terms of a syllogism, the predicate and subject of the conclusion, as distinct from the middle term with which they are compared in the premises [Logic]; the first and last terms of a proportion [Math.]. **extreme unction,** the sacrament of anointing a person believed to be about to die with oil. (O.Fr. from L. *extremus*, superlative of *exterus*, outward.)
extremely, *ad.* in the utmost degree.
extremeness, *n.* eks-*treem*-ness, the quality of being extreme.
extremism, *n.* eks-*treem*-izm, disposition to go to extremes; revolutionism.
extremist, *n.* eks-*treem*-ist, a supporter of extreme doctrines or procedure; a diehard; a revolutionist.
extremity, *n.* eks-*trem*-e-te, the utmost point or

limit; the utmost or highest degree; extreme or utmost distress, straits, or difficulties; the end: *pl.* the feet and hands. (Fr. *extrémité.*)
extricable, *a.* *eks*-trik-a-bl, that can be extricated.
extricate, *v.t.* *eks*-tre-kate, to disengage; to disentangle; to free from difficulties or perplexities. (L. *extricatus*, extricated.)
extrication, *n.* eks-tre-*kay*-shon, the act of extricating; disembarrassment.
extrinsic, *a.* eks-*trin*-sik, external; outward; not contained in or belonging to a body; foreign; not essential. (L. *extrinsecus.*)
extrinsicality, *n.* eks-*trin*-se-*kal*-e-te, the state of being extrinsical.
extrinsically, *ad.* in an extrinsic manner.
extrorse, *a.* eks-*trorse*, opening away from the centre of the flower [Bot.]. (Fr.)
extrospection, *n.* eks-tro-*spek*-shun, interest in, or examination of, matters outside oneself in the reverse of introspection.
extrospective, *a.* eks-tro-*spek*-tiv, given to extrospection.
extroversion, *n.* eks-tro-*ver*-shon, the condition of being turned inside out [Med.]; the opposite of introversion [Psychan.]. (L. *extra-*, and *versum*, turned.)
extrovert, *n.* *eks*-tro-vert, one whose habit is extrospective as opposed to introspective [Psychan.].
extrude, *v.t.* eks-*trood*, to thrust out; to press or force out; to expel. (L. *extrudo*, thrust.)
extrusion, *n.* eks-*troo*-zhon, the act of extruding; violent expulsion; protrusion from within.
extrusive, *a.* eks-*troo*-siv, thrusting, or tending to thrust, out; forced out at the surface (as volcanic rocks) [Geol.].
extuberant, *a.* eks-*tew*-be-rant, swelling out; protuberant.
exuberance, *n.* eks-*yew*-be-rance, an overflowing richness, as of fertility or imagination; luxuriance; overgrowth. (L. *exuberantia.*)
exuberancy, *n.* eks-*yew*-be-ran-se, exuberance.
exuberant, *a.* eks-*yew*-be-rant, abundant; overabundant; superfluous; luxuriant.
exuberantly, *ad.* in great plenty; to a superfluous degree.
exuberate, *v.i.* eks-*yew*-be-rate, to abound; to enjoy or indulge in freely.
exudate, *n.* *eks*-yew-date, a substance discharged by exudation.
exudation, *n.* eks-yew-*day*-shon, the act of exuding; sweating; the matter exuded.
exude, *v.t.* eks-*yewd*, to give off; to discharge through pores, as sweat, or through incisions, as the juices of a plant: *v.i.* to flow from by exudation; to ooze out. (L. *exsudo*, sweat.)
exult, *v.i.* eks-*ult*, to rejoice exceedingly at success or victory; to triumph. (L. *exsulto*, leap.)
exultancy, *n.* eks-*ult*-an-se, exultation.
exultant, *a.* eks-*ult*-ant, rejoicing triumphantly; displaying exultation.
exultantly, *ad.* in an exultant manner.
exultation, *n.* eks-ul-*tay*-shon, lively joy at success, victory, or advantage gained; rapturous delight; triumph.
exultingly, *ad.* in an exulting manner.
exuviæ, *n.pl.* eks-*yew*-ve-e, the cast-off skins, shells, or coverings of animals. (L.)
exuvial, *a.* eks-*yew*-ve-al, pertaining to, resembling, or containing exuviæ.
exuviate, *v.t.* eks-*yew*-ve-ate, to shed exuviæ; to moult. (L. *exuo*, strip.)
exuviation, *n.* eks-*yew*-ve-*ay*-shon, the action or process of exuviating.
ex-voto, *n.* eks-*voh*-to (*pl.* **ex-votos**), a votive offering. (L., on account of a vow.)
eyas, *n.* eye-as, an unfledged hawk not yet able to prey for itself. (Fr. *nidis.*)
eyas-musket, *n.* an unfledged sparrow-hawk.
⋆**eye,** *n.* eye, the organ of sight; the eyeball; the socket containing this; the power of vision; sight; view; countenance; look; mien; observation; watch; oversight; inspection; anything resembling the eye in form; a small hole or aperture; a round window; a small catch for a hook; a loop or ring for fastening the rigging of ships; the bud of a plant; the centre, esp. of a target: *v.t.* to fix the eye on; to look on; to view; to observe or watch narrowly. **an eye for an eye,** strict retaliation. **eye of a dome,** the horizontal aperture on its summit, usually covered with a lantern. **in the wind's eye,** directly against the wind. **mind's eye,** mental perception. **to be all eyes,** to be anxiously on the watch. **to find favour in the eyes,** to be graciously received and treated. **to give the glad eye to,** to try to allure by glances one of the opposite sex [Slang]. **to keep an eye on,** to watch closely; to see that all goes well. **to see eye to eye,** to be in perfect agreement with. **to set the eyes on,** to see; to have a sight of. **up to the eyes,** deeply engaged or immersed in, etc. *p.* and *pp.* **eyed.** *ppr.* **eyeing.** (A.S. *eage.*)
eyeball, *n.* *eye*-bawl, the globe or apple of the eye.
eye-bolt, *n.* a bar with an eye at one end used for fastening ropes, etc. [Naut.].
eyebright, *n.* *eye*-brite, a euphrasy, a little plant formerly used in eye complaints.
eyebrow, *n.* *eye*-brou, the hairy arch above the eye.
eyed, *a.* ide, having eyes, as black-eyed.
eyeflap, *n.* *eye*-flap, a blinker on a horse's harness.
eyeful, *n.* *eye*-ful, a completely satisfying sight [Coll.].
eyeglass, *n.* *eye*-glahs, a glass to assist the sight; a monocle; the glass next the eye in an optical instrument; a cup-shaped vessel for applying washes, etc., to the eye.
eyehole, *n.* *eye*-hole, a hole to peep through; the socket containing the eye.
eyelash, *n.* *eye*-lash, the line of hair edging the eyelid; a single hair of this.
eyeless, *a.* *eye*-less, wanting eyes; destitute of sight.
eyelet, *n.* *eye*-let, a small hole or perforation to receive a lace or small rope or cord; a loophole; an ocellus. (O.Fr. *oeillet*, a small eye.)
eyelet-hole, *n.* the hole of an eyelet; a small aperture; a loophole.
eyelid, *n.* *eye*-lid, the upper or lower movable cover of the eye.
eye-opener, *n.* a revelation; a surprising discovery; anything startling.
eyepiece, *n.* *eye*-peece, the lens, or combination of lenses with which the image is viewed in an optical instrument.
eyepit, *n.* *eye*-pit, the socket of the eye.
eyer, *n.* *eye*-er, one who eyes another; one who makes eyes in needles, etc.
eye-salve, *n.* ointment for the eye.
eyeshot, *n.* *eye*-shot, range of vision; view.
eyesight, *n.* *eye*-site, the sight of the eye; vision; observation; the sense of seeing.
eyesore, *n.* *eye*-sawr, anything offensive to the sight.
eyesplice, *n.* *eye*-splice, a loop formed by splicing the end of a rope into itself [Naut.].
eyespot, *n.* *eye*-spot, a spot like an eye, as on a peacock's feather; a rudimentary eye.
eyestrings, *n.pl.* *eye*-strings, the muscles and tendons by which the eye is moved.
eyetooth, *n.* *eye*-tooth, one of the upper canine teeth.
eyewash, *n.* *eye*-wosh, a lotion for the eyes; deception; humbug; flattery.
eyewater, *n.* *eye*-waw-ter, a lotion for the eyes.
eyewitness, *n.* *eye*-wit-ness, one who saw a thing done.
eyne, *n.* ine, obsolete plural of eye.
eyot, *n.* ait, an islet in a river or a lake; an ait.
eyra, *n.* *eye*-rah, a small wild cat of South America, *Felis eyra*, remarkable for its long body, short legs and long tail. (Native name.)
eyre, *n.* air, a journey or circuit; a court of itinerant justices. **justices in eyre,** a former body of itinerant justices. (O.Fr. *eire*, a journey.)
eyrie, *n.* *ire*-er, the nest of a bird of prey; an aerie.

F

F the sixth letter of the English alphabet, has one uniform sound, as in *father, after*, except in *of* (and *thereof*, etc.), when it has the sound of *f*'s corresponding voiced spirant, *v*. F or *fah* (Italian *fa*). in music is the fourth note in the natural scale.
fabaceous, *a.* fa-*bay*-shus, of the *Fabaceæ*, or bean family; resembling a bean.
Fabian, *a. fay*-be-an, awaiting opportunity; wary and wearying out with delay, in imitation of the policy adopted by the Roman general Fabius Maximus against Hannibal: *n.* a member of the Fabian Society, a political group propagating socialism by permeation rather than by direct action, founded in 1884.
Fabianism, *n. fay*-be-a-nizm, the form of socialism advocated by the Fabian Society.
fable, *n. fay*-bl, a story in which inferior creatures are usually introduced and speak and act like human beings in order to enforce some moral lesson; an apologue; the plot, or connected series of events, in an epic or dramatic poem; a fabrication: *v.i.* to write fables; to tell falsehoods: *v.t.* to devise and speak of as true or real. (Fr.)
fabled, *a. fay*-bld, celebrated in fables; legendary; fictitious.
fabler, *n. fay*-bler, a writer of fables.
fabliau, *n. fab*-le-o (*pl.* **fabliaux**), a short metrical tale for recitation, popular in France about the 12th and 13th cents., dealing in an epigrammatic vein with current topics.
fabric, *n. fab*-rik, anything framed by art and labour; structure; texture; a woven structure; a building, as an edifice; any system composed of connected parts; mode or construction or workmanship. (Fr. *fabrique.*)
fabricant, *n. fab*-re-kant, a manufacturer. (Fr.)
fabricate, *v.t. fab*-rik-ate, to form by art and labour; to manufacture; to put together sections made elsewhere; to forge; to devise falsely. (L. *fabricatus.*)
fabrication, *n. fab*-re-*kay*-shon, construction; manufacture; forgery; that which is fabricated; something trumped up; a falsehood.
fabricator, *n. fab*-re-kay-tor, one who fabricates; a flint tool of the Stone Age.
fabulist, *n. fab*-yew-list, an inventor or writer of fables; an inventor of falsehoods.
fabulize, *v.i. fab*-yew-lize, to invent, relate, or speak in fables.
fabulosity, *n.* fab-yew-*los*-e-te, fabulousness; a fable; a fictitious story.
fabulous, *a. fab*-yew-lus, fictitious; related or celebrated in fable; invented; unreal; as incredible as a fable. **the fabulous age,** the age in which myth and legend served as history. (L. *fabulosus.*)
fabulously, *ad.* in a fabulous manner.
fabulousness, *n.* the quality of being fabulous.
façade, *n.* fa-*sahd*, the front view or elevation of a building; a building's principal front. (Fr.)
***face,** *n.* face, the surface or side which presents itself to the view; the front of a thing; the front part of the head; the visage; aspect of the face; look; look, as of anger or favour; the plane surface or side of a solid; visible state; appearance; confidence; effrontery; presence; sight; the dial of a timekeeper; the operative surface of a tool, implement, etc.; an exposed surface in mine-workings. **face cards,** the king, queen, and knave. **face to face,** in immediate presence. **face value,** nominal value; apparent value. **in the face of,** in spite of. **to lose face,** to suffer a loss in dignity. **to make faces,** to distort the features. **to save one's face,** to preserve one's prestige or dignity. **to set the face against,** to oppose. (Fr.)
face, *v.t.* face, to meet in front; to oppose with firmness; to resist, or to meet for the purpose of stopping or opposing; to stand with the face or front toward; to cover in front; to smooth the surface of; to make appear of superior quality: *v.i.* to look in a certain direction; to turn the face. **to face down,** to oppose boldly or impudently. **to face out,** to brave unblushingly. **to face the enemy,** to meet him in front, and oppose him with determination. **to face the music,** to meet unpleasantness resolutely. **to face up to,** to meet boldly.
faced, *a.* fayst, with a face; face upwards; covered in front; dressed on the surface.
face-guard, *n.* defensive guard for the face.
face-hammer, *n.* a hammer with a flat peen.
face-lifting, *n.*, a minor operation performed in beauty-parlours for the elimination of wrinkles, etc.
facer, *n. face*-er, a blow in the face; an unlooked-for setback; a serious difficulty.
facet, *n. fas*-et, a small surface; the plane surface of a crystal, or one artificially cut; an individual segment of a compound eye [Entom.]; a facette: *v.t.* to cut facets on. (Fr. *facette*, a tiny face.)
faceted, *a. fas*-e-ted, having facets.
facetiæ, *n.pl.* fa-*see*-she-e, witticisms conceived in a spirit of pleasantry; curious or indecent books.
facetious, *a.* fa-*see*-shus, overflowing with wit and good humour; full of pleasantry; witty; jocose. (L. *facetia*, wit.)
facetiously, *ad.* in a facetious way.
facetiousness, *n.* the quality of being facetious.
facette, *n.* fa-*set*, a flat projection between the flutings of a column [Arch.].
facia, *n. fay*-she-a, the name-board over a shop-window; a flat projecting band or fillet [Arch.]. (L. *fascia*, band.)
facial, *a. fay*-shal, pertaining to the face. **the facial angle,** the angle formed by the intersection of a line drawn (1) horizontally from the nostril to the ear with one drawn perpendicularly from the nostril to the most prominent part of the forehead, or (2) over the most prominent parts of the face with one from the occipital condyle to the base of the nose. (Late L. *facialis.*)
facially, *ad.* with reference to the face.
facies, *n. fay*-she-es, external appearance; facial expression [Path.]; aspect, among the rocks and their contents, of any area or period [Geol.]. (L.)
facile, *a. fas*-ile, easy to be done; easily conquerable; easy of access or converse; easily persuaded; pliant ready. (Fr.)
facilitate, *v.t.* fas-*sil*-e-tate, to make easy or less difficult; to lessen the labour of. (Fr. *faciliter.*)
facilitation, *n.* fa-*sil*-e-*tay*-shon, the act of facilitating.
facility, *n.* fa-*sil*-e-te, ease of performance; dexterity proceeding from practice; easiness of access; pliability; means by which anything is rendered easy; convenient opportunity. (Fr. *facilité.*)
facing, *a. face*-ing, fronting: *n.* a covering in front for ornament, defence, etc.; the cuff and collar of a coat: *pl.* movements to the right, left, etc. [Mil.]; trimmings on uniforms [Mil.]; adulteration (esp. of tea) to disguise inferior quality.
facinorous, *a.* fa-*sin*-o-rus (in Shakespeare **facinerious**), infamous, atrocious. (L. *facinus*, a bad deed.)
facsimile, *n.* fak-*sim*-e-le, an exact reproduction, as of handwriting, etc.: *v.t.* to copy exactly. (L. *fac simile*, make thou like.)
facsimilist, *n.* fak-*sim*-e-list, one who makes facsimiles.
***fact,** *n.* fakt, a deed or anything done; an event or anything that comes to pass; reality; truth; the assertion of a thing as a fact. (L. *factum*, done.)
factice, *n. fak*-tis, a rubber substitute and ingredient prepared by vulcanizing vegetable oils with sulphur or sulphur chloride. (Fr., artificial.)
faction, *n. fak*-shon, a combination of persons, esp. a political party acting for purposes of their own in opposition to the government or public good; a clique; tumult; dissension. (Fr.)
factional, *a. fak*-shon-al, pertaining to a faction; characterized by faction.

factionary, *n.* *fak*-shon-a-re, a member of a faction; *a.* pertaining to or taking part in a faction.
factionist, *n.* *fak*-shon-ist, one who promotes faction; a factionary.
factious, *a.* *fak*-shus, given to faction; pertaining to or proceeding from faction; turbulent. (L. *factiosus.*)
factiously, *ad.* in a factious manner.
factiousness, *n.* the spirit of faction; tendency to oppose.
factitious, *a.* fak-*tish*-us, produced by art, not nature; artificial; got up. (L. *factitus,* artificial.)
factitiously, *ad.* in a factitious manner.
factitiousness, *n.* the quality of being factitious.
factitive, *a.* *fak*-te-tiv, causative; producing a change in the condition; applied to the relationship between an active verb and its object when the former has a causative effect, as in "Manners make the man."
factor, *n.* *fak*-tor, an agent; a dealer; a steward; one of the quantities from the multiplication of which is obtained the product [Math.]; anything contributing to a result. **coal factor,** a middleman between colliery and wholesaler. **factor of safety,** the ratio that the breaking load bears to the working load in any structure. (L., a doer.)
factorage, *n.* *fak*-to-raj, the service of, or commission paid to, a factor.
factorial, *a.* fak-*taw*-re-al, pertaining to factors [Math.], or to a factor or steward: *n.* the product of a series of factors in arithmetical progression; the product of an integer multiplied into its lower integers.
factorize, *v.t.* *fak*-to-rize, to resolve into factors [Math.]; to attach goods belonging to a debtor in the hands of a third person [U.S.A.].
factory, *n.* *fak*-to-re, a manufactory; a trading settlement abroad; the body of traders in a trading settlement. **factory hand,** a person employed in a factory. (Fr. *factorie.*)
factotum, *n.* fak-*toh*-tum, a person employed to do all kinds of work; a confidential servant. (L. *factotum,* do all.)
factual, *a.* *fak*-tew-al, pertaining to facts; real.
factum, *n.* *fak*-tum (*pl.* **facta**), a deed; anything stated and made certain [Law]. (L.)
facula, *n.* *fak*-yew-la (*pl.* **faculæ,** -lee), a very bright spot on the sun's disk [Astron.]. (L., a little torch.)
facular, *a.* *fak*-yew-lar, pertaining to faculæ.
facultative, *a.* *fak*-ul-tay-tiv, imparting, or pertaining to, a faculty; permissive; optional.
faculty, *n.* *fak*-ul-te, the ability to do anything or to perform any action, natural, vital, or animal; the skill derived from practice, or practice aided by nature; special power; privilege; a right, power, or authorization granted to a person; the individuals constituting a learned profession, or a branch of one; the graduates of certain universities; one of the departments of a university. **the faculty,** the medical profession. **the Faculty of Advocates,** in Scotland, the incorporated body of barristers, headed by the **Dean of the Faculty.** (Fr. *faculté.*)
fad, *n.* fad, a hobby; a crotchet; a craze. (Origin unknown.)
faddiness, *n.* the state of being faddy.
faddish, *a.* *fad*-dish, prone to be faddy.
faddishness, *n.* the state of being faddish.
faddist, *n.* *fad*-dist, one given to fads.
faddy, *a.* *fad*-de, given to fads; crotchety.
fade, *v.i.* fade, to wither, as a plant; to lose strength, freshness, colour, or lustre gradually; to perish or disappear gradually: *v.t.* to cause to become faded. **to fade in** or **out,** to cause a picture on the screen to become more and more or less and less distinct [Cinema]. (Fr. *fade,* insipid.)
fadeless, *a.* *fade*-less, unfading.
fadge, *v.i.* faj, to suit; to fit; to agree; to jog along. (Origin unknown.)
fæcal, *a.* *fee*-kal, consisting of fæces; excremental.
fæces, *n.pl.* *fee*-seez, the excrements of animals; sediment; dregs. (L.)
fæcula, *n.* *fee*-kew-la, fecula.
faerie, *n.* and *a.* *fay*-e-re, fairy; fairyland; visionary.
fag, *n.* fag, one who labours as a drudge; a schoolboy whose duty it is to do odd jobs for a senior; a fag-end; the stub of a cigar; an inferior cigarette [Slang]: *v.t.* to tire out; to work (a boy) as a fag: *v.i.* to drudge as a fag; to labour to weariness; to become weary. (Perhaps from *flag.*)
fagaceous, *a.* fa-*gay*-shus, belonging to the beech family; resembling the beech [Bot.]. (L. *fagus,* beech.)
fag-end, *n.* *fag*-end, the end of a web of cloth, generally of coarser materials; the latter or meaner part of anything; the untwisted end of a rope [Naut.]. **to fag out,** to become untwisted [Naut.].
fagging, *n.* *fag*-ging, enforced drudging for another.
faggot, *n.* *fag*-got, a bundle of sticks, twigs, or small branches of trees, used for fuel, in road-making, filling ditches, etc.; anything like a bundle of dry sticks; a bundle of iron or steel for re-manufacture; a slatternly or disreputable old woman; a sausage of pig's liver, etc., seasoned and baked: *v.t.* to bind in a bundle or as a faggot. **faggot vote,** a vote formerly created by the nominal transfer of land to one unqualified to vote. (Fr. *fagot.*)
fagine, *n.* *fay*-jin, a narcotic substance obtained from beech-nuts of the common beech. (L. *fagus,* a beech-tree.)
fagotto, *n.* fa-*got*-to, the bassoon. (It.)
fahlerz, *n.* *fah*-lairts, grey copper ore, tetrahedrite. (Ger. *fahl,* fawn-coloured, *erz,* ore.)
Fahrenheit, *a.* *fahr*-en-hite, pertaining to the thermometric scale, which fixes the freezing-point at 32° and the boiling-point at 212°: *n.* this scale, or a thermometer read by it. (G. D. *Fahrenheit,* Ger. inventor, *d.* 1736.)
faience, *n.* (App.), a kind of glazed pottery embellished with painted designs, said to have been first manufactured at Faenza, in Romagna.
fail, *n.* fale, omission; failure. *v.i.* to become deficient; to cease to be abundant; to be wanting in; to decay; to sink; to become weaker; to be entirely wanting; to cease; to perish; to die; not to produce the effect; to miscarry; to be neglectful; to be unsuccessful, as in an examination; to become insolvent or bankrupt: *v.t.* to desert; to disappoint; to cease or neglect to afford aid, supply, or strength; to be wanting to; not to perform. (Fr. *faillir.*)
failing, *a.* *fale*-ing, decaying; declining; becoming insolvent: *n.* the act of failing; a foible; an imperfection: *prep.* in default of.
faille *n.* fale *or* fay, a fine corded silk fabric. (Fr.)
failure, *n.* *fale*-yur, a failing; deficiency; cessation of supply; omission; non-performance; decay, or defect from decay; want of success; insolvency.
fain, *a.* fane, glad; inclined; content for want of something better: *ad.* gladly; with joy or pleasure: *v.i.* to wish or desire. (A.S. *fægen,* joyful.)
fainéant, *a.* fa-nay-*ahn* (*see* App.), do-nothing, applied to certain weak Merovingian kings of France who were subject to the mayors of the palace: *n.* any one of these kings; an idler. (Fr.)
faint, *a.* faynt, weak; feeble; enfeebled with exhaustion; inclined to swoon; not bright or vivid; not loud; not striking; cowardly; not vigorous; not active; dejected: *v.i.* to become feeble; to swoon; to lose courage or spirit. (Fr. *feint,* unreal.)
faint-hearted, *a.* faynt-*har*-ted, timorous; easily depressed or yielding to fear.
faintish, *a.* *faynt*-ish, slightly faint.
faintly, *ad.* *faynt*-le, in a faint or feeble manner.
faintness, *n.* *faynt*-ness, the state of being faint.
fair, *a.* fare, clear; free from blemish; free from a dark hue; pleasing to the eye; beautiful; handsome; pure; light-haired; free from clouds or rain; favourable; prosperous; unobstructed; open; open to attack or access; frank; honest; just; equitable; not effected by insidious or unlawful methods; not foul; candid; not sophistical; honourable; civil; pleasing; moderately good; plain; legible; *ad.* openly; frankly; civilly; candidly; honestly; equitably; happily; successfully; on good terms; *n.* a beautiful woman: *v.t.* to become fair (of the weather). **fair and square,** just in dealing; honest. **fair copy,** a copy made after final correction. **fair play,** even-handed justice. **fair trade,** reciprocity; free trade with countries only in so far as they allow free imports. **fair wind,** a wind that does not make it necessary for a vessel to tack. **the fair,** women generally, the one who is fair or fairest. **to bid fair,** to be. (A.S. *fæger.*)
fair, *n.* fare, a stated market in a particular town or city; a stated meeting of buyers and sellers for trade. **fancy fair,** a sale or bazaar of fancy

articles, etc., for social, religious, or charitable purposes. (O.Fr. *feire.*)
fairing, *n. fare*-ring, a present bought at a fair.
fairing, *n. fare*-ring, a structural addition to an aircraft to reduce head-resistance; streamlining.
fairish, *a. fare*-rish, reasonably fair.
fairly, *ad. fare*-le, in a fair manner; clearly; completely; nearly; moderately.
fair-minded, *a.* impartial; judging fairly.
fairness, *n. fare*-ness, the quality or character of being fair.
fair-seeming, *a.* appearing fair.
fair-spoken, *a.* using fair speech; bland.
fairway, *n. fare*-way, the navigation channel of a river; the smooth way between rough and hazards, from green to green, on a golf course.
fairweather, *a. fare*-weth-er, unfit for storm or trouble; active or of service only in time of prosperity.
fairy, *n. fare*-re, a supernatural being of diminutive size, fabled to assume human form, dance in meadows, steal infants, and play pranks in a spirit of humour rather than mischief; an enchantress: *a.* of or belonging to fairies; fairylike; unreal. **fairy godmother,** a very generous friend. (O.Fr. *faerie,* magic.)
fairydom, *n. fare*-re-dom, fairyland.
fairy-fingers, *n.* the foxglove.
fairyhood, *n. fare*-re-hood, the state of being a fairy; fairies collectively.
fairyism, *n. fare*-re-izm, belief in fairies; fairy character; enchantment.
fairyland, *n. fare*-re-land, the imaginary abode of the fairies; an enchanted region.
fairylike, *a. fare*-re-like, resembling a fairy; imitating the manner of fairies.
fairy-ring, *n. fare*-re-ring, an annular band of grass differently coloured from that in which it grows due to the action of subterranean fungi, formerly thought to be caused by the dancing of fairies.
fairy-tale, *n. fare*-re-tale, a tale about fairies; an incredible fiction; a fib.
faith, *n.* fayth, belief or trust in the statement or word of another, such that we accept and act upon it with full assurance; belief without proof; belief or trust in a religious system, as extending into and pervading the unseen; that which is believed; the religion believed in; fidelity; word or honour pledged; credibility or truth: *int.* on my faith; in truth. **faith cure,** faith-healing. **in good faith,** honestly. (O.Fr. *feid.*)
faithful, *a. fayth*-ful, full of faith; loyal to one's faith, duty, engagement, promise, or vow, etc.; conformable to truth; true; accurate; worthy of belief. **the faithful,** those who are loyal to their religious belief.
faithfully, *ad.* in a faithful manner.
faithfulness, *n.* the quality of being faithful.
faith-healing, *n. fayth*-heel-ing, the practice of attempting to cure sickness by faith and prayer without the use of drugs, surgery, or medical science.
faithless, *a. fayth*-less, destitute of faith; not believing; disloyal; not true to one's engagement, promise, or vow, etc.; inconstant; deceptive.
faithlessly, *ad.* in a faithless manner.
faithlessness, *n.* the quality or state of being faithless.
faix, *int.* fayks, by my faith; verily [Irish].
fake, *n.* fake, a dodge; a cheat; one of the coils of a cable or hawser [Naut.]: *v.t.* to counterfeit or make a counterfeit of; to doctor; to falsify; to cheat [Slang]; to coil a rope or cable.
fakement, *n. fake*-ment, a makeshift; a contrivance; a counterfeit article.
faker, *n. fake*-er, one who fakes, esp. furniture, antiques, etc.
fakir, *n.* fa-*keer,* a member of a Moslem sect of mendicants and ascetics, esp. in India; one who practises or affects a life of self-mortification; a magician; a conjurer. (Ar. *fakir,* poor.)
Falangist, *n.* fa-*lan*-jist, a member of the party in Spain analogous to the Fascists of Italy. (Sp. *falange,* phalanx.)
falbala, *n. fal*-ba-la, a trimming; a furbelow.
falcate, *a. fal*-kate, bent like a sickle, as the moon, crescent or waning; hooked [Bot.]. (L. *falcatus,* furnished with scythes.)
falcated, *a. fal*-kay-ted, falcate (of the moon).
falchion, *n. fawl*-shon, a short sword with a broad slightly curved blade. (O.Fr. *fauchon.*)
falciform, *a. fal*-se-form, in the shape of a sickle.
falcon, *n. fawl*-kon *or faw*-kon, a diurnal bird of prey of the sub-family Falconinæ; a hawk trained in falconry; a female falcon; an obsolete name for a small cannon. (Fr. *faucon.*)
falconer, *n. faw*-ko-ner *or fawk*-ner, one who breeds and trains hawks; one who hunts with hawks.
falconet, *n. faw*-ko-net, a small breed of falcon; a small Australian shrike; an ancient cannon of small size.
falcon-gentle, *n. faw*-kon-*jen*-tl, the female of the peregrine falcon.
falconry, *n. faw*-kon-re, the art of training hawks; the sport of hawking. (O.Fr. *faulconerie.*)
falculate, *a. fal*-kew-late, resembling a small sickle (esp. of claws) [Zool.]. (L.)
faldage, *n. fawl*-daj, former right of a lord of the manor to his tenants' provision of sheep to manure his land.
faldstool, *n. fawld*-stool, a folding stool like a camp-stool, the armless chair of a bishop, when not in his own cathedral; a kneeling stool; a small desk at which the litany is read. (Late L. *faldistolium.*)
Falernian, *a.* fa-*ler*-ne-an, pertaining to the wine of Mt. Falernus, in Italy: *n.* the wine itself.
fall, *v.i.* fawl, to drop from a higher place by the power of gravity; to drop from an erect posture; to discharge itself; to lapse from faith or rectitude; to die by plague or sword; to come to an end suddenly; to sink into disgrace or misery; to decline in power, wealth, or glory; to pass into a worse state; to come; to sink; to be diminished in weight or value; not to amount to the full; to be rejected; to decline from violence to calmness; to pass into a new state; to sink into an air of dejection, discontent, anger, sorrow, or shame; to befall; to light on; to assail; to come unexpectedly; to rush or hurry to; to pass by chance, lot, distribution, inheritance, or otherwise, as possession or property; to become the property of; to be uttered carelessly; to become feeble or faint; to be brought forth; to issue; to terminate: *v.t.* to fell; to cut down [U.S.A.]. **fall aboard of,** to strike against, as one vessel coming into collision with another [Naut.]. **fall across,** to meet by chance. **fall astern,** to drop rearward [Naut.]. **fall away,** to lose flesh; to pine; to renounce allegiance; to revolt; to renounce the faith; to apostatize; to sink into wickedness; to perish; to be lost; to fade; to languish. **fall back,** to recede; to give way; not to fulfil. **fall back upon,** to have recourse to. **fall down,** to prostrate oneself in worship; to drop to the ground; to bow down as a suppliant; to come to grief. **fall flat,** to be disappointing; to fail of the intended effect. **fall for,** to be much attracted to; to take a great fancy for [Slang]. **fall foul,** to attack; to make an assault. **fall from,** to depart from; not to adhere to, as an agreement; to depart from allegiance or duty. **fall from grace,** to backslide. **fall in,** to agree with; to comply; to join, as a procession. **fall in with,** to meet, as a ship. **fall off,** to withdraw; to die away; to abandon; to drop; to depreciate. **fall on,** to begin suddenly and eagerly; to assail; to drop on; to descend on. **fall on one's feet,** to emerge successfully from a difficulty. **fall out,** to quarrel; to happen. **fall short,** to be deficient. **fall to,** to begin hastily and eagerly; to apply oneself to. **fall to the ground,** to collapse completely. **fall under,** to come under or within the limits of; to be subjected to; to become the subject of; to come within; to be ranged or reckoned with. (A.S. *feallan.*)
*★***fall,** *n.* fawl, the act of falling; descent by gravity; tumbling from an erect posture; death; destruction; overthrow; downfall; declension of greatness, power, or dominion; ruin; diminution; decrease of price or value; a sinking of tone; cadence; declivity; descent of water; a cascade; a cataract; the outlet or discharge of a river or current of water into the sea or into a lake or pond; the distance which anything falls; the fall of the leaf; autumn; that which falls; a falling; the act of felling or cutting down [U.S.A.]. **the fall,** the eating by Adam and Eve of the forbidden fruit and the consequent introduction of sin into the world.

fallacious, *a.* fa-*lay*-shus, founded on fallacy; deceptive and misleading; producing disappointment. (L. *fallaciosus.*)
fallaciously, *ad.* in a fallacious manner; sophistically.
fallaciousness, *n.* the quality of being fallacious.
fallacy, *n.* *fal*-la-se, an unsound and misleading though plausible argument; a deceptive mode of reasoning; an error: a sophism; sophistry. (Fr. *fallace.*)
fal-lals, *n.pl.* *fal*-lalz, showy trifles.
fallen, *a.* *faw*-len, degraded; ruined. **the fallen,** those slain in battle.
fallibility, *n.* fal-e-*bil*-e-te, liability to error.
fallible, *a.* *fal*-le-bl, liable to err; liable to be deceived. (Late L. *fallibilis.*)
fallibly, *ad.* *fal*-ib-le, in a fallible manner.
falling, *n.* *faw*-ling, the action of *to fall*; prolapse [Path.]. **falling sickness,** epilepsy. **falling star,** a meteor, aerolite, or shooting star.
Fallopian, *a.* fa-*loh*-pe-an, pertaining to Fallopius, a 16th-century Italian anatomist. **Fallopian tubes,** two membranous ducts by which ova are conveyed to the uterus, mistakenly regarded as discovered by Fallopius.
fallow, *a.* *fal*-lo, of a pale red or pale yellowish colour. **fallow deer,** a species of small semi-domesticated deer of this colour. (A.S. *fealu.*)
fallow, *a.* *fal*-lo, untilled; left unsown after ploughing; uncultivated; neglected: *n.* land that has lain a year or more untilled or unseeded: *v.t.* to plough, harrow, and break land without seeding it. **green fallow,** fallow land rendered mellow and clean from weeds by a green crop, as turnips, etc. (A.S. *fælging,* M.E. *falme,* ploughed land.)
fallow-crop, *n.* crop from fallow ground.
fallowfinch, *n.* *fal*-lo-finch, the wheat-ear.
fall-trap, *n.* *fawl*-trap, a trap with a door which falls and imprisons.
★**false,** *a.* fawlse, not true; not conformable to fact; unfounded; not according to the lawful standard; substituted for another; supposititious; counterfeit; not genuine; not solid or sound; not agreeable to rule or propriety; not fair; unfaithful; inconstant; treacherous; feigned; made or assumed for the purpose of deception; not in tune [Mus.]: *ad.* not truly; not honestly; falsely. **false colours,** flags used unlawfully on a ship for purposes of deception; hence deception generally. **false imprisonment,** unlawful imprisonment; unlawful restraint of a person's freedom of movement [Law]. **false keel,** a protective keel below the real keel. **false pretences,** acts calculated to deceive and thereby defraud a person [Law]. **false quantity,** incorrect metrical use of a vowel or syllable; faulty scansion or pronunciation. **false roof,** the part between the ceiling of the upper floor and the rafters of a roof [Arch.]. (O.Fr. *fals.*)
falsehood, *n.* *fawlse*-hood, an untrue assertion; a lie; want of truth, or of honesty; deceitfulness; false appearance; imposture.
falsely, *ad.* not truly; treacherously; erroneously.
falseness, *n.* the state of being false.
falsetto, *n.* fawl-*set*-to, a pitch or range of voice above the natural compass, produced by tightening the ligaments of the glottis. (It.)
falsifiable, *a.* *fawl*-se-*fy*-a-bl, that may be falsified.
falsification, *n.* *fawl*-se-fe-*kay*-shon, the act of falsifying; making a thing appear to be something which it is not; confutation. (Fr.)
falsifier, *n.* *fawl*-se-*fy*-er, one who falsifies, or gives a thing a false appearance; one who proves a thing to be false.
falsify, *v.t.* *fawl*-se-fy, to make or prove to be false; to counterfeit or forge; to confute.
falsity, *n.* *fawl*-se-te, the quality of being false; untruthfulness; a false assertion.
Falstaffian, *a.* fawl-*staf*-e-an, convivial, coarsely humorous, or otherwise resembling Shakespeare's Sir John Falstaff.
falter, *v.i.* *fawl*-ter, to stumble; not to be firm and steady in action; to hesitate in speech; to fail in any act of the understanding; to waver: *v.t.* to utter in a hesitating way.
falteringly, *ad.* in a faltering manner.
falx, *n.* falks, a membranous sickle-shaped process of the dura mater, the *falx cerebri* [Anat.]. (L., a sickle.
fame, *n.* fame, public rumour; renown; reputation; celebrity for something distinguished, usually good. (Fr., from L. *fama,* fame.)
famed, *a.* faymd, much talked of; renowned.
familiar, *a.* fa-*mil*-yar, well acquainted with; intimate; domestic; affable; not formal or distant; well versed in; well known or understood by frequent use; unceremonious; unconstrained; pertaining to a family; intimate in an unlawful degree: *n.* an intimate; one long acquainted; a demon or spirit fabled to attend at call. (Fr. *familier.*)
familiarism, *n.* fa-*mil*-ya-rizm, an expression, action, etc. proper only to or among intimates.
familiarity, *n.* fa-mil-e-*a*-re-te, close intimacy; affability; freedom from ceremony: *pl.* actions assuming too great familiarity. (Fr. *familiarité.*)
familiarization, *n.* fa-*mil*-ya-ry-*zay*-shon, a making or becoming familiar.
familiarize, *v.t.* fa-*mil*-ya-rize, to make or render familiar; to accustom; to habituate.
familiarly, *ad.* in a familiar manner.
★**family,** *n.* *fam*-e-le, those living in one house under one head, including parents, children, and servants; household; the children of a household; those who descend from one progenitor; a tribe or race; kindred; lineage; course of descent; genealogy; line of ancestors; honourable descent; noble or respectable stock; a brotherhood of persons or group of peoples having some common bond; a group of animals or plants, more extensive than a genus and less so than an order; an order [Bot.]. **family Bible,** a large Bible with blank pages for recording births, marriages, and deaths. **family man,** one whose wife and children form a chief interest; a domesticated man. **family tree,** a genealogical table. **Holy Family,** the child Jesus and his parents; a picture of these. **in a family way,** without ceremony; domestically. **in the family way,** pregnant. (L. *familia,* from *famulus,* a servant.)
famine, *n.* *fam*-in, a general scarcity of food or want of provisions; starvation. (Fr.)
famish, *v.t.* *fam*-ish, to starve; to reduce by starving: *v.i.* to suffer extreme hunger. (L. *fames* hunger.)
famishing, *a.* *fam*-ish-ing, starving; hungry.
famous, *a.* *fay*-mus, renowned; much talked of and praised; distinguished; notable. (Fr. *fameux.*)
famously, *ad.* so as to render or become famous.
famousness, *n.* the quality of being famous.
famulus, *n.* *fam*-yew-lus, the assistant of a magician or scholar. (L., a servant.)
fan, *n.* fan, an implement for causing a current of air; something in the form of a lady's fan when spread; something which acts as a fan, as in winnowing grain, quickening a flame, etc., anything which stirs up or intensifies zeal or passion; a small vane or sail, used to keep the large sails of a windmill always at right angles to the wind; the blade of a propeller; a propeller screw: *v.t.* to cool with a fan; to ventilate or to blow on; to winnow; to stimulate or quicken. **to fan out,** to spread, or be spread, out like a lady's opened fan. (A.S. *fann,* L. *vannus.*)
fan, *n.* fan, a fanatic for outdoor sports, the cinema, or any other craze; an enthusiastic spectator. **fan mail,** letters from their fans and autograph hunters received by celebrities. [U.S.A. slang].
fanatic, *a.* fa-*nat*-ik, affected with or prompted by excessive and exclusive, especially religious, zeal; animated by or proceeding from fanaticism: *n.* one affected with fanaticism. (L. *fanaticus,* relating to a temple.)
fanatical, *a.* fa-*nat*-e-kal, fanatic.
fanatically, *ad.* in the manner of a fanatic.
fanaticism, *n.* fa-*nat*-e-sizm, extravagant and exclusive zeal or devotion.
fanaticize, *v.t.* fa-*nat*-e-size, to render fanatic: *v.i.* to become a fanatic.
fancied, *a.* *fan*-sid, imaginary; favoured; liked.
fancier, *n.* *fan*-se-er, a connoisseur; a breeder of and dealer in birds, dogs, household pets, etc.
fanciful, *a.* *fan*-se-ful, guided, dictated by, or indulging in fancy; fantastical; whimsical; visionary.
fancifully, *ad.* in a fanciful manner; according to fancy.
fancifulness, *n.* quality of being fanciful.
fancy, *n.* *fan*-se, the faculty which the mind has of

forming to itself images or representations of things at pleasure, often synonymous with imagination; fantasy; the resulting image or representation; an opinion or notion; taste; conception; inclination; liking; conceit; whim; something that pleases or entertains without real use or value: *a.* ornamental; merely pleasing to the taste or fancy: *v.i.* to believe or suppose: *v.t.* to portray in the mind; to conceive a liking for; to be pleased with. **fancy ball,** a ball at which allegorical or historical costumes are worn; a masquerade. **fancy dress,** costume for a fancy ball. **fancy fair,** a bazaar. **fancy man,** a sweetheart; a prostitute's protector [Slang]. **fancy price,** an exorbitant price. **fancy work,** ornamental needlework. **the fancy,** patrons of boxing. (O.Fr. *fantaisie*)

fancy-free, *a.* not in love.

fancy-goods, *n.pl.* ribbons, silks, and small ornamental, as distinct from plain and useful, articles.

fandangle, *n.* fan-*dang*-gl, a trumpery ornament; balderdash.

fandango, *n.* fan-*dang*-go, an old Spanish dance, the dancers beating time with castanets; the music for this. (Sp.)

fane, *n.* fane, a temple or church; a place consecrated to religion. (L. *fanum*, a temple.)

fanfare, *n.* *fan*-fare, a short flourish of trumpets, as on one coming into the lists, etc.; a lively piece performed on hunting-horns. (Fr.)

fanfaron, *n.* *fan*-fa-ron, a swaggering bully; one who blows his own trumpet. (Fr.)

fanfaronade, *n.* *fan*-fa-ro-*nade*, ostentation; vain boasting; bluster: *v.i.* to bluster. (Fr.)

fang, *n.* fang, a tusk, esp. of a beast of prey; a long pointed tooth; the grooved tooth of a serpent down which the venom flows; the root of a tooth; the point of a claw or other seizing device; anything by which hold is taken. (A.S.)

fanged, *a.* fangd, furnished with fangs.

fangless, *a.* *fang*-less, having no fangs; toothless.

fanlight, *n.* *fan*-lite, a window over a house-door, esp. one shaped like an open fan.

fanner, *n.* *fan*-ner, one who or that which fans; a contrivance for producing a current of air, as in a window, etc.; a machine for winnowing corn.

fanning-mill, *n.* a winnowing machine.

fanon, *n.* *fan*-on, in the Roman Catholic Church, an embroidered scarf worn about the left arm of a priest at the eucharist; a maniple; a corporal. (O.Fr., a napkin.)

fan-palm, *n.* a palm with fan-shaped leaves, esp. the talipot *Corypha umbraculifera.*

fantail, *n.* *fan*-tale, a variety of pigeon, also an Australian bird, with a fan-shaped tail; a gas-burner which emits a fan-like flame.

fantan, *n.* *fan*-tan, a Chinese gambling game played with coins concealed under a bowl; also newmarket or a similar gambling game with cards. (Chin.)

fantasia, *n.* fan-*tay*-ze-a, an improvised instrumental piece; an extravaganza or potpourri [Mus.]. (It.)

fantast, *n.* *fan*-tast, one who indulges in fantasies.

fantastic, *a.* fan-*tas*-tik, fantastical: *n.* a whimsical person; a fop.

fantastical, *a.* fan-*tas*-te-kal, produced or existing only in the imagination or fancy; not real; of the nature of a phantom; apparent only; whimsical; capricious; odd; grotesque. (Fr. *fantastique.*)

fantastically, *ad.* in a fantastical manner.

fantasticalness, *n.* the state of being fantastical.

fantasy, *n.* *fan*-ta-se, the power of fancy; imagination; an illusion; an imaginary impossibility; a whim or caprice; a fantasia [Mus.]. (O.Fr. *fantaisie.*)

Fantee *or* **Fanti,** *n.* *fan*-tee, a member of a Gold Coast tribe of Negroes. **to go fantee,** to run amuck; to go native.

fantoccini, *n.pl.* fan-to-*chee*-ne, dramatic representations in which puppets are used as performers; marionettes. (It.)

fan-tracery, *n.* elaborate carved work on a vaulted roof in the form of a fan [Arch.]

faquir, *n.* fa-*keer*, a fakir.

***far,** *a.* fahr, distant, in any direction; remote; remote from or contrary to design or wish; remote in affection or obedience; alienated; more distant of two: *ad.* to a great distance, in space, time, or proportion; remotely; interrogatively, to what distance; in great part; very much; to a certain point. **a far cry,** a long distance. **by far,** in a great degree; very much. **far and away,** completely; by a great deal. **far from,** at a great distance. **far from it,** by no means. **far off,** at or to a great distance. **far other,** very different. **from far,** from a great distance; from a remote place. (A.S. *feor.*)

farad, *n.* *fa*-rad, the unit of electrical capacity, named after Faraday.

faradaic, *a.* fa-ra-*day*-ik, inductive [Elect.].

faradization, *n.* *fa*-ra-dy-*zay*-shon, a method of treating disease by the application of faradaic electric currents.

faradize, *v.t.* *fa*-ra-dize, to stimulate the nerves and muscles with faradaic currents [Med.].

farandole, *n.* *fa*-ran-dole, a lively Provençal dance in six-eight measure. (Fr.)

faraway, *a.* *fahr*-a-way, distant; as though from a distance.

farce, *n.* fahrce, a short play in which qualities and actions are greatly exaggerated for the purpose of exciting laughter; a piece of ridiculous parade; an absurdity. (Fr. from *farcir*, to stuff.)

farceur, *n. masc.* (App.) (*fem.* **farceuse**), a jester, joker, or buffoon. (Fr.)

farcical, *a.* *fahr*-se-kal, belonging or appropriate to a farce; ludicrous; ridiculous.

farcicality, *n.* *fahs*-se-*kal*-e-te, farcical nature.

farcically, *ad.* in a farcical manner.

farcin, *n.* *fahr*-sin, farcy.

farcing, *n.* *fahr*-sing, edible stuffing; forcemeat.

farcy, *n.* *fahr*-se, a contagious disease affecting horses, and allied to glanders. (Fr.)

fardel, *n.* *fahr*-del, a bundle or pack. (O.Fr.)

fare, *n.* fare, the price of passage or the sum for conveying a person; the person conveyed; food; provisions of the table: *v.i.* to be in any state, good or bad; to feed; to be entertained; to experience; to succeed: to happen well or ill; to go; to pass or move on. (A.S. *faran*, go.)

farewell, *n.* fare-*wel*, adieu; good-bye; *int.* may you fare well; good-bye.

far-fetched, *a.* brought from a remote place; not naturally deduced or introduced; forced.

farina, *n.* fa-*ree*-na, the pollen of plants; the flour of any species of corn or starchy root, such as the potato; starch. (L., ground corn.)

farinaceous, *a.* fa-re-*nay*-shus, consisting of or containing farina or flour; mealy.

farinaceously, *ad.* in a mealy-like manner. (Late L.)

farinose *a.* *fa*-re-nohs, producing farina; covered with a sort of white mealy dust.

farl, *n.* fahrl, a thin circular oatmeal cake cut into quarters and baked. (Scots.)

***farm** *n.* fahrm, a portion of land with buildings necessary for the business of farming and usually under one management; land within definite boundaries, arable or pasture; a farmhouse: *v.t.* to let out, as lands, to a tenant on condition of paying rent; to take at a certain rent; to let for hire; to lease or let, as taxes, impost, or other duties, at a certain sum or rate per cent.; to cultivate, as land: *v.i.* to engage in farming. **to let to farm,** to lease on rent. (O.Fr. *ferme.*)

farmable, *a.* *fahrm*-a-bl, that may be farmed.

farmer, *n.* *fahrm*-er, one who cultivates a farm; a husbandman; formerly one who collected taxes, customs, excise, or other duties, for payment made or on commission. **farmers general,** under the French monarchy, those to whom the right of levying certain taxes in a particular district was farmed out. (O.Fr. *fermer.*)

farmery, *n.* *fahrm*-er-re, a farmhouse with its outbuildings, yards, etc.

farmhouse, *n.* fahrm-house, the principal house on a farm; the farmer's residence.

farming, *n.* *fahrm*-ing, the business of cultivating land.

farm-labourer, *n.* a working man employed about a farm.

farmstead, *n.* *fahrm*-sted, a farm with all its buildings.

farmyard, *n.* *fahrm*-yard, the yard or enclosure attached to or surrounded by the farm-buildings.

faro, *n.* *fare*-ro, a game of hazard played with cards. (From *Pharaoh*, whose likeness was perhaps depicted on one of the cards used.)

farouche, *a.* fa-*roosh*, shy; sullen; untamed. (Fr.)

farraginous, *a.* fa-*raj*-in-us, formed of various materials; mixed; miscellaneous.
farrago, *n.* fa-*ray*-go, a mass composed of various materials confusedly mixed; a medley; a hodge-podge. (L. *farrago*, a mixture of ground cereals.)
far-reaching, *a.* comprehensive; including much.
farrier, *n.* *fa*-re-er, a shoeing smith; a veterinary surgeon: *v.i.* to practise as a farrier. (O.Fr. *ferrier*, an iron-worker.)
farriery, *n.* *fa*-re-e-re, the business of a farrier; a farrier's shop.
farrow, *n.* *fa*-ro, a litter of pigs: *v.t.* and *i.* to bring forth pigs. A.S. *fearh*, a pig.)
far-sighted, *a.* seeing to a great distance; having foresight; providing for remote issues.
far-sightedness, *n.* far-*site*-ed-ness, the quality or state of being far-sighted.
fart, *v.i.* fahrt, to break wind: *n.* an emission of wind from the anus [Vulg.]. (A.S. *feortan.*)
farther, *a.* and *ad.* *fahr*-ther, *comp. deg.* of *far*; more remote; longer; at a greater distance; further.
farthermost, *a.* *fahr*-ther-most, farthest.
farthest, *a.* *fahr*-thest, the most distant.
farthing, *n.* *farthe*-ing, the smallest British coin, the fourth of a penny, of silver mediævally, later of copper, and since 1860 of bronze. (A.S. *feorthing*, a fourth-part.)
farthingale, *n.* *farthe*-ing-gale, a skirt or petticoat distended by whalebone hoops. (O.Fr. *verdugalle.*)
fasces, *n.pl.* *fas*-eez, the ancient insignia of the Roman lictors, consisting of a bundle of rods bound round the helve of an axe, the head of which projected, as an emblem of authority. (L.)
fascia, *n.* *fash*-ya (*pl.* **fasciæ**), a band, sash, or fillet; a ribbon-like band between mouldings [Arch.]; a facia; the instrument-board of a motor-car or aeroplane; the belt of a planet, as those of Jupiter [Astron.]; a bandage, roller, or ligature [Surg.]; the thin fibrous tissue surrounding a muscle, etc. [Anat.]. (L.)
fascial, *a.* *fash*-e-al, pertaining to the fasciæ [Anat.].
fasciated, *a.* *fash*-e-ay-ted, growing abnormally into a close bundle [Bot.]; broadly striped [Zool.].
fasciation, *n.* *fash*-e-*ay*-shon, the act or manner of binding up diseased parts [Anat.]; a union of stems or branches in a flattened ribbon-like form [Bot.].
fascicle, *n.* *fas*-se-kl, a little bundle; a close cluster or tuft [Bot.]; a fasciculus [Anat.]
fascicled, *a.* *fas*-se-kld, clustered in a fascicle.
fascicular, *a.* fa-*sik*-yew-lar, growing in clusters; united in a bundle. (L. *fasciculus*, a little bundle.)
fascicularly, *ad.* fa-*sik*-yew-lar-le, in the form of bundles.
fasciculate, *a.* fa-*sik*-yew-lat, growing in bundles or bunches from the same point [Bot.].
fascicule, *n.* *fas*-se-kewl, a fascicle or fasciculus.
fasciculus, *n.* fa-*sik*-yew-lus, a bunch; a little bundle of nerve fibres [Anat.]; a single part of a serial publication. (L.)
fascinate, *v.t.* *fas*-e-nate, to charm; to enchant; to act on by some irresistible influence; to captivate; to excite and allure irresistibly or powerfully. (L. *fascinatus*, charmed.)
fascinating, *a.* *fas*-e-nay-ting, very attractive; charming; captivating.
fascination, *n.* fas-e-*nay*-shon, the act or power of fascinating or spell-binding; a mysterious, irresistible, alluring influence.
fascinator, *n.* *fas*-e-nay-tor, one who or that which fascinates.
fascine, *n.* fas-*een*, a long faggot or bound bundle of young branches, brushwood, etc. [Fort.]. (Fr.)
Fascism, *n.* *fash*-izm, an anti-communist, anti-democratic, and totalitarian form of dictatorship originating in Italy in 1922; the principles or organization of this; imitations and adaptations of this elsewhere. (It. *fascismo*, a bundle, group.)
Fascist, *n.* *fash*-ist (*pl.* **fascisti**, fa-*shis*-tee), an adherent of fascism, esp. a member of the Italian nationalist party; a blackshirt: *a.* pertaining to Fascism, to the Fascisti, or to the Fascist party.
fash, *v.t.* fash, to bother; to annoy; *v.i.* to reckon a bother; to be vexed. (Fr. *facher*, to trouble.)
fashion, *n.* *fash*-on, the make or form of anything; model; pattern; method; manner; mode; prevailing mode; the cut or shape of an article of dress; the prevailing mode of dress; upper society: *v.t.* to form; to mould; to accommodate; to make according to custom. (O.Fr. *fachon*, shape.)
fashionable, *a.* *fash*-on-a-bl, according to or observant of the prevailing fashion or mode; well-bred: *n.* a person of fashion.
fashionableness, *n.* the state of being fashionable.
fashionably, *ad.* in a manner according to fashion.
fashious, *a.* *fash*-yus, vexatious. (As *fash.*)
fast, *a.* fahst, firm; strong; firmly fixed; close; sound (as sleep); firm in adherence; swift; quick; promoting rapidity (as a cricket-pitch); acting quickly; dissipated; dissolute: *n.* that which fastens or holds; the rope securing a vessel to a wharf, etc.: *ad.* firmly; swiftly; with quick steps or progression. **fast and loose,** slippery in dealing; unreliable. **fast by** or **fast beside,** close or near to. **stand fast,** stand firm. (A.S. *fæst.*)
fast, *n.* fahst, abstinence from food, esp. on religious grounds; going without food; the time of fasting: *v.i.* to abstain from food wholly or partially; to abstain from food as a means of mortifying desire, etc. **fast day,** a day appointed for a fast; in Scotland, a day of prayer preparatory to Holy Communion.
fasten, *v.t.* *fah*-sen, to fix firmly or make fast; to secure, as by lock, bolt, bar, etc.; to cement or unite closely in any way; to lay on with strength: *v.i.* to become fast; to fix oneself on; to seize and hold on. (A.S. *fæstnian.*)
fastener, *n.* *fah*-sen-er, a clasp, catch, press-button, etc.; a fastening.
fastening, *n.* *fahs*-ning, anything that makes fast.
faster, *n.* *fah*-ster, one who fasts.
Fasti, *n.* *fas*-ty, the Roman register of days on which legal business might be transacted; hence, a calendar or almanac. **Fasti annales,** historical records. (L. *fasti dies*, lawful days.)
fastidious, *a.* fas-*tid*-e-us, over-nice in tastes; difficult to please. (L. *fastidiosus*, disdainful.)
fastidiously, *ad.* in a fastidious manner.
fastidiousness, *n.* quality of being fastidious.
fastigiate, *a.* fas-*tij*-e-at, narrowed to the top: tapering to a point, like a pyramid [Bot.]. (L. *fastigatus*, sloping down.)
fastigium, *n.* fas-*tij*-e-um, the summit, apex, or ridge of a house or pediment; the peak of temperature in a fever [Med.]. (L.)
fasting, *n.* *fahst*-ing, abstinence from, or the act of abstaining from, food.
fastish, *a.* *fahst*-ish, somewhat prone to dissipation.
fastness, *n.* *fahst*-ness, the state of being swift; the state of being fast and firm; firm adherence; strength; security; a stronghold. (A.S. *fæstness.*)
★**fat,** *a.* fat, fleshy; plump; corpulent; gross; dull; heavy; stupid; rich; producing a large income; fertile; nourishing; abounding in spiritual grace and comfort; denoting composition containing much blank space and that therefore pays well [Printing]; broad [Naut.]: *n.* an oily substance found in animals and plants; the best or richest of anything; composition containing much blank space paid for at composing rates [Printing]: *v.t.* and *i.* to fatten. (A.S. *fætt.*)
fatal, *a.* *fay*-tal, causing death or ruin; fraught with ruin; calamitous; fated; fateful; ominous. (O.Fr.)
fatalism, *n.* *fay*-tal-izm, the doctrine that all things are subject to fate and inevitable; submission to such doctrine. (Fr. *fatalisme.*)
fatalist, *n.* *fay*-tal-ist, a believer in the inevitable; *a.* fatalistic.
fatalistic, *a.* *fay*-tal-*is*-tik, involving fatalism.
fatalistically, *ad.* fay-ta-*lis*-te-ka-le, in a fatalistic manner.
fatality, *n.* fa-*tal*-e-te, necessity; a calamity; a fatal event. (Fr. *fatalité.*)
fatally, *ad.* *fay*-ta-le, so as to be fatal.
fate, *n.* fate, that destiny which foredooms everything and which there is no evading; predestined lot; final event; death; destruction. **the Fates,** the three goddesses, Clotho, Lachesis, and Atropos, who presided over the destinies of individuals [Myth.]. (L. *fatum*, spoken, and so irrevocable, from *fari*, speak.)
fated, *a.* *fay*-ted, doomed; destined.
fateful, *a.* *fate*-ful, bearing fatal power; producing fatal events.
fatefully, *ad.* *fate*-ful-le, in a fateful manner.
fatefulness, *n.* *fate*-ful-ness, state of being fateful.

fathead, *n.* *fat*-hed, a stupid fellow.
fat-headed, *a.* fat-*hed*-ed, dull, lacking intelligence [Coll.]; fuddled through alcoholic indulgence [Slang].
★father, *n.* *fah*-ther, a male parent; a forefather; an appellation of respect to an old man; one who exercises paternal care over another; a contriver or originator; the senior member of a profession; the First Person in the Trinity; the title given to dignitaries of the Church, superiors of convents, and often to Roman Catholic priests: *v.t.* to adopt; to claim to be the author of; to ascribe or charge to one as his offspring or production. **father of the chapel,** the elected chairman of a printing-house chapel. **Fathers of the Church,** the ecclesiastical writers of the first centuries. **Father General,** the title of the supreme head of the Jesuits, the "black pope." **gathered to one's fathers,** dead and buried. (A.S. *fæder.*)
fatherhood, *n.* *fah*-ther-hood, the state of being a father; the character or authority of a father.
father-in-law, *n.* the father of one's husband or wife.
fatherland, *n.* *fah*-ther-land, one's native land; the land of one's fathers.
father-lasher, *n.* *fah*-ther-*lash*-er, the sea-bullhead, *Cottus scorpius*, a small fish, allied to the miller's thumb.
fatherless, *a.* *fah*-ther-less, destitute of a living father; without a known author.
fatherliness, *n.* fatherly kindness.
fatherly, *a.* *fah*-ther-le, like a father in affection and care; tender; pertaining to a father.
fathom, *n.* *fath*-um, a measure of six feet, the linear extent of a man's outstretched arms (used chiefly in sounding); a measure of timber (six ft. square in cross-section and of varying length); *v.t.* to comprehend; to try the depth or find the bottom of: to encompass with the extended arms. (A.S. *fæthm*, the embracing arms.)
fathomable, *a.* *fath*-um-a-bl, capable of being fathomed.
fathomless, *a.* *fath*-um-less, not to be fathomed.
fatidical, *a.* fa-*tid*-e-kal, interpretative of fate or destiny; prophetic. (L. *fatidicus*, prophetic.)
fatigue, *n.* fa-*teeg*, weariness or exhaustion from exertion of either body or mind; the cause of weariness, as labour or toil; labour of a non-military character performed by soldiers: *v.t.* to weary or exhaust with labour of either mind or body; to weary by importunity; to harass. (O.Fr. *fatiguer.*)
Fatimite, *n.* *fat*-e-mite, a descendant of Fatima, daughter of Mohammed, esp. one of a dynasty reigning in N. Africa during the 10th–12th cent.: *a.* pertaining t o this dynasty.
fatling, *n.* *fat*-ling, a young animal fattened for slaughter; a fat animal.
fatness, *n.* *fat*-ness, the quality or state of being fat; richness; fruitfulness; fertility.
fatted, *a.* *fat*-ted, fattened; made fat.
fatten, *v.t.* *fat*-tn, to make fat; to feed for slaughte r; to make fertile and fruitful: *v.i.* to grow or become fat, plump, or fleshy. (A.S. *gefatnian.*)
fattener, *n.* *fatt*-ner, one who or that which fattens.
fattiness, *n.* *fat*-te-ness, the state of being fatty.
fattish, *a.* *fat*-tish, somewhat fat.
fatty, *a.* *fat*-te, having the qualities of fat; greasy; adipose. **fatty degeneration,** a diseased state of body, distinguished by a more or less partial transformation into fat of certain tissues, especially the muscular fibres of the heart [Med.]. **fatty tissue,** a tissue composed of minute cells or vesicles, in which the animal fat is deposited [Anat.].
fatuitous, *a.* fa-*tew*-e-tus, characterized by fatuity.
fatuity, *n.* fa-*tew*-e-te, feebleness of intellect; silliness; foolishness. (L. *fatuitatis.*)
fatuous, *a.* *fat*-yew-us, idiotic; witless; silly; illusory. (L. *fatuus*, silly.)
fat-witted, *a.* *fat*-wit-ted, dull; stupid.
faubourg, *n.* *foh*-boorg, a suburb in French cities, or what was originally such. (Fr.)
faucal, *a.* *faw*-kal, pertaining to the fauces; deeply guttural.
fauces, *n.pl.* *faw*-seez, the back of the mouth, terminated by the pharynx and the larynx; an orifice [Bot. and Malac.]. (L.)
faucet, *n.* *faw*-set, a tap or tube inserted in a cask for drawing liquid. (O.Fr. *fausset.*)
faugh, *int.* faw, exclamation of contempt, etc.
fault, *n.* fawlt, whatever impairs excellence, as a flaw, blemish, defect, or mistake; any slip in conduct or propriety, whether in the way of defect, neglect, or deviation; responsibility for such a slip; an interruption in the continuity of a stratum (or strata), causing a displacement of its level though not of its direction [Geol. and Mining]; a wrong placing of the ball or feet at tennis; loss of scent in hunting; a leak or a defective point, esp. in an electric circuit: *v.i.* to err; to commit a fault: *v.t.* to accuse. **at fault,** puzzled, off the scent; open to blame. **to find fault,** to express blame; to complain. **to find fault with,** to blame. (O.Fr. *faute.*)
faulted, *a.* *fawl*-ted, displaced [Geol.].
faultfinder, *n.* *fawlt*-fynd-er, one given to find fault.
faultfinding, *n.* fawlt-*fynd*-ing, the practice or habit of finding fault: *a.* unreasonably censorious.
faultily, *ad.* *fawl*-te-le, in a faulty manner.
faultiness, *n.* the state of being faulty.
faultless, *a.* *fawlt*-less, without fault or blemish.
faultlessly, *ad.* in a faultless manner.
faultlessness, *n.* freedom from faults.
faulty, *a.* *fawl*-te, containing faults; imperfect; guilty of a fault; blamable; worthy of censure.
faun, *n.* fawn, a Roman deity of the woods and fields and guardian of the flocks, later confounded with the Greek god Pan; a satyr, half man and half beast. (L. *Faunus.*)
fauna, *n.* *faw*-na, the animal life of any region or geological period. (L. *Fauna*, a female faun.)
faunistic, *a.* faw-*nis*-tik, pertaining to a fauna.
fauteuil, *n.* (App.), a theatre stall; an arm-chair seat in a pullman, passenger aeroplane, etc.; membership of the French Academy. (Fr.)
fauvette, *n.* fo-*vet*, a warbler; the garden warbler, *Sylvia hortensis.* (Fr. *fauve*, fawn-coloured.)
faveolate, *a.* fa-*vee*-o-lat, cellular, like honeycomb [Bot.]. (L. *favus*, honeycomb.)
faveolus, *n.* fa-*vee*-o-lus, a small cell resembling that of honeycomb, esp. in rock.
favonian, *a.* fa-*voh*-ne-an, pertaining to the west wind; mild; favouring. (L. *Favonius*, the west wind.)
favose, *a.* fa-*vohs*, resembling, or pitted as, a honeycomb [Bot.]. (L.)
favour, *n.* *fay*-vur, kindness; countenance; a disposition to aid, befriend, support, or justify; a kind act or an act of grace; lenity; leave; good will; the object of kind regard; something bestowed as evidence of kind feeling; a festive knot of ribbons; something worn as a token of affection; advantage; convenience afforded for success; partiality; bias; a business communication: *v.t.* to regard with kindness; to support; to countenance; to befriend; to afford advantages for success to; to single out and adopt; to facilitate; to resemble in features. (O.Fr.)
favourable, *a.* *fay*-vur-ra-bl, friendly; propitious; conducive to; tending to promote; advantageous; affording means to facilitate. (Fr.)
favourableness, *n.* the quality or state of being favourable; partiality; conduciveness.
favourably, *ad.* in a favourable manner; propitiously.
favoured, *a.* *fay*-vurd, having a certain appearance, as **ill-favoured, well-favoured,** looking ill- or well-conditioned.
favourer, *n.* *fay*-vur-rer, one who or that which favours; a promoter of a movement, etc.
favouring, *a.* *fay*-vur-ring, wishing well to; promoting; resembling in features.
favourite, *n.* *fay*-vur-rit, a person or thing regarded with favour; one greatly beloved; one regarded with undue preference; the competitor expected to win [Sport]: *a.* regarded with special favour or fondness; preferred. (It. *favorito.*)
favouritism, *n.* *fay*-vur-re-tizm, the disposition to favour one or more to the neglect of others having equal claims; partiality.
favus, *n.* *fay*-vus, a scalp-disease characterized by dry, yellowish incrustations somewhat resembling honeycomb, due to a fungus. (L., a honeycomb.)
fawn, *n.* fawn, a young deer; a fallow deer of the first year; a cub: *a.* of a light brown or reddish-yellow colour: *v.i.* to bring forth a fawn. (O.Fr. *faon.*)

fawn, *v.i.* fawn, to cringe in order to gain favour; to show delight; to caress. (A.S. *fagnian*, glad.)
fawner, *n.* *fawn*-er, a cringer.
fawning, *a.* *fawn*-ing, courting servilely; flattering by cringing and meanness: *n.* gross flattery.
fawningly, *ad.* in a cringing, servile way.
fay, *n.* fay, a fairy; an elf. (Fr. *fée.*)
fay, *v.i.* fay, to fit closely: *v.t.* to fit two pieces of wood together [Ship-building]. (A.S. *fegan*, to join.)
fayalite, *n.* *fay*-a-lite, an iron silicate of the chrysolite group. (*Fayal* in the Azores, where first found.)
feal, *a.* feel, faithful [Scot.].
fealty, *n.* *fee*-al-te, fidelity or faithful adherence, esp. of a tenant or vassal to his lord; loyalty. (O.Fr. *fealte.*)
★**fear,** *n.* feer, a painful emotion excited by the apprehension of evil or impending danger; anxiety; the cause or object of fear; dread; awe; reverence; respect: *v.t.* to regard with fear; to anticipate with fear; to have a reverential awe of; to suspect: *v.i.* to be apprehensive of evil; to be afraid; to doubt. (A.S. *fær*, danger.)
fearful, *a.* *feer*-ful, affected by fear; afraid; wanting courage; timid; impressing fear; dreadful; to be reverenced; awful.
fearfully, *ad.* in fear; in a way to impress fear.
fearfulness, *n.* state of being fearful; timidity.
fearless, *a.* *feer*-less, free from fear; intrepid.
fearlessly, *ad.* in a fearless manner.
fearlessness, *n.* the state of being fearless.
fearnought, *n.* *feer*-nawt, a thick shaggy woollen stuff, used esp. for lining port-holes in ships.
fearsome, *a.* *feer*-sum, inspiring fear by being seen.
fearsomely, *ad.* in a fearsome way.
feasibility, *n.* *fee*-ze-*bil*-e-te, practicability.
feasible, *a.* *fee*-ze-bl, practicable; possible; manageable [Coll.]. (Fr. *faisable.*)
feasibleness, *n.* *fee*-ze-bl-ness, practicability.
feasibly, *ad.* *fee*-ze-ble, practicably.
feast, *n.* feest, a sumptuous repast of which a number partake; a banquet; something delicious to the palate; periodical or stated celebration of some event; a festival; anything bringing great pleasure to the mind or the heart: *v.i.* to eat sumptuously; to be highly gratified or delighted: *v.t.* to entertain sumptuously; to delight; to gratify luxuriously. **feast day,** a day of feasting; a festival. (O.Fr. *feste*, from L. *festum*, a holiday, a festival.)
feaster, *n.* *feest*-er, a participant at a feast; a guest; one who entertains magnificently.
feastful, *a.* *feest*-ful, festive; sumptuous; luxurious; given to feasting.
feat, *n.* feet, an act or deed, especially of extraordinary strength, skill, or courage; an achievement; a stunt. (Fr. *fait*, done.)
★**feather,** *n.* *feth*-er, one of the plumes which form the covering of a bird; one of these used as an ornament, part of a head-dress, etc., or on the shaft of an arrow or dart to steady its flight; hairy fringe on a dog's leg; a tongue on a board fitting into a groove in another; the act of feathering [Rowing]: *v.t.* to dress in feathers; to cover with feathers or such like; to adorn; to flemish (of hounds). **a feather in the cap,** an honour achieved. **in full feather,** elaborately dressed; up to the mark. **in high feather,** in high spirits; elated. **to feather one's nest,** to collect wealth; to make oneself financially secure. **to feather the oar,** to turn its edge horizontally on raising it from the water. **to show the white feather,** to give indications of cowardice. (A.S. *fether*, Ger. *feder.*)
feather-alum, *n.* alunogen.
feather-bed, *n.* a mattress filled with feathers. **feather-bed soldier,** one who has not seen, or has no intention of seeing, active service.
feather-boarding, *n.* weather-boarding in which the edge of one board overlaps that of another, like the feathers of a bird.
feathered, *a.* *feth*-erd, covered with feathers; winged; fitted or furnished with feathers; smoothed like down or feathers; having feathery or feather-like appendages.
feather-edge, *n.* the thinner edge of a piece of feather-boarding.
featherfew, *n.* *feth*-er-few, the feverfew.
featherfoil, *n.* *feth*-er-foyl, the water-violet.
feather-grass, *n.* *feth*-er-grahs, a species of grass with narrow, single-flowered spikelets, *Stipa pennata.*
featheriness, *n.* the state of being feathery.
feathering, *n.* *feth*-er-ing, the turning of the blade of an oar or scull to the horizontal as it leaves the water [Boating]: *pl.* ornamental cusps formed by the junction of small arcs in architectural enrichments [Arch.].
featherless, *a.* *feth*-er-less, destitute of feathers; deprived of feathers; unfledged.
featherman, *n.* *feth*-er-man, a dealer in plumes and feathers.
featherstar, *n.* *feth*-er-star, the common crinoid, *Antedon rosacea.*
featherstitch, *n.* *feth*-er-stitch, a style of needlework in which the stitches are made in a series of branching zigzags.
featherweight, *n.* *feth*-er-wate, a boxer of from 8 st. 6 lb. to 9 st.; the least weight that can be put on a horse when running [Racing]; weight so exact that a feather would turn it.
feathery, *a.* *feth*-er-e, clothed or covered with feathers; having the appearance of feathers; light; insubstantial; trivial.
featly, *ad.* *feet*-le, neatly; dexterously; adroitly.
featness, *n.* *feet*-ness, dexterity; adroitness.
featural, *a.* *feet*-yewr-ral, pertaining to the features, or to a feature.
feature, *n.* *feet*-yewr, the cast of any part of the face; the make or cast of the body; the appearance; the make or form of any part of the surface of a thing; a prominent, conspicuous, or distinguishing part; a special or distinctive article or series in a newspaper, etc.; the principal picture at a cinema entertainment: *v.t.* to make or be a feature of; to give special prominence to (esp. Cinema). (O.Fr. *faiture.*)
featureless, *a.* *feet*-yewr-less, having no distinctive features or shape; plain and ugly.
featurely, *a.* *feet*-yewr-le, good-featured; rather handsome.
feaze, *v.t.* feez, to untwist the end, as of a rope; to unravel [Naut.].
febricula, *n.* feb-*rik*-yew-lah, a slight fever of no specified type and short duration. (L.)
febriculose, *a.* feb-*rik*-yew-lose, feverish.
febrific, *a.* feb-*rif*-ik, producing fever; feverish.
febrifugal, *a.* feb-re-*few*-gal *or* feb-*rif*-yew-gal, having the quality of mitigating or curing fever; antifebrile.
febrifuge, *n.* *feb*-re-fewj, any medicine that mitigates or removes fever. (L. *febris*, and *fugo*, put to flight.)
febrile, *a.* *fee*-brile, pertaining to, indicating, or produced by fever.
Febronianism, *n.* fe-*broh*-ne-a-nizm, an 18th-cent. heretical movement in the Rom. Cath. Church towards the restriction of papal power, esp. in relation to the national churches. (Justinius *Febronius*, pseudonym of its leading advocate, Johann von Hontheim.)
February, *n.* *feb*-roo-a-re, the second month in the year. (L. *Februarius*, the month of purification and expiation.)
fecal, *a.* *fee*-kal, fæcal.
fecial, *n.* and *a.* *fee*-she-al, fetial.
fecit, *fee*-sit, he did it, a word inscribed on a work of art after the name of the artist. (L.)
feckless, *a.* *fek*-less, flabby; inefficient; good-for-nothing. (Etym. uncertain.)
fecklessness, *n.* *fek*-les-ness, ineffectualness; feebleness; worthlessness.
fecula, *n.* *fek*-yew-la, starch; farina. (L.)
feculence, *n.* *fek*-yew-lence, the quality of being feculent; feculent matter.
feculency, *n.* *fek*-yew-len-se, feculence.
feculent, *a.* *fek*-yew-lent, containing or abounding in lees or sediment; muddy; turbid. (L. *fæculentus.*)
fecund, *a.* *fee*-kund, fruitful; prolific. (Fr. *fecond.*)
fecundate, *v.t.* *fee*-kun-date, to make fruitful; to impregnate. (L. *fecundatus*, fertilized.)
fecundation, *n.* *fee*-kun-*day*-shon, the act of fecundating; impregnation.
fecundity, *n.* fee-*kun*-de-te, the quality of being fruitful or prolific; fertility; the property of germinating; power or richness of invention.
fed, fed, *p.* of feed. **fed up,** having had enough; sated; thoroughly bored [Slang].
federacy, *n.* *fed*-er-ra-se, a federation; a confederacy.

federal, *a. fed*-er-al, pertaining to or founded on a league or contract, esp. between states; upholding the federation; pertaining to or based upon the Covenant of Grace [Theol.]: *n.* a supporter of the federal principle in the constitution of the United States. **the Federal Parliament,** the parliament of the Commonwealth of Australia. **federal union,** a union of several internally independent states under a common central government in which they are severally represented. (Fr. *fédéral.*)

federalism, *n. fed*-er-al-izm, the federal principle; the principles of the federalists.

federalist, *n. fed*-er-al-ist, a federal.

federalize, *v.t.* and *v.i. fed*-er-al-ize, to unite in compact, as different states, for political purposes; to federate.

federate, *a. fed*-er-ate, joined in confederacy: *v.t.* to join together on a federal basis. (L. *fæderatus*, leagued.)

federation, *n. fed*-er-*ray*-shon, the act of combining in a confederacy; a confederation.

federative, *a. fed*-er-a-tiv, pertaining to or forming a confederacy; joining in a league.

fee, *n.* fee, recompense or compensation for services, esp. for professional services, prescribed in many cases by law or custom; an estate held of a superior on certain conditions; an heritable or inherited estate: *v.t.* to pay a fee to; to hire; to keep in hire. (O.Fr. *fé*, connected with A.S. *feoh*, cattle, property.)

★feeble, *a. fee*-bl, weak; infirm; weakened by disease or wanting vigour; faint; dull. (Fr. *faible.*)

feeble-minded, *a.* weak in mind; wanting firmness; irresolute; slightly deficient.

feebleness, *n. fee*-bl-ness, the state of being feeble.

feeblish, *a. fee*-blish, rather feeble.

feebly, *ad. fee*-ble, in a feeble manner.

feed, *n.* feed, a certain allowance of provender given to a horse, cow, etc.; food; pasturage; a meal; the act of giving food, or of supplying machinery with material; the means by which a machine is supplied; the amount supplied: *v.t.* to give food to; to supply with anything wanting or necessary; to graze or to pasture; to nourish; to delight; to entertain; to fatten: *v.i.* to take good; to prey; to pasture; to grow fat; to subsist. (A.S. *fēdan*, from A.S. *foda*, food.)

feeder, *n. feed*-er, one who gives good or supplies nourishment; an encourager; one who fattens cattle; a fountain, stream, or channel that supplies a main canal with water; supply or anything that increases it, as of traffic on a railway; the supplying part of a machine; a feeding-bottle; an infant's bib; a bowler at baseball or rounders.

feeding, *n. feed*-ing, that which is caten; pasture: *a.* nourishing; sustaining. **feeding storm,** a storm gradually increasing in violence.

feeding-bottle, *n.* a bottle with a teat from which babies take liquid nourishment.

feed-pipe, *n.* a pipe which feeds or supplies the boiler of a steam-engine, etc., with water.

feed-pump, *n.* the force-pump employed in supplying the boilers of steam-engines [Mech.].

fee-estate, *n. fee*-es-*tate*, estate held on some service or acknowledgment to the superior.

fee-farm, *n. fee*-fahrm, a kind of feudal tenure without homage, fealty, or other service or condition except as stipulated in the feoffment.

fee-faw-fum, *int.* fee-faw-*fum*, a humorously bloodthirsty exclamation: *n.* nonsensical spoof meant to impose on the foolish or ignorant. (The ogre's cry in "Jack the Giant-killer.")

feel, *n.* feel, the sense of touch sensation; perception caused by the touch: *v.t.* to perceive by the touch; to have a sense of or be conscious of; to suffer or experience; to know or to have a real and just view of; to test: *v.i.* to know by the touch; to have the emotions excited; to excite a sensation of being; to be conscious of being. **to feel after,** to search for. **to feel for,** to try to find by the touch; to have sympathy with or compassion for. (A.S. *fēlan.*)

feeler, *n. feel*-er, one who or that which feels; an organ of touch, an antenna; a remark or hint thrown out to ascertain the views of others.

★feeling, *a. feel*-ing, perceiving by the touch; conscious; expressive of keen sensibility; affecting; possessing keen sensibility; easily or deeply affected: *n.* the sense of touch; perception by the touch; sensation or perception by any of the senses; sensibility; susceptibility; emotion.

feelingly, *ad.* in a sympathetic manner.

fee-simple, *n. fee*-sim-pl, an estate held by a person in his own right, and descendible to the heirs in general; freehold.

feet, feet, *n.pl.* of foot.

fee-tail, *n. fee*-tale, an estate entailed to the possessor's heirs, and thus held conditionally.

Fehmic, *a. fay*-mik, Vehmic.

feign, *v.t.* fane, to fashion or fabricate; to affect or pretend; to simulate; to fable. (Fr. *feindre.*)

feigned, *a.* faynd, pretended; counterfeited. **feigned issue,** an action got up to try a question of right [Law].

feignedly, *ad. fay*-ned-le, in pretence.

feint, *n.* faynt, a pretence; a misleading attack; an appearance of aiming at one part when another is intended to be struck: *v.i.* to make a feint or pretended attack [Mil. and Fencing]. (Fr. *feinte.*)

feint, *n.* faynt, faint; ruled in pale ink. (As *faint*).

feldspar, *n. feld*-spahr, felspar.

feldspathic, *a.* feld-*spath*-ik, pertaining to felspar; containing or consisting of felspar.

felicide, *n. fel*-e-side, the killing of a cat. (L. *felis.*)

felicific, *a.* fel-e-*sif*-ik, producing or promoting happiness. (L. *felix*, happy, *facio*, make.)

felicitate, *v.t.* fe-*lis*-e-tate, to congratulate; to make happy. (L. *felicitatis*, of success.)

felicitation, *n.* fe-lis-e-*tay*-shon, congratulation.

felicitator, *n.* fe-*lis*-e-tay-tor, a congratulator.

felicitous, *a.* fe-*lis*-e-tus, very happy; ingenious; most appropriate; successful.

felicitously, *ad.* in a felicitous manner.

felicitousness, *n.* state of being felicitous.

felicity, *n.* fe-*lis*-e-te, happiness; bliss; a blessing or source of happiness; a happy faculty. (O.Fr. *felicité*, from L. *felix*, happy.)

felid, *n. fee*-lid, one of the Felidæ, the family containing the cats, lions, tigers, etc. [Zool.]. (L. *felis*, a cat.)

feline, *a. fee*-line, pertaining to cats or the cat-kind; cat-like; stealthy; wily: *n.* a member of the cat family. (L. *felinus.*)

felinity, *n.* fe-*lin*-e-te, cattishness.

fell, *a.* fel, cruel; fierce; savage; bloody; deadly. (O.Fr. *fel.*)

fell, *n.* fel, the hide or skin of an animal, esp. with the hair; a fleece; a matted mass of hair. (A.S. *fel.*)

fell, *n.* fel, a mountain side; a barren or stony hill; a wild stretch of moorland. (Ice. *fjall.*)

fell, *v.t.* fel, to cause to fall; to bring to the ground by cutting or striking; to hem or finish with a fell: *n.* a hem laid level with the cloth. (A.S. *fiellan.*)

fell, fel, *p.* of *fall.*

fellah, *n. fel*-la (*pl.* **fellahin,** fel-la-*heen*), one of the peasants or labouring class in Egypt. (Ar., a peasant.)

feller, *n. fel*-ler, one who cuts down trees; one who, or a sewing-machine attachment which, fells seams.

fellic, *a. fel*-lik, pertaining to, or designating an acid present in, human bile. (L. *fel*, bile.)

fellmonger, *n. fel*-mung-ger, a dealer in skins, esp. sheepskins; a worker in skins.

felloe, *n. fel*-lo, one of the curved pieces of wood which are joined together to form the rim of a wheel; the rim of a wheel. (A.S. *felge.*)

fellow, *n. fel*-lo, a companion; an associate; one of the same kind; an equal; one of a pair; one equal to or like another; a person; a term of disparagement for one lightly esteemed; a member of a college that shares its revenues; a member of any incorporated society; a college trustee [U.S.A.]: *a.* in composition, along with, in a given respect: *v.t.* to pair with; to match. (Ice. *felagi*, a partner in goods.)

fellow-commoner, *n.* an undergraduate who, at certain colleges, has the right to dine with the fellows.

fellow-feeling, *n. fel*-lo-*feel*-ing, sympathy.

fellowship, *n. fel*-lo-ship, the state of being a fellow; companionship; society; familiar intercourse; communion; partnership; association; frequency of intercourse; fitness and fondness for festive entertainments; an endowment in colleges for

the maintenance of a fellow; the status and dignity of a fellow; the rule by which profit or loss is divided among partners in proportion to their investments [Arith.].
felly, *n. fel*-le, a felloe.
felo-de-se, *n. fee*-lo-de-*see*, one who commits suicide when sane; this felony. (L., a felon of himself.)
felon, *n. fel*-on, a person who has committed felony; a malefactor; a whitlow: *a.* malignant; fierce; traitorous. (Fr., a traitor.)
felonious, *a.* fe-*loh*-ne-us, wicked; worthy of a felon; done with the deliberate purpose to commit a crime [Law].
feloniously, *ad.* in a felonious manner.
feloniousness, *n.* the quality of being felonious.
felonry, *n. fel*-on-re, the felon or convict class.
felony, *n. fel*-on-e, a grave misdemeanour, formerly a crime punishable by total forfeiture of lands or goods (or both), to which capital or other punishment might be added; any grave crime. (Fr. *félonie.*)
felsite, *n. fel*-site, any fine-grained igneous rock of acid composition containing quartz and felspar.
felspar, *n. fel*-spahr, a widely distributed group of rock-forming aluminium silicates, combined with potassium, calcium, sodium, or barium, which form a constituent part of many igneous and metamorphic rocks. (Ger. *feld*, field, *spath*, spar.)
felspathic, *a.* fel-*spath*-ik, pertaining to or containing felspar.
felspathose, *a.* fel-*spath*-ose, pertaining to or containing felspar.
felstone, *n. fel*-stone, felsite.
felt, *n.* felt, a stuff of wool, or wool and hair, which is matted into a fabric by beating, rolling, suction, and pressure; a hat made of felt: *v.t.* to make into, or cover with felt; to cause to mat together: *v.i.* to become felted. (A.S.)
felt, felt, *p.* and *pp.* of the verb *to feel.*
felter, *v.t.* and *i. fel*-ter, to tangle, or become tangled or matted together.
felt-grain, *n. felt*-grane, the grain of cut timber, which is transverse to the annular rings [Carp.].
felting, *n. felt*-ing, the process of making felt; felt.
felty, *a. fel*-te, of the nature of felt.
felucca, *n.* fe-*luk*-ka, a small vessel with oars and lateen sails, used in the Mediterranean. (It.)
felwort, *n. fel*-wurt, a name of some of the gentians, esp. the yellow gentian, *G. amarella.*
★**female,** *a. fee*-male, pertaining to women, to the sex which bears offspring or eggs, or, among plants, to the sex which bears the pistil and receives the pollen of the male flowers; feminine; soft; delicate; bearing the pistil [Bot.]: *n.* a female generally; a woman or girl. **female die,** the concave die into which the male or convex die is struck. **female screw,** the spiral-threaded cavity into which a screw works [Mech.]. **female rhymes,** rhymes which consist of a long syllable and a short, as *plumber, summer,* or *chuck it, bucket.* (O.Fr. *femelle.*)
feme, *n.* fem, a woman [Law]. **feme coverte,** a married woman. **feme sole,** a spinster, a widow, or a woman having property in her own right.
femerell, *n. fem*-er-el, a roof-lantern with louvres serving as a chimney or ventilator. (O.Fr. *fumeraille.*)
femicide, *n. fem*-e-side, the slaying of a woman; one who unlawfully kills a woman.
feminality, *n.* fem-e-*nal*-e-te, a female characteristic or peculiarity; a triviality appealing specially to womankind.
femineity, *n. fem*-e-*nee*-e-te, womanliness.
feminine, *a. fem*-e-nin, pertaining to or characteristic of women of the female sex; tender; effeminate; of the **feminine gender,** that gender which denotes the female sex. **feminine rhyme,** *see* **rhyme.** (O.Fr. *feminin.*)
femininely, *ad. fem*-e-nin-le, in a feminine manner.
femininity, *n.* fem-e-*nin*-e-te, manners and character becoming to a woman; womanishness; women collectively.
feminism, *n. fem*-e-nizm, the advocacy of women's political and economic claims.
feminist, *n. fem*-e-nist, an advocate of women's claims; an authority on female psychology.
feminize, *v.t.* and *i. fem*-e-nize, to make or become feminine or effeminate.
femoral, *a. fem*-o-ral, belonging to the thigh: *n.* the femoral artery. (L. *femoralis*, relating to the thigh.)
femur, *n. fee*-mur, the thigh bone; the third segment of an insect's leg [Entom.]. (L.)
fen, *n.* fen, low marshy land; a marsh; a bog. (A.S.)
fenberry, *n. fen*-be-re, the cranberry.
fence, *n.* fence, a wall, hedge, or line of posts and rails or wire, to confine animals or protect land; a guard or guide in various tools, implements, machinery, etc.; the art of fencing; skill in debate; repartee; a receiver of stolen goods [Slang]: *v.t.* to enclose with a fence; to guard; to fortify: *v.i.* to practise with foil or sword; to raise a fence; to equivocate. **on the fence,** non-committal, hesitating between two opinions. **ring fence,** a fence which encircles a whole estate. (Abbr. for *defence.*)
fenceless, *a. fence*-less, unenclosed; open.
fence-month, *n. fence*-munth, the breeding season for deer, when their hunting is illegal; any close-time for game or fish.
fencer, *n. fence*-er, one who fences or teaches fencing; a maker of fences.
fencible, *a. fence*-e-bl, capable of defence or defending; *n.pl.* soldiers enlisted for home defence. (Abbr. for *defensible.*)
fencing, *n. fence*-ing, materials used in making fences; a casing round machinery in factories; the art of skilfully using sword or foil in attack or defence; equivocating; parrying in debate.
fend, *v.t.* fend, to keep or ward off; to maintain, to provide for [Scot.]: *v.i.* to act in opposition; to resist; to parry. (Abbr. for *defend.*)
fender, *n. fen*-der, a frame round a hearth to confine the ashes; a cushion of rope, etc., to protect the side of a vessel when it comes in contact with another or with the wharf, etc.; any protection from injury by contact.
fen-duck, *n. fen*-duk, the shoveller duck.
fenestella, *n.* fen-es-*tel*-la, a window-like niche in the wall on the south side of an altar [Arch.].
fenestra, *n.* fe-*nes*-tra (*pl.* **fenestræ**), a small opening in a bone [Anat.]; a transparent spot in the wings of certain moths [Entom.]. (L., a window.)
fenestral, *a.* fe-*nes*-tral, pertaining to, or having, fenestræ.
fenestrate, *a.* fe-*nes*-trat, pierced with holes like windows; marked with, or as with, windows.
fenestration, *n.* fen-es-*tray*-shon, architecture or arrangement as regards windows.
fen-goose, *n. fen*-goose, the greylag goose.
Fenian, *n. fee*-ne-an, a member of a former organization formed to overthrow English rule and establish a republic in Ireland. (*Fionn*, an Irish legendary hero.)
Fenianism, *n. fee*-ne-an-izm, the principles and methods of the Fenians.
fenks, *n.* fenks, manure prepared from the refuse of whale's blubber.
fenlander, *n. fen*-lan-der, a dweller among fens, esp. those of eastern England.
fennec, *n. fen*-nek, a small North African large-eared fox, *Vulpes zerda.* (Ar.)
fennel, *n. fen*-nel, an aromatic umbelliferous plant with finely divided leaves, *Fœniculum vulgare.* (A.S. *fenol.*)
fennel-flower, *n.* a plant of the genus *Nigella*, love-in-a-mist.
fenny, *a. fen*-ne, marshy; inhabiting, characteristic of, or abounding in, fens.
fent, *n.* fent, an opening or slit left in a garment, as a shirt-sleeve, for ease in putting on. (Fr. *fente*, a cleft.)
fenugreek, *n. fen*-yew-greek, a leguminous plant allied to clover, *Trigonella fœnum græcum.*
feod, *n.* fewd, a fief or feud.
feodary, *a. few*-da-re, held by feudal tenure.
feoff, *n.* feff, a fief: *v.t.* to enfeoff.
feoffee, *n.* fef-*fee*, a person who is enfeoffed.
feoffment, *n. fef*-ment, the conveyance or grant of a fief.
feoffor, *n. fef*-for, one who grants a fief.
feracious, *a.* fe-*ray*-shus, fertile; yielding abundantly. (L. *ferax*, fruitful.)
feracity, *n.* fe-*ras*-e-te, fruitfulness; fecundity.
feral, *a. feer*-ral, wild; savage; escaped from domestication. (L. *fera*, a wild beast.)
feral, *a. eer*-ral, deadly, fatal; funereal; pertaining to the dead. (L. *feralis.*)

fer-de-lance, *n.* *fare*-de-lahnce, a large venomous snake, *Bothrops atrox*, allied to the rattle-snake, of Cent. and S. America and the West Indies. (Fr.)

fere, *n.* *feer*, a mate, comrade. (A.S. *gefera*.)

feretory, *n.* *fe*-re-to-re, a shrine for containing the relics of saints when carried in processions. (O.Fr. *feretre*.)

fergusonite, *n.* *fer*-gus-son-ite, a rare brownish-black mineral, consisting chiefly of columbate and tantalate of yttrium. (Robert *Ferguson*.)

ferial, *a.* *feer*-re-al, pertaining to holidays, or to week days not being Church feasts or fasts (applied formerly in Scotland to non-court days). (L. *feria*, a holiday.)

ferine, *a.* *feer*-rine, wild; untamed; savage. (L. *ferinus*.)

Feringhee, *n.* fe-*ring*-ge, the Hindu name for Europeans, usually with derogatory implication. (Hind. corruption of *rank*.)

ferment, *n.* *fer*-ment, an enzyme; leaven; any substance causing fermentation; internal motion of the constituent parts of a fluid; commotion; heat; tumult; agitation. (L. *ferveo*, boil.)

ferment, *v.t.* fer-*ment*, to excite fermentation in; to stir up; to inflame: *v.i.* to be in a state of fermentation internally; to be excited or agitated; to work. (L. *fermentum*.)

fermentable, *a.* fer-*men*-ta-bl, capable of fermentation.

fermentation, *n.* fer-men-*tay*-shon, chemical change by the agency of enzymes resulting in the formation of alcohols; mental agitation caused by some disturbing influence that tends materially to modify the ideas or feelings.

fermentative, *a.* fer-*men*-ta-tiv, causing, produced by, or consisting in, fermentation.

fermentescible, *a.* fer-men-*tes*-e-bl, fermentable; able to cause fermentation.

fern, *n.* fern, a cryptogamic plant with its sporangia, or reproductive organs, on the back or margin of its fronds. (A.S. *fearn*.)

fernery, *n.* *fern*-er-re, a place where ferns are cultivated; a collection of growing ferns.

fern-owl, *n.* *fern*-oul, the goatsucker or night-jar.

ferny, *a.* *fern*-e, abounding with ferns.

ferocious, *a.* fer-*roh*-shus, fierce or savage in disposition or expression; barbarous. (L. *ferox*, wild.)

ferociously, *ad.* in a ferocious manner.

ferociousness, *n.* quality of being ferocious.

ferocity, *n.* fer-*ros*-e-te, savage cruelty of disposition; fierceness indicating a savage heart; barbarous inhumanity. (Fr. *férocité*.)

ferox, *n.* *fe*-roks, the great lake trout, *Salmo fario*.

ferrara, *n.* fer-*rah*-rah, a broadsword of high quality. (Andrea *Ferrara*, Italian swordsmith.)

ferrate, *n.* *fe*-rate, a combination of ferric acid with a base. (L. *ferrum*, iron.)

ferreous, *a.* *fe*-re-us, containing or pertaining to iron; resembling or consisting of iron.

ferret, *n.* *fe*-ret, a domesticated variety of the polecat used in unearthing rabbits; a glass-makers' testing iron: *v.t.* to drive out of a lurking place; to hunt out; to search for. (O.Fr. *furet*, from L. *fur*, a thief.)

ferret, *n.* *fe*-ret, a kind of narrow tape made of cotton or silk. (It. *fioretti*, floss silk.)

ferreter, *n.* *fe*-ret-er, one who ferrets or who ferrets out.

ferrety, *a.* *fe*-ret-e, characteristic of a ferret.

ferriage, *n.* *fe*-re-aj, the fare paid for conveyance by ferry.

ferric, *a.* *fe*-rik, pertaining to, containing, or derived from iron. **ferric oxide,** a compound containing two atoms of iron to three of oxygen; hæmatite.

ferriferous, *a.* fe-*rif*-er-us, producing or yielding iron. (L. *ferrum*, and *fero*, bear.)

ferro-alloy, *n.* *fe*-ro-a-*loy*, an alloy containing iron.

ferrocalcite, *n.* fe-ro-*kal*-site, calcite containing iron carbonate.

ferro-concrete, *n.* fe-ro-*kon*-kreet, concrete reinforced with steel bars.

ferrocyanate, *n.* *fe*-ro-*sy*-a-nate, ferrocyanide.

ferrocyanic, *a.* *fe*-ro-sy-*an*-ik, designating an acid obtained by treating ferrocyanides with acids.

ferrocyanide, *n.* *fe*-ro-*sy*-a-nide, a salt of ferrocyanic acid.

ferro-magnetic, *a.* acting like iron in a magnetic field; extremely magnetic opposed to diamagnetic: *n.* a substance that acts like iron in a magnetic field.

ferro-print, *n.* a photographic print made from salts of iron sensitizers.

ferrotype, *n.* *fe*-ro-tipe, a positive photograph on a japanned iron plate; tintype.

ferrous, *a.* *fe*-rus, pertaining to iron. **ferrous oxide,** a compound having one atom of iron to one of oxygen.

ferruginous, *a.* fe-*roo*-jin-us, containing iron; of the colour of iron rust. (L. *ferruginius*.)

ferrule, *n.* *fe*-rool, a small ring or cap of metal to protect an end of a stick, tool, etc. (Fr. *virole*.)

ferrumination, *n.* fe-*roo*-me-*nay*-shon, the act of cementing or soldering together. (L. *ferrumen*, cement.)

ferry, *n.* *fe*-re, a boat serving as a floating bridge; the place of passage where one may be taken across water by ferry-boat; the right of ferrying and charging toll: *v.t.* to carry or transport over a river, strait, or other water, in a boat; to maintain an aerial transport service: *v.i.* to pass over water in a boat. (A.S. *ferian*, go.)

ferry-boat, *n.* a boat for conveyance across a ferry.

ferryman, *n.* *fe*-re-man, one who keeps or works at a ferry.

***fertile,** *a.* *fer*-tile, fruitful; productive; rich in resources; inventive. (Fr.)

fertilely, *ad.* in a fertile manner.

fertileness, *n.* the quality of being fertile.

fertility, *n.* fer-*til*-e-te, productiveness; prolificness; richness; fertileness.

fertilization, *n.* *fer*-te-ly-*zay*-shon, the process of rendering fertile; fecundation; impregnation.

fertilize, *v.t.* *fer*-te-lize, to render fertile or productive; to enrich, as soil; to pollinate.

fertilizer, *n.* *fer*-te-*ly*-zer, an agent in fertilizing; an artificial manure.

ferula, *n.* *fe*-roo-la, a ferule; (*cap.*) a genus of umbelliferous plants including the giant fennel. (L., a rod.)

ferulaceous, *a.* fe-roo *ay*-she-us, pertaining to reeds or canes; having a reed-like stem.

ferule, *n.* *fe*-rool, a cane used to punish children in school: *v.t.* to punish with this. (L. *ferula*.)

fervency, *n.* *fer*-ven-se, the state of being fervent; ardour; zeal; warmth of devotion.

fervent, *a.* *fer*-vent, hot; ardent; glowing; warm in temper; vehement; zealous. (O.Fr., from L. *fervens*, boiling.)

fervently, *ad.* in a fervent manner.

ferventness, *n.* the quality of being fervent.

fervescent, *a.* fer-*ves*-sent, growing hot.

fervid, *a.* *fer*-vid, impassioned; burning; very warm in zeal. (L. *fervidus*.)

fervidly, *ad.* with glowing warmth.

fervidness, *n.* glowing heat; warm zeal.

fervour, *n.* *fer*-vur, heat or warmth; ardour; zeal.

fescennine, *a.* *fes*-sen-nine, licentious. **fescennine verses,** verse dialogues of a scurrilous or licentious character, one of the earliest forms of Italian poetry. (Pertaining to ancient festivals held at *Fescennium*, Etruria.)

fescue, *n.* *fess*-kew, a twig; a pointer used to indicate letters to children when learning to read. **fescue grass,** a grass of the genus *Festuca*, the stem of which was used as a pointer. (L. *festuca*, a straw.)

fess, *n.* fess, fesse.

fesse, *n.* fess, a broad band crossing the shield horizontally and occupying the third part of it [Her.]; one of the nine honourable ordinaries [Her.]. **fesse-point,** the centre of an escutcheon [Her.]. (O.Fr.)

festal, *a.* *fes*-tal, pertaining to a feast or festival; holiday-like; joyous; gay.

festally, *ad.* in a festive manner. (O.Fr.)

fester, *n.* *fes*-ter, a purulent inflamed tumour: *v.i.* to suppurate; to rankle; to grow more virulent: *v.t.* to cause to fester. (O.Fr. *festre*.)

festinate, *a.* *fês*-te-nate, hasty; hurried: *v.t.* and *i.* to hasten or hurry. (L. *festinatus*, hastened.)

festination, *n.* fes-te-*nay*-shon, an involuntary tendency to walk rapidly, noticeable in some nervous disorders [Med.].

festival, *a.* *fes*-te-val, pertaining to or characteristic of a feast; joyous; mirthful: *n.* a festive or joyous celebration; a church holy-day or anniversary; a series of periodically recurring musical or dramatic entertainments; revelry. (O.Fr., from L. *festum*, feast.)

festive, *a. fes*-tiv, pertaining to or becoming a feast; merry; joyous.
festively, *ad.* in a festive manner.
festivity, *n.* fes-*tiv*-e-te, feasting; joy as at a feast; a merrymaking; a festival. (L. *festivitas.*)
festivous, *a. fes*-te-vus, festive.
festoon, *n.* fes-*toon*, a garland of flowers, etc., hanging in an elliptic curve with the ends depending; an ornament of carved work, in imitation of such [Sculp.]: *v.t.* to form in or adorn with festoons. (Fr. *feston.*)
festoonery, *n.* fes-*toon*-er-re, decoration in festoons.
fet, *v.* fet, an obsolete form of **fetched.**
fetal, *a.* fœtal.
fetation, *n.* fœtation.
fetch, *v.t.* fetch, to go and bring; to derive; to bring or draw; to make or to perform; to heave; to attain or come to; to obtain as its price: *v.i.* to move or turn; to reach or attain [Naut.]: *n.* a stratagem, dodge, or trick; a powerful effort; a deep sigh. **fetch a compass,** to go in a roundabout way. **fetch a pump,** to pour water in to make it draw. **fetch out,** to bring or draw out; to cause to appear. **fetch to,** to revive, as from a swoon. **fetch up,** to cause to come up; to overtake. (A.S. *feccan.*)
fetch, *n.* fetch, a wraith or double; a ghost. (Origin unknown.)
fetch-candle, *n.* a light seen at night, as of a moving candle, believed to bode death.
fetcher, *n. fetch*-er, one who fetches; that which attracts.
fetching, *a. fetch*-ing, fascinating; of attractive appearance.
fête, *n.* fate, a festival or holiday; the festival of the saint after whom one is named: *v.t.* to entertain; to honour with a fête or festivities. **en fête** in holiday-making mood or state. **fête champêtre** (App.), an open-air entertainment; a large scale picnic. (Fr.)
fetial, *a. fee*-shal, pertaining to declarations of war and treaties of peace. (L. *Fetiales*, a college of priests responsible for diplomatic negotiations.)
fetid, *a. fet*-id *or fee*-tid, having a strongly offensive smell. (L. *fetidus*, stinking.)
fetidness, *n.* the quality of being fetid.
fetish, *n. fee*-tish *or fet*-ish, an object superstitiously invested with divine, demonic, or erotic power, and as such held in awe and usually worshipped; an idol, juju, or any false object of worship or adoration. (Port. *feitico*, magic.)
fetishism, *n. fet- or fee*-tish-izm, the worship of or belief in fetishes; erotic interest in some object intimately connected with a person adored [Psychan.].
fetishistic, *a. fet- or fee*-tish-*is*-tik, pertaining to fetishism.
fetlock, *n. fet*-lok, the tuft of hair growing behind the pastern joints of horses; the part where it grows; a fetterlock. (Etym. doubtful.)
fetor, *n. fee*-tor, any strong offensive smell. (L.)
fetter, *n. fet*-ter, a chain or shackle for the feet; anything that confines or restrains from motion: *v.t.* to shackle the feet with a chain; to confine ; to restrain; to impede. (A.S. *fetor.*)
fettered, *a. fet*-terd, having the feet stretched backward and unfit for walking (as seals, etc.) [Zool.].
fetterless, *a. fet*-ter-less, free from fetters.
fetterlock, *n. fet*-ter-lok, a shackle for a horse.
fettle, *n. fet*-tl, good condition; fitness: *v.t.* to set right; to tidy; to manage.
fetus, *n. fee*-tus; a fœtus.
fetwa, *n. fet*-wa, a written decision by a Mohammedan judge. (Ar.)
feu, *n.* few, formerly, a tenure under which the tenant performed certain services or made certain payments; now, a perpetual lease at a fixed rent; the land, etc., so held [Scots. Law]: *v.t.* to let or lease in feu. (From *fee.*)
feuar, *n. few*-ar, a holder of real estate on payment of feu-duty.
feud, *n.* fewd, a contention or quarrel; a deadly quarrel between parties, families, or clans to avenge a wrong. (O.Fr. *feide.*)
feud, *n.* fewd, a fief; the right to lands, etc., held by feu; lands so held. (O.Fr. *feu.*)
feudal, *a. few*-dal, pertaining to or consisting of feuds or fiefs; embracing tenures by military services. **feudal system,** the political and economic system prevailing over most of Europe during the Middle Ages, by which vassals held their lands from a lord on condition of performing military service when required.
feudalism, *n. few*-da-lizm, the feudal system; the principles, etc., on which this was based.
feudalist, *n. few*-da-list, a supporter of feudalism; a specialist in feudal history, law, etc.
feudalistic, *a.* few-da-*lis*-tik, pertaining to or characteristic of feudalism.
feudality, *n.* few-*dal*-e-te, the state or quality of being feudal; feudal principles or constitution; a fief.
feudalization, *n. few*-da-ly-*zay*-shon, the act of feudalizing.
feudalize, *v.t.* and *i. few*-da-lize, to reduce to a feudal tenure; to make subject to or conform to feudalism.
feudally, *ad.* in the feudal manner.
feudary, *a. few*-da-re, holding or held of a superior: *n.* a feudatory; a former officer in the court of wards.
feudatory, *n. few*-da-to-re, a vassal who held his lands of a superior on military tenure; holding by feudal tenure; subject; under alien suzerainty.
feudist, *n. few*-dist, a writer on feudal law.
feuilleton, *n.* (App.) the space in a French journal, usually the lower part of the page, devoted to light literature or criticism; a serial or short story in a newspaper. (Fr.)
fever, *n. fee*-ver, a state of body characterized by high temperature, an accelerated pulse, impaired functions, diminished strength, and often excessive thirst; heat; agitation; excitement by anything that strongly affects the passions: *v.t.* to put in a fever: *v.i.* to become feverish. (A.S. *fefer.*)
feverfew, *n. fee*-ver-few, the plant *Pyrethrum parthenium*, and other species of the same genus.
feverish, *a. fee*-ver-ish, slightly fevered; indicating or abounding in fever; inconstant; excited.
feverishly, *ad.* in a feverish manner.
feverishness, *n.* the state of being feverish.
feverous, *a. fee*-ver-us, pertaining to fever; feverish.
few, *a.* few, not many; small in number: *n.* a small number of. (A.S. *feawe.*)
fewness, *n.* smallness of number; paucity.
fey, *a.* fey, doomed to die; dying; on the verge of death; elfin; visionary. (A.S. *fæge.*)
fez, *n.* fez, a tall red cap without a brim. (*Fez*, in Morocco.)
fiacre, *n.* fe-ahkr, a French hackney-cab. (Fr.)
fiancé, *n.masc.* (*fem.* **fiancée**) (App.), one's betrothed. (Fr.)
fianchetto, *n.* fee-ang-*ket*-to, in chess, an opening in which either knight's pawn is advanced and the bishop developed on the long diagonal; a position in which such advance is the operative factor: *v.t.* to attack thus. (It., diminutive of *fianco*, side.)
fiar, *n. fee*-ar, the holder of the fee-simple of an estate [Scots. Law].
fiars, *n.pl. fee*-arz, prices of grain in each county for the current year determined by the sheriff as a basis for certain rates [Scots. Law].
fiasco, *n.* fe-*as*-koh, any signal failure, esp. in a public performer; an abortive attempt. (It., a flask.)
fiat, *n. fy*-at, a command to do something; a decree. (L., let it be done.)
fib, *n.* fib, a falsehood; a harmless inexactitude: *v.i.* to lie. (Origin uncertain.)
fibber, *n. fib*-ber, one who tells fibs.
fibre, *n. fy*-ber, a filament in plants and animals; the raw material in textile manufacture [Comm.]; grit, character, strength. (Fr.)
fibred, *a. fy*-berd, consisting of or having fibres.
fibriform, *a. fy*-bre-form, resembling a fibre.
fibril, *n. fy*-bril (*pl.* **fibrillæ,** fy-*bril*-lee), a small fibre; a very slender thread; one of the absorbent hairs which cover the roots of young plants [Bot.]. (L.)
fibrillated, *a. fy*-bre-*lay*-ted, furnished with fibrillæ; of a fibrous structure.
fibrillose, *a. fy*-bre-lose, fibrillated.
fibrin, *n. fy*-brin, an albuminoid substance present in the blood, without which clotting cannot take place; a similar substance in plants which forms into extremely delicate filaments.
fibrination, *n.* fy-bre-*nay*-shon, formation in the blood of excess of fibrin.
fibrinosis, *n.* fy-bre-*noh*-sis, a diseased condition characterized by excess of fibrin in the blood [Med.].
fibrinous, *a. fi*-bre-nus, of the nature of fibrin.

fibrocellular, *a.* fy-bro-*sel*-yew-lar, consisting of fibrous and cellular tissues.
fibroid, *a. fy*-broyd, resembling fibre.
fibroin, *n. fy*-bro-in, the chief constituent of silk, cobwebs, etc.
fibrolite, *n. fy*-bro-lite, sillimanite.
fibroma, *n.* fy-*broh*-ma, a fibrous tumour [Path.].
fibromuscular, *a.* fy-bro-*mus*-kew-lar, consisting of muscular and connective tissue [Anat.].
fibrosis, *n. fy-broh*-sis, a growth of fibrous matter; fibrous degeneration [Med.].
fibrositis, *n. fy*-bro-*sy*-tis, inflammation of fibrous tissue [Med.].
fibrous, *a. fy*-brus, composed of, containing fibres, or of the nature of fibres; sinewy.
fibrousness, *n.* the state of being fibrous.
fibrovascular, *a.* fy-bro-*vas*-kew-lar, consisting of ducts and woody fibres [Bot.].
fibster, *n. fib*-ster, a fibber [Coll.].
fibula, *n. fib*-yew-la, the outer and smaller bone of the leg [Anat.]; an antique brooch, clasp, or buckle. (L., a clasp.)
fibular, *a. fib*-yew-lar, pertaining to the fibula.
ficaria, *n.* fe-*kare*-re-a, pilewort or little celandine.
ficelle, *a.* fe-*sel*, string-coloured. (Fr., string.)
fichu, *n. fee*-shoo, a small three-cornered silk or lace cape or shawl. (Fr.)
fickle, *a. fik*-kl, changeable; irresolute; inconstant. (A.S. *ficol.*)
fickleness, *n.* the quality of being fickle.
fico, *n. fee*-ko, a snap of the fingers, as much as to say, "a fig for you." (It., a fig.)
fictile, *a. fik*-til *or* -tyl, moulded or mouldable into form by the potter; suitable for the potter or for pottery. (L. *fictilis.*)
★**fiction,** *n. fik*-shon, the act or art of feigning, inventing, or imagining; something feigned, invented, or imagined, esp. a feigned story; the literature of imagination; an assumption [Law]; a fib [Coll.]. (Fr.)
fictional, *a. fik*-shon-al, grounded on or characterized by fiction; fictitious.
fictionist, *n. fik*-shon-ist, a writer of fiction; a novelist; a romancer.
fictitious, *a.* fik-*tish*-us, feigned; imaginary; not real; counterfeit.
fictitiously, *ad.* by fiction; falsely.
fictitiousness, *n.* quality of being fictitious.
fictive, *a. fik*-tiv, feigned; imaginary; founded on fiction; imaginative.
fid, *n.* fid, a wooden pin used as a splicing tool; a bar of wood or iron put through a hole to keep a spar in its place [Naut.].
fiddle, *n. fid*-dl, a violin [Coll.]; a framework to keep plates, etc., on the table during bad weather [Naut.]: *v.i.* to play on a fiddle; to play with the hands, like one playing on a fiddle; to trifle; to fidget; to cheat, peculate, or act dishonesty [Slang]; *v.t.* to play a tune on a fiddle. **as fit as a fiddle,** in the best of condition. **to play second fiddle,** to take a subordinate part. (A.S. *fithele.*)
fiddleblock, *n.* a long block with two sheaves in the same plane [Naut.].
fiddle-bow, *n. fid*-dl-boh, the stringed bow with which the fiddle is played.
fiddle-de-dee, *int. fid*-dl-de-*dee*, nonsense!
fiddle-faddle, *n. fid*-dl-*fad*-dl, trifling talk: *a.* trifling; making a bustle about nothing.
fiddle-head, *n.* an ornament on the prow of a ship, shaped off like the head of a fiddle.
fiddler, *n. fid*-ler, one who fiddles; a violinist; one who fritters time away; a small burrowing crab of the genus *Uca*, with one claw much enlarged [U.S.A.]; a swindler, a dishonest person [Slang].
fiddle-stick, *n.* a fiddle-bow; *pl.* used as an interjection signifying nonsense.
fiddle-string, *n.* a string of the fiddle.
fiddle-wood, *n. fid*-dl-wood, a tropical American tree of the genus *Citharexylum*, yielding durable timber.
fiddley, *n. fid*-le, an iron framework round the opening of a hatchway or stokehole [Naut.].
fiddling, *a. fid*-ling, playing the fiddle; trifling in a fussy way; fidgety; petty; swindling, cozening [Slang].
fideism, *n. fy*-de-izm, the anti-rationalistic theory that divine revelation is the only dependable guide [Phil.].
fidelity, *n.* fy-*del*-e-te, faithfulness in observance of duty or performance of obligations; firm adherence to a person, party, cause, etc., with which one is united or to which one is bound; observance of the marriage covenant; adherence to truth. (O.Fr. *fidelité.*)
fidget, *n. fidj*-et, a state of nervous restlessness; one who fidgets: *v.i.* to move about restlessly or nervously. (Scand.)
fidgetiness, *n.* a state of being fidgety.
fidgety, *a. fidj*-e-te, restless; uneasy.
fidibus, *n. fid*-e-bus, a paper spill. (Ger.)
fiducial, *a.* fe-*dew*-she-al, founded on faith; confident; undoubting; of the nature of a trust; taken as a datum line or point. (Late L. *fiducialis*, from L. *fiducia*, trust.)
fiducially, *ad.* in a fiducial way.
fiduciary, *a.* fe-*dew*-she-a-re, fiducial; held in, or founded on, trust: *n.* one who holds a thing in trust; a trustee; one who depends on faith for salvation without works. **fiduciary issue,** notes or currency issued by a government or central bank backed not by a reserve of bullion but solely by the credit of the issuer.
fie, *int.* fy, expressing disapproval or disgust.
fief, *n.* feef, a fee; a feud; an estate held of a superior under feudal tenure. (O.Fr.)
★**field,** *n.* feeld, a piece of land enclosed for tillage or pasture; the open country; outdoor work; the locality of a battle, a battle itself, also the area of military operations; a mining district; wide expanse; room for action or operation; range within vision; range; magnetic, electrical, or gravitational, etc., range of influence [Physics]; special subject of knowledge; a playing ground; the players other than the batsmen [Cricket]; the horses in a race other than the favourite; the party of fox-hunters hunting; the ground or blank space on which figures are drawn; the whole surface of a shield [Her.]: *v.i.* and *t.* to scout at cricket; to bet on the field. **field events,** athletic contests other than racing, as jumping, wrestling, throwing the hammer, etc. **field of view,** the space within which objects are visible, esp. in an optical instrument adjusted to its focus. **to take the field,** to begin operations [Mil.]. (A.S. *feld.*)
field-allowance, *n.* an extra payment to commissioned and warrant officers for expenses incurred while on field duty.
field-artillery, *n.* artillery for acting with infantry in the field.
field-battery, *n.* a battery of field-guns.
field-book, *n.* a book used in surveying, in which are set down the angles, distances, etc.
field-club, *n.* a club for nature study in the field.
field-day, *n.* a day when troops are drawn out for instruction in field exercises and evolutions; a day when all take the field; a specially important day.
field-dressings, *n.pl.* surgical dressings and appliances for first-aid use [Mil.].
field-duck, *n.* the little bustard, *Otis tetrax.*
fielder, *n. feeld*-er, a scout at cricket; one of the side not batting; one who fields at baseball.
fieldfare, *n. feeld*-fare, a migratory bird of the thrush family, *Turdus pilaris*, visiting Britain during the winter. (A.S. *feldefare.*)
field-glass, *n. feeld*-glahs, the lens of an eyepiece nearest the object; a portable binocular telescope; a large opera-glass.
field-gun, *n. feeld*-gun, a gun for use on the battle field as distinct from a siege-gun.
field-hospital, *n.* a hospital near the front line at which early treatment to casualties is given [Mil.].
field-marshal, *n.* in the British and certain other armies an officer of the highest rank.
field-mouse, *n.* a vole, a rodent of the genus *Microtus.*
field-officer, *n.* a military officer of the rank of brigadier, colonel, lieutenant-colonel, or major.
field-piece, *n.* a field-gun.
field-preacher, *n.* one who preaches at the open-air religious gatherings.
fieldsman, *n. feeldz*-man, one who fields at cricket.
field-sports, *n.pl.* diversions of the field, as shooting and hunting.
field-works, *n.pl.* works thrown up in besieging or defending a place.
fiend, *n.* feend, a devil; a being animated with malice or hate. (A.S. *feond*, Ger. *feind*, a foe.)

fiendish, *a. feend*-ish, like a fiend; diabolical; malicious.
fiendishly, *ad.* in a fiendish manner.
fiendishness, *n.* the quality of being fiendish.
fiendlike, *a. feend*-like, resembling a fiend.
fierce, *a.* feerce, vehement; violent; savage; easily enraged; vehement in rage; fierce-looking; very eager or zealous. (O.Fr. *fers.*)
fiercely, *ad.* in a fierce manner.
fierceness, *n.* the quality of being fierce.
fieri-facias, *n. fy*-er-ry-*fay*-she-as, a writ of execution requiring a sheriff to levy in behalf of one who has recovered in debt or damages [Law]. (L., see it done.)
fierily, *ad. fy*-er-re-le, in a fiery way.
fieriness, *n.* the quality of being fiery.
fiery, *a. fy*-er-re, consisting of fire; on fire; flaring; blazing; apt to take fire; containing coal-gas in the atmosphere (of mines); vehement; ardent; passionate; irritable; spirited; like fire. **fiery cross,** a partially burnt cross or stick sent round in the Highlands to summon the clans to war.
fiesta, *n. fyes*-tah, a holiday; a festivity. (Sp.)
fife, *n.* fyf, a small shrill flute used chiefly in martial music with drums: *v.i.* to play on a fife. **fife-major,** a former non-commissioned officer in charge of the fifers of a battalion. (Ger. *pfeife.*)
fifer, *n. fyf*-er, one who plays on a fife.
fife-rail, *n. fyf*-rale, the rail round a ship's mast fitted with belaying pins [Naut.].
fifteen, *a.* fif-teen, five and ten: *n.* a side at Rugby football. **the 'Fifteen,** the Jacobite rebellion in 1715. (A.S. *fiftyne.*)
fifteenth, *a.* fif-teenth, the fifth after the tenth; forming one part in fifteen: *n.* a fifteenth part; the interval of the double octave [Mus.]; a 2-ft. organ-stop [Mus.]. (A.S. *fifteotha.*)
fifth, *a.* fifth, the ordinal of five; the next to the fourth; forming one part in five: *n.* one of five equal parts of a whole; an interval of three tones and a semitone [Mus.]. **fifth column,** *see* **column. fifth monarchy men,** a fanatical sect which appeared in Britain towards the close of the Protectorate proclaiming a fifth world-wide monarchy (following the Assyrian, Persian, Greek, and Roman), during which Christ should reign on earth a thousand years. (A.S. *fifta.*)
fifthly, *ad. fifth*-le, in the fifth place.
fiftieth, *a. fif*-te-eth, the ordinal of fifty.
fifty, *a. fif*-te, five times ten. (A.S. *fiftig.*)
fifty-fifty, *a.* a half each: *n.* halves [Slang].
fig, *n.* fig, the fig-tree, *Ficus carica*; the fruit of the fig-tree; a thing of no worth; a spongy excrescence on the foot of a horse following a bruise; a piece of tobacco [U.S.A. Slang]. (Fr. *figue.*)
fig, *v.t.* fig, to dress; to rig out; to furbish: *n.* condition, as in "in fine fig." (Ger. *fegen,* to furbish.)
fig-eater, *n.* fig-*ee*-ter, the beccafico or garden warbler, a species of *Sylvia.*
★**fight,** *n.* fite, a battle; a contest: *v.i.* to contend for victory in battle or in single combat; to contend in arms; to contend or strive; to act as a soldier: *v.t.* to carry on, as a battle; to win by a struggle; to war against; to cause to fight. **fight off,** to repel. **fight out,** to decide by fighting; to fight to a finish. **fight shy of,** purposely to avoid meeting or facing up to. *p.* and *pp.* **fought.** (A.S. *feohtan.*)
fighter, *n. fite*-er, one who fights; a combatant; a warrior; a military aeroplane designed solely for combat in the air. **fighter-bomber,** a fighter equipped with bomb carrying and dropping apparatus.
fighting, *a. fite*-ing, trained to fight; engaged in war: *n.* contention; strife. **a fighting chance,** a chance that is possible but not obtainable without a struggle.
fighting-fish, *n.* any of the small pugnacious freshwater fish of the genus *Bette,* abounding in Siam.
fighting-top, *n.* a gun-platform surrounding the head of a warship.
fig-leaf, *n.* the leaf of a fig-tree; a thin covering [Fig.].
fig-marigold, *n. see* **mesembryanthemum.**
figment, *n. fig*-ment, an invention; a fiction; something feigned or imagined. (L. *figmentum.*)
figuline, *a. fig*-yew-line, fictile: *n.* potter's clay; pottery. (L. *figulus,* potter.)
figurable, *a. fig*-yew-ra-bl, capable of being fashioned or moulded into a fixed shape; describable.
figural, *a. fig*-yew-ral, represented by or pertaining to figure or delineation. (O.Fr.)
figurant, *n.masc.* (*fem.* **figurante**) (App.), a ballet dancer; an actor who appears on the stage but has no speaking part. (Fr.)
figurate, *a. fig*-yew-rate, of or after a determinate form; metaphorical; embellished, florid [Mus.]. **figurate numbers,** numbers formed according to certain laws, and having peculiar relations to different geometrical figures, as triangles, squares, pentagons, etc. (L. *figuratus,* formed.)
figuration, *n.* fig-yew-*ray*-shon, the act of giving figure or determinate form; determination to a certain form; florid or ornamental treatment by use of passing-notes, etc. [Mus.].
figurative, *a. fig*-yew-ra-tiv, representing something else; representing by resemblance; metaphorical, not literal or direct; abounding in figures of speech; flowery. (Late L. *figurativus.*)
figuratively, *ad.* in a figurative manner or sense.
figurativeness, *n.* state of being figurative.
figure, *n. fig*-ur, the form of anything in outline; shape; distinguished appearance; appearance of any kind; magnificence; representation in painting, drawing, etc.; a statue; an image; a price [Coll.]; the form of a syllogism with respect to the disposition of the middle term [Logic]; a symbol denoting a number [Arith.]; a diagram [Geom.]; a horoscope [Astrol.]; type, representative, or symbol [Theol.]; a mode of speaking or writing, in which words are deflected from their ordinary signification [Rhet.]; the several steps or movements which the dancer makes in accordance with the music; a combination of movements in which a skater starts and finishes at the same point; any distinct phrase or group of notes [Mus.]: *v.t.* to form into any determinate shape; to make a resemblance of; to cover or adorn with figures; to diversify; to represent typically or figuratively; to image in the mind; to calculate; to note by characters: *v.i.* to cipher; to make a figure. (Fr. from L. *figura,* from *fingo,* form.)
figured, *a. fig*-urd, adorned with or represented by figures; with ornamental grain (of timber). **figured bass,** thorough bass. **figured muslin,** a thin fabric in which a pattern or design is wrought.
figure-head, *n.* the figure, statue, or bust on the projecting part of the prow of a ship; a nominal chief, esp. one whose name gives confidence.
figure-of-eight, *n.* a design made, esp. in skating, in the form of the figure 8.
figure-weaving, *n.* the process of weaving patterns or designs as produced in damask, etc.
figurine, *n. fig*-yew-reen, a small statuette. (Fr.)
figwort, *n. fig*-wurt, a plant of the genus *Scrophularia*; pile-wort.
filament, *n. fil*-a-ment, a slender thread or fibre, such as animal and vegetable tissues and certain mineral structures, are composed of; the stalk of a stamen [Bot.]; a thread-like series of cells set end to end [Bot.]; the thread-like conductor rendered incandescent in an electric lamp; the heated electrode in a thermionic valve [Wire.]. **filament battery,** the battery or cell connected across a thermionic valve filament. **filament current,** the current flowing in a thermionic valve. **filament lamp,** an incandescent electric lamp. (Fr.)
filamentary, *a. fil*-a-*men*-ta-re, of the nature of a filament; formed of a filament or filaments.
filamentous, *a. fil*-a-*men*-tus, like a thread; bearing filaments; consisting of fine filaments.
filanders, *n.pl.* fe-*lan*-derz, intestinal thread-worms, esp. in hawks; the disease due to these.
filar, *a. fy*-lar, pertaining to or furnished with threads.
filaria, *n.* fe-*lare*-re-a (*pl.* **filariæ**), a threadworm parasitic in man and other animals; a genus of Filariidæ. (L. *filum,* thread.)
filarial, *a.* fe-*lare*-re-al, pertaining to the filariæ.
filarian, *a.* fe-*lare*-re-an, filarial.
filariasis, *n.* fil-a-*ry*-a-sis, a disease caused by infestation with filariæ [Path.].
filariform, *a.* fe-*lare*-re-form, shaped like a thread; resembling filaria.
filasse, *n.* fe-*lass,* vegetable fibre prepared for manufacture.
filature, *n. fil*-a-tewr, the reeling of silk from cocoons; the reel used; an establishment for reeling silk. (Late L. *filatura.*)

filbert, *n.* *fil*-bert, the fruit of the cultivated hazel, *Corylus avellanc.* (Fr., after St. Philibert.)
filch, *v.t.* filch, to pilfer; commit a petty theft. (Origin unknown.)
filcher, *n.* *filch*-er, one guilty of petty theft.
file, *n.* file, a line or wire on which papers are strung; the papers so strung or otherwise arranged in order; a jacket in which papers are kept for ready reference; a bundle of papers tied together, with the title of each indorsed; a list or catalogue; a row of soldiers ranged one behind another, from front to rear; a row of squares on a chess-board running at right angles to the ranks and from player to player: *v.t.* to string or fasten, as papers, on a wire, etc., for preservation; to arrange papers in a bundle and in order; to present or exhibit officially or for trial: *v.i.* to march in a file or line, as soldiers. **rank and file,** the common soldiers; a body of men under leaders. **to file off,** to wheel off by files and march in length. (O.Fr. *file.*)
file, *n.* file, a steel tool with little furrows on the surface, used in cutting or smoothing metals, ivory, or wood; a polishing apparatus; an artful dodger [Slang]: *v.t.* to smooth or cut, as with a file; to polish. (A.S. *feol.*)
file, *v.t.* file, to defile, sully or spot. (A.S. *fylan.*)
file-cutter, *n.* a maker of files.
file-fish, *n.* any fish of the genus *Balistes,* so called because the skin is granulated like a file.
filemot, *n.* *fil*-e-mot, a yellowish-brown, the colour of a faded leaf: *a.* of this colour. (Fr. *feuille,* leaf, *morte,* dead.)
filet, *n.* fe-*let,* a lace or net with a square mesh. (Fr., a net.)
filial, *a.* *fil*-e-al, pertaining to a son or daughter; suitable to a child in relation to his parents. (Late L. *filialis.*)
filially, *ad.* *fil*-e-a-le, in a filial manner.
filiation, *n.* fil-e-*ay*-shon, the relation of a child to a father, correlative to paternity; adoption; descent from; affiliation [Law].
filibeg, *n.* *fil*-e-beg, a kilt, esp. the small kilt as distinguished from the older kilt which enveloped the whole body. (Gael. *feileadh-beag,* a small kilt.)
filibuster, *n.* fil-e-*bus*-ter, a military adventurer, esp. one who illegally invades and occupies foreign territory; a buccaneer; a national representative who obstructs legislation or action by dilatory tactics in the assembly [U.S.A.]: *v.i.* to act as a filibuster. (Sp.)
filibusterism, *n.* fil-e-*bus*-ter-rizm, the practice, or the support, of filibustering.
filical, *a.* *fil*-e-kal, pertaining to the Filicales, the order or group containing the ferns. (L. *filix,* fern.)
filiciform, *a.* fe-*lis*-e-form, fern-shaped.
filicoid, *a.* *fil*-e-koyd, fern-like: *n.* a plant resembling a fern. (L. *filix,* and *eidos,* like.)
filiform, *a.* *fil*-e-form, having the form of a thread.
filigree, *n.* *fil*-e-gree, a kind of ornamental lacework in gold or silver wire; light and delicate tracery of any kind; a lacework pattern: *a.* pertaining to, resembling, or composed of filigree. (Fr. *filigrane.*)
filigreed, *a.* *fil*-e-greed, ornamented with filigree.
filings, *n.pl.* *file*-ingz, fragments or particles rubbed off by the act of filing.
Filipino, *n.masc.* fil-e-*pee*-no (*fem.* **Filipina,** fil-e-*pee*-na), a native of the Philippine Islands: *a.* pertaining to the Filipinos, their culture, etc.
fill, *n.* fil, as much as supplies want or satisfies; that which fills, filling: *v.i.* to pour out liquor for drinking; to become full or distended; to be satisfied: *v.t.* to make full; to put or pour in till the space is full; to supply with abundance; to cause to abound; to satisfy; to glut; to supply with an incumbent; to possess and perform the duties of; to brace the yards so that the wind will act upon and distend the sails [Naut.]. **fill out,** to extend or enlarge to the desired limit. **fill up,** to make full; to engage or employ; to complete; to become full. **filled gold,** thin sheet gold with a base metal backing. (A.S. *fyllan.*)
filler, *n.* *fill*-er, one who or that which fills; a tube, vessel, etc., used in filling bottles, casks, etc.; material added to compositions, etc., to impart strength or better working properties.
fillér, *n.* fil-*ayr,* a Hungarian currency unit, one-hundredth of a forint.
fillet, *n.* *fill*-et, a small band to tie about the hair of the head; meat or fish that has had the bones removed; the undercut of a loin; meat boned, rolled, and tied; the loins of a horse; a narrow flat band between mouldings [Arch.]; a plain band on the back of a book-binding; any small scantling less than a batten [Carp.]; a little rule or reglet of leaf-gold [Print. and Gild.]: *v.t.* to bind or adorn with a fillet; to remove the bones. **fillet of beef,** the undercut; a steak. **fillet of veal,** the fleshy part of the thigh tied round in a roll. (O.Fr.)
filling, *a.* *fill*-ing, satisfying: *n.* something which fills up. **filling-in pieces,** short timbers, less than the full length, fitted against the roofs and groins of partitions [Carp.]. **filling-station,** a roadside depot for supplying petrol, oil, etc., to motorists.
fillip, *n.* *fill*-ip, a jerk of the finger forced suddenly from the thumb; an incitement: *v.t.* to strike with the nail of the finger, forced from the thumb with a sudden spring. (Imit., or from *flip.*)
fillister, *n.* *fill*-is-ter, a plane for cutting a groove or rabbet; the rabbet on the outer edge of a window sash.
filly, *n.* *fil*-le, a female foal. (Ice. *fylja.*)
film, *n.* film, a thin skin; a pellicle; a very slender thread; celluloid sensitized for photography; a cinematograph picture: *pl.* the production and exhibition of these: *v.t.* to cover with a film; to take a moving picture of; to photograph subjects for cinematographic reproduction. (A.S. *fylmen.*)
film-fan, *n.* *film*-fan, an enthusiastic devotee of the films or "pictures."
filminess, *n.* *film*-e-ness, the state of being filmy.
filmize, *v.t.* *film*-ize, to make a motion picture of; to adapt (a novel, etc.) for the cinema.
film-pack, *n.* a number of photographic films so wrapped that they may be loaded into or taken from a camera as a unit in daylight.
film-star, *n.* *film*-star, an actor or actress playing a leading part in motion pictures.
filmy, *a.* *film*-e, composed of films; obscured by or resembling a film. **filmy fern,** any fern of the genus *Hymenophyllum.*
filoplume, *n.* *fil*-lo-ploom, a hair-like feather; a slender feather having apparently no shaft. (L. *filum,* thread, *pluma,* feather.)
filose, *a.* *fy*-lohs, ending in a thread-like process [Zool. and Bot.].
filoselle, *n.* *fil*-lo-sel, floss silk. (Fr.)
filter, *n.* *filt*-er, a substance or apparatus for clearing liquids from matter held in suspension; a device used in air-conditioning systems which purifies abnormally polluted air; a device for discriminating between currents of different frequencies in communication circuits, eliminates interference, etc. [Elect.]; a translucent sheet interposed across a beam of light to alter the relative intensity of its different wave-lengths [Phot.]: *v.t.* to purify liquor, etc., by passing it through a filter; to effect by means of a filter [Phot., Elect., etc.]: *v.i.* to pass through by filtering; to percolate; to pass into or by means of another lane of traffic [Transport]. **filter-paper,** a porous paper for filtering. **filter-passer,** a disease-germ so minute that it is microscopically invisible and no known filter can stop it. (Fr. *filtrer.*)
filterable, *a.* *fil*-ter-ra-bl, capable of being filtered or of passing through a filter. **filterable virus,** a filter-passer.
filter-bed, *n.* a double-bottomed tank used for filtering sewage, etc. through sand or gravel.
filth, *n.* filth, any foul matter; anything that defiles; dirt; foul language. (A.S. *fylth.*)
filthily, *ad.* in a filthy manner.
filthiness, *n.* the state of being filthy.
filthy, *a.* *fil*-the, foul; dirty; morally impure; disgusting. **filthy lucre,** dishonourable gain; money.
filtrate, *n.* *fil*-trate, the liquid which has been passed through a filter: *v.t.* and *i.* to filter.
filtration, *n.* fil-*tray*-shon, the act or process of filtering; percolation; diffusion.
fimbria, *n.* *fim*-bre-a, the denticulated ring of the operculum of mosses [Bot.]; the fringe-like extremity of the Fallopian tube [Anat.]. (L., a fringe.)
fimbriate, *a.* *fim*-bre-at, fimbriated: *v.t.* to hem; to fringe. (L. *fimbriatus.*)
fimbriated, *a.* *fim*-bre-ay-ted, fringed; bordered; ornamented, as an ordinary, with a narrow border of another tincture [Her.].
fimbricate, *a.* *fim*-bre-kat, fimbriated.

fimetarious, *a.* fim-e-*tare*-re-us, growing on or among dung [Bot.]. (L. *fimetus*, a dunghill.)
fin, *n.* fin, the organ of locomotion in fishes and cetaceans; a keel like a vertical fin; a fin-like part to secure stability, as in aircraft, kite-balloons, etc.; anything like a fin; a thin excrescence on the surface of a casting [Moulding]; a blade of whalebone [Comm.]: *v.t.* to carve or cut up, as a chub. (A.S.)
finable, *a. fine*-a-bl, subject to a fine or penalty.
final, *a. fine*-al, last; ultimate; conclusive; decisive as regards the ultimate design; *n.* the end; the last heat in a match; the last match or examination in a series; the last edition of a daily or weekly paper. **final cause,** the ultimate end or object contemplated, esp. in the creation of the universe. (O.Fr., from L. *finis*, end.)
finale, *n.* fe-*nah*-le, the last passage in a piece of music; that which closes a concert; close of any performance; the end. (It.)
finalism, *n. fine*-a-lizm, teleology; the belief that the limit has been reached.
finalist, *n. fine*-a-list, a contestant in the final round of a competition, etc.; a believer in finalism: *a.* teleological.
finality, *n.* fy-*nal*-e-te, state of being final or settled for good; teleology; the doctrine that everything has been conceived and arranged in connexion with the execution of a predetermined plan.
finally, *ad. fine*-a-le, lastly; completely.
finance, *n.* fi-*nance*, the science or system of managing money matters: *pl.* the revenue of a state; the funds in the public treasury; the income or resources of individuals: *v.t.* to provide or procure the capital for. (O.Fr.)
financial, *a.* fi-*nan*-shal, pertaining to finance. **financial year,** the fiscal year.
financially, *ad.* in relation to finances.
financier, *n.* fi-*nan*-se-er, one skilled or engaged in finance.
finback, *n. fin*-bak, a finner.
finch, *n.* finch, a general term for members of a large group of small seed-eating birds including the goldfinch, chaffinch, and sparrow, and the crossbills. (A.S. *finc.*)
find, *n.* fynd, something found: *v.t.* to discover, either by chance, search, study, experiment, or trial, etc.; to gain; to perceive; to detect; to enjoy; to discover and declare; to fall in with; to provide for: *v.i.* to determine and declare an issue [Law]; to start a fox [Hunting]. *p.* and *pp.* **found. all found,** with all necessaries provided. **to find a bill,** to establish grounds of accusation, as by grand jury [Law]. **to find fault with,** to censure. **to find in,** to supply or to furnish with. **to find oneself,** to be; to fare in regard to health, etc.; to become aware of one's own capacities; to supply one's own needs. **to find out,** to discover; to sound; to understand; to comprehend; to detect. (A.S. *findan.*)
findable, *a. fynd*-a-bl, discoverable.
finder, *n. fynd*-er, one who or that which finds; an optical appliance for sighting or localizing an object.
find-fault, *n.* a censurer; a caviller.
finding, *n. fynd*-ing, discovery; the act of discovering; the return of a grand jury to a bill; a verdict [Law]: *pl.* things found; the tools, etc., which a workman has himself to supply.
findon, *n. fin*-on, trade term for the smoke-dried haddocks first cured at Finnan, Kincardineshire.
fine, *a.* fine, small; thin; slender; minute; subtle; keen; not coarse; pure; refined; nice; delicate; delicately dextrous; beautiful in thought; handsome; accomplished; excellent; noble; showy; splendid: *v.t.* to clarify; to purify; to refine; to taper or make fine. **fine arts,** the arts which depend chiefly on the imagination, and whose object is to please, as poetry, music, dancing, painting, and sculpture. (O.Fr. *fin.*)
fine, *n.* fine, a sum of money imposed by way of penalty for an offence; a payment for renewing a lease: *v.t.* to impose a fine on; to punish by fine. **in fine,** in conclusion. (L. *finis*, an end.)
fine-draw, *v.t.* to sew up a rent with such nicety that it is not perceived.
fine-drawn, *a.* drawn fine; spun too fine; oversubtle; reduced by training [Sport].
finely, *ad. fine*-le, in a fine manner or state.
fineness, *n. fine*-ness, the state of being fine: the proportion of purity [Metal.].
finer, *n. fine*-er, one who refines metals.
finery, *n. fine*-er-re, showy qualities; splendour; fine showy things in way of dress or ornament; a furnace in which iron is made malleable; the art of refining.
fine-spoken, *a.* using fine phrases.
fine-spun, *a.* drawn to a fine thread; elaborated with subtlety or with over-refinement; unpractical.
finesse, *n.* fe-*ness*, subtlety of contrivance to gain a point; artfulness: *v.i.* to use artifice; to attempt to take a trick with a low card so as to make sure of a second with a higher. (Fr.)
finesser, *n.* fe-*ness*-er, one who finesses.
fine-stuff, *n.* slaked lime, etc., as material for the second coat in plastering.
fin-fish, *n. fin*-fish, a finner.
fin-foot, *n.* a family of tropical aquatic birds of the order Gruiformes, allied to the rails.
fin-footed, *a.* web-footed, as waterfowl.
★**finger,** *n. fing*-ger, a digit of the hand; one of the four longer digits, the fifth being the thumb; a part of a glove covering a finger; a finger's breadth; an index, or anything pointing like a finger; skill in using the fingers, esp. in playing a keyed instrument: *v.t.* to touch or handle with the fingers; to interfere with; to pilfer; to play, as an instrument; to perform with the fingers, as delicate work: *v.i.* to dispose the fingers aptly in playing an instrument. **fingers and toes,** the plant disease anbury. **to burn one's fingers,** to suffer through rash speculation or intermeddling. **to have a finger in the pie,** to be mixed up in the affair. **to have at one's finger ends,** to be quite ready with. **to slip through the fingers,** to escape unexpectedly. **your fingers are all thumbs,** you are very clumsy handed. (A.S.)
finger-alphabet, *n. fing*-ger-*al*-fa-bet, the signs made on the hands by deaf-mutes as a means of communication.
fingerboard, *n. fing*-ger-board, the board at the neck of a violin, guitar, or the like, where the fingers act on the strings; a keyboard.
finger-bowl, *n.* a glass containing water for dipping the fingers in at the dinner-table.
fingered, *a. fing*-gerd, having fingers; digitate [Bot.]. **light-fingered,** addicted to pilfering.
fingering, *n. fing*-ger-ing, the act of touching lightly or handling; the manner of touching an instrument or music; signs on music to guide the player; delicate work made with the fingers; a loose-twisted wool for knitting.
fingerling, *n. fing*-ger-ling, any fish of under finger length, esp. a young salmon or parr.
finger-nail, *n.* a nail growing on a finger.
finger-plate, *n.* a plate fixed on a door to protect the paint.
finger-post, *n.* a post with a finger or fingers pointing out the directions; a sign-post.
finger-print, *n.* an impression of the pattern of the skin of a finger-tip, esp. one taken as a means of identification for police purposes.
finger-ring, *n.* an ornamental circlet of precious metal worn on the finger and frequently jewelled.
finger-stall, *n.* a cover as protection for the finger when hurt or in surgical operations.
finger-tip, *n.* the tip of the finger. **to the finger-tips,** completely; thoroughly; from end to end.
finial, *n. fin*-e-al, the ornamental finishing of a pinnacle or gable; the pinnacle itself [Arch.]. (L. *finis.*)
finical, *a. fin*-e-kal, particular to excess, esp. over trifles or matters of mere detail; over nice; fastidious.
finically, *ad.* in a finical manner.
finicalness, *n.* the quality of being finical; extreme nicety.
finicking, *a. fin*-e-king, precise in trifles; idly busy; niggling.
finicky, *a. fin*-e-ke, finical; fussy.
fining, *n. fine*-ing, the process of refining or purifying; the clarifying of wines, etc.; the solution, generally of gelatine, used for this.
fining-pot, *n.* a crucible in which metals are refined.
finis, *n. fy*-nis, the end; conclusion. (L.)
finish, *n. fin*-ish, the end; the minute labour bestowed on a work of art with a view to render it as perfect as possible; the final stage of an operation,

as the last coat of plaster on a wall: *v.i.* to come to an end: *v.t.* to bring to an end; to complete; to work at elaborately, with a view to make as perfect as possible. (O.Fr. *finiss*, from *ppr.* of *finir.*)
finish, *a. fine*-ish, more or less fine.
finished, *a. fin*-isht, complete, perfect, said of work, either in itself as work, or in its effect as art.
finisher, *n. fin*-ish-er, one who or that which finishes; a final blow.
finishing, *a. fin*-ish-ing, completing; giving a finish to. **finishing coat,** the last coating of paint, etc.
finite, *a. fy*-nite, having a limit; limited, in contrast with infinite; limited as regards number and person, in contrast with infinitive [Gram.]. (L. *finitus.*)
finitely, *ad. fy*-nite-le, in a limited degree.
finiteness, *n. fy*-nite-ness, the state of being limited.
finitude, *n. fin*-e-tude, finite state; finiteness.
finless, *a. fin*-less, destitute of fins.
finlet, *n. fin*-let, a small fin.
Finn, *n.* fin, a native of Finland. (A.S. *Finnas.*)
finnan, *n. fin*-nan, a findon haddock.
finned, *a.* find, having fins; having broad edges on either side.
finner, *n. fin*-ner, a whale of the genus *Balænoptera*; a rorqual.
Finnic, *a. fin*-nik, pertaining to the group of peoples of which the Finns are typical: Finnish.
Finnish, *n. fin*-nish, the language of the Finns: *a.* pertaining to Finland, its people, or language.
finnoc, *n. fin*-ok, the white trout of certain Scottish rivers. (Gael. *fionn*, white.)
finny, *a. fin*-ne, furnished with fins; pertaining to or abounding in fish.
Finsen-light, *n. fin*-sen-*lite*, ultra-violet or other highly actinic light used in treatment of lupus, etc.; the apparatus producing this. (From N. R. *Finsen*, *d.* 1904, the Danish originator.)
fin-whale, *n.* a rorqual; a finner.
fiord, *n.* fyord, a deeply indented, narrow, and rock-bound inlet due to ice-action and partly filled by the sea, as in Norway. (Dan.)
fiorin, *n. fy*-o-rin, the white bent-grass, *Agrostis alba.* (Ice. *fiorthan*, coarse grass.)
fiorite, *n.* fe-*oh*-rite, opaline silica with pearly lustre occurring as incrustations near hot springs. (Sta. *Fiora*, Tuscany, where found.)
fioritura, *n. fee*-o-re-*too*-ra, embellishment of a melody in music. (It.)
fir, *n.* fir, any of several species of cone-bearing trees, esp. of the genus *Abies*, highly valued for their timber; the wood of these; in the Bible, the cedar, cypress, etc. **douglas fir,** the Oregon pine, *Pseudotsuga douglasii*, a large conifer with valuable timber, of western N. America. **Scotch fir,** a pine, *Pinus sylvestris*, of N. Europe and Asia. (Scand.).
***fire,** *n.* fire, heat and light emanating from a body burning; fuel burning on a hearth, etc.; combustion; the burning of a house or town; a conflagration; the discharge of fire-arms; light; lustre; incandescence; that which inflames or irritates the passions; ardour or violence of passion; glow of imagination; severe trial; trouble; affliction: *v.t.* to set on fire; to inflame; to irritate; to animate; to shoot; to cause to explode; to discharge; to supply (a furnace) with fuel; to cauterize; to sack or dismiss [Slang]: *v.i.* to take fire; to become irritated or inflamed; to discharge fire-arms; to ring a peal of bells simultaneously. **Greek fire,** a highly inflammable artificial combustible said to have been used by the Byzantine Greeks against the Saracens. **Kentish fire,** *see* **Kentish. St. Elmo's fire, a** luminosity due to discharges of atmospheric electricity occasionally seen in stormy weather at mast-heads, steeple-tops, etc. **to be on fire,** to be in a state of ignition; to be highly excited. **to be under fire,** to be fired upon by an enemy [Mil.]. **to set on fire,** to kindle; to excite violent action. (A.S. *fyr.*)
fireable, *a. fire*-ra-bl, capable of being ignited; capable of being discharged (of guns).
fire-alarm, *n.* an apparatus, automatic or otherwise, for giving warning of a fire.
fire-arm, *n.* a weapon with which a missile is discharged by the force generated by the ignition of an explosive.
fireback, *n. fire*-bak, the iron plate at the back of a fireplace; a pheasant of S.E. Asia of the genus *Euplocamus.*
fire-ball, *n.* a sack filled with combustibles to be thrown among enemies; a bolide, or exploding meteor; a form of St. Elmo's fire.
fire-balloon, *n. fire*-ba-loon, a balloon which ascends by the rarefaction of its contained air by the burning of a light substance attached to its open mouth.
fire-bar, *n.* one of the bars of a furnace on which the fuel rests.
fire-basket, *n.* a small portable grate.
fire-blast, *n.* a disease in plants, esp. in which they acquire a burnt appearance.
fire-board, *n.* a chimney-board used to close a fireplace in summer.
fire-box, *n.* the furnace of a locomotive engine.
firebrand, *n. fire*-brand, a piece of wood kindled or on fire; one who inflames factions.
fire-brick, *n.* a brick that will sustain intense heat without fusion.
fire-brigade, *n.* a trained body of firemen, with or without auxiliary women.
fireclay, *n. fire*-klay, a kind of clay that will sustain intense heat, used in making firebricks.
fire-control, *n.* control of fire or firing, esp. the system by which the guns of a ship can be controlled from one centre.
firecrest, *n. fire*-krest, the wren *Regulus ignicapillus*, which has a flame-coloured crest.
firedamp, *n. fire*-damp, the explosive carburetted hydrogen of coal-mines; methane.
fire-dog, *n.* an andiron.
fire-drill, *n.* a primitive device for producing fire by twirling a pointed stick on a piece of wood; exercise in fighting fire, or in procedure in case of fire.
fire-eater, *n.* a showman who pretends to swallow fire; a fighting character, bully, or duellist.
fire-engine, *n.* a mobile machine for throwing water to extinguish fire.
fire-escape, *n.* fixed or mobile apparatus or machine for effecting escape from the upper part of a building on fire.
firefly, *n. fire*-fly, a small nocturnal luminous winged beetle.
fire-guard, *n.* a framework placed in front of a fireplace; a firewatcher or organized body of these.
fire-hose, *n.* the portable piping through which a fire-engine pumps the water.
fire-insurance, *n.* insurance against loss from fire.
fire-irons, *n.pl.* the implements belonging to a fireplace, as the shovel, tongs, and poker.
fireless, *a. fire*-less, destitute of fire; effected, or producing effect, without the use of fire (as fireless cookery).
firelight, *n. fire*-lite, the light from the fire in a fireplace.
fire-lighter, *n.* a combustible substance to kindle a fire with.
firelock, *n. fire*-lok, a musket or other gun having a lock with a steel and flint to strike fire.
fireman, *n. fire*-man, a man whose business is to extinguish fires, esp. a member of a fire-brigade; one who tends the fires of a steam-engine, etc.
fire-new, *a.* brand-new.
fire-office, *n.* a fire-insurance office.
fire-opal, *n.* a variety of opal showing flame-like internal coloration.
fire-pan, *n.* a pan for holding or conveying fire; a brazier; the priming part of a firelock.
fireplace, *n. fire*-place, the part of a chimney appropriated to the fire; a grate; a hearth.
fire-plug, *n.* the valve in a water-main with which the fire-hose is connected.
fire-policy, *n.* a certificate of insurance against loss by fire, granted by an insurance office.
fireproof, *a. fire*-proof, proof against fire.
firer, *n. fire*-rer one who or that which fires; an incendiary.
fire-raising, *n.* the crime of arson; incendiarism.
fire-screen, *n.* a movable screen placed before a fire to ward off the heat; a protection against fire.
fireship, *n. fire*-ship, a vessel, filled with combustibles, sent among an enemy's ships to fire them.
fireside, *n. fire*-side, the hearth; home.
fire-step, *n.* a ledge along the front of a trench for firing from [Mil.].
fire-stick, *n.* the obtusely pointed stick component of a fire-drill; a burning brand.
fire-stone, *n.* iron pyrites; any stone which bears a great degree of heat.

firetail, *n.* *fire*-tale, the redstart.
firetrap, *n.* *fire*-trap, a device to prevent the spread of fire, as in a cinema projector; a building in which the means of escape from fire are inadequate.
fire-warden, *n.* a firewatcher; one having authority to direct others in the extinguishing of fires; an officer protecting forests from fire [U.S.A.].
firewatch, *v.i.* *fire*-wotch, to perform the duties of a firewatcher: *n.* the duty, or a spell of duty, of firewatching.
firewatcher, *n.* *fire*-wotch-er, a member of an organized civilian body trained to notify, and to prevent the spread of, fires caused by enemy action.
firewater, *n.* *fire*-waw-ter, the Red Indian name for ardent spirits.
fire-weed, *n.* any of several weeds growing quickly where brushwood has been burned.
firewood, *n.* *fire*-wood, wood for fuel.
fireworks, *n.pl.* *fire*-wurks, preparations of explosives and combustibles for the production of a brilliant display for general exhibition or at times of public rejoicing, etc.; similar devices employed for signalling and incendiary purposes [Mil.]; a sparkling display of virtuosity, etc. [Fig.].
fire-worship, *n.* the worship of fire, esp. of the sun as the most emphatic expression and exhibition of beneficent divine power.
fire-worshipper, *n.* one who worships fire, esp. a Zoroastrian.
firing, *n.* *fire*-ing, fuel; the discharge of fire-arms; the process of replenishing a furnace; the ignition of an explosive mixture, as in an internal combustion engine; excessive heating of a bearing [Mech.]; the application of a cautery [Farriery]. **firing-line,** the line of trenches, or of troops, nearest to the enemy. **firing-step,** a fire-step.
firk, *v.t.* ferk, to defeat; to trounce; to arouse. (A.S. *fercian.*)
firkin, *n.* *fer*-kin, a beer measure of 9 imperial gallons; the fourth part of a barrel; a cask of this capacity. (Mid. Dut. *vierdekyn,* fourth part.)
firm, *a.* ferm, fixed; compact; solid; constant; not easily moved; resolute; steady (of prices): *ad.* firmly: *v.t.* to fix; to make firm; to confirm; to establish. (Fr. *ferme.*)
firm, *n.* ferm, a partnership of two or more persons for transacting business; a business house. **long firm,** a swindling group which fraudulently obtains goods on credit and sells them for cash. (Late L. *firma,* a signature.)
firmament, *n.* *fer*-ma-ment, the sky regarded as a solid expanse with stars fixed in it; the region of the air. (L. *firmamentum.*)
firmamental, *a.* *fer*-ma-*men*-tal, pertaining to the firmament; celestial; being of the upper regions.
firman, *n.* *fer*-man, a decree or mandate issued by certain Oriental rulers; a passport; a licence to trade, etc. (Per.)
firmly, *ad.* solidly; compactly; steadfastly.
firmness, *n.* the state or quality of being firm.
firn, *n.* fern, compacted snow occurring above the snow-line; névé.
***first,** *a.* ferst, the ordinal of one; foremost in place, time, rank, dignity, or excellence; earliest in occurrence; *ad.* before anything else in time, place, rank, consideration, etc.; in preference, sooner: *n.* one who or that which comes first; the first mentioned; the winner of a race, competition, or examination, the first place, or a place in the first class of such; a first edition [Coll.]; the upper part in concerted signing, the chief instrument of its class in an orchestra, etc. [Mus.]. **at first,** at the beginning. **first or last,** at one time or another; at the beginning or end. (A.S. *fyrst.*)
first-aid, *n.* *ferst*-ade, preliminary or emergency treatment given to a sick or wounded person.
firstborn, *n.* *ferst*-born, the eldest child.
first-class, *a.* of the best quality; first-rate: **first class,** *n.* a place in the highest division of an examination list, or the division itself; the best type of accommodation for travellers.
first-day, *n.* Sunday, as the first day in the week.
first-floor, *n.* the story next above the ground-floor; in the U.S.A., the ground-floor.
first-foot, *n.* in Scotland, the first caller at a house on New Year's Day; the first person met on setting out on some important venture.
firstfruits, *n.pl.* *ferst*-froots, the produce first matured and collected in any season; the first effects; the first profits of anything; the profits of every clerical living for one year, originally paid to the pope but afterwards taken by Henry VIII, and by Queen Anne applied to the augmentation of clerical livings as "Queen Anne's Bounty."
first-hand, *a.* obtained direct from the maker or producer. **at first hand,** directly, without a medium; of one's own knowledge; by personal study or observation.
firstling, *n.* *ferst*-ling, the first offspring; the thing first thought or done.
firstly, *ad.* *ferst*-le, in the first place.
first-nighter, *n.* one habitually present at the opening performances of theatrical productions.
first-rate, *a.* *ferst*-rate, of the highest excellence; pre-eminent in quality, size, or esteem: *n.* formerly a ship of war of the most powerful class: *ad.* excellently [Coll.].
first-water, *n.* *ferst*-waw-ter, the purest quality (used esp. of uncoloured and unflawed diamonds).
firth, *n.* ferth, a frith; a narrow arm of the sea. (Scots. from O.Norse.)
fisc, *n.* fisk, a state or public treasury. (L. *fiscus,* purse.)
fiscal, *a.* *fis*-kal, pertaining to the public revenue; financial: *n.* a treasurer; in Scotland, an officer who acts as public prosecutor in criminal cases. (O.Fr.)
***fish,** *n.* fish, a vertebrate animal that lives in water, moves by fins, and breathes by means of gills; fishes in general; the flesh of fish, used as food; a counter used at cards; a piece of wood fastened to another to strengthen it; a fish-block; a person (derogatively) [Slang]: *v.i.* to try to catch fish, as by angling or drawing nets; to seek to obtain by artifice or indirectly: *v.t.* to try to catch fish from; to search by dragging or sweeping; to strengthen, as a mast or yard, with a piece of timber [Naut.]; to draw out or up. **fish out,** to draw out by artifice. **fish the anchor,** to draw the flukes up to the gunwale. (A.S. *fisc.*)
fishable, *a.* *fish*-a-bl, capable of being fished.
fish-basket, *n.* a basket for carrying fish; a creel.
fish-block, *n.* a block to raise the flukes of an anchor to the gunwale.
fish-bolt, *n.* a bolt used to secure two fishplates.
fish-cake, *n.* a fried cake of fish and potato.
fisher, *n.* *fish*-er, one who is employed in catching fish; a fishing-boat; an animal that fishes, esp. the pekan, or fisher marten.
fisherman, *n.* *fish*-er-man, one whose occupation is to catch fish; an angler; a vessel employed in fishery. **fisherman's bend,** a knot used esp. to fasten a hawser to an anchor.
fishery, *n.* *fish*-er-re, the business of catching fish; a place where fish are caught or where fishing is carried on.
fish-garth, *n.* a weir for stopping fish.
fish-gig, *n.* a spear with barbed prongs used for striking fish at sea.
fish-glue, *n.* glue made by boiling down the skins of fishes; isinglass.
fish-hawk, *n.* the osprey.
fish-hook, *n.* a barbed hook for catching fish; a large hook used in fishing an anchor [Naut.].
fishiness, *n.* *fish*-e-ness, the quality of being fishy.
fishing, *n.* *fish*-ing, the art or practice of catching fish; the sport of angling; a fishery.
fishing-boat, *n.* a boat used in catching fish.
fishing-frog, *n.* the angler, a large-headed spinous-finned sea-fish, *Lophius piscatorius.*
fishing-line, *n.* a line with hook for catching fish.
fishing-net, *n.* a net of twine or cord for catching fish.
fishing-rod, *n.* a jointed tapering rod for angling.
fishing-tackle, *n.* apparatus for angling.
fish-joint, *n.* a joint made with fishplates.
fish-kettle, *n.* a large oval kitchen utensil for boiling fish whole.
fish-knife, *n.* a silver or plated knife for use at the table with fish; a fish-slice.
fish-ladder, *n.* a contrivance for helping fish to ascend a weir or other fall on their way upstream.
fish-louse, *n.* any of several small crustaceans parasitic upon aquatic animals.
fish-meal, *n.* a fertilizer and animal food prepared from fish and fish refuse.
fishmonger, *n.* *fish*-mung-ger, a seller of fish.
fish-oil, *n.* oil obtained from fish, whales, etc.

fishplate, *n. fish*-plate, the steel plate by which the rails are joined together on a railroad.
fish-pond, *n.* a pond in which fishes are kept or bred.
fish-royal, *n.* the sturgeon, to which the sovereign is entitled when caught within the realm [Law].
fish-sauce, *n.* a sauce to be eaten with fish.
fish-skin, *n.* the skin of a fish, esp. of shark, etc., for polishing wood. **fish-skin disease,** ichthyosis [Med.].
fish-slice, *n. fish*-slice, a broad knife for serving or dishing up fish; a utensil for turning fish in process of frying.
fish-sound, *n.* the swimming bladder of a fish.
fish-spear, *n.* a spear for stabbing fish.
fish-strainer, *n.* a metal colander with handles for taking fish from the fish-kettle; a perforated dish to drain off water from fish.
fish-tackle, *n.* tackle for raising the flukes of an anchor to the gunwale [Naut.].
fish-tail, *a.* of the shape of a fish's tail. **fish-tail burner,** a gas-jet producing a flame of fish-tail shape.
fishwife, *n. fish*-wife, a woman that cries fish for sale; a scurrilous or bad-tempered woman.
fishy, *a. fish*-e, consisting of fish; inhabited by fish; like fish; seedy; questionable, dubious [Coll.].
fissibility, *n.* fis-e-*bil*-e-te, fissibility.
fissile, *a. fis*-sil, splitting naturally, as wood in the direction of the grain. (L. *fissilis.*)
fissilingual, *a. fis*-e-*ling*-gwal, having the tongue divided. (L. *fissus*, a cleft, *lingua*, tongue.)
fissility, *n.* fis-*sil*-e-te, the quality of being easily cleft fissile.
fission, *n. fish*-on, a cleaving or breaking up into parts; the process by which animal and vegetable cells, and certain simple organisms, spontaneously divide into two independent ones; the process by which binary stars are held to develop from a single gaseous body. **nuclear fission,** the splitting of the atom, resulting in the release of enormous energy.
fissionable, *a. fish*-on-a-bl, capable of being split, esp. by nuclear fission.
fissiparism, *n.* fis-*sip*-a-rizm, reproduction by fission.
fissiparous, *a.* fis-*sip*-a-rus, propagating by fission. (L. *fissus*, and *pario*, produce.)
fissiparously, *ad.* in a fissiparous manner.
fissiped, *a. fis*-e-ped, having separate toes: *n.* any carnivorous mammal whose toes are separate, or not connected by a membrane. (L. *fissus*, and *pes*, a foot.)
fissirostral, *a.* fis-e-*ros*-tral, having a bill with a deep cleft, like the swallows and goatsuckers.
fissure, *n. fish*-yewr, a cleft; a narrow chasm or opening; a deep narrow depression, dividing the anterior and middle lobes of the cerebrum on each side [Anat.]: *v.t.* to cleave; to crack or fracture: *v.i.* to become cleft or split. (O.Fr.)
fist, *n.* fist, the hand clenched; handwriting [Slang]; a printers' mark [☛] used to direct special attention to a passage, etc.: *v.t.* to strike or to grip with the fist. (A.S. *fyst.*)
fistic, *a. fis*-tik, pertaining to pugilism
fisticuffs, *n.pl. fis*-te-kufs, a combat with the fists; boxing; a boxing-match.
fistula, *n. fis*-tew-la, a narrow sinuous pipe-like ulcer [Surg.]; a pipe-like duct or passage in insects, whales, etc. [Zool.]. **fistula in ano,** fistula of the rectum. (L., a pipe.)
fistular, *a. fis*-tew-lar, reed-like; tubular; pertaining to or resembling a fistula.
fistuliform, *a.* fis-*tew*-le-form, fistular in form; tubular; in round hollow columns, as a mineral.
fistulose, *a. fis*-tew-lose, fistulous [Bot.].
fistulous, *a. fis*-tew-lus, of the nature of a fistula; hollow, like a pipe or reed.
fit, *n.* fit, a group of verses in a ballad; a canto. (A.S. *fitt*, a song.)
fit, *n.* fit, a sudden and violent attack, in which the body is often convulsed, and sometimes inanimate; a paroxysm; any sudden impulsive intermittent exertion; a temporary attack; a transient humour. **by fits and starts,** intermittently; impulsively. (A.S. *fitt.*)
fit, *n.* fit, adjustment, as of dress to the body; the way in which anything fits: *a.* suitable; agreeable to some standard; adapted to a purpose; qualified; prepared; in good condition, healthy: *v.t.* to adapt; to make suitable; to accommodate a person with anything; to prepare; to qualify; to suit: *v.i.* to be proper or becoming; to suit; to be adapted. **fit out,** to furnish; to equip. **fit up,** to furnish with things suitable for reception or use. (Scand.)
fitch, *n.* fitch, a chick-pea; a vetch. (Dial. Eng.)
fitch, *n.* fitch, the fur of the fitchew; a brush made of the hair from this. (Dut. *vitsche*, fitchew.)
fitchet, *n. fitch*-et, the fitchew.
fitchew, *n. fitch*-oo, the polecat. (O.Fr. *fissel.*)
fitchy, *a. fitch*-e, pointed at the base, esp. of a cross that is fixable in the ground [Her.].
fitful, *a. fit*-ful, characterized by sudden impulses; suddenly changeable; capricious.
fitfully, *ad. fit*-ful-le, by fits.
fitfulness, *n. fit*-ful-ness, instability.
fitly, *ad. fit*-le, in a fit manner.
fitment, *n. fit*-ment, an article of equipment; a piece of built-in furniture: *pl.* fittings.
fitness, *n. fit*-ness, the state of being fit; good condition.
fitter, *n. fit*-ter, one who adjusts or puts together the parts of a machine; one who fits on articles of dress; one who adjusts ready-made garments to the purchaser's fit; a coal-factor.
fitting, *a. fit*-ting, fit or appropriate: *n.* the act of making fit; a necessary fitment or fixture.
fittingly, *ad. fit*-ting-le, suitably.
fittingness, *n. fit*-ting-ness, suitableness.
five, *a.* five, the half of ten, the number between four and six; the symbol (5, v) representing this; the fifth of a series. **five hundred,** a variety of euchre, the score being 500 points. **five-year plan,** a period of five years devoted, esp. in the U.S.S.R., to a given course of economic development. (A.S. *fif.*)
five-finger, *n. five*-fing-ger, cinquefoil, and other plants: *pl.* a species of star-fish. **five-finger exercises,** exercises on the pianoforte to improve the touch in playing.
fivefold, *a. five*-fohld, five times repeated.
fiveleaf, *n. five*-leef, cinquefoil, *Potentilla reptans.*
fiver, *n. five*-er, a five-pound note of the Bank of England; a five-dollar bill [Slang].
fives, *n.* fyvz, a game with a small hard ball played against walls. **fives court,** the walled court in which the game of fives is played.
fix, *n.* fiks, a dilemma: *v.t.* to make firm or fast; to establish; to attach firmly; to fasten; to deprive of volatility; to give permanency to [Phot.]; to transfix; to withhold from motion; to adjust: *v.i.* to settle down permanently; to become firm; to congeal; to become hard and malleable. **fix on,** to determine on. (O.Fr.)
fixable, *a. fiks*-a-bl, that may be fixed.
fixation, *n.* fik-*say*-shon, the act of fixing; the state of being fixed; the act or process of depriving of volatility; solidification; that firm state of a substance which resists evaporation or volatilization. (Fr.)
fixative, *a. fiks*-a-tiv, tending to fix: *n.* anything that will fix, esp. a substance used to give permanence to colours.
fixature, *n. fiks*-a-tewr, a gummy composition for fixing or stiffening the hair.
*__fixed,__ *pp.* and *a.* fikst, settled; established; firm. **fixed acid,** one not evaporable without decomposition. **fixed air,** an obsolete name of carbonic acid gas. **fixed bodies,** those which bear great heat without becoming volatilized. **fixed oils,** or **alkalies,** those which are unchanged by heat or distillation. **fixed point,** one about which rotation can, or can be assumed to, take place [Math.]. **fixed stars,** such stars as always retain the same apparent position with respect to each other.
fixedly, *ad. fiks*-ed-le, firmly.
fixedness, *n. fiks*-ed-ness, a state of being fixed; the state of a substance that resists volatilization.
fixer, *n. fiks*-er, a fixative, esp. a chemical for fixing negatives or positives [Phot.].
fixings, *n.pl. fiks*-ingz, equipment; outfit; trimmings.
fixity, *n. fiks*-e-te, fixedness; permanence.
fixture, *n. fiks*-tewr, state of being fixed; one who or that which is permanently attached to something; an engagement or sporting event fixed for a certain date; the date of such appointment.
fizgig, *n. fiz*-gig, a fishgig; a firework of damp powder; a flighty girl.
fizz, *n.* fiz, a hissing sound or a thing that fizzes; an

effervescing drink, esp. champagne [Slang]: *v.i.* to make a hissing sound; to effervesce.
fizzle, *n. fiz*-zl, a failure: *v.i.* to fizz feebly. **fizzle out,** to become a failure.
fizzy, *a. fiz*-e, characterized by fizzing; effervescent.
flabbergast, *v.t. flab*-ber-gahst, to astonish, confound, or strike with amazement.
flabbily, *ad. flab*-be-le, in a flabby manner.
flabbiness, *n.* the state of being flabby.
flabby, *a. flab*-be, wanting firmness; limp; soft and yielding; hanging loose. (*Flap.*)
flabellate, *a.* fla-*bel*-lat, in the form of an open fan [Bot.]. (L. *flabelium*, fan.)
flabelliform, *a.* fla-*bel*-le-form, fan-shaped.
flabellum, *n.* fla-*bel*-lum, a fan, esp. used to drive off flies during the celebration of the Eucharist; a fan-shaped appendage or organ [Zool. and Bot.]. (L.)
flaccid, *a. flak*-sid, flabby; soft and yielding; loose; limp. (L. *flaccidus.*)
flaccidity, *n.* flak-*sid*-e-te, flaccidness.
flaccidly, *ad. flak*-sid-le, in a flaccid manner.
flaccidness, *n.* the state of being flaccid.
flag, *n.* flag, any of several herbaceous plants of the genus *Iris*, with sword-shaped leaves growing in damp places; also *Acorus calamus*, the sweet flag.
flag, *v.i.* flag, to hang loose; to grow spiritless or languid; to droop; to become dull. (M.E. *flakken*; cp. L. *flaccidus*, limp.)
flag, *n.* flag, a flat stone used for paving: *v.t.* to pave or lay with flat stones. (A.S. *flake.*)
***flag,** *n.* flag, a piece of plain or coloured bunting or other fabric, with or without a national or other emblem, used as a sign or indication, in signalling, as a decoration, etc.; a small metal indicator showing whether or not a taxicab is disengaged: *v.t.* to decorate, mark out, or signal with a flag or flags; to cover with a flag. **black flag,** the flag of piracy; used also to signify that no quarter will be given, and that a death-sentence has been executed. **red flag,** a sign of defiance or challenge to battle; a signal indicating danger; the emblem of revolution, adopted by advanced Socialists and Communists. **yellow flag,** a sign of quarantine and infectious illness on board. **white flag,** the flag of truce; indication of surrender. **flag flying,** overbidding at bridge. **to strike the flag,** to pull it down in token of respect or submission. (Scand., cf. Swed. *flagg.*)
flag-captain, *n.* the captain of a flagship.
flag-day, *n.* a day on which street collectors give a small flag in exchange for charitable contributions; any day on which the Union Jack is officially flown (royal birthdays, etc.)
flagella, *n.pl.* fla-*jel*-la, *pl.* of *flagellum.*
flagellant, *n. flaj*-e-lant, one who scourges himself in religious discipline; a member of a widespread fanatical sect, which arose in Italy in the 13th cent. and thought by self-flagellation to atone for sin and avert judgment. (L. *flagellans*, scourging.)
flagellate, *v.t. flaj*-e-late, to whip; to scourge: *a.* having flagella [Zool. and Bot.].
flagellation, *n. flaj*-e-*lay*-shon, a flogging or whipping; the act of scourging; the development of flagella among protozoa.
flagellator, *n. flaj*-e-la-tor, one who flagellates.
flagelliform, *a.* fla-*jel*-e-form, like a whip-lash.
flagellum, *n.* fla-*jel*-lum (*pl.* **flagella**), a creeping shoot [Bot.]; a minute whip-like process or appendage [Zool.]. (L., a whip.)
flageolet, *n.* flaj-o-*let* or flaj-o-lay, a dwarf kidney bean. (Fr.)
flageolet, *n.* flaj-o-*let* or *flaj*-o-let, a wooden wind instrument ending in a straight mouthpiece. (Fr.)
flagging, *n. flag*-ging, the act of laying with flagstones; flag-stones, or a pavement of these; signalling, or decorating, with flags: *a.* languid.
flaggy, *a. flag*-ge, weak; flexible; insipid; abounding with flag-plants, or with flag-stones.
flagitate, *v.t. flaj*-e-tate, to demand with violence and importunity. (L.)
flagitious, *a.* fla-*jish*-us, deeply criminal or grossly wicked; guilty of atrocious crimes. (L. *flagitiosus*, shameful.)
flagitiously, *ad.* with extreme wickedness.
flagitiousness, *n.* extreme wickedness.
flag-lieutenant, *n.* the naval officer on a flag-officer's staff who acts as his personal assistant.
flag-officer, *n.* the commander of a fleet or of a squadron; an admiral, vice-admiral, or rear-admiral.
flagon, *n. flag*-on, a large cup with handle, lid, and a narrow mouth, used for holding and conveying liquors; a flattened bottle. (Fr. *flacon.*)
flagrancy, *n. flay*-gran-se, the quality of being flagrant; enormity; excess.
flagrant, *a. flay*-grant, glaring; notorious; outrageous; monstrous. (Fr.)
flagrantly, *ad.* in a flagrant manner.
flag-ship, *n.* the ship in which is the commander of a squadron, and which carries his flag.
flag-staff, *n.* the staff that carries the flag.
flag-stone, *n.* a flat stone for pavements.
flagwagging, *n. flag*-wag-ing, hand-signalling with flags [Slang].
flag-worm, *n. flag*-wurm, a grub found among sedges and flags; the green gentle of anglers.
flail, *n.* flale, a wooden implement for threshing grain by hand: *v.t.* and *i.* to thresh or strike with or as with a flail. (O.Fr. *flaël.*)
flair, *n.* flayr, instinctive appreciation; keen perception; aptitude. (Fr.)
flak, *n.* flak, anti-aircraft fire; ack-ack, or shells, etc., from this. (Ger., abbr. of *flugzeugabwehrkanone*, gun for the warding off of aircraft.)
flake, *n.* flake, a small slice or tuft of anything, as of snow or wool, such as floats lightly in the air; any light scaly substance; a carnation striped with two colours only: *v.t.* to form into flakes: *v.i.* to separate in flakes; to peel off. (Scand. ?)
flake, *n.* flake, a sort of scaffold or platform made of hurdles used for drying fish; a platform hung over the side for calking a ship [Naut.].
flake-white, *n.* a pigment made from the purest white lead in a flaky or scaly form.
flakiness, *n. flake*-e-ness, state of being flaky.
flaky, *a. flake*-e, consisting of flakes; breaking off in flakes.
flam, *n.* flam, a freak or whim; a falsehood; an imposition; a deception: *v.t.* to deceive; to delude.
flambeau, *n. flam*-boh (*pl.* **flambeaux,** *flam*-boze), a lighted torch. (Fr.)
flamboyancy, *n.* flam-*boy*-an-se, over-ornateness; turgidity.
flamboyant, *a.* flam-*boy*-ant, denoting a Gothic style that prevailed in France in the 15th and 16th cents., so named from its flame-like tracery; florid to excess; showy. (Fr., flaming.)
***flame,** *n.* flame, gases in combustion, glowing with light and heat; fire in general; heat or blaze of passion or excitement; ardour of temper; glow of imagination; warmth of affection; a sweetheart, one beloved [Coll.]; the colour of flame: *v.i.* to blaze; to shine like burning gas; to break out in violence of passion. (O.Fr.)
flame-coloured, *a.* of the colour of flame; of a bright yellow colour.
flame-flower, *n. flame*-flou-er, the red-hot poker plant, of the genus *Kniphofia.*
flameless, *a. flame*-less, burning without flame.
flamen, *n. flay*-men, a priest devoted to some special god [Rom. Antiq.]. (L.)
flaming, *a. flame*-ing, blazing; bright red or yellow; florid; exciting the passions. **flaming onion,** a projectile used by or against aircraft and composed of a number of fire-balls linked together [Coll.].
flamingly, *ad.* in a flaming manner.
flamingo, *n.* fla-*ming*-go, a genus of birds, *Phœnicopterus*, with very long necks and legs, and palmated feet, and, when in full plumage, of a colour almost entirely rosy red. **flamingo plant,** a plant of the genus *Anthurum*, with a slender scarlet or yellow spadix. (Sp. *flamenco.*)
flaminical, *a.* fla-*min*-e-kal, pertaining to a flamen.
flammable, *a. flam*-a-bl, inflammable.
flammenwerfer, *n. flam*-en-*ver*-fer, an instrument of war projecting a long jet of flame. (Ger.)
flamy, *a. flame*-e, of the nature or colour of flame.
flan, *n.* flan, an open fruit or custard tart. (Fr.)
flanch, *n.* flansh, one of the honourable ordinaries formed by an arched line drawn from the corners of the chief [Her.]; a flange [Mech.]. (*Flank.*)
flanconnade, *n.* flang-ko-*nade*, a kind of thrust in the flank or side [Fencing]. (Fr.)
Flanders, *n. flahn*-ders, place name, used attributively of things originally from or connected with Flanders, as **Flanders-brick,** a stone similar to bath-brick; **Flanders horse, Flanders lace,** etc.; **Flanders poppy,** the corn-poppy, adopted as the

floral emblem of those who fell in the War of 1914–18; also an artificial imitation sold on behalf of ex-servicemen's funds.

flânerie, *n.* (App.), idling; the lounging habit. (Fr.)

flâneur, *n.* (App.), an idling man-about-town. (Fr.)

flange, *n.* flanj, a projecting edge, esp. that on the rim of a railway carriage wheel, to prevent it from slipping off the line. (*Flank.*)

flange-rail, *n.* a rail with a flange to prevent wheels running off.

flank, *n.* flank, the fleshy part of the side of an animal between the ribs and hip; a side, as of a building [Arch.] or of an army or body of troops [Mil.]; that part of a bastion which reaches from the curtain to the face [Fort.]: *v.t.* to attack or be in position to attack the flank of; to post troops so as to attack the flank: *v.i.* to border; to touch; to be posted on the side. **flank company,** the company drawn up on the right or left of a battalion [Mil.]. **flank files,** the first two men of the right and the last two on the left [Mil.]. (Fr. *flanc.*)

flanker, *n. flang*-ker, one who or that which flanks or is stationed on the flanks: *pl.* skirmishers thrown out to protect the flanks of a line of march [Mil.].

flannel, *n. flan*-el, a soft woollen cloth of loose texture; a piece of this used for cleaning, polishing, etc.: *pl.* underclothes of flannel or the like; flannel trousers for sports-wear. (Fr. *flanelle.*)

flannelette, *n.* flan-el-*let*, a cotton fabric resembling fine flannel. (Fr.)

flannel-flower, *n.* the mullein.

flannelled, *a. flan*-eld, wearing flannels, esp. at cricket or sports.

flannelly, *a. flan*-el-e, resembling flannel.

flap, *n.* flap, anything broad and flexible kept in place on one side only; the motion and noise of it, as a loose sail in the wind; the tail of a coat; the cover to a pocket, limp brim of a hat, hinged extension to a table, etc.; a pivoted section of a wing for modifying drag, etc. [Av.]; a piece of partly severed flesh [Surg.]; a contrivance for driving off flies: *pl.* a disease in the lips of horses: *v.t.* to beat or move with a flap; to let fall, as the brim of a hat: *v.i.* to move as wings, with a flap; to fall, as the brim of a hat or other broad thing. (From the sound.)

flapdoodle, *n.* flap-*doo*-dl, nonsense; bosh [Slang].

flap-dragon, *n.* the game of snapdragon.

flap-jack, *n.* a griddle-cake; an apple puff; a special kind of somersault.

flapper, *n. flap*-er, he who or that which flaps; a young bird; a girl in her teens [Slang]; the hand [Slang].

flare, *n.* flare, a strong unsteady light; a blazing torch, or a torch-like signal light; a sudden outburst; a spreading outward, or the part that spreads: *v.i.* to burn with a waving flame; to flutter with a showy glare; to be exposed to too much light; to spread outward. (Norw. *flara,* blaze.)

flaring, *a. flare*-ring, with glaring display; over-ostentatious; shining fitfully; curving upward.

flash, *a.* flash, showy; counterfeit; pertaining to thieves or the underworld: *n.* a sudden momentary outburst of light; a sudden burst, as of wit or merriment; a short transient state; a body of water driven by violence; a sluice on navigable rivers for raising the water while vessels are passing; slang, jargon; a preparation of burnt sugar and cayenne pepper used for colouring rum and brandy; an ornamental black ribbon worn on the tunic at the back of the neck by officers of the Royal Welch Fusilers; a bright tag to the garter, used when wearing plus-fours, kilt, etc.; an electric torch: *v.i.* to break or burst forth, as a sudden gleam of light; to burst out violently; to pass like a flash; to gleam with a flash; to glitter: *v.t.* to emit in flashes; to cause to flash. **flash in the pan,** an abortive effort, a flash and nothing more. (Origin uncertain.)

flasher, *n. flash*-er, one who or that which flashes; an automatic device for lighting and extinguishing electric lamps.

flashily, *ad.* in a flashy manner; ostentatiously.

flashiness, *n* the state of being flashy.

flashing, *n. flash*-ing, a strip of sheet lead or other metal lapping over a junction on a roof or wall to render it watertight [Arch.].

flash-lamp, *n.* a filament low-voltage electric light for use with a dry battery; a lamp adapted to signalling by flashes.

flashlight, *n. flash*-lite, an intermittent signal-light; a light used for a snapshot photograph; a small electric torch.

flash-point, *n.* the temperature to which oils, etc., must be heated to give off vapour that will ignite.

flashy, *a. flash*-e, showy but empty; dazzling for a moment; gaudy; impulsive; insipid; vapid.

flask, *n.* flahsk, a kind of bottle; a flat, covered pocket-bottle for spirits; a vessel for gunpowder. (A.S. *flasc.*)

flasket, *n. flahs*-ket, a long shallow basket; a small flask. (O.Fr. *flasquet.*)

***flat,** *a.* flat, having an even surface; level; without, or with but a moderate, inclination; prostrate; laid low; ruined; wanting relief or prominence of the figures [Paint.]; insipid; dull; without point or spirit; depressed; dejected; unpleasing; peremptory; absolute; downright; not sharp, low in pitch [Mus.]; low, as the prices of goods, or dull, as sales: *ad.* positively; decisively; flatly: *n.* a level plain; a shoal or shallow; the broad flat side of anything; a floor in a house; a suite of rooms on one floor, esp. a self-contained residence on one floor of a block containing similar residences; a piece of stage scenery extending from the side; a broad flat-bottomed boat; a low-crowned broad-brimmed straw hat [U.S.A.]; a mark of depression in sound, thus ♭ which lowers a note a semitone; one who is easily duped [Slang]: *v.t.* and *i.* to flatten. **flat spin,** a nearly horizontal spin liable to be developed by an aeroplane temporarily out of control. (Scand.)

flatfish, *n. flat*-fish, a fish with a flat body, which, when mature, swims on the side and has both eyes on the upper side, as the flounder, halibut, etc.

flat-footed, *a.* having flat-soled feet; splay-footed.

flat-iron, *n.* the implement used in the laundry, etc. for smoothing clothes.

flatly, *ad.* in a flat manner; plainly; positively.

flatness, *n.* the state of being flat; insipidity.

flat-out, *n.* a complete failure; a bad ending [U.S.A.].

flat-race, *n.* a race over open ground as distinguished from a steeplechase.

flat-rate, *n.* a fixed tariff applicable to all alike.

flatten, *v.t. flat*-en, to make or lay flat; to make vapid or insipid; to depress; to dispirit; to render less acute or sharp [Mus.]: *v.i.* to become flat, or tasteless, or spiritless; to render a sound less sharp; to depress the voice [Mus.]. **flatten out,** to come into the horizontal position, esp. after a sudden descent [Av.]. **flatten a sail,** to make a sail set flat by shortening in the sheet or, in square-rig, by hauling in the aftmost clew.

flatter, *v.t. flat*-er, to please by artful praise so as to induce or foster self-satisfaction; to praise falsely; to encourage by favourable notice; to raise false hopes by representations not well-founded; to gratify: *v.i.* to use flattery. (Etym. doubtful.) (O.Fr. *flater,* to flatter.)

flatterable, *a. flat*-er-ra-bl, open to flattery.

flatterer, *n. flat*-er-rer, one who flatters.

flattering, *a. flat*-er-ring, pleasing to pride or vanity; encouraging hope; uttering false praise.

flatteringly, *ad.* in a flattering manner.

flattery, *n. flat*-er-re, false praise; excessive or insincere compliment. (O.Fr. *flaterie.*)

flatting, *n. flat*-ing, the act or process of flattening, as in rolling out metals by cylindrical pressure; a mode of internal decoration in which the paint-work is left flat, or without gloss; a method of preserving gilding unburnished by touching it with size.

flattish, *a. flat*-ish, somewhat flat.

flatulence, *n. flat*-yew-lence, windiness due to gases generated in a weak stomach and intestines; verbosity. (Fr.)

flatulency, *n. flat*-yew-len-se, flatulence.

flatulent, *a. flat*-yew-lent, windy; affected with flatulency; turgid with air; generating or apt to generate wind in the stomach; empty; vain; without substance or reality. (Fr., from L. *flatus.*)

flatulently, *ad.* in a flatulent manner.

flatus, *n. flay*-tus, a breath; a puff of wind; gas generated in the alimentary canal; flatulence. (L.)

flatwise, *a.* and *ad.* *flat*-wize, with the flat side; not edgewise.
flat-worm, *n.* one of a sub-order of small, flat, fresh- or salt-water worms allied to the flukes; a planarian.
flaunt, *n.* flawnt, a boast, or anything displayed for show: *v.i.* to flourish about and make an ostentatious display; to carry a pert or saucy appearance: *v.t.* to display ostentatiously. (Scand.)
flaunter, *n.* *flawnt*-er, one that flaunts.
flauntingly, *ad.* *flawnt*-ing-le, in a flaunting way.
flautist, *n.* *flawt*-ist, a player on the flute.
flavescent, *a.* fla-*ves*-sent, turning yellow; yellowish [Bot.]. (L. *flavescens*, turning yellow.)
flavin, *n.* *flav*-in, a fine olive-yellow dye-stuff prepared from quercitron bark. (L. *flavus*, yellow.)
flavorous, *a.* *flay*-vu-rus, of a pleasant flavour; sapid; imparting flavour.
flavour, *n.* *flay*-vur, the quality of a substance which pleasantly affects the taste or smell; savour; relish: *v.t.* to communicate a flavour to; to render pleasing to the taste or smell. (O.Fr. *flaur*, smell or savour.)
flavoured, *a.* *flay*-vurd, having a definite, or a particular, flavour.
flavouring, *n.* *flay*-vu-ring, that which gives flavour: the act of imparting flavour.
flavourless, *a.* *flay*-vur-less, without flavour.
flavoursome, *a.* *flay*-vur-sum, of specially pleasing flavour.
flaw, *n.* flaw, a break; a crack; a defect; a sudden gust; *v.t.* to break; to crack; to render invalid: *v.i.* to crack; to chip. (Scand.)
flawless, *a.* *flaw*-less, without defect.
flawy, *a.* *flaw*-e, full of flaws; defective; faulty; subject to sudden gusts of wind.
flax, *n.* flaks, an annual plant, *Linum usitatissimum*, the stalks of which yield a fibre used for making thread and linen, cambric, lawn, lace, etc.; the fibrous part of the plant when broken and cleaned. **flax weed**, a weed like flax. **New Zealand flax**, the liliaceous plant, *Phormium tenax*, the leaves of which yield a fibre, used in the manufacture of cordage. (A.S. *fleax*.)
flax-comb, *n.* a heckle for preparing flax.
flax-dresser, *n.* a cleaner of flax.
flaxen, *a.* *flaks*-en, made of or resembling flax; of the colour of flax; pale yellow; fair and silky.
flax-mill, *n.* a factory where flax is spun.
flax-seed, *n.* linseed, the seed of flax.
flaxy, *a.* *flaks*-e, like flax; of a light colour; fair.
flay, *v.t.* flay, to strip off the skin; to reprove or criticize unmercifully. (A.S. *flean*.)
flayer, *n.* *flay*-er, one who or that which flays.
flay-flint, *n.* a skinflint; a miser.
flea, *n.* flee, an insect of the genus *Pulex*, remarkable for its agility and its blood-sucking bite. **black flea**, the turnip-fly. (A.S. *fleah*.)
flea-bane, *n.* certain species of *Erigeron* and *Pulicaria*, and other plants formerly supposed to be efficacious in driving away fleas.
flea-beetle, *n.* any small leaping beetle destructive to plants.
flea-bite, *n.* the bite of a flea or the red spot caused by it; a negligible trouble or annoyance.
flea-bitten, *a.* bitten by a flea; harbouring fleas; mean; worthless; having small reddish-brown spots on a light ground (of horses).
fleam, *n.* fleem, a lancet or other sharp instrument used for bleeding cattle [Vet.]. (O.Fr. *flieme*.)
flea-wort, *n.* flea-bane.
flèche, *n.* flaysh, a slender spire, generally central [Arch.]; a simple redan, usually constructed at the foot of a glacis [Fort.]. (Fr., an arrow.)
fleck, *n.* flek, a spot; a streak; a speckle: *v.t.* to spot; to streak or stripe; to variegate; to dapple. (Scand.)
flecker, *v.t.* *flek*-er, to fleck.
flection, *n.* *flek*-shon, flexion.
fled, fled, *p.* of *flee*.
fledge, *v.t.* flej, to rear (a bird) until it is able to fly; to furnish with feathers, as an arrow: *v.i.* to grow feathers. (A.S. *flycge*.)
fledgeling, *n.* *flej*-ling, a young bird just fledged: a raw or immature person.
flee, *v.i.* flee, to run away; to hasten, as from danger or expected evil: *v.t.* to shun; to keep at a distance from. (A.S. *fleon*.)
fleece, *n.* fleece, the woolly covering of a sheep; the coat of wool shorn from a sheep at one time; any similar covering; a lining fabric with a silky pile; a web of carded cotton or wool: *v.t.* to shear wool from; to strip; to plunder by severe exactions; to spread over, as with wool. **Golden Fleece**, see *Golden*. (A.S. *fleos*.)
fleeceless, *a.* *fleece*-less, having no fleece.
fleecer, *n.* *fleece*-er, one who fleeces or plunders.
fleecy, *a.* *fleece*-e, covered with wool; soft and woolly; resembling a fleece.
fleer, *n.* fleer, derision or mockery expressed by words or looks; a leer: *v.i.* to mock; to grin in scorn; to grin with an air of civility: *v.t.* to mock; to flout. (Norw. *flira*, to titter.)
fleeringly, *ad.* *fleer*-ing-le, in a fleering manner.
fleet, *n.* fleet, a creek, a bay, a river, as in Fleet Street, or Northfleet. **fleet-dike**, *n.* an embankment for preventing inundation. **Fleet Street**, journalism, or pertaining to journalism (Fleet Street, London, being the centre of the newspaper world). (A.S. *fleot*, a creek.)
fleet, *n.* fleet, a navy or a squadron of ships; a number of ships in company for one object or destination, esp. warships; a navy; a number of ships, aircraft, passenger- or delivery-cars, etc., under one ownership. (A.S. *fleot*, a ship.)
fleet, *a.* fleet, swift of pace; nimble; moving with celerity; shallow; not penetrating deep, as soil; skimming the surface: *v.i.* to move or pass swiftly; to hasten; to vanish: *v.t.* to change the position of [Naut.]; to pass (time) rapidly; to pass lightly, or in mirth, etc. **fleet-footed**, *a.* swift of foot; able to run fast. (A.S. *fleotig*.)
fleeting, *a.* *fleet*-ing, passing quickly; transient.
fleetingly, *ad.* *fleet*-ing-le, in a fleeting manner.
fleetly, *ad.* *fleet*-le, swiftly.
fleetness, *n.* *fleet*-ness, swiftness.
Fleming, *n.* *flem*-ing, a native of Flanders. (Dut. *Vlaming*.)
Flemish, *a.* *flem*-ish, pertaining to Flanders: *n.* the people of Flanders; the language of Flanders.
flemish, *v.i.* *flem*-ish, to make a quivering movement of the tail and body when finding the trail (of hounds).
flench, *v.t.* flensh, to flense.
flense, *v.t.* flens, to cut the blubber out of a whale or seal, etc. (Dan.)
flesh, *n.* flesh, the muscles and fat of an animal body; animal food, in distinction from vegetable; the bodies of beasts and birds used as food, distinct from fish; the body, as distinguished from the soul; animals of all kinds; mankind; human nature; bodily appetites; carnality; the present state of existence; kindred; the soft pulpy substance of fruit [Bot.]: *v.t.* to train to an appetite for, as hawks or dogs, by feeding them with the first game they take; to harden; to accustom; gratify; to clean hides of fat and flesh. **flesh and blood**, human nature, man as he is; one's kith and kin. (A.S. *flæsc*.)
flesh-brush, *n.* a brush for exciting action in the skin by friction.
flesh-coloured, *a.* of the colour of flesh; pale yellowish pink.
fleshed, *a.* flesht, furnished with flesh; fleshy; initiated; accustomed; sated.
flesher, *n.* *flesh*-er, a butcher; a butcher's knife.
flesh-fly, *n.* a blow-fly whose larva feeds on flesh.
flesh-hook, *n.* a hook to draw flesh from a pot; a hook on which meat is hung.
fleshiness, *n.* *flesh*-e-ness, the state of being fleshy.
fleshings, *n.pl.* *flesh*-ingz, flesh-coloured tights worn by acrobats, dancers, etc.
fleshless, *a.* *flesh*-less, destitute of flesh; lean.
fleshliness, *n.* *flesh*-le-ness, state of being fleshly; carnal passions and appetites.
fleshly, *a.* *flesh*-le, pertaining to the flesh; corporeal; carnal; lascivious; animal, not vegetable; human, not spiritual or divine.
fleshmonger, *n.* *flesh*-mung-ger, one who deals in flesh; a pimp; a sensualist.
flesh-pot, *n.* a vessel in which flesh is cooked; *pl.* high living [Fig.]; abundance of good things [Fig.].
flesh-wound, *n.* a wound in the flesh only.
fleshy, *a.* *flesh*-e, full of flesh; fat; corpulent; gross; corporeal; pulpy, as fruit.
fletch, *v.t.* fletch, to feather an arrow.
fletcher, *n.* *fletch*-er, an arrow-maker; a manufacturer of bows and arrows. (As *fledge*.)

fleur-de-lis, *n.* (App.), the iris; the conventionalized heraldic lily, esp. as the royal emblem of France. (Fr. *fleur*, flower, *lis*, lily.)
fleuret, *n.* flu-*ret*, a small flower-like ornament.
fleuron, *n.* (App.), a flower-shaped ornament, esp. as a terminal; a tail-piece [Print.]. (Fr.)
fleury, *a.* *fler*-re, decorated with fleur-de-lis [Her.].
flew, floo, *p.* of *fly*.
flewed, *a.* flood, deep-mouthed; having flews.
flews, *n.pl.* flooz, the large chaps of a deep-mouthed hound.
flex, *n.* fleks, flexible tube or insulated wire; a bend: *v.t.* to bend, as a muscle flexes the arm. [L. *flexus*, bent.)
flexibility, *n.* flek-se-*bil*-e-te, flexibleness; pliability.
flexible, *a.* *flek*-se-bl, easily bent; easily persuaded to comply; pliant; tractable; manageable. (O.Fr.)
flexibleness, *n.* the state of being flexible.
flexibly, *ad.* *flek*-se-ble, in a flexible manner.
flexile, *a.* *flek*-sil, easily bent; pliant or pliable; supple. (L. *flexilis*.)
flexion, *n.* *flek*-shon, the act of bending; a bending; a fold; a turn or inclination; inflexion [Gram.]; flexure [Math.]; the bending movement of a limb, etc. (L. *flexio*, a bend.)
flexor, *n.* *flek*-sor, a muscle that bends the part to which it belongs, opposed to an extensor [Anat.].
flexuose, *a.* *flek*-sew-ose, flexuous.
flexuosity, *n.* *flek*-sew-*os*-e-te, the state of being flexuous; a winding part.
flexuous, *a.* *flek*-sew-us, winding; wavering; curving; having bends or curvatures [Bot. and Zool.]. (L.)
flexure, *n.* *flek*-sewr, the act of bending; state of being bent; a bending; incurvation; the part bend; the folding of strata under pressure [Geol.]. **flexure of a curve,** a curving, either concave or convex, with respect to a given straight line [Math.]. (L. *flexura*.)
flibbertigibbet, *n.* *flib*-er-te-*jib*-et, a flighty, restless individual; a gossip; an imp.
flick, *n.* flik, a light jerk with a whip: *v.t.* to keep striking lightly with a whip. **the flicks,** the cinema [Slang]. (From the sound.)
flicker, *n.* *flik*-er, the act of flickering: *v.i.* to fluctuate unsteadily; to twinkle; to burn fitfully; to flap the wings without flying; to waver. **the flickers,** the movies, pictures, or flicks [Slang]. (A.S. *flicorian*.)
flickeringly, *ad.* in a flickering manner.
flickermouse, *n.* *flik*-er-mouse, the flittermouse.
flickery, *a.* *flik*-er-re, characterized by flickering; unsteady (of light).
flier, *n.* *fly*-er, a flyer.
flies, *n.* flize, *pl.* of *fly*: *third person sing. pres. ind.* of the verb *to fly*.
***flight,** *n.* flite, the act of fleeing; a hasty departure; movement through the air by means of wings, planes, or otherwise; manner of flying; removal by flying; a voyage in an aircraft; distance flown; the birds produced in the same season; a number, esp. of birds, flying together; a R.A.F. unit consisting (in peace-time) of three aeroplanes with personnel; a volley, as of arrows; a soaring; a migration; an excursion; an extravagant sally, as of folly: a series of stairs between landings, of canal-locks, etc.: *v.i.* to take flight; to migrate: *v.t.* to shoot while flying in company (of birds); to fletch (arrows). **flight-lieutenant,** a commissioned officer of the R.A.F. equal in rank to a naval lieutenant and army captain. **flight officer,** a W.A.A.F. commissioned rank, corresponding to flight-lieutenant or army captain. (A.S. *flyht*.)
flight-feather, *n.* one of the larger wing-feathers used in flying [Ornith.].
flightily, *ad.* capriciously; in a flighty manner.
flightiness, *n.* *flite*-e-ness, the state of being flighty.
flighty, *a.* *flite*-e, capricious; imaginative; volatile; giddy.
flimflam, *n.* *flim*-flam, nonsense; humbug.
flimsily, *ad.* in a flimsy manner.
flimsiness, *n.* quality of being flimsy.
flimsy, *a.* *flim*-ze, without strength or substance; weak; of loose or unsubstantial texture; *n.* thin paper; a reporter's script (Journalism); a carbon copy; a bank note [Slang]. (Perhaps *film*.)
flinch, *v.i.* flinch, to shrink from weakness when in pain or difficulty; to wince; to fail. (O.Fr. *flenchir*.)
flinch, *v.t.* flinch, to flense.
flincher, *n.* *flinch*-er, one who flinches or fails.
flinchingly, *ad.* in a flinching manner.
flinder, *n.* *flin*-der, a fragment or splinter.
fling, *n.* fling, a throw; a cast from the hand; a taunt; a sneer; a carouse; a round of pleasure; a plunge or kick; a Highland dance: *v.t.* to cast or throw from the hand; to hurl; to send forth; to throw to the ground; to baffle; to defeat: *v.i.* to flounce; to fly into violent and irregular motions; to cast in the teeth; to sneer; to plunge out (of horses, etc.). **to fling away,** to reject; to discard. **to fling down,** to demolish; to ruin; to throw or cast to the ground. **to fling in,** to throw in; to make an allowance or deduction. **to fling off,** to baffle in the chase. **to fling open,** to open suddenly or with violence. **to fling out,** to utter, to grow unruly or obstreperous. **to fling up,** to relinquish or abandon. **to have a fling at,** to make an attempt at. **to have one's fling,** to act unrestrainedly; to indulge in dissipation. (Scand.)
flint, *n.* flint, a dense and tough variety of quartz composed essentially of silica, which strikes fire with steel, and is used in the manufacture of fine glass and earthenware; a piece of this shaped as a strike-a-light or (by primitive or prehistoric man) as an implement; extreme hardness; anything proverbially hard. (A.S.)
flint-glass, *n.* a superior kind of table glass originally made from calcined flints.
flint-hearted, *a.* having a hard unfeeling heart.
flintiness, *n.* the quality of being flinty.
flint-lock, *n.* an arrangement of flint and steel for igniting the priming of a fire-arm by spark; a musket furnished with this.
flintwood, *n.* *flint*-wood, the extremely hard timber of the Australian tree, *Eucalyptus pilularis*.
flinty, *a.* *flint*-e, consisting of, containing, or like, flint; very hard; not impressible; unfeeling.
flip, *n.* flip, a sweetened mixture of beer and spirit warmed; a slight quick stroke, as of a whip; a short flight in an aeroplane [Slang]: *v.t.* to flick; to jerk; to toss with the thumb.
flipflap, *n.* *flip*-flap, the repeated stroke and noise of something broad and loose; a kind of large mechanical swing in use at amusement grounds, etc.: *ad.* with a repeated flapping noise.
flippancy, *n.* *flip*-an-se, light thoughtless fluency or pertness of speech; superficial assurance.
flippant, *a.* *flip*-ant, lightly, carelessly, or thoughtlessly voluble; wanting in seriousness; expressing oneself pertly. (*flip*.)
flippantly, *ad.* in a flippant manner.
flippantness, *n.* state or quality of being flippant.
flipper, *n.* *flip*-er, a swimming-limb, as of a seal, turtle, or penguin; the fore-limb of a whale, etc.; a broad side-fin; the hand [Slang].
flipperty-flopperty, *a.* *flip*-er-te-*flop*-er-te, loosely dropping; dangling; flopping.
flirt, *n.* flert, a sudden jerk; one (esp. a girl) who plays at courtship; a coquette: *v.i.* to play at courtship; to run and dart about; to act with giddiness, or ostentatiously: *v.t.* to throw with a sudden jerk; to move to and fro briskly as a fan. (Probably imitative.)
flirtation, *n.* fler-*tay*-shon, the behaviour of a flirt; playing at courtship.
flirtatious, *a.* fler-*tay*-shus, flirty.
flirtingly, *ad.* *flert*-ing-le, in a flirting manner.
flirty, *a.* *flert*-e, given to flirting.
flisk, *n.* flisk, a horsehair brush, a whisk; a large-toothed comb; a flick or fillip.
flit, *v.i.* flit, to fly quickly; to flutter on the wing; to migrate; to remove from one habitation to another [Coll.]; to be unstable or easily moved: *n.* an act of flitting; a removal. (M.E. *flitten*, from Scand.)
flitch, *n.* flitch, a side of bacon salted and cured; a halibut steak; a large plank, esp. one from the outer side of the trunk: *v.t.* to cut into flitches. (A.S. *flicce*.)
flitter, *v.i.* *flit*-ter, to flit about; to flutter.
flittermouse, *n.* *flit*-ter-mous, the bat.
flittern, *n.* *flit*-tern, a young oak, or its bark or timber, as distinguished from that of old ones. (Dial. Eng.)
flitting, *n.* *flit*-ting, a fluttering; a removal from one habitation to another.
flivver, *n.* *fliv*-er, a cheap or antiquated motor-car [Slang.]

flix, *n.* fliks, the under-fur of certain animals, esp. the beaver.
flixweed, *n. fliks*-weed, the hedge mustard.
float, *n.* flote, anything buoyed up on the surface of a fluid; cork supporting fishing-nets; the cork or quill on an angling line; a raft; the hollow portions of the under-carriage of a sea-plane giving it buoyancy; the water-gauge of a steam-boiler, attached to the valve in a steam-pipe; a light hollow ball regulating the supply of water to a cistern; a kind of rule or trowel to smooth the plastering on walls; a smooth file; a fish's bladder; surplus small coin in hand to serve as change; one of the transverse boards of a paddle- or water-wheel; a broad wagon: *pl.* the footlights at a theatre: *v.i.* to be buoyed up on the surface of a liquid or in the air; to glide or swim on a liquid; to move with a light, irregular course; to drift: *v.t.* to cause to float; to bear upon the surface; to launch (esp. a company); to put into circulation; to cover or flood with water; to start and set agoing. (A.S. *flotian.*)
floatable, *a. flote*-a-bl, capable of being floated.
floatage, *n. flote*-aj, the state of floating; the power to float; flotsam.
floatation, *n.* floh-*tay*-shon, flotation.
float-board, *n.* the float of a paddle-wheel.
floater, *n. flote*-er, one who or that which floats; a security easily dealt with.
floating, *n. flote*-ing, the action of the verb *to float*: *a.* resting buoyant on the surface of a fluid; circulating, not fixed; of uncertain amount; available for use; unattached, working freely [Mech.]; unfunded. **floating battery,** one or more warships used for coastal defence, as cover for landing-parties, etc. **floating bridge,** a bridge supported wholly by the water; a kind of double bridge, used for carrying troops over narrow channels; a large ferry boat. **floating capital,** capital not represented by permanent investments [Econ.] **floating debt,** *see* **debt. floating dock,** *see* **dock. floating harbour,** a breakwater formed of heavy timbers fastened together, which rise and fall with the tide. **floating island,** a mass of vegetation detached from the bank or bottom of a stream or lake. **floating kidney,** an abnormally mobile kidney [Med.]. **floating light,** a light-ship; a lighted life-buoy for use at night. **floating pier,** a landing-place which rises and falls with the tide. **floating ribs,** ribs which do not reach the sternum (in man, the last two pairs).
float-seaplane, *n.* a seaplane fitted with a pair of main floats.
float-stone, *n.* opal of spongy texture, light enough to float on the surface of water.
flocci, *flok*-sy, *pl.* of *floccus.*
floccillation, *n. flok*-se-*lay*-shon, a plucking of the bedclothes by one in delirium [Med.]. (L. *floccus.*)
floccose, *a. flok*-ose, tufted; covered with little tufts like wool [Bot.]. (L.)
floccule, *n. flok*-yewl, a small flock of wool or other matter. (Late L. *flocculus,* a tiny flock of wool.)
flocculence, *n. flok*-yew-lence, the state of being flocculent.
flocculent, *a. flok*-yew-lent, woolly; consisting of or resembling loosened wool.
flocculose, *a. flok*-yew-lose, woolly; tufty.
flocculous, *a. flok*-yew-lus, flocculose.
flocculus, *n. flok*-yew-lus (*pl.* **flocculi**), a floccula; a tuft of cloudy luminosity as in the sun or a nebula [Astron.]. (L.)
floccus, *n. flok*-us (*pl.* **flocci,** *flok*-sy), a flock of wool; a tuft of downy hairs [Bot.]; the long tuft of hair which terminates the tails of certain mammalia [Zool.]; the down of unfledged birds. (L.)
flock, *n.* flok, an assemblage or collection of birds, sheep, or small animals; a congregation, as under a pastor: *v.i.* to gather in companies or crowds. (A.S.)
flock, *n.* flok, a lock of wool or hair; wool or cotton refuse used in upholstery; wool dust used as a coating for flock-paper; a flock bed. **flock bed,** a bed stuffed with locks of coarse wool or wool refuse. (L. *floccus*).
flockmaster, *n. flok*-mahs-ter, a sheepfarmer.
flock-paper, *n.* wallpaper dusted, after printing with a sticky substance, with fine wool shreds or dust.
flocky, *a. flok*-e, resembling or abounding with flocks: flocculose.

floe, *n.* floh, a flat mass of floating ice. (Scand.)
flog, *v.t.* flog, to whip; to thrash; to strike with a rod; to lash (as a stream in fly-fishing); to sell or exchange, esp. illicitly [Mil. slang]. (L. *flagellare*)
flogging, *n. flog*-ging, a whipping for punishment.
flong, *n.* flong, papier-mâché used for moulding matrices in stereotyping.
flood, *n.* flud, a body of water rising, swelling, and overflowing land not usually under water; the incoming tide; high-water [Naut.]; a deluge, an inundation; a superabundant quantity: *v.t.* to overflow; to inundate. **flood tide,** *see* **tide** (A.S.)
flood-gate, *n.* a contrivance for admitting, excluding or releasing water, or for regulating its flow; a sluice.
flooding, *n. flud*-ing, an abnormal discharge of blood from the uterus; inundation.
floodlight, *v.t. flud*-lite, to illuminate, esp. architectural exteriors, so that shadows are eliminated: *n.* one of the set of brilliant electric lights effecting this. **floodlighting,** the action or result of illuminating thus: floodlights collectively.
flood-mark, *n.* high-water mark.
floodometer, *n.* flud-*om*-e-ter, a gauge for measuring the height of a flood.
★**floor,** *n.* flore, that part of a building or room on which we walk; a platform, as of boards or planks laid on timbers; a story in a building; the part of a legislative chamber, etc., occupied by the members; the sea-bed; the surface of the bottom of anything; the bottom of a vessel on each side of the keelson, nearly horizontal: *v.t.* to furnish with a floor; to strike down; to beat; to put to silence by argument; to discomfit; to finish. **to take the floor,** to address the assembly; to assume a leading rôle. (A.S. *flor.*)
floor-cloth, *n.* linoleum, or other heavy fabric for covering floors.
floorer, *n. flore*-rer, one who or that which floors or leads to defeat; a poser; a knockdown blow.
flooring, *n. flore*-ring, the bottom of a room or building; materials for floors.
floor-walker, *n.* a shop-walker [U.S.A.].
flop, *n.* flop, a dull thud; a sudden fall; a failure [Coll.]: *v.t.* to let down the brim of a hat; to plump down suddenly and limply.
floppiness, *n. flop*-pe-ness, limpness.
floppy, *a. flop*-pe, flaccid; tending to flop.
flora, *n. flore*-ra, a description of the plants, or the plants themselves, of a district or period. (L., the Roman goddess of flowers, from *flos, floris,* a flower.
floral, *a. flore*-ral, of or belonging to flora; pertaining to flowers. **floral envelope,** the calyx and corolla which envelop the inner part of a flower [Bot.] (Fr.)
florally, *ad. flore*-ra-le, like a flower; with flowers.
florence, *n. flo*-rence, a kind of wine, so called from Florence; a former dress material of silk; a florin, esp. the gold one of Edward III. **florence flask,** a thin glass bottle with a long neck. (The English name of *Firenze,* a city of N. Italy.)
Florentine, *n. flo*-ren-tine, a native of Florence a twilled cotton cloth for wear in the tropics: *a.* from or pertaining to Florence. **Florentine fresco** a kind of painting for decorating walls. **Florentine iris,** the white or pale-blue iris. **Florentine mosaic,** a mode of inlaying plane surfaces.
florescence, *n.* flo-*res*-sence, the blossoming of a plant; the flowering season. (L. *florescens,* beginning to blossom.)
floret, *n. flo*-ret, one of the small flowers in composite blossoms; a floweret. (O.Fr.)
floriated, *a. flore*-re-ay-ted, ornamented with floral designs.
floriation, *n.* flo-re-*ay*-shon, conventional floral ornamentation.
floricultural, *a. flo*-re-*kul*-tew-ral, pertaining to floriculture.
floriculture, *n. flo*-re-kul-tewr, the cultivation of flowering plant. (L. *flos,* and *cultura,* cultivation.)
floriculturist, *n. flo*-re-*kul*-tew-rist, a cultivator of flowers.
florid, *a. flo*-rid, bright in colour; splendid; brilliant; of a lively red; highly embellished [Art, Mus., Rhet.]. **florid style,** a highly ornamented and elaborate form, esp. of Gothic architecture. (L. *floridus.*)
floridity, *n.* flo-*rid*-e-te, floridness.

floridly, *ad.* in a florid manner.
floridness, *n.* the quality of being florid; lavish ornamentation.
floriferous, *a.* flo-*rif*-rer-us, bearing or producing flowers. (L. *florifer*, flowery.)
florification, *n.* flo-re-fe-*kay*-shon, the act or process of flowering
floriform, *a. flor*-re-form, in the form of a flower.
florilegium, *n.* flo-re-*lee*-je-um, a collection of flowers; an anthology. (L. *florilegus*, flower-culling.)
florin, *n. flo*-rin, a British silver coin worth 2*s.*; a Continental coin, ranging in value from 1*s.* 6*d.* to 2*s.* 4*d.*, originally of gold and coined at Florence, with on one side a fleur-de-lys. (O.Fr.)
florist, *n. flo*-rist, a nurseryman; one skilled in flowers; a dealer in flowers. (Fr. *fleuriste.*)
floristic, *a.* flo-*ris*-tik, pertaining to flora, flowers, or floral emblems.
flory, *a. flor*-re, fleury [Her.].
floscular, *a. flos*-kew-lar, consisting of or bearing tubular florets or floscules [Bot.].
floscule, *n. flos*-kewl, a floret of a composite flower [Bot.]. (L. *flosculus*, a little flower.)
flosculous, *a. flos*-kew-lus, floscular.
floss, *n.* floss, a downy silk enveloping a cocoon; the silky substance in the husks of certain plants, as the bean; fine untwisted silk filaments used in embroidery. (Perhaps O.Fr. *flosche.*)
flossy, *a. flos*-se, consisting of or like floss; downy.
flota, *n. floh*-ta, a trading fleet, esp. that which formerly sailed every year from Vera Cruz in Mexico to Spain. (Sp.)
flotage, *n. floh*-taj, floatage.
flotant, *a. floh*-tant, floating in the air, as a flag [Her.]. (O.Fr., floating.)
flotation, *n.* flo-*tay*-shon, the act or condition of floating; the launching and financing of a company, project, etc.; a process of ore concentration [Metal.]. **flotation gear,** a contrivance to enable aeroplanes, not specially built for the purpose, to alight and float on water. (Fr.)
flotilla, *n.* flo-*til*-la, a fleet of small vessels; a small fleet. (Sp.)
flotsam, *n. flot*-sam, goods lost by shipwreck, and found floating [Law]; anything drifting about. (O.Fr. *flotaison*, a flooding.)
flounce, *n.* flounce, a sudden jerking motion of the body: *v.i.* to throw about the limbs and body; to struggle and flounder about; to throw oneself with jerks or agitation. (Perhaps Scand. *flunsa*, to plunge.)
flounce, *n.* flounce, a narrow piece of material on a dress, petticoat, etc., with the lower border loose and spreading: *v.t.* to deck with a flounce. (O.Fr. *fronce*, a gather.)
flouncing, *n. floun*-sing, flounces; material for making flounces.
flounder, *n. floun*-der, the small flat-fish, *Pleuronectes flesus*, living in estuaries, etc. (Swed. *flundra.*)
flounder, *v.i. floun*-der, to toss and tumble about; to proceed with difficulty; to struggle along: *n.* act or motion of floundering; a blundering attempt. (Scand.)
flour, *n.* flour, the finer portion of ground corn or grain; any similar powdery substance: *v.t.* to reduce to or sprinkle with flour. (As *flower.*)
flour-dredger, *n.* a perforated tin case for sprinkling flour on meat, etc.
flourish, *n. flu*-rish, showy splendour; showy embellishment; a rhetorical parade; florid diction; a figure formed by fanciful strokes in drawing, etc.; a brandishing; the waving of a weapon or other thing; decorative notes added for the sake of effect, also a fanfare [Mus.]: *v.i.* to thrive; to increase in wealth, honour, etc.; to prosper; to be florid in speech, writing, music, etc.; to make free sweeping strokes or dashes with a pen, etc.; to live or be working (about the date named): *v.t.* to expand in a flowery way; to brandish; to parade about. **flourish of trumpets,** a fanfare, esp. when receiving some notable person; any ostentatious announcement. (O.Fr. *florir.*)
flourishing, *a.* thriving; prosperous; making a show.
flourishingly, *ad.* with flourishes; ostentatiously.
floury, *a. flour*-re, covered with flour; like flour.
flout, *n.* flout, a mock; an insult: *v.t.* to mock or insult; to treat with contempt: *v.i.* to sneer; to behave with contempt. (Origin uncertain.)
flouter, *n. flout*-er, one who flouts; a mocker.
floutingly, *ad.* with flouting; insultingly.
flow, *n.* floh, act or state of flowing; a stream; a current; the rise of the tide; abundance; copiousness; free outflow; an undulation: *v.i.* to move or run, as a fluid; to melt; to proceed or issue; to abound; to glide along smoothly; to rise, as the tide; to circulate, as the blood; to move in a stream; to abound. (A.S. *flowan.*)
★**flower,** *n. flou*-er, the blossom of a plant; the organs of reproduction in seed-plants; the period of youthful vigour; the choicest part of a thing; figure or ornament of speech: *pl.* substances in a fine powdery state due to sublimation [Chem.]; menstrual discharge: *v.i.* to blossom; to flourish; to be at the prime; to come as cream from the surface: *v.t.* to cause to flower; to make flowery or florid. (O.Fr. *fleur.*)
flowerage, *n. flou*-er-raj, flowers collectively; the process of flowering.
flower-de-luce, *n. flou*-er-de-*loos*, fleur-de-lis.
flowered, *a. flou*-erd, expanded into flowers; embellished with figures of flowers.
flowerer, *n. flou*-er-rer, a flowering plant.
floweret, *n. flou*-er-ret, a small flower.
flower-fence, *n.* a tropical evergreen shrub, ***Poinciana** pulcherrima*, with showy flowers.
flower-head, *n.* that mode of inflorescence in which all the florets are combined, as in a daisy.
floweriness, *n.* the state of being flowery.
flowering, *a. flou*-er-ring, bearing conspicuous flowers; flowery. **flowering almond,** the Japanese shrub, *Amygdalus japonica.* **flowering ash,** the manna-ash, *Fraxinus ornus.* **flowering fern,** the king fern, *Osmunda regalis.* **flowering rush,** the aquatic plant, *Butomus umbellatus.*
flower-pot, *n.* an earthenware or china pot for holding growing plants.
flower-show, *n. flou*-er-shoh, a horticultural display, generally including competitions for prizes.
flowery, *a. flou*-er-re, abounding with flowers or blossoms; highly embellished with figurative language; florid.
flowing, *a. floh*-ing, moving as a fluid; brimming; fluent or smooth; hanging loose and waving.
flowingly, *ad.* in a flowing manner; with abundance.
flown, flone, *pp.* of *fly*; *a.* inflated [Milton].
flu, *n.* floo, short for influenza.
fluctuant, *a. fluk*-tew-ant, wavering; unsteady; floating on the waves.
fluctuate, *v.i. fluk*-tew-ate, to float backward and forward; to waver; to rise and fall; to be unsteady; to be irresolute. (L. *fluctuatus*, fluctuated.)
fluctuation, *n. fluk*-tew-*ay*-shon, moving hither and thither; a rising and falling like a wave; unsteadiness; a sudden rise or fall.
flue, *n.* floo, a passage or pipe for allowing the escape of smoke or for conveying heat.
flue, *n.* floo, soft down, fur, or hair; fluff.
fluency, *n. floo*-en-se, the quality of being fluent.
fluent, *a. floo*-ent, flowing; having a ready command and flow of words; voluble; smooth: *n.* a variable quantity, considered as increasing or diminishing [Math.]. (L. *fluentia.*)
fluently, *ad. floo*-ent-le, with fluency.
fluey, *a. floo*-e, downy; fluffy.
fluff, *n.* fluf, a light down, such as rises from beds, cotton, etc., when shaken; free or loosened nap: *v.t.* to make into or cover with fluff; to dress the hair loosely.
fluffiness, *n.* the state or quality of being fluffy.
fluffy, *a. fluf*-fe, consisting of or resembling fluff; fluffed out (of hair, etc.).
flugelman, *n. floo*-gl-man, a fugleman. (Ger. *flügelmann.*)
fluid, *a. floo*-id, that may flow, like water or air; liquid or gaseous; unstable: *n.* a substance whose particles readily move and change their relative position; a liquid. (O.Fr. *fluide.*)
fluidify, *v.t.* floo-*id*-e-fy, to convert to fluid form.
fluidity, *n.* floo-*id*-e-te, the quality of being fluid; a fluid state. (Fr. *fluidité.*)
fluidness, *n. floo*-id-ness, fluidity.
fluke, *n.* flook, the broad triangular plate inside the bill or point of an anchor which holds the ship; the tip of a whale's tail; the barbed head of a harpoon; a chance successful hit: *v.i.* and *t.* to score (as at billiards, etc.) or make a success by chance; to make a lucky shot.

fluke, *n.* flook, a flounder or other flatfish, as the witch, megrim, etc.; a rot or a parasitic disease of sheep, etc.; a variety of kidney potato. (A.S. *flōc.*)
flukily, *ad.* *flook*-e-le, more by luck than judgment.
flukiness, *n.* *flook*-e-ness, chance; accident.
fluky, *a.* *flook*-e, having the form of a fluke; characterized by chance shots; accidentally good.
flume, *n.* floom, the passage or channel for the water that drives a mill-wheel; any artificial water-channel: *v.t.* to carry away, or to drain, by means of a flume. (O.Fr. *flum.*)
flummery, *n.* *flum*-me-re, a mixture of whisked cream, gelatine, wine, sugar, and lemon juice; anything insipid or not to the purpose; nonsense; humbug; flattery. (W. *llymrig*, raw.)
flummox, *v.t.* *flum*-muks, to bewilder; to disconcert; to hoax [Slang].
flung, flung, *pp.* of *fling.*
flunkey, *n.* *flung*-ke, a livery servant; a footman; one who apes the aristocracy; a snob; a toady. (Scots., through Fr. *flanqueur*, allied to *flank.*)
flunkeydom, *n.* *flung*-ke-dum, the world or characteristics of flunkeys.
flunkeyism, *n.* *flung*-ke-izm, the character or quality of a flunkey or snob.
fluor, *n.* *floo*-or, fluor-spar; formerly any mineral containing fluorine. (L., a flowing.)
fluorene, *n.* *floo*-o-reen, a crystalline hydrocarbon occurring in coal-tar and giving violet fluorescence.
fluoresce, *v.i.* floo-o-*res*, to become fluorescent.
fluorescein, *n.* floo-o-*res*-e-in, a green-yellow chemical dye-stuff giving green fluorescence.
fluorescence, *n.* floo-o-*res*-ence, coloured luminosity which certain substances exhibit when exposed to the action of the sun, or to ultra-violet radiation, or to electronic bombardment.
fluorescent, *a.* floo-o-*res*-ent, having, due to, or resembling fluorescence.
fluoric, *a.* floo-*o*-rik, pertaining to or obtained from fluor-spar.
fluoride, *n.* *floo*-o-ride, any salt of hydrofluoric acid.
fluorine, *n.* *floo*-o-rin, a non-metallic yellowish and poisonous gaseous element of the halogen group present in fluor-spar.
fluorite, *n.* *floo*-o-rite, a former name of fluor-spar.
fluoroscope, *n.* *floo*-o-ro-skohp, an instrument for showing or observing fluorescence, esp. one for the examination of objects under the action of X-rays.
fluoroscopy, *n.* floo-o-*ros*-ko-pe, X-ray examination, or the process of such examination, by means of the fluoroscope.
fluorotype, *n.* *floo*-o-ro-tipe, a former photographic process in which silver fluoride was employed.
fluor-spar, *n.* *floo*-or-spar, calcium fluoride, a translucent crystalline mineral of various colours.
flurry, *n.* *flu*-re, a sudden gust; spasmodic commotion; bustle; the convulsive movements of a harpooned whale: *v.t.* to agitate; to bewilder. (Imitative.)
flush, *n.* flush, a sudden flow of blood to the face; the redness induced; sudden impulse or excitement; bloom; abundance; cards of the same suit; birds suddenly started in flight; a flow of water, as in flushing a sewer; a complete bedding of masonry or brickwork, so as to leave no vacant space; *v.i.* to flow and spread suddenly; to come with a rush (of blood); to become suddenly red; to take wing (of game-birds): *v.t.* to cause to blush; to cause birds to take to flight; to excite the spirits of; to clean out with a rush of water. (Probably imitative.)
flush, *a.* flush, fresh and full of vigour; abounding; well supplied with, as money; even or level in respect to surface: *ad.* in manner to be level with. A **flush deck**, a deck with a continuous level floor from stem to stern [Naut.].
flushness, *n.* *flush*-ness, state or quality of being flush; freshness; abundance.
fluster, *n.* *flus*-ter, agitation; confusion: *v.i.* to be in a state of agitation; to bustle: *v.t.* to make hot and red in the face, as with drinking; to agitate and confuse. (Scand.)
flustra, *n.* *flus*-tra, the sea-mat, a species of polyzoa.
flute, *n.* floot, a wood-wind instrument with finger-holes and keys; an organ-stop of similar tone; a furrow or channel cut along the shaft of a column or pilaster; any similar furrowing, as in a skirt or ruffle: *v.i.* to play on, or as on, a flute: *v.t.* to form flutes or channels in; to sound as a flute. (O.Fr. *flaute.*)
fluted, *a.* *floo*-ted, channelled; fine or flute-like, as the upper notes of a soprano voice [Mus.].
fluter, *n.* *floo*-ter, one who cuts, or an implement for cutting, flutes in columns, etc; a flautist [Coll.].
flutina, *n.* floo-*teen*-a, a small instrument of accordion or concertina type [Mus.].
fluting, *n.* *floo*-ting, fluted work; a shallow groove in a column, or in a ruffle or frock, etc.
flutist, *n.* *floo*-tist, a performer on a flute; a flautist.
flutter, *n.* *flut*-ter, quick and irregular motion; vibration; hurry and agitation of the mind; confusion; a gamble: *v.i.* to move or flap the wings spasmodically, without flying, or with only short flights; to move about in a bustling way; to quiver; to move with quick vibrations; to be in agitation; to be in uncertainty: *v.t.* to agitate; to throw into confusion. (A.S. *flotorian*, to float about in).
flutterer, *n.* *flut*-ter-rer, one who flutters.
flutteringly, *ad.* in a fluttering manner.
fluty, *a.* *floo*-te, like a flute in tone.
fluvial, *a.* *floo*-ve-al, pertaining to, or [Geol.] caused by a river; inhabiting rivers [Bot. and Zool.]. (L. *fluvialis*, relating to a river.)
fluvialist, *n.* *floo*-ve-a-list, one holding that certain geological phenomena are attributable mainly to the action of rivers.
fluviatic, *a.* floo-ve-*at*-ik, caused by rivers.
fluviatile, *a.* *floo*-ve-a-tile, growing or living in rivers [Bot. and Zool.]; due to river action [Geol.]
fluviograph, *n.* *floo*-ve-o-graf, an instrument that measures and records the rise and fall of rivers.
fluviology, *n.* floo-ve-*ol*-o-je, the science that treats of rivers and streams.
fluviomarine, *a.* *floo*-ve-o-ma-*reen*, estuarine.
flux, *n.* fluks, the act of flowing; the motion of a fluid; the moving or passing of anything in continued succession; any flow or issue of matter that which flows or is discharged; a liquid state from the action of heat; the flow of the tide; any substance or mixture used to promote the fusion of metals or minerals [Metal.]: *v.t.* to melt; to purge (O.Fr.)
fluxible, *a.* *fluk*-se-bl, capable of being melted or fused.
fluxility, *n.* fluk-*sil*-e-te, possibility of being fused or liquefied. (L. *fluxilis*, fluid.)
fluxion, *n.* *fluk*-shon, the act of flowing; the matter that flows; fusion; an abnormal flow of blood or humour; variation: *pl.* Newton's name for that branch of mathematics, which he first formulated now known as differential and integral calculus (L. *fluxion*, a flow.)
fluxional, *a.* *fluk*-shon-al, pertaining to fluxions.
fluxionary, *a.* *fluk*-shon-a-re, fluxional; variable.
fly, *v.i.* fly, to move through the air on or as on wings; to move through the air; to travel by air in aircraft; to move swiftly; to pass away; to burst; to flee: *v.t.* to quit or avoid by flight; to cause to float in the air; to flutter, as a flag in the wind; to pass over by flying; to carry by flight. **to fly at** to rush or fall on suddenly. **to fly in the face,** to insult; to assail; to set at defiance. **to fly off** to separate or depart suddenly. **to fly open,** to open suddenly or with violence. **to fly out,** to rush out; to burst into a passion; to break out into licence; to issue with violence. **to let fly,** to discharge; to let go suddenly and entirely [Naut.]. *p.* **flew.** *pp.* **flown.** (A.S. *fleogan.*)
★**fly,** *n.* fly, a dipterous insect; the common house-fly a fly-wheel, or similar regulating device [Mech.] that part of a vane which points and shows which way the wind blows; the extent of a flag, pennant etc., from the staff, also its outer end that flutters loose; a one-horse hackney carriage; a hook dressed like a fly; a flap to cover buttonholes; one who or that which takes the sheets from the press or machine [Print.]; (usu. *pl.*) the place above the stage from which scenery is worked [Theat.] (A.S. *fleoge.*)
fly, *a.* fly, knowing; artful [Slang].
fly-away, *a.* loose and streaming; flighty.
fly-bitten, *a.* marked by or as by the bites of flies.
fly-blow, *n.* *fly*-bloh, the egg or larva of a fly: *v.t.* to taint by deposit of flies' eggs.
fly-blown, *a.* contaminated by flies or fly-blows sullied, besmirched [Fig.].

fly-book, *n.* a case or book for anglers' flies.
flycatcher, *n. fly*-katch-er, a bird of the genus *Muscicapa*, which catches insects in its flight; Venus's fly-trap, or other plant that ensnares flies [Bot.].
flyer, *n. fly*-er, one who flies or flees; a fugitive; a flying jump; a fly-wheel; a high-flyer; an airman: *pl.* a straight flight of steps.
fly-fishing, *n.* angling for fish with flies.
fly-flap, *n.* an implement to drive away flies.
flying, *n. fly*-ing, the action of the verb *to fly*; aviation: *a.* that flies, or travels swiftly; resembling that which flies, rapid, speedy; not settled; not lasting. **flying squad,** *see* **squad.**
flying-bomb, *n.* a powerful long-range jet-propelled bomb, having planes and launched from a special ramp.
flying-bridge, *n.* a temporary bridge, esp. one of pontoons [Mil.].
flying-buttress, *n.* an arched brace carrying the thrust of a vault horizontally across a space, esp. in a Gothic edifice [Arch.].
flying-colours, *n.pl.* show of triumph.
flying-column, *n.* a body of specially mobile troops used as scouts, for harassing the enemy, etc.
flying-fish, *n.* a marine fish having the power of sustaining itself temporarily in the air by means of its long pectoral fins.
flying-fox, *n.* a fruit-bat or fox-bat of the genus *Pteropus.*
flying-jib, *n. fly*-ing-jib, the next sail forward of the jib; the third jib [Naut.].
flying-lemur, *n.* an arboreal insectivorous mammal of Malaya and the Philippines having folds of skin extending from behind the throat to the toes and the tip of the tail by means of which it glides from tree to tree.
flying-machine, *n.* an aircraft of any kind.
flying-officer, *n.* an officer in the Royal Air Force equal in rank to a sub-lieutenant in the Navy and a lieutenant in the Army
flying-phalanger, *n.* a phalanger provided with a membrane extending from the fore- to the hind-foot, with which it supports itself when leaping.
flying-squirrel, *n.* any of several squirrels having an expansive skin reaching on each side from the fore- to the hind-legs by which it is borne up in leaping; (in Australia) the flying-phalanger.
flying-start, *n.* the start of a race in which the starting-point is passed after the competitors are in motion.
fly-leaf, *n.* a leaf of blank paper at the beginning and end of a book.
flyman, *n. fly*-man, the driver of a hackney fly; a scene-shifter or other worker in the flies [Theat.].
fly-net, *n.* a net to protect from flies.
fly-nut, *n.* a screw with wings.
fly-over, *n.* and *a.* denoting a road-traffic expedient enabling one road to cross another by means of a bridge connected by ramps to each.
flypaper, *n. fly*-pay-per, paper with an adhesive coating for catching or poisoning flies.
fly-posting, *n.* the open-air display of public notices, etc., at any place other than a recognized bill-posting site.
fly-sheet, *n.* a handbill or broadside; a tract.
fly-trap, *n.* a trap for catching flies; the pitcher-plant, or other insectivorous plant, as Venus's fly-trap.
flyweight, *n. fly*-wate, a boxer weighing 8 stone or less.
fly-wheel, *n.* a heavy wheel that regulates and equalizes the motion of a machine.
foal, *n.* fole, the young of the horse or ass, a colt or filly: *v.t.* and *i.* to bring forth a colt or filly, as a mare or a she-ass. (A.S. *fola.*)
foalfoot, *n. fole*-foot, the colt's-foot and certain other plants.
foam, *n.* fome, the collection of bubbles formed on the surface of liquids by fermentation or violent agitation; froth; spume; a suspension of a gas in a liquid [Chem.]: *v.i.* to gather foam; to be in a rage: *v.t.* to throw out with rage or violence. **to foam at the mouth,** to be furious with anger. (A.S. *fam.*)
foamy, *a. foh*-me, covered with foam; frothy.
fob, *n.* fob, a little pocket for a watch. (Low Ger. *fobke*, a little pocket.)
fob, *v.t.* fob, to impose on. **to fob off,** to shift off, or delude with a trick. (M.E. *fobbere*, one who cheats.)

focal, *a. foh*-kal, pertaining to or situated at a focus **focal distance,** the distance between the centre of a lens and the point where the rays converge. **focal plane,** the plane in which a sharp image is formed by a lens [Opt.].
focalize, *v.t. foh*-ka-lize, to bring to a focus.
focimetry, *n.* foh-*sim*-e-tre, the art of measuring the focal distance of a lens or system of lenses.
fo'c'sle, *n. foh*-k'sl, the forecastle of a ship.
focus, *n. foh*-kus (*pl.* **foci,** *foh*-sy), a point in which the rays of light meet, after being reflected or refracted [Optics]; the point at which sound waves meet; a point in the parabola, ellipse, or hyperbola, where rays reflected from all their parts meet [Geom.]; a central point or point of convergence: *v.t.* to bring to a focus. *pp.* **focused.** (L., a hearth.)
fodder, *n. fod*-der, food for horses, cattle, or sheep, as hay, straw, etc.: *v.t.* to furnish with fodder. (A.S. *fodor.*)
foe, *n.* foh, a personal enemy; an enemy in war; an opponent; an ill-wisher. (A.S. *fah.*)
Foehn, *n.* fern, a dry, hot wind of mountainous districts, esp. the Northern Alps. (Ger.)
foeman, *n. foh*-man, an enemy in war.
fœtal, *a. fee*-tal, pertaining to the fœtus.
fœtation, *n.* fee-*tay*-shon, the formation of a fœtus; pregnancy.
fœticide, *n. fee*-te-side, the destruction of a fœtus; the act of causing abortion. (L. *fœtus*, and *cædo*, kill.)
fœtid, *a. fee*-tid, fetid.
fœtor, *n. fee*-tur, an offensive smell; the effluvia of putrescence.
fœtus, *n. fee*-tus, the young of viviparous animals before their birth, and of oviparous ones in the shell, after the embryo has developed. (L.)
fog, *n.* fog, a dense watery vapour near the surface of the land or water; a state of haze; a state of perplexity: *v.t.* to surround with, or as with, a fog; to perplex: *v.i.* to become foggy, or [Phot.] cloudy. (Scand.)
fog, *n.* fog, aftermath; a growth of grass after the hay is cut in autumn; rank long grass; moss [Scots.]: *v.t.* to feed on fog. (Scand.)
fog-bank, *n.* a dense mass of fog at sea, resembling land at a distance.
fogey, *n. foh*-ge, an alternative spelling of **fogy.**
foggily, *ad. fog*-ge-le, mistily; cloudily.
fogginess, *n. fog*-ge-ness, the state of being foggy.
foggy, *a. fog*-ge, abounding with fog; misty; damp; clouded in understanding; stupid.
foghorn, *n. fog*-hawn, a horn to give warning in a fog.
fogle, *n.* fohgl, a silk handkerchief [Slang].
fog-signal, *n.* any audible signal of danger in a fog, esp. a detonator placed on a railway, which, on exploding, gives notice of danger ahead; a shrill railway whistle; the sound of a foghorn, siren, or steam-whistle, used by ships during a fog.
fogy, *n. foh*-ge, an elderly old-fashioned fellow [Humorous or disrespectful].
fogydom, *n. foh*-ge-dom, the state or condition of a fogy.
foh, *int.* fo, faugh, an exclamation of abhorrence or contempt.
Föhn, *n.* fern, the Foehn. (Ger.)
foible, *n. foy*-bl, a weak point in one's character; a weakness; the half of a foil- or sword-blade nearer the point. (O.Fr., feeble.)
foil, *n.* foyl, a rapier with a leather-covered button at the point, used in fencing; failure of success when on the point of being secured; the track or trail of game when pursued: *v.t.* to frustrate; to defeat; to baffle; to blunt; to dull. (O.Fr. *fouler*, trample upon.)
foil, *n.* foyl, a leaf or thin plate of metal, as tinfoil; a small rounded leaf-like form in window tracery [Arch.]; a thin leaf of metal placed under precious stones to increase their brilliancy; anything of different colour or quality serving to the advantage of, or as contrast to, another; a thin amalgam of tin and quicksilver laid on the back of a mirror to cause reflection. (O.Fr. *feuille*, leaf.)
foiled, *a.* foyld, having or resemblin foils [Arch.].
foiling, *n. foyl*-ing, a foil in tracery [Arch.]; the track or slot of a passing deer.
foin, *n.* foyn, a push; a thrust: *v.i.* to thrust in fencing. (O.Fr.)
foison, *n. foy*-zn, plenty; abundance. (O.Fr.)

foist, *v.t.* foyst, to insert surreptitiously or wrongfully; to palm off in an underhand way something bad. (Dut. *vuisten*, to take in the fist.)
foister, *n. foys*-ter, one who foists; a cheat.
fold, *n.* fohld, a pen or enclosure for sheep; a flock of sheep; a flock of believers: *v.t.* to pen or enclose in or as in a fold. (A.S., *fald.*)
***fold,** *n.* fohld, the doubling of any flexible substance, as cloth; a folding, bend, or doubling; a curve or flexure in stratification; one part turned or laid on another; in composition, times repeated, as fourfold: *v.t.* to double; to lay one or one part over another: *v.i.* to close over another of the same kind. (A.S. *fealdan*, to fold.)
foldage, *n. fohl*-daj, the right of folding sheep; the folding of leaves close over one another.
folded, *a. fohl*-ded, doubled; laid in pleats.
folder, *n. fohl*-der, an instrument used in folding paper; a jacket for papers; a folded leaflet or advertisement; (*pl.*) folding eyeglasses.
folding-doors, *n.pl.* two doors hung on opposite side-posts and opening in the middle.
folding-joints, *n.pl.* double hinges which fold together.
folding-machine, *n.* a machine for folding printed matter.
folding-screen, *n.* an upright portable screen which folds in several leaves.
folding-stool, *n.* a camp-stool.
foliaceous, *a.* foh-le-*ay*-shus, leafy in appearance; leaf-bearing; having leaves mixed with flowers; consisting of, or splitting into, thin laminæ. (L. *foliaceus.*)
foliage, *n. foh*-le-aj, leaves; leaves collectively; a cluster of leaves, flowers, and branches, particularly in representation: *v.t.* to work or form into the representation of leaves. (O.Fr. *fueillage.*)
foliar, *a. foh*-le-ar, pertaining to, resembling, or consisting of leaves.
foliate, *a. foh*-le-ate, furnished with or resembling leaves [Bot.]: *v.t.* to beat into a leaf or thin plate; to embellish with leaf-like patterns; to spread over with a thin coat of tin and quicksilver, etc.; to number the leaves or folios of a book consecutively. (L. *foliatus*, leaved.)
foliated, *a. foh*-le-ay-ted, spread or covered with a thin plate or foil; consisting of plates or thin layers [Min.].
foliation, *n. foh*-le-*ay*-shon, the leafing of plants [Bot.]; the act or operation of foliating; ornamentation with leaf-like tracery [Arch., etc.]; the quality of the metamorphic rocks of cleaving into laminæ [Geol.].
foliature, *n. foh*-le-a-tewr, a cluster of leaves; leaf-like ornamentation.
foliferous, *a.* fo-*lif*-er-rus, bearing or producing leaves. (L. *folium*, and *fero*, produce.)
folio, *n. foh*-le-oh, a sheet of paper folded once; a volume formed of sheets folded once only, hence a book of the largest size; a page of manuscript or printed matter [Print.]; the page-number of a book [Print.]; both the right- and left-hand pages of an account-book, bearing the same number [Comm.]; seventy-two, eighty, or ninety words of manuscript [Law]: *a.* having the paper folded only once: *v.t.* to paginate. (L. *folium*, a leaf.)
foliobranchiate, *a. foh*-le-o-*brang*-ke-at, having leaf-like gills [Zool.].
foliole, *n. foh*-le-ohl, a leaflet of a compound leaf; a small leaf-like appendage [Zool.].
foliose, *a. foh*-le-ohs, foliaceous; well provided with leaves.
folious, *a. foh*-le-us, leafy; thin; unsubstantial; having leaves intermixed with flowers [Bot.].
folk, *n.* foke, people in general; relatives; those collectively of a distinct group, as of nationality, language, social status, etc.; certain people discriminated from others, as old folks. **folk etymology,** the popular but often unsound derivation of a word. (A.S. *folc.*)
folkland, *n. foke*-land, in feudal law, the public land, which could not be alienated from the people.
folk-lore, *n. foke*-lor, the body of popular superstitions; legendary traditions prevailing among a people respecting themselves or their original beliefs and practices; the comparative study of these.
folklorist, *n. foke*-lor-rist, a systematic student of folk-lore.
folkmote, *n. foke*-mote, the national assembly of all classes of freemen to administer the law and consult respecting public affairs in feudal times. (A.S. *folc*, and *mote*, meeting.)
folkright, *n. foke*-rite, the common law of England before the Conquest, administered in the hundred court and folkmote.
folk-song, *n.* a traditional song or ballad originating among the common people of a country or locality.
folk-speech, *n. foke*-speech, dialect; dialect in which ancient idioms are preserved.
follicle, *n. fol*-le-kl, a one-celled pod-like fruit opening on one side only, usually the ventral [Bot.]; a vessel distended with air; a small sac or gland [Anat.]. (L. *folliculus*, a tiny bag.)
follicular, *a.* fo-*lik*-yew-lar, in the form of a follicle.
folliculated, *a.* fo-*lik*-yew-lay-ted, having follicular seed vessels [Bot.].
folliculitis, *n.* fo-*lik*-yew-*ly*-tis, inflammation of a follicle or follicles.
folliculous, *a.* fo-*lik*-yew-lus, having or producing follicles; abounding in follicles.
follow, *v.t. fol*-lo, to go or come after, or behind; to pursue in order to overtake or obtain; to accompany; to adhere to, and go along with; to result from; to pursue with the eye; to imitate; to pay close attention to; to attend to closely; to obey: *v.i.* to come after another; to result. **follow on,** to continue pursuit or endeavour; of a side at cricket, to take their second innings immediately after their first, owing to their not having scored enough runs. **follow suit,** to play a card of the same suit. **follow up,** to be near to help; to pursue steadily. (A.S. *folgian.*)
follower, *n. fol*-lo-er, one who or that which goes after another in the same course; one who takes another as his guide in doctrines, opinions, or example; a lover; a disciple; an attendant; a subordinate.
following, *a. fol*-lo-ing, being next after; succeeding: *n.* body of followers.
folly, *n. fol*-le, want of sense; a foolish act; an extravagant or unprofitable undertaking. (O.Fr. *folie.*)
foment, *v.t.* fo-*ment*, to apply warm lotions to; to cherish; to excite. (Fr. *fomenter.*)
fomentation, *n.* foh-men-*tay*-shon, the act of fomenting; the lotion applied; instigation; encouragement. (Fr.)
fomenter, *n.* fo-*men*-ter, one who foments.
fomes, *n. foh*-meez (*pl.* **fomites,** fo-*my*-teez), any porous substance absorbent of contagious matter [Med.]. (L., touchwood.)
fond, *a.* fond, foolish; silly; foolishly tender and loving; weakly indulgent; loving ardently; relishing highly. (M.E. *fonned.*)
fondant, *n. fon*-dant (or App.), a kind of sweetmeat. (Fr.)
fondle, *v.t. fon*-dl, to treat with tenderness; to caress. (As *fond.*)
fondler, *n. fon*-dler, one who fondles.
fondling, *n. fon*-dling, a person or thing fondled.
fondly, *ad. fond*-le, in a fond manner.
fondness, *n.* the state or quality of being fond.
fondu, *a.* (App.), blended imperceptibly with each other (of colours on textiles, wallpaper, etc.). (Fr., melted.)
font, *n.* font, a basin or vessel to contain water for baptism; a fountain. (A.S.)
font, *n.* font, a fount of printing types.
fontal, *a. fon*-tal, pertaining to a fount or source; baptismal. (Late L. *fontalis.*)
fontanel, *n. fon*-ta-nel, any of the intervals between the parietal bones of the cranium of an infant or fœtus [Anat.]. (Fr.)
***food,** *n.* food, whatever is eaten by animals or absorbed by plants as nutriment; edibles as distinct from beverages; something that sustains, nourishes, and augments. (A.S. *foda.*)
food-card, *n.* a card entitling the holder to his specified food rations.
food-controller, *n.* an officer appointed to regulate food supplies, esp. in times of national stress.
food-fish, *n.* any fish commonly used for human consumption.
foodfull, *a. food*-full, rich in feeding content; notably nutritious.
foodstuff, *n. food*-stuf, anything used as food.
fool, *n.* fool, a person of weak intellect; a person who acts foolishly; a buffoon; a jester: *v.i.* to

trifle; to toy; to spend time unprofitably: *v.t.* to make a fool of; to disappoint; to deceive; to cheat. **a fool's errand,** the pursuit of the impossible; an absurd undertaking. **a fool's paradise,** a state of unreasoning happiness which will shortly be shattered. **the feast of fools,** a mediæval festival, somewhat similar to the Saturnalia of the Romans. **to fool away,** to spend in trifles, idleness, folly, or without advantage; to expend improvidently. **to make a fool of,** to make ridiculous; to frustrate; to defeat. **to play the fool,** to act the buffoon; to act like one void of understanding. (O.Fr. *fol.*)

fool, *n.* fool, a compound, generally, of gooseberries scalded and crushed with cream. (O.Fr. *fol.*)

foolery, *n. fool*-e-re, habitual folly; attention to trifles; any act of folly; absurdity.

foolhardily, *ad.* with foolhardiness.

foolhardiness, *n.* fool-*har*-de-ness, courage without sense or judgment; mad rashness.

foolhardy, *a.* fool-*har*-de, daring without judgment; madly rash; foolishly bold. (O. Fr. *fol hardi.*)

***foolish,** *a. fool*-ish, weak in intellect; without judgment or discretion; ridiculous; proceeding from or marked with folly; deserving of ridicule; indiscreet.

foolishly, *ad.* in a foolish manner; like a fool.

foolishness, *n. fool*-ish-ness, folly.

foolocracy, *n.* fool-*lok*-ra-se, government by, or a government of, fools.

fool-proof, *a. fool*-proof, incapable of being misused, misunderstood, etc.; completely secured against accident.

foolscap, *n. foolz*-kap, the cap and bells of a jester; a size of paper, about 17 inches by 14, so called as originally watermarked with this.

***foot,** *n.* foot (*pl.* **feet**), that part of the leg on which a vertebrate animal stands and walks; the organ of locomotion of invertebrates; anything like a foot in shape or office; the part of a stocking or boot which receives the foot; the lower part, base, or footing; soldiers who march and fight on foot; a lineal measure of 12 in. (roughly the length of a man's foot); a certain number of syllables constituting part of a verse: *v.i.* to dance to music; to pace; to travel on foot: *v.t.* to kick; to spurn; to add the numbers in a column and set the sum at the foot; to add a foot to (a stocking, etc.). **by foot, or on foot,** by walking. **cubic foot,** a cube with sides of one square foot, containing 1728 cubic inches. **foot-and-mouth disease,** a contagious febrile disease affecting cattle and other ungulates. **square foot,** a square whose side is one foot containing 144 square inches. **to foot it,** to walk. **to foot the bill,** to pay the cost. **to put one's foot in,** to spoil and get into a scrape. **to set on foot,** to originate, to put in motion. (A.S. *fot.*)

footage, *n. foot*-aj, length or quantity as measured by the foot; the length of a sound-film in feet [Cinema].

football, *n. foot*-bawl, an inflated ball of thin rubber, cased in leather and played with by the feet; either of the two games (Rugby or Association) played with it.

footballer, *n. foot*-bawl-er, one who plays football, esp. as a gainful occupation.

footboard, *n. foot*-bord, a support for the feet; the step of a vehicle; a treadle; a board at the foot of a bed; a gang-board.

footboy, *n. foot*-boy, a page; a liveried attendant.

foot-bridge, *n.* a bridge for foot-passengers only.

footed, *a. foot*-ed, having a foot or feet.

footer, *n. foot*-er, football [Slang].

footfall, *n. foot*-fawl, the sound of a footstep.

foot-fault, *n.* failure to serve from behind the base-line or without maintaining contact with the ground: *v.i.* and *t.* to commit, or to penalize for, a foot-fault [Lawn tennis].

footgear, *n. foot*-gear, boots, stockings, or other wear for the feet.

foot-guards, *n.pl.* the five infantry regiments of the British household troops.

foot-halt, *n. foot*-hawlt, a disease incident to sheep.

foot-hill, *n.* a hill at the foot of a mountain or mountain-range.

foothold, *n. foot*-hohld, that which sustains the feet or on which one may tread or rest securely.

foothot, *ad. foot*-hot, immediately [Hunting].

footing, *n. foot*-ing, the action of the verb *to foot*; ground for the foot; firm foundation to stand on; settlement; basis; foundation; relative condition; a fine or forfeit by way of entrance. **war footing,** *see* **war.**

foot-iron, *n. foot*-i-urn, a carriage step; a fetter.

footle, *n. foo*-tl, twaddle; foolishness: *v.i.* to talk nonsense; to act frivolously; to potter about.

footless, *a. foot*-less, without feet.

footlights, *n.pl. foot*-lites, the row of lights along the front of a stage [Theat.].

footling, *a. foot*-ling, trifling, piffling [Slang].

footman, *n. foot*-man, a male domestic servant in livery; an infantryman.

footmark, *n. foot*-mark, a footprint.

footnote, *n. foot*-note, a note at the foot of a page.

foot-pace, *n.* a slow step, as in walking.

footpad, *n. foot*-pad, a highwayman or robber on foot.

foot-passenger, *n. foot*-pas-sen-jer, a pedestrian.

footpath, *n. foot*-path, a narrow path or way for foot-passengers only.

footplate, *n. foot*-plate, the platform for the driver and fireman of a locomotive.

foot-pound, *n.* the unit of energy, *i.e.*, that which will raise 1 pound avoirdupois through 1 foot.

footprint, *n. foot*-print, the impression of a foot.

footrace, *n. foot*-race, a race on foot.

foot-rope, *n.* the rope along a yard on which men stand when reefing; that part of the bolt-rope at the foot of a sail [Naut.].

foot-rot, *n.* an infectious soil disease caused in the feet of sheep, etc., by a bacillus.

foot-rule, *n.* a measure twelve inches long.

foots, *n.pl.* foots, refuse or sediment, as at the bottom of an oil or sugar cask.

foot-slogger, *n.* a pedestrian; a soldier in a foot regiment [Slang].

foot-slogging, *n.* walking as opposed to riding; marching: *a.* pertaining to this [Slang].

foot-soldier, *n.* an infantryman.

footsore, *a. foot*-sore, with the feet sore and tender through walking.

footstalk, *n. foot*-stawk, a petiole; a stem supporting the leaf [Bot.]; the peduncle of a crinoid [Zool.].

footstep, *n. foot*-step, an impression of the foot; the sound made by the foot in walking; trace of a course pursued; track.

footstool, *n. foot*-stool, a stool for the feet.

foot-warmer, *n.* a vessel into which hot water is put for warming the feet.

footway, *n. foot*-way, a footpath.

footwear, *n. foot*-ware, footgear; boots and shoes.

foot-worn, *a.* footsore; tired of foot.

footy, *a. foot*-e, containing foots or sediment.

foozle, *n. foo*-zl, a failure; a bungle: *v.t.* to mis-hit; to strike clumsily [Slang].

fop, *n.* fop, a coxcomb; one vain of dress; a dandy. (M.E.)

fopling, *n. fop*-ling, a petty fop.

foppery, *n. fop*-pe-re, coxcombry; vanity in dress and manners; folly; idle affectation.

foppish, *a. fop*-pish, finically stylish and vainly showy in dress; affectedly fine in manners.

foppishly, *ad. fop*-pish-le, in a foppish manner.

foppishness, *n.* the quality of being foppish.

***for,** *prep.* for, in the place of; instead of; as being; towards; for the sake of; on account of; in favour of; leading or inducing to; toward the obtaining of; adapted for; against; by reason of; with respect to; through a certain space; during a certain time; in quest of; in order to obtain; according to; in return for; notwithstanding; in spite of: *conj.* because; since. (A.S.)

for-, prefix signifying thoroughly, negation or privation, wrong, and before. (A.S.)

forage, *n. fo*-raj, food of any kind for horses and cattle; the act of providing forage; search for provisions: *v.i.* to wander about in search of spoil; to ravage; to feed on spoil: *v.t.* to strip of provisions for horses, etc.; to provide forage for. (O.Fr. *fourage.*)

forage-cap, *n.* an undress military cap.

forager, *n. fo*-ra-jer, one who goes out foraging.

foraging, *n. fo*-ra-jing, an incursion for forage.

foramen, *n.* fo-*ray*-men (*pl.* **foramina**), a small natural opening, or a perforation in a bone for a vessel to pass through [Anat.]; the orifice of an ovule [Bot.]. (L.)

foraminate, *a.* fo-*ram*-e-nat, having foramina.

foraminifera, *n.pl.* fo-*ram*-e-*nif*-er-ra, a group of protozoa enclosed in many-chambered calcareous shells perforated by foramina. (L. *foramen*, and *fero*, bear.)
foraminiferous, *a.* fo-*ram*-e-*nif*-er-rus, pertaining to the foraminifera.
forane, *a.* fo-*rain*, *see* **vicar forane.**
forasmuch, *conj.* for-az-*mutch*, because that; considering that.
foray, *n. fo*-ray, a raid; a predatory excursion in border warfare: *v.t.* to plunder; to ravage: *v.i.* to make a raid. (M.E. *forreier*, forager.)
forbade, for-*bad*, *p.* of *forbid*.
forbear, *v.i.* for-*bare*, to hold oneself in check; to refrain; to be patient: *v.t.* to abstain from; to spare; to treat with indulgence and patience. *p.* **forbore.** *pp.* **forborne.** (A.S. *forberan*.)
forbear, *n. for*-bare, an ancestor. (*Fore*, and *be-er*, one who exists.)
forbearance, *n.* for-*bare*-rance, the act of forbearing; abstinence; command of temper; exercise of patience; lenity.
forbearingly, *ad.* in a forbearing manner.
forbid, *v.t.* for-*bid*, to command not to do; to prohibit; to command not to enter; to hinder; to obstruct: *v.i.* to utter a prohibition. *p.* **forbade.** *pp.* **forbidden. forbidden fruit,** the fruit that Adam and Eve were forbidden to eat, hence, anything coveted but unlawful; applied also to grape-fruit and others of the citrus group. (A.S. *forbēodan*.)
forbiddance, *n.* for-*bid*-ance, prohibition.
forbidder, *n.* for-bid-er, one who forbids.
forbidding, *a.* for-*bid*-ing, repulsive; raising aversion or dislike; disagreeable; unpleasant.
forbiddingly, *ad.* in a forbidding manner.
for-by, *prep.* for-*by*, near to; adjacent; besides: *ad.* moreover [Scots.].
★**force,** *n.* force, power, or a power that produces or tends to produce change; energy; active power; momentum; compulsory power; moral power to convince the mind; validity; power to bind or hold; troops; a body organized for action, esp. of an offensive military nature; necessity; any unlawful violence to person or property [Law]. **equilibrium of forces,** the action of forces which balance each other. **external forces,** those which act upon bodies of matter at sensible distances, as gravitation. **lines of force,** the lines along which magnetic and electric forces act. **mechanical force,** any cause which tends to alter a body's state of rest or of uniform motion in a straight line. (O.Fr.)
force, *v.t.* force, to constrain to do or to forbear by the exertion of a power not resistible; to overpower by strength; to draw or push by main strength; to compel by strength of evidence; to take by force; to violate; to overstrain; to distort; to cause to ripen prematurely; to stimulate artificially. **forced bid,** a bid made from expediency only [Contract]. **the Force,** the police. **to force a card,** by one's own play to compel another to play a certain card or in a certain way. **to force from,** to wrest from. **to force out,** to drive out; to compel to issue out or to leave.
force, *v.t.* force, to stuff; to farce. (As *farce*.)
force, *n.* force, a rush of water through a narrow channel ending in a fall; a waterfall. (Ice. *fors*.)
forceable, *a. force*-a-bl, that can be forced.
forced, *a.* forst, affected; overstrained; unnatural. **forced draught,** a draught produced in a furnace by artificial pressure from beneath the grates. **forced march,** a rapid march made in an emergency. **forced move,** the only move possible (esp. in chess).
forcedly, *ad. force*-ed-le, in a forced manner.
forceful, *a. force*-ful, full of force; driven with force; acting with power; violent; impetuous.
forcefully, *ad. force*-ful-le, violently; impetuously.
forcefulness, *n.* the quality of being forceful; vigour; enthusiasm.
forcemeat, *n. force*-meet, meat chopped fine and highly seasoned, as a stuffing. (As *farce*.)
forceps, *n. for*-seps, pincers or small tongs for seizing and extracting anything; the pincer-like organs of certain crustaceans, insects, etc. [Zool.]. (L.)
force-pump, *n.* a pump by which water, etc., is delivered under pressure.
forcible, *a. force*-e-bl, powerful; efficacious; driving forward by force; impetuous; done by force; binding. **forcible entry and detainer,** a taking or keeping possession of lands, etc., without authority [Law]. **forcible-feeble,** *a.* affectedly vigorous, really weak.
forcibleness, *n.* the quality of being forcible.
forcibly, *ad.* in a forcible manner.
forcing-house, *n.* a hothouse [Hort.].
forcing-pit, *n.* a sunken pit of wood or masonry, for containing the fermenting materials used to produce bottom heat in forcing plants [Hort.].
forcipated, *a. for*-se-*pay*-ted, formed like a pair of pincers, to open and enclose [Zool.].
forcipiform, *a.* for-*sip*-e-form, having the shape of pincers or forceps [Zool.].
ford, *n.* ford, a place where a river or other water may be crossed by wading: *v.t.* to cross a river or other water by wading. (A.S.)
fordable, *a. ford*-a-bl, that may be forded.
fordo, *v.t.* for-*doo*, to destroy; to undo; to overpower. *p.* **fordid.** *pp.* **fordone.**
fordone, *a.* for-*dun*, tired out; exhausted with labour.
fore, *a.* fore, advanced in place; coming first; antecedent; being in front or toward the face; near the bow [Naut.]: *ad.* before; previously. **fore and aft,** *see* **aft. fore and after,** a sailing vessel that is not square rigged [Naut.]. (A.S.)
fore, *int.* fore, beware; a warning to any person in the line of flight of the ball [Golf].
fore-, a prefix signifying before, or in front of [A.S.].
forearm, *n. fore*-arm, the part of the arm between elbow and wrist [Anat.]: *v.t.* (fore-*arm*) to arm beforehand; to make preparations in advance.
forebear, *n. fore*-bare, a forbear or ancestor.
forebode, *v.t.* fore-*bode*, to foretell or prognosticate; to have a premonition of something (usually evil) impending. (A.S. *forebodian*.)
forebodement, *n.* fore-*bode*-ment, the act of foreboding; a foreshadowing of coming evil.
foreboding, *n.* fore-*bode*-ing, a presentiment.
forebodingly, *ad.* in the way of anticipating evil.
fore-cabin, *n.* a cabin in the forepart of a ship.
forecast, *n. fore*-kahst, a prediction or anticipation, esp. of the weather: *v.t.* to calculate beforehand; to predict; to foresee; to plan before execution: *v.i.* to form a scheme beforehand. *p.* and *pp.* **forecast** or **forecasted.**
forecastle, *n. foh*-k'sl, the part of the upper deck of a vessel forward of the foremast; the forward part of a merchant vessel under the deck [Naut.].
foreclose, *v.t.* fore-*kloze*, to preclude; to stop; to prevent. **to foreclose a mortgage,** to deprive a mortgager of the power of redeeming the mortgage by a judgment of court [Law]. (O.Fr. *forclos*.)
foreclosure, *n.* fore-*kloze*-yewr, the act of foreclosing.
forecourt, *n. fore*-kort, the first enclosure within the precincts of a building.
foredeck, *n. fore*-dek, the bow part of a ship's deck.
foredone, *pp.* fore-*dun*, fordone.
foredoom, *n.* fore-*doom*, previous doom or sentence: *v.t.* to doom beforehand; to predestinate.
fore-edge, *n. fore*-edj, the front edge, esp. of a book or leaf.
forefather, *n. fore*-fah-ther, an ancestor.
forefeeling, *n. fore*-feel-ing, presentiment.
forefinger, *n. fore*-fing-ger, the finger next to the thumb.
forefoot, *n. fore*-foot, a front foot; a piece of timber which terminates the keel at the fore-end [Naut.].
forefront, *n. fore*-frunt, the foremost or front part.
forego, *v.t.* fore-*goh*, to go before (in time, place, or order). *p.* **forewent.** *pp.* **foregone.** (A.S. *forgān*, pass over.)
foregoer, *n.* fore-*goh*-er, one who goes before another; a predecessor.
foregoing, *a.* fore-*goh*-ing, going before in time or place; previous; antecedent.
foregone, *a.* fore-*gon*, past; determined beforehand.
foreground, *n. fore*-ground, the part (esp. of a vista or picture) nearest the observer.
fore-hammer, *n. fore*-ham-mer, a sledge-hammer.
forehand, *n. fore*-hand, the upper hand or advantage; that part of a horse which is before the rider: *a.* done sooner than is regular; done beforehand; foremost.

forehanded, *a. fore*-han-ded, prudent [U.S.A.]; well off [U.S.A.]; not backhanded (of strokes at lawn tennis, etc.).
forehead, *n. fore*-hed *or fo*-rid, the front of the face above the eyes; impudence; confidence; assurance. (A.S. *forheáfod.*)
foreign, *a. fo*-ren, belonging to another nation or country; alien; remote; not connected with; not to the purpose. (O.Fr. *forain*, strange.)
foreigner, *n. fo*-ren-er, a native of a foreign country; an alien; an outsider.
foreignism, *n. fo*-ren-izm, a phrase, idiom, etc., of foreign origin.
foreignness, *n.* the quality of being foreign.
forejudge, *v.t.* fore-*judj*, to prejudge, or judge before hearing the facts and proof.
forejudgment *or* **forejudgement,** *n.* fore-*judj*-ment, judgment previously formed.
foreknow, *v.t.* fore-*noh*, to know beforehand.
foreknowable, *a.* that may be foreknown.
foreknowingly, *ad.* with knowledge beforehand.
foreknowledge, *n.* fore-*nol*-ij, knowledge of a thing before it happens; prescience.
forel, *n. fo*-ril, a thin kind of parchment. (Fr.)
forelady, *n. fore*-lay-de, a forewoman [U.S.A.].
foreland, *n. fore*-land, a point of land extending into the sea; a headland.
forelay, *v.t.* fore-*lay*, to contrive antecedently.
foreleg, *n. fore*-leg, a front leg.
forelock, *n. fore*-lok, the lock of hair that grows from the fore-part of the head; a flat piece of iron driven through the end of a bolt to prevent its drawing: *v.t.* to secure by this. **to take time by the forelock,** to seize an opportunity.
foreman, *n. fore*-man, the chief man; the chief man of a jury, who acts as their speaker; one in charge of a department, etc.; an overseer, esp. of workmen; a ganger.
foremast, *n. fore*-mahst, the mast near the bow except in yawls and ketches, which have no foremast.
forementioned, *a. fore*-men-shond, aforementioned.
foremost, *a. fore*-mohst, first in place; most advanced; first in dignity. (A.S.)
forename, *n. fore*-name, a name preceding the surname; a Christian name.
forenoon, *n. fore*-noon, the former part of the day, from sunrise to noon.
forensic, *a.* fo-*ren*-sik, pertaining to courts of judicature; used in courts of legal proceedings or in debates. **forensic medicine,** the science which applies the principles and practice of medicine to the elucidation of questions in judicial proceedings; medical jurisprudence. (L. *forensis*, pertaining to the forum.)
foreordain, *v.t.* fore-or-*dane*, to ordain beforehand.
foreordination, *n. fore*-or-de-*nay*-shon, previous ordination; predetermination; predestination.
fore-part, *n. fore*-part, the part most advanced in place or time.
forepeak, *n. fore*-peek, the part of a vessel close to the bow [Naut.].
foreplane, *n. fore*-plane, the plane intermediate between the jack- and the jointing- or smoothing-plane [Carp.].
forequarter, *n. fore*-kwor-ter, the front part of half a carcase (of beef, mutton, etc.).
foreran, fore-*ran*, *p.* of *forerun*.
fore-rank, *n. fore*-rank, the first rank; the front.
fore-reach, *v.t.* fore-*reech*, to gain upon; to go ahead on a wind and shoot up to windward [Naut.].
forerun, *v.t.* fore-*run*, to precede; to advance before.
forerunner, *n.* fore-*run*-ner, a messenger sent before; a harbinger; a prognostic.
foresaid, *pp.* and *a. fore*-sed, mentioned before.
foresail, *n. fore*-sl, the largest and principal sail on the foremast [Naut.].
foresee, *v.t.* fore-*see*, to see beforehand; to foreknow. *p.* **foresaw.** *pp.* **foreseen.** (A.S. *foreséon.*)
foreseeingly, *ad.* fore-*see*-ing-le, with foresight.
foreshadow, *v.t.* fore-*shad*-o, to shadow or typify beforehand; to prefigure; to forecast.
foresheet, *n. fore*-sheet, the rope by which the foresail is adjusted: *pl.* the inner part of a boat's bow forward of the bow-oar's thwart.
foreship, *n. fore*-ship, the fore-part of a ship.
foreshore, *n. fore*-shore, the part of the seashore lying between high- and low-water marks; a built-up or cultivated strip of land adjoining the shore.
foreshorten, *v.t.* fore-*shor*-tn, to represent objects as they appear in perspective [Paint.].
foreshortening, *n.* fore-*shor*-tning, representation or appearance of objects when foreshortened.
foreshow, *v.t.* fore-*shoh*, to show beforehand; to prognosticate; to predict.
foreside, *n. fore*-side, the front side; a specious outside.
fore-sight, *n. fore*-site, the sight on the muzzle of a gun; the height shown by the levelling staff when placed forward of the instrument.
foresight, *n. fore*-site, prescience; foreknowledge; provident care of futurity; prudence.
foresighted, *a. fore*-sy-ted, possessing foresight.
foresignify, *v.t.* fore-*sig*-ne-fy, to signify or betoken previously; to foreshow; to typify.
foreskin, *n. fore*-skin, the prepuce, the skin covering the glans penis.
foreskirt, *n. fore*-skirt, the loose and pendulous part of a coat in front.
foresleeve, *n. fore*-sleev, the portion of a coat or gown sleeve from wrist to elbow.
forespeak, *v.t.* fore-*speek*, to predict; to foretell.
forest, *n. fo*-rest, an extensive wood, or a large tract of land covered with trees; an uncultivated tract more or less covered with trees, or once so covered; an unenclosed royal hunting ground: *a.* pertaining to a forest; sylvan; rustic: *v.t.* to afforest. **forest laws,** laws for the governing and regulating of forests, and the preservation of game. (Late L. *forestis.*)
forestaff, *n. fore*-staff, the cross-staff.
forestage, *n. fo*-res-taj, an ancient service paid by foresters to the king; the rights of foresters.
forestal, *a. fo*-res-tal, of or pertaining to a forest.
forestall, *v.t.* fore-*stawl*, to anticipate; to employ before the time; to preoccupy; to hinder by preoccupation; to buy commodities of any kind before they are publicly offered, with intent to enhance the price [Comm.].
forestaller, *n.* fore-*stawl*-er, one who forestalls, esp. in the commercial sense.
forestation, *n.* fo-res-*tay*-shon, afforestation.
forestay, *n.* fore-*stay*, a strong rope, on which the fore-staysail is hoisted, reaching from the fore-mast head toward the bow to support the mast [Naut.].
forester, *n. fo*-res-ter, an officer who has charge of a forest; an inhabitant of a forest; one skilled in forestry; a forest tree or animal; (*cap.*) a member of the Ancient Order of Foresters; popular name of certain moths. (O.Fr. *forestier.*)
forest-fly, *n.* a species of fly, *Hippobosca equina*, very troublesome to horses.
forest-marble, *n. fo*-rest-*mar*-bl, an oolitic limestone abounding in marine fossils and susceptible of a fine polish, so called as occurring in Wychwood Forest, Oxfordshire.
forest-oak, *n. fo*-rest-*oak*, the trade name for an Australian tree of the genus *Casuarina*.
forestry, *n. fo*-res-tre, the art of cultivating and managing forests or growing timber.
foretackle, *n.* fore-*tak*-kl, the tackle on the foremast of a ship.
foretaste, *n. fore*-taste, a taste beforehand; anticipation: *v.t.* to taste or sample before acquisition; to anticipate.
foretell, *v.t.* fore-*tel*, to tell before an event happens; to foretoken: *v.i.* to prophesy.
foreteller, *n.* fore-*tel*-er, one who foretells.
forethought, *n. fore*-thawt, a thought or care beforehand; provident care.
foretime, *n. fore*-time, the past; the days of old.
foretoken, *n.* fore-*toh*-ken, a prognostic: *v.t.* to foreshow; to prognosticate.
foretooth, *n. fore*-tooth, a front tooth; an incisor.
foretop, *n. fore*-top, the hair on the fore-part of the head; that part of a head-dress that is forward; the platform at the head of the foremast [Naut.].
fore-topgallant, *n.* fore-top-*gal*-lant, the mast above the fore-topmast.
foretop-man, *n.* a man stationed in the foretop to attend to the smaller sails and keep the upper rigging in order.
fore-topmast, *n.* the mast rising from the head of the foremast, and surmounted by the fore-topgallant mast.
foretype, *n. fore*-tipe, an antitype.
forever, *ad.* for-*ev*-er, for ever; through endless ages [U.S.A.]: *n.* eternity.

forewarn, *v.t.* fore-*worn*, to warn or give notice beforehand.
forewent, fore-*went*, *pp.* of *forego*.
forewind, *n.* *fore*-wind, a favouring wind.
forewoman, *n.* *fore*-woom-an, a female foreman; the woman in charge of a group or department.
foreword, *n.* *fore*-wurd, a preface; a note before the preface; an introduction.
foreyard, *n.* *fore*-yard, the lowest yard on the foremast [Naut.].
forfeit, *n.* *for*-fit, that which is forfeited; a penalty; a deposit that is redeemable: *a.* lost or alienated for an offence or crime: *v.t.* to lose through fault, crime, negligence, or breach of conditions. (O.Fr. *forfait.*)
forfeitable, *a.* *for*-fit-a-bl, subject to forfeiture.
forfeiter, *n.* *for*-fit-er, one who forfeits.
forfeiture, *n.* *for*-fit-yewr, the act of forfeiting; that which is forfeited; fine, penalty, or amercement. (O.Fr. *forfaiture.*)
forfend, *v.t.* for-*fend*, to avert: to fend or ward off; to prevent the approach of. (As *fend.*)
forfex, *n.* *for*-feks, the forceps of certain insects, etc. [Entom.]. (L., a pair of scissors.)
forficate, *a.* *for*-fe-kate, resembling scissor-blades [Entom.]; deeply forked, as the tail of some birds.
forficulate, *a.* for-*fik*-yew-lat, forficate [Zool.].
forgat, *p.* for-*gat*, old variant of *forgot*.
forgather, *v.i.* for-*gath*-er, to meet together; to talk with each other.
forgave, for-*gave*, *p.* of *forgive*.
forge, *n.* forj, a furnace in which iron or other metal is heated in order to be hammered into form; a smith's workshop in which such work is done; a workshop or place where anything is made; the manufacture of metal-work: *v.t.* to form by heating and hammering; to form any way into shape; to make or imitate fraudulently or falsely; to counterfeit; to fabricate: *v.i.* to be guilty of forgery. (O.Fr.)
forge, *v.i.* forj, to move slowly; to advance [Naut.]. **to forge ahead,** gradually to draw near the leading position.
forgeman, *n.* *forj*-man, a superior kind of smith, esp. one with a hammerman under him.
forger, *n.* *fore*-jer, one who forges; one guilty of forgery.
forgery, *n.* *fore*-jer-re, the act or crime of forging, esp. in writing; that which is forged. (Fr. *forgerie.*)
forget, *v.t.* for-*get*, to lose remembrance of; to fail to remember; to slight or neglect. *p.* **forgot.** *pp.* **forgotten.** (A.S. *forgetan.*)
forgetful, *a.* for-*get*-ful, apt to forget; neglectful; inattentive; causing to forget.
forgetfully, *ad.* in a forgetful manner.
forgetfulness, *n.* the quality of being forgetful; a ceasing to remember; oblivion; neglect.
forgetive, *a.* *for*-je-tiv, that may forge; inventive.
forget-me-not, *n.* for-*get*-me-not, a small blue flowered plant of the genus *Myosotis*.
forgettable, *a.* for-*get*-a-bl, liable to be forgotten.
forgetter, *n.* for-*get*-er, one who forgets; a heedless person.
forging, *n.* *for*-jing, the act of beating into shape; forged work; the work as it leaves the forge.
forgivable, *a.* for-*giv*-a-bl, that may be pardoned.
forgive, *v.t.* for-*giv*, to pardon; to remit, as an offence of debt; to overlook an offence, and treat the offender as not guilty. *p.* **forgave.** *pp.* **forgiven.** (A.S. *forgefan.*)
forgiveness, *n.* for-*giv*-ness, the act of forgiving; pardon; remission; willingness to forgive.
forgiver, *n.* for-*giv*-er, one who pardons or remits.
forgiving, *a.* for-*giv*-ing, disposed to forgive; mild, merciful, or compassionate.
forgivingness, *n.* a disposition to forgive.
forgo, *v.t.* for-*goh*, to go without. *p.* **forwent.** *pp.* **forgone.**
forgotten, for-*got*-en. *pp.* of *forget*.
forint, *n.* *for*-int, since 1946 the monetary unit of Hungary, nominally equivalent to slightly over 5*d.*
forisfamiliate, *v.i.* *for*-ris-fa-*mil*-e-ate, to resign all further claim on the paternal estate: *v.t.* to separate from the family on receiving a certain part of one's lawful inheritance [Scots. Law]. (L. *foris*, out of doors, *familia*, the family.)
***fork,** *n.* fork, an implement terminating in two or more prongs, and used for various purposes; anything that branches like a fork; a bifurcation; the place of meeting of two diverging limbs, roads, rivers, etc.: *v.i.* to divide into two branches; to shoot into blades, as corn: *v.t.* to raise or pitch with a fork, as hay; to dig and break ground with a fork; to make bifurcate, fork-shaped, or forked; to attack two pieces simultaneously with one [Chess, etc.]. **fork lunch,** a light lunch (table-knives being unnecessary) **to fork out,** to pay up, to hand over [Coll.]. (A.S. *forca.*)
forkbeard, *n.* *fork*-beard, a popular name of certain fish of the hake family.
forked, *a.* forkt, opening into two or more parts, points, or shoots; divided like a fork; furcated.
forkedness, *n.* *fork*-ed-ness, the state of being forked.
fork-head, *n.* the barbed head of an arrow; the double head of a knuckle-joint.
forkiness, *n.* *fork*-e-ness, the quality of being forky.
forktail, *n.* *fork*-tale, local name for a salmon in its fourth year's growth, also for a species of kite and other birds.
forky, *a.* *fork*-e, forked; fork-shaped.
forlorn, *a.* fo-*lorn*, forsaken; helpless; wretched. **forlorn hope,** a detachment of men appointed to lead in an assault or perform other service attended with uncommon peril; any bold desperate enterprise. (A.S. *forloren*, utterly lost; *hope*, here=Dut. *hoop*, band or troop.)
forlornly, *ad.* in a forlorn manner; disconsolately.
forlornness, *n.* fo-*lorn*-ness, the state of being forlorn.
***form,** *n.* form, the shape or external appearance of a body; disposition of particular things; model; a mould; formula; beauty; behaviour; mere external appearance; established practice; ceremony; determinate shape; likeness; manner; system, as of government; manner of arrangement; record of career; a long seat or bench; a class; the bed of a hare; a forme [Print.]; condition; condition fit for a purpose. **essential** or **substantial form,** that mode of existence which cannot cease without destroying a thing. (O.Fr. *forme.*)
form, *v.t.* form, to make; to give shape to; to mould; to plan; to arrange; to settle; to contrive; to make up; to frame; to combine; to establish; to compile; to constitute; to make by derivation, or by affixes or prefixes [Gram.]: *v.i.* to take a form.
formal, *a.* *for*-mal, according to form or established mode; strictly ceremonious; punctilious; exact to affectation; done in due form; having the form without the substance; depending on customary forms; having the power of making a thing what it is; essential; proper. (L. *formalis.*)
formaldehyde, *n.* for-*mal*-de-hide, a colourless disinfectant, and preservative gas generated by the partial oxidation of methyl alcohol. (*Form(ic)* and *aldehyde.*)
formalin, *n.* *for*-ma-lin, trade name of a solution of formaldehyde.
formalism, *n.* *for*-ma-lizm, the quality of resting in mere external forms, especially of religion.
formalist, *n.* *for*-ma-list, one who observes external forms; one who trusts in external religious forms. (Fr. *formaliste.*)
formalistic, *a.* for-ma-*lis*-tik, characterized by formalism.
formality, *n.* for-*mal*-e-te, the precise observance of forms; mere conformity to customary modes; conventionality; established order; mode; external appearance or form.
formalization, *n.* *for*-ma-ly-*zay*-shon, the act of putting into form.
formalize, *v.t.* *for*-ma-lize, to formulate: *v.i.* to affect formality.
formally, *ad.* *for*-ma-le, in a formal manner.
format, *n.* *for*-mat *or* *for*-mah, the size, shape, and external appearance in which a book is produced. (Fr.)
formate, *n.* *for*-mate, a salt of formic acid.
formation, *n.* for-*may*-shon, the act of forming or making; generation; production; the manner in which a thing is formed; structure; arrangement, esp. [Mil.] of a body of troops; a group of strata united by community of age, origin, or composition [Geol.]. (Fr.)
formational, *a.* for-*may*-shon-al, pertaining to formation or to a formation.
formative, *a.* *for*-ma-tive, giving form; having the

power of giving form; serving to form; inflexional, not radical [Gram.]: *n.* that which serves merely to give form (as prefixes, etc.) and is no part of the root [Gram.].
forme, *n.* form, an assemblage of type arranged in order, disposed into pages, and locked in a chase to receive an impression [Print.].
former, *a.* *for*-mer, preceding in time; earlier; near the beginning; previously mentioned. (A.S. *forma.*)
formerly, *ad.* in time past; of old; heretofore.
formic, *a.* *for*-mik, pertaining to or produced by ants. **formic acid,** a fatty acid obtained originally from red ants, but now usually by absorption of carbon mon-oxide in soda-lime. (L. *formica,* an ant.)
formicant, *a.* *for*-me-kant, weak (of the pulse when almost imperceptible) [Med.].
formicarium, *n.* *for*-me-*kare*-re-um, a vivarium for the study of ants under approximately natural conditions.
formicary, *n.* *for*-me-ka-re, an ant-hill; a colony of ants.
formicate, *a.* *for*-me-kate, resembling the ant; *v.i.* to crawl like ants.
formication, *n.* *for*-me-*kay*-shon, a sensation resembling that made by the creeping of ants on the skin [Med.].
formidability, *n.* *for*-me-da-*bil*-e-te, formidableness.
formidable, *a.* *for*-me-da-bl, exciting fear; adapted to excite fear. (Fr.)
formidableness, *n.* quality of being formidable.
formidably, *ad.* so as to impress fear.
formless, *a.* *form*-less, without determinate form; chaotic.
formlessness, *n.* the state of being formless.
formula, *n.* *form*-yew-la (*pl.* **formulæ** *or* **formulas**), a prescribed form; a prescription [Med.]; a formal statement of accepted doctrines, or beliefs [Eccles.]; a general expression for solving certain cases or problems [Math.]; a set of symbols representing the constituents of a compound body [Chem.]. (L.)
formulable, *a.* *form*-yew-labl, that may be formulated.
formularization, *n.* *for*-mew-la-ry-*zay*-shon, the act of formularizing; a formularized expression.
formularize, *v.t.* *for*-mew-la-rize, to express as a formula; to formulate.
formulary, *n.* *for*-mew-la-re, a book of stated and prescribed forms, as of oaths, declarations, prayers, etc.; a formula or prescribed form: *a.* of the nature of a formula; prescribed; ritual.
formulate, *v.t.* *for*-mew-late, to express in a formula; to express in clear definite compendious terms.
formulism, *n.* *for*-mew-lizm, the study of formulas.
formulist, *n.* *for*-mew-list, a student of formulas.
formulization, *n.* *for*-mew-ly-*zay*-shon, reduction to an abstract intelligible form.
formulize, *v.t.* *for*-mew-lize, to formulate; to reduce to a formula.
fornicate, *v.i.* *for*-ne-kate, to commit fornication; fornicated [Bot.]. (L. *fornicatus,* fornicated, from *fornix,* a vault, a brothel.)
fornicated, *a.* *for*-ne-kay-ted, arched; vaulted; arching over [Bot.]. (L. *fornicatus,* arched.)
fornication, *n.* *for*-ne-*kay*-shon, illicit sexual intercourse between unmarried persons or between persons other than spouses; adultery; incest; idolatry, or the worshipping of idols [Bible].
fornicator, *n.* *for*-ne-kay-tor, one guilty of fornication. (L.)
fornicatress, *n.* *for*-ne-kay-tress, a woman given to fornication.
fornix, *n.* *for*-niks, the excavated part of a shell beneath the umbo [Malac.]; a triangular lamina which extends into each lateral ventricle of the brain [Anat.]. (L., an arch.)
forrader, *ad.* *fo*-ra-der, more forward [Slang]. **to get no forrader,** to make no progress.
forrel, *n.* *fo*-rel, forel.
forsake, *v.t.* for-*sake,* to leave entirely; to abandon; to withdraw from. *p.* **forsook.** *pp.* **forsaken.** (A.S. *forsacan.*)
forsakenly, *ad.* for-*say*-ken-le, as if forsaken.
forsooth, *ad.* for-*sooth,* in truth; indeed; doubtless. (A.S. *for sōthe.*)
forspend, *v.t.* for-*spend,* to exhaust; to weary out.
forsterite, *n.* *for*-ste-rite, a crystalline silicate of magnesium allied to olivine. (Ger. traveller, J. H. *Forster, d.* 1798.)
forswear, *v.t.* for-*sware,* to renounce or disown upon oath: *v.i.* to swear falsely. **to forswear oneself,** to perjure oneself. *p.* **forswore.** *pp.* **forsworn.** (A.S. *forswerian.*)
forswearer, *n.* for-*sweare*-er, one who forswears.
forsworn, *a.* for-*sworn,* perjured. (As *forswear.*)
fort, *n.* fort, a fortified place or outpost; a castle; a frontier trading station [U.S.A.]. (O.Fr.)
fortalice, *n.* *for*-ta-lis, a small fort or outwork; a block-house. (Late L. *fortalitia.*)
forte, *ad.* *for*-te, with loudness or force [Mus.]. (It.)
forte, *n.* fort, the part of a sword-blade between the hilt and the middle; hence, one's strong point; that in which one excels. (Fr.)
forth, *ad.* forth, forward; onward in time, place, or order; out into view; abroad; away. (A.S.)
forthcoming, *n.* *forth*-kum-ing, a coming forth: *a.* about to appear.
forthgoing, *n.* *forth*-goh-ing, a going forth or utterance; a proceeding from: *a.* going forth.
forth-issuing, *a.* coming forward, as from a covert.
forthright, *ad.* *forth*-rite, straight forward; straightway: *a.* direct; straightforward; downright: *n.* a straight path. (A.S.)
forthwith, *ad.* forth-*with,* immediately; without delay.
fortieth, *a.* *for*-te-eth, the ordinal of forty: *n.* one of forty equal parts.
fortifiable, *a.* *for*-te-*fy*-a-bl, that may be fortified.
fortification, *n.* *for*-te-fe-*kay*-shon, the act of fortifying; the art or science of fortifying places to defend them against an enemy; a place fortified; *pl.* works erected to defend a place against attack; the strengthening of wine, etc., with spirits. (Fr.)
fortifier, *n.* *for*-te-fy-er, one who or that which fortifies.
fortify, *v.t.* *for*-te-fy, to strengthen and secure by forts or batteries; to strengthen against any attack; to strengthen; to strengthen with alcohol; to confirm: *v.i.* to raise strong places. (O.Fr. *fortifier.*)
fortissimo, *ad.* for-*tis*-se-mo, with the utmost strength or loudness [Mus.]. (It.)
fortitude, *n.* *for*-te-tewd, resolution; endurance; that courage or strength of mind which enables one to bear up calmly under opposition, adversity, or affliction. (Fr.)
fortitudinous, *a.* for-te-*tew*-de-nus, having or characterized by fortitude.
fortlet, *n.* *fort*-let, a little fort.
fortnight, *n.* *fort*-nite, the space of fourteen days; two weeks. (A.S. *feowertyne niht.*)
fortnightly, *a.* and *ad.* *fort*-nite-le, (happening) once a fortnight.
fortress, *n.* *fort*-ress, any permanently garrisoned and fortified place; a place of defence or security: *v.t.* to defend by a fortress. (O.Fr. *forteresce.*)
fortuitism, *n.* for-*tew*-e-tizm, belief that natural causes are due to chance rather than to design.
fortuitist, *n.* for-*tew*-e-tist, one holding the doctrine of fortuitism.
fortuitous, *a.* for-*tew*-e-tus, happening by chance; accidental; incidental. (L. *fortuitus.*)
fortuitously, *ad.* accidentally; casually.
fortuitousness, *n.* quality of being fortuitous.
fortuity, *n.* for-*tew*-e-te, chance; accident; a chance occurrence.
fortunate, *a.* *for*-tew-nat, coming by good luck; lucky; bringing or boding good luck or success; auspicious. (L. *fortunatus.*)
fortunately, *ad.* luckily; successfully.
fortunateness, *n.* quality of being fortunate.
fortune, *n.* *for*-tewn, chance or luck; the good or ill that befalls one; lot in life; good luck or success; private means; wealth: *v.i.* to happen; to come casually to pass: *v.t.* to provide with a fortune.
fortune-hunting, *n.* the seeking of a fortune by marriage.
fortuneless, *a.* *for*-tewn-less, luckless; destitute of a fortune or a dowry.
fortune-teller, *n.* one who tells or pretends to tell the future events of one's life.
forty, *a.* and *n.* *for*-te, four times ten. **forty-niner,** an adventurer in the Californian goldfield during the gold-rush of 1849. **forty winks,** a short nap. **the Forty,** the French Academy. **the forties,** the

years of one's life, or of any century, between 39 and 50. **the roaring forties,** the region of the Atlantic Ocean between 40° and 50° N. lat., notorious for its storms. **the Forty-five,** the Jacobite rebellion of 1745 [British Hist.]. (A.S. *feowertig.*)
fortyfold, *a. for*-te-fohld, forty times.
forum, *n. for*-rum, market-place; a public place in Roman cities, where causes were judicially tried, and orations delivered to the people; place of common judgment or justice. (L.)
***forward,** *ad. for*-ward, toward what is before or in front; onward; progressively; a word of command given when troops are to resume their march after a temporary interruption [Mil.]; towards the fore-part [Naut.]: *a.* near or at the fore-part; in advance of something else; ready; too ready; ardent; bold; presumptuous; advanced for the season; precocious: *n.* one who plays in the front line of his side [Football, etc.]: *v.t.* to advance; to help onward; to accelerate; to send forward; to transmit. (A.S. *foreweard.*)
forward, *a. fo*-rard, at or near the bow of the ship [Naut.].
forwarder, *n. for*-ward-er, he that promotes; one who helps or sends forward; a forwarding merchant [U.S.A.]; forrader [Slang].
forwardly, *ad. for*-ward-le, in a forward manner.
forwardness, *n. for*-ward-ness, the quality of state of being forward.
forwards, *ad. for*-wardz, forward.
forwent, for-*went*, *p.* of *forgo.*
forworn, *a.* for-*worn*, tired out.
fossa, *n. fos*-sa, a cavity in a bone, with a large aperture; a depression [Anat.]. (L., a ditch.)
fossa, *n. fos*-sa, a small species of civet, *Cryptoprocta ferox*, peculiar to Madagascar.
fosse, *n.* foss, a ditch or moat [Fort.]; a fossa [Anat.]. (L. *fossa*, a ditch.)
fossette, *n.* fos-*set*, a dimple; a slight depression; a small fossa [Anat.].
fossick, *v.i. fos*-ik, to rummage; to hunt about in quest of things [Austral.].
fossicker, *n. fos*-e-ker, one who rummages about, esp. a gold-seeker in worked-out diggings.
fossil, *a. fos*-sil, dug out of the earth; in the state of a fossil; petrified; antiquated: *n.* animal or vegetable remains, or traces, impressions, etc., of such, preserved in the strata of the earth's surface [Geol.]; an antiquated person [Slang]. (O.Fr. *fossile.*)
fossiliferous, *a.* fos-se-*lif*-er-rus, containing fossilized organic remains. (*Fossil*, and *fero*, bear.)
fossilist, *n. fos*-e-list, one conversant with fossils; a palæontologist.
fossilization, *n. fos*-e-ly-*zay*-shon, the act or process of converting into a fossil; a fossilized state.
fossilize, *v.t. fos*-e-lize, to turn into a fossil; to reduce to a fossil or fixed state: *v.i.* to be changed into a fossil or fixed state.
fossorial, *a.* fos-*saw*-re-al, digging; made for digging; burrowing; pertaining to the burrowing mammals or insects [Zool.]. (L. *fossus*, *pp. fodere*, to dig.)
foster, *v.t. fos*-ter, to nourish or nurse; to bring up; to cherish; to encourage. (A.S. *fostrian*, to nourish.)
fosterage, *n. fos*-ter-raj, the act or custom of fostering; the state of being fostered; the rearing of a foster-child.
foster-brother, *n.* a brother by nursing but not by birth.
foster-child, *n.* a child nursed by a woman not the mother, or brought up by a man not the father.
foster-daughter, *n.* a daughter by nursing, but not by birth.
fosterer, *n. fos*-ter-rer, a nurse; one who feeds and nourishes in the place of parents; a patron.
foster-father, *n.* one who takes the place of a father in rearing a child.
foster-land, *n.* one's adopted country.
fosterling, *n. fos*-ter-ling, a foster-child.
foster-mother, *n.* a woman who takes the place of a mother; a wet-nurse.
foster-parent, *n.* a foster-father or foster-mother.
foster-sister, *n.* a sister by nursing, but not by birth.
foster-son, *n. fos*-ter-sun, one brought up as a son, though not a son by birth.
fostress, *n. fos*-tress, a foster-mother.
fother, *n. foth*-er, a former measure of weight (for lead, 19½ cwt., for coal, 17⅔ cwt.); hence, any large weight. (A.S.)
fother, *v.t. foth*-er, to endeavour to stop a leak in the bottom of a ship, while afloat, by means of a sail filled with yarn and oakum to be sucked into the crack. (Ice. *fodhra.*)
fou, *a.* foo, drunk [Scots.]. (*full.*)
fougasse, *n.* foo-*gahs*, a small mine for destroying minor fortifications [Mil.]. (Fr.)
fought, fawt, *p.* and *pp.* of *fight.*
foul, *a.* foul, filthy; not clean; turbid; muddy; impure; scurrilous, obscene, or profane; defiling; detestable; unfair; loathsome; disgraceful; full of gross humours or impurities; full of weeds; entangled, hindered from motion, opposed to clear [Naut.]; covered with weeds or barnacles, as a ship's bottom; not favourable (of wind or weather); not safe: *n.* a wilful breach of the rules [Boxing, etc.]; illegal play [Billiards, etc.]: *v.t.* to make filthy; to defile; to soil; to collide with: *v.i.* to become foul; to come into collision. **fall foul,** to rush on with haste, rough force, and unseasonable violence; to run against. **foul anchor,** an anchor entangled with another or with a cable. **foul brood,** a bacillary disease destructive to the larvæ of the honey-bee. (A.S. *ful.*)
foulard, *n.* foo-*lahrd*, a thin dress-material of silk or silk and cotton; a silk kerchief. (Fr.)
fouling, *n. foul*-ling, a making foul; anything that clogs or makes foul; deposit left inside the bore of a fire-arm after firing [Mil.].
foully, *ad. foul*-le, in a foul manner.
foul-mouthed, *a.* foul-spoken; accustomed to use bad language.
foulness, *n. foul*-ness, the state of being foul.
foul-spoken, *a.* using profane, scurrilous, or obscene language.
foumart, *n. foo*-mart, the polecat. (A.S. *ful*, foul, *mearth*, marten.)
found, *v.t.* found, to lay the basis of; to begin and build; to establish; to fix firmly; to endow; to originate: *v.i.* to rest (on). (Fr. *fonder.*)
found, *v.t.* found, to cast; to form by melting a metal and pouring it into a mould. (Fr. *fondre.*)
foundation, *n.* foun-*day*-shon, the act of founding or beginning to build; the base or groundwork of anything; origin; endowment appropriated to support an institution; an endowed institution; *pl.* that part of a structure below the level of the ground. **foundation muslin,** an open-worked stiffened fabric. **foundation scholar,** one whose fees are a charge on the school endowment. **foundation stone,** a stone laid with ceremony to celebrate the founding of a building. (Fr. *fondation.*)
foundational, *a.* foun-*day*-shon-al, fundamental.
foundationer, *n.* foun-*day*-shon-er, a foundation scholar.
founder, *n. foun*-der, one who founds or originates anything; one who endows or furnishes a permanent fund for the support of an institution.
founder, *n. foun*-der, one who casts metal. **founder's dust,** a powder ground fine for casting purposes. **founder's sand,** a fine sand for making foundry moulds.
founder, *v.i. foun*-der, to fill or be filled with water and sink, as a ship; to fail or give way; to miscarry; to fall lame (of horses): *v.t.* to cause internal inflammation and great soreness in the feet of a horse: *n.* laminitis, inflammation in a horse's foot. (O.Fr. *fondrer.*)
founderous, *a. foun*-der-rus, liable to founder or to cause foundering.
foundling, *n. found*-ling, a deserted child of unknown parents.
foundress, *n. foun*-dress, a female founder.
foundry, *n. foun*-dre, the process of casting metals; the place where metals are cast. (Fr. *fonderie.*)
foundryman, *n.* a workman in a foundry.
fount, *n.* fount, a source or spring; a fountain; a well. (O.Fr. *font.*)
fount, *n.* fount, a complete assortment of printing types of one size and face. (Fr. *fonte.*)
fountain, *n. foun*-tan, a spring of water; a jet of water; the structure connected with a basin kept supplied with spouting water; a source or first principle. (Fr. *fontaine.*)
fountain-head, *n.* a primary source.
fountain-pen, *n.* a pen with a reservoir for ink.

four, *a.* and *n.* fore, twice two: *n.* a four-oared boat or its crew; a race rowed in such a boat: *pl.* a formation (of men) four deep [Mil.]. **on all fours,** on hands and knees or hands and feet. (A.S. *feower.*)
four-ale, *n.* ale formerly retailed at fourpence a quart.
fourchette, *n.* foor-*shet*, a bifurcated gusset between the fingers of a glove; a small fork-shaped instrument used in operations on the tongue [Surg.]; the merrythought of a bird; the combination of the card next above and next below that led, held by one player [Cards]. (Fr., table-fork.)
fourfold, *a.* *fore*-fohld, quadruple; four times as much or as many.
four-footed, *a.* having four feet.
fourgon, *n.* *foor*-gon, a baggage or ammunition wagon; a luggage van. (Fr.)
four-handed, *a.* having four hands (as all Primates except man); for four players (of games) or two executants (of music).
four-horse, *a,* *fore*-horse, with four horses.
Fourierism, *n.* *foo*-re-er-izm, a socialistic system propounded by the French philosopher Charles Fourier (*d.* 1837); phalansterianism.
four-in-hand, *a.* and *ad.* with four horses managed by one driver: *n.* a vehicle so drawn and managed; a coach; a kind of neck-tie.
fourling, *n.* *fore*-ling, one of four children born at the same time.
fourneau, *n.* *foor*-noh, the chamber of a mine in which the powder is lodged [Mil.]. (Fr.)
four-oar, *a.* propelled by four oars.
fourpence, *n.* *fore*-pence, a groat; four pennies, or a sum equal to this.
fourpenny, *n.* *fore*-pe-ne, a groat: *a.* fourpennyworth.
four-poster, *n.* a large square bedstead with upright pillars at each corner supporting a canopy.
fourscore, *a.* *fore*-skore, four times twenty; of eighty years.
four-seater, *n.* a vehicle, plane, etc., seated for four.
foursome, *n.* *fore*-sum, a game or dance in which four persons take part in two pairs; in golf, two players on each side who play the ball alternately: *a.* done by four persons.
four-square, *a.* having four sides and four angles equal; square; on a firm foundation.
fourteen, *a.* and *n.* *fore*-teen, four and ten.
fourteenth, *a.* *fore*-teenth, the ordinal of fourteen: *n.* one of fourteen equal parts of a whole; the octave of the seventh [Mus.].
fourth, *a.* forth, the ordinal of four: *n.* one of four equal parts of a whole; an interval composed of two tones and a semi-tone [Mus.]. **the Fourth Estate,** the newspaper press. (A.S. *feortha.*)
fourthly, *ad.* *forth*-le, in the fourth place.
four-wheeler, *n.* a vehicle, esp. a horse-cab plying for hire, with four wheels.
foussa, *n.* foo-sa, the fossa of Madagascar [Zool.].
fovea, *n.* *foh*-ve-a (*pl.* **foveæ**), a fossa [Anat.]. (L.)
foveate, *a.* *foh*-ve-at, having foveæ; pitted [Bot. and Anat.).
foveolated, *a.* *foh*-ve-o-lay-ted, having small depressions or pits [Bot. and Zool.]. (L. *fovea*, a pit.)
fovilla, *n.* fo-*vil*-la, the fine fertilizing substance contained in pollen [Bot.]. (L. *foveo*, cherish.)
***fowl,** *n.* foul, a bird; birds collectively; a domestic game-bird; poultry; the flesh of such: *v.i.* to catch or kill wildfowl for sport. (A.S. *fugol.*)
fowler, *n.* *foul*-er, one who shoots wildfowl for sport or food; a bird-catcher.
fowling-net, *n.* a net for bird-catching.
fowling-piece, *n.* a light gun for shooting birds.
fox, *n.* foks, the carnivore *Canis vulpes*, remarkable for cunning; the dressed pelt of any variety of fox; a sly, cunning fellow; a small strand of rope made by twisting and tarring several rope-yarns together [Naut.]: *v.t.* to make sour; to repair, as boots [U.S.A.]; to play the fox, esp. to sham sleep; to be cunning [Slang]: *v.i.* to turn sour during fermentation; to become discoloured (of paper, prints, etc.). (A.S.)
fox-bat, *n.* the flying-fox.
fox-brush, *n.* a fox's tail.
fox-earth, *n.* the burrow or den of a fox.
foxed, *a.* fokst, stained, as timber; spotted, as paper in printed books: soured, as beer; repaired, as boots.
fox-evil, *n.* alopecia, a disease in which the hair falls off.
foxglove, *n.* *foks*-gluv, a valuable medicinal plant, *Digitalis purpurea*, with flowers shaped somewhat like the fingers of a glove.
foxhound, *n.* *foks*-hound, a hound for chasing foxes.
fox-hunt, *n.* the chase of a fox with hounds.
fox-hunter, *n.* one who follows the hounds.
fox-hunting, *n.* the hunting of foxes with hounds: *a.* pertaining to or engaged in hunting the fox.
foxiness, *n.* *fok*-se-ness, craftiness; shrewdness; the condition of foxed paper, etc.
foxish, *a.* *fok*-sish, pertaining to foxes; resembling a fox in qualities; cunning.
fox-shark, *n.* the sea-fox or thresher.
fox-sleep, *n.* a simulated sleep.
foxtail, *n.* *foks*-tale, the tail of a fox; various species of grass, esp. of the genus *Alopecurus*.
fox-terrier, *n.* a small smooth- or wire-haired dog, originally bred to dig foxes.
fox-trot, *n.* short steps taken by a horse when changing its pace; an American ball-room dance.
foxy, *a.* *fok*-se, pertaining to foxes; wily; having a dun, faded, or fox-like colour (esp. of paper and prints); sour; not completely fermented.
foy, *n.* foy, a feast, stirrup-cup, or the like given by or to one about to depart. (Dut. *fooi.*)
foyer, *n.* (App.), a crush room at a theatre, concert-hall, etc.; an anteroom. (Fr.)
fracas, *n.* *frak*-ah (U.S.A., *fray*-kas), an uproar; a noisy quarrel. (Fr. from *fracasser*, to shatter.)
frack, *n.* frak, a waiter's dress-suit. (Ger.)
fractile, *a.* *frak*-tile, pertaining to or indicating cleavage; fragile [U.S.A.].
fraction, *n.* *frak*-shon, the act of breaking, or state of being broken, especially by violence; a fragment; one or more of aliquot parts into which a whole number is divided [Math.] (*see* **decimal,** and **vulgar fraction**); one of the parts resulting from fractionation [Chem.]. (Fr.)
fractional, *a.* *frak*-shon-al, pertaining to or constituting a fraction or fractions; fragmentary; inconsiderable.
fractionary, *a.* *frak*-shon-a-re, fractional.
fractionate, *v.t.* *frak*-shon-ate, to separate the components of liquid mixtures by distillation [Chem.].
fractionation, *n.* frak-sho-*nay*-shon, the process or action of fractionating [Chem.].
fractionist, *n.* *frak*-shon-ist, a leader or member of a dissident group [Polit.].
fractionize, *v.t.* *frak*-shon-ize, to break up into divisions or fractions.
fractious, *a.* *frak*-shus, apt to break out in passion or to quarrel; cross; petulant; splenetic.
fractiously, *ad.* snappishly; in a fractious manner.
fractiousness, *n.* a cross or snappish temper.
fracture, *n.* *frak*-tewr, a breaking of any body, especially a breach caused by violence; a rupture of a solid body; a crack; the breaking of a bone, called simple when the bone merely is divided, compound when also the integuments are lacerated [Surg.]; the manner in which a mineral breaks, and by which its texture is displayed; the surface, as broken [Min.]: *v.t.* to break; to separate continuous parts. (Fr.)
frænulum, *n.* *free*-new-lum, a frænum, a membranous fold [Anat.]; a bristle or bunch of bristles with which certain lepidoptera lock together their fore- and hind-wings during flight.
frænum, *n.* *free*-num, a small restraining ligament, esp. that of the tongue [Anat.]. (L., a bridle.)
fragile, *a.* *fraj*-ile, easily broken; brittle; delicate. (L. *fragilis.*)
fragileness, *n.* fragility.
fragility, *n.* fra-*jil*-e-te, the quality of being fragile; brittleness.
fragment, *n.* *frag*-ment, a part broken off; a small detached or uncompleted portion; anything left unfinished. (Fr.)
fragmental, *a.* frag-*men*-tal, fragmentary.
fragmentary, *a.* *frag*-men-ta-re, pertaining to or composed of fragments. **fragmentary rocks,** rocks formed of the fragments of other rocks, as conglomerates, sandstones, etc. [Geol.].
fragmented, *a.* *frag*-men-ted, broken into fragments; in detached pieces.
fragor, *n.* *fray*-gor, a loud, harsh, or sudden sound; a crash. (L.)
fragrance, *n.* *fray*-grance, sweetness of smell; pleasing scent; grateful odour.
fragrancy, *n.* *fray*-gran-se, the quality of being fragrant; fragrance.

fragrant, *a. fray*-grant, diffusing an agreeable odour; sweet-smelling. (L. *fragrans*, smelling.)
fragrantly, *ad.* with sweet scent.
frail, *n.* frale, a basket made of rushes, for holding dried fruit; a certain quantity, about 75 lb., that this will contain.
frail, *a.* frale, fragile; infirm; deficient in strength or firmness; weak in mind or resolution. (Fr. *frêle.*)
frailly, *ad. frale*-le, in a frail manner.
frailness, *n.* the quality of being frail.
frailty, *n. frale*-te, weakness in resisting temptation; infirmity; a foible.
fraise, *n.* fraze, a defence consisting of pointed stakes driven into the rampart in a horizontal or inclined position [Fort.]; a reamer [Mech.]: *v.t.* to defend or fortify with a fraise. (Fr.)
Fraktur, *n. frahk*-toor, the black-letter style of type used in Germany before its supersession by Roman faces [Print.]. (Ger.)
framable, *a. frame*-a-bl, that may be framed.
frambœsia, *n.* fram-*bee*-ze-a, the yaws, a contagious tropical disease. (Fr. *framboise*, raspberry.)
★**frame,** *n.* frame, fabric, or structure composed of parts fitted and united; any kind of case or structure made for admitting, enclosing, or supporting things; a wooden or other surround for a picture, window, etc.; a portable glazed cover for protecting plants; a framework; form; system; shape; skeleton; temper or disposition of mind; a sort of loom on which linen, silk, etc., is stretched for quilting or embroidering; a stand to support the cases in which the types are distributed [Print.]; a kind of mould for castings [Founding]: *v.t.* to construct by fitting parts together; to fit one thing to another; to provide with a frame; to make; to compose, as laws; to form by thought; to plan; to fabricate; to attempt to incriminate by means of a frame-up [Slang]. (A.S. *fremman*, to make.)
frame-bridge, *n.* a bridge so framed as to secure great strength with the least material.
frame-house, *n.* a house constructed of a framework of timber covered with shingles or boards.
framer, *n. frame*-er, one who frames; a contriver.
frame-saw, *n.* a ribbon saw stretched and kept rigid in a hand-frame.
framework, *n. frame*-wurk, the frame which supports or encloses a thing; the skeleton; structure as framed.
frame-up, *n. frame*-up, concocted evidence of guilt against a presumably innocent person; a prearranged conspiracy; a faked result [U.S.A. slang].
framing-chisel, *n.* a chisel with a socket shank used for making mortises.
franc, *n.* frank, a silver coin of France; the French monetary unit of the former value of about ninepence halfpenny. (Fr.)
franchise, *n. fran*-chize, a particular privilege or right legally granted by a sovereign or government to an individual, or to a number of persons; an immunity so granted; the district or jurisdiction to which a particular privilege extends; the limits of an immunity; citizenship; the statutory right to vote, esp. for a member of parliament; the qualification for such vote: *v.t.* to enfranchise. (O.Fr.)
Franciscan, *a.* fran-*sis*-kan, belonging to the order of St. Francis: *n.* a member of the order of St. Francis of Assisi, called also Minorities and Grey Friars.
Francize, *v.t. fran*-size to Frenchify.
francolin, *n. frang*-ko-lin, a bird allied to the partridge, found in S. Europe, in S. Asia, and N. Africa. (Fr.)
francolite, *n. frang*-ko-lite, a variety of apatite.
Francophile, *n. frang*-ko-fil, a non-French partisan of France and French things: *a.* friendly to France.
Francophobe, *n. frang*-ko-fobe, one who dreads or detests France and French influence: *a.* hating France.
Francophobia, *n.* frang-ko-*foh*-be-a, unreasoning dread or hatred of France and things French.
franc-tireur, *n.* (App.), a French irregular infantryman; a sniper; a partisan [Mil.]. (Fr., unattached rifleman.)
frangibility, *n. fran*-je-*bil*-e-te, the state or quality of being frangible. (L. *frangere*, to break.)
frangible, *a. fran*-je-bl, easily broken; fragile.
frangibleness, *n. fran*-je-bl-ness, frangibility.
frangipane, *n. fran*-je-pane, a kind of almond pastry or cake. (*Frangipani*, Ital. originator.)
frangipani, *n. fran*-je-*pah*-ne, a perfume prepared from the flowers of *Plumeria rubra*, the red jasmine of the West Indies. (As *frangipane.*)
frank, *a.* frank, free and open in manner or expression; liberal; sincere; generous; without conditions or compensation; unrestrained: *n.* a letter which is exempted from postage, or the writing which renders it free: *v.t.* to send, as a letter, exempt from postage; to mark with a postage meter machine as indication that postage is prepaid. (Fr. *franc*, free).
Frank, *n.* frank, a member of the powerful Germanic tribe that conquered Gaul in the 6th cent.; in the Near East a name given to Western Europeans. (O.E. [from Teut.] *franca*, a javelin.)
frankalmoign, *n. frank*-al-moyn, a tenure by which a religious corporation holds lands in perpetuity on condition of praying for the soul of the donor and his heirs. (*frank*, and O.Fr. *almoignes*, alms.)
Frankenstein, *n. frang*-ken-stine, the constructor of a human monster in Mrs. Shelley's story of this name (1818), who is ultimately destroyed by it, misapplied to an object or situation that has become beyond the control of its originator.
franker, *n. frang*-ker, a machine or stamp for franking postal matter; a postage meter machine.
Frankfort-black, *n. frank*-fort-*blak*, a jet-black pigment used in copperplate printing.
frankfurter, *n. frank*-fur-ter, a small highly seasoned smoked German sausage. (Ger., of Frankfort.)
frankincense, *n. frang*-kn-sense, gum-olibanum, a resinous substance emitting a fragrant smell when burning, obtained from E. African trees of the genus *Boswellia*. (O.Fr. *franc encens*, pure incense.)
Frankish, *a. frang*-kish, relating to the Franks.
franklin, *n. frank*-lin, a mediæval English freeholder, originally one who held his lands direct of the crown; a yeoman. (Anglo-Fr. *fraunkeleyn.*)
franklinite, *n. frank*-lin-ite, a crystalline magnetic oxide of iron, zinc, and manganese, named from Franklin, New Jersey, where found.
frankly, *ad. frank*-le, in a frank manner.
frankness, *n. frank*-ness, the quality of being frank; plainness of speech.
frank-pledge, *n. frank*-plej, a feudal surety for the behaviour of freemen, esp. connoting the common responsibility of all the members of a tithing.
frank-service, *n.* service performed in feudal times by freemen.
frantic, *a. fran*-tik, driven mad or furious with passion or distraction; characterized by violence, fury, and disorder; wild. (O.Fr. *frenetique.*)
frantically, *ad. fran*-te-ka-le, in a frantic manner.
franticly, *ad. fran*-tik-le, frantically.
frap, *v.t.* frap, to pass a rope or line round anything to keep it together; to undergird; to draw together by ropes crossing each other, with a view to secure and strengthen [Naut.]. (Fr. *frapper*, strike.)
frappé, *a.* frah-pay, iced [Cookery]. (Fr.)
frass, *n.* fras, excrement or powdered refuse left by larvæ [Zool.]. (Ger. *fressen*, to devour.)
fraternal, *a.* fra-*ter*-nal, brotherly; pertaining to brethren; suitable for brothers. (O.Fr. *fraternel*, L. *frater*, brother.)
fraternally, *ad.* in a fraternal manner.
fraternity, *n.* fra-*ter*-ne-te, the state of being brothers, or being fraternal; brotherhood; a body of men associated for a common interest; men of the same class or profession. (O.Fr. *fraternité.*)
fraternization, *n. frat*-er-ny-*zay*-shon, the act of fraternizing; friendly or brotherly relations.
fraternize, *v.i. frat*-er-nize, to associate with as brothers; to seek or hold friendly fellowship; to have, as an occupier, social relations with the members (esp. the women) of an occupied country. (Fr. *fraterniser.*)
fratery, *n. fray*-te-re, the refectory of a monastery.
fratricidal, *a.* frat-re-*sy*-dal, pertaining to fratricide.
fratricide, *n. frat*-re-side, the murder of a brother; one who murders a brother. (O.Fr.)
fratry, *n. fray*-tre, a fratery.
fratting, *n. frat*-ing, fraternization with women (of troops, etc.) [Mil. slang].
Frau, *n.* frow, the German equivalent of Mrs.; a German or Dutch housewife. (Ger.)

fraud, *n.* frawd, an artifice by which the right or interest of another is injured; a stratagem intended to obtain some undue advantage; an imposition or imposter; cheating. (O.Fr. *fraude.*)
fraudful, *a.* *frawd*-ful, characterized by fraud; containing fraud.
fraudfully, *ad.* in a manner to defraud.
fraudulence, *n.* *fraw*-dew-lence, the act or quality of being fraudulent; trickiness in bargaining. (O.Fr.)
fraudulent, *a.* *fraw*-dew-lent, practising fraud in making contracts; founded on or proceeding from fraud; obtained by fraud; deceitful. (O.Fr.)
fraudulently, *ad.* in a fraudulent manner.
fraught, *a.* frawt, freighted, as a vessel; filled; stored; laden. (Dan. *fragte.*)
Fräulein, *n.* *froy*-line, the German equivalent of Miss; a young or unmarried German woman; in England, a German governess. (Ger.)
Fraunhofer, *n.* *froun*-hoh-fer, name of a German optician (1787–1826) designating the dark lines ("Fraunhofer's lines") of the spectrum of sunlight.
fraxinella, *n.* *frak*-se-*nel*-a, a cultivated species of dittany.
fray, *n.* fray, a broil; a violent riot; an affray.
fray, *n.* fray, a fret or chafe in cloth; a place injured by rubbing: *v.t.* to wear into loose ends by rubbing. (Fr. *frayer*, from L. *frico*, rub.)
fraying, *n.* *fray*-ing, the velvet frayed from a deer's horn.
frazil, *n.* *fraz*-il, ice formed beneath water; anchor ice. (French-Canadian.)
frazzle, *n.* *fraz*-zl, shreds; tatters; an exhausted or a badly beaten state: *v.t.* and *i.* to fray or become frayed out. **to beat to a frazzle,** to defeat completely [Coll.].
freak, *n.* freek, a sudden capricious change or turn of the mind; a capricious prank; an abnormality; a monstrosity: *v.t.* to variegate; to checker: *a.* unnatural, not normal. (Etym. uncertain.)
freakish, *a.* *freek*-ish, apt to change the mind suddenly; whimsical; capricious.
freakishly, *ad.* capriciously.
freakishness, *n.* capriciousness; whimsicalness.
freckle, *n.* *frek*-kl, a spot of a brownish colour on the skin due to the action of the sun's rays; any small spot or discoloration: *v.t.* to mark with freckles: *v.i.* to become freckled. (Scand.)
freckly, *a.* *frek*-kle, full of freckles.
***free,** *a.* free, at liberty; not under necessity or restraint; not under arbitrary government or foreign domination; instituted by a free people; not imprisoned; not under compulsion or control; not connected with the State (of a Church); not chemically combined; allowed; not obstructed; unrestrained; frank; unreserved; unconventional; liberal; not parsimonious; generous; lavish; gratuitous; guiltless; exempt; not encumbered with; open to all; invested with franchises or certain immunities; possessing without vassalage; liberated from the control of parent, guardian, or master: *ad.* freely: *v.t.* to rid; to strip; to clear; to set at liberty; to deliver; to disengage; to exempt; to release. **free and easy,** *n.* an informal gathering; a smoking concert: *a.* unconventional; quite at home. **free breakfast-table,** unrestricted import of tea, coffee, sugar, etc. [Econ.]. **free city,** a city independent of any State, esp. one forming a state in itself under the Holy Roman Empire. **free house,** a public house not belonging to a brewer. **free lance,** one of an armed band who sold their services to fight on either side; one who fights on his own; an unattached journalist or politician. **free port,** a port where ships pay no duty for loading or unloading. **free trade,** the free international exchange of commodities; freedom from import duties; formerly, smuggling. **free verse,** vers libre. (A.S. *freo.*)
free-bench, *n.* a widow's dower in a copyhold [Law].
freeboard, *n.* *free*-bord, the part of a vessel's hull that extends from the waterline upwards; a margin, as on the outer side of a fence; the space between ground-level and the under-carriage of a car.
freebooter, *n.* *free*-boot-er, one who wanders about for plunder; a roving marauder. (Dut. *vrijbuiter.*)
freebootery, *n.* *free*-boot-er-re, robbery by a freebooter.

free-born, *a.* born free; not in vassalage.
freedman, *n.* *freed*-man, a man who has been a slave and is manumitted.
freedom, *n.* *free*-dom, the state of being free; a state of exemption from the power or control of another; liberty; exemption from slavery, servitude, or confinement; franchise; immunity; exemption from fate, necessity, or any constraint, in consequence of predetermination or otherwise; ease or facility of doing anything; frankness; licence; improper familiarity. **freedom of a city,** rights of citizenship with participation in its privileges. **freedom of the press,** liberty of publication without state control or censorship, subject only to penalty for matter that is seditious, libellous, or contrary to public morals. (A. S. *freōdōm.*)
free-fight, *n.* a mêlée; a promiscuous scrap in which bystanders join.
free-for-all, *n.* an open competition; a free-fight.
freehand, *a.* *free*-hand, drawn without measurements or instruments.
free-handed, *a.* liberal in giving; generous.
freehold, *n.* *free*-hohld, an estate or tenement held in fee-simple, fee-tail, or for term of life; such a tenure; an office held for life: *a.* held by freehold.
freeholder, *n.* *free*-hohl-der, the possessor of a freehold.
free-living, *n.* full gratification of the appetites; not attached; parasitic [Biol.].
free-love, *n.* sexual intercourse without marriage; the practice or doctrine of overt cohabitation without legal marriage.
freely, *ad.* *free*-le, in a free manner; voluntarily.
freeman, *n.* *free*-man, one not a slave or a vassal; one possessing municipal privileges or the freedom of a city.
freemartin, *n.* *free*-mar-tin, a sexually imperfect female calf, twin with a male. (Etym. unknown.)
freemason, *n.* *free*-may-son, one of an ancient and secret fraternity, probably of mediæval origin, at first composed of guilds of masons or builders in stone, but now consisting of men united for brotherly love, charity, and mutual assistance.
freemasonry, *n.* *free*-may-son-re, the spirit and institutions of freemasons.
freeness, *n.* *free*-ness, the state of being free.
freer, *n.* *free*-er, one who gives freedom: *a.* more free.
freesia, *n.* *free*-ze-a, a sweet-scented greenhouse plant of the iris family, originally from S. Africa. (E. M. *Fries*, Swed. botanist, *d.* 1878.)
free-soil, *a.* opposed to the extension of slavery into new territory [U.S.A.].
free-spoken, *a.* accustomed to speak without reserve.
freest, *a.* *free*-est, most free.
freestone, *n.* *free*-stone, any building-stone which, having no grain, can be cut in any direction; a stone (or fruit having such) that does not adhere to the flesh, as in some peaches.
freethinker, *n.* *free*-think-ker, a rationalist; an agnostic; a deist who discarded revelation.
freethinking, *n.* *free*-thing-king, freethought: unbelief; deism: *a.* sceptical; unbelieving.
freethought, *n.* free-thawt, rejection of authority and of revelation in religion; rationalism.
free-trader, *n.* a supporter of free trade; formerly, a smuggler or vessel engaged in smuggling.
free-warren, *n.* a royal franchise or exclusive right of killing beasts and fowls of warren within certain limits [Law].
free-wheel, *n.* a device in a bicycle or other mechanism which allows the wheels to run free of the driving-gear when desired: *v.i.* to allow wheels to run free of driving-gear; to coast.
free-will, *n.* the power of directing one's own actions, unconstrained by necessity or fate; voluntariness: *a.* voluntary; spontaneous.
free-woman, *n.* *free*-woom-an, a woman not a slave.
freezable, *a.* *freez*-a-bl, that can be frozen.
freeze, *v.i.* freez, to be congealed into ice by cold; to be chilled; to become stand-offish [Coll.]: *v.t.* to congeal or harden into ice; to kill by cold; to chill; to render insensitive by cold [Surg.]; to stabilize a price; to make unavailable for current use [Comm.]. **to freeze out,** to boycott; to drive into retirement. *p.* **froze**; *pp.* **frozen.** (A.S. *freosan.*)
freezer, *n.* *freez*-er, a freezing apparatus.

freezing-mixture, *n.* a mixture of substances which, in uniting, absorb heat from contiguous bodies and thus produce intense cold.

freezing-point, *n.* the temperature at which water freezes, being marked 32° on Fahrenheit's thermometer and 0° on the centigrade and Réaumur; the solidifying temperature of any liquid.

freight, *n.* frate, the cargo or any part of the cargo of a ship; the sum charged or paid for the transportation of goods; goods transported by railway [U.S.A.] or air: *v.t.* to load with goods, as a ship, etc., for transportation; to hire for this purpose. **freight car,** an American goods wagon. **freight train,** a goods train. (O.Fr. *fret,* a ship's freight.)

freightage, *n. frate*-aj, charge for freight; freight.

freighter, *n. frate*-er, one who freights a ship; one who transports goods by rail; a ship or aircraft designed for transport of freight.

freightless, *a. frate*-less, destitute of freight.

fremescent, *a.* fre-*mes*-ent, breaking out into loud and louder complaints. (L. *fremens,* murmuring.)

French, *a.* french, pertaining to France or its inhabitants: *n.* the language spoken by the inhabitants of France; the people of France. **French Canadian,** a Canadian descended from the original French colonists; French as spoken by these. (A.S. *frencisc.*)

french-bean, *n.* the kidney bean, *Phaseolus vulgaris.*

french-chalk, *n.* a hardened talc of a pearly white or greyish colour, used in drawing lines on cloth.

french-fake, *n.* a method of coiling a rope by laying it in parallel bends [Naut.].

french-horn, *n.* a brass wind instrument of circular shape with a range of three octaves.

Frenchify, *v.t. french*-e-fy, to make French; to imbue with the manners of the French; to Gallicize.

french-leave, *n.* leave without permission asked; surreptitious departure or abstraction.

Frenchman, *n. french*-man, a man of the French nation, either born or naturalized; a ship under the French flag.

french-polish, *n.* a spirit polish used on furniture, cabinet-work, etc.

french-roll, *n.* a light kind of fancy bread.

french-roof, *n.* a mansard roof.

french-white, *n.* finely pulverized talc.

french-window, *n.* a long casement window opening like folding-doors.

Frenchwoman, *n.* a woman of the French nation.

frenulum, *n. fren*-yew-lum, a frænulum.

frenum, *n. free*-num, a frænum.

frenzied, *pp.* and *a. fren*-zid, affected with madness; delirious.

frenzy, *n. fren*-ze, excitement of mind, as in delirium or madness; fury: *v.t.* to render mad or drive delirious. (O.Fr. *frenisie.*)

frequency, *n. free*-kwen-se, occurrence often at short intervals; the number of repetitions in a given time; the rate of recurrence; in acoustics, the number of vibrations in a second; the number of complete periods per second of an alternating electric current [Elect.]; the number of recurrences of a periodic motion per time-unit (esp. second) [Math.]. **audio frequency,** the frequency at which a transmitted wave becomes audible. **high frequency,** periodic motion recurring at very short intervals; a frequency well above that of the audio range [Wire.]. **low frequency,** periodic motion recurring at relatively long intervals; relating to waves of audio frequency [Wire.]. **natural frequency,** the frequency with which an object or an electric current will oscillate if started by an impulse and left free. **radio frequency,** the frequency of the wave emitted by the transmitter [Wire.].

★frequent, *a. free*-kwent, repeated often; repeating often; full; crowded. (L. *frequens.*)

frequent, *v.t.* free-*kwent,* to resort to often.

frequentation, *n. free*-kwen-*tay*-shon, the habit of visiting often.

frequentative, *a.* and *n.* fre-*kwen*-ta-tiv, a term applied to verbs signifying the frequent repetition of an action [Gram.]. (L. *frequentativus.*)

frequenter, *n.* fre-*kwen*-ter, one who often or habitually visits.

frequently, *ad. free*-kwent-le, often; commonly.

frequentness, *n. free*-kwent-ness, the quality of being frequent.

frescade, *n. fres*-kayd, a cool walk; an alley or shady place. (Fr.)

fresco, *n. fres*-koh, a method of painting durably on walls with water-colours on fresh plaster, or on mortar not yet dry: *v.t.* to paint in fresco. **al fresco,** *see* **alfresco.** (It., fresh.)

fresh, *a.* fresh, brisk, healthy, and strong; looking young and vigorous; lively (of horses); not faded; recently grown; not impaired by time; in a good state; not stale; not forgotten or obliterated; not salted; pure and cool; not warm or vapid; in a state like that of recent growth; having new vigour; slightly intoxicated [Slang]; cheeky, forward [U.S.A. Slang]: *n.* a freshwater river; a freshet; *pl.* the mingling of fresh water with salt water in rivers or bays; a flood. (A.S. *fersc.*)

fresh-blown, *a.* newly blown.

freshen, *v.t. fresh*-en, to make fresh; to refresh; to take saltness from; to shift the part of a rope exposed to friction by slacking it [Naut.]: *v.i.* to grow fresh; to lose saltness; to grow brisk or strong.

freshener, *n. fresh*-en-er, that which refreshes.

fresher, *n. fresh*-er, a freshman [Univ. Slang].

freshet, *n. fresh*-et, a flooding of a river by means of heavy rains or melted snow; a flood. (O.Fr.)

freshly, *ad.* in a fresh manner; newly; briskly.

freshman, *n. fresh*-man, a novice; one in the rudiments of knowledge, esp. a student in his first year, or first term, at a university.

freshmanship, *n.* the state of a freshman.

freshness, *n.* the state or quality of being fresh.

fresh-run, *a.* newly arrived in a river from the sea (of salmon, etc.)

freshwater, *a. fresh*-waw-ter, formed or living in fresh water; accustomed to sail on fresh water only, or in the coasting trade; raw; unskilled.

fret, *n.* fret, agitation of the surface of a fluid; a rippling on the surface; irritation; vexation; a chafing of the skin [Med.]; herpes [Med.]; fretwork; an ornament consisting of small fillets intersecting each other at right angles [Arch.]; one of the short ridges fixed on the finger-board of guitars, etc., under and at right angles to the strings [Mus.]; a figure consisting of narrow bends crossed and interlaced saltirewise [Her.]: *v.i.* to be worn away; to eat or wear into; to be agitated; to be chafed or irritated; to utter peevish expressions: *v.t.* to wear away by friction; to wear away, so as to impair; to eat into; to irritate; to chafe; to gall; to agitate; to make rough; to cause to ripple; to form into or ornament with raised work; to variegate; to provide with frets. (A.S. *fretan,* to gnaw.)

fretful, *a. fret*-ful, disposed to fret; in a state of irritation; peevish.

fretfully, *ad.* peevishly; captiously.

fretfulness, *n.* peevishness.

fretsaw, *n. fret*-saw, the small ribbonsaw used in fretwork.

fretted, *a. fret*-ted, ornamented with fretwork; intersected with small grooves; interlaced [Her.].

fretter, *n. fret*-ter, one who frets; that which irritates or chafes.

fretting, *n. fret*-ting, the process or action of irritating; a state of chafing.

fretty, *a. fret*-te, adorned with fretwork; fretted [Her.].

fretwork, *n. fret*-wurk, interlaced ornament; wood in which the pattern has been cut out by a thin fine saw; work adorned with frets.

Freudian, *a. froy*-de-an, pertaining to or in accordance with the psychoanalytical doctrines of Sigmund Freud (1856–1939): *n.* an adherent of these doctrines.

friability, *n.* fry-a-*bil*-e-te, the quality of being friable.

friable, *a. fry*-a-bl, crumbling easily; easily reduced to powder. (L. *friabilis.*)

friableness, *n. fry*-a-bl-ness, friability.

friar, *n. fry*-ar, a member of one of the religious mendicant orders, viz. the Grey Friars or Franciscans, the Augustinians, the Black Friars or Dominicans, the White Friars or Carmelites, and the former Crutched Friars; a patch on a page which has not received the ink [Printing]. (O.Fr. *frere,* brother.)

friarly, *a. fry*-ar-le, like a friar; untaught in the affairs of life.

friar's-balsam, *n.* compound tincture of benzoin, a popular specific for the healing of wounds.

friar's-cowl, *n.* the plant wake-robin, *Arum maculatum.*
friar's-lantern, *n.* will-o'-the-wisp.
friary, *n. fry*-a-re, a monastery of a mendicant order; a convent of friars.
fribble, *a. frib*-bl, frivolous; trifling: *n.* a frivolous contemptible fellow: *v.i.* to trifle. (L. *frivolus.*)
fribbler, *n. frib*-bler, a trifler.
fricandeau, *n. frik*-an-do, a thick slice of meat, esp. veal, stewed with vegetables: *v.t.* to make into a fricandeau. (Fr.)
fricassee, *n. frik*-a-see, a stew of disjointed poultry or other small animals, cooked in a frying-pan or stewed: *v.t.* to dress in fricassee. (Fr. *fricassée.*)
fricative, *n. frik*-a-tiv, a consonant, such as *f* or *th*, produced by the friction of the breath as it passes through a narrow opening: *a.* produced thus. (L. *fricatus,* rubbed.)
friction, *n. frik*-shon, the act of rubbing the surface of one body against that of another; attrition; abrasion; the resistance which a moving body meets with from the surface on which or the medium in which it moves [Mech.]; the act of rubbing any part of the surface of the body to promote circulation [Med.]. (Fr.)
frictional, *a. frik*-shon-al, relating to or caused by friction.
friction-balls, *n.pl.* the small balls used in ball-bearings for reducing friction.
friction-clutch, *n.* a power-transmission clutch that is operated by friction [Mech.].
friction-drive, *n.* a system of power-transmission in motor-cars in which surface friction takes the place of gear-wheels.
friction-wheel, *n. frik*-shon-wheel, a wheel communicating motion by frictional contact.
Friday, *n. fry*-day, the sixth day of the week, formerly consecrated to Frigga, wife of Odin, the Scandinavian god. **Good Friday,** the Friday before Easter, kept sacred by Christians in memory of the death of Christ. **man Friday,** *see* **man.** (A.S. *frige-dæg.*)
fried, fride, *p.* and *pp.* of the verb *to fry.*
★**friend,** *n.* frend, one who is attached to another by affection; an acquaintance; an adherent or favourer; a term of salutation; (*cap.*) a Quaker, or member of the Society of Friends: *v.t.* to befriend; to favour or countenance. **friend at court,** one who has sufficient interest to serve another. **Society of Friends,** a Christian sect that originated in England about 1650, distinguished for plainness of speech and manners, pacifism, rejection of paid clergy, disavowal of the necessity of sacraments, and their teaching that divine revelation or inward light is given to every man. (A.S. *fréond.*)
friended, *a. fren*-ded, befriended.
friendless, *a.* destitute of friends; forlorn.
friendlessness, *n.* the state of being friendless.
friend-like, *a.* like or becoming a friend.
friendlily, *ad. frend*-le-le, in a friendly way.
friendliness, *n.* a friendly disposition or act.
friendly, *a. frend*-le, having the disposition of a friend; kind; favourable; disposed to peace; amicable; not hostile; propitious; played or contested not for stakes or in formal competition [Sport]: *n.* a friendly lead; a friendly game: *ad.* in the manner of friends; amicably. **friendly lead,** an entertainment held to raise funds for one in trouble. **friendly society,** a voluntary association of individuals for the purpose of mutual assistance in sickness, old age, or distress.
friendship, *n. frend*-ship, an attachment to a person, proceeding from acquaintance and a reciprocation of kind offices; mutual attachment; favour; friendly aid.
frier, *n. fry*-er, one who fries (as in *fish-frier*); a frying-pan.
Friesian, *a.* and *n. free*-ze-an, Frisian.
frieze, *n.* freez, a coarse woollen cloth or stuff with a nap on one side. (Fr. *drap de frise,* cloth of Friesland.)
frieze, *n.* freez, that part of the entablature of a column which is between the architrave and cornice, and generally ornamented; a decorative band round a wall, usually close to the ceiling [Arch.]. (O.Fr. *frise.*)
friezed, *a.* freezd, shaggy with nap or frieze.
frieze-panel, *n.* an upper panel of a six-panelled door.
frieze-rail, *n.* a rail beneath a frieze; a picture-rail.
frigate, *n. frig*-at, a ship of war, formerly rating next below a ship of the line and originally carrying her guns on the maindeck and on a raised quarterdeck and forecastle; an escort vessel. (Fr.)
frigate-bird, *n.* a large and rapacious tropical sea-bird, the man-of-war bird.
frigatoon, *n. frig*-a-toon, an obsolete Venetian vessel, with a square stern, and only a mainmast and mizenmast. (It. *fregatone.*)
fright, *n.* frite, a sudden temporary attack of fear or terror; an incident to shock one; a sudden alarm; anything unsightly or of extraordinary appearance [Coll.]: *v.t.* to frighten. (A.S. *fyrhtu.*)
frighten, *v.t. fry*-t'n, to affright or terrify; to scare.
frightful, *a. frite*-ful, terrible; dreadful; full of what excites fear; shocking; awful [Coll.].
frightfully, *ad.* in a manner to frighten or shock.
frightfulness, *n. frite*-ful-ness, the quality of being frightful; action to cause terror; atrocious activity.
frigid, *a. frij*-id, cold; wanting heat or warmth; lacking warmth of affection; wanting zeal or animation; stiff; formal; forbidding. **frigid zones,** the parts of the earth between the N. and S. Poles and the Arctic and Antarctic Circles respectively. (L. *frigidus,* cold.)
Frigidaire, *n.* frij-e-*dare,* proprietary name of a make of electric refrigerator.
frigidity, *n.* fre-*jid*-e-te, coldness; a manner of stiff formality.
frigidly, *ad. frij*-id-le, in a frigid manner.
frigidness, *n.* the quality of being frigid; frigidity.
frigorific, *a. frig*-o-*rif*-ik, producing or generating cold. (L. *frigorificus,* cooling.)
frill, *n.* fril, a crimped or fluted edging on a garment, etc.; a ruffle; a paper ornamented round a hambone; an ornamental fringe of hair, feathers, paper, etc.; superfluous showiness (Coll.]: *v.t.* to provide with a frill; to serve as a frill: *v.i.* to pucker at the edge. (O.Fr. *vrille,* a tendril, and O.Fr. *friller,* to shiver.)
frilled, *a.* frild, decked with or as with a frill.
frillery, *n. fril*-e-re, frills collectively.
frilling, *n. fril*-ling, edging material.
frilly, *a. fril*-e, having or resembling frills: *n.pl.* frilled undergarments [Slang].
fringe, *n.* frinj, an ornamental appendage consisting of hanging threads or tassals; something resembling a fringe; front hair cut straight and overhanging the forehead; an edging; a border: *pl.* coloured bands seen when a beam of light is transmitted through a slit [Opt.]: *v.t.* to border with fringe or a loose edging. (Fr. *frenge.*)
fringe-tree, *n. frinj*-tree, a small white-flowered tree of the southern United States, *Chionanthus virginica.*
Fringilla, *n.* frin-*jil*-la, a genus of song-birds comprising the finches.
fringillaceous, *a.* frin-jil-*lay*-she-us, pertaining to the finches.
fringing, *a. frinj*-ing, bordering; encircling as coral reefs round an island: *n.* a border.
fringy, *a. frin*-je, adorned with fringes.
fripper, *n. frip*-per, a dealer in old clothes or frippery. (O.Fr. *fripier.*)
frippery, *n. frip*-pe-re, old clothes, second-hand goods; tawdry finery; trumpery; the place where old clothes are sold; trade in old clothes: *a.* trifling; contemptible. (Fr. *friperie.*)
frisette, *n.* fre-*zet,* a row of small artificial curls worn on the forehead. (Fr.)
friseur, *n.* fre-*zoor,* a hairdresser. (Fr. *friser,* to curl.)
Frisian, *a. friz*-e-an, pertaining to, or native to, Friesland: *n.* a native, or the language, of Friesland. (L. *Frisii.*)
frisk, *n.* frisk, a frolic; a fit of wanton gaiety: *v.i.* to dance, skip, caper about, or gambol in frolic and gaiety. (Fr. *frisque,* lively, fresh.)
frisket, *n. fris*-ket, the light frame by which a sheet of paper is confined to the tympan to be laid on the forme for impression [Print.]. (Fr. *frisquette.*)
friskful, *a. frisk*-ful, brisk; lively.
friskily, *ad. fris*-ke-le, in a frisky manner.
friskiness, *n. fris*-ke-ness, the quality of being frisky.
frisky, *a. fris*-ke, jumping with gaiety; frolicsome; lively.
frit, *n.* frit, the material of which glass is made after it has been calcined, or baked in a furnace, but before

fusion; the material for glazing pottery: *v.t.* to expose to dull red heat for the purpose of expelling moisture, etc., from materials for glass. (Fr. *fritte.*)
frit-fly, *n.* a small fly destructive to growing wheat.
frith, *n.* frith, a firth; an inlet of the sea at the mouth of a river; an estuary. (Ice. *fiorthr.*)
frith, *n.* frith, formerly a forest or woody place. (A.S.)
fritillary, *n.* fre-*til*-a-re, a liliaceous plant of the genus *Fritillaria*, including the crown imperial, *F. imperialis*; various butterflies whose wing-coloration resembles the petals of the plant. (L. *fritillus*, a dice-box.)
fritter, *n. frit*-ter, a pancake of fruit in fried batter; a fragment: *v.t.* to cut into small pieces to be fried; to break into small pieces or fragments. **to fritter away,** to waste away by degrees in a frivolous manner. (O.Fr. *friture*, a frying.)
Fritz, *n.* frits, a German; a German soldier, aeroplane, etc. [Slang]. (Ger., form of *Friedrich.*)
frivol, *v.i. friv*-ol, to trifle; to act foolishly: *n.* one who frivols; a fribbler.
frivolity, *n.* fre-*vol*-e-te, frivolousness; levity.
frivolize, *v.t. friv*-o-lize, to make frivolous: *v.i.* to act frivolously.
frivolous, *a. friv*-o-lus, of little weight, worth, or importance; trifling; given to unbecoming levity or to trifling; silly. (L. *frivolus*, silly, empty.)
frivolously, *ad.* in a frivolous manner.
frivolousness, *n.* the quality of being frivolous.
frizz, *n.* friz, that which is curled: *v.t.* to curl; to crisp; to form the nap of cloth into little hard burrs, prominences, or knobs. (Fr. *friser*, to curl.)
frizzle, *n. friz*-zl, tightly curled hair; a crisped lock of hair: *v.t.* to curl; to burn crisp; to fry: *v.i.* to sputter; to curl.
frizzy, *a. friz*-e, frizzed.
fro, *ad.* froh, from; away; back or backward. (Scand.)
frock, *n.* frok, a light, indoor gown or dress worn by women; a child's indoor dress; formerly, a loose overall worn by men over their other clothes; a garment worn by monks and priests. (O.Fr. *froc.*)
frock-coat, *n.* a man's double-breasted coat with skirts reaching to about the knees.
froe, *n.* froh, a tool for splitting laths or shingles, or for splitting staves.
Froebelian, *a.* fru-*bel*-e-an, pertaining to F. W. A. Froebel (*d.* 1852), or to his kindergarten system of education: *n.* a supporter or teacher of this system.
Froebelism, *n. fru*-bel-izm, the Froebelian theory or practice of kindergarten education.
frog, *n.* frog, a tailless amphibian of the genus *Rana*; a converging and forking junction of railway-lines resembling, in plan, a frog's hind-leg. **frog march,** a way of carrying a person face downwards, four men each holding a limb. (A.S. *frocga.*)
frog, *n.* frog, a sort of tender horn that grows in the middle of the sole of a horse's foot.
frog, *n.* frog, a cloak button, swelling in the middle; the attachment to the belt by which the sword is held; a coat-fastening used on uniforms. (Port. *froco.*)
frogbit, *n. frog*-bit, the small aquatic plant, *Hydrocharis morsus-ranæ.*
frog-fish, *n.* the angler, and certain other similarly furnished sea-fish.
frogged, *a.* frogd, fastened or decorated with frogs (of garments).
froggery, *n. frog*-er-re, frogs in general; a natural or artificial breeding-place of frogs; a place where frogs abound.
froggy, *a. frog*-e, abounding with frogs.
frog-hopper, *n.* any small leaping insect living on plants whose larvæ are enveloped in cuckoo-spit.
frogmouth, *n. frog*-mouth, a name given to certain E. Asian and Australasian wide-mouthed birds allied to the goatsuckers.
froise, *n.* froyz, an omelet or pancake containing bacon. (Perhaps connected with *fry.*)
frolic, *a. frol*-ik, gay; full of levity; dancing, playing or frisking about; full of pranks: *n.* a wild prank; gaiety and mirth; a scene of gaiety and mirth; a merrymaking: *v.i.* to play pranks; to play tricks of mirth and gaiety. (Dut. *vrolijk.*)
frolicsome, *a. frol*-ik-sum, full of gaiety and mirth; given to pranks; sportive.
frolicsomely, *ad.* in a frolicsome manner.
frolicsomeness, *n.* quality of being frolicsome.
★**from,** *prep.* from, away; out of; by reason of; since. **from above,** from a superior position; from heaven. **from afar,** from a distance. **from behind,** from a place or position in the rear. **from below,** from a lower place. **from beneath,** from a place or region below. **from on high,** from an upper region, or from heaven. **from within,** from the interior or inside. **from without,** from the outside; from abroad. (A.S. *fram.*)
frond, *n.* frond, the leaf, or combined leaf and stem of a fern and certain other cryptogams [Bot.]; the flattened expanded thallus of the liverwort and of some seaweeds. (L. *frons, frondis*, a leaf.)
frondage, *n. fron*-daj, fronds collectively; leafage.
Fronde, *n.* frawnd, a party in France opposed to the Court in the minority of Louis XIV; hence, any clique of malcontents. (Fr., a sling.)
frondescence, *n.* fron-*des*-sence, the opening of leaves; the act of putting forth leaves [Bot.]. (L. *frondesco*, to become leafy.)
frondescent, *a.* fron-*des*-ent, unfolding or putting forth leaves or fronds.
Frondeur, *n.* frawn-*door*, a member of the Fronde; an implacable rebel.
frondiferous, *a.* fron-*dif*-er-rus, producing fronds. (L. *frondifer*, leaf-bearing.)
frondivorous, *a.* fron-*div*-o-rus, feeding on leaves [Zool.].
frondose, *a. fron*-dose, full of fronds, resembling fronds. (L. *frondosus*, leafy.)
frondous, *a. fron*-dus, leafy; having both leaves and flowers on the same branch [Bot.].
frons, *n.* fronz, the forehead; the part of the skull between the orbits and the vertex [Anat.]. (L.)
★**front,** *n.* frunt, the forehead; the whole face; the forehead or face, as expressive of the temper or disposition, esp. that of boldness or effrontery; the fore-part of anything; the most conspicuous part; the van of an army or a body of troops; the scene of operations, esp. the firing-line [Mil.]; the principal face of a building [Arch.]; the auditorium of a theatre, etc.; a seaside promenade; a dicky or separate shirt-front; a false hair frontlet: *a.* belonging to or in the front; foremost: *v.t.* to oppose face to face; to stand opposite to, or over against; to furnish with a front: *v.i.* to stand foremost; to have the face toward any point. **front door,** the principal entrance. **in front of,** before. (L. *frons, frontis*, the forehead.)
frontage, *n. frun*-taj, the front part of an edifice; the side of a piece of land that abuts on a road or river; the building line.
frontager, *n. frun*-ta-jer, the owner of a frontage on a road, river, etc.
frontal, *a. fron*-tal, pertaining to the forehead [Anat.]; in front: *n.* (*frun*-tal) something worn on the forehead, esp. as an ornament; a hanging or ornamental panel in front of an altar [Eccles.]; a little pediment or front piece over a small door or window [Arch.]. (L. *frontalia*, a frontlet.)
frontate, *a. fron*-tat, growing broader and broader, as a leaf [Bot.].
fronted, *a. frun*-ted, formed with a front.
frontier, *n. frun*-teer *or fron*-teer, the part of a country bordering on another country: *a.* connected with or lying on the frontier. (O.Fr.)
frontiersman, *n. frun- or fron*-teerz-man, a settler on the frontier; a backwoodsman.
frontispiece, *n. frun*-tis-peece, an illustration facing the title page of a book; the principal face of a building [Arch.]. (Fr. *frontispice.*)
frontlet, *n. frunt*-let, a fillet or band worn on the forehead; a phylactery; the margin of the head behind the bill of birds, generally clothed with rigid bristles [Ornith.].
fronton, *n. frun*-ton, a pediment, a frontal [Arch.].
frontward, *ad. frunt*-ward, towards the front.
frore, *a.* fror, frozen: *ad.* frostily. (A.S. *froren.*)
frost, *n.* frost, temperature at or below 32° Fahrenheit which causes freezing of water; the act or state of freezing; the state of the air that produces freezing; rime, frozen dew; frigidity; a failure [Coll.]: *v.t.* to cover with anything resembling hoar-frost; to injure by frost-bite; to roughen, as the shoe of a horse, in frost. **black frost,** a frost unattended with hoar-frost. (A.S. *forst*)
frost-bite, *n.* an inflammation, usually of the

extremities, due to exposure in severe cold: *v.t.* to produce frost-bite in.
frost-bitten, *a.* *frost*-bit-tn, nipped by frost; injured by, or affected with, frost-bite.
frost-bound, *a.* confined by frost.
frosted, *a.* *fros*-ted, covered with a composition resembling hoar-frost or with frosting; injured by frost; having a roughened surface (of glass or metal).
frostily, *ad.* *fros*-te-le, coldly.
frostiness, *n.* the state of being frosty.
frosting, *n.* *fros*-ting, the icing of a cake; a lustreless finish given to glass and metal; a roughening of surface to render glass non-transparent.
frost-nail, *n.* *frost*-nale, a nail driven into a horse-shoe, to prevent the horse from slipping on ice.
frost-work, *n.* *frost*-wurk, the patterns of hoar-frost deposited on window-panes, etc.
frosty, *a.* *fros*-te, producing, accompanied by, or containing frost; extremely cold; affected by frost; covered with or resembling hoar-frost; without warmth of affection or courage; grey-haired. (A.S. *fyrstig.*)
froth, *n.* froth *or* frawth, foam; the bubbles caused in liquids by fermentation or agitation; any empty, senseless show of wit or eloquence; light, unsubstantial matter: *v.t.* to cause froth on; to cover with froth; to emit as no better than froth: *v.i.* to throw out, as foam or bubbles. (Ice. *frotha.*)
frothily, *ad.* *froth*-e-le, in a frothy or empty manner.
frothiness, *n.* quality or state of being frothy.
frothy, *a.* *froth*-e, full of froth; consisting of froth; empty; unsubstantial.
frou-frou, *n.* *froo*-froo, a rustling, or as of silk. (Fr.)
frounce, *n.* frounce, a wrinkle; a flounce; a curl; a disease in hawks: *v.t.* to gather into plaits or wrinkles; to frizzle the hair; to fringe: *v.i.* to frown. (O.Fr.)
frouzy, *a.* *frou*-ze, frowzy.
frow, *n.* froh, a froe.
frow, *n.* frou, a Dutch or German woman; a Frau. (Dut. *vrouwe*: Ger. *Frau.*)
froward, *a.* *froh*-ard, not willing to yield to or comply with what is required; perverse; wayward; peevish. (Scand.)
frowardly, *ad.* *froh*-ard-le, in a froward manner.
frowardness, *n.* *froh*-ard-ness, a froward disposition; perversity.
frower, *n.* *froh*-er, a sharp cleaving tool; a froe.
frown, *n.* froun, a knitting of the brows in displeasure; any expression of displeasure: *v.i.* to express displeasure by contracting the brow; to look displeased; to look threatening: *v.t.* to repel by expressing displeasure; to rebuke. (O.Fr. *frongnier.*)
frowningly, *ad.* *froun*-ing-le, with a look of displeasure.
frowst, *n.* froust, fusty heat; fug; stuffiness: *v.i.* to loaf about in such [Coll.]. (*frowzy.*)
frowzy, *a.* *frou*-ze, musty; fusty; ill-smelling; untidy. (Origin unknown.)
froze, frohz, *p.* of *freeze.*
frozen, *pp.* and *a.* *froh*-zn, congealed by cold; chilled; cold in affection; void of natural heat or vigour; temporarily unrealizable (of credits, etc.). (A.S. *freosan.*)
fructescent, *a.* fruk-*tes*-ent, beginning to bear fruit.
fructiferous, *a.* fruk-*tif*-er-rus, bearing or producing fruit. (L. *fructifer*, fruitful.)
fructification, *n.* *fruk*-te-fe-*kay*-shon, the act or process of fructifying; the organs of reproduction of a plant; the fruit and its appendages [Bot.]. (L. *fructificatio*, a bearing of fruit.)
fructiform, *a.* *fruk*-te-form, of the form or appearance of fruit.
fructify, *v.t.* *fruk*-te-fy, to make fruitful; to fertilize: *v.i.* to bear fruit. (L. *fructifico*, produce.)
fructivorous, *a.* fruk-*tiv*-o-rus, feeding on fruit.
fructose, *n.* *fruk*-tose, sugar as occurring in ripe fruit; fruit-sugar.
fructuous, *a.* *fruk*-tew-us, fruitful; fertile; productive. (L. *fructuosus*, fruitful.)
frugal, *a.* *fru*-gal, economical in the use of means; sparing; thrifty; saving. (Fr.)
frugality, *n.* fru-*gal*-e-te, prudent economy; thrift.
frugally, *ad.* *fru*-ga-le, with economy.
frugalness, *n.* the quality of being frugal.
frugiferous, *a.* fru-*jif*-er-rus, producing fruit or corn. (L. *frugifer*, fertile.)
frugivorous, *a.* fru-*jiv*-o-rus, feeding on fruit [Zool.]. (L. *frux*, and *voro*, devour.)
***fruit,** *n.* froot, the produce of a tree or other plant; the matured ovary or seed-vessel of plants, or the part that contains the seeds [Bot.]; that which is produced; offspring; effect or consequence; good derived; profit: *v.i.* and *t.* to bear or to cause to produce fruit. (O.Fr.)
fruitage, *n.* *froo*-taj, fruit collectively; product.
fruitarian, *n.* froo-*tayr*-re-an, one whose main diet is fruit.
fruit-bearing, *a.* producing fruit.
fruit-bud, *n.* the bud that produces fruit.
fruit-cake, *n.* a cake containing dried fruit.
fruiter, *n.* *froot*-er, a fruit-grower; a tree that bears fruit; a ship equipped for carrying fruit.
fruiterer, *n.* *froot*-er-rer, one who deals in fruit.
fruit-fly, *n.* a small black fly whose larvæ feed on fruit.
fruitful, *a.* *froot*-ful, producing fruit in abundance; bearing children; productive.
fruitfully, *ad.* in a fruitful manner; abundantly.
fruitfulness, *n.* the quality of being fruitful.
fruitiness, *n.* *froot*-e-ness, fruity quality or flavour.
fruition, *n.* froo-*ish*-on, realization, accompanied with pleasure; enjoyment; the pleasure derived from use or possession. (O.Fr.)
fruitist, *n.* *froo*-tist, a fruit-grower.
fruitive, *a.* *froo*-e-tiv, enjoying; pertaining to fruition.
fruit-knife, *n.* a knife for paring and cutting fruit.
fruitless, *a.* *froot*-less, not bearing fruit; destitute of fruit; barren; productive of no advantage or good effect; useless.
fruitlessly, *ad.* in a fruitless manner; unprofitably.
fruitlessness, *n.* the quality of being fruitless.
fruitlet, *n.* *froot*-let, a small fruit; a single unit of a collective fruit [Bot.].
fruit-pigeon, *n.* *froot*-pij-en, a large frugivorous pigeon of India, the Malay Archipelago, and Australasia.
fruit-sugar, *n.* sugar as occurring in fruit and honey.
fruit-tree, *n.* a tree cultivated for its fruit.
fruity, *a.* *froo*-te, having the flavour of the fruit; rich; tasting of the grape (of wine); risqué, somewhat scandalous [Slang]; of exaggerated tone or quality (of the voice) [Coll.].
frumentaceous, *a.* *froo*-men-*tay*-she-us, made of, like, or of the nature of corn. (L. *frumentum*, corn.).
frumenty, *n.* *froo*-men-te, a dish made of wheat boiled in milk, with spice, sugar, etc. (O.Fr. *fromentee.*)
frump, *n.* frump, a dowdy old woman; an old fogy.
frumpish, *a.* *frump*-ish, old-fashioned; ill-natured.
frumpy, *a.* *frump*-e, frumpish.
frush, *n.* frush, the frog in a horse's foot; a discharge of a fetid matter from it.
frush, *a.* frush, brittle; easily broken [Scots.].
frustrate, *a.* frus-*trate* or *frus*-trate, vain; void; of no effect: *v.t.* to render of no effect; to bring to nothing; to baffle. (L. *frustratus*, frustrated.)
frustration, *n.* frus-*tray*-shon, the act of frustrating; disappointment; defeat.
frustule, *n.* *frus*-tewl, the two-valved siliceous shell of a diatom. (L. *frustulum*, a small piece.)
frustum, *n.* *frust*-um (*pl.* **frusta**), that part of a solid next the base, formed by cutting off the top; the part of any solid, as of a cone, pyramid, etc., between two planes [Geom.]. (L., a fragment.)
frutescent, *a.* froo-*tes*-sent, shrubby; like a shrub.
frutex, *n.* *froo*-teks, a shrub [Bot.]. (L.)
fruticetum, *n.* froo-te-*see*-tum, a collection of growing shrubs.
fruticose, *a.* *froo*-te-kose, branching like a shrub [Zool.]; pertaining to shrubs; shrubby.
fruticulose, *a.* froo-*tik*-yew-lose, branching like a small shrub [Zool.].
fry, *n.* fry, a dish of anything fried; the liver, viscera, etc., of a pig or lamb; a state of agitation [Coll.]: *v.t.* to cook in boiling fat: to cook in a frying-pan: *v.i.* to be cooked in a frying-pan. (Fr. *frire.*)
fry, *n.* fry, a swarm; little fish just spawned; a crowd of young people; a swarm of trifling objects; a salmon smolt. (Ice. *fræ*, spawn.)
fryer, *n.* *fry*-er, a frier.
frying-pan, *n.* *fry*-ing-pan, a shallow pan with a long handle, for frying meat and vegetables. **out of the frying-pan into the fire,** out of one trouble into a worse.

fub, *v.t.* fub, to cheat; to fob.
fubby, *a. fub*-be, plump; chubby.
fubsy, *a. fub*-ze, fubby.
fuchsia, *n. few*-sha, an ornamental hardy and half-hardy plant, with pendulous flowers. (L. *Fuchs*, Ger. botanist, *d.* 1566.)
fuchsine, *n. fook*-seen, the dye magenta.
fuchsite, *n. fook*-zite, a variety of white mica containing chromium.
fucivorous, *a.* few-*siv*-o-rus, feeding on seaweeds [Zool.]. (L. *fucus*, and *voro*, devour.)
fucoid, *a. few*-koyd, resembling seaweed: *n.* a fossil seaweed.
fucoidal, *a.* few-*koy*-dal, pertaining to seaweed; like seaweed. (L. *fucus*, and Gr. *eidos*, like.)
Fucus, *n. few*-kus (*pl.* **fuci**), a large genus of seaweeds [Bot.]; (*l.c.*) seaweeds generally; false show. (L.)
fuddle, *v.t. fud*-dl, to make foolish with drink; to intoxicate; to confuse: *v.i.* to tipple: *n.* a drunken bout; drink [Slang]; mental confusion.
fuddler, *n. fud*-dler, a tippler; a drunkard.
fudge, *n.* and *int.* fudj, a made-up story; stuff; nonsense; a soft, creamy sweetmeat (U.S.A.); stop-press news in a newspaper; a fudge-box [Print.]: *v.t.* to do by guess-work; to fabricate; to fake. (Probably *fadge.*)
fudge-box, *n.* an attachment to a rotary newspaper machine enabling late news to be inserted during the run [Print.].
fuel, *n. few*-el, combustible material; firing; wood, coals, gas, etc.; anything that serves to feed flame, heat, or excitement: *v.t.* to feed with fuel; to store with fuel: *v.i.* to obtain fuel. **fuel oils,** residual oils obtained in the distillation of petroleum. (O.Fr. *fouaille.*)
fuelling, *n. few*-el-ling, fuel; firing.
fuff, *n.* fuf, a puff: *v.i.* to puff; to spit (of cats) [Scots.].
fuffy, *a. fuf*-fe, puffy; light and soft.
fug, *n.* fug, unhealthy stuffiness in a room, etc.; reek; fluff and dust: *v.i.* to frowst [Coll.].
fugacious, *a.* few-*gay*-shus, fleeting; volatile; soon falling away [Bot. and Zool.]. (L. *fugax*, fleet.)
fugacity, *n.* few-*gas*-e-te, the quality of being fugacious; uncertainty; instability.
fugal, *a. fewg*-al, pertaining to a fugue or to the fugue mould.
fugato, *ad.* fu-*gah*-toh, in the fugal style: *n.* a short composition somewhat in the style of the fugue [Mus.]. (It.)
fuggy, *a. fug*-ge, badly ventilated; unhealthily stuffy.
fugitive, *a. few*-je-tiv, volatile; apt to flee away; readily escaping or disappearing; fleeting; not fixed or durable; fleeing from danger, pursuit, or duty; wandering; vagabond: *n.* one who flees from his station, duty, or danger; one who has taken refuge from punishment under another power; one not easily caught. **fugitive compositions,** occasional works written for some temporary purpose and not intended for permanence. (O.Fr. *fugitif.*)
fugitiveness, *n.* the quality of being fugitive.
fugleman, *n. few*-gl-man, a trained soldier acting as example during drill; one whose example is followed by others. (Ger. *flügel*, wing, *mann*, man.)
fugue, *n.* fewg, a contrapuntal composition on one or more short themes, each of which is equally important, each part repeating the subject at a certain interval above or below the preceding part [Mus.]. (Fr., from L. *fuga*, flight.)
fuguist, *n. fewg*-ist, a musician who composes fugues or performs them.
Führer, *n. foor*-rer, a dictator; a demagogic leader having absolute power. (Ger., leader; title borne by Adolf Hitler, 1933–45, as head of the Nazi organization.)
fulcrate, *a. ful*-krate, furnished with or supported by fulcra [Bot.].
fulcrum, *n. ful*-krum (*pl.* **fulcra**), the support on which a lever works [Mech.]; (*pl.*) accessory organs serving as defence or support [Bot. and Zool.]. (L., a prop.)
fulfil, *v.t.* full-*fil*, to accomplish; to complete, or carry into effect; to perform what is required. (A.S. *fulfyllan.*)
fulfiller, *n.* one who fulfils or accomplishes.
fulfilling, *n.* full-*fil*-ling, fulfilment.
fulfilment, *n.* full-*fil*-ment, accomplishment; completion; performance.
fulgency, *n. ful*-jen-se, brightness; effulgence.
fulgent, *a. ful*-jent, shining; dazzling; exceedingly bright. (L. *fulgens*, shining.)
fulgently, *ad. ful*-jent-le, in a fulgent manner.
fulgor, *n. ful*-gor, splendour; dazzling brightness. (L., lightning; poet. form of *fulgur.*)
fulgorous, *a. ful*-go-rus, flashing; dazzling. (L.)
fulguration, *n. ful*-gew-*ray*-shon, the sudden brightening of a fused globule of gold, etc., when the last film of dross leaves its surface [Assaying]; lightning-flash. (L. *fulgur*, a lightning flash.)
fulgurite, *n. ful*-gew-rite, a vitrified tube formed by lightning striking the surface of sand, rock, etc.; a variety of dynamite.
fuliginosity, *n.* few-*lij*-e-*nos*-e-te, the quality or state of being fuliginous.
fuliginous, *a.* few-*lij*-e-nus, sooty; smoky; dusky. (L. *fuliginosus*, sooty.)
***full,** *a.* full, having all it can contain; having no empty space; well supplied or furnished; abounding with; supplied; plump; stated; filled, as regards the imagination or memory; that fills, as a meal; complete; mature; perfect; strong; not faint; clear; exhibiting the whole surface illuminated (of the moon); high (of tides); copious; ample: *n.* complete measure; the highest state or degree; the whole; the period of full moon: *ad.* quite; to the same degree; with the whole effect; completely; directly: *v.i.* to become full: *v.t.* to make full or (of garments, etc.) more roomy. (A.S.)
full, *v.t.* full, to scour and make compact, as cloth in a mill: *v.i.* to become fulled. (O.Fr. *fuler.*)
full-aged, *a. full*-ayjd, of mature age.
full-blooded, *a.* strong; vigorous.
full-blown, *a.* fully expanded.
full-bottomed, *a. full*-bot-tomd, having a large bottom, as a wig.
full-cry, *a.* in eager chase, esp. as a mob.
full-dress, *n.* full uniform for state or other ceremonies; evening dress: *a.* at which this is expected; dressed for company.
full-drive, *ad.* at great speed [Coll.].
fuller, *n. full*-er, one whose occupation is to full cloth.
fuller, *n. full*-er, a blacksmith's set-hammer used for making grooves in iron; a groove so made: *v.t.* to make a groove thus.
fuller's-earth, *n.* a non-plastic clay consisting chiefly of hydrated silicate of calcium and magnesium, which absorbs grease and was originally used in fulling cloth.
fuller's-thistle *or* **-weed,** *n.* a teasel, *Dipsacus fullonum*, the burrs of which were used in fulling cloth.
full-eyed, *a. full*-ide, with large prominent eyes.
full-face, *a.* and *ad.* with the subject directly facing the artist or camera (of portraits).
full-faced, *a. full*-fayst, with a full broad face; with the whole face shown; bold-faced [Print.]: *n.* a fount of capitals occupying the whole of the body [Print.].
full-fashioned, *a.* so knitted as to fit the contours of the limb or figure (of garments).
full-house, *n.* a hand of cards at poker of which three are of the same value and the other two form a pair.
fulling-mill, *n.* a mill for fulling cloths.
full-length, *a.* extending the whole length; showing the whole figure (of portraits).
fullness, *n. full*-ness, the state of being full; completeness.
full-pitch, *n.* a ball that pitches inside the popping crease [Cricket].
full-rigged, *a. full*-rigd, having at least three masts each with its full complement of square-sails.
full-stop, *n.* the period (.) used in punctuation; the end; an abrupt finish.
full-swing, *ad.* full-*swing*, at full speed.
fully, *ad. full*-e, in full manner; completely. **fully fashioned,** full-fashioned.
fulmar, *n. full*-mar, an Arctic sea-bird, *Fulmarus glacialis*, allied to the petrels.
fulminant, *a. ful*-me-nant, fulminating; coming on suddenly (of diseases): *n.* a fulminating or explosive substance.
fulminate, *n. ful*-me-nate, a salt of fulminic acid; a detonating compound containing this: *v.i.* to detonate; to hurl forth ecclesiastical censures as with the force of a thunderbolt; to thunder:

v.t. to utter or send out, as a denunciation or censure; to cause to explode. **fulminating oil,** nitro-glycerine. **fulminating powder,** an explosive compound, esp. one containing nitre, carbonate of potash, and sulphur. (L. *fulminatus*, thundered.)
fulmination, *n.* ful-me-*nay*-shon, the act of fulminating; denunciation of censure or threats; a threat denounced.
fulminatory, *a.* *ful*-me-na-to-re, thundering; striking terror.
fulmine, *v.i.* and *v.t.* *ful*-min, to speak as though fulminating. (Fr. *fulminer.*)
fulminic, *a.* ful-*min*-ik, pertaining to or designating a nitrogenous acid that forms highly explosive salts.
fulsome, *a.* *full*-sum, disgusting by excess or grossness; over-obsequious. (M.E. *fulsum.*)
fulsomely, *ad.* *full*-sum-le, in a fulsome manner.
fulsomeness, *n.* the quality of being fulsome.
fulvid, *a.* *ful*-vid, fulvous.
fulvous, *a.* *ful*-vus, tawny; of a tawny yellow. (L. *fulvus.*)
Fum, *n.* fum, the Chinese phœnix, one of the former imperial emblems. (Chin. *feng-hwang.*)
fumacious, *a.* few-*may*-shus, smoky; connected with smoke; addicted to smoking. (L. *fumus*, smoke.)
fumade, *n.* few-*mahd*, a smoked pilchard. (Sp.)
fumage, *n.* *few*-maj, a tax on chimneys; hearth-money.
fumarole, *n.* *few*-ma-role, a hole from which smoke issues in a volcano or sulphur-mine; a femerelle. (It. *fumaruolo.*)
fumatorium, *n.* *few*-ma-*taw*-re-um, a fumatory.
fumatory, *n.* *few*-ma-to-re, a fumigating chamber: *a.* fumacious.
fumble, *v.i.* *fum*-bl, to grope about; to handle awkwardly; to turn over and over aimlessly; to stammer: *v.t.* to manage awkwardly; to crowd or tumble together. (Dut. *fommelen.*)
fumbler, *n.* *fum*-bler, one who fumbles.
fumblingly, *ad.* *fum*-bling-le, in a fumbling manner.
fume, *n.* fewm, smoke; vapour; narcotic or alcoholic exhalation; breaking out of anger or passion; anything unsubstantial: *v.i.* to emit smoke; to pass off in vapours; to chafe, to be in suppressed rage: *v.t.* to dry in smoke; to cure, stain, or darken with smoke; to perfume; to disperse in vapours; to flatter much. (O.Fr. *fum*, from L. *fumus.*)
fumeless, *a.* *fewm*-less, free from fumes.
fumet, *n.* *few*-met, the dung of deer, etc.
fumette, *n.* fu-*met*, scent of overkept game, or of meat when cooking. (Fr.)
fumid, *a.* *few*-mid, smoky; vaporous.
fumidity, *n.* few-*mid*-e-te, smokiness.
fumidness, *n.* *few*-mid-ness, fumidity.
fumiferous, *a.* few-*mif*-er-rus, producing smoke. (L. *fumifer*, smoking.)
fumifugist, *n.* few-*mif*-yew-jist, he who or that which drives away fumes. (L. *fumus*, and *fugo*, put to flight.)
fumigant, *n.* *few*-me-gant, a substance used for fumigation.
fumigate, *v.t.* *few*-me-gate, to disinfect by smoke or vapour; to perfume. (L. *fumigatus*, smoked.)
fumigation, *n.* few-me-*gay*-shon, the action of producing odorous fumes; the act or process of fumigating.
fumigator, *n.* *few*-me-gay-tor, one who or that which fumigates; an apparatus for cleansing, disinfecting, etc., by means of fumes.
fumingly, *ad.* *few*-ming-le, in a fuming manner; angrily; in a rage.
fumishness, *n.* *few*-mish-ness, fretfulness.
fumitory, *n.* *few*-me-to-re, a hardy annual plant of the genus *Fumaria.* (Fr. *fumeterre.*)
fumose, *a.* few-*mohs*, producing fumes or vapours; fumy; of smoke colour [Bot.]. (L. *fumosus*, smoky.)
fumy, *a.* *few*-me, smoky; composed of or abounding in fumes.
fun, *n.* fun, matter for laughter; sport; merriment; frolicsome amusement. **for** *or* **in fun,** not with serious intent. **to make fun of,** to turn to ridicule; to twit or quiz. (Prob. connected with *fond.*)
funambulation, *n.* few-*nam*-bew-*lay*-shon, rope-dancing. (L. *funis*, a rope, *ambūlare*, to walk.)
funambulatory, *a.* few-*nam*-bew-la-to-re, pertaining to tight-rope performances.
funambulist, *n.* few-*nam*-bew-list, a performer on the tight-rope; a rope-dancer.
function, *n.* *funk*-shon, office, employment or duty belonging to a particular station or character; the doing, executing, or performing of anything; a public or official ceremony; an elaborate social occasion; the specific use of any organ [Anat., Zool., Bot.] or of mind or body; power; a quantity so connected with another that any change in the one correspondingly affects the other [Math.]: *v.t.* to operate; to fulfil its function. (Fr.)
functional, *a.* *funk*-shon-al, pertaining to some function; official; affecting functions but not structure; performed by the functions.
functionalism, *n.* *funk*-shon-a-lizm, the theory or practice of adapting method, materials, etc. to the end in view [esp. Arch.].
functionalistic, *a.* funk-shon-a-*lis*-tik, of or pertaining to functionalism.
functionally, *ad.* by means of the functions.
functionary, *n.* *funk*-shon-a-re, a public official; anyone authorized to perform a duty: *a.* functional; formal.
functionate, *v.i.* *funk*-shon-ate, to function; to do its work; to officiate.
functionless, *a.* *funk*-shon-less, without a function.
fund, *n.* fund, a stock or capital; assets; a sum of money, or of money and securities, the amount of which is unvarying and the income of which is appropriated as the foundation of some commercial or other operation: (*pl.*) money lent to a government to constitute a national debt or the stock of a national debt; money collected and set apart for some object; any store laid up for use; abundance; *v.t.* to provide and appropriate a fund for paying interest; to convert into bonds; to change a floating or unsecured debt into a permanent loan; to place money in a fund. (Fr. *fond.*)
fundable, *a.* *fun*-da-bl, that can be funded.
fundament, *n.* *fun*-da-ment, the seat of the body; the buttocks; the anus. (O.Fr. *fondement.*)
fundamental, *a.* fun-da-*men*-tal, pertaining to or serving for the foundation or basis; primary; radical; essential: *n.* a primary or radical principle; that which serves as the groundwork of a system; an essential; the root of a chord [Mus.]. **fundamental bass,** a bass formed of fundamentals; the generating tone of a series of harmonics.
fundamentalism, *n.* fun-da-*men*-ta-lizm, a belief in the literal accuracy of the Bible, esp. with reference to the Creation, the miracles, the Virgin Birth, and the physical resurrection of Christ.
fundamentalist, *n.* fun-da-*men*-ta-list, one who believes in fundamentalism.
fundamentality, *n.* *fund*-a-men-*tal*-e-te, the quality or state of being fundamental.
fundamentally, *ad.* fun-da-*men*-ta-le, in a fundamental manner; essentially.
funded, *pp.* and *a.* *fun*-ded, placed in the funds; deposited as a fund for the payment of interest. **funded debt,** that part of the public debt for the payment of the interest of which certain funds are appropriated.
fundless, *a.* *fund*-less, destitute of funds.
funebrial, *a.* few-*nee*-bre-al, pertaining to funerals.
funeral, *n.* *few*-ne-ral, solemn and ceremonious burial; the ceremony of burying a deceased person; the procession of persons attending the burial of the dead: *a.* pertaining to or used at a burial. **it's not my funeral,** it is no concern of mine. [Slang]. (O.Fr. from L.)
funerary, *a.* *few*-ne-re-re, pertaining to or associated with burial.
funereal, *a.* few-*neer*-re-al, suiting or pertaining to a funeral; dismal; mournful. (L. *funereus.*)
funereally, *ad.* in a funereal manner.
fungaceous, *a.* fung-*gay*-shus, pertaining to the fungi; of the nature of a fungus.
fungal, *a.* *fung*-gal, fungaceous: *n.* a fungus.
fungate, *v.i.* *fung*-gate, to grow in the manner or the form of a fungus [Med.].
fungi, *n.pl.* *fun*-jy, *pl.* of *fungus.*
fungibles, *n.pl.* *fun*-je-blz, movable goods, estimable by number, measure, or weight, that can be replaced by others in the execution of an order [Scots. Law]. (Late L. *fungibilis.*)
fungic, *a.* *fun*-jik, pertaining to or obtained from fungi.

fungicide, *n.* *fun*-je-side, a preparation for destroying fungi. (L. *fungus*, and *cædo*, kill.)
fungiform, *a.* *fun*-je-form, round-headed like a mushroom.
fungin, *n.* *fun*-jin, a variety of cellulose occurring in fungi.
fungivorous, *a.* fun-*jiv*-o-rus, feeding on fungi. (L. *fungus*, and *voro*, devour.)
fungoid, *a.* *fung*-goyd, of the nature of a fungus; having the appearance of a mushroom; fungous. (L. *fungus*, and *eidos*, like.)
fungoidal, *a.* fung-*goy*-dal, of the nature of or resembling fungus.
fungologist, *n.* fung-*gol*-o-jist, a student of fungi.
fungology, *n.* fung-*gol*-o-je, the science treating of fungi. (L. *fungus*, and Gr. *logos*, science.)
fungosity, *n.* fung-*gos*-e-te, a fungoid growth or excrescence [Med.].
fungous, *a.* *fung*-gus, like a fungus; excrescent; spongy; of mushroom growth and unsubstantial.
fungus, *n.* *fung*-gus (*pl.* **fungi** *or* **funguses**), a member of a large natural class of cellular and flowerless plants, comprehending the several varieties of mushrooms, toadstools, and the microscopic plants which form mildew, mould, etc.; a spongy excrescence, as proud-flesh formed in wounds [Med.]. (L., a mushroom.)
fungusy, *a.* *fung*-gus-e, resembling fungi; having a fungoid growth or disease [Path.].
funicle, *n.* *few*-ne-kl, a funiculus [Bot.].
funicular, *a.* few-*nik*-yew-lar, pertaining to, dependent on, or worked by a rope or cable; a funicular railway. **funicular railway,** one worked by means of a cable, esp. on a mountain.
funiculus, *n.* few-*nik*-yew-lus (*pl.* **funiculi**), a cord or bundle of fibres, as esp. the umbilical or the spermatic cord [Anat.]; the stalk connecting the ovule and placenta [Bot.]. (L., a little cord.)
funis, *n.* *few*-nis, the umbilical cord [Anat.]. (L.)
funk, *n.* funk, fear; timidity; one who funks: *v.t.* to be afraid of; to avoid through fear. **funk-hole,** a place of refuge; a hide-out [Slang].
funky, *a.* *fung*-ke, in a funk; easily frightened; disposed to kick (of a horse).
funnel, *n.* *fun*-el, an inverted hollow cone with a pipe for conveying fluids into close vessels; a metal chimney, esp. of a steamship or steam-engine; the inside of a flue. (M.E. *fonel*, L. *fundere*, to pour.)
funnelled, *a.* *fun*-eld, having a funnel or funnels; funnel-shaped.
funnily, *ad.* *fun*-e-le, in a funny manner.
funniment, *n.* *fun*-e-ment, drollery; a joke.
funning, *n.* *fun*-ing, waggishness; drollery.
funniosity, *n.* fun-e-*os*-e-te, waggery, jocularity; a comicality [Coll.].
funny, *a.* *fun*-e, droll; comical; full of fun; queer; *n.* a light clinker-built sculling boat.
funny-bone, *n.* *fun*-e-bone, the point of the elbow.
fur, *n.* fur, the short, fine, soft hair of certain animals, growing thick on the skin; the skins of certain wild animals with the fur; strips of dressed skin with fur, used on garments for lining or as trimming; a coat of morbid matter collected on the tongue, esp. in fever; a coating on the interior of boilers, etc., deposited by hard water; a fungoid growth on stale food, old wine-bottles, etc.: *a.* consisting of fur: *v.t.* to line, face, or cover with fur; to cover with morbid matter, as the tongue; to nail small strips of board on joists, rafters, etc., in order to make a level surface [Carp.]: *v.i.* to become encrusted with fur. (O.Fr. *forre.*)
furacious, *a.* few-*ray*-shus, thievish. (L. *fur*, a thief.)
furbelow, *n.* *fur*-be-lo, a puckered flounce attached as trimming to a gown, petticoat, etc.; the seaweed, *Laminaria bulbosa*: *v.t.* to put a furbelow on. (Dial. Fr. *farbala.*)
furbish, *v.t.* *fur*-bish, to rub or scour to brightness; to polish; to burnish. (Fr. *fourbir.*)
furbisher, *n.* *fur*-bish-er, one who or that which furbishes or cleans.
furcate, *a.* *fur*-kate, forked; branching like the prongs of a fork: *v.i.* to fork; to ramify. (L. *furca*, a fork.)
furcation, *n.* fur-*kay*-shon, a branching like a fork.
furcula, *n.* *fur*-kew-la, that part of the shoulder-girdle of a bird which is formed by the united clavicles; the merrythought. (L.)
furcular, *a.* *fur*-kew-lar, pertaining to or resembling the furcula.
furfur, *n.* *fur*-fur, dandruff; scurf. (L., bran.)
furfuraceous, *a.* fur-few-*ray*-shus, scaly; scurfy.
furfural, *n.* *fur*-few-ral, a colourless oil obtained by distillation from bran, starch, etc. [Chem.].
furfuration, *n.* fur-few-*ray*-shon, the falling of scurf from the head.
furioso, *ad.* foo-re-*oh*-zoh, with great passion or energy [Mus.]. (It.)
furious, *a.* *fewr*-re-us, rushing with impetuosity; transported with passion; frenzied. (L. *furiosus.*)
furiously, *ad.* *fewr*-re-us-le, in a furious manner.
furiousness, *n.* the quality of being furious.
furl, *v.t.* furl, to roll up, as a sail, close to the yard, stay, or mast; to roll up closely: *n.* a curl or roll of anything furled. (Perhaps from O.Fr. *fardeler*, to truss.)
furlong, *n.* *fur*-long, the eighth of a mile; 40 poles; 220 yards (a furrow long). (A.S.)
furlough, *n.* *fur*-loh, leave of absence, esp. to a soldier: *v.t.* to grant leave of absence to. (Dut. *verlof*, Ger. *verlaub*, permission.)
furmety, *n.* *fur*-me-te, frumenty.
furnace, *n.* *fur*-nace, any enclosed fireplace for high temperatures; a firebox; severe affliction, conceived as sent to purify: *v.t.* to cast into or to heat in a furnace. (O.Fr. *fornaise.*)
furnish, *v.t.* *fur*-nish, to supply with anything necessary; to equip; to fit up; to supply. (O.Fr. *fournir*, to furnish.)
furnisher, *n.* *fur*-nish-er, one who furnishes; a dealer in household furniture.
furnishment, *n.* *fur*-nish-ment, the act of supplying; supplies.
furniture, *n.* *fur*-ne-ture, that with which anything is furnished; movable articles added to the interior of a house or apartment for use or convenience; chattels; outfit; equipment, as of a knight, or a horse; decorations; the implements of an art; pieces of wood or metal placed between and around pages in a forme to keep the type in place and allow of margins [Print.]; the brasswork, locks, etc., of windows, doors, shutters, etc., of a house [Arch.]; the masts, rigging, tackle, etc., of a ship [Naut.]. (Fr. *fourniture.*)
furor, *n.* *few*-ror, fury; rage; madness. (L.)
furore, *n.* foo-*raw*-ray, an outburst of enthusiasm; a craze. (It.)
furrier, *n.* *fu*-re-ur, a dealer in furs; one who dresses or manufactures furs. (O.Fr. *fourreur.*)
furriery, *n.* *fu*-re-ur-re, furs in general; the business of a furrier; trade in furs.
furring, *n.* *fur*-ring, trimming, etc., with furs; fur deposited inside boilers, on decaying food, etc.; small slips nailed on joists or rafters to level a surface; doubling planks on the side of a ship.
furrow, *n.* *fu*-ro, a trench made by a plough; a trench or groove in wood or metal; a rut; a wrinkle on the face: *v.t.* to make furrows or grooves in; to plough; to wrinkle. **furrow-drain,** *n.* a deep open channel made by a plough to carry off water. (A.S. *furh.*)
furrowy, *a.* *fu*-ro-e, in furrows.
furry, *a.* *fur*-re, covered with, clad in, or resembling fur; consisting of fur or skins; coated with a deposit of fur.
further, *a.* *fur*-ther, farther; more distant; additional: *ad.* to a greater distance or degree; besides: *v.t.* to help forward; to promote. (A.S. *furthrian.*)
furtherance, *n.* *fur*-ther-ance, promotion; advancement.
furtherer, *n.* *fur*-ther-er, one who helps forward.
furthermore, *ad.* *fur*-ther-more, moreover; besides.
furthermost, *a.* *fur*-ther-most, remotest.
furthersome, *a.* *fur*-ther-sum, helping forward; tending to promote; advantageous.
furthest, *a.* *fur*-thest, most distant either in time or place: *ad.* at the greatest distance.
furtive, *a.* *fur*-tiv, stealthy; sly; surreptitious. (Fr. *furtif.*)
furtively, *ad.* in a furtive manner; by stealth.
furtiveness, *n.* stealth; underhandedness.
furuncle, *n.* *few*-rung-kl, a superficial inflammatory tumour suppurating with a central core; a boil. (L., a tiny thief.)
furunculoid, *a.* few-*rung*-kew-loyd, pertaining to or resembling a furuncle.

furunculosis, *n.* few-*rung*-kew-*loh*-sis, the condition of being affected with boils [Path.].
fury, *n.* *fewr*-re, rage; madness; frenzy; (*cap.*) one of the goddesses of vengeance [Myth.]; a passionate, violent woman. (Fr. *furie.*)
furze, *n.* furz, gorse; whin; a thorny, yellow-flowered, evergreen shrub of the genus *Ulex*. (A.S. *fyrs.*)
furze-chat, *n.* the whinchat, *Saxicola rubetra.*
furzeling, *n.* *furz*-ling, the Dartford warbler, *Melizophilus undatus.*
furzy, *a.* *fur*-ze, overgrown with furze.
fusain, *n.* *few*-zane, a charcoal-like constituent of coal forming a chief cause of dust in mines. (Fr.)
fusarole, *n.* *few*-sa-role, a moulding placed next below the echinus of columns in the Doric, Ionic, and Corinthian orders [Arch.]. (It.)
fusc, *a.* fusk, fuscous.
fuscous, *a.* *fus*-kus, brownish black; dusky; dingy. (L. *fuscus*, swarthy.)
fuse, *v.t.* fewz, to melt; to liquefy by heat; to unite as by melting together: *v.i.* to be melted; to be liquefied. (L. *fusus*, poured.)
fuse, *n.* fewz, a small tube filled with combustible matter; a device to explode a shell, etc., after its discharge, either in its flight (**time-fuse**), on striking its objective (**percussion fuse**), or at a given time after its striking (**delayed action fuse**); a safety device of fusible metal, esp. a wire inserted in a circuit with a maximum current-carrying capacity lower than the safe current-carrying capacity of the rest of the circuit [Elect.]. (L. *fusus.*)
fusee, *n.* few-*zee*, the grooved conical wheel of a watch or clock, round which the chain is wound; a match not easily extinguished when lighted; a fuse. (L. *fusus*, a spindle.)
fusee, *n.* few-*zee*, a light musket; a fusil.
fuselage, *n.* *few*-se-laj, the body or framework of an aeroplane, carrying the wings and tail-unit. (Fr. *fuselé*, spindle-shaped.)
fusel-oil, *n.* *few*-zl-oyl, a malodorous and nauseous spirit, distilled from fermented potatoes, rye, etc., and consisting chiefly of amyl alcohol. (Ger. *fusel*, inferior spirits.)
fusibility, *n.* *few*-ze-*bil*-e-te, the quality of being fusible.
fusible, *a.* *few*-ze-bl, that may be fused or melted; easily melted. **fusible metal,** any alloy of bismuth, lead, and tin which melts at the heat of boiling water, or is so compounded as to melt at different definite temperatures. (Fr.)
fusiform, *a.* *few*-ze-form, shaped like a spindle; tapering to each end [Bot.]. (L. *fusus*, and *form.*)
fusil, *n.* *few*-zil, a light flint-lock musket. (O.Fr. *fuisil*, flint-lock steel.)
fusil, *n.* *few*-zil, a bearing of a rhomboidal figure [Her.]. (Fr., from L. *fusus*, a spindle.)
fusilier, *n.* few-ze-*leer*, a soldier of an infantry regiment originally armed with fusils. (Fr.)
fusillade, *n.* few-ze-*lade*, a continuous discharge of firearms; any rapid discharge (as of questions, etc.); *v.t.* to subject to a fusillade. (Fr.)
fusion, *n.* *few*-zhon, the operation of melting by heat; the state of being melted by heat; coalition. (Fr.)
fusionist, *n.* *few*-zhon-ist, one in favour of fusion, esp. political coalition.
fuss, *n.* fuss, a tumult; bustle; unnecessary ado about trifles: *v.i.* to make a fuss. (Imit.)
fussily, *ad.* *fus*-se-le, in a fussy manner.
fussiness, *n.* the state of being fussy.
fussy, *a.* *fus*-se, busy about trifles; making a fuss; very fastidious [Coll.]; over-elaborate [Art].
fust, *n.* fust, a strong musty smell; the shaft of a column [Arch.]: *v.i.* to become mouldy; to smell ill. (O.Fr. *fuste*, a cask.)
fustanella, *n.* *fus*-ta-*nel*-la, a white plaited linen kilt forming part of the distinctive male costume of certain Albanians and modern Greeks. (As *fustian.*)
fusteric, *n.* *fus*-ter-rik, the yellow colouring matter of fustic.
fustet, *n.* *fus*-tet, the young, or European, fustic.
fustian, *n.* *fus*-te-an, a kind of coarse thick twilled cotton cloth; an inflated style of writing; bombast: *a.* made of fustian; swelling above the dignity of the thoughts or subject; ridiculously tumid; bombastic. (*Fustat*, a suburb of Cairo, where it was made.)
fustianist, *n.* *fus*-te-a-nist, one who writes bombast.
fustic, *n.* *fus*-tik, the wood of either *Chlorophora tinctoria*, a tropical American tree, or *Cotinus coggygria*, of Europe, each of which affords a yellow dye. (Fr. *fustoc.*)
fustigate, *v.t.* *fus*-te-gate, to beat with a cudgel. (L. *fustigatus*, cudgelled.)
fustigation, *n.* fus-te-*gay*-shon, cudgelling.
fustilarian, *n.* fus-te-*lare*-re-an, a low fellow; a scoundrel; a low, frouzy woman.
fustilug, *n.* *fus*-te-lug, a gross, fat, unwieldly person.
fustiness, *n.* *fus*-te-ness, a fusty state or quality; ill smell from mouldiness, or mouldiness itself.
fusty, *a.* *fus*-te, mouldy; ill-smelling.
futchel, *n.* *futch*-el, the beam along the bottom of a carriage which supports the pole and splinter-bar.
futhorc, *n.* *footh*-ork, the Runic alphabet, so called from the first six letters, *f, u, th, o, r*, and *k*.
futile, *a.* *few*-tile, trifling; useless; frivolous; of no avail. (L. *futilis*, leaky.)
futilely, *ad.* *few*-tile-le, in a futile manner.
futility, *n.* few-*til*-e-te, worthlessness; uselessness.
futtock, *n.* *fut*-ok, one of the crooked timbers forming the lower part of the compound rib of a ship [Naut.]. **futtock plates,** iron plates at the head of a lower mast to which the futtock shrouds and the dead eyes of the topmast rigging are secured. **futtock shrouds,** the short shrouds running inwards to a lower mast from the futtock plates above [Naut.].
***future,** *a.* *few*-tewr, that is to come; expressing action not yet taking place [Gram.]: *n.* time to come; the future tense [Gram.]; prospective state or condition, etc.; one's future spouse [Coll.]; (*pl.*) stocks or commodities dealt in under a contract to be fulfilled at some future date. **future perfect,** expressing the past in reference to an assumed future. **future tense,** the modification of a verb which expresses a future act or event [Gram.]. (O.Fr. *futur.*)
futurism, *n.* *few*-tewr-izm, a short-lived, violently anti-tradition art movement originating in Italy about 1910.
futurist, *n.* *few*-tewr-ist, a practiser of futurism; one who maintains that the scriptural prophecies have yet to be fulfilled [Theol.]: *a.* futuristic.
futuristic, *a.* few-tewr-*ris*-tik, pertaining to or characterized by futurism.
futurition, *n.* few-tewr-*rish*-on, the state of being to come hereafter; a futurity.
futurity, *n.* few-*tewr*-re-te, future time; time to come; event to come; the state of being yet to come.
fuzee, *n.* few-*zee*, a fusee; a fusil.
fuzz, *n.* fuz, fine, light particles; fluff; loose, volatile matter: *v.i.* to fly off in minute particles: *v.t.* to cover with fuzz.
fuzz-ball, *n.* a puff-ball.
fuzzle, *v.t.* *fuz*-zl, to fuddle or intoxicate.
fuzzy, *a.* *fuz*-ze, having a fuzz; fluffy; woolly; blurred; muzzy.
fy, *int.* fy, fie!
fyke, *n.* fike, a long hooped bag-net for catching sea-fish. (Dut. *fuik*, net.)
fylfot, *n.* *fil*-fot, the swastika, a rectangular cross with the arms bent at right angles.
fyrd, *n.* furd, the full military force of Britain under the Anglo-Saxons. (A.S.)
fytte, *n.* fit, a fit, or short canto.

G

G jee, the seventh letter and the fifth consonant of the English alphabet. It has two principal sounds, the hard or close, as in *gave, got, gut, glue, grow*, and the soft or *j* sound, as in *gem, gibbet, rage*; and a third (that of *zh*, as in *azure*) in certain French words, as *rouge, garage*. It is silent in some words, as *benign* and *gnat*. **G-man,** a Federal Government police-agent [U.S.A.]. **G-suit,** a garment designed to prevent an airman from blacking out in a spin, etc. ("G" here = "gravity"). In music, G is the fifth note of the natural scale, corresponding to Italian *sol*. **G clef,** treble clef.

gab, *n.* gab, empty talk; the mouth: *v.i.* to talk much and idly. (Dut. *gabberen*, to chatter.)

gabardine, *n.* *gab*-ar-deen, gaberdine.

gabble, *n.* *gab*-bl, loud or rapid talk without meaning; inarticulate sounds rapidly uttered: *v.i.* to talk fast and without meaning; to utter inarticulate sounds with rapidity. (As *gab*.)

gabbler, *n.* *gab*-bler, one who gabbles.

gabbro, *n.* *gab*-bro, any of a large group of granular igneous rocks mainly composed of felspar and augite. (It.)

gabby, *a.* *gab*-be, loquacious [U.S.A.].

gabelle, *n.* ga-*bel*, a tax or excise duty, levied before the Revolution, on salt in France. (Fr.)

gaberdine, *n.* *gab*-er-deen, a woollen material similar to serge; a twill fabric; a coarse frock or loose upper garment, esp. as worn by Jews in the Middle Ages; a mean dress. (O.Fr. *gauvardine*.)

gaberlunzie, *n.* gab-er-*lun*-ze, a wandering beggar; a beadsman [Scots].

gabion, *n.* *gay*-be-on, a cylindrical basket of wicker work or other material, filled with earth [Fort.]. (Fr.)

gabionade, *n.* *gay*-be-o-*nade*, an obstruction formed by gabions.

gable, *n.* *gay*-bl, the triangular end of a building, from the eaves to the top; an architectural feature of this appearance. (Fr.)

gable-end, *n.* *gay*-bl-end, the outside end wall of a house when there is a gable.

gablet, *n.* *gay*-blet, a small ornamental gable-shaped canopy, etc. [Arch.].

gable-window, *n.* a window in a gable.

gaby, *n.* *gay*-be, a silly foolish person.

gad, *n.* gad, a sharp metal spike; a goad; a gadling; a wedge or ingot of steel or iron; a pointed mining chisel; a rod. (Ice. *gaddr*.)

gad, *v.i.* gad, to rove idly for pleasure or without any fixed purpose; to straggle (of plants). (Etym. doubtful.)

gadabout, *n.* *gad*-a-bout, an idler who roves much abroad; a runabout.

gadder, *n.* *gad*-er, one who roves about idly.

gaddish, *a.* *gad*-ish, disposed to gad about.

gadfly, *n.* *gad*-fly, the horse-fly; a dipterous insect whose sting is often maddening to animals; a gadder; a persistent tormentor [Fig.].

gadget, *n.* *gaj*-et, a contrivance of any sort, or any small part of a machine.

Gadhelic, *a.* ga-*del*-ik, pertaining to the Gaelic branch of the Celts or the Celtic language: *n.* the language of the Gaelic Celts. (Gael. *Gaidhealach*.)

gadling, *n.* *gad*-ling, a small steel spike on mailed gauntlets [Antiq.].

gadoid, *a.* *gay*-doyd, of or pertaining to the codfish family: *n.* one of the codfish family. (L. *gadus*, and Gr. *eidos*, like.)

gadolinite, *n.* *gad*-o-lin-ite, a rare black or brownish silicate of beryllium, iron, and yttrium. (John *Gadolin*, Finnish chemist, *d.* 1852.)

gadolinium, *n.* gad-o-*lin*-e-um, a rare metallic element (of the rare earth group), discovered in 1886 and present in gadolinite, black monazite, etc.

gadroon, *n.* ga-*droon*, an ornamental edge of inverted fluting [Arch.].

gadwall, *n.* *gad*-wawl, the large freshwater migratory duck, *Anas streperus*.

gadzooks, *int.* gad-*zooks*, an obsolete oath or expletive. (*God*, and perhaps *houghs* or *hooks*.)

Gaekwar, *n.* *gike*-wahr, the title of the ruling prince of Baroda. (Marathi, literally, cowherd.)

Gael, *n.* gayl, one of the early Celtic inhabitants of Ireland and Scotland; a member of the Gaelic speaking branch of the Celts.

Gaelic, *a.* *gay*-lik *or* *gal*-lik, pertaining to the Gaels: *n.* the language of the Gaels, still spoken in the Highlands of Scotland. (Gael. *Gaidhealach*.)

gaff, *n.* gaf, a boat-hook or light spear used by fishermen; a boom or yard, working on jaws, to extend the upper edge of a fore-and-aft sail: *v.t.* to secure (a fish) with a gaff. (Fr. *gaffe*.)

gaff, *n.* gaf, a low-grade theatre or music-hall, etc.

gaff, *n.* gaf, outcry; conversation. **to blow the gaff,** to divulge information, esp. without authority; to betray a confidence [Slang].

gaffe, *n.* gaf, a social error, indiscretion, or solecism; a bloomer. (Fr.)

gaffer, *n.* *gaf*-fer, an old rustic, usually in familiarity or contempt; an overseer. (*grandfather*.)

gaffle, *n.* *gaf*-fl, an artificial spur, put on cocks when set to fight; a steel lever to bend cross-bows. (Dut. *gaffel*, fork.)

gag, *n.* gag, something thrust into the mouth to prevent speaking; an instrument inserted in the mouth to keep it open [Surg.]; an interpolation by an actor to his verbal part; in Parliament, the closure: *v.t.* to stop, or [Surg.] to keep open, the mouth by thrusting something into it; to silence forcibly; to add to a speech, as by an actor. (Imit.)

gaga, *a.* *gah*-gah, fatuous; slightly idiotic; daft [Slang].

gage, *n.* gaje, a pledge; a security forfeited on non-fulfilment of the pledge; a challenge; something thrown down as a challenge, to be taken up by the acceptor: *v.t.* to pledge or deposit as a pledge; to bind by pledge; to risk or wager; to guarantee. (O.Fr.)

gage, *n.* and *v.t.* gaje, gauge.

gage, *n.* gaje, a greengage, a variety of plum.

gagger, *n.* *gag*-ger, one who gags; a lifting implement used by founders.

gaggle, *n.* *gag*-gl, a flock of geese on the water; a mob of women (in contempt): *v.i.* to make a noise like a goose; to cackle.

gahnite, *n.* *gah*-nite, zinc aluminate, a grey crystalline mineral of the spinel group.

gaiety, *n.* *gay*-e-te, the state of being gay; merriment; (*pl.*) festivities; finery; show. (Fr. *gaieté*.)

gaily, *ad.* *gay*-le, in a gay manner; showily.

gain, *n.* gane, something obtained as an advantage; acquisition, esp. of wealth; increase in value; profit; interest: *v.t.* to obtain by industry or the employment of capital; to acquire; to earn; to obtain by superiority or success; to win; to obtain; to win to one's side or over; to reach: *v.i.* to have profit; to encroach or advance on; to gain ground on; to prevail against or have the advantage; to obtain influence with. **to gain ground,** to advance in any undertaking. **to gain over,** to draw to one's party or interest. **to gain the wind,** to attain the windward side of another ship [Naut.]. **to gain upon,** to overtake little by little. (O.Fr.)

gainable, *a.* *gane*-a-bl, that may be gained.

gainer, *n.* *gane*-er, one who gains advantage, profit, or interest.

gainful, *a.* *gane*-ful, profitable; advantageous.

gainfully, *ad.* *gane*-ful-le, with increase of wealth. **gainfully employed,** in work or office for which payment is received.

gainfulness, *n.* *gane*-ful-ness, profit; advantage.

gainings, *n.pl.* *gane*-ingz, profits; what one has gained by labour or successful enterprise.

gainless, *a.* *gane*-less, bringing no profit or advantage.

gainly, *a.* *gane*-le, comely; shapely; elegant.

gainsay, *v.t.* *gane*-say, to contradict; to deny what another says; to dispute. *p.* and *pp.* **gainsaid,** gane-*sed.* (Ice. *gegn,* against, and *say.*)

gainsayer, *n.* *gane*-say-er, one who gainsays; an opposer.

gair-fowl, *n.* *gare*-fowl, the gare-fowl.

gait, *n.* gate, manner of moving on foot; carriage. (Scand.)

gait, *n.* gate, a single sheaf of reaped corn bound at the top: *v.t.* to set up in gaits (of corn).

gaited, *a.* *gate*-ed, having a particular gait.

gaiter, *n.* *gate*-er, a covering for the calf and ankle, usually fitting down upon the shoe: *v.t.* to dress with gaiters. (Fr. *guêtre.*)

gal, *n.* gal, girl [Slang].

gala, *n.* *gah*-la, festivity; a fête or festival. **gala dress,** festive or bright-coloured attire. (It.)

galactagogue, *n.* ga-*lak*-ta-gog, a medicine which promotes the secretion of milk: *a.* having this action. (Gr. *gala,* milk, *ago,* lead.)

galactic, *a.* ga-*lak*-tik, lactic; pertaining to the galaxy or Milky Way. (Gr. *gala, galaktos,* milk.)

galactin, *n.* ga-*lak*-tin, a nitrogenous substance obtained from milk and from the sap of certain plants.

galactocele, *n.* ga-*lak*-to-seel, a tumour in the breast induced by an obstruction in the mammary glands [Path.]. (Gr. *galaktos,* milk, *kēlē,* tumour.)

galactometer, *n.* gal-lak-*tom*-e-ter, a lactometer.

galactophagist, *n.* gal-lak-*tof*-a-jist, one who subsists on milk. (Gr. *gala,* and *phago,* eat.)

galactophagous, *a.* gal-lak-*tof*-a-gus, feeding on milk.

galactophore, *n.* ga-*lak*-to-for, a milk-duct [Anat.].

galactopoietic, *a.* ga-*lak*-to-poy-*et*-ik, increasing the flow of milk: *n.* a substance that effects this [Med.]. (Gr. *gala,* and *poieo,* make.)

galactorrhœa, *n.* ga-lak-to-*ree*-ah, excessive secretion of milk [Med.]. (Gr. *gala,* and *rheo,* flow.)

galactosis, *n.* gal-ak-*toh*-sis, the secretion of milk.

Galago, *n.* ga-*lay*-go, a genus, or (*l.c.*) a member of the genus, of nocturnal African lemurs.

galah, *n.* ga-*lah,* a species of Australian cockatoo.

galalith, *n.* *gal*-a-lith, trade-name of a hard-setting plastic material manufactured on a basis of casein. (Gr. *gala,* milk, *lithos,* stone.)

Galanthus, *n.* ga-*lan*-thus, the snowdrop genus of plants. (Gr. *gala,* and *anthos,* a flower.)

galantine, *n.* gal-an-*teen,* a dish of veal, chicken, or other white meat, freed from bones, minced, tied up, boiled, and served cold in its jelly. (Fr.)

galanty-show, *n.* ga-*lan*-te-shoh, a puppet-show. (It. *galante,* gallant.)

galatea, *n.* gal-la-*tee*-a, a striped cotton fabric. (L.)

galaxy, *n.* *gal*-ak-se, the Milky Way [Astron.]; an assemblage of brilliant persons or things. (Fr. *galaxie.*)

galbanum, *n.* *gal*-ban-um, the gum or inspissated juice from a species of *Ferula,* used in medicine. (L.)

gale, *n.* gale, a strong breeze or wind, less vehement than a tempest [Naut.]. **equinoctial gales,** the storms which take place about the time of the sun's crossing the equator. (Dan. *gal,* furious.)

gale, *n.* gale, a money payment such as rent or interest which is paid at definite times.

gale, *n.* gale, the bog myrtle, *Myrica gale.* (A.S. *gagel.*)

galea, *n.* *gay*-le-a, any organ resembling a helmet [Zool.]; the upper lip of a labiate flower [Bot.]; an appendix to the maxilla of certain insects. (L., a helmet.)

galeate, *a.* *gay*-le-ate, covered as with a helmet; having a flower or a crest like a helmet [Bot. and Zool.].

galeeny, *n.* ga-*lee*-ne, a guinea-fowl. (L. *gallina,* hen.)

galena, *n.* ga-*lee*-na, native sulphide of lead, the principal lead-ore. (L.)

galenic, *a.* ga-*len*-ik, pertaining to or containing galena; (*cap.*) relating to or according to Galen, the celebrated Greek physician (*d.* A.D. 200).

Galenism, *n.* *gay*-len-izm, the Galenic system.

Galenist, *n.* *gay*-len-ist, a follower of Galen.

galenoid, *a.* ga-*lee*-noyd, resembling galena.

Galeopithecus, *n.* *gay*-le-o-pe-*thee*-kus, the genus containing the flying lemurs. (Gr. *gale,* a weasel, *pithecus,* an ape.)

galette, *n.* ga-*let,* a flat French cake. (Fr.)

Galilean, *n.* gal-e-*lee*-an, a native of Galilee; one of an anti-Roman sect among the Jews named after Judas, a Galilean; a Christian: *a.* belonging to Galilee; pertaining to or according to Galileo, the Ital. astronomer (1564-1642). **Galilean law,** the law according to which bodies fall with a uniform acceleration. **Galilean telescope,** a telescope with a concave lens in the eye-piece, invented by Galileo.

galilee, *n.* *gal*-e-lee, a porch or chapel, usually at the west end of a church [Eccles. Antiq.].

galimatias, *n.* gal-e-*may*-she-as, confused nonsensical talk; gibberish. (Fr.)

galingale, *n.* *gal*-ling-gale, the aromatic root-stock of certain plants allied to the ginger family; an English sedge, *Cyperus longus.*

galiongee, *n.* gal-yon-*jee,* a Turkish sailor, esp. on a galleon. (Turk.)

galiot, *n.* *gal*-le-ot, a galliot.

galipot, *n.* *gal*-e-pot, a white, viscid resin prepared from the exudation of the fir, *Pinus maritimus.* **galipot varnish,** a strong varnish made from this, pounded glass, and turpentine. (Fr.)

Galium, *n.* *gay*-le-um, bed-straw, a genus of herbaceous plants. (L. *galion.*)

gall, *n.* gawl, the bile, a bitter yellowish-green fluid, secreted in the glandular substance of the liver; the gall-bladder; anything extremely bitter; rancour; malignity; bitterness of mind. **gall of glass,** sandiver. (Fr. *galle.*)

gall, *n.* gawl, a hard round excrescence caused on plants by insects, fungi, or bacteria: *v.t.* to impregnate with a decoction of gall-nuts. (L. *galla.*)

gall, *n.* gawl, a wound in the skin, caused by rubbing; *v.t.* to fret, hurt, or break the skin by rubbing; to wear away; to tease; to chagrin; to harrass; to annoy: *v.i.* to fret. (A.S. *gealla.*)

gallant, *a.* *gal*-lant, brave; high-spirited; noble; chivalrous. (O.Fr. *galant.*)

gallant, *a.* gal-*lant,* courtly; polite and attentive to ladies; courteous: *n.* a man polite and attentive to ladies; a suitor; a libertine: *v.t.* to attend on, as on a lady; to flirt with.

gallantly, *ad.* *gal*-lant-le, in a gallant manner.

gallantness, *n.* the quality of being gallant.

gallantry, *n.* *gal*-lan-tre, splendour of appearance; show; bravery; nobleness; generosity; polite attention to ladies, with or without evil intent.

gallate, *n.* *gal*-late, a salt of gallic acid.

gall-bladder, *n.* a small pear-shaped membranous sac on the under-side of the liver which receives the bile.

galleass, *n.* *gal*-e-ass, a galliass.

galleon, *n.* *gal*-e-on, a large sailing ship with three or four decks, formerly used by the Spaniards between their S. American possessions and Spain. (Sp.)

galleried, *a.* *gal*-le-rid, fitted with galleries.

gallery, *n.* *gal*-le-re, a corridor or long apartment serving to communicate with others; an exhibition room, also its contents; an upper floor or balcony with seats in a church, theatre, hall, etc.; the highest and cheapest seats in a place of entertainment, also the persons occupying them; any body of spectators; a passage made by burrowing animals; a ring to support a lamp-shade; a sunk and covered communication or passage-way [Fort.]; a narrow passage-way underground, an adit [Mining]; a covered projecting balcony at the stern [Naut.]: *v.t.* to furnish with a gallery. **to play to the gallery,** to court popular applause; to pander to the least intelligent. (Fr. *galerie.*)

galleryite, *n.* *gal*-le-re-ite, a playgoer who usually sits in the gallery [Coll.].

galley, *n.* *gal*-le, an ancient war vessel propelled by oars; a low, flat-built vessel with one deck, and worked, usually by slaves or convicts, with oars and sails; hence, a place of enforced penal toil; a light open boat; a large row-boat carried by a warship; the cook-room or kitchen of a ship; an oblong frame on which the lines of type are placed as they are composed [Print.]. (Fr. *galée.*)

galley-proof, *n.* an impression taken from the matter in a printer's galley.

galley-slave, *n.* one condemned to work at the oar on board a galley; a drudge.

gall-fly, *n.* an insect, esp. of the genus *Cynips,* that punctures plants and occasions galls.

galliambic, *a.* gal-e-*am*-bik, relating to a swift-timed Ionic metre called galliambicus [Pros.]: *n.* a galliambic verse. (L.)
galliard, *n. gal*-e-ard, a gay fellow; a lively 16th-cent. dance: *a.* gay; valiant.
galliass, *n.* gal-e-ass, a low-built mediæval warship, like but larger than a galley.
Gallic, *a. gal*-lik, pertaining to Gaul or France. (L. *Gallicus.*)
gallic, *a. gawl*-lik, pertaining to galls or oak apples; derived from galls. (As *gall.*)
Gallican, *a. gal*-e-kan, Gallic; pertaining to Gallicanism; *n.* an upholder of Gallicanism; a member of the Gallican Church.
Gallicanism, *n. gal*-e-ka-nizm, the doctrine defining the relationship between the national Church of France and to Papacy; resistance to papal encroachments or domination in France.
gallicism, *n. gal*-e-sizm, a French idiom.
gallicize, *v.t. gal*-e-size, to change into the French idiom; to make French.
galligaskins, *n.pl.* gal-e-*gas*-kinz, large open hose or breeches; leggings worn by sportsmen. (O.Fr. *garguesques.*)
gallimatias, *n.* gal-e-*may*-she-as, galimatias.
gallimaufry, *n.* gal-e-*maw*-fre, a hash; any inconsistent or ridiculous medley. (Fr.)
gallinaceous, *a.* gal-e-*nay*-shus, pertaining to domestic fowls or pheasants, partridges, etc. (L.)
galling, *a. gawl*-ing, fretting; vexing; annoying.
gallinipper, *n. gal*-le-nip-per, a large mosquito.
gallinule, *n. gal*-e-newl, the water-hen, *Gallinula chloropus*, a bird allied to the coot and rail.
Gallio, *n. gal*-le-o, one who refuses to interest himself in things that do not directly concern him. (*Gallio* of Acts xviii, 17, who "cared for none of these things.")
galliot, *n. gal*-le-ot, a small galley or boat; a former Dutch trading-vessel.
gallipot, *n. gal*-le-pot, a small glazed earthenware pot, esp. one for ointments.
gallium, *n. gal*-le-um, a bluish-white and very fusible metallic element occurring in iron ores.
gallivant, *v.i.* gal-le-*vant*, to go gallanting, flirting or idling about; to philander.
gallivat, *n. gal*-le-vat, a large swift two-masted boat formerly used by Malay pirates. (Port.).
galliwasp, *n. gal*-le-wosp, a small West Indian lizard.
gallization, *n. gal*-ly-*zay*-shon, the practice of adding water and sugar to grape-juice to enhance the quality and quantity of the wine. (From the inventor, Dr. *Gall.*)
gallize, *v.t. gal*-lize, to carry out the process of gallization.
gall-nut, *n.* a gall produced on the oak, used in the making of ink, etc.
galloglass, *n. gal*-o-glahs, an armed retainer or foot-soldier of the former Irish chieftains. (Ir. *galloglach.*)
Gallomania, *n.* gal-o-*may*-ne-a, a strong or irrational bias in favour of French fashions, customs, art, etc. (L. *Gallia*, and *mania.*)
gallon, *n. gal*-lon, a measure of capacity, usually for liquids, containing four quarts or 277·463 cu. inches; the **U.S.A. gallon** is five-sixths of the imperial gallon. (O.Fr.)
galloon, *n.* ga-*loon*, a kind of close braid of silk or worsted thread, or both. (Fr. *galon.*)
gallop, *n. gal*-lop, the rapid springing movement of a quadruped, esp. a horse; a galop: *v.i.* to run with leaps, as a horse; to ride or run at a galloping pace: *v.t.* to cause to gallop. **galloping consumption,** a form of pulmonary tuberculosis very rapid in its effects. (Fr. *galoper.*)
gallopade, *n.* gal-lop-*ade*, an Hungarian dance; the music appropriate to it: *v.i.* to dance this, or to dance in a galop. (Fr. *galopade.*)
galloper, *n. gal*-lop-er, a horse, man, etc., that gallops or makes haste; an aide-de-camp; a mounted orderly; a cavalry field-piece [Mil.].
Gallophobia, *n.* gal-lo-*foh*-be-a, intense dread of the French or what is French.
gallow, *v.t. gal*-lo, to gally.
galloway, *n. gal*-lo-way, a hardy species of horse of a small size, originally bred in Galloway, in Scotland; a largish pony.
gallowglass, *n. gal*-lo-glahs, galloglass.
gallows, *n. gal*-ohz, a wooden structure on which criminals are executed by hanging; execution by hanging; a gallows-shaped framework; a wretch deserving the gallows. (A.S. *galga*, a cross or gibbet.)
gallows-bird, *n.* one who deserves the gallows.
gallows-bitts, *n.pl. gal*-lus-bits, a frame of timber, forming a support for the spare spars, etc. [Naut.].
gallows-top, *n. gal*-lus-top, a crosspiece of timber placed at the top of the gallows-bitts [Naut.].
gallows-tree, *n.* the gallows.
gall-stone, *n.* a morbid calcareous concretion formed in the gall-bladder.
gally, *a. gawl*-e, like gall; bitter as gall.
gally, *v.t. gal*-le, to terrify; to stupefy. (A.S. *gaelan.*)
galoot, *n.* ga-*loot*, an uncouth fellow; a lout [Slang].
galop, *n.* gal-*op*, a quick dance in two-four time; music for this: *v.i.* to dance a galop. (As *gallop.*)
galore, *ad.* ga-*lore*, in abundance: *n.* abundance; very many. (Ir. *goleor.*)
galosh, *n.* ga-*losh*, a rubber shoe worn over another shoe to keep the foot dry; the lower part of the upper of a boot. (Fr.)
galumph, *v.i.* ga-*lumf*, to dance about joyfully. (Coined by Lewis Carroll, perhaps from *gallop* and *triumph.*)
galvanic, *a.* gal-*van*-ik, pertaining to or produced by galvanism.
galvanism, *n. gal*-va-nizm, dynamic electricity due to chemical action, especially that of acids on metals; the branch of physics dealing with this; its application, esp. in therapeutics. (*Galvani*, Ital. scientist, 1737-98.)
galvanist, *n. gal*-va-nist, one versed in galvanism.
galvanize, *v.t. gal*-va-nize, to stimulate or rouse into activity by or as by galvanic shock; to coat one metal with another by means of an electric current. **galvanized iron,** iron in plates galvanized with zinc to resist the effects of moisture.
galvanograph, *n. gal*-va-no-graf, a printing-plate produced by galvanography.
galvanography, *n.* gal-va-*nog*-ra-fe, the production of printing-plates by means of the electrotype process.
galvanometer, *n.* gal-va-*nom*-e-ter, an instrument for determining the presence and measuring the intensity of electric current. (*galvanism*, and Gr. *metron*, measure.)
galvanoplastic, *a.* gal-va-no-*plas*-tik, pertaining to electrotyping. (*galvanism*, and Gr. *plasso*, fashion.)
galvanoplasty, *n.* gal-va-no-*plas*-te, the coating of objects with a deposit of metal by means of an electric current. (*galvanism*, and Gr. *plassein*, to mould.)
galvanoscope, *n. gal*-va-no-skope, an instrument to determine the presence and direction of an electric current. (*galvanism*, and Gr. *skopeo*, view.)
galvanotropism, *n. gal*-va-no-*trop*-izm, reaction of an organism to electric stimulus [Biol. and Bot.].
gam, *n.* gam, a school of whales.
gama-grass, *n. gah*-ma-grahs, a tall and exceedingly productive fodder-grass of Mexico and the Southern States, *Tripsacum dactyloides.*
gamba, *n. gam*-ba, a viola da gamba; a viol-like organ-stop. (It.)
gambade, *n.* gam-*bahd*, a spring of a horse; a fantastic caper; a grotesque prank. (Sp.)
gambadoes, *n.pl.* gam-*bay*-dohz, leather leggings. (It. *gamba*, a leg.)
gambeson, *n. gam*-be-zon, a stuffed and quilted doublet, formerly worn under armour.
gambet, *n. gam*-bet, former name of a bird of the redshank family. (It. *gamba*, leg.)
gambier, *n. gam*-be-er, catechu or cutch, an extract from the leaves of a species of *Uncaria*, used as a dyeing and tanning agent.
gambist, *n. gam*-bist, a player on the viola da gamba.
gambit, *n. gam*-bit, the sacrifice, or offer of sacrifice, of a pawn or piece at the opening of a game of chess, with a view to ultimate advantage; a smart opening move in negotiations, etc. [Fig.]. (It. *gambetto*, a tripping up.)
gamble, *v.i. gam*-bl, to play or game for money; to indulge in risk or speculation: *n.* a risky proceeding or action. (As *game.*)
gambler, *n. gam*-bler, one who gambles; a reckless speculator.

gambling-house, *n.* a gaming-house.

gamboge, *n.* gam-*bohdj* or gam-*boodj*, the gum-resin of various trees of the genus *Garcinia*, much used as a yellow pigment. (*Cambodia*, Indo-China.)

gambol, *n.* *gam*-bol, a skipping or leaping about in frolic: *v.i.* to dance and skip about in sport; to frisk. (Fr. *gambade*, from It. *gamba*, the leg.)

gambrel, *n.* *gam*-brel, horse's hock; a stick or iron crooked like a horse's hind leg, used by butchers for suspending carcases. **gambrel roof,** a mansard roof. (O.Fr. *gambe*, a leg.)

gambroon, *n.* gam-*broon*, a twilled linen cloth for linings. (*Gambroon*, earlier name of Bandar Abbas, Persia.)

game, *n.* game, an exercise or play for amusement or winning a stake; a single match at play; the number of points required to win; advantage in play; conquest in play; sport of any kind; diversion; animals or wild birds pursued or taken in the chase or in the sports of the field, esp. those protected by law; the flesh of such; pluck or intrepidity: *pl.* public diversions or contests exhibited as spectacles [Antiq.]: *a.* pertaining to game; plucky; keeping up one's pluck: *v.i.* to play at games of chance; to play for a stake or prize; to practise gambling. **are you game?** are you willing? **big game,** the larger animals shot for sport. **ground game,** hares and rabbits. **none of your games,** play no tricks, or make no bother. **the game's not worth the candle,** the risk is disproportionate to the expected reward. **the game is up,** the plan is a failure. **to make game of,** to ridicule. **to play the game,** to do the proper thing. **what is your game?** What is your intention? (A.S. *gamen*, sport.)

game, *a.* game, lame or disabled (of leg or arm).

gamecock, *n.* *game*-kok, a cock bred to fight.

gameful, *a.* *game*-ful, full of game; sportive.

gamekeeper, *n.* *game*-keep-er, one employed to look after game-preserves and to protect them against poachers.

game-laws, *n.pl.* laws for the protection of game.

gamely, *ad.* *game*-le, intrepidly; courageously.

gameness, *n.* *game*-ness, intrepidity; courage.

game-preserve, *n.* a tract of land on which game can breed undisturbed.

gamesome, *a.* *game*-sum, gay; sportive; playful.

gamesomely, *ad.* in a gamesome manner.

gamesomeness, *n.* the quality of being gamesome.

gamester, *n.* *game*-ster, a person addicted to gaming; a gambler.

gametal, *a.* *gam*-e-tal, gametic.

gamete, *n.* *gam*-eet or gam-*eet*, a sexual reproductive cell capable of uniting with another to produce a new individual [Biol.]. (Gr. *gamete*, wife.)

game-tenant, *n.* the renter of a shoot.

gametic, *a.* ga-*met*-ik, pertaining to or of the nature of gamets.

gametogenesis, *n.* *gam*-e-to-*jen*-e-sis, the formation of gametes. (*gamete*, and Gr. *genesis*, origin.)

gametophyte, *n.* ga-*met*-o-fite, a plant in that phase which produces the sexual organs [Bot.]. (Gr. *gamete*, wife, *phyton*, plant.)

gamic, *a.* *gam*-ik, pertaining to sex; sexual; developing after fertilization. (Gr. *gamos*, marriage.)

gamin, *n.* *gam*-min, a neglected street urchin. (Fr.)

gaming-house, *n.* *game*-ing-house, a house where gaming is carried on as a business.

gamma, *n.* *gam*-ma, the third letter of the Greek alphabet; an instrument for cauterizing a hernia, so called from its resemblance to this (γ). **gamma rays,** short-wave rays, similar to X-rays, given off by certain radioactive substances and used in the treatment of cancer. (Gr.)

gammadion, *n.* ga-*may*-de-on, the swastika or fylfot, formed by the junction of four capital gammas. (Gr.)

gammer, *n.* *gam*-mer, an old woman, correlative of gaffer. (*Grandmother.*)

gammon, *n.* *gam*-mon, the hind leg of a pig cured with the side as bacon: *v.t.* to make bacon; to pickle and dry in smoke. (Fr. *jambon*, a ham.)

gammon, *n.* *gam*-mon, the game of backgammon, also the winning of a game before the opponent has borne a man from the board; a hoax: *v.t.* by fortunate throws of the dice, or by superior skill, to withdraw all one's men from the board before one's antagonist has been able to get his men home and withdraw any of them from his table; to hoax: *v.i.* to practise imposition. (A.S. *gamen*, a game.)

gammy, *a.* *gam*-me, lame; halt and maimed; injured [Coll.].

gamogenesis, *n.* *gam*-mo-*jen*-e-sis, sexual reproduction. (Gr. *gamos*, marriage, *gennao*, produce.)

gamopetalous, *a.* *gam*-mo-*pet*-a-lus, having the petals united [Bot.].

gamosepalous, *a.* *gam*-mo-*sep*-a-lus, having the sepals united [Bot.].

gamp, *n.* gamp, a clumsy or badly rolled umbrella. (Mrs. *Gamp* in Dickens's "Martin Chuzzlewit.")

gamut, *n.* *gam*-ut, a scale on which notes are written or printed and to which Guido applied the monosyllables *ut, re, mi, fa, sol, la*; the first or deepest note in Guido's scale of music; the modern scale [Mus.]; the complete series of musical notes; range; scope. (*gamma*, the Greek *g*, and *ut*.)

gamy, *a.* *game*-e, with the taste of game; "high" from being kept long in store; game, pugnacious.

-gamy, *suffix*, ga-me, denoting marriage, or [Biol.] union for reproductive purpose.

ganch, *v.t.* gansh, to execute by impaling, esp. to drop from a height on to sharp stakes. (It. *ganchio*, a hook.)

gander, *n.* *gan*-der, the male of the goose; a simpleton. (A.S. *gandra*.)

gang, *v.i.* gang, to go; to walk [Scots.]. (A.S. *gangan*.)

gang, *n.* gang, a number of persons associated for a particular purpose, often in a bad sense; a select number of workmen, etc., appointed for a particular service; gangue: *v.t.* to dispose in a gang; to amalgamate or couple [Mech. and Wire.] (A.S.)

gang-board, *n.* a gangway or plank with cleats used as a temporary bridge between ship and shore.

gang-days, *n.pl.* (also called **gang-week**), the days in Rogation week when formerly the clergy and leading parishioners beat the parish bounds.

gange, *v.t.* ganj, to cover a fish-hook and the adjacent end of line with fine wire.

ganger, *n.* *gang*-er, the foreman or overseer of a gang of labourers, esp. of platelayers on a railway.

Gangetic, *a.* gan-*jet*-ik, pertaining to the river Ganges or its basin.

gangliac, *a.* *gang*-gle-ak, pertaining to a ganglion.

gangliform, *a.* *gang*-gle-form, having the form of a ganglion.

ganglion, *n.* *gang*-gle-on (*pl.* **ganglia**), an aggregation of nerve-cells from which nerve fibres lead; a glandiform organ; an enlargement in the course of a nerve [Anat.]; an encysted tumour situated in the sheath of a tendon [Med.]. (Gr.)

ganglionary, *a.* *gang*-gle-o-na-re, composed of ganglia.

ganglionic, *a.* *gang*-gle-*on*-ik, gangliac; composed of or furnished with ganglia.

gangrel, *n.* *gang*-rel, a vagabond. (Dial. Eng.)

gangrene, *n.* *gang*-green, mortification at its first stage in part of a living animal body; putrefaction; *v.t.* to mortify: *v.i.* to become mortified; to corrupt. (O.Fr.)

gangrenescent, *a.* *gang*-gre-*nes*-sent, becoming gangrenous; tending to mortification.

gangrenous, *a.* *gang*-gre-nus, affected with gangrene.

gangster, *n.* *gang*-ster, a member of a gang, esp. in the criminal underworld [U.S.A.].

gangue, *n.* gang, the earthy or mineral substance in which ore is embedded [Mining]; veinstone.

gangway, *n.* *gang*-way, a passage or way into or out of any place, as a ship; a passage along each side of the interior of a ship; an opening for entrance or exit in a vessel; a passage running across the House of Commons, separating the independent members from the supporters of the Government and the Opposition. **to bring to the gangway,** to inflict punishment on a seaman by tying him up and flogging him [Naut.].

gang-week, *see* **gang-days.**

ganister, *n.* *gan*-is-ter, a hard close-grained sandstone from the Upper Carboniferous, used for grindstones and furnace hearths.

ganja, *n.* *gan*-ja, a dried extract from Indian hemp smoked as a narcotic. (Hind.)

gannet, *n.* *gan*-net, a large sea-bird, esp. the solan goose, *Sula bassana*. (S.A. *ganot*.)

ganoid, *a.* *gan*-oyd, having shiny scales of bone;

belonging to the *Ganoidei*, or sturgeon family: *n.* a fish of this family. (Gr. *ganos*, splendour, *eidos*, like.)

gantlet, *n.* *gawnt*-let, a gauntlet. (O.Fr. *gantelet*.)

gantlope, *n.* *gant*-lope, a gauntlet. (Swed. *gatlopp*.)

gantry, *n.* *gan*-tre, a framework carrying a travelling crane; a light bridge over a railway-line carrying several signals; a stillion or stand for casks.

Ganymede, *n.* *gan*-ne-meed, a cupbearer; a waiter. (L., the cupbearer to Zeus.)

gaol, *n.* jale, a prison; a jail.

gaoler, *n.* *jay*-lor, the chief of a gaol; a jailor.

gap, *n.* gap, an opening in anything made by breaking or parting; a cleft; a mountain pass; a vacant place; a deficiency: *v.t.* to make a gap in. **to stand in the gap**, to expose oneself for the protection of something. **to stop a gap**, to secure a weak point; to repair a defect. (As *gape*.)

gap-toothed, *a.* with interstices between the teeth.

gape, *n.* gape, the act of gaping; the width of the mouth when opened, as of a bird, also the part of the beak that opens [Zool.]: *pl.* a disease of young poultry, attended with much gaping; a spasm of yawning: *v.i.* to open the mouth wide in expression of drowsiness, desire, wonderment, etc.; to yawn; to open the mouth for food, as young birds; to open in a fissure or crevice. **to gape at**, to gaze with open-mouthed astonishment. **to gape for or after**, to desire earnestly; to crave. (Ice. *gapa*.)

gaper, *n.* *gape*-er, one who or that which gapes, esp. as applied to certain bivalve molluscs and sea-fish.

gapeworm, *n.* gape-wurm, the parasitic nematoid worm that causes the gapes in birds.

gapingly, *ad.* *gape*-ing-le, in a gaping fashion.

gappy, *a.* *gap*-pe, with gaps.

gar, *n.* gar, a garfish.

garage, *n.* *ga*-raj *or* ga-*rahzh*, a building, shed, or repair-shop for motor-vehicles: *v.t.* to house or put in a garage. (Fr.)

garancine, *n.* *ga*-ran-seen, a dye-stuff made by treating madder with strong sulphuric acid. (Fr. *garance*, madder.)

garb, *n.* gahrb, dress; fashion or mode, especially of dress; exterior appearance: *v.t.* to dress, esp. distinctively. (O.Fr.)

garb, *n.* gahrb, a sheaf of grain [Her.]. (Fr. *gerbe*.)

garbage, *n.* *gahr*-baj, refuse of any kind; offal. (Fr.)

garble, *v.t.* *gahr*-bl, to pick out such parts as may serve a purpose; to give a disconnected or erroneous account of anything; to separate the fine or valuable parts from the coarse or useless. (Ar. *gharbala*, to sift.)

garboard, *n.* *gahr*-bord, the plank next to the keel [Naut.]. (O.Dut. *gaarboord*.)

garçon, *n.* (App.), a waiter. (Fr.)

gardant, *a.* *gahr*-dant, said of a beast, full-faced and looking right forward [Her.]. (Fr.)

★**garden**, *n.* *gahr*-den, a piece of ground appropriated to the cultivation of plants, fruits, and flowers; a rich, well-cultivated spot or tract: (*pl.*) a public pleasure-ground: *a.* pertaining to a garden; cultivated, not wild: *v.i.* to undertake the cultivation of a garden. **garden white**, the cabbage butterfly. **to lead one up the garden**, to humbug, or mislead, him [Slang]. (O.Fr. *gardin*.)

garden-city, *n.* a town built on a systematized and pre-arranged plan combining the advantages of town and country.

gardener, *n.* *gahr*-den-er, one whose occupation is to cultivate and dress a garden.

gardenia, *n.* gahr-*dee*-nya, a tropical and subtropical hothouse shrub cultivated for its beautiful flowers. (Alex. *Garden*, *d.* 1791, Amer. botanist.)

gardening, *n.* *gahr*-den-ing, horticulture.

garden-party, *n.* a social gathering held in a garden.

garden-plot, *n.* a spot laid out as a garden.

garden-stuff, *n.* esculent plants, herbs, etc., grown in a garden.

gardyloo, *int.* gahr-de-*loo*, a warning to beware of the fall of slops emptied from a window [Scots.]. (Fr. *gare l'eau*, look out for the water.)

gare, *n.* gare, a French railway-station. (Fr.)

gare-fowl, *n.* *gare*-foul, the greak auk.

garfish, *n.* *gahr*-fish, a sea-fish of the genus *Belone*, with beak-like jaws, the upper being sharp and pointed. (A.S. *gar*, spear, and *fish*.)

garganey, *n.* *gahr*-ga-ne, a sea-duck, *Querquedula circia*, allied to the teal.

gargantuan, *a.* gahr-*gan*-tew-an, prodigious. (After *Gargantua*, the giant-king, in Rabelais.)

gargarism, *n.* *gahr*-ga-rizm, a gargle.

gargarize, *v.t.* *gahr*-ga-rize, to gargle. (Gr. *gargarizo*.)

garget, *n.* *gahr*-jet, a disease in cattle and swine affecting the throat; a diseased condition of the udders of cows. (O.Fr. *gargate*, throat.)

gargle, *n.* *gahr*-gl, any liquid preparation for washing the mouth and throat: *v.t.* to rinse the throat and mouth with such, preventing its passage down the throat by a gentle expiration; to have a drink [Slang]. (Fr. *gargouille*, the throat.)

gargoyle, *n.* *gahr*-goyl, the projecting spout of a roof-gutter when in the form of a grotesque figure. (Fr. *gargouille*.)

garibaldi, *n.* *ga*-re-*bawl*-de, a blouse-like jacket such as was worn by Garibaldi's "Red-shirts."

garish, *a.* *gare*-rish, gaudy; showy; extravagantly gay; flashy. (Probably M.E. *gaure*, to stare.)

garishly, *ad.* in a garish manner.

garishness, *n.* the quality of being garish.

garland, *n.* *gahr*-land, a wreath or chaplet made of branches or flowers; a similar decoration in stone, plastics, ribbon, etc.; the chief prize; an anthology: *v.t.* to deck or crown with a garland. (Fr.)

garland, *n.* *gahr*-land, a wreath or chaplet made of branches or flowers; a similar decoration in stone, plastics, ribbon, etc.; the chief prize; an anthology: *v.t.* to deck or crown with a garland. (Fr.)

garlic, *n.* *gahr*-lik, a culinary bulb with a pungent taste and scent, *Allium sativum*. (A.S. *gar*, a lance, *leac*, a leek.)

garlicky, *a.* *gahr*-le-ke, like or containing garlic; smelling of garlic.

garlic-pear, *n.* *gahr*-lik-pare, a Jamaican tree, *Cratæva gynandra*, with a garlic-smelling fruit.

garment, *n.* *gahr*-ment, any article of clothing; dress. (O.Fr. *garniment*.)

garmented, *a.* *gahr*-men-ted, clad in, or as in, a garment.

garner, *n.* *gahr*-ner, a granary, a bin; a repository: *v.t.* to store in, or as in, a granary; to gather together. (O.Fr. *gernier*, granary.)

garnet, *n.* *gahr*-net, a group of minerals, crystallizing in the cubic system, of varied composition, colour, and quality, the deep-red translucent variety of which is valued as a gem. (O.Fr. *grenat*.)

garnetiferous, *a.* gahr-ne-*tif*-e-rus, containing garnets [Geol.].

garnish, *n.* *gahr*-nish, ornament; decoration; edible and decorative trimmings round a dish; a fee formerly paid by a prisoner to his jailor: *v.t.* to adorn; to embellish with trimmings, as a dish; to furnish; to supply; to warn; to give notice [Law]. (O.Fr. *garnir*, to furnish.)

garnishee, *n.* *gahr*-ne-*shee*, one on whom notice is served attaching the property of a debtor: *v.t.* to issue the notice making one a garnishee; to attach (funds, etc.) by garnishment [Law].

garnisher, *n.* *gahr*-nish-er, one who or that which garnishes.

garnishing, *n.* *gahr*-nish-ing, the act of embellishing; that which garnishes.

garnishment, *n.* *gahr*-nish-ment, ornament; embellishment; warning given to a party to appear in court, or not to pay money to another [Law].

garniture, *n.* *gahr*-ne-tewr, ornamental appendages; trimmings; furniture; dress. (Fr.)

garotte, *n.* and *v.t.* ga-*rot*, garrotte.

garous, *a.* *gare*-rus, resembling garum.

garpike, *n.* *gahr*-pike, the garfish.

garran, *n.* *ga*-ran, a small horse; a Highland horse; a galloway. (Gael., a gelding.)

garret, *n.* *ga*-ret, a room with sloping ceilings immediately under the roof. (O.Fr. *garite*, watch-tower.)

garreteer, *n.* ga-re-*teer*, one who lives in a garret; a penniless author, a hack.

garrison, *n.* *ga*-ris-son, a body of troops stationed in a fort or fortified town; a fort or fortified town furnished with troops to defend it: *v.t.* to furnish as a fortress with soldiers; to defend by fortresses manned with troops. **garrison town**, a town in which soldiers are permanently stationed. (O.Fr. *garison*.)

garron, *n.* *ga*-ron, a garran.

garrot, *n.* *ga*-rot, a tourniquet [Surg.]. (As *garrotte.*)
garrot, *n.* *ga*-rot, a sea-duck of the genus *Clangula.*
garrotte, *n.* ga-*rot*, a former Spanish method of execution by strangling with a cord twisted tight by turning a stick, or by means of an iron collar tightened by a screw, the point of which penetrated to the spine; the collar so employed: *v.t.* to execute with the garrotte; to throttle so as to render helpless, and rob. (Sp. *garrote*, a cudgel.)
garrotter, *n.* ga-*rot*-er, one practising garrotting.
garrotting, *n.* ga-*rot*-ing, punishment by strangulation; throttling.
garrulity, *n.* ga-*roo*-le-te, talkativeness; loquacity.
garrulous, *a.* *ga*-roo-lus, talkative; loquacious. (L. *garrulus.*)
garrulously, *ad.* in a talkative manner.
garrulousness, *n.* the quality or habit of being garrulous.
garter, *n.* *gahr*-ter, a string or band used to hold the stocking to the leg; (*cap.*) the badge of the highest order of knighthood in Great Britain, called the **Order of the Garter,** instituted by Edward III; the order itself: *v.t.* to fasten with a garter; to invest with the Order of the Garter. **Garter King of Arms,** the principal king of arms. (O.Fr. *gartier.*)
garter-fish, *n.* the scabbard-fish, or other fish having a long thin body.
garter-snake, *n.* a harmless striped snake, of the American genus *Eutænia.*
garth, *n.* gahrth, a lawn surrounded by cloisters; a close; a weir for catching fish; a yard. (Ice.)
garum, *n.* *gayr*-rum, a sauce, much prized by the ancient Romans, prepared from small marinated fish.
garvie, *n.* *gar*-ve, the sprat.
gas, *n.* gas, a permanently elastic aeriform fluid; popularly, that obtained from coal and used for purposes of lighting and heating; any combustible gaseous mixture; petrol or gasoline [U.S.A., Coll.]; laughing-gas; any poison-gas; a gas-jet [Coll.]; empty or foolish talk: *v.t.* to treat, poison, or asphyxiate with gas; to talk boastfully, volubly, or at great length [Coll.]. **to tread on the gas,** to accelerate [U.S.A. motoring slang]. (Coined by Van Helmont, *d.* 1644, Belgian chemist.)
gas-attack, *n.* a preparatory assault, or an air-raid, in which poison-gas is used [Mil.].
gas-bag, *n.* a bag for holding gas; a ballonet; a talkative person [Slang].
gas-bracket, *n.* a fixed or jointed horizontal gaspipe, supplied with a burner.
gas-buoy, *n.* a buoy in which is a gas-reservoir for maintaining a gas-flare alight.
gas-burner, *n.* the jet fitted at the end of a gas-pipe, from which the flame issues.
gas-carbon, *n.* a hard and almost pure carbon deposited in the retorts of gas-works.
gas-coal, *n.* *gas*-koal, bituminous coal from which gas is produced; anthracite.
gas-coke, *n.* the residuum of gas-coal after the gas has been extracted.
gas-colic, *n.* tympanites.
Gascon, *n.* *gas*-kon, a native of Gascony, France, whose inhabitants are noted for boasting; a boaster.
gasconade, *n.* *gas*-ko-*nade*, boasting; bravado; bragging: *v.i.* to boast; to brag.
gasconader, *n.* *gas*-ko-*nay*-der, a great boaster.
gas-condenser, *n.* an apparatus for purifying gas from tar.
gas-cooker, *n.* a stove in which the cooking is done by gas.
gas-disease, *n.* a disease among fish, due to excess of dissolved gas in the water, of which a symptom is bulging eyeballs.
gaseity, *n.* gas-*see*-e-te, state of being gaseous.
gaselier, *n.* *gas*-e-leer, a gas chandelier.
gas-engine, *n.* an engine in which the explosion of gas provides the motive power.
gaseous, *a.* *gay*-se-us *or* *gas*-e-us, in the form of gas; like gas.
gaseousness, *n.* state of being gaseous.
gas-fire, *n.* *gas*-fire, an apparatus consuming gas for the provision of warmth.
gas-fitter, *n.* a workman who fits up pipes and burners for gas.
gas-fittings, *n.pl.* the fittings necessary for burning gas.
gas-gauge, *n.* a device for testing gas pressure.
gash, *n.* gash, a deep and long cut, particularly in flesh: *v.i.* to make a gash. (O.Fr. *garser.*)
gas-helmet, *n.* a gas-mask covering the whole head, or, for infants, the whole head and body.
gashly, *a.* *gash*-le, frightful; ghastly [Scots.].
gas-holder, *n.* a gasometer; a receptacle for gas.
gasification, *n.* *gas*-e-fe-*kay*-shon, conversion into gas.
gasiform, *a.* *gas*-e-form, having the form of gas.
gasify, *v.t.* *gas*-e-fy, to convert into gas. (*gas*, and L. *facio*, make.)
gas-jet, *n.* a gas-burner; a jet of flame from this.
gasket, *n.* *gas*-ket, packing for pipe-joints, pistons, etc., made of plaited hemp, leather, asbestos, rubber, etc. [Mech.]; a cord used to furl the sail to the yard [Naut.]. (It. *gaschetta*, rope's-end.)
gaskins, *n.pl.* *gas*-kinz, galligaskins; wide open hose.
gaslight, *n.* *gas*-lite, light afforded by the combustion of carburetted hydrogen gas, as procured by the distillation of coal; a gas-jet. **gaslight paper,** slow-speed bromide paper that can be used in gaslight [Phot.].
gas-lime, *n.* lime after being used as a filter in the manufacture of coal-gas.
gas-main, *n.* a pipe which conducts gas direct from a gas-works.
gasman, *n.* *gas*-man, the employee of a gas company; a gas-fitter.
gas-mantle, *n.* a network of very light fabric, cylindrically shaped, over a gas-jet so that, when lighted, it gives an incandescent light.
gas-mask, *n.* an airtight respirator protecting the wearer against noxious gas.
gas-meter, *n.* a mechanical contrivance for measuring and recording the quantity of gas passing through a pipe in any given time.
gasogene, *n.* *gas*-o-jeen, a gazogene.
gasoline, *n.* *gas*-o-leen, a volatile inflammable liquid derived from crude petroleum; petrol.
gasometer, *n.* ga-*som*-e-ter, a reservoir for the storage and distribution of gas; an apparatus for the quantitative measurement of gas. (*gas*, and Gr. *metron*, measure.)
gasometric, *a.* gas-o-*met*-rik, pertaining to gasometry.
gasometry, *n.* gas-*om*-e-tre, the science, art, or practice of measuring gases.
gasoscope, *n.* *gas*-o-skope, an apparatus for indicating the presence of gas, esp. in mines. (*gas*, and Gr. *skopeo*, view.)
gasp, *n.* gahsp, a convulsive painful effort to catch the breath. **at the last gasp,** at the limit of one's powers; dying: *v.i.* to gape in order to catch breath, or in laborious respiration; to breathe laboriously; *v.t.* to emit with gasping breath. (Ice. *geispa*, yawn.)
gasper, *n.* *gahs*-per, one who gasps; an inferior cigarette [Slang].
gaspingly, *ad.* *gahs*-ping-le, in a gasping manner.
gas-retort, *n.* a vessel used for holding the material of which gas is being made.
gas-ring, *n.* a metal ring pierced with holes through which gas emerges to be burnt for cooking purposes.
gassed, *a.* gast, affected by poison-gas.
gas-shell, *n.* an explosive projectile filled with gas [Mil.].
gassing, *n.* *gas*-sing, subjection to gaseous action, esp. the process of singeing lace for the removal of the hairy filaments.
gas-stove, *n.* a cooking-stove heated by gas.
gassy, *a.* *gas*-se, gaseous; containing gas; inflated.
gas-tar, *n.* coal-tar.
gasteropod, *n.* *gas*-ter-ro-pod, any member of the Gasteropoda [Zool.].
Gasteropoda, *n.pl.* *gas*-ter-*rop*-o-da, the class of univalve molluscs, including the snails, etc. (Gr. *gaster*, the belly, *pous*, the foot.)
gasteropodous, *a.* *gas*-ter-*rop*-o-dus, belonging to or characteristic of the Gasteropoda.
gas-tight, *a.* *gas*-tite, impenetrable by gas.
gastræa, *n.* gas-*tree*-a, the presumed primordial ancestor of the Metazoa. (As *gastrula.*)
gastral, *a.* *gas*-tral, gastric.
gastralgia, *n.* gas-*tral*-je-a, an unpleasant pain in the stomach; stomach-ache [Med.]. (Gr. *gaster*, and *algos*, pain.)
gastric, *a.* *gas*-trik, pertaining to the stomach or to the whole digestive system. **gastric fever,** typhoid or enteric fever. **gastric juice,** a thin, pellucid liquor secreted in the mucous membrane of the

stomach, principal agent in digestion. **gastric ulcer,** an ulcer on the inner wall of the stomach.
gastricism, *n. gas*-tre-sizm, the theory that assigns to derangement of the digestive system the root-cause of most diseases [Med.].
gastritis, *n.* gas-*try*-tis, inflammation of the stomach or its mucous membrane.
gastrocele, *n. gas*-tro-seel, hernia of the stomach [Med.]. (Gr. *gastēr*, and *kēlē*, hernia.)
gastrocnemius, *n. gas*-trok-*nee*-me-us, the largest muscle in the calf of the leg.
gastrodynia, *n.* gas-tro-*din*-e-a, gastralgia [Med.]. (Gr. *gaster*, and *odyne*, pain.)
gastro-enteritis, *n. gas*-tro-en-ter-*ry*-tis, inflammation of the stomach and intestines [Med.].
gastrology, *n.* gas-*trol*-o-je, the science treating of the stomach; gastronomy. (Gr. *gaster*, and *logos*, a word.)
gastromancy, *n. gas*-tro-man-se, divination by ventriloquism or means of words seeming to proceed from the belly. (Gr. *gaster*, and *manteia*, divination.)
gastronome, *n. gas*-tro-nome, an epicure.
gastronomer, *n.* gas-*tron*-o-mer, a gastronomist.
gastronomic, *a.* gas-tro-*nom*-ik, pertaining to gastronomy.
gastronomist, *n.* gas-*tron*-o-mist, one who likes good living; an epicure.
gastronomy, *n.* gas-*tron*-o-me, the art or science of good eating. (Gr. *gaster*, and *nomos*, a rule.)
gastrophile, *n. gas*-tro-fil, a lover of good food.
gastropod, *n. gas*-tro-pod, one of the Gasteropoda.
gastroscope, *n. gas*-tro-skohp, an instrument for interior examination of the stomach [Surg.]. (Gr. *gaster*, and *skopeo*, view.)
gastroscopy, *n.* gas-*tros*-ko-pe, examination of the stomach by means of the gastroscope [Surg.].
gastrosoph, *n. gas*-tro-sof, a gastronomist.
gastrostomy, *n.* gas-*tros*-to-me, an operation to introduce food directly into the stomach in the case of stricture of the gullet [Surg.]. (Gr. *gaster*, and *stoma*, the mouth.)
gastrotomy, *n.* gas-*trot*-o-me, the operation of cutting into or opening the abdomen [Surg.]. (Gr. *gaster*, and *-tomia*, from *temnein*, to cut.)
gastro-vascular, *a.* pertaining to digestion and circulation.
gastrula, *n.* gas-*troo*-la, the cup stage in the embryonic development of the Metazoa. (L., diminutive from Gr. *gaster*, stomach.)
gas-works, *n.pl.* a manufactory for the production of coal-gas.
gat, gat, *p.* of *get* (obsolete).
gat, *n.* gat, a ship-channel, esp. through sandbanks [Naut.]; an opening in cliffs. (O. Scand., a passage-way.)
gate, *n.* gate, the passage into a city, an enclosure, or a large edifice; the movable barrier which opens or closes the passage; the frame which stops the passage of water through a lock; the guide for the gear-change lever in a motor-car; any means of entrance or exit; a mountain pass; the number of a crowd who have paid entrance money at a sports meeting, etc.; the amount of money so taken: *v.t.* to confine (Oxford or Cambridge undergraduates) to college. (A.S. *geat*, a gate, a way.)
gâteau, *n. gah*-to, a fancy cake. (Fr.)
gate-bill, *n. gate*-bill, a record of fines imposed on undergraduates who have been gated.
gate-crash, *v.t.* and *i. gate*-krash, to attend a social gathering without invitation or authorization [Coll.].
gate-crasher, *n.* an uninvited guest at a social or other function.
gated, *a. gate*-ed, having gates; confined to college for some misdemeanour (of undergraduates).
gatehouse, *n. gate*-house, a house at or over a gate; a porter's lodge.
gatekeeper, *n. gate*-keep-er, the attendant at a swing-gate at a railway level crossing; the porter at a park-lodge; the lessee or collector at a toll-gate.
gate-legged, *a. gate*-legd (of tables) having leaves that drop down when the movable legs are folded back against the frame.
gate-money, *n. gate*-mun-e, money paid for admission, esp. at entrance to a sporting event.
gate-post, *n.* the upright on each side of a gate.
gateway, *n. gate*-way, a passage-way that may be closed by a gate; an entrance.
gather, *n. gath*-er, a fold in cloth, made by drawing together: *v.t.* to bring together; to collect; to pluck; to acquire; to accumulate; to contract; to pucker; to draw together in folds by a thread passing through; to deduce by inference; to haul in the slack of a rope: *v.i.* to collect; to increase; to generate pus or matter; to ripen. **to gather breath,** to have respite. **to gather way,** to get moving so as to be steerable [Naut.]. (A.S. *gaderian*.)
gatherable, *a. gath*-er-a-bl, that may be gathered.
gatherer, *n. gath*-er-er, one who or that which gathers.
gathering, *n. gath*-er-ing, the act of collecting or assembling; collection; an assembly; that which is gathered; a tumour suppurated or maturated; an abscess.
Gatling, *n. gat*-ling, a machine-gun of American invention, named after the inventor (*d.* 1903).
gauche, *a.* gohsh, clumsy; awkwardly tactless; uncouth. (Fr., left hand.)
gaucherie, *n. gohsh*-ree, awkwardness; boorishness; bungling. (Fr. *gauche*, left-handed, awkward.)
Gaucho, *n. gou*-cho, a native of the Argentine pampas, of mixed Spanish and Indian descent, famous for horsemanship and skill with the lasso. (Sp.)
gaud, *n.* gawd, a trinket; a showy ornament: (*pl.*) showy display. (L. *gaudium*, joy.)
gaudeamus, *n.* gaw-de-*ay*-mus, a college students' festival. (L., let us be merry.)
gaudery, *n. gaw*-der-re, finery; showy things.
gaudily, *ad. gaw*-de-le, in a gaudy manner.
gaudiness, *n.* the quality of being gaudy.
gaudy, *a. gaw*-de, showy; gay; tastelessly smart; unrefined: *n.* an annual or other festival. **gaudy-day,** a day on which a gaudy is held; a holiday.
gauffer, *v.t.* and *n. goh*-fer, goffer.
gauge, *n.* gaje, a measure; a standard of measure; a graduated instrument showing certain quantities, as amount of water or steam-pressure in a boiler, or of petrol in a tank, the height of a river, the strength of wind, etc.; the depth to which a ship sinks in the water [Naut.]; the position of one vessel with respect to another (**weather-gauge** being to windward, **lee-gauge** to leeward) [Naut.]; a piece of hardwood variously notched, used to adjust the dimensions of the various sorts of letters [Print]; an instrument for striking a line parallel to the straight side of a board [Carp.]; the width between the rails (British standard gauge 4 ft. 8½ in.) [Railways]: *v.t.* to ascertain the dimensions, capacity or content of; to measure or appraise in respect to capability; to estimate. (O.Fr.)
gaugeable, *a. gaje*-a-bl, that may be gauged.
gauger, *n. gaje*-er, one who or that which gauges; an officer whose business is to ascertain the contents of casks; an exciseman.
gauging, *n. gaje*-ing, the art of measuring the contents of vessels of any form. **gauging rod, rule, stick,** etc., instruments used in gauging.
Gaul, *n.* gawl, ancient France; one of its inhabitants; hence, a Frenchman. (O.Fr. *Gaule*.)
Gauleiter, *n. gou*-ly-ter, the political, cultural, and economic head of a province of the Nazi Reich, or of an occupied territory. (Ger. *Gau*, province, *leiter*, leader.)
Gaulish, *a. gawl*-ish, pertaining to Gaul; French: *n.* the Celtic language of ancient Gaul.
gault, *n.* gawlt, the series of beds of clay between the Upper and Lower Greensands.
Gaultheria, *n.* gawl-*theer*-re-a, a genus of evergreen herbs of the heath family. **gaultheria oil,** wintergreen oil.
gaum, *v.t.* gawm, to smear.
gaunt, *a.* gawnt, lean; thin; emaciated; pinched-looking. (Perhaps Scand.)
gauntlet, *n. gawnt*-let, a gantlet, or a large armoured glove formerly worn by knights and men-at-arms; a stout glove with an extension coming up over the wrist; a bandage wrapping hand and wrist [Surg.]. **run the gauntlet,** a naval or military punishment, in which the offender was compelled to run between two lines of men armed with cords or rods, who struck him as he passed. **take up the gauntlet,** to accept the challenge. **throw down the gauntlet,** to challenge to combat. (O.Fr. *gantelet*.)
gauntleted, *a. gawnt*-let-ed, wearing gauntlets.

gauntly, *ad.* *gawnt*-le, in a gaunt manner.
gauntness, *n.* the state of being gaunt.
gauntry, *n.* *gawn*-tre, a gantry.
gaur, *n.* gour, a wild ox, *Bos gaurus*, of the mountain forests of India. (Hind.)
gauss, *n.* gouse, the c.g.s. unit of magnetic flux density, equal to 1 line per sq. cm., and of the intensity of a magnetic field [Elect.]. (K. F. *Gauss*, Ger. mathematician, *d.* 1855.)
gauze, *n.* gawz, a very thin, slight, transparent stuff, of silk, linen, or cotton; any similar material of hard-spun fibre, wire, etc. (Fr. *gaze.*)
gauzy, *a.* *gawz*-e, like gauze; thin as gauze.
gavage, *n.* (App.), forcible feeding with a stomach-pump; cramming of poultry. (Fr.)
gavel, *n.* *gav*-el, tribute: rent. (A.S. *gafel.*)
gavel, *n.* *gav*-el, a chairman's or an auctioneer's hammer; a wooden mallet; a mason's maul.
gavelkind, *n.* *gav*-el-kynd, an ancient system of land tenure in England under which all sons shared alike, finally abolished in 1925. (A.S. *gafel*, tribute, *kind*, nature.)
gavial, *n.* *gay*-ve-al, an Asiatic species of crocodile, *Gavialis gangeticus*, having a long narrow muzzle. (Hind. *ghariyāl.*)
gavotte, *n.* ga-*vot*, a dance like but livelier than the minuet; music for this. (Fr.)
gawk, *n.* gawk, a fool; a simpleton; a clumsy fellow; a gawky: *v.i.* to gape or stare at [U.S.A.].
gawky, *a.* *gawk*-e, awkward; clownish: *n.* a tall awkward stupid fellow.
gay, *a.* gay, in bright spirits; lively; mirthful; showy; devoted to pleasure; wanton. (Fr. *gai.*)
gayal, *n.* *gy*-al, a species of ox extensively domesticated in the East, *Bos frontalis*. (Bengali.)
gaysome, *a.* *gay*-sum, full of gaiety; merry.
gaze, *n.* gaze, a fixed look; a look of eagerness, wonder, or admiration; formerly, the object gazed at: *v.i.* to look (at) fixedly. **at gaze,** arrested in wonderment; full-faced [Her.].
gazebo, *n.* ga-*zee*-bo, a balcony, lantern or turret from which a view may be had; a projecting window. (Satirically formed from *gaze.*)
gaze-hound, *n.* a hound, as the greyhound, that hunts by sight rather than by scent.
gazelle, *n.* ga-*zel*, one of a genus (*Gazella*) of small, swift antelopes, having large, soft, black eyes, and a distinctive dark triangle on the forehead. **gazelle hound,** the saluki. (Ar. *ghazal.*)
gazer, *n.* *gaze*-er, one who gazes.
gazette, *n.* ga-*zet*, a newspaper. **the Gazette,** the official British journal in which are published public notices, appointments, honours, bankruptcies, etc.: *v.t.* to publish in the Gazette. (It. *gazzetta*, a small Venetian coin, perhaps the price of the first gazette.)
gazetteer, *n.* gaz-et-*teer*, a geographical dictionary; a writer in a gazette. (It. *gazzettiere*, a journalist.)
gazing-stock, *n.* an object exposed to be gazed at; an object of curiosity or contempt.
gazogene, *n.* *gaz*-o-jeen, an apparatus for making aerated beverages. (Fr. *gazogène.*)
gean, *n.* geen, the wild cherry, *Prunus avium*. (Fr. *guigne.*)
gear, *n.* geer, apparatus; harness; tackle; dress; accoutrements; goods or riches [Scots.]; the blocks and ropes belonging to any particular spar or sail [Naut.]; mechanical appliances; a toothed wheel, a train of these, or connexion by means of them [Mech.]; the mechanism by which the revolutions of a driving-wheel are related to the stroke of a piston, pedal, etc.; working adjustment or relation: *v.t.* to put on or in gear; to harness. **first, second, top** (etc.) **gear,** the gear ratio in the mechanism of any vehicle or engine to the speed required. **three-speed gear,** a device which allows three speed ratios between the driving and driven wheels. (M.E. *gēre.*)
gear-box, *n.* the gear-changing mechanism in a power-transmission system; a gear-case.
gear-case, *n.* a protective covering for the gearing of machinery, esp. the case that encloses the chain and cogs of a bicycle.
gear-cutter, *n.* a manufacturer of toothed wheels; a machine for the purpose.
gearing, *n.* *geer*-ing, working parts; tackle [Naut.]; a train of toothed wheels for transmitting motion in machinery [Mech.].
gear-wheel, *n.* a wheel with cogs; the wheel that transmits motion, esp. in a cycle.
gebur, *n.* ge-*boor*, a tenant farmer in an Early English settlement. (A.S.)
Gecko, *n.* *gek*-o, a genus of small insectivorous wall-lizards, with suckers on their feet, and of more or less nocturnal habits. (Malay, *gekog*, from its cry.)
ged, *n.* ged, the freshwater fish, the pike.
gee, *v.i.* jee, to turn to the off side or from the driver: *int.* (or **gee-up**) go faster. **gee-gee,** *n.* a horse.
geese, geese, *n.pl.* of *goose.*
Geez, *n.* ge-*ez* or geez, an archaic Semitic dialect surviving in southern Arabia; Abyssinian; Ethiopic.
geezer, *n.* *gee*-zer, an old man or woman; an elderly eccentric [Slang]. (Perhaps *guiser*, a mummer.)
gegenschein, *n.* *gay*-gen-shine, a faint luminosity sometimes observable in the heavens opposite the position of the sun [Astron.]. (Ger., counter-glow.)
Gehenna, *n.* ge-*hen*-na, hell or hell fire. (Lit., the valley of Hinnom, near Jerusalem, where children were once sacrificed to Moloch, and which became afterwards a place of abomination.)
geisha, *n.* *gay*-sha, a Japanese professional dancing and singing girl. (Jap.)
Geiger counter, *n.* *gy*-ger *koun*-ter, a form of ionization chamber designed to trace electrically the path of particles ejected by radioactive material. (Hans *Geiger*, Ger. physicist, *b.* 1882.)
geitonogamy, *n.* gy-to-*nog*-a-me, pollination by one flower of another on the same plant. (Gr. *geiton*, neighbour, *gamia*, marriage.)
gel, *n.* jel, a jelly-like material formed in a colloidal solution by coagulation [Chem.].
gelastic, *a.* je-*las*-tik, connected with the action of laughter; causing laughter. (Gr. *gelastikos.*)
gelatigenous, *a.* *jel*-a-tij-e-nus, producing gelatine. (*gelatine*, and Gr. *gennao*, produce.)
gelatinate, *v.i.* and *t.* je-*lat*-e-nate, to be converted into or to convert into gelatine or the like.
gelatination, *n.* je-*lat*-e-*nay*-shon, the process of converting or being turned into gelatine.
gelatine, *n.* *jel*-at-een, a substance of a jelly consistence obtained by boiling the connective tissues, as the muscles, cartilages, horns, and bones, of animals. (Fr. *gélatine.*)
gelatiniform, *a.* *jel*-a-*tin*-e-form, having the form of gelatine.
gelatinify, *v.t.* jel-a-*tin*-e-fy, to convert into gelatine.
gelatinize, *v.t.* and *i.* je-*lat*-e-nize, to gelatinate.
gelatinoid, *a.* je-*lat*-e-noyd, resembling gelatine.
gelatinous, *a.* je-*lat*-e-nus, of the nature of gelatine.
gelation, *n.* je-*lay*-shon, solidification by freezing; congelation.
geld, *n.* geld or gelt, a pre-Conquest (and later) land-tax paid to the English crown. (A.S., money.)
geld, *v.t.* geld, to castrate; to emasculate; to deprive of any essential part; to expurgate. (Ice. *gelda.*)
geldable, *a.* *geld*-a-bl, that may be gelded.
gelder-rose, *n.* the guelder-rose.
gelding, *n.* *geld*-ing, the act of castrating; a castrated animal, esp. a horse. (Ice.)
gelid, *a.* *jel*-id, icy cold; very cold. (L. *gelidus*, cold).
gelidity, *n.* je-*lid*-e-te, extreme cold.
gelidly, *ad.* *jel*-id-le, very coldly.
gelidness, *n.* *jel*-id-ness, extreme coldness.
gelignite, *n.* *jel*-ig-nite, gelatine dynamite. (*gel*, from *gelatine*, and L. *ignis*, fire.)
gelose, *n.* *jel*-ohs, an amorphous gelatinous carbohydrate present in agar-agar.
gelotometer, *n.* jel-o-*tom*-e-ter, an appliance for measuring laughter. (Gr. *gēlos*, laughter.)
gelsemium, *n.* jel-*see*-me-um, a climbing plant of the genus *Gelsemium*, allied to *Buddleia*, including *G. sempervirens*, the Carolina or yellow jasmine.
gem, *n.* jem, a precious stone, esp. when cut for ornament, as the diamond; anything like a gem for lustre, beauty, or value; a gemma [Bot. and Zool.]: *v.t.* to adorn with, or as with, gems: *v.i.* to bud. (L. *gemma*, a jewel.)
Gemara, *n.* ge-*mah*-ra, the second part of the Talmad, or the commentary on the Mishna, or text. (Heb. *gamar*, to learn, or to complete.)
Gemaric, *a.* ge-*mah*-rik, pertaining to the Gemara.
Gemarist, *n.* ge-*mah*-rist, one skilled in the study and teaching of the Gemara.
gemel, *n.* *jem*-el, a finger-ring divisible into two or more; a pair of parallel bars [Her.]. (O.Fr.)
geminate, *a.* *jem*-e-nate, disposed in pairs from the same point [Bot. and Zool.]: *v.t.* to duplicate: *v.i.* to occur in pairs. (L. *geminus*, twin.)

gemination, *n.* jem-e-*nay*-shon, **duplication**; repetition; a doubling.
Gemini, *n.pl. jem*-e-ny, the Twins, the third zodiacal constellation containing the two bright stars Castor and Pollux [Astron.]. (L., twins.)
gemma, *n. jem*-ma (*pl.* **gemmæ**), **a leaf-bud**; a minute cellular body in certain mosses, etc. [Bot.]; a bud-like excrescence on certain polyps, etc., which ultimately develops into a separate individual [Zool.]. (L., a bud.)
gemmaceous, *a.* jem-*may*-shus, relating to or having the nature or appearance of leaf-buds.
gemmate, *a. jem*-mat, reproducing by gemmation [Zool.]; having buds [Bot.]: *v.i.* to propagate itself by buds.
gemmation, *n.* jem-*may*-shon, the process of reproduction by buds or by gemmæ; the act of budding; the disposition of buds. (L. *gemmatus*, budded.)
gemmeous, *a. jem*-me-us, pertaining to or like gems; scintillating. **gemmeous dragonet,** the sea-fish *Callionymus lyra*.
gemmiferous, *a.* jem-*mif*-e-rus, producing or containing gems; producing or reproducing by buds. (L. *gemma*, and *fero*, bear.)
gemmiform, *a. jem*-me-form, resembling a bud.
gemminess, *n.* the state of being gemmy.
gemmiparity, *n. jem*-me-*pa*-re-te, reproductiveness by buds. (L. *gemma*, and *pario*, produce.)
gemmiparous, *a.* jem-*mip*-a-rus, producing buds; reproducing by gemmæ, as in polyps.
gemmology, *n.* jem-*mol*-o-je, the science of gems.
gemmule, *n. jem*-mewl, the point of growth of an embryo, or the reproductive cell of a cryptogam [Bot.]; a small bud, gemma, or spore. (Late L. *gemmula*, little bud.)
gemmuliferous, *a. jem*-mew-*lif*-e-rus, bearing gemmules. (L. *gemmula*, and *fero*, bear.)
gemmy, *a. jem*-me, glittering; full of gems.
gemot, *n.* ge-*mot*, a meeting; a council; the court of a hundred in pre-Conquest England. (A.S.)
gemsbok, *n. gemz*-bok, a large South African antelope, *Oryz gazella*, with long straight horns extending back in a line with the forehead. (Ger. *gemse*, chamois, and *bock*, buck.)
gem-stone, *n.* a semi-precious stone; any mineral which, when cut and polished, is used in jewellery.
gen, *n.* jen, any general information, esp. from a reliable source [Airman's slang].
gena, *n. jee*-na, the side of the head [Anat.]. (L., cheek.)
genal, *a. jee*-nal, pertaining to the gena or the cheek.
genappe, *n.* je-*nap*, a smooth worsted yarn used in the manufacture of fringes. (*Genappe*, in Belgium.)
gendarme, *n.* (App.) a member of the gendarmerie. (Fr., man-at-arms.)
gendarmerie, *n.* (App.) the body of police, drilled and armed as a semi-military organization, in France, Belgium, and elsewhere.
gender, *n. jen*-der, classification according to, esp. of words as representing sex [Gram.]: *v.t.* to beget; to engender: *v.i.* to copulate; to breed. (O.Fr. *gendre*.)
gene, *n.* jeen, the hypothetical unit of a chromosome that transmits the hereditary factors [Biol.].
genealogical, *a. jen*-e- *or jee*-ne-a-*loj*-e-kal, pertaining to or exhibiting genealogy; according to genealogy.
genealogically, *ad.* in a genealogical manner.
genealogist, *n. jen*-e- *or jee*-ne-*al*-o-jist, one versed in genealogies.
genealogize, *v.i. jen*-e- *or jee*-ne-*al*-o-jize, to inquire into or relate the history of descents; to trace a pedigree.
genealogy, *n. jen*-e- *or jee*-ne-*al*-o-je, a history or investigation of the descent of a person or family; the record of this; a pedigree. (Fr. *généalogie*, from Gr. *genea*, race.)
genera, *jen*-er-ra, *n.pl.* of *genus*.
generable, *a. jen*-er-ra-bl, that may be generated.
★**general,** *a. jen*-er-ral, relating to a whole class; comprehending many species; not special; not restricted to a particular import, or not specific; common; not directed to a single object; vague; usual: *n.* the whole; the chief part; the majority; the common people; the commander of an army; the army officer ranking next below field-marshal (applied also to lieutenant-generals and major-generals); particular beat of drum or march, which, in the morning, gives notice for the infantry to be ready to march [Mil.]; the chief of an order of monks, or of all the houses or congregations under the same rule; a general servant; (*pl.*) general principles. **general election,** a parliamentary election covering all constituencies. **general practitioner,** *see* **practitioner. general servant,** a female domestic where only one is kept; a maid-of-all-work. **general term,** a term denoting a whole class [Logic]. **in general,** in the main; for most part. (O.Fr.)
generalism, *n. jen*-er-ra-lizm, a general opinion, statement, etc.; a generalization.
generalissimo, *n. jen*-er-ra-*lis*-e-mo, the chief commander of an army of allies, or of a force composed of two or more of the three services. (It.)
generality, *n.* jen-er-*ral*-e-te, the state or quality of being general, and not specific; a statement that is so; the greater part. (Fr. *généralité*.)
generalizable, *a.* that can be generalized.
generalization, *n. jen*-er-ra-ly-*zay*-shon, the act of generalizing, or of reducing particulars to generals, or species to genera; the result of generalizing; an inference of general applicability.
generalize, *v.t. jen*-er-ra-lize, to extend from particular to general, or species to genus; to infer a general principle from particular instances: *v.i.* to draw general conclusions or form general ideas; to reason by induction; to speak vaguely. (Fr. *généraliser*.)
generally, *ad. jen*-er-ral-le, in general; ordinarily; usually; extensively; most frequently; in the whole taken together.
generalship, *n. jen*-er-ral-ship, the rank of a general; military skill, esp. in command; strategy; dexterous management; management.
generalty, *n. jen*-er-ral-te, generality. (Fr.)
generant, *n. jen*-er-rant, that which generates; a point, a line, or a surface conceived of as, by its motion, generating a line, a surface, or a solid [Math.]: *a.* generating; producing.
generate, *v.t. jen*-er-rate, to beget; to produce a being similar; to cause to be; to bring into life; to produce. **generating station,** an electric power-house. (L. *generatus*, begotten.)
generation, *n. jen*-er-*ray*-shon, the act of generating; propagation; production; a single succession in natural descent, as the children of the same parents; progeny; a period of one-third of a century; the people living at the same time; a series of descendants from the same stock; a race. (O.Fr.)
generative, *a. jen*-er-ra-tiv, having the power of generating or propagating; productive.
generator, *n. jen*-er-ray-ter, he who or that which generates or produces; an apparatus for the production of power; a dynamo or other machine for converting mechanical into electric energy; the principal sound or sounds by which others are produced [Mus.]; a point, line, or surface which by its motion can produce a line, area, or solid [Math.]. (L.)
generatrix, *n.* jen-er-*ray*-triks, a generant [Math.].
generic, *a.* je-*ne*-rik, pertaining to or comprehending a genus; comprehensive.
generically, *ad.* je-*ne*-re-ka-le, with regard to a genus.
generosity, *n.* jen-er-*ros*-e-te, the quality of being generous; liberality; nobleness; magnanimity. (Fr. *générosité*.)
generous, *a. jen*-er-rus, bountiful; munificent; courageous; of noble nature; magnanimous; honourable; full of spirit; invigorating; overflowing; abundant. (O.Fr.)
generously, *ad.* in a generous manner.
generousness, *n.* quality of being generous.
Genesiac, *a.* je-*nee*-se-ak, pertaining to the Book of Genesis.
genesic, *a.* je-*nee*-sik, pertaining to origin, or to genesis.
genesiology, *n.* je-nes-e-*ol*-o-je, the science of generation or heredity; genetics.
genesis, *n. jen*-e-sis, the act of producing or endowing with origin; mode of formation; (*cap.*) the first Book of the Old Testament.
genet, *n. jen*-et, any of the genus *Genetta*, small carnivores allied to the civet; the fur of this, or cat-skin, etc., disguised as such. (Fr.)
genethliac, *n.* je-*neth*-le-ak, one who casts horoscopes; a birthday poem; (*pl.*) the prediction of one's future from the stars; astrology: *a.* pertaining to horoscopes. (Gr. *genethle*, birth.)

genetic, *a.* je-*net*-ik, pertaining to the origin or generation of a thing or the mode of it. (L. *genesis*.)
genetically, *ad.* in a genetic manner.
geneticist, *n.* je-*net*-e-sist, a specialist in genetics.
genetics, *n.* je-*net*-iks, the branch of biology dealing with heredity.
geneva, *n.* je-*nee*-va, a spirit distilled from grain, flavoured with juniper: Hollands. (Fr. *genièvre*, juniper.)
Genevan, *a.* je-*nee*-van, pertaining to Geneva or to Calvinism; Calvinistic: *n.* an inhabitant of Geneva; a Calvinist, Calvin having lived at Geneva.
Genevese, *n.* *jen*-e-veez, a native or the people of Geneva: *a.* Genevan.
genevrette, *n.* *jen*-e-vret, a wine made on the Continent, from juniper berries. (Fr.)
genial, *a.* *jee*-ne-al, kindly; cheerful; sympathetic; enlivening; contributing to life and cheerfulness. (L. *genialis*.)
genial, *a.* *jee*-ne-al, pertaining to or situated near the chin. (Gr. *geneion*.)
geniality, *n.* je-ne-*al*-e-te, cheerfulness; the quality of being genial.
genialize, *v.t.* *jee*-ne-a-lize, to make genial.
genially, *ad.* *jee*-ne-a-le, in a genial manner.
genic, *a.* *jen*-ik, pertaining to or of the nature of genes.
genicular, *a.* je-*nik*-yew-lar, pertaining to the knee or its surroundings [Anat.].
geniculate, *a.* je-*nik*-yew-late, kneed; knee-jointed; having joints a little bent, like the knee [Bot.]: *v.t.* to form a joint or knot in. (L. *genu*, knee.)
geniculation, *n.* je-*nik*-yew-*lay*-shon, knottiness; the state or quality of having knots or joints.
genie, *n.* *jee*-ne (*pl.* **genii**, *jee*-ne-eye), a djinn, a sprite in Arabian folk-lore.
genioplasty, *n.* *jee*-ne-o-*plas*-te, plastic surgery of the chin.
genipap, *n.* *jen*-e-pap, an edible fruit of tropical America of the size of an orange; the tree bearing it, *Genipa americana*. (Tupi.)
Genista, *n.* je-*nis*-ta, a genus of leguminous shrubs with yellow flowers. (L.)
genital, *a.* *jen*-e-tal, pertaining to procreation or generation: *n.pl.* the external organs of procreation. (O.Fr., from L.)
genitival, *a.* jen-e-*ty*-val, having genitive form; deriving from the genitive case.
genitive, *a.* *jen*-e-tiv, applied to the case of a noun from which something else proceeds, or to which it belongs [Gram.]: *n.* the possessive case [Gram.]. (L. *genitivus*.)
geniture, *n.* *jen*-e-tewr, procreation: begetting birth. (O.Fr., from L.)
genius, *n.* *jee*-ne-us (*pl.* **geniuses**), natural endowment; natural faculty or aptitude of mind for a particular study or course of life; uncommon powers of intellect, and specially of inventive combination; a man endowed with such powers; peculiar character. (*pl.* **genii**), a good or evil spirit supposed to preside over the life of a man or a nation. **genius loci**, the presiding or ruling spirit of a place or of a public institution, etc. (L., a tutelary spirit.)
genocide, *n.* *jen*-o-side, deliberate and systematic extermination of racial or national groups. (L. *genus*, and *cædere*, to kill.)
Genoese, *a.* jen-o-*eez*, relating to Genoa: *n.* an inhabitant, or the people of Genoa, Italy.
genotype, *n.* *jen*-o-type, a group of individuals having the same genetic characters; the type species of a genus [Bot. and Zool.].
genre, *n.* (App.) a kind or sort of anything; a manner or style of painting, etc., esp. of works of art depicting scenes or subjects of everyday life. (Fr., a kind.)
genro, *n.pl.* *jen*-roh, Japanese "elder statesmen," or confidential advisers of the emperor. (Jap., old men.)
gens, *n.* jenz, a clan among the ancient Romans. (L.)
gent, *n.* jent, a gentleman or a would-be gentleman [Slang].
genteel, *a.* jen-*teel*, having the manners of well-bred people; elegant in manner or dress; refined; polite; affected; mincing. (Fr. *gentil*.)
genteelly, *ad.* jen-*teel*-le, in a genteel manner.
genteelness, *n.* the state or quality of being genteel.
gentian, *n.* *jen*-shan, any plant of the genus *Gentiana*. esp. the yellow gentian (*G. lutea*), source of a very bitter tonic. (*Gentius*, king of ancient Illyria, said to have discovered its use in medicine.)
gentianella, *n.* jen-she-a-*nel*-la, a dwarf species of gentian, *Gentiana acaulis*, with deep-blue flowers.
gentianin, *n.* *jen*-sha-nin, the bitter principle of the root of the yellow gentian [Chem.].
gentile, *n.* *jen*-tile, one who is not a Jew; formerly, a heathen: *a.* pertaining to a non-Jewish nation; indicative of a race or nationality [Gram.]. (L. *gentilis*.)
gentiledom, *n.* *jen*-tile-dom, Gentiles, or the regions occupied by them, in general.
gentilism, *n.* *jen*-tile-izm, heathenism; paganism.
gentilitial, *a.* *jen*-te-*lish*-e-al, peculiar to a people; national; peculiar to the gentility.
gentility, *n.* jen-*til*-e-te, politeness; the manners of well-bred persons; people of gentle birth, the gentry.
gentle, *a.* *jen*-tl, of good birth; not rough, harsh, or severe; placid, bland, and mild in manner; moderate: *v.t.* to tame or break in (of horses). **the gentle sex**, women. (Fr. *gentil*, noble.)
gentle, *n.* *jen*-tl, the larva of the bluebottle fly.
gentlefolk, *n.pl.* *jen*-tl-foke, those of gentle birth; persons of good breeding and family.
gentlehood, *n.* *jen*-tl-hood, the position of being gentle in nature or birth.
gentleman, *n.* *jen*-tl-man, a man of good birth; every man above the rank of yeoman, comprehending noblemen; a man entitled to bear arms [Her.]; a man of good breeding and politeness, as distinguished from the vulgar and clownish; one of the gentry; a man of chivalrous character. **gentleman's agreement**, a pact binding by honour only, not by law. **gentleman's gentleman**, a valet.
gentleman-at-arms, *n.pl.* one of the sovereign's bodyguard on state occasions.
gentleman-commoner, *n.* the highest class of commoner at Oxford University.
gentlemanlike, *a.* *jen*-tl-man-like, gentlemanly.
gentlemanliness, *n.* *jen*-tl-man-le-ness, behaviour of a well-bred man.
gentlemanly, *a.* *jen*-tl-man-le, becoming or like a man of birth and good breeding.
gentleman-usher, *n.* a gentleman who introduces others into the presence of royalty or some great personage.
gentleness, *n.* *jen*-tl-ness, softness; mildness; the quality of being gentle.
gentlewoman, *n.* *jen*-tl-woom-an, the female counterpart of a gentleman; a woman who waits about the person of one of high rank.
gentlewomanly, *a.* befitting a gentlewoman.
gently, *ad.* *jent*-le, in a gentle manner.
Gentoo, *n.* jen-*too*, a non-Moslem inhabitant of India; (*l.c.*) an Antarctic penguin, *Pygosceles tæniata*. (Port.)
gentry, *n.* *jen*-tre, untitled people of good birth and education; gentlefolk. (O.Fr. *genterise*.)
genual, *a.* *jen*-yew-al, pertaining to the knee. (L. *genu*, the knee.)
genuflect, *v.i.* *jen*-yew-flekt, to bend the knee in reverence. (L. *genu*, and *flectere*, to bend.)
genuflectory, *a.* jen-yew-*flek*-to-re, pertaining to or characterized by genuflexion.
genuflexion, *n.* jen-yew-*flek*-shon, the bending of the knee, particularly in worship.
genuine, *a.* *jen*-yew-in, belonging to the original stock; real; pure; not spurious, counterfeited, or adulterated. (L. *genuinus*.)
genuinely, *ad.* *jen*-yew-in-le, in a genuine manner.
genuineness, *n.* state or quality of being genuine.
genus, *n.* *jee*-nus (*pl.* **genera**), a group of one or more species possessing certain structural characters in common, by which they are distinguished [Zool. and Bot.]; kind, or sort; a class made up of two or more species [Logic]. **subaltern genus**, a genus which is a species to another [Logic]. **summum genus**, a genus not subordinate, as a species, to any higher genus [Logic]. (L., a kind.)
geo-, *comb. f.* jee-o-, pertaining to the earth. (Gr. *ge*, the earth.)
geo-botany, *n.* the science or study of plants in relation to their geographical distribution.
geocentric, *a.* jee-o-*sen*-trik, as seen or reckoned from the earth; having the earth for centre; having reference or pertaining to the earth's centre. (Gr. *ge*, the earth, and *centre*.)

geocentrically, *ad.* in a geocentric manner.
geocentricism, *n.* jee-o-*sen*-tre-sizm, the theory that the earth is the centre of the universe.
geocyclic, *a.* jee-o-*sy*-klik, pertaining to the revolution of the earth. (Gr. *ge*, and *cyclic*.)
geode, *n. jee*-ode, a small rounded nodule containing a cavity lined with crystals; the cavity itself. [Min.]. (Gr. *geōdēs*, earthy.)
geodesic, *a.* jee-o-*des*-ik, geodetic.
geodesy, *n.* jee-*od*-e-se, the science of measuring such large tracts of the earth that curvature has to be allowed for. (Gr. *geodaisia*, science of measurement.)
geodetic, *a.* jee-o-*det*-ik, pertaining to geodesy or its measurements.
geodic, *a.* je-*od*-ik, resembling a geode.
geodiferous, *a.* jee-o-*dif*-er-rus, producing geodes.
geodynamic, *a.* jee-o-dy-*nam*-ik, pertaining to those forces which act from within the earth's surface: *n.pl.* the science treating of such forces.
geognostic, *a.* jee-og-*nos*-tik, pertaining to geognosy.
geognosy, *n.* jee-*og*-no-se, the science of the constitution and structure of the earth; local geology; petrography. (Gr. *ge*, and *gnosis*, knowledge.)
geogonic, *a.* jee-o-*gon*-ik, pertaining to geogony.
geogony, *n.* jee-*og*-o-ne, the study of the formation of the earth. (Gr. *ge*, and *gone*, generation.)
geographer, *n.* je-*og*-ra-fer, one who is versed in geography, or who compiles a treatise on the subject.
geographic, *a.* jee-o-*graf*-ik, relating to or containing a description of the earth; pertaining to geography.
geographical, *a.* jee-o-*graf*-e-kal, geographic.
geographically, *ad.* in a geographical manner.
geography, *n.* je-*og*-ra-fe, the science and study of the earth's surface, with its physical features, political divisions, distribution of its products and inhabitants, etc.; a description of the earth or part thereof. (L. *geographia*.)
geolatry, *n.* je-*ol*-a-tre, earth-worship. (Gr. *ge*, and *latreia*, service.)
geological, *a.* jee-o-*loj*-e-kal, pertaining to geology.
geologist, *n.* je-*ol*-o-jist, one versed in geology.
geologize, *v.i.* je-*ol*-o-jize, to study geology; to make geological investigations.
geology, *n.* je-*ol*-o-je, the science which treats of the constitution and structure of the earth's crust with its rocks and their inorganic and organic contents, the successive changes these have undergone, and the causes thereof; a treatise dealing with this. (Gr. *ge*, and *logos*, science.)
geomancer, *n. jee*-o-man-ser, one learned in geomancy.
geomancy, *n. jee*-o-man-se, divination from figures or lines, originally from natural or artificial configurations on the earth's surface. (Gr. *ge*, and *manteia*, divination.)
geomantic, *a.* je-o-*man*-tik, pertaining to geomancy.
geometer, *n.* je-*om*-e-ter, one skilled in geometry; one of a species of the looper moths [Entom.].
geometric, *a.* jee-o-*met*-rik, geometrical. **geometric pen,** an instrument with a revolving arm for drawing geometrical curves. **geometric spider,** any of the spiders that spin a circular web.
geometrical, *a.* jee-o-*met*-re-kal, pertaining to geometry; according to or done by geometry. **geometrical progression,** the increase of a quantity by a common multiplier, as 1, 2, 4, 8, 16, or decrease by a common divisor, as 16, 8, 4, 2, 1. **geometrical staircase,** a spiral staircase.
geometrically, *ad.* according to geometry.
geometrician, *n.* je-*om*-e-*trish*-an, one skilled in geometry.
geometrize, *v.i.* je-*om*-e-trize, to act according to the laws of geometry; to perform geometrically.
geometry, *n.* je-*om*-e-tre, the science of magnitude in general; the mensuration of lines, surfaces, and solids, with their various relations. (Literally, land-measurement, O.Fr. *geometrie*, from Gr.)
geomorphology, *n. jee*-o-mor-*fol*-o-je, the study or theory of the conformation of the earth's crust.
Geomys, *n. jee*-o-mis, a genus of burrowing rodents including the pocket gophers of North America.
geophagous, *a.* je-*of*-a-gus, earth-eating.
geophagy, *n.* je-*of*-a-je, the practice among some primitive peoples of eating clay or earth; a morbid tendency to eat earth [Path.]. (Gr. *ge*, and *phago*, eat.)
geophysical, *a.* jee-o-*fiz*-e-kal, pertaining to geophysics.
geophysics, *n.* jee-o-*fiz*-iks, the science dealing with the physical characteristics, modifications, and properties of the earth.
geopolitics, *n.* jee-o-*pol*-e-tiks, the science or study of international relations with reference, chiefly, to geographical conditions. (Ger. *Geopolitik*, from Gr.)
geoponic, *a.* jee-o-*pon*-ik, relating to agriculture.
geoponics, *n.* jee-o-*pon*-iks, the art or science of cultivating the earth. (Gr. *ge*, and *ponos*, labour.)
georama, *n.* jee-o-*rah*-ma, a hollow sphere exhibiting, from the interior, a geographical view of the earth's surface. (Gr. *ge*, and *horama*, view.)
Geordie, *n. jor*-de, a coal-miner; a collier [Naut.]; a miner's safety-lamp.
George, *n.* jorj, a figure of St. George on horseback, slaying the dragon, worn by knights of the Garter. **George Cross,** a British civilian and military decoration for gallantry, instituted 1940 by King George VI and ranking next after the Victoria Cross. **George noble,** a gold coin in the time of Henry VIII, with a George on the reverse, then worth 6*s.* 8*d.* **St. George's cross,** *see* **cross.**
georgette, *n.* jor-*jet*, a semi-transparent silk crêpe of very fine texture.
Georgian, *a. jor*-je-an, belonging to or characteristic of the reign or period of any of the English Georges; pertaining to Georgia, a Soviet Socialist Republic of Transcaucasia, or to Georgia, one of the southern states of the U.S.A.: *n.* a native of either of these.
georgic, *a. jor*-jik, relating to agricultural and rural affairs: *n.* a poetical composition on rural husbandry. (L. *georgicus*, relating to husbandry.)
geoselenic, *a.* jee-o-se-*len*-ik, connected with or relating to both the earth and the moon. (Gr. *ge*, and *selene*, the moon.)
geostatic, *a.* jee-o-*stat*-ik, relating to downward pressure exerted by a heavy body [Civil Eng.].
geostatics, *n.* jee-o-*stat*-iks, the statics of rigid bodies [Mech.].
geostrophic, *a.* jee-o-*strof*-ik, pertaining to deflexion due to the earth's rotation [Meteor.]. (Gr. *ge*, and *strophikos*, a turning.)
geotectonic, *a.* jee-o-tek-*ton*-ik, pertaining to the structure of the earth. (Gr. *ge*, and *tekton*, builder.)
geothermic, *a.* jee-o-*ther*-mik, pertaining to the internal heat of the earth. (Gr. *ge*, and *thermos*, heat.)
geothermometer, *n.* jee-o-ther-*mom*-e-ter, an instrument for measuring the earth's heat at different depths, as in artesian wells, mines, etc. (Gr. *ge*, and *thermometer*.)
geotropism, *n.* je-*ot*-ro-pizm, the tendency of roots to turn downwards. (Gr. *ge*, and *trepo*, turn.)
gerah, *n. jee*-rah, an ancient Jewish weight, one-twentieth of a shekel. (Heb.)
Geranium, *n.* je-*ray*-ne-um, a large genus of hardy herbaceous plants, including the cranesbills; (*l.c.*) the popular name for several cultivated species of *Pelargonium*. **geranium oil,** an essential oil prepared from various species of *Pelargonium*, used in perfumery, as flavouring, etc. (Gr. *geranos*, a crane.)
geratology, *n. je*-ra-*tol*-o-je, the science treating of the phenomena of deterioration and decay. (Gr. *geras*, age, *logos*, science.)
gerbil, *n. jer*-bil, a small jerboa-like rodent of N. African and Asian deserts.
gerent, *n. je*-rent, one who rules; the holder of an office.
gerfalcon, *n. jer*-faw-kn, a large falcon of the Arctic belonging to the sub-genus *Hierofalco*. (O.Fr. *gerfaucon*.)
germ, *n.* jerm, origin; the origin of an embryo; the rudimentary form of an organism; the seed-bud [Bot.]; any micro-organism causing disease [Coll.]; that from which anything springs. **germ cell,** a cell upon which the perpetuation of the race is directly dependent [Biol.]. (Fr. *germe*.)
German, *a. jer*-man, of or from Germany: *n.* a native of Germany; one of German stock; the German language. **High German,** the literary and official language. **Low German,** the dialects of the German lowlands, including Flemish and Dutch. (L. *Germanus*, German.)
german, *a. jer*-man, germane; having the same grandparents; born of the same parents, as sisters german: *n.* one of the same stock; a first cousin. (O.Fr. *germain*.)
germander, *n.* jer-*man*-der, a labiate plant of the

genus *Teucrium*. **germander speedwell,** the blue-flowered wild plant, *Veronica chamædrys*. (O.Fr. *germandree*.)
germane, *a*. jer-*mane*, related; relevant; appropriate. (O.Fr. *germain*.)
Germanic, *a*. jer-*man*-ik, pertaining to Germany, the Germans, or the Teutonic race: *n*. the primitive Teutonic language.
Germanism, *n*. *jer*-man-izm, a German idiom; a German trait or characteristic; devotion to Germany, German ideals, etc.
germanium, *n*. jer-*may*-ne-um, a brittle, grey, metallic element resembling both silicon and tin.
Germanization, *n*. jer-ma-ny-*zay*-shon, the act of making German; the state of being Germanized.
Germanize, *v.t.* and *i*. *jer*-ma-nize, to make or become German (in style, taste, ideals, etc.); to translate into German.
German-measles, *n*. rubella, a mild, infectious disease.
German-millet, *n*. a grass, *Setaria germanica*, which yields an edible grain.
Germanomania, *n*. jer-ma-no-*may*-ne-a, excessive admiration for or devotion to Germany and things German.
Germanophile, *a*. jer-*man*-o-fil, approving the Germans, their way of life, ideals, etc.: *n*. one of Germanophile principles.
Germanophobia, *n*. jer-ma-no-*foh*-be-a, hatred or fear of Germans, German institutions, etc.
German-paste, *n*. a food for certain cage-birds, made of hempseed, pea-meal, lard, and honey or treacle.
German-sausage, *n*. a sausage of partly cooked meat; breakfast sausage.
German-silver, *n*. a white alloy of copper, zinc, and nickel; nickel silver.
German-tinder, *n*. amadou.
germen, *n*. *jer*-men, an ovary [Bot.].
germicidal, *a*. jer-me-*sy*-dal, germicide.
germicide, *n*. *jer*-me-side, that by which germs can be killed: *a*. destroying germs, esp. those propagating disease. (*germ*, and L. *cædo*, kill.)
germifuge, *a*. *jer*-me-fewj, expelling germs [Med.].
germinal, *a*. *jer*-me-nal, pertaining to or of the nature of a germ; in the first stage of development. (L. *germen*, germ.)
germinant, *a*. *jer*-me-nant, sprouting; developing.
germinate, *v.i.* *jer*-me-nate, to sprout; to bud; to shoot; to develop: *v.t.* to cause to sprout. (L. *germinatus*, sprouted.)
germination, *n*. jer-me-*nay*-shon, the beginning of vegetation in a seed or plant; the act or process of germinating.
germinative, *a*. *jer*-me-na-tiv, germinal. (L.)
germ-plasm, *n*. the matter in the cell-protoplasm through which heredity was supposed to be transmitted.
germule, *n*. *jer*-mewl, a small germ [Biol.].
gerontocracy, *n*. ge-ron-*tok*-ra-se, government by the aged; a government composed of such. (Gr. *geron*, old man, *kratos*, power.)
gerontology, *n*. je-ron-*tol*-o-je, the scientific study of old age or of the disease of the aged.
geropiga, *n*. je-ro-*py*-ga, a compound of unfermented grape juice, colouring matter, etc., employed to adulterate port wines. (Port.)
gerrymander, *n*. *je*-re-man-der, unfair manipulation of anything, orig. of constituences in the U.S.A. so as to put a particular party or candidate at a disadvantage: *v.t.* to manipulate or divide an electoral district for such a purpose. (Elbridge *Gerry*, a governor of Massachusetts, 1812, and *-mander*, from *salamander*.)
gerund, *n*. *je*-rund, a participial noun, expressing the action of the verb [Gram.]. (L. *gerundium*.)
gerundial, *a*. je-*run*-de-al, pertaining to or like a gerund.
gerundival, *a*. je-run-*dy*-val, pertaining to or like a gerundive.
gerundive, *n*. je-*run*-div, in Latin, the future participle passive, used as a gerund; in English, a participial noun, as governed by or governing another word [Gram.]: *a*. gerundival. (Late L. *gerundivus*.)
gesso, *n*. *jes*-so, gypsum, or plaster of Paris, specially made for use in sculpture and painting. (It.)
gest, *n*. jest, a mediæval tale of adventure; an exploit.
Gestapo, *n*. *ges*-tah-*poh*, the secret political police of Nazi Germany (organized 1933); hence, a brutal secret service. (Ger. *Ge*heime *Sta*ats*po*lizei.)
gestation, *n*. jes-*tay*-shon, the act of carrying young in the womb; pregnancy; the period of this. (L. *gestatio*, bearing.)
gestatorial, *a*. jes-ta-*taw*-re-al, suitable for carrying (used only of the chair in which the Pope is borne on ceremonial occasions).
gestatory, *a*. *jes*-ta-to-re, pertaining to gestation or pregnancy.
gestic, *a*. *jes*-tik, pertaining to dancing.
gesticulate, *v.i.* jes-*tik*-yew-late, to make gestures, esp. when, or in place of, speaking: *v.t.* to express by gesture. (L. *gesticulatus*, gesticulated.)
gesticulation, *n*. jes-*tik*-yew-*lay*-shon, the act of gesticulating to express passion or enforce sentiments; a gesture; an antic.
gesticulator, *n*. jes-*tik*-yew-lay-tor, one who gesticulates.
gesticulatory, *a*. jes-*tik*-yew-la-to-re, representing in gestures.
gestural, *a*. *jest*-yewr-ral, consisting of or pertaining to gesture.
gesture, *n*. *jest*-yewr, physical movements expressing emotion or ideas; any movement of the body or limbs: *v.t.* to accompany with gesture: *v.i.* to gesticulate. (Late L. *gestura*, a mode of action.)
gestureless, *a*. *jest*-yewr-less, free from gestures.
★**get,** *v.t.* get, to gain possession of; to have; to earn; to beget, as offspring; to learn; to prevail on; to procure to be; to betake (oneself); to be obliged [Coll.]; to catch or outwit [Coll.]: *v.i.* to go; to arrive at; to profit; to succeed [Coll.]. **to get above,** to surmount. **to get ahead,** to advance; to prosper. **to get along,** to proceed; to advance. **to get among,** to arrive in the midst of. **to get at,** to reach; to tamper with or suborn [Coll.]. **to get away** or **away from,** to quit; to disengage oneself from. **to get back,** to return. **to get behind,** to fall in the rear. **to get clear,** to disengage oneself; to be released. **to get down,** to descend. **to get loose** or **free,** to disengage oneself. **to get near,** to approach within a small distance. **to get off,** to put off; to pull off, as a coat; to remove, as a stranded vessel; to dispose of; to alight; to escape. **to get on,** to put on; to draw or pull on; to proceed; to prosper. **to get out,** to draw forth; to draw out; to disengage; to escape. **to get over,** to surmount; to recover from. **to get religion,** to be converted [Coll.]. **to get rid of,** to disengage oneself from; to remove. **to get round,** to evade; to wheedle [Coll.]. **to get through,** to pass through and reach a point beyond; to finish. **to get to,** to reach. **to get together,** to collect or amass; to meet for consultation or common action. **to get under way,** to start; to begin to move [Naut.]. **to get up,** to bring forward; to ascend; to rise, as from bed or a seat. *p*. and *pp*. **got.** (Ice. *geta*.)
getable, *a*. *get*-a-bl, that which can be obtained or reached.
get-at-able, *a*. get-*at*-a-bl, accessible; obtainable.
getaway, *n*. *get*-a-way, the act of starting, as of horses in a race, a car from a dead stop, etc.; the breaking of game from cover; an escape [Slang].
getter, *n*. *get*-ter, one who gets, or one who begets; a hewer at the face [Mining and Quarrying].
getting, *n*. *get*-ting, acquisition; gain.
get-up, *n*. *get*-up, style of dress; style.
Geum, *n*. *jee*-um, a hardy genus of plants belonging to the rose family. (L., the herb bennet.)
gew-gaw, *n*. *gew*-gaw, a showy trifle; a bauble: *a*. showy without value. (Perhaps from *give-gove*, reduplicate of A.S. *gifu*, gift.)
geyser, *n*. *gee*-zer, an eruptive fountain, due to volcanic agency, which sends forth intermittent jets of hot water and steam; a metal contrivance for heating bath-room water quickly. (Ice. *geysir*.)
gharry, *n*. *ga*-re, a hired horsed carriage in common use in India. (Hind. *gari*.)
ghastliness, *n*. *gahst*-le-ness, the state of being ghastly.
ghastly, *a*. *gahst*-le, deathlike; haggard; horrible; shocking. (A.S. *gæstan*, to terrify.)
ghat *or* **ghaut,** *n*. gawt, in India, a mountain pass; a chain of mountains; stairs descending to a river. (Hind. *ghât*, a passage or gate.)
Ghazi, *n*. *gah*-zee, a title of honour bestowed on Mohammedan fanatics. (Ar. *ghaza*, battle.)

Gheber, *n.* *gee*-ber or *gay*-ber, a Guebre.
ghee, *n.* ge, butter made in India from the milk of buffaloes and clarified by boiling. (Hind.)
gherkin, *n.* *gir*-kin, a small or immature cucumber used for pickling. (Dut. *agherkin.*)
ghetto, *n.* *get*-toh, the Jewish quarter in a city; a town or location set aside for the immurement of Jews. (It.)
Ghibellines, *n.pl.* *gib*-e-leenz, in mediæval Italy, the political party of the German emperors in opposition to that of the Pope. (Ger. *Waiblingen,* a hamlet in Wurtemberg.)
ghost, *n.* gohst, the soul of a deceased person; the soul or spirit separate from the body; a phantom; a false image; one who does work, esp. literary or artistic, for which another gets the credit. **not a ghost of a chance,** no possibility [Coll.]. **the ghost walks,** pay is being handed out [Theat. slang]. **The Holy Ghost,** the Third Person of the Trinity. **to give up the ghost,** to die. (A.S. *gast,* Ger. *geist,* a spirit.)
ghostlike, *a.* *gohst*-like, like a ghost; ghastly.
ghostliness, *n.* the quality of being ghostly.
ghostly, *a.* *gohst*-le, spiritual; relating to the soul or to religious matters; pertaining to apparitions; fit for ghosts.
ghost-moth, *n.* the moth *Hepialus humuli.*
ghost-story, *n.* a tale about ghosts; an eerie tale of the supernatural.
ghost-word, *n.* a spurious word, due usually to a printer's or copyist's error.
ghoul, *n.* gool, a demon of Oriental legend fabled to feed on the dead: a revoltingly cruel person. (Ar.)
ghoulish, *a.* fiendish; like a ghoul.
Ghurka, *n.* *goor*-ka, a Gurkha.
ghyll, *n.* gill, a ravine.
giallolino, *n.* jal-o-*lee*-no, a fine yellow pigment, also known as Naples yellow. (It.)
giant, *n.* *jy*-ant, a mythical being of superhuman size and strength; a man of extraordinary bulk and stature; one of great physical or intellectual powers; any animal or plant of abnormal size: *a.* like a giant; gigantic. (O.Fr.)
giantess, *n.* *jy*-an-tess, a female giant.
giantism, *n.* *jy*-an-tizm, gigantism.
giant-like, *a.* *jy*-ant-like, gigantic; huge.
giant-powder, *n.* a kind of dynamite.
giantship, *n.* *jy*-ant-ship, the state, quality, or character of a giant.
giant-stride, *n.* a pole with a revolving top from which ropes are suspended, by means of which the holders can take large strides round the pole.
giaour, *n.* jour, the Turkish name for an infidel or non-Moslem, esp. a Christian. (Pers.)
gib, *n.* jib, the arm of a crane; a wedge, bolt, or pin [Mech.].
gib, *n.* gib, a gib-cat. (Abbrev. from *Gilbert,* a cat's name.)
gibber, *v.i.* *jib*-ber *or* *gib*-ber, to speak rapidly and inarticulately; to jabber.
gibberish, *n.* *gib*-ber-ish, rapid inarticulate talk; unmeaning words: *a.* unmeaning, as words.
gibbet, *n.* *jib*-bet, a gallows; a post with a projecting arm at the top on which the body of an executed person was hung in chains; formerly, the projecting beam of a crane: *v.t.* to hang and expose on, or as on, a gibbet; to expose to infamy or public contempt. (O.Fr.)
gibble-gabble, *n.* *gib*-bl-*gab*-bl, gabble; gibberish.
gibbon, *n.* *gib*-bon, a long-armed anthropoid ape of the genus *Hylobates.* (Fr.)
gibbose, *a.* gib-*bose,* humped; gibbous.
gibbosity, *n.* gib-*bos*-e-te, the state of being gibbous; a protuberance; convexity.
gibbous, *a.* *gib*-bus, protuberant; convex, as the moon between half-full and full; hump-backed. (L. *gibbosus.*)
gibbously, *ad.* *gib*-bus-le, in a gibbous form.
gib-cat, *n.* *gib*-kat, a he-cat, esp. when castrated.
gibe, *n.* jibe, a sneer or taunt; censure mingled with contempt: *v.i.* to cast reproaches and sneering expressions; to rail or sneer at: *v.t.* to use contemptous words to; to scoff at. (Perhaps Scand. *geipa,* to talk nonsense.)
Gibeonite, *n.* *gib*-e-o-nite, an inhabitant of Gibeon; a menial of the lowest grade; a drudge. (Josh. ix. 27.)
giber, *n.* *jibe*-er, one who jibes.
gibingly, *ad.* *jibe*-ing-le, with jibes; scornfully.
giblet, *a.* *jib*-let, made of giblets, as a giblet-pie.
giblets, *n.pl.* *jib*-lets, the feet, neck, and edible entrails of poultry. **giblet-pie,** a pie containing these. (Fr. *gibelet.*)
gibus, *n.* (App.), an opera, or collapsible, hat. (Maker's name.)
gid, *n.* gid, sturdy, a disease in sheep. (As *giddy.*)
giddily, *ad.* *gid*-de-le, with a giddy feeling; in a giddy manner.
giddiness, *n.* the state of being giddy; vertigo.
giddy, *a.* *gid*-de, dizzy; having in the head a sensation of reeling, vertigo, or dizziness; that induces giddiness; whirling; inconstant; changeable; headless; thoughtless; tottering; unfixed; elated to thoughtlessness; over-excited. (A.S. *gidig,* insane.)
giddy-brained, *a.* careless; thoughtless.
giddy-head, *n.* a thoughtless person.
giddy-paced, *a.* *gid*-e-payst, moving irregularly.
gier-eagle, *n.* *jeer*-ee-gl, an unidentified bird of prey mentioned in the Bible (Lev. and Deut.) as unclean, probably the small Egyptian vulture. (Dut. *gier,* vulture.)
gift, *n.* gift, the act of giving; anything given; a donation; a bribe; a natural endowment: *v.t.* to endow with any gift or faculty; to bestow. (A.S.)
gifted, *a.* *gif*-ted, endowed with intellectual gifts.
gift-horse, *n.* a horse that is given as a gift.
gig, *n.* gig, a small harpoon; a fishgig: *v.t.* to fish with a gig or fishgig.
gig, *n.* gig, any little thing that is whirled round in play; a light two-wheeled one-horse carriage; a ship's rowing boat designed for speed; a racing boat: *pl.* swellings on the insides of a horse's lips; rotary cylinders covered with wire teeth, for teazling woollen cloth [Mech.].
gigantean, *a.* jy-gan-*tee*-an, like a giant; mighty.
gigantesque, *a.* jy-gan-*tesk,* as if by a giant; befitting a giant; gigantean.
gigantic, *a.* jy-*gan*-tik, like a giant; enormous; colossal.
gigantically, *ad.* in a gigantic manner.
gigantism, *jy*-gan-tizm, the state or quality of being a giant, abnormally large development due to excessive activity of the pituitary gland [Med.].
gigantology, *n.* jy-gan-*tol*-o-je, a treatise on giants. (Gr. *gigas,* a giant, *logos,* account.)
gigantomachy, *n.* jy-gan-*tom*-a-ke, the contest of the giants against Zeus [Myth.]; hence, any war of giants. (Gr. *gigas,* and *mache,* a battle.)
giggle, *n.* *gig*-gl, a silly laugh: *v.i.* to laugh with short catches of the breath, or in a silly puerile manner. (Imit.)
giggler, *n.* *gig*-gler, one who giggles or titters.
gig-lamps, *n.pl.* *gig*-lamps, spectacles [Slang].
giglet, *n.* *gig*-let, a giglot.
giglot, *a.* *gig*-lot, giddy; inconstant; wanton: *n.* a silly or a wanton girl.
gigman, *n.* *gig*-man, one who drives a gig; hence, one who is ambitious to seem respectable [Carlyle].
gigmanity, *n.* gig-*man*-e-te, the smug respectability of a gigman; the class of gigmen [Carlyle].
gig-mill, *n.* *gig*-mill, a device for raising a nap upon cloth; the factory in which this is done. (*gig,* a spinning-top.)
gigolo, *n.* *jig*-o-loh, a paid dancing partner; a lounge-lizard. (Fr., *masc.* of *gigolette,* woman of easy virtue.)
gigot, *n.* *jig*-ot, a leg of mutton. (Fr.)
gigue, *n.* jeeg, a lively tune or jig. (It. *giga,* fiddle.)
gila, *n.* *hee*-lah, *or* **gila monster,** a large venomous lizard, *Heloderma suspectum,* of the Gila valley in Arizona and New Mexico.
Gilbertian, *a.* gil-*ber*-te-an, grotesquely topsy-turvy; farcical humour, like that of W. S. Gilbert in his Bab Ballads and Savoy operas.
gild, *v.t.* gild, to overlay with gold; to colour, as with gold; to adorn with lustre; to give a fair and agreeable external appearance to. **gilded youth,** wealthy young men-about-town. **the Gilded Chamber,** the House of Lords. *participial* **a. gilt.** (A.S. *gyldan.*)
gild, *n.* gild, a guild.
gilder, *n.* *gild*-er, one who gilds.
gilding, *n.* *gild*-ing, the art or practice of overlaying with gold; that which is laid on in, or as in, overlaying with gold. **gilding metal,** an alloy of copper, brass, and tin. **gilding size,** size used by gilders.
gill, *n.* gil, the organ of respiration in fishes and certain amphibia; the organ of similar function in certain aquatic insects; the pendent flap below the beak of a fowl; the flesh under the chin [Slang]. (Scand.)

gill, *n.* jil, a measure, containing ¼-pint. (Fr.)
gill, *n.* jil, a gillian.
gill, *n.* gil, a ravine; a narrow valley; a ghyll. (Ice.)
gillaroo, *n.* gil-lar-*roo*, a species of trout, *Salmo stomachicus*, found in Ireland.
gill-cover, *n.* *gil*-kuv-er, the bony flap covering a fish's gills.
gill-flirt, *n.* *jil*-flirt, a flirt; a wanton girl.
gillian, *n.* *jil*-le-an, a girl; a sweetheart; a flirt. (L. *Juliana*.)
gillie, *n.* *gil*-le, a sportsman's attendant in the Highlands; a servant. (Gael. *gille*, a lad.)
gillyflower, *n.* *jil*-le-flour, the common name for the carnation, *Dianthus caryophyllus*, and the stock, *Matthiola incana*. **wall gillyflower**, the wall-flower, *Cheiranthus cheiri*. (Fr. *giroflée*.)
gilt, *a.* gilt, gilded; adorned with or as with gold: *n.* gold laid on the surface; gilding.
gilt, *n.* gilt, a young sow. (Scand.)
gilt-edged, *a.* *gilt*-edjd, having the edges gilded, as a book. **gilt-edge securities**, securities of the highest reputation; trustee stock.
gilt-head, *n.* *gilt*-hed, a fish of the wrasse family, one of the sea-breams, and other brightly coloured marine fish.
gimbals, *n.pl.* *jim*-balz, two brass rings which move within each other, each perpendicularly to its plane, used in suspending the mariner's compass; a universal joint. (O.Fr. *gemel*, twin.)
gimcrack, *a.* *jim*-krak, showy but valueless; trumpery; *n.* a trivial mechanism; a gew-gaw; a toy.
gimcrackery, *n.* jim-*krak*-e-re, trumpery knick-knack; useless ornaments; worthless show.
gimlet, *n.* *gim*-let, a small tool with a pointed screw at the end, for boring holes in wood: *v.t.* to bore with; to turn round, as a gimlet. (O.Fr. *gimbelet*.)
gimmal, *n.* *jim*-mal, a series of interlocking rings which can move within each other; a gemel-ring; a gimbal. **gimmal bit**, the double bit of a bridle.
gimmer, *n.* *gim*-mer, a ewe between one and two years old. (Ice. *gymbr*.)
gimp, *n.* gimp, a kind of trimming or edging, usually stiffened by wire; thread or wire whipped with thread. (O.Fr. *guimpe*.)
gimp, *a.* jimp, smart; spruce; jimp.
gin, *n.* jin, the spirituous drink geneva or hollands. **gin palace, gin shop**, a low-class public-house selling spirits.
gin, *n.* *jin*, a snare or trap; a machine of various kinds, esp. one for hoisting or one for separating the fibre from cotton seeds: *v.t.* to clear cotton of its seed; to catch in a trap. (O.Fr. *engin*, a mechanical device.)
gin, *n.* jin, an Australian aboriginal woman. (Austral.)
gin-fizz, *n.* jin-*fiz*, a drink of soda-water, gin, and lemon, with or without sugar.
gingal, *n.* *jin*-gal, a large musket, formerly used in the East and fired from a rest; a swivel-gun.
ginger, *n.* *jin*-jer, the tropical plant *Zuigiber officinale*; its root-stock, which has hot and spicy qualities and is used as a sweetmeat, in cookery, and in medicine; a red-haired person [Slang]; energy, mettle [Slang]: *v.t.* to impart "go" to; to make mettlesome [Slang]; to dose (a horse) with ginger: *a.* carroty, of bright-red colour (of hair) [Coll.]. **ginger-ale** and **ginger-beer**, non-intoxicating beverages flavoured with ginger. **ginger wine**, a fermented liquor impregnated with ginger. (Fr. *gingembre*.)
gingerade, *n.* *gin*-jer-ade, a non-alcoholic aerated drink with a ginger taste.
ginger-brandy, *n.* a spirituous cordial spiced with ginger.
gingerbread, *n.* *jin*-jer-bred, a cake composed of flour, butter, and sweetened ginger. **gingerbread tree**, the doum-palm; the W. African fan-palm, *Hyphæne thebaica*, with edible fruit. **gingerbread work**, work cut in varied and fanciful shapes. **to take the gilt off the gingerbread**, to disillusion.
gingerly, *ad.* *jin*-jer-le, daintily; gently; cautiously: *a.* cautious; fastidious. (Prob. O.Fr. *genzor*, delicate.
ginger-pop, *n.* ginger-beer.
gingery, *a.* *jin*-je-re, resembling ginger in taste or colour; hot-flavoured.
gingham, *n.* *ging*-am, a kind of striped cotton cloth; an umbrella [Slang]. (Fr. *guingan*, from Malay *ginggang*, striped.)
gingili, *n.* *jin*-jil-e, the oil yielded by *Sesamum indicum*; the plant itself.
ginging, *n.* *jing*-ing, the brick or masonry lining of a mine-shaft; the process of constructing this.
gingival, *a.* jin-*jy*-val, pertaining to the gums [Anat.]. (L. *gingiva*, the gums.)
gingivitis, *n.* jin-je-*vy*-tis, inflammation of the gums.
gingko, *n.* *ging*-koh, the maidenhair tree of Japan, *Gingko biloba*. (Jap.)
ginglymoid, *a.* *ging*-gle-moyd, like or pertaining to a ginglymus.
ginglymus, *n.* *ging*-gle-mus, a hinge-like articulation allowing movement in one plane only [Anat.]. (Gr. *ginglumos*, a hinge.)
gin-horse, *n.* a horse that turns a mill.
gin-house, *n.* an establishment where cotton is ginned.
ginnery, *n.* *jin*-e-re, a gin-house.
ginning, *n.* *jin*-ning, the operation by which cotton is separated from its seeds.
ginny-carriage, *n.* *jin*-ne-*ka*-rij, a small strong car for conveying materials on a railway.
ginseng, *n.* *jin*-seng, a plant, *Aralia ginseng*, the aromatic root of which is used medicinally in China. (Chin.)
gin-sling, *n.* a drink of gin and sweetened water.
gip, *v.t.* jip, to take out the entrails of herrings.
gipsy, *n.* *jip*-se, a widely diffused nomadic people of Indo-Caucasian origin, first appearing in Europe in the 14th cent.; their language; a reproachful name for one of a dark complexion; a tricky or cunning person; a hussy [Coll.]; a brunette [Coll.]: *a.* pertaining to or resembling the gipsies. (*Egyptian*, as the gipsies were supposed to have come from Egypt.)
gipsy-cart, *n.* the roofed van or caravan in which gipsy families live and move about.
gipsydom, *n.* *jip*-se-dom, the world of gipsies; gipsy life.
gipsyism, *n.* *jip*-se-izm, the arts and practices of gipsies; the state of a gipsy.
giraffe, *n.* je-*rahf*, a very long-necked ruminant African ungulate of several sub-species. (Fr. *girafe*.)
girandole, *n.* *ji*-ran-dole, a branched candlestick or chandelier; a revolving firework or jet of water; a pendent jewel with others set round it. (Fr.)
girasol, *n.* *ji*-ra-sol, the fire-opal, a precious stone. (Fr.)
girasole, *n.* *ji*-ra-sole, a sunflower; the Jerusalem artichoke. (It.)
gird, *v.t.* gird, to bind round with any flexible substance; to make fast by binding; to fasten on; to surround as with a girdle; to clothe. (A.S. *gyrdan*.)
gird, *v.t.* gird, to gibe; to reproach: *v.i.* to gibe; to sneer: *n.* a biting remark; a taunt. (M.E. *girden*, to pierce.)
girder, *n.* *gird*-er, a beam supported at both ends and usually used as a support; the main beam of timber or steel in a floor [Arch.].
girding, *n.* *gird*-ing, that which girds; girders.
girdle, *n.* *gir*-dl, a band or belt, especially for the waist; the bony support of a limb [Anat.]; enclosure; the line which encompasses the stone horizontally [Jewellery]; a circular band or fillet round the shaft of a column [Arch.]: *v.t.* to bind with or as with a girdle; to enclose; to make a circular incision through the bark in a tree so as to kill it [U.S.A.]. (A.S. *gyrdel*.)
girdle, *n.* *gir*-dl, a round metal plate for cooking cakes on; a griddle.
girdler, *n.* *gir*-dler, one who girdles; a maker of girdles.
★**girl**, *n.* girl, a female child; a young unmarried woman; a maidservant. **Girl Guide**, the female equivalent in Great Britain (**Girl Scout** in **U.S.A.**) of a Boy Scout. **one's best girl**, one's sweetheart. **principal girl**, the leading actress in a pantomime, etc. (M.E. *gerle*, a child of either sex.)
girlhood, *n.* *girl*-hood, state or time of being a girl.
girlish, *a.* *girl*-ish, of or like a girl.
girlishly, *ad.* *girl*-ish-le, in the manner of a girl.
girlishness, *n.* girlish character or ways.
girn, *v.i.* girn, to grumble; to be fretful [Scots.].
girnel, *n.* *girn*-el, a meal chest; a granary [Scots.].
Girondist, *n.* (App.), one of a moderate Republican party in the French Revolution, the leaders of which represented the Gironde, the French department of which Bordeaux is the capital.

girouette, *n.* (App.), a weathercock; one of unstable politics, principle, etc.; a trimmer. (Fr., weathercock.)
girt, *a.* girt, bound; girded; moored so taut as not to be able to swing to wind or tide (of ships) [Naut.]: *n.* a small girder; a girth.
girth, *n.* girth, the band or strap by which a saddle, etc., on a horse's back is made fast by passing under the belly; a surcingle; a circular bandage; measure round; circumference: *v.t.* to bind, fit, or secure with a girth; to measure the girth of. (Scand.)
girt-line, *n. girt*-line, a rope to lift up the rigging to the mast-head [Naut.].
gist, *n.* jist, the main point of a question or argument; the essence. (O.Fr.)
gitano, *n.masc.* he-*tah*-no *or* je-*tah*-no (*fem.* **gitana**), a gipsy, esp. of Spain. (Sp.)
gîte, *n.* zheet, a place of shelter; a place where one sleeps or resides. (Fr.)
gittern, *n. git*-tern, a cithern, a kind of guitar.
giusto, *ad. joos*-to, in steady correct time [Mus.]. (It.)
★**give,** *v.t.* giv, to bestow; to grant without requiring a recompense; to deliver; to impart; to communicate; to pay; to yield; to grow soft; to quit; to grant; to expose; to allow; to permit; to afford; to furnish; to empower; to pay or render; to pronounce; to show; to emit; to apply; to admit: *v.i.* to yield to pressure; to begin to melt; to grow soft; to move; to recede: *n.* absence of resistance; the state of giving way; resilience. **to give and take,** to play fair; to compromise. **to give away,** to transfer; to betray; to divulge inadvertently [Coll.]. **to give back,** to return. **to give chase,** to pursue. **to give ear,** to pay attention to. **to give forth,** to publish. **to give ground,** to retire. **to give in,** to allow by way of abatement; to yield. **to give in to,** to yield assent. **to give it to one,** to set about or to punish him [Coll.]. **to give off,** to emit. **to give oneself up,** to despair of one's recovery; to abandon. **to give out,** to utter publicly; to report; to become exhausted. **to give over,** to abandon; to desist. **to give tongue,** to bay as a hound. **to give up,** to resign; to surrender; to relinquish. **to give way,** to yield; to recede; to break down. *p.* **gave.** *pp.* **given.** (A.S. *giefan.*)
giveable, *a. giv*-a-bl, that may be given.
given, *a. giv*-en, bestowed. **given name,** the Christian, fore-, or personal name. **given to,** addicted to.
giver, *n. giv*-er, one who gives or bestows.
gizzard, *n. giz*-ard, the strong muscular second stomach of a bird. **to stick in one's gizzard,** to be extremely unpalatable. (O.Fr. *gezier.*)
glabrate, *a. glay*-brat, glabrous [Bot. and Zool.].
glabrescent, *a.* gla-*bres*-ent, becoming hairless; almost without down or hairs [Bot.].
glabrous, *a. glay*-brus, smooth; without hair or down. (L. *glaber.*)
glacé, *a. glas*-ay, made shiny; polished; coated with icing (as cakes and fruit). (Fr.)
glacial, *a. glay*-shal, of or pertaining to ice; due to ice; like ice. (L. *glacialis,* ice-like.)
glacialist, *n. glay*-shal-ist, one who refers certain geological phenomena to the action of ice.
glaciate, *v.i. glay*-she-ate *or glas*-e-ate, to cover with or abrade with ice: *v.i.* to become converted into ice. (L. *glaciatus,* iced.)
glaciation, *n.* glay-she- *or* glas-e-*ay*-shon, the act of freezing; the ice formed; the action of ice.
glacier, *n. glas*-e-er *or glay*-she-er, frozen snow formed on mountains and moving down valleys, fed with semi-melted snow at the top and forming streams at lower altitudes. (Fr.)
glaciology, *n.* glay-she-*ol*-o-je, the scientific study of the geological action of ice.
glacis, *n. glay*-sis *or glas*-se, a gentle slope cleared round a fortress; a sloping bank; the parapet of the covered way [Fort.]. (Fr.)
glad, *a.* glad, affected with pleasure or moderate joy; pleased; cheerful; bright; affording pleasure: *v.t.* to make glad: *v.i.* to be glad. **to give the glad eye,** to ogle [Slang]. **glad rags,** evening dress [Slang]. (A.S. *glæd,* bright.)
gladden, *v.t. glad*-en, to make glad; to cheer: *v.i.* to become glad; to rejoice.
glade, *n.* glade, a green open space in a wood; an avenue through a wood. (A.S. *glæd.*)
gladiate, *a. glay*-de-at, sword-shaped [Bot.]. (L. *glădius,* a sword.)
gladiator, *n. glad*-e-ay-tor, in the Roman amphitheatre, a professional fighter against men or beasts for the entertainment of the people; a prizefighter; a violent controversialist [Fig.]. (L.)
gladiatorial, *a.* glad-e-a-*taw*-re-al, pertaining to gladiators or their combats.
gladiatorship, *n. glad*-e-ay-tor-ship, the art or business of a gladiator.
gladiolus, *n.* glad-e-*oh*-lus *or glad*-e-o-lus, a large genus of iridaceous plants including the sword-lilies and corn-flags; the mesosternum [Anat.]. (L. *gladiolus,* a little sword.)
gladius, *n. glay*-de-us, the pen or internal bone of some cuttle-fishes. (L. *gladius.*)
gladly, *ad. glad*-le, with pleasure.
gladness, *n. glad*-ness, the state of being glad.
gladsome, *a. glad*-sum, pleased; joyful; cheerful; causing joy; pleasing.
gladsomely, *ad.* in a gladsome manner.
gladsomeness, *n.* the state of being gladsome.
gladstone, *n. glad*-ston, a leather double-sided travelling bag on a rigid frame, also known as a **gladstone bag.** (After W. E. *Gladstone.*)
Glagol, *n. glag*-ol, the Glagolitic alphabet.
Glagolitic, *a.* glag-o-*lit*-ik, pertaining to or designating the earliest Slavonic alphabet.
glair, *n.* glare, the white of an egg, used as a varnish; any similar viscous transparent substance: *v.t.* to smear or varnish with glair. (Fr. *glaire,* from L. *clarus,* clear.)
glaireous, *a. glare*-re-us, like glair.
glairy, *a. glare*-re, of the nature of glair.
glaive, *n.* glave, a broadsword or falchion: a sword blade fixed to a pole. (Fr.)
glamorous, *a. glam*-o-rus, filled with glamour; fascinating; bewitching.
glamour, *n. glam*-or, bewitchment of the physical or mental sight, by which things appear different from, esp. more delightful than, what they are; enchantment: *v.t.* to affect with glamour; to enchant. (Scots. corruption of *gramarye.*)
glance, *n.* glahnce, a darting of the eye or sight; a quick momentary view; a sudden shoot of light; a stroke from the side; a passing allusion: *v.i.* to look with a sudden rapid cast of the eye; to dart a ray of light; to fly off obliquely; to allude to in passing: *v.t.* to shoot or dart suddenly or obliquely; to cast (a look) rapidly or momentarily. (Of obscure origin.)
glance, *v.t.* glahnce, to polish, to burnish. (Dut. *glanzen,* to polish.)
glance, *n.* glahnce, lead or other mineral sulphide having a metallic lustre. **glance coal,** a hard lustrous coal; anthracite. **glance pitch,** a high-quality asphalt. (Ger. *Glanz,* lustre.)
glancingly, *ad. glahn*-sing-le, in a glancing manner.
gland, *n.* gland, an organ of secretion [Anat.]; a secretory organ, also a small protuberance, in plants [Bot.]. (Fr. *glande.*)
gland, *n.* gland, the part of a stuffing-box that holds the packing to prevent leakage [Mech.].
glandered, *a. glan*-derd, affected with glanders.
glanderous, *a. glan*-der-rus, having or resembling glanders.
glanders, *n. glan*-derz, a contagious and malignant disease of the mucous membrane in horses and a malignant febrile and contagious disease in man, due in both cases to *Bacillus mallei* [Med.].
glandiferous, *a.* glan-*dif*-er-rus, bearing acorns or nuts; producing nuts or mast. (L. *glandifer.*)
glandiform, *a. glan*-de-form, in the shape of an acorn; resembling a gland. (L. *gland,* and *form.*)
glandular, *a. glan*-dew-lar, having, consisting of, or pertaining to glands; of the nature of glands.
glandularly, *ad.* from the glandular point of view.
glandulation, *n. glan*-dew-*lay*-shon, the situation and structure of the glandules in plants [Bot.].
glandule, *n. glan*-dewl, a small gland.
glanduliferous, *a. gland*-yew-*lif*-er-us, bearing glands. (*glandule,* and *fero,* bear.)
glandulose, *a. glan*-dew-lose, glandular [Bot.].
glandulous, *a. glan*-dew-lus, glandular [Anat.].
glans, *n.* glanz, the rounded end of the penis; an acorn, beach-nut, etc.; a glandular structure [Zool.]. (L.)
glare, *n.* glare, a bright dazzling light; a lustre that dazzles the eyes; a fierce piercing look: *v.i.* to shine with a dazzling light; to look with fierce piercing eyes; to be ostentatiously splendid: *v.t.*

to shoot a dazzling light. (A.S. *glær*, any pellucid substance.)
glareous, *a. glare*-re-us, glaireous.
glaring, *a. glare*-ring, shining with dazzling light; over-conspicuous; very clear; barefaced.
glaringly, *ad. glare*-ring-le, in a glaring manner.
glaringness, *n.* a dazzling lustre or brilliancy.
glary, *a. glare*-re, having a dazzling lustre.
★glass, *a.* glahs, made of glass: *n.* a hard, brittle, transparent substance, formed by fusing siliceous matter with fixed alkalies in varying proportions; a utensil, esp. a drinking vessel, of glass; the quantity of liquor that a glass contains; strong drink; a mirror; a lens or optical instrument through which an object is viewed; a telescope; a barometer; a sand- or hour-glass; a window, esp. of a vehicle; panes, as of greenhouses; (*pl.*) spectacles: *v.t.* to mirror; to case in glass; to cover with glass; to glaze. **cut glass,** ware of flint-glass ornamented by cutting and polishing. **glass cloth,** a fine linen cloth for drying glasses; a woven fabric of fine-spun glass. **glass eye,** an artificial eye made of glass; a kind of blindness in horses [Vet.]. **glass of antimony,** red vitreous oxy-sulphide of antimony when fused. **ground glass,** glass that has been roughened by acid or the sand-blast and is no longer transparent. **potash, soda glass,** types of glass containing potassium or sodium salts. **safety glass,** glass toughened by rapid chilling during manufacture, or reinforced internally by wire mesh. **triplex glass,** trade-name of a glass consisting of adhering laminations of glass and a transparent plastic substance. (A.S. *glæs.*)
glass-blower, *n.* one whose business is to blow and fashion glass.
glass-cloth, *n.* a soft cloth for polishing glass.
glass-coach, *n.* a superior coach having many glass panels allowing good view from within and without.
glass-crab, *n.* a larval form of a shrimp or small crustacean mistaken for an adult animal.
glass-cutting, *n.* the process by which glass is cut or ground into ornamental forms.
glassful, *n. glahs*-ful, as much as a glass holds.
glass-furnace, *n.* a furnace in which the materials of glass are melted.
glass-gall, *n.* sandiver; the saline scum on molten glass.
glasshouse, *n. glahs*-house, a factory for glass; a conservatory; a military prison [Slang].
glassily, *ad. glahs*-e-le, in a glassy manner.
glassiness, *n.* the quality of being glassy.
Glassite, *n. glahs*-ite, a member of a religious sect founded in Scotland, in 1725, by John Glas; a Sandemanian.
glass-metal, *n.* glass in fusion during manufacture.
glass-painting, *n.* the art of producing coloured designs on glass, esp. by burning the pigments in.
glass-paper, *n.* paper coated with pulverized glass for abrasive purposes.
glass-snake, *n.* the blind-worm; the American limbless lizard *Ophisaurus ventralis.*
glass-soap, *n.* the black oxide of manganese.
glass-sponge, *n.* any sponge having silicious fibres resembling spun glass.
glassware, *n. glahs*-ware, articles made of glass.
glasswort, *n. glahs*-wurt, any soda-yielding plant, esp. *Salicornia herbacea,* formerly used in making glass.
glassy, *a. glahs*-e, vitreous; resembling glass in its properties; immobile (of the eye).
Glaswegian, *a.* glas-*wee*-je-an, pertaining to Glasgow, Scotland: *n.* a native or inhabitant of Glasgow.
glauberite, *n. glaw*-ber-ite, a yellow-greyish mineral consisting of sulphate of soda and sulphate of lime. (J. R. *Glauber,* a German chemist, *d.* 1668.)
glauber-salt, *n. glaw- or glou*-ber-sawlt, sulphate of soda, a powerful cathartic, named after its discoverer, Glauber.
glaucescence, *n.* glaw-*ses*-sence, the quality of being glaucescent.
glaucescent, *a.* glaw-*ses*-sent, of a bluish or sea-green appearance; tending to become glaucous.
glaucodote, *n. glaw*-ko-dote, a greyish-white sulpharsenide of iron and cobalt [Min.].
glaucolite, *n. glaw*-ko-lite, a silicate of aluminium, calcium, and sodium; green wernerite [Min.].
glaucoma, *n.* glaw-*koh*-ma, a disease in the eye giving it a bluish-green colour and causing opacity with ultimate blindness. (L.)
glaucomatous, *a.* glaw-*koh*-ma-tus, of the nature of glaucoma.
glauconite, *n. glaw*-ko-nite, a hydrous silicate of iron and potassium abundant in the greensands.
glaucous, *a. glaw*-kus, of a sea-green colour; having a down of this colour [Bot.]. **glaucous gull,** a large gull of northern waters, *Larus glaucus*; the burgomaster. (Gr. *glaukos.*)
Glaucus, *n. glaw*-kus, a genus of nudibranchiate mollusca, abundant in the Atlantic. (L.)
Glaux, *n.* glawks, the genus of plants comprising only the sea-milkwort. (Gr.)
glaze, *n.* glaze, the vitreous coating or glazing of potter's ware, paper, confectionery, etc.; a coating of jelly: *v.t.* to furnish with glass or with windows; to cover or encrust with a glassy surface; to give a smooth and glassy surface to; to coat with jelly. (M.E. *glasen.*)
glazer, *n. glay*-zer, a workman who glazes earthenware; a calico-smoother; a wooden wheel for grinding or polishing knives.
glazier, *n. glay*-ze-er, one who fixes glass in frames.
glaziery, *n. glay*-ze-e-re, glazier's work.
glazing, *n. glay*-zing, the operation of setting glass; the art of crusting with a vitreous substance; the vitreous substance with which potter's ware is encrusted; the process of applying semi-transparent colours over other colours to modify their effect [Paint.].
glazy, *a. glay*-ze, shiny.
gleam, *n.* gleem, a beam of light; a transient ray; brightness: *v.i.* to shoot or dart, as rays of light; to shine; to flash; to glitter. (A.S. *glæm.*)
gleamy, *a. gleem*-e, characterized by gleams.
glean, *v.i.* gleen, to gather grain left by reapers: *v.t.* to gather, as grain which reapers leave behind them; to collect things lightly scattered. (O.Fr. *glener.*)
gleaner, *n. gleen*-er, one who gleans; one who gathers slowly and with labour.
gleaning, *n. gleen*-ing, the act of gathering after reapers; that which is collected by gleaning.
glebe, *n.* gleeb, land belonging to a parish church and forming part of the benefice of the incumbent; a piece of land containing ore [Mining]. (O.Fr.)
glede, *n.* gleed, the kite, *Milvus regalis.* (A.S. *glida.*)
gledge, *v.i.* gledj. to squint. (Scots.)
glee, *n.* glee, joy; mirth; gaiety; a composition for several voices, usually in two or more movements [Mus.]. (A.S. *gleo,* joy, sport.)
gleed, *n.* gleed, a burning coal or cinders; an ember. (A.S. *gled.*)
gleeful, *a. glee*-ful, merry; gay; joyous.
gleek, *n.* gleek, a trick; a scoff; a game at cards for three players. (O.Fr. *glic.*)
gleeman, *n. glee*-man, an itinerant musician.
gleesome, *a. glee*-sum, merry; joyous.
gleet, *n.* gleet, the flux of a diseased humour from the urethra due to gonococcal infection; a thin ichor running from a sore [Med.]: *v.i.* to flow in a thin, limpid humour. (O.Fr.)
gleety, *a. gleet*-e, thin; limpid; serous.
glen, *n.* glen, a narrow valley. (Gael. *gleann.*)
glene, *n.* gleen, the eye-ball [Anat.]; a small socket in a bone [Anat.] cavity. (Gr., the eye-ball.)
glengarry, *n.* glen-*ga*-re, a woollen boat-shaped cap with two streamers of ribbon hanging at the back, and a cockade at the side, worn by certain Highland regiments. (Valley in Inverness-shire.)
glenoid, *a. glee*-noyd, having a slight depression to receive the head or condyle of a bone [Anat.]; socket-shaped [Anat.]. (Gr. *glene,* and *eidos,* like.)
gley, *a.* glay, askew: *v.t.* to squint.
gliadine, *n. gly*-a-din, a protein constituent of gluten [Chem.]. (Gr. *agli,* glue.)
glib, *a.* glib, smooth; slippery; moving easily; fluent; voluble. (Dut. *glibberen,* to slide.)
glibly, *ad. glib*-le, in a glib manner.
glibness, *n. glib*-ness, the quality of being glib.
glide, *n.* glide, the act of gliding; a sliding step in dancing; the steady downward flight of an aeroplane; the flight of an engineless aeroplane; the unarticulated slur joining two successive sounds [Mus.]; the sound produced when, in speech, the vocal organs pass from one position to another [Phon.]: *v.i.* to flow gently; to move along smoothly and easily; to dance with a glide; to fly in an engineless aeroplane or in an aeroplane with engines stopped [Av.]. (A.S. *glidan.*)

glider, *n.* *glide*-er, one who glides; an engineless aeroplane.
glidingly, *ad.* *glide*-ing-le, in a gliding manner.
glim, *n.* glim, a light or candle [Slang].
glimmer, *n.* glim-mer, a faint, unsteady light; a glimpse; an uncertain indication: *v.i.* to shed a faint light. (M.E. *glimeren.*)
glimmering, *n.* *glim*-mer-ing, a glimmer; a transient view; an inkling.
glimmery, *a.* *glim*-me-re, suggestive of glimmering.
glimpse, *n.* glimps, a momentary gleam of light; a short transitory view; a faint resemblance: *v.i.* to appear faintly or by glimpses: *v.t.* to see by a glimpse. (M.E. *glimsen.*)
glint, *n.* glint, a gleam of light; a sparkle: *v.i.* to gleam; to flash out. (M.E. *glenten,* to shine.)
glissade, *n.* glis-*sahd,* a particular method of sliding down an ice- or snow-slope; a glide to one side in dancing: *v.i.* to move by either method. (Fr.)
glisten, *v.i.* *glis*-sen, to shine in the light; to sparkle with light: *n.* a glistening; a reflected sparkle. (A.S. *glisnian.*)
glister, *n.* *glis*-ter, glitter; lustre: *v.i.* to shine; to be bright; to sparkle. (A.S. *glisian.*)
glitter, *n.* *glit*-ter, brilliancy; lustre; specious attractiveness: *v.i.* to sparkle with light; to glisten; to be brilliant; to be showy. (A.S. *glitinian.*)
glitteringly, *ad.* *glit*-ter-ing-le, in a glittering manner.
glittery, *a.* glit-te-re, characterized by glittering.
gloam, *v.i.* glome, to begin to grow dark; to gloom.
gloaming, *n.* *gloam*-ing, twilight; the dusk. (A.S. *glomung.*)
gloat, *v.i.* gloat, to gaze on in malevolent triumph. **to gloat over,** to contemplate with pleasure, exultation, or avarice. (Scand. *glotta,* to smile in scorn.)
gloatingly, *ad.* *gloat*-ing-le, in a gloating manner.
global, *a.* *gloh*-bal, spherical; pertaining to the earth; world-wide.
globate, *a.* *gloh*-bate, having the form of a globe; spherical; spheroidal. (L. *globatus,* made into a ball.)
globe, *n.* globe, a sphere; the earth; a sphere representing the earth, called a terrestrial globe, or the heavens, called a celestial globe: *v.t.* to gather into globular form: *v.i.* to become globular. (L. *globus.*)
globe-amaranth, *n.* a tropical amaranth with heads of red and white flowers, *Gomphrena globosa.*
globe-fish, *n.* any fish which can inflate itself into a globular shape, esp. *Tetrodon lagocephalus,* of the diodon family.
globe-flower, *n.* the ranunculaceous plant *Trollius europæus,* bearing handsome globular flowers.
globe-thistle, *n.* any plant of the thistle-like genus *Echinops,* of the aster family.
globe-trotter, *n.* one who travels extensively and hurriedly as a sightseer.
Globigerina, *n.* gloh-be-je-*ry*-na, a genus of small Foraminifera with small many-chambered shells. **globigerina ooze,** the soft mud of deep-sea bottoms, composed largely of these dead shells.
globoid, *a.* *gloh*-boyd, globose: *n.* a globoid body.
globose, *a.* glo-*bose,* round; spherical; globular.
globosity, *n.* glo-*bos*-e-te, the quality of being globose.
globular, *a.* *glob*-yew-lar, having the form of a small globe or ball; nearly spherical [Bot.]; composed of globules. **globular projection,** a kind of map in which the eye is supposed to be at a given distance from the globe. **globular sailing,** the sailing from one place to another over the arc of a great circle, or the shortest distance between two places [Naut.].
globularity, *n.* glob-yew-*la*-re-te, the state or quality of being globular.
globularly, *ad.* in a globular form.
globule, *n.* *glob*-yewl, a small spherical particle of matter; a blood corpuscle [Phys.]; a very small pill; a rounded drop. (L.)
globulin, *n.* *glob*-yew-lin, with hæmatin, the principal constituent of hæmoglobin [Phys.]; minute vesicular granules in plant-cells [Bot.].
globy, *a.* *gloh*-be, globular; like a globe.
glochidiate, *a.* glo-*kid*-e-at, having doubly barbed hairs [Bot.]. (Gr. *glochidion,* an arrow-tip.)
glockenspiel, *n.* *glok*-en-speel, a carillon; an instrument of harmonica type in which metal tubes, rods, or bells are struck with two hammers. (Ger. *glocke,* bell, *spiel,* play.)
glome, *n.* glome, a roundish head of flowers [Bot.]. (L. *glomus,* a yarn-ball.)
glomerate, *v.t.* and *i.* *glom*-mer-rate, to gether or become gathered into a ball; *a.* growing in rounded or massive forms [Bot.]; growing in a cluster [Anat.]. (L. *glomeratus,* made into a ball.)
glomeration, *n.* *glom*-mer-*ray*-shon, the act of gathering into a ball; a body formed into a ball.
glomerule, *n.* *glom*-mer-rool, a cluster of blood-vessels [Anat.]; a glome [Bot.].
gloom, *n.* gloom, obscurity; partial darkness; thick shadiness; dejection of mind; melancholy; sullenness; darkness of prospect or aspect: *v.i.* to be cloudy, threatening, or obscure; to be sadly or sullenly dejected: *v.t.* to obscure; to make dismal. (A.S. *glōm,* twilight.)
gloomily, *ad.* *gloom*-e-le, in a gloomy manner.
gloominess, *n.* *gloom*-e-ness, the quality of being gloomy; a state of gloom.
gloomy, *a.* *gloom*-e, dark, dim, or dusky; dismal; wearing the aspect of sorrow; melancholy; dejected; threatening (of weather or outlook).
gloria, *n.* *glaw*-re-a, a hymn founded on Luke ii, 14; a doxology to be intoned or sung; the music for either; a glossy textile containing silk. (L., glory.)
glorification, *n.* *glaw*-re-fe-*kay*-shon, the act of glorifying; exaltation to honour and dignity; a spree [Slang]. (Late L. *glorificatio.*)
glorify, *v.t.* *glaw*-re-fy, to magnify and honour in worship; to ascribe glory or honour to; to make glorious; to exalt to glory; to praise; to beautify [Coll.]. (Fr. *glorifier.*)
gloriole, *n.* *glaw*-re-ole, a circle of light; an aureole. (L. *gloriola,* dim. of *gloria.*)
glorious, *a.* *glaw*-re-us, of exalted excellence and splendour; illustrious; conferring glory or renown; entitled to honour; hilarious; tipsy [Slang]. (O.Fr.)
gloriously, *ad.* in a glorious manner.
gloriousness, *n.* the state or quality of being glorious.
glory, *n.* *glaw*-re, brightness; splendour; magnificence; praise ascribed in adoration; honour; renown; the felicity of heaven; heaven; pride; matter of pride or boasting; a halo; a background of rays to the figures of saints [Paint.]: *v.i.* to exult with joy; to boast; to take pride (in). (O.Fr. *glorie.*)
glory-hole, *n.* a cupboard, closet, drawer, etc., for odds and ends [Slang].
gloss, *n.* glos, brightness or lustre, as from a polished surface; sheen; external show that might mislead: *v.t.* to give a superficial lustre to; to make glossy; to give a specious appearance to. (Ice. *glossi,* a blaze.)
gloss, *n.* glos, comment; explanation; an explanatory note; a translation: *v.t.* to explain; to render clear and evident comments; to annotate: *v.i.* to make explanatory remarks. (L. *glossa.*)
glossalgia, *n.* glos-*sal*-je-a, neuralgic pain in the tongue [Med.]. (Gr. *glossa,* tongue.)
glossarial, *a.* glos-*sare*-re-al, of the nature of or pertaining to a glossary.
glossarist, *n.* *glos*-sa-rist, a writer of glosses or comments; the compiler of a glossary.
glossary, *n.* *glos*-sa-re, a vocabulary, esp. one explaining antiquated, local, or technical words. (L. *glossarium.*)
glossator, *n.* glos-*say*-tor, a mediæval writer of glosses.
glosser, *n.* *glos*-ser, a writer of glosses; a polisher.
glossily, *ad.* *glos*-e-le, in a glossy manner.
glossiness, *n.* the lustre of a smooth surface.
glossitis, *n.* glos-*sy*-tis, inflammation of the tongue.
glossocele, *n.* *glos*-so-seel, swollen tongue [Med.]. (Gr. *glossa,* the tongue, *kele,* a swelling.)
glossographer, *n.* glos-*sog*-ra-fer, a writer of glosses; a scholiast. (Gr.)
glossography, *n.* glos-*sog*-ra-fe, the writing of commentaries and glosses; the making of technical dictionaries; a description of the tongue.
glossologist, *n.* glos-*sol*-o-jist, one who defines technical terms; one versed in glossology. (Gr. *glossa,* and *logos,* science.)
glossology, *n.* glos-*sol*-o-je, the explanation of technical terms; the comparative science of language. (Gr. *glossa,* and *logos,* science.)
glossophorous, *a.* glos-*sof*-o-rus, having a tongue or radula [Zool.]; pertaining to the Glossophora, a large division of the Mollusca.

glossotomy, *n.* glos-*sot*-o-me, dissection, incision, or removal of the tongue [Surg.]. (Gr. *glossa*, and *tome*, cutting.)
glossy, *a.* *glos*-se, smooth and shining; highly polished; plausible.
glottal, *a.* *glot*-tal, pertaining to or produced in the glottis.
glottic, *a.* *glot*-ik, glottal; linguistic.
glottis, *n.* *glot*-tis, the opening from the pharynx into the windpipe, which can be dilated at will and by means of which the tones of the voice are modulated. (Gr.)
glottology, *n.* glot-*tol*-o-je, comparative philology; glossology. (Gr.)
★**glove,** *n.* gluv, a cover for the hand, esp. one having a separate sheath for each finger: *v.t.* to cover with a glove. **the gloves,** boxing-gloves. **to take up** or **throw down the glove,** to accept or to issue a challenge. (A.S. *glof.*)
glover, *n.* *gluv*-er, one who makes or sells gloves.
glove-stretcher, *n.* an instrument for opening the fingers of gloves, in order that they may be drawn on the hand more easily.
glow, *n.* gloh, shining or white heat; brightness of colour; ardour; passion; bodily warmth produced by exercise: *v.i.* to shine with intense heat; to be flushed with heat or animation, or by activity; to feel the heat of passion; to be ardent; to burn with intense passion. (A.S. *glōwan.*)
glower, *v.i.* *glou*-er, to scowl, or look menacingly at: *n.* a savage scowl.
glowingly, *ad.* *gloh*-ing-le, with great brightness, heat, or passion; vehemently; ardently.
glow-lamp, *n.* an incandescent electric lamp.
glow-worm, *n.* the female of the beetle, *Lampyris noctiluca*, which glows with phosphorescence in the dark.
Gloxinia, *n.* glok-*sin*-e-a, a tropical American genus of plants with large bell-shaped flowers. (B. P. *Gloxin*, 18th-cent. Ger. botanist.)
gloze, *n.* gloze, flattery; adulation: *v.i.* to smooth over; to palliate; to wheedle; to talk smoothly; to expound. **to gloze over,** to palliate by specious representation. (Fr. *gloser.*)
glucic, *a.* *gloo*-sik, pertaining to or derived from glucose.
glucina, *n.* gloo-*sy*-na, beryllia, or oxide of glucinum, so named from the sweetness of its salts. (Gr. *glykys*, sweet.)
glucinum, *n.* *gloo*-se-num, an alternative name of beryllium.
glucohæmia, *n.* gloo-ko-*hee*-me-a, glucosuria.
glucose, *n.* *gloo*-kose, grape-sugar; starch-sugar; the sugar present in the urine of diabetics [Med.]. (Gr. *glykys*, sweet.)
glucosid, *n.* *gloo*-ko-sid, glucoside.
glucoside, *n.* *gloo*-ko-side, a substance yielding glucose or a sugar when decomposed [Chem.]; a compound of sugar with other substances.
glucosuria, *n.* gloo-ko-*sewr*-re-a, a diabetic condition characterized by a large secretion of urine containing glucose [Med.]. (Gr. *glykys*, and *ouron*, urine.)
glue, *n.* gloo, coarse gelatine used when hot as an adhesive; other viscous adhesives: *v.t.* to join with glue; to unite; to hold together. *ppr.* **gluing.** (O.Fr. *glu.*)
gluey, *a.* *gloo*-e, viscous; glutinous.
glueyness, *n.* *gloo*-e-ness, the quality of being gluey.
gluish, *a.* *gloo*-ish, somewhat gluey; of the nature of glue.
glum, *a.* glum, frowning; sullen; dejected. (As *gloom.*)
glumaceous, *a.* gloo-*may*-shus, having glumes; of the nature of a glume [Bot.].
glume, *n.* gloom, a small bract with a flower in the axil, as in grasses; the husk or chaff of grain. (L. *gluma*, a husk.)
glumiferous, *a.* gloo-*mif*-er-rus, bearing flowers enclosed by glumes.
glumly, *ad.* *glum*-le, in a glum manner.
glumness, *n.* *glum*-ness, gloom; sulkiness.
glumous, *a.* *gloo*-mus, glumaceous.
glut, *n.* glut, a surfeit; plenty, to loathing; superabundance; over supply, esp. of a market: *v.t.* to swallow greedily; to gorge; to cloy; to sate; to delight to satiety; to saturate (as a market). (O.Fr. *gloutir.*)
glutæus, *n.* gloo-*tee*-us, any one of the three muscles of the buttock. (Gr. *gloutos*, rump.)
gluteal, *a.* gloo-*tee*-al, pertaining to the glutæus muscles or to the region of the buttocks.
gluten, *n.* *gloo*-ten, a viscid, elastic albuminous substance present in wheaten flour. (L.)
glutinative, *a.* *gloo*-te-na-tiv, having the quality of cementing; tenacious; an adhesive agent.
glutinize, *v.t.* *gloo*-te-nize, to render gluey.
glutinosity, *n.* gloo-te-*nos*-e-te, the quality of being glutinous.
glutinous, *a.* *gloo*-te-nus, viscous; resembling glue; smeared with sticky moisture [Bot.].
glutton, *n.* *glut*-ton, one who indulges to excess in eating, or in anything; the wolverine, a carnivore allied to the weasel. (O.Fr. *glouton.*)
gluttonish, *a.* *glut*-ton-ish, like a glutton; gluttonous.
gluttonize, *v.i.* *glut*-ton-ize, to eat voraciously; to indulge appetite to excess.
gluttonous, *a.* *glut*-ton-us, given to gluttony; consisting in gluttony; gluttonish.
gluttonously, *ad.* in a gluttonous manner.
gluttony, *n.* *glut*-ton-e, excess in eating; voracity.
glyceride, *n.* *glis*-ser-ride, an ester of glycerine.
glycerine, *n.* *glis*-ser-rin, a viscid colourless liquid of sweet taste, obtained from animal and vegetable fats and oils. (Gr. *glykeros*, sweet.)
glycerol, *n.* *glis*-ser-role, glycerine [Chem.].
glycocoll, *n.* *gly*-ko-kol, an amino-acetic acid, a sweetish crystalline acid obtained from certain proteins [Chem.]. (Gr. *glykus*, sweet, *kolla*, glue.)
glycogen, *n.* *gly*-ko-jen, animal starch, an amorphous carbohydrate present in the liver and other organs. (Gr. *glykus*, and *gennao*, produce.)
glycogenesis, *n.* *gly*-ko-*jen*-e-sis, the process by which glucose is formed in the liver, etc.
glycol, *n.* *gly*-kol, a colourless, inodorous, sweetish liquid, prepared from ethylene compounds as used to prevent freezing. (*gly*cerine and alcoh*ol*.)
glyconic, *a.* gly-*kon*-ik, denoting a kind of verse of four feet in Latin poetry: *n.* a glyconic verse. (*Glykon*, Greek poet.)
glycosuria, *n.* gly-ko-*sewr*-re-a, glucosuria [Med.].
glycyrrhizin, *n.* glis-e-*ry*-zin, a glucoside present in liquorice-root.
glyph, *n.* glif, a vertical fluting, esp. in the Doric Frieze [Arch.]. (Gr. *glyphe*, carving.)
glyphic, *n.* *glif*-ik, a hieroglyph: *a.* carved; pertaining to sculpture or glyphs.
glyphograph, *n.* *glif*-o-graf, a plate formed by glyphography; an impression from such a plate: *v.t.* and *i.* to engrave by glyphography. (Gr. *glypho*, carve, *grapho*, write.)
glyphographer, *n.* gle-*fog*-ra-fer, one skilled in or a worker in glyphography.
glyphography, *n.* gle-*fog*-ra-fe, a process for producing engravings in relief, in the manner of electrotype, after etching on a prepared ground.
glyptic, *a.* *glip*-tik, pertaining to engraving on gems; figured [Min.]: *n.pl.* the art of engraving figures on precious stones. (Gr. *glyptikos*, from *glyptos*, engraved.)
glyptodon, *n.* *glip*-to-don, a large extinct mammal of the armadillo family, with teeth longitudinally fluted. (Gr. *glyptos*, and *odous*, a tooth.)
glyptography, *n.* glip-*tog*-ra-fe, the art of engraving on precious stones; a treatise on this. (Gr. *glyptos* and *grapho*, write.)
glyptology, *n.* glip-*tol*-o-je, the scientific study of engraved gems.
glyptotheca, *n.* glip-to-*thee*-ka, a room for the preservation and display of works of sculpture. (Gr. *glyptos*, and *theka*, a repository.)
gmelinite, *n.* *mel*-e-nite, a whitish zeolite consisting of hydrated silicate of aluminium, sodium, and calcium. (C. A. *Gmelin*, Ger. chemist, *d.* 1860.)
Gnaphalium, *n.* na-*fay*-le-um, a composite genus of woolly plants comprising the cudweeds.
gnar, *v.i.* nahr, to gnarl.
gnarl, *n.* nahrl, a knarl, a knot in wood.
gnarl, *v.i.* nahrl, to growl or snarl; to mutter; to gnaw. (Imit.)
gnarled, *a.* nahrld, knarled; full of knots.
gnash, *v.t.* nash, to grind the teeth together in rage or anguish; to champ: *v.i.* to grind the teeth thus. (M.E. *gnasten*, to gnash.)
gnat, *n.* nat, a small two-winged insect of the genus *Culex*, the females of which are blood-suckers; a mosquito; a trifle [Fig.]. (A.S. *gnæt.*)

gnathic, *a.* *nath*-ik, pertaining to the jaw. (Gr. *gnathos*, the jaw.)
gnathism, *n.* *nath*-izm, the formation of the upper jaw; the classification of mankind according to this.
gnathitis, *n.* na-*thy*-tis, inflammation of the upper jaw or cheek [Med.]. (Gr. *gnathos*, the jaw.)
Gnathonic, *a.* na-*thon*-ik, parasitical; flattering. (*Gnatho*, a character in Terence's play, "Eunuchus.")
gnathostomatous, *a.* nath-o-*stoh*-ma-tus, having the mouth provided with jaws (of certain crustaceans) [Zool.].
gnatty, *a.* *nat*-e, infested with gnats.
gnaw, *v.t.* naw, to bite off little by little with the fore teeth; to bite in agony or rage; to fret; to torment: *v.i.* to use the teeth in biting. (A.S. *gnagan.*)
gnawer, *n.* *naw*-er, he who or that which gnaws; a rodent animal.
gnawingly, *ad.* *naw*-ing-le, in a gnawing manner.
gneiss, *n.* nice, a laminated rock of the composition of granite. (Ger.)
gneissic, *a.* *nice*-ik, resembling gneiss in structure.
gneissoid, *a.* *nice*-oyd, of the nature of gneiss.
gneissose, *a.* nice-ohs, gneissic; gneissoid.
gnome, *n.* nome, an imaginary being, often misshapen and diminutive, of subterranean habitat and supposed to preside over the mineral and other treasures. (Gr. *gnome*, intelligence.)
gnome, *n.* nome, an aphorism; a brief reflection or maxim. (Gr. *gnōmē.*)
gnomic, *a.* *nome*-ik, containing maxims or single detached thoughts; didactic.
gnomish, *a.* *nome*-ish, resembling a gnome or sprite.
gnomology, *n.* no-*mol*-o-je, a collection of maxims; a treatise on maxims; gnomic writing. (Gr. *gnome*, and *logos*, account.)
gnomon, *n.* *no*-mon, the style or pin, which by its shadow shows the hour of the day [Dialling]; a style erected perpendicular to the horizon, for making astronomical observations [Astron.]; the index of the hour-circle of a globe; the part of a parallelogram which remains when one of the parallelograms about its diagonal is removed [Geom.]. (Gr. *gnomon*, an index.)
gnomonic, *a.* no-*mon*-ik, pertaining to gnomonics. **gnomonic projection,** a projection of the sphere from the centre.
gnomonically, *ad.* no-*mon*-e-ka-le, according to the principles of dialling or of the gnomonic projection.
gnomonics, *n.* no-*mon*-iks, the art or science of dialling.
gnosiology, *n.* noh-ze-*ol*-o-je, the theory of the nature and validity of cognition; epistemology [Phil.]. (*gnosis* and *-logy.*)
gnosis, *n.* *noh*-sis (*pl.* **gnoses,** *noh*-seez), ascertained knowledge; esoteric knowledge. (Gr., knowledge.)
Gnostic, *n.* *nos*-tik, one belonging to a sect of the early Christian Church that adopted Gnosticism: *a.* relating to knowledge; pertaining to the Gnostics or to Gnosticism; having esoteric knowledge. (Gr. *gnostikos*, knowing.)
Gnosticism, *n.* *nos*-tis-sizm, a religious philosophy of diverse shades and theosophic tendencies which grew up in the early Church out of the fragments of Oriental speculative systems in connexion with the profession of Christianity, and affected to expound its presumed esoteric doctrines.
gnu, *n.* noo *or* new, any of several large African antelopes of the genus *Connochætes*; the wildebeest. (Bushman.)
go, *n.* goh, movement; dash; enterprise; the mode or fashion; an attempt; a turn; a drink of liquor; inability to play to a card (Cribbage).
★**go,** *v.i.* goh, to move; to pass from one place, state, or station to another; to walk; to travel; to depart; to proceed; to advance; to apply; to have recourse to; to be about to do; to pass; to circulate; to flow; to proceed by some principle or rule; to be freed from restraint; to lead in any direction; to extend; to avail; to be accounted in value; to happen; to turn out; to fare. **to go about,** to set oneself to a business; to tack [Naut.]. **to go abroad,** to go to foreign parts; to leave the house; to be made public. **to go against,** to oppose; to march to attack. **to go aside,** to withdraw into a private situation; to err. **to go astray,** to stray; to sin. **to go away,** to depart. **to go between,** to mediate. **to go by,** to pass near and beyond. **to go down,** to descend in any manner; to fall, to sink (of ships). **to go for nothing,** to have no meaning or efficacy. **to go forth,** to issue or depart out of a place. **to go forward,** to advance. **to go hard with,** to be in great danger. **to go ill with,** not to prosper. **to go in,** to enter. **to go in for,** to pursue, as a calling, hobby, etc. **to go into,** to enter; to investigate. **to go it,** to behave recklessly or uproariously. **to go off,** to depart to a distance; to die; to explode. **to go on,** to advance forward; to continue; to complain; to enter on the stage. **to go out,** to issue forth; to go on an expedition; to become extinct. **to go over,** to read; to examine; to pass from one party to another. **to go the whole hog,** to act wholeheartedly and without reserve. **to go through,** to pass through; to examine; to accomplish; to undergo. **to go through with,** to perform thoroughly. **to go under,** to fail completely; to be submerged; to be known (as). **to go upon,** to proceed as on a principle. **to go well with,** to have good fortune. **to go with,** to accompany; to side. **to go without,** to be or remain destitute; to put up with the lack of. **to go without saying,** to be self-evident. **go to,** come; move; begin. *third pers. sing.* **goes.** *p.* **went.** *pp.* **gone.** (A.S. *gān.*)
go, *n.* goh, the Japanese game of gobang. (Jap.)
goad, *n.* gode, a pointed instrument to urge a beast to move faster; a stimulus: *v.t.* to drive with a goad; to urge forward; to stimulate. (A.S. *gad.*)
goaf, *n.* gohf, place in a mine that is worked out; the waste material in old workings [Mining].
go-ahead, *a.* *go*-a-hed, pushing; enterprising.
goal, *n.* goal, the point set to limit a race; the mark; the end or aim; the winning-post; the posts between which the ball has to be driven in football, hockey, lacrosse, etc.; the point won for the passage of the ball through the goal. (A.S. *gal.*)
goalie, *n.* *goal*-e, a goalkeeper [Coll.].
goalkeeper, *n.* *goal*-keep-er, the player whose duty it is to guard the goal [Football, etc.]
goal-line, *n.* *goal*-line, the line between the goal-posts extended in either direction to form the boundary of each end of the playing-field [Football, etc.].
goal-posts, *n.pl.* *goal*-pohsts, the posts forming the goal in football, etc.
goanna, *n.* go-*an*-na, any large monitor lizard [Austral.]. (As *iguana.*)
★**goat,** *n.* goat, a hollow-horned ruminant ungulate of the genus *Capra*. **the sheep and the goats,** the righteous and the wicked. (A.S. *gat.*)
goatee, *n.* goat-*ee*, a small pointed beard like a goat's.
goatherd, *n.* *goat*-herd, a minder of goats.
goatish, *a.* *goat*-ish, resembling a goat; of a rank smell; lustful.
goatishly, *ad.* *goat*-ish-le, in a goatish manner.
goatishness, *n.* the quality of being goatish.
goatling, *n.* *goat*-ling, a young or little goat.
goat-milker, *n.* the nightjar [Ornith.].
goat-moth, *n.* *goat*-moth, a large British moth, *Cossus ligniperda*.
goat's-beard, *n.* *goats*-beerd, salsify, a plant of the genus *Tragopon*.
goatskin, *n.* *goat*-skin, the prepared skin of a goat: *a.* made of this.
goat's-rue, *n.* *goats*-roo, a leguminous plant of the genus *Galega*.
goat's-thorn, *n.* *goats*-thorn, one of several thorny shrubs of the genus *Astragalus*.
goatsucker, *n.* *goat*-suk-er, the nightjar or fern-owl, a bird erroneously supposed to suck goats.
gob, *n.* gob, a little; a mouthful; goaf [Mining]; a clot of saliva [Slang]. **gob fire,** a fire in a worked-out area [Mining].
gobang, *n.* go-*bang*, a Japanese game played with coloured counters on a square board of 361 squares. (Jap. *goban*, chequer-board.)
gobbet, *n.* *gob*-bet, a small piece, as of meat; a mouthful; a lump. (O.Fr. *gobet*, a morsel.)
gobbing, *n.* *gob*-bing, the gob, or refuse, left in excavations after removal of the coal [Mining].
gobble, *n.* *gob*-bl, the cry of the turkey; a putt which, while resulting in the ball being holed, would ordinarily have overrun it [Golf]: *v.t.* to swallow in lumps; to swallow hastily: *v.i.* to make a noise in the throat, as a turkey. (Fr. *gober*, to swallow.)
gobble-gut, *n.* *gob*-bl-gut, a voracious feeder.

gobbler, *n.* *gob*-bler, one who swallows in haste; a gormandizer; a turkey-cock.
Gobelin, *n.* *goh*-be-lin (*or* App.), a rich French tapestry, first manufactured by the brothers Gobelin, in Paris, in the 16th century.
gobemouche, *n.* *gobe*-moosh, a credulous person; one who spreads sensational gossip. (Fr.)
go-between, *n.* an intermediate agent between parties; an intervening thing.
goblet, *n.* *gob*-let, a stemmed drinking cup without a handle. (Fr. *gobelet.*)
goblin, *n.* *gob*-lin, a mischievous elf fabled to haunt places, esp. mines and dwellings; a phantom. (O.Fr. *gobeline.*)
goby, *n.* *goh*-be, a small marine fish of the genus *Gobius*, allied to the blenny, having ventral fins forming suctorial discs. (L. *gobius*, gudgeon.)
go-by, *n.* *goh*-by, evasion; a passing without notice; a thrusting away; a shifting off. **to give a thing the go-by,** to evade it or set it aside.
go-cart, *n.* a framework with casters, in which children learn to walk; a small two-wheeled hand-cart or toy perambulator.
God, *n.* god, the self-existing supreme Deity; (*l.c.*) a divinity; an idol; any person or thing deified or too much honoured: *pl.* the occupants of the gallery in a theatre. (A.S.)
godchild, *n.* *god*-chyld, one for whom a person becomes sponsor at baptism.
goddaughter, *n.* *god*-daw-ter, a girl for whom one becomes sponsor at baptism.
goddess, *n.* *god*-ess, a female deity; a woman of superior attraction, beauty, or charms.
godet, *n.* *goh*-day, a wedge-shaped piece of material for widening a skirt, glove, etc. (Fr., a gore.)
Godetia, *n.* go-*dee*-sha, a genus of hardy herbaceous plants united with *Œnothera*, the evening primroses. (C. H. *Godet*, a Swiss botanist.)
godfather, *n.* *god*-fah-ther, a man who is sponsor for a child at baptism: *v.t.* to act as godfather.
godfearing, *a.* *god*-feer-ing, having devout awe of God.
godforsaken, *a.* *god*-for-say-ken, desolate, remote; abandoned; neglected; destitute of resources.
Godhead, *n.* *god*-hed, deity, divine nature.
Godhood, *n.* *god*-hood, divinity; divine qualities.
godless, *a.* *god*-less, with no fear of God; ungodly.
godlessly, *ad.* *god*-less-le, in a godless manner.
godlessness, *n.* the state of being godless.
godlike, *a.* *god*-like, resembling a god.
godlily, *ad.* *god*-le-le, in a godly manner.
godliness, *n.* the quality of being godly.
godly, *a.* *god*-le, pious; righteous.
godmother, *n.* *god*-muth-er, a woman who becomes sponsor for a child at baptism.
godown, *n.* go-*doun*, a warehouse or general store in the Far East. (Malay, *godong.*)
godparent, *n.* *god*-pare-rent, a sponsor at baptism.
godroon, *n.* go-*droon*, gadroon.
God's-acre, *n.* *godz*-ay-ker, a burial-ground.
godsend, *n.* *god*-send, an unexpected acquisition of good fortune.
godship, *n.* *god*-ship, a deity; the rank of a god.
godson, *n.* *god*-sun, a boy for whom one has been sponsor at the font.
God-speed, *int.* god-speed, a wish for success, esp. at setting out.
godward, *a.* *god*-ward, toward God.
godwit, *n.* *god*-wit, a marsh or shore bird of the genus *Limosa*. (Origin unknown.)
goer, *n.* *goh*-er, one who goes, walks, etc.; an expert [Coll.]; a high-flyer [Slang].
gofer, *n.* *goh*-fer, a thin cake baked between two hinged plates.
Goethian, *n.* *ger*-te-an, a follower or admirer or student of Goethe, his life and his works. (*Goethe*, Ger. poet and philosopher, 1749-1832.)
goffer, *v.t.* *gof*-fer, to crimp; to flute at the edge: *n.* a fluting or plaiting; a ruffle; a goffering-iron.
goffering, *n.* *gof*-fer-ing, goffer work. **goffering-iron,** an implement for goffering.
go-getter, *n.* *goh*-get-ter, a pushful person; a hustler; a thruster [Amer. slang].
goggle, *n.* *gog*-gl, a strained or affected rolling of the eye; *pl.* *gog*-glz, instruments used to cure squinting [Surg.]; large round spectacles; blinkers for horses: *a.* having prominent staring eyes: *v.i.* to strain or roll the eyes. (Origin unknown.)
goggle-eyed, *a.* *gog*-gl-ide, having prominent, staring, or rolling eyes.
goglet, *n.* *gog*-let, a pottery or earthenware vessel for keeping water cool.
Goidel, *n.* *goy*-del, one belonging to the Gadhelic branch of the Celtic family.
Goidelic, *a.* goy-*del*-ik, designating or belonging to the Gaels: *n.* the language of the Gaels.
going, *a.* *goh*-ing, departing; serviceable, in working order; current: *n.* the act of moving or walking; departure; the state of the road; procedure; course of life; behaviour. **going concern,** a business in full working order. **going forth,** outlet; boundary. **going out,** end; journeying or departing. **goings on,** conduct, proceedings (esp. in bad sense). **while the going's good,** when everything is favourable. [Coll.]
goitre, *n.* *goy*-ter, a morbid swelling of the thyroid gland causing deformity of neck; bronchocele. (Fr.)
goitred, *a.* *goy*-terd, affected with goitre.
goitrous, *a.* *goy*-trus, pertaining to or characterized by goitre; goitred.
gola, *n.* a cyma [Arch.]. (It., the throat.)
Golconda, *n.* gol-*kon*-da, an inexhaustible mine; any place of surpassing wealth. (Town in India, formerly fabled for its riches.)
★**gold,** *n.* gohld, a chemical element and precious metal of a yellow colour, for long the standard of value; money; riches; wealth; something genuine and of value; a bright yellow colour; gilding: *a.* made of or consisting of gold; of the colour of gold. **gold digger,** one who mines for gold; a money-seeking adventuress [Coll.]. **gold diggings,** a place where gold is found. **gold dust,** gold in very fine particles. **gold fever,** a mania for gold-seeking. **gold lace,** a lace wrought with gold wire. **gold leaf,** gold beaten into thin leaf. **gold mine,** a mine from which gold is obtained, hence any rich source of wealth or knowledge. **gold plate,** dishes and table services of gold. **gold point,** the rate of foreign exchange at which the cost of shipment of gold equals that of buying exchange [Finance]. **gold size,** a size used as an adhesive in gilding. **gold standard,** a method of establishing international exchange values by fixing currency units in given weights of gold. **Gold Stick,** a court official (usually a colonel of the Household Cavalry) who carries a gilt rod and attends the British sovereign on state occasions. **gold thread,** thread formed of flattened gold laid over a thread of silk. **gold tissue,** tissue through which gold threads are woven. **gold washer,** one who or that which washes refuse from gold ore. (A.S.)
goldbeater, *n.* one whose occupation is to beat gold into gold leaf for gilding. **goldbeater's skin,** a membrane prepared from the intestine of an ox for laying between gold leaves while being beaten.
goldbeating, *n.* the act or occupation of beating gold into leaf.
goldcrest, *n.* *gohld*-krest, the golden-crested wren.
golden, *a.* *gohl*-dn, made or consisting of gold; bright; shining; of a gold colour or lustre; excellent; most valuable; pre-eminently favourable. **golden age,** a fabled period of innocence in which man and every creature lived at peace with every other [Myth.]; the brightest or best period of a people's history, literature, or art. **golden-crested wren,** *Regulus cristatus*, the smallest of British birds. **golden eagle,** the largest British eagle, *Aquila chrysaëtus*, nesting in the Scottish mountains. **golden fleece,** the fleece of gold taken from the ram that bore Phryxus through the air to Colchis, and in quest of which Jason undertook the Argonautic expedition [Myth.]; (*caps.*) a former Austrian and Spanish order of knighthood originating in 1429. **golden mean,** just right, neither too much nor too little. **golden-mouthed,** eloquent. **golden number,** a number showing the place of any year in the Metonic cycle, from which the date of Easter is computed [Chron.]. **golden rain,** a firework producing a shower of yellow sparks; a yellow-flowered shrub of the genus *Forsythia*. **golden rule,** the rule of three [Arith.]; the rule that we should do as we would be done by. **golden syrup,** refined treacle. **golden wedding,** the fiftieth anniversary of a marriage. (A.S. *gylden.*)
golden-eye, *n.* either of the British sea-ducks, *Fuligula cristata* or *Clangula glaucion*.
golden-rod, *n.* a plant of the genus *Solidago*.
goldfields, *n.pl.* *gohld*-feelds, a district where gold is found; gold diggings.

gold-filled, *a.* coated with gold; covered with a thin layer of gold.
goldfinch, *n.* *gohld*-finch, a song-bird, *Carduelis elegans*, named from the colour of its wings.
goldfinny, *n.* *gohld*-fin-ne, a brightly-coloured sea-fish of the wrasse family, *Crenilabrus cornubicus*; the gilthead.
goldfish, *n.* *gohld*-fish, a freshwater fish of the carp family, usually of a golden-red colour in the upper part, *Carassius auratus*.
goldilocks, *n.* *gohl*-de-loks, the composite plant, *Chrysochroma linosyris*; also *Ranunculus auricomus*.
goldsinny, *n.* *gohld*-sin-ne, error for "goldfinny."
goldsmith, *n.* *gohld*-smith, a worker in gold and silver; a dealer in gold plate.
golf, *n.* golf *or* goff, a game played with special clubs and a small ball, on a grass course, in which the player who drives the ball into a series of small holes (9 or 18) in the ground with the fewest strokes is the winner: *v.i.* to play golf. (Perhaps Dut. *kolf*, a club.)
golf-club, *n.* *golf*-klub, a stick for golfing with; an association of golf-players; their building.
golfer, *n.* *golf*-er, a player at golf.
golf-links, *n.pl.* *golf*-links, land laid out for the purpose of playing golf; a golf course.
goliard, *n.* *goh*-le-ard, a vagrant student-writer of satirical Latin verse in the Middle Ages. (O.Fr.)
goliath-beetle, *n.* go-*ly*-ath-*bee*-tl, a tropical beetle nearly four inches long, *Goliathus giganteus*.
golliwog, *n.* *gol*-le-wog, a black-faced doll of grotesque appearance.
golly, *int.* *gol*-le, euphemistic for "by God!"
golosh, *n.* go-*losh*, a galosh.
goluptious, *a.* gol-*lup*-shus, luscious; delicious [Slang].
gombeen, *n.* gom-*been*, money-lending; usury. (Ir. *gaimbin.*)
gombeenism, *n.* gom-*bee*-nizm, the practice of usury.
gombeen-man, *n.* a money-lender; a mortgagee.
gombroon, *n.* gom-*broon*, a Persian pottery ware. (A port on the Persian Gulf.)
gomphiasis, *n.* gom-*fy*-a-sis, a disease of the teeth, causing them to loosen. (Gr., toothache.)
gomphosis, *n.* gom-*foh*-sis, a form of immovable articulation, as in the case of the teeth. (Gr.)
gomuti, *n.* go-*moo*-te, a fibre resembling horse-hair obtained from the sago-palm, and used for making cordage, etc. (Malay.)
gonad, *n.* *gon*-ad, an hermaphroditic germ-gland acting both as ovary and spermary [Biol.].
gonagra, *n.* go-*nag*-ra, gout in the knee. (Gr.)
gonalgia, *n.* go-*nal*-je-a, pain in the knee. (Gr. *gonē*, knee, *algos*, pain.)
gondola, *n.* *gon*-do-la, a long, black, narrow boat with prow and stern curving high above the water, and a covered shelter amidships, used esp. at Venice; the car of an airship; a flat-bottomed boat for carrying produce [U.S.A.]. (It.)
gondolier, *n.* gon-do-*leer*, a man who works a gondola.
gone, gon, *pp.* of *go*, departed; ruined; dead.
goner, *n.* *gon*-er, one who is past recovery or is ruined [Slang].
gonfalon, *n.* *gon*-fa-lon, a banner with two or three streamers hung from a horizontal bar held up by a pole. (Fr.)
gonfalonier, *n.* *gon*-fa-lo-*neer*, standard-bearer; formerly the chief magistrate of certain mediæval Italian republics. (It.)
gong, *n.* gong, a metal tambourine-like disc which, when struck with a padded mallet, emits a loud sonorous sound; a spiral steel spring on which, in many clocks, a hammer strikes the hours; a bell with a curved vertical section: *v.t.* and *i.* to use a gong as a means of attracting attention. (Malay.)
Gongorism, *n.* *gong*-go-rizm, a euphuistic affected literary style based on that of the Spanish poet Luis de Gongora y Argote (*d.* 1627).
goniatite, *n.* *goh*-ne-a-tite, a fossil of the amnionite family having a shell with lobed sutures.
gonidium, *n.* go-*nid*-e-um (*pl.* **gonidia**), one of the algal cells in the thallus of lichens; a reproductive cell in algæ.
goniometer, *n.* goh-ne-*om*-e-ter, an instrument for measuring solid angles, as of crystals; a radio-goniometer. **reflecting goniometer,** one for measuring the angles of crystals by reflection. (Gr. *gonia*, an angle, *metron*, measure.)
goniometry, *n.* goh-ne-*om*-e-tre, the measurement of angles; the use of the goniometer.
gonoblast, *n.* *gon*-o-blast, a cell or bud taking part in reproduction [Biol.]. (Gr. *gonos*, procreation, *blastos*, a sprout.)
gonococcus, *n.* gon-o-*kok*-us, the pus-producing bacterium present in the gonorrhœal discharge.
gonorrhœa, *n.* gon-o-*ree*-ah, a contagious venereal disease, attended by inflammation of the urethra and a secretion of a contagious purulent mucoid fluid [Med.]. (Gr. *gonorrhoia.*)
gonorrhœal, *a.* gon-o-*ree*-al, relating to or affected with gonorrhœa.
***good,** *a.* good, valid; sufficiently perfect in its kind; having the qualities, physical or moral, best adapted to its design and use; virtuous; pious; proper; fit; seasonable; expedient; sound; wholesome; palatable; salutary; beneficial; full; useful; competent; convenient; able; skilful; kind; benevolent; faithful; pleasant; honourable; unblemished; cheerful; considerable; polite; serious; companionable; brave; well-formed; mild; not irritable; friendly. **as good as,** equally; no better than; the same as. **as good as his word,** equalling in fulfilment what was promised. **good behaviour,** obligation to keep the peace. **good breeding,** polite manners, formed by good education; a polite education. **good day,** salutation at meeting or parting in daytime. **good fellow,** a jolly or boon companion; a pleasant companion. **Good Friday,** a fast in memory of Christ's sufferings, kept on the Friday of Passion-week. **good humour,** a cheerful temper. **good lack,** *int.* exclamation of wonder. **good looks,** handsome appearance. **good luck,** *n.* and *int.* prosperity; may all go well. **good manners,** propriety of behaviour; politeness. **good morrow,** good morning. **good nature,** natural mildness and kindness of disposition. **good neighbour,** one who respects the rights of others. **good night,** a kind wish at parting in the evening. **good sense,** sound judgment. **good temper,** equable disposition. **Good Templar,** a member of a society pledged to teetotalism and its promotion. **good time,** a considerable period; an enjoyable event or experience. **in good time,** at the proper time; punctually. **good turn,** an act of kindness. **in good sooth,** in very truth. **to make good,** to perform; to fulfil; to confirm or establish; to supply deficiency; to revert from backsliding. (A.S. *gōd.*)
good, *n.* good, that which contributes to diminish pain, or to increase happiness or prosperity; advantage; welfare; prosperity; spiritual advantage or improvement; earnestness; moral qualities; virtue; richness; abundance. **as good,** *ad.* as well; with equal advantage: *int.* well! right! **for good and all,** finally.
good-bye, *int.* good-by, farewell! (a salutation at parting): *n.* a farewell. ("God be with ye!")
good-fellowship, *n.* pleasant company; conviviality.
good-folk, *n.* *good*-foke, the fairies.
good-for-nothing, *a.* worthless; useless: *n.* a ne'er-do-well; an idle loafer.
good-humoured, *a.* of a cheerful temper.
good-humouredly, *ad.* with good humour.
goodish, *a.* *good*-ish, rather good; of fairly considerable quantity.
goodliness, *n.* *good*-le-ness, goodly quality; beauty of form; elegance.
good-looking, *a.* of handsome appearance.
goodly, *a.* *good*-le, being of a handsome form; beautiful; pleasant; agreeable; considerable.
goodman, *n.* *good*-man, a rustic term of compliment; a husband; the master of the house [Archaic.].
good-natured, *a.* naturally mild in temper.
good-naturedly, *ad.* with mildness of temper.
good-naturedness, *n.* the quality of being good-natured or not easily provoked.
goodness, *n.* *good*-ness, the state of being good; kindness (used also as an *int.*, as **goodness gracious! goodness knows! goodness me!**).
goods, *n.pl.* goodz, household furniture; movable property; articles of merchandise. **goods and chattels,** personal property. **goods train,** a railway train conveying luggage or general merchandise. **goods truck,** a railway wagon for goods. **the goods,** exactly what was wanted [Slang]. **to**

deliver the goods, to fulfil one's promise ; to come up to expectation [Slang].
good-tempered, *a.* not prone to anger.
goodwife, *n. good*-wife, the mistress of a house.
goodwill, *n.* good-*wil*, kindly feeling ; the extrinsic and intangible assets of a business, as reputation, personality, drawing power, locality, etc. [Comm.].
goody, *n. good*-e, a term of civility to a poor woman [Archaic] : *pl.* sweets or cakes, etc. [Coll.].
goody-goody, *a.* well-meant, but weak ; namby-pamby ; sanctimoniously pious.
goofy, *a. goo*-fe, foolish ; daft [Slang].
google, *v.t. goo*-gl, to bowl googlies: *v.i.* to have a googly effect (of the ball) [Cricket].
googly, *n. goo*-gle, a ball bowled at cricket which breaks contrary to the bowler's apparent action.
goor, *n.* goor, a coarse variety of sugar. (Hind.)
goosander, *n.* goo-*san*-der, the merganser.
goose, *n.* goos (*pl.* **geese**), a web-footed bird of the genus *Anser*, larger than a duck ; a stupid, silly creature ; the female, as distinct from a gander ; (*pl.* **gooses**) a tailor's smoothing iron. **wild-goose chase,** *see* **wild.** (A.S. *gos.*)
gooseberry, *n. gooz*-be-re, the berry of *Ribes grossularia* ; the shrub itself. **Cape gooseberry,** *see* **cape. to play gooseberry,** to act as chaperon to lovers. (*goose* and *berry*, cf. O.Fr. *grosele.*)
gooseberry-fool, *n.* scalded gooseberries forced through a sieve and beaten up with cream. (Fr. *foulé.*)
goose-corn, *n.* a species of coarse rush, *Juncus squarrosum.*
goose-flesh, *n.* a roughened state of the skin caused by contraction due to cold or fear.
goose-foot, *n.* a herb of the genus *Chenopodium.*
goose-grass, *n.* the plant cleavers, *Galium aparine*, or *Potentilla anserina*, silverweed.
goose-herd, *n.* one who tends geese.
gooseneck, *n. goos*-nek, a piece of bent iron fitted to the end of a boom [Naut.].
goosequill, *n. goos*-kwil, the large quill of a goose, or a pen made of it.
goosery, *n. goos*-er-re, an enclosure, or farm, for geese ; tomfoolery, silliness [Coll.].
goose-step, *n.* a formal parade step used in the German army ; the step of marking time.
goosewing, *n. goos*-wing, a lower corner of a foresail or mainsail when the centre or body of a sail is furled [Naut.].
goosewinged, *a. goos*-wingd, having fore-and-aft sails set on opposite sides when running before the wind [Naut.].
goosy, *a. goos*-e, foolish ; very nervous ; affected with goose-flesh.
gopher, *n. goh*-fer, prairie squirrel ; any of several species of American burrowing rodents. (Fr. *gaufre.*)
gopher, *n. goh*-fer, the wood of which Noah's ark was made, said to be cypress. (Heb.)
goral, *n. goh*-ral, the Himalayan goat-antelope, *Nemorhædus goral.* (Nepalese.)
goramy, *n. go*-rah-me, the gourami.
gorcock, *n. gawr*-kok, the male red grouse [Scot.].
gorcrow, *n. gawr*-kroh, the carrion crow. (A.S. *gor*, dung.)
Gordian, *a. gawr*-de-an, intricate ; difficult. **Gordian knot,** a knot in the harness of the chariot of Gordius, king of Phrygia, which Alexander cut with his sword on hearing the declaration of the oracle that he who undid it would be lord of all Asia ; hence, an apparently inextricable difficulty.
Gordius, *n. gawr*-de-us, a genus of parasitic hair-worms, so called from the knots which they form.
gore, *n* gore, blood effused from the body ; clotted blood ; blood. (A.S. *gor.*)
gore, *n.* gore, a wedge-shaped or triangular piece of cloth, let into a garment, balloon, globe, etc., to widen it ; a shaped longitudinal segment of a globe, or of the envelope of an airship, parachute, etc.; a triangular piece of land ; an abatement denoting a coward [Her.] : *v.t.* to pierce with anything pointed ; to fit with a gore. (A.S. *gara.*)
gorge, *n.* gorj, the throat ; the gullet ; that which is gorged or swallowed ; the act of gorging ; a huge meal [Coll.] ; a narrow pass between cliffs or mountains, or its entrance ; the entrance into a bastion or other outwork [Fort.] : *v.t.* to swallow with greediness ; to glut : *v.i.* to feed greedily ; to surfeit. (O.Fr.)
gorged, *a.* gorjd, having a gorge ; surfeited ; bearing a crown or the like about the neck [Her.].
gorgeous, *a. gor*-jus, showy ; splendid ; magnificent. (O.Fr. *gorgias.*)
gorgeously, *ad. gor*-jus-le, in a gorgeous manner.
gorgeousness, *n.* the state of being gorgeous.
gorget, *n. gor*-jet, a piece of armour for defending the throat or neck ; a kind of breast-plate like a crescent moon ; a metallic ornament formerly worn by officers on the breast ; a ruff formerly worn by women. (Fr.)
gorgio, *n. gor*-je-o, (*pl.* **gorgios**), to a gipsy, one who is not a gipsy. (Romany, *gaja.*)
Gorgon, *n. gor*-gon, one of three fabled sisters of such horrible aspect that anyone beholding them turned to stone [Myth.]; any very ugly and repulsive creature, esp. a woman. (L.)
gorgoneion, *n.* gor-goh-*ny*-on (*pl.* **gorgoneia,** -*ny*-a), a mask carved in imitation of the Gorgon Medusa's snake-haired head [Arch.].
Gorgonia, *n.pl.* gor-*goh*-ne-a, the sea-fans, a family of flexible corals, growing in the form of shrubs, twigs, and reticulate fronds [Zool.]. (L., coral.)
gorgonian, *a.* gor-*goh*-ne-an, like a Gorgon ; pertaining to Gorgons, or to the sea-fans.
gorgonize, *v.t. gor*-go-nize, to gaze or stare at as though to petrify.
gorgonzola, *n. gor*-gon-*zoh*-la, a strongly flavoured cheese, originally made at Gorgonzola, near Milan.
gorhen, *n. gawr*-hen, the female of the red grouse [Scot.].
gorilla, *n.* go-*ril*-la, the largest anthropoid ape. (Used as from native name by the Carthaginian navigator, Hanno, 6th cent. B.C.)
gormand, *n. gor*-mand, a gourmand.
gormandize, *v.i. gor*-man-dize, to eat largely or greedily ; to gorge.
gormandizer, *n.* a greedy eater ; a glutton.
gorse, *n.* gors, furze or whin, a yellow-flowered shrub of the genus *Ulex.* (A.S. *gorst.*)
gorsechat, *n. gors*-chat, the whinchat.
Gorsedd, *n. gor*-sethe, the ancient assembly of the Welsh bards ; an assembly at an Eisteddfod.
gorsy, *a. gors*-e, covered with gorse.
gory, *a. gaw*-re, covered with clotted blood ; bloody. **gory dew,** a viscous reddish patch occurring on damp walls and consisting of the alga *Palmella cruenta.*
gosh, *int.* gosh, By God ! (*God.*)
goshawk, *n. gos*-hawk, the large short-winged bird of prey, *Astur palumbarius.* (A.S. *goshafoc.*)
gosling, *n. goz*-ling, a young goose ; a callow greenhorn. (A.S. *gos*, goose.)
gospel, *n. gos*-pl, any of the first four books of the New Testament, giving the history of the life and doctrines of Christ ; a selection from these books used in the Church services ; a system, principle, or creed professed or preached ; the truth. **gospel side,** the north side of the chancel or altar, where the priest stands when reading the gospel. **gospel truth,** certain or unquestionable truth. (A.S. *godspell*, glad tidings.)
gospeller, *n. gos*-pl-ler, an evangelist ; the priest who reads the gospel in the Communion service.
gossamer, *n. gos*-sa-mer, the fine, filmy cobweb spun by small spiders, floating in the air or on bushes in calm weather ; any gauze-like fabric. (M.E. *gossomer*, goose-summer.)
gossamery, *a. gos*-sa-me-re, like gossamer ; diaphanous ; flimsy.
gossan, *n. gos*-san, oxidized sulphide ore occurring in mineral lodes at shallow depths. (Perhaps Cornish.)
gossip, *n. gos*-sip, trifling talk ; idle rumour ; one who runs about tattling ; a tippling companion ; a sponsor : *v.i.* to run about and tattle ; to chat ; to talk much. (A.S. *godsib*, sponsor.)
gossipry, *n. gos*-sip-re, talk of the nature of gossip ; a coterie of gossips.
gossipy, *a. gos*-sip-e, talkative ; full of gossip ; like gossip.
gossoon, *n.* gos-*soon*, a boy ; a lad, esp. as a servant. (Ir., from Fr. *garçon.*)
Gossypium, *n.* gos-*sip*-e-um, a tropical genus of plants of the mallow order, including the cotton plants.
got, got, *pp.* of *get.* **got up,** dressed up for show, disguised, falsified [Slang].
Goth, *n.* goth, one of an ancient tribe of Teutons, who are first recorded as pouring down upon S. Europe from the north in the 3rd and 4th cents. A.D. ; a rude

or uncivilized person; a barbarian. (Late L. *Gothus*, a Goth.)
Gothamist, *n.* *goh*-ta-mist, a wiseacre. (*Gotham*, a Nottinghamshire village famed in legend for the stupidity of its inhabitants.)
Gothamite, *n.* *goh*-ta-mite, a Gothamist; an inhabitant of New York City [Jocular].
Gothic, *a.* *goth*-ik, pertaining to the Goths; denoting a style of architecture with high and sharply pointed arches; black-letter [Print.]; rude; barbarous: *n.* the language of the Goths; the Gothic style; black-letter [Print.]. (Late L. *Gothicus*.)
Gothically, *ad.* *goth*-e-ka-le, in the Gothic style.
Gothicism, *n.* *goth*-e-sizm, rudeness of manners; a Gothic idiom; conformity to the Gothic style.
Gothicize, *v.t.* *goth*-e-size, to make Gothic; to bring back to barbarism.
gotten, *got*-ten, *old* and *U.S.A. p.* of *get*.
gouache, *n.* (App.), a method of water-colour painting, using opaque colours in which gum and honey have been mixed. (Fr.)
gouda, *n.* *gou*-dah, a kind of Dutch cheese. (*Gouda*, in Holland.)
gouge, *n.* gouj, a hollow-bladed chisel, used to cut holes or grooves; a cheat, a swindle or fraud [Slang]: *v.t.* to scoop out, as with a gouge; to force out the eye, as with the thumb; to cheat [U.S.A. slang]. (Fr.)
gouge-slip, *n.* a hone for sharpening gouges.
goulard, *n.* goo-*lard*, a lotion containing sub-acetate of lead used to reduce inflammation. (T. *Goulard*, an 18th-cent. French surgeon.)
goulash, *n.* *goo*-lash, a stew of beef or veal and vegetables highly seasoned with paprika; in contract bridge, a deal following one in which no bid has been made, the cards as dealt being arranged by the players in suits and then re-dealt without shuffling. (Hung. *gulyás*.)
Goura, *n.* *goor*-rah, a genus of large pigeons of New Guinea; (*l.c.*) the crowned pigeon. (Papuan.)
gourami, *n.* *goor*-ro-me *or* goo-*ray*-me, a food fish of the East Indies, *Osphromenus olfax*.
gourd, *n.* goord, a trailing plant of the order *Cucurbita*, comprising the cucumber, pumpkin, melon, etc.; its fruit; the hard rind of any of these, used to hold liquids, etc. (Fr. *gourde*.)
gourd-worm, *n.* the liver-fluke.
gourdy, *a.* *goor*-de, swollen, esp. of a diseased condition of a horse's legs.
gourmand, *n.* *goor*-mand, a greedy or ravenous eater; a glutton. (Fr.)
gourmet, *n.* *goor*-may, a connoisseur of delicate wines and fare; an epicure in food. (Fr.)
gout, *n.* gout, a metabolic disease accompanied by painful paroxysms, acute inflammation in the smaller joints, and the deposition of sodium urate around these; a disease in corn crops caused by *Chlorops tæniopus*, the gout fly. (Fr. *goutte*, from L. *gutta*, a drop.)
goût, *n.* goo, taste; relish. (Fr. *goût*, L. *gustus*, taste.)
goutiness, *n.* *gout*-e-ness, the state of being gouty.
gout-weed, *n.* the common weed *Ægopodium podagraria*, with white flower and grooved hollow stem.
gouty, *a.* *gout*-e, affected with or pertaining to the gout; subject to gout; swollen.
govern, *v.t.* *guv*-ern, to direct and control; to regulate by authority; to influence; to restrain; to require a particular case, mood, etc. [Gram.]: *v.i.* to exercise authority; to administer the laws; to have the control. (Fr. *gouverner*, from L. *guberno*, steer a ship.)
governable, *a.* *guv*-er-na-bl, that may be governed.
governance, *n.* *guv*-er-nance, government; direction; control; management.
governess, *n.* *guv*-er-ness, a woman who has the care of young children or girls, especially educationally; an instructress. **governess cart,** a two-wheeled carriage with facing side-seats only.
★**government,** *n.* *guv*-ern-ment, direction; regulation; control; the exercise of authority; the administration of public affairs; the system of polity in a state; the territory governed; the right of governing; the council or body of persons governing. (Fr. *gouvernement*.)
governmental, *a.* guv-ern-*men*-tal, pertaining to government; made by government.
governmentalism, *n.* guv-ern-*men*-ta-lizm, the over-extension of the legitimate sphere of civil government.
governor, *n.* *guv*-er-nor, one who or that which governs; a ruler; the chief officer of a garrison, prison, etc.; the representative of the monarch in a colony or dependency; one of a governing body; a tutor; familiar name for a father, employer, or master; a regulator; a pair of heavy balls, or other device, connected with machinery and designed to equalize the speed of the engine, etc., by operating on its throttle-valve [Mech.]. (Fr. *gouverneur*.)
governor-general, *n.* a viceroy, esp. of Canada, the Commonwealth of Australia, and, formerly, India.
governorship, *n.* *guv*-er-nor-ship, the office of a governor.
gowan, *n.* *gou*-an, the daisy [Scots.]. (Scand.)
gowk, *n.* gouk, the cuckoo; a fool [Scots.]. (Scand.)
gown, *n.* goun, a woman's upper garment; a dress; a long, loose robe, esp. as worn by professional or university men, the civil magistracy, etc.: *v.t.* to dress in a gown. (O.Fr. *goune*.)
gowned, *a.* gound, dressed in a gown.
gownsman, *n.* *gounz*-man, one whose professional habit is a gown, esp. a university man; a civilian, as distinct from one in the forces.
grab, *v.t.* grab, to grasp or seize suddenly: *v.i.* to clutch at: *n.* a sudden grasp or clutch; a mechanical clutcher; dishonest or extortionate acquisition; a simple card game. (Perhaps Swed. *grabba*.)
grabber, *n.* *grab*-er, one who or that which grabs.
grabble, *v.i.* *grab*-bl, to grope; to sprawl. (*grovel*.)
grace, *n.* grace, favour; good will; divine influence; mercy; pardon; privilege; elegance or ease of form or manner; natural or acquired excellence; beauty; embellishment; an interposition of grace-notes [Mus.]; the form of address of a duke or archbishop; a short prayer at meal times; in some English universities, an act, vote, or decree of the governing body: *v.t.* to adorn; to favour; to honour. **day of grace,** time of probation [Theol.]. **days of grace,** the days allowed for the payment of a bill after it becomes due [Comm.]. **good graces,** favour or friendship. **with a good (bad) grace,** graciously, gracefully (or the reverse). **the Graces,** the three goddesses of radiant life—Aglaia, the shining one, Thalia, the blooming one, and Euphrosyne, the cheerful one [Myth.]. (O.Fr.)
grace-cup, *n.* the loving-cup passed round the table after grace.
graceful, *a.* *grace*-ful, dignifiedly elegant and easy in manner or deportment.
gracefully, *ad.* *grace*-ful-le, in a graceful manner.
gracefulness, *n.* quality of being graceful.
graceless, *a.* *grace*-less, wanting in grace or saving virtue; abandoned; profligate.
gracelessly, *ad.* *grace*-less-le, in a graceless manner.
gracelessness, *n.* condition of being graceless.
grace-note, *n.* an extra note added to a composition as an ornamental flourish [Mus.].
gracile, *a.* *gras*-il, slender. (L.)
gracility, *n.* gra-*sil*-e-te, slenderness.
graciosity, *n.* gras-e-*os*-e-te, affected or exaggerated graciousness.
gracious, *a.* *gray*-shus, expressive of grace or kindness; affable; disposed to forgive; proceeding from divine grace; endowed with grace; virtuous; favourable. (O.Fr. *gracios*.)
graciously, *ad.* *gray*-shus-le, in a gracious manner.
graciousness, *n.* the quality of being gracious.
grackle, *n.* *grak*-kl, any bird of the genus *Gracula*, esp. the myna of the E. Indies, allied to the glossy starlings.
gradate, *v.t.* gra-*date*, to arrange colours so that one passes gradually into another: *v.i.* to blend; to shade insensibly into each other (of colours).
gradation, *n.* gra-*day*-shon, ascension, progression, or arrangement step by step in regular order; a single step in a series; regular arrangement, as in the gradual blending of one tint into another [Paint.]; a diatonic ascending or descending succession of chords [Mus.]. (Fr.)
gradational, *a.* gra-*day*-shon-al, by gradations.
gradationed, *a.* gra-*day*-shond, formed by gradation; in gradation.
gradatory, *a.* *grad*-a-to-re, proceeding step by step; gradational: *n.* a flight of steps, esp. from cloisters into a church [Arch.].
grade, *n.* grade, a step or degree in rank, dignity, order, or any series; degree of slope in a road: *v.t.*

to arrange in regular series; to class by quality, etc.; to improve by cross-breeding (of cattle); to adjust the rate of slope in a road. (Fr.)
gradely, *a. grade*-le, decent; orderly; really good: *ad.* well; handsomely; decently [Lancashire].
gradient, *n. gray*-de-ent, the degree of ascent or descent in a road, railway, etc.; an incline; the variation in height of thermometric or barometric recordings [Meteor.]. (L. *gradiens*, going.)
gradine, *n. gray*-din, a toothed chisel used by sculptors; a tier, or one of a tier, of seats. (Fr. *gradin.*)
gradual, *a. grad*-yew-al, proceeding step by step; regular and slow; not steep or abrupt: *n.* the antiphon, or part of the mass between the epistle and the gospel, so called because chanted on the steps of the altar; a book containing such antiphons. (L. *gradus*, a step.)
gradually, *ad. grad*-yew-a-le, in a gradual manner.
graduate, *n. grad*-yew-at, one who has received a degree in a college or university: *v.t.* to mark with or divide into degrees; to form shades or nice differences; to temper by degrees; to bring fluids to a certain degree of consistency [Chem.]; to award an academic degree to: *v.i.* to receive a degree from a college or university; to pass or change by degrees. (Late L. *graduatus*, admitted to a degree.)
graduation, *n.* grad-yew-*ay*-shon, the act of graduating; regular progression by degrees; the conferring or receiving of academic degrees; a division of any space into small regular intervals; the reduction of a liquid to a certain consistence by evaporation [Chem.].
graduator, *n. grad*-yew-ay-tor, one who or an apparatus which graduates; an instrument for dividing lines into small regular intervals.
graduction, *n.* gra-*duk*-shon, the division of circular arcs into degrees, minutes, etc. [Astron.]. (L. *gradus*, and *ductus*, lead.)
gradus, *n. gray*-dus, a dictionary of Greek or Latin prosody, a "Gradus ad Parnassum." (L., a step.)
Græcism, *n. gree*-sizm, a Greek idiom; Greek style or thought; imitation of anything Greek. (Fr. *grĕcisme*, from L. *Græcus*, Greek.)
Græcize, *v.t. gree*-size, to Hellenize; to imitate the Greeks in any way; to give a Greek term or form to anything.
Graf, *n.* grahf (*fem.* **Gräfin**), a German count. (Ger.)
graffiti, *n.pl.* grah-*fee*-te (*sing.* **graffito**), ancient inscriptions made by scribbling with a stylus on a wall. (It., scratchings.)
graft, *n.* grahft, a small shoot of a tree inserted into another as the stock which is to support and nourish it; transplantation of living tissue, as bone or skin [Med.]: *v.t.* to insert a shoot, as into a tree; to insert or transplant after the manner of a graft: *v.i.* to practise engrafting. (Fr. *graffe*, from Gr. *graphion*, a style.)
graft, *n.* grahft, a spadeful.
graft, *n.* grahft, shady or dishonest practice; advancing by dishonest means; a swindle; the misappropriation of public funds; political jobbery. [U.S.A. slang.]
grail, *n.* grale, a gradual, or church service book.
Grail, *n.* grale, the vessel said to have been used by Christ at the Last Supper and in which Joseph of Arimathea caught up His blood when He was taken from the cross. (O.Fr. *greal*, a dish.)
***grain,** *n.* grane, any small hard mass; a single hard seed of a plant, particularly of those kinds whose seeds are used for food; corn collectively, as wheat, rye, barley, oats, and maize; (*pl.*) malt refuse after brewing; a minute particle; the 20th part of the scruple in apothecaries' weight, and the 24th of a pennyweight troy (either equal to 0·0648 gramme); a very small quantity; the veins or fibres of wood or other fibrous substances; the body or substance of wood as modified by the fibres; texture; state of the grit of any body composed of grains; the dye made from cochineal insects; the heart and temper: *v.t.* to paint in imitation of wood fibre; to form into grains, as powder: *v.i.* to become granulated. **against the grain,** contrary to natural inclination; unwillingly. **grain colours,** the dyes made from cochineal. **grain of allowance,** a small allowance or indulgence. **grains of paradise,** a pungent tropical W. African spice, also known as Guinea grains. **to dye in grain,** to dye in the raw material. (O.Fr.)
grainage, *n. grane*-aj, mangy tumours on the legs of horses.
grainer, *n. grane*-er, an infusion of pigeons' dung in water, used by tanners as bate; one who paints in imitation of the grain of wood; a brush or other implement used in graining.
graining, *n. grane*-ing, painting in imitation of the grain of wood; a process in tanning; indentation; a fish resembling the dace.
grainy, *a. grane*-e, full of grains or corn; resembling the grain of wood.
graip, *n.* grape, a broad-pronged fork. (Scots.)
Grallæ, *n.pl. gral*-lee, the wading birds characterized by long naked legs and, as a rule, long necks and bills. (L. *grallæ*, stilts.)
Grallatores, *n.pl.* gral-a-*taw*-reez, the Grallæ [Ornith.]
grallatorial, *a.* gral-a-*taw*-re-al, pertaining to the Grallæ or waders.
grallic, *a. gral*-lik, grallatorial.
gralloch, *n. gral*-lokh, the entrails of a deer: *v.t.* to remove these. (Gael. *grealoch*, entrails.)
gram, *n.* gram, the metric unit of weight, equal to 15·4323 grains. **gram-atom** or **-molecule,** as many grams of an element (or substance) as are equivalent to the number of its atomic (or molecular) weight.
gram, *n.* gram, any pea or bean cultivated in India for fodder. (Port. *grâo.*)
gramarye, *n. gram*-ma-re, necromancy; magic.
gramercy, *int.* gra-*mer*-se, formerly used to express thankfulness with surprise. (Fr. *grand merci*, great thanks.)
graminaceous, *a.* gram-e-*nay*-shus, pertaining to the grasses: of the nature of grass. (L. *gramen*, grass.)
gramineous, *a,* gra-*min*-e-us, graminaceous.
graminifolious, *a. gram*-in-e-*foh*-le-us, bearing leaves like grass. (L. *gramen*, and *folium*, a leaf.)
graminivorous, *a. gram*-e-niv-o-rus, subsisting on grass or vegetable food. (L. *gramen*, and *voro*, devour.)
graminology, *n.* gram-e-*nol*-o-je, the branch of botany treating of the grasses.
grammalogue, *n. gram*-ma-log, a word symbolized by a single sign or logogram; a logogram [Phonography]. (Gr. *gramma*, letter, *logos*, word.)
grammar, *n. gram*-mar, the principles of language; a system of general principles and of particular rules for correctly speaking or writing a language; a book containing these principles and rules; an elementary treatise; the rudiments of a subject. **grammar school,** a school preparatory to colleges and universities, originally endowed for the teaching of Latin grammar. (O.Fr. *gramaire.*)
grammarian, *n.* gra-*mare*-re-an, one versed in grammar; a philologist; one who teaches grammar.
grammatic, *a.* gra-*mat*-ik, grammatical.
grammatical, *a.* gra-*mat*-e-kal, belonging to grammar; according to the rules of grammar. (Fr.)
grammatically, *ad.* gra-*mat*-e-ka-le, according to the rules of grammar.
grammaticalness, *n.* gra-*mat*-e-kal-ness, the state of being grammatical.
grammaticaster, *n.* gra-*mat*-e-*kas*-ter, a pedant.
grammaticism, *n.* gra-*mat*-e-sizm, a point of grammar.
grammaticize, *v.t.* gra-*mat*-e-size, to render grammatical.
grammatist, *n. gram*-a-tist, a grammarian (usually in disparagement).
gramme, *n.* gram, a gram (metric weight). (Fr.)
gramophone, *n. gram*-o-fone, an instrument for reproducing vocal and other sounds. (Gr. *gramma*, and *phone*, sound.)
grampus, *n. gram*-pus, the killer whale, *Orca gladiator*; a cetacean, *Grampus griseus*, allied to the dolphins. (O.Fr. *gras peis*, great fish.)
granadilla, *n.* gran-a-*dil*-la, the passion-flower; the edible fruit of some species of this; the wood of the granadilla tree. **granadilla tree,** the West Indian tree, *Brya ebenus*. (Sp., a small pomegranate.)
granary, *n. gran*-a-re, a store-house for threshed grain; a region producing much grain [Fig.]. (L. *granarium.*)
grand, *a.* grand, great; illustrious; high in power and dignity; splendid; magnificent; chief; noble; conceived or expressed with great dignity; fashionable; aristocratic [Coll.]; final; in the second

degree, as in grandfather: *n.* a grand piano; a Grand Master [Coll.]. **Grand Duchess,** the female ruler of a Grand Duchy, or wife of a Grand Duke. **Grand Duchy,** the territory, jurisdiction, or rank of a Grand Duke. **Grand Duke,** title of the hereditary ruler of Luxemburg, certain former European ruling princes, and the brothers of the Russian Tsar. **Grand Inquisitor,** the chief of a Court of Inquisition. **grand jury,** a jury whose duty it is to decide whether there are grounds for an accusation to justify a trial (abolished, except for a few special purposes, 1933). **Grand Lodge,** the governing body of the freemasons. **Grand Master,** the head of certain orders of knighthood, of the freemasons, etc. **grand piano,** a large piano with horizontal frame. **Grand Seignor,** a title of the former Sultans of Turkey. **grand slam,** the taking of all the tricks at bridge, etc. **grand stand,** the principal stand on a racecourse or sports ground. **Grand Vizier,** formerly the chief minister of Turkey. (O.Fr.)

granddad, *n.* *gran*-dad, an affectionate abbreviation of grandfather.

grandam, *n.* *gran*-dam, a grandmother; an old woman.

grand-aunt, *n.* the sister of a grandfather or grandmother.

grandchild, *n.* *grand*-chyld, a son's or daughter's child.

granddaughter, *n.* *gran*-daw-ter, a son's or daughter's daughter.

grandee, *n.* gran-*dee*, a nobleman of Spain or Portugal of the first rank; a man of elevated rank or station. (Sp. *grande.*)

grandeur, *n.* *gran*-dewr, vastness; that combination of qualities in an object which elevates or expands the mind, and excites pleasurable emotions; splendour of appearance; elevation of thought, sentiment, or deportment; majesty. (Fr.)

grandfather, *n.* *gran*-fah-ther a father's or mother's father. **grandfather clock,** a clock in a tall case with pendulum and weights.

grandiloquence, *n.* gran-*dil*-o-kwence, the quality of being grandiloquent.

grandiloquent, *a.* gran-*dil*-o-kwent, speaking in a lofty or bombastic style; pompous. (L. *grandis*, great, and *loquens*, speaking.)

grandiloquently, *ad.* in a grandiloquent manner.

grandiose, *a.* *gran*-de-ose, affectedly imposing; pompous; turgid. (Fr.)

grandiosity, *n.* gran-de-*os*-e-te, the quality of being grandiose.

Grandisonian, *a.* gran-de-*soh*-ne-an, distinguished by exquisite courtesy; wearisomely polite. ("Sir Charles *Grandison*," by Richardson.)

grandly, *a.* *grand*-le, in a grand manner.

grandmother, *n.* *gran*-muth-er, the mother of one's father or mother.

grandnephew, *n.* *grand*-nev-yew, the grandson of one's brother or sister.

grandness, *n.* *grand*-ness, grandeur; the quality of being grand.

grandniece, *n.* *grand*-neece, the grand-daughter of a brother or sister.

grandparent, *n.* *grand*-pare-rent, a parent's parent.

grandsire, *n.* *grand*-sire, a grandfather; a male ancestor; a particular sequence in change-ringing [Campanology]. (O.Fr. *grantsire.*)

grandson, *n.* *grand*-sun, a son's or daughter's son.

grand-uncle, *n.* the brother of one's grandfather or grandmother.

grange, *n.* graynj, an outlying farm; the farm of a monastery; a commercial association of farmers [U.S.A.]. (O.Fr.)

granger, *n.* *grayn*-jer, a farm bailiff; a member of a grange [U.S.A.].

grangerism, *n.* *grayn*-jer-izm, the practice of grangerizing.

grangerize, *v.t.* *grayn*-jer-ize, to add illustrations to a book by fixing into it prints, etc., usually cut from other books; to extra-illustrate. (After *Granger*, who published a "History of England" designed to be so illustrated.)

graniferous, *a.* gra-*nif*-er-rus, bearing grain, or seeds like grain. (L. *granum*, grain, *fero*, bear.)

graniform, *a.* *gran*-e-form, like grains of corn.

granite, *n.* *gran*-it, a hand igneous crystalline rock composed mainly of quartz, felspar, and mica. (It. *granito.*)

granitic, *a.* gra-*nit*-ik, pertaining to granite; having the nature or consisting of granite.

granitification, *n.* gra-*nit*-e-fe-*kay*-shon, formation into granite. (*Granite*, and L. *facio*, make.)

granitiform, *a.* gra-*nit*-e-form, resembling granite.

granitoid, *a.* *gran*-e-toyd, resembling granite.

granivorous, *a.* gra-*niv*-o-rus, feeding on seeds. (L. *granum*, and *voro*, devour.)

grannom, *n.* *gran*-om, a grandmother; a four-winged aquatic fly, or angler's imitation thereof.

granny, *n.* *gran*-ne, familiar name for grandmother. **granny knot,** a knot in which one end is passed over the bend instead of under it.

granolithic, *a.* gran-o-*lith*-ik, composed of cement and fine granite chippings: *n.* a concrete of this composition.

granophyre, *n.* *gran*-o-fire, a fine-grained porphyritic igneous rock having similar constituents to those of granite

grant, *n.* grahnt, a bestowing; the thing bestowed; a gift; a concession or admission of something as true; a conveyance in writing [Law]; the thing conveyed: *v.t.* to give or bestow without compensation in answer to request; to transfer the title of a thing to another, for a good or valuable consideration; to confer (a privilege, etc.); to admit as true what is not proved; to concede. (O.Fr. *graunter.*)

grantable, *a.* *grahn*-ta-bl, that may be granted.

grantee, *n.* grahn-*tee*, the person to whom a grant or conveyance is made [Law].

granter, *n.* *grahn*-ter, one who grants.

grantor, *n.* *grahn*-tor, one who makes a conveyance [Law].

granular, *a.* *gran*-yew-lar, granulated; small and compact. **granular limestone,** a white variety of limestone used as statuary marble. (L. *granum*, grain.)

granularity, *n.* *gran*-yew-*la*-re-te, the condition of being granular.

granularly, *ad.* in a granular manner.

granulate, *a.* *gran*-yew-lat, having numerous small elevations, like shagreen; consisting of or resembling grains: *v.i.* to collect or be formed into grains: *v.t.* to collect or form into grains or small masses; to make rough on the surface.

granulated, *a.* *gran*-yew-*lay*-ted, consisting of grains; having the form of grains.

granulation, *n.* gran-yew-*lay*-shon, the act or process of forming into grains, esp. of metals by pouring them in molten state into water through a sieve: *pl.* small grain-like formations in healing sores [Med.].

granule, *n.* *gran*-yewl, a little grain; a small particle. (Late L. *grannulum.*)

granuliferous, *a.* *gran*-yew-*lif*-er-rus, full of granules or granulations. (*granule*, and *fero*, bear.)

granuliform, *a.* gra-*new*-le-form, having an irregular granular structure [Min.].

granulous, *a.* *gran*-yew-lus, granuliferous.

grape, *n.* grape, the fruit of the vine; grape-shot: *pl.* a mangy tumour on the leg of a horse. (O.Fr.)

grapefruit, *n.* *grape*-froot, a small variety of shaddock, *Citrus decumana*, a large hard-rinded citrus fruit growing, like grapes, in clusters.

grape-hyacinth, *n.* grape-*hy*-a-sinth, the liliaceous plant, *Muscari racemosum.*

grapery, *n.* *grape*-er-re, a vinery.

grape-shot, *n.* a cluster of small shot, arranged in tiers between plates round a wire, and dispersing when fired.

grape-stone, *n.* the stone or seed of the grape.

grape-sugar, *n.* dextrose, a waxy dextro-rotatory glucose, present in grapes and prepared commercially from starch.

grape-vine, *n.* the vine which yields the grape, *Vitis vinifera.*

grape-wort, *n.* the baneberry, a poisonous plant, *Actæa spicata.*

graph, *n.* graf, a diagram by means of which mathematical, chemical, or other relationships can be illustrated; a hectograph, or gelatine copying slab: *v.t.* to represent by a graph; to reproduce by hectograph. (Gr. *graphē*, writing.)

graphic, *a.* *graf*-ik, pertaining to the art of writing or delineating; indicating by means of graphs; well delineated; describing picturesquely; life-like. **graphic arts,** drawing, engraving, painting, etc. **graphic granite,** a rock composed of felspar and quartz. (L. *graphicus.*)

graphically, *ad.* *graf*-e-ka-le, in a graphic manner.
graphicalness, *n.* *graf*-e-kal-ness, the quality of being graphic.
graphics, *n.* *graf*-iks, the use of graphs; the art of mathematical drawing. (L. *graphicus.*)
graphiology, *n.* graf-e-*ol*-o-je, graphology.
graphite, *n.* *graf*-ite, plumbago, a form of carbon, also known as blacklead. (Gr. *graphē*, writing.)
graphitic, *a.* gra-*fit*-ik, resembling, derived from, or pertaining to graphite.
graphium, *n.* *graf*-e-um, a stylus for writing on wax-covered tablets. (L., a style.)
grapholite, *n.* *graf*-o-lite, a kind of writing slate.
graphology, *n.* gra-*fol*-o-je, the study of handwriting, or of judging character by means of handwriting; the system of graphical notation.
graphometer, *n.* gra-*fom*-e-ter, a surveying instrument for measuring the degrees in an angle.
graphotype, *n.* *graf*-o-tipe, a method of engraving in which the drawing was made on compressed chalk with a special ink which remained in relief when the chalk intervals were brushed away from it.
grapnel, *n.* *grap*-nel, a small anchor fitted with three or more flukes; a grappling-iron. (O.Fr. *grappe*, a hook.)
grapple, *n.* *grap*-pl, a seizing; a close hug in a contest; close fight; a grappling-iron or other clutching appliance: *v.t.* to lay fast hold of: *v.i.* to contend or struggle in close fight. (O.Fr. *grappil*, a grapple.)
grappling-iron, *n.* an implement for grappling and holding fast; a grapnel.
graptolite, *n.* *grap*-to-lite, a fossil hydrozoan, with its cells arranged on one or both sides of a slender stem. (Gr. *graptos*, written, *lithos*, a stone.)
graptolitic, *a.* grap-to-*lit*-ik, relating to or containing graptolites.
grapy, *a.* *grape*-e, like grapes; made of grapes; affected with grapes (of horses).
grasp, *n.* grahsp, a grip of the hand; reach of the arms; the power of seizing; hold; intellectual capacity: *v.t.* to seize and hold by clasping or embracing; to catch at: *v.i.* to try to seize; to catch; to comprehend. (M.E. *grapsen.*)
graspable, *a.* *grahsp*-a-bl, that can be grasped.
grasper, *n.* *grahsp*-er, one who grasps.
grasping, *a.* *grahsp*-ing, greedy to possess; avaricious.
graspingly, *ad.* in a grasping manner.
***grass,** *n.* grahs, pasture; a pasture plant; plants with simple leaves, a stem generally jointed and tubular, a husky calyx, and the seed single [Bot.]: *v.t.* to cover with grass or turf; to graze (cattle, etc.); to expose on grass for bleaching; to bring to the ground [Sports]. **grass of Parnassus,** a plant of the saxifrage family, *Parnassia palustris*. (A.S. *græs.*)
grass-blade, *n.* a blade or leaf of grass.
grass-cloth, *n.* an Eastern fabric made of the fibres of various plants.
grass-cutter, *n.* one who or an implement which cuts grass; in India, one who provides provender for the army cattle and horses.
grass-green, *a.* dark-green: *n.* the colour of grass.
grass-grown, *a.* overgrown with grass.
grasshopper, *n.* *grahs*-hop-per, a straight-winged jumping insect of the locust family. **grasshopper beam,** the beam of an engine pivoted at one end instead of the centre. **grasshopper warbler,** the small bird, *Locustella nævia*.
grassiness, *n.* *grahs*-se-ness, the state of being grassy.
grassland, *n.* *grahs*-land, land that is, naturally or artificially, constantly under grass.
grass-oil, *n.* an essential oil obtained from various scented grasses in India.
grass-plot, *n.* a plot of ground covered with grass.
grass-snake, *n.* the common British non-venomous snake, of the colubrine group, *Natrix natrix*.
grass-tree, *n.* an Australian liliaceous plant, of the genus *Xanthorrhœa*, yielding a resin.
grass-widow, *n.* a woman whose husband is temporarily absent; a divorced woman (hence, **grass-widower**).
grass-wrack, *n.* the eel-grass, a pond-weed, *Zostera marina*, growing in shallow salt water.
grassy, *a.* *grahs*-e, covered with grass; resembling grass; green.

grate, *n.* grate, a frame of parallel or cross bars, with interstices; a frame of iron bars for holding fuel for a fire: *v.t.* to furnish with grating; to make fast with cross bars. (L. *cratis*, a hurdle.)
grate, *v.t.* grate, to rub, as a body with a rough surface against another body; to make a harsh sound by the friction of rough bodies; to offend; to fret; to irritate: *v.i.* to rub hard, so as to offend; to make a harsh sound by friction of rough bodies. (O.Fr. *grater.*)
grateful, *a.* *grate*-ful, having or implying a due sense of benefits; affording pleasure; gratifying. (L. *gratus*, pleasing.)
gratefully, *ad.* in a grateful manner.
gratefulness, *n.* the quality of being grateful.
grater, *n.* *grate*-er, a kitchen utensil with a rough surface for rubbing down a substance.
graticulation, *n.* gra-*tik*-yew-*lay*-shon, the division of a design or drawing into squares, for the purpose of reducing or enlarging it. (L. *cratēs*, hurdles.)
graticule, *n.* *grat*-e-kewl, a design treated by graticulation; a glass marked with hair-lines inserted in a telescope, etc., for use in measuring or location [Opt.].
gratification, *n.* *grat*-e-fe-*kay*-shon, the act of gratifying; that which gratifies; delight; recompense. (L. *gratificatio.*)
gratifier, *n.* *grat*-e-fy-er, one who or that which gratifies.
gratify, *v.t.* *grat*-e-fy, to please; to indulge; to humour; to satisfy; to recompense. (Fr. *gratifier.*)
gratin, *n.* (App.) a brown crust formed on dishes cooked with a cover of buttered bread-crumbs or grated cheese. **au gratin,** baked thus. (Fr.)
grating, *n.* *grate*-ing, a partition of bars; lattice-work; a series of parallel lines ruled or engraved close together for optical or spectroscopic work; a graticule.
gratingly, *ad.* in an irritating or grating manner.
gratis, *ad.* *gray*-tis, for nothing; without payment. (L.)
gratitude, *n.* *grat*-e-tewd, a sentiment of gratefulness to a benefactor. (Fr.)
gratuitous, *a.* gra-*tew*-e-tus, free; voluntary; granted without claim or merit; without reason, warrant, or proof. (L. *gratuitus.*)
gratuitously, *ad.* in a gratuitous manner.
gratuitousness, *n.* the quality of being gratuitous.
gratuity, *n.* gra-*tew*-e-te, something given voluntarily in return for a favour, service, etc.; a tip; a bounty paid on retirement. (Fr. *gratuité.*)
gratulate, *v.t.* *grat*-yew-late, to congratulate.
gratulation, *n.* grat-yew-*lay*-shon, congratulation.
gratulatory *a.* *grat*-yew-*lay*-to-re, congratulatory.
gravamen, *n.* gra-*vay*-men (*pl.* **gravamina**), the substantial cause of an action [Law]; the most serious part of a charge. (L. from *gravis*, heavy.)
grave, *n.* grave, a pit dug to bury a dead body; any place of burial; a tomb; a place of great slaughter or mortality; death or destruction: *v.t.* to engrave; to carve or cut on stone, etc., with a chisel or edged tool: *v.i.* to carve; to engrave. (A.S. *grafan.*)
grave, *v.t.* grave, to clean a wooden ship's hull by burning off. (Origin uncertain.)
grave, *a.* grave, of weight; of importance; of a serious character; not gay or showy; solemn; sedate; low or depressed, as opposed to acute [Mus.]; heavy or long-sounding, not acute (of accents) [Gram.]. (Fr. from L. *gravis*, heavy.)
grave-clothes, *n.pl.* the shroud or clothes in which the dead are interred.
grave-digger, *n.* one whose occupation is to dig graves; the burying-beetle.
gravel, *n.* *grav*-el, small stones, often intermixed with particles of sand, etc.; a disease characterized by minute calculous concretions in the urinary organs [Med.]: *v.t.* to cover with gravel; to stick in the sand; to embarrass; to perplex. (O.Fr. *gravele*, from *grève*, a shingly shore.)
gravel-blind, *a.* half-blind; a stage worse than sand-blind.
gravelling, *n.* *grav*-el-ing, a covering of gravel.
gravelly, *a.* abounding with gravel.
gravel-pit, *n.* a place where gravel is dug.
gravely, *ad.* *grave*-le, in a grave manner.
graven, *a.* *gray*-vn, carved; sculptured; inscribed. **graven image,** an idol.
graveness, *n.* *grave*-ness, the state or quality of being grave.

graveolence, *n.* gra-*vee*-o-lence, a strong and offensive smell.
graveolent, *a.* gra-*vee*-o-lent, fetid; having a strong offensive odour. (L. *gravis*, and *olens*, smelling.)
graver, *n.* *grave*-er, an engraver; an engraving tool.
Graves, *n.* grahv, a white wine grown at Les Graves, a gravelly district of the Gironde, France.
gravestone, *n.* *grave*-stone, a stone laid over a grave, or erected near it, as a monument.
graveyard, *n.* *grave*-yard, a burying-ground.
gravid, *a.* *grav*-id, pregnant [Med.]. (L. *gravidus.*)
gravidity, *n.* gra-*vid*-e-te, the state of being pregnant [Med.].
gravied, *a.* *gray*-vid, covered with gravy.
gravigrade, *a.* *grav*-e-grade, stepping heavily like an elephant; pertaining to the *Gravigrada*, or ground-sloths. (L. *gravis*, heavy, *gradus*, step.)
gravimeter, *n.* gra-*vim*-e-ter, a form of hydrometer. (L. *gravis*, and Gr. *metron*, measure.)
gravimetric, *a.* grav-e-*met*-rik, measured by weight; pertaining to measurement by weight.
graving-dock, *n.* a dry dock in which ships are laid up for cleaning, repairs, and overhaul.
gravitate, *v.i.* *grav*-e-tate, to be acted on or attracted by gravity; to tend in a downward direction; to be irresistibly drawn towards. (L. *gravis.*)
gravitation, *n.* grav-e-*tay*-shon, the force under which bodies attract and tend to each other; mutual attraction; the process of gravitating.
gravitational, *a.* grav-e-*tay*-shon-al, pertaining to or due to gravity.
gravitative, *a.* *grav*-e-ta-tiv, tending to gravitate.
gravity, *n.* *grav*-e-te, heaviness; weight; importance; seriousness; solemnity; enormity; lowness of pitch [Mus.]; the tendency, causing weight, of a mass of matter to attract and be attracted by another. **centre of gravity,** *see* **centre. specific gravity,** the relative weight of a body compared with that of another of equal volume, taken as a standard. (Fr. *gravité.*)
gravure, *n.* gra-*vewr*, an engraving; a photogravure.
gravy, *n.* *gray*-ve, the juice from flesh while roasting; a sauce resembling this. (M.E. *gravey*, origin uncertain.)
gray, *a.* gray, grey.
grayling, *n.* *gray*-ling, a freshwater fish of the salmon family, resembling the trout in shape, *Thymallus vulgaris*.
graze, *n.* graze, a light touch in passing; an abrasion: *v.t.* to rub, brush, or touch lightly in passing.
graze, *v.t.* graze, to feed with grass; to furnish pasture for; to feed on; to tend while grazing: *v.i.* to eat grass; to browse; to supply grass. (A.S. *grasian.*)
grazer, *n.* *graze*-er, an animal that grazes.
grazier, *n.* *graze*-yer, one who pastures cattle, and rears them for market.
grazing, *n.* *graze*-ing, feeding on grass; a pasture.
grazioso, *ad.* grat-se-*oh*-zo, gracefully and elegantly [Mus.]. (It.)
grease, *n.* greece, animal fat in a soft state; oily matter of any kind; an inflammation in the legs of a horse. **grease gun,** a syringe for injecting grease into the moving parts of mechanism. **grease paint,** tinted tallow used in making up. (Fr. *graisse*, from *gras*, fat.)
grease, *v.t.* greeze, to lubricate; to bribe; to corrupt with presents.
greaser, *n.* *greeze*-er, one who or that which greases; a lubricator; a Mexican or Spanish-American [U.S.A. Slang].
greasily, *ad.* *gree*-ze-le, in a greasy manner; with or as with grease.
greasiness, *n.* the state of being greasy.
greasy, *a.* *gree*-ze, oily; fat; unctuous; like or smeared with grease; gross; indelicate; indecent.
★**great,** *a.* grate, large; of large amount; long-continued; weighty; chief; of vast power and excellence; supreme; vast; wonderful; able; accomplished; distinguished; eminent; dignified; magnanimous; magnificent; sublime; noble; proud; pregnant; difficult; distant by one more generation, in the ascending or descending line, as **great-grandfather**; pre-eminent: *n.* the whole; the gross; the lump; people of rank or distinction. **Great Bear,** the northern constellation Ursa Major. **great circle,** a circle the plane of which passes through the centre of the terrestrial or celestial sphere. **great Dane,** a large boarhound. **great go,** the final examination at Cambridge for the B.A. degree. **Great Powers,** the leading States of the world at any particular period. **Great Seal,** the principal seal of a kingdom, in Great Britain held by the Lord Chancellor. (A.S.)
greatcoat, *n.* *grate*-kote, an overcoat.
great-hearted, *a.* having a great and generous heart; high-spirited; noble.
greatly, *ad.* *grate*-le, in a great degree or manner.
greatness, *n.* the state or quality of being great.
greats, *n.pl.* grayts, the final examination at Oxford for the degree of B.A.
greaves, *n.pl.* greevz, armour for the legs. (Fr.)
greaves, *n.pl.* greevz, the fibrous sediment of melted tallow; cracklings. (Low Ger. *greven.*)
grebe, *n.* greeb, a bird of the genus *Podiceps* with short wings, and very expert at diving. (Fr. *grèbe.*)
Grecian, *a.* *gree*-shan, pertaining to Greece or its people: *n.* a native of Greece; one well versed in the Greek language; a Greek by adoption; a member of the Sixth Form at Christ's Hospital.
Grecianize, *v.i.* *gree*-sha-nize, to græcize. (Rare.)
Grecism, *n.* *gree*-sizm, a græcism.
grecize, *v.t.* *gree*-size, to græcize. (Fr. *Gréciser.*)
gree, *n.* gree, a step; a degree, as of rank; pre-eminence. (Scots.)
greed, *n.* greed, greediness; avarice; eager longing.
greedily, *ad.* *gree*-de-le, in a greedy manner.
greediness, *n.* the quality of being greedy.
greedy, *a.* *gree*-de, having a keen appetite for food or drink; gluttonous; voracious; eagerly desirous to obtain. (A.S. *grædig.*)
Greek, *a.* greek, pertaining to Greece: *n.* a native of Greece; the language of Greece; something one does not understand [Coll.]. **Greek calends,** *see* **calends. Greek Church,** the Orthodox or Eastern Church. **Greek cross,** a cross having limbs of equal length. **Greek fire,** *see* **fire. Greek gift,** a gift bestowed with a sinister motive. **Greek orders,** the Doric, Ionic, and Corinthian [Arch.]. (A.S. *Grēcas*, a Greek.)
★**green,** *a.* green, of a colour composed of blue and yellow, or that of growing plants and herbage; fresh; recent; flourishing; undecayed; not dry; not seasoned; half-raw; unripe; young; callow; inexperienced; pale; sickly: *n.* a colour composed of blue and yellow; the colour of growing grass; a green pigment; a grass-plot or lawn: *v.t.* and *i.* to make or become green. **green belt,** a zone surrounding a town, building in which is subject to consent of the local authority. **green cloth,** formerly a court of justice connected with the royal household; a department under the Lord Steward, controlling household matters. **green crop,** vegetables used for food when green. **green goose,** a young goose fattened for eating. **green sickness,** chlorosis, a disease of young women characterized by paleness, languor, and indigestion. **green stuff,** greens. **green table,** a gaming table. **green tea,** tea-leaves cured before fermentation. **green vitriol,** crystallized sulphate of iron. (A.S. *grene.*)
greenback, *n.* *green*-bak, legal-tender paper money of the United States, first issued in 1862, the back being green; a green frog.
greenery, *n.* *green*-er-re, verdure; green plants, or a place for growing them.
green-eyed, *a.* jealous; having green or jaundiced eyes.
greenfinch, *n.* *green*-finch, a British and European singing-bird of the genus *Ligurinus*.
green-fly, *n.* any green aphis destructive to growing plants.
greengage, *n.* green-*gaje*, a kind of yellowish green plum with green pulp. (*green*, and *gage*, from Sir W. *Gage*, who introduced it into England.)
greengrocer, *n.* *green*-groh-ser, a dealer in vegetables, fruit, etc.
greengrocery, *n.* *green*-groh-se-re, the occupation, shop, or wares of a greengrocer.
greenheart, *n.* *green*-hahrt, a hard-timbered West Indian and S. American tree of the genus *Nectandra*.
greenhorn, *n.* *green*-horn, a novice; a raw youth.
greenhouse, *n.* *green*-house, a glass house for tender or exotic plants.
greening, *n.* *green*-ing, an apple, green when ripe; an oyster of a greenish tint.
greenish, *a.* *green*-ish, somewhat green.

greenishness, *n.* quality of being greenish.
green-keeper, *n.* one employed to tend a golf-course.
Greenlander, *n.* *green*-lan-der, a native or inhabitant of Greenland. **Greenland spar,** cryolite. **Greenland whale,** the Arctic right whale, *Balæna mysticetus*.
greenlet, *n.* *green*-let, any of several small greenish N. American song-birds.
greenly, *ad.* *green*-le, with a green colour ; in a green manner.
greenness, *n.* *green*-ness, the quality of being green.
greenockite, *n.* green-o-*kite*, crystalline sulphide of cadmium.
green-room, *n.* a room near the stage, to which actors retire during the intervals of their parts.
greens, *n.pl.* greenz, cabbages, sprouts, and other plants boiled in their green state for food.
greensand, *n.* *green*-sand, a sandstone formation of the Cretaceous series lying between the chalk and the wealden beds [Geol.].
greenshank, *n.* *green*-shank, a species of sandpiper of the genus *Totanus*.
green-stick, *n.* a fracture in which only one side of the bone is broken [Surg.].
greenstone, *n.* *green*-stone, a kind of jade ; an old name for diorites and dolerites.
greensward, *n.* *green*-swawrd, grassy turf.
greenth, *n.* greenth, verdure ; green growth.
greenweed, *n.* *green*-weed, dyer's weed, *Genista tinctoria*.
Greenwich, *n.* *grin*-ij, the town in Kent in which the Royal Observatory was situated from 1675 to 1949. **Greenwich Mean Time,** mean time of the meridian of Greenwich, the standard British time.
greenwood, *n.* *green*-wood, woodland when green, as in summer : *a.* pertaining to forest land or conditions, or to outlawry.
greeny, *a.* *gree*-ne, greenish.
greet, *v.t.* greet, to salute with expressions or signs of kind wishes ; to send kind wishes to ; to meet with greetings : *v.i.* to meet and salute. (A.S. *grētan*.)
greet, *v.i.* greet, to weep or cry. (Scots.)
greeting, *n.* *greet*-ing, expression of kindness or joy ; a welcome ; a salutation.
greffier, *n.* *gref*-fe-er, a notary or registrar in the Channel Islands. (O.Fr.)
gregarianism, *n.* gre-*gare*-re-a-nizm, the practice of crowding together in herds, etc. ; gregariousness.
gregarious, *a.* gre-*gare*-re-us, going or living in flocks or herds ; belonging to the herd or common crowd ; growing in clusters [Bot.]. (L. *gregarisus*, belonging to a flock.)
gregariously, *ad.* in a gregarious manner.
gregariousness, *n.* the state or quality of being gregarious.
Gregorian, *a.* gre-*gaw*-re-an, arranged or invented by Gregory. **Gregorian calendar,** the regulation of the year according to the reformation introduced by Pope Gregory XIII in 1582. **Gregorian chant,** plainsong, choral music named after Pope Gregory I. **Gregorian telescope,** a common form of the reflecting telescope, so named from its inventor, James Gregory, about 1662. **Gregorian year,** the year as now reckoned according to the Gregorian calendar.
Gregory-powder, *n.* *greg*-o-re-*pou*-der, a compound of magnesia, ginger and rhubarb used as an aperient. (Dr. J. *Gregory*, *d.* 1822.)
gremial, *a.* *gree*-me-al, belonging to the lap or bosom : *n.* an apron worn by Roman Catholic bishops during certain ceremonies. (L. *gremium*, lap.)
gremlin, *n.* *grem*-lin, a supposititious imp of mischief infesting aircraft and responsible for minor mishap [Slang]. (Said to be compounded from *goblin* and *Fremlin*, name of a brewer.)
grenade, *n.* gre-*nade*, a small explosive shell used at short range ; a chemical-filled glass container for extinguishing fires. (Fr., from Sp. *granada*, a pomegranate.)
grenadier, *n.* gren-a-*deer*, originally a soldier who threw grenades, esp. a member of the specially selected first company of every battalion of foot ; a soldier of the First Regiment of Guards in the British army. (Fr.)
grenadine, *n.* *gren*-a-deen, a dish of veal or chicken larded and glazed ; a dress-material of silk or silk and wool ; a syrup made from pomegranates ; a variety of highly scented dwarf carnation [Hort.]. (Fr.)
gressorial, *a.* gre-*saw*-re-al, adapted for walking [Zool.] ; having three toes of the feet forward, two of them connected, and one behind [Ornith.]. (L. *gressus*, stepping.
grew, *p.* groo, p. of *grow*.
★**grey,** *a.* gray, white with a mixture of black ; ashy ; a neutral tint compounded of several colours : *n.* a horse, badger, or other grey-coloured animal. **Grey Friar,** a Franciscan. **grey goose,** the grey-lag. **grey matter,** the greyish cortical substance of the brain [Anat.].
greybeard, *n.* *gray*-beard, an old man ; a large earthenware jar ; a variety of lichen.
grey-hen, *n.* the female of the black grouse.
greyhound, *n.* *gray*-hound, a hound of thin, high build, length of limb, and great swiftness, used for hunting hares and racing. **ocean greyhound,** a swift liner. (A.S. *grighund*.)
greyish, *a.* *gray*-ish, rather grey.
grey-lag, *n.* the grey-lag goose, *Anser cinereus*.
greyness, *n.* *gray*-ness, the state of being grey.
greystone, *n.* *gray*-stone, a greyish or greenish rock mainly composed of felspar and augite.
greywacke, *n.* *gray*-wak-a, a gritty kind of dark-coloured sandstone of palæozoic age [Geol.]. (Ger. *grauwacke*.)
greywethers, *n.pl.* *gray*-weth-erz, large detached blocks of compact sandstone ; sarsen stones.
grice, *n.* grice, a sucking-pig ; a young wild boar. (Ice.)
grid, *n.* grid, a grating ; a gridiron ; a frame of bars ; graticulation on a plan, etc. [Surv.] ; the central electrode in a thermionic valve, interposed between the filament and the plate [Wire.] ; the system by which electric current is transmitted from high-power generating stations through subsidiary stations to the distributing companies. **screen grid valve,** a four-electrode thermionic valve having two grids, a filament, and an anode [Wire.). (As *gridiron*.)
griddle, *n.* *grid*-dl, a round iron plate for baking cakes on ; a wire-bottomed sieve [Mining.] (O.Fr. *gredil*.)
griddle-cake, *n.* a cake baked on a griddle.
gride, *v.t.* gride, to grate harshly ; to jar : *n.* a grating sound. (As *gird*, orig. sense, *to pierce*.)
gridelin, *n.* *grid*-e-lin, a colour mixed of white and red, or a grey violet. (Fr. *gris de lin*, grey of flax.)
gridiron, *n.* *grid*-i-urn, a frame of iron bars for broiling flesh or fish over a fire ; a grill ; a framework for various uses ; a network of railway tracks. (M.E. *gridire*, a griddle.)
grief, *n.* greef, pain of mind produced by loss, misfortune, misconduct, or evil, whether suffered or done ; sorrow ; cause of sorrow ; regret ; that which afflicts ; affliction. **to come to grief,** to be injured ; to fail ; to end badly. (O.Fr.)
grief-shot, *a.* *greef*-shot, sorrow stricken.
grievance, *n.* *greev*-ance, a hardship and injustice ; a ground of complaint. (O.Fr.)
grieve, *v.t.* greev, to give pain of mind to ; to afflict ; to make sorrowful ; to mourn over : *v.i.* to feel grief ; to sorrow ; to mourn. (O.Fr. *grever*.)
grievous, *a.* *greev*-us, causing grief or pain ; burdensome ; hard to be borne ; heinous ; serious ; full of complaint ; hurtful. (O.Fr. *grevus*.)
grievously, *ad.* *greev*-us-le, in a grievous manner.
grievousness, *n.* *greev*-us-ness, oppressiveness ; affliction ; atrociousness.
griffin, *n.* *grif*-fin, a fabulous monster with the body and legs of a lion, the wings and beak of an eagle, and a pair of listening ears. (Fr. *griffon*.)
griffin, *n.* *grif*-fin, a novice ; a newly arrived European ; a pony entered for its first race [Anglo-Indian].
griffon, *n.* *grif*-fon, a griffin [Her.] ; a rough-haired European dog of four or five varieties. **Brussels griffon,** a small, rough-haired, short-nosed dog. **griffon vulture,** *Gyps fulvus*. (Fr.)
grig, *n.* grig, a sand-eel ; a cricket. **a merry grig,** a lively frolicsome fellow. (Dial. Eng.)
grill, *n.* gril, a gridiron ; a piece of meat, etc., grilled : *v.t.* to broil on a gridiron ; to torment, as if by broiling ; to subject to severe cross-examination [Slang]. (Fr. *griller*.)
grillage, *n.* *gril*-aj, an arrangement of cross-beams, bedded in loose soil, as a building foundation. (Fr.)

grille, *n.* gril, a grating; a screen of metal lattice-work; a grille; the square opening in the end hazard side wall of a tennis-court. (Fr.)
grill-room, *n.* a place where a grill is installed and grilled food served.
grilse, *n.* grils, a young salmon in its second year, after its first return from the sea. (Scots.)
grim, *a.* grim, stern; forbidding; fierce; horrible. **like grim death,** with inflexible determination. (A.S., fierce.)
grimace, *n.* gre-*mace*, distortion of the face: *v.i.* to make grimaces.
grimalkin, *n.* gre-*mawl*-kin, an old she-cat; a spiteful old woman. (*grey* and *malkin.*)
grime, *n.* grime, foul matter leaving a black stain; ingrained dirt: *v.t.* to soil with grime. (M.E. *grīm*, from Low Ger.)
grimily, *ad.* *gry*-me-ly, in a grimy manner.
griminess *n.* *gry*-me-ness, the state or quality of being grimy.
grimly, *ad.* *grim*-le, fiercely; in a grim manner.
grimness, *n.* *grim*-ness, the state of being grim.
grimy, *a.* *gry*-me, full of grime; foul.
grin, *n.* grin, the act of closing the teeth and showing them; a forced smile: *v.i.* to show the teeth, as in laughter or pain; to smile derisively or maliciously: *v.t.* to express by grinning. (A.S. *grennian.*)
grind, *n.* grynd, the act or process of grinding; hard and tedious study for an examination; any hard or tedious task: *v.t.* to reduce to small pieces or powder by friction; to wear down, sharpen, or smoothe by friction; to grate; to oppress; to harass; to teach (a pupil) or study laboriously for an examination, etc.: *v.i.* to be rubbed together; to perform the operation of grinding; to be pulverized, polished, or sharpened by grinding; to study laboriously [Slang]. *p.* and *pp.* **ground.** (A.S. *grindan.*)
grinder, *n.* *gryn*-der, one who grinds; a tooth that grinds the food, a molar; a crammer for examinations.
grindery, *n.* *gryn*-der-re, materials or tools for leather-workers, or a shop where they are sold; a place where tools may be ground.
grindstone, *n.* *grynd*-stone, a revolving circular stone for grinding tools.
gringo, *n.* *gring*-go, among Spanish Americans, an Englishman or American (derogatively).
grinningly, *ad.* *grin*-ning-le, with a grinning laugh.
***grip,** *n.* grip, grasp with the hand; a holding fast; a handle; a clutching tool or part of mechanism; a handbag or suit-case [U.S.A.]: *v.t.* to grasp. (A.S. *gripe.*)
grip, *n.* grip, a small ditch or furrow: *v.t.* to trench; to drain.
gripe, *n.* gripe, grasp; fast hold with the hand; squeeze; pressure; oppression; pinching distress; a lever, clutch, or brake by which motion can be stopped or retarded [Mech.]: *pl.* pain in the bowels; colic [Med.]; the fore-foot or piece of timber at the fore-end of the keel [Naut.]; a series of ropes, dead-eyes, and hooks, fastened to the deck to secure boats [Naut.]: *v.t.* to catch with the hand and clasp closely with the fingers; to seize and hold fast; to clutch; to pinch; to give pain to the bowels; to distress: *v.i.* to seize and hold fast; to get money by hard bargains; to feel the colic; to come up too close to the wind [Naut.]. (A.S. *grīpan.*)
griper, *n.* *gripe*-er, an oppressor; an extortioner.
griping, *a.* *gripe*-ing, grasping; greedy; pinching the bowels.
gripingly, *ad.* *gripe*-ing-le, in a griping manner.
grippe, *n.* grip, influenza. (Fr.)
gripper, *n.* *grip*-per, one who or that which grips.
Griqua, *n.* *gree*-kwa, one of mixed Bushman and Hottentot race in Griqualand, S. Africa; also, half-caste of Dutch and native descent.
grisaille, *n.* gre-*zayl* (*or* App.), a painting, esp. on glass, in grey tints to represent solid bodies in relief; grey used as a background. (Fr.)
griseous, *a.* *griz*-e-us, bluish-grey. (Fr. *gris*, grey.)
grisette, *n.* gre-*zet*, a gay young girl of the working class; a young woman of easy virtue. (Fr., a grey cloth worn by shop-girls.)
griskin, *n.* *gris*-kin, the lean part of a loin of pork (*grice.*)
grisliness, *n.* *griz*-le-ness, quality of being grisly.
grisly, *a.* *griz*-le, inspiring fear; grim. (A.S. *grislic.*)
grison, *n.* *gree*-zn, a South American carnivore, *Grison vittatus*, allied to the marten. (Fr., grey.)
grist, *n.* grist, corn for grinding, or corn ground at one time; malt for a brewing; provision. (A.S.)
grist, *n.* grist, the thickness of rope or yarn.
gristle, *n.* *gris*-sl, cartilage, a smooth, solid, elastic substance in animal bodies. (A.S. *gristel.*)
gristliness, *n.* *gris*-le-ness, the state of being gristly.
gristly, *a.* *gris*-sle, consisting of gristle; like gristle; cartilaginous.
grist-mill, *n.* a mill for grinding grain.
grit, *n.* grit, the coarse part of meal; oats hulled or coarsely ground; rough hard particles; a hard gritty sandstone; quality as regards grittiness; firm texture; firmness of character, intrepidity, pluck [Coll.]: *v.i.* and *t.* to be ground together; to grate or grind; to annoy [Coll.]. (A.S. *grēot.*)
gritstone, *n.* *grit*-stone, a gritty sandstone.
grittiness, *n.* *grit*-te-ness, the quality of being gritty.
gritty, *a.* *grit*-te, containing or consisting of small hard particles; plucky, persistent [Coll.].
grivet, *n.* *griv*-et, a long-tailed monkey of equatorial Africa, *Cercopithecus sabæus.*
grizzle, *a.* *griz*-zl, grey: *n.* a grey colour; grey hair; a grey wig, or animal. (O.Fr. *grisel.*)
grizzle, *v.i.* and *v.t.* *griz*-zl, to complain or grumble; to fret; to grin. (Dial. Eng.)
grizzled, *a.* *griz*-zld, grey; having hair mixed with grey.
grizzly, *a.* *griz*-zle, somewhat grey: *n.* a grizzly bear. **grizzly bear,** *Ursus horribilis*, a large and ferocious bear of Western North America.
groan, *n.* grone, a deep mournful sound, uttered in pain, sorrow, or anguish; any low rumbling sound; *v.i.* to utter a deep moaning, as in pain or sorrow; to be oppressed or afflicted; to long earnestly. (A.S. *grānian.*)
groaningly, *a.* *groh*-ning-le, with groans; mournfully.
groat, *n.* grote, a coin or money of account, equal to 4*d.*; a silver fourpenny-piece; any small sum. (Dut. *groot*, great, the original coin being thick.)
groats, *n.pl.* grohts, oats or wheat with the hulls taken off; grain hulled and cracked. (A.S. *grūt.*)
Grobian, *n.* *groh*-be-an, a clumsy careless person; a lout. (Ger.)
grocer, *n.* *groh*-ser, a dealer in tea, sugar, spices, household articles, etc. (O.Fr. *grossier*, a wholesale dealer.)
grocery, *n.* *groh*-ser-re, the commodities sold by grocers; a grocer's shop. (O.Fr. *grosserie.*)
grog, *n.* grog, a mixture of spirit, originally rum, and cold water; any spirituous liquor. **grog blossom,** a redness of the nose or face due to continued over-indulgence in liquor. ("Old Grog," Admiral Vernon, who introduced it into the navy, so called from his wearing a grogram cloak.)
groggery, *n.* *grog*-ger-re, a grog-shop [U.S.A.].
grogginess, *n.* *grog*-ge-ness, the state of being groggy; an arthritic disease of horses.
groggy, *a.* *grog*-ge, tipsy; staggering; having a hobbling gait (of horses).
grogram, *n.* *grog*-ram, a coarse stuff made of silk and mohair. (Fr. *gros*, coarse, and *grain.*)
grog-shop, *n.* *grog*-shop, a place where spirits are sold and consumed.
groin, *n.* groyn, the depressed part of the body between the body and the thigh; the angular curve made by the intersection of two arches [Arch.]; a groyne [U.S.A.]: *v.t.* to form into or to furnish with groins. (M.E. *grynde*—of doubtful origin.)
groined, *a.* groynd, having an angular curve made by the intersection of two arches [Arch.]
gromel, *n.* *grom*-el, gromwell.
grommet, *n.* *grom*-met, a grummet; a metal-lined eyelet-hole. (Fr.)
gromwell, *n.* *grom*-wel, a trailing herb of the genus *Lithospermum.* (O.Fr. *grémil.*)
groom, *n.* groom, a young man-servant, esp. one having charge of horses; a bridegroom; a title of several officers of the royal household, chiefly in the Lord Chamberlain's department: *v.t.* to feed and take care of, as a groom does horses; to make neat. (M.E. *grōm*, boy, perhaps from O.Fr. *gromet*, man-servant.)
groomsman, *n.* *groomz*-man, a bachelor who attends the bridegroom; the best man.
groove, *n.* groov, a furrow or long hollow cut by a tool; a channel or fluting; a rut: *v.t.* to cut a furrow or groove in. (Dut. *groeve.*)
groover, *n.* *groo*-ver, one who makes, or a tool for making, grooves.

grope, *v.i.* grope, to search for something, like one in the dark, or blind, by feeling with the hands; to seek blindly: *v.t.* to search by feeling in the dark; to try to find out. (A.S. *grāpian.*)
gropingly, *ad. grope*-ing-le, in a groping manner.
grosbeak, *n. grohs*-beak, the hawfinch, a thick-billed bird.
groschen, *n. groh*-shen, a former German coin, worth little over 1*d.*; a bronze coin of Austria (introduced 1925). (Ger.)
grosgrain, *a. groh*-grane, having a large grain or cord (of silk fabrics). (Fr.)
gross, *a.* grohs, thick; bulky; corpulent; coarse; rough; vulgar; sensual; obscene; impure; unrefined; great; palpable; enormous; shameful; stupid; total, not net; without discount: *n.* the sum total or main body; twelve dozen. **gross weight,** the weight of goods with their container. **in** or **by the gross,** the whole undivided; all parts taken together. (Fr. *gros*, from L. *grossus*, thick.)
gross-headed, *a.* thick-skulled; stupid.
grossly, *ad. grohs*-le, in a gross manner.
grossness, *n.* the quality of being gross.
grossulaceous, *a.* gros-yew-*lay*-shus, of or belonging to the gooseberry family. (Late L. *grossula.*)
grossular, *a. gros*-yew-lar, pertaining to or resembling a gooseberry: *n.* a variety of green garnet.
grot, *n.* grot, a grotto [Poet.].
grotesque, *a.* gro-*tesk*, extravagantly and whimsically formed; of incongruous parts; fantastic; absurd: *n.* a whimsically designed ornamentation composed of fanciful distortions of plants and animals; a sans-serif type-face of square outline [Print.]; (*pl.*) whimsical scenery or figures. (Fr.)
grotesquely, *ad.* gro-*tesk*-le, in a grotesque manner.
grotesqueness, *n.* state of being grotesque.
grotto, *n. grot*-to, a small, picturesque natural or artificial cave; an artificial cavern ornamented with shells, etc. (It. *grotta.*)
grotto-work, *n.* ornamental work, as in a grotto; a garden rockery.
grouch, *n.* grouch, a grumble, a peevish complaint; an ill-feeling (towards); a confirmed grumbler: *v.i.* to grumble; to sulk. [U.S.A.].
grouchy, *a. grou*-che, grumpy [U.S.A.].
ground, *n.* ground, the surface of the earth; territory; land; the surface of a floor or pavement; foundation; cause or reason; first principle; that which is first put on the surface on which a figure or object is represented [Paint.]; the principal colour, to which others are ancillary [Manufactures]; the composition, impervious to acid, used in etching; field or place of action; a composition in which the bass, consisting of a few bars of independent notes, is continually repeated to a continually varying melody [Mus.]: *v.t.* to lay or set on the ground; to base; to instruct in first principles; to run aground [Naut.]: *v.i.* to run aground [Naut.]. **break ground,** to be the first to open up. **down to the ground,** thoroughly [Coll.]. **fall to the ground,** come to nothing. **forbidden ground,** a reserved area, topic, etc. **gain ground,** to advance; to proceed forward; to gain credit; to prevail. **give ground,** to recede; to yield advantage. **lose ground,** to retire; to retreat; to lose credit; to decline. **shift one's ground,** to adopt a different argument; to try another method or approach. (A.S. *grund.*)
ground, *a.* ground, pulverized by grinding or crushing; treated, fashioned, or sharpened by grinding. **ground glass,** *see* **glass.** *pp.* of *grind.*
groundage, *n. groun*-daj, dues paid by a ship for the space occupied while in port.
ground-ash, *n.* a sapling of ash.
ground-bait, *n.* bait dropped to the bottom of the water to attract fish: *v.t.* to prepare (a stream, etc.) for angling by laying ground-bait.
ground-bass, *n. ground*-bace, bass of a few bars continually repeated with varied melody and harmony [Mus.].
groundedly, *ad. groun*-ded-le, upon firm principles.
grounder, *n. groun*-der, a ball that keeps low or on the ground [Cricket, Baseball]; a knock-down blow [Slang].
ground-floor, *n.* the floor of a house level with the main entrance (the "first floor" in the U.S.A.); an advantageous situation [Slang].
ground-game, *n.* running game as compared with flying game; hares and rabbits.
ground-hog, *n.* the woodchuck; the aardvark.
ground-ice, *n.* anchor ice; ice formed at the bottom of the water.
grounding, *n. groun*-ding, the act of running a ship aground; a thorough instruction in the elements of a subject; a background.
ground-ivy, *n.* the purple-flowered creeping plant, *Nepeta glechoma.*
ground-landlord, *n.* the owner of land leased for building purposes.
groundless, *a. ground*-less, without ground, reason, or warrant; unfounded.
groundlessly, *ad. ground*-less-le, without ground.
groundlessness, *n.* the quality of being groundless.
groundling, *n. ground*-ling, a fish that keeps at the bottom, such as the spiny loach, *Cobitis tænia*, or the rock goby, *Gobius niger*; a creeping plant; one of the common herd, so called because in theatres such formerly stood on the ground.
ground-nut, *n.* the earth-nut, *Bunium esculentum*; the pea-nut, *Arachis hypogæa.*
ground-oak, *n.* a sapling of oak.
ground-parrot, *n.* the kakapo.
ground-plan, *n.* the plan of the ground story of a building in horizontal section.
ground-plane, *n.* the situation of the original plane in the supposed level of the horizon [Perspective].
ground-plot, *n.* the ground on which a building is placed.
ground-rent, *n.* the rent paid to a ground-landlord for the use of his land for building.
grounds, *n.pl.* groundz, dregs; lees; reasons; private enclosed lands attached to a house.
groundsel, *n. groun*-sel, the composite plant *Senecio vulgaris.* (A.S. *grundeswylige.*)
groundsel, *n. ground*-sel, the timber of a building next to the ground; a threshold. (*ground* and *sill.*)
groundsman, *n. groundz*-man, the man responsible for the state of the turf in a cricket-field or sports ground.
ground-squirrel, *n.* a species of *Tamias*; a chipmuck.
ground-staff, *n.* those employed on the upkeep of sports grounds; aerodrome or Air Force personnel whose duties do not include flying.
ground-swell, *n.* a broad, deep, heavy swell of the sea, due to a spent or distant storm.
ground-tackle, *n.* everything necessary to secure a vessel at anchor.
groundwork, *n. ground*-wurk, the work which forms the foundation of anything; first principle.
★**group,** *n.* groop, a cluster; an assemblage; a coterie of persons of similar interests; an assemblage of figures forming an artistic whole [Paint. and Sculp.]; a class scientifically connected: *v.t.* to form into a group. **Group Captain,** an officer in the R.A.F. equal in rank to a naval captain or army colonel. (Fr. *groupe.*)
grouper, *n. groop*-er, a marine food-fish allied to the sea-bass; one who groups; a member of a group, esp. a Buchmanite [Coll.].
grouping, *n. groop*-ing, the action of placing in groups; the arrangement of the component factors of a group.
grouse, *n.* grouce, a group of game-birds including the red grouse, *Lagopus scoticus*, the black grouse, *L. tetrix*, the capercaillie, *L. urogallus*, and the ptarmigan, *L. mutus*, and others: *v.i.* to seek or shoot grouse. (Origin unknown.)
grouse, *v.t.* grouce, to complain or grumble [Slang].
grouser, *n. grouce*-er, a grumbler [Slang].
grout, *n.* grout, coarse meal; pollard; a kind of wild apple; a thin coarse mortar for pouring into masonry or brickwork joints; a finer material for finishing ceilings: *pl.* dregs, grounds: *v.t.* to fill in or finish with grout; to dig up with the snout. (A.S. *grūt.*)
grouting, *n. grout*-ing, the process of filling in or finishing with grout; the grout thus filled in; plaster for ceilings.
grove, *n.* grove, a small shady wood; a wood of small extent; an avenue of trees. (A.S. *graf.*)
grovel, *v.i.* grovl, to crawl on the earth; to cringe; to be low or mean. (M.E. *grufelinge.*)
groveller, *n. grov*-vler, one who grovels.
grovelling, *a. grov*-vling, abject; without dignity.
grow, *v.i.* groh, to increase in size by natural organic development; to be produced by vegetation; to

flourish; to increase; to advance; to be changed from one state to another; to arise; to become: *v.t.* to cultivate; to raise. **to grow on one,** to become accustomed to, to become increasingly affected by. **to grow out of,** to issue from, as plants from the soil. **to grow together,** to close and adhere to. **to grow up,** to advance to full maturity; to become prevalent. *p.* **grew.** *pp.* **grown.** (A.S. *growan.*)
growable, *a. groh*-a-bl, that may be grown.
grower, *n. groh*-er, one who grows; that which grows.
growl, *n.* groul, the snarl of an angry dog; a dog-like grumbling; a muttered complaint: *v.i.* to murmur or snarl, as a dog; to grumble; to utter an angry, grumbling sound: *v.t.* to express by a growl. (Of Teutonic origin.)
growler, *n. grou*-ler, a snarling cur; a grumbler; a North American perch, *Grystes salmonoides,* so called from the sound it emits; a four-wheeled cab [Slang].
growlery, *n. grou*-ler-re, growling; a private den in which one can grouse or grumble.
growlingly, *ad.* in a growling manner.
grown, grone, *pp.* of *grow,* advanced; increased in growth; arrived at full size.
grown-up, *n. grone*-up, an adult [Coll.]: *a.* grone-*up,* mature; fully developed.
★**growth,** *n* grohth, the process of growing that goes on in plants and animals; increase; advancement; progress; improvement; that which has grown; a tumour or other morbid formation; anything produced.
groyne, *n.* groyn, a structure across a beach to resist the encroachment of the sea. (Perhaps as *groin* O.Fr. *groin,* pig's snout.)
grub, *n.* grub, food.
grub, *n.* grub, the larva of a moth, beetle, or other insect; a squat man; a drudge; a dwarf, in contempt; food [Slang]: *v.i.* to dig up; to clear by tearing up; to drudge; to consume food [Slang]: *v.t.* to clear of roots, etc.; to provide with food [Slang]; to grope in dirt. **to grub up,** to dig up by the roots. (Perhaps O. Scand. *gryfja,* a pit.)
grubber, *n. grub*-ber, one who grubs; an instrument to stir up the soil and clear out weeds; a machine for tearing up tree-roots, etc.
grubbiness, *n. grub*-be-ness, state of being grubby.
grubbing-hoe, *n.* an instrument for digging up trees, shrubs, etc., by the roots.
grubby, *a. grub*-be, grimy; dirty; full of grubs.
Grub-Street, *n. grub*-street, a street (now Milton Street) in Moorfields, London, inhabited in 17th cent. by jobbing literary men; authors of this class of hack writers: *a.* produced by such; mean, paltry; needy.
grudge, *n.* gruj, ill-will; secret enmity; unwillingness; reluctance to benefit another: *v.t.* to regard with envy and discontent; to give or take unwillingly or reluctantly: *v.i.* to complain; to be unwilling or reluctant; to be envious; to cherish ill-will. (O.Fr. *groucher.*)
grudger, *n. gruj*-er, one who grudges; a murmurer.
grudgingly, *ad. gruj*-ing-le, with reluctance.
gruel, *n. groo*-el, thin porridge. **to get one's gruel,** to be severely punished. (O.Fr., groats.)
gruelling, *a. groo*-el-ing, exhausting; severe: *n.* an exhausting endeavour or defeat; harsh treatment [Slang].
gruesome, *a. groo*-sum, horrible. (Dan. *gru,* horror.)
gruff, *a.* gruf, of a rough surly manner; ungracious; having a hoarse voice. (Dut. *grof,* coarse.)
gruffly, *ad. gruf*-le, in a gruff manner.
gruffness, *n. gruf*-ness, a gruff manner.
gru-gru, *n. groo*-groo, the edible larva of a large beetle infesting the **gru-gru palm,** a species of *Acrocomia* of tropical America.
gruine, *a. groo*-ine, pertaining to or resembling the cranes [Zool.].
grum, *a.* grum, morose; surly; guttural. (A.S. *grom.*)
grumble, *v.i. grum*-bl, to murmur with discontent; to growl; to mutter; to rumble. (Fr. *grommeler.*)
grumbler, *n. grum*-bler, one who grumbles.
grume, *n.* groom, a fluid of a thick viscid consistence; a clot, as of blood. (O.Fr.)
grumly, *ad. grum*-le, in a grum manner; turbid [Scots.].
grummet, *n. grum*-met, a ring of rope [Naut.]; any mixture for making joints watertight [Plumbing].
grumness, *n. grum*-ness, the quality of being grum.
grumous, *a. groo*-mus, thick; concreted; clotted; in the form of little clustered grains [Bot.].
grumpily, *ad. grum*-pe-le, in a grumpy manner.
grumpy, *a. grum*-pe, gruff; surly; out of humour.
Grundyism, *n. grun*-de-izm, prudish or unintelligent conventionality. **Mrs. Grundy,** prudishness personified as an old wife passing judgment. (Character in Morton's "Speed the Plough," 1798.)
grunt, *n.* grunt, a deep guttural sound, as of a hog: *v.i.* to make a sound like a hog: *v.t.* to utter in a grunting manner.
grunter, *n. grunt*-er, one who grunts; any of several fish that make a grunting noise.
gruntingly, *ad. grunt*-ing-le, with grunting.
gruntling, *n. grunt*-ling, a young hog.
gruyère, *n. groo*-yare, a pale skim-milk cheese, full of holes, originally made at Gruyère, Switzerland.
gryposis, *n.* gry-*poh*-sis, abnormal inward curvature of the nails [Med.]. (Gr. *grypos,* bent.)
grysbock, *n. grice*-bok, the small S. African antelope, *Nototragus melanotis.* (Dut.)
guacharo, *n. gwah*-cha-roh, the oil-bird, *Steatornis caripensis,* a South American nocturnal frugivorous bird.
guacho, *n. gwah*-choh, a gaucho.
guaiacol, *n. gwy*-a-kol, an odorous liquid distilled from guaiacum and creosote and used as an expectorant. (*guaiacum* and *-ol.*)
Guaiacum, *n. gwy*-a-kum, a genus of tropical American trees, the wood of one species of which, *G. officinale,* is lignum vitæ; (*l.c.*) the wood of this tree; a drug prepared from its resin. (Sp. *guayacan.*)
guan, *n.* gwahn, a S. American bird of the species *Penelope,* allied to the curassows.
guanaco, *n.* gwah-*nah*-ko, a South American ungulate, *Lama huanacos,* allied to the llama. (Sp.)
Guanche, *n. gwahn*-chay, one of the extinct aboriginal Canary Islanders.
guaniferous, *a.* gwa-*nif*-er-rus, yielding or producing guano. (*guano,* and *fero,* bear.)
guanine, *n. gwah*-nin, a nitrogenous compound allied to uric acid found in guano, in animal excreta, in the liver, etc., and in plants [Chem.].
guano, *n. gwah*-no, a rich manure, composed chiefly of the excrement of seabirds; a similar artificial preparation. (Peruvian, *huanu,* dung.)
guaracha, *n.* gwa-*rah*-chah, an old Spanish dance in which the dancer plays the guitar.
guarana, *n.* gwah-*rah*-na, Brazilian cocoa, a preparation from certain seeds used in Brazil as an astringent and as a flavouring. (Native name.)
guarani, *n.* gwa-*rah*-ne, since 1943 the currency unit of Paraguay (1956, about 200 to the £ stg.).
guarantee, *n.* ga-ran-*tee,* a warranty; an engagement by a third person to see an agreement fulfilled; one who becomes surety (an incorrect use); a thing given as security; the person to whom the pledge is given: *v.t.* to become surety for; to undertake to see another perform what he has stipulated; to secure against risk or damage; to indemnify. (O.Fr. *garantie.*)
guaranteed, *a.* ga-ran-*teed,* warranted.
guarantor, *n. ga*-ran-tor, one who guarantees.
guaranty, *n. ga*-ran-te, the act of guaranteeing; an undertaking to answer for payment of debt, etc., by another person; basis of security.
guard, *n.* gahrd, security or defence against attack or injury; a man or body of men on guard or protecting a place, person, etc.; a man in charge of a railway train, coach, etc.; a watch-chain; a state of caution or vigilance; the part of a sword-hilt which protects the hand; an act or a posture of defence: *pl.* (*cap.*) household troops, including Foot and Life Guards and Royal Horse Guards: *v.t.* to defend or protect from danger or attack: *v.i.* to watch by way of caution; to be cautious. **advance guard,** the vanguard [Mil.]. **mount guard,** to take sentry-duty. **rearguard,** a body of troops that march in the rear of an army, etc., for its protection. **relieve guard,** to take another's place in sentry-duty. (O.Fr. *guarde.*)
guardable, *a. gahrd*-a-bl, that may be protected.
guardant, *a. gahrd*-ant, acting as a guardian; gardant [Her.].
guard-boat, *n. gahrd*-boat, an official harbour-boat to enforce regulations; a boat on guard duty with a fleet.

guardedly, *ad.* *gahr*-ded-le, with circumspection; cautiously; warily.
guardedness, *n.* circumspection.
guard-house, *n.* a station for housing a military guard or the detention of prisoners.
guardian, *n.* *gahr*-de-an, a warden; one who guards; one to whose care or protection anything is committed; one appointed to take charge of the estate and education of an orphan minor [Law]: *a.* protecting; performing the office of a protector. **Board of Guardians**, a board for administering the poor laws by the Ministry of Health through the local authority. (O.Fr. *gardien.*)
guardianship, *n.* *gahr*-de-an-ship, the office of a guardian; protection; care; watch.
guard-rail, *n.* a rail placed on the inside of a main rail at curves, etc., as a safeguard against derailment [Railway]; any protecting rail.
guard-room, *n.* a guard-house [Mil.].
guard-ship, *n.* a warship protecting a port and accommodating seamen waiting to join their ships.
guardsman, *n.* *gahrdz*-man, a soldier or officer of the household troops.
guava, *n.* *gwah*-va, a tree of warm climates of the genus *Psidium*; its succulent pear-shaped fruit. (Sp. *guayaba.*)
guayule, *n.* gwah-*yew*-lay, a plant, *Parthenium argentatum*, of sub-tropical N. America, cultivated for its rubber; the rubber. (Aztec, *quauitl*, plant, *ulli*, gum.)
gubernatorial, *a.* *gyew*-ber-na-*taw*-re-al, pertaining to government, to a governor, or to control. (L. *gubernator*, a governor.)
gudgeon, *n.* *gud*-jon, a small freshwater fish, *Gobio fluviatilis*, of the carp family; a person easily cheated; a bait; allurement. **sea gudgeon**, the black goby, or rock-fish. (Fr. *goujon.*)
gudgeon, *n.* *gud*-jon, the bearing of a shaft; the axle which turns in the collar [Mech.]; a clamp on which the rudder turns [Naut.]. (O.Fr. *gougeon.*)
gudgeon-pin, *n.* a pin holding two blocks of stone or metal together; the pin which attaches the connecting rod of an engine to the piston. [Eng.].
Guebre, *n.* *gee*- or *gay*-ber, a fire-worshipper; a Parsee; a Zoroastrian.
gudok, *n.* *goo*-dok, a Russian three-stringed fiddle.
guelder-rose, *n.* *gel*-der-roze, the snowball tree, *Viburnum opulus*, having large globular, white heads of flowers. (*Gelderland*, in Holland.)
Guelph (or **Guelf**), *n.* gwelf, a member of a potent mediæval Italian faction, supporters of the Pope and the independence of Italy and opposed to the Emperor. (It. *Guelfo*, Ger. *Welf*; the Saxon house opposed to Frederick of Suabia.)
Guelphic, *a.* *gwel*-fik, belonging to the Guelphs. **Guelphic order**, a Hanoverian order of knighthood, instituted in 1815, discontinued in 1866.
guenon, *n.* *gay*-non, a member of the group of monkeys comprised in the genus *Cercopithecus*.
guerdon, *n.* *ger*-don, a reward; recompense: *v.t.* to reward. (Fr.)
guereza, *n.* ge-*ree*-za, a beautiful African thumbless monkey, *Colobus guereza*.
guerilla, *n.* ge- *il*-la, guerrilla.
guernsey, *n.* *gern*-ze, a thick jersey; (*cap.*) a breed of light-coloured dairy cattle, giving very rich milk, originally bred in Guernsey.
guerrilla, *n.* ge-*ril*-a, irregular warfare; a mode of carrying on war by the constant attacks of small detached bands; a member of one of these bands: *a.* consisting of or carried out by guerrillas; waged irregularly (of war). (Sp. from *guerra*, war.)
guess, *n.* ges, judgment without certain evidence or grounds; a conjecture; an estimate: *v.t.* to surmise, imagine, or conclude on imperfect grounds; to divine; to hit upon; to be inclined to believe: *v.i.* to conjecture; to judge at random. (M.E. *gessen.*)
guessable, *a.* *ges*-a-bl, capable of being guessed.
guesser, *n.* *ges*-er, one who guesses.
guesswork, *n.* *ges*-wurk, calculation done at hazard, or by mere conjecture; result so obtained.
guest, *n.* gest, a visitor or a friend entertained in the house or at the table of another; one staying at a hotel, boarding-house, etc. (Ice. *gestr*, a stranger.)
guest-chamber, *n.* an apartment appropriated to the entertainment of guests; a spare room.
guest-house, *n.* a boarding-house; an inn.
guest-rope, *n.* an extra steadying line from a ship to a boat being towed astern; a rope for boats coming alongside.
guffaw, *n.* guf-*faw*, a loud boisterous laugh. (Imit.)
guggle, *n.* *gug*-gl, a gurgle: *v.i.* to gurgle.
guichet, *n.* *gee*-shay, a grille, grating, or wicket opening, as of a booking-office window. (Fr.)
guidable, *a.* *gide*-a-bl, that may be guided.
guidage, *n.* *gide*-aj, payment given a guide; guidance.
guidance, *n.* *gide*-ance, the act of guiding; direction; government.
***guide**, *n.* gide, a person who leads or directs another in his way or course; a conductor of tourists, etc.; a director; a regulator; that which guides; a guide-book; one of a company of Guides [Mil.]; a Girl Guide: *v.t.* to lead or direct by conducting; to regulate and manage; to influence and direct another in his conduct; to instruct; to superintend. (Fr. *guider.*).
guide-bars, *n.pl.* the bars on which guide-blocks work and are kept true in their motion.
guide-blocks, *n.pl.* blocks guided by and sliding upon guide-bars [Mech.].
guide-book, *n.* a book for tourists, describing routes, places, and objects of interest, etc.
guide-post, *n.* a direction post on roads; a finger-post.
guider, *n.* *gide*-er, one who or that which guides; a senior Girl Guide.
guide-rail, *n.* an additional rail for keeping wheels on the line [Railway]; the track of a sliding door.
guide-rope, *n.* a lateral rope to direct the motion of a rope by which anything is being hauled, etc.
guidon, *n.* *gy*-don, a cavalry flag with a pointed or indented fly; a standard-bearer. (Fr.)
guild, *n.* gild, an incorporated association for the promotion and protection of a common civic, industrial, or other interest; a corporation of craftsmen or tradesmen. **guild socialism**, the theory advocating state ownership of industries and their individual management by guilds consisting of representatives of all branches of each. (A.S. *gild*, money payment.)
guild-brother, *n.* one of the same guild.
guilder, *n.* *gil*-der, a Dutch florin, the gulden.
guildhall, *n.* *gild*-hawl, the hall where a guild or corporation usually assembles; a town-hall.
guildry, *n.* *gil*-dre, a guild [Scot.].
guile, *n.* gile, craft; artifice; duplicity. (O.Fr.)
guileful, *a.* *gile*-ful, crafty; deceitful; insidious; treacherous.
guilefully, *ad.* *gile*-ful-le, in a guileful manner.
guilefulness, *n.* the quality of being guileful.
guileless, *a.* *gile*-less, free from guile; artless.
guilelessly, *ad.* in a guileless manner.
guilelessness, *n.* *gile*-less-ness, freedom from guile.
guillemot, *n.* *gil*-le-mot, a sea-bird of either the *Uria* or *Cepphus* genus, allied to the auks. (Fr.)
guilloche, *n.* gil-*lohsh*, an ornament resembling intertwining ribbons [Arch.]. (Fr.)
guillotine, *n.* *gil*-lo-teen, a machine for decapitation fitted with a weighted knife blade running in grooves; a paper-cutting machine; a surgical instrument; a method of curtailing Parliamentary debates: *v.t.* to behead, or to cut (sheets of paper), with the guillotine. (Dr. *Guillotin*, who suggested its use in the French Revolution.)
guilt, *n.* gilt, criminality; the state of having committed a crime; state of liability to penalty for crime. (A.S. *gylt*, from *gildan*, to pay.)
guiltily, *ad.* *gil*-te-le, in a guilty manner.
guiltiness, *n.* *gil*-te-ness, the state of being guilty.
guiltless, *a.* *gilt*-less, free from guilt; innocent; having no experience.
guiltlessly, *ad.* *gilt*-less-le, without guilt.
guiltlessness, *n.* the state of being guiltless.
guilty, *a.* *gil*-te, having committed a crime; characterized by or betraying guilt. (A.S. *gyltig.*)
guinea, *n.* *gin*-ne, a gold coin, coined in Great Britain, 1663–1813, worth 21*s.*, so called as first coined in gold from Guinea, in Africa.
Guinea-corn, *n.* durra, Indian millet, *Sorghum vulgare*.
guinea-fowl, *n.* the gallinaceous galeeny, *Numida meleagris*, a West African game-bird now domesticated. **black guinea-fowl**, *Phasidus niger*.
Guinea-grass, *n.* a West African fodder plant, *Panicum maximum*.
Guinea-pepper, *n.* a species of *Capsicum*, the source

of cayenne; the fruit of the West African tropical tree, *Xylopia æthiopica*.

guinea-pig, *n.* a small domesticated variety of cavy, originally from Brazil and Guiana; a company director, etc., who accepts fees for no work. (*Guiana-pig.*)

Guinea-worm, *n.* the nematode worm, *Dracunculus medinensis*, common on the Guinea coast and parasitic in man and quadrupeds; the disease it causes.

guipure, *n.* gip-*poor*, a kind of lace-work held together by threads. (Fr.)

guise, *n.* gize, external appearance; garb; habiliments; manner. (Fr.)

guiser, *n.* *gize*-er, a person in disguise; a mummer.

guitar, *n.* ge-*tahr*, a lute with a flat back and six strings, played with the fingers. (Sp. *guitarra*, from Gr. *kithara*, a lyre.)

guitarist, *n.* ge-*tah*-rist, one who plays the guitar.

Gujarati, *n.* goo-ja-*rah*-te, the language of Gujarat and neighbouring states north of Bombay, India.

gular, *a.* *gew*-lar, pertaining to or situated in the gullet. (L. *gula*, throat.)

gulch, *n.* gulch, a deep ravine, esp. one formed by the action of a torrent [Western U.S.A.].

gulden, *n.* *gool*-den, a florin, formerly current in the Netherlands and Austria-Hungary. (*golden*, the original coin having been of gold.)

gulder, *n.* *gool*-der, since 1946 the monetary unit of Hungary, then exchangeable at 96·34 to the £ (gold) approx. 2½*d*.

gules, *n.* gewlz, the tincture red [Her.]. (Fr. *gueules.*)

gulf, *n.* gulf, a large deep bay or arm of the sea; a deep place in the earth; an abyss; a wide space; a whirlpool; that which engulfs; anything impassable. (Fr. *golfe*, from Gr. *kolphos.*)

Gulf-stream, *n.* a broad warm current passing from the Gulf of Mexico across the Atlantic and to the north of Great Britain.

gulf-weed, *n.* a tropical sea-weed of the genus *Sargassum*, found in the Gulf-stream.

gulfy, *a.* *gul*-fe, full of whirlpools; like a gulf.

gull, *n.* gul, a seabird, with long wings and a square tail, of which there are many species; a trick; one easily cheated; a dupe: *v.t.* to deceive; to cheat; to impose upon. (Cornish *gwillan*, from Celtic.)

gull-catcher, *n.* *gul*-katch-er, one who entraps silly people; a confidence trickster.

gullery, *n.* *gul*-ler-re, a place where gulls breed; cheating; imposture; trickery.

gullet, *n.* *gul*-let, the passage by which food enters the stomach; any similar channel; the space between adjacent saw-teeth. (O.Fr. *goulet.*)

gullibility, *n.* *gul*-e-*bil*-e-te, the being gullible.

gullible, *a.* *gul*-e-bl, easily gulled; over-credulous.

gullied, *a.* *gul*-id, having a hollow worn by water.

gully, *n.* *gul*-e, a channel or hollow worn by water; a ditch; an iron tram-plate or tram-rail: *v.t.* to wear a gully in; to furrow. (O.Fr. *goulet.*)

gully-hole, *n.* an opening where gutters empty their contents into the sewer.

gulosity, *n.* gew-*los*-e-te, greediness; voracity. (L. *gulositas*, from L. *gulosus*, greediness.)

gulp, *n.* gulp, a swallow, or as much as is swallowed at once; an attempt to swallow: *v.t.* to swallow eagerly or in large draughts: *v.i.* to make a noise as in trying to swallow; to come near choking. **to gulp up,** to disgorge. (Dut. *gulpen.*)

gum, *n.* gum, the fleshy substance of the jaws, in which the teeth are imbedded. (A.S. *goma.*)

gum, *n.* gum, a more or less soluble resinous exudation from trees, used to stick things together and to stiffen them; gum-resin; gum-tree; chewing-gum: *v.t.* to smear with gum; to unite by a viscous substance. **gum arabic,** a gum obtained from certain species of acacia, used in calico printing, mucilages, confectionery, and medicine. **gum boot,** a long-legged rubber boot. (Fr. *gomme.*)

gum, *n.* gum, as in oaths, By gum! (*God.*)

gumbo, *n.* *gum*-bo, the okra plant; a stew or soup made from the young capsules of this, seasoned and served with melted butter. (U.S.A. Negro.)

gumboil, *n.* *gum*-boyl, an abscess on the gum.

gum-dragon, *n.* tragacanth.

gum-elastic, *n.* india-rubber; caoutchou.

gum-juniper, *n.* the resin, sandarac.

gumma, *n.* *gum*-a (*pl.* **gummata,** *gum*-a-ta), a syphilitic tumour containing gummy matter. (L.)

gummatous, *a.* *gum*-a-tus, relating to or of the nature of gummata.

gummiferous, *a.* gu-*mif*-er-rus, producing gum. (*Gum*, and L. *fero*, bear.)

gumminess, *n.* *gum*-me-ness, the state or quality of being gummy or gummous.

gumming, *n.* *gum*-ming, a disease in certain fruit trees (esp. cherry and plum) in which a morbid exudation of gum tends to the destruction of the tree.

gummosity, *n.* gum-*mos*-e-te, the quality of being gummous.

gummous, *a.* *gum*-mus, gum-like; gummy.

gummy, *a.* *gum*-me, consisting of gum; of the nature of gum; productive of or covered with gum.

gumption, *n.* *gump*-shon, shrewd sense; tact. (Scots.)

gum-rash, *n.* red gum; strophulus [Med.].

gum-resin, *n.* a vegetable secretion of mixed gum and resin.

gum-tree, *n.* any gum-yielding tree; in Australia, any species of *Eucalyptus*. **up a gum-tree,** in a quandary.

★**gun,** *n.* gun, a fire-arm from which projectiles are discharged by a propellant; a cannon, rifle, shotgun, etc.; a pistol [U.S.A. Coll.]; a member of a shooting-party. **big** or **great gun,** a person of importance. **blow great guns,** blow a gale. **son of a gun,** a man, a fellow; a rascal. **stick to one's guns,** maintain one's position. (Scand.)

gun-barrel, *n.* the barrel or tube of a gun.

gunboat, *n.* *gun*-boat, a naval vessel of light draught, armed with one or more heavy guns.

gun-carriage, *n.* the wheeled mount of a mobile cannon.

guncotton, *n.* *gun*-kot-ton, a highly explosive substance obtained by soaking vegetable fibre in nitric and sulphuric acids and carefully drying it.

gun-fire, *n.* *gun*-fire, firing of guns; the hour at which morning or evening guns are fired.

gunlock, *n.* *gun*-lok, the mechanism by means of which the charge in certain fire-arms is ignited.

gunman, *n.* *gun*-man, an armed desperado [U.S.A.].

gunmetal, *n.* *gun*-met-al, an alloy of copper and tin.

gunnel, *n.* *gun*-nel, gunwale; the butterfish, *Centronotus gunnellus*, related to the blenny.

gunner, *n.* *gun*-ner, one who works a gun; an artilleryman; a naval warrant-officer in charge of the ship's guns, fire-arms, ammunition, and everything pertaining thereto.

gunnery, *n.* *gun*-ner-re, the science of artillery; ballistics; the firing of guns.

gunning, *n.* *gun*-ning, shooting, esp. of game.

gunny, *n.* *gun*-ne, a coarse sackcloth manufactured of jute or hemp. (Hind.)

gunpowder, *n.* *gun*-pou-der, a composition of nitre, sulphur, and charcoal, mixed and reduced to a fine powder, then granulated and dried, and used as an explosive; a fine kind of green tea.

gun-reach, *n.* gunshot.

gun-room, *n.* *gun*-room, an apartment occupied by junior officers as a mess-room [Naut.].

gun-runner, *n.* one engaged in gun-running.

gun-running, *n.* illegally introducing fire-arms into a country.

gunshot, *n.* *gun*-shot, the range of a gun; the distance of the point-blank range of a cannon shot.

gun-shy, *a.* easily frightened by the noise of shooting.

gunsmith, *n.* *gun*-smith, one who makes or repairs small fire-arms.

gunsmithery, *n.* gun-*smith*-er-re, the business or workshop of a gunsmith; the art of making small fire-arms.

gunstock, *n.* *gun*-stok, the wooden stock in which the barrel and mechanism of a gun is fixed.

gunter, *n.* *gunt*-er, a Gunter's scale or chain; a sliding arrangement of mast and rigging [Naut.]. **Gunter's chain,** the 66-ft. chain divided into 100 links used for measuring land. **Gunter's line,** a logarithmic line, used for performing the multiplication and division of numbers mechanically. **Gunter's scale,** a large flat rule having various scales and numbers engraved on it, by means of which problems in surveying, navigation, etc., are solved with the aid of compasses. (Inventor, Edmund *Gunter*, *d.* 1626, Engl. mathematician.)

gunwale, *n.* *gun*-el, the upper edge of a boat's side: the uppermost plank of a ship. (*gun* and *wale.*)

gunyah, *n.* *gun*-yah, an aboriginal's hut; any rough hut in the bush. (Austral. native.)
gurgitation, *n.* *ger*-je-*tay*-shon, violent surging of a liquid, as when boiling; ebullition.
gurgle, *n.* *gur*-gl, a flowing; a sound of flowing: *v.i.* to flow in a broken, noisy current; to flow with a purling, bubbling sound. (It. *gurgulio*, gullet.)
gurgoyle, *n.* *gur*-goyl, gargoyle.
gurjun, *n.* *ger*-jun, an Indian balsam resembling copaiba, from several species of *Dipterocarpus*.
Gurkha, *n.* *goor*-kah, one of a warlike Rajput race that settled in the province of Gurkha, Nepal, late in the 18th century.
gurly, *a.* *gur*-le, stormy [Scots.].
gurnard, *n.* *gur*-nard, a gurnet.
gurnet, *n.* *gur*-net, a sea-fish of the genus *Trigla*. (O.Fr. *gornard*, grunter.)
gurrah, *n.* *gu*-rah, a plain coarse Indian muslin.
gurry, *n.* *gu*-re, a small fort. (East Indies.)
gurry, *n.* *gu*-re, fish offal [U.S.A.].
guru, *n.* *goo*-roo, a teacher, esp. religious. (Hind.)
gush, *n.* gush, a violent and copious issue of a fluid from an enclosed place; the fluid thus emitted; an outburst; effusively sentimental talk: *v.i.* to issue with violence, as a fluid; to follow copiously: *v.t.* to emit in copious effusion; to talk effusively of a person or thing [Slang]. (Ice. *gusa.*)
gusher, *n.* *gush*-er, that which or one who gushes; an oil-well flowing naturally and not needing pumps; a geyser.
gushing, *a.* *gush*-ing, flowing copiously; effusive; extravagant in talk; demonstrative to excess.
gushingly, *ad.* *gush*-ing-le, in a gushing manner.
gushy, *a.* *gush*-e, gushing; effusive.
gusset, *n.* *gus*-set, a small triangular piece of cloth inserted in a garment to strengthen or enlarge some part; a similar piece of iron for strengthening angles. (Fr. *gousset.*)
gust, *n.* gust, the sense or the pleasure of tasting; relish; gratification; enjoyment; intellectual taste. (L. *gustus*, taste.)
gust, *n.* gust, a sudden squall; a violent blast of wind; a violent burst of passion. (Ice, *gustr.*)
gustative, *a.* *gus*-ta-tiv, affecting or pertaining to the sense of taste.
gustatory, *a.* *gus*-ta-to-re, pertaining to the sense of taste: *n.* one of the two lingual nerves of taste.
gustiness, *n.* *gus*-te-ness, state of being gusty.
gusto, *n.* *gus*-to, relish; taste; enjoyment; zest. (It.)
gusty, *a.* *gus*-te, subject to gusts or sudden outbursts; stormy; passionate.
gut, *n.* gut, the intestinal canal extending, with many circumvolutions, from the pylorus to the anus, or a part of it; the intestines; catgut; a string made of gut; a narrow channel: *pl.* the bowels or stomach; courage, pluck [Coll.]; the essentials [Coll.]: *v.t.* to eviscerate; to plunder of contents. (A.S., a channel.)
gutta, *n.* *gut*-ta, a hydrocarbon forming the chief constituent of guttapercha and balata [Chem.]: *pl.* **guttæ,** small ornaments resembling drops, used in the Doric entablature. **gutta serena,** amaurosis [Med.]. (L., a drop.)
guttapercha, *n.* *gut*-ta-*per*-cha, the hardened latex of several Malayan trees resembling india-rubber and used as insulating material, etc. (Malay, *gatah*, gum, *percha*, the tree yielding it.)
guttate, *a.* *gut*-at, spotted; speckled [Bot., Zool.].
guttee, *a.* *gut*-te, gutty [Her.].
gutter, *n.* *gut*-ter, a channel for conveying away water; a conduit; a narrow groove; the back margin [Print.]: *v.t.* to cut into small hollows: *v.i.* to become channelled; to run away in drops, as a burning candle. (O.Fr. *goutiere.*)
guttering, *n.* *gut*-ter-ing, gutters, or a series of gutters; a forming into hollows; material for gutters.
guttersnipe, *n.* *gut*-ter-snipe, a street arab.
guttiferous, *a.* gut-*tif*-er-us, yielding gum or resin. (L. *gutta*, a drop, *fero*, bear.)
guttiform, *a.* *gut*-e-form, drop-shaped.
guttle, *v.t.* and *i.* *gut*-tl, to swallow or devour greedily; to gobble up.
guttural, *a.* *gut*-ter-ral, pertaining to the throat; formed in the throat; husky: *n.* a velar, or letter (as *k*) pronounced in the throat [Gram.]. (Fr.)
gutturally, *ad.* *gut*-ter-ra-le, in a guttural manner.
gutturalness, *n.* the quality of being guttural.

gutty, *a.* *gut*-te, sprinkled with drops [Her.]. (O.Fr. *goute.*)
gutty, *n.* *gut*-te, a guttapercha golf-ball [Coll.].
gutwort, *n.* *gut*-wurt, an African plant of the genus *Globularia*, with violently purgative leaves.
guy, *n.* gy, a rope or chain attached to anything to steady it [Naut.]. (O.Fr. *guye*, as *guide.*)
guy, *n.* gy, a grotesque effigy of Guy Fawkes or other person, on Gunpowder Plot day; a badly dressed person; a fellow, a chap [U.S.A. Slang]. **to do a guy,** to bolt, to decamp [Slang].
guzzle, *v.i.* *guz*-zl, to swallow liquor greedily; to drink frequently: *v.t.* to swallow much or often, or with immoderate gusto. (Perhaps O.Fr. *gosillier*, to retch.)
guzzler, *n.* *guz*-zler, one who guzzles.
gwyniad, *n.* *gwin*-e-ad, a freshwater salmonoid fish of the genus *Coregonus*. (W., *gwyn*, white.)
gybe, *v.t.* jibe, to swing the boom of a fore-and-aft sail across a vessel when running before the wind: *v.i.* (of a sail) to swing from one side of the mast to the other; to take the wind on the other quarter: *n.* the act or process of gybing [Naut.].
gyle, *n.* gile, quantity of one brewing of ale or beer. (Dut. *gijl*, unfermented beer.)
gym, *n.* jim, gymnastics; a gymnasium [Coll.].
gymbals, *n.pl.* *jim*-balz, gimbals.
gymkhana, *n.* jim-*kah*-nah, an athletic meeting, especially for races. (Anglo-Indian name.)
gymnasiarch, *n.* jim-*nay*-ze-ark, one who presided at the ancient Grecian games; a sports leader; a great athlete. (L. *gymnasiarchus.*)
gymnasium, *n.* jim-*nay*-ze-um *or* -*nay*-zhum, a place where physical exercises are performed; on the Continent, a school for the higher branches of literature and science. (L.)
gymnast, *n.* *jim*-nast, an expert in gymnastic exercises. (Gr. *gymnastes.*)
gymnastic, *a.* jim-*nas*-tik, pertaining to athletic exercises; involving athletic effort: *n.pl.* exercises for the development of physical powers; the gymnastic art; gymnastic feats.
gymno-, *comb.f.* jim-no, indicating nakedness, bareness [Bot. etc.]. (Gr. *gymnos*, naked.)
gymnocarpous, *a.* *jim*-no-*kahr*-pus, having naked fruit [Bot.]. (Gr. *gymnos*, and *karpos*, fruit.)
gymnogen, *n.* *jim*-no-jen, a gymnosperm.
gymnogenous, *a.* jim-*noj*-e-nus, naked when hatched [Ornith.].
gymnogynous, *a.* jim-*noj*-e-nus, with a naked ovary [Bot.].
gymnorhinal, *a.* *jim*-no-*ry*-nal, with unfeathered nostrils [Ornith.].
gymnosophist, *n.* jim-*nos*-o-fist, one of an ancient school of Indian contemplative ascetics, so called by the Greeks from their going with bare feet, or with little clothing. (Gr. *gymnos*, and *sophos*, wise.)
gymnosophy, *n.* jim-*nos*-o-fe, the doctrines of the gymnosophists.
gymnosperm, *n.* *jim*-no-sperm, a plant that bears naked seeds [Bot.]. (Gr. *gymnos*, and *sperma*, seed.)
gymnospermous, *a.* jim-no-*sperm*-us, having naked seeds [Bot.].
gymnospore, *n.* *jim*-no-spore, a naked spore. [Bot.].
Gymnotus, *n.* jim-*noh*-tus, a genus of apodal fishes with eel-shaped bodies, including the electric eel. (Gr. *gymnos*, and *notos*, the back.)
gynæceum, *n.* jy-*nee*-se-um, women's apartments in a house [Antiq.]; the pistils or female organs of a seed-plant [Bot.]. (L.)
gynæcian, *a.* jy-*nee*-se-an, relating to women.
gynæcocracy, *n.* jy-ne-*kok*-ra-se, government by women or a woman. (Gr. *gyne*, and *kratos*, power or sway.)
gynæcology, *n.* jy-ne-*kol*-o-je, the branch of medicine treating of the diseases of women. (Gr. *gyne*, and *logos*, science.)
gynæolatry, *n.* jy-ne-*ol*-a-tre, the worship of women. (Gr. *gyne*, and *latria*, worship.)
gynandria, *n.pl.* jy-*nan*-dre-a, plants whose stamens are united with the pistil [Bot.]. (Gr. *gyne*, a woman, *aner*, a man.)
gynandrian, *a.* jy-*nan*-dre-an, gynandrous.
gynandrous, *a.* jy-*nan*-drus, having stamens adherent to the carpels in the pistils.
gynandry, *n.* jy-*nan*-dre, hermaphroditism.
gynarchy, *n.* *jy*-nar-ke, gynæcocracy. (Gr. *gyne*, and *archo*, rule.)

gynœcium, *n.* jy-*nee*-se-um, gynæcium [Bot.].
gynophobia, *n.* jy-no-*foh*-be-a, fear or dislike of women. (Gk. *gyne*, woman, *phobos*, fear.)
gynophore, *n.* *jy*-no-fore, the pedicel supporting the carpels, as in the passion flower [Bot.]. (Gr. *gyne*, and *phero*, bear.)
gyp, *n.* jip, a male servant at Cambridge and Durham Universities. (Probably from *gypsy*.)
gypseous, *a.* *jip*-se-us, of the nature of gypsum.
gypsiferous, *a.* jip-*sif*-er-rus, containing or producing gypsum. (*Gypsum*, and L. *fero*, bear.)
gypsoplast, *n.* *jip*-so-plast, a plaster-of-Paris cast. (*Gypsum*, and Gr. *plasso*, fashion.)
gypsum, *n.* *jip*-sum, hydrous sulphate of lime, yielding, when dehydrated and burnt, plaster of Paris, used in the arts. (L.)
gypsy, *n.* *jip*-se, gipsy.
gyral, *a.* *jire*-ral, gyratory ; pertaining to a gyrus.
gyrate, *a.* *jire*-rat, winding, as in a circle [Bot.]; convoluted : *v.i.* to revolve round a central point, as a tornado ; to whirl in a circle or spiral. (L. *gyratus*, circled.)
gyration, *n.* jy-*ray*-shon, a turning or whirling round ; a circular motion.
gyratory, *a.* *jire*-ra-to-re, whirling around ; moving in a circle ; rotary (of traffic).
gyre, *n.* jire, a gyration ; a circle described by a moving body ; a turn : *v.t.* and *i.* to whirl, to move circlewise. (Gr. *gyros*, a circle or ring.)
gyrfalcon, *n.* *jer*-faw-kn, the gerfalcon.
gyroidal, *a.* jy-*roy*-dal, arranged or moving spirally. (Gr. *gyros*, and *eidos*, like.)
gyromancy, *n.* *jire*-ro-man-se, divination performed by walking round in a circle or ring until dizziness causes the walker to fall. (Gr. *gyros*, and *manteia*, divination.)
gyron, *n.* *jire*-ron, a triangular subordinary having an angle at the fesse-point and the opposite side at the escutcheon edge [Her.]. (Fr. *giron*.)
gyronny, *a.* *jire*-ro-ne, divided into gyrons, forming a series of triangles based on the outer edges [Her.].
gyroplane, *n.* *jire*-ro-plane, a flying machine supported and balanced by rapidly rotating horizontal planes.
gyropter, *n.* jire-*rop*-ter, a form of helicopter or rotaplane. (Gr. *gyros*, and *pteron*, wing.)
gyroscope, *n.* *jire*-ro-skope, an instrument on the principle of the spinning top in which the axis retains its direction, applied to the mariner's compass, the steering of torpedoes, etc. (Gr. *gyros*, and *skopeo*, view.)
gyroscopic, *a.* jire-ro-*skop*-ik, pertaining to or like the gyroscope.
gyrose, *a.* jire-roz, marked with wavy lines ; undulate ; bent like a crook [Bot.].
gyrostat, *n.* *jire*-ro-stat, a form of gyroscope for demonstrating the dynamics of rotation ; an appliance for maintaining horizontality in a moving submarine.
gyrostatics, *n.* jire-ro-*stat*-iks, the branch of physics that treats of the phenomena of rotating bodies.
gyrus, *n.* *jire*-us, a convolution, esp. of the brain [Anat.].
gyve, *n.* jive, a fetter or shackle : *v.t.* to fetter. (M.E.)

H

H, aitch, eighth letter of alphabet, is pronounced initially with an audible expiration of breath, as in *harm, hear, heat.* The *h* is sometimes mute, as in *honour, fight, ayah, dhow, antirrhinum, yacht*; and when united with certain consonants sometimes modifies them, as in *each, tough, graph, short, thin, then, when.*
ha, *int.* hah, an exclamation denoting surprise, joy, grief, or laughter: *v.i.* to express surprise; to hesitate. (Imit., cf. O.Fr. *ha,* O.Frisian, *haha.*)
haar, *n.* hahr, a cold damp sea mist. (Scots.)
Habeas Corpus, *n. hay*-be-as-*kor*-pus, a writ to produce a prisoner from prison, and show reason for his detention, with a view to judge of its justice. (L., you must have the body.)
haberdasher, *n. hab*-er-dash-er, a dealer in small drapery, as ribbons, tapes, etc. (Fr.)
haberdashery, *n. hab*-er-dash-er-re, the goods sold by a haberdasher.
haberdine, *n. hab*-er-din, stockfish; cod salted and dried in the sun.
habergeon, *n.* ha-*ber*-jon, chain armour from neck to waist, without sleeves. (O.Fr. *haubergeon.*)
habiliment, *n.* ha-*bil*-e-ment, a garment; clothing; equipment. (Fr. *habiller,* to dress.)
habit, *n. hab*-it, ordinary condition or state; a tendency or aptitude acquired by custom or frequent repetition; involuntary tendency; practice; custom; ordinary manner; dress; lady's riding-dress; characteristic manner or general appearance [Bot. and Zool.]: *v.t.* to dress; to array; to inhabit. (O.Fr.)
habitability, *n. hab*-e-ta-*bil*-e-te, habitableness.
habitable, *a. hab*-e-ta-bl, that may be dwelt in. (Fr.)
habitableness, *n.* the state of being habitable.
habitably, *ad. hab*-it-a-ble, in a habitable manner.
habitancy, *n. hab*-e-tan-se, inhabitancy; permanent abode.
habitant, *n. hab*-e-tant (but *see* App. for Fr. Canadian), an inhabitant; in Canada, a descendant of the early French settlers.
habitat, *n. hab*-e-tat, the natural abode or locality of an animal or a plant. (L., it dwells.)
habitation, *n. hab*-e-*tay*-shon, act of inhabiting or dwelling; place of abode; natural locality. (Fr.)
habit-shirt, *n.* a kind of chemisette with collar formerly worn by women.
habitual, *a.* ha-*bit*-yew-al, formed or acquired by habit, frequent use, or custom; customary. (Fr. *habituel.*)
habitually, *ad.* by habit; customarily.
habitualness, *n.* the state of being habitual.
habituate, *v.t.* ha-*bit*-yew-ate, to accustom; to make familiar by frequent practice or repetition. (L. *habituatus.*)
habituation, *n.* ha-*bit*-yew-*ay*-shon, the state of being habituated or act of habituating.
habitude, *n. hab*-e-tewd, customary manner or mode; habit; propensity.
habitué, *n.* a-*bee*-too-ay, one who constantly frequents a place. (Fr.)
hachure, *n. hash*-yewr, a short line in engraving to represent shadows; the line method of mountain-shading on maps: *v.t.* to add hachures to. (Fr.)
hacienda, *n.* ah-*syen*-dah, an estate; a farm; an establishment. (Sp.)
hack, *n.* hak, a notch; a cut; a kick, or its result (esp. on the shin); a pick or mattock [Mining]: *v.t.* to cut irregularly and into small pieces; to notch; to mangle or chop; to kick on the shin: *v.i.* to cough drily and intermittently. (A.S. *haccian.*)
hack, *n.* hak, a horse kept for hire; a hackney; a horse worn out with hard work; a drudge (esp. at literary work): *v.t.* to let out on hire: *v.i.* to drudge; to work as a hack: *a.* hired out; suitable for a hack. (As *hackney.*)
hack, *n.* hak, a frame or rack for various purposes.
hackberry, *n. hak*-be-re, a tree of the genus *Celtis,* allied to the elm; its edible fruit; the hagberry.
hackbut, *n. hak*-but, a form of harquebus.
hackee, *n. hak*-kee, the ground-squirrel or chipmunk of N. America. (From its call.)
hackery, *n. hak*-er-re, a two-wheeled street cart drawn by oxen in Bengal.
hacking, *n. hak*-ing, the action of the verb *to hack,* in various senses: *a.* mangling; short and interrupted, as a cough.
hackle, *n. hak*-kl, an instrument with sharp teeth for hackling; any soft flimsy substance, as raw silk; a fly for angling, dressed with feathers or silk; a cock's neck-plumage: *v.t.* to separate the coarse part of flax or hemp with a hackle; to tear asunder; to dress (a fly) with a hackle. (M.E. *hachele.*)
hackler, *n. hak*-kler, one who hackles flax.
hacklet, *n. hak*-let, the kittiwake.
hackly, *a. hak*-kle, jagged; broken as if hacked; having fine, short, and sharp points on the surface [Min.].
hackmatack, *n. hak*-ma-tak, the timber-tree tamarack or American larch. (Algonq.)
hackney, *n. hak*-ne, a horse kept for hire; a horse for riding or driving; a hackney carriage or coach (*i.e.,* one kept for hire); a hireling; a drudge: *v.t.* to use much; to make trite. (O.Fr. *haquenée.*)
hackneyed, *a. hak*-nid, much used; trite.
hack-saw, *n.* a fine-toothed saw for metal, the narrow blade of which is stretched in a frame.
hacqueton, *n. hak*-ton, an acton, or wadded jacket.
had, had, *p.* of *have.*
haddock, *n. had*-ok, a sea-fish, *Gadus æglefinus,* with a black lateral line, allied to the cod.
hade, *n.* hade, deviation from the vertical of a fault or vein: *v.i.* to incline from the vertical [Mining]. (Origin doubtful.)
Hades, *n. hay*-deez, the abode of the dead; the infernal regions. (Gr. *a-,* not, *idein,* to see.)
Hadith, *n. had*-ith, the body of oral tradition respecting Mohammed, appended to the Koran. (Ar.)
hadj, *n.* haj, a pilgrimage to Mecca. (Ar.)
hadji, *n. haj*-ee, one who has performed his hadj.
hæcceity, *n.* hek-*see*-e-te, specificness; the quality of being individual [Phil.].
hæma-, *comb.f. hee*-ma, connoting blood. (Gr. *haima,* blood.)
hæmachrome, *n. hee*-ma-krome, the colouring matter of the blood. (Gr. *haima,* blood, *chroma,* colour.)
hæmacyte, *n. hee*-ma-site, a blood corpuscle.
hæmal, *a. hee*-mal, pertaining to the blood; pertaining to the side of the body on which are the heart and chief blood-vessels [Anat.].
hæmatemesis, *n. hee*-ma-*tem*-e-sis, a vomiting of blood from the stomach [Med.]. (Gr. *haima,* and *emeo,* vomit.)
hæmatic, *a.* he-*mat*-ik, pertaining to or containing blood; acting on the blood; of the colour of blood.
hæmatin, *n. hee*-ma-tin, an amorphous iron-containing constituent of hæmoglobin.
hæmatinic, *a.* hee-ma-*tin*-ik, acting upon the blood [Med.].
hæmatite, *n. hem*-a-tite, red or brown ferric oxide, a valuable iron ore. (Gr. *haima,* the blood.)
hæmatitic, *a.* hem-a-*tit*-ik, pertaining to or resembling hæmatite.
hæmatoid, *a. hee*-ma-toyd, resembling blood.
hæmatology, *n. hee*-ma-*tol*-o-je, the branch of physiology treating of blood.
hæmatosin, *n.* hee-ma-*toh*-sin, hæmatin.
hæmatosis, *n. hee*-ma-*toh*-sis, formation into blood; formation of blood corpuscles.
hæmatoxylin, *n. hee*-ma-*tok*-se-lin, the colouring principle of logwood, used as a dye.
hæmatozoon, *n. hee*-ma-to-*zoh*-on (*pl.* **hæmatozoa**), any parasite living in the blood. (Gr. *haima,* and *zoon,* an animal.)
hæmaturia, *n. hee*-ma-*tewr*-re-a, presence of blood

in the urine; hæmorrhage from the urinary organs [Med.]. (Gr. *haima*, and *ouron*, urine.)
hæmocœle, *n.* *hee*-mo-seel, a cavity in which hæmolymph circulates [Zool.].
hæmoglobin, *n.* *hee*-mo-*gloh*-bin, a red fluid substance in the red corpuscles of the blood. (Gr. *haima*, and L. *globus*, a ball.)
hæmolymph, *n.* *hee*-mo-limf, the whitish blood, devoid of red corpuscles, of the higher invertebrates [Zool.].
hæmophilia, *n.* *hee*-mo-*fil*-e-a, a constitutional and usually hereditary tendency to hæmorrhage. (Gr. *haima*, and *philos*, inclined to.)
hæmophiliac, *n.* *hee*-mo-*fil*-e-ak, a person subject to hæmophilia.
hæmoptysis, *n.* hee-*mop*-te-sis, a coughing up of blood from the lungs [Med.]. (Gr. *haima*, and *ptyo*, spit.)
hæmorrhage, *n.* *hem*-o-raj, any discharge of blood from a blood vessel. (Gr. *haima*, and *rhēgnynai*, to burst forth.)
hæmorrhagic, *a.* *hem*-o-*raj*-ik, pertaining to a flux of blood; pertaining to hæmorrhage.
hæmorrhoidal, *a.* hem-o-*roy*-dal, pertaining to hæmorrhoids.
hæmorrhoids, *n.pl.* *hem*-o-roydz, piles. (Gr. *haimorrhoides phlebes*, bleeding veins.)
hæmostasis, *n.* hee-*mos*-ta-sis, congestion of blood; the arrest or stoppage of bleeding.
hæmostat, *n.* *hee*-mo-stat, a hæmostatic.
hæmostatic, *a.* hee-mo-*stat*-ik, relating to stagnation of the blood; serving to arrest hæmorrhage: *n.* an instrument or medicine effecting this; a styptic.
haffet, *n.* *haf*-fet, the side of the head [Scots.].
hafiz, *n.* *hah*-fiz, a title given by Moslems to one who knows the Koran by heart (Per.).
hafnium, *n.* *haf*-ne-um, a rare metallic element discovered in association with zirconium, 1922. (*Hafnia*, L. form of *Haven*, early name of Copenhagen.)
haft, *n.* hahft, a handle, esp. of a weapon or tool: *v.t.* to furnish with a handle. (A.S. *hæft.*)
hag, *n.* hag, an ugly old woman; a witch; a fury; the hagfish: *v.t.* to harass; to overwork. (A.S. *hægtis*, a fury.)
hag, *n.* hag, a patch of firm ground in a bog; a hole cut out of peat in a bog: *v.t.* and *i.* to hack.
hagberry, *n.* *hag*-be-re, the bird-cherry, *Prunus padus*, or its fruit.
hagfish, *n.* *hag*-fish, a cyclostome allied to the lamprey, *Myxine glutinosa.*
haggard, *a.* *hag*-gard, wild or intractable; lean and hollow-eyed from age, or want, or suffering: *n.* an untrained or refractory hawk. (O.Fr. *hagard.*)
haggardly, *ad.* *hag*-gard-le, in a haggard manner.
haggis, *n.* *hag*-gis, a Scotch dish made of the heart, liver, etc., of a sheep, chopped fine with suet and oatmeal, highly seasoned and boiled in the sheep's stomach. (Scots.)
haggish, *a.* *hag*-gish, like a hag; ugly.
haggle, *v.t.* *hag*-gl, to cut unskilfully; to mangle: *v.i.* to raise difficulties in bargaining; to higgle.
haggler, *n.* *hag*-gler, a difficult bargainer.
hagiarchy, *n.* *hag*-e-ar-ke, government by priests or saints. (Gr. *hagios*, holy, *archo*, rule.)
hagio-, *comb.f.* *hag*-e-o, holy; sacred. (Gr. *hagios.*)
hagiographal, *a.* hag-e-*og*-ra-fal, pertaining to the Hagiographa, that part of the Jewish Scriptures not included in the Law and the Prophets.
hagiographer, *n.* *hag*-e-*og*-ra-fer, a writer of a hagiography; a hagiologist.
hagiography, *n.* *hag*-e-*og*-ra-fe, a collection of lives of the saints; the study or compilation of such biographies. (Gr. *hagios*, and *grapho*, write.)
hagiolatry, *n.* *hag*-e-*ol*-a-tre, the invocation or excessive adoration of saints. (Gr. *hagios*, and *latreia*, worship.)
hagiologist, *n.* *hag*-e-*ol*-o-jist, one expert in hagiology.
hagiology, *n.* *hag*-e-*ol*-o-je, literature recording legends of the saints; a list of the saints. (Gr. *hagios*, and *logos*, account.)
hagioscope, *n.* *hag*-e-o-skope, an oblique opening in a church to afford a glimpse of the altar; the squint. (Gr. *hagios*, holy, *skopeo*, view.)
hag-ridden, *a.* afflicted with night-mare.
hah, *int.* hah, an expression of surprise or effort; ha.
ha-ha, *n.* *hah*-hah, a sunk fence or wall, a hawhaw.
hail, *n.* hale, a shower of rain in the form of ice; frozen drops of rain: *v.i.* to rain hail. (A.S. *hagol.*)
hail, *n.* hale, a salutation; call: *int.* health to you: *v.t.* to call to one at a distance to arrest his attention; to greet as: *v.i.* to come from. (Scand.)
hail-fellow, *n.* an intimate companion. **hail fellow well met,** on very familiar terms.
hailstone, *n.* *hale*-stone, a single frozen raindrop.
hailstorm, *n.* *hale*-storm, a violent fall of hail.
haily, *a.* *hale*-le, consisting of hail.
★**hair,** *n.* hare, a small filament, with a bulbous root, growing from the skin of a mammal; the mass of filaments growing thus and forming an integument or covering; anything very small or fine; a minute hair-like filament on the surface of plants [Bot.]: *v.t.* to remove the hair from. **keep your hair on**! [Slang], don't get excited. **not to turn a hair,** to keep cool and unruffled. **to split hairs,** to quibble; to be over-meticulous. (A.S. *hær.*)
hairbell, *n.* *hare*-bell, the popular name of *Campanula rotundifolia*, the bluebell of Scotland, so called from the slender peduncle.
hairbreadth, *n.* *hare*-bredth, the breadth of a hair; a very small distance.
hair-brush, *n.* a brush for the hair.
hair-cloth, *n.* a textile made chiefly or wholly of hair.
hairdresser, *n.* *hare*-dres-er, one who cuts and dresses hair.
haired, *a.* haird, having hair.
hair-grass, *n.* any tall tufted grass, esp. one of the genus *Aira.*
hairiness, *n.* *hare*-re-ness, the state of being hairy.
hairless, *a.* *hare*-less, destitute of hair; bald.
hairline, *n.* *hare*-line, a very fine line; a hair-stroke; the edge of the growth of hair on the scalp.
hair-net, *n.* a net of very fine thread worn by women for confining the hair.
hair-oil, *n.* oil for dressing the hair.
hair-pencil, *n.* a brush made of very fine hair for painting.
hairpin, *n.* *hare*-pin, a pin used in keeping the hair in place. **hairpin bend,** an acute-angled curve; the doubling back on itself (of a road, etc.).
hair-raising, *a.* calculated to inspire terror.
hair-salt, *n.* epsomite when occurring in fine silky fibres; alunogen.
hair-slide, *n.* a clip of metal, plastic, etc. for keeping women's hair tidy.
hair-space, *n.* the thinnest printers' space.
hair-splitting, *n.* and *a.* making minute distinctions in argument; quibbling.
hair-spring, *n.* a very fine steel spring regulating the balance-wheel of a watch.
hair-stroke, *n.* a fine, esp. upward, stroke of the pen; a serif.
hair-trigger, *n.* a secondary trigger allowing a firearm to be discharged by very slight pressure.
hairworm, *n.* *hare*-wurm, a thread-like freshwater worm esp. of the genera *Gordius* and *Mermis.*
hairy, *a.* *hare*-re, covered with, consisting of, or resembling hair.
hake, *n.* hake, a marine food-fish, *Merlucius vulgaris*, allied to the cod. (Scand.)
Hakenkreutz, *n.* *hah*-ken-kroytz, the swastika. (Ger., hooked cross.)
hakim, *n.* *hah*-kim, a Moslem judge, or physician. (Ar.)
halation, *n.* ha-*lay*-shon, fogging; a halo-like blur on a negative, due to reflection during exposure [Phot.].
halberd, *n.* *hal*-berd, a military weapon partly battle-axe, partly spear, mounted on a long shaft. (O.Fr. *halebarde.*)
halberdier, *n.* hal-ber-*deer*, one armed with a halberd.
halcyon, *n.* *hal*-se-on, the kingfisher, whose breeding season was fabled to be always accompanied with calm weather; (*cap.*) a genus of Australian wood kingfishers [Zool.]: *a.* calm; peaceful. **halcyon days,** days of quiet prosperity; the seven days preceding and the seven succeeding the winter solstice, when the kingfisher was supposed to breed. (L., kingfisher.)
hale, *v.t.* hale, to haul; to drag along. (Fr. *haler.*)
hale, *a.* hale, sound in body; healthy; robust. (A.S. *hāl*, whole.)
haleness, *n.* *hale*-ness, the state of being hale.
half, *n.* hahf (*pl.* **halves,** hahvz), one of two equal parts; a moiety; a term or half-year; half a pint [Coll.]: *a.* consisting of a half: *v.t.* to halve: *ad.*

in part, or in an equal part or degree; imperfectly. **to cry halves,** to claim an equal share. **better half,** one's wife. **by halves,** not whole-heartedly; without enthusiasm. **to go halves,** to have an equal share. (A.S. *healf.*)

half-and-half, *n.* one, a mixture, usually of stout and ale; a hesitating, indifferent, or insincere person: *a.* listless; feeble.

half-back, *n.* a player next behind the forwards at Association football.

half-baked, *a. hahf*-baykd, insufficiently baked; not properly thought out; inexperienced; half-witted.

half-blood, *n.* relationship between offspring of the same father or mother, but not of both; one so related; a half-breed.

half-blooded, *a.* proceeding from a male and female of different breeds.

half-blue, *n.* at Oxford and Cambridge, a representative of certain minor sports; the colours awarded to such.

half-bound, *a.* of a book, bound with leather only on back and corners.

half-breed, *a.* half-blooded: *n.* one born of parents of different races.

half-brother, *n.* a brother by one parent, but not by both.

half-caste, *n. hahf*-kahst, a half-breed, esp. a Eurasian: *a.* of mixed race.

half-cock, *n.* the position of the cock of a gun when retained by the first notch.

halfcrown, *n.* hahf-*croun*, a coin worth two shillings and sixpence.

half-dead, *a.* almost dead; completely tired out.

half-decked, *a.* hahf-*dekt*, partly decked and partly open [Naut.].

half-dollar, *n.* a silver coin worth 50 cents [U.S.A.]; a halfcrown [Coll.].

half-face, *n.* the profile.

half-guinea, *n.* a former English gold coin worth 10*s.* 6*d.*

half-hearted, *a.* lukewarm; only half zealous.

half-hitch, *n.* a simple variety of seaman's knot.

half-holiday, *n.* cessation from work for one afternoon and evening.

half-length, *a.* showing only the upper part of the body: *n.* a portrait which does so.

half-light, *n.* twilight; gloaming; the subdued light of an interior.

half-mark, *n.* hahf-*mark*, an old coin of 6*s.* 8*d.* sterling.

halfmast, *n. hahf*-mahst, halfway up the mast: *a.* flying at this position in sign of mourning.

half-moon, *n.* the moon at the quarters, when only half of its disk is illuminated; anything in the shape of a half-moon; a demilune.

half-mourning, *n.* black relieved by grey or white.

half-nelson, *n.* hahf-*nel*-son, a strong hold in wrestling, one arm being thrust under the corresponding arm of the opponent, and the hand pressed on the back of his neck.

half-note, *n.* a minim; a semitone [Mus.].

half-past, *ad.* half an hour past.

half-pay, *n.* reduced pay to an officer when retired from service, temporarily or permanently: *a.* receiving or entitled to it.

halfpenny, *n. hayp*-ne (*pl.* **halfpence,** *hay*-pence), a copper coin of the value of half a penny; its value: *a.* of the price or value of half a penny.

half-price, *n.* a charge reduced by one-half.

half-rater, *n.* a small racing yacht under 5 metres in length on the water-line.

half-round, *a.* semicircular: *n.* a semicircular moulding.

half-seas, *a.* half-way [Naut.]. **half-seas over,** tipsy; getting on for drunk [Slang].

half-shift, *n.* a move of the hand upward on a violin, to reach a high note.

half-sister, *n.* a sister by one parent, but not by both.

half-sovereign, *n.* a former English gold coin worth ten shillings.

half-timbered, *a.* having the foundations and principal supports of stout timber, and the intervening spaces in front filled with plaster or brickwork.

half-time, *n.* half the usual time or the time allotted; the midway interval in football, hockey, etc., when the teams change ends.

half-timer, *n.* a pupil who spends half a day at school and the rest at work for wages; a worker engaged for half-time only.

half-title, *n.* the title, or shortened title, of a book printed on the right-hand page preceding the title-page; this page.

half-tone, *n. hahf*-tone, a process block obtained by photographing the object through a screen or network of fine lines.

halfway, *ad.* in the middle; at half the distance: *a.* equally distant from the extremes.

half-wit, *n. hahf*-wit, a simpleton; a moron.

half-witted, *a.* weak in intellect.

half-yearly, *a.* happening once in six months: *ad.* twice in a year; semi-annually.

halibut, *n. hal*-e-but, *Hippoglossus vulgaris,* the largest of the flat-fishes. (A.S. *halig,* holy, and *butte,* a flounder.)

halicore, *n. hal*-e-kore, the dugong. (Gr. *hals,* salt, *kore,* a maid.)

halidom, *n. hal*-e-dom, holiness; a small relic; a mascot. (A.S. *haligdom.*)

halieutic, *a.* hal-e-*yew*-tik, pertaining to fishing: *pl.* the art of fishing. (Gr. *halieutikos.*)

haliotis, *n.* hal-e-*oh*-tis, the sea-ear [Zool.].

halite, *n. hal*-ite *or hay*-lite, native salt; the naturally occurring form of sodium chloride.

halitosis, *n.* hal-e-*toh*-sis, foul or offensive breath. (Lat. *halitus,* breath.)

halituous, *a.* ha-*lit*-yew-us, like breath; vaporous; slightly moist [Med.]. (L. *halitus,* breath.)

halitus, *n. hal*-e-tus, exhalation; breath. (L.)

hall, *n.* hawl, a room at the entrance of a house; a building in which courts of justice are held; the chief apartment of a castle, manor-house, etc.; a mansion; a college [Scot.]; the edifice of a college; a room for a corporation, guild, etc.; a place to dine in common. (A.S. *heal,* a shelter.)

hall-door, *n.* the front-door.

Hallelujah, *n.* hal-le-*loo*-yah, a Hebrew word, used in songs of praise, signifying, Praise the Lord.

halliard, *n. hal*-yard, a halyard.

hall-mark, *n. hawl*-mark, an official stamp on gold and silver articles impressed at the assay offices, to attest their standard: *v.t.* to stamp with this; to guarantee as genuine.

hallo, *int.* ha-*loh,* halloo; hello, a call for attention.

halloo, *int.* ha-*loo,* an exclamation to invite attention or to urge on: *n.* a cry to call attention; a hunting cry: *v.i.* to cry halloo: *v.t.* to encourage or chase with shouts; to call or shout to. (Imit.)

hallow, *v.t. hal*-lo, to set apart for sacred use; to reverence or honour as sacred. (A.S. *halgian.*)

Halloween, *n. hal*-lo-een, the eve of All-Saints Day.

Hallowmass, *n. hal*-lo-mas, All-Saints Day.

hallucinate, *v.t.* ha-*lew*-se-nate, to induce hallucinations in.

hallucination, *n.* ha-*lew*-se-*nay*-shon, an illusion; the false belief in sensations that have no foundation in fact; the sensation itself. (L.)

hallucinatory, *a.* ha-*lew*-se-*nay*-to-re, partaking of or tending to produce hallucination.

hallux, *n. hal*-uks (*pl.* **halluces,** *hal*-yew-seez), in man, the great toe; in mammals, the first digit of the hind limb; in birds, the hind toe. (Late L. *allex.*)

halma, *n. hal*-ma, a game played with pieces on a board of 256 squares. (Gr., a leap.)

halo, *n. hay*-lo, a luminous and sometimes coloured circle occasionally surrounding the sun or moon; a nimbus; the glory in which enthusiasm invests an object: *v.t.* to invest with a halo: *v.i.* to form into a halo. (Gr., a round threshing-floor.)

halogen, *n. hal*-o-jen, a substance which, by combination with a metal, forms a salt, as chlorine [Chem.]. (Gr. *hals,* salt, *gennao,* produce.)

halogenous, *a.* ha-*loj*-e-nus, of the nature of halogen.

haloid, *a. hal*-oyd, resembling common salt: *n.* a salt formed by the combination of a halogen and a metal.

halophile, *a. hal*-o-fil, halophilous.

halophilism, *n.* ha-*lof*-e-lizm, adaptation to life in saline conditions [Bot.].

halophilous, *a.* ha-*lof*-e-lus, adapted to life in saline conditions [Bot.].

halophobe, *n. hal*-o-fobe, a plant that will not grow in salty soil.

halophyte, *n. hal*-o-fite, a plant living in salt soil or salt water.

halt, *a.* hawlt, lame; stopping in walking: *n.* a stoppage; a stopping place; a stop in marching; the act of limping; lame persons collectively: *v.i.* to limp; to stop in marching or walking; to stand in doubt whether to proceed or what to do; to hesitate; to falter: *v.t.* to stop; to cause to cease marching. (A.S. *healt*, lame.)

halter, *n.* *hawl*-ter, a rope or strap for leading or holding a horse; a rope for hanging malefactors; a strong cord: *v.t.* to put a halter on; to catch or tie up with a halter. (A.S. *hælftre.*)

halteres, *n.pl.* hal-*teer*-eez, the second pair of wings in flies modified into thread-like antennæ and thought to serve as balancers. (Gr. *halteres*, dumb-bells.)

haltingly, *ad.* *hawl*-ting-le in a hesitating manner.

halve, *v.t.* hahve, to divide into two equal parts. (As *half.*)

halyard, *n.* *hal*-yard, a running rope for hoisting or lowering yards, sails, or flags.

ham, *n.* ham, the inner or hind part of the thigh; the thigh of an animal, esp. of a pig, salted and dried in smoke. (A.S. *hamm.*)

hamadryad, *n.* ham-a-*dry*-ad, a wood-nymph identified with a tree, whose existence was co-extensive with that of the tree [Myth.]; the venomous snake, the king cobra of India, *Naja hannah bungarus*; the Arabian or sacred baboon, *Cynocephalus hamadryas.* (Gr. *hama*, together, *drys*, a tree.)

hamartiology, *n.* ha-mar-te-*ol*-o-je, the doctrine of sin. (Gr. *hamartia*, sin.)

hamate, *a.* *hay*-mat, hooked, or set with hooks [Bot.]. (L. *hamatus*, from *hamus*, a hook.)

hamble, *v.i.* *ham*-bl, to mutilate the foot, esp. of hounds. (A.S. *hamelian*, mutilate.)

Hamburg, *n.* *ham*-berg, a small breed of domestic fowl; a black variety of hothouse grape.

Hamburger, *n.* *ham*-ber-ger, minced beef fried with onion, seasoning, etc. (also known as **Hamburg steak**); a variety of breakfast sausage.

hame, *n.* hame, one of the two curved bars of metal or wood to which the trace is attached on the collar of a draught horse. (M.E.)

hamiform, *a.* *hay*-me-form, shaped like a hook. (L.)

hamirostrate, *a.* hay-me-*ros*-trat, having a hooked beak [Ornith.].

Hamitic, *a.* ha-*mit*-ik, pertaining to Ham, son of Noah, to his supposed descendants, or their languages: *n.* any one of the Hamitic languages.

hamlet, *n.* *ham*-let, a small village; a little cluster of houses in the country. (O.Fr.)

hammam, *n.* ha-*mahm*, a hummum, or Turkish bath. (Ar.)

★**hammer,** *n.* *ham*-mer, a tool for driving nails, beating metals, etc.; that which resembles a hammer in form or action, as the striker of a clock, the gavel of an auctioneer, etc.; the cock of a gun-lock; the padded striker of the wires in a piano: *v.t.* to beat or forge with a hammer; to conceive and produce with labour: *v.i.* to work; to make a noise like hammering; to labour in contrivance. **hammer and tongs,** with noise and vigour. **hammered,** proclaimed as a defaulter on the Stock Exchange. **to bring to the hammer,** to put up to auction. (A.S. *hamor.*)

hammer-beam, *n.* a beam projecting horizontally from a wall to support roof-timbers in place of a tie-beam.

hammer-cloth, *n.* the cloth which covers the box of a coach or carriage.

hammerer, *n.* *ham*-mer-er, a worker with a hammer.

hammerhead, *n.* *ham*-mer-hed, the striking part of a hammer; a species of shark, *Zygæna malleus*; the umbrette, a S. African bird.

hammerless, *a.* *ham*-mer-less, without a visible hammer (of fire-arms).

hammer-lock, *n.* a wrestling position in which the opponent's arm is held twisted and bent behind his back.

hammerman, *n.* *ham*-mer-man, one who works with a hammer; a smith.

hammer-toe, *n.* a malformation of the foot entailing angular flexion of one or more toes.

hammock, *n.* *ham*-mok, a hanging bed, usually of canvas or network, suspended by cords from hooks. **hammock chair,** a folding chair with canvas to sit or recline in. (Sp. *hamaca.*)

hammy, *a.* *ham*-me, tasting of ham.

hamose, *a.* *hay*-mose, hamous.

hamous, *a.* *hay*-mus, having the end hooked [Bot.].

hamper, *n.* *ham*-per, a large basket with a lid, used for package: *v.t.* to put in a hamper. (O.Fr. *hanapier.*)

hamper, *n.* *ham*-per, that which hampers; a fetter or shackle, heavy spars, rigging, etc. [Naut.]: *v.t.* to shackle; to impede; to tangle; to perplex; to embarrass. (M.E. *hampren.*)

hamshackle, *v.t.* *ham*-shak-kl, to fasten the head of an animal to one of its forelegs.

hamster, *n.* *ham*-ster, a rodent of the genus *Cricetus*, having two cheek-pouches for holding grain. (Ger.)

hamstring, *n.* *ham*-string, one of the tendons behind the knee: *v.t.* to lame by cutting the tendons of the leg. *pp.* **hamstrung.**

hamular, *a.* *ham*-yew-lar, resembling a small hook.

hamulate, *a.* *ham*-yew-lat, having a small hook [Bot.].

hamulus, *n.* *ham*-yew-lus, a small hook. (L.)

hanaper, *n.* *han*-a-per, a wicker travelling-case or basket holding money, documents, or valuables; a former Chancery department where charters, etc. were sealed. (O.Fr. *hanapier*, a case to hold a *hanap*, or drinking cup.)

hance, *n.* hance, the haunch of an elliptical arch.

★**hand,** *n.* hand, the organ of prehension, forming the extremity of the human arm and consisting of the palm and fingers; a similar organ in apes, etc.; a measure of four inches; side part, right or left; performance; workmanship; handiwork; skill; power or manner of acting or performance; agency; possession; power; a player's share of a pack of cards; a game at cards, or a part in it; an innings; an index, or that which performs the office of a pointing finger, as of a watch, etc.; a workman; a servant on a farm; a man employed on board ship; style of workmanship or penmanship; handwriting; a shoulder of pork: *v.t.* to give or transmit with the hand; to lead; to conduct; to furl, as a sail. **at hand,** near; not distant. **hand and,** or **in, glove,** intimate and familiar. **hand in hand,** in union; conjointly. **hand over hand,** by passing the hands alternately one before or above another. **hand over head,** negligently; rashly. **hands off!** don't touch; don't interfere. **hand's turn,** a job a spell of manual work. **hand to hand,** in close fight; in close union. **hand to mouth,** without provision beforehand. **in hand,** remaining unspent; in a state of execution. **on hand,** in present possession; under one's care or management. **out of hand,** ready payment, with regard to the payer; at once; directly; out of control. **to bear a hand,** to take part in quickly. **to bear in hand,** to keep in expectation. **to hand,** in readiness; already prepared. **to have a hand in,** to be concerned in. **to lend a hand,** to give assistance. **to set the hand to,** to undertake. **to take in hand,** to lay hold of or deal with; to undertake. **under his hand,** with the proper signature. **wash the hands of,** *see* **wash. with clean hands,** blameless. (A.S.)

handbag, *n.* *hand*-bag, a reticule; a small bag for carrying on the wrist or in the hand.

handball, *n.* *hand*-bawl, an ancient game in which the ball was hit between goals by the hand.

hand-barrow, *n.* a barrow with handles at each end borne between two men; a wheeled barrow pushed by one man; a coster's mobile stall.

handbell, *n.* *hand*-bel, a small bell rung by the hand.

handbill, *n.* *hand*-bil, a loose sheet containing some printed announcement.

handbook, *n.* *hand*-book, a manual; a guide-book.

handbreadth, *n.* *hand*-bredth, a length equal to the breadth of the hand.

hand-cart, *n.* a cart pushed or drawn by hand.

handcuff, *n.* *hand*-kuf, one of a pair of chained iron manacles for the wrists: *v.t.* to manacle the hands.

handed, *a.* *hand*-ed, having hands or a certain kind of hand. **left-, right-handed,** most dexterous with the left or the right hand.

handfast, *n.* *hand*-fahst, hold; custody; betrothal; *v.t.* to pledge; to bind by contract; to betroth.

handful, *n.* *hand*-ful, as much as the hand will grasp or contain; a small quantity; a troublesome person or job [Coll.].

hand-gallop, *n.* a slow and easy gallop.
hand-glass, *n.* a glass used for protecting and fostering plants; a small mirror, or magnifying-glass, with a handle.
handgrip, *n.* *hand*-grip, a grasp.
handicap, *n.* *han*-de-kap, a penalty or allowance so adjusted as to give all the competitors an equal chance; allowance made to the weaker in any contest: *v.t.* to allot the penalties or allowances for competitors; to place impediments upon. (*Hand in cap*, from a way of drawing lots.)
handicapper, *n.* *han*-de-kap-er, a racing or sports official who determines handicaps.
handicraft, *n.* *han*-de-krahft, skill in working with the hands; a manual occupation: *a.* pertaining to manual labour. (A.S. *handcræft.*)
handicraftsman, *n.* *han*-de-krahfts-man, one skilled or employed in manual occupation.
handily, *ad.* *han*-de-le, skilfully; quickly.
handiness, *n.* *han*-de-ness, readiness; versatility.
handiwork, *n.* *han*-de-wurk, work done by the hands or by skill of hand; the product of one's work. (A.S. *handgeweorc.*)
handkerchief, *n.* *hang*-ker-chif, a square of linen, or silk, etc., for wiping the nose, face, etc.
handle, *n.* *han*-dl, that part which is held in the hand when used; that of which use is made; a means by which something is effected: *v.t.* to touch, to feel, or wield with the hand; to discourse on; to deal with; to use well or ill. **a handle to one's name,** a title. (A.S. *handlian.*)
handler, *n.* *han*-dler, one who handles.
handline, *n.* *hand*-line, a fishing-line used without a rod.
handling, *n.* *han*-dling, use by the hand; treatment; the manipulation or characteristic style peculiar to an artist [Paint.].
handmade, *n.* *hand*-made, made by hand, not by factory methods.
handmaid (*or* **-maiden**), *n.* *hand*-made (-maydn), a female servant.
handmill, *n.* *hand*-mil, a mill worked by the hand; a quern.
hand-picked, *a.* *hand*-pikt, especially selected [Coll.].
handpress, *n.* *hand*-pres, a press, esp. a small printing-press, worked by hand.
handrail, *n.* *hand*-rale, a rail to hold by; a protecting rail on a staircase, etc.
handsaw, *n.* *hand*-saw, a saw used with one hand.
handscrew, *n.* *hand*-skrew, any screw device worked by hand, esp. a clamp or a lifting jack.
handsel, *n.* *han*-sel, first sale or use; earnest-money, deposit; a present for luck; foretaste: *v.t.* to use or do anything for the first time; to give a handsel to. (Scand. *handsale.*)
handsome, *a.* *han*-sum, good-looking; graceful; becoming; ample; liberal; generous. (A.S. *hand*, and suffix *-sum.*)
handsomely, *ad.* *han*-sum-le, in a handsome manner; steadily or gradually [Naut.].
handsomeness, *n.* the quality of being handsome.
handspike, *n.* *hand*-spike, a bar used as a lever.
handstaff, *n.* *hand*-stahf, a javelin.
handwriting, *n.* *hand*-ry-ting, that which is written by hand; personal style of penmanship.
handy, *a.* *han*-de, dexterous; skilful; ready to hand; near; convenient.
handy-dandy, *n.* a game in which children change the place of a thing, and challenge one to guess where it is.
handyman, *n.* *han*-de-man, a man-of-all-work; a jack-of-all-trades.
hang, *v.t.* hang, to suspend; to fasten as on a hinge; to put to death by suspending by the neck; to cover or decorate by anything suspended: *v.i.* to be suspended; to dangle; to depend; to bend forward; to project (over); to cling to; to hover; to linger; to have a steep declivity; to be executed by hanging. **hang about** or **around,** to loiter [Coll.]. **hang down,** to droop; to let fall below the proper situation. **hang fire,** said of a gun when the charge does not rapidly ignite; to hesitate. **hang in doubt,** to be in suspense. **hang on** or **upon,** to adhere to; to adhere obstinately; to rest; to be dependent on; to hold fast without belaying [Naut.]. **hang to,** to cling. **hang together,** to be closely united. **hang up,** to place on something fixed on high; to leave undecided; to defer. **to hang out,** to display. *pp.* **hung** (A.S. *hangian.*)
hang, *n.* hang, slope; drift; mode of connexion or dependence; the way in which one thing depends on another; knack. **get the hang of,** to understand the connexion; to acquire the knack.
hangar, *n.* *hang*-ar, an aircraft shed. (Fr.)
hangbird, *n.* *hang*-bird, the Baltimore oriole, *Icterus galbula*, which builds a hanging nest, or other member of the genus *Icterus.*
hang-dog, *a.* looking like a sneak; sullen; *n.* a base, disreputable fellow.
hanger, *n.* *hang*-er, that on which a thing is hung; that which hangs or is suspended; an ess-curve in writing; a short broadsword, curved towards the point, so called because hung from the belt; a wood on the slope of a hill.
hanger-on, *n.* one who dangles after another in expectation of favours; a retainer.
★**hanging,** *n.* *hang*-ing, death by the hangman; *pl.* drapery hung on the walls of a room; display; exhibition. **hanging committee,** the body responsible for the hanging of pictures in an exhibition. **hanging gardens,** gardens in terraces rising behind one another.
hanging-guard, *n.* a defensive position in broad-sword exercise.
hangman, *n.* *hang*-man, a public executioner.
hangnail, *n.* *hang*-nale, an agnail.
hangnest, *n.* *hang*-nest, any bird whose nest is built to suspend from a bough, etc.; such a nest; the hangbird.
hang-net, *n.* *hang*-net, a net with a large mesh hung between stakes.
hang-over, *n.* a surviving trait, custom, etc.; the after-effects of alcoholic dissipation [Coll.].
hank, *n.* hank, a coil; seven skeins of silk or thread tied together; 560 yards of worsted yarn; 300 yards of linen yarn; a loop; one of the rings of wood, etc., attached to a sail for holding its luff close up to a stay [Naut.]: *v.t.* to form into hanks; to fasten. (Scand.)
hanker, *v.i.* *hang*-ker, to long for with a keen desire.
hankering, *n.* *hang*-ker-ing, a keen appetite that causes uneasiness till it is gratified.
hankeringly, *ad.* in a hankering manner.
hanky-panky, *n.* *hang*-ke-*pang*-ke, hocus-pocus; jugglery; deceptive action.
Hanoverian, *a.* han-o-*veer*-re-an, pertaining to Hanover, or to the family of the Dukes of Hanover and their descendants, esp. the dynasty that occupied the British throne 1714–1901: *n.* a native of Hanover; a supporter of the Hanoverian dynasty.
Hansard, *n.* *han*-sahrd, a merchant of a Hanse town.
Hansard, *n.* *han*-sahrd, the official record of the proceedings and debates of the British Parliament, published originally by Luke Hansard, printer.
Hanse, *n.* hans, a merchant guild, esp. that of a Hanse town. **Hanse towns,** certain cities of Germany, associated in the Middle Ages for the protection of commerce. (Ger.)
Hanseatic, *a.* han-se-*at*-ik, pertaining to the Hanse towns.
hansom, *n.* *han*-sum, a light two-wheeled cab seated for two, with the driver mounted behind. (Name of inventor, Jos. Aloysius *Hansom*, an architect.)
hanuman, *n.* hun-oo-*mahn*, the entellus monkey, *Semnopithecus entellus.* (Hind.; name of the monkey-god.)
hap, *n.* hap, that which happens by chance: *v.i.* to happen; to befall by chance. (Scand. *happ.*)
haphazard, *n.* hap-*haz*-ard, chance; accident: *a.* dependent upon chance; random: *ad.* in a haphazard way.
hapless, *a.* *hap*-less, luckless; unfortunate; unlucky.
haplodont, *a.* *hap*-lo-dont, having molars with simple, not ridged, crowns: *n.* the sewellel, a rodent of the genus *Haplodon* [Zool.]. (Gr. *haploos*, simple, *odous*, *odontis*, tooth.)
haplography, *n.* hap-*log*-ra-fe, the unintentional slip whereby adjacent letters are omitted in the writing of a word, as *suppositious* for *supposititious.*
haply, *ad.* *hap*-le, by chance; perhaps.
ha'p'orth, *n.* *hay*-perth, halfpennyworth.
happen, *v.t.* *hap*-pen, to chance; to fall out; to take place. (As *hap.*)
happily, *ad.* *hap*-pe-le, in a happy manner; by good fortune.

happiness, *n.* *hap*-pe-ness, the state of being happy; good fortune.

★**happy,** *a.* *hap*-pe, fortunate; successful; enjoying pleasure from the possession or fruition of good; in secure possession of good; blessed; agreeable; dexterous; well-adapted to a purpose; felicitous; living in concord; propitious. **happy dispatch,** hara-kiri.

happy-go-lucky, *a.* thoughtless and light-hearted; improvident.

haquebut, *n.* *hak*-but, a hackbut. (Fr.)

hara-kiri, *n.* *hah*-ra-*keer*-re, honourable suicide by self-disembowelment; happy dispatch. (Jap.)

harangue, *n.* ha-*rang*, a vehement and declamatory speech addressed usually to a crowd; a tirade: *v.i.* to deliver an harangue: *v.t.* to address by an harangue. (Fr.)

haranguer, *n.* ha-*rang*-er, one who harangues.

harass, *v.t.* *ha*-ras, to weary; to fatigue to excess; to annoy by repeated attacks. (Fr.)

harasser, *n.* *ha*-ras-er, one who harasses.

harassment, *n.* *ha*-ras-ment, state of being harassed.

harbinger, *n.* *har*-bin-jer, a forerunner; originally one who goes before to provide lodgings: *v.t.* to precede as a harbinger. (O.Fr. *herbergere.*)

★**harbour,** *n.* *har*-bur, a port or haven for ships; a refuge; a shelter; security: *v.t.* to shelter; to foster; to entertain; to indulge: *v.i.* to lodge; to receive entertainment. (M.E. *herbege*, from Scand. *herbyrgi*, army-shelter.)

harbourage, *n.* *har*-bu-raj, a place of shelter; refuge; sheltering.

harbour-bar, *n.* a shoal at a harbour entrance.

harbourer, *n.* *har*-bu-rer, one who harbours another.

harbour-master, *n.* an officer who has charge of the mooring of ships, etc., at a harbour.

★**hard,** *a.* hard, firm; solid; not easily pressed, penetrated, or broken; difficult to understand, or solve, do, get over, or bear; painful; laborious; oppressive; exacting; unfeeling; unkind; severe; unjust; stiff; distressing: *ad.* close; near; diligently; laboriously; earnestly: *n.* a landing place; a jetty. **die hard,** to die with a struggle or impenitent. **hard-a-lee, -a-port, -a-starboard,** an order to put the helm close to the named side of the ship [Naut.]. **hard by,** close by; near. **hard cash,** ready money. **hard coal,** anthracite. **hard drinker,** a drunkard. **hard fern,** a plant of the genus *Blechnum*, or *Lomaria*. **hard hit,** seriously affected or damaged; pecuniarily embarrassed. **hard labour,** compulsory labour imposed on convicted criminals. **hard lines,** undeserved bad luck. **hard of hearing,** slightly deaf. **hard up,** in want of money or means. **hard water,** water unsuitable for washing purposes through holding mineral salts in solution. (A.S. *heard.*)

hardbake, *n.* *hard*-bake, a toffee almond cake.

hardbeam, *n.* *hard*-beem, the hornbeam.

hard-bitten, *a.* tough in fight; resolute.

hard-boiled, *a.* boiled until the whole content is solidified (of eggs); unyielding; impervious to argument; practical.

hard-core, *n.* *hard*-kawr, broken brick, clinker, etc., used in road foundations.

harden, *v.t.* *har*-dn, to make hard or harder; to confirm in effrontery, obstinacy, or in wickedness; to make unfeeling; to inure: *v.i.* to become hard or harder; to become unfeeling; to become inured. (A.S. *heardian.*)

hardener, *n.* *hard*-ner, one who or that which hardens; one who tempers tools.

hardfaced, *a.* *hard*-fayst, stern looking; having coarse forbidding features.

hardfisted, *a.* hard-*fis*-ted, grasping; close-handed.

hard-fought, *a.* closely and vigorously contested.

hard-gotten, *a.* obtained with difficulty.

hard-handed, *a.* having hard hands, as a labourer; severe.

hard-headed, *a.* unsentimental; practical.

hard-hearted, *a.* cruel; unfeeling.

hard-heartedly, *ad.* hard-*har*-ted-le, in a hard-hearted manner.

hardihood, *n.* *har*-de-hood, boldness; effrontery.

hardily, *ad.* *har*-de-le, in a hardy manner.

hardiment, *n.* har-de-ment, hardihood; courage.

hardiness, *n.* *har*-de-ness, the state or quality of being hardy.

hardish, *a.* *hard*-ish, rather hard.

hardly, *ad.* *hard*-le, with difficulty; not quite; harshly; unfavourably.

hard-mouthed, *a.* hard-*mouthed*, not sensible to the bit; not easily governed; harsh in reproof.

hardness, *n.* *hard*-ness, the state or quality of being hard; solidity; compactness.

hardock, *n.* *har*-dok, the burdock, *Arctium lappa.*

hard-pan, *n.* *hard*-pan, a subsoil composed of clay, sand or gravel; unbroken ground; bed-rock [U.S.A.].

hard-pressed, *a.* *hard*-prest, in straits.

hards, *n.pl.* hardz, the refuse of flax or wool; coarse hemp or flax.

hard-set, *a.* rigid; inflexible; hard-pressed.

hardshell, *a.* *hard*-shel, having a hard shell; uncompromising; strictly orthodox.

hardship, *n.* *hard*-ship, anything hard to bear; severe labour or want; injustice; oppression.

hard-tack, *n.* ship's biscuit; rough fare generally.

hardware, *n.* *hard*-ware, ironmongery; metal ware.

hardwareman, *n.* *hard*-ware-man, a maker or seller of hardware.

hardwood, *n.* *hard*-wood, close-grained wood.

hardy, *a.* *har*-de, bold; resolute; confident; inured to fatigue; standing exposure (esp. of plants): *n.* an ironsmith's metal-cutting chisel. **half-hardy.** capable of bearing exposure except in winter (of plants). **hardy annual,** a plant from seed that can be sown in the open air; a constantly recurring debatable topic. (Fr. *hardi.*)

hare, *n.* hare, a rodent of the genus *Lepus*, with long ears, a short tail, soft hair, and a cleft upper lip: *v.i.* to run fast, like a hare. **Belgian hare,** a breed of the domesticated rabbit. **hare's ear,** the plant *Bupleurum rotundifolium.* **hare's eye,** the red campion. **hare's foot,** a species of clover. **hare's tail,** the grass *Lagurus ovatus.* **hare thistle,** the sow-thistle. **jumping hare,** a jerboa-like animal of South Africa, *Pedetes capper.* (A.S. *hara.*)

hare-and-hounds, *n.* cross-country running; a steeplechase on foot; a paper-chase.

harebell, *n.* *hare*-bel, the hairbell.

harebrained, *a.* *hare*-braynd, rash; flighty; shallow; volatile.

harehound, *n.* *hare*-hound, a hound for hunting hares; a harrier.

hareld, *n.* *ha*-reld, the long-tailed sea-duck, *Harelda glacialis.* (Ice.)

harelip, *n.* *hare*-lip, a congenital malformed fissure of the upper lip, like that of the hare.

harem, *n.* *hare*-rem *or* hah-*reem*, the apartments in the larger dwelling-houses of the East allotted to women; its inmates. (Turk.)

haricot, *n.* *ha*-re-koh, the kidney-bean, the French bean, *Phaseolus vulgaris*; a stew of meat with the seeds of the French bean, etc. (Fr.)

hari-kari, *n.* *ha*-re-*ka*-re, hara-kiri.

hark, *v.i.* hark, to listen; to lend an ear: *int.* listen! **hark back!** a call to hounds when they have overrun the scent. **to hark back,** to return to some previous point; to make a fresh start. (A.S. *hercnian.*)

harken, *v.t.* *har*-kn, to hearken.

harl, *n.* harl, any fibrous substance; the filaments of flax or hemp. (Low Ger.)

Harleian, *a.* *har*-le-an, pertaining to or collected by Robert Harley, Earl of Oxford (*d.* 1724): *n.* his collection of books and manuscripts; name of a society, founded, 1869, in his honour.

harlequin, *n.* *har*-le-kwin, the mute dancing lover in a pantomime, dressed in parti-coloured clothes, who plays tricks to divert the audience; a buffoon. **harlequin duck,** an Arctic species of sea-duck, *Cosmonetta histrionica.* (Fr.)

harlequinade, *n.* *har*-le-kwe-*nade*, the part of a pantomime in which a harlequin appears; buffoonery.

harlot, *n.* *har*-lot, a prostitute. (O.Fr.)

harlotry, *n.* *har*-lot-re, the trade or practice of prostitution; prostitution; incontinence.

harm, *n.* harm, injury; damage; moral wrong; detriment: *v.t.* to hurt; to injure. (A.S.)

harmattan, *n.* har-*mat*-tan, a hot, dry, withering wind, blowing to the Atlantic from the interior of Africa in the dry season. (Ar.)

harmel, *n.* *har*-mel, wild rue. (Ar. *harmil.*)

harmful, *a.* *harm*-ful, hurtful; injurious.

harmfully, *ad.* *harm*-ful-le, in a harmful manner.

harmfulness, *n.* the quality of being harmful.
harmless, *a.* *harm*-less, not injurious; innocent; non-venomous; unharmed.
harmlessly, *ad.* *harm*-less-le, in a harmless manner.
harmlessness, *n.* the quality of being harmless; innocence.
harmonic, *a.* har-*mon*-ik, relating to harmony or music; concordant; consonant: *n.* a sound produced by a vibrating string when it is divided into aliquot parts [Mus.]. **harmonic progression,** a series of numbers the reciprocals of which are in arithmetical progression [Math.]. **harmonic proportion,** *see* **proportion. harmonic triad,** the common chord, or the chord of a note consisting of its third and perfect fifth [Mus.]. (L. *harmonicus.*)
harmonica, *n.* har-*mon*-e-ka, an instrument developed from the "musical glasses"; an instrument of plates of glass or metal, of graduated lengths, played with a small mallet. **mouth harmonica,** the mouth-organ. (L.)
harmonical, *a.* har-*mon*-e-kal, harmonic.
harmonically, *ad.* in an harmonic manner.
harmonicon, *n.* har-*mon*-e-kon, an harmonica.
harmonious, *a.* har-*moh*-ne-us, adapted to each other; symmetrical; concordant; living in peace and friendship. (L. *harmonia.*)
harmoniously, *ad.* in an harmonious manner.
harmoniousness, *n.* quality of being harmonious.
harmoniphon, *n.* har-*mon*-e-fon, a wind-instrument in which the metal reed-pipes are played from a keyboard [Mus.]. (Gr. *harmonia,* and *phone,* sound.)
harmonist, *n.* *har*-mo-nist, one skilled in harmony; a composer of music; one who brings together corresponding passages to show their agreement.
harmonistic, *a.* har-mo-*nis*-tik, harmonizing characteristic of a harmony or harmonist.
harmonium, *n.* har-*moh*-ne-um, a wind-instrument, with free metal reeds, played with keys [Mus.]. (Gr. *harmonion.*)
harmonization, *n.* har-mo-ny-*zay*-shon, the act of harmonizing or state of being in harmony; anything that is harmonized.
harmonize, *v.i.* *har*-mo-nize, to agree in sound; to be in peace and friendship; to agree: *v.t.* to adjust in fit proportions; to cause to agree; to make musical.
harmonizer, *n.* *har*-mo-nize-er, one who harmonizes; a harmonist.
harmonometer, *n.* har-mo-*nom*-e-ter, an instrument for measuring relative pitch. (Gr. *harmonia,* and *metron,* measure.)
***harmony,** *n.* *har*-mo-ne, the just adaptation of parts to each other, in any system or composition of things, intended to form a connected whole; just proportion of sound; musical concord; concord; a work pointing out the accordance between different authors or seeking to harmonize what seems discordant. (Gr. *harmonia.*)
harmotome, *n.* *har*-mo-tome, a hydrous silicate of baryta and alumina, called also cross-stone. (Gr. *harmos,* joint, *temno,* cut.)
harness, *n.* *har*-ness, the equipment of a draught-horse or other draught-animal; the whole accoutrements or armour of a knight; an arrangement of straps; tackle: *v.t.* to equip with armour; to put the harness on. (O.Fr. *harneis,* armour.)
harness-cask, *n.* a cask on board ship for keeping the salt meat at hand for daily use.
harnesser, *n.* *har*-ness-er, one who harnesses.
harness-maker, *n.* one whose business it is to make harness for horses.
harp, *n.* harp, a stringed instrument of music, of a triangular figure, and commonly plucked by the fingers: *v.t.* to play on the harp. **to harp on,** to dwell on tediously. (A.S. *hearpe.*)
harper, *n.* *harp*-er, a harpist; a minstrel.
harpings, *n.pl.* *harp*-ingz, battens used to keep a ship's frames in position before the planking is put on.
harpist, *n.* *harp*-ist, a player on the harp.
harpoon, *n.* har-*poon,* a barbed spear for striking and killing whales: *v.t.* to strike with a harpoon. (Fr.)
harpooner, *n.* har-*poon*-er, one who uses a harpoon; the man in a whale-boat who throws the harpoon.
harp-shell, *n.* *harp*-shel, the beautiful shell of the tropical genus *Harpa.*
harpsichord, *n.* *harp*-se-kord, a primitive form of piano in which the strings are plucked by jacks. (Fr. *harpechorde.*)
harpy, *n.* *harp*-e, a fabulous winged monster of extreme ravenousness, living in filth and defiling everything, having the body of a woman and the wings and claws of a bird [Myth.]; any one of the harpy-eagles of Central and S. America of which the largest is *Thrasaetus harpyia*; any ravenous animal; an extortioner; a plunderer. (O.Fr. *harpie.*)
harquebus, *n.* *har*-kwe-bus, an early form of musket fired from a tripod or forked rest.
harquebusier, *n.* *har*-kwe-bus-*seer,* a soldier armed with a harquebus.
harr, *n.* hahr, a haar. (Scots.)
harridan, *n.* *ha*-re-dan, an old vixen; a decayed prostitute; a hag. (Fr.)
harrier, *n.* *ha*-re-er, a hound for hunting hares; a cross-country runner. (As *hare.*)
harrier, *n.* *ha*-re-er, a hawk of the genus *Circus*; one who harries.
Harrovian, *n.* ha-*roh*-ve-an, a past or present pupil of Harrow School: *a.* of or pertaining to Harrow School.
harrow, *n.* *ha*-roh, an agricultural implement of wood or iron, set with teeth, for levelling ploughed land and covering seed: *v.t.* to draw a harrow over; to break or tear with a harrow; to lacerate or torment. (Origin obscure.)
harrowing, *a.* *ha*-roh-ing, lacerating to the feelings.
harry, *v.t.* *ha*-re, to pillage; to harass: *v.i.* to make predatory incursions. (A.S. *hergian,* lay waste.)
harsh, *a.* harsh, rough to the touch, taste, or ear; rugged; grating; discordant; austere; peevish; severe; unfeeling. (Scand.)
harshly, *ad.* *harsh*-le, in a harsh manner.
harshness, *n.* the quality of being harsh..
hart, *n.* hart, a stag from its fifth year. (A.S. *heort.*)
hartal, *n.* *har*-tal, in India, a concerted strike or boycott, esp. as a protest against governmental action. (Hind. *hāt,* shop, *tālā,* lock.)
hartebeest, *n.* *har*-te-beest, a S. African antelope of the genus *Bubalis.* (Dut.)
hartshorn, *n.* *harts*-horn, the horn of the hart; spirit of hartshorn; carbonate of ammonia. **spirit of hartshorn,** a solution of ammonia in water.
hart's-tongue, *n.* a fern of the genus *Scolopendrium.*
harum-scarum, *a.* *hare*-um-*skare*-um, hare-brained; flighty; rash. (*hare* and *scare.*)
haruspex, *n.* ha-*rus*-peks (*pl.* **haruspices,** ha-*rus*-pe-seez), one who divines from the entrails of slaughtered victims. (L.)
haruspicy, *n.* ha-*rus*-pe-se, the art or practices of a haruspex.
harvest, *n.* *har*-vest, the season of reaping and gathering in crops; the ripe corn or grain collected; the product of labour; consequence: *v.t.* to reap or gather ripe corn and other fruits. (A.S. *hærfest.*)
harvest-bug, *n.* a harvestman.
harvester, *n.* *har*-ves-ter, a reaper; a reaping machine; a harvest-mite or harvestman.
harvest-festival, *n.* a church service of thanksgiving for the harvest.
harvest-home, *n.* the in-gathering of harvest; the festival at its completion.
harvest-lord, -lady, *n.* the first and second reaper sin a row.
harvestman, *n.* *har*-vest-man, an arachnid feeding upon spiders and insects.
harvest-mite, *n.* the scarlet harvest-bug, *Trombidium holosericeum.*
harvest-moon, *n.* the moon near the full, about the time of the autumnal equinox.
harvest-mouse, *n.* the smallest of the European field-mice, *Micromys minutus.*
harvest-queen, *n.* an image or person representing Ceres, formerly paraded on the last day of harvest.
has, haz, *third pers. sing. pres.* of *have.* **has-been,** a person or thing that is—or should be—superannuated; one past his heyday [Coll.].
hash, *n.* hash, a dish of meat, esp. cooked meat, and vegetables chopped small and stewed; a further working of old matter; a muddle: *v.t.* to chop small and mix; to slice; to cook a second time. (Fr. *hacher,* to mince.)
hashish, *n.* *hash*-ish, a narcotic preparation of Indian hemp, *Cannabis sativa*; bhang. (Ar.)

haslet, *n. has*-let, the entrails, heart and liver of an animal, esp. a pig. (O.Fr. *hastelet.*)
hasp, *n.* hahsp, a clasp that passes over a staple to be fastened by a padlock, etc.; a clasp: *v.t.* to shut or fasten with a hasp. (A.S. *hæpse.*)
hassock, *n. has*-sok, a stuffed footstool; a cushion to kneel on in church; a tuft of grass. (A.S. *hassuc.*)
hast, hast, former *second pers. sing. pres.* of *have.*
hastate, *a. has*-tat, spear-shaped [Bot.]. (L. *hasta,* a spear.)
haste, *n.* hayst, speed; quickness; hurry; impulsive inconsiderateness: *v.t.* to hasten. (O.Fr. *haste.*)
hasten, *v.t. hay*-sn, to urge forward; to push on; to expedite: *v.i.* to move with speed.
hastener, *n. hay*-sner, one who urges forward; that which hastens.
hastiform, *a. has*-te-form, hastate.
hastily, *ad. hays*-te-le, in a hasty manner.
hastiness, *n. hays*-te-ness, the state or quality of being hasty; irritability.
hasting, *a. hays*-ting, hurrying; ripening early: *n.* a fruit or vegetable that reaches maturity early.
hasty, *a. hays*-te, quick; speedy; eager; precipitate; easily excited to wrath; ripening early.
hasty-pudding, *n.* meal or flour with water or milk boiled thinly together; porridge.
★**hat,** *n.* hat, a covering for the head with a crown and brim; a woman's headgear with or without a brim; the dignity of a cardinal, from his ceremonial scarlet hat. **I'll eat my hat if . . . ,** an expression adding strong emphasis to the statement. **to pass the hat round,** to make a collection. (A.S. *hæt.*)
hatable, *a. hate*-a-bl, deserving of hatred; odious.
hatband, *n. hat*-band, a band round the crown of a hat, esp. one in token of mourning.
hatch, *n.* hatch, a brood; the act of hatching; that which is hatched: *v.t.* to produce young from eggs by natural or artificial incubation; to contrive or plot: *v.i.* to produce young; to emerge from the egg; to be developed from ova. (M.E. *hacchen.*)
hatch, *v.t.* hatch, to shade in a drawing or an engraving with lines crossing each other; one of the fine lines of hatching. (Fr. *hacher,* to hack.)
hatch, *n.* hatch, a half door working independently of the other half; a wicket; a hatchway, or its covering; a grated weir. **under hatches,** confined below; in distress, or slavery. (A.S. *hæce,* gate.)
hatch-boat, *n.* a kind of half-decked fishing-boat; one which has a well for keeping fish.
hatchel, *n. hatch-el,* a hackle, an instrument for combing flax, etc.: *v.t.* to hackle; to heckle.
hatcher, *n. hatch*-er, one who hatches; a plotter; an incubator.
hatchery, *n. hatch*-er-re, a place where eggs, esp. of poultry or fish, are hatched artificially.
hatchet, *n. hatch*-et, a small one-handed axe with a short handle. **to bury or take up the hatchet,** to make peace or war. (Fr. *hachette,* a tiny axe.)
hatchet-face, *n.* a face with sharp prominent features.
hatching, *n. hatch*-ing, shading by courses of lines crossing each other at an angle more or less acute; the production of young from eggs.
hatchment, *n. hatch*-ment, a copy of the armorial bearings of the dead placed temporarily on the house or tomb; an achievement [Her.].
hatchway, *n. hatch*-way, an opening in the deck of a ship for lowering cargo or passage below [Naut.].
★**hate,** *n.* hate, great dislike or aversion; hatred; a strafe, or exhibition of hatred [Slang]: *v.t.* to dislike greatly; to regard with ill-will; to detest; to loathe. (A.S. *hatian.*)
hateful, *a. hate*-ful, exciting hate; odious; full of hate.
hatefully, *ad. hate*-ful-le, in a hateful manner.
hatefulness, *n.* the quality of being hateful.
hater, *n. hate*-er, one who hates.
hath, hath, former *third pers. sing. pres.* of *have.*
hatless, *a. hat*-less, with head uncovered.
hatpin, *n. hat*-pin, a pin to fasten a hat to the hair.
hatred, *n. hate*-rid, great dislike; hate; enmity.
hatted, *a. hat*-ted, covered with or wearing a hat.
hatter, *n. hat*-ter, a maker or seller of hats; a miner who works without a partner [Austral. slang]. **mad as a hatter,** very eccentric.
hatteria, *n.* hat-*teer*-re-a, the tuatara, or sphenodon lizard of New Zealand.
hatti-sherif, *n. hat*-te-she-*reef,* an irrevocable order countersigned personally by the Sultan. (Turk.)
hat-trick, *n.* the feat of taking three wickets with successive balls [Cricket]; any threefold success.
hauberk, *n. haw*-berk, a coat of mail, sometimes sleeveless, formed of interwoven steel rings. (O.Fr. *hauberc.*)
haugh, *n.* haw, a low meadow by a river; a fertile meadow. (Scots.)
haughtily, *ad. haw*-te-le, in a haughty manner.
haughtiness, *n.* the quality of being haughty.
haughty, *a. haw*-te, proud and disdainful; supercilious; proceeding from pride mingled with contempt. (Fr. *haut,* high.)
haul, *n.* hawl, a pulling with force; the length hauled; draught of a net; what is caught at once; acquisition: *v.t.* to pull or draw with force; to drag; to cart. **to haul the wind,** to turn the head of a ship nearer to the point from which the wind blows [Naut.]. (Fr. *haler,* to haul a boat.)
haulage, *n. hawl*-aj, the act or process of hauling; charge for hauling.
hauler, *n. hawl*-er, one who or that which hauls.
haulier, *n. hawl*-e-er, a hauler; a carter; a lorry owner; one who hauls up, esp. in mines.
haulm, *n.* hawm, the stalk of grain of any kind, or of peas, beans, etc.; straw; stubble. (A.S. *healm.*)
haunch, *n.* hawnch, that part of the body which lies between the last ribs and the thigh; the fleshy part of the hip; the buttock; the leg and loin as one cut [Butchery]; the part of an arch between the springing and the crown [Arch.]. (O.Fr. *hanche.*)
haunched, *a.* hawncht, having haunches.
haunt, *n.* hawnt, a place of frequent resort; a place customarily visited by certain animals: *v.t.* to frequent; to trouble with frequent visits, as an apparition: *v.i.* to be often about. (Fr. *hanter.*)
haunted, *a. hawn*-ted, reputed to be the haunt of ghosts.
haunter, *n. hawn*-ter, one who or that which haunts.
hauriant, *a. haw*-re-ant, represented in a perpendicular position, as if rising for air (of fishes) [Her.]. (L. *hauriens,* drawing.)
Hausfrau, *n. house*-frou, a housewife. (Ger.)
haustellate, *a. haw*-stel-lat, having a haustellum; suctorial.
haustellum, *n.* haw-*stel*-lum, the suctorial organ of certain insects and crustaceans. (L. *haustus,* drawn.)
haustorium, *n. haw*-staw-re-um, the sucker of parasitic plants, as dodder, certain fungi, etc. [Bot.].
hautboy, *n. hoh*-boy, the oboe; a tall variety of strawberry. (Fr. *hautbois.*)
hauteur, *n.* hoh-*ter,* haughtiness; disdain. (Fr.)
haut-goût, *n.* hoh-*goo,* strong relish or flavour; high seasoning. (Fr.)
haut-ton, *n.* (App.), highly fashionable society; high social position. (Fr.)
Havana, *n.* ha-*van*-a, a cigar made at Havana or in Cuba.
★**have,** *v.t.* hav, to possess; to hold; to take; to be obliged; to contain; to receive: *n.* one (or a nation, etc.) holding property or possessions of value [Coll.]. **had rather,** wish rather. **to have a care,** to take care. **to have after,** to pursue. **to have at,** to assail; to enter into competition with. **to have away,** to remove; to take away. **to have in,** to contain. **to have it out,** finally to settle a dispute or quarrel. *p.* and *pp.* **had.** *third pers. sing. pres.* **has.** (A.S.)
havelock, *n. hav*-lok, a white cap-cover with a flap behind as a sunshade, so called after Sir Henry Havelock (*d.* 1857), of the Indian Mutiny.
haven, *n. hay*-vn, an inlet; a harbour; a station for ships; a place of safety. (Scand.)
have-not, *n. hav*-not, one (or a nation, etc.) without worldly goods or possessions [Coll.].
haver, *v.i. hay*-ver, to maunder; to talk nonsense: *n.* (or **havers**), twaddle; maundering. (Scots.)
havercake, *n. hay*-ver-kake, an oatcake. (Scots.)
haversack, *n. hav*-er-sak, a bag of strong cloth for provisions, carried by soldiers, etc. (Fr. *havresac.*)
Haversian, *a.* ha-*ver*-se-an, discovered by C. Havers

(Eng. 17th-cent. physician). **Haversian canals,** a net-work of canals in bones, protecting the blood-vessels [Anat.].
havildar, *n. hav*-il-dar, a native sergeant in a native Indian regiment under British rule. (Hind.)
havoc, *n. hav*-ok, devastation; wide and general destruction: *int.* a hunting- and war-cry, the signal for indiscriminate slaughter. (O.Fr. *havot.*)
haw, *n.* haw, the third eyelid in a dog, horse, etc.; an inflammation of this [Vet.].
haw, *n.* haw, the hawthorn berry; a hedged enclosure; a yard. (A.S. *haga.*)
haw, *n.* haw, a hesitation or intermission of speech: *v.i.* to speak so. (From the sound.)
Hawaiian, *a.* ha-*wy*-an, pertaining to Hawaii and the other islands of the Sandwich group: *n.* a native or the language of Hawaii.
hawfinch, *n. haw*-finch, the grosbeak, *Coccothraustes vulgaris,* a finch distinguished by its large beak. (A.S. *haga,* a hedge.)
hawhaw, *n. haw*-haw, a fence sunk between slopes, and not perceived till approached. (Fr. *haha.*)
haw-haw, *n. haw*-haw, a loud laugh; a guffaw; an affected accent in speaking.
hawk, *n.* hawk, one of many species of birds of prey, allied to the falcons and eagles; a falcon; a rapacious person; a swindler: *v.i.* to hunt birds with trained hawks; to attack on the wing: *v.t.* to hunt on the wing, as a hawk. (A.S. *hafoc.*)
hawk, *n.* hawk, an effort to force up phlegm from the throat: *v.i.* to make such an effort. (Imit.)
hawk, *v.t.* hawk, to cry, or to carry about, for sale.
hawk, *n.* hawk, a plasterer's board.
hawk-bell, *n.* a bell on the foot of a hunting-hawk.
hawkbit, *n. hawk*-bit, any plant of the genus *Leontodon,* esp. *L. Hispida.*
hawk-eagle, *n.* a bird of prey of the genus *Nisaëtus.*
hawker, *n. hawk*-er, one who offers goods for sale in the street; a pedlar. (Ger.)
hawker, *n. hawk*-er, a falconer.
hawk-eyed, *a. hawk*-ide, having a keen eye.
hawkmoth, *n. hawk*-moth, a large quick-darting moth of the family *Sphingidæ,* so called from hovering like a hawk.
hawk-nosed, *a. hawk*-nohzd, aquiline-nosed.
hawk-owl, *n. hawk*-oul, the short-eared owl.
hawksbeard, *n. hawks*-beerd, a composite plant of the genus *Crepis.*
hawksbill, *n. hawks*-bil, a marine turtle, of the species *Eretmochelys imbricata,* common in tropical waters.
hawkweed, *n. hawk*-weed, a yellow-flowered composite plant of the genus *Hieracium.*
hawse, *n.* hawz, the part of a ship's bow in which are the holes for the cables; the situation of the cables in front of a ship's bow, when she is moored with two anchors forward [Naut.]. (Scand.)
hawse-hole, *n.* the cable hole in a ship's bow.
hawser, *n. haw*-zer, a large rope for use in working and mooring [Naut.]. (O.Fr. *haucier,* to hoist.)
hawthorn, *n. haw*-thorn, the may or whitethorn, *Cratægus oxygacantha,* the tree bearing the haw.
hay, *n.* hay, grass cut and dried for fodder. (A.S. *hieg.*)
hay, *n.* hay, a rustic dance of Elizabethan times.
hay-band, *n.* a rope of twisted hay.
hay-box, *n.* a box packed with hay in which food can be kept hot and be cooked.
haycock, *n. hay*-kok, a conical pile of hay in a field.
hay-fever, *n.* an allergic catarrhal disorder, usually occurring annually in summer and caused or aggravated by the inhalation of pollen.
hayfield, *n. hay*-feeld, a field where hay is gathered.
hay-fork, *n.* a fork for turning over or pitching hay.
hayloft, *n. hay*-loft, a loft for hay in a barn.
haymaker, *n. hay*-make-er, one who makes hay; a machine for making or tossing hay.
haymaking, *n. hay*-make-ing, the work of cutting grass and curing it for fodder.
hay-mow, *n.* a mass of hay in a barn; a hay-rick.
hay-rick, *n.* a shaped mass of hay in the open air for preservation.
haystack, *n. hay*-stak, a large thatched hay-rick.
hayward, *n. hay*-ward, a former parish official in charge of commons and enclosures.
haywire, *n. hay*-wire, wire used for binding hay; a tangle of this when discarded [U.S.A.]; anything amiss or uncontrollable. **to go haywire,** to become completely disorganized or out of hand; to run amok [Coll.].
hazard, *n. haz*-ard, chance; accident; risk; a game with dice: a stroke at billiards, etc. in which a ball is potted; any part of a golf-course subject to a restriction: *v.t.* to expose to chance; to risk: *v.i.* to try the chance; to run the risk. **at all hazards,** whatever the risk. **to hazard a guess, etc.,** to venture to make it. (Fr. *hasard.*)
hazardous, *a. haz*-ar-dus, that exposes to peril or danger of loss; dangerous; risky.
hazardously, *ad.* in a hazardous manner.
hazardousness, *n.* the state of being hazardous.
haze, *n.* haze, mistiness, generally due to dust or heat, which renders the air thick; mist; obscurity: *v.t.* to make hazy.
haze, *v.t.* haze, to punish or harass with unnecessary work [Naut.]; to annoy by practical joking; to rag [U.S.A. slang]. (O.Fr. *haser,* annoy.)
hazel, *n. hay*-zl, the small tree or shrub, *Corylus avellana,* bearing the hazel-nut; a reddish brown colour: *a.* of this colour, like the hazel-nut. **hazel-eyed,** having eyes of this colour. (A.S. *hæsel.*)
hazel-grouse *or* **hazel-hen,** *n.* the European ruffed grouse, *Bonasa betulina.*
hazelly, *a. hay*-zl-e, of a reddish brown colour like that of a hazel-nut.
hazel-nut, *n.* the nut or fruit of the hazel.
hazel-wort, *n. hay*-zl-wort, the stemless herb, *Asarum europæum*; asarabacca.
hazily, *ad. hay*-ze-le, obscurely; in a general and confused manner.
haziness, *n. hay*-ze-ness, the state of being hazy.
hazy, *a. hay*-ze, thick with haze; misty; mentally confused.
★**he,** hee, *pron. third pers. sing. masc.*: *n.* the man: in combination denoting of the male genders as *he-goat.* (A.S.)
★**head,** *n.* hed, the uppermost or the foremost part of anything, esp. that part of the body of a man or animal where are the brain, visage, etc.; fore part; top; source; a chief or leader; a headmaster; an individual; the place of honour or command; countenance; brain; understanding; spontaneous will or resolution; a promontory; height, culmination, or pitch; topic of discourse; froth on liquor; the capital of a column [Arch.]; available steam-, water-, or other pressure; freedom from restraint; a headache [Coll.]: *v.t.* to lead; to act as leader to; to go in front of; to furnish with a head; to strike with the head; to oppose [Naut.]: *v.i.* to form a head; to go, point, or tend in a certain direction: *a.* principal; coming from the front, as a head wind. **head and ears,** wholly. **head and shoulders,** by force; far. **head voice,** the higher notes in a singer's range [Mus.]. **to go over the head of,** to take action without the knowledge of (the person concerned). (A.S. *heafod.*)
headache, *n. hed*-ake, pain in the head.
headachy, *a. hed*-ay-ke, with a headache.
headband, *n. hed*-band, a band for the head, as ornament, or for connecting earphones, etc.; the band at top and bottom of the spine of a book.
headborough, *n. hed*-bu-ro, the chief of a tithing; a petty constable.
head-cheese, *n.* brawn; parts of the head or feet of swine, cooked, chopped, and pressed [Amer.].
head-dress, *n.* a covering or ornament for the head.
headed, *a. hed*-ed, with a head; having understanding, as clear-headed, thick-headed, etc.
header, *n. hed*-er, one who puts heads on anything; a dive head-foremost; a brick laid lengthwise across a wall.
headfast, *n. hed*-fahst, a rope at the head of a ship with which to make fast [Naut.].
head-first, *ad.* with the head foremost; precipitately.
headgear, *n. hed*-geer, covering for the head; the framework supporting the winding wheels of a mine.
headhunter, *n. hed*-hunt-er, a member of a tribe practising headhunting.
headhunting, *n. hed*-hunt-ing, the practice of procuring and keeping the heads of enemies, formerly prevalent among the Dyaks of Borneo.
headily, *ad. hed*-e-le, hastily; impetuously; in a heady manner.
headiness, *n. hed*-e-ness, the quality of being heady.
heading, *n. hed*-ing, the action of the verb *to head*; that which stands at the head; a headline; material for the head of a cask; an adit [Mining];

taking a ball with the head [Football]. **heading course,** a visible course of bricks made up of headers [Building].

headlamp, *n. hed*-lamp, a headlight.

headland, *n. hed*-land, a promontory; a strip of unploughed land at the ends of furrows or near a fence.

headless, *a. hed*-less, without a head; without a leader; without prudence or consideration; lacking in brains.

headlight, *n. hed*-lite, a powerful light carried at the front of a locomotive, motor-car, etc.; a light at the masthead [Naut.].

headline, *n. hed*-lyne, line at the head of a chapter, page, column, or paragraph; a prominently displayed heading [Print.]: *v.t.* to provide with a headline.

headlong, *ad. hed*-long, head-foremost; without thinking; hastily; *a.* precipitous; precipitate.

headman, *n. hed*-man, chief; leader; chief man.

headmaster, *n.* hed-*mahs*-ter, the chief master of a school, the principal.

headmistress, *n.* hed-*mis*-tress, the chief mistress of a school.

headmoney, *n. hed*-mun-ne, a capitation tax; prize-money for the capture of a wanted person.

headmost, *a. hed*-mohst, most advanced; furthest forward.

headnote, *n. hed*-note, a note at the head of a page or chapter.

head-on, *a.* with the head to the front; facing (esp. of collisions): *ad.* from diametrically opposite directions.

headphone, *n. hed*-fone, a receiver of a telephone or wireless set to fix to the head; an earphone.

headpiece, *n. hed*-peece, armour for the head; the head [Coll.]; a headstall; an engraving at the head of a page or chapter.

headquarters, *n.pl.* hed-*kwor*-terz, the quarters of the commander-in-chief of an army; the centre of administration or authority; a chief office. **headquarters staff,** the staff of the commander-in-chief of an army.

headrest, *n. hed*-rest, a support for the head to rest on.

head-room, *n.* space under an arch, etc. to allow of passage beneath.

headship, *n. hed*-ship, the rank, dignity, or office of a head; supreme authority.

headsman, *n. hedz*-man, an executioner.

headspring, *n. hed*-spring, the main source.

headstall, *n. hed*-stawl, a bridle without the bit; a halter.

headstock, *n. hed*-stok, the part of a machine supporting a revolving part, esp. of a lathe that holds the spindle.

headstone, *n. hed*-stone, the stone at the head of a grave. **head stone,** the principal stone; the corner stone.

headstrong, *a. hed*-strong, obstinately self-willed.

headstrongness, *n.* the quality or condition of being headstrong; obstinacy.

headway, *n. hed*-way, motion ahead; progress or rate of progress; head-room.

head-wind, *n. hed*-wind, a contrary wind.

headwork, *n. hed*-wurk, mental or intellectual labour; an ornamental keystone [Arch.].

heady, *a. hed*-e, rash; precipitate; impetuous; affecting the head; intoxicating.

heal, *v.t.* heel, to cure; to restore to health: *v.i.* to grow sound, whole, or healthy. (A.S. *hælan.*)

healable, *a. heel*-a-bl, that may be healed.

heald, *n.* heeld, a heddle.

healer, *n. heel*-er, he who or that which heals.

healing, *a. heel*-ing, tending to heal; mollifying.

healingly, *ad. heel*-ing-le, in a healing manner.

health, *n.* helth, wholeness or soundness of body or of mind, a state in which each organ performs its proper function and acts in harmony with every other; physical condition; a toast wishing prosperity, etc. (A.S. *hælth.*)

healthful, *a. helth*-ful, promoting health; wholesome; edifying; salubrious.

healthfully, *ad. helth*-ful-le, in a healthful manner.

healthfulness, *n.* state of being healthful.

healthily, *ad. helth*-e-le, in a healthy manner.

healthiness, *n. helth*-e-ness, state of being healthy.

★**healthy,** *a. helth*-e, in a sound state; conducive to health; salubrious.

heap, *n.* heep, a mass of things thrown into a pile; a collection; a crowd; a quantity: *v.t.* to throw or lay in a heap; to accumulate. **all of a heap,** in confusion; overwhelmed; flabbergasted [Coll.]. (A.S.)

heapy, *a. heep*-e, lying in heaps; full of heaps.

hear, *v.t.* heer, to perceive by the ear; to listen to; to obey; to attend to and regard; to grant an answer to prayer: *v.i.* to have the sense of hearing; to attend; to receive by report. *p.* and *pp.* **heard,** herd. (A.S. *hieran.*)

hearable, *a. heer*-a-bl, that can be heard.

hearer, *n. heer*-er, one who hears; one of an audience.

★**hearing,** *n. heer*-ing, the act of perceiving sound; the sense by which it is perceived; attention; opportunity to be heard; judicial trial; the range of the ear.

hearken, *v.i. hark*-en, to listen; to attend with eagerness or curiosity to what is uttered; to hark.

hearkener, *n. hark*-ner, a listener.

hearsay, *n. heer*-say, anything heard or overheard; evidence at second hand; rumour; common talk: *a.* on the mere testimony of others.

hearse, *n.* herse, a carriage for conveying a corpse to the grave; a framework supporting a pall: *v.t.* to carry or enclose in a hearse. (Fr. *herse.*)

hearsecloth, *n. herse*-kloth, a pall.

hearselike, *a. herse*-like, suitable to a funeral.

★**heart,** *n.* hart, the muscular organ, situated in the thorax, the rhythmic contraction and dilatation of which determines the circulation of the blood; the core or inner part of anything; the chief or vital part; the seat of the affections and passions, or of the understanding or the will; the moral sense; secret purpose; love; courage; spirit; disposition of mind; efficacy; anything shaped like a heart; *pl.* a suit of cards marked with red conventional hearts. **at heart,** at bottom. **to find in the heart,** to be willing or disposed. **to get** or **learn by heart,** to commit to memory. **to have in the heart,** to purpose. **to set the heart at rest,** to make oneself quiet. **to set the heart on,** to fix the desires on. **to take** or **lay to heart,** to be much affected. (A.S. *heorte.*)

heartache, *n. hart*-ake, anguish of mind; sorrow.

heart-breaking, *a.* causing, or afflicted by, overwhelming sorrow.

heart-broken, *a. hart*-bro-ken, crushed with grief.

heartburn, *n. hart*-burn, a burning sensation in the digestive tract due to indigestion; cardialgia.

heart-burning, *a. hart*-burn-ing, distressing the heart: *n.* discontent; enmity.

heart-disease, *n.* any morbid or abnormal condition of the heart.

hearted, *a. har*-ted, having a heart, as *sound-hearted, hard-hearted.*

hearten, *v.t. har*-tn, to encourage; to animate: *v.i.* to take courage.

heartfelt, *a. hart*-felt, deeply felt or affecting.

hearth, *n.* harth, part of the floor on which a fire is made; the lowest part of a blast furnace or of a smith's forge; the part of a reverbatory furnace in which the ore is exposed to the flames; the fireside; the home; the family circle. (A.S. *heorth.*)

hearth-money, *n.* a tax on hearths.

hearth-rug, *n.* a rug laid in front of the fender.

hearthstone, *n. harth*-stone, stone forming the hearth; friable sandstone for cleaning hearths, etc.

heartily, *ad. har*-te-le, sincerely; cordially.

heartiness, *n. har*-te-ness, the state of being hearty.

heartless, *a. hart*-less, without heart; without feeling; without courage; unfeeling; cruel.

heartlessly, *ad. hart*-less-le, in a heartless manner.

heartlessness, *n.* the state of being heartless.

heartlet, *n. hart*-let, a little heart.

heart-rending, *a.* heart-breaking; deeply afflictive.

heart's-blood, *n.* the blood of the heart; life; life-blood; essence.

heartsease, *n. harts*-eez, a species of violet, the wild pansy or love-in-idleness; peace of mind.

heart-sick, *a.* deeply despondent; much afflicted.

heartsome, *a. hart*-sum, cheering; cheerful; lively.

heart-strings, *n.pl.* the deepest affections.

heart-to-heart, *a.* unreserved; frank; outspoken.

heartwater, *n. hart*-waw-ter, a dangerous infection of livestock in S. Africa transmitted by the tick, *Amblyomma hebræum.*

heart-whole, *a.* not, or not deeply, in love ; sincere.
heart-wood, *n.* the hard central part of the trunk of a tree.
hearty, *a. har*-te, proceeding from the heart ; good-natured ; sincere ; open and free ; healthy ; strong ; having a keen appetite : *n.* a good fellow ; a bluff and jovial man ; one given to sport rather than study [Univ. slang].
★**heat,** *n.* heet, the sensation produced by a hot body ; that in the body which causes the sensation ; warm temperature ; warmest time ; pungency of flavour ; sexual excitement in animals in the breeding season ; utmost violence ; ardour ; exasperation ; a division of competitors, the winner of which qualifies for the next round [Sports] : *v.t.* to make hot ; to make feverish ; to agitate ; to excite : *v.i.* to grow hot. (A.S. *hætu.*)
heat-apoplexy, *n.* sunstroke.
heated, *a. hee*-ted, warmed or made hot ; animated, with passion [Fig.].
heater, *n. hee*-ter, one who or that which heats ; any thing or apparatus for heating, as a stove, radiator, piece of iron heated and inclosed in a box, etc.
heath, *n.* heeth, a plant of the genus *Erica* ; a tract of waste land ; a moor. (A.S. *hæth.*)
heath-cock, *n.* the blackcock, *Tetrao tetrix,* a species of grouse which frequents heaths.
heathen, *n. hee*-then, one who is neither Christian, Moslem, nor Jew ; a rude, barbarous, irreligious person : *a.* pagan ; without the knowledge or fear of God ; barbarous. (A.S. *hæthen.*)
heathendom, *n. hee*-then-dom, the lands where heathenism prevails ; heathens collectively.
heathenish, *a. hee*-then-ish, belonging to pagans ; idolatrous ; rude ; barbarous.
heathenishly, *ad.* after the manner of heathens.
heathenishness, *n.* state of being heathenish.
heathenism, *n. hee*-then-izm, the religious and moral state or practices of the heathen.
heathenize, *v.t. hee*-then-ize, to render heathen.
heathenry, *n. hee*-then-re, heathendom ; heathenism.
heather, *n. heth*-er, the common heath of the genus *Calluna* ; the ling.
heather-ale, *n.* a strong liquor formerly brewed from or flavoured with flowers of the heather.
heather-bell, *n.* the cross-leaved heather ; a blossom of the heath.
heather-mixture, *n.* a woollen cloth of speckled or mixed colour.
heathery, *a. heth*-er-re, abounding in heather.
heath-pea, *n.* a species of bitter vetch.
heath-pout, *n.* the female, or young, of the heath-cock.
heathy, *a. heeth*-e, abounding with heath ; resembling heath.
heating, *a. hee*-ting, imparting heat ; stimulating.
heat-spot, *n.* a freckle ; a small pimple.
heat-wave, *n.* a wave of radiant heat ; a period of high temperature passing on from one area to another.
heaume, *n.* home, a large heavy helmet.
heave, *n.* heev, an effort upward ; a rising swell or distention ; a throw ; an effort to vomit : *v.t.* to lift up ; to raise ; to cause to swell ; to force from the breast ; to throw ; to hoist : *v.i.* to swell, distend, or dilate ; to pant ; to make an effort to vomit. **to heave down,** to careen [Naut.]. **to heave in sight,** to appear [Naut.]. **to heave out,** to throw out. **to heave to,** to bring the ship's head to the wind, and stop her motion [Naut.]. (A.S. *hebban.*)
heaven, *n. hev*-en, the sky ; the place of the immediate divine presence ; the home of the blessed ; the powers above ; supreme felicity. **tree of heaven,** *see* **tree.** (A.S. *heofon.*)
heaven-born, *a.* sent by heaven ; inspired.
heaven-directed, *a.* pointing to the sky ; guided by the celestial powers.
heavenliness, *n.* the quality of being heavenly.
heavenly, *a. hev*-en-le, pertaining to heaven ; as in heaven ; supremely excellent : *ad.* in a manner like that of heaven ; by the influence of heaven. **heavenly bodies,** the sun, moon, and stars. **heavenly host,** the angels.
heavenly-minded, *a. hev*-en-le-*myn*-ded, having the affections placed on heavenly things.
heavenward, *ad. hev*-en-ward, towards heaven.
heaver, *n. hee*-ver, one who or that which heaves or lifts, as a coal-heaver ; a dock-labourer.
heaves, *n.* heevz, broken wind, a disease of horses.
heavies, *n.pl. hev*-iz, heavy cavalry, esp. the Dragoon Guards ; heavy artillery.
heavily, *ad. hev*-e-le, weightily ; grievously.
heaviness, *n. hev*-e-ness, weight ; sorrow.
Heaviside-layer, *n. hev*-e-side-*lay*-er, an ionized stratum in the upper atmosphere that reflects wireless waves back. (O. *Heaviside, d.* 1925, Engl. physicist.)
heavy, *a. hev*-e, weighty ; ponderous ; sad ; downcast ; distressing ; oppressive ; dull ; drowsy ; indolent ; slow ; wearisome ; loaded ; not easy to digest ; clayey ; difficult ; large and swelling ; large in amount ; dense ; not well leavened (of bread) ; loud : *ad.* with great weight. **heavy water,** water in which the hydrogen is the heavy isotope of at.wt. 2 ; deuterium oxide (D_2O). (A.S. *hefig.*)
heavy, *a. hee*-ve, affected with heaves (of horses).
heavy-handed, *a.* not dexterous ; oppressive.
heavy-laden, *a.* laden with a heavy burden ; sorely oppressed.
heavy-spar, *n. hev*-e-spar, barytes.
heavy-weight, *n. hev*-e-wayt, any person or animal of more than average weight ; a boxer weighing not less than 158 lb.
hebdomadal, *a.* heb-*dom*-a-dal, consisting of seven days ; occurring weekly. (L. *hebdomadalis.*)
hebdomadary, *a.* heb-*dom*-a-da-re, hebdomadal : *n.* a member of a chapter or convent whose week it is to officiate.
Hebe, *n. hee*-be, the goddess of youth, cupbearer to the gods [Myth.] ; a barmaid. (Gr., youth.)
hebetant, *a. heb*-e-tant, making blunt or dull.
hebetate, *v.t. heb*-e-tate, to make dull ; to blunt ; to stupefy. (L. *hebetatus,* blunted.)
hebetation, *n.* heb-e-*tay*-shon, the act of making blunt, dull, or stupid ; the state of being so.
hebetic, *a.* he-*bet*-ik, pertaining to or occurring at puberty [Med.].
hebetude, *n. heb*-e-tewd, dulness ; stupidity.
Hebraic, *a.* he-*bray*-ik, pertaining to the Hebrews, their manner of thinking, or their language ; characteristic of the Jews.
Hebraically, *ad.* he-*bray*-e-ka-le, after the Hebrew manner.
Hebraism, *n. hee*-bray-izm, a Hebrew characteristic or idiom ; Judaism ; Hebrew institutions.
Hebraist, *n. hee*-bray-ist, one versed in the Hebrew language and learning ; an adherent of Judaism.
Hebraistic, *a. hee*-bray-*is*-tik, Hebraic.
Hebraize, *v.t. hee*-bray-ize, to convert into the Hebrew idiom ; to make Hebrew : *v.i.* to speak Hebrew, or to conform to Hebrew institutions or idiom.
Hebrew, *n. he*-broo, a Jew ; the ancient Jewish language : *a.* pertaining to the Hebrews. (Aramaic *hebrai,* an immigrant.)
Hebridean, *a.* heb-re-*dee*-an *or* he-*brid*-e-an, pertaining to the Hebrides ; *n.* a native of the Hebrides.
hecatomb, *n. hek*-a-toom, the sacrifice of a large number of victims, literally a hundred ; any great sacrifice or slaughter. (Gr.)
heck, *n.* hek, a grating for catching fish, or for keeping them back ; a rack for holding fodder ; a door latch. (A.S. *hæce,* hatch.)
heckle, *v.t. hek*-kl, to comb ; to dress flax or hemp ; to worry with awkward questions. (M.E. *hachele.*)
heckler, *n. hek*-kler, one who heckles ; a political opponent who asks embarrassing questions.
heckymal, *n. hek*-e-mal, the blue tit, *Parus obscurus.*
hectare, *n. hek*-tair, a metric measure containing 100 ares, or 2·471 English acres.
hectic, *a. hek*-tik, constitutional ; pertaining to or affected with hectic fever ; consumptively feverish ; wildly exciting [Coll.] : *n.* hectic fever, a remittent fever attendant on consumption ; one suffering from this ; a consumptive. (Fr. *hectique,* from Gr. *hexis,* habit of body.)
hectically, *ad. hek*-te-ka-le, in a hectic manner.
hectocotylus, *n. hek*-to-*kot*-e-lus, a modified arm serving as a reproductive organ in cuttle-fish and other cephalopods.
hectogramme, *n. hek*-to-gram, a metric weight containing 100 grammes, or 3·527 oz. (Gr. *hekaton,* a hundred, and *gramme.*)

hectograph, *n.* *hek*-to-graf, an apparatus for duplicating copies from a gelatine pad: *v.t.* to duplicate by means of this. (Gr. *hekaton*, and *grapho*, write.)
hectolitre, *n.* *hek*-to-lee-ter, a metric measure of capacity containing 100 litres, or 22 gallons. (Gr. *hekaton*, and *litre*.)
hectometre, *n.* *hek*-to-mee-ter, a metric measure of 100 metres, or approx. 328 English feet. (Gr. *hekaton*, and *metron*, measure.)
hector, *n.* *hek*-tor, a bully; one who teases or vexes: *v.t.* to bully; to treat with insolence; to torment by words: *v.i.* to play the bully. (Gr. *Hector*, of Troy.)
hectorly, *a.* *hek*-tor-le, blustering; insolent.
hectostere, *n.* *hek*-to-steer, a metric solid measure of 100 cubic metres, or 130·8 cubic yards.
heddle, *n.* *hed*-dl, the loop that works a warp thread. (A.S. *hefeld*.)
hederaceous, *a.* *hed*-e-*ray*-shus, pertaining to or resembling ivy. (L. *hedera*, ivy.)
hederiferous, *a.* *hed*-e-*rif*-er-rus, producing ivy.
hedge, *n.* hedj, a line of bushes fencing a field, etc.: a barrier: *v.t.* to fence with or separate by a hedge; to surround; to guard against loss by betting both ways: *v.i.* to cut or repair hedges; to hide, as in a hedge; to skulk; to trim or prevaricate. (A.S *hecg*.)
hedge-bill, *n.* a cutting hook for dressing hedges.
hedge-born, *a.* of low, illegitimate, or obscure birth.
hedge-creeper, *n.* one who skulks under hedges; a sneaking vagabond.
hedge-garlic, *n.* garlic mustard, the cruciferous plant *Sisymbrium alliaria*.
hedgehog, *n.* *hedj*-hog, an insectivorous mammal, *Erinaceus europæus*, the upper part of whose body is covered with spines; applied also to certain fish, etc. with spines; a strongly fortified outpost in enemy country [Mil.]; an irritable person [Fig.].
hedgehog-thistle, *n.* a popular name for plants of the genus *Echinocactus*.
hedge-hopping, *n.* flying so low as apparently only just to clear the hedges [Airmen's slang].
hedge-hyssop, *n.* a bitter herb of the genus *Gratiola*, or *Scutellaria minor*.
hedge-marriage, *n.* a secret or irregular marriage.
hedge-mustard, *n.* the cruciferous plant, *Sisymbrium officinale*.
hedge-priest, *n.* a poor, bogus, or uneducated priest.
hedger, *n.* *hedj*-er, one who makes or trims hedges.
hedgerow, *n.* *hedj*-roh, a row or series of shrubs or trees planted for the enclosure or separation of fields.
hedge-school, *n.* a poor country school such as was formerly held in the open.
hedge-sparrow, *n.* the small passerine warbler, *Accentor modularis*.
hedonic, *a.* he-*don*-ik, pertaining to or consisting in pleasure; professing hedonism: *n.pl.* the branch of ethics treating of the relation between duty and pleasure.
hedonism, *n.* *hee*-do-nizm, the doctrine that pleasure or happiness is the chief good and chief end of man; devotion to pleasure. (Gr. *hedone*, pleasure.)
hedonist, *n.* *hee*-do-nist, an adherent of hedonism; one who lives a life of pleasure: *a.* hedonistic.
hedonistic, *a.* *hee*-do-*nis*-tik, pertaining to or characterized by hedonism.
hedonology, *n.* *hee*-do-*nol*-o-je, hedonics.
heed, *n.* heed, care; attention; caution: *v.t.* to regard with care; to take notice of; to attend to. (A.S. *hedan*.)
heedful, *a.* *heed*-ful, attentive; observant; cautious.
heedfully, *ad.* *heed*-ful-le, in a heedful manner.
heedfulness, *n.* the state of being heedful.
heedless, *a.* *heed*-less, inattentive; thoughtless.
heedlessly, *ad.* *heed*-less-le, in a heedless manner.
heedlessness, *n.* the state of being heedless.
heehaw, *n.* *hee*-haw, the bray of an ass; a loud and empty guffaw: *v.i.* to make such a sound. (Imit.)
heel, *n.* heel, the hind part of the foot, or of a covering for the foot; a built-up block forming part of a shoe, etc. and raising its hinder end; a heel-shaped protuberance, knob, or part; the after end of anything; the end: *v.t.* to add a heel to; to kick backwards; to arm a cock with spurs: *v.i.* to dance. **be at the heels,** to pursue closely. **heel of Achilles,** the one vulnerable spot. **down at heel,** shabby; in poor circumstances. **have the heels of,** to outrun. **Heel and toe,** walking as distinct from running. **lay by the heels,** to seize and hold. **show,** or **take to the heels,** to betake to flight. (A.S. *hela*.)
heel, *v.i.* heel, to lean on one side: *v.t.* to cause (a ship) to do this. (A.S. *hyldan*, to incline.)
heel-ball, *n.* a mixture of wax and lamp-black used by shoemakers, and for taking rubbings of brasses, etc.
heel-piece, *n.* a piece of leather on a shoe-heel; armour for the heel; a finishing piece.
heel-tap, *n.* a single layer of leather in a shoe-heel; liquor left in a glass.
heft, *n.* heft, the act of heaving; a lift; an effort. (As *heave*.)
heft, *n.* heft, a haft.
heftily, *ad.* *hef*-te-le, strongly; vigorously.
heftiness, *n.* *hef*-te-ness, strength; vigour.
hefty, *a.* *hef*-te, strong; vigorous.
Hegelian, *a.* he-*gee*-le-an, pertaining to Hegel or his philosophy: *n.* one who accepts this philosophy.
Hegelianism, *n.* he-*gee*-le-an-izm, the philosophical system of the German philosopher G. F. W. Hegel (*d.* 1831), which resolves being into thought, as primarily unconsciously implicit in Nature, and finally explicit in the self-consciousness of man.
hegemonic, *a.* hej-e-*mon*-ik, ruling; predominant; pertaining to or exercising hegemony.
hegemony, *n.* *hej*-e-mon-e, *or* he-*jem*-o-ne, leadership; preponderating power. (Gr. *hegemonia*).
Hegira, *n.* *hej*-e-rah, the flight of Mohammed, commemorated on 16 July, A.D. 622, the date from which the Mohammedan era begins; any precipitate flight. (Ar., separation.)
heifer, *n.* *hef*-er, a young cow. (A.S. *heahfore*.)
heigh, *int.* hay, an expression of encouragement.
heigh-ho, *int.* hay-hoh, an expression of surprise or weariness.
height, *n.* hite, elevation above the ground; the altitude of an object; stature; an eminence; elevation in excellence or rank; highest degree; the top. (A.S. *hiehthu*.)
heighten, *v.t.* *hite*-en, to raise higher; to advance; to improve; to increase; to exaggerate; to emphasize; to make prominent by touches of light or brilliant colours [Paint.].
heinous, *a.* *hay*-nus, characterized by great wickedness; hateful; atrocious. (Fr. *haineux*.)
heinously, *ad.* *hay*-nus-le, in a heinous manner.
heinousness, *n.* the quality of being heinous.
heir, *n.* air, one who succeeds, or is to succeed another, in the possession of a property by descent; one who inherits; one entitled to possess. **heir apparent, presumptive,** *see* these words. **heir at law,** a legal heir, as distinct from a legatee, etc. (O.Fr.)
heirdom, *n.* *air*-dom, succession by inheritance; an inheritance; condition of an heir.
heiress, *n.* *air*-ess, a female heir.
heirless, *a.* *air*-less, destitute of an heir.
heirloom, *n.* *air*-loom, any chattel which descends with the estate to the heir [Law]; anything that has belonged to a family for some generations.
heirship, *n.* *air*-ship, the state or rights of an heir; right of inheriting.
Hejira, *n.* *hej*-e-ra *or* he-*jire*-ra, the Hegira.
helcoid, *a.* *hel*-koyd, resembling an ulcer; ulcerous. (Gr. *helkos*, ulcer, *eidos*, like.)
helcology, *n.* hel-*kol*-o-je, the branch of pathology dealing with ulcers.
helcosis, *n.* hel-*koh*-sis, ulceration [Med.].
held, held, *p.* and *pp.* of *hold*.
heliacal, *a.* he-*ly*-a-kal, close to the sun; emerging from or passing into the sun's light. (Gr. *helios*, the sun.)
heliacally, *ad.* he-*ly*-a-ka-le, in a heliacal manner.
Helianthemum, *n.* *hee*-le-*an*-the-mum, the rock-rose genus of plants.
Helianthus, *n.* *hee*-le-*an*-thus, the sun-flower genus of plants. (Gr. *helios*, and *anthos*, a flower.)
helical, *a.* *hel*-e-kal, spiral; like or pertaining to a helix. **helical gears,** gear-wheels in which the teeth are set at an angle with the wheel axis. (Gr. *helix*, a spiral.)
heliciform, *a.* hel-*lis*-e-form, shaped like a snail's shell; spirally wound.
helicoid, *a.* *hel*-e-koyd, spiral; screw-shaped;

coiled like a flat spring [Biol.]: *n.* a geometrical spirally curved figure. (Gr. *helikocides.*)
helicon, *n. hel*-e-kon, a bass brass wind-instrument used in military bands.
Heliconian, *a.* hel-e-*koh*-ne-an, pertaining to Helicon, the sacred seat of the Muses, or to the Muses themselves. (*Helicon*, a mountain in Bœotia.)
helicopter, *n.* hel-e-*kop*-ter, an aircraft supported by propellers that rotate round a vertical axis, driving a stream of air down-wards and giving the machine a hovering flight. (Gr. *helikos*, and *pteron*, wing.)
heliocentric, *a. hee*-le-o-*sen*-trik, as seen from the sun's centre. (Gr. *helios*, and *centre.*)
heliochrome, *n. hee*-le-o-krome, a photograph taken by heliochromy.
heliochromoscope, *n. hee*-le-o-*kroh*-mo-skope, a photographic instrument for producing pictures in natural colour.
heliochromy, *n.* hee-le-*ok*-ro-me, the process of obtaining photographs in natural colours; colour photography. (Gr. *helios*, and *chroma*, colour.)
heliogram, *n. hee*-le-o-gram, a message flashed by heliograph.
heliograph, *n. hee*-le-o-graf, a signalling instrument which acts by flashing the sun's rays from a mirror; a photograph or photo-engraving; an instrument for photographing the sun; a photograph of the sun: *v.i.* to signal with a heliograph.
heliographic, *a. hee*-le-o-*graf*-ik, pertaining to heliography or to the heliograph.
heliographically, *ad.* by means of the heliograph.
heliography, *n. hee*-le-*og*-ra-fe, the geographical description of the sun; the art of signalling by heliograph; a process of photo-engraving. (Gr. *helios*, and *grapho*, write.)
heliogravure, *n. hee*-le-o-gra-*vewr*, photo-engraving by heliography; a print so obtained.
heliolater, *n. hee*-le-*ol*-a-ter, a sun-worshipper.
heliolatry, *n. hee*-le-*ol*-a-tre, the worship of the sun. (Gr. *helios*, and *latreia*, worship.)
heliology, *n. hee*-le-*ol*-o-je, the science or study of the sun. (Gr. *helios* and *logos.*)
heliometer, *n. hee*-le-*om*-e-ter, an instrument for measuring the angular distances in the celestial sphere. (Gr. *helios* and *metron.*)
heliophilous, *a. hee*-le-*of*-e-lus, attracted by or bending towards the sun [Bot.].
helioscope, *n. hee*-le-o-skope, a reflecting telescope for viewing the sun. (Gr. *helios*, and *skopeo*, view.)
heliosis, *n.* hee-le-*oh*-sis, sunstroke; the production of discolorations on leaves by the action of the sun [Bot.]. (Gr. *heliosmai*, suffer from sunstroke.)
heliostat, *n. hee*-le-o-stat, a mirror on a clockwork stand for directing a sunbeam continuously to the same spot; a surveying instrument in which the sun's rays are reflected by a mirror. (Gr. *helios*, and *statos*, fixed.)
heliotherapy, *n. hee*-le-o-*the*-ra-pe, treatment by exposure to the action of sunlight [Med.].
heliotrope, *n. hee*-le-o-trope, the sunflower, or any of several plants, whose flowers turn with the sun, among them being the cherry-pie, *Heliotropium peruvianum*; the purplish colour, or a perfume, reminiscent of this; a siliceous mineral, the bloodstone. (Gr. *heliotropion*, sundial.)
heliotropic, *a. hee*-le-o-*trop*-ik, pertaining to heliotropism; turning towards the light.
heliotropism, *n.* hee-le-*ot*-ro-pizm, the turning of a growing plant towards the light.
heliotype, *n. hee*-le-o-tipe, a method of printing photographs from a gelatine surface; a print so obtained. (Gr. *helios*, and *typos*, an impression.)
helium, *n. hee*-le-um, an inert, non-inflammable, gaseous element, first discovered (1868) in the sun's atmosphere, and because of its buoyancy used in balloons. (Gr. *helios*, sun.)
helix, *n. hee*-liks (*pl.* **helices,** *hel*-e-seez), a spiral line, as of wire in a coil; a spiral ornament [Arch.]; the external margin of the ear [Anat.]; (*cap.*) the largest genus of land snails [Zool.]. (Gr.)
hell, *n.* hel, the place of the dead, or of souls after death; the place of punishment for the wicked after death; the infernal powers; a haunt of vice, esp. a gambling house; used also as an imprecation, as **hell's bells! what the hell! hell for leather,** at top speed [Coll.]. (A.S.)
hellbender, *n. hel*-ben-der, the menopome, a voracious N. American salamander.

hell-broth, *n.* something concocted for an evil or a magical purpose.
hell-cat, *n. hel*-kat, a hag; a witch.
hellebore, *n. hel*-le-bore, any plant of the genus *Helleborus*, as the Christmas rose. (O.Fr. *ellebore.*)
helleborine, *n. hel*-e-bo-reen, an orchid of the genus *Epipactis*. **white helleborine,** an orchid of the genus *Cephalamthera*.
Hellene, *n.* he-*leen or hel*-leen, an ancient Greek of pure race; a modern Greek subject.
Hellenic, *a.* he-*len*-ik, pertaining to the Hellenes, or inhabitants of Greece.
Hellenism, *n. hel*-len-izm, a Greek idiom; Greek culture; the taste for Greek literature and art. (Gr. *Hellenismos.*)
Hellenist, *n. hel*-len-ist, one skilled in the Greek language and literature; one of another nation, esp. a Jew, who adopted the customs, etc. of the ancient Greeks.
Hellenistic, *a.* hel-len-*is*-tik, derived from or pertaining to the Hellenists; pertaining to Greek culture of the period after Alexander the Great.
Hellenize, *v.i. hel*-len-ize, to use the Greek language or customs, etc.: *v.t.* to give a Greek character to.
heller, *n. hel*-er, Hungarian money of account, one-hundredth part of a gulder.
hellhound, *n. hel*-hound, an agent of hell.
hellish, *a. hel*-lish, pertaining to hell; inspired by hell; extremely wicked.
hellishly, *ad. hel*-lish-le, in a hellish manner.
hellishness, *n. hel*-lish-ness, extreme wickedness.
hello, *int. hel*-lo, hallo; hullo.
helm, *n.* helm, the tiller, wheel, or other apparatus by which a rudder is worked; place of direction or management. (A.S. *helma.*)
helm, *n.* helm, a helmet. (A.S.)
helmet, *n. hel*-met, armour for the head; a representation of this bearing the crest [Her.]; a domed metal hat worn as a protection at fires, during air-raids, and by soldiers, police, etc.; a policeman's head-dress; a light hat of pith, etc., worn as protection against the sun; the hooded upper lip of some flowers [Bot.]. (A.S.)
helmeted, *a. hel*-met-ed, furnished with a helmet.
helminth, *n. hel*-minth, an intestinal worm. (Gr. *helmins.*)
helminthagogue, *n.* hel-*min*-tha-gog, a medicine to expel parasitic worms. (Gr. *helmins*, worm, *ago*, drive.)
helminthiasis, *n.* hel-min-*thy*-a-sis, any disease in which internal parasitic worms are present [Med.].
helminthic, *a.* hel-*min*-thik, relating to parasitic worms; expelling worms: *n.* a vermifuge.
helminthoid, *a.* hel-*min*-thoyd, worm-shaped. (Gr.)
helminthological, *a.* hel-*min*-tho-*loj*-e-kal, pertaining to helminthology.
helminthologist, *n.* hel-min-*thol*-o-jist, one who is versed in helminthology.
helminthology, *n.* hel-min-*thol*-o-je, the study of worms. (Gr. *helmins*, and *logos*, science.)
helminthous, *a.* hel-*min*-thus, infested with parasitic worms [Med.].
helmless, *a. helm*-less, without a helm.
helmsman, *n. helmz*-man, a steersman.
heloderm, *n.* hee-lo-*derm*, one of the *Heloderma*, the genus of venomous lizards that includes the gila monster. (Gr. *helos*, nail, *derma*, skin.)
heloma, *n.* he-*loh*-ma, a corn [Med.].
helot, *n. hel*-ot, a slave in ancient Sparta; a slave or serf. (L. *Helotae.*)
helotism, *n. hel*-o-tizm, Spartan slavery; the system of serfdom.
helotomy, *n.* he-*lot*-o-me, corn cutting [Med.].
helotry, *n. hel*-ot-re, helots collectively; serfs.
★**help,** *n.* help, aid; assistance; that which gives assistance; remedy; a hired servant: *v.t.* to aid; to assist; to lend strength or means toward effecting a purpose; to relieve; to remedy; to share out; to carve and distribute; to prevent; to forbear: *v.i.* to lend aid; to contribute; to be of service. **help forward** or **on,** to advance by assistance. **help out,** to aid in delivering from difficulty, or in completing a design. **help over,** to enable to surmount. **help to,** to supply with. (A.S. *helpan.*)
helper, *n. help*-er, one who helps; an unskilled worker assisting a skilled.
helpful, *a. help*-ful, that gives help; useful.
helpfulness, *n.* assistance; usefulness.

helping, *n. help*-ing, a share; a portion of food.
helpless, *a. help*-less, without help in oneself; wanting help.
helplessly, *ad. help*-less-le, in a helpless manner.
helplessness, *n.* the state of being helpless.
helpmate, *n. help*-mate, a companion; a helper; a partner; a wife.
helpmeet, *n. help*-meet, a helpmate; a suitable help.
helter-skelter, *ad.* and *a. hel*-ter-*skel*-ter, in hurry and confusion: *n.* hurry; confusion.
helve, *n.* helv, the handle of a tool or weapon: *v.t.* to furnish with a helve. (A.S. *helfe.*)
helve-hammer, *n.* a ponderous power hammer for manufacturing wrought iron; a trip-hammer.
Helvetian, *a.* hel-*vee*-shan, Helvetic: *n.* one of the ancient Helvetic; a Swiss.
Helvetic, *a.* hel-*vet*-ik, pertaining to the Helvetii or inhabitants of Switzerland; Swiss. (L. *Helvetius.*)
hem, *n.* hem, the border of a garment, doubled and sewn to strengthen it; edge; border: *v.t.* to form a hem on; to edge. **to hem in,** to shut in; to enclose. (A.S.)
hem, *int.* hem, a sort of voluntary half cough: *v.i.* to utter the sound hem.
he-man, *n. hee*-man, a specially virile fellow; a bit of a thug [Coll.].
hemastatic, *a. hem*-a-*stat*-ik, hæmostatic.
hematin, *n. hem*-a-tin, hæmatin.
hematite, *n. hee*-ma-tite, hæmatite.
hematocele, *n. hem*-a-to-seel, a tumour filled with blood [Med.]. (Gr. *haima*, and *kele*, a tumour.)
hematosin, *n.* hem-a-*toh*-sin, hæmatosin.
hemeralopia, *n.* hem-e-ral-*oh*-pe-a, the abnormal condition in which the sight is better in a faint than in a good light [Med.].
hemi-, *hem*-e, a Greek prefix, signifying half.
hemianopia, *n.* hem-e-an-*oh*-pe-a, blindness affecting one half only of the field of vision [Med.].
hemicrania, *n. hem*-e-*kray*-ne-a, headache affecting only one side of the head. (Gr. *hemi-*, and *kranium*, the skull.)
hemicycle, *n. hem*-e-sy-kl, a semicircle; a semicircular space, room, etc. (Gr. *hemi-*, and *cycle.*)
hemigale, *n. hem*-e-gale, a small Malayan mammal allied to the civets and mongooses. (Gr. *hemi-*, half and *galē*, weasel.)
hemihedral, *a. hem*-e-*hee*-dral, having only half the normal number of faces (of crystals) [Min.]. (Gr. *hemi*, and *hedra*, a side.)
hemiplegia, *n. hem*-e-*plee*-je-a, paralysis limited to one half the body [Med.]. (Gr.)
Hemiptera, *n.pl.* he-*mip*-ter-ra (*sing.* **hemipteron**), the order of insects comprising the bugs, lice, etc., most of which have four wings, the upper being partly coriaceous, and partly membranous. (Gr. *hemi-*, and *pteron*, a wing.)
hemipteral, *a.* he-*mip*-ter-ral, hemipterous.
hemipterology, *n.* hem-ip-te-*rol*-o-je, the branch of entomology treating of the Hemiptera.
hemipterous, *n.* he-*mip*-ter-rus, pertaining to or resembling the Hemiptera.
hemisphere, *n. hem*-e-sfeer, half a sphere or globe, bisected by a plane passing through its centre; a map of half a sphere. (L. *hemisphærium.*)
hemispheric, *a.* hem-e-sfe-rik, hemispherical.
hemispherical, *a.* hem-e-sfe-re-kal, of the form of, or containing, half a sphere or globe.
hemistich, *n. hem*-e-stik, half a poetic verse, or a verse not completed. (L. *hemistichium.*)
hemistichal, *a.* hem-*is*-te-kal, pertaining to or of the nature of a hemistich.
hemitrope, *a. hem*-e-trope, of a twinned structure (of crystals): half turned round. (Gr. *hemi-*, and *tropos*, turn.)
hemitropic, *a.* hem-e-*trop*-ik, hemitrope [Cryst.].
hemlock, *n. hem*-lok, the poisonous umbelliferous plant, *Conium maculatum*; the poison yielded by this. (A.S. *hemlic.*)
hemlock-spruce, *n. hem*-lok-sprooce, the American tree, *Tsuga canadensis.*
hemmer, *n. hem*-mer, one who hems; the hemming attachment to a sewing-machine.
hemophilia, *n.* hem-o-*fil*-e-a, hæmophilia.
hemorrhage, *n. hem*-o-raj, hæmorrhage.
hemorrhoids, *n.pl. hem*-o-roydz, hæmorrhoids.
hemp, *n.* hemp, a plant of the genus *Cannabis*, whose fibre is used for cloth and cordage; the fibre, prepared for spinning; hashish. **hemp agrimony,** a composite plant, *Eupatorium cannabirium*, with coarse hemp-like foliage. (A.S. *henep.*)
hempen, *a. hemp*-en, made of hemp.
hemp-nettle, *n.* the annual labiate plant, *Galeopsis tetrahit.*
hempseed, *n. hemp*-seed, the seed of hemp; a candidate for the gallows [Coll.].
hempy, *a. hemp*-e, like hemp.
hemstitch, *n. hem*-stitch, a broad hem so stitched as to leave a row of holes along the inner edge: *v.t.* to hem in this way.
hen, *n.* hen, the female of any bird, but especially of the domestic fowl. (A.S.).
henbane, *n. hen*-bane, several species of herbs of the genus *Hyoscamus*, so called because *H. niger* is poisonous; the poison itself.
henbit, *n. hen*-bit, a species of dead nettle; one of the speedwells, *Veronica hederifolia.*
hence, *ad.* hence, from this place; from this time; in the future; from this source; consequently; for this reason: *int.* begone! be off! (A.S. *heonan.*)
henceforth, *ad. hence*-forth, from this time forward.
henceforward, *ad. hence*-for-ward, henceforth.
henchman, *n. hench*-man, a page; a servant. (A.S. *hengst*, horse, and *man.*)
hen-coop, *n.* a coop or cage for fowls.
hendecagon, *n.* hen-*dek*-a-gon, a plane figure of eleven sides and angles [Geom.]. (Gr. *hendeka*, eleven, *gonia*, an angle.)
hendecagynous, *a.* hen-de-*kaj*-e-nus, having eleven pistils [Bot.]. (Gr. *hendeka*, and *gyne*, female.)
hendecandrian, *a.* hen-de-*kan*-dre-an, having eleven stamens [Bot.]. (Gr. *hendeka*, and *aner*, a male.)
hendecaphyllous, *a.* hen-de-*kaf*-e-lus, having a compound leaf, with eleven leaflets [Bot.]. (Gr. *hendeka*, and *phyllon*, a leaf.)
hendecasyllable, *n.* hen-*dek*-a-*sil*-a-bl, a line of eleven syllables in poetry. (Gr.)
hendiadys, *n.* hen-*dy*-a-dis, a figure in which the idea is given by two nouns connected by a conjunction instead of by noun qualified by an adjective [Rhet.]. (Gr. *hen dia dyoin*, one by means of two.)
hen-driver, *n.* the hen-harrier.
henequen, *n. hen*-e-ken, sisal. (Sp. *jeniquen.*)
hen-harrier, *n.* the hawk, *Circus cyaneus.*
hen-house, *n.* a house or shelter for fowls.
henism, *n. hen*-izm, the doctrine that all things are of one kind (*e.g.*, mind, matter) only; monism. (Gr. *heis*, *henos*, one.)
hen-mould, *n.* black, spongy mould or soil.
henna, *n. hen*-na, a tropical shrub, *Lawsonia inermis*, cultivated in Egypt; a reddish-orange dye and cosmetic prepared from this. (Ar. *hinna.*)
hennery, *n. hen*-e-re, a poultry farm.
henotheism, *n.* hen-o-*thee*-izm, belief in one god without denying the existence of others. (Gr. *heis*, *henos*, one, and *theism.*)
henotic, *a.* he-*not*-ik, tending to reconcile. (Gr.)
hen-party, *n.* a social gathering of women only [Coll.].
henpecked, *a. hen*-pekt, governed, or nagged at, by one's wife.
hen-roost, *n.* a place where poultry roost.
henry, *n. hen*-re, the electrical unit of induction, so called after Joseph Henry (U.S.A., *d.* 1878).
henwife, *n. hen*-wife, a woman in charge of poultry.
heortology, *n.* hee-or-*tol*-o-je, the science or historical study of the Christian festivals. (Gr. *heorte*, feast.)
hep, *n.* hep, a hip, the fruit of the dog-rose.
hepat-, *hep*-at-, **hepato-,** *comb. forms* connoting the liver. (L., from Gr. *hepar*, *hepat-*, the liver.)
hepatectomy, *n.* hep-a-*tek*-to-me, the removal of part of the liver [Surg.].
hepatic, *a.* he-*pat*-ik, pertaining to or good for the liver; of a liver colour: *n.* a medicine for the liver. (L. *hepaticus*, relating to the liver.)
hepatica, *n.* he-*pat*-e-ka (*pl.* **hepaticæ**, he-*pat*-e-see), the plant, *Anemone hepatica*; a group of cryptogams comprising the liverworts. (L.)
hepatite, *n. hep*-a-tite, fetid sulphate of baryta.
hepatitis, *n.* hep-a-*ty*-tis, inflammation or congestion of the liver.
hepatization, *n. hep*-a-ty-*zay*-shon, conversion (esp. of the lungs) into a substance resembling the liver [Med.].
hepatize, *v.t. hep*-a-tize, to gorge (the lungs) with effused matter [Med.].

hepatocele, *n.* he-*pat*-o-seel, hernia of the liver [Med.]. (Gr. *hepar*, and *kele*, a tumour.)
hepatogenous, *a.* hep-a-*toj*-e-nus, originating in the liver [Med.].
hepatorrhœa, *n.* *hep*-at-o-*ree*-a, a diseased flow of bile [Med.]. (Gr. *hepar*, and *rheo*, flow.)
hepatoscopy, *n.* hep-a-*tos*-ko-pe, divination by inspecting the liver of animals. (Gr. *hepar*, and *skopeo*, view.)
hepatotomy, *n.* hep-a-*tot*-o-me, surgical incision of the liver.
Hepplewhite, *n.* *hepl*-white, a delicate style of furniture originated in the late 18th cent. by George Hepplewhite.
hepta-, *comb.f.* connoting seven. (Gr.)
heptachord, *n.* *hep*-ta-kord, a seven-stringed lyre; a series of seven notes; the interval of a seventh [Mus.]. (Gr. *hepta*, seven.)
heptad, *n.* *hep*-tad, the sum or number of seven; a group of seven; a week. (Gr. *hepta*, seven.)
heptaglot, *n.* *hep*-ta-glot, a book in seven languages. (Gr. *hepta*, and *glotta*, a tongue.)
heptagon, *n.* *hep*-ta-gon, a plane figure consisting of seven sides and seven angles [Geom.]. (Gr.)
heptagonal, *a.* hep-*tag*-o-nal, having seven angles.
Heptagynia, *n.pl.* hep-ta-*jin*-e-a, an order comprising plants having seven pistils [Bot.]. (Gr. *hepta*, and *gyne*, a female.)
heptagynian, *a.* hep-ta-*jin*-e-an, heptagynous.
heptagynous, *a.* hep-*taj*-e-nus, pertaining to the Heptagynia [Bot.].
heptahedron, *n.* *hep*-ta-*hee*-dron, a solid figure with seven sides. (Gr. *hepta*, and *hedra*, a side.)
heptahexahedral, *a.* *hep*-ta-*hek*-sa-*hee*-dral, presenting seven ranges of faces one above another, each range containing six faces. (Gr. *hepta*, and *hexahedral*.)
heptamerous, *a.* hep-*tam*-e-rus, having seven parts; having the parts of the flowers in sevens [Bot.].
heptameter, *n.* hep-*tam*-e-ter, a metrical line of seven feet.
heptandria, *n.pl.* hep-*tan*-dre-a, a group comprising plants having seven stamens [Bot.]. (Gr. *hepta*, and *aner*, a man.)
heptangular, *a.* hep-*tang*-gew-lar, having seven angles. (Gr. *hepta*, and *angular*.)
heptaphyllous, *a.* hep-*taf*-e-lus, having seven leaves [Bot.]. (Gr. *hepta*, and *phyllon*, a leaf.)
Heptarchy, *n.* *hep*-tar-ke, a government by seven rulers; a country, esp. Saxon England, under seven kings. (Gr. *hepta*, and *arche*, rule.)
heptaspermous, *a.* *hep*-ta-*sper*-mus, containing seven seeds [Bot.]. (Gr. *hepta* and *sperma*, seed.)
heptasyllabic, *a.* *hep*-ta-se-*lab*-ik, having seven syllables.
Heptateuch, *n.* *hep*-ta-tewk, the first seven books of the Old Testament. (Gr. *hepta*, and *teuchos*, a book.)
her, her, *pron. third. pers. sing. fem.*: *a.* of or belonging to a female. (A.S. *hire*.)
herald, *n.* *he*-rald, an officer of the College of Arms or Heralds' College whose business is to marshal and conduct ceremonies at coronations, royal marriages, installations, creations of peers, declarations of war, proclamations of peace, and to record and blazon the arms of the nobility and gentry, and to regulate abuses therein, and to record pedigrees; a proclaimer; a forerunner: *v.t.* to introduce, as by a herald; to proclaim. (O.Fr. *heralt*.)
heraldic, *a.* he-*ral*-dik, pertaining to heralds or heraldry.
heraldically, *ad.* in an heraldic manner.
heraldry, *n.* *he*-ral-dre, the art of a herald and of armorial bearings; emblazonment; heraldic ceremony. (O.Fr. *heralderie* or *heraulderie*.)
herb, *n.* herb, a plant with a soft or succulent stem or stems that die to the roots every year; a culinary or medicinal plant; a simple. **herb bennet,** bennet. **herb carpenter,** selfheal. **herb Christopher,** baneberry. **herb Paris,** the woodland plant, *Paris quadrifolia*. **herb Robert,** ragged robin. **herb trinity,** the pansy. (Fr. *herbe*.)
herbaceous, *a.* her-*bay*-shus, pertaining to herbs; of the nature of a herb. (L.)
herbage, *n.* *her*-baj, herbs collectively; grass; pasture; right of pasture [Law]. (Fr.)
herbal, *n.* *her*-bal, a book containing the names of plants with their descriptions, medicinal properties, etc; a collection of specimens of plants dried and preserved: *a.* pertaining to herbs. (O.Fr.)
herbalist, *n.* *her*-ba-list, one skilled in herbs; a collector of plants; a dealer in medicinal herbs.
herbarium, *n.* her-*bayr*-re-um, a classified collection of dried and preserved plants; a building or case for such collection.
herbary, *n.* *her*-ber-re, an herbarium; a vegetable-garden.
herbescent, *a.* her-*bes*-sent, growing into a herb; becoming herbaceous.
herbiferous, *a.* her-*bif*-er-rus, bearing herbs.
Herbivora, *n.pl.* her-*biv*-o-ra, animals subsisting on plants. (L. *herba*, and *voro*, devour.)
herbivore, *n.* *her*-be-vor, any of the Herbivora.
herbivorous, *a.* her-*biv*-o-rus, subsisting on plants.
herborist, *n.* *her*-bo-rist, a herbalist.
herborization, *n.* *her*-bo-ry-*zay*-shon, botanical research; arborization [Min.].
herborize, *v.i.* *her*-bo-rize, to botanize; to gather herbs or plants. (Fr. *herboriser*.)
herbous, *a.* *her*-bus, herby.
herb-woman, *n.* a woman who sells herbs.
herby, *a.* *her*-be, like or of the nature of herbs; abounding in herbs.
Herculean, *a.* her-*kew*-le-an, pertaining to Hercules or his labours; very great, difficult, or dangerous; of superhuman strength.
Hercules, *n.* *her*-kew-leez, a hero of Greek fable, distinguished for his prodigious strength, which he employed through twelve labours in a superhuman manner; hence, a man of extraordinary strength. (Gr. *Herakles*.)
Hercules-beetle, *n.* a very large beetle of tropical America, *Dynastes hercules*, the male bearing pincer-like projections on the head and thorax.
herd, *n.* herd, beasts feeding or driven together; a collection of cattle of the same stock; a company of people, in contempt; a rabble; one who minds cattle; a herdsman: *v.i.* to associate; to associate as beasts: *v.t.* to form into a herd; to tend (cattle). **herd instinct,** gregariousness; the tendency of a crowd to act as an individual. (A.S. *heord*.).
herd-book, *n.* a book containing the pedigrees of stud cattle.
herdsman, *n.* *herdz*-man, one employed in tending herds of cattle.
★**here,** *ad.* heer, in this place; hither; in the present life or state. **here and there,** in one place and another. **here, there, and everywhere,** dispersed; all about. **neither here nor there,** neither in one place nor in another; bearing neither on this nor that; of no consequence; not to the point. (A.S.)
hereabouts, *ad.* *heer*-a-bouts, near here.
hereafter, *ad.* heer-*ahf*-ter, from this time forwards: *n.* a future state. **the hereafter,** the future life; the next world.
hereat, *ad.* heer-*at*, at this point.
hereby, *ad.* heer-*by*, by this.
heredipety, *n.* he-re-*dip*-e-te, legacy-hunting. (L. *heredium*, legacy, *petere*, to seek.)
hereditability, *n.* he-*red*-e-ta-*bil*-e-te, the state of being inheritable.
hereditable, *a.* he-*red*-e-ta-bl, that may be inherited.
hereditament, *n.* he-re-*dit*-a-ment, any kind of property that may be inherited; real or personal property. (Late L. *herditamentum*.)
hereditarian, *n.* he-*red*-e-*tay*-re-an, one who emphasizes the biological importance of heredity.
hereditarily, *ad.* he-*red*-e-ta-re-le, by inheritance.
hereditary, *a.* he-*red*-e-ta-re, descending by inheritance; holding through inheritance; transmitted by descent from parent to offspring. (L. *hereditarius*.)
heredity, *n.* he-*red*-e-te, transmission of the characters or qualities of parents to their offspring.
herein, *ad.* heer-*in*, in this.
hereinafter, *ad.* *heer*-in-*ahf*-ter, later on; below.
hereinto, *ad.* heer-*in*-to, into this.
hereof, *ad.* heer-*ov*, of this.
hereon, *ad.* heer-*on*, on this.
heresiarch, *n.* he-*ree*-se-ark, the leader of an heretical sect; an arch-heretic. (Gr. *hairesiarches*.)
heresiographer, *n.* he-*ree*-se-*og*-ra-fer, one who writes on heresies. (Gr. *heresy*, and *grapho*, write.)
heresiography, *n.* he-*ree*-se-*og*-ra-fe, a treatise on heresy or heresies.

heresy, *n.* *he*-re-se, an unorthodox doctrine in any particular Church [Theol.]; any opinion held in opposition to that generally accepted, as in politics. (O.Fr. *heresie.*)
heretic, *n.* *he*-re-tik, a person who holds heretical opinions, esp. in religion; one who is not orthodox. (Fr. *hérétique.*)
heretical, *a.* he-*ret*-e-kal, containing heresy; contrary to orthodox belief.
heretically, *ad.* in a heretical manner.
hereticate, *v.t.* he-*ret*-e-kate, to pronounce heretical.
hereto, *ad.* *heer*-to, in addition; to this time or place.
heretofore, *ad.* *heer*-to-*for*, formerly; till now.
hereunto, *ad.* heer-*un*-to, unto this.
hereupon, *ad.* *heer*-up-on, upon this.
herewith, *ad.* heer-*with*, with this.
heriot, *n.* *he*-re-ot, a fine in kind or cash, payable to the lord of the manor on the decease of the owner, landholder, or vassal [Law]. (A.S. *heregeatu*, military accoutrements.)
heriotable, *a.* *he*-re-o-ta-bl, subject to the payment of a heriot.
herisson, *n.* *he*-re-son, a bar armed with iron spikes for obstructing a passage [Fort.]. (Fr., a hedgehog.)
heritable, *a.* *he*-re-ta-bl, that may be inherited; passing by inheritance; capable of inheriting by descent. (O.Fr.)
heritably, *ad.* *he*-re-ta-ble, by inheritance.
heritage, *n.* *he*-re-taj, an estate that passes from an ancestor to an heir by descent; that which is inherited. (O.Fr.)
heritor, *n.* *he*-re-tor, one who inherits.
herling, *n.* *her*-ling, the sea-trout, *Salmo trutta*, esp. when young. (Scots.)
herma, *n.* *her*-ma (*pl.* **hermæ**), a rough quadrangular pillar surmounted by a sculptured head, esp. that of Hermes.
hermaphrodism, *n.* her-*maf*-fro-dizm, hermaphroditism.
hermaphrodite, *n.* her-*maf*-ro-dite, an animal having both male and female sexual organs usually imperfectly developed [Biol.]; monoclinous [Bot.]: *a.* with both sexes in the same individual. **hermaphrodite brig,** a brigantine. (Gr. *Hermaphrodites*, the son of Hermes and Aphrodite.)
hermaphroditic, *a.* her-*maf*-fro-*dit*-ik, characteristic of hermaphroditism; partaking of both sexes; uniting discordant elements.
hermaphroditism, *n.* her-*maf*-fro-dy-tizm, the state or condition of being hermaphrodite.
hermeneutic, *a.* her-men-*yew*-tik, interpreting; explanatory.
hermeneutically, *a.* her-men-*yew*-te-ka-le, in a hermeneutic manner.
hermeneutics, *n.* her-men-*yew*-tiks, the science of interpretation, especially of the Scriptures. (Gr. *hermeneus*, an interpreter, from *Hermes.*)
Hermes, *n.* *her*-meez, the Greek Mercury, the ever-ready swift-winged messenger and interpreter of the gods; a herma [Arch.].
hermetic, *a.* her-*met*-ik, pertaining to alchemy; perfectly close and air-tight. (L. *hermeticus.*)
hermetically, *ad.* her-*met*-e-ka-le, so closely as to be air-tight.
hermit, *n.* *her*-mit, a religious recluse living apart in contemplation; one retired from society and living in solitude. (Fr. *hermite.*)
hermitage, *n.* *her*-me-taj, the dwelling or cell of a hermit; (*cap.*) a red or white French wine (from a hermitage near Valence).
hermit-crab, *n.* a decapod crustacean generally occupying the shell of a whelk or other mollusc.
hermitical, *a.* her-*mit*-ik-al, pertaining to a hermit; suited for a hermit.
hern, *n.* hern, a heron.
hernia, *n.* *her*-ne-a, the abnormal protrusion of part or the whole of an organ from its natural cavity; a rupture [Med.]. (L.)
hernial, *a.* *her*-ne-al, pertaining to hernia.
herniotomy, *n.* her-ne-*ot*-o-me, the operation for strangulated hernia.
hernshaw, *n.* *hern*-shaw, a heronshaw.
hero, *n.* *heer*-ro, a demigod, or semi-mythological man of supposed divine descent; a great, illustrious, or extraordinary man, or one of exceptional valour; the chief male character in a play, novel, etc. (Gr.)
heroic, *a.* he-*roh*-ik, becoming or worthy of a hero; having the qualities of a hero; respecting heroes; productive of heroes; larger than life: *n.pl.* heroic verse; extravagant or bombastic expressions or language. **heroic age,** the period of the heroes of Greek antiquity. **heroic verse,** iambic verse of ten syllables, esp. the classical hexameter or the verse of Milton's "Paradise Lost."
heroically, *ad.* he-*roh*-e-ka-le, in the manner of a hero.
heroi-comic, *a.* he-*roh*-e-*kom*-ik, consisting of the heroic and the ludicrous; burlesque.
heroi-comical, *a.* he-*roh*-e-*kom*-e-kal, heroi-comic.
heroin, *n.* he-*roh*-in *or* *he*-ro-in, a drug prepared from morphia.
heroine, *n.* *he*-ro-in, a female hero; a woman of a brave spirit; principal female character. (O.Fr.)
heroism, *n.* *he*-ro-izm, the qualities characteristic of a hero; a hero's conduct.
heroize, *v.t.* *he*-ro-ize, to make a hero of; to regard as heroic: *v.i.* to parade or masquerade as a hero.
heron, *n.* *he*-ron, a wading bird of the genus *Ardea*, with long legs and neck. (O.Fr. *hairon.*)
heronry, *n.* *he*-ron-re, a place where herons breed.
heron's-bill, *n.* a plant of the genus *Erodium*, its fruit somewhat resembling a heron's bill.
heronshaw, *n.* *he*-ron-shaw, a young heron.
herpes, *n.* *her*-peez, acute inflammation of the skin and mucous membranes accompanied by vesicular eruptions. **herpes zoster,** shingles [Med.]. (L., from Gr. *herpein*, to creep).
herpetic, *a.* her-*pet*-ik, pertaining to herpes; resembling herpes.
herpetism, *n.* *her*-pe-tizm, constitutional predisposition to herpes [Med.].
herpetoid, *a.* *her*-pe-toyd, of the shape of a snake. (Gr. *herpeton*, reptile, *eidos*, like.)
herpetological, *a.* *her*-pe-to-*loj*-e-kal, pertaining to herpetology.
herpetologist, *n.* *her*-pe-*tol*-o-jist, a person versed in herpetology.
herpetology, *n.* *her*-pe-*tol*-o-je, the natural history of reptiles. (Gr. *herpeton*, a reptile, *logos*, science.)
Herr, *n.* hair, the German equivalent for "Mr."
herring, *n.* *he*-ring, a sea fish, *Clupea harengus*, swimming in shoals, and much used for food. **herring gull,** the robber gull, *Larus argentatus*. **herring pond,** the open sea, esp. the North Atlantic. **king of the herrings,** the chimæra [Ichth.]. **red herring,** *see* **red.** (A.S. *hæring.*)
herring-bone, *a.* arranged, like the bones of a herring, esp. of stitchery and of building in which the bricks or stones are laid diagonally to ensure a better bond.
Herrnhuter, *n.* *hair*-noo-ter, one of the sect of Moravians, settled at first at Herrnhut, near Bautzen, in Germany.
hers, *pron.* herz, possessive of *her*.
herschelite, *n.* *her*-shel-ite, a silicate of alumina with soda and potash (Sir John *Herschel*).
herse, *n.* herse, a portcullis, in the form of a harrow, set with iron spikes, for blocking a gateway, etc. [Fort.]. (Fr., a harrow.)
herself, her-*self*, *recip. pron. third pers. fem. sing.*
Hertzian, *a.* *hert*-se-an, pertaining to H. Hertz, the German physicist (*d.* 1894), or to his discoveries, experiments, etc. **Hertzian wave,** an electric wave, esp. as used in radio communication.
hesitancy, *n.* *hez*-e-tan-se, the act of hesitating.
hesitant, *a.* *hez*-e-tant, hesitating; undecided.
hesitantly, *ad.* *hez*-e-tant-le, in a hesitating manner.
hesitate, *v.i.* *hez*-e-tate, to pause in doubt; to be in suspense; to waver; to stammer. (L. *hæsitatus*, stuck.)
hesitatingly, *ad.* *hez*-e-*tay*-ting-le, with hesitation.
hesitation, *n.* hez-e-*tay*-shon, the act or fact of hesitating; vacillation; stammering.
hesitative, *a.* *hez*-e-tay-tiv, showing hesitation.
hesitator, *n.* *hez*-e-tay-tor, one who hesitates; a waverer.
Hesper, *n.* *hes*-per, the planet Venus, esp. as the evening star. (L. *Hesperus.*)
Hesperian, *a.* hes-*peer*-re-an, western; situated at the west: *n.* an inhabitant of a western country.
Hesperides, *n.pl.* hes-*pe*-re-deez, sisters who guarded the golden apples given by Ge to Hera on her marriage with Zeus [Myth.]. (Gr.)
Hesperornis, *n.* *hes*-per-*or*-nis, a genus of extinct toothed birds found in the Cretaceous deposits in Kansas.

Hessian, *a.* *hes*-se-an, relating to Hesse, in Germany: *n.* (*l.c.*) a coarse hempen cloth; a coarse fabric of jute: *pl.* high boots with tassels, Hessian boots.
Hessian-fly, *n.* a small fly, *Cecidomyia destructor,* whose larvæ are destructive to wheat.
hest, *n.* hest, command; behest.
Hesychast, *n.* *hee*-se-kast, one of a sect of quietist mystics of the 14th century. (Gr. *hesychos,* quiet.)
hetærism, *n.* he-*teer*-rizm, concubinage; community of women within the tribe. (Gr. *hetaira,* a concubine.)
hetero-, *comb.f.* signifying other, different. (Gr. *heteros,* the other of two.)
heterocarpous, *a.* het-er-o-*kar*-pus, bearing more than one kind of fruit [Bot.].
heterocercal, *a.* *het*-er-o-*ser*-kal, having the upper fork of the tail longer than the lower [Ichthy.]. (Gr. *heteros,* and *kerkos,* a tail.)
heterochromus, *a.* *het*-er-o-*kroh*-mus, of different colours [Bot.]. (Gr. *heteros,* and *chroma,* colour.)
heteroclite, *a.* *het*-er-o-klite, heteroclitic: *n.* a word which is irregular or anomalous [Gram.]; any thing or person deviating from common forms. (Gr. *heteroclitus.*)
heteroclitic, *a.* *het*-er-o-*klit*-ik, irregular; anomalous; deviating from ordinary forms or rules.
heterodactyl, *a.* *het*-er-o-*dak*-til, having the digits irregular in number or form [Zool.]. (Gr. *heteros,* and *dactylos,* finger.)
heterodont, *a.* *het*-er-o-dont, having teeth of different forms: *n.* a heterodont animal.
heterodox, *a.* *het*-er-o-doks, contrary to accepted opinion; holding opinions contrary to the orthodox; heretical. (Gr. *heteros,* and *doxa,* opinion, from *dokeo,* seem.)
heterodoxy, *n.* *het*-er-o-dok-se, opinion or doctrine contrary to the orthodox; heresy.
heterodyne, *a.* *het*-er-o-dyne, pertaining to the method by which a wave of different length is imposed on a transmitted wave to produce beat-notes of audible frequency: *n.* an auxiliary generator adapted to heterodyne reception [Wire.]. (Gr. *heteros,* another, *dynamis,* power.)
heteroepy, *n.* *het*-er-o-*ee*-pe, pronunciation not in accordance with the normal.
heterogamous, *a.* het-er-*rog*-a-mus, having sexually different flowers or florets [Bot.]. (Gr. *heteros,* and *gamos,* marriage.)
heterogeneity, *n.* *het*-ter-o-je-*nee*-e-te, heterogeneousness; difference in kind.
heterogeneous, *a.* *het*-ter-o-*jee*-ne-us, unlike or dissimilar in kind; of different kinds; incommensurable [Math.]. (Gr. *heteros,* and *genos,* kind.)
heterogeneously, *ad.* *het*-ter-o-*jee*-ne-us-le, in a heterogeneous manner.
heterogeneousness, *n.* *het*-ter-o-*jee*-ne-us-ness, the state of being heterogeneous.
heterogenesis, *n.* *het*-ter-o-*jen*-e-sis, production of offspring differing from the parent; spontaneous generation; alternate generation. (Gr. *heteros,* and *gennao,* produce.)
heterogeny, *n.* het-ter-*roj*-en-e, heterogenesis.
heterography, *n.* het-ter-*rog*-ra-fe, employment of the same letter to represent different sounds, as the *c* in *face* and *fact*; wrong spelling. (Gr. *heteros,* and *grapho,* write.)
heterologous, *a.* het-ter-*rol*-o-gus, differing in structure or type. (Gr. *heteros,* and *logos,* plan).
heteromerous, *a.* het-ter-*rom*-er-rus, diversiform; differing in composition [Chem.]. (Gr. *heteros,* and *meros,* a part.)
heteromorphic, *a.* *het*-ter-o-*mor*-fik, differing in type or from the normal; of different form at different stages, as the butterflies.
heteromorphism, *n.* *het*-ter-o-*mor*-fizm, the quality of being heteromorphic; existence in different forms. (Gr. *heteros,* and *morphe,* shape.)
heteronomous, *a.* het-ter-*ron*-o-mus, subject to the law of another power; not autonomous; diverging from type [Biol.]. (Gr. *heteros,* and *nomos,* law.)
heteronomy, *n.* het-te-*ron*-o-me, the condition of being heteronomous; wanting self-determination; subjection to something else [Phil.]. (Gr. *heteros,* and *nomos,* law.)
heteronym, *n.* *het*-ter-o-nim, a word of the same spelling but of different sound and meaning, as *slough* (slou), swamp, and *slough* (sluf) a cast skin. (Gr. *heteronymos,* from *heteros,* and *onyma,* name.)
heteroousian, *a.* *het*-ter-o-*ou*-se-an, of a different nature of substance, esp. of an Arian sect. that held that the Son was of different essence from the Father. (Gr. *heteros,* and *ousia,* being.)
heteropathy, *n.* het-ter-*rop*-a-the, allopathy.
heterophyllous, *a.* het-ter-*rof*-e-lus, having differently shaped leaves on the same stem [Bot.]. (Gr. *heteros,* and *phyllon,* a leaf.)
heteropod, *n.* *het*-ter-o-pod, one of a group of marine molluscs the foot of which is modified into a fin-like organ. (Gr. *heteros,* and *pous,* foot.)
heteroscian, *a.* *het*-ter-*ros*-e-an, said of a part of the globe where the shadows fall in an opposite direction relatively to another part: *n.* one whose shadow so falls. (Gr. *heteros,* and *skia,* a shadow.)
heterosexuality, *n.* *het*-ter-o-seks-zew-*al*-e-te, normal sexuality as opposed to homosexuality.
heterotomous, *a.* het-ter-*rot*-o-mus, having an abnormal cleavage [Min.]. (Gr. *heteros,* and *tome,* cutting.)
heterotropia, *n.* *het*-er-o-*troh*-pe-a, strabismus [Med.].
heterotypic, *a.* het-er-o-*tip*-ik, differing from the normal condition [Zool.].
hetman, *n.* *het*-man, a Cossack commander-in-chief.
heugh, *n.* hewh, a ravine; a crag; a mine-shaft.
heulandite, *n.* *hew*-lan-dite, a mineral consisting of silica, alumina, and lime, occurring in amygdaloidal rocks and metalliferous veins, so called after Heuland, an English mineralogist.
heuristic, *a.* hew-*ris*-tik, leading to discovery; serving to find out. (Gr. *heurisko,* discover.)
Hevea, *n.* *hee*-ve-a, a genus of S. American trees yielding rubber, *Hevea brasiliensis.*
hew, *v.t.* hew, to cut with an axe or pickaxe; to hack; to chop; to shape. *pp.* **hewed** or **hewn.** (A.S. *heawan.*)
hewer, *n.* *hew*-er, one who hews wood, coal, or stone.
hexachord, *n.* *heks*-a-kord, a scale or series of six notes; an interval of four tones and a semitone [Mus.]. (Gr. *hex,* six, and *chord.*)
hexad, *n.* *heks*-ad, a series or group of six.
hexadactylous, *a.* *heks*-a-*dak*-til-us, having six fingers or toes. (Gr. *hex,* and *daktylos,* a finger.)
hexagon, *n.* *heks*-a-gon, a plane figure of six sides and angles [Geom.]. (Gr. *hex,* and *gonia,* an angle.)
hexagonal, *a.* heks-*ag*-on-al, having six sides and angles.
hexagram, *n.* *heks*-a-gram, a figure formed of two intersecting equilateral triangles; the seal of Solomon. (Gr. *hexagrammatos,* six-lettered.)
Hexagynia, *n.pl.* *heks*-a-*jin*-e-a, an order of plants having six pistils [Bot.]. (Gr. *hex,* and *gyne,* a female.)
hexagynian, *a.* *heks*-a-*jin*-e-an, having six pistils [Bot.].
hexahedral, *a.* heks-a-*hee*-dral, of the figure of a hexahedron.
hexahedron, *n.* heks-a-*hee*-dron *or* -*hed*-ron, a regular solid body of six sides; a cube. (Gr. *hex,* and *hedra,* a side.)
hexahemeron, *n.* *heks*-a-*hee*-mer-ron, hexameron.
hexameron, *n.* heks-*am*-er-ron, the six days of the Creation; an account of, or a treatise on, this. (Gr. *hex,* and *hemera,* a day.)
hexameter, *n.* heks-*am*-e-ter, a metrical line of six feet of dactyls and spondees. (Gr. *hex,* and *metron,* measure.)
hexametrical, *a.* heks-a-*met*-re-kal, consisting of six metrical feet.
Hexandria, *n.pl.* heks-*an*-dre-a, an order of plants having six stamens [Bot.]. (Gr. *hex,* and *aner,* a male.)
hexandrian, *a.* heks-*an*-dre-an, having six stamens.
hexangular, *a.* heks-*ang*-gew-lar, having six corners.
hexapetalous, *a.* heks-a-*pet*-a-lus, having six petals or flower-leaves [Bot.]. (Gr. *hex,* and *petal.*)
hexaphyllous, *a.* heks-*af*-e-lus, having six leaves [Bot.]. (Gr. *hex,* and *phyllon,* a leaf.)
hexapla, *n.* *heks*-a-pla, an edition of the Scriptures in six versions, esp. that of Origen. (Gr., six-fold.)
hexaplar, *a.* *heks*-a-plar, sextuple; in six columns.
hexapod, *a.* *heks*-a-pod, having six feet: *n.* a six-legged animal; any one of the Hexapoda, or true insects. (Gr. *hex,* and *pous,* foot.)
hexastich, *n.* *heks*-a-stik, a poem of six lines or verses. (Gr. *hex,* and *stichos,* a line or verse.)
hexastyle, *a.* *heks*-a-stile, having six columns [Arch.]: *n.* a portico or building with six columns. (Gr. *hex,* and *stylos,* a pillar.)

hexasyllable, *n.* *heks*-a-*sil*-a-bl, a word of six syllables.
Hexateuch, *n.* *heks*-a-tewk, the first six books of the Bible. (Gr. *hex*, and *teuchos*, book.)
hey, hay, *int.* of joy, exhortation, or interrogation, etc.
heyday, *hay*-day, *int.* of frolic, wonder, or exultation : *n.* a period of vigour ; a wild or frolicsome season.
hi, *int.* hy, a word for calling attention.
hiatus, *n.* hy-*ay*-tus, an opening ; a gap ; a chasm ; a lacuna ; the concurrence of two vowel sounds in two successive syllables [Gram.]. (L.)
hibernaculum, *n.* hy-ber-*nak*-yew-lum, the winter leaf-bud [Bot.] ; winter lodging or shelter. (L.)
hibernal, *a.* hy-*bern*-al, belonging to winter. (Fr.)
hibernate, *v.i.* *hy*-bern-ate, to winter, or pass the winter season in torpor or sleep ; to withdraw to seclusion or inactivity. (L. *hibernatus*, hibernated.)
hibernation, *n.* *hy*-ber-*nay*-shon, the act of hibernating.
Hibernian, *a.* hy-*bern*-e-an, pertaining to Ireland : *n.* a native of Ireland. (L. *Hibernia*, Ireland.)
Hibernicism, *n.* hy-*bern*-e-sizm, an Irish idiom.
Hibernicize, *v.t.* hy-*bern*-e-size, to render Irish.
Hiberno-Celtic, *n.* hy-*bern*-o-*kel*-tik, the native language of the Irish ; Erse : *a.* pertaining to the Irish Celts.
Hibiscus, *n.* hy-*bis*-kus, a genus of beautifully flowered mallows, mostly tropical. (Gr.)
hicatee, *n.* hik-a-*tee*, a fresh-water tortoise of the West Indies.
hiccough, *n.* and *v.* *hik*-up, hiccup.
hiccup, *n.* *hik*-up, a convulsive sort of cough due to spasmodic contraction of the diaphragm : *v.i.* to have a hiccup : *v.t.* to utter with hiccups. (From the sound.)
hickory, *n.* *hik*-o-re, any of several American nut-bearing trees of the genus *Carya* ; its tough elastic wood. (N. Amerind.)
hickwall, *n.* *hik*-wawl, the hickway.
hickway, *n.* *hik*-way, a woodpecker of a small species, *Picus minor*. (Dial. Eng.)
hid, hid, *pp.* of *hide*.
hidage, *n.* *hy*-daj, a tax formerly paid to the kings of England for every hide of land. (*hide*.)
hidalgo, *n.* he-*dal*-goh, a Spanish nobleman of the lowest rank. (Sp.)
hidden, *a.* *hid*-en, *pp.* of *to hide* ; occult, secret ; not obvious.
hiddenly, *ad.* *hid*-en-le, in a hidden manner.
hide, *v.t.* hide, to withhold or withdraw from sight : to conceal ; to screen ; to suppress ; not to confess : *v.i.* to lie concealed : *n.* a hiding-place [Coll.]. **hide and seek,** a children's game. *p.* **hid.** *pp.* **hidden.** (A.S. *hydan.*)
hide, *n.* hide, the skin of an animal ; a dressed and prepared skin : *v.t.* to flog. *p.* **hided.** (A.S. *hyd.*)
hide, *n.* hide, a portion of land in Saxon times (60 to 120 acres) sufficient to support one family. (A.S.)
hidebound, *a.* *hide*-bound, with a tightly bound skin or bark, preventing movement or growth ; bigoted ; narrow-minded ; crabbed.
hideosity, *n.* hid-e-*os*-e-te, hideousness ; a hideous object.
hideous, *a.* *hid*-e-us, frightful ; shocking to the eye or ear ; horrible ; grim. (O.Fr. *hidos.*)
hideously, *ad.* *hid*-e-us-le, to a hideous degree.
hideousness, *n.* the state of being hideous.
hide-out, *n.* a hiding-place [Coll.].
hider, *n.* *hide*-er, one who hides or conceals.
hiding, *n.* *hide*-ing, a flogging ; a heavy defeat [Coll.].
hiding-place, *n.* a place of concealment.
hidrosis, *n.* hy-*droh*-sis, excessive perspiration ; any skin-disease accompanied by this [Med.]. (Gr. *hidros*, sweat.)
hidrotic, *a.* hy-*drot*-ik, provoking perspiration : *n.* a sudorific. (Gr. *hidros*, sweat.)
hie, *v.i.* hy, to hasten. *ppr.* **hying.** (A.S. *higian.*)
hiemal, *a.* *hy*-e-mal, belonging to winter ; wintry.
hierarch, *n.* *hy*-er-rark, one with authority in sacred things ; the head of a sacred order ; a chief priest. (Gr. *hieros*, sacred, *archo*, rule.)
hierarchic, *a.* hy-er-*rar*-kik, pertaining to a hierarch or a hierarchy.
hierarchical, *a.* hy-er-*rar*-ke-kal, hierarchic.
hierarchism, *n.* hy-er-*rar*-kizm, government by a hierarchy ; hierarchic principles.
hierarchy, *n.* *hy*-er-rar-ke, an order of sacred persons, or of angels ; ecclesiastical government ; an organization of ruling priests ; any graded body of officials [Coll.]. (O.Fr. *hierarchie.*)
hieratic, *a.* hy-er-*rat*-ik, pertaining to priests or to the priesthood ; applied, esp. to a mode of writing of the ancient Egyptians and to their early conventionalized art. (L. *hieraticus.*)
hierocracy, *n.* hy-er-*rok*-ra-se, government by ecclesiastics ; hierarchy. (Gr. *hieros*, and *kratos*, power, rule.)
hieroglyph, *n.* *hy*-er-ro-glif, a hieroglyphic : *v.t.* to represent in hieroglyphics. (Gr. *hieros*, and *glypho*, carve.)
hieroglyphic, *n.* *hy*-er-ro-*glif*-ik, a species of writing, esp. of the ancient Egyptians, in which the figures of objects are employed to represent words, letters, or ideas ; a symbolic or emblematic figure : *pl.* hieroglyphic writing : *a.* marked with hieroglyphics : hieroglyphical.
hieroglyphical, *a.* *hy*-er-ro-*glif*-e-kal, after the manner of a hieroglyph ; emblematic ; esoteric.
hieroglyphically, *ad.* in a hieroglyphic manner.
hieroglyphist, *n.* *hy*-er-*rog*-le-fist, one versed in hieroglyphics.
hierogram, *n.* *hy*-er-ro-gram, a sacred letter or symbol ; a hieroglyphic. (Gr. *hieros*, and *gramma*, a letter.)
hierogrammatic, *a.* *hy*-er-ro-gra-*mat*-ik, written in sacred or sacerdotal characters ; of the nature of a hierogram.
hierogrammatist, *n.* *hy*-er-ro-*gram*-a-tist, a writer or interpreter of hierograms.
hierograph, *n.* *hy*-er-ro-graf, a hierogram.
hierography, *n.* *hy*-er-*rog*-ra-fe, writing on sacred subjects ; a treatise on religion. (Gr. *hieros*, and *grapho*, write.)
hierolatry, *n.* *hy*-er-*rol*-a-tre, the worship of saints. (Gr. *hieros*, and *latreia*, worship.)
hierological, *a.* *hy*-er-ro-*loj*-e-kal, belonging to the study of hierology.
hierologist, *n.* *hy*-er-*rol*-o-jist, one versed in hierology.
hierology, *n.* *hy*-er-*rol*-o-je, sacred literature ; the body of religious belief of a people ; hagiology. (Gr. *hieros*, and *logos*, science.)
hieromancy, *n.* *hy*-er-ro-man-se, divination from things offered in sacrifice. (Gr. *hieros*, and *manteia*, divination.)
hierophant, *n.* *hy*-er-ro-fant, a priest, esp. as instructor on religious matters ; an initiator. (Gr. *hierophantes*, showing the ritual.)
hierophantic, *a.* *hy*-er-ro-*fan*-tik, pertaining to or of the nature of a hierophant.
hieroscopy, *n.* *hy*-er-*ros*-ko-pe, hieromancy.
higgle, *v.i.* *hig*-gl, to carry provisions about for sale ; to be hard in bargaining ; to dispute about trifles. (*haggle.*)
higgledy-piggledy, *ad.* *hig*-gl-de-*pig*-gl-de, in confusion : *n.* a jumble.
higgler, *n.* *hig*-gler, one who higgles.
*****high,** *a.* hy, elevated ; lofty ; tall ; elevated in rank, condition, or office ; exalted in character or excellence ; difficult ; boastful ; ostentatious ; arrogant ; loud ; threatening or angry ; violent ; powerful ; luxurious ; strong ; remote from the equator ; intense ; far-advanced ; noble ; honourable ; possessed of supreme power ; dear in price ; tainted ; remote in past time ; ritualistic ; acute ; sharp [Mus.] : *ad.* aloft ; to a great altitude ; eminently ; greatly ; powerfully : *n.* an elevated place ; a top level (esp. of prices) [Coll.] ; an area of high pressure, an anticyclone [Meteor.]. **high altar,** the principal altar. **high and dry,** applied to the situation of a vessel when aground above water-mark ; left stranded or behind. **High Commissioner,** the chief representative in London of one of the Dominions or of India. **high day, high noon,** the time when the sun is in the meridian. **high Dutch,** German. **high living,** rich or dainty living. **High Mass,** *see* **Mass. High School,** a secondary school. **high seas,** the ocean beyond certain limits from the coast. **high table,** a table on a dais, a table of honour. **high tea,** a meat tea. **high tide,** the tide at its full ; high-water ; the time of this ; a culminating point [Fig.]. **high time,** quite time, time it was attended to ; a spree or carousal [Slang]. **high treason,** *see* **treason. on high,** aloft. (A.S. *heah.*)
highball, *n.* *hy*-bawl, iced whisky and soda served in a tall glass [U.S.A. Coll.]

highbinder, *n.* *hy*-byn-der, a rowdy, a gangster [U.S.A. slang].
highbindery, *n.* *hy*-byn-der-re, rowdyism, lawlessness produced by gangsters. [U.S.A. slang].
highborn, *a.* *hy*-born, of noble birth.
highbred, *a.* *hy*-bred, bred in high life; refined; of pure extraction; thoroughbred.
highbrow, *n.* *hy*-brou, an intellectual; a superior person in his own estimation: *a.* suited to such persons [all Coll.].
High-Church, *a.* in the Church of England, attaching great importance to the authority of the priesthood, the efficacy of the sacraments, and matters of ritual; ritualistic.
High-Churchman, *n.* one who holds High-Church principles.
high-class, *a.* of a superior class.
high-coloured, *a.* florid; lurid; having a strong or glaring colour.
highday, *n.* *hy*-day, a holiday: *a.* befitting a holiday.
high-explosive, *n.* an explosive of great power used esp. in shells and bombs and for disruption.
highfalutin, *a.* *hy*-fa-*loo*-tin, high-flown; pretentious: *n.* bombastic rubbish [U.S.A. slang].
high-fed, *a.* pampered; fed luxuriously.
high-flown, *a.* proud; turgid; highfalutin.
high-flyer, *n.* *hy*-fly-er, a high-flying bird [Shooting]; hence, a person inclined to go to extremes.
high-flying, *a.* extravagant in claims or opinions; taking undue risks.
high-frequency, *n.* of a relatively rapid frequency [Elect.]; in Wireless, any frequency above the audible range.
high-handed, *a.* violent or overbearing; arbitrary.
highjacker, *n.* *hy*-jak-er, a highwayman; a hold-up man (*and see* **hijacker**) [U.S.A. slang].
highland, *n.* *hy*-land, a hilly country, esp. (*cap.*) in Scotland: *a.* pertaining to highlands.
Highlander, *n.* *hy*-lan-der, a native of the Highlands or of highlands; a soldier in a kilted regiment.
high-life, *n.* the upper classes; their mode of life.
high-light, *n.* *hy*-lite, the brightest or lightest part in a painting, photographic print, etc.; any detail of outstanding merit or interest [Fig.].
highlow, *n.* *hy*-loh, a kind of laced boot.
highly, *ad.* *hy*-le, in a high manner.
high-mettled, *a.* having high spirits; ardent.
high-minded, *a.* proud; magnanimous.
highness, *n.* *hy*-ness, the state of being high; (*cap.*) a title of honour given to princes, princesses, and certain others of high rank (*e.g.* with poss. pron., *His Highness*, etc.).
high-pressure, *a.* having or involving pressure much in excess of that of the atmosphere (usually over 50 lb. per sq. in.); intense. **at high pressure,** exerting full or great power.
high-priest, *n.* a chief priest, esp. among the Jews.
highroad, *n.* *hy*-rode, a highway.
high-seasoned, *a.* enriched with spices or other seasoning; piquant; somewhat obscene.
high-sounding, *a.* pompous; ostentatious.
high-spirited, *a.* having a high spirit or keen sense of honour; bold; mettlesome.
high-stepper, *n.* a horse that lifts its feet well in moving; a smart, dashing person.
high-stomached, *a.* haughty; proud.
hight, *a.* hite, called or named. (A.S.)
high-tension, *n.* and *a.* a term denoting any voltage over 650 volts [Elect.].
high-toned, *a.* high in sound; of rigid principles.
high-water, *n.* the point, in space or time, reached by the tide at its full. **high-water mark,** the highest point reached by the tide; a mark showing this; a culminating point.
highway, *n.* *hy*-way, a much frequented public road; a way open to all; course; train of action.
highwayman, *n.* *hy*-way-man, one who robs on the public highway; a footpad.
high-wrought, *a.* *hy*-rawt, wrought with exquisite art or skill; strongly inflamed.
hijacker, *n.* *hy*-jak-er, a highjacker, esp. one who preys on bootleggers or smugglers [U.S.A. slang].
hike, *n.* hike, a ramble; a walking-tour: *v.i.* to go on a ramble or tramp: *v.t.* to jerk or swing; to hoist.
hiker, *n.* *hyk*-er, one who hikes.
hilar, *a.* *hy*-lar, pertaining to the hilum [Bot.].
hilarious, *a.* he-*lair*-re-us, mirthful; merry. (L.)
hilarity, *n.* he-*la*-re-te, pleasurable excitement of the animal spirits; merriment; gaiety. (Fr. *hilarité.*)
Hilary, *n.* *hil*-a-re, one of the four English law-court terms, January 11–31, so called from the festival of St. Hilary.
hill, *n.* hil, an eminence on the earth of less elevation than a mountain; a small heap; a mound: *v.t.* to raise earth about plants. (A.S. *hyll,* L. *collis.*)
hillbilly, *n.* *hil*-bil-e, a backwoodsman [U.S.A.].
hill-farming, *n.* the work, or the technique, of agriculture and sheep-farming in hilly districts.
hill-fort, *n.* a prehistoric fortification on a hilltop.
hilliness, *n.* *hil*-le-ness, the state of being hilly.
hillman, *n.* *hil*-man, one dwelling among the hills; a mountaineer.
hillo, *int.* *hil*-lo, hallo.
hillock, *n.* *hil*-lok, a small hill.
hillside, *n.* *hil*-side, the side or declivity of a hill.
hilltop, *n.* *hil*-top, the top of a hill.
hilly, *a.* *hil*-le, abounding with hills; steep.
hilsah, *n.* *hil*-sah, an anadromous fish of Indian waters, allied to the shad and much esteemed for food. (Hind.)
hilt, *n.* hilt, the handle of a sword, dagger, etc. (A.S. *helt.*)
hilted, *a.* *hilt*-ed, having a hilt.
hilum, *n.* *hy*-lum, the eye of a bean or other seed where it separates from the placenta [Bot.]; a small aperture or notch on an organ for the entrance of a nerve, duct, etc. [Anat.]. (L.)
him, *pron.* him, the objective case of *he.*
himation, *n.* he-*mat*-e-on, the rectangular cloth worn as an outer garment by the ancient Greeks. (Gr.)
himself, him-*self, recip. pron. third pers. masc. sing.* **by himself,** alone; sequestered.
Himyaritic, *a.* *him*-yah-*rit*-ik, pertaining to the Himyarites, a Semitic tribe of S.W. Arabia: *n.* their language. (*Himyar*, one of their legendary kings.)
hin, *n.* hin, a Hebrew liquid measure of about 6 quarts. (Heb.)
hind, *n.* hynd, the female of the red deer. (A.S.)
hind, *n.* hynd, a farm servant or agricultural labourer; a peasant; a rustic. (A.S. *hina,* a domestic.)
hind, *a.* hynd, backward; pertaining to the rear or part behind. (A.S.)
hindberry, *n.* *hynd*-be-re, the wild raspberry.
hinder, *a.* *hyn*-der, pertaining to the rear.
hinder, *v.t.* *hin*-der, to prevent; to delay; to obstruct: *v.i.* to interpose obstacles or impediments. (A.S. *hindrian.*)
hinderer, *n.* *hin*-der-rer, one who or that which hinders.
hindermost, *a.* *hynd*-er-most, hindmost.
Hindi, *n.* *hin*-dee, the Indo-Aryan language forming the vernacular of Northern India. (Pers. *Hind,* India.)
hindmost, *a.* *hynd*-most, last; furthest behind.
hindrance, *n.* *hin*-drance, the act of hindering; that which hinders; obstruction.
Hindu, *n.* *hin*-doo, a native of Hindustan other than one of Parsee, Islamic, or Christian descent: *a.* pertaining to the Hindus.
Hinduism, *n.* *hin*-doo-izm, the doctrines and rites of the Hindus; Brahmanism as affected by Buddhism.
Hindustani, *n.* hin-doo-*stah*-nee, the common and official language of India; Urdu: *a.* of or pertaining to Hindustan, or to the language.
hinge, *n.* hinj, the hook or joint on which a door, gate, etc., turns; that on which anything depends or turns: *v.t.* to furnish with hinges: *v.i.* to stand, depend, or turn, as on a hinge. **off the hinges,** in a state of disorder or irregularity. (M.E. *heng.*)
hinny, *v.i.* *hin*-ne, to whinny. (L. *hinnio.*)
hinny, *n.* *hin*-ne, the offspring of a stallion and a she-ass. (L. *hinnus,* mule.)
hint, *n.* hint, a distant allusion; slight indication; suggestion: *v.t.* to bring to mind by a slight allusion; to allude to; to suggest; to imply. **to hint at,** to make a remote allusion to; to mention slightly. (A.S. *hentan,* to seize.)
hinterland, *n.* *hin*-ter-land, the back country; the region remote from the coast. (Ger.)
hintingly, *ad.* in a hinting manner.
hip, *n.* hip, the projecting part of an animal, formed

by the haunch bone; the haunch; the external angle, or the rafter at the angle, where two sloping roofs meet [Arch.]: *v.t.* to sprain the hip; to furnish with a hip [Arch.]; to throw by a hip-lock. **to have on the hip,** to have the advantage over one. **to smite hip and thigh,** completely to overthrow or defeat. (A.S. *hype.*)
hip, *n.* hip, the fruit of the dog-rose. (A.S. *heope,* dog-rose.)
hip, *int.* hip, the first note of a general cheer.
hip, *n.* hip, a state of despondency; "the blues": *v.t.* to render melancholy. (*hypochondria.*)
hip-bone, *n.* the innominate bone [Anat.].
hip-lock, *n.* the cross-buttock throw [Wrestling].
hipparion, *n.* hip-*pair*-re-on, an extinct three-toed collateral ancestor of the modern horse, of the Miocene and Pliocene. (Gr., pony.)
hipped, *a.* hipt, made melancholy.
hippic, *a. hip*-pik, pertaining to horses.
hippish, *a. hip*-ish, inclined to be melancholy; downcast.
hippo, *n. hip*-o, a hippopotamus [Coll.].
Hippocampus, *n. hip*-o-*kam*-pus, a genus of osseous fishes with a head and neck like a horse's, and a tapering prehensile tail; the sea-horse. (Gr. *hippos,* a horse, *kampos,* a sea-monster.)
hippocentaur, *n. hip*-o-*sen*-tawr, a centaur.
hippocras, *n. hip*-o-krass, a medicinal drink of wine with an infusion of spices, etc. (*Hippocrates.*)
Hippocratic, *a. hip*-o-*krat*-ik, pertaining to the Greek physician Hippocrates (5th cent. B.C.); applied, esp. to the appearance of the face of one utterly exhausted and dying, as described by him.
hippocrepian, *a. hip*-o-*kree*-pe-an, shaped like a horse-shoe [Zool.]. (Gr. *hippos,* and *krepis,* a shoe.)
hippodrome, *n. hip*-o-drome, a circus for equestrian exercises. (Gr. *hippos,* a horse, and *dromos,* running.)
hippogriff, *n. hip*-o-grif, a fabulous compound of horse and griffin. (Fr. *hippogriffe.*)
hippology, *n.* hip-*pol*-o-je, the study of horses.
hippomancy, *n. hip*-o-man-se, divination from the neighing of horses.
hippopathology, *n. hip*-o-pa-*thol*-o-je, the science of veterinary medicine; the pathology of the horse. (Gr. *hippos,* and *pathology.*)
hippophagous, *a.* hip-*pof*-a-gus, feeding on horse-flesh.
hippophagy, *n.* hip-*pof*-a-je, the practice of eating horseflesh. (Gr. *hippos,* and *phago,* eat.)
hippophile, *n. hip*-o-file, a lover of horses. (Gr. *hippos,* and *philos,* affection.)
hippopotamus, *n. hip*-o-*pot*-a-mus, a large pachydermatous non-ruminant ungulate of aquatic habits allied to the hogs, of which there are two species, both African. (Gr. *hippos,* and *potamos,* a river.)
hippuric, *a.* hip-*pewr*-rik, obtained from the urine of horses, etc. (Gr. *hippos,* and *ouron,* urine.)
hippurite, *n. hip*-ew-rite, an extinct bivalve mollusc occurring in the chalk. (Gr. *hippouris,* mare's tail.)
hippy, *a. hip*-e, broody; hypochondriac [Coll.].
hip-roof, *n.* a roof whose ends slant back at the same angle with the adjacent sides [Arch.].
hirable, *a. hire*-ra-bl, that may be hired.
hircine, *a. her*-sine, like a goat; hircinous: *n.* a fatty substance in goats to which their odour is attributed. (L. *hircinus.*)
hircinous, *a. her*-se-nus, smelling like a goat.
hire, *n.* hire, the price paid for the temporary use of anything; recompense for personal service; wages; a bribe: *v.t.* to procure or lend the services or use of at a certain price, and for a certain term; to engage for a reward. (A.S. *hyr,* wages.)
hireless, *a. hire*-less, gratuitous; without reward; unbribable.
hireling, *n. hire*-ling, one who serves for wages; a mercenary: *a.* serving for wages; mercenary.
hire-purchase, *n.* a contract under which goods are hired, the hirer agreeing to pay a stated number of stated sums at stated intervals, on the completion of which the goods hired become his property; purchase by instalments: *a.* pertaining to hire-purchase.
hirer, *n. hire*-rer, one who hires or lets on hire.
hirrient, *a. hi*-re-ent, strongly trilled: *n.* a strongly trilled letter or sound [Phonetics].
hirsute, *a. her*-sewt, rough with hair; set with softish bristles; boorish. (L. *hirsutus.*)
hirsuteness, *n.* the quality of being hirsute.
hirsutism, *n. her*-sew-tizm, abnormal growth of hair [Med.].
hirudine, *a.* hi-*roo*-dine, pertaining to the Hirudinea, or leeches; like a leech.
hirundine, *a.* hi-*rund*-in, like or pertaining to a swallow. (L. *hirundo,* a swallow.)
his, *pron.* hiz, possessive of *he.*
Hispanic, *a.* his-*pan*-ik, pertaining to Spain or its language or people. (L. *Hispania,* Spain.)
Hispanicism, *n.* his-*pan*-e-sizm, a Spanish idiom.
hispid, *a. hiss*-pid, rough with stiff bristles; bristly. (L.)
hiss, *n.* hiss, the sound made by hissing, or in sounding *s*; an expression of contempt or disapprobation: *v.i.* to make a sound by driving the breath between the tongue and the upper teeth; to express derision or disapprobation by hissing; to sound like *s*; to whiz: *v.t.* to condemn by hissing; to procure hisses or disgrace. (From the sound.)
hissingly, *ad. his*-sing-le, with a hissing sound.
hist, *int.* hist, be silent; hush.
histic, *a. his*-tik, pertaining to tissue.
histogenetic, *a. his*-to-je-*net*-ik, able to form tissue; relating to histogeny.
histogeny, *n.* his-*toj*-e-ne, the formation of the organic tissues; the science of the origin of tissues. (Gr. *histos,* a web, or tissue, *gennao,* produce.)
histography, *n.* his-*tog*-ra-fe, a description of the organic tissues. (Gr. *histos,* and *grapho,* write.)
histological, *a. his*-to-*loj*-e-kal, pertaining to histology; histogenetic.
histologist, *n.* his-*tol*-o-jist, one versed in histology.
histology, *n.* his-*tol*-o-je, the science or study of organic tissues. (Gr. *histos,* and *logos,* science.)
histolysis, *n.* his-*tol*-e-sis, dissolution of the organic tissues. (Gr. *histos,* and *lyo,* loosen.)
historian, *n.* his-*taw*-re-an, a writer of history; one versed in history.
historiated, *a.* his-*taw*-re-ay-ted, decorated with figures of natural objects as apart from flourishes, etc.
historic, *a.* his-*to*-rik, recorded in history; constituting history; notable. (Fr. *historique.*)
historical, *a.* his-*to*-re-kal, pertaining to, contained in, deduced from, or representing history; belonging to the past. **historical painting,** that branch of the art which depicts events of history. **historical sense,** the faculty of construing and reproducing an historical situation.
historically, *ad.* his-*to*-re-ka-le, in the manner of history; according to history; by way of narration.
historicity, *n.* his-to-*ris*-e-te, the state or quality of being historic; genuineness.
historiette, *n.* his-taw-re-*et,* a tale or short history. (Fr.)
historiographer, *n.* his-taw-re-*og*-ra-fer, an official historian. (Gr. *historiographia.*)
historiographical, *a.* his-*taw*-re-o-*graf*-e-kal, relating to historiography.
historiography, *n.* his-taw-re-*og*-ra-fe, the art or employment of an historian; the study of historical sources; the writing of history.
★**history,** *n. his*-to-re, a chronological narrative of events, esp. in the development of men and nations, with their causes and effects; a treatise dealing with some portion of the past; past events generally, a knowledge of facts. **natural history,** *see* **natural.** (L. *historia,* knowledge acquired through research.)
histrion, *n. his*-tre-on, a stage-player. (L.)
histrionic, *a. his*-tre-*on*-ik, pertaining to actors; stagy: *n.pl.* the theatrical art; dramatic representation; staginess; bombast. (L. *histrionicus.*)
histrionically, *ad.* in histrionic manner.
histrionism, *n. his*-tre-o-nizm, stage-playing; theatrical style; histrionics.
hit, *n.* hit, a stroke; a wound; a chance; a lucky chance; a happy remark; a success: *v.i.* to strike; to come in contact; to succeed; to suit: *v.t.* to strike, touch, or attain to, especially what is aimed at; to suit. **to hit off,** to represent or describe exactly. **to hit on,** to light on; to come to or fall on by chance. (Ice. *hitta.*)
hitch, *n.* hich, a catch or anything that holds; a jerk up; a stop or halt; an impediment; a break; a holding knot or noose in a rope: *v.i.* to move by jerks, or with stops; to become hooked or entangled; to interfere, or hit the legs together (as horses): *v.t*

to hook; to catch by a hook; to fasten; to pull up with jerks [Naut.]. (M.E. *hicchen.*)

hitch-hike, *v.i.* to go hiking with the intention of getting lifts from passing vehicles.

hithe, *n.* hithe, a port or small haven. (A.S.)

hither, *ad.* *hith*-er, to this place: *a.* toward the speaker. **hither and thither,** to this place and that. (A.S. *hider.*)

hithermost, *a.* *hith*-er-mohst, nearest on this side.

hitherside, *n.* *hith*-er-side, the nearer side.

hitherto, *ad.* *hith*-er-too, to this time; till now; to this place.

hitherward, *ad.* *hith*-er-ward, toward this place.

Hitlerism, *n.* *hit*-ler-izm, the extreme nationalistic and other political doctrines and practices of Adolf Hitler, German Führer, 1933–45; German fascism.

Hitlerite, *a.* *hit*-ler-ite, of or pertaining to Hitler or Hitlerism: *n.* a National Socialist of Germany; one imbued with Hitlerism.

Hittite, *n.* *hit*-tite, a member of an ancient civilization which flourished in Asia Minor about 3000–1200 B.C.; the language of the Hittites: *a.* pertaining to this people or their language. (Heb. *Khittim.*)

hive, *n.* hive, an artificial living-place for bees; a swarm of bees inhabiting a hive; a busy company or society: *v.t.* to collect into a hive; to store up: *v.i.* to take shelter together; to reside in a body. (A.S. *hyfe.*)

hiver, *n.* *hive*-er, one who hives; one who collects bees into a hive.

hives, *n.* hyvz, any skin-disease; an inflammation, as of the bowels (enteritis) or the larynx (croup) [Med.].

ho, *int.* hoh, a call to excite attention.

hoa, *int.* *hoh*-a *or* hoh, ho; whoa.

hoactzin, *n.* ho-*akt*-zin, the hoatzin.

hoar, *a.* hor, white; greyish white; white with age; hoary: *n.* hoariness; rime; antiquity. (A.S. *har.*)

hoard, *n.* hord, a store or large quantity of anything, esp. money, laid up; a hidden stock; a treasure: *v.t.* to collect and lay up in store: *v.i.* to store up. (A.S. *hord.*)

hoarder, *n.* *hord*-er, one who hoards up.

hoarding, *n.* *hord*-ing, a fence or screen enclosing a house and materials while builders are at work; a screen for displaying advertisement posters. (Dut. *horde,* hurdle.)

hoar-frost, *n.* the white particles of frozen dew.

hoarhound, *n.* *hor*-hound, horehound.

hoariness, *n.* *haw*-re-ness, the state of being hoary.

hoarse, *a.* horse, having a harsh grating voice, as from a cold; harsh; discordant. (A.S. *hās.*)

hoarsely, *ad.* *horse*-le, in a hoarse manner.

hoarseness, *n.* the state of being hoarse.

hoarstone, *n.* *hor*-stone, a landmark; a stone designating the bounds of an estate.

hoary, *a.* *haw*-re, white or grey with age; venerable; greyish white through being covered by very short dense hairs [Bot.].

hoatzin, *n.* ho-*at*-zin, a S. American bird of the genus *Opisthocomus,* of which the young have claws on the first and second fingers of the wings by which they climb trees. (Sp., from Native.)

hoax, *n.* hohks, a trick played off in sport; a practical joke; a deception; a misleading statement: *v.t.* to play a trick upon for sport; to dupe. (*hocus-pocus.*)

hoaxer, *n.* *hohk*-ser, one who hoaxes.

hob, *n.* hob, the nave of a wheel; the flat part at the side of a grate where things are kept warm; the peg or mark in quoits, etc.; a hobnail. (*hub.*)

hob, *n.* hob, a rustic; an elf or fairy. (*Robert.*)

Hobbism, *n.* *hob*-bizm, the philosophy of Thomas Hobbes (*d.* 1679), esp. the doctrine that submission to the will of the State, as vested in the Sovereign, is the supreme rule for the regulation of the individual.

Hobbist, *n.* *hob*-bist, a follower of Hobbes.

hobble, *n.* *hob*-bl, an unequal, halting, awkward gait; a clog or fetter for a horse, etc.; difficulty; perplexity: *v.i.* to walk as if lame; to walk awkwardly; to move irregularly: *v.t.* to clog; to shackle the legs (of a horse, etc.). **hobble bush,** the American wayfaring-tree. **hobble skirt,** a woman's skirt cut very narrow round the knees. (M.E. *hobelen.*)

hobbledehoy, *n.* *hob*-bl-de-*hoy,* a youth between boyhood and manhood.

hobbler, *n.* *hob*-bler, one who hobbles: a hoveller. (As *hobble.*)

hobbler, *n.* *hob*-bler, formerly, a soldier mounted on a hobby, or one who, by his tenure, maintained a hobby for military service. (O.Fr. *hobeler.*)

hobblingly, *ad.* *hob*-bling-le, in a hobbling manner.

hobby, *n.* *hob*-be, a small species of falcon, *Falco subbuteo.* (O.Fr. *hobet.*)

hobby, *n.* *hob*-be, a horse of a middle size; a pacing horse; a hobby-horse; any favourite pursuit or subject. (O.Fr. *hobin.*)

hobby-horse, *n.* *hob*-be-horse, an imitation horse with a wickerwork body; a wooden horse, or stick with a horse's head, on which children ride; a rocking-horse; a hobby.

hobgoblin, *n.* hob-*gob*-lin, a goblin; a mischievous imp; an alarming apparition.

hobnail, *n.* *hob*-nale, a nail with a thick strong head, for heavy boots; a clownish person; hobnailed liver [Med.].

hobnailed, *a.* *hob*-nayld, set or as set with hobnails; rough. **hobnailed liver,** an indurated human liver covered with small projections, a result of a form of cirrhosis [Med.].

hobnob, *n.* *hob*-nob, a friendly conversation; a familiar call to drink: *v.i.* to drink or associate familiarly with. (A.S. *habban,* to have, *nabban,* not to have.)

hobo, *n.* *hoh*-boh, a tramp [U.S.A.].

hock, *n.* and *v.t.* hok, hough. (A.S. *hok.*)

hock, *n.* hok, a white Rhenish wine, so called from Hochheim on the Main.

hockey, *n.* *hok*-ke, an outdoor game between opposite sides played with a ball and sticks of ash curved at the end. (*hook.*)

Hock-tide, *n.* *hok*-tide, the Monday and Tuesday in the second week after Easter, two days of feasting formerly held in England, allegedly to commemorate an overthrow of Danish invaders.

hocus, *n.* *hoh*-kus, a cheat; a stupefying draught: *v.t.* to cheat; to drug; to cheat after drugging.

hocus-pocus, *n.* *hoh*-kus-*poh*-kus, a juggler; a juggler's trick; conjurers' jargon: *v.t.* to cheat; to trick (Mock Latin of the 17th cent.)

hod, *n.* hod, a trough on a long handle for carrying mortar and bricks on the shoulder. (Fr. *hotte.*)

hodden, *n.* *hod*-dn, coarse cloth made of undyed wool in its natural state. **hodden grey,** the colour of hodden; rustic; homely.

hodge, *n.* hodj, a rustic; the class of agricultural labourers.

hodge-podge, *n.* *hodj*-podj, a hotchpotch.

hodiernal, *a.* *hoh*-de-*er*-nal, belonging to to-day. (L. *hodiernus.*)

hodman, *n.* *hod*-man, a man who carries a hod.

hodmandod, *n.* *hod*-man-dod, a snail. (*dodman.*)

hodograph, *n.* *hoh*-do-graf, a curve the radius vector of which represents in direction and magnitude the velocity of a moving point. (Gr. *hodos,* way, *grapho,* write.)

hodometer, *n.* ho-*dom*-e-ter, a contrivance connected with the axle, and provided with a dial and index to show the distance a vehicle has travelled. (Gr. *hodos,* a way, *metron,* measure.)

hoe, *n.* hoh, a garden tool for cutting up weeds and loosening the earth: *v.t.* to cut or clean with a hoe: *v.i.* to use a hoe. (Fr. *houe.*)

hoe-cake, *n.* a cake of Indian meal, originally baked on a hoe [U.S.A.]

hog, *n.* hog, a swine, a general name of that species of animal; a castrated boar; a sheep or a bullock of a year old; one who is mean and filthy; a scrubbing-broom for scraping a ship's bottom under water [Naut.]; a stone that fails to pass the hog-score [Curling]: *v.t.* to scrape a ship's bottom under water [Naut.]; to cut the hair short: *v.i.* to bend, so as to resemble a hog's back. (A.S.)

hogbacked, *a.* *hog*-bakt, shaped like a hog's back.

hogged, *a.* hogd, higher in the middle than at the ends [Naut.].

hoggerel, *n.* *hog*-grel, a sheep of the second year.

hogger, *n.* *hog*-ger, a footless stocking worn by coal-miners when at work.

hogger-pump, *n.* the top pump in the sinking pit of a mine.

hoggery, *n.* *hog*-er-re, a pig-farm; swine collectively; the characteristic behaviour of hogs.

hogget, *n.* *hog*-get, a sheep two years old; a colt of a year old; a boar of the second year. (Dial. Eng.)

hoggish, *a.* *hog*-gish, like a hog; brutish; gluttonous; filthy; meanly selfish.
hoggishly, *ad.* *hog*-gish-le, in a hoggish manner.
hoggishness, *n.* the quality of being hoggish.
hogmanay, *n.* *hog*-ma-nay, in Scotland, the last day of the year; a present given on this day.
hog-plum, *n.* any of several tropical trees of the genus *Spondias*, or its plum-like fruit.
hog-reeve, *n.* a parish officer who adjudicated regarding the trespasses of swine.
hog-ringer, *n.* one whose business is to put rings in the snouts of swine.
hog-score, *n.* the distance-line across a curling rink which a stone in play must pass.
hogshead, *n.* *hogz*-hed, a large cask, esp. one of 54 gall. for beer, or 63 gall. for wine.
hogwash, *n.* *hog*-wosh, kitchen or brewery refuse; swill for swine.
hogweed, *n.* *hog*-weed, cow parsnip, sow thistle, hedge parsley, or other coarse weed.
hoiden, *n.* *hoy*-den, a hoyden.
hoist, *n.* hoyst, the act of raising; an elevator or apparatus for hoisting the perpendicular height of a flag or sail; a string of signalling flags: *v.t.* to raise with tackle; to heave; to run up a flag; to heighten a sail [Naut.]. (O.Dut. *hyssen.*)
hoity-toity, *int.* *hoy*-te-*toy*-te, surprise or disapprobation with some degree of contempt.
hokey-pokey, *n.* *hoh*-ke-*poh*-ke, cheap ice-cream; hanky-panky [Slang].
hokum, *n.* *hoh*-kum, action or method designed to sway followers, an audience, etc. in some desired direction; buncombe, bunk [U.S.A. slang].
holarctic, *a.* hol-*ark*-tik, pertaining to the arctic regions [Zool.]. (Gr. *holos*, whole, and *arctic.*)
hold, *v.t.* hohld, to retain with a grasp; to keep in a certain way; to consider or judge; to contain; to retain; to maintain; to possess; to keep; to entertain; to restrain; to keep fast; to keep from running or flowing out; to continue; to celebrate: *v.i.* to remain fixed; to be true or not fail; to stand; to continue unbroken or unsubdued; to last; to endure; to continue; to adhere: *n.* a grasp with the hand or arms; grasp or gripe; something for support; power of keeping; a place of confinement; custody; a fortified place; a mark directing the performer to rest on the note over which it is placed [Mus.]. **hold forth,** to offer; to harangue; to declaim; to speak in public. **hold in,** to restrain. **hold of,** to derive title from. **hold off,** to keep at a distance. **hold on,** to continue in; to continue; to cling to. **hold one's own,** to keep good one's present condition. **hold out,** to stretch forth; to offer; to endure; to maintain position. **hold over,** to keep in reserve; to defer; to remain in after one's term has expired [Law]. **hold to,** to cling or cleave to; to bind by. **hold together,** to be joined; to keep in union. **hold up,** to raise or sustain; to support oneself; to cease or cause to cease; to continue the same speed; to keep fine (of weather); to carry out a hold-up. **hold with,** to side with. *p.* and *pp.* **held.** (A.S. *healdon.*)
hold, *n.* hohld, the interior cavity of a ship, where the cargo is stowed. (Dut. *hol*, a cavity.)
hold, *int.* hohld, stop! forbear! be still!
hold-all, *n.* a roll-up wrapper with pockets for carrying clothes, etc., when travelling.
hold-back, *n.* check; hindrance; drag.
holder, *n.* *hohl*-der, one who holds; a tenant; the payee of a bill of exchange, etc. [Comm.]; something that will hold.
holder-forth, *n.* one who harangues.
holdfast, *n.* *hohld*-fahst, a contrivance for securing and holding a thing in its place, as a nail, a catch, etc.; a support.
holding, *n.* *hohl*-ding, anything held; a farm held of a superior; a small-holding; tenure; hold; influence.
hold-up, *n.* a temporary traffic block; forcible obstruction or detention, esp. on the highway, for purpose of robbery [Amer.].
★**hole,** *n.* hole, a hollow place or cavity; an excavation; a pit; a perforation; a mean habitation; means of escape; a difficulty; a small pit into which a player is to send his ball, also a point scored by doing this [Golf]: *v.i.* to go into a hole; to drive one's ball into a hole [Golf]: *v.t.* to make holes in; to drive into a hole. **hole and corner,** underhand; not quite honest. **(A.S. *hol.*)**
holey, *a.* *hoh*-le, holed; abounding in holes.
holibut, *n.* *hol*-e-but, a halibut.
holiday, *n.* *hol*-e-day, a cessation of work; a day set apart for commemorating some important event; a day or period of general rejoicing; vacation: *a.* pertaining to a holiday: *v.i.* to take a holiday. (*holy* and *day.*)
holily, *ad.* *hoh*-le-le, in a holy way; piously.
holiness, *n.* *hoh*-le-ness, sanctity; devotion. **his Holiness,** a title of the Pope.
holing-axe, *n.* a narrow axe for cutting holes in posts.
holism, *n.* *hol*-izm, the formation by creative evolution in Nature of wholes that are greater than the sum of the parts [Phil.]. (Gk. *holos*, whole.)
holistic, *a.* ho-*lis*-tik, pertaining to holism.
holla, *int.* hol-*lah*, hallo! attend here!: *n.* a loud call: *v.i.* to call out loudly to one at a distance. (Fr. *ho*, ho, *là*, there.)
holland, *n.* *hol*-land, a coarse linen, first made in Holland. **brown holland,** unbleached holland.
Hollander, *n.* *hol*-lan-der, a native of Holland; a Dutch vessel.
Hollandish, *a.* *hol*-lan-dish, Dutch.
hollands, *n.* *hol*-landz, a gin made in Holland; schnapps.
holloa, *v.i.* hol-*loh*, to holla or hallo.
★**hollow,** *a.* *hol*-lo, containing an empty space; vacant; not solid; concave; sunken; deep; not sincere; not sound; easy: *n.* a cavity; a depression; a cave; a hole; a valley or channel: *v.t.* to make hollow, as by digging; to excavate. **hollow square,** a body of soldiers drawn up in the form of a square with an empty space in the middle. (A.S. *holh.*)
hollow-eyed, *a.* having sunken eyes.
hollowly, *ad.* *hol*-lo-le, in a hollow manner; insincerely.
hollowness, *n.* the state of being hollow; insincerity.
hollow-ware, *n.* pots, kettles, etc., esp. those made of cast-iron.
holly, *n.* *hol*-le, an evergreen tree of the genus *Ilex*, with prickly leaves and scarlet berries. (A.S. *holen.*)
hollyhock, *n.* *hol*-le-hok, a tall plant of the mallow order, *Althæa rosea.* (*holy*, and A.S. *hoc*, a mallow.)
holm, *n.* home, the evergreen oak, *Quercus ilex.*
holm, *n.* home, a low flat tract of rich land on the banks of a river; an islet in a river. (Ice. *holmr*, islet.)
holmia, *n.* *hol*-me-a, oxide of holmium [Chem.].
holmic, *a.* *hol*-mik, pertaining to chemical salts containing holmium [Chem.].
holmium, *n.* *hol*-me-um, a rare-earth metallic element of the yttrium sub-group. (Stock*holm*, where found in gadolinite.)
holm-oak, *n.* *home*-oke, the evergreen oak. *Quercus ilex.*
holo-, *comb.f.* *hol*-lo, whole, entire. (Gr. *holos.*)
holoblastic, *a.* *hoh*-lo-blas-tik, entirely germinal; undergoing complete cleavage (of the cells of ova). [Biol.]. (Gr. *holos*, and *blastos*, a sprout.)
holocaust, *n.* *hol*-o-kawst, a burnt sacrifice, of which the whole was consumed; a great slaughter. (Gr. *holos*, and *kaustos*, burned.)
holocryptic, *a.* hoh-lo-*krip*-tik, wholly secret; indecipherable. (Gr. *holos*, and *krupto*, hide.)
holograph, *n.* *hol*-o-graf, a document entirely in the handwriting of the person who signs it: *a.* written thus. (Gr. *holos*, and *grapho*, write.)
holographic, *a.* hol-o-*graf*-ik, written wholly by the author, esp. as testator; pertaining to a holograph.
holohedral, *a.* hol-o-*hee*-dral, perfectly symmetrical (of crystals) [Min.]. (Gr. *holos*, and *hedra*, a side.)
holometabola, *n.pl.* *hoh*-lo-me-*tab*-o-la, those insects that undergo complete metamorphosis [Entom.]. (Gr. *holos*, and *metabole*, change.)
holometer, *n.* ho-*lom*-e-ter, an instrument for taking all kinds of measurements; a pantometer. (Gr. *holos*, and *metron*, measure.)
holophotal, *a.* hol-o-*foh*-tal, reflecting all the light unbroken. (Gr. *holos*, and *phos*, light.)
holosericeous, *a.* *hoh*-lo-se-*rish*-e-us, wholly covered with silky down [Bot.]. (Gr. *holos*, and L. *sericeus*, silken.)
holothurian, *n.* ho-lo-*thewr*-re-an, an echinoderm of the class Holothuroidea, which includes the sea-

cucumbers, sea-slugs, and trepang. (Gr. *holos*, and *thyra*, a door.)
holpen, *hole*-pen, old *pp.* of *help.*
holster, *n.* *hole*-ster, a leather case for a pistol, carried by a belt or attached to the saddle. (Dut.)
holt, *n.* hohlt, a copse; a wooded hill. (A.S.)
holt, *n.* hohlt, a burrow; a hole. (As *hold.*)
holy, *a.* *hoh*-le, pure in heart; free from sin; set apart to a sacred use; sacred; religious. **Holy Cross Day,** 14 Sept., commemorating the return of the true Cross to Jerusalem, A.D. 628 **holy day,** any day commemorating a religious event. **Holy Ghost,** or **Holy Spirit,** the Divine Spirit, the Third Person of the Trinity. **the Holy Land,** Palestine. **Holy of Holies,** the innermost apartment of the Jewish tabernacle or temple, where the ark was kept; an inmost shrine. **Holy Office,** the Inquisition. **holy orders,** deacons, priests, and bishops. **Holy Roman Empire,** *see* **Roman. holy rood,** the Crucifix; a cross over the entrance to a chancel. **Holy Saturday,** the Saturday in Holy Week. **the Holy See,** the see of Rome, as established by St. Peter; hence, papal authority. **Holy Spirit,** the Holy Ghost. **Holy Thursday,** the day on which the Ascension is commemorated. **holy water,** water for sprinkling after being consecrated by the priest. **Holy Week,** the week before Easter, in which the Passion is commemorated. **Holy Writ,** the Bible. (A.S. *halig*, holy.)
holystone, *n.* *hoh*-le-stone, a soft sandstone used to scrub the decks of ships: *v.t.* to scour with holystone.
homage, *n.* *hom*-aj, the submission and service which a tenant promised to his feudal superior; the act of fealty; respect paid by external action; devout affection or reverence: *v.t.* to pay respect; to subject. (O.Fr.)
homager, *n.* *hom*-a-jer, one who does homage, or who holds land of another by homage.
Homburg, *n.* *hom*-berg, a soft felt hat with narrow brim. (Ger. place-name.)
home, *n.* home, the abode of the family; habitat; where one stays; one's own country; where one is at rest; the grave; a charitable or public institution where something like home comfort is provided; a goal or station in certain games: *a.* connected with one's dwelling or country; domestic; close up; pointed; personal: *ad.* to one's habitation or country; pointedly; closely: *v.i.* to come home. **at home,** at one's house; in one's country; conversant with, or familiar. **home counties,** the five counties adjacent to Greater London. **Home Guard,** the British citizen army established (as the Local Defence Volunteers) in 1940; a member of this. **Home Office,** the department of State dealing with domestic affairs not covered by other departments. **Home Rule,** national self-government. **home signal,** the signal at the entrance to a block of the block system indicating whether or not it is clear [Rlys.]. **home truth,** an unpleasant truth, one that thrusts home. (A.S. *ham.*)
homeborn, *a.* *home*-born, native; domestic.
homebred, *a.* *home*-bred, bred at home; natural; domestic; not foreign; uncultivated; unpolished.
homecoming, *n.* *home*-kum-ing, arrival at home.
homecraft, *n.* *home*-krahft, the art or occupation of housekeeping; household management.
home-farm, *n.* a farm on a large estate attached to the owner's dwelling-house.
homefelt, *a.* *home*-felt, felt in one's own breast; inward; private.
homekeeping, *a.* *home*-keep-ing, staying at home; domesticated; untravelled.
homeland, *n.* *home*-land, one's native country; the Mother Country of an overseas dominion.
homeless, *a.* *home*-less, without a home.
homelessness, *n.* the state of having no home.
homelike, *a.* *home*-like, like home; homely.
homelily, *ad.* *home*-le-le, in a homely way.
homeliness, *n.* *home*-le-ness, the state of being homely; plainness; rudeness.
homely, *a.* *home*-le, domestic; of plain features; not handsome; plain; rude.
homelyn, *n.* *home*-lin, the spotted ray, *Raia maculata*, a fish of the same genus as the skate.
homemade, *a.* *home*-made, made at home; not the product of a factory; plain.
homeopathy, *n.* hoh-me-*op*-a-the, homœopathy.
homer, *n.* *hoh*-mer, an ancient Hebrew measure equal, at various times, to 6–8 bushels (dry), or 47–64 gallons (liquid).
homer, *n.* *home*-er, a homing pigeon.
Homeric, *a.* ho-*me*-rik, pertaining to Homer, or to his poetry; resembling Homer's verse. **Homeric laughter,** irrepressible laughter.
homesick, *a.* *home*-sik, longing for home; grieved at absence from home.
homesickness, *n.* *home*-sik-ness, depression of spirits occasioned by a separation from one's home or country; nostalgia [Med.].
home-speaking, *n.* direct and forcible speaking.
homespun, *a.* *home*-spun, spun at home; plain; rude; homemade; not elegant: *n.* cloth of homespun yarn; an unpolished, rustic person.
homestead, *n.* *home*-sted, a farm with its buildings.
homesteader, *n.* *home*-sted-er, a holder of a homestead.
homeward, *ad.* *home*-ward, towards home.
homework, *n.* *home*-wurk, work to be done at home; lessons prepared at home or not in class.
homey, *a.* *home*-e, homy.
homicidal, *a.* *hom*-e-sy-dal, pertaining to homicide; murderous; bloody.
homicide, *n.* *hom*-e-syd, the killing of one man by another; a manslayer. (Fr.)
homiletical, *a.* hom-e-*let*-e-kal, pertaining to homiletics.
homiletics, *n.* hom-e-*let*-iks, the art of preaching; pulpit eloquence. (Gr. *homiletikos*, talkative.)
homilist, *n.* *hom*-e-list, one who preaches to a congregation; a composer of homilies.
homily, *n.* *hom*-e-le, a moralizing discourse; a sermon. **Book of Homilies,** a collection of sermons prepared at the time of the Reformation for reading in churches. (Gr. *homilia*, converse.)
homing, *a.* *home*-ing, home-returning. **homing pigeon,** a carrier-pigeon trained to return home from a distance.
hominoid, *n.* *hom*-e-noyd, a man-like animal.
hominy, *n.* *hom*-e-ne, boiled maize. (Indian.)
homish, *a.* *home*-ish, like home [Coll.].
hommock, *n.* *hom*-mok, a hummock.
homo-, *comb.f.* *hoh*-mo, of the same sort, the same. (Gr. *homos*, same.)
homocarpous, *a.* *hoh*-mo-*kar*-pus, bearing fruits all alike. (Gr. *homos*, same, *karpos*, fruit.)
homocentric, *a.* *hoh*-mo-*sen*-trik, having the same centre. (Gr. *homos*, and *centric.*)
homocercal, *a.* *hoh*-mo-*ser*-kal, with both tail lobes equal [Ichth.]. (Gr. *homos*, and *kerkos*, a tail.)
homochromous, *a.* ho-*mok*-ro-mus, of uniform colour; with florets of the same colour [Bot.].
homodont, *a.* *hoh*-mo-dont, having the teeth all alike.
homodromous, *a.* ho-*mod*-ro-mus, taking the same direction.
homœopathic, *a.* *hoh*-me-o-*path*-ik, of or pertaining to homœopathy.
homœopathist, *n.* hoh-me-*op*-a-thist, one who practises or believes in homœopathy.
homœopathy, *n.* hoh-me-*op*-a-the, a system which professes to cure diseases by the administration in minute doses of medicines that would induce these diseases or similar symptoms in healthy persons. (Gr. *homoiopatheia*, sympathy.)
homœozoic, *a.* hoh-me-o-*zoh*-ik, containing similar forms of life. (Gr. *homoios*, like, *zoe*, life.)
homogamous, *a.* hoh-*mog*-a-mus, having hermaphroditic essential parts of fructification; with pistils and stamens ripening at the same time [Bot.]. (Gr. *homos*, the same, *gamos*, marriage.)
homogamy, *n.* hoh-*mog*-a-me, state of being homogamous [Bot.]; inbreeding [Zool.].
homogeneal, *a.* hoh-mo-*jee*-ne-al, homogeneous.
homogeneity, *n.* hoh-mo-je-*nee*-e-te, sameness of kind, nature, or structure.
homogeneous, *a.* hoh-mo-*jee*-ne-us, of the same kind or nature; consisting of similar parts or elements of like nature; commensurable [Math.]. (Gr. *homos*, and *genos*, kind.)
homogeneously, *ad.* in a homogeneous manner.
homogeneousness, *n.* homogeneity.
homogenesis, *n.* hoh-mo-*jen*-e-sis, the doctrine that in the higher organisms the offspring passes through the same cycle of changes as the parent; reproduction characterized by the likeness of successive generations [Biol.]. (Gr. *homos*, and *genesis.*)
homogenetic, *a.* hoh-mo-je-*net*-ik, pertaining to or

exhibiting homogenesis [Biol.]; similar in structural relations [Geol.].

homogenize, *v.t.* hoh-*moj*-e-nize, to make homogeneous; mechanically to break up the fat globules, etc., of milk to increase digestibility.

homogenous, *a.* hoh-*moj*-e-nus, having similarity of structure due to common descent [Biol.].

homograph, *n. hoh*-mo-graf, a homonym.

homoiousian, *a.* hoh-moy-*ou*-se-an, of similar, but not the same, nature: *n.* one who maintained that Christ was of a similar, but not the same, nature with God [Theol.]. (Gr. *homoios*, like, *ouisa*, being.)

homologate, *v.t.* ho-*mol*-o-gate, to admit; to approve; to confirm.

homological, *a. hoh*-mo-*loj*-e-kal, pertaining to homology; with parts corresponding.

homologize, *v.i.* and *t.* ho-*mol*-o-jize, to be or to make homologous.

homologous, *a.* ho-*mol*-o-gus, corresponding in position, proportion, value, or structure.

homologue, *n. hoh*-mo-log, the same organ in form and function in different animals.

homology, *n.* ho-*mol*-o-je, correspondence; affinity of structure, as between the human arm, animal's foreleg, and bird's wing [Biol.]. (Gr. *homos*, and *lovos*, proportion.)

homomorphous, *a. hoh*-mo-*mor*-fus, very similar in form; analagous. (Gr. *homos*, and *morphe*, shape.)

homonym, *n. hom*-o-nim, a word the same in sound but different in derivation and sense, as *cleave*, to adhere to, and *cleave*, to part asunder. (Gr. *homos*, and *onyma*, a name.)

homonymous, *a.* ho-*mon*-e-mus, having the same name; of the nature of a homonym.

homonymy, *n.* ho-*mon*-e-me, the state of being homonymous; sameness between words which differ in signification; ambiguity.

homoousian, *a.* hoh-mo-*ou*-se-an, of the same, and not merely similar nature: *n.* one who maintained that Christ was of the same nature with God. (Gr. *homos*, and *ouisa*, being.)

homophone, *n. hom*-o-fone, a letter representing or a word having the same sound as another. (Gr. *homos*, and *phone*, sound.)

homophonic, *a.* hom-o-*fon*-ik like or similar in sound; not polyphonic [Mus.].

homophonous, *a.* ho-*mof*-o-nus, having the same sound; homophonic.

homophony, *n.* ho-*mof*-on-e, quality of being homophonous; sameness of sound; unison, as opposed to polyphony [Mus.].

homoplastic, *a. hoh*-mo-*plas*-tik, similarly formed but not essentially the same. (Gr. *homos*, and *plastos*, shaped.)

homoptera, *n.pl.* ho-*mop*-te-ra, an order of insects whose fore wings and hind wings are alike [Entom.]. (Gr. *homos*, and *pteron*, a wing.)

homosexual, *a.* hoh-mo-*seks*-yew-al, attracted sexually by those of one's own sex: *n.* a person addicted to homosexuality; a sodomite.

homosexuality, *n.* hoh-mo-*seks*-yew-*al*-e-te, sexual attraction for members of the same sex; sodomy.

homotaxial, *a. ho*-mo-*taks*-e-al, characterized by homotaxis [Geol.]; containing a similar assemblage of fossils.

homotaxis, *n. ho*-mo-*taks*-is, similarity in the relative arrangement of strata [Geol.]. (Gr. *homos*, and *taxis*, order.)

homotonous, *a.* ho-*mot*-o-nus, equable; of the same tenor. (Gr. *homos*, and *tone*.)

homotropal, *a.* ho-*mot*-ro-pal, turning in the same direction; having the same direction as the body to which they belong [Bot.]. (Gr. *homos*, and *trepo*, turn.)

homotype, *n. hoh*-mo-tipe, an organ, etc., of the same type of structure [Biol.].

homotypic, *a.* hoh-mo-*tip*-ik, conforming to the normal condition [Zool.]

homunculus, *n.* ho-*mung*-kewl-us, a little man; a dwarf; a nonentity [Coll.]. (L. *homo*, a man.)

homy, *a. home*-e, homelike; intimate [Coll.].

hone, *n.* hone, a whetstone; a stone of a fine grit, used for sharpening instruments: *v.t.* to sharpen on a hone. (A.S. *han.*)

honest, *a. on*-est, fair in dealing with others; just and upright; free from fraud; sincere; unreserved; honourable or suitable; chaste (of women); respectable; faithful. (O.Fr. *honeste.*)

honestly, *ad. on*-est-le, with honesty.

honesty, *n. on*-es-te, the state or quality of being honest; an upright disposition; integrity; honour; sincerity; a cruciferous plant of the genus *Lunaria*, with purple flowers and semi-transparent elliptical seed pods.

honey, *n. hun*-e, a sweet viscid substance, collected by bees from flowers; sweetness; lusciousness; a sweetheart; a word of tenderness: *v.i.* and *t.* to flatter; to cover with honey. (A.S. *hunig.*)

honey-bag, *n.* the honey-bee's receptacle for honey.

honey-bear, *n.* the Indian sloth-bear; the kinkajou of S. America.

honey-bee, *n.* a bee that makes honey.

honey-buzzard, *n.* a hawk, *Pernis apivorus*, that feeds on the larvæ of bees, etc.

honeycomb, *n. hun*-e-kome, a waxy substance formed by bees into hexagonal cells for storing honey; decoration of similar pattern; flaws in metal castings, etc.: *v.t.* to make full of holes or cavities like honey-comb. (A.S. *hunigcamb.*)

honeydew, *n. hun*-e-dew, a saccharine exudation of plant leaves; a similar substance secreted by aphides on leaves; cavendish tobacco.

honey-eater, *n.* any of the Meliphagidæ, a number of Australasian birds having a long extensile tongue, including the parson-bird and stitch-bird of New Zealand.

honeyed, *a. hun*-id, sweet; flattering.

honey-flower, *n.* an evergreen plant of the genus *Melianthus*; the bee-orchis.

honeyguide, *n. hun*-e-gide, a S. African cuckoo of the genus *Indicator*, whose cry is said to indicate the nests of bees.

honey-locust, *n.* a sub-tropical tree of the genus *Gleditschia*, having a thorny stem.

honeymoon, *n. hun*-e-moon, the first month after marriage; the holiday of a newly married pair; *v.i.* to take such a holiday.

honey-mouthed, *a.* soft or smooth in speech.

honey-stone, *n.* mellite.

honeysuckle, *n. hun*-e-suk-kl, a climbing plant of the genus *Lonicera*, celebrated for the beauty and fragrance of its flowers; the woodbine. **Australian honeysuckle,** a shrub of the genus *Banksia*. **French honeysuckle,** a leguminous plant of the genus *Hedysarum*.

honey-tongued, *a. hun*-e-tungd, using soft speech.

honeywort, *n. hun*-e-wurt, a plant of the borage family with flowers very attractive to bees.

hong, *n.* hong, a trading factory or commercial establishment in the Far East. (Chin.)

honied, *a. hun*-id, honeyed.

Honiton, *n. hon*-e-ton, a lace of the kind made by hand at Honiton, in Devonshire.

honk, *n.* honk, the hoarse hoot of a motor-car's horn: *v.i.* to make this sound.

honorarium, *n.* on-o-*rare*-re-um, a recompense or fee, esp. to a professional man. (L.)

honorary, *a. on*-o-ra-re, conferring honour, or intended merely to confer honour; obtained without passing examinations; possessing a title or office without performing service or receiving payment. (L. *honorariys.*)

honorific, *a. on*-o-*rif*-ik, conferring honour; implying honour.

honour, *n. on*-ur, the esteem due or paid to worth; a testimony of esteem; exalted rank; distinction; reverence; veneration; reputation; nobleness of mind; any virtue much valued; dignity of mien; that which honours; a high mark of distinction; privileges of rank or birth; a group of manors under a lord paramount: *pl.* the four highest cards in a suit: *v.t.* to respect; to venerate; to confer honour; to exalt; to glorify; to treat with civility; to accept and pay when due, as a draft [Comm.]. **debt of honour,** *see* **debt.** **honours of war,** distinctions granted to a vanquished enemy. **roll of honour,** *see* **roll.** **upon my honour,** words accompanying a declaration which pledges one's honour for the truth of it. (L. *honor*, esteem.)

honourable, *a. on*-ur-a-bl, of distinguished rank: illustrious: actuated by honour; conferring honour: consistent with honour or reputation: with tokens of honour; not base; without hypocrisy or deceit; worthy of respect; becoming men of rank and character: *n.* (*cap.*) a title of distinction borne by the younger children of earls, and all children of barons and viscounts, also by maids of honour, certain judges, and certain high Indian and Dominion officials and in the U.S.A. to members of Congress and certain State and municipal officials. **Most Honourable,** a title of marquises. **Right Honourable,** a title of barons, viscounts, earls, Privy Councillors, certain Lord Mayors, and the chairman of the London County Council.

honourableness, *n. on*-ur-a-bl-ness, the state or condition of being honourable; conformity to honourable principles.

honourably, *ad. on*-ur-a-ble, in an honourable manner.

honourer, *n. on*-ur-er, one who honours.

honour-point, *n. on*-ur-poynt, the point immediately above the centre of the shield [Her.].

hooch, *n.* hooch, raw or crude spirits; any synthetic alcoholic drink [U.S.A. slang]. (N.Amerind. *hutsnuwu.*)

hood, *n.* hood, a covering for the head; a cowl; anything drawn over the head to cover it; a cover, the cowl worn over the gown to show the graduate's degree; anything resembling a hood: *v.t.* to put a hood on; to cover; to blind. (A.S. *hod.*)

hooded, *a. hood*-ed, covered with or as with a hood; blinded; in the form of a hood; cucullate [Bot.].

hoodlum, *n. hood*-lum, a street rowdy; a hooligan [U.S.A. slang].

hoodman-blind, *n. hood*-man-blind, blind-man's buff.

hood-moulding, *n.* the upper moulding over a door or window; the drip-stone [Arch.].

hoodoo, *n. hoo*-doo, a cause of bad luck: a person who brings bad luck; voodoo: *v.t.* to cast an evil spell on: *a.* unlucky [U.S.A. coll.].

hoodwink, *v.t. hood*-wink, to blind by covering the eyes; to impose on; to deceive.

hooey, *n. hoo*-e, nonsense; ballyhoo [U.S.A. slang].

hoof, *n.* hoof (*pl.* **hoofs** *or* **hooves**), the horny substance on the feet of certain animals: *v.i.* to walk, as cattle: *v.t.* to kick; to attack with the hoofs. **to hoof it,** to go afoot [Coll.]. **to hoof out,** to eject or dismiss summarily [Coll.]. (A.S. *hof.*)

hoof-bound, *a.* having a painful dryness and contraction of the hoof.

hoofed, *a.* hooft, furnished with hoofs.

★**hook,** *n.* hook, a sharply curved piece, usually of metal, for catching and holding anything; a snare; a curved instrument for cutting grain; a sickle; that part of a hinge which is fixed or inserted in a post; a forked timber in a ship, placed on the keel; a promontory; a blow delivered with the elbow bent [Boxing]: *v.t.* to catch with a hook; to draw, as with a hook; to ensnare: *v.i.* to bend; to fit on by a hook. **by hook or by crook,** by right means or by wrong. **hook it!** or **take your hook!** clear off! begone! [Slang]. **hooks and eyes,** dress-fasteners consisting of a hook and a loop. **off the hooks,** out of sorts; dead [Slang]. (A.S. *hoc.*)

hookah, *n. hook*-ah, a Turkish tobacco pipe, in which the smoke passes through water. (Ar.)

hooked, *a.* hookt, shaped like a hook; fitted with hooks.

hookedness, *n. hook*-ed-ness, the state of being bent like a hook.

hooker, *n. hook*-er, one who hooks; a thief [Slang]; a front row player in a scrimmage who tries to secure the ball with his foot [Rugby Football].

hooker, *n. hook*-er, a single-masted trading boat; an Irish fishing boat. (Dut. *hoek.*)

hook-nosed, *a.* having an aquiline nose.

hook-up, *n.* a connexion or assemblage of apparatus for some specific or temporary purpose (esp. of simultaneous radio transmission).

hook-worm, *n.* a species of worm parasitic to the intestines of man and other mammals, the best known being *Ankylostoma duodenale.*

hooky, *a. hook*-e, full of hooks; hook-shaped; pertaining to hooks. **to play hooky,** to play truant.

hooligan, *n. hoo*-le-gan, a street rough; a hoodlum; a cruel ruffian [Slang].

hoop, *n.* hoop, a band of wood or metal formed into a ring to fasten the staves of casks together; a similar band trundled by children; a piece of whalebone or cane formerly used to extend petticoats; one of the arches used in croquet; anything like a hoop: *v.t.* to bind with hoops; to encircle. (A.S. *hop.*)

hoop, *n.* and *v.i.* hoop, whoop.

hooper, *n. hoop*-er, one who hoops casks or tubs.

hooping-cough, *n. hoop*-ing-kof, whooping-cough.

hoop-iron, *n. hoop*-i-urn, thin iron in narrow lengths used for strengthening cases, barrels, etc.

hoop-la, *n. hoop*-lah, a game played at fairs, small prizes being won by throwing rings over them.

hoopoe, *n. hoo*-poh, a bird of the genus *Upupa,* with a large crest. (L. *upupa.*)

hoop-stick, *n.* a stick for trundling a child's hoop.

hoosh, *n.* hoosh, a stew, or thick soup [Slang].

hoot, *n.* hoot, a cry or shout in contempt; the sound of a syren or motor-horn: *v.i.* to shout in contempt; to cry as an owl; to use a horn or syren: *v.t.* to shout at with contempt; to signal by syren or horn.

hooter, *n. hoot*-er, a steam whistle; a horn for signalling sounded by steam or compressed air; a syren; one who hoots.

hoove, *n.* hoove, a cattle disease due to eating an excess of green fodder.

Hoover, *n. hoo*-ver, proprietary name of a type of electric vacuum-cleaner: *v.t.* to clean with this.

hop, *n.* hop, a leap on one leg; a jump; a spring; a dancing party [Slang]: *v.i.* to leap or spring on one leg; to skip; to limp; to bounce. (A.S. *hoppian.*)

hop, *n.* hop, a climbing plant, *Humulus lupulus,* the fruit of which, used in brewing, imparts a bitter flavour to beer: *v.t.* to impregnate with hops: *v.i.* to pick hops. (Dut. *hoppe.*)

hop-bine, *n.* the stem of the hop; the hop-vine.

★**hope,** *n.* hope, a desire of some good, accompanied with expectation of obtaining it; confidence in a future event; anticipation; he in whom or that in which we have hope; what is hoped for: *v.i.* to cherish a desire with expectation of fulfilment; to place confidence in; to trust confidently: *v.t.* to desire with expectation of good, or a belief that it may be obtained. (A.S. *hopa.*)

hope, *n.* hope, a combe; a small enclosed valley; a small bay or coastal inlet. (A.S. *hop.*)

hopeful, *a. hope*-ful, of a nature to excite hope; full of hope; encouraging. **young hopeful,** a child or youth [Coll.].

hopefully, *ad.* in a manner to raise hope.

hopefulness, *n.* state or quality of being hopeful.

hopeless, *a. hope*-less, destitute of hope; yielding no hope; desponding.

hopelessly, *ad. hope*-less-le, without hope.

hopelessness, *n.* a state of being hopeless.

hop-fly, *n.* an aphid destructive of hops, *Phorodon humuli.*

hop-garden, *n.* a plantation of hops.

hopingly, *ad. hope*-ing-le, with hope.

hop-kiln, *n.* a kiln for drying hops; an oast.

hoplite, *n. hop*-lite, a heavy-armed soldier of ancient Greece. (Gr.)

hop-o'-my-thumb, *n. hop*-o-me-thum, a dwarf, a pigmy. (From the nursery-tale character.)

hopper, *n. hop*-per, one who hops or leaps on one leg; a hop-picker [Coll.]; a trough or funnel through which grain passes into a mill; a similar apparatus in machinery; a hopping insect: *pl.* a game in which the players hop.

hopper-boy, *n.* a rake moving in a circle, to draw meal over an opening, through which it falls.

hoppet, *n. hop*-pet, a hand-basket; a large bucket used as an elevator in mines.

hop-picker, *n.* a paid worker who gathers hops.

hop-pillow, *n.* a pillow stuffed with hops, said to induce sleep.

hopple, *n. hop*-pl. a fetter for horses or other animals when turned out to graze: *v.t.* to tie the feet near together so as to prevent straying; to hobble. (Prob. M. Dut. *hoppeln.*)

hop-pocket, *n.* a large sack for holding hops; a measure of 168 lb. used for hops.

hop-pole, *n.* a pole used to support hops.

hoppy, *a. hop*-pe, tasting of hops: *n.* hop-scotch.

hop-scotch, *n. hop*-skotch, a widespread children's game in which a pebble, etc., is kicked from one division to another of a small marked area while the player hops on one leg. (*Hop,* and *scotch,* scratch.)

hop-vine, *n.* hop-bine.

horal, *a. haw*-ral, relating to an hour; horary.

horary, *a. haw*-ra-re, pertaining to or noting the hours; for an hour; hourly. (L. *hora,* hour.)

Horatian, *a.* ho-*ray*-shan, pertaining to the Latin poet Horace (*d.* 8 B.C.), or his verse.

horde, *n.* hoard, a nomadic tribe; a great host; a gang: *v.i.* to form a horde; to live in hordes. (Fr.)
hordein, *n. hor*-de-in, a substance analogous to starch, found in barley. (L. *hordeum*, barley.)
hordeolum, *n.* hor-*dee*-o-lum, a sty or inflamed swelling on the eyelid. (L., barleycorn.)
horehound, *n. hor*-hound, a bitter labiate plant, *Marrubium vulgare*, used as a tonic. (A.S., from its hoary appearance.)
horizon, *n.* ho-*ry*-zon, a circle bounding the view where the earth and sky seem to meet, called the **visible horizon,** as distinguished from the great circle parallel to it, the centre of which is the centre of the earth, called the **rational horizon. artificial horizon,** a horizontal reflecting surface, *e.g.* mercury, used instead of the actual horizon in taking sextant readings [Naut.]. (Fr.)
horizontal, *a.* ho-re-*zon*-tal, pertaining or relating to the horizon; parallel to the horizon; near the horizon; in the direction of the horizon.
horizontality, *n. ho*-re-zon-*tal*-e-te, the state of being horizontal.
horizontally, *ad.* in an horizontal direction.
hormone, *n. hor*-mone, one of the internal secretions of the ductless glands which are carried by the blood and stimulate certain organs [Physiol.]. (Gr. *hormaein*, to excite.)
*__horn,__ *n.* hawrn, a hard pointed or curved protuberance, or its substance, growing on the heads of certain (esp. cloven-footed) animals; anything like a horn; a wind musical instrument made out of a horn or of brass; a motor-car hooter: the loud-speaker of a gramophone or radio; an extremity of the moon when it is waxing or waning; the feeler of a snail; a drinking cup; a branch of a lake, etc.; a wing of an army: *v.t.* to furnish with horns; to attack or gore with horns. **horn of plenty,** a cornucopia. **the horns of a dilemma,** a position of extreme difficulty. **to draw in one's horns,** to become reticent or wary; to restrain one's ardour. (A.S.)
horn-bar, *n.* the cross-bar of a carriage.
horn-beak, *n.* the garfish or mackerel guide.
hornbeam, *n. hawrn*-beem, a tree, *Carpinus betulus*, with a wood of horny toughness.
hornbill, *n. hawrn*-bill, a large tropical bird of the family Bucerotidæ, having a very large bill surmounted by a horny process.
hornblende, *n. hawrn*-blend, a mineral consisting of silica, magnesia, lime, iron and alumina. **hornblende-schist,** hornblende rock of a schistose structure. (Ger. *horn*, and *blende*, to dazzle.)
horn-book, *n.* a child's first reading-book, originally a printed sheet backed with board and covered with horn.
horn-distemper, *n.* a disease of cattle affecting the internal substance of the horn.
horned, *a.* hawrnd, furnished with horns. **horned frog,** a S. American amphibian of the genus *Ceratophrys*, having a triangular appendage on the eyelid. **horned horse,** the gnu. **horned owl,** one of several owls having tufts of feathers on their heads like horns. **horned poppy,** the yellow poppy. **horned screamer,** the kamichi, a South American bird with a horn on its forehead, and a shrill note. **horned toad,** a harmless lizard of the genus *Phrynosoma* of the arid regions of Mexico and the western U.S.A. having horn-like spines on the head and body. **horned viper,** the cerastes.
horner, *n. hawrn*-er, one who works or deals in horns; one who blows a horn.
hornet, *n. hawr*-net, a large wasp, *Vespa crabro*, whose sting gives severe pain. **a hornet's nest,** a pack of trouble. (A.S. *hyrnet*.)
Hornie, *n. hawr*-ne, the Devil [Scots.].
horning, *n. hawrn*-ing, the appearance of the crescent moon; a summons to a debtor to pay within a given time or forfeit his freedom [Old Scots. Law].
hornish, *a. hawrn*-ish, somewhat like horn; hard.
hornito, *n.* hawr-*nee*-to, a smoking fumarole or oven-shaped mound near volcanoes. (Sp.)
horn-owl, *n. hawrn*-oul, the horned owl.
hornpipe, *n. hawrn*-pipe, an obsolete musical instrument; a lively air; a lively British dance; a sailor's dance; music for such dance.
horn-rims, *n.* spectacles with frames of real or artificial tortoiseshell or horn.
horn-silver, *n.* old name of native chloride of silver.
hornstone, *n. hawrn*-stone, a brittle flinty variety of quartz; chert.
hornwort, *n. hawrn*-wurt, a rootless water-plant, *Ceratophyllum demersum*.
hornwrack, *n. hawrn*-rak, a polyzoan of the genus *Flustra*; the sea-mat.
horny, *a. hawrn*-e, like horn; hard; callous; abounding in horns.
horography, *n.* ho-*rog*-ra-fe, the art of constructing clocks, watches, dials, etc. (Gr. *hora*, an hour, *grapho*, write.)
horologe, *n. ho*-ro-lohzh, any instrument that indicates the hour of the day. (O.Fr.)
horological, *a.* ho-ro-*loj*-e-kal, pertaining to horology; showing the hours.
horologiography, *n. ho*-ro-*loj*-e-*og*-ra-fe, an account of instruments that show the hour of the day; the art of constructing such instruments. (Gr. *horologion*, sundial, *grapho*, write.)
horologist, *n.* ho-*rol*-o-jist, an adept in horology.
horology, *n.* ho-*rol*-o-je, the art of measuring time, or of constructing machines for measuring and indicating time.
horometrical, *a.* ho-ro-*met*-re-kal, belonging to horometry.
horometry, *n.* ho-*rom*-e-tre, the art or practice of measuring time. (Gr. *hora*, and *metron*, measure.)
horoscope, *n. ho*-ro-skope, a scheme or figure of the twelve houses or signs of the zodiac, on which is marked a celestial chart at a given time; an observation of the heavens at the time of one's birth. (Fr.)
horoscopic, *a.* ho-ro-*skop*-ik, pertaining to a horoscope, or to horoscopy.
horoscopy, *n.* ho-*ros*-ko-pe, the art of constructing horoscopes with the view to predicting future events.
horrent, *a. ho*-rent, standing erect, as bristles; bristling. (L. *horrens*, bristling.)
horrible, *a. ho*-re-bl, exciting or tending to excite horror; dreadful; unpleasant. (O.Fr.)
horribleness, *n.* the state of being horrible.
horribly, *ad. ho*-re-ble, in a manner to excite horror excessively.
horrid, *a. ho*-rid, fitted to excite horror; frightful; very unpleasant, offensive, or disgusting. (L. *horridus*.)
horridly, *ad.* in a manner to excite horror.
horridness, *n.* the state of being horrid.
horrific, *a.* ho-*rif*-ik, causing horror; terrifying.
horrify, *v.t. ho*-re-fy, to strike with horror; seriously to perturb [Coll.]. (L. *horrifico*, terrorize.)
horripilation, *n. ho*-rip-e-*lay*-shon, a sensation as of the bristling of the hair due to disease, terror, or cold; goose-flesh. (L. *horreo*, stand on end, *pilus*, the hair.)
horrisonant, *a.* ho-*ris*-o-nant, having a dreadful sound. (L. *horreo*, and *sonus*, sound.)
horror, *n. ho*-ror, a shivering or shuddering; excessive fear; dread with shrinking or loathing; that which excites horror. **the horrors,** the "blues"; extreme agitation due to excess in drinking. (L.)
horror-stricken, *a.* overwhelmed with horror.
hors, *ad.* and *prep.* hawr, beyond; out of it; additional. **hors concours,** not in the competition. **hors de combat,** out of the fight; disabled. **hors d'œuvre,** a relish taken at the beginning of or during a meal. (Fr.)
*__horse,__ *n.* horse, the ungulate *Equus caballus*; a male of the species; cavalry; that by which something is supported; a clothes-horse; a vaulting block; a frame on which soldiers were made to ride as a punishment; a foot-rope along a yard to support sailors while at work on the sails; a bar on which the sheet of a fore-and-aft sail travels [Naut.]: *v.t.* to provide with a horse; to sit astride; to carry on the back; to cover a mare: *v.i.* to get on horseback. **horse artillery,** mounted gunners with light guns to act with cavalry. **Horse Guards,** the headquarters in Whitehall of the London and Eastern military districts; the military authorities of the British Army; the Blues, or third regiment of household cavalry, the Royal Horse Guards. **horse latitudes,** the area of tropical calms bordering the trade winds. **horse mackerel,** the scad, the cavally, and other fish. **to take horse,** to set out to ride on horseback. (A.S. *hors*.)
horseback, *n. horse*-bak, the back of a horse. **on horseback,** mounted on a horse.

horsebane, *n.* *horse*-bane, one of the water drop-worts, *Œnanthe phellandrium*, formerly thought to cause palsy in horses.
horse-bean, *n.* a small bean on which horses feed; the tick bean, a variety of *Faba vulgaris*.
horse-block, *n.* a block or raised step to assist persons in mounting and dismounting from a horse.
horse-boat, *n.* *horse*-boat, a boat for conveying horses over water; a boat drawn by horses.
horse-box, *n.* a van, or a pen on board-ship, for horses.
horse-boy, *n.* a stable-boy.
horse-breaker, *n.* one whose employment is to train horses.
horse-chestnut, *n.* a tree, *Æsculus hippocastanum*, or its fruit.
horse-cloth, *n.* a rug or cloth to cover a horse.
horse-doctor, *n.* a farrier; a veterinary surgeon.
horse-drench, *n.* a dose of physic for a horse.
horse-elder, *n.* the plant elecampane.
horse-faced, *a.* having a long coarse face.
horseflesh, *n.* *horse*-flesh, the flesh of a horse, esp. as food; horses collectively.
horse-fly, *n.* any large fly that stings horses.
horsehair, *n.* *horse*-hare, the long mane- and tail-hair of horses: *a.* made of this, esp. when woven.
horse-laugh, *n.* a loud boisterous laugh.
horse-leech, *n.* a large leech; a bloodsucker; a horse-doctor.
horseless, *a.* *horse*-less, without a horse; not needing a horse (of vehicles).
horse-litter, *n.* a litter hung on poles, borne between two horses; bedding for horses.
horse-mackerel, *n.* the scad, a common sea-fish of the genus *Caranx*.
horseman, *n.* *horse*-man, a rider on horseback; a skilled rider.
horsemanship, *n.* *horse*-man-ship, the art of riding; the art of training and managing horses.
Horse-marine, *n.* a member of a mythical corps (of jocular allusion); an awkward person; one out of his element.
horsemeat, *n.* *horse*-meet, food for horses; provender; horseflesh.
horse-milliner, *n.* one who supplies ribbons or other decorations for horses.
horse-mint, *n.* the wild mint, *Mentha sylvestris*.
horse-parsley, *n.* the large-leaved umbelliferous plant, *Smyrnium olusatrum*, alexanders.
horseplay, *n.* *horse*-play, rough play.
horse-pond, *n.* a pond for watering horses.
horse-power, *n.* the power of a horse; the engineering unit of power, equivalent to 550 foot-pounds a second; mechanical power expressed in such units.
horse-race, *n.* *horse*-race, a race by horses.
horse-radish, *n.* a cruciferous plant with a pungent root, *Cochtearia armoracia*, used as a condiment.
horse-sense, *n.* common sense.
horseshoe, *n.* *horse*-shoo, a shoe for horses; a curve or thing of the same shape: *a.* in the shape of a horseshoe.
horseshoe-crab, *n.* the king-crab, so called from the shape of its shell.
horseshoeing, *n.* *horse*-shoo-ing, the act or employment of shoeing horses.
horseshoe-vetch, *n.* the yellow-flowered leguminous plant *Hippocrepis comosa*.
horse-tail, *n.* a plant of the genus *Equisetum*; a horse's tail formerly used (in varying numbers) as a Turkish emblem of rank.
horsewhip, *n.* *horse*-whip, a whip for driving horses: *v.t.* to lash; to thrash with a horsewhip.
horsewoman, *n.* *horse*-woom-an, a woman rider; a woman skilled in stable management.
horsiness, *n.* *horse*-e-ness, the state or quality of being horsy.
horsy, *a.* *horse*-e, pertaining to horses or horse-racing; fond of horses; imitating the dress and manners of a groom.
hortation, *n.* hor-*tay*-shon, exhortation.
hortative, *a.* *hor*-ta-tiv, giving exhortation or advice; inciting; encouraging. (L., as *exhort.*)
hortatory, *a.* *hor*-ta-to-re, hortative.
horticultural, *a.* *hor*-te-*kul*-tewr-ral, pertaining to horticulture.
horticulture, *n.* *hor*-te-kul-tewr, the art of cultivating gardens. (L. *hortus*, a garden, and *culture.*)
horticulturist, *n.* *hor*-te-*kul*-tewr-rist, one who is skilled in the art of cultivating gardens.
hosanna, *n.* ho-*zan*-na, an exclamation of praise, or an invocation for blessings. (Heb., save, we pray.)
hose, *n.* hoze (*pl.* **hose**), covering for the leg, or for leg and foot; stockings; socks; (*pl.* **hoses**) a flexible pipe for conveying water: *v.t.* to water with a hose. (A.S. *hosa.*)
hose-reel, *n.* a reel on which hose is kept in readiness for use.
hosier, *n.* *hoze*-yer, one who deals in hosiery.
hosiery, *n.* *hoze*-ye-re, hose or stockings in general; knit or woven underclothing; a manufactory of such.
hospice, *n.* *hos*-pis, a convent, etc., esp. on the Alps, for the entertainment of travellers. (Fr., from L. *hospes*, a guest, a host.)
hospitable, *a.* *hos*-pit-a-bl, entertaining strangers with kindness; showing or implying hospitality.
hospitableness, *n.* quality of being hospitable.
hospitably, *ad.* with kindness to strangers.
* **hospital,** *n.* *hos*-pit-al, an institution for the reception of the sick and injured; an establishment of the Hospitallers; an almshouse; a charity school or other charitable institution. (O.Fr.)
hospitalism, *n.* *hos*-pit-al-izm, the hospital system; bad conditions due to defective hospital management.
hospitality, *n.* *hos*-pit-*al*-e-te, friendly reception of, or kindness to, strangers.
hospitalization, *n.* *hos*-pit-a-ly-*zay*-shon, consignment to, or accommodation in, a hospital for treatment.
hospitalize, *v.t.* *hos*-pit-a-lize, to place in a hospital for treatment.
hospitaller, *n.* *hos*-pit-al-ler, the officer of a religious house charged with the reception of strangers; a member of a brotherhood devoted to the care of the sick. the **Hospitalers,** the Knights of St. John, a mediæval order of religious monks, who (about 1050) built a hospital at Jerusalem for pilgrims.
hospodar, *n.* *hos*-po-dar, former title of the governors under the Sultan, of Moldavia and Wallachia. (Slav., lord.)
host, *n.* hohst, one who entertains another; an innkeeper; a living organism on which another is parasitic [Biol.]. (O.Fr.)
host, *n.* hohst, a number of men embodied for war; a multitude; a large number. (L. *hostis*, an enemy.)
Host, *n.* hohst, the consecrated wafer of the Eucharist, offered in sacrifice. (O.Fr.)
hostage, *n.* *hos*-taj, a person delivered to, or kept or taken by, an enemy as a pledge for the fulfilment of certain conditions. (O.Fr.)
hostel, *n.* *hos*-tel, an inn; a residential hall; a lodging house for students, organized wayfarers, etc. (O. Fr.)
hosteller, *n.* *hos*-tl-ler, the manager of a hostel; one residing in a hostel; a frequenter of Youth or other hostels.
hostelry, *n.* *hos*-tl-re, an inn.
hostess, *n.* *hohs*-tess, a female host.
hostile, *a.* *hos*-tile, belonging to an enemy; showing enmity; unfriendly. (L. *hostilis.*)
hostilely, *ad.* *hos*-tile-le, in a hostile manner.
hostility, *n.* hos-*til*-e-te, enmity: *pl.* warfare; acts of war.
hostler, *n.* *host*-ler, an ostler.
hot, *a.* hot, having much heat; ardent in temper; easily excited; violent; eager; acrid; pungent; rutting (of animals); lustful; on the scent, very near; rhythmically over-elaborated (of dance-music); recent, up-to-date (of news): *v.t.* to make hot [Coll.]. **hot air,** exaggerated talk; bombast. **hot favourite,** a horse or competitor well up in the betting. **in hot water,** in for, or having, a very unpleasant time; in bad trouble. **to make it hot for one,** to rebuke him severely; to make him thoroughly uncomfortable. (A.S. *hat.*)
hotbed, *n.* *hot*-bed, a bed of mould heated by fermenting manure for raising early plants; a place favourable to the rapid growth or development of anything.
hot-blast, *n.* a current of heated air injected into a furnace to increase its heat.
hot-blooded, *a.* hot-*blud*-id, excitable; irritable.
Hotchkiss, *n.* *hotch*-kiss, a type of quick-firing machine-gun, patented in the 1890's. (Name of Amer. inventor.)

hotchpot, *n.* *hotch*-pot, the throwing into common stock of property for equal division, esp. among the heirs of an intestate person. (Fr. *hochepot.*)
hotchpotch, *n.* *hotch*-potch, a mingled mass; a mixture of ingredients.
hot-cockles, *n.pl.* a game in which one covers his eyes and guesses who strikes him.
hotel, *n.* ho-*tel*, a superior inn or house for entertaining strangers or travellers; in France, a palace or dwelling of persons of rank. **Hôtel-Dieu,** a hospital in France. **hôtel de ville,** the guildhall of a French town. (Fr.)
hotelier, *n.* ho-*tel*-e-er, the proprietor or manager of an hotel.
hot-foot, *ad.* in haste: *a.* going swiftly; fleeting.
hot-headed, *a.* of ardent passions; violent; impetuous.
hot-house, *n.* a glass house artificially warmed, for the sheltering of tender plants from the cold air.
hotly, *ad.* *hot*-le, with heat.
hotness, *n.* *hot*-ness, the state of being hot.
hot-plate, *n.* a heater on which cooked food is kept hot.
hot-pot, *n.* a peppery stew of meat and vegetables cooked in a casserole in an oven.
hot-press, *v.t.* to press, as paper or linen, between heated plates, in order to give a smooth and glossy surface: *n.* a machine for this purpose.
hot-short, *a.* brittle when hot (of iron).
hotspur, *n.* *hot*-spur, a violent or precipitate man: *a.* hot-headed; impetuous. (*Hotspur* from " Henry IV," Shakespeare.)
Hottentot, *n.* *hot*-en-tot, one of an aboriginal negroid race of South Africa; the language of this race; a brutish individual. (From the stammering the language seemed to the early Dutch settlers.)
Hottentotism, *n.* *hot*-en-tot-izm, a characteristic or quality of the Hottentots, esp. their peculiar stammering.
hot-wall, *n.* a wall with flues for conducting heat to hasten the ripening of fruit trained to it.
houdah, *n.* *hou*-dah, a howdah.
hough, *n.* hok, the joint on the hind-leg of an ungulate corresponding to the ankle-joint in man; the back of the knee-joint in man; the ham: *v.t.* to hamstring. (A.S. *hoh*, the heel.)
hound, *n.* hound, a generic name of the dog, specifically a hunting dog; a dog that hunts by scent; a pursuer in a paper-chase; a mean, despicable fellow [Coll.]: *pl.* a hunt with hounds: *v.t.* to set on the chase; to hunt; to incite. (A.S. *hund.*)
hound, *n.* hound, one of the projections at the masthead to support the trestle-trees [Naut.]; a bar in a vehicle connecting a fore- and hind-carriage. (O.Scand. *hunn*, knob.)
hound-fish, *n.* a dogfish; the garfish.
hound's-tongue, *n.* a succulent plant, *Cynoglossum officinale.* (From the form of its leaves.)
★**hour,** *n.* our, a space of sixty minutes, equal to one twenty-fourth part of a day; the time indicated by a clock, etc.; particular time: *pl.* times of attendance at work, office, etc.; in the Roman Catholic Church, prayers at stated hours of the day; the goddesses of the seasons and hours [Myth.]. **at the eleventh hour,** very late; at the last moment. **now is the hour,** this is the expected time, or the opportunity. **to keep good hours,** to be punctual; to be at home in good time. (L. *hora.*)
hour-angle, *n.* the angular distance of a heavenly body east or west of meridian [Astron.].
hour-circle, *n.* any line of meridian, esp. one of the twelve at intervals of 15°, or one hour; the graduated circle of an equatorial telescope on which is read sidereal time and right ascension.
hour-glass, *n.* an instrument for measuring intervals of time by the running of sand between two glass bulbs.
hour-hand, *n.* the hand on a timepiece which shows the hour.
houri, *n.* *hoor*-re, among Mohammedans, a nymph of paradise; a seductive young woman. (Per.)
hourly, *a.* *our*-le, happening or done every hour; continual: *ad.* every hour; frequently.
hour-plate, *n.* the dial of a timepiece.
housage, *n.* *house*-aj, the housing or storage of goods; the charge for this.
house, *v.t.* houze, to provide houses for; to shelter; to store; to lower or run in, as a topmast or bowsprit: *v.i.* to take shelter or lodgings; to reside.
★**house,** *n.* house, a building for dwelling in; a dwelling-place; an edifice appropriated to the service of God; a temple; a church; a monastery; a college; a family or race; a household; a school boarding-house, or its boarders collectively; a body of men united in their legislative capacity; a quorum of a legislative body; a firm or commercial establishment; a theatre; an audience; a public-house; the station of a planet in the heavens, or the twelfth part of the heavens [Astrol.]; a gambling game resembling lotto. **house of call,** a house where journeymen of a particular trade assemble when out of work, for the purpose of obtaining employment; a public-house [Coll.]. **house of correction,** a reformatory; a prison for idle and disorderly persons. **house of God,** a church. **house organ,** a periodical issued by, and dealing with the interests of, a particular firm, business, or concern. **to bring down the house,** to provoke a general burst of applause. **to keep house,** to do the housekeeping for, and manage, a household. (A.S. *hus.*)
house-agent, *n.* one employed to look after, or to sell and let, household property.
house-boat, *n.* a covered boat for use as a dwelling; a moored pontoon with living-rooms built on it.
housebote, *n.* *house*-boat, the amount of wood allowed to be taken by a tenant to repair his house and for fuel [Law].
housebreaker, *n.* *house*-brake-er, one who breaks into and robs a house between sunrise and sunset; one who pulls down houses.
housebreaking, *n.* *house*-brake-ing, the breaking or opening and entering of a house by daylight, with intent to commit a felony; the demolition of buildings.
housecraft, *n.* *house*-krahft, the art of household management.
housed, *a.* houzd, provide with living accommodation, or with housings.
house-dog, *n.* a dog kept to guard the house.
house-flag, *n.* the flag denoting the ownership of a ship.
house-fly, *n.* the dipterous insect, *Musca domestica.*
household, *n.* *house*-hohld, those who dwell under the same roof and compose a family; *pl.* a variety of flour not of the finest quality: *a.* belonging to the house and family; domestic. **the Household,** the royal household. **household stuff,** the furniture of a house; the vessels, utensils, and goods of a family. **Household troops,** the regiments of life-guards, horse-guards, and foot-guards, specially employed about the Sovereign.
householder, *n.* *house*-hohl-der, the responsible head of the household.
housekeeper, *n.* *house*-kee-per, one in charge of the housekeeping; a servant who has the chief care of the house; a head caretaker or janitor.
housekeeping, *a.* *house*-kee-ping, domestic: *n.* care of domestic concerns; domestic economy.
housel, *n.* *hou*-zl, the Eucharist: *v.t.* to administer the Eucharist to. (A.S.)
houseleek, *n.* *house*-leek, a plant of the genus *Sempervivum*, with succulent leaves, that grows on walls and roofs.
house-line, *n.* a small line formed of three strands, used for seizings [Naut.].
housemaid, *n.* *house*-made, a female servant employed to keep a house clean, etc. **housemaid's knee,** inflammation affecting the patella, due to overmuch kneeling.
house-master, *n.* a schoolmaster in charge of a house in a boarding school.
house-party, *n.* a party of guests staying in a country house.
house-physician, *n.* a junior resident physician in a hospital.
house-proud, *a.* proud of one's house or housewifery.
house-room, *n.* *house*-room, room in a house; space for accommodation.
house-sparrow, *n.* the common sparrow, *Passer domesticus.*
house-steward, *n.* one who manages the household affairs of a large establishment.
house-surgeon, *n.* a surgeon resident in a hospital.
house-tax, *n.* a tax on inhabited houses.
house-warming, *n.* a feast or merrymaking at the time of a move into a new house.

housewife, *n.* *house*-wife, the mistress of a family; a female domestic manager; (*huz*-if) a small hold-all for pins, needles, and thread, etc.
housewifely, *a.* *house*-wife-le, pertaining to a housewife or good female management: *ad.* like a good housewife; thriftily.
housewifery, *n.* *huz*-if-re, *house*-wy-fe-re, *or house*-wif-e-re, the business of a housewife; female management of domestic concerns.
housework, *n.* *house*-wurk, the domestic work attaching to the management of a household; the work of a housewife.
housing, *n.* *houz*-ing, the providing of houses, esp. for the working classes; provision of shelter; accommodation in houses.
housing, *n.* *houz*-ing, a covering, esp. for a horse; a saddle-cloth; the trappings of a horse. (O.Fr. *huche*, prob. from Ar. *ghushiah*, a veil.)
Hova, *n.* *huv*-a (*pl.* **Hovas**), the leading native tribe of Madagascar; a member of this tribe. (Malagasy.)
hove, *p.* hove, did heave (obsolete).
hovel, *n.* *hov*-el or *huv*-el, an open cattle-shed; a poor mean house: *v.t.* to shelter in a hovel. (M.E., perhaps from A.S. *hof*, house.)
hoveller, *n.* *huv*-el-ler, a longshoreman; one who saves life or property from or who robs wrecks; an east-coast lugger.
hovelling, *n.* *huv*-el-ling, a mode of preventing chimneys smoking; the occupation of a hoveller.
hover, *v.i.* *hov*-er *or huv*-er, to float stationary in the air; to flutter over or about; to stand in suspense; to loiter about; to waver: *n.* an act of hovering. (M.E. *hoven.*)
hover, *v.t.* *hov*-er, to pack loosely (esp. of hops): *a.* of loose texture; light (of soil). (Dial.)
hoveringly, *ad.* in a hovering manner.
★**how,** *ad.* hou, in what manner; to what extent; for what reason; by what means. (A.S. *hu*, from *hwa*, who.)
how, *n.* hou, a small hill; a tumulus. (Scand.)
howbeit, *ad.* hou-*bee*-it, be it as it may; nevertheless.
howdah, *n.* *hou*-da, a seat usually canopied, for two or more riders on an elephant's back. (Hind.)
howdie, *n.* *hou*-de, a midwife. (Scots.)
howe, *n.* hou, a narrow hollow; a dell. (Scots.)
however, *ad.* hou-*ev*-er, in whatever manner or degree; at all events; notwithstanding.
howitzer, *n.* *hou*-it-zer, a gun of high trajectory and low muzzle velocity. (Ger. *haubitze.*)
howker, *n.* *houk*-er, a hooker (sailing vessel).
howl, *n.* houl, the cry of a dog or wolf, or of a human being in distress: *v.i.* to cry as a dog or wolf; to utter a loud, prolonged, mournful sound, expressive of distress; to wail; to roar: *v.t.* to utter with outcry. (M.E. *houlen.*)
howler, *n.* *houl*-er, one who howls; a keener; a monkey of the genus *Alouatta*; a bad or a ludicrous mistake [Slang].
howling, *a.* *houl*-ing, filled with howls or howling beasts; dreary (of deserts); extreme [Slang].
howsoever, *ad.* hou-so-*ev*-er, in what manner soever; although; however.
hoy, *n.* hoy, a one-masted coasting ketch; a barge. (Dut.)
hoy, *int.* hoy, for calling attention; ho! (Imit.)
Hoya, *n.* *hoy*-a, a genus of Australasian climbing plants with yellow, pink, or white flowers; the wax-plants. (Thos. *Hoy*, *d.* 1821. Engl. gardener.)
hoyden, *n.* *hoy*-dn, a rude or uncouth girl: a tomboy; a country girl: *a.* bold; rude; rustic: *v.i.* to romp roughly or rudely.
hoydenish, *a.* *hoy*-dn-ish, having the manners of a hoyden.
huanaco, *n.* wah-*nah*-koh, the guanaco.
hub, *n.* hub, the nave of a wheel; a centre of attraction; a hilt; a mark in quoits; any protuberance.
hubble-bubble, *n.* *hun*-bl-*bub*-bl, a hookah, or tobacco-pipe, in which the smoke is drawn through water with bubbling; a bubbling sound.
hubbub, *n.* *hub*-bub, a great noise of many confused voices; a tumult. (Imit.)
hubbubboo, *n.* *hub*-bub-*boo*, a howling; a hubbub.
hubby, *n.* *hub*-be, diminutive of *husband*.
hubris, *n.* *hew*-bris, wanton and insolent arrogance; violent behaviour due to this. (Gr.)
hubristic, *a.* hew-*bris*-tik, proud and insolent. (Gr. *hybristikos*, insolent.)
huckaback, *n.* *huk*-a-bak, a strong rough-surfaced fabric, sometimes with raised figures on it, used for towels. (Origin uncertain.)
huckle, *n.* *huk*-kl, the hip or haunch. (M.E. *hoke.*)
huckle-backed, *a.* having round shoulders.
huckleberry, *n.* *huk*-kl-be-re, a whortleberry; an American plant of the genus *Gaylussacia*.
huckle-bone, *n.* the hip-bone.
huckster, *n.* *huk*-ster, a retailer of small articles; a mean, trickish fellow; *v.i.* to deal in small articles. (M. Dut. *heukster.*)
huddle, *n.* *hud*-dl, a crowd; tumult; confusion: *v.i.* to crowd or gather together confusedly; to hurry: *v.t.* to throw confusedly together; to perform or do in haste and disorder. (Origin unknown.)
Hudibrastic, *a.* hew-de-*bras*-tik, similar in style to Samuel Butler's poem, "Hudibras" (1678); of the nature of a lampoon; doggerel.
hue, *n.* hew, colour; tint; dye. (A.S. *hiw*, appearance.)
hue, *n.* hew, shouting; a clamour. **hue and cry,** the pursuit of a felon or offender [Law]. (O.Fr. *hu.*)
hued, *a.* hewd, of a certain hue, as *dark-hued*.
hueless, *a.* *hew*-less, destitute of colour.
huer, *n.* *hew*-er, the lookout on shore who shouts and signals the movements of a shoal of fish. (*Hue.*)
huff, *n.* huf, a swell of sudden anger or arrogance; a fit of peevishness; the act of huffing (at draughts): *v.t.* to puff up; to bully; to remove an adversary's piece from the board in draughts when he refuses to take one in his power: *v.i.* to take offence; to bluster. (Imit.)
huffer, *n.* *huf*-er, a blusterer; one who huffs.
huffily, *ad.* *huf*-e-le, in a huffy way.
huffiness, *n.* the state of being huffy.
huffing, *n.* *huf*-ing, the action of the verb *to huff*; blustering; swashbuckling.
huffish, *a.* *huf*-ish, huffy; disposed to bluster.
huffishly, *ad.* *huf*-ish-le, in a huffish manner.
huffishness, *n.* the state of being huffish.
huffy, *a.* *huf*-e, huffish; inclined to quarrel; apt to take offence.
hug, *n.* hug, a close embrace; a particular grip in wrestling: *v.t.* to embrace closely; to cherish with fondness; to hold fast; to cling to; to keep close to [Naut.]; to crowd together. **hug oneself,** congratulate oneself.
huge, *a.* hewj, of immense size; enormous. (O.Fr. *ahuge.*)
hugely, *ad.* *hewj*-le, enormously; immensely.
hugeness, *n.* *hewj*-ness, enormous bulk.
hugeous, *a.* *hewj*-us, huge [Coll.].
hugger-mugger, *n.* *hug*-ger-*mug*-ger, secrecy; confusion; slovenliness: *a.* clandestine; in disorder: *ad.* secretly; in a muddle. (Probably rhyming duplicate of *hug.*)
Huguenot, *n.* *hew*-ge-no, a French Protestant of the 16th and 17th centuries. (Fr., perhaps from Ger. *eidgenoss*, confederate.)
Huguenotism, *n.* *hew*-ge-no-tizm, the principles or religious system of the Huguenots; Calvinism.
huh, *int.* huh, expressing some suppressed feeling.
huia, *n.* *hoo*-e-a, a New Zealand bird, *Neomorpha acutirostris*, of the starling family. (From its cry.)
hula, *n.* *hoo*-lah, a native mimetic and suggestive dance of Hawaiian women. (Hawaiian.)
hulk, *n.* hulk, the body of a ship, especially an old one, unfit for sea. **the hulks,** old ships, formerly used as prisons for convicts. (A.S. *hulc.*)
hulking, *a.* *hulk*-ing, big; ungainly; clumsy.
hull, *n.* hull, the frame or body of a ship, as distinct from her masts and rigging: *v.t.* to pierce the hull with a projectile: *v.i.* to float or drive on the water, like a mere hull. **hull down,** said of a ship when her hull is concealed by the convexity of the sea. (Perhaps Dut. *hol.*)
hull, *n.* hull, the outer covering of anything, particularly of a nut or of grain; a pod: *v.t.* to strip off the hull. (A.S. *hulu*, a covering.)
hullabaloo, *n.* *hull*-a-ba-*loo*, noisy confusion.
huller, *n.* *hull*-er, a machine for stripping the hulls from grain.
hullo, *int.* hul-*loh*, hallo.
hum, *n.* hum, the noise of bees or other insects; any low dull droning sound; a murmuring sound; an unpleasant odour [Slang]: *v.i.* to make a low, droning, murmuring sound; to become inarticulate (in speaking); to reek [Slang]: *v.t.* to sing with closed lip or very softly: *int.* an inarticulate

sound, implying doubt or deliberation. **hum and haw,** to stutter; to hesitate to give decided answer. (Imit.)
hum, *n.* hum, a humbug; a sham.
human, *a.* *hew*-mun, belonging to or characteristic of a man or of mankind; having the qualities of a man: *n.* a human being [Coll.]. (Fr. *humain.*)
humane, *a.* hew-*mane*, having the feelings proper to man; tender; merciful; kind; humanizing. (L. *humanus.*)
humanely, *ad.* hew-*mane*-le, in a humane manner.
humaneness, *n.* hew-*mane*-ness, the quality of being humane.
humanify, *v.t.* hew-*man*-e-fy, to make human; to incarnate.
humanism, *n.* *hew*-mu-nizm, the study of the moral and intellectual interests of mankind as a whole; humanitarianism; polite learning; culture developed from the study of the classics.
humanist, *n.* *hew*-mu-nist, a student or upholder of the humanities; one of the classical scholars of the Renaissance; a student of human nature and its history.
humanistic, *a.* *hew*-mu-*nis*-tik, pertaining to humanity or to humanism.
humanitarian, *n.* *hew*-man-e-*tare*-re-an, one who believes in humanity as the crown of being, and in its self-sufficiency as it is to realize its own ideal; a perfectionist; a philanthropist; (*cap.*) one holding that Christ was a mere man: *a.* humane; pertaining to the Humanitarians.
humanitarianism, *n.* *hew*-man-e-*tare*-re-a-nizm, regard for the interests of humanity; the doctrine of the Humanitarians.
humanity, *n.* hew-*man*-e-te, the nature peculiar to man; mankind; the kind feelings, dispositions, and sympathies of man; benevolence. **the humanities,** classical learning and literature, including grammar, rhetoric, the Latin and Greek languages, and poetry. (Fr. *humanité.*)
humanization, *n.* *hew*-mu-ny-*zay*-shon, the act of humanizing.
humanize, *v.t.* *hew*-mu-nize, to render human or humane; to give human character to: *v.i.* to become civilized or more humane. **humanized milk,** cow's milk brought approximately to the same content and quality as human milk.
humankind, *n.* hew-mun-*kynd*, mankind.
humanly, *ad.* *hew*-mun-le, after the manner of men; as a man.
humanness, *n.* *hew*-mun-ness, state of being human.
humble, *a.* *hum*-bl, of low condition; unpretending; modest; meek: *v.t.* to lower; to abase; to abase the pride of; to make humble. (Fr.)
humble-bee, *n.* a species of the genus *Bombus*, a group of social bees humming loudly; the bumble-bee. (M.E. *humbylbee*, from *hum.*)
humbleness, *n.* *hum*-bl-ness, the state of being humble; humility.
humble-pie, *n.* a pie made of umbles, the internal organs of the deer. **to eat humble-pie,** to submit to humiliation; to make humble apology (because formerly at a hunting-feast the umbles were given to the hunt-servants).
humble-plant, *n.* *Mimosa pudica*, a species of sensitive plant.
humbly, *ad.* *hum*-ble, in a humble manner.
humbug, *n.* *hum*-bug, an imposition under fair pretences; a hoax; one who imposes; a genial imposter; a peppermint sweetmeat: *v.t.* to impose upon; to hoax. (Origin unknown.)
humdrum, *a.* *hum*-drum, dull; commonplace: *n.* a stupid fellow; a dronish tone.
humectant, *a.* hew-*mek*-tant, moistening; augmenting the fluidity of the blood: *n.* a substance with this effect; a diluent [Med.].
humectation, *n.* hew-mek-*tay*-shon, the act of moistening, wetting, or watering. (L. *humectatio.*)
humeral, *a.* *hew*-me-ral, pertaining to the shoulder. **humeral veil,** a veil worn over the shoulders by certain priests at High Mass.
humerus, *n.* *hew*-me-rus, the bone of the upper arm from shoulder to fore-arm; the analogous bone of a forelimb. (L.)
humhum, *n.* *hum*-hum, a coarse Indian cotton cloth. (Ar.)
humic, *a.* *hew*-mik, pertaining to or formed from humus.
humid, *a.* *hew*-mid, moist; damp. (Fr. *humide.*)
humidifier, *n.* hew-*mid*-e-fy-er, an apparatus for maintaining humidity in the air [Air-conditioning].
humidify, *v.t.* hew-*mid*-e-fy, to make moist.
humidity, *n.* hew-*mid*-e-te, the state of being humid; moisture. (Fr. *humidité.*)
humidor, *n.* *hew*-me-dor, a contrivance for keeping the air moist or controlling its humidity; a case, etc., for storing cigars.
humification, *n.* *hew*-me-fe-*kay*-shon, the transformation of organic matter into humus [Bot.]; moistening.
humify, *v.t.* *hew*-me-fy, to render humid; to damp; to moisten.
humiliate, *v.t.* hew-*mil*-e-ate, to humble; to lower in condition; to abase. (Late L. *humiliatus.*)
humiliating, *a.* hew-*mil*-e-ay-ting, humbling; depressing; abating pride; reducing self-confidence.
humiliation, *n.* hew-mil-e-*ay*-shon, act of humbling; state of being humbled; abasement; mortification.
humility, *n.* hew-*mil*-e-te, state of being humble, modest, or submissive; humbleness of mind; act of submission. (Fr. *humilité.*)
humite, *n.* *hew*-mite, a group of crystalline minerals consisting of basic magnesium fluo-silicates. (Sir A. *Hume*, *d.* 1839).
hummel, *a.* *hum*-mel, having no horns (of cattle); awnless (of grain): *v.t.* to remove the awn from barley after it has been thrashed. (Ger.)
hummeller, *n.* *hum*-mel-ler, an instrument for hummelling grain.
hummer, *n.* *hum*-mer, one who hums; a humming insect, etc.
humming, *a.* *hum*-ming, murmuring; brisk; strong (of liquor); spirited; vigorous (of blows): *n.* the sound made when anything hums.
humming-bird, *n.* a species of small brightly-coloured tropical American birds, the Trochilidæ, the pulsation of whose wings in flight causes a humming sound.
humming-top, *n.* *hum*-ming-top, a hollow top with a hole at the side which hums when spun.
hummock, *n.* *hum*-mok, a hillock; a knoll; a small conical tree-covered eminence; a hillock of ice. (*Hump.*)
hummocky, *a.* *hum*-mok-e, of the nature of or abounding in hummocks.
hummum, *n.* *hum*-mum, a sweating place or bath; a Turkish bath. (Ar. *hamham.*)
humoral, *a.* *hew*-mo-ral, pertaining to or proceeding from the humours. **humoral pathology,** humoralism [Med.]. (L. *humor.*)
humoralism, *n.* *hew*-mo-ra-lizm, the doctrine that diseases have their seat in the humours [Med.].
humoralist, *n.* *hew*-mo-ra-list, one who favoured the humoral pathology.
humoresque, *n.* hew-mo-*resk*, a humorous musical composition; a caprice: *a.* humorous in style.
humorism, *n.* *hew*-mo-rizm, humorousness; a piece of humour; humoralism.
humorist, *n.* *hew*-mo-rist, one who displays humour; one having a playful fancy or odd conceits; a droll; a humorous entertainer.
humoristic, *a.* *hew*-mo-*ris*-tik, characteristic of a humorist.
humorless, *a.* *hew*-mor-less, destitute of humour.
humorous, *a.* *hew*-mo-rus, full of humour; governed by humour; adapted to excite laughter; capricious; whimsical.
humorously, *ad.* in a humorous manner.
humorousness, *n.* the state or quality of being humorous.
humorsome, *a.* *hew*-mor-sum, humorous; influenced by the humour of the moment.
humorsomely, *ad.* in a humorsome manner.
* **humour,** *n.* *hew*-mor turn of mind or peculiarity of disposition; temper; caprice; whim; a sympathetic sense of the laughable and the sad; formerly moisture, an animal fluid: *v.t.* to fall in with the humour of; to indulge by compliance. (L. *humor*, moisture.)
humous, *a.* *hew*-mus, contained in or derived from vegetable mould; containing much humus.
hump, *n.* hump, a protuberance on the back; a hillock; a heap; a fit of depression or petulance [Slang]: *v.t.* to make hump-shaped; to depress [Slang]; to hoist on the back and carry. **hump the swag,** to tramp the country [Austral. slang]. (Dut. *homp.*)

humpback, *n.* *hump*-bak, a back with a hump; a humpbacked person; a species of whale of the genus *Megapterus*; a small salmon of the Pacific coasts.
humpbacked, *a.* *hump*-bakt, having a humpback.
humped, *a.* humpt, having a hump; peeved; humpy.
humph, *int.* humf, an exclamation of doubt, disapproval, or contempt, etc.
humpless, *a.* *hump*-less, without a hump.
humpy, *a.* *hump*-e, having a hump or humps; out of humour; ill-tempered.
humus, *n.* *hew*-mus, soil; vegetable mould; a blackish-brown powder formed by the action of the air on decaying organic matter. (L., soil.)
Hun, *n.* hun, one of a fierce Tartar race that overran Europe in the 5th century, and gave its name to Hungary; a barbarian. (Late L. *Hunni.*)
hunch, *n.* hunch, a hump; a thick slice; a push or jerk with the fist or elbow; a presentiment or suspicion [U.S.A. slang]: *v.t.* to bend upwards; to push with a sudden jerk; to crook the back. (Perhaps *hump.*)
hunchback, *n.* *hunch*-bak, a humpback.
hunchbacked, *a.* *hunch*-bakt, having a humpback.
hundred, *a.* *hun*-dred, ten multiplied by ten: *n.* the number of ten times ten; a division of a county, perhaps one originally containing a hundred families. **Chiltern Hundreds,** a Buckinghamshire district, the acceptance of the stewardship of which (a Crown office) by a member of Parliament allows him to resign his seat without penalties. (A.S.)
hundreder, *n.* *hun*-dred-er, the chief municipal officer of a hundred; one living in and paying dues to a hundred [Old Law].
hundredth, *a.* *hun*-dredth, the ordinal of a hundred: *n.* one of a hundred equal parts. **the Old Hundredth,** the tune (of about 1550) to which the Doxology is usually sung.
hundredweight, *n.* *hun*-dred-wate, a weight of 112 lb. avoirdupois, or 50·802 kilogrammes.
hung, hung, *p.* of *hang.* **hung beef,** beef slightly salted and hung up to dry.
Hungarian, *a.* hung-*gare*-re-an, pertaining to Hungary; *n.* a native of Hungary; the Magyar language.
hungary-water, *n.* *hung*-ge-re-*waw*-ter, a distilled water prepared from the tops of flowers of rosemary, etc.
hunger, *n.* *hung*-ger, a sensation caused by want of food; craving for food; any strong desire: *v.i.* to feel the pain occasioned by want of food; to crave food: *v.t.* to subject to hunger; to compel by hunger. (A.S.)
hunger-march, *n.* an organized march of unemployed workpeople to call attention to their distress.
hunger-strike, *n.* the refusal of food by prisoners: *v.i.* to refuse food by way of protest.
hunger-striker, *n.* one who hunger-strikes.
hunger-weed, *n.* a name of various plants flourishing on poor soil, esp. *Ranunculus acris* and *Alopecurus agrestis.*
hungrily, *ad.* *hung*-gre-le, in a hungry manner.
hungry, *a.* *hung*-gre, having a keen appetite or desire; suffering from hunger; emaciated; poor; barren. (A.S. *hungrig.*)
hunk, *n.* hunk, a large slice or lump. (*hunch.*)
hunker, *v.i.* *hung*-ker, to crouch so as to rest on the calves or heels: *n.* (*usu. pl.*) the haunch; the ham. **on one's hunkers,** in a squatting position. (Scots.)
hunks, *n.* a covetous man; a niggard.
Hunnish, *a.* *hun*-ish, pertaining to or having the manners of the Huns; barbarian; uncultured.
hunt, *n.* hunt, the chase; a chasing of wild animals; pursuit; a pack of hounds; an association of hunting men; a terrain hunted by these: *v.t.* to chase wild animals; to search after; to pursue; to employ in hunting: *v.i.* to follow the chase; to search. **to hunt counter,** to trace the scent backward in hunting, or the wrong way. **to hunt down,** to destroy by persecution or violence. **to hunt out** or **up,** to seek; to search for. (A.S. *huntian.*)
hunter, *n.* *hunt*-er, one who hunts; a horse used in fox-hunting; a watch with a hinged metal cover protecting the glass. **hunter's moon,** the full moon next after the harvest-moon.
hunting-box, *n.* a residence used during the hunting season.
hunting-crop, *n.* a stick with a loop at one end for a whip-thong, and a handle at the other for lifting gate-latches, catching reins, etc.
hunting-ground, *n.* a district in which hunting is followed; any likely place for a search. **happy hunting grounds,** the heaven of the North American Indians.
huntress, *n.* *hun*-tress, a female hunter.
huntsman, *n.* *hunts*-man, the manager of a pack of hounds at the hunt; a hunter.
huntsmanship, *n.* the art or practice of hunting.
hurdies, *n.pl.* *hur*-diz, the buttocks. (Scots.)
hurdle, *n.* *hur*-dl, a texture of twigs, osiers, or split sticks; a movable framework of this serving for gates, inclosures, etc. [Agric.]; a sledge on which criminals were dragged to execution: *v.t.* to make up, hedge, cover, or close with hurdles: *v.i.* to compete in hurdle races. (A.S. *hyrdel.*)
hurdler, *n.* *hurd*-dler, a maker of hurdles; a runner of hurdle races.
hurds, *n.* hurdz, hards, flax refuse.
hurdy-gurdy, *n.* *hur*-de-*gur*-de, a mechanical violin worked by a wooden wheel instead of a bow; a primitive form of barrel-organ.
hurl, *n.* hurl, the act of throwing with violence; the club used in hurley: *v.t.* to throw with violence; to utter with vehemence: *v.i.* to move rapidly; to whirl; to play at hurling. (From *hurtle.*)
hurlbone, *n.* *hurl*-bone, the whirlbone.
hurler, *n.* *hurl*-er, one who hurls, or plays at hurling.
hurley, *n.* *hurl*-e, hockey; shinty; hurling; a hockey stick. (Ir.)
hurling, *n.* *hurl*-ing, an old Cornish game of the football kind, in which the ball is thrown and carried; (in Eire) hockey.
hurly-burly, *n.* *hur*-le-*bur*-le, tumult; bustle; confusion. (Perhaps O.Fr. *hurlee,* an outcry.)
hurrah, hoo-*rah,* *int.* of joy or applause: *v.t.* to shout "Hurrah." (*huzza.*)
hurricane, *n.* *hu*-re-kan, a tropical cyclone; a violent tempest; a gale of 75 miles per hour. **hurrican deck,** an upper deck, usually above the saloon. **hurricane lamp,** a lamp specially protected from the wind. (Sp. *huracan.*)
hurriedly, *ad.* *hu*-rid-le, in a hurried manner.
hurriedness, *n.* state of being hurried.
hurrier, *n.* *hu*-re-er, one who hurries.
hurry, *n.* *hu*-re, undue haste; urgency; confusion; a chute by which coal is shot into ships: *v.i.* to move or act with haste: *v.t.* to urge forward; to hasten. (Scand.)
hurryingly, *ad.* in a hurrying manner.
hurry-scurry, *ad.* *hu*-re-*sku*-re, confusedly; in a bustle: *n.* confused bustle: *v.i.* to act thus.
hurst, *n.* hurst, a thicket; a wooded hill. (A.S.)
hurt, *n.* hurt, anything that gives pain to the body; an injury; a wound; a detriment: *v.t.* to give pain; to damage or cause loss to; to wound. *p.* and *pp.* **hurt.** (O.Fr. *hurter,* to knock against.)
hurtful, *a.* *hurt*-ful, occasioning loss or destruction; tending to impair or destroy; injurious; mischievous.
hurtfully, *ad.* *hurt*-ful-le, in a manner to hurt.
hurtfulness, *n.* the quality of being hurtful.
hurtle, *v.i.* *hur*-tl, to clash in collision; to sound like a clash: *v.t.* to move noisily or forcibly: *n.* a collision; a sound as of clashing.
hurtleberry, *n.* *hur*-tl-be-re, the whortleberry.
hurtless, *a.* *hurt*-less, doing or receiving no injury; harmless.
husband, *n.* *huz*-band, a man joined to a woman by marriage; a ship's agent for keeping her in repair [Naut.]; a good manager; a farmer; *v.t.* to manage with frugality; to cultivate; to supply with a husband; to wed. (A.S. *husbonda,* from *hus,* a house, Ice. *bondi,* inhabiting.)
husbandage, *n.* *huz*-ban-daj, commission paid to a ship's husband.
husbandman, *n.* *huz*-band-man, a farmer; a cultivator or tiller of the ground.
husbandry, *n.* *huz*-ban-dre, the business of a farmer; agriculture; domestic economy; frugality.
hush, *int.* hush; silence! be still! *n.* quietude; stillness: *v.t.* to silence; to calm: *v.i.* to be still; to be silent. **to hush up,** to suppress. (From the sound.)
hushaby, *int.* *hush*-a-by, used in hushing an infant to sleep.

hush-hush, *a.* very private; done or made in secrecy [Coll.].
hush-money, *n.* a bribe to secure silence.
husk, *n.* husk, the external covering of many fruits or seeds; any worthless part: *v.i.* to strip the husks from. (From A.S. *hus*, house.)
husked, *a.* huskt, having or covered with a husk; stripped of husks.
huskily, *ad. hus*-ke-le, in a husky manner; roughly.
huskiness, *n. hus*-ke-ness, a roughness of the voice; the state of being husky.
husky, *a. hus*-ke, abounding with husks; consisting of husks; rough; rough in sound; hoarse.
husky, *n. hus*-ke, an Eskimo; a sledge dog; any well-developed man: *a.* stalwart; of rough and vigorous personality [Canadian slang].
hussar, *n.* hoo-*zahr*, a light cavalryman, originally of Croatia and Hungary; a member of certain British cavalry (now armoured) regiments. (O. Serbian, *husar*, a freebooter.)
hussif, *n. huz*-if, a housewife or holdall for haberdashery.
Hussite, *n. huss*-ite, a follower of John Huss (burned at the stake, 1415), the Bohemian reformer.
hussy, *n. huz*-e, a pert or ill-behaved girl.
hustings, *n.pl. hus*-tingz, formerly, a wooden erection with a platform for the nomination and election of parliamentary representatives; hence, election proceedings. **Court of Hustings,** an ancient civic court of law, still held ceremonially in the City of London. (Ice. *hus*, a house, *thing*, an assembly.)
hustle, *n. hus*-sl, hurry; bustle; a show of energy: *v.i.* to shove and push, esp. in a crowd: *v.t.* to shake together in confusion; to push along; to jostle; to cause rapid progress. (Dut. *hutselen*, to shake.)
hustler, *n. hus*-sler, one who hustles; a man of energy; one who gets things done.
hut, *n.* hut, a small house, hovel, or cabin; a cottage; a small temporary camp erection [Mil.]: *v.t.* to place in huts: *v.i.* to lodge in huts. (Fr. *hutte.*)
hutch, *n.* hutch, a chest, box, or bin; a coop or cage for small animals; a trough for washing ore; a bolting-hutch: *v.t.* to lay up, as in a chest; to wash ore. (O.Fr. *huche.*)
hutia, *n. hoo*-te-a, a West Indian rodent of the genus *Capromys*, allied to the coypu. (Native name.)
hutment, *n. hut*-ment, a hut or a camp of huts.
huzza, *n.* huz-*zah*, a shout of joy; hurrah: *v.i.* to utter a loud shout of joy: *v.t.* to receive or attend with shouts of joy. (Ger. *hussa.*)
hyacinth, *n. hy*-a-sinth, a bulbous-rooted flowering plant of the genus *Hyacinthus*; the gem-stone jacinth. (Gr. *Hyakinthos*, a youth killed by Apollo and changed into a flower.)
hyacinthine, *a.* hy-a-*sin*-thine, resembling the hyacinth in colour.
Hyades, *n.pl. hy*-a-deez, a cluster of five stars in the constellation Taurus, supposed to bring rain when they rose with the sun (Astron.]. (L.)
hyæna, *n.* hy-*ee*-na, the hyena. (L.)
hyalescent, *a.* hy-a-*les*-ent, becoming hyaline or glassy; somewhat glassy.
hyaline, *a. hy*-a-lin, resembling or consisting of glass; glassy; translucent [Bot.]. (Gr. *hyalos*, glass.)
hyalite, *n. hy*-a-lite, a colourless variety of opal.
hyalography, *n.* hy-a-*log*-ra-fe, the art of engraving on glass. (Gr. *hyalos*, and *grapho*, write.)
hyaloid, *a. hy*-a-loyd, resembling glass; hyaline.
hyalopterous, *a.* hy-a-*lop*-ter-rus, having transparent wings [Entom.].
hybrid, *a. hy*-brid, mongrel; produced from different species: *n.* a mongrel; an animal or plant produced from two species; a word compounded from different languages; anything of heterogeneous composition. (L. *hybrida.*)
hybridism, *n. hy*-brid-izm, the state of being hybrid; hybridization.
hybridity, *n.* hy-*brid*-e-te, hybridism.
hybridization, *n. hy*-bri-dy-*zay*-shon, the act or process of interbreeding.
hybridize, *v.t. hy*-bri-dize, to render hybrid; to procreate by hybrids: *v.i.* to produce or to be capable of producing hybrids.
hydatid, *n. hy*-da-tid, a cyst produced by certain tapeworms in the larval stage. (Gr. *hydatis*, a watery vesicle.)
hydatism, *n. hy*-da-tizm, sound proceeding from an effusion of fluid in a cavity of the body [Med.].
hydatoid, *a. hy*-da-toyd, like water (esp. of the aqueous humour of the eye).
hydra, *n. hy*-dra, a water serpent, slain by Hercules, which had many heads, each of which when cut off was replaced by two [Myth.]; any manifold evil; a genus of freshwater polyps which multiply when divided; a water-snake; a southern constellation. (Gr. from *hydor*, water.)
hydragogue, *n. hy*-dra-gog, a purgative that occasions a fluid discharge. (Gr. *hydor*, and *ago*, lead.)
hydra-headed, *a. hy*-dra-*hed*-ed, having many heads or roots; hence, difficult to extirpate.
hydrangea, *n.* hy-*drayn*-je-a, any deciduous ornamental shrub of the genus *Hydrangea* of the saxifrage family, some of them climbing. (Gr. *hydor*, and *angeion*, a vessel.)
hydrant, *n. hy*-drant, a pipe by which water is discharged; a fire-plug in a water-main.
hydrargyric, *a.* hy-*drahr*-je-rik, pertaining to or containing mercury.
hydrargyrism, *n.* hy-*drahr*-je-rizm, poisoning by mercury or one of its compounds [Med.].
hydrargyrum, *n.* hy-*drahr*-je-rum, the element mercury; quicksilver. (Gr. *hydor*, and *argyros*, silver.)
hydrate, *n. hy*-drate, a compound in which a definite quantity of water is combined with some other element: *v.t.* to combine with water [Chem.].
hydration, *n.* hy-*dray*-shon, the action of hydrating; the addition of atmospheric or magmatic water to anhydrous minerals [Geol.].
hydraulic, *a.* hy-*draw*-lik, pertaining to fluids in motion or to the power they exert; worked by water pressure. **hydraulic cement,** a cement having the property of hardening under water. **hydraulic glue,** a glue having strong water-resisting properties. **hydraulic press,** a machine for obtaining great pressure through the agency of water. **hydraulic ram,** a kind of force pump by which water, through its own momentum, raises a portion of its bulk to a height above that of its source. (Fr. *hydraulique.*)
hydraulically, *ad.* by means of hydraulics.
hydraulician, *n.* hy-draw-*lish*-an, an hydraulic engineer.
hydraulics, *n.* hy-*draw*-liks, the science of fluids in motion; the art of the use of water-power in mechanics and engineering. (Gr. *hydor*, and *aulos*, a pipe.)
hydric, *a. hy*-drik, of or containing hydrogen.
hydride, *n. hy*-dride, a compound of hydrogen with another element or with a radical [Chem.].
hydriodate, *n. hy*-dre-o-date, a salt of hydriodic acid.
hydriodic, *a. hy*-dre-*od*-ik, containing hydrogen and iodine [Chem.].
hydro, *n. hy*-dro, a hydropathic establishment [Coll.].
hydro-aeroplane, *n.* a seaplane.
hydro-barometer, *n.* an instrument for determining the depth of the sea by its pressure.
hydrobromate, *n. hy*-dro-*broh*-mat, a salt of hydrobromic acid.
hydrobromic, *a. hy*-dro-*broh*-mik, composed of hydrogen and bromine [Chem.].
hydrocarbon, *n. hy*-dro-*kar*-bon, a compound of hydrogen and carbon [Chem.].
hydrocele, *n. hy*-dro-seel, a tumour containing serous fluid, esp. in the scrotum [Med.]. (Gr. *hydor*, and *kele*, a tumour.)
hydrocephalic, *a. hy*-dro-se-*fal*-ik, pertaining to hydrocephalus.
hydrocephalus, *n. hy*-dro-*sef*-al-us, dropsy of, or water on, the brain [Med.]. (Gr. *hydor*, and *kephale*, the head.)
hydrochlorate, *n. hy*-dro-*klaw*-rate, a salt of hydrochloric acid.
hydrochloric, *a. hy*-dro-*klo*-rik, composed of chlorine and hydrogen. **hydrochloric acid,** spirits of salts, or muriatic acid, an aqueous solution of hydrogen chloride gas.
hydrocyanate, *n.* hy-dro-*sy*-a-nate, salt of hydrocyanic acid.
hydrocyanic, *a. hy*-dro-sy-*an*-ik, formed by the combination of hydrogen and cyanogen. **hydrocyanic acid,** prussic acid.
hydrodynamic, *a. hy*-dro-dy-*nam*-ik, pertaining to hydrodynamics; derived from the force or pressure of water. (Gr. *hydor*, and *dynamic.*)

hydrodynamics, *n.* *hy*-dro-dy-*nam*-iks, that branch of physics which treats of fluid pressures.
hydro-electric, *a.* pertaining to electricity generated by water-power or by high-pressure steam.
hydro-electricity, *n.* electricity generated by means of water-power.
hydro-extractor, *n.* *hy*-dro-eks-*trak*-tor, a machine for separating moisture from textiles by centrifugal action.
hydrofluoric, *a.* *hy*-dro-floo-*o*-rik, consisting of fluorine and hydrogen.
hydrogel, *n.* *hy*-dro-jel, a jelly consisting of a colloidal substance and water.
hydrogen, *n.* *hy*-dro-jen, the lightest known body, a highly inflammable gaseous element combining with oxygen to produce water. (Gr. *hydor*, and *gennao*, produce.)
hydrogenate, *v.t.* *hy*-dro-je-nate *or* hy-*droj*-e-nate, to hydrogenize.
hydrogenation, *n.* hy-dro-je-*nay*-shon, the act or process of hydrogenizing.
hydrogenic, *a.* hy-dro-*jen*-ik, similar to hydrogen [Physics]; formed by the action of water [Geol.].
hydrogenize, *v.t.* *hy*-dro-je-nize, to combine or cause to combine with hydrogen.
hydrogenous, *a.* hy-*droj*-en-us, pertaining to or containing hydrogen.
hydrographer, *n.* hy-*drog*-ra-fer, a student or practitioner of hydrography; a maker of charts.
hydrographic, *a.* *hy*-dro-*graf*-ik, relating to hydrography.
hydrography, *n.* hy-*drog*-ra-fe, the art of surveying and describing the sea, lakes, rivers, and other waters; the construction of charts. (Gr. *hydor*, and *grapho*, write.)
hydrohæmatite, *n.* *hy*-dro-*hee*-ma-tite, turgite.
hydroid, *a.* *hy*-droyd, hydrozoan; hydra-like [Zool.]: *n.* a hydrozoan. (L. *hydra*, and Gr. *eidos*, like.)
hydrokinetics, *n.* *hy*-dro-ke-*net*-iks, that branch of physics which treats of fluids in motion or under the action of force. (Gr. *hydor*, and *kinetics*.)
hydrological, *a.* *hy*-dro-*loj*-e-kal, pertaining to hydrology.
hydrology, *n.* hy-*drol*-o-je, the science of water, its properties, distribution, laws, etc. (Gr. *hydor*, and *logos*, science.)
hydrolysis, *n.* hy-*drol*-e-sis, a process of decomposition in which the elements of water become fixed in distinct compounds [Chem.]. (Gr. *hydor*, and *lysis*, easing or loosening.)
hydrolyst, *n.* *hy*-dro-list, a hydrolyzing agent.
hydrolyze, *v.t.* and *i.* *hy*-dro-lize, to subject to or to undergo hydrolysis.
hydromancy, *n.* *hy*-dro-man-se, divination by water. (Gr. *hydor*, and *manteia*, divination.)
hydromania, *n.* *hy*-dro-*may*-ne-a, a morbid craving for water.
hydromechanics, *n.* *hy*-dro-me-*kan*-iks, the branch of physics treating of the laws of motion and equilibrium of liquids.
hydromel, *n.* *hy*-dro-mel, a drink consisting of honey and water. (L.)
hydrometeorology, *n.* *hy*-dro-*mee*-te-o-*rol*-o-je, the branch of meteorology treating of rain, hail, snow, clouds, etc.
hydrometer, *n.* hy-*drom*-e-ter, an instrument for determining the specific gravity of liquids, and consequently the strength of spirituous liquors. (Gr. *hydor*, and *metron*, measure.)
hydrometric, *a.* *hy*-dro-*met*-rik, pertaining to hydrometry.
hydrometrical, *a.* hydrometric.
hydrometry, *n.* hy-*drom*-e-tre, the art of determining the specific gravity of liquids, and hence the strength of spirituous liquors.
hydromotor, *n.* *hy*-dro-*moh*-tor, a machine for propelling ships by the emission of jets of water.
hydropathic, *a.* *hy*-dro-*path*-ik, pertaining to hydropathy: *n.* an establishment for the treatment of ailments by means of medicinal waters [Coll.].
hydropathist, *n.* hy-*drop*-a-thist, one who practises or believes in hydropathy.
hydropathy, *n.* hy-*drop*-a-the, a mode of treating diseases by the use of water or medicinal waters. (Gr. *hydor*, and *pathos*, suffering.)
hydrophane, *n.* *hy*-dro-fane, a variety of opal that becomes translucent on immersion in water [Min.]. (Gr. *hydor*, and *phaino*, show.)
hydrophanous, *a.* hy-*drof*-a-nus, becoming translucent or transparent when immersed in water.
hydrophilic, *a.* hy-dro-*fil*-ik, having a strong affinity for water (of certain colloids) [Chem.].
hydrophilous, *a.* hy-*drof*-e-lus, water-loving; dependent upon water (of plants, insects, etc.).
hydrophobia, *n.* *hy*-dro-*foh*-be-a, a morbid aversion to water, a symptom of rabies due to inoculation with the saliva of a rabid animal; the disease itself. (Gr. *hydor*, and *phobos*, fear.)
hydrophobic, *a.* *hy*-dro-*foh*-bik, pertaining to hydrophobia; forming a solution in water only with difficulty (of certain colloids) [Chem.].
hydrophone, *n.* *hy*-dro-fone, an instrument for detecting by sound objects moving in water; an apparatus for detecting leaks by sound. (Gr. *hydor*, and *phone*, sound.)
hydrophore, *n.* *hy*-dro-fore, an instrument for obtaining specimens of water from any particular depth. (Gr. *hydor*, and *phoreo*, bear.)
hydrophthalmia, *n.* *hy*-drof-*thal*-me-a, enlargement of the eye-ball due to excess of any of the humours within it [Med.]. (Gr. *hydor*, and *ophthalmos*, the eye.)
hydrophyte, *n.* *hy*-dro-fite, any aquatic plant. (Gr. *hydor*, and *phyton*, a plant.)
hydrophytic, *a.* *hy*-dro-*fit*-ik, pertaining to the hydrophytes; resembling a hydrophyte.
hydrophytology, *n.* *hy*-dro-fy-*tol*-o-je, the branch of botany treating of aquatic plants. (*hydrophyte*, and Gr. *logos*, science.)
hydropic, *a.* hy-*drop*-ik, dropsical; like dropsy.
hydroplane, *n.* *hy*-dro-plane, a light motor-boat that skims along the water at high speed; the plane by which this is raised partly from the water; a plane or fin regulating the vertical direction of a submarine.
hydroponics, *n.* *hy*-dro-*pon*-iks, the growing of vegetable, cereal, or floral crops by use of water containing the necessary nutrient salts instead of in soil. (Gr. *hydor*, and *ponos*, labour.)
hydropsy, *n.* *hy*-drop-se, dropsy. (Fr. *hydropisie*.)
hydroscope, *n.* *hy*-dro-skope, a form of clepsydra; a hygroscope.
hydrosphere, *n.* *hy*-dro-sfeer, the atmospheric moisture enveloping the globe [Meteor.]; the whole body of water of the earth.
hydrostat, *n.* *hy*-dro-stat, an apparatus for preventing the explosion of steam-boilers; an electrical device for detecting the presence of water; a form of bathysphere.
hydrostatic, *a.* *hy*-dro-*stat*-ik, relating to hydrostatics. **hydrostatic balance,** a balance for weighing substances in water, for ascertaining their specific gravities. **hydrostatic press,** an hydraulic press.
hydrostatical, *a.* *hy*-dro-*stat*-e-kal, hydrostatic.
hydrostatically, *ad.* according to hydrostatic principles.
hydrostatics, *n.* *hy*-dro-*stat*-iks, the science which treats of fluids at rest. (Gr. *hydrostates*.)
hydrosulphuric, *a.* *hy*-dro-sul-*fewr*-rik, containing or consisting of hydrogen and sulphur in combination [Chem.].
hydrotherapeutic, *a.* *hy*-dro-the-ro-*pew*-tik, pertaining to the curative effect of waters.
hydrotherapeutics, *n.pl.* *hy*-dro-the-ro-*pew*-tiks, a method of medical treatment by baths, mineral waters, etc.; hydrotherapy.
hydrotherapy, *n.* *hy*-dro-*the*-ra-pe, the treatment of disease by water; hydropathy.
hydrothermal, *a.* *hy*-dro-*ther*-mal, pertaining to the action of heated water, or to hot springs.
hydrothorax, *n.* *hy*-dro-*thaw*-raks, dropsy in the chest. (Gr. *hydor*, and *thorax*, the chest.)
hydrotic, *a.* hy-*drot*-ik, causing a discharge of water or phlegm: *n.* a medicine that does so.
hydrotimeter, *n.* hy-dro-*tim*-e-ter, an apparatus for ascertaining the hardness of water.
hydrotropic, *a.* *hy*-dro-*trop*-ik, exhibiting or affected by hydrotropism.
hydrotropism, *n.* hy-*drot*-ro-pizm, tendency to turn towards or away from moisture [Bot.]. (Gr. *hydor*, and *trepo*, turn.)
hydrous, *a.* *hy*-drus, containing water [Chem.].
hydroxide, *n.* *hy*-*drok*-side, a compound of an element or radical with water [Chem.].
hydrozincite, *n.* *hy*-dro-*zing*-kite, zinc-bloom.
hydrozoan, *a.* hy-dro-*zoh*-an, pertaining to the

Hydrozoa, a class of cœlenterates comprising polyps, medusæ, and jelly-fish : *n.* a member of this class.
hyena, *n.* hy-*ee*-na, a nocturnal carnivore of the family Hyænidæ of Africa and S.E. Asia, allied to the dog.
hyetal, *a. hy*-e-tal, pertaining to rain or to statistics, etc., of rainfall. (Gr. *hyetos*, rain.)
hyetograph, *n. hy*-e-to-graf, a chart of rainfall in different regions. (Gr. *hyetos*, and *grapho*, write.)
hyetography, *n. hy*-e-*tog*-ra-fe, the branch of meteorology treating of rainfall.
hyetology, *n. hy*-e-*tol*-o-je, the science treating of the precipitation of rain.
hyetometer, *n.* hy-e-*tom*-e-ter, a rain-gauge.
hygeian, *a.* hy-*jee*-an, relating to health.
hygiene, *n. hy*-jeen *or hy*-je-een, the science of health. (Fr. *hygiene*, from L. *Hygea*, the goddess of health.)
hygienic, *a. hy*-je-*en*-ik, pertaining to health or hygiene : *n.pl.* hygiene.
hygienist, *n. hy*-je-e-nist, one versed in hygiene.
hygrology, *n.* hy-*grol*-o-je, the science of the phenomena of atmospheric humidity. (Gr. *hygros*, moist, *logos*, science.)
hygrometer, *n.* hy-*grom*-e-ter, an instrument for measuring the moisture of the atmosphere.
hygrometric, *a. hy*-gro-*met*-rik, pertaining to hygrometry.
hygrometry, *n.* hy-*grom*-e-tre, the art of measuring moisture content, esp. that of the air.
hygrophyte, *n. hy*-gro-fite, a plant which thrives under conditions of great moisture.
hygroplasm, *n. hy*-gro-plazm, the fluid part of protoplasm.
hygroscope, *n. hy*-gro-skope, an instrument to test the presence or the degree of moisture in the air. (Gr. *hygros*, and *skopeo*, view.)
hygroscopic, *a. hy*-gro-*skop*-ik, relating to the hygroscope ; readily absorbing and retaining moisture from the atmosphere.
hygroscopicity, *n. hy*-gro-sko-*pis*-e-te, sensitiveness to moisture [Bot.].
hygrostat, *n. hy*-gro-stat, an instrument for regulating humidity.
hygrostatics, *n. hy*-gro-*stat*-iks, the science of comparing or measuring degrees of moisture.
hying, *hy*-ing, *ppr.* of *hie.*
hylic, *a. hy*-lik, pertaining to matter ; material as opposed to spiritual [Phil.]. (Gr. *hyle*, matter.)
hylicizm, *n. hy*-le-sizm, hylism.
hylicist, *n. hy*-le-sist, an adherent of hylism ; a materialist.
hylism, *n. hy*-lizm, materialism ; the theory that matter is the basic principle of evil. (Gr. *hyle*, matter.)
hylobate, *n. hy*-lo-bate, a gibbon or long-armed anthropoid ape. (Gr. *hylobatēs*, a wood-walker.)
hyloist, *n. hy*-lo-ist, a hylicist.
hylopathism, *n.* hy-*lop*-a-thizm, the doctrine that spirit and matter can affect each other. (Gr. *hyle*, and *pathos*, feeling.)
hylotheism, *n. hy*-lo-*thee*-izm, the doctrine which assigns to deity a material basis, or that identifies God with matter. (Gr. *hyle*, and *theos*, god.)
hylozoic, *a. hy*-lo-*zoh*-ik, pertaining to or believing in hylozoism ; materialistic.
hylozoism, *n. hy*-lo-*zoh*-izm, the doctrine that life is inherent in matter, or is matter self-vivified ; materialism. (Gr. *hyle*, and *zoe*, life.)
hylozoist, *n. hy*-lo-*zoh*-ist, one who holds hylozoism.
Hymen, *n. hy*-men, the Greek god of marriage ; (*l.c.*) the membrane partly closing the orifice of the vagina [Anat.]. (Gr.)
hymeneal, *a. hy*-men-*nee*-al, pertaining to marriage : *n.* a marriage song.
hymenean, *a. hy*-men-*nee*-an, hymeneal.
hymenogeny, *n. hy*-men-*oj*-e-ne, the production of artificial membranes from liquids in contact. (Gr. *hymen*, a membrane, *gennao*, produce.)
Hymenoptera, *n.pl. hy*-men-*op*-ter-ra, the very extensive order of four-winged insects including the bees, wasps, ants, and many parasitic flies. [Entom.]. (Gr. *hymen*, and *pteron*, a wing.)
hymenopteran, *a. hy*-men-*op*-ter-ran, having four membranous wings : *n.* any of the hymenoptera.
hymenopterous, *a. hy*-men-*op*-ter-rus, belonging to the Hymenoptera ; hymenopteran.
hymenotomy, *n. hy*-men-*ot*-o-me, the cutting or dissection of membranes.
hymn, *n.* him, a song of praise or adoration : *v.t.* to praise in song ; to worship by singing hymns : *v.i.* to sing in praise or adoration. (Gr. *hymnos*, hymn.)
hymnal, *n. him*-nal, a collection of hymns for a hymn-book : *a.* pertaining to hymns.
hymnary, *n. him*-na-re, a hymnal.
hymn-book, *n. him*-book, a book of hymns.
hymnic, *a. him*-nik, relating to hymns.
hymnist, *n. him*-nist, a composer of hymns.
hymnodist, *n. him*-no-dist, a writer of hymns.
hymnody, *n. him*-no-de, the composition or singing of hymns ; hymns collectively. (Gr. *hymnodia.*)
hymnographer, *n.* him-*nog*-ra-fer, a writer about hymns ; a hymnist.
hymnologist, *n.* him-*nol*-o-jist, one conversant with hymns ; a composer of hymns.
hymnology, *n.* him-*nol*-o-je, the study of hymns ; the composition or singing of hymns ; hymns collectively. (Gr. *hymnologia.*)
hyodont, *a. hy*-o-dont, having teeth on the hyoid bone (of certain fish).
hyoid, *a. hy*-oyd, U-shaped, esp. as designating the bone supporting the tongue [Anat.]. (Greek *v.* and *eidos*, like.)
hyoscine, *n. hy*-o-sine, trade-name of a variety of scopolamine, used as a narcotic.
hyoscyamine, *n. hy*-o-*sy*-a-min, a crystalline alkaloid obtained from henbane, *Hyoscyamus niger.*
hyp, *n.* hip, melancholia, the hip : *v.t.* to depress the spirits [Slang].
hypæthral, *a.* hy-*pee*-thral, open to the sky, esp. of a temple without a roof. (Gr. *hypo-*, under, *aither*, the sky.)
hypallage, *n.* hy-*pal*-la-je, interchange in the relationship of terms in a sentence ; with no essential difference in meaning [Gram.]. (Gr.)
hyper-, *hy*-per, a Greek prefix signifying over, beyond, or excess.
hyperacute, *a. hy*-per-a-*kewt*, unusually acute.
hyperæmia, *n. hy*-per-*ee*-me-a, excess of blood [Med.]. (Gr. *hyper-*, and *aima*, blood.)
hyperæsthesia, *n. hy*-per-es-*thee*-ze-a, excessive sensibility of the nerves [Med.]. (Gr. *hyper-*, and *aisthesis*, sensation.)
hyperalgesic, *a. hy*-per-al-*jee*-sik, excessively sensitive to pain [Med.].
hyperbatic, *a. hy*-per-*bat*-ik, transposed (of words or phrases) [Rhet.].
hyperbaton, hy-*per*-ba-ton, a transposition of wording [Rhet.], as " Came the dawn " for " the dawn came." (Gr. *hyper-*, and *bainen*, to go.)
hyperbola, *n.* hy-*per*-bo-la, a curve in which the plane is at a greater angle to the base than that made by the side of the cone [Geom.]. (Gr. *hyperbole.*)
hyperbole, *n.* hy-*per*-bo-le, a figure of speech which expresses more or less than the truth ; extravagant exaggeration [Rhet.]. (Gr.)
hyperbolic, *a. hy*-per-*bol*-ik, belonging to or having the nature of the hyperbola or hyperbole ; exaggerative ; exceeding the truth. (L. *hyperbolicus.*)
hyperbolical, *a. hy*-per-*bol*-e-kal, hyperbolic.
hyperbolically, *ad. hy*-per-*bol*-e-kal-le, in the form of a hyperbola or hyperbole ; with exaggeration.
hyperboliform, *a.* hy-per-*bol*-e-form, of the shape or appearance of a hyperbola.
hyperbolism, *n.* hy-*per*-bo-lizm, the use of hyperbole ; a hyperbolic expression.
hyperbolist, *n.* hy-*per*-bo-list, one who uses hyperboles.
hyperbolize, *v.i.* hy-*per*-bo-lize, to speak with exaggeration : *v.t.* to exaggerate or extenuate.
hyperboloid, *a.* hy-*per*-bo-loyd, hyperboliform : *n.* a solid formed by the revolution of a hyperbola about its axis. (Gr. *hyperbola*, and *eidos*, like.)
hyperborean, *a. hy*-per-*baw*-re-an, far northern ; very cold : *n.* (*cap.*) one of a mythical race living in the extreme north in perpetual youth and health ; anyone of Arctic habitat. (Gr. *hyperboreas*, beyond the north wind.)
hypercatalectic, *a. hy*-per-kat-a-*lek*-tik, having a syllable or two beyond the regular measure of a verse [Pros.]. (Gr. *hyper-*, and *catalectic.*)
hypercatalexis, *n. hy*-per-kat-a-*lek*-sis, the state of being hypercatalectic [Pros.].
hypercritic, *n. hy*-per-*krit*-ik, one who is overcritical; a captious censor. (Gr. *hyper-*, and *critic.*)

hypercritical, *a.* *hy*-per-*krit*-e-kal, over-critical; excessively exact; finical.
hypercritically, *ad.* *hy*-per-*krit*-e-ka-le, in a hypercritical manner.
hypercriticism, *n.* *hy*-per-*krit*-e-sizm, excessive rigour of criticism.
hyperdimensional, *a.* *hy*-per-dy-*men*-shon-al, pertaining to space of more than three dimensions [Math.].
hyperdulia, *n.* *hy*-per-*dew*-le-a, the superior dulia, or veneration, paid to the Virgin Mary.
hyperemesis, *n.* *hy*-per-em-*ee*-sis, excessive vomiting (esp. in pregnancy) [Med.]. (Gr. *hyper-*, and *emesis.*)
hypergeometry, *n.* *hy*-per-jee-*om*-e-tre, the geometry of hyperdimensional spaces.
Hypericum, *n.* hy-*pe*-re-kum, the genus of plants including the St. John's worts. (L.)
hyperinosis, *n.* *hy*-per-e-*noh*-sis, excess of fibrine in the blood [Med.]. (Gr. *hyper-*, and *is, inos*, fibre.)
hypermetrical, *a.* *hy*-per-*met*-re-kal, exceeding the common measure [Pros.]; having a redundant syllable [Pros.].
hypermetropia, *n.* *hy*-per-me-*troh*-pe-a, abnormally long sight. (Gr. *hyper-*, *metron*, and *ops*, eye.)
hypermetropic, *a.* *hy*-per-me-*trop*-ik, very long-sighted.
hyperopia, *n.* hy-per-*oh*-pe-a, the condition of long-sightedness [Opt.].
hyperparasite, *n.* *hy*-per-*pa*-ra-site, a superparasite.
hyperpiesia, *n.* *hy*-per-py-*ee*-ze-a, the condition occasioned by hyperpiesis [Med.]. (Gr. *hyper-*, and *piesis*, pressure.)
hyperpiesis, *n.* *hy*-per-py-*ee*-sis, abnormally high blood-pressure.
hyperphasia, *n.* *hy*-per-*fay*-ze-a, inability to control the organs of speech.
hyperphysical, *a.* *hy*-per-*fiz*-e-kal, supernatural.
hyperplasia, *n.* *hy*-per-*play*-ze-a, excessive cell-formation; abnormal growth due to this [Med.].
hyperpyrexia, *n.* *hy*-per-py-*rek*-se-a, abnormally high fever [Med.].
hypersensitive, *a.* *hy*-per-*sen*-se-tiv, over-sensitive.
hypersthene, *n.* *hy*-per-stheen, a mineral of the pyroxene group, allied to hornblende. (Gr. *hyper-*, and *sthenos*, strength.)
hypersthenia, *n.* *hy*-per-*sthee*-ne-a, a condition of excessive excitement of vital phenomena [Med.]. (Gr. *hyper-*, and *sthenos*, force.)
hypertrophied, *a.* hy-*per*-tro-fid, excessively developed; affected by hypertrophy [Med.].
hypertrophy, *n.* hy-*per*-tro-fe, a condition of morbid enlargement through excessive use, etc.: *v.t.* and *i.* to affect with, or be affected by, hypertrophy. [Med.]. (Gr. *hyper-*, and *trophe*, nourishment.)
hypha, *n.* *hy*-fa (*pl.* **hyphæ,** *hy*-fee), one of the filamentous components of the mycelium of a fungus [Bot.]. (Gr. *hype*, a web.)
hyphen, *n.* *hy*-fen, a dash, thus (-), connecting words or syllables: *v.t.* to connect with a hyphen. (Gr. *hypo-*, under, *hen*, one.)
hyphenate, *v.t.* *hy*-fen-*ate*, to hyphen. **hyphenated,** *a.* joined by a hyphen, esp. of nationality names, as German-American.
hypnoid, *a.* *hip*-noyd, pertaining to hypnosis; resembling sleep.
hypnoid, *a.* *hip*-noyd, belonging to, characteristic of, or resembling the large genus of mosses, *Hypnum.*
hypnology, *n.* hip-*nol*-o-je, a treatise on sleep; the study or science of the phenomena of sleep. (Gr. *hypnos*, sleep, *logos*, science.)
hypnosis, *n.* hip-*noh*-sis, a hypnotic sleep in which the sleeper obeys external suggestions.
hypnotic, *a.* hip-*not*-ik, producing sleep; pertaining to or inducing hypnotism: *n.* a medicine that induces sleep; an opiate; a hypnotized, or readily hypnotized, person. (Gr. *hypnotikos.*)
hypnotism, *n.* *hip*-no-tizm, an artificially induced state of sleep; the method by which this is attained; mesmerism.
hypo-, *hy*-po, a Greek prefix, signifying under or beneath; used in chemistry to form names of oxygen compounds lower in the series than those with the simple names.
hypo, *n.* *hy*-po, sodium thiosulphate, or other fixing solution [Phot.].
hypobole, *n.* hy-*pob*-o-le, a figure in which several points apparently telling against an argument are adduced and then refuted [Rhet.]. (Gr. *hypo-*, and *ballo*, throw.)
hypocaust, *n.* *hip*-o- *or* *hy*-po-kawst, the hot-air chamber under a Roman bath; a stove or hot-house. (L. *hypocaustum.*)
hypochondria, *n.* *hy*-po- *or* *hip*-o-*kon*-dre-a, mental derangement accompanied by melancholy; excessive and unnecessary anxiety about one's health [Med.]. (Late L.)
hypochondriac, *a.* *hy*-po- *or* *hip*-o-*kon*-dre-ak, pertaining to hypochondria, or the hypochondrium; affected with depression of spirits: *n.* a person affected with hypochondria. (Fr. *hypochondriaque.*)
hypochondriacal, *a.* *hy*-po- *or* *hip*-o-kon-*dry*-a-kal, hypochondria.
hypochondriacally, *ad.* in a hypochondriacal way.
hypochondriacism, *n.* *hip*-o-kon-*dry*-a-sizm, hypochondriasis.
hypochondriasis, *n.* *hip*-o-kon-*dry*-a-sis, hypochondria [Med.].
hypochondrium, *n.* *hy*-po- *or* *hip*-o-*kon*-dre-um, either of the two regions of the abdomen situated below the short ribs and above the lumbar regions [Anat.]. (L.)
hypochromat, *n.* hip-o-*kroh*-mat, a colour-blind person.
hypocist, *n.* *hip*-o-sist, an astringent inspissated juice obtained from the parasitic plant *Cytinus hypocistis.*
hypocoristic, *a.* *hy*-po-ko-*ris*-tik, pertaining to pet names (as "Winnie" for "Winston") or their use. (Gr. *hypo-*, and *korizesthai*, to pet.)
hypocrisy, *n.* hip-*pok*-re-se, a feigning to be what one is not, esp. pretence to virtue; dissimulation. (O.Fr. *hypocrisie.*)
hypocrite, *n.* *hip*-o-krit, one who practises hypocrisy; a dissembler. (Fr.)
hypocritical, *a.* *hip*-o-*krit*-e-kal, counterfeiting a virtuous or religious character; concealing one's real motives.
hypocritically, *ad.* in a hypocritical manner.
hypodermic, *a.* *hy*-po-*der*-mik, pertaining to the parts immediately under the skin: *n.* a drug for injecting beneath the skin. **hypodermic needle, syringe,** implements for effecting hypodermic injections. (Gr. *hypodermis*, under the skin.)
hypogastric, *a.* hy-po-*gas*-trik, relating to the hypogastrium.
hypogastrium, *n.* hy-po-*gas*-tre-um, the lowest median area of the abdomen [Phys.]. (Gr. *hypo-*, and *gaster*, belly.)
hypogean, *a.* *hy*-po-*jee*-an, subterranean; existing under the ground. (Gr. *hypo-*, and *ge*, the earth.)
hypogene, *a.* *hy*-po-jeen, hypogean; not formed near the surface (of certain rocks) [Geol.]. (Gr. *hypo-*, and *gennao*, produce.)
hypogeum, *n.* *hy*-po-*jee*-um, all the parts of a building beneath the level of the ground [Antiq.]. (L.)
hypoglossal, *a.* *hy*-po-*glos*-al, situated under the tongue [Anat.]. (Gr. *hypo-*, and *glossa*, tongue.)
hypognathous, *a.* hy-*pog*-na-thus, with the lower mandible longer than the upper [Ornith.].
hypogynous, *a.* hy-*poj*-e-nus, growing from beneath the ovary [Bot.]. (Gr. *hypo-*, and *gyne*, female.)
hypophosphite, *n.* *hy*-po-*fos*-fite, a compound of hypophosphorous acid with a base.
hypophosphorous, *a.* *hy*-po-*fos*-fo-rus, designating a certain white crystalline acid of phosphorus.
hypophysis, *n.* hy-*pof*-e-sis, the pituitary body [Anat.]; the cell from which the root of a seed-plant is developed [Bot.]. (Gr., undergrowth.)
hyposcope, *n.* *hy*-po-skope, a form of periscope.
hypostasis, *n.* hy-*pos*-ta-sis, the assumed substratum or common basis of being; essential substance; the essence or divinity of the Godhead [Theol.]; congestion of or sediment in the blood [Med.]. (Gr. *hypo-*, and *stasis*, standing.)
hypostatic, *a.* hy-po-*stat*-ik, relating to hypostasis; constitutive; constituting a distinct substance or personality. **hypostatic union,** the indivisible union in Christ of the divine and human natures [Theol.].
hypostatize, *v.t.* hy-*pos*-ta-tize, to treat as a distinct substance or person; to attribute a personal existence to.
hypostrophe, *n.* hy-*pos*-tro-fe, a return from a digression [Rhet.]; a relapse in illness [Med.]. (Gr., turning around.)
hypostyle, *a.* *hy*-po-stile, having the roof supported by pillars: *n.* a pillared court, covered colonnade, etc. (Gr. *hypo-*, and *stylos*, pillar.)

hypotaxis, *n.* *hy*-po-*tak*-sis, dependent construction [Gram.].
hypotenuse, *n.* hy-*pot*-e-newce, the side of a right-angled triangle opposite the right angle [Geom.]. (Fr. *hypoténuse.*)
hypothec, *n.* hip- *or* hy-*poth*-ek, the security which a creditor has over goods in respect of a debt due by their owner [Scots. Law]. (Fr. *hypothèque.*)
hypothecary, *a.* hip- *or* hy-*poth*-e-ka-re, pertaining to or secured by a hypothec or pledge.
hypothecate, *v.t.* hy-*poth*-e-kate, to pledge as security for a debt or money borrowed; to mortgage.
hypothecation, *n.* hy-*poth*-e-*kay*-shon, the act of pledging as a security for debt.
hypothecator, *n.* hy-*poth*-e-kay-tor, one who hypothecates or pledges; a mortgagor.
hypothesis, *n.* hy-*poth*-e-sis, a supposition; something assumed for the purpose of argument; an assumption in explanation of a fact which may or may not be found to be true. (L., from Gr.)
hypothetic, *a.* *hy*-po-*thet*-ik, hypothetical.
hypothetical, *a.* *hy*-po-*thet*-e-kal, founded on, or assumed by way of, hypothesis; conjectural.
hypothetically, *ad.* by way of hypothesis.
hypotyposis, *n.* *hy*-po-te-*poh*-sis, vivid presentation as in actual vision [Rhet.]. (Gr.)
hypozoic, *a.* *hy*-po-*zoh*-ik, situated under the strata that contain organic remains [Geol.]. (Gr. *hypo-*, and *zoe*, life.)
hyppish, *a.* *hip*-ish, affected with the hyp or hypochondria; melancholy.
hypsography, *n.* hip-*sog*-ra-fe, that branch of geography treating of altitudes.
hypsometer, *n.* hip-*som*-e-ter, an instrument for measuring altitudes by determining the local atmospheric pressure. (Gr. *hypsos*, height, *metron*, measure.)
hypsometry, *n.* *hip*-som-e-tre, the art of measuring heights with the hypsometer.
hypural, *a.* hy-*pewr*-ral, situated below the tail [Ichth.]. (Gr. *hypo*, and *oura*, tail.)
hyrax, *n.* *hy*-raks, a small ungulate of the genus *Hyrax* comprising the conies and rock-rabbits of Africa and S.W. Asia. (Gr., shrew-mouse.)
hyson, *n.* *hy*-sun, a Chinese green tea. (Chin.)
hyssop, *n.* *his*-up, the labiate plant, *Hyssopus officinalis*, formerly used in medicine; the popular name of several aromatic herbs. (O.Fr.)
hysteranthous, *a.* *his*-ter-*an*-thus, having leaves that appear after the flowering [Bot.]. (Gr. *husteros*, late, *anthos*, flower.)
hysteresis, *n.* his-te-*ree*-sis, magnetic retardation or inertia; the resultant lagging when forces acting upon a body are changed [Physics]. (Gr. *husteros*, late.)
hysteria, *n.* his-*teer*-re-a, a nervous disorder occurring in paroxysms, characterized by emotional excitability and often simulating other diseases. (Gr. *hystera*, the womb, as its assumed origin.)
hysteric, *a.* his-*te*-rik, hysterical.
hysterical, *a.* his-*te*-re-kal, affected with, due to, or resembling hysteria; emotionally excitable. (L. *hystericus.*)
hysterically, *ad.* in a hysterical manner.
hysterics, *n.* his-*te*-riks, hysteria; fits, or a fit, of hysteria.
hysteritis, *n.* his-ter-*ry*-tis, inflammation of the uterus. (Gr. *hystera*, the womb, and *-itis.*)
hysteroid, *a.* *his*-te-royd, like hysteria.
hysterology, *n.* his-te-*rol*-o-je, the branch of medical science treating of the uterus.
hysteron-proteron, *n.* *his*-ter-on-*prot*-er-on, an inversion of thought or expression in which the consequent is placed before the antecedent. (Gr., last first.)
hysterotomy, *n.* his-te-*rot*-o-me, the Cæsarian section; surgical removal of or incision of the womb. (Gr. *hystera*, and *tome*, cutting.)
hythe, *n.* hithe, a port; a hithe.

I

I is the ninth letter and third vowel of the English alphabet, and has three main sounds: the first, long, open, and diphthongal, as in *fine*; the second, short and acute, as in *sit*; the third, close and slender, though long (like the Italian), as in *fatigue*; *i* may also have the half-close mixed front-back sound, as in *stir*, and the consonantal *y* sound, as in *bunion*.
***I**, i, *pron. first pers. sing.* myself; *pl.* **we.** (A.S. *ic.*)
iamb, *n.* *i*-amb, an iambus.
iambic, *n.* i-*am*-bik, a poetic foot consisting of a short or unaccented syllable followed by a long or accented one: *pl.* (i-*am*-biks), verses composed of iambics: *a.* consisting of iambic feet or measure. (L. *iambicus.*)
iambist, *n.* i-am-*bist*, a writer of iambic verse.
iambus, *n.* i-*am*-bus, an iambic foot. (Gr.)
iatraliptic, *a.* *i*-at-ra-*lip*-tik, pertaining to the treatment of disease by the application of unguents. (Gr. *iatros*, physician, *aleiptos*, anointer.)
iatrical, *a.* i-*at*-re-kal, medical; pertaining to medicine or physicians. (Gr. *iatros*, a physician.)
Iberian, *a.* i-*beer*-re-an, pertaining to ancient Iberia, *i.e.* Spain and Portugal; Spanish: *n.* an inhabitant or the language of ancient Iberia. **Iberian Peninsula**, Spain and Portugal together.
Iberis, *n.* i-*beer*-ris, a genus of cruciferous plants comprising the candytufts. (Gr., cress.)
ibex, *n.* *i*-beks, a wild goat of many species of the genus *Capra* inhabiting mountain regions of Europe, Asia, and N. Africa. (L.)
ibidem, *ad.* ib-*i*-dem, in the same place (usually abbreviated as *ibid.*). (L.)
ibis, *n.* *i*-bis, a wading bird of a genus allied to the storks, one species of which, the sacred ibis, *Ibis æthiopica*, was worshipped in Egypt. (L.)
Icarian, *a.* i-*kare*-re-an characteristic of Icarus; aiming too high, too venturesome. (*Icarus*, of Greek myth, in flight soared too near the sun and fell into the sea, the sun having melted the wax attaching his wings to his body.)
***ice**, *n.* ice, frozen water; ice-cream; concreted sugar: *v.t.* to cover with ice; to convert into ice; to chill; to freeze; to coat with icing. **ice age**, any of the geological periods during which large parts of the N. Hemisphere were under ice. **to break the ice**, to make the first opening in any attempt. (A.S. *is.*)
ice-anchor, *n.* a grapnel for holding ships to the ice.
ice-axe, *n.* mountaineer's axe for cutting steps in ice.
iceberg, *n.* *ice*-berg, a hilly mass of floating ice. (*ice*, and Ger. *berg*, a mountain.)
ice-bird, *n.* one of several Arctic sea-birds, as the black guillemot, glaucous gull, little auk, etc.
iceblink, *n.* *ice*-blink, the reflection of ice from below the horizon.
iceboat, *n.* *ice*-boat, an ice-breaker; a boat to travel on ice.
icebound, *a.* *ice*-bound, surrounded with ice so as to be incapable of motion.
ice-box, *n.* a simple form of refrigerator.
ice-breaker, *n.* a steamer strongly built for the purpose of opening a way through an ice-field or through floating ice.
ice-cap, *n.* the sheet of land ice formed round the pole in the glacial periods.
ice-cream, *n.* flavoured cream or custard, etc., congealed by a freezing mixture.
ice-field, *n.* a large expanse of ice-bound sea; a wide area of floating ice.
ice-floe, *n.* a flat mass of floating ice.
ice-hockey, *n.* hockey played on skates.
icehouse, *n.* *ice*-house, a store to keep ice in; an igloo.
Icelander, *n.* *ice*-land-er, a native of Iceland.
Icelandic, *a.* ice-*land*-ik, pertaining to Iceland: *n.* the language of Iceland.
Iceland-moss, *n.* a lichen, *Cetraria islandica*, common in the northern and mountainous districts of Europe, used in medicine and as food.
Iceland-spar, *n.* a transparent variety of calcite.
ice-pack, *n.* an ice-floe or aggregation of ice-floes.
icepail, *n.* *ice*-pale, a wine-cooler.
ice-plant, *n.* a species of *Mesembryanthemum*, whose leaves glisten as though covered with frost.
ice-sheet, *n.* the land ice during a glacial period.
ice-spar, *n.* rhyacolite, a transparent or translucent orthoclase with a vitreous lustre.
ichneumon, *n.* ik-*new*-mon, a small carnivore of the genus *Herpestes*, allied to the mongoose and found in Egypt, where it was anciently worshipped as a destroyer of crocodiles' eggs. **ichneumon fly**, one of a large genus of parasitic hymenopterous insects. (L.)
ichnite, *n.* *ik*-nite, an ichnolite.
ichnographic, *a.* *ik*-no-*graf*-ik, pertaining to ichnography; describing a ground plan.
ichnography, *n.* ik-*nog*-ra-fe, a horizontal section of a building or other object; the art of making ground-plans [Arch.]. (Gr. *ichnos*, a track, *grapho*, write.)
ichnolite, *n.* *ik*-no-lite, a fossil footmark [Geol.]. (Gr. *ichnos*, and *lithos*, a stone.)
ichnolithology, *n.* ik-no-le-*thol*-o-je, ichnology.
ichnology, *n.* ik-*nol*-o-je, the scientific study of fossil footprints. (Gr. *ichnos*, and *logos*, discourse.)
ichor, *n.* *i*-kor, an ethereal fluid that supplied the place of blood in the veins of the gods [Myth.]; a thin watery humour like serum; a colourless matter from an ulcer, wound, etc. (Gr., juice.)
ichorous, *a.* *i*-ko-rus, like ichor; thin; serous.
ichthyic, *a.* *ik*-the-ik, pertaining to fishes; like a fish; (Gr. *ichthys*, a fish.)
ichthyocol, *n.* *ik*-the-o-kol, fish-glue; isinglass. (Gr. *ichthys*, and *kolla*, glue.)
ichthyodorulite, *n.* *ik*-the-o-*do*-ru-lite, a fossil fish-spine.
ichthyography, *n.* *ik*-the-*og*-ra-fe, a treatise on fishes. (Gr. *ichthys*, and *grapho*, write.)
ichthyoid, *a.* *ik*-the-oyd, having many of the characters of a fish: *n.* a fish-like animal. (Gr. *ichthys*, and *eidos*, like.)
ichthyolatry, *n.* ik-the-*ol*-a-tre, the worship of a fish-like idol.
ichthyolite, *n.* *ik*-the-o-lite, a fossil fish or its impression. (Gr. *ichthys*, and *lithos*, a stone.)
ichthyological, *a.* *ik*-the-o-*loj*-e-kal, pertaining to ichthyology.
ichthyologist, *n.* *ik*-the-*ol*-o-jist, one versed in ichthyology.
ichthyology, *n.* *ik*-the-*ol*-o-je, the branch of zoology treating of fishes. (Gr. *ichthys*, and *logos*, science.)
ichthyophagist, *n.* *ik*-the-*of*-a-jist, one who habitually eats fish. (Gr. *ichthys*, and *phago*, eat.)
ichthyophagous, *a.* *ik*-the-*of*-a-gus, subsisting on fish.
ichthyophagy, *n.* *ik*-the-*of*-a-je, the practice of eating or living on fish.
ichthyornis, *n.* *ik*-the-*or*-nis, an extinct toothed bird of the American Cretaceous. (Gr. *ichthys*, and *ornis*, bird.)
ichthyosaurus, *n.* *ik*-the-o-*saw*-rus, one of an order of gigantic extinct marine reptiles, chiefly of the Lias, having a fish-like body. (Gr. *ichthys*, and *sauros*, lizard.)
ichthyosis, *n.* *ik*-the-*oh*-sis, congenital roughness and thickness of the skin; xeroderma.
ichthyotomy, *n.* *ik*-the-*ot*-o-me, the dissection of fishes. (Gr. *ichthys*, and *tome*, cutting.)
icicle, *n.* *ice*-e-kl, a slender pendent mass of ice, formed by the freezing of dripping water. (A.S. *is-gicel.*)
icily, *ad.* *ice*-e-le, in an icy manner.
iciness, *n.* *ice*-e-ness, coldness.
icing, *n.* *ice*-ing, a covering of concreted sugar.
icon, *n.* *i*-kon, a sacred portrait, image, or representation, esp. in the Orthodox Church. (Gr. *eikon.*)
iconoclasm, *n.* i-*kon*-o-klazm, the breaking of images or idols; the practices of iconoclasts.
iconoclast, *n.* i-*kon*-o-klast, a breaker of images or

idols; one who scorns or attacks cherishes beliefs. (Gr. *eikon*, and *klastēs*, a breaker or destroyer.)
iconoclastic, *a.* i-*kon*-o-*klas*-tik, pertaining to iconoclasm or iconoclasts.
iconography, *n.* *i*-ko-*nog*-ra-fe, the science or art of representation, esp. on ancient sculptures, coins, etc., by images or pictures; a treatise on this. (Gr.)
iconolatry, *n.* *i*-ko-*nol*-a-tre, image-worship. (Gr. *eikon*, and *latreia*, worship.)
iconology, *n.* *i*-ko-*nol*-o-je, the doctrine of images, esp. as religious symbols; the science or study of icons; iconography. (Gr. *eikon*, and *logos*, science.)
iconomachy, *n.* i-ko-*nom*-a-ke, war against, or strong opposition to, the veneration of images. (Gr. *eikon*, and *machia*, fighting.)
iconomatic, *a.* *i*-ko-no-*mat*-ik, told by pictures and not by letters. (Gr. *eikon*, and *onoma*, name.)
iconometer, *n.* i-ko-*nom*-e-ter, a specialized form of photographic view-finder.
icosahedral, *a.* *i*-ko-sa-*hee*-dral, with twenty equal sides. (Gr. *eikosi*, twenty, *hedra*, a side.)
icosahedron, *n.* *i*-ko-sa-*hee*-dron, a regular solid bounded by twenty equilateral triangles.
icteric, *n.* ik-*te*-rik, a remedy for the jaundice: *a.* affected with or efficacious against jaundice. (L. *icterus*, jaundice.)
icterine, *a.* *ik*-ter-rine, yellow. **icterine warbler,** the tree warbler, *Hypolais icterina*.
icteritious, *a.* ik-ter-*rish*-us, jaundiced [Med. and Fig.].
ictus, *n.* *ik*-tus, stress of voice in reading; accentuation; the beat of the pulse [Med.]. (L.)
icy, *a.* *ice*-e, like or abounding with ice; cold; freezing; destitute of affection; indifferent.
id, *n.* id, the basic inherited instinctive impulses of a person [Psychan.].
ide, *n.* ide, a freshwater fish allied to the roach.
★**idea,** *n.* i-*dee*-a, an image or a conception of a thing in the mind; a notion; a thought; an impression; an opinion; a plan or intention. (L.)
ideal, *a.* i-*dee*-al, consisting or pertaining to ideas; existing in idea or conception; existing only in idea; visionary; phenomenal; the best conceivable; perfect: *n.* an intellectual or imaginary conception or standard. (O.Fr.)
idealess, *a.* i-*dee*-a-less, destitute of ideas.
idealism, *n.* i-*dee*-a-lizm, the philosophic theory, of which there are various phases, that resolves the universe into ideas as the only existences; the practice of forming ideals or of idealizing; in art and literature, the tendency opposed to realizm.
idealist, *n.* i-*dee*-a-list, an upholder of idealism in philosophy or in art, literature, etc.; one who idealizes; a visionary: *a.* idealistic.
idealistic, *a.* i-dee-a-*lis*-tik, pertaining to idealists or idealism.
ideality, *n.* i-de-*al*-e-te, quality of being ideal; capacity for the ideal; ideal state; an idealization.
idealization, *n.* i-*dee*-a-ly-*zay*-shon, the act of forming in idea, or after an ideal; that which is idealized.
idealize, *v.i.* i-dee-a-lize, to form ideals; to make ideal: *v.t.* to represent after an ideal; to attribute ideal characteristics to.
ideally, *ad.* i-*dee*-a-le, in an ideal manner; perfectly; intellectually; mentally.
ideate, *v.t.* i-*dee*-ate, to form in idea; to imagine: *v.i.* to form ideas: *n.* the object forming the basis of an idea.
ideation, *n.* i-de-*ay*-shon, the act of power of forming ideas.
idem, *ad.* *i*-dem, the same. (L.)
identic, *a.* i-*den*-tik, identical. **identic note,** a note sent by one government to two or more others in precisely similar terms. **identic twins,** twins derived from a single ovum.
identical, *a.* i-*den*-te-kal, the same; not different. (Late L. *identicus*.)
identically, *ad.* in an identical manner.
identicalness, *n.* the state of being identical.
identifiable, *a.* i-*den*-te-*fy*-a-bl, that may be identified.
identification, *n.* i-*den*-te-fe-*kay*-shon, the act of making or proving to be the same; recognition; that by which identity is established.
identify, *v.t.* i-*den*-te-fy, to ascertain or prove to be the same; to consider as the same in effect; to recognize as. (Late L. *identicus*.)
identity, *n.* i-*den*-te-te, the state of being identical; personality or individuality. (Fr. *identité*.)
ideogram, *n.* *id*-e-o-gram, an ideograph.
ideograph, *n.* *id*-e-o-graf, a graphic symbol of an idea of an object. (*idea*, and Gr. *grapho*, write.)
ideographic, *a.* *id*-e-o-*graf*-ik, pertaining to ideography; composed of ideographs.
ideography, *n.* i-de-*og*-ra-fe, the representation of ideas by ideographs; the study of ideographs.
ideological, *a.* i-de-o-*loj*-e-kal, pertaining to ideology.
ideologist, *n.* *i*-de-*ol*-o-jist, one who treats of ideas; one who indulges in speculative theories; one versed in ideology; one who propounds mere ideas.
ideologue, *n.* i-*dee*-o-log, an ideologist; an impractical dreamer.
ideology, *n.* i-de-*ol*-o-je, the science of ideas; visionary theorizing. (*idea*, and Gr. *logos*, science.)
ideopraxist, *n.* *i*-de-o-*prak*-sist, one who carries out an idea.
Ides, *n.pl.* idez, in ancient Rome, the 15th of March, May, July and October, and the 13th of the other months. (Fr., from L. *idūs*, ides.)
idiocrasy, *n.* id-e-*ok*-ra-se, idiosyncrasy.
idiocy, *n.* *id*-e-o-se the state of being an idiot or defective in intelligence; weakness of intellect.
idiograph, *n.* *id*-e-o-graf, a private mark; a trade-mark. (*idea*, and Gr. *grapho*, write.)
idiom, *n.* *id*-e-om, peculiarity of expression or phraseology; a characteristic mode of expression [Mus.]. (Fr. *idiome*.)
idiomatic, *a.* *id*-e-o-*mat*-ik, proper or peculiar to a language; expressed in idioms; vernacular.
idiomatically, *ad.* in an idiomatic manner.
idiomorphic, *a.* *id*-e-o-*mor*-fik, having its own distinctive form (esp. of crystals) [Min.].
idiopathic, *a.* *id*-e-o-*path*-ik, indicating a disease not consequent upon another.
idiopathy, *n.* id-e-*op*-a-the, a primary or spontaneous disease, or one not the result of another. (Gr. *idiopatheia*.)
idiosyncrasy, *n.* *id*-e-o-*sin*-kra-se, peculiarity of constitution, temperament, or character; a characteristic. (Gr. *idios*, one's own, *syn*, with, and *krasis*, mixing.)
idiosyncratic, *a.* *id*-e-o-sin-*krat*-ik, of temper or disposition peculiar to the individual.
idiot, *n.* *id*-e-ot, a person of weak intellect; a defective: *a*: idiotic. (Fr.)
idiotcy, *n.* *id*-e-ot-se, the state of being an idiot; idiocy.
idiotic, *a.* id-e-*ot*-ik, like an idiot; weak in intellect; foolish. (Gr. *idiotikos*.)
idiotically, *ad.* id-e-*ot*-e-ka-le, in an idiotic manner.
idiotism, *n.* *id*-e-ot-izm, an idiom; an idiosyncrasy; idiocy.
idiotize, *v.i.* *id*-e-ot-ize, to become stupid: *v.t.* to make an idiot, or a fool, of.
idle, *a.* *i*-dl, not employed; doing nothing; useless; not occupied; unfruitful; unprofitable; of no use or importance; vain: *v.i.* to lose or spend time in inaction. **to idle away,** to spend in idleness. (A.S. *idel*, vain.)
idleness, *n.* *i*-dl-ness, quality or state of being idle; triviality; abstinence from, or having no, work.
idler, *n.* *i*-dler, one who spends his time in idleness.
idle-wheel, *n.* a gear-wheel between two others, simply transferring motion [Mech.].
idly, *ad.* *i*-dle, in an idle manner; indolently.
ido, *n.* *ee*-doh, an artificial universal language based (1907) on Esperanto.
idocrase, *n.* *id*-o-krays, a basic silicate of calcium and aluminium occurring in translucent crystals exhibiting double refraction; vesuvianite. (Gr. *eidos*, form, *krasis*, mixture.)
idol, *n.* *i*-dol, a visible image representative of an unseen object of worship; an object of worship; a false idea; a person loved and honoured to adoration. (O.Fr. *idole*.)
idolater, *n.* i-*dol*-a-ter, a worshipper of idols; a great or extravagant admirer. (O.Fr. *idolatre*.)
idolatress, *n.* i-*dol*-a-tress, a female idolater.
idolatrous, *a.* i-*dol*-a-trus, of the nature of idolatry; given to idolatry.
idolatrously, *ad.* i-*dol*-a-trus-le, in an idolatrous manner.
idolatry, *n.* i-*dol*-a-tre, the worship of idols; excessive attachment. (O.Fr. *idolatrie*.)
idolization, *n.* *i*-do-ly-*zay*-shon, the act or practice of idolizing; the making an idol of.

idolize, *v.t.* *i*-do-lize, to worship as an idol; to make an idol of; to adore; to love to excess.
idolizer, *n.* *i*-do-ly-zer, one who idolizes.
idoloclast, *n.* i-*dol*-o-klast, an iconoclast.
idolum, *n.* i-*doh*-lum, a mental image. (L.)
idrialite, *n.* *id*-re-a-lite, a bituminous crystalline hydrocarbon from the mines of Idria, Italy.
idyll, *n.* *i*-dil *or* *id*-il, a short descriptive poem of everyday life, esp. in rural or pastoral surroundings; a fitting scene for such a poem. (L. *idyllium.*)
idyllic, *a.* *i*- *or* i-*dil*-ik, of the nature of an idyll; picturesquely simple.
***if,** *conj.* if, supposing that; in case that. (A.S. *gif.*)
igloo, *n.* *ig*-loo, an Eskimo's house of frozen snow, wood, or other material; the hole in the snow made by seals over their breathing holes in the ice. (Eskimo.)
igneous, *a.* *ig*-ne-us, of the nature of or consisting of fire; produced by volcanic action. (L. *igneus,* from *ignis,* fire.)
ignescent, *a.* ig-*nes*-sent, emitting sparks when struck. (L. *ignescens,* burning.)
igniferous, *a.* ig-*nif*-er-rus, producing fire. (L.)
ignigenous, *a.* ig-*nij*-e-nus, produced by fire. (L. *ignis,* and *gigno,* produce.)
ignis-fatuus, *n.* *ig*-nis-*fat*-yew-us, phosphorescence appearing in the night over marshy places, due to the decomposition of organic matter under water; will-o'-the-wisp. (L., foolish fire.)
ignite, *v.t.* ig-*nite,* to kindle or set on fire; to make red with heat: *v.i.* to take fire; to become red with heat.
igniter, *n.* ig-*ny*-ter, any device used to fire an explosive charge.
ignitible, *a.* ig-*ny*-te-bl, capable of being ignited.
ignition, *n.* ig-*nish*-on, the act of igniting; the state of being ignited; the process of or electrical apparatus used in igniting the mixture in an internal combustion engine.
ignobility, *n.* *ig*-no-*bil*-e-te, ignobleness.
ignoble, *a.* ig-*noh*-bl, of low birth or family; of mean character; dishonourable. (Fr.)
ignobleness, *n.* ig-*noh*-bl-ness, the state or quality of being ignoble; meanness of birth or character.
ignobly, *ad.* ig-*noh*-ble, in an ignoble manner or state.
ignominious, *a.* ig-no-*min*-e-us, incurring or deserving disgrace or ignominy; despicable. (L. *ignominiosus.*)
ignominiously, *ad.* meanly; disgracefully.
ignominiousness, *n* ig-no-*min*-e-us-ness, the quality of being ignominious; ignominy.
ignominy, *n.* *ig*-no-min-e, public disgrace; dishonour; infamy. (Fr. *ignominie.*)
ignomy, *n.* *ig*-no-me, old form of *ignominy.*
ignoramus, *n.* ig-no-*ray*-mus, an ignorant person; a dolt; a blockhead. (L. "We do not know," an indorsement on the back of a bill by a grand jury when there was not evidence to support the charge.)
ignorance, *n.* *ig*-no-rance, want of knowledge (of); the state of being ignorant. (Fr.)
ignorant, *a.* *ig*-no-rant, without knowledge; uninformed; unconscious (of); uneducated. (Fr.)
ignorantism, *n.* *ig*-no-ran-tizm, obscurantism.
ignorantly, *ad.* *ig*-no-rant-le, without knowledge.
ignore, *v.t.* ig-*nore,* to affect not to know; to disregard wilfully; to reject a bill by the grand jury for want of evidence [Law]. (Fr. *ignorer.*)
iguana, *n.* ig-*wah*-na, any one of a family of American pleurodont lizards having short, thick non-protractile tongues. (Carib. *yuana,* a lizard.)
iguanodon, *n.* ig-*wah*-no-don, an extinct gigantic herbivorous dinosaur of the early Cretaceous. (*iguana,* and *odous, odontos,* a tooth.)
ihlang-ihlang, *n.* e-*lang*-e-*lang,* ylang-ylang.
ileac, *a.* *il*-e-ak, iliac.
ileum, *n.* *il*-e-um, the last portion of the small intestine [Anat.]. (L.)
ilex, *n.* *i*-leks, the holly [Bot.]; *Quercus ilex,* the evergreen or holm oak. (L., holm-oak.)
iliac, *a.* *il*-e-ak, pertaining to the ileum, or to the ilium. **iliac passion,** colic of a dangerous type, in which the peristaltic action of the small intestines is inverted. **iliac region,** the region of the abdomen between the ribs and the hips. (Fr. *iliaque.*)
Iliad, *n.* *il*-e-ad, an epic poem ascribed to Homer, the incidents of which belong to the last year of the ten years' siege of Troy; a long account, esp. of woes (L. *Ilias,* the Iliad.)
ilium, *n.* *il*-e-um, the upper partly flattened part of the hip-bone. (L.)
ilk, *a.* ilk, the same. **of that ilk, denotes that a** person's surname is the same as that of his estate or territory. (A.S. *ylc,* from *i,* he, and *lic,* like.)
***ill,** *a.* il, bad or evil; contrary to good; producing evil; cross; sick, not well, indisposed; suggestive of evil; unfavourable; rude; unpolished; not proper: *n.* wickedness; evil; misfortune: *ad.* not well; not rightly; with difficulty. **ill at ease,** uncomfortable; embarrassed. **ill fame,** bad repute. **house of ill fame,** a brothel. **ill turn,** an unkind or ungenerous act. (Scand.)
ill-advised, *a.* injudicious; due to not taking sufficient forethought.
ill-affected, *a.* unfavourably disposed.
illapse, *n.* il-*laps,* a sliding in; the entrance of one thing into another; sudden seizure: *v.i.* to glide into. (L. *illapsus,* gliding.)
illation, *n.* il-*lay*-shon, deduction; inference; an inference. (L. *illatio.*)
illative, *a.* *il*-a-tiv, that may be inferred; expressive of inference: *n.* that which denotes inference. (L. *illativus.*)
illaudable, *a.* il-*lawd*-a-bl, not laudable.
ill-blood, *n.* state of resentment or enmity.
ill-bred, *a.* badly brought up; uncivil.
ill-breeding, *n.* want of good breeding.
ill-conditioned, *a.* in a bad condition; badly disposed.
illegal, *a.* il-*lee*-gal, contrary to or not according to law; unlawful. (Late L. *illegalis.*)
illegality, *n.* il-le-*gal*-e-te, unlawfulness; the quality or state of being illegal.
illegalize, *v.t.* il-*lee*-ga-lize, to render illegal.
illegally, *ad.* il-*lee*-ga-le, unlawfully.
illegibility, *n.* il-*lej*-e-*bil*-e-te, state of being illegible.
illegible, *a.* il-*lej*-e-bl, that cannot be read.
illegibly, *ad.* il-*lej*-e-ble, in a manner to be illegible.
illegitimacy, *n.* il-le-*jit*-e-ma-se, state of being illegitimate; bastardy.
illegitimate, *a.* il-le-*jit*-e-mat, born out of wedlock; unlawful; illogical: *n.* a bastard: *v.t.* to render illegitimate. (L. *il* for *in,* not, and *legitimate.*)
illegitimately, *ad.* in an illegitimate manner.
illegitimation, *n.* il-le-jit-e-*may*-shon, the act of illegitimating; illegitimacy.
ill-fated, *a.* fated to misfortune.
ill-favoured, *a.* ill-looking; ugly; deformed.
ill-got, *a.* got dishonestly.
ill-humour, *n.* bad temper.
illiberal, *a.* il-*lib*-er-ral, not liberal; not generous; not ingenuous; narrow-minded; uncultured.
illiberality, *n.* il-*lib*-er-*ral*-e-te, narrowness of mind; contractedness; meanness.
illiberalize, *v.t.* il-*lib*-er-ra-lize, to make illiberal.
illiberally, *ad.* il-*lib*-er-ra-le, in an illiberal manner.
illicit, *a.* il-*lis*-it, prohibited; not allowed; unlawful. (L. *illicitus,* forbidden.)
illicitly, *ad.* il-*lis*-it-le, in an illicit manner.
illicitness, *n.* il-*lis*-it-ness, the state of being illicit.
illimitable, *a.* il-*lim*-it-a-bl, that cannot be limited.
illimitableness, *n.* state of being illimitable.
illimitably, *ad.* il-*lim*-it-a-ble, without possibility of being limited.
illimited, *a.* il-*lim*-it-ed, unbounded; not limited.
illinition, *n.* il-lin-*ish*-on, a coating of foreign matter, esp. on minerals; a rubbing in of ointment; the ointment rubbed in. (L. *illinitus,* smeared.)
illinium, *n.* il-*lin*-e-um, an element of the cerium sub-group of the rare earth metals, discovered at Illinois University in 1926. (From *Illinois.*)
illiquid, *a.* il-*lik*-wid, not liquid (of assets, etc.) [Comm.]; not made clear and certain (of claims, etc.) [Law].
illiteracy, *n.* il-*lit*-er-a-se, the state of being illiterate or ignorant; ignorance; a case of ignorance.
illiterate, *a.* il-*lit*-er-at, unlearned; unable to read or write: *n.* one who can neither read nor write. (L. *illiteratus.*)
illiterateness, *n.* the state of being illiterate.
ill-judged, *a.* unwise; foolish; injudicious.
ill-mannered, *a.* badly behaved; rude.
ill-nature. *n.* habitual bad temper; want of kindness.
ill-natured, *a.* il-*nay*-tewrd, of habitual bad temper; peevish; cross.

ill-naturedly, *ad.* in an ill-natured manner.
illness, *n.* *il*-ness, the state of being ill; physical indisposition; sickness; moral perversity.
illogical, *a.* il-*loj*-e-kal, not conforming or not conformable to the rules of logic.
illogically, *ad.* in an illogical manner.
illogicalness, *n.* the state of being illogical.
ill-omened, *a.* il-*oh*-mend, foredoomed to failure: inauspicious.
ill-sorted, *a.* not well matched; badly arranged.
ill-starred, *a.* fated to misfortune; born under an unpropitious star.
ill-tempered, *a.* cross in temper; ill-conditioned in temper or body.
ill-treat, *v.t.* to treat badly or cruelly; to maltreat.
illude, *v.t.* il-*lewd*, to play upon by artifice; to deceive. (L. *illuder.*)
illume *v.t.* il-*lewm*, to illumine; to brighten: to elucidate. (O.Fr. *illumer.*)
illuminable, *a.* il-*lew*-me-na-bl, that may be illuminated.
illuminant, *n.* il-*lew*-me-nant, that which illuminates: *a.* illuminating; affording light. (L. *illuminans*, lighting.)
illuminate, *v.t.* il-*lew*-me-nate, to enlighten; to throw light on; to adorn with festal lamps or bonfires; to adorn with ornamental letters or illustrations: *a.* enlightened. (L. *illuminatus*, lighted.)
Illuminati, *n.pl.* il-*lew*-me-*nay*-te *or* -*nah*-te, a, name given to several sects affecting superior enlightenment, esp. to those priding themselves on their superiority to certain superstitions, or on their merely negative attitude to existing creeds and systems. (L.)
illumination, *n.* il-*lew*-me-*nay*-shon, the act of illuminating; state of being illuminated; a display of lights; brightness; splendour; that which gives light; the practice of adorning manuscripts and books with ornamental letters and pictures, also, the decoration so supplied; divine inspiration. (L. *illuminatio.*)
illuminative, *a.* il-*lew*-me-na-tiv, tending to give light or enlightenment. (L. *illuminativus.*)
illuminator, *n.* il-*lew*-me-*nay*-tor, he who or that which illuminates or gives light; one whose occupation is to illuminate manuscripts and books.
illumine, *v.t.* il-*lew*-min, to light up; to enlighten. (Fr. *illuminer.*)
Illuminism, *n.* il-*lew*-me-nizm, the principles of the Illuminati.
illusion, *n.* il-*lew*-zhon, the act of deceiving; deceptive appearance; false show; deception; a conjuring trick. (L. *illusio.*)
illusionism, *n.* il-*lew*-zhon-izm, the doctrine that all phenomena external to oneself are wholly illusory; the art of creating illusions.
illusionist, *n.* il-*lew*-zhon-ist, an adherent of illusionism; one who practises illusion.
illusive, *a.* il-*lew*-siv, tending to deceive; illusory.
illusively, *ad.* il-*lew*-siv-le, in an illusive manner.
illusiveness, *n.* the quality of being illusive.
illusory, *a.* il-*lew*-so-re, deceiving or tending to deceive by false appearances; fallacious.
illustrate, *v.t.* *il*-lus-trate, to explain by example; to explain or adorn pictorially; to display the glory of. (L. *illustratus.*)
illustration, *n.* il-lus-*tray*-shon, the act of illustrating; explanation; that which illustrates; a picture designed to illustrate. (L. *illustratio.*)
illustrational, *a.* il-lus-*tray*-shon-al, illustrative.
illustrative, *a.* il-*lus*-tra-tiv, serving or tending to illustrate.
illustratively, *ad.* by way of illustration.
illustrator, *n.* *il*-lus-tray-tor, one who illustrates.
illustratory, *a.* il-*lus*-tra-to-re, illustrative.
illustrious, *a.* il-*lus*-tre-us, distinguished; conspicuous; eminent; conferring lustre or honour; glorious. (L. *illustris.*)
illustriously, *ad.* in an illustrious manner.
illustriousness, *n.* il-*lus*-tre-us-ness, the quality of being illustrious.
ill-will, *n.* il-*wil*, unkind or hostile feeling; enmity.
ill-wisher, *n.* one who wishes ill to befall another.
ilmenite, *n.* *il*-men-ite, an oxide of iron and titanium, so called from the Ilmen mountains in the Urals.
ilvaite, *n.* *il*-va-ite, a black or brownish-black crystalline silicate of iron and calcium found in Elba. (L. *Ilva*, Elba.)
image, *n.* *im*-aj, a material representation or likeness of anything, as a statue; a likeness; an idol; appearance; an idea or conception; a mental picture; a lively description of anything in discourse [Rhet.]; the figure of any object made by rays of light [Optics]: *v.t.* to form an image of; to form a likeness mentally; to symbolize. (Fr.)
imageable, *a.* *im*-aj-a-bl, that may be imaged.
imageless, *a.* *im*-aj-less, having no image.
imagery, *n.* *im*-aj-er-re, images collectively; show: appearance; forms of the fancy; rhetorical figures.
image-worship, *n.* idolatry; worship of statutes or pictures.
imaginable, *a.* im-*aj*-e-na-bl, that may be imagined.
imaginably, *ad.* in an imaginable manner.
imaginal, *a.* im-*aj*-e-nal, pertaining to the imagination; of the nature of an image or [Entom.] an imago.
imaginary, *a.* im-*aj*-e-na-re, existing only in imagination or fancy; not real. (L. *imaginarius.*)
imagination, *n.* im-*aj*-e-*nay*-shon, an imagining; the power or process of imagining; a mental image; the poetic or creative faculty, esp. as exhibited in the vivid conceptions and combinations of the fine arts; idea; contrivance or device; a groundless or fanciful opinion. (Fr.)
imaginationalism, *n.* im-aj-e-*nay*-shon-a-lizm, idealism.
imaginative, *a.* im-*aj*-e-na-tiv, gifted with imagination; proceeding from imagination. (Fr. *imaginatif.*)
imaginativeness, *n.* the quality of being imaginative.
imagine, *v.t.* im-*aj*-in, to form a mental image; to contrive; to fancy or think: *v.i.* to conceive; to suppose. (Fr. *imaginer.*)
imaginer, *n.* im-*aj*-e-ner, one who imagines.
Imagism, *n.* *im*-a-jizm, the literary practices and doctrines of the Imagists.
Imagist, *n.* *im*-a-jist, one of a modern school of poets which uses vers libre, avoids the mystical, and seeks to attain clarity of expression through a logical succession of definite images: *a.* pertaining to this mode of writing or this school.
imago, *n.* im-*ay*-go (*pl.* **imagines,** im-*ay*-je-neez), the adult state of an insect [Entom.]. (L.)
imam, *n.* im-*ahm*, or **imaum**, im-*awm*, a Mohammedan priest or spiritual instructor; a title in certain Moslem states. (Ar.)
imamate, *n.* im-*ah*-mate, the territory under the jurisdiction of an imam.
imbalance, *n.* im-*bal*-ance, lack of balance [Med.].
imbecile, *a.* *im*-be-seel, feeble-minded; fatuous; mentally weak: *n.* one who is imbecile. (O.Fr.)
imbecilitate, *v.t.* *im*-be-*sil*-e-tate, to enfeeble; to make imbecile.
imbecility, *n.* *im*-be-*sil*-e-te, the state of being imbecile; feebleness of mind; debility. (O.Fr.)
imbed, *v.t.* im-*bed*, to embed.
imbibe, *v.t.* im-*bibe*, to drink in or absorb; to receive into the mind. (L. *imbibo*, drink.)
imbiber, *n.* im-*bibe*-er, he who or that which imbibes.
imbibition, *n.* im-be-*bish*-on, absorption; the act or process of imbibing.
imbricate, *v.t.* *im*-bre-kate, to lap (leaves, scales, etc.) one over another like tiles on a roof: *v.i.* to overlap thus: *a.* overlapped in this way. (L. *imbricatus*, covered with tiles, from *imbrex*, a tile.)
imbrication, *n.* *im*-bre-*kay*-shon, an overlapping as of tiles; decorative work on this pattern.
imbroglio, *n.* im-*broh*-le-oh, a complicated plot; a confused and perplexing state of things. (It.)
imbrue, *v.t.* im-*broo*, to wet or moisten; to drench, as in blood; to stain with. (O.Fr. *embruer.*)
imbrute, *v.t.* im-*broot*, to degrade to the state of a brute: *v.i.* to sink to the state of a brute.
imbue, *v.t.* im-*bew*, to saturate with; to tinge deeply; to inspire; to prejudice. (O.Fr. *imbuer.*)
imburse, *v.t.* im-*burse*, to supply with money.
imide, *n.* *im*-ide, an organic compound derived from an acid anhydride by replacement of the hydrogen with a metal or radical [Chem.].
imitability, *n.* *im*-e-ta-*bil*-e-te, the quality of being imitable.
imitable, *a.* *im*-e-ta-bl, that may be imitated; worthy of imitation. (L. *imitabilis.*)
imitate, *v.t.* *im*-e-tate, to follow in manners; to copy in form, colour or quality; to ape; to simulate. (L. *imitatus.*)
imitation, *n.* im-e-*tay*-shon, the act of imitating; mimicking; likeness; mimicry; a copy; a parody.

imitational, *a.* im-e-*tay*-shon-al, pertaining to imitation; used for imitative purposes.
imitative, *a.* *im*-e-ta-tiv, inclined to imitate; aiming at imitation; formed after a model.
imitatively, *ad.* in the way of imitation.
imitativeness, *n.* the quality of being imitative.
imitator, *n.* *im*-e-tay-tor, one who imitates or copies.
immaculate, *a.* im-*mak*-yew-lat, spotless; pure; unstained. **Immaculate Conception,** the Roman Catholic doctrine that in her conception the Virgin Mary was preserved free from original sin. (L. *immaculatus.*)
immaculately, *ad.* with spotless purity.
immaculateness, *n.* spotless purity.
immalleable, *a.* im-*mal*-le-a-bl, not malleable.
immanacle, *v.t.* im-*man*-a-kl, to put manacles on: to restrain from free action. (L. *in*, in, and *manacle*)
immanation, *n.* im-ma-*nay*-shon, a flowing or entering in. (L. *in-*, into, *mano*, flow.)
immanence, *n.* *im*-ma-nence, the state of being immanent; inherence; the omnipresent indwelling spirit of God in the universe.
immanency, *n.* *im*-ma-nen-se, the quality of being immanent; immanence.
immanent, *a.* *im*-ma-nent, having the quality of immanence; remaining within; inherent; non-transient. (L. *immanens*, staying near.)
immarcescible, *a.* im-mar-*ses*-e-bl, unfading, incorruptible. (L. *marcescere*, languish.)
immarginate, *a.* im-*mar*-je-nat, without a border.
immaterial, *a.* im-ma-*teer*-re-al, not consisting of matter; incorporeal; spiritual; unimportant.
immaterialism, *n.* im-ma-*teer*-re-a-lizm, the doctrine which affirms the existence of spirit independently of matter, or which denies the existence of matter independently of mind; spiritism; idealism.
immaterialist, *n.* im-ma-*teer*-re-a-list, one who professes immaterialism.
immateriality, *n.* im-ma-*teer*-re-*al*-e-te, the state or quality of being immaterial.
immaterialize, *v.t.* im-ma-*teer*-re-a-lize, to render immaterial.
immaterially, *ad.* in an immaterial manner.
immature, *a.* im-ma-*tewr*, not mature or ripe; not perfect; premature. (L. *immaturus.*)
immaturely, *ad.* in an immature manner.
immaturity, *n.* im-ma-*tewr*-re-te, the state of being immature; unripeness.
immeability, *n.* im-e-a-*bil*-e-te, want of power to pass or flow through a channel. (L. *meabilis*, passable.)
immeasurable, *a.* im-*mezh*-yew-ra-bl, that cannot be measured.
immeasurableness, *n.* the state of being immeasurable.
immeasurably, *ad.* to an immeasurable extent.
immediacy, *n.* im-*mee*-de-a-se, immediateness.
immediate, *a.* im-*mee*-de-at, with nothing intervening, no space, or time, or medium; proximate; instant; direct. (O.Fr. *immediat.*)
immediately, *ad.* in an immediate manner; proximately; instantly; directly.
immediateness, *n.* the state of being immediate.
immedicable, *a.* im-*med*-e-ka-bl, not to be healed. (L. *immedicabilis*, incurable.)
immemorable, *a.* im-*mem*-o-ra-bl, not to be remembered; not worth remembering.
immemorial, *a.* im-me-*maw*-re-al, beyond the reach of memory or record.
immemorially, *ad.* beyond memory.
immense, *a.* im-*mense*, vast in extent; very great; very large; immeasurable. (Fr.)
immensely, *ad.* im-*mense*-le, to an immense degree.
immenseness, *n.* the quality of being immense.
immensity, *n.* im-*men*-se-te, extent not to be measured; infinity; hugeness; an immense or immeasurable thing. (L. *immensitas.*)
immensurable, *a.* im-*men*-sew-ra-bl, immeasurable.
immerge, *v.t.* im-*merj*, to immerse: *v.i.* to disappear behind, or in the shadow of, another heavenly body [Astron.]. (L. *immergo.*)
immerse, *v.t.* im-*merse*, to plunge into a fluid; to dip; to baptize by immersion; to engage or involve deeply. (L. *immersus*, plunged.)
immersible, *a.* im-*mer*-se-bl, capable of being immersed or of functioning when immersed.
immersion, *n.* im-*mer*-shon, the act of immersing; the state of being immersed or deeply engaged; baptism by being plunged under water; the disappearance of a celestial body behind, or in the shadow of, another [Astron.]. (L. *immersio.*)
immesh, *v.t.* im-*mesh*, to enmesh.
immethodical, *a.* im-me-*thod*-e-kal, having no method of regular arrangement.
immethodically, *ad.* without method.
immethodicalness, *n.* want of method.
immew, *v.t.* im-*mew*, to mew up; to confine.
immigrant, *n.* *im*-e-grant, one who immigrates: *a.* immigrating. (L. *immigrans*, going into.)
immigrate, *v.i.* *im*-e-grate, to pass into a country other than one's own for the purpose of permanent residence. (L. *immigratus.*)
immigration, *n.* *im*-e-*gray*-shon, the act of immigrating.
imminence, *n.* *im*-min-ence, the state or quality of being imminent; nearness. (L. *imminentia.*)
imminent, *a.* *im*-min-ent, impending; threatening; close at hand. (L. *imminens*, overhanging.)
imminently, *ad.* *im*-min-ent-le, in an imminent manner or degree.
immingle, *v.t.* im-*ming*-gl, to mingle; to mix.
immiscibility, *n.* im-*mis*-e-*bil*-e-te, the property of not mixing; incapacity of being mixed.
immiscible, *a.* im-*mis*-e-bl, that cannot be mixed.
immitigable, *a.* im-*mit*-e-ga-bl, incapable of being mitigated; unappeasable. (L. *immitigabilis.*)
immitigably, *ad.* in an immitigable manner.
immixture, *n.* im-*mik*-stewr, the action of mixing up; a commingling; a state of involvement.
immobile, *a.* im-*moh*-bile, not mobile; motionless; immovable; impassible. (Fr.)
immobility, *n.* im-mo-*bil*-e-te, state or quality of being immobile; unmovableness; fixedness.
immobilize, *v.t.* im-*moh*-bil-ize, to render (troops) incapable of mobilization [Mil.]; to withdraw (coin, etc.) from circulation; to render stationary; to make immovable.
immoderate, *a.* im-*mod*-er-rat, exceeding due or usual bounds; excessive; exorbitant. (L. *immoderatus.*)
immoderately, *ad.* to an immoderate degree.
immoderateness, *n.* the state of being immoderate.
immoderation, *n.* im-*mod*-er-*ray*-shon, excess; want of moderation.
immodest, *a.* im-*mod*-est, not modest; wanting in regard for moderation or modesty; indecent. (L. *immodestus.*)
immodestly, *ad.* im-*mod*-est-le, without modesty.
immodesty, *n.* im-*mod*-es-te, want of modesty.
immolate, *v.t.* *im*-mo-late, to kill as a sacrifice; to offer in sacrifice. (L. *immolatus*, sprinkled with sacrificial meal.)
immolation, *n.* im-mo-*lay*-shon, sacrificing; killing for sacrifice; a sacrifice offered. (L. *immolatio.*)
immolator, *n.* *im*-mo-lay-tor, one who offers in sacrifice. (L.)
immomentous, *a.* im-mo-*men*-tus, unimportant.
immoral, *a.* im-*mo*-ral, not moral; inconsistent with moral rectitude or purity; licentious.
immorality, *n.* im-mo-*ral*-e-te, the quality of being immoral; unchastity; an immoral action.
immorally, *ad.* in violation of morality.
immortal, *a.* im-*mor*-tal, not mortal or subject to death, or oblivion; imperishable; relating to immortality: *n.* one who is immortal; a god or deified hero. (L. *immortalis.*)
immortality, *n.* *im*-mor-*tal*-e-te, exemption from death or oblivion; continued existence after death. (L. *immortalitas.*)
immortalization, *n.* im-*mor*-ta-ly-*zay*-shon, act of immortalizing; the state of being immortalized.
immortalize, *v.t.* im-*mor*-ta-lize, to render immortal: *v.i.* to become immortal.
immortally, *ad.* with endless existence.
immortelle, *n.* im-mor-*tel*, a flower whose petals last long; an everlasting flower, a species of either *Helichrysum*, *Ammobium*, *Achyrachæna*, *Helipterum*, or *Antennaria*; a wreath of such flowers. (Fr.)
immortification, *n.* im-*mor*-te-fe-*kay*-shon, lack of mortification, or subjection, of the passions.
immovability, *n.* im-*moov*-a-*bil*-e-te, the state or quality of being immovable; fixedness.
immovable, *a.* im-*moov*-a-bl, that cannot be moved from a place, or in purpose, or in feeling, or so as to be altered; steadfast; unalterable; not liable to be removed [Law]: *n.pl.* things which cannot be legally taken away in leaving a house or estate, etc. [Law].

immovableness, *n.* quality of being immovable.
immovably, *ad.* in a manner not to be moved.
immune, *a.* im-*mewn*, secure against attack; protected against infection [Med.]: *n.* one not liable to infection [Med.]. (L. *immunis.*)
immunity, *n.* im-*mew*-ne-te, exemption from any obligation, duty, or tax; privilege; freedom from risk of infection. (L. *immunitas*, freedom from taxes.)
immunization, *n.* *im*-mew-ny-*zay*-shon, the act of immunizing, or condition of being immunized.
immunize, *v.t.* *im*-mew-nize, to render immune.
immunology, *n.* im-mew-*nol*-o-je, the science treating of the phenomena of immunity from infection [Path.].
immure, *v.t.* im-*mewr*, to enclose within walls; to confine. (O.Fr. *enmurer.*)
immurement, *n.* im-*mewr*-ment, confinement; the act of immuring, or state of being immured.
immutability, *n.* im-*mew*-ta-*bil*-e-te, unchangeableness.
immutable, *a.* im-*mew*-ta-bl, unchangeable; unalterable; invariable.
immutably, *ad.* im-*mew*-ta-ble, unchangeably.
imp, *n.* imp. a little demon or mischievous sprite; a mischievous child: *v.t.* to graft; to extend or repair by something inserted or added; to strengthen. (A.S. *impa*, a graft.)
impacable, *a.* im-*pak*-a-bl, not to be appeased or quieted. (L. *in*, not, *paco*, pacify.)
impact, *v.t.* im-*pakt*, to press or drive firmly together: *n.* *im*-pakt, impulse by contact; collision. **impacted fracture,** a fracture resulting in one broken end being driven into the other [Surg.]. (L. *impactus.*)
impaction, *n.* im-*pak*-shon, the state of being impacted.
impaint, *v.t.* im-*paynt*, to depict with colours.
impair, *v.t.* im-*pare*, to make worse; to lessen in quantity, value, or excellence; to enfeeble; to injure: *n.* impairment. (O.Fr. *empeirer.*)
impairer, *n.* im-*pare*-rer, one who or that which impairs.
impairment, *n.* im-*pare*-ment, state of being impaired; deterioration. (O.Fr. *empeirement.*)
impala, *n.* im-*pah*-la, a large South African antelope of the genus *Æpyceros*. (Zulu.)
impale, *v.t.* im-*pale*, to put to death by fixing on an upright sharp stake; to enclose with palings; to divide a shield into halves by a vertical line [Her.]. (Late L. *impalare.*)
impalement, *n.* im-*pale*-ment, a fencing or enclosing with stakes; a putting to death by thrusting a stake into the body; two coats-of-arms on a shield, divided by a central vertical line. [Her.]. (Fr.)
impalpability, *n.* im-*pal*-pa-*bil*-e-te, the quality of being impalpable.
impalpable, *a.* im-*pal*-pa-bl, not palpable to touch or to apprehension; intangible.
impalpably, *ad.* in a manner not to be palpable.
impaludism, *n.* im-*pal*-yew-dizm, a form of malaria to which dwellers in marshy districts are liable. [Path.]. (L. *palus*, *paludis*, a marsh.)
impanate, *a.* im-*pay*-nat, embodied in bread: *v.t.* to embody in bread. (L. *in*, into, and *panis*, bread.)
impanation, *n.* *im*-pa-*nay*-shon, the doctrine that the body of Christ, without change in any substance, is included in the bread and wine of the Eucharist.
impanel, *v.t.* im-*pan*-el, to empanel.
imparadise, *v.t.* im-*pa*-ra-dice, to put in a place of supreme felicity; to make perfectly happy.
imparidigitate, *a.* im-*pa*-re-*dij*-e-tate, having an uneven number of toes [Zool.]. (L. *impar*, unequal, *digitatus*, having toes.)
imparipinnate, *a.* im-*pa*-re-*pin*-nate, pinnate with an odd leaflet at the end (of leaves) [Bot.]. (L. *impar*, and *pinnatus*, winged.)
imparisyllabic, *a.* im-*pa*-re-se-*lab*-ik, not having the same number of syllables in all the cases [Gram.] (L. *impar*, and *syllabic.*)
imparity, *n.* im-*pa*-re-te, inequality; disproportion; indivisibility into equal parts; difference of degree, rank, or excellence. (L. *impariter.*)
impark, *v.t.* im-*park*, to enclose as a park; to confine in or as in a park.
imparlance, *n.* im-*par*-lance, leave for conference; the continuance of a cause to another day [Old Law]. (O.Fr. *emparlance.*)

impart, *v.t.* im-*part*, to bestow a portion of; to bestow; to make known; to communicate: *v.i.* to give part. (O.Fr. *impartir.*)
impartance, *n.* im-*par*-tance, the act of imparting; communication; the giving of a share.
impartation, *n.* im-par-*tay*-shon, impartance.
imparter, *n.* im-*par*-ter, one who imparts.
impartial, *a.* im-*par*-shal, not favouring one party more than another; unprejudiced; disinterested; just.
impartiality, *n.* im-*par*-she-*al*-e-te, the quality of being impartial.
impartially, *ad.* in an impartial manner.
impartibility, *n.* im-par-te-*bil*-e-te, the state or quality of being impartible.
impartible, *a.* im-*par*-te-bl, not subject to or capable of partition; indivisible.
impartite, *a.* im-*par*-tite, undivided.
impartment, *n.* im-*part*-ment, the act of imparting; that which is imparted or communicated.
impassable, *a.* im-*pahs*-sa-bl, that cannot be passed.
impassableness, *n.* im-*pahs*-sa-bl-ness, the state of being impassable.
impassably, *ad.* im-*pahs*-sa-ble, in a manner so as not to be passable.
impasse, *n.* *im*-pahs, a deadlock; a blind alley. (Fr.)
impassibility, *n.* im-*pas*-se-*bil*-e-te, the condition or quality of being impassible; insensibility to pain or suffering.
impassible, *a.* im-*pas*-se-bl, incapable of feeling or passion; impassive. (L. *impassibilis.*)
impassibleness, *n.* im-*pas*-se-bl-ness, impassibility.
impassion, *v.t.* im-*pash*-on, to move or affect strongly with passion or ardour.
impassionable, *a.* im-*pash*-o-na-bl, susceptible of strong passion.
impassionate, *a.* im-*pash*-o-nat, impassioned (*formerly also* dispassionate).
impassioned, *a.* im-*pash*-ond, moved with or displaying passion or deep feeling; animated.
impassive, *a.* im-*pas*-siv, not susceptible of, or not exhibiting, feeling; apathetic.
impassively, *ad.* in an impassive manner.
impassiveness, *n.* the state of being impassive.
impassivity, *n.* *im*-pas-*siv*-e-te, impassiveness.
impastation, *n.* *im*-pas-*tay*-shon, the act of impasting; a concretion of substances by means of cements. (Late L. *impastatio.*)
impaste, *v.t.* im-*payst*, to knead; to make into paste; to decorate with impasto; to lay on colours thickly and boldly [Paint.].
impasto, *n.* im-*pas*-to, the application of colour laid on thickly; the body of colour so applied. (It.)
impatience, *n.* im-*pay*-shence, want of patience; restless irritability. (L. *impatientia.*)
impatient, *a.* im-*pay*-shent, not patient under suffering or restraint; not enduring pain or delay; without forbearance. (L. *impatiens.*)
impatiently, *ad.* im-*pay*-shent-le, with impatience.
impavid, *a.* im-*pav*-id, fearless. (L. *impavidus.*)
impawn, *v.t.* im-*pawn*, to pledge; to deposit as security.
impayable, *a.* im-*pay*-a-bl, beyond price; not to be paid for. (Fr.)
impeach, *v.t.* im-*peech*, to call in question; to call to account; to charge with a crime or misdemeanour, esp. in administration or for treason (Law). (Fr. *empêcher*, to hinder.)
impeachable, *a.* im-*peech*-a-bl, liable to impeachment; chargeable with a crime; accountable.
impeacher, *n.* im-*peech*-er, one who impeaches.
impeachment, *n.* im-*peech*-ment, the act of impeaching; an accusation in or as in impeaching; a calling in question.
impearl, *v.t.* im-*perl*, to form into or make like pearls; to decorate with or as with pearls.
impeccability, *n.* *im*-pek-a-*bil*-e-te, the quality of being incapable of sinning.
impeccable, *a.* im-*pek*-a-bl, not liable to sin; faultless; not blameworthy. (L. *impeccabilis.*)
impeccancy, *n.* im-*pek*-an-se, impeccability.
impeccant, *a.* im-*pek*-ant, sinless. (L. *impeccantia.*)
impecuniosity, *n.* im-pe-kew-ne-*os*-e-te, the state of being without money.
impecunious, *a.* im-pe-*kew*-ne-us, without money; hard up. (L. *in*, not, *pecunia*, money.)

impedance, *n.* im-*pee*-dance, that which opposes an alternating electric current, either by resistance or reactance.
impede, *v.t.* im-*peed,* to hinder; to obstruct. (L. *impedio.*)
impedient, *a.* im-*pee*-de-ent, obstructive.
impediment, *n.* im-*ped*-e-ment, hindrance; obstruction; that which prevents distinct articulation.
impedimenta, *n.pl.* im-*ped*-e-*men*-ta, baggage; anything hindering progress. (L.)
impedimental, *a.* im-*ped*-e-*men*-tal, hindering; obstructing.
impeditive, *a.* im-*ped*-e-tiv, tending to obstruct; causing hindrance.
impel, *v.t.* im-*pel,* to drive or urge forward; to excite to action; to instigate. (L. *impello.*)
impellent, *a.* im-*pel*-lent, having the quality of impelling: *n.* an impulsive power or agent. (L. *impellens,* urging forward.)
impeller, *n.* im-*pel*-ler, he who or that which impels.
impen, *v.t.* im-*pen,* to pen; to shut in or enclose.
impend, *v.i.* im-*pend,* to hang over; to threaten; to be imminent. (L. *impendeo.*)
impendence, *n.* im-*pen*-dence, the state of impending or being imminent.
impendency, *n.* im-*pen*-den-se, impendence.
impendent, *a.* im-*pen*-dent, imminent.
impenetrability, *n.* im-*pen*-e-tra-*bil*-e-te, the quality of being impenetrable; that quality of matter by which it excludes all other matter from the space it occupies [Physics]; insusceptibility of impression in intellect or feeling.
impenetrable, *a.* im-*pen*-e-tra-bl, that cannot be pierced; not admitting any other substance into the same place; unimpressible, mentally or emotionally. (L. *impenetrabilis.*)
impenetrableness, *n.* impenetrability.
impenetrably, *ad.* so as not to be penetrated.
impenetrate, *v.t.* im-*pen*-e-trate, to penetrate deeply into.
impenitence, *n.* im-*pen*-e-tence, want or absence of penitence.
impenitency, *n.* im-*pen*-e-ten-se, impenitence.
impenitent, *a.* im-*pen*-e-tent, not penitent; not contrite: *n.* one who does not repent; a hardened sinner.
impenitently, *ad.* with impenitence.
impennate, *a.* im-*pen*-nat, wingless; having short unfeathered wings, as penguins. (L. *in,* not, *pennatus,* feathered.)
imperatival, *a.* im-*pe*-ra-*ty*-val, imperative; pertaining to the imperative mood.
imperative, *a.* im-*pe*-ra-tiv, authoritative; commanding; absolutely necessary: *n.* that form of the verb which expresses command, exhortation, etc. [Gram.]. **categorical imperative,** *see* **categorical.** (L. *imperativus.*)
imperatively, *ad.* in an imperative manner.
imperator, *n.* im-pe-*ray*-tor, a chief commander under the Roman Republic; later, the title of the head of the state. (L.)
imperatorial, *a.* im-*pe*-ra-*taw*-re-al, commanding; relating to the emperor.
imperceptibility, *n.* im-per-*sep*-te-*bil*-e-te, the quality of being imperceptible.
imperceptible, *a.* im-per-*sep*-te-bl, not perceptible or discernible; very small. (Late L. *imperceptibilis.*)
imperceptibleness, *n.* imperceptibility.
imperceptibly, *ad.* im-per-*sep*-te-ble, in an imperceptible manner; so as not to be perceived.
imperception, *n.* im-per-*sep*-shon, lack of perception.
imperceptive, *a.* im-per-*sep*-tiv, without perception.
impercipient, *a.* im-per-*sip*-e-ent, not perceiving or having power to perceive: *n.* one who is unperceiving.
imperfect, *a.* im-*per*-fekt, not perfect or complete; defective; subject to defect; liable to err; wanting either stamens or pistils [Bot.]; incomplete [Mus.]; denoting action in time past, then present, but not finished [Gram.]. **imperfect number,** one which is not equal to the sum of its aliquot parts [Arith.]. (L. *imperfectus.*)
imperfectible, *a.* im-per-*fek*-te-bl, incapable of being made perfect.
imperfection, *n.* im-per-*fek*-shon, defect; shortcoming; fault. (Fr.)
imperfectly, *ad.* im-*per*-fekt-le, in an imperfect manner or degree.
imperfectness, *n.* im-*per*-fekt-ness, the state of being imperfect.
imperforable, *a.* im-*per*-fo-ra-bl, that cannot be perforated.
imperforate, *a.* im-*per*-fo-rat, imperforated.
imperforated, *a.* im-*per*-fo-*ray*-ted, without holes or pores.
imperforation, *n.* im-*per*-fo-*ay*-shon, the state of being without perforation, pore, or aperture.
imperial, *a.* im-*peer*-re-al, pertaining to an empire an emperor or supreme ruler; befitting or like an emperor; majestic; pertaining to an empire (esp. the British Empire) as a whole, as distinguished from any one of its component parts: *n.* a tuft of hair on a man's lower lip and chin; a soldier or adherent of the Holy Roman Empire; a former Russian gold coin of 15 roubles; a size of paper of 30 by 22 in. **Imperial Conference,** a conference of the prime ministers and other representatives of the British mother-country, and members of the Commonwealth and Empire, held in London or elsewhere periodically. **Imperial Service Order,** an order restricted to members of the administrative and clerical branches of the Home and Imperial Civil Services, instituted in 1902. (O.Fr. *emperial.*)
imperialism, *n.* im-*peer*-re-a-lizm, government by an emperor; an emperor's state, authority, etc.; the encouragement of the close federation and interdependence of an empire; the doctrine that the British Empire as a whole is of more importance than the United Kingdom by itself; imperial state and its support; the desire for empire.
imperialist, *n.* im-*peer*-re-a-list, a soldier or adherent of an empire, esp. the Holy Roman Empire; an advocate of imperial rule, or of the doctrine of imperialism: *a.* imperialistic.
imperialistic, *a.* im-peer-re-a-*lis*-tik, pertaining to imperialism or imperialists; of imperialist principles or tendencies; advocating imperialism.
imperiality, *n.* im-*peer*-re-*al*-e-te, imperial power or right. (L. *imperialiter.*)
imperialize, *v.t.* im-*peer*-re-a-lize, to render imperial.
imperially, *ad.* im-*peer*-re-a-le, in an imperial way.
imperil, *v.t.* im-*pe*-ril, to endanger.
imperilment, *n.* im-*pe*-ril-ment, the act of imperilling; the state of being imperilled.
imperious, *a.* im-*peer*-re-us, haughtily dictatorial or overbearing; authoritatively commanding; urgent; pressing; not to be resisted. (L. *imperiosus.*)
imperiously, *ad.* in an imperious manner.
imperiousness, *n.* quality of being imperious.
imperishability, *n.* im-*pe*-re-sha-*bil*-e-te, the quality of being imperishable.
imperishable, *a.* im-*per*-rish-a-bl, not subject to decay; indestructible.
imperishableness, *n.* im-*pe*-rish-a-bl-ness, the quality of being imperishable.
imperishably, *ad.* in an imperishable manner.
imperium, *n.* im-*peer*-re-um, sovereign authority; absolute power; empire. (L.)
impermanence, *n.* im-*per*-ma-nence, want of permanence.
impermanent, *a.* im-*per*-ma-nent, not permanent.
impermeability, *n.* im-*per*-me-a-*bil*-e-te, the state or quality of being impermeable.
impermeable, *a.* im-*per*-me-a-bl, not permitting passage to a fluid.
impermeably, *ad.* in an impermeable manner.
impermissible, *a.* *im*-per-*mis*-se-bl, not permissible.
imperscriptible, *a.* *im*-per-*skrip*-te-bl, without written authority. (L. *im-,* and *perscribo,* write out.)
impersonal, *a.* im-*per*-son-al, not personal; without personality; said of a verb which is used only in the third person singular [Gram.]: *n.* an impersonal verb. (L. *impersonalis.*)
impersonality, *n.* im-*per*-so-*nal*-e-te, want of personality.
impersonally, *ad.* in an impersonal manner.
impersonate, *v.t.* im-*per*-so-nate, to invest with personality; to personify; to pretend to be someone else.
impersonation, *n.* im-*per*-so-*nay*-shon, investment with personality; the act or an instance of personifying or of personating.
impersonator, *n.* im-*per*-so-nay-tor, one who impersonates, esp. as a stage act.

imperspicuity, *n.* *im*-per-spe-*kew*-e-te, obscurity; inexactness.
impersuadable, *a.* im-per-*sway*-da-bl, not to be moved by persuasion or argument.
impertinence, *n.* im-*pert*-in-ence, that which is not pertinent; an impertinent act; rudeness.
impertinency, *n.* im-*pert*-in-en-se, impertinence; the quality of being impertinent.
impertinent, *a.* im-*pert*-in-ent, not pertaining to the matter in hand; irrelevant; intrusive; rude; saucy; unmannerly; trifling: *n.* an intruder; one who meddles or interferes. (L. *impertinens, -entis*, not pertaining to.)
impertinently, *ad.* im-*pert*-in-ent-le, in an impertinent manner.
imperturbability, *n.* im-per-*tur*-ba-*bil*-e-te, the quality of being imperturbable. (L. *imperturbabilis.*)
imperturbable, *a.* im-per-*tur*-ba-bl, not to be disturbed, agitated, or ruffled; calm and cool.
imperturbation, *n.* im-*per*-tur-*bay*-shon, freedom from agitation of mind; calmness. (L.)
imperturbed, *a.* im-per-*turbd*, not perturbed.
impervertible, *a.* im-per-*ver*-te-bl, not capable of being perverted.
imperviability, *n.* im-*per*-ve-a-*bil*-e-te, imperviousness.
imperviable, *a.* im-*per*-ve-a-bl, impervious.
impervious, *a.* im-*per*-ve-us, not to be penetrated or passed through; impenetrable; deaf (to argument, etc.). (L. *impervius.*)
imperviously, *ad.* in a manner not penetrable.
imperviousness, *n.* state of being impervious.
impetiginous, *a.* im-pe-*tij*-en-us, of the nature of impetigo; affected with impetigo.
impetigo, *n.* im-pe-*ty*-go, a contagious skin disease characterized by an eruption of yellow-scaled pustules [Med.]. (L.)
impetrate, *v.t.* *im*-pe-trate, to obtain by request or entreaty. (L. *impetratus*, effected as by entreaty.)
impetration, *n.* im-pe-*tray*-shon, the act of obtaining by petition.
impetrative, *a.* *im*-pe-tra-tiv, possessing the quality of obtaining by entreaty.
impetratory, *a.* *im*-pe-*tray*-to-re, impetrative.
impetuosity, *n.* im-*pet*-yew-*os*-e-te, sudden violence of action; dash; vehemence.
impetuous, *a.* im-*pet*-yew-us, rushing with force; vehement or violent in feeling; hasty in decision; hot-headed; precipitate. (L. *impetuosus.*)
impetuously, *ad.* in an impetuous manner.
impetuousness, *n.* the quality of being impetuous; vehemence or violence of temper.
impetus, *n.* *im*-pe-tus, driving force; momentum; the force with which a body moves or is driven or impelled. (L.)
impeyan, *n.* *im*-pe-an, a brilliantly plumaged Himalayan pheasant, *Lophophorus impeyanus*, named after the wife of Sir Elijah Impey, C.J. of Bengal, 1774–89.
impi, *n.* *im*-pe, a Kafir regiment. (Zulu.)
impiety, *n.* im-*py*-e-te, want of piety; ungodliness; want of filial piety; an impious act. (L. *impieta.*)
impignorate, *v.t.* im-*pig*-no-rate, to mortgage; to pledge or pawn: *a.* pawned. (L. *in-*, and *pignus*, a pledge.)
impinge, *v.i.* im-*pinj*, to fall or dash against; to come into collision with; to touch upon. (L. *impingo*, drive into.)
impingement, *n.* im-*pinj*-ment, act of impinging.
impingent, *a.* im-*pin*-jent, impinging.
impious, *a.* *im*-pe-us, irreverent; irreligious; profane. (L. *impius.*)
impiously, *ad.* *im*-pe-us-le, with impiety.
impiousness, *n.* the quality of being impious.
impish, *a.* *imp*-ish, having the qualities of an imp.
implacability, *n.* im-*plak*-a-*bil*-e-te, the state or quality of being implacable.
implacable, *a.* im-*plak*-a-bl, not to be appeased; inexorable; irreconcilable. (L. *implacabilis.*)
implacableness, *n.* implacability.
implacably, *ad.* to an implacable degree.
implacental, *a.* *im*-pla-*sen*-tal, without a placenta.
implant, *v.t.* im-*plahnt*, to set, plant, or infix, for the purpose of growth; to graft; to instil; to infuse.
implantation, *n.* *im*-plahn-*tay*-shon, the act of implanting, esp. in the mind or heart.
implausibility, *n.* im-*plaw*-ze-*bil*-e-te, the state or quality of not being plausible.
implausible, *a.* im-*plaw*-ze-bl, not wearing the appearance of truth or credibility.
implausibly, *ad.* in an implausible manner.
impleach, *v.t.* im-*pleech*, to interweave.
implead, *v.t.* im-*pleed*, to institute and prosecute a suit at law; to impeach: *v.i.* to bring an action [Law]. (O.Fr. *emplaidier.*)
impledge, *v.t.* im-*plej*, to pawn; to pledge.
implement, *n.* *im*-ple-ment, a tool or instrument; a utensil: *v.t.* to give effect to; to accomplish; to fulfil. (Late L. *implementum.*)
implemental, *a.* *im*-ple-*men*-tal, of the nature of an implement; serving as an implement.
implementation, *n.* im-ple-men-*tay*-shon, the action of implementing; performance; accomplishment.
implementiferous, *a.* im-ple-men-*tif*-er-rus, containing prehistoric implements [Archæol.].
impletion, *n.* im-*plee*-shon, the act of filling; the state of being full. (L. *in-*, and *pleo*, fill.)
implicate, *v.t.* *im*-ple-kate, to infold; to involve; to entangle: *n.* that which is implied or involved. (L. *implicatus.*)
implication, *n.* *im*-ple-*kay*-shon, the act of implicating; state of being implicated; entanglement; something implied. (L. *implicatio.*)
implicative, *a.* *im*-ple-ka-tiv, tending to imply or to implicate.
implicit, *a.* im-*plis*-sit, implied; tacitly comprised; to be understood, though not expressed; trusting without questioning or reserve. (L. *implicitus.*)
implicitly, *ad.* im-*plis*-sit-le, in an implicit manner.
implicitness, *n.* the state of being implicit.
implied, *a.* im-*plide*, contained virtually, though not expressed; understood.
impliedly, *ad.* im-*ply*-ed-le, by implication.
implode, *v.i.* im-*plode*, to burst inward; to utter with implosion [Phon.]. (*im-* and [*ex*]*plode.*)
imploration, *n.* im-plaw-*ray*-shon, earnest supplication.
imploratory, *a.* im-*plaw*-ra-to-re, imploring.
implore, *v.t.* im-*plawr*, to ask or supplicate earnestly: *v.i.* to entreat; to beg. (Fr. *implorer.*)
implorer, *n.* im-*plaw*-rer, one who earnestly prays or supplicates.
imploringly, *ad.* im-*plaw*-ring-le, with earnest supplications.
implosion, *n.* im-*ploh*-zhon, a bursting inwards; the formation of sounds (*p, t, k*) by compression of air between the glottis and the mouth and nose passages, all being closed [Phon.].
implosive, *a.* im-*ploh*-siv, formed by implosion: *n.* a sound thus formed [Phon.].
impluvium, *n.* im-*ploo*-ve-um, a cistern in the entrance-hall of a Roman house, in which the rain-water from the roof was received. (L.)
imply, *v.t.* im-*ply*, to involve or contain by implication; to import or signify. (O.Fr. *empleier.*)
impocket, *v.t.* im-*pok*-et, to pocket.
impolder, *v.t.* im-*pol*-der, to reclaim (land) by making a polder.
impolicy, *n.* im-*pol*-e-se, inexpedience; the quality of being unsuitable to the end proposed.
impolite, *a.* *im*-po-*lite*, of unpolished manners; uncivil. (L. *impolitus*, rough.)
impolitely, *ad.* im-po-*lite*-le, not politely.
impoliteness, *n.* want of good manners.
impolitic, *a.* im-*pol*-it-ik, not wise in policy; inexpedient; not calculated to serve the purpose.
impoliticly, *ad.* in an impolitic manner.
imponderability, *n.* im-*pon*-der-ra-*bil*-e-te, imponderableness.
imponderable, *a.* im-*pon*-der-ra-bl, not having sensible weight; very tenuous: *n.* an imponderable body or agent, such as light, or heat.
imponderableness, *n.* im-*pon*-der-ra-bl-ness, state or quality of being imponderable.
imponderous, *a.* im-*pon*-der-rus, imponderable; without perceptible weight.
imponent, *a.* im-*poh*-nent, that imposes: *n.* one who imposes.
imporous, *a.* im-*paw*-rus, destitute of pores; very compact in texture.
import, *v.t.* im-*pawrt*, to bring from a foreign country or jurisdiction; to introduce; to convey; to signify; to be of moment or consequence to; to concern. (L. *importo*, carry.)
import, *n.* *im*-pawrt, that which is conveyed in

words; signification; drift; that which is imported into a country: importance; consequence.
importable, *a.* im-*pawr*-ta-bl, capable of being imported. (O.Fr.)
importance, *n.* im-*pawr*-tance, the quality of being important or of moment; significance; estimation; self-esteem. (Fr.)
***important,** *a.* im-*pawr*-tant, of great import or consequence; momentous; pretentious. (Fr.)
importantly, *ad.* to an important degree.
importation, *n.* *im*-paw-*tay*-shon, the act or practice of importing; commodities imported.
importunacy, *n.* im-*pawr*-tew-na-se, importunity.
importer, *n.* im-*pawr*-ter, one who imports goods.
importunate, *a.* im-*pawrt*-yew-nat, unreasonably urgent in solicitation; pertinacious: *v.t.* to importune.
importunately, *ad.* with importunity.
importunateness, *n.* im-*pawrt*-yew-nat-ness, the quality of being importunate; importunity.
importune, *v.t.* im-pawr-*tewn*, to request with troublesome urgency; to beg persistently: *a.* persistently pressing in solicitation. (O.Fr.)
importuner, *n.* one who importunes.
importunity, *n.* im-pawr-*tew*-ne-te, importunateness; pertinacious persistency in solicitation. (Fr. *importunité.*)
imposable, *a.* im-*poze*-a-bl, that may be imposed.
impose, *v.t.* im-*poze*, to lay on; to enjoin; to obtrude; to arrange the pages for printing, and prepare the forme for the press [Print.]. **to impose on,** to deceive. (Fr. *imposer.*)
imposer, *n.* im-*poze*-er, one who imposes.
imposing, *a.* im-*poze*-ing, stately; grandiose; adapted to impress: *n.* the putting of the pages of a sheet in proper order and preparing them to be printed. **imposing stone,** the flat surface on which the pages of type are imposed.
imposingly, *ad.* in an imposing manner.
imposition, *n.* *im*-po-*zish*-on, the act of imposing or laying on, such as hands in ordination; a task as a punishment; that which is imposed, as a tax, toll, or duty; a deception or imposture. (Fr.)
impossibility, *n.* im-*pos*-se-*bil*-e-te, the quality or state of being impossible; a thing impossible. (L. *impossibilis.*)
impossible, *a.* im-*pos*-se-bl, not possible; that cannot be or be done; impracticable; difficult to consort with (of persons) [Coll.]. (Fr.)
impost, *n.* *im*-post, a tax or duty imposed by authority; the moulding on the top of a pillar or pier, from which an arch springs [Arch.]; the weight carried by a horse in a handicap [Slang]. (O.Fr.)
impostor, *n.* im-*pos*-tor, one who practises imposition or swindles; a cheat. (L.)
impostumate, *v.i.* im-*pos*-tew-mate, to form an abscess; to gather: *v.t.* to affect with an abscess.
impostumation, *n.* im-*pos*-tew-*may*-shon, the act of forming an abscess; an impostume.
impostume, *n.* im-*pos*-tewm, an abscess; a collection of purulent matter in any part of an animal body. (O.Fr. *apostume.*)
imposture, *n.* im-*post*-yur, deception practised under a false or assumed character; an imposition or swindle. (L. *impostura.*)
impotence, *n.* *im*-po-tence, the state or quality of being impotent. (Fr.)
impotency, *n.* *im*-po-ten-se, impotence.
impotent, *a.* *im*-po-tent, wanting strength or power; wanting the power of procreation; wanting the power of self-restraint: *n.* one who is sexually impotent. (Fr.)
impotently, *ad.* in an impotent manner.
impound, *v.t.* im-*pound*, to put in the pound; to confine; to confiscate; to hold in security.
impoverish, *v.t.* im-*pov*-er-ish, to make poor; to exhaust resources or fertility. (O.Fr. *empovris*, from *empovrir*, impoverish.)
impoverisher, *n.* im-*pov*-er-ish-er, one who makes poor; that which impairs fertility.
impoverishment, *n.* im-*pov*-er-ish-ment, reduction to poverty; exhaustion of resources or fertility.
impracticability, *n.* im-*prak*-te-ka-*bil*-e-te, impracticableness.
impracticable, *a.* im-*prak*-te-ka-bl, that cannot be done in the circumstances; not feasible; unmanageable; stubborn.
impracticableness, *n.* im-*prak*-te-ka-bl-ness, the state or quality of being impracticable.
impracticably, *ad.* im-*prak*-te-ka-ble, in a manner to be impracticable.
impractical, *a.* im-*prak*-te-kal, unpractical; impracticable.
imprecate, *v.t.* *im*-pre-kate, to invoke, as an evil; to pray that a curse fall on. (L. *imprecatus*, prayed.)
imprecation, *n.* *im*-pre-*kay*-shon, the act of imprecating; a prayer that a curse may fall on one.
imprecatory, *a.* *im*-pre-*kay*-to-re, containing a curse; maledictory.
imprecision, *n.* *im*-pre-*sizh*-on, want of precision.
impregnability, *n.* im-*preg*-na-*bil*-e-te, the state or quality of being impregnable.
impregnable, *a.* im-*preg*-na-bl, not to be captured by assault; able to withstand any attack; invincible. (Fr. *imprenable.*)
impregnably, *ad.* in a manner to resist assault.
impregnate, *v.t.* im-*preg*-nate, to make pregnant, as a female animal; to fecundate; to infuse the particles or qualities of one thing into another; to imbue. (L. *impraegnatus*, impregnated.)
impregnation, *n.* im-preg-*nay*-shon, the act of impregnating; fertilization; that with which anything is impregnated.
impresa, *n.* im-*pres*-a, an heraldic or other device, as on a seal, etc. (Ir.)
impresario, *n.* *im*-pre-*sah*-re-o, one who organizes or conducts an opera or a body of musicians. (It.)
imprescriptibility, *n.* *im*-pre-*skrip*-te-*bil*-e-te, the state of being imprescriptible.
imprescriptible, *a.* *im*-pre-*skrip*-te-bl, that cannot be lost or impaired by prescription or by lapse of time; inalienable; independent of external authority.
impress, *v.t.* im-*press*, to mark by pressure; to print; to mark; to fix deeply; to affect forcibly; to force (esp. seamen) into public service. (L. *impressare.*)
impress, *n.* *im*-press, a mark, figure, or image made by pressure; stamp; likeness; device; motto.
impressibility, *n.* im-*pres*-se-*bil*-e-te, the quality of being impressible.
impressible, *a.* im-*pres*-se-bl, capable of being impressed; susceptible.
impression, *n.* im-*presh*-on, the act of impressing; mark made by pressure; copy of an engraving; a whole printing of a book from standing type without change; effect of an object on the sense or mind; indistinct remembrance; sensible effect. (Fr.)
impressionability, *n.* im-*presh*-o-na-*bil*-e-te, the quality of being impressionable; susceptibility to impressions.
impressionable, *a.* im-*presh*-o-na-bl, susceptible of impression; easily influenced.
impressionism, *n.* im-*presh*-o-nizm, a non-academic style in art in which the general tone and effect are rendered without elaborate detail; so called in derision of the work of certain French artists of the 1860's.
impressionist, *a.* im-*presh*-o-nist, pertaining to impressionism: *n.* an artist who, in his work, adheres to the methods of impressionism.
impressionistic, *a.* im-presh-o-*nis*-tik, pertaining to or characterized by impressionism.
impressive, *a.* im-*pres*-siv, calculated to make an impression on the mind.
impressively, *ad.* in an impressive manner.
impressiveness, *n.* im-*pres*-siv-ness, the condition or quality of being impressive.
impressment, *n.* im-*press*-ment, the act of impressing into public service; seizure for public use.
imprest, *n.* *im*-prest, a cash advance made to an official for use on the public business. **Imprest Office,** an Admiralty department from which advances were made to paymasters.
imprimatur, *n.* im-pre-*may*-tur, an official licence to print a book; approval. (L., let it be printed.)
imprimis, *ad.* im-*pry*-mis, in the first place. (L.)
imprint, *v.t.* im-*print*, to impress; to stamp; to print; to fix on the mind.
imprint, *n.* *im*-print, the name of the printer or publisher of a book, with the place (and sometimes the date) of publication as given in the book.
imprison, *v.t.* im-*priz*-on, to put into and confine in a prison; to confine or restrain. (O.Fr. *emprisonner.*)
imprisonable, *a.* im-*priz*-on-a-bl, capable of being, or liable to be, imprisoned.

imprisonment, *n.* im-*priz*-on-ment, act of imprisoning; confinement in a place; restraint of liberty. **false imprisonment,** illegal restraint or confinement under colour of law.
improbability, *n.* *im*-prob-a-*bil*-e-te, the quality of being improbable; unlikelihood.
improbable, *a.* im-*prob*-a-bl, not likely to be true; un kely. (L. *improbabilis.*)
i nprobably, *ad.* in an improbable manner.
improbation, *n.* im-pro-*bay*-shon, an action for the setting aside of a deed on account of falsehood or forgery [Scots. Law]. (L. *improbatio*, blame.)
improbity, *n.* im-*proh*-be-te, dishonesty; want of probity. (L. *improbitas.*)
impromptu, *a.* and *ad.* im-*promp*-tew, off-hand; extempore; without previous study: *n.* a piece of wit, music, etc., produced off-hand or purporting to be so. (L. *in promptu*, in readiness.)
improper, *a.* im-*prop*-er, not proper; not suitable; unfit; unbecoming; incorrect; indecorous. **improper fraction,** a fraction whose numerator is equal to or greater than its denominator. (Fr. *impropre.*)
improperly, *ad.* in an improper manner.
impropriate, *a.* im-*proh*-pre-at, vested in the hands of a layman: *v.t.* to appropriate to private use; to place ecclesiastical property in the hands of a layman. (L. *in-*, and *propriatus*, appropriated.)
impropriation, *n.* im-proh-pre-*ay*-shon, the act of impropriating; the benefice impropriated.
impropriator, *n.* im-*proh*-pre-ay-tor, a layman in possession of church lands or an ecclesiastical living.
impropriety, *n.* im-pro-*pry*-e-te, unsuitableness; an improper or indelicate act or expression. (Fr. *impropriété.*)
improvability, *n.* im-*proo*-va-*bil*-e-te, the state or quality of being improvable.
improvable, *a.* im-*proo*-va-bl, susceptible of improvement; that may be used to advantage.
improve, *v.t.* im-*proov*, to make better; to advance in value or good qualities; to employ to profit; to make productive; to correct; to apply to practical purposes; to employ; to cultivate: *v.i.* to grow better or advance in goodness, knowledge, wisdom, or other excellence; to increase. **to improve on,** to make additions or amendments to; to point the moral from. (O.Fr. *aproer*, benefit.)
improvement, *n.* im-*proov*-ment, the act of improving; advancement in worth, learning, wisdom, skill or other excellence; employment or application to good purpose or profit; enhancement; a betterment to a house or land.
improver, *n.* im-*proo*-ver, one who or that which improves; an apprentice; a learner at a trade.
improvidence, *n.* im-*prov*-e-dence, want of providence or provision beforehand; extravagance.
improvident, *a.* im-*prov*-e-dent, thriftless; careless; wanting in foresight.
improvidently, *ad.* without foresight.
improving, *a.* im-*proo*-ving, becoming better; tending to improve (esp. the morale).
improvingly, *ad.* in a manner to improve.
improvisate, *v.t.* im-*prov*-e-zate, to improvise.
improvisation, *n.* im-pro-ve-*zay*-shon, the act of improvising; that which is improvised.
improvisator, *n.* im-*prov*-e-*zay*-tor, an improviser.
improvise, *v.i.* *im*-pro-vize, to improvisate; to do anything offhand, or on the spur of the moment. (Fr. *improviers.*)
improviser, *n.* *im*-pro-vy-zer, one who improvises.
imprudence, *n.* im-*proo*-dence, want of prudence or caution; an imprudent act. (L. *imprudentia.*)
imprudent, *a.* im-*proo*-dent, wanting prudence or discretion; incautious; inconsiderate.
imprudently, *ad.* without prudence.
impuberty, *n.* im-*pew*-ber-te, the state of not having reached the age of puberty; immaturity.
impubescent, *a.* im-pew-*bes*-ent, not pubescent; immature.
impudence, *n.* *im*-pew-dence, the quality of being impudent. (Fr.)
impudent, *a.* *im*-pew-dent, wanting modesty; shameless; insolent; impertinent. (Fr.)
impudently, *ad.* in an impudent manner.
impudicity, *n.* im-pew-*dis*-se-te, immodesty; shamelessness. (Fr. *impudicité.*)
impugn, *v.t.* im-*pewn*, to attack by words or arguments; to contradict; to call in question. (Fr. *impugner.*)
impugnable, *a.* im-*pew*-na-bl, that may be questioned.
impugner, *n.* im-*pew*-ner, one who impugns.
impuissance, *n.* im-*pew*-e-sance, impotence; powerlessness. (Fr.)
impuissant, *a.* im-*pew*-e-sant, impotent; feeble. (Fr.)
*****impulse,** *n.* *im*-pulse, the act of impelling; impulsion; force suddenly communicated; impetus; influence acting suddenly on the mind. (L. *impulsus*, an impulse.)
impulsion, *n.* im-*pul*-shon, the act of impelling; the effect of an impelling force; impulse.
impulsive, *a.* im-*pul*-siv, having the power to impel; rash, actuated by impulse rather than by reason; acting by impulse [Mech.].
impulsively, *ad.* im-*pul*-siv-le, by impulse.
impulsiveness, *n.* the quality of being impulsive.
impunity, *n.* im-*pew*-ne-te, exemption from penalty, injury, or loss. (Fr. *impunité.*)
impure, *a.* im-*pewr*, not pure; mixed with extraneous substance; obscene; unchaste; defiled by sin or guilt; unholy; ceremonially unclean. (L. *impurus*, unclean.)
impurely, *ad.* im-*pewr*-le, in an impure manner; with impurity.
impurity, *n.* im-*pewr*-re-te, the state of being impure. want of purity; anything impure.
imputability, *n.* im-*pew*-ta-*bil*-e-te, the quality of being imputable.
imputable, *a.* im-*pew*-ta-bl, that may be imputed, charged or attributed.
imputation, *n.* im-pew-*tay*-shon, the act of imputing; the charge against one; the attribution of the guilt or the righteousness of one to another, who is by natural or spiritual descent of the same stock [Theol.]. (L. *imputatio.*)
imputative, *a.* im-*pew*-ta-tiv, coming or transferred by imputation; imputable.
imputatively, *ad.* by imputation.
impute, *v.t.* im-*pewt*, to ascribe; to charge; to attribute. (Fr. *imputer.*)
imputer, *n.* im-*pew*-ter, one who imputes.
imputrescible, *a.* im-pew-*tres*-e-bl, not subject to putrefaction or corruption.
in-, in, a Latin prefix, which assumes the form of *ig-*, *il-*, *im-*, *ir-*, and signifies in, into, on, etc., in verbs and nouns, and of un- or not in adjectives.
*****in,** *prep.* in, presence in place, time or state; within; during; by, or through, means of: *ad.* within; not out; into. **in-and-in,** bred from the same stock, inbred. **in-and-out,** alternating between in and out; both inside and outside. (A.S., Ger., L., etc.)
inability, *n.* in-a-*bil*-e-te, the act of being unable; incapacity.
inabstinence, *n.* in-*ab*-ste-nence, lack of abstinence.
inaccessibility, *n.* in-ak-*ses*-se-*bil*-e-te, impossibility of access; unaccessibleness.
inaccessible, *a.* in-ak-*ses*-se-bl, not to be reached, obtained, or approached. (L. *inaccessabilis.*)
inaccessibleness, *n.* in-ak-*ses*-se-bl-ness, the state of being inaccessible; inaccessibility.
inaccessibly, *ad.* so as not to be accessible.
inaccuracy, *n.* in-*ak*-kew-ra-se, want of accuracy; a mistake or error.
inaccurate, *a.* in-*ak*-kew-rat, not accurate; erroneous; untrue.
inaccurately, *ad.* in an inaccurate manner.
inaction, *n.* in-*ak*-shon, want of action; forbearance of labour; idleness; sluggishness; rest.
inactive, *a.* in-*ak*-tiv, not active; inert; indisposed to action or effort; indolent; not acting or operating [Med.].
inactively, *ad.* in an inactive manner.
inactivity, *n.* *in*-ak-*tiv*-e-te, want of action or exertion; inertness; indolence.
inadaptable, *a.* in-a-*dap*-ta-bl, incapable of adaptation, lacking adaptability.
inadequacy, *n.* in-*ad*-e-kwa-se, inadequateness.
inadequate, *a.* in-*ad*-e-kwate, not adequate; not equal to the purpose; insufficient.
inadequately, *ad.* in-*ad*-e-kwat-le, not sufficiently.
inadequateness, *n.* in-*ad*-e-kwat-ness, the quality of being inadequate; insufficiency.
inadherent, *a.* *in*-ad-*heer*-ent, not adherent [Bot.].
inadhesion, *n.* in-ad-*hee*-zhon, want of adhesion.
inadmissibility, *n.* in-ad-*mis*-se-*bil*-e-te, impossibility of admission.

inadmissible, *a.* in-ad-*mis*-se-bl, not admissible.
inadvertence, *n.* in-ad-*vert*-ence, a lack of advertence or attention; heedlessness; an effect of inattention; an oversight.
inadvertency, *n.* in-ad-*vert*-en-se, inadvertence.
inadvertent, *a.* in-ad-*vert*-ent, not turning the mind to; inattentive; negligent.
inadvertently, *ad.* in-ad-*vert*-ent-le, with inattention; unintentionally.
inadvisable, *a.* in-ad-*vize*-a-bl, unadvisable.
inalienability, *n.* in-*ay*-le-en-a-*bil*-e-te, the state of being inalienable.
inalienable, *a.* in-*ay*-le-en-a-bl, that cannot be alienated or transferred.
inalienably, *ad.* in-*ay*-le-en-a-ble, in a manner that forbids alienation.
inalterability, *n.* in-*awl*-ter-ra-*bil*-e-te, the quality of being unalterable.
inalterable, *a.* in-*awl*-ter-ra-bl, unalterable.
inamorato, *n.masc.* in-am-o-*rah*-to (*fem.* **inamorata,** in-am-o-*rah*-tah), one who is loved or beloved; a lover; a sweetheart. (It.)
inane, *a.* in-*ane*, empty; void; brainless: *n.* an infinite void space. (L. *inanis*, empty.)
inanely, *ad.* in an inane manner.
inanimate, *a.* in-*an*-im-ate, without life or animation.
inanimation, *n.* in-*an*-im-*ay*-shon, want of animation.
inanition, *n.* in-an-*ish*-on, emptiness; exhaustion and bodily wasting from want of food. (Fr.)
inanity, *n.* in-*an*-e-te, the state of being inane; senselessness. (Fr. *inanité*.)
inappeasable, *a.* in-ap-*peez*-a-bl, not to be appeased.
inappellable, *a.* in-ap-*pel*-a-bl, not appealable from; absolute; final.
inappetence, *n.* in-*ap*-pe-tence, want of appetence or appetite; lack of disposition to seek nutriment.
inappetent, *a.* in-*ap*-pe-tent, not having appetite or desire.
inapplicability, *n.* in-*ap*-le-ka-*bil*-e-te, the quality of being inapplicable; unfitness.
inapplicable, *a.* in-*ap*-le-ka-bl, not applicable.
inapplicably, *ad.* in an inapplicable manner.
inapplication, *n.* in-ap-le-*kay*-shon, want of application; inapplicability.
inapposite, *a.* in-*ap*-po-zit, not apposite; not pertinent.
inappositely, *ad.* in a manner not apposite.
inappreciable, *a.* in-a-*pree*-she-a-bl, not appreciable.
inappreciative, *a.* in-a-*pree*-she-a-tiv, not appreciative.
inapprehensible, *a.* *in*-ap-re-*hen*-se-bl, not intelligible. (L. *inapprehensibilis*.)
inapprehensive, *a.* *in*-ap-re-*hen*-siv, not apprehensive; regardless (of).
inapproachable, *a.* in-a-*proach*-a-bl, unapproachable; inaccessible.
inappropriate, *a.* *in*-a-*proh*-pre-ate, not appropriate; unsuitable.
inappropriately, *ad.* not appropriately.
inappropriateness, *n.* unsuitableness.
inapt, *a.* in-*apt*, not suitable; not ready; inept.
inaptitude, *n.* in-*ap*-te-tewd, want of aptitude.
inaptly, *ad.* in-*apt*-le, unfitly; unsuitably.
inaptness, *n.* in-*apt*-ness, unfitness.
inarable, *a.* in-*a*-ra-bl, not arable; not fit for ploughing.
inarch, *v.t.* in-*arch*, to graft a scion without separating it from its parent tree into a stock standing near.
inarticulate, *a.* *in*-ar-*tik*-yew-*lat*, not uttered with distinct articulation; not jointed or articulated [Bot. and Zool.]. (L. *inarticulatus*.)
inarticulately, *ad.* *in*-ar-*tik*-yew-lat-le, in an inarticulate manner.
inarticulateness, *n.* the condition of being inarticulate.
inarticulation, *n.* *in*-ar-*tik*-yew-*lay*-shon, inarticulateness; indistinctness of utterance.
inartificial, *a.* *in*-art-e-*fish*-al, not artificial; not characterized by art or skill; simple; artless. (L. *inartificialis*.)
inartificially, *ad.* in an inartificial manner.
inartistic, *a.* *in*-ar-*tis*-tik, unskilled in art; crude.
inartistically, *ad.* *in*-ar-*tis*-te-ka-le, crudely; clumsily; showing no skill in art.
inasmuch, *ad.* in-az-*much*, seeing that: this being so; because.
inattention, *n.* in-at-*ten*-shon, the want of attention; heedlessness; neglect.
inattentive, *a.* in-at-*tent*-iv, not attentive; heedless; negligent.
inattentively, *ad.* without attention.
inaudibility, *n.* in-*aw*-de-*bil*-e-te, the quality or state of being inaudible.
inaudible, *a.* in-*aw*-de-bl, that cannot be heard. (L. *inaudibilis*.)
inaudibly, *ad.* in an inaudible manner.
inaugural, *a.* in-*aw*-gewr-ral, pertaining to, made or pronounced at, an inauguration; introductory: *n.* an address made by one at his inauguration [U.S.A.].
inaugurate, *v.t.* in-*aw*-gewr-rate, to induct into office with suitable ceremonies; to commence or introduce formally; to set in motion. (L. *inauguratus*, consecrated with augury.)
inauguration, *n.* in-*aw*-gewr-*ray*-shon, the act or ceremony of inaugurating. (L. *inauguratio*.)
inaugurator, *n.* in-*aw*-gewr-ray-tor, one who inaugurates.
inauguratory, *a.* in-*aw*-gewr-ray-to-re, inaugural.
inauspicious, *a.* *in*-aw-*spish*-us, ill-omened; unlucky; unfavourable.
inauspiciously, *ad.* with ill omens.
inauspiciousness, *n.* unluckiness.
inbeing, *n.* *in*-bee-ing, inherence; inherent existence.
inboard, *a.* and *ad.* *in*-bord, within the ship.
inbond, *a.* *in*-bond, laid with the long way across (of bricks).
inborn, *a.* *in*-born, innate; implanted by nature.
inbound *a.* *in*-bound, inward bound (of traffic).
inbreak, *n.* *in*-brake, the act of breaking in or into; an inroad.
inbreathe, *v.t.* in-*breethe*, to breathe into.
inbred, *a.* *in*-bred, bred in-and-in; bred within; innate; natural.
inbreed, *v.t.* in-*breed*, to breed in-and-in.
inca, *n.* *ing*-kah, one of the ruling family of Peru before the Spanish Conquest; the family or clan itself.
incalculable, *a.* in-*kal*-kew-la-bl, not calculable.
incalculableness, *n.* in-*kal*-kewl-a-bl-ness, incapability of being calculated.
incalculably, *ad.* in-*kal*-kew-la-ble, in a degree beyond calculation.
incalescence, *n.* *in*-ka-*les*-sence, the state or quality of being incalescent.
incalescent, *a.* *in*-ka-*les*-sent, growing warm; increasing in heat. (L. *incalescens*, growing warm.)
incameration, *n.* *in*-kam-e-*ray*-shon, the uniting of lands, revenues, or other rights to the Pope's domain. (L. *in*-, and *camera*, a chamber.)
incandesce, *v.i.* and *t.* in-kan-*dess*, to become or cause to become incandescent; to glow through heat.
incandescence, *n.* *in*-kan-*des*-sense, the state of being incandescent; a white heat.
incandescent, *a.* *in*-kan-*des*-sent, glowing with heat; luminous with heat. **incandescent-lamp,** a filament or other lamp in which the light is produced by the raising of a medium to a glowing heat. **incandescent-mantle,** a gas-mantle. (L. *incandescens*, glowing.)
incantation, *n.* *in*-kan-*tay*-shon, the utterance of a spell; a magical chant; a magic spell. (L. *incantatio*.)
incantatory, *a.* in-*kan*-ta-to-re, of the nature of incantation.
incapability, *n.* *in*-kay-pa-*bil*-e-te, the quality or state of being incapable; incapacity.
incapable, *a.* in-*kay*-pa-bl, not capable physically, intellectually, or morally; not in a state to undergo; legally unqualified or disqualified. (Fr.)
incapably, *ad.* in an incapable manner.
incapacious, *a.* in-ka-*pay*-shus, having small containing space; narrow, not roomy; of deficient or limited mental capacity.
incapaciousness, *n.* in-ka-*pay*-shus-ness, the state or quality of being incapacious.
incapacitate, *v.t.* in-ka-*pas*-e-tate, to render unfit or incapable; to disqualify; to disable.
incapacitation, *n.* in-ka-*pas*-e-*tay*-shon, the act of incapacitating; the state of being incapacitated; disqualification.
incapacity, *n.* in-ka-*pas*-e-te, want of capacity; inability; legal disqualification.
incarcerate, *v.t.* in-*kar*-ser-rate to imprison; to confine. (Late L. *incarceratus*.)

incarceration, *n.* in-*kar*-ser-*ay*-shon, imprisonment; abnormal retention of a part, esp. through constriction about the hernial sac [Med.].
incarnadine, *a.* in-*kar*-na-dine, flesh-coloured: *v.t.* to dye red or of a flesh-colour. (Fr. *incarnadin.*)
incarnate, *a.* in-*kar*-nate, invested with or embodied in flesh: *v.t.* to clothe with or embody in flesh. (L. *incarnatus.*)
incarnation, *n.* *in*-kar-*nay*-shon, the act of incarnating; exhibition in human form or embodiment; the process of healing wounds and filling the part with new flesh [Surg.]. **the Incarnation,** the assumption by Christ of a human body and the nature and state of a human being. (Fr.)
incase, *v.t.* in-*kase*, to encase.
incatinate, *v.t.* in-*kat*-e-nate, to put in chains; to fetter. (L. *in-*, and *catena*, a chain.)
incaution, *n.* in-*kaw*-shon, want of caution.
incautious, *a.* in-*kaw*-shus, not cautious or considerate; indiscreet.
incautiously, *ad.* in an incautious manner.
incautiousness, *n.* quality of being incautious.
incavate, *v.t.* *in*-ka-vate, to hollow out. (L.)
incavation, *n.* in-ka-*vay*-shon, the act of making hollow; a hollow made. (L. *in-*, and *cavus*, hollow.)
incavo, *n.* in-*kay*-voh, the sunken part of an intaglio. (It.)
incendiarism, *n.* in-*sen*-de-a-rizm, the act or practice of an incendiary.
incendiary, *n.* in-*sen*-de-a-re, one who maliciously sets fire to another home or other property; one who inflames factions and promotes quarrels; he who or that which excites: *a.* pertaining to the malicious burning of a dwelling; tending to excite or inflame sedition or quarrels. **incendiary bomb,** a bomb that contains chemicals that ignite and cause a conflagration on its bursting. (L. *incendiarius*, causing a conflagration.)
incensation, *n.* in-sen-*say*-shon, the act of ceremonially offering incense; censing.
incense, *n.* *in*-sence, a mixture of *Styrax* and other resins and spices burned in religious rites; the smoke or the odour from this; any fragrant disinfectant; flattery: *v.t.* to offer incense to; to perfume with incense. (Fr. *encens.*)
incense, *v.t.* in-*sence*, to inflame to violent anger; to enrage. (L. *incensus*, set on fire.)
incensement, *n.* in-*sence*-ment, wrath; exasperation; irritation of the passions.
incensory, *n.* in-*sen*-so-re, a censer.
incentive, *a.* in-*sen*-tiv, inciting; encouraging: *n.* that which prompts to good or ill; stimulus; incitement. (L. *incentivus.*)
incept, *v.t.* in-*sept*, to take in; to intussuscept [Biol.]: *v.i.* at Cambridge University, to complete admission to the degree of Master or Doctor: *n.* the rudiment of an organ [Bot.].
inception, *n.* in-*sep*-shon, beginning; the act or ceremony of incepting (at Cambridge).
inceptive, *a.* in-*sep*-tiv, primary; beginning: *n.* that which is inceptive; a verb denoting the beginning of an action [Gram.]. (O.Fr. *inceptif.*)
inceptor, *n.* in-*sep*-tor, a beginner; one about to incept (at Cambridge).
incertain, *a.* in-*ser*-tan, uncertain.
incertitude, *n.* in-*ser*-te-tewd, uncertainty.
incessably, *ad.* in-*ses*-a-ble, without cessation. (L. *incessabilis.*)
incessancy, *n.* in-*ses*-an-se, the state or quality of being incessant; unbroken continuance.
incessant, *a.* in-*ses*-ant, perpetual; unceasing; uninterrupted.
incessantly, *ad.* in-*ses*-ant-le, without ceasing.
incest, *n.* *in*-sest, sexual intercourse within the degrees of affinity. (Fr. *inceste.*)
incestuous, *a.* in-*ses*-tew-us, guilty of incest; pertaining to or involving incest.
incestuously, *ad.* in an incestuous manner.
inch, *n.* inch, the twelfth part of a lineal foot; 2·54 centimetres; the depth of an inch, as measurement of rainfall; the air pressure of an inch; a small degree; (pl.) stature: *v.t.* to mark in inches; to drive by small degrees: *v.i.* to advance or retire by small degrees. **by inches,** by slow degrees. **to inch out,** to eke out. (A.S. *ynce*, L. *uncia*, a twelfth part.)
inch, *n.* inch, in Scotland, a small island. (Gael.)
inchmeal, *ad.* *inch*-meel, by inches; gradually. (*inch*, and A.S. *maelum*, quantity taken at one time.)
inchoate, *a.* *in*-ko-ate, begun; incipient; undeveloped. (L. *inchoatus.*)
inchoately, *ad.* in an incipient degree.
inchoation, *n.* in-ko-*ay*-shon, beginning; an inception.
inchoative, *a.* in-*koh*-a-tiv, inceptive; rudimentary.
inchpin, *n.* *inch*-pin, the sweetbread of a deer.
incidence, *n.* *in*-sid-ence, a falling upon; the manner of falling; the direction in which a body falls on another. **angle of incidence,** the angle which a ray of light, etc., falling on a surface makes with a perpendicular to that surface.
incident, *a.* *in*-se-dent, falling on; casual; belonging or appertaining to; naturally occurring: *n.* that which falls out or takes place; an occurrence or event; subordinate action. (Fr.)
incidental, *a.* in-se-*den*-tal, coming without design; not essential; accidental; occasional; naturally connected with.
incidentally, *ad.* in an incidental manner.
incinerate, *v.t.* in-*sin*-er-rate, to burn to ashes: *v.i.* to be consumed by fire. (L. *in-*, and *cinis*, *cineris*, ashes.)
incineration, *n.* in-*sin*-er-*ray*-shon, the act of incinerating; reduction to ashes.
incinerator, *n.* in-*sin*-er-ray-tor, a furnace for incinerating or cremating; an iron basket for burning garden refuse; one who incinerates.
incipience, *n.* in-*sip*-e-ence, the state or fact of being incipient; commencement.
incipient, *a.* in-*sip*-e-ent, in the early stages; beginning to appear. (L. *incipiens*, beginning.)
incipiently, *ad.* in a way of commencing.
incircle, *v.t.* in-*ser*-kl, to encircle.
incise, *v.t.* in-*syz*, to cut in; to engrave; to scribe. (Fr. *inciser.*)
incised, *a.* in-*syzd*, cut; made by a cut; regularly and deeply notched [Bot. and Zool.].
incisiform, *a.* in-*sy*-se-form, resembling an incisor; shaped for cutting.
incision, *n.* in-*sizh*-on, the act of incising; a cut; a gash; pointed or trenchant expressiveness. (Fr.)
incisive, *a.* in-*sy*-siv, having the quality of cutting sharply into; trenchant; penetrating.
incisor, *n.* in-*sy*-zor, a tooth adapted for cutting, esp. any of the three between the canine teeth in both jaws of mammals.
incisorial, *a.* in-sy-*zaw*-re-al, incisory; sharp; incisive.
incisory, *a.* in-*sy*-zo-re, adapted for cutting.
incisure, *n.* in-*sy*-zewr, a deep cut or notch; an incision. (L. *incisura.*)
incitant, *n.* in-*sy*-tant, that which incites; a stimulant: *a.* exciting.
incitation, *n.* in-se-*tay*-shon, the act of inciting; incitement; instigation; motive.
incite, *v.t.* in-*syt*, to move to action; to stir up; to prompt; to stimulate. (Fr. *inciter.*)
incitement, *n.* in-*syt*-ment, that which incites; motive; stimulant.
inciter, *n.* in-*sy*-ter, he who or that which incites.
incitingly, *ad.* in-*sy*-ting-le, in a way to incite.
incivility, *n.* *in*-se-*vil*-e-te, want of courtesy; an act of rudeness or discourtesy. (L. *incivilitas.*)
incivilization, *n.* in-*siv*-e-ly-*zay*-shon, an uncivil condition.
incivism, *n.* *in*-siv-izm, neglect of duty as a citizen; lack of patriotism. (Fr. *incivisme.*)
in-clearing, *n.* *in*-kleer-ing, the amount chargeable to a bank by the clearing-house.
inclemency, *n.* in-*klem*-en-se, want of clemency; harshness; storminess or severity of weather. (L. *inclementia.*)
inclement, *a.* in-*klem*-ent, not clement; harsh; stormy; very boisterous. (L. *inclemens.*)
inclemently, *ad.* in an inclement manner.
inclinable, *a.* in-*klyn*-a-bl, having a tendency; tending; somewhat disposed. (L. *inclinabilis.*)
inclinableness, *n.* favourable disposition.
inclination, *n.* in-kle-*nay*-shon, a leaning or bending towards, esp. downwards; bent, tendency, or proneness; disposition more favourable to one thing than to another; slope; a deviation from the normal; magnetic dip; the angle made by two lines or planes which meet, or would meet if produced [Geom.]. (L. *inclinatio.*)
inclinatorium, *n.* in-kly-na-*taw*-re-um, the dipping needle; an inclinometer.
incline, *n.* *in*-klyn, an inclined plane; a declivity; a slope or gradient.

incline, *v.i.* in-*klyne,* to deviate from an erect or parallel line towards any object; to tend; to have some desire; to be disposed; *v.t.* to cause to deviate from an erect or parallel line; to give a leaning to; to dispose; to cause to bend; to bow. **inclined plane,** a plane at an angle with the plane of the horizon less than a right angle; a sloping plane [Mech.]. (Fr. *incliner.*)
incliner, *n.* in-*klyn*-er, one who or that which inclines; an inclined dial.
inclinometer, *n.* in-klin-*om*-et-er, an instrument for determining magnetic inclination; a clinometer. (L. *inclino,* bend, Gr. *metron,* measure.)
inclose, *v.t.* in-*kloze,* to enclose.
inclosure, *n.* in-*kloze*-yewr, enclosure.
incloud, *v.t.* in-*kloud,* to encloud.
include, *v.t.* in-*klood,* to confine within; to contain; to comprise; to comprehend. (L. *includo,* shut.)
included, *a.* in-*klood*-ed, enclosed; comprised; not projecting [Bot.].
includible, *a.* in-*klood*-e-bl, that may be included.
inclusion, *n.* in-*kloo*-zhon, the act of including; that which is included; a minute foreign body enclosed in a mineral or by solid metal [Min. and Metal.].
inclusive, *a.* in-*kloo*-siv, inclosing; encircling; comprehended in the number or sum.
inclusively, *ad.* in-*kloo*-siv-le, so as to include the thing mentioned.
incoagulable, *a.* *in*-ko-*ag*-yew-la-bl, not coagulable.
incoercible, *a.* in-ko-*er*-se-bl, not to be coerced or restrained; irrepressible.
incog, *ad.* in-*kog,* incognito.
incogitable, *a.* in-*koj*-e-ta-bl, inconceivable. (L.)
incogitant, *a.* in-*koj*-e-tant, not thinking; thoughtless.
incogitative, *a.* in-*koj*-e-ta-tiv, not thinking; lacking the power of thought.
incognita, *n.* in-*kog*-ne-tah, a woman in disguise or unknown. **terra incognita,** *see* **terra.** (It.)
incognito, *ad.* in-*kog*-ne-toh, under an assumed name or a title seldom used; in disguise, so as not to be recognized: *n.* a person disguised or of unknown identity: *a.* unknown; of concealed identity. (It., from L. *in-,* not, and *cognitus,* known.)
incognizable, *a.* in-*kog*-ne-za-bl *or* in-*kon*-ne-za-bl, that cannot be recognized, known, or distinguished.
incognizance, *n.* in-*kog*-ne-zance, want of knowledge; unawareness.
incognizant, *a.* in-*kog*-ne-zant, not having knowledge of; unaware or unconscious of.
incognoscible, *a.* *in*-kog-*nos*-se-bl, unknowable; not cognoscible. (L. *incognoscibilis.*)
incoherence, *n.* in-ko-*heer*-rence, want of coherence or cohesion; want of connexion; incongruity.
incoherency, *n.* *in*-ko-*heer*-ren-se, incoherence.
incoherent, *a.* *in*-ko-*heer*-rent, wanting cohesion; unconnected; incongruous; inconsistent.
incoherently, *ad.* in an incoherent manner.
incoincident, *a.* in-ko-*in*-se-dent, not coinciding; not identical.
incombustibility, *n.* *in*-kom-*bus*-te-*bil*-e-te, the quality of being incombustible.
incombustible, *a.* *in*-kom-*bus*-te-bl, not to be burned, decomposed, or consumed by fire.
incombustibly, *ad.* so as to resist combustion.
income, *n.* *in*-kum, gain, profit, or interest which accrues from labour, business, property, pension, or investment of any kind; revenue; annual receipts. **income tax,** a tax levied annually by the state on all incomes above a certain low level.
incomer, *n.* *in*-kum-mer, a resident who was not born in the district; an immigrant; an intruder; a successor.
incoming, *a.* *in*-kum-ing, coming in, esp. as a tenant or occupier, or as successor; accruing: *n.* arrival; *pl.* income.
incommensurability, *n.* *in*-kom-*men*-sew-ra-*bil*-e-te, quality or state of being incommensurable.
incommensurable, *a.* *in*-kom-*men*-sew-ra-bl, having no common measure; surd [Math.]; not worthy or fit to be measured with.
incommensurably, *ad.* *in*-kom-*men*-sew-ra-ble, so as not to admit of being measured.
incommensurate, *a.* *in*-kom-*men*-sew-rat, inequivalent; not adequate.
incommensurately, *ad.* in-kom-*men*-sew-rat-le, in an incommensurate degree.
incommiscible, *a.* in-kom-*mis*-e-bl, immiscible.
incommode, *v.t.* *in*-kom-*mode,* to cause inconvenience or trouble to; to annoy or disturb. (Fr. *incommoder.*)
incommodious, *a.* *in*-kom-*moh*-de-us, not commodious; inconvenient; incommoding.
incommodiously, *ad.* *in*-kom-*moh*-de-us-le, in an incommodious manner.
incommodiousness, *n.* *in*-kom-*moh*-de-us-ness, the state of being incommodious.
incommodity, *n.* *in*-kom-*mod*-e-te, inconvenience; incommodiousness; a cause of this.
incommunicability, *n.* *in*-kom-*mew*-ne-ka-*bil*-e-te, the quality of not being communicable.
incommunicable, *a.* *in*-kom-*mew*-ne-ka-bl, that cannot be communicated or imparted to others.
incommunicably, *ad.* *in*-kom-*mew*-ne-ka-ble, in a manner not to be communicated.
incommunicado, *a.* *in*-kom-mew-ne-*kah*-do, in solitary confinement. (Sp., without means of communication.)
incommunicative, *a.* *in*-kom-*mew*-ne-ka-tiv, not communicative; not disposed to social intercourse.
incommunicatively, *ad.* in-kom-*mew*-ne-ka-tiv-le, in an incommunicative manner.
incommutability, *n.* *in*-kom-*mew*-ta-*bil*-e-te, the quality of being incommutable.
incommutable, *a.* *in*-kom-*mew*-ta-bl, not capable of being commuted or exchanged.
incommutably, *ad.* without reciprocal change.
incompact, *a.* *in*-kom-*pakt,* not compact; not solid.
incomparable, *a.* in-*kom*-pa-ra-bl, not to be compared with; peerless; matchless.
incomparableness, *n.* in-*kom*-pa-ra-bl-ness, excellence beyond comparison.
incomparably, *ad.* beyond comparison.
incompatibility, *n.* *in*-kom-*pat*-e-*bil*-e-te, the quality or state of being incompatible.
incompatible, *a.* *in*-kom-*pat*-e-bl, not compatible; that cannot subsist with something else; incongruous; inconsistent: *n.* one who or that which is incompatible, esp. [Chem.] a substance which, in solution with another, involves mutual decomposition.
incompatibleness, *n.* incompatibility.
incompatibly, *ad.* so as to be incompatible.
incompetence, *n.* in-*kom*-pe-tence, want of sufficient power or authority; want of adequate means, knowledge, or qualification; inability.
incompetency, *n.* in-*kom*-pe-ten-se, incompetence.
incompetent, *a.* in-*kom*-pe-tent, wanting adequate power or authority; incapable; wanting the legal or constitutional qualifications. (L. *incompetens.*)
incompetently, *ad.* in an incompetent manner.
incomplete, *a.* *in*-kom-*pleet,* not complete; imperfect. **incomplete flower,** a flower lacking either the calyx or corolla, or both. (L. *incompletus.*)
incompletely, *ad.* in an incomplete manner.
incompleteness, *n.* an unfinished state.
incompletion, *n.* *in*-kom-*plee*-shon, want of completion; incompleteness.
incomplex, *a.* in-kom-*pleks or* in-*kom*-pleks, simple; uncompounded.
incompliance, *n.* in-kom-*ply*-ance, indisposition to comply.
incompliant, *a.* *in*-kom-*ply*-ant, unyielding to request or solicitation; not disposed to comply.
incomposite, *a.* in-*kom*-po-zite, not composite; simple. **incomposite number,** a prime number.
incompossible, *a.* *in*-kom-*pos*-se-bl, not possible to be or subsist with something else; logically incompatible.
incomprehensibility, *n.* in-*kom*-pre-*hen*-se-*bil*-e-te, inconceivableness; boundlessness.
incomprehensible, *a.* in-*kom*-pre-hen-se-bl, boundless; that cannot be comprehended or understood; inconceivable. (L. *incomprehensibilis.*)
incomprehensibleness, *n.* incomprehensibility.
incomprehensibly, *ad.* inconceivably.
incomprehension, *n.* in-*kom*-pre-*hen*-shon, failure to understand.
incomprehensive, *a.* in-kom-pre-*hen*-siv, not comprehensive.
incompressibility, *n.* *in*-kom-*pres*-e-*bil*-e-te, the quality or power of resisting compression.
incompressible, *a.* *in*-kom-*pres*-e-bl, incapable of compression; unsqueezable.
incomputable, *a.* *in*-kom-*pew*-ta-bl, incalculable.
inconceivability, *n.* in-kon-*seev*-a-*bil*-e-te, inconceivableness; something that is inconceivable.

inconceivable, *a.* in-kon-*seev*-a-bl, incomprehensible; unimaginable; incredible [Coll.].
inconceivableness, *n.* in-kon-*seev*-a-bl-ness, the quality of being inconceivable.
inconceivably, *ad.* in-kon-*seev*-a-ble, in a manner beyond comprehension.
inconcinnity, *n.* in-kon-*sin*-ne-te, lack of concinnity; incongruity: unsuitableness.
inconclusive, *a.* *in*-kon-*kloo*-siv, not conclusive; not producing a conclusion; not settling a point in debate.
inconclusively, *ad.* in an inconclusive manner.
inconclusiveness, *n.* *in*-kon-*kloo*-siv-ness, the state of being inconclusive.
incondensability, *n.* in-kon-*dense*-a-*bil*-e-te, the quality of not being condensable.
incondensable, *a.* *in*-kon-*dense*-a-bl, not condensable.
incondite, *a.* in-*kon*-dite, ill-arranged; confused; crude. (L. *inconditus*, uncreated.)
inconformable, *a.* in-kon-*for*-ma-ble, not conformable; indisposed to conformity.
inconformity, *n.* *in*-kon-*for*-me-te, want of conformity; nonconformity; unconformity.
incongealable, *a.* *in*-kon-*jeel*-a-bl, not congealable.
incongruence, *n.* in-*kong*-groo-ence, incongruity.
incongruent, *a.* in-*kong*-groo-ent, incongruous.
incongruity, *n.* *in*-kong-*groo*-e-te, want of congruity; inconsistency; inharmony; unsuitableness.
incongruous, *a.* in-*kong*-groo-us, not congruous; unsuitable; inconsistent. (L. *incongruus.*)
incongruously, *ad.* in an incongruous manner.
incongruousness, *n.* the equality of being incongruous; incongruity.
inconscient, *a.* in-*kon*-shent, not conscious; done unconsciously.
inconsecutive, *a.* in-kon-*sek*-yew-tiv, not consecutive; inconsequent.
inconsequence, *n.* in-*kon*-se-kwence, quality or condition of being inconsequent; irrelevance; lack of logical sequence.
inconsequent, *a.* in-*kon*-se-kwent, not following from the premises; disconnected; illogical.
inconsequential, *a.* in-*kon*-se-*kwen*-shal, not regularly following from the premises; not of importance; of no consequence.
inconsequentiality, *n.* in-*kon*-se-*kwen*-she-*al*-e-te, state of being inconsequential.
inconsequentially, *ad.* in-*kon*-se-*kwen*-she-al-le, without logical sequence.
inconsiderable, *a.* *in*-kon-*sid*-er-ra-bl, not worthy of consideration; unimportant; insignificant; trivial.
inconsiderableness, *n.* quality of being inconsiderable; trivial amount; small importance.
inconsiderably, *ad.* *in*-kon-*sid*-er-ra-ble, in a small degree; to a small amount.
inconsiderate, *a.* *in*-kon-*sid*-er-rat, not considerate; thoughtless; incautious; inattentive.
inconsiderately, *ad.* *in*-kon-*sid*-er-rat-le, in an inconsiderate manner.
inconsiderateness, *n.* inconsideration; the quality of being inconsiderate.
inconsideration, *n.* *in*-kon-*sid*-er-*ray*-shon, want of due consideration or thought; inattention to consequences.
inconsistency, *n.* *in*-kon-*sis*-ten-se, the state of being inconsistent; an instance of inconsistent action, or character, etc.
inconsistent, *a.* *in*-kon-*sis*-tent, not consistent; not congruous; incompatible; self-contradictory; not uniform.
inconsistently, *ad.* in an inconsistent manner.
inconsolable, *a.* *in*-kon-*sole*-a-bl, not to be consoled; disconsolate. (L. *inconsolabilis.*)
inconsolably, *ad.* *in*-kon-*sole*-a-ble, in a manner or degree that does not admit of consolation.
inconsonance, *n.* in-*kon*-so-nance, disagreement; discordance.
inconsonant, *a.* in-*kon*-so-nant, not consonant with; disagreeing; disagreeing; discordant.
inconsonantly, *ad.* not consonantly.
inconspicuous, *a.* *in*-kon-*spik*-yew-us, not conspicuous; hardly or not clearly discernible.
inconspicuously, *ad.* *in*-kon-*spik*-yew-us-le, so as not to be clearly discerned.
inconspicuousness, *n.* in-kon-*spik*-yew-us-ness, the quality or condition of being inconspicuous.
inconstancy, *n.* in-*kon*-stan-se, the quality of being inconstant; fickleness.
inconstant, *a.* in-*kon*-stant, subject or prone to change; fickle; changeable. (Fr.)
inconstantly, *ad.* in an inconstant manner.
inconsumable, *a.* *in*-kon-*sew*-ma-bl, that cannot be consumed; not intended for consumption; indestructible.
inconsumably, *ad.* so as not to be consumable.
incontaminate, *a.* in-kon-*tam*-e-nate, not contaminated; undefiled.
incontestable, *a.* *in*-kon-*tes*-ta-bl, not admitting of question; undeniable.
incontestably, *ad.* in an incontestable manner.
incontinence, *n.* in-*kon*-te-nence, the state of being incontinent; want of self-restraint; inability to restrain discharges or evacuations [Med.]. (Fr.)
incontinent, *a.* in-*kon*-te-nent, not restraining the passions or appetites; unchaste; unable to restrain discharges [Med.]: *n.* one who is unchaste: *ad.* at once; forthwith.
incontinently, *ad.* in-*kon*-te-nent-le, in an incontinent manner; at once; immediately.
incontinuity, *n.* *in*-kon-te-*new*-e-te, lack of continuity.
incontrollable, *a.* *in*-kon-*trole*-a-bl, not controllable.
incontrollably, *ad.* *in*-kon-*trole*-a-ble, in a manner that admits of no control.
incontrovertible, *a.* in-*kon*-tro-*ver*-te-bl, too clear or certain to admit of dispute.
incontrovertibly, *ad.* in-*kon*-tro-*ver*-te-ble, in a manner that precludes controversy.
inconvenience, *n.* *in*-kon-*vee*-nyence, the being inconvenient; want of convenience; that which inconveniences: *v.t.* to put to inconvenience; to incommode; to trouble.
inconvenient, *a.* *in*-kon-*vee*-nyent, causing trouble or embarrassment; unseasonable; incommodious; unsuitable; unfit.
inconveniently, *ad.* in an inconvenient manner.
inconvertibility, *n.* *in*-kon-ver-te-*bil*-e-te, quality of not being convertible into something else.
inconvertible, *a.* *in*-kon-*ver*-te-bl, not convertible; not exchangeable for coin.
inconvincible, *a.* *in*-kon-*vince*-e-bl, not convincible.
incoordination, *n.* *in*-ko-*or*-de-*nay*-shon, want of coordination, esp. in regard to muscular movements.
incorporable, *a.* in-*kor*-po-ra-bl, capable of being incorporated.
incorporate, *a.* in-*kor*-po-rate, made into a corporation; united as a single body; closely united: *v.t.* to form or combine into one body or mass; to unite; to embody; to form into a body politic or corporation: *v.i.* to become united so as to make a part of another body; to be mixed or blended. (L. *incorporatus*, united to.)
incorporation, *n.* in-*kor*-po-*ray*-shon, the act of incorporating; the state of being incorporated; intimate union; embodiment; formation or association in a body politic or a corporate body; a corporation.
incorporative, *a.* in-*kor*-po-ra-tiv, incorporating or tending to incorporate; running a number of words into one so as to form a sentence.
incorporeal, *a.* *in*-kor-*paw*-re-al, not in a body or bodily form; immaterial.
incorporeality, *n.* in-kor-*paw*-re-*al*-e-te, incorporeity.
incorporeally, *ad.* in-kor-*paw*-re-a-le, without body; immaterially.
incorporeity, *n.* in-*kor*-paw-*ree*-e-te, the quality of being incorporeal; immateriality.
incorrect, *a.* *in*-ko-*rekt*, not correct; inaccurate; not according to copy, fact, or rule; indecorous.
incorrectly, *ad.* *in*-ko-*rekt*-le, not correctly.
incorrectness, *n.* *in*-ko-*rekt*-ness, the state or fact of being incorrect.
incorrigibility, *n.* in-*ko*-re-je-*bil*-e-te, the state or quality of being incorrigible.
incorrigible, *a.* in-*ko*-re-je-bl, that cannot be corrected or amended; too depraved to be reformed; *n.* an incorrigible person.
incorrigibleness, *n.* the quality of being incorrigible.
incorrigibly, *ad.* to an incorrigible degree.
incorrodible, *a.* *in*-ko-*roh*-de-bl, that cannot be corroded.

incorrupt, *a.* *in*-ko-*rupt*, not corrupt; sound; untainted; above being bribed.
incorruptibility, *n.* *in*-ko-*rup*-te-*bil*-e-te, the quality of being incapable of corruption.
incorruptible, *a.* *in*-ko-*rup*-te-bl, incapable of corruption; that cannot be bribed; inflexibly just.
incorruptibly, *ad.* to an incorruptible degree.
incorruption, *n.* *in*-ko-*rup*-shon, incapability of being corrupted; freedom from corruption.
incorruptness, *n.* *in*-ko-*rupt*-ness, exemption from decay or corruption; integrity; honesty.
incrassate, *a.* in-*kras*-sate, made thick or thicker; fattened; thickened toward the flower [Bot.]: *v.t.* to make thick; to inspissate [Pharm.]. (L. *incrassatus*, made thick.)
incrassation, *n.* *in*-kras-*say*-shon, the act of thickening; a thickened formation.
increasable, *a.* in-*krees*-a-bl, susceptible of increase; that may be increased.
increase, *v.i.* in-*krees*, to become greater; to grow; to advance; to multiply: *v.t.* to make greater; to add; to extend; to intensify; to aggravate. (O.Fr. *encreistre.*)
★**increase,** *n.* *in*-krees, augmentation; growth; increment; profit; produce; progeny.
increasingly, *ad.* in-*krees*-ing-le, growingly.
increate, *a.* *in*-kre-at, uncreated; divine.
increative, *a.* in-kre-*ay*-tiv, incapable of creating.
incredibility, *n.* in-*kred*-e-*bil*-e-te, the quality of being incredible; an unbelievable statement, etc.
incredible, *a.* in-*kred*-e-bl, not credible; passing belief; marvellous.
incredibleness, *n.* in-*kred*-e-bl-ness, incredibility.
incredibly, *ad.* in an incredible manner.
incredulity, *n.* in-kre-*dew*-le-te, the quality of being incredulous; scepticism; indisposition to believe.
incredulous, *a.* in-*kred*-yew-lus, not disposed to believe; sceptical. (L. *incredulus.*)
incredulously, *ad.* with incredulity.
incredulousness, *n.* in-*kred*-yew-lus-ness, the quality or state of being incredulous.
increment, *n.* *in*-kre-ment, the act of increasing; augmentation; that by which a thing is increased; increase; the finite increase of a variable quantity [Math.]. (L. *incrementum.*)
incremental, *a.* in-kre-*men*-tal, pertaining to or resulting from increase or increment.
increscent, *a.* in-*kres*-sent, increasing; growing; in the shape of the moon in its first quarter.
incriminate, *v.t.* in-*krim*-e-nate, to charge with crime; to involve in a criminal charge. (Late L. *incriminatus.*)
incrimination, *n.* in-*krim*-e-*nay*-shon, the act of incriminating or condition of being incriminated.
incriminatory, *a.* in-*krim*-e-na-to-re, tending to incriminate.
incrust, *v.t.* in-*krust*, to encrust. (L. *incrusto.*)
incrustation, *n.* in-krus-*tay*-shon, the act of incrusting; the state of being incrusted; a crust or coat of anything on a surface; a covering or inlaying of marble, mosaic, or other substance.
incubate, *v.i.* *in*-kew-bate, to sit, as on eggs, for hatching. (L. *incubatus*, hatched.)
incubation, *n.* in-kew-*bay*-shon, the act of incubating or hatching; brooding; the period between infection and the first symptoms of a disease [Med.].
incubator, *n.* *in*-kew-bay-tor, an apparatus for hatching eggs by artificial means; an apparatus for the development of bacteria, etc.
incubous, *a.* *in*-kew-bus, with the leaf imbricated over the one above [Bot.]. (L. *incubo*, lie upon.)
incubus, *n.* *in*-kew-bus (*pl.* **incubi**), the oppression of nightmare; a demon fabled to cause oppression; anything that oppresses like a nightmare; an incumbrance. (L.)
inculcate, *v.t.* *in*-kul-kate, to impress or enforce by frequent repetition. (L. *inculcatus*, rammed down.)
inculcation, *n.* in-kul-*kay*-shon, the action of inculcating.
inculcator, *n.* *in*-kul-kay-tor, one who inculcates.
inculpable, *a.* in-*kul*-pa-bl, not blameworthy; innocent.
inculpate, *v.t.* *in*-kul-pate, to blame; to censure; to incriminate. (L. *inculpatus.*)
inculpation, *n.* *in*-kul-*pay*-shon, the act of inculpating; blame; censure.
inculpatory, *a.* in-*kul*-pa-to-re, imputing blame.
incult, *a.* in-*kult*, uncultivated; lacking culture or refinement.
incumbency, *n.* in-*kum*-ben-se, the state of being incumbent; the holding of an office, or the possession of a benefice; the period of this.
incumbent, *a.* in-*kum*-bent, lying or resting on; lying on, as a duty; so disposed as to lie one over the other (of anthers) [Bot.]; lying folded along the body (of the wings of insects) [Entom.]: *n.* the person in present possession of a benefice or of an office. (L. *incumbens*, lying down.)
incumbrance, *n.* in-*kum*-brance, encumbrance.
incunable, *n.* in-*kew*-na-bl, a single specimen of incunabula.
incunabula, *n.pl.* *in*-kew-*nab*-yew-la, examples of books printed in the infancy of printing, prior generally to 1500. (L., swaddling clothes.)
incur, *v.t.* in-*kur*, to become liable for; to bring upon oneself [Law]. (L. *incurro*, run into.)
incurability, *n.* in-*kewr*-ra-*bil*-e-te, the state of being incurable; impossibility of cure.
incurable, *a.* in-*kewr*-ra-bl, that cannot be cured; irremediable: *n.* one beyond cure. (L. *incurabilis.*)
incurableness, *n.* in-*kewr*-ra-bl-ness, the state of being incurable.
incurably, *ad.* in an incurable manner or degree.
incuriosity, *n.* in-*kewr*-re-*os*-e-te, want of curiosity.
incurious, *a.* in-*kewr*-re-us, not curious to know. (L. *incuriosus.*)
incuriously, *ad.* without inquisitiveness.
incuriousness, *n.* want of curiosity.
incurrable, *a.* in-*kur*-ra-bl, that may be incurred.
incurrence, *n.* in-*ku*-rence, the act or fact of incurring.
incursion, *n.* in-*kur*-shon, a hostile irruption or inroad. (L. *incursio.*)
incursive, *a.* in-*kur*-siv, making incursions.
incurvate, *a.* in-*kur*-vat, curved inward or upward: *v.t.* to cause to turn from a straight line. (L. *incurvatus*, bent.)
incurvation, *n.* *in*-kur-*vay*-shon, the act or process of incurvating; the state of being incurvated; crookedness. (L. *incurvatio.*)
incurvature, *n.* in-*kur*-va-tewr, incurvation.
incurve, *v.t.* in-*kurv*, to cause to bend inwards; to make crooked. (L. *incurvo.*)
incurvity, *n.* in-*kur*-ve-te, state of being bent.
incus, *n.* *in*-kus, the ossicle of the middle ear that receives vibrations from the malleus. (L., an anvil.)
incuse, *v.t.* in-*kewz*, to impress a coin with a hammer or a die: *n.* a stamped or hammered impression: *a.* stamped or hammered in. (L. *incusus*, forged.)
incut, *n.* *in*-kut, a block inserted in a page in the space left for it.
indaba, *n.* in-*dah*-ba, a tribal council or conference of, or with, S. African natives. (Bantu, an affair.)
indagate, *v.t.* *in*-da-gate, to investigate; to search out. (L. *indagatus.*)
indebted, *a.* in-*det*-ted, in debt; under obligation.
indebtedness, *n.* in-*det*-ted-ness, the state of being indebted.
indecency, *n.* in-*dee*-sen-se, the state of being indecent; an immodest or obscene action or expression. (Fr. *indécence.*)
indecent, *a.* in-*dee*-sent, not decent; unbecoming; offensive to morals or to modesty; obscene.
indecently, *ad.* in-*dee*-sent-le, in a manner to offend decency.
indeciduate, *a.* *in*-de-*sid*-yew-ate, not deciduate [Zool.].
indeciduous, *a.* *in*-de-*sid*-yew-us, not falling, as leaves in autumn; evergreen [Bot.].
indecipherable, *a.* in-de-*sy*-fer-ra-bl, not decipherable; illegible.
indecision, *n.* *in*-de-*sizh*-on, want of decision; irresolution.
indecisive, *a.* *in*-de-*sy*-siv, not decisive; wavering.
indecisively, *ad.* in an indecisive manner.
indecisiveness, *n.* the state of being undecided.
indeclinable, *a.* in-de-*kly*-na-bl, having no inflexion; not varied by inflexion: *n.* an indeclinable word [Gram.]. (L. *indeclinabilis.*)
indeclinably, *ad.* in an indeclinable manner.
indecomposable, *a.* *in*-de-kom-*poze*-a-bl, incapable of decomposition.
indecorous, *a.* in-de-*kaw*-rus, in violation of good manners; unbecoming. (L. *indecorus.*)
indecorously, *ad.* in an indecorous manner.
indecorousness, *n.* quality of being indecorous.

indecorum, *n.* in-de-*kaw*-rum, want or violation of decorum or propriety; an indecorous act. (L.)

indeed, *ad.* in-*deed*, in reality; in truth; in fact: *int.* of surprise.

indefatigability, *n.* *in*-de-*fat*-e-ga-*bil*-e-te, a being indefatigable; unweariedness; persistency.

indefatigable, *a.* in-de-*fat*-e-ga-bl, not yielding to fatigue; unwearied. (L. *indefatigabilis.*)

indefatigableness, *n.* indefatigability.

indefatigably, *ad.* in an indefatigable manner.

indefeasibility, *n.* *in*-de-*fee*-ze-*bil*-e-te, the state of being indefeasible.

indefeasible, *a.* *in*-de-*fee*-ze-bl, that cannot be defeated, forfeited, or made void.

indefeasibly, *ad.* in an indefeasible manner.

indefectible, *a.* *in*-de-*fek*-te-bl, not liable to defect, failure, or decay; unfailing.

indefensibility, *n.* *in*-de-*fen*-se-*bil*-e-te, the quality or state of not being defensible.

indefensible, *a.* *in*-de-*fen*-se-bl, that cannot be defended or justified.

indefensibly, *ad.* in an indefensible manner.

indefinable, *a.* *in*-de-*fine*-a-bl, that cannot be defined.

indefinably, *ad.* so as not to be definable.

indefinite, *a.* in-*def*-e-nit, not defined or determinate; not precise or certain; that has no determinate or certain limits [Math.]; not defining or determining [Gram.]; not constant in number (of stamens) [Bot.]. (L. *indefinitus.*)

indefinitely, *ad.* in an indefinite manner.

indefiniteness, *n.* quality of being indefinite.

indefinitude, *n.* *in*-de-*fin*-e-tewd, indefiniteness.

indehiscent, *a.* *in*-de-*his*-sent, not dehiscent; not opening spontaneously when ripe [Bot.].

indeliberate, *a.* in-de-*lib*-er-rat, unpremeditated; not thought out beforehand.

indelibility, *n.* in-*del*-e-*bil*-e-te, the quality of being indelible.

indelible, *a.* in-*del*-e-bl, not to be blotted out or effaced. (L. *indelebilis.*)

indelibly, *ad.* in-*del*-e-ble, in an indelible manner.

indelicacy, *n.* in-*del*-e-ka-se, want of delicacy; coarseness of manners or language.

indelicate, *a.* in-*del*-e-kat, not delicate; offensive to modesty, propriety, or decency.

indelicately, *ad.* in an indelicate manner.

indemnification, *n.* in-*dem*-ne-fe-*kay*-shon, the act of indemnifying; that which indemnifies.

indemnify, *v.t.* in-*dem*-ne-fy, to secure against loss, damage, or penalty; to compensate for loss or injury sustained. (L. *indemnis*, uninjured.)

indemnitee, *n.* in-dem-ne-*tee*, one who receives an indemnity.

indemnitor, *n.* in-*dem*-ne-tor, an indemnifier.

indemnity, *n.* in-*dem*-ne-te, a contract against loss, damage, or penalty; indemnification or compensation for loss or injury. (Fr. *indemnité.*)

indemonstrable, *a.* *in*-de-*mon*-stra-bl, that cannot be proved. (L. *indemonstrabilis.*)

indent, *n.* *in*-dent, a notch in the margin of anything; an indentation; an indenture; an official requisition; an order for goods, supplies, etc.: *v.t.* in-*dent*, to notch; to cut on the edge into points like teeth; to bind by indenture; to begin further in from the margin than the rest of a paragraph [Print.]; to make a requisition or give an order for: *v.i.* to be notched; to run in and out; to make an indent or order. (Fr. *endenter.*)

indentation, *n.* in-den-*tay*-shon, a notching; a notch in a margin; a recess or depression in any border; a zigzag edge or moulding.

indented, *a.* in-*den*-ted, cut on the edge into points like teeth; serrated [Her.]; bound by indenture.

indenter, *n.* *in*-den-ter, a machine or appliance for indenting.

indention, *n.* in-*den*-shon, indentation; the indenting of a line, or the space so left. [Print.].

indentor, *n.* in-*den*-tor, one who indents.

indenture, *n.* in-*den*-tewr, a writing containing a contract, so called from the two copies being originally indented, so as to correspond with each other; a deed made by two or more parties; an indentation: *v.t.* to indent; to bind by indentures.

independence, *n.* in-de-*pen*-dence, the quality or state of being independent of others; that which enables one to be independent; adequate income. **Independence Day,** the anniversary of the American Declaration of Independence, July 4, 1776, kept as a legal holiday in U.S.A.

independency, *n.* in-de-*pen*-den-se, independence; the doctrines of the Congregationalists or Independents.

independent, *a.* in-de-*pen*-dent, not dependent; not subject to the control of others; not subordinate not holding possessions at the will of another; affording the means of independence; not subject to influence; not obsequious; free; unconstrained; irrespective: *n.* one who is independent; (*cap.*) a member of a Congregational or other Christian church which is subject to no superior authority.

independently, *ad.* *in*-de-*pen*-dent-le, in an independent manner.

indescribable, *a.* *in*-des-*kry*-ba-bl, that cannot be described.

indesignate, *a.* in-*dez*-ig-nate, with no indication of quantity; not quantified [Logic].

indestructibility, *n.* *in*-de-*struk*-te-*bil*-e-te, the quality of being indestructible.

indestructible, *a.* *in*-de-*struk*-te-bl, not capable of being destroyed.

indestructibly, *ad.* in an indestructible manner.

indeterminable, *a.* *in*-de-*term*-e-na-bl, that cannot be determined or defined; that does not terminate.

indeterminably, *ad.* *in*-de-*term*-e-na-ble, in an indeterminable manner.

indeterminate, *a.* *in*-de-*term*-e-nate, not precise; not fixed; uncertain; having no fixed value [Math.].

indeterminately, *ad.* *in*-de-*term*-e-nate-le, in an indeterminate manner; indefinitely.

indeterminateness, *n.* *in*-de-*term*-e-nate-ness, the state or quality of being indeterminate.

indetermination, *n.* *in*-de-*term*-e-*nay*-shon, want of determination; wavering; vacillation.

indetermined, *a.* *in*-de-*ter*-mind, not determined.

indeterminism, *n.* *in*-de-*ter*-me-nizm, the doctrine that human action does not entirely depend on motives and that the will is free to choose between motives.

indevotion, *n.* *in*-de-*voh*-shon, want of devotion.

indevout, *a.* in-de-*vout*, not devout; undevout.

index, *n.* *in*-deks (*pl.* **indexes,** *in*-dek-sez, *or* [Math. and Science] **indices,** *in*-de-seez), that which points out, manifests, or indicates; the hand (of timepiece, etc.) or pointer that points to anything; a gnomon; an alphabetical table of contents giving page numbers; the forefinger or pointing finger [Anat.]; the exponent of a power [Math.]; a ratio between the dimensions of an object, esp. of the skull: *v.t.* to provide with an index; to put in the Index. **the Index,** the list of books the reading of which by its members is either forbidden or restricted by the Holy Office of the Roman Catholic Church. **index of a logarithm,** the integral part of the logarithm; the characteristic. **index of refraction,** the number that expresses the ratio of the sines of the angles of incidence and refraction [Opt.]. **index number,** a percentage, used esp. in statistical comparison of prices, etc. at different times. (L., from *indico*, point out.)

indexer, *n.* *in*-deks-er, one who makes an index.

indexical, *a.* in-*dek*-se-kal, pertaining to or like an index.

Indiaman, *n.* *in*-de-a-mn, a large ship employed in trade with India; formerly, one belonging to the East India Company.

Indian, *a.* *in*-de-an, pertaining to either of the Indies, East or West, or to the aborigines of America: *n.* a native of the East or West Indies, or an aboriginal of America. **Indian berry,** the East Indian evergreen twining shrub *Anamirta cocculus.* **Indian club,** a wooden club used in physical drill. **Indian corn,** maize. **Indian cress,** the nasturtium, a plant of the genus *Tropæolum.* **Indian date,** the tamarind. **Indian fig,** the prickly pear, also the banyan tree. **Indian file,** single file. **Indian ink,** a substance made of lampblack and animal glue, formerly brought chiefly from the Far East, used for water-colours and line-drawing. **Indian madder,** *Rubia cordifolia,* of the East Indies, much used in dyeing. **Indian red,** a species of ochre; a yellowish-red pigment or colour. **Indian reed,** the *Canna indica.* **Indian summer,** a summer-like

spell in late autumn, esp. in the northern United States. **Indian tobacco,** a species of *Lobelia* furnishing an antispasmodic; hemp. **Indian weed,** tobacco. **Indian yam,** a tropical American yam, *Dioscorea trifida.* **Indian yellow,** purree.
indianite, *n.* *in*-de-a-nite, a grey variety of anorthite occurring in the Carnatic, India.
Indianize, *v.t.* *in*-de-a-nize, to make Indian in character, etc.
Indianization, *n.* *in*-de-a-ny-*zay*-shon, the act, process, or policy of Indianizing.
india-paper, *n.* *in*-de-a-*pay*-per, a fine, originally Chinese, paper, used by engravers; a thin, tough, and opaque printing-paper.
india-rubber, *n.* *in*-de-a-*rub*-ber, caoutchouc; rubber; a milky coagulated exudation obtained from a number of tropical trees.
indicant, *a.* and *n.* *in*-de-kant, pointing out, or that which points out (used esp. of a remedy to a disease). (L. *indicans,* pointing out.)
indicate, *v.t.* *in*-de-kate, to point out; to show; to mark out; to suggest; to point to as the remedy [Med.]. (L. *indicatus.*)
indication, *n.* *in*-de-*kay*-shon, the act of pointing out; that which points out; symptom in a disease which serves to direct to suitable remedies [Med.].
indicative, *a.* in-*dik*-a-tiv, pointing out, as a sign or intimation: *n.* the indicative mood. **indicative mood,** the form of the verb that affirms, denies, or interrogates, as regards matters of fact.
indicatively, *ad.* in an indicative manner.
indicator, *n.* *in*-de-kay-tor, he who or that which points out or indicates; a pressure gauge; an apparatus showing the working of steam in the cylinder or for measuring pressure in the cylinders of an internal-combustion engine; a registering dial; a substance indicating by colour change the presence of an alkali or acid, etc. [Chem.].
indicatory, *a.* *in*-de-*kay*-to-re, serving to indicate.
indicial, *a.* in-*dish*-al, of the nature of an indication, or of an index.
indicolite, *n.* in-*dik*-o-lite, an indigo-blue variety of tourmaline. (*indigo,* and Gr. *lithos,* a stone.)
indict, *v.t.* in-*dite,* to charge with a crime or misdemeanour, esp. by means of an indictment. (Fr. *indite.*)
indictable, *a.* in-*dite*-a-bl, that may be indicted; that exposes to indictment.
indictee, *n.* in-dy-*tee,* a person who is indicted.
indicter, *n.* in-*dite*-er, one who indicts.
indiction, *n.* in-*dik*-shon, declaration; proclamation; a cycle of fifteen years, instituted for fiscal purposes by Constantine the Great as from Sept. 1, 312, and used throughout the Middle Ages as a period in chronology; a Roman imperial land-tax imposed at the opening of each of these periods. (L. *indictio,* an impost.)
indictive, *a.* in-*dik*-tiv, proclaimed; declared.
indictment, *n.* in-*dite*-ment, the act of indicting; a written accusation; formal charge of a crime or misdemeanour, preferred by a grand jury under oath to a court; the document containing this.
indifference, *n.* in-*dif*-e-rence, the state of being indifferent; unconcern; freedom from prepossession or bias; state in which there is no difference; mediocrity; inferior quality.
indifferent, *a.* in-*dif*-e-rent, neutral; impartial; unconcerned; of no importance; of no account; of rather inferior quality. (O.Fr.)
indifferentism, *n.* in-*dif*-e-ren-tizm, state of indifference; the tenets of those who are indifferent in matters of religion.
indifferentist, *n.* in-*dif*-e-ren-tist, one who professes indifferentism.
indifferently, *ad.* in an indifferent manner.
indigenal, *a.* in-*dij*-e-nal, indigenous: *n.* an indigene.
indigence, *n.* *in*-de-jence, state of being indigent; extreme poverty. (Fr.)
indigency, *n.* *in*-de-jen-se, indigence.
indigene, *n.* *in*-de-jene, one native-born; a native animal or plant. (Fr. *indigène.*)
indigenous, *a.* in-*dij*-e-nus, native; not exotic. (L. *indigenus.*)
indigent, *a.* *in*-de-jent, in need; destitute of means of subsistence. (Fr.)
indigently, *ad.* *in*-de-jent-le, with indigence.
indigested, *a.* in-de-*jes*-ted, not digested; not arranged in due order; crude.

indigestible, *a.* in-de-*jes*-te-bl, not digestible; not to be received or patiently endured.
indigestibly, *ad.* in-de-*jes*-te-ble, not digestibly.
indigestion, *n.* in-de-*jes*-tyon, want of digestion or due digestive power; dyspepsia; the state of being crude or unorganized. (L. *indigestio.*)
indign, *a.* in-*dine,* unworthy; despicable.
indignant, *a.* in-*dig*-nant, affected with anger and scorn; exasperated, esp. by wrong or injustice. (L. *indignans,* being indignant.)
indignantly, *ad.* in-*dig*-nant-le, with indignation.
indignation, *n.* *in*-dig-*nay*-shon, scorn at base or unworthy conduct; anger, mingled with contempt and abhorrence.
indignity, *n.* in-*dig*-ne-te, unmerited contumely; an act of incivility with insult.
indigo, *n.* *in*-de-go, a deep-blue dye, prepared chiefly synthetically but formerly from the leaves and stalks of the indigo plant. (Sp.)
indigotic, *a.* in-de-*got*-ik, pertaining to or of the colour of indigo.
indigotin, *n.* in-*dig*-o-tin, indigo blue, the essential colouring principle of indigo [Chem.].
indirect, *a.* in-dy-*rekt,* not direct or straight; not tending directly to the point; not straightforward; not fair or honest. **indirect tax,** a tax paid directly by one who does not ultimately bear it; a customs or excise tax. (L. *indirectus.*)
indirection, *n.* in-dy-*rek*-shon, indirect course or action; devious means; malpractice.
indirectly, *ad.* in-dy-*rekt*-le, in an indirect manner.
indirectness, *n.* the quality of being indirect.
indiscernible, *a.* in-de-*zern*-e-bl, not discernible: *n.* a thing that cannot be discerned.
indiscernibly, *ad.* in-de-*zern*-e-ble, in a manner not to be discerned or distinguished.
indiscerptibility, *n.* in-dis-*serp*-te-*bil*-e-te, the quality or condition of being indiscerptible.
indiscerptible, *a.* in-dis-*serp*-te-bl, incapable of destruction by separation of parts.
indisciplinable, *a.* in-*dis*-e-plin-a-bl, not capable of discipline, or of being improved by discipline.
indiscipline, *n.* in-*dis*-e-plin, want of discipline.
indiscoverable, *a.* *in*-dis-*kuv*-er-ra-bl, not discoverable.
indiscreet, *a.* *in*-dis-*kreet,* not exercising discretion; injudicious.
indiscreetly, *ad.* *in*-dis-*kreet*-le, not discreetly.
indiscreetness, *n.* *in*-dis-*kreet*-ness, the quality of being indiscreet; indiscretion.
indiscrete, *a.* in-dis-*kreet,* not discrete or separated.
indiscretion, *n.* *in*-dis-*kresh*-on, want of discretion; rashness; an imprudent act.
indiscriminate, *a.* *in*-dis-*krim*-e-nate, not discriminating; withou making any distinction; promiscuous.
indiscriminately, *ad.* without discrimination.
indiscriminating, *a.* *in*-dis-*krim*-e-nay-ting, not making any distinction.
indiscrimination, *n.* *in*-dis-*krim*-e-*nay*-shon, want of discrimination or distinction.
indiscriminative, *a.* *in*-dis-*krim*-e-na-tiv, making no distinction.
indispensability, *n.* *in*-dis-*pense*-a-*bil*-e-te, indispensableness.
indispensable, *a.* *in*-dis-*pense*-a-bl, that cannot be done without.
indispensableness, *n.* *in*-dis-*pense*-a-bl-ness, the state or quality of being indispensable.
indispensably, *ad.* *in*-dis-*pense*-a-ble, necessarily; not to be dispensed with.
indispose, *v.t.* *in*-dis-*pohz,* to disincline; to render indisposed; to render unfit; to make unwell.
indisposed, *a.* *in*-dis-*pohzd,* disinclined; averse; slightly unwell.
indisposition, *n.* in-*dis*-po-*zish*-on, disinclination; aversion; slight illness.
indisputable, *a.* in-*dis*-pew-ta-bl, too evident to admit of dispute.
indisputableness, *n.* in-*dis*-pew-ta-bl-ness, the state or quality of being indisputable.
indisputably, *ad.* in-*dis*-pew-ta-ble, beyond dispute.
indissociable, *a.* *in*-dis-*soh*-she-a-bl, that cannot be separated. (L. *indissociabilis.*)
indissolubility, *n.* in-*dis*-sol-yew-*bil*-e-te, indissolubleness.
indissoluble, *a.* in-*dis*-sol-yew-bl *or* in-de-*sol*-yew-bl, not dissoluble or dissolvable; not violable; always binding. (L. *indissolubilis.*)

indissolubleness, *n.* in-de-*sol*-yew-bl-ness, the state or quality of being indissoluble.
indissolubly, *ad.* in-de-*sol*-yew-ble, in an indissoluble manner.
indissolvable, *a.* *in*-de-*zolv*-a-bl, not dissolvable.
indistinct, *a.* in-dis-*tingkt*, not distinct or clear; not clearly defined. (L. *indistinctus.*)
indistinction, *n.* in-dis-*tingk*-shon, want of distinction; the fact or condition of not being distinguished.
indistinctly, *ad.* in an indistinct manner.
indistinctness, *n.* *in*-dis-*tingkt*-ness, the state or quality of being indistinct.
indistinguishable, *a.* *in*-dis-*ting*-gwish-a-bl, not distinguishable.
indistributable, *a.* in-dis-*trib*-yew-ta-bl, that cannot be distributed.
indite, *v.t.* in-*dite*, to compose; to write down or describe in formal style. (O.Fr. *enditer.*)
inditer, *n.* in-*dite*-er, a writer.
indium, *n.* *in*-de-um, a very rare silver-white malleable metallic element found in small amounts in association with zinc, tungsten, etc., discovered 1863. (L. *indicum*, indigo.)
indivertible, *a.* *in*-de-*vert*-e-bl, not to be turned aside.
individual, *a.* in-de-*vid*-yew-al, subsisting as a distinct, indivisible being; single; one; pertaining to one only: *n.* a single person, animal, or thing; a single as distinct from a compound organism [Biol.]; a person [Coll.]. (L. *in-*, not, *dividuus*, divisible.)
individualism, *n.* in-de-*vid*-yew-al-izm, egoism; idiosyncrasy; individuality; undue attachment to individual interest; a social and political system aiming at the maintenance of personal rights in government, industrial organization, etc., as against authoritarian or communistic State control.
individualist, *n.* in-de-*vid*-yew-a-list, one who acts as an independent individual; an adherent of individualism.
individualistic, *a.* in-de-*vid*-yew-a-*lis*-tik, pertaining to the individual; like, characteristic of, or favouring individualism.
individuality, *n.* in-de-*vid*-yew-*al*-e-te, separate and distinct existence; oneness; distinctness of character.
individualization, *n.* in-de-*vid*-yew-a-ly-*zay*-shon, the act of individualizing; the state of being individualized.
individualize, *v.t.* *in*-de-*vid*-yew-a-lize, to distinguish individually; to connect with an individual.
individually, *ad.* in-de-*vid*-yew-al-le, separately.
individuate, *v.t.* *in*-de-*vid*-yew-ate, to make individual in character; to distinguish individually.
individuation, *n.* *in*-de-*vid*-yew-*ay*-shon, the act or process of individuating; the state of being an individual; individuality.
indivisibility, *n.* *in*-de-*viz*-e-*bil*-e-te, indivisibleness.
indivisible, *a.* *in*-de-*viz*-e-bl, not divisible; not exactly divisible [Math.]: *n.* one of the parts, infinitely small and incapable of further subdivision, into which a whole may be resolved [Math.]. (L. *indivisibilis.*)
indivisibleness, *n.* *in*-de-*viz*-e-bl-ness, the state or quality of being indivisible.
indivisibly, *ad.* so as not to be divisible.
Indo-, *in*-doh, a combining form denoting a combination of which an Indian origin, race, language, etc., forms part, as **Indo-Chinese, Indo-Germanic,** etc.
indocile, *a.* in-*doh*-sile, not docile; not disposed to be taught. (L. *indocilis.*)
indocility, *n.* *in*-do-*sil*-e-te, intractableness.
indoctrinate, *v.t.* in-*dok*-tre-nate, to instruct in any doctrine or imbue with the principles of any system. (L. *in-*, and *doctrinatus*, taught.)
indoctrination, *n.* in-*dok*-tre-*nay*-shon, instruction in or inoculation with the principles of any system.
Indo-European, *a.* *in*-doh-yew-ro-*pee*-an, Aryan; pertaining to the large family of languages spoken in western Asia and most of Europe: *n.* the Indo-European group of languages; a descendant of a people of whom one of these languages was the original speech.
indolence, *n.* *in*-do-lence, habitual laziness. (Fr.)
indolent, *a.* *in*-do-lent, habitually lazy; slothful; causing little or no pain (of ulcers, etc.) [Med.]. (L. *in-*, not, *dolens*, painful.)
indolently, *ad.* *in*-do-lent-le, in an indolent manner.
indomitable, *a.* in-*dom*-it-a-bl, that cannot be subdued; untamable. (L. *in-*, and *domitus*, tamed.)
Indonesian, *a.* in-doh-*neez*-yan, of the East Indian islands: *n.* a pre-Malayan inhabitant, a native, or the language, of these islands; a Malay of Indian type.
indoor, *a.* *in*-dor, within the house (*ad.* **indoors,** in-*dorz*).
indorsation, *n.* in-dor-*say*-shon, endorsement; the act or process of endorsing.
indorse, *v.t.* in-*dorse*, to endorse.
indraught, *n.* *in*-drahft, an inlet; influx below; air drawn in.
indrawn, *a.* *in*-drawn, drawn in.
indri, *n.* *in*-dre, the largest of the Madagascan lemurs, the babacoote, *Indris brevucaudata.* (Malagasy.)
indubious, *a.* in-*dew*-be-us, not doubtful; not doubting.
indubitable, *a.* in-*dew*-be-ta-bl, not to be doubted; clear or certain beyond question. (L. *indubitabilis.*)
indubitableness, *n.* in-*dew*-be-ta-bl-ness, state of being indubitable.
indubitably, *ad.* in-*dew*-be-ta-ble, undoubtedly.
induce, *v.t.* in-*dewce*, to prevail on; to bring on; to actuate; to cause; to cause, as an electric or magnetic condition, by mere proximity [Physics]; to infer by induction, as opposed to deduction [Logic]. (L. *induco, inductum*, lead.)
inducement, *n.* in-*dewce*-ment, anything that induces the mind to will or to act; an incentive; a recompense; a statement of facts introducing other material facts [Law].
inducer, *n.* in-*dewce*-er, he who or that which induces.
induct, *v.t.* in-*dukt*, to introduce into a benefice or office; to invest with such office. (L. *inductus.*)
inductance, *n.* in-*duk*-tance, the property of a circuit by which electromotive force is induced [Elect.].
inductile, *a.* in-*duk*-tile, not ductile, as a metal.
inductility, *n.* *in*-duk-*til*-e-te, the quality of being inductile.
induction, *n.* in-*duk*-shon, the act or process of inducting; adduction; the process of reasoning from particulars to generals, or the conclusion thus attained [Logic]; introduction or instalment into a benefice or office; the production of magnetic or electrical influence without direct contact [Physics]; an introduction or prologue to a play. **induction coil,** an apparatus for transforming a direct to an alternating current by induction [Elect.]. **induction pipe,** the pipe by which the steam, or other source of power, is admitted to the cylinder [Eng.]. **mutual induction,** the property by which a change in current in one circuit induces a current in a neighbouring circuit [Elect.]. (Fr.)
inductional, *a.* in-*duk*-shon-al, pertaining or due to induction.
inductive, *a.* in-*duk*-tiv, tending to induce; leading to inferences; characterized or proceeding by induction [Logic]; pertaining to or producing induction [Elect.]. **inductive method,** the process, as distinct from the deductive, of reasoning, from particular instances to general principles.
inductively, *ad.* in-*duk*-tiv-le, by induction or inference.
inductivity, in-duk-*tiv*-e-te, inductive capacity [Elect.].
inductor, *n.* in-*duk*-tor, one who inducts another into a benefice or office; any part of an electrical equipment that acts inductively [Elect.].
indue, *v.t.* in-*dew*, to endue.
indulge, *v.t.* in-*dulj*, to gratify by concession to; to yield to the wishes of; not to check or restrain: *v.i.* to allow oneself; to partake freely of intoxicants [Coll.]. (L. *indulgeo.*)
indulgence, *n.* in-*dul*-jence, the practice of indulging; forbearance of restraint; permission; gratification; favour granted; in the Rom. Cath. Church, remission granted to a penitent of a temporal punishment, due to an act of sin; in Engl. Hist., a relaxation of anti-Nonconformist legislation offered by the late Stuart kings. (L. *indulgentia.*)
indulgent, *a.* in-*dul*-jent, yielding to the wishes of those under us; complaint; not severe; kind. (L. *indulgens*, being kind.)
indulgently, *ad.* in an indulgent manner.
indulger, *n.* in-*dul*-jer, one who indulges in.
induline, *n.* *in*-dew-leen, any of a group of blue-

black or bluish aniline dyestuffs from coal tar products.
indumentum, *n.* *in*-dew-*men*-tum, a covering of hair or feathers [Zool.]; any downy covering [Bot.]. (L., a garment.)
induna, *n.* in-*doo*-nah, the chief of an impi. (Zulu.)
induplicate, *a.* in-*dew*-plik-ate, with edges bent towards the axis [Bot.].
indurate, *v.i.* *in*-dewr-rate, to become hard; to become insensible: *v.t.* to make hard; to deprive of sensibility; to render obdurate. (L. *induratus*, hardened.)
induration, *n.* *in*-dewr-*ray*-shon, the act of hardening, or process of growing hard; hardened state; hardness of heart; obduracy.
indusial, *a.* in-*dew*-ze-al, composed of the fossil larva-cases of certain insects [Geol.].
indusium, *n.* in-*dew*-ze-um (*pl.* **indusia**), a hairy cup inclosing a stigma [Bot.]; the cover of the sori in ferns [Bot.]; the case or covering of certain larvæ [Entom.]. (L., an under-garment.)
industrial, *a.* in-*dust*-re-al, consisting in, pertaining to, or intended for use in industry; pertaining to productiveness or produce: *n.* a worker in a trade or industry: (*pl.*) shares, etc., in a joint-stock industrial company. **the Industrial Revolution,** the gradual supersession of handicrafts and small-scale labour by machinery and mass production, esp. that which began in England in the late 18th century.
industrialism, *n.* in-*dust*-re-a-lizm, a social system of which large-scale industrial pursuits are the chief characteristic.
industrialist, *n.* in-*dust*-re-a-list, a manufacturer; one engaged in an industry.
industrialize, *v.t.* in-*dust*-re-a-lize, to make industrial; to hand over to industry.
industrially, *ad.* with reference to industry.
industrious, *a.* in-*dust*-re-us, given to industry; diligent in business or study; habitually occupied in business; assiduous; active. (L. *industriosus.*)
industriously, *ad.* in an industrious manner.
★**industry,** *n.* *in*-dus-tre, habitual diligence in any employment; steady application to labour; assiduity; manufacturing or mechanical occupations as distinct from agriculture, the professions, etc.; any branch of such. (Fr. *industrie.*)
induviæ, *n.pl.* in-*dew*-ve-ee, withered leaves remaining on the stems of some plants [Bot.]. (L., clothing.)
indwell, *v.t.* *in*-dwel, to dwell or abide in.
indweller, *n.* *in*-dwel-ler, an inhabitant.
inebriant, *a.* in-*ee*-bre-ant, intoxicating: *n.* anything that intoxicates. (L.)
inebriate, *n.* in-*ee*-bre-ate, an habitual drunkard: *a.* drunk: *v.t.* to make drunk; to intoxicate. (L. *inebriatus*, drunk.)
inebriation, *n.* in-*ee*-bre-*ay*-shon, inebriety.
inebriety, *n.* in-e-*bry*-e-te, habitual intoxication; drunkenness.
inebrious, *a.* in-*ee*-bre-us, drunk; causing or addicted to drunkenness.
inedible, *a.* in-*ed*-e-bl, uneatable; not fit for human consumption.
inedited, *a.* in-*ed*-e-ted, unpublished; not revised.
ineffability, *n.* *in*-ef-fa-*bil*-e-te, the quality of being ineffable.
ineffable, *a.* in-*ef*-fa-bl, inexpressible in words. (L. *ineffabilis*, unutterable.)
ineffableness, *n.* ineffability.
ineffably, *ad.* in a manner not to be expressed in words; indescribably.
ineffaceable, *a.* *in*-ef-*face*-a-bl, not effaceable.
ineffaceably, *ad.* in-ef-*face*-a-ble, not effaceably.
ineffective, *a.* *in*-ef-*fek*-tiv, without effect; inefficient; not efficacious; useless.
ineffectively, *ad.* *in*-ef-*fek*-tiv-le, not effectively.
ineffectiveness, *n.* *in*-ef-*fek*-tiv-ness, the quality of being ineffective.
ineffectual, *a.* *in*-ef-*fek*-tew-al, not producing or not able to produce its effect; inefficient.
ineffectuality, *n.* *in*-ef-*fek*-tew-*al*-e-te, the condition or fact of being ineffectual.
ineffectually, *ad.* *in*-ef-*fek*-tew-al-le, without effect; in vain.
ineffectualness, *n.* in-ef-*fek*-tew-al-ness, want of effect, or of power to produce it.
ineffervescence, *n.* *in*-ef-fer-*vess*-ence, absence of effervescence; the state of not effervescing.
inefficacious, *a.* in-ef-fe-*kay*-shus, not efficacious; of inadequate power or force; unproductive of result.
inefficaciously, *ad.* without efficacy.
inefficaciousness, *n.* inefficacy.
inefficacy, *n.* in-*ef*-fe-ka-se, want of efficacy.
inefficiency, *n.* in-ef-*fish*-en-se, want of power, ability, or capacity.
inefficient, *a.* in-ef-*fish*-ent, not efficient: *n.* an inefficient person.
inefficiently, *ad.* in-ef-*fish*-ent-le, without effect.
inelaborate, *a.* in-e-*lab*-o-rat, not elaborate; somewhat crude.
inelastic, *a.* *in*-e-*las*-tik, wanting elasticity; incompressible.
inelasticity, *n.* *in*-e-las-*tis*-e-te, want of elastic property or power.
inelegance, *n.* in-*el*-e-gance, want of elegance; want of beauty, symmetry, or refinement: an inelegant quality.
inelegancy, *n.* in-*el*-e-gan-se, inelegance.
inelegant, *a.* in-*el*-e-gant, not elegant.
inelegantly, *ad.* in an inelegant manner.
ineligibility, *n.* in-*el*-e-je-*bil*-e-te, the state or quality of being ineligible.
ineligible, *a.* in-*el*-e-je-bl, not eligible; not capable or worthy of being elected or chosen.
ineligibly, *ad.* in-*el*-e-jib-le, in an ineligible manner.
ineloquent, *a.* in-*el*-o-kwent, not eloquent; having small command of words.
ineluctable, *a.* in-e-*luk*-ta-bl, irresistible; unavoidable; not to be overcome. (L. *in-*, not, *eluctari*, to struggle against.)
ineludible, *a.* in-e-*lew*-de-bl, that cannot be eluded.
inenarrable, *a.* in-e-*na*-ra-bl, that cannot be narrated; indescribable.
inept, *a.* in-*ept*, not apt or fit; unsuitable; absurd. (L. *ineptus*, not apposite.)
ineptitude, *n.* in-*ep*-te-tewd, unfitness; foolishness.
ineptly, *ad.* in-*ept*-le, in an inept manner.
ineptness, *n.* in-*ept*-ness, the state of being inept.
inequable, *a.* in-*ee*-kwa-bl, not equable.
inequality, *n.* in-e-*kwol*-e-te, want of equality; difference; unevenness; disparity; incompetence.
inequilateral, *a.* in-*ek*-we-*lat*-er-ral, having unequal sides.
inequitable, *a.* in-*ek*-we-ta-bl, not equitable; unjust.
inequity, *n.* in-*ek*-we-te, injustice; partiality.
inequivalvular, *a.* in-ek-we-*val*-vew-lar, having valves of unequal sizes (of bivalves) [Conch.].
ineradicable, *a.* in-e-*rad*-e-ka-bl, not eradicable.
ineradicably, *ad.* so as not to be eradicable.
inergetical, *a.* in-er-*jet*-e-kal, being devoid of energy; sluggish.
inergetically, *ad.* in-er-*jet*-e-ka-le, without energy.
inerm, *a.* in-*erm*, destitute of prickles or thorns, as a leaf [Bot.]. (L. *inermis*, armless.)
inerrability, *n.* in-*er*-ra-*bil*-e-te, infallibility.
inerrable, *a.* in-*er*-ra-bl, that cannot err; infallible. (L. *inerrabilis.*)
inerrably, *ad.* in-*er*-ra-ble, infallibly.
inerrancy, *n.* in-*e*-ran-se, freedom from error.
inerrant, *a.* in-*e*-rant, free from error; inerratic [Old Astron.].
inerratic, *a.* *in*-e-*rat*-ik, not erratic; fixed.
inert, *a.* in-*ert*, destitute of the power of moving itself, or of active resistance to motion; indisposed to act; inactive; sluggish; having no chemical effect; neutral [Chem.]. (L. *iners*, from *in-*, not, and *ars*, art.)
inertia, *n.* in-*er*-she-a, that property of matter by which, in absence of external force, it tends to preserve a state of rest when still and of uniform motion when moving [Physics]; inertness. **vis inertiæ,** the passive resistance of matter to an operating force. (L.)
inertion, *n.* in-*er*-shon, inert condition; sluggishness; sloth.
inertly, *ad.* in-*ert*-le, sluggishly; lifelessly.
inertness, *n.* in-*ert*-ness, the state or quality of being inert; indisposition to exertion; sluggishness.
inerudite, *a.* in-*e*-roo-dite, unlearned.
inescapable, *a.* *in*-es-*kay*-pa-bl, not to be escaped.
inescutcheon, *n.* *in*-es-*kutch*-on, a small shield borne within a shield [Her.].
inessential, *a.* *in*-es-*sen*-shal, unessential; not really necessary: *n.* that which is inessential.
inestimable, *a.* in-*es*-te-ma-bl, that cannot be estimated; beyond all price in value. (Fr.)

inestimably, *ad.* in an inestimable manner or degree.
ineunt, *a.* *in*-e-unt, entering; going in. (L.)
inevasible, *a.* *in*-e-*vay*-ze-bl, that cannot be evaded.
inevident, *a.* in-*ev*-e-dent, not evident; not obvious.
inevitability, *n.* in-*ev*-e-ta-*bil*-e-te, inevitableness.
inevitable, *a.* in-*ev*-e-ta-bl, that admits of no escape or evasion; unavoidable; customary [Coll.]. (L. *inevitabilis.*)
inevitableness, *n.* in-*ev*-e-ta-bl-ness, the state or quality of being inevitable.
inevitably, *ad.* in-*ev*-e-ta-ble, unavoidably.
inexact, *a.* in-ek-*zakt*, not precisely correct.
inexactitude, *n.* in-ek-*zak*-te-tewd, want of exactitude; inexactness; **terminological inexactitude**, a falsehood.
inexactness, *n.* in-ek-*zakt*-ness, want of precision.
inexcusable, *a.* *in*-eks-*kew*-za-bl, not to be excused or justified.
inexcusableness, *n.* *in*-eks-*kew*-za-bl-ness, the quality of being inexcusable.
inexcusably, *ad.* *in*-eks-*kew*-za-ble, to a degree beyond excuse or justification.
inexecutable, *a.* in-*ek*-se-*kew*-ta-bl, not capable of being done or performed.
inexecution, *n.* in-*ek*-se-*kew*-shon, non-performance.
inexertion, *n.* in-ek-*zer*-shon, want of exertion or effort; defect of action.
inexhausted, *a.* in-eg-*zaws*-ted, not exhausted.
inexhaustible, *a.* *in*-eg-*zaws*-te-bl, that cannot be exhausted; unfailing.
inexhaustibleness, *n.* *in*-egs-*zaws*-te-bl-ness, the state of being inexhaustible.
inexhaustibly, *ad.* *in*-egs-*zaws*-te-ble, in an inexhaustible manner.
inexhaustive, *a.* *in*-egs-*zaws*-tiv, not to be exhausted or spent.
inexistent, *a.* in-eg-*zis*-tent, not existing; existent in or within.
inexorability, *n.* in-*eks*-o-ra-*bil*-e-te, the state or quality of being inexorable.
inexorable, *a.* in-*eks*-o-ra-bl, not to be moved by entreaty; inflexible; unrelenting. (O.Fr. from L.)
inexorably, *ad.* in-*eks*-o-ra-ble, so as to be immovable by entreaty.
inexpansible, *a.* *in*-ex-*pan*-se-bl, incapable of being expanded.
inexpectant, *a.* *in*-ex-*pek*-tant, not expectant.
inexpediency, *n.* *in*-eks-*pee*-de-en-se, want of fitness; unsuitableness to the purpose.
inexpedient, *a.* *in*-eks-*pee*-de-ent, not expedient; not tending to promote a purpose; unfit.
inexpediently, *ad.* not expediently.
inexpensive, *a.* *in*-eks-*pen*-siv, not expensive.
inexperience, *n.* *in*-eks-*peer*-re-ence, want of experience, or of knowledge through experience. (Late L. *inexperientia.*)
inexperienced, *a.* *in*-eks-*peer*-re-enst, not having experience; unskilled.
inexpert, *a.* in-eks-*pert*, not expert; not skilled.
inexpertness, *n.* in-eks-*pert*-ness, want of expertness.
inexpiable, *a.* in-*eks*-pe-a-bl, that admits of no atonement or satisfaction. (L. *inexpiabilis.*)
inexpiably, *ad.* to an inexpiable degree.
inexplicability, *n.* in-*eks*-ple-ka-*bil*-e-te, the state or quality of being inexplicable.
inexplicable, *a.* in-*eks*-ple-ka-bl, that cannot be explained.
inexplicably, *ad.* so as not to be explicable.
inexplicit, *a.* in-eks-*plis*-it, not explicit or clear.
inexplorable, *a.* in-eks-*plore*-a-bl, not explorable.
inexplosive, *a.* in-ex-*ploh*-siv, not explosive.
inexpressible, *a.* in-eks-*pres*-se-bl, not to be expressed: *n.pl.* trousers [jocular].
inexpressibly, *ad.* unutterably.
inexpressive, *a.* in-eks-*pres*-siv, not expressive.
inexpressiveness, *n.* the state of being inexpressive.
inexpugnable, *a.* in-eks-*pug*-na-bl, not to be taken by assault; impregnable; invincible; fixed.
inextensible, *a.* in-eks-*ten*-se-bl, not capable of extension.
inextinguishable, *a.* in-eks-*ting*-gwish-a-bl, that cannot be extinguished; unquenchable.
inextirpable, *a.* in-eks-*ter*-pa-bl, that cannot be rooted out.
inextricable, *a.* in-*eks*-tre-ka-bl, not extricable; incapable of being disengaged.
inextricably, *ad.* in-*eks*-tre-ka-ble, in an inextricable manner.
infall, *n.* *in*-fawl, an inroad; an incursion; a confluence; the entrance place of water to a reservoir, etc.
infallibilism, *n.* in-*fal*-le-bil-izm, the doctrine of papal infallibility.
infallibilist, *n.* in-*fal*-le-bil-ist, an adherent of infallibilism.
infallibility, *n.* in-*fal*-le-*bil*-e-te, the quality of being infallible, esp. on behalf of the Pope when speaking *ex cathedra* in regard to faith and morals.
infallible, *a.* in-*fal*-le-bl, incapable of erring; exempt from liability of failure; certain. (Late L. *infallibilis.*)
infallibleness, *n.* in-*fal*-le-bl-ness, infallibility.
infallibly, *ad.* in-*fal*-le-ble, in an infallible manner.
infamize, *v.t.* *in*-fa-mize, to render infamous.
infamous, *a.* *in*-fa-mus, of ill report; having a reputation of the worst kind; notoriously vile; disgraceful; publicily branded with infamy [Law.].
infamously, *ad.* *in*-fa-mus-le, to an infamous degree.
infamy, *n.* *in*-fa-me, ill-fame; loss of reputation; public disgrace; extreme vileness; loss of character or status incurred by a convict [Law]. (Fr. *infamie.*)
infancy, *n.* *in*-fan-se, the state or period of being an infant; the period till the age of twenty-one [Law]; the early period of existence. (L. *infantia.*)
infant, *n.* *in*-fant, a baby; a very young child; a person under the age of twenty-one [Law]: *a.* pertaining to infancy; young; tender. **infant prodigy**, an exceptionally precocious young scholar, performer, etc. **infant school**, a school or kindergarten for children under seven years. (L. *infans*, from *in*, not, and *fans*, speaking.)
infanta, *n.* in-*fan*-ta, in the former Iberian monarchies, any princess of the blood royal, except an heiress apparent.
infante, *n.* in-*fan*-te, in the former Iberian monarchies, any son of the king except the heir apparent.
infanticidal, *a.* in-*fan*-te-*sy*-dal, pertaining to infanticide.
infanticide, *n.* in-*fan*-te-side, the murder or the murderer of a new-born infant. (L. *infant*, and *cædo*, kill.)
infantile, *a.* *in*-fan-tile, pertaining to infancy or infants, or to the first period of life. **infantile paralysis**, febrile inflammation and degeneration of the motor-cells of the spinal cord due to infection by a filter-passing virus; acute anterior poliomyelitis [Med.]. (L. *infantilis.*)
infantilism, *n.* in-*fan*-te-lizm, the condition of arrested development, mental, physical, or emotional [Med.].
infantine, *a.* *in*-fan-tine, infantile.
infantry, *n.* *in*-fan-tre, soldiers trained, armed, and equipped for fighting on foot. (Fr. *infanterie.*)
infatuate, *v.t.* in-*fat*-yew-ate, to make foolish; to affect with folly; to deprive of sound judgment; to infect with a foolish passion. (L. *infatuatus*, made a fool of.)
infatuation, *n.* in-*fat*-yew-*ay*-shon, the act or state of being infatuated; besotted folly.
infaust, *a.* in-*fawst*, unlucky. (L. *infaustus.*)
infeasibility, *n.* in-*fee*-ze-*bil*-e-te, the quality of being impracticable; impracticability.
infeasible, *a.* in-*fee*-ze-bl, not feasible; impracticable.
infect, *v.t.* in-*fekt*, to taint with disease; to taint or affect with morbid or noxious matter; to communicate disease; to imbue with any (esp. bad) quality; to corrupt. (O.Fr.)
infecter, *n.* in-*fek*-ter, he who or that which infects.
infectible, *a.* in-*fek*-te-bl, capable of being infected.
infection, *n.* in-*fek*-shon, act of or process infecting; a diseased state due to invasion of the body-tissue by micro-organisms [Med.]; that which infects or taints.
infectious, *a.* in-*fek*-shus, having the quality of infecting or tainting; apt to spread; liable to be communicated by air or water; pestilential; corrupting.
infectiously, *ad.* in-*fek*-shus-le, by infection.
infectiousness, *n.* the quality of being infectious.
infective, *a.* in-*fek*-tiv, infectious; able to infect.
infecund, *a.* in-*fek*-und, not fruitful; unproductive.
infecundity, *n.* in-fe-*kun*-de-te, barrenness [Med.].
infeftment, *n.* in-*feft*-ment, the act of symbolically

putting one in possession of an hereditament [Scots. Law].
infelicitous, *a.* in-fe-*lis*-e-tus, not felicitous; unhappy; inapt.
infelicity, *n.* *in*-fe-*lis*-e-te, unhappiness; misery; unfavourableness; inaptness. (L. *infelicitas.*)
infelt, *a.* *in*-felt, experienced within; heartfelt.
infer, *v.t.* in-*fer*, to deduce; to derive, as a fact or consequence; to imply. (O.Fr. *inferer.*)
inferable, *a.* in-*fer*-ra-bl, that may be inferred from premises; deducible.
inference, *n.* *in*-fer-ence, the act of inferring; that which is inferred; deduction; conclusion.
inferential, *a.* *in*-fer-*ren*-shal, deduced or deducible by inference.
inferentially, *ad.* by way of inference.
inferiæ, *n.pl.* in-*feer*-re-ee, sacrifices offered by the ancient Romans in honour of the dead. (L.)
inferior, *a.* in-*feer*-re-or, lower in place, station, rank, or quality, etc.; subordinate; secondary; below; within the earth's orbit [Astron.]; growing under another organ [Bot.]: *n.* one who is inferior or of a lower rank; a subordinate. (L. comparative of *inferus*, low.)
inferiority, *n.* in-*feer*-re-*o*-re-te, the state of being inferior. **inferiority complex,** a morbid sense of inferiority masked by a show of aggressiveness, exaggerated self-importance or timidity, etc.
infernal, *a.* in-*fer*-nal, pertaining to hell or the lower regions; worthy of hell; diabolical: *n.* a denizen of hell; a fiend. **infernal machine,** an explosive machine contrived for assassination, etc. (L. *infernus*, lower.)
infernally, *ad.* in a detestable and infernal way.
inferno, *n.* in-*fer*-noh, hell, esp. as depicted in Dante's "Divine Comedy"; any place or situation resembling the popular conception of hell. (It.)
inferrible, *a.* in-*fe*-re-bl, inferable.
infertile, *a.* in-*fer*-tile, not fertile; barren.
infertility, *n.* *in*-fer-*til*-e-te, sterility.
infest, *v.t.* in-*fest*, to trouble greatly; to plague; to overrun. (Fr. *infester.*)
infestation, *n.* *in*-fes-*tay*-shon, the state of being infested, esp. [Med.] by parasites; molestation.
infeudation, *n.* *in*-few-*day*-shon, the act of putting one in possession of an estate in fee; enfeoffment; the granting of tithes to laymen.
infibulate, *v.t.* in-*fib*-yew-late, to fasten with a clasp or buckle. (L. *in*-, and *fibula*, a clasp.)
infibulation, *n.* in-*fib*-yew-*lay*-shon, a clasping; the confining or enclosing of the sexual organs in such a way as to prevent copulation. (L. *infibulatus*, fastened with a clasp.)
infidel, *a.* *in*-fe-del, disbelieving, esp. in Christianity *n.* one who disbelieves or has no faith in a given religious creed, esp. the Christian; a sceptic; a deist; a Mohammedan. (O.Fr. *infidele.*)
infidelity, *n.* *in*-fe-*del*-e-te, want of faith, esp. in the Christian creed; scepticism; a violation of the marriage covenant; breach of trust; treachery. (Fr. *infidélité.*)
infield, *n.* *in*-feeld, the portion of a farm which is manured and kept in crop; the part of the ground near the wicket, also the fieldsmen in this part [Cricket]; in Baseball, the square area (with 90 ft. sides) within the base lines: *v.t.* to enclose as a field.
infighting, *n.* *in*-fite-ing, fighting or boxing at such close quarters that blows from the shoulder are not possible [Sport].
infiltrate, *v.i.* and *t.* in-*fil*-trate, to enter or to cause to enter by penetrating the pores or interstices of a substance; to enter enemy territory by passing small detachments through the enemy lines [Mil.]: *n.* that which infiltrates.
infiltration, *n.* in-fil-*tray*-shon, the process or act of infiltrating; a substance infiltrated.
infinite, *a.* *in*-fe-nit, without limit; boundless; endless; great beyond measure; greater or less than any assignable quantity [Math.]: *n.* infinity; an infinite space; something infinite; an infinite quantity [Math.]. **the Infinite,** God. (O.Fr. *infinit.*)
infinitely, *ad.* *in*-fe-nit-le, to an infinite degree.
infiniteness, *n.* *in*-fe-nit-ness, the state of being infinite.
infinitesimal, *a.* *in*-fin-e-*tes*-e-mal, infinitely small; less than any assignable quantity: *n.* a quantity that is so.
infinitesimally, *ad.* *in*-fin-e-*tes*-e-mal-le, by quantities infinitely small.
infinitival, *a.* *in*-fin-e-*ty*-val, pertaining to the infinitive mood.
infinitive, *a.* in-*fin*-e-tiv, not limiting; expressing the mere action of the verb without limitation of person or number [Gram.]: *n.* the infinitive mood. (L. *infinitus.*)
infinitude, *n.* in-*fin*-e-tewd, infinity; boundlessness; uncountable quantity.
infinity, *n.* in-*fin*-e-te, infiniteness; infinite extent; infinite number.
infirm, *a.* in-*firm*, lacking strength or vigour, esp. through old age or disease; feeble; irresolute; not stable. (L. *infirmus*, weak.)
infirmary, *n.* in-*firm*-a-re, a hospital or place where sick or suffering people are lodged and nursed.
infirmity, *n.* in-*firm*-e-te, a weakness; a diseased state of the body; a disease; a failing.
infirmly, *ad.* in-*firm*-le, in an infirm manner.
infirmness, *n.* in-*firm*-ness, the state of being infirm; weakness.
infix, *v.t.* in-*fiks*, to fix or to fasten in; to implant, as a principle or idea: *n.* *in*-fiks, a modifying element inserted in the body of a word [Gram.].
inflame, *v.t.* in-*flame*, to set on fire; to excite or kindle into violent action; to excite excessive action in the blood; to cause heat, redness, and swelling; to provoke; to exasperate: *v.i.* to burst into flame; to become inflamed or affected with inflammation [Med.]. (L. *inflammo.*)
inflamer, *n.* in-*flame*-er, one who or that which inflames.
inflammability, *n.* in-*flam*-ma-*bil*-e-te, inflammableness.
inflammable, *a.* in-*flam*-ma-bl, that may be easily set on fire; susceptible of combustion; irascible.
inflammableness, *n.* in-*flam*-ma-bl-ness, the quality of being inflammable.
inflammably, *ad.* in an inflammable manner.
inflammation, *n.* *in*-fla-*may*-shon, the act of inflaming; state of being inflamed; the reaction of living tissues to injury, entailing tenderness, swelling, and increased vascularity [Med. and Surg.].
inflammatory, *a.* in-*flam*-ma-to-re, tending to excite heat or inflammation; accompanied by inflammation; tending to excite tumult or sedition.
inflatable, *a.* in-*flay*-ta-bl, that may be inflated.
inflate, *v.t.* in-*flate*, to swell by injecting air; to puff up; to increase or expand artificially, esp. with intent to raise the level of prices [Econ.]. (L. *inflatus*, puffed up.)
inflated, *a.* in-*flay*-ted, distended with air; turgid; hollow and distended [Bot.].
inflation, *n.* in-*flay*-shon, act of inflating; state of being inflated; distension; pompous pretension; the causing a fall in money value and rise in prices by the increase in the quantity of money and/or credit relative to the volume of exchange transactions [Econ.].
inflationist, *a.* in-*flay*-shon-ist, pertaining to or characterized by inflation: *n.* one favouring a policy of inflation [Econ.].
inflect, *v.t.* in-*flekt*, to bend; to turn from a direct line or course; to vary terminations for purposes of declension or conjugation [Gram.]; to modulate, as the voice. (L. *inflecto*, bend.)
inflected, *a.* in-*flek*-ted, subject to inflexion [Gram.]; inflexed [Bot.[.
inflection, *n.* in-*flek*-shon, inflexion.
inflective, *a.* in-*flek*-tiv, capable of bending.
inflexed, *a.* in-*flekst*, bent inwards [Bot.].
inflexibility, *n.* in-*flek*-se-*bil*-e-te, inflexibleness.
inflexible, *a.* in-*flek*-se-bl, that cannot be bent; that will not yield or be persuaded to change; unbending; unyielding; unrelenting. (L. *inflexibilis.*)
inflexibleness, *n.* quality of being inflexible.
inflexibly, *ad.* in-*flek*-se-ble, to an inflexible degree.
inflexion, *n.* in-*flek*-shon, the act of inflecting; state of being inflected; the variation in termination of nouns by declension, and of verbs by conjugation [Gram.]; diffraction [Opt.]; modulation of the voice.
inflexional, *a.* in-*flek*-shon-al, pertaining to grammatical inflexions.
inflict, *v.t.* in-*flikt*, to lay on; to impose as punishment or disgrace. (L. *inflictus*, struck.)

inflicter, *n.* in-*flik*-ter, he who inflicts.
infliction, *n.* in-*flik*-shon, the act of inflicting; the punishment applied; trouble.
inflictive, *a.* in-*flik*-tiv, tending to inflict; causing infliction.
inflorescence, *n.* in-flo-*res*-sence, the act or mode of flowering; manner in which flowers are supported on the foot-stalk [Bot.]; collective blossoms. (Fr.)
inflow, *n.* *in*-flo, a flowing in: *v.i.* to flow in.
influence, *n.* *in*-floo-ence, power which affects men or things, whether physically, morally, or spiritually; one who or that which exercises such power; sway; authority: *v.t.* to move, affect, or direct; to sway. (O.Fr.)
influent, *a.* *in*-floo-ent, flowing in: *n.* a tributary; that which flows in.
influential, *a.* in-floo-*en*-shal, having or exerting influence or power.
influentially, *ad.* by means of influence.
influenza, *n.* in-floo-*en*-za, an infectious and contagious epidemic catarrh, attended by fever and great weakness. (It.)
influx, *n.* *in*-fluks, a flowing in; infusion; intromission; a coming in; importation in abundance. (L. *influxus*, a pouring in.)
influxion, *n.* in-*fluk*-shon, the act of flowing in; an influx.
infold, *v.i.* in-*fohld*, to enfold.
inform, *v.t.* in-*form*, to give form to; to animate or give life to; to communicate knowledge to; to apprize; to acquaint: *v.i.* to give intelligence. **to inform against,** to communicate facts by way of accusation. (Fr. *informer.*)
informal, *a.* in-*form*-al, not in the proper, usual or customary form; without ceremony.
informality, *n.* *in*-for-*mal*-le-te, want of regular or customary form; an irregularity.
informally, *ad.* in-*form*-al-le, in an informal manner.
informant, *n.* in-*form*-ant, one who informs.
information, *n.* in-for-*may*-shon, intelligence communicated; knowledge acquired; news; a preliminary complaint or accusation made to a magistrate or court. (Fr.)
informative, *a.* in-*form*-a-tiv, conveying information; having power to animate.
informatory, *a.* in-*form*-a-to-re, instructive; containing or conveying information.
informed, *a.* in-*formed*, having knowledge of the facts; educated.
informer, *n.* in-*form*-er, one who makes a business of informing against others, esp. one who communicates to a magistrate a knowledge of a violation of law.
infortune, *n.* in-*for*-tewn, misfortune.
infra, *prep.* *in*-fra, below. **infra dig,** beneath one's dignity (L. *infra dignitatum*). **infra red,** denoting the invisible and non-actinic rays lying just beyond the red end of the visible spectrum [Physics].
infracostal, *a.* *in*-fra-*kos*-tal, situated below the ribs.
infraction, *n.* in-*frak*-shon, violation; infringement.
infrahuman, *a.* *in*-fra-*hew*-man, lower than human.
infralapsarian, *n.* and *a.* *in*-fra-lap-*sare*-re-an, sublapsarian.
inframaxillary, *a.* *in*-fra-mak-*sil*-a-re, relating to the lower jaw; under the jaw in place: *n.* the lower jaw-bone.
inframedian, *a.* *in*-fra-*mee*-de-an, at a depth of between fifty and a hundred fathoms.
infrangibility, *n.* *in*-fran-*je*-*bil*-e-te, the quality or condition of being infrangible.
infrangible, *a.* in-*fran*-je-bl, that cannot be broken; not to be violated.
infra-orbital, *a.* placed below the orbit of the eye.
infra-scapular, *a.* *in*-fra-*skap*-yew-lar, situated under the shoulder-blade.
infrequency, *n.* in-*free*-kwen-se, the state of being infrequent; rareness. (L. *infrequentia.*)
infrequent, *a.* in-*free*-kwent, rare; uncommon; seldom happening.
infrequently, *ad.* in-*free*-kwent-le, not frequently; seldom.
infringe, *v.t.* in-*frinj*, to break (a rule, contract, etc.); to violate; to transgress; to neglect to fulfil or obey. (L. *infringere*, break into.)
infringement, *n.* in-*frinj*-ment, act of infringing; violation; infraction.
infringer, *n.* in-*frinj*-er, one who infringes.
infructuous, *a.* in-*fruk*-tew-us, not bearing fruit; barren; unprofitable. (L. *infructuosus.*)
infula, *n.* *in*-few-la, a fillet worn as a badge of priestly, sacrificial, or royal consecration [Rom. Antiq.]; the hanging ornament at the back of a mitre. (L.)
infundibular, *a.* *in*-fun-*dib*-yew-lar, having the form of a funnel. (L. *infundibulum*, a funnel.)
infundibuliform, *a.* in-*fun*-de-*bew*-le-form, having the shape of a funnel, as a corolla [Bot.].
infundibulum, *n.* in-fun-*dib*-yew-lum, any funnel-shaped organ [Anat. and Zool.]. (L., a funnel.)
infuriate, *v.t.* in-*fewr*-re-ate, to render furious or mad; to enrage: *a.* enraged; raging. (It. *infuriato.*)
infuriation, *n.* in-*fewr*-re-*ay*-shon, state of being infuriated; act of infuriating.
infuse, *v.t.* in-*fewz*, to pour in; to instil, as principles; to introduce; to steep in liquor for extracting the soluble qualities. (Fr. *infuser.*)
infuser, *n.* in-*few*-zer, one who or that which infuses.
infusibility, *n.* in-*few*-ze-*bil*-e-te, the capacity of being infused; the incapability of being fused.
infusible, *a.* in-*few*-ze-bl, that may be infused; incapable of fusion.
infusion, *n.* in-*few*-zhon, the act or process of infusing; instillation; that which is extracted from vegetable matter in water by infusion; the liquid used in steeping; the introduction of a solution into a vein [Surg.].
infusive, *a.* in-*few*-siv, having the power of infusing.
infusoria, *n.pl.* *in*-few-*zaw*-re-a, microscopic organisms developed in infusions of decaying animal or vegetable matter; the motile protozoans. (L.)
infusorial, *a.* *in*-few-*zaw*-re-al, pertaining to, composed of, or containing infusoria. **infusorial earth,** a siliceous deposit of fossil diatoms.
infusorian, *n.* in-*few*-*zaw*-re-an, a protozoan.
infusory, *a.* in-*few*-zo-re, infusorial.
ingate, *n.* *in*-gate, an aperture in a mould for pouring in metal; a way in.
ingathering, *n.* *in*-gath-er-ing, a collecting and securing, esp. of the fruits of the earth; harvest.
ingeminate, *a.* in-*jem*-e-nate, redoubled; repeated: *v.t.* to double; to reiterate. (L. *ingeminatus*, redoubled.)
ingemination, *n.* in-*jem*-e-*nay*-shon, repetition.
ingenerable, *a.* in-*jen*-er-ra-bl, that cannot be engendered.
ingenerate, *a.* in-*jen*-er-rat, innate; inbred: *v.t.* to generate or produce within. (L. *ingeneratus.*)
ingenious, *a.* in-*jee*-ne-us, possessed of genius or the faculty of invention; skilful to invent, contrive, or combine; showing ingenuity; of skilful contrivance; witty. (L. *ingeniosus.*)
ingeniously, *ad.* with ingenuity; with skill.
ingeniousness, *n.* quality of being ingenious.
ingénue, *n.* (App.) a naïve or ingenuous girl, esp. as a stage character. (Fr.)
ingenuity, *n.* *in*-je-*new*-e-te, ingeniousness; the power of ready invention; quickness or aptness in combining ideas; curiousness in design, the effect of ingenuity. (L. *ingenuitas.*)
ingenuous, *a.* in-*jen*-yew-us, artless; open; frank; generous; of honourable extraction. (L. *ingenuus*, free-born.)
ingenuously, *ad.* in an ingenuous manner.
ingenuousness, *n.* the quality of being ingenuous.
ingest, *v.t.* in-*jest*, to take food into the stomach. (L. *in-*, and *gerere*, to carry.)
ingesta, *n.pl.* in-*jes*-ta, that which is taken into the stomach; food.
ingestible, *a.* in-*jes*-te-bl, capable of being ingested.
ingestion, *n.* in-*jes*-chun, the act or process of ingesting.
ingestive, *a.* in-*jes*-tiv, pertaining to the act of injestion.
ingle, *n.* *ing*-gl, a fire burning on a hearth (also used incorrectly of a fireplace.) **ingle-nook,** a chimney corner. (Gael.)
ingle, *n.* *ing*-gl, a male paramour.
inglorious, *a.* in-*glaw*-re-us, not bringing honour; shameful; disgraceful.
ingloriously, *ad.* in an inglorious manner.
ingloriousness, *n.* state of being inglorious.
ingluvies, *n.* in-*gloo*-ve-eez, the crop or craw of birds; the stomach of ruminants. (L.)
ingoing, *a.* *in*-goh-ing, going in: *n.* entrance; *pl.* money paid by an ingoing tenant for fixtures, etc.
ingot, *n.* *in*-got, a mass of unwrought gold, silver, steel, or other metal, cast in a mould. (A.S. *in*, into, *geotan*, to pour.)

ingraft, *v.t.* in-*grahft,* to engraft.
ingrain, *v.t.* in-*grane,* to engrain.
ingrain, *a.* *in*-grane, dyed in the grain; imbued thoroughly: *n.* a yarn, etc., dyed with fast colours before manufacture.
ingrained, *a.* in-*graynd,* engrained; dyed in the grain; inherent; inveterate.
ingrate, *a.* *in*-grate, unpleasant; unpleasing to the sense: *n.* an ungrateful person. (Fr. *ingrat.*)
ingratiate, *v.t.* in-*gray*-she-ate, to commend (usually oneself) to another's good will; to curry favour with. (L. *in-*, and *gratia,* favour.)
ingratitude, *n.* in-*grat*-e-tewd, want of gratitude.
ingravescent, *a.* *in*-gra-*ves*-sent, gradually getting worse [Med.]. (L. *ingravescens,* becoming heavier.)
ingredient, *n.* in-*gree*-de-ent, that which enters into a compound; a component part. (Fr.)
ingress, *n.* *in*-gress, entrance, act of entering; power of means of entrance. (L. *ingressus.*)
ingression, *n.* in-*gresh*-on, entering; entrance.
ingrowing, *a.* *in*-groh-ing, growing inwards; growing into the flesh (of a nail).
ingrowth, *n.* *in*-grohth, growth inwards; growth into the flesh.
inguinal, *a.* *in*-gwe-nal, pertaining to or near the groin. (L. *inguinalis.*)
ingurgitate, *v.t.* in-*gur*-je-tate, to swallow up greedily; to engulf: *v.i.* to gorge; to drink to excess. (L. *ingurgitatus,* engulfed.)
ingurgitation, *n.* in-*gur*-je-*tay*-shon, the act of swallowing greedily or in great quantity.
inhabit, *v.t.* in-*hab*-it, to live or dwell in; to occupy as a residence: *v.i.* to dwell. (O.Fr. *inhabiter.*)
inhabitable, *a.* in-*hab*-e-ta-bl, habitable.
inhabitancy, *n.* in-*hab*-e-tan-se, residence for a considerable period; domiciliation.
inhabitant, *n.* in-*hab*-e-tant, one who resides in a place; one legally treated as such. (O.Fr.)
inhabitation, *n.* in-*hab*-e-*tay*-shon, the act of inhabiting; state of being inhabited; dwelling-place.
inhabitativeness, *n.* *in*-hab-e-*tay*-tiv-ness, the propensity to remain long in one dwelling.
inhalant, *a.* in-*hay*-lant, inhaling: *n.* a medicament for inhaling. (L. *inhalans,* breathing.)
inhalation, *n.* in-ha-*lay*-shon, the act of inhaling; an inhalant.
inhale, *v.t.* in-*hale,* to draw into the lungs, as air: *v.i.* to draw cigarette-smoke into the lungs. (L. *inhalo,* breathe.)
inhaler, *n.* in-*hale*-er, one who inhales; an apparatus for inhaling vapours; a respirator.
inharmonic, *a.* in-har-*mon*-ik, inharmonious.
inharmonious, *a.* *in*-har-*moh*-ne-us, not harmonious; unmusical; discordant.
inharmoniously, *ad.* without harmony.
inharmony, *n.* in-*har*-mo-ne, want of harmony.
inhere, *v.i.* in-*heer,* to exist in naturally; to belong to; to be an essential part of. (L. *inhæreo,* stick.)
inherence, *n.* in-*heer*-rence, existence in something else; a fixed state of being in another body or substance.
inherency, *n.* in-*heer*-ren-se, inherence.
inherent, *a.* in-*heer*-rent, existing in something else and inseparable from it; innate. (L. *inhærens.*)
inherently, *ad.* in-*heer*-rent-le, by inherence.
inherit, *v.t.* in-*he*-rit, to come into possession of from an ancestor by right of succession; to possess by natural descent; to take as a possession by gift: *v.i.* to take or have possession as an heir. (O.Fr. *enheriter.*)
inheritability, *n.* in-*he*-re-ta-*bil*-e-te, the quality of being inheritable.
inheritable, *a.* in-*he*-re-ta-bl, capable of inheriting; that may be inherited.
inheritably, *ad.* in-*he*-re-ta-ble, by inheritance.
inheritance, *n.* in-*he*-re-tance, that which is inherited; an estate derived from an ancestor by succession; possession by descent.
inheritor, *n.* in-*he*-re-tor, an heir.
inheritrix, *n.* in-*he*-re-triks, a female heir.
inhesion, *n.* in-*hee*-zhon, inherence.
inhibit, *v.t.* in-*hib*-it, to restrain; to hinder; to prohibit; to interdict. (L. *inhibitus,* held in.)
inhibition, *n.* in-he-*bish*-on, the act of inhibiting; the state of being inhibited; prohibition; a prohibitory writ of various kinds [Law]; the sentence by which a clergyman is prohibited from performing his customary duties; the restraining of the working of an organ, etc. [Med.]; any psychic impediment to freedom of volition.
inhibitor, *n.* in-*hib*-e-tor, one who or that which inhibits; an agent that prevents or retards a chemical reaction [Chem.].
inhibitory, *a.* in-*hib*-e-to-re, prohibitory; of the nature of an inhibition.
inhospitable, *a.* in-*hos*-pe-ta-bl, not hospitable; affording no kindly entertainment to strangers; forbidding; desolate. (O.Fr.)
inhospitableness, *n.* in-*hos*-pe-ta-bl-ness, want of hospitality; inhospitality.
inhospitably, *ad.* unkindly to strangers.
inhospitality, *n.* in-*hos*-pe-*tal*-e-te, the state or quality of being inhospitable.
inhuman, *a.* in-*hew*-man, destitute of kindly feeling towards human beings; cruel; brutal; barbarous. (L. *inhumanus.*)
inhumane, *a.* in-hew-*mane,* not humane.
inhumanity, *n.* *in*-hew-*man*-e-te, quality or state of being inhuman; cruelty.
inhumanly, *ad.* in-*hew*-man-le, with inhumanity.
inhumation, *n.* *in*-hew-*may*-shon, the act of burying in the ground; interment. (L. *inhumo,* bury.)
inhume, *v.t.* in-*hewm,* to bury in the ground.
inia, *n.* *in*-ya, the freshwater dolphin of the Amazon.
inimical, *a.* in-*im*-e-kal, having the disposition of an enemy; unfriendly; unfavourable. (L. *inimicalis.*)
inimically, *ad.* in-*im*-e-kal-le, in an inimical manner.
inimitability, *n.* in-*im*-e-ta-*bil*-e-te, the quality or state of being inimitable. (L. *inimitabilis.*)
inimitable, *a.* in-*im*-e-ta-bl, that cannot be imitated.
inimitably, *ad.* in an inimitable manner.
inion, *n.* *in*-e-on, the external ridge of the occiput [Anat.]. (Gr., nape of the neck.)
iniquitous, *a.* in-*ik*-we-tus, characterized by iniquity; unrighteous; unjust; wicked.
iniquitously, *ad.* in an iniquitous manner.
iniquity, *n.* in-*ik*-we-te, injustice; wickedness; sin. (Fr. *iniquité.*)
initial, *a.* in-*ish*-al, placed at the beginning; incipient: *n.* the first letter of a word or name: *v.t.* to put one's initials to, esp. as a sign of ownership or a guarantee. (Fr.)
initially, *ad.* in-*ish*-al-le, at the beginning; in the first place.
initiate, *a.* in-*ish*-e-ate, initiated: *n.* one who is, or is to be, initiated: *v.i.* to perform the first act or rite: *v.t.* to instruct in the first principles or beginnings; to introduce into a new state or society. (L. *initiatus.*)
initiation, *n.* in-*ish*-e-*ay*-shon, the act or process of initiating, esp. of acquainting one with principles before unknown; admission into a society, by instructing one in its rules, etc.
initiative, *a.* in-*ish*-e-a-tiv, serving to initiate; introductory: *n.* an introductory or first step; right to take the first step, esp. in legislation; aptitude to exercise self-reliance or to take the lead.
initiatory, *a.* in-*ish*-e-a-to-re, introductory; initiating or serving to initiate.
inject, *v.t.* in-*jekt,* to throw in; to force in by injection, as a liquid. (L. *injectus,* thrown.)
injection, *n.* in-*jek*-shon, the act of injecting, esp. fluids into the body by means of a syringe; that which is injected; a clyster; the forcing of cold water into the cylinder of a steam-engine to condense the steam. **injection cock,** the cock which admits cold water into the condenser [Mech.]. **injection engine,** a steam-engine in which the steam is condensed thus. (L. *injectio.*)
injector, *n.* in-*jek*-tor, any apparatus for injecting, esp. the mechanism by which water is forced into a boiler against the pressure of the steam.
injudicial, *a.* *in*-joo-*dish*-al, not in legal form.
injudicious, *a.* *in*-joo-*dish*-us, not judicious; not acting with judgment; not done with proper judgment; unwise.
injudiciously, *ad.* without judgment.
injudiciousness, *n.* quality of being injudicious.
injunction, *n.* in-*junk*-shon, the act of enjoining; command; order; direction; exhortation; an order of the court forbidding a person from doing a wrongful act, or requiring him to do a rightful one [Law]. (L. *injunctio.*)
injure, *v.t.* *in*-jer, to harm or hurt; to damage; to impair; to violate; to do wrong to. (Fr. *injurier.*)

injurer, *n.* *in*-jer-er, one who injures.
injurious, *a.* in-*joor*-re-us, tending to injure; harmful; damaging; unjust. (Fr. *injurieux.*)
injuriously, *ad.* so as to injure.
injuriousness, *n.* quality of being injurious.
injury, *n.* *in*-jer-re, any wrong or damage done to the person, rights, reputation, or goods of another; harm. (Fr. *injure.*)
injustice, *n.* in-*jus*-tis, the quality of being unjust; disregard or violation of what is right or due; wrong. (Fr.)
***ink,** *n.* ink, a coloured fluid for writing or printing; the protective exudation of a cuttle-fish: *v.t.* to colour or blacken with ink; to mark with ink; to apply ink to. (L. *encaustum,* the purple-red ink of the Roman emperors, from Gr. *encaustos,* burnt in.)
ink-bag, *n.* *ink*-bag, the sac from which the cuttle-fish discharges its ink.
ink-bottle, *n.* a bottle to hold ink.
inker, *n.* *ink*-er, an appliance that inks; an inking-roller [Print.].
inkhorn, *n.* *ink*-horn, a small vessel for ink; a portable writing-case: *a.* pedantic.
inkiness, *n.* *ing*-ke-ness, state or quality of being inky.
inking-roller, *n.* a roller covered with a composition for inking printing types.
inking-table, *n.* *ing*-king-*tay*-bl, a slab for supplying the inking-roller with ink during printing.
inkle, *n.* *ing*-kl, a kind of broad linen tape.
inkling, *n.* *ing*-kling, a hint or whisper; an intimation; inclination.
inkpot, *n.* *ink*-pot, a small vessel for ink.
inkslinging, *n.* *ink*-sling-ing, slapdash authorship or journalism [Slang.].
inkstand, *n.* *ink*-stand, a stand for holding ink and pens.
inkwell, *n.* *ink*-well, a small cup for ink fitting a hole in a desk.
inky, *a.* *ing*-ke, resembling or of the nature of ink; smeared or blackened with ink; black as ink.
inlace, *v.t.* in-*lace,* to lace; to enlace.
inlaid, *a.* in-*lade,* fitted in flush on the surface; decorated with a design by this means.
inland, *a.* *in*-land, remote from the sea; carried on within a country; confined to a country: *ad.* in or towards the land or the interior: *n.* the interior part of a country. **inland navigation,** navigation on rivers, canals, and lakes. **Inland Revenue,** the branch of the civil service responsible for revenue derived from income-tax, estate duties, stamps, and other internal imposts; (*l.c.*) such revenue.
inlander, *n.* *in*-lan-der, one who lives inland.
in-laws, *n.pl.* in-lawz, relatives by marriage [Coll.].
inlay, *v.t.* in-*lay,* to ornament by laying in pieces of fine wood, ivory, etc., flush with the surface of the ground-work. *p.* and *pp.* **inlaid.**
inlay, *n.* *in*-lay, pieces of wood, ivory, etc., inlaid; inlaid work.
inlayer, *n.* in-*lay*-er, one who inlays.
inlaying, *n.* in-*lay*-ing, the act or the occupation of one who inlays.
inlet, *n.* *in*-let, a passage by which there is ingress; a small entrance; a small bay or creek; something let in or inserted.
inlet, *v.t.* in-*let,* to insert or let in.
inlier, *n.* *in*-ly-er, an isolated exposure of underlying rocks.
inly, *a.* *in*-le, inward; secret: *ad.* inwardly.
inmate, *n.* *in*-mate, one who dwells in the same house with another; an occupant. (*in* and *mate.*)
inmost, *a.* *in*-mohst, deepest or farthest within. (A.S.)
inn, *n.* in, a public-house licensed for the lodging and refreshment of travellers; an hotel. **Inns of Court,** four corporate societies of lawyers in London possessing the exclusive privilege of qualifying for the bar; the buildings belonging severally to these societies. (A.S. *inn,* a house, from *in,* within.)
innate, *a.* in-*nate,* inborn; native; derived from within; inherent; natural. (L. *innatus,* born.)
innately, *ad.* in-*nate*-le, in an innate manner.
innateness, *n.* the quality of being innate.
innavigable, *a.* in-*nav*-e-ga-bl, not navigable.
inner, *a.* *in*-ner, further in; interior; inward; nearer the centre; at bottom; obscure; esoteric: *n.* the circle of a target next outside the bull's-eye; a shot striking this. (A.S. *innera.*)
innermost, *a.* *in*-ner-most, farthest inward; deepest within.
innervate, *v.t.* in-*ner*-vate, to give nervous energy to; to stimulate; to supply with nerves.
innervation, *n.* *in*-ner-*vay*-shon, act or process of innervating or strengthening; state of being innervated; the distribution of nerves [Zool.].
innerve, *v.t.* in-*nerv,* to give nerve to; to invigorate.
innholder, *n.* *in*-hohl-der, an innkeeper.
inning, *n.* *in*-ning, the ingathering of grain: *pl.* turn for batting in cricket or in baseball; the period of retention of power by a person or party. (A.S. *innung.*)
innkeeper, *n.* *in*-kee-per, a person who keeps an inn; the holder of the licence of an inn or tavern.
innocence, *n.* *in*-no-sence, harmlessness; guiltlessness; perfect moral purity, integrity, or simplicity. (Fr.)
innocent, *a.* *in*-no-sent, harmless; free from guilt or sin; guiltless; lawful; guileless; not malignant [Med.]; without, not having [Coll.]: *n.* one innocent; an imbecile. (Fr.)
innocently, *ad.* in an innocent manner.
innocuous, *a.* in-*nok*-yew-us, harmless in effect; not venomous [Zool.]. (L. *innocuus.*)
innocuously, *ad.* without harm.
innocuousness, *n.* in-*nok*-yew-us-ness, harmlessness.
innominable, *a.* in-*nom*-e-na-bl, unmentionable; not fit to be named.
innominate, *a.* in-*nom*-e-nate, having no name. **innominate artery,** an artery rising from the arch of the aorta. **innominate bone,** the hip-bone, or lateral half of the pelvic girdle. (Late L. *innominatus.*)
innovate, *v.t.* *in*-no-vate, to change by introducing something new: *v.i.* to introduce novelties or alterations in a thing established. (L. *innovatus.*)
innovation, *n.* in-no-*vay*-shon, change in an established practice by the introduction of new methods, etc.
innovator, *n.* *in*-no-vay-tor, one who makes innovations; an introducer of changes.
innoxious, *a.* in-*nok*-shus, harmless; innocuous.
innoxiously, *ad.* in-*nok*-shus-le, harmlessly.
innoxiousness, *n.* in-*nok*-shus-ness, harmlessness.
innuendo, *n.* in-new-*en*-do (*pl.* **innuendoes**), an oblique hint; a suggestive allusion; an indirect intimation or reference; an insinuation. (L.)
Innuit, *n.* *in*-yew-it, an American, as distinct from an Asiatic, Eskimo. (Eskimo, men.)
innumerability, *n.* in-*new*-mer-ra-*bil*-e-te, the quality of being innumerable.
innumerable, *a.* in-*new*-mer-ra-bl, that cannot be counted; indefinitely numerous. (O.Fr.)
innumerably, *ad.* without number.
innumerous, *a.* in-*new*-mer-rus, innumerable.
innutrition, *n.* *in*-new-*trish*-on, want of nutrition.
innutritious, *a.* *in*-new-*trish*-us, not nutritious.
innutritive, *a.* in-*new*-tre-tiv, innutritious.
inobservance, *n.* *in*-ob-*zer*-vance, failure to observe; non-observance.
inobservant, *a.* *in*-ob-*zer*-vant, not observant.
inobtrusive, *a.* in-ob-*troo*-siv, unobtrusive.
inoculable, *a.* in-*ok*-yew-la-bl, that may be inoculated; not immune; transmissible by inoculation.
inoculate, *v.t.* in-*ok*-yew-late, to render immune by the introduction into the body of the disease in a mild and controllable form; to infect or imbue with; to insert the bud of a tree in another as a graft: *v.i.* to practise inoculation; to propagate by budding. (L. *inoculatus,* engrafted.)
inoculation, *n.* in-*ok*-yew-*lay*-shon, the act, process, or practice of inoculating.
inoculator, *n.* in-*ok*-yew-lay-tor, one who inoculates.
inoculum, *n.* in-*ok*-yew-lum, the virus or other matter used in inoculation.
inodorous, *a.* in-*oh*-do-rus, having no scent or odour. (L. *inodorus.*)
inoffensive, *a.* *in*-of-*fen*-siv, giving no offence or provocation; harmless.
inoffensively, *ad.* in an inoffensive manner.
inoffensiveness, *n.* *in*-of-*fen*-siv-ness, the quality of being inoffensive or unobjectionable.
inofficious, *a.* *in*-of-*fish*-us, regardless of natural obligation; contrary to natural duty; inoperative.
inoperable, *a.* in-*op*-er-ra-bl, that cannot be operated upon [Surg.].

inoperative, *a.* in-*op*-er-a-tiv, producing no effect ; having no force.
inopportune, *a.* in-*op*-por-tune, not opportune.
inopportunely, *ad.* unseasonably.
inordinacy, *n.* in-*or*-de-na-se, inordinateness ; an inordinate act.
inordinate, *a.* in-*or*-de-nate, irregular ; immoderate ; excessive ; arranged in no definite order [Bot.]. (L. *inordinatus.*)
inordinately, *ad.* in an inordinate manner.
inordinateness, *n.* in-*or*-de-nate-ness, the quality of being inordinate ; deviation from order or rule prescribed ; irregularity.
inorganic, *a.* in-or-*gan*-ik, not organic ; not possessed of organs of life ; not organized ; void of organs, as earths, metals, etc. **inorganic chemistry**, *see* **chemistry**.
inorganically, *ad.* in-or-*gan*-e-kal-le, without organization.
inorganization, *n.* in-*or*-ga-ny-*zay*-shon, absence of organization.
inornate, *a.* in-or-*nate*, not elaborate.
inosculate, *v.i.* and *t.* in-*os*-kew-late, to unite or cause to become united by inosculation. (L. *in-*, and *osculum*, a little mouth.)
inosculation, *n.* in-*os*-kew-*lay*-shon, the union of two vessels in an animal body by a duct or by the mouth of one fitting into that of the other ; anastomosis.
in-patient, *n.* *in*-pay-shent, a patient lodged within a hospital for treatment.
input, *n.* *in*-poot, the amount of energy received by a machine [Mech.] ; a contribution [Scots.].
inquest, *n.* *in*-kwest, inquiry ; judicial inquiry, esp. by a coroner ; a jury. **coroner's inquest**, a judicial investigation into the cause of a death held before a coroner and jury. **grand inquest of the nation**, the House of Commons [Coll.]. (O.Fr. *enqueste.*)
inquietude, *n.* in-*kwy*-e-tewd, disturbed state or uneasiness, either of body or mind. (Fr.)
inquiline, *n.* *in*-kwe-line, an animal living in the abode and on the food of another ; a commensal [Zool.].
inquirable, *a.* in-*kwire*-a-bl, subject to inquiry.
inquire, *v.i.* in-*kwire*, to ask a question ; to make investigation : *v.t.* to ask about ; to seek by asking. **to inquire into**, to make examination. (Fr. *enquérir.*)
inquirendo, *n.* in-kwe-*ren*-do, an authority given to someone to inquire into something for the sovereign's advantage. (L.)
inquirer, *n.* in-*kwire*-er, one who makes inquiry.
inquiring, *a.* in-*kwire*-ing, given to inquiry.
inquiringly, *ad.* in-*kwire*-ing-le, by way of inquiry ; in an inquisitive manner.
inquiry, *n.* in-*kwire*-re, enquiry ; the act of inquiring ; interrogation ; search for information ; examination into facts or principles. **court of inquiry**, a body appointed by the military authorities to decide whether, on any given charge, a court-martial shall be held. **writ of inquiry**, a writ commanding the sheriff to summon a jury to inquire into the damages due from defendant to plaintiff in a given action.
inquisition, *n.* *in*-kwe-*zish*-on, inquiry ; examination ; inquest ; the treatment of heresy as carried out by the Court of Inquisition. **Court of Inquisition**, a tribunal of the Rom. Cath. Church established for the examination and punishment of heretics and now dealing chiefly with heretical publications ; the Holy Office. (Fr.)
inquisitional, *a.* *in*-kwe-*zish*-on-al, making inquiry ; prying ; inquisitorial.
inquisitive, *a.* in-*kwiz*-e-tiv, curious to know ; prying : *n.* a person who is inquisitive. (Fr. *inquisitif.*)
inquisitively, *ad.* in an inquisitive manner.
inquisitiveness, *n.* quality of being inquisitive.
inquisitor, *n.* in-*kwiz*-e-tor, one who inquires, specially officially ; a functionary of the Court of Inquisition. **Grand Inquisitor**, the president of this Court. **Inquisitor-General**, the head of the Inquisition in Spain.
inquisitorial, *a.* in-*kwiz*-e-*taw*-re-al, pertaining to inquiry, or to the Court of Inquisition ; searching.
inquisitorially, *ad.* after the manner of an inquisitor.
inrigged, *a.* *in*-rigd, with rowlocks on the gunwale.
inro, *n.* *in*-ro, a small box or nest of boxes for sweetmeats, medicines, etc., carried by Japanese on the belt. (Jap.)
inroad, *n.* *in*-rode, hostile entrance into an enemy's country ; a sudden or desultory irruption ; attack ; an encroachment.
inrush, *n.* *in*-rush, a rushing in ; an irruption.
insalivate, *v.t.* in-*sal*-e-vate, to mix food with saliva in masticating.
insalivation, *n.* in-*sal*-e-*vay*-shon, the mixing of the saliva with the food when eating.
insalubrious, *a.* *in*-sa-*lew*-bre-us, unhealthy.
insalubrity, *n.* *in*-sa-*lew*-bre-te, want of salubrity.
insalutary, *a.* in-*sal*-yew-ta-re, having a deleterious effect, esp. mentally or socially.
insane, *a.* in-*sane*, not of a sound mind ; deranged in mind ; for the insane : *n.* insane persons collectively. (L. *insanus.*)
insanely, *ad.* in an insane manner ; foolishly.
insaneness, *n.* in-*sane*-ness, insanity.
insanitary, *a.* in-*san*-e-ta-re, not sanitary ; unhealthy.
insanitation, *n.* in-*san*-e-*tay*-shon, defective sanitary conditions or arrangements.
insanity, *n.* in-*san*-e-te, the state of being unsound in mind ; lunacy ; derangement.
insatiability, *n.* in-*say*-she-a-*bil*-e-te, insatiableness.
insatiable, *a.* in-*say*-she-a-bl, incapable of being satisfied or appeased. (L. *insatiabilis.*)
insatiableness, *n.* in-*say*-she-a-bl-ness, the quality or state of being insatiable.
insatiably, *ad.* in-*say*-she-a-ble, with greediness not to be satisfied.
insatiate, *a.* in-*say*-she-ate, insatiable.
insaturable, *a.* in-*sat*-yew-ra-bl, incapable of being saturated.
inscribable, *a.* in-*skribe*-a-bl, that may be inscribed.
inscribe, *v.t.* in-*skribe*, to write on ; to engrave ; to imprint deeply ; to address as a dedication ; to mark with letters, characters, or words ; to draw a figure within another [Geom.]. (L. *inscribere*, write.)
inscriber, *n.* in-*skribe*-er, one who inscribes.
inscription, *n.* in-*skrip*-shon, the act or process of inscribing ; that which is inscribed ; something inscribed for transmission of information ; the title to an illustration, etc. ; address by way of dedication.
inscriptional, *a.* in-*skrip*-shon-al, pertaining to an inscription ; inscriptive.
inscriptive, *a.* in-*skrip*-tiv, of the nature of an inscription.
inscrutability, *n.* in-*skroo*-ta-*bil*-e-te, the quality of being inscrutable.
inscrutable, *a.* in-*skroo*-ta-bl, incapable of being found out by searching or by reason ; mysterious ; incomprehensible. (Fr.)
inscrutably, *ad.* to an inscrutable degree.
***insect**, *n.* *in*-sekt, any of the Insecta, a very large and widely distributed class of arthropodous animals having the body in three sections—head, thorax and abdomen—and six legs ; any small or contemptible person. (L. *insectum.*)
insectarium, *n.* *in*-sek-*tare*-re-um, a place for keeping a collection of insects ; such a collection.
insecticide, *n.* in-*sek*-te-side, a preparation that destroys insects but is harmless to plants or the skin. (L. *insectum*, insect, *cædo*, kill.)
insectiform, *a.* in-*sek*-te-form, having the shape or appearance of an insect.
insectifuge, *n.* in-*sek*-te-fewj, a preparation for keeping insects away. (L. *insectum*, and *fugo*, drive away.)
insectile, *a.* in-*sek*-til, of the nature of insects ; resembling insects.
insection, *n.* in-*sek*-shon, an incision ; a cutting in.
insectivore, *n.* in-*sek*-te-vor, any of the Insectivora, an order of mammals, including the shrews and hedgehog, that feed on insects. (L. *insectum*, insect, *voro*, devour.)
insectivorous, *a.* *in*-sek-*tiv*-o-rus, feeding on insects.
insectology, *n.* *in*-sek-*tol*-o-je, economic entomology.
insecure, *a.* in-se-*kewr*, not secure ; unsafe ; not confident of safety ; not effectually protected.
insecurely, *ad.* in-se-*kewr*-le, without security.
insecurity, *n.* in-se-*kewr*-re-te, want of safety or of confidence in safety ; uncertainty ; exposure to destruction or loss.

inseminate, *v.t.* in-*sem*-e-nate, to sow, as seed; to impregnate; to implant, as in the mind. (L. *inseminatus.*)
insemination, *n.* *in*-sem-e-*nay*-shon, the act or process of inseminating; impregnation.
insensate, *a.* in-*sen*-sate, destitute of sense; wanting sensibility; stupid.
insensibility, *n.* in-*sen*-se-*bil*-e-te, state of being insensible; want of the power to be moved or affected; absence of susceptibility of emotion and passion.
insensible, *a.* in-*sen*-se-bl, without feeling, power of feeling, or sensibility; unconscious; not susceptible of emotion or passion; apathetic; imperceptible to the senses.
insensibly, *ad.* in-*sen*-se-ble, imperceptibly; by slow degrees; gradually.
insensitive, *a.* in-*sen*-se-tiv, not sensitive.
insensitiveness, *n.* in-*sen*-se-tiv-ness, the condition or quality of not being sensitive.
insensuous, *a.* in-*sen*-sew-us, not sensuous; not pertaining to the senses.
insentient, *a.* in-*sen*-she-ent, not having perception; devoid of consciousness.
inseparability, *n.* in-*sep*-a-ra-*bil*-e-te, the quality of being inseparable.
inseparable, *a.* in-*sep*-a-ra-bl, that cannot be separated. **inseparable accident,** an attribute inseparable from an individual [Logic]. (L. *inseparabilis.*)
inseparableness, *n.* in-*sep*-a-ra-bl-ness, inseparability.
inseparably, *ad.* to an inseparable degree.
insert, *v.t.* in-*sert*, to set in or among; to thrust in; to introduce into; to ornament with insertions. (L. *insertus*, joined.)
inserted, *a.* in-*sert*-ed, growing out of or attached to [Bot.].
insertion, *n.* in-*ser*-shon, the act of inserting; the state of being inserted; the thing or matter inserted; lace or embroidery to be inserted in dresses and other articles of women's wear; the place where one part grows out of another, or the manner in which it does so [Bot. and Anat.].
Insessores, *n.pl.* in-ses-*saw*-reez, an order of birds that perch; perchers [Ornith.]. (Late L.)
insessorial, *a.* in-ses-*saw*-re-al, belonging to the Insessores; perching.
inset, *v.t.* in-*set*, to infix or implant.
inset, *n.* *in*-set, an insertion; something set in, as extra pages in a book, a small map, etc., within a larger one.
inseverable, *a.* in-*sev*-er-a-bl, that cannot be severed.
inshore, *ad.* *in*-shore, near the shore from the sea: *a.* situated near the shore.
inside, *n.* *in*-side, the interior part of a thing; the bowels; a passenger in the inside of a vehicle.
inside, *prep.* in-*side*, within: *ad.* into the interior: *a.* internal; situated within.
insider, *n.* in-*side*-er, one in the secret; one with inside knowledge.
insidious, *a.* in-*sid*-e-us, lying in wait; watching an opportunity to ensnare; treacherous; deceitful; intended to ensnare or betray; working secretly; coming on gradually (of illness) [Med.]. (Fr. *insidieux.*)
insidiously, *ad.* in an insidious manner.
insidiousness, *n.* in-*sid*-e-us-ness, the quality of being insidious.
insight, *n.* *in*-site, clear vision or perception into the true nature or character of a thing.
insignia, *n.pl.* in-*sig*-ne-a, badge of office or honour; distinguishing marks. (L.)
insignificance, *n.* *in*-sig-*nif*-e-kance, want of significance, meaning, or importance.
insignificancy, *n.* *in*-sig-*nif*-e-kan-se, insignificance.
insignificant, *a.* *in*-sig-*nif*-e-kant, destitute of meaning; of no importance; without weight of character; contemptible.
insignificantly, *ad.* *in*-sig-*nif*-e-kant-le, without meaning or importance.
insincere, *a.* in-sin-*seer*, not sincere; dissembling; hypocritical; deceitful; false. (L. *insincerus.*)
insincerely, *ad.* in-sin-*seer*-le, without sincerity.
insincerity, *n.* *in*-sin-*se*-re-te, want of sincerity; hypocrisy; deceitfulness; hollowness.
insinuate, *v.t.* in-*sin*-yew-ate, to introduce gently or artfully; to hint or suggest by remote allusion; to instil: *v.i.* to enter gently or imperceptibly; to gain on the affections by gentle or artful means. (L. *insinuatus*, wound in.)
insinuatingly, *ad.* in an insinuating way.
insinuation, *n.* in-*sin*-yew-*ay*-shon, suggestion by allusion; the act or power of insinuating; that which is insinuated; a hint.
insinuative, *a.* in-*sin*-yew-a-tiv, insinuating.
insinuator, *n.* in-*sin*-yew-ay-tor, one who insinuates.
insipid, *a.* in-*sip*-id, tasteless; wanting animation or interest; dull; spiritless. (L. *insipidus.*)
insipidity, *n.* *in*-se-*pid*-e-te, tastelessness; want of spirit or interest.
insipidly, *ad.* in-*sip*-id-le, tastelessly; spiritlessly.
insipidness, *n.* in-*sip*-id-ness, insipidity.
insipience, *n.* in-*sip*-e-ence, the quality of being insipient; foolishness.
insipient, *a.* in-*sip*-e-ent, wanting sense or wisdom. (L. *in-*, not, *sapiens*, wise.)
insist, *v.i.* in-*sist*, to persist in; to urge as a command; to dwell on (as in discourse). (Fr. *insister.*)
insistence, *n.* in-*sis*-tence, the quality of being insistent; act of insisting on.
insistent, *a.* in-*sis*-tent, insisting; persevering; dwelling or dilating on.
insistently, *ad.* in-*sis*-tent-le, in an insistent manner.
insobriety, *n.* in-so-*bry*-e-te, absence of sobriety; intemperance.
insociably, *ad.* in-*soh*-she-a-ble, unsociably.
insolate, *v.t.* *in*-so-late, to dry in the sun. (L. *insolatus.*)
insolation, *n.* in-so-*lay*-shon, the act or process of exposing to the rays of the sun; the radiation received from the sun [Meteor.]; sunstroke [Med.].
insole, *n.* *in*-sole, the inner sole in footwear.
insolence, *n.* *in*-so-lence, pride or haughtiness manifested in contemptuous and overbearing treatment; contemptuous impertinence. (Fr.)
insolent, *a.* *in*-so-lent, haughty and contemptuous; proceeding from insolence; offensively insulting.
insolently, *ad.* *in*-so-lent-le, in an insolent manner.
insolidity, *n.* in-so-*lid*-e-te, absence of solidity; weakness; frailty.
insolubility, *n.* in-*sol*-yew-*bil*-e-te, the quality of being insoluble.
insoluble, *a.* in-*sol*-yew-bl, that cannot be dissolved; that cannot be explained. (L. *insolubilis.*)
insolubleness, *n.* in-*sol*-yew-bl-ness, insolubility.
insolubly, *ad.* in an insoluble manner.
insolvable, *a.* in-*sol*-va-bl, that cannot be solved or explained; that cannot be cashed (as notes, etc.).
insolvency, *n.* in-*sol*-ven-se, state of being insolvent; inability to pay.
insolvent, *a.* in-*sol*-vent, not able or sufficient to pay all debts; relating to debtors: *n.* a debtor unable to pay his debts.
insomnia, *n.* in-*som*-ne-a, prolonged or abnormal sleeplessness. (L.)
insomuch, *ad.* *in*-so-*mutch*, so that; to such a degree.
insouciance, *n.* in-*soo*-se-ance, unconcern. (Fr.)
insouciant, *a.* in-*soo*-se-ant, careless; unconcerned.
inspan, *v.t.* in-*span*, to yoke. (Dut. *inspannen.*)
inspect, *v.t.* in-*spekt*, to look into; to examine officially or critically. (L. *inspecto.*)
inspection, *n.* in-*spek*-shon, the act of inspecting; close or careful survey; official oversight or examination.
inspectioneer, *n.* in-*spek*-sho-*neer*, a specksioneer.
inspective, *a.* in-*spek*-tiv, given to inspecting.
inspectoscope, *n.* in-*spek*-to-skope, an X-ray apparatus by means of which the contents of an unopened package or container may be examined.
inspector, *n.* in-*spek*-tor, one who inspects; an overseer or superintendent; an official examiner; a police officer next below a superintendent. **Inspector-General,** a chief of inspectors, esp. a high military departmental officer. (L.)
inspectorate, *n.* in-*spek*-to-rat, the office of inspector; a body of inspectors.
inspectorial, *a.* *in*-spek-*taw*-re-al, pertaining to an inspector or his duties.
inspectorship, *n.* in-*spek*-tor-ship, the office, status, or period of office of an inspector.
inspirable, *a.* in-*spire*-ra-bl, that may be inhaled.
inspiration, *n.* in-spe-*ray*-shon, the act of drawing air into the lungs; the suggestion of thoughts; supernatural influence on the human mind; supernatural influence, tending to raise the soul above

itself; the resulting elevation; an idea or impression received in this elevated state. (Fr.)
inspirational, *a.* in-spe-*ray*-shon-al, able or tending to inspire; pertaining to inspiration.
inspirationist, *n.* in-spe-*ray*-shon-ist, one believing in the divine inspiration of the Scriptures.
inspirator, *n.* *in*-spe-ray-tor, an apparatus for sucking in air or vapour; an injector [Eng.].
inspiratory, *a.* in-*spire*-a-to-re, pertaining to or aiding inspiration; respiratory.
inspire, *v.i.* in-*spire*, to draw in the breath: *v.t.* to breathe into; infuse by breathing; to infuse or instil into the mind; to infuse or communicate by divine inspiration; to animate or elevate supernaturally; to inhale. (O.Fr. *enspirer.*)
inspired, *a.* in-*spired*, directed or proceeding by or as by divine influence; emanating from above; authoritative but anonymous.
inspirer, *n.* in-*spire*-er, he who inspires.
inspiringly, *ad.* in-*spire*-ing-le, in an inspiring manner; in a way to infuse spirit or courage.
inspirit, *v.t.* in-*spi*-rit, to infuse spirit into; to give new life to; to invigorate.
inspissate, *a.* in-*spis*-sat *or* *in*-spe-sate, rendered thicker or more dense; *v.t.* to thicken, as a fluid substance, by boiling or evaporation. (L. *inspissatus.*)
inspissation, *n.* in-spe-*say*-shon, the act or process of inspissating or thickening.
instability, *n.* in-sta-*bil*-e-te, absence of stability; want of firmness; inconstancy; fickleness.
install, *v.t.* in-*stawl*, to place or establish in an office; to invest with any charge, office, or rank, with the customary ceremonies; to have fittings or apparatus, etc., put in for use. (Fr. *installer.*)
installation, *n.* *in*-staw-*lay*-shon, the act of installing; induction to office; that which is installed, esp. mechanical or electrical apparatus.
instalment, *n.* in-*stawl*-ment, the act of installing; such part of a total sum as is payable at stated intervals; one of the parts of anything, esp. a publication, issued at intervals. **instalment system,** hire-purchase.
instance, *n.* *in*-stance, a case occurring; example; occurrence; a solicitation: *v.t.* to mention as an example or case. (Fr.)
instancy, *n.* *in*-stan-se, urgency.
instant, *a.* *in*-stant, pressing; urgent; making no delay; present, in the current month, as on the 10th instant: *n.* a point in duration; a moment; a particular time. (L. *in-*, and *sto*, to stand.)
instantaneity, *n.* *in*-stan-ta-*nee*-e-te, instantaneousness.
instantaneous, *a.* *in*-stan-*tay*-ne-us, done or happening in an instant; lasting only for an instant.
instantaneously, *ad.* *in*-stan-*tay*-ne-us-le, in an instant; in a moment.
instantaneousness, *n.* *in*-stan-*tay*-ne-us-ness, the quality of being instantaneous.
instanter, *ad.* in-*stan*-ter, immediately. (L.)
instantly, *ad.* *in*-stant-le, immediately; eagerly.
instar, *n.* *in*-star, the form assumed by an insect at any given stage in development. [Zool.]. (L., an appearance.)
instate, *v.t.* in-*state*, to set or place; to establish.
instauration, *n.* in-staw-*ray*-shon, the restoration of a thing; renewal; repair. (L. *instauro*, renew.)
instead, *ad.* in-*sted*, in the stead, place, or room of.
instep, *n.* *in*-step, the fore-part of the upper side of the foot, near its junction with the leg; the corresponding part of footwear; that part of the hind-leg of a horse reaching from the ham to the pastern-joint.
instigate, *v.t.* *in*-ste-gate, to set or urge on; to incite, esp. to what is bad. (L. *instigatus*, goaded on.)
instigation, *n.* in-ste-*gay*-shon, the act of instigating; incitement; impulse to evil.
instigator, *n.* *in*-ste-gay-tor, one who incites to evil.
instil, *v.t.* in-*stil*, to pour in by drops; to infuse slowly into the mind. (Fr. *instiller.*)
instillation, *n.* in-stil-*lay*-shon, the act or process of instilling; that which is instilled.
instiller, *n.* in-*stil*-ler, one who instils.
instilment, *n.* in-*stil*-ment, the act of instilling; anything instilled.
instinct, *n.* *in*-stinkt, natural propensity in animals to do what is necessary for existence, preservation, and propagation; unreasoned prompting; innate impulse: *a.* animated or moved from within; full of; charged with. (Fr.)
instinctive, *a.* in-*stink*-tiv, prompted by instinct; spontaneous; determined by natural impulse.
instinctively, *ad.* by force or instinct.
instipulate, *a.* in-*stip*-yew-late, without stipules [Bot.].
institute, *n.* *in*-ste-tewt, anything instituted; a society established for some scientific, literary, or public object; an established law, precept, or principle; a book of principles, esp. in jurisprudence or medicine: *v.t.* to set up in; to establish; to found; to originate; to commence; to invest with the spiritual part of a benefice [Eccles.]. (L. *institutus*, established.)
institution, *n.* *in*-ste-*tew*-shon, the act of instituting; that which is instituted; establishment; an established law, enactment, or custom, etc.; a society established for promoting any object, public or social; the act or ceremony of investing a clergyman with the spiritual part of a benefice [Eccles.]; a workhouse, or poor-law institution [Coll.].
institutional, *a.* in-ste-*tew*-shon-al, pertaining to or finding expression through an institution; instituted by authority.
institutionalism, *n.* *in*-ste-*tew*-shon-a-lizm, the use of institutions, esp. for charitable or reformatory purposes; this system, or its advocacy; attachment to established institutions.
institutionalist, *n.* in-ste-*tew*-shon-a-list, an upholder of established institutions, esp. those of the Church.
institutionalize, *v.t.* in-ste-*tew*-shon-a-lize, to make institutional.
institutionary, *a.* in-ste-*tew*-shon-a-re, pertaining to institutions, esp. ecclesiastical.
institutive, *a.* *in*-ste-*tew*-tiv, tending to institute; depending on institution.
institutor, *n.* *in*-ste-*tew*-tor, one who institutes, esp. a society or scheme; one who institutes a clergyman into a parish. (L.)
instruct, *v.t.* in-*strukt*, to impart knowledge to one who is destitute of it; to teach; to direct; to furnish with orders or instructions; to inform. (L. *instructus*, instructed.)
instruction, *n.* in-*struk*-shon, the act of instructing; teaching; information; direction; order; mandate.
instructional, *a.* in-*struk*-shon-al, pertaining to, containing, or purveying instruction.
instructive, *a.* in-*struk*-tiv, serving to instruct or inform; conveying instruction.
instructively, *ad.* so as to afford instruction.
instructiveness, *n.* quality of being instructive.
instructor, *n.* in-*struk*-tor, a teacher; one who instructs; a book containing instruction. (L.)
instructress, *n.* in-*struk*-tress, a female instructor.
***instrument,** *n.* *in*-stroo-ment, a tool, implement, or other means by which work is done or effects are produced; an agent or means employed as a tool for a purpose; a contrivance for producing musical sounds by means of vibration (stringed instrument) or by direct air-currents (wind-instrument); a writing containing the terms of a contract [Law]: *v.t.* to prepare a score for musical instruments. (Fr., from L. *instruere*, to instruct.)
instrumental, *a.* *in*-stroo-*men*-tal, conducive, as an instrument or means, to some end; contributing; pertaining to music arising from instruments.
instrumentalist, *n.* *in*-stroo-*men*-ta-list, one who plays a musical instrument.
instrumentality, *n.* *in*-stroo-men-*tal*-e-te, subordinate or auxiliary agency; usefulness, as means to an end.
instrumentally, *ad.* *in*-stroo-*men*-tal-le, by means of an instrument; with instruments of music.
instrumentation, *n.* *in*-stroo-men-*tay*-shon, the arranging of music for a combination of instruments: manner of playing in concert; the use of surgical or other instruments; instrumentality.
insuavity, *n.* in-*swav*-e-te, lack of suavity; harshness.
insubjection, *n.* *in*-sub-*jek*-shon, insubordination.
insubmissive, *a.* in-sub-*miss*-iv, not submissive; rebellious against control.
insubordinate, *a.* *in*-sub-*or*-de-nat, not subordinate or submissive to authority; unruly.
insubordination, *n.* in-sub-*or*-de-*nay*-shon, want of subordination; disobedience to lawful authority.
insubstantial, *a.* *in*-sub-*stan*-shal, unsubstantial.

insubstantiality, *n.* *in*-sub-*stan*-she-*al*-e-te, the quality of being insubstantial.
insufferable, *a.* in-*suf*-fer-a-bl, that cannot be suffered or endured; intolerable; detestable.
insufferably, *ad.* to an insufferable degree.
insufficiency, *n.* *in*-suf-*fish*-en-se, the quality of being insufficient; inadequateness; incompetency.
insufficient, *a.* *in*-suf-*fish*-ent, not sufficient; inadequate; incapable; unfit. (O.Fr.)
insufficiently, *ad.* in an insufficient manner.
insufflate, *v.t.* *in*-suf-flate, to blow on to or into, esp. [Med.] to blow powder or vapour into the lungs. (L. *insufflatus*, blown into.)
insufflation, *n.* *in*-suf-*flay*-shon, the act of insufflating [Med.].
insufflator, *n.* *in*-suf-flay-tor, an appliance used for insufflating [Med.].
insulant, *n.* *in*-sew-lant, any insulating material [Elect.].
insular, *a.* *in*-sew-lar, belonging to an island; surrounded by water; isolated; narrow-minded. (L. *insularis*, from *insula*, an island.)
insularity, *n.* in-sew-*la*-re-te, the state of being insular.
insularly, *ad.* *in*-sew-lar-le, in an insular manner.
insulate, *v.t.* *in*-sew-late, to place in a detached situation so as to break continuity or prevent communication; to isolate; to separate or isolate by a non-conducting substance [Elect.]. (L. *insulatus.*)
insulated, *a.* *in*-sew-lay-ted, standing by itself; not being contiguous to other bodies [Arch.]; separated by a non-conductor [Elect.].
insulation, *n.* *in*-sew-*lay*-shon, act of insulating; state of being insulated, esp. by a non-conductor.
insulator, *n.* *in*-sew-lay-tor, that which insulates, esp. an appliance used to insulate a conductor from earth or from another conductor [Elect.].
insulin, *n.* *in*-sew-lin, proprietary name of a hormone prepared from the pancreas and used in the treatment of diabetes.
insult, *n.* *in*-sult, abuse, either by word or action; affront; indignity; outrage; insolent treatment. (Fr. *insulter.*)
insult, *v.t.* in-*sult*, to treat with abuse or insolence; to affront: *v.i.* to behave with insolent triumph.
insultable, *a.* in-*sult*-a-bl, capable of appreciating an insult.
insulter, *n.* in-*sult*-er, one who insults.
insultingly, *ad.* in-*sult*-ing-le, with insolence.
insuperability, *n.* in-*sew*-per-a-*bil*-e-te, the quality of being insuperable or insurmountable.
insuperable, *a.* in-*sew*-per-a-bl, that cannot be overcome or surmounted. (O.Fr.)
insuperably, *ad.* to an insuperable degree.
insupportable, *a.* in-sup-*por*-ta-bl, insufferable; intolerable.
insupportably, *ad.* *in*-sup-*por*-ta-ble, to an insupportable degree.
insuppressible, *a.* *in*-sup-*pres*-se-bl, not to be suppressed.
insuppressibly, *ad.* so as not to be suppressed.
insuppressive, *a.* in-sup-*pres*-siv, insuppressible.
insurable, *a.* in-*shure*-ra-bl, that may be insured against loss or damage; proper to be insured.
★**insurance,** *n.* in-*shure*-rance, the act of insuring against damage or loss; a contract by which one engages, for a stipulated premium, to make up a loss which may be sustained or to pay an agreed amount at a death or other contingency; the premium paid. **insurance broker,** a broker acting as agent for the insured, esp. in marine insurance. **insurance company,** a company whose business is to insure persons against loss or damage.
insurant, *n.* in-*shure*-rant, one who insures; the holder of an insurance policy.
insure, *v.t.* in-*shure*, to contract for a premium to secure against loss: *v.i.* to take out an insurance policy. (O.Fr. *enseurer.*)
insurer, *n.* in-*shure*-rer, one who insures; the insured (person).
insurgence, *n.* in-*sur*-jence, the act of rebelling; a rising.
insurgency, *n.* in-*sur*-jen-se, the state or quality of being insurgent; insurgence; insurrection.
insurgent, *a.* in-*sur*-jent, rising in opposition to authority: *n.* one who actively rebels against constituted authority or openly resists the execution of some law; a rebel. (Fr.)
insurmountable, *a.* *in*-sur-*moun*-ta-bl, that cannot be surmounted or overcome.
insurmountably, *ad.* to an insurmountable degree.
insurrection, *n.* *in*-sur-*rek*-shon, a rising up against constituted government or lawful authority; an open and active resistance to the execution of some law.
insurrectional, *a.* in-sur-*rek*-shon-al, insurrectionary.
insurrectionary, *a.* in-sur-*rek*-shon-a-re, pertaining to or consisting in insurrection: *n.* one participating in an insurrection; a rebel.
insurrectionist, *n.* *in*-sur-*rek*-shon-ist, one who favours or engages in insurrection.
insusceptibility, *n.* *in*-sus-*sep*-te-*bil*-e-te, absence of susceptibility.
insusceptible, *a.* *in*-sus-*sep*-te-bl, not susceptible; not capable of being affected, or of receiving impression.
inswinger, *n.* *in*-swing-er, that which swings inwards, esp. [Cricket] a ball from the off side.
intact, *a.* in-*takt*, untouched by adverse influence; entire; unimpaired. (L. *intactus.*)
intagliated, *a.* in-*tal*-yay-ted, engraved in or as in intaglio; incised.
intaglio, *n.* in-*tah*-lyo, a figure hollowed out in a gem or other substance; a precious stone with a figure or device cut into it. **intaglio printing,** printing done from an incised or engraved plate. (It., cutting in.)
intake, *n.* *in*-take, a tract of enclosed land; the inlet of a pipe; the point where a tube narrows; an inhalation.
intangibility, *n.* in-*tan*-je-*bil*-e-te, the quality of being intangible.
intangible, *a.* in-*tan*-je-bl, not tangible; not perceptible to the touch; unsubstantial.
intangibleness, *n.* in-*tan*-je-bl-ness, intangibility.
intangibly, *ad.* in-*tan*-je-ble, so as to be intangible.
intarsia, *n.* in-*tar*-se-a, an inlay of wood of one or more colours upon a darker or lighter ground. (It. *in*, and *tarsia*, marquetry.)
integer, *n.* *in*-te-jer, a whole, complete in itself; a whole number [Arith.]. (L. from *in*, not, and *tango*, touch.)
integrable, *a.* *in*-te-gra-bl, capable of being integrated.
integral, *a.* *in*-te-gral, comprising all the parts; whole; entire; not fractional; pertaining to or consisting of a whole: *n.* a whole; an entire thing; the result of the integration of a function or equation [Math.]. **integral calculus,** *see* **calculus.**
integrality, *n.* in-te-*gral*-e-te, integral quality or state.
integrally, *ad.* *in*-te-gra-le, wholly; completely.
integrand, *n.* *in*-te-grand, an expression to be integrated [Math.].
integrant, *a.* *in*-te-grant, making part of a whole; necessary to constitute an entire thing. **integrant parts,** the small particles of which any substance is composed, each being of the same composition. (L. *integrans.*)
integrate, *v.t.* *in*-te-grate, to make entire; to give the total; to find the integral of [Math.]. (L. *integratus*, made whole.)
integrate, *a.* *in*-te-grat, made up of integrant parts; complete; entire.
integration, *n.* in-*te-gray*-shon, the act, process, or operation of integrating; the blending of diverse psychological characteristics to form a complete whole.
integrative, *a.* *in*-te-gra-tiv, tending to integrate.
integrator, *n.* *in*-te-gray-tor, one who integrates; an instrument or device for performing integrations.
integrity, *n.* in-*teg*-re-te, wholeness; entireness; unbroken or unimpaired state; moral soundness; uprightness; honesty.
integument, *n.* in-*teg*-yew-ment, that which naturally invests or covers, as skin (of animals) or rind, husk (of seeds, etc.). (L. *integumentum.*)
integumentary, *a.* in-*teg*-yew-*men*-ta-re, belonging to, resembling, or composed of integuments.
intellect, *n.* *in*-te-lekt, the mind or understanding; that faculty by which the mind perceives and comprehends things in themselves and their relations, as distinct from the faculties of feeling and willing; the faculty of thinking; intellectual persons collectively. (O.Fr.)
intellection, *n.* *in*-te-*lek*-shon, the act of understanding; simple apprehension of ideas.

intellective, *a.* *in*-te-*lek*-tiv, having power to understand; produced by, perceptible by, or pertaining to, the intellect.
intellectual, *a.* *in*-te-*lek*-tew-al, markedly endowed with intellect; relating to the or performed by the intellect; existing in the intellect: *n.* one who is intellectual; a member of the intelligentsia.
intellectualism, *n.* *in*-te-*lek*-tew-a-lizm, the more or less exclusive culture of intellect; the philosophical doctrine that all knowledge is derived from pure reason.
intellectualist, *n.* *in*-te-*lek*-tew-a-list, an advocate of intellectual culture; a supporter of philosophic intellectualism.
intellectuality, *n.* *in*-te-*lek*-tew-*al*-e-te, the state of being intellectual; intellectual power.
intellectualize, *v.t.* and *i.* *in*-te-*lek*-tew-a-lize, to render or to become intellectual.
intellectually, *ad.* in-te-*lek*-tew-a-le, by means of the understanding.
intelligence, *n.* in-*tel*-le-jence, intellectual capacity, skill, or power; acquired knowledge; news; information; or spiritual being possessing intellect. **Intelligence Department,** the branch of a business, army, etc., charged with compiling and supplying necessary information. **intelligence test,** any test to determine the mental capacity of, or the degree of intelligence possessed by, the person tested. (Fr.)
intelligencer, *n.* in-*tel*-le-jen-ser, one who or that which conveys intelligence; a spy.
intelligent, *a.* in-*tel*-le-jent, quick to learn; endowed with understanding or reason; endowed with superior intelligence; sagacious. (Fr.)
intelligential, *a.* in-*tel*-le-*jen*-shal, pertaining to or having intelligence; intellectual.
intelligently, *ad.* in an intelligent manner.
intelligentsia, *n.pl.* in-*tel*-le-*jen*-se-a, the educated or professional classes; persons of culture collectively (often used in derision).
intelligibility, *n.* in-*tel*-le-je-*bil*-e-te, the quality or state of being intelligible.
intelligible, *a.* in-*tel*-le-je-bl, that may be understood; clear. (Fr.)
intelligibly, *ad.* in a manner to be understood.
intemperance, *n.* in-*tem*-per-ance, want of moderation or due restraint; excess in any kind of action or indulgence; habitual over-indulgence in intoxicating liquors. (L. *intemperantia.*)
intemperate, *a.* in-*tem*-per-ate, not restrained within due limits; indulging to excess any appetite or passion; addicted to excessive drinking; immoderate; violent. (L. *intemperatus.*)
intemperately, *ad.* to an immoderate degree.
intemperateness, *n.* in-*tem*-per-at-ness, the quality or condition of being intemperate.
intend, *v.t.* in-*tend*, to mean; to design; to purpose; to have a certain intention. (Fr. *entendre.*)
intendancy, *n.* in-*ten*-dan-se, the office or district of an intendant; a body of intendants.
intendant, *n.* in-*ten*-dant, a superintendent. (Fr.)
Intendant-General, *n.* a chief intendant, esp. of the administrative branch of an army's Staff; a supreme Quartermaster-General.
intended, *n.* in-*ten*-ded, an affianced lover [Coll.].
intendedly, *ad.* in-*ten*-ded-le, purposely.
intendment, *n.* in-*tend*-ment, signification; the true meaning of any legal instrument [Law].
intensative, *a.* in-*ten*-sa-tiv, intensifying: *n.* an intensive.
intense, *a.* in-*tense*, strained or raised to a high degree; extreme; excessive; very severe or keen; ardent; emotional; kept on the stretch; anxiously attentive. (O.Fr.)
intensely, *ad.* in-*tense*-le, to an intense degree.
intenseness, *n.* the state of being intense.
intensification, *n.* in-*tense*-e-fe-*kay*-shon, the action of making intense.
intensifier, *n.* in-*tense*-e-fy-er, that which intensifies; a chemical agent for intensifying a negative [Phot.].
intensify, *v.t.* in-*ten*-se-fy, to make intense or more intense; to increase the contrast and density of a negative [Phot.].
intension, *n.* in-*ten*-shon, the act of stretching or making more tense; the state of being stretched; intensity; the sum of attributes implied in a term [Logic].
intensity, *n.* in-*ten*-se-te, quality of being intense; intenseness; sum of energy; very high degree. (L. *intensus.*)
intensive, *a.* in-*ten*-siv, admitting of intension; or increase of degree; concentrated; marked by increasing intensity; giving or serving to give force or emphasis: *n.* a word used for increasing emphasis. **intensive agriculture,** the effort to obtain the greatest possible yield per acre.
intensively, *ad.* in an intensive manner.
intent, *a.* in-*tent*, anxiously diligent; having the mind strained or bent on an object; fixed closely; sedulously applied: *n.* the thing aimed at or intended; aim; purpose. **to all intents,** for all practical purposes. (O.Fr. *entente.*)
intention, *n.* in-*ten*-shon, design; purpose; end or aim; closeness of application; fixedness of attention: *pl.* designs regarding future marriage [Coll.]. (Fr.)
intentional, *a.* in-*ten*-shon-al, done designedly.
intentionally, *ad.* in-*ten*-shon-al-le, by design.
intentioned, *a.* in-*ten*-shond, having intentions; meant.
intently, *ad.* in-*tent*-le, fixedly; earnestly.
intentness, *n.* the state of being intent.
inter-, *in*-ter, Latin prefix, among or between.
inter, *v.t.* in-*ter*, to bury. (Fr. *enterrer.*)
interact, *n.* *in*-ter-*akt*, an interlude; a short piece between the acts of a play: *v.t.* to act upon each other.
interaction, *n.* in-ter-*ak*-shon, reciprocal action.
interactive, *a.* *in*-ter-*ak*-tiv, interacting.
interagent, *n.* *in*-ter-*ay*-jent, an intermediate agent.
interarticular, *a.* *in*-ter-ar-*tik*-yew-lar, situated between the joints or articulations [Anat.].
interaxal, *a.* *in*-ter-*ak*-sal, pertaining to or situated in the interaxis [Arch.]
interaxillary, *a.* *in*-ter-ak-*sil*-a-re, situated within the axils of leaves [Bot.].
interaxis, *n.* *in*-ter-*ak*-sis, the space between the axes in columnar erections [Arch.].
interblend, *v.t.* *in*-ter-*blend*, to blend with each other.
interbreed, *v.t.* *in*-ter-*breed*, to cross-breed: *v.i.* to breed together.
intercalary, *a.* in-*ter*-ka-la-re, inserted between or among others; denoting a month (Feb.) or a year (leap year) to which an extra day has been added.
intercalate, *v.t.* in-*ter*-ka-late, to insert between or among, esp. a day in the calendar; to interpolate. (L. *intercalatus*, inserted.)
intercalation, *n.* *in*-ter-ka-*lay*-shon, the act or result of intercalating.
intercede, *v.t.* *in*-ter-*seed*, to mediate; to plead in favour of one. (L. *intercedo*, go between.)
interceder, *n.* *in*-ter-*see*-der, one who intercedes.
intercellular, *a.* *in*-ter-*sel*-yew-lar, lying between or among the cells [Bot.].
intercept, *v.t.* *in*-ter-*sept*, to seize by the way; to stop on its passage; to interrupt communication with; to include between [Math.]. (Fr. *interceptor.*)
intercepter, *n.* *in*-ter-sep-ter, one who intercepts.
interception, *n.* *in*-ter-*sep*-shon, the act of intercepting; obstruction; hindrance.
interceptor, *n.* *in*-ter-*sep*-tor, one who or that which intercepts; a trap for gas [Sewerage]; a lightly armed single-seated fighter designed for making early contact with enemy aircraft [Air warfare].
intercerebral, *a.* *in*-ter-*se*-re-bral, connecting the hemispheres of the brain.
intercession, *n.* *in*-ter-*sesh*-on, the act of interceding; mediation with a view to reconciliation. (L. *intercessio.*)
intercessional, *a.* containing intercession.
intercessor, *n.* *in*-ter-*ses*-sor, one who goes between; one who intercedes; one who administers a see pending the election of a new bishop.
intercessorial, *a.* *in*-ter-ses-*saw*-re-al, pertaining to intercession or to an intercessor.
intercessory, *a.* *in*-ter-*ses*-so-re, serving to intercede.
interchange, *v.t.* in-ter-*chaynj*, to change reciprocally; to give and take; to exchange; to succeed alternately. (Fr. *entrechanger.*)
interchange, *n.* *in*-ter-chaynj, reciprocal exchange; alternate succession.
interchangeability, *n.* *in*-ter-*chaynj*-a-*bil*-e-te, state or quality of being interchangeable.

interchangeable, *a.* *in*-ter-*chaynj*-a-bl, that may be interchanged; following each other alternately.
interchangeably, *ad.* *in*-ter-*chaynj*-a-ble, in an interchangeable manner.
interclavicle, *n.* *in*-ter-*klav*-e-kl, a membraneous bone lying between the clavicles in certain lower vertebrates [Zool.].
interclude, *v.t.* *in*-ter-*klood*, to intercept; to cut off; to confine. (L. *intercludo*, shut.)
intercollegiate, *a.* *in*-ter-kol-*lee*-je-at, existing or carried on between colleges.
intercolonial, *a.* *in*-ter-ko-*loh*-ne-al, taking place between or among colonies.
intercolumnar, *a.* *in*-ter-ko-*lum*-nar, placed between columns [Arch.].
intercolumniation, *n.* *in*-ter-ko-*lum*-ne-*ay*-shon, the spacing of or the space between the columns of a colonnade [Arch.]. (L. *intercolumnium.*)
intercom, *n.* *in*-ter-kom, the intercommunication system between the captain and crew of an aeroplane [Av. slang].
intercommune, *v.i.* *in*-ter-kom-*mewn*, to commune together.
intercommunicable, *a.* *in*-ter-kom-*mew*-ne-ka-bl, that may be mutually communicated; suitable for intercommunication.
intercommunicate, *v.i.* *in*-ter-kom-*mew*-ne-kate, to hold mutual communication; to have free access to each other.
intercommunication, *n.* *in*-ter-kom-*mew*-ne-*kay*-shon, reciprocal communication.
intercommunion, *n.* *in*-ter-kom-*mew*-nyon, mutual communion; the partaking in common of Holy Communion by members of different Christian denominations.
intercommunity, *n.* *in*-ter-kom-*mew*-ne-te, quality of being held in common.
interconnect, *v.t.* and *v.i.* *in*-ter-ko-*nekt*, to join together reciprocally.
interconnector, *n.* *in*-ter-ko-*nek*-tor, a cable connecting generating or sub-stations along which power may be transmitted in either direction [Elect.].
intercontinental, *a.* *in*-ter-*kon*-te-*nen*-tal, subsisting or carried on between continents.
interconvertible, *a.* *in*-ter-kon-*ver*-te-bl, interchangeable.
intercostal, *a.* *in*-ter-*kos*-tal, situated between the ribs: *n.* the part lying between the ribs: *pl.* the intercostal muscles. (L. *inter-*, and *costa*, a rib.)
intercourse, *n.* *in*-ter-koarse, connexion by reciprocal dealings; communion; fellowship; mutual communication; sexual connexion.
intercrop, *v.t.* and *i.* *in*-ter-krop, to grow different crops in alternate rows: *n.* a crop raised in this manner.
intercross, *v.t.* *in*-ter-kross, to cross mutually; to cause to interbreed: *v.i.* to interbreed: *n.* a crossbreed. (O.Fr. *entrecours.*)
intercurrent, *a.* *in*-ter-*ku*-rent, occurring between or among; intervening. (L. *intercurrens*, running between.)
interdenominational, *a.* *in*-ter-de-nom-e-*nay*-shonal, existing between or partaken by two denominations.
interdepartmental, *a.* *in*-te-*dee*-part-*men*-tal, carried on or exchanged between departments.
interdepend, *v.t.* *in*-ter-de-*pend*, to depend upon each other.
interdependence, *n.* *in*-ter-de-*pen*-dence, mutual dependence.
interdependent, *a.* *in*-ter-de-*pen*-dent, mutually dependent.
interdict, *v.t.* in-ter-*dikt*, to forbid; to place under an interdict; to debar from communion.
interdict, *n.* *in*-ter-dikt, prohibition; a prohibiting decree; an injunction [Law]; a sentence debarring specified persons or bodies, etc., from participation in public worship, the Sacrament, Christian burial, etc. [Rom. Cath. Ch.]. (L. *interdictum*, a decree.)
interdiction, *n.* *in*-ter-*dik*-shon, the act of interdicting; state of being under an interdict.
interdictive, *a.* *in*-ter-*dik*-tiv, interdictory.
interdictory, *a.* *in*-ter-*dik*-to-re, pertaining to or conveying interdiction; serving to prohibit.
interdigital, *a.* *in*-ter-*dij*-e-tal, situated between the fingers. (L. *inter-*, and *digitus*, a finger.)
interdigitate, *v.i.* *in*-ter-*dij*-e-tate, to interlock, like the fingers of the two clasped hands.
interequinoctial, *a.* *in*-ter-*ek*-we-*nok*-shal, coming between the vernal and autumnal equinoxes: *n.* either of the solstices.
★**interest,** *n.* *in*-ter-rest, personal concern; sympathetic attention; advantage; good; influence over others; share; those concerned in a particular industry, etc. [Collect.]; premium paid for the use of money: *v.t.* to awaken concern in; to excite emotion or passion, usually in favour of; to engage special attention; to give a share in. **compound interest**, *see* **compound. simple interest,** *see* **simple.** (O.Fr. *interesser.*)
interested, *pp.* *in*-ter-*res*-ted, having the interest excited: *a.* having an interest; taking an interest; concerned in a cause or its consequences, and liable to be biased.
interestedly, *ad.* *in*-ter-*res*-ted-le, in a manner evincing interest.
interesting, *a.* *in*-ter-res-ting, engaging the attention or curiosity; exciting emotions or passions.
interestingly, *ad.* *in*-ter-*res*-ting-le, in an interesting manner.
interfacial, *a.* *in*-ter-*fay*-shal, included between the faces of two planes [Geom.].
interfemoral, *a.* *in*-ter-*fem*-o-ral, situated or extending between the thighs.
interfenestral, *a.* *in*-ter-fe-*nes*-tral, situated between windows [Arch.].
interfenestration, *n.* *in*-ter-*fen*-e-*stray*-shon, the spacing of windows [Arch.].
interfere, *v.i.* *in*-ter-*feer*, to interpose; to intermeddle; to come in collision; to act reciprocally, so as to modify the result [Physics]; in a horse, to strike the hoof against the opposite fetlock. (Fr. *interférer.*)
interference, *n.* *in*-ter-*feer*-ence, the action or process of interfering; interposition; intermeddling; the resultant interaction of the meeting of two beams of light or two series of waves [Physics].
interferential, *a.* *in*-ter-fer-*ren*-shal, pertaining to or dependent on interference [Physics].
interferer, *n.* *in*-ter-*feer*-er, one who interferes.
interfering, *a.* *in*-ter-*feer*-ing, inclined to interfere; meddling: *n.* interference.
interferingly, *ad.* by interference.
interferometer, *n.* *in*-ter-feer-*rom*-e-ter, an instrument utilizing the phenomena of interference in the measurement of light waves [Physics].
interfluent, *a.* in-*ter*-floo-ent, flowing between, or into each other; intermingling. (L. *inter-*, and *fluo*, to flow.)
interfluous, *a.* in-*ter*-floo-us, interfluent.
interfold, *v.t.* *in*-ter-*fohld*, to fold into each other.
interfoliaceous, *a.* *in*-ter-*foh*-le-*ay*-shus, situated alternately between opposite leaves, [Bot.]. (L. *inter-*, and *folium*, a leaf.)
interfoliate, *v.t.* *in*-ter-*foh*-le-ate, to interleave.
interfuse, *v.t.* in-ter-*fewz*, to blend; to mix in; to melt with. (L. *interfusus.*)
interfusion, *n.* *in*-ter-*few*-zhon, interfused state.
interglacial, *a.* *in*-ter-*glay*-shal, occurring between the glacial periods.
interglandular, *a.* *in*-ter-*gland*-yew-lar, situated between glands.
intergradation, *n.* *in*-ter-gra-*day*-shon, the act of changing or passing into by degrees; the condition of being graded.
intergrowth, *n.* *in*-ter-grohth, a growing of one into another; the condition or result so produced.
interim, *n.* *in*-ter-im, the meantime; time intervening: *a.* preliminary; provisional. (L.)
interior, *a.* in-*teer*-e-or, inner; internal; remote from the frontier or shore; inland: *n.* the inside; the inland part of a country; (*cap.*) the Home Department of a state, or its business. (O.Fr.)
interiorly, *ad.* in-*teer*-e-or-le, internally; inwardly.
interjacent, *a.* *in*-ter-*jay*-sent, lying between; intervening. (L. *interjacens*, lying between.)
interjaculate, *v.t.* *in*-ter-*jak*-yew-late, to make an exclamation when others are conversing.
interject, *v.t.* *in*-ter-*jekt*, to throw between; to insert. (L. *interjectus*, thrown between.)
interjection, *n.* *in*-ter-*jek*-shon, the act of interjecting; a word thrown in between others to express some emotion or passion; a sudden exclamation.
interjectional, *a.* *in*-ter-*jek*-shon-al, thrown in between other words; of the nature of an interjection.

interjectory, *a.* in-*ter*-jek-to-re, characterized by interjection; interjectional.
interknit, *v.t.* and *i.* *in*-ter-*nit*, to knit together; to intertwine; to become intimately united.
interlace, *v.t.* *in*-ter-*lace*, to intermix; to put or insert one thing with another; to lace together: *v.i.* to intersect. (O.Fr. *entrelacer.*)
interlacement, *n.* *in*-ter-*lace*-ment, intermixture or insertion within; an interlacing.
interlard, *v.t.* *in*-ter-lard, to run in as strips of fat into poultry; to interpose; to insert between; to diversify. (O.Fr. *entrelarder.*)
interleaf, *n.* *in*-ter-leef, a blank leaf inserted between other leaves.
interleave, *v.t.* *in*-ter-*leev*, to insert a blank leaf or blank leaves in a book, between other leaves.
interline, *v.t.* *in*-ter-*line*, to write or print between lines; to print in alternate lines.
interlineal, *a.* *in*-ter-*lin*-e-al, interlinear; arranged in alternate lines.
interlinear, *a.* *in*-ter-*lin*-e-ar, written or printed between lines.
interlineary, *a.* *in*-ter-*lin*-e-a-re, interlinear: *n.* a book or writing having interlineations.
interlineation, *n.* *in*-ter-*lin*-e-*ay*-shon, the act of interlining; that which is interlined.
interlink, *v.t.* *in*-ter-*link*, to connect by uniting links: *n.* an intermediate link.
interlocation, *n.* *in*-ter-lo-*kay*-shon, interposition.
interlock, *v.t.* and *i.* *in*-ter-*lok*, to embrace or communicate with one another; to connect firmly by reciprocal action.
interlocution, *n.* *in*-ter-lo-*kew*-shon, discourse; cross talk; an intermediate decree before final decision [Law]. (L. *interlocutio.*)
interlocutor, *n.* *in*-ter-*lok*-yew-tor, one who speaks in dialogue; an interim judgment [Scots. Law].
interlocutory, *a.* *in*-ter-*lok*-yew-to-re, consisting of dialogue; intermediate; not final or definitive [Law].
interlocutress, *n.* *in*-ter-*lok*-yew-tress, a woman as interlocutor.
interlope, *v.t.* *in*-ter-*lope*, to run between parties, and intercept the advantage that one should gain from the other; to traffic illegally.
interloper, *n.* *in*-ter-*lope*-er, one who interlopes; one who infringes upon another's rights; an intruder. (Dut. *enterlooper.*)
interlude, *n.* *in*-ter-lewd, a short performance between the acts of a play, or between the play and the after-piece; a short piece of music played between stanzas; any intervening incident or pause. (O.Fr. *entrelude.*)
interlunar, *a.* *in*-ter-*lew*-nar, belonging to the time when the moon, about the change, is invisible. (L. *inter-*, and *luna*, the moon.)
intermarriage, *n.* *in*-ter-*ma*-raj, marriage between people of two families or castes, tribes, races, etc.; marriage between near relatives.
intermarry, *v.i.* *in*-ter-*ma*-re, to marry; to become connected by marriage.
intermaxillary, *a.* *in*-ter-mak-*sil*-la-re, situated between the jaw-bones.
intermeddle, *v.i.* *in*-ter-*med*-dl, to meddle in the affairs of others; to meddle officiously; to interfere.
intermeddler, *n.* in-ter-*med*-ler, one who intermeddles.
intermediary, *a.* *in*-ter-*mee*-de-a-re, lying between: *n.* that which is intermediate; an agent.
intermediate, *a.* *in*-ter-*mee*-de-at, lying or being in the middle between extremes; interposed: *n.* that which is intermediate; one who intervenes; *v.i.* to mediate. (Fr. *intermediat.*)
intermediately, *ad.* *in*-ter-*mee*-de-at-le, by way of intervention or medium.
intermediation, *n.* *in*-ter-mee-de-*ay*-shon, intervention.
intermedium, *n.* *in*-ter-*mee*-de-um, an intermediate agent or agency; that which transmits energy through space. (L.)
interment, *n.* in-*ter*-ment, the act of interring; burial; sepulture. (O.Fr. *enterrement.*)
intermezzo, *n.* *in*-ter-*met*-zo, an interlude. (It.)
intermigration, *n.* *in*-ter-my-*gray*-shon, reciprocal migration.
interminable, *a.* in-*ter*-min-a-bl, without end or limit; illimitable; tediously protracted.
interminableness, *n.* in-*ter*-min-a-bl-ness, state of being interminable.
interminably, *ad.* without end or limit.
interminate, *a.* in-*ter*-min-at, infinite; recurring (of decimal fractions).
intermingle, *v.t.* *in*-ter-*ming*-gl, to mingle together: *v.i.* to be mixed or incorporated.
intermission, *n.* *in*-ter-*mish*-on, cessation for a time; interval; pause; the temporary cessation or subsidence of a fever, paroxysm, etc. [Med.].
intermissive, *a.* *in*-ter-*mis*-siv, intermittent; coming by fits or after temporary cessations.
intermit, *v.t.* *in*-ter-*mit*, to cause to cease for a time; to suspend: *v.i.* to cease for a time. (L. *intermitto*, send.)
intermittent, *a.* *in*-ter-*mit*-tent, ceasing and recurring at intervals: *n.* an intermittent fever.
intermittently, *ad.* with intermissions.
intermix, *v.t.* *in*-ter-*miks*, to mix together; to intermingle: *v.i.* to be mixed together.
intermixture, *n.* *in*-ter-*miks*-tewr, a mass formed by mixture; admixture.
intermodillion, *n.* *in*-ter-mo-*dil*-yon, the space between two modillions [Arch.].
intermontane, *a.* *in*-ter-*mon*-tane, situated between mountains.
intermundane, *a.* *in*-ter-*mun*-dane, subsisting or being between worlds.
intermural, *a.* *in*-ter-*mew*-ral, lying between walls.
intermuscular, *a.* *in*-ter-*mus*-kew-lar, situated between the muscles.
intermutation, *n.* *in*-ter-mew-*tay*-shon, interchange. (Late L. *intermutatus*, interchanged.)
intern, *v.t.* in-*tern*, to oblige to reside within the confines of a country; to keep under restraint, esp. during time of war, guiltless persons whom it is undesirable to leave at liberty; to detain in port: *n.* a resident doctor at a hospital. (Fr. *interner.*)
internal, *a.* in-*ter*-nal, inward; interior; in the heart; intrinsic; real; domestic; not foreign. **internal-combustion engine,** an engine that derives its motive force from the explosion of mingled air and gas in the cylinders. (O.Fr. *internel.*)
internality, *n.* *in*-ter-*nal*-e-te, the quality of being internal; inner character.
internally, *ad.* in-*ter*-na-le, inwardly.
international, *a.* *in*-ter-*nash*-on-al, pertaining to, carried on between, or interacting upon different nations: *n.* a player representing his country in any sport, as football; a sporting contest between representatives of different countries.
International, *n.* *in*-ter-*nash*-on-al, an organization of communistic socialists open to members of all nations—esp. the First International, founded by Karl Marx and others, 1864; the Second, founded 1889; and the Third, or Comintern, founded in Moscow, 1919, disbanded 1943, re-established 1947. (Fr. *internationale.*)
Internationale, *n.* *an*-ter-*nah*-syo-*nahl*, the rallying and marching song of communists and members of the International. (Fr.)
internationalism, *n.* in-ter-*nash*-o-na-lizm, the principle of community of interests, etc., between nations; a system of international control; the principles of the International.
internationalist, *n.* *in*-ter-*nash*-o-na-list, one who places the common interests of the world above national interests; an expert in the Law of Nations; (*cap.*) a member of the International.
internationality, *n.* *in*-ter-*nash*-o-*nal*-e-te, the quality or condition of being international.
internationalize, *v.t.* *in*-ter-*nash*-o-na-lize, to make international.
internationally, *ad.* in-ter-*nash*-o-na-le, from an international viewpoint; between different nations; in an international way.
internecine, *a.* *in*-ter-*nee*-sine, mutually destructive; deadly. (L. *internecīnus.*)
internee, *n.* in-ter-*nee*, one who is lawfully interned.
interneural, *a.* *in*-ter-*newr*-ral, situated between the neural processes or between two nerves.
internment, *n.* in-*tern*-ment, restraint for safe custody; the state of being interned.
internodal, *a.* *in*-ter-*noh*-dal, intervening between nodes, joints, etc.
internode, *n.* *in*-ter-node, the space between two joints of a plant [Bot.]. (L. *internodium.*)
internuncial, *a.* *in*-ter-*nun*-shal, pertaining to a messenger or nuncio; communicating between different parts (of nerves) [Phys.].

internuncio, *n.* *in*-ter-*nun*-she-o, a messenger between two parties; the Pope's representative at certain minor courts. (It.)
interoceanic, *a.* *in*-ter-*oh*-she-*an*-ik, extending or situated between two oceans.
interocular, *a.* *in*-ter-*ok*-yew-lar, situated between the eyes.
interosculant, *a.* *in*-ter-*os*-kew-lant, interosculating; intersecting; constituting a connecting link through certain affinities.
interosculate, *v.t.* *in*-ter-*os*-kew-late, to link up into each other, as in the case of two species or genera or other systematic groupings [Bot. and Zool.]. (L. *inter-*, and *osculor*, kiss.)
interosseous, *a.* *in*-ter-*os*-se-us, situated between bones [Anat.]. (L. *inter-*, and *os*, a bone.)
interpage, *v.t.* in-ter-*page*, to insert pages between other pages; to interleave.
interpellant, *a.* in-ter-*pel*-lant, interrupting: *n.* one who interpellates.
interpellate, *v.t.* *in*-ter-*pel*-ate *or* in-*ter*-pe-late, to interrogate; to interrupt a debate in order to question a minister [Parl.]. (L.)
interpellation, *n.* *in*-ter-pel-*lay*-shon, a question put to the government during a debate in parliament; interruption; an earnest address.
interpenetrate, *v.t.* *in*-ter-*pen*-e-trate, to penetrate mutually.
interpenetration, *n.* *in*-ter-*pen*-e-*tray*-shon, mutual penetration.
interpetiolar, *a.* *in*-ter-*pet*-e-o-lar, being between petioles [Bot.].
interplanetary, *a.* *in*-ter-*plan*-e-ta-re, between the planets.
interplay, *n.* *in*-ter-play, interaction; reciprocation.
interplead, *v.i.* *in*-ter-pleed, to take action with reference to a point incidentally arising or one in which a third party has an interest [Law].
interpleader, *n.* *in*-ter-*plee*-der, one who interpleads; a suit pleaded between two interpleading parties [Law].
interpleural, *a.* *in*-ter-*ploor*-ral, situated between the pleuræ of the lungs.
interpolable, *a.* in-*ter*-po-la-bl, that may be interpolated.
interpolar, *a.* *in*-ter-*pole*-ar, between the poles (esp. of an electric cell or battery).
interpolate, *v.i.* in-*ter*-po-late, to foist in; to insert, as a spurious word or passage in a writing; to throw in (a remark); to corrupt; to insert intermediate terms of a series [Math.]. (L. *interpolatus*, patched.)
interpolation, *n.* in-*ter*-po-*lay*-shon, the act of interpolating a word or passage; a word, etc., inserted; a method employed for filling up the intermediate terms of a series of numbers or observations by numbers which follow the same law [Math.].
interpolator, *n.* in-*ter*-po-la-tor, one who or that which interpolates.
interposal, *n.* *in*-ter-*poze*-al, interposition.
interpose, *v.t.* *in*-ter-*poze*, to place between or among; to thrust in; to offer, as aid, in some emergency: *v.i.* to step in and mediate between parties at variance; to intervene; to put in by way of interruption. (Fr. *interposer*, put between.)
interposer, *n.* *in*-ter-*poze*-er, one who interposes.
interposition, *n.* *in*-ter-po-*zish*-on, the act of interposing; intervention; mediation; anything interposed. (Fr.)
interpret, *v.t.* in-*ter*-pret, to explain, unfold, or present the meaning of; to translate from one language into another; to put into intelligible words. (O.Fr. *interpreter*.)
interpretable, *a.* in-*ter*-pre-ta-bl, that may be interpreted.
interpretation, *n.* in-*ter*-pre-*tay*-shon, the act of interpreting; the exposition or translation given; rendering; the power of explaining.
interpretational, *a.* *in*-ter-pre-*tay*-shon-al, pertaining to interpretation.
interpretative, *a.* in-*ter*-pre-tay-tiv, collected or known by interpretation; explanatory.
interpretatively, *ad.* in-*ter*-pre-tay-tiv-le, in an interpretative manner.
interpreter, *n.* in-*ter*-pre-ter, one who interprets, esp. between persons when speaking different languages.
interpretive, *a.* in-*ter*-pre-tiv, interpretative.
interprovincial, *a.* *in*-ter-pro-*vin*-shal, carried on or subsisting between provinces.
interpunctuation, *n.* *in*-ter-*punk*-tew-*ay*-shon, punctuation within the sentence.
interracial, *a.* *in*-ter-*ray*-she-al, between races.
interracialism, *n.* *in*-ter-*ray*-she-a-lizm, the principle of community of interest, etc., between persons of different racial origin.
interradial, *a.* *in*-ter-*ray*-de-al, between radii.
interregnum, *n.* *in*-ter-*reg*-num, the time between two reigns, governments, or ministries; a period of irregular rule, or of anarchy. (L. *inter-*, and *regnum*, reign or rule.)
interreign, *n.* *in*-ter-rane, an interregnum.
interrelated, *a.* *in*-ter-re-*lay*-ted, having a mutual relationship; correlative.
interrelation, *n.* *in*-ter-re-*lay*-shon, mutual relation.
interrex, *n.* *in*-ter-reks, a regent; one who governs during an interregnum. (L. *inter*, and *rex*, king.)
interrogable, *a.* in-*te*-ro-ga-ble, capable of being interrogated.
interrogant, *n.* in-*te*-ro-gant, an interrogator.
interrogate, *v.t.* in-*te*-ro-gate, to question; to examine formally: *v.i.* to ask questions. (L. *interrogatus*, asked.)
interrogation, *n.* in-*te*-ro-*gay*-shon, the act of interrogating; a question put; a note that marks a question, thus (?).
interrogational, *a.* in-te-ro-*gay*-shon-al, interrogative; of the nature of a question.
interrogative, *a.* *in*-ter-*rog*-a-tiv, denoting a question; expressed in the form of a question: *n.* a word used in asking questions [Gram.].
interrogatively, *ad.* *in*-ter-*rog*-a-tiv-le, in the form of a question; by way of questioning.
interrogator, *n.* in-*te*-ro-*gay*-tor, a questioner.
interrogatory, *n.* *in*-ter-*rog*-a-to-re, a question or inquiry: *a.* containing or expressing a question.
interrupt, *v.t.* *in*-ter-*rupt*, to stop or hinder by breaking in upon; to block; to break continuity: *v.i.* to interpolate; to make interruption. (L. *interruptus*, broken.)
interruptedly, *ad.* *in*-ter-*rup*-ted-le, with breaks or interruptions.
interrupter, *n.* *in*-ter-*rup*-ter, one who interrupts; any device for making and breaking a current [Elect.].
interruption, *n.* *in*-ter-*rup*-shon, the act of interrupting; intervention; hindrance; intermission. (Fr.)
interruptive, *a.* *in*-ter-*rup*-tiv, characterized by interrupting; tending to interrupt.
interscapular, *a.* *in*-ter-*skap*-yew-lar, situated between the shoulder-blades.
intersect, *v.t.* *in*-ter-*sekt*, to cut or cross mutually: *v.i.* to cross each other. (L. *intersectus*, cut.)
intersection, *n.* in-ter-*sek*-shon, the act of intersecting; the point or line in which two lines or two planes cut each other [Geom.].
intersectional, *a.* *in*-ter-*sek*-shon-al, pertaining to intersection.
intersegmental, *a.* *in*-ter-seg-*men*-tal, situated between segments [Anat.].
intersex, *n.* *in*-ter-seks, an intermediate sex; an individual whose sex, at a certain stage in its development, has undergone transformation [Biol.].
intersexual, *a.* in-ter-*seks*-yew-al, between the sexes; pertaining to intersexuality or to an intersex.
intersexuality, *n.* *in*-ter-*seks*-yew-*al*-e-te, the sexual condition of an intersex.
intersow, *v.t.* in-ter-*soh*, to intersperse.
interspace, *n.* *in*-ter-space, a space between; an interval: *v.t.* to space out.
interspecific, *a.* *in*-ter-spe-*sif*-ik, common to two or more species [Biol.].
intersperse, *v.t.* *in*-ter-*sperse*, to scatter or set here and there; to diversify by interspersion. (L. *interspersus*, sprinkled amongst.)
interspersion, *n.* *in*-ter-*sper*-shon, the act of interspersing.
interspinal, -spinous, *a.* *in*-ter-*spy*-nal, -*spy*-nus, situated between spines [Anat.].
interstate, *a.* *in*-ter-*state*, subsisting or carried on between states; including different states.
interstellar, *a.* in-ter-*stel*-lar, situated among the stars. (L. *inter-*, and *stella*, a star.)
interstellary, *a.* in-ter-*stel*-la-re, interstellar.
interstice, *n.* in-*ter*-stis, a small space between

things closely set, or between the component parts of a body. (Fr.)
interstitial, *a.* *in*-ter-*stish*-al, pertaining to or containing interstices.
interstratified, *a.* *in*-ter-*strat*-e-fide, stratified between other strata.
intertangle, *v.t.* *in*-ter-*tang*-gl, to intertwist.
intertentacular, *a.* *in*-ter-ten-*tak*-yew-lar, situated between tentacles [Zool.].
interterritorial, *a.* *in*-ter-*te*-re-*taw*-re-al, being, transacted, etc. between territories.
intertexture, *n.* *in*-ter-*teks*-tewr, the act of interweaving; the state of being interwoven.
intertidal, *a.* *in*-ter-*ty*-dal, living between high- and low-water marks [Zool.].
intertie, *n.* *in*-ter-*ty*, a short horizontal timber connecting posts in partitions, etc.
intertribal, *a.* *in*-ter-try-bal, carried on or existing between different tribes.
intertrigo, *n.* *in*-ter-*try*-go, inflammation of the skin due to chafing together of moist parts.
intertropical, *a.* *in*-ter-*trop*-e-kal, pertaining to tropical regions; lying within the tropics.
intertwine, *v.t.* *in*-ter-*twine*, to twine or twist together: *v.i.* to be intertwisted.
intertwist, *v.t.* *in*-ter-*twist*, to twist together.
interval, *n.* *in*-ter-val, a space (in time or distance) between; the extent of such interruption; a gap; the distance between two notes of different pitch [Mus.]. (O.Fr. *intervalle.*)
intervale, *n.* *in*-ter-vale, a tract of low ground between hills or beside a river [U.S.A.].
intervallic, *a.* in-ter-*val*-ik, pertaining to an interval or intervals [esp. Mus.].
interveined, *a.* *in*-ter-*vaned*, intersected with or as with veins.
intervene, *v.i.* *in*-ter-*veen*, to come, be, or lie between; to occur between points of time or events; to occur so as to interrupt; to interpose; to interfere. (L. *intervenio*, come.)
intervenient, *a.* *in*-ter-*veen*-e-ent, lying between; interposing; extraneous.
intervention, *n.* *in*-ter-*ven*-shon, interposition; agency of persons; agency or instrumentality; mediation. **war of intervention,** a war undertaken from outside to put an end to a civil war or settle internal disorders.
interventionist, *n.* in-ter-*ven*-shon-ist, one who favours or takes part in intervention, or in a war of intervention: *a.* involving or relating to intervention.
interventor, *n.* in-ter-*ven*-tor, an administrator temporarily appointed in time of revolution or emergency, esp. in Latin America.
interventricular, *a.* *in*-ter-ven-*trik*-yew-lar, situated between the ventricles [Anat.].
intervertebral, *a.* *in*-ter-*ver*-te-bral, being between the vertebræ [Anat.].
interview, *n.* *in*-ter-vew, a meeting and conference face to face; a visit and interrogation by the representative of a newspaper, etc., or of the police: *v.t.* to meet and confer face to face; to visit a person to ascertain certain facts, or his opinions, etc., for the purpose of publication. (Fr. *entrevue.*)
interviewer, *n.* *in*-ter-*vew*-er, one who interviews.
intervisible, *a.* *in*-ter-*viz*-e-bl, visible from each to the other (of two stations) [Surv.].
intervocalic, *a.* *in*-ter-vo-*kal*-ik, between vowels.
intervolve, *v.t.* *in*-ter-*volv*, to involve one within another. (L. *inter-*, and *volvo*, roll.)
inter-war, *a.* *in*-ter-*wawr*, relating to a period between wars, esp. 1918–39.
interweave, *v.t.* *in*-ter-*weev*, to weave together; to intermingle. *p.* **interwove.** *pp.* **interwoven.**
interwork, *v.t.* *in*-ter-*wurk*, to work things together or into each other: *v.i.* to interact.
intestacy, *n.* in-*tes*-ta-se, the state or the fact of dying intestate.
intestate, *a.* in-*tes*-tat, without having made a will; not disposed of by will: *n.* a person who dies without making a valid will. (L. *intestatus.*)
intestinal, *a.* *in*-tes-ty-nal, pertaining to the intestines of an animal body.
intestine, *a.* in-*tes*-tin, internal, domestic, not foreign (of a state or country): *n.* the part of the alimentary canal terminating in the anus: *pl.* the bowels. (L. *intestinus*, inward.)
inthral, *v.t.* in-*thrawl*, to enthral.
intimacy, *n.* *in*-te-ma-se, close familiarity; friendship; irregular sexual intercourse [Coll.].
intimate, *a.* *in*-te-mat, inward; internal; near; close; close in friendship or acquaintance: *n.* a familiar friend or associate: *v.t.* *in*-te-mate, to hint; to make known; to indicate; to announce. (L. *intimatus*, announced.)
intimately, *ad.* *in*-te-mat-le, in an intimate or a close manner.
intimation, *n.* *in*-te-*may*-shon, an indirect suggestion or notice; a hint; an announcement.
intimidate, *v.t.* in-*tim*-e-date, to make timid or fearful; to cow; to dishearten; to dispirit. (Late L.)
intimidation, *n.* *in*-tim-e-*day*-shon, the act of intimidating; the state of being intimidated.
intimidatory, *a.* in-*tim*-e-day-to-re, serving or tending to intimidate.
intimity, *n.* in-*tim*-e-te, the quality of being intimate; inwardness. (L. *intimus*, innermost.)
intinction, *n.* in-*tink*-shon, the act or practice of dipping the bread into the wine in the administration of the sacrament [Eccles.]. (L. *intinctus*, moistened.)
intitule, *v.i.* in-*tit*-yewl, to entitle. (Fr. *intituler.*)
into, *prep.* *in*-too, noting passage from the outside to inside, or from one state to another. (A.S. *in tō.*)
intoed, *a.* *in*-tode, with toes turned inward.
intolerable, *a.* in-*tol*-er-a-bl, not to be borne or endured; insufferable. (L. *intolerabilis.*)
intolerableness, *n.* in-*tol*-er-a-bl-ness, the quality of being intolerable.
intolerably, *ad.* to a degree beyond endurance.
intolerance, *n.* in-*tol*-er-ance, a being intolerant; want of capacity to endure; want of toleration. (L. *intolerantia.*)
intolerant, *a.* in-*tol*-er-ant, not able to endure; not enduring or refusing to tolerate difference of opinion or conduct; bigoted: *n.* one who is opposed to toleration; a bigot. (L. *intolerans.*)
intolerantly, *ad.* in an intolerant manner.
intoleration, *n.* *in*-tol-er-*ay*-shon, intolerance; refusal to tolerate others in their opinions or conduct.
intonable, *a.* in-*toh*-na-bl, capable of being intoned.
intonate, *v.i.* *in*-to-nate, to sound musical notes; to modulate the voice: *v.t.* to intone. (Late L. *intonatus.*)
intonation, *n.* in-to-*nay*-shon, the modulation or intoning of the voice, esp. in reading in church; intoning; the opening phrase of a Gregorian chant; the action of sounding the notes of the scale with the voice; the manner of sounding or tuning the notes of a musical scale.
intone, *v.i.* in-*tone*, to chant or recite in a monotone; to utter a deep, protracted sound: *v.t.* to chant; to read in a singing, recitative style. (Late L. *intono*, sing in tone.)
intorsion, *n.* in-*tor*-shon, a winding, bending, or twisting, esp. [Bot.] of any part of a plant.
intort, *v.t.* in-*tort*, to twist; to wreathe; to wind; to involve. (L. *intortus*, twisted.)
intoxicant, *n.* in-*tok*-se-kant, anything intoxicating: *a.* intoxicating.
intoxicate, *v.t.* in-*tok*-se-kate, to make drunk; to excite to enthusiasm, frenzy, or madness. (Late L. *intoxicatus*, made drunk.)
intoxicating, *a.* in-*tok*-se-kay-ting, having qualities that produce intoxication.
intoxication, *n.* in-*tok*-se-*kay*-shon, the act of intoxicating; the state of being intoxicated; excitement to enthusiasm; unusual exhilaration.
intra-, *in*-tra, a Latin prefix, signifying within.
intracellular, *a.* in-tra-*sel*-yew-lar, within the cell [Biol.].
intractability, *n.* in-*trak*-ta-*bil*-e-te, intractableness.
intractable, *a.* in-*trak*-ta-bl, ungovernable; unmanageable; stubborn. (L. *intractabilis.*)
intractableness, *n.* in-*trak*-ta-bl-ness, the quality of being intractable.
intractably, *ad.* in an intractable manner.
intractile, *a.* in-*trak*-tile, not easily manipulated; intractable.
intrados, *n.* in-*tray*-dos, the interior and lower line or curve of an arch [Arch.]. (Sp., entrance.)
intramolecular, *a.* *in*-tra-mo-*lek*-yew-lar, existing or occurring within the molecule.
intramundane, *a.* *in*-tra-*mun*-dane, within the material world.

intramural, *a.* *in*-tra-*mew*-ral, within the walls, as of a city or university.
intranquillity, *n.* *in*-trang-*kwil*-e-te, lack of tranquillity; inquietude.
intransigency, *n.* in-*tran*-se-jen-se, the quality of being intransigent; irreconcilable opposition.
intransigent, *a.* in-*tran*-se-jent, uncompromising in opposition: *n.* an irreconcilable. (Sp. *intransigente.*)
intransitive, *a.* in-*tran*-se-tiv, expressing an action limited to the agent, or not passing over to an object [Gram.]: *n.* an intransitive verb. (Late L. *intransitivue.*)
intransitively, *ad.* in an intransitive manner.
intransmissible, *a.* *in*-trans-*mis*-se-bl, not transmissible.
intransmutability, *n.* *in*-trans-mew-ta-*bil*-e-te, the quality of being intransmutable.
intransmutable, *a.* *in*-trans-*mew*-ta-bl, that cannot be transmuted or changed into another substance.
intrant, *n.* *in*-trant, one who enters a college, or some office, etc. (L. *intrans*, entering.)
intrench, *v.t.* in-*trench*, to entrench.
intrenchant, *a.* in-*tren*-chant, not capable of being cut.
intrepid, *a.* in-*trep*-id, without fear; undaunted. (L. *intrepidus*, unafraid.)
intrepidity, *n.* *in*-tre-*pid*-e-te, fearlessness; undaunted courage.
intrepidly, *ad.* in-*trep*-id-le, in an intrepid manner.
intricacy, *n.* *in*-tre-ka-se, the state of being entangled or involved; complication; perplexity.
intricate, *a.* *in*-tre-kat, entangled; involved; complicated. (L. *intricatus*, perplexed.)
intricately, *ad.* in an intricate manner.
intricateness, *n.* *in*-tre-kat-ness, intricacy.
intrigant, *n.* *in*-tre-gant (*or* App.), an intriguer. (Fr.)
intrigue, *n.* in-*treeg*, a plot of a complicated nature; a secret plot for some party purpose; a secret illicit love affair: *v.i.* to form a plot, esp. for a bad or secret purpose; to carry on illicit love: *v.t.* to puzzle; to arouse curiosity. (Fr. *intriguer.*)
intriguer, *n.* in-*treeg*-er, one who intrigues.
intriguing, *a.* in-*treeg*-ing, addicted to intrigue; provoking curiosity [Coll.].
intriguingly, *ad.* in-*treeg*-ing-le, with intrigue.
intrinsic, *a.* in-*trin*-sik, inward; inherent; essential; genuine; actual. (L. *intrinsecus*, on the inside, from *intra.*)
intrinsical, *a.* in-*trin*-se-kal, intrinsic.
intrinsicality, *n.* *in*-trin-se-*kal*-e-te, the quality of being intrinsic.
intrinsically, *ad.* in-*trin*-se-ka-le, inherently.
intro-, *in*-tro, a Latin prefix signifying within.
introcession, *n.* *in*-tro-*sesh*-on, a sinking of parts inward [Med.]. (L. *intro-*, and *cessio*, yielding.)
introduce, *v.t.* *in*-tro-*dewce*, to lead or bring in; to conduct or usher in; to put in; to bring to be acquainted; to import; to open to notice; to bring before the public. (L. *introduco*, lead.)
introducer, *n.* in-tro-*dewce*-er, one who introduces.
introduction, *n.* in-tro-*duk*-shon, the action of conducting or ushering into a place; the act of making persons known to each other; the act of bringing something into notice, practice, or use; a preface or preliminary discourse; an elementary treatise.
introductive, *a.* *in*-tro-*duk*-tiv, introductory.
introductorily, *ad.* *in*-tro-*duk*-to-re-le, by way of introduction; in the way of introducing.
introductory, *a.* *in*-tro-*duk*-to-re, serving to introduce something else; preliminary.
introflexed, *a.* *in*-tro-*flekst*, bent inward [Bot.].
introit, *n.* in-*troh*-it, the verse or psalm sung or chanted while the priest approaches the altar rails at the beginning of the Mass or Communion Service. (L. *introitus*, entered.)
intromission, *n.* *in*-tro-*mish*-on, the act of intromitting; sending into; intermeddling with the effects of another [Scots. Law].
intromit, *v.t.* *in*-tro-*mit*, to send within; to insert; to admit; to allow to enter; to be the medium by which a thing enters: *v.i.* to intermeddle with the effects of another [Scots. Law]. (L. *intromitto*, send.)
intromittent, *a.* *in*-tro-*mit*-tent, allowing to pass within; used as an intromitting agent.
introrse, *a.* *in*-*trorse*, facing inwards; turned towards the axis [Bot.]. (L. *introrsus*, turned.)
introspect, *v.t.* *in*-tro-*spekt*, to look within or inwardly; to examine one's own thoughts, etc. (L. *introspecto*, from *introspicio*, view.)
introspection, *n.* *in*-tro-*spek*-shon, inspection inwardly or of one's own thoughts and feelings; self-inspection.
introspective, *a.* *in*-tro-*spek*-tiv, given or pertaining to introspection.
introsusception, *n.* *in*-tro-sus-*sep*-shon, intussusception. (L. *intro-*, and *susceptio*, taking up.)
introversion, *n.* *in*-tro-*ver*-shon, the act of introverting; the state of being introverted.
introversive, *a.* *in*-tro-*ver*-siv, turning inwards; characterized by introspection.
introvert, *v.t.* *in*-tro-*vert*, to turn inward to invaginate: *n.* one given to introspection [Psychan.]; an organ that is or may be introverted [Zool.] (L. *intro-*, within, *verto*, turn.)
introvertive, *a.* *in*-tro-*ver*-tiv, introversive.
intrude, *v.i.* in-*trood*, to thrust oneself in; to enter without invitation; to encroach; to trespass: *v.t.* to thrust in without right; to force in with violence. (L. *intrudo*, thrust.)
intruder, *n.* in-*trood*-er, one who intrudes. **intruder patrol,** a small force of bombers with a strong escort of fighters, manned and equipped for making lightning attacks [Air warfare].
intrusion, *n.* in-*troo*-zhon, the act of intruding; the penetrating of rock, while in a melted state, through or among other rocks [Geol.].
intrusive, *a.* in-*troo*-siv, apt to intrude; entering without right; forced, while molten, into the cavities or between layers of other rocks [Geol.].
intrusively, *ad.* in an intrusive manner.
intrusiveness, *n.* quality of being intrusive.
intrust, *v.t.* in-*trust*, to entrust.
intubate, *v.t.* *in*-tew-bate, to insert a tube [Surg.].
intubation, *n.* in-tew-*bay*-shon, the introduction of a tube into the larynx or other cavity [Surg.].
intuit, *v.t.* *in*-tew-it, to know intuitively.
intuition, *n.* *in*-tew-*ish*-on, the act or power of direct or immediate perception; instinctive knowledge; an object or a truth of direct or immediate perception. (Fr.)
intuitional, *a.* *in*-tew-*ish*-on-al, pertaining to, derived from, or characterized by, intuition.
intuitionalism, *n.* *in*-tew-*ish*-on-al-izm, the doctrine that the perception of truth is by intuition.
intuitionism, *n.* *in*-tew-*ish*-on-izm, intuitionalism.
intuitionist, *n.* *in*-tew-*ish*-on-ist, an adherent of intuitionalism.
intuitive, *a.* in-*tew*-e-tiv, possessing intuition; perceived or perceiving by intuition; intuitional. (Late L. *intuitivus.*)
intuitively, *ad.* in-*tew*-e-tiv-le, by immediate perception; without reasoning.
intuitivism, *n.* in-*tew*-e-tiv-izm, the opinion that ethical principles are intuitional.
intumesce, *v.i.* *in*-tew-*mess*, to swell; to enlarge or expand with heat. (L. *intumesco*, swell.)
intumescence, *n.* *in*-tew-*mess*-ence, the action of swelling; a swelling; a tumid state.
intumescent, *a.* *in*-tew-*mess*-ent, swelling up.
intussusception, *n.* *in*-tus-sus-*sep*-shon, reception within; the reception and conversion into tissue of foreign matter by a living organism; invagination [Med.]. (L. *intus*, within, *suscipio*, take up.)
intwine, *v.t.* and *i.* in-*twine*, to entwine.
inulin, *n.* *in*-yew-lin, the carbo-hydrate of elecampane, *Inula helenium.*
inunction, *n.* in-*unk*-shon, act of anointing; state of being anointed. (L. *inunctio.*)
inundant, *a.* in-*un*-dant, inundating; overflowing.
inundate, *v.t.* *in*-un-date, to flood; to overflow; to fill to superfluity; to deluge. (L.)
inundation, *n.* in-un-*day*-shon, a flood; an overflow; an overflowing or superfluous abundance.
inurbane, *a.* in-ur-*bane*, uncivil; discourteous; unpolished. (L. *in-*, not, and *urbane.*)
inurbanely, *ad.* in-ur-*bane*-le, without urbanity.
inurbanity, *n.* in-ur-*ban*-e-te, want of urbanity; incivility.
inure, *v.t.* in-*yewr*, to apply or expose in practice till use does not inconvenience; to habituate; to accustom: *v.i.* to take or have effect; to serve to the use or benefit of [Law]. (*in-*, and O.Fr. *eure*, work.)

inurement, *n.* in-*yewr*-ment, practice; habituation.
inurn, *v.t.* in-*urn*, to put in an urn; to bury.
inutile, *a.* in-*yew*-til, of no use.
inutility, *n.* in-yew-*til*-e-te, uselessness; unprofitableness.
invade, *v.t.* in-*vade*, to enter a country with hostile intentions; to attack; to violate; to seize upon: *v.i.* to make an invasion. (L. *invado*, go.)
invader, *n.* in-*vade*-er, one who invades; an assailant; an encroacher.
invaginate, *v.t.* in-*vaj*-e-nate, to put into or as into a sheath; to effect introversion.
invagination, *n.* in-*vaj*-e-*nay*-shon, the reception of one part within another, as of an upper segment of the intestine into the lower by accidental displacement [Med.]. (L. *in-*, and *vagina*, a sheath.)
invalid, *a.* in-*val*-id, not valid; of no force, weight, or cogency; void; null. (L. *invalidus.*)
invalid, *n.* *in*-va-leed, a person who is weak or sickly; one disabled or worn out in service: *a.* disabled through ill-health; infirm: *v.t.* to make invalid; to enrol on the list of invalids: *v.i.* to become an invalid. (Fr. *invalide.*)
invalidate, *v.t.* in-*val*-e-date, to weaken or lessen the force of; to destroy the validity of.
invalidation, *n.* in-*val*-e-*day*-shon, the act of invalidating.
invalidhood, *n.* *in*-va-leed-hood, the state of being an invalid.
invalidism, *n.* *in*-va-leed-izm, chronic ill-health; valetudinarianism.
invalidity, *n.* *in*-va-*lid*-e-te, want of cogency; want of legal force.
invalidly, *ad.* in-*val*-id-le, without validity.
invalidness, *n.* in-*val*-id-ness, invalidity.
invaluable, *a.* in-*val*-yew-a-bl, precious above estimation; inestimable; priceless.
invaluably, *ad.* in-*val*-yew-a-ble, inestimably.
invar, *n.* *in*-var, proprietary name of an alloy of nickel and steel. (From its invariability.)
invariability, *n.* in-*vare*-re-a-*bil*-e-te, constancy of state, condition, or quality; unchangeableness.
invariable, *a.* in-*vare*-re-a-bl, not variable; constant in the same state; unchangeable.
invariableness, *n.* in-*vare*-re-a-bl-ness, invariability.
invariably, *ad.* in-*vare*-re-a-ble, constantly; uniformly.
invariant, *a.* in-*vare*-re-ant, constant; not subject to change: *n.* a quantity that is itself, as apart from its constituents, invariable [Math.].
invasion, *n.* in-*vay*-zhon, a hostile entrance into the possessions of another; an attack on the territory of another; infringement or violation; attack of a disease. (L. *invasus.*)
invasive, *a.* in-*vay*-siv, making invasion; aggressive.
invection, *n.* in-*vek*-shon, invective; vituperation.
invective, *n.* in-*vek*-tiv, something uttered or written with heat by way of opprobrium, censure, or reproach: *a.* abusive; railing. (Fr. *invectif.*)
invectively, *ad.* in-*vek*-tiv-le, abusively.
inveigh, *v.i.* in-*vay*, to rail against with warmth and bitterness; to reproach. (L. *invehi*, to abuse.)
inveigher, *n.* in-*vay*-er, one who inveighs.
inveigle, *v.t.* in-*vee*-gl *or* in-*vay*-gl, to entice; to seduce; to wheedle. (Fr. *aveugler*, blind.)
inveiglement, *n.* in-*vee*- *or* in-*vay*-gl-ment, seduction to evil; enticement.
inveigler, *n.* in-*vee*- *or* in-*vay*-gler, one who inveigles.
invendible, *a.* in-*ven*-de-bl, not vendible or saleable.
invent, *v.t.* in-*vent*, to devise something original; to contrive; to discover; to fabricate. (Fr. *inventer.*)
inventful, *a.* in-*vent*-ful, full of inventiveness.
★**invention,** *n.* in-*ven*-shon, that which is invented; an original contrivance; fiction; fabrication; the power of imaginative conception; imaginative faculty or ability. **Invention of the Cross,** the discovery of the Cross (A.D. 326) by St. Helena, or the festival (3 May) commemorating this. (L. *inventio.*)
inventive, *a.* in-*ven*-tiv, able to invent; quick at contrivance; ready at expedients. (Fr. *inventif.*)
inventively, *ad.* by the power of invention.
inventiveness, *n.* the faculty of inventing, or of making use of expedients.
inventor, *n.* in-*ven*-tor, one who invents; one who contrives and produces anything not before existing.
inventorially, *ad.* *in*-ven-*taw*-re-a-le, in the manner of an inventory.
inventory, *n.* *in*-ven-to-re, a list of goods or chattels; the articles listed: *v.t.* to make an inventory of; to enter in an inventory.
inveracity, *n.* *in*-ve-ras-e-te, untruthfulness.
invermination, *n.* *in*-ver-me-*nay*-shon, helminthiasis; the condition of infestation by worms [Path.].
Inverness, *n.* in-ver-*ness*, a long sleeveless outdoor cloak with removable cape. (Town in Scotland.)
inverse, *a.* *in*-verse, inverted; reciprocal: *n.* that which is inverted; the exact opposite; the result of inversion [Math.]. **inverse proportion,** an equality between a direct ratio and an inverse ratio; the rule of three or proportion, applied in a reverse or contrary order [Math.]. **inverse ratio,** the ratio of the reciprocals of two quantities [Math.]. (Fr.)
inversely, *ad.* in-*verse*-le, in an inverted order or manner.
inversion, *n.* in-*ver*-shon, change of an order, or of position, into the inverse; a turning backward or a contrary order of operation; the inverting of the terms of a proportion by changing the antecedents into consequents and the consequents into antecedents [Math.]; a change of the natural order of words [Gram.]; the change of position either of a subject, an interval, or a chord [Mus.].
inversive, *a.* in-*ver*-siv, exhibiting inversion.
invert, *v.t.* in-*vert*, to turn upside down; to place in a contrary order or method; to reverse. **invert sugar,** a mixture of dextrose and lævulose prepared from cane sugar. (L. *inverto*, turn.)
invert, *n.* *in*-vert, an inverted arch [Arch]; one addicted to homosexual practices [Psychan.].
invertebrata, *n.pl.* in-*ver*-te-*bray*-ta, a division of the animal kingdom which includes all those animals not possessed of a backbone. (L.)
invertebrate, *a.* in-*ver*-te-brat, destitute of a backbone or vertebral column: *n.* an animal having no vertebral column. (L. *in-*, and *vertebrata.*)
invertedly, *ad.* in-*ver*-ted-le, in an inverted order.
invertible, *a.* in-*ver*-te-bl, capable of inversion.
invest, *v.t.* in-*vest*, to clothe; to array; to clothe with office or authority; to place in possession of an office, rank, or dignity; to enclose; to surround; to block up; to lay siege to; to place or lay out money in some species of property: *v.i.* to make an investment. (Fr. *investir*, clothe.)
investigable, *a.* in-*ves*-te-ga-bl, capable of being investigated.
investigate, *v.t.* in-*ves*-te-gate, to search into; to examine into with care. (L. *investigatus*, traced.)
investigation, *n.* in-*ves*-te-*gay*-shon, the act of investigating; examination; research.
investigative, *a.* in-*ves*-te-gay-tiv, addicted to investigation; curious to find out.
investigator, *n.* in-*ves*-te-gay-tor, one who investigates.
investigatory, *a.* in-*vest*-e-gay-to-re, pertaining to investigation.
investitive, *a.* in-*ves*-te-tiv, having the property of, or pertaining to, vesting (a right) [Law].
investiture, *n.* in-*ves*-te-ture, the act, ceremony, or right of investing or putting in possession; the state of being invested; vesture. (Fr.)
investment, *n.* in-*vest*-ment, the act of investing, esp. a place with an armed force, or money in some species of property; that in which anything is invested; integument [Zool.]; investiture. (Late L. *investimentum.*)
investor, *n.* in-*ves*-tor, one who invests.
inveteracy, *n.* in-*vet*-er-a-se, the state of being inveterate; long continuance.
inveterate, *a.* in-*vet*-er-at, long-established; fixed by long habits; deep-rooted; obstinate. (L. *inveteratus*, retained for a great while.)
inveterately, *ad.* in an inveterate manner.
inveterateness, *n.* in-*vet*-er-at-ness, the quality of being inveterate, or confirmed by time or habit.
invidious, *a.* in-*vid*-e-us, likely to incur ill-will or to provoke envy; unfairly discriminating. (L. *invidiosus.*)
invidiously, *ad.* in an invidious manner.
invidiousness, *n.* quality of being invidious.
invigilate, *v.i.* in-*vij*-e-late, to watch over candidates at an examination. (L. *invigilatus*, watched keenly.)
invigilation, *n.* in-vij-e-*lay*-shon, the act of invigilating.

invigilator, *n.* in-*vij*-e-lay-tor, one who superintends an examination.
invigorate, *v.t.* in-*vig*-o-rate, to give vigour to; to strengthen; to impart life and energy to; to encourage. (L. *in*-, and *vigor*, strength.)
invigoration, *n.* in-*vig*-o-*ray*-shon, the action of invigorating; state of being invigorated.
invincibility, *n.* in-*vin*-se-*bil*-e-te, the quality of being invincible.
invincible, *a.* in-*vin*-se-bl, not to be conquered or subdued. (Fr.)
invincibleness, *n.* in-*vin*-se-bl-ness, invincibility.
invincibly, *ad.* in-*vin*-se-ble, in an invincible manner.
inviolability, *n.* in-*vy*-o-la-*bil*-e-te, the quality or state of being inviolable. (L. *inviolabilis.*)
inviolable, *a.* in-*vy*-o-la-bl, not violable; not to be violated, profaned, broken, or injured.
inviolableness, *n.* in-*vy*-o-la-bl-ness, inviolability.
inviolably, *ad.* in-*vy*-o-la-ble, so as not to be violable.
inviolacy, *n.* in-*vy*-o-la-se, the state or quality of being inviolate.
inviolate, *a.* in-*vy*-o-late, unprofaned; unbroken; uninjured. (L. *inviolatus.*)
inviolateness, *n.* in-*vy*-o-lat-ness, inviolacy.
invious, *a.* *in*-ve-us, impassable; untrodden. (L. *in*-, not, *via*, a way.)
invisibility, *n.* in-viz-e-*bil*-e-te, the state of being invisible.
invisible, *a.* in-*viz*-e-bl, not visible; imperceptible. **invisible exports,** factors other than goods, bullion, or specie that help to balance imports, *e.g.* loans raised abroad, shipping dues from foreigners, expenditure by foreign tourists in the country, etc. **invisible ink,** sympathetic ink.
invisibleness, *n.* in-*viz*-e-bl-ness, invisibility.
invisibly, *ad.* in-*viz*-e-ble, so as not to be visible.
invitation, *n.* in-ve-*tay*-shon, the act of inviting; the missive or message inviting one; solicitation. (Fr.)
invitatory, *a.* in-*vy*-ta-to-re, containing or conveying invitation.
invite, *v.t.* in-*vite*, to ask; to request the company of; to induce by pleasure or hope; to allure; to offer for attack: *n.* an invitation [Coll.]. (L. *invito.*)
inviter, *n.* in-*vy*-ter, one who invites.
inviting, *a.* in-*vy*-ting, attractive; tempting.
invitingly, *ad.* in-*vy*-ting-le, in an inviting manner.
invitrifiable, *a.* in-*vit*-re-*fy*-a-bl, not capable of being vitrified.
invocate, *v.t.* *in*-vo-kate, to invoke.
invocation, *n.* in-vo-*kay*-shon, act of addressing or of calling on in prayer; the customary phrase prefactory to a sermon; a prayerful address. (Fr.)
invocatory, *a.* in-*vok*-a-to-re *or* in-vo-*kay*-to-re, pertaining to invocation.
invoice, *n.* *in*-voyce, a detailed account of goods delivered: *v.t.* to enter in an invoice. (Fr. *envois.*)
invoke, *v.t.* in-*voke*, to address in prayer; to call on for assistance and protection; to implore; to appeal to as an authority. (Fr. *invoquer.*)
involucel, *n.* in-*vol*-yew-sel, a secondary involucre as in umbelliferous plants. (L., a little envelope.)
involucral, *a.* in-vo-*lew*-kral, pertaining to an involucre.
involucrate, *a.* *in*-vo-*lew*-krate, with an involucre.
involucre, *n.* in-vo-*lewkr*, the whorl of bracts enclosing flowers in their unexpanded state; the whorl of leaves below a flower and on the same axis, as in *Anemone*, etc.; the indusium of ferns [Bot.]. (L., an envelope.)
involucrum, *n.* in-vo-*lew*-krum, the membranous covering of certain organs [Anat.]; the new bone formed about a decayed or diseased bone [Med.].
involuntarily, *ad.* in-*vol*-un-ta-re-le, in an involuntary manner.
involuntariness, *n.* in-*vol*-un-ta-re-ness, the quality of being involuntary.
involuntary, *a.* in-*vol*-un-ta-re, having no will or choice; unwilling; not by an act of will; not done willingly or spontaneously; without intention.
involute, *a.* *in*-vo-lewt, involuted: *n.* a curve traced by the end of a string unwinding itself from another curve. (L. *involutus*, involved.)
involuted, *a.* *in*-vo-lew-ted, rolled spirally inward; turned inward at the margin [Bot. and Malac.].
involution, *n.* in-vo-*lew*-shon, the act of involving or enfolding; the state of being involved or entangled; complication; the insertion of one or more clauses or members of a sentence in a way which involves the construction [Gram.]; the raising of a quantity to any given power [Math.].
involutional, *a.* in-vo-*lew*-shon-al, pertaining to or characterized by involution.
involve, *v.t.* in-*volv*, to envelop on all sides; to imply; to connect intimately; to include in; to entangle; to overwhelm; to enwrap; to complicate; to raise a quantity to any given power [Math.]. (L. *involvo*, roll.)
involvement, *n.* in-*volv*-ment, the act of involving; the state of being involved.
invulnerability, *n.* in-*vul*-ner-a-*bil*-e-te, the quality of being invulnerable.
invulnerable, *a.* in-*vul*-ner-a-bl, that cannot be wounded, injured, or impeached; not having won a game towards rubber [Contract].
invulnerably, *ad.* so as to be invulnerable.
invultuation, *n.* in-vul-tew-*ay*-shun, the practice of stabbing the wax or clay image of an enemy that he may suffer a speedy and painful death [Witchcraft]. (L. *in*-, and *vultus*, face.)
inward, *a.* *in*-werd, placed or being within; internal; seated in the mind or soul; intimate; domestic; familiar: *ad.* toward the inside or interior; into the mind or thoughts. (A.S. *inweard.*)
inwardly, *ad.* in the inner parts; privately.
inwardness, *n.* the state of being inward; intimacy; inner nature; inner significance.
inwards, *ad.* *in*-werdz, inward: *n.* the inner parts, esp. the entrails, etc. of an animal.
inweave, *v.t.* in-*weev*, to weave together; to intermix or intertwine by weaving.
inwick, *n.* *in*-wik, a cannon off another stone resulting in a close approach to the tee [Curling].
inwit, *n.* *in*-wit, instinctive knowledge; conscience.
inwrap, *v.t.* in-*rap*, to enwrap.
inwrought, *pp.* and *a.* in-*rawt*, wrought or worked in or among other things; having wrought in ornamentation.
inyala, *n.* in-*yah*-la, the antelope *Tragelephas angari* of Central Africa. (Native.)
iodal, *n.* *eye*-o-dal, an oleaginous liquid obtained from the action of alcohol and nitric acid on iodine.
iodate, *n.* *eye*-o-date, a salt of iodic acid: *v.t.* to iodize.
iodic, *a.* eye-*od*-ik, belonging to or containing iodine.
iodide, *n.* *eye*-o-dide, a compound of iodine with another element or radical.
iodine, *n.* *eye*-o-din, a solid non-metallic element of the halogen group, the salts of which are widely used in medicine and photography; named from the violet colour of its vapour. (Gr. *iōdēs*, violet-coloured.)
iodism, *n.* *eye*-o-dizm, a morbid state induced by injudicious use of iodine or its compounds.
iodize, *v.t.* *eye*-o-dize, to treat, permeate, or coat with iodine.
iodoform, *n.* eye-*oh*-do-form, an antiseptic made from iodine.
iodotherapy, *n.* eye-*oh*-do-*the*-ra-pe, medical treatment by means of iodine or its compounds.
iodyrite, *n.* eye-*oh*-de-rite, native iodide of silver.
iolite, *n.* *eye*-o-lite, a transparent or translucent silicate of aluminium and magnesium with some iron. (Gr. *ion*, and *lithos*, a stone.)
ion, *n.* *eye*-on, the electrified particle produced when an atom loses or gains one or more electrons by electrolytic dissociation, or when a molecule of a gas loses an electron through X-ray action. (Gr., going.)
Ionian, *a.* eye-*oh*-ne-an, relating to Ionia or its inhabitants: *n.* a member of the Ionian branch of the ancient Greeks. (L. *Ionius.*)
Ionic, *a.* eye-*on*-ik, Ionian; pertaining to the Ionic order. **Ionic dialect,** the Greek dialect anciently used in Ionia. **Ionic order,** that order whose distinguishing feature is the ram's horn volute on either side of its capital [Arch.]. **Ionic school,** the philosophic school founded by Thales of Miletus, from whom Hegel dated the birth of philosophy. (L. *Ionicus.*)
ionic, *a.* eye-*on*-ik, pertaining to an ion or ions.
ionium, *n.* eye-*oh*-ne-um, a radioactive isotope of thorium.
ionization, *n.* *eye*-on-ize-*ay*-shon, the creation of ions in a gas or liquid; the state of being ionized.

ionize, *v.t.* and *i.* *eye*-o-nize, to convert or be converted into ions.
ionosphere, *n.* eye-*on*-o-sfeer, the region of the Heaviside-layer [Wireless].
iota, *n.* eye-*oh*-ta, the Greek letter ι, the smallest in the alphabet; hence, a very small quantity. (Gr.)
I.O.U., *n.* eye-o-*yew*, a written acknowledgment of a loan, containing a note of the amount, the signature, and the letters I O U (*I owe you*).
ipecacuanha, *n.* *ip*-e-*kak*-yew-*an*-na, a South American creeping plant from the dried root of which is prepared a purgative and emetic. (Port.)
Ipomœa, *n.* *eye*-po-*mee*-a, a genus of plants allied to *Convolvulus*, consisting of many species, among which are the sweet potato and the jalap. (Gr. *ips*, worm, *homoios*, like.)
ipseity, *n.* ip-*see*-e-te, personal identity; selfhood.
iracund, *a.* *ire*-ra-kund, irascible. (L. *iracundus*.)
irade, *n.* i-*rah*-de, a written decree of a Moslem ruler, esp. a former Turkish sultan. (Turk.)
Iranian, *a.* eye-*ray*-ne-an, belonging to Iran, or Persia. (Pers. *Iran*, Persia.)
Iraqi, *n.* eye-*rah*-ke, a native of Iraq, formerly Mesopotamia; the Arabic dialect of the Iraqui: *a.* belonging to Iraq, its people, or its dialect.
irascibility, *n.* i-*ras*-se-*bil*-e-te, the quality of being irascible.
irascible, *a.* i-*ras*-se-bl, susceptible of anger; easily provoked; irritable. (Fr.)
irascibleness, *n.* i-*ras*-se-bl-ness, irascibility.
irascibly, *ad.* i-*ras*-se-ble, in an irascible manner.
irate, *a.* *ire*-rate, angry; enraged. (L. *iratus*, enraged.)
ire, *n.* ire, anger; wrath; keen resentment. (L. *ira*.)
ireful, *a.* *ire*-ful, angry; wroth.
irefully, *ad.* *ire*-ful-le, in an angry manner.
irenical, *a.* ire-*ren*-e-kal, pacific; promoting peace. (Gr. *eirinikos*, peaceful.)
irenicon, *n.* ire-*ren*-e-kon, an eirenicon. (Gr.)
irian, *a.* *ire*-re-an, pertaining to the iris (of the eye) [Anat.].
Iricism, *n.* *ire*-re-sizm, an Irishism.
iridaceous, *a.* *ire*-re-*day*-shus, belonging to the order that includes the genera *Iris*, *Crocus*, *Gladiolus*, etc.
iridal, *a.* *ire*-re-dal, pertaining to the iris of the eye, or to the rainbow.
iridescence, *n.* i-re-*des*-sence, the exhibition of interference colours like those of the rainbow.
iridescent, *a.* i-re-*des*-sent, showing iridescence; having rainbow colours.
iridin, *n.* *ire*-e-din, the active principle of the iris or flag; a purgative prepared from this.
iridium, *n.* i-*rid*-e-um, a very heavy metallic element of whitish colour, found associated with platinum. (From the variety of colours of its compounds.)
iridize, *v.t.* *ire*-re-dize, to make iridescent; to tip with iridium.
iridosmine, *n.* ire-re-*doz*-min, a native iridium osmium alloy, used in pointing gold pen-nibs.
iris, *n.* *ire*-ris, the rainbow; an appearance resembling the rainbow; the coloured circle which surrounds the pupil of the eye; (*cap.*) a genus of plants including the flags and *Iris florentina*, the orris root. **iris diaphragm,** a diaphragm the diameter of the central opening of which is readily adjustable (Opt. and Phot.]. (Gr. *iris*, the rainbow.)
irisated, *a.* *ire*-re-say-ted, exhibiting prismatic colours.
iriscope, *n.* *ire*-re-skope, an instrument for exhibiting the prismatic colours. (Gr. *iris*, and *skopeo*, view.)
irised, *a.* *ire*-rist, having colours like the rainbow.
Irish, *a.* *ire*-rish, pertaining to Ireland or its people: *n.* the natives of Ireland; the old native language of the Irish. **Irish bull,** a ludicrous verbal blunder or contradiction in terms. **Irish moss,** carrageen, which contains a gelatine used in medicine. **Irish stew,** a rich stew of meat, potatoes, and onions. (A.S. *Irisc*.)
Irishism, *n.* *ire*-rish-izm, an Irish peculiarity, esp. of speech; an Irish bull.
Irishman, *n.* *ire*-rish-man, one of Irish race; a native of Eire, as distinct from an Ulsterman.
Irishry, *n.* *ire*-rish-re, the people of Ireland.
iritis, *n.* ire-*ry*-tis, inflammation of the iris of the eye.
irk, *v.t.* irk, to weary; to give pain to. (M.E. *irken* —origin unknown.)
irksome, *a.* *irk*-sum, wearisome; tedious; troublesome; vexatious.
irksomely, *ad.* *irk*-sum-le, in an irksome manner.
irksomeness, *n.* the quality of being irksome.
★**iron,** *n.* *eye*-urn, a widespread metallic element, the most useful of all the metals; an instrument or utensil of iron; a flat-iron; a metal-headed lofting club [Golf]: *pl.* chains; metal supports to correct malformation of the legs; stirrups; climbing-irons: *a.* made or consisting of iron; resembling iron; harsh; rude; severe; binding fast; not to be broken; firm; robust; hard of understanding: *v.t.* to smooth with a hot flat- or box-iron; to shackle with irons; to furnish or arm with iron. **iron age,** the last of the four ages, being that of enforced toil [Myth.]; the last of the three prehistoric ages, when iron came into use [Archæol.]. **Iron Cross,** a German (and formerly Austrian) war decoration for gallantry. **Iron crown,** the jewelled gold crown of the mediæval Lombard kings, said to contain one of the nails of the Cross, possession of which is fabled to ensure the dominion of Italy. **iron curtain,** an impenetrable barrier purposefully fixed [Fig.]. **iron ration,** the ration carried by a soldier for use only in emergency, hence [Fig.] short commons. (A.S. *iren*.)
ironbark, *n.* *eye*-urn-bahrk, a species of *Eucalyptus*.
ironbound, *a.* *eye*-urn-bound, bound or encircled with or as with iron, or with rocks; rigid.
ironclad, *a.* *eye*-urn-klad, plated with thick iron: *n.* a warship that is so protected.
ironer, *n.* *i*-urn-er, one who irons; a machine that irons.
iron-founder, *n.* one who makes iron castings.
iron-foundry, *n.* the place where iron castings are made.
iron-grey, *n.* the colour of iron just fractured: *a.* of this colour.
iron-hearted, *a.* unfeeling; cruel.
ironic, *a.* eye-*ron*-ik, ironical. (Gr. *eironikos*.)
ironical, *a.* eye-*ron*-e-kal, of the nature of irony; expressing one thing and meaning another.
ironically, *ad.* eye-*ron*-e-kal-le, by way of irony.
ironing, *a.* *eye*-urn-ing, smoothing with a hot flat- or box-iron. **ironing board,** a board for ironing on.
ironist, *n.* *ire*-ron-ist, one who relies on irony for effect; an ironical writer.
iron-liquor, *n.* acetate of iron, used in dyeing as a mordant.
ironmaster, *n.* *eye*-urn-*mahs*-ter, a manufacturer of iron.
ironmonger, *n.* *eye*-urn-mung-ger, a dealer in hardware or ironware.
ironmongery, *n.* *eye*-urn-mung-ge-re, ironware; the business, or the place of business, of an ironmonger.
iron-mould, *n.* a stain on cloth, etc., made by ink or rusty iron.
Ironside, *n.* *eye*-urn-side, one of Cromwell's veterans; hence, any hardy veteran or resolute person.
ironsmith, *n.* *eye*-urn-smith, a worker in iron.
ironstone, *n.* *eye*-urn-stone, an impure ore of iron, containing much clay; siderite.
ironware, *n.* *eye*-urn-ware, iron utensils, tools, etc.; hardware.
ironweed, *n.* *eye*-urn-weed, knapweed.
ironwood, *n.* *eye*-urn-wood, any of several trees with particularly hard, tough, or heavy wood; the timber of such trees.
ironwork, *n.* *eye*-urn-wurk, anything made of iron: *pl.* a factory where iron or steel is wrought, smelted, etc.; an iron-foundry.
irony, *a.* *eye*-urn-e, made or consisting of iron; partaking of iron; resembling iron.
irony, *n.* *ire*-ro-ne, an expression having the opposite of its ostensible meaning; satire in which, while the terms are commendatory, the tones are sarcastic; censure disguised as praise. (Fr. *ironie*.)
irradiance, *n.* i-*ray*-de-ance, emission of rays of light on an object; beams of light emitted; lustre.
irradiant, *a.* i-*ray*-de-ant, emitting rays of light; shining brightly.
irradiate, *v.t.* i-*ray*-de-ate, to illuminate; to brighten; to enlighten intellectually; to decorate with shining ornaments: *v.i.* to emit rays. (L. *irradiatus*, shone upon.)
irradiation, *n.* i-*ray*-de-*ay*-shon, the act of emitting beams of light; illumination; brightness; intellectual or spiritual illumination.
irrational, *a.* i-*rash*-on-al, not rational; illogical; void of reason or contrary to reason; absurd; not expressible as an integer; surd [Math.]: *n.* a surd, or an irrational number. (L. *irrationalis*.)

irrationality, *n.* i-*rash*-o-*nal*-e-te, the quality of being irrational.
irrationally, *ad.* without reason; absurdly.
irrationalize, *v.t.* i-*rash*-o-na-lize, to render irrational.
irrealizable, *a.* i-ree-a-*ly*-za-bl, not able to be realized; not convertible into money.
irrebuttable, *a.* i-re-*but*-a-bl, not rebuttable.
irreceptive, *a.* i-re-*sep*-tiv, unreceptive.
irreciprocal, *a.* i-re-*sip*-ro-kal, not reciprocal.
irreclaimable, *a.* i-re-*klame*-a-bl, that cannot be reclaimed; incorrigible.
irreclaimably, *ad.* i-re-*klame*-a-ble, so as not to admit of reformation.
irrecognizable, *a.* i-*rek*-og-*ny*-za-bl, unrecognizable.
irreconcilable, *a.* i-*rek*-on-*sile*-a-bl, incapable of being reconciled, harmonized, or atoned for.
irreconcilableness, *n.* i-*rek*-on-*sile*-a-bl-ness, the quality of being irreconcilable.
irreconcilably, *ad.* i-*rek*-on-*sile*-a-ble, in a manner that precludes reconciliation.
irrecoverable, *a.* i-re-*kuv*-er-a-bl, not to be recovered; irreparable.
irrecoverableness, *n.* i-re-*kuv*-er-a-bl-ness, the state of being irrecoverable.
irrecoverably, *ad.* beyond recovery.
irrecusable, *a.* i-re-*kew*-za-bl, not liable to be rejected.
irredeemability, *n.* i-re-*deem*-a-*bil*-e-te, the quality of not being redeemable.
irredeemable, *a.* i-re-*deem*-a-bl, that cannot be redeemed; not subject to be paid at the nominal value.
irredeemably, *ad.* so as not to be redeemable.
irredentism, *n.* i-re-*den*-tizm, policy of irredentists.
irredentist, *n.* i-re-*den*-tist, one of an Italian party of the late 1870's working for the annexation to Italy of adjoining Italian-speaking districts; hence, a person or party in any state seeking to re-incorporate lost territorial possessions: *a.* pertaining to irredentism or irredentists. (It. *irredentista.*)
irreducible, *a.* i-re-*dew*-se-bl, not reducible.
irreducibleness, *n.* ir-re-*dew*-se-bl-ness, the quality of being irreducible.
irreducibly, *ad.* in a manner not reducible.
irreflective, i-re-*flek*-tiv, not reflective; unthinking.
irreformable, *a.* i-re-*form*-a-bl, not capable of being reformed; incapable of revision.
irrefragability, *n.* i-*ref*-ra-ga-*bil*-e-te, the quality of being irrefragable.
irrefragable, *a.* i-*ref*-ra-ga-bl, that cannot be refuted; incontrovertible. (Fr.)
irrefragably, *ad.* in an irrefragable manner.
irrefrangible, *a.* i-re-*franj*-e-bl, inviolable: incapable of being refracted [Opt.].
irrefutable, *a.* i-re-*few*-ta-bl *or* i-*ref*-yew-ta-bl, that cannot be refuted. (Late L. *irrefutabilis.*)
irrefutably, *ad.* beyond refutation.
irregular, *a.* i-*reg*-yew-lar, not regular; not according to rule, common form, established principles, or custom; not conformable to nature, or the operation of natural laws; not according to the rules of art; not in conformity to law, human or divine; deviating from the rules of moral rectitude; not straight; not uniform; asymmetric; deviating from the normal in inflexion [Gram.]; not in the regular army [Mil.]; not ending upon the tonic chord (of cadences) [Mus.]: *n.* one who does not conform to the rule or standard; an irregular noun or verb [Gram.]: *pl.* troops not forming part of the regular army [Mil.].
irregularity, *n.* i-*reg*-yew-*la*-re-te, deviation from a straight line, or from rule or order; that which is irregular; inordinate practice; vice.
irregularly, *ad.* without rule, method, or order.
irrelative, *a.* i-*rel*-a-tiv, not relative; unrelated; unconnected.
irrelatively, *ad.* i-*rel*-a-tiv-le, unconnectedly.
irrelevancy, *n.* i-*rel*-e-van-se, the quality of being irrelevant; inapplicability.
irrelevant, *a.* i-*rel*-e-vant, not applicable or pertinent; inapposite.
irrelevantly, *ad.* without being to the purpose.
irreligion, *n.* i-re-*lij*-on, opposition to religion; disregard or contempt of religion.
irreligionist, *n.* i-re-*lij*-on-ist, one who has hostility to or contempt of religion.
irreligious, *a.* i-re-*lij*-us, destitute of religion; ungodly. (Late L. *irreligiosus.*)
irreligiously, *ad.* in an irreligious manner.
irreligiousness, *n.* state of being irreligious.
irremeable, *a.* i-*ree*-me-a-bl *or* i-re-*mee*-a-bl, not admitting of return. (L. *in-*, not, *re-*, back, and *meo*, go.)
irremediable, *a.* i-re-*mee*-de-a-bl, incapable of remedy, redress, or correction. (L. *irremediabilis.*)
irremediableness, *n.* i-re-*mee*-de-a-bl-ness, state of being irremediable.
irremediably, *ad.* i-re-*mee*-de-a-ble, to an irremediable degree.
irremissible, *a.* i-re-*mis*-se-bl, not to be remitted or pardoned.
irremissibly, *ad.* so as not to be remissible.
irremovability, *n.* i-re-*moov*-a-*bil*-e-te, the quality or state of being irremovable.
irremovable, *a.* i-re-*moov*-a-bl, not removable or movable; fixed; permanent.
irremovably, *ad.* so as not to admit of removal.
irreparability, *n.* i-*rep*-a-ra-*bil*-e-te, irreparableness.
irreparable, *a.* i-*rep*-a-ra-bl, that cannot be remedied, repaired, or recovered. (L. *irreparabilis.*)
irreparableness, *n.* i-*rep*-a-ra-bl-ness, the quality or state of being irreparable, or beyond repair.
irreparably, *ad.* i-*rep*-a-ra-ble, in a manner or degree that precludes recovery or repair.
irrepealability, *n.* i-re-*peel*-a-*bil*-e-te, the state or quality of being irrepealable.
irrepealable, *a.* i-re-*peel*-a-bl, that cannot be repealed.
irrepealably, *ad.* i-re-*peel*-a-ble, beyond repeal.
irreplaceable, *a.* i-re-*place*-a-bl, that cannot be replaced.
irreprehensible, *a.* i-*rep*-re-*hen*-se-bl, that cannot be blamed. (Late L. *irreprehensabilis.*)
irrepresentable, *a.* i-*rep*-re-*zen*-ta-bl, incapable of representation.
irrepressible, *a.* i-re-*pres*-se-bl, not to be repressed; unquenchable.
irrepressibly, *ad.* so as not to be repressible.
irreproachable, *a.* i-re-*proach*-a-bl, blameless; faultless; upright.
irreproachableness, *n.* i-re-*proach*-a-bl-ness, the quality or state of being irreproachable.
irreproachably, *ad.* i-re-*proach*-a-ble, in an irreproachable manner.
irreproducible, *a.* i-*rep*-ro-*dew*-sa-bl, that cannot be reproduced.
irreprovable, *a.* i-re-*proov*-a-bl, blameless; upright.
irreprovably, *ad.* i-re-*proov*-a-ble, in an irreprovable manner.
irresistance, *n.* i-re-*zis*-tance, forbearance to resist; non-resistance; passive submission.
irresistibility, *n.* i-re-*zis*-te-*bil*-e-te, the quality of being irresistible.
irresistible, *a.* i-re-*zis*-te-bl, that cannot be successfully resisted or opposed.
irresistibly, *ad.* in an irresistible manner.
irresoluble, *a.* i-*rez*-o-lew-bl, incapable of being dissolved, or resolved into its elements; insoluble.
irresolute, *a.* i-*rez*-o-lewt, wavering; undecided; not firm in purpose. (L. *irresolutus.*)
irresolutely, *ad.* without firmness of mind.
irresoluteness, *n.* irresolution.
irresolution, *n.* i-*rez*-o-*lew*-shon, want of firm determination or resolution; fluctuation of mind.
irresolvability, *n.* i-re-*zol*-va-*bil*-e-te, the state or quality of not being resolvable.
irresolvable, *a.* i-re-*zol*-va-bl, not resolvable.
irrespective, *a.* i-re-*spek*-tiv, not having regard to; not taking into account: *ad.* irrespectively.
irrespectively, *ad.* i-re-*spek*-tiv-le, without regard to; not taking into consideration; independently.
irrespirable, *a.* i-res-*spire*-ra-bl *or* ir-*res*-pe-ra-bl, unfit for respiration.
irresponsibility, *n.* i-re-*spon*-se-*bil*-e-te, want of responsibility.
irresponsible, *a.* i-re-*spon*-se-bl, not responsible; not liable or able to answer for consequences; unaccountable; untrustworthy.
irresponsibly, *ad.* so as not to be responsible.
irresponsive, *a.* i-re-*spon*-siv, not responsive.
irrestrainable, *a.* i-re-*strane*-a-bl, not capable of being restrained.
irretentive, *a.* i-re-*ten*-tiv, not retentive.
irretraceable, *a.* i-re-*trace*-a-bl, not retraceable.

irretrievability, *n.* i-re-*treev*-a-*bil*-e-te, the state or quality of being irretrievable.
irretrievable, *a.* i-re-*treev*-a-bl, not to be retrieved or repaired; irreparable.
irretrievably, *ad.* irreparably; irrecoverably.
irrevealable, *a.* i-re-*veel*-a-bl, not to be revealed.
irreverence, *n.* i-*rev*-er-ence, an irreverent state of mind; irreverent behaviour or action.
irreverent, *a.* i-*rev*-er-ent, wanting in reverence; proceeding from irreverence.
irreverently, *ad.* in an irreverent manner.
irreversibility, *n.* i-re-*ver*-se-*bil*-e-te, the quality or state of being irreversible.
irreversible, *a.* i-re-*ver*-se-bl, that cannot be reversed or annulled.
irreversibly, *ad.* so as to be irreversible.
irrevocability, *n.* i-*rev*-o-ka-*bil*-e-te, the quality or state of being irrevocable.
irrevocable, *a.* i-*rev*-o-ka-bl, not to be revoked, recalled, or reversed. (L. *irrevocabilis.*)
irrevocableness, *n.* irrevocability.
irrevocably, *ad.* i-*rev*-o-ka-ble, beyond recall.
irrigable, *a.* *i*-re-ga-bl, capable of being irrigated; suitable for irrigation.
irrigant, *a.* *i*-re-gant, irrigating: *n.* a channel for irrigation.
irrigate, *v.t.* *i*-re-gate, to water; to moisten; to cause to flow over in channels. (L. *irrigatus,* flooded.)
irrigation, *n.* i-re-*gay*-shon, the act of irrigating; the artificial watering of lands for agricultural purposes.
irrigational, *a.* i-re-*gay*-shon-al, pertaining to irrigation.
irrigator, *n.* *i*-re-*gay*-tor, one who irrigates; any appliance used for irrigation.
irriguous, *a.* i-*rig*-yew-us, well-watered; damp; irrigated.
irrision, *n.* i-*rizh*-on, mockery; derision. (L. *irrisus,* laughed at.)
irritability, *n.* *i*-re-ta-*bil*-e-te, the state or quality of being irritable; susceptibility to irritation.
irritable, *a.* *i*-re-ta-bl, susceptible of irritation; easily inflamed or exasperated; receptive of and responsive to external stimuli [Med.]. (L. *irritabilis.*)
irritableness, *n.* *i*-re-ta-bl-ness, irritability.
irritably, *ad.* *i*-re-ta-ble, in an irritable manner.
irritancy, *n.* *i*-re-tan-se, the state of being irritant; nullification [Scots. Law].
irritant, *a.* *i*-re-tant, irritating: *n.* that which causes irritation.
irritate, *v.t.* *i*-re-tate, to excite impatience in; to make angry or fretful; to provoke; to heighten excitement in; to cause irritation or an uneasy sensation in. (L. *irritatus,* excited.)
irritate, *v.t.* *i*-re-tate, to render null [Scots. Law]. (L. *in-,* not, *ratus,* established.)
irritatingly, *ad.* *i*-re-tay-ting-le, in an irritating or annoying manner.
irritation, *n.* i-re-*tay*-shon, excitement of anger or passion; excitement of muscular action by stimuli operating on the nervous system, also the abnormal condition occasioned by this [Med.].
irritative, *a.* *i*-re-tay-tiv, serving to irritate; attended with irritation; annoying.
irruption, *n.* i-*rup*-shon, a bursting in; a sudden invasion or incursion. (Fr.)
irruptive, *a.* i-*rup*-tiv, rushing in or upon.
irruptively, *ad.* in an irruptive manner.
is, *v.i.* iz, *third person sing. pres. ind.* of the verb *to be.* (A.S.)
isabel, *a.* and *n.* *iz*-a-bel, greyish yellow. (From the female personal name—for some reason unknown.)
isabelline, *a.* iz-a-*bel*-ine, of isabel colour. **isabelline bear,** a small yellowish-brown bear of the Himalayas.
isagogic, *a.* *eye*-sa-*goj*-ik, introductory [Theol.]; *n.pl.* the department of theology introductory to the literary and historical study of the Bible. (Gr. *eisagogikos.*)
isagogical, *a.* eye-sa-*goj*-e-kal, isagogic.
isagon, *n.* *eye*-sa-gon, an isogon.
isandrous, *a.* i-*san*-drus, with similar stamens equal in number to the petals.
isanthous, *a.* i-*san*-thus, with regular flowers.
isatin, *n.* *eye*-sa-tin, a reddish crystalline compound obtained by oxidizing indigo. (L. *isatis,* woad.)
ischial, *a.* *is*-ke-al, pertaining to or in the region of the posterior bone of the pelvic girdle, *i.e.* that on which one sits.
ischialgia, *n.* *is*-ke-*al*-je-a, pain in the hip; sciatica. (Gr. *ischion,* the hip, *algos,* pain.)
ischiatic, *a.* *is*-ke-*at*-ik, pertaining to the hip or the region of the hip; pertaining to sciatica. (Gr.)
ischuretic, *a.* *is*-kew-*ret*-ik, of a quality to relieve ischuria: *n.* a medicine adapted to relieve ischuria.
ischuria, *n.* *is*-*kewr*-re-a, a stoppage, suppression, or morbid retention of urine. (Gr. *ischo,* keep back, *ouron,* urine.)
isenergic, *a.* is-e-*ner*-jik, having equal energy.
iserine, *n.* *eye*-ze-rin, a variety of ilmenite [Min.]. (Ger. *eisen,* iron.)
Ishmaelite, *n.* *ish*-ma-lite, a social outcast, esp. as a rebel against convention. (*Ishmael,* Gen. xvi, 12.)
isidium, *n.* i-*sid*-e-um, a coralliform outgrowth on the thallus of certain lichens [Bot.].
isinglass, *n.* *eye*-zing-glahs, a firm, whitish, gelatinous substance prepared from the air-bladder of the sturgeon; fish-glue. (Dut. *huizen,* sturgeon, *blase,* bladder.)
Islam, *n.* *iz*-lam, Mohammedanism, as the religion which hinges all on submission to the will of God; the Mohammedan world. (Ar., submission.)
Islamic, *a.* iz-*lam*-ik, Moslem; pertaining to Islam.
Islamism, *n.* *iz*-la-mizm, Mohammedanism.
Islamitic, *a.* iz-la-*mit*-ik, Islamic.
Islamize, *v.t.* *iz*-la-mize, to convert to Mohammedanism.
***island,** *n.* *eye*-land, a tract of land surrounded by water; a floating mass; anything isolated like an island; a small protected safety area in a traffic way.: *a.* pertaining to an island or islands; insular: *v.t.* to make into an island; to set with islands; to insulate. **islands of the blest,** islands fabled to lie in the region of the setting sun, and regarded as the abode of the souls of dead heroes [Myth.]. (A.S. *igland.*)
islanded, *a.* *eye*-land-ed, isolated as an island; studded as with islands.
islander, *n.* *eye*-land-er, an inhabitant of an island.
isle, *n.* ile, an island. (O.Fr. *isle.*)
islesman, *n.* *ilez*-man, an islander, esp. a native of the Hebrides or of the Orkneys or Shetlands.
islet, *n.* *eye*-let, a small island.
ism, *n.* izm, a theory or doctrine (in depreciation). (From *-ism,* a suffix denoting theory.)
iso-, *eye*-so, a prefix or combining form denoting, esp. in scientific terms, similarity, equality, or identity. (Gr. *isos,* equal.)
isobar, *n.* *eye*-so-bar, a line on a map connecting places of equal mean barometrical height at sea-level [Meteor.]; an isobare [Chem.]. (Gr. *isos,* equal, *baros,* weight.)
isobare, *n.* *eye*-so-bare, each of two atoms having the same atomic weight but differing in chemical properties [Chem.].
isobaric, *a.* *eye*-so-*ba*-rik, having equal barometric pressure; pertaining to isobars [Meteor.] or to isobares [Chem.].
isobarometric, *a.* *eye*-so-*ba*-ro-*met*-rik, isobaric [Meteor.].
isobathytherm, *n.* *eye*-so-*bath*-e-therm, a line on a vertical section of the sea joining the points of equal temperature. (Gr. *isos,* *bathos,* deep, *therme,* heat.)
isocheim, *n.* *eye*-so-kime, an isochimenal line. (Gr. *isos,* equal, *cheima,* winter.)
isocheimal, *a.* *eye*-so-*ky*-mal, isochimenal.
isochimenal, *a.* *eye*-so-*ky*-men-al, having the same mean winter temperature. **isochimenal lines,** lines passing through places having the same mean winter temperature.
isochromatic, *a.* *eye*-so-kro-*mat*-ik, having the same colour. (Gr. *isos,* and *chroma,* colour.)
isochronal, *a.* i-*sok*-ro-nal, isochronous.
isochronism, *n.* i-*sok*-ro-nizm, equality of time; the quality of being done in equal times.
isochronous, *a.* i-*sok*-ro-nus, uniform in time; of equal time. (Gr. *isos,* and *chronos,* time.)
isochroous, *a.* i-*sok*-ro-us, of uniform colour throughout. (Gr. *isos,* and *chroa,* colour.)
isoclinal, *a.* eye-so-*kly*-nal, having equal inclination. (Gr. *isos,* and *klino,* bend.)
isoclinic, *a.* eye-so-*klin*-ik, isoclinal.
isodiametric, *a.* *eye*-so-*dy*-a-*met*-rik, having equal diameters.
isodomon, *n.* i-*sod*-o-mon, a method of building

among the ancient Greeks with stones of equal thickness and equal length [Arch.]. (Gr. *isos*, and *dome*, building.)
isodont, *a.* *eye*-so-dont, with the teeth all alike.
isodynamic, *a.* *eye*-so-dy-*nam*-ik, having equal force. (Gr. *isos*, and *dynamic*.)
isogeny, *n.* i-*soj*-e-ne, general similarity of origin [Biol.]. (Gr. *isos*, and *gennao*, be born.)
isogeotherm, *n.* *eye*-so-*jee*-o-therm, a line connecting points of equal temperature in the interior of the earth. (Gr. *isos*, *ge*, the earth, and *therme*, heat.)
isognathous, *a.* i-*sog*-na-thus, with molar teeth alike in both jaws.
isogon, *n.* *eye*-so-gon, a figure all of whose angles are equal.
isogonal, *a.* i-*sog*-o-nal, isogonic; having equal angles: *n.* an isogonic line.
isogonic, *a.* *eye*-so-*gon*-ik, relating to places on the earth's surface in which the magnetic declination is the same [Geog.]: *n.* a line on a chart, etc. connecting such places.
isogram, *n.* *eye*-so-gram, a line on a chart, etc., indicating equality in the given characteristic, phenomenon, etc.
isohel, *n.* *eye*-so-hel, a line on a map joining places having the same amount of sunshine.
isohyetal, *n.* *eye*-so-*hy*-e-tal, a line joining places with equal rainfall.
isolate, *v.t.* *eye*-so-late, to place in a detached situation; to insulate; to put in quarantine [Med.]: *a.* isolated; in isolation. (It. *isolato*.)
isolation, *n.* *eye*-so-*lay*-shon, the act of isolating; state of being isolated; loneliness. **isolation hospital**, a hospital treating only infectious cases.
isolationism, *n.* *eye*-so-*lay*-shon-izm, a policy involving isolation, esp. aloofness from international commitments.
isolationist, *a.* *eye*-so-*lay*-shon-ist, pertaining to isolationism: *n.* one favouring isolationism.
isomer, *n.* *eye*-so-mer, a compound isomeric with another or others [Chem.].
isomeric, *a.* *eye*-so-*me*-rik, composed of the same elements and in the same proportions, but having different chemical properties or physical characteristics [Chem.]. (Gr. *isos*, and *meros*, part.)
isomerism, *n.* i-*som*-er-izm, the state or quality of being isomeric.
isometric, *a.* *eye*-so-*met*-rik, with equality of measure. (Gr. *isos*, and *metric*.)
isomorphism, *n.* *eye*-so-*mor*-fizm, the state or quality of being isomorphous.
isomorphous, *a.* *eye*-so-*mor*-fus, of like or identical form; having the same crystalline form but different constituent elements [Chem.] (Gr. *isos*, and *morphe*, shape.)
isonomy, *n.* i-*son*-o-me, equality of rights and privileges. (Gr. *isos*, and *nomos*, law.)
isoperimetrical, *a.* *eye*-so-*pe*-re-*met*-re-kal, having equal perimeters.
isoperimetry, *n.* *eye*-so-pe-*rim*-e-tre, the science of figures having equal perimeters or boundaries [Geom.]. (Gr. *isos*, and *perimeter*.)
isopod, *n.* *eye*-so-pod, any of that group of the crustacea having seven pairs of legs, usually similar and equal. (Gr. *isos*, and *pous*, the foot.)
isopodous, *a.* i-*sop*-o-dus, having the characteristics of an isopod.
isopyre, *n.* *eye*-so-pyre, an impure variety of opal.
isosceles, *a.* i-*sos*-se-leez, having two sides equal (of triangles) [Geom.]. (L.)
isoseismal, *n.* *eye*-so-*size*-mal, the line connecting places where earthquake shock was of equal intensity.
isostasy, *n.* i-*sos*-ta-se, the quality of being isostatic, esp. [Geol.] with reference to its influence on the stability of the earth's crust.
isostatic, *a.* *eye*-so-*stat*-ik, maintaining equilibrium through equality of pressure on all sides; subjected to such pressure.
isostemonous, *a.* *eye*-so-*stem*-o-nus, having stamens of equal number or numerically equal to the parts of the perianth [Bot.]. (Gr. *isos*, and *temon*, a stamen.)
isotheral, *a.* i-*soth*-e-ral, indicating the same mean summer temperature: *n.* an isothere. (Gr. *isos*, and *theros*, summer.)
isothere, *n.* *eye*-so-theer, an isotheral line as drawn on a map.
isotherm, *n.* *eye*-so-therm, a line on which places have the same mean summer temperature.
isothermal, *a.* *eye*-so-*ther*-mal, having an equal degree of heat. **isothermal line**, an isotherm.
isotonic, *a.* *eye*-so-*ton*-ik, having equal tones or tension; having the same osmotic pressure [Phys.]. (Gr. *isos*, and *tonus*, tone.)
isotope, *n.* *eye*-so-tope, each of two or more elements or atoms having the same chemical properties and atomic number, and differing only in their atomic weight and radioactive transformations. (Gr. *isos*, and *topos*, place.)
isotropic, *a.* *eye*-so-*trop*-ik, having the same physical properties in all directions.
isotropy, *n.* i-*sot*-ro-pe, the condition or quality of being isotropic.
isotype, *n.* *eye*-so-type, an animal or plant common to two or more regions; a typical specimen of a local species [Biol.].
Israelite, *n.* *iz*-ra-el-ite, a descendant of Israel, a Jew. (Heb. *Ysrael*, a champion of God.)
Israelitic, *a.* *iz*-ra-e-*lit*-ik, Israelitish.
Israelitish, *a.* *iz*-ra-e-*ly*-tish, pertaining to Israel; Jewish; Hebraic.
issuable, *a.* *ish*-yew-a-bl, that may issue or be issued; relating to an issue.
issuance, *n.* *ish*-yew-ance, the act of issuing; an issue, or a dealing out.
issue, *n.* *ish*-yew, the act of passing or flowing out; a sending out; a giving out; egress; outlet; consequence; that which issues or is issued; end or ultimate result; offspring; progeny; produce of the earth; profits of land or other property; a discharge, as of blood; an official allowance [Mil. and Nav.]; the point of matter depending in a suit, on which the parties join [Law]; the point in debate: *v.i.* to pass or flow out; to proceed; to come to a point in fact or law, on which the parties join and rest the decision of the cause; to close; to result: *v.t.* to send out; to put into circulation; to deliver for use. **at issue**, in debate; at variance. **house of issue**, the bank underwriting and offering to the public a new issue of stock, bonds, etc. [Comm.]. **to join issue**, to take opposite sides in a suit or debate. (L. *ex-*, out, *eo*, go.)
issueless, *a.* *ish*-yew-less, having no issue or progeny.
issuer, *n.* *ish*-yew-er, one who issues or emits.
-ist, suffix denoting one who does, professes, adheres to, or makes a practice of something, as art*ist*, athe*ist*, telepath*ist*, violin*ist*, etc.
isthmian, *a.* *isth*-me-an, pertaining to an isthmus. **Isthmian Canal**, the Panama Canal. **Isthmian Games**, games held every two years in ancient Greece on the Isthmus of Corinth.
isthmus, *n.* *is-*, *ist-*, or *isth*-mus, a narrow neck of land connecting two larger portions; a contracted passage or part between two cavities or parts [Anat.]. (L., from Gr. *isthmos*, a narrow pass.)
istle, *n.* *ist*-le, a tough fibre obtained from various tropical American plants, esp. from a species of *Agave*. (Mex. *ixtli*.)
it, it, *pron. third pers. sing. neut.*: *n.* the very thing, the acme [Coll.]; personal attractiveness, sexual appeal [Slang]. (A.S. *hit*.)
itacolumite, *n.* *it*-a-*kol*-yew-mite, flexible sandstone, a schistose quartzite frequently forming the matrix of Brazilian diamonds. (*Itacolumi*, in Brazil.)
Italian, *a.* i-*tal*-yan, pertaining to Italy; *n.* a native of Italy; the Italian language. **Italian warehouseman**, a grocer dealing in olive-oil, macaroni, and other Italian produce. (L. *Italia*, Italy.)
Italianate, *a.* i-*tal*-yan-ate, having Italian characteristics.
Italianize, *v.i.* i-*tal*-yan-ize, to ape the Italian: *v.t.* to render Italian in character.
Italic, *a.* i-*tal*-ik, relating to ancient Italy or its peoples other than Roman; (*l.c.*) applied to a leaning type (*as this*), first used by Aldus Manutius, of Venice, in 1501: *n.pl.* italic type or letters.
italicize, *v.t.* i-*tal*-e-size, to write or print in italics; to underline.
Italiot, *n.* i-*tal*-e-ot, one of the ancient Greek colonists of Magna Græcia, in Southern Italy: *a.* pertaining to these, or to the colonies.
itch, *n.* itch, scabies, an irritating skin disease, due to the mite *Sarcoptes scabiei*; the sensation caused by the disease; a constant, teasing desire, as for novelty, etc.: *v.i.* to feel that uneasiness in the skin that calls for scratching; to have a constant desire or teasing inclination. (A.S. *giccan*.)

itchy, *a.* *itch*-e, having an itching sensation; resembling or infected with the itch.
item, *ad.* *eye*-tem, likewise; also: *n.* an article; a separate particular or entry in an account, etc.; a newspaper paragraph. (L., likewise.)
itemize, *v.t.* *eye*-tem-ize, to codify in detail; to state the items of.
iterant, *a.* *it*-er-ant, repeating; iterating.
iterate, *v.t.* *it*-er-ate, to utter or do a second time; to repeat. (L. *iteratus*, repeated.)
iteration, *n.* *it*-er-*ray*-shon, repetition.
iterative, *a.* *it*-er-a-tiv, repeating.
ithyphallic, *a.* ith-e-*fal*-ik, of the nature of the obscenities of the Bacchic rites; grossly obscene. (Gr. *ithus*, straight, and *phallus*.)
itineracy, *n.* i-*tin*-er-a-se, itinerancy.
itinerancy, *n.* i-*tin*-er-an-se, the state of being itinerant; the practice of itinerating, esp. in discharge of official duty.
itinerant, *a.* i-*tin*-er-ant, passing or travelling from place to place; pertaining to journeying relative to some special business or duty: *n.* one who travels from place to place, as an itinerant preacher or player. (Late L. *itinerans*, travelling.)
itinerary, *n.* eye-*tin*-e-ra-re, an account of travels, or of places and their distances on a road; a plan for a tour, etc.: *a.* pertaining to routes or travelling.
intinerate, *v.i.* i-*tin*-er-ate, to travel from place to place, esp. as a preacher or player; to tour or wander about. (Late L. *itineratus*, travelled.)
-itis, *eye*-tis, a suffix denoting inflammation of the part, organ, or region indicated, as, *bronchitis*, inflammation of the bronchia [Med.]. (Gr. *itis*, like.)
its, *pron.* its, the possessive of *it*.
itself, *pron.* it-*self*, the neuter reciprocal pronoun.
ivied, *a.* *eye*-vid, overgrown with ivy.
ivory, *n.* *eye*-vo-re, a hard, fine-grained, creamy-white substance composing the tusks of the elephant, walrus, etc.; the dentine of teeth; the colour of ivory: *pl.* (in slang use) the teeth, piano-keys, dice, billiard balls, etc.: *a.* consisting of or made of ivory; creamy-white, hard, or smooth like ivory. **ivory black,** a kind of charcoal in powder, made by charring ivory or bones. **ivory nut,** the nut-like seed of a S. American palm, often as large as a hen's egg, consisting of a hard close-grained substance resembling ivory. **ivory turner,** a worker in ivory. **vegetable ivory,** *see* **vegetable.** (O.Fr. *ivurie*.)
ivy, *n.* *eye*-ve, a climbing and creeping plant, *Hedera helix*, having aerial rootlets by which it clings. **ivy tree,** the New Zealand tree, *Panax colensoi*. **poison ivy,** the American sumac or climbing vine. (A.S. *ifig*.)
ixolite, *n.* *ik*-so-lite, a mineral resin occurring in bituminous coal.
izard, *n.* *iz*-ard, a Pyrenean antelope of the chamois family. (Fr. *isard*.)
izzard, *n.* *iz*-erd, the letter Z. **from A to izzard,** from beginning to end.

J

J, jay, the tenth letter and seventh consonant was, until early 19th cent., interchangeable with *i*. In English words it has the sound of the softened *g*, as in *genuine*; in some foreign words (as *allelujah*, *junker*) that of consonantal *y*, and in French words (as *déjeuner*) the *zh* sound as in *treasure*.
jab, *n.* jab, a poke; a stab; *v.t.* to dig with a stick; to stab.
jabber, *n.* *jab*-ber, rapid talk with indistinct utterance: *v.t.* to utter rapidly or indistinctly: *v.i.* to talk rapidly or indistinctly; to chatter. (*Imitative.*)
jabberer, *n.* *jab*-er-rer, one who jabbers.
jabberingly, *ad.* *jab*-er-ring-le, in a jabbering manner.
jabiru, *n.* *jab*-e-roo, a S. American wading bird of the genus *Mycteria*, allied to the storks; a stork of the genus *Xenorhynchus*. (Tupi.)
jaborandi, *n.* *jab*-o-*ran*-de, a plant of the genus *Pilocarpus* yielding alkaloids used in medicine.
jabot, *n.* *zhah*-boh, a frill or bow on the front of a bodice or shirt. (Fr.)
jaca, *n.* *zhah*-ka, a large East Indian tree, *Artocarpus integra*, allied to the bread-fruit; its fruit, also its close-grained timber. (Port., from Malay, *cakka.*)
jacamar, *n.* *jak*-a-mar, one of several tropical American birds of the genus *Galbula*, with brilliant plumage, allied to the kingfisher. (Fr.)
jacana, *n.* *jak*-a-nah, one of several tropical American wading birds of the genus *Parra*. (Brazilian.)
Jacaranda, *n.* *jak*-a-*ran*-da, a genus of S. American hardwood trees yielding valuable timber; (*l.c.*) Brazilian rose-wood. (Brazilian.)
jacchus, *n.* *jak*-kus, one of the marmosets.
jacinth, *n.* *jas*-inth, the blue sapphire or other gemstone of the ancients; a transparent reddish-orange variety of zircon. (O.Fr.)
Jack, *n.* jak, a diminutive of *John*; (*l.c.*) a saucy or paltry fellow; a sailor; a bootjack; a portable appliance for raising weighty objects; an oscillating or other lever in various machines; a contrivance to turn a spit; a young pike; a coat of mail; a black-jack, or leather pitcher; a small white ball thrown out for a mark in bowls; a wooden frame on which wood is sawn; a wooden wedge used in coal-mining; the knave at cards; a jack-staff [Naut.]; the small flag flown from the jack-staff. **Jack-a-lantern**, the will-o'-the-wisp. **Jack by the hedge**, hedge garlic, *Sisymbrium alliaria*. **Jack Frost**, frost personified. **Jack in office**, one who assumes airs on account of his office. **Jack in the box**, the tropical tree *Hernandia sonora*, the seeds of which rattle in the seed-vessel; a large wooden male screw, turning in a female one; a figure made to start out of a box; a kind of firework. **Jack in the green**, a sweep disguised in a cone of green boughs in which he took part in May-day festivities. **Jack Ketch**, the common hangman. **Jack of all trades**, one who can turn his hand to any kind of work. **jack rabbit**, a large, very long-eared hare of N. America. **jack tree**, the jaca. **Union Jack**, *see* **Union.**
jack, *n.* jak, the fruit of the jaca, the seeds of which are eaten.
jack, *v.t.* jak, to lift with a jack. **to jack up** (a job, etc.), to resign, to give it up [Slang].
jack-a-dandy, *n.* jak-a-*dan*-de, a little foppish fellow.
jackal, *n.* *jak*-awl, a gregarious carnivore, *Canis aureus*, allied to the dog, fabled to forage for the lion, and so called the lion's provider; one who does menial work or drudgery for another's benefit. (Turk., from Per.)
jackanapes, *n.* *jak*-a-napes, a monkey, a coxcomb; a mischievous fellow. (From *Jack Napes*, nickname of Wm. de la Pole–executed 1450—whose badge was the chain and clog used for tame apes.)
jackaroo, *n.* *jak*-a-roo, a newcomer in the Australian bush; a greenhorn [Austral. slang].
jackass, *n.* *jak*-ass, the male of the ass; a blockhead. **laughing jackass**, the Australian kingfisher, *Dacelo gigantea*.
jack-boots, *n.pl.* large boots with extensions covering the knee and protecting the thighs.
jackdaw, *n.* *jak*-daw, a small bird of the crow family, *Corvus monedula*.
jacket, *n.* *jak*-et, a short coat; an outer covering; a dust-cover: *v.t.* to clothe in or cover with a jacket; to thrash [Slang]. (Fr. *jaquette.*)
jack-knife, *n.* a large clasp-knife for the pocket.
jack-plane, *n.* a plane for preparing wood for the trying-plane.
jackpot, *n.* *jak*-pot, a pool at the card game of poker; a round or hand in which this is played for.
jack-pudding, *n.* a merry-andrew, a buffoon.
jack-screw, *n.* a screw-jack.
jack-snipe, *n.* the small snipe, *Gallinago gallinula*, also the dunlin, *Tringa alpina*.
jack-staff, *n.* a short flagstaff at a ship's bow for flying the jack.
jackstays, *n.pl.* *jak*-stayz, ropes or strips of wood or iron stretched along a ship's yard to bend the sails to.
jack-straw, *n.* a mere man of straw; one worth nothing in himself. (Nickname of leader of the Peasant's Revolt, 1381.)
jack-tar, *n.* a common sailor, esp. of the Navy.
jack-towel, *n.* a roller towel.
jackwood, *n.* *jak*-wood, the wood of the jaca, much used in cabinet making.
jackyard, *n.* *jak*-yard, the extending boom at the foot of a gaff-topsail.
jacobean, *a.* *jak*-o-*bee*-an, of the reign of James I; in the style of this period (esp. of furniture).
Jacobin, *n.* *jak*-o-bin, a friar of the Order of St. Dominic; a member of an extreme republican party which took a prominent lead during the French Revolution, so called from their meeting-place being the hall of the Jacobin friars; hence, an extreme revolutionary; a variety of hooded pigeon: *a.* Jacobinic. (L. *Jacobus*, Fr. *Jacques*, name of the street in Paris containing the Dominican convent.)
Jacobinic, *a.* jak-o-*bin*-ik, pertaining to or resembling the Jacobins; revolutionary.
Jacobinism, *n.* *jak*-o-bin-izm, Jacobin principles.
Jacobite, *n.* *jak*-o-bite, a partisan or adherent of James II of England after his expulsion, or of his descendants: *a.* pertaining to, or of the opinions of, the Jacobites. (L. *Jacobus*, James.)
Jacobitical, *a.* jak-o-*bit*-e-kal, pertaining to the Jacobites.
Jacobitism, *n.* *jak*-o-bit-izm, the principles of the Jacobites.
Jacob's-ladder, *n.* *jay*-kubz-*lad*-der, the border plant with bright blue flowers, *Polemonium cæruleum*; a rope-ladder, with wooden steps [Naut.].
Jacob's-staff, *n.* *jay*-kubz-*stahf*, a cross-staff, an instrument formerly used by surveyors.
jacobus, *n.* ja-*koh*-bus, popular name of a gold coin (value 20*s.*) struck in the reign of James I.
jaconet, *n.* *jak*-o-net, a light, soft muslin, of an open texture. (Hind. *Jagganath*, as *Juggernaut.*)
Jacquard, *n.* *jak*-kard, a Jacquard loom, a loom with a device for weaving figured fabrics. (Name of inventor, a mechanician of Lyons, early 19th cent.)
Jacquerie, *n.* *zhak*-ree, the peasant insurrection in France against the nobles in 1357-58; hence, any peasant revolt. (Fr. *Jacques*, a peasant.)
jactation, *n.* jak-*tay*-shon, the act of throwing; a nervous rocking of the body [Med.]. (L. *jactatio.*)
jactitation, *n.* *jak*-te-*tay*-shon, a tossing of the body, restlessness [Med.]; a false pretension to marriage [Law].
jade, *n.* jade, a mean, poor, or tired horse; a worthless nag; a mean woman; any young woman [Slang]: *v.t.* to tire with over-driving; to fatigue; to weary with hard service. (O. Scand. *jalda*, mare.)
jade, *n.* jade, a silicate of magnesia and lime, of a

greenish colour and dull, greasy aspect, used for ornamental purposes. (Fr.)
jadeite, *n.* *jay*-dite, a valuable greenish variety of jade found in Burma.
jadish, *a.* *jade*-ish, of jade-like behaviour.
jaeger, *n.* *yay*-ger, a German or Austrian rifleman; a sharpshooter; the great skua, one of the pirate gulls. (Ger. *Jaeger*, a hunter.)
jaeger, *n.* *yay*-ger, trade-name of a pure woollen material and of clothing made therewith. (Patentee's name.)
Jaffa, *n.* *jaf*-a, a variety of orange grown near Jaffa (Joppa), Palestine.
jag, *n.* jag, a notch; a ragged protuberance; a cleft or division: *v.t.* to cut into notches or teeth like those of a saw. **on the jag,** on the spree, tipsy [Slang].
jagged, *a.* *jag*-ged, notched; sharply indented; cut coarsely [Bot.].
jaggedness, *n.* *jag*-ged-ness, state of being jagged.
jagger, *n.* *jag*-ger, an implement for notching; a notched chisel; a brass wheel with notched edge for cutting cakes, etc.
jaggery, *n.* *jag*-ger-re, sugar got by inspissation from palm sap. (Hind.)
jaggy, *a.* *jag*-ge, set with teeth; notched; uneven.
jaghir, *n.* jah-*geer*, in India, assignment of land or a share in the produce, granted to an individual, generally for military purposes. (Hind.)
jaghirdar, *n.* jah-geer-*dar*, the holder of a jaghir. (Hind.)
jaguar, *n.* *jag*-yew-ar *or* *jag*-war, the largest of the American carnivores, *Felis onca*. (Brazilian.)
Jah, *n.* jah *or* yah, Jehovah. (Heb. *Yah.*)
Jahvist, *n.* *jah*-vist *or* *yah*-vist, name assigned by Biblical critics to the presumed writer of those portions of the Hexateuch in which the word Jehovah rather than Elohim is used (*see* **Elohist**). (Heb.)
jail, *n.* jale, a prison; a building or place for the confinement of persons arrested for crime. **jail delivery,** the order empowering a judge on assize to try prisoners and relieve the jail of them, also the action taken under this. **jail fever,** typhus fever. (O.Fr. *gaiole*, from L. *cavea*, a coop.)
jailbird, *n.* *jale*-bird, a prisoner; one who has been confined in prison.
jailor, *n.* *jale*-or, the keeper of a prison.
Jainism, *n.* *jane*-izm, the religion of an Indian body of dissenters from Hinduism of unknown antiquity, but pre-Buddhist. (*Jina*, the victorious.)
jakes, *n.* jakes, a privy.
jalap, *n.* *jal*-ap, the root of *Ipomœa purga*, used in medicine as a cathartic. (*Jalapa*, in Mexico.)
jalapin, *n.* *jal*-a-pin, the purgative glucoside constituent of jalap.
jalousie, *n.* *zhal*-oo-zee, a blind of movable, sloping wooden slats; a Venetian blind. (Fr.)
jam, *n.* jam, a conserve of fruits boiled with sugar; anything pleasant [Slang]. (Origin doubtful.)
jam, *n.* jam, a block or squeeze: *v.t.* to press; to crowd; to squeeze tight; to cause, or to be affected by, interference [Wire. and Physics]. (M.E.)
Jamaica-pepper, *n.* ja-*may*-ka-*pep*-per, allspice, *Pimenta officinalis*.
jamb, *n.* jam, the sidepiece or post of a door or fireplace; a piece of leg armour. (Fr. *jambe*, leg.)
jambone, *n.* *jam*-bone, the exposed hand in certain varieties of euchre [Card-playing].
jamboree, *n.* jam-bo-*ree*, a jolly gathering; an international or large general gathering of boy-scouts; a spree [Slang]; name of one of the varieties of euchre [Card-playing].
jamdani, *n.* *jam*-da-nee, a fine figured muslin woven in India. (Hind.)
jamming, *n.* *jam*-ing, interference with reception due to another transmitting station working on the same wavelength [Wire.].
jammy, *a.* *jam*-e, sticky; covered or as though covered with jam.
jampan, *n.* *jam*-pan, a kind of sedan chair used in the hills, India. (Hind.)
jane, *n.* jane, jean; any young woman [Slang].
jangle, *n.* *jang*-gl, discordant sound; bickering; babble: *v.i.* to sound discordantly; to quarrel; to wrangle: *v.t.* to cause to sound or to utter discordantly; to twitter (of birds). (O.Fr. *jangler.*)
jangler, *n.* *jang*-gler, a wrangling noisy fellow.
jangling, *n.* *jang*-gling, a noisy dispute; a wrangling.
janitor, *n.* *jan*-e-tor, a doorkeeper. (L.)
janizary, *n.* *jan*-e-za-re *or* *yan*-e-za-re, a soldier of the Turkish foot-guards, disbanded in 1826, formed originally of captured Christian youths. (Fr. *janissaire.*)
jannock, *a.* *jan*-nok, excellent; straightforward: *n.* fair play; an oaten cake *or* bread. (Dial. Eng.)
Jansenism, *n.* *jan*-sen-izm, the doctrine of the Jansenists, a Rom. Cath. party which maintained, in opposition to the Jesuits, the Augustinian principle of the sovereign and irresistible nature of divine grace. (*Jansen*, Bp. of Ypres, *d.* 1638.)
Jansenist, *n.* *jan*-sen-ist, a supporter of Jansenism.
jantu, *n.* *jun*-too, a primitive water-raising device in use in Bengal for irrigation. (Hind.)
January, *n.* *jan*-yew-a-re, the first month of the year. (L. *Januarius mensis*, the month of Janus.)
Janus, *n.* *jane*-us, the Italic deity of doors, represented with two faces looking opposite ways, the gates of whose temple were kept open when the Romans were at war. (L.)
Janus-faced, *a.* having two faces; double-dealing.
Jap, *a.* jap, Japanese: *n.* a Japanese.
japan, *n.* ja-*pan*, work varnished and figured in the Japanese manner; the very hard varnish used: *v.t.* to cover with a thick coat of this; to black and gloss. **Japan earth,** catechu.
Japanese, *a.* jap-a-*neez*, pertaining to Japan or its inhabitants: *n.* a native of Japan, or the language.
japanner, *n.* ja-*pan*-ner, one who varnishes in the manner of the Japanese.
jape, *n.* jayp, a joke; a jest: *v.i.* to make jokes; to jest. (O.Fr. *japer.*)
japery, *n.* *jay*-pe-re, the tricks of a jester; buffoonery.
Japhetic, *a.* ja-*fet*-ik, pertaining to Japheth, Noah's second son, or his descendants; Caucasian.
Japonic, *a.* ja-*pon*-ik, Japanese.
japonica, *n.* ja-*pon*-e-ka, the Japanese quince, a hardy ornamental shrub with scarlet flowers; the camellia.
Japonicize, *v.t.* and *i.* ja-*pon*-e-size, to make or become Japanese.
jar, *n.* jar, a rattling vibration of sound; a harsh sound; clash of interests or opinions: discord; debate; a harsh vibration: *v.i.* to sound or vibrate harshly or discordantly; to be inconsistent; to clash; to quarrel: *v.t.* to shake; to cause to tremble; to cause a short tremulous motion in. (Imit.)
jar, *n.* jar, a glass or earthenware pot, generally circular and upright; what a jar holds. (Ar.)
jar, *n.* jar, only in phrase **on the jar,** almost shut. (*ajar.*)
jararaca, *n.* *zhah*-ra-*rah*-ka, the venomous snake, fer-de-lance. (Tupi.)
jardinière, *n.* (App.), an ornamental flower-stand. (Fr.)
jargon, *n.* *jar*-gon, speech that is unintelligible or full of unfamiliar words; made-up speech; terminology peculiar to some profession, trade, or sport, etc. (O.Fr.)
jargonelle, *n.* *jar*-gon-*el*, a variety of pear. (Fr.)
jargonize, *v.i.* *jar*-gon-ize, to utter jargon: *v.t.* to put into jargon.
jargoon, *n.* jar-*goon*, a translucent yellowish variety of zircon. (Fr.)
jarl, *n.* yarl, a leader; a Norse earl or nobleman. (Scand.)
jarrah, *n.* *ja*-rah, the wood of Australian mahogany-like tree *Eucalyptus marginata*. (Austral.)
jarringly, *ad.* *jar*-ring-le, in a jarring or harshly discordant manner.
jarvey, *n.* *jar*-ve, a driver of an Irish car; a cab-driver [Slang].
jasey, *n.* *jay*-ze, a worsted wig; a wig. (*jersey.*)
jasmine, *n.* *jas*-min, jessamine; a plant of the genus *Jasminum*, many species of which are climbing and very fragrant. (Fr. *jasmin*, Pers. *yasmin.*)
jasper, *n.* *jas*-per, an opaque variety of quartz of various colours, of earthy fracture, and taking a high polish. (O.Fr. *jaspre.*)
jaspery, *a.* *jas*-per-re, having the qualities of jasper.
jaspideous, *a.* jas-*pid*-e-us, like jasper; consisting of jasper; jaspery.
jaundice, *n.* *jawn*- or *jahn*-dis, icterus; a yellow coloration of the eyes and skin, caused by an excess of bile pigment in the blood, and its escape into tissue cells [Med.]: *v.i.* to become affected with jaundice; to become prejudiced. (O.Fr. *jaunisse.*)

jaunt, *n.* jawnt, a short journey, tour or excursion: *v.i.* to ramble here and there; to make an excursion. (O.Fr. *jancer*, to stir a horse.)
jauntily, *ad.* *jawn*-te-le, in a jaunty manner.
jauntiness, *n.* *jawn*-te-ness, the quality of being jaunty; vivacity; animation.
jaunting-car, *n.* a low light car, with seats back to back, used in Ireland.
jaunty, *a.* *jawn*-te, airy; sprightly; perky.
jaup, *v.t.* jawp, to dash and splash; to bespatter. (Scots.)
Javanese, *a.* *jah*-va-*neez* or *jav*-a-neez, pertaining to Java: *n.* a native of Java, or the language.
javelin, *n.* *jav*-e-lin, a short light spear with a barbed pyramidal head; a slender 8½-ft. wooden shaft for throwing in athletic sports. **javelin men**, the judge's escort at assizes. (O.Fr.)
jaw, *n.* jaw, the bones of the mouth in which the teeth are fixed; the mouth; anything like the jaw; the inner end of a boom or gaff [Naut.]; offensive talk, abuse [Slang]: *v.t.* and *i.* to talk, esp. rapidly; to scold; to lecture; to hold forth [Slang]. (Of doubtful origin.)
jawbone, *n.* *jaw*-bone, the bone of the lower jaw.
jaw-breaker, *n.* a word of difficult pronunciation [Coll.].
jawed, *a.* jawd, having jaws.
jawfallen, *a.* *jaw*-fawl-en, depressed in spirits.
jaw-lever, *n.* an instrument for opening the mouth and administering medicine to cattle.
jawy, *a.* *jaw*-e, relating to the jaws; garrulous. [Coll.].
jay, *n.* jay, a chattering bird of the crow family, *Garrulus glandarius*, and of other genera; a foolish person; a jade or loose woman; a simpleton. (O.Fr.)
jay-walker, *n.* *jay*-wawk-er, a heedless pedestrian [Amer. slang.]
jazerant, *n.* *jaz*-er-ant, a jesserant.
jazz, *n.* jaz, syncopated ragtime music; a dance to this music: *v.i.* play or dance jazz; to dance to jazz: *a.* pertaining to or composed of jazz; harsh in tone; gaudy in colour and design.
jazz-band, *n.* a band employing the instruments and syncopation necessary to produce jazz.
jealous, *a.* *jel*-us, uneasily apprehensive that love, favour, etc., may be or has been withdrawn or transferred from one; inclined to suspect, or intolerant of, rivalry; envious; suspiciously vigilant; anxiously careful. (O.Fr. *jalous*.)
jealously, *ad.* *jel*-us-le, with jealousy.
jealousy, *n.* *jel*-us-e, the state or quality of being jealous; the uneasiness arising from jealous suspicions; apprehension of rivalry; envy; suspicious fear or vigilance.
jeames, *n.* jeemz, a lackey of the old style. (*Jeames*, from "Yellowplush Papers," Thackeray.)
jean, *n.* jane, a twilled cotton cloth: *pl.* overalls or trousers of this. (Fr., from Ital. *Genova* (Genoa) cloth.)
jeep, *n.* jeep, a small utility motor truck designed (1941) for use in the U.S.A. Army. (Named from maker's identification symbol, G.P.—for "general purposes" car.)
jeer, *n.* jeer, railing remark; mockery; derision: *v.i.* to utter severe, sarcastic reflections: *v.t.* to treat with derision; to make a mock of; to scoff at. (Possibly *cheer*.)
jeerer, *n.* *jeer*-er, a scoffer; a railer.
jeeringly, *ad.* *jeer*-ing-le, in a jeering manner.
jeffersonite, *n.* *jef*-fer-son-ite, a dark-green pyroxene containing manganese and zinc. (Thomas *Jefferson*, 3rd President, U.S.A.)
jehad, *n.* je-*hahd*, jihad.
Jehovah, *n.* je-*hoh*-va, the God of Israel; the Lord; Yahveh. (Heb. *Yahovah*, the Lord.)
jehovist, *n.* je-*hoh*-vist, one who maintains that the vowel-points annexed to the word JHVH, in Hebrew, express the true pronunciation; a Jahvist.
jehovistic, *a.* *jee*-ho-*vis*-tik, containing the name Jehovah, and written by the Jahvist.
jehu, *n.* *jee*-hew, a driver, esp. a reckless coachman. (2 Kings ix, 20.)
jejune, *a* je-*joon*, empty; void of interest; meagre; barren. (L. *jejunus*, fasting, hungry.)
jejunely, *ad.* je-*joon*-le, in a jejune manner.
jejuneness, *n.* the quality of being jejune.
jejunum, *n.* je-*joo*-num, the part of the small intestine between the duodenum and the ileum.

jellied, *a.* *jel*-led, brought to the consistence of jelly; cased in jelly.
jellify, *v.i.* and *t.* *jel*-le-fy, to turn, or convert, into jelly.
***jelly**, *n.* *jel*-le, anything gelatinous or glutinous; the inspissated juice of fruit boiled with sugar; a transparent, sizy substance, obtained from animal substances by decoction: *v.i.* and *t.*, to turn or be converted into jelly. (Fr. *gelée*.)
jellybag, *n.* *jel*-le-bag, the conical bag through which jelly is strained.
jellyfish, *n.* *jel*-le-fish, a medusa or similar cœlenterate animal; a person lacking "backbone."
jellygraph, *n.* *jel*-le-graf, a duplicating device in which impressions are taken from a gelatinous sheet.
jemadar, *n.* jem-a-*dar*, a native lieutenant in the Indian army.
jemminess, *n.* *jem*-me-ness, spruceness.
jemmy, *a.* *jem*-me, spruce; well dressed.
jemmy, *n.* *jem*-me, a small crowbar used by house-breakers; a baked sheep's head [Slang]. (*James*.)
jennet, *n.* *jen*-net, a small Spanish horse; a female donkey. (O.Fr. *genette*.)
jenneting, *n.* *jen*-net-ing, a species of early apple. (Fr. *jeanneton*.)
jenny, *n.* *jen*-ne, a machine for spinning; a locomotive crane; a stroke at billiards by which the ball is put into a pocket from an unfavourable position near a side cushion. (*Jenny*, a woman's name.)
jeofail, *n.* je-*fale*, an oversight in pleading or other proceeding [Law]. (Fr. *j'ai failli*, I have mistaken.)
jeopardize, *v.t.* *jep*-ard-ize, to expose to jeopardy.
jeopardous, *a.* *jep*-ard-us, exposed to danger.
jeopardy, *n.* *jep*-ard-e, exposure to loss or injury; peril. (Fr. *jeu parti*, divided play, even chance.)
jequirity, *n.* je-*kwi*-re-te, Indian liquorice, a tropical shrub with black-and-scarlet beans; its bean, also a medicinal infusion from this.
jerboa, *n.* jer-*boh*-a, a small rodent, *Dipus jaculus*, with long hind legs and great jumping power. (Ar.)
jereed, *n.* je-*reed*, djerid.
jeremiad, *n.* je-re-*my*-ad, lamentation or complaining, esp. over modern decadence. (*Jeremiah*, the prophet.)
jerfalcon, *n.* *jer*-fawl-kon, the gerfalcon.
jerid, *n.* je-*reed*, djerid. (Ar.)
jerk, *n.* jerk, a quick throw, pull, or knock; a spasm: *v.t.* to give a sudden pull, twitch, thrust, or push to; to throw underhand with a quick, smart movement.
jerk, *v.t.* jerk, to cut into pieces, as beef, and dry in the sun. **jerked beef**, charqui. (Sp.-Amer. from Peruv. *charqui*.)
jerker, *n.* *jer*-ker, one who jerks; a jerquer.
jerkily, *ad.* *jer*-ke-le, in a jerky manner.
jerkin, *n.* *jer*-kin, a man's sleeveless leather jacket; a short coat; a close waistcoat. (Origin doubtful.)
jerkin, *n.* *jer*-kin, a male gerfalcon.
jerkiness, *n.* the state or quality of being jerky.
jerky, *a.* *jer*-ke, with jerks; marked by abrupt breaks or transitions.
jeroboam, *n.* *je*-ro-*boh*-am, a large bowl or breaker; a very large wine-bottle, esp. one containing two magnums or more. (Heb., increaser.)
jerque, *v.t.* jerk, to search a vessel, or examine her papers, for contraband, etc. (Origin doubtful.)
jerquer, *n.* *jer*-ker, a Customs searcher.
jerry, *n.* *je*-re, anything inferior or put to mean uses; a chamber-pot [Slang]; a German (esp. a soldier or airman) [Slang]. **jerry builder**, one who uses materials of the cheapest and commonest kind.
jerrymander, *v.t.* *je*-re-*man*-der, to gerrymander.
jersey, *n.* *jer*-ze, fine yarn of wool; a close-fitting knitted body-garment; a breed of cattle used for dairy produce. (*Jersey*, in the Channel Islands.)
Jerusalem-artichoke, *n.* je-*roo*-sa-lem-*ar*-te-choke, *see* **artichoke**.
jervin, *n.* *jer*-vin, a poisonous crystalline alkaloid obtained from the white hellebore. (Sp.)
jess, *n.* jes, a short strap round the legs of a hawk, by which she is held and let fly. (O.Fr. *ges*.)
jessamine, *n.* *jes*-sa-min, jasmine. (O.Fr. *jessemin*.)
jessamy, *a.* *jes*-sa-me, perfumed with jasmine; foppish: *n.* a dandy.
jesse, *n.* *jes*-se, a many-branched candlestick, spreading out like the genealogical tree of Jesse;

a stained glass window representing Jesse's pedigree (Eccles.].

jesserant, *n. jes*-se-rant, a jacket armoured with thin slips of steel and forming a sort of corset. (O.Fr.)

jest, *n.* jest, something ludicrous, meant only to excite laughter; something uttered in sport; a joke; a pleasantry; the object of laughter or sport: *v.i.* to make merriment; to joke. (O.Fr. *geste*, an exploit.)

jester, *n. jest*-er, one who jests; a buffoon; a merry-andrew. (L. *gesta.*)

jestful, *a. jest*-ful, given to jesting; full of jokes.

jestingly, *ad. jest*-ing-le, in a jesting manner; not in earnest.

Jesuit, *n. jez*-yew-it, a member of the Society of Jesus, founded by Ignatius Loyola, in 1534; a crafty casuist; an intriguer. **Jesuit's bark,** quinine. **Jesuit's drops,** friar's balsam. **Jesuit's nut,** the fruit of the water caltrops.

Jesuitess, *n. jez*-yew-it-ess, a member of an order of nuns suppressed by Urban VIII, 1630.

Jesuitic, *a. jez*-yew-*it*-ik, Jesuitical.

Jesuitical, *a. jez*-yew-*it*-e-kal, pertaining to the Jesuits or the principles ascribed to them; designing; cunning; deceitful; prevaricating.

Jesuitically, *ad. jez*-yew-*it*-e-ka-le, craftily.

Jesuitism, *n. jez*-yew-it-izm, the principles and practices attributed to the Jesuits; cunning; deceit; prevarication.

Jesuitry, *n. jez*-yew-it-re, Jesuitism.

jet, *n.* jet, a hard variety of lignite of velvet-black colour, much used for ornaments. (O.Fr. from *Gagas*, in Lycia, where it was obtained.)

jet, *n.* jet, a spouting and shooting, as of water or flame; the pipe of issue; that which issues; a tube for running melted metal into a mould: *v.i.* to shoot forward; to jut: *v.t.* to spout. (O.Fr. *jetter*, from L. *jacio*, throw.)

jet-black, *a.* black as jet; of deepest black.

jetsam, *n. jet*-sum, goods thrown overboard to lighten a ship, esp. those that have sunk before being washed ashore.

jettiness, *n.* jet-e-ness, the condition or quality of being jet-black.

jettison, *n. jet*-e-son, the act of throwing goods overboard so as to lighten a ship in distress: *v.t.* to treat cargo thus; to discard as an encumbrance. (O.Fr. *getaison.*)

jetton, *n. jet*-on, a counter used in table-games; a brass check. (O.Fr.)

jetty, *n. jet*-e, a projection; a small pier: *v.i.* to jut: *v.t.* to provide with a jetty.

jetty, *a. jet*-e, made of jet; black as jet.

Jew, *n.* joo, a descendant of the tribe of Judah; a Semite of Hebrew race; one whose religion is Judaism; applied to a close bargainer, an extortionate moneylender, etc.: *v.t.* to defraud or dupe [Coll.]. (O.Fr. *Jeu*, from L. *Judæus*, from Heb. *Yehûdāh*, Judah.)

Jew-baiting, *n.* persecuting the Jews.

★**jewel,** *n. joo*-el, an ornament of dress, usually containing a precious stone; a precious stone; anything highly valued or dear to one: *v.t.* to dress or adorn with, or as with jewels; to furnish with a jewel. **jewel block,** one of two small blocks suspended at the extremity of the main and foretopsail yards [Naut.]. (O.Fr. *jouel.*)

jeweller, *n. joo*-el-ler, a worker or dealer in jewels.

jewellery, *n. joo*-el-re, jewels in general; the art or trade of a jeweller.

jewelry, *n. joo*-el-re, jewellery.

Jewess, *n. joo*-ess, a female Jew.

jew-fish, *n.* the tarpon.

Jewish, *a. joo*-ish, pertaining to or characteristic of the Jews or their rites or customs; Israelitish.

Jewishness, *n. joo*-ish-ness, Jewish quality; the state of being Jewish.

Jewry, *n. joo*-re, Judæa; a ghetto or Jewish quarter; Jews collectively. (O.Fr. *juerie.*)

Jew's-ear, *n.* an edible gelatinous fungus shaped like an ear, *Hirneola auricula-judæ.*

Jew's-harp, *n.* a small harp-shaped musical instrument with a metal tongue, which, when placed between the teeth and struck by the finger, gives modulated sounds.

Jew's-mallow, *n.* a yellow-flowered plant, *Corcorus olitorius*, used in the East as a pot-herb.

Jew's-myrtle, *n.* the butcher's-broom.

jezebel, *n. jez*-e-bel, a vicious unscrupulous woman; a much painted or bedizened woman. (Ahab's wife, 1 Kings xvi.)

jib, *n.* jib, the foremost sail of a ship, extending from the outer end of the jib-boom; the extended arm of a crane: *v.i.* to move restively backwards or sideways; to refuse to go further; to shy; to shirk. **flying jib,** a sail on a boom rigged out beyond the jib-boom. **middle jib,** a sail set between the jib and flying-jib. (Scand.)

jibbah, *n. jib*-a, a long outer garment as worn by Moslems; a smock.

jibber, *n. jib*-ber, one who, or a horse that, jibs: *v.i.* to gibber.

jib-boom, *n.* a spar forming an extension to the bowsprit. **flying jib-boom,** a boom extended beyond the jib-boom.

jib-door, *n.* a door standing flush with the wall.

jibe, *v.t.* and *i.* jibe, to taunt; to sneer; to gibe.

jiboya, *n.* je-*boh*-ya, the boa-constrictor, or other large S. American boa. (Tupi.)

jib-topsail, *n.* a small jib extending between topmast-head and end of jib-boom.

jiffy, *n. jif*-fe, an instant [Slang].

jig, *n.* jig, a lively, light, quick tune; a quick dance suited to it; a weighted fish-hook; any of several mechanical devices: *v.i.* to dance a jig; to dance or jerk about: *v.t.* to jerk up and down rapidly; to sieve or separate by means of a jigger; to hoax [Coll.]. (Perhaps Fr. *gigue*, a fiddle, a dance.)

jigger, *n. jig*-ger, one who dances jigs; a potter's wheel; a miner who cleans ores in a sieve, also the sieve itself; any small mechanical device, esp. a device for holding the heaved cable; a small mizen abaft the sternpost [Naut.].

jigger, *n. jig*-ger, the chigoe or sand-flea.

jiggered, *a. jig*-gerd, confounded (a mild oath), as *Well, I'm jiggered!* I'm most astonished! [Coll.].

jiggery-pokery, *n. jig*-e-re-*poh*-ke-re, humbug; a hoax; underhand dealing [Slang].

jigging, *n. jig*-ing, the process of sorting ore by passing it through a wire-bottomed sieve [Mining].

jiggish, *a. jig*-ish, suitable to a jig; frisky.

jiggle, *v.t. jig*-gl, to jerk or wriggle about.

jig-saw, *n. jig*-saw, a saw for cutting fretwork, etc. **jigsaw puzzle,** a dissected puzzle; a picture pasted on thin board and cut into diverse fanciful shapes to be fitted together.

jihad, *n.* je-*hahd*, a Mohammedan holy war; a war opposing some principle or doctrine. (Arab.)

jill, *n.* jil, a young woman; a gillian; **jill-flirt,** a light, wanton woman. (Dial.)

jillet, *n. jil*-et, a flighty young woman; a jilt.

jilt, *n.* jilt, a woman who gives her lover hopes and capriciously disappoints him; a coquette: *v.t.* to discard a sweetheart: *v.i.* to play the jilt. (*jill.*)

jimjams, *n. jim*-jamz, delirium tremens [Slang].

jimmy, *n. jim*-e, a jemmy; a sovereign [Slang].

jimp, *a.* jimp, neat; handsome; elegantly shaped; of short measure; scant. (Scots.)

jingal, *n.* jing-*gawl*, a gingal. (Hind.)

jingle, *n. jing*-gl, a clinking sound, as of little bells or pieces of metal; that which jingles; a little bell or rattle; correspondence of sound in rhymes; a covered two-wheeled public car of southern Ireland and Australia: *v.i.* to sound with a jingle: *v.t.* to cause to jingle. **jingling Johnny,** a set of small bells on a portable stand. (Imit.)

jingo, *n. jing*-go, a bellicose patriot, esp. one who in 1877 insisted that England should join the Turks against Russia (from a contemporary popular song representing them eager to fight "by jingo"). **by jingo,** a mild oath. (Probably a conjurer's nonsense word.)

jingoism, *n. jing*-go-izm, the boastfully bellicose spirit of jingoes; chauvinism.

jingoistic, *a.* jing-go-*is*-tik, of the nature of, or expressing, jingoism.

jinks, *n.* jinks, merrymaking. **high jinks,** lively entertainment, uproarious sport. (Scots.)

jinn, *n.pl.* jin (*sing.* **jinni,** jin-*nee*), an order of spirits in Mohammedan demonology. (Ar.)

jinricksha, *n. jin*-rik-shaw, a Japanese two-wheeled carriage drawn by a man between the shafts. (Jap.)

jirgah, *n. jur*-gah, a council of Afghan tribal chiefs.

jitterbug, *n. jit*-ter-bug, one addicted to jitters; a modern style of dancing [U.S.A.].

jitters, *n. jit*-terz, extreme nervousness; unreasonable terror [U.S.A. slang].

jittery, *a.* *jit*-er-re, trembling with fear; panicky [U.S.A. slang].
jiu-jitsu, joo-*jit*-soo, ju-jitsu.
jo, *n.* joh, a sweetheart. (Scots.)
job, *n.* job, a piece of work, esp. temporary and for a stated sum; anything to be done; occupation; situation; an undertaking professedly for the public good, but really for one's own; a criminal enterprise; *a.* at a special price; bought cheap: *v.t.* to let out, as work for execution, or horses for hire; to hire; to buy up and retail: *v.i.* to buy and sell as a broker; to engage in business as a stockjobber; to do job-work or jobbing; to hire or let; to act in the public service for one's own ends. **job lot,** a miscellaneous assortment, esp. one bought cheap for profitable retailing. **to do the job for one,** to kill him. (Fr. *gobet,* a small piece, a mouthful, from Celt. *gob,* a mouth.)
job, *n.* job, a sudden stab or jab with a pointed instrument: *v.t.* to strike or stab with a sharp instrument. (Prob. imit.)
jobation, *n.* joh-*bay*-shon, a scolding; a long tedious reproof. (*Job,* the prophet.)
jobber, *n.* *job*-ber, one who does small jobs; a worker by the job; a stockjobber; one who lets out carriages or horses; one who serves his own ends in office; one who engages in underhand dealings.
jobbernowl, *n.* *job*-ber-noul, a blockhead [Slang].
jobbery, *n.* *job*-ber-e, corrupt practices; intriguing for private profit.
jobmaster, *n.* *job*-mahs-ter, one who lets out horses and carriages; a livery-stable keeper.
job's-comforter, *n.* *johbz-kum*-for-ter, one who reproaches while he sympathizes.
job's-tears, *n.* a grass, *Coix lachryma,* used as a cereal in India and a drug in China; its seeds.
Jock, *n.* jok, a Scot; *pl.* Highland troops [Slang].
jockey, *n.* *jok*-e, a professional rider of racehorses; one who deceives or takes undue advantage in trade: *v.t.* to play the jockey to; to outwit; to cheat; to jostle by riding against one. **Jockey Club,** the supreme horseracing authority in Great Britain. (*Jacky,* from *Jack.*)
jockeyism, *n.* *jok*-e-izm, the practice of jockeys.
jockeyship, *n.* *jok*-e-ship, the art or practice of riding horses in races; trickery.
jocko, *n.* *jok*-ko, a chimpanzee.
jocose, *a.* jo-*kohs*, given to jokes and jesting; containing a joke; humorous; facetious. (L. *jocosus.*)
jocosely, *ad.* jo-*kohs*-le, in a jocose manner.
jocoseness, *n.* the quality of being jocose.
jocosity, *n.* jo-*kos*-e-te, jocoseness; an act or instance of this.
jocular, *a.* *jok*-yew-lar, containing jokes; humorous; given to jesting or pleasantry. (L. *jocularis.*)
jocularity, *n.* *jok*-yew-*la*-re-te, jocular behaviour; merriment; jesting.
jocularly, *ad.* *jok*-yew-lar-le, in a jocular manner.
jocund, *a.* *jok*-und, sportive; merry; cheerful; lighthearted. (O.Fr. *jocond.*)
jocundity, *n.* jo-*kun*-de-te, the quality or state of being jocund; mirthfulness.
jocundly, *ad.* *jok*-und-le, in a jocund manner.
jodhpurs, *n.pl.* *jod*-poorz, long riding-breeches fitting closely from knee to ankle. (*Jodhpur,* town in Rajputana.)
joey, *n.* *joh*-e, a young kangaroo [Austral. coll.]; a fourpenny piece [Slang].
jog, *n.* jog, a push; a slight shake; a shake or push to awaken attention: *v.t.* to push with the elbow or hand; to excite attention by a slight push: *v.i.* to move by jogs or small shocks, as in a slow trot; to move along slowly. (Origin doubtful.)
jogger, *n.* *jog*-ger, one who jogs.
joggle, *n.* *jog*-gl, a notch in a joint to prevent slipping: *v.t.* to shake slightly; to give a sudden but slight push; to indent as at the joinings of stones to prevent sliding; to unite with joggles; *v.i.* to shake.
jog-trot, *a.* monotonous: *n.* a slow formal regular pace.
Johannine, *a.* joh-*han*-nine, pertaining to the writer of the Fourth Gospel, St. John.
Johannisberger, *n.* joh-*han*-nis-berg-er, a variety of hock. (*Johannisberg,* near Wiesbaden.)
johannite, *n.* joh-*han*-nite, a grass-green sulphate of uranium and copper. (*John,* Archduke of Austria, 1782–1859.)
John, *n.* jon, a man's name. **John Bull,** a humorous impersonation of the English people, conceived of as well-fed, good-natured, honest-hearted, justice-loving, and plain-spoken. **John Company,** the East India Company personified. **John Dory,** a fish, the dory. (Heb. *Yokhanan,* the grace of the Lord.)
johnny, *n.* *jon*-ne, a would-be fashionable young man-about-town. **johnny cake,** a cake made of maize. **johnny raw,** a beginner.
Johnsonese, *n.* jon-so-*neez,* a ponderous style of writing, so called after Dr. Johnson.
Johnsonian, *a.* jon-*soh*-ne-an, in the style of Dr. Johnson: *n.* an admirer or student of Dr. Johnson.
⋆**join,** *n.* joyn, act of joining; point of junction; a seam: *v.i.* to connect; to unite; to associate; to engage in; to enter; to annex: *v.t.* to grow to; to adhere; to be contiguous or in contact; to unite with in marriage, league, confederacy, partnership, or society. (O.Fr. *joindre.*)
joinder, *n.* *joyn*-der, a joining, as of parties or claims, etc., in one suit or action [Law]. **joinder in demurrer,** the acceptance by a partner of the challenge in his adversary's demurrer [Law].
joiner, *n.* *joyn*-er, one whose occupation is to construct things by joining pieces of wood; a wood-worker; a builder's carpenter.
joinering, *n.* *joyn*-er-ring, the work of a joiner.
joinery, *n.* *joyn*-er-re, the art of a joiner; the woodwork in buildings.
joint, *n.* joynt, the part where two or more things join; a joining; a knot; a node or internode [Bot.]; a juncture of parts which admit of motion; a hinge; the union of two bones [Anat.]; an articulation, as the elbow; a piece of meat with bone as cut by the butcher for the table; a fissure dividing rock masses into blocks [Geol.]; any low haunt, esp. a drinking- or gambling-den [U.S.A. Slang]: *a.* shared by two or more; united in the same profession or interest; united; combined; acting in concert: *v.t.* to form with joints or articulations; to unite by joints; to cut or divide (meat) into joints and quarters; to smooth the edges of boards, so that they may fit close to each other; to fit closely. **joint action,** an action in which several wrongs or claims are joined in one writ [Law]. **joint and several,** each both independently and jointly. **out of joint,** dislocated; not in adjustment. (O.Fr.)
jointed, *pp.* and *a.* *joynt*-ed, having joints; formed with articulations.
jointedly, *ad.* *joynt*-ed-le, connectedly.
jointer, *n.* *joynt*-er, a long smoothing-plane used by joiners; tool used by masons, etc., at joinings; one who makes joints, esp. in wiring.
joint-heir, *n.* an heir having a joint interest with another.
jointing, *n.* *joynt*-ing, the making of a joint. **jointing plane,** a jointer. **jointing rule,** a straight edge used by bricklayers for regulating the direction and course of the jointer.
jointly, *ad.* *joynt*-le, together; unitedly; in concert.
jointress, *n.* *joyn*-tress, a woman who has a jointure.
joint-stock, *n.* stock or capital held jointly by several share- or stock-holders. **joint-stock company,** a company having the stock or capital divided into shares, which are transferable by each owner without the consent of the others.
joint-stool, *n.* a stool made of parts inserted in each other.
joint-tenancy, *n.* a tenure of estate by unity of interest, title, time, and possession.
joint-tenant, *n.* one who holds by joint-tenancy.
jointure, *n.* *joynt*-yewr, an estate in lands or tenements, settled on a woman in consideration of marriage, and to be enjoyed by her after her husband's decease [Law]: *v.t.* to settle a jointure upon. (Fr.)
joist, *n.* *joyst,* one of the parallel timbers to which the boards of a floor or the laths of a ceiling are nailed: *v.t.* to fit with joists. (O.Fr. *giste,* couch.)
joke, *n.* joke, a jest to raise a laugh; something witty or sportive; something not serious or in earnest: *v.i.* to jest; to sport: *v.t.* to rally; to make merry with. **in joke,** in jest, not in earnest. **practical joke,** *see* **practical.** (L. *jocus.*)
jokelet, *n.* *joke-let,* a trifling or feeble joke.
joker, *n.* *joke*-er, a jester; a merry fellow; an extra

card in a pack, usually ranking as any card and above the highest trump.
jokingly, *ad. joke*-ing-le, in a joking way.
jollification, *n. jol*-le-fe-*kay*-shon, noisy festivity and merriment.
jollify, *v.t. jol*-le-fy, to make jolly: *v.i.* to make merry.
jollily, *ad. jol*-le-le, in a jolly manner; with noisy mirth.
jolliness, *n. jol*-le-ness, jollity.
jollity, *n. jol*-le-te, the quality of being jolly; merriment; joviality.
jolly, *a. jol*-le, merry; lively; full of life and mirth; expressing mirth or inspiring it; plump and cheerful, agreeable [Coll.]: *ad.* very: *v.t.* and *i.* to banter; to chaff; to treat a person pleasantly with some ulterior object [U.S.A. slang]. **Jolly Roger,** the pirate flag. (Fr. *joli*, pretty, from Ice. *jol*, feast at Yule.)
jolly, *n. jol*-le, a marine [Naut.].
jollyboat, *n. jol*-le-boat, a small four-oared ship's boat. (Port. *galeota.*)
jolt, *n.* johlt, a shock or shake by a sudden jerk: *v.i.* to move with jolts: *v.t.* to shake with sudden jerks, as a vehicle on rough ground.
jolter, *n. johlt*-er, he who or that which jolts.
jolter-head, *n.* a dunce; a dolt.
joltingly, *ad. johlt*-ing-le, so as to jolt or shake.
Jonah, *n. joh*-na, a bringer of bad luck. (Named after *Jonah*, the prophet.)
Jonathan, *n. jon*-a-than, Brother Jonathan, the American people viewed collectively; an individual of the American type of character, so called after Washington's friend, Jonathan Trumbull; (*l.c.*) a variety of dessert apple.
jongleur, *n. jong*-gler, a wandering minstrel. (O.Fr.)
jonquil, *n. jong*-kwil, the pale yellow daffodil, *Narcissus jonquilla.* (Fr. *jonquille.*)
jordan, *n. jawr*-dan, a chamber-pot [Slang]. (Probably the river Jordan, water of which was brought home in vessels by pilgrims for baptisms.) **jordan almond,** the cultivated almond (Probably Fr. *jardin*).
jorum, *n. jaw*-rum, a full bowl; a large drinking vessel, or its contents (*Joram*, 2 Sam. viii, 10.)
joseph, *n. joh*-zef, a woman's riding-coat or habit, with buttons down the skirts. (Probably an allusion to the coat Joseph left with Potiphar's wife.)
joss, *n.* joss, a Chinese idol; a self-important person. (Pidgin-Eng. from Port. *deos*, God.)
josser, *n. joss*-er, a foolish fellow; a chap (generally old) [Slang.]
joss-house, *n.* a Chinese temple.
joss-stick, *n.* a small perfumed reed, burned by Chinese before their idols.
jostle, *v.t. jos*-sl, to push against; to shove about or hustle: *n.* an act of jostling; a hasty shove.
jot, *n.* jot, an iota; a tittle: *v.t.* to set down; to make a memorandum of. (L. *iota.*)
jotting, *n. jot*-ting, a memorandum.
joule, *n.* jool, the electrical unit of energy, *i.e.* that expended in one second by a current of one ampere against a resistance of one ohm. (J. P. *Joule*, Engl. physicist, *d.* 1889.)
jounce, *n.* jounce, a jolt, bump, or bounce: *v.t.* to shake up and down; to jolt.
journal, *n. jur*-nal, a diary; an account of daily or current transactions and events, or the book containing such account; a book in which entries are made of transfers from one account to another [Comm.]; a daily register of the ship's course and distance, the winds, weather, etc. [Naut.]; a newspaper or other periodical publication, esp. one recording the progress of discovery or the transactions of a society. (Fr., from L. *diurnalis.*)
journal, *n. jur*-nal, the neck or the bearing portion of the shaft in machinery. **journal box,** the fitting on which the journal works. (Origin doubtful.)
journalese, *n.* jur-na-*leez*, the literary style of journalism [Derogatory].
journalism, *n. jur*-na-lizm, daily or periodical literature, with its conduct and influence; the business of a journalist; writing suitable for periodicals.
journalist, *n. jur*-na-list, a contributor to, or a conductor of, a public journal; formerly also, a diarist.
journalistic, *a. jur*-na-*lis*-tik, pertaining to or characteristic of journals or journalism.
journalize, *v.t.* and *i. jur*-na-lize, to enter in, or to keep, a journal.
★**journey,** *n. jur*-ne, travel or passage from one place to another: *v.i.* to travel from place to place. (Fr. *journée*, a day, day's work, or day's travel, from *jour*, a day.)
journeyer, *n. jur*-ne-er, one who journeys.
journeyman, *n. jur*-ne-man, a mechanic who has served his apprenticeship and is qualified; one hired from day to day; a hack.
journey-work, *n. jur*-ne-wurk, work done for hire, esp. by a mechanic in his proper occupation.
joust, *n.* joost, a mock encounter of armed knights or men-at-arms on horseback: *v.i.* to engage in a joust; to tilt. (O.Fr. *jouster.*)
Jove, *n.* johv, Jupiter, the supreme deity among the Romans, the Greek Zeus; tin [Alchemy]. (L. *Jovis.*)
jovial, *a. joh*-ve-al, full of mirth and gladness; joyous; merry; jolly. (O.Fr.)
joviality, *n. joh*-ve-*al*-e-te, jovialness; jollity.
jovially, *ad. joh*-ve-a-le, in a jovial manner.
jovialness, *n. joh*-ve-al-ness, the quality of being jovial; jolly good fellowship.
Jovian, *a. joh*-ve-an, pertaining to the planet Jupiter; pertaining to Jove.
jowl, *n.* joul, the cheek; the jaw; the cheek of a pig salted; the crop of a fowl; the head part of a fish. **cheek by jowl,** tête-a-tête. (A.S. *ceafl.*)
jowler, *n.* joul-er, any dog with large jowls.
joy, *n.* joy, the passion or emotion excited by the acquisition or expectation of cherished good; gladness; exhilaration of spirits; happiness: the cause of joy or happiness: *v.i.* to rejoice; to be glad; to exult: *v.t.* to give joy to; to gladden. **joy ride,** a motor ride for pleasure or excitement, esp. taken surreptitiously. (O.Fr. *joye.*)
joyance, *n. joy*-ance, gaiety; festivity.
joyful, *a. joy*-ful, full of joy; very glad; merry; happy.
joyfully, *ad. joy*-ful-le, in a joyful manner.
joyfulness, *n. joy*-ful-ness, the state of being joyful; great gladness; joy.
joyless, *a. joy*-less, wanting joy; giving no joy.
joylessly, *ad. joy*-les-le, without joy.
joylessness, *n. joy*-les-ness, state of being joyless.
joyous, *a. joy*-us, joyful; giving joy. (O.Fr.)
joyously, *ad. joy*-us-le, in a joyous manner.
joyousness, *n. joy*-us-ness, the state of being joyous.
joystick, *n. joy*-stik, the control lever of an aeroplane [Slang].
juba, *n. joo*-ba, a mane, or similar growth; a loose panicle or tuft [Bot.]. (L., a mane.)
juba, *n. joo*-ba, an old negro dance.
jubate, *a. joo*-bat, having a mane, or growth like a mane [Zool.].
jubbah, *n. jub*-bah, a jibbah.
jube, *n. joo*-be, a rood-loft; the screen dividing choir from nave [Arch.]. (L., bid thou; first word of a prayer there uttered.)
jubilant, *a. joo*-be-lant, uttering songs of triumph; shouting with joy; rejoicing. (L. *jubilans*, rejoicing.)
jubilation, *n. joo*-be-*lay*-shon, the act of declaring triumph; shouting in triumph; exultation. (L. *jubilatio.*)
jubilee, *n. joo*-be-lee, a festive period among the ancient Jews, proclaimed by trumpet, celebrated every fiftieth year to commemorate the deliverance from Egypt, and marked by the liberation of slaves, etc.; fiftieth anniversary; a season of festivity and great public joy; a solemnity or ceremony, usually celebrated every twenty-fifth year at Rome, at which the Pope grants plenary indulgence. **diamond jubilee,** a sixtieth anniversary. (Fr. *jubilé*, from Heb. *yobel*, the blast of a trumpet.)
Judaic, *a.* joo-*day*-ik, Judaical.
Judaical, *a.* joo-*day*-e-kal, pertaining to the Jews.
Judaically, *ad.* joo-*day*-e-ka-le, after the Jewish manner.
Judaism, *n. joo*-da-izm, the religious doctrines and rites of the Jews; conformity to the Jewish rites.
Judaization, *n. joo*-da-eye-*zay*-shon, act of Judaizing.
Judaize, *v.i.* and *v.t. joo*-da-ize, to conform to Jewish doctrines, rites or modes of thinking; to force (Gentiles) to conform to them.
Judaizer, *n. joo*-da-eye-zer, one who Judaizes; one

of the Christianized Jews of Apostolic times who conformed to certain of the Mosaic laws and observances.

Judas, *n. joo*-das, a double-dyed traitor; a Judas-hole. (Name of the disciple who betrayed Christ.)

Judas-hole, *n. joo*-das-hole, a hole to pry secretly into a chamber.

Judas-tree, *n. joo*-das-tree, the leguminous tree, *Cercis siliquastrum*, on which, by tradition, Judas hanged himself.

★**judge,** *n.* judj, a civil officer invested with authority to hear and determine causes, civil or criminal, between parties; one skilled in judging merit or worth; one competent to give an opinion; among the ancient Jews, a chief magistrate having both civil and military powers: *v.i.* to hear and determine, as in causes on trial; to pass sentence; to distinguish; to compare facts or ideas, and perceive their agreement or disagreement, and thus to distinguish truth from falsehood: *v.t.* to hear and determine a cause; to examine and pass sentence on; to try; to pass severe sentence upon; to reckon; to consider. **Judge-Advocate,** a legal adviser to the court at a British, and the prosecutor at a United States, court-martial. **Judge-Advocate-General,** a barrister in charge of the administration of military and R.A.F. law, and acting as legal adviser to both Secretaries of State in matters regarding courts-martial (title changed, 1949, to Chief Judge Martial). (Fr. *juge.*)

judgement, *n. judj*-ment, judgment.

judger, *n. judj*-er, one who judges.

judgeship, *n. judj*-ship, the office, status, or dignity of a judge.

judgment, *n. judj*-ment, the act of judging; the faculty, act, or process of the mind in comparing ideas and determining their relation; discrimination; criticism; determination; opinion; the sentence pronounced in any cause; the right or power of passing sentence; the spirit of wisdom and prudence, enabling one to discern right and wrong; an extraordinary calamity inflicted by God on sinners; a divine statute or dispensation. **judgment creditor,** a creditor in favour of whom a judgment has been given for the paying of a debt. **Judgment Day,** the day of final judgment; the final trial of the human race. **judgment debt,** a security debt, legalized by a judge's order, under which execution can at any time be issued. **judgment seat,** the seat or bench on which the judges sit; a court or tribunal. **judgment summons,** a summons issued against a debtor whose debts remain unpaid. (Fr. *jugement.*)

Judica, *n. joo*-de-ka, Passion Sunday, the psalm for which commences "Judica me."

judicable, *a. joo*-de-ka-bl, capable of being, or liable to be, judged.

judication, *n.* joo-de-*kay*-shon, the action of judging; judgment.

judicative, *a. joo*-dik-a-tiv, having the function of judging; judicial.

judicatory, *a. joo*-de-ka-to-re, dispensing or pertaining to the administration of justice: *n.* a court of justice; a tribunal; the administration of justice.

judicature, *n. joo*-de-ka-tewr, the power of administrating justice by legal trial and determination; the body of judges; a court of justice; jurisdiction.

judicial, *a.* joo-*dish*-al, pertaining to justice or to courts of justice; practised in the distribution of justice; proceeding from or issued by a court of justice; inflicted as the result of judgment; critical; impartial. **judicial separation,** legal separation of man and wife, neither being free to remarry during the lifetime of the other. (L. *judicialis.*)

judicially, *ad.* joo-*dish*-al-le, in a judicial manner; in legal form.

judiciary, *a.* joo-*dish*-e-a-re, passing judgment; pertaining to the courts of judicature: *n.* that branch of government which is concerned in the trial and determination of controversies; the judicial department; the judges collectively.

judicious, *a.* joo-*dish*-us, according to a sound judgment; possessing sound judgment; directed by reason and wisdom. (Fr. *judicieux.*)

judiciously, *ad.* in a judicious manner.

judiciousness, *n.* the quality of being judicious.

judo, *n. joo*-do, an advanced form of ju-jitsu. (Jap.)

jug, *n.* jug, a vessel usually with a swelling body, narrow mouth, and a handle, for holding liquors: *v.t.* to stew in or as in a jug: *v.i.* to utter a sound resembling this word (as of certain birds). **stone jug,** gaol [Slang]. (Origin unknown.)

jugal, *a. joo*-gal, pertaining to the cheek or cheek-bone. (L. *jugalis.*)

jugate, *a. jew*-gate, coupled together; ha-ing leaflets in pairs [Bot.]. (L. *jugatus.*)

jugful, *n. jug*-ful, the quantity that a jug will hold.

juggernaut, *n. jug*-ger-nawt, the eighth avatar of Vishnu; his idol at Puri, Orissa, which, on a chariot, was taken periodically in procession when thousands, it is said, sacrificed themselves under the wheels; any cause by which a devotee is destroyed or for which he blindly sacrifices himself. (Sans. *Jagannâtha*, the master of the world.)

juggins, *n. jug*-ginz, a silly fellow; a dupe [Slang].

juggle, *n. jug*-gl, a piece of juggling; an imposture: *v.i.* to amuse by sleight of hand; to practise artifice or imposture: *v.t.* to deceive by trick or artifice. (O.Fr. *jogler.*)

juggler, *n. jug*-gler, one who juggles, esp. as an entertainer; a deceiver; a trickish fellow.

jugglery, *n. jug*-gler-e, juggling; legerdemain; underhand practice; trickery.

juggling, *n. jug*-gling, a feat of dexterity in which illusion is effected by sleight of hand; such entertainment.

Juglans, *n. joo*-glanz, the genus of trees comprising the walnut and butternut. (L.)

Jugoslav, *see* **Yugoslav.**

jugular, *a. joo*-gew-lar, pertaining to the neck or throat: *n.* a jugular vein [Anat.]. **jugular vein,** one of the large veins which bring back the blood from the head. (L. *jugulum*, the collar-bone.)

juice, *n.* jooce, the sap of vegetables; organic fluid; the essence of a thing; petrol, or electricity [Slang]. (L. *jus*, broth.)

juiceless, *a. jooce*-less, destitute of juice.

juiciness, *n. joo*-se-ness, succulence; the state of being juicy.

juicy, *a. joo*-se, abounding with juice; succulent.

ju-jitsu, *n.* joo-*jit*-soo, Japanese wrestling, in which one's opponent's weight and strength is turned to one's own advantage. (Jap.)

juju, *n. joo*-joo, a fetish; an amulet; the beliefs and practices of animism. (W. African.)

jujube, *n. joo*-joob, the berry-like fruit of any of the species of *Zizyphus*; a confection of gum arabic and sugar; a kind of lozenge. (Fr.)

julep, *n. joo*-lep, a sweet drink, esp. one serving as a vehicle to medicine; a spirituous drink with water, sugar, and a seasoning of mint, etc. (Fr.)

Julian, *a. joo*-le-an, pertaining to Julius Cæsar. **Julian Calendar,** the calendar devised by him in 46 B.C. (superseded in England in 1752 by the Gregorian year), based on the **Julian year** of 365 days 6 hours.

julienne, *n. joo*-le-en, clear soup with shredded vegetables; a variety of pear. (Fr.)

July, *n.* joo-*ly*, the seventh month of the year. (From *Julius* Cæsar, who was born in this month.)

jumart, *n. joo*-mart, the supposed offspring of a bull and a mare, or a horse and a cow. (Fr.)

jumble, *n. jum*-bl, a confused mixture; disorder; a thin, crisp, sweet cake: *v.t.* to throw together without order: *v.i.* to mix or unite in a confused manner. **jumble sale,** a sale of miscellaneous things for charitable purposes. (Probably imit.)

jumblement, *n. jum*-bl-ment, confused mixture.

jumbo, *n. jum*-bo, anything very large or clumsy. (Name of a famous show elephant accidentally killed, 1885).

★**jump,** *n.* jump, the act of jumping; a leap; a bound; a gap; a sudden rise (in price, etc.); a fault [Geol.]; *pl.* involuntary twitchings: *ad.* exactly: *v.i.* to leap; to spring; to jolt; to agree with; to start rising suddenly (of prices): *v.t.* to pass by a leap; to skip or cause to skip over. **jumped-up,** upstart; parvenu. **to jump a claim,** to take possession of a claim in mining. (Probably imit.)

jumper, *n. jump*-er, one who or that which jumps; a sailor's loose jacket; a woman's outer garment worn with a skirt but not tucked in; a man's sweater or pull-over; a long iron boring-tool used by masons and miners; a jumping insect or maggot; (*cap.*) one of an 18th-cent. Calvinistic sect, from their practice of jumping in worship; a ticket-inspector on a public conveyance [Coll.].

jumpiness, *n.* *jump*-e-ness, nervousness.
jumpy, *a.* *jump*-e, twitching involuntarily; nervous; irritable.
juncaceous, *a.* jung-*kay*-shus, resembling the rushes; belonging to the rush family (Bot.]. (L. *juncus*, a rush.)
juncous, *a.* *jung*-kus, juncaceous.
junction, *n.* *junk*-shon, the act of joining; the state of being joined; union; coalition; the place or point of union; a place where railways meet or send off branches. (L. *junctio*.)
juncture, *n.* *junk*-tewr, a joining; union; the line or point at which two bodies are joined; a seam; point of time, esp. a critical moment. (L. *junctura*.)
June, *n.* joon, the sixth month of the year. (L. *Junius*, one of the Roman gens; O.Fr. *juin*.)
jungle, *n.* *jung*-gl, land covered with dense vegetation, esp. in India. (Hind. *jangal*.)
jungle-fever, *n.* malaria.
jungle-fowl, *n.* an East Indian bird of the genus *Gallus*; a mound-bird of Australia.
jungly, *a.* *jung*-gle, consisting of jungles; abounding with jungles.
junior, *a.* *joon*-yor, younger in years or practice: *n.* one who is younger in either way; a subordinate. (L., comp. of *juvenis*, young.)
juniority, *n* joo-ne-*o*-re-te, state of being junior.
juniper, *n.* *joo*-ne-per, a small evergreen conifer, genus *Juniperus*, bearing berries the oil of which is used to give flavour to gin. (L. *juniperus*.)
junk, *n.* junk, any miscellaneous rubbish, esp. pieces of old cordage used as oakum for filling the seams of ships, etc.; hard salt beef formerly supplied for long voyages. (Origin unknown.)
junk, *n.* junk, a flat-bottomed vessel with one or more pole masts and flat matting sails used in Chinese waters. (Port.)
Junker, *n.* *yoong*-ker, a young German nobleman, esp. a member of the reactionary and exclusive Prussian aristocracy. (Ger., young Herr.)
junket, *n.* *jung*-ket, curds and cream sweetened and flavoured; a delicacy: *v.i.* to feast; to picnic: *v.t.* to entertain to a feast. (O.Fr. *jonkette*, rush-basket in which a sweetmeat was made.)
junketing, *n.* *jung*-ke-ting, a festive entertainment; a merrymaking.
junk-ring, *n.* a steam-tight packing round the piston of a steam-engine.
Juno, *n.* *joo*-noh, the wife of Jupiter and queen of heaven; a regal-looking woman. (L.)
junta, *n.* *jun*-ta, an administrative or deliberative council, esp. in Spain or Italy. (Sp.)
junto, *n.* *jun*-toh, a cabal or faction; a union of persons for some common purpose, usually political.
jupe, *n.* joop, a skirt; a petticoat; a pelisse or short mantle, formerly worn by women. (Fr.)
Jupiter, *n.* *joo*-pe-ter, the supreme deity of the Romans; Jove; the largest of the planets. (L. *Jove*, and *pater*, father.)
jupon, *n.* *joo*-pon, a surcoat; a petticoat; a short close-fitting sleeveless coat worn over armour. (Fr.)
jural, *a.* *joor*-ral, pertaining to law; juristic.
Jurassic, *a.* joor-*ras*-ik, pertaining to the middle division of the Secondary rocks, succeeding the Triassic and including the Lias and Oolite. (*Jura* mountains, where first studied.)
jurat, *n.* *joor*-rat, a municipal officer; a magistrate in the Channel Islands and certain corporations; the record of the time, place, and before whom an affidavit was sworn. (Fr.)
juratory, *a.* *joo*-ra-to-re, comprising an oath.
juridical, *a.* joor-*rid*-e-kal, pertaining to or acting in the administration of justice; pertaining to a judge; used in law courts. (L. *juridicus*.)
juridically, *ad.* in a judicial manner.
jurisconsult, *n.* *joor*-ris-*kon*-sult, one learned in law, esp. in Roman jurisprudence. (L. *jurisconsultus*.)
jurisdiction, *n.* *joor*-ris-*dik*-shon, legal power or authority to execute the laws and distribute justice; legal authority; the territorial limit within which power may be exercised. (O.Fr.)
jurisdictional, *a.* pertaining to jurisdiction.
jurisdictive, *a.* *joor*-ris-*dik*-tiv, having jurisdiction.
jurisprudence, *n.* *jew*-ris-*proo*-dence, the science of law; the knowledge of the laws, customs, and rights of men in states or communities; any national legal system. **medical jurisprudence,** the inter-relation of medical and legal science. (L. *juris-prudentia*.)

jurisprudent, *a.* *joor*-ris-*proo*-dent, understanding legal principles: *n.* one versed in jurisprudence.
jurisprudential, *a.* *joor*-ris-proo-*den*-shal, pertaining to jurisprudence.
jurist, *n.* *joor*-rist, one versed in law, esp. civil or international law; a writer on law. (Fr. *juriste*.)
juristic, *a.* joor-*ris*-tik, relating to, dependent upon, or recognized by, law; pertaining to jurisprudence.
juror, *n.* *joor*-ror, a member of a jury. (Fr. *jureur*.)
jury, *n.* *joor*-re, a number of persons selected and sworn to inquire into and try any matter of fact; any body of judges, esp. one selected to adjudicate at public exhibitions, etc. (O.Fr. *jurée*.)
jury-box, *n.* the enclosure in which the jury sit.
juryman, *n.* *joor*-re-man, one impanelled on a jury; a juror.
jury-mast, *n.* a temporary mast erected in place of one carried away. **jury-rigged,** *a.* rigged for a temporary purpose [Naut.]. (Origin unknown.)
jussive, *a.* *juss*-iv, in the nature of a command. (L. *jussus*, commanded.)
just, *a.* just, true; acting agreeably to right, or law, or engagement; impartial; righteous; faithful; agreeable to fact, or truth, or justice; agreeable to what is due, or proper, or proportionate; merited; deserved: *ad.* close or closely; nearly; exactly; barely. (Fr. *juste*.)
justice, *n.* *jus*-tis, justness; giving or rendering to every one what is his due; rectitude, esp. in reciprocal dealings; honesty; accordance with truth or fact; impartiality; agreeableness to right; just desert; one commissioned to hold courts, or to try and decide controversies, and administer justice to individuals; a judge of the High Court [Law]. **justice of the peace,** one appointed by royal commission to try cases of summary jurisdiction. (Fr.)
justiceship, *n.* *jus*-tis-ship, the office, dignity, or rank of a justice.
justiciable, *a.* jus-*tish* e-a-bl, liable to be, or proper to be, examined in a court of justice. (Fr.)
Justiciar, *n.* jus-*tish*-e-ar, in Norman and Plantagenet times the chief political officer and administrator of justice.
Justiciary, *a.* jus-*tish*-e-a-re, pertaining to the administration of justice. **the High Court of Justiciary,** in Scotland, the court of supreme jurisdiction in criminal cases.
justifiable, *a.* *jus*-te-*fy*-a-bl, that may be proved to be just; defensible; excusable. **justifiable homicide,** non-criminal deprivation of another's life, as in self-defence or in the execution of the law. (Fr.)
justifiableness, *n.* *jus*-te-*fy*-a-bl-ness, the quality of being justifiable; rectitude.
justifiably, *ad.* so as to be justifiable; rightly.
justification, *n.* *jus*-te-fe-*kay*-shon, the act of justifying; vindication; defence; the showing of a sufficient reason in court for bringing an action [Law]; the divine act of acquitting a sinner, and accepting him as just [Theol.]; the act of adjusting type or lines [Print.].
justificative, *a.* *jus*-te-fe-kay-tiv, justifying; that has power to justify.
justificatory, *a.* *jus*-te-fe-*kay*-to-re, vindicatory.
justifier, *n.* *jus*-te-fy-er, one who justifies; one who vindicates, pardons, or absolves; an appliance for justifying type [Print.].
justify, *v.t.* *jus*-te-fy, to prove or show to be just; to vindicate; to absolve; to accept and treat as just on faith and repentance [Theol.]; to space out lines or type to even length, and thus make every line range [Print.]: *v.i.* to conform exactly; to range (of type). (Fr. *justifier*.)
justle, *v.i.* *jus*-sl, to jostle.
justly, *ad.* *just*-le, in a just manner; accurately.
justness *n.* *just*-ness, the quality of being just; correctness; uprightness; justice.
jut, *n.* jut, a projection: *v.i.* to shoot forward; to project beyond the main body. (*jet*.)
jute, *n.* joot, the fibre of the inner bark of *Corchorus capsularis* or *C. olitorius*, from which coarse and other fabrics are woven; gunny. (Bengali.)
Jutes, *n.pl.* joots, the invaders from Jutland, under Hengist, who settled in Kent. (A.S. *Jutas*, Jutes.)
jutty, *n.* *jut*-te, a jetty.
juvenescence, *n.* *joo*-ve-*nes*-ence, a becoming young.

juvenescent, *a.* *joo*-ve-*nes*-ent, becoming or being young. (L. *juvenescens*, growing young.)
juvenile, *a.* *joo*-ve-nile, youthful; pertaining or suited to youth; *n.* a youth or young person. (L. *juvenis*, young: Fr. *juvenil.*)
juvenileness, *n.* *joo*-ve-*nile*-ness, youthfulness.
juvenilia, *n.pl.* *joo*-ve-*nil*-e-a, works written in youth. (L.)
juvenility, *n.* *joo*-ve-*nil*-e-te, the state of being young; the manner of a youth; youthfulness.
juxtapose, *v.t.* juks-ta-*poze*, to place near to.
juxtaposition, *n.* *juks*-ta-po-*zish*-on, the state of being placed in nearness or contiguity. (L. *juxta*, nigh to, and *position.*)
juzail, *n.* joo-*zale*, a large musket formerly used by the Afghans. (Afghan.)

K

K, kay, a voiceless guttural consonant, borrowed from Greek; it is invariably pronounced hard, except before the letter *n*, when it is silent, as in *knee*, *knife*.
kaaba, *n.* ka-*ah*-ba *or* *kah*-ba, the shrine at Mecca containing the sacred Black Stone (traditionally given by Gabriel to Abraham) towards which Moslems turn in prayer. (Ar., the square building.)
kaama, *n.* *kah*-ma, the hartebeest. (S. African name.)
kabbala, *n.* *kab*-a-la, cabbala.
Kabyle, *n.* ka-*bile*, one of the agricultural Berbers living in the highlands of Algeria; the dialect of the Kabyles. (Fr.)
kaddish, *n.* *kad*-ish, a part of the Jewish religious service, used esp. for mourning. (Aramaic.)
kadi, *n.* *kah*-de, cadi.
Kaffir, *n.* *kaf*-fir, a native of Kaffraria, in Cape Province, S. Africa; a Bantu; the language of these people: *n.pl.* South African mining shares [Stock Exchange slang]. (Ar., infidel.)
kafila, *n.* *kaf*-e-la, a caravan; a train of camels.
Kafir, *n.* *kaf*-fir, a native of Kafiristan, in Eastern Afghanistan.
kaftan, *n.* *kaf*-tan, a caftan.
kago, *n.* *kah*-go, in Japan, a palanquin. (Jap. *kango.*)
kagu, *n.* *kah*-goo, a bird, *Rhinochetus jubatus*, allied to the cranes, peculiar to New Caledonia.
kail, *n.* kale, a curly cabbage; kale; cole.
kailyard, *n.* *kale*-yard, a kale-yard. **Kailyard School,** a group of early 20th-cent. Scots writers treating of humble Scottish life with much use of local colour and vernacular.
kainite, *n.* *kay*-nite, a fertiliser consisting of magnesium sulphate and potassium chloride. (Gr. *kainos*, new.)
kainozoic, *a.* and *n.* ky-no-*zoh*-ik, cainozoic.
kaiser, *n.* *ky*-zer, the title taken by the sovereigns of the Holy Roman Empire, in imitation of the Cæsars; an emperor, esp. of the former German Empire (1871–1918). (L. *Cæsar.*)
kaiserism, *n.* *ky*-zer-rizm, autocratic rule, policy, etc.
kaka, *n.* *kah*-ka, the New Zealand parrot, *Nestor meridionalis.*
kakapo, *n.* *kah*-ka-po, the owl parrot of New Zealand, *Stringops habroptilus*, a flightless nocturnal bird nesting in burrows.
kakemono, *n.* kah-ke-*moh*-no, a Japanese hanging picture, unrolling vertically. (Jap.)
kakistocracy, *n.* *kak*-is-*tok*-ra-se, government by the worst men. (Gr. *kakistos*, very bad, *krateo*, rule.)
kakodyl, *n.* *kak*-o-dil, cacodyl.
kala-azar, *n.* *kah*-la-a-*zahr*, a very dangerous non-malarial remittent fever of parts of India, Burma, etc. (Assam, *kālā*, black, *āzār*, disease.)
kale, *n.* kale, a curly-leafed cabbage; colewort; a vegetable soup, esp. containing kale [Scot.]; sea-kale, a culinary vegetable of the genus *Crambe.*
kaleidoscope, *n.* ka-*ly*-do-skope, an optical instrument, which, by the movement of internal reflecting surfaces, presents to the eye a variety of colours and symmetrical forms. (Gr. *kalos*, beautiful, *eidos*, form, and *skopeo*, view.)
kaleidoscopic, *a.* ka-*ly*-do-*skop*-ik, pertaining to or formed by the kaleidoscope; changeful in colour or appearance.
kalendar, *n.* *kal*-en-dar, calendar.
kalends, *n.* *kal*-endz, calends.
Kalevala, *n.* *kah*-lay-*vah*-la, a collection of ancient Finnish epics. (Finnish, literally, land of heroes.)
kale-yard, *n.* a kitchen-garden [Scot.].
kali, *n.* *kay*-le, a species of saltwort, the ashes of which were used in making glass. (Ar.)
kalif, *n.* *kay*-lif, caliph.
kaligenous, *a.* kal-*lij*-e-nus, forming alkalies [Chem.].
kalinite, *n.* *kal*-e-nite, native alum.
kalium, *n.* *kay*-le-um, potassium.
kalmia, *n.* *kal*-me-a, any evergreen shrub of a small genus including the American laurel, *Kalmia latifolia.* (Peter *Kalm*, Swed. botanist, *d.* 1779.)
Kalmuck, *n.* *kal*-muk, one of a Mongolian tribe of nomads that has spread east and west from Central Asia. (Russ. *kalmiukār.*)
kalong, *n.* *kah*-long, the Malay fox-bat, *Pteropus edulis.*
kalpa, *n.* *kal*-pa, in the Hindu chronology, the period of 4,320,000,000 solar years separating one destruction of the world from the next. (Sans.)
kam, *a.* kam, cam; awry. (Gael.)
kamarband, *n.* *kum*-mer-bund, a cummerbund.
kame, *n.* kame, an esker.
Kamerad, *n.* kam-er-*rahd*, comrade (Ger.); used in the War of 1914–18 by German soldiers offering surrender.
kamichi, *n.* *kah*-me-she, the horned screamer, *Palamedes cornuta*, of the swamps of Guiana and Brazil. (Tupi.)
kampong, *n.* kam-*pong*, a Malay village. (Malay.)
kamptulicon, *n.* kamp-*tew*-le-kon, a floor-cloth composed of cork and rubber, or a substitute, and canvas. (Gr. *kamptos*, bendable, *oulos*, thick.)
kamsin, *n.* kam-*seen*, the khamsin.
Kanaka, *n.* ka-*nak*-a, a native of the Sandwich Islands; formerly, one of these under contract as a labourer in Australia. (Hawaiian, a man.)
kangaroo, *n.* *kang*-ga-roo, any species of *Macropus*, a leaping marsupial with fore-legs short and hind-legs long and powerful. **brush kangaroo,** a wallaby, any small species of *Macropus.* **rat kangaroo,** any species of *Potorous.* **rock kangaroo,** any species of *Petrogale.* **tree kangaroo,** any species of *Dendrolagus.* (Origin uncertain, but perhaps a native name.)
kangaroo-apple, *n.* the oval, yellow fruit of *Solanum aviculare.*
kangaroo-grass, *n.* the tall Australian forage grass, *Thernida trianadra.*
kangaroo-rat, *n.* the potoroo, or rat kangaroo; a nocturnal burrowing rodent of the genus *Dipodomys*, of the deserts of the western U.S.A.
Kantian, *a.* *kant*-e-an, pertaining to the German philosopher Emmanuel Kant (1724–1804), or to his philosophical system: *n.* a Kantist.
Kantianism, *n.* *kant*-e-an-izm, a Kantian view or theory; Kantian criticism.
Kantist, *n.* *kant*-ist, a disciple or follower of Kant.
Kanuck, *n.* ka-*nuk*, a Canuck, a French Canadian.
kaolin, *n.* *kay*-o-lin, china-clay, obtained chiefly from decomposed feldspar. (Chin. *Kaoling*, place where first found.)
kaolinize, *v.t.* *kay*-o-le-nize, to make into kaolin.
kapnography, *n.* kap-*nog*-ra-fe, the art of designing with a fine point on a smoked surface. (Gr. *kapnos*, smoke, *graphia*, writing.)
kapok, *n.* *kah*-pok, a light oily fibre of the silk-cotton tree. (Malay *kāpoq.*)
kaput, *a.* ka-*poot*, finished; all gone; dead [Slang]. (Ger.)
karagan, *n.* *ka*-ra-gan, the corsac. (Russ.)
Karaite, *n.* *kay*-ra-ite, a Jew adhering strictly to Scriptural as opposed to rabbinical tradition. (Heb.)
karakul, *n.* *ka*-ra-kul, caracul.
karma, *n.* *kahr*-ma, the Buddhist theory that all causations produce inevitable consequences and that the conditions of one's future existence are predetermined by his past actions. (Sans. *karma*, work.)
Karmathian, *n.* kahr-*may*-the-an, one of a Mohammedan rationalistic sect, founded by Al-Karmat in the ninth century: *a.* pertaining to this.
karoo, *n.* ka-*roo*, an elevated, arid table-land, esp. the Great Karoo of central S. Africa. (Hottentot.)
kaross, *n.* ka-*ross*, a South African native rug or cloak made of furs. (Not native; perhaps as *cuirass.*)
karri, *n.* *ka*-re, a deep-red and very tough Australian wood, similar to jarrah.

karyokinesis, *n.* *ka*-re-o-ke-*nee*-sis, mitosis. (Gr. *karyo*, nut, *kinesis*, movement.)
karyoplasm, *n.* *ka*-re-o-plazm, the protoplasm of the nucleus of a cell [Biol.].
katabatic, *a.* kat-a-*bat*-ik, pertaining to the downward motion of air [Meteor.]. (Gr. *katabainein*, to go down.)
katabolism, *n.* ka-*tab*-o-lizm, the breaking down of complex organic compounds into simpler compounds; the process by which this change is effected. (Gr. *kataballein*, to throw down.)
katydid, *n.* *kay*-te-did, a green tree-grasshopper of N. America, so called from the stridulating sound it makes with its wing-covers.
kauri, *n.* *kaw*-re, a New Zealand conifer of the genus *Agathis*; its valuable timber or resin. (Maori.)
kava, *n.* *kah*-va, an intoxicating Polynesian drink prepared from certain species of pepper. (Maori.)
kavass, *n.* ka-*vass*, a Turkish armed constable, guard, or courier. (Turk.)
kayak, *n.* *ky*-ak, an Eskimo canoe made of seal-skin over a wooden frame.
kayles, *n.pl.* kaylz, the game of ninepins [Scot.].
kea, *n.* *kee*-a, the New Zealand parrot, *Nestor notabilis*, which feeds on carrion and kills sheep. (Maori.).
keblah, *n.* *keb*-lah, the direction of the temple at Mecca.
keck, *n.* kek, a retching: *v.i.* to retch, as in an effort to vomit. (Imit.)
keckle, *v.i.* *kek*-kl, to cackle; to chuckle [Scots.]. (Imit.)
keckle, *v.t.* *kek*-kl, to wind rope, etc., round a cable to prevent its being chafed [Naut.].
keckling, *n.* *kek*-ling, rope or chain, etc., wound round cables to keep them from chafing [Naut.].
kecks, *n.* keks, kex [Bot.].
kedge, *n.* kedj, a small anchor used in warping: *v.t.* to warp, as a ship; to move by means of a kedge. (Perhaps as *cadge*.)
kedger, *n.* *kedj*-er, a kedge.
kedgeree, *n.* *kedj*-er-ree, a spiced Indian stew of rice, peas, onions, and butter, etc.; a European breakfast-dish made with cold fish or meat, rice, eggs, and condiments. (Hind. *khichri*.)
keek, *v.i.* keek, to peep; to look pryingly. (Scots.)
keel, *n.* keel, the lowest part of a ship's structure, extending from stem to stern and supporting the whole; a ship in general; a flat-bottomed barge; the lowest petal of a papilionaceous corolla [Bot.]; a projecting ridge [Anat.]: *v.t.* to plough with a keel; to navigate; to turn up the keel; to show the bottom: *v.i.* to run on the keel. **false keel,** a second keel bolted under the main keel. **sliding keel,** a centre-board. (Ice. *kjölr*, keel.)
keelage, *n.* *keel*-aj, duty required for a ship entering certain harbours.
keel-boat, *n.* *keel*-bote, a large covered river-boat with a keel but no sails [U.S.A.].
keeled, *a.* keeld, having a keel; carinated [Bot.].
keeler, *n.* *keel*-er, a small shallow tub; a salt-box used in salting mackerel. (A.S. *cēlan*, to cool.)
keel-haul, *v.t.* to haul under the keel of a ship, esp. to punish by drawing the culprit under the bottom of a vessel by ropes from the yardarms on each side.
keeling, *n.* *keel*-ing, a small cod, or a codling.
keelivine, *n.* *keel*-e-vin, a lead pencil [Scots.].
keelless, *a.* *keel*-less, not having a keel [esp. Anat.].
keelman, *n.* *keel*-man, a man who works a keel or barge; a dealer in keels; a lighterman on the Tyne.
keelson, *n.* *kel*-sun, the kelson [Naut.].
keen, *a.* keen, eager; sharp; having a very fine edge; piercing; severe; bitter; acute of mind. **keen prices,** prices allowing barely a margin for profit. **keen as mustard,** extremely eager. (A.S. *cene*.)
keen, *n.* keen, a wail; lamentation over a corpse: *v.i.* to raise a keen. (Ir. *caoine*.)
keener, *n.* *keen*-er, a professional mourner [Ir.].
keenly, *ad.* *keen*-le, in a keen manner.
keenness, *n.* *keen*-ness, the quality of being keen.
keen-witted, *a.* discerning; quick at repartee.
***keep,** *v.t.* keep, to hold or retain; to have in custody for security; to preserve; to protect; to detain; to tend and look after; to supply with necessaries of life; to maintain; to attend to; to conduct; to fulfil; to perform; to observe; to have in pay; to remain in; to lodge; to have in stock; to keep in. **keep a term,** in English universities, to reside during a term. **keep back,** to reserve; to withhold; to restrain. **keep company with,** to associate with; to accompany. **keep down,** to prevent from rising. **keep from,** to restrain; to prevent approach. **keep house,** to maintain a family state; to be confined to the house; to housekeep. **keep in,** to prevent from escape; to restrain; to subdue. **keep off,** to hinder from approach or attack. **keep on foot,** to maintain ready for action. **keep out,** to hinder from entering or taking possession. **keep time,** *see* **time. keep under,** *see* **under. keep up,** to maintain; to prevent from falling or diminution. *p.* and *pp.* **kept.** (A.S. *cepan*.)
keep, *v.i.* keep, to remain in any state; to last; to endure; to lodge; to dwell. **keep from,** to abstain; to refrain. **keep on,** to go forward; to proceed. **keep to,** to adhere strictly. **keep up,** to remain unsubdued; to continue; not to cease. *p.* and *pp.* **kept.**
keep, *n.* keep, care; maintenance; necessary nutriment, or the expense of this; that which protects; the strongest tower of a castle, the place of final retreat for a garrison; a donjon; a place of confinement. **for keeps,** for good; for permanent possession [Coll.].
keeper, *n.* *keep*-er, he who or that which keeps; one who holds or has possession of anything; one who retains in custody; one who has the care of a park or other enclosure; one who has the care, custody, or superintendence of anything; a ring to guard a wedding ring; a lock-nut, or other holding device. **Keeper of the Great Seal,** the officer entrusted with the Great Seal of England, now the Lord Chancellor. **Keeper of the King's Conscience,** the Lord Chancellor.
keepership, *n.* *keep*-er-ship, the office of keeper.
keeping, *n.* *keep*-ing, a holding; restraint; custody; guard; preservation; maintenance; keep; just proportion; congruity; consistency.
keeping-room, *n.* the sitting-room in which a family generally lives [U.S.A.].
keepsake, *n.* *keep*-sake, anything kept or given to be kept for the sake of the giver; a token of remembrance.
keeshond, *n.* *kays*- or *kees*-hond, a small thick-coated dog, formerly used on Dutch barges. (Dut. *kees*, terrier, *hond*, dog.)
keeve, *n.* keev, a large tub for fermenting liquors in; a mash-tub: *v.t.* to set in a keeve for fermentation; to tip up a cart. (A.S. *cyf*, a tub.)
keg, *n.* keg, a small cask or barrel. (Ice. *kaggi*.)
keir, *n.* keer, a boiler or vat for liquor used in bleaching. (Ice. *ker*.)
keitloa, *n.* *kate*-lo-a, a variety of S. African rhinoceros with two horns of nearly equal length. (Sechuana.)
kelk, *n.* kelk, the roe of a fish. (Dial.)
kell, *n.* kel, the caul or omentum; a cobweb; a woman's hair-net. (*caul*.)
kelp, *n.* kelp, a coarse seaweed; calcined ash of this, formerly used in glass- and soap-making, now in the manufacture of iodine.
kelpie, *n.* *kel*-pe, an imaginary water-sprite, generally in the form of a horse. (Scots.)
kelson, *n.* *kel*-sun, the inner keel; the part of a ship's structure that rests on the keel. (From *keel*, but origin doubtful.)
kelt, *n.* kelt, a spent salmon; cloth of native black wool. (Both Scots, and of unknown origin.)
Kelt, *n.* kelt, a Celt.
kelter, *n.* *kel*-ter, good order or condition (Dial.)
kelvin, *n.* *kel*-vin, the commercial unit of energy, or Board of Trade Unit of 3,600 joules; the kilowatt hour [Elect.]. (Lord *Kelvin*, *d.* 1907, British physicist.)
kemp, *n.* kemp, the coarse rough hairs of wool.
kempy, *a.* *kemp*-e, abounding in kemps.
ken, *n.* ken, view; reach of sight or knowledge: *v.t.* to know; to see and recognize at a distance; to descry: *v.i.* to look round. (A.S. *cennan*, to declare.)
Kendal-green, *n.* *ken*-dal-green, a green woollen cloth made originally at Kendal.
kennel, *n.* *ken*-nel, a shelter for a dog; a building and enclosure for a pack of hounds; a pack of hounds; the hole of a fox, etc.; a haunt: *v.t.* and *i.* to confine or live in or as in a kennel. (O.Fr. *chenil*.)

kennel, *n.* *ken*-nel, the watercourse of a street; a gutter. (M.E. *canel*, canal.)
kennel-book, *n.* a book in which is entered the details of the breeding of dogs.
kennel-coal, *n.* cannel coal.
kennel-maid, *n.* a woman employed in the tending and breeding of dogs.
kenning, *n.* *ken*-ing, mental knowledge or recognition; any metaphorical term as used in ancient Norse poetry to denote some common thing [Literature].
kenosis, *n.* ke-*noh*-sis, the laying aside by Christ of his divinity on his incarnation. (Gr., emptying.)
Kentish, *a.* *kent*-ish, belonging to Kent. **Kentish balsam,** dog's-mercury. **Kentish fire,** ironic or barracking clapping, three strokes at a time. **Kentish man,** a native of West Kent, as distinct from a native of East Kent (the Medway being the boundary), known as a "Man of Kent." **Kentish rag,** a limestone of the lower greensand found in Kent.
kentledge, *n.* *kent*-ledj, scrap iron; pigs of iron used as ballast [Naut.]. (Origin unknown.)
képi, *n.* *kep*-e, a French military peaked cap. (Fr.)
keramic, *a.* ke-*ram*-ik, ceramic, pertaining to pottery.
kerargyrite, *n.* ke-*rahr*-je-rite, native silver chloride; horn-silver. (Gr. *keras*, horn, *argyros*, silver.)
keratin, *n.* *ke*-ra-tin, the chief chemical constituent of hair, feathers, nails, and horn.
keratinize, *v.t.* and *i.* ke-*rat*-e-nize, to make or to become keratinous.
keratinous, *a.* ke-*rat*-e-nus, horny.
keratitis, *n.* ke-ra-*ty*-tis, acute or chronic inflammation of the cornea. (Gr. *keras*, a horn.)
keratogenous, *a.* ke-ra-*toj*-e-nus, horn-producing [Anat.].
keratose, *a.* *ke*-ra-tohs, horny: *n.* the horny substance of the skeleton of certain sponges, etc.
keraunograph, *n.* ke-*raw*-no-graf, an instrument for detecting and recording distant thunderstorms; a figure impressed by lightning on an object struck. (Gr. *keraunos*, thunderbolt, and *graph.*)
kerb, *n.* kerb, the edge of the pavement; the curb. **kerb market,** a stock market conducted near a Stock Exchange after its closing hour.
kerbstone, *n.* *kerb*-stone, the stone of which the kerb is made.
kerchief, *n.* *ker*-chif, a square piece of cloth to cover the head. (O.Fr. *covrechef*, head-cover.)
kerchiefed, *a.* *ker*-chift, hooded; covered.
kerf, *n.* kerf, the slit or channel made by a saw or cutting instrument; the place where a cut has been made; that which is cut off. (A.S. *cyrf*, cutting.)
kermes, *n.* *ker*-meez, a stuff yielding a crimson dye from the dried bodies of *Coccus ilicis*; the dried bodies, also the pregnant female, of this insect. **kermes mineral,** trisulphide of antimony, red in colour.
kermess, *n.* *ker*-mess, a fair in Germany and the Low Countries. (Dut. *kermis.*)
kern, *n.* kern, an Irish or Celtic foot-soldier; an idle vagabond [Old Law]. (Ir. *ceatharn.*)
kern, *n.* kern, that part of a type which hangs over the body or shank [Print.]. (Fr. *carne*, edge.)
kern, *v.i.* kern, to harden; to take the form of corns; to granulate. (*Kernel.*)
kernel, *n.* *ker*-nl, the enclosure in a husk or shell; the edible contents of a nut or fruit-stone; the central part, the nucleus, or the essential point [Fig.]: *v.i.* to harden or ripen into kernels. (A.S. *cyrnel*, a little corn.)
kernelled, *a.* *ker*-nld, having a kernel.
kernelly, *a.* *ker*-nl-e, full of or resembling kernels.
kerosene, *n.* *ke*-ro-seen, paraffin oil, a refined petroleum. (Gr. *keros*, wax.)
kerria, *n.* *ke*-re-a, the rosaceous yellow-flowered hardy deciduous shrub, *Kerria japonica*. (M. Kerr, early 19th-cent. Engl. botanist in Ceylon.)
kersey, *n.* *ker*-ze, a smooth-faced cloth, so called from Kersey, in Suffolk, where once made.
kerseymere, *n.* *ker*-ze-meer, cassimere.
kestrel, *n.* *kes*-trel, the small hawk or falcon, *Falco tinnunculus*. (O.Fr. *quercerelle.*)
ket, *n.* ket, carrion; any sort of filth. (Dial. Eng.)
ketch, *n.* ketch, a small vessel with two masts, the short mizen stepped forward of the sternpost. (M.E. *cache*, catch.)
ketchup, *n.* *ketch*-up, a sauce made of mushrooms, tomatoes, or walnuts. (Malay.)
ketone, *n.* *kee*-tone, a hydrocarbon derivative; a member of a group of organic compounds produced by the dry distillation of certain acids or by the oxidation of secondary alcohols. (Variation of *acetone.*)
★**kettle,** *n.* *ket*-tl, a vessel of iron or other metal for heating and boiling liquids, esp. water; a pot-hole [Geol.]. **a pretty kettle of fish,** a mess. (Scand.)
kettledrum, *n.* *ket*-tl-drum, a copper or brass hemispherical drum with a parchment head.
kettle-holder, *n.* a protector for the hand in holding a hot kettle.
keuper, *n.* *koy*-per, the upper portion of the Triassic system, chiefly marls and sandstones [Geol.]. (Ger.)
kevel, *n.* *kev*-el, one of a pair of pegs or cleats for belaying ropes [Naut.]; a stone-breaker's hammer.
kex, *n.* keks, kecks, fool's parsley, *Æthusa cynapium*; dried stalks of certain umbelliferous plants. (Origin unknown.)
★**key,** *n.* kee, an implement for opening and closing a lock; that by which something is screwed or turned; a keystone [Arch.]; a little lever or piece by which the fingers play on an instrument or operate a typewriter or mechanical contrivance; a system of tones based on their relation to a key-note from which it is named [Mus.]; that which serves to explain anything difficult to be understood; a solution; a translation; a place which, by its prominence or other advantage, is used to control land, sea, etc.; a piece of wood or metal let into the back of a board to prevent warping; a cotter; a winged fruit, as that of the ash: *v.t.* to fasten with a key or bolt [Mech.]. **House of Keys,** the Manx legislature. **key industry,** an industry without the activity of which others could not survive. **key man,** an indispensable worker in an industry, etc. **key map,** a map in outline supplementary to a fuller map. **key money,** a premium paid by a new tenant on entering into possession. **key move,** the opening move, esp. in the solution of a chess problem. **key position,** a place the occupancy of which secures the possession of some area [Mil.]. **key signature,** the sign indicating the key in which music is written. **key up,** to bring up to tone. **Power of the Keys,** the ecclesiastical authority of the Papacy. (O.E. *cæg.*)
key, *n.* kee, a ledge of rocks near the surface of the water; a cay.
keyboard, *n.* *kee*-bord, a range of the keys, as those of a pianoforte, organ, carillon, typewriter, etc.
keybolt, *n.* *kee*-bohlt, a bolt held by a cotter.
key-bugle, *n.* *kee*-bew-gl, a bugle fitted with keys, usually six.
keyed, *a.* keed, furnished with keys; set to a key; fastened, wound, etc. by a key; having a keystone.
keyhole, *n.* *kee*-hole, the aperture in a door or lock for receiving a key. **keyhole saw,** a very narrow bladed saw for cutting keyholes.
keyless, *a.* *kee*-less, having no key; fashioned to be wound up without a detachable key (of watches, etc.).
key-note, *n.* *kee*-note, the fundamental and lowest note of a scale [Mus.]; the basis or central fact (of a policy, etc.).
key-ring, *n.* *kee*-ring, a ring for a bunch of keys.
keystone, *n.* *kee*-stone, the central stone of an arch which binds the whole [Arch.].
khaddar, *n.* *kad*-ar, an Indian homespun cloth. (Hind.)
khaki, *a.* *kah*-ke, brownish greyish yellow; *n.* a twilled fabric of this colour used for army uniforms; woollen material for these. (Hind. *khak*, dust.)
khamsin, *n.* *kam*-sin, kam-*seen*, a hot southerly sand-bearing wind blowing in Egypt for about 50 days from mid-March. (Ar. fifty.)
Khan, *n.* kahn, title of a governor or other dignitary in Persia, Afghanistan, etc. (Pers., prince.)
khan, *n.* kahn, an unfurnished rest-house or caravansary in the Near East. (Turk.)
khanate, *n.* *kahn*-ate, the jurisdiction of, or the territory ruled by, a khan.
kheddah, *n.* *ked*-da, an enclosure for the capture of wild elephants. (Hind.)
Khediva, *n.* ke-*dee*-va, the wife of a Khedive.
Khedival, *a.* ke-*dee*-val, pertaining to a Khedive.
Khedivate, *n.* ke-*dee*-vat, the office, term of office, or jurisdiction of a Khedive.
Khedive, *n.* ke-*deev*, the official title of the Viceroy

in Egypt from 1867 until its supersession by "Sultan" in 1914. (Turk.)
Khedivial, *a.* ke-*dee*-ve-al, Khedival.
khidmutgar, *n. kid*-mut-gar, a man-servant who waits at table. (Hind.)
khus-khus, *n. koos*-koos, an Indian grass, *Andropogon iwaranchusa*, yielding an essential oil; its fibrous aromatic root, used for making mats, baskets, etc.
kiang, *n.* ke-*ang*, the Tibetan wild ass. (Native.)
kibble, *n. kib*-bl, an iron bucket for raising ore from a mine; a well-bucket. (Dial.)
kibe, *n.* kibe, a chap occasioned by cold; an ulcerated chilblain, esp. on the heel. (Origin unknown.)
kibed, *a.* kybd, affected with chilblains.
kibitka, *n.* ke-*bit*-ka, a rude covered vehicle for use in winter; a nomad Tartar tent. (Russ.)
Kiblah, *n. kib*-lah, keblah.
kibosh, *n. ky*-bosh, absurdity. **put the kibosh on,** to dispose of, to silence or squelch [Slang].
kiby, *a. ky*-be, affected with kibes.
*****kick,** *n.* kik, a blow with or thrust of the foot; recoil: *v.t.* to strike with the foot; to strike backwards or upwards; to thrust out the foot or feet with violence; to manifest opposition; to resist; to recoil. **to kick against,** to be strongly opposed to, to resist. (Origin doubtful.)
kicker, *n. kik*-er, one who kicks; a horse that kicks; a third card kept with a pair [Poker].
kick-off, *n. kik*-off, the first kick of the ball in football; the commencement of anything.
kickshaw, *n. kik*-shaw, anything fantastic or uncommon; a light dainty dish. (Fr. *quelque chose*, something.)
kid, *n.* kid, a young goat; kidskin; a child; a term of address or endearment [Slang]: *pl.* gloves of kid: *v.t.* to bring forth, as a goat; to deceive; to humbug [Slang].
kid, *n.* kid, a faggot; a bundle of heath and furze.
kid, *n.* kid, a small wooden tub or vessel [Naut.].
kidder, *n. kid*-der, one who makes a corner in corn to enhance the price.
Kidderminster *n. kid*-der-min-ster, a reversible carpeting so called from the town where it was originally manufactured.
kiddle, *n. kid*-dl, a wicker fish-weir. (Dial. Eng.)
kiddy, *n. kid*-e, a small child.
kidling, *n. kid*-ling, a young kid.
kidnap, *v.t. kid*-nap, to seize and forcibly carry away any person. (*kid*, a child, *nab*, to steal.)
kidnapper, *n. kid*-nap-per, a man-stealer.
kidney, *n. kid*-ne, one of two oblong flattened glands, situated in the rear region of the loins, and embedded in fatty tissue, which secrete the urine and pass it into the bladder; anything like a kidney; sort, kind, or disposition. (Origin unknown.) (A.S.)
kidney-bean, *n.* a bean of kidney shape; the French bean; the scarlet runner. **Chinese kidney-bean,** wistaria.
kidney-vetch, *n. kid*-ne-vetch, the leguminous plant lady's finger, *Anthyllis vulneraria*.
kidney-wort, *n.* local name for pennywort, navelwort, star saxifrage, etc.
kief, *n.* keef, the drowsy condition produced by using bhang, etc.; pleasant idleness; Indian hemp smoked to bring about this state. (Ar.)
kiekie, *n. kee*-kee, a climbing shrub of New Zealand; its fleshy edible berry.
kier, *n.* keer, a boiler; a vat in which textile fabrics are boiled in bleaching.
kieselguhr, *n. kee*-zel-*goor*, a diatomaceous earth used chiefly as a heat insulator and for polishing purposes. (Ger. *Kiesel*, flint, *Guhr*, earthy deposit.)
kilderkin, *n. kil*-der-kin. a cask of half-barrel, or 18 gallons, capacity; this measure. (Dut. *kinderkin.*)
kilerg, *n. kil*-erg, a thousand ergs (a unit of work) [Physics].
kill, *v.t.* kil, to deprive of life; to slay; to slaughter; to suppress; to deaden; to make neutral by using contrast; to pass (time) idly; to overwhelm with charms, etc.; to hit a ball so strongly that it cannot be returned [Tennis]: *v.i.* to put to death; to fascinate [Fig.]: *n.* the act of killing; an animal, or animals, killed. **in at the kill,** present at the finish. (Origin unknown.)
killadar, *n. kil*-la-dar, the commandant or governor of a fort in India. (Hind.)
killas, *n. kil*-las, clay-slate [Geol.]. (Cornish name.)
killdeer, *n. kil*-deer, the North American migratory plover, *Ægialitis vociferus*. (Imit. of cry.)
killer, *n. kil*-ler, one who kills or slaughters; a homicidal maniac; the voracious dolphin, *Orca gladiator*.
killick, *n. kil*-lik, a small anchor, or a stone used as such.
killinite, *n. kil*-in-ite, a greenish amorphous mineral formed by decomposition of spodumene. (*Killiney*, Eire, where found.)
killjoy, *n. kil*-joy, a gloomy person whose presence has a depressing effect.
kill-time, *n.* an occupation, etc., merely to pass time.
kiln, *n.* kil *or* kiln, a furnace, oven, or pile for drying, burning, or hardening anything. (A.S. *cyln.*)
kiln-dry, *v.t. kil*-dry *or kiln*-dry, to dry in a kiln.
kilo-, *kil*-o, a prefix denoting that the measure with which it is combined is multiplied by one thousand. (Gr. *chilioi*, a thousand.)
kilocycle, *n. kil*-o-*sy*-kl, a thousand cycles, or alternations, in a second (the unit of frequency employed for sound and radio waves).
kilogramme, *n. kil*-o-gram, a thousand grammes, or 2·204 lb. avoirdupois. (Fr.)
kilogrammetre, *n. kil*-o-*gram*-me-ter, the energy required to raise a kilogramme to the height of one metre, or about 7·25 foot-pounds.
kilolitre, *n. kil*-o-lee-ter, a thousand litres, or 220 gallons.
kilometre, *n. kil*-o-mee-ter, a thousand metres, or ·62137 (slightly under five-eighths) of a mile.
kilowatt, *n. kil*-o-wot, a thousand watts [Elect.].
kilt, *n.* kilt, a short thickly pleated skirt-like garment worn chiefly by Scotsmen: *v.t.* kilt, to tuck up, as the clothes; to gather into pleats. (Scand.)
kilter, *n. kil*-ter, kelter.
kiltie, *n. kil*-te, a nickname for a soldier in a kilted regiment.
kimmer, *n. kim*-er, a woman neighbour, a cummer [Scots].
Kimmeridge clay, *n. kim*-mer-ij-*klay*, an oolitic clay found at Kimmeridge, in the Isle of Purbeck.
kimono, *n.* ke-*moh*-noh, a loose wide-sleeved outer robe; a light dressing-gown. (Jap.)
kin, *n.* kin, relatives, esp. by consanguinity; kindred; persons of the same race: *a.* of the same nature; kindred; congenial. (A.S. *cynn.*)
kinæsthesis, *n.* ky-nees-*thee*-sis, the sense by which, through the muscles, tendons, etc., bodily movement, weight, pressure, posture, etc. are perceived. (Gr. *kinein*, to move, *aisthesis*, perception.)
kinæsthetic, *a.* ky-nees-*thet*-ik, pertaining to kinæsthesis.
kinchin, *n. kin*-chin, a child. **kinchin lay,** practice of robbing children sent on errands [both Slang].
kincob, *n. king*-kob, a heavy silk with gold or silver thread-work. (Anglo-Indian word.)
*****kind,** *n.* kynd, race; genus; sort or species; nature; natural propensity or determination; *a.* disposed to do good to others and to make them happy; proceeding from tenderness or goodness of heart; benevolent; gentle; indulgent. **a kind of,** a sort of; falling roughly into the class of. **in kind,** payment in goods instead of money; repayment of manner, etc., in the same way in which it was given. (A.S. *cynd*, nature.)
kindergarten, *n. kin*-der-*gar*-ten, an infant school in which education is imparted by games and object lessons. (Ger. *Kinder*, children, *Garten*, garden.)
kindle, *v.t. kin*-dl, to set fire to or to light; to inflame, as the passions; to provoke; to excite to action; to animate: *v.i.* to take fire; to become excited; to be roused. (Scand.)
kindle, *v.i. kin*-dl, to bring forth young: *n.* a litter or brood. (*kind.*)
kindler, *n. kin*-dler, he who or that which kindles.
kindliness, *n. kynd*-le-ness, the state of being kindly; affectionate disposition.
kindling, *n. kin*-dling, the act of kindling; fuel for kindling.
kindly, *a. kynd*-le, kind; benevolent; beneficial: *ad.* in a kind manner.
kindness, *n. kynd*-ness, the quality of being kind; sympathy; goodness.
kindred, *n. kin*-dred, relationship by birth or marriage; relatives: *a.* related; congenial; of the like nature. (A.S. *cynn*, kin, *ræden*, state.)

kine, *n.pl.* kine, cows. (A.S. *cy*, cows.)
kinema, *n. kin*-e-ma, cinema, a picture palace.
kinematic, *a.* kin-e-*mat*-ik, belonging to kinematics: *n.pl.* the science of pure motion, irrespective of the force producing it. (Gr. *kinema*, motion.)
kinematograph, *n. kin*-e-*mat*-o-graf, cinematograph.
kinesiatrics, *n.* kin-e-sy-*at*-riks, kinesipathy.
kinesipathy, *n.* kin-e-*sip*-a-the, the treatment of disease by muscular movement. (Gr. *kinesis*, movement, *pathos*, suffering.)
kinetic, *a.* ke-*net*-ik, of or belonging to motion: *n.pl.* the science of the action of forces in causing motion. (Gr. *kinetikos.*)
kinetoscope, *n.* ke-*net*-o-skope, an early form of cinematograph.
king, *n.* king, the sovereign of a nation, usually hereditary; the monarch; the chief; a card having the conventional picture of a king; the chief piece in the game of chess: *v.t.* to supply with a king or make royal: *v.i.* to act as a king. **king cobra,** the large and very venomous serpent *Naja hannah*, of S. Asia. **king fern,** the royal fern, *Osmunda regalis*. **king of arms,** any of the chief officers of the College of Heralds, viz. Garter, Norroy, and Clarenceux (England), and Lyon (Scotland). **King of Kings,** the Deity; Christ; a title used by various Oriental monarchs. **king of the herrings,** the rabbit fish, *Chimæra monstrosa*. **king penguin,** a large variety of penguin found in the Antarctic and the Falkland Islands. **King's Bench,** *see* **bench. king's colour,** in the British army, the Union Jack carried on the right of the regimental colour. **King's Counsel,** *see* **counsel. King's English,** *see* **English. king's evidence,** *see* **evidence. king's evil,** scrofula. **King's messenger,** *see* **messenger. king vulture,** the large and brilliantly coloured American vulture, *Sarcorhampus papa.* (A.S. *cyning*, from *cyn*, a tribe.)
kingbird, *n. king*-berd, any of the American tyrant fly-catchers of the genus *Tyrannus*.
kingbolt, *n. king*-bohlt, a principal connecting bolt [Mech.].
king-crab, *n.* large tropical crab of the genus *Limulus*.
kingcraft, *n. king*-krahft, the business of kings; the art of governing.
kingcup, *n. king*-kup, the marsh-marigold.
kingdom, *n. king*-dum, the state, authority, or power of a king; the territory, country, or dominion subject to a king; domain ruled over; one of the comprehensive groups in which natural objects are classified, viz. animal, vegetable, and mineral. **kingdom come,** the next world [Slang]. (A.S. *cynedom.*)
kingfish, *n. king*-fish, popular name of several seafish, including the opah.
kingfisher, *n. king*-fish-er, the halcyon, a brilliantly plumaged bird of the genus *Alcedo*.
kinghood, *n. king*-hood, state of being a king.
kingless, *a. king*-less, having no king.
kinglet, *n. king*-let, a petty king; the golden-crested wren.
kinglike, *a. king*-like, like a king.
kingliness, *n. king*-le-ness, a state of being kingly.
kingly, *a. king*-le, pertaining to a king; royal; monarchial; becoming a king: *ad.* with an air of royalty; with a superior dignity.
kingpin, *n.* king-pin, a kingbolt; the centre-pin of the frame [Bowls]; the central or leading figure in an organization, etc. [Fig.].
kingpost, *n. king*-pohst, the binding beam in the frame of a roof rising from the tie-beam to the ridge.
kingship, *n. king*-ship, the state or dignity of a king.
kingwood, *n. king*-wood, Jamaica ebony, *Brya ebenus*, also the Brazilian *Dalbergia cearensis*, hard variegated woods used in cabinet-work.
kinic, *a. ky*-nik *or kin*-ik, quinic.
kink, *n.* kink, the twist in a rope or thread when doubled; a whim or crotchet: *v.i.* to wind into a kink; to twist spontaneously. (Scand.)
kinkajou, *n. king*-ka-joo, a small nocturnal carnivore of Cent. and S. America, of the genus *Cercoleptes*, allied to the racoons. (Native name.)
kinky, *a. king*-ke, abounding in kinks.
kinless, *a. kin*-less, without kin; uninfluenced by kinship.
kinnikinnick, *n. kin*-ne-*kin*-nik, the bearberry; sumach-leaves or the bark of cornel or willow used for smoking.
kino, *n. kee*-no, an astringent substance obtained from the stem of several tropical shrubs and trees. (W. African.)
kinsfolk, *n.pl. kinz*-foke, persons of the same family.
kinship, *n. kin*-ship, blood relationship.
kinsman, *n. kinz*-man, a male relation.
kinswoman, *n. kinz*-woom-an, a female relation.
kiosk, *n.* ke-*osk*, an open summer-house; a covered stall; a highway telephone call-box. (Turk.)
kip, *n.* kip, leather from the skin of young cattle.
kip, *n.* kip, a cheap lodging-house, or a bed in one. **to kip down,** to go to bed [Slang].
kipe, *n.* kipe, a basket for catching fish. (Dial.)
kipper, *n. kip*-per, a salmon after spawning; a fish, esp. a herring, split down the back, salted, and dried: *v.t.* to cure, as fish. (Origin doubtful.)
kirk, *n.* kerk, in Scotland, a church; an ecclesiastical body, specially the Established Church and the Free Church. **auld kirk,** the established Church of Scotland. **kirk session,** the lowest court of a Scottish Presbyterian Church, composed of the minister and lay elders. **kirkyard,** a graveyard. (O.N. *kirkja*, a church.)
kirschwasser, *n. keersh*-vas-ser, an alcoholic cordial made in Germany from morello cherries. (Ger.)
kirtle, *n. ker*-tl, an outer garment; a gown, or skirt; a short jacket; a mantle. (A.S. *cyrtel.*)
kirtled, *a. ker*-tld, wearing a kirtle.
Kisleu, *n. kis*-lew, the third month of the Jewish ecclesiastical year and ninth of the civil. (Heb.)
kismet, *n. kiz*-met, fate or destiny. (Per. and Ar.)
★**kiss,** *n.* kiss, a salute given with the lips; passing contact of the balls in billiards: *v.t.* to salute with the lips; to treat with fondness; to caress; to touch gently; to touch a ball in passing in billiards (of another ball): *v.i.* to salute with the lips. **to kiss the dust,** to yield; to die. **to kiss the rod,** to accept punishment meekly. (A.S. *cyssan.*)
kiss-curl, *n.* a small curl on the temple or forehead.
kisser, *n. kis*-ser, one who kisses; the mouth [Slang].
kissing-crust, *n.* the soft crust of a loaf that has touched another loaf during baking.
kiss-me-quick, *n.* a small old-fashioned bonnet; the wild pansy; a kiss-curl.
kistvaen, *n. kist*-vane, a sepulchral chamber made of flat stones; a cist. (W. *cistfaen*, stone cist.)
kit, *n.* kit, a small wooden tub; a small violin; an outfit; a set; equipment. (Dut. *kitte*, bowl.)
kit-bag, *n.* a bag or valise for a soldier's or traveller's kit.
kitcat, *n. kit*-kat, a size for portraits, 36 inches by 28, three-quarter length. (Name of an 18th-cent. London club which had portraits of its members of this size.)
kitchen, *n. kitch*-en, the room of a house appropriated to cookery; any place where food is regularly cooked. **kitchen dresser,** a frame with shelves and drawers for keeping crockery. **kitchen garden** a piece of ground used for appropriated to raising culinary vegetables. **kitchen range,** a fire-grate and stove with oven and boiler, for cooking. **kitchen stuff,** kitchen requisites; fat collected from pots and dripping pans. (A.S. *cycene.*)
kitchener, *n. kitch*-en-er, a cooking range.
kitchenette, *n.* kitch-e-*net*, a diminutive kitchen.
kitchenmaid, *n. kitch*-en-made, a female assistant to a cook.
kitchen-midden, *n.* a prehistoric refuse heap. (Dan.)
kite, *n.* kite, a hawk of the genus *Milvus*; a name of reproach, denoting rapacity; a flying device attached to a string; an accommodation bill: *v.i.* to fly a kite: *v.t.* to raise money on an accommodation bill. **to fly a kite,** to try to ascertain the trend of public opinion. (A.S. *cyta.*)
kite-balloon, *n.* a captive balloon.
kite-flying, *n.* the dealing in accommodation paper for the purpose of raising money.
kith, *n.* kith, acquaintance; friends. **kith and kin,** friends and relations. (A.S. *cyththu.*)
kitten, *n. kit*-tn, a young cat: *v.i.* to bring forth young, as a cat. (M.E. *kitoun.*)
kittenish, *a. kit*-tn-ish, playful; like a kitten.
kittiwake, *n. kit*-te-wake, a three-toed species of sea-gull, *Rissa tridactyla*, so called from its cry.
kittle, *a. kit*-tl, difficult to manage or get on with; ticklish; precarious.
kittle-cattle, *a. kit*-tl-*kat*-tl, capricious; unreliable.

kittlish, *a.* *kit*-tlish, ticklish; awkward to manage.
kitty, *n.* *kit*-te, a kitten; the pool, or the part of it set on one side [Card-games]; the jack [Bowls].
kive, *n.* kive, a mashing vat. (Dial. Eng.)
kiwi, *n.* *kee*-wee, the apteryx, a New Zealand flightless bird.
klaxon, *n.* *klak*-sun, the proprietary name of an electric motor-horn.
Klepht, *n.* kleft, one of the former Greek opponents to Turkish rule. (Gr. *kleptēs*, thief.)
kleptomania, *n.* klep-to-*may*-ne-a, insane or morbid condition characterized by an irresistible propensity to steal. (Gr. *klepto*, steal, and *mania*.)
kleptomaniac, *n.* klep-to-*may*-ne-ak, one afflicted with kleptomania.
klipspringer, *n.* *klip*-spring-er, a small African antelope of the genus *Oreotragus*.
kloof, *n.* kloof, a narrow gorge. (Dut., a chasm.)
knack, *n.* nak, a petty contrivance; a toy; special dexterity; the trick of anything. (Imit.)
knacker, *n.* *nak*-er, a maker of toys or knick-knacks; *pl.* a pair of castanets.
knacker, *n.* *nak*-er, one who buys worn-out horses for slaughter and sells the flesh for dog's meat; one who deals in old ships, second-hand goods, etc.
knackery, *n.* *nak*-er-re, a slaughter-house for animals not intended for human food.
knacky, *a.* *nak*-e, having a knack; ingenious.
knag, *n.* nag, a knot in wood; a wart; a peg; a snag. (Perhaps Scand. *knagge*, peg.)
knaggy, *a.* *nag*-e, knotty; rough in temper.
knap, *n.* nap, a protuberance; a knob; a swelling.
knap, *v.t.* nap, to snap off in pieces; to flake or chip flint: *v.i.* to make a short, sharp sound. (Imit.)
knapper, *n.* *nap*-per, a maker of flint flakes, gun flints, etc.; a stone-breaker.
knapsack, *n.* *nap*-sak, a travelling bag carried on the back. (Dut. *knapzak*.)
knapweed, *n.* *nap*-weed, a composite plant of the genus *Centaurea*.
knar, *n.* nahr, a knarl.
knarl, *n.* nahrl, a knot in wood; a gnarl; a protuberance on the bark of a tree.
knarled, *a.* nahrld, knotted; gnarled.
knarry, *a.* *nah*-re, having knarls; gnarled.
knaur, *n.* nawr, a knarl on the trunk of a tree.
knave, *n.* nave, a false, deceitful fellow; a dishonest man or boy; the jack in a pack of cards. (A.S. *cnafa*, and Ger. *Knabe*, a boy.)
knavery, *n.* *nave*-er-re, dishonesty; petty villainy; fraud; mischievous tricks or practices.
knavish, *a.* *nave*-ish, dishonest; fraudulent; waggish; mischievous.
knavishly, *ad.* *nave*-ish-le, in a knavish manner.
knavishness, *n.* *nave*-ish-ness, the quality or habit of being knavish.
knead, *v.t.* need, to work into a mass, usually with the hands; to work into dough; to blend together; to massage as though kneading. (A.S. *cnedan*.)
kneading, *n.* *need*-ing, the act of working into dough or any similar movement of the hands.
kneading-trough, *n.* a trough or tray in which dough is worked or mixed.
★**knee,** *n.* nee, the joint of the thigh and leg bones; the corresponding part in animals; the part of a garment covering the knee; a knee-like structure in carpentry, etc., esp. piece of timber or metal connecting the beams of a ship with her sides. **on the knees of the gods,** beyond human control. **to bow the knee to Baal,** to conform to prevailing custom, etc.; to be ultra-conventional. (A.S. *cnēow*.)
knee-breeches, *n.pl.* breeches reaching just below the knee.
kneecap, *n.* *nee*-kap, a small, flat, heart-shaped bone, the patella, situated at the fore-part of the knee-joint; a cover for the knee.
kneed, *a.* need, having knees; forming an obtuse angle, like the knee [Bot.].
knee-deep, *a.* rising to or sunk to the knees.
knee-high, *a.* rising to the knees.
knee-holly, *n.* butcher's-broom, *Ruscus aculeatus*.
knee-jerk, *n.* the reflex extension of the leg produced by a slight tap on the tendon below the kneecap [Med.].
knee-joint, *n.* the joint of the knee; a joint between hinged pieces in carpentry, etc.
kneel, *v.i.* neel, to bend the knee; to fall on the knees. *p.* and *pp.* **knelt.** (A.S. *cnēowlian*, kneel.)
kneeler, *n.* *neel*-er, one who kneels; a hassock or stool for kneeling on.
knee-pan, *n.* the kneecap, or its socket.
knee-piece, *n.* the portion of armour protecting the knee; a piece of timber bent to connect beams or rafters.
knee-stop, *n.* a knee-swell.
knee-swell, *n.* *nee*-swell, a lever worked by the knee in the American organ for increasing and decreasing the volume of sound.
knee-tribute, *n.* *nee*-trib-yewt, reverence shown or tribute paid by kneeling.
knell, *n.* nel, the stroke of a bell, especially at a death or funeral; a tolling; a death signal: *v.i.* to sound as a tolling bell; to toll: *v.t.* to announce by tolling. (A.S. *cynllan*, to knock.)
knew, new, *p.* of *know*.
Knickerbocker, *n.pl.* *nik*-er-*bok*-er, a New Yorker, esp. a descendant of the early Dutch settlers; *pl.* (*l.c.*) loose breeches gathered in below the knee; knickers. (Washington Irving's Dutchman, Diedrich *Knickerbocker*.)
knickers, *n.pl.* *nick*-erz, a loose-fitting man's outer garment for the legs gathered in at the knee; a similar undergarment for women.
knick-knack, *n.* *nik*-nak, any trifle or toy. (*knack*.)
knick-knackery, *n.* nik-*nak*-er-re, knick-knacks collectively.
★**knife,** *n.* nife (*pl.* **knives**), an instrument with a sharp edge for cutting, usually with a handle; a blade in a cutting machine: *v.t.* to cut or stab with a knife. **to have one's knife into,** to be actively hostile or unfriendly to. **war to the knife,** relentless opposition, unremitting hostility. (A.S. *cnif*, knife.)
knifeboard, *n.* *nife*-bord, a piece of wood for cleaning knives on; a seat longways on top of an early form of omnibus.
knife-edge, *n.* a sharp edge of steel, serving as the axis of a balance; a narrow ridge.
knife-grinder, *n.* one who sharpens knives.
knife-rest, *n.* a small stand for keeping carving knife and fork from soiling the tablecloth.
knife-switch, *n.* a hinged switch for making or breaking contact or transferring current [Elect.]
knight, *n.* nite, in feudal times, one admitted to a certain military rank; now, a non-hereditary title of honour, conferred by the sovereign and carrying the appellation *Sir* before the Christian name; one admitted to this rank, coming next below that of baronet; a chess-piece with a horse's head: *v.t.* to dub or create a knight. **knight bachelor,** a member of the order of knights but not of one of the orders of knighthood. **knight banneret,** formerly, one created knight on the battlefield and ranking above other knights. **knight hospitaller,** *see* **hospitaller. knight's fee,** the amount of land possession of which entailed knight-service. **knight of the road,** a highwayman. **knight of the shire,** formerly, the representative of a county in Parliament. **Knight Templar,** *see* **templar.** (A.S. *cniht*, a servant, Ger. *Knecht*.)
knightage, *n.* *nite*-aj, the body of knights; an annotated register of knights.
knight-errant, *n.* a knight who travelled in search of adventures, to show his military prowess and gallantry (*pl.* **knights-errant**).
knight-errantry, *n.* practices of knights-errant.
knight-head, *n.* one of two timbers in a ship rising on each side of the stem, and supporting the bowsprit between them [Naut.].
knighthood, *n.* *nite*-hood, the character or dignity of a knight; qualities befitting a knight; the body of knights. **order of knighthood,** a distinctive body of knights, formerly bound by military and religious rules; in Great Britain, one of the nine orders of chivalry of which all, or all the higher, members are knights or dames.
knightliness, *n.* *nite*-le-ness, the quality of being knightly.
knightly, *a.* *nite*-le, pertaining to a knight; becoming a knight: *ad.* in a manner becoming a knight.
knight-service, *n.* a tenure of lands held on condition of military service.
knit, *v.t.* nit, to tie together; to unite or connect into a kind of network, by looping yarn with eyeless needles; to cause to grow together; to unite closely; to draw together, or to contract: *v.i.* to

weave by knitting; to grow together; to unite closely. (A.S. *cnyttan*, to knot.)
knitter, *n.* *nit*-ter, one who or that which knits.
knitting, *n.* *nit*-ting, the work of a knitter; network thus formed; union or junction. **knitting machine,** a machine on which knitting is done. **knitting needle,** a long eyeless needle of metal, wood, or bone, etc., used for knitting.
knittle, *n.* *nit*-tl, a string that draws together a purse, etc.; a small line to sling hammocks with on board ship. (*knit.*)
knitwear, *n.* *nit*-ware, knitted garments.
knives, *n.pl.* nyvz, plural of *knife.*
knob, *n.* nob, a hard protuberance; a hard swelling; a bunch; a boss; a knoll [U.S.A.]; a door-handle; a turning-handle on a wireless set; a rounded terminal. (*knop.*)
knobbed, *a.* nobd, containing knobs; full of knobs; shaped into a knob.
knobbiness, *n.* *nob*-be-ness, the quality or condition of being knobby.
knobble, *n.* nobl, a small knob.
knobbly, *a.* *nobl*-e, knobby; of the nature of knobbles.
knobby, *a.* *nob*-be, full of knobs; knotty; stubborn.
knobkerrie, *n.* *nob*-ke-re, a round-topped stick used as a weapon or missile, esp. by the Kaffirs. (Taal, *knopkirie.*)
knobstick, *n.* *nob*-stik, a knobkerrie; a blackleg [Slang].
knock, *v.i.* nok, to strike with something hard or heavy; to drive or be driven against; to clash; to rap; to make a knocking noise (of machinery). **to knock about,** to idle about. **to knock off,** to stop work. **to knock under,** to yield; to submit; to acknowledge oneself beaten. (A.S. *cnucian.*)
knock, *v.t.* nok, to strike; to drive against; to drive. **to knock down,** to strike down; to fell; to sell at a reduction; to sell to a bidder (at an auction). **to knock off,** to strike off; to deduct; to drink up [Slang]. **to knock on the head,** to dispatch or stun; to defeat. **to knock out,** to force out by a blow or blows; to eliminate by competition; to render temporarily unconscious. **to knock together,** to construct hastily and roughly. **to knock up,** to arouse by knocking; to exhaust with excessive toil; to make in rough and ready fashion; to improvise.
knock, *n.* nok, a blow; a stroke with something hard or heavy; a stroke on a door for admittance; a rap.
knockabout, *a.* *nok*-a-bout, noisily comic and more or less acrobatic; suitable for daily or rough use; bohemian: *n.* that which, or one who, is knockabout.
knockdown, *a.* *nok*-doun, of sufficient strength to overcome; reduced to the lowest limit (of prices): *n.* anything so constructed that it can easily be taken to pieces; a free fight.
knocker, *n.* *nok*-er, one who knocks; a kind of hammer hinged to a door for knocking.
knocking, *n.* *nok*-ing, the action of the verb *to knock*; the recurrent sound due to faulty combustion in a petrol engine, or to a worn bearing in a reciprocating engine.
knock-knee, *n.* *nok*-nee, the condition in which the legs curve inwards and the knees touch in walking: (*pl.*) knees in this condition.
knock-kneed, *a.* with knees that knock against each other in walking; weak.
knock-out, *a.* *nok*-out, felling, stunning: *n.* a knock-out blow; a tournament in which a defeated player must retire; an auction in which the bids are arranged beforehand by confederates who later resell the goods among themselves and share the profits.
knock-up, *n.* *nok*-up, a bout of practice before a game of tennis, etc.; something made hurriedly or to fill an immediate need; any improvisation.
knoll, *v.t.* and *i.* nole, to knell. (*knell.*)
knoll, *n.* nole, the rounded top of a hill; a rounded hillock. (A.S. *cnol.*)
knoller, *n.* *nole*-er, one who tolls a bell.
knop, *n.* nop, a knob; a tufted top; an ornamental bunch; a button. (A.S. *cnæp.*)
knopper, *n.* *nop*-per, a gall formed by a gall-fly on the immature flower-cups of the oak, used in tanning. (Ger.)
knosp, *n.* nosp, an ornament resembling a flower-bud [Arch.]. (Ger. *Knospe.*)
***knot,** *n.* not, the complication of a thread or cord, made by tying or interlacing; an ornamental bow of ribbon, etc.; a porter's shoulder-pad; hard part of wood due to the fibres interlacing; a protuberant joint [Bot.]; a nodule; a figure, the lines of which frequently interlace each other; difficulty; intricacy; something not easily solved; a bond of association or union; a cluster; a collection; a group, as of persons; a division of the log-line, serving to measure a vessel's rate of travel [Naut.]; the speed of one nautical mile (6,080 ft.) per hour: *v.t.* to complicate or tie in a knot; to entangle; to perplex; to unite closely: *v.i.* to form knots or joints [Bot.]; to knit knots or fringe. **granny knot, porters' knot,** *see* these words. **square knot,** *see* **square,** *a.* **surgeon's knot, truelove knot,** *see* these words. (A.S. *cnotta.*)
knot, *n.* not, the small sandpiper, *Tringa canutus.* (Origin unknown.)
knotgrass, *n.* *not*-grahs, any many-jointed weed, esp. *Illecebrum verticillatum* and *Polygonum aviculare.*
knotless, *a.* *not*-less, free from knots.
knotted, *a.* *not*-ted, full of knots; having knots with intersecting lines; having knots in relief.
knottiness, *n.* *not*-te-ness, the state or quality of being knotty.
knotting, *n.* *not*-ting, the tying or splicing of knots; fancy-work of twisted and knotted thread; the filling of knots in wood, or a composition for this.
knotty, *a.* *not*-te, full of knots; hard; rugged; difficult; intricate.
knout, *n.* nout, a leather and wire whip formerly used for the punishment of criminals in Russia; punishment with the knout: *v.t.* to punish with the knout. (Russ.)
know, *v.t.* noh, to perceive with certainty; to have a clear and certain idea of notion of; to be aware of; to have an assured conviction of; to distinguish; to recognise by recollection, remembrance, representation, or description; to be acquainted or familiar with; to have sexual commerce with [Bible]: *v.i.* to have a clear and certain perception; not to be doubtful; to be informed; to take cognizance of; to learn. **in the know,** having special or "inside" information. **to know a thing or two,** *see* **thing. to know what's what,** to know the ins and outs, or all about something; to be cute. *p.* **knew.** *pp.* **known.** (A.S. *cnawan.*)
knowable, *a.* *noh*-a-bl, that may be known; that may be discovered, understood, or ascertained.
knowableness, *n.* *noh*-a-bl-ness, the quality of being knowable.
know-all, *n.* a pretender to very extensive knowledge; a "walking encyclopædia" [Coll.].
knower, *n.* *noh*-er, one who knows.
knowing, *a.* *noh*-ing, skilful; well informed; intelligent; cunning, artful; stylish [Slang].
knowingly, *ad.* *noh*-ing-le, with knowledge.
knowingness, *n.* the quality of being knowing.
***knowledge,** *n.* *nol*-lej, a clear and certain perception of that which exists; that which is known; cognition; learning; erudition; skill from practice; acquaintance with any fact or person; information. **carnal knowledge,** sexual intercourse. **tree of knowledge,** *see* **tree.**
knowledgeable, *a.* *nol*-lej-a-bl, well informed; possessing intelligence or shrewdness [Coll.].
knowledgeably, *n.* *nol*-lej-a-ble, in knowledgeable fashion.
known, *a.* nohn, perceived; understood; recognized.
knub, *n.* nub, a small lump or knob; *pl.* inferior silk from the innermost part of the cocoon. (*knob.*)
knuckle, *n.* *nuk*-kl, a joint of a finger, esp. that at the base; the knee-joint of an animal; a joint of meat consisting of this, with the adjoining parts; anything in machines, etc., shaped like a knuckle: *v.t.* to touch or hit with the knuckles: *v.i.* to yield; to submit, as beaten. **to knuckle down, or under,** to acknowledge oneself beaten; to behave submissively. **to knuckle down to,** to settle steadily to (work, etc.). **near the knuckle,** bordering on indecency.
knuckle-bones, *n.pl.* a game played with the bones of sheep's knuckles.
knuckle-bow, *n.* *nuk*-kl-boh, the curved part of a sword-hilt that protects the knuckles.
knuckle-duster, *n.* a glove or bar across the knuckles, studded with metal, to render a blow from the fist more formidable.

knuckle-joint, *n.* a hinged joint shaped like a knuckle [Mech.].
knur, *n.* nur, a gnarl, as in a tree-trunk; a wooden ball. **knur-and-spell,** trap-ball, a game played with a knur, a spell (wooden trap), and a trap-stick. (M.E. *knurre*, Swed. *knurr*.)
knurl, *n.* nurl, a knot, lump, or protuberance; an ornamental bead or milling, as on the edge of a coin: *v.t.* to make knurls; to mill the edge of a coin. (Perhaps from *knur*.)
koa, *n. koh*-a, the tree *Acacia koa*, of Hawaii, or its valuable mahogany-like timber. (Native name.)
koala, *n.* ko-*ah*-la, the Australian sloth-like arboreal marsupial rodent, *Phascolarctus cinereus*. (Native name.)
kob, *n.* kohb, *or* **koba,** *koh*-ba, a large African antelope of the genus *Adensta*, allied to the water-bucks. (Native name.)
kobang, *n. koh*-bang, an oblong, round-cornered gold plate circulating in Japan as money in the 17th to 19th cents. (Jap.)
kobold, *n. koh*-buld *or kob*-uld, a household goblin or brownie; an elf frequenting mines. (Ger.)
kodak, *n. koh*-dak, a patented type of portable film camera: *v.t.* to photograph by snapshot. (Trade name.)
koff, *n.* kof, a small two-masted Dutch vessel. (Dut.)
koft, *n.* koft, koftgari.
koftgar, *n. koft*-gar, a worker in koftgari.
koftgari, *n.* koft-*gah*-re, Indian damascene-work in which gold is inlaid on steel. (Per.)
Koh-i-noor, *n. koh*-e-noor, a large diamond, the property of the British Crown since 1849; anything very splendid, magnificent, or supreme in its class. (Per., "mountain of light.")
kohl, *n.* kole, a preparation, esp. of powdered antimony, used as a cosmetic for darkening eye-brows, etc. (Ar.)
kohl-rabi, *n.* kole-*rah*-be, the edible turnip-stemmed cabbage, *Brassica oleracea*. (Ger., kale-turnip.)
kokra-wood, *n. kok*-ra-wood, the hard wood of the Burmese tree, *Aporosa dioica*, used in the manufacture of flutes. (Native name.)
kola, *n. koh*-la, a tropical African tree of the genus *Cola*, or its bitter chestnut-like nut; a beverage prepared from these nuts.
Kolarian, *n.* koh-*lare*-re-an, a member of any of the pre-Aryan tribes of Central India: *a.* pertaining to these tribes. (Hind. *Kol*.)
kolinsky, *n.* ko-*lin*-ske, a furriers' name for the fur of certain minks. (*Kola* peninsula, N. Russia.)
koniscope, *n. kon*-e-skope, a device for measuring the quantity of dust in the atmosphere.
konker, *n. kong*-ker, a conker.
koodoo, *n. koo*-doo, the kudu. (Native name.)
koolah, *n. koo*-la, the koala. (Native Austral.)
kopeck, *n. koh*-pek, a Russian bronze coin, one-hundredth of a rouble. (Russ.)
kopje, *n. kop*-pe, a low hill. (Dut.)
Koran, *n.* ko-*rahn*, the sacred book of the Mohammedans, containing the whole rule for Moslem observance and conduct of life. (Ar., "The Book.")
Koranic, *a.* ko-*ran*-ik, pertaining to the Koran.
kosher, *a. koh*-sher, pure; clean, as fulfilling requirements of the sacred law: *n.* food specially prepared for Jews; a shop for the sale of this: *v.t.* to make (food) kosher. (Heb. *kasher*, right.)
koto, *n. koh*-toh, a Japanese zither-like instrument with thirteen silk strings. (Jap.)
kotow, *n.* ko-*tou*, the Chinese custom of kneeling and touching the ground with the forehead as a mark of reverence: *v.i.* to perform the kotow. (Chin. *k'o-t'ou*, knock the head.)
kotwal, *n. kot*-wahl, a native town-magistrate or chief of police in India. (Hind.)
koumiss, *n. koo*-mis, spirituous liquor made among the Tartars by fermenting mare's milk. (Russ.)
kourbash, *n. koor*-bash, a whip made from the hide of a rhinoceros or hippopotamus. (Ar.)
kousso, *n. koos*-so, the N. African tree *Hagenia abyssinica*, from the flowers of which an anthelmintic is prepared. (Abyssinian.)
kowtow, *n.* and *v.i.* kou-*tou*, kotow.
kraal, *n.* krahl, an enclosed group of native huts in South Africa; an enclosure for cattle, etc.: *v.t.* to enclose in a kraal. (Dut.)
kraft, *n.* krahft, strong brown paper made from sulphate wood pulp. (Ger., strength.)
krait, *n.* krite, the venomous Indian snake, *Bungarus cœruleus*, related to the cobras.
kraken, *n. kray*-ken, a mythical octopus of the northern seas. (Dan.)
kran, *n.* kran, a former Persian silver coin (superseded 1932) of 71 grains, value 2*s.* 6*d.*
krang, *n.* krang, the fleshy part of the whale after the blubber has been taken off. (Dan. *kreng*, carcase.)
krantz, *n.* krants, a precipitous overhanging wall of rocks. (Taal from Dut.)
krasis, *n. kray*-sis, Eucharistic wine mixed with water; the act or practice of mixing water with the wine [Eccl.]. (Gr., mixing.)
kraurosis, *n.* kraw-*roh*-sis, shrivelling and dryness of a part, or of mucous membrane [Med.]. (Gr. *krauros*, brittle.)
kraut, *n.* krout, sauerkraut.
kreatine, *n. kree*-a-tin, creatine [Anat.].
Kremlin, *n. krem*-lin, in Russia, the inner city or citadel of a town or city, esp. that of Moscow; hence the ruler, government, or governmental system of Russia. (Russ.)
kreng, *n.* kreng, krang.
Kreutzer, *n. kroyt*-ser, a coin, value about one farthing, formerly in circulation in Austria and Germany. (Ger. *Kreuz*, a cross.)
Kriegspiel, *n. kreeg*-speel, a game used in training military officers, in which pieces representing army units are manœuvred. (Ger., war game.)
kris, *n.* kreece, a Malay dagger with wavy blade. (Malay.)
Krishna, *n. krish*-na, a Hindu male deity, the eighth incarnation of Vishnu. (Hind., the black one.)
kromesky, *n.* kro-*mes*-ke, chicken or other meat minced, and fried in rolls of bacon. (Russ.)
krone, *n. kroh*-ner, a former monetary unit of several Cent. European and still of Scandinavian countries (value about 1*s.* 1½*d.*); the former German gold ten-mark piece. (Dan., crown.)
Kroo, *n.* kroo, a member of a negro tribe of the Guinea coast.
krummhorn, *n. kroom*-hawrn, the cromorne, an obsolete wood-wind instrument of clarinet type; an organ-stop of this type. (Ger. *krumm*, curved, and *horn*.)
kryometer, *n.* kry-*om*-e-ter, a thermometer for measuring exceptionally low temperatures. (Gr. *kryos*, cold, *metron*, measure.)
krypton, *n. krip*-ton, an inert gaseous element occurring in minute quantities in the air. (Gr. *kryptos*, hidden.)
Kshatriya, *n. kshat*-re-yah, the former second or military and governing caste in India; one belonging to this. (Sans.)
kudos, *n. kew*-doss, fame; credit. (Gr., glory.)
kudu, *n. koo*-doo, the large African antelope, *Strepsiceros kudu*, with corkscrew horns. (Kaffir.)
Kufic, *n. kew*-fik, the early Arabic character, so called from Kufa, on the Euphrates.
Ku-Klux-Klan, *n. kew*-kluks-klan, a secret society originally formed about 1865 in U.S.A., to suppress negro ambitions, and revived in 1915 as The Invisible Empire. (Gr. *kyklos*, circle.)
kukri, *n. kook*-re, the Gurkha knife. (Hind.)
kulak, *n.* koo-*lahk*, a prosperous Russian peasant farmer, esp. one who objected to co-operation with the Soviet government. (Russ., fist.)
Kultur, *n. kool*-toor, culture (*ironically*). (Ger.)
kumiss, *n. koo*-mis, koumiss.
kümmel, *n. kim*-mel, a liqueur flavoured with caraway seeds and cumin or anise. (Ger.)
kumquat, *n. kum*-kwot, the small fruit, like an orange, of *Citrus japonica*. (Chin.)
kunkur, *n. koon*-kur, an Indian nodular limestone used in road-making, etc. (Hind. *kankar*.)
Kuomintang, *n.* gwoh-min-*tang*, from 1905 to 1948 the nationalist and progressive party of China. (Chin., People's National Party.)
kupfernickel, *n. koop*-fer-*nik*-el, niccollite, one of the chief ores of nickel. (Ger.)
Kurd, *n.* kurd, a native of Kurdistan. (Ar.)
Kurdish, *a. kurd*-ish, pertaining to the Kurds or their language: *n.* the language of the Kurds.
kursaal, *n. koor*-sahl, a public hall, esp. for visitors at a watering-place. (Ger.)

kutch, *n.* kutch, cutch; catechu.
kvass, *n.* kvass, a thin sour beer made in Russia from rye. (Russ.)
kyanite, *n. ky*-a-nite, cyanite, a crystalline silicate of aluminium.
kyanize, *v.t. ky*-a-nize, to immerse wood in a solution of corrosive sublimate to prevent dry-rot. (*Kyan*, the inventor of the process.)
kye, *n.pl.* ky, old plural of *cow*. (A.S. *cy*.)
kyle, *n.* kyl, a narrow channel between islands or between island and mainland, esp. in W. Scotland. (Gael. *caol*, a narrow strait.)
kylin, *n. kee*-lin, the unicorn of Chinese legend. (Chin. *chi*, male, *lin*, female.)
kylix, *n. ky*-liks, a flat and shallow two-handled stemmed drinking-vessel of ancient Greece. (Gr.)
kyllosis, *n.* ky-*loh*-sis, congenital deformity of the foot; club-foot. (Gr., crippling.)
kyloe, *n. ky*-loh, one of a breed of small Highland black cattle.
kymograph, *n. ky*-mo-graf, an instrument for recording oscillations, curves of pressure, etc. (Gr. *kyma*, a wave, *grapho*, write.)
kymoscope, *n. ky*-mo-skope, an instrument used in examination of the flow of the blood [Med.]. (Gr. *kyma*, a wave, *skopein*, to view.)
kyphosis, *n.* ky-*foh*-sis, the condition of being humpbacked; angular curvature of the spine [Path.]. (Gr. *kyphos*, humpbacked.)
kyphotic, *a.* ky-*fot*-ik, pertaining to kyphosis.
Kyrie, *n. ky*-re-e, the Kyrie eleison (Late L., from Gr., Lord, have mercy upon us!), a petition or response used in various liturgies; a musical setting for this.
kyriologic, *a.* ki-re-o-*loj*-ik, pertaining to the hieroglyphic representation of objects by pictures rather than by symbolic characters. (Gr. *kyriologia*, using words in their proper literal senses.)

L

L, el, twelfth letter of the alphabet, a liquid consonant with, normally, only one sound in English, as in *like, canal.* It is syllabic in such words as *circle, double, thistle, coddled*; is pronounced as single though printed double (*hollow, spelling,* etc.), except in certain combinations, as *soulless, wholly*; and in some words, as *calf, salmon, folk, would,* etc., it is silent.

la, *int.* law, look; see; behold. (A.S.)

la, *n.* lah, the sixth note in Guido's scale. (It.)

laager, *n. lah*-ger, a camp defended by wagons: *v.t.* and *i.* to form into a laager; to encamp. (S. African Dut.)

labarum, *n. lab*-a-rum, the standard, surmounted by the monogram of Christ, adopted by the Emperor Constantine after his conversion to Christianity. (Late L.)

labdanum, *n. lab*-da-num, ladanum.

labefaction, *n.* lab-e-*fak*-shon, a weakening or loosening; decay. (L. *labefactus.*)

label, *n. lay*-bl, a narrow slip affixed to anything, denoting its contents, ownership, or destination; an adhesive stamp; a descriptive term; a paper annexed to a document, esp. a codicil to a will; a fillet, with pendants or points, borne on the family arms by an eldest or only son while the father is still living [Her.]; a brass rule with sights, formerly used to take altitudes; a drip-stone, or moulding over doorways, etc. [Arch.]: *v.t.* to affix a label to; to attach a seal to; to describe by a word or phrase. (O.Fr.)

labellum, *n.* la-*bel*-lum, the lower petal of the flower in plants of the orchid family [Bot.]. (L., a small lip.)

labia, *n.pl. lay*-be-a, *see* **labium.**

labial, *a. lay*-be-al, pertaining to the lips; formed by the lips or like lips or lip-like parts: *n.* a sound (or letter representing this) formed with the lips, as *b, p.* (Late L. *labialis,* from L. *labium,* a lip.)

labialism, *n. lay*-be-a-lizm, the habit of labializing; labial pronunciation [Phon.].

labialize, *v.t. lay*-be-a-lize, to render labial in quality (of sounds) [Phon.].

labially, *ad.* by means of the lips; with labial enunciation [Phon.].

labiate, *a. lay*-be-at, having lips or lip-like parts, esp. [Bot.] an irregular, monopetalous corolla, the lower lip being three-lobed.

labile, *a. lab*-ile, unstable; liable to change; passing over [Elect.].

labiodental, *a. lay*-be-o-*den*-tal, pronounced by both the lips and teeth, as *f* and *v*: *n.* a labiodental letter or sound [Phon.]. (L. *labium,* and *dental.*)

labium, *n. lay*-be-um (*pl.* **labia**), any organ resembling a lip, esp. the external parts of the vulva in Primates [Anat.]; the inner lip of the aperture in gastropods [Conch.]. (L., a lip.)

laboratory, *n. lab*-o-ra-to-re *or* la-*bor*-a-to-re, a room or building fitted with apparatus for practical scientific work; a place where anything is elaborated or prepared. (Late L. *laboratorium.*)

laborious, *a.* la-*baw*-re-us, using exertion; given to labour; industrious; involving or requiring much work; toilsome; not easy; laboured. (Fr. *laborieux.*)

laboriously, *ad.* in a laborious manner.

laboriousness, *n.* quality of being laborious.

labour, *n. lay*-bur, toilsome exertion of either body or mind, specially in one's calling or occupation; toil; difficulty; task; the class of workers, artisans, and labourers; work, or its share in production; the pangs of childbirth: *v.i.* to exert muscular strength; to toil; to work as a labourer; to exert one's powers of body or mind in the prosecution of any design; to be hard pressed; to be burdened; to pitch and roll in a heavy sea [Naut.]; to suffer the pangs of childbirth: *v.t.* to work at; to deal with at length; to elaborate; to form or fabricate with exertion. **Labour Exchange,** a local office under the Ministry of Labour and National Service for apportioning available labour and administering the national Unemployment Insurance scheme. **labour market,** the supply of the labour in relation to the demand. **Labour Party,** a socialist party formed to promote democratic institutions and the social and political interests of the working class. (O.Fr.)

laboured, *a. lay*-burd, bearing marks of labour or effort in the execution.

labourer, *n. lay*-bo-rer, one who labours in a toilsome occupation or does unskilled manual work.

labourism, *n. lay*-bo-rizm, the principles, policy, etc., of labour organizations.

Labourite, *n. lay*-bo-rite, a member or supporter of a Parliamentary Labour Party.

labour-saving, *a.* adapted to diminish or supersede labour.

laboursome, *a. lay*-bur-sum, made with or entailing great labour; apt to labour (of a ship).

Labrador, *n. lab*-ra-dor, a black variety of Newfoundland dog. (Name of peninsula in British N. America.)

labradorite, *n. lab*-ra-do-rite, a variety of lime-soda felspar in which change in direction of reflected light causes brilliant colour changes. (Labrador.)

labret, *n. lay*-bret, a lip-ornament worn among certain primitive races.

labrum, *n. lay*-brum (*pl.* **labra**), the upper lip of insects and crustaceans; a lip-like part, a labium [Anat.]. (L.)

laburnum, *n.* la-*bur*-num, a small tree of the genus *Cytisus,* with hanging racemes of yellow flowers. (L.)

labyrinth, *n. lab*-e-rinth, a maze; a structure composed of intricate winding passages, which render it difficult to find the way in either direction; an inexplicable difficulty; an intricate pattern; the cavities of the internal ear [Anat.]; a series of troughs conveying water for washing pulverized ore in a stamping mill [Metal.]. (Fr. *labyrinthe.*)

labyrinthian, *a.* lab-er-*rin*-the-an, labyrinthine.

labyrinthic, *a.* lab-er-*rin*-thik, like a labyrinth.

labyrinthiform, *a.* lab-er-*rin*-the-form, having the tortuous form of a labyrinth.

labyrinthine, *a.* lab-er-*rin*-thyn, of the nature of a labyrinth; winding; intricate.

labyrinthodont, *n.* lab-e-*rin*-tho-dont, any of a suborder of extinct gigantic amphibians characterized by teeth of labyrinthine structure. (Gr. *labyrinthos,* and *odous,* a tooth.)

lac, *n.* lak, a resinous substance produced by *Coccus lacca,* which yields a fine red dye; ware coated with lac. (Hind.)

lac, *n.* lak, in India, 100,000 (esp. of rupees). (Hind. *lakh.*)

laccic, *a. lak*-sik, produced from lac.

laccin, *n. lak*-sin, the colouring principle of lac.

laccolith, *n. lak*-o-lith, an intrusive mass of igneous rock having a flattened base and dome-like upper surface [Geol.].

lace, *n.* lace, a delicate ornamental network, the meshes of which are formed of threads knotted together; a string or thong that fastens by being interwoven and tied; ornamental braid (esp. of gold or silver wire) for trimming uniforms, etc.: *v.t.* to fasten with a string through eyelet-holes; to compress by means of tight corsets; to adorn with lace; to embellish with stripes; to beat or lash [Coll.]; to strengthen a drink with a little alcohol: *v.i.* to fasten with a lace or laces; to wear tight corsets. (O.Fr. *las,* a snare.)

lace-bark, *n.* the lace-like bark of the West Indian tree *Lagetta lintearia*; the tree itself.

lace-coral, *n.* any coral of the Fenestella group.

lace-frame, *n.* a machine for making lace.

laceman, *n. lace*-man, a man who deals in lace.

lacerable, *a. las*-ser-a-bl, that may be lacerated.

lacerate, *v.t. las*-ser-ate, to tear; to rend; to wound painfully. (L. *laceratus,* torn.)

lacerate, *a. las*-ser-at, lacerated; deeply and irregularly indented (of leaves, etc.) [Bot.].

laceration, *n.* las-er-*ray*-shon, the act of tearing; the breach made by rending.
lacerative, *a.* *las*-er-ra-tiv, tearing; having power to tear.
Lacerta, *n.* la-*ser*-ta, a genus of reptiles comprising most of the lizards. (L.)
lacertian, *a.* la-*ser*-she-an, pertaining to the lizards: *n.* a lizard.
lacertilian, *n.* and *a.* las-er-*til*-e-an, lacertian.
lacertine, *a.* la-*ser*-tine, resembling a lizard; lacertian.
lacet, *n.* la-*set*, lace with inserted tape or braid.
lacewing, *n.* *lace*-wing, any of many neuropterous insects with long lace-like wings and very bright eyes.
laches, *n.* *lash*-ez, negligence [Law]. (O.Fr.)
Lachesis, *n.* *lak*-e-sis, the Fate who spins the thread of life; (*l.c.*) a venomous serpent of the rattle-snake family; the bushmaster. (L.)
Lachryma Christi, *n.* *lak*-re-ma *kris*-te, a sweet, rich wine of southern Italy.
lachrymal, *a.* *lak*-re-mal, pertaining to or secreting tears; conveying tears. (L. *lacrima*, a tear.)
lachrymary, *a.* and *n.* *lak*-re-ma-re, lachrymatory.
lachrymation, *n.* lak-re-*may*-shon, the act of shedding tears.
lachrymator, *n.* *lak*-re-may-tor, any substance causing tears to flow; tear-gas.
lachrymatory, *a.* *lak*-re-*may*-to-re, pertaining to tears; causing tears to flow: *n.* a bottle deposited in ancient tombs, possibly for tears of the mourners, but probably for perfumes and ointments.
lachrymose, *a.* *lak*-re-mohs, shedding tears; mournful; tearful.
lachrymosely, *ad.* in a lachrymose manner.
lacing, *n.* *lace*-ing, a fastening with a lace through eyelet holes; a cord used in drawing tight or fastening; any interlacing structure; a dash of spirits to strengthen or flavour a drink; a thrashing.
lacinia, *n.* la-*sin*-e-a (*pl.* **laciniæ**), an incised segment in a leaf or petal [Bot.]; the inner terminal lobe of the maxilla in insects. (L.)
laciniate, *a.* la-*sin*-e-at, fringed; with a fringed border [Bot.]. (L. *lacinia*, a lappet.)
lack, *n.* lak, want; deficiency: *v.t.* to want; to be destitute of: *v.i.* to be in want; to be wanting.
lackadaisical, *a.* *lak*-a-*day*-ze-kal, affectedly pensive; sentimental.
lackadaisically, *ad.* in a languishing way.
lack-a-day, *int.* *lak*-a-day, alack-a-day.
lackey, *n.* *lak*-e, a footman; a male servant; a toady or servile follower: *v.t.* to attend as lackey; to attend servilely: *v.i.* to pay servile attendance. (Fr. *laquais.*)
lack-lustre, *a.* wanting lustre or brightness.
lac-lake, *n.* a dye or pigment obtained from lac.
laconic, *a.* la-*kon*-ik, expressing much in few words; concise; pithy; pertaining to or like Sparta (Laconia), or its people.
laconically, *ad.* la-*kon*-e-ka-le, in a laconic manner.
laconicism, *n.* la-*kon*-e-sizm, a laconic saying; a sententious phrase or expression.
lacquer, *n.* *lak*-er, a varnish, usually of a solution of shellac in alcohol with added colouring; a hard varnish for wood; articles coated with this: *v.t.* to varnish; to apply lacquer to. (Fr. *lacre.*)
lacquerer, *n.* *lak*-er-er, one who applies lacquer.
lacrosse, *n.* lah-*kross*, a Canadian game played with a hard ball and a long-handled racket or stringed bat, called a crosse.
lactarine, *n.* *lak*-ta-rin, a preparation of casein from milk, used by calico printers as a fixing agent. (L. *lactarius*, milky.)
lactate, *n.* *lak*-tate, a salt of lactic acid.
lactation, *n.* lak-*tay*-shon, the act of giving suck; the time of suckling; the secreting of milk. (L. *lactatus*, suckled.)
lacteal, *a.* *lak*-te-al, pertaining to milk; conveying chyle: *n.* one of the lymphatic vessels which convey chyle from the intestines to the thoracic duct [Anat.]. **lacteal fever,** milk-fever. (L. *lacteus*, milky.)
lacteous, *a.* *lak*-te-us, resembling milk; milky.
lactescence, *n.* lak-*tes*-sence, the state of being lactescent; the sap exuding from a plant when wounded [Bot.].
lactescent, *a.* lak-*tes*-sent, turning to milk; turning milky; yielding milk or a milk-like juice. (L. *lactescens*, turning to milk.)
lactic, *a.* *lak*-tik, pertaining to milk; in or procured from sour milk, as lactic acid. (L. *lac*, milk.)
lacticiferous, *a.* lak-te-*sif*-er-rus, containing latex [Bot.].
lactiferous, *a.* lak-*tif*-er-rus, bearing or conveying milk or milk-like juice. (L. *lac*, and *fero*, bear.)
lactifuge, *n.* *lak*-te-fewj, a medicine to check or diminish the secretion of milk.
lactine, *n.* *lak*-tin, lactose.
lactometer, *n.* lak-*tom*-e-ter, a hydrometer adapted for the determination of the quality of milk. (L. *lac*, and Gr. *metron*, measure.)
lactoscope, *n.* *lak*-to-skope, an instrument for estimating the amount of cream in milk by its opacity. (L. *lac*, and Gr. *skopeo*, view.)
lactose, *n.* *lak*-tohs, sugar formed from evaporating the whey of milk; sugar of milk.
Lactuca, *n.* lak-*tew*-ka, the genus of plants including *L. sativa*, the lettuce. (L.)
lactucic, *a.* lak-*tew*-sik, pertaining to *Lactuca*.
lacuna, *n.* la-*kew*-na (*pl.* **lacunæ**), a gap; a void space; a hiatus; a small cavity in bone [Anat.]; an air-cell [Bot.]. (L.)
lacunal, *a.* la-*kew*-nal, pertaining to or having lacunæ; pitted.
lacunar, *n.* la-*kew*-nar, a ceiling or under surface consisting of compartments sunk or hollowed without spaces or bands between the panels [Arch.].
lacunose, *a.* la-*kew*-nohs, lacunal.
lacustral, *a.* la-*kus*-tral, lacustrine.
lacustrian, *a.* la-*kus*-tre-an, lacustrine: *n.* an inhabitant of a lake dwelling.
lacustrine, *a.* la-*kus*-trin, pertaining to lakes; living in or on lakes. (L. *lacus*, a lake.)
lacy, *a.* *lay*-se, resembling lace; made of lace.
lad, *n.* lad, a boy or youth; a dashing fellow of any age [Coll.]. **lad's love,** southernwood. **lads of the village,** boon companions [Coll.]. (M.E.)
ladanum, *n.* *lad*-an-um, the resinous exudation of *Cistus creticus* and *Cistus ladaniferus*. (L.)
ladder, *n.* *lad*-der, a frame consisting of two side-pieces, connected by rungs or steps by which one may ascend or descend; means of rising or ascending; a parting of the material, as in silk stockings: *v.i.* to run, as a thread in stockings. **accommodation ladder,** *see* **accommodation. Jacob's ladder,** *see* **Jacob's. ladder-back chair,** a chair having a back made of horizontal pieces of wood. **ladder-proof,** *a.* that has been subjected to a special process designed to prevent "ladders" forming in materials. **ladder-stitch,** a crossbar embroidery stitch. (A.S. *hlæder.*)
laddie, *n.* *lad*-de, a little lad (term of endearment.)
lade, *v.t.* layd, to load; to burden; to freight; throw in or out, as a fluid with a ladle. *pp.* **laden.** *ppr.* **lading,** bill of **lading,** *see* **bill.** (A.S. *hladan*, load.)
ladify, *v.t.* *lay*-de-fy, to make a lady of; to make ladylike or effeminate.
Ladin, *n.* la-*deen*, any of certain dialects of the Engadine and neighbouring parts of N. Italy. (L. *Latinus*, Latin.)
lading, *n.* *lay*-ding, cargo; freight. **bill of lading,** *see* **bill.**
Ladino, *n.* la-*dee*-no, the mixed Hebrew and Spanish dialect spoken by Jews of the Sephardim; in Latin America, a partly Spanish cross-breed, a mestizo.
ladle, *n.* *lay*-dl, a cup-like receptacle with a long handle for lifting or serving out liquid; a similar implement for conveying molten metal from a furnace; the float-board of a mill-wheel: *v.t.* to lift or serve out with a ladle. (A.S. *hlædel.*)
lady, *n.* *lay*-de, a gentlewoman; any woman of refined manners and education; the mistress of a house; a wife; a title borne by peeresses in their own right, by the wife of one of not lower rank than knight (duchesses excepted), and by the daughters of noblemen not lower than earl. **lady almoner, doctor,** etc., a woman qualified for the duty indicated. **lady in waiting,** a lady of a royal household in attendance upon the queen or a princess. **Lady Mayoress,** the wife of a Lord Mayor. **lady's maid,** a female valet to a woman: also used in the names of many wild flowers, as:—**lady's bower,** *Clematis vitalba*; **lady's finger,** *Anthyllis vulneraria*; **lady's glove,** *Inula conyza*; **lady's hair,** *Briza media*; **lady's mantle,** *Alchemilla vulgaris*; **lady's nightcap,** *Convolvulus sepium*; **lady's pin-**

cushion, *Armeria maritima*; **lady's seal,** *Tamus communis*; **lady's slipper,** any *Cypripedium*; **lady's smock,** *Cardamine pratensis*; **lady's thimble,** *Campanula rotundifolia*; **lady's thistle,** *Carduus marianus*; **lady's thumb,** *Polygonum persicaria*; **lady's tresses,** *Neottia spiralis* or any *Spiranthes*. (A.S. *hlæf-dige*, from *hlæf*, a loaf, and *dige*, giver, or *hlæfweardige*, from *hlæf*, and *weardian*, to look after.)

Lady-altar, *n.* an altar in a Lady-chapel.

lady-bird, *n.* a small beetle of the genus *Coccinella*, of a brilliant red or yellow colour and spotted. (Our Lady's bird.)

Lady-chapel, *n.* a chapel, usually in a church or cathedral, dedicated to the Virgin Mary.

lady-cow, *n.* the lady-bird.

Lady-day, *n.* the first quarter-day, the Feast of the Annunciation of the Virgin Mary, March 25th.

lady-fern, *n.* the fern *Asplenium filix-fœmina*.

ladyfy, *v.t. lay*-de-fy, ladify.

lady-help, *n.* a lady undertaking domestic duties for pay.

ladyism, *n. lay*-de-izm, the characteristics, enunciation, or manners of a lady.

lady-killer, *n.* a man who supposes no woman can resist him.

ladylike, *a. lay*-de-like, like a lady in manners; genteel; well-bred; soft; delicate.

ladylove, *n. lay*-de-luv, a sweetheart or mistress.

ladyship, *n. lay*-de-ship, the quality of being a lady; the rank of a lady; used with "your" or "her" of one bearing the title "Lady."

lady's-maid, *n.* a female servant attending to the toilet, clothes, and personal needs of a lady.

lævo-, pref. *lee*-vo, denoting a leftward direction as opposed to dextro-. (L. *lævus*, left.)

lævogyrate, *a.* lee-vo-*jyr*-rat, lævorotatory.

lævorotatory, *a.* lee-vo-ro-*tay*-to-re, turned or rotating towards the left, esp. of rays of polarized light.

lævulose, *n. lee*-vew-lohs, fructose, or fruit sugar, differentiated from dextrose by its lævorotatory property.

lag, *a.* lag, coming behind; long-delayed: *n.* the fag-end; he who or that which comes behind; retardation; a convict [Slang]: *v.i.* to move slowly; to stay behind; to loiter. (Celt.)

lag, *n.* lag, a stave of a cask, etc.; lagging, or material for this: *v.t.* to cover (esp. a boiler) with lagging. (Swed. *lagg*.)

lagan, *n. lag*-an, goods sunk in the sea with a buoy attached in order to be found again [Law].

lager, *n. lah*-ger, a light German beer. (Ger. *lagerbier*, store-beer.)

laggard, *a. lag*-gard, slow; sluggish; backward: *n.* one who falls behind; a loiterer; an idler.

lagging, *n. lag*-ging, a non-conducting covering; a term of imprisonment [Slang]: *a.* loitering.

laggingly, *ad. lag*-ging-le, in a lagging manner.

Lagomys, *n. lag*-o-mis, the genus consisting of the pikas [Zool.]. (Gr. *lagos*, a hare, *mys*, a mouse.)

lagoon, *n.* la-*goon*, a shallow stretch of water near the sea or a river, formed by the overflowing or the infiltration of the waters of the sea; the water-area enclosed by an atoll. (It. *lagone*.)

lagophthalmia, *n.* lag-of-*thal*-me-a, an affection of the eyelids preventing their perfect closure. (Gr. *lagos*, hare, *opthalmos*, eye; hares being fabled to sleep with their eyes open.)

lagopodous, *a.* la-*gop*-o-dus, having feet well covered with hair or feathers. (Gr. *lagos*, hare, *pous*, *podos*, foot.)

lagostoma, *n.* la-*gos*-to-ma, hare-lip. (Gr. *lagos*, and *stoma*, the mouth.)

laic, *a. lay*-ik, lay, not clerical: *n.* a layman. (Gr. *laikos*, from *laos*, the people.)

laical, *a. lay*-e-kal, laic; belonging to the laity.

laicize, *v.t. lay*-e-size, to throw open to the laity; to render secular.

laid, lade, *p.* and *pp.* of *lay*; deposited. **laid up,** stored away; confined to bed; dismantled, as a ship. **laid paper,** writing paper with a ribbed surface marked by the wires on which the pulp is laid.

lain, lane, *p.* and *pp.* of *lie*.

lair, *n.* lare, a place to lie down and rest in; the den or bed of a wild beast; a pen for cattle on the way to market or at an abbatoir. (A.S. *leger*.)

lairage, *n. lare*-raj, lairs for cattle, or the placing of cattle in them.

laird, *n.* layrd, a Scottish landowner. (*lord*.)

laissez-aller, *n. lay*-say-*al*-lay freedom from conventionality; lack of restraint. (Fr.)

laissez-faire, *n. lay*-say-*fare* the principle of non-interference by the Government, esp. in industry and trade. (Fr.)

laity, *n. lay*-e-te, the people, as distinguished from the clergy; those not of some particular profession as distinguished from its members.

lake, *n.* lake, a stretch of water, surrounded by land. **lake dwelling,** a prehistoric hut or house built on piles in shallow lakes. **Lake-country,** or **Lake-land,** the mountainous districts of Cumberland, Lancashire, and Westmorland in which lie the English lakes. (L. *lacus*, a lake.)

lake, *n.* lake, a purplish-red pigment, generally consisting of an aluminous earth coloured with lac or cochineal. (Fr. *laque*.)

lakelet, *n. lake*-let, a little lake.

lakh, *n.* lak, a lac; a hundred thousand. (Hind.)

laky, *a. lake*-e, pertaining to or like a lake.

lallation, *n.* lal-*lay*-shon, the pronunciation of the letter *r* like *l*. (Fr.)

lam, *v.t.* lam, to beat; to thrash; to wallop [Coll.].

lama, *n. lah*-ma, a Tibetan or Mongolian Buddhist priest. (Tib. *blama*, spiritual teacher.)

Lamaism, *n. lah*-ma-izm, Buddhism as professed in Tibet and neighbouring countries, or conceived of as prelatically incarnated in the priesthood.

lamantin, *n.* la-*man*-tin, the manatee. (Fr.)

lamasery, *n. lah*-ma-se-re *or* la-*mah*-se-re, a Tibetan monastery.

lamb, *n.* lam, the young of the sheep; one who is meek and gentle; a member of a church flock: *v.t.* to bring forth young, as sheep. **the Lamb, the Lamb of God,** Christ. **lamb's tails,** hazel catkins. (A.S.)

lamb-ale, *n.* a feast at a sheep shearing.

lambdacism, *n. lam*-da-sizm, an imperfect pronunciation of the letter *l*; lallation. (Gr. *lambda*, the Greek *l*.)

lambdoidal, *a.* lam-*doy*-dal, in the form of the Greek lambda (Λ).

lambency, *n. lam*-ben-se, the state or quality of being lambent.

lambent, *a. lam*-bent, playing on the surface; touching lightly; flickering. (L. *lambens*, licking.)

lambkin, *n. lam*-kin, a small lamb.

lamblike, *a. lam*-like, like a lamb; gentle; meek.

lambrequin, *n. lam*-bre-kin, the covering of a helmet; the conventional representation of this [Her.]; drapery over a door or window. (Fr.)

lambskin, *n. lam*-skin, the prepared skin or skin and fleece of the lamb; a textile imitation of this.

lamb's-wool, *n.* wool from lambs; ale mixed with sugar, nutmeg, and the pulp of roasted apples.

lame, *a.* laym, disabled in a limb, esp. a leg or foot; crippled; hobbling; imperfect; unsatisfactory; not proceeding smoothly: *v.t.* to make lame; to cripple or disable. **lame duck,** one crippled financially; a defaulter on the Stock Exchange. (A.S. *lama*.)

lamé, *n. lah*-may, a rich woven material of or including metallic threads. (Fr.)

lamella, *n.* la-*mel*-la (*pl.* **lamellæ**), a thin plate or scale [Bot. and Zool.]. (L.)

lamellar, *a.* la-*mel*-lar, composed of or disposed in lamellæ.

lamellate, *a. lam*-el-lat, composed of or furnished with lamellæ.

lamellibranch, *n.* la-*mel*-e-brank, any of a class of bivalve molluscs having two pairs of lamelliform gills. (L. *lamella* and *branchia*.)

lamellibranchiate, *a.* la-*mel*-e-*brang*-ke-at, belonging to the Lamellibranchiata, the class of molluscs comprising the lamellibranchs.

lamellicorn, *a.* la-*mel*-e-korn, having short antennæ ending in a lamellate club [Entom.]: *n.* any of a group of lamellicorn beetles.

lamelliferous, *a.* lam-el-*lif*-er-rus, having a lamellar or foliated structure.

lamelliform, *a.* la-*mel*-le-form, having the form of a plate or scale. (L. *lamella*, and *forma*, shape.)

lamellirostral, *a.* la-*mel*-le-*ros*-tral, having the margin of the beak furnished with numerous lamellæ, as the swan. (L. *lamella*, and *rostrum*, a beak.)

lamellose, *a.* la-*mel*-lohs, lamellar; stratified.

lamely, *ad. laym*-le, like a cripple; in a lame manner.

lameness, *n. laym*-ness, the condition of being lame.
lament, *n.* la-*ment*, sorrow expressed in complaints; an elegy; a dirge: *v.i.* to grieve; to express sorrow; to regret deeply: *v.t.* to bewail; to mourn for; to deplore. (Fr. *lamenter*.)
lamentable, *a. lam*-en-ta-bl, to be lamented; deserving sorrow; expressing sorrow; mournful; miserable; pitiful.
lamentably, *ad.* in a lamentable manner.
lamentation, *n. lam*-en-*tay*-shon, the act of bewailing; expression of sorrow; cries of grief: *pl.* (*cap.*) a book of Scripture, containing dirges on the fall of Jerusalem ascribed to Jeremiah.
lamenter, *n.* la-*men*-ter, one who laments.
lamentingly, *ad.* la-*men*-ting-le, with lamentation.
lametta, *n.* la-*met*-ta, foil or wire of gold, silver, or brass. (It.)
lamia, *n. lay*-me-a, a sorceress; a witch. (L.)
lamina, *n. lam*-in-a (*pl.* **laminæ**), a thin plate; a layer or coat lying over another. (L.)
laminable, *a. lam*-in-a-bl, capable of being formed into thin plates.
laminar, *a. lam*-in-ar, in, or consisting of, laminæ.
laminarian, *a.* lam-in-*ayr*-re-an, belonging to the genus of seaweeds comprising those with flat ribbon-like fronds. (L. *lamina*.)
laminate, *v.t. lam*-in-ate, to roll, cut, or form into thin plates: *v.i.* to split off in layers: *a.* consisting of laminæ over one another.
lamination, *n.* lam-in-*nay*-shon, state of being laminated; a laminated formation.
laminiferous, *a.* lam-in-*nif*-er-rus, having a structure consisting of laminæ. (L. *lamina*, and *fero*, bear.)
laminitis, *n.* lam-in-*ny*-tis, founder; inflammation of the fleshy laminæ of a horse's foot.
lamish, *a. laym*-ish, somewhat lame.
Lammas, *n. lam*-mas, the first of August, as the day of first fruits. **old Lammas Day,** the twelfth of August, when grouse shooting begins. (A.S. *hlaf*, loaf or bread, and *mæsse*, feast.)
lammergeyer, *n. lam*-mer-gy-er, a vulture of the genus *Gypaëtus*. (Ger.)
lamp, *n.* lamp, an apparatus for producing light, esp. by the combustion of oil; any source of artificial light; that which enlightens. **lamp glass,** the upright glass tube or chimney for a lamp. (Fr. *lampe*.)
lampadist, *n. lam*-pa-dist, the winner of an ancient Greek torch-race. (Gr. *lampadedromia*, torch-race.)
lampas, *n. lam*-pas, a fleshy swelling behind the fore teeth, in the palate of a horse. (Fr.)
lampas, *n. lam*-pas, a flowered silk. (Fr.)
lampblack, *n. lamp*-blak, a fine soot, formed by the condensation of the smoke of burning pitch, oil, or a resinous substance.
lampern, *n. lam*-pern, the river lamprey.
lampion, *n. lam*-pe-on, a small coloured glass vessel with oil and wick, formerly used in illuminations. (Fr.)
lampless, *a. lamp*-less, unlighted, dark.
lamplight, *n. lamp*-lite, the light of a lamp.
lamplighter, *n. lamp*-lite-er, a lighter of lamps.
lampoon, *n.* lam-*poon*, a personal satire in writing: *v.t.* to abuse with personal satire; to satirize. (O.Fr. *lampon*, a drinking song.)
lampooner, *n.* lam-*poon*-er, a writer of lampoons.
lampoonery, *n.* lam-*poon*-er-re, the practice of writing lampoons.
lampoonist, *n.* lam-*poon*-ist, a lampooner.
lamppost, *n. lamp*-post, the pillar supporting a lamp, esp. for external illumination.
lamprey, *n. lam*-pre, a sea- and river-fish with circular suctorial mouth, resembling the eel in shape. (O.Fr. *lampreie*.)
lamp-shade, *n.* a covering to soften, concentrate, or intercept the light of a lamp.
lamp-shell, *n.* any brachiopod, esp. one of the genus *Terebratula*.
lana, *n. lay*-na, the close-grained wood of the genipap tree. **lana dye,** a pigment from the fruit of the lana. (S. American Ind.)
lanarkite, *n. lan*-ark-ite, a rare monoclinic basic of lead found in Lanarkshire.
lanate, *a. lay*-nat, woolly; covered with curly hair or hair-like filaments [Bot. and Zool.] (L. *lanatus*.)
Lancasterian, *a.* lan-kas-*teer*-re-an, relating to the monitorial system of teaching by advanced pupils introduced by Joseph Lancaster about 1800.
Lancastrian, *a.* lan-*kas*-tre-an, pertaining to the House of Lancaster, descended from John of Gaunt, Duke of Lancaster: *n.* a member or adherent of this; in the Wars of the Roses, a supporter of the Red Rose; a native of Lancashire.
lance, *n.* lahnce, a spear; an offensive weapon with a wooden shaft and a sharp steel point; a lancet; a spear used by whalers: *v.t.* to pierce with a lance or a sharp-pointed instrument; to open with a lancet. (Fr.)
lance-corporal, *n.* a non-commissioned officer ranking between private and corporal.
lancelet, *n. lahnce*-let, a small translucent marine protochordate with laterally compressed body, of the genus *Branchiostoma*.
lanceolar, *a. lan*-se-o-lar, lanceolate.
lanceolate, *a. lan*-se-o-lat, gradually tapering toward the outer extremity, or [Bot.] toward each end. (L. *lanceolatus*, having a spiked end.)
lancer, *n. lahnce*-er, a cavalry soldier armed with a lance: *pl.* a quadrille-like square dance. (Fr. *lancier*.)
lance-sergeant, *n.* a corporal appointed to act as, or on probation as, a sergeant.
lancet, *n. lahnce*-et, a sharp two-edged surgical instrument, used in venesection, opening abscesses, etc.; a lancet window. **lancet arch,** a narrow pointed Gothic arch. **lancet window,** a high and narrow window, pointed like a lancet. (Fr. *lancette*.)
lancewood, *n. lahnce*-wood, the tough elastic wood of certain tropical American trees.
lanciform, *a. lan*-se-form, shaped like a lance or lancet.
lancinate, *v.t. lan*-se-nate, to tear; to lacerate. (L. *lancinatus*, torn.)
lancination, *n. lan*-se-*nay*-shon, a tearing; laceration; a piercing or shooting pain [Med.].
***land,** *n.* land, earth; the solid portion of the surface of the globe, or any portion of it; the mainland; a country or district; ground; soil; real estate; a nation or people: *v.t.* to set on shore; to set down from a vehicle or aircraft; to place; to strike a blow; to acquire or make sure of [Coll.]: *v.i.* to go on shore; to arrive, alight, or disembark. **land force,** a military force serving on land. **land o' the leal,** *see* **leal. land service,** military as distinct from naval service; service ashore. **make (the) land,** to discover land from the sea as the ship approaches it. **set the land,** to see by the compass how it bears from the ship [Naut.]. **shut in the land,** to lose sight of the land left, by the intervention of a point or promontory. (A.S.)
Land, *n.* lahnt, in Germany, a country, state, or large administrative division. (Ger.)
land-agent, *n.* one who manages land for the owner; one who sells landed property.
landamman, *n. land*-am-man, the chief magistrate of some of the Swiss cantons. (Ger.)
landau, *n. lan*-daw, a carriage with a roof that folds back. (*Landau*, in Bavaria, where first made.)
landaulet, *n.* lan-daw-*let*, a small landau; a motor-car with a landau body.
land-breeze, *n.* a current of air setting from the land toward the sea.
land-crab, *n.* a crab living mainly on land, esp. one of the genus *Gecarcinus*.
lande, *n.* lahnd, a large extent of moorland. (Fr.)
landed, *a. land*-ed, having an estate in land; consisting in real estate or land; disembarked; left without a way out.
lander, *n. land*-er, one who lands; the miner who receives the bucket of ore at the pit-head.
landfall, *n. land*-fawl, a sudden or unexpected inheritance of property in land; the first land sighted after a voyage [Naut.]; a coming to land (of aircraft); a landslip. **a good** (or **bad**) **landfall,** the arrival at journey's end according (or not according) to intention.
land-girl, *n.* a woman worker in farming or agriculture, esp. as a member of the Women's Land Army.
landgrave, *n. land*-grave, a title borne by certain nobles having territorial jurisdiction in the mediæval German empire. (Ger. *Land*, land, *Graf*, a count.)
landgraviate, *n.* land-*grave*-e-at, the territory held, or administered, by a landgrave.
landgravine, *n. land*-gra-veen, the wife of a landgrave. (Ger. *Landgräfin*.)

landholder, *n.* *land*-hohl-der, a freeholder; a landowner.
landing, *n.* *land*-ing, the act of going or setting on shore, or [Av.] on earth; the place for disembarking or alighting; the level part of a staircase which connects one flight with another. **landing ground,** a flat unobstructed area prepared or suitable for the landing of aircraft. **landing net,** a small hoop-net, used by anglers for securing their fish. **landing run,** the run of a landing plane from the point at which it touches ground to that at which it comes to rest. **landing speed,** the lowest speed at which a plane can be safely landed. **landing stage,** a floating platform. **landing surveyor** and **waiter,** Custom-house officers controlling the landing of dutiable goods.
land-jobber, *n.* one who speculates in land.
landlady, *n.* *land*-lay-de, a woman who lets apartments; the mistress of an inn; a female landlord.
landless, *a.* *land*-less, destitute of land; not being a landowner.
landlocked, *a.* *land*-lokt, enclosed by land, so as to be protected from the winds and sea; not descending to the sea (of certain salmon, etc.).
landloper, *n.* *land*-lope-er, a vagabond or vagrant [Scot.]. (Dut.).
landlord, *n.* *land*-lord, the owner of land or houses, esp. one who lets his property to tenants; the master of an inn, etc., or of a lodging-house.
landlordism, *n.* *land*-lord-izm, land-ownership with its rights, interests, and influence; the proceedings of landlords in respect to their tenants.
landlubber, *n.* *land*-lub-ber, a landsman [Naut.].
landmark, *n.* *land*-mark, a mark to designate the boundary of land, or of an epoch; an object that serves as a guide; a notable event: *v.t.* to provide with a landmark.
land-mine, *n.* an explosive mine used to destroy advancing troops, tanks, etc.; a powerful bomb dropped by parachute from aircraft and designed to cause widespread devastation by explosion on contact.
landocracy, *n.* lan-*dok*-ra-se, landowners collectively.
landowner, *n.* *land*-ohn-er, a proprietor of land.
land-rail, *n.* the corncrake, *Crex pratensis.*
landscape, *n.* *land*-skape, a view over a portion of the country; a picture of such scenery. **landscape gardening,** the art of laying out grounds, and arranging flower-beds, etc. (Dut. *landschap.*)
landscapist, *n.* *land*-skape-ist, a painter of landscapes.
land-shark, *n.* one who preys on sailors ashore.
landslide, *n.* *land*-slide, a landslip; a serious political debacle.
landslip, *n.* *land*-slip, the slipping of a portion of land to a lower level; the land that has thus slipped.
landsman, *n.* *landz*-man, one who lives on the land, opposed to a seaman; a sailor on his first voyage [Naut.].
land-spring, *n.* a spring which comes into action only after heavy rains.
land-steward, *n.* one in charge of the management of a landed estate.
Landsting, *n.* *lahn*-sting, the upper house of the Danish legislative assembly.
Landsturm, *n.* *lahnt*-shtoorm, a former militia of Germany and elsewhere, serving only in its own district, and only in case of actual invasion; the final reserve; the general levy of the nation. (Ger. *Land,* country, *Sturm,* storm.)
land-surveyor, *n.* one who measures and draws plans of landed estates, etc.
Landtag, *n.* *lahnt*-tahg, the legislative assembly of certain former German states.
land-tax, *n.* a tax assessed on land and buildings.
land-waiter, *n.* an officer of the Customs whose duty is to wait or attend on landed goods.
landward, *ad.* *land*-ward, towards the land.
Landwehr, *n.* *lahnt*-vare, that part of the army in Germany (and certain other states) which had finished its service with the colours but was still liable to be called out for active service; the second line of defence. (Ger. *Land,* country, *Wehr,* defence.)
land-wind, *n.* a wind blowing from the land.
lane, *n.* lane, a narrow way or passage; a narrow street; a country by-road; a passage between lines of people standing on each side; a prescribed or recognized ocean route. **the red lane,** the throat [Slang]. (A.S.)
langite, *n.* *lang*-gite, a rare native hydrated copper sulphate allied to brochantite. (von *Lang,* 19th-cent. Austrian physicist.)
langrage, *n.* *lan*-graj, case-shot formerly used for damaging rigging, etc.
Langshan, *n.* *lang*-shan, a breed of black poultry, brought originally from China. (Chin.)
langsyne, *ad.* lang-*syne,* long ago: *n.* the days of old. (Scots.)
***language,** *n.* *lang*-gwaj, the expression of ideas by words or articulate sounds; speech; dialect; any manner of expression; phraseology; literary style. **bad language,** oaths; vulgar abuse. **strong language,** forcible expressions. (Fr. *langage,* from L. *lingua,* the tongue.)
languaged, *a.* *lang*-gwajd, having a language; expert in language.
languet, *n.* *lang*-gwet, any tongue-shaped part or implement; one of the tongue-like processes on the bronchial sac of some ascidians [Zool.]. (Fr. *languette.*)
languid, *a.* *lang*-gwid, faint; indisposed to exertion; listless; feeble; slow; without animation. (L. *languidus,* feeble.)
languidly, *ad.* *lang*-gwid-le, in a languid manner.
languidness, *n.* the state of being languid.
languish, *n.* *lang*-gwish, act of languishing; a soft and tender look: *v.i.* to become listless or languid; to lose strength or animation; to pine, droop, or wither; to look with tenderness or wistfulness. (Fr. *languissant,* languishing.)
languishingly, *ad.* *lang*-gwish-ing-le, in a languishing manner.
languishment, *n.* *lang*-gwish-ment, the act or state of languishing; softness of look or mien; languor; inertness; mental depression.
languor, *n.* *lang*-gor, slackness; want of interest; heaviness; dullness; lassitude; listlessness; softness. (Fr. *langueur.*)
languorous, *a.* *lang*-go-rus, characterized by, or inducing, languor.
langur, *n.* *lang*-gur, a slender, long-tailed monkey of the genus *Semnopithecus.* (Hind.)
laniard, *n.* *lan*-yard, a lanyard.
laniary, *a.* *lan*-e-a-re, lacerating; adapted for tearing. (L. *laniarius,* pertaining to a butcher.)
laniferous, *a.* la-*nif*-er-rus, bearing or producing wool. (L. *lana,* wool, *fero,* bear.)
lanigerous, *a.* la-*nij*-er-rus, bearing wool; woolly.
lank, *a.* lank, loose or lax; flabby; tall and thin; limp; languid. (A.S. *hlanc.*)
lankiness, *n.* state of being lanky; slenderness.
lankly, *ad.* *lank*-le, in a lank manner; limply.
lankness, *n.* the state of being lank.
lanky, *a.* *lang*-ke, tall and thin; lean and spare.
lanner, *n.* *lan*-ner, the female of the falcon, *Falco feldeggi.* (Fr. *lanier.*)
lanneret, *n.* lan-ner-*ret,* the male lanner, as smaller.
lanolin, *n.* *lan*-o-lin, wool grease, an unctuous product of wool used in ointments, cosmetics, etc. (L. *lana,* and *oleum,* fat or oil.)
lansquenet, *n.* *lance*-ke-net, formerly, a German foot-soldier, usually in foreign service; a gambling card-game. (Fr., from Ger. *Land,* country, *Knecht,* a servant.)
lantern, *n.* *lan*-tern, a case (usually portable) for holding a light; a dome raised over the roof of a building to light the interior and crown the exterior; an architectural structure for the illumination from without of a gallery, etc.; the chamber containing the light in a lighthouse; a magic lantern; a lantern pinion. **Chinese lantern,** a collapsible lantern of thin paper. **dark lantern,** one which may be closed so as entirely to hide the light. **lantern fly,** any of several tropical insects of the genera *Laternaria, Fulgora,* etc. formerly supposed to emit light in the dark. **lantern jaws,** long thin jaws; a thin visage. **lantern pinion** or **wheel,** a kind of pinion on which the teeth of the main wheel act [Mech.]. **magic lantern,** an optical instrument by which magnified pictures on glass are projected on a screen or prepared surface. (Fr. *lanterne,* from Gr. *lampo,* shine.)
lanthanum, *n.* *lan*-tha-num, a metallic element of the cerium sub-group of the rare earth metals. (Gr. *lanthano,* be hid.)
lanthorn, *n.* *lan*-tern, a lantern.

lanuginous, *a.* la-*new*-je-nus, downy; covered with down, or fine soft hair. (L. *lana*, wool.)

lanyard, *n.* *lan*-yard, a short piece of cord or line made fast to anything as a handle or to secure it. (O.Fr. *lanière*, a leather thong.)

Laodicean, *a.* *lay*-o-de-*see*-an, pertaining to the Christians of Laodicea in ancient Phrygia, or its inhabitants, esp. lukewarm in religion, etc.: *n.* a native of Laodicea; one who is half-hearted or indifferent in matters of religion, politics, etc. (Rev. iii, 15).

lap, *n.* lap, a loose overhanging flap; the part of a garment that hangs loosely and lies on the knees when the wearer sits; the part of the body covered by this; a roll of textile fibre for carding; a disk or wheel on which leather is secured, used for burnishing, etc.; a length of wound material making one circuit of the reel; a single circuit of a racing-track: *v.t.* to fold; to bend and lay over or on; to place one thing upon another, so as partially to cover it; to wrap round; to infold; to polish with a lap: *v.i.* to be spread or laid; to be turned over; to complete a lap in a race. **lap weld,** a weld in which the parts joined overlap. (A.S. *læppa.*)

lap, *n.* lap, a licking, or the sound of the act: *v.t.* to lick up with the tongue: *v.i.* to feed or drink by licking; to sound as if lapping. (A.S. *lapian.*)

laparotomy, *n.* lap-a-*rot*-o-me, the operation of cutting into the abdominal cavity, esp. for the purpose of examination [Surg.].

lap-dog, *n.* *lap*-dog, a small pet dog.

lapel, *n.* la-*pel* or *lap*-el, a part of a garment that folds over, esp. the continuation of a coat collar. (Diminutive of *lap.*)

lapful, *n.* *lap*-ful, as much as the lap can hold.

lapidary, *a.* *lap*-e-da-re, pertaining to the art of cutting stones: *n.* a cutter and polisher of ornamental stones; a dealer in precious stones; one skilled in these or in lapidary work. **lapidary bee,** a bumble-bee, *Bombus lapidarius*, which nests among stones. **lapidary style,** the style proper for monumental or other inscriptions. **lapidary's wheel,** the lathe on which precious stones are ground and polished. (L. *lapidarius*, a stonemason.)

lapidation, *n.* *lap*-e-*day*-shon, stoning to death. (L.)

lapideous, *a.* la-*pid*-e-us, of the nature of stone.

lapidescent, *a.* *lap*-e-*des*-sent, turning to stone; petrifying: *n.* a substance which petrifies.

lapidification, *n.* la-*pid*-e-fe-*kay*-shon, the operation of forming or converting into a stony substance.

lapidify, *v.t.* la-*pid*-e-fy, to form into stone: *v.i.* to turn into stone. (L. *lapis*, and *facio*, make.)

lapidose, *a.* *lap*-e-dohs, stony; abounding in stones.

lapilli, *n.pl.* la-*pil*-ly, small stones or ashes erupted from a volcano. (L.)

lapilliform, *a.* la-*pil*-le-form, pebble shaped.

lapis-lazuli, *n.* *lap*-is-*laz*-yoo-le, a deep-blue ornamental crystalline stone composed largely of lazurite; an ultramarine pigment made from this. (L.)

lap-joint, *n.* *lap*-joynt, an overlapping joint, as that in a clinker-built boat.

Laplander, *n.* *lap*-land-er, an inhabitant of Lapland, in North Scandinavia.

Lapp, *n.* lap, a Laplander; a member of a dwarfish race in Scandinavia; the language of this race: *a.* pertaining to this race. (Swed.)

lapper, *n.* *lap*-per, one who laps, wraps, or folds; a worker with a lapidary's lap.

lappet, *n.* *lap*-pet, a loose flap on a dress or head-dress; the lobe of an ear; a wattle. (Diminutive of *lap.*)

Lappic, *a.* *lap*-ik, pertaining to Lapland or the Lapps: *n.* the Lapp language.

lapsable, *a.* *lap*-sa-bl, that may lapse or be lapsed.

lapse, *n.* laps, a flowing or passing gradually; an imperceptible gliding; a slip, mistake, or fault; a failing in duty; omission; deviation from truth or rectitude; the termination of a right or privilege through omission to exercise it within the allotted period [Law]; the fall of Adam [Theol.]: *v.i.* to glide or slip; to pass by degrees; to slide or slip in moral conduct; to fail in duty; to fall from a state of innocence, of truth, faith or rectitude; to fall or pass from one to another by negligence, omission, or desuetude; to become void [Law]. **lapsed legacy,** a legacy which lapses to the heirs at law from the death of a legatee, or other cause. (L. *lapsare*, slide down.)

lapstone, *n.* *lap*-stone, a shoemaker's stone, placed in his lap, on which he hammers his leather.

Laputan, *a.* la-*pew*-tan, visionary; extravagantly absurd: *n.* an inhabitant of Laputa; a romantic Utopian. (*Laputa*, flying island in "Gulliver's Travels.")

lapwing, *n.* *lap*-wing, the peewit, a bird of the plover family. (A.S. *hleàpewince*, from *hleàpan*, to leap.)

lapwork, *n.* *lap*-wurk, work in which parts overlap.

Lar, *n.* lar (*pl.* **Lares**, *lare*-reez), a household god or ancestral spirit, reverenced as guardian of a household; (*l.c.*; *pl.* **lars**) the Malayan gibbon *Hylobates lar*. **Lares and Penates,** *see* **Penates.** (L.)

larboard, *n.* *lar*-bord, the side of a ship to the left of a person looking from the stern; the port side: *a.* pertaining to this side. (Derivation uncertain.)

larcener, *n.* *lar*-se-ner, a thief.

larcenous, *a.* *lar*-se-nus, of the nature of theft.

larceny, *n.* *lar*-se-ne, theft [Law]. (Fr. *larcin.*)

larch, *n.* larch, a conifer of the genus *Larix*; the tough timber of this. (Ger. *lärche*, from L.)

lard, *n.* lard, the melted fat (and formerly the flesh) of swine: *v.t.* to thread strips of bacon fat into; to smear with lard; to interlard. (Fr.)

lardaceous, *a.* lar-*day*-she-us, of the nature of, or consisting of, lard.

larder, *n.* *lard*-er, a room or place where meat and other perishable provisions are kept; loosely, a pantry.

lardon, *n.* *lard*-on, a strip of fat bacon used in larding. (Fr.)

lardy, *a.* *lard*-e, containing, or full of, lard.

lardy-dardy, *a.* *lard*-e-*dard*-e, foppish; affected.

Lares, *n.pl.* *lare*-reez, *see* **Lar.**

large, *a.* larj, great in size, quantity, number, extent, or capacity, etc.; bulky; abundant; numerous; ample; diffuse; wide; extensive; capacious; comprehensive; liberal; generous: *ad.* by a great deal; fully, at length. **at large,** without restraint or confinement; diffusely; fully. **by and large,** *see* **by.** (Fr.)

large-hearted, *a.* having a liberal or generous disposition.

largely, *ad.* *larj*-le, to a large extent.

large-minded, *a.* magnanimous.

largen, *v.i.* and *t.* *lar*-jen, to grow or to make large or larger.

largeness, *n.* the state or quality of being large.

largess, *n.* *lar*-jes, a gift, esp. from a superior; a bounty; alms thrown to a crowd. (Fr. *largesse.*)

larghetto, *ad.* lar-*get*-to, somewhat slowly [Mus.]: *n.* a larghetto movement [Mus.]. (It.)

largish, *a.* *lar*-jish, somewhat large.

largo, *ad.* *lar*-go, slowly [Mus.]: *n.* a piece or movement in this time [Mus.]. (It.)

lariat, *n.* *la*-re-at, a lasso rope for picketing horses: *v.t.* to catch or secure with this. (Sp. *lariata.*)

lark, *n.* lark, any small bird of the genus *Alauda*; the skylark, *A. arvensis*, remarkable for its lively song: *v.i.* to catch larks. (A.S. *lawerce*, or *laferce.*)

lark, *n.* lark, a frolic; a prank; a spree: *v.i.* to indulge in a frolic. (Origin doubtful.)

larkiness, *n.* *lark*-e-ness, the quality of being larky; playful merriment.

lark's-heel, *n.* *larks*-heel, the nasturtium.

larkspur, *n.* *lark*-spur, a plant of the genus *Delphinium*.

larky, *a.* *lark*-e, inclined for a spree; sportive.

larmier, *n.* *lar*-me-er, a corona or drip-stone [Arch.]; a tear-pit, the lachrymal fossa [Anat.]. (Fr.)

larrikin, *n.* *la*-re-kin, a hooligan; a rowdy youngster; a street Arab. (Austral. Slang.)

larrup, *v.t.* *la*-rup, to beat or flog. (Dial.)

larum, *n.* *la*-rum, alarum; tumultuous uproar.

Larus, *n.* *lare*-rus, a genus of sea-birds comprising the gulls and terns. (Gr. *laros*, sea-bird.)

larva, *n.* *lar*-va (*pl.* **larvæ**), an insect in the stage of caterpillar, grub, or maggot. (L., a mask.)

larval, *a.* *lar*-val, pertaining to or characteristic of a larva or larvæ.

larvicide, *n.* *lar*-ve-side, the large-scale destruction of the larvæ of pests.

larviform, *a.* *lar*-ve-form, of larva shape.

larviparous, *a.* lar-*vip*-a-rus, bringing forth young as larvæ; produced in the form of larvæ.

laryngeal, *a.* la-*rin*-je-al, pertaining to the larynx.

laryngectomy, *n.* la-ring-*gek*-to-me, removal of the larynx by surgical operation.
laryngismus, *n.* la-ring-*gis*-mus, a spasmodic affection of the glottis. (Gr. *larynx.*)
laryngitis, *n.* la-ring-*jy*-tis, inflammation of the larynx.
laryngologist, *n.* la-ring-*gol*-o-jist, a specialist in disorders of the larynx [Med.].
laryngophony, *n.* la-ring-*gof*-o-ne, the sound of the voice as heard through the stethoscope over the larynx. (Gr. *larynx,* and *phone,* voice.)
laryngoscope, *n.* lar-*ring*-go-skope, an instrument with a reflecting mirror for examining the larynx and throat. (Gr. *larynx,* and *skopeo,* view.)
laryngoscopy, *n.* *la*-ring-*gos*-ko-pe, the employment of, or the technique of using, the laryngoscope.
laryngotomy, *n.* *la*-ring-*got*-o-me, the operation of cutting into the larynx. (Gr. *larynx,* and *tome,* cutting.)
larynx, *n.* *la*-rinks, the upper part of the windpipe, a cartilaginous cavity containing the vocal chords and serving to modulate the sound of the voice [Anat.]. (Gr.)
lascar, *n.* *las*-kar, a native East Indian sailor. (Hind., camp follower, from Per. *lashkar,* camp.)
lascivious, *a.* la-*siv*-e-us, lustful; lewd; wanton; exciting lust. (L. *lascivus.*)
lasciviously, *ad.* in a lascivious manner.
lasciviousness, *n.* quality of being lascivious.
lash, *n.* lash, a thong, esp. of a whip; a whip or scourge; a stroke with a whip or anything pliant; a stroke of satire; a bitter sarcasm or retort; an eyelash: *v.t.* to strike with a lash or anything pliant; to whip; to throw up with a sudden jerk; to dash against; to tie or bind with a rope or cord; to scourge with censure, satire, or sarcasm: *v.i.* to ply the whip; to attack severely. **lash out,** to be extravagant or unruly. (M.E. *lasshe.*)
lasher, *n.* *lash*-er, one who whips or lashes; a weir, the water rushing over it, or the pool beneath it; applied also to certain marine fish as the sculpin and the father lasher, or the sea-scorpion.
lashing, *n.* *lash*-ing, a piece of rope for binding or making fast one thing to another; castigation or chastisement: *pl.* a great deal of anything, as lashings of milk [Slang].
lashkar, *n.* *lash*-kar, a body of tribal troops, esp. on the N.-W. Frontier. (Hind.)
lasket, *n.* *las*-ket, a small loop sewn to a sail to fasten it on to its bonnet [Naut.].
lass, *n.* lass, a young woman; a girl; a sweetheart. (M.E. *lasce.*)
lassie, *n.* *lass*-e, a young lass.
lassitude, *n.* *las*-se-tewd, the condition of weariness; heaviness; languor. (Fr.)
lasso, *n.* *las*-so, a rope, with a noose, for catching cattle and wild horses: *v.t.* to catch with the lasso. (O.Sp. *laso,* from L. *laqueus,* a noose.)
***last,** *a.* lahst, that comes after all the others; latest; hindmost; next before the present; utmost; ultimate; lowest; least likely: *ad.* the last time; the time before the present; in the end. **at last,** at the end. **to the last,** to the end. (*lætest,* superlative of A.S. *læt,* late.)
last, *v.i.* lahst, to continue in time; to endure; to continue unimpaired; to hold out: *n.* lasting (the fabric). (A.S. *last,* a foot-track.)
last, *n.* lahst, a load; a cargo; a local weight or measure. (A.S. *hlæst,* a weight.)
last, *n.* lahst, a model of the human foot on which shoes are formed. (A.S. *læst,* a footprint.)
lastage, *n.* *lahs*-taj, ballast; the lading of a ship; the dues paid for the right of lading a ship.
lasting, *a.* *lahs*-ting, continuing; durable: *n.* endurance; a durable woollen stuff formerly used in making women's shoes.
lastingly, *ad.* *lahs*-ting-le, in a lasting manner.
lastingness, *n.* quality or state of long continuance.
lastly, *ad.* in the last place; finally; in conclusion.
lat, *n.* lat, the franc of the Latvian Republic, equal to about 9½*d.* at par.
latakia, *n.* lat-a-*kee*-a, a high grade of Turkish tobacco exported from Latakia, near Beyrut.
latch, *n.* latch, a movable catch for a door, gate, or lid; a spring lock; a lasket [Naut.]: *v.t.* to fasten with a latch. (A.S. *læccan,* seize.)
latchet, *n.* *latch*-et, a shoe fastening. (O.Fr.)
latchett, *n.* *latch*-et, a fishmongers' name for the gurnard.
latch-key, *n.* a key for opening the latch of a door.
***late,** *a.* late, coming after the usual time; slow; tardy; long-delayed; far-advanced; existing not long ago, but not now; departed or deceased; not long past; recent: *ad.* after the usual time; not long ago; lately; far in the night, day, week or other particular period. **late fee,** an extra charge for transmission by a mail after its time of closing. **of late,** in time not long past. **too late,** not in due time. (A.S. *læt,* slow.)
lateen, *n.* la-*teen,* a triangular sail, extended by a long yard at a slope of about 45°. (Fr. *latine.*)
lately, *ad.* *late*-le, not long ago; recently.
latency, *n.* *lay*-ten-se, the state of being latent.
lateness, *n.* *late*-ness, the condition of being late.
latent, *a.* *lay*-tent, dormant; concealed; not visible or apparent. **latent heat,** heat which enters into a body while changing its form from a solid to a liquid, or from a liquid to a vapour, without altering its temperature. (L. *latens,* lying hid.)
lateral, *a.* *lat*-er-ral, pertaining to, towards, or proceeding from the side; (of consonants) uttered with the tongue free on one or both sides, its tip touching the palate, as *l* in *late, plate,* etc. [Phon.]. (L. *lateralis.*)
laterality, *n.* lat-er-*ral*-e-te, the quality of being lateral; over-development on one side [Med.].
lateralize, *v.t.* *lat*-er-ra-lize, to direct to, or localize on, one side; to render lateral or [Phon.] laterally.
laterally, *ad.* *lat*-er-ra-le, in a lateral manner or direction.
Lateran, *n.* *lat*-er-ran, the cathedral church of the Pope, as Bishop of Rome. **Lateran Council,** any of the five general councils held therein. **Lateran Pact,** the concordat of 1929 between the Papacy and the Kingdom of Italy by which the Vatican State was established. (Roman family of *Laterani,* owners of a palace formerly on this site.)
laterifolious, *a.* *lat*-er-re-*foh*-le-us, growing on the side of a leaf at the base [Bot.]. (L. *latus,* side, *folium,* a leaf.)
laterite, *n.* *lat*-er-rite, a red clay composed chiefly of hydroxides of iron and aluminium. (L. *later,* a brick.)
latest, *a.* *late*-est, the most recent.
latex, *n.* *lay*-teks, the milky juice of certain plants; the viscous fluid obtained by tapping rubber trees and coagulating into rubber; a rubber solution used to toughen paper. (L., a fluid.)
lath, *n.* lahth, a thin narrow strip of wood used for the support of tiles or plaster, also in Venetian blinds, for trellis-work, etc.: *v.t.* to cover or line with laths. (A.S. *lætt.*)
lathe, *n.* laythe, one of the five administrative divisions of the county of Kent. (A.S.)
lathe, *n.* laythe, a machine tool for holding and rotating material to be turned, chased, polished, bored, etc.; a potter's wheel; the batten in a loom. **lathe-bed,** the lower framework of a lathe having a slot for adjustment. (Origin doubtful.)
lather, *n.* *lah*-ther *or* *lath*-er, froth made by soap moistened with water, or produced from profuse perspiration: *v.i.* to form such a froth or foam; to become froth or frothy matter: *v.t.* to spread over with lather; to thrash [Coll.]. (A.S. *leathor.*)
lathi, *n.* *lah*-the, the staff-like truncheon of the Indian native police. (Hind.)
lath-work, *n.* a lining or covering of laths for receiving plaster.
lathy, *a.* *lahth*-e, thin as a lath; long and slender.
laticiferous, *a.* *lat*-e-*sif*-er-rus, bearing or conveying latex. (L. *latex,* and *fero,* bear.)
laticlave, *n.* *lat*-e-klave, the broad purple stripe on the tunic, the distinctive badge of a Roman senator. (L. *latus,* broad, *clavus,* a stripe.)
laticostate, *a.* *lat*-e-*kos*-tat, broad-ribbed [Zool.]. (L. *latus,* and *costa,* a rib.)
latidentate, *a.* *lat*-e-*den*-tat, broad-toothed. (L.)
latifoliate, *a.* *lat*-e-*foh*-le-at, latifolious.
latifolious, *a.* *lat*-e-*foh*-le-us, having broad leaves. (L. *latus,* and *folium,* a leaf.)
Latin, *a.* *lat*-in, pertaining to ancient Latium, in Italy, or its people; Roman; of or pertaining to the Latin language or one of the languages derived from this: *n.* a native of Latium; the language of the ancient Romans. **Latin America,** those parts of America under the rule of one of the Latin peoples. **Latin Church,** the Roman Catholic branch of the Catholic Church. **Latin Empire,** the Byzantine Empire under the rule of the

Crusaders (1204–1261). **Latin Kingdom,** the Kingdom of Jerusalem under the rule of the Crusaders (1099–1187). **Latin peoples,** the Italians, French, Spanish, and Portuguese. **Latin Quarter,** a district of Paris near the Sorbonne, on the south side of the Seine, frequented chiefly by students. **Latin Union,** a monetary alliance, subsisting among certain European countries 1865–1926, to maintain and regulate a uniform bimetallic currency based on the French franc. **dog Latin,** illiterate Latin. **law Latin,** *see* **law. thieves' Latin,** secret language used by thieves. (L. *Latinus*, pertaining to *Latium.*)

latine, *ad.* la-*tee*-ne, in Latin.

Latinism, *n.* *lat*-in-izm, a Latin idiom.

Latinist, *n.* *lat*-in-ist, one skilled in Latin.

latinity, *n.* la-*tin*-e-te, purity of the Latin style or idiom; the Latin tongue or idiom.

latinize, *v.t.* *lat*-in-ize, to give Latin terminations to; to put into Latin; to render comformable to the ideas, etc., of the Romans, the Latin races, or the Latin Church: *v.i.* to use words or phrases borrowed from the Latin.

latipennate, *a.* *lat*-e-*pen*-nat, having broad wings.

latirostral, *a.* *lat*-e-*ros*-tral, having a broad beak. (L. *latus*, and *rostrum*, a beak.)

latiseptate, *a.* lat-e-*sep*-tat, having a broad septum or dissepiment [Bot., Zool.].

latish, *a.* *late*-ish, somewhat late.

latitude, *n.* *lat*-e-tewd, angular distance on a meridian N. or S. from the equator; the angular distance of a heavenly body from the ecliptic [Astron.]; breadth; width; space; scope; extent of meaning; freedom from rules or limits; laxity. **high latitudes,** regions in the neighbourhood of either pole. **low latitudes,** regions near the equator. (Fr.)

latitudinal, *a.* *lat*-e-*tew*-de-nal, pertaining to latitude; in the direction of latitude.

latitudinarian, *a.* *lat*-e-*tew*-de-*nare*-re-an, not restrained; not confined within narrow or established limits in religious principles or views; freethinking: *n.* one who is latitudinarian or unorthodox, esp. [Theol.] one who indulges in undue latitude of thinking and interpretation. (L. *latitudo*, breadth.)

latitudinarianism, *n.* *lat*-e-*tew*-de-*nare*-re-a-nizm, freedom or laxness of opinion in theology.

latitudinous, *a.* *lat*-e-*tew*-de-nus, having latitude or breadth; characterized by latitudinarianism.

latria, *n.* la-*tre*-a, the highest kind of worship, or that paid to God. (Gr. *latreia*, service.)

latrine, *n.* la-*treen*, a privy, esp. in barracks and camps. (L. from *lavo*, wash.)

latrobite, *n.* *lat*-ro-bite, a variety of pink anorthite found only in Labrador. (C. J. *Latrobe*, discoverer.)

-latry, a suffix denoting worship of, or excessive devotion to, as *autolatry*, *bardolatry*. (Gr. *latreia*, service.)

latten, *n.* *lat*-ten, a fine brass formerly used for crosses and memorial plates; sheet brass, or plates of mixed metal: *a.* made of latten. (O.Fr. *laton.*)

latter, *a.* *lat*-ter, coming or happening after something else; last named of two; lately done or past. **latter-day,** modern. **Latter-day Saints,** the Mormons.

latterly, *ad.* *lat*-ter-le, of late; in time not long past; lately; at last.

lattice, *n.* *lat*-tis, a network made by crossing laths, rods, or bars; anything, as a window, of lattice: *a.* consisting of cross pieces; furnished with lattice-work: *v.t.* to form with cross bars and open work; to furnish with a lattice. **lattice-girder,** a girder the flanges of which are connected by iron lattice-work. **lattice-work,** the arrangement of laths or bars, etc. forming a lattice. (Fr. *lattis.*)

Latvian, *a.* *lat*-ve-an, pertaining to Latvia: *n.* an inhabitant of Latvia.

laud, *n.* lawd, praise; eulogy; that part of divine worship which consists in praise: *pl.* the first of the day-hours in the liturgy of the Church: *v.t.* to praise in words alone, or with words and singing; to celebrate. (L. *laudo*, praise.)

laudability, *n.* *lawd*-a-*bil*-e-te, laudableness.

laudable, *a.* *lawd*-a-bl, praiseworthy.

laudableness, *n.* *lawd*-a-bl-ness, the quality of being laudable.

laudably, *ad.* *lawd*-a-ble, in a laudable manner.

laudanum, *n.* *lod*-a-num, opium prepared in spirits of wine; tincture of opium. (L. *ladanum.*)

laudation, *n.* law-*day*-shon, praise; honour paid.

laudative, *a.* *lawd*-a-tiv, laudatory.

laudatory, *a.* *lawd*-a-to-re, containing praise; expressing praise. (Late L. *laudatorius.*)

***laugh,** *n.* lahf, an audible and convulsive expression of mirth, ridicule, scorn, etc., peculiar to the human species; the act or manner of making this expression; the sound of laughter: *v.i.* to make the noise and exhibit the features which sudden mirth creates; to be gay, cheerful, or lively; to ridicule or deride: *v.t.* to express by laughing; to utter with laughter. **laugh at,** to ridicule. **laugh off,** to dismiss or ward off with pleasantry. **laugh in one's sleeve,** *see* **sleeve. laugh to scorn,** to deride; to treat with mockery. (A.S. *hlihan.*)

laughable, *a.* *lahf*-a-bl, exciting or fitted to excite laughter; ludicrous.

laughableness, *n.* *lahf*-a-bl-ness, the quality of being laughable.

laughably, *ad.* *lahf*-a-ble, so as to excite laughter.

laugher, *n.* *lahf*-er, one who laughs.

laughing-gas, *n.* the anæsthetic nitrous oxide which induces laughing spasms when inhaled. **laughing gull,** the peewit gull. **laughing hyena,** the spotted hyena. **laughing jackass,** *see* **jackass.**

laughingly, *ad.* *lahf*-ing-le, in a merry way.

laughing-stock, *n.* an object of ridicule.

laughter, *n.* *lahf*-ter, the partly involuntary vocal and facial actions, expressive of mirth, etc., produced by laughing. **Homeric laughter,** *see* **Homeric.**

laumontite, *n.* *law*-mon-tite, a zeolite, composed chiefly of hydrated silicate of aluminium and calcium. (Named from its discoverer, G. *Laumont*, 1805.)

launce, *n.* lahns, a sand-eel of the genus *Ammodytes.*

launch, *n.* lawnch *or* lahnch, the act of moving, or the movement of, a ship from the land into the water; a long, flat-bottomed boat, now generally motor-propelled; a pleasure-boat; the largest boat of a warship: *v.t.* to throw, as a lance; to send forth; to cause to slide into the water; to set going a person or enterprise; *v.i.* to glide or shoot into the water; to go forth; to expatiate in language. **to launch out,** to rush into expense; to commence an undertaking; to break out into strong language. (Sp. *lancha.*)

launder, *n.* *lawn*-der *or* *lahn*-der, a long, hollow trough, used in washing ore: *v.t.* to wash and iron; to work in a laundry. (O. Fr. *lavendiere*, a washer-woman.)

launderer, *n.* *lawn*-der-rer, a man who, or firm that, undertakes laundry-work.

laundress, *n.* *lawn*-dres *or* *lahn*-dres, a washer-woman; a woman caretaker in legal chambers.

laundry, *n.* *lawn*-dre *or* *lahn*-dre, the works or room where clothes, linen, etc., are washed; clothes, etc., to be washed. **laundryman,** a male worker in a laundry. **laundry-maid,** a female servant who attends to the laundry. **laundry-work,** the business or operation of washing and getting up clothes, linen, etc.

laura, *n.* *law*-ra, a group of cells for recluses, esp. in the desert. (Gr., a narrow way.)

laureate, *a.* *law*-re-at, crowned with laurel; worthy to be so crowned; eminent: *n.* one crowned with laurel; a poet laureate (*see* **poet**). (L. *laureatus*, crowned with a laurel-wreath.)

laureateship, *n.* *law*-re-at-ship, the office, rank, or dignity of laureate.

laureation, *n.* *law*-re-*ay*-shon, the act of conferring a degree in a university.

laurel, *n.* *lo*-rel, the bay-tree, *Laurus nobilis*, dedicated to Apollo and used in making wreaths for victors; a wreath of laurel; a distinctive honour; *a.* consisting of laurel. **garden laurel,** a shrub of the genus *Prunus.* **laurel water,** the leaves of the laurel distilled with water, and used medicinally. **Portugal laurel,** *Cerasus lusitanicus.* **spurge laurel,** *Daphne laureola.* **to look to one's laurels,** to take care not to lose one's pre-eminence. **to win or reap laurels,** to win distinction. **to rest on one's laurels,** to cease from efforts; to retire. (Fr. *laurier.*)

laurelled, *a.* *lo*-reld, crowned with laurel.

lauriferous, *a.* law-*rif*-er-rus, producing or bringing laurel. (L. *laurus*, and *fero*, bear.)

laurin, *n.* *law*-rin, an acrid, fatty substance, contained in the berries of the laurel. (L. *laurus.*)

laurite, *n.* *law*-rite, a sulphide of ruthenium and osmium. (L. *laurus.*)
laurustinus, *n.* *law*-rus-*ty*-nus, an ornamental evergreen shrub of southern Europe, *Viburnum tinus.* (L. *laurus,* and *tinus,* plant.)
lautu, *n.* *lou*-too, llautu.
lava, *n.* *lah*-va, molten rock matter issuing in streams from the vent of a volcano; such matter solidified. **lava cone,** a volcanic cone built up by successive flows of lava. (It. *lava,* a stream.)
lavabo, *n.* la-*vay*-bo, a formal or ritual washing of hands; the basin, or towel, used in this. (L., I will wash.)
lavage, *n.* *lay*-vaj, the cleansing by irrigation of the stomach, colon, or other organ [Med.]. (Fr.)
lavation, *n.* la-*vay*-shon, the act of washing or cleansing. (L. *lavatio.*)
lavatorial, *a.* *lav*-a-*taw*-re-al, pertaining to washing, or to lavatories.
lavatory, *n.* *lav*-a-to-re, a place for washing the hands and face; a water-closet; a urinal; a public convenience. (Late L. *lavatorium.*)
lave, *v.t.* lave, to wash; to flow past or against: *v.i.* to wash oneself; to bathe. (L. *lavare,* to wash.)
lavender, *n.* *lav*-en-der, the odoriferous flowering shrub, *Lavandula vera*; its dried flowers, etc., used to scent newly washed linen, etc.; a greyish blue colour. **lavender water,** a perfume composed of spirits of wine, essential oil of lavender and ambergris. **sea lavender,** a plant of the genus *Statice.* (Late L. *lavendula,* of uncertain origin.)
laver, *n.* *lay*-ver, a brazen vessel used in Jewish ritual washing; a large basin.
laver, *n.* *lay*-ver, various marine seaweeds of the genera *Porphyra* and *Ulva,* some of which are edible.
laverock, *n.* *lav*-er-ok, the skylark [Scot.].
lavish, *a.* *lav*-ish, expending or bestowing with profusion; liberal to a fault; prodigal; unrestrained; wasteful: *v.t.* to expend or bestow with profusion; to squander. (O.Fr. *lavasse,* a deluge.)
lavishly, *ad.* *lav*-ish-ly, in a lavish manner.
lavishness, *n.* the quality of being lavish.
lavolta, *n.* la-*vol*-ta, an old dance involving much turning and capering. (It. *la volta,* the turn.)
***law,** *n.* law, a rule of action, established by the supreme power of a state; a statute; the body of rules governing a community; legal knowledge; a rule in regulation of anything; a theoretical principle; a rule or principle of science or art; a settled principle; jurisprudence; judicial process; the legal profession. **canon, civil, common law,** *see* these words. **law-abiding,** submitting to or keeping the law. **law-breaker,** one who violates the law. **law-hand,** the script formerly used in legal documents. **law Latin,** the barbarous Latin of legal documents. **law-lord,** a peer of the House of Lords specially qualified and appointed to take part in its legal business. **law merchant,** a former loosely recognized international code of commercial law. **law-stationer,** one who sells legal stationery and accepts documents for engrossing. **law-term,** a word, etc., used in law; one of the recurrent periods during which the Law Courts sit. **to go to law,** to take legal proceedings. **to lay down the law,** to talk or act dictatorially. **to take the law into one's own hands,** to obtain redressment of one's wrongs by force. **written law,** law enacted by statute. (A.S. *lagu.*)
lawful, *a.* *law*-ful, conformable to or allowed by law; constituted by law; rightful.
lawfully, *ad.* in a lawful manner; legally.
lawfulness, *n.* the quality of being lawful.
lawgiver, *n.* *law*-giv-er, one who makes or enacts laws; a legislator.
lawgiving, *a.* *law*-giv-ing, making or enacting laws.
lawless, *a.* *law*-less, not subject to law; unrestrained by law; contrary to law; illegal; uncontrolled.
lawlessly, *ad.* *law*-less-le, in a lawless manner.
lawlessness, *n.* quality or state of being lawless.
lawmaker, *n.* *law*-make-er, a lawgiver.
lawmaking, *a.* *law*-make-ing, legislative; enacting laws.
lawmonger, *n.* *law*-mung-ger, a pettifogger.
lawn, *n.* lawn, a space of ground covered with grass, and kept closely mown; formerly, a glade in forestland. **lawn-mower,** a machine for mowing a lawn. **lawn tennis,** *see* **tennis.** (O.Fr. *lande.*)
lawn, *n.* lawn, a fine linen or cambric, specially used for the wide sleeves of the Anglican bishops' rochet: *a.* made of lawn. (Linen of *Laune,* now *Laon,* town in N. France.)
lawny, *a.* *lawn*-e, having or resembling a lawn; made of or like lawn.
lawsuit, *n.* *law*-sewt, an action at law.
law-writer, *n.* a lawyer's copying-clerk; a writer of books on law.
lawyer, *n.* *law*-yer, one versed in or one who practises law; an expounder of the Mosaic law [Bible]; applied to various birds, fish, climbing plants, etc.
lawyering, *n.* *law*-yer-ing, the profession, or the following the profession, of the law [Coll.].
lawyerly, *ad.* *law*-yer-le, in the manner of a lawyer.
lax, *a.* laks, loose; flabby; slack; not tight; of loose texture; not rigidly exact; vague; not strict; loose in the bowels. (L. *laxus,* loose.)
laxation, *n.* lak-*say*-shon, the act of loosening or slackening; the state of being loose or slackened.
laxative, *a.* *laks*-a-tiv, having the power of loosening the bowels: *n.* a medicine that has this effect.
laxativeness, *n.* *laks*-a-tiv-ness, the quality or state of being laxative.
laxity, *n.* *laks*-e-te, laxness; looseness; inexactness; slackness in morals.
laxly, *ad.* *laks*-le, in a lax manner.
laxness, *n.* the state or quality of being lax.
lay, *v.t.* lay, to put or place; to beat down; to settle, as dust; to place in order; to spread on a surface; to calm; to appease; to spread and set in order; to wager; to produce eggs; to impose; to charge; to enjoin; to present (a claim, accusation, etc.); to set; to contrive; to aim. **lay a cable,** to twist or unite the strands. **lay about one,** to fight vigorously. **lay aside,** to put off or away; to discontinue. **lay away,** to put aside for preservation. **lay bare,** to strip; to reveal. **lay before,** to exhibit. **lay by,** to reserve for future use. **lay down,** to deposit; to resign; to relinquish; to offer or advance. **lay heads together,** to confer. **lay hold of,** to seize; to catch; to make a pretext of. **lay in,** to store; to treasure. **lay off,** to measure off; to cease to employ, or cease work; to hedge (a bet); to move from the shore, or further away [Naut.]; to desist [Slang]. **lay on,** to apply with force; to inflict. **lay open,** to make bare; to uncover. **lay out,** to expend; to plan; to dispose in order; to prepare (a corpse) for burial. **lay over,** to spread over; to encrust. **lay siege to,** to besiege. **lay the course,** to sail toward the intended place without tacking [Naut.]. **lay the land,** to cause the land to appear to sink by sailing from it [Naut.]. **lay to,** to charge upon; to impute; to apply with vigour; to check the motion of a ship. **lay together,** to collect; to bring to one place. **lay to heart,** to regard or treat seriously. **lay under,** to subject to. **lay up,** to store; to hoard; to dismantle and place in dock [Naut.]. **lay waste,** to destroy; to desolate. *p.* and *pp.* **laid.** (A.S. *lecgan.*)
lay, *v.i.* lay, to produce eggs; to contrive; to wager. **lay about,** to strike or throw the arms on all sides; to act with vigour. **lay in for,** to make overtures for; to engage or secure the possession of. **lay on,** to strike; to beat; to deal blows with vehemence; to act with vehemence. **lay out,** to purpose; to intend; to take measures. **lay up,** to be confined to bed. *p.* and *pp.* **laid.**
lay, *n.* lay, that which is laid; a layer; the direction in which the strands of a rope are twisted; share of profit [U.S.A.]; the direction or position in which a country, object, etc., is situated; a scheme, a particular job or occupation [Slang].
lay, *n.* lay, a narrative poem; a song or ballad; the singing of birds. (Fr. *lai,* song.)
lay, *a.* lay, pertaining to the laity, as distinct from the clergy; not clerical; unprofessional. **lay baptism,** baptism administered by a layman. **lay communion,** the communion of the laity; membership as a layman of the church. (Gr. *laikos,* the people.)
lay-brother, *n.* a male inmate of a monastery under the three vows but not in holy orders.
lay-by, *n.* *lay*-by, a slack part of a stream; a place where barges, rolling-stock, etc. may be laid by when temporarily not in use.
lay-clerk, *n.* a layman who leads the responses in the church-service.

lay-days, *n.pl. lay*-daze, days allowed for the loading or unloading of cargo [Comm.].
lay-elder, *n.* in the Presbyterian Church, a non-ministerial church manager.
layer, *n. lay*-er, one who or that which lays. **layer-on,** one who feeds sheets into a printing machine. **layer-out,** one who expends money; one who lays out a corpse. **layer up,** one who deposits for future use.
layer, *n.* lare *or lay*-er, a stratum; a bed; an undetached shoot laid under ground for propagation: *v.t.* to propagate by layers [Hort.].
layering, *n. lay*-er-ing, propagation by layers. [Hort.].
layette, *n.* lay-*et,* a baby's outfit. (Fr.)
lay-figure, *n.* an artist's jointed dummy made in imitation of the human body; hence, a nonentity.
laying, *n. lay*-ing, the first coat of plaster on laths of two-coat work; the act or period of laying eggs; the eggs laid; the process of twisting the strands of a rope.
layland, *n. lay*-land, lea-land.
layman, *n. lay*-man, a man who is not a clergyman; one of the laity; a man who is not in the profession.
lay-off, *n. lay*-off, the act of temporarily discharging from work; a period of temporary unemployment; that part of a bet laid off.
lay-out, *n. lay*-out, a plan of buildings or gardens; a ground plan; a plan or make-up [Print.].
lay-shaft, *n.* a subsidiary or intermediate shaft, esp. the counter-shaft of a motor-car [Mech.].
laystall, *n. lay*-stawl, a heap of dung or refuse, or place where this is laid; a place where milch-cows are kept.
lazar, *n. laz*-ar, a pauper infected with leprosy or other pestilential disease. (*Lazarus,* Luke xvi.)
lazaret, *n. laz*-a-ret, a lazaretto.
lazaretto, *n. laz*-a-*ret*-to, a hospital for persons affected with infectious diseases; a place of quarantine. (It.)
lazar-house, *n. laz*-ar-house, a lazaretto.
Lazarist, *n. laz*-a-rist, a lazarite.
Lazarite, *n. laz*-a-rite, a member of a religious congregation founded by St. Vincent de Paul in 1624. (From its centre, the college St. *Lazare,* Paris.)
laze, *v.i.* laze, to loaf; to live in idleness: *v.t.* to waste in sloth.
lazily, *ad. lay*-ze-le, in a lazy manner.
laziness, *n. lay*-ze-ness, the state of being lazy.
lazulite, *n. laz*-yew-lite, blue spar, a light, indigo-blue mineral, chemically a hydrous phosphate of aluminium and magnesium. (Late L. *lazulus.*)
lazurite, *n. laz*-yew-rite, the chief component of lapis-lazuli, chemically a sodium, calcium, aluminium sulpho-chloro-silicate.
lazy, *a. lay*-ze, disinclined to exertion; indolent; slothful; sluggish. **lazy-bed,** a bed in which seed potatoes are laid on the surface and earth thrown on them. **lazy-bones,** a lazy fellow. **lazy tongs,** a series of scissor-like bars, each pair fitted on to the end of the other, by which things at a distance may be seized. (Origin not known.)
lazzaroni, *n.pl. lats*-a-*roh*-ne, those forming an idly disposed, outcast class once numerous and formidable in Naples. (It. *lazzarone,* a beggar.)
lea, *n.* lee, a meadow or pasture. (A.S. *leah.*)
leach, *n.* leech, a quantity of wood-ashes, through which water passes, and thus imbibes the alkali; a vessel in which ashes are leached; the solution obtained after leaching: *v.t.* to wash, as ashes, by percolation, or causing water to pass through them, and thus to separate from them the alkali. (A.S. *leccan,* to lave.)
★**lead,** *n.* led, common metallic element, bluish-grey, malleable, ductile, and very heavy; a plummet [Naut.]; a thin strip of metal for spacing made-up lines of type [Print.]; a small stick of plumbago used in pencils: *pl.* sheets of lead for covering roofs; a flat roof so covered: *a.* made or consisting of lead: *v.t.* to cover or fit with lead; to make or widen spaces between lines with leads [Print.]. **red lead,** oxide of lead. **white lead,** carbonate of lead. (A.S.)
lead, *n.* leed, the act of leading; guidance; leadership; the leading role; an example; a dog-chain or the like; an artificial watercourse; the first card played in a game, or the right to play this; the principal part in a play, film, etc.; a conductor conveying electricity to the place where it is to be used [Elect.]: *v.i.* to go before and show the way; to go first; to conduct, as a chief or commander; to draw; to have a tendency to; to exercise dominion: *v.t.* to guide by the hand; to guide by showing the way; to conduct; to direct; to govern; to precede; to allure; to induce; to prevail on. **lead astray,** to guide in a wrong way or into error. **lead captive,** to carry into captivity. **lead off,**, to begin; [Slang] to rant, to lose one's temper. *p.* and *pp.* **led.** (A.S. *lædan.*)
lead-arming, *n. led*-arm-ing, tallow pressed into the socket of a plummet to test the nature of the bottom [Naut.].
leaded, *pp.* and *a. led*-ed, fitted with or set in lead; separated by leads [Print.].
leaden, *a. led*-en, made of or characteristic of lead; indisposed to action; heavy; dull; depressing.
leader, *n. leed*-er, one who or that which leads or goes first; a conductor; a chief; the chief counsel for the defence or prosecution [Law]; a performer who leads a choir, etc.; a branch of ore leading to the lode; the principal editorial article in a newspaper; a row of dots leading across a page; the principal wheel in machinery; a leading horse in a tandem or team; the top bud.
leaderette, *n.* leed-er-*ret,* a short editorial leader or paragraph.
leadership, *n. leed*-er-ship, the office of a leader; direction.
lead-glance, *n.* galena; native lead sulphide.
leadhillite, *n. led*-hill-ite, a mineral composed of sulphate and carbonate of lead. (*Leadhills,* Scotland.)
lead-in, *n.* leed-in, an electrical conductor, esp. one connecting an aerial to a receiving-set [Wire.].
leading, *a. leed*-ing, chief; important; most influential; showing the way by going first: *n.* guidance. **leading case,** a case the decision in which is regarded as a precedent to be followed [Law]. **leading lady,** the star actress in a theatrical production. **leading question,** a question framed with intent to evoke a certain answer. **leading-strings,** strings or leads formerly used to support children when learning to walk. **in leading-strings,** in a state of dependence on, or under the control of, others.
lead-pencil, *n.* a writing and drawing implement consisting of a rod of graphite or black-lead, enclosed generally in wood.
leadsman, *n. ledz*-man, the man who heaves the lead in taking soundings [Naut.].
leadwort, *n. led*-wurt, thrift, sea-lavender, or other plant of the genus *Plumbago* [Bot.].
leady, *a. led*-de, containing or like lead.
★**leaf,** *n.* leef (*pl.* **leaves,** leevz), the thin, flat appendage of a plant's axis, in which the sap is elaborated and transpiration effected; anything resembling this; tobacco leaves collectively; a part of a book comprising two pages; the side of a shutter, screen, or folding-door, etc.; a very thin plate; a layer of leaf-fat; a movable section of a table-top; a tooth of a gear pinion [Mech.]: *v.i.* to shoot out or produce leaves. **leaf insect,** any of certain tropical orthopterous insects of the family Phasmidæ the formation and coloration of which resembles foliage. (A.S.)
leafage, *n. leef*-aj, leaves collectively; foliage.
leaf-bridge, *n.* a drawbridge, as having a platform on each side which rises and falls.
leaf-bud, *n.* a bud developing into a leaf, not a flower.
leafed, *a.* leeft, having leaves.
leaf-fat, *n. leef*-fat, fat lying in layers, esp. about the kidneys of a hog.
leafiness, *n. leef*-e-ness, state of being leafy.
leafing, *n. leef*-ing, the process of producing or developing leaves.
leafless, *a. leef*-less, destitute of leaves.
leaflet, *n. leef*-let, a folded but non-stitched pamphlet; a handbill; a little leaf, one of the divisions of a compound leaf; a foliole [Bot.].
leaf-metal, *n.* foil for giving a brilliant surface to metal or other goods.
leaf-mould, *n.* mould formed by decayed leaves.
leafstalk, *n. leef*-stawk, the petiole or stalk supporting a leaf.
leafy, *a. leef*-e, abounding in leaves; made of or resembling leaves; laminate.
league, *n.* leeg, alliance or union for the promotion of a common interest; confederacy: *v.i.* to unite

in a league; to confederate: *v.t.* to join together with. **league football,** football as played by a league of clubs competing against each other for the championship. **League of Nations,** a league of sovereign states established under the Treaty of Versailles, 1919, to maintain world peace, promote international collaboration, administer certain mandates, etc., and succeeded by the United Nations, 1946. (Fr. *ligue.*)

league, *n.* leeg, a measure of length containing, in English-speaking countries, three miles. **sea league,** three nautical miles. (O.Fr. *legue.*)

leaguer, *n. leeg*-er, one who unites in a league; an adherent of a league.

leaguer, *n. leeg*-er, a siege; a camp of besiegers: *v.t.* to beleaguer. (Dut. *leger,* a camp.)

leak, *n.* leek, a crevice or fissure, esp. in a vessel, through which liquid may pass; the oozing of a fluid through such: *v.i.* to let water or other liquor into or out of a vessel through a leak. **leak out,** to find vent; to escape privately. **spring a leak,** to open or crack so as to let in water. (Scand.)

leakage, *n. leek*-aj, a leak or leaking; the quantity of liquid thus passing; allowance of a certain rate per cent. for leaking; loss unaccounted for, or allowance for this [Comm.].

leakiness, *n. leek*-e-ness, state of being leaky.

leaky, *a. leek*-e, letting liquid pass in or out; not watertight; apt to disclose secrets; tattling.

leal, *a.* leel, loyal; faithful; true. **land of the leal,** the realm of the saints, heaven. (O.Fr. *leial.*)

lea-land, *n.* fallow land; land lying untilled or in pasture.

lean, *n.* leen, a slope; an inclination: *v.i.* to incline or bend; to deviate from a straight or perpendicular line; to incline towards; to be partial to; to rest against: *v.t.* to incline; to cause to lean. **lean-to,** *n.* a building with the rafters supported by another building: *a.* of, or belonging to, this kind of building. *p.* and *pp.* **leaned,** leend, *or* **leant,** lent. (A.S. *hlænan.*)

lean, *a.* leen, wanting flesh; not fat; thin; not rich; poor; barren of thought and interest; jejune: *n.* flesh or meat consisting of muscular tissue without fat. (A.S. *hlæne.*)

***leaning,** *n. leen*-ing, inclination; propensity; tendency towards.

leanness, *n. leen*-ness, the state or quality of being lean.

leap, *n.* leep, a jump; a bound; space passed in leaping; an abrupt transition; formerly, copulation of animals: *v.i.* to spring upward or forward; to jump; to vault; to rush with force: *v.t.* to spring or bound over; to cause to leap. **leap in the dark,** a risky proceeding. *p.* and *pp.* **leaped,** leept, *or* **leapt,** lept. (A.S. *hleapan.*)

leaper, *n. leep*-er, one who or that which leaps.

leap-frog, *n.* a boys' game in which one stoops down and another leaps over him, straddled.

leapingly, *ad. leep*-ing-le, by leaps.

leap-year, *n. leep*-yer, the intercalary year of 366 days occurring every fourth year; so called because each day after the added day (29 Feb.) falls two days (instead of one) later than the corresponding day of the previous year, thus appearing to "leap" a day.

learn, *v.t.* lern, to acquire knowledge of; to acquire skill in, or a faculty of performing by, practice: *v.i.* to gain knowledge; to receive instruction. *p.* and *pp.* **learned,** lernd, *or* **learnt,** lernt. (A.S. *leornian.*)

learnable, *a. lern*-a-bl, that may be learnt.

learned, *a. lern*-ed, having acquired learning from study; erudite; well acquainted with an art; knowing; containing and showing learning. **the learned,** men of erudition; literati. **the learned professions,** the Church, the Law, and Medicine.

learnedly, *ad. lern*-ed-le, in a learned manner.

learnedness, *n. lern*-ed-ness, state of being learned.

learner, *n. lern*-er, one who is learning; a tyro; an apprentice.

***learning,** *n. lern*-ing, that which is to be learnt; knowledge acquired by study, esp. of literature; erudition; scholarship; knowledge acquired from others.

leasable, *a. leece*-a-bl, that may be leased.

lease, *n.* leece, a letting of tenements for a term of years; the contract for such letting; any tenure: *v.t.* let or hold on lease. **lease-lend,** *see* **lend-lease.** (Fr. *laisser,* let.)

lease, *n.* leece, the plan on which warp and weft cross in weaving. (*leash.*)

leasehold, *a. leece*-hohld, held by lease: *n.* a tenure by lease; property so held.

leaseholder, *n.* leece-*hohl*-der, a tenant under a lease.

leaser, *n. leez*-er, a gleaner. (A.S. *lesan,* to glean.)

leash, *n.* leesh, a thong or line by which a hawk or a hound is held; a brace and a half, three (of three greyhounds, foxes, etc.); a band to tie anything with: *v.t.* to bind; to hold by a leash. (O.Fr. *lesse.*)

leasing, *n. leez*-ing, falsehood; lies. (A.S. *lĕasung.*)

leasowe, *n. lee*-soh, a pasture; meadow-land.

least, *a.* leest: *superl.* of *little,* smallest; little beyond others: *ad.* in the smallest or lowest degree; in a degree below all others: *n.* the least amount or degree. **at least,** at or in the lowest degree; at all events. **not in the least,** not in the slightest degree, not at all.

leastwise, *ad. leest*-wize, anyhow; at least [Coll.].

leat, *n.* leet, a watercourse leading to or from a mill. (A.S. *lædan,* lead.)

***leather,** *n. leth*-ther, the skin of an animal dressed and prepared for use; dressed hides in general; a person's skin [Coll.]; the ball in cricket or football; imperviousness to ideas, etc.: *pl.* breeches, leggings; *v.t.* to equip or cover with leather; to thrash [Slang]: *a.* made of or consisting of leather. (A.S.)

leather-back, *n.* the soft-shelled marine turtle *Sphargis coriacea.*

leather-cloth, *n.* a name of various fabrics dressed in imitation of leather.

leather-coat, *n.* an apple with a tough rind.

leather-dresser, *n.* one who dresses leather or prepares hides for use.

leatherette, *n. leth*-ther-*ret,* a paper, or cloth and paper, imitation of leather.

leather-jacket, *n.* an Australian tree, *Eucalyptus resinifera;* any of several fishes of the Pacific; the larva of the daddy-longlegs.

leathern, *a. leth*-thern, made of, consisting of, or resembling leather.

leatheroid, *n. leth*-ther-royd, proprietary name of an artificial leather consisting chiefly of vulcanized fibre.

leatherwood, *n. leth*-ther-wood, a North American shrub, *Dirca palustris,* or its tough bark used for cordage and baskets; any ironwood.

leathery, *a. leth*-ther-re, resembling leather; tough.

leave, *n.* leev, liberty granted; permission; departure; a formal parting of friends; farewell; permission to be absent from duties, hence, holidays; the position of the balls at the end of a break in billiards: *v.t.* to depart from; to abandon; to commit; to suffer to remain; to have remaining at death; to bequeath; to permit; to forbear; to refer: *v.i.* to cease; to desist. **leave alone,** to have nothing to do with. **leave behind,** to outstrip. **leave in the dark,** keep unaware of. **leave of absence,** period of permitted absence from duty. **leave off,** to desist from; to cease wearing; to abandon. **leave out,** to omit. **leave over,** to allow to stand for future consideration. **on leave,** absent from duty. **take leave,** *see* **take.** *p.* and *pp.* **left.** (A.S. *læfan.*)

leaved, *a.* leevd, leafed; having leaves. (*leaf.*)

leaven, *n. lev*-en, any ferment, esp. fermenting dough, used to produce fermentation or to impart a spongy texture to bread; yeast; barm; anything which pervades a mass and changes its nature, esp. for the worse: *v.t.* to raise with leaven; to imbue; to taint; to modify; to temper. (Fr. *levain.*)

leavening, *n. lev*-en-ing, that which leavens; the act of fermenting or making light, esp. with leaven.

leavenous, *a. lev*-en-us, having the characteristics of leaven.

leaver, *n. leev*-er, one who leaves (in any sense).

leaves, *n.* leevz, *pl.* of *leaf.*

leave-taking, *n.* a farewell; parting compliments.

leavings, *n.pl. leev*-ingz, things left, or left over; relics; refuse.

lecher, *n. letch*-er, a man given to lewdness: *v.i.* to practise lewdness. (O.Fr. *lecheor.*)

lecherous, *a. letch*-er-rus, lustful; provoking lust.

lecherously, *ad. letch*-er-rus-le, lustfully.

lecherousness, *n. letch*-er-rus-ness, lust.

lechery, *n.* *letch*-er-re, lewdness.
lecithin, *n.* *lee*-se-thin, a fatty, phosphoric constituent of protoplasm, the brain, yolk of egg, etc.
lecotropal, *a.* le-*kot*-ro-pal, shaped like a horseshoe [Bot.]. (Gr. *lekos*, dish, *tropos*, turning.)
lectern, *n.* *lek*-tern, a reading desk for large books, esp. one from which the lessons are read [Eccles.]; the precentor's desk [Scot.]. (O.Fr. *letrun.*)
lection, *n.* *lek*-shon, a variant in a manuscript, etc.; a Scripture lesson read in divine service. (L. *lectio.*)
lectionary, *n.* *lek*-shon-a-re, a service-book containing portions of Scripture to be read.
lector, *n.* *lek*-tor, formerly, a cleric in minor orders who read the lessons [Eccles.]. (L.)
lecture, *n.* *lek*-tewr, a discourse of a methodical nature on any subject; a reading with a tutor; an exposition; a reprimand [Coll.]: *v.t.* to instruct by discourses; to reprimand [Coll.]: *v.i.* to give lectures. (Fr.)
lecturer, *n.* *lek*-tew-rer, one who lectures, esp. at a college or university.
lectureship, *n.* *lek*-tewr-ship, the office of a lecturer.
lecythus, *n.* *les*-e-thus, a narrow-necked ceramic oil cruet of the ancient Greeks. (Gr.)
led, *a.* led, guided; drawn: *p.* and *pp.* of the verb *to lead.* **led captain,** an obsequious follower. **led horse,** a pack-horse or spare horse.
ledge, *n.* ledj, a shelf on which to lay things; anything similar; a part rising or projecting beyond the rest; a ridge; an inshore submarine reef; a small moulding [Arch.]; a lode [Mining]. (M.E. *legge*, as *lay.*)
ledger, *n.* *ledj*-er, the principal book of account, into which the items of the other accounts are entered on debtor and creditor sides in a summary form; a piece of timber to support the platform of scaffolding; a horizontal covering slab [Arch.]; the sinker used in bottom fishing; a ledger-line. (Probably as *ledge.*)
ledger-line, *n.* a fishing line with a sinker near the hook; a leger-line [Mus.].
ledgy, *a.* *ledj*-e, abounding in ledges.
lee, *n.* lee, the quarter opposite to that against which the wind blows; the sheltered side; shelter: *a.* pertaining to the side away from the wind. **lee board,** a plank let down from the lee side of a flat-bottomed vessel to prevent it drifting leeward. **lee gauge,** the position, as regards another ship, of a ship to leeward of it. **lee lurch,** a sudden and violent roll of a ship to leeward in a high sea. **lee shore,** the shore under the lee of a ship. **lee side,** the side of a vessel farthest from the point whence the wind blows. **lee tide,** a tide running in the direction of the wind. **under the lee,** defended from the wind. (A.S. *hleow*, shelter.)
leech, *n.* leech, any aquatic blood-sucking worm of the order Annelida and class Hirudinea, some of which are used in blood-letting; a physician: *v.t.* to bleed with leeches: *v.i.* to apply leeches. **stick like a leech,** cling persistently. (A.S. *læce*, a physician.)
leech, *n.* leech, any edge of a square sail; the after edge of a fore-and-aft sail. (Scand.)
leechcraft, *n.* *leech*-krahft, the art of healing.
leechee, *n.* *lee*-chee, the litchi.
leefange, *n.* lee-*fanj*, a horse, or transverse bar on deck, on which slide the sheets of a fore-and-aft sail [Naut.]. (Probably *lee*, shelter, and *fang.*)
leek, *n.* leek, the culinary vegetable, *Allium porrum*, allied to the onion; the old national emblem of Wales. **to eat the leek,** to retract. (A.S. *leac.*)
leemost, *a.* *lee*-mohst, farthest to leeward.
leer, *n.* leer, a sidelong look expressive of contempt, defiance, sly archness, amorousness, or malignity, etc.: *v.i.* to look with a leer: *v.t.* to glance at obliquely or with a leer. (A.S. *hleor*, the cheek.)
leeringly, *ad.* *leer*-ring-le, in a leering manner.
leery, *a.* *leer*-re, sly; wide-awake [Slang].
lees, *n.pl.* leez, the dregs which have settled at the bottom of liquor; refuse. (Fr. *lie.*)
leet, *n.* leet, a court-leet; the jurisdiction of this. **leet ale,** a feast or merrymaking at the holding of this court. (Scand.)
leet, *n.* leet, in Scotland, a list of selected candidates for an office. (*list.*)
leeward, *a.* *lew*-ard, in the direction towards which the wind blows: *ad.* towards the lee.
leeway, *n.* *lee*-way, the lateral movement of a ship to the leeward of her course; arrears of work.
***left,** *a.* left, opposed to the right of the body; revolutionary, communistic [Coll.]: *n.* the side opposite the right; the party opposed to the government in a legislative assembly, as sitting on the left of the chair; the opposition; the advanced or innovating party or section of a party, school, etc. The **left bank of a river** is that which is on the left-hand of a person looking in the direction of the flow. (A.S.)
left-hand, *n.* the left side: *a.* lefthanded; situated on the left; done with the left hand.
lefthanded, *a.* left-*hand*-ed, using the left hand more readily than the right; to the left; having a counter-clockwise direction or action (of screws, twist in rope, etc.); implying the opposite; awkward; unlucky. **lefthanded compliment,** apparent praise but actual depreciation. **lefthanded marriage,** a morganatic marriage.
lefthandedness, *n.* left-*hand*-ed-ness, the quality of being lefthanded.
lefthander, *n.* left-*hand*-er, a lefthanded person; a blow with the left hand; a ball bowled from the left hand.
leftist, *a.* *lef*-tist, having a bias towards the political left: *n.* an adherent or member of a party of the left [Coll.].
leftward, *a.* *left*-ward, to the left.
***leg,** *n.* leg, limb by which an animal walks; that which covers the leg; a leg-like support; the side of a triangle; a limb of a pair of compasses; the part of the on side of the field behind the extended popping-crease [Cricket]; a single round at darts, etc.; a tack in sailing to windward [Naut.]; a blackleg [Slang]. **a leg up,** help, assistance. **leg theory,** bowling intended to result in the batsman being caught to leg. **to leg it,** to walk, also to run away [Slang]. **to make a leg,** to bow and scrape. **to pull one's leg,** to hoax or play a trick on one [Slang]. **to stand on one's own legs,** to depend on one's own efforts without aid. (Ice. *leggr*, a leg.)
legacy, *n.* *leg*-a-se, a bequest left by will; anything bequeathed. **legacy duty,** a government tax on testamentary bequests. **legacy hunter,** one who flatters and courts in expectation of legacies. (L. *legatum.*)
legal, *a.* *lee*-gal, pertaining to or according to law; lawful; created by law; according to the law that salvation is by works, not by faith [Theol.]. **legal tender,** coin that by law a creditor must accept. (L. *legalis*, relating to the law.)
legalism, *n.* *lee*-gal-izm, the doctrine of strict adherence to law or legal system or [Theol.] the theory of justification by works.
legalist, *n.* *lee*-gal-ist, a stickler for law; one who relies for salvation on works [Theol.].
legality, *n.* le-*gal*-e-te, lawfulness; conformity to law; reliance on works or the letter of the law for salvation [Theol.].
legalize, *v.t.* *lee*-gal-ize, to make lawful; to render conformable to law; to authorize; to sanction.
legally, *ad.* *lee*-gal-le, in a legal manner.
legate, *n.* *leg*-at, an ambassador, esp. (and now only) one representing the Vatican at a foreign court; in ancient Rome, a provincial governor or deputy. (O.Fr. *legat.*)
legatee, *n.* *leg*-a-*tee*, one to whom a legacy is bequeathed. **residuary legatee,** the legatee to whom the remainder of the property is left after the settlement of all claims.
legateship, *n.* *leg*-at-ship, the office of a legate.
legatine, *a.* *leg*-a-tine, pertaining to or proceeding from a legatee.
legation, *n.* le-*gay*-shon, the act of commissioning or sending one as legate; the embassy of a diplomatist not of ambassadorial rank; the person or persons sent as envoys; the official residence of a diplomatic representative abroad. (Fr. *légation.*)
legato, *ad.* le-*gah*-to, in a smooth, gliding manner [Mus.]. (It.)
leg-bail, *n.* escape from custody [Slang].
leg-bye, *n.* a run made when the ball touches any part of a batsman except his hand [Cricket].
legend, *n.* *ledj*-end, a chronicle or register of the lives of saints, formerly read at matins and in religious houses; a traditional, historically unauthentic relation or narrative, generally more or less marvellous or incredible; a myth; an inscription or the motto on a shield, medal, or coin, etc.; the caption of an illustration [Print.]. (O.Fr. *legende.*)

legendary, *a.* *ledj*-en-da-re, in the form of legend; romantic; fabulous: *n.* a book of legends; a relater of legends.
leger, *a.* *ledj*-er, of small size or weight: *n.* the ledger used in bottom fishing. (Fr. *léger.*)
legerdemain, *n.* *ledj*-er-de-*mane*, sleight of hand; jugglery; a deceptive performance which depends on dexterity of hand. (Fr., light of hand.)
leger-line, *n.* a line added to the staff for designating notes ascending or descending [Mus.]; a ledger-line [Angling].
legged, *a.* legd, having legs, as two-legged.
legger, *n.* *leg*-ger, one formerly employed to float a barge through a canal tunnel by pushing his feet against the side walls.
legging, *n.* *leg*-ging, a covering for the leg; a long gaiter.
leggy, *a.* *leg*-ge, with very long legs.
leghorn, *n.* *leg*-horn, a plait of smooth straw for bonnets and hats; a hat, etc., made of this; a breed of poultry. (Town in Italy.)
legibility. *n.* *ledj*-e-*bil*-e-te, the quality or state of being legible.
legible, *a.* *ledj*-e-bl, that may be read; clear and distinct; easily discoverable or decipherable. (L.)
legibleness, *n.* *ledj*-e-bl-ness, legibility.
legibly, *ad.* *ledj*-e-ble, so as to be legible.
legion, *n.* *lee*-jon, in the ancient Roman army, a body of from 3,000 to 6,000 men divided into cohorts, maniples and centuries; a military force; a great number; a vast host. **British Legion,** a national association of ex-service men established in 1921 and incorporated by royal charter, 1925. **Foreign Legion,** a corps extra-national of volunteers attached to certain armies, esp. the French. **Legion of Honour,** an order instituted in France, by Napoleon I, as a reward for merit, civil or military. (O.Fr. from L. *legio*, collect.)
legionary, *a.* *lee*-jon-a-re, relating to or consisting of a legion or legions; containing a great number: *n.* one of a legion; a member of the Legion of Honour. (L. *legionarius.*)
legionnaire, *n.* lee-jo-nare, a legionary. (Fr.)
legislate, *v.i.* *lejd*-is-late, to make or enact a law or laws. (L. *lex, legis*, a law, *latus*, passed.)
legislation, *n.* *ledj*-is-*lay*-shon, the act of legislating; the laws enacted.
legislative, *a.* *ledj*-is-la-tiv, enacting law or the laws; pertaining to or effected by legislation; having power to legislate: *n.* the legislature.
legislatively, *ad.* in a legislative manner.
legislator, *n.* *ledj*-is-lay-tor, one who makes laws; a member of a legislature. (L.)
legislatorship, *n.* the office of a legislator.
legislatress, *n.* *ledj*-is-lay-tress, a female legislator or member of a legislative body.
legislature, *n.* *lejd*-is-lay-tewr, the assembly in a state invested with power to make, repeal, alter, and suspend the laws. (L. *lex, legis*, and *latura*, a connection.)
legist, *n.* *lee*-jist, one skilled in the law. (Fr.)
legitim, *n.* *ledj*-e-tim, that portion of the estate of a deceased father to which the children are legally entitled.
legitimacy, *n.* le-*jit*-e-ma-se, condition or quality of being legitimate; genuineness; lawfulness of birth; logical deduction.
legitimate, *a.* le-*jit*-e-mat, in accordance with law or usage, or an accepted standard; following logically or naturally; lawfully begotten: *v.t.* to make lawful; to render (the illegitimate) legitimate; to invest with the rights of a lawful heir. (Late L. *legitimatus*, declared lawful, from L. *legitimus*, according to law.)
legitimately, *ad.* in a legitimate manner.
legitimateness, *n.* le-*jit*-e-mat-ness, legitimacy.
legitimation, *n.* le-*jit*-e-*may*-shon, the act or process of rendering legal or legitimate.
legitimatize, *v.t.* le-*jit*-e-ma-tize, to legitimate.
legitimism, *n.* le-*jit*-e-mizm, the principles, or adherence to the principles, of legitimists.
legitimist, *n.* le-*jit*-e-mist, one who supports legitimate authority, esp. hereditary royal right.
legless, *a.* *leg*-less, having no legs.
leg-pull, *n.* a hoax; a "sell" [Slang].
legume, *n.* le-*gewn*, a fruit which splits into two halves and has the seeds attached to the ventral suture; the pod of a leguminous plant. (L. *legumen*, pulse.)
legumin, *n.* le-*gew*-min, an albumin obtained from leguminous plants; vegetable casein.
leguminous, *a.* le-*gew*-me-nus, pertaining to the Leguminosæ, the order of plants bearing legumes; pulse-like; bearing legumes.
Leibnitzian, *a.* lyb-*nit*-se-an, of, or pertaining to Leibnitz or his philosophy: *n.* a follower of Leibnitz. (G. W. *Leibnitz.*)
leiotrichous, *a.* ly-*ot*-re-kus, smooth-haired. (Gr. *leios*, smooth, *thrix*, hair.)
leipoa, *n.* ly-*poh*-a, the mallee-bird. (Gr. *leipo*, leave, *oon*, an egg.)
leister, *n.* *les*-ter, a fishing spear with three prongs. (Ice.)
leisurable, *a.* *lezh*-ur-a-bl, not occupied.
leisurably, *ad.* *lezh*-ur-a-ble, in a leisurely manner; deliberately.
leisure, *n.* *lezh*-ur, freedom from occupation; time free from employment: *a.* unoccupied. (Fr. *loisir.*)
leisured, *a.* *lezh*-urd, characterized by leisure; free from occupation.
leisurely, *a.* *lezh*-ur-le, done at leisure; deliberate: *ad.* not in haste; slowly; deliberately.
leitmotif, *n.* *lyte*-mo-teef, the principal theme in a musical composition. (Ger.)
leman, *n.* *lem*-an, a sweetheart: a mistress or paramour; a gallant. (A.S. *leof*, dear, *mann*, man.)
lemma, *n.* *lem*-ma, a proposition demonstrated for the purpose of being used in the demonstration of some other proposition [Math.]; a subject used for an article, an annotation, etc., prefixed as a heading. (Gr., anything that is taken.)
lemming, *n.* *lem*-ming, a small migratory rodent, *Myodes lemmus*, of N. Europe. (Norw.)
Lemnian, *a.* *lem*-ne-an, pertaining to the island of Lemnos in the Ægean.
lemniscate, *n.* lem-*nis*-kate, a curve in the form of the figure 8. (L. *lemniscus*, a ribbon.)
lemniscus, *n.* lem-*nis*-kus, a ribbon-like band of fibre [Anat.]; the sign ÷ [Print.].
★**lemon,** *n.* *lem*-on, the acid fruit of *Citrus limonum*; the tree that produces this; its light yellow colour; any person (*e.g.* an attractive girl) or object that suggests sour fruit [Slang]: *a.* of lemon colour, pale yellow: *v.t.* to flavour with lemon. **lemon dab,** a small lemon sole. **lemon-drop,** a sweet flavoured with lemon. **lemon grass,** a species of *Andropogon*, *A. schœnanthus*. **lemon kali,** an effervescent drink of soda bicarbonate and tartaric acid. **lemon-plant,** the lemon-scented verbena. **lemon sole,** a trade name for several species of *Pleuronectes*. **lemon-squash,** a drink of lemon-juice, sugar, and water. **lemon-squeezer,** an instrument used to extract the juice of lemons. **salt of lemon,** binoxalate of potash, or potash combined with oxalic acid. **the answer's a lemon,** a derisive, but otherwise meaningless, retort [Slang]. (Fr. *limon*, from Pers. *limūn.*)
lemonade, *n.* lem-on-*ade*, a drink of lemon juice or a lemon substitute mixed with water and sweetened; an aerated drink of similar flavour. (Fr. *limonade.*)
lemur, *n.* *lee*-mur, an arboreal nocturnal mammal allied to the monkeys. (L. *lemur*, ghost.)
lemures, *n.pl.* *lem*-yew-reez, ghosts or spectres among the Romans; shades or spirits of the departed. (L.)
Lemurian, *a.* le-*mewr*-re-an, pertaining to Lemuria, a supposititious land of which Madagascar is a remnant; (*l.c.*) lemurine.
lemurine, *a.* *lem*-yew-rin, pertaining to or resembling the lemurs.
lemuroid, *a.* *lem*-yew-royd, lemurine: *n.* any one of the lemurs.
lend, *v.t.* lend, to grant for temporary use; to grant on condition that the thing or its equivalent be returned; to grant or accord; to do; to let for hire; to loan. **lend-lease,** the method adopted in 1941 under which the U.S.A. lent anti-Axis belligerents munitions, defence articles, etc., on indefinite lease, such loans to be eventually returned in good condition or replaced in kind, thus obviating money debts. *p.* and *pp.* **lent.** (A.S. *lænan.*)
lendable, *a.* *lend*-a-bl, that may be lent.
lender, *n.* *lend*-er, one who lends; a moneylender.
lending, *n.* *lend*-ing, the act of giving on loan; that which is lent or furnished. **lending library,** *see* **library.**

length, *n.* length, extent from end to end; the longest line which can be drawn through a body; long continuance; detail; distance; flight distance of a bowled ball [Cricket]; more than the average number of cards in one suit [Bridge, etc.]. **at length,** in full; at last; at the end or conclusion. **at arm's length,** so as to avoid intimacy. **go to any length,** to be very thorough in action; to stop at no obstacle. (A.S.)

lengthen, *v.t. length*-en, to extend in length; to elongate; to draw out: *v.i.* to grow longer.

lengthily, *ad. length*-e-le, at great length.

lengthiness, *n.* the state of being lengthy.

lengthwise, *ad. length*-wize, in the direction of the length.

lengthy, *a. length*-e, long; rather long; not short; not brief.

leniency, *n. lee*-ne-en-se, the quality of being lenient.

lenient, *a. lee*-ne-ent, softening; mitigating; emollient; not severe; mild. (L. *leniens*, soothing.)

leniently, *ad. lee*-ne-ent-le, in a lenient manner.

lenify, *v.t. len*-e-fy, to make supple; to mitigate; to assuage. (L. *lenis*, mild, *ficare*, to make.)

Leninism, *n. len*-in-izm, the principles and doctrines of V. I. Ulyanov Lenin (1870-1924), Russian Communist leader and founder of the U.S.S.R.

Leninist, *n. len*-in-ist, an adherent to the doctrines of Leninism: *a.* of, or belonging to, Lenin or his party.

lenitic, *a.* le-*nit*-ik, pertaining to or living in still waters [Zool.].

lenitive, *a. len*-e-tiv, having the quality of softening or mitigating; assuasive; emollient: *n.* a medicine or application that eases pain; that which soothes or allays excitement; a palliative. (L. *lenitus*, soothed.)

lenity, *n. len*-e-te, mildness of treatment; clemency.

leno, *n. lee*-no, a cross-woven open-work fabric used for window-curtains, etc.; gauze. (Fr. *leinon*, lawn.)

lens, *n.* lenz (*pl.* **lenses**), a piece of glass or other transparent substance, so shaped that rays of light passing through it are made to change their direction, and to magnify or diminish objects at a certain distance; the crystalline body in the eye that focuses light-rays upon the retina. **compound lens,** *see* **compound.** (L. *lens*, a lentil.)

Lent, *n.* lent, a fast of forty days, observed as a time of mortification in commemoration of the fasting of Christ in the wilderness, commencing with Ash Wednesday, and continuing till Easter. **Lent lily,** the daffodil. (A.S. *lencten*, the spring.)

lent, lent, *p.* and *pp.* of *lend.*

lentamente, *ad. len*-ta-*men*-ta, slowly [Mus.]. (It.)

lentando, *ad.* len-*tan*-do, with slackening [Mus.].

Lenten, *a. len*-ten, pertaining to, or used in, Lent; sparing; unostentatious.

lenticular, *a.* len-*tik*-yew-lar, resembling a lentil; of the form of a double-convex lens; pertaining to the lens of the eye. (L. *lenticula.*)

lenticularly, *ad.* in the manner of a lens.

lentiform, *a. len*-te-form, lenticular.

lentigerous, *a.* len-*tij*-er-rus, having a crystalline lens [Zool.].

lentiginous, *a.* len-*tij*-e-nus, freckly; scurfy. (Late L. *lentiginosus.*)

lentigo, *n.* len-*ty*-go, a freckly appearance of or eruption on the skin. (L. *lens, lentis*, lentil.)

lentil, *n. len*-til, a leguminous plant, *Lens esculenta*, and its seed resembling in shape a lens convex on both sides. (O.Fr. *lentille*, from L. *lens, lentis.*)

lentisk, *n. len*-tisk, the mastic-tree, *Pistacia lentiscus.* (L. *lentiscus.*)

lento, *ad. len*-toh, slowly [Mus.]. (It.)

lentoid, *a. len*-toyd, shaped like a lens.

lentor, *n. len*-tor, tenacity; viscousness; slowness; sluggishness. (L.)

Leo, *n. lee*-oh, the zodiacal constellation, the Lion; the fifth sign of the zodiac. (L.)

leonid, *a. lee*-o-nid, pertaining to the constellation Leo, from which the November meteors appear to diverge: *n.* (*pl.* **leonides,** lee-*on*-e-deez), one of these meteors radiating from Leo.

leonine, *a. lee*-o-nine, of or like a lion.

Leonine, *a. lee*-o-nine, pertaining to any of the Popes named Leo: *n.* an elegiac verse containing an internal rhyme as, "Arethusa arose from her couch of snows" (said to be named after *Leoninus*, a 12th-century canon of Paris). the Leonine City, the Vatican, originally walled by Leo IV about 850.

leopard, *n. lep*-ard, a large and ferocious carnivore of the cat group, *Felis pardus*, known by its spots; the panther. **American leopard,** the jaguar. **hunting leopard,** the cheetah. **leopard cat,** a small handsome cat of South-Eastern Asia, *Felis bengalensis.* **leopard's bane,** a plant of the genus *Doronicum*; also herb Paris, *Paris quadrifolia.* **snow leopard,** the ounce, *Felis uncia.* (O.Fr.)

leopardess, *n. lep*-ard-ess, the female leopard.

Lepcha, *n. lep*-chah, a member of a Mongoloid Buddhist people of Sikkim; their language.

leper, *n. lep*-er, one affected with leprosy. (Fr. *lèpre.*)

lepid, *a. lep*-id, pleasant; jocose. (L. *lepidus*, jolly.)

Lepidodendron, *n. lep*-e-do-*den*-dron, a genus of fossil trees, common in the coal-measures, so named from the scaly appearance of the stem. (Gr. *lepis*, a scale, *dendron*, a tree.)

lepidoid, *a. lep*-e-doyd, ganoid. (Gr.)

lepidolite, *n.* le-*pid*-o-lite, a species of mica, usually of a lilac or rose colour, containing lithia and rubidium. (Gr. *lepis*, and *lithos*, a stone.)

lepidomelane, *n. lep*-e-do-me-*lane*, a variety of mica containing much iron.

Lepidoptera, *n.pl. lep*-e-*dop*-ter-ra, an order of insects, including butterflies and moths, having four wings, covered with minute powder-like scales. (Gr. *lepis*, and *pteron*, a wing.)

lepidopteral, *a.* lep-e-*dop*-ter-ral, lepidopterous.

lepidopteran, *a.* lep-a-*dop*-ter-ran, lepidopterous: *n.* any member of the Lepidoptera.

lepidopterous, *a.* lep-e-*dop*-ter-rus, of or belonging to the Lepidoptera.

lepidosiren, *n. lep*-e-do-*syr*-ren, the South American mud-fish, *Lepidosiren paradoxa.* (Gr. *lepis*, and *siren.*)

leporine, *a. lep*-o-rine, pertaining to or of the nature of the hare. (L. *leporinus*, pertaining to a hare.)

lepra, *n. lee*-pra, leprosy; formerly any scaly affection of the skin.

leprechaun, *n.* lep-re-*kawn*, a benevolent, helpful brownie. (Ir.)

leprosy, *n. lep*-ro-se, a bacillary disease eating away the body-tissues and causing scales to form on the skin; a chronic constitutional disease. *Elephantiasis Græcorum*; moral foulness or contagion.

leprous, *a. lep*-rus, infected with, or pertaining to, leprosy.

leprousness, *n. lep*-rus-ness, the state of being leprous; leprous disease.

leptocephalus, *n.* lep-to-*sef*-a-lus, the larval form of members of the eel family.

leptodactyl, *n. lep*-to-*dak*-til, having slender toes (esp. of certain birds). (Gr. *leptos*, slender, *daktylos*, a toe.)

lepton, *n. lep*-ton, the smallest ancient Greek coin; a money of account in modern Greece equivalent to the hundredth of a drachma. (Gr.)

leptorrhine, *a. lep*-to-rine, having a slender nose.

Lesbian, *a. lez*-be-an, of, or pertaining to, Lesbos: *n.* a native of Lesbos: (*l.c.*) *a.* of, or pertaining to lesbianism: *n.* one addicted to lesbianism. (Gr., the island of Lesbos, the home of Sappho.)

lesbianism, *n. lez*-be-a-nizm, homosexuality between women; Sapphism.

lese-majesty, *n. leez-maj*-es-te, treason against the state; high treason. (Fr. *lèse-majesté.*)

lesion, *n. lee*-zhon, morbid change in the structure of an organ; a wound or injury. (Fr.)

lesional, *a. lee*-zhon-al, pertaining to or characterized by a lesion [Path.].

less, *a.* less, comparative of little; smaller; not so large or great: *ad.* in a smaller or lower degree: *n.* not so much; a smaller portion; the inferior or younger: *prep.* minus, deducting. **nothing less,** anything else; anything rather than. (A.S. *læssa.*)

-less, suffix denoting not having, destitute of (*senseless, supperless*), beyond the scope of (*numberless*), or without ability to effect (*tameless*).

lessee, *n.* les-*see*, the person to whom a lease is granted. (O.Fr. *lessé.*)

lessen, *v.t. less*-en, to make less in bulk, quantity, amount, degree, state, or quality; to bring down in dignity; to degrade; to underrate: *v.i.* to become less in bulk, quantity, degree, intensity, etc.

lesser, *a.* *les*-ser, comparative of little; less; smaller; inferior.
lesson, *n.* *less*-on, as much instruction as a pupil is given at one time; anything learned or that may be learned; a portion of Scripture read in divine service; precept; reproof. (Fr. *leçon.*)
lessor, *n.* *les*-sor, one who grants a lease. (O.Fr.)
lest, *conj.* lest, for fear that; that . . . not. (A.S.)
⋆**let,** *v.t.* let, to allow, permit, or suffer; to give leave or power to; to lease; to grant possession and use for a compensation; in the imperative, followed by the first and third persons, it expresses desire or wish; by the first person plural, exhortation or entreaty; by the third person, it implies permission or command addressed to an inferior: *n.* a letting [Coll.]. **let alone,** *see* **alone. let blood,** to open a vein and suffer the blood to flow out. **let down,** to permit to sink or fall; to lower; to fail or disappoint (one). **let fly,** to send forth or discharge with violence, as an arrow or stone; to break forth in a tirade [Coll.]. **let go,** to release from holding. **let in** or **into,** to permit to enter. **let loose,** to free from restraint. **let off,** to discharge; to let fly or cause to explode; to excuse; to pardon. **let on,** to show knowledge; to betray (a confidence, etc.) [Coll.]; to behave excitedly [Coll.]. **let out,** to suffer to escape; to lease or let to hire; to divulge; to hit out [Coll.]. **let slip,** to allow to slip; to overlook. *p.* and *pp.* **let**; *ppr.* **letting.** (A.S. *lettan.*)
let, *n.* let, hindrance; a retarding; obstruction of the ball in certain ways, so that it must be served again [Tennis, etc.]: *v.i.* to hinder; to prevent [Archaic]. *p.* and *pp.* **let.** (A.S. *lettan.*)
letch, *v.t.* letch, to leach: *n.* a stream running through boggy ground.
letch, *n.* letch, a desire; a craving.
lethal, *a.* *lee*-thal, deadly; fatal. **lethal chamber,** an enclosure in which animals are killed painlessly. (L. *lethalis,* death-like.)
lethality, *n.* lee-*thal*-e-te, the condition or property of being lethal; deadliness.
lethargic, *a.* le-*thar*-jik, affected with lethargy or morbid drowsiness; dull; apathetic.
lethargical, *a.* le-*thar*-je-kal, lethargic.
lethargically, *ad.* in a lethargic manner.
lethargize, *v.t.* *leth*-ar-jize, to make lethargic.
lethargy, *n.* *leth*-ar-je, a heavy, unnatural, or morbid drowsiness; dullness; a state of inaction or inattention. (L. *lethargia.*)
Lethe, *n.* *lee*-the, one of the rivers of the nether world of the Greeks, a draught of whose water was said to induce oblivion of the past; oblivion; forgetfulness. (Gr., oblivion.)
Lethean, *a.* le-*thee*-an, pertaining to or having the effect of the waters of Lethe; inducing forgetfulness.
lethiferous, *a.* le-*thif*-er-us, bringing death; deadly. (L. *lethum,* death, *fero,* bring.)
let-off, *n.* *let*-off, an act of letting off; an unexpected escape, excusal, or deliverance.
Lett, *n.* let, a native of Latvia (Livonia). (Ger. *Lette.*)
⋆**letter,** *n.* *let*-ter, an alphabetic character as the symbol of a sound; a manually or mechanically written communication sent by post or otherwise; the literal meaning; a single type [Print.]: *pl.* learning; literary culture; erudition: *v.t.* to impress or form letters on. **letter of advice,** a letter notifying the dispatch of goods, etc. **letter of marque,** *see* **marque. letter-board,** a board on which pages of type are placed for distribution [Print.]; a board on which letters for members or visitors are placed until claimed. **letter-book,** a book containing copies of letters for reference. **letter-card,** a postcard that can be folded and stuck together at the edges. **letter-founder,** a typefounder. **letter-lock,** a lock in which rings of letters can be combined so that it can be opened only by those who know the combination. **letter-paper,** paper used for writing letters; notepaper. **letter-perfect,** accurate in the recital of words committed to memory. **letter-scale** a scale used to weigh letters. **letter-weight,** a paper-weight. **letter-writer,** one who writes letters; a book to teach letter-writing. **letters patent,** a writing executed and sealed, by which power and authority are granted to a person to do some act or enjoy some right. (Fr. *lettre.*)
lettered, *a.* *let*-terd, marked with letters; educated; versed in literature; belonging to or suited for learning.
lettering, *n.* *let*-ter-ing, the act of impressing or otherwise marking with letters; the letters impressed, painted, or drawn, etc.; titling.
letterless, *a.* *let*-ter-less, illiterate; unlearned.
letterpress, *n.* *let*-ter-press, surface printing from type or blocks; printed matter exclusive of illustrations, etc.
letterwood, *n.* *let*-ter-wood, the wood of the S. American tree *Brosimum aubletii,* used for cabinet-work and veneering.
Lettic, *a.* *let*-tik, pertaining to the group of languages that includes Lettish, Lithuanian, and Old Prussian; Lettish.
Lettish, *a.* *let*-tish, pertaining to the Letts, or to Latvia; Lettic: *n.* the language of the Letts.
lettuce, *n.* *let*-is, a succulent plant of the genus *Lactuca,* used as a salad. (L. *lactuca.*)
leu, *n.* *le*-oo (*pl.* **lei,** lay), the monetary unit of Roumania, nominally equivalent to about ⅓rd of a penny. (Roumanian.)
leucæthiopia, *n.* *lew*-se-the-*oh*-pe-a, the condition of albinism among Negroes.
leucæthiopic, *a.* lew-se-the-*op*-ik, relating to, or characterized by, leucæthiopia.
leuchæmia, *n.* lew-*kee*-me-a (*or* **leucæmia,** lew-*see*-me-a), leukæmia.
leucine, *n.* *lew*-sin, a white flaky substance produced by the decomposition of protein during digestion. (Gr. *leukos,* white.)
leucism, *n.* *lew*-sizm, leucosis.
leucite, *n.* lew-*site,* a silicate of potassium and aluminium, a mineral of a dull, glassy appearance, found in the volcanic rocks of Italy.
leucitic, *a.* lew-*sit*-ik, containing, or pertaining to, leucite.
leucocyte, *n.* *lew*-ko-site, a white blood-corpuscle. (Gr. *leukos,* and *kytos,* a cell.)
leucocythemia, *n.* *lew*-ko-se-*thee*-me-a, leukæmia [Med.]. (Gr. *leukos, kytos,* a cell, *haima,* blood.)
leucoderma, *n.* *lew*-ko-*der*-ma, abnormal whiteness of the skin. (Gr. *leukos,* and *derma,* skin.)
leucoma, *n.* lew-*koh*-ma, an opacity of the cornea due to ulceration or injury. (Gr.)
leucopathy, *n.* lew-*kop*-a-the, albinism. (Gr. *leukos,* and *pathos,* affection.)
leucorrhœa, *n.* *lew*-kor-*ree*-a, a mucous discharge from the lining of the uterus or of the vaginal canal; the whites. (Gr. *leukos,* and *rheo,* flow.)
leucosis, *n.* lew-*koh*-sis, the abnormal pallor of albinism.
leucous, *a.* *lew*-kus, white-skinned; having the pallor of an albino.
leukæmia, *n.* lew-*kee*-me-a, a disease, usually fatal, characterized by numerical increase of white and decrease of red blood-corpuscles.
lev, *n.* lef (*pl.* **leva,** *lev*-a), the monetary unit of Bulgaria, nominally equivalent to about ⅓rd of a penny. (Bulgarian.)
Levant, *n.* le-*vant,* the eastern coasts of the Mediterranean Sea; (*l.c.*) a levanter; a high-class variety of morocco leather. (It. *levante,* the east wind.)
levant, *v.i.* le-*vant,* to decamp. (Sp. *levantar.*)
levanter, *n.* le-*van*-ter, a strong easterly wind on the North African coast; one who levants, a welsher: (*cap.*) a Levantine.
Levantine, *a.* le-*van*-tine, pertaining to the Levant: *n.* a native of the Levant; (*l.c.*) a kind of silk cloth.
levator, *n.* le-*vay*-tor, a muscle that serves to raise some part, as the eyelid [Anat.]; an instrument used to raise a depressed piece of bone [Surg.]. (L.)
levee, *n.* le-*vee or lev*-ee, a dyke; an artificial river bank; a wharf. (Fr.)
levee, *n.* *lev*-e *or lev*-ay, a reception by a prince or great personage in the morning; a royal reception at which only men are presented; any reception; the time of rising. (Fr.)
⋆**level,** *a.* *lev*-el, horizontal; even; flat; even with anything else of the same height; on the same line or plane; equal in rank or degree; well balanced; uniform: *n.* a horizontal line or plane; a surface without inequalities; usual elevation; a state of equality; the line of direction; an instrument by which to find the horizontal [Mech.] or [Surveying.]: *v.t.* to make horizontal; to make even; to obtain a perfectly horizontal line of sight between two points: *v.t.* to make horizontal; to make even, flat, or smooth; to make equal; to aim; to lay low;

to raze: *v.i.* to aim at; to be aimed. **level best,** very best [Coll.]. **level crossing,** the place where a road crosses a railway line at the same level. **level-headed,** possessed of common sense; thoughtful; judicious. **level race,** a race in which the difference between the leading competitors is very slight.

leveller, *n. lev*-el-ler, one who levels; one who would destroy all social distinctions.

levelling, *n. lev*-el-ling, the reduction of uneven surfaces to a level; the art or process of ascertaining the different elevations of objects. **levelling instrument,** a surveyors' level. **levelling screw,** a screw for adjusting the level of a machine, instrument, etc.

levelly, *ad. lev*-el-le, in a horizontal direction or position.

levelness, *n. lev*-el-ness, condition of being level.

lever, *n. lee*-ver, a bar of metal, wood, or other substance, working on a support (fulcrum) and contrived originally to raise heavy weights; a lever-watch; anything bringing power to bear: *v.t.* to lift or move with a lever: *v.i.* to use a lever. **lever escapement,** an escapement in which the pallet and the balance are connected by two levers. **lever watch,** a watch with a lever escapement. (Fr. *leveur.*)

leverage, *n. lee*-ver-raj, mechanical advantage gained by use of the lever; the action of a lever.

leveret, *n. lev*-er-ret, a hare in its first year. (O.Fr.)

leverwood, *n. lee*-ver-wood, the North American tree, *Ostrya virginica.*

leviable, *a. lev*-e-a-bl, that may be levied or assessed and collected.

leviathan, *n.* le-*vy*-a-than, a gigantic sea-monster mentioned in the Bible (Job xl, 1, etc.); anything huge or monstrous. (Heb.)

levigable, *a. lev*-e-ga-bl, that can be levigated.

levigate, *a. lev*-e-gate, made smooth: *v.t.* to reduce to a fine impalpable powder [Pharm. and Chem.]; to smooth by polishing. (L. *levigatus,* made smooth.)

levigation, *n. lev*-e-*gay*-shon, the operation or act of levigating.

levin, *n. lev*-in, a flash of lightning. (Perhaps Scand.)

levirate, *n. lee*-ve-rate, the custom, according to the Hebrew law, which required a man to marry the widow of a brother who died without issue. (L. *levir,* a husband's brother.)

levitate, *v.i. lev*-e-tate, to rise and float in the air: *v.t.* to cause to float in air. (L. *levitas,* lightness.)

levitation, *n.* lev-e-*tay*-shon, the act or process of levitating. (L.)

Levite, *n. lee*-vite, one of the tribe or family of Levi, esp. one acting as assistant to a Jewish priest; a priest.

Levitical, *a.* le-*vit*-e-kal, pertaining to the Levites; priestly. **Levitical degrees,** relationships preclusive of marriage under Hebrew law.

Levitically, *ad.* after the manner of the Levites.

Leviticus, *n.* le-*vit*-e-kus, the book of the Old Testament containing Levitical laws and regulations.

levity, *n. lev*-e-te, lightness of temper or conduct; inconstancy; want of due consideration or seriousness; lightness of weight. (L. *levitas,* lightness.)

levo-, *pref. leev*-o, *see* **lævo-.**

levy, *v.t. lev*-e, to raise; to collect, as an army, compulsory contribution or tax; to seize for debt. **levy a fine,** to commence and carry on a suit for assuring the title to lands or tenements. **levy war,** to raise or begin war; to attack. (Fr. *levée.*)

levy, *n. lev*-e, that which is levied, whether in men, taxes, or contributions, etc.; the act of collecting such; troops called up for service. **capital levy,** a compulsory and proportionate levy on capital in addition to income tax, etc. **levy in mass,** a requisition for service of all liable to bear arms. (Fr. *levée.*)

lewd, *a.* lewd, given to the unlawful indulgence of lust; licentious; profligate; obscene. (A.S. *læwede,* ignorant.)

lewdly, *ad. lewd*-le, in a lewd manner.

lewdness, *n. lewd*-ness, the quality of being lewd.

lewdster, *n. lewd*-ster, a lecher.

lewis, *n. lew*-is, an appliance for raising large stones, thin wedges of iron being let into the stone, so as to form a dovetail: *v.t.* to fasten in the manner of a lewis.

Lewis gun, *n.* a light automatic machine-gun of various patterns. (Name of inventor.)

lewisite, *n. lew*-is-ite, a calcium titanate and antimonate crystallizing in the isometric system [Min.]. (W. J. *Lewis, d.* 1926, Engl. mineralogist.)

lewisite, *n. lew*-is-ite, a strongly vesicant and persistent poison-gas containing arsenic and smelling of geraniums. (W. L. *Lewis,* U.S.A. chemist.)

lexical, *a. leks*-e-kal, connected with words as distinct from grammar; pertaining to a lexicon or to lexicography.

lexicographer, *n. leks*-e-*kog*-ra-fer, a dictionary maker. (Gr. *lexikographos,* a writer of words.)

lexicographic, *a. leks*-e-ko-*graf*-ik, pertaining to lexicography.

lexicography, *n. leks*-e-*kog*-ra-fe, the art of compiling dictionaries. (Gr. *lexicon,* of words, and *grapho,* write.)

lexicologist, *n. leks*-e-*kol*-o-jist, one skilled in lexicology.

lexicology, *n. leks*-e-*kol*-o-je, that branch of study which treats of the derivation, signification, and application of words. (Gr. *lexicon,* and *logos,* science.)

lexicon, *n. leks*-e-kon, a dictionary, esp. one of Greek or an Oriental language. (Gr.)

lexigraphic, *a. leks*-e-*graf*-ik, pertaining to lexigraphy.

lexigraphy, *n.* leks-*ig*-ra-fe, the system of writing in which each character represents a whole word. (Gr. *lexis,* a word, *grapho,* write.)

lexiphanic, *a.* leks-e-*fan*-ik, addicted to the use of long words or pretentious phraseology. (Gr. *lexis,* word, *phanein,* to show.)

ley, *n.* lee, a lea; a meadow. **ley farming,** the systematic ploughing and cropping of grassland to ensure high production with maintenance of fertility [Agr.]. (A.S. *leah.*)

ley, *n.* lee, lye.

Leyden-jar, *n. lay*-den-jar, a glass condenser formerly used for storing statical electricity. (Invented, 18th cent., at Univ. of *Leyden.*)

li, *n.* lee, a Chinese measure of weight (about ⅓rd oz.) and of length (varying in different periods and areas). (Chin.)

liability, *n.* ly-a-*bil*-e-te, the state or condition of being liable: *pl.* pecuniary obligations. **limited liability,** responsibility for debts, etc., only to a limited amount. **limited (liability) company,** a company whose members accept only limited liability.

liable, *a. ly*-a-bl, bound; obliged in law or equity; responsible; subject; obnoxious; exposed (to). (Fr. *lier,* tie.)

liaise, *v.i.* le-*ayze,* to make liaison with; to form a working alliance. (Back-formation from *liaison.*)

liaison, *n.* le-*ay*-zon, a union or bond of union; an intimacy, usually of an illicit nature; co-ordination between allies, usually military; sounding of the final silent consonant before a vowel or a mute *h.* **liaison officer,** an officer who is a go-between for allied forces; one acting as a connecting link. (Fr.)

liana, *n.* le-*ah*-na, any climbing plant of tropical America. (Fr. *liane.*)

liar, *n. ly*-er, one given to lying; one who knowingly utters falsehoods. (A.S. *leogare.*)

liard, *n.* lee-ar, a former French farthing. (O.Fr.)

lias, *n. ly*-as, an argillaceous limestone immediately below the oolitic series of rocks; the series of strata (the oldest of the Jurassic) characterized by this. (Fr.)

liassic, *a.* ly-*ass*-ik, pertaining to the lias formation.

libation, *n.* ly-*bay*-shon, a sacrifice by the pouring of a liquid, usually wine, in honour of some deity; the liquid so poured. (Fr.)

libatory, *a. ly*-ba-to-re, pertaining to libation.

libel, *n. ly*-bel, a defamatory writing; a lampoon; any book, writing, or picture containing representations maliciously made or published, tending to bring a person into contempt or to expose him to public hatred and derision; an obscene, blasphemous, or seditious publication; a written statement of the plaintiff's allegations [Law]; the act of publishing a libel: *v.t.* to defame by a libel; to lampoon; to proceed against by a written complaint [Law]: *v.i.* to spread libels. (O.Fr.)

libellant, *n. ly*-bel-lant, one who institutes a suit in an admiralty or ecclesiastical court.

libeller, *n. ly*-bel-ler, one who libels; a lampooner.

libellous, *a. ly*-bel-lus, being, containing, or of the nature of a libel; defamatory.

libellously, *ad.* *ly*-bel-lus-le, in libellous manner.
liber, *n.* *ly*-ber, the innermost bark, or phloem, of exogenous plants [Bot.]. (L., bark.)
liberal, *a.* *lib*-er-ral, giving largely; munificent; generous; ample; large; not selfish or narrow; embracing other interests than one's own; refined; free; open; candid; not too literal; favourable to democratic reforms: *n.* (*cap.*) one who advocates greater freedom in political institutions, and the extension of political power among the people at large; the party-name adopted by the Whigs in 1830. **Liberal Conservative,** a Conservative in politics who is not averse to reforms. **Liberal Party,** the party advocating democratic changes, etc., forming, till 1918, the parliamentary opposition to the Conservative party. **Liberal Unionist,** one of the Liberals who broke from the party in 1886 on the question of Home Rule for Ireland. (O.Fr., from L.)
liberalism, *n.* *lib*-er-ra-lizm, liberal principles, esp. those of the Liberal Party.
liberalist, *n.* *lib*-er-ra-list, one who advocates liberalism; a liberal.
liberalistic, *a.* *lib*-er-ra-*lis*-tik, pertaining to liberalism; of liberal leanings.
liberality, *n.* *lib*-er-*ral*-e-te, the quality of being liberal; munificence; generosity; largeness of mind; impartiality; a particular act of generosity; a liberal donation. (Fr. *libéralité.*)
liberalization, *n.* *lib*-er-ra-ly-*zay*-shon, the process or act of liberalizing; the fact, or state, of being liberalized.
liberalize, *v.t.* *lib*-er-ra-lize, to render liberal; to free from control, or from narrow views and prejudices.
liberally, *ad.* *lib*-er-ra-le, bountifully; largely.
liberate, *v.t.* *lib*-er-rate, to set free; to release from restraint, confinement, or bondage. (L. *liberatus.*)
liberation, *n.* *lib*-er-*ray*-shon, the act of liberating; deliverance from constraint.
liberationism, *n.* lib-er-*ray*-shon-izm, the principles or theories of the liberationists.
liberationist, *n.* lib-er-*ray*-shon-ist, one advocating the disestablishment of the Church of England.
liberator, *n.* *lib*-er-ray-tor, one who sets free, esp. the deliverer of a people from oppression.
liberee, *n.* lib-er-*ree*, a liberated person, esp. one from a prisoner-of-war camp.
libertarian, *a.* *lib*-er-*tare*-er-an, pertaining to liberty; upholding the doctrine of free-will as opposed to that of necessity: *n.* one holding the doctrine of the freedom of the will.
libertarianism, *n.* *lib*-er-*tare*-re-a-nizm, the principles or doctrines of the libertarians.
liberticidal, *a.* le-*ber*-te-*sy*-dal, characterized by liberticide; destructive of liberty.
liberticide, *n.* le-*ber*-te-side, destruction of liberty; a destroyer of liberty: *a.* destroying liberty. (L. *libertas*, and *cædo*, kill.)
libertinage, *n.* *lib*-er-te-naj, libertinism; the behaviour of a libertine.
libertine, *n.* *lib*-er-teen, one of loose moral or religious opinions; one who leads a dissolute, licentious life; a rake; a debauchee; formerly, a freed slave: *a.* licentious; dissolute; not under the restraint of law or religion. (L. *libertinus*, a freedman.)
libertinism, *n.* *lib*-er-te-nizm, licentiousness of opinion or practice; an unrestrained indulgence of lust; debauchery; lewdness. (Fr. *libertinisme.*)
liberty, *n.* *lib*-er-te, freedom from restraint; leave; permission granted; immunity enjoyed by prescription or by grant; privilege; space within which one has privilege or freedom; permission to go about; a breach of decorum or courtesy; freedom of action or speech beyond the ordinary bounds of civility or decorum; as opposed to necessity, the power of an agent to do or forbear any particular action [Metaphysics]; a district beyond the city walls but subject to its jurisdiction; a district within which certain privileges are granted; prior to 1850, a district having a commission of the peace not under the jurisdiction of the sheriff of the county. **at liberty,** free from restraint; not occupied or engaged. **civil liberty,** liberty abridged and restrained only so far as is necessary and expedient for the safety and interest of the society, state, or nation. **Liberty Hall,** a house in which all are free to do as they like. **liberty-man,** a sailor who has received leave to go ashore [Naut.]. **liberty of the press,** *see* **freedom of the press. natural liberty,** freedom of action uncontrolled, except by the laws of nature. **political liberty,** the enjoyment of just and equal participation in the government of the state of which one is a member, and of freedom under its laws. **religious liberty,** the right of adopting, enjoying, and disseminating opinions on religious subjects, and worshipping according to the dictates of conscience. **set at liberty,** to deliver from confinement or restraint. **take the liberty,** to use freedom not specially granted in saying or doing anything. (Fr. *liberté.*)
libethenite, *n.* le-*beth*-en-ite, an olive-green hydrous phosphate of copper. (First found at *Libethen*, Hungary.)
libidinal, *a.* le-*bid*-e-nal, pertaining to libido.
libidinous, *a.* le-*bid*-e-nus, having or implying an inordinate desire for sexual indulgence; lewd. (L. *libidinosus*, filled with passion.)
libidinously, *ad.* le-*bid*-e-nus-le, with lewd desire.
libidinousness, *n.* le-*bid*-e-nus-ness, the state or quality of being libidinous.
libido, *n.* le-*bee*-do, vital energy (*Jung*); desire or other energy derived from the sexual impulse (*Freud*) [Psychan.]; characterized by libidinousness. (L., desire.)
Libra, *n.* *ly*-bra, the seventh sign in the zodiac, which the sun enters at the autumnal equinox. (L., a balance.)
librarian, *n.* ly-*brayr*-re-an, the custodian of a library.
librarianship, *n.* ly-*brayr*-re-an-ship, the office or duties of a librarian; the science or art of conducting a library.
*****library,** *n.* *ly*-bra-re, a collection of books; an edifice or an apartment containing a collection of books; a theatre-ticket agency [Coll.]. **circulating library,** *see* **circulating. lending library,** a library which lends books to read and return within a specified time. **public library,** a library, generally rate-supported, open to the general public; a municipal library. **reference library,** a library in which the books are for consultation but not for taking away. (Fr. *librairie.*)
librate, *v.t.* *ly*-brate, to poise; to balance: *v.i.* to be balanced; to move, as a balance; to oscillate. (L. *libratus*, balanced.)
libration, *n.* ly-*bray*-shon, the act of balancing; state of being balanced or in equipoise; vibratory motion, as of a balance before it comes to rest [Astron.].
libratory, *a.* *ly*-bra-to-re, oscillating.
librettist, *n.* le-*bret*-tist, the writer of a libretto.
libretto, *n.* le-*bret*-to (*pl.* **libretti**), the written words of a musical play; the book containing them. (It., a little book.)
libriform, *a.* *ly*-bre-form, resembling or of the nature of liber [Bot.].
Libyan, *a.* *lib*-yan, of, or pertaining to, Libya, in N. Africa: *n.* a native of Libya; a language of the ancient or modern Libyans.
lice, *n.pl.* lyce, *pl.* of *louse.*
licence, *n.* *ly*-sense, leave; permission granted by some competent authority; a certificate giving such permission; excess or abuse of liberty; departure from rule or custom (in art, etc.). **off-licence,** a licence empowering the holder to sell by retail excisable liquor for consumption off the premises only. (Fr. *licence.*)
licensable, *a.* *ly*-sens-a-bl, that may be permitted by a legal grant.
license, *v.t.* *ly*-sense, to permit by grant of authority; to authorize. **licensed victualler,** the holder of a licence authorizing him to sell excisable liquors by retail to be drunk on the premises; an innkeeper or publican.
licensee, *n.* ly-sen-*see*, the holder of a licence; a licensed victualler.
licenser, *n.* *ly*-sen-ser, one who grants a licence.
licentiate, *n.* ly-*sen*-she-at, one licensed by a University or analogous body to practise a profession; among the Presbyterians, one who has been licensed to preach and is eligible for a charge: *v.t.* to give a licence to. (Late L. *licentiatus.*)
licentiation, *n.* *ly*-sen-she-*ay*-shon, the granting of a licence, esp. for the practice of medicine.
licentious, *a.* ly-*sen*-shus, immoral; dissolute; indulging lust to excess; not restrained by law, rule, or custom. (Fr. *licencieux*).

licentiously, *ad.* in a licentious manner.
licentiousness, *n.* quality of being licentious.
lich, *n.* litch, a dead body or corpse. (A.S. *lic,* body.)
lichen, *n. ly*-ken *or litch*-en, a parasitic fungus growing as a shaggy crust on rocks, trees, etc.; applied to symptoms of several obstinate papular skin diseases [Med.]. (Gr.)
lichenaceous, *a.* ly-ken-*ay*-shus, pertaining to or of the nature of the lichens.
lichenic, *a.* ly-*ken*-ik, lichenous; obtained from lichen.
lichenin, *n. ly*-ken-in, a starch-like demulcent carbohydrate extracted from Iceland-moss; moss starch.
lichenoid, *a. ly*-ken-oyd, lichenaceous.
lichenography, *n. ly*-ken-*og*-ra-fe, a description of lichens. (Gr. *lichen,* and *grapho,* write.)
lichenology, *n. ly*-ken-*ol*-o-je, the study of lichens. (Gr. *lichen,* and *logos,* science.)
lichenous, *a. ly*-ken-us, of or like a lichen.
lich-gate, *n. litch*-gate, a porch at the entrance of a churchyard to rest the bier in while part of the service is being read. (A.S. *lic,* and *gate.*)
lich-owl, *n. litch*-oul, a screech-owl, as supposed to bode death.
lich-wake, *n. litch*-wake, a watching at night with the dead.
licit, *a. lis*-it, lawful. (L., it is allowed.)
licitly, *ad. lis*-it-le, lawfully.
licitness, *n. lis*-it-ness, lawfulness.
lick, *n.* lik, the act of licking; a daub; a little; a salt-lick (U.S.A.): *v.t.* to pass or draw the tongue over; to take in by the tongue; to lap; to chastise; to flog; to beat. **a lick and a promise,** a hasty wash; a slovenly piece of work. **lick into shape,** to trim; to give form or method to. **lick the dust,** to be slain; to perish in battle; to be humbled. **lick up,** to devour; to consume entirely. (A.S. *liccian.*)
lickerish, *a. lik*-er-ish, nice in the choice of food; greedy; having a keen relish; tempting the appetite; lecherous. (*lick.*)
lickerishly, *ad. lik*-er-ish-le, in a lickerish manner.
lickerishness, *n. lik*-er-ish-ness, the state or quality of being lickerish.
lickerous, *a. lik*-er-us, lickerish.
licking, *n. lik*-ing, the action of the verb *to lick*; a thrashing, a beating [Coll.].
lickspittle, *n. lik*-spit-tl, a mean flatterer; a toady.
licorice, *n. lik*-o-ris, liquorice.
lictor, *n. lik*-tor, one of the civil officers who bore the fasces before a Roman magistrate. (L.)
lid, *n.* lid, a movable cover; that which shuts a vessel or box; the cover of the eye, or eyelid. **put the lid on,** to surpass; to act as the culmination of. **with the lid off,** having horrors exposed to view [Slang]. (A.S. *hlid.*)
lidded, *a. lid*-ed, having a lid or (of the eyes) lids.
lidless, *a. lid*-less, having no lid; unclosed (of the eye).
lido, *n. lee*-do, an outdoor bathing pool for public use; a waterside place of alfresco entertainment. (Name of bathing beach, Venice.)
lie, *n.* ly, an intentional falsehood uttered for the purpose of deception; an intentional violation of truth; a fiction; anything that misleads: *v.i.* to utter falsehood with an intention to deceive; to say or do that which deceives another. **give the lie,** to charge with falsehood. **white lie,** a lie told without evil intent; a fib. *ppr.* **lying.** (A.S. *leogan.*)
lie, *v.i.* ly, to rest in a reclining posture; to lean; to press on; to be situated; to be; to abide; to consist; to be sustainable (of an action, etc.) [Law.]: *n.* a lair; how a thing lies; position, as the lie of the ball in golf. **lie at the heart,** to be fixed as an object of affection or anxiety. **lie by,** to rest; to be near. **lie down,** to lay the body on the ground or couch, etc.; to go to rest. **lie hard** or **heavy,** to oppress; to burden. **lie in,** to be in childbed. **lie in one,** to be in the power of; to belong to. **lie in the way,** to be an obstacle or impediment. **lie in wait,** to wait for in concealment or in ambush. **lie low,** to await an opportunity; to conceal one's intentions so as to forestall or outwit. **lie on** or **upon,** to be a matter of obligation or duty. **lie on hand** or **on the hands,** to remain unsold or in possession. **lie on the head,** to be imputed. **lie over,** to be deferred; to remain unpaid when overdue. **lie under,** to be subject to; to suffer. **lie with,** to lodge or sleep with; to have carnal knowledge of; to belong to. **the lie of the land,** the general outlook; prospects. *p.* **lay.** *pp.* **lain.** *ppr.* **lying.** (A.S. *licgan.*)
Lieberkuhn, *n. lee*-ber-koon, a reflector fixed at the object-glass end of a microscope to focus the light on an opaque object. (Name of inventor.)
Lied, *n.* leet (*pl.* **lieder,** *lee*-der), a German song or lyric [Mus.]; a folk-song. (Ger.)
lief, *a.* leef, dear; beloved; willing: *ad.* gladly; willingly. (A.S. *leof,* L. *libet,* it pleases.)
liege, *a.* leej, bound by feudal tenure, whether sovereign or subject, lord or vassal; faithful; subject: *n.* a vassal holding a fee by which he is bound to perform certain services and duties to his lord; a lord or superior who has lieges. (O.Fr.)
liegeman, *n. leej*-man, a vassal.
lien, *n. lee*-en, a right to hold another's property in satisfaction of a claim [Law]. (Fr.)
lienal, *a.* ly-*ee*-nal, pertaining to the spleen. (L. *lien,* the spleen.)
lienitis, *n.* ly-en-*ny*-tis, inflammation of the spleen.
lienteric, *a. ly*-en-*te*-rik, pertaining to a lientery.
lientery, *n. ly*-en-te-re, a diarrhœa, in which aliments are discharged undigested [Med.]. (Gr. *leienteria,* from *leios,* smooth, *enteron,* an intestine.)
lierne, *n.* le-*ern,* a short connecting rib in Gothic vaulting [Arch.]. (Fr.)
lieu, *n.* lew, place; stead. (Fr., from L. *locus,* a place.)
lieutenancy, *n.* lef-*ten*-an-se, the office, command, or commission of a lieutenant; the body of lieutenants or deputy lieutenants.
lieutenant, *n.* lef-*ten*-ant, a deputy; an officer who supplies the place of a superior in his absence; a commissioned officer in the Army next below a captain, and in the Navy (lu-*ten*-ant) next below a lieutenant-commander and ranking with an Army captain. **lieutenant governor,** a deputy governor. **deputy lieutenant,** the deputy of the lord-lieutenant of a county. **second lieutenant,** the lowest commissioned officer in the British Army. (Fr. from *lieu tenant,* in the sense of L. *locum tenens.*)
lieutenant-colonel, *n.* the Army officer of the rank next below colonel, usually in command of a regiment or battalion.
lieutenant-commander, *n.* the naval officer of the rank next below commander.
lieutenant-general, *n.* the officer of the rank next below general.
lieutenantship, *n.* lef-*ten*-ant-ship, a lieutenancy, esp. in the Navy or Army.
life, *n.* life (*pl.* **lives**), that state of an animal and a plant in which it is capable of performing its natural functions; the time from birth to death; period of existence; the present state of existence; state of existence after death; manner of living; conduct in regard to morals; course of living; source of living; living things in general; spirit; animation; resolution; the living form; general state of man, or of social manners; rank in society; human affairs; a person; a biographical narration; supreme felicity; a quickening principle; a point to which in certain games a player is or may be entitled; a person insured [Coll.]. **life annuity,** a yearly sum paid to a person after a specified age. **life assurance,** a contract for the payment of a certain sum on a person's death. **life insurance,** life assurance. **life interest,** an interest or estate which lasts during the life of the named person or persons. **life-estate,** an estate that continues during the life of the possessor. **life-history,** the development of an organism from the cell to maturity. **life-jacket,** a buoyant jacket for support in water. **life-peer,** a peer whose title lasts only the duration of his life. **life-preserver,** any apparatus for preserving life in cases of shipwreck or fire; a cudgel weighted at one end. **life-rate,** the rate at which a human life is insured. **life-rocket,** the rocket carrying the line fired over a wreck to effect communication with the shore. **life-sentence,** a term of imprisonment, etc., intended to cease only at death. **life-size,** of the same size as that of the object reproduced. **life-spring,** a source of life. **life-table,** a table of the

statistics of the expectations of life at various ages. **life-work,** the work on which one expends one's time and energy. **for dear life,** as if life depended upon. **such is life,** an expression indicative of the passive acceptance of events. **to the life,** as if the original, of a painting, etc., were before one; with great fidelity. (A.S. *lif.*)

lifebelt, *n. life*-belt, a belt for support in the water.

lifeblood, *n. life*-blud, the blood necessary to life; that which constitutes or gives strength and energy.

lifeboat, *n. life*-boat, a boat for saving lives in cases of shipwreck.

lifebuoy, *n. life*-boy, a buoyant ring for saving life at sea.

lifegiving, *a. life*-giv-ing, giving life or spirit.

lifeguard, *n. life*-gard, a contrivance attached to engines, machinery, and motor vehicles, to prevent accidents; a bodyguard, as the Lifeguards, two cavalry regiments forming part of the royal body-guard in England; a member of either of these regiments, a **lifeguardsman.**

lifehold, *a. life*-hohld, held for life: *n.* property held by lease for life.

lifeless, *a. life*-less, destitute of life; deprived of life; destitute of power, force, vigour, or spirit; vapid; insipid; torpid.

lifelessly, *ad. life*-less-le, in a lifeless manner.

lifelessness, *n.* the state of being lifeless.

lifelike, *a. life*-like, resembling life.

lifeline, *n. life*-line, a rope for saving life.

lifelong, *a. life*-long, all through life.

lifer, *n. life*-er, a sentence of penal servitude for life; a convict undergoing this [Slang].

life-saving, *a.*, designed for the prevention of the loss of life: *n.* act or operation of saving life.

lifetime, *n. life*-time, duration of life; period of efficiency or activity.

lift, *v.t.* lift, to raise; to elevate; to exalt; to elate; to take and carry away; to hit the ball in the air [Cricket]; to appropriate or steal [Coll.]: *v.i.* to try to raise; to rise; to disperse (of fog, etc.). **lift the elbow,** to drink. **lift up the eyes,** to fix the eyes on; to direct the desires to God. **lift up the face,** to look to with confidence, cheerfulness, and comfort. **lift up the hand,** to swear; to raise the hands in prayer; to rise in opposition to; to shake off sloth and engage in duty. **lift up the head,** to raise from a low condition; to rejoice; to rally; to renew one's courage. **lift up the voice,** to call out either in grief or joy. (O. Scand. *lypta.*)

★**lift,** *n.* lift, the act of lifting; that which is to be raised; assistance in lifting or otherwise; anything which lifts; an elevator; a rope from masthead to yardarm; a rise; a degree of elevation; the distance through which anything is lifted; the upward force exerted perpendicularly to the flight path of any aircraft; a layer of leather in a boot-heel: a ride in a vehicle [Coll.]. **disposable lift,** ballast, fuel, stores, etc., carried in aircraft [Av.]. **dynamic lift,** lift due to forward motion. **static lift,** lift due to buoyancy.

lift, *n.* lift, the sky; the upper regions. (A.S. *lyft.*)

liftable, *a. lift*-a-bl, that can be lifted.

lifter, *n. lift*-er, one who or that which lifts; a thief [Slang].

lifting-bridge, *n.* a drawbridge which lifts.

ligament, *n. lig*-a-ment, anything that binds; a strong fibrous band connecting a movable joint [Anat.]. (Fr.)

ligamental, *a.* lig-a-*men*-tal, of the nature of a ligament; binding.

ligamentous, *a.* lig-a-*men*-tus, ligamental.

ligan, *n. ly*-gan, lagan.

ligate, *v.t. ly*-gate, to tie with a ligature [Surg.]. (L. *ligatus*, tied.)

ligation, *n.* le-*gay*-shon, the act of binding; state of being bound; the operation of tying (esp. an artery) [Surg.]; the thing that binds.

ligature, *n. lig*-a-tewr, anything that binds; a thread or wire which binds; a band; the act of binding; a line connecting notes [Music]; the state of being bound; a single type formed of two or more letters, as ff, ffi, also a stroke connecting two letters [Print.]. (Fr.)

★**light,** *n.* lite, the radiation that stimulates the sense of sight through the eye; that which gives light, natural or artificial; anything from which it emanates; anything of the nature of light or its source; amount of illumination; knowledge; enlightenment; that which constitutes day; the dawn of day; one who can enlighten; a visible state; public view; conspicuous position; that which admits light; a window, a pane or a division of a window or sky-light, etc.; a point of view; the manner in which the light strikes upon a picture; the illuminated part of a picture [Paint.]: *a.* bright; not dark; whitish; fair: *v.i.* to set fire to; to give light to; to spread; to kindle; to ignite; to enlighten: *v.i.* to catch fire; to become lit; to brighten up. **come to light,** to be detected. **light dues,** dues levied on ships navigating certain waters towards keeping up the lighthouses in them. **light of the countenance,** favour; smiles. **red light,** *see* **red. see the light,** to come into being; to be published. **stand in one's own light,** to be the means of preventing one's own good. **throw light upon,** to explain; to elucidate. *p.* and *pp.* **lighted, lit.** (A.S. *leoht.*)

light, *a.* lite, not heavy; not of legal weight; easy to be endured, performed, digested, etc.; not heavily armed; carrying what is light; active; nimble; not encumbered; not laden; not important; not dense; not copious; not violent; moderate; easily influenced; gay; indulging in levity; unchaste; loose; sandy; giddy: *ad.* lightly; cheaply. **light engine,** an engine running without a train. **light literature,** reading matter for recreation or entertainment. **light marching order,** military equipment comprising immediate necessities only. **light railway,** a railway or tram-way for light traffic, usually on or adjacent to a road. **make light of,** to treat as of little consequence; to disregard. **set light by,** to undervalue; to treat as of no importance. (A.S. *leoht.*)

light, *v.i.* lite, to alight; to stoop from flight; to settle; to rest. **light on,** to happen to find. (A.S. *lihtan.*)

lightable, *a. lite*-a-bl, that can be lighted.

light-armed, *a.* armed with light weapons.

lighten, *v.i. ly*-tn, to flash, as lightning; to grow light or brighter: *v.t.* to make light; to fill with light; to enlighten; to illuminate with knowledge.

lighten, *v.t. ly*-tn, to make lighter or less heavy; to alleviate; to cheer: *v.i.* to become less heavy.

lighter, *n. lite*-er, a large, open, flat-bottomed boat, used in loading and unloading ships. (Dut. *lichter*, from *lichten*, to unload.)

lighter, *n. lite*-er, one who kindles, as lamplighter; an appliance for producing a light, esp. one at which tobacco, gas-jets, etc., may be ignited.

lighter, *a. lite*-er, more light. **lighter-than-air,** not so heavy as the air displaced (of aircraft).

lighterage, *n. lite*-er-raj, price paid for unloading ships by, or act of unloading into, lighters.

lighterman, *n. lite*-er-man, a boatman of a lighter.

light-fingered, *a.* thievish; given to stealing.

light-footed, *a.* nimble on the feet; active.

light-handed, *a.* having a light touch; tactful; with too small a crew [Naut.].

light-headed, *a.* thoughtless; heedless; unsteady; disordered in the head; delirious.

light-headedness, *n.* state, condition, or character of being light-headed.

light-hearted, *a.* free from grief or anxiety; cheerful; merry.

light-heartedly, *ad.* with a light heart.

light-heartedness, *a.* lite-*har*-ted-ness, the state of being light-hearted.

lighthouse, *n. lite*-house, a tower or building with a light to direct navigation at night; a pharos.

lighting, *n. lite*-ing, illumination; artificial supply of light; disposition of light [Paint.].

lightish, *a. lite*-ish, rather light.

lightkeeper, *n. lite*-keep-er, one having charge of a lighthouse or lightship.

light-legged, *a.* nimble; swift of foot.

lightless, *a. lite*-less, destitute of light; dark.

lightly, *ad. lite*-le, in a light manner; carelessly.

light-minded, *a.* frivolous; unsteady; volatile.

lightness, *n. lite*-ness, want of weight, buoyancy, grace; state or quality of illumination.

lightning, *n. lite*-ning, a flash, or succession of flashes, of light due to atmospheric electricity. **lightning-arrester,** a contrivance for protecting telegraphic apparatus. **lightning conductor,** a lightning rod. **lightning glance,** a sudden flash of lightning; a flash of the eye. **lightning rod,** a metallic rod projecting from the top of a building,

mast, etc., to protect the structure from lightning. **lightning strike,** a sudden unexpected strike of workers. **like lightning,** with the greatest speed.
light-o'-love, *n.* lite-o-*luv*, a flirtatious woman; a wanton; a prostitute.
lights, *n.pl.* lites, the lungs of cattle, pigs, etc., used as food for animals.
lightship, *n. lite*-ship, a floating lighthouse.
lightsome, *a. lite*-sum, luminous; not dark; gay; airy; cheering.
lightsomeness, *n. lite*-sum-ness, the quality of being lightsome.
light-spirited, *a.* cheerful; buoyant.
lightweight, *n. lite*-wayt, a man or beast under weight; a boxer not weighing more than 135 lb.: *a.* of light weight.
light-year, *n. lite*-year, an astronomical unit equal to the distance traversed by light in a year, about 5 billion 900 thousand million miles.
lign-aloes, *n.* lin-*al*-oze, agalloch, *Aquillaria agallocha.* (L. *lignum aloes*, wood of aloes.)
ligneous, *a. lig*-ne-us, made of, consisting of, or resembling wood; woody. (L. *ligneus*, wooden.)
ligniferous, *a.* lig-*nif*-er-rus, yielding or producing wood. (L. *lignum*, wood, *fero*, bear.)
lignification, *n. lig*-ne-fe-*kay*-shon, the process of lignifying; state of being lignified.
ligniform, *a. lig*-ne-form, like wood.
lignify, *v.t. lig*-ne-fy, to convert into wood: *v.i.* to become wood. (L. *lignum*, and *facio*, make.)
lignin, *n. lig*-nin, the essential part of woody fibre.
ligniperdous, *a.* lig-ne-*per*-dus, destructive of wood (of many insects) [Entom.]. (L. *lignum*, and *perdere*, to destroy.)
lignite, *n. lig*-nite, brown-coal, a natural deposit resembling coal and containing a greater percentage of hydrocarbons.
lignitic, *a.* lig-*nit*-ik, containing or like lignite.
lignose, *n. lig*-nohs, lignin; an explosive made of wood fibre and nitro-glycerine: *a.* ligneous.
lignum-vitæ, *n. lig*-num-*vy*-tee, the exceedingly hard, dark-coloured, and close-grained wood of *Guaiacum officinale*, of tropical America; other hard woods, as of *Metrosideros buxifolia*, an Australasian climber. (L., wood of life, *i.e.* durability.)
ligroin, *n. lig*-ro-in, a purified petroleum distillate from petroleum, used as a solvent for fats, resins, etc. [Chem. and Pharm.].
ligula, *n. lig*-yew-la, a tongue-like organ or appendage; the flat part of the leaf of a grass; a strap-shaped petal [Bot.]. (L., a little tongue, from *lingua*, the tongue.)
ligulate, *a. lig*-yew-late, having a ligula; shaped like a strap [Bot.].
ligulated, *a. lig*-yew-lay-ted, ligulate.
ligule, *n. lig*-yewl, a ligula.
ligurite, *n. lig*-yew-rite, a transparent pea-green variety of sphene. (From *Liguria*, Italy.)
***like,** *a.* like, equal in quantity, quality, or degree; having resemblance; similar; likely: *n.* some person, thing, or incident resembling another; a copy; a stroke that equalizes the number of strokes played by each side [Golf]: *ad.* in the same manner; likely. **like-minded,** *a.* having a like purpose or disposition. **something like,** approximate; nearly resembling; (*said emphatically*) excellent! very good indeed! [Coll.]. **the like,** the same kind of thing. **the likes of him,** a depreciatory reference to the type or class of person indicated [Coll.]. (A.S. *ge-tic*, resembling in form, from *lic*, form.)
like, *n.* like, what pleases one, liking (*usually in pl.*): *v.t.* to be pleased with; to enjoy; to approve: *v.i.* to be pleased; to choose. (A.S. *lician*, to please.)
likeable, *a. like*-a-bl, that one can like; attractive.
likeableness, *n.* the quality of being likeable.
likelihood, *n. like*-le-hood, probability.
likeliness, *n.* the quality of being likely.
likely, *a. like*-le, such as may have taken place; probable; like what is wanted; suitable; such as may be liked; pleasing: *ad.* probably.
liken, *v.t. like*-en, to represent as resembling or similar; to compare.
likeness, *n. like*-ness, resemblance; similarity; a portrait; a picture.
likewise, *ad. like*-wize, in like manner; also.
likin, *n. lee*-kin, a Chinese transport duty. (Chin.)
liking, *n. like*-ing, the state of being pleased; inclination; pleasure.
lilac, *n. ly*-lak, a fragrant flowering shrub, of the genus *Syringa*, originally from Persia; its colour, a very pale and faintly pink purple. (Ar. *lilak.*)
lilacine, *n. ly*-la-sin, former name of syringin.
liliaceous, *a. lil*-e-*ay*-shus, pertaining to lilies.
lilied, *a. lil*-led, resembling the lily in pallor; embellished with lilies.
Lilliputian, *n.* lil-le-*pew*-shan, a dwarfish inhabitant of Lilliput, in "Gulliver's Travels"; one of very small size: *a.* pigmy-like; of very small size.
lilt, *n.* lilt, a cheery song; a catchy tune: *v.i.* and *t.* to sing or play cheerfully; to do anything cleverly or quickly. (M.E. *lulte.*)
lily, *n. lil*-le, any plant of the herbaceous genus *Lilium*, esp. the **tiger-lily** (*L. tigrinum*) and **madonna lily** (*L. candidum*); applied also to several other species; the heraldic fleur-de-lis; a person or object of special whiteness or purity: *a.* white as a lily; pure. **lily of the mountain,** *Polygonatum multiflorum.* **lily of the valley,** the beautiful flowering plant, *Convallaria majalis.* (A.S. *lilie.*)
lily-handed, *a.* with white delicate hands.
lily-livered, *a.* white-livered; cowardly.
lily-pad, *n.* the floating leaf of a water-lily.
lily-white, *a.* pure white, as white as the lily.
limaceous, *a.* ly-*may*-she-us, like or pertaining to the slugs. (L. *limax*, a slug or snail.)
limaciform, *a.* ly-*mas*-e-form, resembling a slug.
limacoid, *a. ly*-ma-koyd, like a slug: *n.* any of the slugs.
limation, *n.* ly-*may*-shon, the act of filing, or [Fig.] freeing from imperfections. (L. *limare*, to file.)
limb, *n.* lim, the arm or leg; a branch of a tree; a member; a mischievous child or young person [Slang]: *v.t.* to supply with limbs; to dismember. **limb of the law,** a member of the legal profession; a policeman [Coll.]. (A.S. *lim.*)
limb, *n.* lim, an edge or border, as of the sun or moon [Astron.]; the border of a monopetalous corolla [Bot.]; the graduated arc of a sextant. (L. *limbus*, a border.)
limbate, *a. lim*-bat, bordered; having one colour surrounded by an edging of another [Bot. and Zool.]. (Late L. *limbatus*, edged.)
limbec, *n. lim*-bek, an alembic.
limbed, *a.* limd, having limbs.
limber, *a. lim*-ber, flexible; pliant: *v.t.* to render supple or pliant. (Origin uncertain.)
limber, *n. lim*-ber, the detachable front part of a gun-carriage [Mil.]: *v.t.* to attach the limber to. (Perhaps from Fr. *limonière*, pair of shafts.)
limberness, *n. lim*-ber-ness, the quality or condition of being limber.
limbic, *a. lim*-bik, pertaining to or of the nature of, a limbus [Bot., etc.]; marginal [Surg.].
limbo, *n. lim*-boh, the region of the next world, placed on the edge of Hell, for the souls of unbaptized infants and of the just who died before the coming of Christ; Milton's "paradise of fools"; a place of restraint; a glory-hole. (L. *limbus*, a border.)
limbus, *n. lim*-bus, limbo; a border of differentiated colour or structure [Bot., Zool., etc.]; a margin [Anat.] (L. *limbus.*)
lime, *n.* lime, birdlime, a viscous substance used for catching birds: *v.t.* to smear this; to ensnare.
lime, *n.* lime, oxide of calcium, the earthy residue of burnt limestone; quicklime: *v.t.* to treat or manure with lime; to cement. **slaked lime,** calcium hydroxide, or hydrated lime, formed by slaking quicklime. (A.S. *lim*, bitumen.)
lime, *n.* lime, the linden-tree. (A.S. *lind.*)
lime, *n.* lime, the W. Indian tree, *Citrus medica*; its acid, lemon-like fruit. (Fr.)
lime-burner, *n.* one who burns limestone to make lime.
lime-hound, *n.* a lyam-hound.
lime-juice, *n.* a beverage made with the juice of *Citrus medica.*
limekiln, *n. lime*-kiln, a furnace in which limestone is exposed to a strong heat, and reduced to lime.
limelight, *n. lime*-lite, a powerful light caused by making a stream of ignited oxygen and hydrogen play on a ball or cylinder of lime. **in the limelight,** prominent by publicity.
limen, *n. ly*-men, the limit below which any given stimulus ceases to be perceptible; the smallest quantity of nerve excitation required to produce sensation [Psych.].

lime-pit, *n.* a limestone quarry; a pit for dressing leather hides with lime.
Limerick, *n. lim*-er-rik, a verse of five lines, the first and second rhyming with the fifth, and the third with the fourth; a nonsense verse.
limestone, *n. lime*-stone, a sedimentary rock of which the chief constituent is carbonate of lime.
lime-twig, *n.* a twig smeared with birdlime.
lime-wash, *n.* a mixture of lime and water used in whitewashing: *v.t.* to treat (walls, etc.) with this.
lime-water, *n.* a solution of slaked lime used medicinally and as a chemical reagent.
limewort, *n. lime*-wurt, various plants, including a species of pink, brooklime, and *Lychnis viscaria,* allied to ragged robin.
limicolous, *a.* li-*mik*-o-lus, living in mud [Zool.].
liminal, *a. lim*-e-nal, at the threshold; on the verge of consciousness.
liming, *n. lime*-ing, a coating of lime.
★**limit,** *n. lim*-it, boundary; utmost extent; restriction; almost beyond what is possible or believable [Slang]: *v.t.* to set bounds to; to confine within certain bounds; to restrain; to restrict. **limit man,** a competitor having a maximum handicap, the opposite of scratch. **the limit,** the last straw. (Fr. *limite.*)
limitable, *a. lim*-e-ta-bl, that may be limited, circumscribed, bounded, or restricted.
limitarian, *a. lim*-e-*tare*-re-an, tending to limit: *n.* one holding that redemption extends to a limited portion of mankind only [Theol.].
limitary, *a. lim*-e-ta-re, placed at the limit, esp. as a guard; restrained within limits; limiting.
limitation, *n. lim*-e-*tay*-shon, the act of limiting; state of being limited; restriction; that which limits, restricts, or qualifies; the period within which an action can be raised [Law]. (Fr.)
limited, *a. lim*-it-ed, narrow; circumscribed; restricted. **limited company, limited liability,** *see* **liability. limited monarchy,** a monarchy in which the sovereign must keep within the limits of the constitution.
limitedly, *ad. lim*-it-ed-le, with limitation.
limitedness, *n. lim*-it-ed-ness, state of being limited.
limiter, *n. lim*-it-er, he who or that which limits; a limitour.
limitless, *a. lim*-it-less, boundless; immense.
limitour, *n. lim*-e-toor, a friar licensed to beg or perform duties within a limited area.
limitrophe, *a. lim*-e-trohf, on or near the boundary. (L. *limis,* a boundary, Gr. *tropho,* feed.)
limmer, *n. lim*-mer, a hussy; a jade; a rascal.
limn, *v.t.* lim, to draw; to paint, specially in water-colours; to illuminate, as a book. (O.Fr. *luminer.*)
limner, *n. lim*-ner, an artist or delineator, esp. a portrait painter or miniaturist.
limnetic, *a.* lim-*net*-ik, living in fresh water [Zool.].
limnite, *n. lim*-nite, a variety of bog-ore [Min.].
limnology, *n.* lim-*nol*-o-je, the scientific study of inland waters; the study of pond life. (Gr. *limne,* a lake, *logos,* science.)
limonite, *n. ly*-mo-nite, bog-ore or brown hæmatite, hydrous ferric oxide. (Gr. *leimon,* a pasture.)
limous, *a. ly*-mus, muddy; slimy.
limousine, *n. lim*-oo-zeen, a closed motor-car with fixed roof extending over the driver's seat. (Fr.)
limp, *a.* limp, flexible; wanting stiffness; flaccid; wanting firmness. (O.Scand. *limpa.*)
limp, *n.* limp, a halting walk or step; the act of limping: *v.i.* to halt; to walk lamely. (A.S. *lemp-healt.*)
limpet, *n. lim*-pet, a univalve mollusc of the genus *Patella,* adhering to rocks; one who clings too long to office [Coll.]. (A.S. *lempedu.*)
limpid, *a. lim*-pid, clear; pellucid; bright; pure; perspicuous. (Fr. *limpide.*)
limpidity, *n.* lim-*pid*-e-te, limpidness.
limpidness, *n.* the quality of being limpid.
limpingly, *ad. limp*-ing-le, in a limping manner.
limpkin, *n. limp*-kin, the courlan.
limply, *ad. limp*-le, in a limp or flaccid fashion.
limpness, *n. limp*-ness, the quality of being limp.
limy, *a. ly*-me, viscous; glutinous; containing, resembling, or having the qualities of lime.
lin, *n.* lin, a linn.
linage, *n. lyne*-aj, the number of printed or written lines; work estimated by this; payment for contributions by the line.
linarite, *n. lin*-a-rite, hydrous sulphate of lead and copper, a deep-blue crystalline mineral. (*Linares,* in Spain.)
linch, *n.* linch, a linchet; a linch-pin.
linchet, *n. linch*-et, an unploughed strip of land, esp. as a boundary; a ridge or terrace, as on a chalk down. (A.S. *hlinc,* link.)
linch-pin, *n.* a pin to keep a wheel on an axle. (*linch* and *pin*).
Lincoln-green, *n. lin*-kon-green, the bright green colour of a cloth formerly made in Lincoln.
lincrusta, *n.* lin-*krus*-ta, proprietary name of a fabric treated with linoxyn, resin, etc., and used as floor-cloth and on walls.
linctus, *n. link*-tus, a syrupy medicament to be taken by licking [Med.]. (L., licked.)
linden, *n. lin*-den, the lime-tree, *Tilia europæa.*
★**line,** *n.* lyne, a slender string or cord; a thread-like stroke or trace; the equator; that which has length without breadth or thickness; a row, as of letters, words or soldiers; a fleet of merchant ships, or other transport service as of aircraft or omnibuses; a railroad; a verse; a series in regular succession; lineage; outline; lineament; a short missive; a trench or rampart; the twelfth part of an inch; disposition; method; occupation; description of goods; goods ordered; the present stock of a class of goods; course; direction; a mark limiting a court, etc., in games: *pl.* method of procedure; a marriage certificate [Coll.]; an actor's spoken part; a plan or draught, as of a ship; a school imposition. **all along the line,** at every point. **bring into line,** to cause to agree or co-operate. **draw the line,** to determine the limit; to decide to refuse to act beyond a certain limit. **equinoctial line,** the equator of the earth or heavens. **hard lines,** bad luck; undeserved misfortune. **in one's line,** in one's branch of work; in accord with one's capacity. **line block,** a printing block photographically reproduced direct from a black-and-white drawing with no intermediate tones other than tints. **line of battle,** the disposition of an army or fleet. **line of communication,** *see* **communication. line of life,** the most important of the lines in the hand from which deductions are drawn in palmistry. **on the line,** not definitely one way or the other; doubtful. **read between the lines,** to deduce from a statement a concealed or not obvious meaning. **right line,** a straight line, the shortest that can be drawn between two points. **ship of the line,** a ship of war large enough to have a place in the line of battle. **toe the line,** *see* **toe.** (A.S., from L. *linea,* a thread of flax or linen.)
line, *v.t.* lyne, to mark with lines; to cover on the inside; to put in as a lining; to cram; to place in a line.
line, *v.t.* lyne, to copulate with; to fecundate (of dogs only). (Fr. *aligner.*)
lineage, *n. lin*-e-aj, descendants in a line from a common progenitor; race; family. (Fr. *lignage.*)
lineage, *n. lyne*-aj, linage.
lineal, *a. lin*-e-al, in length; composed of lines; in the direction of a line; in a direct line to or from an ancestor. (L. *linealis.*)
lineality, *n.* lin-e-*al*-e-te, quality of being lineal.
lineally, *ad. lin*-e-al-le, in a direct line.
lineament, *n. lin*-e-a-ment, distinguishing outline of a body or figure, esp. of the face; feature. (O.Fr.)
linear, *a. lin*-e-ar, pertaining to a line; consisting or having the form of lines; in a straight direction; like a line; slender [Bot.]. **linear perspective,** perspective showing only the positions, magnitudes, and forms of objects. (L. *linearis.*)
linearity, *n.* lin-e-*a*-re-te, quality of being linear.
linearly, *ad. lin*-e-ar-le, in a linear manner.
lineate, *a. lin*-e-at, marked longitudinally with depressed parallel lines [Bot.] (L. *lineatus,* lined.)
lineation, *n.* lin-e-*ay*-shon, the act of marking with lines; arrangement of lines.
lined, *a.* lynd, marked with lines; having wrinkles; fitted with a lining.
lineman, *n. lyne*-man, one employed in the erection or maintenance of a line, as of telephone, telegraph, railway, etc.
★**linen,** *n. lin*-en, cloth or thread made of flax; sheets, tablecloths, underclothing, etc., as usually of linen: *a.* made of flax; resembling linen; white; pale. (A.S.)
linen-draper, *n.* a retail dealer in linens, calicoes, etc., and articles made of these.

linenette, *n.* lin-en-*et*, imitation linen made of cotton.
liner, *n. ly*-ner, a vessel belonging to a regular line of passenger ships; a large passenger aeroplane engaged on regular flights; anything which serves as a lining; an implement for making lines; a newspaper writer paid by the line.
linesman, *n. lynz*-man, a referee's assistant in certain outdoor games; a soldier of the line; a lineman on a railway track, etc.
ling, *n.* ling, an edible sea-fish of the cod family, *Molva vulgaris*. (A.S. *lang*, long.)
ling, *n.* ling, the common heather, *Calluna vulgaris*. (Ice. *lyng*.)
lingam, *n. ling*-gam, the phallus or phallic symbol among the Hindus. (Hind.)
ling-bird, *n.* a local name of the meadow-pipit.
lingel, *n. ling*-gel, cobbler's waxed thread. (Scots.)
linger, *v.i. ling*-ger, to delay; to remain long; to hesitate: *v.t.* to protect; to prolong wearisomely. (A.S. *lengan*.)
lingerer, *n. ling*-ger-er, one who lingers.
lingerie, *n.* (App.), linen articles generally, but esp. women's underwear. (Fr.)
lingeringly, *ad. ling*-ger-ing-le, tardily; in a lingering manner.
lingo, *n. ling*-go, language; speech; technical jargon. (L. *lingua*, speech.)
linguadental, *a.* and *n. ling*-gwa-*den*-tal, dentilingual.
lingua-franca, *n. ling*-gwah-*frang*-ka, the international language of the Levant, consisting of a mixture of Italian, Arabic, modern Greek, and other words; any international patois.
lingual, *a. ling*-gwal, pertaining to the tongue; formed by the tongue; tongue-like; *n.* a lingual letter, as *l*.
linguiform, *a. ling*-gwe-form, having the form or shape of the tongue.
linguist, *n. ling*-gwist, one skilled in languages.
linguistic, *a.* ling-*gwis*-tik, pertaining to linguistics; *n.pl.* the science of languages in their relations and affinities.
linguistically, *adv.* ling-*gwis*-te-ka-le, in regard to linguistics or languages.
lingula, *n. ling*-gew-la, a tongue-like process; a small lobule of the cerebellum [Anat. and Zool.].
linhay, *n. lin*-ne, an open shed on a farm. (Perhaps from A.S. *hlinian*, to lean.)
liniment, *n. lin*-e-ment, a medicated liquid for rubbing in to relieve pain or strain. (Fr. from L.)
lining, *n. lyne*-ing, the covering of the inner surface of anything; that which is within. (*line*.)
link, *n.* link, a ring or loop of which two or more form a chain; anything doubled and closed like a link; a bend in a river; any thing or person acting as a connexion or closing a gap; a measure of 7·92 inches: *v.t.* to unite or connect by something, as by a link; to connect: *v.i.* to be connected. **missing link,** a connexion that is lacking, esp. a type in a zoological or other system. (Ice. *hlekkr*.)
link, *n.* link, a torch made of tow and pitch. (Dut. *lont*, a match.)
linkage, *n. ling*-kaj, state of being linked or manner of linking; a system of links.
link-boy, *n.* a boy or man who carried a torch.
links, *n.pl.* links, a sandy stretch of ground near the sea; a golf course. (A.S. *hlinc*, an earth-ridge.)
linn, *n.* lin, a pool caused by a waterfall; a waterfall; a precipitous gorge. (Gael. *linne*.)
Linnæan, *a.* lin-*nee*-an, pertaining to Linnæus (the celebrated Swedish botanist Linné, *d.* 1778), or to his system of classification, now superseded.
linnet, *n. lin*-net, the small song-bird, *Linota cannabina*, so called as feeding on flax. **mountain linnet,** the finch *Linota flavirostris*, of Great Britain and N. Europe. (A.S. *linece*.)
lino, *n. ly*-noh, linoleum (Coll.].
linocut, *n. ly*-noh-kut, a design cut in relief on linoleum-like material; a print from this [Print.].
linoleum, *n.* li-*noh*-le-um, a durable fabric used as floorcloth, etc., made of hessian or canvas treated with linoxyn, resins, cork dust, etc. (L. *linum*, and *oleum*, oil.)
linotype, *n. ly*-no-tipe, proprietary name of a type-setting machine in which the matter is cast in lines as it is set. (L. *linea*, line, and *type*.)
linoxyn, *n.* li-*nok*-sin, oxidized linseed oil, a resinous substance used in the manufacture of linoleum, etc.

Linsang, *n. lin*-sang, a genus of small carnivores of Malaya and the East Indies, allied to the civets. (Javanese.)
linseed, *n. lin*-seed, the seed of the flax plant (*Linum*). **linseed cake,** the mass left after the oil has been pressed out of flax-seed. **linseed meal,** meal of linseed. **linseed oil,** oil obtained by pressure from flax-seed. **linseed tea,** a mucilaginous drink made from infused linseed. (A.S. *lin*, flax, and *seed*.)
linsey, *n. lin*-ze, linsey-woolsey.
linsey-woolsey, *n. lin*-ze-*wool*-ze, a coarse textile material made of linen and wool mixed; an unsuitable or incongruous mixture; a jargon.
linstock, *n. lin*-stok, a forked stick to hold a lighted match for firing a gun. (Dut. *lontstok*.)
lint, *n.* lint, scraped or fleecy linen used for dressing wounds [Surg.]. (A.S. *lin*.)
lintel, *n. lin*-tel, the transverse beam or head-piece over a door or casement. (O.Fr.)
linters, *n.pl. lin*-terz, the short fibres left on cotton seeds after removal of the long ones by ginning.
lintie, *n. lin*-te, the linnet. (Scots.)
lintwhite, *n. lint*-white, a linnet. (A.S. *linetwige*.)
liny, *a. line*-e, streaky; wrinkled.
lion, *n. ly*-on, the carnivore *Felis leo*, remarkable for its roar; Leo, a sign of the zodiac; an object of interest and curiosity; a celebrity [Coll.]; a symbol of power, courage, and virtue. **lion's mouth,** a position of danger [Fig.]. **lion's provider,** a jackal. **lion's skin,** a deceptive show of courage [Fig.]. (O.F. *leon*, from L. *leo*, *leonem*.)
lioncel, *n. ly*-on-sel, a small lion [Her.]. (O.Fr.)
lionesque, *a.* ly-o-*nesk*, like, or in the manner of, the lion.
lioness, *n. ly*-on-ess, the female of the lion.
lionet, *n. ly*-on-et, a young lion.
lion-heart, *n. ly*-on-hart, one of great courage.
lion-hearted, *a. ly*-on-*har*-ted, courageous.
lion-hunter, *n.* one who hunts lions; one who seeks intimacy with celebrities for personal ostentation [Fig.].
lionism, *n. ly*-on-izm, the practice of lionizing; treatment of any one as a lion.
lionize, *v.t. ly*-on-ize, to treat or visit as an object of curiosity: *v.i.* to act the lion-hunter; to visit the objects of curiosity in a place.
***lip,** *n.* lip, the edge or border of the mouth; the edge of a precipice, orifice, etc.; one of the two opposite divisions of a labiate coral [Zool.]; the edge of the aperture of a univalve shell [Conch.]: *v.t.* to kiss; to utter; to lap; to mutter. **lip deep,** superficial; not sincere. **lip language,** a language for the deaf and dumb in which the movements of the lips form the words. **lip reading,** the understanding of lip language by watching the lip movements of a person. **lip salve,** ointment for the lips. **lip service,** assistance offered but not forthcoming. **lip worship,** insincere worship. **hang on one's lips,** listen with reverence. **make a lip,** to drop the under lip in sullenness or contempt. **none of your lip,** none of your impudence [Slang]. **stiff upper lip,** fortitude; courage. (A.S. *lippa*, that which laps.)
lipæmia, *n.* li-*pee*-me-a, lipohæmia.
liparocele, *n.* li-*pa*-ro-seel, a fatty tumour, esp. of the scrotum [Med.]. (Gr. *liparos*, oily, *kele*, a tumour.)
liparous, *a. lip*-a-rus, obese [Med.].
lipase, *n.* li-*pace*, any enzyme that digests fats by means of hydrolysis.
liplet, *n. lip*-let, a small lip-like part [Entom.].
lipogenic, *a.* lip-o-*jen*-ik, producing, or tending to produce, fat.
lipogram, *n. lip*-o-gram, a writing in which a particular letter is wholly omitted. (Gr. *leipo*, leave, *gramma*, a letter.)
lipography, *n.* li-*pog*-ra-fe, accidental omission of a letter or syllable in writing; haplography.
lipohæmia, *n.* lip-o-*hee*-me-a, a fatty condition of the blood [Path.]. (Gr. *lipos*, fat, *haima*, blood.)
lipoid, *a. lip*-oyd, of the nature of fat: *n.* a fat-like organic substance insoluble in water [Med.].
lipoma, *n.* li-*poh*-ma, a fatty tumour [Med.]. (Gr. *lipos*, fat.)
lipoxenous, *a.* li-*pok*-se-nus, abandoning the host before completion of development (of parasites) [Bot. and Zool.]. (Gr. *leipein*, to leave, *xenos*, host.)

lipped, *a.* lipt, having lips; having a raised or rounded edge like a lip; labiate [Bot.].
lipper, *n. lip*-per, a rippling; surface roughness (of the sea) [Naut.].
lippitude, *n. lip*-pe-tewd, chronic soreness of eyes; marginal blepharitis [Med.]; blearedness. (L. *lippitudo*, blear-eyed.)
lippy, *n. lip*-e, a former Scottish measure of half a gallon or about 1¼ lb.
lipstick, *n. lip*-stik, a stick of cosmetic for reddening the lips.
liquate, *v.t.* and *v.i. ly*-kwate, to liquefy. (L.)
liquation, *n.* li-*kway*-shon, the separation of the constituents of an alloy when cooling from the molten state; the process of separating, by means of heat, an easily fusible metal from one less fusible. [Metal.].
liquefacient, *a. lik*-we-*fay*-she-ent, serving to liquefy: *n.* an agent that promotes liquefaction. (L. *liquefaciens*, making liquid.)
liquefaction, *n.* lik-we-*fak*-shon, act or process of melting or dissolving; state of being melted.
liquefiable, *a.* lik-we-*fy*-a-bl, that may be liquefied.
liquefier, *n. lik*-we-fy-er, that which liquefies; an apparatus for liquefying.
liquefy, *v.t. lik*-we-fy, to convert to liquid form, esp. by the agency of heat; to melt; to dissolve: *v.i.* to become liquid. (Fr. *liquéfier.*)
liquescence, *n.* li-*kwes*-ense, aptness to melt.
liquescent, *a.* li-*kwes*-sent, melting; becoming fluid. (L. *liquescens*, being liquid.)
liqueur, *n.* li-*kewr*, a spirituous, sweetened, and flavoured cordial; a mixture of wine and sugar used for flavouring champagne: *v.t.* to flavour champagne in this way. **liqueur brandy,** a special quality of brandy used as a liqueur. **liqueur glass,** a very small glass used in drinking liqueurs. (Fr.)
★**liquid,** *a. lik*-wid, fluid; flowing; soft; clear; transparent; smooth, as in pronunciation; readily convertible into cash; unstable: *n.* a fluid or flowing substance; a letter which has a smooth sound, as *l* and *r* [Phon.]. (Fr. *liquide.*)
Liquidambar, *n. lik*-wid-*am*-bar, a genus of trees, some species of which yield the balsam storax; (*l.c.*) the resin from these trees. (L. *liquidus*, fluid, *ambar*, amber.)
liquidate, *v.t. lik*-we-date, to make clear the amount of (indebtedness, etc.); to adjust; to pay, as a debt; to wind up, as a bankrupt estate; to convert into cash [Coll.]; finally to dispose of; to destroy completely, to annihilate: *v.i.* to have assets, liabilities, etc., liquidated (of a company). (Late L. *liquidatus*, clarified.)
liquidation, *n. lik*-we-*day*-shon, the act of settling and adjusting debts, or ascertaining their amount; the clearing and settling of the affairs between debtor and creditor in a bankrupt estate; the act or process of finally getting rid of.
liquidator, *n. lik*-we-day-tor, he who or that which settles; one who effects a liquidation.
liquidity, *n.* li-*kwid*-e-te, liquidness.
liquidize, *v.t. lik*-we-dize, to render liquid.
liquidly, *ad. lik*-wid-le, in a liquid manner.
liquidness, *n.* quality or condition of being liquid.
liquor, *n. lik*-ur, a liquid or fluid substance, commonly spirituous: *v.t.* to moisten; to oil: *v.i.* to take spirits. **in liquor,** tipsy, fuddled. **worse for liquor,** drunk. (Fr. *liqueur.*)
liquorice, *n. lik*-o-ris, a perennial plant, *Glycyrrhiza glabra*, common in the South of Europe, from the rhizome of which a sweet mucilaginous juice, used medicinally and as a sweetmeat, is prepared. (O.Fr. from Gr. *glykys*, sweet, *rhiza*, root.)
liquorish, *a. lik*-o-rish, fond of liquor.
lira, *n. leer*-ra (*pl.* **lire,** *leer*-ray), the Italian monetary unit, nominally equivalent to the French franc. (It.)
liripoop, *n. li*-re-poop, a hood or scarf formerly worn by graduates and clergy; learning; wit; a trick; a silly person [Slang].
liroconite, *n.* li-*rok*-o-nite, a rare blue or green copper ore containing oxide of arsenic and aluminium. (Gr. *leiros*, wan, *konia*, dust.)
Lisbon, *n. liz*-bon, a sweet wine exported from Lisbon.
lisle, *n.* leel *or* lyl, lisle thread; a fabric made of this. **lisle thread,** a hard-twisted, fine cotton thread originally made at Lille (formerly Lisle), France.
lisp, *n.* lisp, the pronunciation of *s* like *th*; a slight sound as of lisping: *v.i.* to speak with a lisp; to articulate or speak imperfectly, as a child: *v.t.* to pronounce with a lisp. (A.S. *wlispian.*)
lisper, *n. lisp*-er, one who lisps.
lispingly, *ad. lisp*-ing-le, with a lisp.
lisse, *n.* leece, the warp in tapestry.
lissom, *a. lis*-sum, lithe; agile. (*lithesome.*)
lissomness, *n. lis*-sum-ness, state of being lissom.
lissotrichous, *a.* lis-*sot*-re-kus, leiotrichous.
★**list,** *n.* list, the edge or selvedge of cloth; a strip of cloth; a fillet; a listel [Arch.]; a roll or catalogue; a limit or boundary; the barriers of a tournament ground, also the ground itself, and hence a scene or arena of contest: *v.t.* to place in a list; to enlist; to sew together; to form a border: *v.i.* to enlist. **to enter the lists,** to come forward and engage in a contest. (A.S. *liste*, a border.)
list, *v.t.* and *i.* list, to desire or choose; to please; to have pleasure in: *n.* desire; inclination. (A.S. *lystan*, to please.)
list, *n.* list, a leaning over to one side [Naut., etc.]: *v.i.* to incline to one side.
list, *v.i.* list, to listen: *v.t.* to listen to. (A.S. *hlystan.*)
listel, *n. lis*-tel, a fillet or facette [Arch.]. (Fr.)
listen, *v.i. lis*-sen, to hearken; to give ear; to hear; to attend to. **to listen in,** to pay attention to broadcasting; to intercept a telephonic communication. (A.S. *hlystan.*)
listener, *n. lis*-e-ner, one who listens or hearkens, esp. to broadcasting.
listening-post, *n.* a station or position at which sentries listen to the doings of, or for the approach of, the enemy.
lister, *n. lis*-ter, one who makes a list or roll.
listerine, *n. lis*-ter-reen, proprietary name of an antiseptic preparation used as a disinfectant, etc.
Listerism, *n. list*-er-rizm, the method or principles of antiseptic surgery as introduced by Lord Lister (*d.* 1912).
listing, *n. lis*-ting, list (selvedge); the sapwood cut from the edges of a board [Carp.].
listless, *a. list*-less, indifferent to what is passing; not attending; not interested; languid.
listlessly, *ad. list*-less-le, in a listless manner.
listlessness, *n.* the state of being listless.
lit, *n.* lit, the Lithuanian litas.
lit, lit, *p.* and *pp.* of *light.* **lit up,** hilarious through drink [Slang].
litany, *n. lit*-a-ne, a solemn form of supplication used in public worship; a collection of short prayers, with responses from the congregation. (Fr. *litanie.*)
litas, *n. lee*-tas, the monetary unit of the former Lithuanian republic, nominally nearly equal to 5*d.*
litchi, *n. lee*-chee, the fruit of the Chinese tree, *Litchi chinensis*, of the soapberry family; the tree itself. (Chin.)
literacy, *n. lit*-er-ra-se, ability to read and write.
literal, *a. lit*-er-ral, according to the letter; real; not figurative; following the letter or exact words; not free, as a translation; prosaic; lacking imagination; expressed in letters [Alg.]: *n.* a misprint of a letter. (Fr. *littéral.*)
literalism, *n. lit*-er-ral-izm, adherence to the letter or to the precise literal meaning.
literalist, *n. lit*-er-ral-ist, one practising literalism.
literality, *n. lit*-er-*ral*-e-te, condition or quality of being literal; literal meaning.
literalize, *v.t. lit*-er-ra-lize, to interpret in the literal sense; to make literal.
literally, *ad. lit*-er-ral-le, in a literal sense.
literalness, *n. lit*-er-ral-ness, literality.
literary, *a. lit*-er-ra-re, pertaining to letters or literature; respecting or derived from learning or learned men; versed in letters; consisting of letters or written or printed compositions. **literary man,** an author; a man of letters. (L. *literarius.*)
literate, *a. lit*-er-rat, acquainted with letters or learning: *n.* one able to read and write; one admitted to holy orders not having graduated. (L. *literatus*, lettered.)
literati, *n.pl. lit*-er-*ray*-ty, the learned; men of erudition; men of letters. (L.)
literatim, *ad.* lit-er-*ray*-tim, letter for letter; hence, literally. (L.)
literature, *n. lit*-er-ra-tewr, books generally; the collective body of literary productions of a country or an age, in general or in some special department,

esp., more narrowly, that part which, as distinct from philosophical, scientific, or journalistic work, is occupied mainly with that which is spiritual in its nature and imaginative in its form; belles-lettres; the profession of letters. (O.Fr.)

lith, *n.* lith, a limb or joint; a terminal finger-joint; a division; one of the rings at the base of a cow's horn; a section of an orange. (A.S.)

litharge, *n. lith*-arj, lead monoxide, used in the manufacture of flint-glass, in the rubber industry, as a paint drier, etc. (Fr.)

lithate, *n. lith*-ate, a salt of lithic acid.

lithe, *a.* lythe, easily bent; limber; active. (A.S.)

lithe, *n.* lythe, the lythe or pollack.

litheness, *n. lythe*-ness, the quality of being lithe.

lither, *a. lith*-er, pliant; supple; nimble.

lithesome, *a. lythe*-sum, lissom; nimble; limber.

lithia, *n. lith*-e-a, lithium monoxide. **lithia water,** a mineral water containing lithium salts.

lithiasis, *n.* li-*thy*-a-sis, the disease of stone, esp. in the bladder or kidneys [Med.]. (Gr.)

lithic, *a. lith*-ik, pertaining to lithiasis; pertaining to or derived from lithium.

lithium, *n. lith*-e-um, a tough, silver-white metal, the lightest of the metallic elements, specific gravity 0·534. (Gr. *litheion*, stony, from *lithos*, a stone.)

lithocarp, *n. lith*-o-karp, a fossil fruit.

lithochromatics, *n. lith*-o-kro-*mat*-iks, chromolithography; printing in oil colours from stone.

lithoclast, *n. lith*-o-klast, a lithotrite.

lithodome, *n. lith*-o-dome, a small mollusc living in a hole in a rock that it has bored. (Gr. *lithos*, and *domos*, a house.)

lithodomous, *a.* li-*thod*-o-mus, burrowing in rock; living in rocks [Zool.].

lithofracteur, *n. lith*-o-*frak*-toor, a blasting explosive composed chiefly of dynamite. (Gr. *lithos*, and L. *fractum*, broken.)

lithofractor, *n. lith*-o-*frak*-tor, a lithotrite.

lithogenous, *a.* li-*thoj*-e-nus, forming stone or coral. (Gr. *lithos*, and *gennao*, produce.)

lithoglyph, *n. lith*-o-glif, an engraving on a gem. (Gr. *lithos*, and *glypho*, carve.)

lithoglyphite, *n.* li-*thog*-li-fite, a fossil deceptively appearing as though fashioned by man.

lithoglyptics, *n.* lith-o-*glip*-tiks, gem-engraving.

lithograph, *n. lith*-o-graf, a print from a drawing on stone: *v.t.* to trace on stone and transfer to paper, etc., by printing. (Gr. *lithos*, and *grapho*, write.)

lithographer, *n.* li-*thog*-ra-fer, one who practises lithography.

lithographic, *a.* lith-o-*graf*-ik, pertaining to lithography.

lithographically, *ad.* lith-o-*graf*-e-ka-le, by the lithographic art.

lithography, *n.* li-*thog*-ra-fe, the art of drawing, writing, etc., on stone, and printing from ink impressions taken from the lithographic stone.

lithoid, *a. lith*-oyd, lithoidal.

lithoidal, *a.* lith-*oy*-dal, resembling stone; having a stone structure. (Gr. *lithos*, and *eidos*, like.)

litholabe, *n. lith*-o-labe, an instrument for holding fast the stone in the operation of lithotomy. (Gr. *lithos*, and *labein*, take.)

lithological, *a.* lith-o-*loj*-e-kal, pertaining to lithology.

lithologist, *n.* li-*thol*-o-jist, one skilled in lithology.

lithology, *n.* li-*thol*-o-je, the science of the constitution, structure, and classification of rocks; the science treating of the nature of calculi [Med.]. (Gr. *lithos*, and *logos*, science.)

litholysis, *n.* li-*thol*-e-sis, the dissolution of stone in the bladder [Med.].

lithomancy, *n. lith*-o-man-se, divination by means of stones. (Gr. *lithos*, and *manteia*, divination.)

lithomarge, *n. lith*-o-marj, a former name of kaolin and allied clays. (Gr. *lithos*, and L. *marga*, marl.)

lithontriptic, *a.* lith-on-*trip*-tik, dissolving or destroying stone in the bladder: *n.* a lithontriptic medicine. (Gr. *lithos*, and *thryptikos*, crushed small.)

lithontriptor, *n.* lith-on-*trip*-tor, a lithotrite.

lithophagous, *a.* li-*thof*-a-gus, swallowing stones or gravel, as the ostrich; perforating stones, as certain molluscs. (Gr. *lithos*, and *phago*, eat.)

lithophane, *n. lith*-o-fane, an ornamental porcelain adapted to transparencies. (Gr. *lithos*, and *phanos*, clear.)

lithophosphor, *n.* lith-o-*fos*-for, a stone or mineral that becomes phosphorescent when heated.

lithophosphoric, *a. lith*-o-fos-*fo*-rik, becoming phosphorescent under the influence of heat.

lithophotography, *n. lith*-o-fo-*tog*-ra-fe, photolithography.

lithophyll, *n. lith*-o-fil, a fossil leaf or its impression. (Gr. *lithos*, and *phyllon*, a leaf.)

lithophyte, *n. lith*-o-fite, a coral; a plant growing on rock or stone [Bot.]. (Gr. *lithos*, and *phyton*, a plant.)

lithopone, *n. lith*-o-pone, a mixture of sulphide of zinc and sulphate of barium used as a non-poisonous substitute for white lead.

lithosis, *n.* li-*thoh*-sis, a disease of stonemasons, in which pieces of stone are found in the lungs.

lithosphere, *n. lith*-o-sfeer, the solid crust of the earth. (Gr. *lithos*, a stone, *sphaira*, a ball.)

lithotint, *n. lith*-o-tint, the lithographic production of a coloured picture; the picture itself.

lithotome, *n. lith*-o-tome, a stone so formed naturally as to appear as if cut artificially; a lithotomic instrument. (Gr. *lithos*, and *tome*, cutting.)

lithotomic, *a.* lith-o-*tom*-ik, pertaining to or performed by lithotomy [Surg.].

lithotomist, *n.* li-*thot*-o-mist, one skilled in lithotomy.

lithotomous, *a.* li-*thot*-o-mus, boring in stone, as certain molluscs.

lithotomy, *n.* li-*thot*-o-me, operation of cutting for stone in the bladder. (Gr. *lithos*, and *tome*, cutting.)

lithotripsy, *n. lith*-o-trip-se, the operation of removing stone from the bladder by crushing and irrigation [Surg.]. (Gr. *lithos*, and L. *tribus*, rubbed.)

lithotriptor, *n.* lith-o-*trip*-tor, a lithotrite.

lithotrite, *n. lith*-o-trite, the crushing implement used in lithotripsy [Surg.]

lithotritist, *n.* li-*thot*-re-tist, one who performs the operation of lithotripsy.

lithotrity, *n.* li-*thot*-tre-te, lithotripsy.

lithotype, *n. lith*-o-tipe, a kind of stereotype plate; a stone printing surface with design etched in relief; a print from such.

lithotypy, *n. lith*-o-ty-pe, the art of producing lithotype. (Gr. *lithos*, and *type*.)

lithoxyl, *n.* li-*thok*-sil, wood-opal. (Gr. *lithos*, and *xulon*, wood.)

Lithuanian, *a.* lith-yew-*ay*-ne-an, pertaining to Lithuania: *n.* a native or the language of Lithuania.

lithy, *a. ly*-the, supple; pliant; easily bent.

litigable, *a. lit*-e-ga-bl, contestable in law.

litigant, *a. lit*-e-gant, contending in law; engaged in a lawsuit: *n.* one engaged in a lawsuit.

litigate, *v.t. lit*-e-gate, to contest in a lawsuit: *v.i.* to carry on a lawsuit. (L. *litigatus*, disputed.)

litigation, *n. lit*-e-*gay*-shon, the act, process, or habit of litigating; a lawsuit.

litigiosity, *n.* le-*tij*-e-*os*-e-te, litigiousness; the character of being litigious.

litigious, *a.* le-*tij*-us, inclined to engage in lawsuits; quarrelsome; contentious; pertaining to or subject to contention. (Fr. *litigieux*.)

litigiously, *ad.* le-*tij*-us-le, in a litigious manner.

litigiousness, *n.* le-*tij*-us-ness, the condition or quality of being litigious.

litmus, *n. lit*-mus, a colouring matter obtained from several lichens. **litmus paper,** unsized paper stained with litmus, which is turned red by acids and blue by alkalies. (Dut. *lakmoes*, a blue dye, from *lak*, lacquer, *moes*, pulp.)

litotes, *n. ly*-to-teez, an understatement, esp. an affirmation expressed by the negative of the contrary (as "not at all bad" for "very good"), or a mild expression for the naked truth (as "he was put to sleep" for "killed") [Rhet.]. (Gr., simplicity, from *litos*, simple.)

litre, *n. lee*-ter, a French measure equal to 1·7598 (slightly over 1¾) pints.

litter, *n. lit*-ter, a covered bed or couch hung between shafts for carrying; a stretcher; straw, hay, or the like used as bedding for horses, etc.; a brood of animals, such as pigs or puppies; waste matter, shreds, fragments, etc., scattered about; confusion: *v.t.* to bring forth young, as swine; to scatter over carelessly with shreds, fragments, and the like; to cover or supply with litter or straw. (O.Fr. *litière*.)

litterateur, *n. lit*-ter-a-*ter*, a literary man. (Fr.)

littery, *a. lit*-ter-re, covered with litter; untidy; of the nature of litter.

***little,** *a. lit*-tl, small in size, quantity, or extent;

brief; of small dignity, power, or importance; of small force or effect; inconsiderable; mean; base: *n.* a small quantity or amount; a mere trifle: *ad.* in a small quantity or degree; not much; slightly. **little by little,** gradually; by degrees. **Little Englander,** a Briton who maintains that the Mother Country should restrict her Imperial responsibilities. **little hours,** the liturgical "hours" of prime to nones. **little Mary,** the stomach [Coll.]. **little people,** the fairies. **little season,** a fashionable period, preceding the "season," in London. **you little know,** you are far from knowing. (A.S. *lytel.*)

little-go, *n.* popular name for the preliminary examination for the B.A. degree at Cambridge.

littleness, *n. lit*-tl-ness, the state or quality of being little.

littoral, *a. lit*-to-ral, belonging to the shore: *n.* a coastal strip. (L. *litoralis.*)

liturgic, *a.* le-*tur*-jik, liturgical.

liturgical, *a.* le-*tur*-je-kal, pertaining to a liturgy or to public worship.

liturgically, *ad.* according to the liturgy.

liturgics, *n.* le-*tur*-jiks, the study of liturgies, or of the art of conducting public worship.

liturgiology, *n.* le-*tur*-je-*ol*-o-je, the science treating of, or a treatise on, liturgies.

liturgist, *n. lit*-ur-jist, an advocate of a liturgy; one versed in liturgies.

liturgy, *n. lit*-ur-je, a body of ritual or established formulæ for public worship; the Mass; the Office for the Celebration of the Holy Communion. (O.Fr. *liturgie.*)

livable, *a. liv*-a-bl, liveable.

live, *v.i.* liv, to be alive; to continue in life; to spend life; to dwell or reside; to enjoy life; to subsist; to be nourished and supported in life; to gain a livelihood; to continue functioning; to use life fully; to live in the memory; to subsist spiritually: *v.t.* to spend; to conform to. **live down,** to cause to be forgotten by one's manner of living. **live in,** to reside in the premises where one works. **live in a small way,** to live a quiet, inexpensive kind of life. **live on air,** to seem to take little food. **live out,** to live away from one's work. **live well,** to eat choice food. (A.S. *libban,* to live, to stay behind.)

live, *a.* lyve, having life; living; not dead; effective; ready for use; on fire; ignited; vivid; charged with (explosive, electric, or other power, etc.); full of energy. **live axle,** an axle through which power is transmitted. **live cartridge,** one loaded with ball. **live feathers,** or **hair,** feathers or hair plucked from the living animal. **live oak,** *see* **oak. live rail,** the rail of an electric railway system which conveys the current to the trains. **live wire,** a wire along which an electric current is passing; an intelligent energetic person.

liveable, *a. liv*-a-bl, that may be lived; endurable; conducive to a pleasant existence.

lived, *a.* livd, having a particular length or kind of life, as *short-lived, well-lived.*

livelihood, *n. lyve*-le-hood, means of supporting life.

livelily, *ad. lyve*-le-le, in a lively manner.

liveliness, *n.* quality or state of being lively.

livelong, *a. liv*-long, lasting; all through: *n.* the orpine, *Sedum telephium.*

lively, *a. lyve*-le, brisk; vigorous; gay; sprightly; representing life; strong and active; vivid.

liven, *v.i. ly*-ven, to cheer up: *v.t.* to enliven.

liver, *n. liv*-er, a resident; one who lives in a certain specified way.

liver, *n. liv*-er, an organ of a glandular structure whose office is to secrete the bile; the fleshy part of this in animals used for food; a diseased state of the liver: *a.* of the colour of the liver, dark red. **liver of sulphur,** a liver-coloured insecticide obtained by the fusion of potassium carbonate with sulphur. **liver-opal,** menillite.

liver, *n. ly*-ver, a bird of doubtful identity in the arms of the city of Liverpool.

livered, *a. liv*-erd, having a liver, as *white-livered.*

liver-fluke, *n. liv*-er-flook, the parasitic worm, *Distomum hepaticum,* sometimes infesting man and causing the rot in sheep.

liveried, *a. liv*-er-rid, wearing a livery, as servants.

liverish, *a. liv*-er-rish, bilious; testy.

Liverpudlian, *n.* liv-er-*pud*-le-an, a native or inhabitant of Liverpool.

liverwort, *n. liv*-er-wurt, any member of the Hepaticæ, cryptogamic plants allied to the mosses.

livery, *n. liv*-er-re, a uniform or form of dress by which the servants of a particular family are distinguishable from those of others (originally, the feeding and entire maintenance of retainers); a garb appropriate or peculiar to particular persons or things, as the city guilds, etc.; the collective body of liverymen in London; the act of delivering possession of property, or the writ by which possession is obtained [Law]: *v.t.* to clothe in livery. **at livery,** kept for owner at a contract rate. **Livery Company,** a City Company, members of each of which formerly wore a distinctive costume. (Fr. *livrie.*)

livery, *a. liv*-er-re, liverish [Coll.].

liveryman, *n. liv*-er-re-man, a member of a Livery Company and a freeman of the City of London having, among other privileges, the right of voting for lord mayor, sheriff, and other corporation officials; an attendant in or keeper of a livery-stable.

livery-stable, *n.* a jobmaster's stable where horses are kept at livery or for hire.

live-stock, *n. lyve*-stok, domestic animals, esp. such as are kept for profit or use; fleas, lice, or other body vermin [Slang].

livid, *a. liv*-id, black and blue; of a lead colour; discoloured. (Fr. *livide.*)

lividity, *n.* le-*vid*-e-te, the state of being livid.

lividness, *n. liv*-id-ness, livid discoloration; lividity.

***living,** *a. liv*-ing, having life; contemporary; running or flowing; operative; quickening; true to life: *n.* livelihood or means of livelihood; power of continuing life; the benefice of a clergyman; manner of life. **cost of living,** the average consumer's expenditure on certain necessities as deduced from official statistics [Econ.]. **living rock,** rock in its native state or location. **living-room,** a sitting-room. **living pictures,** tableaux vivants. **living wage,** a wage that reaches the standard of living. **standard of living,** the scale of income necessary to enable an individual to maintain himself and his family with respect as members of his social group [Econ.].

livingly, *ad. liv*-ing-le, in a living manner; vividly.

livingness, *n. liv*-ing-ness, the condition or quality of being alive; vivacity; vividness.

livor, *n. ly*-vor, lividity [Med.]; discoloration as of a bruise. (L.)

livraison, *n.* (App.), a single part of a literary work delivered from time to time. (Fr., delivery.)

livre, *n.* leevr, a former French coin equal, when superseded by the franc (1795), to about 9½*d.* (Fr.)

lixivial, *a.* lik-*siv*-e-al, pertaining to lye; obtained by lixiviation.

lixiviate, *v.t.* lik-*siv*-e-ate, to form into lye; to separate soluble from insoluble matter by means of water or leaching.

lixiviation, *n.* lik-siv-e-*ay*-shon, the process of lixiviating; leaching.

lixivious, *a.* lik-*siv*-e-us, lixivial.

lixivium, *n.* lik-*siv*-e-um, lye; water impregnated with alkaline salts. (L., lye.)

lizard, *n. liz*-ard, a reptile of the genus *Lacerta,* having a long body and tail, a scaly hide and four legs; a greenish variety of canary. (O.Fr. *lesarde.*)

lizard-stone, *n. liz*-ard-stone, serpentine found in Cornwall, near Lizard Point.

llama, *n. lah*-ma, a South American ally of the camel, *Lama huanacus glama,* domesticated as a beast of burden; its wool; a fabric made with or in imitation of this. (Peruv.)

llanero, *n.* lyah-*nay*-ro, an inhabitant of a llano; a cowboy. (Sp.)

llano, *n. lah*-noh, one of the vast level plains in northern South America. (Sp.)

llautu, *n. lou*-too, a cord of vicuña wool worn with feathers about the head by incas and nobles of ancient Peru. (Peruv.)

Lloyd's, *n.* loydz, the headquarters of the London underwriters and marine (and other) insurance brokers. **Lloyd's register,** an annual publication of lists of ships with their respective classes. (From *Lloyd's* coffee-house, their original meeting-place.)

lo, *int.* loh, look; see; behold. (A.S. *lā.*)

loach, *n.* lohkh, a small river fish of the genus *Cobitis* or *Nemachilus.* (Fr. *loche.*)

load, *n.* lode, that which is laid on or put in anything for conveyance; a burden; a charge; weight; a cargo or freight; as much as can be carried at once; that which is borne with pain or difficulty; anything oppressive or depressing; violence; a measure of hay (36 trusses), grain (40 bushels), etc.: *pl.* heaps, a large quantity (of): *v.t.* to lay a burden on; to lay on as much as can be carried; to lay on or lade too much; to oppress; to embarrass; to encumber; to make heavy by something added; to charge a gun; to adulterate or fortify (esp. wines). (A.S. *lād.*)
loader, *n.* *lode*-er, one who puts on a load; a hunt-attendant who loads guns; a machine for loading.
loading, *n.* *lode*-ing, a cargo; a burden; anything that makes part of a load; added strengthening; a filler [papermaking, etc.]; an addition to an insurance premium for expenses, contingencies, etc.
load-line, *n.* a line on the side of a ship to indicate the limit of loading [Naut.].
load-shedding, *n.* cessation or diminution of current to avoid excessive loading of generating plant [Elect.].
loadstar, *n.* *lode*-star, lodestar.
loadstone, *n.* *lode*-stone, a natural oxide of iron which has the power of attracting iron. (A.S. *lād,* way, and *stone.*)
loaf, *n.* lofe (*pl.* **loaves,** lohvz), a mass of bread when baked; a conical mould of sugar; a lump or any thick mass; the rounded head of a cabbage, etc.; the head [Slang]. **loaf sugar,** sugar refined and formed into a conical mass. (A.S. *hlaf.*)
loaf, *v.i.* and *v.t.* lofe, to spend or pass time lazily and idly: *n.* an idling. (Origin uncertain.)
loafer, *n.* *lofe*-er, an idler; a ne'er-do-well; one who seeks his living by mean expedients.
loam, *n.* lome, a sandy, clayey, vegetable mould: *v.t.* to cover with loam. (A.S. *lam.*)
loamy, *a.* *lome*-e, consisting of or resembling loam.
loan, *n.* lone, the act of lending; state of being lent; anything lent, esp. money on interest; permission to use; grant of the use: *v.t.* to lend. **loan word,** a word borrowed from another language and partly naturalized. (A.S. *læn.*)
loath, *a.* lohth, unwilling; reluctant. (A.S. *lath.*)
loathe, *v.t.* lohthe, to abhor; to feel disgust at.
loather, *n.* *lohthe*-er, one who loathes.
loathful, *a.* *lohthe*-ful, loathsome.
loathfully, *ad.* *lohthe*-ful-le, in a loathful manner.
loathfulness, *n.* *lohthe*-ful-ness, the quality or state of being loathful.
loathing, *a.* *lohthe*-ing, feeling or evincing disgust: *n.* extreme disgust; abhorrence.
loathingly, *ad.* *lohthe*-ing-le, with extreme disgust.
loathliness, *n.* *lohthe*-le-ness, loathsomeness.
loathly, *a.* *lohthe*-le, exciting disgust; loathsome: *ad.* reluctantly.
loathness, *n.* *lohth*-ness, unwillingness; reluctance.
loathsome, *a.* *lohthe*-sum, exciting disgust or abhorrence; abominable; nauseating.
loathsomely, *ad.* in a loathsome manner.
loathsomeness, *n.* quality of being loathsome; repulsiveness.
lob, *n.* lob, a dull, sluggish person; something thick and heavy; a ball sent underhand at cricket, or high up in tennis: *v.t.* to bowl underhand at cricket; to hit high at lawn tennis; to pitch; to let fall heavily. **lob's pound,** a prison; the stocks [Slang]. (Probably imit.)
lobar, *a.* *loh*-bar, belonging to a lobe.
lobate, *a.* *loh*-bat, lobed [Bot. and Zool.].
lobation, *n.* loh-*bay*-shon, the state of being lobed; the formation of lobes.
lobby, *n.* *lob*-be, a passage opening into several apartments; a hall serving as an ante-room or waiting-room; a hall in certain parliament-houses used for interviews between outsiders and members, also, lobbyists collectively, and one of two corridors in which the voting is done; a confined place for cattle, near the farm-yard [Agr.]: *v.t.* to seek to influence the members of a legislative assembly in order to secure the passage of a bill: *v.i.* to seek votes. (Late L. *lobia.*)
lobbyist, *n.* *lob*-be-ist, one, other than a member, who frequents the lobby of a house of legislation.
lobcock, *n.* *lob*-kok, a rustic, bumpkin, lubber.
lobe, *n.* lobe, a rounded projecting part; a division of the brain, lungs, liver, or other organ; the lower soft part of the ear; a division of a leaf; the cotyledon of a seed. (Fr.)
lobed, *a.* lohbd, having or consisting of lobes; characterized by lobes. (Gr. *lobos,* a lobe.)
lobelia, *n.* lo-*bee*-le-a, any of a large genus, *Lobelia,* of hardy and half-hardy herbaceous plants in which the flower is twisted halfway round on its axis. (From M. de *Lobel,* Flemish botanist, physician to James I.)
lobelin, *n.* lo-*bee*-lin, an emetic and diaphoretic alkaloid obtained from *Lobelia inflata.*
loblolly, *n.* *lob*-lol-le, water-gruel, or spoon meat [Naut.]; a lout or rustic. **loblolly bay,** an ornamental evergreen tree, *Gordonia lasianthus,* of the southern U.S.A., whose bark is used in tanning. **loblolly boy,** a surgeon's attendant on shipboard [Naut.]. **loblolly pine,** *Pinus tæda,* of the southern U.S.A., or its timber. **loblolly tree,** name of several trees of tropical America.
lobscouse, *n.* *lob*-skouce, a dish of salt meat stewed with vegetables and ship's biscuits [Naut.].
lobster, *n.* *lob*-ster, an edible decapod crustacean of the genus *Homarus,* bluish black when alive, scarlet when boiled. **lobster pot,** a wickerwork trap for lobsters. (A.S. *loppestre.*)
lobular, *a.* *lob*-yew-lar, of the nature of a lobule.
lobulation, *n.* lob-yew-*lay*-shon, the formation of lobules.
lobule, *n.* *lob*-yewl, a small lobe. (*lobe.*)
lobworm, *n.* *lob*-wurm, any of several annelids of the genus *Arenicola,* burrowing in sandy shores; the lugworm.
local, *a.* *loh*-kal, pertaining to a place; confined to a spot, place, or definite district; relating to what is local; not general: *n.* a short-distance train; a local newspaper, tavern, team, etc. [Coll.]. **local colour,** realistic emphasis on local peculiarities and characteristics [Literature]; colour belonging to an object as distinct from that imparted (*e.g.* by reflection) [Painting]. **local government,** direct administration of the domestic affairs of a community by representatives locally elected. **Local Government Board,** a British department of State superseded, 1919, mainly by the Ministry of Health. **local option,** regulation (esp. of the liquor traffic) by a majority of the voters of a district. (Fr.)
locale, *n.* loh-*kahl,* a particular place or locality. (Fr.)
localism, *n.* *loh*-kal-izm, the state of being local; affection for a place; a local peculiarity.
locality, *n.* loh-*kal*-e-te, existence in or limitation to a place; a particular position or situation.
localization, *n.* loh-ka-ly-*zay*-shon, the act of localizing; state of being localized.
localize, *v.t.* *loh*-ka-lize, to make local; to put into a place; to determine the seat of.
locally, *ad.* *loh*-ka-le, with respect to place; in some particular place; in the neighbourhood.
locate, *v.t.* loh-*kate,* to set in a particular spot or position; to select, survey, and settle the bounds of a particular tract of land; to discover the position of; to fix on the site of [U.S.A.]. (L. *locatus,* placed.)
location, *n.* loh-*kay*-shon, the art of locating, placing or designating the limits of; situation; relative situation; that which is located; a place apart from the studio at which a localized scene is "shot" [Cine.].
locative, *a.* *lok*-a-tiv, pertaining to the case denoting place or position: *n.* this case [Gram.].
loch, *n.* lokh, a lake; a long, narrow arm of the sea. (Gael.)
Locahber-axe, *n.* lo-*khah*-ber-*aks,* a large hooked halberd formerly used in the Highlands. (Place in Inverness-shire, Scotland.)
lochia, *n.pl.* *lok*-e-a, the uterine and vaginal discharge following childbirth [Med.].
loci, *n.pl.* *loh*-sy, plural of *locus.*
★**lock,** *n.* lok, anything that fastens; an instrument for fastening doors, boxes, etc.; a means of stopping or checking motion; the part of a fire-arm by which it is discharged; an air-lock; an enclosure in a canal, where the level changes, with gates at each end, for raising or lowering vessels; the relative freedom of fore and rear wheels of a vehicle in turning; a jam, or state of being blocked; a grapple in wrestling; a lock-hospital: *v.t.* to fasten with a lock; to fasten, so as to impede motion; to make fast by interlocking; to shut up or confine; to close fast; to embrace closely; to provide with locks; to seize the sword-arm of an antagonist [Fencing]: *v.i.* to become locked; to become fast by interlocking; to engage [Fencing]. **lock, stock,**

and barrel, the whole lot. **locks and keys,** the fruit of the ash, or of the sycamore maple. (A.S. *loc,* a fastening.)
lock, *n.* lok, a tuft of hair; a tuft of wool, hay, or like substance; a ringlet of hair. (A.S. *locc,* curl.)
lockage, *n. lok*-aj, works which form a canal lock; toll paid for passing the locks; amount of ascent and descent of the locks.
lock-chamber, *n.* the basin of a canal lock.
locker, *n. lok*-er, one who or that which locks; a place that may be closed with a lock; a drawer; a cupboard. **Davy Jones's locker,** the ocean, as the grave of those drowned at sea. **a shot in the locker,** a last resource, a stand-by.
locket, *n. lok*-et, a small lock; a catch to fasten a necklace, etc.; a little case with a miniature or a lock of hair, worn as an ornament. (Fr. *loquet.*)
lock-gate, *n. lok*-gate, the gate of a lock-chamber.
lock-hospital, *n.* a hospital where venereal diseases are treated. (Origin uncertain.)
Lockian, *a. lok*-e-an, pertaining to the school of philosophy founded by John Locke (*d.* 1704) or to the Lockists: *n.* a Lockist.
Lockist, *n. lok*-ist, a philosopher of the school of John Locke: *a.* Lockian.
lock-jaw, *n.* a violent contraction of the muscles of the jaw, by which its motion is suspended; a variety of tetanus.
lock-keeper, *n.* one who attends the locks of a canal.
lock-out, *n. lok*-out, a suspension of work by order of employers pending the acceptance of their terms by the workers.
lockram, *n. lok*-rum, a kind of coarse linen cloth. (*Locronan,* in France.)
lock-sill, *n.* a beam at the bottom of a lock, against which the gates shut.
locksmith, *n. lok*-smith, one who makes locks.
lock-stitch, *n.* a stitch (esp. by a sewing-machine) by which two threads are locked together.
lock-up, *n. lok*-up, a place for the temporary confinement of persons under arrest; a shop, building, etc., without living accommodation; capital on long-term investment; the action or time of locking a place up: *a.* that can be locked up.
loco, *a. loh*-ko, crazy; eccentric: *n.* a diseased condition in cattle, etc., due to eating locoweed [Vet.]; locoweed [U.S.A.]
locoism, *n. loh*-ko-izm, the disease loco [Vet.].
locomobile, *n. loh*-ko-mo-*beel,* a motor-car.
locomotion, *n. loh*-ko-*moh*-shon, the act or power of moving from place to place; travel; travelling. (L. *locus,* a place, and *motion.*)
locomotive, *a. loh*-ko-*moh*-tiv, moving or changing from place to place; affecting locomotion; pertaining to travel: *n.* an engine moving along on wheels by its own power; a railway-engine.
locomotor, *a. loh*-ko-*moh*-tor, pertaining to movement. **locomotor ataxy,** a nervous disease (tabes dorsalis), due to syphilis, characterized by lack of co-ordination of muscular movements, loss of reflexes, etc.
locomotory, *a. loh*-ko-*moh*-to-re, pertaining to locomotion; self-moving.
locoweed, *n. loh*-ko-weed, any of several poisonous leguminous plants having a deleterious effect on livestock [U.S.A.].
loculament, *n. lok*-yew-la-ment, one of the cells of a pericarp in which the seed is lodged; a loculus [Bot.]. (L. *loculamentum.*)
locular, *a. lok*-yew-lar, pertaining to or having loculi.
loculose, *a. lok*-yew-lohs, having cells; divided internally into cells [Bot.]. (L. *loculosus.*)
loculus, *n. lok*-yew-lus (*pl.* **loculi,** *lok*-yew-ly), a small recess or cavity; a small cell [Bot., Anat., etc.]. (L., a little place.)
locum-tenens, *n. lo*-kum-*tee*-nenz, a deputy. (L.)
locus, *n. loh*-kus (*pl.* **loci,** *loh*-sy), locality; the line generated by a point, or the surface generated by a line, moving according to a fixed law [Geom.]. **locus classicus** the original or authoritative literary source. **locus standi** (L., a place of standing), recognized position; a right to be heard in court [Law]. (L., a place.)
locust, *n. loh*-kust, an orthopterous insect, allied to the grasshopper, which migrates in vast hordes, and is very destructive to vegetation; applied also to the fruit of the locust-tree. **honey locust,** a tree of the genus *Gleditschia.* (L. *locusta.*)
locust-tree, *n.* the false acacia, *Robinia pseudacacia*; the carob; and certain other trees.
locution, *n.* lo-*kew*-shon, a mode of expression; a phrase. (L. *locutio.*)
locutory, *n. lok*-yew-to-re, the visitors' reception room at a monastery or nunnery; the grille through which conversation takes place.
lode, *n.* lode, a mineral vein, or any regular vein or course [Mining]; a reach of water; an open ditch. (A.S. *lad.*)
lodestar, *n. lode*-star, the pole-star, the star that guides. (A.S. *lād,* way, and *star.*)
lodestone, *n. lode*-stone, loadstone.
lodge, *n.* lodj, a temporary habitation; a hut or cot; a gate-keeper's cottage; a small house in a park; a room at an entrance for a concierge or porter; the home of an American Indian; a den; a retreat for otters, beavers, etc.; a secret local association, as of freemasons, and the place where they meet: *v.t.* to deposit temporarily; to provide with a temporary habitation; to harbour; to plant; to infix or settle; to beat down, as growing crops: *v.i.* to reside for a time; to settle; to be laid flat, as crops. (O.Fr. *loge.*)
lodgement, *n. lodj*-ment, lodgment.
lodger, *n. lodj*-er, one who lodges, specially in hired furnished apartments.
lodging, *n. lodj*-ing, a temporary habitation; hired apartment; harbour; cover.
lodging-house, *n. lodj*-ing-house, a house let out by the tenant in separate apartments.
lodgment, *n. lodj*-ment, act of lodging, or state of being lodged; accumulation of something deposited or remaining at rest; position taken up by a besieging party, and the works to maintain it [Mil.].
loess, *n. loh*-ess, an alluvial and wind-borne post-tertiary deposit of fine buff-coloured silt and marl occurring in certain arid regions [Geol.]. (Ger.)
loft, *n.* loft, a room or space immediately under the roof; a gallery in a church or large hall; a pigeon-house; a flock of pigeons; the backward slope of a lofter: *v.t.* to provide (pigeons) with a loft; to hit a ball high. (Scand.)
lofter, *n. lof*-ter, a club with an iron head used at golf to lift the ball up high.
loftily, *ad. lof*-te-le, in a lofty manner.
loftiness, *n.* state or quality of being lofty.
lofty, *a. lof*-te, extending high up; elevated in place, condition, character, demeanour, or style, etc.; dignified; haughty.
log, *n.* log, a bulky piece of unshaped timber; an apparatus for measuring the rate of a ship's motion; a daily record at sea; a log-book or diary: *v.t.* to fell timber; to cut into logs; to enter in a log-book; to record or make a note of [Coll.]. (M.E. *logge.*)
log, *n.* log, a Hebrew liquid measure, variously reckoned at ½ or ⅛ of a pint. (Heb.)
log, *n.* log, a logarithm.
loganberry, *n. loh*-gan-*be*-re, a hybrid between a blackberry and a raspberry. (Introduced 1881 by J. H. *Logan,* Amer. botanist.)
logan-stone, *n. log*-an-stone, a rocking-stone.
logarithm, *n. log*-a-rithm, a number related to a number so that addition serves for multiplication, and subtraction for division [Math.]. (Gr. *logos,* ratio, and *arithmos,* number.)
logarithmetical, *a. log*-a-rith-*met*-e-kal, logarithmic.
logarithmic, *a.* log-a-*rith*-mik, pertaining to or consisting of logarithms.
logarithmical, *a.* log-a-*rith*-me-kal, logarithmic.
log-board, *n.* two boards hinged together on which the course, speed, etc., of a ship and other details were chalked before transcription in the logbook [Naut.].
log-book, *n.* the official record of the daily events of a ship's voyage [Naut.]; a book containing a daily record.
log-cabin, *n.* a hut built of logs of timber.
loge, *n.* lohzh, a box in a theatre. (Fr.)
loggat, *n. log*-at, one of the sticks thrown in loggats: *pl.* an old English game resembling nine-pins.
logger, *n. log*-er, a hewer of timber; a lumberer.
loggerhead, *n. log*-er-hed, a blockhead; a spherical mass of iron with a long handle formerly used for melting tar; a species of turtle, *Thalassochelys caretta*; the chub, miller's thumb, etc. **at loggerheads,** at variance; quarrelling; come to blows. (*log* and *head.*)

logger-headed, *a.* log-er-*hed*-ed, dull-witted; thick-headed.
loggia, *n.* *loj*-e-a, a gallery or arcade in front of a building; a balcony. (It.)
logia, *n.pl.* *log*-e-a, traditional sayings, esp. an early collection of the sayings of Christ. (Gr. *logion*, a saying.)
logic, *n.* *loj*-ik, the study of reasoning, esp. of inference; the science of the formal and necessary laws of thought and demonstration; a treatise on this; reasoning. (Fr. *logique*.)
logical, *a.* *loj*-e-kal, belonging to or connected with logic; according to the rules of logic; skilled in logic; consistent; discriminating.
logicality, *n.* loj-e-*kal*-e-te, logical character.
logically, *ad.* according to the rules of logic.
logician, *n.* lo-*jish*-an, one versed or skilled in logic.
logicize, *v.i.* *loj*-e-size, to employ logic; to reason from premises.
-logist, a suffix formed by adding *-ist* to nouns in *-logy*, signifying one who is skilled in a subject, as *biologist*, *zoologist*.
logistic, *a.* lo-*jis*-tik, pertaining to calculation or proportion. **logistic logarithms,** certain logarithms of sexagesimal numbers or fractions, used in astronomical calculations. (Gr. *logistikos*.)
logistics, *n.pl.* lo-*jis*-tiks, the art of disposing troops, munitions, etc., in the right quantities in the right place at the right time [Mil.]. (Fr. *logis*, quarters.)
log-line, *n.* a cord about 100 fathoms in length connecting the log-ship to the log-reel and divided by knots into equal spaces [Naut.].
logogram, *n.* *log*-o-gram, a shorthand character representing a word; a puzzle in verse made up of anagrams of the word or phrase to be found out. (Gr. *logos*, a word, *gramma*, letter.)
logography, *n.* lo-*gog*-ra-fe, a method of printing with logotypes. (Gr. *logos*, and *grapho*, write.)
logogriph, *n.* *log*-o-grif, a species of anagrammatic logogram.
logomachy, *n.* lo-*gom*-a-ke, a war of words; contention about words. (Gr. *logos*, and *mache*, a fight.)
logomania, *n.* *log*-o-*may*-ne-a, a form of insanity characterized by uncontrollable loquacity.
logopathia, *n.* log-o-*path*-e-a, any disorder of the speech [Path.].
Logos, *n.* *log*-os, the Divine Word incarnate; the active principle of the world [Theol.]. (Gr.)
logotype, *n.* *log*-o-tipe, a single type on which two or more letters are cast. (Gr. *logos* and *typos*.)
log-reel, *n.* the reel of a log-line [Naut.].
log-roll, *v.i.* *log*-role, to conduct or assist in log-rolling. **log-rolling,** mutual advertisement, esp. of authors and journalists; covert combination for political or literary purposes [Slang].
log-ship, *n.* the float at the end of the log-line distant from the reel.
logwood, *n.* *log*-wood, a tree of tropical America, *Hæmatoxylon campechianum*, the deep-red wood of which furnishes an extensively used dye.
-logy, a suffix forming the names of sciences and branches of learning (*biology*, *espistemology*, etc.), and nouns denoting speaking or saying (*apology*, *neology*, etc.). (Gr. *logos*, word.)
lohoch, *n.* *loh*-hok, an opaque oily linctus or emulsion [Med.]. (Ar.)
loimic, *a.* *loy*-mik, relating to the plague or contagious disorders. (Gr. *loimos*, a plague.)
loimology, *n.* loy-*mol*-o-je, the science or study of epidemic contagious diseases.
loin, *n.* loyn, one of the lateral portions of the lumbar regions just above the haunch bone; a joint of meat that includes the loin in sheep, etc. **loin-cloth,** the cloth worn round the loins by many primitive peoples in hot climates. (O.Fr. *logne*.)
loiter, *v.i.* *loy*-ter, to be slow in moving; to linger or delay. (Dut. *leuteren*.)
loiterer, *n.* *loy*-ter-rer, an idler; one who delays.
loiteringly, *ad.* *loy*-ter-ring-le, in a loitering manner.
Loligo, *n.* *lol*-e-go, a genus of cuttlefishes with narrow shells; a calamary or squid. (L.)
loll, *v.i.* lol, to lounge or lie lazily about; to hang out from the mouth: *v.t.* to thrust out, as the tongue. (Perhaps O.Scand. *lolla*, to act lazily.)
Lollard, *n.* *lol*-lard, one of a sect of early Reformers in Germany; a follower of Wycliffe in England. (O.Dut. *lollaerd*, a mumbler—as of prayers, etc.)
Lollardy, *n.* *lol*-lar-de, the teaching of the Lollards.
lollipop, *n.* *lol*-le-pop, a sweetmeat.
lollop, *v.i.* *lol*-lop, to move heavily; to lounge or loll about. (*loll*.)
Lombard, *n.* *lom*-bard, a native of Lombardy; a moneylender or banker, a profession first exercised in London by the Lombards. **Lombard Street,** the bankers' headquarters in London; hence, the money-market, the monied interest.
loment, *n.* *loh*-ment, a legume divided into small cells, with a seed attached to the under suture [Bot.]. (L. *lomentum*, a perfume.)
lomentaceous, *a.* loh-men-*tay*-shus, having loments; like a loment.
lomentum, *n.* lo-*men*-tum, a loment [Bot.].
lomonite, *n.* *lom*-on-ite, laumontite.
Londoner, *n.* *lun*-dun-er, a person born or living in London, the capital of England.
Londonism, *n.* *lun*-dun-izm, mannerism, mode of speech, etc., peculiar to Londoners.
Londonize, *v.t.* *lun*-dun-ize, to give a London character to.
London pride, *n.* the plant none-so-pretty, *Saxifraga umbrosa*, cultivated in gardens.
lone, *a.* lone, solitary; retired; unfrequented; standing by itself; companionless. *alone*.)
loneliness, *n.* *lone*-le-ness, the state of being lonely.
lonely, *a.* *lone*-le, lone; addicted to solitude or seclusion; sad in solitude.
loneness, *n.* *lone*-ness, the quality or state of being lone; loneliness.
lonesome, *a.* *lone*-sum, solitary; secluded from society; unfrequented.
lonesomely, *ad.* *lone*-sum-le, in a lonesome manner.
lonesomeness, *n.* the state of being lonesome.
***long,** *a.* long, extended in length; extended in time; protracted; stressed (of vowels, etc.); slow in coming; lingering; extending far in prospect; far-seeing; lengthy; verbose: *ad.* to a great extent in space or time; at a point of duration far distant; for or by a long time: *v.i.* to desire earnestly; to have a craving appetite. **long-breathed,** having the power of retaining the breath for a long time. **long face,** a sad or miserable expression. **long firm,** *see* **firm. long-headed,** shrewd; discerning; dolichocephalic. **long home,** the grave; death. **long-period,** of or pertaining to that which continues for a long time. **long pull,** an over-measure to increase trade given in public-houses. **long-range,** of or pertaining to anything (esp. missile weapons) which extends over a long range. **in the long run,** in the final result; as the outcome of ripe experience. **long-sighted,** sagacious; seeing distant objects distinctly, but not near ones [Opt.]. **long-suffering,** forbearing long; long patience. **long-tongued,** prating; babbling. **long-wave,** applied to a station, etc., having a wave-length of 1,000 or more metres [Wire.]. **long-winded,** tedious in speaking; taking long credit; long-breathed. (A.S. *lang*.)
long-ago, *n.* *long*-a-goh, the distant past.
longan, *n.* *long*-gan, the Indo-Malayan tree, *Nephelium longana*, cultivated for its fruit. (Chin.)
longanimity, *n.* long-ga-*nim*-e-te, capacity of forbearance; long-suffering.
longboat, *n.* *long*-bote, the strongest and largest boat belonging to a merchant sailing vessel.
longbow, *n.* *long*-boh, the large and powerful bow, formerly used by English archers; the bow as distinct from the cross-bow. **to draw the long bow,** to exaggerate.
longcloth, *n.* *long*-kloth, a fine cotton cloth used chiefly for underwear and shirting.
long-clothes, *n.* *long*-kloathz, the first clothes worn by infants in arms.
long-dozen, *n.* long-*duz*-en, thirteen.
longe, *n.* lonj, a lunge or thrust with a sword. (Fr.)
longer, *n.* *long*-er, one who longs.
longeron, *n.* *lon*(*g*)-zha-ron(g) (or App.), the main longitudinal member of the fuselage of an aeroplane of girder construction. (Fr.)
longeval, *a.* lon-*jee*-val, long-lived. (L. *longævus*.)
longevity, *n.* lon-*jev*-e-te, great length of life; long duration of life. (L. *longævitas*.)
longevous, *a.* lon-*jee*-vus, long-lived; having lived long.
long-field, *n.* that part of a cricket-field to the rear of the bowler; a player fielding here, long-on on bowler's right, long-off on his left.
longhand, *n.* *long*-hand, ordinary handwriting.

long-headed, *a.* dolichocephalic [Ethn.]; of keen discernment or foresight [Fig.].
long-hop, *n.* *long*-hop, in cricket, fives, etc., a short-pitched ball that makes a long bounce.
long-hundred, *n.* one hundred and twenty.
longicorn, *a.* *lon*-je-korn, having long antennæ; of or pertaining to the group of beetles so furnished: *n.* one of such beetles. (Lat. *longus*, long, *cornu*, horn.)
longiloquence, *n.* lon-*jil*-o-kwence, speaking at tedious length. (L. *longus*, and *loquentia*, speaking.)
longimanous, *a.* lon-*jim-a*-nus, long-handed (of some apes). (L. *longus*, and *manus*, the hand.)
longing, *n.* *long*-ing, eager desire: *a.* earnestly desiring; yearning.
longingly, *ad.* *long*-ing-le, with eager desire.
longipennate, *a.* *lon*-je-*pen*-nat, with long wings. (L. *longus*, and *penna*, a wing.)
longirostral, *a.* *lon*-je-*ros*-tral, having a long beak, as the snipe. (L. *longus*, and *rostrum*, a beak.)
longish, *a.* *long*-ish, somewhat long.
longitude, *n.* *lon*-je-tewd, angular distance of a place east or west from a given meridian, generally that of Greenwich, expressed in degrees [Geog.]; distance from the vernal equinox reckoned eastward on the ecliptic all round the celestial sphere [Astron.]. (L. *longitudo*, length.)
longitudinal, *a.* lon-je-*tew*-de-nal, pertaining to longitude or length; running lengthwise.
longitudinally, *ad.* lengthwise.
long-measure, *n.* *long*-mezh-ur, linear measure.
long-moss, *n.* *long*-moss, an epiphytic moss of the genus *Tillandsia* found in tropical America.
Longobard, *n.* *long*-go-bard, a Lombard.
long-primer, *n.* long-*prim*-er, a printing type of a size between small pica and bourgeois; 10-point.
longshoreman, *n.* *long*-shore-man, one who earns his living in or about boats along the shore.
long-sighted, *a.* long-*sy*-ted, able to distinguish objects at a great distance; far-sighted; sagacious [Fig.].
long-sightedness, *n.* long-*sy*-ted-ness, the state, condition, or quality of being long-sighted.
longsome, *a.* *long*-sum, lengthy; somewhat long; tedious.
long-stop, *n.* *long*-stop, the player who fields behind the wicket-keeper: *v.i.* to field in this position [Cricket].
long-suffering, *a.* patiently forbearing; enduring or tolerating much: *n.* patient and sustained endurance.
longtail, *a.* *long*-tale, having the tail uncut: *n.* an animal (esp. dog) in this state.
longways, *ad.* *long*-wayz, lengthwise.
long-winded, *a.* long-*win*-ded, tedious in speaking; dilatory in action; able to continue without becoming out of breath.
long-windedness, *n.* the quality of being long-winded; longiloquence.
Lonicera, *n.* lo-*nis*-er-ra, the genus of hardy deciduous shrubs comprising honeysuckles. (After *Lonicer*, 16th-cent. Ger. botanist.)
loo, *n.* loo, a round game at cards; the pool at this also the penalty: *v.t.* to beat at the game by winning every trick. (Fr. *lanterlu*.)
looby, *n.* *loo*-be, an awkward young oaf. (*lubber*.)
loof, *n.* loof, the palm of the hand. (O.Scand. *lofe*.)
loofah, *n.* *loo*-fah, the fibrous skeleton of the fruit of a species of *Luffa*, a genus of cucurbitaceous tropical climbing plants, used as a sponge, etc. (Ar.)
look, *v.i.* look, to direct the eye at an object; to direct the mind or attention to; to consider; to examine; to expect; to take care; to seem; to face; to front: *v.t.* to express or influence by look or presence. **look about,** to look on all sides or in different directions. **look about one,** to be on the watch, or vigilant. **look after,** to take care of; to search; to expect. **look down,** to overawe by the appearance assumed. **look down upon,** to despise. **look for,** to expect; to search. **look in the face,** to face or meet with boldness. **look into,** to inspect closely. **look on,** to regard; to view; to be a mere spectator. **look out,** to be on the watch; to select; to search for and discover. **look over,** to examine one by one. **look sharp,** to make haste. **look through,** to penetrate with the eye or the understanding. **look to,** to take care of; to depend on. **look up,** to give an upward glance; to visit; to search for (a reference, etc.). (A.S. *locian*.)
*__look,__ *n.* look, the act of looking or seeing; a glance; aspect: *pl.* general appearance.
looker, *n.* *look*-er, one who looks; an inspector. **a good looker,** one of handsome appearance [Coll.].
looker-on, *n.* *look*-er-*on*, a mere spectator.
looking-glass, *n.* a mirror.
look-out, *n.* a careful looking out or watching for any object or event; a place to look out from; the person on the look-out.
loom, *n.* loom, a weaving machine; the shaft of an oar inboard. (A.S. *geloma*, an implement.)
loom, *v.i.* loom, to appear above the horizon; to rise to view enlarged and through, or as through, haze; to appear in large, faint outline in the distance.
loom, *n.* *loom*, the guillemot, loon, or other sea-bird.
looming, *n.* *loom*-ing, the indistinct and magnified appearance of objects seen in particular states of the atmosphere; a form of mirage.
loon, *n.* loon, a base or worthless fellow; a child. (Scots. *lown*, perhaps from Dut. *loen*.)
loon, *n.* loon, the great northern diver, *Colymbus glacialis*, or any species of *Colymbus*; the crested grebe, *Podicipes cristatus*. (Scand.)
loony, *a.* and *n.* *loo*-ne, lunatic [Slang].
loop, *n.* loop, a doubling of a string or cord; a bight or bend; a noose through which a cord may be run for fastening; a curved piece forming an eye, hook, fastener, etc., a stitch in knitting; a loophole; a loop-line; the curve traced in looping the loop [Av.], or by skating on one edge only on a track that crosses itself: *v.t.* to make into or fasten with a loop: *v.i.* to make a loop. **loop the loop,** to make a plane describe a vertical circle [Av.]. (Origin unknown.)
loop, *n.* loop, part of a block of cast iron melted off for the forge or hammer [Metal.]. (Fr. *loupe*.)
looper, *n.* *loop*-er, a hook that loops; one who or that which loops. **looper-moth,** the geometer, the larvæ of which form a loop when crawling.
loophole, *n.* *loop*-hohl, a hole in a wall, ship's bulk-head, etc., through which small-arms may be discharged; a way or means of escape: *v.t.* to make such holes. (Low Ger. *lupen*, to peep.)
loopholed, *a.* *loop*-hohld, provided with one or more loopholes.
loop-line, *n.* a short line (railway, telegraph, etc.) running from and returning to the main line.
*__loose,__ *a.* loose, unbound; slack; not tight; not compact; not concise; not grammatical; vague; not strict; lax; slovenly; unconnected; having a flux from the bowels; unrestrained; licentious; containing unchaste language; free: *v.t.* loose, to unbind; to free from any fastening; to relax; to liberate; to free from obligation; to relieve; to undo; to remit; to absolve: *v.i.* to set sail. **at a loose end,** having nothing definite to do. **break loose,** to escape from confinement or restraint. **give loose to,** to give vent to; to let go. **let loose,** to set at liberty. **on the loose,** having a spree [Slang]. (Scand.).
loose, *ad.* loose, loosely. **fast and loose,** *see* **fast.**
loose-box, *n.* a stall in a stable in which the horse is not tied up.
loose-leaf, *a.* having each leaf removable and replaceable (of books, ledgers, etc.).
loosely, *ad.* *loose*-le, in a loose manner.
loosen, *v.t.* *loose*-en, to render loose; to render less dense; to free from restraint: *v.i.* to become loose; to become less tight or compact.
looseness, *n.* *loose*-ness, state of being loose.
loosestrife, *n.* *loose*-strife, either of the plants *Lysimachia vulgaris* (yellow) or *Lythrum salicaria* (red or purple).
loot, *n.* loot, plunder, esp. from a conquered city; booty: *v.i.* and *t.* to plunder or seek for loot; to pillage. (Hind.)
looter, *n.* *loot*-er, one who loots.
lop, *n.* lop, that which is lopped, or cut from trees: *v.t.* to shorten; to cut off the ends or the useless parts of, or trim by this means. (Origin not known.)
lop, *v.t.* lop, to let fall: *v.i.* to hang down. (Imit.)
lope, *v.i.* lope, to run with long easy strides. (O. Scand. *hlaupa*, leap.)
lop-eared, *a.* *lop*-eerd, with hanging ears.
lophobranchiate, *a.* loh-fo-*brang*-ke-at, having tufted gills like the sea-horses. (Gr. *lophos*, a crest, *branchia*, arm.)

lopper, *n.* *lop*-per, a trimmer of trees.
lopper, *v.i.* *lop*-per, to curdle, to turn sour (of milk): *v.t.* to turn to curds: *n.* a curdled state. (O. Scand. *hloup*, a coagulation.)
loppings, *n.pl.* *lop*-pingz, portions lopped or cut off; trimmings.
lopsided, *a.* lop-*sy*-ded, heavier on one side than the other.
loquacious, *a.* lo-*kway*-shus, talkative; noisy; blabbing. (L. *loquax*, from *loquor*, speak.)
loquaciously, *ad.* in a loquacious manner.
loquaciousness, *n.* lo-*kway*-shus-ness, loquacity.
loquacity, *n.* lo-*kwas*-e-te, the quality or habit of being loquacious; an instance of this; the gift of the gab.
loquat, *n.* *loh*-kwat, an Asiatic tree of the genus *Eriobotrya*, bearing a fruit about the size of a large gooseberry; the fruit. (Chin.)
loral, *a.* *law*-ral, pertaining to the lore, as of a bird [Anat. and Zool.].
lorate, *a.* *law*-rat, strap-shaped; ligulate.
lorcha, *n.* *lor*-ka, a Chinese vessel of European build, rigged like a junk. (Port.)
lord, *n.* lord, a master; a sovereign or ruler; a husband [Coll.]; the proprietor of a manor; a peer of the realm; a nobleman, esp. a baron; a title of honour given to certain sons of peers other than barons and viscounts; an honorary title bestowed on certain officials, as Lord Chancellor, Lord of the Admiralty, Lord of Appeal, and others; a title applied in general parlance to all ranks of the peerage below a duke: *v.t.* to invest with the dignities and privileges of a peer: *v.i.* to domineer; to rule with arbitrary or despotic sway. **House of Lords,** the upper legislative chamber in the parliament of Great Britain, composed of the lords spiritual and temporal. **Lord High Commissioner,** the representative of the sovereign at the General Assembly of the Church of Scotland. **Lord Lieutenant,** the principal official of a county, appointed by the sovereign originally to manage its military concerns. **Lord Mayor,** the chief magistrate of certain cities. **lord of misrule,** one formerly chosen to preside over the sports and revels of a family during certain holidays. **Lord Rector,** the head of certain Scottish Universities. **Lord's day,** Sunday. **lord spiritual,** an archbishop or bishop of the Church of England, esp. one sitting in the House of Lords. **Lord's supper,** the eucharist. **lord temporal,** a lay member of the House of Lords. **our Lord,** Jesus Christ. **the Lord,** the Supreme Being, also Jesus Christ. **lords and ladies,** cuckoo-pint or wake-robin, the wild arum, *Arum maculatum*. (A.S. *hlaford*, from *hlaf*, loaf, *weard*, to keep.)
lordliness, *n.* *lord*-le-ness, quality of being lordly; dignity; pride.
lordling, *n.* *lord*-ling, a little lord; a would-be lord.
lordly, *a.* *lord*-le, becoming or befitting a lord; haughty; imperious; overbearing: *ad.* proudly; imperiously.
lordolatry, *n.* lor-*dol*-a-tre, excessive deference paid to a peer or the peerage.
lordosis, *n.* lor-*doh*-sis, curvature of the bones, esp. anterior curvature of the spine [Anat.]. (Gr.)
Lord's, *n.* lordz, the headquarters of cricket and of the Marylebone Cricket Club (M.C.C.) in north-west London. (T. *Lord*, original owner of ground.)
lordship, *n.* *lord*-ship, a title of honour given to noblemen or persons in high authority; dominion; power; the territory of a lord; domain.
lore, *n.* lore, knowledge; learning; the body of traditional knowledge of a subject. (A.S. *lar.*)
lore, *n.* lore, the space between a bird's bill and its eye, or between a snake's eye and nostril. (Fr.)
lorette, *n.* lo-*ret*, a stylish Parisienne of the demi-monde; a courtesan. (Fr., from Notre Dame de *Lorette*, Paris.)
lorgnette, *n.* lor-*nyet*, a pair of eyeglasses on a handle; a small opera-glass. (Fr.)
lorica, *n.* lo-*ry*-ka, the cuirass of the ancient Romans; a carapace [Zool.]. (L. from *lorum*, a thong.)
loricate, *a.* *lo*-re-kat, having a lorica; naturally protected by plates or scales, etc. [Zool.]. (L. *loricatus*, clad in mail.)
lorication, *n.* lo-re-*kay*-shon, the state of being loricate; having a plate or crust for defence [Zool.].
lorikeet, *n.* lo-re-*keet*, a small arboreal lory of the Malay Archipelago.
loriner, *n.* *lo*-re-ner, a maker of bits and bridles.
loriot, *n.* *lo*-re-ot, the golden oriole. (Fr.)
loris, *n.* *lor*-ris, either of two slow-moving lemurs of Eastern India and the Malay Archipelago. (Fr.)
lorn, *a.* lorn, lost; undone; forsaken; forlorn. (A.S.)
lorry, *n.* *lo*-re, a long four-wheeled wagon without sides; a goods truck for road work.
lory, *n.* *lore*-re, any of several brilliant Australasian parrots having a brush tongue. (Malay.)
losable, *a.* *looz*-a-bl, that may be lost.
lose, *v.t.* looz, to cease to have; to be deprived of; not to gain; to fail to obtain; to possess no longer; to forfeit; to waste; to squander; to destroy; to cause to perish; to miss; to bewilder; to fail to see or find: *v.i.* to forfeit anything in contest; not to win; to decline; to fail. **lose oneself,** to be bewildered; to have the memory and reason suspended. **lose time,** *see* **time.** *p.* and *pp.* **lost.** (A.S. *leosan*, to lose.)
losel, *a.* *loz*-el, wasteful; slothful: *n.* a wasteful or worthless fellow. (A.S. *lēosan.*)
loser, *n.* *looz*-er, one who loses or does not win; a losing hazard [Billiards].
losing, *a.* *looz*-ing, bringing or causing loss. **losing hazard,** a hazard in which one's own ball is potted [Billiards].
***loss,** *n.* loss, failure to keep; privation; deprivation; failure to win; damage; ruin; defeat; waste; that which is lost. **at a loss,** puzzled; unable to determine. **bear a loss,** to sustain a loss without sinking under it. (A.S. *los.*)
lost, *a.* lost, that cannot be found; forfeited; wasted; perplexed; ruined; alienated; shipwrecked.
lot, *n.* lot, chance; destiny; that by which the fortune of one is determined; that which falls to one by fortune; a distinct portion or parcel of things (as at an auction) or of land; a quantity of things, persons, animals, etc.; a considerable quantity, a great deal [Coll.]; the studio and grounds of a producing unit [Cinema]: *v.t.* to allot; to catalogue. **a bad lot,** one of bad or dubious character. **cast lots,** to decide by a throw of the dice or in some similar way. **draw lots,** to determine an event by drawing one thing from a number whose marks are concealed from the drawer. (A.S. *hlot.*)
lota, *n.* *loh*-tah, a spheroidal brass or copper pot for drinking or cooking purpose [Anglo-Ind.] (Hind.).
loth, *a.* loath, loath; unwilling; reluctant.
Lothario, *n.* lo-*thar*-ne-oh, a libertine. (Character in Rowe's "The Fair Penitent," 1703.)
lotion, *n.* *lo*-shun, a fluid preparation for outward use [Med.]; drink [Slang]. (L. *lotio*, washing.)
lottery, *n.* *lot*-er-re, a distribution of prizes by chance; a mere chance. (M.E. *lot.*)
lotto, *n.* *lot*-to, a table game in which numbers are drawn from a bag and placed on cards having numbered spaces. (It.)
lotus, *n.* *loh*-tus, a fruit of ancient legend fabled to induce happy forgetfulness; either of the African water-lilies *Nymphæa lotus* (the sacred lotus of Egypt), or *Nelumbium speciosum*; a genus of leguminous plants including the bird's-foot trefoil, *L. corniculatus*; an ornament derived from the African lotus [Arch.]. **lotus eater,** one given to indolent enjoyment; an idle voluptuary. (L.)
***loud,** *a.* lowd, high-sounding; striking the ear with great force; noisy; clamorous; ostentatious; showy: *ad.* loudly. (A.S. *hlud.*)
loudish, *a.* *lowd*-ish, somewhat loud.
loudly, *ad.* *lowd*-le, in a loud manner.
loudness, *n.* *lowd*-ness, the quality of being loud.
loud-speaker, *n.* lowd-*speek*-er, an electrical appliance for magnifying sound, esp. in a radio receiver.
lough, *n.* lokh, a lake, or an arm of the sea (esp. in Ireland). (Ir. *loch.*)
louis-d'or, *n.* loo-e-*dore*, a French gold coin, now superseded, equivalent in different periods to about from 16*s.* 6*d.* to 19*s.* **louis heel,** an extra high curved heel for ladies' shoes. (Fr.)
lounge, *n.* lounj, the act of lounging; a kind of sofa: a place for lounging; a reception-room; a superior bar in a hotel, etc.: *v.i.* to spend time lazily; to move idly about; to recline at ease. **lounge-lizard,** *n.* a male adventurer frequenting lounges in expectation of illicit gain, esp. from women [Slang]. **lounge suit,** a man's suit for business or informal wear. (O.Fr. *longis*, a dullard.)

lounger, *n.* *lounj*-er, one who lounges; an idler.
loup, *v.i.* loop, to leap [Scots.]; to lope. (*lope.*)
loupgarou, *n.* *loo*-ga-roo, a werewolf.
lour, *v.i.* *lou*-er, to appear dark and gloomy; to frown; to threaten a storm: *n.* a sour or sullen look; gloominess.
loury, *a.* *lou*-er-re, cloudy; gloomy; threatening.
louse, *n.* louse (*pl.* **lice**), a wingless parasitic insect of the order Anoplura and genus *Pediculus.* (A.S. *lus.*)
louse, *v.t.* and *i.* louze, to clean from lice.
lousewort, *n.* *louse*-wurt, a plant of the genus *Pedicularis,* esp. the marsh red rattle.
lousily, *ad.* *louz*-e-le, in a mean, paltry manner.
lousiness, *n.* *louz*-e-ness, the state of being lousy.
lousy, *a.* *louz*-e, afflicted with lice; mean; low; contemptible; unpleasant.
lout, *n.* lout, a mean, awkward fellow; a bumpkin; a clown. (A.S. *lutan,* to stoop.)
loutish, *a.* *lout*-ish, awkward; clumsy; uncouth.
loutishly, *ad.* *lout*-ish-le, in a loutish manner.
loutishness, *n.* the quality of being loutish.
louver *or* **louvre,** *n.* *loo*-ver, an open turret or lantern on ancient roofs, for the escape of smoke; a louver board; a louvre window. **louver board,** one of a set of sloping boards fixed in an unglazed window opening to deflect falling rain. **louver window,** an opening, as in a belfry, fitted with louver boards. (O.Fr. *lover.*)
lovable, *a.* *luv*-a-bl, worthy of love; amiable.
lovage, *n.* *luv*-aj, name of various umbelliferous plants, esp. *Ligusticum scoticum.*
★**love,** *n.* luv, an affectionate devoted attachment, esp. that passionate all-absorbing form directed towards one of the opposite sex; strong affection and regard mingled with strong desire; the object beloved; a term of endearment; Cupid, the god of love; a scoring term signifying none [Tennis, etc.]: *v.i.* to be in love; to be tenderly attached: *v.t.* to like; to be pleased with; to regard with affection; to be in love with. (A.S. *lufu,* Sans. *lubh,* to desire.)
love-apple, *n.* the tomato.
love-bird, *n.* a small parakeet, so called from its affection to its mate.
love-child, *n.* an illegitimate child.
love-feast, *n.* the agape or service analogous to this; a banquet for common rejoicing.
love-in-a-mist, *n.* the fennel-flower.
love-in-idleness, *n.* heartsease, *Viola tricolor.*
loveknot, *n.* *luv*-not, a double knot with two interlacing bows.
Lovelace, *n.* *luv*-lace, a well-bred libertine. (Hero of Richardson's "Clarissa Harlowe," 1748.)
loveless, *a.* *luv*-less, void of love; not loved.
love-letter, *n.* a letter of courtship.
love-lies-bleeding, *n.* a species of amaranth.
lovelily, *ad.* *luv*-le-le, in a lovely manner.
loveliness, *n.* *luv*-le-ness, state or condition of being lovely; gentle beauty.
love-lock, *n.* a tress or curl worn on the forehead.
love-lorn, *a.* forsaken by one's love; jilted.
lovely, *a.* *luv*-le, such as to excite love or admiration; beautiful.
lovemaking, *n.* *luv*-make-ing, courtship.
loveman, *n.* *luv*-man, a name of goose-grass, *Galium aparine.*
lover, *n.* *luv*-er, one in love; one who loves; one fond of anything; a paramour.
lovesick, *a.* *luv*-sik, languishing with love.
loving, *a.* *luv*-ing, entertaining or expressing love for; affectionate.
loving-kindness, *n.* tender regard.
lovingly, *ad.* *luv*-ing-le, affectionately.
lovingness, *n.* *luv*-ing-ness, affection; kind regard.
★**low,** *a.* loh, not high; depressed below any given surface or place; depressed to the utmost; below the usual height; deep; not loud; grave; dejected; depressed or lacking in vigour; in a mean condition; abject; base; not exalted in thought or diction; vulgar; submissive; weak; moderate; cheap; low church; in poor circumstances; plain; simple: *ad.* not on high; cheaply; meanly; not loudly; near the present; near the equator; near the horizon (of heavenly bodies); in a state of subjection, backward civilization, or disgrace: *n.* that which is low, as a low level of price [Comm.], or an area of low pressure [Meteor.]. **low birth,** obscure or humble parentage. **low church,** that section of the Church of England which, as contrasted with the High Church party, lays particular stress on evangelical principles. **low comedy,** a comedy of an almost farcical character. **low gear,** the gear used for the lowest speed in motors and cycles. **low life,** life among the least cultured classes. **low Mass,** *see* **Mass. low pitch,** a low key or tone [Mus.]. **low Sunday,** the next Sunday after Easter. **low-water,** the lowest point of the ebb or receding tide; hence, **in low-water,** in difficulties (esp. financial). **low wine,** a liquor produced by the first distillation of alcohol. (Scand.)
low, *v.t.* loh, to bellow, as an ox: *n.* a moo. (A.S. *hlōwan.*)
low, *n.* loh, a mound. (A.S. *hlāw.*)
low-bred, *a.* ill-bred; born in humble circumstances.
low-brow, *n.* *loh*-brow, one of uncultured or non-intellectual tastes: *a.* having such tastes; suitable for such persons.
low-browed, *a.* loh-*broud,* having little forehead; beetling.
lowdown, *a.* *loh*-doun, mean; rascally [Coll.]. **the low-down,** information of a private or intimate nature [Slang].
lower, *v.t.* *loh*-er, to let down; to bring down; to humble; to diminish: *v.i.* to fall; to sink; to grow less.
lower, *v.i.* *lou*-er, to lour.
lower, *a.* *loh*-er, comparative of *low.* **lower case,** the case which contains the minuscules or small letters; small letters [Print.]. **Lower Chamber** or **House,** the second of two parliamentary chambers; the House of Commons. **lower deck,** the lowest deck of a ship where are usually the crew's quarters; the crew exclusive of officers [Naut.]. **Lower Empire,** the Byzantine Empire. **Lower School,** in English public schools, any class below the fifth form.
lowermost, *a.* *loh*-er-most, lowest.
lowery, *a.* *lou*-er-re, loury.
lowing, *a.* *loh*-ing, bellowing as an ox: *n.* the bellowing or cry of cattle.
lowland, *n.* *loh*-land, level or low land: *pl.* (*cap.*) the less mountainous parts of S. and S.E. Scotland: *a.* pertaining to, or of, a lowland or the Lowlands.
lowlander, *n.* *loh*-land-er, a native or resident of lowlands.
lowlily, *ad.* *loh*-le-le, in a lowly manner.
lowliness, *n.* state of being lowly; humility.
lowly, *a.* *loh*-le, humble; modest; meek; low; not elevated in place: *ad.* lowlily.
low-minded, *a.* mean; base.
low-necked, *a.* *loh*-nekt, cut low in the neck (of dresses, etc.); décolleté.
lowness, *n.* *loh*-ness, depression; dejection.
low-pressure, *a.* *loh*-*presh*-ur, said of steam as exerting, and of steam engines as employing, a pressure on the piston of under 50 lb. to the square inch: *n.* a small degree of expansive force.
low-spirited, *a.* dejected; depressed in spirits.
loxa-bark, *n.* *lok*-sa-bark, the bark of *Cinchona officinalis,* an important source of quinine. (*Loja,* province of Ecuador.)
loxodromic, *a.* lok-so-*drom*-ik, pertaining to oblique sailing: *pl.* the art of oblique sailing by the rhumb line. **loxodromic curve,** a line which always makes an equal angle with every meridian; the rhumb line. (Gr. *loxos,* oblique, *dromos,* a course).
loxotomy, *n.* lok-*sot*-o-me, amputation by cutting obliquely through the limb [Surg.]. (Gr. *loxos,* oblique, *tomē,* a cutting.)
loy, *n.* loy, a long narrow spade or digger [Ireland and U.S.A.]. (Ir. *laighe.*)
loyal, *a.* *loy*-al, faithful in allegiance, esp. to king or country or those over one; true to plighted faith or duty: *n.* one remaining loyal in a time of troubles. (Fr.)
loyalist, *n.* *loy*-al-ist, one who maintains his allegiance to his prince or who is true to his country.
loyally, *ad.* *loy*-al-le, in a loyal manner.
loyalty, *n.* *loy*-al-te, state of being loyal; fidelity to a trust, a principle, a superior, etc.; devotion to a prince or sovereign or to a husband or lover.
lozenge, *n.* *loz*-enj, a figure with four equal sides, having two acute and two obtuse angles; a rhomb; anything similarly shaped; a diamond-shaped figure, or a square set diagonally [Her.]; a medicament or sweetmeat of tablet shape to be dissolved by sucking. (Fr.)

lozengy, *a. loz*-en-je, divided into lozenge-shaped areas (of the field, etc.) [Her.].
lubber, *n. lub*-ber, a heavy, clumsy fellow; a sturdy, lazy fellow; a bad seaman. (*lob.*)
lubberly, *a.* and *ad. lub*-ber-le, like a lubber; bulky and clumsy.
lubra, *n. loo*-brah, an aboriginal Australian woman; a gin. (Native Tasmanian.)
lubric, *a. lew*-brik, slippery. (L. *lubricus*, slippery.)
lubricant, *a. lew*-bre-kant, lubricating: *n.* that which lubricates. (L.)
lubricate, *v.t. lew*-bre-kate, to make smooth or slippery; to lessen friction, esp. with oil or grease. (L. *lubricatus*, made slippery.)
lubrication, *n. lew*-bre-*kay*-shon, the act of lubricating; state of being lubricated.
lubricator, *n. lew*-bre-kay-tor, one who or that which lubricates; an oil-cup or other contrivance for supplying grease.
lubricity, *n.* lew-*bris*-e-te, smoothness; slipperiness; instability; lasciviousness; lewdness.
lubricous, *a. lew*-bre-kus, slippery; having a slippery surface [Bot.]; unstable.
Lucan, *a. loo*-kan, pertaining to St. Luke or his writings.
lucarne, *n. lew*-karn, a dormer window; a window in a spire. (Fr.)
luce, *n.* lewce, a pike, *Esox lucius*, when full grown. (L. *lucius.*)
lucency, *n. lew*-sen-se, brilliancy; the quality of being lucent.
lucent, *a. lew*-sent, bright; shining; clear. [L. *lucens*, shining.)
lucernal, *a.* lew-*ser*-nal, pertaining to a lamp. **lucernal microscope,** a microscope in which the object is illuminated by means of a lamp. (L. *lucerna*, lamp.)
lucerne, *n.* lew-*sern*, the purple medick, a plant cultivated for fodder, *Medicago sativa.* (Fr.)
lucid, *a. lew*-sid, shining; bright; shedding light; clear; transparent; radiant with reason; easily understood. **lucid interval,** a sane period (in insanity). (L. *lucidus*, bright.)
lucidity, *n.* lew-*sid*-e-te, lucidness.
lucidly, *ad. lew*-sid-le, in a lucid manner.
lucidness, *n.* state or quality of being lucid.
Lucifer, *n. lew*-se-fer, the planet Venus, as morning star; Satan, before his fall; (*l.c.*) a match tipped with some combustible substance, and ignited by friction; a Mexican humming-bird, *Calothorax lucifer.* (L., light bringer, from *lux*, and *fero*, bring.)
Luciferian, *a. lew*-se-feer-re-an, pertaining to Lucifer.
luciferous, *a.* lew-*sif*-er-rus, giving or affording light or mental illumination.
lucimeter, *n.* lew-*sim*-e-ter, a photometer. (L. *lux*, and Gr. *metron*, measure.)
luck, *n.* luk, chance; fortune, good or bad; good fortune; some object conferring good fortune on its possessor. (Dut. *luk.*)
luckily, *ad. luk*-e-le, fortunately.
luckiness, *n. luk*-e-ness, the state of being lucky.
luckless, *a.* unfortunate; without good luck.
lucklessly, *ad. luk*-less-le, in a luckless manner.
luck-penny, *n.* a small sum returned to the buyer by one receiving money under a contract or bargain.
lucky, *a. luk*-e, characterized by good luck; fortuitously meeting with success; fortunate; happy by chance; auspicious. **to touch lucky,** to have a bit of good luck [Slang].
lucrative, *a. lew*-kra-tiv, bringing gain; profitable. (Fr. *lucratif.*)
lucratively, *ad.* in a lucrative manner.
lucre, *n. lew*-ker, gain, specially base gain; gain in money; profit. (Fr.)
lucubrate, *v.i. lew*-kew-brate, to work or study by candle-light or at night: *v.t.* to produce by lucubration. (L. *lucubratus*, worked by lamp-light.)
lucubration, *n. lew*-kew-*bray*-shon, study by candle-light; a work so produced, or as the fruit of study.
luculent, *a. lew*-kew-lent, lucid; clear; manifest; transparent. (L. *luculentus.*)
Lucullian, *a.* loo-*kul*-e-an, relating to or like Lucullus and his sumptuous feasts.
lucullite, *n.* lew-*kul*-ite, an ornamental black variety of limestone. (Named from the consul, L. *Lucullus.*)
Luddite, *n. lud*-ite, a member of a band of unemployed workers who, about 1811–16, destroyed machinery, burned factories, etc. (*Ludd*, name of a leader.)
ludicrous, *a. lew*-de-krus, adapted to raise laughter or ridicule; laughable. (L. *ludicrus.*)
ludicrously, *ad.* in a ludicrous manner.
ludicrousness, *n. lew*-de-krus-ness, the quality of being ludicrous.
ludlamite, *n. lud*-lam-ite, a brilliant green hydrous ferrous phosphate [Min.] (H. *Ludlam*, Engl. mineralogist, *d.* 1880.)
ludo, *n. lew*-do, a game played on a board with counters. (L. *ludo*, play.)
ludwigite, *n. lud*-wig-ite, a blackish-green fibrous borate of magnesium and iron [Min.]. (E. *Ludwig*, Austrian mineralogist.)
lues, *n. lew*-eez, the plague or similar disease; syphilis. (L.)
luetic, *a.* lew-*et*-ik, pertaining to or suffering from lues; syphilitic.
luff, *n.* luf, the weather-gauge; towards the wind; the act of sailing close to the wind; the weather leech of a sail: *v.i.* to sail nearer the wind [Naut.]. (Dut. *loef.*)
luffer, *n. luf*-fer, a louver.
luff-tackle, *n.* luf-*tak*-kl, a large tackle, composed of a double and single block [Naut.].
Luftwaffe, *n. looft*-vof-er, the German Air Force. (Ger. *Luft*, air, *Waffe*, arm or weapon.)
lug, *v.t.* lug, to drag; to pull with difficulty: *v.i.* to drag; to move heavily. (Swed. *lugga*, to pull by the hair.)
lug, *n.* lug, a thing which projects, as the ear; the handle of a jug; a loose-hanging flap. (Perhaps Swed. *lug*, the forelock.)
lug, *n.* lug, a lugworm.
luggage, *n. lug*-aj, baggage, esp. of a traveller; anything lugged, or cumbersome and heavy to be carried.
lugger, *n. lug*-ger, a small vessel carrying two or three masts with a running bowsprit and lugsails.
lug-mark, *n.* a mark cut in the ear of an animal to identify it. (*lug*, ear.)
lugsail, *n. lug*-sale, a sail, set fore-and-aft, bent upon a yard that hangs obliquely to the mast.
lugubrious, *a.* lew-*gew*-bre-us, mournful; funeral. (L. *lugubris.*)
lugubriously, *ad.* in a lugubrious manner.
lugworm, *n. lug*-wurm, a lobworm, a marine worm burrowing in sand.
Lukan, *a. loo*-kan, Lucan.
lukewarm, *a. lewk*-wawrm, moderately warm; tepid; not zealous; indifferent. (M.E. *luke*, perhaps from Dut. *leuk*, warm, and *warm.*)
lukewarmly, *ad.* in a lukewarm manner.
lukewarmness, *n.* state of being lukewarm.
lull, *n.* lul, that which soothes; a calm spell after tumult; a lulled condition: *v.t.* to quiet; to compose; to rest; to soothe: *v.i.* to subside; to become calm. (Swed. *lulla*, to sing to sleep.)
lullaby, *n. lul*-a-by, a song to lull a child to sleep: *v.t.* to sing to sleep.
lumbaginous, *a.* lum-*bay*-je-nus, characteristic of or pertaining to lumbago.
lumbago, *n.* lum-*bay*-go, a rheumatic affection of the muscles about the lumbar region [Med.]. (L.)
lumbar, *a. lum*-bar, pertaining to or situated near the loins. **lumbar region,** the hinder part of the body, from the false ribs down to the haunch bone. (L. *lumbaris*, from *lumbus*, loin.)
lumber, *n. lum*-ber, anything useless and cumbersome; junk or refuse; timber sawn or split for use: *v.t.* to heap together; to fill with lumber; to encumber; to cut and dress timber. **lumber dealer,** a timber-merchant. (*Lombard.*)
lumber, *v.i. lum*-ber, to move heavily or clumsily; to make a rumbling noise. (Scand. *lomra*, rumble.)
lumberer, *n. lum*-ber-rer, one engaged in cutting and getting lumber from the forest.
lumbering, *n. lum*-ber-ring, the occupation of a lumberer.
lumbering, *a. lum*-ber-ring, moving in a clumsy, awkward manner; heavy.
lumberman, *n. lum*-ber-man, a lumberer; a timber merchant.
lumber-room, *n.* a place for the reception of useless lumber.
lumbrical, *a. lum*-bre-kal, pertaining to or resembling a worm; vermiform: *n.* a muscle of the

fingers or toes, so named from its resembling a worm. (L. *lumbricus*, a worm.)
lumbriciform, *a.* lum-*bris*-e-form, vermiform; in shape like a worm.
lumbricine, *a.* *lum*-bre-syn, pertaining to the earthworms.
lumen, *n.* *lew*-men, a unit of luminosity; the amount of luminous flux emitted by an ideal source having in all directions a luminous intensity of one candle-power; the opening or cavity of a passage-way or cell [Anat. and Bot.].
luminant, *a.* *lew*-me-nant, luminous: *n.* an illuminant.
luminary, *n.* *lew*-me-na-re, a body that gives light, especially a heavenly body; one distinguished for enlightening others. (Fr. *luminaire.*)
luminescence, *n.* lew-me-*nes*-ence, any emission of light other than that produced by incandescence.
luminescent, *a.* *lew*-me-*nes*-ent, giving out light without being hot.
luminiferous, *a.* *lew*-me-*nif*-er-rus, producing or transmitting light. (L. *lumen*, light, *fero*, bring.)
luminism, *n.* *lew*-me-nizm, a form of impressionism in which representation of lighting effects is of prime importance [Painting].
luminosity, *n.* *lew*-me-*nos*-e-te, luminousness.
luminous, *a.* *lew*-me-nus, emitting light; bright; clear; lucid; perspicuous. **luminous flux,** the rate of transference of light. (L. *luminosus*, radiant.)
luminously, *ad.* in a luminous manner.
luminousness, *n.* quality of being luminous.
★**lump,** *n.* lump, a small mass of matter of no definite shape; a confused heap; a bump or swelling; a dullard: *v.t.* to throw into a mass; to take in the gross; to put up with: *v.i.* to collect in lumps; to lumber or move clumsily. **in the lump,** in gross. **lump sugar,** loaf sugar broken into small cubes. **lump sum,** complete amount (esp. as opposed to instalments). (Scand.)
lumper, *n.* *lump*-er, one who loads or unloads ships; a contractor in a small way.
lumpfish, *n.* *lump*-fish, a heavily built suctorial sea-fish of the genus *Cyclopterus.*
lumping, *a.* *lump*-ing, bulky; heavy; plentiful.
lumpish, *a.* *lump*-ish, like a lump; heavy; dull.
lumpishly, *ad.* *lump*-ish-le, in a lumpish manner.
lumpishness, *n.* the quality of being lumpish.
lumpsucker, *n.* *lump*-suk-er, the lumpfish.
lumpy, *a.* *lum*-pe, full of lumps.
lunacy, *n.* *lew*-na-se, a species of insanity, often with lucid intervals, formerly supposed to depend upon the phases of the moon; great folly; senselessness. (L. *luna*, the moon.)
lunar, *a.* *lew*-nar, pertaining to the moon; measured by the revolutions of the moon; resembling or influenced by the moon. **lunar caustic,** nitrate of silver. **lunar cycle,** the metonic cycle. **lunar month,** the time in which the moon completes a revolution about the earth (22 d. 12¾ hr.) **lunar observation,** an observation of the moon's distance from a star to find the longitude. **lunar rainbow,** a faint rainbow occasioned by the refraction of the light of the moon. **lunar year,** the period of 12 synodic lunar months (354 d. 10 hr. 8 min.). (L. *lunaris.*)
lunarian, *n.* lew-*nare*-re-an, one who studies the moon; a supposed inhabitant of the moon.
lunarium, *n.* lew-*nare*-re-um, a mechanism representing the motions and phases of the moon.
lunary, *a.* *lew*-na-re, lunar: *n.* the moonwort; the cruciferous plant honesty.
lunate, *a.* *lew*-nat, formed like a half-moon. (L. *lunatus*, shaped like a crescent.)
lunatic, *a.* *lew*-na-tik, affected by lunacy; crazy: *n.* a person affected by insanity. (Fr. *lunatique.*)
lunation, *n.* lew-*nay*-shon, a lunar month, the period from one new moon to the next.
lunch, *n.* lunch, luncheon: *v.i.* to take lunch.
luncheon, *n.* *lunch*-un, a repast between breakfast and dinner. (*lump* and *nuncheon.*)
lune, *n.* lewn, any crescent-shaped figure or object. (Fr.)
lunette, *n.* lew-*net*, an advanced work composed of two faces and two flanks [Fort.]; a horse-shoe docked of its extremities [Farriery]; a blinker for a vicious horse; an aperture for the admission of light into a concave ceiling, also a semicircular space or panel [Arch.]; a watch-glass flattened at the centre; a spectacle lens; the hole in a guillotine for the victim's neck. (Fr.)
lung, *n.* lung, the respiratory organ in an air-breathing animal; an open space in or near a city. **coal lung,** pneumoconiosis due to inhalation of coal-dust. **iron lung,** a respirator for the artificial maintenance of breathing, esp. in cases of infantile paralysis. (A.S. *lungen.*)
lunge, *n.* lunj, a sudden thrust, esp. with a sword; a plunge: *v.i.* to make a lunge; to strike from the shoulder [Boxing]. (*allonge.*)
lunge, *v.t.* lunj, to train or exercise a horse at the end of a long rope or rein: *n.* the rope used for this. (Fr. *longe.*)
lunged, *a.* lungd, having lungs.
lungfish, *n.* *lung*-fish, any fish of the order Dipnoi, in which the air-bladder is elongated and performs the function of a lung.
lung-grown, *a.* having lungs that adhere to the pleura [Med.].
lungless, *a.* *lung*-less, having no lungs.
lungwort, *n.* *lung*-wurt, a plant of the genus *Pulmonaria*, formerly a specific for disorders of the lungs; a lichen growing on tree-trunks.
luniform, *a.* *lew*-ne-form, crescent-shaped; lunate.
lunisolar, *a.* *lew*-ne-*soh*-lar, pertaining to both sun and moon, or compounded of their revolutions. **lunisolar period** or **year,** the period of 532 years, at the end of which the series of eclipses, new moons, etc., recur on the same day of the year as in the previous period. (L. *luna*, the moon, *sol*, the sun.)
lunkah, *n.* *lung*-kah, a strong Indian cheroot. (Hind.)
lunt, *n.* lunt, a fuse or slow-match; smoke: *v.t.* to light; to kindle. (Dut. *lont*, a match.)
lunula, *n.* *lew*-new-la (*pl.* **lunulæ**), a small luniform ornament; a crescent-shaped organ or mark [Anat. and Bot.]. (L., a small moon.)
lunular, *a.* *lew*-new-lar, lunulate.
lunulate, *a.* *lew*-new-lat, like the new moon; shaped like a small crescent [Bot.]; marked with lunulæ.
lunule, *n.* *lew*-newl, a lunula; the whitish mark at the base of a finger-nail.
lunulet, *n.* *lew*-new-let, a semi-circular spot on insects, of a different colour from the rest [Entom.].
Lupercalia, *n.pl.* lew-per-*kay*-le-a, an ancient festival (Feb. 15) among the Romans, originally a purification ceremony and later connected with the legend of Romulus and Remus. (L. *Lupercus*, the protecting deity of shepherds.)
lupine, *a.* *lew*-pin, pertaining to or resembling the wolf. (L. *lupus*, a wolf.)
lupine, *n.* *lew*-pin, a leguminous fodder and garden plant with spikes of coloured flowers. (Fr., from L. *lupus.*)
lupinine, *n.* *lew*-pin-ine, a slightly poisonous alkaloid extracted from the leaves of certain lupines.
lupinosis, *n.* lew-pe-*noh*-sis, a disease among cattle caused by eating certain lupines.
lupoid, *a.* *loo*-poyd, resembling lupus [Med.].
lupous, *a.* *loo*-pus, affected with or pertaining to lupus; lupoid [Med.].
lupulin, *n.* *lew*-pew-lin, the bitter principle of hops. (Med. L. *lupulus*, from L. *lupus*, hop-plant.)
lupus, *n.* *loo*-pus, a tuberculous skin disease occurring chiefly on the face. (L., wolf.)
lurch, *n.* lurch, a sudden roll of a ship to one side [Naut.]; unsteadiness, esp. in walking: *v.i.* to lie in ambush; to lurk; to shift; to play tricks; to roll or pitch suddenly to one side, as a ship in a heavy sea. (*lurk.*)
lurch, *n.* lurch, a losing position in the game of cribbage. **leave in the lurch,** to leave in a difficult situation. (O.Fr. *lourche.*)
lurcher, *n.* *lurch*-er, one who lurks, esp. lies in wait to ensnare or steal; a breed of dog, said to be a cross between greyhound and collie.
lure, *n.* lewr, an enticement; a bait: *v.t.* to entice; to attract. (O.Fr. *loirre*, a lure to recall a hawk.)
lurid, *a.* *lewr*-rid, pale yellow; ghastly pale; unearthly; wan; gloomy; sensational. (L. *luridus.*)
lurk, *v.i.* lurk, to lie in wait; to lie concealed. (Origin unknown.)
lurker, *n.* *lurk*-er, one who lurks.
lurry, *n.* *lu*-re, an inarticulate utterance; patter; a confused throng.
Lusatian, *a.* lew-*say*-she-an, pertaining to Lusatia

a region of mediæval N.E. Germany, or to its Wendish people: *n.* an inhabitant of Lusatia.
luscious, *a.* *lush*-us, very sweet; delicious; rich in flavour; fulsome. (Fr.)
lusciously, *ad.* *lush*-us-le, in a luscious manner.
lusciousness, *n.* the state of being luscious.
lush, *a.* lush, luxuriant; juicy; luscious; *n.* liquor; drink [Slang]: *v.t.* and *i.* to drink or ply with drink [Slang].
lushy, *a.* *lush*-e, lush; intoxicated [Slang].
Lusitanian, *a.* *lew*-se-*tay*-ne-an, pertaining to Lusitania, an ancient Hispanic province, or to Portugal, its modern equivalent: *n.* an inhabitant of Lusitania or of Portugal.
lusk, *a.* lusk, sluggish; listless; inert.
lust, *n.* lust, eagerness to possess or enjoy; concupiscence; depraved sexual desire: *v.i.* to desire eagerly; to have irregular, inordinate, or extravagant sexual desire. (A.S. *lust*, pleasure.)
lustful, *a.* *lust*-ful, having lust; inciting to lust; lascivious.
lustfully, *ad.* *lust*-ful-le, in a lustful manner.
lustfulness, *n.* the state of being lustful.
lustihood, *n.* *lus*-te-hood, the quality of being lusty; vigour of body.
lustily, *ad.* *lus*-te-le, in a lusty manner; vigorously.
lustiness, *n.* the state of being lusty; robustness.
lustral, *a.* *lus*-tral, pertaining to or used in purification; pertaining to a lustrum.
lustrate, *v.i.* *lus*-trate, to purify ceremoniously.
lustration, *n.* lus-*tray*-shon, the act of purifying; ceremonial purification, esp. by sacrifice from defilement by crime. (L. *lustratus*, purified.)
lustrative, *a.* *lus*-tra-tiv, pertaining to lustration.
lustre, *n.* *lus*-ter, brightness; splendour; distinction; renown; the quality and intensity of light reflected from mineral surfaces; a pendant of cut glass; a lustrous fabric; metallic glass applied to pottery. (Fr.)
lustre, *n.* *lus*-ter, a lustrum.
lustreless, *a.* *lus*-ter-less, destitute of lustre.
lustring, *n.* *lus*-tring, an obsolete make of species of glossy silk fabric. (Fr. *lustrine*.)
lustrous, *a.* *lus*-trus, bright; shining; luminous.
lustrously, *ad.* in a lustrous manner.
lustrum, *n.* *lus*-trum, a period of five years; originally, a sacrificial purification of the Roman people every five years. (L., a purification.)
lustwort, *n.* *lust*-wurt, the sundew.
lusty, *a.* *lus*-te, full of life and vigour; robust.
lusus, *n.* *lew*-sus, an exception; a sport; a freak. (L. *lusus naturæ*, a freak of nature.)
lutanist, *n.* *lew*-tan-ist, one who plays on the lute.
lute, *n.* lewt, a stringed instrument of music like the guitar. (O.Fr. *lut*.)
lute, *n.* lewt, a composition of clay, or other tenacious substance, for making vessels air-tight, or for coating and protecting them when exposed to fire: *v.t.* to close or coat with lute. (O.Fr. *lut*, from L. *lutum*, mud.)
lutecium, loo-*tee*-she-um, an element of the rare-earth group, occurring in gadolinite, etc., and discovered in 1907.
lutein, *n.* *loo*-te-in, a yellowish pigment found in the yolk of eggs, butter, etc. (L. *luteous*, yellow.)
luteolin, *n.* *loo*-te-o-lin, a yellow colouring matter found in dyer's weed, *Reseda luteola*. (Fr. *lutéoline*.)
luteolous, *a.* loo-*tee*-o-lus, yellowish [Bot. and Zool.].
luteous, *a.* *lew*-te-us, of a brownish-yellow or clay colour. (L. *luteus*, yellow.)
lutescent, *a.* lew-*tes*-ent, tending towards yellow.
lutestring, *n.* *lewt*-string, a string for a lute; a glossy silk fabric; lustring. (Fr. *lustrine*.)
Lutetian, *a.* loo-*tee*-shan, pertaining to Paris. (L. *Lutetia*, ancient name of Paris.)
Lutheran, *a.* *loo*-ther-an, pertaining to Luther, his doctrine, or his Church: *n.* a disciple or follower of Luther; a member of the Lutheran Church. (Martin *Luther*, Ger. Protestant reformer, *d.* 1546.)
Lutheranism, *n.* *lew*-ther-an-izm, the principles of Luther, or the Lutherans.
luthern, *n.* *lew*-thern, a dormer-window.
luting, *n.* *lew*-ting, lute, or any material with which to lute; the application of lute.
lutist, *n.* *lew*-tist, one who plays on the lute.
lutose, *a.* *lew*-tose, miry; covered with clay.
lutrine, *a.* *lew*-trine, resembling or pertaining to the otter. (L.)
lux, *n.* luks, the unit of light power, equal to 1 lumen per sq. metre. (L., light.)
luxate, *v.t.* *luk*-sate, to put out of joint; to displace (L. *luxatus*, displaced.)
luxation, *n.* luk-*say*-shon, dislocation.
luxuriance, *n.* lug-*zewr*-re-ance, state or quality of being luxuriant; vigorous or excessive growth; exuberance.
luxuriancy, *n.* lug-*zewr*-re-an-se, luxuriance.
luxuriant, *a.* lug-*zewr*-re-ant, exuberant in growth; abundant; superfluous in abundance; florid in style; rank. (L. *luxurians*, abounding.)
luxuriantly, *ad.* in a luxuriant manner.
luxuriate, *v.i.* lug-*zewr*-re-ate, to grow exuberantly; to feed or live luxuriously; to expatiate with delight. (L. *luxuriatus*.)
luxurious, *a.* lug-*zewr*-re-us, indulging in luxury; administering to luxury; furnished with luxuries; softening by luxury.
luxuriously, *ad.* in a luxurious manner.
luxuriousness, *n.* lug-*zewr*-re-us-ness, the state or quality of being luxurious.
luxury, *n.* *luk*-shu-re, the indulgence of dainty and expensive pleasures; anything delightful, especially to appetite; a dainty. (O.Fr. *luxurie*.)
lyam, *n.* *ly*-am, a leash for holding a hound. (O.Fr. *liem*.)
lyam-hound, *n.* a dog used in hunting the wild boar; a bloodhound. (*lyam* and *hound*.)
lycanthrope, *n.* *ly*-kan-thrope, one affected with lycanthropy; a werewolf.
lycanthropy, *n.* ly-*kan*-thro-pe, a species of insanity in which the patient imagines himself to be a wolf or other animal. (Gr. *lykos*, a wolf, *anthropos*, a man.)
lyceum, *n.* ly-*see*-um, a place appropriated to instruction by lectures; an association for literary improvement; a French secondary school (*lycée*). (L.; the gymnasium at Athens where Aristotle taught.)
lychgate, *n.* *litch*-gate, a lichgate.
Lychnis, *n.* *lik*-nis, the genus of plants comprising the campions, ragged robin, etc. (Gr.)
lychnoscope, *n.* *lik*-no-skope, a low side window in a church, formerly supposed to afford lepers sight of the altar lamps. (Gr. *lychnos*, lamp, and *-scope*.)
Lycoperdon, *n.* *ly*-ko-*per*-don, a genus of puff-ball fungi, some of which are edible. (Gr. *lykos*, wolf, *perdesthai*, to break wind.)
lycopod, *n.* *ly*-ko-pod, any species of lycopodium.
lycopodium, *n.* *ly*-ko-*poh*-de-um, a club-moss; a yellow powder in the spores of this, used in surgery, etc. (Gr. *lykos*, and *pous*, a foot.)
lyddite, *n.* *lid*-ite, a high explosive used as a bursting charge for shells and consisting chiefly of picric acid. (First tested at *Lydd* in Kent.)
Lydian, *a.* *lid*-e-an, soft, effeminate. **Lydian stone,** a hard black slate with flat-conchoidal fracture; touchstone. (*Lydia*, in Asia Minor, famed for the luxury of its ancient kings.)
lye, *n.* ly, an alkaline solution, esp. one consisting of dissolved potash; a detergent. (A.S. *leah*.)
lygon, *n.* *ly*-gon, the hybrid offspring of a lion and a tigress.
lying, *a.* *ly*-ing, prostrate; the state or act of being recumbent. **low-lying,** situated at a low level.
lying, *a.* *ly*-ing, wilfully deceiving.
lying-in, *n.* *ly*-ing-*in*, childbirth.
lyke-wake, *n.* *like*-wake, lich-wake.
lyme-grass, *n.* *lime*-grahs, the grass, *Elymus arenarius*, used for binding shifting sand.
lymph, *n.* limf, a colourless fluid in animal bodies [Phys.]; morbid exudation from a sore, etc.; any morbid matter used in vaccination or inoculation [Med.]. (L. *lympha*, pure, spring water.)
lymphad, *n.* *lim*-fad, a one-masted galley forming a charge in certain Scottish arms [Her.]. (Gael. *longfhada*.)
lymphadenomatous, *a.* *lim*-fad-e-*noh*-ma-tus, containing or consisting of an abnormal development of lymphoid tissue [Path.].
lymphangitis, *n.* lim-fan-*jy*-tis, inflammation of the lymphatics.
lymphatic, *a.* lim-*fat*-ik, pertaining to, conveying, or secreting lymph; flabby; phlegmatic: *n.pl.* the vessels absorbing or conveying lymph [Anat.]
lymphocyte, *n.* *lim*-fo-syt, one of the colourless cells, resembling the leucocytes, present in lymph.
lymphoid, *a.* *lim*-foyd, pertaining to or resembling lymph or the tissue of the lymph glands.

lymphy, *a.* *lim*-fe, containing or resembling lymph.
lyncean, *a.* *lin*-se-an, pertaining to the lynx; lynx-eyed. (Gr. *lynkeios.*)
lynch, *v.t.* linch, to punish without the form of law, as by an American mob. **lynch law,** a summary punishment illegally inflicted by private individuals. (Charles *Lynch*, *d.* 1796, a Virginian who used such methods during the American War of Independence.)
lyncher, *n.* *lin*-cher, one who lynches.
lynchet, *n.* *lin*-chet, a linchet.
lynx, *n.* links, a feline carnivore with tufted ears, proverbial for its acuteness of vision; the dressed skin of this. **lynx-eyed,** *a.* keen of vision. (L. and Gr.)
Lyon, *n.* *ly*-on, the chief Scottish herald, known as Lord Lyon, and Lyon King of Arms. (From Scottish lion of the royal arms.)
Lyra, *n.* *lyr*-ra, the northern constellation, the lyre, in which is the bright star Vega.
Lyraid, *n.* *lyr*-ra-id, a Lyrid.
lyrate, *a.* *lyr*-rat, lyre-shaped [Bot.].
lyre, *n.* lyr, an early form of harp; a stringed instrument of music, used by the ancients as an accompaniment to poetry; the constellation Lyra. **lyre bird,** an Australian bird of the genus *Menura*, with a lyre-shaped tail. **lyre tree,** the tulip tree, *Liriodendron tulipiferum*, from its lyrate leaf. (L. *lyra.*)
lyric, *a.* *lyr*-ik, pertaining to the lyre; fit to be sung to the lyre; appropriate for singing; composing lyric poetry: *n.* an example of lyric poetry: (*pl.*) verses in the lyric style. **lyric poetry,** that kind of poetry in which the poet sympathetically sings of his own thoughts and emotions. (L. *lyricus.*)
lyrical, *a.* *li*-re-kal, lyric.
lyricism, *n.* *li*-re-sizm, quality of being lyrical; a lyric composition.
Lyrid, *n.* *lyr*-rid, one of the meteors that appear to start from the constellation Lyra.
lyrist, *n.* *lyr*-rist, a writer of lyrics; a poet; a musician who plays on the lyre.
lysis, *n.* *ly*-sis, the gradual abatement of an acute disease. (Gr.)
lysol, *n.* *ly*-sol, the trade name of a special mixture of cresole and oil, used for disinfecting. (Gr.)
lyssa, *n.* *lis*-sa, hydrophobia; canine madness. (Gr., madness.)
lyssophobia, *n.* lis-so-*foh*-be-a, morbid dread of rabies. (*lyssa* and *-phobia.*)
lythe, *n.* lythe, the pollack. (Scots.)
lytta, *n.* *lit*-a, the worm, a worm-like structure lying longitudinally beneath the tongue of dogs and certain other carnivores, removal of which was supposed to prevent madness. (Gr. *lyssa*, madness.)

M

M, em, thirteenth letter of the English alphabet, a labial nasal of uniform sound (as in *maim, emerge*), except that it is occasionally silent before *n* (as in *mnemonics*), and that as a final in certain words of Greek origin (*logarithm, chasm, microcosm*, etc.) it has a syllabic value.
ma, *n.* mah, mother; a contraction of mamma.
ma'am, *n.* mam, a contraction of madam; when used in addressing the Queen or a royal princess, pronounced "mahm."
maar, *n.* mahr, a crater formed in a volcano by a gaseous explosion. (Ger.)
Mab, *n.* mab, the queen of the fairies.
macabre, *a.* ma-*kahbr*, gruesomely grotesque, as a *danse macabre*, or dance of death. (Fr.)
macaco, *n.* ma-*kay*-ko, applied to several lemurs, macaques, and S. American monkeys. **macaco wood,** wood of the Brazilian shrub, *Tococa guianensis*. **macaco worm,** the larva of the S. American bot-fly, *Dermatobia noxialis*, parasitic on man and monkeys.
macadam, *n.* ma-*kad*-am, small broken granite for forming a smooth, hard surface to roadways; a surface so made. (Inventor's name.)
macadamize, *v.t.* ma-*kad*-a-mize, to make or cover a roadway with macadam.
macaque, *n.* ma-*kahk*, any of several Asiatic monkeys of the genus *Macacus*. (Fr., from Port.)
macarize, *v.t. mak*-a-rize, to call down blessings on. (Gr.)
macaroni, *n.* mak-a-*roh*-ne, the dough of the flour of a hard glutinous wheat formed into long slender tubes and other shapes; a fop of the later 18th cent. (It.)
macaronic, *a.* mak-a-*ron*-ik, consisting of a mixture or jumble of incongruous words, as of modern words Latinized, or Latin words modernized: *n.* a jumble; macaronic verse.
macaroon, *n.* mak-a-*roon*, a small cake, composed chiefly of white of egg, almonds, and sugar. (Fr. *macaron*.)
macartney, *n.* ma-*kart*-ne, a crested fire-back pheasant of the genus *Euplocamus*, described by Lord Macartney, envoy to China, 1792.
macassar, *n.* ma-*kas*-sar, an oil for the hair, expressed from various seeds and berries and originally imported from Macassar in Celebes.
macaw, *n.* ma-*kaw*, a group of large and beautiful S. American parrots. **macaw tree,** the tropical American palm of the genus *Acromia*, the fruit of which yields a valuable oil. (Port.)
Maccabean, *a.* mak-ka-*bee*-an, pertaining to the Maccabees, a line of Jewish princes which flourished two centuries before Christ, the story of whom is told in the Books of the Maccabees, two of which are included in the Apocrypha.
mace, *n.* mace, a kind of club; a staff of authority; a mace-bearer; a flat-headed cue formerly used in billiards and bagatelle. (O.Fr.)
mace, *n.* mace, a spice; the aril of the nutmeg, *Myristica fragrans*. (Fr. *macis*.)
mace-ale, *n. mace*-ale, ale spiced with mace.
mace-bearer, *n.* a man who carries the mace at ceremonies, in procession, etc.
macedoine, *n.* (App.) a jelly embedding pieces of fruit; a dish of mingled vegetables. (Fr.)
macer, *n. mace*-er, a mace-bearer; an usher in the law courts [Scot.].
macerate, *v.t. mas*-ser-ate, to make lean; to cause to wither; to soften and separate the parts of by steeping. (L. *maceratus*, softened.)
maceration, *n.* mas-ser-*ray*-shon, the act of macerating; the state of being macerated.
mach, *n.* makh, the unit of velocity of sound at any given altitude (*e.g.* 762 m.p.h. at sea-level, 660 at 40,000 ft.), used esp. in expressing supersonic speeds [Av.]. (Ernst *Mach*, Austrian physicist, *d.* 1916.)
machairodus, *n.* ma-*kyr*-ro-dus, the sabre-toothed tiger, now extinct. (Gr. *machaira*, a sword.)
machete, *n.* mah-*chay*-ta, a heavy cutting tool with a cutlass blade used in South America and the West Indies. (Sp.)
Machiavellian, *a.* mak-e-a-*vel*-e-an, pertaining or according to Machiavelli, or his principles; politically cunning; crafty; double-dealing: *n.* one who adopts the principles of Machiavelli, Italian diplomatist and political writer, 1469–1527.
machiavellism, *n.* mak-e-a-*vel*-izm, the principles of Machiavelli, or the doctrine more especially, that, in upholding order in a state, the ruler should hold himself bound by no scruple.
machicolated, *a.* ma-*chik*-o-lay-ted, having machicolations or overhanging battlements with openings between the corbels for dropping stones, pitch and molten lead on the assailants. (O.Fr. *machicolie*.)
machicolation, *n.* ma-*chik*-o-*lay*-shon, a machicolated battlement.
machinable, *a.* ma-*sheen*-a-bl, capable of being machined.
machinate, *v.t. mak*-e-nate, to plan; to contrive; to scheme to do evil. (L. *machinatus*.)
machination, *n.* mak-e-*nay*-shon, the act of planning a scheme for executing some purpose, esp. an evil one; a plot or intrigue; an artful design, formed with evil intent.
machinator, *n. mak*-e-nay-tor, an intriguer.
★**machine,** *n.* ma-*sheen*, any contrivance consisting of a combination of the mechanical powers; an engine; a sewing- or other machine; a vehicle dependent upon mechanism; supernatural agency in a poem; one who can only do as he is bid; any organization acting mechanically or controlled by a party boss: *v.t.* to fashion, or to finish, with a machine; to work with a machine: *v.i.* to be employed with machinery. **machine gun,** a light gun supported on a tripod that discharges automatically continuous rounds of rifle ammunition. **machine ruler,** a machine which lines or rules paper. **machine tool,** a power-operated implement for a specific purpose, comprising a number of intricate parts and largely self-acting. (Fr.)
machiner, *n.* ma-*sheen*-er, one who works a machine.
machinery, *n.* ma-*sheen*-er-re, machines in general; mechanical combination; the parts of a machine; superhuman agency introduced into a poem for the purpose of solving difficulties. (Fr. *machinerie*.)
machinist, *n.* ma-*sheen*-ist, a constructor of machines and engines; one versed in the principles of machines; one who works a machine.
mackerel, *n. mak*-er-el, the edible sea-fish *Scomber scombrus*. **mackerel gale,** a fresh, rippling breeze. **mackerel-guide,** the garfish. **mackerel-shark,** the porbeagle. **mackerel sky,** a sky in which the clouds are broken up into fleecy masses. (O.Fr. *makerel*.)
mackintosh, *n. mak*-in-tosh, a waterproof fabric made of cloth and rubber; an ulster or overcoat made of this. (Name of inventor.)
mackite, *n. mak*-ite, a fire-resisting building material composed of asbestos and plaster of Paris.
mackle, *n. mak*-kl, a blurred impression giving the appearance of double printing [Print.]: *v.t.* to spoil (paper) by blurring in printing. (Fr., as *macula*.)
macle, *n. mak*-kl, a twin crystal; a mascle [Her.].
macled, *a. mak*-ld, hemitrope; of twinned structure [Min.].
Macon, *n. mak*-kon, a red Burgundy wine produced in Macon.
maconochie, *n.* ma-*kon*-o-ke, a stew tinned and ready for eating when heated, used largely as an army ration. (Name of manufacturer.)
macramé, *n.* ma-*krah*-may, a fringe or corded edging. (It.)
macrobiosis, *n. mak*-ro-by-*oh*-sis, longevity. (Gr. *makros*, long, *bios*, life.)
macrobiotic, *a. mak*-ro-by-*ot*-ik, long-lived: *n.pl.* the art of prolonging life. (Gr.)

macrocephalism, *n.* mak-ro-*sef*-a-lizm, the condition of being macrocephalous.
macrocephalous, *a.* mak-ro-*sef*-a-lus, having an abnormally large head.
macrocosm, *n. mak*-ro-kozm, the universe; the complete whole. (Gr. *makros*, great, *kosmos*, world.)
macrocosmology, *n. mak*-ro-koz-*mol*-o-je, a treatise on the macrocosm.
macrodactylic, *a. mak*-ro-dak-*til*-ik, having long toes [Ornith.]. (Gr.)
macrognathic, *a.* mak-ro-*nath*-ik, having prominent jaws. (Gr. *makros*, and *gnathos*, the jaw-bone.)
macrology, *n.* ma-*krol*-o-je, verbosity.
macrometer, *a.* ma-*krom*-e-ter, an instrument to measure the size and distance of inaccessible objects by means of two reflectors on a common sextant. (Gr. *makros*, and *metron*, measure.)
macron, *n. may*-kron, a mark placed over a vowel (as ē) to show that it has a long sound. (Gr.)
macropia, *n.* ma-*kroh*-pe-a, a defect in vision causing objects to appear enlarged.
macropsia, *n.* ma-*krop*-se-a, macropia.
macropterous, *a.* ma-*krop*-ter-rus, having long wings or fins. (Gr. *makros*, and *pteron*, a wing.)
macroscopic, *a. mak*-ro-*skop*-ik, visible without magnification.
Macrotheerium, *n. mak*-ro-*theer*-re-um, a genus of huge extinct ungulates of the Miocene. (Gr. *makros* great, *therion* wild beast.)
macrurous, *a.* ma-*kroor*-rus, having a long tail; belonging to the *Macrura*, the group of crustaceans including the lobsters, shrimps, etc.
mactation, *a.* mak-*tay*-shon, the act of killing a victim for sacrifice. (L. *mactatio*.)
macula, *n. mak*-yew-la (*pl.* **maculæ,** *mak*-yew-lee), a spot on the skin or on the surface of the sun. (L.)
maculate, *v.t. mak*-yew-late, to spot; to stain: *a.* spotted; stained. (L. *maculatus*, spotted.)
maculation, *n. mak*-yew-*lay*-shon, a spotting; a stain; a spotted condition [Path.].
macule, *n. mak*-yewl, a spot; a stain; a mackle.
mad, *a.* mad, disordered or distracted in intellect; insane; crazed; exceedingly foolish; proceeding from madness; infatuated; furious; wild with excitement; inflamed with anger: *v.i.* to be or go mad: *v.t.* to drive mad. (A.S. *gemæded*, driven mad.)
Madam, *n. mad*-am, a complimentary title or form of address accorded to married or elderly ladies; (*l.c.*) a pert or forward young woman [Coll.]. (Fr. *ma dame*, my lady.)
madapollam, *n.* mad-a-*pol*-am, a coarse kind of calico. (Name of place, in India, of original manufacture.)
madar, *n.* ma-*dar*, the shrub and medicament mudar [Hind.]
madarosis, *n.* mad-a-*roh*-sis, falling off of the hair, especially the eyebrows or eyelashes [Med.]. (Gr.)
madcap, *n. mad*-kap, a wild, hare-brained, frolicsomely eccentric person: *a.* eccentric; freakish.
madden, *v.t. mad*-dn, to make or drive mad; to enrage: *v.i.* to become mad; to act as if mad.
madder, *n. mad*-der, a plant of the genus *Rubia*, also its root and a red dyestuff prepared from this. (A.S. *mædere*.)
madding, *a. mad*-ding, raging; furious.
made, made, *p.* and *pp.* of *make*.
Madeira, *n.* ma-*deer*-ra, a rich wine made in Madeira. **Madeira cake,** a rich cake containing peel but no fruit. **Madeira nut,** a thin-shelled walnut.
Mademoiselle, *n.* mad-mwah-*zel*, a title given to an unmarried lady; miss. (Fr.)
madhouse, *n. mad*-house, a house or asylum for the cure or restraint of the insane.
madia, *n. may*-de-a, a South American composite plant, *Madia sativa*, the tar-weed, cultivated for its oil. (Native name.)
madid, *a. mad*-id, damp, moist. (L. *madidus*.)
madly, *ad. mad*-le, in a mad way.
madman, *n. mad*-man, a maniac; one who is mad.
madness, *n. mad*-ness, the state of being mad.
Madonna, *n.* ma-*don*-na, the Virgin Mary; a picture of the Madonna. **Madonna lily,** the common white lily, *lilium candidum*. (It., my lady.)
madoqua, *n. mad*-o-kwa, an Abyssinian antelope, *Cephalophus abyssinicus*, the smallest of horned mammals, about the size of a hare. (Amharic.)
Madrasi, *n.* ma-*dras*-e, a native (esp. a coolie) of Madras.
madrepore, *n. mad*-re-pore, a variety of reef-coral. (It., mother-stone.)
madreporite, *n. mad*-re-po-rite, fossil madrepore; columnar carbonate of lime; a tubercle in starfish, etc.
madrigal, *n. mad*-re-gal, a short love-lyric; vocal composition in five or six parts; an unaccompanied part song. (It. *mardigale*.)
Madrilenian *a.* mad-re-*lee*-ne-an, pertaining to Madrid: *n.* native or inhabitant of Madrid.
Madura foot, *n.* ma-*door*-ra foot, a form of mycetoma endemic in India. (*Madura*, a town in Madras.)
madwort, *n. mad*-wurt, *Alyssum calycinum*, *Asperugo procumbens*, or other plant formerly supposed to cure hydrophobia.
Mæcenas, *n.* me-*see*-nass, a patron of the arts. (Name of a wealthy 1st-cent. Roman.)
Maelstrom, *n. male*-strohm, a dangerous whirlpool off the W. coast of Norway; hence (*l.c.*), a wide-spread and disorderly commotion. (Norw., whirling stream.)
mænad, *n. mee*-nad, a Bacchante; a frenzied or infuriated woman. (Gr. *mainomai*, to rave.)
maestoso, *ad.* mah-es-*toh*-so, with grandeur and strength [Mus.].. (It.)
maestro, *n.* ma-*es*-troh, a master in any art, esp. music; an eminent composer or conductor. (It.)
Mae West, *n.* may-*west*, an inflated breast-piece used as a life-saving jacket, esp. by airmen. (Name of a film-star.)
mafia, *n.* mah-*fee*-yah, violent popular hostility to law and order; (*cap.*) the body of persons taking part in, or the secret society organizing, this. (Sicilian.)
mafflck, *v.i. maf*-fik, to rejoice or celebrate an event riotously. (From the excitement with which the relief of *Mafeking* was hailed in London, May, 1900.)
mag, *n.* mag, a magpie: *v.i.* to gossip [Slang].
magazine, *n.* mag-a-*zeen*, a warehouse; a depot for arms and ammunition; a gunpowder room [Naut.]; the supply chamber or cartridge holder of a rifle, automatic gun, etc., or its contents; a periodical containing miscellaneous compositions; a light-tight container for films [Phot.]. (Fr. *magazin*, from Ar. *makhazin*, a storehouse.)
magdalen, *n. mag*-da-len, a reformed prostitute; (*cap.*) a home for such. (Mary *Magdalene*, in Luke vii.)
Magdalenian, *a. mag*-da-*lee*-ne-an, of the upper Palæolithic age that succeeded the Solutrian, first studied at La Madeleine, in Dordogne, France.
mage, *n.* mayj, a magician. (Fr.)
magellanic, *a.* mag-el-*lan*-ik, discovered by Magellan, the navigator. **magellanic clouds,** two conspicuous nebulæ near the south celestial pole.
magenta, *n.* ma-*jen*-ta, a purplish-red aniline dye discovered in the year of the battle of Magenta, 1859; fuchsine.
maggot, *n. mag*-got, the larva of a fly or beetle; a soft-bodied grub; a whim. (W. *maceiad*.)
maggotiness, *n.* the state of being maggoty.
maggoty, *a. mag*-got-e, full of maggots; whimsical.
Magi, *n.pl. may*-jy, wise men, esp. of the East; the sacerdotal and learned class among the Medes and Persians, who studied and practised magic. **the Magi,** the three wise men who brought gifts to the infant Christ. (L.)
Magian, *a. may*-je-an, pertaining to the Magi: *n.* one of the Magi; (*l.c.*) a magician.
Magianism, *n. may*-je-a-nizm, the principles and philosophy of the Magians.
magic, *n. maj*-ik, the pretended art of bringing into action the agency of supernatural beings; a wonderful effect produced in some mysterious way; sorcery; witchcraft: *a.* magical; produced by magic. **magic lantern,** *see* **lantern. magic square,** numbers arranged in a square so that their total is the same by horizontal, vertical or diagonal addition. **black magic,** magic calculated to cause death or serious injury. **white** or **natural magic,** the art of employing the powers of nature to produce effects apparently supernatural. (L. *magicus*, as *Magi*.)
magical, *a. maj*-e-kal, pertaining to, or used by magic; employing magic; as if done by magic.
magically, *ad. maj*-e-ka-le, in a magical way.
magician, *n.* ma-*jish*-an, one skilled in magic; a necromancer; a conjurer.

magilp, *n.* ma-*gilp*, megilp.
magirology, *n.* *maj*-ire-*rol*-o-je, the art or science of cookery. (Gr. *mageiros*, cook, and *-logy*.)
magism, *n.* *may*-gizm, magianism.
magisterial, *a.* maj-is-*teer*-re-al, pertaining to or befitting a master, a magistrate, or a magistracy; authoritative; dignified; proud; imperious.
magisteriality, *n.* *maj*-is-*teer*-re-*al*-e-te, magisterial office, position, or character.
magisterially, *ad.* in a magisterial way.
magistracy, *n.* *maj*-is-tra-se, the office or dignity of a magistrate; a magistrate's district; magistrates collectively.
magistral, *a.* *maj*-is-tral, magisterial; prescribed by special prescription [Med.].
magistrand, *n.* *maj*-is-trand, a student in his fourth or final year in a Scottish (esp. Aberdeen) university.
magistrate, *n.* *maj*-is-trate, a public civil officer, invested with a certain judicial and executive authority; a Justice of the Peace. (Fr. *magistrat*.)
magistratical, *a.* *maj*-is-*trat*-e-kal, pertaining to magistrates, or to their powers; proper to a magistrate.
magistrature, *n.* *maj*-is-tra-tewr, the position of a magistrate; the term of office of a magistrate; magistrates as a class.
Maglemosian, *a.* *mag*-le-*moh*-ze-an, pertaining to the late palæolithic European culture represented by implements, etc. found at Maglemose, Denmark [Ethn.].
magma, *n.* *mag*-ma, the semi-molten rock covered by the lithosphere [Geog.]; a mixture of mineral or organic matter in a thin, pasty state; a residuum. (Gr.)
magmatic, *a.* mag-*mat*-ik, of or pertaining to magma.
Magna Charta, *n.* *mag*-na *kar*-ta, the English charter of rights, liberties, and principles extracted from King John, A.D. 1215; any fundamental constitution guaranteeing rights and privileges. (L., Great Charter.)
magnalium, mag-*nay*-le-um, a light tough aluminium alloy containing from 2½ to 10 per cent. magnesium.
magnanerie, *n.* mah-*nyah*-ne-re (or App.), the art of sericulture; a place in which silk-worms are reared. (Fr.)
magnanimity, *n.* mag-na-*nim*-e-te, greatness or generous nobility of mind; high-mindedness.
magnanimous, *a.* mag-*nan*-e-mus, high-minded; elevated in soul; disinterested; heroic; exhibiting nobleness of soul. (L. *magnanimus*.)
magnanimously, *ad.* mag-*nan*-e-mus-le, in a magnanimous manner.
magnascope, *n.* *mag*-na-skope, a combination of lenses to increase the size of a projected picture [Cine.].
magnate, *n.* *mag*-nate, a person of rank, wealth, or distinction; a leader in some branch of commerce. (L. *magnus*, great.)
magnesia, *n.* mag-*nee*-she-a, oxide of magnesium, a white and tasteless substance, used in pharmacy and as a refractory. **fluid magnesia,** a solution of magnesium bicarbonate. (*Magnesia*, district of ancient Greece.)
magnesian, *a.* mag-*nee*-she-an, pertaining to, containing, or resembling, magnesia.
magnesite, *n.* *mag*-ne-site, native magnesium carbonate.
magnesium, *n.* mag-*nee*-ze-um, a silver-white metallic element giving an intense white light when burnt, and used much in aluminium alloys.
magnet, *n.* *mag*-net, the loadstone; a piece of magnetized iron or steel; a thing or person having strong attractive power. (O.Fr. *magnete*.)
magnetic, *a.* mag-*net*-ik, pertaining to the magnet or to magnetism; having the properties of the magnet; attractive: *n.* any metal capable of being magnetized. **magnetic battery,** a combination of magnets with their poles similarly disposed. **magnetic circuit,** the path through which the lines of magnetic force due to a magnet spread. **magnetic dip,** *see* **dip. magnetic equator,** the line round the globe where the needle has no dip. **magnetic field,** a region of magnetic influence. **magnetic flux,** the total number of lines of force in a magnetic field. **magnetic induction,** power in a magnet of imparting its qualities to certain other substances. **magnetic meridian,** *see* meridian. **magnetic pole,** the place where the needle dips vertically. **magnetic screen,** an iron shield or cover to localize or restrict the field of influence of a magnet. **magnetic storm,** an unpredictable disturbance of terrestrial magnetic conditions associated with sunspots and the Aurora Borealis.
magnetically, *ad.* by magnetism.
magnetiferous, *a.* mag-net-*tif*-e-rus, exhibiting or conducting magnetism.
magnetism, *n.* *mag*-net-izm, that property of certain substances (as iron) the possession of which renders them capable of being magnetized; an attractive and repulsive force; the branch of science treating of magnetic phenomena; power of attraction. **animal magnetism,** mesmerism. **residual magnetism,** the magnetic flux remaining in a body after removal of the magnetizing force. **terrestrial magnetism,** the magnetic influence exerted by the earth.
magnetist, *n.* *mag*-net-ist, one versed in magnetism; a mesmerist.
magnetite, *n.* *mag*-net-ite, a magnetic oxide of iron crystallizing in the cubic system.
magnetization, *n.* *mag*-ne-ty-*zay*-shon, the act of magnetizing; state of being magnetized.
magnetize, *v.t.* *mag*-ne-tize, to communicate magnetic properties to; to render magnetic; to attract, as by a magnet; to mesmerize: *v.i.* to become magnetic.
magnetizer, *n.* *mag*-ne-ty-zer, one who or that which imparts magnetism.
magneto, *n.* mag-*nee*-to, the generator of current for electric ignition in internal combustion engines.
magneto-electric, *a.* electro-magnetic.
magneto-electricity, *n.* electricity evolved by magnets; electro-magnetism.
magnetogram, *n.* mag-*net*-o-gram, the record made by a magnetograph.
magnetograph, *n.* mag-*net*-o-graf, an instrument for registering magnetic states. (Gr. *magnet*, and *grapho*, write.)
magnetometer, *n.* *mag*-ne-*tom*-e-ter, an instrument to ascertain the force of terrestrial magnetism. (Gr. *magnet*, and *metron*, measure.)
magnetomotor, *n.* *mag*-net-o-*moh*-tor, a voltaic series of large plates producing electricity of low tension.
magneto-optics, *n.* the branch of optics dealing with the action of a magnetic field on light rays.
magnetophone, *n.* mag-*nee*-to-fone, a type of resonance-eliminating microphone amplifier [Wire.].
magnetoscope, *n.* mag-*nee*-to-skope, an appliance for detecting magnetic force.
magnetotherapy, *n.* *mag*-ne-to-*ther*-ra-pe, the treatment of disease by magnetic electricity.
magnetron, *n.* *mag*-ne-tron, a thermionic valve in which an internal magnetic field causes the deflexion of the rapidly moving electrons.
magnifiable, *a.* *mag*-ne-*fy*-a-bl, that may be magnified; worthy of being magnified or extolled.
magnific, *a.* mag-*nif*-ik, grand; splendid; would-be impressive. (L. *magnificus*.)
Magnificat, *n.* mag-*nif*-e-kat, the song of the Virgin Mary, Luke i, 46–55, so called from its opening word in the Vulgate. (L. *magnificare*, to esteem highly.)
magnification, *n.* *mag*-ne-fe-*kay*-shon, the act or the result of magnifying.
magnificence, *n.* mag-*nif*-e-sense, grandeur or splendour of appearance.
magnificent, *a.* mag-*nif*-e-sent, grand in appearance; splendid; characterized by or exhibiting grandeur; impressive. (L. *magnificens*, doing wonderful deeds.)
magnificently, *ad.* in a magnificent manner.
magnifico, *n.* mag-*nif*-e-ko, a grandee of Venice; hence, any person giving himself airs. (It.)
magnifier, *n.* *mag*-ne-fy-er, one who magnifies; an optical instrument which magnifies.
magnify, *v.t.* *mag*-ne-fy, to make greater; to make appear greater or larger; to exaggerate; to praise or extol: *v.i.* to have the power of increasing apparent size. (Fr. *magnifier*.)
magniloquence, *n.* mag-*nil*-o-kwence, a pompous style of speech or writing. (L. *magniloquentia*.)
magniloquent, *a.* mag-*nil*-o-kwent, speaking loftily or pompously; bombastic.
magniloquently, *ad.* in a magniloquent manner.
magnitude, *n.* *mag*-ne-tewd, extent; size; bulk;

amount; quantity; that which is extended in length, breadth, and thickness; greatness; grandeur; importance; degree of comparative brilliance of a celestial body [Astron.]. (L. *magnitudo.*)

Magnolia, *n.* mag-*noh*-le-a, a genus of beautiful flowering trees of Asia and N. America. **magnolia metal,** a lead alloy containing from 16 to 20 per cent. of antimony. (P. *Magnol, d.* 1715, French botanist.)

magnum, *n. mag*-num, a wine-bottle holding two quarts.

magnum-bonum, *n. mag*-num-*boh*-num, applied to large and good kinds of plum, potato, etc. (L., large, good.)

magot, *n. mag*-ot *or* mah-*goh*, the Barbary ape of N. Africa and Gibraltar; a grotesque figure in porcelain, ivory, bronze, etc. [Chin. and Jap. art]. (Fr.)

magpie, *n. mag*-py, the corvine bird *Pica rustica*; a species of pigeon; a chatterer; the outermost circle but one of a target, or a shot hitting this. (*Mag*, from Fr. *Margot*, Margaret, and O.Fr. *pie*, from L. *pica*, a bird.)

maguey, *n. mag*-way, various species of Mexican agave, esp. *Agave atrovirens.* (Mexican word.)

Magyar, *n. mag*-yar *or mod*-yah, a Hungarian or member of the Magyar race that settled in Hungary in the 9th century A.D.; a woman's bodice cut in magyar style: *a.* of, or pertaining to, this race; applied to a style of dress which has the sleeves cut in one piece with the garment. (Hungarian.)

mahaleb, *n. mah*-ha-leb, a cherry, whose inedible fruit yields a violet dye and a fermented liquor like kirschwasser. (Ar.)

Maharaja, *n. mah*-ha-*rah*-jah, the title of certain Hindu sovereign princes. (Sans., great king.)

Maharanee, *n. mah*-ha-*rah*-nee, the consort of a Maharaja; a Hindu sovereign princess. (*Maharani.*)

mahatma, *n.* ma-*hat*-ma, an adept in esoteric Buddhism; any person of outstanding virtue or deep philosophy. (Sans.)

Mahdi, *n. mah*-de, the Saviour of the Mohammedan belief; the leader that is to come. (Ar., leader.)

mah-jong, *n.* mah-*jong*, a Chinese game played with tiles and counters. (Chin., sparrows.)

mahlstick, *n. mahl*-stik, a maulstick.

mahogany, *n.* ma-*hog*-a-ne, the wood of *Swietenia mahogani*, a tree of tropical America; the tree itself; the brownish-yellow colour of the wood. **the mahogany,** a dining-table. (W. Indian, *mahagoni.*)

Mahometan, *a.* ma-*hom*-e-tan, Mohammedan.

mahout, *n.* ma-*hoot*, an elephant-driver. (Hind.)

mahseer, *n. mah*-seer, a very large sporting- and food-fish, *Barbus mosal*, of Indian rivers, allied to the barbel. (Hind., big-head.)

maid, *n.* mayd, a maiden; a female domestic servant. **lady's maid,** *see* **lady. maid of honour,** an attendant upon the Queen bearing the prefix Honourable; a chief bridesmaid [U.S.A.]; a kind of small cheesecake.

maidan, *n.* may-*dahn*, a parade-ground in India, etc. (Pers.)

maiden, *n.* maydn, a girl; an unmarried woman; a virgin; a maiden over; a horse that has never won a race; an instrument like the guillotine formerly used in Scotland: *a.* pertaining to a young woman or virgin; consisting of maidens; fresh; new; unused. **maiden assize,** an assize at which there are no criminal cases. **maiden city,** a city that has never been captured. **maiden name,** the surname of a woman before marriage. **maiden over,** an over at cricket in which no runs are made. **maiden pink,** the plant *Dianthus deltoides*. **maiden race,** a race for horses that have never won a prize. **maiden speech,** the first speech of a member in a public body. (A.S. *mægden.*)

maidenhair, *n. maydn*-hare, a species of fern of the genus *Adiantum*. **maidenhair tree,** the gingko, whose leaves resemble those of the fern.

maidenhead, *n. maydn*-hed, virginity; the hymen [Anat.].

maidenhood, *n. maydn*-hood, the state of being a maid; virginity; purity; newness; freshness.

maidenish, *a. maydn*-ish, maidish.

maidenly, *a. maydn*-le, like a maid or young girl; gentle; modest.

maidhood, *n. mayd*-hood, virginity; maidenhood.

maidish, *a. mayd-ish*, resembling or characteristic of a maid. **old maidish,** straight-laced; prim and proper.

maidism, *n. may*-dizm, maize-poisoning; pellagra [Med.]. (*maize.*)

maidservant, *n. mayd*-ser-vant, a female domestic servant.

maieutic, *a.* mah-*yew*-tik, delivering, as in childbirth; applied to the method by which Socrates forced his interlocutors to demonstrate for themselves the truth of his teaching. (Gr., obstetric.)

maigre, *a. mayg*-er, vegetarian, and so suitable for fast-days (of food); pertaining to fast-days: *n.* the Mediterranean food-fish, *Sciæna aquila.* (Fr., thin, skinny.)

mail, *n.* male, defensive armour of chains, rings, or scales: *v.t.* to clothe in or as with mail. (O.Fr. *maille.*)

mail, *n.* male, a bag for the conveyance of letters and papers; the post; the postal system; postal business; a conveyance or ship that carries mails: *v.t.* to send by mail; to post. **mail order,** an order for goods received and dispatched by mail; the system by which goods are bought through the post [Comm.]. (O.Fr. *male*, a bag.)

mailable, *a. male*-a-bl, that may be mailed.

mail-boat, *n.* a mail-steamer.

mail-cart, *n.* a vehicle for the carriage of mail by road; a light kind of perambulator for children.

mail-coach, *n.* a coach that conveyed the public mails.

mailed, *a.* mayld, clothed with mail; protected by an external covering of scales, etc.

mail-steamer, *n.* a steamship that carries the mails.

mail-train, *n.* a train that carries the mails.

maim, *v.t.* mame, to deprive of the use of a limb; to mutilate; to cripple; to disable: *n.* a crippling defect or mutilation; injury. (O.Fr. *mahaigner*, to cripple.)

main, *a.* mane, principal; chief; leading; first in importance; vast; sheer: *n.* the chief part; the gross; the bulk; the ocean; a main pipe, sewer, electric cable, etc. **in the main,** for the most part. **main chance,** the most important issue; private advantage. **with might and main,** with all one's strength. (O.Fr. *maine.*)

main, *n.* mane, a match at cockfighting; in dicing, the number called before casting. (Origin unknown.)

mainboom, *n.* mane-*boom*, the boom at the foot of a fore-and-aft mainsail.

main-brace, *n.* the rope by which the mainyard is worked. **splice the main-brace,** *see* **splice.**

main-deck, *n.* the principal deck; the deck between the poop and forecastle [Naut.].

mainland, *n. mane*-land, the principal land, as opposed to adjacent islands; the continent.

mainly, *ad. mane*-le, chiefly; principally; in the main.

mainmast, *n. mane*-mahst, the principal mast of a ship.

mainour, *n. may*-noor, stolen property found in the hands of the thief [Law]. (*manœuvre.*)

mainpernor, *n. mane*-per-nor, a person who is surety for another's appearance before a court; one giving mainprize. (O.Fr.)

mainprize, *n. mane*-preez, suretyship; the act of procuring bail by becoming surety. **writ of mainprize,** a writ ordering a sheriff to find surety for a person's appearance in court [Law]. (O.Fr.)

mainsail, *n. mane*-sl, the principal sail in a ship.

main-sheet, *n.* the rope that extends the mainsail; the rope by which the mainboom is worked.

mainspring, *n. mane*-spring, the principal spring in a clock or watch; hence, a chief motive.

mainstay, *n.* mane-stay, the stay that extends from the maintop to the deck; a chief support.'

maintain, *v.t.* mane-*tane*, to hold, preserve, or keep in condition; to hold; to keep up; to continue; to support; to defend; to vindicate; to support by assertion or argument. (Fr. *maintenir.*)

maintainable, *a.* mane-*tay*-na-bl, that may be maintained, supported, or defended.

maintainer, *n.* mane-*tay*-ner, one who or that which maintains; one guilty of maintenance [Law.].

maintenance, *n. mane*-te-nance, the act of maintaining; sustenance; support; continuance; defence; means of support; officious intermeddling in a suit in which one has no interest [Law]. **cap of maintenance,** *see* **cap.** (Fr.)

maintop, *n.* mane-*top*, a platform at the top of the mainmast to which shrouds, etc., are fixed [Naut.].

mainyard, *n.* mane-*yard*, the yard by which the mainsail is supported [Naut.].
maisonette, *n.* may-zo-*net*, a self-contained domicile forming part of a larger building but not, like a flat, on one floor.
maître d'hôtel, *n.* maytr-do-tel, a major-domo; a hotel manager. (Fr., house-master.)
maize, *n.* maze, Indian corn, *Zea mays.* (Sp. *maiz.*)
maizena, *n.* ma-*zee*-na, trade name for a foodstuff prepared from maize.
majestic, *a.* ma-*jes*-tik, having majesty or dignity of person or appearance; splendid; sublime; stately.
majestical, *a.* ma-*jes*-te-kal, majestic.
majestically, *ad.* in a majestic manner.
majesty, *n.* *maj*-es-te, impressive grandeur; greatness; dignity; elevation of manner; (*cap.*) a title of emperors, kings, and queens. (O.Fr. *majestet.*)
majolica, *n.* ma-*jol*-e-ka *or* ma-*yol*-e-ka, an ornate enamelled kind of pottery said to have been introduced into Italy from Majorca.
major, *a.* *may*-jor, greater in number, quantity, extent, or importance; designating the modes in which the third is four semitones above the tonic or key-note, and also intervals consisting of four semitones [Mus.]: *n.* an army officer next in rank above a captain, and below a lieutenant-colonel; a person of full age (21 years) to manage his own concerns [Law]; that premise of a syllogism which contains the major term [Logic]. (L., greater.)
majorat, *n.* ma-*zhaw*-rah, the right of succession to property according to age; primogeniture. (Fr.)
majorate, *n.* *may*-jo-rat, a major's office or rank.
major-domo, *n.* *may*-jor-*doh*-mo, a man who holds the place of master of the house; a steward. (Sp.)
major-general, *n.* a military officer next in rank below a lieutenant-general.
majority, *n.* ma-*jo*-re-te, the greater number; more than half; amount by which one number exceeds another; full age, above 21 years; the office, rank, or commission of a major. **to join the majority,** to die. (Fr. *majorité.*)
majorship, *n.* *may*-jor-ship, majorate.
majuscule, *n.* ma-*jus*-kewl, a capital letter, as distinguished from a minuscule, or small letter. (L.)
make, *v.t.* make, to cause to exist; to frame; to fashion; to compose; to cause to become; to produce or effect; to compel or constrain; to procure; to execute; to establish; to raise to good fortune; to commit; to gain; to collect; to arrive in sight of, as land; to reach; to gain by advance; to provide; to place; to turn; to represent; to induce; to fabricate. **make account of,** to esteem. **make amends,** to compensate. **make away with,** to kill; to destroy. **make bold,** *see* **bold. make free with,** to treat with freedom. **make good,** to defend; to accomplish; to make compensation for; to succeed. **make light of,** to consider as of no consequence. **make love,** to court. **make merry,** *see* **merry. make much of,** to treat with fondness or esteem. **make of,** to understand by; to produce from. **make out,** to learn; to understand clearly; to prove; to furnish. **make over,** to transfer the title of. **make ready,** *see* **ready. make sail,** to increase the quantity of sail already set [Naut.]. **make sure of,** to consider as certain; to secure to one's possession. **make up,** to reconcile; to repair; to supply what is wanting; to complete by assembly of parts, etc.; to shape; to compensate; to adjust: to arrange (type) in page form. **make water,** to leak; to discharge urine. **make way,** to clear a passage; to make progress. *p.* and *pp.* **made.** (A.S. *macian.*)
make, *v.i.* make, to tend; to move; to contribute; to rise; to flow towards land. **make against,** to tend to injury. **make as if,** to appear. **make away,** to hurry off. **make for,** to move toward; to favour. **make off,** to decamp. **make out,** to succeed. **make up,** to approach; to prepare oneself for an impersonation (of actors); to use make-up. **make up for,** to compensate. **make up with,** to settle differences; to become friends **make with,** to concur. *p.* and *pp.* **made.**
***make,** *n.* make, structure; texture; shape; style; disposition; making of contact or completing a circuit [Elect.]. **make-and-break,** a device that automatically makes and breaks an electric circuit. **on the make,** on the look-out for the main chance; out to make personal profit [Slang].

make-believe, *n.* persuasion that a thing is which it is not; a pretence; a sham: *a.* sham.
maker, *n.* *make*-er, one who makes; the declarer (at Bridge, etc.); (*cap.*) the Creator.
makeshift, *n.* *make*-shift, a temporary expedient: *a.* made or used for a temporary purpose.
make-up, *n.* *make*-up, the parts out of which the whole is formed; the arrangement of galleys of type into pages; lay-out [Print.]; grease-paint; the disguise assumed by an actor.
makeweight, *n.* *make*-wayt, that which is thrown into a scale to make up the weight; a stopgap.
makimono, *n.* mah-ke-*moh*-no, a Japanese hanging picture or writing unrolling horizontally.
making, *n.* *make*-ing, composition; workmanship; quantity; material; (*pl.*) earnings; profit. **making up,** the reduction of spirits to a standard of strength; the putting together of the types in the form of pages [Print.]; the actor's art of assuming make-up; reconciliation. **making-up day,** contango day [Stock Exchange].
malacca, *n.* ma-*lak*-a, a dark brown to light brown cane from the rattan palm, *Calamus scipionum,* of Malaysia; a walking-stick of this. (*Malacca,* in the Malay peninsula.)
malachite, *n.* *mal*-a-kite, a bright green monoclinic basic carbonate of copper. (Gr. *malache,* mallow, the colour of the leaf.)
malacodermous, *a.* ma-lak-o-*der*-mus, soft-skinned [Zool.].
malacia, *n.* ma-*lay*-she-a, any morbid softening of the tissues; a depraved appetite [Path.]. (Gr. *malakia,* softness.)
malacoid, *a.* *mal*-a-koyd, soft-bodied [Zool.]; of soft texture [Bot., etc.].
malacolite, *n.* *mal*-a-ko-lite, a light-coloured variety of diopside. (Gr. *malache,* and *lithos,* a stone.)
malacologist, *n.* *mal*-a-*kol*-o-jist, one versed in malacology.
malacology, *n.* *mal*-a-*kol*-o-je, the study of the mollusca. (Gr. *malachos,* soft, *logos,* science.)
malacopterygian, *a.* *mal*-a-kop-ter-*rij*-e-an, belonging to the division of fishes having soft fin-rays: *n.* any one of these fishes. (Gr. *malachos,* and *pteryz,* a fin.)
malacostomous, *a.* *mal*-a-*kos*-to-mus, having soft jaws without teeth [Ichth.]. (Gr. *malachos,* and *stoma,* the mouth.)
malacostraca, *n.pl.* *mal*-a-*kos*-tra-ka, the sub-class of crustaceans, including the lobsters, crabs, etc. (Gr. *malachos,* and *ostraca,* shells.)
malacostracous, *a.* mal-a-*kos*-tra-kus, having a soft shell [Zool.].
maladjustment, *n.* *mal*-ad-*just*-ment, a bad or wrong adjustment. (L. *male,* bad, and *adjustment.*)
maladministration, *n.* *mal*-ad-min-is-*tray*-shon, bad management, esp. of public affairs.
maladroit, *a.* *mal*-a-droyt, clumsy; unskilful. (Fr.)
maladroitly, *ad.* in a maladroit manner.
maladroitness, *n.* the quality of being maladroit.
malady, *n.* *mal*-a-de, disease, esp. a lingering or deep-seated disorder, either of body or mind. (Fr.)
Malaga, *n.* *mal*-a-ga, a white muscatel wine imported from Malaga.
Malagasy, *a.* *mal*-a-*gas*-e, relating to Madagascar, its inhabitants, or their language: *n.* an inhabitant or native of Madagascar; their language.
malaise, *n.* ma-*layz,* a vague feeling of uneasiness or physical discomfort, often heralding an illness. (Fr.)
malanders, *n.pl.* *mal*-an-derz, mallenders.
malapert, *a.* *mal*-a-pert, pert; saucy; impudent; forward: *n.* a pert, saucy person. (O.Fr. *mal,* and *apert,* open, ready, expert.)
malapertly, *ad.* in a malapert manner.
malapertness, *n.* the quality of being malapert.
malapropism, *n.* *mal*-a-pro-pizm, misapplication of fine words. (Fr. *mal à propos,* with reference to Mrs. *Malaprop* in Sheridan's "The Rivals.")
malapropos, *ad.* mal-ah-pro-*poh,* out of place; badly timed; unreasonably: *a.* inappropriate: *n.* an inopportune remark, event, etc. (Fr., ill for the purpose.)
malar, *a.* *may*-lar, pertaining to the cheek: *n.* the cheek-bone. (L. *mala,* the cheek.)
malaria, *n.* ma-*lare*-re-a, noxiously infected air; miasma; an intermittent and remittent fever caused by infection from the bite of the *Anopheles* mosquito; ague. (It. *mala aria,* bad air.)

malarial, *a.* ma-*lare*-re-al, pertaining to or infected by malaria.
malariology, *n.* ma-*lare*-re-*ol*-o-je, the study of malaria.
malarious, *a.* ma-*lare*-re-us, malarial.
malassimilation, *n.* *mal*-a-sim-e-*lay*-shon, imperfect assimilation or nutrition.
malate, *n.* *mal*-ate, a salt of malic acid.
malaxation, *mal*-ak-*say*-shon, the process of softening by kneading [Massage, etc.].
Malay, *a.* ma-*lay*, relating to the Malay Peninsula, or its inhabitants: *n.* an inhabitant of the Malay Peninsula; the Malay language.
Malayalam, *n.* mal-a-*yah*-lam, the Dravidian language, akin to Tamil, of the Malabar coast of India.
Malayalim, *n.pl.* mal-a-*yah*-lim, the Dravidian people speaking Malayalam. (Native name.)
Malayan, *a.* and *n.* ma-*lay*-an, Malay.
Malaysian, *a.* ma-*lay*-ze-an, pertaining or belonging to Malaysia, *i.e.* the Malay Archipelago.
malconformation, *n.* *mal*-kon-for-*may*-shon, imperfect conformation; disproportion of parts.
malcontent, *a.* *mal*-kon-tent, discontented, especially with the laws or the administration of government: *n.* one who is malcontent. (O.Fr.)
mal de mer, *n.* mal-de-mare, seasickness.
★**male,** *a.* male, pertaining to the sex that begets; bearing stamens but not fruit [Bot.]; virile; denoting a screw whose thread enter the grooves of the corresponding, or female screw [Mech.]: *n.* a male animal or plant. **male fern,** *Nephrodium filix-mas.* **male rhymes,** those in which only final syllables rhyme. (Fr. *mâle*, from L. *masculus*, a diminutive of *mas*, a male.)
malediction, *n.* mal-e-*dik*-shon, denunciation of evil; a curse. (Fr.)
malefactor, *n.* *mal*-e-fak-tor, an evil-doer; one who commits a crime; a criminal. (L. *male*, ill, *facio*, do.)
malefic, *a.* ma-*lef*-ik, maleficent.
maleficence, *n.* ma-*lef*-e-sence, evil-doing.
maleficent, *a.* ma-*lef*-e-sent, doing harm or injury. (L. *maleficus.*)
maleic, *a.* ma-*lee*-ik, designating a crystalline acid obtained by the dry distillation of malic acid.
malenders, *n.* *mal*-en-derz, mallenders.
malevolence, *n.* ma-*lev*-o-lence, ill-will; spitefulness.
malevolent, *a.* ma-*lev*-o-lent, wishing ill; ill-disposed towards others; envious; spiteful; malicious. (L. *malevolens.*)
malevolently, *ad.* in a malevolent spirit.
malfeasance, *n.* mal-*fee*-zance, evil conduct; wrong; illegal conduct, esp. by a public official. (Fr. *malfaisance.*)
malformation, *n.* *mal*-for-*may*-shon, wrong formation; irregular or anomalous formation or structure.
malformed, *a.* mal-*formd*, misshapen; ill-shaped; irregularly made.
malic, *a.* *mal*-ik, derived from the apple or other fruit (only of **malic acid,** an acid present in the juice of unripe fruit). (L. *malum*, an apple.)
malice, *n.* *mal*-is, a disposition to injure others; ill-will; unprovoked spite; premeditated intention to cause injury [Law]. (Fr.)
malicious, *a.* ma-*lish*-us, harbouring malice; spiteful; dictated by malice. (Fr. *malicieuse.*)
maliciously, *ad.* ma-*lish*-us-le, with malice.
maliciousness, *n.* quality of being malicious.
malign, *a.* ma-*line*, having a very evil disposition towards others; malicious; unfavourable; pernicious: *v.t.* to speak evil of; to traduce; to defame: *v.i.* to entertain malice. (O.Fr. *maligne.*)
malignancy, *n.* ma-*lig*-nan-se, extreme malevolence; malice; unfavourableness; virulence; tendency to mortification or a fatal issue [Med.].
malignant, *a.* ma-*lig*-nant, having extreme malevolence; unpropitious or exerting pernicious influence; virulent; dangerous to life; tending to a fatal issue [Med.]: *n.* one evilly-disposed (applied esp. by the Puritans to a royalist supporter). (L. *malignans.*)
malignantly, *ad.* in a malignant manner.
maligner, *n.* ma-*line*-er, one who maligns another; a traducer.
malignity, *n.* ma-*lig*-ne-te, extreme enmity or malice; evil nature; virulence.
malignly, *ad.* ma-*line*-le, in a malign manner.
malinger, *v.i.* ma-*ling*-ger, to feign illness in order to avoid duty. (Fr. *malingre*, sickly.)
malingerer, *n.* ma-*ling*-ger-rer, one who malingers.
malism, *n.* *may*-lizm, the doctrine that evil exceeds good in the world. (L. *malus*, evil.)
malison, *n.* *mal*-e-zon, malediction; a curse. (O.Fr.)
malkin, *n.* *maw*-kin, amop; a dirty drab; a scare-crow; a kitchen-maid. (*Mald-kin*, diminutive of *Maud* or *Matilda.*)
mall, *n.* mal, the mallet used in pall-mall; hence, a place for playing this game, as Pall Mall, in London, and hence, a shaded public promenade. (*maul.*)
mallard, *n.* *mal*-lard, the common wild duck, *Anas boscas*, esp. the drake. (O.Fr.)
malleability, *n.* *mal*-le-a-*bil*-e-te, the capability of being hammered or pressed into thin sheets. (L. *malleus*, a hammer.)
malleable, *a.* *mal*-le-a-bl, that may be extended by hammering. (Fr.)
malleate, *v.t.* *mal*-le-ate, to extend into a plate or leaf by beating, etc.: *a.* hammer-shaped [Zool.].
malleation, *n.* *mal*-le-*ay*-shon, extension by action of hammering or rolling.
mallee, *n.* *mal*-lee, one of several Australian scrub-plants, esp. *Eucalyptus dumosa.*
mallee-bird, *n.* *mal*-lee-bird, the Australian mound-bird *Leipoa ocellata*, of the genus *Megapodius.*
mallemuck, *n.* *mal*-e-muk, the fulmar, or other large sea-bird. (Dut. *mallemok*, foolish gull.)
mallenders, *n.* *mal*-en-derz, a scaly eczematous eruption occurring in horses at the bend of the knee and on the inside of the hock of the foreleg (*cf.* **sallenders**) [Vet.]. (Through Fr. from L. *malandria*, sores.)
malleolar, *a.* mal-*lee*-o-lar, relating or belonging to the malleolus [Anat.].
malleolus, *n.* mal-*lee*-o-lus, one of two bony processes that project from the leg on either side of the ankle. (L., a small hammer.)
mallet, *n.* *mal*-let, a wooden hammer; the long-handled striker used in croquet and polo. **mallet-finger,** a fixed flexion of the terminal phalanx of a finger. **mallet-toe,** hammer-toe. (Fr. *maillet.*)
malleus, *n.* *mal*-le-us, the hammer-shaped ossicle of the middle ear. (L.)
mallow, *n.* *mal*-loh, the downy-leaved plant *Malva sylvestis*; also *Althæa officinalis*, the marsh mallow, and *Lavatera arborea*, the tree mallow. (A.S. *malwe*, connected with Gr. *malache*, soft.)
malm, *n.* mahm, a light loamy soil composed of friable chalky rock: *v.t.* to treat or mix with this. (A.S. *mealm.*)
Malmaison, *n.* mal-*may*-zon, a variety of carnation; a dark-pink Bourbon rose. (Name of a palace of the Empress Josephine.)
malmsey, *n.* *mahm*-ze, Malvoisie, a strong sweet wine, now made principally in Spain, Madeira, and the Azores. (*Malvasia*, in the Morea.)
malnutrition, *n.* *mal*-new-*trish*-on, insufficient or faulty nutrition.
malodorous, *a.* mal-*oh*-do-rus, having an offensive odour, stinking.
malodour, *n.* mal-*oh*-dor, an offensive odour.
Malpighian, *a.* mal-*pig*-e-an, relating to Marcello Malpighi (*d.* 1694), Ital. anatomist; applied esp. to certain vessels, tubes, tissue, etc., first investigated by him [Anat.].
malpractice, *n.* mal-*prak*-tis, illegal or immoral conduct; wrong or unskilful treatment [Med.].
malpresentation, *n.* *mal*-prez-en-*tay*-shun, faulty presentation of the fœtus at birth.
malt, *n.* mawlt, barley or other grain steeped in water till it germinates, dried in a kiln, and used in brewing or distilling: *a.* made with or containing malt: *v.t.* to convert to or treat with malt: *v.i.* to become malt. (A.S. *mealt*, from *meltan*, to melt.)
Malta, *n.* *mawl*-ta, a British island and naval base in the Mediterranean. **Malta fever,** an undulant or remittant fever, formerly prevalent in Mediterranean lands, and due to a micrococcus conveyed by the milk of the Maltese goat.
maltase, *n.* *mawl*-tace, an enzyme present in the digestive juices, the liver, etc., and in yeast [Chem.].
Maltese, *n.* mawl-*teez*, a native or the natives of Malta; their language; a Maltese terrier: *a.* pertaining to Malta or its people. **Maltese cross,** a cross having equal arms, each expanding from their junction and being bifurcated at the extremity, thus giving eight points; wrongly applied to the cross patée. **Maltese fever,** Malta fever. **Maltese**

terrier, a small lapdog of spaniel appearance with straight silky hair.
malt-floor, *n.* a floor on which malt is laid for germinating.
maltha, *n. mal*-tha, a former cement of some kind; a tarry variety of asphalt. (Gr.)
Malthusian, *a.* mal-*thew*-ze-an, according to the principle of Malthus: *n.* an advocate of his doctrine, that as population tends to increase at a greater rate than the means of subsistence, some check on the rate of human reproduction is necessary. (T. R. *Malthus*, Engl. economist, *d.* 1834.)
malt-liquor, *n.* a liquor prepared by an infusion of malt, esp. beer of any kind.
maltman, *n. mawlt*-man, a maltster.
maltose, *n. mawl*-tohs, a dextrorotatory sugar obtained from starch by the action of diastase.
maltreat, *v.t.* mal-*treet*, to treat badly; to abuse; to treat rudely or with unkindness. (Fr. *maltraiter.*
maltreatment, *n.* mal-*treet*-ment, ill treatment; ill usage; abuse.
maltster, *n. mawlt*-ster, a malt maker.
maltworm, *n. mawlt*-wurm, a tippler [Slang].
malty, *a. mawl*-te, containing or tasting of malt.
malvaceous, *a.* mal-*vay*-shus, pertaining to mallows, or the group they belong to. (L. *malva*, a mallow.)
malversation, *n. mal*-ver-*say*-shon, fraudulent tricks; corruption in office. (Fr.)
malvoisie, *n. mal*-vwah-zee, malmsey wine.
mamba, *n. mam*-ba, the large venomous tree cobra of tropical Africa, of the genus *Dendraspis*. (Zulu.)
mamelon, *n. mam*-e-lon, a rounded hillock or mound. (Fr., nipple.)
Mameluke, *n. mam*-e-look, a formidable military force in Egypt, of white slave origin, destroyed by Mehemet Ali in 1811. (Ar., a slave.)
mamilla, *n.* ma-*mil*-la, the teat or nipple; a nipple-shaped organ or part [Anat. and Bot.]. (L.)
mamillary, *a. mam*-mil-la-re, pertaining to the breast; resembling a nipple; mammiform.
mamillated, *a. mam*-mil-lay-ted, having mammiform protuberances.
mamma, *n.* ma-*mah*, a childish name for mother.
mamma, *n. mam*-ma, the breast; the mammary gland in the female mammal; an udder. (L.)
mammal, *n. mam*-mal, any one of the mammalia.
mammalia, *n.pl.* ma-*may*-le-a, the highest class of the vertebrates, including man and all animals which suckle their young. (L. *mammalis*, from *mamma*, breast.)
mammalian, *a.* ma-*may*-le-an, pertaining to or characteristic of the mammalia: *n.* a mammal.
mammaliferous, *a. mam*-ma-*lif*-er-rus, containing mammalian remains [Geol.].
mammalogist, *n.* ma-*mal*-o-jist, one versed in the study of the mammalia.
mammalogy, *n.* ma-*mal*-o-je, the scientific study of mammals.
mammary, *a. mam*-a-re, pertaining to the breasts. **mammary gland,** one of the milk-secreting glands of the female mammal.
mammee, *n.* mam-*mee*, the fruit of the West Indian tree, *Mammea americana*; applied also to the fruit of the marmalade-tree and the sapodilla.
mammet, *n. mam*-et, a puppet; a dressed figure.
mammifer, *n. mam*-e-fer, a mammal. (L. *mamma*, and *ferre*, to bear.)
mammiform, *a. mam*-e-form, breast-shaped.
mammon, *n. mam*-on, the god of riches or spirit of the world; the personification of wealth. (Aramaic.)
mammonish, *a. mam*-on-ish, characteristic of mammon; money-grubbing.
mammonism, *n. mam*-on-izm, pursuit of riches; the service of mammon.
mammonist, *n. mam*-on-ist, a person devoted to the acquisition of wealth; a worldling.
mammose, *a. mam*-moce, having full breasts.
mammoth, *n. mam*-moth, one of several extinct species of elephant of Pleistocene times, some of which were gigantic: *a.* of immense size. **mammoth tree,** the Wellingtonia or giant sequoia. (Russ. *mammot.*)
mammula, *n. mam*-yew-la, a small mamilla or nipple-like process [Zool.].
mammy, *n. mam*-e, nursery name for mother; a coloured nurse or servant-girl [U.S.A.].
***man,** *n.* man (*pl.* **men**), a human being; an adult male of the human species; one with manly qualities; mankind; a male servant, valet, or attendant; a workman; a private soldier; a husband; a word of familiar address; a vassal; a liege subject or tenant; one of the movable pieces at chess or draughts; the obverse of a tossed coin [Slang]: *v.t.* to furnish with men; to fortify or strengthen. **best man,** *see* **best. inner man,** the soul or intellect. **man about town,** a moneyed frequenter of society functions, fashionable resorts, etc. **man Friday,** a factotum; a servile follower. **man in the street,** the hypothetical normal, or average, man. **man of God,** a prophet; an ecclesiastic. **man of letters,** a scholar; a literary man. **man of sorrows,** the Messiah, Christ. **man of straw,** a person of no reliability; a fictitious person. **man to man,** openly; frankly. (A.S. *mann.*)
mana, *n. mah*-na, supernatural power, esp. that attributed to the forces of nature; magical power. (Maori.)
manacle, *n. man*-a-kl, a handcuff; a shackle for the wrist or hand: *v.t.* to put manacles on; to shackle; to confine. (O.Fr. *manicle.*)
manage, *v.t. man*-aj, to conduct; to direct; to control; to wield; to have under command; to make subservient; to husband; to treat judiciously: *v.i.* to conduct affairs; to do, or get on or along (with or without): *n.* management; handling. (It. *maneggiare*, to manage.)
manageability, *n. man*-aj-a-*bil*-e-te, the quality of being manageable.
manageable, *a. man*-aj-a-bl, easy to be managed; tractable.
manageably, *ad. man*-aj-a-ble, in a manageable way.
management, *n. man*-aj-ment, manner of directing or carrying on; conduct; administration; skilful conduct; dealing; managing body.
***manager,** *n. man*-aj-er, one who manages; an overseer or director; a good economist in household affairs; one appointed to look after a business in the interest of creditors, etc. [Law].
manageress, *n. man*-aj-er-*ress*, a female manager.
managerial, *a.* man-a-*jeer*-re-al, relating to management; characteristic of a manager.
manakin, *n. man*-a-kin, any of a group of small brightly coloured birds of the genus *Pipra*, found in Central and South America; a manikin.
man-at-arms, *n.* a heavily-armed mounted soldier, esp. of mediæval times.
manatee, *n. man*-a-tee, a large herbivorous sirenian of American rivers, allied to the dugong; the sea-cow. (Sp.)
manche, *n.* mansh, an old-fashioned long-hanging sleeve, esp. in heraldic representation. (Fr.)
Manchester, *a. man*-ches-ter, relating to Manchester, the centre, in England, of the cotton trade. **Manchester goods,** cotton textiles. **Manchester School,** believers in free-trade and laissez-faire, first led at Manchester by Cobden and Bright in mid-19th cent. **Manchester terrier,** a long-legged lightly built dog with a short-haired black-and-tan coat.
manchet, *n. man*-chet, a small loaf of fine bread. (Fr.)
man-child, *n. man*-chyld, a boy.
manchineel, *n.* man-che-*neel*, the poisonous tropical American tree, *Hippomane mancinella*, valued for cabinet-work. (Sp., a little apple.)
Manchu, *n.* man-*choo*, a member of a Manchurian branch of the Tungus that conquered China in the 17th century and provided the ruling dynasty till 1912; their language: *a.* pertaining to Manchuria or the Manchus.
manciple, *n. man*-se-pl, a steward; a purveyor of stores. (O.Fr.)
Mancunian, *a.* man-*kew*-ne-an, of or relating to Manchester: *n.* a native or inhabitant of Manchester. (L. *Mancunium*, Manchester.)
-mancy, *man*-se, suffix signifying divination by, as in *arithmancy*, *chiromancy*. (Gr. *manteia*, divination.)
mandamus, *n.* man-*day*-mus, a command or writ officially directing a person, corporation, or inferior court to do some act appertaining to their office and duty [Law]. (L., we command.)
mandarin, *n. man*-da-rin, a Chinese or higher official under the Chinese Empire; the more prevalent Chinese dialect; a tangerine orange; a liqueur flavoured with this, also a dye of its colour. **mandarin duck,** a duck of Eastern Asia, *Aix galericulata*. (Sans. *mantra*, counsel.)

mandatary, *n.* *man*-da-ta-re, one to whom a mandate or charge is given.
mandate, *n.* *man*-date, an official or authoritative command; a charge; a commission to act on another's behalf; a rescript of the pope; an order from the League of Nations (1919–39) entrusting a state with the governance of a conquered territory: *v.t.* to assign to a mandatary. **mandated territory,** a country or territory administered under a mandate. (O.Fr. *mandat*, order.)
mandatory, *a.* *man*-da-to-re, containing a command; perceptive; directory; pertaining to a League of Nations mandate.
mandelic, *a.* man-*del*-ik, amygdalic; designating an acid occurring naturally in amygdalin. (Ger. *Mandel*, almond.)
mandible, *n.* *man*-de-bl, the jaw, applied to both jaws in birds, the under jaw in mammals, and to the anterior pair in insects. (L. *mandibula*, jaw.)
mandibular, *a.* man-*dib*-yew-lar, belonging to the jaw.
mandibulate, *a.* man-*dib*-yew-late, provided with mandibles, as many insects.
mandioc, *n.* *man*-de-ok, manioc; cassava.
mandoline, *n.* *man*-do-lin, a guitar-like instrument having a pear- or almond-shaped body and metal strings played with a plectrum. (It.)
mandragora, *n.* man-*drag*-o-ra, the mandrake; (*cap.*) a small genus of plants allied to the potato.
mandrake, *n.* *man*-drake, any plant of the genus *Mandragora*, esp. *M. officinarum*, which has narcotic qualities; the white bryony, *Bryonia dioica*. (Gr. *mandragoras*, mandrake.)
mandrel, *n.* *man*-drel, the shank of a lathe on which the substance to be turned is fixed; a cylindrical rod or core on which metal is shaped or cast. (Fr. *mandrin*.)
mandrill, *n.* *man*-dril, the fierce W. African baboon, *Cynocephalus mormon*. (*man*, and *drill*, baboon.)
manducable, *a.* *man*-dew-ka-bl, eatable; that can be chewed.
manducate, *v.t.* *man*-dew-kate, to chew. (L. *manducatus*, chewed.)
manducation, *n.* man-dew-*kay*-shon, the act of eating, esp. the sacramental bread.
manducatory, *a.* man-dew-*kay*-to-re, pertaining to or employed in chewing.
mane, *n.* mane, the hair on the upper side of the neck of a horse or certain other animals. (A.S. *manu*.)
maned, *a.* maynd, having a mane.
manège, *n.* ma-*nayzh*, horsemanship or the training of horses; a school for teaching horsemanship or for training horses. (Fr.)
manes, *n.pl.* *may*-neez, the ghosts or spirits of the dead, esp. of one's ancestors. (L.)
mane-sheet, *n.* a covering for the upper part of a horse's head.
manful, *a.* *man*-ful, having the spirit of a man; bold; courageous; noble.
manfully, *ad.* *man*-ful-le, in a manful manner.
manfulness, *n.* the quality of being manful.
mangabey, *n.* *mang*-ga-be, a W. African monkey with bare eyelids, a species of *Cercocebus*. (Erroneously from Mangabey, in Madagascar.)
manganate, *n.* *mang*-ga-nate, a compound of manganic acid with a base.
manganese, *n.* *mang*-ga-neez, a hard, brittle metallic element of a silvery-grey colour; any of its oxides, esp. pyrolusite. **manganese steel,** a steel alloy of great hardness. (Fr. *manganèse*, corruption of *magnesia*.)
manganesian, *a.* mang-ga-*nee*-ze-an, pertaining to, consisting of, or containing manganese.
manganic, *a.* mang-*gan*-ik, manganesian; resembling manganese; designating the acid which, with a base, forms manganates.
manganin, *n.* *mang*-ga-nin, a copper alloy containing 13–18 per cent. manganese with a little nickel, used for resistance coils [Elect.].
manganite, *n.* *mang*-ga-nite, hydrous oxide of manganese, one of its ores.
manganosite, *n.* mang-ga-*noh*-site, the protoxide of magnesium, occurring in green isometric crystals.
mange, *n.* maynj, a contagious parasitic skin-disease in dogs and beasts. (O.Fr. *mangeson*.)
mangel-wurzel, *n.* *mang*-gl-*wur*-zl, the large beet, *Beta vulgaris*, cultivated for feeding cattle. (Ger. *Mangold*, beet, *Wurzel*, root.)
manger, *n.* *mane*-jer, a trough for horses and cattle to eat out of. (O.Fr. *mangeure*.)
manginess, *n.* *mane*-je-ness, the state of being mangy.
mangle, *v.t.* *mang*-gl, to cut and hack or hash; to tear in cutting; to mutilate; to spoil; to mar. (O.Fr. *mahangler*.)
mangle, *n.* *mang*-gl, a rolling-press for smoothing damp linen: *v.t.* to smooth linen with a mangle; to calender. (Dut. *mangel*, a rolling pin.)
mangler, *n.* *mang*-gler, one who mangles.
mango, *n.* *mang*-goh, the tropical tree, *Mangifera indica*, and its fruit; a green musk-melon pickled [U.S.A.]. (Malay.)
mango-fish, *n.* a tropical sea-fish of the order *Polyneumus*, of India and Malaysia.
mangold, *n.* *mang*-guld, mangel-wurzel. (Ger.)
mangonel, *n.* *mang*-go-nel, a mediæval military engine used for battering walls with stones. (O.Fr.)
mangosteen, *n.* *mang*-go-steen, an Indian tree, *Garcinia mangostana*; its fruit, about the size of an orange. (Malay.)
mangrove, *n.* *mang*-grove, any of several tropical trees of different genera, esp. *Rhizophora mangle*, growing near or in water and having many aerial interlacing roots. (Malay.)
mangy, *a.* *mane*-je, infected with the mange; mean.
man-handle, *v.t.* to move anything without mechanical help; to treat another roughly.
manhole, *n.* *man*-hole, a hole through which a man may enter a drain, or boiler, etc.
manhood, *n.* *man*-hood, the state of being a man, esp. as distinct from a woman or boy; manliness. **manhood suffrage,** the political enfranchisement of all male adult citizens not disqualified by lunacy or crime, etc.
man-hour, *n.* the amount of work done by one man in one hour, used as a unit in costing.
mania, *n.* *may*-ne-a, madness; acute mental derangement; vehement desire; a craze. (Gr., frenzy.)
-mania, *may*-ne-a, a suffix denoting some special form of insanity, as *megalomania*, or a morbid or irresistible craving for, as *dipsomania*.
maniac, *n.* *may*-ne-ak, a madman.
maniacal, *a.* ma-*ny*-a-kal, affected with madness; connected with madness.
Manichæan, *n.* man-e-*kee*-an, one of a sect who believed in two eternal and equal principles of being, good or light, and evil or darkness: *a.* pertaining to Manichæism.
Manichæism, *n.* *man*-e-*kee*-izm, the religious system of the Manichæans, founded by the Persian Mani, who was crucified by the Magians about 276 A.D.
Manichee, *n.* *man*-e-kee, a Manichæan.
manicure, *n.* *man*-e-kewr, the care of the hands and finger-nails; a manicurist: *v.t.* to treat the finger-nails and hands: *v.i.* to practise as a manicurist. (L. *manus*, hand, *cura*, care.)
manicurist, *n.* *man*-e-kewr-rist, one whose business it is to manicure.
manifest, *a.* *man*-e-fest, clearly visible or intelligible; clear; evident: *n.* an invoice of a cargo for customs purposes: *v.t.* to show plainly; to reveal. (Fr. *manifeste*.)
manifestation, *n.* *man*-e-fes-*tay*-shon, the act of disclosing or manifesting; exhibition; revelation.
manifestly, *ad.* *man*-e-fest-le, in a manifest manner.
manifestness, *n.* quality of being manifest.
manifesto, *n.* man-e-*fes*-toh, a public declaration in regard to some political intention or measure.
manifold, *a.* *man*-e-fohld, of different kinds; numerous; multiplex; multifarious: *n.* a copy made by manifolding: *v.t.* to multiply copies of letters, documents, etc., mechanically. **manifold paper,** thin paper used in duplicating.
manifoldly, *ad.* in a manifold manner.
manifoldness, *n.* *man*-e-fohld-ness, the state of being manifold; multiplicity.
Manihot, *n.* *man*-e-hot, the large genus of S. American plants of the spurge family including the manioc.
manikin, *n.* *man*-e-kin, a little man; a pygmy; a model of the human body for anatomical and surgical studies; a dummy for displaying garments. (Fr. *mannequin*.)
manilla, *n.* ma-*nil*-la, a metal ring worn by natives of the West African coast, on the arm or leg; a piece of copper money in use among certain native West Africans. (Sp.)
Manilla, *n.* ma-*nil*-la, a kind of cheroot made at

Manilla, in the Philippine Islands. **Manilla hemp,** abaca, a fibrous material from which ropes and cables are made, obtained from the plantain, *Musa textilis*. **Manilla paper,** a strong paper made from sulphite wood-pulp with about 35 per cent. Manilla hemp fibre.
manioc, *n.* *man*-e-ok, the S. American tree, *Manihot aipi*, from the roots of which cassava and tapioca are prepared. (Port.)
maniple, *n.* *man*-e-pl, a kind of scarf worn on the left wrist, originally a napkin for wiping the chalice [Eccles.]; a company in a Roman legion. (L. *manipulus*, handful.)
manipular, *a.* ma-*nip*-yew-lar, pertaining to a maniple; manipulatory: *n.* a soldier of a manible.
manipulate, *v.t.* ma-*nip*-yew-late, to handle skilfully; to treat; to manage; to falsify [Coll.]: *v.i.* to use one's hands with skill.
manipulation, *n.* ma-*nip*-yew-*lay*-shon, the act of manipulating; skilful use of the hands in scientific operations; falsification [Coll.].
manipulative, *a.* ma-*nip*-yew-la-tiv, pertaining to or of manipulation. **manipulative surgery,** the treatment of displacements malformations, adhesions, etc., by manipulation without the use of the knife; osteopathy.
manipulator, *n.* ma-*nip*-yew-*lay*-tor, one who manipulates; a contrivance for assisting manipulation.
manipulatory, *a.* ma-*nip*-yew-la-to-re, performed by manipulation; manipulative.
Manis, *n.* *may*-nis, the genus of edentates comprising the pangolins or scaly ant-eaters. (L. *manes.*)
Manitou, *n.* *man*-e-too, a N. American Indian personification of one of the great forces of nature; (*l.c.*) a totem, fetish or amulet. (Algonquian.)
manitrunk, *n.* *man*-e-trunk, the anterior segment of the body of an insect. (L. *manus*, hand, *truncus*, trunk.)
mankind, *n.* man-*kynd*, the human race.
manless, *a.* *man*-less, destitute of men; not manned.
manliness, *n.* manly quality; courage.
manly, *a.* *man*-le, manlike; becoming a man; brave; dignified; characteristic of a man.
man-made, *a.* *man*-made, made by man; handmade as distinguished from machine-made.
manna, *n.* *man*-na, the food divinely supplied to the Israelites in the wilderness; spiritual nourishment; a sweet, mildly laxative juice exuding from incisions in the ash, esp. *Fraxinus ornus*. (Heb. *man.*)
manned, *pp.* mand, furnished with men.
mannequin, *n.* *man*-e-kin, a lay-figure for displaying dresses and clothes; a woman paid to display newly designed clothes by wearing them. (Fr. *mannequin.*)
manner, *n.* *man*-ner, way of performing anything; method; fashion; style; habit; custom; mannerism; sort: *pl.* ways of acting; morals; behaviour; deportment; politeness. (Fr. *manière*, from L. *manus*, the hand.)
mannered, *a.* *man*-nerd, having manners (as *well-mannered, ill-mannered*); displaying mannerisms.
mannerism, *n.* *man*-ner-izm, peculiarity of style or manner, often constrained and affected.
mannerist, *n.* *man*-ner-ist; one given to mannerisms; an artist, etc., with a distinctive style.
mannerless, *a.* having no manners; rude.
mannerliness, *n.* quality of being mannerly.
mannerly, *a.* *man*-ner-le, of good address and deportment; complaisant; civil; respectful.
mannikin, *n.* *man*-e-kin, a manikin.
mannish, *a.* *man*-nish, masculine; befitting or characteristic of a man rather than a woman.
mannishly, *ad.* *man*-nish-le, in a mannish manner.
mannite, *n.* *man*-nite, a sweet crystalline compound obtained from the manna ash and other plants.
manœuvrable, *a.* ma-*noo*-vra-bl, capable of being manœuvred, esp. of aircraft, tanks, etc.
manœuvrability, *n.* ma-noo-vra-*bil*-e-te, capacity of being manœuvrable.
manœuvre, *n.* ma-*noo*-ver, an evolution; an adroit movement; skilful management; stratagem; *pl.* field exercises of considerable forces in mimic warfare; similar naval exercises: *v.i.* and *t.* to move or change positions among troops or ships; to manage with address. (Fr., handwork, from *main*, hand, *œuvre*, work.)
manœuvrer, *n.* ma-*noo*-vrer, one who manœuvres.
man-of-war *n.* a naval vessel, esp. one of large size, built, equipped, and employed for purposes of war. **man-of-war bird,** the frigate-bird; applied also to the albatross and arctic skua.
manometer, *n.* ma-*nom*-e-ter, an instrument for measuring the elastic force of gases; a pressure gauge. (Gr. *manos*, rare, *metron*, measure.)
manometric, *a.* *man*-o-*met*-rik, pertaining to, or effected by means of, the manometer.
manor, *n.* *man*-or, a demesne estate which held, or was entitled to hold, a court-baron; an estate held in copyhold; the house and land belonging to the holder of such, known as the **lord of the manor.** (O.Fr. *manoir.*)
manorial, *a.* ma-naw-re-al, pertaining to a manor.
man-power, *n.* power supplied by man unaided by the machine; the collective force of personnel available for a given purpose.
manqué, *a.* (App.), that comes short of perfection or expectation; abortive. (Fr., spoilt.)
man-rope, *n.* a side-rope at a ship's gangway.
mansard, *n.* *man*-sard, a roof with two stages of different slopes, the lower steeper than that above. (François *Mansard*, noted Fr. architect, *d.* 1666.)
manse, *n.* manse, the residence of a Presbyterian or Free Church minister, esp. in Scotland. (O.Fr.)
man-servant, *n.* a domestic male servant.
mansion, *n.* *man*-shon, a house of some size and pretension; an astrological "house"; *pl.* a group of residential flats. **the Mansion House,** the Lord Mayor of London's official residence. (O.Fr.)
manslaughter, *n.* *man*-slaw-ter, the killing of a man; the unlawful killing of a man without malice aforethought [Law].
man-slayer, *n.* one who has slain a human being or has committed manslaughter.
mansuetude, *n.* *man*-swe-tewd, gentleness; tameness. (L.)
mantel, *n.* *man*-tel, a beam or slab resting on the jambs of a fireplace; a mantelpiece; the whole ornamental finish to a fireplace. (O.Fr.)
mantelet, *n.* *mant*-let, a small sleeveless mantle; a moveable bullet-proof shield for defence.
mantelpiece, *n.* *man*-tel-peece, an ornamental shelf above the mantel over a fireplace.
mantic, *a.* *man*-tik, pertaining to divination; prophetic. (Gr. *mantis*, a prophet.)
mantilla, *n.* man-*til*-la, a small mantle; a hood; a lace veil worn by women over the head and shoulders in Spain. (Sp.)
mantis, *n.* *man*-tis, any of the genus comprising the stick insects; the praying mantis, *Mantis religiosa*.
mantissa, *n.* man-*tis*-sa, the decimal part of a logarithm. (L., an addition.)
mantle, *n.* *man*-tl, a cloak or loose outer garment; a covering; a mantling [Her.]; a gas-mantle; a covering part, esp. the external fold of the skin of a mollusc [Zool.]: *v.t.* to cloak; to disguise: *v.i.* to be expanded; to be coated over; to be suffused. **incandescent mantle,** a gas-mantle. (O.Fr. *mantel.*)
mantlet, *n.* *mant*-let, a mantelet.
mantling, *n.* *mant*-ling, a material for mantles; a lambrequin, or representation of a mantle, as background to a shield [Her.]; a foaming or blushing.
mantra, *n.* *man*-tra, a Vedic hymn.
man-trap, *n.* a trap for catching trespassers.
mantua, *n.* *man*-tew-a, a loose-bodied gown worn by women in the early 18th century. **mantua-maker,** *n.* a dressmaker. (Fr. *manteau.*)
manual, *a.* *man*-yew-al, pertaining to or performed by the hand: *n.* a handbook or handy compendium; the Roman Catholic service-book; a fire-engine operated by hand; the keyboard of an organ. (Fr. *manuel.*)
manually, *ad.* *man*-yew-al-le, with the hand.
manucode, *n.* *man*-yew-kode, any of a group of Australasian birds, allied to the birds of paradise, with glossy steel-blue plumage. (Malay *manuk-dewata*, bird of the gods.)
manufactory, *n.* *man*-yew-*fak*-to-re, a place where goods are manufactured; a factory.
manufactural, *a.* relating to manufactures.
manufacture, *n.* *man*-yew-*fak*-tewr, the process of manufacturing into a form suitable for use; the article manufactured: *v.t.* to make or fabricate from raw or partly wrought materials, esp. with machinery and on a large scale: *v.i.* to be occupied in manufacturing; to be capable of being manufactured. (Fr.)

manufacturer, *n.* *man*-yew-*fak*-tewr-rer, one who manufactures; the owner of a manufactory.
manufacturing, *a.* *man*-yew-*fak*-tewr-ring, pertaining to or employed in manufacture.
manumission, *n.* *man*-yew-*mish*-on, liberation of a slave.
manumit, *v.t.* *man*-yew-*mit*, to release from slavery; to free. (L. *manumittere*, release.)
manure, *n.* ma-*newr*, dung, compost, or any preparation which fertilizes land: *v.t.* to fertilize or enrich by manuring. (Contracted from *manœuvre.*)
manurer, *n.* ma-*newr*-rer, one who or that which distributes manure over the ground.
manuscript, *a.* *man*-yew-skript, written with the hand: *n.* a book or paper written with the hand; copy for printing. (Late L. *manuscriptum.*)
manward, *a.* and *ad.* *man*-ward, toward or directed toward man; in relation to man.
Manx, *n.* manks, the Celtic language, or the people, of the Isle of Man: *a.* pertaining to the Isle of Man or its people. **manx cat,** a breed of cat with only a rudimentary tail. **manx shearwater,** the sea bird *Puffinus puffinus.*
many, *a.* *men*-e, comprising a great number; numerous: *n.* a great number; many people. **the many,** the majority; the common herd. (A.S. *manig.*)
manyplies, *n.* *men*-e-plyz, the omasum, or third stomach of ruminants. (*many*, and *plies*, folds.)
many-sidedness, *n.* *men*-e-*side*-ed-ness, the quality of having many sides, or of being of a wide range of sympathy and capability.
manzanilla, *n.* man-za-*nil*-la, a dry brown sherry; a small and bitter olive. (Sp.)
manzanita, *n.* *man*-za-*nee*-ta, a Californian shrub of the genus *Arctostaphylos.*
Maori, *n.* *mah*-re *or* *mou*-re, a native of the Polynesian race of New Zealand; the language of these Polynesians: *a.* of, or pertaining to, the Maoris. (Literally, native.)
★**map,** *n.* map, a representation on a plane of a portion of the surface of the earth or the heavens; a chart; any delineation: *v.t.* to draw or delineate in, or as in, a map; to describe distinctly. **off the map,** in an insignificant position; in oblivion. **on the map,** in an important position. (L. *mappa.*)
maple, *n.* *may*-pl, a tree of the genus *Acer*; its timber. **maple sugar,** sugar obtained by evaporation from the sap of certain maples, esp. *Acer saccharum.* (A.S. *mapol.*)
mapper, *n.* *map*-er, a map-maker; one who maps.
maqui, *n.* *mah*-kee, the Chilean evergreen shrub *Aristotelia maqui*; a flavouring made from its berries. (Native name.)
maquis, *n.* *mah*-kee, brushwood-covered heath, esp. in Corsica. **to take to the maquis,** to be "on the run," to go into hiding (hence used of the underground movement in France during the German occupation, 1940–44). (Fr., from Ital. *macchie*, thickets.)
mar, *v.t.* mar, to injure; to blemish; to disfigure; to interrupt: *n.* a defect. (A.S. *merran*, to hinder.)
marabou, *n.* *ma*-ra-boo, a large African adjutant stork of the genus *Leptoptilus.*
marabout, *n.* *mah*-ra-boot, one of a N. African Mohammedan priestly caste; a Mohammedan saint or hermit. (Fr., from Ar. *mūrabit*, through Port.)
maranatha, *n.* mah-rah-*nah*-tha, a kind of anathema (Aramaic, the Lord cometh to judge.)
marantic, *a.* ma-*ran*-tik, due to or pertaining to marasmus [Med.].
maraschino, *n.* *ma*-ra-*skee*-no, a spirit distilled from *Prunus cerosus marasca*, the bitter wild cherry. (It. *marasca*, from L. *amarus*, bitter.)
marasmatic, *a.* *ma*-raz-*mat*-ik, affected with marasmus [Med.].
marasmus, *n.* ma-*raz*-mus, emaciation; wasting away of the body [Med.]. (Gr.)
Marathi, *n.* ma-*rah*-the, the language (derived from Sanskrit) of the Mahrattas of Western India.
marathon, *n.* *ma*-ra-thon, a long-distance foot race (properly of 26 miles 385 yds., commemorating Pheidippides's run from Marathon to Athens announcing the Persian defeat, 490 B.C.).
maraud, *v.i.* and *t.* ma-*rawd*, to rove in quest of plunder; to pillage. (O.Fr. *marault*, rogue.)
marauder, *n.* ma-*raw*-der, one who marauds.
maravedi, *n.* *ma*-ra-*vay*-dee, a small Spanish copper coin; a doit. (Sp.)
marble, *n.* *mar*-bl, a limestone of compact texture, and susceptible of a high polish; a little ball used in certain games; *pl.* sculpture or statuary of marble: *a.* made of marble; veined like marble; hard; unfeeling: *v.t.* to stain or vein like marble. (O.Fr. *marbre*, from Gr. *marmaros*, a sparkling stone.)
marbled, *a.* *mar*-bld, veined like marble.
marble-edged, *a.* with marbled edges.
marble-hearted, *a.* hard-hearted.
marbler, *n.* *mar*-bl-er, one who veins paper or other material in imitation of marble.
marbling, *n.* *mar*-bl-ing, the art or practice of variegating like marble; a variegation like marble.
marbly, *ad.* *mar*-bl-e, resembling, or of the nature of, marble.
marc, *n.* mark, the refuse or cake after expressing the oil or juice from fruits or seeds. (Fr.)
marcasite, *n.* *mar*-ka-site, white iron pyrites, orthorhombic disulphide of iron. (Fr.)
marcasitic, *a.* *mar*-ka-*sit*-ik, pertaining to marcasite.
marcel, *v.t.* mar-*sel*, to impart a marcel wave to (of the hair). **marcel-wave,** *n.* the ripple given to straight hair by the process invented by Marcel, a French hairdresser (early 20th cent.).
marceline, *n.* *mar*-sel-in, a thin silk fabric. (Fr.)
marcescence, *n.* mar-*ses*-ence, state of being marcescent; a fading.
marcescent, *a.* mar-*ses*-ent, fading; withering without falling off [Bot.]. (L. *marcescens*, withering.)
marcessible, *a.* mar-*ses*-e-bl, that may wither.
March, *n.* march, the third month of the year. (L. *Martius*, dedicated to Mars.)
march, *n.* march, the border of a country or district: *v.i.* to border. **ride the marches,** to traverse the border lines. (O.Fr. *marche.*)
march, *n.* march, regular measured movement, esp. of troops; a piece of music to march by; the distance marched over; onward movement: *v.i.* to move in a military manner; to walk in a grave, deliberative, or stately manner: *v.t.* to cause to march or go. (Fr. *marcher.*)
marcher, *n.* *march*-er, a warder or defender of the marches; one living in a borderland.
marchioness, *n.* *mar*-shon-ess, the wife of a marquess; a woman holding the rank in her own right. (Late L. *marcionissa.*)
marchpane, *n.* *march*-pane, old name of marzipan.
marcid, *a.* *mar*-sid, wasting; withered; causing or attended by wasting [Med.]. (L. *marcidus.*)
marconigram, *n.* mar-*koh*-ne-gram, a wireless message over the Marconi system. (G. *Marconi*, It. scientist, *d.* 1937, and L. *gramma*, letter.)
mardi-gras, *n.* mar-de-*grah*, Shrove-Tuesday, the last day of carnival. (Fr., fat Tuesday.)
mare, *n.* mare, the female of the horse. **mare's nest,** a new discovery that proves to be old or a hoax; something ridicuously absurd. **mare's tail,** a long, streaky cloud; an aquatic plant of the genus *Hippuris*; the plant horsetail. (A.S. *mere.*)
maremma, *n.* ma-*rem*-ma, a flat, fertile, but marshy and unhealthy district, esp. on the coast. (It.)
margarate, *n.* *mar*-ga-rat, a salt of margaric acid.
margaric, *a.* mar-*ga*-rik, pertaining to pearl; pearly. **margaric acid,** an acid obtained from several oily compounds, the deposits of which have a pearly aspect. (Gr. *margarites*, a pearl.)
margarine, *n.* *mar*-ga-reen (erroneously *mar*-ja-reen), an artificial butter prepared from certain vegetable and animal oils. (Fr., from Gr. *margarites*, pearl.)
margarite, *n.* *mar*-ga-rite, pearl mica, a hydrated silicate of aluminium and lime.
margaritiferous, *a.* *mar*-ga-re-*tif*-er-rus, producing pearls. (Gr. *margarites*, and L. *fero*, bear.)
margarodite, *n.* mar-*ga*-ro-dite, a hydrated mica with pearly lustre.
margay, *n.* *mar*-gay, the tiger-cat, *Felis tigrina*, of Central and South America.
margin, *n.* *mar*-jin, the edge or border of anything; the blank edge of the page of a book; reserve or allowance for contingencies; difference between cost and selling price [Stock Exchange, etc.]; the smallest profit on which an industry or business can be kept going; a limit: *v.t.* to furnish with a margin; to write on the margin. (L. *margo.*)

marginal, *a.* *mar*-je-nal, on the margin; pertaining to a margin.
marginalia, *n.pl.* *mar*-je-*nay*-le-a, marginal notes.
marginally, *ad.* *mar*-je-na-le, in the margin.
marginate, *a.* *mar*-je-nat, having a margin: *v.t.* to provide with a margin. (L. *marginatus.*)
margosa, *n.* mar-*goh*-sa, the Indian tree *Melia azedarach*, valuable for the tonic quality of its bark and the oil in its seeds. (Port. *amargoso*, bitter.)
margrave, *n.* *mar*-grave, a German title of nobility, originally bestowed on defenders of the marches; the title borne by some hereditary princes of the Holy Roman Empire. (Ger. *Mark*, a march, *Graf*, a count.)
margraviate, *n.* mar-*gray*-ve-at, a margrave's domain.
margravine, *n.* *mar*-gra-veen, the wife of a margrave.
marguerite, *n.* mar-ger-*reet*, the ox-eye daisy.
Marian, *a.* *mare*-re-an, connected with the Virgin Mary, or with Mary I of England or Mary Queen of Scots.
marigold, *n.* *ma*-re-gohld, a composite plant bearing a showy yellow flower, *Calendula officinalis*. **African marigold,** *Tagetes erecta*. **corn marigold,** *Chrysanthemum segetum*. **field marigold,** *Calendula arvensis*. **fig marigold,** any species of *Mesembryanthemum*. **French marigold,** *Tagetes patula*. **marsh marigold,** the kingcup, *Caltha palustris*. (Virgin *Mary* and *gold*.)
marigraph, *n.* *ma*-re-graf, a tide-gauge.
marikina, *n.* ma-re-*kee*-na, a long-tusked marmoset or tamarin of the genus *Midas*.
marimba, *n.* ma-*rim*-ba, a musical instrument of the xylophone kind. (Native W. African.)
marinade, *n.* ma-re-*nade*, pickled fish in vinegar; a highly flavoured pickle or sauce: *v.t.* to pickle in marinade. (Fr.)
marinate, *v.t.* *ma*-re-nate, to marinade.
marine, *a.* ma-*reen*, pertaining to the sea; living or found in the sea; for use at sea; near the sea: *n.* a soldier who serves on board ship; the whole navy of a state; the maritime interest generally. **marine engine,** an engine for propelling a steamship. **marine glue,** a water-resisting cement containing india-rubber and shellac. **marine store,** a place where old ships' stores, etc., are bought and sold. **mercantile marine,** sea-going vessels used for commercial purposes as contrasted with a navy. (Fr. *marin.*)
mariner, *n.* *ma*-re-ner, a sailor, esp. in the merchant service. **master mariner,** a seaman qualified to command a merchant ship. (Fr. *mariner.*)
Marinism, *n.* *ma*-rin-izm, the florid literary style of Giov. Battista Marini, Italian poet, 1569–1625.
Mariolatry, *n.* mare-re-*ol*-a-tre, idolatrous worship of the Virgin Mary. (*Mary*, and Gr. *latreia*, worship.)
marionette, *n.* ma-re-o-*net*, a puppet made to perform motions by means of attached strings. (Fr. *marionnette*, diminutive of *Marie.*)
mariput, *n.* *ma*-re-put, the zorilla. (Native African.)
marish, *n.* *ma*-rish, a marsh. (O.Fr. *mareis.*)
marital, *a.* *ma*-re-tal, pertaining to a husband or to married life; matrimonial. (L. *maritalis.*)
maritally, *ad.* *ma*-re-ta-le, in a marital manner.
maritime, *a.* *ma*-re-time, connected with the sea; bordering on the sea; nautical; living by the sea [Bot. and Zool.].
marjoram, *n.* *mar*-jo-ram, an aromatic plant of the genus *Origanum*, used in seasoning food, and as a tonic and stimulant. (O.Fr. *marjorane.*)
★**mark,** *n.* mark, a stroke, dot, impression, etc., leaving a visible sign; distinction; a visible effect; any note of distinction; an indication, symbol, device, trade-mark, etc.; an evidence; a thing aimed at; something serving as a guide; a limit or boundary; a character made by one unable to sign; a unit awarded to examination candidates to indicate degree of merit; the jack [Bowls]; the pit of the stomach [Boxing]: *v.t.* to make a mark on; to single out; to note or observe; to pay attention to; to be a feature of; to award marks in an examination: *v.i.* to note; to observe critically. **below the mark,** not up to standard. **beside the mark,** having failed to attain an end; irrelevant. **black mark,** a mark of disfavour, censure, or reproof for bad conduct, etc. **man of mark,** a distinguished man. **mark time,** *see* **time.** (A.S. *mearc*, a mark, a bound.)
mark, *n.* mark, a former weight (about ½ lb.) used for gold and silver; an obsolete coin of various countries (originally of 1 mark weight); a German silver coin (about 11¾*d.*) superseded, 1924, by the Reichsmark. (A.S. *marc.*)
marked, *a.* markt, distinguished; unmistakable.
markedly, *ad.* *mar*-ked-le, in a marked or unmistakable manner.
marker, *n.* *mar*-ker, one who or that which marks; a counter used in card-playing; one who marks the score at billiards.
★**market,** *n.* *mar*-ket, a meeting for purchase and sale; a public place for buying and selling; assemblage at a market; sale; the demand for goods, etc., also value ascertained by this; an organization, or a building for the use, of dealers in commodities, securities, etc.: *v.i.* to deal at a market: *v.t.* trade in. **black market,** *see* **black.** **market cross,** a cross set up where a market is held. **market overt,** the public offering of goods for sale. **market place,** the place where cattle, provisions, goods, etc., are exposed for sale. **market price,** the current price of commodities at any given time. **market town,** a town that has the privilege of a public market. (A.S.)
marketable, *a.* *mar*-ket-a-bl, saleable.
marketableness, *n.* state of being marketable.
market-day, *n.* the day of a public market.
market-garden, *n.* a plot on which garden fruits and vegetables are grown for market.
marketing, *n.* *mar*-ket-ing, the act of buying at a market; goods bought at market.
markhor, *n.* *mar*-kor, the wild goat, *Capra falconeri*, of the Himalayas and Afghanistan.
marking, *n.* *mar*-king, impression with a mark; a mark: *a.* having the quality to produce a mark. **marking ink,** indelible ink for the marking of fabrics. **marking nut,** the nut of the East Indian *Semecarpus anacardium*, from which marking ink is made.
markka, *n.* *mar*-kah (*pl.* **markkaa**), the Finnish unit of currency, nominally equal to 1·24*d.*
marksman, *n.* *marks*-man, one skilful in hitting the mark; first-class shot.
marksmanship, *n.* skill in shooting.
marl, *n.* marl, a rich fertilizing earth containing clay, sand, and lime: *v.t.* to manure with marl. (O.Fr.)
marl, *v.t.* marl, to fasten or bind with marline [Naut.].
marline, *n.* *mar*-lin, small two-stranded cord used for winding round a rope [Naut.]. (Dut. *marren*, to bind, and *line.*)
marline-spike, *n.* a pointed iron tool for opening the strands of rope in splicing; a fid.
marlite, *n.* *mar*-lite, a variety of marl.
marlitic, *a.* mar-*lit*-ik, of the nature of marlite.
marl-pit, *n.* a pit where marl is dug.
marlstone, *n.* *marl*-stone, the calcareous and sandy strata dividing the Upper from the Lower Lias clays.
marly, *a.* *mar*-le, of or resembling marl.
marmalade, *n.* *mar*-ma-lade, jam made of pulp and peel from such fruit as the orange, lemon, etc., esp. from the orange. **marmalade tree,** the dicotyledonous tree, *Achras zapota*, of Central America, yielding the **marmalade plum,** or mammee. (Fr., from Port., from L. *marmelo*, quince.)
marmarize, *v.t.* *mar*-ma-rize, to convert into marble.
marmarosis, *n.* mar-ma-*roh*-sis, the process by which limestone is naturally converted into marble.
marmatite, *n.* *mar*-ma-tite, a ferruginous sulphide of zinc found at Marmato in Colombia.
marmite, *n.* *mar*-mite, an earthenware pot for cooking or boiling, also one in which soup is served; an explosive shell of this shape [Mil. Slang]. (Fr.)
marmolite, *n.* *mar*-mo-lite, a variety of green serpentine. (Gr. *marmairein*, to glitter.)
marmoraceous, *a.* *mar*-mo-*ray*-shus, like marble.
marmoreal, *a.* mar-*maw*-re-al, made of or resembling marble.
marmorean, *a.* mar-*maw*-re-an, marmoreal.
marmose, *n.* *mar*-mohs, any one of the *Marmosa*, a genus of mouse-like opossums of Cent. and S. America.
marmoset, *n.* *mar*-mo-zet, a small bushy-tailed

American monkey of the family *Hapalidæ*. (O.Fr. a grotesque figure.)

marmot, *n.* *mar*-mot, a rodent of the genus *Arctomys* of the size of a rabbit, and allied to the squirrels; the woodchuck of N. America. **prairie marmot,** the prairie-dog. (Fr. *marmotte.*)

marocain, *n.* *ma*-ro-kane, a material with a grain surface woven from silk or wool specially twisted. (Fr. *maroquin.*)

Maronite, *n.* *ma*-ron-ite, one of an ancient body of Christians, in communion with Rome since the early 17th cent., and now widely distributed from their centre on Mount Lebanon: *a.* pertaining or belonging to the Maronites.

maroon, *n.* ma-*roon*, a brownish crimson colour: *a.* of this colour; an explosive firework. (Fr. *marron*, a chestnut.)

maroon, *n.* ma-*roon*, a runaway negro slave, living in woods or mountains: *v.t.* to put ashore and leave on a desolate island. (Fr., Sp. *cimarron*, wild.)

marooning, *n.* ma-*roon*-ing, camping-out [U.S.A.].

maroquin, *n.* *ma*-ro-kin, morocco leather.

marplot, *n.* *mar*-plot, one who, by officious interference, mars a design or plot.

marque, *n.* mark, mark; a letter of marque. **letter of marque** (*usually in pl.*), a licence granted by one state to make reprisals at sea on the subjects of another; a ship thus commissioned. (Fr.)

marquee, *n.* mar-*kee*, a large tent. (Fr. *marquise*, as originally used for a notable personage.)

marquess, *n.* *mar*-kwess, a title of the British peerage next in rank below that of a duke; formerly a similar title in France and elsewhere; originally the defender of a frontier. (O.Fr. *markis*, Sp. *marques.*)

marquetry, *n.* *mar*-ket-re, wood mosaic; cabinet work inlaid with choice woods, tortoiseshell, ivory, etc. (Fr. *marqueterie.*)

marquis, *n.* *mar*-kwiss, marquess.

marquisate, *n.* *mar*-kwi-sat, the seigniory, dignity, or lordship of a marquis.

marquise, *n.* mar-*keez*, a marchioness; a marquise-ring. **marquise-ring,** a finger-ring in which the gems, usually diamonds, are set in a pointed cluster. (Fr.)

marram, *n.* *ma*-ram, a coarse bent or reed, *Psamma arenaria*, common on sandhills.

marrano, *n.* ma-*rah*-no, a Jew or Moor of mediæval Spain professing Christianity. (Sp.)

marrer, *n.* *mar*-rer, one who mars, hurts, or impairs.

marriage, *n.* *ma*-raj, the legal union of a man and woman as husband and wife; wedlock; a marriage ceremony; intimate union; in certain card games, the holding of king and queen of the same suit. **companionate marriage,** *see* **companionate. marriage articles,** the contract on which a marriage is founded. **marriage licence,** a licence to marry without proclamation of banns. **marriage lines,** the marriage certificate [Coll.]. **marriage of convenience,** a marriage contracted for purposes of social or financial advantage. **marriage settlement,** a legal contract securing property to a wife or husband (and sometimes children) in the event of the decease of either spouse.

marriageable, *a.* *ma*-raj-a-bl, of age for marriage; fit to be married.

***married,** *pp.* and *a.* *ma*-red, united in wedlock; pertaining to wedded life.

marron, *n.* *ma*-ron(g), a chestnut. **marron glacé,** a sugar-coated chestnut. (Fr.)

marrow, *n.* *ma*-ro, a partner or mate; a spouse; one of a pair [Scots.].

marrow, *n.* *ma*-ro, a soft fatty tissue contained in the cavities of the bones; the pith; the essence; the vegetable marrow, the fruit of *Cucurbita ovifera*. (A.S. *mearh.*)

marrowbone, *n.* *ma*-ro-bone, a bone containing enough marrow to be used in cookery: *pl.* the knees.

marrowfat, *n.* *ma*-ro-fat, the rounceval, a rich variety of pea.

marrowless, *a.* *ma*-ro-less, destitute of marrow; weakly; ineffective.

marrowy, *a.* *ma*-ro-e, full of marrow; pithy.

marry, *v.t.* *ma*-re, to unite in wedlock; to take for husband or wife; to wed; to unite intimately: *v.i.* to enter into the married state. (Fr. *marier.*)

marry, *int.* *ma*-re, indeed! (*By Mary.*)

Mars, *n.* marz, the Roman god of war; **a planet, the fourth in distance from the sun. (L.)**

Marsala, *n.* mar-*sah*-la, a strong, sweet wine resembling sherry, from Marsala, in Sicily.

Marseillaise, *n.* mar-se-*laze*, the national anthem of the French Republic, first sung by revolutionists of Marseilles, written and composed (1792) by Rouget de l'Isle.

marsh, *n.* marsh, a tract of low boggy or waterlogged land; a swamp. (A.S. *merse.*)

marshal, *n.* *mar*-shal, one who regulates rank and order at an assembly, or directs the order of procession on state occasions; a harbinger; a pursuivant; the presiding officer at tournaments; a military officer of high rank (in France the highest military officer of the state, in the British army the highest rank of general officers, a Field-Marshal, and in the R.A.F. applied to three senior officers, see **air**); an Earl Marshal; a provost-marshal; a civil officer with powers similar to a sheriff [U.S.A.]: *v.t.* to arrange in a suitable manner; to arrange the several parts of an escutcheon or shield [Her.]. **earl marshal,** *see* **earl.** (O.Fr. *mareschal.*)

marshalcy, *n.* *mar*-shal-se, the office or rank of a marshal.

marshalling-yard, *n.* a large group of railway sidings with necessary sheds, equipment, offices, etc.

Marshalsea, *n.* *mar*-shal-see, a prison formerly belonging to the marshal of the royal household.

marshalship, *n.* *mar*-shal-ship, marshalcy.

marsh-beetle, *n.* the reed-mace, *Typha latifolia.*

marsh-cinquefoil, *n.* the plant *Comarum palustre.*

marsh-elder, *n.* the guelder rose.

marsh-gas, *n.* methane; fire-damp from marshes.

marsh-harrier, *n.* the moor buzzard, *Circus æruginosus.*

marsh-hen, *n.* the moorhen, *Gallinula chloropus*; the Virginia rail, *Rallus virginianus.*

marshiness, *n.* *mar*-she-ness, swampiness.

marshland, *n.* *marsh*-land, boggy, marshy country.

marsh-mallow, *n. see* **mallow.**

marsh-marigold, *n. see* **marigold.**

marsh-parsley, *n.* wild celery, *Apium graveolens.*

marsh-tit, *n.* the small black-headed tomtit, *Parus palustris.*

marsh-trefoil, *n.* the buckbean.

marsh-warbler, *n.* the small bird, *Acrocephalus palustris.*

marshy, *a.* *mar*-she, swampy; boggy; produced in marshes.

marsipobranchiate, *a.* *mar*-se-po-*brang*-ke-at, with purse gills, like the lampreys.

marsupial, *a.* mar-*sew*-pe-al, resembling a pouch [Anat.]; carrying immature young in an external pouch, as the kangaroos, etc. [Zool.]: *n.* a marsupial mammal. (Gr. *marsupion*, a bag.)

marsupialization, *n.* mar-*sew*-pe-a-ly-*zay*-shon, the operation of converting a portion of the abdomen into an open cavity [Surg.].

marsupite, *n.* *mar*-sew-pite, a fossil crinoid of purse-like shape.

marsupium, *n.* mar-*sew*-pe-um, the abdominal pouch of marsupials enclosing the teats and mammary glands.

mart, *n.* mart, a market; a centre of trade; an auction-room. (Dut. *markt*, a market.)

martagon, *n.* *mar*-ta-gon, the Turk's cap lily, *Lilium martagon*, with small purple flowers. (It.)

martello, *n.* mar-*tel*-lo, a small circular stone fort of two stories erected on the English coast as a defence against invasion during the French Revolutionary Wars. (*Mortella*, in Corsica.)

marten, *n.* *mar*-ten, any of several small carnivores of the genus *Mustela*, esp. the pine-marten (*M. martes*), the beech-marten (*M. foina*), the sable (*M. zibellina*, and *M. Americana*), all yielding valuable furs; this fur. (O.Fr. *martrine.*)

martial, *a.* *mar*-shal, pertaining to war; military; warlike; bellicose; pertaining to the planet Mars [Astrol.]. **martial law,** military government, which, when proclaimed, applies to civilians in cases of disaffection or public danger. (Fr.)

martially, *ad.* *mar*-shal-le, in a martial manner.

Martian, *n.* *mar*-shan, a supposititious inhabitant of the planet Mars: *a.* of, or pertaining to, Mars or the Martians.

martin, *n.* *mar*-tin, a species of swallow, esp. the common European martin, *Chelidon urbica*, and the sand-martin. (St. *Martin.*)

martinet, *n.* mar-te-*net*, a strict disciplinarian. (Gen. *Martinet*, a strict officer of Louis XIV.)

martinet, *n.* *mar*-te-net, a short line fastened to the back of a sail [Naut.]. (Fr.)
martingale, *n.* *mar*-ting-gale, a strap fastened to a horse's girth to hold its head down; the stay extended by the dolphin striker [Naut.]; a system of doubling stakes as a means of recouping losses [Gambling]. (Fr.)
Martini, *n.* mar-*tee*-ne, an early make of breech-loading rifle. (Name of inventor, 1872.)
martini, *n.* mar-*tee*-nee, a sweetened cocktail of gin, vermouth, and bitters. **dry martini,** the same unsweetened.
Martinmas, *n.* *mar*-tin-mass, the feast of St. Martin, the 11th November. (*Martin* and *mass.*)
martlet, *n.* *mart*-let, the martin; the heraldic representation of this. (Fr. *merlette.*)
martyr, *n.* *mar*-ter, one who, by death, bears witness to the sincerity of his or her faith; one who endures great suffering or sacrifice for a cause; a constant sufferer from disease, etc.: *v.t.* to put to death for belief; to subject to grievous suffering. (A.S.)
martyrdom, *n.* *mar*-ter-dom, the death of a martyr; great or continual suffering.
martyrization, *n.* *mar*-te-ry-*zay*-shon, the making a martyr of; the act of causing to suffer for the sake of a cause, opinion, etc.
martyrological, *a.* *mar*-te-ro-*loj*-e-kal, pertaining to martyrology.
martyrologist, *n.* mar-te-*rol*-o-jist, a historian of martyrs.
martyrology, *n.* *mar*-te-*rol*-o-je, a history or a register of martyrs. (*martyr,* and Gr. *logos,* account.)
marvel, *n.* *mar*-vel, anything wonderful or astonishing: *v.i.* to be astonished at; to feel wonder. **marvel of Peru,** the greenhouse plant, *Mirabilis jalapa,* originally from S. America. (Fr. *merveille.*)
marvellous, *a.* *mar*-vel-lus, exciting wonder; surpassing belief. (O.Fr. *merveillos.*)
marvellously, *ad.* in a marvellous manner.
Marxian, *a.* *marks*-e-an, relating to Karl Marx, the German communist writer (*d.* 1883), or his theories: *n.* a believer in the Marxian doctrine.
Marxism, *n.* *marks*-izm, the body of Marxian political and economic doctrine.
Marxist, *n.* *marks*-ist, an adherent of Karl Marx or of his theories: *a.* Marxian.
marybud, *n.* *mare*-re-bud, the marigold.
marzipan, *n.* mar-ze-*pan*, a sweetmeat made of crushed almonds and sugar, flavoured and beaten to a paste, marchpane. (Fr. *massepain.*)
mascara, *n.* mas-*kah*-ra, a cosmetic for dyeing the eyelids.
mascaron, *n.* *mas*-ka-ron(g), a grotesque mask, as on a keystone, etc. [Arch.]. (Fr.)
mascle, *n.* *mas*-kl, a lozenge voided [Her.]; one of the plates of which scale armour was composed. (O.Fr.)
mascot, *n.* *mas*-kot, any person or thing supposed to bring good luck; a charm; a talisman. (Fr.)
masculine, *a.* *mas*-kew-lin, having the qualities of or resembling a man; strong; robust; manly; coarse; denoting the male gender [Gram.]: *n.* the masculine gender [Gram.]. **masculine rhyme,** a monosyllabic rhyme, both words ending in a consonant. (Fr. *masculin.*)
masculinely, *ad.* in a masculine manner.
masculinity, *n.* *mas*-kew-*lin*-e-te, the quality of being masculine.
mash, *n.* mash, a mass made by crushing; a mixture of ingredients, beaten together; a mixture of bran and hot water given to horses; ground malt or grain steeped in hot water [Brewing]: *v.t.* to crush by pressure; to mix into a mash. (A.S.)
mash, *v.t.* mash, to act with intent to excite love; to ogle: *n.* the person to whom such action is directed. **mashed on,** infatuated with [Slang].
masher, *n.* *mash*-er, a foppish lady-killer; a dandy.
mashie, *n.* *mash*-e, a golf-club with a lofted face, used to lift the ball out of a bunker, or for playing short approach shots with back-spin. **mashie-niblick,** *n.* an exceptionally lofted mashie [Golf].
mash-tub, or **-vat,** *n.* a tub in which the mash is made [Brewing].
mashy, *a.* *mash*-e, like mash; produced by bruising.
mask, *n.* mahsk, a cover to conceal, protect, or disguise the face; a visor; a gas-mask; a disguise or pretence; a masque, masked entertainment, or masquerade; a piece of mummery; an architectural feature resembling a face; an opaque screen or border [Phot.]; the head of a fox, etc.: *v.t.* to conceal with a mask; to disguise; to camouflage: *v.i.* to take part in a masque or masquerade; to be disguised. (Fr. *masque.*)
masker, *n.* *mahs*-ker, a masquer.
maskinonge, *n.* *mas*-ke-nonj, the muskelonge, a species of pike [Ichth.].
maslin, *n.* *maz*-lin, a mixture of wheat and rye; bread made of this. (Dial. Eng.)
masochism, *n.* *maz*-o-kizm, sexual perversion characterized by delight in suffering inflicted on oneself by the loved person. (L. von Sacher-*Masoch, d.* 1895, Austrian novelist, who described it.)
masochist, *n.* *maz*-o-kist, one who has contracted masochism.
masochistic, *a.* *maz*-o-*kis*-tik, characterized by, or tending towards, masochism.
mason, *n.* *may*-son, a worker in stone; one who builds in stone; a freemason: *v.t.* to build or construct of masonry. (O.Fr. *masson.*)
masonic, *a.* ma-*son*-ik, pertaining to freemasonry.
masonry, *n.* *may*-son-re, the art or occupation of a mason; mason's work, or what is built of it; freemasonry.
Masora, *n.* ma-*saw*-ra, the Massorah.
Masorite, *n.* *mas*-o-rite, Massorete.
masque, *n.* mahsk, a masquerade; a histrionic entertainment comprising dancing, singing, and, in its later form, dialogue in verse.
masquer, *n.* *mahs*-ker, one who takes part in a masque.
masquerade, *n.* mahs-ker-*rade*, a revel or dance at which people wear masks; disguise: *v.t.* to join in a masquerade; to go in disguise. (Fr.)
masquerader, *n.* mahs-ker-*ray*-der, a participant in a masquerade; one disguised; one dissembling his true character.
★**mass,** *n.* mass, a lump; a body of matter concreted, collected, or formed into a heap; a collective body; a heap; magnitude; an assemblage; the body or main body; quantity of matter: *v.i.* and *t.* to collect into a mass or body. (Fr.)
Mass, *n.* mass, in the Roman Church, the consecration and oblation of the host in the Eucharist; the celebration of this; the office of the Mass, or music composed for it. **High Mass,** that which is publicly performed with music on high occasions or festivals. **Low Mass,** that which is merely read. **Mass book,** the missal, or Roman service-book. (A.S. *mæsse.*)
massacre, *n.* *mas*-sa-ker, indiscriminate slaughter, esp. of unarmed persons: *v.t.* to slaughter or murder wholesale and with barbarity. (Fr.)
mass-action, *n.* chemical action as determined by the masses of the respective substances interacting.
massage, *n.* *mas*-sahzh, the treatment of the body for remedial or curative purposes by manipulation: *v.t.* to manipulate a patient's muscles, etc. [Med.]. (Fr.)
massagist, *n.* *mas*-sa-jist, one who practises massage.
massé, *n.* *mas*-say, a stroke with the cue held in an upright position [Billiards]. (Fr.)
masseter, *n.* *mas*-se-ter, the muscle which raises the under jaw, the muscle of mastication [Anat.]. (Gr. *massaomai,* to chew.)
masseur, *n.* mas-*sur*, a male massagist. (Fr.)
masseuse, *n.* (App.), a female massagist. (Fr.)
massicot, *n.* *mas*-se-kot, litharge, or lead monoxide, used as a yellow pigment. (Fr.)
massif, *n.* *mas*-sif, the highest and central group in a range of mountains, or in a mountain ridge. (Fr.)
massiness, *n.* *mas*-se-ness, the state of being massy; massiveness.
massive, *a.* *mas*-siv, heavy; bulky; having crystalline structure without regular form [Min.]: *n.* massif. (Fr. *massif.*)
massively, *ad.* *mas*-siv-le, in a mass; heavily.
massiveness, *n.* hugeness; ponderousness.
mass-meeting, *n.* a public meeting with no charge for admission.
mass-production, *n.* the mechanical manufacture of goods to one pattern in quantity.
Massorah, *n.* ma-*saw*-ra, the body of notes appended to the Massoretic text by the Massoretes codifying and expounding the traditional Hebrew interpretation of the Scriptural text. (Heb., tradition.)

Massorete, *n.* *mas*-o-reet, one of the scribes who, about the 6th to 8th cent. A.D. compiled and edited the Massoretic text; one learned in the Massorah.

Massoretic, *a.* mas-o-*ret*-ik, relating to the Massorah or the Massoretes. **Massoretic points,** the Hebrew vowel-points and accents invented by the Massoretes. **Massoretic text,** the earliest MS. form of the Hebrew text of the Old Testament as finally edited from traditionary sources by the Massoretes.

massotherapy, *n.* *mas*-o-*the*-ra-pe, remedial treatment by means of massage [Med.].

massoy, *n.* *mas*-oy, the aromatic bark of an East Indian tree, *Cinnamomum kiamis.* (Papuan, *masui.*)

massy, *a.* *mas*-se, massive.

mast, *n.* mahst, the long upright spar for supporting the yards and booms; a similar vertical post for a flag, aerial, etc.: *v.t.* to supply with masts. (A.S. *mæst,* the stem of a tree.)

mast, *n.* mahst, the fruit of the oak and beech, or other forest trees. (A.S. *mæst,* mast in this sense.)

mastaba, *n.* *mas*-ta-ba, an early Egyptian form of tomb having sloping sides and a flat roof; a stone bench outside an oriental dwelling. (Ar.)

mastalgia, *n.* mas-*tal*-je-a, pain in the breast. (Gr. *mastos,* breast, *algia,* pain.)

master, *n.* *mahs*-ter, a man who rules, governs or directs; a director; owner; ruler; commander; the captain of a merchant ship; an officer who navigated the ship under the captain [Navy]; the head of a household, or of a school or college; a teacher; an appellation of respect; an appellation given to young gentlemen; an expert or proficient; a great artist; a university degree; the chief of a society; a courtesy title of the eldest sons of Scottish viscounts and barons: *a.* pertaining to a master; employing or in charge of workmen; chief; principal: *v.t.* to conquer or subdue; to make oneself master of; to become thoroughly competent in. **master clock,** a clock that regulates others, esp. by electricity. **master of ceremonies,** *see* **ceremony. master of foxhounds,** the person who manages a pack of hounds. **Master of the Horse,** the third in precedence of the great officers of the British Royal Household. **Master of the Rolls,** the judge who has the keeping of the records and is next in precedence after the Lord Chief Justice of England. **master switch,** a switch for controlling other switches [Elect.]. (O.Fr. *maistre.*)

master, *n.* *mahs*-ter, a ship with more than one mast, as a three-master or four-master.

master-at-arms, *n.* the officer of police on board a warship.

master-builder, *n.* *mahs*-ter-*bild*-er, the chief builder; builder employing workmen.

masterdom, *n.* *mahs*-ter-dom, dominion; rule.

masterful, *a.* *mahs*-ter-ful, expressing mastery; domineering.

masterfully, *ad.* in a masterful way.

masterfulness, *n.* quality of being masterful.

master-key, *n.* a key that opens many locks, hence, that which resolves difficulties.

masterless, *a.* *mahs*-ter-less, destitute of a master; vagrant; ungovernable.

masterliness, *n.* *mahs*-ter-le-ness, the quality of being masterly.

masterly, *a.* *mahs*-ter-le, executed with superior skill: *ad.* with the skill of a master.

master-mind, *n.* a ruling mind; the originator or leader of an enterprise, etc.

masterpiece, *n.* *mahs*-ter-peece, a first-rate performance in literature or art, etc.; a supreme achievement.

mastership, *n.* *mahs*-ter-ship, the office of master; superior skill; pre-eminence.

master-spring, *n.* the spring which moves or regulates the whole.

master-stroke, *n.* the achievement of a master; a masterly performance.

masterwort, *n.* *mahs*-ter-wurt, name of various plants including cow-parsley and *Peucedanum ostruthium.*

mastery, *n.* *mahs*-ter-re, the act of mastering; pre-eminence; victory; eminent skill; attainment of skill or power; dominion.

masthead, *n.* *mahst*-hed, the upper part of a mast above the rigging, esp. of the topmast [Naut.].

mastic, *n.* *mas*-tik, a resin exuding from *Pistacia lentiscus,* chiefly used for varnish; a distilled liquor flavoured with this; a very durable cement. (Fr. from L. *mastichum,* chewing-gum.)

masticable, *a.* *mas*-te-ka-bl, that can be masticated.

masticate, *v.t.* *mas*-te-kate, to chew; to grind with the teeth. (L. *masticatus.*)

mastication, *n.* mas-te-*kay*-shon, the act of chewing.

masticator, *n.* *mas*-te-kay-tor, one who or that which masticates; a machine for masticating or mincing.

masticatory, *a.* *mas*-te-ka-to-re *or* *mas*-te-*kay*-to-re, adapted for chewing; pertaining to the organs of mastication: *n.* a substance to be chewed [Med.].

masticin, *n.* *mas*-te-sin, the portion of mastic insoluble in alcohol.

mastiff, *n.* *mas*-tif, a large smooth-coated dog of great strength and courage, one of the oldest of British breeds. (O.Fr. *mestif.*)

masting, *n.* *mahs*-ting, the masts in a ship collectively, or their disposition.

mastitis, *n.* mas-*ty*-tis, inflammation of the breast, esp. of its glandular substance [Med.]. (Gr. *mastos,* breast.)

mastless, *a.* *mahst*-less, having no mast, as a vessel.

mastodon, *n.* *mas*-to-don, an extinct species of elephant, earlier than and contemporary with the mammoth. (Gr. *mastos,* and *odous,* a tooth.)

mastodynia, *n.* *mas*-to-*din*-e-a, pain in the breast.

mastoid, *a.* *mas*-toyd, resembling the nipple or breast; pertaining to the mastoid process, or protruding part, of the temporal bone [Anat.]: *n.* mastoiditis [Coll.]; the mastoid process. (Gr. *mastos,* and *eidos,* like.)

mastoiditis, *n.* mas-toy-*dy*-tis, inflammation of the cavities in the mastoid process.

masturbate, *v.i.* *mas*-ter-bate, to excite the genital organs and cause venereal orgasm by artificial means, esp. with the hand. (L. *masturbatus.*)

masturbation, *n.* mas-ter-*bay*-shon, the act of masturbating; self-abuse; onanism.

masurium, *n.* ma-*zewr*-re-um, a rare metallic element discovered spectroscopically in association with platinum in 1925. (From *Masurenland,* then in East Prussia.)

mat, *n.* mat, a texture of sedge, rushes, straw, or other coarse fibrous material; a tangled mass; a small rug; a piece of material laid as a protection on tables or floors; a web of rope-yarn: *v.t.* and *i.* to cover or lay with mats; to twist together; to tangle or become tangled. (A.S. *meatte.*)

mat, *a.* mat, dull; unpolished: *n.* a mat or lustreless surface or border, etc.: *v.t.* to dull; to impart a lustreless surface to.

matador, *n.* *mat*-a-dor, the man who kills the bull in a bull-fight; one of the three principal cards at ombre and quadrille; one of the games played with dominoes. (Sp., killer.)

matamata, *n.* *mat*-a-*mah*-ta, the South American river-turtle, *Chelys fimbriata.*

★**match,** *n.* match, anything easily kindled and used for lighting; a lucifer; a fuse for firing artillery, mines, etc. (Fr. *mèche.*)

match, *n.* match, anything which tallies with or equals another; one able to cope with another; an equal; a contest; union by marriage; one to be married or gained in marriage: *v.t.* to equal; to show an equal to; to oppose as equal; to suit: *v.i.* to correspond; to tally. **match point,** the last point needed to win a match. (A.S. *mæcca,* mate.)

matchable, *a.* *match*-a-bl, suitable; fit to be matched.

match-boarding, *n.* boards fitting into one another by means of a tongue on one edge and a groove on the other.

matchbox, *n.* *match*-boks, a box for holding matches.

matchet, *n.* *match*-et, a machete.

matchless, *a.* *match*-less, having no match or equal.

matchlessly, *ad.* in a matchless manner.

matchlessness, *n.* quality of being matchless.

matchlock, *n.* *match*-lok, the lock of a musket, containing a match for firing it; a musket so fired.

matchmaker, *n.* *match*-make-er, one who makes matches; one who brings about a marriage.

matchwood, *n.* *match*-wood, wood from which matches are made; any thin or splintered wood.

mate, *n.* mate, a companion; a comrade; an equal; a husband or wife; the male or female of animals going in pairs; the officer of a ship whose duty is to assist the captain and command in his stead; an assistant: *v.t.* to match; to couple; to join in marriage: *v.i.* to pair (esp. of birds). (O.Ger.)
mate, *n.* and *v.t.* mate, checkmate. (Per. *mat*, dead.)
maté, *n.* *mat*-ay, the shrub, *Ilex paraguayensis*, the leaves of which are used in S. America as a substitute for tea; Brazilian holly. (Sp.)
matelassé, maht-lah-say, having a quilted appearance (of textiles, etc.): *n.* a brocade-like cloth of silk or mixture with quilted ornamentation. (Fr., padded.)
mateless, *a.* *mate*-less, having no mate or companion.
matelot, *n.* *mat*-loh, a French able-bodied seaman; [Slang] a sailor. (Fr.)
matelote, *n.* *mat*-e-loht, a dish of fish stewed with herbs, claret, and vinegar. (Fr. *matelot*, a sailor.)
mater, *n.* *may*-ter, mother (esp. as a schoolboy term). **Alma Mater,** one's school, college, or university. (L., fostering mother.) **dura mater,** the outermost, **pia mater,** the innermost of the three membranes surrounding the brain and spinal cord in vertebrates, the arachnoid intervening [Anat.]. **Mater Dolorosa,** the Virgin Mary as the grief-stricken mother. (L., mother.)
materfamilias, *n.* *may*-ter-fa-*mil*-e-as, the mother of the family, or mistress of the house. (L.)
materia, *n.* ma-*teer*-re-a, matter. **materia medica,** a general name for all substances used in the composition of medicines; the science which treats of them and their action. (L.)
***material,** *a.* ma-*teer*-re-al, consisting of or pertaining to matter; corporeal; not spiritual; substantial; essential; more or less necessary; important in the matter: *n.* the substance of which anything is made; component parts of; data for use in a finished work; a fabric. (Fr. *matériel.*)
materialism, *n.* ma-*teer*-re-a-lizm, the theory which refers all spiritual and mental as well as other phenomena to a material origin; respect for material or secular to the neglect or exclusion of spiritual interests.
materialist, *n.* ma-*teer*-re-a-list, one who in theory or by implication accepts materialism.
materialistic, *a.* ma-*teer*-re-a-*lis*-tik, imbued with materialism.
materiality, *n.* ma-*teer*-re-*al*-e-te, quality or condition of being material; material existence; importance.
materialization, *n.* ma-*teer*-re-a-ly-*zay*-shon, the act of making material or (in spiritualism) visible; the materialized object.
materialize, *v.t.* ma-*teer*-e-a-lize, to reduce to a state of matter; to render materialistic; to cause a spirit to assume bodily shape [Spiritualism].
materially, *ad.* in a material manner or degree.
materialness, *n.* state of being material.
matériel, *n.* ma-*tay*-re-*el*, working appliances generally, esp. the baggage and munitions of an army as distinct from the personnel. (Fr.)
maternal, *a.* ma-*ter*-nal, pertaining to a mother or to motherhood; related on the mother's side. (Fr. *maternel.*)
maternally, *ad.* in a maternal manner.
maternity, *n.* ma-*ter*-ne-te, motherhood; the state of being a mother; motherliness. **maternity hospital,** a hospital for women about to be confined. **maternity nurse,** a nurse who attends confinements. (Fr. *maternité.*)
matey, *a.* *may*-te, sociable; characteristic of a mate [Slang]. (*mate.*)
matfellon, *n.* *mat*-fel-lon, knapweed. (O.Fr.)
mathematical, *a.* *math*-e-*mat*-e-kal, pertaining or according to the principles of mathematics; accurate. **mathematical instruments,** instruments used for drawing and measuring. (L. *mathematicus.*)
mathematically, *ad.* *math*-e-*mat*-e-ka-le, in a mathematical manner.
mathematician, *n.* *math*-e-ma-*tish*-an, one versed in mathematics.
mathematics, *n.* *math*-e-*mat*-iks, the science which treats of magnitude and number, or of whatever can be measured or numbered. **applied** *or* **mixed mathematics** considers these in their application to concrete entities, as in mensuration, astronomy, etc. **pure mathematics** treats of them and their relations in the abstract.
mathesis, *n.* ma-*thee*-sis, learning, esp. mathematical science. (Gr.)
matico, *n.* *mat*-e-koh, the tropical American shrub *Piper angustifolium*, the leaves of which are used as a stimulant, tonic, and styptic. (Sp.)
matin, *a.* *mat*-in, pertaining to morning; matinal.
matinal, *a.* *mat*-e-nal, belonging to the morning or to matins.
matinée, *n.* *mat*-e-nay, an afternoon dramatic performance; a daytime reception or entertainment. (Fr.)
matins, *n.pl.* *mat*-inz, the first of the canonical hours; morning worship or service; the early song of birds. (Fr., mornings.)
matlockite, *n.* *mat*-lok-ite, oxychloride of lead, first found near Matlock, Derbyshire.
matrass, *n.* *mat*-rass, a long-necked round-bottomed flask formerly used by alchemists. (Fr.)
mat-reed, *n.* *mat*-reed, the bulrush or reed-mace.
matriarch, *n.* *may*-tre-ark, a woman having the status of a patriarch; the mother as head of a family or tribe. (L. *mater*, mother, Gr. *archos*, rule.)
matriarchal, *a.* may-tre-*ar*-kal, pertaining to matriarchy or a matriarch; reckoning kinship on the female side only.
matriarchate, *n.* may-tre-*ar*-kat, a community ruled by, or the rulership of, a matriarch.
matriarchy, *n.* *may*-tre-ar-ke, the primitive social organization in which the mother is looked upon as head of the family or tribe, and in which kinship and inheritance are traced through her.
matricidal, *a.* mat-re-*sy*-dal, pertaining to matricide.
matricide, *n.* *mat*-re-side, the murder or murderer of a mother. (L. *matricida.*)
matricular, *a.* ma-*trik*-yew-lar, relating to matriculation, to a matrix, or to the womb.
matriculate, *n.* ma-*trik*-yew-late, one who is matriculated: *a.* matriculated: *v.t.* to enrol as a member of some body, esp. as a student at a university: *v.i.* to be enrolled as a member or a student. (L. *matriculatus*, from *matricula*, a register.)
matriculation, *n.* ma-*trik*-yew-*lay*-shon, the act of matriculating; the examination for this [Coll.].
matrilineal, *a.* mat-re-*lin*-e-al, pertaining to kinship on the mother's side or in the female line.
matrimonial, *a.* mat-re-*moh*-ne-al, relating to or connected with marriage.
matrimonially, *ad.* in a matrimonial connection.
matrimony, *n.* *mat*-re-mo-ne, marriage; the nuptial state; a simple card-game like Pope Joan. (O.Fr. *matrimonie.*)
matrix, *n.* *may*-triks *or* *mat*-riks (*pl.* **matrixes** *or* **matrices,** *may*-tre-seez), the womb; any hollow place in which a thing is formed; a mould; the substance in which a mineral, etc., is embedded, or the impression left by such mineral. (L., the uterus).
matron, *n.* *may*-tron, a married woman or widow; an elderly lady; a head nurse; a female superintendent of an institution. (L. *matrona.*)
matronage, *n.* *may*-tron-aj, matronhood; matronly supervision; matrons as a body.
matronal, *a.* *may*-tron-al, pertaining to a matron; motherly; sedate.
matronhood, *n.* state or condition of a matron.
matronize, *v.t.* *may*-tron-ize, to render matron-like; to act as a matron to.
matronly, *a.* *may*-tron-le, matron-like; grave; sedate.
matronymic, *n.* *mat*-ro-*nim*-ik, metronymic.
matt, *a.* mat, mat: *n.* a dull finish.
matte, *n.* mat, any metal containing sulphide after smelting, esp. crude copper. (Fr.)
matted, *a.* *mat*-ted, laid with mats; entangled.
matter, *n.* *mat*-ter, that which occupies space, and is perceptible to any one of the senses; anything having mass; the substance of all physical objects; material; the subject treated of, or that occupies us; the substance of what is said; affair; business; importance; thing; indefinite amount; that which suppurates from a tumour, boil, or abscess; pus [Med.]; set-up type [Printing]: *v.i.* to be of importance; to signify; to form pus. **matter of course,** that which may be expected in the natural course of things. **matter of fact,** an actual occurrence; (*adjectivally*) concerned only with crass

realities or tangible interests, or adhering to and insisting on the mere literal facts. (O.Fr. *matiere.*)
mattery, *a.* *mat*-ter-re, purulent; generating pus.
matting, *n.* *mat*-ting, material for mats; mats collectively.
mattock, *n.* *mat*-tok, a sort of pickaxe combining axe and adze. (A.S. *mattuc.*)
mattoid, *n.* *mat*-oyd, a semi-lunatic; a crank; a paranoiac. (It. *matto,* insane.)
mattress, *n.* *mat*-tress, a bed stuffed and quilted; an under-bed; a spring or wire mattress; strong wire mesh for reinforcing concrete roadways, etc. **spring mattress,** an arrangement of spiral springs supporting a stuffed mattress. **wire mattress,** a framework of wire upon which a mattress is laid. (O.Fr. *materas.*)
maturant, *n.* *mat*-yew-rant, a maturative.
maturate, *v.t.* *mat*-yew-rate, to promote suppuration in: *v.i.* to suppurate perfectly [Med.]. (*mature.*)
maturation, *n.* mat-yew-*ray*-shon, the process of ripening or [Med.] of suppurating.
maturative, *a.* *mat*-yew-ra-tiv, conducing to ripeness, or to the formation of matter in an abscess: *n.* an application to accelerate suppuration in an inflamed part [Med.].
mature, *a.* ma-*tewr,* perfected in growth or development; ripe; completed; ready; arrived at suppuration [Med.]; now payable: *v.t.* to ripen; to bring to perfection: *v.i.* to become ripe; to become payable. (L. *maturus,* ripe.)
maturely, *ad.* with ripeness; with full deliberation.
matureness, *n.* the state of being mature.
maturescence, *n.* mat-yew-*res*-ens, the process of reaching maturity. (L. *maturescens.*)
maturity, *n.* ma-*tewr*-re-te, matureness.
matutinal, *a.* mat-*yew*-te-nal, pertaining to the morning; early. (L. *matutinus.*)
matzoth, *n.* *mat*-zoth, unleavened bread or biscuit eaten by Jews at the Passover. (Heb.)
maud, *n.* mawd, a plaid of wool worn by Scottish shepherds; a travelling-rug.
maudlin, *a.* *mawd*-lin, foolishly sentimental; silly or partly fuddled with drink (tearful, like Mary Magdalene).
maugre, *ad.* *maw*-ger, notwithstanding. (Fr. *malgré,* from L. *male,* badly, *gratus,* agreeable.)
maul, *n.* mawl, a heavy hammer; a large wooden mallet or beetle: *v.t.* to beat and bruise, as with a maul; to wound in a rough manner. (O.Fr. *mail,* L. *malleum.*)
maulstick, *n.* *mawl*-stik, a long rest used by painters to steady the hand in painting; a mahlstick. (Dut. *maalstok.*)
maund, *n.* mawnd, a weight of varying amount used throughout India and the East. (Hind.)
maunder, *v.t.* and *i.* *mawn*-der, to mutter; to drivel. **to maunder along,** to wander aimlessly.
maunderer, *n.* *mawn*-der-rer, one who mumbles; a discontented, grumbling person.
Maundy, *n.* *mawn*-de, the Thursday before Good Friday, when a royal bounty is dispensed to certain poor people at Westminster Abbey; the special silver coins included in this bounty; the ceremony of washing the feet of the poor on this day. (L. *mandatum,* the word with which the service of the day begins: O.Fr. *mandé.*)
mauresque, *a.* and *n.* maw-*resk,* moresque.
Maurist, *n.* *maw*-rist, a monk of the former Benedictine order of St. Maur.
Mauser, *n.* *mouz*-er, proprietary name of various small-arms the repeating action of which was the invention of Paul Mauser (Ger. 1838–1914.)
mausolean, *a.* maw-so-*lee*-an, pertaining to mausoleums; of the nature of, or resembling, a mausoleum.
mausoleum, *n.* maw-so-*lee*-um, a stately sepulchral monument. (Gr. *mausoleion,* a tomb erected in memory of *Mausolus,* King of Caria, 4th cent. B.C., one of the Seven Wonders of the World.)
mauve, *n.* mohv, an aniline purple dye; the colour it produces: *a.* of a lilac or light purple colour. (Fr. a mallow, from L. *malva.*)
maverick, *n.* *mav*-e-rik, an unbranded calf; anything obtained by misappropriation: *v.t.* and *i.* to steal unbranded cattle; to take unlawfully [U.S.A.]. (Personal name.)
mavis, *n.* *may*-vis, the throstle, or song-thrush. (Fr. *mauvis.*)
mavourneen, *n.* ma-*voor*-neen, my darling; an Irish term of endearment. (Ir.)
maw, *n.* maw, the crop of birds; the stomach of mammals; the human mouth or stomach (in contempt). (A.S. *maga.*)
mawkish, *a.* *mawk*-ish, apt to cause satiety or loathing; squeamish; weakly sentimental. (Scand.)
mawkishly, *ad.* *mawk*-ish-le, in a mawkish way.
mawkishness, *n.* feeble sentimentality.
mawseed, *n.* *maw*-seed, the seed of the opium poppy, esp. as food for moulting cage-birds. (Ger.)
mawworm, *n.* *maw*-wurm, an intestinal worm.
maxilla, *n.* maks-*il*-la, the upper jawbone. (L.)
maxillary, *a.* maks-*il*-la-re, pertaining to the jaw or jawbone: *n.* any of the maxillary bones.
maxilliform, *a.* maks-*il*-le-form, in the form of a maxilla.
maxillipede, *n.* maks-*il*-e-peed, foot-jaw, one of the masticating and mobile limbs of crustacea.
maxim, *n.* *maks*-im, an axiom; a general truth; an aphorism. (Fr. *maxime.*)
Maxim, *n.* *maks*-im, a quick-firing machine gun invented by Sir Hiram Maxim (*d.* 1916).
maximal, *a.* *maks*-e-mal, pertaining to or consisting of a maximum.
Maximalist, *n.* *maks*-e-mal-ist, a member of a former Russian extremist group which seceded from the Social Revolutionaries in 1905.
maximize, *v.t.* *maks*-e-mize, to increase to the utmost.
maximum, *a.* *maks*-e-mum, greatest: *n.* the greatest amount; the greatest number or quantity attainable in any given case [Math.]. (L. *maximus,* greatest.)
maxixe, *n.* mak-*seeks,* a two-step dance, originally Brazilian.
maxwell, *n.* *maks*-wel, the international unit of magnetic flux. (Jas. Clerk *Maxwell,* Scot. physicist, *d.* 1879.)
***may,** *v.aux.* may, to be able; to be possible; to be free to; to be allowed. *p.* **might** (no infinitive or participles in use). (A.S. *mæg,* first pers. sing. of *mugan.*)
May, *n.* may, the fifth month of the year; the early part of life; (*l.c.*) hawthorn blossom: *v.i.* to gather flowers in May. (L. *Maius.*)
Mayan, *a.* *mah*-yan, pertaining to the Mayas, an ancient and highly civilized race of Central America.
May-apple, *n.* *may*-ap-pl, the fruit of the North American plant *Podophyllum peltatum.*
maybe, *ad.* *may*-be, perhaps: *n.* a possibility.
May-bug, *n.* *may*-bug, the cockchafer.
May-day, *n.* *may*-day, the first day of May.
mayduke, *n.* *may*-dewk, a hybrid cherry from the sweet and sour varieties.
mayflower, *n.* *may*-flou-er, the North American plant *Epigæa repens*; the cuckoo-flower, *Cardamine pratensis.*
mayfly, *n.* *may*-fly, a species of *Ephemera.*
mayhap, *ad.* *may*-hap, perhaps.
mayhem, *n.* *may*-hem, the crime of maiming a person [Law]. (As *maim.*)
maying, *n.* *may*-ing, May-day observances.
May-lady, *n.* the May-queen.
May-lily, *n.* the lily of the valley.
mayonnaise, *n.* may-o-*nayz,* a dressing or sauce made of yolk of eggs, vinegar, and olive-oil, flavoured with condiments. (Fr.)
mayor, *n.* mare, the chief of a municipal corporation. **Lord Mayor,** *see* **lord. mayor of the palace,** the prime minister of the early Frankish kings; hence, a power behind the throne. (L. *major,* greater, comparative of *magnus,* great.)
mayoral, *a.* *mare*-ral, pertaining to a mayor or mayoralty.
mayoralty, *n.* *mare*-ral-te, the office, or the period of office, of a mayor.
mayoress, *n.* *mare*-ress, the wife of a mayor, or woman officially deputizing as such.
maypole, *n.* *may*-pole, a pole to dance round on May day.
May-queen, *n.* a girl crowned with flowers and acting as president of the May-games on the first of May.
mayst, *v.aux.* mayst, *second person singular* of *may.*
mayweed, *n.* *may*-weed, the fetid camomile *Anthemis cotula.*
mazard, *n.* *maz*-ard, the bird-cherry, *Prunus avium.*
mazarine, *n.* maz-a-*reen,* a deep blue colour. (Perhaps after Cardinal *Mazarin.*)

Mazdaism, *n.* *maz*-da-izm, Zoroastrianism. (*Ormazd*, the principle of good and supreme deity of Persian mythology.)
maze, *n.* maze, a confusion of intricate windings and turnings; a labyrinth; perplexed state of things; intricacy: *v.t.* to bewilder; to confuse. **in a maze,** bewildered. (M.E. *maren*, to puzzle.)
mazer, *n.* *may*-zer, a bowl or goblet of hard wood, esp. maple. (O.Fr.)
mazily, *ad.* *may*-ze-le, in a mazy manner.
maziness, *n.* *may*-ze-ness, the state of being mazy.
mazuma, *n.* ma-*zoo*-ma, money [U.S.A. Slang]. (Yiddish.)
mazurka, *n.* ma-*zoor*-ka, a lively Polish dance; music for this. (Pol., a woman from Mazoyia.)
mazut, *n.* ma-*zoot*, the liquid residue of Russian petroleum, used as a lubricant. (Russ.)
mazy, *a.* *may*-ze, winding; perplexed; intricate.
me, *pron.* mee, the *objective case* of *I.* (A.S.)
meable, *a.* *mee*-a-bl, readily permeable. (L. *meabilis*, that can be penetrated.)
meacock, *n.* *mee*-kok, a cowardly, effeminate person.
mead, *n.* meed, a fermented liquor consisting of honey and water, usually spiced. (A.S. *medu.*)
mead, *n.* meed, a meadow. (A.S. *mæd.*)
meadow, *n.* *med*-oh, grass land, land appropriated to the production of hay; any rich land, esp. near a river. (A.S. *mædw*, dative case of *mæd.*)
meadow-cress, *n.* lady's smock, *Cardamine pratensis.*
meadow-crocus, *n.* the meadow-saffron.
meadow-drake, *n.* the landrail or corncake.
meadow-grass, *n.* any pasture grass, esp. of the genus *Poa* or *Schlerochloa.*
meadow-lark, *n.* the meadow-pipit; a N. American song-bird of the genus *Sturnella.*
meadow-pink, *n.* the plant, ragged robin.
meadow-pipit, *n.* the common pipit, *Anthus pratensis.*
meadow-saffron, *n.* autumn crocus, the bulbous medicinal plant *Colchicum autumnale.*
meadowsweet, *n.* *med*-oh-sweet, the fragrant, white-flowered rosaceous plant *Spiræa ulmaria.*
meadowy, *a.* *med*-oh-e, resembling a meadow; abounding in meadows.
meagre, *a.* *mee*-ger, thin; lean; destitute of vitality, richness, fertility, vigour, etc.; barren; poor. (Fr. *maigre*, from L. *macer*, lean.)
meagrely, *ad.* *mee*-ger-le, poorly; thinly.
meagreness, *n.* the state of being meagre.
***meal,** *n.* meel, a repast taken at a particular time; the food taken on such an occasion, or the time of this: *v.t.* and *i.* to give or take a meal; to feed. **square meal,** a satisfying meal. (A.S. *mæl*, a stated time.)
***meal,** *n.* meel, the edible part of grain, or pulse ground into flour; a substance resembling this, as linseed meal. (A.S. *melu.*)
mealie, *n.* *mee*-le, an ear of maize: *pl.* maize; Indian corn. (S.Afr. Dut. *milje*, as *millet.*)
mealiness, *n.* the quality of being mealy.
mealman, *n.* *meel*-man, a dealer in meal.
meal-time, *n.* the usual time for a meal.
meal-worm, *n.* the larva of any beetle infesting granaries, etc., esp. *Tenebrio molitor.*
mealy, *a.* *meel*-le, farinaceous; sprinkled with meal; farinose [Bot.]. **mealy bug,** any insect pest in greenhouses, on fruit-trees, etc., esp. of the genus *Pseudococcus.* **mealy mouth,** the willow wren. **mealy redpoll,** the lesser redpoll, *Linota linaria.* **mealy tree,** the wayfaring tree.
mealy-mouthed, *a.* *meel*-le-mouthd, using soft words; unwilling to be blunt in speech; euphemistic.
mean, *a.* meen, low in rank or birth; ignoble; sordid; of little value; low in esteem; contemptible; poor. (A.S. *mæne*, common.)
mean, *a.* meen, in or having a middle position; moderate; intervening: *n.* the middle point, rate, or degree; mediocrity; intervening time; the medium, instrument, or agent through which something is done; an average, or a quantity having an intermediate value between several others [Math.]: *pl.* instrumentality; method; resources, income, revenue, or estate. **by all means,** without fail. **by means of,** through the instrumentality of. **by no means,** not at all. **mean time,** *see* **time.** **means test,** investigation into personal resources, esp. to ascertain the financial position of one eligible for benefit under state insurance. (O.Fr. *meien.*)
mean, *v.t.* meen, to have in the mind or in view; to signify; to intend, purpose, or design: *v.i.* to have thought or meaning; to be disposed. *p.* and *pp.* **meant** (ment). (A.S. *mænan*, to intend.)
meander, *n.* me-*and*-er, a winding course; a maze; a tortuous bend; a design composed of such: *v.i.* to flow in a winding course; to be intricate. (Gr. *Meander*, a winding river in Phrygia.)
meandrine, *a.* me-*an*-drine, characterized by windings (esp. of the brain-corals, a genus of corals with meandering cavities and ridges.
meaning, *a.* *meen*-ing, significant: *n.* that which is meant; signification; import.
meaningless, *a.* *meen*-ing-less, having no meaning.
meaningly, *ad.* *meen*-ing-le, significantly.
meanly, *ad.* in a mean or a stingy manner; ignobly; scurvily.
meanness, *n.* *meen*-ness, baseness; paltriness.
meant, ment, *p.* and *pp.* of the verb *to mean.*
meantime, *ad.* *meen*-time, in the intervening time: *n.* the time between two stated times.
meanwhile, *ad.* *meen*-while, during the intervening time between two stated times: *n.* meantime.
mease, *n.* meez, a fish-trade measure containing five "hundreds" of, usually, from 100 to 124 each. (O.F.)
measled, *a.* *mee*-zld, infected or marked with or as with measles.
measles, *n.* *mee*-zlz, a contagious disease of the human body characterized by a patchy crimson rash upon the skin; a disease of swine and cattle due to infestation by certain parasite larvæ. (A.S. *mæsle*, a spot.)
measly, *a.* *mee*-zle, infected with measles (esp. of pork); stingy [Slang].
measurable, *a.* *mezh*-ur-ra-bl, that may be measured; moderate. (Fr. *mesurable.*)
measurably, *ad.* *mezh*-ur-ra-ble, in a limited degree.
***measure,** *n.* *mezh*-ur, the extent or dimensions of a thing; that by which extent or dimension is ascertained or expressed; a definite quantity; determined extent; a standard of measurement; an instrument for, or a system of, measuring; proportion; lot or portion; extent of ability; degree; just degree; moderation; means to an end; the width of a line or column, etc. [Print.]; that division by which motion in music is regulated; time [Music]; metre; a stately dance: *pl.* a group or series of strata [Geol.]: *v.i.* to have a certain extent; to take measurements: *v.t.* to ascertain or express the dimensions of; to estimate; to compute by a standard; to mark out; to pass or travel over; to allot or distribute by measure. (O.F. *mesure.*)
measured, *a.* *mezh*-urd, of a definite measure; steady; uniform; rhythmical; well considered.
measureless, *a.* without measure; boundless.
measurement, *n.* *mezh*-ur-ment, act or result of measuring; dimension ascertained by measuring.
measurer, *n.* *mezh*-ur-rer, one who or that which measures.
***meat,** *n.* meet, food; flesh dressed and used as food (other than fish and fowl); the edible interior of nuts, eggs, lobsters, etc. **meat-fly,** a bluebottle. **meat offering,** a Jewish sacrifice of flour with oil and frankincense. **meat safe,** a small cupboard, generally of perforated zinc, for meat and other food. **meat salesman,** an agent who receives carcases and sells them to retail butchers. (A.S. *mete.*)
meatiness, *n.* *meet*-e-ness, the condition of being meaty, or of being filled with thought.
meatless, *a.* *meet*-less, containing no meat. **meatless day,** a day on which meat is not served or eaten.
meatus, *n.* mee-*ay*-tus, a passage in the body, or opening in such passage. [Anat.]. (L., passage or way.)
meaty, *a.* *meet*-e, fleshy, but not fat; like meat; full of matter, as a solid discourse.
Mecca, *n.* *mek*-ka, the Arabian city where Mohammed was born, and goal of Mohammedan pilgrims; hence any much desired object of attainment.
meccano, *n.* me-*kah*-noh, proprietary name of miniature metal constructional material for children.
mechanic, *n.* me-*kan*-ik, one employed in a craft or in a mechanical occupation; an artisan or operative: *a.* mechanical. (O.Fr. *mechanique.*)
mechanical, *a.* me-*kan*-e-kal, pertaining to or constructed according to the principles of mechanics;

applying to machines; acting as a mere machine; done in the manner of a machine, or by force of mere habit; pertaining to artisans or mechanics; acting by physical power without chemical change. **mechanical advantage,** the ratio of the force applied, as of a lever, to the force generated or weight moved. **mechanical drawing,** drawing done with instruments. **mechanical powers,** the lever, the wheel and axle, the pulley, the inclined plane, the wedge, and the screw—the elementary bases of machinery. **mechanical transport,** carriage by mechanical as distinguished from horse transport.

mechanically, *ad.* in a mechanical manner.

mechanician, *n.* mek-a-*nish*-an, one skilled in mechanics; one skilled in constructing machines.

mechanics, *n.* me-*kan*-iks, the branch of physical science treating of the action of force upon matter; the science of machinery.

mechanism, *n.* *mek*-an-izm, the interrelated parts of a machine; machinery; mechanical construction or (in art, etc.) execution.

mechanist, *n.* *mek*-an-ist, a mechanician; one holding that natural phenomena are the effects of solely mechanical causes [Phil.].

mechanistic, *a.* mek-a-*nis*-tik, pertaining to mechanism, or to the philosophic tenets of the mechanists.

mechanization, *n.* mek-a-ny-*zay*-shon, the result or action of mechanizing.

mechanize, *v.t.* *mek*-an-ize, to form mechanically; to make mechanical; to replace human or animal labour with machinery; to substitute tanks, etc., for cavalry [Mil.]. **mechanized warfare,** hostilities in which results are chiefly obtained by the use of mechanical transport and machine weapons, etc., of offence and defence.

mechanotherapy, *n.* me-*kan*-o-*the*-ra-pe, the treatment of injury or disease by mechanical means.

Mechlin, *n.* *mek*-lin, Flemish lace, a light lace made at Mechlin (Malines), Belgium.

mecometer, *n.* me-*kom*-e-ter, an instrument for measuring lengths. (Gr. *mēkos,* length, *metron,* measure.)

meconate, *n.* *mek*-o-nate, a salt of meconic acid.

meconic, *a.* me-*kon*-ik, obtained from the poppy. **meconic acid,** a bitter acid contained in opium. (Gr. *mekon,* a poppy.)

meconin, *n.* *mek*-o-nin, a neutral crystalline substance present in opium.

meconium, *n.* me-*koh*-ne-um, the first discharge from the bowels of infants. (L.)

medal, *n.* *med*-al, a small metal decoration, usually coin- or cross-shaped, cast or stamped with some figure or device in commemoration of an illustrious person or event. (O.Fr. *médaille.*)

medalet, *n.* *med*-a-let, a miniature medal.

medallic, *a.* me-*dal*-lik, pertaining to medals.

medallion, *n.* me-*dal*-yon, a large medal; a tablet, esp. round or oval, with figures in relief. (Fr. *médaillon.*)

medallist, *n.* *med*-al-ist, one skilled in medals; a maker, engraver, or collector of medals; one who has gained a medal by way of prize.

meddle, *v.i.* *med*-dl, to interfere in other people's affairs; to interpose. (O.Fr. *mesler.*)

meddler, *n.* *med*-dler, one who meddles; an officious busybody.

meddlesome, *a.* *med*-dl-sum, given to meddling.

meddlesomeness, *n.* officious interference.

meddlingly, *ad.* *med*-dling-le, in a meddlesome manner.

Mede, *n.* meed, an inhabitant of Media, a powerful state of N.W. Persia about the 6th cent. B.C.

media, *n.* *mee*-de-a, the middle coat of the wall of any vessel [Anat.]; a voiced mute [Phonetics]. (L.)

media, *n.pl.* *mee*-de-a, a plural of *medium.*

mediacy, *n.* *mee*-de-a-se, mediateness.

mediæval, *a.* med-e-*ee*-val, belonging to or characteristic of the Middle Ages: *n.* one who lived in this period. (L. *medius,* the middle, *ævum,* an age.)

mediævalism, *n.* med-e-*ee*-va-lizm, mediæval spirit, method, or practice; a survival from the Middle Ages.

mediævalist, *n.* med-e-*ee*-va-list, one who admires or retains the practices of the Middle Ages; a student or historian of this period.

mediævalize, *v.t.* med-e-*ee*-va-lize, to render mediæval.

mediævally, *ad.* in a mediæval manner.

medial, *a.* *mee*-de-al, intermediate; pertaining to or noting a mean or average; relating to a medium: *n.* a media [Phonetics]. (L. *medialis.*)

medially, *ad.* *mee*-de-a-le, in a medial position.

median, *a.* *mee*-de-an, being in or relating to the middle or the average; traversing the middle lengthwise [Anat.]: *n.* that which is median; a median quantity; each line bisecting the angles of a triangle and meeting within it. [L. *medianus.*]

Median, *a.* *mee*-de-an, pertaining to the Medes or to ancient Media.

mediant, *n.* *mee*-de-ant, a tone between the final and dominant, the third tone in the modern diatonic scale [Mus.]. (It. *mediante.*)

mediastinum, *n.* *mee*-de-as-*ty*-num, the membranous septum of the chest, dividing the cavity into two parts and separating the right and left lung. (L.)

mediate, *a.* *mee*-de-ate, between two extremes; intervening; acting as a medium; effected by a medium; not immediate: *v.i.* to interpose between parties with a view to reconciliation: *v.t.* to effect by mediation. (L. *mediatus.*)

mediately, *ad.* *mee*-de-at-le, in a mediate way.

mediateness, *n.* the state of being mediate.

mediation, *n.* me-de-*ay*-shon, the act of mediating; intercession; interposition.

mediatization, *n.* *mee*-de-a-ty-*zay*-shon, the act of mediatizing.

mediatize, *v.t.* *mee*-de-a-tize, to deprive of independence; to annex a small state to a larger one while allowing its ruler to retain certain rights and privileges.

mediator, *n.* *mee*-de-ay-tor, one who mediates or interposes between parties at variance, for the purpose of reconciling them; an intercessor.

mediatorial, *a.* *mee*-de-a-*taw*-re-al, belonging to a mediator.

mediatorially, *ad.* by mediation.

mediatorship, *n.* *mee*-de-ay-tor-ship, the office of a mediator.

mediatory, *ad.* *mee*-de-a-to-re, pertaining to mediation.

mediatrix, *n.* *mee*-de-a-triks, a woman mediator.

medic, *n.* *med*-ik, medick.

medicable, *a.* *med*-ik-a-bl, capable of medicinal cure or relief. (L. *medicabilis.*)

***medical,** *a.* *med*-ik-al, pertaining to or connected with the art or practice of healing diseases; pertaining to medicine as apart from surgery; tending to cure: *n.* a medical man or student [Coll.]. **medical jurisprudence,** forensic medicine. **medical man,** a medical practitioner. **medical officer of health,** a legally qualified medical man appointed by the Ministry of Health or a Local Authority to supervise the public health, hygiene, sanitation, etc., of a district. **medical practitioner,** a fellow, member, or licentiate of a recognized college of physicians or surgeons; a graduate in medicine of a university or a licentiate of the Society of Apothecaries; a family doctor. **medical treatment,** treatment by a physician as distinguished from treatment by a surgeon. (Fr. *médical.*)

medically, *ad.* *med*-ik-al-le, according to the rules of medicine or of the medical profession.

medicament, *n.* me-*dik*-a-ment, a healing application. (L. *medicamentum.*)

medicamental, *a.* *med*-e-ka-*men*-tal, relating to medicaments.

medicaster, *n.* *med*-e-*kas*-ter, a quack doctor. (L. *medicus,* a doctor, *aster,* partial resemblance.)

medicate, *v.t.* *med*-e-kate, to tincture with anything medicinal; to treat with medicine. (L. *medicatus.*)

medication, *n.* *med*-e-*kay*-shon, impregnation with medicinal substances; medical treatment.

medicative, *a.* *med*-e-ka-tiv, curative.

Medicean, *a.* med-e-*chee*-an, relating to the Medici, the ruling family of Florence about 1430–1530.

medicinal, *a.* me-*dis*-e-nal, pertaining to medicine; adapted to cure or mitigate disease.

medicinally, *ad.* in the manner of medicine.

medicine, *n.* *med*-e-sin, any substance administered (esp. internally) in the treatment of disease; a drug; the art of preventing, curing, or alleviating disease by medical, as distinct from surgical means; among N. American Indians, a spell, enchantment, magical power. **forensic medicine,** *see* **forensic. medicine man,** one who professes supernatural

powers, and practises enchantment; a tribal magician. **proprietary medicine,** *see* **proprietary.** (O.Fr.)
medick, *n. med*-ik, a fodder plant, *Medicago sativa*, allied to clover; lucerne.
medico, *n. med*-e-koh, a doctor or medical student [Slang]; in combination implying "medical and," as in *medico-legal*.
medieval, *a.* med-e-*ee*-val, mediæval.
mediocre, *a. mee*-de-oh-ker, of moderate quality; middling. (Fr. *médiocre.*)
mediocrity, *n. mee*-de-*ok*-re-te, a moderate degree; moderation; a person of only ordinary ability.
mediolateral, *a. mee*-de-o-*lat*-er-ral, pertaining to the middle and the side.
meditate, *v.i. med*-e-tate, to dwell on anything in thought; to muse; to think over: *v.t.* to plan; to contrive; to intend. (L. *meditatus.*)
meditation, *n.* med-e-*tay*-shon, the act of meditating; close or continued thought.
meditative, *a. med*-e-ta-tiv, addicted to or indicative of meditation.
meditatively, *ad.* in a meditative manner.
meditativeness, *n.* state of being meditative.
Mediterranean, *a. med*-e-ter-*ray*-ne-an, belonging to or situated about the Mediterranean Sea: *n.* the Mediterranean Sea. **Mediterranean fever,** Malta fever. (L. *mediterraneus*, located in the midst of land.)
medium, *a. mee*-de-um, middling; moderate; average in quality, degree, etc.: *n.* (*pl.* **media** *or* **mediums**) anything that intervenes; a mean; middle place, stage, or degree; agency; agent; transmitting substance or vehicle; means or instrument; one said to be able to transmit communications from supernatural agencies [Spiritualism]; a fluid or semi-fluid in which bacteria are cultivated; a preservative substance; a size of paper between demy and royal; the mean or middle term of a syllogism [Logic]. **medium wave,** any electromagnetic wave of a wavelength between 200 and 1000 metres [Wire.]. (L.)
mediumistic, *a. mee*-de-u-*mis*-tik, relating to spiritualistic mediums and their work.
Medjidie, *n. medj*-e-dee, name of a former Turkish order of knighthood (1851–1920), and of the former silver 20-piastre piece, equal to 3*s.* 7·36*d.* (Abdul *Medjid*, Sultan 1840–61.)
medlar, *n. med*-lar, a roseaceous tree, *Pyrus germanica*, the fruit of which is eaten when half rotten. (O.Fr. *meslier.*)
medley, *n. med*-le, a mingled and confused mass or collection; a miscellany, literary or musical: *a.* motley; mixed: *v.t.* to make a medley of. (O.Fr. *medle.*)
Médoc, *n.* may-*dok*, a red claret from Médoc, France.
medulla, *n.* me-*dul*-a, the marrow in the cavities of the bones; the internal part of an organ; the lowermost part of the brain or **medulla oblongata** [Anat.]; the pith of hair, also of plants (L.)
medullary, *a.* me-*dul*-a-re, pertaining to, consisting of, or resembling marrow; pertaining to the medulla oblongata; filled with pith. **medullary ray,** one of the small tubes conveying urine through the medulla of the kidneys [Anat.]; a layer of cells lying between the xylem and phlœm in the stem and root of most plants [Bot.].
medusa, *n.* me-*dew*-sa (*pl.* **medusæ** me-*dew*-see), a jellyfish. (Name of the Gorgon of Greek myth, whose head, cut off by Perseus, turned every one who looked on it into stone.)
meed, *n.* meed, reward; recompense. (A.S. *mēd.*)
meek, *a.* meek, mild; gentle; submissive; forbearing. (A.S. *mēoc*, from Scand.)
meeken, *v.t.* and *i.* to make or become meek.
meekly, *ad. meek*-le, in a meek manner.
meekness, *n. meek*-ness, the quality of being meek.
meerkat, *n. meer*-kat, the small South African mammal, *Suricata tetradactyla*, with long soft hair, allied to the civet.
meerschaum, *n. meer*-shum, a fine clay-like hydrated silicate of magnesium used in making tobacco-pipes; a tobacco-pipe made of this. (Ger. *Meer*, the sea, *Schaum*, foam.)
meet, *a.* meet, fitting; suitable; proper. (A.S. *gemæte.*)
meet, *n.* meet, a meeting for a hunt or other sporting event; the place of this: *v.t.* to come face to face with; to join; to encounter; to come together with; to find; to receive; to fit in with; to satisfy: *v.i.* to encounter; to come together; to assemble; to come in contact. *p.* and *pp.* **met.** (A.S. *mētan.*)
*__meeting,__ *n. meet*-ing, a coming together; an assembly, esp. for public worship; a congregation; a race-meeting; an encounter; a conflux; a joining.
meeting-house, *n.* a nonconformist chapel; a Quakers' place of worship.
meetly, *ad. meet*-le, fitly; suitably.
meetness, *n. meet*-ness, fitness; propriety.
mega-, *meg*-a, prefix signifying great or large, and, in the metric system and technics, one million times the unit named, as *mega-cycle*, *mega-dyne*, *mega-erg*, *mega-farad*, etc. (Gr.)
megacephalous, *a.* meg-a-*sef*-a-lus, large-headed. (Gr. *megas*, great, *kephale*, the head.)
megalith, *n. meg*-a-lith, any very large stone used in prehistoric buildings or monuments. (*mega-*, and Gr. *lithos*, a stone.)
megalithic, *a.* meg-a-*lith*-ik, pertaining to or composed of megaliths.
megalomania, *n. meg*-a-lo-*may*-ne-a, a form of mental disorder in which the patient has the delusion that he is a great personage or is possessed of great genius. (Gr. *megalo-*, *comb.f.* of *megas*, great, and *mania*, madness.)
megalomaniac, *n. meg*-a-lo-*may*-ne-ak, a victim of megalomania: *a.* characterized by this.
megalopsia, *n.* meg-a-*lop*-se-a, macropia.
megalosaur, *n. meg*-a-lo-sor, one of an extinct order of gigantic carnivorous lizards of the Jurassic. (Gr. *megale*, and *sauros*, lizard.)
megaphone, *n. meg*-a-fone, an instrument for amplifying sound, esp. of the voice; a long-distance speaking trumpet: *v.i.* and *t.* to use, or to utter by means of, a megaphone. (Gr. *megas*, great, *phone*, voice.)
megapode, *n. meg*-a-pode, any of the large mound-building gallinaceous birds of the Pacific islands and Australia. (*mega-*, and Gr. *pous*, *podos*, foot.)
megascope, *n. meg*-a-skope, an apparatus for throwing enlarged pictures upon a screen. (Gr. *megas*, and *skopeo*, view.)
megass, *n.* me-*gass*, bagasse, refuse stalks of the sugar-cane.
megatherium, *n.* meg-a-*theer*-re-um, an extinct gigantic edentate of the Pleistocene of S. America. (*mega-*, and Gr. *therion*, a wild animal.)
megger, *n. meg*-er, proprietary name of an instrument for measuring the resistance of electrical insulation.
megilp, *n.* me-*gilp*, a compound of linseed-oil and mastic-varnish, used by artists as a vehicle of colours.
megohm, *n. meg*-ohm, a million ohms, the unit of electrical resistance. (*mega-* and *ohm.*)
megrim, *n. mee*-grim, the flat-fish *Lepidorhombus megastoma*, the whiff or merry-sole.
megrim, *n. mee*-grim, migraine; the staggers, an attack under which a horse at work reels and sometimes falls: *pl.* depression of spirits. (Fr. *migraine.*)
meionite, *n. my*-o-nite, a variety of scapolite. (Gr. *meion*, less.)
meiosis, *n.* my-*oh*-sis, a species of hyperbole, representing a thing less than it is, litotes [Rhet.]; the stage of a disease when the symptoms begin to diminish [Path.]; the nuclear changes accompanying the maturation of germ-cells [Biol.]. (Gr. *meion*, less.)
meiotic, *a.* my-*ot*-ik, pertaining to or characterized by meiosis.
Meistersinger, *n.* my-ster-*sing*-er, one of a class of poets and musicians of certain German cities in the 14th to 16th centuries. (Ger., master-singer.)
mekometer, *n.* me-*kom*-e-ter, a form of range-finder, esp. for use with small-arms. (Gr. *mekos*, length, and *-metre.*)
melaconite, *n.* me-*lak*-o-nite, an earthy black oxide of copper. (Gr. *melas*, black, *konis*, powder.)
melæna, *n.* me-*lee*-na, an intestinal evacuation mixed with altered blood, often black, and sometimes like tar; black vomit [Med.]. (Gr.)
melanæmia, *n.* mel-a-*nee*-me-a, an abnormally dark condition of the blood, due to the presence of melanin.
melancholia, *n.* mel-an-*koh*-le-a, a form of insanity

marked by fits of profound depression, often preceding mania. (L., from Gr., as *melancholy.*)
melancholic, *a.* mel-an-*kol*-ik, affected with melancholy; depressed in spirits; expressive of melancholy; mournful.
melancholily, *ad.* *mel*-an-ko-le-le, with melancholy.
melancholious, *a.* mel-an-*koh*-le-us, inclined to, or suggestive of, melancholy; melancholic.
melancholize, *v.i.* *mel*-an-ko-lize, to become gloomy in mind: *v.t.* to make melancholy.
melancholy, *n.* *mel*-an-ko-le, a diseased state of mind, characterized by great depression and gloomy apprehensions, formerly thought to be due to an excess of black bile; a gloomy state of mind; depression of spirits: *a.* depressed in spirits; gloomy; sad. (O.Fr. *melancolie,* from Gr. *melas, melanos,* black, *cholos,* bile.)
Melanesian, *a.* mel-a-*nee*-ze-an, pertaining to Melanesia, a group of S. Pacific islands so called from the blackness of the natives: *n.* a native or the language of Melanesia.
mélange, *n.* may-*lahnzh,* a confused mixture; a medley. (Fr.)
melanian, *a.* me-*lay*-ne-an, of dark pigmentation; negroid.
melanic, *a.* me-*lan*-ik, melanian; melanotic.
melanin, *n.* *mel*-a-nin, the black colouring matter contained in certain tissues, as in hair, the skin of Negroes, etc. (Gr. *melas,* black.)
melanism, *n.* *mel*-a-nizm, excess of dark colouring matter in the skin, fur, or feathers; black coloration. (Gr. *melas.*)
melanite, *n.* *mel*-a-nite, a black variety of garnet.
Melanochroi, *n.* *mel*-a-*nok*-ro-eye, that class of the white races characterized by dark hair and pale complexion. (Gr. *melas,* and *ochroi,* pale.)
melanosis, *n.* mel-a-*noh*-sis, a condition characterized by the morbid deposition of black pigment or melanin [Med.].
melanotic, *a.* mel-a-*not*-ik, pertaining to or characterized by melanosis.
melanotrichous, *a.* mel-a-*not*-re-kus, dark-haired.
melanotype, *n.* me-*lan*-o-tipe, a kind of ferrotype.
melanterite, *n.* me-*lan*-ter-ite, native copperas.
melanure, *n.* *mel*-an-yewr, the gilt-head, a brightly-coloured sea-bream. (Gr. *melas,* black, *oura,* tail.)
melanuria, *n.* mel-a-*new*-re-a, a disorder in which the urine contains black pigment [Med.].
melaphyre, *n.* *mel*-a-fire, a variety of very dark porphyry. (Gr. *melas,* and *porphyrites.*)
melasma, *n.* me-*laz*-ma, a morbid dark discoloration of the skin; a form of chloasma in which the patches are blackish; a black spot sometimes occurring on the tibia of old people. (Gr.)
meld, *n.* meld, any of certain scoring combinations of cards in the games of pinochle, canasta, etc.: *v.i.* to form one of these combinations. (Ger. *melden,* to notify.)
mêlée, *n.* *mel*-ay, a confused fight or scuffle. (Fr.)
Melibœan, *a.* mel-e-*bee*-an, alternately answering. (L. *Melibœus,* in Virgil's eclogue.)
melic, *a.* *mel*-ik, lyric; intended for singing. (Gr. *melikos,* from *melos,* song.)
meliceris, *n.* me-*lis*-er-ris, an encysted tumour filled with a honey-like matter [Med.]. (Gr. *meli,* honey, *keros,* wax.)
melilite, *n.* *mel*-e-lite, a native honey-coloured silicate of calcium, magnesium, aluminium, etc.
melilot, *n.* *mel*-e-lot, a sweet-scented clover of the genus *Melilotus.* **blue melilot,** *Trigonella cærulea,* one of the fenugreeks. (Gr. *melilotos.*)
melinite, *n.* *mel*-e-nite, lyddite. (Fr. *mélinite.*)
meliorant, *n.* *mee*-le-o-rant, that which meliorates.
meliorate, *v.t.* *mee*-le-o-rate, to make better; to improve: *v.i.* to grow better. (Late L. *melioratus.*)
melioration, *n.* *mee*-le-o-*ray*-shon, improvement.
meliorism, *n.* *mee*-le-o-rizm, the theory that good in the world outweighs evil and must eventually prevail; the philosophical halfway house between optimism and pessimism. (L. *melior,* better.)
meliorist, *n.* *mee*-le-o-rist, an adherent of meliorism: *a.* pertaining to meliorism.
meliphagous, *a.* me-*lif*-a-gus, feeding on honey; pertaining to the honey-eaters, an Australasian group of birds. (Gr. *meli,* and *phago,* eat.)
melliferous, *a.* me-*lif*-er-rus, producing honey. (L.)
mellification, *n.* *mel*-e-fe-*kay*-shon, the production of honey. (L. *mel,* and *facio,* make.)
mellifluence, *n.* me-*lif*-loo-ence, a sweet flow.
mellifluent, *a.* me-*lif*-loo-ent, flowing as with honey; smooth; sweetly flowing; mellisonant. (Late L. *mellifluus,* flowing sweetly.)
mellifluous, *a.* me-*lif*-loo-us, mellifluent.
mellisonant, *a.* me-*lis*-o-nant, sweet-sounding.
mellit, *n.* *mel*-it, a dry scab on the heel of a horse.
mellite, *n.* *mel*-ite, a yellow compound of aluminium found in lignite; honey-stone; any preparation containing honey [Pharm.]. (L. *mel,* honey, Gr. *lithos,* a stone.)
mellivorous, *a.* me-*liv*-o-rus, eating honey.
mellow, *a.* *mel*-oh, soft with ripeness; fully ripe; soft to the senses; softened by age; genial with drink [Coll.]: *v.t.* to ripen; to bring to maturity; to soften; *v.i.* to become soft; to be ripened. (A.S. *melwe.*)
mellowly, *ad.* *mel*-oh-le, in a mellow manner.
mellowness, *n.* *mel*-oh-ness, the quality of being mellow; softness; maturity.
mellowy, *a.* *mel*-oh-e, soft; unctuous.
melodeon, *n.* me-*loh*-de-on, a musical instrument with metallic reeds, on the same principle as the harmonium. (L. *melodia,* melody.)
melodic, *a.* me-*lod*-ik, relating to or containing melody. (Gr. *melodikos.*)
melodicon, *n.* me-*lod*-e-kon, a form of metallophone.
melodious, *a.* me-*loh*-de-us, full of melody. (Fr. *mélodieux.*)
melodiously, *ad.* in a melodious manner.
melodiousness, *n.* quality of being melodious.
melodist, *n.* *mel*-o-dist, a composer or singer of melodies (used also of a collection of melodies).
melodize, *v.t.* *mel*-o-dize, to make melodious; to compose a melody for: *v.i.* to make melody.
melodrama, *n.* *mel*-o-drah-ma, a sensational drama with a happy ending and with or without incidental music; a sensational story, or incident. (Fr. *mélodrame.*)
melodramatic, *a.* mel-o-dra-*mat*-ik, pertaining to or suitable for melodrama; sensational.
melodramatist, *n.* mel-o-*dram*-a-tist, one skilled in melodramatic acting; a writer of melodramas.
melody, *n.* *mel*-o-de, a rhythmical and pleasing succession of musical sounds; the air or tune of a musical piece; music. (L. *melodia.*)
melomania, *n.* mel-o-*may*-ne-a, insane or inordinate love of music.
melon, *n.* *mel*-on, the gourd of *Cucumis melo,* the musk-melon, or of *Citrullus vulgaris,* the water-melon, of which several varieties are cultivated. **melon thistle,** a melon-shaped cactus, *Melocactus communis.* (Gr. *melon,* an apple.)
meloplasty, *n.* *mel*-o-*plas*-te, the surgical replacement of a cheek by transference of tissue. (Gr. *mela,* cheeks, *plasso,* shape.)
Melpomene, *n.* mel-*pom*-e-ne, the muse of tragedy [Myth.]. (Gr. *melpomai,* sing.)
melt, *v.t.* melt, to make liquid; to dissolve; to mollify; to waste away; to dissipate: *v.i.* to become liquid; to dissolve; to blend; to be softened to sympathy; to be subdued; to be dispersed or dissipated: *n.* molten metal; quantity of metal melted at one operation. (A.S. *meltan.*)
melter, *n.* *mel*-ter, one who melts anything.
melting, *a.* *mel*-ting, dissolving; deeply affecting; affected to tenderness: *n.* act of dissolving or softening or rendering tender. **melting-point,** the temperature at which a solid becomes liquid. **melting-pot,** a crucible. **in the melting-pot,** [Coll.], in a state of dissolution or suspense.
meltingly, *ad.* in a manner to melt or soften.
melton, *n.* *mel*-ton, a stout, smooth-faced woollen cloth for coatings, etc. (*Melton* Mowbray, an English hunting centre.)
member, *n.* *mem*-ber, the limb of an animal with a special function; any part with a special office; a clause; a part of a verse; a part of a whole; either side of an equation [Alg.]; one belonging to a community or society. **member of parliament,** a person representing a constituency in the House of Commons. (Fr. *membre.*)
membered, *a.* *mem*-berd, having limbs.
membership, *n.* *mem*-ber-ship, the state of being a member; community; society.
membral, *a.* *mem*-bral, pertaining to the limbs.
membranaceous, *a.* mem-bra-*nay*-shus, membranous.
membrane, *n.* *mem*-brane, a thin, pliable animal or vegetable tissue, serving to line or cover the parts or organs [Anat. and Bot.]; a single piece of parch-

ment or vellum forming part of a roll [Palæography]. (Fr.)
membraneous, *a.* mem-*bray*-ne-us, membranous.
membraniform, *a.* mem-*bray*-ne-form, of the form of a membrane.
membranous, *a.* *mem*-bra-nus, belonging to, consisting of, or like a membrane. (L. *membrana*, the skin covering a member of the body.)
memento, *n.* me-*men*-to, something which reminds; a keepsake; a souvenir. **memento mori** [L.], a reminder of death. (L., remember.)
memo, *n.* *mem*-oh, a memorandum [Coll.].
memoir, *n.* *mem*-wahr, a written account of recollections; a biographical sketch; a record of researches; an account of some investigation submitted to a learned society. (Fr. *mémoire.*)
memoirist, *n.* *mem*-wah-rist, a writer of memoirs or of a memoir.
memorabilia, *n.pl.* *mem*-o-ra-*bil*-e-a, things worthy of remembrance or record. (L.)
memorability, *n.* *mem*-o-ra-*bil*-e-te, the state or quality of being memorable.
memorable, *a.* *mem*-o-ra-bl, worth remembering, remarkable. (L. *memorabilis.*)
memorableness, *n.* *mem*-o-ra-bl-ness, memorability.
memorably, *ad.* in a manner to be remembered.
memorandum, *n.* mem-o-*ran*-dum (*pl.* **memorandums** *or* **memoranda**), a note to help the memory; a brief note or record; a summary account; a draft or summary of a legal document. **memorandum of association,** the charter or legal articles of incorporation of a limited company. (L.)
memorative, *a.* *mem*-o-ra-tiv, adapted to preserve the memory of anything.
memorial, *a.* me-*maw*-re-al, commemorative; preservative of memory; preserved in memory: *n.* that which preserves the memory of something; a monument; a written representation of facts; an informal state paper used in international negotiations. (L. *memorialis.*)
memorialist, *n.* me-*maw*-re-a-list, one who writes or subscribes to a memorial, or who presents one to a legislative body; a writer of memoirs.
memorialize, *v.t.* me-*maw*-re-a-lize, to petition by memorial; to address a memorial to.
memoria-technica, *n.* me-*maw*-re-a-*tek*-ne-ka, an artificial aid to memorizing. (L.)
memorize, *v.t.* *mem*-o-rize, to cause to be remembered; to learn by heart.
★**memory,** *n.* *mem*-o-re, the faculty of the mind by which it retains and can recall previous ideas and impressions; the state, or the period, of being remembered; anything remembered; remembrance; recollection. (O.Fr. *memorie.*)
Memphian, *a.* *mem*-fe-an, pertaining to Memphis, the ancient capital of Lower Egypt; Egyptian; very dark: *n.* an Egyptian; an inhabitant of Memphis.
memsahib, *n.* *mem*-sah-ib, the Hindu "madam," or address of respect to a white woman. (*mem*, and Hind. *sahib*, lord.)
men, men, *n.pl.* of *man.*
menaccanite, *n.* me-*nak*-a-nite, ilmenite, or sand consisting of this. (*Menaccan*, in Cornwall.)
menace, *n.* *men*-as, a threat; a threatening; a presage of coming evil; one who or that which menaces: *v.t.* to threaten. (O.Fr.)
menacer, *n.* *men*-a-ser, one who threatens.
menacingly, *ad.* *men*-a-sing-le, in a threatening manner.
ménage, *n.* me-*nahzh*, a household; household management. (Fr.)
menagerie, *n.* me-*nadj*-e-re, a place in which wild animals are kept; a collection of wild animals. (Fr.)
menagogue, *n.* *men*-a-gog, a medicine that promotes menstruation. (Gr. *menes*, menses, *ago*, bring.)
mend, *v.t.* mend, to repair; to improve; to correct; to augment: *v.i.* to grow better; to improve: *n.* the act or process of mending; a mended place; improvement. **mend the fire,** to put fresh coal on. **on the mend,** improving, getting better.
mendable, *a.* *men*-da-bl, capable of being mended.
mendacious, *a.* men-*day*-shus, lying; false; given to deception. (L. *mendax*, false.)
mendacity, *n.* men-*das*-e-te, falsehood; lying; deceit. (L. *mendacitas.*)
Mendelian, *a.* men-*dee*-le-an, relating to Mendel or to Mendelism: *n.* a follower of Mendel.
Mendelism, *n.* *men*-del-izm, the theory elaborated by Gregor Mendel (*d.* 1884, biologist and abbot of Brunn, Austria), of the inheritance in animals and plants of certain characteristics in accordance with a definite law.
mender, *n.* *men*-der, one who mends or repairs.
mendicancy, *n.* *men*-de-kan-se, beggary; the state of being a mendicant.
mendicant, *a.* *men*-de-kant, begging; practising beggary: *n.* a beggar; one of a religious order, without private property, and subsisting on alms. (L. *mendicans*, begging.)
mendicity, *n.* men-*dis*-e-te, mendicancy; the life of a beggar. (O.Fr. *mendicite.*)
mending, *n.* *men*-ding, the act of repairing; articles needing repair; wool or thread for darning with; a mended place.
mendipite, *n.* *men*-dip-ite, an oxychloride of lead found in the Mendip Hills, Somerset.
menhaden, *n.* men-*hay*-den, a marine fish, *Brevoortia tyrannus*, of the Atlantic coasts of N. America, related to the shads.
menhir, *n.* *men*-heer, a prehistoric monument consisting of a single unhewn upright stone. (Celt. *maen*, a stone, *hir*, high.)
menial, *a.* *mee*-ne-al, pertaining to servants; servile; mean: *n.* a domestic servant; one doing servile work; one of a servile spirit. (O.Fr. *mesne*, a household, from L. *manei*, stay.)
menilite, *n.* *men*-e-lite, a brownish variety of opal; liver-opal. (*Ménil*-montant, place near Paris, where found.)
meningeal, *a.* me-*nin*-je-al, pertaining to the meninges.
meninges, *n.pl.* me-*nin*-jeez, *plural* of *meninx.*
meningitis, *n.* men-in-*jy*-tis, inflammation of the meninges, esp. of the pia mater and arachnoid [Med.].
meninx, *n.* *men*-inks, any one of the three membranes (dura mater, arachnoid, and pia mater) enveloping the brain and spinal cord. (Gr., a membrane.)
meniscal, *a.* me-*nis*-kal, pertaining to a meniscus.
meniscus, *n.* me-*nis*-kus (*pl.* **meniscuses**), a lens, convex on one side and concave on the other, with the concavity sharper than the convexity; the curved top of a column of liquid (as in a barometer). (Gr. *meniskos*, little moon.)
menisperm, *n.* *men*-e-sperm, any plant of the family Menispermaceæ, esp. moonseed. (Gr. *mēnē*, the moon, *sperma*, seed.)
menispermine, *n.* men-e-*sperm*-in, a tasteless, white, opaque crystalline alkaloid obtained from various menisperms.
mennad, *n.* *men*-nad, the minnow.
Mennonite, *n.* *men*-on-ite, a member of an evangelical sect of Protestants founded by Menno Simons in Switzerland in the 16th century, who believe in the New Testament as the sole inspirational guide to conduct.
menology, *n.* me-*nol*-o-je, a register of months; a calendar of saints and festivals of the Greek Church; a martyrology. (Gr. *men*, a month, *logos*, list.)
menopause, *n.* *men*-o-pawz, the change of life, or final cessation of the menses, in women.
menopome, *n.* *men*-o-pome, a voracious carnivorous crypto-branchiate amphibian of certain N. American rivers; the hellbender or mud-devil. (Gr. *menein*, to remain, *poma*, lid.)
menorrhagia, *n.* men-o-*ray*-je-a, immoderate menstrual discharge [Med.]. (Gr. *men*, a month, *rhegnunai*, to burst forth.)
menorrhœa, *n.* men-o-*ree*-a, normal flow of the menses; excessive or long-continued menstrual flow [Med.]. (Gr. *men*, a month, *rheo*, flow.)
mensal, *a.* *men*-sal, pertaining to or used at the table or at meals. (L. *mensa*, a table.)
mensal, *a.* *men*-sal, monthly. (L. *mensis*, a month.)
menses, *n.pl.* *men*-seez, the catamenial or monthly discharges from the uterus. (L., months.)
Menshevik, *n.* *men*-she-vik, a member of the moderate socialist party in tsarist Russia which, in opposition to the Bolsheviks, favoured co-operation with the bourgeoisie. (Russ., the lesser, the minority.)
menstrual, *a.* *men*-stroo-al, recurring once a month; monthly; pertaining to the menses, or to a menstruum.
menstruant, *a.* *men*-stroo-ant, subject to menses; menstruating.

menstruate, *v.i.* *men*-stroo-ate, to discharge the menses.
menstruation, *n.* men-stroo-*ay*-shon, the act or the time of menstruating.
menstruous, *a.* *men*-stroo-us, having or pertaining to the menses; catamenial. (L. *menstruus.*)
menstruum, *n.* *men*-stroo-um (*pl.* **menstrua**), a solvent or dissolving substance, so called by the alchemists from some supposed connexion of its action with the menstrual flow. (Late L.)
mensurability, *n.* *men*-sew-ra-*bil*-e-te, capability of being measured. (L. *mensuranbilis.*)
mensurable, *a.* *men*-sew-ra-bl, measurable.
mensural, *a.* *men*-sew-ral, pertaining to measure. (Late L. *mensuralis.*)
mensuration, *n.* men-sew-*ray*-shon, the act, process, or art of measuring. (L. *mensuratio.*)
-ment, ment, an O.Fr. suffix denoting state, result, or action, as in *displacement, garnishment, lodgement.* For words ending in *-ment* not included in this vocabulary, reference should be made to the first part of the word. (L. *-mentum.*)
mentagra, *n.* men-*tag*-ra, sycosis, an eruption on the chin [Path.]. (L. *mentum,* chin, Gr. *agra,* a catching.)
mental, *a.* *men*-tal, pertaining to the mind; intellectual; pertaining to or affected by mental disease; demented. **mental arithmetic,** unwritten arithmetic. **mental defective,** a moron; a feeble-minded individual. **mental disease,** lunacy; insanity. **mental hospital,** a place where feeble-minded or insane patients are treated. **mental nurse,** a nurse who looks after insane or weak-minded persons. (L. *mens, mentis,* the mind.)
mental, *a.* *men*-tal, pertaining to the chin. (L. *mentum,* the chin.)
mentality, *n.* men-*tal*-e-te, intellectuality; the whole intellectual powers of a person; the character of a mind or of one's intelligence.
mentally, *ad.* *men*-tal-le, in the mind; in idea.
mentation, *n.* men-*tay*-shon, the action of the brain; cerebration.
menthol, *n.* *men*-thol, peppermint camphor; a mild local anodyne prepared from oil of peppermint. (L. *mentha,* mint.)
menticulture, *n.* men-te-*kul*-tewr, the culture or improvement of the mind. (L. *mens,* mind, and *culture.*)
mention, *n.* *men*-shon, a brief notice; a cursory remark or notice: *v.t.* to notice incidentally; to name. **honourable mention,** an examination award to a candidate whose work has been rather better than "good." **mentioned in dispatches,** officially reported to the War Office for specially meritorious action [Mil.]. (Fr.)
mentionable, *a.* *men*-shon-a-bl, that may be mentioned.
mentor, *n.* *men*-tor, a wise and faithful monitor and adviser. (Name of the friend of Ulysses and tutor of Telemachus.)
mentorial, *a.* men-*taw*-re-al, containing advice.
menu, *n.* *men*-oo, a list of the dishes provided at a meal or banquet; a bill of fare. (Fr.)
Mephistophelian, *a.* *mef*-e-sto-*fee*-le-an, in the spirit and style of Mephistopheles in Goethe's "Faust"; sceptical, cynical, and enticing to evil. (Gr. *me,* not, *phos,* a brilliance or light, and *phileo,* love.)
mephitic, *a.* me-*fit*-ik, offensive to the smell; foul; noxious; pestilential.
mephitis, *n.* me-*fy*-tis, foul, offensive, or noxious exhalations from decomposing substances. (L.)
mephitism, *n.* *mef*-e-tizm, poisoning caused by noxious exhalations.
mercantile, *a.* *mer*-kan-tile, pertaining to the usages, laws, etc., of buying and selling; commercial. **mercantile marine,** the merchant navy or service. **mercantile system,** the theory and practice of mercantilism. (O.Fr. *mercantil.*)
mercantilism, *n.* *mer*-kan-til-izm, the theory of trade; a former economic system depending for success chiefly upon a favourable balance of trade.
mercaptan, *n.* mer-*kap*-tan, any of a group of compounds resembling the alcohols but in which oxygen is replaced by sulphur. (L. *mercurium captans,* seizing mercury.)
Mercator's projection, *see* **projection.**
mercenarily, *ad.* *mer*-se-na-re-le, in a mercenary manner.
mercenariness, *n.* *mer*-se-na-re-ness, quality of being mercenary.
mercenary, *a.* *mer*-se-na-re, hired or procured with money; actuated by the love of money or gain; venal; greedy of gain; done for money: *n.* a professional soldier hired into foreign service. (Fr. *mercenaire.*)
mercer, *n.* *mer*-ser, a dealer in silks, cottons, linens, and woollen cloths. (Fr., a trader.)
mercerization, *n.* *mer*-ser-ry-*zay*-shon, the process of treating cotton yarns and fabrics with caustic alkali to give a glossy finish. (John *Mercer, d.* 1866, the inventor.)
mercerize, *v.t.* *mer*-ser-rize, to subject (cotton goods) to mercerization to give them a lustrous appearance.
mercery, *n.* *mer*-ser-re, the commodities or goods in which a mercer deals; the trade of a mercer.
merchandise, *n.* *mer*-chan-dize, wares, goods, or commodities bought or sold. (Fr.)
merchant, *n.* *mer*-chant, one who traffics or carries on trade, esp. with foreign countries or on a large scale; a trader: *a.* pertaining to trade; mercantile. **merchant marine,** or **service,** the mercantile marine, the body of ships engaged in commerce. **law merchant,** *see* **law.** (Fr. *marchand.*)
merchantable, *a.* *mer*-chant-a-bl, fit for market; marketable; saleable.
merchantman, *n.* *mer*-chant-man, a ship in the merchant service.
merchantry, *n.* *mer*-chant-re, the business of a merchant; merchants as a body.
merciful, *a.* *mer*-se-ful, having mercy; disposed to pity and forgive; compassionate; humane.
mercifully, *ad.* with compassion or pity.
mercifulness, *n.* the quality of being merciful.
merciless, *a.* *mer*-se-less, without mercy; unfeeling; cruel.
mercilessly, *ad.* in a merciless manner.
mercilessness, *n.* *mer*-se-less-ness, want of mercy.
mercurial, *a.* mer-*kewr*-re-al, pertaining to, consisting of, or due to quicksilver; like the god Mercury; active; flighty; fickle; changeable: *n.* any preparation containing mercury [Med.].
mercurialism, *n.* mer-*kewr*-re-a-lizm, poisoning attributable to prolonged mercurial treatment [Med.].
mercurialist, *n.* mer-*kewr*-re-a-list, a practitioner advocating the use of mercury for venereal disease.
mercuriality, *n.* *mer*-kewr-re-*al*-e-te, the state or quality of being mercurial or flighty.
mercurialize, *v.t.* mer-*kewr*-re-a-lize, to affect or treat with mercury [Med. and Phot.].
mercurially, *ad.* mer-*kewr*-re-a-le, in a fickle or lively manner.
mercuric, *a.* mer-*kewr*-rik, of or containing mercury.
mercurify, *v.t.* to treat or mix with mercury; to mercurialize.
mercurous, *a.* *mer*-kew-rus, mercuric; designating a compound in which mercury is a univalent. **mercurous chloride,** calomel.
Mercury, *n.* *mer*-kew-re, the swift ready messenger of the gods, and god of eloquence, theft, merchandise and trade [Myth.]; the planet nearest the sun; (*l.c.*) the metallic element quicksilver; a preparation of quicksilver. **dog's mercury,** the herbaceous plant *Mercurialis perennis.* **mercury vapour lamp,** an electric lamp in which a luminous electric discharge takes place in an atmosphere of mercury vapour. (Fr. *mercure.*)
mercy, *n.* *mer*-se, disposition to pity and forgive or spare; an act of mercy or kindness; goodwill; clemency; compassion. **Sister of Mercy,** a woman bound in religious community, and consecrated to works of mercy. (Fr. *merci,* favour, from L. *merces,* reward.)
mercy-seat, *n.* *mer*-se-seet, the covering of the Jewish ark of the covenant; the throne of God.
mere, *a.* meer, only this and nothing else; simple; absolute; entire. (L. *merus,* pure, unmixed.)
mere, *n.* meer, a pool or lake. (A.S.)
mere, *n.* meer, a boundary; a landmark. (A.S.)
merely, *ad.* *meer*-le, only; thus and no other way; simply.
meretricious, *a.* me-re-*trish*-us, showy and attractive; gaudy; pertaining to prostitutes. (L. *meretricius,* relating to a prostitute.)
meretriciously, *ad.* in a meretricious manner.
meretriciousness, *n.* the quality of being meretricious; deceitful allurement.

merganser, *n.* mer-*gan*-ser, a diving duck of the genus *Mergus*. (L. *mergus*, diver, *anser*, goose.)
merge, *v.t.* merj, to immerse; to sink; to cause to be swallowed up; to bring about a merger [Law]: *v.i.* to be sunk, swallowed, or lost. (L. *mergo*, dive.)
merger, *n.* *merj*-er, one who or that which merges: the absorption or extinguishment of a small property or estate by a greater [Law]; absorption; a combine or many commercial companies.
meri, *n.* *me*-re, a Maori war-club.
mericarp, *n.* *me*-re-karp, one of the two carpels of the fruit of umbelliferous plants.
meridian, *n.* me-*rid*-e-an, a great circle supposed to pass through the poles of the earth, and the zenith and nadir of any given place, intersecting the equator at right angles, and dividing the hemisphere into eastern and western [Geog. and Astron.]; the time when a heavenly body crosses this [Astron.]; midday; noon; the highest point: *a.* pertaining to the meridian or at mid-day, or to the highest point, or to the magnetic meridian. **magnetic meridian**, a great circle, parallel with the direction of the magnetic needle, and passing through its poles. (L. *meridianus*, from *meridies*, midday.)
meridional, *a.* me-*rid*-e-o-nal, pertaining to the meridian or to the highest point; southerly; having a southern aspect, or a north-south trend (as a mountain-range): *n.* (*cap.*) a dweller in the south (esp. S. France). (O.Fr.)
meridionality, *n.* me-*rid*-e-o-*nal*-e-te, the state of being on the meridian; aspect toward the south.
meridionally, *ad.* in the direction of the meridian.
meringue, *n.* mer-*rang*, white of egg beaten up with sugar as a garnishment for puddings; a hollow confection of this filled with whipped cream. (Fr.)
merino, *n.* mer-*ree*-no, a variety of fine-wooled sheep, originally from Spain; a fabric of merino wool; a fine wool yarn used in hosiery: *a.* pertaining to or made of this wool. (Sp., moving from pasture to pasture.)
merismatic, *a.* me-riz-*mat*-ik, dividing by the formation of internal partitions [Biol.]. (Gr. *merisma*, part.)
meristem, *n.* *me*-ris-tem, the tissue of dividing and growing cells; formative tissue [Bot.].
merit, *n.* *me*-rit, the quality or fact of deserving (esp. well); excellence entitling to honour or reward; worth; value; reward deserved; a mark (in examinations) recognizing merit: *pl.* question at issue: *v.t.* to deserve; to earn; to have a right to claim as reward; to have a just title to. **merit system**, method of promotion according to competence and proficiency only. **Order of Merit**, a British order of two divisions, military and civil, for men and women of conspicuous eminence, conferring no precedence and limited to 24 members (O.M.). (O.Fr. *merite.*)
meritorious, *a.* me-re-*taw*-re-us, deserving of reward or honour; praiseworthy. (L *meritorious.*)
meritoriously, *ad.* so as to deserve reward.
meritoriousness, *n.* state of deserving reward.
merk, *n.* merk, the former Scottish mark, a silver coin.
merle, *n.* merl, the blackbird. (O.Fr.)
merlin, *n.* *mer*-lin, the smallest of the European falcons, *Falco æsalon*. (O.Fr. *esmerillon.*)
merling, *n.* *mer*-ling, the whiting. (Fr. *merlan.*)
merlon, *n.* *mer*-lon, that part of a parapet which lies between two embrasures [Fort.]. (Fr.)
mermaid, *n.* *mer*-mayd, an imaginary marine animal, resembling a woman in the upper parts and a fish below. **mermaid's purse**, the egg capsule of a skate or dogfish. (A.S. *mere*, a lake, and *maid.*)
merman, *n.* *mer*-man, the male of the mermaid.
meroblast, *n.* *me*-ro-blast, a meroblastic ovum [Biol.].
meroblastic, *a.* me-ro-*blas*-tik, characterized by incomplete cleavage (of ova) [Biol.]; developing from part only of the spore [Bot.]. (Gr. *meros*, part, *blastos*, a shoot.)
merogenesis, *n.* me-ro-*jen*-e-sis, reproduction by segmentation [Biol.].
merome, *n.* *me*-rome, a metamere [Zool.].
meropidan, *a.* me-*rop*-e-dan, belonging to the family Meropidæ, comprising the bee-eaters [Orinth.].
Merovingian, *a.* me-ro-*vin*-je-an, relating to the ruling dynasty of the Franks, founded by Clovis and succeeded by the Carolingians, from about 486 to 751: *n.* any one of these kings.
merrily, *ad.* *me*-re-le, with mirth; jovially.
merriment, *n.* *me*-re-ment, gaiety with laughter or noise; mirth; jollity.
merriness, *n.* *me*-re-ness, merriment.
merry, *a.* *me*-re, gay and noisy; causing laughter or mirth; sportive; cheerful; pleasant; slightly drunk [Coll.]. **merry dancers**, the aurora borealis. **make merry**, to be jovial; to feast with mirth. (A.S. *myrige.*)
merry, *n.* *me*-re, the gean, or wild cherry.
merry-andrew, *n.* *me*-re-*an*-droo, a buffoon.
merry-go-round, *n.* a circular revolving frame mounted with seats, model horses, etc., for people to be carried round on.
merrymaking, *a.* *me*-re-make-ing, producing mirth: *n.* a festival; a meeting for mirth.
merryman, *n.* *me*-re-man, a buffoon.
merry-sole, *n.* *me*-re-sole, the megrim (fish).
merrythought, *n.* *me*-re-thawt, the united clavicles of a fowl's breast.
mersion, *n.* *mer*-shon, baptismal immersion.
meruline, *a.* *me*-roo-line, of or pertaining to the blackbird, *Turdus merula*, or related birds. (L.)
merycism, *n.* *me*-re-sizm, rumination in cattle, etc.; a nervous disorder in which this takes place [Med.]. (Gr. *mērukizein*, to ruminate.)
mesa, *n.* *may*-sa, a broad, flat, rocky tableland; a terrace-like hill rising from the surrounding level, esp. in southern U.S.A. (Sp.)
mésalliance, *n.* may-zah-*ly*-ans (or App.), a marriage in which one of the partners is of inferior social position to the other. (Fr.)
mesaraic, *a.* mes-a-*ray*-ik, mesenteric.
mescal, *n.* *mes*-kal, the maguey: also, a small Mexican cactus, and a mild intoxicant prepared from this [Sp.].
mesdames, *n.* may-*dahm*: *pl.* of *madame*. (Fr.)
meseems, *v.i.* me-*seemz*, it seems to me.
mesembryanthemum, *n.* mes-*em*-bre-*an*-the-mum, any of a genus of succulent greenhouse plants, mainly from S. Africa, including the fig-marigold, *M. roseum*, the hottentot fig, *M. edule*, and the ice plant, *M. crystallinum*. (Gr. *mesos*, middle, *hemera*, a day, and *anthemon*, a flower.)
mesencephalon, *n.* mes-en-*sef*-a-lon, the middle brain of vertebrates.
mesenteric, *a.* *mes*-en-*te*-rik, pertaining to the mesentery.
mesenteritis, *n.* *mes*-en-te-*ry*-tis, inflammation of the mesentery.
mesentery, *n.* *mes*-en-ter-re, a membranous fold of the peritoneum investing the small intestines and attaching them to the abdominal wall [Anat.]. (Gr. *mesos*, middle, *enteron*, intestines.)
★**mesh**, *n.* mesh, the space between the knots in a net or the dividing wires, etc., of a sieve; the gauge on which the net is made: *pl.* a net; network: *v.t.* to catch in a net; to enmesh; to engage (of gear-wheels etc.) [Mech.]. (A.S. *max*, a net.)
meshwork, *n.* *mesh*-wurk, network.
meshy, *a.* *mesh*-e, formed like network; consisting of meshes; reticulated.
mesial, *a.* *mee*-se-al, middle, esp. of the longitudinal line dividing the body, or any member or organ, into two equal parts [Anat.]. (Gr. *mesos*, the middle.)
mesitite, *n.* *mes*-e-tite, a variety of magnesite containing up to 50 per cent. of iron carbonate.
mesmeric, *a.* mez-*me*-rik, from or relating to mesmerism.
mesmerism, *n.* *mez*-mer-rizm, hypnotism; animal magnetism; the power by which one person induces in another a state of hypnosis. (F. A. *Mesmer*, *d.* 1815, a German physician, who practised this.)
mesmerist, *n.* *mez*-mer-rist, one who practises or advocates mesmerism.
mesmerization, *n.* *mez*-mer-ry-*zay*-shon, the act of mesmerizing; the mesmerized state.
mesmerize, *v.t.* *mez*-mer-rize, to hypnotize.
mesnalty, *n.* *mee*-nal-te, the estate of a mesne lord.
mesne, *a.* meen, intermediate. **mesne lord**, a landlord having tenants but himself holding of a superior [Feudal Law]. **mesne process**, such as intervenes between the beginning and end of a suit [Law]. **mesne profits**, the profits of an estate received by one who is wrongfully in possession. (O.Fr., middle.)

meso-, *pref.* mes-o, signifying middle. (Gr. *mesos*, middle.)
mesobar, *n. mes*-o-bar, a region of normal pressure [Meteor.].
mesoblast, *n. mes*-o-blast, the middle germinal layer of the embryo. (Gr. *mesos*, middle, *blastos*, a shoot.)
mesocarp, *n. mes*-o-karp, the middle layer of a pericarp [Bot.].
mesocephalic, *a. mes*-o-se-*fal*-lik, relating to the middle region of the head; possessing a skull of average size. (Gr. *mesos*, and *kephale*, head.)
mesocolon, *n. mes*-o-*koh*-lon, the fold of the mesentery connecting the colon to the abdominal wall [Anat.]. (Gr. *mesos*, and *colon*.)
mesoderm, *n. mes*-o-derm, the mesoblast. (Gr. *mesos*, and *derma*, skin.)
mesogastric, *a.* mes-o-*gas*-trik, pertaining to the umbilical region, or middle of the belly [Anat.]. (Gr. *mesos*, and *gaster*, the belly.)
mesolite, *n. mes*-o-lite, a zeolite intermediate between natrolite and scolecite [Min.].
mesolithic, *a.* mes-o-*lith*-ik, of or pertaining to the Stone Age period between the palæolithic and neolithic.
mesophlœum, *n.* mes-o-*flee*-um, the middle bark in exogens [Bot.].
mesophyll, *n. mes*-o-fil, the inmost cellular tissue in plants [Bot.]. (Gr. *mesos*, and *phyllon*, leaf.)
mesophyte, *n. mes*-o-fite, a plant to which either excess or scarcity of moisture is inimical. (Gr. *mesos*, and *phyton*, a plant.)
mesosperm, *n. mes*-o-sperm, the middle covering of a seed [Bot.].
mesosternum, *n.* mes-o-*ster*-num, the middle portion of the sternum or breastbone [Anat.].
mesothorax, *n.* mes-o-*thaw*-raks, the middle segment of the thorax [Entom.].
mesothorium, *n.* mes-o-*thaw*-re-um, a radioactive isotope of thorium used in medicine and as a constituent of luminous paints.
mesozoic, *a.* mes-o-*zoh*-ik, pertaining to the period during which the secondary rocks were formed: *n.* the period between the Permian and Tertiary, comprising the Triassic, Jurassic, and Cretaceous systems [Geol.].
Mespot, *n. mes*-pot, Mesopotamia [Army slang].
mesquite, *n. mez*-keet, a spiny Mexican shrub, *Prosopis juliflora*, the pods of which are used for fodder. (Sp.)
mess, *a.* mess, a dish or a quantity of food served up at one time; a number of persons who eat together, as amongst sailors and soldiers; a confused mixture; a state of dirt and confusion; confusion: *v.i.* to eat in company, as seamen, etc.; to muddle; to potter about: *v.t.* to soil or dirty; to jumble; to make a mess of; to supply with a mess. (O.Fr. *mes*, from L. *missum*, sent.)
message, *n. mes*-aj, any communication sent from one person to another; a communication sent by messenger; the teaching or principles of one inspired. (Fr.)
messenger, *n. mes*-sen-jer, one who bears a message; a forerunner; a cable used in weighing anchor [Naut.]. **King's (Queen's) Messenger**, a Foreign Office official employed to take and deliver dispatches abroad.
Messiah, *n.* mes-*sy*-a, Christ, the Saviour of the World. (Heb. *mashiah*, anointed.)
Messianic, *a.* mes-se-*an*-ik, relating to the Messiah.
messieurs, *n.pl.* (App.) (*sing.* **monsieur**), sirs; gentlemen. (Fr.)
messiness, *n. mes*-se-ness, the state of being untidy.
messmate, *n. mes*-mate, a member of the same mess; a table companion.
messroom, *n. mes*-room, a room in which a mess assembles.
messrs., *n.pl. mes*-erz, a title placed before the name of a firm, or list of men's names. (Abbr. *messieurs*.)
messuage, *n. mes*-swaj, a dwelling-house with outbuildings and garden [Law]. (O.Fr. *mesuage*.)
messy, *a. mes*-se, in a mess; dirty; untidy. (*mess*.)
mestee, *n.* mes-*tee*, a mustee.
mestizo, *n.* mes-*tee*-zoh, a half-breed, esp. the offspring of a Spanish-American and a native Indian. (Sp.)
met, met, *p.* and *pp.* of *meet*.
meta-, *met*-a, a Greek prefix signifying beyond, after, with, or among, and frequently expressing change.
metabasis, *n.* me-*tab*-a-sis, transition from one subject to another [Rhet.]; change of remedy [Med.]. (Gr.)
metabolian, *n.* met-a-*bol*-e-an, one of the class of insects which undergo a complete metamorphosis.
metabolic, *a.* met-a-*bol*-ik, capable of or undergoing metamorphosis; due to change; pertaining to or characterized by metabolism. (Gr. *metabole*, change.)
metabolism, *n.* me-*tab*-o-lizm, the process by which the body makes use of nutriment for its constructive and destructive requirements.
metabolite, *n.* me-*tab*-o-lite, any product of metabolism.
metabolize, *v.t.* me-*tab*-o-lize, to subject to or alter by metabolism.
metacarpal, *a.* met-a-*kar*-pal, belonging to the metacarpus.
metacarpus, *n.* met-a-*kar*-pus, the part of the hand between the wrist and the fingers [Anat.]. (Gr. *meta-*, and *karpos*, the wrist.)
metacentre, *n.* met-a-*sen*-ter, a point in a floating body on the position of which its stability depends.
metachronism, *n.* me-*tak*-ro-nizm, the chronological error of postdating an event. (Gr. *meta-*, and *kronos*, time.)
metachrosis, *n. met*-a-*kroh*-sis, the power of certain animals (esp. lizards) to change colour.
metacism, *n. met*-a-sizm, mytacism.
metage, *n. mee*-taj, official measurement of weight, content, etc., or charge made for this. (*mete*.)
metagenesis, *n.* met-a-*jen*-e-sis, alternation of generations. (Gr. *meta-*, and *genesis*.)
metagenetic, *a.* met-a-je-*net*-ik, pertaining to metagenesis.
***metal**, *n. met*-al, one of a class of elementary substances which are insoluble in water, fusible by heat, good conductors of heat and electricity, malleable, ductile, and (mercury excepted) solid at ordinary temperatures; an alloy or compound of such substances; gold or silver [Her.]; glass in a state of fusion; stones broken small for roads; the effective power of guns borne by a warship; the essential quality of a person's character: *pl.* rails of a railway: *v.t.* to furnish or cover with metal; to repair a road with metal. (O.Fr.)
metalepsis, *n.* met-a-*lep*-sis, the conjunction of two or more different figures in the same word [Rhet.]. (Gr., alternation.)
metaleptic, *a.* met-a-*lep*-tik, pertaining to metalepsis; transverse.
metallic, *a.* me-*tal*-ik, pertaining to or of the nature of a metal; containing or consisting of metal. **metallic lustre**, the lustre peculiar to metals. **metallic oxide**, a metal combined with oxygen. **metallic salts**, salts which have a metallic oxide as their base.
metallicity, *n. met*-a-*lis*-e-te, the quality of being metallic.
metalliferous, *a.* met-a-*lif*-er-rus, producing or yielding metal. (*metal*, and L. *fero*, bear.)
metalliform, *a.* me-*tal*-e-form, having the form of metal.
metalline, *a. met*-a-line, metallic; metalliferous; made of metal.
metalling, *n. met*-a-ling, stone or other material used to give solidity to roads, railways, etc.; the process of making or repairing roads, etc.
metallist, *n. met*-a-list, a worker in metal.
metallization, *n.* met-a-ly-*zay*-shon, the act or process of metallizing.
metallize, *v.t. met*-a-lize, to form into metal; to give metallic properties to; to vulcanize.
metallogeny, *n.* met-a-*loj*-e-ne, the science or study of the origin of ore deposits.
metallography, *n.* met-a-*log*-ra-fe, the study of the internal structure of metals and alloys. (*metal*, and Gr. *grapho*, write.)
metalloid, *a. met*-a-loyd, having the appearance of a metal: *n.* a non-metallic element; an element (as arsenic, antimony, etc.) having certain metallic properties.
metallophone, *n.* me-*tal*-o-fohn, a xylophone with metallic instead of wooden bars.
metallurgical, *a.* met-a-*lur*-je-kal, pertaining to metallurgy.
metallurgist, *n.* me-*tal*-ur-jist, a student or practitioner of metallurgy.
metallurgy, *n. met*-a-lur-je, the extraction of metal from the ore; the art of working metals from the native state to the utensil. (Gr. *ergon*, work.)

metalogical, *a.* met-a-*loj*-e-kal, beyond the scope of logic.
metamer, *n.* *met*-a-mer, a metameric compound [Chem.]; a phytomer [Bot.].
metamere, *n.* *met*-a-meer, a somite; any one of the homologous segments of a metameric animal [Zool.].
metameric, *a.* met-a-*me*-rik, having the same chemical elements in the same proportion and atomic weight, but with different properties and structure; isomeric [Chem.]; having a body composed of a series of similar segments disposed along a central axis, as in the earthworms [Zool.]. (Gr. *meta-*, and *meros*, a part.)
metamerism, *n.* me-*tam*-er-rizm, the state or quality of being metameric. [Chem. and Zool.]
metamorphic, *a.* met-a-*mor*-fik, involving transformation; transformed, esp. of stratified rocks that, since deposition, have undergone structural change through heat, chemical action, or pressure, etc. [Geol.].
metamorphism, *n.* met-a-*mor*-fizm, quality or state of being metamorphic.
metamorphopsia, *n.* *met*-a-mor-*fop*-se-a, a defect of vision causing apparent distortion or wrong location of objects.
metamorphose, *v.t.* met-a-*mor*-foze, to change into a different form. (Gr. *meta-*, and *morphe*, form.)
metamorphosis, *n.* met-a-*mor*-fo-sis, change of form, shape, or condition, etc.; transformation, as of the pupa into a winged insect. (L.)
metaphor, *n.* *met*-a-for, a figure of speech in which an epithet usually attached to one kind of object is analogically attached to another, as "a barrage of questions"; a condensed simile [Rhet.]. (Gr. *metaphora*, transference, from *meta-*, and *phero*, bear.)
metaphoric, *a.* met-a-*fo*-rik, metaphorical.
metaphorical, *a.* met-a-*fo*-re-kal, pertaining to metaphor; comprising a metaphor; figurative.
metaphorically, *ad.* met-a-*fo*-re-ka-le, in a metaphorical manner.
metaphorist, *n.* *met*-a-fo-rist, one who uses metaphors.
metaphrase, *n.* *met*-a-fraze, a rendering into other words; a literal translation: *v.t.* to render into other words; to make a metaphrase of. (Gr. *metaphrasis.*)
metaphrast, *n.* *met*-a-frast, one who rewrites in different wording, or who translates literally.
metaphrastic, *a.* met-a-*fras*-tik, of the nature of a metaphrase; literal in translation.
metaphysic, *a.* met-a-*fiz*-ik, metaphysical.
metaphysical, *a.* met-a-*fiz*-e-kal, pertaining or relating to metaphysics; analytic of pure being or thought; ontological; abstract; visionary.
metaphysically, *ad.* met-a-*fiz*-e-ka-le, in the manner of metaphysics.
metaphysician, *n.* met-a-fe-*zish*-an, one versed in metaphysics.
metaphysics, *n.* met-a-*fiz*-iks, the philosophy of mind; the science of knowing, being, and causation; the theoretical principles of any science. (L. *metaphysica.*)
metaplasia, *n.* met-a-*play*-zhe-a, the change of one form of tissue into another [Biol.].
metaplasm, *n.* *met*-a-plazm, the protoplasm containing the formative material [Biol.]; a change made in a word by alteration of a syllable or letter [Gram.]. (L. *metaplasmus.*)
metaplastic, *a.* met-a-*plas*-tik, relating to metaplasia [Biol.].
metapolitics, *n.* *met*-a-*pol*-it-iks, theoretical political science.
metapophysis, *n.* met-a-*pof*-e-sis, a mammillary process of the vertebræ.
metapsychics, *n.* met-a-*sy*-kiks, the scientific study of abstruse psychical phenomena.
metasomatism, *n.* met-a-*soh*-ma-tizm, metasomatosis. (Gr. *meta-*, and *soma*, body.)
metasomatosis, *n.* met-a-*soh*-ma-*toh*-sis, chemical change in rocks by the replacement of one constituent by another.
metastasis, *n.* me-*tas*-ta-sis (*pl.* **metastases**), change in the seat of a disease; a change; metabolism. (Gr. *meta-* and *stasis.*)
metatarsal, *a.* met-a-*tar*-sal, belonging to the metatarsus.
metatarsus, *n.* met-a-*tar*-sus, the part of the foot between the ankle and the toes. (Gr. *meta-*, and *tarsos*, the sole of the foot.)
metathesis, *n.* me-*tath*-e-sis, transposition, esp. of the letters or syllables of a word [Gram.]; removal of a morbific cause [Med.]. (L.)
metathetical, *a.* met-a-*thet*-e-kal, pertaining to metathesis.
metathorax, *n.* met-a-*thaw*-raks, the last or posterior segment of the thorax [Entom.]. (Gr.)
metatome, *n.* *met*-a-tome, the space between one dentil and another [Arch.]. (Gr. *meta-*, and *tome*, cutting.)
metayage, *n.* met-ay-*ahzh*, a system of farming in which the produce is shared (usually equally) between farmer and landowner, the latter providing seed, stock, implements, etc. (Fr. *métayage.*)
metayer, *n.* met-*tay*-yer, a tenant-farmer working on the metayage system. (Fr. *métayer*, from L. *medietarius*, one taking a moiety.)
Metazoa, *n.pl.* met-a-*zoh*-a, the zoological group comprising the multicellular animals, or all animals other than Protozoa.
mete, *v.t.* meet, to measure; to appraise: *n.* measure; limit; boundary. (A.S. *metan.*)
metempiric, *a.* met-em-*pi*-rik, transcendental [Metaphysics]. (Gr. *meta-*, beyond, and *empiric.*)
metempiricism, *n.* met-em-*pi*-re-sizm, the science of pure, abstract reason; transcendentalism.
metempsychosis, *n.* met-*em*-se-*koh*-sis, transmigration of the soul after death from one body to another, esp. from a human being to an animal. (Gr.)
metemptosis, *n.* met-em-*toh*-sis, the solar equation necessary to prevent the new moon from happening a day too late or the suppression of the bissextile once in 134 years. (Gr. *meta*, and *en*, on, *ptosis*, falling.)
metensomatosis, *n.* met-en-*soh*-ma-*toh*-sis, a re-embodiment of the soul, esp. as in Buddhist doctrine. (Gr.)
meteor, *n.* *mee*-te-or, a transitory luminous body passing through the atmosphere; a shooting star; formerly, any atmospheric phenomenon; any transiently dazzling or astonishing object. (Gr.)
meteoric, *a.* mee-te-*o*-rik, pertaining to or consisting of meteors; formed in the atmosphere; like a meteor; illustrious for a brief period. **meteoric iron,** iron as found in meteors. **meteoric showers,** periodical occurrences of shooting stars.
meteorism, *n.* *mee*-te-o-rizm, excessive accumulation of gas in the intestines; tympanites [Med. and Vet.]. (Gr. *meteorizein*, to elevate.)
meteorite, *n.* *mee*-te-o-rite, a fallen meteor; an aerolite.
meteorograph, *n.* *mee*-te-o-ro-*graf*, an instrument for recording simultaneously and automatically several different meteorological phenomena.
meteorography, *n.* *mee*-te-o-*rog*-ra-fe, the science of meteors; the recording of meteorological phenomena. (Gr. *meteor*, and *grapho*, write.)
meteroid, *n.* *mee*-te-o-royd, a particle moving through space which forms a meteor when entering the earth's atmosphere. (*meteor*, and Gr. *eidos*, like.)
meteorolite, *n.* *mee*-te-o-ro-lite, a meteorite. (Gr. *meteor*, and *lithos*, a stone.)
meteorological, *a.* *mee*-te-o-ro-*loj*-e-kal, pertaining to the atmosphere and its phenomena.
meteorologist, *n.* *mee*-te-o-*rol*-o-jist, one skilled in meteorology.
meteorology, *n.* *mee*-te-o-*rol*-o-je, the science which treats of the atmosphere and its phenomena; the study of, also the general character of, the weather. (Gr. *meteorologia.*)
meter, *n.* *mee*-ter, one who or that which measures; a machine for registering the consumption of gas, electricity, or water, or any other fluid.
metewand, *n.* *meet*-wond, an old name for a measuring-rod or yardstick. (*mete* and *wand.*)
methane, *n.* *meth*-ane, marsh-gas, a light colourless gas composed of one atom of carbon to four of hydrogen.
methanol, *n.* *meth*-a-nol, an extremely volatile, poisonous, and inflammable liquid resembling alcohol, obtained from the distillation of wood, and used in the manufacture of formaldehyde, etc.; methyl alcohol.
metheglin, *n.* me-*theg*-lin, a beverage made of fermented honey and water; mead. (W. *meddyg*, healing, *llyn*, liquor.)

methinks, *v.i.* me-*thinks*, it seems to me; I think. (A.S. *me thynceth.*)
method, *n. meth*-od, mode of procedure; logical arrangement; orderly arrangement; system; classification. (Fr., from Gr. *methodos.*)
methodic, *a.* me-*thod*-ik, methodical.
methodical, *a.* me-*thod*-e-kal, arranged with method; orderly; systematic. (L. *methodicus.*)
methodically, *ad.* in a methodical manner.
methodics, *n.* me-*thod*-iks, methodology.
Methodism, *n. meth*-o-dizm, the principles and practice of the Methodists.
Methodist, *n. meth*-o-dist, one of a body of Protestant dissenters, originally founded within the Church of England by John and Charles Wesley about 1740 and administered generally on Presbyterian and congregational principles; (*l.c.*) a strict observer of method; a physician who practises by method or theory: *a.* pertaining to the Methodists; Methodistical.
Methodistical, *a. meth*-o-*dis*-te-kal, resembling the Methodists; strictly or over-piously religious.
methodize, *v.t. meth*-o-dize, to reduce to method or arrange properly.
methodology, *n.* meth-o-*dol*-o-je, the science of scientific method or classification; the branch of logic dealing with the method and principles of procedure. (Gr. *methodos*, and *logos*, science.)
methought, me-*thawt*, *p.* of *methinks.*
methyl, *n. meth*-il, the hydrocarbon radical containing one atom of carbon to three of hydrogen forming a constituent of many organic compounds [Chem.]. **methyl alcohol,** methanol. (Gr. *methu*, wine, *hulē*, wood).
methylate, *v.t. meth*-e-late, to treat or mix with methyl alcohol. **methylated spirit,** rectified spirit mixed with wood naphtha or methyl alcohol.
methylene, *n. meth*-e-leen, a hypothetical hydrocarbon radical containing one atom of carbon to two of hydrogen forming a constituent of many compounds; a former name of methanol.
methylic, *a.* me-*thil*-ik, pertaining to methyl.
metic, *n. met*-ik, a foreign resident in a city of ancient Greece. (Gr. *metoikos.*)
meticulous, *a.* me-*tik*-yew-lus, careful in details; over-particular. (L. *meticulosus*, from *metus*, fear.)
métier, *n. met*-e-ay, profession; trade; calling; that for which one has an aptitude. (Fr.)
metis, *n. may*-tis, a Canadian half-breed of American Indian and European parentage. (Fr. *métis.*)
metonic, *a.* me-*ton*-ik, designating the cycle of the moon, or period of nineteen years, in which the lunations of the moon return to the same days of the month, so called from Meton, the 5th-cent. B.C. Athenian astronomer.
metonym, *met*-o-nim, a word used in metonymy.
metonymic, *a.* met-o-*nim*-ik, used by way of metonymy.
metonymy, *n.* me-*ton*-e-me, a trope in which one word is put for another related to it, as effect for cause, or an author for his works. (Gr. *metonymia.*)
metope, *n. met*-o-pe, the space between the triglyphs of the Doric frieze [Arch.]. (Gr. *meta-*, and *opē*, opening.)
metope, *n. met*-ope, the face, or mid-frontal portion, of a crab [Zool.]. (Gr. *metopon*, forehead.)
metoposcopist, *n.* met-o-*pos*-ko-pist, one skilled in metoposcopy.
metoposcopy, *n.* met-o-*pos*-ko-pe, fortune-telling or character-reading by study of the physiognomy. (Gr. *metopon*, forehead, and *-scope.*)
metre, *n. mee*-ter, a rhythmic arrangement of syllables in verse; the rhythm of music measured by bars and beats; the unit of length of the metrical system, equal to 39·37 inches. (O.Fr.)
metric, *a. met*-rik, according to the decimal system of weights and measures legally adopted in France in 1801 (and since in most European and Latin American countries), and founded on the metre, the ascending series multiplying and the descending series dividing by ten; metrical. **metric ton,** 1,000 kilograms, or 2,204·62 lb.
metrical, *a. met*-re-kal, pertaining to measure or to metre; in metre.
metrically, *ad. met*-re-ka-le, in a metrical manner.
metrician, *n.* me-*trish*-an, a metrist.
metrics, *n. met*-riks, the theory and art of verse-composition; the scientific theory of measurement.
metrify, *v.i. met*-re-fy, to versify.
metrist, *n. met*-rist, a composer of verses.
metritis, *n.* me-*try*-tis, inflammation of the uterus [Med.]. (Gr. *metra*, womb, and *-itis.*)
metrological, *a.* met-ro-*loj*-e-kal, relating to metrology.
metrologist, *n.* me-*trol*-o-jist, a student of or writer on metrology.
metrology, *n.* me-*trol*-o-je, the science of weights and measures. (Gr. *metron*, and *logos*, science.)
metromania, *n.* met-ro-*may*-ne-a, a passion for writing verses. (Gr. *metron*, metre, and *mania.*)
metronome, *n. met*-ro-nome, an instrument with a short pendulum to beat time at the rate required [Music]. (Gr. *metron*, and *nomos*, law.)
metronomic, *a.* met-ro-*nom*-ik, pertaining to the metronome.
metronymic, *n.* met-ro-*nim*-ik, a person's maternal name, or a name taken from the mother's family: *a.* derived from one's mother or a maternal ancestor (of names). (Gr. *meter*, mother, *onyma*, name.)
metropolis, *n.* me-*trop*-o-lis, the chief or capital city of a country; a metropolitan see, or chief ecclesiastical city. (L., a mother-city.)
metropolitan, *a.* met-ro-*pol*-e-tan, belonging to a metropolis or an archbishopric; pertaining to, or being, the mother-country; *n.* the bishop of a metropolis; the bishop who presides over the other bishops of a province; an ecclesiastic of the Greek church ranking above an archbishop and below a patriarch. **Metropolitan Borough,** *see* **borough.** (L. *metropolitanus.*)
metropolitanate, *n.* met-ro-*pol*-e-tan-ate, the see or office of a metropolitan bishop.
metropolitical, *a. met*-ro-po-*lit*-e-kal, pertaining to a metropolis; metropolitan.
metrostyle, *n. met*-ro-stile, the mechanism of a pianola by which speed and tone are regulated.
mettle, *n. met*-tl, character; courage; constitutional ardour. **to put one on his mettle,** to test his endurance or temperament. (*metal.*)
mettled, *a. met*-tld, mettlesome.
mettlesome, *a. met*-tl-sum, high-spirited; full of fire; brisk.
mettlesomely, *ad.* in a mettlesome manner.
mettlesomeness, *n.* state of being mettlesome.
meum, *n. mee*-um, mine (used only in the saying "*meum* and *tuum*," mine and thine). (L.)
meuse, *n.* mewz, a gap in a hedge, etc., in a run made by hares or other animals; a means of escape. (O.Fr. *muce.*)
mew, *n.* mew, a cage for birds, esp. for moulting hawks; an enclosure; a place of confinement: *pl.* stables (named from the former royal stables in London, built near where the king's hawks were mewed): *v.t.* to shed or cast; to moult; to confine in or as in a cage. (O.Fr. *mue.*)
mew, *n.* mew, the cry of a cat: *v.i.* to cry this. (Imit.)
mew, *n.* mew, baldmoney, the umbelliferous plant *Meum athamanticum.*
mew, *n.* mew, a seagull, esp. the common gull, *Larus canus.* (A.S. *mæw.*)
mewl, *v.i.* mewl, to cry, as an infant; to squall; to mew as a cat. (Imit.)
mewler, *n. mewl*-er, a crying child or animal.
Mexican, *a. mek*-se-kan, pertaining to, or of, Mexico: *n.* a native or the language of Mexico; a heavy bleached calico fabric.
mezereon, *n.* me-*zeer*-re-on, a small hardy shrub of the laurel family, *Daphne mezereum.* (Fr. *mézéréon.*)
mezquit, *n. mez*-kit, mesquite.
mezzanine, *n. met*-za-nin, a story of small height introduced between two higher ones; a window in it [Arch.]. (Fr.)
mezzo, *a. met*-zoh (*fem.* **mezza**), middle; mean. **mezzo-forte,** moderately loud [Mus.]. **mezzo relievo,** middle relief. **mezzo-soprano,** a voice between soprano and contralto; a person gifted with that voice. **mezzo voce,** a medium fullness of voice. (It.)
mezzotint, *n. met*-zoh-tint, a mode of engraving on steel or copper, in imitation of painting in Indian ink, lights being produced by scraping on a deeply burred ground; a print taken from this: *v.i.* to engrave in this way. (It. *mezzo*, half, *tinto*, tinted.)
mho, *n.* moh, the unit of electrical conductance, the reciprocal of the ohm. (*ohm* transposed.)
mi, *n.* mee, the third note in the diatonic scale, E in the scale of C [Mus.].

miaow, *v.i.* me-*ou*, to mew, or cry like a cat: *n.* a cry of, or as of, a cat.
miasma, *n.* my-*az*-ma (*pl.* **miasmata**, my-*az*-ma-ta), infectious matter floating in the air; a malarial exhalation. (Gr.)
miasmal, *a.* my-*az*-mal, miasmatic.
miasmatic, *a.* my-az-*mat*-ik, pertaining to or containing miasma; malarial; noxious.
miasmology, *n.* my-az-*mol*-o-je, the study or science of miasma.
miau, miauw, *v.i.* and *n.* me-*ou*, miaow.
miaul, *n.* me-*awl*, a mew, or cat-call: *v.i.* to make this cry.
mica, *n.* *my*-ka, a group of silicates readily split unto flexible transparent leaves that are used in place of glass in stove-doors, etc. (L. *mica*, a crumb.)
micaceous, *a.* my-*kay*-shus, containing, consisting of, or resembling mica.
mica-schist, *n.* *my*-ka-shist, schist consisting chiefly of mica and quartz.
Micawberism, *n.* me-*kaw*-ber-rizm, the habit of unfounded and inconsiderate optimism. (Mr. *Micawber*, in Dickens's "David Copperfield.")
mice, *n.* myce: *pl.* of *mouse*.
Michaelmas, *n.* *mik*-el-mas, the feast of St. Michael, celebrated Sept. 29—a quarter-day; autumn. **michaelmas daisy**, the composite plant *Aster tripolium*. (*Michael*, and *mass*, festival.)
miche, *v.i.* mitch, to lie hid; to skulk; to sneak; to play truant. (Perhaps O.F. *muchier*, to hide.)
micher, *n.* *mitch*-er, one who mitches; an habitual truant; a miker.
mickle, *a.* *mik*-kl, much; great; muckle: *n.* a large quantity [Scots.]. (A.S. *micel*.)
micracoustic, *n.* *my*-kra-*kou*-stik, an instrument to assist hearing: *a.* serving to augment small sounds. (Gr.)
micrencephalous, *a.* my-kren-*sef*-a-lus, having a small brain. (*micr(o)*- and *encephalous*.)
micro-, *my*-kroh-, prefix denoting very small, on a very small scale, or enlarging from a small size; and in the metric system, one millionth of the unit specified. (Gr. *mikros* small.)
microbe, *n.* *my*-krobe, any minute organism or germ, esp. one causing disease or fermentation. (Gr. *mikros*, small, *bios*, life.)
microbial, *a.* my-*kroh*-be-al, relating to or like microbes.
microbic, *a.* my-*kroh*-bik, microbial.
microbicide, *n.* my-*kroh*-be-side, a preparation for destroying microbes.
microbiology, *n.* *my*-kro-by-*ol*-o-je, the scientific study of microbes or other microscopic organisms.
microbism, *n.* *my*-kro-bizm, infestation by microbes [Med.].
microcephalic, *a.* *my*-kro-se-*fal*-ik, having an uncommonly small skull. (Gr. *mikros*, and *kephale*, head.)
microcephalous, *a.* my-kro-*sef*-a-lus, microcephalic.
microcephaly, *n.* my-kro-*sef*-a-le, the condition of possessing a microcephalic head.
microcline, *n.* *my*-kro-kline, a silicate of potassium and aluminium resembling orthoclase.
micrococcus, *n.* my-kro-*kok*-us (*pl.* **micrococci**), one of a group of very minute spherical bacteria.
microcosm, *n.* *my*-kro-kozm, man considered as an epitome of the world or macrocosm; anything small as representative of the universe; the universe in little. (Gr. *mikros*. and *kosmos*, world.)
microcosmic, *a.* *my*-kro-*koz*-mik, pertaining to or after the fashion of a microcosm. **microcosmic salt**, a triple salt of soda, ammonia, and phosphoric acid.
microcosmography, *n.* *my*-kro-koz-*mog*-ra-fe, the description of man as a little world.
microcrith, *n.* *my*-kro-krith, the weight of the hydrogen atom [Chem.].
microfarad, *n.* *my*-kro-*fa*-rad, one millionth of a farad [Elect.].
microgram, *n.* *my*-kro-gram, one millionth of a gram.
micrograph, *n.* *my*-kro-graf, a graphic delineation of an object as observed through a microscope; an instrument for producing very small writing or engraving.
micrographic, *a.* *my*-kro-*graf*-ik, relating to micrography.
micrography, *n.* my-*krog*-ra-fe, the description of microscopic objects; the art or practice of very minute handwriting. (Gr. *mikros*, and *grapho*, write.)
microhm, *n.* *my*-krohm, the millionth of an ohm [Elect.].
microhmmeter, *n.* my-*kroh*-me-ter, a specially sensitive kind of ohmmeter. [Elect.]
microlith, *n.* *my*-kro-lith, a minute stone implement of the palæolithic age.
micrology, *n.* my-*krol*-o-je, hair-splitting; arguing over trivialities; the art of managing microscopic objects.
micrometer, *n.* my-*krom*-e-ter, an attachment to the telescope or microscope for measuring small objects or spaces; a micrometer caliper [Eng.]. **micrometer adjustment**, a device enabling a machine, etc., to be set with a very high degree of precision. **micrometer caliper**, a caliper fitted with a micrometer screw by means of which measurements correct to $\frac{1}{10,000}$th of an inch can be taken. **micrometer screw**, the very fine-pitch graduated adjusting screw of a micrometer. (Gr. *mikros*, and *metron*, measure.)
micrometrical, *a.* my-kro-*met*-re-kal, pertaining to or ascertained by the micrometer.
micrometry, *n.* my-*krom*-e-tre, the art of measuring with a micrometer.
micromicron, *n.* *my*-kro-*my*-kron, one millionth of a micron, or ten angstrom units.
micromotoscope, *n.* *my*-kro-*moh*-to-skope, an apparatus for photographing moving micro-organisms.
micron, *n.* *my*-kron, the millionth part of a metre. (Gr. *mikros*.)
Micronesian, *a.* my-kro-*nee*-ze-an, of, or pertaining to, the lesser islands of the Southern Pacific between Australasia and the Malay Peninsula: *n.* a native of Micronesia; the language of Micronesia. (Gr. *mikros*, and *nesos*, island.)
micro-organism, *n.* any organism of microscopic size, esp. among the bacteria and protozoa [Biol.]
micropathology, *n.* my-kro-pa-*thol*-o-je, the science treating of the relation of bacteria to disease.
microphone, *n.* *my*-kro-fone, an electrical instrument for intensifying and transmitting sounds, esp. in telephony and broadcasting. (Gr. *mikros*, and *phone*, sound.)
microphonics, *n.* my-kro-*fon*-iks, the science treating of the microphone, or of the magnification of sound.
microphotography, *n.* *my*-kro-fo-*tog*-ra-fe, photomicrography.
microphyte, *n.* *my*-kro-fite, a microscopic vegetable parasite or bacterium. (Gr. *mikros*, and *phyton*, a plant.)
micropodal, *a.* my-*krop*-o-dal, having abnormally small feet [Zool.].
micropsia, *n.* my-*krop*-se-a, a defect of the vision causing apparent diminution of objects.
micropyle, *n.* *my*-kro-pile, any minute opening [Anat. and Zool.]; the mouth of the foramen of an ovule, forming the closed orifice of the seed [Bot.]. (Gr. *mikros*, and *pyle*, a gate.)
microscope, *n.* *my*-kro-skope, an optical instrument for magnifying and rendering visible minute objects, esp. those invisible to the naked eye. (Gr. *mikros*, and *skopeo*, view.)
microscopic, *a.* my-kro-*skop*-ik, microscopical.
microscopical, *a.* my-kro-*skop*-e-kal, pertaining to the microscope or microscopy; resembling a microscope; very small.
microscopically, *ad.* *my*-kro-*skop*-e-ka-le, by or as by the microscope.
microscopist, *n.* my-*kros*-ko-pist *or* *my*-kro-skoh-pist, one skilled in microscopy.
microscopy, *n.* my-*kros*-ko-pe, the use of the microscope; microscopic investigation.
microsmatism, *n.* my-*kroz*-ma-tizm, the condition of having organs of smell only partially developed [Zool.]. (Gr. *mikros*, and *osmē*, a smell.)
microsome, *n.* *my*-kroh-sohm, one of the minute granules present in the protoplasm of a vegetable cell.
microspore, *n.* *my*-kro-spore, the spore acting as the pollen-grain of a fern.
microtome, *n.* *my*-kro-tome, an instrument for cutting thin sections for examination with the microscope. (Gr. *mikros*, and *tome*, cutting.)
microvolt, *n.* *my*-kro-volt, the millionth of a volt [Elect.].

microwave, *n.* *my*-kro-wave, an electro-magnetic wave having a wavelength of less than 20 centimetres [Wire.].
microzoa, *n.pl.* *my*-kro-*zoh*-a, the protozoans and other microscopic animals.
microzyme, *n.* *my*-kro-zime, a zymotic microbe thought to constitute the germ of certain epizootic and epidemic diseases. (Gr. *mikros*, and *zyme*, leaven.)
micturate, *v.i.* *mik*-tewr-rate, to pass urine.
micturition, *n.* mik-tewr-*rish*-on, the act of passing urine. (L. *micturire*, to urinate, make water often.)
mid, *a.* mid, middle; at equal distance from extremes; intervening. (A.S. *mid.*)
midbrain, *n.* *mid*-brain, the mesencephalon [Anat.].
midday, *a.* and *n.* *mid*-day, noon.
midden, *n.* *mid*-den, a refuse heap; a dunghill. (Scand.)
***middle,** *a.* *mid*-dl, equally distant from the extremes; intermediate: reflexive [Gram.]: *n.* the point or part equally distant from the extremities; the centre; the midst; the waist; a middle article: *v.t.* to put in the middle; to fold in the middle; to pass (the ball) to the centre [Football]. **middle age,** the period of human life between youth and old age. **Middle Ages,** the period in European history from about the 5th to the 15th centuries. **middle article,** a leader that originally followed the chief leader in a newspaper, generally on some literary or non-political subject. **middle C,** the note midway between the bass and treble staves [Mus.]. **middle class,** the social group between the upper and lower classes: *a.* of, or pertaining to, this class. **middle distance,** the part of a picture or vista between the foreground and the background. **middle ear,** the tympanum [Anat.]. **Middle East,** *see* **East. Middle English,** spoken or written English of the second period, *i.e.* about 1100 to 1500. **Middle Kingdom,** the former Chinese Empire. **middle term,** that term in the premises with which those of the conclusion are successively compared [Logic]. **Middle West,** the part of the U.S.A. between the Alleghenies and Rocky Mountains and north of Oklahoma, Arkansas, and the R. Ohio. (A.S. *middel.*)
middleman, *n.* *mid*-dl-man, an agent between two parties; a go-between; a broker; a distributor.
middlemost, *a.* *mid*-dl-most, nearest the middle.
middle-rail, *n.* the current-carrying rail of an electric railway.
middle-weight, *n.* a boxer of between 10 stone 7 lb. and 11 stone 6 lb. in weight: *a.* of this weight.
middling, *a.* *mid*-ling, of middle rank, size, or quality; about equally distant from the extremes; moderate: *n.pl.* the coarser part of flour; second-rate or inferior goods.
middlingly, *ad.* in middling fashion.
middy, *n.* *mid*-de, a midshipman [Coll.].
midge, *n.* midj, any minute fly or gnat. (A.S. *mycg.*)
midget, *n.* *midj*-et, a dwarf or diminutive person; a small size in photographs: *a.* small; miniature; puny.
midinette, *n.* mid-e-*net*, a young French working girl, esp. in dressmaking, millinery, etc.
midland, *a.* *mid*-land, being in the interior of a country; distant from the coast. **the Midlands,** the counties of central England.
mid-life, *n.* *mid*-life, the middle years of an average lifetime.
midmost, *a.* *mid*-mohst, middlemost.
midnight, *n.* *mid*-nite, 12 o'clock at night; the middle of the night: *a.* being in the middle of the night; very dark. **midnight oil,** *see* **oil. midnight sun,** the sun shining at midnight during either polar summer.
mid-off, *n.* mid-*off*, the fieldsman stationed half-right to the batsman and to rear of the bowler; this position [Cricket].
mid-on, *n.* mid-*on*, the fieldsman or position corresponding to mid-off on the left side of the pitch. [Cricket.]
Midrash, *n.* *mid*-rash, an ancient Jewish commentary on the Hebrew scriptures, the commentaries that remain being contained in the Mishna. (Heb.)
midrib, *n.* *mid*-rib, central vein of a leaf, a continuation of the petiole [Bot.].
midriff, *n.* *mid*-rif, the diaphragm [Anat.]. (A.S.)
midship, *a.* *mid*-ship, situated in the middle of a ship: *n.* the middle part of a ship.
midshipman, *n.* *mid*-ship-man, a naval officer ranking below a sub-lieutenant.
midshipmite, *n.* *mid*-ship-mite, a midshipman.
midships, *ad.* *mid*-ships, in the middle of a ship [Naut.].
midst, *n.* midst, the middle: *ad.* in the middle. **in the midst,** among; involved in; overwhelmed by.
mid-stream, *n.* the middle of the stream.
midsummer, *n.* *mid*-sum-mer, the summer solstice, about June 21. **midsummer day,** the feast of the nativity of St. John the Baptist, June 24—a quarter-day. **midsummer eve,** June 23. **midsummer madness,** utter folly and recklessness.
midway, *n.* *mid*-way, the middle of the way: *a.* being in the middle distance: *ad.* half-way.
midwife, *n.* *mid*-wife (*pl.* **midwives,** *mid*-wyvz), a woman professionally trained to supervise or assist in childbirth. (A.S. *mid*, with, and *wife.*)
midwifery, *n.* *mid*-wif-re, the art or practice of assisting women in childbirth; obstetrics.
midwinter, *n.* *mid*-win-ter, the winter solstice, about December 21.
mien, *n.* meen, external appearance; look; demeanour. (Fr. *mine.*)
miff, *n.* mif, a tiff; a feeling of slight annoyance or irritation [Slang].
miffed, *a.* mift, slightly annoyed [Slang].
might, mite, *p.* of the verb *may.*
might, *n.* mite, strength; force; power. **with might and main,** with the utmost strength. (A.S. *miht.*)
mightily, *ad.* *my*-te-le, with great power or strength; vigorously; greatly.
mightiness, *n.* *my*-te-ness, the state of being mighty; power; greatness; a title of dignity formerly used by the States-General of the Netherlands.
mightst, mytst, *second pers. sing. p.* of the verb *may.*
mighty, *a.* *my*-te, having great power; potent; valiant; very great; important; momentous; showing great power; wonderful: *ad.* in a great degree.
mignon, *a.* *min*-yun (*or* App.), delicately shaped; dainty; pretty. (Fr., favourite.)
mignonette, *n.* min-yo-*net*, a sweet-scented plant of the species *Reseda*, esp. the garden plant *R. odorata.* (Fr. *mignon*, favourite.)
migraine, *n.* *mee*-grane, a neuralgic pain or nervous headache in one side of the head; megrim. (Fr.)
migrant, *a.* *my*-grant, migratory; *n.* a migrating animal or bird.
migrate, *v.i.* *my*-grate, to make a seasonal passage from one climate to another [Zool.]; to pass from one country or place to another [Coll.]. (L. *migratus*, migrated.)
migration, *n.* my-*gray*-shon, the act of migrating.
migratory, *a.* *my*-gra-to-re, removing or accustomed to remove from one country to another; wandering.
mihrab, *n.* me-*rahb*, a niche in a mosque showing the direction of Mecca. (Ar.)
Mikado, *n.* me-*kah*-doh, a title used by foreigners of the Tenno, or Emperor of Japan. (Jap., "exalted gate.")
mike, *n.* myk, only in phrases, as "on the mike," idling, "to do a mike," etc.: *v.t.* to shirk work; to loiter about [Slang]. (Perhaps from *miche.*)
mike, *n.* myk, a microphone, or microscope [Slang].
miker, *n.* *my*-ker, one who mikes; an habitually work-shy person.
mil, *n.* mil, one-thousandth of an inch, a unit used for wire-gauges; a millilitre.
Milanese, *a.* mil-a-*neez*, relating to, or of, Milan; made of Milanese silk: *n.* an inhabitant of Milan in Italy. **Milanese silk,** a material made of silk or artificial silk with a very fine weave.
milch, *a.* miltch, yielding milk. **milch-cow,** a cow yielding milk; a person from whom money is obtained with ease. (*milk.*)
mild, *a.* myld, gentle; not acrid, corrosive, or drastic; not acrimonious; not fierce, rough, or angry; placid; calm; moderate. (A.S. *milde.*)
mildew, *n.* *mil*-dew, a fungoid growth appearing on living plants and certain organic substances as paper, cloth, etc., exposed to damp: *v.t.* to taint with mildew: *v.i.* to be affected with mildew. (A.S. *mele*, honey, and *dew.*)
mildewy, *a.* *mil*-dew-e, resembling mildew; tainted with mildew.

mildly, *ad.* *myld*-le, in a mild manner.
mildness, *n.* *myld*-ness, gentleness ; softness.
mile, *n.* mile, a measure of length or distance, the English statute mile being 1,760 yards (5,280 ft.), and the geographical (and nautical) mile one-sixtieth of a degree of latitude at the equator, or 6,080 ft. (A.S. *mil.*)
mileage, *n.* *mile*-aj, distance, or rate of travel, in miles ; charge or travelling expenses per mile.
milepost, *n.* *mile*-post, a post at the end of each mile ; a milestone.
miler, *n.* *mile*-er, one who runs a mile-race ; anything travelling at a stated number of miles per hour.
Milesian, *a.* my-*lee*-zhe-an, relating to the followers of Milesius, a legendary Spanish king fabled to have conquered Ireland about the 11th cent. B.C. : *n.* a member of this tribe ; an Irishman.
Milesian, *a.* my-*lee*-zhe-an, of Miletus, an ancient city of Caria, Asia Minor : *n.* an inhabitant of Miletus. **Milesian tales,** short bawdy stories current about the 1st cent. B.C.
milestone, *n.* *mile*-stone, a stone milepost ; some important point in a career, course, etc.
milfoil, *n.* *mil*-foyl, the yarrow, *Achillea millefolium*, remarkable for its finely divided leaves. **water milfoil,** a plant of the genus *Myriophyllum*. (L. *mille*, a thousand, *folium*, a leaf.)
miliaria, *n.* mil-e-*ayr*-re-a, a skin complaint characterized by inflammation and itching ; miliary fever ; prickly heat ; sudamina.
miliary, *a.* *mil*-ya-re, accompanied by an eruption resembling millet-seeds [Med.] : having granulations like these : *n.* miliaria. (L. *miliarus*, pertaining to millet.)
milieu, *n.* *meel*-yew (*or* App.), environment social or otherwise ; condition in life. (Fr.)
Miliola, *n.pl.* me-*ly*-o-la, a genus of microscopic foraminifera of the Tertiary strata. (L. *milium*, millet.)
milioline, *a.* *mil*-e-o-line, pertaining to the *Miliola* : *n.* a member of the genus *Miliola* [Zool.].
miliolite, *a.* *mil*-e-o-lite, formed of miliolæ : *n.* a fossil foraminifer of the genus *Miliola*.
militancy, *n.* *mil*-e-tan-se, militant spirit ; state of being militant.
militant, *a.* *mil*-e-tant, warlike ; of a fighting temperament ; employing violent methods : *n.* a militant person ; a fighter. **Church militant,** the Christian Church on earth as opposing spiritual enemies. (L. *militans*, serving as a soldier.)
militantly, *ad.* *mil*-e-tant-le, in a fighting manner.
militarily, *ad.* *mil*-e-ta-re-le, in military manner.
militarism, *n.* *mil*-e-ta-rizm, military predominance or government ; national desire for military glory ; the exaltation of and reliance on belligerency. (Fr. *militarisme.*)
militarist, *n.* *mil*-e-ta-rist, an advocate of militarism or of a warlike policy ; a student of military science.
militaristic, *a.* mil-e-ta-*ris*-tik, characterized by militarism.
militarization, *n.* *mil*-e-ta-ry-*zay*-shon, the act of militarizing.
militarize, *v.t.* *mil*-e-ta-rize, to convert to a military purpose or to militarism.
★**military,** *a.* *mil*-e-ta-re, pertaining to soldiers or to arms ; warlike ; becoming a soldier ; martial : *n.* soldiers ; soldiery ; the army. **Military Cross,** decoration awarded to captains, lieutenants, and first-class warrant-officers in the British and Colonial Armies, for bravery and devotion in action (inst. 1915). **Military Medal,** awarded since 1916 to men of the British Army (women later included) under commissioned rank for bravery and devotion under fire. **military tenure,** a tenure of land on condition of performing military service. (L. *militaris*, warlike.)
militate, *v.i.* *mil*-e-tate, to oppose ; to operate against or act in opposition. (L. *militatus*, served as a soldier.)
militia, *n.* me-*lish*-a, a voluntary force of partly trained citizen soldiers for service in an emergency ; a conscripted force (1939) receiving training as auxiliaries for home defence. (L.)
militiaman, *n.* me-*lish*-a-man, a member of a militia.
★**milk,** *n.* milk, a white fluid, secreted by certain glands in female mammals, for the nourishment of their young ; the white juice of certain plants ; an emulsion made by bruising seeds : *v.t.* to draw milk from ; to extract from, esp. surreptitiously or unfairly : *v.i.* to yield milk. **milk-bar,** a shop or counter at which milk and milk products are sold and consumed. **milk-fever,** a transitory fever which sometimes accompanies first lactation. **milk of human kindness,** goodness or warmth of heart. **milk of magnesia,** a suspension of magnesium hydroxide in water. **milk-shake,** a drink consisting of milk, aerated water, etc., mixed and shaken up. **milk-sugar,** lactose. (A.S. *meolc.*)
milk-and-water, *a.* namby-pamby ; insipid ; twaddling.
milker, *n.* *milk*-er, one who or that which milks.
milkily, *ad.* *milk*-e-le, after the manner of milk.
milkiness, *n.* *milk*-e-ness, softness ; having the characteristics of milk.
milking, *n.* *milk*-ing, the act of drawing milk from a milk gland ; the quantity of milk so drawn. **milking stool,** the stool on which the milker sits.
milk-leg, *n.* *milk*-leg, a painful swelling in the leg of pregnant women.
milk-livered, *a.* *milk*-liv-erd, timorous ; cowardly.
milkmaid, *n.* *milk*-mayd, a woman who milks or is employed in a dairy.
milkman, *n.* *milk*-man, a man who sells milk.
milk-punch, *n.* a mixture of milk and spirits sweetened.
milk-round, *n.* the district served by one delivering household milk.
milk-sickness, *n.* a disease in cattle due to poisoning by certain herbs, and in humans partaking of the meat or milk of such cattle.
milksop, *n.* *milk*-sop, a piece of bread sopped in milk ; a soft, effeminate, feeble-minded youth.
milk-teeth, *n.pl.* the fore-teeth of a foal ; also of children, which are shed in childhood.
milk-thistle, *n.* the plant *Silybum marianum*.
milk-tree, *n.* *milk*-tree, a name of various trees yielding an abundance of milky juice.
milk-vetch, *n.* a plant of the genus *Astragalus*.
milk-weed, *n.* a plant of the genus *Asclepias* ; the sow-thistle, *Sonchus oleraceus*, or the milk parsley, *Peucedanum palustre*.
milkwort, *n.* *milk*-wurt, a plant of the genus *Polygala*. **sea milkwort,** *Glaux maritima*.
milky, *a.* *milk*-e, made of, full of, or resembling milk ; yielding milk ; mild ; gentle ; timorous. **Milky Way,** the galaxy, a broad luminous belt of very distant stars in the heavens.
mill, *n.* mil, a machine for grinding and reducing to fine particles ; a manufactory employing machinery ; a fight with the fists [Slang] : *v.t.* to grind ; to make indentations round the edge of a coin ; to stamp [Coining] ; to full, as cloth ; to whip or churn, as chocolate ; to beat severely with the fists. **go through the mill,** to have a hard struggle for a livelihood, or to undergo any unpleasant experience. (A.S. *myln.*)
mill, *n.* mil, a money or account, the thousandth part of a dollar [U.S.A.]. (L. *mille*, a thousand.)
millboard, *n.* *mil*-bord, board for bookbinding made of wood-pulp or substitutes.
mill-dam, *n.* a dam to obstruct a watercourse and divert it into a millrace ; the millpond formed by such.
milled, *pp.* and *a.* mild, passed through a mill ; serrated by milling, as a coin ; fulled.
millenarian, *a.* mil-e-*nare*-re-e-an, lasting a thousand years ; pertaining to the millennium : *n.* one who believes in the thousand-year reign of Christ.
millenarianism, *n.* mil-e-*nare*-re-a-nizm, the doctrine of millenarians ; belief in the coming of the millennium ; chiliasm.
millenary, *a.* *mil*-e-na-re, consisting of a thousand, esp. years : *n.* the space of a thousand years ; a millenarian. (L. *millenarius.*)
millennial, *a.* mil-*len*-ne-al, pertaining to the millennium.
millennium, *n.* mil-*len*-ne-um, a thousand years, esp. that during which (Rev. xx, 1–5) Christ is to reign in person on earth. (L.)
millepede, *n.* *mil*-le-peed, any segmented myriapod, esp. of the genus *Julus* ; the woodlouse. (L. *mille*, and *pes*, a foot.)
millepore, *n.* *mil*-le-pore, any of the shallow-water reef-corals of the genus *Millepora*. (L. *mille*, and *porus*, channel.)
miller, *n.* *mil*-ler, the owner or manager of a flour

mill; various moths with white powdered wings, esp. *Acronycta leporina.* **miller's thumb,** a small fish, *Cottus gobio*, the river bull-head.
millerite, *n. mil*-ler-rite, native sulphide of nickel.
millesimal, *a.* mil-*les*-e-mal, thousandth; consisting of thousandths. (L. *millesimus.*)
millet, *n. mil*-let, the edible grain of several species of grass, esp. *Panicum miliaceum.* (Fr.)
mill-hand, *n.* a worker in a factory.
milliampere, *n. mil*-le-*am*-pare, one thousandth part of an ampere [Elect.].
milliard, *n. mil*-yard, a thousand millions. (Fr.)
milliary, *a. mil*-le-a-re, pertaining to a Roman mile; denoting a mile: *n.* a milestone. (L. *milliarus.*)
millibar, *n. mil*-le-bar, the thousandth part of a bar of atmospheric pressure.[Meteor.]. (Fr.)
millier, *n. meel*-yay, the metric ton, or 2,204·62 lb. (Fr.)
milligramme, *n. mil*-le-gram, the thousandth part of a gramme, ·0154 of a grain troy. (Fr.)
millilitre, *n. mil*-le-*lee*-ter, the thousandth part of a litre, ·06103 cubic inches. (Fr.)
millimetre, *n. mil*-le-*mee*-ter, the thousandth part of a metre, ·03937 inches. (Fr.)
milliner, *n. mil*-in-er, one who makes, trims, or sells head-gear for women. (*Milaner*, a dealer in Milan goods.)
millinery, *n. mil*-in-er-re, articles made or sold by milliners.
milling, *n. mil*-ling, the action of the verb *to mill*; the serrations on the edge of a milled coin; partaking in a fistic or glove contest.
million, *n.* and *a. mil*-yon, a thousand thousands; a very great number. **the million,** the general public; the masses. (Fr.)
millionaire, *n. mil*-yo-*nair*, one owning a million or more francs, dollars, or pounds; a very rich man. (Fr. *millionnaire.*)
millionairess, *n. mil*-yo-*nair*-res, a female millionaire.
millionary, *a. mil*-yo-na-re, pertaining to, consisting of, or possessing a million or millions.
millionfold, *a. mil*-yon-fohld, a million times the quantity: *ad.* a million times in quantity.
millionth, *a. mil*-yonth, a ten hundred thousandth: *n.* one of a million parts.
millipede, *n. mil*-e-peed, a millepede.
millpond, *n. mil*-pond, a reservoir of a water-mill.
millrace, *n. mil*-race, the current of water that drives a mill-wheel.
mill-rind, *n. mil*-rynd, the iron in which the spindle of an upper millstone works; a moline.
millstone, *n. mil*-stone, either of two circular stones between which grain is ground; the material of these: *a.* millstone about one's neck, a grievous burden. **millstone grit,** a formation of hard coarse gritty sandstone. **to see far into a millstone,** to be sharp-sighted.
milltail, *n. mil*-tale, the rush of water when it has turned the mill-wheel; the channel through which this flows.
mill-wheel, *n.* the water-driven wheel that operates the machinery of a mill.
millwright, *n. mil*-rite, one who constructs mills or their machinery.
milreis, *n. mil*-race, a former coin, superseded in Portugal by the escudo and in Brazil by the cruzeiro (*see* **reis.**)
milsey, *n. mil*-say, a sieve for straining milk. (Scot.)
milt, *n.* milt, the spleen; the reproductive glands of male fish; the secretion, or " soft roe," from these: *v.t.* to impregnate the roe or spawn of the female fish. (A.S. *milte.*)
milter, *n. mil*-ter, a male fish when spawning.
Miltonic, *a.* mil-*ton*-ik, like or belonging to John Milton or his works; hence, majestic.
milvine, *a. mil*-vine, pertaining to birds of the kite family: *n.* a kite. (L. *milvus*, kite.)
mime, *n.* mime, a kind of farce among the Greeks and Romans; an actor in such; a mimic: *v.t.* to mimic: *v.i.* to play in a mime. (L. *mimus.*)
mimeograph, *n. mim*-e-o-graf, proprietary name of a device for duplicating manuscript or typewritten matter by means of a stencil: *v.t.* to duplicate with this.
mimesis, *n.* mime-*ee*-sis, mimicry, esp. that of animals [Zool.]; imitation of the voice or gestures of another [Rhet.]. (Gr.)
mimetic, *a.* mime-*et*-ik, imitative; apt to imitate; characterized by imitation.
mimetically, *ad.* mime-*et*-e-ka-le, in an imitative manner.
mimetite, *n. mime*-e-tite, a lead arsenate and chloride resembling pyromorphite. (Gr. *mimētes*, imitator.)
mimic, *a. mim*-ik, imitating; imitative; inclined to imitate or to ape: *n.* one who mimics; a buffoon: *v.t.* to ape; to imitate for sport.
mimicker, *n. mim*-e-ker, one who mimics.
mimicry, *n. mim*-e-kre, imitation, esp. for sport or ridicule; likeness among animals or birds to each other, or to their environment [Zool.].
miminy-piminy, *a. mim*-e-ne-*pim*-e-ne, finical; over-nice or fastidious: *n.* prose, writing, etc., of this nature.
mimosa, *n.* me-*moh*-za, any of a genus of leguminous shrubs and trees, including the sensitive plant *Mimoso pudica.* (Gr. *mimos*, mime.)
mimulus, *n. mim*-yew-lus, a genus of plants including *M. luteus*, the monkey flower, and *M. moschatus*, the musk plant. (L., a mime.)
mina, *n. my*-na, an ancient unit of weight and money; among the Greeks 100 drachmæ, and among the Jews 50 shekels. (L.)
mina, *n. my*-na, the myna.
minacious, *a.* min-*ay*-shus, threatening; minatory.
minaret, *n. min*-a-ret, a tall turret attached to a mosque, with one or more balconies from which the muezzin summons the people to prayer. (Ar. *manarah*, lighthouse.)
minatory, *a. min*-a-to-re, threatening. (L. *minatorius.*)
minauderie, *n.* me-*noh*-de-re, simpering ways; coquettishness. (Fr.)
mince, *v.t.* mince, to cut or chop into very small pieces; to extenuate or palliate; to restrain oneself (in speaking, etc.); to pronounce in an affected way: *v.i.* to walk with short steps; to speak with affected nicety: *n.* minced meat; mincemeat. **to mince matters,** to minimize the unpleasant; to represent things in the least disagreeable light. (O.Fr. *mincier.*)
mincemeat, *n mince*-meet, a mixture of raisins and currants with chopped candied peel and suet.
mince-pie, *n.* a pie or tartlet made of mincemeat.
mincer, *n. mince*-er, one who minces; a mincing machine.
mincing, *a. mince*-ing, over-cautious, prudishly delicate; walking or speaking in an affected manner. **mincing-machine,** *n.* a mechanical device for mincing anything, esp. meat.
mincingly, *ad.* with affectation.
★**mind,** *n.* mynd, the thinking faculty; the spiritual principle or the soul in man; intention; purpose; inclination; desire; thought; opinion; memory; remembrance; disposition; the heart or seat of affection: *v.t.* and *i.* to attend to; to obey; to take care or charge of; to see to; to object to; to watch out for; to beware of. **I've a good mind to,** I'm almost decided to. **mind your eye,** beware! be on your guard! **to be in two minds,** to be undecided. **to speak one's mind,** openly to utter one's thoughts. (A.S. *gemynd*, memory.)
minded, *a. myn*-ded, having a mind; disposed; inclined.
minder, *n. myn*-der, one employed as a guardian or watcher of anything, esp. the working of a machine.
mindful, *a. mynd*-ful, attentive; bearing in mind.
mindfully, *ad. mynd*-ful-le, attentively.
mindfulness, *n.* attention; heedfulness.
mindless, *a. mynd*-less, lacking in intelligence; unmindful; heedless.
mind-reading, *n.* the faculty of apprehending what is passing in the mind of another, whether present or absent; transference of thought.
mine, *pron.* mine, possessive case of *I*, belonging to me: *a.* my (before vowels and *h*, as *mine host*). (A.S. *min.*)
★**mine,** *n.* mine, an excavation in the earth out of which minerals are dug; a deposit of mineral awaiting digging; a subterranean passage dug under a fortification, etc., to blow it up [Mil.]; an explosive charge, with detonator, in a metal container, used, either moored or free-floating at sea or lying on or under the surface on land, to destroy or impede enemy vessels, troops, tanks, etc. [Mil.]; a rich source of wealth, valuables, or information, etc.:

v.i. to dig a mine in the earth; to burrow; to practise secret means of injury: *v.t.* to sap; to supply with a mine; to sow with mines; to undermine. **acoustic mine,** a floating mine activated by the sound of the passing of ships through water. **land mine,** a large high-explosive charge for exploding on land, usually by an electrically operated detonator; a similar charge dropped by parachute from aircraft and exploding on contact. **magnetic mine,** a floating mine activated by the steel of a passing vessel setting up an electrical contact in its detonator. (Fr.)

minefield, *n. mine*-feeld, an area on land or at sea which has been sown with mines [Mil.].

minelayer, *n. mine*-lay-er, a vessel equipped for sowing mines at sea.

miner, *n. mine*-er, one who digs for minerals; one who digs a mine; one who lays mines [Mil.]. **miner's phthisis,** anthracosis [Med.].

mineral, *n. min*-er-ral, an inorganic body with a definite chemical composition found in the earth; *pl.* mineral waters: *a.* pertaining to or consisting of minerals; impregnated with mineral matter. **mineral acid,** an inorganic acid. **mineral caoutchouc,** elaterite, an elastic mineral pitch. **mineral green,** ground malachite used as a pigment. **mineral jelly,** crude petroleum jelly. **mineral kingdom,** the third grand division of natural objects, embracing all inorganic substances. **mineral oil,** petroleum, shale oil, or other hydrocarbon oil. **mineral salt,** a salt of a mineral acid. **mineral waters,** waters naturally or artificially impregnated with mineral matter; aerated waters. (O.Fr.)

mineralization, *n. min*-er-ra-ly-*zay*-shon, the act or process of mineralizing.

mineralize, *v.t. min*-er-ra-lize, to convert into a mineral; to impregnate with mineral matter; to combine with a metal in forming an ore: *v.i.* to become mineralized; to engage in the study or collection of minerals.

mineralizer, *n. min*-er-ra-ly-zer, a substance which mineralizes another.

mineralogical, *a. min*-er-ra-*loj*-e-kal, pertaining to mineralogy.

mineralogically, *ad.* according to mineralogy.

mineralogist, *n. min*-er-*ral*-o-jist, one versed in mineralogy.

mineralogy, *n.* min-er-*ral*-o-je, the study of the nature, properties, classification, etc., of minerals. (Fr. *minéralogie.*)

Minerva, *n.* me-*ner*-va, the goddess of wisdom, war, and the liberal arts [Rom. Myth.]. (L.)

minestrone, *n.* mee-na-*stroh*-na, a thick vegetable soup containing vermicelli, etc. (It.)

minesweeper, *n. mine*-sweep-er, a vessel equipped for clearing an enemy minefield.

mine-thrower, *n.* a trench-mortar.

Ming, *n.* ming, the ruling dynasty in China, 1368–1644: *a.* pertaining to this period, esp. of works of art. (Chin.)

mingle, *v.t. ming*-gl, to mix; to unite in one mass; to join in mutual intercourse; to debase by mixture: *v.i.* to be united; to be united with. (A.S. *mengan.*)

mingle-mangle, *n. ming*-gl-*mang*-gl, general confusion; a medley.

minglement, *n. ming*-gl-ment, the act of mingling; state of being mixed.

mingler, *n. ming*-gler, one who mingles.

mingy, *a. min*-je, mean; miserly; exiguous [Slang]. (*stingy.*)

miniate, *v.t. min*-e-ate, to tinge with vermilion; to illuminate (MSS., etc.). (L. *miniatus.*)

miniature, *n. min*-e-a-tewr, a small-sized painting or portrait, in oil or water-colours; the art of such painting; anything on a small scale: *a.* on a small scale: *v.t.* to embellish with miniature-work; to represent in miniature; to diminish the size of. (It. *miniatura.*)

miniaturist, *n. min*-e-a-tewr-rist, a painter of miniatures.

minify, *v.t. min*-e-fy, to diminish; to depreciate. (L. *minus,* less.)

minikin, *a. min*-e-kin, very small; elegantly affected: *n.* a favourite; a minion; a tiny pin. (Dut. *minnikyn,* little love.)

minim, *n. min*-im, a dwarf; a note equal to two crotchets [Mus.]; a down-stroke in writing; the smallest liquid measure, the sixtieth of a fluid drachm; a single drop. (L. *minimus,* the least.)

Minim, *n. min*-im, one of a former mendicant order founded by St. Francis of Paula in 1453. (L. *Minimi Fratres,* the Least among Brethren.)

minimal, *a. min*-e-mal, of the smallest amount, quantity, etc., possible or required.

Minimalist, *n. min*-e-mal-ist, a member of a moderate revolutionary party in pre-Soviet Russia.

minimization, *n. min*-e-my-*zay*-shon, the action or process of minimizing.

minimize, *v.t. min*-e-mize, to reduce to the smallest possible; to make the least of; to depreciate.

minimum, *n. min*-e-mum, the least quantity in a given case: *a.* least or lowest possible. **minimum wage,** the lowest wage on which a worker can maintain himself and family in his social status with respect. (L., least.)

minimus, *n. min*-e-mus, the smallest; the lowest or most junior in rank or age. (L.)

mining, *n. mine*-ing, the art, act, or occupation of working mines.

minion, *n. min*-yon, a favourite; a servile flatterer; a former size of type between nonpareil and brevier, about 7-point [Print.]. (Fr. *mignon,* a darling.)

minister, *n. min*-is-ter, an agent who transacts business under the authority of another; one entrusted with the direction of affairs of state; the representative of a government at a foreign court; one who conducts service at public worship; a nonconformist clergyman; a servant: *v.i.* to perform service in any office, sacred or secular; to afford supplies; to be conducive to. (Fr. *ministre.*)

ministerial, *a.* min-is-*teer*-re-al, pertaining to service, official, clerical, or ecclesiastical; acting under superior authority; pertaining to a minister or to the ministry.

ministerialist, *n.* min-is-*teer*-re-a-list, a supporter of the ministry in power.

ministerially, *ad.* min-is-*teer*-re-a-le, in a ministerial manner.

ministrant, *a. min*-is-trant, ministering; conducting divine service: *n.* one who ministers. (L. *ministrans,* serving.)

ministration, *n.* min-is-*tray*-shon, act of performing service as a minister; the office of a minister.

ministress, *n. min*-is-tress, a female minister.

ministry, *n. min*-is-tre, the act of ministering; instrumentality; the office, duties, or functions of a minister; the body of ministers of state; term of office. (Fr. *ministère.*)

minium, *n. min*-e-um, red oxide of lead, red-lead, a deep-red pigment. (L.)

miniver, *n. min*-e-ver, a white fur, esp. ermine, as used in trimming judges' robes. (O.Fr. *menu vair,* little fur.)

mink, *n.* mink, any of several members of the genus *Putorius,* large semi-aquatic mammals of polecat type of northern parts of both hemispheres; the vision; the fur of these. (Perhaps Swed. *menk.*)

minnesinger, *n. min*-ne-*sing*-er, one of a body of lyric poets and singers in Germany, 12th to mid-14th cents., whose chief theme was love. (Ger. *Minne,* love, and *singer.*)

minnie, *n. min*-e, a trench-mortar; its projectile [Mil. slang]. (Ger. *Minenwerfer,* trench-mortar.)

minnikin, *a.* and *n. min*-e-kin, minikin.

minnow, *n. min*-noh, a small cyprinoid river fish, *Phoxinus phoxinus.* (A.S. *myne.*)

Minoan, *a.* me-*noh*-an, relating to the prehistoric civilization of Crete: *n.* a Cretan of the Minoan Period; his language. **Minoan Period,** approximately 3000–1150 B.C. (Gr. *Minos,* a legendary Cretan king.)

minor, *a. my*-nor, less; smaller; petty; inconsiderable; lower; less by a semitone [Mus.]: *n.* a person of either sex under age; the term forming, or the premise containing, the subject of the conclusion [Logic]. **minor canon,** a clergyman who officiates in the services of a cathedral but is not a member of the chapter. **minor key,** a key whose third is minor, chiefly used for solemn or mournful subjects [Mus.]. **Minor prophets,** those whose Books form the last twelve of the Old Testament. (L., less.)

Minorca, *n.* me-*nor*-ka, a breed of domestic fowl originally from Spain. (One of the Balearic Isles.)

Minorite, *n. my*-no-rite, a Franciscan friar. (L. *Fratres Minores,* the Lesser Brothers.)

minority, *n.* my-*no*-re-te, the state or period of being under age; the smaller number, esp. in two parties of voters. **minority report,** a separate report made by those members dissenting from the majority.
minotaur, *n.* *min*-o-tawr, a fabled monster, half man and half bull, confined in the labyrinth of Crete. (O.Fr. from Gr. *Minos,* king of Crete, *tauros,* bull.)
minster, *n.* *min*-ster, the church of an existing or former monastery; a cathedral church; any large church. (A.S. *mynster.*)
minstrel, *n.* *min*-strel, a singer who accompanies himself on an instrument; in the Middle Ages, one who subsisted by the arts of poetry and music, and sang to the harp; a musician. **nigger minstrels,** a group of entertainers performing with blackened faces. (O.F. *menestral.*)
minstrelsy, *n.* *min*-strel-se, the art or occupation of minstrels; instrumental music; a body of musicians or minstrels; a collection of glees, etc. (O.Fr. *menestralsie.*)
mint, *n.* mint, an aromatic plant of the genus *Mentha,* from which is distilled an odoriferous and pungent essential oil. (A.S. *minte.*)
mint, *n.* mint, the place where money is coined by public authority; a place of invention or fabrication; a source of abundant supply: *v.t.* to coin; to invent (a phrase, etc.); to fabricate; to forge. (A.S. *mynet,* money.)
mintage, *n.* *mint*-aj, the act or process of coining; that which is minted; the duty paid for coining.
minter, *n.* *mint*-er, one who mints, or coins money.
mint-julep, *n.* a drink of brandy, sugar, and pounded ice flavoured with mint.
mint-sauce, *n.* *mint*-sawce, a sauce for roast lamb made of mint chopped up with vinegar and sugar.
minuend, *n.* *min*-yew-end, the number from which another is to be subtracted [Arith.]. (L. *minuendus,* to be lessened.)
minuet, *n.* min-yew-*et,* a slow graceful dance; the tune accompanying it. (Fr. *menuet.*)
minus, *n.* *my*-nus, the subtractive sign (—); a minus quantity; a deficiency: *a.* and *prep.* less; less by; short of. (L.)
minuscule, *a.* me-*nus*-kewl, minute: *n.* a small letter, as distinguished from a capital. (L.)
minute, *a.* my-*newt,* very small; attending to small things; precise; particular. (L. *minuta.*)
***minute,** *n.* *min*-it, a small portion of time, the sixtieth part of an hour; an exact instant of time; the sixtieth part of a degree [Geom.]; a brief jotting or note to aid the memory: *pl.* the official record of proceedings at a conference, etc.: *v.t.* to jot down a short note or memorandum. **minute book,** a book in which the minutes of a meeting are recorded. (Fr.)
minute-glass, *n.* a sand-glass constructed to measure a minute.
minute-gun, *n.* a gun discharged at intervals of a minute, as a signal of distress or mourning.
minute-hand, *n.* the long hand of a clock or watch marking off the minutes.
minutely, *ad.* my-*newt*-le, in a minute manner.
minuteness, *n.* my-*newt*-ness, extreme smallness.
minuter, *n.* *min*-e-ter, one who takes the minutes.
minute-watch, *n.* a watch having a minute-hand, and the minutes marked.
minutiæ, *n.pl.* me-*new*-she-e, matters of small moment; less important particulars or details. (L.)
minx, *n.* minks, a pert, saucy girl. (Origin unknown.)
Miocene, *a.* *my*-o-seen, designating the middle division of the Tertiary rocks [Geol.]. (Gr. *meion,* less, *kainos,* new.)
miosis, *n.* my-*oh*-sis: *see* **meiosis** and **myosis.**
mir, *n.* meer, a partly autonomous village community of pre-Soviet Russia. (Russ., world, universe.)
mirabilite, *n.* mi-*rab*-e-lite, Glauber salt, hydrated sodium sulphate. (L. *sal mirabilis,* wonderful salt.)
miracle, *n.* *mi*-ra-kl, anything wonderful; a prodigy; a supernatural effect or event. **miracle play,** a mediæval play in which sacred subjects are represented. (Fr.)
miraculous, *a.* mi-*rak*-yew-lus, of the nature of a miracle; performed supernaturally; wonderful; extraordinary. (Fr. *miraculeux.*)
miraculously, *ad.* by miracle.
miraculousness, *n.* the state or quality of being miraculous.
mirador, *n.* *mi*-ra-dor a, balcony, turret, or window commanding an extensive view. (Sp.)
mirage, *n.* me-*rahzh,* an optical illusion seen mainly in deserts, and due to refraction of light-rays by heated atmospheric layers; some visionary object of desire. (Fr.)
mirbane, *n.* *mir*-bane, trade-name of a mixture of benzoic and nitric acid having the scent of bitter almonds.
mire, *n.* mire, deep mud; boggy ground: *v.t.* to plunge and fix in mire; to soil or daub with mud: *v.i.* to sink in mire. (Ice. *myrr,* a swamp.)
mire-crow, *n.* the common black-headed gull, *Larus ridibundus.*
miriness, *n.* *mire*-re-ness, muddiness.
miriti, *n.* *mi*-re-te, the lofty Brazilian palm, *Mauritia flexuosa;* the moriche. (Tupi.)
mirk, *a.* and *n.* merk, murk.
mirror, *n.* *mi*-ror, a looking-glass or speculum; a pattern; an exemplar: *v.t.* to reflect as in a mirror. (O.Fr. *mireor.*)
mirth, *n.* merth, high excitement of pleasurable feelings; noisy gaiety; merriment; gladness. (A.S. *myrgth.*)
mirthful, *a.* *merth*-ful, merry; jovial; festive.
mirthfully, *ad.* *merth*-ful-le, in a mirthful manner.
mirthfulness, *n.* *merth*-ful-ness, mirth.
mirthless, *a.* *merth*-less, without mirth or hilarity.
mirthlessness, *n.* absence of mirth.
miry, *a.* *mire*-re, abounding in or covered with mire.
Mirza, *n.* *mer*-zah, Persian title of honour signifying a scholar when placed before a name, and a prince when placed after. (Per., son of an emir.)
mis-, mis, a prefix signifying wrong or ill. (A.S.)
misadventure, *n.* mis-ad-*vent*-yur, an unlucky accident; mischance; misfortune; disaster.
misadventurous, *a.* mis-ad-*vent*-yur-rus, pertaining to misadventure; disastrous; unlucky.
misadvised, *a.* mis-ad-*vized,* ill-advised or directed.
misalliance, *n.* mis-al-*ly*-ance, improper alliance, connexion or association; a mésalliance.
misanthrope, *n.* *mis*-an-thrope, a misanthropist.
misanthropic, *a.* mis-an-*throp*-ik, hating mankind.
misanthropist, *n.* mi-*san*-thro-pist, a hater of mankind. (Gr. *misanthropos,* hating man.)
misanthropy, *n.* mi-*san*-thro-pe, hatred or morbid dislike of mankind.
misapplication, *n.* *mis*-ap-le-*kay*-shon, a wrong application.
misapply, *v.t.* mis-a-*ply,* to apply wrongly.
misappreciated, *a.* mis-a-*pree*-she-ay-ted, not appreciated properly or fully.
misapprehend, *v.t.* mis-ap-re-*hend,* to misunderstand.
misapprehension, *n.* mis-ap-re-*hen*-shon, wrong apprehension of one's meaning; misconception.
misapprehensive, *a.* mis-ap-re-*hen*-siv, apt to misapprehend.
misappropriate, *v.t.* mis-a-*proh*-pre-ate, to apply to a wrong purpose, such as a trust to one's own benefit; to take unlawfully [Coll.].
misappropriation, *n.* *mis*-a-proh-pre-*ay*-shon, wrong appropriation.
misarrange, *v.t.* mis-a-*raynj,* to arrange wrongly.
misbecome, *v.t.* *mis*-be-*kum,* to suit ill or not become.
misbecoming, *ppr.* and *a.* mis-be-*kum*-ing, unseemly.
misbecomingly, *ad.* in an unseemly manner.
misbegotten, *pp.* and *a.* mis-be-*got*-en, unlawfully or irregularly begotten.
misbehave, *v.i.* mis-be-*hayv,* to behave ill or improperly.
misbehaved, *a.* mis-be-*hayvd,* guilty of ill behaviour.
misbehaviour, *n.* mis-be-*hayv*-yur, improper behaviour; misconduct.
misbelief, *n.* mis-be-*leef,* erroneous or false belief.
misbelieve, *v.t.* mis-be-*leev,* to believe erroneously.
misbeliever, *n.* mis-be-*leev*-er, one who believes wrongly or falsely.
misbeseem, *v.t.* mis-be-*seem,* to suit ill; to misbecome.
misbeseeming, *a.* mis-be-*seem*-ing, unbecoming.
misbirth, *n.* mis-*berth,* an abortion.
misborn, *a.* mis-*born,* of illegitimate birth; born to evil or misfortune.
miscalculate, *v.t.* and *i.* mis-*kal*-kew-late, to calculate erroneously.

miscalculation, *n.* mis-*kal*-kew-*lay*-shon, erroneous calculation.
miscall, *v.t.* mis-*kawl*, to name improperly; to misname; to abuse [Coll.].
miscarriage, *n.* mis-*ka*-raj, unfortunate issue of an undertaking; failure; premature delivery, esp. within 28 weeks of pregnancy [Med.]. **miscarriage of justice,** a judicial error by reason of which justice is not done.
miscarry, *v.i.* mis-*ka*-re, to go wrong; to be unsuccessful; to suffer defeat; to abort, or bring forth young before the proper time.
miscast, *n.* mis-*kahst*, an erroneous cast or reckoning: *v.t.* to cast or reckon erroneously; to allot the parts of a play to unsuitable actors; to play or to be given a stage part unsuited to one's abilities.
miscasting, *n.* mis-*kahst*-ing, the action of giving the parts in a play or film to unsuitable actors; the allotting of stage parts inappropriately.
miscegenation, *n.* *mis*-sej-e-*nay*-shon, mingling of races, esp. intermarriage between whites and blacks. (L. *misceo*, mix, *genus*, race.)
miscellanea, *n.pl.* mis-se-*lay*-ne-a, a collection of odds and ends. (L.)
miscellaneous, *a.* mis-se-*lay*-ne-us, mixed; c-onsisting of several kinds.
miscellaneously, *ad.* with variety or mixture.
miscellaneousness, *n.* mis-se-*lay*-ne-us-ness, the state of being miscellaneous.
miscellanist, *n.* mis-*sel*-an-ist, a compiler of miscellanea or of miscellanies.
miscellany, *n.* mis-*sel*-a-ne, a mixture of various kinds; a collection of compositions of various kinds or on various subjects; a magazine. (L. *misceo*, to mix.)
mischance, *n.* mis-*chahnce*, ill-luck; misfortune; accident. (O.Fr. *meschance*.)
mischarge, *n.* mis-*chahrj*, an erroneous charge: *v.t.* to make a mistake in charging an account.
mischief, *n.* *mis*-chif, harm; injury; damage; vexatious affair; wrong or harmful conduct; a troublesome child. **make mischief,** cause ill-feeling between people. (O.Fr. *meschief*.)
mischief-maker, *n.* one who makes mischief or sets people at variance.
mischief-making, *a.* exciting enmity: *n.* behaviour or action that causes ill-feeling.
mischievous, *a.* *mis*-che-vus, making mischief; inclined to mischief; given to annoying pranks. (O.Fr. *meschevous*.)
mischievously, *ad.* so as to harm; with evil intention.
mischievousness, *n.* *mis*-chev-us-ness, harmfulness; disposition to do harm, or to annoy.
mischoose, *v.t.* mis-*chooz*, to make a wrong choice.
miscibility, *n.* mis-se-*bil*-e-te, state of being miscible.
miscible, *a.* *mis*-se-bl, mixable. (L. *misceo*.)
miscitation, *n.* mis-sy-*tay*-shon, a wrong citation.
miscite, *v.t.* mis-*site*, to quote erroneously.
misclaim, *n.* mis-*klame*, a mistaken claim: *v.t.* to claim erroneously.
miscolour, *v.t.* mis-*kul*-or, to give a false appearance to; to misrepresent.
miscomprehend, *v.t.* mis-kom-pre-*hend*, to comprehend wrongly; to misapprehend.
miscomprehension, *n.* mis-kom-pre-*hen*-shon, misunderstanding.
misconceive, *v.t* and *i.* mis-kon-*seev*, to form or have a false conception of; to misapprehend.
misconception, *n.* mis-kon-*sep*-shon, wrong conception; misapprehension.
misconduct, *n.* mis-*kon*-dukt, ill behaviour; ill management; adultery.
misconduct, *v.t.* mis-kon-*dukt*, to mismanage; to conduct badly: *v.i.* to commit adultery.
misconstruction, *n.* mis-kon-*struk*-shon, wrong interpretation of words or things.
misconstrue, *v.t.* mis-*kon*-stroo, to construe or interpret erroneously; to misapprehend.
miscorrect, *v.t.* mis-ko-*rekt*, to alter erroneously with intent to correct.
miscounsel, *v.t.* mis-*koun*-sel, to advise wrongly.
miscount, *n.* mis-*kount*, an erroneous counting, esp. of votes at an election: *v.t.* to mistake in counting; *v.i.* to make a wrong reckoning.
miscreant, *n.* *mis*-kre-ant, a vile wretch; an unprincipled fellow; formerly, an unbeliever or infidel: *a.* villainous, vile, scoundrelly. (O.Fr., misbelieving.)
miscreation, *n.* mis-kre-*ay*-shon, a monstrous, unnatural, or misshapen creation.
miscreative, *a.* mis-kre-*ay*-tiv, tending to wrong creation.
miscue, *n.* mis-*kew*, a stroke at billiards foiled by the slipping of the cue: *v.i.* to make a miscue.
misdate, *n.* mis-*date*, a wrong date: *v.t.* to date erroneously.
misdeal, *n.* mis-*deel*, a faulty or unlawful distribution (of cards): *v.t.* to deal a pack of cards wrongly.
misdealing, *n.* mis-*deel*-ing, an act of distributing wrongfully; improper or evil conduct.
misdeed, *n.* mis-*deed*, an evil deed; a wicked action; a crime.
misdeem, *v.t.* mis-*deem*, to judge erroneously.
misdemean, *v.t.* mis-de-*meen*, to behave ill.
misdemeanant, *n.* mis-de-*mee*-nant, a person guilty of a misdemeanour [Law].
misdemeanour, *n.* mis-de-*mee*-nur, ill-behaviour; misbehaviour; an indictable offence, but of a less serious nature than a felony.
misderive, *v.t.* mis-de-*rive*, to err in deriving.
misdescribe, *v.t.* mis-de-*skribe*, to describe wrongly.
misdirect, *v.t.* mis-dy-*rekt*, to direct wrongly.
misdirection, *n.* mis-dy-*rek*-shon, a wrong direction.
misdo, *v.t.* mis-*doo*, to do improperly: *v.i.* to do wrong; to commit a crime.
misdoer, *n.* mis-*doo*-er, one who does wrong.
misdoing, *n.* mis-*doo*-ing, a wrong done; a fault.
misdoubt, *n.* mis-*dout*, suspicion; distrust: *v.t.* to regard with doubts or misgiving; to suspect.
mise, *n.* meez, cost; expense; issue in a real action [Law]; a treaty, or arbitral award, as the Mise of Lewes between Simon de Montfort and Henry III in 1264. (Fr.)
miseducate, *v.t.* mis-*ed*-yew-kate, to educate wrongly.
mise-en-scène, *n.* meez-on(g)-*sayn*, the staging of a play; the arrangement of actors in regard to the scenery; external environment. (Fr.)
misemploy, *v.t.* mis-em-*ploy*, to employ uselessly or to a wrong purpose.
misemployment, *n.* mis-em-*ploy*-ment, the act of misemployment; improper employment.
misentry, *n.* mis-*en*-tre, a wrong entry or charge.
miser, *n.* *my*-zer, an extremely covetous person; a sordid wretch; a niggard; one who though wealthy enjoys hoarding. (L., wretched.)
miser, *n.* *my*-zer, a large boring tool used in well-sinking. (Origin unknown.)
miserable, *a.* *miz*-er-ra-bl, wretched; very unhappy; fraught with misery; very poor or mean; despicable; worthless: *n.* a wretch. (O.Fr.)
miserableness, *n.* *miz*-er-ra-bl-ness, the condition of being miserable.
miserably, *ad.* to a miserable degree.
misère, *n.* mi-*zare*, the declaration in certain card-games by which declarer undertakes to play his hand without making a trick. **misère ouverte,** a similar call, declarer exposing his cards after playing to the first trick. (Fr.)
miserere, *n.* *miz*-er-*rare*-re, the 51st Psalm, beginning in the Vulgate with this word; a musical composition adapted to this psalm; a lamentation; a projection from the under side of a folding seat in the stall of a church, used as a rest. (L., have pity.)
misericord, *n.* mi-*ze*-re-kord, a dispensation granted to a monk in respect of food, also a small refectory for monks having such; the miserere of a folding seat; a slender dagger for inflicting a death-thrust. (O.Fr.)
miserliness, *n.* *my*-zer-le-ness, the state or quality of being miserly.
miserly, *a.* *my*-zer-le, very covetous; avaricious; penurious.
misery, *n.* *miz*-er-re, wretchedness; great unhappiness; extreme pain; distress; misfortune.
misestimate, *v.t.* mis-*es*-te-mate, to estimate erroneously.
misfeasance, *n.* mis-*fee*-zance, trespass; wrong-doing; the improper execution of an act which is lawful [Law]. (O.Fr. *mesfaisance*.)
misfire, *n.* mis-*fire*, the failure of the explosive charge of a fire-arm, or of an internal-combustion engine, effectively to ignite; an abortive attempt [Coll.]: *v.i.* to fail to go off or explode.
misfit, *n.* *mis*-fit, a bad fit; a badly fitting garment;

a person ill-suited to his surroundings: *v.t.* and *i.* to fit badly.
misform, *v.t.* mis-*form,* to put in an ill shape; to form badly.
misformation, *n.* *mis*-for-*may*-shon, an irregularity of formation; a malformation.
misfortunate, *a.* mis-*for*-tew-nat, unfortunate.
misfortune, *n.* mis-*for*-tewn, ill luck; a mishap; calamity.
misgive, *v.t.* mis-*giv,* to fill with doubt; to fail: *v.i.* to go wrong; to have doubts; to misfire.
misgiving, *n.* mis-*giv*-ing, a sense of lack of confidence; mistrust.
misgotten, *a.* mis-*got*-en, ill-gotten; unlawfully obtained.
misgovern, *v.t.* mis-*guv*-ern, to govern, manage, or administer ill.
misgovernment, *n.* mis-*guv*-ern-ment, ill-administration of public affairs; irregularity; disorder.
misgrowth, *n.* mis-*grohth,* an abnormal growth.
misguidance, *n.* mis-*gy*-dance, wrong direction.
misguide, *v.t.* mis-*gide,* to lead or guide into error.
misguidingly, *ad.* mis-*gy*-ding-le, in a way to mislead.
mishandle, *v.t.* mis-*han*-dl, to handle badly; to maltreat.
mishap, *n.* mis-*hap,* ill chance; misfortune.
mishear, *v.t.* mis-*heer,* to mistake in hearing: *p.* and *pp.* **misheard,** mis-*herd.*
mishit, *v.t.* mis-*hit,* to hit in a faulty or ill-directed manner: *n.* a stroke so made or delivered.
mishmash, *n.* *mish*-mash, a medley; a hotch-potch.
mishmi, *n.* *mish*-me, a drug used by natives obtained from the root of *Coptis teeta,* a small herb found in the Mishmi mountains, Assam.
Mishna, *n.* *mish*-na, the body of traditions, etc., forming the basis of the Talmud; the doctrine therein contained. (Heb.)
mishnaic, *a.* mish-*nay*-ik, pertaining to the Mishna.
misinform, *v.t.* mis-in-*form,* to give wrong information to.
misinformant, *n.* mis-in-*for*-mant, a misinformer.
misinformation, *n.* mis-*in*-for-*may*-shon, wrong information; false account or intelligence received.
misinformer, *n.* mis-in-*for*-mer, one who gives wrong information.
misinstruct, *v.t.* mis-in-*strukt,* to instruct wrongly; to provide with erroneous orders or directions.
misinstruction, *n.* mis-in-*struk*-shon, wrong instruction.
misintelligence, *n.* mis-in-*tel*-le-jence, wrong information.
misinterpret, *v.t.* and *v.i.* mis-in-*ter*-pret, to interpret erroneously; to arrive at a false conclusion.
misinterpretation, *n.* *mis*-in-*ter*-pre-*tay*-shon, the act of misinterpreting.
misjoin, *v.t.* mis-*joyn,* to join improperly or badly.
misjoinder, *n.* mis-*joyn*-der, the incorrect union of parties or demands, etc., in an action [Law].
misjudge, *v.t.* and *i.* mis-*judj,* to judge or estimate erroneously or unjustly.
misjudgment, *n.* mis-*judj*-ment, a wrong determination; a misconstruction.
misknow, *v.t.* mis-*noh,* to know imperfectly; to misunderstand; to fail or to refuse to recognize.
mislabel, *v.t.* mis-*lay*-bl, to label wrongly.
mislay, *v.t.* mis-*lay,* to lay in a wrong place, or a place which one has forgotten; to lose. *p.* and *pp.* **mislaid,** mis-*lade.*
mislead, *v.t.* mis-*leed,* to lead wrong or astray; to deceive. *p.* and *pp.* **misled,** mis-*led.* (A.S.)
mislike, *n.* mis-*like,* dislike; aversion: *v.t.* and *i.* to dislike; to disapprove; to feel aversion.
mislippen, *v.t.* and *v.i.* mis-*lip*-en, to disappoint purposely; to deceive; to fail to keep a promise; to distrust; to neglect [Scots.].
mismanage, *v.t.* mis-*man*-aj, to manage ill.
mismanagement, *n.* mis-*man*-aj-ment, bad or improper management.
mismarry, *v.t.* and *i.* mis-*ma*-re, to marry unsuitably or unfortunately.
mismatch, *v.t.* mis-*match,* to match unsuitably.
mismated, *a.* mis-*may*-ted, unsuitably matched.
mismeasure, *v.t.* and *v.i.* mis-*mezh*-ur, to measure or estimate incorrectly.
misname, *v.t.* mis-*name,* to call by the wrong name.
misnomer, *n.* mis-*noh*-mer, a misnaming; a wrong or wrongly applied name. (O.Fr. *mesnommer.*)
misogamist, *n.* mi-*sog*-a-mist, a hater of marriage.
misogamy, *n.* mi-*sog*-a-me, hatred of marriage. (Gr. *misogamos,* disliking marriage.)
misogynist, *n.* mi-*soj*-e-nist, woman-hater.
misogyny, *n.* mi-*soj*-e-ne, hatred of the female sex. (Gr. *misogynia,* hatred of women.)
misologist, *n.* mi-*sol*-o-jist, a hater of logic, reason, or discussion.
misoneism, *n.* mis-o-*nee*-izm, hatred of what is new. (Gr. *mis(ein),* to hate, *nĕos,* new.)
misopædist, mis-o-*pee*-dist, one having a morbid aversion for children. (Gr. *mis(ein),* to hate, *pais, paidos,* a child.)
mispickel, *n.* *mis*-pik-kl, a crystalline ore of arsenic, a compound of arsenic, sulphur, and iron [Min.]. (Ger.)
misplace, *v.t.* mis-*place,* to put in a wrong place; to place on an improper object.
misplacement, *n.* mis-*place*-ment, act of misplacing: wrong position.
mispoint, *v.t.* mis-*poynt,* to punctuate improperly.
mispolicy, *n.* mis-*pol*-e-se, wrong policy; impolicy.
misprint, *n.* mis-*print,* a mistake in printing; a typographical error: *v.t.* to make a mistake in printing.
misprisal, *n.* mis-*pry*-zal, scorn; contempt.
misprision, *n.* mis-*prizh*-on, neglect, esp. of official duty; mistake or oversight; any serious misdemeanour bordering upon the degree of a capital crime [Law]. **misprision of felony,** or **of treason,** wilful concealment of the crime without being a party to or assenting to it. (O.Fr. *mesprison,* an error, wrongful action.)
misprize, *v.t.* mis-*prize,* to slight or undervalue.
mispronounce, *v.t.* and *i.* mis-pro-*nounce,* to pronounce erroneously.
mispronunciation, *n.* *mis*-pro-nun-se-*ay*-shon, wrong pronunciation.
misproportion, *n.* mis-pro-*por*-shon, lack of proportion.
misquotation, *n.* mis-kwo-*tay*-shon, an erroneous quotation.
misquote, *v.t.* mis-*kwote,* to quote wrongly.
misrate, *v.t.* mis-*rate,* to rate erroneously.
misread, *v.t.* mis-*reed,* to read a thing wrongly.
misreckon, *v.t.* mis-*rek*-on, to reckon wrongly.
misrelate, *v.t.* mis-re-*late,* to relate inaccurately or falsely.
misrelation, *n.* mis-re-*lay*-shon, a faulty or false relation.
misremember, *v.t.* mis-re-*mem*-ber, not to remember correctly; to forget [Coll.].
misreport, *n.* mis-re-*pawrt,* a false or erroneous report: *v.t.* to report erroneously.
misrepresent, *v.t.* *mis*-rep-re-*zent,* to represent falsely, improperly, or incorrectly.
misrepresentation, *n.* *mis*-rep-re-zen-*tay*-shon, erroneous or false representation.
misrepute, *n.* mis-re-*pewt,* doubtful reputation: *v.t.* to hold in wrong estimation.
misrule, *n.* mis-*rool,* disorder; confusion; tumult from insubordination: *v.t.* and *i.* to rule badly or foolishly. **master, lord,** or **abbot of misrule,** a mediæval leader of the Christmas revels.
miss, *n.* mis (*pl.* **misses**), an unmarried lady; a girl; (*cap.*) the title of address prefixed to the name of such. (*Mistress* contracted.)
miss, *n.* mis, failure to hit or reach; loss; want; lack: *v.t.* to fail to hit, reach, find, or see; to omit; to pass by; to go without; to feel the want or need of: *v.i.* to fail to hit; to deviate from the true direction. **a miss is as good as a mile,** a narrow escape is still an escape, or a failure a failure. **to give a miss to,** to avoid, or to cease, doing; to leave out; to ignore. **to miss stays,** to fail in going about from one tack to another [Naut.]. (A.S. *missan.*)
missal, *n.* *mis*-sal, the Roman Catholic mass-book or prayer-book; a mediæval illuminated manuscript. (Late L. *missale.*)
missay, *v.t.* mis-*say,* to say wrongly; to slander.
misseeming, *a.* mis-*see*-ming, unbecoming.
missel-thrush, *n.* *mis*-sel-thrush, mistle-thrush.
missend, *v.t.* mis-*send,* to send wrongly, or to a wrong address.
misserve, *v.t.* mis-*serv,* to serve unfaithfully.
misshape, *v.t.* mis-*shape,* to shape ill; to deform.
misshapen, *a.* mis-*shape*-en, ill-shapen; deformed.
missile, *a.* *mis*-sil *or* *mis*-sile, that may be thrown; capable of being thrown or projected from the hand

or an instrument: *n.* a weapon or other object for throwing or projecting thus. (L. *missilis.*)
missing, *a. mis*-ing, lost; lacking; not present. **missing link,** *see* **link. the missing,** casualties unaccounted for [Mil.].
mission, *n. mish*-on, a sending or being sent; what one is sent or appointed to do; a message; errand or commission; those commissioned; a vocation; a journey for the propagation of religion; a series of religious services; a body or organization of missionaries; a station of missionaries. (O.Fr.)
missionary, *n. mish*-on-a-re, one sent on a mission, esp. to propagate religion: *a.* pertaining to missions. (Late L. *missionarius.*)
missioner, *n. mish*-on-er, one in charge of a parochial mission.
missis, *n. mis*-sis, an abbreviation of mistress used by servants; also a familiar way of speaking of a wife; missus.
missish, *a. mis*-sish, having a schoolgirlish manner.
missive, *a. mis*-siv, such as is sent or thrown: *n.* a written message; a letter. (Fr.)
missoy-bark, *n. mis*-oy-bark, massoy.
misspell, *v.t.* mis-*spel*, to spell wrongly.
misspelling, *n.* mis-*spel*-ling, a wrong spelling.
misspend, *v.t.* mis-*spend*, to spend amiss; to waste.
misspent, *a.* mis-*spent*, expended to no purpose, as "a misspent youth."
misstate, *v.i.* mis-*state*, to state incorrectly; to misrepresent.
misstatement, *n.* mis-*state*-ment, an erroneous or incorrect statement.
misstay, *v.i.* mis-*stay*, to miss stays [Naut.].
missus, *n. mis*-sus, missis; one's wife [Coll.].
missy, *n. mis*-e, a young girl; a miss.
★**mist,** *n.* mist, visible aqueous vapour in the atmosphere near the surface of the earth; anything, esp. a watery condensation, that obscures or intercepts vision: *v.t.* to cover with or as with mist: *v.i.* to become blurred, dim, or misty; to gather in mist. (A.S.)
mistakable, *a.* mis-*take*-a-bl, capable of being mistaken or misunderstood.
mistake, *n.* mis-*take*, an error of any kind; a blunder; misconception; misapprehension: *v.t.* to misunderstand; to take one thing or person for another: *v.i.* to err in opinion or judgment. *p.* **mistook**; *pp.* **mistaken.** (Scand.)
mistaken, *a.* mis-*tay*-kn, wrong; erroneous; incorrect.
mistakenly, *ad.* mis-*tay*-kn-le, by mistake.
misteach, *v.t.* mis-*teech*, to teach wrongly.
mistell, *v.t.* mis-*tel*, to tell erroneously.
Mister, *n. mis*-ter, a title of address to men of all classes not having other titles, expressed in writing by the abbreviation Mr. (*master.*)
misterm, *v.i.* mis-*term*, to denominate erroneously.
mistful, *a. mist*-ful, clouded with mist.
mistigris, *n. mis*-te-gris, the joker [Card-playing]; a variety of poker with this included. (Fr. *mistigri*, knave of clubs.)
mistily, *ad. mis*-te-le, in a misty manner.
mistime, *v.t.* mis-*time*, to time wrongly; to do at a wrong or inappropriate time.
mistiness, *n. mis*-te-ness, the state of being misty.
mistitle, *v.t.* mis-*ty*-tl, to call by a wrong title.
mistle-thrush, *n. mis*-sel-thrush, the largest of the European thrushes, *Turdus viscivorus*, which eats the berries of the mistletoe.
mistletoe, *n. mis*-sel-toh, the plant, *Viscum album*, parasitic on various trees, esp. the apple, and venerated by the ancient Druids when found on the oak. (A.S. *misteltan.*)
mistral, *n. mis*-tral, the cold, dry northerly wind of the south of France. (Fr.)
mistranslate, *v.t. mis*-trans-*late*, to translate wrongly.
mistranslation, *n. mis*-trans-*lay*-shon, a wrong translation.
mistress, *n. mis*-tress, a woman who controls or governs; the female head of a family or a school; a woman beloved and courted; a concubine; (*cap.*) a form of address to a married woman (abbreviated to Mrs.). **Mistress of the Robes,** the highest lady member (always a Duchess) of the Household of a British Queen, Queen Consort, or Queen Mother.
mistrial, *n.* mis-*try*-al, a trial rendered non-effective through a flaw in its proceedings; an inconclusive trial.
mistrust, *n.* mis-*trust*, distrust; want of confidence: *v.t.* to suspect or doubt.
mistrustful, *a.* mis-*trust*-ful, suspicious; doubting.
mistrustfully, *ad.* mis-*trust*-ful-le, with mistrust.
mistrustfulness, *n.* suspicion; doubt.
mistrustingly, *ad.* mis-*trus*-ting-le, with distrust.
mistune, *v.t.* mis-*tewn*, to tune erroneously.
misty, *a. mist*-e, overspread with mist; obscure.
misunderstand, *v.t. mis*-un-der-*stand*, to take in a wrong sense; to mistake the meaning of.
misunderstanding, *n. mis*-un-der-*stand*-ing, misconception; disagreement; dissension.
misusage, *n.* mis-*yew*-zaj, ill-usage; abuse; wrong or improper use.
misuse, *n.* mis-*yewce*, ill-treatment; improper use.
misuse, *v.t.* mis-*yewz*, to treat or use improperly; to maltreat or misapply.
misuser, *n.* mis-*yew*-zer, use otherwise than in accordance with one's right [Law].
misvaluation, *n. mis*-val-yew-*ay*-shon, a faulty valuation.
misword, *v.t.* mis-*werd*, to word incorrectly. **miswording,** *n.* erroneous or wrong wording.
miswrite, *v.t.* mis-*rite*, to write incorrectly.
miswrought, *a.* mis-*rawt*, badly wrought.
misyoke, *v.t.* mis-*yoke*, to yoke improperly.
mitcheline, *n. mitch*-el-ine, a cotton fabric of firm texture with an embossed pattern, used for counterpanes, etc.; patent satin.
mitchell-grass, *n. mitch*-el-grahs, an Australian fodder grass of the genus *Astrebla*.
mite, *n.* mite, a small arachnid of the order *Acarina*; a cheese-mite, harvest-mite, etc. (O.Fr.)
mite, *n.* mite, a very small coin, worth about a third of a farthing; anything very small; a tiny child. (Dut. *mijt.*)
Mithraic, *a.* mith-*ray*-ik, pertaining to Mithraism or to Mithra.
Mithraism, *n. mith*-ra-izm, the worship of Mithra, the sun-god of the ancient Persians.
mithridate, *n. mith*-re-date, any antidote against poison. **mithridate mustard,** a name of candytuft, pennycress, and certain other cresses. (*Mithridates* VI, King of Pontus (?132–63 B.C.), said to have made himself immune to poisons.)
mithridatic, *a.* mith-re-*dat*-ik, pertaining to a mithridate or to Mithridates.
mithridatism, *n. mith*-re-da-tizm, immunity to poison. (*mithridate.*)
mitigable, *a. mit*-e-ga-bl, that may be mitigated.
mitigant, *a. mit*-e-gant, softening; lenitive.
mitigate, *v.t. mit*-e-gate, to alleviate; to make less severe; to moderate. (L. *mitigatus.*)
mitigation, *n.* mit-e-*gay*-shon, alleviation; abatement.
mitigative, *a. mit*-e-ga-tiv, tending to alleviate.
mitigator, *n. mit*-e-ga-tor, he who or that which mitigates.
mitigatory, *a. mit*-e-gay-to-re, serving to mitigate; palliative.
mitogenetic, *a.* my-to-je-*net*-ik, produced by mitosis [Biol.].
mitosis, *n.* my-*toh*-sis, indirect cell-division; the series of changes undergone by a nucleus during this; karyokinesis [Biol.]. (Gr. *mitos*, thread, and *-osis.*)
mitotic, *a.* my-*tot*-ik, pertaining to, or characterized by, mitosis [Biol.].
mitraille, *n.* (App.), small shot or missiles as ammunition for a mitrailleuse. (Fr., grapeshot.)
mitrailleur, *n.* (App.), a gunner who works a mitrailleuse; a mitrailleuse. (Fr.)
mitrailleuse, *n.* (App.), a breach-loading machine-gun consisting of several barrels which can be discharged in quick succession. (Fr.)
mitral, *a. my*-tral, pertaining to or like a mitre or the mitral valve. **mitral valve,** the valve of the heart preventing the return of blood from the ventricle.
mitre, *n. my*-ter, the cleft head-dress worn as a symbol of office by bishops; the dignity of a bishop; an angle of 45°, or a joint at this angle [Carp.]: *v.t.* to join at an angle of 45° [Carp.]. **mitre flower,** a plant of the genus *Cyclamen*. (O.Fr.)
mitred, *a. my*-terd, wearing a mitre; having the rank of bishop [Eccles.]; cut or joined at an angle of 45° [Carp.].
mitriform, *a. my*-tre-form, mitre-shaped [Bot. and Zool.].

mitt, *n.* mit, a mitten: *pl.* boxing-gloves, the clenched fists [Slang]. **the frozen mitt,** the "cold shoulder," frigid neglect or contempt [Slang].
mitten, *n. mit*-en, a cover for the hand, from the knuckles to the wrist; a glove having a thumb but no fingers. **the mitten,** dismissal; rejection; the sack [Slang]. **the mittens,** a pair of boxing-gloves [Slang]. (Fr. *mitaine.*)
mittimus, *n. mit*-te-mus, a warrant from a justice of commitment to prison; a writ to transfer a record from one court to another [Law]. (L., we send.)
mity, *a. my*-te, having or abounding in mites.
mix, *v.t.* miks, to unite or blend promiscuously two or more ingredients; to join; to associate: *v.i.* to become united or blended promiscuously; to mingle. **mix up,** to confuse; to mix unsuitably; to entangle in a "shady" affair; a muddle, a state of confusion. (L. *mixtus,* mixed.)
mixable, *a. miks*-a-bl, capable of being mixed.
★**mixed,** *a.* mikst, not clear; consisting of different things. **mixed bathing,** public bathing of both sexes together. **mixed doubles,** a match (esp. lawn tennis) contested by a man and woman on each side. **mixed foursome,** a similar match at golf. **mixed income,** one partly earned and partly unearned. **mixed marriage,** a marriage in which the partners are of different creeds or races.
mixedly, *ad. miks*-ed-le, in a mixed manner.
mixen, *n. miks*-en, a midden. (A.S.)
mixer, *n. miks*-er, one who or that which mixes; a device in which ingredients are mixed; a person considered as a social unit, as "a good mixer" [Coll.].
mixtilinear, *a. miks*-te-*lin*-e-ar, containing or formed by both straight and curved lines.
mixture, *n. miks*-tewr, the act of mixing, or state of being mixed; a compound or preparation of two or more commingled ingredients; the explosive combination of gas and air operating an internal-combustion engine. (L. *mixtura.*)
mizen, *n.* mizn, the aftermost of the fore-and-aft sails of a ship. **mizen mast,** the aftermost mast of a ship having three or more masts. **mizen rigging,** the shrouds of the mizen mast. (Fr. *misaine.*)
mizzle, *n. miz*-zl, fine rain; drizzle: *v.t.* to rain in very fine drops. (*mist.*)
mizzle, *v.t. miz*-zl, to go away; to clear off [Slang].
mizzly, *a. miz*-le *or mizl*-le, drizzling; misty.
mizzonite, *n. miz*-o-nite, one of the scapolite minerals, containing silicates of aluminium, calcium, etc.
mizzy, *n. miz*-ze, a bog or quagmire. (Dial. Eng.)
mnemonic, *a.* ne-*mon*-ik, assisting the memory: *n.* an aid to the memory.
mnemonics, *n.* ne-*mon*-iks, the art of assisting the memory; a system for improving or training the memory. (Gr. from *mnēmon,* mindful.)
mnemotechny, *n.* nem-o-*tek*-ne, mnemonics. (Gr.)
mo, *n.* moh, a moment [Slang]
moa, *n. moh*-a, any of a group of large extinct flightless birds of New Zealand of the genus *Dinornis.* (Maori.)
moan, *n.* mone, a low audible expression of pain or sorrow; a restrained wail: *v.i.* to utter a low sound from, or as from, pain or grief; to grumble: *v.t.* to lament; to deplore. (A.S. *mænan.*)
moanful, *a. mone*-ful, expressing sorrow.
moanfully, *ad. mone*-ful-le, with lamentation.
moat, *n.* mote, a protecting ditch round a fortress or other building: *v.t.* to surround with a ditch. (O.Fr. *mote,* a dike.)
mob, *n.* mob, a mob-cap. **mob-cap,** a woman's cap with broad frills and a puffy crown, completely covering the hair. (O.Dut. *mop,* a coif.)
mob, *n.* mob, a promiscuous or disorderly multitude; the populace; the rabble: *v.t.* to attack as a mob or in a disorderly manner. **mob law,** rule of the mob; lynch law. **swell mob,** *see* **swell-mob.** (Abbrev. of L. *mobile vulgus,* fickle crowd.)
mobbish, *a. mob*-bish, like a mob; tumultuous.
mobby, *n. mob*-be, fruit juice from which brandy is distilled; such brandy [U.S.A.].
mobile, *a. moh*-bile, movable; easily moved; characterized by easy movement; having a high degree of fluidity. **mobile gun,** a piece of artillery mounted on a motorized carriage. **mobile warfare,** warfare characterized by rapid movements from place to place. **to go mobile,** to be furnished with mechanized transport (of infantry, etc.) [Mil.]. (Fr.)
mobility, *n.* mo-*bil*-e-te, state or condition of being mobile; susceptibility of motion; ready changeability; moveableness.
mobilization, *n. moh*-be-ly-*zay*-shon, act of mobilizing.
mobilize, *v.t. moh*-be-lize, to render moveable; to gather together and prepare for use; to put armed forces on a war footing [Mil.]. (Fr. *mobiliser.*)
moble, *v.t. moh*-bl, to wrap in a hood.
mobocracy, *n.* mob-*ok*-ra-se, government by the mob, or the lower orders of a community. (*mob,* and Gr. *krateia,* rule.)
mobsman, *n. mobz*-man, a member of a mob, esp. a swell-mob.
moccasin, *n. mok*-a-sin, a heel-less covering for the feet of soft leather, worn by American Indians and many primitive peoples; any soft house slipper made in the same fashion. **moccasin snake,** the copper-head or any venomous American pit-viper of the genus *Ancistrodon.* (Algonquian.)
Mocha, *n. moh*-kah, a special quality of coffee brought from Mocha in Arabia. **Mocha-stone,** *n.* moss-agate, a dendritic variety of chalcedony; a moth of the genus *Ephyra.*
mock, *a.* mok, false; counterfeit; imitating reality, but not real: *v.t.* to mimic, esp. in derision; to laugh at; to deride; to befool; to disappoint: *v.i.* to make sport in contempt. **to make a mock of,** to treat with ridicule or contempt. (O.Fr. *mocquer.*)
mocker, *n. mok*-er, one who mocks; a scoffer.
mockery, *n. mok*-er-re, the act of mocking; derision; that which deceives; false show; a futile attempt.
mock-heroic, *a.* burlesquing the heroic style.
mocking-bird, *n.* an American bird of the thrush family, *Mimus polyglottus,* that imitates the song of other birds.
mockingly, *ad. mok*-ing-le, by way of derision.
mock-orange, *n.* the deciduous shrub *Philadelphus coronarius,* commonly called syringa.
mock-sun, *n.* any one of the luminous spheres appearing on a halo surrounding the sun under certain atmospheric conditions in which ice-crystals are present; a parhelion.
mock-turtle, *n.* a soup made chiefly of calf's head, veal, and condiments.
mock-up, *n.* a fabricated approximation of a finished article [Comm.].
moco, *n. moh*-koh, the rock cavy, a large South American guinea-pig. (Native name.)
Mod, *n.* mod, an annual Highland festival for the encouragement of literature and the arts. (Gael. an assembly, a moot.)
modal, *a. moh*-dal, pertaining to a mode or mood. **modal proposition,** one in which an assertion or denial is made with a limitation or restriction [Logic]. (Late L. *modlisa.*)
modalism, *n. moh*-da-lizm, the tenets of the modalists.
modalist, *n. moh*-da-list, one who regards the distinction of person in the Trinity as a mere distinction in the mode of divine being.
modality, *n.* mo-*dal*-e-te, the quality of being modal.
modally, *ad. moh*-dal-e, in a modal manner.
mode, *n.* mode, manner; method; form; fashion; alamode, a kind of silk; the arrangement of the intervals in a musical scale originating in ancient Greece. (Fr.)
model, *n. mod*-el, a pattern to copy; a copy, esp. on a small scale; example; something to imitate; one who poses for a painter or sculptor; a lay-figure which, or a mannequin who, wears and displays clothes for sale: *v.t.* and *i.* to form or work after or for a model, esp. in some plastic material; to give shape to; to make models; *a.* serving or capable of serving as a model. (O.Fr. *modelle.*)
modeller, *n. mod*-el-er, one who models.
modelling, *n. mod*-el-ing, the art of making models; the representation, in painting, etc., of solidity.
modena, *n.* mo-*dee*-na, a purplish crimson colour. (*Modena,* in Italy.)
moderate, *a. mod*-er-rat, temperate; observing reasonable bounds; not excessive or extreme; not violent; of middle rate or quality: *n.* one who is

moderate or accommodating in his views: *v.t.* *mod*-er-rate, to keep within bounds; to restrain; to regulate: *v.i.* to become less violent or intense; to officiate as moderator. (L. *moderatus*, regulated.)
moderately, *ad.* in a moderate manner.
moderateness, *n.* the quality of being moderate.
moderation, *n.* mod-er-*ray*-shon, act of moderating; state of being moderate; freedom from excess; calmness of mind; temperance: *pl.* (*cap.*) the first public examinations for the B.A. degree at Oxford.
moderatism, *n.* *mod*-er-ra-tizm, moderate opinions in religion or politics; the principles of the moderates.
moderato, *ad.* mod-e-*rah*-toh, moderately [Mus.]. (It.)
moderator, *n.* *mod*-er-ray-tor, one who or that which moderates; one who presides over a meeting, esp. of a Presbyterian council; an examiner for Moderations (Oxford), and for the mathematical tripos (Cambridge); one who superintends the University examinations for honours and degrees; at Trinity College, Dublin, a candidate obtaining an honours pass in the examination for the B.A. degree. **moderator lamp,** a lamp with an arrangement for moderating the supply of oil to the wick.
moderatorship, *n.* *mod*-er-ray-tor-ship, the office of a moderator.
modern, *a.* *mod*-ern, pertaining to the present time; recent or new: *n.* a person of modern times; one who is up-to-date. **modern face,** a style of roman letter having right-angled serifs and marked differentiation between thick and thin strokes [Print.]. **modern languages,** those commonly taught in schools other than Latin and Greek, viz. French, and German. **modern side,** the division of a school specializing in modern languages and science as contrasted with classics. (Fr. *moderne.*)
modernism, *n.* *mod*-ern-izm, modern cast, manner, or practice; something recently formed; (*cap.*) a rationalistic theology based on the findings of modern biblical criticism and scientific research.
modernist, *n.* *mod*-ern-ist, an admirer of the moderns, or what is modern; an advocate of modern methods, esp. in education; (*cap.*) a teacher or supporter of Modernism.
modernistic, *a.* mod-er-*nis*-tik, modernist; tending towards Modernism.
modernity, *n.* mo-*der*-ne-te, the quality of being modern.
modernization, *n.* mod-er-ny-*zay*-shon, the act or result of modernizing.
modernize, *v.t.* *mod*-ern-ize, to render modern; to adapt to modern taste, style, or usage, etc.
modest, *a.* *mod*-est, restrained by a sense of propriety; not forward, presumptuous or arrogant; unobtrusive; diffident; bashful; not loose or lewd; chaste; moderate. (Fr. *modeste.*)
modestly, *ad.* *mod*-est-le, in a modest manner.
modesty, *n.* *mod*-es-te, the quality of being modest; the temper which accompanies a moderate estimate of one's worth and importance; lack of presumption; unpretentiousness; purity of manners; the wild plant, hare's ear.
modicum, *n.* *mod*-e-kum, a small quantity or allowance. (L.)
modifiable, *a.* mod-e-*fy*-a-bl, that may be modified.
modification, *n.* *mod*-e-fe-*kay*-shon, the act of modifying; state of being modified; a modified form; umlaut [Gram.]. (Fr.)
modificative, *a.* *mod*-e-fe-*kay*-tiv, tending to modify: *n.* that which modifies.
modificatory, *a.* *mod*-e-fe-*kay*-to-re, modifying.
modifier, *n.* *mod*-e-fy-er, he who or that which modifies.
modify, *v.t.* and *i.* *mod*-e-fy, change the form or external qualities of; to vary; to qualify; to change by umlaut [Gram.]: *v.i.* to undergo modification. (Fr. *modifier.*)
modillion, *n.* mo-*dil*-yon an ornamental bracket under the cornice of the Corinthian and composite order [Arch.]. (Fr.)
modiolar, *a.* mo-*dy*-o-lar, pertaining to the modiolus [Anat.].
modiolus, *n.* mo-*dy*-o-lus, the conical axial bone of the cochlea of the ear [Anat.]. (L.)
modish, *a.* *mode*-ish, fashionable.
modishly, *ad.* *mode*-ish-le, in a modish manner.
modishness, *n.* the state of being modish.
modiste, *n.* mo-*deest*, one who makes fashionable dresses; a dressmaker; a milliner. (Fr.)
Mods, *n.* modz, Moderations (at Oxford Univ.).
modulate, *v.t.* *mod*-yew-late, to adjust; to vary or inflect in tone; to change the key or mode: *v.i.* to pass from one key to another [Mus.]. (L. *modulatus.*)
modulation, *n.* mod-yew-*lay*-shon, act of modulating; state of being modulated; the change of one key into another.
modulator, *n.* *mod*-yew-lay-tor, he who or that which modulates; a chart to indicate the modulations in the tonic sol-fa system [Mus.].
module, *n.* *mod*-yewl, a standard of measurement, esp. a unit of proportion for regulating the dimensions of the various parts of a column [Arch.]. (Fr.)
modulus, *n.* *mod*-yew-lus, a constant factor in a function of a variable quantity [Math.]. (L.)
modus, *n.* *moh*-dus, a mode; a compensation in lieu of tithes. **modus operandi,** the way of working or manner of procedure. **modus vivendi,** manner of living; hence, compromise, or means of carrying on by temporary adjustment. (L.)
moellon, *n.* (App.), rough stones and mortar used as a filling in masonry. (Cr.)
Mœso-Gothic, *a.* *mee*-so-*goth*-ik, pertaining to the Goths of Mœsia, an ancient Roman province of the northern Balkans: *n.* their language.
mofette, *n.* mo-*fet*, a fissure in the earth's surface through which a noxious gas emanates; an exhalation of this nature. (It.)
moff, *n.* mof, a marking-off tool consisting of a combined compass and caliper. (Corruption of *hermaphrodite.*)
moff, *n.* mof, a silk stuff from Caucasia.
mofussil, *n.* mo-*fus*-il, the countryside as contrasted with the urban areas: *a.* provincial; rural. (Hind.)
mogigraphia, *n.* moj-e-*graf*-e-a, writers' cramp. (Gr. *mōgis*, with difficulty, *graphein*, to write.)
Mogul, *n.* mo-*gul*, a Mongol, esp. as one of the ruling race in India, 16th–18th cents. **the Great Mogul,** a sovereign of the Mogul Empire in India. (Pers. *Mugul*, Mongol.)
mohair, *n.* *moh*-hare, the hair of the Angora goat; cloth made of this; a wool and cotton imitation of this. (Ar.)
Mohammedan, *a.* mo-*ham*-e-dan, pertaining to Mohammed or Mohammedanism: *n.* a follower of Mohammed, the prophet of the Arabs (about 570–632); an adherent of Islam. **Mohammedan Era,** the era used in Mohammedan countries, dating from the Hegira (in A.D. 622). (Ar. *Muhammad*, the praised, from *hamad*, praise.)
Mohammedanism, *n.* mo-*ham*-e-dan-izm, Islam, the religion of Mohammed.
Mohawk, *n.* *moh*-hawk, a member of a N.-American Indian tribe formerly settled in the north of New York State; their language; a figure in skating; a Mohock: *a.* pertaining to the Mohawks or to their language.
Mohican, *n.* *moh*-e-kan, a member of a warlike group of small tribes of Algonquian Indians living east of New York State, now nearly extinct.
Mohock, *n.* *moh*-hok, one of a class of aristocratic rakes who infested the London streets in the 18th cent. (*Mohawk.*)
mohr, *n.* mohr, the swift gazelle of northern Africa, one of the largest of the gazelles. (Ar. *muhr.*)
mohur, *n.* *moo*-hur, a former gold coin of British India equivalent to 15 rupees. (Pers.)
moider, *v.t.* *moy*-der, to confuse; to bemuddle or bewilder: *v.i.* to ramble aimlessly; to talk foolishly. (Scots.)
moidore, *n.* moy-*dore*, a former gold coin of Portugal and Brazil, nominally valued at £1 7*s.* (Port., money of gold.)
moiety, *n.* *moy*-e-te, one of two equal parts; a half; a half share. (O.Fr. *moitié.*)
moil, *v.t.* moyl, to tire out; to weary; to make dirty: *v.i.* to toil amid dirt; to wallow; to drudge. (O.Fr. *moiller*, to wet.)
moiré, *a.* *mwah*-ray, having a watered appearance: *n.* watered or clouded silk; a watered or clouded appearance on metals or textures: *v.t.* to impart this appearance to. **moiré antique,** a species of figured silk. (Fr.)
moirette, *n.* mwah-*ret*, imitation moiré. (Fr.)
moist, *a.* moyst, moderately wet; damp; inclined to rain; discharging matter [Med.]. (O.Fr. *moiste.*)
moisten, *v.t.* and *i.* *moy*-sn, to make or become damp; to wet slightly.
moistener, *n.* *moy*-sn-er, that which moistens.

moistness, *n.* *moyst*-ness, dampness; humidity.
moisture, *n.* *moys*-tewr, diffused or condensed water in the atmosphere; a moderate degree of wetness.
moistureless, *a.* *moys*-tewr-less, arid; destitute of moisture.
moke, *n.* amoke, dolt; slang for a donkey [Engl.], a Negro [U.S.A.], or a broken-down horse [Austral.].
mol, *m.* mol, a gram-molecule [Chem.].
molar, *a.* *moh*-lar, pertaining to a mass. **molar volume,** the volume of one gram-molecule of a gas at normal temperature and pressure [Physics]. (L. *moles*, mass.)
molar, *a.* *moh*-lar, having power to grind; grinding: *n.* a grinding tooth. (L. *mola*, a mill.)
molarity, *n.* mo-*la*-re-te, molar concentration [Chem.].
molasse, *n.* mo-*lahs*, a greenish fossiliferous sandstone found in the Alps. (Fr.)
molasses, *n.* mo-*las*-sez, the dark-brown viscid syrup which drains from cane sugar; crude treacle. (Port. *melaço*.)
mold, *n.* mohld, mould.
mole, *n.* mole, a small dark-brown congenital spot on the human body, usually permanent and protuberant; a nævus; a blemish. (A.S. *mal*.)
mole, *n.* mole, a mound of large stones laid in the sea before a port for protection; a jetty serving as a breakwater. (Fr. *môle*.)
mole, *n.* mole, a small, soft-furred burrowing insectivore of the genus *Talpa*, esp. *T. europæa*; the grey colour of moleskin. (Perhaps A.S. *myl*, dust; not from *mouldwarp*.)
molecast, *n.* *mole*-kahst, a molehill.
mole-cricket, *n.* an insect of the genus *Gryllotalpa* which burrows underground.
molecular, *a.* mo-*lek*-yew-lar, pertaining to, consisting of, or existing between, molecules. **molecular weight,** the sum of the atomic weights of the elements composing a molecule [Chem.].
molecularity, *n.* mo-lek-yew-*la*-re-te, condition of being molecular.
molecule, *n.* *moh*-le-kewl, the smallest portion of a substance capable of independent existence while retaining the properties of that substance; a union of two or more atoms; a minute particle. (Fr. *molécule*.)
mole-eyed, *a.* having very small eyes or imperfect vision.
molehill, *n.* *mole*-hill, a little hillock thrown up by moles; in burrowing; a trumpery obstacle, objection, etc. [Bot.]. (L. *molendinium*, mill-house.)
mole-rat, *n.* the burrowing rodent, *Spalax typhlus*.
mole-shrew, *n.* any of several small insectivores allied to the desman [Zool.].
moleskin, *n.* *mole*-skin, the skin of the mole dressed for fur; a strong twilled cloth resembling this in colour and texture.
molest, *v.t.* mo-*lest*, to disturb; to annoy; to injure by interfering with. (Fr. *molester*.)
molestation, *n.* mol-es-*tay*-shon, act of molesting; state of being molested; annoyance.
molester, *n.* mo-*lest*-er, one who molests.
molimen, *n.* mo-*ly*-men, a physiological effort, as in motion of the bowels. (L.)
moline, *a.* *moh*-line, of the shape of a mill-rind, the end of which curves outwards in two branches: *n.* a mill-rind; a cross moline. **cross moline,** a cross each arm of which terminates in two curved branches. (O.Fr. *molin*, mill.)
Molinism, *n.* *mol*-in-izm, the teaching of Miguel de Molina (*d.* 1697), a Spanish Jesuit, that the efficacy of grace is dependent on voluntary acceptance; quietism.
Molinist, *n.* *mol*-in-ist, an adherent of Molinism.
Mollah, *n.* *mol*-lah, a Mullah.
mollifiable, *a.* *mol*-le-*fy*-a-bl, that may be softened or soothed.
mollification, *n.* *mol*-le-fe-*kay*-shon, the act of mollifying; mitigation.
mollifier, *n.* *mol*-le-fy-er, a softener; a mitigator.
mollify, *v.t.* *mol*-le-fy, to soften, assuage, or pacify; to appease. (Fr. *mollifier*.)
mollipilose, *a.* *mol*-e-*py*-lohs, having soft plumage; downy. (L. *mollis*, soft, *pilosus*, hairy.)
mollusc, *n.* *mol*-usk, one of the Mollusca. (L. *molluscus*, from *mollis*, soft.)
Mollusca, *n.pl.* mo-*lus*-ka, the division of soft-bodied invertebrates without segmentation which includes the snails and slugs, etc., cuttlefish, and all shellfish other than crustaceans. (L.)
molluscan, *a.* mo-*lus*-kan, pertaining to the Mollusca: *n.* a mollusc.
molluscoid, *a.* mo-*lus*-koyd, resembling a mollusc.
molluscum, *n.* mol-*lus*-kum, a chronic skin-disease with pulpy tumours [Path.].
molluscous, *a.* mo-*lus*-kus, molluscan; pertaining to molluscum [Path.].
molly, *n.* *mol*-le, a milksop; a man who does the housework; an effeminate man. (Form of *Mary*.)
molly-coddle, *n.* *mol*-e-kod-dl, an effeminate, pampered individual: *v.t.* and *i.* to pamper; to take excessive care of one's health.
mollymoke, *n.* *mol*-e-moke, the mallemuck.
Moloch, *n.* *moh*-lok, a Phœnician deity to whom children were sacrificed, their bodies being burnt; hence anything demanding unnatural rites or sacrifices; (*l.c.*) the Australian spiny lizard *Moloch horridus*. (Heb., king.)
molossus, *n.* mo-*los*-us, a foot of three syllables, each being long [Pros]. (Gr. *molossos*.)
molten, *a.* *mole*-tn, melted; made of melted metal.
molto, *ad.* *mol*-toh, much; very [Mus.]. (It.)
moly, *n.* *moh*-le, a fabulous herb given to Ulysses as a countercharm against the spells of Cire; a species of wild garlic. *Allium moly*. (Gr.)
molybdate, *n.* mo-*lib*-date, a salt of molybdic acid.
molybdenite, *n.* mo-*lib*-den-ite, disulphide of molybdenum, a valuable source of the metal.
molybdenous, *a.* mo-*lib*-den-us, pertaining to or containing molybdenum.
molybdenum, *n.* mo-*lib*-den-um, a metallic element physically similar to iron, and much used as a steel alloy and, as wire, in electrical equipment. (L. *molybdæna*, galena.)
molybdic, *a.* mo-*lib*-dik, pertaining to or obtained from molybdenum.
moment, *n.* *moh*-ment, the most minute part of time; instant. **moment of a force,** the measure of its power in causing rotation. **of moment,** of consequence or importance. (Fr.)
momental, *a.* mo-*men*-tal, pertaining to moment or momentum [Mech.].
momentarily, *ad.* *moh*-men-ta-re-le, for a moment; every moment.
momentary, *a.* *moh*-men-ta-re, done in a moment; instantaneous; lasting a very short time.
momently, *a.* *moh*-ment-le, at any moment; for a moment.
momentous, *a.* mo-*men*-tus, important; weighty. (L. *momentosus*.)
momentously, *ad.* mo-*men*-tus-le, in an important manner; weightily.
momentousness, *n.* mo-*men*-tus-ness, quality of being momentous; great importance.
momentum, *n.* mo-*men*-tum, impetus due to the mass of a body multiplied by the velocity of its motion. (L.)
Momus, *n.* *moh*-mus, the god of ridicule and censure [Myth.]; a carping or censorious person. (Gr.)
Monacan, *a.* and *n.* *mon*-a-kan, Monegasque.
monachal, *a.* *mon*-a-kal, pertaining to monks; monastic. (L. *monachus*, a monk.)
monachism, *n.* *mon*-a-kizm, monasticism; monastic life; monkery.
monad, *n.* *mon*-ad, a unit or atom [Phil.]; an elementary organism [Biol.]; a zoospore moving by means of flagella [Zool.]; an element which combines with only one equivalent of another [Chem.]. (Gr. *monas*, unity.)
monadelphian, *a.* mon-a-*del*-fe-an, having the filaments of the stamens united into a single tube [Bot.]. (Gr. *monos*, alone, *adelphos*, a brother.)
monadic, *a.* mo-*nad*-ik, of the nature of a monad.
monadical, *a.* mo-*nad*-e-kal, monadic.
monadism, *n.* *mon*-a-dizm, the doctrine of monads, esp. as expounded by Leibnitz [Phil.].
monal, *n.* mo-*nawl*, any of the brilliantly plumaged pheasants of the genus *Lophophorus*.
monandrian, *a.* mon-*an*-dre-an, having one stamen only. (Gr. *monos*, and *aner*, a male.)
monandrous, *a.* mon-*an*-drus, monandrian.
monandry, *n.* mon-*an*-dre, the condition of being monandrian [Bot.]; the custom of having one husband only at a time [Anthrop.]. (Gr. *monos*, and *aner*, a man.)
monanthous, *a.* mon-*an*-thus, one-flowered.
monarch, *n.* *mon*-ark, the supreme ruler (usually

hereditary) of a state; a king, queen, tsar, emperor, etc.; the chief of its class; a large black and red butterfly. (Fr. *monarque*, from L., from Gr. *monos*, alone, *archein*, to rule.)
monarchal, *a.* mon-*ar*-kal, pertaining to a monarch or to monarchy; sovereign; regal.
Monarchian, *n.* mo-*nar*-ke-an, a member of any of the heretical unitarian Christian sects of the 2nd and 3rd centuries: *a.* pertaining to these heretics or to their doctrine.
Monarchianism, *n.* mo-*nar*-ke-a-nizm, the heretical doctrines of the Monarchians.
monarchic, *a.* mo-*nar*-kik, monarchal; characteristic of a monarch; under, or vested in, a single ruler.
monarchism, *n.* *mon*-a-kizm, the principles of monarchy; a preference for monarchy.
monarchist, *n.* *mon*-a-kist, an advocate of monarchy.
monarchize, *v.i.* *mon*-a-kize, to play the king; *v.t.* to rule over, as a monarch.
monarchy, *n.* *mon*-a-ke, a government in which the supreme power is vested in a monarch; a kingdom; monarchic or supreme rule. (L. *monarchia*.)
monarticular, *a.* mon-ar-*tik*-yew-lar, pertaining to one joint only [Anat.].
monasterial, *a.* mon-as-*teer*-re-al, monastical.
monastery, *n.* *mon*-as-te-re, a house of religious retirement; the residence of a community of monks; a convent. (L. *monasterium*.)
monastic, *a.* mo-*nas*-tik, monastical: *n.* a monk.
monastical, *a.* mo-*nas*-te-kal, pertaining to monasteries, monks, and nuns; recluse. (Fr. *monastique*.)
monastically, *ad.* in a monastic manner.
monasticism, *n.* mo-*nas*-te-sizm, monastic life.
monasticize, *v.t.* mo-*nas*-te-size, to train in, or convert to, monastic rules of life.
monasticon, *n.* mo-*nas*-te-kon, a book on monasteries. (Gr.)
monatomic, *a.* *mon*-a-*tom*-ik, consisting of or saturating one atom; univalent.
monazite, *n.* *mon*-a-zite, a native phosphate of cerium in association with other rare earths, esp. thorium.
mondaine, *n.* *mon*-dane, a woman of fashion: *a.* worldly; clinging to material things.
Monday, *n.* *mun*-day, the second day of the week. (A.S. *monan dæg*, the moon-day.)
Mondayish, *a.* *mun*-day-ish, tired-out; slack, disinclined to work, as after a holiday.
monde, *n.* mond, society; the world of fashion; one's own circle. (Fr., world.)
Monegasque, *a.* mon-e-*gask*, pertaining to Monaco: *n.* native or inhabitant of Monaco. (Fr. *monégasque*.)
monel, *n.* moh-*nel*, an alloy of nickel and copper with small quantities of iron, manganese, silicon, and carbon, of high strength and tensility. (Name of inventor, *d.* 1921.)
monetary, *a.* *mun*-e-ta-re, of or relating to money or the coinage. **monetary unit,** the unit of measure of the value of the money of a state, as the pound sterling of Great Britain. (L. *monetarius*.)
monetization, *n.* mun-e-ty-*zay*-shon, assigning a standard value to a metal or a coinage.
monetize, *v.t.* *mun*-e-tize, to give a basic value to a metal currency; to coin bullion; to convert (tokens, etc.) into legal tender.
***money,** *n.* *mun*-e, any metal coin, usually gold, stamped and issued by public authority, used as the medium of exchange; bank-notes, bank bills, bills of credit, etc., legally representing coin; wealth. **money of account,** a denomination in which accounts are kept, representing or not actual coin, as the sovereign and guinea (Great Britain), the dollar and mill (U.S.A.). **money order,** a post-office order authorizing payment of a specified amount (not exceeding £50) to its lawful holder. (O.Fr. *moneie*.)
moneybox, *n.* *mun*-e-boks, a slotted receptacle for collecting or storing coin.
money-broker, *n.* a money-changer or -lender.
money-changer, *n.* a broker who deals in the exchange of currencies.
moneyed, *a.* *mun*-ed, rich in money; wealthy; derived from money.
moneyer, *n.* *mun*-e-er, an authorized coiner of money; a master of a mint.
money-grubber, *n.* a miserly person; one making money by doubtful practices.
moneylender, *n.* *mun*-e-lend-er, a person who lends money at interest.
moneylending, *n.* *mun*-e-*lend*-ing, a moneylender's occupation.
moneyless, *a.* *mun*-e-less, destitute of money.
money-making, *a.* engaged in acquiring money; profitable: *n.* the act or process of accumulating wealth.
money-market, *n.* the world of finance; the field of operation of those who deal in stocks, shares, etc.
money-matter, *n.* an affair concerned with money; *pl.* financial concerns.
money-spinner, *n.* the small spider, *Aranea scenica*, supposed to bode good luck; one who makes large sums of money by speculation.
money's-worth, *n.* something that will bring money; full value.
money-wort, *n.* *mun*-e-wurt, the plant creeping-jenny, *Lysimachia nummularia*. **Cornish money-wort,** the plant *Sibthorpia europæa*.
monger, *n.* *mung*-ger, a dealer, generally used in combination, as fishmonger, etc. (A.S. *mangere*.)
Mongol, *n.* *mong*-gol, a member of a tribe native to Mongolia, or of the Mongolian race; the language of the Mongols: *a.* Mongolian.
Mongolian, *n.* mong-*goh*-le-an, a Mongol; the Mongol language: *a.* of or pertaining to the Mongols or Mongolia, or to Mongolism. **Mongolian race,** the largest division of mankind, comprising the straight-haired, yellow-skinned Asiatics and their offshoots in N. and E. Europe with, probably, some Amerinds and Eskimos.
Mongolism, *n.* *mong*-go-lizm, a congenital condition in which the child has Mongolian physical characteristics and is usually mentally deficient [Med.].
Mongoloid, *a.* mong-go-*loyd*, belonging to the Mongolian race; having Mongolian characteristics.
mongoose, *n.* *mung*-goose, mungoose.
mongrel, *a.* *mung*-grel, of a mixed breed: *n.* anything of mixed breed, esp. a dog; a cur. (Perhaps A.S. *mengan*, to mix.)
mongrelize, *v.t.* *mung*-grel-ize, to render mongrel.
moniliform, *a.* mo-*nil*-e-form, shaped like a necklace. (L. *monile*, necklace, *forma*, shape.)
monism, *n.* *moh*-nizm, the doctrine that the whole universe and all its activities have developed from a single substance or principle connoting belief in the identity of matter and mind; any philosophic system opposed to dualism. (Gr. *monos*, single.)
monist, *n.* *moh*-nist, a believer in monism.
monistic, *a.* mo-*nis*-tik, pertaining to monism.
monition, *n.* mo-*nish*-on, admonition; warning; notice. (Fr.)
monitor, *n.* *mon*-e-tor, one who warns or admonishes; a senior pupil selected to superintend and sometimes instruct younger ones; a large lizard of the genus *Varanus*; a heavily-armed ironclad of shallow draught; a monitor-man [Cine.]; one whose business is monitoring, also, an electrical apparatus enabling this to be effected [Wire.]: *v.i.* to tap a circuit without disturbing the transmission [Elect.], esp. to tap and record radio communications or broadcasts. (L.)
monitorial, *a.* mon-e-*taw*-re-al, monitory; relating to school monitors.
monitorially, *ad.* mon-e-*taw*-re-a-le, by way of monition; in the manner of a school monitor.
monitor-man, *n.* an operator controlling the sound-recording currents [Cine.]
monitory, *a.* *mon*-e-to-re, giving admonition; warning: *n.* a letter containing admonition [Eccl.].
monitress, *n.* *mon*-e-tress, a girl monitor.
monk, *n.* munk, one who separates himself, singly or in community, from the world, and devotes himself to religion; a member of a religious order; a monkfish; an ink-stain in printing. **monk seal,** the seal *Monachus albiventer*, of the Mediterranean and Black Seas. (L. *monachus*, a monk.)
monkery, *n.* *mung*-ker-re, the life or principles of monks; monks collectively; monasticism (a term of contempt).
***monkey,** *n.* *mung*-ke, a mammal of the families between the apes and lemurs; a young imp or rogue (esp. as an affectionate term); the striker of a pile-driver; £500 [Racing slang]: *v.i.* to act the monkey; to ape or mimic. **to get one's monkey**

up, to excite him to wrath. **to monkey about with**, to play about with, esp. in a damaging way. (Possibly It. *monicchio*, from *monna*, an ape.)
monkey-block, *n.* a small single block strapped with a swivel [Naut.].
monkey-boat, *n.* a half-decked river boat.
monkey-bread, *n.* the fruit of the baobab.
monkey-engine, *n.* an engine for working the monkey in pile-driving.
monkey-flower, *n.* any plant of the genus *Mimulus*; also, the common toadflax.
monkey-gaff, *n.* a gaff working on a topmast.
monkeyism, *n.* *mung*-ke-izm, monkey-like character or behaviour; apishness.
monkey-jacket, *n.* a thick pea-jacket; a close-fitting jacket.
monkey-nut, *n.* the peanut.
monkey-pot, *n.* a S. American tree of the genus *Lecythis*, the empty fruit of which is used as a monkey-trap; this fruit.
monkey-puzzle, *n.* the coniferous tree, *Araucaria imbricata*.
monkey-rail, *n.* a light rail a short distance above the quarter-rail [Naut.].
monkey-rope, *n.* a rope by which a sailor is secured when working in dangerous places.
monkey-wrench, *n.* a wrench or spanner with an adjustable jaw.
monkfish, *n.* *munk*-fish, the angler, *Lophius piscatorius*, or the angel fish, *Rhina squatina*.
monkhood, *n.* *munk*-hood, the condition or character of a monk; monks collectively.
monkish, *a.* *mung*-kish, characteristic of a monk; monastic.
monkshood, *n.* *munks*-hood, aconite, so called from the shape of its flowers.
mono-, *comb.f.* *mon*-o-, with one only; single, alone. (Gr. *monos*.)
monobasic, *a.* mon-o-*bay*-sik, having only one hydrogen atom replaceable by a metal or basic radical, thereby forming a salt [Chem.]. (Gr. *monos*, and *basic*.)
monoblepsia, *n.* *mon*-o-*blep*-se-a, a condition in which vision is normal only when a single eye is used. (Gr. *monos*, and *blepsis*, vision.)
monocardian, *a.* mon-o-*kar*-de-an, having a heart with a single auricle and ventricle. (Gr. *monos*, and *kardia*, the heart.)
monocarp, *n.* *mon*-o-karp, an annual plant, or one which perishes after it has once borne fruit. (Gr. *monos*, and *karpos*, fruit.)
monocarpic, *a.* mon-o-*kar*-pik, bearing fruit but once [Bot.].
monocarpous, *a.* mon-o-*kar*-pus, having or consisting of a single carpel; monocarpic [Bot.].
monocephalous, *a.* mon-o-*sef*-a-lus, having a single head of flowers [Bot.]. (Gr. *monos*, and *kephale*, the head.)
monoceros, *n.* mo-*nos*-er-ros, a one-horned animal; the unicorn. (Gr. *monos*, and *keras*, a horn.)
monochlamydeous, *a.* *mon*-o-kla-*mid*-e-us, having a perianth with only one whorl [Bot.]. (Gr. *monos*, and *chlamys*, a cloak.)
monochord, *n.* *mon*-o-kord, a musical instrument of one string; an apparatus to exhibit the mathematical proportions of musical intervals. (Gr. *monokordon*.)
monochromatic, *a.* mon-o-kro-*mat*-ik, of only one colour; in monochrome. (L. *monochromatos*.)
monochromatism, *n.* mon-o-*kroh*-ma-tizm, total colour-blindness.
monochrome, *n.* *mon*-o-krome, an illustration, painting, etc., in a single colour. (Gr. *monochromos*, one colour.)
monocle, *n.* *mon*-o-kl, an eye-glass for one eye. (Fr.)
monoclinal, *a.* mon-o-*kly*-nal, sloping in one direction [Geol.]. (Gr. *monos*, and *klino*, bend.)
monocline, *n.* *mon*-o-kline, a monoclinal fold [Geol.].
monoclinic, *a.* mon-o-*klin*-ik, having three axes, two of which are perpendicular to the third though oblique to each other (of crystals).
monoclinous, *a.* mon-o-*kly*-nus, having stamens and carpels in the same flower [Bot.]; monoclinal [Geol.].
monocoque, *n.* *mon*-o-koke, a type of body construction in which structural stresses are taken chiefly by the skin [Av.]. (Gr. *monos*, sole, Fr. *coque*, shell.)
monocotyledon, *n.* *mon*-o-kot-e-*lee*-don, any plant having a single cotyledon or seed-leaf [Bot.]. (Gr. *monos*, and *cotyledon*.)
monocotyledonous, *a.* *mon*-o-kot-e-*lee*-do-nus, having only one cotyledon.
monocracy, *n.* mo-*nok*-ra-se, government by a single person. (Gr. *monos*, and *krateo*, govern.)
monocrat, *n.* *mon*-o-krat, an absolute ruler; an adherent of monocracy.
monocratic, *a.* mon-o-*krat*-ik, pertaining to monocracy.
monocular, *a.* mo-*nok*-yew-lar, with one eye only; for the use of one eye only. (L. *monoculus*.)
monodactylous, *a.* mon-o-*dak*-til-us, having only one finger, toe, or claw. (Gr. *monos*, and *dactylos*, a finger.)
monodic, *a.* mo-*nod*-ik, pertaining to or resembling a monody.
monodist, *n.* *mon*-o-dist, one who writes, sings, or composes monodies.
monodrama, *n.* *mon*-o-drah-ma, a dramatic performance by a single person.
monodramatic, *a.* mon-o-dra-*mat*-ik, pertaining to a monodrama.
monody, *n.* *mon*-o-de, a mournful ode or song for recitation or singing by one person only. (Gr. *monodia*.)
monœcious, *a.* mo-*nee*-shus, having the stamens and pistils in separate flowers of the same plant [Bot.]; hermaphrodite [Zool.]. (Gr. *monos*, and *oikos*, a house.)
monogamist, *n.* mo-*nog*-a-mist, a man with one wife; one who disapproves of second marriages.
monogamous, *a.* mo-*nog*-a-mus, having one wife only; mating with one only [Zool.].
monogamy, *n.* mo-*nog*-a-me, the practice of having but a single spouse, esp. of not remarrying; pairing with one mate only [Zool.]. (Gr. *monogamia*.)
monogenesis, *n.* mon-o-*jen*-e-sis, the theory that all living things have their derivation from a single cell [Biol.]; monogony. (Gr. *monos*, and *genesis*.)
monogenetic, *a.* mon-o-je-*net*-ik, relating to monogenesis [Biol.]; producing but one colour (of dye-stuffs).
monoglot, *a.* *mon*-o-glot, using, knowing, or written in a single language.
monogony, *n.* mo-*nog*-o-ne, non-sexual reproduction or propagation.
monogram, *n.* *mon*-o-gram, a character or cipher composed of two or more letters interwoven. (L. *monogramma*.)
monogrammatic, *a.* *mon*-o-gra-*mat*-ik, pertaining to or of the nature of a monogram.
monograph, *n.* *mon*-o-graf, a treatise on a special limited subject. (Gr. *monos*, and *grapho*, write.)
monographer, *n.* mo-*nog*-ra-fer, a writer of a monograph.
monographic, *a.* mon-o-*graf*-ik, pertaining to a monograph.
monographist, *n.* mo-*nog*-ra-fist, a monographer.
monogynian, *a.* mon-o-*jin*-e-an, having only one pistil [Bot.]. (Gr. *monos*, and *gyne*, a female.)
monogynous, *a.* mo-*noj*-e-nus, having but one wife; monogynian [Bot.]; mating with but one female [Zool.].
monogyny, *n.* mo-*noj*-e-ne, marriage to one wife only; state of being monogynous. (Gr. *monos*, and *gyne*, a woman.)
monolith, *n.* *mon*-o-lith, a monument, etc., consisting of a single stone. (L. *monolithus*.)
monolithic, *a.* mon-o-*lith*-ik, consisting of a single stone or of monoliths.
monolocular, *a.* mon-o-*lok*-yew-lar, having but one cell [Biol. etc.].
monologist, *n.* mo-*nol*-o-jist, one who soliloquizes; one who monopolizes the conversation.
monologue, *n.* *mon*-o-log, a soliloquy; a literary or dramatic composition for a single performer. (Fr.)
monologuist, *n.* mo-*nol*-o-gist, one who performs in or delivers monologues; one given to soliloquy.
monology, *n.* mo-*nol*-o-je, the habit of talking to oneself.
monomachy, *n.* mo-*nom*-a-ke, single combat. (Gr.)
monomania, *n.* mon-o-*may*-ne-a, mental derangement with regard to a particular subject. (Gr. *monos*, and *mania*.)

monomaniac, *a.* mon-o-*may*-ne-ak, affected by monomania : *n.* a person affected by monomania.
monomark, *n.* *mon*-o-mark, proprietary name of a combination of letters and figures registered with the proprietors as an identification mark of a particular individual.
monomerous, *a.* mo-*nom*-er-rus, having a single member in each whorl [Bot.]; single-jointed [Entom.].
monometallic, *a.* mon-o-me-*tal*-ik, using, or pertaining to the use of, a single metal for currency purposes.
monometallism, *n.* mon-o-*met*-al-izm, the system or practice of basing the currency of a state on a single metal as the unit of value.
monometallist, *n.* mon-o-*met*-al-ist, an advocate of monometallism.
monometer, *n.* mo-*nom*-e-ter, a rhythmical series of a single metre. (Gr. *monos*, and *metron*, measure.)
monometric, *a.* mon-o-*met*-rik, written in monometer; isometric [Min.].
monomial, *n.* mo-*noh*-me-al, a quantity expressed by one term only [Alg.]: *a.* consisting of a single term [Alg.]. (Gr. *monos*, and *onyma*, a name.)
monomineralic, *a.* *mon*-o-min-er-*ral*-ik, consisting essentially of but one mineral (of certain rocks) [Geol.].
monomorphic, *a.* mon-o-*mor*-fik, unchanging in structure or form, esp. [Zool.] through successive stages of development.
monopathic, *a.* mon-o-*path*-ik, affecting only one organ or function [Med.].
monopathy, *n.* mo-*nop*-a-the, disease or derangement in only one organ or function [Med.]. (Gr. *monos*, and *pathos*, suffering.)
monopetalous, *a.* mon-o-*pet*-a-lus, having the corolla undivided into petals [Bot.]. (Gr. *monos*, and *petalon*, a petal.)
monophagous, *a.* mo-*nof*-a-gus, subsisting on one kind of food only [Zool.].
monophobia, *n.* mon-o-*foh*-be-a, morbid dread of being alone.
monophthong, *n.* *mon*-of-thong, a single vowel sound. (Gr. *monos*, and *phthongos*, sound.)
monophyllous, *a.* mon-o-*fil*-lus, consisting of a single leaf. (Gr. *monos*, and *phyllon*, a leaf.)
Monophysite, *n.* mo-*nof*-e-site, one of an Eastern Christian sect maintaining that in the person of Christ was only a single nature in which the human and divine were fused. (Gr. *monos*, and *physis*, nature.)
Monophysitism, *n.* mo-*nof*-e-se-tizm, the doctrine of the Monophysites.
monoplane, *n.* *mon*-o-plane, an aircraft with one sustaining surface.
monoplegia, *n.* mon-o-*plee*-je-a, paralysis affecting only one part, limb, or organ [Med.].
monopodial, *a.* *mon*-o-*poh*-de-al, pertaining to a monopodium.
monopodium, *n.* mon-o-*poh*-de-um, a form of branching in which the branches are developed laterally in succession below the apex of the growing point of the stem [Bot.].
monopolism, mo-*nop*-o-lizm, the monopolistic system or policy; the practices of monopolists.
monopolist, *n.* mo-*nop*-o-list, one who monopolizes or has a monopoly: *a.* monopolistic.
monopolistic, *a.* mo-nop-o-*lis*-tik, connected with or characteristic of monopolies.
monopolization, *n.* mo-*nop*-o-ly-*zay*-shon, the act of monopolizing.
monopolize, *v.t.* mo-*nop*-o-lize, to purchase or obtain the monopoly of; to engross the whole of.
monopolizer, *n.* mo-*nop*-o-ly-zer, a monopolist.
monopoly, *n.* mo-*nop*-o-le, the sole power of dealing in anything; exclusive possession; state charter or licence to exclusive trade in an article; privilege given by patents and copyrights; a commodity covered by, and a party or company, etc., holding, a monopoly. (L. *monopolium*.)
monopolylogue, *n.* *mon*-o-*pol*-e-log, an entertainment in which one performer plays all the parts.
monopteral, *a.* mo-*nop*-te-ral, of the nature of a monopteron [Arch.]; having but one wing or fin [Zool.].
monopteron, *n.* mo-*nop*-te-ron, an open or circular shrine or temple, surmounted by a dome supported on one circle of columns. (Gr. *monos*, and *pteron*, a wing.)
monorail, *n.* *mon*-o-rale, a single rail on which balanced cars are run.
monorganic, *a.* *mon*-or-*gan*-ik, affecting one organ or set of organs only [Med.].
monorhyme, *n.* *mon*-o-rime, a composition in which all the lines end with the same rhyme: *a.* having only one rhyme.
monosepalous, *a.* mon-o-*sep*-a-lus, having a single sepal [Bot.].
monospermous, *a.* mon-o-*sper*-mus, single-seeded [Bot.]. (Gr. *monos*, and *sperma*, seed.)
monostich, *n.* *mon*-o-stik, a composition of one verse. (Gr. *monos*, and *stichos*, a verse.)
monostichous, *a.* mo-*nos*-te-kus, consisting of or arranged in a single row on one side of the axis [Bot.]
monostrophic, *a.* mon-o-*strof*-ik, having one strophe only. (Gr. *monos*, and *strophe*.)
monostyle, *a.* *mon*-o-stile, of one shaft [Arch.]; of the same style throughout [Arch.]. (Gr. *monos*, and *style*.)
monosyllabic, *a.* *mon*-o-sil-*lab*-ik, composed of, or speaking in words of, only one syllable.
monosyllable, *n.* mon-o-*sil*-la-bl, a word of one syllable. (L. *monosyllabus*.)
monothalamous, *a.* mon-o-*thal*-a-mus, one-chambered [Conch. and Entom.]. (Gr. *monos*, and *thalamos*, a chamber.)
monotheism, *n.* *mon*-o-*thee*-izm, the doctrine that there is only one God. (Gr. *monos*, and *theos*, god.)
monotheist, *n.* *mon*-o-thee-ist, an adherent of monotheism.
monotheistic, *a.* mon-o-thee-*is*-tik, pertaining to monotheism.
Monothelete, *n.* mo-*noth*-e-leet, one of an Eastern 7th-cent. sect maintaining that Christ had one will only. (Gr. *monos*, and *thelein*, to will.)
monotint, *n.* *mon*-o-tint, a picture painted or reproduced in a single colour only.
monotomous, *a.* mo-*not*-o-mus, having cleavage distinct in only one direction [Min.]. (Gr. *monos*, and *tome*, cutting.)
monotone, *n.* *mon*-o-tone, a succession of sounds on the same pitch; unvaried tone; monotony; a monotint: *v.t.* and *i.* to intone on a single note; to utter or sing without change of tone. (Gr. *monotonos*.)
monotonic, *a.* mon-o-*ton*-ik, uttered in a monotone; having but a single tone [Mus.].
monotonous, *a.* mo-*not*-o-nus, continued in one tone; tedious; with dull uniformity.
monotonously, *ad.* with one uniform tone.
monotonousness, *n.* quality of being monotonous.
monotony, *n.* mo-*not*-o-ne, a dull uniformity of tone or sound; an irksome sameness or want of variety.
monotrematous, *a.* mon-o-*trem*-a-tus, belonging to or characteristic of the monotremes.
monotreme, *n.* *mon*-o-treem, one of the Monotremata, the lowest sub-class of mammals comprising the Ornithorhynchidæ and Echidnidæ, which lay eggs and have a single external opening for reproductive organs and the excretions. (Gr. *monos*, and *trema*, a perforation.)
monotriglyph, *n.* *mon*-o-*trig*-lif, an intercolumniation of only one triglyph and two metopes [Arch.]. (Gr. *monos*, and *triglyph*.)
monotropic, *a.* mon-o-*trop*-ik, existing in only one stable physical form [Chem.].
monotype, *n.* *mon*-o-tipe, proprietary name of a combined key-board type-setting machine and a machine casting individual types [Print.]; the only representative of its kind [Nat. Hist.]. (Gr. *monos*, and *typos*.)
monotypic, *a.* mon-o-*tip*-ik, of or pertaining to a genus having only one species.
monovalent, *a.* mon-o-*vay*-lent, univalent.
monoxenous, *a.* mo-*nok*-se-nus, remaining with one host only (of parasites) [Biol.]. (Gr. *monos*, and *xenos*, stranger.)
monoxide, *n.* mon-*ok*-side, an oxide containing one atom of oxygen in the molecule.
Monroeism, *n.* *mun*-ro-izm, the doctrine first formulated (1823) by Pres. Monroe, U.S.A., that America should not entangle itself with the affairs of the Old World, that there should be no addition to European possessions in the Americas, nor interference in the concerns of their independent governments.
Monseigneur, *n.* (App.), a title given to the high

dignitaries of France before the Revolution; a cardinal's title of address. (Fr., my lord.)

Monsieur, *n.* (App.) (*pl.* **Messieurs**), Sir; **Mr.**; a Frenchman. (Fr.)

Monsignor, *n.* (App.), my lord; the courtesy title of a Roman Catholic prelate. (It.)

monsoon, *n.* mon-*soon*, a periodical wind of southern Asia and the Indian Ocean, blowing from S.W. from April to October, and from N.E. from October to April; a similar wind. (It. *monsone.*)

monster, *n.* *mon*-ster, a monstrosity; an actual or fabulous unnatural production; a teratism; an animal or object of abnormal size; something greatly deformed; a person unnaturally wicked or vicious: *a.* very large. (Fr. *monstre.*)

monstrance, *n.* *mon*-strance, in the Roman Church, a transparent pyx containing the consecrated wafer, carried in procession or exposed on the altar. (O.Fr.)

monstrosity, *n.* mon-*stros*-e-te, the state or quality of being monstrous; an unnatural production or formation; a teratism. (Fr. *monstruosité.*)

monstrous, *a.* *mon*-strus, unnatural in form; enormous; horrible. (Fr. *monstrueux.*)

monstrously, *ad.* *mon*-strus-le, hideously; horribly.

monstrousness, *n.* state of being monstrous.

montage, *n.* mon-*tahzh*, the final result of the selection and arrangement of a series of photographs for a film, as shown on the screen [Cine.]. (Fr., mounting.)

montane, *a.* mon-*tane*, pertaining to mountains; living among mountains [Nat. Hist.].

Montanism, *n.* *mon*-tan-izm, the tenets of the followers of Montanus, a millenarian 2nd-cent. heretic of Phrygia.

montbretia, *n.* mon-*breesh*-ya, a garden plant of the iris family. (From Coquebert de *Montbret*, *d.* 1801, Fr. botanist.)

monte, *n.* *mon*-te, or **monte bank,** a variation of faro played with a pack omitting the 8's, 9's, and 10's. (Sp.)

monteith, *n.* mon-*teeth*, a vessel in which wine-glasses are cooled or punch is served. (Inventor's name.)

Montem, *n.* *mon*-tem, an obsolete custom among the boys at Eton of going on Whit-Tuesday, every third year, to a neighbouring hillock to collect money from passers-by for the university expenses of the senior scholar. (L. *ad montem*, to the hill.)

Montenegrin, *a.* mon-te-*nee*-grin, relating or belonging to Montenegro: *n.* a native of Montenegro, now a federative unit of Yugoslavia.

montero, *n.* mon-*teer*-ro, a cap formerly worn by huntsmen. (Sp.)

Montessorian, *a.* mon-te-*saw*-re-an, pertaining to a form of infant education devised about 1900–1910 by Dr. Maria Montessori, of which the basic principles are " free discipline " and self-education.

***month,** *n.* munth, a period comprising approximately one-twelfth of the year, called the **calendar month**; the period of one revolution of the moon, called a **lunar month,** approximately 29½ days; four weeks. **month of Sundays,** a long but indefinite time [Coll.]. (A.S. *monath.*)

monthling, *n.* *munth*-ling, an animal at the age of one month.

monthly, *a.* *munth*-le, continued for or performed in a month; relating to the menses [Med.]: *n.* a publication appearing once a month: *ad.* in every month. **monthly nurse,** an attendant on women during and after confinement.

monticle, *n.* *mon*-te-kl, a little mount; a hillock; a small volcanic cone. (L. *monticulus.*)

monticule, *n.* *mon*-te-kewl, a monticle.

monticulose, *a.* mon-*tik*-yew-lohs, having many small projections [Anat. and Zool.].

montoir, *n.* *mon*-twawr, horse-block. (Fr.)

monture, *n.* *mon*-tewr, a setting or mounting, esp. of a gem. (Fr.)

monument, *n.* *mon*-yew-ment, anything by which the memory of a person, event, etc., is preserved or perpetuated; a permanent structure serving as a memorial; a permanent example of record. (Fr.)

monumental, *a.* mon-yew-*men*-tal, serving as, or of the nature of, a monument.

monumentally, *ad.* by way of memorial.

moo, *n.* moo, the call of a cow: *v.i.* to call like a cow; to low. (Imit.)

mooch, *v.i.* mootch, to dally or loiter: *n.* a spell of loitering about. [Slang.]

moocher, *n.* mootch-er, one who mooches; a loafer.

mood, *n.* mood, a variation of form in a verb to express the manner in which the action or fact denoted is conceived in connexion with the subject [Gram.]: the form of a syllogism as regards the quantity and quality of its propositions when arranged in the first figure [Logic]; mode [Mus.]. (*mode.*)

mood, *n.* mood, temper of mind; humour or disposition. (A.S. *mod*, mind, feeling.)

moodily, *ad.* *moo*-de-le, in a moody manner.

moodiness, *n.* quality or state of being moody.

moody, *a.* *moo*-de, indulging in moods or fits of temper; out of humour; angry; fretful; sullen; gloomy.

Moolvie, *n.* *mool*-ve, a Mullah; any learned Mohammedan. (Urdu, from Ar. *maula.*)

***moon,** *n.* moon, the satellite which revolves round the earth; the satellite of a planet; a month; a moon-shaped object: *v.i.* to day-dream; to wander aimlessly. The moon is said to be **new** when visible through being in conjunction with the sun, and **full** when the earth is between her and the sun and her face is fully illuminated. **moon year,** the lunar year. (A.S. *mona.*)

moonbeam, *n.* *moon*-beam, a ray of light from the moon.

mooncalf, *n.* *moon*-kahf, a monstrosity; a congenital idiot; a stupid fellow.

moon-daisy, *n.* the ox-eye daisy.

moondog, *n.* *moon*-dog, a paraselene.

mooneye, *n.* *moon*-eye, a large-eyed North American lake fish of the genus *Hiodon.*

moonface, *n.* *moon*-face, a face round and full.

moonfish, *n.* *moon*-fish, name given to several fish with the tail-fin shaped like a half-moon, and to others with broad and compressed bodies.

moonflower, *n.* *moon*-flou-er, the moon-daisy, climbing plants of the genus *Ipomœa*, the wood-anemone, the S. African tree *Datura arborea*, and other plants.

moonish, *a.* *moon*-ish, like the moon; changeable; fickle.

moonless, *a.* *moon*-less, not favoured with moonlight.

moonlet, *n.* *moon*-let, a small moon.

moonlight, *a.* *moon*-lite, illuminated by the moon: *n.* the light afforded by the moon. **moonlight flit,** the clandestine removal of household goods with intent to avoid paying rent.

moonlighter, *n.* *moon*-lite-er, one who engaged in moonlighting, esp. a member of a secret society for that purpose.

moonlighting, *n.* *moon*-lite-ing, the perpetration of outrages, raids, etc., by night, esp. of agrarian crimes in Ireland about the 1880's.

moonlit, *a.* *moon*-lit, lighted or irradiated by the moon.

moonraker, *n.* *moon*-rake-er, a bumpkin [Coll.]; a sail above a skysail [Naut.].

moonseed, *n.* *moon*-seed, any climbing plant of the genus *Menispermum.* (Named from its crescent-shaped seed.)

moonshee, *n.* *moon*-shee, a munshi. (Ar.)

moonshine, *n.* *moon*-shine, the light of the moon; anything visionary or without reality; nonsense; smuggled or illicit spirits [Slang].

moonshiner, *n.* *moon*-shine-er, a rum-runner, or illicit distiller [U.S.A. Slang].

moonshiny, *a.* *moon*-shine-e, moonlit; visionary; unreal.

moonstone, *n.* *moon*-stone, an opalescent or translucent variety of felspar.

moonstruck, *a.* *moon*-struk, mentally affected by the supposed influence of the moon; lunatic.

moon-trefoil, *n.* an evergreen shrub, *Medicago arborea*, of Southern Europe.

moonwort, *n.* *moon*-wurt, the fern *Botrychium lunaria.* **blue moonwort,** *Soldanella Alpina*, of the family Primulaceæ.

moony, *a.* *moon*-e, crescent-shaped; resembling moonlight; moonstruck; dreamy; insane.

moor, *n.* moor, an extensive barren waste, covered with heath, and sometimes marshy. (A.S. *mor.*)

Moor, *n.* moor, a native of Morocco; one of a mixed Arab and Berber race living in N.W. Africa. (Fr. *More.*)

moor, *v.t.* moor, to secure, as a ship, with anchors or cables, etc.: *v.i.* to anchor. (Origin doubtful.)

moorage, *n.* *moor*-raj, a place for mooring; the charge payable for mooring.
moorberry, *n.* *moor*-be-re, the cranberry.
moor-buzzard, *n.* the marsh harrier.
moorcock, *n.* *moor*-kok, the male of the red grouse.
moorfowl, *n.* *moor*-foul, the red grouse.
moor-game, *n.* grouse, red or black.
moor-grass, *n.* any grass common on moors; the sundew; the blue grass, *Sesleria cœrulea.*
moor-hawk, *n.* the marsh harrier.
moorhen, *n.* *moor*-hen, the small coot-like bird, *Gallinula chloropus*: the female of the red grouse.
mooring, *n.* *moor*-ing, a fastening to keep a ship in a given position: *n.pl.* the anchors, chains, and bridles laid athwart the bottom of a river or harbour for mooring ships; place of mooring. **mooring-mast,** *n.* the mast or tower to which an airship is secured.
moorish, *a.* *moor*-ish, of the nature of a moor.
Moorish, *a.* moor-ish, pertaining to the Moors; in the style of the Moors [Arch., etc.].
moorland, *n.* *moor*-land, land with much heather; heathland; peaty soil: *a.* pertaining to or inhabiting moors.
moorstone, *n.* *moor*-stone, a species of granite found in Cornwall and other parts of England.
moor-tit, *n.* the stonechat; the meadow pipit.
mooruk, *n.* *moor*-ruk, the cassowary, *Casuarius bennetti,* peculiar to New Britain.
moorwort, *n.* *moor*-wurt, the marsh plant, *Andromeda polifolia.*
moory, *a.* *moor*-e, marshy; fenny; boggy; of the nature of a moor.
moose, *n.* moos, the North American elk, *Alces Americana,* the largest of the deer. (Algonquian.)
moot, *n.* moot, a meeting of freemen: *a.* reserved for discussion; subject to argument: *v.t.* to raise for discussion; a law-students' debate upon a supposed case: *v.i.* to argue or plead on a supposed cause. **moot case** or **point,** a case or point to be debated; an unsettled question. (A.S. *mot,* a meeting.)
mootable, *a.* *moot*-a-bl, capable of being debated.
moot-court, *n.* a meeting held for the purpose of discussing points of law or supposed cases.
mooter, *n.* *moot*-er, one who argues at a moot.
moot-hall, *n.* a hall of judgment, or for holding moots.
mop, *n.* mop, a grin or grimace: *v.i.* to grimace.
mop, *n.* mop, a collection of thrums or rags fastened to a handle, and used for cleaning floors, washing dishes, etc.; a tangled mass of hair; a mop-fair: *v.t.* to rub or wipe with or as with a mop. (Fr. *moppe,* napkin.)
mope, *n.* mope, a dull or low-spirited person: *v.i.* to pine; to be dull or spiritless. (Perhaps Dut. *moppen,* to be sulky.)
mope-eyed, *a.* short-sighted; purblind.
mop-fair, *n.* an annual statute fair formerly attended by disengaged servants wishing to be hired.
mopish, *a.* *mope*-ish, dull; spiritless; gloomy.
mopishly, *ad.* *mope*-ish-le, in a mopish manner.
mopishness, *n.* dejection; dullness; stupidity.
mopoke, *n.* mo-*poke,* name of various Australasian nightjars and owls. (From their cry.)
moppet, *n.* *mop*-pet, a rag doll; a darling; a pet name for a girl.
mopsy, *n.* *mop*-se, a dowdy or slatternly woman [Slang].
mopus, *n.* *moh*-pus, a small coin; money [Slang].
moquette, *n.* mo-*ket,* a carpet fabric of fine quality with short velvety pile. (Fr.)
mora, *n.* *maw*-ra, a tree of tropical S. America, *Dimorphandra mora*; its valuable timber, used in shipbuilding and for wharves, etc. (Port.)
mora, *n.* *maw*-ra, an ancient game in which the correct number of fingers held up is to be guessed. (It.)
moraine, *n.* mo-*rane,* accumulated stones and other debris at the foot, along the edges, or down the middle of glaciers. (Fr.)
moral, *a.* *mo*-ral, relating to manners or conduct; agreeable to what is right; capable of right or wrong; subject to the moral law; virtuous; just; sufficient for practical purposes [Coll.]: *n.* the practical lesson taught by a fable or gained through an incident, etc.; (*pronounced* mo-*rahl*) morale: *pl.* the doctrine or practice of the duties of life; moral behaviour, esp. in matters of sex; moral philosophy. **moral law,** the law which prescribes the moral or social duties. **moral philosophy,** ethics, the science which treats of moral duties and social relations. **moral pressure,** pressure which influences the conduct of persons by means of the moral sense. **moral victory,** a result which is claimed as a victory on account of its moral effects. (Fr.)
morale, *n.* mo-*rahl,* mental or moral condition or disposition, esp. in a crisis and as affecting self-confidence. (Fr.)
moralism, *n.* *mo*-ra-lizm, moral teaching; morality considered apart from religious implications.
moralist, *n.* *mo*-ra-list, a writer on or student of ethics; one practising the moral virtues.
moralistic, *a.* mo-ra-*lis*-tik, pertaining to or characterized by moralism.
morality, *n.* mo-*ral*-e-te, the doctrine or the practice of moral duties; ethics; virtue; moral quality; a play in which the characters personify virtues and vices. (O.Fr. *moralité.*)
moralization, *n.* *mo*-ra-ly-*zay*-shon, moral reflection.
moralize, *v.t.* *mo*-ra-lize, to explain or apply in a moral sense: to draw a moral from; to render moral: *v.i.* to make moral reflections.
moralizer, *n.* *mo*-ra-ly-zer, one who moralizes.
morally, *ad.* *mo*-ra-le, in a moral or ethical sense; agreeably to moral rule; in a practical or empirical point of view.
morass, *n.* mo-*rass,* a marsh; a swamp. (Dut. *moeras.*)
morat, *n.* *maw*-rat, a former drink made of mixed honey and mulberry juice.
moratorium, *n.* *mo*-ra-*taw*-re-um, a period of temporary legal suspension or deferment of payments due. (L.)
moratory, *a.* *mo*-ra-to-re, pertaining to a moratorium, or to delay of any kind.
Moravian, *n.* mo-*ray*-ve-an, one of the United Brethren, a religious society originated by the Hussites of Moravia about 1450 and re-formed in Saxony about 1727; a Herrnhuter: *a.* pertaining to this sect, or to Moravia or its people.
moray, *n.* mo-*ray,* any eel of the genus *Murena* [U.S.A.].
morbid, *a.* *mor*-bid, sickly; unhealthy; characteristic of, or connected with, disease. **morbid anatomy,** the study of diseased structures. (Fr. *morbide.*)
morbidezza, *n.* mor-be-*det*-sa, a soft, delicate flesh-colouring [Paint.]. (It.)
morbidity, *n.* mor-*bid*-e-te, condition of ill-health; rate of disease [Statistics]; morbidness.
morbidly, *ad.* *mor*-bid-le, in a morbid manner.
morbidness, *n.* a state of being morbid.
morbific, *a.* mor-*bif*-ik, causing or tending to cause disease or a morbid state. (L. *morbifre,* that brings disease.)
morceau, *n.* *mor*-so, a bit; a morsel; a small piece [Mus., etc.]. (Fr.)
morcellation, *n.* mor-sel-*lay*-shon, the act of dividing, esp. [Surg.] the removal of a diseased part in fragments. (O.Fr. *morcel,* a morsel.)
morcellement, *n.* (App.), division of lands or estates into small portions. (Fr.)
mordacious, *a.* mor-*day*-shus, biting; given to biting; bitterly sarcastic. (L. *mordax,* biting.)
mordaciously, *ad.* in a very sarcastic manner.
mordacity, *n.* mor-*das*-e-te, the quality or state of being mordacious. (Fr. *mordacité.*)
mordancy, *n.* *mor*-dan-se, mordacity.
mordant, *a.* *mor*-dant, mordacious; caustic; acting as a mordant: *n.* a corrosive, esp. as used in etching; a substance having a chemical affinity for colouring matter and serving to fix dyes; a glue to make gold-leaf adhere. (Fr.)
mordantly, *ad.* *mor*-dant-le, in a mordant manner.
mordent, *n.* *mor*-dent, a short trill made by the rapid alternation of a note with the one half a tone below it [Mus.]. (Ger.)
mordicate, *v.t.* *mor*-de-kate, to corrode; to give pain to by biting.
more, *a.* mor, greater in quality, degree, amount, or number; added to some former number; additional; further: *ad.* in or to a greater degree; again: *n.* a greater quantity, amount, or number; something in addition. **more and more,** with

continual increase. **more or less,** to an undetermined extent. **much more,** in a greater degree. **no more,** no longer existing. (A.S. *mara.*)
moreen, *n.* mo-*reen,* a coarse woollen fabric, frequently watered. (Fr. *moire,* or from *mohair.*)
moreish, *a. more*-rish, creating appetite for more [Coll.].
morel, *n.* mo-*rel,* an edible fungus of the genus *Morchella*; the latticed mushroom. (Fr.)
morel, *n.* mo-*rel,* any of the nightshades, esp. the black, *Solanum nigrum.*
morelles, *n.* mo-*relz,* the old game of nine men's morris (*see* **morris**). (Origin unknown.)
morello, *n.* mo-*rel*-lo, a variety of sour cherry.
moreover, *ad.* more-*oh*-ver, beyond what has been said; besides.
morepork, *n.* more-*pork,* mopoke.
Moresque, *a.* mo-*resk,* Moorish: *n.* a Moorish or arabesque style of decoration. (It. *moresco.*)
morganatic, *a.* mor-ga-*nat*-ik, pertaining to or designating a marriage formerly contracted between princes (esp. in Germany) and ladies of inferior rank, in which neither the wife nor her children shared in the princely status, property, or succession; a left-handed marriage. (Ger. *morgengabe,* morning gift, *i.e.* that given to a wife on the morning after such a marriage.)
morgay, *n. mor*-gay, the dogfish. (Cornish.)
morgue, *n.* morg, a public mortuary or dead-house, esp. in France; haughtiness; coldness of manner. (Fr.)
moribund, *a. mo*-re-bund, in a dying state: *n.* a dying person. (L. *moribundus.*)
moriche, *n.* mo-*ritch*-e, the miriti palm. (Carib.)
morigerous, *a.* mo-*rij*-er-rus, obedient; obsequious. (L. *morigerus.*)
morillon, *n.* mo-*ril*-un, a species of duck, the golden-eye; a variety of vine, and its fine black grape. (Fr.)
moringa, *n.* mo-*ring*-ga, the horse-radish tree. *Moringa oleifera,* which yields the ben nut. (Malay.)
morion, *n. mo*-re-on, a hat-shaped helmet having no protection for the face. (Sp.)
Morisco, *a.* mo-*ris*-ko, Moorish; Moresque: *n.* a Christianized Moor of mediæval Spain; the Moorish language; a morris dance, or dancer. (Sp.)
morkin, *n. mor*-kin, a beast that has died by sickness or mischance. (F. *morticina,* carrion.)
morling, *n. mor*-ling, wool cut from a dead sheep.
mormo, *n. mor*-mo, a bugbear; a false terror. (Gr.)
Mormon, *n. mor*-mon, a member of the Church of Jesus Christ of Latter-day Saints, a sect founded in the United States in 1830 by Joseph Smith, and taking its name from the alleged author of a 5th-cent. A.D book of "scripture" which was committed into Smith's hands by the angel of the Lord in 1827; a polygamist (polygamy having been one of their practices).
Mormonism, *n. mor*-mon-izm, the principles and practices of the Mormons.
morn, *n.* morn, the first part of the day; morning.
★**morning,** *n. morn*-ing, the first part of the day, beginning at twelve o'clock at night, and extending to noon, or the time from daybreak to noon; the forenoon; an early part: *a.* pertaining to the first or early part of the day. **morning coat,** a tailcoat with cutaway front. **morning dress,** clothes worn in the day; dress other than evening dress. **morning gown,** a loose gown worn in the morning. **morning prayer,** the Church of England service of Matins. **morning sickness,** a nausea which occurs in the morning, during the early period of pregnancy. **morning star,** any planet, esp. Venus, which visibly precedes the sun in rising. (A.S. and Ger. *morgen.*)
morning-glory, *n.* the climbing plant, *Ipomœa purpurea.*
morning-room, *n.* a sitting-room for use in the morning.
morning-star, *n.* a ball with spikes, attached to or suspended from a staff, and used in mediæval times against armour.
Moroccan, *a.* mo-*rok*-kan, pertaining to Morocco.
morocco, *n.* mo-*rok*-ko, or **morocco leather,** a fine kind of grained leather prepared from goatskin. (*Morocco,* whence first brought to Europe.)
moron, *n. maw*-ron, one mentally deficient, esp. an adult whose mental development has been arrested; a degenerate. (Gr. *moros,* dull.)
morose, *a.* mo-*rohs,* of a sour temper; sullen; austere; gloomy. (L. *morosus.*)
morosely, *ad.* mo-*rohs*-le, in a morose manner.
moroseness, *n.* the quality of being morose.
moroxite, *n.* mo-*rok*-site, a bluish crystallized variety of apatite [Min.].
Morpheus, *n. mor*-fe-us, the god of sleep and dreams [Myth.]. (Gr. shaper, from *morphe,* shape, form.)
morphia, *n. mor*-fe-a, an alkaloid extracted from opium, of which it constitutes the narcotic principle, used in medicine as a sedative and analgesic.
morphiate, *v.t. mor*-fe-ate, to treat or impregnate with morphia.
morphine, *n. mor*-feen, morphia.
morphinism, *n. mor*-fe-nizm, the morbid state induced by prolonged use or overdoses of morphia.
morphinist, *n. mor*-fe-nist, a morphinomaniac.
morphinomaniac, *n. mor*-fin-o-*may*-ne-ak, one whose craving for morphia is uncontrollable.
morphogenesis, *n. mor*-fo-*jen*-e-sis, the origin and development of an organ [Biol.].
morphological, *a.* mor-fo-*loj*-e-kal, belonging to morphology; structural.
morphologist, *n.* mor-*fol*-o-jist, a student of morphology.
morphology, *n.* mor-*fol*-o-je, the study of organic form [Biol.], or of the development of the forms of words [Gram.]; geomorphology. (Gr. *morphe,* form, *logos,* science.)
morphonomy, *n.* mor-*fon*-o-me, the science concerned with the laws of form in relation to animals, plants, and crystals.
morphosis, *n.* mor-*foh*-sis, mode of morphological development [Biol.]. (Gr.)
morris, *n. mo*-ris, a grotesque dance; a country dance, often performed in Robin Hood period dress. **morris-dancer,** one who dances in a morris. **nine men's morris,** an old game played between two opponents having nine counters each, on a marked board.
Morris-tube, *n. mo*-ris-*tewb,* a steel tube fitted within the bore of a firearm to allow of use of a smaller charge and projectile. (Named from the inventor.)
morrow, *n. mo*-roh, the day next after the present; the next day. **good morrow,** good morning. **to-morrow,** next day; on the morrow. (A.S. *morgen.*)
morse, *n.* mawrs, the walrus. (Lapp. *morsha.*)
morse, *n.* mawrs, a clasp used on a cope or other ecclesiastical vestment. (L. *morsus,* clasp.)
Morse, *n.* mawrs, the code used in signalling or telegraphy, and consisting of variations in dots and dashes, so named after the inventor. **Morse lamp,** a flash-lamp used for signalling in Morse.
morsel, *n. mor*-sel, a bite; a mouthful; a small piece of food; a small piece; a piece. (O.Fr.)
mort, *n.* mort, the call at the death sounded by a hunting-horn. (L. *mors, mortis,* death.)
mort, *n.* mort, a salmon in its third year. (Origin unknown.)
mort, *n.* mort, a quantity, as of people; a great deal. (Dial. Eng.)
mortal, *a. mor*-tal, subject to death; involving death; deadly; fatal; implacable; pertaining to man, who is mortal; extreme; tedious: *n.* a being subject to death; a human being: *ad.* excessively. (O.Fr. from L. *mors, mortis,* death.)
mortality, *n.* mor-*tal*-e-te, the quality of being subject to death or the necessity of dying; death; death rate; human nature; power of destruction. **bill of mortality,** *see* **bill.** (O.Fr. *mortalité.*)
mortalize, *v.t. mor*-tal-ize, to make mortal.
mortally, *ad. mor*-ta-le, as a mortal; in a manner that must cause death; grievously.
mortar, *n. mor*-tar, a vessel in which substances are pounded with a pestle; a short cannon of large calibre and very high angle of projection for firing shells at low muzzle velocity; a mixture of lime and sand with water, used as a cement for uniting stones and bricks in walls. **hydraulic mortar,** a cement which becomes extremely hard under water. (A.S. *mortere.*)
mortar-board, *n.* a square, flat board on which mortar is held by a mason; the familiar name for the square college cap.
mortgage, *n. mor*-gaj, the temporary grant or pledge of an estate as security for the payment of a debt: *v.t.* to grant an estate in fee as security for money

lent, and contracted to be paid at a certain time; to pledge. (O.Fr.)

mortgagee, *n.* mor-ga-*jee*, the person to whom an estate is mortgaged.

mortgagor, *n.* *mor*-ga-*jor*, the person who grants an estate as security for a debt.

mortice, *n.* *mor*-tis, a mortise.

mortician, *n.* mor-*tish*-an, an undertaker; a funeral director [U.S.A.].

mortification, *n.* *mor*-te-fe-*kay*-shon, act of mortifying; a mortified state; the death of a part of an animal body while the rest is alive, gangrene; the act of subduing the passions and appetites by penance or abstinence; humiliation or vexation; the act of giving or bequeathing land for charitable or public uses, also such gift or bequest [Scots. Law.] (Fr.)

mortifier, *n.* *mor*-te-fy-er, he who or that which mortifies.

mortify, *v.t.* *mor*-te-fy, to destroy the organic texture and vital functions of some part of a living animal; to subdue or bring into subjection bodily appetites or inordinate passions, by self-denial or abstinence; to humble; to affect with vexation; *v.i.* to lose vitality; to become gangrenous; to be subdued; to practise austerities for religious motives. (O.Fr. *mortifier.*)

mortifyingly, *ad.* *mor*-te-fy-ing-le, in a humiliating manner.

mortise, *n.* *mor*-tis, a hole made in a piece of wood, to receive the tenon of another piece: *v.t.* to cut or make a mortise in; to join by a tenon and mortise. **mortise lock,** a lock set in a mortise cut in the thickness of a door. (Fr. *mortaise.*)

mortling, *n.* *mort*-ling, morling; wool taken from a dead sheep.

mortmain, *n.* *mort*-mane, possession of lands or tenements in hands from which they cannot be alienated, such as an ecclesiastical or other corporation [Law]. (Fr. *mort*, dead, *main*, hand.)

mortuary, *n.* *mor*-tew-a-re, a place where the bodies of persons found dead and unknown are deposited; heriot or claim formerly preferred by a parish minister on the death of a parishioner: *a.* pertaining to death, or to the burial of the dead. (L. *mortuarius.*)

morula, *n.* *mo*-roo-la, a spherical mass of cells formed by cleavage of the partly developed ovum [Biol.].

mosaic, *n.* moh-*zay*-ik, a design consisting of small cut pieces of coloured glass, marble, or stone cemented on to a stucco ground or inlaid in metal; tesselation; a literary or artistic composition of small separate parts: *a.* tesselated; consisting of mosaic. **mosaic gold,** stannic sulphide, used as a pigment; ormolu. (Gr. *mousaikos*, belonging to the Muses.)

Mosaic, *a.* moh-*zay*-ik, pertaining to Moses, or his laws.

Mosaism, *n.* moh-*zay*-izm, the system peculiar to Moses.

mosaicist, *n.* moh-*zay*-e-sist, a dealer, or a worker, in mosaics.

mosasaurus, *n.* mos-a-*saw*-rus, an extinct marine reptile whose remains are found in the chalk formation. (*Mosa*, the Meuse, Gr. *sauros*, a lizard.)

moschatel, *n.* *mos*-ka-tel, a small British plant, with pale-green flowers of a musky smell, *Adoxa moschatellina*. (Fr. *moscatelle.*)

moschiferous, *a.* mos-*kif*-er-rus, producing musk. (L. *moschus*, musk.)

moschine, *a.* *mos*-kin, pertaining to, or resembling members of, the Moschinæ, the family comprising the musk-deer: *n.* an animal of this family [Zool.].

moselle, *n.* mo-*zel*, a light French wine, from the district of the Moselle.

Moslem, *n.* *moz*-lem, a mussulman; an orthodox Mohammedan: *a.* Mohammedan. (Ar. *muslim.*)

moslings, *n.pl.* *mos*-lingz, the thin shreds of leather shaved off by the currier in dressing skins.

mosque, *n.* mosk, a Mohammedan place of worship. (Fr. *mosquée*, from Ar. *masjid.*)

mosquito, *n.* mos-*kee*-to, any species of the *Culex*, insects with a proboscis which punctures the skin and sucks the blood of animals; a gnat. (Sp.)

mosquito-net, *n.* a fine gauze hanging used in the tropics to exclude mosquitoes.

moss, *n.* mos, a cryptogamic plant with simple leaves; lichen; Iceland-moss; a bog; a place where peat is found: *v.t.* to cover with moss. (A.S. *mos.*)

moss-agate, *n.* mocha-stone.

moss-campion, *n.* the tufted plant *Silene acaulis*.

moss-cheeper, *n.* *mos*-cheep-er, the meadow-pipit.

moss-clad, *a.* clad or covered with moss.

moss-grown, *a.* overgrown with moss.

mossiness, *n.* *mos*-e-ness, state of being mossy.

moss-pink, *n.* the plant *Phlox subulata*.

moss-rose, *n.* a fragrant variety of cabbage-rose, *Rosa centifolia muscosa*.

moss-rush, *n.* the plant *Juncus squarrosus*.

moss-trooper, *n.* one of a band of 17th-cent. raiders in the border country between England and Scotland.

mossy, *a.* *mos*-se, overgrown with or like moss.

most, *a.* mohst, greatest in quality, degree, amount, or number: *ad.* in the greatest or highest degree: *n.* the greatest number or amount. **at the most,** at the utmost extent; at furthest. (A.S. *maest.*)

mostly, *ad.* *mohst*-le, for the greatest part.

mot, *n.* moh, a witty saying. (Fr.)

motatorious, *a.* moh-ta-*taw*-re-us, maintaining an almost continual motion (as the antennæ of certain insects) [Entom.].

mote, *n.* mote, a small particle; anything proverbially small; a spot; a speck. (A.S.)

motet, *n.* mo-*tet*, a short musical composition of a sacred character. (Fr.)

moth, *n.* moth, one of an order of nocturnal lepidopterans differing slightly from the butterflies, the caterpillar of certain species of which feeds on and destroys furs and woollen fabrics; that which gradually and silently eats away or wastes anything. (A.S. *moththe.*)

moth-ball, *n.* *moth*-bawl, a ball of naphthalene or other chemical used for keeping moths from clothes.

moth-eaten, *a.* *moth*-ee-tn, eaten away by or as by moths; full of moths.

***mother,** *n.* *muth*-er, a female parent; a woman who has borne a child; a producer; a motherly woman; a woman superior in a religious house: *a.* native; natural; received, as from one's mother; giving birth, or acting, as a mother: *v.t.* to adopt as a son or daughter; to protect like a mother. **Mother Carey's chicken,** *see* **chicken.** **Mother-Church,** a church from which other churches have sprung, esp. that of the original parish, each subdivision of which now has its own church. **mother country,** the county of one's origin or ancestors; the country from which the founders of a colony emigrated. **Mother Earth,** the earth personified as a great mother. **mother liquor,** the residual liquid after the salts have been crystallized out [Chem.]. **mother of thousands,** one of the toad-flaxes, *Linaria cymbalaria*. **mother of thyme,** the lemon-scented thyme, *Thymus serpyllum*. **mother right,** the custom of tracing relationship by the maternal side [Ethn.]. **mother ship,** a naval vessel escorting and supplying smaller ships. **mother wit,** native wit; common sense. (A.S. *modor.*)

mother, *n.* *muth*-er, a thick slimy substance forming on the surface of certain liquors in fermentation: *v.i.* to become mothery. (Perhaps O.Dut. *modder*, mud.)

mother-cell, *n.* a cell that, by division, produces other cells [Biol.].

mothercraft, *n.* *muth*-er-krahft, the duties or business of a mother; the art of rearing a family.

motherhood, *n.* *muth*-er-hood, the state of being a mother; motherly quality or character.

mothering, *n.* *muth*-er-ing, the old custom of visiting one's parents on Mid-Lent, or Mothering, Sunday.

mother-in-law, *n.* the mother of a husband or wife.

motherland, *n.* *muth*-er-land, one's native land.

motherless, *a.* *muth*-er-less, without a mother.

motherliness, *n.* *muth*-er-le-ness the quality of being motherly.

mother-lodge, *n.* the lodge at which a freemason was initiated into freemasonry.

motherly, *a.* *muth*-er-le, pertaining to, or having the manner of, a mother; tender; parental: *ad.* in the manner of a mother.

mother-of-pearl, *n.* nacre; the hard, iridescent, internal layer of several kinds of shells, particularly oysters.

mother-superior, *n.* head of a convent.

mother-tongue, *n.* one's native tongue.

mother-water, *n.* mother liquor.
motherwort, *n. muth*-er-wurt, the hardy herbaceous perennial *Leonurus cardiaca.*
mothery, *a. muth*-er-re, having formed mother, or partaking of the nature of mother (of fermenting liquors).
mothy, *a. moth*-e, full of moths; moth-eaten.
motif, *n. moh*-teef, the predominant feature in a piece of music or any work of art; an ornamental design used as a trimming for a dress. (Fr.)
motile, *a. moh*-tile, having motility. (Fr.)
motility, *n.* moh-*til*-e-te, the capacity of spontaneous movement; contractility [Phys.]. (Fr., from L. *motum*, moved.)
***motion,** *n. moh*-shon, act of moving; change of position; the passing of a body from one place to another; a movement; power of movement; impulse; a proposal made in a deliberate assembly; action of the bowels, or the evacuated fæces [Med.]; the works of a machine; an application to the court for some rule or order which has become necessary in the progress of the cause [Law]: *v.t.* and *i.* to make a significant movement or gesture, as with the hand; to make proposals. **accelerated motions,** motions having a velocity that increases or decreases as distinct from one that is equable or uniform. **angular motion,** the motion of a body as referred to a centre about which it revolves. **in motion,** moving; in a state of activity. **laws of motion,** Newton's three axioms, viz.: (1) every body perseveres in its state of rest or uniform motion in a straight line, until a change is effected by the agency of some external force; (2) any change effected in the quiescence or motion of a body, is in the direction of the force impressed and is proportional to it in quantity; and (3) action and reaction are equal and in contrary directions. **motion pictures,** pictures produced and reproduced by cinematography; the films. **to put in motion,** to set going; to put into operation (O.Fr., from L. *motio*, from *movere*, to move.)
motional, *a. moh*-shon-al, kinetic; characterized by motion.
motionless, *a. moh*-shon-less, wanting motion; being at rest.
motivate, *v.t. moh*-te-vate, to supply a motive to; to incite; to cause to come into action.
motivation, *n.* moh-te-*vay*-shon, the act of instigation, or of arousing an interest.
motive, *a. moh*-tiv, causing motion; having power or tending to move; pertaining to movement: *n.* that which incites to action or determines choice; inducement; the object of a work of art, or the idea which pervades it; motif: *v.i.* to act as, or incite by, a motive; to motivate. **motive force,** the sum of force which tends to promote motion. **motive power,** impelling power; electricity, steam, or other mechanical energy used to drive machinery. (Fr. *motif*, as *motion*.)
motiveless, *a. moh*-tiv-less, without motive or aim.
motivity, *n.* moh-*tiv*-e-te, the power of producing motion.
motley, *a. mot*-le, variegated in colour; of different colours; diversified; of diverse elements or qualities: *n.* a dress of different colours; the costume of the fool or clown. (Origin unknown.)
mot-mot, *n. mot*-mot, one of a racket-tailed family of birds of Central and South America.
motor, *a. moh*-tor, imparting or causing motion; fitted with or pertaining to a motor or motors; of or pertaining to motor nerves [Anat.]; imparting an impulse that leads to motion [Phys.]: *n.* that which moves or produces motion; a rotatory machine transforming electrical into mechanical energy; an internal combustion engine; a motor-car: *v.t.* to convey in a motor-vehicle: *v.i.* to travel by motor-car. **motor-bandit,** a thief who uses a motor-car. **motor-dynamo,** a dynamotor.
motor-boat, *n.* a boat propelled by an internal combustion engine or by electric power.
motor-bus, *n.* a mechanically propelled omnibus.
motor-car, *n.* a carriage propelled by a motor operated either by petrol, electricity, or steam; the car housing the motor of an electric train.
motor-coach, *n.* a superior class of motor-bus for long-distance travel; a coach with its own motor for use on electric railways.
motor-cycle, *n.* a mechanically propelled bicycle: *v.i.* to travel by motor-cycle.
motordrome, *n. moh*-tor-drome, a testing-track, or a race-track, for motor-vehicles.
motorial, *a.* mo-*taw*-re-al, motory, pertaining to or transmitting motion.
motoring, *n. moh*-to-ring, the act of using or driving a motor-car, esp. for recreation.
motorist, *n. moh*-to-rist, one who habitually drives or uses a motor-car.
motorize, *v.t. moh*-to-rize, to supply with a motor or with motor-cars; to supplant horse-drawn by motor-propelled vehicles.
motor-launch, *n.* a launch propelled by an internal combustion engine.
motor-lorry, *n.* a lorry propelled by a motor.
motorman, *n. moh*-tor-man, an artisan in control of a motor or of an electric locomotive; the driver of a mechanically propelled vehicle.
motory, *a. moh*-to-re, giving motion; designating a nerve conveying to a muscle an impulse causing motion [Phys.].
mottle, *n. mot*-tl, a coloured patch; a variegated appearance caused by coloured blotches: *v.t.* to variegate with spots.
mottled, *a. mot*-tld, blotched with spots of different colours or shades of colour; dappled.
motto, *m. mot*-toh (*pl.* **mottoes**), a suggestive sentence, phrase, or word, adopted as a device to signify usually motive or intent; a sentimental couplet printed on the wrapping of a sweetmeat, etc., for amusement. (It. *motto*, a saying.)
mottoed, *a. mot*-tohd, having a motto.
mouch, *v.i.* mouch, to mooch or loaf; to skulk.
moucher, *n. mouch*-er, a skulker; a loafer.
moue, *n.* moo, a pout; a grimace. (Fr.)
mouflon, *n. moo*-flon, a species of wild sheep, esp. that of Corsica and Sardinia, *Ovis musimon.*
moujik, *n. moo*-jik, mujik.
mould, *n.* mohld, fine soft earth, or earth easily pulverized, such as constitutes soil and is rich in decayed vegetable or animal matter; earth, ground, hence the tomb: *v.t.* to cover with mould. (A.S. *molde*.)
mould, *n.* mohld, the matrix in which anything is cast and receives its form; the frame on which handmade paper is made; pattern; cast; form; shape; a moulding [Arch.]; a vessel in which a jelly or sweet is shaped, or a sweet so shaped: *v.t.* to form into a particular shape; to shape; to fashion; to knead. (O.Fr. *modle*.)
mould, *n.* mohld, a woolly superficial fungoid growth on damp or decaying animal or vegetable matter; a fungus producing this: *v.i.* to become mouldy. (Origin uncertain.)
mouldable, *a. mohld*-a-bl, that may be moulded.
mould-board, *n. mohld*-board, the curved iron plate in a plough which turns up the furrow.
moulder, *n. mohld*-er, one who moulds or casts, esp. metal.
moulder, *v.i. mohld*-er, to turn to dust by natural decay; to crumble; to waste away gradually: *v.t.* to turn to dust; to crumble; to waste.
mouldiness, *n. mohld*-e-ness, state of being mouldy.
moulding, *n. mohld*-ing, the act or process of forming in a mould, or of making moulds; anything so formed; ornamental woodwork, as for picture frames, etc.; a projection beyond a wall, column, or wainscot [Arch.].
mould-loft, *n.* a large room in which the moulds for ships are drawn full-size.
mouldwarp, *n. mohld*-worp, a mole, so called as casting up mounds of mould. (A.S.)
mouldy, *a. mohld*-e, overgrown with mould or fungoid growth; fusty; stale: *n.* a torpedo [Naval slang].
moulin, *n. moo*-lan(g), a crevasse or shaft in a glacier due to the action of surface water. (Fr.)
moulinage, *n. moo*-lin-aj, the operation of spinning, twisting, and doubling raw silk. (Fr.)
moulinet, *n. moo*-le-net, the drum of a crane or capstan. (Fr., a winch.)
moult, *n.* mohlt, the action of moulting (of birds); *v.i.* to shed the hair, feathers, skin, or horns, as an animal. (A.S. *mutian*, change.)
mound, *n.* mound, an artificial bank of earth, originally for defence; a hillock, or natural elevation; a tumulus: *v.t.* to heap in a mound; to protect with a mound. (Origin uncertain.)
mound, *n.* mound, a small globe surmounted by a cross, forming a symbol of sovereignty. (L. *mundus*, the world.)

mound-bird, *n.* any of the megapodes, esp. the brush-turkey.

mound-builder, *n.* a member of an early race of North American Indians who were builders of certain curious moundlike structures in the Southern States; a mound-bird.

mount, *n.* mount, a mountain or hill; a mound for defence or attack; the representation of a grassy mound with trees on the base of a shield [Her.]; cardboard, etc., to which a drawing is fixed; the setting of a gem; a riding-horse; a horse-block: *v.i.* to rise on high; to ascend; to rise or tower aloft; to get on horseback, or on anything; to rise in amount: *v.t.* to raise aloft or on high; to climb or to ascend; to furnish with a horse or horses; to copulate with (of quadrupeds); to affix, as drawings, stamps, gems, etc., to a background or in a setting; to prepare a skin or skeleton for exhibition; to equip a stage piece with properties, etc.; to set a piece of ordnance upon the carriage. **mounted infantry,** infantry trained to manœuvre on horseback. **mounted police,** police mounted on horses. (A.S. *munt,* from L. *mons, montis,* mountain.)

mountable, *a. mount*-a-bl, that may be ascended or mounted.

***mountain,** *n. mount*-an, a lofty hill; a great mass; any very large object: *pl.* a mountainous region: *a.* pertaining to a mountain; growing or dwelling on a mountain; vast. **the Mountain,** the extreme section in the French Revolution, as occupying the highest seats in the National Convention. **mountain cork** or **leather,** varieties of asbestos having properties resembling those of the objects named. **mountain cure,** the cure of illness by living at a high elevation. **mountain railway,** a railway with special devices, racks, and pinions, etc., for use among mountains; a funicular railway. **mountain sickness,** indisposition caused by breathing the rarefied air of high regions. (O.Fr. *montaine.*)

mountain-ash, *n.* the rowan-tree.

mountain-dew, *n.* Scotch whisky, formerly secretly distilled in the mountains of Scotland.

mountaineer, *n.* mount-a-*neer,* an inhabitant of a mountainous district; a mountain climber. (O.Fr. *montanier.*)

mountaineering, *n.* mount-a-*neer*-ing, the climbing of mountains for sport or scientific purposes.

mountain-flax, *n.* a name given to various plants, as centaury, spurry, and quaking-grass.

mountain-fringe, *n.* the climbing fumitory, *Adlumia cirrhosa.*

mountain-limestone, *n.* the carboniferous limestone between the old red sandstone and the coal measures.

mountainous, *a. mount*-a-nus, full of mountains; large as a mountain; huge; inhabiting mountains. (L. *montaniosus.*)

mountainousness, *n. mount*-a-nus-ness, the state of being mountainous.

mountain-rice, *n.* various forage grasses of the genus *Oryzopsis*; rice grown without irrigation on mountain slopes.

mountain-soap, *n.* a soft, earthy, brownish-black mineral, used in crayon painting.

mountain-sorrel, *n.* the plant *Oxyria digyna.*

mountain-widow, *n.* either of the plants *Geranium phæum* or *Scabiosa atrapurpurea.*

mountant, *a. mount*-ant, rising high: *n.* an adhesive used in mounting photographs, etc. (Fr.)

mountebank, *n. mount*-e-bank, a circus performer; a humbug; a quack; any boastful pretender: *v.t.* to cheat by boasting and charlatanism; to gull. (It. *montambanco.*)

mountebankery, *n. mount*-e-bank-er-re, the wiles of the mountebank; quackery.

mounter, *n. mount*-er, one who mounts.

mounting, *n. mount*-ing, the act of mounting; the act of furnishing or setting, or of preparing for use; equipment; embellishment; the frame of a picture or map, etc.

Mounty, *n. moun*-te, a member of the Royal Canadian Mounted Police [Coll.].

mourn, *v.i.* moarn, to express grief or sorrow; to grieve; to be sorrowful; to wear the customary habit of sorrow: *v.t.* to grieve for; to utter in a sorrowful manner. (A.S. *murnan.*)

mourner, *n. moarn*-er, one who mourns.

mournful, *a. moarn*-ful, expressive of sorrow; causing sorrow; feeling grief; sorrowful.

mournfully, *ad.* in a mournful manner.

mournfulness, *n. moarn*-ful-ness, sorrow; act or state of mourning.

mourning, *a. moarn*-ing, grieving; lamenting; expressive of grief: *n.* lamentation; the act of sorrowing or expressing grief; the dress worn by mourners.

mourning-coach, *n.* a coach used by mourners attending a funeral.

mourning-dove, *n.* the N. American wild dove, *Columba carolinensis,* so called from its plaintive note.

mouse, *n.* mous (*pl.* **mice**), a small rodent of the genus *Mus,* esp. the common house-mouse (also used incorrectly of certain voles, etc.); a discoloured bruise, a black eye [Slang]: *v.i.* (mouz), to watch for or catch mice; to watch for slyly: *v.t.* to tear, as a cat devours a mouse. (A.S. *mūs,* from L. *mus.*)

mouse-barley, *n.* wall-barley, *Hordeum murinum.*

mouse-colour, *n.* the bluish-grey shade of a mouse's coat.

mouse-deer, *n. mous*-deer, the chevrotain.

mouse-ear, *n.* a name of several herbs, on account of the shape and velvety surface of their leaves.

mousehole, *n. mous*-hole, a hole where mice enter or pass.

mouser, *n. mou*-zer, a cat that catches mice.

mousetail, *n. mous*-tale, an annual plant, *Myosurus minimus,* with seeds resembling the tail of a mouse.

mousetrap, *n. mous*-trap, a trap for catching mice.

mousmee, *n. moos*-may, an unmarried girl in Japan; a waitress in a tea-garden. (Japanese.)

mousquetaire, *n.* moos-ke-*tare,* a member of the bodyguard of the French kings. (Fr.)

mousse, *n.* moos, a kind of blanc-mange, usually iced. (Fr.)

mousseline, *n. moos*-s'-lin, muslin; a fine-blown glass. **mousseline - de - laine,** an untwilled woollen, or cotton and woollen, fabric of light texture. (Fr.)

moustache, *n.* mus-*tahsh,* hair grown on the upper lip. (Fr.)

Mousterian, *a.* moos-*teer*-re-an, belonging to the early Palæolithic period named after remains found in the Moustier cave, France.

mousy, *a. mous*-e, overrun with mice; like a mouse.

moutan, *n. moo*-tan, the tree-peony, *Pæonia moutan,* of China.

***mouth,** *n.* mouth, the aperture in the head of an animal, by which it utters sound and receives food; the cavity within the lips; the opening of a vessel or of a river; the opening or entrance of a cave, pit, well, or den; instrument of speaking; principal speaker; voice. **down in the mouth,** dejected [Coll.]. **keep the mouth shut,** maintain silence. **make mouths,** to distort the mouth; to pout. **stop the mouth,** to put to silence. (A.S. *mūth.*)

mouth, *v.t.* mouthe, to utter with a voice affectedly big or swelling; to seize with the mouth; to chew; to devour; to accustom to the use of a bit (of horses): *v.i.* to speak with a full, swelling, affected voice; to vociferate; to rant; to make mouths.

mouthed, *a.* with a particular kind of mouth (in composition, as, foul-mouthed, hard-mouthed.)

mouther, *n. mouthe*-er, one who mouths; an affected speaker or declaimer.

mouthful, *n. mouth*-ful, as much as the mouth contains at once; a small quantity.

mouthing, *n. mouthe*-ing, affected utterance.

mouthless, *a. mouth*-less, destitute of a mouth.

mouth-organ, *n.* the Pandean pipes; a musical wind instrument consisting of metallic reeds of varying lengths.

mouthpiece, *n. mouth*-peece, a tube for use by the mouth; the mouth of a wind instrument; one who delivers the opinions of others.

mouthwash, *n. mouth*-wosh, an antiseptic liquid preparation for cleansing the mouth and teeth.

mouthy, *a. mouth*-e, affected or ranting in speech; bombastic.

moutonnée, *a.* moo-to-*nay,* rounded like the back of a sheep (of glacier-worn rocks).

movability, *n. moo*-va-*bil*-e-te, the state of being movable.

movable, *a. moo*-va-bl, that may be moved; changing from one date to another: *pl.* goods, wares, commodities, furniture; any species of property not fixed; personal, as distinguished from heritable,

property [Scots. Law]. **movable feast,** an ecclesiastical feast depending on the date of Easter.
movableness, *n.* *moo*-va-bl-ness, the state or quality of being movable; mobility; susceptibility of motion.
movably, *ad.* *moo*-va-ble, so that it may be moved.
★**move,** *n.* moov, the act of moving; right to move (in games); a movement; step; procedure; change of residence: *v.t.* to carry, convey, or draw from one place to another; to excite into action; to agitate or rouse; to affect; to prevail on; to excite tenderness or pity; to irritate; to excite to tumult; to influence; to propose: *v.i.* to change place or posture; to stir; to have action, or the power of action; to walk; to change residence; to take action; to propose something for consideration and determination. (O.Fr. *movoir.*)
moveless, *a.* *moov*-less, motionless; fixed.
movement, *n.* *moov*-ment, motion; a passing, progression, or flowing; change of position; manner of moving; excitement; agitation; any single strain having the same measure or time [Mus.]; the entire wheel-work of a clock or watch; a military evolution [Mil.]. **in the movement,** playing a part in the general trend; in the swim. (O.Fr.)
mover, *n.* *moo*-ver, he who or that which gives motion, or impels to action; the proposer of a resolution. **prime mover,** the originator of, or driving force in, anything.
movie, *a.* *moo*-ve, of, or pertaining to, the movies, as in movie picture, movie screen.
movies, *n.pl.* *moo*-viz, cinematograph pictures; an exhibition of such pictures [Coll.].
movietone, *n.* *moo*-ve-tohn, trade name of a system used in producing sound films, by which sound and photographs are recorded simultaneously.
moving, *a.* *moo*-ving, urging or persuading to move or act; exciting the emotions; pathetic. **moving coil,** a coil of conducting wire about an axis capable of rotation. **moving pictures,** the movies. **moving staircase,** an escalator.
movingly, *ad.* in a moving manner.
movingness, *n.* power of moving or affecting.
mow, *n.* mou, a heap of hay or sheaves of grain deposited in a barn: *v.t.* to lay hay or sheaves of grain in a heap. (A.S. *mūga.*)
mow, *v.t.* moh, to cut down with a scythe or machine; to cut the grass from; to cut down indiscriminately or in great numbers: *v.i.* to cut grass; to practise mowing. *p.* **mowed.** *pp.* **mowed** or **mown.** (A.S. *mawan.*)
mow, *n.* *moh* or *mou,* a wry face: *v.i.* to make grimaces. (Fr. *moue.*)
mowburnt, *a.* *moh*-bernt, spoilt by becoming overheated in the rick (of stacked corn, etc.).
mower, *n.* *moh*-er, one who mows; a mowing-machine.
mowing, *n.* *moh*-ing, the act of cutting with a scythe or a mowing machine; land from which grass is cut: *a.* intended to be mown.
moxa, *n.* *mok*-sa, a fluffy material prepared from the leaves of *Artemisia moxa,* used in the Far East to effect cauterization; the plant that yields it; any material used similarly as a counter-irritant [Med.]. (Jap.)
moxibustion, *n.* mok-se-*bus*-tyun, cauterization by means of moxa [Med.].
moya, *n.* *moy*-a, local name of mud ejected from certain South American volcanoes.
Mozarab, *n.* moz-*a*-rab, a Spaniard who retained his Christian faith as a subject of the Moors during the Moorish occupation of Spain.
Mozarabic, *a.* moz-*a*-ra-bik, pertaining to the Mozarabs, and esp. to their liturgy.
moze, *v.t.* mohz, to raise the nap on (cloth), as in a gig-mill.
mozetta, *n.* mo-*zet*-ta, a short cape having a small hood worn by the Pope and other prelates of the Roman Catholic Church. (It.)
mozo, *n.* *moh*-tho, a man-servant or labourer in Spanish America. (Sp.)
Mpret, *n.* m-*pret,* title of the ruler of Albania in 1913. (Albanian, from L. *imperator,* emperor.)
Mr., *n.* *mis*-ter, an abbreviation of *master.*
Mrs., *n.* *mis*-siz, an abbreviation of *mistress.* **Mrs. Grundy,** the personification of prudish propriety and conventionality.
mu, mew, *n.* the twelfth letter (μ, *m*) of the Greek alphabet.
mucedine, *n.* *mew*-se-dine, a fungus that forms mould or mildew. (L. *mucedo.*)
mucedinous, *a.* mew-*sed*-e-nus, resembling mould or mildew.
★**much,** *a.* mutch, great in quantity or amount; long in duration: *ad.* in a great degree; by far; nearly; often or long: *n.* a great quantity; a great matter. **as much** or **so much,** an equal quantity. **make much of,** to value, or esteem; to fondle. **too much,** an excessive quantity. (A.S. *micel.*)
muchly, *ad.* *mutch*-le, exceedingly [Coll.].
muchness, *n.* *mutch*-ness, the state of being much. **much of a muchness,** very similar; nearly the same.
mucic, *a.* *mew*-sik, obtained from the oxidation of sugar, gums, etc. (L. *mucus,* mucus.)
mucid, *a.* *mew*-sid, musty; mouldy; slimy.
mucidity, *n.* mew-*sid*-e-te, state of being mucid.
mucific, *a.* mew-*sif*-ik, producing mucus. (L. *mucus,* and *facio,* make.)
mucilage, *n.* *mew*-se-laj, a viscous substance present in many fruits, seeds, roots, etc. [Bot.]; a fluid solution of gum, gelatine, or glue. (Fr.)
mucilaginous, *a.* mew-se-*laj*-e-nus, pertaining to mucilage; gummy; slimy.
muciparous, *a.* mew-*sip*-a-rus, secreting or producing mucus. (L. *mucus,* and *pario,* produce.)
mucitis, *n.* mew-*sy*-tis, inflammation of a mucous membrane.
mucivorous, *a.* mew-*siv*-o-rus, feeding on the mucilage or gum of plants, as certain insects. (L. *mucus,* and *voro,* devour.)
muck, *n.* muk, dung in a moist state; something mean or filthy; refuse: *v.t.* to manure with moist dung; to make a mess of. **to muck about,** to potter about. (Scand.)
mucker, *n.* *muk*-er, a bad fall; a cropper. [Slang.]
muck-heap, *n.* a heap of muck; a dunghill.
muckiness, *n.* *muk*-e-ness, filthiness; nastiness.
muckle, *a.* and *n.* *muk*-kl, mickle. (Scots.)
muckna, *n.* *muk*-na, a male elephant in which tusks are absent or merely rudimentary. (Hind. *makhna.*)
muck-rake, *n.* a rake for collecting muck.
muck-sweat, *n.* profuse perspiration.
muckweed, *n.* *muk*-weed, the plant white goosefoot, *Chenopodium album.*
muck-worm, *n.* *muk*-wurm, a worm that lives in dunghills; a miser.
mucky, *a.* *muk*-e, filthy with muck; nasty.
mucoid, *a.* *mew*-koyd, resembling mucus.
Mucor, *n.* *mew*-kor, a genus including many of the mucedinous fungi. (L.)
mucose, *a.* *mew*-kohs, slimy [Bot.].
mucosity, *n.* mew-*kos*-e-te, the state of being mucous.
mucous, *a.* *mew*-kus, pertaining to mucus; mucoid; slimy; viscous; secreting mucus. **mucous membrane,** the membranous lining of the canals and cavities of the body. (L. *mucosus.*)
mucro, *n.* *mew*-kro (*pl.* **mucrones,** mew-*kroh*-neez), a stiff sharp point [Bot. and Zool.]. [L.)
mucronate, *a.* *mew*-kro-nat, narrowed to a point [Bot. and Zool.].
mucronately, *ad.* *mew*-kro-nat-le, in a mucronate or sharp-pointed manner. (L. *mucronatus.*)
muculent, *a.* *mew*-kew-lent, like mucus; slimy; somewhat viscous.
mucus, *n.* *mew*-kus, a viscid fluid secreted by the mucous membrane; any viscid animal secretion; mucilage [Bot.]. (L., secretion from the nose.)
mud, *n.* mud, decomposed or finely detrited material from the rocks; moist earth; slimy earth; mire; *v.t.* to bury in or besmear with mud; to muddy. (Low Ger.)
mudar, *n.* moo-*dar,* an East Indian shrub of the genus *Calotropis,* containing a juice used medicinally as an emetic and purgative; the medicinal extract itself. (Hind. *madar.*)
mudarine, *n.* *mew*-da-reen, the principle contained in mudar, which has the property of softening by cold and hardening by heat.
mud-bath, *n.* a bath of certain curative muds taken for rheumatic affections, etc.
mud-cart, *n.* *mud*-kart, a scavenger's cart for removing dirt from the streets.
mud-devil, *n.* the menopome.
muddily, *ad.* *mud*-de-le, turbidly; cloudily.
muddiness, *n.* *mud*-de-ness, turbidness; cloudiness; intellectual dullness.

muddle, *n.* *mud*-dl, a confused or turbid state; a mess: *v.t.* to make muddy or foul; to fuddle with drink; to confuse or bewilder; to squander; to bungle; to mismanage. **muddle along,** to manage in a haphazard way. **muddle through,** to attain an end in spite of repeated blunders. (*mud.*)
muddle-headed, *a.* with one's wits confused.
muddlesome, *a.* *mud*-dl-sum, given to muddling; unmethodical.
muddy, *a.* *mud*-de, foul with dirt or mud; containing mud; turbid; gross; impure; of the colour of mud; cloudy in mind; stupid; obscure: *v.t.* to soil with mud; to dirty; to cloud.
mudfish, *n.* *mud*-fish, any fish burrowing in mud or living in muddy water, as the loach and the bowfin; also, any lung-fish.
mudguard, *n.* *mud*-gard, a shield over the wheels of a vehicle or bicycle to catch mud as it is thrown up.
mud-hole, *n.* *mud*-hole, a hollow in the road holding mud; a mud-valve.
mudir, *n.* *moo*-deer, a provincial governor in Egypt or the Sudan. (Ar.)
mudlark, *n.* *mud*-lark, one who plays in the mud; a guttersnipe; one who cleans out sewers, docks, etc., for things lost in them.
mud-plantain, *n.* a North American aquatic plant of the genus *Heteranthera.*
mud-scow, *n.* a flat-bottomed vessel for carrying mud from a dredger.
mud-slinging, *n.* the use of calumny, offensive epithets, or ill-natured gossip, esp. in place of argument.
mud-valve, *n.* *mud*-valv, the hole by which sediment, etc., is removed from a boiler.
mudwort, *n.* *mud*-wurt, the small plant *Limosella aquatica.*
muezzin, *n.* moo-*ez*-in, the Moslem crier of the hour of prayer. (Ar.)
muff, *n.* muf, a warm cover for both hands, usually of fur, formerly carried by women. (Dut. *mof.*)
muff, *n.* muf, a simpleton; a clumsy stupid fellow; a failure; a bungled action, esp. (in games) failure to catch the ball: *v.t.* to bungle; to fail to catch the ball in games: *v.i.* to fail; to miss the ball.
muff, *n.* muf, the whitethroat, *Sylvia cinerea.*
muffetee, *n.* muf-e-*tee*, a mitten that covers the wrist.
muffin, *n.* *muf*-fin, a light, round, spongy cake eaten hot. **muffin man,** an itinerant vendor of muffins. (Origin unknown.)
muffineer, *n.* muf-e-*neer*, a covered dish to keep toasted muffins hot; a cruet with a perforated top for sprinkling salt on muffins.
muffle, *n.* *muf*-fl, a muffler; a boxing-glove; anything used to deaden sound; the internal fire-clay oven of a muffle-furnace: *v.t.* to cover from inclement weather; to blindfold; to conceal; to deaden the sound of. (O.Fr. *moufle*, a fur glove.)
muffle, *n.* *muf*-fl, the hairless flabby end of the muzzle in ruminants and certain other animals [Zool.]. (Fr. *mufle.*)
muffle-furnace, *n.* a furnace in which the articles fired are protected by a muffle from the flames.
muffler, *n.* *muf*-fler, a scarf or wrapper for the throat; a stuffed glove; anything that deadens sound.
muffling, *n.* *muf*-fl-ing, anything with which an object is muffled; a contrivance for deadening sound.
mufti, *n.* *muf*-te, an official expounder or doctor of Mohammedan law; plain clothes as distinct from uniform or ceremonial attire. (Ar.)
mug, *n.* mug, a straight-sided earthen or metal drinking-vessel; the contents of this; a tankard. (Origin uncertain.)
mug, *n.* mug, the face; the mouth; an inexperienced person (esp. at games); a fool or simpleton; one who studies hard. **to mug up,** to study assiduously [All Slang]. (Origin unknown.)
mugger, *n.* *mug*-er, the East Indian crocodile, *Crocodilus palustris.*
muggins, *n.* *mug*-inz, a mug or simpleton, a juggins [Slang]; a children's game of cards; a game of dominoes.
muggish, *a.* *mug*-ish, muggy.
Muggletonian, *n.* mug-gl-*toh*-ne-an, one of a sect of Christians founded in 1651 by Lodowicke Muggleton, a fanatical tailor, who posed as one of the witnesses of Rev. xi, 3.
muggy, *a.* *mug*-e, damp, warm, close; foggy. (Perhaps Ice. *mugga*, a soft, drizzling mist.)
mugwort, *n.* *mug*-wurt, the plant *Artemisia vulgaris*; also the crosswort, *Galium cruciatum.*
mugwump, *n.* *mug*-wump, a superior or distinguished person; a "big noise" [Slang]. (Algonquian, "great chief.")
Muhammadan, *a.* and *n.* moo-*ham*-a-dan, Mohammedan.
muir, *n.* mewr, a moor [Scots.].
mujik, *n.* *moo*-jik, a Russian peasant, rustic, or boor. (Russ.)
mulatto, *n.* mew-*lat*-to, the offspring of a white and a pure Negro: *a.* of the mulatto class, or colour; tawny. (Sp. *mulato*, from L. *mulus*, a mule.)
mulberry, *n.* *mul*-be-re, any tree of the genus *Morus* bearing fruit like large blackberries and having leaves which are used for feeding silkworms; the fruit; the bluish-red colour of mulberry-juice. (M.E. *murberie*, from the L. name *morus*, and *berry.*)
mulch, *n.* mulsh, half-rotten straw or manure spread on the surface to keep the soil moist and protect the roots from frost: *v.t.* to cover with mulch; apply mulch to. (A.S.)
mulct, *n.* mulkt, a fine, usually in money, imposed for some offence: *v.t.* to fine. (L. *mulcta*, a fine.)
mulctuary, *a.* *mulk*-tew-a-re, imposing, consisting of, or punishable by, a pecuniary penalty.
mule, *n.* mewl, the offspring of a mare by a male ass (used also of a hinny); any hybrid, esp. of a canary; a machine for cotton-spinning; a motor-tractor for hauling canal-boats [U.S.A.]. (O.Fr., from L. *mūlus.*)
mule, *n.* mewl, a low heelless shoe for women. (Fr., slipper.)
mule-deer, *n.* the N. American deer, *Cariacus macrotis.*
mule-spinner, *n.* one who spins on a mule.
muleteer, *n.* *mewl*-e-teer, one who drives mules. (Fr. *muletier.*)
mulewort, *n.* *mewl*-wurt, a fern of the genus *Hemionitis.*
mulga, *n.* *mul*-ga, an Australian species of acacia, *Acacia aneura*; a club or shield made of its wood. **mulga scrub,** thickets of mulga trees.
muliebrity, *n.* mew-le-*eb*-re-te, womanhood; femininity. (L. *muliebritas.*)
mulish, *a.* *mewl*-ish, like a mule; sullen; stubborn.
mulishly, *ad.* *mewl*-ish-le, in a mulish manner.
mulishness, *n.* quality or state of being mulish.
mull, *v.t.* mul, to heat, sweeten, and season wine or liquor with spices. (Origin unknown.)
mull, *n.* mul, a snuff-box, esp. one made of the small end of a ram's horn. (*mill.*)
mull, *n.* mul, a cape or headland (in Scotland). (Gael. *maol.*)
mull, *n.* mul, a miss; a mistake; a failure: *v.t.* to bungle; to make a failure of.
mull, *n.* mul, a thin, soft kind of muslin. (Hind. *malmal.*)
Mullah, *n.* *mul*-a *or* *moo*-lah, one learned in Mohammedan rites and laws; a teacher of these. (Turk., from Ar. *maula.*)
mullein, *n.* *mul*-len, any plant of the genus *Verbascum*, esp. the great mullein, Aaron's rod, *V. thapsus.*
muller, *n.* *mul*-ler, a flat-bottomed pestle for grinding colours, etc., and other matters on a slab; a vessel in which liquor is mulled.
mullet, *n.* *mul*-let, the name of several fishes, mostly of the genera *Mullus* and *Mugil.* **mullet hawk,** the osprey. (O.Fr. *mulet.*)
mullet, *n.* *mul*-let, an heraldic figure in shape like the rowel of a spur. (O.Fr. *molette*, rowel.)
mulligatawny, *n.* mul-e-ga-*taw*-ne, a kind of curry soup. (Tamil, *milagu-tannir*, water of pepper.)
mulligrubs, *n.* *mul*-le-grubz, pain in the intestines; colic; hence, disagreeableness [Slang].
mullion, *n.* *mul*-yon, an upright bar in a window-frame. (Perhaps Fr. *moignon*, stump.)
mullioned, *a.* *mul*-yond, having mullions; divided by mullions, as a window.
mullock, *n.* *mul*-lok, rubbish; refuse, esp. from a mine; rock containing no gold [Austral.]. (*mull.*)
mulse, *n.* mulss, a drink of heated wine and honey. (L. *mulsum*, sweetened.)
multangular, *a.* mul-*tang*-gew-lar, having many angles. (L. *multangulus.*)

multangularly, *ad.* with many angles.
multarticulate, *a.* mult-ar-*tik*-yew-lat, having many joints. (L. *multus*, and *articulatus*.)
multeity, *n.* mul-*tee*-e-te, state or quality of being manifold; multiplicity. (L. *multus*, many.)
multi-, *mul*-te, Latin prefix signifying many, manifold, in many ways, as in *multipolar*, *multilingual*, *multilocation*. For words in *multi-* not here given reference should be made to the subsequent part of the word.
multicapsular, *a.* mul-te-*kap*-sew-lar, having many capsules [Bot.]. (L. *multus*, and *capsular*.)
multicarinate, *a.* mul-te-*ka*-re-nat, with many keel-like ridges [Conch.]. (L. *multus*, and *cariba*, a keel.)
multicavous, *a.* mul-te-*kay*-vus, having many cavities. (L. *multicavus*.)
multicellular, *a.* mul-te-*sel*-yew-lar, many-celled [Biol., etc.].
multicipital, *a.* mul-te-*sip*-e-tal, many-headed. (L. *multus*, and *caput*, a head.)
multicolour, *a.* *mul*-te-kul-or, in several colours; many-coloured.
multicostate, *a.* mul-te-*kos*-tat, many-ribbed. (L. *multus*, and *costa*, a rib.)
multicuspidate, *a.* mul-te-*kus*-pe-dat, having many cusps. (L. *multus*, and *cuspis*, a point.)
multi-cycle, *n.* mul-te-*sy*-kl, a velocipede with four or more wheels, or one carrying a number of riders.
multidentate, *a.* mul-te-*den*-tat, with numerous teeth or teeth-like processes. (L. *multus*, and *dens*, a tooth.)
multidigitate, *a.* mul-te-*dij*-e-tat, with many digits or finger-like processes. (L. *multus*, and *digitus*, a finger.)
multifarious, *a.* mul-te-*fare*-re-us, having great multiplicity; having great diversity or variety; manifold. (L. *multifarius*.)
multifariously, *ad.* with great variety.
multifariousness, *n.* mul-te-*fare*-re-us-ness, multiplied diversity.
multifid, *a.* *mul*-te-fid, multifidous.
multifidous, *a.* mul-*tif*-e-dus, having many lobes or divisions; many-cleft; divided into terminal strips. (L. *multifidus*.)
multiflorous, *a.* mul-te-*flaw*-rus, having many flowers. (L. *multus*, and *flos*, *floris*, a flower.)
multifoil, *a.* *mul*-te-foyl, with over five foils, or rounded leaf-like divisions (esp. of windows: *n.* an ornament consisting of more than five such foils [Arch.]. (L. *multus*, and *folium*, a leaf.)
multifold, *a.* *mul*-te-fohld, many times doubled.
multiform, *a.* *mul*-te-form, having many forms or shapes. (L. *multiformis*.)
multiformity, *n.* mul-te-*form*-e-te, state of being multiform; diversity of forms.
multigraph, *mul*-te-graf, proprietary name of a printing machine intended for office use.
multigyrate, *a.* mul-te-*jire*-rat, much convoluted.
multijugous, *a.* mul-te-*joo*-gus, having many pairs of leaflets [Bot.]. (L. *multijugus*.)
multilateral, *a.* mul-te-*lat*-er-al, having many sides. (L. *multus*, and *latus*, *lateris*, a side.)
multilineal, *a.* mul-te-*lin*-e-al, having many lines. (L. *multus*, and *linea*, a line.)
multilobate, *a.* mul-te-*loh*-bat, with many lobes.
multilocular, *a.* mul-te-*lok*-yew-lar, having many cells or chambers. (L.)
multiloquence, *n.* mul-*til*-o-kwence, use of many words; loquaciousness.
multiloquous, *a.* mul-*til*-o-kwus, speaking much; loquacious. (L. *multiloquens*.)
multinodate, *a.* mul-te-*noh*-dat, having many knots. (L. *multinodus*, having many knots.)
multinomial, *a.* mul-te-*noh*-me-al, having many names or terms, used esp. of an expression denoting several terms connected by the sign of addition or subtraction (+ or −): *n.* an expression of this nature [Alg.]. (L. *multinominis*.)
multinominal, *a.* mul-te-*nom*-e-nal, having many names.
multipara, *n.* mul-*tip*-a-ra, a woman who has borne two or more children [Med.].
multiparity, *n.* mul-te-*pa*-re-te, the production of several at a birth.
multiparous, *a.* mul-*tip*-a-rus, producing many at a birth; pertaining to a multipara, or [Bot.] to a cyme having three or more lateral axes. (L. *multus*, and *pario*, produce.)
multipartite, *a.* mul-te-*par*-tite, divided into many parts. (L. *multipartitus*.)
multiped, *a.* *mul*-te-ped, with many feet: *n.* an animal with many feet, as a centipede. (L. *multipeda*.)
multiphase, *a.* *mul*-te-fayz, polyphase [Elect.].
multiplane, *n.* *mul*-te-plane, an aeroplane with more than two supporting planes.
multiple, *a.* *mul*-te-pl, containing many times: *n.* a quantity which contains another a certain number of times without a remainder [Math.]. **common multiple,** one which contains two or more different numbers exactly. **least common multiple,** the lowest that will contain two or more numbers exactly. **multiple fruit,** an aggregation of fruits from a combination of flowers. **multiple shop,** one of a number of retail shops under the same ownership and central management, and selling similar goods. **multiple values,** symbols which fulfil the algebraical conditions of a problem when different values are given them [Alg.]. (L. *multus*, and *plico*, fold.)
multiplepoinding, *n.* *mul*-te-pl-*poyn*-ding, an action to decide the ownership of property, etc. to which there are several claimants [Scots. Law]. (*multiple* and *poind*.)
multiplex, *a.* *mul*-te-pleks, manifold; designating a transmission system by which several messages are carried simultaneously [Teleg., Wire., etc.]. (L.)
multipliable, *a.* *mul*-te-*ply*-a-bl, that can be multiplied.
multiplicable, *a.* *mul*-te-plik-a-bl, multipliable. (L.)
multiplicand, *n.* *mul*-te-ple-*kand*, the number or quantity to be multiplied [Arith.].
multiplicate, *a.* *mul*-te-plik-at, consisting of many; multiplex. (L. *multiplicatus*.)
multiplication, *n.* *mul*-te-ple-*kay*-shon, the act or process of multiplying; state of being multiplied; a rule or operation by which any given number is multiplied, or added to itself a given number of times [Arith.]. (L. *multiplicatio*.)
multiplicative, *a.* *mul*-te-plik-a-tiv, tending to multiply or increase; capable of multiplying.
multiplicator, *n.* *mul*-te-ple-*kay*-tor, a multiplier or intensifier of electrical forces, current, etc.
multiplicity, *n.* mul-te-*plis*-e-te, a great number; many of the same kind.
multiplier, *n.* *mul*-te-ply-er, one who or that which multiplies or increases; the number by which another is multiplied; an instrument for intensifying the force of an electric current.
multiply, *v.t.* *mul*-te-ply, to increase in number; to make more by natural generation, or production, or addition; to add any given number to itself a given number of times: *v.i.* to grow or increase in number; to increase in extent. **multiplying glass,** a glass with many facets giving many reflections of a single object. (Fr. *multiplier*.)
multiply, *ad.* *mul*-te-ple, in a multiple way; in the manner of a multiple.
multi-ply, *n.* plywood of more than three layers: *a.* constructed thus, or of this.
multipolar, *a.* *mul*-te-*poh*-lar, having more than one pair of poles [Elect.].
multipotent, *a.* mul-*tip*-o-tent, having power to do many things. (L. *multipotens*, very mighty.)
multipresence, *n.* *mul*-te-prez-ence, the power or act of being present in many places at once.
multipresent, *a.* *mul*-te-prez-ent, having the power of multipresence.
multiradiate, *a.* mul-te-*ray*-de-at, having many rays. (L. *multus*, and *radius*, a ray.)
multisect, *v.t.* *mul*-te-sekt, to divide into a number of segments. (L. *multus*, and *sectum*, cut.)
multisiliquous, *a.* mul-te-*sil*-e-kwus, having many pods. (L. *multus*, and *siliqua*, a pod.)
multisonous, *a.* mul-*tis*-o-nus, having many sounds, or sounding much. (L. *multisonus*.)
multispiral, *a.* mul-te-*spire*-ral, with many spirals or whorls, as in the opercula of univalve shells.
multistaminate, *a.* *mul*-te-*stam*-e-nat, with many stamens.
multisulcate, *a.* *mul*-te-*sul*-kat, much furrowed.
multisyllable, *n.* mul-te-*sil*-la-bl, a polysyllable.
multituberculate, *a.* *mul*-te-tew-*ber*-kew-lat, with many tubercles.
multitubular, *a.* *mul*-te-*tew*-bew-lar, with many tubes.

multitude, *n.* *mul*-te-tewd, a great number; a crowd; an assemblage; the common people. (Fr.)
multitudinous, *a.* mul-te-*tew*-de-nus, consisting of a great number or extent; of the multitude.
multitudinously, *ad.* mul-te-*tew*-de-nus-le, after the manner of a multitude.
multivagant, *a.* mul-*tiv*-a-gant, addicted to wandering (*multi-*, and L. *vagus*, wandering.)
multivalent, *a.* mul-*tiv*-a-lent, having more than two valencies; having a valence of several units [Chem.].
multivalve, *a.* *mul*-te-valv, with many valves: *n.* a mollusc with a shell of many valves; a multivalve shell.
multivalvular, *a.* mul-te-*valv*-yew-lar, multivalve.
multivious, *a.* mul-*tiv*-e-us, leading in many directions; having many paths. (*multi-*, and L. *via*, way.)
multivocal, *a.* mul-*tiv*-o-kal, ambiguous; equivocal: *n.* an ambiguous word.
multiwire, *a.* *mul*-te-wire, having a number of horizontal parallel wires (of antennæ) [Wire.].
multocular, *a.* mul-*tok*-yew-lar, having many eyes.
multum, *n.* *mul*-tum, a compound extract of quassia and liquorice formerly used as an adulterant of beer. (L., much.)
multungulate, *a.* mul-*tung*-gew-late, having the hoof divided into more than two parts, as the elephant [Zool.]. (L. *multus*, and *ungula*, a hoof.)
multure, *n.* *mul*-tewr, the fee for grinding grain at a mill [Law.] (O.Fr.)
mum, *a.* mum, silent: *int.* hush! be silent. **mum budget,** an expression denoting secrecy, as well as silence. **mum's the word**! keep silence (about this; it's secret)! (From the sound.)
mum, *n.* mum, abbreviation of mummy, an infantile term for mother.
mum, *n.* mum, a kind of ale, originally brewed in Germany from wheat. (Ger. *mumme.*)
mumble, *v.i.* *mum*-bl, to mutter; to speak inarticulately; to chew softly, or eat with the lips close: *v.t.* to utter with a low inarticulate voice; to mouth gently: *n.* an indistinct utterance. (*mum.*)
mumblement, *n.* *mum*-bl-ment, inarticulate speech.
mumbler, *n.* *mum*-bler, one who mumbles.
mumblingly, *ad.* *mum*-bling-le, in a mumbling way.
mumbo-jumbo, *n.* *mum*-bo-*jum*-bo, a grotesque West African idol; any similar object of reasonless veneration. (Jargon, possibly from a native source.)
mumchance, *n.* *mum*-chahnce, a game of hazard with cards; tongue-tied; a fool: *a.* silent; tongue-tied.
mummer, *n.* *mum*-mer, an actor in dumb-show; one who masks himself and makes diversion in disguise; an actor. (*mum.*)
mummery, *n.* *mum*-mer-re, masquerading; buffoonery; empty parade.
mummied, *a.* *mum*-ed, embalmed or mummified.
mummification, *n.* *mum*-me-fe-*kay*-shon, the process of mummifying; the act of making into a mummy.
mummiform, *a.* *mum*-me-form, shaped like a mummy.
mummify, *v.t.* *mum*-me-fy, to make into a mummy; to embalm and dry as a mummy: *v.i.* to become shrivelled like a mummy [Med.].
mumming, *n.* *mum*-ming, the sports of mummers.
mummy, *n.* *mum*-me, mother; mamma [Childish].
mummy, *n.* *mum*-me, a dead body embalmed with myrrh and spices, and dried after the manner of the ancient Egyptians; a shrivelled, dried up person; a sort of wax used in grafting and planting trees; a bituminous substance, giving a rich brown tint: *v.t.* and *i.* to mummify. **beat to a mummy,** to beat soundly. **mummy wheat,** an Egyptian wheat alleged to be grown from seed found in mummy-cases. (Fr. *momie*, from Ar. *mum*, wax used in embalming.)
mump, *v.t.* and *i.* mump, to move the lips with the mouth almost closed; to nibble; to chew with continued motion; to grin; to whine or deceive as a beggar. (Perhaps, M.Dut. *mompelen*, to whine.)
mumper, *n.* *mump*-er, a whining beggar.
mumpish, *a.* *mump*-ish, dull; heavy; sullen.
mumpishly, *ad.* *mump*-ish-le, in a mumpish manner.
mumps, *n.pl.* mumps, epidemic parotitis; a contagious swelling or inflammation of the salivary glands, and specially of the parotid gland. (*mump.*)
mumpsimus, *n.* *mump*-se-mus, a mistake or opinion adhered to after it has been proved to be wrong.
munch, *v.t.* and *i.* munsh, to chew eagerly and noisily, esp. with the mouth shut. (Imit.).
Munchausen, *n.* mun-*chaw*-zen, a braggart; an incredible yarn. (After the sham autobiography of "Baron *Munchausen*" by R. E. Raspe, 1785.)
muncher, *n.* *munsh*-er, one who munches.
mundane, *a.* *mun*-dane, pertaining to this world or its affairs; worldly. (Fr. *mondain.*)
mundanely, *ad.* in a mundane reference.
mundic, *n.* *mun*-dik, iron pyrites (so called by Cornish miners). (Probably Corn.)
mundificant, *a.* *mun-dif*-e-kant, cleansing and healing; *n.* a cleansing agent.
mundification, *n.* *mun*-dif-e-*kay*-shon, the operation of cleansing.
mundificative, *a.* mun-*dif*-e-ka-tiv, having the power to cleanse: *n.* a medicine having this property.
mundify, *v.t.* *mun*-de-fy, to cleanse, esp. [Med.] to deterge. (L. *mundificare*, to make clean.) (Fr. *mondifier.*)
mundivagant, *a.* mun-*div*-a-gant, wandering over the world. (L. *mundus*, the world, *vagans*, wandering.)
mundungus, *n.* mun-*dung*-gus, any rank tobacco with an unpleasant smell.
mungo, *n.* *mung*-go, a shoddy-like cloth made from woollen rags.
mungoose, *n.* *mung*-goose (*pl.* **mungooses**), a small weasel-like carnivore of the genus *Herpestes*, esp. the Indian mungoose, *H. mungo*, famed as a snake-killer.
municipal, *a.* mew-*nis*-e-pal, pertaining to a town, city, or state, or to local government. **municipal borough,** *see* **borough. municipal law,** the general or common law of a country or of a city. (Fr. *municipal*, from L. *municipium*, a free town with the rights of Roman citizenship, from *munia*, duties, functions, *capio*, take.)
municipalism, *n.* mew-*nis*-e-pa-lizm, local government; municipal institutions; local patriotism.
municipality, *n.* mew-nis-e-*pal*-e-te, a town or district having self-governing powers; a municipal corporation.
municipalization, *n.* mew-*nis*-e-pa-ly-*zay*-shon, the act or process of making a municipality.
municipalize, *v.t.* mew-*nis*-e-pa-lize, to constitute a municipality; to comprise within a municipal area.
municipally, *ad.* in a municipal manner. (Fr.)
munificence, *n.* mew-*nif*-e-sence, the quality of being munificent; liberality; generosity. (Fr.)
munificent, *a.* mew-*nif*-e-sent, giving liberally or generously; manifesting liberality. (L. *munificus.*)
munificently, *ad.* liberally.
muniment, *n.* *mew*-ne-ment, a record by which claims and rights are maintained; title-deed; formerly, a means or place of defence. **muniment room,** a strong fire-proof building or apartment for preserving muniments, charters, etc. (O.Fr.)
munition, *v.t.* mew-*nish*-on, to equip (as an army); to furnish with stores and arms.
munitions, *n.pl.* mew-*nish*-onz, materials used in war; military stores; requisites, or necessary equipment, for an undertaking. (Fr.)
munjeet, *n.* mun-*jeet*, the Siberian madder, *Rubia cordifolia*, the root of which yields a red dye. (Hind.)
munnion, *n.* *mun*-yon, a mullion.
munshi, *n.* *moon*-she, a teacher, usually of languages, in the East; an interpreter; a secretary. (Hind.)
muntin, *n.* *munt*-in, the middle upright dividing the panels of a framed door. (Fr. *montant*, rising.)
muntjak, *n.* munt-*jak*, the East Indian barking deer, *Cervulus muntjac.* (Malay.)
muntz-metal, *n.* *muntz*-met-al, an alloy of 60 parts copper, and 40 zinc, so called from the inventor.
Muræna, *n.* mew-*ree*-na, a genus of voracious tropical marine eels. (L.)
murage, *n.* *mewr*-raj, a toll formerly levied for maintaining the walls of a town. (Fr.)
mural, *a.* *mew*-ral, pertaining to or resembling a wall; attached to a wall [Med.]. **mural arc** or **circle,** a circle formerly attached to a wall in the plane of the meridian for measuring distances from the pole or zenith. **mural crown,** an embattled crown bestowed among the Romans on the foremost soldier in scaling the wall of a besieged city. (Fr.)

murder, *n.* *mur*-der, the act of unlawfully killing a human being with premeditated malice: *v.t.* to kill a human being thus; to slay; to destroy; to mar and disfigure. (A.S. *morthor.*)
murderer, *n.* *mur*-der-er, one who commits murder.
murderess, *n.* *mur*-der-ess, a female murderer.
murderous, *a.* *mur*-der-us, guilty of, consisting in, or attended with, murder.
murderously, *ad.* in a murderous manner.
mure, *v.t.* mewr, to immure, to surround with walls.
murex, *n.* *mew*-reks (*pl.* **murices,** *mew*-re-seez), a genus of marine whelk-like molluscs, one species of which yielded the purple Tyrian dye of the ancients. (L.)
murexide, *n.* mew-*reks*-ide, the crystalline ammonium salt of purpuric acid formerly used for dyeing purple. (*murex.*)
muriate, *n.* *mew*-re-ate, a salt of hydrochloric acid.
muriated, *a.* *mew*-re-ay-ted, combined or impregnated with chlorine; soaked in brine.
muriatic, *a.* mew-re-*at*-ik, hydrochloric. (L. *muriaticus*, brine-soaked.)
muricate, *a.* *mew*-re-kat, furnished with sharp points or prickles [Bot. and Zool.]. (L. *muricatus*, prickly.)
muriculate, *a.* mew-*rik*-yew-lat, with very short prickles [Bot. and Zool.].
muriform, *a.* *mew*-re-form, resembling the arrangement of bricks in a wall (of cells) [Bot.]. (L. *murus*, a wall, *forma*, shape.)
murine, *a.* *mew*-rin, resembling a mouse; pertaining to the mice. (L. *mus*, *muris*, a mouse.)
muriti, *n.* moor-*ree*-te, the Brazilian fan-palm, *Mauritia vinifera*, allied to the miriti. (Tupi.)
murk, *n.* murk, darkness; gloom. (A.S. *murc.*)
murkily, *ad.* *murk*-e-le, in a murky manner.
murkiness, *n.* *murk*-e-ness, the state of being murky.
murky, *a.* *murk*-e, dark; obscure; gloomy.
murmur, *n.* *mur*-mur, an indistinct sound, continually repeated, as that of a running stream; a half-suppressed complaint; hushed voices; the sound (esp. when abnormal) heard in auscultation of the heart [Med.]: *v.i.* to make a low, continued noise or hum; to grumble; to complain; to mutter discontentedly. (Fr. *murmure.*)
murmurer, *n.* *mur*-mur-er, one who murmurs; a grumbler.
murmuringly, *ad.* *mur*-mur-ing-le, with a murmuring sound; in a non-complaisant way.
murmurous, *a.* *mur*-mur-us, characterized by or exciting murmur or complaint; murmuring.
murphy, *n.* *mur*-fe, a potato [Slang].
murrain, *n.* *mu*-ran, an infectious disease among cattle: *a.* affected with this. (O.Fr. *morine.*)
murre, *n.* murr, the razorbill, or any guillemot.
murrey, *a.* *mu*-re, of a purplish red colour like the mulberry: *n.* this colour, cloth of this colour. (O.Fr. *morée.*)
murrhine, *a.* *mu*-rin, an epithet given to a delicate kind of ancient ware, made of fluor-spar. (L.)
Musca, *n.* *mus*-ka (*pl.* **Muscæ**), a genus of dipterous insects, including the house-flies. **muscæ volitantes,** imaginary motes floating before the eye [Med.]. (L.)
muscadel, *n.* *mus*-ka-del, muscatel.
muscadine, *n.* *mus*-ka-din, a variety of grape with a slight odour of musk; the wine muscatel.
muscal, *a.* *mus*-kal, pertaining to the mosses.
muscardine, *n.* *mus*-kar-din, a fungus or rot destructive to silkworms; the disease caused by this. (Fr.)
muscarin, *n.* *mus*-ka-rin, a tasteless poisonous crystalline alkaloid present in certain fungi. (L. *muscarius*, pertaining to flies.)
muscat, *n.* *mus*-kat, muscatel.
muscatel, *n.* *mus*-ka-tel, a rich, sweet wine; the grapes which produce it, esp. the malaga grape; a dessert raisin. (O.Fr. *muscadel*, from It. *moscato*, musk.)
muschelkalk, *n.* *mush*-el-kalk, shell limestone, belonging to the middle beds of the German Triassic [Geol.]. (Ger. *Musckel*, mussel, *Kalk*, lime.)
musci, *n.pl.* *mus*-sy, the mosses. (L.)
muscite, *n.* *mus*-site, a fossil moss, esp. as found in amber.
★**muscle,** *n.* *mus*-sl, an animal organ of motion, contractile and extensile, consisting of fibres wrapped in a sheath of connective tissue; muscular strength: *v.i.* to force (in or through) by brute strength [Coll.]. **to muscle in,** to break in where one has no right or is unwelcome; to intrude against opposition [Coll.]. (Fr.)
muscled, *a.* *mus*-sld, having (well-developed) muscles.
muscoid, *a.* *mus*-koyd, moss-like: *n.* a moss-like flowerless plant. (L. *muscus*, moss, *eidos*, like.)
muscology, *n.* mus-*kol*-o-je, that part of botany which treats of mosses.
muscose, *a.* *mus*-kohs, like moss.
muscovado, *n.* mus-ko-*vay*-do, raw or unrefined sugar from cane juice. (Sp.)
Muscovite, *n.* *mus*-ko-vite, a native of Muscovy, *i.e.* Russia; (*l.c.*) common mica, also known as Muscovy glass [Min.]: *a.* (*cap.*) Russian. **Muscovy duck,** the tropical American duck, *Cairina moschata.*
muscular, *a.* *mus*-kew-lar, pertaining to a muscle; consisting of or dependent on muscles; strong; brawny; vigorous; robust; active. (L. *musculus.*)
muscularity, *n.* mus-kew-*la*-re-te, the state of being muscular.
muscularly, *ad.* *mus*-kew-lar-le, in a muscular manner; with strength of muscle.
musculation, *n.* mus-kew-*lay*-shon, the whole muscular system.
musculature, *n.* *mus*-kew-la-tewr, a set of muscles; musculation.
Muse, *n.* mewz, one of the nine sister goddesses, daughters of Zeus and Mnemosyne, that presided each over one of the nine liberal arts of the ancient Greeks, being Clio (history); Euterpe (lyric poetry); Thalia (comedy); Melpomene (tragedy); Terpsichore (choral dance and music); Erato (erotic poetry); Polyhymnia (harmony and song); Urania (astronomy); Calliope (epic poetry) [Myth.]; poetical genius; the power of song. (Fr.)
muse, *n.* mewz, meditation; absence of mind: *v.i.* to ponder; to think closely; to study in silence; to be abstracted in mind: *v.t.* to meditate on. (Fr. *muser.*)
museful, *a.* *mewz*-ful, silently thoughtful.
muser, *n.* *mewz*-er, one given to musing.
musette, *n.* mew-*zet*, a soft, sweet, musical air; a rustic dance; a small bagpipe. (Fr.)
museum, *n.* mew-*zee*-um, a repository of natural, scientific, artistic, or literary specimens and objects of interest. **museum piece,** an object suitable for exhibition in a museum; a first-class specimen; a person or thing of particular interest. (L.)
mush, *n.* mush, the meal of maize boiled; any pulpy mass; hasty pudding: *v.t.* and *i.* to mash; to reduce to mush. (*mash*).
mush, *n.* mush, an umbrella [Slang]. (*mushroom.*)
mush, *v.i.* mush, to proceed by dog sled [U.S.A.]. (Fr. *marche.*)
mushiness, *n.* *mush*-e-ness, a state of being mushy; sponginess; sickly sentimentality.
mushroom, *n.* *mush*-room, an edible fungus, esp. *Agaricus campestris*; an upstart: *a.* like a mushroom in sudden growth and decay; upstart; of mushroom shape: *v.i.* to gather mushrooms; to grow or expand like a mushroom; to bulge upwards. **mushroom spawn,** the spores of the mushroom. (O.Fr. *mousseron.*)
mushy, *a.* *mush*-e, pulpy; moist and soft; insipid; over-sentimental; milk-soppy.
★**music,** *n.* *mew*-zik, melody or harmony; any succession of sound so modulated as to please the ear; the science of harmonic sounds, or the art of producing such; rhythmic order; musical taste. (Fr. *musique*, from L. *musica.*)
musical, *a.* *mew*-ze-kal, belonging to or producing music or agreeable sounds; fond of music; melodious; pleasing to the ear. **musical-box,** a mechanical device by which a set selection of tunes may be played. **musical clock,** a clock which plays tunes at the hours. **musical comedy,** a light dramatic entertainment, with dancing, singing, and dialogue linked together by a slender plot. **musical glasses,** a musical instrument consisting of a number of glass goblets. **musical ride,** a military exercise performed on horseback to music.
musicale, *n.* mew-ze-*kahl*, a musical party; an informal concert. (Fr.)
musicality, *n.* *mew*-ze-*kal*-e-te, musicalness.
musically, *ad.* *mew*-ze-ka-le, in a musical manner.
musicalness, *n.* *mew*-ze-kal-ness, the quality of being musical.

music-book, *n.* a book containing tunes or songs.
music-hall, *n.* a hall in which revues, vaudeville, and light variety shows are given.
musician, *n.* mew-*zish*-an, a professional performer on instruments of music; one skilled in the science of music; a composer. (Fr. *musicien.*)
musicianly, *a.* mew-*zish*-an-ly, characterized by the qualities, or exhibiting the taste, of a skilled musician.
musicology, *n.* mew-ze-*kol*-o-je, the historical and scientific study of music.
musicomania, *n.* *mew*-ze-ko-*may*-ne-a, morbid or inordinate love of music.
music-paper, *n.* paper printed with lines for the transcription of music.
music-stand, *n.* a light frame for holding a piece or book of music.
music-stool, *n.* a stool or seat for one who performs on the pianoforte.
musingly, *ad.* *mew*-zing-le, in a musing or meditative way.
musk, *n.* musk, a strong-scented secretion obtained from the musk-deer, used as a basis of perfumes; a scent as of musk; the musk-deer; the plant, *Mimulus moschatus,* and similarly scented plants. (Fr. *musc.*)
musk-beaver, *n.* the musk-rat.
musk-deer, *n.* the small Central Asian deer, *Moschus moschiferus,* that yields musk.
musk-duck, *n.* the Muscovy duck, also the Australian duck, *Biziura lobata.*
muskelonge, *n.* *mus*-ke-lunj, the large pike of the N. American lakes, *Esox masquinongy,* reaching 70 lb. or more. (Ojibway, *mashkinoje.*)
musket, *n.* *mus*-ket, the muzzle-loading smooth-bore firearm formerly used by infantry. (O.Fr. *mousquet.*)
musketeer, *n.* mus-ke-*teer,* a soldier armed with a musket. (Fr. *mousquetaire.*)
musketoon, *n.* mus-ke-*toon,* a short thick musket, or blunderbuss; one so armed. (Fr. *mousqueton.*)
musketry, *n.* *mus*-ke-tre, muskets, or musketeers, collectively; the art of using a musket; musket fire; the theory and practice of rifle-shooting. (Fr. *mousqueterie.*)
muskiness, *n.* *mus*-ke-ness, the scent of musk.
musk-mallow, *n.* the plant *Malva moschata*; also the abelmosk.
musk-melon, *n.* the melon *Cucurbita melo.*
musk-orchis, *n.* the musk-scented orchid, *Herminium monorchis.*
musk-ox, *n.* the bovine ungulate *Ovibos moschatus,* inhabiting Greenland and Arctic America.
musk-pear, *n.* a musk-scented pear.
musk-rat, *n.* the musquash, *Fiber zibethicus,* a destructive North American aquatic rodent allied to the beaver.
musk-rose, *n.* a species of rambling rose with a musky scent.
musk-shrew, *n.* an East Indian insectivore of the genus *Crocidura.*
musk-thistle, *n.* the plant *Carduus nutans.*
musk-wood, *n.* a name of various trees or timbers having a musky smell.
musky, *a.* *mus*-ke, having the odour of musk; like musk; fragrant.
Muslim, *n.* and *a.* *mus*-lim, Moslem.
muslin, *n.* *muz*-lin, a fine thin cotton cloth: *a.* made of muslin. **muslin-de-laine,** *see* **mousseline.** (Fr. *mousseline,* from *Moseil,* in Irak, where first made.)
muslinet, *n.* muz-lin-*et,* a sort of coarse muslin.
musmon, *n.* *mus*-mon, the mouflon.
musnud, *n.* *moos*-nud, the throne of cushions used by Indian and Persian princes. (Hind. *masnad.*)
musquash, *n.* *mus*-kwosh, the musk-rat; the dressed skin of this. (Algonquian.)
muss, *n.* mus, a scramble; a confused struggle: *v.t.* to disarrange [U.S.A.]. (*mess.*)
mussal, *n.* moo-*sahl,* a torch made of rags. (Urdu.)
mussel, *n.* *mus*-sl, any bivalve mollusc of the marine genus *Mytilus* or of the freshwater genera *Unio* and *Anodonta.* (A.S. *muscelle* or *muxle,* as *muscle.*)
mussitation, *n.* mus-e-*tay*-shon, a mumbling; a movement, as in mumbling; the inarticulate muttering of delirium. (L.)
Mussulman, *n.* *mus*-sul-man (*pl.* **Mussulmans**), an adherent of Islam; a Mohammedan. (Per., true believer.)

must, *v.aux.* must, obliged or necessitated. (A.S.)
must, *n.* must, mustiness; mould; wine from the grape not fermented: *v.i.* to grow mouldy and sour: *v.t.* to make mouldy and sour.
must, *a.* must, mad, frenzied (esp. of male elephants): *n.* the state or condition of frenzy. (Hind.)
mustachio, *n.* mus-*tahsh*-e-oh, moustache.
mustachioed, *a.* mus-*tahsh*-e-ode, having moustaches.
mustang, *n.* *mus*-tang, the half-wild horse of the American prairies. (Sp. *mestengo,* stray.)
mustard, *n.* *mus*-tard, the plant of the genus *Sinapis* (esp. *S. alba*) and its seeds; a pungent condiment prepared from the seeds; that which improves the flavour of anything; a piquant person or thing [Slang]. **French mustard,** table mustard prepared with vinegar, etc. **mustard and cress,** a salad composed of *S. alba* and *Lepidium sativum.* **mustard gas,** a poison gas having an irritant and blistering action and a faint smell of mustard or horse-radish. **mustard plaster,** a counter-irritant poultice of mustard. **oil of mustard,** a pungent oil obtained from the seeds of black mustard, *S. nigra.* (O.Fr. *mostarde.*)
mustard-pot, *n.* a small receptacle for holding mustard at table.
mustee, *n.* mus-*tee,* the offspring of a white person and a quadroon, esp. in the West Indies.
Mustela, *n.* mus-*tee*-la, the genus of small carnivores comprising the weasels.
musteline, *a.* and *n.* *mus*-te-lin, pertaining to, or a member of, the weasel family.
muster, *n.* *mus*-ter, an assembling of troops; a review; a display; a roll of troops mustered; a collection or the act of collecting: *v.t.* to assemble troops, persons, or things generally for review: *v.i.* to meet in one place. **pass muster,** to be accepted, after inspection, as satisfactory. (O.Fr. *mostre.*)
muster-book, *n.* a book in which military forces are registered.
musterer, *n.* *mus*-ter-rer, one who rounds up livestock [Austral.].
muster-master, *n.* one who takes an account of troops and of military equipment.
muster-roll, *n.* a roll or register of troops, or a ship's company, etc.
mustily, *ad.* *mus*-te-le, in a mouldy manner; sourly.
mustiness, *n.* *mus*-te-ness, the quality of being musty.
musty, *a.* *mus*-te, mouldy; sour; stale; having an ill flavour; vapid; spiritless. (L. *musteus.*)
mutability, *n.* mew-ta-*bil*-e-te, the quality of being mutable; changeableness; instability.
mutable, *a.* *mew*-ta-bl, susceptible of change; changeable; inconstant; unstable. (L. *mutabilis.*)
mutably, *ad.* *mew*-ta-ble, in a mutable manner.
mutacism, *n.* *mew*-ta-sizm, mytacism. (Gr. *mu,* m.)
mutage, *n.* *mew*-taj, a process for checking fermentation in the must of grapes. (Fr.)
mutant, *n.* *mew*-tant, anything that has undergone mutation; a species resulting from mutation [Biol.]: *a.* of, or belonging to, mutation.
mutate, *v.i.* *mew*-tate, to undergo mutation [Philol.]: *n.* a mutant.
mutation, *n.* mew-*tay*-shon, the act or process of changing; alteration; a permanent change in organism effecting a new species, and a species so produced [Biol.]: umlaut [Philol.]. (L. *mutare,* to change.)
mutative, *a.* *mew*-ta-tiv, changeable; pertaining to mutation; tending to mutate [Biol.].
mutch, *n.* mutch, a woman's linen or muslin coif or cap. (M.Dut. *mutse.*)
mutchkin, *n.* *mutch*-kin, a Scottish liquid measure of about ¾ pint. (M.Dut. *mudseken.*)
mute, *n.* mewt, the dung of fowls: *v.i.* to eject the contents of the bowels, as birds. (O.Fr. *mutir.*) (Dial. Eng.)
mute, *a.* mewt, silent; not uttering words; uttering no sound; dumb; not sounded [Gram.]: *n.* one who cannot speak; one who remains silent; one employed by undertakers as an attendant at a funeral; a letter that represents no sound [Gram.]; a consonant which stops the sound [Gram.]; one speechless when he should plead [Law]; a sordine, an appliance for deadening or softening sound [Mus.]: *v.t.* to deaden or soften (sound); to subdue or diminish (light). (L. *mutus,* dumb.)

mutely, *ad.* *mewt*-le, in a mute manner.
muteness, *n.* *mewt*-ness, the state of being mute.
muticate, *a.* *mew*-te-kat, not having an awn or point [Bot.]; devoid of the defensive parts [Zool.]. (L. *muticus*, docked.)
mutilate, *v.t.* *mew*-te-late, to cut off a limb or an essential part of; to maim; to render imperfect, esp. by excision. (L. *mutilatus*, maimed.)
mutilation, *n.* mew-te-*lay*-shon, the act of mutilating; a maimed state.
mutilator, *n.* *mew*-te-lay-tor, one who mutilates.
mutineer, *n.* mew-te-*neer*, one guilty of mutiny. (O.Fr. *mutinier*.)
muting, *n.* *mewt*-ing, the dung or droppings of birds.
mutinous, *a.* *mew*-te-nus, disposed to mutiny; guilty of mutiny; seditious.
mutinously, *ad.* in a mutinous manner.
mutinousness, *n.* state of being mutinous.
mutiny, *n.* *mew*-te-ne, an insurrection against constituted authority, specially of soldiers or seamen against their commanders: *v.i.* to rise or stir up revolt against lawful authority. **the Mutiny,** the Indian Mutiny of 1857–58. (Fr. *mutin*.)
mutism, *n.* *mewt*-izm, the condition of the dumb; speechlessness; an inability to hear and to speak or articulate audibly.
mutograph, *n.* *mew*-to-graf, an early form of apparatus for exhibiting pictures of objects in motion.
mutoscope, *n.* *mew*-to-skope, an early form of apparatus for the projection of cinematographic pictures. (L. *mutare*, change.)
mutt, *n.* mut, a fool; a simpleton; a stupid person [U.S.A. slang]. (*muttonhead*.)
mutter, *n.* *mut*-ter, murmur; obscure utterance: *v.i.* to utter words with a low voice and compressed lips, with sullenness and complaint; to grumble; to murmur; to sound with a low, rumbling noise: *v.t.* to utter with imperfect articulations or a low, murmuring voice. (Probably imit.)
mutterer, *n.* *mut*-ter-er, one who mutters.
mutteringly, *ad.* *mut*-ter-ing-le, with a low voice.
mutton, *n.* *mut*-ton, the flesh of sheep as human food. **to return to one's muttons,** to come back to the subject. (Fr. *mouton*, a sheep.)
mutton-bird, *n.* any of several large Antarctic petrels or shearwaters [Austral.].
mutton-chops, *n.* side whiskers having an outline resembling that of a mutton-chop [Coll.].
mutton-fist, *n.* a large, brawny hand.
mutton-ham, *n.* a leg of mutton salted and cured as a ham.
muttonhead, *n.* *mut*-ton-hed, a dull person.
muttonheaded, *a.* *mut*-ton-*hed*-ed, dull, stupid.
muttony, *a.* *mut*-ton-e, resembling mutton in taste.
mutual, *a.* *mew*-tew-al, reciprocal; interchanged; given and received; shared by each of two towards each other. (O.Fr. *mutuel*.)
mutualism, *n.* *mew*-tew-a-lizm, the doctrine that well-being is secured only by mutual dependence; symbiosis in which the associated organisms are beneficial to each other [Biol.].
mutuality, *n.* mew-tew-*al*-e-te, the state of being mutual; reciprocation.
mutualize, *v.t.* and *i.* *mew*-tew-a-lize, to make or become mutual.
mutually, *ad.* *mew*-tew-al-le, reciprocally.
mutule, *n.* *mew*-tewl, a projecting block under the corner of the Doric cornice. (L. *mutulus*.)
Muzarab, *n.* mooz-*a*-rab, Mozarab.
muzhik, *n.* *moo*-zhik, a mujik [Russ.].
muzzily, *ad.* *muz*-ze-le, in a muzzy manner.
muzziness, *n.* drunkenness; muddle-headedness.
muzzle, *n.* *muz*-zl, a snout; the mouth of anything; a guard over the mouth which hinders from biting; the mouth of a rifle, gun, etc.: *v.t.* to fasten the mouth to prevent biting; to restrain from hurting: *v.i.* to feel or root about with the snout; to nuzzle. (O.Fr. *musel*.)
muzzle-loader, *n.* a firearm loaded through the muzzle.
muzzy, *a.* *muz*-ze, confused in mind; fuddled; tipsy.
my, *a.* my, *poss. pron.* belonging to me. (A.S. *min*.)
Mya, *n.* *my*-a, a genus of gaping bivalves including many of the clams. (L., a sea-mussel.)
myalgia, *n.* my-*al*-je-a, stiffness or pain in the muscles; muscular rheumatism [Med.]. (Gr. *mys*, a muscle, *algos*, pain.)
myalism, *n.* *my*-a-lizm, a form of West Indian sorcery practised to counteract obeahism. (Native name.)
myall, *n.* *my*-awl, the Australian tree *Acacia pendula*; a wild blackfellow.
mycelium, *n.* my-*see*-le-um, the vegetative mass of a fungus; mushroom spawn. (Gr. *mykos*, a mushroom.)
Mycenæan, *a.* my-se-*nee*-an, pertaining to Mycenæ, a city of ancient Argolis, in Greece, or to the civilization or art of its prime, about the 15th to 12th cent. B.C.
mycetes, *n.pl.* my-*see*-teez, the group of organisms commonly called microbes. (Gr., fungi.)
mycetismus, *n.* my-se-*tiz*-mus, mushroom-poisoning.
mycetoma, *n.* my-se-*toh*-ma, a fungoid skin-disease affecting esp. the feet; Madura foot [Med.]. (Gr. *mykēs*, a mushroom.)
Mycetozoa, *n.pl.* *my*-se-to-*zoh*-a, a group of minute organisms generally included in the Myxomycetes.
mycoderm, *n.* *my*-ko-derm, a fungous organism forming the mother of fermenting liquids. (Gr. *mykēs*, and *derma*, a skin.)
mycologic, *a.* *my*-ko-*loj*-ik, pertaining to mycology, or to fungi in general.
mycologist, *n.* my-*kol*-o-jist, one who studies fungi.
mycology, *n.* my-*kol*-o-je, the scientific study and classification of fungi. (Gr. *mykēs*, and *logos*, science.)
mycophagist, *n.* my-*kof*-a-jist, a fungus-eater.
mycophagy, *n.* my-*kof*-a-je, the eating of fungi.
mycosis, *n.* my-*koh*-sis, a fungoid growth within the body; the disease caused by this.
mydriasis, *n.* me-*dry*-a-sis, abnormal dilatation of the pupil of the eye.
mydriatic, *a.* my-dre-*at*-ik, causing dilatation of the pupil: *n.* an agent effecting this.
myectopy, *n.* my-*ek*-to-pe, abnormal displacement of a muscle. (Gr. *mys*, a muscle, and *ectopia*.)
myelitis, *n.* my-e-*ly*-tis, inflammation of the spinal cord. (Gr. *myelos*, marrow.)
myeloid, *a.* *my*-e-loyd, pertaining to the spinal cord; pertaining to or resembling marrow.
myelomeningitis, *n.* *my*-e-lo-*men*-in-*jy*-tis, inflammation of the membranes of the spinal cord.
Mygale, *n.* *mig*-a-lee, a genus of large S. American spiders. (L., a field-mouse.)
myiasis, *n.* my-e-*ay*-sis, any disease caused by the presence in or on the body of insect larvæ. (Gr.)
Mylodon, *n.* *my*-lo-don, an extinct genus of gigantic sloths. (Gr. *mylos*, a mill, *odous*, a tooth.)
mylohyoid, *a.* *my*-lo-*hy*-oyd, pertaining to the hyoid bone and the molar teeth.
myna, *n.* *my*-nah, the Indian starling, *Acridotheres tristis*; also, the grackle and other birds of allied genera.
mynheer, *n.* mine-*heer*, a Dutchman. (Dut. *mijn heer*, my lord.)
myocarditis, *n.* *my*-o-kar-*dy*-tis, inflammation of the myocardium.
myocardium, *n.* my-o-*kar*-de-um, the muscular substance of the heart [Med.]. (Gr. *mys*, a muscle, *kardia*, the heart.)
myodynamics, *n.* *my*-o-dy-*nam*-iks, the physiology of muscular action. (Gr. *mys*, and *dynamics*.)
myogenic, *a.* my-o-*jen*-ik, contracting spontaneously without nervous stimulation (of muscles) [Anat.].
myogenous, *a.* my-*oj*-e-nus, originating in muscle.
myographical, *a.* my-o-*graf*-e-kal, descriptive of the muscles.
myographist, *n.* my-*og*-ra-fist, one who describes the muscles.
myography, *n.* my-*og*-ra-fe, a description of the muscles. (Gr. *mys*, and *grapho*, write.)
myoid, *a.* *my*-oyd, resembling muscular tissue.
myological, *a.* my-o-*loj*-e-kal, descriptive of the muscles.
myologist, *n.* my-*ol*-o-jist, one versant in myology.
myology, *n.* my-*ol*-o-je, the study of the muscles. (Gr. *mys*, and *logos*, science.)
myomancy, *n.* *my*-o-*man*-se, divination from the actions of mice. (Gr. *mys*, a mouse, and *-mancy*.)
myonicity, *n.* *my*-o-*nis*-e-te, the contractile power or faculty of the muscles.
myopathy, *n.* my-*op*-a-the, disease of the muscles. (Gr. *mys*, and *pathos*, suffering.)
myope, *n.* *my*-ohp, a short-sighted person.
myopia, *n.* my-*oh*-pe-a, short-sightedness.

myopic, *a.* my-*op*-ik, relating to myopia.
myopy, *n.* *my*-o-pe, myopia. (Gr. *myo*, shut, *ops*, the eye.)
myosis, *n.* my-*oh*-sis, abnormal contraction of the pupil of the eye.
myositis, *n.* my-o-*sy*-tis, inflammation of the muscles.
Myosotis, *n.* my-o-*soh*-tis, the genus of plants including the forget-me-nots. (Gr.)
myotic, *a.* my-*ot*-ik, pertaining to or affected by myosis; inducing myosis: *n.* a drug effecting this.
myotomy, *n.* my-*ot*-o-me, dissection of the muscles. (Gr. *mys*, and *tome*, cutting.)
myriad, *n.* *mi*-re-ad, ten thousand; a multitude: *a.* innumerable. (Gr. *myrios*, innumerable.)
myriametre, *n.* mi-re-*am*-e-ter, ten thousand metres (=6 miles 376 yds.). (Fr.)
myriapod, *n.* *mi*-re-a-pod, a centipede or millipede.
Myriapoda, *n.pl.* mi-re-*ap*-o-da, a class of the Arthropoda, including such as have an indeterminate number of jointed feet [Zool.]. (Gr. *myrios*, and *pous*, a foot.)
Myrica, *n.* mi-*ry*-ka, a genus of plants including the candleberry myrtle, *M. cerifera*. (Gr. *myrike*, tamarisk.)
myricin, *n.* mi-*ry*-sin *or* *mire*-re-sin, a crystalline constituent of beeswax; the substance of beeswax digested in alcohol [Pharm.].
myriophyllous, *a.* mi-re-*of*-e-lus, with very many leaves [Bot.] (Gr. *myria*, and *phyllon*, a leaf.)
myriorama, *n.* mi-re-o-*rah*-ma, a variety of scenes produced from combinations of sections of views (Gr. *myrios*, and *horama*, a view.)
myrmecology, *n.* mer-me-*kol*-o-je, the scientific study of ants. (Gr. *myrmekos*, an ant.)
myrmecophagous, *a.* mer-me-*kof*-a-gus, feeding on ants [Zool.].
myrmidon, *n.* *mer*-me-don, a desperate soldier or ruffian under some daring leader, so called from the Myrmidons who accompanied Achilles to the Trojan war; an unscrupulous executioner of justice. (Gr.)
myrmidonian, *a.* mer-me-*doh*-ne-an, like to myrmidons.
myrobalan, *n.* my-*rob*-a-lan, the tropical plum-tree, *Terminalia chebula*, or its astringent fruit, used in dyeing and tanning. (Gr. *myron*, an unguent, *balanos*, an acorn.)
myrrh, *n.* mer, the resin from several of the fifty species of *Commiphora*; sweet cicely, *Myrrhis odorata*. (O.Fr. *mirre*.)
myrrhic, *a.* *mer*-rik, obtained from or pertaining to myrrh.
myrrhine, *a.* *mer*-rin, murrhine.
myrrhy, *a.* *mer*-re, abounding in, or having the scent of, myrrh.
myrtaceous, *a.* mer-*tay*-shus, belonging to or characteristic of the myrtle family [Bot.].
myrtiform, *a.* *mer*-te-form, resembling the myrtle-leaf or myrtle-berry in shape.
myrtle, *n.* *mer*-tl, an evergreen shrub of the genus *Myrtus*. **myrtle flag,** the sweet flag, *Acorus calamus*. (O.Fr. *mirtil*.)
myrtle-berry, *n.* the fruit of the myrtle.
myrtle-wax, *n.* a concrete oil or vegetable wax from *Myrica cerifera*.
myself, *pron.* my-*self*, a compound of *my* and *self*, used after "I" for emphasis; used reflexively as an object after a verb.
mysophobia, *n.* my-so-*foh*-be-a, morbid dread of dirt or contamination [Med.]. (Gr. *mysos*, uncleanness, and *-phobia*.)
mystagogic, *a.* mis-ta-*goj*-ik, connected with mystagogy.
mystagogue, *n.* *mis*-ta-gog, one who initiates into or interprets mysteries. (Gr. *mystes*, one initiated in sacred mysteries, *agogos*, a leader.)
mystagogy, *n.* *mis*-ta-goj-e, the interpretation of, or initiation into, mysteries.
mysterial, *a.* mis-*teer*-re-al, containing a mystery.
mysteriarch, *n.* mis-*teer*-re-ark, one who presides over mysteries. (Gr. *mysterion*, and *archo*, rule.)
mysterious, *a.* mis-*teer*-re-us, hidden from the understanding; not revealed; obscure; difficult to understand. (L. *mysterium*.)
mysteriously, *ad.* [mis-*teer*-re-us-le, in a mysterious manner.
mysteriousness, *n.* mis-*teer*-re-us-ness, the quality of being mysterious; obscurity.
mystery, *n.* *mis*-ter-re, a secret; something not comprehensible; an enigma; a trade or handicraft; a mediæval drama of a religious nature portraying characters and events drawn from sacred history and the lives of the saints: *pl.* sacred rites and ceremonies into which only the initiated were admitted; in combination (as **mystery-man, -ship, -story,** etc.), denoting connexion with a mystery, or something of which full particulars have not been revealed. (Gr. *mysterion*.)
mystic, *a.* *mis*-tik, pertaining to or involving mystery or mysticism; obscure; secret; allegorical; emblematical: *n.* one who holds the doctrines of mysticism; endeavouring by self-surrender and contemplation to attain to union with, or absorption into, God; one holding that truths beyond the understanding of man may be apprehended spiritually.
mystical, *a.* *mis*-te-kal, mystic.
mysticality, *n.* mis-te-*kal*-e-te, mysticalness.
mystically, *ad.* in a mystical manner.
mysticalness, *n.* *mis*-te-kal-ness, the state or quality of being mystical.
mysticism, *n.* *mis*-te-sizm, a profession of a higher and more intimate knowledge of divine or spiritual things, which can only express itself in terms that to the uninitiated are obscure; the doctrine that direct knowledge of and contact with God are attainable through contemplation alone.
mystification, *n.* *mis*-te-fe-*kay*-shon, the act of mystifying, or state of being mystified.
mystify, *v.t.* *mis*-te-fy, to involve in mystery; to bewilder. (Fr. *mystifier*.)
mytacism, *n.* *my*-ta-sizm, a defect in utterance of the letter *m*, or the continual repetition of that letter. (Late L. *mytacismus*.)
myth, *n.* mith, a legend, magnified by tradition, and given out as historical, affecting the origin of a race or a religion, and expressive of primitive beliefs or forms of belief; a fable; an invention; a fictitious event or person, etc. (Gr. *mythos*, fable.)
mythic, *a.* *mith*-ik, mythical.
mythical, *a.* *mith*-e-kal, pertaining to myth; fabulous; legendary. (L. *mythicus*.)
mythically, *ad.* *mith*-e-ka-le, in a mythical manner.
mythicize, *v.t.* *mith*-e-size, to render in a mythical form.
mythoclast, *n.* *mith*-o-klast, one who discredits or destroys myths. (*myth*, and Gr. *klastes*, breaker.)
mythogony, *n.* my-*thog*-o-ne, the science of the origin of myths.
mythographer, *n.* my-*thog*-ra-fer, a writer of fables or myths. (Gr. *mythos*, and *grapho*, write.)
mythological, *a.* mith-o-*loj*-e-kal, relating to mythology; fabulous.
mythologically, *ad.* by the use of myths.
mythologist, *n.* mi-*thol*-o-jist, one versed in mythology.
mythologize, *v.i.* mi-*thol*-o-jize, to relate or explain fabulous history.
mythology, *n.* mi-*thol*-o-je, a system of myths respecting national or tribal deities and the early beliefs of a people relative to their origin, heroes, etc.; scientific investigation of myths; a treatise on myths. (Fr. *mythologie*.)
mythonomy, *n.* mi-*thon*-o-me, the science of the laws governing the evolution of myths.
mythopœic, *a.* mith-o-*pee*-ik, making, or tending to evolve, myths. (Gr. *mythopoios*.)
mythopoesis, *n.* *mith*-o-po-*ee*-is, the making of myths.
mythus, *n.* *my*-thus, a myth. (L.)
mytilite, *n.* *mit*-il-ite, a fossil mussel-shell [Geol.].
mytiloid, *a.* *mit*-il-oyd, resembling or pertaining to mussels.
Mytilus, *n.* *mit*-il-us, the genus of bivalve molluscs which includes the marine mussels. (L.)
Myxine, *n.* *miks*-ine, a genus of cyclostomous fishes including the hag.
myxœdema, *n.* miks-e-*dee*-ma, a morbid condition due to insufficiency of thyroid secretion and characterized by dryness of skin, loss of hair, and impaired mentality. (Gr. *mucus*, slime, and *œdema*.)
Myxomycetes, *n.pl.* *miks*-o-my-*see*-teez, a group of low organisms allied to the thallophytes, including the slime fungi.
Myzontes, *n.pl.* my-*zon*-teez, the Cyclostomata. [Zool.]. (Gr.)

N

N, en, the fourteenth letter of the English alphabet, is a nasal dental. After *m* at the end of a word it is usually silent, as in *hymn, condemn*; when preceded by *g, k, m,* or *p,* the *n* alone is sounded, as in *gnat, knife, mnemonic, pneumonia*; and when preceding *g* or *k* it frequently has the value of *ng,* as in *linger, link.* It is used by printers as a unit in casting up composition, being half the width of the type-body, and in mathematics to indicate an indefinite number or power, etc.

nab, *n.* nab, a rocky ledge below water; the projecting top of a ridge or hill; the projection on the bolt of a lock that the key catches in turning. (O.Scand. *nabbr.*)

nab, *v.t.* nab, to catch or seize suddenly. (Perhaps Scand.)

nabob, *n. nay*-bob, a deputy ruler under the Mogul emperors; a man who has made his fortune in India; a man of great wealth. (Hind. *nawob.*)

nacarat, *n. nak*-a-rat, a pale red colour; a red shown in iridescence; a fine linen or crape dyed of the colour. (Fr.)

nacelle, *n.* na-*sel,* the body of an aeroplane; the car of an airship. (Fr.)

nacre, *n. nay*-ker, any shell-fish yielding mother-of-pearl; mother-of-pearl. (Fr.)

nacré, *a.* na-*kray,* having the iridescence of mother-of-pearl [Art].

nacreous, *a. nay*-kre-us, consisting of nacre; having an iridescent lustre.

nacrite, *n. nay*-krite, anhydrous silicate of alumina, a clay mineral chemically similar to kaolin.

nadir, *n. nay*-deer, that point of the heavens directly under our feet, or directly opposite the zenith; the lowest point. (Ar.)

nævoid, *a. nee*-voyd, pertaining to or resembling a nævus.

nævus, *n. nee*-vus, a congenital mark on the skin; a birthmark; a mole. (L., a spot.)

nag, *n.* nag, a small saddle-horse. (Origin unknown.)

nag, *v.t.* and *v.i.* nag, to find fault constantly; to scold: *n.* the act of nagging; persistent querulousness. (Scand.)

Naga, *n. nah*-gah, an ancient Indian people now inhabiting the borders of Assam and Burma; a Hindu deity, half man, half serpent, the emblem of eternity; (*l.c.*) the cobra, or any venomous Indian snake. (Hind.)

nagana, *n.* na-*gah*-na, a parasitic disease in live-stock disseminated by the tsetse fly. (Zulu.)

Nagari, *n.* na-*gah*-ri, *see* **Devanagari.**

nagger, *n. nag*-er, one who nags.

naggy, *a. nag*-e, contentious; disposed to bicker and find fault.

nagor, *n. nay*-gor, the Senegal reedbuck or antelope, *Cervicapra redunca.* (Coined by Buffon, 1760.)

naiad, *n. ny*-ad, a nymph of fountains, streams, and lakes [Gr. Myth.]; any water-plant of the genus *Naias*; any of the freshwater mussels; the nympha of certain aquatic insects. (Gr. *naias.*)

naiant, *a. ny*-ant, floating; natant, or in a horizontal position (of fish only) [Her.]. (O.Fr.)

naib, *n. nah*-ib, a deputy governor or law officer in India. (*nawab.*)

naik, *n. nah*-ik, an Indian title of honour; a governor; a native corporal of infantry in the Indian army. (Hind.)

★**nail,** *n.* nale, the horny substance at the end of the human fingers and toes; the claw or talon of an animal; a small pointed piece of metal used as a fastening; a measure of length, one-sixteenth of a yard or 2¼ inches; an obsolete weight of from 7 to 10 lb.: *v.t.* to fasten or stud with nails; to spike; to seize or steal [Slang]. **hard as nails,** in very fit condition; pitiless. **hit the nail on the head,** to touch or seize the exact point. **to nail to the counter,** to show up as false or spurious. **on the nail,** at once. (A.S. *nægel.*)

nailbourne, *n. nale*-boorn, an intermittent spring or stream. (Formerly *eyle-* [of doubtful origin], and *bourn.*)

nailbrush, *n. nale*-brush, a toilet brush for cleaning the finger-nails.

nailer, *n. nale*-er, a maker of nails; one who or that which nails.

nailery, *n. nale*-er-re, a place where metal nails are made.

nailfile, *n. nale*-file, a small file for smoothing the finger-nails.

nail-head, *n.* the head of a nail; an ornament of this shape [Arch.].

nailwort, *n. nale*-wurt, the whitlow grass.

nainsook, *n. nane*-sook, a thick sort of jaconet muslin, originally made in India. (Hind.)

naissant, *a. nay*-sant, issuing out of the midst of an ordinary, esp. a fesse, with only the fore-parts of the body visible [Her.]. (Fr.)

naïve, *a.* na-*eev,* unaffectedly simple; artless; ingenuous; unsophisticated. (Fr.)

naïvely, *ad.* na-*eev*-le, with unaffected simplicity.

naïveté, *n.* na-*eev*-tay, the quality of being naïve; native simplicity; ingenuousness. (Fr. *naïveté.*)

naked, *a. nay*-ked, devoid of clothing; nude; uncovered; bare; unarmed; defenceless; exposed; open to view; not concealed; destitute; without disguise, ornament, or exaggeration; evident; mere; unaided (of the eye). **naked lady,** the meadow saffron, *Colchicum autumnale.* (A.S. *nacod.*)

nakedly, *ad. nay*-ked-le, without covering; simply.

nakedness, *n. nay*-ked-ness, nudity; the state of being naked.

naker, *n. nay*-ker, a kettle-drum. (Ar.)

namable, *a. name*-a-bl, nameable.

namby-pamby, *a. nam*-be-*pam*-be, weakly sentimental: *n.* talk or writing that is so. (Applied to the sentimental poems of *Ambrose Philips, d.* 1749.)

★**name,** *n.* name, the word by which a person or a thing is called and distinguished; the discriminative appellation of an individual; reputation; renown; family; appearance or profession (as opposed to actuality); a noun [Gram.]: *v.t.* to give an appellation to; to speak of by name; to mention; to designate; to reprimand by naming. **in the name of,** on behalf of, or on the authority of. **name day,** the day sacred to the saint whose name one bears; the second day of the Stock Exchange account, when the purchasing broker gives names of buyers to the selling jobber. **to name the day,** to fix the date of her wedding (of a woman). (A.S. *nama.*)

nameable, *a. name*-a-bl, that may be named.

nameless, *a. name*-less, without a name; unknown; unnoted; unnameable.

namelessly, *ad. name*-les-le, in a nameless manner.

namely, *ad. name*-le, that is to say.

name-plate, *n.* a brass or other plate on a door or doorway bearing the name of the occupant of the house or room.

namer, *n. name*-er, one who gives a name to, or who calls by name.

namesake, *n. name*-sake, one having the same name, or named after another.

Nancy, *n. nan*-se, a very effeminate man; a nancy-boy: *a.* given to homosexual practices (of men only) [Slang].

nancy-boy, *n.* a catamite; a male homosexual [Slang].

nandine, *n. nan*-din, an arboreal civet of W. Africa, *Nandinia binotata.* (Native.)

nandu, *n. nan*-doo, the rhea (esp. *R. americana*), of South America. (Port., from the native name.)

nanism, *n. nane*-izm, the condition of dwarfishness. (L. *nanus,* a pigmy.)

nanization, *n.* nay-ny-*zay*-shon, artificial dwarfing, esp. of trees [Hort.].

nankeen, *n.* nan-*keen,* a cotton fabric, originally from China, generally brownish yellow. (*Nankin.*)

nanny, *n.* *nan*-ne, a female goat; a children's nurse.
nanoid, *a.* *nay*-noyd, dwarfish. (L. *nanus*, a pigmy.)
naos, *n.* *nay*-os, the inner sanctuary of a Greek temple. (Gr.)
nap, *n.* nap, Napoleon, a game of cards; a call in the game by which a player undertakes to make all the tricks. **go nap,** to risk everything on a single chance. (*Napoleon.*)
nap, *n.* nap, a short light sleep or slumber: *v.i.* to have a short sleep; to be careless or off one's guard. (A.S. *hnæppian*, to doze.)
nap, *n.* nap, the woolly or villous surface of certain textile fabrics; the substance of this; the downy growth on many plants. (Perhaps A.S. *hnæppan*, to strike.)
nape, *n.* nape, the hind part of the neck. (Perhaps A.S. *cnæp*, hill-top.)
napery, *n.* *nay*-per-re, linen for domestic use, esp. at table. (O.Fr. *naperie.*)
naphtha, *n.* *naf*-tha *or* *nap*-tha, a fluid inflammable oil obtained from the dry distillation of bituminous shale or other organic substances.
naphthalene, *n.* *naf*-tha-lin, a benzene hydrocarbon obtained from the dry distillation of coal tar.
naphthalic, *a.* naf-*thal*-ik, pertaining to or obtained from naphthalene.
naphthalize, *v.t.* *naf*-tha-lize, to saturate or otherwise treat with naphtha.
naphthene, *n.* *naf*-theen, a liquid hydrocarbon present in shale oil and certain petroleums, etc.
naphthol, *n.* *naf*-thol, either of two antiseptic phenols prepared from naphthalene.
naphthous, *a.* *naf*-thus, resembling or pertaining to naphtha.
napiform, *a.* *nay*-pe-form, having the shape of a turnip. (L. *napus*, a turnip, *forma*, shape.)
napkin, *n.* *nap*-kin, a small towel or cloth for wiping the hands; a serviette; an infant's sanitary binder. (O.Fr. *nape*, a cloth.)
napless, *a.* *nap*-less, without nap; threadbare.
Naples-yellow, *n.* *nay*-plz-*yel*-lo, antimoniate of lead, a brilliant reddish-yellow pigment.
Napoleon, *n.* na-*poh*-le-on, a former French gold coin of the value of twenty francs; the card-game generally known as nap. (Fr. *Napoléon.*)
Napoleonic, *a.* na-poh-le-*on*-ik, pertaining to Napoleon, his family, or his period, etc.
napoleonite, *n.* na-*poh*-le-o-nite, corsite; a gabbro containing hornblende and felspars [Min.].
napoo, *int.* nap-*poo*, no more; no good; finished; lost [Army slang]. (Fr. *il n'y a plus*, there is no more.)
nappiness, *n.* *nap*-pe-ness, the condition of having nap; abundance of nap, as on cloth.
nappy, *n.* *nap*-pe, a round flat-bottomed dish with sloping sides [U.S.A.].
nappy, *a.* *nap*-pe, covered with a good deal of nap; strong, foaming (of ale): *n.* strong drink, esp. ale.
nappy, *n.* *nap*-pe, an infant's napkin [Coll.].
narceine, *n.* *nar*-se-in, an alkaloid obtained from opium. (Gr. *narke*, drowsiness.)
narcissism, *n.* *nar*-se-sizm, excessive admiration of one's own person; erotic emotion arising from this [Psychan.]. (*Narcissus.*)
narcissist, *n.* *nar*-se-sist, one affected with narcissism.
narcissistic, *a.* nar-se-*sis*-tik, pertaining to or characterized by narcissism.
Narcissus, *n.* nar-*sis*-us, a genus of bulbous-rooted plants, comprising the daffodils. **narcissus fly,** the fly whose larva feeds on daffodil bulbs, *Merodon clavipes*. (L., the name of a self-enamoured youth [Myth.].)
narcolepsy, *n.* nar-ko-*lep*-se, a nervous condition marked by short sudden spells of sleep [Med.]. (Gr. *narkē*, torpor, and (epi)*lepsy.*)
narcomania, *n.* nar-ko-*may*-ne-a, irresistible craving for narcotics.
narcosis, *n.* nar-*koh*-sis, stupor induced by the use of narcotics; the effect of a narcotic; narcotism. (Gr.)
narcotic, *a.* nar-*kot*-ik, having the properties of a narcotic: *n.* a drug that induces stupor, allaying pain, causing sleep, and, in excess, death. (Fr. *narcotique.*)
narcotine, *n.* *nar*-ko-tin, an alkaloid present in opium.
narcotism, *n.* *nar*-ko-tizm, the effect of a narcotic, esp. of its prolonged use; addiction to narcotics; narcosis.
nard, *n.* nard, an aromatic unguent prepared from spikenard; the plant itself. (Fr.)
nardoo, *n.* *nar*-doo, the Australian plant, *Marsilea macropus*, the spores of which serve the aborigines as bread or porridge. (Austral.)
nares, *n.pl.* *nare*-reez, the nostrils [Anat. and Med.]. (L.)
narghile, *n.* *nar*-gil-e, a small hookah in which the smoke is passed through water. (Per.)
narial, *a.* *nare*-re-al, pertaining to the nostrils or nasal passages. (L. *naris*, a nostril.)
nark, *n.* nark, a police spy; an informer: *v.t.* and *i.* to act as a nark [Slang]. (Romany, *nāk*, nose.)
narrate, *v.t.* na-*rate*, to tell, recite, or write, as a story. (L. *narratus*, told.)
narration, *n.* na-*ray*-shon, the act of narrating; a statement in words or writing; a narrative.
narrative, *a.* *na*-ra-tiv, in the form of a story; relating an event or story: *n.* a story; an account of an event; a narration.
narrator, *n.* na-*ray*-tor, one who narrates.
***narrow,** *a.* *na*-roh, of little breadth; not wide or broad; very limited; straitened; covetous; contracted; not liberal; narrow-minded; near; close; scrutinizing; barely sufficient to avoid evil: *n.* a narrow or contracted passage; a strait: *v.t.* to lessen the breadth of; to contract in extent; to draw into a smaller compass; to confine: *v.i.* to become less broad; to contract; not to take ground enough (of a horse). **narrow gauge,** the British national gauge in which the rails are placed 4 ft. 8½ in. apart [Railways]. **narrow goods,** ribbons, braid, etc. **narrow work,** excavations of not more than 3 yds. wide. (A.S. *nearu.*)
narrower, *n.* *na*-roh-er, the person or thing which narrows or contracts.
narrowly, *ad.* in a narrow manner; closely.
narrow-minded, *a.* prejudiced; bigoted; illiberal in sentiment.
narrow-mindedness, *n.* illiberality; the state or quality of being narrow-minded.
narrowness, *n.* *na*-roh-ness, smallness of breadth.
narthex, *n.* *nahr*-theks, a large porch at the west door of a church, to the inside section of which catechumens and penitents were admitted; (*cap.*) an umbelliferous genus of plants, one species of which produces asafœtida. (Gr.)
narwhal, *n.* *nar*-wal, a large arctic cetacean, *Monodon monoceros*, of the dolphin family, having one large tusk, and sometimes two. (Scand.)
nasal, *a.* *nay*-zal, pertaining to the nose; sounded through the nose: *n.* a letter sounded through the nose; a nasal bone; the nose-piece of a helmet. (L. *nasus*, nose.)
nasalis, *n.* na-*zay*-lis, the proboscis monkey, remarkable for its enormous nose.
nasalism, *n.* *nay*-za-lizm, nasality.
nasality, *n.* na-*zal*-e-te, the state of being nasal, esp. in enunciation.
nasalization, *n.* *nay*-za-ly-*zay*-shon, the act of uttering with a nasal enunciation; an instance of this.
nasalize, *v.i.* *nay*-za-lize, to speak through the nose; *v.t.* to sound or enunciate nasally.
nasally, *ad.* *nay*-za-le, through the nose.
nascency, *n.* *nas*-en-se, the process of beginning; birth.
nascent, *a.* *nas*-ent, coming into existence; beginning to grow; springing up. (L. *nascens*, being born.)
naseberry, *n.* *naze*-be-re, the sapodilla plum of the West Indies. (Sp. *nispero*, a medlar tree.)
nasicorn, *a.* *nay*-ze-korn, having a horn or horns on the nose. (L. *nasus*, and *cornu*, a horn.)
nasiform, *a.* *nay*-ze-fawrm, in the shape of the nose.
nasology, *n.* na-*sol*-o-je, the study of noses.
nastily, *ad.* *nahs*-te-le, filthily; objectionably; disagreeably; spitefully.
nastiness, *n.* *nahs*-te-ness, filthiness; objectionable dirtiness; dirt; indecency.
Nasturtium, *n.* nas-*tur*-shum, the genus of cruciferous plants including the watercresses; (*l.c.*) Indian cress, and other trailing plants of the genus *Tropæolum*. (L.)

nasty, *a.* *nahs*-te, very dirty; defiled: indecent; disagreeable; unpleasant; spiteful. (Scand.)
natal, *a.* *nay*-tal, of or pertaining to birth. (L. *natalis*, from natus, born.)
natal, *a.* *nay*-tal, pertaining to the buttocks, or nates. (L. *nates.*)
natality, *n.* na-*tal*-e-te, birth; birthrate.
natant, *a.* *nay*-tant, swimming; floating [Bot.]; represented as swimming (of fish) [Her.]. (L. *natans*, swimming.)
natation, *n.* na-*tay*-shon, the act or art of swimming. (L. *natatio.*)
Natatores, *n.pl.* *nay*-ta-*taw*-reez, the order including the ducks, gulls, and other swimming birds.
natatorial, *a.* *nay*-ta-*taw*-re-al, swimming; pertaining to or adapted to swimming.
natatory, *a.* *nay*-ta-to-re, characterized by swimming; enabling to swim.
natch, *n.* natch, the part of an ox between the loins; the rump. (Dial. Eng.)
nates, *n.* *nay*-teez, the buttocks. (L.)
natheless, *ad.* *nayth*-less, nevertheless. (O.F. *na*, no, *the*, and *less.*)
★**nation,** *n.* *nay*-shon, a people owing a common allegiance and inhabiting the same country; people of the same blood and having the same language, history, etc., usually occupying some special territory. **the nation,** the country as a whole.
national, *a.* *nash*-on-al, pertaining to or common to a nation; public; general; attached to one's country: *n.* a member of a particular country; a fellow-countryman. **national anthem,** the patriotic song officially adopted as distinctive of the nation. **national debt,** money borrowed from individuals or corporations for national purposes and due by a nation. **National Socialism,** the political and economic creed of Hitlerite Germany, based on extreme nationalism, anti-democratic and racialist doctrines, and complete subjection to an autocratic and demagogic leader. **National Socialist,** a Nazi.
nationalism, *n.* *nash*-on-al-izm, the state or character of being national; national peculiarity; national independence; zealous and exclusive patriotism; the principle in direct opposition to internationalism; advocacy of the nationalization of industry.
nationalist, *a.* *nash*-o-na-list, supporting nationalism; *n.* a believer in or worker for nationalism or national independence; an opponent of internationalism.
nationality, *n.* *nash*-o-*nal*-e-te, condition or quality of being a nation; national character; national attachment; nation.
nationalization, *n.* *nash*-on-a-ly-*zay*-shon, the act or process of nationalizing.
nationalize, *v.t.* *nash*-on-a-lize, to transfer the individual control of property (esp. land, mines, communications, etc.) to the state; to naturalize, or allow into, a nation; to form into a nation.
nationally, *ad.* *nash*-o-na-le, in a national way; as a nation.
native, *a.* *nay*-tiv, produced by nature; original; natural; not acquired; not artificial; conferred by birth; pertaining to one's birthplace, or to the natives of a locality; born with; congenial; uncombined with another chemical element: *n.* a denizen by birth; an oyster raised in home waters, esp. in an artificial bed. (L. *nativus.*)
natively, *ad.* *nay*-tiv-le, by birth; naturally.
nativeness, *n.* *nay*-tiv-ness, state of being native.
nativity, *n.* na-*tiv*-e-te, birth; coming into life or the world; time, place, or manner of birth; a representation of the positions of the heavenly bodies at the moment of a man's birth [Astrol.]. **the Nativity,** the birth of Christ; a festival commemorating this, or the birth of the Virgin; a picture of Christ in the manger. (Fr. *nativité.*)
natrolite, *n.* *nat*-ro-lite, one of the zeolites, a silicate of alumina and soda. (Ar. *natron*, and Gr. *lithos*, a stone.)
natron, *n.* *nat*-ron or *nay*-tron, native carbonate of soda. (Ar.)
natterjack, *n.* *nat*-er-jak, the yellow-striped toad, *Bufo calamita*, remarkable for its running motion.
nattily, *ad.* *nat*-e-le, in a natty manner; neatly.
natty, *a.* *nat*-e, neatly fine; trim; spruce. (*neat.*)
★**natural,** *a.* *nat*-yew-ral, pertaining to, produced by, by way of, or in course of, nature; not artificial; not far-fetched; such as nature dictates; according to the life; consonant with nature; derived from nature; discoverable by reason; affectionate by nature; unaffected; unassumed; illegitimate (of children); native; vernacular: *n.* an idiot; a character corrective of the previous power of a sharp or flat [Mus.]. (♮) **natural note,** one which is according to the usual order of the scale [Mus.]. **natural history,** the study of the earth and its productions; zoology. **natural order,** a group the members of which have definite resemblances and affinity [Bot.]. **natural philosophy,** the study of nature in general; physics. **natural religion,** religion based on reason and independent of supernatural revelation. **natural rights,** rights recognized by the law as belonging to man by reason of his human status. **natural scale,** a scale having no sharp or flat [Mus.]. **natural science,** the science of things physical as distinct from things psychical, logical, or ethical. **natural selection,** *see* **selection.** (Fr.)
natural-born, *a.* being a subject of one's country by birth, not by naturalization.
naturalism, *n.* *nat*-yew-ra-lizm, mere state of nature; adherence to nature; natural religion; unbelief in the supernatural; the theory which regards mythological fancies as originally deifications and personifications of the powers of nature.
naturalist, *n.* *nat*-yew-ra-list, a student of natural history, esp. zoology; a believer in naturalism; a dealer in live pets or natural history specimens [Coll.].
naturalistic, *a.* *nat*-yew-ra-*lis*-tik, pertaining to naturalism; realistic.
naturalistically, *ad.* *nat*-yew-ra-*lis*-te-ka-le, in a naturalistic style or manner.
naturalization, *n.* *nat*-yew-ra-ly-*zay*-shon, the act of investing an alien with the rights of a citizen.
naturalize, *v.t.* *nat*-yew-ra-lize, to confer on an alien the rights and privileges of a native; to make natural; to adapt to a different climate or to strange conditions; to adopt.
naturally, *ad.* *nat*-yew-ra-le, according to nature; of course.
naturalness, *n.* *nat*-yew-ral-ness, state of being natural; conformity to nature.
nature, *n.* *nay*-tewr, the universe; the essence or essential qualities of a thing; the established or regular course of things; natural law; constitution; disposition; natural affection; species; particular character. **in a state of nature,** with no additions; naked; as at birth. **nature study,** natural history studied in the field. (Fr.)
naturecraft, *n.* *nay*-tewr-krahft, nature study; natural history, esp. as a hobby.
nature-printing, *n.* a process of producing a print of a flower, etc., from an impression obtained from the object.
naturopathy, *n.* nat-ew-*rop*-a-the, a system of treating disease, deformity, etc., without the use of drugs or surgical instruments.
naught, *n.* nawt, nothing: *ad.* in no degree: *a.* worthless. (A.S. *na*, no, *wiht*, a whit.)
naughtily, *ad.* *naw*-te-le, in a naughty manner.
naughtiness, *n.* *naw*-te-ness, the state, or an instance, of being naughty; misbehaviour.
naughty, *a.* *naw*-te, wicked; perverse; mischievous; badly behaved.
naumachia, *n.* naw-*may*-ke-a, a sea-fight, or its representation. (Gr. *naus*, ship, *machē*, battle.)
nauplius, *n.* *naw*-ple-us, a larval stage in the development of certain crustaceans. (L.)
nausea, *n.* *naw*-se-a, a sickness of the stomach accompanied with a propensity to vomit; seasickness; loathing. (L., sea-sickness.)
nauseant, *n.* *naw*-se-ant, a substance which produces nausea [Med.]: *a.* producing nausea.
nauseate, *v.i.* *naw*-se-ate, to become squeamish; to feel nausea or disgust: *v.t.* to loathe or reject with disgust; to affect with disgust. (L. *nauseatus*, sea-sick.)
nauseation, *n.* *naw*-se-*ay*-shon, sickness; the act of nauseating.
nauseous, *a.* *naw*-se-us, loathsome; sickening; disgusting. (L. *nauseosus.*)
nauseously, *ad.* *naw*-se-us-le, loathsomely.
nauseousness, *n.* *naw*-se-us-ness, loathsomeness.
nautch, *n.* nawch, an exhibition of Indian dancing provided by **nautch girls,** *i.e.* professional dancing girls. (Hind.)

nautical, *a.* *naw*-te-kal, pertaining to ships, navigation, and seafaring. **nautical almanac,** a government publication containing tables and calculations for navigators and astronomers published annually in advance. **nautical mile,** the sixtieth of a degree of longitude. (L. *nauticus*, nautical.)
nautically, *ad.* in a nautical manner.
nautilite, *n.* *naw*-te-lite, a fossil nautilus.
nautiloid, *a.* *naw*-te-loyd, resembling the nautilus: *n.* any member of the Nautiloidea, an order of (mainly extinct) tetrabranchiate cephalopods. (L. *nautilus*, and Gr. *eidos*, like.)
nautilus, *n.* *naw*-te-lus, any marine cephalopod mollusc of the order Tetrabranchia, esp. the pearly nautilus, *Nautilus pompilius*, and the paper nautilus, *Argonauta argo*. (Gr. and L., a sailor.)
naval, *a.* *nay*-val, consisting of or pertaining to warships or to a navy; effected by a navy. **naval base,** a port equipped for maintaining a fleet in constant readiness. **naval brigade,** a naval detachment taking part in operations on land. (L. *navis*, a ship.)
navalism, *n.* *nay*-val-izm, the doctrine of sea power; the policy of maintaining this.
nave, *n.* nave, the middle or body of a church, extending from the chancel or choir to the principal entrance. (L. *navis*, a ship.)
nave, *n.* nave, the centre of a wheel, through which the axle passes; the hub. (A.S. *nafu*, a boss.)
navel, *n.* *nay*-vel, the depression in the abdomen, marking the position of the umbilical cord; the umbilicus; the centre. **navel orange,** a large type of orange having an indentation at the apex. (A.S. *nafela*.)
navel-string, *n.* the umbilical cord.
navelwort, *n.* *nay*-vel-wurt, the marsh pennywort, and other plants.
navette, *n.* na-*vet*, a variety of rape-plant, *Brassica napus*; a marquise finger-ring. (Fr.)
navew, *n.* *nay*-vew, the wild turnip, *Brassica campestris*.
navicert, *n.* *nav*-e-sert, a document issued by a belligerent to neutral shipping granting free passage to it and its cargo through a traffic zone under the belligerent's control. (*naval* and *certificate*.)
navicular, *a.* na-*vik*-yew-lar, relating to small ships or boats; shaped like a boat [Anat. and Bot.]. **navicular bone,** the scaphoid bone of the foot or the wrist. **navicular disease,** inflammation in the navicular bone of horses. (L. *navicula*, a little ship.)
navigability, *n.* *nav*-e-ga-*bil*-e-te, navigableness.
navigable, *a.* *nav*-e-ga-bl, that may be navigated.
navigableness, *n.* state or quality of being navigable.
navigably, *ad.* *nav*-e-ga-ble, in a navigable manner.
navigate, *v.i.* *nav*-e-gate, to voyage in ships; to sail; to manage a ship: *v.t.* to pass over or through in a ship; to conduct a vessel on the sea or in the air. (L. *navigatus*, sailed.)
navigation, *n.* nav-e-*gay*-shon, the act or art of navigating; nautical astronomy; the science of finding a vessel's position, and the art of conducting her from point to point; management of aircraft in flight; an inland waterway. (Fr.)
navigator, *n.* *nav*-e-gay-tor, one skilled in navigation; one who directs the course of a ship; (formerly) a navvy.
navvy, *n.* *nav*-ve, originally a labourer employed in cutting canals for navigation; now one engaged in the construction of railways, docks, drains, and other engineering works, etc. **steam navvy,** an excavating machine; a bull-dozer. (*navigator*.)
navy, *n.* *nay*-ve, a fleet of ships; the sea defence force of a nation; the warships of a nation; these together with their officers, men, dockyards, and establishment; navy blue. **merchant navy,** the trans-ocean shipping of a country. **navy bills,** bills issued by the Admiralty in payment for stores for ships and dockyards; also those drawn by naval officers for their pay. **navy blue,** the dark blue colour of British naval uniforms, etc. **navy cut,** tobacco compressed into cakes and cut into thin strips. **Navy League,** an organization (founded 1894) for promoting the interests of Great Britain as the leading sea-Power. (L. *navis*, a ship.)
nawab, *n.* na-*wahb*, a Mohammedan ruler in India corresponding to a Hindu rajah; a nabob. (*nabob*.)
nay, *ad.* nay, no, a term expressive of negation or refusal; not only so; not this alone: *n.* denial; a refusal. (Ice. *nei*.)
nayword, *n.* *nay*-wurd, a bye-word; a watch-word.
Nazarene, *n.* naz-a-*reen*, a native of Nazareth, applied esp. to Christ and, later, to the early Christian converts; an early Judaizing sect. of Christians. (*Nazareth*.)
Nazarite, *n.* *naz*-a-rite, a Jew of ancient times consecrated to the service of God and bound to austerity of life. (Heb. *nazar*, to separate oneself.)
Nazaritism, *n.* *naz*-a-ry-tizm, the practices of a Nazarite.
naze, *n.* naze, a cape or headland. (Scand.)
Nazi, *a.* *naht*-se, denoting or pertaining to the former German National Socialist party; Hitlerite: *n.* a member of this party. (Ger. *Nationalsozialist*.)
Naziism, *n.* *naht*-se-izm, the principles, theories, or methods of the Nazis; Hitlerism.
Nazirite, *n.* *naz*-eer-rite, a Nazarite.
Neanderthal, *a.* ne-*an*-der-tahl, pertaining to the valley of that name near Dusseldorf; having, or resembling, the low skull of Neanderthal man. **Neanderthal Man,** the palæolithic race represented by a very primitive type of skull discovered in 1857 in a cave in the Neanderthal valley.
Neanderthaloid, *a.* ne-*an*-der-ta-loyd, having or resembling the skull of the Neanderthal Man.
neap, *a.* neep, low (of tides only): *n.* the tide at the beginning of the moon's second and fourth quarters. (A.S. *nep*.)
neaped, *a.* neept, left aground between high tides; wanting sufficient depth of water.
Neapolitan, *a.* ne-a-*pol*-e-tan, pertaining to Naples: *n.* an inhabitant or native of Naples. **Neapolitan fever,** Malta fever. **Neapolitan ice,** ice-cream in two or more differently flavoured layers.
★**near,** *a.* neer, nigh; not far distant; closely related; intimate; united in close ties; dear; affecting one's interest or feelings; close; parsimonious; stingy; next to one; on the left (of horses, etc., and vehicles): *ad.* almost; within a little; parsimoniously: *v.t.* to approach; to come nearer to: *v.i.* to draw near. (A.S.)
near-by, *ad.* *neer*-by, adjacent; close at hand.
nearctic, *a.* ne-*ark*-tik, of or belonging to Greenland and the Arctic and northern parts of America. (Gr. *neos*, new, and *arctic*.)
nearly, *ad.* *neer*-le, not quite; closely; almost; in a niggardly manner.
nearness, *n.* *neer*-ness, closeness; propinquity; parsimony.
near-sighted, *a.* short-sighted.
near-sightedness, *n.* short-sightedness; myopia.
neat, *n.* neet, cattle; any bovine animal: *a.* belonging to bovine animals. **neat's foot oil,** a lubricant oil obtained by boiling the bones of cattle. (A.S. *neat*, cattle.)
neat, *a.* neet, tidy; trim; well shaped; adroit; pure; undiluted; simple. (Fr. *net*.)
neath, *prep.* neeth, beneath.
neat-handed, *a.* *neet*-han-ded, skilful and quick.
neatherd, *n.* *neet*-herd, a cowherd.
neatly, *ad.* *neet*-le, with neatness; nicely.
neatness, *n.* *neet*-ness, cleanliness; tidiness.
neb, *n.* neb, the nose; a beak; a nib. (A.S. *nebb*, face.)
nebris, *n.* *neb*-ris, the skin of a fawn as worn by votaries of Bacchus. (Gr.)
nebula, *n.* *neb*-yew-la (*pl.* **nebulæ**), a faint and misty appearance, dimly visible in the heavens, and resolvable into groups of stars, or a mass of gaseous matter; a white spot or slight opacity of the cornea [Med.]. (L.)
nebular, *a.* *neb*-yew-lar, pertaining to nebulæ. **nebular hypothesis,** the theory that the heavenly bodies originated through the gradual contraction of one vast nebula.
nebularization, *n.* neb-yew-la-ry-*zay*-shon, the act or process of becoming nebular.
nebulium, *n.* ne-*bew*-le-um, the hypothetical element shown by certain lines in the spectra of some nebulæ, now identified as oxygen.
nebulosity, *n.* *neb*-yew-*los*-e-te, state of being nebulous, cloudy, or obscure.
nebulous, *a.* *neb*-yew-lus, like a nebula; obscure; formless; hazy.
nebulousness, *n.* *neb*-yew-lus-ness, nebulosity.

nebuly, *a.* *neb*-yew-le, ornamented with, or shaped in, wavy lines indicative of cloud-formation. [Her.].
necessarian, *a.* and *n.* *nes*-e-*sare*-re-an, necessitarian.
necessarianism, *n.* *nes*-e-*sare*-re-a-nizm, necessitarianism.
necessarily, *ad.* *nes*-e-sa-re-le, by necessity.
★**necessary,** *a.* *nes*-e-sa-re, indispensable; essential; inevitable; requisite; acting from necessity: *n.* something necessary; a water-closet [Coll.]: *pl.* requisites; things necessary. **the necessary,** ready cash [Slang]. (O.Fr. *necessaire.*)
necessitarian, *n.* ne-*ses*-e-*tare*-re-an, an advocate of the doctrine of philosophical necessity; one opposing the doctrine of free-will.
necessitarianism, *n.* ne-*ses*-e-*tare*-re-a-nizm, the doctrine of philosophical necessity, or that which denies the freedom of the will.
necessitate, *v.t.* ne-*ses*-e-tate, to render necessary or unavoidable; to compel. (Late L. *necessitatus,* rendered certain.)
necessitation, *n.* ne-*ses*-e-*tay*-shon, act of making necessary; compulsion.
necessitous, *a.* ne-*ses*-e-tus, needy; indigent.
necessitously, *ad.* in a necessitous manner.
necessitousness, *n.* extreme poverty or destitution.
necessitude, *n.* ne-*ses*-e-tewd, need; poverty.
necessity, *n.* ne-*ses*-e-te, that which is necessary; compulsion; inevitableness; extreme indigence: *pl.* things requisite for a purpose. (Fr. *nécessité.*)
★**neck,** *n.* nek, the part of the body connecting the head and trunk; any narrow connecting portion, as of land; the long slender part of any vessel; an isthmus: *v.t.* to kill by beheading or strangulation; to couple (oxen, etc.) by the neck; to swallow [Slang]; to hug, to cuddle [U.S.A. slang]. **neck and crop,** completely. **neck and neck,** equal. **neck or nothing,** at great risk. **to break the neck of,** to lame the power of. **to get it in the neck,** to be severely reprimanded; to experience unpleasantness. (A.S. *hnecca.*)
neck-band, *n.* the part of a shirt, etc., fitting round the neck.
neck-cloth, *n.* a piece of cloth worn round the neck; a cravat.
necked, *a.* nekt, having a neck.
neckerchief, *n.* *nek*-er-chif, a kerchief for the neck.
necking, *n.* *nek*-ing, the part of a column between the capital and shaft; an annulet [Arch.]; the act or action of one who necks.
necklace, *n.* *nek*-lace, a string of beads or other ornaments worn round the neck.
necklaced, *a.* *nek*-layst, wearing or having the appearance of wearing a necklace.
necklet, *n.* *nek*-let, a thin necklace; a small fur neck-wrap.
neck-moulding, *n.* *nek*-mohld-ing, a moulding at the junction of the shaft and capital of a column [Arch.].
neck-piece, *n.* *nek*-peece, a frill or boa for the neck; a piece of armour protecting the neck.
necktie, *n.* *nek*-ty, a scarf or bow for the neck.
necrobiosis, *n.* *nek*-ro-by-*oh*-sis, an intermediate stage before complete degeneration of tissue, etc.; the theory that organic decomposition is productive of life. (Gr. *nekros,* dead body, *bios,* life, and *-osis.*)
necrobiotic, *a.* *nek*-ro-by-*ot*-ik, pertaining to or characterized by necrobiosis.
necrogenous, *a.* ne-*kroj*-e-nus, living in or proceeding from the bodies of dead animals [Biol.].
necrolatry, *n.* ne-*krol*-a-tre, excessive veneration of the dead. (Gr. *nekros,* and *latreia,* worship.)
necrological, *a.* nek-ro-*loj*-e-kal, pertaining to or giving an account of the dead or deaths.
necrologist, *n.* ne-*krol*-o-jist, a writer of obituary notices.
necrology, *n.* ne-*krol*-o-je, a register of deaths; a collection of obituaries. (Gr. *nekros,* and *logos,* account.)
necromancer, *n.* *nek*-ro-man-ser, one who practises necromancy.
necromancy, *n.* *nek*-ro-man-se, divination by means of pretended communication with the dead; black magic; enchantment. (O.Fr. *nigromance.*)
necromantic, *a.* nek-ro-*man*-tik, pertaining to or performed by necromancy or conjuration.
necronite, *n.* *nek*-ro-nite, a variety of orthoclase exhaling a fetid odour.
necrophagous, *a.* ne-*krof*-a-gus, eating or feeding on carrion [Zool.]. (Gr. *nekros,* and *phago,* eat.)
necrophilia, *n.* nek-ro-*fil*-e-a, necrophilism.
necrophilism, *n.* ne-*krof*-e-lizm, an unnatural love for the dead. (Gr. *nekros,* and *phileo,* love.)
necrophilous, *a.* ne-*krof*-e-lus, affected with necrophilism; necrophagous [Zool.].
necrophobia, *n.* nek-roh-*foh*-be-a, a morbid horror of dead bodies or of death. (Gr. *nekros,* and *phobos,* fear.)
necrophorous, *a.* ne-*krof*-o-rus, bearing away the bodies of dead animals (esp. of burying-beetles) [Zool.].
necropolis, *n.* ne-*krop*-o-lis, a cemetery, esp. a large or an ancient burial-place. (Gr., a city of the dead).
necropsy, *n.* ne-*krop*-se, an autopsy; a post-mortem examination [Med.].
necroscopic, *a.* nek-ro-*skop*-ik, relating to a necropsy. (Gr. *nekros,* and *skopeo,* view.)
necrosed, *a.* ne-*krohzd,* affected with necrosis.
necrosis, *n.* ne-*kroh*-sis, mortification of tissue (esp. in bone) due to interference with blood supply [Med.]; a disease of plants caused by cold or fungi [Bot.]. (Gr., condition of death.)
necrotic, *a.* ne-*krot*-ik, pertaining to or affected with necrosis.
necrotize, *v.i.* *nek*-ro-tize, to become affected with necrosis: *v.t.* to cause necrosis.
necrotomy, *n.* ne-*krot*-o-me, dissection of dead bodies.
nectar, *n.* *nek*-tar, the drink of the gods [Myth.]; any very sweet beverage; the sweet secretion in flowers providing the source of honey. (L.)
nectarean, *a.* nek-*tare*-re-an, resembling or pertaining to nectar; sweet as nectar.
nectared, *a.* *nek*-tard, imbued with nectar.
nectareous, *a.* nek-*tare*-re-us, nectarean.
nectarial, *a.* nek-*tare*-re-al, pertaining to or of the nature of a nectary.
nectariferous, *a.* nek-ta-*rif*-er-rus, producing nectar. (Gr. *nectar,* L. *fero,* bear.)
nectarine, *a.* *nek*-ta-rin, nectarean; sweet as nectar: *n.* a smooth-skinned variety of peach.
nectarium, *n.* nek-*tare*-re-um, the nectary of a flower.
nectarous, *a.* *nek*-ta-rus, nectarean.
nectary, *n.* *nek*-ta-re, the honey, or nectar-secreting, gland of a flower.
nectocalyx, *n.* nek-to-*kay*-liks, a swimming-bell [Zool.].
nectopod, *n.* *nek*-to-pod, an organ adapted for swimming [Zool.]. (Gr. *nectos,* swimming, *pous, podis,* foot.)
Neddy, *n.* *ned*-e, a donkey [Coll.].
née, *a.* nay, born (indicating the maiden name of a married woman). (Fr.)
★**need,** *n.* need, want; necessity; state that requires relief; urgent want; want of the means of subsistence; indigence: *v.t.* to want; to lack: *v.i.* to be wanted or necessary. (A.S. *nīed.*)
needer, *n.* *need*-er, one who wants.
need-fire, *n.* *need*-fire, fire procured from friction, formerly a counter-charm against sorcery; a beacon-fire.
needful, *a.* *need*-ful, needy; necessary; requisite: *n.* that which is needful. **the needful,** money [Coll.].
needfully, *ad.* *need*-ful-le, necessarily.
needfulness, *n.* *need*-ful-ness, the quality of being needful; necessity.
needily, *ad.* *need*-e-le, necessitously.
neediness, *n.* *need*-e-ness, want; indigence.
★**needle,** *n.* *nee*-dl, a small tool, pointed at one end, with an eye at the other to receive a thread, used in sewing; a small pointed piece of steel, as used in the mariner's compass; a pointed etching tool; a sharp rock; the end of a hypodermic syringe; the striker of a needle-gun; the point by which the vibrations of a gramophone record are received and transmitted; the long stiff leaf of the pine and related trees; any needle-shaped object: *v.t.* and *i.* to form needle-shaped crystals; to sew, embroider, or do needlework. **needle bath,** a bath in which fine and strong jets are directed on the body [Med.]. **needle chervil,** the wild plant *Scandix pecten.* **needle lace,** point lace. **needle match, game,** etc., a contest (esp. boxing) into which ill-feeling enters; a game upon which much depends. **needle whin,** the plant *Genista*

anglica. **to give,** or **get, the needle,** to annoy; to become annoyed or irritated. (A.S. *nædel.*)
needle-book, *n.* a book-like case with fabric leaves to put needles into.
needle-case, *n.* a case for holding needles; a needle-book.
needle-fish, *n.* the garfish; the greater pipefish; and others of similar appearance.
needleful, *n.* *nee*-dl-full, the ordinary length of thread that a needle is worked with.
needle-furze, *n.* the prickly shrub, *Genista anglica.*
needle-gun, *n.* an obsolete fire-arm in which the cartridge was exploded by a needle-shaped striker actuated by the trigger.
needle-point, *n.* the point of a needle; any very fine point; point lace.
needlespar, *n.* *nee*-dl-spar, aragonite.
needless, *a.* *need*-less, not wanted; unnecessary.
needlessly, *ad.* *need*-less-le, without necessity.
needlessness, *n.* *need*-less-ness, unnecessariness.
needlewoman, *n.* *nee*-dl-woom-an, a seamstress.
needlework, *n.* *nee*-dl-wurk, work executed with a needle; embroidery; the business of a seamstress.
needments, *n.pl.* *need*-ments, necessities; things needed.
needs, *ad.* needz, necessarily; indispensably.
needy, *a.* *need*-e, necessitous; indigent; very poor.
neem, *n.* neem, the East Indian tree, margosa, with medicinal properties; the oil from this. (Hind. *nīm.*)
neep, *n.* neep, a turnip [Scots.]. (A.S. *næp.*)
ne'er, *ad.* nare, a contraction of *never.*
ne'er-do-well, *n.* *nare*-do-well, a mere loafer; a good-for-nothing; one never likely to do well.
neeze, *v.i.* neez, to sneeze.
nef, *n.* nef, a silver model of a ship, often serving as a case for a knife, fork and spoon. (Fr., ship.)
nefandous, *a.* ne-*fan*-dus, abominable; atrocious; very wicked. (L. *nefandus.*)
nefarious, *a.* ne-*fare*-re-us, impious or wicked in the extreme; abominable. (L. *nefarius.*)
nefariously, *ad.* in a nefarious manner.
nefariousness, *n.* quality of being nefarious.
negate, *v.t.* ne-*gate,* to nullify; to deny. (L. *negatus,* denied.)
negation, *n.* ne-*gay*-shon, denial; declaration that something is not. (L. *negatio,* a denial.)
negationist, *n.* ne-*gay*-shon-ist, one who opposes on merely negative grounds.
negative, *a.* *neg*-a-tiv, implying denial, absence, or refusal; having the power of vetoing; acid [Chem.]; denoting the opposite [Math. and Elect.]; of the nature of a photographic negative; affording no confirmation of the suspected condition [Med.]: *n.* a proposition by which something is denied; a word that denies; the right of veto; the opposite of the affirmative; a photograph in which the lights and shades are the reverse of those in nature; the cathode in the electric circuit: *v.t.* to veto; to reject by vote; to refuse to sanction; to reverse (a previous decision, or a positive statement, etc.); to disprove; to counteract: **negative electricity,** the type of electricity in which the electrons outnumber the protons. **negative quantity,** a minus quantity [Alg.]. (L. *negativus.*)
negatively, *ad.* in a negative manner; with or by a negative; without producing the expected result.
negativeness, *n.* the quality of being negative.
negatron, *n.* *neg*-a-tron, a four-electrode thermionic valve for obtaining negative resistance [Wire.].
neglect, *n.* ne-*glekt,* omission; forbearance to do anything that should be done; slight; habitual want of regard; inattention; negligence; state of disregard: *v.t.* to omit by carelessness or design; to disregard; to slight; not to notice. (L. *neglectus,* neglected.)
neglectable, *a.* ne-*glek*-ta-bl, that may be neglected.
neglectedness, *n.* neg-*lek*-ted-ness, state of being neglected.
neglecter, *n.* ne-*glek*-ter, one who neglects.
neglectful, *a.* ne-*glekt*-ful, heedless; inattentive; treating with neglect; indicating neglect.
neglectfully, *ad.* ne-*glekt*-ful-le, with neglect.
negligé, *n.* *neg*-le-zhay, loose, easy clothes; a state of undress.
negligee, *n.* *neg*-le-jee, a woman's loose gown; a long necklace of beads or coral. (Fr.)
negligence, *n.* *neg*-le-jence, neglect; carelessness.
negligent, *a.* *neg*-le-jent, careless; unheedful; inattentive. (O.Fr.)
negligently, *ad.* *neg*-le-jent-le, carelessly.
negligibility, *n.* *neg*-le-je-*bil*-e-te, the state or quality of being negligible.
negligible, *a.* *neg*-le-je-bl, that need not be noticed; of little value.
negotiability, *n.* ne-*goh*-she-a-*bil*-e-te, the quality of being negotiable.
negotiable, *a.* ne-*goh*-she-a-bl, that may be negotiated or transferred by assignment; transferable by endorsement. (Fr. *négociable.*)
negotiant, *n.* ne-*goh*-she-ant, a negotiator.
negotiate, *v.i.* ne-*goh*-she-ate, to transact business; to treat with another respecting purchase and sale; to treat with respecting peace or commerce: *v.t.* to procure by mutual intercourse and agreement; to transfer for value; to surmount (as an obstacle) [Coll.]. (L. *negotiatus,* negotiated.)
negotiation, *n.* ne-*goh*-she-*ay*-shon, the transacting of business; treating with another. (Fr. *négociation.*)
negotiator, *n.* ne-*goh*-she-ay-tor, one who negotiates or treates with others.
negotiatory, *a.* ne-*goh*-she-a-to-re, of or pertaining to negotiation.
Negress, *n.* *nee*-gress, a female Negro.
Negrillo, *n.* ne-*gril*-oh, a Bushman; a Negrito.
Negrito, *n.* ne-*gree*-toh, a member of any short-statured negroid race, as certain tribes of the Philippines and Malaysia, and the Bushmen and Pygmies of S. Africa. (Sp., diminutive *negro,* black.)
Negro, *n.* *nee*-gro, one of the black-skinned races of mankind with woolly hair and protruding lips, found chiefly in Africa: *a.* (*l.c.*) relating to Negroes; black. (Sp., from L. *niger,* black.)
negrohead, *n.* *nee*-gro-hed, strong dark tobacco softened in molasses and pressed into cakes.
negroid, *a.* *nee*-groyd, of negro type. (Sp. *negro,* and Gr. *eidos,* like.)
negroism, *n.* *nee*-gro-izm, an idiom characteristic of Negroes; advocacy of the rights of Negroes.
negrophile, *n.* *nee*-gro-file, a friend of the Negro. (Sp. *negro,* and Gr. *philos,* love.)
negrophilist, *n.* nee-*grof*-e-list, a negrophile.
negrophobe, *n.* *nee*-gro-fobe, one strongly averse to Negroes. (Sp. *negro,* and Gr. *phobos,* dread.)
negrophobia, *n.* *nee*-gro-*foh*-be-a, unreasoning aversion toward, or morbid dread of, Negroes.
negundo, *n.* ne-*gun*-doh, the box elder, *Acer negundo.* (Malayalam.)
Negus, *n.* *nee*-gus, the native title of the sovereign of Abyssinia. (Native word.)
negus, *n.* *nee*-gus, a hot drink of wine, water, and sugar, with nutmeg or lemon. (Col. *Negus, d.* 1732, its inventor.)
neigh, *n.* nay, the cry of a horse; a whinnying: *v.i.* to utter this cry; to whinny. (A.S. *hnægan.*)
neighbour, *n.* *nay*-bor, one who lives near; one having a claim upon his fellow-man: *a.* near to another; adjoining: *v.t.* to adjoin; to be near to: *v.i.* to border upon; to live near to. (A.S. *neah,* near, *bur,* a dweller.)
neighbourhood, *n.* *nay*-bor-hood, a place near; the adjoining district; the state of being near; inhabitants living near each other [Collect.].
neighbouring, *a.* *nay*-bor-ing, living or being near.
neighbourliness, *n.* *nay*-bor-le-ness, the state of being neighbourly.
neighbourly, *a.* *nay*-bor-le, becoming a neighbour; kind; civil; cultivating familiar intercourse; social: *ad.* with social civility.
neither, *a., pron.,* and *conj.* *ny*-ther *or* *nee*-ther, not either. (A.S.)
nek, *n.* nek, a narrow ridge connecting two hills [S. African]. (Dut.)
nekton, *n.* *nek*-ton, free-swimming aquatic organisms, esp. as opposed to plankton [Zool.]. (Gr., swimming.)
nelumbium, *n.* ne-*lum*-be-um, a species of water-lily; the sacred Egyptian bean of Pythagoras, *N. speciosum*; the Indian and Chinese lotus.
nemalite, *n.* *nem*-a-lite, a fibrous variety of brucite [Min.]. (Gr. *nema,* thread, *lithos,* stone.)
nemathecium, *n.* nem-a-*thee*-she-um, in certain algæ, a cushion-like prominence on the thallus bearing the reproductive organs. (Gr. *nema,* and *theke,* sheath.)

nematocyst, *n.* ne-*mat*-o-sist, the stinging organ of jellyfish and allied species.

nematode, *n.* *nem*-a-tohd, a threadworm; one of a class of entozoans with filiform elongated bodies, many of which are parasitic in animals and plants [Zool.]: *a.* thread-like.

nematoid, *a.* *nem*-a-toyd, like a thread. (Gr. *nema*, a thread, *eidos*, like.)

Nemertea, *n.pl.* ne-*mer*-te-a, a group of marine annelids, remarkable for their ribbon-like body. (Gr. *Nemertes*, one of the sea-nymphs.)

nemertid, *n.* *nem*-er-tid, any member of the Nemertea [Zool.].

Nemesis, *n.* *nem*-e-sis, the goddess of vengeance or retributive justice. (Gr.)

Nemophila, *n.* ne-*mof*-e-la, a genus of Californian herbaceous annuals with showy blue or white flowers. (Gr. *nemos*, grove, *phileo*, to love.)

nemoral, *a.* *nem*-o-ral, pertaining to a wood; growing in groves. (L. *nemoralis*, from *nemus*, a grove.)

nenuphar, *n.* *nen*-yew-far, the white water-lily, *Nymphæa alba*. (Sans.)

neo-, *pref.* *nee*-o, a combining form signifying modern, recent, later, etc. (Gr. *neos*, new.)

Neocomian, *a.* ne-o-*koh*-me-an, pertaining to or denoting the lower, or earliest, division of the Cretaceous strata [Geol.). (L. *Neocomium*, Neuchatel, Switzerland, where present.)

neocosmic, *a.* ne-o-*koz*-mik, pertaining to the existing condition of the universe. (Gr. *neos*, new, *kosmos*, universe.)

neocracy, *n.* ne-*ok*-ra-se, government by new or inexperienced men. (Gr. *neos*, and *kratein*, rule.)

neodymium, *n.* nee-*o-dim*-e-um, a metallic element of the rare earth group occurring in monazite, cerite, etc.

neogæan, *a.* nee-o-*je*-an, of, or pertaining to, the New World or the western hemisphere. (Gr. *neogenes*, recently born.)

neogene, *a.* *nee*-o-jeen, belonging to the Miocene and Pliocene systems of rocks [Geol.]. (Gr. *neogenes*, recently born.)

neogenetic, *a.* *nee*-o-je-*net*-ik, appearing not in the embryo but during development [Biol.].

neo-impressionism, *n.* a later development of impressionism; pointillism [Art].

neolite, *n.* *nee*-o-lite, a green silicate of aluminium and magnesium. (Gr. *neos*, and *lithos*, stone.)

neolithic, *a.* nee-o-*lith*-ik, pertaining to or denoting the later Stone Age, when implements were polished. (Gr. *neos*, and *lithos*, a stone.)

neologian, *a.* nee-o-*loh*-je-an, neological: *n.* a neologist.

neological, *a.* nee-o-*loj*-e-kal, pertaining to neology; employing new words.

neologically, *ad.* in a neological manner.

neologism, *n.* ne-*ol*-o-jizm, a word or expression that is new or of new significance; the use of such; theological neology.

neologist, *n.* ne-*ol*-o-jist, one addicted to the use of neologisms; an introducer of new doctrines, esp. in theology.

neologistical, *a.* nee-o-lo-*jis*-te-kal, neological.

neologize, *v.i.* ne-*ol*-o-jize, to use or introduce new terms; to practise or advance new theological doctrines.

neology, *n.* ne-*ol*-o-je, the introduction of new words or new meanings; a new doctrine; rationalistic theology. (Gr. *neos*, and *logos*, a word.)

neon, *n.* *nee*-on, a colourless and odourless gaseous element present in minute quantities in the atmosphere. **neon light,** a light obtained by the electrical discharge in a glass tube of a mixture of gases containing a large percentage of neon. (Gr. *neos*.)

Neonomian, *n.* ne-o-*noh*-me-an, one holding the doctrine that Christianity introduced a new law supplanting that of Moses. (Gr. *neos*, and *nomos*, a law.)

Neonomianism, *n.* ne-o-*noh*-me-a-nizm, the doctrine of the Neonomians.

neontology, *n.* ne-on-*tol*-o-je, the study of existing species, as opposed to palæontology.)

neophobia, *n.* ne-o-*foh*-be-a, dread or hatred of anything new. (Gr. *neos*, and *phobos*, fear.)

neophron, *n.* *nee*-o-fron, the white Egyptian vulture, *N. percnopterus*.

neophyte, *n.* *nee*-o-fite, a new convert or proselyte; a novice; a tyro. (Gr. *neos*, and *phutos*, grown.)

neoplasm, *n.* *nee*-o-plazm, any new and abnormal formation of tissue or of a tumour [Med.].

neoplastic, *a.* nee-o-*plas*-tik, pertaining to neoplasm, or to neoplasty. (Gr. *neos*, and *plasso*, form.)

neoplasty, *n.* *nee*-o-plas-te, restoration of tissue, etc., by any plastic method; autoplasty [Surg.].

Neoplatonic, *a.* nee-o-pla-*ton*-ik, pertaining to Neoplatonism.

Neoplatonism, *n.* nee-o-*play*-to-nism, a synthesis of Oriental and Platonic philosophy, first fully formulated by Plotinus of Alexandria in the third century A.D. (Gr. *neos*, and *Plato*.)

Neoplatonist, *n.* nee-o-*play*-to-nist, an upholder of the Neoplatonic philosophy.

neoteinia, *n.* nee-o-*ty*-ne-a, neoteny.

neoteny, *n.* ne-*ot*-o-ne, a condition of arrested development, esp. between a larval and mature stage [Zool.].

neoteric, *a.* nee-o-*te*-rik, new; recent in origin: *n.* an up-to-date, modern-minded person, esp. author, artist, etc. (Gr. *neoterikos*, young.)

neotropical, *a.* nee-o-*trop*-e-kal, pertaining to or characteristic of all tropical and South America with the adjacent islands [Geog. and Zool.].

Neozoic, *a.* nee-o-*zoh*-ik, denoting the formations from the beginning of the Tertiary up to the most recent [Geol.]. (Gr. *neos*, and *zoe*, life.)

nep, *n.* nep, small irregularly formed knots in cotton-fibre, or a bunch of these.

Nepalese, *a.* nep-a-*leez*, belonging to Nepal: *n.* a native of Nepal.

Nepali, *n.* nep-a-*lee*, one of the Indo-Chinese dialects spoken in Nepal.

nepenthe, *n.* ne-*pen*-the, any drug that relieves pain or banishes care; any of the pitcher-plants, members of the Malayan order *Nepenthes* [Bot.]. (Gr. *nepenthes*, not sorrowful.)

nephalism, *n.* *nef*-a-lizm, teetotalism. (Gr. *nephalismos*, sobriety.)

nepheline, *n.* *nef*-el-in, a silicate of aluminium, sodium, and potassium occurring in some volcanic rocks and lavas. (Gr. *nephele*, a cloud.)

nephelite, *n.* *nef*-el-ite, nepheline.

nepheloid, *a.* *nef*-el-oyd, cloudy, turbid [Med.]. (Gr. *nephele*, and *eidos*, like.)

nephew, *n.* *nev*-yew, the son of a brother or sister. (O.Fr. *neveu*.)

nephology, *n.* ne-*fol*-o-je, the branch of meteorology treating of clouds.

nephoscope, *n.* *nef*-o-skope, an instrument for determining the altitude, etc., of the clouds. (Gr. *nephos*, cloud, *skopeo*, view.)

nephralgia, *n.* ne-*fral*-je-a, pain in the kidneys [Med.]. (Gr. *nephros*, a kidney, *algos*, pain.)

nephrectomy, *n.* ne-*frek*-to-me, the surgical excision of a kidney. (Gr. *nephros*, and *ektomē*, to cut out.)

nephrite, *n.* *nef*-rite, a variety of jade, formerly worn as a remedy for kidney trouble. (Gr. *nephros*, a kidney.)

nephritic, *a.* ne-*frit*-ik, pertaining to the kidneys; affected with or relieving disorders of the kidneys: *n.* one affected with nephritis.

nephritis, *n.* ne-*fry*-tis, inflammation of the kidneys.

nephrocele, *n.* *nef*-ro-seel, hernia of the kidneys [Med.]. (Gr. *nephros*, and *kele*, a tumour.)

nephrogenic, *a.* nef-ro-*jen*-ik, arising in the kidneys.

nephrography, *n.* ne-*frog*-ra-fe, a description of the kidneys. (Gr. *nephros*, and *grapho*, write.)

nephroid, *a.* *nef*-royd, kidney-shaped. (Gr. *nephros*, and *eidos*, like.)

nephrology, *n.* ne-*frol*-o-je, the branch of anatomy treating of the kidneys; a treatise on the kidneys. (Gr. *nephros*, and *logos*, science.)

nephrotomy, *n.* ne-*frot*-o-me, the act of cutting into a kidney, esp. for extracting a stone [Surg.]. (Gr. *nephros*, and *tome* cutting.)

nepotic, *a.* ne-*pot*-ik, pertaining to or evincing nepotism.

nepotism, *n.* *nee*-po-tizm, favouritism toward relatives, esp. in the bestowal of patronage. (L. *nepos*, a grandson, a nephew.)

nepotist, *n.* *nee*-po-tist, one who practises nepotism.

Neptune, *n.* *nep*-tewn, the god of the sea [Roman Myth.]; the large planet beyond Uranus, having one known moon (Astron.]. (L. *Neptunus*, the sea-god.)

Neptunian, *a.* nep-*tew*-ne-an, pertaining to Neptune, or to the ocean; formed by water or aqueous solution. **Neptunian theory,** the obsolete theory

which referred the formation of all rocks and strata to the agency of water [Geol.]: *n.* a Neptunist.
Neptunist, *n.* *nep*-tew-nist, one who adopted the Neptunian theory.
neptunium, *n.* nep-*tew*-ne-um, the unstable trans-uranium chemical element (No. 93) produced by the emission of one electron from the uranium nucleus [Phys.].
Nereid, *n.* *neer*-re-id, a sea-nymph, any one of the fifty daughters of Nereus, the wise old man of the sea [Myth.]; (*l.c.*) a marine annelid of the genus *Nereis*. (Gr. *Nereus*, from *neros*, wet.)
nerite, *n.* *neer*-ryt, a mollusc of the genus *Nerita*.
neritic, *a.* ner-*rit*-ik, pertaining to shallow coastal waters, as opposed to oceanic [Zool.].
neroli, *n.* *ne*-ro-le, a scent prepared from essential oil of orange flowers. (Personal name.)
nervate, *a.* *ner*-vate, ribbed; veined [Bot.].
nervation, *n.* ner-*vay*-shon, the arrangement of nerves or veins; the venation of leaves.
★**nerve,** *n.* nerv, a fibre or fibres conveying impulses from or to the various parts of the body; a vein in the leaf of a plant; strength; firmness of mind; fortitude; courage; impudence [Coll.]: *v.t.* to give strength or vigour to. (Fr. *nerf*.)
nerve-cell, *n.* a protoplasmic cell branching into processes and occurring in the brain, spinal cord, ganglia, etc. [Anat.].
nerve-centre, *n.* an aggregation of nerve-cells, a ganglion [Anat.]; a central directing authority, factor, or power [Fig.].
nerved, *pp.* and *a.* nervd, having nerves as indicated; full of vigour.
nerveless, *a.* *nerv*-less, destitute of strength or nerve; feeble; weak.
nervine, *a.* *ner*-vin, able to act on or to soothe the nerves: *n.* a medicine that soothes the nerves; a nerve tonic. (L. *nervinus*, composed of sinews.)
nervose, *a.* *ner*-vohs, having nerves; nervate [Bot.].
nervous, *a.* *ner*-vus, strong; vigorous; pertaining to, composed of, or affecting the nerves; having easily agitated nerves; sensitive; abnormally excitable [Med.].
nervously, *ad.* *ner*-vus-le, timidly; with agitation.
nervousness, *n.* *nerv*-us-ness, the quality or state of being nervous; weakness of nerve.
nervure, *n.* *ner*-vewr, the ramification of veins in leaves [Bot.]; the corneous divisions in the wings of insects [Entom.].
nervy, *a.* *ner*-ve, nervous; jumpy, "on edge"; (formerly also) vigorous, courageous.
nescience, *n.* *nes*-yence, want of knowledge; ignorance. (L. *nescientia*.)
nescient, *a.* *nes*-yent, ignorant; unaware of; agnostic. (L. *nesciens*, unknowing.)
nesh, *a.* nesh, soft; delicate; squeamish. (A.S. *hnesce*.)
ness, *n.* ness, a promontory or cape. (A.S. *næss*.)
-ness, *suffix*, ness, denoting condition, state, or quality, as in *badness*, *likeness*, *richness*. (A.S.)
nest, *n.* nest, the shelter prepared by a bird for the reception and hatching of its eggs and the rearing of its young; hence, any receptacle for incubation; an abode; a retreat; a snug residence; a set of cases, etc., inserted in each other: *v.i.* to build and occupy a nest. (A.S.)
nest-egg, *n.* an egg left in the nest to prevent the hen from forsaking it; something laid up as a beginning [Fig.].
nestle, *v.i.* *nes*-sl, to lie close and snug, as a bird in her nest: *v.t.* to house in or as in a nest; to cherish; to cuddle. (A.S. *nestlian*.)
nestling, *n.* *nes*-sling *or* *nest*-ling, a young bird that has not yet left the nest; a young child.
Nestor, *n.* *nes*-tor, a wise counsellor; the genus of New Zealand parrots that includes the kaka and kea. (Homer's king of Pylos, in Greece.)
Nestorian, *n.* nes-*taw*-re-an, a follower of Nestorius, heretical patriarch of Constantinople in A.D. 428, who maintained the co-existence, but not the union, of the divine and human in the person of Christ: *a.* relating to Nestorius or his doctrine.
★**net,** *n.* net, a device for catching fish, birds, or wild beasts, or for protecting, confining, carrying, etc., formed with twine or other fibre or wire-knotted in meshes; anything similar in form or purposes; a hair-net; the network used in tennis, netball, or other games; a snare: *v.t.* to make into a net or network; to capture with or as with a net. (A.S.)
net, *a.* net, clear of discount and all deductions or charges; unadulterated: *v.t.* to realize as clear profit. (Fr. clear.)
netball, *n.* *net*-bawl, an outdoor ball-game played with the hands only, in which the goals are bottomless bags of network suspended from an elevated iron ring.
nether, *a.* *neth*-er, lower, opposed to upper; belonging to the regions below. **nether garments,** clothing for the lower limbs. **the nether world,** Hades; hell. (A.S. *neothera*, nether.)
nethermost, *a.* *neth*-er-mohst, lowest.
Nethinim, *n.pl.* *neth*-e-nim, the menial servants of the ancient Jewish temple. (Heb., those given.)
netsuke, *n.* *net*-soo-kay, a small decorative button-like ornament worn by the Japanese. (Jap.)
nett, *a.* *net*, net, without discount.
netting, *n.* *net*-ing, net-making; network. **netting needle,** a long needle, slotted at each end, to wind the twine or thread on.
nettle, *n.* *net*-tl, a plant of the genus *Urtica*, covered with hairlike stinging prickles: *v.t.* to fret; to irritate. (A.S. *netele*.)
nettle, *n.* *net*-tl, variant of *knittle*.
nettle-cloth, *n.* a thick tissued cotton fabric japanned and used as a leather substitute.
nettler, *n.* *net*-tl-er, one who nettles or provokes to irritation.
nettle-rash, *n.* urticaria, an irritating eruption upon the skin resembling nettle stings.
nettlesome, *a.* *net*-tl-sum, irritable; apt to be nettled.
nettle-tree, *n.* *net*-tl-tree, a tree allied to the elm *Celtis australis*; in Australia, a tree of the genus *Laportea*, esp. *L. gigas*.
network, *n.* *net*-wurk, a complication of threads, cords, wires, etc., forming interstices between the intersections; netting; anything resembling a net; (fig.) a system of related units.
neum, *n.* newm, a mark indicating a group of notes to be sung to one syllable, also, such a group [Mediæval Mus.]. (O.Fr.)
neural, *a.* *newr*-ral, pertaining to the nerves or the nervous system. (Gr. *neuron*, a nerve.)
neuralgia, *n.* newr-*ral*-je-a, acute paroxysmal pain in a nerve [Med.]. (Gr. *neuron*, and *algos*, pain.)
neuralgic, *a.* newr-*ral*-jik, pertaining to neuralgia.
neurasthenia, *n.* newr-ras-*thee*-ne-a, nervous exhaustion. (Gr. *neuron*, and *asthenia*, weakness.)
neurastheniac, *n.* newr-ras-*thee*-ne-ak, one affected with neurasthenia.
neurasthenic, *a.* newr-ras-*then*-ik, pertaining to or caused by neurasthenia.
neuration, *n.* newr-*ray*-shon, arrangement of nerves, esp. that of nervures in insects' wings [Ent.].
neurectomy, *n.* new-*rek*-to-me, the complete or partial excision of a nerve. (Gr. *neuron*, *ektos*, and *tome*, a cutting.)
neuriatry, *n.* newr-*ry*-a-tre, the treatment of nervous diseases; neurology.
neurilemma, *n.* newr-re-*lem*-a, the sheath investing a nerve [Anat.]. (Gr. *neuron*, and *eitema*, a covering.)
neurine, *n.* *newr*-rin, a poisonous ptomaine present in decaying meat, etc.
neuritic, *a.* newr-*rit*-ik, pertaining to neuritis: *n.* one subject to neuritis.
neuritis, *n.* newr-*ry*-tis, inflammation of a nerve or nerves; the condition occasioned by this.
neuroglia, *n.* newr-*rog*-le-a, the supporting and connective tissue of the central nervous system [Anat.]. (Gr. *neuron*, and *glia*, glue.)
neurography, *n.* newr-*rog*-ra-fe, a description of the nervous system. (Gr. *neuron*, and *grapho*, write.)
neurological, *a.* newr-ro-*loj*-e-*kal*, pertaining to neurology.
neurologist, *n.* newr-*rol*-o-jist, a specialist in neurology [Med.].
neurology, *n.* newr-*rol*-o-je, the scientific study of the nervous system and its special disorders. (Gr. *neuron*, and *logos*, science.)
neurolysis, *n.* newr-*rol*-e-sis, the exhaustion of a nerve or disintegration of nerve-tissue; the freeing of a nerve from adhesions [Surg.].
neuroma, *n.* newr-*roh*-ma, a tumour formed on a nerve or in nerve tissue.
neuron *or* **neurone,** *n.* newr-*rohn*, a nerve-cell with its processes.

neuropath, *n.* *newr*-ro-path, one liable to nervous disorders; a neuropathist. (Gr. *neuron*, and *pathos*, suffering.)
neuropathic, *a.* newr-ro-*path*-ik, pertaining to or affected with neuropathy.
neuropathist, *n.* newr-*rop*-a-thist, a specialist in the treatment of disease through the medium of the nerves [Med.].
neuropathologist, *n.* *newr*-ro-pa-*thol*-o-jist, a practitioner of, or consultant in, neuropathology.
neuropathology, *n.* *newr*-ro-pa-*thol*-o-je, the pathology of the nerves; the study and treatment of nervous diseases.
neuropathy, *n.* newr-*rop*-a-the, any disorder of the nerves. (Gr. *neuron*, and *pathos*, suffering.)
neuropsychosis, *n.* *newr*-ro-sy-*koh*-sis, any combined nervous and mental disease.
Neuroptera, *n.pl.* newr-*rop*-ter-a, an order of insects having four transparent, finely reticulated, membranous wings. (Gr. *neuron*, and *pteron*, a wing.)
neurosis, *n.* newr-*roh*-sis, a morbid affection of the nervous system [Path.]; a change in the nerve-cells effecting an unhealthy or abnormal psychic activity [Psych.].
neurotic, *a.* newr-*rot*-ik, affecting the nervous system; nervous; highly strung: *n.* a medicine useful in disorders of the nerves; a neurotic person, or one suffering from neurosis.
neurotomical, *a.* newr-o-*tom*-e-kal, pertaining to neurotomy.
neurotomist, *n.* newr-*rot*-o-mist, one practised in neurotomy.
neurotomy, *n.* newr-*rot*-o-me, dissection of the nerves; an incision in a nerve. (Gr. *neuron*, and *tome*, cutting.)
neurypnology, *n.* newr-rip-*nol*-o-je, hypnology.
neuter, *a.* *new*-ter, not adhering to, or taking part with, either side; neither male nor female [Bot. and Zool.]; sterile [Ent.]; neither masculine nor feminine [Gram.]; neither active nor passive [Gram.]: *n.* an animal or insect that is neuter; a castrated animal; a plant with neither stamens nor pistils [Bot.]; a neuter word [Gram.]; formerly, a neutral. (L., neither.)
neutral, *a.* *new*-tral, not engaged on either side; not biased on either side; indifferent; neither very good nor bad; having neither stamens nor pistils [Bot.]; neither positive nor negative [Elect.]; vague; indeterminate; greyish: *n.* a non-belligerent; one taking no part in a competition, etc. **neutral salt,** a salt possessing the character neither of an acid nor an alkali [Chem.]. **neutral tint,** a grey or dullish colour. (L. *neutralis*.)
neutrality, *n.* new-*tral*-e-te, the quality or state of being neutral; the condition of immunity from, or liability to, warlike action.
neutralization, *n.* *new*-tra-ly-*zay*-shon, the act of neutralizing, or of reducing to a neutral state.
neutralize, *v.t.* *new*-tra-lize, to render neutral; to render inert, inactive, or of no effect; to exempt or exclude from belligerency.
neutralizer, *n.* *new*-tra-ly-zer, one who or that which neutralizes.
neutrally, *ad.* *new*-tra-le, in a neutral manner.
neutrodyne, *n.* *new*-tro-dyne, proprietary name of a device for neutralizing capacity between the plate and grid in a valve [Wire.]. (L. *neuter*, neither, Gr. *dynamis*, power.)
neutron, *n.* *new*-tron, an electrically neutral particle consisting of an electron and a proton.
névé, *n.* nay-*vay* or nev-*ay*, the granular snow that feeds a glacier; firn. (Fr.)
never, *ad.* *nev*-er, not at any time; in no degree; not ever: *int.* surely not!; you can't mean it! [Coll.]. **on the never,** on credit [Slang]. (A.S. *næfre*.)
nevermore, *ad.* *nev*-er-*mor*, never again.
nevertheless, *ad.* *nev*-er-the-*less*, in spite of that; notwithstanding.
***new,** *a.* new, lately made, invented, produced, or come into being; recent in origin; not before known; recently discovered; modern; not habituated or accustomed; as at first; fresh; not of known or ancient lineage. **New World,** the Americas. (A.S. *niwe*.)
newcomer, *n.* *new*-kum-er, one who has recently arrived; a recruit or novice.
newel, *n.* *new*-el, the upright post about which is formed a winding stair; the post at the head or foot of a flight of stairs to which the handrail is fixed [Arch.]. (O.Fr. *neuil*.)
newfangled, *a.* new-*fang*-gld, formed with the affectation of novelty; fond of novelties. (*new*, and *fangel*, ready to catch at, from A.S. *fangen*, seize.)
newfangledly, *ad.* new-*fang*-gld-le, in a new-fangled manner.
newfangledness, *n.* new-*fang*-gld-ness, the fact of being newfangled; innovation.
Newfoundland, *n.* new-*found*-land or *new*-fn-land, a large variety of dog, originally from Newfoundland.
newish, *a.* *new*-ish, somewhat new.
newly, *ad.* *new*-le, lately; freshly; in a new way.
newmarket, *n.* *new*-mar-ket, a gambling card-game developed from Pope Joan. (Racing centre in Cambridgeshire.)
newness, *n.* *new*-ness, novelty; the state of being new.
***news,** *n.* newz, tidings; fresh information; intelligence; a newspaper. **news agency,** a journalistic organization supplying material to newspapers, etc.
newsagent, *n.* *newz*-ay-jent, a retail dealer in newspapers and periodicals.
newsboy, *n.* *newz*-boy, a boy who vends or delivers newspapers.
newsletter, *n.* *newz*-let-ter, an occasional letter circulating news to subscribers.
newsman, *n.* *newz*-man, one who vends or delivers newspapers; a collector and retailer of news.
newsmonger, *n.* *newz*-mung-ger, one who deals in newspapers and periodicals; a gossip or tale-bearer.
newspaper, *n.* *news*-pay-per, a printed paper publicly issued each day or week, containing contemporary news and opinions, with advertisements, etc., and usually advocating some policy.
newsprint, *n.* *newz*-print, the lowest grade of printing paper, chiefly of wood-pulp, used for newspapers.
news-reel, *n.* a film showing items of current events.
news-vendor, *n.* a seller of newspapers.
news-writer, *n.* one who writes a newsletter; a writer in a newspaper.
newsy, *ad.* *newz*-e, chatty; abounding in news: *n.* a newsboy [U.S.A.].
newt, *n.* newt, a tailed amphibian of the genus *Triton*; an eft. (*An ewt*, from A.S. *efeta*, lizard.)
Newtonian, *a.* new-*toh*-ne-an, pertaining to, or invented, or discovered by Sir Isaac Newton (1642-1727): *n.* a follower of Newton in philosophy.
next, *a.* nekst, nearest in place, time, or degree: *ad.* immediately succeeding. **next best,** second best. **next door to,** very near to. **next-of-kin,** *n.* the nearest blood relative. (A.S. *nēhst*, nigh-est.)
nexus, *n.* *nek*-sus (*pl.* **nexuses,** *nek*-sus-iz, or **nexus,** *nek*-sews), a connecting link or principle. (L.)
nias, *n.* *ny*-ass, a young hawk; an eyas. (O.Fr. *niais*.)
nib, *n.* nib, the bill or beak of a bird; a small pen; the point of anything, particularly of a pen; *pl.* crushed cocoa-seeds: *v.t.* to shape as a nib; to provide a penholder with a nib. (A.S. *neb*.)
nibble, *n.* *nib*-bl, a little bite, or seizing to bite: *v.t.* and *i.* to bite a little at a time; to bite; to carp at. (Of uncertain origin.)
nibbler, *n.* *nib*-bler, one who nibbles.
nibblingly, *ad.* *nib*-bling-le, in a nibbling manner.
niblick, *n.* *nib*-lik, a club used in golf with a round iron head and very lofted face.
niccolite, *n.* *nik*-o-lite, an ore of nickel, composed chiefly of arsenic and the metal. (*nickel*.)
nice, *a.* nice, attractive; pleasing; dainty; delicate; fine; exact; precise; minutely discriminative; requiring scrupulous exactness; subtle; over-exact; fastidious; easily injured; palatable; good to the taste; delightful; delicious. (O.Fr. from L. *nescius*, ignorant.)
nicely, *ad.* *nice*-le, in a nice manner.
Nicene, *a.* ny-*seen*, pertaining to Nicæa, a town of Asia Minor, or to the first and most important general council of the Christian Church, which was held here in A.D. 325. **Nicene creed,** an early statement of Christian doctrine, so called because adopted at this council.
niceness, *n.* *nice*-ness, quality or state of being nice; delicacy of perception; scrupulousness; precision.

nicety, *n.* *nice*-e-te, delicacy ; delicacy of perception ; delicate handling or treatment ; minute accuracy ; fastidiousness ; squeamishness ; precision.
niche, *n.* nitch, a recess in a wall for a statue, etc. ; the surroundings or condition suitable to a person [Fig.]. (Fr., from It. *nicchia*, a nook.)
nick, *n.* nik, a notch cut into anything ; a score to reckon by ; a reckoning ; the exact point of time required by necessity ; the critical time ; a winning throw at dice : *v.t.* to hit or touch luckily, or at the lucky time ; to cut in nicks or notches ; to defeat or cozen, as at dice ; to steal ; to make an incision in a horse's tail to make him carry it higher. (Perhaps as *nock.*)
Nick, *n.* nik, the devil, usually with the epithet "Old" added. (*Nicholas.*)
nick-eared, *a.* *nik*-eerd, crop-eared.
nickel, *n.* *nik*-el, a hard, but malleable and ductile, silvery-white metallic element used chiefly in alloys ; a five-cent piece [U.S.A.] ; any trivial sum of money. (Swed.)
nickelage, *n.* *nik*-el-aj, the art or process of electroplating with nickel.
nickel-glance, *n.* an ore of nickel, composed chiefly of nickel, arsenic, and sulphur.
nickel-green, *n.* a hydrous arsenate of nickel occurring in capillary crystals [Min.].
nickelic, *a.* ni-*kel*-ik, pertaining to or containing nickel.
nickeliferous, *a.* nik-el-*if*-er-us, containing nickel.
nickeline, *n.* *nik*-el-in, niccolite ; also, a variety of nickel-silver.
nickelize, *v.t.* *nik*-el-ize, to plate with nickel.
nickel-ochre, *n.* nickel-green.
nickel-silver, *n.* an alloy of copper, nickel, and zinc.
nicker, *n.* *nik*-er, one who nicks.
nick-nack, *n.* *nik*-nak, knick-knack.
nickname, *n.* *nik*-name, a name given in derision or familiarity : *v.t.* to give a nickname to. (M.E. *an ekename.*)
nicotian, *a.* ni-*koh*-shan, pertaining to tobacco : *n.* a tobacco smoker. (*nicotine.*)
nicotine, *n.* *nik*-o-teen, a poisonous alkaloid of very acrid taste, obtained from tobacco. (*Nicot*, Fr. ambassador to Portugal, who introduced tobacco into France in the 16th cent.)
nicotinism, *n.* *nik*-o-te-nizm, a morbid condition due to the excessive use of tobacco [Med.].
nictitate, *v.t.* *nik*-te-tate, to wink. (L. *nictitatus.*)
nictitation, *n.* nik-te-*tay*-shon, the act of winking.
nidamental, *a.* nid-a-*men*-tal, serving as a receptacle for eggs [Zool.], or as a nest. (L. *nidamentum.*)
niddering, *a.* *nid*-er-ring, mean, vile, contemptible : *n.* a base or abject person ; a coward. (A.S. *nithing.*)
nide, *n.* nide, a brood of pheasants. (L. *nidus*, nest.)
nidge, *v.t.* nij, to dress stones with a pick [Scots.].
nidicolous, *a.* ni-*dik*-o-lus, remaining in the nest for more than the usual period. (L. *nidus*, nest, *colo*, dwell in.).
nidificate, *v.t.* ne-*dif*-e-kate, to build a nest.
nidification, *n.* *nid*-e-fe-*kay*-shon, the building of a nest. (L. *nidificatus*, made a nest.)
nidifugous, *a.* ni-*dif*-ew-gus, leaving the nest soon after hatching. (Lat. *nidus*, nest, *fugere*, to flee.)
nidify, *v.t.* *nid*-e-fy, to nidificate.
nidor, *n.* *ny*-dor, the odour of cooking. (L.)
nidorous, *a.* *nid*-o-rus, resembling the smell or taste of burnt or over-roasted meat. (L. *nidor.*)
nidulant, *a.* *nid*-yew-lant, nestling ; lying loose, as pulp inside a berry [Bot.]. (L. *nidulans*, nesting.)
nidus, *n.* *ny*-dus, a nest ; the place of incubation of a disease [Med.] ; a place in which something is formed or deposited ; a source ; an origin ; a set of eggs, tubercules, etc. (L.)
niece, *n.* neece, the daughter of one's brother or sister. (O.Fr.)
niello, *n.* ne-*el*-lo, a black alloy of sulphur with a metal ; a piece of metal decorated with an incised design filled with this ; this art or process. (It.)
niellure, *n.* nee-el-*yewr*, the art or process of working in niello ; niello-work collectively. (Fr.)
Niersteiner, *n.* *neer*-shty-ner, a white Rhenish hock.
Nietzschean, *a.* *nee*-che-an, of, or pertaining to, the German writer, Friedrich Wilhelm *Nietzsche* (1844–1900), or to his philosophy.
nifty, *a.* *nif*-te, stylish ; fashionable [Slang].
Nigella, *n.* ny-*jel*-la, a genus of annual plant including love-in-a-mist, *N. damascena.* (L.)
niggard, *n.* *nig*-gard, a miser : *a.* miserly ; meanly covetous ; sparing. (Perhaps Scand.)
niggardliness, *n.* the quality of being niggardly.
niggardly, *a.* *nig*-gard-le, meanly avaricious : *ad.* in niggard manner.
nigger, *n.* *nig*-ger, a Negro ; a man of colour (in contempt) ; a nigger minstrel ; a dark brown colour. **nigger minstrel,** a comic entertainer with a blackened face. (Fr. *nègre.*)
niggerhead, *n.* *nig*-ger-hed, a matted tussock projecting above a swamp [U.S.A.] ; popular name of several N. American plants. **niggerhead cactus,** any of the Californian genus *Ferocactus.*
niggle, *v.i.* *nig*-gl, to trifle ; to finick ; to waste time in petty details ; to worry about trifles.
niggler, *n.* *nig*-gler, one who niggles.
niggling, *a.* *nig*-gling, finicking ; petty and over-elaborate : *n.* work of this nature.
niggly, *a.* *nig*-gle, niggling ; petty.
nigh, *a.* ny, near ; not distant ; not remote ; closely allied : *ad.* near ; almost : *prep.* near ; close to. (A.S. *neah.*)
★**night,** *n.* nite, that part of the natural day when the sun is beneath the horizon, or between the end of the evening and beginning of the morning twilight ; darkness ; intellectual and moral darkness ; adversity, or a state of affliction ; obscurity ; death. **a night out,** a night or evening on the spree ; a night off duty. (A.S. *niht.*)
night-blindness, *n.* nyctalopia ; inability to see except in daylight.
night-cap, *n.* a cap worn in bed ; a drink at bedtime.
night-churr, *n.* the nightjar or goatsucker.
night-clothes, *n.pl.* clothes worn in bed.
night-club, *n.* a club for purposes of amusement that does not open till night.
nightdress, *n.* *nite*-dress, a nightgown.
nightfall, *n.* *nite*-fawl, the close of day.
night-fire, *n.* the will-o'-the-wisp.
night-glass, *n.* a telescope specially constructed for use at night.
nightgown, *n.* *nite*-goun, a long shirt-like garment worn in bed.
night-hawk, *n.* the nightjar ; in Australia, the morepork ; one who is up and about habitually at night.
night-heron, *n.* the crepuscular heron *Nycticorax europæus*, or allied American species.
nightie, *n.* *ny*-te, a nightgown.
nightingale, *n.* *nite*-ing-gale, the warbler *Daulias luscinia*, that sings sweetly at night. **mock nightingale,** the blackcap. **Persian nightingale,** the bulbul, *D. hafizi.* (A.S. *nihtegale.*)
nightingale, *n.* *nite*-ing-gale, a kind of bed-jacket used by the sick and aged (Florence *Nightingale.*)
nightjar, *n.* *nite*-jahr, the goatsucker, *Caprimulgus europæus.*
nightless, *a.* *nite*-less, having no night.
night-light, *n.* a short, thick, slow-burning candle to give light at night.
night-line, *n.* a fishing line left to catch fish during the night.
night-long, *a.* throughout the night : *ad.* all night.
nightly, *a.* *nite*-le, done by night or every night ; *ad.* by night ; every night.
nightman, *n.* *nite*-man, one who collects night-soil or empties cesspools in the night.
nightmare, *n.* *nite*-mare, an incubus ; an agonized sense of oppression and helplessness, accompanied by terrifying dreams when asleep ; a sense of dread, or that which inspires it. (A.S. *niht*, and *mære*, nightmare.)
nightmarish, *a.* *nite*-mare-rish, like a nightmare ; temporarily and oppressively terrifying.
night-piece, *n.* a painting adapted to be best seen by artificial light ; a night scene.
night-porter, *n.* a male servant on duty at night in hotels, hospitals, etc.
night-raven, *n.* any bird that flies or cries at night.
night-school, *n.* an organization of evening classes for those employed during the day.
nightshade, *n.* *nite*-shade, several berry-bearing plants, mostly poisonous, of the genus *Solanum*, or *Atropa belladonna.* (A.S. *nihtscada.*)
nightshirt, *n.* *nite*-shert, a man's nightgown.
night-soil, *n.* the contents of privies, esp. for use as manure.

night-stool, *n.* *nite*-stool, a close-stool.
night-walker, *n.* one who walks in his sleep; one who walks with evil designs at night; a prostitute.
night-walking, *n.* somnambulism.
nightward, *a.* and *ad.* *nite*-ward, approaching towards night.
night-watch, *n.* a guard or watch in the night; time of changing the watch or guard at night.
nigrescent, *a.* ny-*gres*-sent, growing black; blackish. (L. *nigrescens*, growing black.)
nigrify, *v.t.* *nig*-re-fy, to blacken.
nigrine, *n.* *ny*-grin, a black variety of rutile containing iron. (L. *niger*, black.)
nigritude, *n.* *nig*-re-tewd, intense darkness; anything black.
nihil, *n.* *ny*-hil, nothing. (L.)
nihilism, *n.* *ny*-hil-izm, any doctrine that negates, or that aims at the desctruction of existing institutions in politics, religion, or morals; the programme or political theories of the revolutionary terrorists of late Tsarist Russia. (L. *nihil*, nothing.)
nihilist, *n.* *ny*-hil-ist, an upholder of nihilism, esp. in pre-Soviet Russia.
nihilistic, *a.* ny-hi-*lis*-tik, pertaining to or characteristic of nihilism.
nihility, *n.* ny-*hil*-e-te, nothingness; the state of being nothing; a nullity.
nil, *n.* nil, nothing. (L., contracted from *nihil.*)
nilgai, *n.* *nil*-gy, an Indian antelope, a species of *Boselaphus*. (Per. *nil*, blue, *gau*, cow.)
nill, *v.i.* nil, to be unwilling. (A.S. *ne*, not, *willan*, to will.)
Nilometer, *n.* nile-*om*-e-ter, a measure for showing the rise of water in the Nile during the state of flood. (Gr. *Neilometron.*)
Nilotic, *a.* nile-*ot*-ik, relating to the Nile.
nimble, *a.* *nim*-bl, light and quick in motion; moving with ease and celerity; brisk. (A.S. *numol*, from *niman*, to steal.)
nimble-fingered, *a.* expert at stealing.
nimble-footed, *a.* speedy; light of foot.
nimbleness, *n.* *nim*-bl-ness, lightness and celerity.
nimble-witted, *a.* quick in reply; quick-witted.
nimbly, *ad.* *nim*-ble, with agility.
nimbus, *n.* *nim*-bus, a shapeless grey layer of cloud from which falls rain or snow [Meteor.]; a disc of light round the heads of divinities, saints, etc., a halo. (L.)
nimiety, *n.* ne-*my*-e-te, state of excessiveness; redundancy. (L. *nimius*, too much.)
niminy-piminy, *a.* *nim*-in-e-*pim*-in-e, with affectation; prim; mincing.
Nimrod, *n.* *nim*-rod, a sportsman; a mighty hunter. (Heb.: Gen. x, 8–10.)
nincompoop, *n.* *nin*-kum-poop, a blockhead. (Origin uncertain, but not L. *non compos mentis.*)
nine, *a.* and *n.* nine, the number composed of eight and one; a card with nine pips. **nine days' wonder,** an incident or person of temporary interest. **nine men's morris,** *see* **morris. the Nine,** the Muses. **to the nines,** to perfection. (A.S. *nigon.*)
ninefold, *a.* *nine*-fohld, nine times repeated.
nine-holes, *n.* a game in which a small ball or marble is played into a series of nine holes.
ninepins, *n.* *nine*-pinz, a kind of skittles in which a round ball is rolled at nine pieces of wood set on end.
nineteen, *a.* and *n.* *nine*-teen, nine and ten united.
nineteenth, *a.* *nine*-teenth, the ordinal of nineteen. **nineteenth hole,** the bar-room of a golf-house (the last hole played being the 18th) [Slang].
ninetieth, *a.* *nine*-te-eth, the ordinal of ninety: *n.* a ninetieth part.
ninety, *a.* and *n.* *nine*-te, nine times ten. (A.S. *nigontig.*)
ninny, *n.* *nin*-ne, a fool; a simpleton. (Imit., or perhaps *an innocent.*)
ninny-hammer, *n.* *nin*-ne-*ham*-mer, a ninny.
ninon, *n.* (App.) a light silky dress material. (Fr.)
ninth, *a.* nineth, ordinal of nine: *n.* a ninth part.
ninthly, *ad.* *nineth*-le, in the ninth place.
niobate, *n.* *ny*-oh-bate, a columbate.
niobite, *n.* *ny*-oh-bite, columbite.
niobium, *n.* ny-*oh*-be-um, a malleable and ductile metallic element occurring, with tantalum, in columbite. (*Niobe* of Greek myth, a daughter of Tantalus, who, weeping for her children, was turned to stone.)
nip, *n.* nip, a pinch with the nails or teeth; a blast; destruction by frost; a biting sarcasm; a sip or small draught: *v.t.* to pinch or bite off the end; to pinch off with the nails; to cut off the end of anything; to blast; to bite: *v.i.* to move or step quickly [Slang]. (M.E.)
nipa, *n.* *nee*-pa, the East Indian palm, *Nipa fruticans*; an alcoholic drink prepared from its sap; also its leaves, used for mats and thatching. (Malay, *nipah.*)
niphablepsia, *n.* nif-a-*blep*-se-a, snow-blindness. (Gr. *nipha*, snow, *blepharon*, eyelid.)
nipper, *n.* *nip*-per, he who or that which nips; a fore-tooth of a horse; a small boy; a street arab; *pl.* a pair of pliers; small pincers.
nipperkin, *n.* *nip*-per-kin, a small cup; a liquor measure of rather under half a pint.
nippiness, *n.* nip-e-ness, agility; nimbleness.
nippingly, *ad.* *nip*-ping-le, so as to nip; with bitter sarcasm.
nipple, *n.* *nip*-pl, the pap by which milk is sucked from the breast; a teat; anything like it. **nipple shield,** a protection for the breast, worn by nursing mothers. (Perhaps dim. of *neb.*)
nipplewort, *n.* *nip*-pl-wurt, a yellow-flowered weed of the genus *Lapsana*.
Nipponism, *n.* *nip*-o-nizm, a peculiarity, etc., of the Japanese; veneration of the Japanese, their customs, art, etc. (*Dai Nippon*, native name of Japan.)
nippy, *a.* *nip*-pe, cold; nimble [Coll.]: *n.* a waitress (esp. of the London caterers, Lyons) [Slang].
Nirvana, *n.* neer-*vah*-na, in Buddhist doctrine, the total extinction of existence as agitated by desire, and the consequential attainment of self-centred composure of being; the state of supreme bliss, or [Theos.] of unconsciousness of the liberated soul. (Sans., extinguished by blowing.)
Nisan, *n.* *ny*-san, the first month of the Jewish sacred calendar, known as Abib before the Captivity. (Heb.)
nisi, *conj.* *ny*-sy, unless; if not. Used after *decree, order, rule*, etc., to denote that it is valid or takes effect provided that sufficient cause to the contrary is not shown before a certain date [Law]; *see* **decree nisi.** (L., unless.)
nisi prius, *n.* *ny*-sy-*pry*-us, the trial of civil causes by the judges of assize [Law]. (L., unless before.)
nisus, *n.* *ny*-sus, an effort; endeavour. (L.)
nit, *n.* nit, the egg of any small insect, esp. a louse or other parasite. (A.S. *hnitu.*)
nitid, *a.* *nit*-id, shining; lustrous; gay. (L. *nitēre*, to shine.)
niton, *n.* *ny*-ton, former name of radon.
nitralloy, *n.* *ny*-tra-loy, any steel that can be case-hardened by the nitriding process.
nitrate, *n.* *ny*-trate, a salt of nitric acid. **nitrate of silver,** a salt obtained by dissolving silver in nitric acid, used in chemistry and photography, and as a hair-dye and indelible ink: *v.t.* to convert into a nitrate; to combine with nitric acid.
nitratine, *n.* *ny*-tra-teen, sodium nitrate in the native state; caliche.
nitration, *n.* ny-*tray*-shon, the act or process of forming a nitrate, esp. in the soil by the action of bacteria.
nitre, *n.* *ny*-ter, saltpetre, or potassium nitrate. **cubic nitre,** sodium nitrate. (Fr.)
nitric, *a.* *ny*-trik, pertaining to or containing nitrogen. **nitric acid,** a compound of hydrogen, nitrogen, and oxygen, a powerful corrosive acid; aquafortis.
nitride, *n.* *ny*-tride, a compound of a metal with nitrogen: *v.t.* to convert into a nitride [Chem.]; to treat by nitriding [Metal.].
nitriding, *n.* *ny*-try-ding, the process of case-hardening special steels by heating in gaseous ammonia.
nitriferous, *a.* ny-*trif*-er-rus, bearing nitre.
nitrification, *n.* ny-trif-e-*kay*-shon, the process of nitrifying; the formation of nitrates, esp. by bacteria. (Fr. *nitre*, and L. *facio*, make.)
nitrify, *v.t.* *ny*-tre-fy, to form into nitre; to combine with nitrogen: *v.i.* to become nitrous. (Fr. *nitre*, and L. *facio*, make.)
nitrite, *n.* *ny*-trite, a salt or ester of nitrous acid.
nitro-bacteria, *n.pl.* bacteria that convert ammonia into nitric acid.
nitro-benzol, *n.* a combination of benzole and nitric acid having the flavour of oil of bitter almonds.

nitro-cellulose, *n.* an ester of nitric acid produced by the action of the acid on cellulose; gun-cotton; pyroxylin.
nitrogen, *n.* *ny*-tro-jen, an inert gaseous chemical element, constituting about 78 per cent. by volume of the atmosphere and serving as the basis of nitric acid and ammonia. (Gr. *nitron*, and *gennao*, produce.)
nitrogenize, *v.t.* *ny*-tro-je-nize, to treat or impregnate with nitrogen or its compounds.
nitrogenous, *a.* ny-*troj*-e-nus, pertaining to or containing nitrogen.
nitro-glycerine, *n.* a highly explosive oily liquid prepared by the action of concentrated nitric and sulphuric acids on glycerine.
nitro-magnesite, *n.* nitrate of magnesia, occurring as an efflorescence on old walls and in limestone caves.
nitrometer, *n.* ny-*trom*-e-ter, an instrument for ascertaining the amount of nitrogen, or of nitrates, etc., present in a substance. (Gr. *nitron*, and *metron*, measure.)
nitro-naphthalene, *n.* a substance prepared by boiling naphthalene in nitric acid.
nitrophilous, *a.* ny-*trof*-e-lus, readily growing in highly nitrogenous soil [Bot.].
nitrous, *a.* *ny*-trus, obtained from, impregnated with, or resembling nitre. **nitrous acid,** a weak acid formed by the action of water on any oxide of nitrogen. **nitrous oxide,** a gaseous mixture of oxygen and nitrogen, widely used as an inhalation anæsthetic; laughing-gas. (L. *nitrosus.*)
nitter, *n.* *nit*-ter, the bot-fly that lays its eggs or nits in horses.
nitty, *a.* *nit*-te, abounding with nits.
nitwit, *n.* *nit*-wit, a feeble-minded or empty-headed person [Coll.].
nitwitted, *a.* nit-*wit*-ed, of feeble intelligence: daft; senseless [Coll.].
nival, *a.* *ny*-val, pertaining to snow; niveous; growing in or under snow [Bot.]. (L. *nivis*, of snow.)
niveous, *a.* *niv*-e-us, snowy; resembling snow; snow-white [Bot.].
nix, *n.* niks, nil, nothing [Coll.]. (Ger. *nichts*, nothing.)
nix, *int.* niks, beware; take care [Slang].
nix, *n.* niks, a water-elf. (Ger.)
nixie, *n.* *nik*-se, a female nix or water-sprite.
Nizam, *n.* ne-*zahm*, the title of the native sovereign of Hyderabad in the Deccan. (Hind.)
*__no,__ *ad.* noh, not in any degree; not at all: *a.* not any; not one: *n.* (*pl.* **noes**), nohz, word of denial or refusal; a saying no: *pl.* those voting on the negative side. **no ball,** a ball delivered by the bowler in a way contrary to the laws [Cricket]. **no go,** an insurmountable obstacle; an indecisive struggle; useless. **no man,** nobody. **no-man's-land,** waste or unowned land; unoccupied land between opposing armies. **no one,** nobody. **no side,** the end of the game [Rugby Football]. **no wonder,** *see* **wonder.** (A.S. *na.*)
no, *n.* noh, an ancient form of Japanese drama accompanied by choral singing. (Jap.)
Noachian, *a.* noh-*ay*-ke-an, pertaining to the patriarch Noah, or his time.
nob, *n.* nob, a swell, a nobleman. (Abbrev. *nobleman.*)
nob, *n.* nob, a knob; the head. **one for his nob,** a point scored for holding the knave of trumps [Cribbage]. (*knob.*)
nobble, *v.t.* *nob*-bl, to render a horse unfit for a race; to obtain possession of dishonestly [Slang].
nobbler, *n.* *nob*-bler, one who nobbles; a blow on the head; a glass of spirits; a thief's or swindler's confederate [Slang].
nobby, *a.* *nob*-be, good enough for a nobleman; smart; grand [Slang].
nobiliary, *a.* no-*bil*-e-a-re, of or belonging to the nobility. (Fr. *nobiliaise.*)
nobility, *n.* no-*bil*-e-te, nobleness; dignity of mind; distinction by birth; peers and their families collectively; the peerage. (Fr. *nobilité.*)
noble, *a.* *noh*-bl, high in excellence or worth; honourable, dignified, or exalted; stately; of an ancient and honourable family; characterized by liberality; of an excellent disposition; choice: *n.* a nobleman; a peer; an old English coin originally worth 6*s.* 8*d.* **the noble art,** boxing. **noble metals,** gold, silver, and platinum. (Fr.)
nobleman, *n.* *noh*-bl-man, a peer; a male member of the nobility; formerly, any piece in the game of chess other than a pawn.
nobleness, *n.* *noh*-bl-ness, the state or quality of being noble; greatness; dignity; stateliness.
noblesse, *n.* no-*bless*, the nobility; persons of noble rank collectively. (Fr.)
noblewoman, *n.* *noh*-bl-woom-an, a woman of noble rank.
nobly, *ad.* *noh*-ble, in a noble manner; of noble extraction; magnificently.
nobody, *n.* *noh*-bod-e, no person; no one; an insignificant person; one of no note.
nocake, *n.* *noh*-kake, a paste of parched maize and water [U.S.A.]. (Amerind. *nookik*, meal.)
nocent, *a.* *noh*-sent, hurtful; mischievous: *n.* a guilty person. (L. *nocens.*)
nock, *n.* nok, a notch; the notch in an arrow, or in the horn of a bow to hold the string; the weather corner of a gaff sail. (Scand.)
noctambulation, *n.* nok-*tam*-bew-*lay*-shon, walking in sleep. (L. *nox*, night, *ambulatus*, walked.)
noctambulism, *n.* nok-*tam*-bew-lizm, somnambulism.
noctambulist, *n.* nok-*tam*-bew-list, a somnambulist.
noctiflorous, *a.* *nok*-te-*flaw*-rus, flowering at night. (L. *nox*, and *flos*, *floris*, a flower.)
Noctiluca, *n.* nok-te-*lew*-ka, a genus of small phosphorescent marine protozoa. (L. *nox*, and *luceo*, shine.)
noctilucent, *a.* nok-te-*lew*-sent, shining by night; phosphorescent.
noctivagant, *a.* nok-*tiv*-a-gant, wandering in the night. (L. *nox*, and *vagans*, wandering.)
noctivagation, *n.* *nok*-tiv-a-*gay*-shon, the act of wandering in the night.
noctograph, *n.* *nok*-to-graf, a writing frame for the blind. (L. *nox*, and Gr. *grapho*, write.)
noctule, *n.* *nok*-tewl, a bat of the genus, *Vesperugo*.
nocturn, *n.* *nok*-turn, in Roman Catholic Church, one of the three divisions of matins. (L. *nocturnus*, nightly.)
nocturnal, *a.* nok-*tur*-nal, pertaining to, done or happening at night.
nocturnally, *ad.* in the night; nightly.
nocturne, *n.* *nok*-turn, a picture of a night scene; a quiet piece of music suitable for playing at night [Mus.]. (Fr.)
nocuous, *a.* *nok*-yew-us, hurtful. (L. *nocuus.*)
nocuously, *ad.* in a hurtful manner.
nod, *n.* nod, a quick declination or inclination, as of the head; a slight obeisance; a command: *v.i.* to incline, as the head, with a quick motion; to be drowsy; to make a slight bow or beckon with the head: *v.t.* to incline or bend. **land of nod,** sleep. **on the nod,** on credit [Slang]. (M.E. *nodden.*)
nodal, *a.* *noh*-dal, pertaining to nodes. **nodal lines,** lines on the surface of a vibrating elastic body which remain at rest. **nodal point,** a point in a string extended between two fixed objects, which, when the string vibrates, remains at rest; the centre of curvature of a spherical lens or refracting surface. (L. *nodus*, a knot.)
nodality, *n.* no-*dal*-e-te, the state of being nodal.
nodder, *n.* *nod*-der, one who nods; a drowsy person.
noddle, *n.* *nod*-dl, the back of the head; the head: *v.t.* and *i.* to nod the head rapidly. (Probably from *nod.*)
noddy, *n.* *nod*-de, a simpleton; a fool; a sea-fowl allied to the terns, *Anous stolidus*, which is easily caught. (*nod.*)
node, *n.* node, a knot; a point of intersection; a knob; a swelling on a tendon or bone, etc.; a hard concretion round gouty parts [Med.]; the point of juncture of leaf and stem [Bot.]; a point where the orbit of a planet intersects the ecliptic [Astron.]; the intrigue or plot of a play, story, etc.; the principal difficulty. (Fr.)
nodical, *a.* *noh*-de-kal, pertaining to nodes [Astron.]. **nodical month,** the mean time of revolution between ascending nodes.
nodiferous, *a.* noh-*dif*-er-rus, bearing nodes. (L.)
nodiform, *a.* *noh*-de-form, resembling nodes.
nodose, *a.* no-*dohs*, knotty; having knots or swelling joints. (L. *nodosus.*)
nodosis, *n.* no-*doh*-sis, the condition of having nodes [Med.].
nodosity, *n.* no-*dos*-e-te, knottiness: a knot or node.

nodular, *a.* *nod*-yew-lar, pertaining to or resembling a nodule or knot; having nodes or nodules.
nodulate, *v.t.* *nod*-yew-late, to become nodulous.
nodulation, *n.* nod-yew-*lay*-shon, the process of nodulating; state of being nodulous; a nodule.
nodule, *n.* *nod*-yewl, a small knot; a rounded concretion. (L. *nodulus.*)
nodulose, *a.* *nod*-yew-lohs, nodulous.
nodulous, *a.* *nod*-yew-lus, having little knots or protuberances [Bot. and Zool.].
nodus, *n.* *noh*-dus, a node [Bot.]; the point of difficulty. (L.)
Noel, *n.* noh-*el*, Christmas; a Christmas carol. (Fr.)
noesis, *n.* noh-*ee*-sis, rational activity; pure thought, intellectual apprehension [Phil.]; cognition [Psych.]. (Gr., from *noos*, mind.)
noetic, *a.* no-*et*-ik, intellectual; relating to, originating in, or performed by the intellect. (Gr. *noetikos*, clever, intellectual.)
nog, *n.* nog, a kind of strong ale; egg-nog.
nog, *n.* nog, a bolt or peg; a piece of wood shaped like and used as a brick. (Scand.)
noggin, *n.* *nog*-gin, a small mug or cup; a quartern, a quarter of a pint; a gill. (Origin unknown.)
nogging, *n.* *nog*-ging, brickwork or other filling in timber framing.
nohow, *ad.* *noh*-hou, in no way [Coll.].
noils, *n.pl.* noylz, the short pieces and knots of wool left after combing. (Origin unknown.)
***noise,** *n.* noyz, sound of any kind; a loud sound; clamour; outcry or uproar; loud, importunate, or continued talk; frequent talk: *v.i.* to sound loud: *v.t.* to spread by rumour or report. (Fr.)
noiseless, *a.* *noyz*-less, making no noise or bustle.
noiselessly, *ad.* without noise.
noiselessness, *n.* state of being noiseless.
noisette, *n.* nwah-*zet*, a choice piece of meat for cooking; the colour hazel. (Fr., hazel-nut.)
noisily, *ad.* *noyz*-e-le, with noise.
noisiness, *n.* *noyz*-e-ness, the state of being noisy.
noisome, *a.* *noy*-sum, noxious to health; hurtful; disgusting. (Fr.)
noisomely, *ad.* with a fetid stench.
noisomeness, *n.* the quality of being noisome.
noisy, *a.* *noyz*-e, clamorous; turbulent; making much noise.
noli-me-tangere, *n.* *noh*-ly-mee-*tan*-je-re, lupus, or other skin disease [Med.]; the name of certain plants, esp. of the genus *Impatiens*; a picture representing the risen Christ as he appeared to Mary Magdalene. (L., touch me not.)
noll, *n.* nol, the head. (A.S. *hnoll.*)
nomad, *n.* *noh*-mad, one of a tribe that leads a wandering life, generally for pasture; a wanderer: *a.* nomadic; pertaining to nomads. (Gr. *nomas*, wandering for grazing.)
nomadic, *a.* no-*mad*-ik, characteristic of nomads; roving.
nomadically, *ad.* in a nomadic manner.
nomadism, *n.* *noh*-ma-dizm, the nomad's way of life; vagabondage.
nomadize, *v.i.* *noh*-ma-dize, to live as nomads.
nomarch, *n.* *nom*-ark, the governor of a nome or nomarchy. (Gr. *nomos*, a province, *archos*, ruler.)
nomarchy, *nom*-ar-ke, one of the provinces of modern Greece. (Gr.)
nombril, *n.* *nom*-bril, the centre of an escutcheon [Her.]. (Fr., the navel.)
nom-de-plume, *n.* *nom*-de-ploom (or App.), a name used by an author in place of his own; an assumed name. (Fr., pen-name.)
nome, *n.* nome, a territorial division of ancient Egypt; a nomarchy of modern Greece. (Gr. *nomos*, a province.)
nomenclative, *a.* *noh*-men-klay-tiv, concerned with nomenclature or naming.
nomenclator, *n.* *noh*-men-klay-tor, one who gives names to or classifies things. (L., a caller of names.)
nomenclatural, *a.* noh-men-*klay*-tewr-ral, pertaining to a nomenclature; nomenclative.
nomenclature, *n.* *noh*-men-klay-tewr, terminology; the system or collection of names for the objects and groups of objects in any branch of science.
nomial, *n.* *noh*-me-al, a single term [Alg.].
nomic, *a.* *nom*-ik, customary (of spelling). (Gr. *nomikos.*)
nominal, *a.* *nom*-e-nal, existing in name only; titular; trivial; not actual; substantival. (L. *nominalis.*)
nominalism, *n.* *nom*-e-na-lizm, the doctrine that a general notion has no existence in nature, only in the mind or in the name, or that there is nothing general but names (antithetical to philosophic realism).
nominalist, *n.* *nom*-e-na-list, an upholder of nominalism, esp. a scholastic philosopher.
nominally, *ad.* *nom*-e-na-le, in or by name only.
nominate, *v.t.* *nom*-e-nate, to name; to mention by name; to denominate; to designate by name or appoint; to name as a candidate for election. (L. *nominatus*, named.)
nominately, *ad.* *nom*-e-nat-le, by name.
nomination, *n.* nom-e-*nay*-shon, the act or the power of nominating; the state of being nominated.
nominative, *n.* *nom*-e-na-tiv, the case of the subject of a verb or sentence: *a.* relating to the subject.
nominatively, *ad.* as a nominative.
nominator, *n.* *nom*-e-nay-tor, one who nominates.
nominee, *n.* nom-e-*nee*, a person named or designate by another; one on whose life an annuity or grant depends.
nomistic, *a.* no-*mis*-tik, based upon law, esp. moral law. (Gr. *nomos*, a law.)
nomography, *n.* no-*mog*-ra-fe, the art of, or a treatise on, drafting laws. (Gr. *nomos*, a law, *grapho*, write.)
nomology, *n.* no-*mol*-o-je, the science of law. (Gr. *nomos*, and *logos*, science.)
nomothetic, *a.* nom-o-*thet*-ik, legislative; enacting laws; based on law. (Gr. *nomos*, and *tithemi*, lay down.)
non-, *ad.* non, not; a prefix implying negation. (The significance of terms with this prefix not appearing here will be deduced from that of the negatived word.) (L.)
non-ability, *n.* a want or lack of ability.
non-acid, *a.* without the qualities of an acid.
nonage, *n.* *non*-aj, minority; state or condition of being under age. (O.Fr.)
nonagenarian, *n.* *non*-a-je-*nare*-re-an, a person of from ninety to ninety-nine years old. (L. *nonagenarius.*)
nonagesimal, *n.* non-a-*jes*-se-mal, the highest point of the ecliptic above the horizon, *i.e.* 90° [Astron.]: *a.* pertaining to this, or to 90. (L. *nonagesimus*, ninetieth.)
non-aggression, *n.* abstention from the use of force. **non-aggressional pact,** an international agreement to settle differences only by negotiation or arbitration.
nonagon, *n.* *non*-a-gon, a nine-angled polygon [Geom.]. (L. *nonus*, nine, Gr. *gonia*, an angle.)
non-appearance, *n.* default of appearance [Law.].
nonary, *a.* *noh*-na-re, based on nine: *n.* a group of nine. (L. *nonas*, ninth.)
non-attendance, *n.* a failure to attend.
non-belligerent, *a.* taking no part, active or passive, in hostilities: *n.* a state, person, etc. that is non-belligerent.
nonce, *n.* nonce, the present time or purpose; the occasion. **nonce word,** a word coined for some special occasion but not adopted for general use, as in "the *treeness* of a tree." (A.S. *then anes*, the once.)
nonchalance, *n.* *non*-sha-lance, indifference; unconcern; coolness. (Fr.)
nonchalant, *a.* *non*-sha-lant, indifferent; casual; lacking in enthusiasm. (Fr.)
non-claim, *n.* a failure to make claim within the time allowed [Law].
non-collegiate, *n.* a student at a university who is not a member of a college: *a.* not belonging to a college; not having a collegiate system.
noncom, *n.* *non*-kom, a non-commissioned officer [Coll.].
non-combatant, *n.* a member of an armed force (esp. a surgeon or chaplain) whose duties do not include fighting; also, any civilian: *a.* pertaining to or consisting of non-combatants.
non-commissioned, *a.* not holding His Majesty's commission, esp. of army and air-force officers under the rank of second lieutenant or pilot officer, and similarly in the women's services.
non-committal, *a.* not being committed or pledged; indicative of indifference: *n.* refusal to commit oneself.

non-compliance, *n.* neglect of compliance; failure to comply [Law].
non-concurrence, *n.* a refusal to concur.
non-conductor, *n.* a substance or medium which does not conduct electricity or heat.
non-conforming, *a.* not conforming, esp. to the established religion.
nonconformist, *n.* non-kon-*for*-mist, one who does not conform, esp. a Protestant dissenter from the established Church of England: *a.* of or pertaining to nonconformists or nonconformity.
nonconformity, *n.* non-kon-*for*-me-te, refusal to conform, esp. to an established church; nonconformists collectively.
non-content, *n.* non-kon-*tent*, in the House of Lords, one who gives a negative vote.
non-delivery, *n.* failure to deliver.
nondescript, *a.* *non*-de-skript, not easily described or classified; strange; abnormal: *n.* one who or that which is nondescript. (L. *non*, and *descriptus* described.)
none, *pron.* nun, not one; not any; not the least portion: *a.* not any: *ad.* in no respect; not at all. (A.S. *nān.*)
non-effective, *a.* not available or qualified for active service [Mil.]: *n.* one who is non-effective.
non-efficient, *a.* non-ef-*fish*-ent, not effective; non-effective.: *n.* a recruit who has not qualified as an efficient soldier.
non-ego, *n.* non-*eg*-oh, the external or objective in perception or thought; the external world. (L., not I.)
non-elect, *a.* not elected: *n.* one not elected, esp. to salvation [Theol.].
non-election, *n.* failure of election.
nonentity, *n.* non-*en*-te-te, non-existence; a thing not existing, or as good as not; a mere figment; a nobody.
nones, *n.pl.* nohnz, in the Roman calendar, the ninth day (inclusive) before the Ides; in the Rom. Cath. Church, the office recited at 3 p.m., *i.e.*, the ninth hour. (L. *nonus*, ninth.)
none-so-pretty, *n.* *nun*-so-*prit*-te, the plant London pride, *Saxifraga umbrosa.*
non-essential, *a.* not essential or necessary: *n.* a thing that can be dispensed with.
nonesuch, *n.* *nun*-such, a thing that has not its like; a nonpareil; the fodder plant medick; a variety of apple.
nonet, *n.* no-*net*, a musical piece for nine singers or players. (L. *nonus.*)
non-execution, *n.* non-performance.
non-existence, *n.* the negation of being; a thing that has no existence.
non-existent, *a.* not having existence.
non-feasance, *n.* non-*fee*-zance, a failure to perform an obligatory act [Law]. (Fr. *non*, and *faire*, do.)
non-ferrous, *a.* not containing, or pertaining to, iron. **non-ferrous alloy,** any alloy based on a metal other than iron. (L. *non*, and *ferrum*, iron.)
non-flam, *n.* *non*-flam, non-flammable cinema film not exceeding 16 mm. in width.
non-flammable, *a.* not inflammable; capable of being burned but not of producing flame.
nonillion, *n.* no-*nil*-yon, a million raised to the ninth power. (L. *nonus*, ninth, and *million.*)
non-importation, *n.* failure or refusal to import.
non-intervention, *n.* refusal to interfere or intervene, esp. internationally by way of arms, sanctions, or threats, etc.
non-interventionist, *n.* one practising, or favouring a policy of, non-intervention.
nonjuring, *a.* non-*jewr*-ing, not swearing allegiance; of or pertaining to the nonjurors.
nonjuror, *n.* non-*jewr*-or, one who refused to take the oath of allegiance to the English crown after the Revolution of 1688.
non-metal, *n.* any element other than a metal.
non-metallic, *a.* not consisting of metal; devoid of metallic properties.
non-moral, *a.* amoral, neither moral nor immoral; having nothing to do with morality.
non-natural, *a.* unnatural; strained; figurative.
non-obedience, *n.* neglect of obedience.
non-observance, *n.* failure to observe or fulfil.
nonpareil, *n.* *non*-pa-rel, excellence unequalled; one whose excellence is so; a sort of apple; an old type-size, approximately 6-point [as this]: *a.* having no equal; peerless. (Fr. *non*, and *pareil*, equal.)
non-performance, *n.* a failure to perform.
non-placental, *a.* without a placenta [Anat.].
nonplus, *n.* *non*-plus, an insuperable difficulty; perplexity: *v.t.* to puzzle; to confound. *p.* and *pp.* **nonplussed.** (L. *non*, and *plus*, more.)
non-ponderous, *a.* having no weight.
non-productive, *a.* not, or not directly, productive.
non-professional, *a.* amateur; not professional; unskilled: *n.* an amateur.
non-proficient, *a.* having failed to acquire proficiency: *n.* one who is non-proficient.
non-provided, *a.* not officially supplied (esp. of schools and school buildings provided otherwise than by the Education Authorities).
non-resident, *a.* not residing on one's estate, or at one's place of office: *n.* an absentee landlord or incumbent.
non-resistance, *n.* the doctrine that injustice, violence, oppression, etc., should not be resisted by force; passive obedience.
non-resistant, *a.* non-re-*zis*-tant, passively obedient: *n.* one who advocates non-resistance.
nonsense, *n.* *non*-sense, no sense; words or language which have no meaning; anything absurd.
nonsensical, *a.* non-*sen*-se-kal, full, or characteristic, of nonsense; absurd; unmeaning.
nonsensically, *ad.* in a nonsensical way.
non-sequitur, *n.* non-*sek*-we-tur, a conclusion which does not follow from the premises [Logic]. (L., it does not follow.)
non-sexual, *a.* asexual; without distinction of sex; without union of the sexes.
nonskid, *a.* non-*skid*, treated or constructed in such a way as to prevent skidding (of tyres, and road surfaces).
non-society, *a.* non-union.
non-solvent, *a.* insolvent: *n.* an insolvent.
non-starter, *n.* one who (or animal, yacht, etc., which) though entered for a race, competition, etc. fails to start.
non-stop, *a.* and *ad.*, not stopping, esp. between the beginning and end of a journey; without a stop: *n.* a train not stopping at intermediate stations.
nonsuch, *n.* *non*-such, nonesuch.
nonsuit, *n.* *non*-sewt, the stoppage of a case owing to the default, neglect, or non-appearance of the plaintiff: *v.t.* to record that an action is estopped for such reason [Law]. (O.Fr. *non suit*, he does not follow it up.)
nontronite, *n.* *non*-tro-nite, a hydrous iron silicate found at Nontron, in France.
non-union, *a.* not belonging to a trade union.
nonuple, *a.* *non*-yew-pl, consisting of nine; nine-fold.
noodle, *n.* *noo*-dl, a simpleton; a blockhead [Slang].
noodle, *n.* *noo*-dl, a paste made of flour, water, and eggs for use in soups. (Ger. *Nudel.*)
nook, *n.* nook, a corner; a narrow place formed by an angle; a secluded retreat. (Origin unknown.)
noon, *n.* noon, the middle of the day; twelve o'clock in the day; meridian height; culmination [Fig.]: *a.* pertaining to noon. (L. *nona*, ninth, *i.e.*, ninth hour, or 3 p.m., which was the noon of the Romans.)
noonday, *n.* *noon*-day, mid-day: *a.* pertaining to or occurring at mid-day.
nooning, *n.* *noon*-ing, noontide; repose, or a meal, at noon.
noontide, *n.* *noon*-tide, the time of noon; mid-day.
noose, *n.* noose *or* nooze, a running knot which binds the closer the more it is drawn: *v.t.* to catch in a noose; to ensnare; to lasso. (O.Fr. *nous*, a knot.)
nopal, *n.* *noh*-pal, a species of *Nopalea*, a genus of thornless cacti; *N. coccinellifera*, the plant on which the cochineal insect feeds. (Mexican.)
nor, *conj.* nor, a word that denies or renders negative the second or subsequent part of a proposition; sometimes used for neither. (A.S. *nother*, neither.)
Norbertine, *a.* and *n.* *nor*-ber-tin, Premonstratensian.
Nordenfelt, *n.* *nor*-den-felt, an obsolete quick-firing machine gun named after the inventor, about 1878.
nordic, *a.* *nor*-dik, of or pertaining to the blond dolichocephalic race typical of Scandinavia: *n.* a member of this race.
Norfolk, *n.* *nor*-fok, the name of an English county: *a.* peculiar to, or characteristic of, Norfolk. **Norfolk**

capon, a red herring [Slang]. **Norfolk Howard,** a bug [Slang]. **Norfolk jacket,** a loose jacket with a belt worn by men.
noria, *n. naw*-re-a, a primitive form of waterwheel, raising water by means of buckets. (Sp.)
norland, *a. nor*-land, northern : *n.* the north country [Scots.].
norm, *n.* norm, the standard ; a rule ; a model ; typical form or structure. (L. *norma*, a carpenter's square.)
★**normal,** *a. nor*-mal, according to rule ; regular ; perpendicular [Geom.] : *n.* the acknowledged standard ; a perpendicular [Geom.]. **normal school,** an institution for training teachers. (L. *normalis.*)
normalcy, *n. nor*-mal-se, normal state or condition ; normality.
normality, *n.* nor-*mal*-e-te, the state or quality of being normal.
normalize, *v.t. nor*-ma-lize, to render normal.
normally, *ad. nor*-ma-le, in a normal manner.
Norman, *a. nor*-man, pertaining to the Normans or Normandy : *n.* a native of Normandy ; one of mixed Frankish and Scandinavian race settled there about the 9th to 11th cents. ; one of Norman descent. **Norman architecture,** a massive architecture characterized by the semicircular arch introduced by the Normans after the Norman Conquest. **Norman Conquest,** the conquest of England by William of Normandy in 1066. (Dan. *Normand*, northman.)
normated, *a. nor*-may-ted, made to conform to a norm or standard.
normative, *a. nor*-ma-tiv, based upon, or establishing, a norm.
Norn, *n.* norn, any one of the three fates of Norse mythology. (Scand.)
Norroy, *n. no*-re, the English king-of-arms whose jurisdiction lies north of the Trent. (*north*, and Fr. *roi*, king.)
Norse, *n.* norse, the language of Norway, or of Scandinavia generally : *a.* pertaining to Norway or its language ; Norwegian. (Ice. *norskr.*)
Norseman, *n. norse*-man, a native of ancient Norway ; a northman.
★**north,** *n.* north, one of the cardinal points, directly opposite to the sun in the meridian ; region to the north : *a.* northern. **North Pole,** the northernmost point of the earth. **North Star,** the pole-star. (A.S.)
north-east, *n.* the point equally distant between north and east : *a.* pertaining to or proceeding from the north-east.
north-easter, *n.* north-*ees*-ter, a north-easterly wind.
north-easterly, *a.* to or (of winds) from the north-east.
north-eastern, *a.* in or toward the north-east.
north-eastward, *a.* toward the north-east.
northerly, *a. north*-er-le, in, from, or toward the north.
northern, *a. north*-ern, in, toward or from the north : *n.* a northerner. (A.S.)
northerner, *n. north*-er-ner, a native of the north.
northernmost, *a. north*-ern-mohst, furtherest north (the superlative of *northern*).
northing, *n. north*-ing, distance or progress northward ; north declination [Astron.].
northman, *n. north*-man, a name given to the inhabitants of the north of Europe ; a Norseman.
northward, *a.* and *ad. north*-ward, being toward the north.
northwardly, *a.* and *ad. north*-ward-le, having a northern direction.
north-west, *n.* the point exactly intermediate between north and west : *a.* pertaining to, being in, or proceeding from this point.
north-wester, *n.* a north-westerly wind.
north-westerly, *a.* toward or from the north-west.
north-western, *a.* pertaining to, in a direction to, or from the north-west.
Norwegian, *a.* nor-*wee*-jan, belonging to Norway : *n.* a native, or the language, of Norway.
★**nose,** *n.* noze, the organ of smell ; the end of anything ; scent ; sagacity : *v.t.* to smell ; to scent ; to speak through the nose ; to feel one's way carefully. **lead by the nose,** to lead blindly. **parson's nose,** the pope's nose (of a fowl). **pay through the nose,** to pay an exorbitant price. **put one's nose out of joint,** to spoil one's plans ; to supplant. **thrust one's nose into,** to busy oneself with what does not concern one. **turn up one's nose,** to show disdain. (A.S. *nosu.*)
nose-bag, *n.* a bag tied to a horse's nose, containing oats, etc. ; a meal carried with one [Slang].
nose-band, *n.* the nose-part of a bridle.
nosed, *a.* nohzd, having a nose, as *snub-nosed.*
nose-dive, *n.* a steep downward swoop by an aeroplane : *v.i.* to make such a descent in an aircraft.
nosegay, *n. noze*-gay, a bunch of sweet-scented flowers ; a bouquet.
noseleaf, *n. noze*-leef, a membranous appendage on the nose of certain bats.
noseless, *a. noze*-less, destitute of a nose.
nose-piece, *n.* a nozzle ; a piece at the nose ; the end of a microscope that carries the object-glass.
nose-ring, *n.* a ring, by way of ornament, for the nose ; the leading-ring of a bull, etc.
nosey, *a. noh*-ze, nosy. **nosey parker,** a prying, inquisitive person [Slang].
nosing, *n. noze*-ing, projecting rounded part of a moulding, as on the edge of a step.
nosocomial, *a.* noh-soh-*koh*-me-al, relating to hospitals. (Gr. *nosos*, disease, *komeo*, attend to.)
nosography, *n.* noh-*sog*-ra-fe, the scientific description of diseases. (Gr. *nosos*, and *grapho*, write.)
nosological, *a.* noh-soh-*loj*-e-kal, pertaining to nosology.
nosologist, *n.* noh-*sol*-o-jist, one skilled in nosology.
nosology, *n.* noh-*sol*-o-je, the science of the classification of diseases ; the defining, naming, and grouping of diseases. (Gr. *nosos*, and *logos*, science.)
nosomania, *n. noh*-soh-*may*-ne-a, monomania in which one has the delusion that he is ill.
nosonomy, *n.* nos-*on*-o-me, the scientific classification of diseases.
nosophobia, *n.* noh-soh-*foh*-be-a, morbid dread of contracting disease. (Gr. *nosos*, and *phobos*, fear.)
nosophyte, *n. noh*-soh-fite, a pathogenic microbe.
nostalgia, *n.* nos-*tal*-je-a, home-sickness. (Gr. *nostos*, return, *algos*, pain.)
nostalgic, *a.* nos-*tal*-jik, pertaining to or characterized by nostalgia.
nostomania, *n.* nos-to-*may*-ne-a, greatly accentuated nostalgia [Path.].
nostril, *n. nos*-tril, one of the apertures of the nose. (A.S. *nosthyrl*, nose-hole.)
nostrum, *n. nos*-trum, a quack medicine or remedy ; a pet scheme for accomplishing something. (L., our own.)
nosy, *a. noh*-ze, having a large nose ; unduly inquisitive.
★**not,** *ad.* not, a word expressing negation, denial, or refusal.
notabilia, *n.pl.* note-a-*bil*-e-a, notable things.
notability, *n.* note-a-*bil*-e-te, the quality of being notable ; remarkableness ; a person of note.
notable, *a. note*-a-bl, worthy of notice ; remarkable ; memorable ; conspicuous ; notorious ; known : *n.* a person of note or distinction : *pl.* state representatives convened in times of emergency in pre-Revolutionary France.
notably, *ad. note*-a-ble, in a notable manner.
notalgia, *n.* no-*tal*-je-a, a pain in the back ; backache. (Gr. *notos*, the back, *algos*, pain.)
notandum, *n.* no-*tan*-dum (*pl.* **notanda**), a memorandum ; a thing to be noted. (L.)
notarial, *a.* no-*tare*-re-al, pertaining to or characteristic of a notary ; done or taken by a notary.
notary, *n. note*-a-re, a professional man authorized to note and protest bills of exchange and to attest writings or contracts of any kind in order to certify their authenticity ; also styled a **notary public.** (L. *notarius.*)
notate, *a. noh*-tate, marked with varicoloured spots or lines, etc. [Bot.].
notation, *n.* noh-*tay*-shon, the act or practice of recording anything by marks ; a system of figures and signs. (L. *notatio.*)
notational, *a.* noh-*tay*-shon-al, of or relating to notation.
notch, *n.* notch, an indentation ; a small nick ; the old term for a run at cricket : *v.t.* to cut small hollows in ; to fit to or fasten by a notch ; to score. (Formerly *an otch*, from O.Fr. *oche*, a nick.)
notch-board, *n.* the notched board which receives the ends of the steps in a staircase.

*__note__, *n.* note, a mark or token; a memorandum; an annotation; notice; a comment; distinction; an account; a short letter; a document promising payment; a diplomatic communication; a character to indicate a sound and its duration, also the sound itself [Mus.]: *v.t.* to notice with particular care; to attend to; to set down in writing; to annotate. (Fr.)
notebook, *n.* *note*-book, a book in which memoranda or notes are written.
noted, *a.* *note*-ed, illustrious; celebrated; well known by reputation.
notedly, *ad.* *note*-ed-le, in a marked degree.
noteless, *a.* *note*-less, undistinguished; not attracting notice; not musical.
notelet, *n.* *note*-let, a short note.
notepaper, *n.* *note*-pay-per, a small-sized writing paper for correspondence.
noteworthy, *a.* *note*-wur-the, notable; worthy of observation.
nothing, *n.* *nuth*-ing, not anything; non-existence; no part; no amount; a thing of no importance; a cipher: *ad.* in no degree. (*no* and *thing*.)
nothingness, *n.* *nuth*-ing-ness, non-existence; worthlessness.
notice, *n.* *noh*-tis, observation by the senses or by the mind; information; intelligence; attention; a review of a book, performance, etc.; consideration; announcement; a document communicating information; a written and dated notification of the termination of a contract or agreement: *v.t.* to observe; to heed or regard; to remark on; to treat with attention. **notice board,** a board for the display of notices. (Fr.)
noticeable, *a.* *noh*-tis-a-bl, that may be noticed; worthy of notice; remarkable.
noticeably, *ad.* remarkably.
notifiable, *a.* noh-te-*fy*-a-bl, such as must be notified (esp. of certain diseases to the authority).
notification, *n.* noh-te-fe-*kay*-shon, the act of notifying; the notice given; the writing which communicates information
notify, *v.t.* *noh*-te-fy, to make known; to give notice of; to inform by notice. (Fr. *notifier*.)
notion, *n.* *noh*-shon, idea; conception; mental apprehension; sentiment; opinion; inclination; an ingenious contrivance [Amer., coll.]. (Fr.)
notional, *a.* *noh*-shon-al, pertaining to notions; ideal; fanciful; conveying an idea [Gram.].
notitia, no-*tish*-e-a, a list or catalogue [esp. Eccl.]. (L., knowledge.)
notobranchiate, *a.* *noh*-to-*brang*-ke-at, having dorsal gills [Ichth.]. (Gr. *notos*, the back, and *branchiate*.)
notochord, *n.* *noh*-to-kord, a rudimentary form of special column present in embryos and certain primitive vertebrates [Biol.]. (Gr. *notos*, the back, and *chord*.)
notonectal, *a.* *noh*-to-*nek*-tal, swimming on the back (of certain water-beetles).
notoriety, *n.* no-to-*ry*-e-te, notoriousness; a celebrated or popular person. (Fr. *notoriété*, distinct.)
notorious, *a.* no-*taw*-re-us, known to disadvantage; manifest to all. (L. *notorius*, distinct.)
notoriously, *ad.* in a notorious degree.
notoriousness, *n.* no-*taw*-re-us-ness, the state or quality of being notorious.
notornis, *n.* no-tor-nis, a gigantic New Zealand wading bird, allied to the coot, extinct or nearly so. (Gr. *notos*, south, *ornis*, a bird.)
notwithstanding, *conj.* *not*-with-*stand*-ing, nevertheless; without hindrance or obstruction from: despite.
nougat, *n.* *noo*-gah, a confection of sugar and almonds. (Fr.)
nought, *n.* nawt, naught; nothing; the cipher, "0." **noughts and crosses,** a children's game in which the one of two playing alternately who first constructs a row of three ciphers or crosses wins. **to set at nought,** *see* **set.**
noumenal, *a.* *nou*-me-nal, pertaining to the noumenon; real as opposed to phenomenal.
noumenon, *n.* *nou*-me-non, a thing, or the conception of a thing, as it is in itself or to pure thought; the real underlying the phenomenal. (Gr., thing as perceived by the *nous*, or intelligence.)
noun, *n.* noun, a substantive, or word forming the name of anything material or immaterial, concrete or abstract, real or imaginary.
nounal, *a.* *noun*-al, pertaining to a noun.
nourish, *v.t.* *nu*-rish, to feed; to support; to maintain by feeding; to encourage; to cherish; *v.i.* to promote growth. **nourishing.** (O.Fr. *nouris*.)
nourishable, *a.* susceptible of nourishment.
nourisher, *n.* a person or a thing that nourishes.
nourishment, *n.* *nu*-rish-ment, that which nourishes; food; nutriment; instruction.
nous, *n.* nouce, intelligent perception; common sense; gumption. (Gr.)
nova, *n.* *noh*-va (*pl.* **novæ,** *noh*-vee), a hitherto unobserved star that suddenly increases in brilliance (L., new.)
novaculite, *n.* no-*vak*-yew-lite, a variety of hard-grained siliceous rock used for hones. (L. *novacula*, a razor.)
novate, *v.t.* and *i.* to convert into, or to make, a novation [Law].
Novatian, *n.* no-*vay*-shan, one of a 3rd-cent. puritanical sect which maintained that the Church had no power to absolve the penitent. (*Novatianus*, their founder.)
novation, *n.* no-*vay*-shon, the acceptance of a new debt or obligation in satisfaction of an old one [Law]. (L. *novatio*.)
novel, *a.* *nov*-el, of recent origin or introduction; unusual; strange: *n.* a fictitious tale or narrative in prose descriptive of life and character; a new or supplemental constitution or decree. [Law]. (O.Fr.)
novelette, *n.* nov-el-*et*, a short novel. (Fr.)
novelist, *n.* *nov*-el-ist, a writer of novels.
novelistic, *a.* nov-el-*is*-tik, characteristic of, or pertaining to, novels.
novelize, *v.t.* *nov*-el-ize, to relate in, or convert into, the form of a novel; to render novel; to make new.
novelty, *n.* *nov*-el-te, newness; something novel.
November, *n.* no-*vem*-ber, the eleventh month of the year, being the ninth of the Roman year, which began in March. (L. *novem*, nine.)
novena, *n.* no-*vee*-na, in the Roman Catholic Church, a form of intercession repeated on each of nine successive days. (Late L.)
novenary, *a.* *noh*-ven-a-re, pertaining to the number nine: *n.* nine collectively; a group of nine. (L. *novenarius*.)
novennial, *a.* no-*ven*-ne-al, done or happening every ninth year. (Late L. *novennis*.)
novercal, *a.* no-*ver*-kal, pertaining to or like a stepmother. (L. *noverca*, a step-mother.)
novice, *n.* *nov*-is, one who is new in any business, etc.; a beginner; one who has entered a religious house but has not yet taken the vow; a probationer; a new convert. (Fr.)
novilunar, *a.* no-ve-*lew*-nar, pertaining to the new moon. (L. *novus*, and *luna*, the moon.)
novitiate, *n.* no-*vish*-e-ate, the state or period of being a novice; a time of probation; a novice.
novocaine, *n.* *noh*-vo-kane, proprietary name of a local anæsthetic derived from coal-tar. (L. *novus*, new, and *cocaine*.)
*__now__, *ad.* nou, at the present time; very lately: *n.* the present time: *conj.* this being the case; after this; but. **now and then,** at one time and another. (A.S. *nu*.)
nowadays, *ad.* *nou*-a-dayz, in these days.
noways, *ad.* *noh*-waze, in no manner or degree.
nowed, *a.* *noh*-id *or* noud, tied or coiled in a knot [Her.]. (Fr. *nœud*, a knot.)
Nowel, *n.* noh-*el*, Noel.
nowel, *n.* *nou*-el, the inner mould of a hollow casting. (O.Fr. *noiel*.)
nowhere, *ad.* *noh*-whare, not in any place or state.
nowise, *ad.* *noh*-wize, not in any manner or degree.
nowt, *n.* nout, nothing; naught [North. dial.].
nowy, *a.* *noh*-e, having a projection in the centre [Her.]. (O.Fr. *noué*, knotted.)
noxious, *a.* *nok*-shus, hurtful; pernicious; injurious. (L. *noxius*.)
noxiously, *ad.* hurtfully; perniciously.
noxiousness, *n.* the quality of being noxious.
noyade, *n.* nwah-*yahd*, a method of execution, during the French Revolution, by wholesale drowning in vessels with a movable bottom. (Fr., from *noyer*, to drown.)
noyau, *n.* nwah-*yoh*, a liqueur prepared from brandy and peach, cherry, or other kernels. (Fr., stone of a fruit.)

nozzle, *n.* *noz*-zl, a projecting mouthpiece; the extremity of anything; a snout. (*nose.*)
nth, *a.* enth, of indefinite but abnormal size (either large or small). **the nth degree,** an indefinite power [Math.]. **to the nth,** to the utmost [Coll.].
nuance, *n.* noo-*ahnce*, each of the different degrees of shade in a colour; a subtle distinction among things of the same kind. (Fr.)
nub, *n.* nub, a small lump; a knob. (*knob.*)
nubbly, *a.* *nub*-ble, in small lumps. (*nub.*)
nubecula, *n.* new-*bek*-yew-la, a cloudy appearance, esp. [Med.] in the urine or over the eye; a nebula [Astron.]. (L., a little cloud.)
nubiferous, *a.* new-*bif*-er-rus, bringing or producing clouds. (L. *nubes*, a cloud, *fero*, bring.)
nubile, *a.* *new*-bil, marriageable. (L. *nubilis.*)
nubility, *n.* new-*bil*-e-te, state of being marriageable.
nucellar, *a.* new-*sel*-lar, pertaining to the nucellus [Bot.].
nucellus, *n.* new-*sel*-lus, the nucleus of the ovule [Bot.]. (L. *nucella*, a tiny nut.)
nuchal, *a.* *new*-kal, pertaining to, or about, the nape of the neck. (L., from Ar.)
nuciferous, *a.* new-*sif*-er-rus, bearing nuts [Bot.].
nuciform, *a.* *new*-se-form, in the shape of a nut. (L. *nux*, a nut, *forma*, shape.)
Nucifraga, *n.* new-*sif*-ra-ga, a genus of birds including the nutcrackers. (L. *nux*, a nut, *frango*, break.)
nucivorous, *a.* new-*siv*-o-rus, feeding on or eating nuts [Zool.].
nuclear, *a.* *new*-kle-ar, pertaining to a nucleus. **nuclear fission,** *see* **fission. nuclear fuel,** any substance from which atomic energy can readily be obtained.
nucleate, *v.t.* and *i.* *new*-kle-ate, to form into, or to form, a nucleus: *a.* nucleated.
nucleated, *a.* *new*-kle-ay-ted, having a nucleus; having nuclei.
nucleiform, *a.* *new*-kle-e-form, like a nucleus.
nucleolar, *a.* new-*klee*-o-lar, pertaining to or of the nature of a nucleolus.
nucleole, *n.* *new*-kle-ole, a nucleolus.
nucleolus, *n.* new-*klee*-o-lus, the nucleus of a nucleus; a small nucleus within another.
nucleus, *n.* *new*-kle-us (*pl.* **nuclei,** *new*-kle-eye), the centre of a cell; the central point of growth; that part of a body round which the rest accumulates; the central part of an atom, usually carrying a positive charge of electricity [Physics]; the body of a comet [Astron.]. (L., a kernel, from *nux*, a nut.)
nude, *a.* newd, bare; naked; void, or of no force [Law]; without drapery [Art]: *n.* that which is nude; the undraped human figure; the condition of being nude (L. *nudus*, naked.)
nudely, *ad.* *newd*-le, in a nude manner.
nudeness, *n.* state of being nude; nudity.
nudge, *v.t.* nuj, to shove gently, as with the elbow: *n.* such a push. (Perhaps Scand. *nugga*, to jostle.) (Scots. *nodge.*)
nudibranch, *n.* *new*-de-brank, a nudibranchiate mollusc.
nudibranchiate, *a.* *new*-de-*brang*-ke-at, having naked gills and no shell (of certain molluscs). (L. *nudus*, and Gr. *branchia*, gills.)
nudism, *n.* *new*-dizm, the cult of going naked. (*nude.*)
nudist, *n.* *new*-dist, one who practises nudism: *a.* pertaining to nudism or its followers.
nudity, *n.* *new*-de-te, nakedness; a nude figure.
nugæ, *n.pl.* *new*-jee, trifles, esp. in literary composition. (L.)
nugatory, *a.* *new*-ga-to-re, trifling; futile; ineffectual. (L. *nugatorius.*)
nuggar, *n.* *nug*-gar, a flat-bottomed barge used on the Nile. (Egyptian.)
nugget, *n.* *nug*-et, a lump of native precious metal, esp. gold.
nuisance, *n.* *new*-sance, that which or one who annoys, gives trouble, or is offensive; an injurious, offensive, or obnoxious practice, etc. [Law]. (Fr.)
null, *a.* nul, void; of no legal validity; ineffectual; expressionless. (Fr. *nul.*)
nullah, *n.* *nul*-la, a watercourse; a ravine. (Hind.)
nullification, *n.* *nul*-e-fe-*kay*-shon, the act of nullifying. (L. *nullus*, none, *facio*, make.)
nullifidian, *a.* nul-e-*fid*-e-an, of no faith: *n.* an unbeliever. (L. *nullus*, and *fides*, faith.)
nullifier, *n.* *nul*-e-*fy*-er, one who makes void.
nullify, *v.t.* *nul*-e-fy, to annul; to make void. (L. *nullus*, and *facio*, make.)
nullipara, *n.* nul-*lip*-a-ra, a woman who has never given birth to a child. (L. *nullus*, and *pario*, bring forth.)
nulliparity, *n.* nul-e-*pa*-re-te, the condition of being nulliparous.
nulliparous, *a.* nul-*lip*-a-rus, having never borne offspring.
nullity, *n.* *nul*-e-te, the state of being null; invalidity; want of force; a nonentity; that which is without legal existence or effect [Law]. (Fr. *nullité.*)
numb, *a.* num, destitute of sensation; torpid: *v.t.* to make torpid; to deaden; to benumb. (A.S. *numen*, taken, from *niman*, to take.)
★number, *n.* *num*-ber, a unit; an assemblage of units; more than one; many; a multitude; any numeral; one of a series; measure, or the order and quantity of syllables constituting feet; (*usually in pl.*) verse; the difference of termination of a word, to express unity or plurality [Gram.]: *pl.* (*cap.*) the fourth book of the Pentateuch, as giving the numbers of the Israelites: *v.t.* to ascertain the units of any sum or multitude; to reckon among; to amount to; to assign a number to, or mark with a number. **abstract, cardinal, golden, ordinal,** and **prime number,** *see* these words. **number one** [Coll.], oneself. **square number,** the product of a number multiplied by itself. **whole number,** an integer as distinct from a fraction. (Fr. *nombre.*)
numberer, *n.* *num*-ber-rer, one who or a machine that numbers.
numberless, *a.* *num*-ber-less, that cannot be counted.
numbles, *n.pl.* *num*-blz, umbles.
numbness, *n.* *num*-ness, the state of being numb.
numdah, *n.* *num*-dah, felt, or a saddle-cloth made of this [Anglo.-Ind.]. (Hind., from Per.)
numen, *n.* *new*-men, the divine will; the potency by reason of which persons or objects are worshipped. (L.)
numerable, *a.* *new*-me-ra-bl, that may be numbered.
numeral, *a.* *new*-me-ral, pertaining to, consisting of, or denoting number: *n.* a figure, group of figures, or word expressing a number. (L. *numeralis.*)
numerally, *ad.* *new*-me-ra-le, according to number.
numerary, *a.* *new*-me-ra-re, belonging to a number or numbers.
numeration, *n.* new-me-*ray*-shon, the act, art, or process of numbering; calculation; the art of writing or reading numbers.
numerative, *a.* *new*-me-ra-tiv, pertaining to numeration.
numerator, *n.* *new*-me-*ray*-tor, one who numbers; a numbering machine; the number above the line in vulgar fractions indicating how many parts of the unit are taken [Arith.].
numeric, *a.* new-*me*-rik, numerical: *n.* the numerical part of an expression [Math.].
numerical, *a.* new-*me*-re-kal, belonging to, denoting or consisting of numbers. **numerical difference,** a difference in respect to number. (Fr. *numérique.*)
numerically, *ad.* with respect to number.
numerology, *n.* new-me-*rol*-o-je, the study of the hidden meanings of numbers.
numerous, *a.* *new*-me-rus, consisting of a great number. (L. *numerosus.*)
numerously, *ad.* *new*-me-rus-le, in great numbers.
numerousness, *n.* quality of being numerous.
numinous, *a.* *new*-me-nus, characteristic of a numen: *n.* the awe-inspiring quality of any object of worship. (*numen.*)
numismatic, *a.* new-miz-*mat*-ik, pertaining to coins or medals.
numismatics, *n.* new-miz-*mat*-iks, the science of coins and medals. (L. *numisma*, a coin.)
numismatist, *n.* new-*miz*-ma-tist, a student of coins or medals.
numismatologist, *n.* new-*miz*-ma-*tol*-o-jist, a numismatist.
numismatology, *n.* new-*miz*-ma-*tol*-o-je, numismatics. (L. *numisma*, and Gr. *logos*, science.)
nummary, *a.* *num*-ma-re, pertaining to or dealing in coins or money. (L. *nummarius.*)
nummiform, *a.* *num*-e-form, coin-shaped.
nummular, *a.* *num*-mew-lar, pertaining to or shaped like coins. (L. *nummularius.*)

nummulary, *a.* *num*-mew-la-re, nummary.
nummulation, *n.* num-yew-*lay*-shon, the natural arrangement, like coins in a pile, of the red blood corpuscles [Path.]; the assuming of a nummular form.
nummuline, *a.* *num*-yew-line, nummulitic.
nummulite, *n.* *num*-yew-lite, a species of *Nummulus*, a fossil genus of foraminifera resembling a coin. (L. *nummulus*, a little coin, Gr. *lithos*, a stone.)
nummulitic, *a.* num-yew-*lit*-ik, composed of or containing nummulites.
numnah, *n.* *num*-nah, the thick pad on which a saddle rests; a saddle-cloth. (Hind., from Pers.)
numskull, *n.* *num*-skul, a dunce; a blockhead. (*numb* and *skull*.)
numskulled, *a.* *num*-skuld, slow witted; stupid.
nun, *n.* nun, a woman devoted to a religious life, living in celibacy in a convent; applied to a variety of pigeon, and to some other birds. **nun's veiling,** a soft woollen dress material. (A.S. *nunne*.)
nun-buoy, *n.* *nun*-boy, a circular buoy tapering at each end.
nuncheon, *n.* *nun*-shon, a luncheon. (A.S. *nōn*, noon, *scenc*, a draught.)
nunciature, *n.* *nun*-she-a-tewr, the office of a nuncio; the period of this.
nuncio, *n.* *nun*-she-oh, a papal ambassador; formerly, a messenger. (It.)
nuncle, *n.* *nung*-kl, old variant of uncle. (Contraction of "myn uncle.")
nuncupate, *v.t.* *nung*-kew-pate, to declare orally (esp. of wills).
nuncupation, *n.* nung-kew-*pay*-shon, the oral declaration of a will.
nuncupative, *a.* *nung*-kew-pay-tiv, nominal; by word of mouth; not written. **nuncupative will,** a will orally made. (L. *nuncupatus*, called by name.)
nuncupatory, *a.* *nung*-kew-*pay*-to-re, nuncupative.
nundinal, *a.* *nun*-de-nal, pertaining to fairs or markets, or to a market day. (L. *nundinæ*, from *novem*, nine, *dies*, a day.)
nunhood, *n.* *nun*-hood, the state of being a nun.
nunnery, *n.* *nun*-er-re, a house for nuns.
nunnish, *a.* *nun*-ish, characteristic of a nun.
nuphar, *n.* *new*-far, the yellow water-lily. (Pers.)
nuptial, *a.* *nup*-shal, pertaining to, done at, or constituting a marriage: *n.pl.* a wedding. (Fr.)
nurl, *v.t.* and *n.* nurl, knurl.
nurse, *n.* nurse, a woman who suckles children, esp. of another; a nursemaid; one who tends the sick or wounded; he who or that which nourishes or protects; the state of being nursed; a tree planted as protection to saplings; a worker ant or bee that tends the young; a nurse-hound; *v.t.* to suckle; to tend in infancy or sickness; to feed (an infant); to bring up; to cherish; to fondle in the arms; to promote growth in; to foster or encourage; to manage with care and economy; to keep the balls together in play [Billiards]. (O.Fr. *norrice*.)
nurse-balloon, *n.* a balloon used as a gas reservoir or to maintain pressure in the envelope of a lighter-than-air craft [Av.].
nurse-hound, *n.* the small shark *Scyllium catulus*.
nursemaid, *n.* *nurse*-mayd, a girl or woman employed to take care of infants or children.
nurser, *n.* *nurse*-er, one who or that which nurses.
nursery, *n.* *nurse*-re, an apartment in a house for children; a place or garden for rearing young plants; a place where anything is fostered and the growth promoted; that which forms and educates; a race for two-year-old horses. **nursery cannons,** a series of cannons made by keeping the balls together [Billiards]. **nursery governess,** a governess for small children. **nursery rhymes,** verses for children's amusement.
nurseryman, *n.* *nurse*-re-man, a grower of plants for sale.
nursling, *n.* *nurse*-ling, an infant; a child.
nurture, *n.* *nur*-tewr, the act of nourishing or rearing; up-bringing; training; nourishment: *v.t.* to nourish; to educate; to bring up. (O.Fr.)
***nut,** *n.* nut, a hard indehiscent pericarp; the fruit of certain trees consisting of a kernel enclosed in a hard shell; a small block of metal or wood containing a concave or female screw; the projection near the eye of an anchor, a person, thing, etc., difficult to cope with; the head [Slang]; a young dandy [Slang]: *v.i.* to gather nuts. **nut gall,** the gall of the oak (used in dyeing). **off his nut** or **he's nuts,** he's crazy [Slang]. **to be nuts on,** to dote on [Slang]. (A.S. *hnutu*.)
nutant, *a.* *new*-tant, nodding; bent down at the top [Bot.]. (L. *nutans*, nodding.)
nutarian, *n.* nut-*tare*-re-an, one who eats nuts as his principal food.
nutation, *n.* new-*tay*-shon, a nodding; a vibratory motion of the earth's axis [Astron.]; a habitual and involuntary motion of the head [Path.]; a bending movement of the tips of plants [Bot.]. (L. *nutatio*.)
nut-brown, *a.* brown as a nut.
nut-butter, *n.* a butter-like substance prepared from vegetable fats, esp. coconut and palm-kernel.
nutcracker, *n.* *nut*-krak-er, any bird of the genus *Nucifraga*; also, the nuthatch: *pl.* an implement for cracking nuts at table. **nutcracker jaws,** toothless jaws causing nose and chin to appear to want to meet.
nuthatch, *n.* *nut*-hatch, the small passerine bird, *Sitta cæsia*, allied to the wren and the tits.
nut-hook, *n.* in nut-gathering, a pole with a hook at the end to pull down the bough.
nutjobber, *n.* *nut*-job-ber, the nuthatch.
nutmeg, *n.* *nut*-meg, the aromatic kernel of the fruit of *Myristica fragrans*, an evergreen of the East Indies, used as a flavouring. **nutmeg butter,** a solid oil extracted from the nutmeg by expression. **nutmeg grater,** a rasp for grating spices. (*nut*, and O.Fr. *mugue*, from L. *moscata*, musk-like.)
nutmegged, *a.* *nut*-megd, spiced with nutmeg.
nutmeggy, *a.* *nut*-meg-ge, smelling or tasting of nutmegs; like nutmegs.
nut-oil, *n.* oil expressed from nuts.
nut-pine, *n.* any species of pine bearing edible seeds.
nutria, *n.* *new*-tre-a, the skin of the coypu, a species of *Myopotamus*. (Sp., an otter.)
nutrient, *a.* *new*-tre-ent, nourishing; promoting growth: *n.* any nutritious substance. (L. *nutriens*, feeding.)
nutriment, *n.* *new*-tre-ment, that which nourishes; food. (L. *nutrimentum*.)
nutrimental, *a.* new-tre-*men*-tal, nutritious.
nutrition, *n.* new-*trish*-on, the function or process of promoting the growth of animal and vegetable bodies; the process of assimilation of food; nutriment.
nutritional, *a.* new-*trish*-o-nal, pertaining to nutrition; nutritious.
nutritious, *a.* new-*trish*-us, nourishing; affording nourishment. (L. *nutritius*, nourishing.)
nutritiously, *ad.* in a nutritious manner.
nutritiousness, *n.* quality of being nutritious.
nutritive, *a.* *new*-tre-tiv, nourishment; concerned in or pertaining to nutrition. (Fr. *nutritif*.)
nutritively, *ad.* so as to nourish.
nutritiveness, *n.* the value as nourishment.
nut-screw, *n.* a nut-wrench.
nutshell, *n.* *nut*-shel, the hard shell covering the kernel; a thing of little value or small compass.
nuttiness, *n.* *nut*-te-ness, the state or quality of being nutty.
nut-tree, *n.* the hazel; any tree that bears nuts.
nutty, *a.* *nut*-te, abounding in or tasting like nuts.
nut-wrench, *n.* an instrument for fixing or removing the nuts on screws.
nux vomica, *n.* nuks *vom*-e-ka, the fruit or seeds of a species of *Strychnos*, from which strychnine is obtained. (L. *nux*, a nut, *vomo*, vomit.)
nuzzer, *n.* *nuz*-zer, a present to one of higher rank. (Hind. *nazr*, a gift.)
nuzzle, *v.t.* *nuz*-zl, to nestle; to house, as in a nest; to suckle; to foster: *v.i.* to hide the head, as a child in the mother's bosom; to root about with the nose. (*nose*.)
nyctalope, *n.* *nik*-ta-lope, one affected with nyctalopia.
nyctalopia, *n.* nik-ta-*loh*-pe-a, night-blindness; failure or imperfection of vision at night or in a dim light; used also (less correctly) for hemeralopia, or day-blindness [Med.]. (Gr. *nyx*, night, *alaos*, blind, and *ops*, eye.)
nyctitropic, *a.* *nik*-te-*trop*-ik, turning in a definite direction at night (esp. of leaves) [Bot.]. (Gr. *nyx*, *nyktos*, night, *tropos*, turn.)

nyctophobia, *n.* nik-to-*foh*-be-a, morbid dread of the night or of darkness.

nye, *n.* ny, a brood or flock of pheasants.

nylghau, *n.* *nil*-gaw, the nilgai.

nylon, *n.* *ny*-lon, a synthetic textile fibre of great strength and toughness derived from coal residues, hydrogen, and nitrogen. (Origin disputed)

nymph, *n.* nimf, one of a class of minor divinities of Greek myth, represented as beautiful maidens presiding over some particular river, fountain, wood, mountain, or sea; a handsome, graceful young woman; a nympha. (Gr. *nymphe*, a bride.)

nympha, *n.* *nim*-fa (*pl.* **nymphæ,** *nim*-fee), a pupa or chrysalis. (L.)

Nymphæa, *n.* nim-*fee*-ah, a genus of aquatic plants, of which *N. alba* is the white water-lily, and *N. lotus* the red Egyptian lotus.

nymphal, *a.* *nim*-fal, nymphean; consisting of nymphs; pertaining to nymphæ [Zool.].

nymphean, *a.* nim-*fee*-an, pertaining to a nymph or nymphs; characteristic of nymphs.

nymphic, *a.* *nim*-fik, pertaining to or characteristic of nymphs.

nympholepsy, *n.* *nim*-foh-lep-se, frenzy due to bewitchment by a nymph; hence, mania caused by desire for the unattainable. (Gr. *nymphe*, and *lambanein*, seize.)

nympholept, *n.* *nim*-foh-lept, one suffering from nympholepsy; a fanatical idealist.

nymphomania, *n.* nim-foh-*may*-ne-a, uncontrollable sexual desire in women. (Gr. *nymphe*, and *mania*.)

nymphomaniac, *n.* nim-foh-*may*-ne-ak, one afflicted with nymphomania.

nystagmus, *n.* nis-*tag*-mus, a continuous rolling movement of the eyeball, generally associated with nervous derangement [Med.]. (Gr. *nystazein*, to nod.)

O

O, oh, is the fifteenth letter and the fourth vowel of the English alphabet. It represents many sounds, of which the chief are—long (*go*), short (*got*), and those heard in *sword, word, son, woman,* and *move.* As a word it is an interjection (*see* **oh**), and (as **o'**) an abbreviation of *of*; and as a symbol is the cipher, nought.

oaf, *n.* ofe, a changeling; a foolish child left by fairies in place of another taken away by them; a dolt; a boor. (*elf.*)

oafish, *a. ofe*-ish, stupid; dull; boorish.

oak, *n.* oke, a stately forest tree of the genus *Quercus,* much esteemed for its timber. **live oak,** any of several N. American evergreen timber trees, esp. *Q. virginiana.* **to sport one's oak,** to close one's outer door against visitors. **the Oaks,** a race for 3-yr.-old fillies held at Epsom on the Friday after the Derby. (A.S. *ac.*)

oak-apple, *n.* a large oak-gall. **Oak-apple** day, the 29th of May (anniversary of the birth, 1630, of Charles II, and in memory of his escape from Cromwell, 1651, by hiding in an oak-tree).

oak-egger, *n. oke*-eg-er, a moth of the family Lasiocampidæ.

oaken, *a. oke*-en, made of or consisting of oak.

oak-fern, *n.* any fern of the genus *Polypodium.*

oak-gall, *n.* a diseased growth on the oak due to either a gall-fly of the *Cynipidæ* or a fungus.

oak-leather, *n.* the fungus *Dædalea giganteum,* found in fissures in old oaks; leather tanned with the bark of oak.

oakling, *n. oke*-ling, a young oak.

oakum, *n. oke*-um, the substance of old ropes untwisted into loose hemp, used for caulking and for stopping leaks. (A.S. *acumba,* tow.)

oaky, *a. oke*-e, resembling oak; firm; strong; abounding in oaks.

oar, *n.* ohr, a long shaft with a flattened blade for rowing boats; an oarsman: *v.t.* to impel by rowing: *v.i.* to row. **lie on one's oars,** to rest on one's oars or from work. **put in an oar,** to intrude, esp. in conversation; to interfere. **ship the oars,** to place them in the rowlocks. (A.S. *ar.*)

oarage, *n. ohr*-raj, a poetical term for rowing; oars collectively; apparatus for rowing.

oared, *a.* ohrd, having oars.

oarfish, *n. ohr*-fish, any of the ribbon-fish.

oarium, *n.* oh-*ayr*-re-um, an ovary [Anat.]. (Gr. *oarion.*)

oarsman, *n. ohrz*-man, one who rows with an oar.

oarsmanship, *n. ohrz*-man-ship, skill in rowing.

oasis, *n.* oh-*ay*-sis (*pl.* **oases**), a fertile spot in a sandy or barren desert. (L.)

oast, *n.* oast, a kiln for drying hops or malt. (A.S. *ast.*)

oast-house, *n.* a building containing an oast-kiln.

oat, *n.* ote (*pl.* **oats;** used also as *sing.*), a grass of the genus *Avena,* the seeds of which are used for food; the seeds. **wild oats,** youthful dissipation. (A.S. *ate.*)

oatcake, *n. ote*-kake, a thin cake made of oatmeal.

oaten, *a. oh*-tn, made of oatmeal, or of oats, or of the straw of oats.

oath, *n.* oath, a solemn affirmation or declaration, made with an appeal to God in witness of the truth of what is affirmed; such an affirmation made according to prescribed form [Law]; a blasphemous or profane imprecation. **oath of abjuration,** an oath introduced after the Revolution of 1688, excluding the Stuarts from the throne. **oath of allegiance,** the oath which binds a subject to bear true allegiance to his sovereign. **oath of supremacy,** the oath establishing the supremacy of the British sovereign over every other power, spiritual or temporal, in the realm. (A.S. *ath.*)

oatmeal, *n. ote*-meel, meal ground from oats.

ob-, ob, a Latin prefix signifying in the way of, towards, before, upon, near, about, etc., also reversal.

obbligato, *n.* ob-ble-*gah*-to, an instrumental accompaniment or part that is essential to the composition: *a.* indispensable [Mus.]. (It.)

obcompressed, *a.* ob-kom-*prest,* flattened in a direction other than normal [Bot. and Zool.].

obconical, *a.* ob-*kon*-e-kal, inversely conical [Zool.].

obcordate, *a.* ob-*kawr*-dat, shaped like a heart, but inverted [Bot.]. (L. *ob-,* and *cor,* the heart.)

obdiplostemonous, *a.* ob-*dip*-lo-*stee*-mo-nus, diplostemonous, but with the two stamen whorls reversed [Bot.].

obdormition, *n.* ob-dor-*mish*-on, numbness, or sense of being "asleep," of a limb, etc. through pressure on a nerve. (*ob-,* and L. *dormire,* to sleep.)

obduracy, *n. ob*-dew-ra-se, stubbornness in feeling or conduct.

obdurate, *a. ob*-dew-rat hardened in heart; hardened against good; stubborn; stubbornly impenitent. (L. *obduratus.*)

obdurately, *ad.* in an obdurate manner.

obdurateness, *n.* the state of being obdurate.

obeah, *n. oh*-be-a, a form of sorcery or magic practised by the Negroes of West African. (Native name.)

obeahism, *n. oh*-be-a-izm, the practices of, or the belief in, obeah.

obedience, *n.* o-*bee*-de-ence, state of being obedient; compliance with a command enjoined by authority; dutifulness. **passive obedience,** implicit obedience to lawful authority, whether exercised lawfully or otherwise. (Fr.)

obedient, *a.* o-*bee*-de-ent submissive to authority; yielding compliance with commands; dutiful; respectful. (O.Fr.)

obediential, *a.* oh-bee-de-*en*-shal, according to the rule of, or characterized by, obedience.

obedientiary, *n.* oh-bee-de-*en*-sha-re, an office-holder in a monastery or convent less in rank than the superior. (Late L. *obedientiarius.*)

obediently, *ad.* o-*bee*-de-ent-le, with obedience.

obeisance, *n.* o-*bay*-sance, a bow or curtsy. **make obeisance to,** to do homage to, or bow down before, a person or thing. (O.Fr.)

obeisant, *a.* o-*bay*-sant, showing respect for; reverencing; obsequious.

obeliscal, *a.* ob-e-*lis*-kal, in the form of an obelisk.

obelisk, *n. ob*-el-isk, a tall four-sided pillar, generally monolithic, gradually tapering as it rises, and terminating in a pointed or pyramidal top; the reference mark "†", the dagger [Print.]. (O.Fr. *obelisque.*)

obelize, *v.t. ob*-e-lize, to designate with an obelus; to mark as doubtful or spurious.

obelus, *n. ob*-el-us, in ancient MSS. a mark expressive of doubt thus – or ÷, so called from its resembling a needle. (Gr. *obelos,* a spit.)

Oberon, *n. oh*-ber-ron, king of the fairies, as personified by Shakespeare (Folklore].

obese, *a.* o-*beece,* extremely fat; corpulent. (L. *obesus.*)

obeseness, *n.* o-*beece*-ness, obesity.

obesity, *n.* o-*beece*-e-te, excessive corpulency, esp. undue accumulation of fat under the integuments [Med.].

obey, *v.t.* o-*bay,* to comply with orders or instructions; to submit to be ruled by, or to the control of; to yield to: *v.i.* to carry out an order or orders. (Fr. *obeir,* from L. *obedire.*)

obeyer, *n.* o-*bay*-er, one who obeys.

obeyingly, *ad.* o-*bay*-ing-le, obediently.

obfuscate, *v.t. ob*-fus-kate, to darken; to obscure; to bewilder. (L. *obfuscatus,* darkened.)

obfuscation, *n. ob*-fus-*kay*-shon, the act of obfuscating; bewilderment; cloudiness.

obi, *n. oh*-be, obeah.

obi, *n. oh*-be, a broad coloured sash worn with the kimono. (Jap.)

obimbricate, *a.* ob-*im*-bre-kate, imbricated in a reverse or downward direction [Bot., etc.].

obit, *n. oh*-bit *or ob*-it, an anniversary service or Mass for the soul of a departed person; funeral

solemnities; an obituary notice or register. (O.Fr.)
obiter, *ad.* *ob*-e-ter, incidentally. **obiter dictum** (*pl.* **obiter dicta**), an incidental remark, esp. a judicial opinion which does not form part of a judgment and has no legal force. (L).
obituarist, *n.* o-*bit*-yew-a-rist, a writer of obituaries.
obituary, *n.* o-*bit*-yew-a-re, an account of persons deceased; a list of the dead, or a register of obitual anniversary days, when service is performed for the dead: *a.* relating to the death of a person. (Late L. *obituarius.*)
object, *n.* *ob*-jekt, that about which any faculty is employed, or to which it is directed; something presented to or before the mind; anything to be looked at; any material thing; end; ultimate purpose; that which follows as acted upon by a transitive verb [Gram.]; someone or something presenting on absurd or pitiable appearance [Coll.]. **object ball,** the ball at which the cue ball is directed [Billiards]. (L. *objectus.*)
object, *v.t.* ob-*jekt,* to oppose: *v.i.* to offer reasons against; to dislike; to disapprove. (L.)
object-finder, *n.* an attachment to the microscope or telescope for locating an object.
object-glass, *n.* *ob*-jekt-glahss, in an optical instrument, the lens placed nearest to the object.
objectification, *n.* ob-*jek*-te-fe-*kay*-shon, the act or process of objectifying; state of being objectified; anything objectified.
objectify, *v.t.* ob-*jek*-te-fy, to regard objectively; to present as an object; to render objective.
objection, *n.* ob-*jek*-shon, the act of objecting; that which is presented in opposition; adverse reason; fault found. (Late L. *objectio.*)
objectionable, *a.* ob-*jek*-shon-a-bl, liable to objection; reprehensible; offensive; undesirable; nasty.
objectionably, *ad.* ob-*jek*-shon-a-ble, in an objectionable manner.
objectival, *a.* ob-jek-*ty*-val, pertaining to or constituting an object.
objective, *a.* ob-*jek*-tiv, belonging to or proceeding from the object itself, as it exists apart from its apprehension or comprehension by the mind; relating to external, as distinct from mental or emotional, objects; actual: *n.* any specially desirable place or object, esp. [Mil.] one towards which a body of troops is seeking to advance; an object-glass. **objective case,** the case following and depending on a transitive verb or preposition [Gram.]. (Late L. *objectivus.*)
objectively, *ad.* in an objective manner.
objectiveness, *n.* the state of being objective.
objectivism, *n.* ob-*jek*-te-vizm, that quality that enables one to dissociate his personality from his work [Art, etc.]; the theory that gives the objective elements in life predominance over the subjective.
objectivist, *a.* ob-*jek*-te-vist, characterized by objectivism: *n.* one who practises or advocates objectivism.
objectivity, *n.* ob-jek-*tiv*-e-te, the condition of being objective.
objectless, *a.* *ob*-jekt-less, having no object.
object-lesson, *n.* a lesson from an object, or a representation of it; a practical illustration.
objector, *n.* ob-*jek*-tor, one who objects or offers opposition to a measure or proposal. **conscientious objector,** see **conscientious.**
object-staff, *n.* a surveyor's staff of the same height as the level; the levelling staff.
object-teaching, *n.* the use of illustrations or actual objects in teaching.
objuration, *n.* ob-joo-*ray*-shon, swearing; a binding by oath. (L. *objuratio.*)
objurgate, *v.t.* *ob*-jur-gate, to chide; to reprove. (L. *objurgatus,* childed.)
objurgation, *n.* ob-jur-*gay*-shon, chiding; reproof.
objurgatory, *a.* ob-*jur*-ga-to-re *or* *ob*-jur-*gay*-to-re, containing censure or reproof.
oblanceolate, *a.* ob-*lan*-se-o-lat, inversely lanceolate; gently tapering towards the base.
oblate, *n.* *ob*-late, one of a society of secular priests founded by St. Charles Borromeo; one not under vows but dedicated to religious work.
oblate, *a.* ob-*late,* flattened or depressed at the poles [Geom.]. **oblate spheroid,** a sphere flattened at the poles, or such a sphere as is produced by the revolution of an ellipse about its shorter axis. (L. *oblatus.*)
oblateness, *n.* ob-*late*-ness, state of being oblate.
oblation, *n.* ob-*lay*-shon, anything offered, or the act of offering, in worship; a gift to a church or religious body; an offering. (Fr.)
oblational, *a.* ob-*lay*-shon-al, relating to oblation.
oblatory, *a.* *ob*-la-to-re, relating to oblation.
obligant, *n.* ob-le-gant, an obligor.
obligate, *v.t.* *ob*-le-gate, to bind, esp. by law; to bring under an obligation; to put under oath: *a.* bound to be such [Zool.], as an obligate parasite. (L. *obligatus.*)
obligation, *n.* ob-le-*gay*-shon, the binding power of a vow, promise, or contract, or of law, independent of a promise; the state of being bound to return some favour or service; a bond with a condition annexed [Law].
obligato, *n.* and *a.* ob-ble-*gah*-to, obbligato.
obligatory, *a.* *ob*-le-ga-to-re *or* ob-*lig*-a-to-re, imposing or constituting an obligation; binding in law or conscience.
oblige, *v.t.* o-*blije,* to constrain by physical, legal, or moral force; to do a favour to; to lay under an obligation of gratitude; to gratify. (Fr. *obliger,*)
obligee, *n.* ob-le-*jee,* the person to whom another is bound or under bond. (Fr.)
obligement, *n.* o-*blije*-ment, obligation; a favour granted.
obliger, *n.* o-*blije*-er, one who obliges.
obliging, *a.* o-*blije*-ing, courteous or complaisant; kind.
obligingly, *ad.* o-*blije*-ing-le, in an obliging manner.
obligingness, *n.* the quality of being obliging.
obligor, *n.* *ob*-le-gor, one bound by a bond [Law].
oblique, *a.* o-*bleek,* slanting; sideways; askew; neither perpendicular nor parallel; indirect; sinister: *v.i.* to move forward to the right or left, by advancing sideways [Mil.]; of or pertaining to cases other than the nominative [Gram.]. **oblique angle,** an angle greater or less than a right angle [Geom.]. **oblique oration,** reported, as contrasted with direct, speech [Rhet.]. **oblique plane,** a plane that declines from the zenith [Dialling]. **oblique sphere,** the terrestrial sphere when its axis is inclined to the horizon of the place [Geog.]. (Fr.)
obliquely, *ad.* o-*bleek*-le, in an oblique manner.
obliqueness, *n.* the state of being oblique.
obliquitous, *a.* o-*blik*-we-tus, characterized by obliquity.
obliquity, *n.* o-*blik*-we-te, obliqueness; a slanting direction; deviation from moral rectitude; irregularity. (Fr. *obliquité.*)
obliterate, *v.t.* o-*blit*-er-ate, to efface; to wear out; to destroy by time or other means; to cause to disappear; to cancel (of postage stamps). (L. *obliteratus.*)
obliteration, *n.* o-blit-er-*ray*-shon, the act of obliterating; state of being obliterated.
oblivion, *n.* o-*bliv*-e-on, forgetfulness; state of being forgotten; remission of punishment, esp. [Law] by an Act of Oblivion. (O.Fr., from L. *oblivisci,* to forget.)
oblivious, *a.* o-*bliv*-e-us, causing forgetfulness; forgetful. (L. *obliviosus.*)
obliviously, *ad.* o-*bliv*-e-us-le, forgetfully.
obliviousness, *n.* forgetfulness; oblivion.
oblong, *a.* *ob*-long, longer than broad: *n.* a figure or thing longer than broad. (Fr.)
oblongish, *a.* *ob*-long-ish, somewhat oblong.
oblongness, *n.* the state of being oblong.
obloquy, *n.* *ob*-lo-kwe, reproachful language; calumny. (L. *obloquium,* speaking against.)
obmutescence, *n.* ob-mew-*tes*-sence, wilful refusal to speak; deliberate silence. (L. *obmutescens.*)
obnoxious, *a.* ob-*nok*-shus, liable (to injury, etc.); reprehensible; offensive; hateful; in disfavour. (L. *obnoxius.*)
obnoxiously, *ad.* in an obnoxious manner.
obnoxiousness, *n.* state of being obnoxious.
obnubilate, *v.t.* ob-*new*-be-late, to cloud; to obscure. (L. *obnubilatus,* clouded.)
obnubilation, ob-new-be-*lay*-shon, the action of darkening as with a cloud; the fact of being obscured.
oboe, *n.* *oh*-boh, an orchestral wood-wind instrument with a double reed and conical bore; an organ

reed-stop of 8 ft. pitch and similar tone. (It., from Fr. *hautbois.*)
oboist, *n.* *o*-boh-ist, one who plays the oboe.
obol, *n.* *ob*-ol, a small coin and weight of ancient Greece equivalent to one-sixth of a drachma. (Gr. *obolos.*)
obovate, *a.* ob-*oh*-vate, inversely ovate; egg-shaped with the small end at the base.
obreption, *n.* ob-*rep*-shon, the act of acquiring secretly or by craft or fraud. (L. *obreptio.*)
obreptitious, *a.* ob-rep-*tish*-us, done or obtained surreptitiously or by obreption.
obscene, *a.* ob-*seen*, offensive to chastity and delicacy; indecent; lewd; filthy; disgusting; ill-omened. (L. *obscenus*, ill-boding, repulsive.)
obscenely, *ad.* ob-*seen*-le, in an obscene manner.
obsceneness, *n.* ob-*seen*-ness, obscenity.
obscenity, *n.* ob-*sen*-e-te, state or quality of being obscene; unchaste speech or action; ribaldry; lewdness.
obscurant, *n.* ob-*skewr*-rant, one who obscures; an opponent of progress or reform; an enemy to science on religious grounds: *a.* obscurantist. (L. *obscurans.*)
obscurantism, *n.* ob-*skewr*-ran-tizm, the principles of an obscurant.
obscurantist, *n.* ob-*skewr*-ran-tist, an obscurant: *a.* obscuring; pertaining to an obscurant.
obscuration, *n.* ob-skewr-*ray*-shon, the act of obscuring or state of being obscured.
obscure, *a.* ob-*skewr*, dark; badly lighted; not easily understood; abstruse; remote from observation; unnoticed or unknown; lowly; not clear or distinct; not easily legible: *v.t.* to darken; to cloud; to make less visible, legible, intelligible, or glorious; to tarnish. (Fr. *obscur.*)
obscurely, *ad.* ob-*skewr*-le, in an obscure manner.
obscurement, *n.* ob-*skewr*-ment, obscuration.
obscureness, *n.* obscurity.
obscurity, *n.* ob-*skewr*-re-te, state or quality of being obscure; darkness; abstruseness; unintelligibleness; lowly condition.
obsecration, *n.* ob-se-*kray*-shon, entreaty; a clause in the Litany beginning with "by." (L. *obsecrare*, to entreat.)
obsequial, *a.* ob-*see*-kwe-al, relating to obsequies.
obsequies, *n.pl.* *ob*-se-kwiz, funeral rites. (O.Fr. *obseques.*)
obsequious, *a.* ob-*see*-kwe-us, compliant to excess; servile. (L. *obsequi*, to comply.)
obsequiously, *ad.* in an obsequious manner.
obsequiousness, *n.* the quality of being obsequious.
observable, *a.* ob-*zer*-va-bl, remarkable; worthy of observation.
observably, *ad.* in an observable manner.
observance, *n.* ob-*zer*-vance, the act of observing, or of complying with, etc.; performance; performance of rites; a rule, practice, etc., to be observed. (Fr.)
observanda, *n.pl.* ob-zer-*van*-da, things or meanings to be observed.
observant, *a.* ob-*zer*-vant, taking notice; watchful; carefully attentive: *n.* (*cap.*) an Observantine.
Observantine, *n.* ob-*zer*-van-tin, a member of a former branch of the Franciscan friars who practised with rigour the rules of the founder.
Observantist, *n.* ob-*zer*-van-tist, an Observantine.
observantly, *ad.* with attentive view.
★**observation,** *n.* ob-zer-*vay*-shon, the act of observing or fixing the mind on anything; that which is observed; a remark; the scientific investigating and noting of an occurrence or phenomenon, esp. angular measurement of distance on the celestial sphere [Astron. and Navig.]. **observation balloon,** a stationary balloon formerly used for watching an enemy's movements [Mil.]. **observation car,** a coach attached to the end of a railway train from which passengers can view the scenery. **observation mine,** a sea- or land-mine electrically exploded by a distant watcher [Mil.]. **observation post,** an advanced position from which the effect of gun-fire can be observed [Mil.]. (Fr.)
observational, *a.* ob-zer-*vay*-shon-al, consisting of remarks or observations.
observative, *a.* ob-*zer*-va-tiv, pertaining to or given to observation; attentive.
observatory, *n.* ob-*zer*-va-to-re, a building or institution equipped for the observation of astronomical, meteorological, or magnetic phenomena.
observe, *v.t.* ob-*zerv*, to notice; to take notice of; to remark; to celebrate; to comply with; to examine and ascertain by scientific observation: *v.i.* to be attentive; to remark. (Fr. *observer.*)
observer, *n.* ob-*zer*-ver, one who observes; a spectator; one who keeps any law or custom; a member of the R.O.C.; a chief assistant to the pilot of a fighting or bombing aircraft. **observer post,** a wartime site permanently manned by the R.O.C. **Royal Observer Corps,** an enrolled body of civilians attached to the R.A.F. whose chief duties are plotting and reporting the course of aircraft.
obsess, *v.t.* ob-*sess*, to besiege; to haunt; to harass as an evil spirit; to preoccupy mentally. (L. *obsessus*, besieged.)
obsession, *n.* ob-*sesh*-on, the condition or state of being obsessed; any persistent or permanent delusion. (L. *obsessio.*)
obsessional, *a.* ob-*sesh*-o-nal, of the nature of, or characterized by, an obsession [Path.].
obsidian, *n.* ob-*sid*-e-an, a volcanic rock with vitreous lustre and conchoidal fracture. (L., from *Obsius*, a personal name.)
obsidional, *a.* ob-*sid*-e-on-al, pertaining to a siege. **obsidional crown,** a crown granted to a general who successfully resisted or who raised a siege [Roman Antiq.]. (L. *obsidionalis.*)
obsignation, *n.* ob-sig-*nay*-shon, act of ratifying.
obsolescence, *n.* ob-so-*les*-sence, the state or process of passing into disuse.
obsolescent, *a.* ob-so-*les*-sent, becoming obsolete.
obsolete, *a.* *ob*-so-leet, gone into disuse; out-of-date; no longer current; atrophied, or not fully developed [Biol.]. (L. *obsoletus*, decayed.)
obsoleteness, *n.* *ob*-so-leet-ness, a state or condition of being obsolete.
obstacle, *n.* *ob*-sta-kl, anything which hinders; an obstruction. **obstacle race,** a foot race in which the competitors have to surmount natural or artificial obstacles. (Fr.)
obstetric, *a.* ob-*stet*-rik, obstetrical.
obstetrical, *a.* ob-*stet*-re-kal, pertaining to midwifery or to childbirth. (L. *obstetricius.*)
obstetrician, *n.* ob-stet-*rish*-an, one skilled in obstetrics.
obstetrics, *n.* ob-*stet*-riks, the science dealing with gestation, pregnancy, and labour [Med.]; midwifery.
obstinacy, *n.* *ob*-ste-na-se, obstinateness; unyielding firmness; dogged perseverance; resolution.
obstinate, *a.* *ob*-ste-nat, pertinaciously adhering to an opinion or purpose; not easily subdued; resolute. (L. *obstinatus*, resolute.)
obstinately, *ad.* in an obstinate manner.
obstinateness, *n.* state of being obstinate.
obstipation, *n.* ob-ste-*pay*-shon, excessive costiveness [Med.]. (L. *obstipatus*, crowded together.)
obstreperous, *a.* ob-*strep*-er-rus, loud; clamorously or turbulently noisy; unruly. (L. *obstreperus.*)
obstreperously, *ad.* in an obstreperous manner.
obstreperousness, *n.* ob-*strep*-er-rus-ness, the quality of being obstreperous; turbulence.
obstriction, *n.* ob-*strik*-shon, the condition of being bound or obligated; an obligation.
obstruct, *v.t.* ob-*strukt*, to block up; to impede; to stop or arrest; to retard; to interrupt; to prevent progress in a debate, etc., esp. in parliament. (L. *obstructus*, piled up.)
obstructer, *n.* ob-*struk*-ter, one who obstructs.
obstruction, *n.* ob-*struk*-shon, act of obstructing; that which impedes progress; an impediment; a block.
obstructionism, *n.* ob-*struk*-shon-izm, the practice of obstructing business, esp. in parliament.
obstructionist, *n.* ob-*struk*-shon-ist, one who practises obstructionism.
obstructive, *a.* ob-*struk*-tiv, tending to obstruct: *n.* one who or that which obstructs; an obstructionist; an impediment.
obstructiveness, *n.* ob-*struk*-tiv-ness, the quality or practice of obstructing.
obstruent, *a.* *ob*-stroo-ent, obstructing; hindering; *n.* anything that obstructs [Med.]; any astringent drug. (L. *obstruens*, piling up.)
obtain, *v.t.* ob-*tane*, to get possession of; to gain or procure; to hold: *v.i.* to be established in practice; to continue in use. (Fr. *obtenir.*)
obtainable, *a.* ob-*tane*-a-bl, that may be obtained.
obtainer, *n.* ob-*tane*-er, one who obtains.

obtainment, *n.* ob-*tane*-ment, the act of obtaining; that which is obtained.
obtected, *a.* ob-*tek*-ted, translucently covered (of certain pupæ) [Entom.]. (L. *obtectus*, hidden.)
obtemper, *v.t.* ob-*tem*-per, to comply with [Scots. Law.]. (L. *obtemperare.*)
obtest, *v.t.* ob-*test*, to beseech; to supplicate: *v.i.* to protest. (O.Fr. *obtester.*)
obtestation, *n.* ob-tes-*tay*-shon, the act of obtesting; supplication; entreaty.
obtrude, *v.t.* ob-*trood*, to thrust in or on; to urge upon against the will: *v.i.* to enter when not invited. (L. *obtrudo*, thrust.)
obtruder, *n.* ob-*trood*-er, one who obtrudes.
obtruncate, *v.t.* ob-*trung*-kate, to lop off; to decapitate. (L. *obtruncatus.*)
obtrusion, *n.* ob-*troo*-zhon, the act of obtruding; an unsolicited or forcible thrusting in; that which is obtruded.
obtrusive, *a.* ob-*troo*-siv, disposed to obtrude, esp. oneself; intrusive.
obtrusively, *ad.* ob-*troo*-siv-le, by way of obtrusion.
obtund, *v.t.* ob-*tund*, to blunt or deaden. (L. *obtundo*, beat.)
obtundent, *a.* ob-*tun*-dent, reducing pain: *n.* a medicine to relieve irritation [Med.].
obturate, *v.t.* *ob*-tewr-rate, to shut up, esp. to close the breech of a gun to prevent the escape of gases. (L. *obturatus*, closed.)
obturation, *n.* ob-tew-*ray*-shon, the method or the action of closing a gun-breech against the escape of gas.
obturator, *n.* *ob*-tew-ray-tor, that which closes or stops a cavity [esp. Anat.]; one of the muscles of the thigh; an appliance preventing escape of gas from the breech of a gun; the shutter of a camera [Phot.]. **obturator ring,** a ring round a piston to ensure that the cylinder in which it works is gas-tight. (L. *obturatus*, closed up.)
obturbinate, *a.* ob-*tur*-be-nat, inversely top shaped [Zool., etc.].
obtuse, *a.* ob-*tewce*, blunt; not pointed or acute; denoting an angle larger than a right angle; mentally dull; not sharp. (L. *obtusus*, beaten.)
obtuse-angled, *a.* having an obtuse angle.
obtusely, *ad.* ob-*tewce*-le, in an obtuse manner.
obtuseness, *n.* ob-*tewce*-ness, the state of being obtuse; dullness of perception.
obtusity, *n.* ob-*tew*-se-te, the quality of being obtuse; obtuseness.
obumbrant, *a.* ob-*um*-brant, projecting, esp. of feathers or other parts [Zool.].
obumbrate, *a.* ob-*um*-brat, beneath an overhanging part. (L. *obumbratus.*)
obvallate, *a.* ob-*val*-lat, walled in. (L. *obvallatus.*)
obvention, *n.* ob-*ven*-shon, an occasional or incidental acquisition.
obverse, *a.* *ob*-verse, facing the observer; narrower at the base than the top [Bot.]: *n.* the side of a coin bearing the head or main device (opposed to reverse); the counterpart (esp. of a statement, etc.). (L. *obversus*, turned.)
obversely, *ad.* *ob*-verse-le, in an obverse form.
obversion, *n.* ob-*ver*-shon, the operation of arriving at the same conclusion from the other side of a statement (as "All Cretans are liars, therefore no Cretan is truthful.") [Log.].
obvert, *v.t.* ob-*vert*, to turn towards; to face. (L. *obverto*, turn.)
obviate, *v.t.* *ob*-ve-ate, to remove out of the way as difficulties or objections; to overcome; to anticipate. (L. *obviatus*, met.)
obvious, *a.* *ob*-ve-us, easily discovered, seen or understood; clear; evident. (L. *obvius*, lying in the path.)
obviously, *ad.* *ob*-ve-us-le, evidently.
obviousness, *n.* *ob*-ve-us-ness, state of being obvious.
obvolent, *a.* ob-*voh*-lent, folded downwards and inwards (of wings) [Entom.].
obvolute, *a.* *ob*-vo-lewt, alternately embracing the straight margin of the opposite leaf [Bot.]. (L. *obvolutus*, rolled.)
oca, *n.* *oh*-ka, a S. American plant of the genus *Oxalis*, with edible tubers. (Native name.)
ocarina, *n.* ok-a-*ree*-na, a toy egg-shaped wind-instrument of the flute family, usually made of pottery. (It.)
Occamism, *n.* *ok*-a-mizm, the doctrines of William of Occam, a 14th-cent. English exponent of nominalism.
occasion, *n.* o-*kay*-zhon, an occurrence; opportunity; favourable time or circumstances; incidental, as distinct from primary or efficient, cause; incidental need; situation of affairs: *v.t.* to cause incidentally; to produce; to influence. (Fr., from L. *occasio.*)
occasional, *a.* o-*kay*-zhon-al, occurring at times; produced by accident; made to mark some special event, or for some special purpose; incidental; casual.
occasionalism, *n.* o-*kay*-zhon-a-lizm, the Cartesian theory accounting for the action of the mind on the body, and of the body on the mind, by assuming that a change of state in the one is the mere occasion of a change of state in the other, the efficient cause in every case being Deity.
occasionalist, *a.* o-*kay*-zhon-a-list, pertaining to or characteristic of occasionalism: *n.* an adherent of this.
occasionality, *n.* o-*kay*-zho-*nal*-e-te, that which is occasional; the state of being occasional.
occasionally, *ad.* o-*kay*-zhon-a-le, in an occasional manner; now and then.
occasioner, *n.* o-*kay*-zhon-er, one who occasions.
Occident, *n.* *ok*-sid-ent, the west, esp. Europe as apart from Asia; European culture, etc., as distinct from oriental. (O.Fr.)
Occidental, *a.* ok-se-*den*-tal, western; (of precious stones) inferior in quality.
Occidentalism, *n.* ok-se-*den*-ta-lizm, the life and civilization of the West.
Occidentalist, *n.* ok-se-*den*-ta-list, a student or adherent of Occidentalism, esp. an Oriental.
Occidentalize, *v.t.* ok-se-*den*-ta-lize, to inculcate with Western notions or habits.
occipital, *a.* ok-*sip*-e-tal, pertaining to the occiput.
occiput, *n.* *ok*-se-put, the back part of the head. (L.)
occlude, *v.t.* ok-*klood*, to shut up; to enclose; to absorb and retain unchanged (of gases by charcoal, etc.) [Chem.]. (L. *occludo*, shut up.)
occlusion, *n.* ok-*kloo*-zhon, a shutting up; a closing; the absorption of gases by solids; a complete closure of the breath passage in vocalization [Phon.]; the overlap of the teeth when the jaws close [Anat.]; the condition arising when warm air has been forced upward on meeting cold air [Meteor.].
occlusive, *a.* ok-*kloo*-siv, tending to occlude; characterized by occlusion: *n.* a sound (or its symbol) occluded in vocalization.
occult, *a.* ok-*kult*, hidden; secret; mysterious; supernatural; unknown: *v.t.* to hide; to cover from view, esp. [Astron.] of a celestial body by the moon. (Fr. *occulte.*)
occultation, *n.* ok-kul-*tay*-shon, temporary concealment or disappearance; the eclipse of a celestial body by another, esp. by the moon.
occultism, *n.* *ok*-ul-tizm, the theory or practice of the occult or mysterious; supernatural or magic power; theosophy; mysticism.
occultist, *n.* *ok*-ul-tist, a believer in, or practiser of, occultism.
occultly, *ad.* ok-*kult*-le, in an occult manner.
occultness, *n.* ok-*kult*-ness, the quality or condition of being occult.
occupancy, *n.* *ok*-kew-pan-se, state of being an occupant; the act of taking or holding possession.
occupant, *n.* *ok*-kew-pant, he who holds possession: the occupier, esp. as tenant. (Fr.)
occupation, *n.* ok-kew-*pay*-shon, the act of taking possession; tenure; possession; employment; vocation. **army of occupation,** an army temporarily occupying the territory of a present or recent enemy. **occupation road,** a private road primarily for the use of the occupiers of its houses. (Fr.)
occupational, *a.* ok-kew-*pay*-shon-al, pertaining to an occupation. **occupational disease,** a disease that directly arises from the conditions of the patient's employment.
occupier, *n.* *ok*-kew-py-er, one who occupies; one in occupation of property.
occupy, *v.t.* *ok*-kew-py, to take possession; to keep in possession; to take up or fill; to employ; to busy oneself; to follow, as business: *v.i.* to hold possession; to follow business. (Fr. *occupier.*)
occur, *v.i.* ok-*kur*, to present itself to the mind; to appear; to be found here and there; to happen. *p.* and *pp.* **occurred**; *ppr.* **occurring.** (L. *occurro*, run.)

occurrence, *n.* ok-*ku*-rence, an event, the fact of occurring. (L.)
ocean, *n.* *oh*-shan, the continuous body of water covering more than five-sevenths of the globe's surface; any one of its main five divisions; an immense expanse: *pl.* a very large quantity [Coll.]; *a.* pertaining to the ocean. **ocean greyhound,** a North Atlantic liner. **ocean lane,** the track regularly followed by steamers crossing an ocean. **the Five Oceans,** the Atlantic, Pacific, Indian, Arctic, and Antarctic Oceans. (O.Fr., from Gr. *okeanos*, the great parent stream fabled to encircle the earth.)
Oceania, *n.* o-she-*ay*-ne-a, the S. Pacific archipelagos not grouped geographically as Asiatic or American.
oceanic, *a.* o-she-*an*-ik, pertaining to, found in, or formed in the ocean. (L. *oceanus.*)
Oceanid, *n.* o-*see*-a-nid, any of the ocean nymphs, daughters of Oceanos [Gr. Myth.].
oceanographer, *n.* o-she-a-*nog*-ra-fer, one learned in oceanography.
oceanography, *n.* o-she-a-*nog*-ra-fe, the science of oceanic phenomena.
Oceanos, *n.* o-*see*-a-nos, the god of the ocean. (Gr.).
ocellar, *a.* o-*sel*-ar, pertaining to or characterized by ocelli or ocellus-like markings.
ocellated, *a.* *os*-e-lay-ted, resembling an eye or ocellus; marked with small eyes. (L. *ocellatus*, from *ocellus.*)
ocellus, *n.* o-*sel*-lus (*pl.* **ocelli,** o-*sel*-le), the simple eye in caterpillars and many insects; a facet of a compound eye; a coloured spot, found on wings, etc., surrounded by rings of other colour [Entom.]. (L. *ocellus*, dim. of *oculus*, eye.)
ocelot, *n.* *oh*-se-lot, the Mexican wild cat, *Felis pardalis.* (Mexican.)
och, *int.* okh *or* awkh, oh or ah. (Scots. and Ir.)
ocherous, *a.* *oh*-ker-rus, ochrous.
ochery, *a.* *oh*-ke-re, ochry.
ochlesis, *n.* ok-*lee*-sis, disease or unhealthiness due to overcrowding, esp. of the sick [Med.]. (Gr., uproar.)
ochlocracy, *n.* ok-*lok*-ra-se, government by the mob; mob-rule; mobocracy. (Gr. *ochlos*, a crowd, *kratos*, rule.)
ochlocrat, *n.* *ok*-lo-krat, a mob-leader; a partisan of ochlocracy.
ochlocratic, *a.* *ok*-lo-*krat*-ik, pertaining to or characteristic of mob-rule.
ochlophobia, *n.* ok-lo-*foh*-be-a, morbid dread of crowds.
ochone, *int.* ukh-*ohn*, a cry of lamentation [Irish].
ochraceous, *a.* o-*kray*-she-us, containing or of the nature of ochre; ochrous.
ochre, *n.* *oh*-ker, a fine clay consisting chiefly of hydrated oxide of iron, widely used as a red, brown, or yellow pigment. (Fr. *ocre.*)
ochrous, *a.* *oh*-krus (*or* **ochreous,** *oh*-kre-us), consisting of or resembling ochre.
ochry, *a.* *oh*-kre, ochrous.
o'clock, o-*klok*, an abbreviation for " of the clock," *i.e.* of the time.
ocrea, *n.* *oh*-kre-ah (*pl.* **ocreæ,** *oh*-kree-ee), a piece of armour protecting the front of the leg from knee to ankle; a tubular sheath at the base of the petiole [Bot.]; an investing growth on the legs of certain birds [Zool.].
ocreate, *a.* *oh*-kre-at, having ocreæ [Bot. and Zool.].
oct-, *pref.* okt, eight. (Gr. *okto.*)
octachord, *n.* *ok*-ta-kawrd, an instrument of eight strings; a system of eight sounds [Mus.]. (Gr. *okto*, eight, and *chord.*)
octad, *n.* *ok*-tad, a series of eight; an element or radical with a combining power of eight [Chem.]. (Gr. *okto.*)
octagon, *n.* *ok*-ta-gon, a polygon of eight sides and eight angles [Geom.]; a room or other place with eight sides. (Gr. *okto*, and *gonia*, an angle.)
octagonal, *a.* ok-*tag*-on-al, having eight sides and eight angles.
octahedral, *a.* ok-ta-*heed*-ral, having the form of an octahedron.
octahedrite, *n.* ok-ta-*heed*-rite, anatase.
octahedron, *n.* ok-ta-*heed*-ron, a solid contained by eight planes, esp. triangular. **regular octahedron,** a solid contained by eight equal and equilateral triangles [Geom.]. (Gr. *okto*, and *hedra*, a side.)
octamerous, *a.* ok-*tam*-er-rus, having parts or organs in groups of eight [Bot. and Zool.].
octameter, *n.* ok-*tam*-e-ter, a line of eight feet [Pros.].
octan, *a.* *ok*-tan, recurring every eight days (of fevers) [Med.].
octandrian, *a.* ok-*tan*-dre-an, having eight distinct stamens [Bot.].
octane, *n.* *ok*-tayn, a paraffin hydrocarbon present in petroleum and an important constituent of fuel oil for aero-motors.
octangular, *a.* ok-*tang*-gew-lar, having eight angles.
octant, *n.* *ok*-tant, the eighth part of a circle; a sextant-like instrument for angular measurement, attached to an arc of 45°; position or aspect of a heavenly body when 45°, or one octant, distant from another [Astron.]. (L. *octans.*)
octarchy, *n.* *ok*-tar-ke, government by eight.
octastich, *n.* *ok*-ta-stik, a poem or stanza of eight lines.
octastyle, *n.* *ok*-ta-stile, a building with eight columns in front. (Gr. *oktastylos.*)
octateuch, *n.* *ok*-ta-tewk, the first eight books of the Old Testament. (Gr.)
octavalent, *a.* ok-ta-*vay*-lent, having a valence of eight [Chem.].
octave, *n.* *ok*-tav, the eighth day after a church festival; a group of eight; an eighth, or an interval of twelve semitones, also the series of notes within this interval [Mus.]; the eighth tone in a musical scale; a small cask for wine, the eighth part of a pipe. (Fr.)
octavo, *a.* ok-*tay*-vo, having eight leaves to the sheet: *n.* a book in which a sheet is folded into sixteen pages. (L. *octavus.*)
octennial, *a.* ok-*ten*-ne-al, happening every eighth year; lasting for eight years. (L. *octo*, and *annus*, year.)
octennially, *ad.* once for every eight years.
octet, *n.* ok-*tet*, a piece of music set for eight voices or instrument; a group of eight, esp. lines [Pros.].
octile, *a.* *ok*-tile, in the octant position [Astron.]: *n.* octant [Astron.].
octillion, *n.* ok-*til*-yon, the number produced by involving a million to the eighth power, represented by a unit followed by 48 ciphers.
octingentenary, *n.* *ok*-tin-jen-*tee*-na-re, an eight hundredth anniversary. (L. *octingenti*, eight hundred.)
octo-, *pref.* *ok*-to, eight. (L. *octo.*)
October, *n.* ok-*toh*-ber, the tenth month of our year, and eighth of the Julian year; a kind of ale brewed in that month. (L.)
octocentenary, *n.* *ok*-to-sen-*tee*-na-re, an eight hundredth anniversary.
octodecimo, *a.* *ok*-to-*des*-e-moh, having eighteen leaves to a sheet: *n.* a book in which a sheet is folded into eighteen leaves. (L.)
octodentate, *a.* *ok*-to-*den*-tat, having eight teeth. (L. *octo*, and *dens*, a tooth.)
octofid, *a.* *ok*-to-fid, cleft or separated into eight segments [Bot.]. (L. *octo*, and *findo*, cleave.)
octogenarian, *n.* *ok*-to-je-*nare*-re-an, one who is eighty or between eighty and ninety years of age: *a.* of this age; pertaining to a person of such age. (L. *octogenarius.*)
octogenary, *a.* ok-*toj*-e-na-re, of eighty or between eighty and ninety years of age. (L.)
octonal, *a.* *ok*-to-nal, octonary.
octonarian, *a.* *ok*-to-*nare*-re-an, consisting of eight metrical feet: *n.* a verse of eight feet [Pros.].
octonary, *a.* *ok*-to-na-re, belonging to the number eight; consisting of eight: *n.* a group of eight; a stanza of eight lines [Pros.].
octopartite, *a.* *ok*-to-*par*-tite, consisting of eight parts, counterparts, or divisions.
octopetalous, *a.* ok-to-*pet*-a-lus, having eight petals. (Gr. *okto*, and *petalon*, a petal.)
octopod, *n.* *ok*-to-pod, any species of octopus: *a.* having eight feet. (Gr. *okto*, and *pous*, the foot.)
octopus, *n.* *ok*-to-pus, one of a genus, *Octopus*, comprising many species, of two-gilled cephalopods, each with eight tapering arms having two rows of suckers; a cuttle-fish.
octoradiate, *a.* ok-to-*ray*-de-at, having eight rays (L. *octo*, and *radius*, a ray.)
octoroon, *n.* ok-to-*roon*, the offspring of a quadroon and a white person; a person with one-eighth negro blood.
octospermous, *a.* ok-to-*sper*-mus, containing eight seeds. (Gr. *okto*, and *sperma*, seed.)
octostyle, *n.* *ok*-to-stile, octastyle.

octosyllabic, *a.* ok-to-sil-*lab*-ik, of eight syllables.
octosyllable, *n.* ok-to-*sil*-la-bl, a word of eight syllables.
octroi, *n.* *ok*-trwah, a tax levied at the gates of cities on articles, esp. provisions, brought in; the place of collection. (Fr.)
octuple, *a.* *ok*-tew-pl, eightfold: *v.t.* and *i.* to make or become eightfold.
ocular, *a.* *ok*-yew-lar, pertaining to or known by the eye; received by actual sight: *n.* the eye-piece of an optical instrument. (L. *oculus*, the eye.)
ocularly, *ad.* by the eye or actual view.
oculate, *a.* *ok*-yew-lat, furnished with eyes or eye-like spots [Zool.].
oculiform, *a.* *ok*-yew-le-form, in the form of an eye.
oculist, *n.* *ok*-yew-list, one skilled in the treatment of diseases, malformations, etc., of the eyes.
od, *n.* od, a supposititious natural magnetic force to account for certain phenomena, as mesmerism. (Coined word.)
odal, *n.* *oh*-dal, an absolute hereditary tenure in land; udal. (Scand.)
odalisque, *n.* *oh*-da-lisk, a woman slave or concubine in a Turkish harem. (Turk.)
odaller, *n.* *oh*-da-ler, one in possession of, or having an hereditary right to, an odal.
odd, *a.* od, not even; not divisible into equal numbers; remaining over after a round number; remaining over; singular; differing from what is usual; not taken into the common account; uncommon; quaint; droll. **odd trick,** the seventh trick in the "book" [Whist, etc.]; hence, any winning stroke. **the odd,** the additional stroke played by one of two players or sides [Golf]; an odd trick [Whist, etc.]. (Ice. *oddi*, a triangle, A.S. *ord*, a point.)
Oddfellow, *n.* *od*-fel-loh, a member of the Independent Order of Odd Fellows, a friendly and benefit society having certain rites analogous to those of the Freemasons.
oddity, *n.* *od*-e-te, a person or thing that is singular; oddness; singularity; strangeness.
oddly, *ad.* *od*-le, in an odd manner.
oddment, *n.* *od*-ment, something left over; a book's preliminaries: *pl.* odds and ends.
oddness, *n.* *od*-ness, the state of being odd.
odds, *n.* odz, inequality; excess of either compared with the other; advantage; probability; chances; the ratio of the sums wagered [Betting]. **at odds,** at variance. **odds and ends,** miscellaneous scraps, remnants, etc.
ode, *n.* ode, a short poem or song; a lyric poem, esp. one to be set to music. (Fr.)
odeon, *n.* *oh*-de-on, an odeum.
odeum, *n.* oh-*dee*-um, among the ancients, a theatre or hall for musical performances. (Gr. *odeion.*)
odic, *a.* *oh*-dik, pertaining to an ode or odes.
Odinism, *n.* *oh*-din-izm, the worship of Odin, the chief god of Norse mythology; the pagan doctrines of the ancient Scandinavians; Teutonic heathenry.
odious, *a.* *oh*-de-us, hateful; offensive; disgusting; hated. (L. *odiosus*, from *odium.*)
odiously, *ad.* *oh*-de-us-le, hatefully.
odiousness, *n.* *oh*-de-us-ness, hatefulness.
odium, *n.* *oh*-de-um, hatred; dislike; hatefulness. **odium theologicum,** the bitterness engendered among theological disputants. (L., hatred.)
odograph, *n.* *oh*-do-graf, a form of pedometer; a hodometer.
odometer, *n.* oh-*dom*-e-ter, an instrument for measuring distances in travelling; a hodometer. (Gr. *hodos*, way, *metron*, measure.)
odontalgia, *n.* oh-don-*tal*-je-a, toothache. (Gr. *odous*, tooth, *algos*, pain.)
odontalgic, *a.* oh-don-*tal*-jik, pertaining to toothache: *n.* a remedy for toothache.
odontatrophy, *n.* oh-don-*tat*-ra-fe, arrest of development of the teeth. (Gr. *odous*, and *atrophy.*)
odontiasis, *n.* *oh*-don-*ty*-a-sis, the cutting of the teeth; dentition.
odontic, *a.* oh-*don*-tik, pertaining to the teeth.
odontogeny, *n.* oh-don-*toj*-en-e, the study of dentition; the development of teeth. (Gr. *odous*, and *gennao*, produce.)
Odontoglossum, *n.* oh-*don*-to-*glos*-um, a large genus of tropical American orchids. (Gk. *odous*, tooth, *glossa*, tongue.)
odontograph, *n.* oh-*don*-to-graf, an instrument for laying off the teeth of gear-wheels. (Gr. *odous*, and *grapho*, write.)
odontography, *n.* oh-don-*tog*-ra-fe, a description of the teeth.
odontoid, *a.* oh-*don*-toyd, tooth-like.
odontology, *n.* oh-don-*tol*-o-je, the science which treats of teeth. (Gr. *odous*, and *logos*, science.)
odontophore, *n.* oh-*don*-to-fore, a ribbon-like structure covered with teeth, forming the masticator organ in certain molluscs. (Gr. *odous*, and *phorein*, to bear.)
odorant, *a.* *oh*-do-rant, odorous; odoriferous.
odoriferous, *a.* oh-do-*rif*-er-us, diffusing odour, or fragrance. (L. *odor*, odour, *fero*, yield.)
odoriferously, *ad.* fragrantly or malodorously.
odoriferousness, *n.* the quality of being odoriferous, fragrance.
odorimetry, *n.* oh-do-*rim*-e-tre, the measurement of the strength and durability of odours.
odorous, *a.* *oh*-do-rus, sweet of scent; fragrant.
odorously, *ad.* *oh*-do-rus-le, fragrantly.
odorousness, *n.* the quality of being odorous; fragrance.
odour, *n.* *oh*-dor, scent; fragrance; perfume; esteem. **odour of sanctity,** the perfume supposedly issuing during life or after death from a saint's body; hence a state of holiness or piety. (L.)
odourless, *a.* *oh*-dor-less, free from odour.
Odyssey, *n.* *od*-e-se, an epic poem by Homer, relating the homeward wanderings of Odysseus (Ulysses) after the capture of Troy; hence, any long, adventurous, and hazardous journey. (Gr.)
œcology, *n.* ee-*kol*-o-je, ecology.
œcumenical, *a.* ee-kew-*men*-e-kal, ecumenical.
œcumenicity, *n.* *ee*-kew-men-*is*-e-te, ecumenicity.
œdema, *n.* ee-*dee*-ma, a swelling in the tissues; localized dropsy. (Gr. *oideo*, swell.)
œdematous, *a.* ee-*dem*-a-tus, of the nature of, or affected by, œdema; dropsical; swollen with fluid [Med.].
Œdipus, *n.* *ee*-de-pus, one who solves riddles, like Œdipus, legendary king of Thebes. **œdipus complex,** an early abnormal attraction between parent and child of opposite sexes (Œdipus in ignorance married his mother, Jocasta).
œil-de-bœuf, *n.* (App.), a circular or oval window in the roof or frieze of a large building. (Fr., ox-eye.)
œillade, *n.* (App.), an amorous glance; an ogle. (Fr.)
œnanthic, *a.* ee-*nan*-thik, having the characteristic odour of wine. (Gr. *oinos*, wine, *anthos*, flower.)
œnolin, *n.* *ee*-no-lin, the red colouring matter of wine.
œnology, *n.* ee-*nol*-o-je, the study or knowledge of wines.
œnomania, *n.* *ee*-no-*may*-ne-a, a morbid craving for intoxicating drinks; dipsomania [Path.].
œnomel, *n.* *ee*-no-mel, a mixture of wine and honey.
œnometer, *n.* ee-*nom*-e-ter, an alcoholometer for use with wines.
Œnothera, *n.* e-*noth*-er-a, a genus of plants including the evening primrose, *Œ. biennis*.
o'er, ore, a contraction of *over*.
oersted, *n.* *er*-sted, the C.G.S. electromagnetic unit of magnetizing force. (Name of Danish physicist, *d.* 1851.)
œsophageal, *a.* ee-so-*faj*-e-al, pertaining to the œsophagus.
œsophagus, *n.* ee-*sof*-a-gus, the gullet; the portion of the alimentary canal connecting the pharynx and the stomach. (Gr.)
œstrous, *a.* *ee*-strous, pertaining to the œstrum.
œstrual, *a.* *ee*-stroo-al, œstrous; pertaining to sexual desire.
œstrum, *n.* *ee*-strum, an overpowering (usually erotic) impulse or desire; the rut in animals.
Œstrus, *n.* *ee*-strus, a genus of insects comprising the gadflies, botflies, etc.
★**of,** *prep.* ov, from or out of; proceeding from; belonging to; from among; concerning. (A.S.)
★**off,** *a.* off *or* awf, most distant; right (of vehicles, horses, etc.); no longer available; state; in bad condition: *ad.* away; not towards: *prep.* not on; distant from: *int.* begone; depart: *n.* the side opposite to that on which the striker stands at cricket. **to be off,** to depart or to recede from an agreement or design; to cancel or be cancelled.

to come off, to escape; to part from; to happen; to be accomplished. **to go off,** to depart; to be discharged (of firearms); to go bad; to fare; to become unconscious; to cease to be noticeable. **off and on,** at odd moments; now and then. **off chance,** the barest possible chance. **off colour,** *see* **colour. off day,** a day on which one cannot work well; a holiday. **off duty,** free from duty or responsibility. **take off, well off,** *see* these words.

offal, *n. of*-al, waste meats; parts of a carcase not commonly used as food; inferior kinds of meat or fish; liver, kidneys, or other edible organs of a beast; carrion; refuse; rubbish. (M.E. from *off* and *fall.*)

offcast, *a. off*-kahst, rejected or discarded as useless or unwanted: *n.* that which is offcast; an outcast.

offcut, *n. off*-kut, the part (esp. of a printed sheet) cut off as being redundant.

offence, *n.* o-*fence*, the act of offending; a violation of the law; displeasure; cause of stumbling; a state or feeding of umbrage; a transgression, or breach of custom; an injury; attack. (Fr.)

offenceless, *a.* o-*fence*-less, not giving offence.

offend, *v.t.* o-*fend*, to displease; to affront; to make angry; to shock; to pain or annoy; to transgress or violate; to cause to stumble or sin: *v.i.* to sin; to scandalize. (Fr. *offendre.*)

offender, *n.* o-*fen*-der, one who offends or commits an offence; a transgressor.

offensive, *a.* o-*fen*-siv, causing displeasure; giving pain; disagreeable; assailant; pertaining to or used in attack; aggressive; making the first attack: *n.* aggressive attitude; the act of attacking; an attack [Mil.].

offensively, *ad.* in an offensive manner.

offensiveness, *n.* quality or being offensive.

★**offer,** *n. of*-er, a proposal to be accepted or rejected; first advance; a bidding of a price, also a price bid: *v.t.* to present for acceptance or rejection; to proffer; to present as an act of worship, sacrifice, or prayer; to present to the mind; to bid as a price; to attempt; to show readiness to act, etc.: *v.i.* to be at hand; to express a willingness; to make an attempt. **offer violence,** to attack. (A.S. *offrian.*)

offerable, *a. of*-er-a-bl, that may be offered.

offerer, *n. of*-er-er, one who offers.

offering, *n. of*-er-ing, something offered; a sacrifice; an oblation.

offertory, *n. of*-er-to-re, the presentation of the elements of the Eucharist; also, the sentences then said or sung, and offerings then made [Eccles.]; any collection taken at a religious service.

offhand, *a.* and *ad. off*-hand *or* off-*hand*, carelessly; wanting deliberation or intention; rudely.

offhanded, *a.* off-*han*-ded rude, careless, or wanton in manner

offhandedness, *n. off*-*han*-ded-ness, rudeness; casualness; carelessness.

★**office,** *n. of*-fis, a duty or employment of a public, a sacred, or a private nature; function; customary duty; employment; service tendered; a formulary of devotion or prescribed act of worship; a house or apartment for business purposes; a business or official staff or organization: *pl.* the kitchen and other apartments where a household's domestics work. **Holy Office,** the Inquisition. **office boy,** a youth engaged for odd jobs and minor clerical work in a business office. (Fr.)

officer, *n. of*-fis-er, one holding office or official position; one commissioned to perform a public duty, esp. one holding H.M.'s commission in the navy, army, or air force; a member of a ship's company ranking above the crew; a bailiff; a policeman [Coll.]: *v.t.* to furnish with officers. (Fr. *officier.*)

official, *a.* o-*fish*-al, pertaining to office; from or under proper authority; duly authorized; characteristic of those in office; officinal [Med.]: *n.* one entrusted with a civil office; one in a position of authority; an ecclesiastical judge.

officialdom, *n.* o-*fish*-al-dom, officials collectively, or their sphere; official routine; officialism.

officialese, *n.* o-fish-a-*leez*, language similar to that used in official documents; a stilted or laboured literary style.

officialism, *n.* o-*fish*-al-izm, bureaucracy; government by officials.

officiality, *n.* o-*fish*-e-*al*-e-te, that which is official; officialism.

officially, *ad.* o-*fish*-al-le, by the proper officer; in an official manner; from an official source.

officialty, *n.* o-*fish*-e-al-te, officiality.

officiant, *n.* o-*fish*-ant, an officiating priest; a celebrant.

officiate, *v.t.* o-*fish*-e-ate, to perform official duties; to act as an official; to conduct public worship.

officinal, *a.* o-*fis*-e-nal, used in the arts or medicine; authorized for use by the pharmacopœia [Med.]. (L. *officina*, workshop.)

officious, *a.* o-*fish*-us, forward in kindness; meddlesome; intermeddling; obtrusive. (Fr. *officieux.*)

officiously, *ad.* o-*fish*-us-le, in an officious manner.

officiousness, *n.* quality of being officious.

offing, *n. off*-ing, the sea at a distance from the shore, esp. halfway or more to the horizon.

offish, *a. off*-ish, distant, reserved, or snobbish in manner [Slang].

offishness, *n. off*-ish-ness, the quality or condition of being offish.

off-licence, *n.* a licence to sell intoxicating liquors not to be drunk on the premises; a house with such a licence only.

off-print, *n.* a separate reprint of an article from a periodical.

offsaddle, *v.t.* and *i. off*-sad-l, to unsaddle.

off-scouring, *n.* that which is scoured off; refuse.

offset, *n. off*-set, a shoot, or a short runner bending up at the end to form a new plant [Bot.]; a short perpendicular measured from the main line [Surveying]; a spur of a mountain-range; a compensation; a sum or value set off against another as an equivalent: *v.t.* to set one account against another as equivalent. **offset printing,** a lithographic process in which the impression is transferred to a rubber cylinder and thence to the paper.

offshoot, *n. off*-shoot, a branch from a main stem; anything dividing off from the original parent stock; a side-issue.

offshore, *a.* and *ad. off*-shore, away from the land.

offside, *n. off*-side, in driving, the right-hand side; in football, etc., between the ball and the other side's goal; the farther side: *a.* in such a position that the reception or playing of the ball is unlawful [Football, etc.].

offspring, *n. off*-spring, progeny; children; any production.

offward, *ad. off*-ward, off or away from the shore [Naut.].

off-white, *a.* nearly, but not quite, white; creamy.

oft, *ad.* oft, often. (A.S.)

often, *ad. of*-en, many times; frequently. (A.S.)

oftentimes, *of*-en-timez, **ofttimes,** *oft*-timez, *ad.* often. [Archaic.]

ogee, *n.* oh-*jee*, a moulding of two members, the one concave and the other convex. **ogee arch,** a pointed arch formed by two ogees meeting at the apex. (F. *ogive.*)

ogham, *n. og*-ham, a primitive alphabet invented and used by the ancient Irish; a character of this (Ir.)

ogival, *a.* oh-*jy*-val, pertaining to or resembling an ogive; pointed.

ogive, *n. oh*-jive, a pointed arch; a diagonal rib of a Gothic arch. (Fr.)

ogle, *n. oh*-gl, an amorous glance or look: *v.i.* to cast amorous glances. (Perhaps Low Ger. *oegelen*, from *oege*, the eye.)

ogler, *n. oh*-gler, one who ogles.

Ogpu, *n.* og-*poo*, the former secret police of Soviet Russia. (Initials of the name of the organization.)

ogre, *n. oh*-ger, a gigantic cannibal of folk-lore; a terrifying monster; one like an ogre. (Fr.)

ogreish, *a. oh*-grish, like an ogre.

ogress, *n. oh*-gress, a female ogre.

Ogygian, *a.* oh-*gij*-e-an, pertaining to Ogyges, a legendary King of Attica and Bœotia, or to a destructive flood said to have occurred in his time; of obscure origin; prehistoric.

oh, *int.* oh, exclamation of surprise, pain, anxiety, etc.

ohm, *n.* ohm, the unit of resistance in electricity, obtained by dividing the volts by the amperes. (G. S. *Ohm*, *d.* 1854, Ger. electrician.)

ohmic, *a. oh*-mik, pertaining to or measured in ohms.

ohmmeter, *n.* oh-*mee*-ter, an instrument for measuring electrical resistances.
oho, *int.* o-*hoh*, exclamation of surprise, doubt, etc.
-oid, *suff.* oyd, a termination denoting having the form of, or resembling, as in *asteroid, spheroid.* (Gr. *eidos*, form.)
oidium, *n.* oh-*id*-e-um (*pl.* **oidea,** oh-*id*-e-a), a parasitic fungus of the genus *Monilia*; the plant-disease or mildew caused by this. (Gr. *oion*, an egg.)
★**oil,** *n.* oyl, a fatty liquid of many kinds, soluble in ether, and derived from animal, vegetable, and mineral sources; any lubricant used for machinery; petroleum [U.S.A.]: *v.t.* to smear, lubricate, anoint, or furnish with oil; to convert (grease, etc.) into oil; to bribe [Slang]: *v.i.* to become like oil; to take in oil (of ships). **burn the midnight oil,** to work or read far into the night. **oil of malt,** whisky [Coll.]. **oil of vitriol,** sulphuric acid. **oiled,** half drunk [Slang]. **oiled silk,** silk waterproofed through being treated with boiled oil. **pour oil on the waters,** to smooth things over. **strike oil,** to find petroleum, hence to reach success or prosperity. (O.Fr. *oile.*)
oil-bird, *n.* *oyl*-berd, any bird yielding oil, esp. the guacharo.
oilcake, *n.* *oyl*-kake, the residue from seed oils prepared as cattle food.
oilcloth, *n.* *oyl*-kloth, canvas fabric treated with oil or paint used as a covering for tables, shelves, etc.; floor-cloth.
oil-colour, *n.* a paint made by grinding a colouring substance in oil.
oiled, *a.* oyld, treated, lubricated, or impregnated with oil; rendered waterproof by means of oil; slightly drunk [Slang].
oil-engine, *n.* an internal combustion stationary or locomotive engine burning vaporized oil as fuel.
oiler, *n.* *oyl*-er, one who or that which oils; an oiling can; an automatic device for oiling engines; a ship carrying oil, or using oil for fuel.
oil-field, *n.* an area rich in deposits of workable oil.
oil-fuel, *n.* any fuel oil used for driving an internal combustion engine.
oil-gas, *n.* inflammable gas procured by the destructive distillation of oil.
oil-gauge, *n.* a device indicating the present oil content of a container; also, an oleometer.
oiliness, *n.* *oyl*-e-ness, the quality of being oily, greasy, or unctuous.
oil-man, *n.* one who deals in oils.
oil-meal, *n.* ground oil-cake.
oil-nut, *n.* any nut yielding oil, esp. the butternut.
oil-painting, *n.* the art of painting in oil-colours; a picture painted in oils.
oil-palm, *n.* the palm *Elæis guineensis* of W. Africa and Brazil, the fruit of which yields palm-oil.
oil-paper, *n.* paper waterproofed or made transparent through treatment with oil.
oil-press, *n.* a machine for extracting oil from nuts, seeds, etc.
oilskin, *n.* *oyl*-skin, cloth waterproofed by means of oil: *pl.* overalls, trousers, etc., made of this.
oilstone, *n.* *oyl*-stone, a kind of hone slate; a fine grained whetstone.
oil-tanker, *n.* a ship carrying oil in tanks, as apart from barrels.
oil-well, *n.* a well yielding petroleum.
oily, *a.* *oyl*-e, consisting of, containing, or like oil; greasy; flattering.
oinomania, *n.* oy-no-*may*-ne-a, œnomania.
ointment, *n.* *oynt*-ment, any unctuous substance applied externally; an unguent. (O.Fr. *oignement.*)
Oireachtas, *n.* *er*-rekh-thas, the National Parliament of Eire, consisting of the President, the Dail Eireann, and the Seanad Eireann. (Irish, assembly.)
O.K. *or* **okay,** *a.* oh-*kay*, good; all right: *v.t.* to pass as correct. **to give the O.K. to,** to certify as being in order or to standard [Slang]. (Probably initials of "oll korrect," for "all correct.")
okapi, *n.* o-*kah*-pe, an ungulate of Central African forests, allied to the giraffes. *Ocapia johnstoni.* (Native.)
okay, *a.* and *v.t.* oh-*kay*, *see* **O.K.**
oke, *int.* oke, O.K. [Slang].
okra, *n.* *ok*-rah, gumbo, the fruit of *Hibiscus esculentus*, used in soups.
-ol, *suff.* ol, a termination, denoting, in chemical nomenclature, one of the alcohols or phenols
-olatry, *suff.* *ol*-a-tre, denoting worship of or devotion to.
★**old,** *a.* ohld, advanced in age; decayed by time; existing long; not new or fresh; ancient; antiquated; of any duration whatever; previous; long practised; experienced; cultivated for long; more than enough; crafty. **old age,** advanced years. **old age pension,** *see* **pension. Old Gentleman, Nick, Harry,** the devil. **Old Glory,** the United States' flag, the Stars and Stripes. **old hand,** a practised or experienced person. **Old Lady of Threadneedle Street,** the Bank of England. **old maid,** an unmarried elderly woman; a bivalve mollusc of the *Myidæ*; a simple card-game; a very precise person. **old man,** the southernwood; an adult male kangaroo [Austral.]. **old man's beard,** the plant *Clematis vitalba*; the long moss *Tillandsia usneoides.* **old red sandstone,** a series of red sandstone rocks lying below the coal formation [Geol.]. **old style,** according to the Julian calendar (used in England to 1752). **Old Testament,** *see* **Testament. old tom,** a kind of gin. **old wife,** a prating old woman; the black sea-bream (*Cantharus lineatus*), the menhaden, and other fish. **old woman,** a fussy, over-particular person; a man like an old woman in his habits [Coll.]; the plant *Artemisia absinthium*; [Slang] one's wife. **Old World,** the Eastern Hemisphere. (A.S. *eald.*)
old-clothesman, *n.* a dealer in old clothes.
olden, *a.* *ohl*-dn, old; ancient: *v.i.* and *t.* to grow, or cause to grow, old.
old-face, *a.* designating the earliest form of roman printing-type, revived in 1844.
old-fashioned, *a.* antiquated; long out of fashion.
oldish, *a.* *ohld*-ish, somewhat old.
oldness, *n.* quality or state of being old.
oldster, *n.* *ohld*-ster, an adult of middle age.
old-time, *a.* pertaining to or characteristic of former times.
old-timer, *n.* one long accustomed (to a position, occupation, etc.); a veteran.
old-world, *a.* antiquated; behind the times or the fashion; pertaining to the Eastern Hemisphere.
oleaginous, *a.* oh-le-*aj*-e-nus, oily; unctuous; insinuating. (L. *oleaginus.*)
oleaginousness, *n.* o-le-*aj*-e-nus-ness, oiliness.
oleander, *n.* o-le-*an*-der, a poisonous evergreen shrub of the genus *Nerium.* (Fr. *oleandre.*)
oleaster, *n.* oh-le-*as*-ter, a species of *Elæagnus.* (L.)
oleate, *n.* *oh*-le-at, a salt of oleic acid.
olefiant, *a.* o-*lef*-e-ant *or* oh-le-*fy*-ant, forming or producing oil. **olefiant gas,** former name of the hydrocarbon constituent of coal-gas which with chlorine and bromine forms oily liquids and is now known as ethylene. (L. *oleum*, and *facio*, make.)
olefine, *n.* *oh*-le-fin, a hydrocarbon of the ethylene series.
oleic, *a.* o-*lee*-ik, pertaining to or derived from oil. **oleic acid,** a colourless liquid obtained chiefly from the saponification of fats. (L. *oleum.*)
oleiferous, *a.* oh-le-*if*-er-rus, producing oil. (L. *oleum*, and *fero*, produce.)
olein, *n.* *oh*-le-in, the liquid portion of fat or oil.
oleograph, *n.* *oh*-le-o-graf, a lithograph imitating an oil painting.
oleomargarine, *n.* *oh*-le-o-*mar*-ga-rin, margarine, esp. that made from high-grade animal fats. (L. *oleum* and *margarin.*)
oleometer, *n.* oh-le-*om*-e-ter, an instrument to ascertain the density or specific gravity of oil. (L. *oleum*, and Gr. *meter.*)
oleon, *n.* *oh*-le-on, an oily liquid obtained by the distillation of a mixture of oleic acid and lime.
oleoresin, *n.* *oh*-le-o-*rez*-in, a natural mixture of an essential oil and a resin. (L. *oleum*, and *resin.*)
oleosaccharum, *n.* *oh*-le-o-*sak*-a-rum, a mixture of an essential oil and sugar [Med.].
oleraceous, *a.* ol-e-*ray*-shus, esculent; of the nature of a pot herb. (L. *oleraceus.*)
olfaction, *n.* ol-*fak*-shon, the sense of smell; the action of smelling.
olfactometer, *n.* ol-fak-*tom*-e-ter, an apparatus for testing the sense of smell.
olfactory, *a.* ol-*fak*-to-re, pertaining to or used in smelling: *n.* an organ of smell. (L. *olfactorius*, from *olere*, to smell, *facere*, to make.)
olibanum, *n.* oh-*lib*-a-num, the gum-resin frankincense, used as a stimulant and expectorant

[Pharm.] (L. *oleum*, and Gr. *libanos*, frankincense.)
oligæmia, *n.* ol-e-*jee*-me-a, deficiency in the volume of blood [Med.]. (Gr. *oligos*, little, *haima*, blood.)
oligarch, *n.* *ol*-e-gark, one of an oligarchy.
oligarchical, *a.* ol-e-*gar*-ke-kal, pertaining to oligarchy.
oligarchy, *n.* *ol*-e-gar-ke, government by the few, or by a small exclusive class; a state so governed. (Gr. *oligos*, small, *archein*, to rule.)
oligist, *n.* *ol*-e-jist, hæmatite. (Gr. *oligistos*, least.)
oligo-, *comb.f.* denoting fewness or scarcity. (Gr. *oligos*, few.)
Oligocene, *n.* o-*lig*-o-seen, the period, or the series of rocks, between the Eocene and Miocene. [Geol.].
oligoclase, *n.* o-*lig*-o-klayz, a triclinic felspar, a silicate of aluminium and soda.
oligocythæmia, *n.* *ol*-e-go-sy-*thee*-me-a, deficiency in the number of red cells in the blood.
olio, *n.* *oh*-le-o, a mixture; a medley; a miscellaneous stew. (Sp.)
oliphant, *n.* *ol*-e-fant, an ancient ivory hunting horn. (Elephant.)
olitory, *a.* *ol*-e-to-re, belonging to pot-herbs, or to the kitchen-garden. (L. *olitorius*.)
olivaceous, *a.* ol-e-*vay*-shus, of olive colour; greyish-green.
olivary, *a.* *ol*-e-va-re, shaped like an olive [Anat.].
olive, *n.* *ol*-iv, a tree of the genus *Olea*, or its fruit; the colour of unripe olives, greyish-green; the metal fastener of a strap; a spindle-shaped button used with a loop: *pl.* rolled slices of meat seasoned and cooked: *a.* of the colour olive; dull greenish-yellow. **olive oil**, oil expressed from the olive. (Fr.)
olive-branch, *n.* the branch of the olive; the emblem of peace; a child.
olivenite, *n.* *ol*-e-ve-nite, native hydrated arsenate of copper.
oliver, *n.* *ol*-e-ver, a small tilt-hammer worked by the foot. **a Roland for an Oliver**, *see* **Roland.**
olivet, *n.* *ol*-e-vet, an olive (button); an imitation pearl made for barter with primitive tribes.
Olivetan, *n.* ol-e-*vee*-tan, a member of a branch of Benedictine monks founded in 1313 by St. Bernard Tolomei on Monte Oliveto, Siena.
olive-yard, *n.* a piece of ground in which olives are cultivated.
olivil, *n.* *ol*-e-vil, a crystalline compound obtained from the gum of the olive tree.
olivine, *n.* *ol*-e-vin, anhydrous silicate of magnesium, a variety of chrysolite; a yellowish-green colour.
olla, *n.* *ol*-la, an olio; an olla-podrida; a Spanish cooking-pot with a wide mouth. (Sp.)
olla-podrida, *n.* *ol*-la-po-*dree*-da, a Spanish dish of meat, poultry, etc., stewed with vegetables; any incongruous mixture. (Sp., putrid pot.)
ology, *n.* *ol*-o-je, for any branch of science [Coll.]. (*-logy*.)
olpe, *n.* *ol*-pee, an ancient Greek cylindrical wine-pitcher.
olympiad, *n.* o-*lim*-pe-ad, in ancient Greece, the space of four years between one celebration of the Olympic games and another (forming the basis of a system of chronology from 776 B.C.).
Olympian, *a.* o-*lim*-pe-an, pertaining to or characteristic of Olympus; godlike: *n.* a dweller on Mt. Olympus, a Greek god; a very important or very stately person [Coll.].
Olympic, *a.* o-*lim*-pik, at or of Olympia; Olympian. **Olympic games**, ancient Greek games held every four years at Olympia in honour of Zeus; an international meeting for athletic games held in a different country every fourth year (with war-time breaks) since 1896.
omadhaun, *n.* *awm*-a-dawn, a fool, a lunatic (esp. as form of abuse). (Ir. *amadan*.)
omasum, *n.* o-*may*-sum, the third stomach in ruminants. (L.)
ombre, *n.* *om*-ber, a Spanish card-game in which the eights, nines, and tens are not used, generally played by three. (Sp. *hombre*, man.)
ombrology, *n.* om-*brol*-o-je, the branch of meteorology concerned with rain and rainfall.
ombrometer, *n.* om-*brom*-e-ter, a rain-gauge. (Gr. *ombros*, rain, *metron*, measure.)
ombrophile, *n.* *om*-bro-file, a plant enduring long-continued rain without injury.
ombrophobe, *n.* *om*-bro-fobe, a plant that cannot endure long continued rain.

omega, *n.* *oh*-me-ga, the last letter of the Greek alphabet. **alpha and omega**, the first and the last. (Gr. *ō mega*, the great *o*.)
omelet, *n.* *om*-let, a kind of pancake or fritter made of beaten eggs. (Fr. *omelette*.)
omen, *n.* *oh*-men, a sign of something to happen, good or bad: *v.i.* to augur. (L.)
omental, *a.* o-*men*-tal, relating to the omentum.
omentitis, *n.* oh-men-*ty*-tis, inflammation of the omentum.
omentum, *n.* o-*men*-tum (*pl.* **omenta**), a free fold of the peritoneum connecting the viscera [Anat.]. (L.)
omer, *n.* *oh*-mer, a Hebrew measure equivalent to slightly over 2½ quarts. (Heb.)
omicron, *n.* o-*my*-kron, the short *o* in the Greek alphabet.
ominous, *a.* *om*-e-nus, foreboding or presaging evil (L. *ominosus*.)
ominously, *ad.* in an ominous manner.
ominousness, *n.* the condition of being ominous.
omissible, *a.* o-*mis*-si-bl, that may be omitted.
omission, *n.* o-*mish*-on, neglect to do something; a leaving out; something left out.
omissive, *a.* o-*mis*-siv, leaving out.
omit, *v.t.* o-*mit*, to neglect; to leave out; to make no mention of: *ppr.* **omitting**; *pp.* **omitted.** (L. *omittere*, let go.)
omnibus, *a.* *om*-ne-bus, covering or containing many things, as an omnibus bill: *n.* a large public passenger vehicle, familiarly called a 'bus. **omnibus bill** a parliamentary bill affecting many different subjects or interests. **omnibus book**, a one-volume collection of similar items or of a single author's works. **omnibus box**, a large box at a theatre. (L., for all.)
omnicompetent, *a.* *om*-ne-*kom*-pe-tent, having jurisdiction or legal capacity to act in all causes or cases.
omnidirectional, *a.* *om*-ne-dy-*rek*-shon-al, transmitting to or receiving from all directions equally [Wire.].
omnifarious, *a.* *om*-ne-*fare*-re-us, of all varieties; of many varieties. (L. *omnis*.)
omniferous, *a.* om-*nif*-er-rus, bearing all kinds of products. (L. *omnis*, all, *fero*, bear.)
omnific, *a.* om-*nif*-ik, all-creating. (L. *omnis*, and *facio*, make.)
omniform, *a.* *om*-ne-form, having every form.
omniformity, *n.* om-ne-*for*-me-te, the quality of having every form.
omnigenous, *a.* om-*nij*-e-nus, consisting of all kinds. (L. *omnis*, and *genus*, kind.)
omniparity, *n.* om-ne-*pa*-re-te, general equality.
omniparous, *a.* om-*nip*-a-rus, producing all things. (L. *omnis*, and *pario*, bring forth.)
omnipatient, *a.* om-ne-*pay*-shent, all-enduring.
omnipercipience, *n.* *om*-ne-per-*sip*-e-ence, perception of everything.
omnipercipient, *a.* *om*-ne-per-*sip*-e-ent, perceiving everything.
omnipotence, *n.* om-*nip*-o-tence, almighty power; unlimited power.
omnipotent, *a.* om-*nip*-o-tent, almighty; possessing unlimited power. **the Omnipotent**, the Almighty. (L. *omnipotens*.)
omnipresence, *n.* om-ne-*prez*-ence, presence everywhere.
omnipresent, *a.* om-ne-*prez*-ent, present in all places at the same time.
omniscience, *n.* om-*nish*-e-ence, the quality of being omniscient; knowledge of everything.
omniscient, *a.* om-*nish*-e-ent, all-knowing; all-seeing (in strictness applied only to the Deity). (L. *omnis*, and *scio*, know.)
omnium, *n.* *om*-ne-um, the aggregate value of the different kind of stocks forming a loan [Stock Exchange]. **omnium gatherum**, a miscellaneous assemblage of all sorts and conditions [Coll.]. (L. *omnis*, and *gather*.)
omnivorous, *a.* om-*niv*-o-rus, feeding on both plants and animals; devouring anything obtainable (both literally and figuratively). (L. *omnis*, and *voro*, devour.)
omnivorously, *ad.* om-*niv*-o-rus-le, in an omnivorous manner.
omophagia, *n.* oh-moh-*fay*-je-a, the practice of eating raw flesh or uncooked food.
omophagous, *a.* oh-*mof*-a-gus, feeding on raw flesh, etc. (Gr.)

omoplate, *n.* *oh*-mo-plate, the shoulder-blade. (Gr. *omos*, the shoulder, and *plate.*)
omphacite, *n.* *om*-fa-site, a green variety of augite.
omphalic, *a.* om-*fal*-ik, pertaining to the umbilicus or navel. (*omphalos.*)
omphalism, *n.* *om*-fa-lizm, centralization, esp. of administration.
omphalocele, *n.* om-*fal*-oh-seel, a rupture at the navel [Med.]. (*omphalos*, and Gr. *kele*, a tumour.)
omphalos, *n.* *om*-fa-los, the navel; any central point or part, esp. [Gr. Myth.] the centre of the earth's surface; the boss of a shield. (Gr., navel.)
omphalotomy, *n.* om-fa-*lot*-o-me, the operation of dividing the navel string.
★**on,** *prep.* on, in contact with the upper part of a thing; upon; at; near; in consequence of: *ad.* forward; onward; not off: *n.* the side on which the striker stands at cricket. **to be a bit on,** to be fuddled through drink. **to get on,** *see* **get. to have a bit on,** to have laid a bet [Coll.].
onager, *n.* *on*-a-jer, a variety of the Asiatic wild ass, *Equus hemionus*; a mediæval military machine by which stones were thrown. (L.)
onanism, *n.* *oh*-nan-izm, self-abuse; masturbation; uncompleted sexual intercourse [Med.]. (*Onan*, Gen. xxxviii.)
once, *ad.* wunce, on one occasion; formerly; as soon as; at any time; some time or other: *conj.* as soon as; when: *n.* one time; doing anything once. **a once-over,** a rapid but comprehensive examination [U.S.A.]. **all at once,** quite suddenly or unexpectedly. **at once,** immediately. **once for all,** finally; once and finished with. **once upon a time,** formerly; at a time long ago. (*one*).
oncer, *n.* *wunce*-er, one who does a thing once [Slang].
oncograph, *n.* *ong*-ko-graf, an instrument for recording variations in the size of organs [Surg.].
oncology, *n.* ong-*kol*-o-je, the study of tumours. [Med.].
oncometer, *n.* ong-*kom*-e-ter, an instrument for measuring variations in bulk, esp. [Surg.] of internal organs. (Gr. *onkos*, bulk.)
oncoming, *a.* and *n.* *on*-kum-ing, approaching.
oncost, *n.* *on*-kost, wages paid in mining to those other than miners (engineers, maintenance staff, etc.).
ondograph, *n.* *on*-do-graf, an instrument for automatically recording the wave-form of alternating currents [Elect.].
ondy, *a.* *on*-de, wavy [Her.].
one, *a.* wun, single in number; some or any; undivided: *n.* the number one, or its symbol; an individual: *pron.* any single person. **all in one,** combined. **at one,** in agreement. **at one time,** formerly. **one too many,** too difficult. **put on one side,** to reserve. (A.S. *ān.*)
oneberry, *n.* *wun*-be-re, herb Paris.
onefold, *a.* *wun*-fohld, single; simple.
one-horse, *a.* inferior; small; poorly equipped.
oneirocritic, *n.* o-*nyr*-ro-*krit*-ik, an interpreter of dreams: *pl.* oneirocriticism. (Gr. *oneiron*, a dream, *kritikos*, critical.)
oneirocritical, *a.* o-*nyr*-ro-*krit*-e-kal, pertaining to, or skilled in the interpretation of, dreams.
oneirocriticism, *n.* o-*nyr*-ro-*krit*-e-sizm, the art of interpretating dreams; oneirocritics.
oneirodynia, *n.* o-*nyr*-ro-*din*-e-a, restlessness in sleep; nightmare; somnambulism. (Gr. *oneiron*, a dream, *odynē*, pain.)
oneirology, *n* o-nyr-*rol*-o-je, the theory of or a treatise on dreams. (Gr. *oneiron*, and *logos*, science.)
oneiromancy, *n.* o-*nyr*-ro-man-se, divination by dreams. (Gr. *oneiron*, and *manteia*, divination.)
one-man, *a.* pertaining to, consisting of, or done by, one man only.
oneness, *n.* *wun*-ness, quality or state of being one or undivided; singleness; identity.
one-piece, *a.* consisting of or made in a single piece (esp. of garments).
oner, *n.* *wun*-er, a stroke that requires no second to follow it; a stroke at cricket that results in a single run; an unusual person or thing [Slang].
onerary, *a.* *on*-er-ra-re, fitted for carrying loads; comprising a burden. (L. *onerarius.*)
onerous, *a.* *on*-er-rus, burdensome; oppressive. (L. *onerosus.*)
onerously, *ad.* *on*-er-rus-le, in a burdensome way; laboriously.
oneself, *pron.* wun-*self*, reflexive form of the indefinite pronoun *one*; one's own personality or ego.
one-sided, *a.* limited to one side; partial.
one-sidedly, *ad.* in a one-sided manner.
one-sidedness, *n.* having regard to one side only.
one-step, *n.* a dance to two-four time; music for this dance.
one-way, *a.* going or permitted to go in one direction only; allowing of motion in only one direction (esp. of traffic).
onfall, *n.* *on*-fawl, a snowstorm, or heavy rainstorm; the approach of night; an attack.
onflow, *n.* *on*-floh, flowing onward.
ongoing, *n.* *on*-goh-ing, proceeding; doing; progress.
oniomania, *n.* *oh*-ne-o-*may*-ne-a a morbid craving to buy things. (Gr. *onios*, for sale, and *mania.*)
onion, *n.* *un*-yon, the bulbous herb, *Allium cepa*; its bulb; the head [Slang]: *v.t.* to treat or flavour with onions. (Fr. *oignon.*)
onionskin, *n.* *un*-yon-skin, the skin of the onion; a thin glazed semi-transparent paper.
oniony, *a.* *un*-yon-e, resembling the onion in smell, taste, or appearance.
oniscoid, *a.* o-*nis*-koyd, shaped like, or allied to, the woodlouse. (Gr. *oniskos*, woodlouse.)
on-licence, *n.* a licence to sell alcoholic beverages to be drunk on the premises.
onliness, *n.* *ohn*-le-ness, uniqueness; singular condition.
onlooker, *n.* *on*-look-er, a spectator.
★**only,** *a.* *ohn*-le, single; one alone: *ad.* singly; merely; solely; barely: *conj.* but; except that. (A.S. *ānlic.*)
onocentaur, *n.* *oh*-no-*sen*-tawr, a fabulous animal, half man, half ass. (Late L. *onocentaurus.*)
onofrite, *n.* o-*noh*-frite, sulpho-selenide of mercury, first found at St. Onofre, Mexico.
onomancy, *n.* *on*-o-man-se, divination by the letters of a name. (Gr. *onoma*, a name, *manteia*, divination.)
onomastic, *a.* on-o-*mas*-tik, pertaining to a name.
onomasticon, *n.* on-o-*mas*-te-kon, a dictionary or vocabulary. (Gr.)
onomatology, *n.* *on*-o-ma-*tol*-o-je, nomenclature; the science of naming; terminology. (Gr. *onoma*, and *logos*, science, account.)
onomatope, *n.* *on*-o-ma-tope, a world formed to represent the sound signified.
onomatopœia, *n.* *on*-o-mat-o-*pee*-a, the formation of words to resemble the sound made by the thing signified; the use of such or the word itself. (Gr. *onoma*, and *poieo*, make.)
onomatopœic, *a.* *on*-o-mat-o-*pee*-ik, formed by or exhibiting onomatopœia; imitative verbally. (Gr. *onomatopoiitikos.*)
onrush, *n.* *on*-rush, an onset; the rapid or sudden approach of anything.
onset, *n.* *on*-set, a violent attack; assault.
onsetting, *n.* *on*-set-ting, a rushing or assaulting.
onslaught, *n.* *on*-slawt, a furious attack; an onset. (Perhaps Dut. *aanslag*, an attempt.)
ontogenesis, *n.* on-to-*jen*-e-sis, the origin of an individual, or its development from the embryo. (Gr. *on*, *ontos*, being, and *genesis.*)
ontogenetic, *a.* on-to-je-*net*-ik, pertaining to ontogenesis.
ontogeny, *n.* on-*toj*-e-ne, ontogenesis; embryology.
ontological, *a.* on-to-*log*-e-kal, pertaining to ontology, or to pure being; metaphysical.
ontologism, *n.* on-*tol*-o-jizm, a mystical philosophy holding that to the intellect cognition of God is essential and intuitive.
ontology, *n.* on-*tol*-o-je, the logic of pure being, or being in the element of pure thought; metaphysics. (Gr. *on*, *ontos*, and *logos*, science.)
onus, *n.* *oh*-nus, an obligation; responsibility. **onus probandi,** the burden of proof. (L., burden.)
onward, *a.* and *ad.* *on*-ward, forward; in advance.
onwards, *ad.* *on*-wardz, on; toward the front; forward.
onychia, *n.* o-*nik*-e-a, an abscess round the finger- or toe-nail; a whitlow [Med.]. (Gr. *onyx*, the nail.)
onychitis, *n.* *oh*-ne-*ky*-tis, inflammation at the side or base of a nail [Med.].
onychomancy, *n.* oh-*ny*-ko-man-se, divination by means of the finger-nails.

onychophagist, *n.* oh-ne-*kof*-a-jist, a person who bites his finger-nails. (Gr.)
onym, *n. on*-im, a technical name or term. (Gr. *onoma,* a name.)
onymous, *a. on*-e-mus, having a name; not anonymous.
onyx, *n. on*-iks, an agate-like stone consisting of alternate streaks of dark and white chalcedony; opacity of the eye due to pus in the cornea [Path.]. (Gr.)
oobit, *n. oo*-bit, a hairy caterpillar, a woubit.
oodles, *n.pl. oo*-dlz, lots; abundance [Slang].
oœcium, *n.* oh-*ee*-se-um, the sac in which fertilization in certain polyzoa is effected. (Gr. *oion,* an egg, *oikon,* a small house.)
oof, *n.* oof, money [Slang].
oofy, *a. oof*-e, rich; wealthy [Slang].
oogamous, *a.* oh-*og*-a-mus, reproducing by the union of male with female cells [Biol.].
oogenesis, *n.* oh-o-*jen*-e-sis, the development of the ovum.
ooidal, *a.* oh-*oyd*-al, egg-shaped; ovoid.
oolite, *n. oh*-o-lite, a coarse-grained limestone; a series of rocks of Jurassic age. (Gr. egg-stone, from *oion,* an egg, *lithos,* a stone.)
oolitic, *a.* oh-o-*lit*-ik, pertaining to the oolite formation [Geol.]; having grains like the roe of a fish (of rocks).
oologist, *n.* oh-*ol*-o-jist, a student of birds' eggs.
oology, *n.* oh-*ol*-o-je, a treatise on, or the study of, birds' eggs. (Gr. *oion,* and *logos,* science.)
oolong, *n. oo*-long, a variety of China tea. (Chinese, black dragon.)
oom, *n.* oom, uncle. (South African Dutch.)
oometer, *n.* oh-*om*-e-ter, an instrument for measuring eggs.
oomiak, *n. oo*-me-ak, umiak. (Eskimo.)
oopak, *n. oo*-pak, a variety of black tea from the province of Hupeh (Chin. *Oopak*), Central China.
oophorectomy, *n. oh*-of-o-*rek*-to-me, excision of an ovary [Surg.].
oorali, *n.* oo-*rah*-le, curare.
oorial, *n. oor*-re-al, the urial, a wild sheep of northern India.
oosperm, *n. oh*-o-sperm, a fertilized ovum [Zool.]; an oospore [Bot.].
oosphere, *n. oh*-o-sfeer, the unfertilized female reproductive cell in certain cryptogams [Bot.].
oospore, *n. oh*-o-spor, a fertilized oosphere [Bot.].
ootheca, *n. oh*-o-*thee*-ka, the purse-like egg-carrying structure of certain molluscs and insects.
ooze, *n.* ooz, soft mud or slime; a deposit on the bed of the ocean; a sluggish flow; the liquor of a tan-vat: *v.i.* to percolate, as a liquid, through the pores of a substance; to flow gently; to escape or exude slowly. (A.S. *wos,* moisture.)
oozily, *ad. ooz*-e-le, in an oozy or slimy manner.
oozy, *a. ooz*-e, miry; resembling ooze.
opacity, *n.* oh-*pas*-e-te, opaqueness; obscurity.
opah, *n. oh*-pah, a large brightly coloured fish, *Lampris guttatus,* of the Atlantic. (West African.)
opal, *n. oh*-pal, hydrate of silica, a gem-stone of many tints and varieties. (Fr. *opale.*)
opalesce, *v.i.* oh-pa-*less,* to give forth a play of colour like the opal.
opalescence, *n.* oh-pa-*less*-ence, the quality of being opalescent.
opalescent, *a. oh*-pa-*less*-ent, exhibiting a play of colours like the opal; reflecting a pearly or milky light from the interior.
opaline, *a. oh*-pa-lin, pertaining to or resembling opal: *n.* a variety of chalcedony; a translucent opalescent glass.
opalize, *v.t.* and *i. oh*-pa-lize, to make or become opalescent or like opal.
opaque, *a.* oh-*pake,* not transparent or translucent; impervious to rays of any kind [Physics]; dull; unintelligible [Fig.]. (Fr.)
opaqueness, *n.* oh-*pake*-ness, condition or quality of being opaque; opacity.
ope, *a., v.i.* and *t.* ope, poetical form of open.
opeidoscope, *n.* oh-*py*-do-skope, an apparatus for showing visually the vibrations caused by musical and other sounds. (Gr. *ops,* voice, *sidos,* form, and *-scope.*)
★**open,** *a. oh*-pen, not shut or closed; spread; expanded; unsealed; not covered; clear; not stopped; not fenced; not frosty; public; frank; free to all comers; not clouded; not hidden; undisguised; manifest; subject to; debatable: *v.t.* to unclose; to unlock; to break the seal of; to part; to rend; to clear; to expand; to begin; to disclose: *v.i.* to unclose itself; to commence; to bark on scent of game. **the open,** the open air or open country; public view. **open air,** out of doors. **open arms,** outstretched arms, esp. as expressing welcome. **to open the ball,** to take the first step. **open city,** a city declared and acknowledged to be unequipped offensively or defensively and to be outside the sphere of warlike operations [Mil.]. **open country,** an unenclosed stretch of land, or a wide sweep of country. **open door,** a welcome to all; (in international politics) availability of commercial or other opportunities to all states upon equal terms. **open face,** ingenuousness. **to open fire,** to start firing [Mil.] **open house,** a house in which hospitality is lavishly dispensed. **open letter,** a letter addressed to an individual but made public by the writer. **open order,** a military or naval formation in which considerable intervals are kept between the men or the ships. **open question,** one about which there must always exist differences of opinion. **open sea,** the main sea; sea unenclosed by land. **open sesame,** a magician's conjuration by which entrance may be gained to closed or secret places (from the story of the Forty Thieves in the "Arabian Nights"). **open verdict,** the finding of a coroner's jury that a crime has been committed by some person or persons unknown. (A.S. *open,* from *up.*)
openable, *a. oh*-pn-a-bl, capable of being opened.
opener, *n. oh*-pn-er, one who or that which opens.
open-eyed, *a. oh*-pen-ide, watchful; vigilant.
open-handed, *a.* generous; liberal.
open-handedness, *n.* generosity in giving.
open-hearted, *a.* candid; frank.
open-heartedness, *n.* frankness.
opening, *a. oh*-pen-ing, first in order: *n.* a breach; an aperture; a commencement; counsel's statement of his case before evidence is produced [Law]: the initial moves in chess, etc.; an opportunity.
openly, *ad. oh*-pn-le, in an open manner.
open-minded, *a.* unprejudiced.
open-mouthed, *a.* gaping; greedy: clamorous.
openness, *n.* frankness; the state of being open.
open-work, *n.* ornamental work with open spaces in its substance.
opera, *n. op*-er-ra, a dramatic composition set to music and sung on the stage. **grand opera,** an opera usually with a tragic theme, which is sung throughout. **opéra comique,** a lighter form of opera in which the dialogue is usually spoken. (It.)
operable, *a. op*-er-ra-bl, practicable; capable of treatment by operation [Surg.].
opéra-bouffe, *n.* op-er-ra-*boof,* a farcical or exaggerated form of opéra comique. (Fr.)
opera-cloak, *n.* a lady's evening dress cloak.
opera-glass, *n.* a small field glass; a short binocular telescope.
opera-hat, *n.* an extensible tall hat that folds into a small compass; a gibus.
opera-house, *n.* a theatre for the performance of operas.
operameter, *n.* op-er-*ram*-e-ter, an instrument for registering the revolutions of a shaft, etc. [Mech.]. (L. *opera,* works, Gr. *metron,* measure.)
operant, *a. op*-er-rant, having power to produce an effect; operative: *n.* one who or that which operates. (L. *operans.*)
operate, *v.i. op*-er-rate, to work; to act; to produce an effect; to perform an act of surgery: *v.t.* to produce by agency; to manage the working of. (L. *operatus.*)
operatic, *a.* op-er-*rat*-ik, pertaining to the opera.
operatically, *ad.* op-er-*rat*-e-ka-le, in an operatic manner; as in opera.
★**operation,** *n.* op-er-*ray*-shon, the act or process of operating; an act of surgery; agency; the exertion of power, physical, mechanical, or moral; manipulation; movement of an army or fleet, or of machinery or any physical body.
operational, *a.* op-er-*ray*-shon-al, relating to operation or an operation.
operative, *a. op*-er-ra-tiv, having the power of acting; exerting force; producing the desired effect: *n.* an artisan, mechanic, or mill-hand.
operatively, *ad. op*-er-ra-tiv-le, so as to operate; effectively; by means of an operation [Surg.].

operatize, *v.t.* *op*-er-ra-tize, to convert into an opera.
operator, *n.* *op*-er-ray-tor, he who or that which operates.
opercular, *a.* o-*per*-kew-lar, operculate; pertaining to the operculum.
operculate, *a.* o-*per*-kew-lat, having an operculum or cover [Bot. and Zool.].
operculiform, *a.* o-*per*-kew-le-form, having the form of an operculum.
operculum, *n.* o-*per*-kew-lum, a lid-like process or part, esp. of a pitcher-form leaf or of the spore-vessel of a moss; the lid of a spiral shell; a gill cover. (L., a lid or cover.)
operetta, *n.* op-er-*ret*-ta, a short musical drama of a light nature. (It.)
operose, *a.* *op*-er-rohs, laborious or tedious; involving labour. (L. *operosus.*)
operosely, *ad.* *op*-er-rohs-le, laboriously.
operoseness, *n.* the state of being operose.
ophic, *a.* *of*-ik, pertaining to serpents.
ophicleide, *n.* *of*-e-klide, a large brass keyed wind instrument, now replaced by the bass tuba. (Gr. *ophis*, a serpent, *kleis*, a key—it succeeded the older serpent, a wood-wind.)
Ophidia, *n.pl.* o-*fid*-e-a, the division of reptiles that includes the snakes.
ophidian, *a.* o-*fid*-e-an, pertaining to snakes; snake-like: *n.* one of the ophidia. (Gr. *ophis.*)
ophidiophobia, *n.* o-*fid*-e-oh-*foh*-be-a, a morbid dread of snakes.
ophioid, *a.* of-e-*oyd*, pertaining to or like snakes.
ophiolater, *n.* of-e-*ol*-a-ter, a serpent worshipper.
ophiolatrous, *a.* of-e-*ol*-a-trus, addicted to serpent worship.
ophiolatry, *n.* of-e-*ol*-a-tre, serpent worship. (Gr. *ophis*, and *latreia*, worship.)
ophiological, *a.* of-e-o-*loj*-e-kal, pertaining to ophiology.
ophiologist, *n.* of-e-*ol*-o-jist, one skilled in ophiology.
ophiology, *n.* of-e-*ol*-o-je, the study of snakes. (Gr. *ophis*, and *logos*, science.)
ophiomancy, *n.* *of*-e-o-man-se, the art of divining from snakes. (Gr. *ophis*, and *manteia*, divination.)
ophiomorphous, *a.* of-e-o-*mor*-fus, having the form of a snake. (Gr. *ophis*, and *morphe*, shape.)
ophiophagous, *a.* of-e-*of*-a-gus, feeding on snakes. (Gr. *ophis*, and *phago*, eat.)
ophiosaurus, *n.* of-e-o-*saw*-rus, any one of the glass-snakes. (Gr. *ophis*, and *sauros*, a lizard.)
Ophite, *n.* *oh*-fite, one of a sect of Gnostics who regarded the serpent as the incarnation of divine wisdom. (Gr. *ophites*, resembling a serpent.)
ophite, *n.* *oh*-fite, serpentine; a variety of dolerite containing diallage and epidote.
ophthalmia, *n.* of-*thal*-me-a, inflammation of the eye or the conjunctiva. (Gr. *ophthalmos*, the eye.)
ophthalmic, *a.* of-*thal*-mik, pertaining to the eye.
ophthalmious, *a.* of-*thal*-me-us, affected with ophthalmia.
ophthalmitis, *n.* of-thal-*my*-tis, ophthalmia.
ophthalmocele, *n.* of-*thal*-mo-seel, protrusion of the eyeball [Path.].
ophthalmologist, *n.* of-thal-*mol*-o-jist, one versed in the treatment of the eyes.
ophthalmology, *n.* of-thal-*mol*-o-je, the science which treats of the eye and its disorders. (Gr. *ophthalmos*, and *logos*, science.)
ophthalmoplegia, *n.* of-*thal*-mo-*plee*-je-a, paralysis of the muscles of the eye.
ophthalmoscope, *n.* of-*thal*-mo-skope, an instrument for the visual examination of the eye. (Gr. *ophthalmos*, and *skopeo*, view.)
ophthalmoscopy, *n.* of-thal-*mos*-ko-pe, examination of the eye with the ophthalmoscope.
ophthalmotomy, *n.* of-thal-*mot*-o-me, dissection or excision of the eye. (Gr. *ophthalmos*, and *tome*, cutting.)
opiate, *n.* *oh*-pe-ate, a narcotic; anything that induces rest or allays uneasiness, esp. a medicine containing opium: *a.* soporific; allaying uneasiness: *v.t.* to treat or mix with opium; to deaden. (Fr.)
opiatic, *a.* oh-pe-*at*-ik, pertaining to opiates; of the nature of an opiate.
opine, *v.i.* and *t.* o-*pine*, to think; to suppose; to be of opinion. (Fr. *opiner.*)
opiniative, *a.* o-*pin*-ya-tiv, opinionative.
★**opinion,** *n.* o-*pin*-yon, persuasion of the mind without proof or certain knowledge; judgment; persuasion; estimation; a formal statement by an expert, esp. medical or legal. (Fr.)
opinionated, *a.* o-*pin*-yon-ay-ted, stiff or obstinate in opinion; opinionative.
opinionative, *a.* o-*pin*-yon-a-tiv, obstinately adhering to one's own opinions or over-valuing them; dogmatic.
opinionatively, *ad.* in an opinionative manner.
opinionativeness, *n.* the quality of being opinionative; undue attachment to one's own opinions.
opinionist, *n.* o-*pin*-yon-ist, one holding an opinion; an opinionated or bigoted person.
opisometer, *n.* oh-pe-*som*-e-ter, an instrument for measuring curved or irregular lines, esp. on maps. (Gr., backwards.)
opisthobranch, o-*pis*-tho-brank, any one of the opisthobranchiate molluscs.
opisthobranchiate, *a.* o-*pis*-tho-*brang*-ke-at, of the order Opisthobranchia, marine molluscs having the gills behind the heart and no operculum. (Gr. *opisthen*, behind, *branchia*, gills.)
opisthocœlian, *a.* o-*pis*-tho-*see*-le-an, opisthocœlous: *n.* an opisthocœlous animal.
opisthocœlous, *a.* o-*pis*-tho-*see*-lus, concave behind (of vertebræ) [Anat.].
opisthocome, *n.* o-*pis*-tho-kohm, the hoatzin, a bird having an occipital crest of feathers. (Gr. *opistho*, behind, *komos*, hair.)
opisthodont, *a.* o-*pis*-tho-dont, having back teeth only [Zool.].
opisthogastric, *a.* o-*pis*-tho-*gas*-trik, behind the stomach.
opisthognathous, *a.* oh-pis-*thog*-na-thus, having retreating jaws.
opisthograph, *n.* o-*pis*-tho-graf, a writing or inscription set out on both sides.
opisthographic, *a.* o-*pis*-tho-*graf*-ik, written or inscribed on both sides.
opisthotonous, *n.* oh-pis-*thot*-o-nus, a form of tetanus in which the trunk is thrown backward and arched upward [Path.]. (Gr., drawn backwards.)
opium, *n.* *oh*-pe-um, a narcotic drug prepared from the dried juice of certain oriental poppies. **opium eater,** one who indulges in opium. (L., from Gr. *opion*, sap.)
opiumism, *n.* *oh*-pe-um-izm, chronic opium poisoning [Med.]; addiction to, or the habit of taking, opium.
opobalsam, *n.* op-o-*bawl*-sam, balm of Gilead, *Commiphora opobalsamum.* (Gr. *opobalsamon.*)
opodeldoc, *n.* oh-po-*del*-dok, soap liniment.
opopanax, *n.* o-*pop*-a-naks, a gum-resin obtained from a herb of this name, used in perfumery and formerly as a drug. (L.)
opossum, *n.* o-*pos*-sum, an American marsupial of the genus *Didelphys*; an Austrian marsupial of the phalanger family; the dressed skin of any of these. **water opossum,** the yapok, of South America. (Algonquian.)
opotherapy, *n.* *oh*-po-*the*-ra-pe, organotherapy.
oppidan, *n.* *op*-e-dan, a boy at Eton College boarded in the town, as distinct from a colleger. (L. *oppidanus*, relating to a town.)
oppilate, *v.t.* *op*-e-late, to obstruct or block up [Med.]. (L. *oppilatus*, stopped up.)
oppilation, *n.* op-e-*lay*-shon, the act of obstructing; an obstruction; constipation [Med.].
oppilative, *a.* *op*-e-la-tiv, obstructive [Med.].
opponency, *n.* op-*poh*-nen-se, the action of the opposition; antagonism; the action or the opening of an academical disputation. (L. *opponens.*)
opponent, *a.* op-*poh*-nent, that opposes; opposite; antagonistic: *n.* one who opposes, esp. in debate or argument.
opportune, *a.* op-por-*tewn*, seasonable; well-timed. (Fr. *opportun.*)
opportunely, *ad.* op-por-*tewn*-le, seasonably.
opportuneness, *n.* seasonableness.
opportunism, *n.* *op*-or-tew-nizm, policy based on opportunity; compromise through sacrifice of principles; making party capital out of the circumstances of the moment.
opportunist, *n.* *op*-or-tew-nist, one who practises opportunism; a seizer of opportunity.
opportunistic, *a.* *op*-or-tew-*nis*-tik, characteristic of opportunism or an opportunist.
opportunity, *n.* op-por-*tew*-ne-te, fit, convenient, or favourable time. (Fr. *opportunité.*)

opposability, *n.* o-*poh*-za-*bil*-e-te, capability of being resisted, or of being placed in opposition.
opposable, *a.* o-*poh*-za-bl, that may be opposed; that can be brought together like thumb and finger. (Fr. *opportunité.*)
oppose, *v.t.* op-*poze*, to act against or in opposition; to resist; to combat; to contradict; to compete with; to dispute: *v.i.* to offer opposition or resistance. (Fr. *opposer.*)
opposeless, *a.* op-*poze*-less, irresistible.
opposer, *n.* op-*poze*-er, one who opposes; an opponent; one who acts in opposition.
★**opposite,** *a. op*-po-zit, situated in front; adverse; contrary; differing directly from; facing each other; growing in pairs, opposed at the same level [Bot.]: *n.* one who or that which is opposed; anything that is contradictory: *ad.* in an opposite direction: *prep.* opposite to. (Fr.)
oppositely, *ad. op*-po-zit-le, in front; adversely.
oppositeness, *n.* state of being opposite.
opposition, *n.* op-po-*zish*-on, a position fronting something else; the act of opposing; obstacle; resistance; contrariety; the collective body of opponents to an administration; the situation of two heavenly bodies when distant in longitude from each other 180°; difference as regards quantity, quality, or both in propositions with the same subject and predicate [Logic]. (Fr.)
oppositional, *a.* op-po-*zish*-on-al, pertaining to or constituting opposition or an opposition.
oppositionist, *n.* op-po-*zish*-on-ist, one of the party that opposes an administration: *a.* oppositional; befitting an opposition.
oppositive, *a.* op-*poz*-e-tiv, characterized by opposing; that may be put in opposition.
oppress, *v.t.* op-*press*, to load or burden by hardship; to overpower; to lie heavy on; to act tyrannically towards. (Fr. *oppresser.*)
oppression, *n.* op-*presh*-on, act of oppressing; state of being oppressed; hardship; calamity; depression; sense of weight pressing. (Fr.)
oppressive, *a.* op-*pres*-siv, unreasonably burdensome; tyrannical; heavy; overwhelming; close and depressive.
oppressively, *ad.* in an oppressive manner.
oppressiveness, *n.* quality of being oppressive.
oppressor, *n.* op-*pres*-sor, one who oppresses.
opprobrious, *a.* op-*proh*-bre-us, reproachful and contemptuous; thoroughly disgraceful; infamous. (L. *opprobriosus.*)
opprobriously, *ad.* op-*proh*-bre-us-le, in an opprobrious manner; scurrilously.
opprobriousness, *n.* op-*proh*-bre-us-ness, reproachfulness with contempt; scurrility.
opprobrium, *n.* op-*proh*-bre-um, reproach with disdain; infamy; disgrace. (L.)
oppugn, *v.t.* op-*pewn*, to oppose; to withstand; to controvert or call in question. (Fr. *oppugner.*)
oppugnancy, *n.* op-*pug*-nan-se, antagonism.
oppugnant, *a.* op-*pug*-nant, opposing; antagonistic. (L. *oppugnans*, fighting against.)
oppugner, *n.* op-*pew*-ner, one who oppugns.
opsimath, *n. op*-se-math, one who begins to study late in life. (Gr. *opse*, late, *mathein*, to learn.)
opsiometer, *n. op*-se-*om*-e-ter, an optometer.
opsomania, *n. op*-so-*may*-ne-a, a morbid craving for some particular food. (Gr. *opson*, rich food, and *mania.*)
opsonic, *a.* op-*son*-ik, pertaining to, or destructible by, opsonin.
opsonin, *n. op*-so-nin, a substance present in the blood serum which renders bacteria more susceptible of destruction by the phagocytes. (Gr. *opsonein*, purchase food.)
opt, *v.i.* opt, to make a choice.
optant, *n. op*-tant, one with the power of opting.
optative, *a. op*-ta-tiv, expressing desire or wish; subject to choice: *n.* the optative mood. **optative mood,** that form of the verb in which wish is expressed [Gram.]. (Fr. *optatif*, from L. *optare*, to choose.)
optic, *a. op*-tik, relating or pertaining to the eye or vision, or to optics: *n.* an eye (in humorous use only). **optic angle,** the angle formed by two straight lines drawn from the extreme points of an object to the centre of the eye; the angle between the optic axes of the eyes when directed to the same object. **optic axis,** the axis of the eye. **optic nerve,** one of the two nerves of sight. (Fr. *optique.*)
optical, *a. op*-te-kal, relating or pertaining to the science of optics, or to the eyesight.
optically, *ad. op*-te-ka-le, in relation to optics or to the sight; by optical means.
optician, *n.* op-*tish*-an, one who makes or sells optical instruments.
optics, *n. op*-tiks, the science which treats of light and the phenomena of vision.
optigraph, *n. op*-te-graf, an instrument formerly used in the mechanical drawing of landscapes. (Gr. *optikos*, relating to sight, *grapho*, write.)
optimacy, *n. op*-te-ma-se, government by an aristocracy; such a government, or class; a state so governed.
optimates, *n.pl.* op-te-*may*-teez, aristocrats generally; primarily the Roman nobility. (L.)
optime, *n. op*-te-me, one of those who passed immediately below the wranglers in the examination for the Cambridge Univ. B.A. degree. (L. *optime*, best.)
optimism, *n. op*-te-mizm, the doctrine that the existing order of things is on the whole the best possible; the doctrine that good will prevail over evil; disposition to take a sanguine or hopeful view of things. (Fr. *optimisme.*)
optimist, *n. op*-te-mist, one addicted to optimism; one who thinks that all is for the best: *a.* optimistic.
optimistic, *a.* op-te-*mis*-tik, characterized by, or given to, optimism; pertaining to optimism.
optimize, *v.i. op*-te-mize, to see everything in its best light; to make the most of.
optimum, *a. op*-te-mum, highest; best: *n.* condition producing the best result. (L. *optimus*, best.)
option, *n. op*-shon, the power of choosing or wishing; the opportunity of choice; a bargain in which a dealer has the right to buy or sell a certain amount of stock within certain limits of price during a certain time. (Fr.)
optional, *a. op*-shon-al, involving an option; left to choice or to one's own discretion.
optionally, *ad. op*-shon-al-le, at one's own choice.
optogram, *n. op*-to-gram, the faint visual image temporarily retained on the retina after death.
optography, *n.* op-*tog*-ra-fe, the chemical fixation of an optogram.
optometer, *n.* op-*tom*-e-ter, an instrument for measuring the limits of distinct vision, used in testing the sight for glasses. (Gr. *optomai*, see, *metron*, measure.)
optometry, *n.* op-*tom*-e-tre, the use of the optometer; the measurement of the range of vision.
optophone, *n. op*-to-fone, an instrument which, by means of the selenium cell, transmutes light into sound, making it possible for the blind to "read" print. (Gr. *optos*, seen, *phone*, voice.)
opulence, *n. op*-yew-lence, wealth; riches. (Fr.)
opulent, *a. op*-yew-lent, wealthy; affluent. (Fr.)
opulently, *ad. op*-yew-lent-le, richly.
Opuntia, *n.* o-*pun*-she-a, a large genus of cactaceous plants including the prickly pear. (L. *Opus*, a town in Locris.)
opus, *n. oh*-pus, a work; a musical composition generally denoted in the series of a composer's works by a number. **magnum opus,** the supreme achievement of a life-work, esp. a great literary work. (L.)
opuscule, *n.* o-*pus*-kewl, a minor musical or literary work. (Fr.)
opusculum, *n.* o-*pus*-kew-lum, an opuscule. (L.)
★**or,** *conj.* awr, a connective marking an alternative, connecting synonyms, or introducing an explanation, etc. (A.S. *other.*)
or, *prep.* and *conj.*, awr, ere, before, esp. [Poet.] in *or ever, or e'er.* (A.S. *œr*, before.)
or, *n.* awr, gold or yellow [Her.]. (Fr.)
-or, awr, a suffix denoting agency, as in actor, creditor, doctor, sailor.
orache, *n. aw*-ratch, the mountain spinach, *Atriplex hortensis*, formerly used in cookery. (Fr. *arroche.*)
oracle, *n. o*-ra-kl, the answer of a god, or his priest, to an enquiry on some matter of moment; the deity who gave the response; the place where it was given; the most holy place in the Jewish Temple; a person reputedly wise; a wise sentence or divine communication. **to work the oracle,** to gain one's end (esp. funds) by craft. (Fr.)
oracular, *a.* o-*rak*-yew-lar, uttering oracles; like an oracle; authoritative; sententious; ambiguous. (Late L. *oracularis.*)

oracularity, *n.* o-*rak*-yew-*la*-re-te, the quality of being oracular.
oracularly, *ad.* in the manner of an oracle.
oracularness, *n.* o-*rak*-yew-lar-ness, oracularity.
oral, *a.* *aw*-ral, pertaining to the mouth; by word of mouth; spoken not written. (L. *os, oris,* the mouth.)
orally, *ad.* *aw*-ra-le, by word of mouth; by the mouth.
orang, *n.* aw-*rang,* the orang-outang.
Orange, *a.* *o*-ranj, of or relating to the Society of Orangemen, a Protestant Royalist party founded in Ulster in 1795, and so named after William of Orange.
★**orange,** *n.* *o*-ranj, the fruit of *Citrus aurantium*; the yellow-red colour of this: *a.* of orange colour. **orange moth,** the geometer moth, *Angerona prunaria.* (O.Fr. *orenge,* from Per. *narang,* orange.)
orangeade, *n.* o-ranj-*ade,* a drink made of, or in resemblance of, orange juice.
orange-bat, *n.* the Australian horseshoe bat, *Rhinonycteris aurantius,* the fur of the male being of an orange hue.
orange-blossom, *n.* the flower of the orange tree (worn esp. by brides), also of the syringa or mock-orange.
Orangeism, *n.* *o*-ranj-izm, the principles, practices, or tenets of the Orangemen; adherence to these.
orange-lily, *n.* a lily with orange flowers.
Orangeman, *n.* *o*-ranj-man, a member of the Society of Orangemen. (*see* **Orange**).
orange-peel, *n.* the rind of an orange.
orangery, *n.* *o*-ranj-re, an orange garden or a house for orange trees.
orange-tawny, *a.* of a colour between yellow and brown.
orange-tip, *n.* the butterfly, *Euchloe cardamines.*
orangey, *a.* *o*-ranj-e, of the taste or colour of an orange.
Orangism, *n.* *o*-ranj-izm, Orangeism.
orangite, *n.* *o*-ranj-ite, a yellow variety of thorite.
orang-outang, *n.* aw-*rang*-oo-*tang,* the large arboreal anthropoid ape, *Simia satyrus,* of Borneo and Sumatra (Malay, *oran,* man, *utan,* wild.)
orarium, *n.* o-*rare*-re-um, a deacon's stole, esp. in the Eastern Church. (L., a napkin or handkerchief.)
orate, *v.i.* aw-*rate,* to harangue (jocular). (L. *oro,* to speak, from *os, oris,* mouth.)
oration, *n.* aw-*ray*-shon, an elaborate speech; a formal discourse on a special occasion. (Fr.)
orator, *n.* *o*-ra-tor, one who makes orations; an eloquent speaker. **Public Orator,** the official of a university who, at a public graduation, pronounces the merits of those receiving academic honours. (Fr. *orateur.*)
oratorial, *a.* o-ra-*taw*-re-al, oratorical; referring to an oratorio.
oratorian, *a.* o-ra-*taw*-re-an, relating to the clergy of an oratory: *n.* (*cap.*) a member of an oratory, esp. that founded by St. Philip Neri in 1564.
oratorical, *a.* *o*-ra-*to*-re-kal, pertaining to an orator or oratory; rhetorical; becoming to an orator.
oratorically, *ad.* in an oratorical manner.
oratorio, *n.* *o*-ra-*taw*-re-oh, a vocal and instrumental semi-dramatic musical composition, usually based on a scriptural theme and presented without stage-setting or costumes. (It.)
oratory, *n.* *o*-ra-to-re, the art of speaking persuasively; eloquence or its exercise; a small chapel, usually for private devotion. **Congregation of the Oratory,** one of a number of religious orders the members of which live in community but without vows, and pursue theological and other sacred studies. (L. *oratoria.*)
oratress, *n.* *o*-ra-tress, a female orator.
orb, *n.* awrb, a globe; a circle; an orbit; a heavenly body; the eye; the golden cross-crowned sphere of the regalia: *v.t.* to form into a circle; to surround (Fr. *orbe.*)
orbed, *a.* awrbd, round; orbicular.
orbicular, *a.* awr-*bik*-yew-lar, in the form of an orb; flat with a circular outline [Bot.]. (Late L. *orbicularis.*)
orbicularly, *ad.* awr-*bik*-yew-lar-le, spherically.
orbicularness, *n.* awr-*bik*-yew-lar-ness, sphericity.
orbiculate, *a.* awr-*bik*-yew-lat, orbicular.
orbiculation, *n.* awr-*bik*-yew-*lay*-shon, orbicular formation.
orbit, *n.* *awr*-bit, the path of a heavenly body in its periodic revolution [Astron.]; the bony cavity of the eye [Anat.]; a sphere of action [Fig.]. (Fr. *orbite,* from L. *orbita,* a circuit.)
orbital, *a.* *awr*-be-tal, pertaining to an orbit.
orc, *n.* awrk, a voracious species of dolphin, *Orca gladiator,* the killer whale. (L. *orca.*)
Orcadian, *a.* awr-*kay*-de-an, belonging to Orkney: *n.* a native of Orkney. (L. *Orcades,* the Orkneys.)
orcanet, *n.* *awr*-ka-net, the plant alkanet. (Fr.)
orcein, *n.* *awr*-se-in, a reddish-purple nitrogenous colouring matter obtained from orcin.
orchard, *n.* *awr*-chard, an enclosure, or a plantation, of fruit trees. **orchard house,** a green-house for the cultivation of fruit trees. (A.S. *orceard.*)
orcharding, *n.* *awr*-chard-ing, the cultivation of orchards; the occupation of an orchardist.
orchardist, *n.* *awr*-chard-ist, a cultivator of orchards.
orchectomy, *n.* awr-*kek*-to-me, the excision of a testicle [Surg.]. (Gr. *orchis,* testicle, *tomsen,* to cut.)
orchesis, *n.* awr-*kee*-sis, the art of dancing, esp. in the ancient Grecian style. (Gr.)
orchestic, *a.* awr-*kes*-tik, relating to dancing: *n.pl.* the art of dancing; orchesis.
orchestra, *n.* *awr*-kes-tra, the part of a theatre or other public place appropriated to the musicians; a company of instrumentalists. **orchestra stalls,** the front rows of stalls in a theatre. (L.)
orchestral, *a.* awr-*kes*-tral, pertaining to an orchestra; suitable for or performed in an orchestra.
orchestrate, *v.t.* *awr*-kes-trate, to arrange or compose a piece for performance by an orchestra.
orchestration, *n.* awr-kes-*tray*-shon, the art of orchestrating; instrumentation.
orchestrina, *n.* awr-kes-*tree*-na, an orchestrion.
orchestrion, *n.* awr-*kes*-tre-on, any mechanical device, esp. an elaborated barrel-organ, imitating an orchestra.
orchialgia, awr-ke-*al*-je-a, pain in the testicles [Path.].
orchid, *n.* *awr*-kid, any member of the Orchidaceæ, a large family of flowering monocotyledonous plants, terrestrial and epiphytic. (Gr. *orchis,* a testicle.)
orchidaceous, *a.* awr-ke-*day*-shus, pertaining to the Orchidaceæ or to the Orchis.
orchideous, *a.* awr-*kid*-e-us, orchidaceous.
orchidist, *n.* *awr*-ke-dist, an expert in, cultivator of, or collector of, orchids.
orchidomania, *n.* *awr*-ke-do-*may*-ne-a, a craze for, or excessive admiration of, orchids.
orchil, *n.* *awr*-kil, a red-violet, purple, or blue dyestuff made from archil; the lichen, a species of *Rocella,* yielding this. (O.Fr.)
Orchis, *n.* *awr*-kis, a large genus of terrestrial orchidaceous plants, many of which have fragrant and beautiful flowers. (Gr., a testicle, from the shape of the tuber.)
orchitis, *n.* awr-*ky*-tis, inflammation of a testicle.
orchotomy, *n.* awr-*kot*-o-me, incision or removal of a testicle; orchectomy; castration. (Gr. *orchis,* and *tomein,* to cut.)
orcin, *n.* *awr*-sin, a crystallizable colouring matter and antiseptic phenol obtained from orchil or the lichen *Rocella.*
ordain, *v.t.* awr-*dane,* to appoint; to decree; to institute. (O.Fr. *ordonner.*)
ordainer, *n.* awr-*dane*-er, one who ordains.
ordainment, *n.* awr-*dane*-ment, act or fact of ordaining; institution; a divine ordinance.
ordeal, *n.* awr-*dee*-al, an ancient form of trial to determine guilt or innocence, as by fire, water, or battle; a severe testing trial. **ordeal bean,** the Calabar bean, *Physostigma venenosum.* **ordeal tree,** the red-water tree of Sierra Leone, *Erythrophleum guineense.* (A.S. *ordel.*)
★**order,** *n.* *awr*-der, regular or methodical arrangement; proper state; adherence to rule laid down; settled mode of proceeding or working; regularity; mandate; a command; a direction to do certain work, supply certain goods, etc.; that which is ordered; a regulation; rank; class; division of men; a religious fraternity; a society of knights, also, its badge; a division intermediate between a class and a family [Bot. and Zool.]; the position of order arms [Mil.]; a system of several members, ornaments, and proportions of columns and pilasters, as the Tuscan, Doric, Ionic, Corinthian, and Compo-

site [Arch.]: *v.t.* to regulate; to methodize; to conduct; to command; to manage: *v.i.* to give command. **holy orders,** the different grades of the priesthood of an episcopal church; the Christian ministry. **order arms!** a command to soldiers to stand at attention with their arms in a certain position. **Order in Council,** an order made by the King on the advice (through the Privy Council) of a minister of the crown. **order of battle,** the arrangement and disposition for action of the different parts of any armed force. **order of the day,** prearranged order of business. **order paper,** the printed schedule of questions, business, etc., to be dealt with during the sitting [Parliament]. **regimental orders,** such orders as proceed immediately from a commanding officer for the observance of the regiment. **take orders,** to be ordained [Eccles.]. (Fr. *ordre.*)

orderer, *n.* *awr*-der-er, one who gives an order.

ordering, *n.* *awr*-der-ing, disposition; distribution.

orderless, *a.* *awr*-der-less, without regularity or method; disordered.

orderliness, *n.* *awr*-der-le-ness, regularity; the condition of being orderly.

orderly, *a.* *awr*-der-le, methodical; regular; in good order; not unruly; pertaining to orders [Mil.]: *n.* a soldier who attends an officer and transmits his orders, etc.; a hospital attendant; a street-cleaner: *ad.* according to due order. **orderly book,** a book for general and regimental orders. **orderly officer,** the officer on duty for the day. **orderly room,** the room in which the administrative work of a regiment, etc., is conducted [Mil.].

ordinal, *a.* *awr*-din-al, denoting order: *n.* a number denoting order; the formulæ of ordination [Eccles.]. (L. *ordinalis,* in order.)

ordinance, *n.* *awr*-din-ance, a rule established by authority; established rite or ceremony. (O.Fr.)

ordinand, *n.* *awr*-din-and, a candidate for ordination.

ordinant, *a.* *awr*-din-ant, ordaining; directing: *n.* a prelate conferring orders.

ordinarily, *ad.* *awr*-din-a-re-le, according to established rules; usually.

ordinariness, *n.* the state of being ordinary.

ordinary, *a.* *awr*-din-a-re, according to established order; common; customary; of common rank; inferior; plain; of little merit: *n.* an ecclesiastical judge; a dinner served to all at a fixed price; an eating-house; a large-wheeled bicycle anterior to the safety; a portion of the escutcheon comprised between straight or other lines, as a bend, chevron, pale, etc. [Her.] **ordinary seaman,** one not yet qualified as an able-bodied seaman. **Lords Ordinary,** the five judges of the Outer House of the Scottish Court of Session. (Fr. *ordinaire.*)

ordinaryship, *n.* *awr*-din-a-re-ship, an ordinary's office or personality [Eccles.].

ordinate, *a.* *awr*-de-nat, methodical; orderly: *n.* a straight line from any point drawn parallel to one co-ordinate axis and meeting the others [Math.]. (L. *ordinatus,* set in order.)

ordination, *n.* awr-de-*nay*-shon, the state of being ordained or appointed; the act of conferring holy orders. (Fr.)

ordinee, *n.* awr-de-*nee,* a newly ordained clergyman.

ordnance, *n.* *awrd*-nance, artillery generally, including cannon, mortars, howitzers, etc. **ordnance datum,** *see* **datum. ordnance map,** a map made by the Ordnance Survey. **Ordnance Survey,** the British government survey of the land, originally under the War Office now a department of the Ministry of Agriculture. (O.Fr.)

Ordovician, *a.* *awr*-do-*vish*-an, pertaining to the period between the Cambrian and the Silurian: *n.* the system of rocks laid down in this period [Geol.]. (L. *Ordovices,* the Roman name for the Welsh.)

ordure, *n.* *awr*-dewr, dung; excrement. (Fr.)

ore, *n.* awr, metal in its natural state combined with some other substance; metal. (A.S. *ora.*)

öre, *n.* (App.) a bronze coin of the Scandinavian countries, one-hundredth of a krone.

oread, *n.* *aw*-re-ad, a mountain nymph. (Gr. *oros,* a mountain.)

orectic, *a.* o-*rek*-tik, pertaining to or stimulating desire; appetitive. (Gr. *orexis.*)

orexis, *n.* o-*rek*-sis, desire [Med.]. (Gr.)

orfe, *n.* orf, a large variety of goldfish. (Ger.)

orfèvrerie, *n.* or-*fay*-vre-re, goldsmith's work; gold and silver plate. (Fr.)

organ, *n.* *awr*-gan, any part of an animal or vegetable body performing some special function; a party newspaper, trade journal, or house organ; a means or medium by or through which some end is attained; the largest of keyboard wind instruments, of general use in cathedral and church services; a mechanically similar instrument used in cinemas; a barrel-organ. **American organ,** a reed instrument resembling the harmonium. **organ loft,** the gallery in which a church or other organ is placed. **organ screen,** an ornamental partition or framework supporting a church organ. (Fr. *organe,* from Gr. *organon,* an implement.)

organ-builder, *n.* one whose occupation is to construct church or cinema organs.

organdie, *n.* *awr*-gan-de, a light muslin fabric with figured patterns. (Fr. *organdi,* book-muslin.)

organelle, *n.* awr-ga-*nel,* any protozoan cell or part performing a special function [Biol.].

organ-grinder, *n.* one who works the handle of a barrel-organ.

organic, *a.* awr-*gan*-ik, pertaining to, of the nature of, or containing organs or organisms; affecting an organ or organs (of disease) [Med.]; pertaining to what has organs, or functional parts; organized; systematic; fundamental; vital. **organic bodies,** such as possess organs with separate functions. **organic chemistry,** *see* **chemistry. organic remains,** the remains of animals or plants. (L. *organicus.*)

organically, *ad.* awr-*gan*-e-ka-le, in an organic manner; with or by means of organs.

organism, *n.* *awr*-ga-nizm, that which lives or has lived; that which has organic structure; a plant or an animal; a whole having related parts comparable with those of a living body.

organist, *n.* *awr*-ga-nist, a player on the organ.

organity, *n.* awr-*gan*-e-te, an organized whole.

organizable, *a.* *awr*-ga-*ny*-za-bl, that may be organized.

★**organization,** *n.* *awr*-ga-ny-*zay*-shon, the act of organizing; state of being organized; an organized business, institution, society, etc.

organizational, *a.* *awr*-ga-ny-*zay*-shon-al, pertaining to organization or an organization.

organize, *v.t.* *awr*-ga-nize, to form or supply with organs; to render organic; to make into an organism; to arrange parts so that the whole shall act as one body; to arrange a scheme of routine; to sing in parts [Mus.].

organizer, *n.* *awr*-ga-ny-zer, one who organizes.

organogeny, *n.* awr-ga-*noj*-e-ne, the development of the organs of living things. (Gr. *organon,* and *gennao,* produce.)

organographical, *a.* awr-gan-o-*graf*-e-kal, pertaining to organography.

organography, *n.* awr-ga-*nog*-ra-fe, a description of the organs of plants or animals.

organology, *n.* awr-ga-*nol*-o-je, the science of organs; the branch of physiology treating of the organs of animals; splanchnology [Med.].

organon, *n.* *awr*-ga-non, a prescribed method of philosophic or scientific inquiry. (Gr., an implement.)

organonomy, *n.* awr-ga-*non*-o-me, the science or study of the laws controlling organic life.

organopathy, *n.* awr-ga-*nop*-a-the, the diseases of an organ; the local action of drugs.

organoplastic, *a.* *awr*-ga-no-*plas*-tik, able to form, or formative of, organic tissue.

organoplasty, *n.* *awr*-ga-no-*plas*-te, the formation or development of the organs. (Gr. *organon,* and *plassein,* to mould.)

organotherapy, *n.* *awr*-ga-no-*the*-ra-pe, the treatment of disease by the administration of animal organs or their extracts [Med.].

organzine, *n.* *awr*-gan-zeen, thrown silk, or a fabric made of this. (Fr. *organsin.*)

orgasm, *n.* *awr*-gazm, immoderate excitement or action, esp. the crisis of venereal excitement. (Gr. *orgasmos.*)

orgeat, *n.* *awr*-zhah, a drink made of barley and sweet almonds. (Fr.)

orgiastic, *a.* awr-je-*as*-tik, pertaining to the Bacchanalian or other orgies. (Gr. *orgiastikos.*)

orgulous, *a.* *awr*-gew-lus, proud; over-bearing. (O.Fr. *orguillous.*)

orgy, *n.* *awr*-je (*pl.* **orgies**), a festival or revels in honour of Bacchus; nocturnal revels; drunken revelry. (Gr. *orgia.*)
orichalc, *n.* *aw*-re-kalk, brass, or some other yellow metal resembling gold. (Gr. *oros,* mountain, *chalkos,* copper.)
oriel, *n.* *aw*-re-el, a large projecting angular window divided by mullions and transoms into different bays; a bay-window. (O.Fr. *oriol.*)
oriency, *n.* *aw*-re-en-se, brightness or strength of colour; orient quality.
orient, *a.* *aw*-re-ent, rising, as the sun; eastern; bright; shining: *n.* the east; between north-east and south-east; a pearl or gem of the highest quality: *v.t.* to orientate. **the Orient,** the lands of the East, esp. those countries to the east of the Mediterranean. (O.Fr., from L. *oriens,* rising.)
oriental, *a.* aw-re-*en*-tal, eastern; situated in, or proceeding from, the east; precious: *n.* (*cap.*) a native of the East; an Asiatic. (Fr.)
orientalism, *n.* aw-re-*en*-ta-lizm, the doctrines of an idiom of the East; acquaintance with oriental literature.
orientalist, *n.* aw-re-*en*-ta-list, one versed in eastern languages, literature, customs, etc.
orientality, *n.* aw-re-en-*tal*-e-te, the state of being oriental.
orientalize, *v.t.* aw-re-*en*-ta-lize, to render oriental.
orientate, *v.t.* and *i.* *aw*-re-en-tate, to turn to, or perform rite facing, the east [Eccles.]; to ascertain or adjust a position primarily with reference to the east; to determine geographical position.
orientation, *n.* aw-re-en-*tay*-shon, eastward position or attitude [Eccles.]; the act of orientating; determination of the compass point; alignment. (Fr.)
orifice, *n.* *o*-re-fis, an aperture; an opening or mouth, as of a tube, etc. (Fr.)
orificial, *a.* o-re-*fish*-al, pertaining to an orifice.
oriflamme, *n.* *o*-re-flam, a battle standard, originally the sacred banner of the abbey of St. Denis, France; hence, any high aim or purpose, a rallying-point. (Fr.).
origan, *n.* *o*-re-gan, wild marjoram, or other herb of the genus *Origanum.* (Fr.)
origin, *n.* *o*-re-jin, the beginning of anything; the source. (Fr. *origine.*)
original, *a.* o-*rij*-e-nal, pertaining to an origin; first in order; primitive; creative; originating; having power to originate; not copied: *n.* origin; that from which anything is copied; archetype; the exact language in which a work was written; an eccentric individual [Coll.]. **original bid,** the first bid made after the deal (Bridge, etc.). **original sin,** the first sin, by which sin was introduced into the world; the natural depravity of man consequential upon this [Theol.]. (Fr.)
originality, *n.* o-rij-e-*nal*-e-te, the state or quality of being original; creativeness.
originally, *ad.* o-*rij*-e-na-le, primarily.
originate, *v.t.* o-*rij*-e-nate, to bring into existence: *v.i.* to have origin; to be derived.
origination, *n.* o-rij-e-*nay*-shon, first production; process or mode of production; invention.
originative, *a.* o-*rij*-e-na-tiv, having power to originate.
originator, *n.* or-*rij*-e-nay-tor, one who originates.
orinasal, *a.* *awr*-e-*nay*-zal, sounded with mouth and nose: *n.* a vowel so sounded.
oriole, *n.* *aw*-re-ole, an Old World passerine bird of the genus *Oriolus,* allied to the shrikes and wagtails; in America, the hangbird. (O.Fr. *oriol.*)
Orion, *n.* o-*ry*-on, one of the chief constellations on the celestial equator, but south of the ecliptic. (Name of a giant hunter of Greek myth.)
orismology *n.* aw-riz-*mol*-o-je, scientific terminology; the study or definition of scientific terms. (Gr. *horismos,* restriction, *logos,* science.)
orison, *n.* *o*-re-zon, a prayer of supplication. (O.Fr.)
orle, *n.* awrl, a narrow bordure not touching the edge of the shield [Her.]; the wreath supporting a crest [Her.]. (O.Fr.)
orleans, *n.* *awr*-le-anz, a cloth of mixed wool and cotton originally made in Orleans; a variety of plum.
orlop, *n.* *awr*-lop, the lowest deck of a ship. (Dut. *over,* and *loopen,* run.)
ormer, *n.* *awr*-mer, the sea-ear, *Haliotis tuberculata.*
ormolu, *n.* *awr*-mo-loo, gilded bronze or brass; mosaic gold; a composition to imitate gold; articles of this. (Fr. *or moulu,* ground gold.)
Ormuzd, *n.* *awr*-muzd, the Zoroastrian impersonation of light or the good principle, in opposition to Ahriman. (Per.)
***ornament,** *n.* *awr*-na-ment, that which adorns: decoration; embellishment; that which confers lustre or credit: *v.t.* to adorn or beautify. (Fr. *ornement.*)
ornamental, *a.* awr-na-*men*-tal, decorative; serving to decorate.
ornamentally, *ad.* awr-na-*men*-ta-le, in ornamental fashion.
ornamentation, *n.* awr-na-men-*tay*-shon, that which ornaments; decoration; use of ornament.
ornate, *a.* awr-*nate,* elaborately adorned; flamboyant, highly embellished (of literary style). (L. *ornatus,* adorned.)
ornately, *ad.* in an ornate manner or style.
ornateness, *n.* the state or quality of being ornate.
ornery, *a.* *awr*-ner-e, mean; low. (Amer. slang, abbrev. of *ordinary.*)
ornithic, *a.* awr-*nith*-ik, pertaining to or characteristic of birds. (Gr. *ornis,* bird.)
ornithichnite, *n.* awr-ne-*thik*-nite, the fossilized print of a birdlike footmark. (Gr. *ornis,* bird, *ichnos,* track.)
ornithocopros, *n.* *awr*-ne-tho-*kop*-ros, bird's dung; guano. (Gr. *ornis,* and *kopros,* dung.)
ornithoid, *a.* *awr*-ne-thoyd, birdlike.
ornitholite, *n.* awr-*nith*-o-lite, the fossil remains of a bird. (Gr. *ornis,* and *lithos,* a stone.)
ornithological, *a.* *awr*-ne-tho-*loj*-e-kal, pertaining to ornithology.
ornithologist, *n.* awr-ne-*thol*-o-jist, one skilled in ornithology.
ornithology, *n.* awr-ne-*thol*-o-je, the branch of zoology treating of birds. (Gr. *ornis,* and *logos,* science.)
ornithomancy, *n.* awr-*nith*-o-man-se, divination from the movements or flight of birds. (Gr. *ornis,* and *manteia,* divination.)
ornithopter, *n.* awr-ne-*thop*-ter, an aeroplane intended to be propelled by flapping wings.
ornithorhynchus, *n.* awr-ne-tho-*ring*-kus, the duckbill or platypus, an Australian egg-laying mammal. (Gr. *ornis,* and *rhynchos,* a snout.)
ornithoscopy, *n.* awr-ne-*thos*-ko-pe, ornithomancy; observation of the habits of birds. (Gr. *ornis,* and *skopeo,* view.)
orographic, *a.* aw-ro-*graf*-ik, pertaining to orography. **orographic rain,** rain due to the impinging upon mountain slopes of winds carrying moisture.
orography, *n.* aw-*rog*-ra-fe, the branch of physical geography treating of mountains and mountain systems. (Gr. *oros,* a mountain, *grapho,* write.)
oroide, *n.* *o*-ro-id, an alloy of tin, copper, and other metals used in cheap jewellery. (Fr. *or,* gold, Gr. *eidos,* like.)
orological, *a.* aw-ro-*loj*-e-kal, pertaining to orology.
orologist, *n.* aw-*rol*-o-jist, a student of orology.
orology, *n.* aw-*rol*-o-je, orography; a treatise on mountains. (Gr. *oros,* and *logos,* word.)
orotund, *a.* *o*-ro-tund, with a full, clear voice; pompous; magniloquent. (L. *os, oris,* the mouth, *rotundus,* round.)
orotundity, *n.* o-ro-*tun*-de-te, the quality of being orotund.
orphan, *n.* *awr*-fan, a child bereaved of both parents or (more rarely) of one only: *a.* being so bereft: *v.t.* to make an orphan of. (Gr. *orphanos,* bereft.)
orphanage, *n.* *awr*-fan-aj, state of an orphan; a home or institution for orphans.
orphaned, *a.* *awr*-fand, left an orphan.
orphanhood, *n.* *awr*-fan-hood, the state of being an orphan.
Orphean, *a.* awr-*fee*-an, pertaining to Orpheus, a mythical musician of Thrace; melodious, enchanting, like the strains of Orpheus.
Orphic, *a.* *awr*-fik, orphean; mystic; oracular.
orphrey, *n.* *awr*-fray, a gold or richly embroidered border on an ecclesiastical vestment. (O.Fr.)
orpiment, *n.* *awr*-pe-ment, a native yellow sulphide of arsenic, used as a pigment and in dyeing. (Fr.)
orpine, *n.* *awr*-pin, the succulent herbaceous plant *Sedum telephium,* named from its colour. (Fr.)

Orpington, *n.* *awr*-ping-ton, a breed of domestic fowl. (Name of town in Kent.)
orrery, *n.* *o*-re-re, a working model demonstrating the motions of the bodies in the solar system; a planetarium. (The Earl of *Orrery*, *d.* 1731, for whom one was made.)
orris, *n.* *o*-ris, *Iris florentina*; its dried rhizome, used in perfumery. (Probably O. Ital. *ireos.*)
orris, *n.* *o*-ris, gold or silver lace. (Perhaps O.F. *orphreis*, orphrey.)
ort, *n.* awrt, a fragment: *pl.* refuse. (A.S.)
orthite, *n.* *awr*-thite, a variety of allanite. (Gr. *orthos*, straight.)
ortho-, *comb.f.* *awr*-tho, correct, regular, normal. (Gr. *orthos*, right, straight.)
orthochromatic, *a.* *awr*-tho-kro-*mat*-ik, giving true colour values, esp. in lights and shades. (Gr. *orthos*, and *chroma*, colour.)
orthoclase, *n.* *awr*-tho-klayz, the common monoclinic potash felspar. (Gr. *orthos*, and *klasis*, breaking.)
orthoclastic, *a.* awr-tho-*klas*-tik, cleaving in directions at right angles to each other [Cryst.].
orthodiagonal, *n.* *awr*-tho-dy-*ag*-o-nal, the inclined lateral axis in the monoclinic system of crystallization.
orthodox, *a.* *awr*-tho-doks, holding the accepted faith, belief, or doctrine; according to the accepted belief or doctrine; not heterodox; conforming to a norm; conventional. **the Orthodox Church,** the Eastern or Greek Church, which seceded from Rome in the 11th cent. (Late L. *orthodoxus.*)
orthodoxly, *ad.* consistent with orthodoxy.
orthodoxness, *n.* the state or quality of being orthodox.
orthodoxy, *n.* *awr*-tho-dok-se, accepted belief or doctrine; consonance with accepted belief or doctrine; that which is orthodox.
orthodromic, *a.* awr-tho-*drom*-ik, pertaining to orthodromy: *n.pl.* orthodromy.
orthodromy, *n.* awr-*thod*-ro-me, the art or act of sailing in a direct course, *i.e.*, on the arc of a great circle. (Gr. *orthos*, and *dromos*, running.)
orthoepic, *a.* awr-tho-*ep*-ik, pertaining to orthoepy.
orthoepist, *n.* awr-tho-*ee*-pist *or* awr-*thoh*-e-pist, one skilled in orthoepy.
orthoepy, *n.* *awr*-tho-ee-pe *or* awr-*thoh*-e-pe, the branch of grammar treating of correct pronunciation. (Gr. *orthoepeia.*)
orthogenesis, *n.* *awr*-tho-jen-e-sis, the theory that biological variations are determined by environment, and are therefore defined, not fortuitous. (Gr. *orthos*, straight, and *genesis.*)
orthogenetic, *a.* *awr*-tho-je-*net*-ik, characterized by or pertaining to orthogenesis.
orthognathous, *a.* awr-*thog*-na-thus, straight-jawed; having a vertical face profile.
orthogon, *n.* *awr*-tho-gon, a rectangular figure. (L. *orthogonius.*)
orthogonal, *a.* awr-*thog*-o-nal, right-angled.
orthographer, *n.* awr-*thog*-ra-fer, one skilled in orthography.
orthographic, *a.* awr-tho-*graf*-ik, pertaining to orthography.
orthographically, *ad.* awr-tho-*graf*-e-ka-le, in orthographic style.
orthographist, *n.* awr-*thog*-ra-fist, an orthographer.
orthography, *n.* awr-*thog*-ra-fe, correct spelling; the art of drawing of elevations, etc., in true projection. (Fr. *orthographie.*)
orthological, *a.* awr-tho-*loj*-e-kal, pertaining to or in accordance with orthology.
orthology, *n.* awr-*thol*-o-je, the art of speaking, or of using words, correctly.
orthometry, *n.* awr-*thom*-e-tre, the laws of correct versification. (Gr. *orthos*, and *metron*, measure.)
orthopædic, *a.* awr-tho-*pee*-dik, pertaining to the prevention or correction of physical deformities, esp. in children.
orthopædist, *n.* awr-tho-*pee*-dist, a specialist in the cure of deformities [Med.].
orthopædy, *n.* awr-tho-*pee*-de, the art of curing physical deformities, esp. those of children. (Gr. *orthos*, and *pais*, a child.)
orthopnœa, *n.* awr-thop-*nee*-a, difficulty of breathing, such that the patient has to sit erect. (L.)
orthopraxy, *n.* *awr*-tho-*prak*-se, right or orthodox action or acts; orthopædic surgery [Med.].
orthopter, *n.* awr-*thop*-ter, any one of the Orthoptera; an ornithopter.
Orthoptera, *n.pl.* awr-*thop*-te-ra, order of insects comprising those with straight wings (grasshoppers, crickets, etc.). (Gr. *orthopteros*, straight-winged.)
orthopterous, *a.* awr-*thop*-te rus, belonging to the Orthoptera; straight-winged.
orthoptic, *a.* awr-*thop*-tik, pertaining to correct vision [Opt.]; relating to tangents that intersect at right angles [Math.]: *n.* a perforated disc used in taking aim in rifle-shooting.
orthorhombic, *n.* *awr*-tho-*rom*-bik, pertaining to forms having three unlike axes at right angles [Cryst.].
orthoscopic, *a.* awr-tho-*skop*-ik, having, or giving, correct vision; seeing correctly.
orthostyle, *a.* *awr*-tho-stile, having columns arranged in a straight line [Arch.]. (Gr. *orthos*. straight, *stylos*, a column.)
orthotomic, *n.* awr-tho-*tom*-ik, intersecting or cutting at right angles [Geom].
orthotropal, *a.* awr-*thot*-ro-pal, orthotropous [Bot.]. (Gr. *orthos*, and *tropos*, turning.)
orthotropism, *n.* awr-*thot*-ro-pizm, the tendency to grow in a vertical direction [Bot.].
orthotropous, *a.* awr-*thot*-ro-pus, growing straight, esp. of ovules and embryonic radicles [Bot.].
orthotypous, *a.* awr-*thot*-e-pus, having a perpendicular cleavage [Min.]. (Gr. *orthos*, and *typto*, strike.)
ortolan, *n.* *awr*-to-lan, the garden bunting, *Emberiza hortulanus*. (Fr., from L. *hortulanus*, gardener.)
-ory, o-re, a suffix used to form nouns denoting place or instrument, as *oratory*, *lavatory*, *factory*; used also to form adjectives, as *accusatory*, *illusory*.
Oryx, *n.* *or*-riks, a genus of straight-horned African antelopes including the gemsbok and beisa. (L.)
os, *n.* os, a bone [Anat.]. (L.)
Oscan, *n.* *os*-kan, a member of a pre-Latin race in Italy; their language: *a.* pertaining to this race or language. (L. *Osci.*)
oscheal, *a.* *os*-ke-al, pertaining to the scrotum.
oscheocele, *n.* *os*-ke-o-seel, scrotal hernia. (Gr. *oschon*, the scrotum, *kele*, a tumour.)
oschitis, *n.* os-*ky*-tis, inflammation of the scrotum.
oscillate, *v.i.* *os*-e-late, to swing; to vibrate; to move up and down or backwards and forwards; to vacillate. (L. *oscillatus*, swung.)
oscillation, *n.* os-e-*lay*-shon, vibration; fluctuation; vibration caused in wireless receiving apparatus by excessive reaction [Wire.].
oscillator, *n.* *os*-e-lay-tor, an instrument or part that oscillates; a device for producing oscillation [esp. Elect.].
oscillatory, *a.* *os*-e-la-to-re, oscillating.
oscillograph, *n.* *os*-e-lo-graf, a device by which the oscillations in an electric current can be graphically recorded.
oscine, *a.* *os*-sine, relating to the *Oscines*, or singing birds: *n.* any one of these. (L.)
oscitancy, *n.* *os*-e-tan-se, the act of yawning; sluggishness.
oscitant, *a.* *os*-e-tant, yawning; drowsy; dull. (L. *oscitans.*)
oscitantly, *ad.* in an oscitant manner.
oscitate, *v.i.* *os*-e-tate, to yawn. (L. *oscitatus.*)
oscitation, *n.* os-e-*tay*-shon, the act of yawning.
osculant, *a.* *os*-kew-lant, kissing; closely approximating; closely adhering. (L. *osculans*, kissing.)
oscular, *a.* *os*-kew-lar, of or relating to the mouth, or hence, to kissing.
osculate, *v.t.* and *i.* *os*-kew-late, to kiss; to touch by osculation [Geom.]. (L. *osculatus.*)
osculation, *n.* *os*-kew-*lay*-shon, the act of kissing; a kiss; the contact between any given curve and its osculatory circle [Geom.]; inosculation, anastomosis [Anat.].
osculatory, *a.* *os*-kew-la-to-re, relating to osculation or to kissing; touching: *n.* a tablet or board bearing an image or symbol of Christ or the Virgin, first kissed by the priest at the Eucharist and then by the people [Eccles.]. **osculatory circle,** a circle having the same curvature with any curve at any given point [Geom.].
oscule, *n.* *os*-kewl, a small bilabiate aperture [Zool.]. (L. *osculum*, kiss.)
-ose, ohs, a suffix used to form adjectives denoting

fullness, abundance, as *grandiose, bellicose.* (L. *-osus.*)

osier, *n. oh*-zheer, the willow, *Salix viminalis,* whose twigs are used for making baskets: *a.* of osier. **osier holt,** a place where willows are cultivated. (Fr.)

osiered, *a. oh*-zheerd, covered with osiers.

-osis, *oh*-sis, suffix indicating state or condition, esp. [Path.] a diseased or abnormal condition. (Gr.)

-osity, *os*-e-te, suffix forming nouns from adjectives in *-ose* and *-ous,* as *jocosity, porosity.*

Osmanli, *a.* oz-*man*-le, relating to the Turks: *n.* a member of the Turkish race. (Turk.)

osmazome, *n. oz*-ma-zome, former name of a substance supposed to be present in muscular fibre to which its taste and smell, when cooked, was due. (Gr. *osme,* smell, *zomos,* gravy.)

osmic, *a. oz*-mik, of or relating to osmium in its higher valency.

osmious, *a. oz*-me-us, relating to osmium in its lower valency.

osmiridium, *n.* oz-mer-*rid*-e-um, iridosmine.

osmium, *n. oz*-me-um, a bluish-grey metallic element of the platinum group, the heaviest substance known, with a specific gravity nearly twice that of lead. (Gr. *osme,* a smell.)

osmology, *n.* oz-*mol*-o-je, the science of odours and the sense of smell; a treatise on odours. (Gr. *osme,* a smell.)

osmometer, *n.* oz-*mom*-e-ter, an instrument for measuring osmotic pressure [Chem.].

osmose, *v.i.* and *t. oz*-mohs, to diffuse by or subject to osmosis.

osmosis, *n.* oz-*moh*-sis, the tendency of two different fluids, when separated by a membrane, to pass through the pores and mingle. (Gr. *osmos,* a pushing.)

osmotic, *a.* oz-*mot*-ik, relating to or having the property of osmosis.

osmund, *n. oz*-mund, the flowering fern *Osmunda regalis,* the royal fern. (Fr. *osmonde.*)

osphresiology, *n. os*-free-ze-*ol*-o-je, the scientific study of odours or of the sense of smell. (Gr. *osphresis,* smelling, *logos,* account.)

osprey, *n. os*-pray, the fish-hawk, *Pandion haliaëtus,* a large sea-bird preying on fish; a plume of the feathers of the white egret (milliners' erroneous term). (L. *ossifragus,* bone-breaking.)

ossein, *n. os*-se-in, a glue-like substance present in bone. (L. *os,* a bone.)

osselet, *n. os*-sel-let, the cuttle-bone of certain cephalopods; an exostosis occurring on certain bones in horses. (Fr.)

osseous, *a. os*-se-us, composed of or resembling bone; bony; containing fossil bones. (L. *osseus.*)

Ossianic, *a.* os-se-*an*-ik, pertaining to Ossian, a legendary Gaelic poet, or in the style of poems ascribed to him.

ossicle, *n. os*-se-kl, a small bone or bony particle. (L. *ossiculum,* a little bone.)

ossiferous, *a.* os-*sif*-er-rus, containing or yielding bones. (L. *os,* and *fero,* bear.)

ossific, *a.* os-*sif*-ik, having power to ossify; generating bone.

ossification, *n. os*-e-fe-*kay*-shon, the formation of, or conversion into, bone or a bony substance.

ossify, *v.t. os*-e-fy, to form into bone or a bone-like substance: *v.i.* to become bone; to become hardened or callous. (Fr. *ossifier.*)

ossivorous, *a.* os-*siv*-o-rus, feeding on bones. (L. *os,* and *voro,* devour.)

ossuary, *n. os*-yew-a-re, a charnel-house; a deposit of bones. (Late L. *ossuarium.*)

osteal, *a. os*-te-al, pertaining to or resembling bone.

osteitis, *n.* os-te-*eye*-tis, inflammation of bone [Med.].

ostensibility, *n. os*-ten-se-*bil*-e-te, the quality of being ostensible.

ostensible, *a.* os-*ten*-se-bl, that may be shown; professed, whether real or not; apparent; plausible. (Fr.)

ostensibly, *ad.* in appearance; professedly.

ostension, *n.* os-*ten*-shon, the exposure of the Host that the congregation may adore it [Eccles.].

ostensive, *a.* os-*ten*-siv, showing; exhibiting.

ostensory, *n.* os-*ten*-so-re, a monstrance.

ostent, *n. os*-tent, appearance; show; a portent. (L. *ostentus,* shown.)

ostentation, *n.* os-ten-*tay*-shon, outward show; pretentious display. (Fr.)

ostentatious, *a.* os-ten-*tay*-shus, making a display from vanity; intended for vain display; fond of show; boastful.

ostentatiously, *ad.* with vain display.

ostentatiousness, *n.* quality of being ostentatious; vain display.

osteo-, *os*-te-o, a combining form meaning bone. (Gr. *osteon,* a bone.)

osteoarthritis, *n. os*-te-o-ar-*thry*-tis, chronic rheumatoid arthritis.

osteoblast, *n. os*-te-o-blast, a bone-forming cell [Anat.].

osteoclasis, *n.* os-te-o-*klay*-sis, the surgical breaking of a bone for correcting a deformity. (*osteo-,* and Gr. *klassein,* to break.)

osteocolla, *n.* os-te-o-*kol*-la, a tufaceous deposit of calcium carbonate on the roots and stems of plants. (*osteo-,* and Gr. *kolla,* glue.)

osteocope, *n. os*-te-o-kope, bone-ache, esp. that due to syphilitic rheumatism [Path.]. (*osteo-,* and Gr. *kopos,* fatigue.)

osteogen, *n. os*-te-o-jen, the soft transparent substance from which bone is formed.

osteogenesis, *n.* os-te-o-*jen*-e-sis, the formation or growth of bone; ossification. (*osteo-,* and Gr. *gennao,* produce.)

osteography, *n.* os-te-*og*-ra-fe, descriptive osteology. (*osteo-,* and Gr. *grapho,* write.)

osteoid, *a. os*-te-oyd, resembling bone.

osteolite, *n. os*-te-o-lite, a massive variety of apatite.

osteological, *a.* os-te-o-*loj*-e-kal, pertaining to osteology.

osteologically, *ad.* according to osteology.

osteologist, *n.* os-te-*ol*-o-jist, one skilled in osteology.

osteology, *n.* os-te-*ol*-o-je, the branch of zoology treating of the bones of vertebrates. (Gr.)

osteoma, *n.* os-te-*oh*-ma, a bony tumour [Med.].

osteomalacia, *n. os*-te-o-ma-*lay*-se-a, a disease characterized by progressive softening of the bones. (Gr. *osteon,* and *malachos,* soft.)

osteopath, *n. os*-te-o-path, an osteopathist.

osteopathic, *a. os*-te-o-*path*-ik, relating to osteopathy.

osteopathist, *n.* os-te-*op*-a-thist, a practitioner of osteopathy; a bone-setter.

osteopathy, *n.* os-te-*op*-a-the, a morbid state of the bones; treatment of disease by manipulative surgery and without drugs; bone-setting. (*osteo-* and Gr. *pathein,* suffer.)

osteosarcoma, *n. os*-te-o-sahr-*koh*-ma, a sarcoma containing osseous tissue.

osteotomy, *n.* os-te-*ot*-o-me, surgical dissection or division of bones. (Gr. *osteon,* and *tome,* cutting.)

ostiolar, *a. os*-te o-lar *or* os-*ty*-o-lar, pertaining to ostioles.

ostiolate, *a. os*-te-o-late, having ostioles.

ostiole, *n. os*-te-ole, a small opening in the conceptacles of algæ and fungi, through which the spores are discharged [Bot.]; an inhalent orifice of a sponge [Zool.]. (L. *ostiolum,* a small opening.)

ostitis, *n.* os-*ty*-tis, osteitis.

ostler, *n. os*-ler, a stableman or groom, esp. at an inn or livery-stables. (*hosteler.*)

Ostmen, *n.pl. ohst*-men, the early Scandinavian settlers in Ireland. (Scand. *ost,* east, and *men.*)

ostosis, *n.* os-*toh*-sis, formation of bone; ossification [Med.].

ostracean, *n.* os-*tray*-she-an, any member of the oyster family: *a.* pertaining to this family. (Gr. *ostrakon,* shell.)

ostracism, *n. os*-tra-sizm, temporary banishment by ostracizing; exclusion by popular consent. (Gr. *ostrakismos.*)

ostracite, *n. os*-tra-site, a fossil oyster-shell. (Gr.)

ostracize, *v.t. os*-tra-size, to exclude from society or its amenities; originally, in Athens, to banish temporarily by popular vote inscribed on a potsherd or a shell. (Gr. *ostrakizo,* ostracize.)

ostracon, *n. os*-tra-kon (*pl.* **ostraca**), a clay tablet or sherd of ancient pottery for use or used as writing material. (Gr. *ostrakon,* potsherd.)

ostreiculture, *n. os*-tre-e-*kul*-tewr, the artificial breeding of oysters. (L. *ostrea,* oyster, and *culture.*)

ostrich, *n. os*-tritch, a flightless ratite bird of the genus *Struthio,* of southern and eastern Africa, esp. *S. camelus,* the largest bird extant; applied also to the rhea. (O.Fr. *ostruce.*)

Ostrogoth, *n. os*-tro-goth, one of the group of

Goths that settled in the East, *i.e.* from the Danube to the Black Sea. (Late L. *ostrogothi*, from Old Ger. *ostar*, eastward.)
otacoustic, *a.* ot-a-*kous*-tik, assisting the sense of hearing: *n.* an instrument to assist the hearing. (Gr. *otakoustes.*)
otacousticon, *n.* ot-a-*kous*-te-kon, an otacoustic.
otalgia, *n.* oh-*tal*-je-a, the ear-ache. (Gr.)
otarian, *a.* oh-*tare*-re-an, pertaining to the Otariidæ, a family of pinnipeds comprising the eared seals, sea-lions, etc. (Gr. *otaros*, having big ears.)
***other,** *a.* *uth*-er, the second of two; not the same; different; not this, but the contrary; noting something besides. (A.S.)
otherguess, *ad.* *uth*-er-gess, of another kind.
otherness, *n.* state of being other.
otherwhere, *ad.* in some other place.
otherwhile, *ad.* at other times.
otherwise, *ad.* *uth*-er-wize, in another manner; by other causes; in other respects: *conj.* this excepted.
otic, *a.* *ot*-ik, pertaining to or in the region of the ear; auditory. (Gr. *otikos*, relating to the ear.)
otiose, *a.* *oh*-she-ohs, fruitless; having no useful function; idle; unemployed. (L. *otiosus.*)
otitis, *n.* oh-*ty*-tis, inflammation of the ear.
otocyst, *n.* *oh*-to-sist, the auditory vesicle or organ of hearing in some invertebrates. (Fr. *otocyste.*)
otography, *n.* o-*tog*-ra-fe, descriptive otology.
otolith, *n.* *oh*-to-lith, an ear-stone, or concretion of lime, present in the labyrinth of the ear of some animals.
otology, *n.* oh-*tol*-o-je, the science treating of the ear, its diseases, etc. (Gr. *ous*, and *logos*, science.)
otorrhœa, *n.* oh-to-*ree*-a, a discharge from the ear [Med.]. (Gr. *ous*, ear, *rheo*, flow.)
otoscope, *n.* *oh*-to-skope, an instrument for visual examination of the ear. (Gr. *ous*, and *skopeo*, view.)
otosis, *n.* oh-*toh*-sis, mishearing, esp. of vocal sounds; alteration of words due to this. (Gr.)
ottar, *n.* *ot*-tar, attar; otto.
ottava-rima, *n.* ot-*tah*-va-*ree*-ma, a form of versification consisting of eight lines, of which the first six rhyme alternately, and the last two form a couplet. (It., eighth rhyme.)
otter, *n.* *ot*-ter, an aquatic fish-eating mammal of the genus *Lutra*; the fur of this; a type of paravane. (A.S. *otor.*)
otto, *n.* *ot*-toh, an essential oil, esp. of roses. (*attar.*)
Ottoman, *a.* *ot*-toh-man, appertaining to the Turks: *n.* a Turk (*l.c.*) a cushioned seat or couch without back or sides. (Fr. *ottomane*, from Turk., *Othman*, founder of the former Turkish empire.)
ouabain, *n.* wah-*bah*-in, a poisonous glucoside obtained from certain African trees, used as an arrow-poison and in pharmacy. (*ouabaio*, Somali name of the trees.)
ouananiche, *n.* wah-na-*neesh*, a small non-anadromous salmon of certain inland Canadian waters. (Algonquian.)
oubit, *n.* *ou*-bit, a hairy caterpillar, a woubit.
oubliette, *n.* oo-ble-*et*, an underground dungeon with access only from above, esp. for person condemned to perpetual imprisonment. (Fr., from *oublier*, forget.)
ouch, *n.* outch, a clasp or buckle; the socket in which a precious stone is set. (O.Fr. *nouche.*)
ought, *n.* awt, aught; anything.
ought, *n.* awt, nought [Coll.]. (Corruption of *nought.*)
ought, *v.aux.* awt, should; to be held or bound in duty or moral obligation; to be necessary; to behove; to be fit or proper. (A.S. *ahte.*)
ouija, *n.* *wee*-jah, a form of planchette used by spiritualistic mediums, etc. for the reception of supernatural messages. (Coined from Fr. *oui*, yes, and Ger. *ja*, yes.)
ouistiti, *n.* wis-*tee*-te, the wistiti.
ounce, *n.* ounce, a weight; in avoirdupois, the sixteenth of a pound (28·350 grammes), and in troy 20 dwts. (31·1035 grammes). (O.Fr. *unce.*)
ounce, *n.* ounce, the snow-leopard, *Felis uncia.* (O.Fr. *once.*)
ouphe, *n.* oof, an elf; a sprite. (*oaf.*)
our, *a.* our, pertaining or belonging to us. (A.S. *ure.*)
ourang-outang, *n.* o-*rang*-oo-*tang*, orang-outang.
ouranography, *n.* oo-ran-*og*-ra-fe, uranography.
ouroscopy, *n.* oo-*ros*-ko-pe, uroscopy.
ours, *poss. pron. pl.* ourz, the possessive case of *we.*
ourself, *pron.* our-*self* (*pl.* **ourselves,** our-*selvz*), an addition after *we* and *us*, sometimes used in the regal style for *myself.*
ousel, *n.* *oo*-zl, the ouzel.
oust, *v.t.* oust, to eject. (O.Fr. *oster*, to remove.)
ouster, *n.* *ous*-ter, dispossession; ejection [Law]. (O.Fr.)
***out,** *ad.* out, without; not within; not at home; at a distance; in a state of disclosure, or extinction, or being exhausted, or destitution; not in office; to the end; loudly; in an error; at a loss; introduced to society: *int.* away! begone: *v.t.* to eject; to expel; as a prefix, it signifies to go beyond, to exceed, or excel. **out of,** proceeding from a place. **out of countenance,** embarrassed. **out of date,** obsolete. **out-of-door,** outdoor; done, existing, etc., in the open air. **out of hand,** immediately; beyond control. **out of pocket,** having lost or spent one's money. **out of print,** no longer on sale by the publisher (of books). **out of the way,** not on the right path; uncommon; sequestered. **out upon you, out upon it,** expressions of dislike or contempt. (A.S. *ute.*)
out-, out, prefix having the force of the adverb *out* in its various senses, and frequently expressing excess, or a going or passing beyond.
outage, *n.* *out*-aj, state of being in disuse; the period during which current supplied is not in use; the amount of such unused supply [Elect.].
out-and-out, *a.* out-and-*out*, thorough; complete: *adv.* thoroughly; without reservation. **out-and-outer,** a thorough-going specimen [Coll.].
outask, *v.t.* *out*-ahsk, to publish the banns of marriage for the last time.
outbalance, *v.t.* to exceed in weight.
outbid, *v.t.* to bid more than.
outboard, *a.* *out*-bord, beyond the side of the ship. **outboard motor,** a small internal combustion engine working a propellor, for occasional use in a sailing- or rowing-boat.
outbound, *a.* *out*-bound, outward bound.
outbrag, *v.t.* out-*brag*, to surpass in boasting.
outbrave, *v.t.* out-*brave*, to surpass in defying.
outbreak, *n.* *out*-brake, a sudden bursting forth; a rebellion; an eruption.
outbreaking, *n.* *out*-brake-ing, an outbreak.
outbreathe, *v.t.* out-*breethe*, to weary by having better breath; to exhale: *v.i.* to be exhaled.
outbuilding, *n.* *out*-bild-ing, an outhouse.
outburst, *n.* *out*-burst, an outbreak; an outcry.
outcast, *a.* *out*-kahst, exiled: *n.* an exile; a vagabond.
outcaste, *n.* *out*-kahst, one expelled from a particular caste: *v.t.* to expel from a caste.
outclass, *v.t.* out-*klahss*, to excel.
outcome, *n.* *out*-kum, issue; result; output.
outcrop, *n.* *out*-krop, the coming up of a stratum to the surface; the position that has outcropped: *v.i.* to come to the surface (of strata) [Geol.].
outcross, *n.* *out*-kros, the progeny of different strains; a hybrid.
outcry, *n.* *out*-kry, a vehement or loud cry; a cry of distress; clamour of opposition.
outdare, *v.t.* out-*dare*, to surpass in venturesomeness; to dare beyond another.
outdistance, *v.t.* out-*dis*-tance, to pass in front of; to get ahead of.
outdo, *v.t.* out-*doo*, to excel; to surpass.
outdoor, *a.* *out*-dawr, that exists or is done, etc., out of doors or in the open air. **outdoor relief,** outside relief.
outdoors, *ad.* out-*dawrz*, out of doors.
outer, *a.* *out*-er, being on the outside; exterior: *n.* a shot that strikes the division of a target farthest from the bull's eye. **outer bar,** the body of utter barristers. (A.S. *utera.*)
outermost, *a.* *out*-er-most, farthest out.
outface, *v.t.* out-*face*, to brave; to confront; to defy.
outfall, *n.* *out*-fawl, the mouth or place of discharge of a river, sewer, etc.
outfield, *n.* *out*-feeld, an outlying field; the fielders at cricket who are farther out than the rest, also their location.
outfit, *n.* *out*-fit, a fitting out or equipment, or the expense of this; mental equipment for a particular calling; a group of persons taken as an entity [U.S.A. slang].

outfitter, *n.* *out*-fit-ter, a tradesman who supplies outfits, esp. of clothes, haberdashery, etc.
outflank, *v.t.* out-*flank*, to get round the side of; to extend beyond the flank of; to gain an advantage over.
outflow, *n.* *out*-floh, process of flowing out; an outfall or outlet.
outfly, *v.t.* out-*fly*, to fly better than.
outgeneral, *v.t.* out-*jen*-er-al, to excel in generalship.
outgo, *n.* out-*goh*, that which goes out; expenditure: *v.t.* to go beyond; to surpass.
outgoer, *n.* *out*-goh-er, one who leaves a place.
outgoing, *n.* *out*-goh-ing, a departure or going out; outlay: *pl.* expenditure.
outgrow, *v.t.* out-*groh*, to surpass in growth; to grow too large or too old for.
outgrowth, *n.* *out*-grohth, that which grows out of some other thing; an excrescence.
outguard, *n.* *out*-gard, a guard at a distance from the main body [Mil.]; any defence at a distance.
outhaul, *n.* *out*-hawl, a rope for hauling out the head or foot of a sail.
out-Herod, *v.t.* out-*he*-rod, to overact the character of Herod; to surpass in enormity or absurdity.
outhouse, *n.* *out*-house, a small house or building detached from but belonging to the main one.
outing, *n.* *out*-ing, a pleasure trip; an airing.
outjockey, *v.t.* out-*jok*-e, to overreach.
outland, *a.* *out*-land, foreign; outlying: *n.* (*usually pl.*) a foreign land.
outlander, *n.* *out*-lan-der, an alien; a stranger.
outlandish, *a.* out-*land*-ish, foreign; not native; strange. (A.S. *utlendisc.*)
outlast, *v.t.* out-*lahst*, to last longer than; to exceed in duration.
outlaw, *n.* *out*-law, a person excluded from the benefit of the law; a bandit: *v.t.* to deprive of the benefit and protection of the law.
outlawry, *n.* *out*-law-re, the act or process of outlawing.
outlay, *n.* *out*-lay, expenditure: *v.t.* out-*lay*, to lay out (money); to surpass in laying (eggs).
outleap, *v.t.* out-*leep*, to leap beyond, or farther than. *pp.* **outleapt,** out-*lept*.
outlet, *n.* *out*-let, passage outward; point of egress or discharge. (A.S. *ut*, out, *latan*, let.)
outlier, *n.* *out*-ly-er, one who does not reside at or in his place of work; an isolated rock visible above water; a small part of a formation separated from the main body [Geol.].
outline, *n.* *out*-line, the line or lines by which a figure is defined; first sketch; a general indication: *v.t.* out-*line*, to draw the exterior line; to sketch.
outlive, *v.t.* out-*liv*, to survive; to outlast.
outlook, *n.* *out*-look, vigilant watch; a lookout; prospect; general appearance of things: *v.t.* out-*look*, to face down; to browbeat.
outlying, *a.* *out*-ly-ing, lying or being at a distance; remote; on the exterior or frontier.
outmanœuvre, *v.t.* out-ma-*noo*-ver, to surpass or get the better of in manœuvring.
outmarch, *v.t.* out-*march*, to march more quickly; to march farther.
outmatch, *v.t.* out-*match*, to be more than the equal of; to be superior to.
outmeasure, *v.t.* out-*mezh*-ur, to exceed in measure.
outmode, *v.t.* out-*mode*, to render unfashionable or obsolete.
outmost, *a.* *out*-mohst, farthest outward; utmost.
outness, *n.* *out*-ness, externality; the state or quality of being outside.
outnumber, *v.t.* out-*num*-ber, to exceed in number.
outpace, *v.t.* out-*pace*, to walk faster than.
outpart, *n.* *out*-part, a part remote from the centre; an exterior part.
out-patient, *n.* *out*-pay-shent, a non-resident patient at a hospital.
out-pensioner, *n.* a non-resident pensioner.
outplay, *v.t.* out-*play*, to beat at a game; to play better than.
outport, *n.* *out*-pawrt, any port not within the boundaries or customs jurisdiction of the chief port of a country.
outpost, *n.* *out*-pohst, a detachment of troops stationed at a distance from the main body.
outpour, *v.t.* out-*pawr*, to pour out.
outpouring, *n.* *out*-paw-ring, abundant effusion.
output, *n.* *out*-poot, the quantity of anything produced; the yearly production of a mine or factory; the energy delivered by a machine, battery, dynamo, etc., to any instrument adapted to make use of it [Mech. and Elect.].
outrage, *n.* *out*-raj, injurious violence; wanton mischief: *v.t.* *out*-rayj, to treat with violence and wrong; to rape: *v.i.* to commit exorbitances. (Fr.)
outrageous, *a.* out-*ray*-jus, violent; furious; exceeding reason or propriety; enormous; atrocious.
outrageously, *ad.* in an outrageous manner.
outrageousness, *n.* quality of being outrageous.
outrange, *v.t.* out-*raynj*, to have a longer range than.
outré, *a.* *oo*-tray, extravagant; bizarre; beyond what is proper, usual, or correct. (Fr.)
outreach, *v.t.* out-*reech*, to reach farther than; to extend farther; to overreach.
out-relief, *n* parish or other relief of one not resident in an institution; outside relief.
outride, *v.t.* out-*ride*, to ride faster than.
outrider, *n.* *out*-ride-er, a servant on horseback attending a carriage or cavalcade.
outrigged, *a.* *out*-rigd, with rowlocks extending beyond the gunwale.
outrigger, *n.* *out*-rig-er, a projecting spar for keeping ropes or sails out from the masts; a counterpoise carried to windward; an outrigged rowlock; a boat with outrigged rowlocks.
outright, *ad.* *out*-rite, at once; frankly, brusquely: *a.* downright; wholly out.
outrun, *v.t.* out-*run*, to run or go beyond; to outstrip; to surpass. **to outrun the constable,** to get into debt [Coll.].
outsail, *v.t.* out-*sale*, to leave behind in sailing.
outsell, *v.t.* out-*sel*, to exceed in amount of sales or in selling price.
outset, *n.* *out*-set, the beginning; the first entrance on any business.
outshine, *v.t.* out-*shine*, to excel; to surpass; to shine more brilliantly than.
outside, *n.* *out*-side, external part; superficial appearance; part that lies outside; the limit: *a.* on the outside; exterior: *ad.* out; excluded: *prep.* beyond; external to. **outside broker,** a stockbroker not being a member of a Stock Exchange. **outside edge,** a lunge with the foot on the outer edge of the skate. **outside market,** the kerb market [Stock Exchange]. **outside relief,** assistance in money or kind accorded by an authority to persons other than inmates of institutions.
outsider, *n.* out-*side*-er, an ill-bred person; an uninitiated person; one outside the indicated class or profession; a competitor not expected to win.
outsize, *a.* *out*-size, unusually large.
outskirt, *n.* (*usually in pl.*) *out*-skert, a border; a place close beyond the boundary; suburb.
outsoar, *v.t.* out-*sore*, to soar higher.
outsole, *n.* *out*-sole, the outer sole (of a shoe, etc.).
outspan, *v.t.* *out*-span, to unyoke, as oxen; to unharness.
outspeak, *v.t.* out-*speek*, to speak boldly; to say more than: *v.i.* to speak out.
outspoken, *a.* *out*-spoh-kn, bold in speech; candid.
outspokenness, *n.* quality of being outspoken.
outspread, *v.t.* out-*spred*, to extend; to diffuse: *a.* *out*-spred, spread out.
outstand, *v.i.* out-*stand*, to project; to stand out: *v.t.* to withstand.
outstanding, *a.* out-*stand*-ing, projecting outward; very conspicuous; not collected; unpaid.
outstare, *v.t.* out-*stare*, to stare out of countenance.
outstay, *v.t.* to stay too long; to overstay. **outstay one's welcome,** stay too long.
outstretch, *v.t.* out-*stretch*, to expand.
outstrip, *v.t.* out-*strip*, to outrun; to advance beyond.
outtalk, *v.t.* out-*tawk*, to talk down; to reduce a person to silence by talking.
outvalue, *v.t.* out-*val*-ew, to exceed in value.
outvote, *v.t.* out-*vote*, to poll more votes than.
outvoter, *n.* *out*-vote-er, a voter living outside the electoral district or division.
outwalk, *v.t.* out-*wawk*, to walk more quickly than.
outward, *a.* *out*-ward, exterior; external; visible; directed or extended toward the exterior; corporeal: *ad.* outwards: *n.* external appearance. **outward bound,** proceeding from a port or country.

outwardly, *ad.* externally; on the outside; to all appearance.
outwardness, *n.* externality; objectivity.
outwards, *ad. out*-wardz, toward the outside; in a direction away from.
outwash, *n. out*-wosh, overwash [Geol.].
outwear, *v.t.* out-*ware,* to last longer in wear.
outweigh, *v.t.* out-*way,* to exceed in value; to weigh more than; to surpass.
outwit, *v.t.* out-*wit,* to surpass in design or stratagem; to frustrate by superior ingenuity.
outwith, *prep. out*-with, outside of; except [Scots.].
outwork, *n. out*-werk, a work constructed beyond the main body of the place [Fort.]; work done away from the place of employment: *v.t.* out-*werk,* to surpass in work or speed of working.
outworn, *a.* out-*worn,* worn-out; antiquated, obsolete.
ouzel, *n. oo*-zl, any of various birds of the thrush family, esp. the blackbird, *Turdus merula,* the ring ouzel, *Turdus torquatus,* or the dipper or water ouzel, *Cinclus aquaticus.*
ova, *n.pl. oh*-va, *pl.* of *ovum.*
oval, *a. oh*-val, elliptical; of the shape of an egg; *n.* an egg-like shape or thing; an oval stadium or sports ground. **the Oval,** the ground of the Surrey County Cricket Club, in south-east London. (Fr. *ovale.*)
ovalbumen, *n.* oh-val-*bew*-men, the albumen or white of an egg.
ovally, *ad. oh*-va-le, in an oval form or manner.
ovarian, *a.* o-*vare*-re-an, belonging to the ovary.
ovariotomist, *n.* o-vare-re-*ot*-o-mist, an expert in ovariotomy.
ovariotomy, *n.* o-vare-re-*ot*-o-me, the surgical removal of an ovary or the ovaries, or of an ovarian tumour. (*overy,* and Gr. *tome,* cutting.)
ovary, *n. oh*-va-re, one of the two genital glands of a female in which the eggs or ova are formed [Anat.]; the vessel in which the seed is formed [Bot.]. (L. *ovum,* egg.)
ovate, *a. oh*-vate, egg-shaped. (L. *ovatus.*)
ovate-oblong, *a.* between ovate and oblong.
ovation, *n.* o-*vay*-shon, in ancient Rome, a lesser triumph; an enthusiastic demonstration of popular applause. (Fr.)
★**oven,** *n. uv*-en, a chamber in which baking and heating, etc., is effected; any apparatus for baking. **dutch oven,** an oven like a small meat-screen, open to the front of the fire. (A.S. *ofn.*)
ovenbird, *n. uv*-en-berd, any bird building a dome-shaped nest on or near the ground, esp. one of the South American genus *Furnarius.*
★**over,** *prep. oh*-ver, from side to side of; above in place, excellence, dignity, value, or authority; opposed to under; through the whole extent of; upon; all through; covering; upwards of: *a.* upper; superior; past: *ad.* from side to side; on the opposite side; from one to another; above the top; in addition; more than the quantity assigned; through-out: *n.* the number of balls the bowler has to deliver before the fielders change over [Cricket]. **all over,** including everything; finished. **over again,** afresh; once more. **over all,** from end to end; taking everything into consideration. **over the head of,** *see* **head.** (A.S. *ofer.*)
over-, *oh*-ver, prefix denoting excess, superiority, or more than enough.
overact, *v.t.* o-ver-*akt,* to overdo; to act too much so as to be unnatural.
overalls, *n. sing.* and *pl. oh*-ver-awlz, trousers or vest and trousers in one worn over others as protection at work or in bad weather; the pantaloons of a cavalryman.
overarch, *v.t.* o-ver-*arch,* to arch over: *v.i.* to cover over as with an arch.
overarm, *a.* and *ad. oh*-ver-arm, with the arm raised above the shoulder (of bowling) [Cricket].
overawe, *v.t.* o-ver-*aw,* to restrain by fear.
overbalance, *v.t.* o-ver-*bal*-ance, to exceed in weight, value, or importance: *n.* overweight.
overbear, *v.t.* o-ver-*bare,* to bear down; to overcome.
overbearing, *a.* haughty and dogmatical; domineering.
overbearingly, *ad.* in an over-bearing way.
overbid, *v.t.* o-ver-*bid,* to outbid; to offer too high a price; to over-call: *n. oh*-ver-bid, a bid in excess of one previously made.
over-blouse, *n.* a blouse which, instead of being tucked in at the waist, comes over the waistband; a jumper.
overblown, *a. oh*-ver-blohn, just past their best bloom (of flowers).
overboard, *ad. oh*-ver-bord, out of a ship.
overbuild, *v.t.* o-ver-*bild,* to build beyond the demand; to build on or over.
overburden, *v.t.* o-ver-*bur*-dn, to burden too heavily.
overbusy, *a.* o-ver-*biz*-e, too officious.
overbuy, *v.t.* and *i.* o-ver-*by,* to buy in quantities too large for the purpose; to buy beyond one's means.
over-call, *n.* an outbidding call; a higher bid than the strength of one's hand warrants [Bridge, etc.]: *v.t.* and *i.* to make such a bid.
over-capitalize, *v.t.* to float a company with too great a capital; to increase the capital of a company too greatly.
overcast, *a. oh*-ver-*kahst,* cloudy, dull, gloomy: *v.t.* o-ver-*kahst,* to cloud; to darken; to rate too high; to sew over slightly.
overcharge, *n. oh*-ver-chahrj, an excessive load or burden; an excessive charge: *v.t.* o-ver-*chahrj,* to charge or load to excess; to surcharge; to charge too much.
overcloud, *v.t.* o-ver-*kloud,* to cover with clouds; to deject: *v.i.* to become overcast.
overcoat, *n. oh*-ver-koat, a coat worn outdoors over a suit.
overcomable, *a.* that may be overcome.
overcome, *v.t.* o-ver-*kum,* to be victorious over.
overcrowd, *v.t.* and *i.* o-ver-*kroud,* to fill or crowd to excess.
over-discharge, *v.t.* to discharge (esp. a battery) [Elect.] in too great a degree or beyond a certain limit.
overdo, *v.t.* o-ver-*doo,* to do or perform too much; to excel; to fatigue with too much labour; to cook too much: *v.i.* to labour too hard or do too much.
overdone, *a.* o-ver-*dun,* cooked to excess; tired out; carried too far.
overdose, *n. oh*-ver-dohs, too large a dose: *v.t.* o-ver-*dohss,* to administer too big a dose.
overdraft, *n. oh*-ver-drahft, the act of overdrawing (at a bank); the amount by which one is indebted to the bank; too large a draft (as of men for an army); the current passing over a furnace.
overdraw, *v.t.* o-ver-*draw,* to draw beyond what is due to one's credit at a bank; to exaggerate.
overdrive, *v.t.* o-ver-*drive,* to drive too hard.
overdue, *a. oh*-ver-dew, more than due; past the time of payment.
overestimate, *n.* o-ver-*es*-te-mate, too high a calculation: *v.t.* to rate too highly.
over-expose, *v.t.* to expose to excess; to subject too long to the action of light [Phot.].
over-exposure, *n.* the act, process, or result of over-exposing [Phot.].
overfeed, *v.t.* and *i.* o-ver-*feed,* to feed immoderately.
overflow, *n. oh*-ver-floh, an inundation; superabundance: *v.t.* o-ver-*floh,* to flow over; to inundate; to deluge: *v.i.* to run over; to abound.
overfreight, *v.t.* o-ver-*frayt,* to load too heavily.
overground, *a. oh*-ver-ground, situated on the ground (opposed to *underground*).
overgrow, *v.t.* o-ver-*groh,* to grow beyond or above; to cover with grasses or growth of any kind.
overgrowth, *n. oh*-ver-grohth, immoderate growth; a growth upon or over anything.
overhand, *a.* and *ad. oh*-ver-hand, with the arm above the shoulder; in this manner. **overhand stitch,** a small close stitch used in joining edges.
overhang, *v.t.* o-ver-*hang,* to project; to put over: *n.* that which overhangs; a projecting part.
over-hasty, *a.* precipitate; unduly hasty.
overhaul, *n. oh*-ver-hawl, inspection; repairs: *v.t.* o-ver-*hawl,* to turn over for examination; to inspect; to examine again; to overtake.
overhead, *ad.* o-ver-*hed,* aloft; above; in the zenith: *n.pl.* overhead expenses, *viz.,* those not chargeable to any one department in a business but to the whole concern: *a.* situated above or over; taken one with another, average; not particularized.
overhear, *v.t.* o-ver-*heer,* to hear by accident; to hear what is meant for another.

overheat, *v.t.* o-ver-*heet,* to heat to excess.
over-issue, *v.t.* to issue more notes than can be paid.
overjoy, *v.t.* o-ver-*joy,* to render very glad; to please excessively.
over-labour, *v.i.* to overwork; to elaborate to too great an extent.
overlade, *v.t.* o-ver-*lade,* to place too heavy a cargo in a ship.
overland, *a.* and *ad.* *oh*-ver-land, across land; by land (*i.e.,* not by sea or air).
overlap, *v.t.* o-ver-*lap,* to lap over: *n.* an overlapping post or object.
overlay, *n.* *oh*-ver-lay, a covering, layer, etc., laid over; paper placed over parts of a block to increase the pressure when being printed [Print.]: *v.t.* o-ver-*lay,* to lay too much upon; to cover; to overwhelm; to smother; to pack for pressure.
overlaying, *n.* o-ver-*lay*-ing, a superficial covering.
overleaf, *ad.* *oh*-ver-leef, on the next page.
overleap, *v.t.* o-ver-*leep,* to leap over or beyond. **to overleap oneself,** to fail through aiming too high.
overlie, *v.t.* o-ver-*ly,* to lie upon; to smother by lying upon: *v.i.* to be placed upon.
overload, *v.t.* o-ver-*lode,* to lay too heavy a load on, or place too heavy a cargo in: *n.* *oh*-ver-lode, an excessive load [esp. Elect.].
overlook, *v.t.* o-ver-*look,* to look over; to stand higher; to inspect; to superintend; to review; to pass by indulgently; to slight.
overlooker, *n.* o-ver-*look*-er, a superintendent.
overlord, *n.* *oh*-ver-lord, a feudal superior; a lord having authority over other lords.
overman, *n.* *oh*-ver-man, a foreman; one in authority.
overmantel, *n.* *oh*-ver-man-tl, the shelf over a mantelpiece.
overmaster, *v.t.* o-ver-*mahs*-ter, to overpower.
overmatch, *n.* o-ver-*match,* one superior in power: *v.t.* to be too powerful or more than a match for.
overmeasure, *n.* *oh*-ver-mezh-ur, excess of measure: *v.t.* to estimate too largely.
overmuch, *a.* *oh*-ver-much, too much; *ad.* in too great a degree: *n.* more than sufficient.
over-nice, *a.* too fastidious or scrupulous.
overnight, *ad.* *oh*-ver-nite, on the night before: through the night.
overpass, *v.t.* o-ver-*pahss,* to pass or to go over.
overpay, *v.t.* o-ver-*pay,* to pay more than is due: *n.* *oh*-ver-pay, excess pay.
over-pitch, *v.t.* to pitch too high; to pitch a ball too far while bowling [Cricket].
overplus, *n.* *oh*-ver-plus, quantity more than enough; the remainder.
overply, *v.t.* o-ver-*ply,* to ply to excess; to exert with too much vigour.
overpower, *v.t.* o-ver-*pou*-er, to vanquish; to be too much for.
overpoweringly, *ad.* o-ver-*pou*-er-ring-le, to an overpowering extent; irresistibly.
overpraise, *n.* *oh*-ver-praze, excessive praise: *v.t.* o-ver-*praze,* to praise too highly.
overprint, *v.t.* *oh*-ver-print, to print on sheets already printed [Print.]; to print too long or too intensely [Phot.]: *n.* that which is overprinted; a surcharge or additional inscription, etc., on a postage-stamp.
overprize, *v.t.* to overrate; to prize excessively.
overproduce, *v.t.* *oh*-ver-pro-*dewce,* to produce more goods than are demanded.
overproduction, *n.* *oh*-ver-pro-*duk*-shon, production in excess of demand.
over-proof, *a.* above proof strength (of alcoholic liquors).
overrate, *v.t.* o-ver-*rate,* to rate at too much.
overreach, *v.t.* o-ver-*reech,* to reach beyond; to outwit; to cheat: *v.i.* to strike the hoof of the hind foot against the fore foot (of horses).
override, *v.t.* o-ver-*ride,* to brush aside; to overcome obstacles as though trampling on them; to overlap (of the ends of a fractured bone) [Surg.].
overrule, *v.t.* o-ver-*rool,* to control; to supersede or reject; to annul another's ruling; to dominate, to prevail over.
overrun, *v.t.* o-ver-*run,* to cover all over; to harass by hostile incursions; to ravage; to outrun; to change the disposition of types, and carry those of one line into another [Print.]: *v.i.* to run over.
overrunner, *n.* o-ver-*run*-ner, one who overruns.

oversea, *a.* *oh*-ver-see, from beyond sea; situated across the seas; colonial; foreign.
overseas, *ad.* o-ver-*seez,* across or beyond the sea; abroad.
oversee, *v.t.* o-ver-*see,* to overlook; to superintend.
overseer, *n.* *oh*-ve-seer, a superintendent; a parish officer administering the former poor-law.
oversell, *v.t.* o-ver-*sel,* to sell more of anything than one actually has; to sell at too high a price.
overset, *v.t.* o-ver-*set,* to upset; to overthrow: *v.i.* to turn over.
oversew, *v.t.* o-ver-*soh,* to sew with close stitches as overhand.
overshade, *v.t.* o-ver-*shade,* to cover with shade.
overshadow, *v.t.* o-ver-*shad*-o, to overshade; to protect; to dominate or tower over.
overshoe, *n.* *oh*-ver-shoo, a shoe of rubber or felt worn over another; a galosh.
overshoot, *v.t.* o-ver-*shoot,* to shoot over or beyond: *v.i.* to fly beyond the mark.
overshot, *a.* o-ver-*shot,* shot over; with the upper jaw projecting beyond the lower (esp. of dogs). **overshot wheel,** a water-wheel turned by water shooting over the top.
oversight, *n.* *oh*-ver-site, watchful care; inadvertence; mistake; error; omission.
overslaugh, *v.t.* o-ver-*slaw,* to pass over; to bar; to hinder: *n.* the passing over of a normal duty for a superior one [Mil.]. (Dut. *overslaan.*)
oversleep, *v.t.* o-ver-*sleep,* to sleep too long.
oversoul, *n.* *oh*-ver-sole, the one all-pervading and all-embracing entity of the transcendentalists, the ideal soul transfusing, though imperfectly, all men.
overspend, *v.t.* o-ver-*spend,* to spend too much or extravagantly; to exhaust: *v.i.* to spend beyond one's income.
overspread, *v.t.* o-ver-*spred,* to spread over; to cover: *n.* that which is spread over.
overspring, *v.t.* *oh*-ver-spring, to leap over; to fit with springs which compress when weight is added.
overstand, *v.t.* o-ver-*stand,* to insist too much on the price or conditions of.
overstate, *v.t.* o-ver-*state,* to exaggerate.
overstatement, *n.* o-ver-*state*-ment, an act or the action of overstating; an exaggeration.
overstay, *v.i.* o-ver-*stay,* to remain too long in a place; to outstay one's welcome.
overstep, *v.t.* o-ver-*step,* to step beyond; to exceed; to transgress.
overstock, *n.* *oh*-ver-stok, superabundance; more than sufficient: *v.t.* o-ver-*stok,* to lay in too large a stock for; to fill too full; to crowd.
overstrain, *n.* o-ver-*strane,* excessive strain: *v.t.* to strain too greatly: *v.i.* to try too hard.
overstrung, *a.* o-ver-*strung,* too highly strung or too sensitive; having two sets of strings crossing obliquely (of pianos).
oversubscribe, *v.t.* *oh*-ver-sub-*skribe,* to apply for more than is issued or allotted (esp. of shares, etc.).
oversubscription, *n.* *oh*-ver-sub-*skrip*-shon, the act of oversubscribing.
over-supply, *n.* a supply which is in excess of the demand: *v.t.* to supply in excess.
overt, *a.* *oh*-vert, open to view; public; apparent. (O.Fr. *ouvert,* open.)
overtake, *v.t.* o-ver-*take,* to come up with; to catch; to come upon; to take by surprise.
overtaker, *n.* *oh*-ver-tay-ker, one who or that which overtakes.
overtask, *v.t.* o-ver-*tahsk,* to place too hard a task upon.
overtax, *v.t.* *oh*-ver-*taks,* to tax too heavily; to demand too much of.
overthrow, *v.t.* o-ver-*throh,* to turn upside down; to throw down; to demolish; to defeat; to subvert; to throw too far: *n.* *oh*-ver-throh, the act or result of overthrowing; state of being overthrown; ruin; subversion; defeat.
overthwart, *ad.* *oh*-ver-thwort, placed transversely or across.
overtime, *n.* *oh*-ver-time, time at work beyond the regular hours.
overtly, *ad.* *oh*-vert-le, in an overt manner.
overtone, *n.* *oh*-ver-tone, a harmonic; the colour of reflected, as opposed to transmitted, light [Paint.]: *v.t.* o-ver-*tone,* to obscure or dominate one tone with another; to give too deep a tone to (esp. a print [Phot.]).

overtop, *v.t.* o-ver-*top*, to rise above the top of; to surpass.
overtrade, *v.i.* o-ver-*trade*, to trade beyond one's capital.
overtrain, *v.t.* o-ver-*train*, to train beyond one's strength or constitution [Athletics].
over-trick, *n.* a trick won in excess of the number declared or needed [Bridge, etc.].
overtrump, *v.t.* o-ver-*trump*, to defect a lower with a higher trump [Cards].
overture, *n.* *oh*-ver-tewr, a proposal; a musical prologue: *v.t.* to lay a proposal before. (O.Fr.)
overturn, *n.* o-ver-*turn*, state of being overturned: *v.t.* to destroy; to subvert.
overvalue, *v.t.* o-ver-*val*-ew, to value at too high a rate.
overwash, *n.* *oh*-ver-wosh, the waterborne detritus carried over frontal moraines [Geol.].
overween, *v.i.* o-ver-*ween*, to think too highly, esp. of oneself; to be arrogant.
overweening, *a.* o-ver-*ween*-ing, with too much conceit; vain; conceited.
overweigh, *v.t.* o-ver-*way*, to exceed in weight; to overbalance.
overweight, *n.* *oh*-ver-wayt, an excess of weight beyond what is legally or customarily permitted; preponderance.
overwhelm, *v.t.* o-ver-*whelm*, to crush; to immerse and bear down.
overwhelmingly, *ad.* in a manner to overwhelm.
overwind, *v.t.* o-ver-*wynd*, to wind too much.
overwork, *n.* *oh*-ver-wurk, work done out of ordinary working hours; extra work; undue work: *v.t.* o-ver-*wurk*, to exhaust by excessive labour; to require too much work from a person or thing: *v.i.* to work excessively.
overwrought, *a.* o-ver-*rawt*, overdone; too elaborate; too laboured.
ovibovine, *a.* oh-ve-*boh*-vine, belonging to the Ovibovinæ, or musk-ox family: any member of this family. (L. *ovis*, sheep, and *bovine.*)
Ovidian, *a.* o-*vid*-e-an, like or relating to Ovid, the Latin poet, and his works.
oviduct, *n.* *oh*-ve-dukt, a passage for the ovum from the ovary [Anat. and Zool.]. (L. *ovum*, and *duct.*)
oviferous, *a.* oh-*vif*-er-rus, egg-bearing. (L. *ovum*, and *fero*, bear.)
ovification, *n.* *oh*-ve-fe-*kay*-shon, the production of ova.
oviform, *a.* *oh*-ve-form, having the figure of an egg.
ovine, *a.* *oh*-vine, pertaining to, or of the nature of, sheep. (L. *ovis.*)
oviparous, *a.* oh-*vip*-a-rus, bringing forth eggs instead of fully developed young (opposed to viviparous).
oviposit, *v.t.* oh-ve-*poz*-it, to lay eggs (esp. of insects). (L. *ovum*, and *positum*, place.)
oviposition, *n.* oh-ve-po-*zish*-on, the laying or depositing of eggs. [Entom.].
ovipositor, *n.* oh-ve-*poz*-e-tor, the tubular organ by which insects deposit their eggs.
ovisac, *n.* *oh*-ve-sak, the receptacle in the ovary which contains the egg or ova. (L. *ovum*, and *sac.*)
ovoid, *a.* *oh*-voyd, of the shape of an egg: *n.* an egg-shaped body. (L. *ovum*, and Gr. *eidos*, like.)
ovoidal, *a.* oh-*voy*-dal, ovoid.
ovolo, *n.* *oh*-vo-lo, a rounded moulding sloping downward [Arch.]. (It.)
ovology, *n.* oh-*vol*-o-je, the branch of embryology treating of ova.
ovoviviparous, *a.* *oh*-vo-ve-*vip*-a-rus, producing eggs which hatch inside the parent [Zool.]. (L. *ovum*, and *viviparous.*)
ovular, *a.* *oh*-vew-lar, pertaining to or of the nature of an ovum or ovule.
ovule, *n.* *oh*-vewl, the rudimentary seed; the seed before it is fertilized [Bot.]; the unimpregnated ovum [Biol.]. (Fr.)
ovuliferous, *a.* oh-vew-*lif*-er-rus, producing ovules.
ovulite, *n.* *oh*-vew-lite, a fossil egg. (L. *ovum*, and Gr. *lithos*, a stone.)
ovum, *n.* *oh*-vum (*pl.* **ova**), the egg-cell which, when impregnated, becomes the embryo and develops into the fœtus [Zool.]; an ovule [Bot.]; an egg-shaped ornament, esp. carvèd on the contour of the ovolo [Arch.]. (L. *ovum*, an egg.)
owe, *v.t.* oh, to be indebted to; to be bound to pay; to be obliged for. (A.S. *agan*, possess.)
owing, *a.* *oh*-ing, due as a debt; ascribable to; imputable to.
owl, *n.* oul, a nocturnal bird of prey of the order Strigiformes, comprising a large number of varieties; a solemn looking fool [Coll.].
owler, *n.* *oul*-er, a person or vessel engaged in owling; a former smuggler.
owlery, *n.* *oul*-er-re, a haunt of owls; owlish quality or character.
owlet, *n.* *oul*-et, a young owl.
owling, *n.* *oul*-ing, smuggling, esp. (17th and 18th cents.) the illegal exportation of wool and sheep from England.
owlish, *a.* *oul*-ish, resembling or characteristic of an owl; foolish-looking.
owl-light, *n.* glimmering or imperfect light.
own, *a.* ohn, belonging or peculiar to; individual; not belonging to another. **on one's own,** independently; without outside assistance. **to get one's own back,** to obtain tit for tat; to be revenged. **to hold one's own,** *see* **hold.** (A.S. *agan.*)
own, *v.t.* ohn, to possess; to have a rightful title to; to avow or admit. **to own up,** to confess frankly and fully. (A.S. *agnian.*)
★**owner,** *n.* *ohn*-er, the rightful proprietor.
ownerless, *a.* *ohn*-er-less, having no known or legal owner.
ownership, *n.* *ohn*-er-ship, proprietorship.
ox, *n.* oks (*pl.* **oxen**), the castrated male of the domesticated cow; applied also to any bovine quadruped. (A.S. *oxa.*)
oxalate, *n.* *oks*-al-ate, a salt of oxalic acid.
oxalic, *a.* oks-*al*-ik, pertaining to or obtained from plants of the genus *Oxalis*; designating an acid present in sorrel and various roots. (L. *oxalis*, sorrel.)
Oxalis, *n.* *oks*-a-lis, a large genus of acaulescent plants typified by the wood-sorrel. (L.)
oxbird, *n.* *oks*-berd, name given to various birds, including the dunlin, sanderling, and sandpiper.
oxbow, *n.* *oks*-boh, the wooden hoop, hanging from the yoke of draught-oxen.
oxen, *n.pl.* *oks*-en, plural of *ox*.
oxer, *n.* *oks*-er, a strong high fence against oxen [Slang].
ox-eye, *n.* *oks*-eye, the marguerite daisy; an oval or circular dormer window [Arch.].
ox-eyed, *a.* *oks*-ide, having large ox-like eyes.
ox-fly, *n.* *oks*-fly, a bot-fly; a fly hatched under the skin of cattle.
Oxford, *n.* *oks*-ford, a university town in England. **Oxford bags,** loose-fitting trousers. **Oxford blue,** a purplish dark blue. **Oxford clay,** a bed of clay that underlies the coral-rag. **Oxford Group,** the name assumed in England by the Buchmanites. **Oxford mixture,** a dark grey suiting. **Oxford Movement,** the High Church revival begun in 1883. **Oxford shoes,** shoes laced over the instep.
Oxfordian, *a.* oks-*for*-de-an, of or pertaining to Oxford, esp. the University; applied to a division of the Jurassic rocks: *n.* an Oxonian.
oxgall, *n.* *oks*-gawl, a fluid secreted by the liver of an ox.
oxgang, *n.* *oks*-gang, an ancient measure of land, the eighth part of a carucate.
oxgate, *n.* *oks*-gate, an oxgang [Scot.].
oxidable, *a.* *oks*-e-da-bl, oxidizable.
oxidate, *v.t.* and *i.* *oks*-e-date, to oxidize.
oxidation, *n.* oks-e-*day*-shon, oxidization.
oxide, *n.* *oks*-ide, a compound formed by the combination of oxygen with another element. (Gr. *oxys*, acid.)
oxidizable, *a.* *ok*-se-*dy*-za-bl, capable of being oxidized, or of being converted into an oxide.
oxidization, *n.* *ok*-se-dy-*zay*-shon, the act or process of oxidizing; the result of being oxidized.
oxidize, *v.t.* *ok*-se-dize, to combine with oxygen; to add oxygen to; to make rusty: *v.i.* to become oxidized; to rust.
ox-like, *a.* *oks*-like, resembling an ox.
oxlip, *n.* *oks*-lip, a hybrid between the primrose and cowslip; also the plant *Primula elatior*.
Oxonian; *n.* oks-*oh*-ne-an, a native of Oxford; a member (past or present) or student of Oxford University.
oxpecker, *n.* oks-*pek*-er, an African bird of the genus *Buphaga*, esp. the beefeater.
oxtail, *n.* *oks*-tale, a beef tail used for making soup.

oxter, *n.* *oks*-ter, the armpit [Scots.]. (A.S. *oxta.*)
ox-tongue, *n.* *oks*-tung, the tongue of an ox (as food); various plants with tongue-shaped leaves, as alkanet, and *Helminthia echioides.*
oxyacanthous, *a.* oks-e-a-*kan*-thus, having sharp thorns or prickles [Bot.].
oxy-acetylene, *a.* containing or consisting of a mixture of oxygen and acetylene.
oxyacid, *n.* *oks*-e-*as*-id, an oxygenated acid.
oxychloride, *n.* oks-e-*klaw*-ride, a basic chloride, a compound of a chloride and an oxide at the same time.
oxygen, *n.* *oks*-e-jen, the most abundant of the elements, an invisible, tasteless, and odourless gas constituting one-fifth of the atmosphere, 86 per cent. of water, 46 per cent. of the earth's crust, and 66 per cent. of human tissue, and the supporter of life and ordinary combustion. (Gr., acid-producer.)
oxygenate, *v.t.* *oks*-e-je-nate, to treat or charge with oxygen; to oxidize.
oxygenation, *n.* *oks*-e-je-*nay*-shon, the act or process of oxygenating.
oxygenic, *a.* oks-e-*jen*-ik, oxygenous.
oxygenize, *v.t.* *oks*-e-je-nize, to oxygenate.
oxygenous, *a.* oks-*ij*-e-nus, pertaining to, resembling, or containing oxygen.
oxygon, *n.* *oks*-e-gon, an acute-angled triangle: *a.* having acute angles.
oxyhydrogen, *a.* oks-e-*hy*-dro-jen, pertaining to, consisting of, or derived from a compound of oxygen and hydrogen; its intensely hot flame, when burning, is used in the production of limelight, for soldering and welding, and for melting platinum. **oxyhydrogen light,** limelight.
oxymel, *n.* *oks*-e-mel, an old medicinal syrup composed of vinegar and honey. (L. *oxymeli.*)
oxymoron, *n.* oks-e-*mor*-ron, a figure of speech in which an epithet of a quite contrary signification is added to a word, as cruel kindness. (Gr. *oxys*, and *moros*, foolish.)
oxymuriate, *n.* oks-e-*mewr*-re-ate, name formerly applied to chlorides and chlorates.
oxymuriatic, *a.* *oks*-e-mewr-re-*at*-ik, pertaining to chlorine (term used when chlorine was known only as oxidized muriatic acid).
oxyopia, *n.* oks-e-*oh*-pe-a, exceptionally acute vision. (Gr. *oxys*, and *opsis*, sight.)
oxyphonia, *n.* oks-e-*foh*-ne-a, shrillness of voice. (Gr. *oxys*, and *phone*, voice.)
oxysalt, *n.* *oks*-e-sawlt, a salt containing oxygen; a salt of an oxyacid.
oxysulphide, *n.* oks-e-*sul*-fide, a compound of oxygen and sulphur with an element or radical [Chem.].
oxytone, *a.* *oks*-e-tone, having an acute accent on the last syllable: *n.* such a word. (Gr. *oxytonos.*)
oyer, *n.* *oy*-yer, the hearing of a law suit [Law]. **oyer and terminer,** a commission formerly granted to judges of assize to hear and determine treasons, felonies, and trespasses [Law]. (Anglo-Fr., hear and determine.)
oyez, *v.imp.* oh-*yess*, hear ye, a call by an usher of the court or a town crier. (Fr., hear ye.)
oyster, *n.* *oys*-ter, an edible bivalve mollusc of the genus *Ostrea*; either of two delicate pieces of meat on a fowl's back. (O.Fr. *oistre.*)
oyster-bed, *n.* a breeding-place for oysters.
oyster-catcher, *n.* the sea-pie, a shore bird of the genus *Hæmatopus.*
oyster-plant, *n.* *oys*-ter-plahnt, salsify, and others whose leaves are reputed to taste like oyster.
ozena, *n.* o-*zee*-na, a fetid ulcer in the nostril, or the discharge from this [Med.]. (L. *ozæna.*)
ozocerite, *n.* o-*zoh*-ser-rite, a natural mineral paraffin wax used in making candles, etc. (Gr. *ozo* smell, *keros*, wax.)
ozokerite, *n.* o-*zoh*-ker-rite, ozocerite.
ozone, *n.* *oh*-zone, an active allotropic variety of oxygen, having three molecules to the atom, occurring in the atmosphere. (Gr. *ozon*, smelling, from its peculiar smell.)
ozonic, *a.* oh-*zoh*-nik, pertaining to ozone.
ozonize, *v.t.* oh-*zoh*-nize, to charge with ozone.
ozonizer, *n.* *oh*-zo-ny-zer, an electrical apparatus for converting oxygen into ozone.
ozonometer, *n.* oh-zo-*nom*-e-ter, an instrument for detecting the presence and quantity of ozone in the atmosphere. (Gr. *ozon*, and *metron*, measure.)

P

P, pee, the sixteenth letter and twelfth consonant of the alphabet, has a labial articulation, except when occurring in the digraph *ph* (which has the sound of *f*), and that in the initial use of the combinations *pn, ps, pt* it is silent, as in *pneumonia, psalm, pterodactyl.* As a musical direction it stands for *piano,* softly, and *pp.* for *piu piano,* more softly.
pa, *n.* pah, papa.
pabular, *a. pab*-yew-lar, pertaining to pabulum.
pabulous, *a. pab*-yew-lus, affording pabulum.
pabulum, *n. pab*-yew-lum, food; aliment; that which nourishes or sustains. (L.)
paca, *n. pah*-ka, a large Central and S. American rodent, *Cœlogenys paca,* allied to the agouti. (Sp.)
pacation, *n.* pa-*kay*-shon, pacification; the act of pacifying.
pacable, *a. pak*-a-bl, appeaseable; placable.
pace, *n.* pace, the space between the two feet in stepping; a lineal measure, usually taken as 30 in. from heel to heel in pacing; in ancient Rome, the space covered by two steps (60 in.); manner of walking or stepping; gait; speed: *v.i.* to go; to walk deliberately or slowly; to amble: *v.t.* to measure by steps; to regulate in motion; to set the speed for. **go the pace,** to go at a great speed; to indulge in dissipation. **put one through one's paces,** to test one's qualities in deeds. (Fr. *pas.*)
pace, *ad. pay*-se, by permission of; notwithstanding (esp. in irony). (L. *in pace,* in peace.)
paced, *a.* payst, having a particular gait; measured by pacing.
pacemaker, *n. pace*-make-er, one who sets the pace in a race.
pacer, *n. pace*-er, one who, or a horse that, paces.
pacha, *n.* pa-*shaw,* a pasha. (Fr.)
pachisi, *n.* pa-*chee*-ze, an Indian four-handed game of backgammon kind. (Hind.)
pachometer, *n.* pa-*kom*-e-ter, a pachymeter.
pachycephalous, *a. pak*-e-*sef*-a-lus, having a thick skull.
pachydactyl, *n.* pak-e-*dak*-til, an animal having thick toes. (Gr. *pachys,* thick, *daktylos,* a toe.)
pachyderm, *n. pak*-e-derm, a non-ruminant ungulate with a thick skin, as the hog, rhinoceros, or or elephant; a thick-skinned person. (Gr. *pachys,* and *derma,* skin.)
pachydermatous, *a.* pak-e-*der*-ma-tus, pertaining to a pachyderm; thick-skinned.
pachydermia, *n.* pak-e-*der*-me-a, thickening of the skin; elephantiasis [Med.].
pachymeter, *n.* pa-*kim*-e-ter, an instrument for measuring thickness, esp. of paper. (Gr. *pachys,* and *metron,* a measure.)
pachyrhizus, *n. pak*-e-*ry*-zus, a genus of leguminous plants of the vine family, cultivated in India for their edible tuberous roots.
pacifiable, *a. pas*-e-*fy*-a-bl, that may be pacified.
pacific, *a.* pa-*sif*-ik, peace-making; conciliatory; appeasing; mild; tranquil; pertaining to the Pacific: *n.* (*cap.*) the great western ocean, so called because found peaceful by Magellan, who first navigated it, 1521. (Fr. *pacifique.*)
pacification, *n. pas*-e-fe-*kay*-shon, the act or process of making peace or of pacifying wrath. (L. *pacificatus,* pacified.)
pacificator, *n.* pa-*sif*-e-kay-tor, a peace-maker.
pacificatory, *a.* pa-*sif*-e-ka-to-re, tending to make peace.
pacificity, *n.* pas-e-*fis*-e-te, pacific quality; pacifism.
pacifier, *n. pas*-e-fy-er, one who pacifies.
pacifism, *n. pas*-e-fizm, opposition to war and militarism; the advocacy of the peaceful settlement of international disputes.
pacifist, *n. pas*-e-fist, an adherent and advocate of pacifism; an opponent of militarism: *a.* pertaining to or characteristic of pacifists or pacifism.
pacify, *v.t. pas*-e-fy, to appease; to calm; to tranquillize; to suppress revolt in a subjugated country: *v.i.* to become calm. (Fr. *pacifier.*)

pack, *n.* pak, a bundle; a burden; a bale; a great number; a wool weight of 240 lbs.; a set of cards; a large quantity of ice floating in the sea; the amount of fruit, fish, etc., packed for the market; a wrapping of blankets (dry or wet) [Med.]; a cosmetic paste for the face, etc.; a number of hounds trained together; a company of wolves, etc.; a scrummage in Rugby football; a number of persons united, esp. in some bad design: *v.t.* to stow in close order; to place and press together; to put together and bind fast; to make joints tight; to add material that makes working parts fit; to send in haste; to load; to put together, as cards, so as unfairly to win; to select and bring together, as persons, to gain some cause unfairly: *v.i.* to be packed; to go in haste; to stow articles in a case, etc., for transportation or travel. (Probably from O.Dut. *pack.*)
package, *n. pak*-aj, a bundle or bale; a large parcel; a carton or container; the act or manner of packing: *v.t.* to make into a package; to enclose in a container.
pack-drill, *n.,* a former punishment drill in full marching order [Mil.].
packer, *n. pak*-er, one who packs.
packet, *n. pak*-et, a small package; a packet-boat; a surprising or knock-down blow, a bit of luck (good or bad), a superfluity (of) [Slang]: *v.t.* to put up in a packet.
packet-boat, *n.* a vessel conveying mails under a government contract; a vessel trading regularly on some route with mails, goods, and passengers.
pack-horse, *n.* a horse employed in carrying packs.
pack-ice, *n.* floating ice broken up and then re-united in a solid mess.
packing, *n. pak*-ing, any material used in packing, or filling up vacant spaces or interstices.
packing-case, *n.* a wooden case in which goods may be packed.
packing-needle, *n.* a curved needle for sewing up packages, bales, etc.
packing-sheet, *n.* a coarse cloth for packing in; a sheet for wrapping a patient in.
packman, *n. pak*-man, a pedlar; a tallyman.
pack-saddle, *n.* a saddle on which packs are laid.
packstaff, *n. pak*-stahf, the tallyman's stick by which he carried the pack on his shoulder.
packthread, *n. pak*-thred, strong thread for tying up parcels.
packwax, *n. pak*-waks, paxwax.
packway, *n. pak*-way, bridle-path for pack-horses.
paco, *n. pah*-ko, the alpaca; a brown oxide of iron of earthy appearance. (Peruv.)
pact, *n.* pakt, a compact; an agreement. (L. *pactum.*)
paction, *n. pak*-shon, a pact.
pactional, *a. pak*-shon-al, by way of agreement.
pad, *n.* pad, an easy-paced horse; a footpad; a robber who infests the road on foot: *v.i.* to trudge; to travel slowly; to rob on foot: *v.t.* to tramp; to travel over. **to pad the hoof,** to go on foot or by foot-slogging. (Dut., a path.)
pad, *n.* pad, anything stuffed with something soft, as a saddle, cushion, or bolster; a protection for any part of the body; a block of writing-, drawing-, or blotting-paper; a cushion-like paw; an adjustable handle for tools of various sorts or sizes: *v.t.* to stuff with padding; to fix colours in dyed material; inartistically to increase the length of a literary production. (L.Ger. *pad,* sole of the foot.)
padcloth, *n. pad*-kloth, a saddlecloth; a cover for a horse's loins.
padding, *n. pad*-ding, material used in stuffing; the impregnation of cloth with a mordant [Dyeing]; something to fill up with; matter inserted merely to extend an article or story, etc.
paddle, *n. pad*-dl, a broad short scull; the blade or broad part of an oar; a float on the circumference of a paddlewheel; a long-handled spade-like tool

for clearing ploughshares, etc. : *v.i.* to dabble in the water with the hands or feet; to walk in water with bare feet; to finger : *v.t.* to row gently; to propel by a paddle.
paddle-board, *n.* one of the floats or projecting flanges on a paddle-wheel.
paddle-box, *n.* the casing over the upper part of the paddle-wheel of a steamboat.
paddler, *n. pad*-dler, one who paddles : *pl.* waterproof overalls or knickers for a child.
paddle-wheel, *n.* a wheel with paddles used in propelling steamboats.
paddock, *n. pad*-dok, a frog or toad [Scots.]. (Scand. *padda.*)
paddock, *n. pad*-dok, a small pasture field near a house or stable; a turfed enclosure for horses at a race-course. (M.E. *parrok.*)
Paddy, *n. pad*-de, an Irishman; a fit of temper, a paddywhack [Slang]. (St. Patrick, patron saint of Ireland.)
paddy, *n. pad*-de, rice, esp. unmilled or in the husk. (East Indian.)
paddy-bird, *n.* the Java sparrow, *Munia oryzivora*; also, a small East Indian heron, and other birds.
paddy-melon, *n.* a small wallaby. (Australian.)
paddywhack, *n. pad*-de-whak, a fit of temper; a rage [Slang].
padella, *n.* pa-*del*-la, a container, formerly used in illuminations, filled with grease of some kind, and provided with a wick. (It.)
padisha, *n. pad*-e-shah, governor-in-chief; a title of certain Oriental rules, esp. the former Turkish sultans and Persian shahs. (Pers.)
padlock, *n. pad*-lok, a detachable lock hung on a staple and held by a link : *v.t.* to fasten with a padlock.
padnag, *n. pad*-nag, an ambling nag.
padouk, *n.* pa-*dook*, the valuable timber of the E. Indian tree *Pterocarpus dalbergioides*; the tree itself. (Burmese.)
padre, *n. pah*-dray *or pah*-dre, a chaplain, esp. an army chaplain; any minister of religion. (Sp., father.)
padrone, *n.* pa-*droh*-nay, the captain of an Italian coaster; an Italian innkeeper; an owner of street-organs who lets them out for hire. (It.)
paduasoy, *n. pad*-yew-a-soy, a corded silk stuff. (Fr. *pou-de-soie*, influenced by *Padua.*)
pæan, *n. pee*-an, a song in honour of Apollo, or some other god; a song of triumph. (Gr.)
pæderast, *n. pee*-de-rast, one addicted to pæderasty.
pæderasty, *n. pee*-de-ras-te, sodomy with a juvenile. (Gr. *paidos*, boy, *eran*, to love.)
pædeutics, *n.pl.* pe-*dew*-tiks, the science of education. (Gr. *paideutikos*, relating to teaching.)
pædiatrics, *n.* pee-de-*at*-riks, the study, or the science treating, of the ailments and health of children.
pædobaptism, *n.* pee-do-*bap*-tizm, baptism of infants. (Gr. *pais*, a child, and *baptism.*)
pædobaptist, *n.* pee-do-*bap*-tist, one who supports infant baptism.
pædology, *n.* pee-*dol*-o-je, the branch of medical science treating of childhood.
pæon, *n. pee*-on, a foot of four syllables, of which only one is long [Pros.].
pæony, *n. pee*-o-ne, peony.
pagan, *n. pay*-gan, a heathen; an idolater; one of no religion : *a.* heathenish; idolatrous; irreligious. (L. *paganus*, a rustic, a country bumpkin.)
paganish, *a. pay*-gan-ish, heathenish.
paganism, *n. pay*-gan-izm, heathenism.
paganize, *v.t. pay*-gan-ize, to make pagan or heathenish : *v.i.* to behave like pagans.
page, *n.* payj, a youth attending on a great person or in a royal household; a young male uniformed attendant; a messenger-boy in livery : *v.t.* to attend as a page; to call the name (in a hotel, suite of offices, etc.) of one whose presence or attention is required. (Fr.)
***page,** *n.* payj, one side of a leaf of paper : *pl.* books or writings : *v.t.* to paginate; to make up type in pages [Print.]. (Fr.)
pageant, *n. paj*-ent, a dramatic representation of historical episodes; a brilliant parade, show, or spectacle; anything merely showy. (M.E. *pagent*, a movable stage, from L. *pagina*, a stage.)
pageantry, *n. paj*-en-tre, pageants generally; that which makes a pageant; a glittering exhibition.
pagehood, *n. payj*-hood, the state of a page or boy in livery.
paginal, *a. paj*-e-nal, pertaining to pages.
paginate, *v.t. paj*-e-nate, to number the pages of.
pagination, *n.* paj-e-*nay*-shon, the act or process of paginating; the number of pages. (Late L. *paginatus*, divided into pages.)
pagoda, *n.* pa-*goh*-da, a Hindu or Chinese tower, tapering upward in stories, usually with a religious object; an imitation of this; a gold coin formerly current in Hindustan. **pagoda tree,** popular name of several trees, including the banyan and *Sophora japonica.* (Port.)
pagodite, *n. pag*-o-dite, agalmatolite, the soft stone which the Chinese cut into images.
pagurian, *a.* pa-*gewr*-re-an, relating to the Paguridæ, the family including the hermit crabs : *n.* any one of these crabs [Zool.]. (L. *pagurus.*)
pah, *n.* pah, a Maori stockade; a native fort or village [New Zealand].
pah, *int.* pah, an expression of disgust.
Pahlavi, *n. pah*-la-ve, the characters in which are written the sacred books of the Persians; old Persian; (*l.c.*) the Persian gold money of account, equivalent to 100 rials or (nominally) 25*s.* (Per., from *Parthava*, Parthia.)
paid, pade, *p.* of *pay.*
paideutics, *n.* py-*dew*-tiks, pædeutics.
paidology, *n.* py-*dol*-o-je, pædology.
paigle, *n. pay*-gl, the cowslip, *Primula veris*, and similar wild-flowers. (Dial. Eng.)
pail, *n.* pale, an open vessel of wood or metal with a bow handle across the top, for carrying liquids, as water or milk; a bucket; a pailful. (A.S. *paegel.*)
pailful, *n. pale*-ful, the quantity a pail will hold.
pailiasse, *n.* pal-*yas*, a palliasse. (Fr.)
paillette, *n. pal*-yet, a spangle.
***pain,** *n.* pane, an uneasy sensation in animal bodies; the result of the excessive stimulation of nerves; an acute ache; laborious effort; labour with care; uneasiness of mind; suffering; *pl.* trouble; labour; conscientious effort; throes of parturition : *v.t.* to cause uneasiness; to afflict; to distress. (Fr. *peine.*)
painful, *a. pane*-ful, full of pain; giving pain to body or mind; difficult; laborious.
painfully, *ad.* in a painful manner.
painfulness, *n.* quality or state of being painful.
painless, *a. pane*-less, free from pain.
painlessly, *ad.* in a manner to incur no pain.
painlessness, *n.* state or quality of being painless.
painstaker, *n. paynz*-take-er, one who takes pains; a laborious person.
painstaking, *a. paynz*-take-ing, taking pains; carefully laborious : *n.* labour with care.
***paint,** *n.* paynt, colouring matter; pigment; rouge; lipstick : *v.t.* to cover or besmear with colour; to represent by colours or images; to form a likeness in colours; to picture or describe : *v.i.* to practise painting; to apply colours to the face; to use cosmetics. **painted lady,** the butterfly *Vanessa cardui*, orange-red blotched with black and white. **pretty as paint,** very pretty indeed. **to paint the town red,** to have a lively spree about town [Slang]. (Fr. *peint*, painted.)
painter, *n. paynt*-er, one whose occupation is to paint; a house-painter; an artist skilled in representing objects or to portray in colours. **painter's colic,** a form of lead-poisoning to which painters and plumbers are subject. **painter-stainer,** *see* **stainer.**
painter, *n. paynt*-er, the rope carried in the bow of a boat to make it fast by. (M.E. *pantere*, a noose.)
painting, *n. paynt*-ing, painter's work; the act or employment of laying on colours; the art of representation in colours; a painted picture.
paintress, *n. paynt*-ress, a woman painter.
painty, *a. paynt*-e, unskilfully painted; overdone with paint.
pair, *n.* pare, two of a kind, similar in form, suited to each other, and used together; an article having two corresponding parts; two of different sexes; an engaged or married couple : *v.i.* to be joined in pairs; to fit as corresponding : *v.t.* to unite in couples; to abstain from voting by arrangement with an opponent who also abstains. **carriage and pair,** a carriage with a pair of horses harnessed side by side. **pair of colours,** the King's Colour (*i.e.* the national flag) and the Regimental Colour,

the two military flags carried by a battalion. **pair of stairs,** a flight of stairs between two floors. **pair off,** to separate from a company in pairs. **pair royal,** three similar things; three playing cards of the same rank. (Fr. *paire.*)
pairing-time, *n.* the time when birds couple.
pakeha, *n.* pa-*kay*-ha, a white man; any foreigner [New Zealand and Australia]. (Maori.)
paktong, *n.* *pak*-tong, a Chinese alloy of nickel, zinc, and copper somewhat resembling silver. (Cantonese.)
pal, *n.* *pal*, a companion; a friend [Slang]. **to pal up with,** to associate closely, or become intimate, with. (Romany, brother.)
pala, *n.* *pah*-la, impala, a S. African antelope.
palabra, *n.* pa-*lah*-bra, a palaver; a talk. (Sp.)
palace, *n.* *pal*-as, a house in which an emperor, king, bishop, or other distinguished person resides; an official residence; a fine mansion. (Fr. *palais.*)
paladin, *n.* *pal*-a-din, a champion of Charlemagne; a true knight; a knight-errant. (Fr.)
palæ- (*or* **palæo-**), *pal*-e (*pal*-e-o-), a prefix signifying that which existed in ancient times (or pertaining to them). (Gr. *palaios*, ancient.)
palæarctic, *n.* *pal*-e-*ark*-tik, the northern temperate region, esp. as characterized by its flora and fauna.
palæichthyology, *n.* *pal*-e-ik-the-*ol*-o-je, the branch of palæontology treating of extinct fishes.
palæobotany, *n.* *pal*-e-o-*bot*-a-ne, the botany of extinct or fossil plants.
palæocrystic, *a.* *pal*-e-o-*kris*-tik, pertaining to ice that has been such since remote antiquity. (*palæo-*, and Gr. *krustallos*, ice.)
palæogeography, *n.* *pal*-e-o-je-*og*-ra-fe, the science or study of prehistoric geographical conditions.
palæograph, *n.* *pal*-e-o-graf, an ancient manuscript or inscription; a palæographer.
palæographer, *n.* pal-e-*og*-ra-fer, one skilled in palæography.
palæography, *n.* pal-e-*og*-ra-fe, the study of ancient writings and inscriptions; the science of deciphering these.
palæolith, *n.* *pal*-e-o-lith, a palæolithic stone implement.
palæolithic, *a.* *pal*-e-o-*lith*-ik, belonging to the age of roughly worked flint implements, or (*cap.*) that division of the Stone Age next following the Eolithic.
palæology, *n.* *pal*-e-*ol*-o-je, archæology; the science of antiquities.
palæontographical, *a.* *pal*-e-on-to-*graf*-e-kal, pertaining to palæontography.
palæontography, *n.* *pal*-e-on-*tog*-ra-fe, the illustration and description of fossils. (*palæo-*, and Gr. *onta*, beings.)
palæontological, *a.* *pal*-e-on-to-*loj*-e-kal, pertaining to palæontology.
palæontology, *n.* *pal*-e-on-*tol*-o-je, the study of fossils; the science of extinct organisms.
palæozoic, *a.* *pal*-e-o-*zoh*-ik, belonging to the oldest fossiliferous rocks. (*paliæo-*, and Gr. *zoë*, life.)
palæstra, *n.* pa-*les*-tra, wrestling; a hall, etc., for wrestling exhibitions. (L.)
palæstric, *a.* pa-*les*-trik, pertaining to wrestling or the palæstra.
palafitte, *n.* *pal*-a-fit, a prehistoric lake-dwelling, esp. in Italy. (It. *palafitta.*)
palagonite, *n.* pa-*lag*-o-nite, a devitrified basaltic glass occurring in certain rocks [Geol.]. (*Palagonia*, Sicily.)
palanquin, *n.* pal-an-*keen*, an enclosed litter borne on the shoulders of four bearers. (Port. *palanquim.*)
palatable, *a.* *pal*-a-ta-bl, agreeable to the taste; savoury.
palatableness, *n.* agreeableness to the taste.
palatal, *a.* *pal*-a-tal, palatine [Anat.]; pertaining to or uttered by the palate: *n.* a sound formed with the tongue and hard palate, as *k*, *j*, *s*.
palatalize, *v.t.* pa-*lat*-a-lize, to pronounce as a palatal [Phonetics].
palate, *n.* *pal*-at, the roof or upper part of the mouth; taste; relish: *v.t.* to try with the palate; to relish. (O.Fr. *palat.*)
palatial, *a.* pa-*lay*-shal, pertaining to or befitting a palace; magnificent. (L. *palatium*, a palace.)
palatiform, *a.* pa-*lat*-e-form, shaped like the palate.
palatinate, *n.* pa-*lat*-e-nat, the province of a palatine; palatinate purple. **the Palatinate,** a Rhenish state of the former German Empire. **palatinate purple,** the lavender colour used distinctively in robes, blazers, etc. of Durham University (Durham being a " county palatine ").
palatine, *a.* *pal*-a-tine, pertaining to a palace, esp. that of the Holy Roman Emperors; possessing royal privileges, such as the counties of Durham and Lancaster: *n.* one invested with royal privileges; a short fur cape. (Fr.)
palatine, *a.* *pal*-a-tine, pertaining to the palate: *n.* either of the two bones forming the hard palate [Anat.].
palatize, *v.t.* *pal*-a-tize, to palatalize.
palaver, *n.* pa-*lah*-ver, idle talk; flattery; talk; conversation; conference: *v.t.* to deceive by words; to flatter: *v.i.* to indulge in palaver. (Port. *palavra*, a word.)
palaverer, *n.* pa-*lah*-ver-er, one who palavers.
palay, *n.* pa-*lay*, a small white-wood tree cultivated in southern India.
pale, *a.* pale, not ruddy or fresh of colour; wan; of a faint lustre: *v.t.* to make pale: *v.i.* to turn pale. (O.Fr.)
pale, *n.* pale, a narrow board used in fencing; a pointed stake; an enclosure; a vertical stripe down the middle of the shield [Her.]. **the Pale,** that part of Ireland acknowledging English rule before the mid-17th cent. **outside the pale,** beyond the limits; not included in. **pale bark,** loxa-bark. (Fr. *pal.*)
palea, *n.* *pay*-le-a, the scaly bract at the base of florets of some composite plants, as in sunflower heads; the inner husk of a grass. (L., chaff.)
paleaceous, *a.* pay-le-*ay*-shus, resembling chaff; covered with chaff-like scales [Bot.]. (L. *palea*, chaff.)
pale-face, *n.* a white man. (Amerind. term.)
palely, *a.* *pale*-le, wanly; not ruddily; dimly.
paleness, *n.* *pale*-ness, wanness; want of freshness.
Palestinian, *a.* pal-es-*tin*-e-an, pertaining to Palestine or its people: *n.* a native of Palestine.
palestra, *n.* pa-*les*-tra, palæstra.
paletot, *n.* *pal*-e-to, a loose overcoat. (Fr.)
palette, *n.* *pal*-et, a small flat board or plate with a thumb-hole, on which painters place and mix their colours. (Fr.)
palfrey, *n.* *pawl*-fre, a small horse fit for ladies; a safe saddle-horse. (Fr. *palefroi.*)
Pali, *n.* *pah*-le, the Sanskrit dialect used in the sacred writings of the Buddhists. (Hind., a line.)
palilogy, *n.* pa-*lil*-o-je, the repetition of a word. (Gr. *palin*, again, *logos*, a word.)
palimpsest, *n.* *pal*-imp-sest, parchment manuscript written on a second time; a writing over imperfectly erased writing. (L. *palimpsestus.*)
palindrome, *n.* *pal*-in-drome, a word or verse that is the same when read backwards or forwards. (Gr. *palin*, and *dromos*, running.)
paling, *n.* *pay*-ling, a fencing pale; a fence formed with pales.
palingenesia, *n.* pal-in-je-*nee*-se-a, a new birth; a regeneration. (Gr. *palin*, and *genesis*, birth.)
palingenesis, *n.* pal-in-*jen*-e-sis, the reproduction of ancestral characters [Biol.]; a regeneration; a revival. (Gr.)
palinode, *n.* *pal*-in-ode, a recantation, esp. one in poetical form. (Fr. *palinodie.*)
palisade, *n.* *pal*-e-sade, a fence or fortification of stakes with pointed tops: *v.t.* to enclose or fortify with stakes. **palisade worm,** a parasite of the horse, *Strongylus equimus.* (Fr. *palissade.*)
palisander, *n.* pal-e-*san*-der, jacaranda, or similar timber. (Brazilian.)
palish, *a.* *pale*-ish, somewhat pale or wan.
palki, *n.* *pawl*-ke, a palanquin. (Hind.)
pall, *n.* pawl, a cloak; a mantle; a pallium; a chalice cover; a cloth to cover a coffin, used at funerals: *v.t.* to cloak; to cover with a pall. (A.S. *pæl.*)
pall, *v.t.* pawl, to make vapid or insipid; to make spiritless; to cloy: *v.i.* to become vapid or insipid. (*appal.*)
Palladian, *a.* pal-*lay*-de-an, in or pertaining to the classical style of architecture introduced by Andrea Palladio (Ital.) in the 16th century.
palladic, *a.* pa-*lad*-ik, pertaining to palladium [Chem.].
palladium, *n.* pa-*lay*-de-um, a hard silvery-white ductile and malleable metallic element of the platinum group [Chem.].

palladium, *n.* pa-*lay*-de-um, a defence or protection. (Gr. *palladion*, a statue of Pallas Athena, the Grecian goddess of wisdom, on the preservation of which the safety of Troy was fabled to depend.)
pallbearer, *n.* *pawl*-bare-rer, one who holds up the funeral pall or attends the coffin at a funeral.
pallet, *n.* *pal*-let, a palette; any of various implements used in pottery, gilding, surgery, etc.; the oscillating lever working on an escapement wheel; the plate of a valve in a pipe or flue. (Fr. *palette.*)
pallet, *n.* *pal*-let, a small bed; a palliasse. (Fr. *paillet.*)
pallial, *a.* *pal*-le-al, pertaining to the pallium of the mollusca. (Late L. *pallialis.*)
palliasse, *n.* pal-le-*yas*, a straw mattress; an under-bed of straw. (Fr. *paillasse.*)
palliate, *a.* *pal*-le-at, having a pallium [Zool.].
palliate, *v.t.* *pal*-le-ate, to cover with excuses; to extenuate; to mitigate. (L. *palliatus*, covered with a mantle.)
palliation, *n.* pal-le-*ay*-shon, the act of palliating; extenuation; mitigation.
palliative, *a.* *pal*-le-a-tiv, extenuating; alleviating; *n.* that which extenuates; that which alleviates pain.
palliatory, *a.* *pal*-le-a-to-re, extenuating.
pallid, *a.* *pal*-lid, pale; wan. (L. *pallidus.*)
pallidity, *n.* pa-*lid*-e-te, pallidness.
pallidly, *ad.* *pal*-lid-le, palely; wanly.
pallidness, *n.* *pal*-lid-ness, paleness; wanness.
pallium, *n.* *pal*-le-um, a cloak of the ancient Greeks; a short white robe bearing red crosses, worn by the Pope and certain prelates; the mantle of a mollusc [Zool.]. (L.)
pall-mall, *n.* pel-*mel*, an old English game in which a ball was driven through an iron ring by a mallet—the ancestor of croquet, and origin of the name of Pall Mall, the street in London. (It. *palla*, a ball, *maglio*, mallet.)
pallone, *n.* pal-*loh*-nay, an Italian game played with a ball and an armguard. (It.)
pallor, *n.* *pal*-or, pallidness; the condition of being pale. (L.)
pally, *a.* *pal*-e, friendly; chummy [Slang]. (*pal.*)
palm, *n.* pahm, the inner part of the hand, or of a glove; a measure of a hand's breadth (3 to 4 in.) or length (7 to 10 in.); a flat broad part, as of an antler, oar, etc.; the fluke of an anchor; the thimble and guard used by sailmakers: *v.t.* to conceal in the palm of the hand; to impose by fraud; to handle; to stroke with the hand. (O.Fr. *paume*, from L. *palma.*)
palm, *n.* pahm, any member of the Palmaceæ, a natural order of endogenous plants containing many species, mostly tropical and native to both hemispheres, the leaves of which have some resemblance to the outstretched palm of the hand; applied also to the Sallow, *Salix caprea*; a palm-branch or leaf in token of victory; triumph; victory. **Palm Sunday,** the Sunday before Easter, when Christ's triumphal entry into Jerusalem is commemorated. (A.S., from L. *palma.*)
palmaceous, *a.* pal-*may*-shus, pertaining to the palm family; resembling a palm [Bot.].
palma-Christi, *n.* *pal*-ma-*kris*-ty, the castor-oil plant, *Ricinus communis.* (L.)
palmar, *a.* *pal*-mar, pertaining to or situated in the palm of the hand.
palmary, *a.* *pal*-ma-re, bearing or deserving the palm as prize; pre-eminent; capital. (L. *palmarius.*)
palmate, *a.* *pal*-mate, having the shape of the outspread hand; web-footed. (L. *palmatus.*)
palmatifid, *a.* pal-*mat*-e-fid, shaped like a hand with short spread fingers. [Bot.].
palmature, *n.* *pal*-ma-tewr, abnormal union of the fingers; webbed fingers.
palm-civet, *n.*, the paradoxure.
palmer, *n.* *pahm*-er, a pilgrim who carried a palm leaf in token of his having been to Palestine; a wandering friar or religious devotee; an angler's imitation of the palmer-worm; one who palms. (O.Fr. *palmier.*)
palmer-worm, *n.* a hairy caterpillar.
palmette, *n.* pal-*met*, an ancient ornamental device of palm-leaf shape.
palmetto, *n.* pal-*met*-toh, the small palm *Sabal palmetto*, or other dwarf fan-palm. (Sp. *palmito.*)
palm-house, *n.* a greenhouse for palms and tropical plants.
palmiferous, *a.* pal-*mif*-er-rus, carrying palm-branches.
palmigrade, *a.* *pal*-me-grade, plantigrade.
palmiped, *a.* *pal*-me-ped, web-footed: *n.* a web-footed swimming bird. (L. *palma*, and *pes*, the foot.)
palmist, *n.* *pahm*-ist, one who practises palmistry.
palmistry, *n.* *pahm*-is-tre, the art of telling fortunes by the lines on the palm of the hand.
palmitate, *n.* *pal*-me-tate, a salt of palmitic acid.
palmitic, *a.* pal-*mit*-ik, pertaining to the palm-tree; designating a fatty acid present in palm-oil.
palmitin, *n.* *pal*-me-tin, the solid crystalline substance of fat.
palm-oil, *n.* an oil obtained from the fruit of several species of palms; a bribe, bribery [Coll.].
palmy, *a.* *pahm*-e, bearing palms; prosperous, flourishing [Fig.].
palolo, *n.* pa-*loh*-loh, an edible annelid, *Palolo viridis*, appearing in vast numbers on the reefs of Polynesia every autumn. (Samoan.)
palp, *n.* palp (*pl.* **palps** *or* **palpi**), a jointed feeler or sense-organ attached to the lower jaw of spiders and crustaceans. (L. *palpo*, stroke gently.)
palpability, *n.* pal-pa-*bil*-e-te, the state of being palpable.
palpable, *a.* *pal*-pa-bl, perceptible to the touch; easily perceived and detected; obvious. (Fr.)
palpableness, *a.* *pal*-pa-bl-ness, the quality of being palpable; palpability.
palpably, *ad.* *pal*-pa-ble, plainly; obviously.
palpal, *a.* *pal*-pal, pertaining to a palp or palpi.
palpate, *v.t.* *pal*-pate, to examine by touch or handling: *a.* *pal*-pat, having tactile organs. (L. *palpatus*, felt.)
palpation, *n.* pal-*pay*-shon, act of palpating; examination or exploration with the hand [Med.].
palpebral, *a.* *pal*-pe-bral, pertaining to the eye-brow or eyelid. (L. *palpebra*, an eyelid.)
palpebrate, *a.* *pal*-pe-brate, having eyelids: *v.i.* to wink.
palpi, *n.pl.* *pal*-pe, *see* **palp.**
palpiform, *a.* *pal*-pe-form, shaped like palpi.
palpigerous, *a.* pal-*pij*-er-rus, having or bearing palpi. (L. *palpus*, and *gero*, bear.)
palpitant, *a.* *pal*-pe-tant, palpitating; throbbing.
palpitate, *v.i.* *pal*-pe-tate, to pulsate; to beat, as the heart. (L. *palpitatus*, throbbed.)
palpitation, *n.* pal-pe-*tay*-shon, a rapid beating of the heart; throbbing.
palsgrave, *n.masc.* *pawlz*-grave (*fem.* **palsgravine,** *pawlz*-gra-veen), a count or earl who had the superintendence of the palace; a count palatine. (Ger. *Pfalz*, palace, *Graf*, a count.)
palsied, *a.* *pawl*-zid, affected with palsy.
palstave, *n.* *pawl*-stave, a bronze axe fitting into a split handle. (Dan. *paalstav.*)
palsy, *n.* *pawl*-ze, paralysis: *v.t.* to affect with paralysis; to paralyze. (Fr. *paralysie.*)
palter, *v.i.* *pawl*-ter, to shuffle; to trifle with; to equivocate. (M.E., perhaps from Scand.)
palterer, *n.* *pawl*-ter-rer, one who palters or dodges; a quibbler.
paltrily, *ad.* in a paltry manner.
paltriness, *n.* the state of being paltry.
paltry, *a.* *pawl*-tre, trivial; mean; insignificant; vile; worthless. (*paltry.*)
paludal, *a.* pa-*lew*-dal *or* *pal*-ew-dal, pertaining to marshes; marshy; malarial. (L. *palus*, a marsh.)
paludinous, *a.* pa-*lew*-de-nus, paludal.
paludism, *n.* *pal*-ew-dizm, impaludism, a malarial disease [Path.].
paludrine, *n.* *pal*-yew-drine, an anti-malarial drug derived from coal-tar.
palustral, *a.* pa-*lus*-tral, resembling malarial fever.
paly, *a.* *pale*-le, pale; wanting colour.
paly, *a.* *pay*-le, divided by pales into four or more equal parts of two alternate colours [Her.]. (O.Fr.)
pam, *n.* pam, the knave of clubs in certain card-games; a game in which this is the highest trump. (Fr. *pamphile.*)
pampas, *n.pl.* *pam*-pas (*sing.* **pampa**), the treeless plains of South America. **pampas grass,** a tall-growing ornamental perennial grass, *Cortaderia argentea*, originally from Brazil. (Sp.)
pamper, *v.t.* *pam*-per, to feed to the full; to glut; to spoil by kindness. (Origin doubtful.)
pampero, *n.* pam-*pare*-roh, a westerly or south-westerly wind that sweeps over the pampas; an Indian of the pampas.

pamphlet, *n.* *pam*-flet, a small publication of one or more printed folded sheets stitched together but not bound, usually on some current topic; a controversial tract.

pamphleteer, *n.* pam-fle-*teer*, a writer of pamphlets: *v.i.* to write or publish pamphlets.

pampiniform, *a.* pam-*pin*-e-form, of the shape of a vine-tendril. (L. *pampinus*, vine-shoot, and *form.*)

pan-, pan, prefix denoting all or every. (Gr.)

pan, *n.* pan, a broad, shallow vessel for domestic or other purposes; the metal dish in which gold and gravel are shaken for separating; the part of a firearm which held the priming; the upper part of the skull; a hollow which becomes a pool in the rainy season: *v.t.* to wash (esp. gold and gravel) in a pan. **to pan out,** to yield (gold); to result; to eventuate. (A.S. *panne.*)

pan, *n.* pan, in timber-framed houses, the beam that supports the rafters; also a compartment between beams filled with brickwork, etc. (Origin uncertain.)

pan, *n.* pahn, betel-leaf; a masticatory of which this is the base. (Hind.)

Pan, *n.* pan, the rural god of the ancient Greeks, half man, half goat, and fond of music [Myth.].

panacea, *n.* pan-a-*see*-a, a universal remedy; a quack medicine. (L.)

panache, *n.* pa-*nahsh*, a plume of feathers worn upright on a helmet; display; swagger. (Fr.)

panada, *n.* pa-*nay*-da, a dish of pulped or soaked bread sweetened and flavoured. (Sp.)

Panama, *n.* pan-a-*mah*, a Panama hat. **Panama hat,** a hat made of plaited strips of the young leaves of *Carludovica palmata*, a palm-like plant of Central America. (The place-name.)

Pan-American, *a.* pertaining to all the states and peoples of North, South, and Central America.

Pan-Anglican, *a.* pertaining to or representing all members of the Anglican churches.

panary, *a.* *pan*-a-re, pertaining to bread.

panatrope, *n.* *pan*-a-trope, an electrical apparatus for reproducing gramophone records through a loud-speaker.

pancake, *n.* *pan*-kake, a thin batter cake fried in a pan; a flattened-out landing due to stalling [Av.]: *v.i.* to make a landing in a stalled condition [Av.].

panchayat, *n.* punt-*shah*-yat, the native council of an East Indian village. (Hind. *panch*, five.)

panchromatic, *a.* pan-kro-*mat*-ik, sensitive to light of all colours (of plates and films) [Phot.].

pancosmism, *n.* pan-*koz*-mizm, the doctrine that nothing exists outside of or apart from the material universe.

pancratic, *a.* pan-*krat*-ik, excelling in gymnastics; athletic; adjustable to many degrees of power (of lenses) [Opt.].

pancratist, *n.* *pan*-kra-tist, one who excels in gymnastics.

pancratium, *n.* pan-*kray*-she-um, an athletic contest in ancient Greece. (Gr. *pankration.*)

pancreas, *n.* *pang*-kre-as, a gland opening into the duodenum and secreting a fluid helpful in digestion; the sweetbread. (Gr. *pankreas.*)

pancreatic, *a.* pang-kre-*at*-ik, pertaining to the pancreas. **pancreatic juice,** the fluid secreted by the pancreas.

pancreatitis, *n.* pang-kre-a-*ty*-tis, inflammation of the pancreas.

panda, *n.* *pan*-da, a carnivorous racoon-like mammal, *Ailurus fulgens*, of the Himalayas. **giant panda,** a rare, black-and-white bear-like mammal, *Aluropoda melanoleuca*, of Tibet and S. China. (Native.)

Pandanus, *n.* pan-*day*-nus, a genus of trees comprising the screw-pines. (Malay, *pandan.*)

Pandean, *a.* pan-*dee*-an, pertaining to Pan. **Pandean pipes,** a musical wind instrument consisting of short reeds of different lengths fastened side by side.

pandect, *n.* *pan*-dekt, a treatise on the whole of a science: *pl.* (*cap.*) the digest of civil or Roman law; any complete code of law. (Gr. *pandektes.*)

pandemic, *a.* pan-*dem*-ik, affecting a whole people; widely epidemic [Med.]. (Gr. *pandemos.*)

pandemonium, *n.* pan-de-*moh*-ne-um, hell, as the abode of all the devils; a place or state of uproar. (Gr. *pan-*, and *daimōn*, devil.)

pander, *n.* *pan*-der, a pimp; a procurer: *v.t.* to procure or pander for: *v.i.* to act as agent for debauchees; to minister to lust or passion; to encourage evil designs. (*Pandarus*, the pimp in the mediæval romance of Troilus.)

panderess, *n.* *pan*-der-ess, a female pander.

panderism, *n.* *pan*-der-izm, the business of a pander.

pandiculation, *n.* *pan*-dik-yew-*lay*-shon, a yawning; a stretching. (L. *pando*, stretch.)

pandit, *n.* *pan*-dit, a pundit.

Pandora, *n.* pan-*daw*-ra, the first woman of Greek mythology, sent from heaven to earth to punish man for thinking he could wield the fire of Jove; a genus of marine bivalves: (*l.c.*) a bandore. **Pandora's box,** the box Pandora brought with her, filled with all good and evil things and from which, when opened by her husband Epimetheus, all escaped except Hope. (Gr. *pan-*, all, *dora*, gifts.)

pandore, *n.* *pan*-dore, a bandore. (Fr.)

pandour, *n.* *pan*-door, a Croatian light infantry soldier of the Austrian Imperial army; any cruel marauder or warrior. (Croatian *pandur*, a constable, a frontier guard.)

panduriform, *a.* pan-*dew*-re-form, fiddle-shaped [Bot. and Ent.]. (*pandore.*)

pandy, *n.* *pan*-de, a stroke on the open hand [Scots.]. (L. *pande palmam*, stretch forth thy hand.)

pane, *n.* pane, a square of glass in a window; a distinct patch; a piece of variegated work: *v.t.* to furnish with panes. (Fr. *pan.*)

panegyric, *n.* pan-e-*ji*-rik, an oration or eulogy in praise of some distinguished person or achievement; an encomium. (Gr. *panegyrikos*, delivered in public, from *pan-*, and *agora*, a gathering.)

panegyrical, *a.* pan-e-*ji*-re-kal, containing praise or eulogy; encomiastic.

panegyrist, *n.* pan-e-*ji*-rist, a eulogist.

panegyrize, *v.t.* *pan*-e-ji-rize, to praise highly: *v.i.* to bestow praises.

panel, *n.* *pan*-el, a thin rectangular board for insertion in a frame; an ornamental piece let into a dress lengthwise; a saddle-pad; a picture tall in proportion to its breadth; a schedule containing names of persons summoned or chosen for certain duties (as a jury), or of insured persons attending a particular doctor; a complete jury; the criminal at the bar [Scots. Law]; a single section of the fabric of a balloon, etc.; a section of a switchboard [Elect.]: *v.t.* to form with panels. **panel doctor,** a medical practitioner having a National Health Insurance panel. (O.Fr.)

paneless, *a.* *pane*-less, without panes of glass.

panelling, *n.* *pan*-el-ing, panels; panelled surfaces generally [Arch.].

pang, *n.* pang, a sudden pain; extreme pain; a fit of sorrow. (Origin unknown.)

pangenesis, *n.* pan-*jen*-e-sis, the theory that heredity is transmitted directly from all parts of both parents through gemmules that multiply by subdivision. (Gr. *pan-*, all, *genesis*, origin.)

Pan-German, *a.* pan-*jer*-man, pertaining to Germans collectively, or to Pan-Germanism.

Pan-Germanism, *n.* pan-*jer*-ma-nizm, the movement for the union of all Germanic peoples in a Greater Germany under a single Führer; German imperialism.

pangolin, *n.* *pang*-go-lin, a scaly ant-eater of the genus *Manis*. (Malay.)

panhandle, *n.* *pan*-han-dl, a straight projecting handle; a narrow promontory or strip of land.

Panhellenic, *a.* *pan*-he-*len*-ik, pertaining to all Greeks, esp. of ancient Greece.

panic, *n.* *pan*-ik, a sudden fright; a state of financial alarm resulting in depreciation: *a.* extreme or sudden; under fright: *v.t.* to affect with panic; *v.i.* to be thus affected; to stampede. (So called as ascribed to *Pan.*)

panic, *n.* *pan*-ik, Italian millet, *Setaria italica*, or other grass of the genus *Panicum*.

panicky, *a.* *pan*-e-ke, prone to panic; groundlessly timid; affected with panic.

panicle, *n.* *pan*-e-kl, a compound raceme, a loose inflorescence [Bot.]. (L. *panicula*, a tiny tuft.)

panicled, *a.* *pan*-e-kld, furnished with panicles.

panic-struck, *a.* struck with panic or sudden fear.

paniculate, *a.* pa-*nik*-yew-late, having the flowers in panicles.

Panicum, *n.* *pan*-e-kum, a genus of grasses including the panic, or panic grass.

panidiomorphic, *a.* pa-*nid*-e-o-*mor*-fik, completely idiomorphic (of crystals).
panification, *n.* pan-e-fe-*kay*-shon, the process of bread-baking or of converting into bread. (L. *panis*, bread, *facio*, make.)
Panislam, *n.* pan-*iz*-lam, Mohammedans collectively; a union of the Mohammedan peoples.
Panislamic, *a.* pan-iz-*lam*-ik, pertaining to Panislam or to all Mohammedans.
Panjandrum, *n.* pan-*jan*-drum, a pompous pretender or official. (Coined by Foote, the actor.)
panlogism, *n.* *pan*-lo-jizm, the philosophical doctrine that thought is the only absolute reality. (Gr. *pan-*, and *logos*, reason.)
pannade, *n.* pa-*nade*, the curvetting of a horse. (Fr.)
pannage, *n.* *pan*-aj, the food of swine in the woods; the right of such feeding, also, the payment for it. (O.Fr. *panage*.)
panne, *n.* pan, a velvety dress-material with a long nap. (Fr., plush.)
pannier, *n.* *pan*-e-er, one of a pair of wicker baskets, primarily a bread-basket, slung over a horse; a dress contrivance for making the hips look larger; a corbel [Arch.]. (Fr. *panier*.)
pannikin, *n.* *pan*-e-kin, a small metal mug.
pannose, *a.* *pan*-nohs, resembling felt or cloth in texture [Bot.]. (L. *pannosus*, rag-like.)
pannosity, *n.* pa-*nos*-e-te, softness of the skin [Med.].
pannus, *n.* *pan*-nus, a condition of vascularity and opacity of the cornea, present esp. in trachoma. (L., a cloth.)
panoistic, *a.* pan-o-*is*-tik, producing ova only [Ent.]. (Gr. *pan-*, and *oion*, an egg.)
panoplied, *a.* *pan*-o-plid, completely armed.
panoply, *n.* *pan*-o-ple, a full suit of armour; any complete protection. (Fr. *panoplie*.)
panopticon, *n.* pan-*op*-te-kon, a prison so constructed that a centrally placed warden can watch all prisoners; an exhibition hall. (Gr. *pan-*, and *optikon*, relating to sight.)
panorama, *n.* pan-o-*rah*-ma, a complete view all round, as seen from a central point; a continuous picture of several scenes unrolled before the spectators. (Gr. *pan-*, and *horama*, a view.)
panoramic, *a.* pan-o-*ram*-ik, belonging to or as in a panorama.
panphobia, *n.* pan-*foh*-be-a, morbid groundless fear of everything.
Pan-pipe, *n.* the pandean pipes; a mouth organ.
pansclerosis, *n.* *pan*-skler-*roh*-sis, complete local thickening and hardening of interstitial tissue. (Gr. *pan-*, and *sklerosis*, hardening.)
pansied, *a.* *pan*-zid, covered with pansies.
Panslavic, *a.* pan-*slah*-vik, pertaining to all the Slavic nations.
Panslavism, *n.* pan-*slah*-vizm, a movement towards union among all the Slavic nations.
pansophical, *a.* pan-*sof*-e-kal, pretending to know everything. (Gr. *pan-*, and *sophia*, wisdom.)
pansophism, *n.* *pan*-so-fizm, pretension to universal knowledge; sciolism.
panspermy, *n.* pan-*sper*-me, the theory accounting for the spread of disease, or for apparent spontaneous generation, by the fortuitous development of airborne germs. (Gr. *pan-*, and *sperma*, seed.)
pansy, *n.* *pan*-ze, a kind of *Viola*, the heart's-ease; a very effeminate young man, a male homosexual [Slang]. (Fr. *pensee*, thought.)
pant, *n.* pant, palpitation of the heart; a gasping for want of breath: *v.i.* to palpitate; to gasp for want of breath; to desire ardently. (Fr. *panteler*.)
pantagraph, *n.* *pan*-ta-graf, pantograph.
Pantagruelian, *a.* *pan*-ta-groo-*el*-e-an, characterized by or pertaining to Pantagruelism; humorously coarse: *n.* one given to Pantagruelism; an admirer or copier of Pantagruel.
Pantagruelism, *n.* *pan*-ta-*groo*-el-izm, coarse humour or buffoonery used as serious satire. (The giant hero of Rabelais's "Pantagruel.")
pantalets, *n.pl.* pan-ta-*lets*, frilled drawers coming below the skirts, as worn by girls in the mid-nineteenth century; detachable frills for drawers; women's knickers. (*pantaloon*.)
pantaloon, *n.* pan-ta-*loon*, a combination of breeches and stockings for men; *pl.* tight-fitting trousers; trousers [U.S.A.]; (*cap.*) the old man character in pantomimes. (Fr. *pantalon*.)
pantatrophia, *n.* pan-ta-*troh*-fe-a, general atrophy [Path.].
pantechnicon, *n.* pan-*tek*-ne-kon, a warehouse for storing furniture; a furniture van. (Gr. *pan-*, and *techne*, art.)
panter, *n.* *pan*-ter, one who pants.
pantheism, *n.* *pan*-the-izm, the doctrine that identifies the universe with God, conceiving of Him as wholly, and in some systems exclusively, immanent in all things; the worship, or toleration of worship, of all the gods. (Gr. *pan-* and *theos*, God.)
pantheist, *n.* *pan*-the-ist, a believer in pantheism.
pantheistical, *a.* pan-the-*is*-te-kal, pertaining to pantheism.
Pantheon, *n.* *pan*-the-on, a temple dedicated to all the gods; a system of deities; a building for entertainments; a bazaar; a building, esp. that in Paris, dedicated to the memory of the great men of a nation. (Gr.)
panther, *n.* *pan*-ther, the leopard; applied also to the puma and jaguar. (O.Fr. *panthere*.)
panties, *n.* *pan*-tiz, a kind of women's knickers.
pantile, *n.* *pan*-tile, a curved roofing tile.
pantingly, *ad.* *pan*-ting-le, in a panting manner.
pantisocracy, *n.* *pan*-te-*sok*-ra-se, a Utopian community in which all are equal in rank and all should have equal rule. (Gr. *pan-*, and *isos*, equal, *kratein*, govern.)
pantler, *n.* *pant*-ler, an officer in charge of the pantry and provisions in large mediæval establishments. (O.F. *panetier*, from L. *panis*, bread.)
pantochronometer, *n.* *pan*-to-kro-*nom*-e-ter, an instrument which combines the compass, sun-dial, and time-dial. (Gr. *pan-*, and *chronometer*.)
pantofle, *n.* pan-*toofl*, a slipper for the foot. (Fr.)
pantograph, *n.* *pan*-to-graf, an instrument consisting of a jointed parallelogram for copying, reducing, or enlarging plans, etc. (Gr. *pan*, and *grapho*, write.)
pantographic, *a.* *pan*-to-*graf*-ik, pertaining to a pantograph.
pantography, *n.* pan-*tog*-ra-fe, general description.
pantological, *a.* *pan*-to-*loj*-e-kal, pertaining to pantology.
pantology, *n.* pan-*tol*-o-je, universal knowledge; general information; an encyclopædia. (Gr. *pan-*, and *logos*, account.)
pantometer, *n.* pan-*tom*-e-ter, an instrument for measuring elevations and angles. (Gr. *pan-*, and *metron*, measure.)
pantomime, *n.* *pan*-to-mime, representation in dumb show, in which the characters are harlequin and columbine, pantaloon and clown; a Christmas theatrical entertainment, generally a travesty of a fairy tale; in ancient Rome, a mute actor: *a.* representing in mute action. (Fr.)
pantomimic, *a.* pan-to-*mim*-ik, pertaining to pantomime.
pantomimist, *n.* *pan*-to-mym-ist, one who acts in pantomime.
pantomorphic, *a.* pan-to-*morf*-ik, assuming all forms; existing in all shapes.
panton, *n.* *pan*-ton, a kind of horseshoe.
pantophagist, *n.* pan-*tof*-a-jist, a man or animal that eats all kinds of food. (Gr. *pan-*, and *phago*, eat.)
pantophagous, *a.* pan-*tof*-a-gus, omnivorous [Zool.].
pantoscope, *n.* *pan*-to-skope, a wide-angled lens [Phot.]. (Gr. *pan*, and *skopeo*, view.)
pantoscopic, *a.* *pan*-to-*skop*-ik, having a wide field of vision; wide-angled (of lenses) [Opt.].
pantoum, *n.* pan-*toom*, a series of quatrains with alternate interlinking rhymes based on a Malayan verse-form [Pros.]. (Fr., from Malay *pantun*.)
pantry, *n.* *pan*-tre, a room for plate, glass, and china; a room or cupboard in which provisions are kept. (O.Fr. *paneterie*.)
pants, *n.pl.* pants, men's underwear from waist to ankles; trousers [U.S.A.]. (*pantaloon*.)
panurgy, *n.* *pan*-ur-je, skill in all kinds of work. (Gr. *pan-*, and *ergon*, a work.)
Panzer, *a.* *punt*-ser, armoured (of troops, mobile guns, etc.) [Mil.]. (Ger., coat of mail.)
pap, *n.* pap, a nipple; a teat; a rounded hill. (Perhaps Scand.)
pap, *n.* pap, soft food for infants; pulp; mental nourishment suitable to the young or foolish. (Infant's cry for food.)

papa, *n.* pa-*pah*, father; a Greek parish priest; the Pope. (Fr. *papa*, and cf. L. *papa*, a pope.)
papacy, *n.* *pay*-pa-se, the office or tenure of office of the Pope; the papal system or authority; the Popes collectively; popery. (O.Fr. *papacie*.)
papal, *a.* *pay*-pal, proceeding from or pertaining to the Pope or the Roman Catholic Church. (Late L. *papalis*.)
papalist, *n.* *pay*-pal-ist, one who upholds the papal system, supremacy, or religion.
papalize, *v.t.* *pay*-pal-ize, to make papal; to spread papal doctrines: *v.i.* to conform to Roman Catholicism.
papaphobia, *n.* *pay*-pa-*foh*-be-a, hatred of the papacy. (L. *papa*, and Gr. *phobos*, terror.)
papaveraceous, *a.* pa-*pav*-er-*ray*-shus, pertaining to the poppies. (L. *papaver*, the poppy.)
papaverous, *a.* pa-*pav*-er-rus, resembling or allied to the poppy.
papaw, *n.* pa-*paw*, a tropical American tree of the genus *Carica*, and its fruit. (Sp.)
★**paper,** *n.* *pay*-per, pulp made into thin sheets, used for writing, printing, and drawing on, for wrapping and packing, etc.; a single sheet or piece of this; a newspaper; a literary contribution; any written instrument; promissory notes; paper money; paper-hangings; a free pass, or those admitted with such: *pl.* documents establishing the identity, etc., of a person or a ship; state papers: *a.* made of or like paper; unreal, having no existence except on paper: *v.t.* to cover, wrap, or supply with paper; to decorate with paper-hangings; to treat with sandpaper or the like. **paper credit,** credit allowed on notes or bills promising payment of money. **paper money,** bank-notes or bills used as currency. **paper nautilus,** *see* **nautilus. paper profits,** hypothetical or prospective profits. (L. *papyrus*.)
paperchase, *n.* *pay*-per-chase, a cross-country run following a trail of paper; hare and hounds.
paper-hanger, *n.* one who affixes wallpapers.
paper-hangings, *n.pl.* wallpaper; paper ornamented with coloured designs for decorating interiors.
paperknife, *n.* *pay*-per-nife, a knife for cutting open the leaves of books, opening envelopes, etc.; a thin blade for folding paper.
paper-stainer, *n.* a manufacturer of wallpaper.
paperweight, *n.* *pay*-per-wate, a weight for keeping papers from being blown about.
papery, *a.* *pay*-per-re, resembling paper.
papeterie, *n.* *pap*-a-tre, a case with paper, envelopes, etc.; a decorated stationery case. (Fr.)
Paphian, *a.* *pay*-fe-an, pertaining to the rites or worship of Venus; lewd: *n.* a native of Paphos; a harlot. (*Paphos*, a Cyprian city, famed for the worship of Venus.)
papier-mâché, *n.* *pap*-ya-*mah*-shay, a strong mouldable material consisting of paper pulp mixed with a hardening substance, as glue, rosin, etc. (Fr., mashed paper.)
papilionaceous, *a.* pa-*pil*-e-o-*nay*-shus, resembling the butterfly; having flowers like the wings of a butterfly [Bot.]. (L. *papilio*, a butterfly.)
papilla, *n.* pa-*pil*-la (*pl.* **papillæ**), a small pap or nipple; a protuberance; a pustule. (L.)
papillary, *a.* *pap*-e-la-re, pertaining to or resembling the nipple: covered with papillæ, pimpled.
papillate, *a.* *pap*-e-lat, papillary.
papilloma, *n.* pap-e-*loh*-ma, a growth (as a corn or wart) formed by enlargement of the papillæ of the skin or mucous membrane [Med.].
papillon, *n.* pa-*pil*-lon, a very small long-haired lap-dog, named from the shape of its ears. (Fr., a butterfly.)
papillose, *a.* *pap*-e-lose, papillary; warty.
papillote, *n.* *pap*-e-lote, a curl-paper. (Fr.)
papillous, *a.* pa-*pil*-lus, covered with papillæ; pimply.
papish, *a.* *pay*-pish, popish (disparagingly).
papism, *n.* *pay*-pizm, popery; Roman Catholicism (used only disparagingly).
papist, *n.* *pay*-pist, a Roman Catholic (disparagingly).
papistic, *a.* pa-*pis*-tik, pertaining to popery or the church of Rome (disparagingly).
papoose, *n.* pa-*poose*, an American Indian baby or small child. (Algonquian, a suckling.)
pappescent, *a.* pa-*pes*-sent, producing a pappus [Bot.].
pappose, *a.* *pap*-ohs, downy; having or resembling a pappus [Bot.]. (L. *pappus*, down.)
pappous, *a.* *pap*-pus, pappose.
pappus, *n.* *pap*-pus, the tuft of down on the seeds of composite plants; the first down on the chin. (L.)
pappy, *a.* *pap*-pe, like pap; succulent: foolishly simple.
paprika, *n.* *pap*-re-ka *or* pa-*pree*-ka, a pungent variety of red pepper. (Hungarian.)
papula, *n.* *pap*-yew-la (*pl.* **papulæ**), a pimple; a fleshy protuberance on a stem, etc. [Bot.]. (L.)
papular, *a.* *pap*-yew-lar, papulose.
papulation, *n.* pap-yew-*lay*-shon, the stage of the formation of pimples [Med.].
papule, *n.* *pap*-yewl, a papula; a small elevation of the skin.
papulose, *a.* *pap*-yew-lohs, full of papulæ.
papulous, *a.* *pap*-yew-lus, papulose.
papyraceous, *a.* *pap*-e-*ray*-shus, belonging to or made of papyrus; papery. (L. *papyrus*.)
papyrograph, *n.* pa-*pyr*-ro-graf, a copying apparatus employing a gelatine pad and paper stencil. (L. *papyrus*, and Gr. *grapho*, write.)
papyrologist, *n.* pap-e-*rol*-o-jist, a student of or expert in papyrology.
papyrology, *n.* pap-e-*rol*-o-je, the study of papyri.
papyrus, *n.* pa-*pyr*-rus, an Egyptian sedge, *Cyperus papyrus*, from which the ancients made paper; (*pl.* **papyri**) a scroll, esp. an ancient text, written on papyrus. (L.)
par, *n.* par, state of equality or parity; equal to face value; equality in condition. (L., equal.)
par, *n.* par, parr, the young of salmon.
para-, *pa*-ra, a Greek prefix, signifying beside or beyond, also wrong, on the other side, irregular.
para, *n.* *pah*-ra, rubber obtained from a S. American tree of the genius *Hevea*. (*Para*, in Brazil.)
para, *n.* pa-*rah*, a Turkish money of account, one-fortieth of a piastre. (Pers.)
parabaptism, *n.* *pa*-ra-*bap*-tizm, uncanonical or irregular baptism.
parabasis, *n.* pa-*rab*-a-sis, in ancient Greek comedy, an ode (esp. on current topics) addressed by the chorus to the audience.
parable, *n.* *pa*-ra-bl, a fable with a moral; an allegory: *v.t.* to represent by a parable. (O.Fr. *parabole*.)
parabiosis, *n.* *pa*-ra-by-*oh*-sis, the functional union of embryos, as in Siamese twins.
parablepsis, *n.* *pa*-ra-*blep*-sis, false vision. (Gr. *para-*, and *blepsis*, vision.)
parabola, *n.* pa-*rab*-o-la, a conic section formed by cutting a cone by a plane parallel to its side. (L.)
parabole, *n.* pa-*rab*-o-le, similitude; comparison.
parabolic, *a.* pa-ra-*bol*-ik, pertaining to or like a parabola; expressed by parable; figurative.
parabolical, *a.* pa-ra-*bol*-e-kal, pertaining to, or expressed by, parable.
parabolically, *ad.* in the form of a parable.
paraboloid, *n.* pa-*rab*-o-loyd, a solid generated by the revolution of a parabola about its axis. (Gr. *parabola*, and *eidos*, like.)
Paracelsian, *a.* *pa*-ra-*sel*-se-an, pertaining to or denoting the medical practice of the Swiss alchemist and philosopher Paracelsus (*d.* 1541): *n.* a follower of Paracelsus.
paracentesis, *n.* *pa*-ra-sen-*tee*-sis, the operation of tapping [Surg.]. (Gr. *para-*, and *kenteo*, pierce.)
paracentral, *a.* pa-ra-*sen*-tral, situated at or near the centre.
parachronism, *n.* pa-*rak*-ro-nizm, a chronological error, esp. by postdating an event. (Gr. *para-*, and *chronos*, time.)
parachute, *n.* *pa*-ra-shoot, a folding umbrella-like device to retard the rate of descent of a falling body, esp. one used in dropping parachutists, supplies, etc., from aircraft in flight; a seed or fruit adapted to dispersal by the wind [Bot.]: *v.i.* to use a parachute.
parachutist, *n.* pa-ra-*shoo*-tist, an expert in the use of the parachute, esp. [Mil.] one trained to alight from aircraft thus, armed and ready for action.
Paraclete, *n.* *pa*-ra-kleet, the Holy Ghost, the Comforter. (Gr., one called to one's aid.)
paracme, *n.* pa-*rak*-me, decadence after reaching the prime. (Gr. *para-*, beyond, and *acme*.)
paracrostic, *n.* *pa*-ra-*kros*-tik, a poetical composition in which the first verse contains in order all the letters which commence the others. (Gr. *para-*, and *acrostic*.)
paracusis, *n.* *pa*-ra-*kew*-sis, disordered hearing. (Gr. *para-*, and *akousis*, hearing.)

paracyanogen, *n.* *pa*-ra-sy-*an*-o-jen, an insoluble substance obtained by heating cyanide of mercury. (Gr. *para-*, and *cyanogen.*)

parade, *n.* pa-*rade,* show ; ostentation ; pompous display or procession ; military display ; the place where troops assemble for parade ; a public thoroughfare or fashionable lounge ; an esplanade : *v.t.* to make a display of ; to array in military order : *v.i.* to go about in military array ; to promenade, or walk about for show. (Fr.)

paradigm, *n.* *pa*-ra-dime, an example ; a model ; a scheme of the inflections of a verb [Gram.]. (Fr. *paradigme.*)

paradigmatic, *a.* *pa*-ra-dig-*mat*-ik, in the form of a paradigm.

paradigmatically, *ad.* by way of a paradigm.

paradisaic, *a.* *pa*-ra-de-*say*-ik, pertaining to paradise ; celestial ; heavenly.

paradisaical, *a.* *pa*-ra-de-*say*-e-kal, paradisaic.

paradise, *n.* *pa*-ra-dice, the garden of Eden ; a place of bliss ; heaven. **bird of paradise,** *see* **bird. paradise fish,** any of several small brightly coloured freshwater fish of China and the East Indies, esp. of the genus *Macropodus.* (Gr. *paradeisos,* a park or pleasure garden, from Pers.)

paradisiac, *a.* *pa*-ra-*diz*-e-ak, paradisaic.

parados, *n.* *pa*-ra-dos, an elevation of earth behind a fortified place to secure it from attack rearward ; a rampart in the rear of a trench [Mil.]. (Fr.)

paradox, *n.* *pa*-ra-doks, a proposition contrary to received opinion ; an assertion, etc., seemingly absurd, yet really true. (Gr. *para-*, and *doxa,* opinion.)

paradoxical, *a.* *pa*-ra-*dok*-se-kal, having the nature of a paradox ; inclined to paradox.

paradoxically, *ad.* in a paradoxical manner.

paradoxicalness, *n.* state of being paradoxical.

paradoxure, *n.* *pa*-ra-*dok*-sewr, any of several long-tailed arboreal civets, esp. of the genus *Paradoxurus,* ranging from India to Formosa ; the palm-civet.

paræsthesia, *n.* pah-rees-*thee*-ze-a, any abnormal tickling or tingling sensation [Med.].

paraffin, *n.* *pa*-ra-fin, a waxy substance, tasteless, inodorous, and colourless when pure, derived from the distillation of wood, petroleum, and various hydrocarbons ; paraffin oil. **paraffin oil,** an illuminant and lubricant obtained with paraffin in the distillation of petroleum, etc. **paraffin wax,** solid paraffin. (L. *parum affinis,* little akin—because non-reactive.)

paragenesis, *n.* *pa*-ra-*jen*-e-sis, hybridism ; the product of characteristics of different species in a single organism [Biol.] ; the formation of minerals in contact, both being affected thereby [Geol.]. (Gr. *para-*, and *genesis.*)

paragenetic, *a.* *pa*-ra-je-*net*-ik, paragenic.

paragenic, *a.* *pa*-ra-*jen*-ik, pertaining to paragenesis ; developed at the commencement, esp. of twinned crystals [Min.]. (Gr. *para-*, and *gennao,* produce.)

parageusia, *n.* *pa*-ra-*gew*-se-a, any abnormality in the sense of taste [Med.]. (Gr. *para-*, and *geusis,* taste.)

paragnathous, *a.* pa-*rag*-na-thus, having the mandibles of equal length [Ornith.].

paragoge, *n.* *pa*-ra-*goh*-je, the addition of a letter or syllable to the end of a word. (Gr. *para-*, and *ago,* lead.)

paragogic, *a.* *pa*-ra-*goj*-ik, pertaining to paragoge.

paragon, *n.* *pa*-ra-gon, a model or pattern of superior excellence or perfection ; a flawless diamond of not less than 100 carats ; an old type-size of about 20 points [Print.] : *v.t.* to compare ; to equal. (O.Fr.)

paragram, *n.* *pa*-ra-gram, a play upon words ; a pun. (Gr. *para-*, and *gramma,* a letter.)

paragrammatist, *n.* pa-ra-*gram*-a-tist, a maker of paragrams.

paragraph, *n.* *pa*-ra-graf, a short passage in type, generally distinguished by a break in the line ; a short passage; the reference-mark ¶ [Print.]. (Fr. *paragraphe.*)

paragraphic, *a.* pa-ra-*graf*-ik, pertaining to or consisting of paragraphs.

paragraphist, *n.* *pa*-ra-graf-ist, one who writes paragraphs ; a columnist.

Paraguay-tea, *n.* *pa*-ra-gway-*tee,* maté, an infusion of the leaves of *Ilex paraguensis.* (*Paraguay,* in South America.)

paraheliotropism, *n.* *pa*-ra-hee-le-*ot*-ro-pizm, the curvature of leaves, etc., towards a plane parallel to the sun's rays, the so-called daily sleep of plants. (*para-* and *heliotropism.*)

parakeet, *n.* *pa*-ra-keet, a small species of long-tailed parrot. (O.Fr. *paroquet.*)

paraldehyde, *n.* pa-*ral*-de-hide, a modification of aldehyde used as a soporific and narcotic.

paraleipsis, *n.* pa-ra-*lipe*-sis, a figure in which a speaker affects to pass over what he is really calling attention to [Rhet.]. (Gr.)

paralexia, *n.* pa-ra-*lek*-se-a, the defect of transposing words or syllables in reading, due to a lesion in the brain. (Gr. *para-*, and *lesis,* speaking.)

paralipomena, *n.pl.* *pa*-ra-ly-*poh*-me-na, matter omitted from, but added as addenda to, a literary work. (Gr. *paraleipein,* to omit.)

parallactic, *a.* *pa*-ra-*lak*-tik, due or pertaining to a parallax.

parallax, *n.* *pa*-ra-laks, apparent displacement due to shifting the point of view, esp. the difference in the position of a heavenly body as seen from a point on the earth's surface and from some other point, as the earth's or the sun's centre. (Gr. *parallaxis,* change.)

★**parallel,** *a.* *pa*-ra-lel, equidistant for any distance ; having the same direction or tendency ; running in accordance with something ; resembling in essentials ; similar : *n.* a line which, throughout its whole extent, is equidistant from another ; direction conformable to that of another line ; likeness ; comparison ; a counterpart ; one of the circles on the terrestrial sphere parallel to the equator and marking degrees of latitude ; a trench in front of a fortified place parallel to the defences [Mil.] ; the reference-mark || [Print.] : *v.t.* to place parallel ; to equal ; to correspond to ; to be equal to ; to compare. **in parallel,** having the ends joined to a pair of common terminals (of electrical components) [Elect.]. **parallel bars,** a gymnastic apparatus consisting of two bars of equal length placed at the same height. **parallel motion,** a linkage by which circular motion is converted into rectilineal motion while keeping the rods parallel. **parallel ruler,** a drawing instrument formed of two equal rulers, movable about joints, but always remaining parallel. (O.Fr. *parallele.*)

parallelepiped, *n.* *pa*-ra-lel-*ep*-e-ped, an oblong solid bounded by six parallelograms, of which the opposite pairs are equal and parallel. (L. *parallelepipedum.*)

parallelism, *n.* *pa*-ra-lel-izm, state of being parallel ; resemblance ; comparison.

parallelogram, *n.* *pa*-ra-*lel*-o-gram, a four-sided figure with opposite parallel sides, generally one of greater length than breadth. (O.Fr. *paralelograme.*)

paralogism, *n.* pa-*ral*-o-jizm, a fallacious argument ; a conclusion not warranted by the premises [Log.]. (Gr. *para-*, and *logos,* reason.)

paralogize, *v.i.* pa-*ral*-o-jize, to reason falsely ; to draw unjustifiable conclusions.

paralogy, *n.* pa-*ral*-o-je, false reasoning.

paralysant, *a.* *pa*-ra-ly-zant, producing paralysis : *n.* an agent effecting this.

paralysation, *n.* *pa*-ra-ly-*zay*-shon, the act or process of paralysing ; condition of being paralysed.

paralyse, *v.t.* *pa*-ra-lize, to affect with paralysis ; to destroy or weaken power of action.

paralysis, *n.* pa-*ral*-e-sis, total or partial inability to control the voluntary muscles ; loss or impairment of sensation or power of motion in one or more parts of the body ; palsy. (L.)

paralytic, *a.* pa-ra-*lit*-ik, pertaining to or affected with paralysis ; inclined to paralysis : *n.* a person affected with paralysis.

paramagnetic, *a.* *pa*-ra-mag-*net*-ik, capable of being attracted towards a magnetic pole (opposed to diamagnetic).

paramatta, *n.* pa-ra-*mat*-a, a twilled cotton fabric with worsted filling used for waterproofs. (*Paramatta,* N.S.W.)

parameter, *n.* pa-*ram*-e-ter, the focal chord at right angles to the axis in each of the three conic sections ; the constant quantity which enters into the equation of a curve [Geom.]. (Gr. *para-*, and *metron,* measure.)

para-military, *a.* civilian, but of a military nature and effect ; overtly civilian, but covertly military.

paramnesia, *n.* *pa*-ram-*nee*-se-a, any disorder of memory, esp. the illusion of having formerly experienced events now first experienced.
paramo, *n.* pa-*rah*-mo, a high-lying desert tract in the Andes. (Sp.)
paramorph, *n.* *pa*-ra-morf, a mineral having the same chemical composition as another but differing physically.
paramount, *a.* *pa*-ra-mount, superior to all others: *n.* the highest in rank; a lord paramount. (O.Fr.)
paramountcy, *n.* *pa*-ra-mount-se, the condition or quality of being paramount.
paramour, *n.* *pa*-ra-moor, a lover; an illicit mistress. (Fr. *par*, by or with, *amour*, love.)
parang, *n.* pah-*rang*, a short sword or sheath-knife used by the Dyaks. (Malayan.)
paranoia, *n.* pa-ra-*noy*-a, a form of lunacy characterized by delusions, hallucinations, etc. (Gr.)
paranoiac, *a.* pa-ra-*noy*-ak, having paranoia: *n.* one affected with paranoia.
paranoid, *a.* *pa*-ra-noyd, resembling paranoia; paranoiac.
paranymph, *n.* *pa*-ra-nimf, a bridesmaid or best man; an abettor. (Gr. *paranymphos*.)
parapet, *n.* *pa*-ra-pet, a wall breast-high; a rampart in front of a trench; a wall or elevation for covering soldiers from observation or attack. (Fr.)
paraph, *n.* *pa*-raf, a flourish attached to a signature: *v.t.* to initial or sign. (Fr. *parapher*.)
paraphernalia, *n.pl.* *pa*-ra-fer-*nay*-le-a, personal belongings; equipment; ornaments; trappings; formerly, the personal property of a married woman other than her dower [Law]. (Gr. *parapherne*, dowry.)
paraphimosis, *n.* *pa*-ra-fy-*moh*-sis, permanent retraction of the prepuce [Med.]. (Gr. *para-*, and *phimosis*, muzzling.)
paraphrase, *n.* *pa*-ra-fraze, a fuller and clearer explanation of a text, etc.; a free translation; a hymn founded on a passage of scripture: *v.t.* to state in clearer or other terms; to translate freely: *v.i.* to make a paraphrase. (O.Fr.)
paraphrasia, *n.* pa-ra-*fray*-ze-a, incoherence of speech [Path.].
paraphrast, *n.* *pa*-ra-frast, one who paraphrases.
paraphrastic, *a.* pa-ra-*fras*-tik, free and ample in explanation; of the nature of a paraphrase.
paraphrenia, *n.* pa-ra-*free*-ne-a, a form of schizophrenia. (Gr. *para-*, and *phrēn*, mind.)
paraplectic, *a.* pa-ra-*plek*-tik, stricken with paraplegia.
paraplegia, *n.* pa-ra-*plee*-je-a, paralysis of the legs and lower parts of the body. (Gr.)
paraplegic, *a.* pa-ra-*plej*-ik, pertaining to or characteristic of paraplegia: *n.* one affected with paraplegia.
parapleuritis, *n.* pa-ra-ploo-*ry*-tis, a mild form of pleurisy.
parapodium, *n.* pa-ra-*poh*-de-um, a foot tubercle in certain annelids. (Gr. *para-*, and *pous*, foot.)
parapophysis, *n.* pa-ra-*pof*-e-sis, the inferior or anterior process on the side of a vertebra.
paraquet, *n.* *pa*-ra-keet, a parakeet.
parasang, *n.* *pa*-ra-sang, an ancient Persian measure of length of about four English miles. (Per.)
parasceve, *n.* *pa*-ra-seev, the eve before the Jewish sabbath. (Gr., preparation.)
paraselene, *n.* *pa*-ra-se-*lee*-ne, a mock moon, sometimes seen with lunar halos. (Gr. *para-*, and *selene*, the moon.)
parasite, *n.* *pa*-ra-site, a hanger-on; a sycophant; one who frequents the tables of the rich, and earns his welcome by flattery; a plant or animal which attaches itself to or in and lives at the expense of another [Bot. and Zool.]. (Fr., from Gr. *parasitos*, eating beside.)
parasitic, *a.* *pa*-ra-*sit*-ik, like a parasite; fawning for bread or favours; living on another.
parasitical, *a.* pa-ra-*sit*-e-kal, parasitic.
parasiticide, *n.* *pa*-ra-*sit*-e-side, an agent used to destroy parasites.
parasitism, *n.* *pa*-ra-sit-izm, the act or practice of a parasite; state of being parasitic.
parasitize, *v.t.* *par*-a-sit-ize, to infest as with or as with parasites.
parasitoid, *a.* *pa*-ra-sit-oyd, resembling parasites.
parasitological, *a.* *par*-a-sit-o-*loj*-e-kal, pertaining to parasitology.
parasitologist, *n.* *par*-a-se-*tol*-o-jist, one who specializes in parasitology.
parasitology, *n.* *pa*-ra-se-*tol*-o-je, the study of parasites. (Gr. *parasites*, and *logos*, science.)
parasitosis, *n.* *pa*-ra-se-*toh*-sis, infestation by parasites [Med.].
parasol, *n.* *pa*-ra-sol, an umbrella used, esp. by women, as a shade from the sun; a sunshade. **parasol plane,** a monoplane with the wings mounted above the fuselage to allow of downward vision [Av.]. (It. *para*, defend, *sole*, sun.)
parasynthesis, *n.* pa-ra-*sin*-the-sis, the process or principle of forming derivatives from compounds [Philology].
parasynthetic, *a.* *pa*-ra-sin-*thet*-ik, formed by parasynthesis: *n.* a parasynthetic derivative.
parasyphilitic, *a.* *pa*-ra-sif-e-*lit*-ik, due indirectly to syphilis [Med.].
parataxis, *n.* pa-ra-*tak*-sis, a loose arrangement of clauses or sentences [Gram.].
parathesis, *n.* pa-*rath*-e-sis, apposition [Gram.]; a parenthetical notice [Rhet.]. (Gr.)
parathyroid, *a.* pa-ra-*thy*-royd, situated near the thyroid gland, esp. of certain other glands [Anat.].
paratroops, *n.* *pa*-ra-troops, an organized body of parachutists [Mil.].
paratrophy, *n.* pa-*rat*-ro-fe, abnormal nutrition [Path.]; hypertrophy. (Gr. *para-*, and *trophe*, food.)
paratyphoid, *n.* par-a-*ty*-foyd, an enteric fever much resembling typhoid.
paravane, *n.* *pa*-ra-vane, a device towed under water for removing mines in sea-ways.
parboil, *v.t.* *par*-boyl, to half cook by boiling, esp. for subsequent cooking. (O.Fr. *parboiller*, cook thoroughly.)
parbuckle, *n.* *par*-bukl, a double sling for hoisting or lowering casks, etc.: *v.t.* to hoist or lower with this. (Fr. *par*, by, and *buckle*.)
Parcæ, *n.pl.* *par*-see, the three Fates [Myth.]. (L.)
***parcel,** *ad.* *par*-sl, partly: half: *n.* a small package; a little part; a separate portion, esp. of land; a quantity; a number (in contempt); to make into a parcel; to divide into parts: *v.t.* to cover a rope with strips of canvas [Naut.]. **parcel post,** a postal service undertaking the conveyance and delivery of parcels. (Fr. *parcelle*.)
parcelling, *n.* *par*-sl-ing, strips of tarred canvas round a rope to prevent chafing. [Naut.].
parcenary, *n.* *par*-se-na-re, co-heirship [Law].
parcener, *n.* *par*-se-ner, a co-heir [Law]. (O.Fr.)
parch, *v.t.* parch, to shrivel by heat; to scorch; to dry to excess: *v.i.* to be parched.
parchedness, *n.* parchd-ness, the state of being parched.
parchment, *n.* *parch*-ment, the skin of a sheep, goat, or calf, dressed and rendered fit for writing on; a deed or other manuscript on this. (O.Fr. *parchemin*, from L. *Pergamenus*, relating to *Pergamum*, where first made.)
parchmentize, *v.t.* *parch*-men-tize, to make (paper) parchment-like by treatment with sulphuric acid.
parcimonious, *a.* *par*-se-*moh*-ne-us, parsimonious.
parclose, *n.* *par*-kloze, an enclosure; a screen, esp. in a church; a railing round a tomb. (O.Fr.)
pard, *n.* pard, the leopard. (L. *pardus*.)
pard, *n.* pard, a partner, a mate [U.S.A. slang].
pardie, *ad.* and *int.* par-*dee*, certainly; in truth.
pardon, *n.* *par*-don, forgiveness; remission of a penalty; a papal indulgence, also a festival on the granting of this; the festival of a patron saint (esp. in Brittany): *v.t.* to forgive; to remit, as a penalty; to excuse, as for a fault. (Fr.)
pardonable, *a.* *par*-don-a-bl, excusable; venial.
pardonably, *ad.* *par*-don-a-ble, excusably.
pardoner, *n.* *par*-don-er, one who forgives; a person formerly licensed to sell papal indulgences.
pare, *v.t.* pare, to cut or shave off; to diminish by little and little. (Fr. *parer*.)
paregoric, *a.* pa-re-*go*-rik, soothing; assuaging pain: *n.* a medicine that mitigates pain, esp. camphorated tincture of opium. (L. *paregoricus*, soothing.)
pareira, *n.* pa-*ryr*-ra, a diuretic prepared from the roots of certain South American plants. (Port. *pareirra*, vine.)
parella, *n.* pa-*rel*-la, the lichen, *Lecanora parella*, which yields litmus and orchil. (Fr. *parelle*.)
parembole, *n.* pa-*rem*-bo-le, an explanation inserted in a sentence [Rhet.]. (Gr.)

parencephalon, *n.* pah-ren-*sef*-a-lon, the cerebellum [Anat.].
parenchyma, *n.* pa-*reng*-ke-ma, the soft cellular tissue of the glandular organs [Anat.]; fruit-pulp or pith of plants [Bot.]. (Gr. *para-*, *en*, in, and *cheo*, pour, the tissue being taken for effused blood.)
parenchymatous, *a.* pa-reng-*kim*-a-tus, like parenchyma; spongy.
parenchymous, *a.* pa-*reng*-ke-mus, parenchymatous.
parenetic, *a.* pa-re-*net*-ik, hortatory; persuasive; advisory. (Gr. *parainetikos*.)
parent, *n. pare*-rent, a father or mother; an ancestor; that which produces; source; cause. (Fr., a blood relation.)
parentage, *n. pare*-ren-taj, extraction; birth.
parental, *a.* pa-*ren*-tal, pertaining to parents; befitting parents; tender; affectionate.
parentally, *ad.* pa-*ren*-ta-le, in a parental way.
parenteral, *a.* pa-*ren*-ter-ral, situated or occurring outside the digestive tract [Med.]. (Gr. *para-*, and *enteron*, intestine.)
parenthesis, *n.* pa-*ren*-the-sis, a clause inserted in a grammatically complete sentence for explanation or confirmation, etc., and usually placed between brackets; an interlude [Fig.]: *pl.* **parentheses,** pa-*ren*-the-seez, a pair of round brackets, thus () [Print.]. (Gr.)
parenthesize, *v.t.* pa-*ren*-the-size, to insert as, or convert into, a parenthesis; to place between parentheses.
parenthetic, *a.* pa-ren-*thet*-ik, parenthetical.
parenthetical, *a.* pa-ren-*thet*-e-kal, expressed in a parenthesis; using parentheses; interposed.
parenthetically, *ad.* in a parenthetical manner.
parenthood, *n.* the state of being a parent.
parenticide, *n.* pa-*ren*-te-side, the murder of a parent; one who murders his parent.
parer, *n. pare*-rer, an instrument for paring.
parergon, *n.* pa-*rer*-gon, a subsidiary work. (L.)
paresis, *n. pa*-re-sis, slight or partial paralysis; general paralysis of the insane. (Gr.)
paretic, *a.* pa-*ret*-ik, pertaining to, affected by, or resembling paresis.
pargasite, *n. par*-ga-site, a green variety of hornblende. (*Pargas*, Finland.)
parget, *n. par*-jet, rough plaster; pargeting: *v.t.* to plaster over, as a wall. (O.Fr. *pargeter*.)
pargeter, *n. par*-je-ter, a plasterer.
pargeting, *n. par*-je-ting, decorative plaster-work.
parhelion, *n.* par-*hee*-le-on (*pl.* **parhelia**), a mock-sun. (L.)
pariah, *n. pah*-re-a *or pare*-re-a, one of the lowest class in India, also one of no caste; a social outcast. **pariah dog,** a homeless mongrel, esp. in India. (Tamil.)
Parian, *a. pare*-re-an, pertaining to the Ægean Isle of Paros, famed for its marble; resembling marble from Paros: *n.* a fine kind of clay used for statuettes.
parietal, *a.* pa-*ry*-e-tal, pertaining to the wall of a body-cavity [Anat.], esp. to the sides and upper part of the skull; growing from the side or wall of another organ [Bot.]: *n.* a parietal bone. **parietal bone,** either of the two membrane bones in the roof of the skull [Anat.]. (L. *parietatis*, relating to a wall.)
pari-mutuel, *n. pa*-re-*mew*-tew-*el* (*pl.* **paris-mutuels**), a form of betting in which winners share the stakes proportionally, less a percentage for expenses; a totalisator. (Fr.)
paring, *n. pare*-ring, that which is pared off; rind; cutting off, or what is cut off, the surface of grass-land for tillage.
Paris, *n. pa*-ris, the capital of France. **herb Paris,** *see* **herb. Paris blue,** bright Prussian blue. **Paris green,** a light-green pigment and a highly poisonous insecticide prepared from aceto-arsenite of copper. **Paris red,** minium; finely divided ferric oxide used as a polishing agent. **Paris white,** a fine grade of whiting used as a pigment and for polishing. **Paris yellow,** light chrome yellow. **plaster of Paris,** *see* **plaster.**
parish, *n. pa*-rish, a minor sub-division of a county under the local government of a Parish Council; a district assigned to a particular church under a rector, vicar, or other minister; those under the charge of a particular pastor [U.S.A.]: *a.* belonging to, or maintained by, a parish. **on the parish,** receiving relief as a pauper. (Fr. *paroisse*.)
parishioner, *n.* pa-*rish*-on-er, a resident in a parish.
Parisian, *a.* pa-*riz*-e-an, pertaining to Paris; characteristic of Paris or its people: *n.fem.* **Parisienne** (App.), a native or French inhabitant of Paris.
parisite, *n. pa*-re-site, a brittle vitreous fluo-carbonate of metals of the cerium group. (Discoverer, J. J. *Paris*, early 19th cent.)
parisyllabic, *a. pa*-re-sil-*lab*-ik, having an equal number of syllables. (L. *par*, equal, and *syllable*.)
parity, *n. pa*-re-te, equality, esp. of rank; equivalence; nominal value being actual value. (Fr. *parité*.)
park, *n.* park, a large piece of ground enclosed for public or private recreation; an enclosure round a mansion; an artillery encampment; the train of artillery or transport belonging to an army; a place for the temporary accommodation of vehicles en route: *v.t.* to enclose in a park; to collect in a park; to leave in or as in a park (of vehicles, etc.). (Fr. *parc*.)
parka, *n. park*-ah, a fur or woollen shirt-like garment with hood attached. (Eskimo.)
parker, *n. park*-er, a park-keeper.
parkin, *n. park*-in, a thin cake made with treacle.
parkinsonism, *n. par*-kin-so-nizm, shaking palsy, or Parkinson's disease, a form of paralysis characterized by muscular rigidity and tremulous movements. (Jas. *Parkinson*, *d.* 1824, Engl. physician.)
parky, *a. par*-ke, chilly, cold [Slang].
parlance, *n. par*-lance, mode of speech; idiom.
parley, *n. par*-le, conference between opponents: *v.i.* to confer or treat with, as an enemy. (Fr. *parler*, speak.)
parleyvoo, *n. par*-le-voo, French; Frenchman: *v.i.* to speak French. [Slang].
Parliament, *n. par*-le-ment, the supreme legislature of the British nation, consisting of the Sovereign, the Lords, and the Commons; a deliberative assembly; a national assembly. (Fr. *parlement*.)
Parliamentarian, *n. par*-le-men-*tare*-re-an, an adherent of the parliament in the time of Charles I; (*l.c.*) one upholding parliamentary institutions, also one versed in these.
parliamentarianism, *n. par*-le-men-*tare*-re-a-nizm, the doctrine or system of parliamentary government.
parliamentary, *a.* par-le-*men*-ta-re, pertaining to, enacted by, or according to the usuages of, parliament.
parlour, *n. par*-lur, a sitting-room; the room in a house which the family usually occupy; a reception room. (O.Fr. *parloir*.)
parlour-maid, *n.* a female domestic servant who waits at table, etc.
parlous, *a. par*-lus, perilous; difficult: *ad.* excessively. (*perilous*.)
Parmesan, *n.* par-me-*zan*, a delicate sort of pressed cheese, first made at Parma, a city of N. Italy: *a.* belonging to Parma.
Parnassian, *a.* par-*nas*-e-an, pertaining to Parnassus, a mountain in Greece, considered sacred to the Muses, or to the Parnassian School: *n.* a member of this School. **Parnassian School,** a group of French poets of about 1865–80, including Catulle Mendès, Baudelaire, and Coppée.
parochial, *a.* pa-*roh*-ke-al, pertaining or restricted to a parish; petty. (L. *parochialis*, relating to a district.)
parochialism, *n.* pa-*roh*-ke-a-lizm, parish government; the condition or quality of being parochial; narrowness of opinion.
parodic, *a.* pa-*rod*-ik, of the nature of parody.
parodist, *n. pa*-ro-dist, one who makes parodies.
parody, *n. pa*-ro-de, a burlesque imitation of a literary work; a travesty: *v.t.* to imitate by way of parody. (L. *parodia*.)
parol, *a. pa*-rol, oral, by word of mouth [Law].
parole, *n.* pa-*role*, word of mouth; word of honour; promise given by a prisoner of war that, on temporary release, he will abide by certain conditions, as return at the time appointed, etc. [Mil.]; a password [Mil.]: *v.t.* to release on parole. (Fr.)
paronomasia, *n. pa*-ro-no-*may*-ze-a, a pun; punning. (Gr.)
paronychia, *n. pa*-ro-*nik*-e-a, a whitlow; inflammation about the nail [Med.]. (Gr.)
paronym, *n. pa*-ro-nim, a paronymous word. (Fr.)
paronymous, *a.* pa-*ron*-e-mus, alike in sound and origin, but different in spelling and meaning. (Gr.)
paroquet, *n. pa*-ro-keet, a parakeet.

parotid, *a.* pa-*rot*-id, pertaining to the parotis; situated near the ear: *n.* the parotis.
parotis, *n.* pa-*roh*-tis (*pl.* **parotides,** pa-*rot*-e-deez), a salivary gland near the ear. (Gr. *para-*, and *ous*, *otos*, the ear.)
parotitis, *n.* pa-ro-*ty*-tis, inflammation of the parotis; mumps.
paroxysm, *n.* *pa*-rok-sizm, a fit or exacerbation of any disease; any sudden violent spasm or action. (Fr. *paroxysme.*)
paroxysmal, *a.* *pa*-rok-*siz*-mal, pertaining to, occurring in, or due to paroxysm.
paroxytone, *n.* pa-*rok*-se-tone, a word with an acute accent on the penultimate syllable. (Gr. *paroxytonos.*)
parpen, *n.* *par*-pen, a large stone extending from one side of a wall to the other and serving as a binder. **parpen-wall,** a partition, or other wall, built of single stones or bricks. (Origin uncertain.)
parquet, *n.* par-*ket* or *par*-ke, parquetry, or a flooring of this; the stalls, or the front part of the pit, in a theatre: *v.t.* to furnish with a floor of parquetry. (Fr.)
parquetry, *n.* *par*-ket-re, inlaid woodwork for flooring. (Fr. *parqueterie.*)
parr, *n.* par, a young salmon in its striped stage before becoming a smolt.
parrakeet, *n.* *pa*-ra-keet, a parakeet.
parrel, *n.* *pa*-rel, a contrivance for preventing yards and gaffs from slipping from the mast. (*apparel.*)
parrhesia, *n.* pa-*ree*-ze-a, free-spokenness. (Gr.)
parricidal, *a.* *pa*-re-*sy*-dal, pertaining to parricide.
parricide, *n.* *pa*-re-side, a murderer, or the murder, of one with whom the murderer is specially connected, as a parent, benefactor, or ruler. (Fr., from L.)
parrot, *n.* *pa*-rot, one of an order of zygodactylous birds of the tropics, Australasia, and Polynesia, remarkable for their hooked beaks, beautiful colours, and in some cases, their imitation of the human voice; one who mechanically and unintelligently repeates opinions, etc.; a talkative person: *v.t.* to imitate mechanically. **parrot-disease,** psittacosis [Med. and Vet.]. **parrot fish,** name given to many brightly coloured fish of tropical seas, having a prominent beak-like jaw. (Fr. *perrot*, from *Pierre*, Peter.)
parrotry, *n.* *pa*-rot-re, servile imitations; unintelligent repetition.
parry, *v.t.* and *i.* *pa*-re, to ward off; to shift off; to evade: *n.* the warding off of a blow, etc., esp. in boxing and fencing; an evasive or defensive movement. (Fr. *parer.*)
parse, *v.t.* parze, to analyse grammatically; to point out the parts of speech in a sentence, and their relations [Gram.]. (L. *pars*, a part.)
parsec, *n.* *par*-sek, a unit of astronomical distance, that at which the distant object has a parallax of one second of arc, *i.e.* 3·26 light-years, or 19 billion 234 thousand million miles (19,234 followed by 9 ciphers). (*par*allax and *sec*ond.)
Parsee, *n.* par-*see*, one of Persian descent and of the religion of Zoroaster, living in India; one of the ancient Persian dialects. (Per. *Parsi*, a Persian.)
Parseeism, *n.* par-*see*-izm, the religion of the Parsees.
Parsi, *n.* par-*see*, Parsee.
parsimonious, *a.* *par*-se-*moh*-ne-us, very sparing in expending money; niggardly.
parsimoniously, *ad.* meanly; sparingly.
parsimoniousness, *n.* the quality of being parsimonious.
parsimony, *n.* *par*-se-mo-ne, closeness in expenditure; niggardliness. (O.Fr. *parsimonie*, from L. *parcere*, to spare.)
parsley, *n.* *par*-sle, a green culinary herb of the genus *Petroselinum.* (Fr. *persil.*)
parsnip, *n.* *par*-snip, the umbelliferous plant *Peucedanum sativum*, also its esculent root. (O.Fr. *pastenaque*, parsnip.)
parson, *n.* *par*-son, the rector or other incumbent of a parish; a clergyman. **parson bird,** the tui or New Zealand honey-eater. **parson gull,** the great black-backed gull, *Larus marinus.* **parson's nose,** the pope's nose. (Late L. *persona*, a dignitary.)
parsonage, *n.* *par*-son-aj, a church benefice; the residence attached to this. (Fr. *personnage.*)
parsonic, *a.* par-*son*-ik, pertaining to or characteristic of a parson.
parsonical, *a.* par-*son*-e-kal, parsonic; befitting a parson.
***part,** *n.* part, a portion, piece, or fragment; portion considered apart; a member or organ [Anat.]; division; ingredient; share; proportional quantity; interest; side; party; role, esp. that played by an actor; an actor's script; one of the melodies in a harmony; a section of a publication issued at intervals; portion which, when multiplied a certain number of times, shall equal the whole: *pl.* qualities; powers; accomplishments: *v.t.* to sever into two or more pieces; to distribute; to separate: *v.i.* to be separated; to quit each other; to break or to be torn asunder. **in good part,** favourably. **in ill part,** unfavourably. **part and parcel,** an essential part. **part of speech,** class of words. [Gram.]. **to part company,** to separate; to diverge from. **to play a part,** to act with cunning. (Fr.)
partakable, *a.* par-*take*-a-bl, capable of being partaken.
partake, *v.i.* par-*take*, to take a part or share, in common with others: *v.t.* to have a part in; to share. *p.* **partook;** *pp.* **partaken.**
partaker, *n.* par-*take*-er, a sharer; a participator.
partan, *n.* *par*-tan, a crab, esp. an edible crab; an ill-favoured person [Celt.].
parted, *a.* *par*-tid, separated, severed; partite [Bot.].
parter, *n.* *par*-ter, one who separates.
parterre, *n.* par-*tare*, a lay-out of flower-beds with intervening spaces to walk on; the back part of the pit in a theatre. (Fr.)
parthenogenesis, *n.* *par*-then-o-*jen*-e-sis, reproduction by means of ova capable of development without male fertilization [Bot. and Zool.]. (Gr. *parthenos*, a virgin, *genesis*, being.)
parthenogenetic, *a.* *par*-the-no-je-*net*-ik, pertaining to parthenogenesis.
parthenogenetically, *ad.* in a parthenogenetic manner.
Parthenon, *n.* *par*-the-non, the temple of Minerva, the virgin goddess, at Athens. (Gr. *parthenos.*)
Parthian, *a.* *par*-the-an, relating to Parthia, an ancient kingdom S. and S.E. of the Caspian Sea. **Parthian thrust** or **shot,** a remark, etc., on parting, as the Parthians used to shoot their arrows when retreating.
partial, *a.* *par*-shal, biased in favour of one party or side; inclined to favour without reason; unfair; affecting a part only. (Fr.)
partiality, *n.* *par*-she-*al*-e-te, inclination to favour one party more than another; an undue bias of mind; special fondness.
partially, *ad.* in a partial manner; not entirely.
partibility, *n.* par-te-*bil*-e-te, the quality of being partible; separability.
partible, *a.* *par*-te-bl, divisible; separable.
participable, *a.* par-*tis*-e-pa-bl, that may be shared.
participant, *a.* par-*tis*-e-pant, sharing; having a part: *n.* a partaker.
participate, *v.i.* par-*tis*-e-pate, to partake; to have: *v.i.* to partake; to share in. (L. *participatus*, shared in.)
participation, *n.* *par*-tis-e-*pay*-shon, the sharing in common with others; possession of a part.
participative, *a.* par-*tis*-e-pa-tiv, capable of participating.
participator, *n.* par-*tis*-e-pay-tor, a partaker.
participial, *a.* *par*-te-*sip*-e-al, having the nature and use of a participle; formed from a participle. (Fr.)
participially, *ad.* in a participial way.
participle, *n.* *par*-te-sipl, a word having the characteristics and function of both an adjective and a verb. (Fr. *participe.*)
particle, *n.* *par*-te-kl, a minute part or portion; an atom; a word not inflected or used alone [Gram.]. (Fr. *particule.*)
parti-coloured, *a.* variegated; of different colours.
particular, *a.* pa-*tik*-yew-lar, pertaining to a single person or thing; single; private; individual; special; singular; nice in taste; peculiar; precise or exact; remarkable: *n.* an item; a single instance; a distinct part: *pl.* details. **in particular,** specially. **particular average,** *see* **average.** **Particular Baptists,** a Christian sect

holding the theological doctrine of particularism. **London particular,** a dense yellow fog [Slang]. (O.F., from L. *particula*, particle.)
particularism, *n.* pa-*tik*-yew-la-rizm, regard for only self or party; the doctrine that the elect comprise only those individually chosen [Theol.]; decentralization in the government of federated states [Polit.].
particularist, *a.* pa-*tik*-yew-la-rist, pertaining to, or characteristic of, particularism: *n.* a believer in, or adherent to, the doctrine of particularism [Theol. and Polit.].
particularity, *n.* pa-*tik*-yew-*la*-re-te, the quality of being particular; a single act or case; minute detail; peculiarity; minuteness in detail.
particularization, *n.* pa-*tik*-yew-la-ry-*zay*-shon, act of particularizing.
particularize, *v.t.* pa-*tik*-yew-la-rize, to mention or enumerate in detail: *v.i.* to be attentive to details.
particularly, *ad.* in a particular manner; specially.
particulate, *a.* par-*tik*-yew-lat, relating to or existing as distinct particles [Chem., etc.]; having characteristics of both parents [Biol.].
partim, *ad.* *par*-tim, in part; partly. (L.)
parting, *a.* *par*-ting, separating; given at separation; departing: *n.* division; separation; rupture; a dividing line. **parting sand,** the sand between two members of a mould to make them come apart easily.
partisan, *n.* *par*-te-zan, an adherent to a party or faction; one of a body of irregular soldiers; a franc-tireur: *a.* adhering to a party: employed in a raid or special enterprise [Mil.]. (Fr.)
partisan, *n.* *par*-te-zan, a kind of halberd; a truncheon; a baton. (O.Fr. *pourtisaine.*)
partisanship, *n.* *par*-te-*zan*-ship, adherence to a party.
partite, *a.* *par*-tite, cleft almost to the base [Bot.]. (L. *partitus*, divided.)
partition, *n.* par-*tish*-on, division into parts; separation; that which separates; a dividing wall; part where separation is made: *v.t.* to divide into parts or shares; to supply with partitions.
partitive, *a.* *par*-te-tiv, denoting a part: *n.* a word denoting partition [Gram.].
partizan, *n.* *par*-te-zan, a partisan (in either sense).
partlet, *n.* *part*-let, a ruff; a band or collar; a hen. (O.Fr. *patelette*, from *pate*, a paw.)
partly, *ad.* *part*-le, in part; not wholly.
partner, *n.* *part*-ner, one who shares with another; a joint owner of stock or capital employed in business; one who dances with another; a player on the same side; a husband or wife: *pl.* the frame between the deck beams which receives and supports the mast [Naut.]: *v.t.* to be or become a partner with. (O.Fr. *parcener.*)
partnership, *n.* *part*-ner-ship, the association of persons for the purpose of business; joint interest.
part-owner, *n.* one of two or more owning something in common.
partridge, *n.* *par*-trij, a game-bird of the genus *Perdix*, or other gallinaceous birds of similar size, appearance, and habits. **partridge-wood,** the reddish mottled wood of the tropical *Andira americana* or other variegated wood used for cabinet-work, etc. (Fr. *perdrix.*)
part-singing, *n.* singing in which parts are taken by different voices to make harmony.
part-song, *n.* a song sung in parts.
part-time, *a.* not engaged or occupied for the whole of the working day, week, etc.; requiring or effected in only part of one's time: *a.* for only part of one's or the usual time.
part-timer, *n.* one engaged or working for less than whole-time.
parturient, *a.* par-*tewr*-re-ant, about to bring forth young; pertaining to parturition. (L. *parturiens*, desiring to bring forth.)
parturifacient, *a.* *par*-tewr-re-*fay*-she-ent, promoting parturition: *n.* a drug or agent that induces parturition. (L. *parturine*, to labour, *faciens*, *-entem*, making.)
parturition, *n.* *par*-tew-*rish*-on, the bringing forth.
party, *n.* *par*-te, a number of persons united in opinion or design; a select company; a social gathering, or the person collectively forming such; a detachment of troops [Mil.]; one of two litigants; one concerned in an affair; a side; a person [Coll.]. **third party,** *see* **third.** (O.Fr. *partie.*)
partyism, *n.* *par*-te-izm, the system of parties (as in politics); devotion to party; party spirit.
party-wall, *n.* a wall separating two properties, the owners of which have equal rights in it [Law].
parure, *n.* pa-*roor*, a set of jewels. (Fr.)
parvanimity, *n.* *par*-va-*nim*-e-te, the reverse of magnanimity; pettiness. (L. *parvus*, little, and *animus*, intellect.)
parvenu, *n.* *par*-ve-new, an upstart. (Fr.)
parvis, *n.* *par*-vis, an enclosed space or cloister in front of a church (incorrectly used of a church porch or a room over it). (O.Fr., paradise.)
pas, *n.* pah, any step in dancing; right of precedence. (Fr.)
pasch, *n.* pahsk, the passover; Easter. **pasch egg,** an Easter egg. (Heb. *pasakh*, he passed over.)
paschal, *a.* *pahs*-kal, pertaining to the passover or Easter. **paschal full moon,** the hypothetical moon on which the date of Easter depends. **paschal moon,** the new moon occurring on or next after the vernal equinox (21 Mar.). (Late L. *paschalis*, through Gr. from Heb.)
pascual, *a.* *pas*-kew-al, pertaining to, or [Bot.] growing in, pastures. (L. *pascuum*, a pasture.)
pasha, *n.* pa-*shah*, a former Turkish title of honour; a governor or commander. (Turk.)
pashalik, *n.* pa-*shah*-lik, jurisdiction of a pasha.
pashm, *n.* pashm, the under-fur of the Tibetan goat, used for shawls, rugs, etc. (Per.)
Pashto, *n.* *push*-toh, Pushtu.
pasigraphy, *n.* pa-*sig*-ra-fe, any system of universal language, the written signs of which represent ideas, not words. (Gr. *pas*, all, *grapho*, write.)
pasque-flower, *n.* *pahsk*-flou-er, a species of anemone. *A. pulsatilla*, flowering about Easter. (O.Fr. *pasque*, Easter.)
pasquil, *n.* *pas*-kwil, a pasquinade.
pasquinade, *n.* pas-kwe-*nade*, a lampoon or coarse satire: *v.t.* to lampoon; to satirize. (Name of an ancient statute in Rome, on which in the 15th-cent. lampoons used to be affixed.)
pass, *v.i.* pahss, to move from one place to another, or from one state to another; to change; to disappear; to elapse; to die; to be enacted (esp. of Parliamentary bills); to be current; to be regarded; to take place; to thrust [Fencing]; to let go unheeded; to go through inspection; to be approved; to be transferred; to go through; to run; to undergo examination satisfactorily; to make no bid [Bridge, etc.]: *v.t.* to go beyond, through or over; to allow to pass; to spend; to cause to move hastily; to transfer (as an object, in conjuring, or a ball, to a player of one's own side, in football); to strain; to utter; to pronounce; to cause to go; to omit [U.S.A.]; to emit; to admit or approve; to enact. **pass away,** to die; to come to an end. **pass degree,** a University degree without honours. **pass muster,** *see* **muster. pass off,** to cease gradually; to impose by fraud; to dispose of fraudulently. **pass on,** to go on; to die. **pass out,** to become unconscious; to die [Coll.]. **pass the buck,** *see* **buck. pass the hat round,** to take up a collection [Slang.]. (Fr. *passer.*)
pass, *n.* pahss, the act or process of passing; a narrow passage, entrance, or avenue; a defile through mountains; a way for fish over a weir; a permission to pass; a free ticket; state of things, esp. extreme state; a thrust [Fencing]; movement of the hands, as by a mesmerist. **sell the pass,** to relinguish an advantage to an opponent; to double-cross.
passable, *a.* *pahss*-a-bl, that may be passed or navigated; current; receivable; tolerable.
passably, *ad.* *pahss*-a-ble, tolerably.
passado, *n.* pas-*sah*-doh, a thrust [Fencing]; a turn or course of a horse backward or forward [Man.]. (Fr.)
passage, *n.* *pas*-saj, act of passing; transition; road; avenue; entrance or exit; right of passing; a voyage or journey, or the duration of such; that which passes or takes place; a heated argument; the alternate raising simultaneously of a hind- and foreleg [Man.]; a short extract from a discourse or book; the enactment of a law; a pass: *v.t.* and *i.* to make a journey or passage; to have a passage at arms; to traverse, or cause a horse to traverse or move sideways, in riding. **bird of passage,** a bird, or [Coll.] person, of migratory

habits. **passage at arms** a fight; a contention (physical or verbal). (Fr.)
passant, *a. pas*-ant, depicted as walking with the dexter foreleg raised and the head facing forward [Her.]. (Fr.)
pass-book, *n.* a book retained by the customer in which the retailer enters his purchases; the book a banker enters up for his client in which are shown the debits and credits of the account.
passé, *a. pas*-ay (*fem.* **passée**), antiquated; faded; out of date. (Fr., passed.)
passementerie, *n.* (App.), trimmings for dress, as gimp, tinsel, gold or silver lace. (Fr.)
passenger, *n. pas*-sen-jer, one who travels in a public conveyance; a traveller; an inefficient member of a team, etc. [Slang]. **passenger mile,** the transporting of one passenger one mile (the unit for passenger traffic). **passenger pigeon,** a North American wild pigeon, *Ectopistes migratorius*, once very abundant but now exterminated. (Fr. *passager*.)
passe-partout, *n. pass*-par-*too*, a light frame for photographs, etc., with easily removable back; adhesive paper or tape used in framing photographs; a master-key. (Fr.)
passer-by, *n. pahss*-er-by, one who goes by or near.
passerine, *a. pas*-er-ine, pertaining to the perching birds; like a sparrow. (L. *passer*, sparrow.)
passibility, *n. pas*-se-*bil*-e-te, the state of being passible.
passible, *a. pas*-se-bl, susceptible of feeling, or of impressions from external agents. (L.)
Passiflora, *n. pas*-se-*flaw*-ra, a large genus of plants, of which the passion-flower is the type. (L. *passus*, and *flos*, *floris*, a flower.)
passim, *a. pas*-sim, here and there; everywhere (esp. in reference to a book or body of writings).
passimeter, *n.* pa-*sim*-e-ter, a pedometer; an automatic machine for the rapid issue of tickets to railway passengers, etc. (*pass* and *meter*.)
passing, *a. pahs*-ing, going by or beyond; departing; transitory: *ad.* exceedingly; surpassingly: *prep.* over: *n.* a departure, esp. by death; a satisfying of examiners; a means of passage.
passing-bell, *n.* a bell tolled at death, to invite people to pray for the passing soul.
passing-note, *n.* a note introduced between essential notes to soften the melody [Mus.].
passion, *n. pash*-on, effect produced by external agency; state of being acted upon; extreme suffering, originally the last agonies of Christ; the Gospel story of Christ's Passion, also a musical setting of this; martyrdom; any strong, deep feeling or excitement, such as desire, fear, joy, grief, love, hatred; ardour; eager desire (esp. sexual): *v.t.* to imbue with passion: *v.i.* to be affected by passion. **Passion Sunday,** the fifth Sunday in Lent. **Passion Week,** rubrically the week before Palm Sunday; popularly Holy Week, the week in which Good Friday comes. (Fr.)
passional, *a. pash*-on-al, pertaining to passion: *n.* a book about martyrs and the suffering of saints.
passionate, *a. pash*-on-at, easily moved to anger; moved, prompted, or inspired by passion or strong emotion; vehement. (Late L. *passionatus*, agitated.)
passionately, *ad.* with passion.
passionateness, *n.* state of being passionate.
passioned, *a. pash*-ond, violently affected; inspired by passion; passionate.
passion-flower, *n.* a climbing plant of the genus *Passiflora*, the three stigmas, five anthers, and other parts of which have a fancied resemblance to the instruments of the Passion of Christ.
Passionist, *n. pash*-on-ist, a member of a religious order instituted to bear witness to the spirit and import of Christ's Passion.
passionless, *a.* not easily excited; calm.
Passion-play, *n.* a drama representing Christ's Passion.
passive, *a. pas*-siv, suffering; not acting; receptive; unresisting; not opposing. **passive obedience,** *see* **obedience. passive resistance,** non-violent resistance, esp. by refraining from any act that might assist authority, or accepting imprisonment rather than comply with some law or direction. **passive verb,** that form of the verb which denotes that the subject is acted upon [Gram.]. (Fr. *passif*.)
passively, *ad.* in a passive way.
passiveness, *n. pas*-siv-ness, state or quality of being passive; unresisting submission.
passivity, *n.* pa-*siv*-e-te, passiveness; inertia.
pass-key, *n.* a master-key; a latch-key.
passman, *n. pahs*-man, one who passes without honours for a university degree.
passometer, *n.* pa-*som*-e-ter, a pedometer.
Passover, *n. pahs*-oh-ver, a feast of the Jews to commemorate the night in Egypt when the destroying angel passed over their houses (Exodus xii).
passport, *n. pahs*-port, an official document guaranteeing the holder's nationality and asking for his protection when in a foreign country; a safe-conduct; a permission to pass; anything procuring admission or acceptance. (Fr. *passeport*.)
password, *n. pahs*-wurd, a watchword.
★**past,** pahst, *pp.* of *pass*: *a.* gone by; spent; ended; accomplished: *n.* past time: *prep.* having lost; beyond; beyond in time.
★**paste,** *n.* payst, a composition of a doughy consistence, whether of flour in baking or of clay in the arts; an adhesive, as of flour and water, etc., boiled; a relish having pounded meat, fish, fowl, etc., as basis or flavouring; a fine glass compounded for artificial gems, strass: *v.t.* to fasten or smear with paste; to thrash [Slang]. (Fr.)
pasteboard, *n. payst*-bord, thick, stiff paper board made by pasting sheets of paper together; a wooden board on which dough is rolled for pastry.
paste-grain, *n.* a thin leather for book-bindings; imitation morocco.
pastel, *n. pas*-tel, woad; a paste composed of a pigment and gum-water; a coloured crayon; a drawing in pastel, also the art of making such drawings. (Fr.)
pastellist, *n. pas*-tel-ist, an artist who works in pastel.
pastern, *n. pas*-tern, the part of a horse's leg between the fetlock and hoof. **pastern joint,** the joint next the hoof. (O.Fr. *pasturon*, tether for a horse at pasture.)
Pasteurism, *n. pas*-tewr-rizm, preventive medicine; the cure or prevention of disease by inoculation; pasteurization. (Louis *Pasteur*, Fr. bacteriologist, *d.* 1895.)
pasteurization, *n.* pas-tewr-ry-*zay*-shon, the art, act, or process of pasteurizing.
pasteurize, *v.t. pas*-tewr-rize, to prevent or cure disease by inoculation in accordance with Pasteur's method; to subject liquids to a high temperature followed by sudden cooling, in order to destroy noxious bacteria.
pasticcio, *n.* pas-*titch*-e-oh, a medley; a work in another's style and manner [Art and Mus.]. (It.)
pastiche, *n.* pas-*teesh*, a pasticcio. (Fr.)
pastille, *n.* pas-*teel*, an aromatic cone, etc., burnt for fumigation; a medicated lozenge. (Fr.)
pastime, *n. pahs*-time, that which amuses or serves to pass the time; amusement; recreation.
pastiness, *n. pay*-ste-ness, quality of being pasty.
past-master, *n.* one who has held the office of master; one long proficient in his art, craft, or occupation, etc.
pastor, *n. pahs*-tor, a minister of the gospel having charge of a congregation; a spiritual guide; the rose-coloured starling. (O.Fr. *pastour*, shepherd.)
pastoral, *a. pahs*-to-ral, pertaining to shepherds or shepherd life; rural; relating to the pastor of a church or the cure of souls; addressed to the clergy: *n.* a poem on shepherd or rural life; a bucolic; a bishop's letter or address to his clergy; a pastorale [Mus.]. **Pastoral Epistles,** those of St. Paul to Timothy and Titus. **pastoral staff,** a crosier, the official staff of a bishop. (Fr.)
pastorale, *n.* pahs-to-*rah*-le, a simple melody in a rustic style or on a rustic theme; a dance. (It.)
pastoralism, *n. pahs*-to-ra-lizm, pastoral quality or style; rural amenity.
pastorate, *n. pahs*-to-rat, the office, or term of office of a pastor; pastors collectively.
pastorless, *a. pahs*-tor-less, having no pastor.
pastry, *n. pay*-stre, baked articles of food made wholly or chiefly of dough paste, bread and rolls excepted. (*paste*.)
pastrycook, *n. pay*-stre-kook, one whose occupation is to make pastry.
pasturable, *a. pahs*-tew-ra-bl, fit for pasture.
pasturage, *n. pahs*-tew-raj, pasture; the right of grazing cattle.

pasture, *n.* *pahs*-tewr, grass for grazing; land on which cattle feed: *v.t.* to feed on grass: *v.i.* to graze. (O.Fr.)

pastureless, *a.* *pahs*-tewr-less, having no pasture.

pasty, *n.* *pas*-te *or* *pahs*-te, a small pie enclosed in pastry and baked without a dish.

pasty, *a.* *pays*-te, like paste; of dull white complexion.

pat, *a.* pat, exactly fitting; apposite: *ad.* fitly; aptly: *n.* a light, quick slap with the hand; a tap; a small mass, as of butter, moulded with pats: *v.t.* to strike gently with the fingers or hand; to tap. **stand pat,** *see* **stand.** (Imit.)

patagium, *n.* pa-*tay*-je-um (*pl.* **patagia**), a wing membrane, as of the bats and flying squirrels. (L., the edging of a mantle.)

patamar, *n.* *pat*-a-mar, a lateen-rigged vessel used on the Indian and Singhalese coasts. (Malay.)

patavinity, *n.* pat-a-*vin*-e-te, provincialism; the use of local idiom. (*Patavium*, Livy's birthplace.)

pat-ball, *n.* inferior lawn-tennis; rounders [U.S.A.].

patch, *n.* patch, a piece of cloth sewed on a garment; anything similar, as metal on metal; a piece of court-plaster on the face or over a wound, or of rubber on a puncture; a small piece of ground; a fool; a jester (in Shakespeare): *v.t.* to mend by sewing on or affixing pieces and shreds; to repair clumsily; to arrange hastily. **patch pocket,** a pocket sewn to the outside of a garment. **not a patch on,** not to be compared with. **strike a bad patch,** to meet with ill-luck. (M.E. *pacche*, of doubtful origin.)

patcher, *n.* *patch*-er, one who patches or botches.

patchery, *n.* *patch*-er-re, bungling work; botchery.

patchily, *ad.* *patch*-e-le, in patches; in a patchy manner.

patchouli, *n.* pa-*choo*-le, the dried branches of an eastern labiate plant, *Pogostemon patchouly*, which are highly odoriferous; the perfume they yield. (Fr.)

patchwork, *n.* *patch*-wurk, work composed of pieces sewn together; clumsy work; any surface composed of unequal or diversified areas.

patchy, *a.* *patch*-e, in patches; not uniform; unequal; spasmodic.

pate, *n.* pate, the head; the crown of the head. (M.E., origin unknown.)

pâté, *n.* *pat*-ay, a very small pie; a patty. (Fr.)

patée, *a.* *pat*-ay, pattée [Her.]. (Fr.)

patella, *n.* pa-*tel*-la, the kneecap; a small dish-like vase; any of the genus of univalvular molluscs containing the limpet. (L., a small pan.)

patellar, *a.* pa-*tel*-lar, pertaining to the kneecap.

patelliform, *a.* pa-*tel*-le-form, shaped like a limpet, or [Bot.] like a small saucer.

paten, *n.* *pat*-en, a plate; plate or vessel on which the consecrated bread in the eucharist is placed; a thin disk of metal, a spangle. (L. *patina*, a dish.)

patency, *n.* *pay*-ten-se, state of being manifest, or [Med.] unobstructed; obviousness.

patent, *a.* *pay*-tent *or* *pat*-ent, open; evident; manifest; secured or protected by patent; spreading [Bot.]: *n.* a privilege granted by letters patent from the Crown, as a title of nobility or the exclusive right to a property in an invention; any patented invention; the document giving such right: *v.t.* to secure by patent. **letters patent,** *see* **letter. patent leather,** japanned leather. **Patent Office,** a government office for the granting of patents for inventions. **patent rolls,** the records or registers of patents. (Fr.)

patentable, *a.* *pay*-ten-ta-bl, that can be patented.

patentee, *n.* pay-ten-*tee*, one who has obtained a patent.

pater, *n.* *pat*-er, a paternoster; (*pay*-ter), a father [Slang]. (L., a father.)

patera, *n.* *pat*-er-ra, a shallow, circular dish; a circular ornament in relief, esp. on a frieze [Arch.]. (L.)

paterfamilias, *n.* *pay*-ter-fa-*mil*-e-as, the father of a family, or head of a household. (L. *pater*, a father, *familia*, a family.)

paternal, *a.* pa-*ter*-nal, fatherly; hereditary, or related, on the father's side. (Fr. *paternel.*)

paternalism, *n.* pa-*ter*-na-lizm, the principle or practice of a fatherly government, esp. its needless intermeddling in domestic affairs.

paternally, *ad.* in a paternal manner.

paternity, *n.* pa-*ter*-ne-te, fatherhood; the state of being a father; source; authorship. (Fr. *paternité.*)

paternoster, *n.* *pat*-er-*nos*-ter, the Lord's Prayer; the eleventh bead in a rosary; a fishing line having a weight at the end and pairs of hooks at equal intervals. (L., our father.)

path, *n.* pahth, a way trodden by the foot of man or beast; a course or track for athletic sports; course of life or action. (A.S.)

Pathan, *a.* pa-*tahn*, of or relating to Afghans; of Afghan descent: *n.* an Afghan.

pathetic, *a.* pa-*thet*-ik, affecting or moving the tender passions; causing pity or grief. (O.Fr. *pathetique*, from Gr. *pathos.*)

pathetically, *ad.* pa-*thet*-e-ka-le, in a pathetic manner.

patheticalness, *n.* pathetic character.

pathfinder, *n.* *pahth*-fyn-der, an explorer, pioneer, or scout; an illuminating flare dropped by an attacking bomber [Mil. Av.].

pathic, *a.* *path*-ik, concerning or pertaining to disease. (Gr. *pathikos*, suffering.)

pathless, *a.* *pahth*-less, having no beaten way.

pathogen, *n.* *path*-o-jen, any pathogenic agent.

pathogenetic, *a.* path-o-je-*net*-ik, pathogenic.

pathogenic, *a.* path-o-*jen*-ik, causing disease; relating to pathogeny or pathogenesis.

pathogeny, *n.* pa-*thoj*-e-ne, the science of the origin and development of disease. (Gr. *pathos*, suffering, *gennao*, produce.)

pathognomonic, *a.* pa-*thog*-no-*mon*-ik, characteristic or indicative of a disease [Med.].

pathognomy, *n.* pa-*thog*-no-me, expression of the passions; the study of their several signs; the science of the signs indicative of disease [Med.]. (Gr. *pathos*, and *gnome*, sign.)

pathological, *a.* path-o-*loj*-e-kal, pertaining to pathology; morbid; caused by disease.

pathologist, *n.* pa-*thol*-o-jist, one versed in pathology.

pathology, *n.* pa-*thol*-o-je, the science or study of disease. (Gr. *pathos*, and *logos*, science.)

pathophobia, *n.* path-o-*foh*-be-a, a morbid or exaggerated dread of disease.

pathos, *n.* *pay*-thos, deep emotion or passion, such as moves others to sympathy; the literary quality that touches the feelings. (Gr., suffering, emotion.)

pathway, *n.* *pahth*-way, a path; a way or course.

patibulary, *a.* pa-*tib*-yew-la-re, pertaining to, resembling, or suggestive of the gallows. (L. *patibulum*, the gallows.)

patience, *n.* *pay*-shence, quality of being patient; calm endurance; forbearance; a game at cards, usually for one. (O.Fr.)

patient, *a.* *pay*-shent, sustaining pain, affliction, or annoyance, without fretfulness, or with calmness; not easily provoked; persevering; waiting with calmness: *n.* a person under medical treatment.

patiently, *ad.* with composure; quietly.

patina, *n.* *pat*-e-na, the green incrustation testifying to age on bronze works of art, etc. (It.)

patinate, *v.t.* and *i.* *pat*-e-nate, to coat or become coated with patina.

patine, *n.* *pa*-teen, a paten.

patio, *n.* *pah*-te-oh, the open courtyard within a large Spanish house. (Sp.)

patisserie, *n.* pa-*tis*-er-re, a pastrycook's shop; the wares sold in this. (Fr.)

patly, *ad.* *pat*-le, fitly; conveniently.

patness, *n.* *pat*-ness, appositeness; suitableness.

patois, *n.* *pat*-wah, a provincial dialect; the language of the uneducated. (Fr.)

patriarch, *n.* *pay*-tre-ark, the head of a family or tribe; a metropolitan dignitary in the Eastern church; a venerable chief or old man. (O.Fr. *patriarche.*)

patriarchal, *a.* pay-tre-*ar*-kal, belonging or subject to a patriarch.

patriarchate, *n.* *pay*-tre-ar-kat, office, jurisdiction, or residence of a patriarch.

patriarchism, *n.* *pay*-tre-ar-kizm, government by a patriarch; the patriarchal system.

patriarchy, *n.* *pay*-tre-ar-ke, patriarchism.

patrician, *a.* pa-*trish*-an, senatorial (in ancient Rome); noble; aristocratic: *n.* a nobleman, esp. of primitive senatorial descent in Rome; one of high rank. (L., from *patres*, "fathers" or senators.)

patriciate, *n.* pa-*trish*-e-at, the aristocratic or patrician class; the status of patrician.

patricidal, *a.* pat-re-*sy*-dal, pertaining to patricide.
patricide, *n.* *pat*-re-side, the murder, or the murderer, of one's own father; a parricide. (L. *pater*, father, *cædo*, slay.)
patrilineal, *a.* pat-re-*lin*-e-al, pertaining to the male or paternal line of descent.
patrimonial, *a.* pat-re-*moh*-ne-al, pertaining to a patrimony; inherited from ancestors.
patrimony, *n.* *pat*-re-mo-ne, an ancestral estate; a church estate or revenue. (L. *patrimonium.*)
patriot, *n.* *pay*-tre-ot *or* *pat*-re-ot, one who loves his country, and is devoted to its interests. (O.Fr. *patriote.*)
patriotic, *a.* pat-re-*ot*-ik, full of, or actuated by, patriotism.
patriotically, *ad.* in a patriotic spirit.
patriotism, *n.* *pat*-re-o-tizm, love of one's country.
patristic, *a.* pa-*tris*-tik, pertaining to the Fathers of the Christian Church: *n.pl.* the study of the writings of the Christian fathers. (Fr. *patristique.*)
patrol, *n.* pa-*trole*, a detachment of reconnoitring troops; a regimental picket; a corporal's guard to keep order at night; a policeman, watchman, fireman, etc., engaged on patrolling, or a detachment of these: *v.i.* and *t.* to go the rounds, esp. in a camp, garrison town, etc. (Fr. *patrouille.*)
patrology, *n.* pa-*trol*-o-je, patristics; a collection of the writings of the Early Church Fathers.
patron, *n.* *pay*-tron *or* *pat*-ron, a protector; advocate; a supporter; a guardian; a regular customer; the holder of an advowson. **patron saint,** the saint to whose protection a country, church, society, or person is dedicated. (Fr.)
patronage, *n.* *pat*-ro-naj, act of patronizing; special countenance or support; guardianship; right of presentation to a church living. (Fr.)
patronal, *a.* *pat*-ro-nal, pertaining to a patron or patron saint.
patroness, *n.* *pat*-ron-ess, a female patron.
patronize, *v.t.* *pat*-ron-ize, to countenance, as a patron; to assume the air of a superior.
patronizer, *n.* *pat*-ro-ny-zer, one who patronizes.
patronymic, *a.* pat-ro-*nim*-ik, derived from the name of a father or ancestor: *n.* a name so derived; the family name. (L. *patronymicus.*)
pattée, *a.* *pat*-ay, having the arms (of a cross) expanding towards the ends [Her.]. (Fr.)
patten, *n.* *pat*-en, a clog mounted on an iron ring; a thick-soled overshoe; the base of a column or pillar [Arch.]. (Fr. *patin.*)
patter, *n.* *pat*-ter, a quick patting sound, as of rain: *v.i.* to strike, as falling drops of water, or move with a quick succession of sharp, light sounds. (*pat.*)
patter, *n.* *pat*-ter, glib talk; professional talk or jargon, as of a quack or entertainer; a succession of words spoken or sung at a very rapid rate: *v.t.* to say (esp. prayers) in a mumbling mechanical way: *v.i.* to talk glibly; to mumble. (*paternoster.*)
pattern, *n.* *pat*-tern, a model to be copied; a decorative design; a specimen or sample; anything cut or formed into a shape to be copied; the distribution of shot on a target: *v.t.* to make in imitation; to match. (Fr. *patron.*)
patternmaker, *n.* *pat*-tern-*make*-er, a maker of wooden patterns for foundry moulds.
pattress, *n.* *pat*-tres, a piece of wood used in fixing gas brackets, etc., to the wall.
patty, *n.* *pat*-te, a little pie. (O.Fr. *paste*, a pasty.)
patty-pan, *n.* a pan to bake patties in.
patulous, *a.* *pat*-yew-lus, having a wide opening; spreading [Bot.]; expanded [Med.]. (L. *patulus.*)
paucity, *n.* *paw*-se-te, fewness; insufficiency; exiguity. (Fr., from L. *paucus*, few.)
pauldron, *n.* *pawl*-dron, the shoulder plate of a coat of armour. (O.Fr. *espauleron.*)
Pauline, *a.* *paw*-line, pertaining to the Apostle Paul or his epistles: *n.* a student at St. Paul's School, London.
paulo-post, *a.* *paw*-lo-pohst, somewhat late.
paulo-post-future, the future perfect tense [Gr. Gram.]. (L., a little after.)
paunch, *n.* pawnch, the belly; in ruminants, the first and largest stomach: *v.t.* to rip the belly of; to eviscerate; to glut. (O.Fr. *panche.*)
paunchy, *a.* *pawn*-che, pot-bellied.
pauper, *n.* *paw*-per, a destitute person; one dependent on public or Poor Law relief. (L., poor.)
pauperism, *n.* *paw*-per-rizm, state of being a pauper.
pauperization, *n.* *paw*-per-ry-*zay*-shon, the act or process of reducing to pauperism.
pauperize, *v.t.* *paw*-per-rize, to reduce to the condition of a pauper.
pause, *n.* pawz, a cessation or intermission in speaking or action; suspense; a break in writing; mark of cessation or an intermission of the voice; a rest, thus indicated 𝄐 or 𝄑 [Mus.]: *v.i.* to stop; to hesitate; to wait. (Fr.)
pavage, *n.* *pay*-vaj, a tax for paving the streets; the laying of pavements. (Fr.)
pavane, *n.* pa-*vahn*, a stately costume dance of Tudor and Stuart times. (It. *pavana.*)
pave, *v.t.* pave, to lay with stone or brick, so as to make a level surface; to put a surface layer on a path or road. **pave a way,** to prepare a way; to facilitate. (Fr. *paver.*)
pavement, *n.* *pave*-ment, a paved path by the side of a road; a paved roadway or floor; a footway; material for paving. (Fr.)
paver, *n.* *pay*-ver, a pavior; a heavy mallet for setting paving-stones.
pavid, *a.* *pav*-id, timid. (L. *pavidus.*)
pavilion, *n.* pa-*vil*-yon, a large tent; a temporary movable habitation; a building, or part of a building, with a tent-shaped roof; a club-house in a field devoted to outdoor games; a covering like a tent; the lower part of a brilliant-cut diamond: *v.t.* to furnish with tents; to shelter with a tent. (Fr. *pavillon.*)
paving, *n.* *pay*-ving, the upper surface of a road or path. **paving-stone,** *n.* a slab of hard-wearing stone dressed flat for use as pavement.
pavior, *n.* *pay*-ve-or, one who lays paving-stones; a very hard brick used for pavements.
pavis, *n.* *pav*-is, a large shield to protect the whole body. (Fr. *pavois*, a great shield.)
pavisade, *n.* pav-e-*sade*, a light defence, esp. one of overlapping pavisades; any defensive screen [Mil. and Nav.].
pavonine, *a.* *pav*-o-nine, like or pertaining to the peacock; resembling a peacock's tail; iridescent.
paw, *n.* paw, the foot of animals with claws; the hand: *v.t.* and *i.* to scrape, clutch, or strike with the fore-foot; to handle clumsily. (O.Fr. *poe.*)
pawky, *a.* *paw*-ke, droll and shrewd; arch [Scots.].
pawl, *n.* pawl, a catch preventing recoil or lifting as it engages; a short bar attached as a catch to a capstan or windlass. (O.Fr. *paul.*)
pawn, *n.* pawn, a pledge: *v.t.* to give or deposit in pledge. **in pawn,** the state of being pledged. (Fr. *pan.*)
pawn, *n.* pawn, a chessman of the lowest rank; an insignificant agent, a mere tool [Fig.].
pawnbroker, *n.* *pawn*-broh-ker, one whose business it is to lend money on the security of articles left in pawn.
pawnbroking, *n.* *pawn*-broh-king, the business of a pawnbroker.
pawnee, *n.* paw-*nee*, a pawnbroker; one who accepts a pledge as security.
pawnee, *n.* *paw*-nee, water [Anglo-Ind.]. (Hind.)
Pawnee, *n.* paw-*nee*, an Indian of a former confederacy of tribes in the Middle West United States.
pawner, *n.* *paw*-ner, one who pledges anything as security for the payment of borrowed money.
pawnshop, *n.* *pawn*-shop, a pawnbroker's shop.
pawn-ticket, *n.* a voucher or receipt for an article pledged at a pawnshop.
pawpaw, *n.* *paw*-paw, the papaw or its fruit.
pax, *n.* paks, an osculatory [Eccles.]. (L., peace.)
paxiuba, *n.* *pah*-she-*oo*-bah, the rasp palm. (Tupi.)
paxwax, *n.* *paks*-waks, a strong tendon in the neck of mammals. (A.S. *feax*, hair, *waxan*, grow.)
pay, *v.t.* pay, to discharge a debt; to fulfil; to render what is due; to recompense; to punish [Slang]: *v.i.* to make payment; to be remunerative; to give an adequate return: *n.* compensation; recompense; salary or wages. **pay as you go,** to pay recurrent debts, etc., as they are incurred (esp. of income tax). **pay for,** to make amends; to give an equivalent. **pay load,** that part of the load for which carriage is paid [Av.]. **pay off,** to pay in full and discharge; to fall to leeward [Naut.]. **pay out,** to let run out [Naut.]. **pay the piper,** to pay the cost. **pay through the nose,** *see* **nose. pay up,** to pay in full. **paying guest,** a boarder in a private home. *p.* and *pp.* **paid.** (Fr. *payer.*)

pay, *v.t.* pay, to coat with pitch or any waterproof composition; to render watertight. *p.* and *pp.* **payed.** (L. *picare*, pitch.)
payable, *a.* *pay*-a-bl, that can be paid; due; capable of being worked at a profit (esp. of mines).
pay-bill, *n.* statement of money to be paid to soldiers, workmen, etc.
pay-day, *n.* the day when payment is to be made or debts discharged.
pay-dirt, *n.* alluvial deposit worth working for the gold in it.
payee, *n.* pay-*ee*, the person to whom money is to be paid.
payer, *n.* *pay*-er, one who pays or has to pay.
paymaster, *n.* *pay*-mahs-ter, one who regularly pays, esp. the wages; an army officer or non-executive naval officer in charge of accounts for stores, messing, etc., and of payments to officers and men. **Paymaster-General,** a member of the British government and head of the office charged with payments on behalf of all departments other than Revenue Departments.
★**payment,** *n.* *pay*-ment, the act of paying; that which is paid; reward; remuneration; pay.
paynim, *n.* *pay*-nim, a pagan; a non-Christian. (O.Fr. *paienime*, heathendom.)
pay-roll, *n.* a pay-bill or pay-sheet.
paysagist, *n.* pay-za-jist, a landscape painter. (Fr. *paysage*, landscape.)
pay-sheet, *n.* a register of names of employees with the wages paid to each.
pea, *n.* pee, the leguminous plant, *Pisum sativum*, and its seed: *pl.* **peas,** but sometimes **pease** when used collectively. **sweet-pea,** *Lathyrus odoratus*. (A.S. *pisa*, L. *pisum*.)
★**peace,** *n.* peece, a state of quiet or tranquillity; freedom from disturbance or agitation; freedom from war or quarrel; quietness of mind; rest; concord; a treaty ending hostilities; a formal reconciliation: *int.* hist! silence! **Justice of the Peace,** *see* **justice. to hold one's peace,** to be silent. **to keep the peace,** to refrain from law-breaking or violence; to prevent strife. (O.Fr. *pais*.)
peaceable, *a.* *peece*-a-bl, tranquil; peaceful; disposed to peace.
peaceableness, *n.* state of being peaceable.
peaceably, *ad.* without tumult or agitation.
peaceful, *a.* *peece*-ful, quiet; pacific; mild; calm; removed from noise or tumult.
peacefully, *ad.* in a peaceful manner.
peacefulness, *n.* peaceful state.
peaceless, *a.* *peece*-less, without peace; disturbed.
peacemaker, *n.* *peece*-make-er, one who makes peace where there was formerly variance.
peace-offering, *n.* an offering that procures or bespeaks peace, friendship, or reconciliation.
peace-officer, *n.* a civil officer whose duty is to preserve the public peace; a constable or policeman.
peacetime, *n.* *peece*-time, a period of freedom from war: *a.* pertaining to such period.
peach, *n.* peech, a rosaceous tree and its fruit *Prunus persica*. **peach coloured,** of the colour of peach blossom, or of a ripe peach. **peach Melba,** a dish of peach and ice-cream flavoured, sometimes, with a liqueur. (Fr. *péche*, from L. *persicum*, of Persia, the peach being a Persian tree.)
peach, *v.i.* peech, to turn informer; to divulge a secret; to tell tales: *n.* an informer. (Abbrev. of *impeach*.)
peacher, *n.* *peech*-er, one who peaches.
peachery, *n.* *peech*-er-re, a glass house in which peaches are grown.
pea-chick, *n.* the young of the peafowl.
peachwort, *n.* *peech*-wurt, either of the weeds *Polygonum persicaria* or *Persicaria mitis*.
peachy, *a.* *peech*-e, resembling a peach, esp. in colour or texture.
peacock, *n.* *pee*-kok, a gamebird of the genus *Pavo*, allied to the pheasant: *n.* a showy, vainglorious person: *v.i.* to pose or strut in an ostentatious way. **peacock-fish,** a brilliantly coloured Mediterranean fish of the wrasse kind. **peacock ore,** bornite. (A.S. *pawe*, L. *pavo*.)
peafowl, *n.* *pee*-foul, a peacock or peahen; any species of the genus *Pavo*.
peahen, *n.* *pee*-hen, the female of the peacock.
pea-jacket, *n.* a stout, loose double-breasted jacket as worn by seamen. (Dut. *pije*, a coarse woollen coat, and *jacket*.)
peak, *n.* peek, a sharp top, esp. of a hill or of anything terminating in a point; a culminating point or period; the projecting shade in front of a cap; the end of a yard or gaff, or the upper corner of a sail extended by it; the bill of an anchor; a ship's hold in the bow [Naut.]: *v.t.* to raise a yard obliquely to the mast; to raise the oars apeak: *a.* reaching the maximum (as *peak load, price*, etc.): *ad.* apeak. (O.Fr. *pec*.)
peak, *v.i.* peek, to look sickly; to pine.
peaked, *a.* peekt, with a peak; pointed.
peakish, *a.* *peek*-ish, looking or feeling sickly.
peaky, *a.* *peek*-e, having peaks; like a peak; peakish.
peal, *n.* peel, a loud sound as of bells or thunder; a set of bells, or the changes rung on them: *v.i.* to sound a peal; to utter loud and solemn sounds: *v.t.* to assail with noise; to celebrate; to sound; to ring a bell violently. (*appeal*.)
peal, *n.* peel, a grilse of under 2 lb.; a sea-trout.
pean, *n.* peen, an heraldic fur in which the field is black and the spots gold. (O.Fr. *panne*, fur.)
peanut, *n.* *pee*-nut, the ground-nut, *Arachis hypogæa*.
pea-ore, *n.* *pee*-awr, limonite in the form of round, smooth grains.
pear, *n.* pare, the fruit of the pear-tree, *Pyrus communis*; the tree itself. (A.S. *pere*.)
pearl, *n.* perl, a silvery-white, smooth and iridescent product of many bivalved molluscs, esp. the pearl-oyster; mother-of-pearl; something round and clear, like a dewdrop; anything very precious; pearl-eye; an old type-size (about 5-point) [Print.]; *a.* pertaining to or made of pearls: *v.t.* to set or adorn with pearls; to convert barley into pearl-barley: *v.i.* to assume the shape of pearls; to fish or dive for pearls. **pearl button,** a button cut from mother-of-pearl. **pearl disease,** tuberculosis in cattle [Vet.]. (Fr. *perle*.)
pearl, *n.* perl, a purl, or fine loop.
pearlaceous, *a.* per-*lay*-shus, perlaceous.
pearl-ash, *n.* impure carbonate of potash.
pearl-barley, *n.* barley reduced to small grains.
pearl-diver, *n.* one who dives for pearl-oysters.
pearled, *a.* perld, set or adorned with pearls.
pearl-eye, *n.* *perl*-eye, a white speck growing on the eye; cataract.
pearlies, *n.pl.* *perl*-iz, pearl buttons as worn on a costermonger's jacket; a suit with such.
pearliness, *n.* *perl*-e-ness, the characteristic quality or appearance of pearl.
pearling, *n.* *perl*-ing, a lace made of silk or fine linen thread [Scots.]. (*purl*.)
pearlite, *n.* *perl*-ite, the eutectoid alloy of carbon and iron, normally occurring as a constituent of steel and cast iron.
pearl-oyster, *n.* any of various species of the marine bivalve molluscs, *Margaritifera*, all of which yield pearls.
pearl-sinter, *n.* florite, an opaline silica.
pearl-spar, *n.* *perl*-spar, a pearly variety of dolomite.
pearl-stone, *n.* perlite.
pearl-white, *n.* a white cosmetic powder prepared from various bismuth compounds.
pearlwort, *n.* *perl*-wurt, a plant of the genus *Sagina*.
pearly, *a.* *perl*-e, containing or resembling pearls; of pearl-like lustre. **pearly nautilus,** *see* **nautilus.**
pearmain, *n.* *pare*-main, a variety of apple (and, formerly, of pear). (O.Fr. *parmain*.)
pear-tree, *n.* any of a number of hardy deciduous trees of the genus *Pyrus*, esp. *P. communis* bearing the pear.
peasant, *n.* *pez*-ant, a countryman; a rustic labourer: *a.* rustic; rural. (O.Fr. *paisant*.)
peasantry, *n.* *pez*-an-tre, peasants as a body.
pease, *n.pl.* peez, peas collectively. **pease meal,** dried peas ground to a meal. **pease pudding,** a dish of boiled pease meal. (A.S. *pise*.)
peasecod, *n.* *peez*-kod, the legume or pericarp of the pea.
peastone, *n.* *pee*-stone, pisolite.
peat, *n.* peet, decaying vegetable matter resembling turf cut from a bog and used as fuel. (M.E. *pete*.)
peat-bog, *n.* a bog containing peat.
peat-hag, *n.* a hole from which peat has been dug.

peat-moss, *n.* any peat-forming moss, esp. of the species *Sphagnum*; a peat-bog.

peaty, *a.* *pee*-te, composed of, resembling, or abounding in peat.

peba, *n.* *pee*-ba, the small nine-banded armadillo, *Dasypus novemcinctus*, ranging from Texas to Paraguay. (Tupi, flat.)

pebble, *n.* *peb*-bl, a small rounded fragment of rock of any kind; a transparent rock crystal, or a lens of this; an agate. (A.S. *papol-stan*, pebble stone.)

pebbled, *a.* *peb*-bld, abounding with pebbles.

pebbly, *a.* *peb*-ble, full of pebbles.

pebrine, *n.* *peb*-rin, a contagious disease of silk-worms, etc., due to internal parasites. (Fr.)

pecan, *n.* pe-*kan*, a species of hickory, *Carya olivæformis*, and its fruit the pecan nut. (Fr. *pacane*.)

peccability, *n.* *pek*-a-*bil*-e-te, capacity of sinning.

peccable, *a.* *pek*-a-bl, liable to sin. (L. *pecco*, sin.)

peccadillo, *n.* *pek*-a-*dil*-lo, a petty fault; a venial or slight offence. (Sp.)

peccancy, *n.* *pek*-an-se, state of being peccant; offence.

peccant, *a.* *pek*-ant, sinning; incorrect; violating rule, etc.; morbid, offensive [Med.]. (L. *peccans*.)

peccary, *n.* *pek*-ka-re, a nocturnal American ungulate allied to the swine. (Carib.)

peccavi, pe-*kay*-vy, a colloquial expression of contrition or error: *n.* a confession of error or sin. (L., I have sinned.)

peck, *n.* pek, the fourth part of a bushel; two gallons in dry measure. (O.Fr. *pek*.)

peck, *v.t.* pek, to strike with the beak or with a pointed instrument; to break into or pick up with the beak; to strike with small and repeated blows; to eat [Coll.]: *n.* a sharp blow with the beak, etc.; the dent made by such; a hurried kiss [Coll.]. (*pick*.)

pecker, *n.* *pek*-er, one who or that which pecks; a woodpecker; appetite [Slang]. **keep your pecker up,** maintain your courage or resolution [Slang].

peckish, *a.* *pek*-ish, hungry [Slang].

Pecksniff, *n.* *pek*-snif, an unctuous canting hypocrite. (Character of that name in Dickens's *Martin Chuzzlewit*.)

pecky, *a.* *pek*-e, showing signs of rot (of timber).

pectate, *n.* *pek*-tate, a salt or ester of pectic acid.

pecten, *n.* *pek*-ten, a vascular membrane on the eyes of birds and some reptiles; a stridulating organ in arachnids; the genus of bivalve molluscs comprising the scallops [Zool.]; the pubic bone [Anat.]. (L., a comb.)

pectic, *a.* *pek*-tik, of the nature of, or derived from, pectin. **pectic acid,** an acid obtained by completely hydrolyzing certain peptins. (Gr. *pektikos*, congealing.)

pectin, *n.* *pek*-tin, any of a group of water-soluble carbohydrates occurring in the cell-walls of plants and forming the gelatinizing principle of certain fruits.

pectinal, *a.* *pek*-te-nal, resembling a comb [esp. Bot. and Zool.]; pectineal [Anat.].

pectinate, *a.* *pek*-te-nat, comb-like; having teeth like those of a comb. (L. *pectinatus*, combed.)

pectinated, *a.* *pek*-te-nay-ted, pectinate.

pectination, *n.* *pek*-te-*nay*-shon, state of being pecinate; a comb-like formation; the act of combing.

pectineal, *a.* pek-*tin*-e-al, pertaining to the pubis [Anat.].

pectinibranchiate, *a.* *pek*-te-ne-*brang*-ke-at, having pectinate gills. (L. *pecten*, and Gr. *branchia*, gills.)

pectiniform, *a.* pek-*tin*-e-form, comb-like; resembling a scallop-shell.

pectoral, *a.* *pek*-to-ral, pertaining to the breast; relating to, or alleviating, diseases of the chest: *n.* a breastplate; a sacerdotal habit worn by the Jewish high priest; a medicine to relieve chest complaints; a pectoral fin. **pectoral arch,** the shoulder-girdle. **pectoral sandpiper,** a small American sandpiper, *Tringa maculata*, an occasional British visitant. (L. *pectoralis*, of the breast.)

pectoriloquism, *n.* pek-to-*ril*-o-kwizm, pectoriloquy.

pectoriloquy, *n.* pek-to-*ril*-o-kwe, sound of the voice coming from the chest as heard with stethoscope, indicative of lung trouble. (L. *pectus*, breast, *loquor*, speak.)

pectose, *n.* *pek*-tohs, an insoluble substance occurring in unripe fruit, ultimately becoming pectin.

peculate, *v.i.* *pek*-yew-late, illegally to appropriate money to one's own use; to embezzle.

peculation, *n.* *pek*-yew-*lay*-shon, embezzlement of money, esp. public money, to one's own use.

peculator, *n.* *pek*-yew-lay-tor, one who peculates.

peculiar, *a.* pe-*kew*-le-ar, characteristic of one person; one's own; solely or specially belonging to; singular; odd: *n.* exclusive property or right; a parish or church exempt from the authority of the bishop in whose diocese it is; any unusual type-character [Print.]. **Court of Peculiars,** a court having authority over the peculiars of the Archbishop of Canterbury. **Peculiar People,** an English evangelical sect (founded 1838) which reject medicine and practises faith-healing. (O.Fr. *peculier*.)

peculiarity, *n.* pe-*kew*-le-*a*-re-te, the quality of being peculiar; something peculiar.

peculiarize, *v.t.* pe-*kew*-le-a-rize, to make peculiar; to individualize.

peculiarly, *ad.* in a peculiar manner.

pecuniarily, *ad.* pe-*kew*-ne-a-re-le, from a money point of view.

pecuniary, *a.* pe-*kew*-ne-a-re, relating to or consisting of money. (L. *pecuniarius*, relating to money.)

ped, *n.* ped, a hamper or wickerwork pannier.

pedagogic, *a.* ped-a-*goj*-ik, pertaining to pedagogy or to a pedagogue.

pedagogics, *n.* ped-a-*goj*-iks, the science of teaching.

pedagogism, *n.* *ped*-a-gog-izm, the business, character, or manners of a pedagogue.

pedagogue, *n.* *ped*-a-gog, a teacher of the young; a schoolmaster; a pedant: *v.t.* to teach with a pedantic air. (Fr. *pédagogue*.)

pedagogy, *n.* *ped*-a-goj-e, the office, art, or manners of a pedagogue; pedagogics. (Gr. *paidagogia*.)

pedal, *a.* *ped*-al, pertaining to the foot; worked by the foot: *n.* a lever worked by the foot; the treadle of a cycle, sewing-machine, etc.; the foot-lever of an organ key, of an apparatus to modify the tone of a piano, etc.: *v.t.* and *i.* to work with a pedal. **pedal note,** a holding-note [Mus.]. **pedal point,** a sustained or stationary base [Mus.]. (L. *pedalis*, relating to the foot.)

pedalist, *n.* *ped*-a-list, one expert in the use of pedals.

pedant, *n.* *ped*-ant, one making a display of book-learning; one who insists on the mere letter; a conceited scholar. (O.Fr.)

pedantic, *a.* pe-*dan*-tik, given to or indicative of pedantry.

pedantically, *ad.* pe-*dan*-te-ka-le, in a pedantic manner.

pedantize, *v.i.* *ped*-an-tize, to play the pedant.

pedantry, *n.* *ped*-an-tre, vain ostentation of learning; blind and obstinate insistence on mere forms. (Fr. *pédanterie*.)

pedate, *a.* *ped*-at, having feet or foot-like organs [Zool.]; palmate, with lobes cleft into digit-like segments [Bot.]. (L. *pedatus*, having feet.)

peddle, *v.i.* *ped*-dl, to go about the country and retail goods; to be busy about trifles: *v.t.* to sell small wares, esp. in travelling about the country.

peddler, *n.* *ped*-dler, one who peddles; a pedlar.

peddlery, *n.* *ped*-le-re *or* *ped*-dl-re, pedlary.

peddling, *a.* *ped*-dling, insignificant; trifling.

pedestal, *n.* *ped*-es-tal, the base of a column, etc.; a stand for a statue; a base or support, as for a knee-hole table. (Sp.)

pedestrial, *a.* pe-*des*-tre-al, suited to walking.

pedestrian, *a.* pe-*des*-tre-an, going on foot; pertaining to walking; slow; prosaic: *n.* one who journeys on foot; one who engages in foot-races; an expert walker. (L. *pedester*, a pedestrian.)

pedestrianism, *n.* pe-*des*-tre-a-nizm, walking; the art or practice of walking, as a pedestrian.

pedestrianize, *v.i.* pe-*des*-tre-a-nize, to practise walking.

pedetentous, *a.* ped-e-*ten*-tus, advancing slowly. (L. *pedetentim*, pace by pace.)

pediatrics, *n.* ped-e-*at*-riks, *see* **pædiatrics.**

pedicel, *n.* *ped*-e-sel, the stalk of each particular flower [Bot.]; a footstalk by which certain invertebrates attach themselves to objects [Zool.]. (O.Fr. *pedecule*.)

pedicellate, *a.* *ped*-e-se-lat, having, or supported by, a pedicel.

pedicle, *n.* *ped*-e-kl, a pedicel or peduncle.

pedicular, *a.* pe-*dik*-yew-lar, pertaining to, or having, lice; lousy. (L. *pediculus*, a louse.)

pedicularis, *n.* pe-*dik*-yew-*lah*-ris, lousewort. (L.)
pediculation, *n.* pe-*dik*-yew-*lay*-shon, the state of being lousy; pediculosis.
pediculosis, pe-dik-yew-*loh*-sis, infestation with lice; phthiriasis.
pediculous, *a.* pe-*dik*-yew-lus, lousy; pedicular.
pedicure, *n.* *ped*-e-kewr, surgical treatment of the feet; a chiropodist. (L. *pes*, a foot, *cura*, care.)
pedigerous, *a.* pe-*dij*-er-rus, having feet or foot-like organs. (L. *pes*, and *gero*, bear.)
pedigree, *n.* *ped*-e-gree, lineage; a chart of ancestry; a genealogical table or family tree: *a.* having a registered ancestry (of live-stock). (O.Fr. *pee de grue*, a crane's foot, the arrow-like mark used in pedigrees resembling this.)
pedimanous, *a.* pe-*dim*-a-nus, having foot-like hands (of lemurs, etc.); quadrumanous. (L. *pes*, and *manus*, the hand.)
pediment, *n.* *ped*-e-ment, a triangular facing as a decoration over the portico of a Greek building. (L. *pedamentum*, a vine-stake.)
pedimental, *a.* *ped*-e-*men*-tal, pertaining to or resembling a pediment.
pedipalp, *n.* *ped*-e-palp, one of an order of arachnids, including most of the scorpions, having feelers like pincers; one of the pair of secondary appendages of arachnids, at either side of the mouth. (L. *pes*, and *palpo*, feel.)
pedlar, *n.* *ped*-lar, a travelling hawker; a peddler.
pedlary, *n.* *ped*-la-re, small-wares sold by pedlars; the occupation of pedlars.
pedobaptism, *n.* *pee*-do-*bap*-tizm, pædobaptism.
pedology, *n.* pe-*dol*-o-je, pædology.
pedometer, *n.* pe-*dom*-e-ter, an instrument for measuring distances covered in walking. (L. *pes*, and Gr. *metron*, measure.)
pedomotor, *n.* *ped*-o-mo-tor, an appliance worked by the foot or for applying foot-power; a velocipede.
pedrail, *n.* *ped*-rail, a heavy wheel with foot-like plates hinged to the periphery, these coming successively into contact with the ground; a tractor or vehicle fitted with such. (L. *pes*, *pedis*, foot, and *rail*.)
pedrero, *n.* ped-*reer*-ro, a perrier; a small gun for firing salutes, etc. (Sp., from L. *petraria*, a machine for hurling stones.)
peduncle, *n.* pe-*dung*-kl, the stalk either of the flower or the cluster [Bot.]; a supporting part [Anat.]; a pedicel [Zool.]. (Late L. *pedunculus*, a tiny foot.)
peduncular, *a.* pe-*dung*-kew-lar, pertaining to a peduncle.
pedunculate, *a.* pe-*dung*-kew-lat, having a peduncle; growing on a peduncle.
pedunculation, *n.* pe-dung-kew-*lay*-shon, the state of being pedunculate.
peek, *v.* peek, to look out; to peer; to look slyly or peep: *n.* a peep.
peel, *n.* peel, the skin or rind: *v.t.* and *i.* to strip off skin, bark, or rind. (Fr. *peler*.)
peel, *n.* peel, the long-handled wooden shovel used by bakers; the blade of an oar. (O.Fr. *pele*.)
peel, *n.* peel, a square fortress tower, esp. on the Scottish border. (O.Fr. *pel*, a pale or stake.)
peeler, *n.* *peel*-er, one who peels.
peeler, *n.* *peel*-er, a policeman [Slang]. (Sir Robert *Peel*, originator of the force, 1839.)
peelings, *n.pl.* *peel*-ingz, that which is peeled off; stripped rind, skin, etc.
peen, *n.* peen, the end of a hammer-head opposite the face. (Ger. *pinne*.)
peep, *n.* peep, the act of peeping; a cautious or furtive look; the first emergence: *v.i.* to look through a crevice; to look narrowly, closely, or slyly; to appear gradually, or make the first appearance.
peep, *n.* peep, the cry of a chicken: *v.i.* peep, to chirp or cry, as young birds. (Imit.)
peep-bo, *n.* *peep*-boh, the child's game bopeep.
peeper, *n.* *peep*-er, a chicken just breaking the shell; one that peeps; the eye [Slang].
peep-hole, *n.* a crevice for peeping through.
peep-o'-day, *n.* daybreak; dawn.
peep-show, *n.* a well-lighted box in which are viewed set scenes, pictures, etc., through a lens fixed in the side.
peep-sight, *n.* an adjustable backsight of a firearm, pierced with a small hole.
peepul, *n.* *pee*-pul, the pipal, or sacred fig.
peer, *n.* peer, one of the same rank; an equal; a nobleman. **Peer of Parliament,** a member of the House of Lords. (O.Fr.)
peer, *v.i.* peer, to peep; to look carefully and intently; to show or appear slightly. (Origin unknown.)
peerage, *n.* *peer*-raj, the ranks of nobility from baron upwards; a book about peers, their lineage and families; the body of peers.
peeress, *n.* *peer*-ress, the consort of a peer; a lady who has inherited a peerage, or upon whom a peerage has been conferred.
peerless, *a.* *peer*-less, matchless; having no equal.
peerlessly, *ad.* in a peerless manner.
peerlessness, *n.* the quality of being peerless.
peeve, *v.t.* peev, to irritate or annoy; to make fretful: *v.i.* to become irritated; to be irritable [all Coll.]. (Abbrev. of *peevish*.)
peevish, *a.* *pee*-vish, fretful; querulous; hard to please; petulant. (Origin unknown; possibly *perverse*.)
peevishly, *ad.* in a peevish manner.
peevishness, *n.* querulousness.
peewit, *n.* *pee*-wit, the lapwing or green plover, *Vanellus cristatus*. **peewit gull,** the black-headed or laughing gull, *Larus ridibundus*. (From its cry.)
peg, *n.* peg, a small wooden pin; a projecting piece on which to hang anything; a dram (of spirits): *v.t.* to fasten with or as with pegs; to score with pegs. **peg away,** to advance gradually and persistently, as in pegging at cribbage. **peg out,** to die [Slang]. **peg prices,** prevent their fluctuation by restricting dealings to a fixed price [Comm.]. **take a peg lower,** or **down,** to lower; to humble. (Scand.)
pegamoid, *n.* *peg*-a-moyd, proprietary name of an imitation leather.
Pegasus, *n.* *peg*-a-sus, the winged horse, sprung from the blood of Medusa, that with a stroke opened a spring in the ground whence the poets were fabled to draw their inspiration [Myth.]; the poetic muse; a northern constellation; a genus of fishes with large pectoral fins [Zool.]. (Gr., of the fountain.)
pegmatite, *n.* *peg*-ma-tite, a coarse-grained variety of granite; graphic granite.
peg-top, *n.* a child's spinning-top: *pl.* trousers having legs that narrow at the ankles.
peignoir, *n.* *pay*-nwahr, a woman's dressing robe or jacket. (Fr.)
peirastic, *a.* py-*ras*-tik, tentative: making trial. (Gr. *peirastikos*, from *peira*, trial.)
Peishwa, *n.* *pesh*-wa, the Peshwa.
pejorate, *v.t.* *pee*-jo-rate, to disparage; to worsen. (L. *pejor*, worse.)
pejoration, *n.* pee-jo-*ray*-shun, a worsening; depreciation.
pejorative, *a.* *pee*-jo-ra-tiv *or* pe-*jo*-ra-tiv, disparaging; tending to become worse; depreciatory: *n.* a depreciatory word.
pejorism, *n.* *pee*-jo-rizm, the belief or doctrine that all things are becoming worse.
pekan, *n.* *pee*-kan, the fisher, a N. American fur-bearing carnivore *Mustela pennanti*, allied to the marten. (Algonquian.)
Pekinese, *n.* *pee*-ke-neez, a breed of Chinese pug-dogs. (*Peking*, China.)
peking, *n.* *pee*-king, a silk material, originally from China. **Peking man,** an extinct human species, *Sinanthropus pekinensis*, deduced from a skull and other indications found near Peking in 1929.
pekoe, *n.* *pek*-oh, a variety of black tea. (Chinese.)
pelage, *n.* *pel*-aj, the coat or covering, fur or otherwise, of a mammal; the hairy system of the body. (Fr.)
pelagian, *a.* pe-*lay*-je-an, pertaining or belonging to the deep sea. (Gr. *pelagos*, the deep sea.)
Pelagian, *n.* pe-*lay*-je-an, a follower of Pelagius, a British monk of the early 5th cent., who denied the doctrine of original sin, and asserted that man can, with divine direction, work out his own salvation: *a.* pertaining to Pelagius or Pelagianism.
Pelagianism, *n.* pe-*lay*-je-an-izm, the doctrines of Pelagius.
pelagic, *a.* pe-*laj*-ik, pertaining to the deep sea.
pelamid, *n.* *pel*-a-mid, a young tunny.
pelargic, *a.* pe-*lar*-jik, pertaining to the storks. (Gr. *pelargos*, a stork.)
pelargonium, *n.* *pel*-ar-*goh*-ne-um, any of a genus

Pelagonium, of ornamental plants allied to the geranium, but having irregular instead of regular flowers and five or fewer stamens instead of ten. (Gr. *pelargos*, stork.)
Pelasgi, *n.pl.* pe-*laz*-jy, a prehistoric people of South-Eastern Europe and Asia Minor. (L.)
Pelasgic, *a.* *pe*-laz-jik, pertaining to the Pelasgi.
pelerine, *n.* *pel*-er-reen, a woman's fur cape with long ends. (Fr., from *pelerin*, a pilgrim.)
pelf, *n.* pelf, petty gains; money, esp. when doubtfully acquired. (O.Fr. *pelfre*, booty.)
pelican, *n.* *pel*-e-kan, a fish-eating bird of the genus *Pelecanus*, allied to the storks, with all four toes pointing forwards and an enormous bill with a large dilatable pouch. (Fr.)
pelisse, *n.* pe-*leece*, a woman's long, sleeved cloak; a child's loose coat. (Fr., from L. *pelliceus*, make of skins.)
pell, *n.* pel, a skin or hide; a roll of parchment; a document on parchment: *pl.* the former office in charge of the Exchequer receipts, etc. (O.Fr. *pel.*)
pellagra, *n.* pel-*ay*-gra *or* pe-*lah*-gra, a chronic disease due to vitamin deficiency, seriously affecting the skin and digestive system, etc. (L. *pellis*, skin, and Gr. *agra*, seizure.)
pellagrous, *a.* pe-*lay*-grus, pertaining to or affected with pellagra.
pellet, *n.* *pel*-let, a little ball; a pillule; a small bullet. (O.Fr. *pelote*, a small ball.)
pellicle, *n.* *pel*-le-kl, a thin skin or crust; a membranous film. (Fr. *pellicule.*)
pellitory, *n.* *pel*-le-to-re, a plant of the genus *Parietaria*, growing on old walls; a plant of the genus *Anacyclus*. (O.Fr. *paritoire.*)
pell-mell, *ad.* *pel*-mel, in disorder; vehemently. (O.Fr. *peslemesle*, chaos.)
pellucid, *a.* pel-*lew*-sid, perfectly clear; transparent. (Fr. *pellucide.*)
pellucidness, *n.* perfect clearness.
pelmanism, *n.* *pel*-man-izm, proprietary name of a specialized system of mnemonics and memory training.
pelmet, *n.* *pel*-met, a decorative fringe, etc., to conceal a curtain rod or fittings. (*palmette.*)
pelorus, *n.* pe-*law*-rus, an instrument serving as a mariner's compass but having no magnetic needle. (*Pelorus*, pilot to Hannibal.)
pelota, *n.* pe-*loh*-ta, a Basque ball game of the tennis kind in which the ball is struck with a wickerwork shield strapped to the forearm. (Sp.)
pelt, *n.* pelt, a skin; a raw hide. **pelt wool,** wool from a sheep or lamb, esp. when plucked after death. (*peltry.*)
pelt, *n.* pelt, a blow from something thrown: *v.t.* to strike, by throwing something: *v.i.* to fall thick and fast (of rain); to hurry. **full pelt,** as quickly as possible. (L. *pello*, drive.)
peltate, *a.* *pel*-tat, shaped like a shield with the stalk in the centre [Bot.]. (L. *peltatus*, furnished with a shield.)
pelter, *n.* *pel*-ter, one who pelts; a rainstorm; a hail, as of missiles.
peltry, *n.* *pel*-tre, pelts collectively; skins with the fur on them. (O.Fr. *pelleterie.*)
pelvic, *a.* *pel*-vik, pertaining to the pelvis. **pelvic arch** (or **girdle**), the bony arch by which the legs are joined to the body, consisting of the sacrum and coccyx with the innominate (or haunch) bone on each side [Anat.].
pelvimeter, *n.* pel-*vim*-e-ter, an instrument for measuring the pelvis.
pelvis, *n.* *pel*-vis, the basin-like cavity forming the lower portion of the abdomen; the bony wall (pelvic arch) enclosing this; the kidney cavity forming the upper end of the ureter [Anat.]. (L. a basin.)
pemmican, *n.* *pem*-e-kan, lean meat dried, pounded, and pressed into cakes for keeping. (N. Amerind.)
pemphigoid, *a.* *pem*-fe-goyd, resembling pemphigus [Path.].
pemphigus, *n.* *pem*-fe-gus, a skin disease, characterized by round or oval blisters of two or three inches diameter. (Gr. *pemphix*, a bubble.)
★**pen,** *n.* pen, an instrument used for writing with ink; a quill; the cuttle-bone of cephalopods: *v.t.* to write; to compose. **pen-and-ink,** *a.* done with a pen and ink, as a drawing. **to live by one's pen,** to maintain oneself by authorship. (O.Fr. *penne*, a feather.)
pen, *n.* pen, an enclosure, esp. for animals: *v.t.* to shut in a pen; to coop. (A.S. *penn.*)
pen, *n.* pen, the female swan. (Origin unknown.)
penal, *a.* *pee*-nal, enacting, inflicting, or incurring punishment for crime; pertaining to, or of the nature of, punishment. **penal servitude,** *see* **servitude.** (O.Fr.)
penalize, *v.t.* *pee*-na-lize, to subject to penalty; to handicap.
penally, *ad.* *pee*-na-le, by way of penalty.
penalty, *n.* *pen*-al-te, legal punishment or forfeit; a fine; a handicap [Sport]. **penalty goal,** in football, a goal scored from a penalty kick or free kick awarded to a team because of a breach of the rules by their opponents. (Fr. *pénalité.*)
penance, *n.* *pen*-ance, the suffering to which a person voluntarily subjects himself as an expression of penitence; in the Roman and Greek Churches, the sacrament consisting of making satisfaction to God for sins confessed and for which absolution has been received. (O.Fr.)
penannular, *a.* pen-*an*-new-lar, almost annular.
Penates, *n.pl.* pe-*nay*-teez, household gods. **Lares and Penates,** the home, and all it means. (L. *penus*, sanctuary.)
pence, *n.pl.* pence, pennies.
penchant, *n.* (App.), inclination; liking. (Fr.)
★**pencil,** *n.* *pen*-sil, a small brush used by painters for laying on colours; a bar of blacklead or coloured chalk in a wooden or metal sheath for writing with; a converging system of rays of light: *v.t.* to mark, paint, or draw with or as with a pencil. **pencil cedar,** any wood, usually of juniper, used for lead pencils. **pencil compass,** a drawing compass with a pencil on one of its legs. (O.Fr. *pincel.*)
pencilled, *pp.* and *a.* *pen*-sild, painted or marked, as with a pencil; having rays or pencils.
penciliform, *a.* pen-*sil*-e-form, shaped like a pencil (esp. of a beam of light).
pencilling, *n.* *pen*-sil-ling, painting or sketching; marking with fine lines.
pencraft, *n.* *pen*-krahft, penmanship.
pendant, *n.* *pen*-dant, anything hanging by way of ornament; a hanging lamp, electrolier, etc.; the stem and ring of a watch; a pennant; a match or counterpart. (Fr., from L. *pendere*, to hang.)
pendency, *n.* *pen*-den-se, suspense; state of pending or of being undecided.
pendent, *a.* *pen*-dent, hanging; pending; appendant.
pendentive, *n.* pen-*den*-tiv, a portion of a vault resting on a pier, and extending from the springing to the apex.
pendently, *ad.* in a pendent manner.
pendicle, *n.* *pen*-de-kl, an appendage or dependency; a subordinate part.
pending, *a.* *pend*-ing, depending; not terminated; awaiting decision: *prep.* during.
Pendragon, *n.* pen-*drag*-on, a chief king or generalissimo among the ancient Britons. (W. *pen*, head, *dragon*, a chief.)
penduline, *a.* *pen*-dew-line, pendulous (of certain bird's nests).
pendulous, *a.* *pen*-dew-lus, hanging so as to swing; oscillating. (L. *pendulus.*)
pendulousness, *n.* state of being pendulous.
pendulum, *n.* *pen*-dew-lum, a weight suspended from a fixed point, and swinging freely under the action of gravity, as in a clock. **compensation pendulum,** *see* **compensation. the swing of the pendulum,** alternation in public opinion, esp. in politics. (L.)
pene-, *comb.f.* *pee*-ne, nearly, almost, as in **penecontemporaneous,** of nearly the same period. (L. *pæne.*)
penelope, *n.* pe-*nel*-o-pe, the guan, a bird of Central and S. America, allied to the curassow. (Gr., Penelope, wife of Ulysses.)
peneplain, *n.* *pen*-e-plane, a tract worn by erosion almost to a plain [Geog.]. (L. *pæne*, nearly, and *plain.*)
penetrability, *n.* *pen*-e-tra-*bil*-e-te, susceptibility of being penetrated by another body.
penetrable, *a.* *pen*-e-tra-bl, that may be penetrated; that may be affected.
penetralia, *n.pl.* pen-e-*tray*-le-a, the interior part of a temple or palace; mysteries. (L.)
penetrancy, *n.* *pen*-e-tran-se, power of entering; penetrativeness.

penetrant, *a.* *pen*-e-trant, penetrating; subtle; able to pierce. (L. *penetrans*, entering.)
penetrate, *v.t.* *pen*-e-trate, to enter into; to pierce; to affect deeply; to discern by the intellect; to pass into the interior: *v.i.* to make way. (L. *penetratus*, fixed within.)
penetrating, *a.* *pen*-e-tray-ting, sharp; subtle; acute; discerning.
penetration, *n.* pen-e-*tray*-shon, the act of penetrating; acuteness; discernment; the act of establishing influence in a foreign country, esp. by repeated diplomatic or commercial intrigue.
penetrative, *a.* *pen*-e-tra-tiv, piercing; penetrating.
penetrativeness, *n.* quality of being penetrative.
pengo, *n.* *peng*-go, the monetary unit of Hungary from 1925 to 1946 (when superseded by the forint), nominally equivalent to about 8½d.
penguin, *n.* *peng*-gwin, any flightless sea-bird of the family Spheniscidæ, found only in the southern hemisphere and having paddle-like wings and scaly feathers. (Perhaps from W. *pen gwyn*, white head.)
penguinery, *n.* *peng*-gwe-ne-re, a haunt of penguins for breeding purposes.
penholder, *n.* *pen*-hohl-der, a holder for a writing pen; a rack for pens.
penial, *a.* *pee*-ne-al, pertaining to the penis.
penicillate, *a.* pe-*nis*-e-lat, having small tufts, or pencil-like markings [Zool.]. (L. *penicillum*, paint-brush.)
penicillation, *n.* *pen*-e-se-*lay*-shun, a tuft-like growth of hairs [Bot. and Zool.]
penicilliform, *a.* *pen*-e-*sil*-e-form, penicillate [Bot. and Zool.]
penicillin, *n.* *pen*-e-*sil*-in, a bacteria-killing drug prepared from the mould *Pencillium notatum*, used against sepsis with blood-poisoning, pneumonia, gangrene, etc.
penile, *a.* *pee*-nile, penial.
peninsula, *n.* pen-*in*-sew-la, a tract of land nearly surrounded by water. (L.)
peninsular, *a.* pen-*in*-sew-lar, in form of a peninsula; pertaining to a peninsula, esp. Spain and Portugal.
peninsularity, *n.* pen-*in*-sew-*la*-re-te, the state of being peninsular; peninsular character.
peninsulate, *v.t.* pen-*in*-sew-late, to encompass almost with water; to form a peninsula of.
penis, *n.* *pee*-nis, the male organ of coition. (L.)
penitence, *n.* *pen*-e-tence, sorrow for sins or offences; repentance; contrition. (O.Fr.)
penitency, *n.* *pen*-e-ten-se, the state of being penitent.
penitent, *a.* *pen*-e-tent, contrite; repentant: *n.* one who repents of sin; one under church censure, but admitted to penance under a confessor; a member of any fraternity in the Roman Catholic Church practising penance and acts of charity. (O.Fr.)
penitential, *a.* pen-e-*ten*-shal, expressing penitence: *n.* a book containing rules for penitents.
penitentiary, *a.* pen-e-*ten*-sha-re, relating to penance; penitential: *n.* a penitent; one who does penance; a house of correction; (*cap.*) a court (also an official) that grants dispensations, absolutions, etc. [Rom. Cath.]. **Grand Penitentiary,** the cardinal presiding over the Penitentiary. (Late L. *pœnitentiarius*.)
penitently, *ad.* *pen*-e-tent-le, with penitence.
penknife, *n.* *pen*-nife, a small pocket knife, originally one for making and mending quill pens.
penman, *n.* *pen*-man, a man who teaches the art of writing, or who writes a good hand; an author.
penmanship, *n.* *pen*-man-ship, the art of using a pen; handwriting.
pen-name, *n.* a pseudonym; a nom-de-plume.
pennant, *n.* *pen*-ant, a pennon; a long strip of bunting flown at the mast-head of vessels of war to show they are in commission; a streamer. (*pennon*.)
pennate, *a.* *pen*-at, winged; pinnate.
penniform, *a.* *pen*-e-form, in the form of a feather. (L. *penna*, a feather, and *form*.)
pennigerous, *a.* pe-*nij*-er-rus, bearing feathers.
penniless, *a.* *pen*-e-less, moneyless; poor.
pennilessness, *n.* *pen*-e-les-ness, destitution.
penninite, *n.* *pen*-e-nite, a silicate of magnesium, monoclinic, but rhombohedral in habit. (The *Pennine* Alps, where found.)
pennon, *n.* *pen*-on, a small narrow flag, forked or swallow-tailed, borne on a knight's lance and often charged with his arms; the distinguishing ensign of lancer regiments. (O.Fr.)
penn'orth, *n.* *pen*-urth, a pennyworth [Coll.].
penny, *n.* *pen*-e, a copper coin, the twelfth of a shilling; a small sum; money; a denarius: *pl.* **pennies,** to denote the number of coins. **pence,** the amount of pennies in value. **a pretty penny,** a considerable amount. **penny bank,** a savings bank at which deposits of one penny are accepted. **penny dreadful,** *see* **dreadful. penny wedding,** a wedding at which the guests pay. **penny wise,** saving small sums; foolishly niggardly. (A.S. *penig*.)
penny-a-liner, *n.* formerly, a journalist or reporter working for absurdly small remuneration.
penny-cress, *n.* any plant of the genus *Thlaspi*.
penny-farthing, *n.* the bicycle, with a large direct-drive front wheel and small rear wheel, that preceded the "safety"; an "ordinary" [Slang].
pennyroyal, *n.* *pen*-e-*roy*-al, the perennial mint *Mentha pulegium*. (L. *pulicium regium*, fleabane.)
pennyweight, *n.* *pen*-e-wate, a troy weight of twenty-four grains, or 1·5552 grammes.
pennywort, *n.* *pen*-e-wurt, any plant of the umbelliferous genus *Hydrocotyle*; the ivy-leaved toad-flax, *Linaria cymbalaria*. **marsh pennywort,** *Cotyledon umbilicus*.
pennyworth, *n.* *pen*-e-wurth, as much as is bought for a penny; any purchase; a good bargain; a small quanitty.
penology, *n.* pe-*nol*-o-je, the study of prison management, discipline, etc. (L. *pœna*, punishment, *logos*, science.)
pensile, *a.* *pen*-sile, hanging; pendulous; building hanging nests [Ornith.]. (L. *pensilis*, pendent.)
pensility, *n.* pen-*sil*-e-te, the condition or quality of being pensile.
pension, *n.* *pen*-shon, a periodical allowance in consideration of past services; an annuity; sum paid to a clergyman instead of tithes: *v.t.* to grant a pension to. **civil list pension,** *see* **civil. old-age pension,** a pension, contributory or non-contributory, granted under various Acts of Parliament and under certain conditions to persons on reaching the stated age. (Fr., from L. *pendere*, to pay.)
pension, *n.* (App.) a boarding-house or boarding-school. **en pension,** board and lodging inclusive. (Fr.)
pensionary, *a.* *pen*-shon-a-re, maintained by a pension; consisting of a pension: *n.* one receiving a pension; formerly, in Holland, a chief magistrate.
pensioner, *n.* *pen*-shon-er, the holder of a pension; a dependant; an undergraduate at Cambridge not holding a university scholarship or a sizarship. **gentlemen pensioner,** former designation of a gentleman-at-arms.
pensive, *a.* *pen*-siv, thoughtful; thoughtful with sadness; expressing melancholy thoughtfulness. (Fr. *pensif*.)
pensively, *ad.* in a pensive manner.
pensiveness, *n.* the state of being pensive.
penstock, *n.* *pen*-stok, a sluice or flood-gate; a trough leading the water to a waterwheel.
pent, *a.* pent, shut up; imprisoned. (*pp.* of *pen*.)
pent-, penta-, *pref.*, denoting that the object consists of five, or has five, of the specified thing. (Gr. *pente*, five.)
pentacapsular, *a.* *pen*-ta-*kap*-sew-lar, having five capsules or seed-vessels [Bot.].
pentachord, *n.* *pen*-ta-kord, a musical scale of five sounds; an instrument of music with five strings.
pentacle, *n.* *pen*-ta-kl, the pentagram, or similar design, used as a symbol. (Late L. *pentaculum*.)
pentacoccous, *a.* *pen*-ta-*kok*-kus, having five seeds, or five cells, with a seed in each [Bot.]. (Gr. *pente*, and *kokkos*, a kernel)
pentacrinite, *n.* pen-*tak*-re-nite, one of the fossil crinoids or stone-lilies. (Gr. *pente*, and *krinon*, a lily.)
pentacrostic, *a.* *pen*-ta-*kros*-tik, containing five acrostics of the same word. (Gr. *pente*, and *acrostic*.)
pentad, *n.* *pen*-tad, a group of five; an element, radical, or atom having a valency of five [Chem.]. (Gr. *pentados*.)
pentadactylous, *a.* *pen*-ta-*dak*-te-lus, having five fingers or toes [Bot. and Zool.].

pentadelphous, *a.* *pen*-ta-*del*-fus, with the stamens grouped in five sets [Bot.].
pentafid, *a.* *pen*-ta-fid, cleft into five [Bot.].
pentagon, *n.* *pen*-ta-gon, a figure or object having five angles. (L. *pentagonus.*)
pentagonal, *a.* pen-*tag*-on-al, having five angles.
pentagram, *n.* *pen*-ta-gram, a figure, formerly used as an ornament and symbolically, formed by producing the sides of a pentagon until they cross and give the outline of a five-pointed star. (Gr. *pente*, and *gramma*, a letter.)
pentahedral, *a.* *pen*-ta-*heed*-ral, of five equal sides.
pentahedron, *n.* *pen*-ta-*heed*-ron, a solid figure having five equal sides. (Gr. *pente*, and *hedra*, a side.)
pentahexahedral, *a.* *pen*-ta-heks-a-*heed*-ral, having five six-faced ranges of facets one above another [Cryst.]. (Gr. *pente*, *hex*, six, and *hedra.*)
pentamerous, *a.* pen-*tam*-er-rus, having its parts in fives [Bot.]; five-jointed [Zool.]. (Gr. *pentameros*, split up into five parts.)
pentameter, *n.* pen-*tam*-e-ter, a verse of five feet; the English iambic verse of ten syllables [Pros.]. (Gr. *pente*, and *metron*, measure.)
pentane, *n.* *pen*-tane, a highly inflammable liquid present in light petroleum, the fifth member of the paraffin series of hydrocarbons.
pentangular, *a.* pen-*tang*-gew-lar, having five angles. (Gr. *pente*, and *angular.*)
pentapetalous, *a.* pen-ta-*pet*-a-lus, having five petals. (Gr. *pente*, and *petalon*, a petal.)
pentaphyllous, *a.* pen-ta-*fil*-lus, having five leaves. (Gr. *pente*, and *phyllon*, a leaf.)
pentarchy, *n.* *pen*-tar-ke, a government of five. (Gr. *pente*, and *archo*, rule.)
pentasepalous, *a.* pen-ta-*sep*-a-lus, having five sepals. (Gr. *pente*, and *sepal.*)
pentaspermous, *a.* pen-ta-*sper*-mus, containing five seeds. (Gr. *pente*, and *sperma*, seed.)
pentastich, *n.* *pen*-ta-stik, a poem or stanza consisting of five lines.
pentastyle, *a.* *pen*-ta-stile, having five columns in front [Arch.]. (Gr. *pente*, and *stylos*, a column.)
Pentateuch, *n.* *pen*-ta-tewk, the first five books of the Old Testament. (L. *pentateuchus.*)
pentathlon, *n.* pen-*tath*-lon, an athletic contest comprising five different events, esp., in ancient Greece, running, wrestling, leaping, throwing the discus, and hurling the spear.
pentatonic, *a.* pen-ta-*ton*-ik, consisting of five tones [Mus.].
Pentecost, *n.* *pen*-te-kost, a solemn festival of the Jews fifty days after the second day of the Passover; Whit-Sunday or Whitsuntide. (Gr. *pentekoste*, fiftieth.)
Pentecostal, *a.* pen-te-*kos*-tal, pertaining to Pentecost; as at Pentecost.
penthouse, *n.* *pent*-house, a shed standing aslope from a main building. (Formerly *pentice*, from O.Fr. *apentis*, a penthouse.)
pentile, *n.* *pen*-tile, a tile so formed as to cover the sloping part of the roof.
pentlandite, *n.* *pent*-lan-dite, a native nickel iron sulphide. (J. B. *Pentland*, its discoverer, 1856.)
pentode, *n.* *pen*-tode, a vacuum tube having five electrodes [Elect.].
pent-roof, *n.* a roof sloping to one side only.
Pentstemon, *n.* pent-*stee*-mon, a genus of showy herbaceous plants including the figworts. (Gr. *pente*, five, *stemon*, stamen.)
penult, *n.* pe-*nult*, the last syllable but one of a word. (L. *pene*, almost, *ultimus*, last.)
penultimate, *a.* pe-*nul*-te-mat, last but one: *n.* penult.
penumbra, *n.* pe-*num*-bra, the imperfect shadow between total shadow and full light, esp. in an eclipse [Astron.]; the area in which light and shade are blended [Painting]. (L. *pene*, almost, *umbra*, a shadow.)
penurious, *a.* pe-*newr*-re-us, excessively saving; sordid; scanty.
penuriously, *ad.* in a penurious manner.
penuriousness, *n.* stinginess; meanness.
penury, *n.* *pen*-yewr-re, indigence; extreme poverty; destitution. (O.Fr. *penurie.*)
penwiper, *n.* *pen*-wy-per, a piece, or assemblage of pieces, of cloth, etc. for wiping ink from pen nibs.
peon, *n.* *pee*-on, in India, a foot-soldier, a policeman; in Latin America, a day labourer; a bondman for debt. (Sp.)
peonage, *n.* *pee*-o-naj, the state of being a peon.
peony, *n.* *pee*-o-ne, a plant of the genus *Pæonia.* (O.Fr. through Gr. *Paion*, the god of healing.)
people, *n.* *pee*-pl, the body of persons constituting a community or nation; the populace; the vulgar; persons of a class; persons generally; kindred; attendants: *v.t.* to stock with inhabitants; to populate; to inhabit. (O.Fr. *peuple.*)
peotomy, *n.* pe-*ot*-o-me, amputation of the penis [Surg.]. (Gr. *peos*, penis, *-toma*, cutting.)
pep, *n.* pep, brisk energy; go; vigour [Slang]. **to pep up**, to liven up, to put dash or "go" into. (*pepper.*)
peperino, *n.* pep-er-*ree*-noh, a dark brown granular tufa, found chiefly near Rome [Geol.]. (It., pepper.)
peplos, *n.* *pep*-los, the shawl-like outer robe worn by women of ancient Greece. (Gr.)
pepo, *n.* *pee*-po, a fruit like a cucumber; a gourd. (L.)
pepper, *n.* *pep*-per, a hot pungent spice, also the plant *Piper nigrum*, from the berry of which this is made: *v.t.* to sprinkle with ground pepper, or season with pepper; to pelt with or as with shot. **pepper-and-salt**, *a.* and *n.* black and white intermingled; dull grey. (A.S. *pipor.*)
pepper-box, *n.* a small box with perforated lid, for sprinkling ground pepper on food.
pepper-caster, *n.* a pepper-box.
peppercorn, *n.* *pep*-per-kawrn, the berry of the pepper-plant; something of inconsiderable value. **peppercorn rent**, a purely nominal rent.
pepper-grass, *n.* a garden cress of the genus *Lepidium*; also pillwort and shepherd's-purse.
pepperidge, *n.* *pep*-er-ridj, a North American tree of the genus *Nyssa.*
peppering, *n.* *pep*-er-ring, a sprinkling with or as with pepper; a hail of missiles, blows, etc.
peppermint, *n.* *pep*-per-mint, the pungent aromatic mint plant, *Mentha piperita*; an essential oil distilled from peppermint, also a drink, sweet, etc., flavoured with this.
pepper-pot, *n.* a pepper-box; a highly seasoned stew.
pepper-tree, *n.* the tropical South American tree *Schinus molle*, which yields mastic; in Australasia, any tree of the genus *Drimys.*
pepperwort, *n.* *pep*-per-wurt, a cruciferous plant of the genus *Lepidium.*
peppery, *a.* *pep*-per-re, having the qualities of pepper; hot; irascible.
pepsin, *n.* *pep*-sin, an enzyme secreted in the stomach, assisting digestion by converting proteins into peptones. (Fr., from Gr. *pepsis*, digestion.)
peptic, *a.* *pep*-tik, pertaining to digestion, or to pepsin; promoting digestion; able to digest: *n.* a substance that promotes digestion. **peptic ulcer**, a gastric ulcer. (Gr. *peptikos.*)
pepticity, *n.* pep-*tis*-e-te, the state of being able to digest; eupepsia.
peptone, *n.* *pep*-tone, any of the albuminoid substances into which the action of pepsin converts the proteids. (Gr. *pepton.*)
peptonemia, *n.* pep-to-*nee*-me-a, the presence of peptone in the blood [Path.].
peptonize, *v.t.* *pep*-ton-ize, to convert into peptone.
per, *prep.* per, by means of; through; to or for each; according to. (L.)
per-, per, a Latin prefix denoting through, by, very, over the whole extent; for each; in chemistry, to the highest degree, as peroxide.
peradventure, *ad.* per-ad-*vent*-yur, by chance; perhaps: *n.* chance; uncertainty.
perambulate, *v.t.* per-*ram*-bew-late, to walk through or round, esp. in order to survey or inspect. (L. *perambulatus*, gone round.)
perambulation, *n.* per-ram-bew-*lay*-shon, the act of passing through; a travelling survey or inspection, also the district assigned for this purpose; a survey or settling of boundaries.
perambulator, *n.* per-*ram*-bew-lay-tor, a light carriage for children, pushed by hand; an hodometer or other instrument for measuring distances traversed.
percale, *n.* per-*kayl*, a closely woven cotton material resembling muslin. (Fr.)
perceivable, *a.* per-*see*-va-bl, perceptible.
perceive, *v.t.* per-*seev*, to apprehend by the senses; to discern; to know; to understand. (O.Fr. *percever.*)

perceiver, *n.* one who perceives or observes.
per cent, per-*sent*, by the hundred; used adjectivally, as in "a three per cent investment," and as a noun (for *percentage*), as in "a small per cent of the regiment." **the three per cents,** a public security yielding three per cent. (L. *per*, and *centum*, a hundred.)
percentage, *n.* per-*sen*-taj, the rate per cent; proportion, esp. of each hundred.
percept, *n.* *per*-sept, that which is mentally perceived [Phil.]. (L. *perceptum*, apprehended.)
perceptibility, *n.* per-*sep*-te-*bil*-e-te, capability of being perceived.
perceptible, *a.* per-*sep*-te-bl, that may be perceived.
perceptibly, *ad.* in a perceptible manner.
perception, *n.* per-*sep*-shon, the act, process, or faculty of perceiving, whether through the senses or mentally; discernment; understanding; intuition. (Fr.)
perceptional, *a.* per-*sep*-shon-al, pertaining to perception.
perceptive, *a.* per-*sep*-tiv, having the faculty of perceiving; perceptional; discerning.
perceptively, *ad.* in a perceptive manner.
perceptiveness, *n.* perceptivity.
perceptivity, *n.* per-sep-*tiv*-e-te, quality of being perceptive; power of perception; intelligence.
perceptual, *a.* per-*sep*-tew-al, pertaining to or involving perception.
perch, *n.* perch, a freshwater fish of the genus *Perca*. **dusky perch,** the sea-fish *Serranus gigas*. (Fr. *perche*, from Gr. *perknos*, dark-coloured.)
perch, *n.* perch, a pole; a roost bar for fowls, cage-birds, etc.; a measure of 5½ yards; a measure of 30¼ square yards: *v.i.* to sit or roost; to light or settle on a fixed body: *v.t.* to place on a perch. (Fr. *perche*, from L. *pertica*, a pole.)
perchance, *ad.* per-*chahnce*, by chance.
percher, *n.* *perch*-er, one who or that which perches; any of the Insessores, or perching birds.
percheron, *n.* *per*-sher-on, a breed of Normandy draught-horses. (Fr. *le Perche*, a former district in Normandy.)
perciform, *a.* *per*-se-form, resembling the perch [Ichth.]
percine, *a.* *per*-sine, belonging to the perch family: *n.* a perch or related fish
percipience, *n.* per-*sip*-e-ence, the act or power of perceiving; cognizance.
percipient, *a.* per-*sip*-e-ent, perceiving; having the faculty of perceiving; pertaining to a perception or a perceiver: *n.* one who perceives; one who receives telepathic or similar communications. (L. *percipiens*, apprehending.)
perclose, *n.* *per*-kloze, a parclose.
percoid, *a.* *per*-koyd, resembling the perch [Ichth.]; of the perch family.
percolate, *v.t.* *per*-ko-late, to strain through; to ooze through: *v.i.* to pass or filter through; to seep. (L. *percolatus*, strained.)
percolation, *n.* per-ko-*lay*-shon, filtration.
percolator, *n.* *per*-ko-lay-tor, a filtering machine; a coffee-pot in which hot water percolates through the coffee.
percurrent, *a.* per-*ku*-rent, running through the whole length [Bot. and Zool.].
percursory, *a.* per-*kur*-so-re, running over slightly; cursory. (Late L. *percursor*.)
percuss, *v.t.* per-*kus*, to strike forcibly; to subject to percussion [Med.]. (O.Fr. *percussir*.)
percussion, *n.* per-*kush*-on, collision; the shock produced by collision of bodies; impression of sound on the ear; the tapping of the body surface to diagnose the state of the underlying organs by the resulting sound [Med.]. **percussion cap,** a small copper cap, containing fulminating powder. **percussion instrument,** a band instrument obtaining its tone by percussion, as the drum, cymbal, or triangle. **percussion lock,** a gun-lock in which the percussion cap is struck by a hammer. (Fr.)
percussive, *a.* per-*kus*-siv, pertaining to percussion; striking against.
percutaneous, *a.* *per*-kew-*tay*-ne-us, acting or effected through the skin [Med.].
perdition, *n.* per-*dish*-on, utter destruction; ruin; damnation; the utter loss of the soul or of happiness in a future state. (Fr.)
perdu, *a.* per-*dew*, hidden; lost or abandoned; employed in desperate purposes [Mil.]: *n.* one placed in ambush; one engaged in a forlorn hope or desperate enterprise. (Fr. *perdu*, lost.)
perdurable, *a.* per-*dewr*-ra-bl, very durable; everlasting. (Fr.)
perdurance, *n.* per-*dewr*-rance, lasting quality; long continuance; permanence.
perduration, *n.* per-dewr-*ray*-shon, an indefinite or continuous duration.
perdure, *v.i.* per-*dewr*, to endure; to continue to last. (L. *perduro*, last long.)
peregrinate, *v.i.* *pe*-re-gre-nate, to travel from place to place or about; to live abroad. (L. *peregrinatus*, travelled.)
peregrination, *n.* *pe*-re-gre-*nay*-shon, travelling from one place to another; a foreign sojourn.
peregrinator, *n.* *pe*-re-gre-nay-tor, a traveller.
peregrine, *a.* *pe*-re-grin, foreign; exotic: *n.* an alien in a foreign land; the peregrine falcon. **peregrine falcon,** the large falcon, *Falco peregrinus*. (L. *peregrinus*, foreign.)
peremptorily, *ad.* pe-*remp*-to-re-le, in a peremptory manner.
peremptoriness, *n.* quality of being peremptory.
peremptory, *a.* pe-*remp*-to-re, in a manner to preclude debate or expostulation; decisive; positive; final; determinate. (O.Fr. *peremptoire*.)
perennial, *a.* pe-*ren*-ne-al, lasting; enduring; continuing more than two years [Bot.]: *n.* a perennial plant [Bot.]. (L. *perennis*, eternal.)
perennially, *ad.* so as to be perennial.
perfect, *a.* *per*-fekt, complete in all its parts; completely skilled; complete morally; faultless; monoclinous [Bot.]: *v.t.* *per*-fekt *or* per-*fekt*, to complete; to finish; to instruct fully; to print the second side of a sheet of paper. **perfect tense,** the tense that expresses complete action [Gram.]. (O.Fr. *parfit*.)
perfecter, *n.* *per*-fek-ter *or* per-*fek*-ter, one who or that which makes perfect.
perfectibilism, *n.* per-*fek*-te-be-lizm, perfectionism.
perfectibilist, *n.* per-*fek*-te-be-list, one who believes in the attainability by man of moral and social perfection.
perfectibility, *n.* per-*fek*-te-*bil*-e-te, the capacity of becoming or of being made perfect; attainability of perfection.
perfectible, *a.* per-*fek*-te-bl, capable of becoming perfect or of being perfected.
perfection, *n.* per-*fek*-shon, the act of making or state of being perfect; a perfect thing, quality, or attribute; the highest excellence. (Fr.)
perfectionism, *n.* per-*fek*-shon-izm, the doctrine of the perfectibilists.
perfectionist, *n.* per-*fek*-shon-ist, a perfectibilist; one satisfied only with perfection.
perfectionment, *n.* per-*fek*-shon-ment, the act of making perfect.
perfective, *a.* per-*fek*-tiv, tending or calculated to make perfect; expressing action as complete [Gram.].
perfectly, *ad.* completely; accurately.
perfectness, *n.* perfection; consummate excellence.
perfervid, *a.* per-*fer*-vid, very fervid; highly impassioned.
perficient, *a.* per-*fish*-ent, effectual: *n.* one who perfects. (L. *perficiens*, finishing.)
perfidious, *a.* per-*fid*-e-us, faithless; false to a vow or a trust; unfaithful; treacherous. (L. *perfidiosus*.)
perfidiously, *ad.* in a perfidious manner.
perfidiousness, *n.* quality of being perfidious.
perfidy, *n.* *per*-fe-de, breach of faith, promise, vow, or allegiance; violation of trust reposed. (Fr. *perfidie*.)
perfoliate, *a.* per-*foh*-le-at, with the leaf united round the stem [Bot.]. (L. *per*-, and *folium*, a leaf.)
perforate, *v.t.* *per*-fo-rate, to bore through; to make a hole by boring: *v.i.* to make perforations; to become perforate: *a.* perforated; umbilicate [Zool.]. (L. *perforatus*, bored through.)
perforation, *n.* per-fo-*ray*-shon, act of boring through; a hole or aperture bored; a series, or one of a series, of holes close together in a line.
perforative, *a.* *per*-fo-ra-tiv, able to pierce; causing or characterized by perforation [Med.].
perforator, *n.* *per*-fo-ray-tor, a perforating machine.
perforce, *ad.* per-*force*, by violence; of necessity.
perform, *v.t.* per-*form*, to execute; to accomplish; to discharge; to fulfil: *v.i.* to do; to give a per-

formance; to act a part; to play. (O.Fr. *parfournir*, perform.)
performable, *a.* per-*form*-a-bl, that may be performed.
performance, *n.* per-*form*-ance, the carrying anything into effect; execution; action; thing done; composition; an entertainment; acting, or an exhibition of character or skill.
performer, *n.* per-*form*-er, one who performs anything, particularly in an art.
perfume, *n. per*-fewm, a substance which emits a sweet odour; sweet odour emitted; fragrance: *v.t.* per-*fewm*, to scent; to fill or impregnate with a grateful odour. (Fr. *parfumer*, to perfume.)
perfumer, *n.* per-*fewm*-er, one who or that which perfumes; a seller of perfumes.
perfumery, *n.* per-*fewm*-er-re, the business of a perfumer; a perfume factory or warehouse; perfumes in general.
perfunctorily, *ad.* per-*funk*-to-re-le, carelessly.
perfunctoriness, *n.* per-*funk*-tor-e-ness, negligent performance; carelessness.
perfunctory, *a.* per-*funk*-to-re, done only for the sake of getting rid of an obligation, duty, etc.; careless; negligent. (L. *perfunctorius.*)
perfuse, *v.t.* per-*fewz*, to sprinkle, pour, or spread over. (L. *perfusus*, poured through.)
perfusion, *n.* per-*few*-zhon, the act of sprinkling or pouring (liquid) over; baptism by affusion.
perfusive, *a.* per-*few*-siv, apt to spread.
pergameneous, *a.* per-ga-*mee*-ne-us, like parchment (esp. of the skin). (L. *pergamena*, parchment.)
pergola, *n. per*-go-la, an arbour or a garden walk with plants climbing at the sides on trellis, etc., and along poles overhead. (It.)
perhaps, *ad.* per-*haps*, by chance; it may be. (*per* and *hap.*)
peri, *n. peer*-re, a beautiful elf, the descendant of a fallen spirit, excluded from Paradise till purged from sin by penance; a fairy, or fairy-like woman [Per. Myth.]. (Per., sprite.)
peri-, *pe*-re, a Greek prefix signifying around, near, about.
perianth, *n. pe*-re-anth, the floral envelope or outer part of a flower. (Gr. *peri-*, and *anthos*, a flower.)
periapt, *n. pe*-re-apt, an amulet; a protective charm. (Gr. *peri-*, and *haptein*, to fasten.)
peribolus, *n.* pe-*rib*-o-lus, a court surrounding a temple. (Gr. *peri-*, and *ballo*, throw.)
pericardiac, *a.* pe-re-*kar*-de-ak, relating to the pericardium.
pericardial, *a.* pe-re-*kar*-de-al, pericardiac.
pericarditis, *n. per*-re-kar-*dy*-tis, inflammation of the pericardium.
pericardium, *n.* pe-re-*kar*-de-um, the sac of serous membrane enveloping the heart [Anat.]. (L.)
pericarp, *n. pe*-re-karp, the seed-vessel of plants [Bot.]. (Gr. *perikarpion.*)
pericarpial, *a.* pe-re-*kar*-pe-al, relating to the pericarp.
perichætium, *n.* pe-re-*kee*-te-um, a cluster of leaflets at the base of the fructification of certain liverworts. (Gr. *peri-*, and *chaite*, flowing hair.)
perichondrium, *n.* pe-re-*kon*-dre-um, the membrane that covers a cartilage. (Gr. *peri-*, and *chondros*, cartilage.)
periclase, *n. pe*-re-klaze, native oxide of magnesium crystallizing in the cubic system. (Gr. *peri-*, and *klasis*, breaking.)
periclasis, *n.* pe-re-*klay*-sis, a comminuted fracture [Surg.]. (Gr. *peri-*, and *klasis*, breaking.)
Periclean, *a.* pe-re-*klee*-an, pertaining to Pericles, or his period (about 470–430 B.C.), the height of Athenian splendour.
periclinal, *a. pe*-re-*kly*-nal, dipping on all sides from a central point [Geol.]. (Gr. *periklinēs*, sloping.)
pericline, *n. pe*-re-kline, a variety of albite.
pericope, *n.* pe-*rik*-o-pe, an extract or selected passage. (Gr. *peri-*, and *kope*, cutting.)
pericranium, *n.* pe-re-*kray*-ne-um, the membrane investing the skull. (Late L. *peri-*, and *cranium.*)
pericystitis, *n. pe*-re-sis-*ty*-tis, inflammation of the tissue round the bladder [Path.].
peridot, *n. pe*-re-dot, a transparent, greenish-yellow form of olivine. (Fr.)
peridrome, *n. pe*-re-drome, the open space between the exterior columns of a building and the walls [Arch.]. (Gr. *peri-*, and *dromos*, a course.)
periganglionic, *a. pe*-re-gang-gle-*on*-ik, around a ganglion.
perigastritis, *n.* pe-re-gas-*try*-tis, inflammation of the peritoneal coat of the stomach [Med.].
perigean, *a.* pe-re-*jee*-an, pertaining to the perigee.
perigee, *n. pe*-re-jee, that point in the orbit of the moon, or a planet, which is nearest the earth. (Gr. *peri-*, and *ge*, the earth.)
periglottis, *n.* pe-re-*glot*-is, the skin or mucous membrane covering the tongue.
perigonium, *n.* pe-re-*goh*-ne-um, the perianth [Bot.]; the membranous sac surrounding the fibres of sponges [Zool.].
perigynous, *a.* pe-*rij*-e-nus, growing around the ovary (of stamens, etc.) [Bot.]. (Gr. *peri-*, and *gyne*, female.)
perihelion, *n.* pe-re-*hee*-le-on, the point in a planet's (or comet's) orbit when it is nearest the sun. (Gr. *peri-*, and *helios*, the sun.)
peril, *n. pe*-ril, danger; risk; exposure to injury, loss, or destruction: *v.t.* to expose to danger. (L. *periculum*, danger, trial.)
perilous, *a. pe*-re-lus, dangerous; hazardous.
perilously, *ad. pe*-re-lus-le, dangerously.
perilousness, *n.* quality of being perilous; dangerousness.
perilymph, *n. pe*-re-limf, the fluid contained in the internal ear [Anat.].
perimeter, *n.* pe-*rim*-e-ter, the outer boundary of a body or figure [Geom.]; an instrument used in the examination of the retina [Opt.]. (Gr. *peri-*, and *meter.*)
perimetrical, *a. pe*-re-*met*-re-kal, pertaining to the perimeter.
perimorph, *n. pe*-re-morf, a mineral enclosing another.
perineum, *n.* pe-re-*nee*-um, the external floor of the pelvis between the anus and genitalia [Anat.].
period, *n. peer*-re-od, a circuit; the time a planet takes to make a complete revolution round the sun; a revolution or series of years by which time is measured; a space of time in which a revolution is completed, and the same course to be begun; any specified portion of time; end or conclusion; any indefinite portion of existence; limit; length of duration; a complete sentence; a full-stop: *pl.* the menses: *a.* belonging to or characteristic of some past period, as *period furniture, period play*, etc. (Gr. *peri-*, and *hodos*, a way.)
periodate, *n.* per-*eye*-o-date, a salt of periodic acid.
periodic, *a.* peer-re-*od*-ik, pertaining to a period; performed by revolution in a certain time; happening or appearing at regular intervals; constituting a complete sentence.
periodic, *a.* per-eye-*od*-ik, designating the highest oxygen acid of iodine, a stronger oxidizing agent than iodic acid.
periodical, *a.* peer-re-*od*-e-kal, periodic; pertaining to a periodical: *n.* a magazine or other publication that is published at stated periods.
periodically, *ad.* at regularly recurring intervals.
periodicity, *n.* peer-re-o-*dis*-e-te, state of being periodical; rhythmic activity [Biol.]; frequency [Elect.].
periœci, *n.* pe-re-*ee*-sy, those living in the same latitude but on opposite sides of the globe. (Gr. *peri-*, and *oikein*, to dwell.)
periosteal, *a.* pe-re-*os*-te-al, situated round a bone; pertaining to the periosteum.
periosteum, *n.* pe-re-*os*-te-um, a nervous vascular membrane investing the bones except at articulations [Anat.]. (Gr. *peri-*, and *osteon*, bone.)
periostitis, *n. pe*-re-os-*ty*-tis, inflammation of the periosteum.
periotic, *a. pe*-re-*oh*-tik, around the inner ear: *n.* a periotic bone or cartilage.
peripatetic, *a.* pe-re-pa-*tet*-ik, walking about; pertaining to the philosophy of Aristotle, who walked about while he taught: *n.* a follower of Aristotle; one who walks, esp. because he cannot afford to ride. (Gr. *peri-*, and *pateo*, to walk.)
peripateticism, *n.* pe-re-pa-*tet*-e-sizm, the system of Aristotle.
Peripatus, *n.* pe-*rip*-a-tus, a genus of soft-bodied worm-like arthropods, living in damp forests and ranking between the Annelida and the Arthropoda.
peripeteia, *n. pe*-re-pe-*ty*-a, an unexpected alteration in circumstances; a change of fortune. (Gr. *peri-*, and *pipto*, to fall.)

peripheral, *a.* pe-*rif*-er-ral, pertaining to or constituting a periphery.
periphery, *n.* pe-*rif*-er-re, perimeter; circumference of a curvilinear figure; outer surface. (Gr. *peri-*, and *phero*, to bear.)
periphlebitis, *n.* *pe*-re-fle-*by*-tis, inflammation of the outer coat of a vein [Path.].
periphrase, *v.t.* *pe*-re-fraze, to express in periphrasis: *v.i.* to use circumlocution. (*peri-*, *phrase*.)
periphrasis, *n.* pe-*rif*-ra-sis, circumlocution.
periphrastic, *a.* pe-re-*fras*-tik, circumlocutory.
periphrastically, *ad.* with circumlocution.
periplus, *n.* *pe*-re-plus, a circumnavigation, or an account of one. (Gr. *peri-*, and *pleo*, sail.)
peripolygonal, *a.* *pe*-re-po-*lig*-o-nal, having a great number of sides [Cryst.].
peripteral, *a.* pe-*rip*-ter-ral, having a single range of columns all round (of a building) [Arch.].
peripterous, *a.* pe-*rip*-ter-rus, feathered all round [Ornith.]; peripteral [Arch.]. (Gr. *peri-*, and *pteron*, a wing.)
perique, *n.* pe-*reek*, a strong, curly tobacco grown in Louisiana, used chiefly in mixtures.
perirhinal, *a.* *pe*-re-*ry*-nal, around the nose.
periscope, *n.* *pe*-re-skope, an optical instrument, esp. for use in trenches and submarines, fitted with lenses and reflectors for observation beyond an obstruction in the direct line of sight. (Gr. *peri-*, and *skopeo*, view.)
periscopic, *a.* pe-re-*skop*-ik, by means of the periscope; viewed on all sides; giving distinctness to objects viewed obliquely; concavo-convex [Optics].
perish, *v.i.* *pe*-rish, to lose life in any manner; to die; to decay; to come to nothing, or be destroyed; to be lost. (O.Fr. *perissant*, from L. *perire*, to go or pass away.)
perishability, *n.* pe-rish-a-*bil*-e-te, perishableness.
perishable, *a.* *pe*-rish-a-bl, liable to perish or decay.
perishableness, *n.* *pe*-rish-a-bl-ness, the state or quality of being perishable.
perishably, *ad.* *pe*-rish-a-ble, in a perishable manner.
perisperm, *n.* *pe*-re-sperm, the thick farinaceous part of the seed of plants; the albumen. (Gr. *peri-*, and *sperma*, seed.)
perispomenon, *a.* pe-re-*spom*-e-non, having a circumflex accent on the last syllable: *n.* such a word. (Gr., circumflexed.)
perissodactyl, *a.* pe-*ris*-so-*dak*-til, odd-toed; pertaining to that division of the ungulates which comprises the horse and rhinoceros.
peristalith, *n.* pe-*ris*-ta-lith, a series of stones around a prehistoric burial mound.
peristalsis, *n.* pe-re-*stal*-sis, the contractile movement by means of which the alimentary canal propels its contents. (Gr. *peri-*, and *stalsis*, contraction.)
peristaltic, *a.* pe-re-*stal*-tik, contracting in successive circles as the worm-like motion of the intestines.
peristeronic, *a.* pe-*ris*-te-*ron*-ik, pertaining to pigeons. (Gr. *peristera*, a pigeon.)
peristeropod, *a.* pe-*ris*-te-ro-pod, having toes like a pigeon: *n.* a pigeon-footed bird.
peristole, *n.* per-*ris*-to-le, peristalsis [Anat.].
peristome, *n.* *pe*-re-stohm, the region around the mouth (of invertebrates); the lip of a spiral shell; the fringe surrounding the orifice of a moss's capsule. (Gr. *peri-*, and *stoma*, mouth.)
peristrephic, *a.* pe-re-*stref*-ik, rotatory; revolving. (Gr. *peri-*, and *strephein*, to turn round.)
peristyle, *n.* *pe*-re-stile, a range of columns round a building or square; a court, etc., so enclosed. (Gr. *peri-*, and *stylos*, column.)
perisystole, *n.* pe-re-*sis*-to-le, the interval between the contraction and dilatation of the heart.
peritomous, *a.* pe-*rit*-o-mus, cleaving in more directions than one parallel to the axis [Min.]. (Gr. *peri-*, and *tome*, cutting.)
peritoneal, *a.* *pe*-re-to-*nee*-al, pertaining to the peritoneum.
peritoneum, *n.* *pe*-re-to-*nee*-um, the serous membrane investing the internal surface of the abdomen, and enveloping more or less completely the abdominal viscera. (Gr. *peri-*, and *teino*, stretch.)
peritonitis, *n.* *pe*-re-to-*ny*-tis, inflammation of the peritoneum.
peritropal, *a.* pe-*rit*-ro-pal, amphitropal [Bot.].
perityphlitis, *n.* *pe*-re-tif-*ly*-tis, inflammation in the region of the cæcum.
perivisceral, *a.* *pe*-re-*vis*-er-ral, surrounding the viscera.
periwig, *n.* *pe*-re-wig, a small wig. (Fr. *perruque*.)
periwinkle, *n.* *pe*-re-wing-kl, a creeping evergreen plant of the genus *Vinca*. (L. *per-*, and *vincio*, bind.)
periwinkle, *n.* *pe*-re-wing-kl, a small univalve mollusc of the genus *Littorina*. (A.S. *wincle*.)
perjure, *v.t.* *per*-jur, to forswear (oneself); to swear falsely. (L. *per-*, and *juro*, swear.)
perjured, *a.* *per*-jurd, forsworn; guilty of perjury.
perjurer, *n.* *per*-jur-rer, a false swearer.
perjurious, *a.* per-*joor*-re-us, pertaining to or characterized by perjury.
perjury, *n.* *per*-jur-re, the crime of false swearing, or act of wilfully giving false evidence on oath.
perk, *a.* perk, smart; trim; spruce: *v.i.* to hold up the head with affected smartness; to peer: *v.t.* to dress; to make trim or smart. (Origin unknown.)
perkin, *n.* *per*-kin, a watery kind of cider. (Perhaps from *perry*.)
perky, *a.* *per*-ke, smart; brisk; lively.
perlaceous, *a.* per-*lay*-shus, like mother-of-pearl; shaped like pearls.
perlite, *n.* *per*-lite, an igneous glass-like rock of perlitic structure; pearl-stone; pitchstone.
perlitic, *a.* per-*lit*-ik, applied to the structure of certain igneous rocks which, owing to concentric cracks due to cooling, break down into pearl-like fragments.
perlustration, *n.* per-lus-*tray*-shon, act of viewing all over. (L. *per-*, and *lustro*, survey.)
perm, *n.* perm, a permanent wave in the hair [Coll.].
permalloy, *n.* *perm*-al-loy, an alloy of soft iron with 78·5 per cent of nickel, used to reduce loss of energy in electrical machinery subject to alternating magnetic fields.
permanence, *n.* *per*-ma-nence, the quality or state of being permanent; continuance in the same state; duration.
permanency, *n.* *per*-ma-nen-se, permanence.
permanent, *a.* *per*-ma-nent, durable; lasting; continuing, or intended to continue, in the same state or without any radical change. **permanent wave,** a special method of hair-dressing the effect of which is intended to be lasting. **permanent way,** the road bed of a railway. (L. *per-*, and *maneo*, remain.)
permanently, *ad.* in a permanent manner.
permanganate, *n.* per-*mang*-ga-nate, any salt of permanganic acid, all of which are oxidizing agents, esp. **permanganate of potash,** potassium permanganate.
permanganic, *a.* per-mang-*gan*-ik, designating a strongly oxidizing acid that contains magnesium in its highest valency.
permeability, *n.* *per*-me-a-*bil*-e-te, the quality or state of being permeable.
permeable, *a.* *per*-me-a-bl, penetrable; that may be passed through as by a fluid.
permeably, *ad.* in a permeable manner.
permeate, *v.t.* *per*-me-ate, to pass through pores or interstices; to penetrate and pass through; to pervade. (L. *per-*, and *meo*, go.)
permeation, *n.* per-me-*ay*-shon, the act or process of passing through pores or interstices; diffusion.
permed, *a.* permd, provided with a permanent wave.
permiameter, *n.* per-me-*am*-e-ter, an instrument for measuring magnetic permeability [Elect.].
Permian, *a.* *per*-me-an, designating or belonging to the series of rocks overlying the Carboniferous and underlying the Trias. (Russian province of *Perm*.)
permissible, *a.* per-*mis*-e-bl, that may be permitted.
permissibly, *ad.* in a permissible manner.
permission, *n.* per-*mish*-on, the act of permitting; formal consent; leave; liberty granted.
permissive, *a.* per-*mis*-iv, allowing; conceding permission or liberty; not prohibited; optional.
permissively, *ad.* by permission.
permissory, *a.* per-*mis*-o-re, depending upon or involving permission.
permit, *v.t.* per-*mit*, to give leave or liberty to by express consent; to allow; to afford ability or means; to tolerate: *v.i.* to allow: *n.* *per*-mit, a warrant; a written permission; a formal authority to shift, export, or land dutiable goods [Comm.]. (L. *per-*, and *mitto*, *missum*, send.)

permittance, *n.* per-*mit*-ance, electrostatic capacity; the ratio of condenser charge to condenser voltage [Elect.].
permittee, *n.* per-mit-*tee*, one who is permitted; the holder of a permit.
permitter, *n.* per-*mit*-er, one who permits.
permutable, *a.* per-*mew*-ta-bl, capable of being exchanged or interchanged.
permutably, *ad.* per-*mew*-ta-ble, by exchange.
permutation, *n.* per-mew-*tay*-shon, exchange of one thing for another; change of order or different combination of any number of quantities; any different arrangement so effected [Math.]; transmutation. (L. *per-*, and *muto*, change.)
permute, *v.t.* per-*mewt*, to change completely; to exchange; to subject to permutation [Math.].
permutite, *n.* *per*-mew-tite, proprietary name of an artificial natrolite used for softening water.
pern, *n.* pern, the honey-buzzard, *Pernis apivorus.*
pernancy, *n.* *per*-nan-se, the receiving or taking of anything, esp. rents or tithes [Law.]. (O.Fr.)
pernicious, *a.* per-*nish*-us, destructive; harmful; tending to injure or destroy; fatal [Path.]. (L. *per-*, and *neco*, kill.)
perniciously, *ad.* in a pernicious manner.
perniciousness, *n.* quality of being pernicious.
pernickety, *a.* per-*nik*-e-te, fastidious; touchy; cantankerous about small matters.
pernoctation, *n.* per-nok-*tay*-shon, a remaining all night; an all-night watching or vigil. (L. *per-*, and *nox, noctis*, night.)
peroneal, *a.* pe-ro-*nee*-al, pertaining to, or near, the fibula [Anat.]. (Gr. *peronē*, the fibula.)
perorate, *v.i.* *per*-o-rate, to make a speech; to make a peroration. (L. *per-*, and *orate.*)
peroration, *n.* per-o-*ray*-shon, the concluding part of a speech or oration.
perovskite, *n.* per-*ov*-skite, titanate of calcium. (Russ., Count L. *Perovsky*, 1839).
peroxide, *n.* per-*oks*-ide, the oxide of the base named which contains the greatest quantity of oxygen: *v.t.* to bleach (esp. hair) with a solution of hydrogen peroxide. **peroxide blonde,** a woman whose hair has been bleached [Slang].
perpend, *v.t.* per-*pend*, to weigh in the mind: *v.i.* to take thought: *n.* a parpen or binding stone [Build.]. (L. *per-*, and *pendo*, weigh.)
perpender, *n.* per-*pen*-der, a coping-stone; a parpen.
perpendicular, *a.* per-pen-*dik*-yew-lar, upright; extending in a straight line towards the earth's centre, or at right angles to the plane of the horizon; vertical; at right angles to a given line or surface [Geom.]: *n.* a perpendicular line; any instrument for determining verticality.
perpendicularity, *n.* per-pen-*dik*-yew-*la*-re-te, the state of being perpendicular.
perpendicularly, *ad.* per-pen-*dik*-yew-lar-le, in a perpendicular position or manner.
perpetrable, *a.* *per*-pe-tra-bl, capable of being perpetrated.
perpetrate, *v.t.* *per*-pe-trate, to perform; to commit. (L. *per-*, and *patro*, bring to pass.)
perpetration, *n.* per-pe-*tray*-shon, the act of committing, esp. a crime; the action perpetrated; an atrocity.
perpetrator, *n.* *per*-pe-tray-tor, one who commits, esp. a crime or evil deed.
perpetuable, *a.* per-*pet*-yew-a-bl, capable of being perpetuated.
perpetual, *a.* per-*pet*-yew-al, continuing for ever; continuing without ceasing; permanent. **perpetual curate,** the vicar of the church of an ecclesiastical district that forms part of an ancient parish. **perpetual motion,** a hypothetical motion perpetually self-renewed without outside intervention. (L. *perpetuus.*)
perpetually, *ad.* per-*pet*-yew-al-le, continually.
perpetuate, *v.t.* per-*pet*-yew-ate, to make perpetual; to preserve from extinction or oblivion.
perpetuation, *n.* per-*pet*-yew-*ay*-shon, the act of perpetuating.
perpetuator, *n.* per-*pet*-yew-ay-tor, one who makes perpetual.
perpetuity, *n.* *per*-pe-*tew*-e-te, endless or indefinite duration; something perpetual; a sum, or the number of years' purchase necessary to buy an annuity.
perplex, *v.t.* per-*pleks*, to make intricate or difficult to understand; to confuse; to embarrass; to puzzle; to tease with suspense, anxiety, or ambiguity (L. *per-*, and *plexus*, entangled.)
perplexedly, *ad.* per-*plek*-sed-le, in a perplexed manner.
perplexedness, *n.* state of being perplexed.
perplexingly, *ad.* per-*plek*-sing-le, so as to perplex.
perplexity, *n.* per-*pleks*-e-te, puzzled condition; embarrassment; confusion.
perquisite, *n.* *per*-kwe-zit, anything obtained by one in employment beyond the ordinary wage (or sometimes in lieu thereof); an additional or incidental gain; a customary tip [Coll.]. (L. *per-*, and *quæsitum*, sought.)
perquisition, *n.* per-kwe-*zish*-on, close inquiry or search.
perrier, *n.* *pe*-re-er, an ancient military machine for hurling stones; a form of catapult. (O.Fr., from *pierre*, a stone.)
perron, *n.* *pe*-ron, an exterior flight of steps leading up to a terrace or entrance [Arch.]. (Fr.)
perruquier, *n.* pe-*roo*-ke-er, a maker of or dealer in perukes; a wigmaker. (Fr.)
perry, *n.* *pe*-re, the fermented juice of pears. (*pear.*)
perscrutation, *n.* per-skroo-*tay*-shon, minute inquiry.
persecute, *v.t.* *per*-se-kewt, to harass with unjust and cruel treatment, esp. on religious grounds; to harass with importunity. (L. *persecutus*, followed after.)
persecution, *n.* per-se-*kew*-shon, the act or practice of persecuting; state of being persecuted; a course or campaign of persecuting.
persecutive, *a.* *per*-se-kew-tiv, of a persecuting nature; given to persecuting.
persecutor, *n.masc.* *per*-se-kew-tor (*fem.* **persecutrix**), one who persecutes.
Perseus, *n.* *per*-sewce, a northern constellation named after the son of Zeus and Danaë, famed for having slain the Medusa and delivered Andromeda [Gr. Myth.].
perseverance, *n.* per-se-*veer*-rance, persistence in anything undertaken; continuance in the state of grace [Theol.].
perseveration, *n.* per-sev-er-*ray*-shon, continued, and meaningless repetition of an action or phrase, etc. [Med. and Psychan.].
persevere, *v.i.* per-se-*veer*, to persist in any business or enterprise undertaken; to be steady in the pursuit of any object. (Fr. *persévérer.*)
perseveringly, *ad.* per-se-*veer*-ring-le, in a persevering manner.
Persian, *a.* *per*-shan, pertaining to Persia or its language; Iranian: *n.* a native or the language of Persia; a kind of thin silk; a male figure in Persian attire supporting an entablature [Arch.]; a Persian cat. **Persian apple,** a peach. **Persian berry,** the berry of the buckthorn. **Persian blinds,** persiennes. **Persian cat,** a species of cat having long silky hair and a bushy tail. **Persian lamb,** the finest grade of astrakhan. **Persian powder,** an insecticide prepared from the flowers of certain species of *Chrysanthemum.* **Persian wheel,** an undershot water-wheel.
persicaria, *n.* per-se-*kare*-re-a, the weed peach-wort.
persicot, *n.* *per*-se-koh, a cordial flavoured with kernels of the peach family.
persiennes, *n.pl.* per-ze-*enz*, outside window-shutters made like venetian blinds.
persiflage, *n.* *per*-se-flahzh, light, quizzing mockery or banter; flippant treatment of serious subjects. (Fr., from L. *per-*, and *sibilo*, hiss.)
persifleur, *n.* *per*-se-floor, one given to persiflage.
persimmon, *n.* per-*sim*-mon, the plum-like fruit of any tree of the species *Diospyros*, esp. the N. American ebony, *D. virginiana*; the tree itself. (Algonquian.)
persist, *v.i.* per-*sist*, to continue steadily in any course; to persevere; to last. (L. *per-*, and *sto*, stand.)
persistence, *n.* per-*sis*-tence, the state of persisting; quality of being persistent; obstinacy.
persistency, *n.* per-*sis*-ten-se, persistence.
persistent, *a.* per-*sis*-tent, persisting; persevering; remaining till the fruit is ripe [Bot.]. **persistent gas,** any poison-gas in liquid form, giving off dangerous fumes over a long period.
persistently, *ad.* per-*sis*-tent-le, in a persistent manner; importunately.

persistive, *a.* per-*sis*-tiv, characterized by persistency; tending to persist.
★**person,** *n.* *per*-son, an individual human being, esp. conceived of as having a distinct personality; the body of a living human being; a human being, or a body corporate having similar rights, etc. [Law]; an individual organism [Zool.]; (*cap.*) any one of the three entities (Father, Son, and Holy Spirit) composing the Godhead [Theol.]; the subject or object of a verb, as speaking, spoken to, or spoken of [Gram.]. **in person,** by oneself, not by an agent. (L. *persona*, an actor's mask, a character, and hence, a person.)
personable, *a.* *per*-son-a-bl, of good appearance.
personage, *n.* *per*-son-aj, a person, esp. one of rank or standing; a character in a play, story, historical situation, etc.
personal, *a.* *per*-son-al, pertaining to a person, not a thing; individual; relating, affecting, peculiar to, or applicable to, a person; pertaining to the external appearance; done in person; private; denoting the person [Gram.]: *n.* movable property [Law]. **personal equation,** the correction due to differences between individuals, esp. in observations with scientific instruments; departure from strict accuracy owing to individual characteristics. **personal estate,** movable property as distinguished from real estate in land and houses [Law].
personalism, *n.* *per*-son-a-lizm, any doctrine or theory stressing the ultimate importance of personality [Phil.].
personality, *n.* per-so-*nal*-e-te, quality or condition of being a person; that which constitutes individuality; self-conscious, self-determining power; an outstanding personage; applicability to a person (of a remark, etc., esp. on his character).
personalization, *n.* *per*-son-a-ly-*zay*-shon, the act or process of personalizing; state of being personalized.
personalize, *v.t.* *per*-son-a-lize, to make personal; to personify.
personally, *ad.* *per*-son-a-le, in person; particularly; as regards oneself.
personalty, *n.* *per*-son-al-te, personal estate [Law].
personate, *a.* *per*-son-ate, bilabiate, with a palate in the throat of the corolla (as the snapdragon) [Bot.]: *v.t.* to represent by an assumed character; to assume the character and act the part of; to impersonate, esp. for a fraudulent purpose.
personation, *n.* per-so-*nay*-shon, the counterfeiting of the person and character of another.
personator, *n.* *per*-son-ay-tor, one who personates.
personification, *n.* per-*son*-e-fe-*kay*-shon, a figure of speech in which inanimate objects or abstractions are conceived of and represented as endowed with personal qualities and faculties; impersonation.
personify, *v.t.* per-*son*-e-fy, to treat or represent as endowed with personal qualities; to typify or embody in one's own person. (L. *persona*, and *facio*, make.)
personnel, *n.* per-so-*nel*, the whole staff of employees of an organization; the collective human resources of a force (as opposed to matériel) [Mil.]. (Fr.)
perspective, *a.* pre-*spek*-tiv, relating to the art of perspective; in perspective: *n.* the art of representing objects on a plane surface with the same effect on the eye as the presentation of the objects themselves; a representation of objects in perspective; view; vista. **angular** or **oblique perspective,** one in which neither side of the principal object is parallel to the plane of delineation. **in perspective,** according to the laws of perspective. (Fr. *perspectif.*)
perspectively, *ad.* in perspective.
perspectograph, *n.* per-*spek*-to-graf, an instrument to assist the correct drawing in perspective. (L. *perspectiva*, and Gr. *grapho*, write.)
perspicacious, *a.* per-spe-*kay*-shus, of acute discernment; mentally keen; quick-sighted.
perspicaciously, *ad.* in a perspicacious way.
perspicaciousness, *n.* perspicacity.
perspicacity, *n.* per-spe-*kas*-e-te, the quality of being perspicacious.
perspicuity, *n.* per-spe-*kew*-e-te, the quality of being perspicuous; clearness; freedom from obscurity or ambiguity.
perspicuous, *a.* per-*spik*-yew-us, clear; not obscure or ambiguous.
perspicuously, *ad.* in a perspicuous manner.
perspicuousness, *n.* perspicuity.
perspirable, *a.* per-*spire*-ra-bl, that may be perspired; capable of perspiring; apt to perspire.
perspiration, *n.* per-spe-*ray*-shon, act of perspiring; matter perspired; sweat.
perspirative, *a.* per-*spire*-ra-tiv, causing perspiration.
perspiratory, *a.* per-*spire*-ra-to-re, performing or concerned in the act of perspiration.
perspire, *v.i.* per-*spire*, to excrete through the pores of the skin; to sweat. (L. *per-*, and *spiro*, breathe.)
perstringe, *v.t.* per-*strinj*, to criticize; to censure. (L. *per-*, and *stringo*, touch upon.)
persuadable, *a.* per-*sway*-da-bl, persuasible.
persuade, *v.t.* per-*swade*, to influence or try to influence by argument, entreaty, or expostulation; to convince by argument; to induce. (Fr. *persuader.*)
persuader, *n.* per-*sway*-der, one who or that which incites or persuades.
persuasibility, *n.* per-*sway*-ze-*bil*-e-te, the state or quality of being persuasible; degree of readiness to be persuaded.
persuasible, *a.* per-*sway*-ze-bl, that may be persuaded.
persuasibleness, *n.* per-*sway*-ze-bl-ness, persuasibility.
persuasion, *n.* per-*sway*-zhon, act of persuading; state of being persuaded; conviction; a religious sect; a sort or kind [Coll.].
persuasive, *a.* per-*sway*-ziv, tending to persuade; having the power of persuading: *n.* that which persuades; an incitement.
persuasively, *ad.*, in a persuasive manner.
persuasiveness, *n.*, quality of being persuasive.
persuasory, *a.* per-*sway*-zo-re, persuasive.
pert, *a.* pert, smart; forward; saucy; impertinent; lively. (O.Fr. *apert*, from L. *apertus*, opened.)
pertain, *v.t.* per-*tane*, to belong to as an attribute; to have reference to. **pertaining to,** having to do with; associated with. (L. *per-*, and *teneo*, hold.)
pertinacious, *a.* per-te-*nay*-shus, obstinate; perversely persistent; resolute.
pertinaciously, *ad.*, in a pertinacious manner.
pertinaciousness, *n.*, pertinacity.
pertinacity, *n.* per-te-*nas*-e-te, the state or quality of being pertinacious.
pertinence, *n.* *per*-te-nence, the quality of being pertinent; fitness; appositeness; suitableness.
pertinency, *n.* *per*-te-nen-se, pertinence.
pertinent, *a.* *per*-te-nent, appropriate to the subject; apposite; relevant; suitable. (L. *pertinens.*)
pertinently, *ad.*, in a pertinent manner.
pertinentness, *n.* *per*-te-nent-ness, pertinence.
pertly, *ad.* *pert*-le, in a pert manner.
pertness, *n.* *pert*-ness, impudent, impertinence.
perturb, *v.t.* per-*turb*, to disturb; to agitate; to bring to a state of disorder. (L. *perturbo.*)
perturbate, *v.t.* *per*-tur-bate, to perturb.
perturbation, *n.* per-tur-*bay*-shon, agitation of mind; disturbance; an irregularity or deviation in the motion of a heavenly body [Astron.].
perturbator, *n.* *per*-tur-bay-tor, a perturber.
perturber, *n.* per-*tur*-ber, one who disturbs or raises commotion.
pertused, *a.* per-*tewzd*, punched out; pierced with holes [Bot.]. (L. *pertusus*, beaten through.)
pertussal, *a.* per-*tus*-sal, pertaining to whooping-cough.
pertussis, *n.* per-*tus*-sis, whooping-cough [Med.]. (L. *per-*, and *tussis*, a cough.)
peruke, *n.* per-*rewk*, an artificial cap of hair; a wig or periwig. (Fr. *perruque*, from L. *pilus*, hair.)
perusal, *n.* per-*rew*-zal, the act of perusing; careful reading.
peruse, *v.t.* per-*rewz*, to read with attention; to inspect or observe carefully. (L. *per*, and *use.*)
peruser, *n.* per-*rew*-zer, one who peruses.
Peruvian, *a.* per-*roo*-ve-an, pertaining to Peru. **Peruvian balsam,** the fragrant, pungent, bitter balsam of *Myroxylon pereiræ*. **Peruvian bark,** the bark of several species of *Cinchona*.
peruvin, *n.* *per*-roo-vin, an alcohol distilled from Peruvian balsam.
pervade, *v.t.* per-*vade*, to pass through; to permeate; to spread or be diffused in. (L. *pervado.*)
pervasion, *n.* per-*vay*-zhon, act of pervading or passing through the whole extent of a thing.
pervasive, *a.* per-*vay*-ziv, able or tending to pervade.

pervenche, *n.* (App.) a shade of light blue. (Fr., periwinkle.)
perverse, *a.* per-*verse*, obstinate in the wrong; stubborn; untractable; cross; disposed to thwart and vex. (L. *perversus*, turned aside.)
perversely, *ad.* per-*verse*-le, in a perverse manner.
perverseness, *n.* state or quality of being perverse.
perversion, *n.* per-*ver*-shon, act of perverting; a turning from truth or propriety; a diverting from the true object; misapplication; pathological aberrancy in sex-relationship [Psychan.]
perversity, *n.* per-*ver*-se-te, perverseness; waywardness; a tendency to thwart or annoy.
perversive, *a.* per-*ver*-siv, tending to pervert.
pervert, *v.t.* per-*vert*, to turn from truth, propriety, or its proper purpose; to turn from the right: *n.* *per*-vert, one who has been perverted, esp. from truth to error; one who has abandoned one creed for another; one having abnormal sexual instincts. (Fr. *pervertir*, from L. *pervertere*, to turn aside.)
perverter, *n.* per-*ver*-ter, one who perverts; a corrupter.
pervertible, *a.* per-*ver*-te-bl, that may be perverted.
pervicacious, *a.* per-ve-*kay*-shus, very obstinate; wilfully contrary. (L. *pervicax*.)
pervicacity, *n.* per-ve-*kas*-e-te, wilful obstinacy.
pervious, *a.* *per*-ve-us, admitting passage; permeable. (L. *per-*, and *via*, a way.)
perviousness, *n.*, the state of being pervious.
pesade, *n.* pe-*sade*, the motion of a horse when he raises his fore-quarters without advancing. (Fr. from *peser*, to weigh.)
peseta, *n.* pe-*say*-ta, a Spanish coin of the approximate value of 8*d.*
Peshito, *n.* pe-*shee*-to, the Syriac translation of the Old Testament and the greater part of the New.
Peshwa, *n.* *pesh*-wah, the former title of the chief minister and (1749–1818) hereditary ruler of the Mahrattas of western India. (Per., chief.)
pesky, *a.* *pes*-ke, troublesome [U.S.A.; Coll.].
peso, *n.* *pay*-so, a former Spanish silver coin; any of several coins in use in Latin America; a Mexican dollar. (Sp.)
pessary, *n.* *pes*-sa-re, a surgical instrument or appliance for preventing a *lapsus uteri*; a vaginal suppository. (L.)
pessimism, *n.* *pes*-e-mizm, the doctrine that evil predominates over good, and that the "ups" of this life can never compensate for the "downs" [Phil.]; the habit of looking, or the disposition to look, on the gloomy side (opposed to optimism). (L. *peshimus*, worst.)
pessimist, *n.* *pes*-e-mist, one who holds the doctrine of pessimism; one habitually expecting the worst; a Job's comforter.
pessimistic, *a.* pes-e-*mis*-tik, pertaining to or characterized by pessimism; hopeless.
pest, *n.* pest, anything noxious or destructive; a pesterer; a pestilence. (L. *pestis.*)
Pestalozzian, *a.* pes-ta-*lot*-se-an, pertaining to the system of Pestalozzi, the Swiss educational reformer (*d.* 1827): *n.* one advocating or working by his system.
pester, *v.t.* *pes*-ter, to trouble; to annoy; to harass (O.Fr. *empaistrer.*)
pesterer, *n.* *pes*-ter-rer, one who pesters.
pest-house, *n.*, a hospital for contagious disease.
pesticide, *n.* *pes*-te-side, any agent for destroying or controlling horticultural or other pests. (*pest*, and L. *cædo*, to kill.)
pestiferous, *a.* pes-*tif*-er-rus, pestilential; noxious to health, peace, or morals; mischievous; conveying contagion. (L. *pestis*, and *fero*, bring.)
pestiferously, *ad.*, in a pestiferous manner.
pestilence, *n.* *pes*-te-lence, any contagious disease that is epidemic and mortal; anything pestilent, physically or morally.
pestilent, *a.* *pes*-te-lent, noxious to health, or to life, morals, society, peace, etc.; mischievous.
pestilential, *a.* pes-te-*len*-shal, of the nature of a plague or infectious disease, or producing such; mischievous; morally contagious.
pestilently, *ad.* in a pestilent manner.
pestle, *n.* *pes*-tl, a tool to pound with in a mortar: *v.t.* to pound with a pestle. (O.Fr. *pestel.*)
pestology, *n.* pes-*tol*-o-je, the study of insect pests.
pet, *n.* pet, a fit of peevishness or fretful discontent; a temper. (Origin uncertain.)
pet, *n.* pet, a fondling; a darling: *v.t.* to treat as a pet; to fondle. (Origin uncertain.)
petal, *n.* *pet*-al, a flower-leaf forming part of a corolla [Bot.]. (Gr. *petalon*, a leaf.)
petaline, *a.* *pet*-al-in, pertaining to a petal; attached to a petal; having petals.
petalism, *n.* *pet*-al-izm, a method of ostracism in ancient Syracuse, the name being written on an olive leaf.
petalite, *n.* *pet*-al-ite, a translucent foliated silicate of aluminium and lithium.
petalody, *n.* *pet*-a-loh-de, the metamorphosis of stamens into petals [Bot.].
petaloid, *a.* *pet*-a-loyd, in the form or with the texture of a petal. (Gr. *petal*, and *eidos*, like.)
petalous, *a.* *pet*-a-lus, having petals.
petard, *n.* pe-*tard*, an explosive device, formerly used for breaking in gates or making breaches. (Fr.)
petasus, *n.* *pet*-a-sus, the winged cap of Mercury; a low-crowned broad-brimmed hat. (L.)
petaurist, *n.* pe-*taw*-rist, any of the flying phalangers [Zool.]. (Gr. *petauristes*, an acrobat.)
petechiæ, *n.pl.* pe-*tee*-ke-e, purple spots due to blood effusion, as in malignant fevers [Med.]. (L.)
petechial, *a.* pe-*tee*-ke-al, pertaining to or characterized by petechiæ.
peter, *n.* *pee*-ter, the blue peter (*see* **blue**); a signal for trumps [Whist, etc.]: *v.i.* to signal to one's partner to play trumps. **peter boat,** a small decked fishing-boat; a dredger with a stern like that of a whaleboat. **Peter's pence,** voluntary contributions (earlier a tax) paid to the Pope. **to rob Peter to pay Paul,** to borrow in order to pay a debt. (From the personal name.)
peter, *v.i.* *pee*-ter, to come to an end. **to peter out,** to give out gradually (esp. of mineral veins) [Slang]. (Origin unknown.)
peterpence, *n.pl.* *pee*-ter-pence, *see* **Peter's pence.**
petersham, *n.* *pee*-ter-sham, a heavy cloth used for overcoats, so called after Visct. Petersham, 4th Earl of Harrington (*d.* 1851).
petiolar, *a.* *pet*-e-o-lar, pertaining to a petiole.
petiolate, *a.* *pet*-e-o-late, having a petiole [Bot.].
petiole, *n.* *pet*-e-ohl, a leaf-stalk. (L. *pes*, *pedis*, the foot.)
petiolule, *n.* *pet*-e-*oh*-lewl, a small petiole.
petit, *a.* *pet*-te, petty. **petit jury, larceny,** etc., *see* **petty. petits fours,** small sponge cakes or fancy biscuits, usually iced. **petit-maître,** a coxcomb, a lady-killer. **petit mal,** a mild form of epilepsy. (Fr.)
petite, *a.* pe-*teet*, small and (usually) trim of figure (of women). (Fr.)
petition, *n.* pe-*tish*-on, a request or prayer; a formal supplication from an inferior to a superior; the paper containing a supplication or solicitation: *v.t.* to make a request to; to solicit. (L. *peto*, ask.)
petitionary, *a.* pe-*tish*-on-a-re, supplicatory; containing a petition.
petitioner, *n.* pe-*tish*-on-er, one who petitions.
petitory, *a.* *pet*-e-to-re, petitioning; pertaining to an action in respect of title to property [Law].
petrean, *a.* pe-*tree*-an, rock-like; pertaining to stone. (L. *petra*, a rock.)
petrel, *n.* *pet*-rel, any of several species of long-winged dark-plumaged sea-birds. **stormy petrel,** Mother Carey's chicken, *Hydrobates pelagicsus* of the N. Atlantic, one of the smallest web-footed birds. (Dim. of name *Peter.*)
petrescence, *n.* pet-*res*-ence, the process of petrifaction.
petrifaction, *n.* pet-re-*fak*-shon, the act or process of petrifying; the state of being petrified; anything petrified; an organized body rendered hard by deposition of stony matter in its cavities; a body incrusted with stony matter; an incrustation.
petrifactive, *a.* pet-re-*fak*-tiv, having power to petrify.
petrification, *n.* pet-re-fe-*kay*-shon, petrifaction; that which is petrified; callousness [Fig.].
petrify, *v.t.* *pet*-re-fy, to convert into stone or a stony substance; to make callous or obdurate; to fix in amazement [Fig.]: *v.t.* to become stone or stony. (Fr. *petrifier.*)
Petrine, *a.* *pet*-rine, pertaining to or derived from the Apostle Peter.
pétrissage, *n.* *pay*-tre-sahzh, the kneading movement in massage. (Fr., kneading.)

petroglyphy, *n.* pe-*trog*-le-fe, the art or operation of writing on or carving in stone.

petrography, *n.* pe-*trog*-ra-fe, the description and classification of rocks; descriptive petrology. (Gr. *petros*, stone, *grapho*, to write.)

petrol, *n.* *pet*-rol, a hydrocarbon obtained by fractional distillation of petroleum, or from synthesized hydrocarbon oils, and forming an explosive gas when air is mixed with its vapour; motor-spirit; gasoline [U.S.A.]. **petrol engine,** an internal combustion engine the gas in which is derived from petrol. **petrol pump,** a small pump automatically transferring petrol from the tank to the carburettor of a motor-car in motion; a pump for delivering petrol to motor-vehicles at garages, etc.

petrolatum, *n.* pet-ro-*lay*-tum, petroleum jelly, or pure vaseline, a tasteless and odourless derivative of distilled petroleum.

petroleum, *n.* pe-*troh*-le-um, crude mineral hydrocarbon oil, existing in natural oil-wells and exuding from rocks; paraffin oil. (L. *petra*, a rock, *oleum*, oil.)

pétroleur, *n.masc.* pet-ro-*ler* (*fem.* **pétroleuse**) (App.), an incendiary who uses petroleum.

petrolic, *a.* pe-*trol*-ik, pertaining to petrol or petroleum.

petrolific, *a.* pet-ro-*lif*-ik, yielding petroleum.

petrolize, *v.t.* *pet*-ro-lize, to impregnate or otherwise treat with petroleum.

petrological, *a.* pet-ro-*loj*-e-kal, pertaining to petrology.

petrologist, *n.* pe-*trol*-o-jist, a student of petrology.

petrology, *n.* pe-*trol*-o-je, the science or study of rocks, their formation, deposition, disintegration, chemical and mineral structure, etc. (Gr. *petros*, stone, *logos*, account.)

petronel, *n.* *pet*-ron-el, an obsolete variety of horse pistol or carbine. (Fr.)

petrosal, *a.* pe-*troh*-sal, hard; stony; pertaining to the petrous bone [Anat.].

petrosilex, *n.* pet-ro-*sy*-leks, felsite. (L. *silex*, flint.)

petrosiliceous, *a.* pet-ro-se-*lish*-us, consisting of or containing petrosilex.

petrous, *a.* *pet*-rus, like stone; hard. **petrous bone,** the lower pyramidal portion of the temporal bone.

pettichaps, *n.* *pet*-te-chaps, the chiff-chaff, garden warbler, or other small singing bird.

petticoat, *n.* *pet*-te-koat, an underskirt; a woman or girl [Fig.]. **petticoat government,** female government. **petticoat insulator,** an insulator shielded by inverted cups placed one above another. (*petty* and *coat*.)

pettifog, *v.i.* *pet*-te-fog, to do small, mean, or questionable business as a lawyer; to act trickily. (*petty* and *fog*.)

pettifogger, *n.* *pet*-te-fog-er, a second-rate lawyer; a shifty solicitor; one whose conduct is quibbling and contemptible.

pettifoggery, *n.* pet-te-*fog*-er-re, the practices of a pettifogger; disreputable trickery; quibbling.

pettifogging, *n.* *pet*-te-fog-ing, mean paltry behaviour; pettifoggery; legal trickery: *a.* acting as, or characteristic of, a pettifogger; shifty.

pettily, *ad.* *pet*-te-le, in a petty manner.

pettiness, *n.* *pet*-te-ness, the state of being petty.

pettish, *a.* *pet*-ish, fretful; peevish; subject to fits of ill temper.

pettishly, *ad.* *pet*-ish-le, in a pet.

pettishness, *n.* the state of being pettish.

pettitoes, *n.pl.* *pet*-e-tohz, the toes or feet of a pig.

petto, *n.* *pet*-toh, the breast. **in petto,** in secrecy, in reserve. (It. from L. *pectus*, the breast.)

petty, *a.* *pet*-te, small in amount, degree, or importance. **petty cash,** minor cash transactions; money in hand to cover such. **petty jury,** a jury for the trial of causes in a court, in distinction from a grand or a special jury. **petty larceny,** the stealing of an article of trifling value. **petty officer,** an officer in the navy of similar rank to a non-commissioned officer in the army. **petty sessions,** *see* **sessions. petty treason,** the crime of murdering one to whom the murderer owes fealty. **petty whin,** rest-harrow, also the needle-furze. (Fr. *petit*, small.)

petulance, *n.* *pet*-yew-lance, freakish passion; peevishness; sauciness.

petulancy, *n.* *pet*-yew-lan-se, petulance.

petulant, *a.* *pet*-yew-lant, peevish; irritable; manifesting or proceeding from petulance; freakish. (L. *peto*, seek, also assail in jest.)

petulantly, *ad.* *pet*-yew-lant-le, with petulance.

petunia, *n.* pe-*tew*-ne-a, an ornamental herbaceous plant of the genus *Petunia*, allied to the potato and tobacco plant. (Braz. native *petun*, tobacco.)

petuntse, *n.* pe-*tun*-tse, a kind of fine clay used in the manufacture of porcelain. (Chin.)

petzite, *n.* *pet*-zite, a grey to blackish telluride of gold and silver.

pew, *n.* pew, an enclosed seat in a church. (O.Fr. *pui*, a raised seat.)

pewit, *n.* *pee*-wit, the peewit.

pewter, *n.* *pew*-ter, an alloy, mainly of tin and lead; utensils made of pewter; a tankard: *a.* made of pewter. (O.Fr. *peautre*.)

pewterer, *n.* *pew*-ter-rer, one who makes utensils of pewter or who works in pewter.

pewtery, *a.* *pew*-ter-re, characteristic of pewter: *n.* pewter utensils collectively.

Pfennig, *n.* *pfen*-nig, a minor German copper coin, one-hundredth of a mark, and approximately five to the penny. (Ger.)

phacitis, *n.* fa-*sy*-tis, inflammation of the crystalline lens. (Gr. *phakos*, the eye-lens.)

phacoidal, *a.* fa-*koy*-dal, of lens-like form; lenticular.

phacometer, *n.* fa-*kom*-e-ter, an instrument for determining the refractive power of lenses.

phænogam, *n.* *fee*-no-gam, a phanerogam.

phænology, *n.* fee-*nol*-o-je, phenology.

phæton, *n.* *fay*-e-ton, an open, four-wheeled carriage. (Gr. *Phæthon*, shining, the name of the son of Phœbus and Clymene, who, being permitted to guide the chariot of the sun, would have set the world on fire had not Jupiter transfixed him with a thunderbolt.)

phagedena, *n.* faj-e-*dee*-na, a rapidly spreading ulcer; gangrenous ulceration [Path.]. (Gr.)

phagedenic, *a.* faj-e-*den*-ik, of the nature of, or affected with, phagedena.

phagocyte, *n.* *fag*-o-site, any leucocyte that ingests and destroys bacteria. (Gr. *phagein*, eat, *kytos*, cell.)

phagocytic, *a.* fag-o-*sit*-ik, pertaining to phagocytes.

phagocytosis, *n.* fag-o-sy-*toh*-sis, the ingestion or destruction of tissue cells or micro-organisms by phagocytes.

phagomania, *n.* fag-o-*may*-ne-a, an insatiable craving for food [Med.].

phakitis, *n.* fa-*ky*-tis, phacitis.

phalange, *n.* *fal*-anj (*pl.* **phalanges,** fa-*lan*-jeez), a small bone of a digit [Anat.]; a joint of the tarsus in insects [Entom.]; a bundle of stamens united by their filaments [Bot.]. (Fr., from Gr. *phalanx*.).

phalangeal, *a.* fa-*lan*-je-al, pertaining to the phalanges.

phalanger, *n.* fa-*lan*-jer, any member of the Phalangistinæ, a sub-family of small Australian marsupials, mainly nocturnal and arboreal. (Fr., from Gr. *phalanx*.)

phalangian, *a.* fa-*lan*-je-an, phalangeal.

phalansterianism, *n.* fal-an-*steer*-re-a-nizm, the system of living in phalansteries; Fourierism.

phalanstery, *n.* *fal*-an-ste-re, a small community living as a social unit, esp. on the system advocated by Fourier. (Fr., from Gr. *phalanx*, and Fr. *monastère*, monastery.)

phalanx, *n.* *fal*-anks (*pl.* **phalanxes,** *fal*-ank-siz, and **phalanges,** fa-*lan*-jeez) the close order of the ancient Macedonian infantry; any body of troops in close formation; a compact body; a phalange [Anat., etc.]. (Gr., battle array.)

phalarope, *n.* *fal*-a-rope, a plover-like swimming and wading shore-bird. (Gr. *phalaris*, a coot, *pous*, foot.)

phallic, *a.* *fal*-lik, pertaining to the phallus, or to phallicism. (Gr. *phallikos*.)

phallicism, *n.* *fal*-e-sizm, the worship of the generative principle or its symbol, the phallus.

phallus, *n.* *fal*-lus, the penis; a representation of the male organ of generation as a symbol of the procreative power of nature; a group of fungi including the stinkhorn. (L.)

phanerogam, *n.* *fan*-er-ro-gam, a plant that flowers. (Gr. *phaneros*, visible, *gamos*, marriage.)

phanerogamous, *a.* fan-er-*rog*-a-mus, having visible flowers [Bot.].

phantascope, *n.* *fan*-ta-skope, an optical instrument for the study of binocular vision; also, a phenakistoscope. (Gr. *phantasma*, image, *skopeo*, view.)

phantasm, *n.* *fan*-tazm, an image created by the

fancy which seems real; a fancied vision; a fancy; a notion. (O.Fr. *fantosme.*)
phantasmagoria, *n.* fan-*taz*-ma-*gaw*-re-a, shadow show of optical illusions by magic lantern; an array or procession of shadowy illusory figures. (Gr. *phantasma*, image, *agora*, an assembly.)
phantasmagorial, *a.* fan-*taz*-ma-*gaw*-re-al, pertaining to a phantasmagoria.
phantasmagoric, *a.* *fan*-taz-ma-*go*-rik, of the nature of phantasmagoria; phantasmagorial; chimerical.
phantasmal, *a.* fan-*taz*-mal, like a phantasm.
phantom, *n.* *fan*-tom, an apparition; a ghost; a fancied vision; an artificial bait resembling a minnow [Angling]. (O.Fr. *fantosme.*)
Pharaoh, *n.* *fare*-ro, the title borne by the kings of ancient Egypt. **Pharaoh's chicken,** the Egyptian vulture, *Neophron percnopterus.* **Pharaoh's rat,** the Egyptian ichneumon. **Pharaoh's serpent,** a pellet of sulpho-cyanide of mercury which, when burned, assumes a long serpentine form. (Egyptian, *Per-aa*, literally, great house.)
phare, *n.* fare, a pharos.
pharisaic, *a.* fa-re-*say*-ik, resembling the Pharisees; making a show of religion; formal; hypocritical.
pharisaical, *a.* fa-re-*say*-e-kal, pharisaic.
pharisaically, *ad.* in a pharisaical manner.
pharisaicalness, *n.*, quality of being pharisaical.
pharisaism, *n.* *fa*-re-say-izm, the doctrines and conduct of the Pharisees; hypocrisy in religion.
Pharisee, *n.* *fa*-re-see, one of a Jewish sect whose religion consisted in a strict observance of rites and ceremonies; a mere formalist. (L. *pharisæus.*)
pharmaceutical, *a.* far-ma-*sew*-te-kal, pertaining to pharmacy; engaged in preparing and dispensing medicines.
pharmaceutics, *n.* far-ma-*sew*-tiks, the science of preparing medicines. (Gr. *pharmakeutikos.*)
pharmaceutist, *n.* far-ma-*sew*-tist, one who prepares medicines; a pharmacist.
pharmacist, *n.* *far*-ma-sist, a druggist; one skilled in pharmacy.
pharmacodynamics, *n.* *far*-ma-koh-dy-*nam*-iks, the science of the action of drugs.
pharmacolite, *n.* far-*mak*-o-lite, native arsenate of calcium. (Gr. *pharmakon*, drug, *lithos*, stone.)
pharmacology, *n.* far-ma-*kol*-o-je, the science or study of the nature and action of drugs. (Gr. *pharmakon*, and *logos*, science.)
pharmacopœia, *n.* *far*-ma-koh-*pee*-a, a book containing authoritative directions for the preparation of medicines, with descriptive lists of the articles of the Materia Medica. (Gr. *pharmakopoiia.*)
pharmacosiderite, *n.* *far*-ma-koh-*sid*-er-ite, arsenate of iron.
pharmacy, *n.* *far*-ma-se, the art of preparing and dispensing medicines; a drug-store. (Gr. *pharmakeia.*)
pharology, *n.* fa-*rol*-o-je, the science of signalling by light from the shore. (Gr. *pharos* and *logos.*)
pharos, *n.* *fare*-ros, a lighthouse; a beacon. (Gr.; so from that on the island of Pharos, Alexandria.)
pharyngeal, *a.* fa-*rin*-je-al, pertaining to or situated near the pharynx.
pharyngitis, *n.* fa-rin-*jy*-tis, inflammation of the membrane of the pharynx.
pharyngology, *n.* fa-ring-*gol*-o-je, the branch of medicine treating of the pharynx.
pharyngoscope, *n.* fa-*ring*-go-skope, an instrument for examining the pharynx.
pharyngotomy, *n.* far-ring-*got*-o-me, the making of an incision into the pharynx [Surg.].
pharynx, *n.* *fa*-rinks (*pl.* **pharynges,** fa-*rin*-jeez), the opening from the mouth into the œsophagus, serving for the transmission of food to the stomach and of air to the respiratory organs. (Gr.)
phase, *n.* faze, appearance to the eye, esp. [Astron.] of the illuminated surface of the moon or a planet; aspect; particular stage of a phenomenon which suffers periodic changes; the stage in the period of an alternating current to which oscillation has advanced, also that part of the cycle through which the current is actually passing [Elect.]. (Late L.)
phasis, *n.* *fay*-sis (*pl.* **phases,** *fay*-ziz), a phase, esp. in the astronomical sense.
pheasant, *n.* *fez*-ant, a game-bird of the genus *Phasianus*, noted for its plumage and the delicacy of its flesh. **pheasant's eye,** the plant *Adonis autumnalis*, also the white narcissus. (O.Fr. *faisan*, from Gr. *Phasis*, a river in Colchis.)
pheasantry, *n.* *fez*-an-tre, a place for rearing pheasants.
phellogen, *n.* *fel*-o-jen, the cambium from which cork tissue is evolved [Bot.].
phelloplastic, *n.* *fel*-lo-*plas*-tik, the art of cutting models in cork; a figure so modelled. (Gr. *phellos*, cork, *plastos*, shaped.)
phenacetin, *n.* fe-*nas*-se-tin, a colourless crystalline anti-pyretic and anti-neuralgic drug prepared from phenol.
phenacite, *fee*-na-site, silicate of glucina. (Gr. *phenax*, a deceiver.)
phenakistoscope, fe-na-*kist*-o-skope, an obsolete zoetrope-like toy giving crude representations of objects in motion. (Gr. *phenakistakos*, false.)
phenate, *n.* *fee*-nate, a salt of phenol.
phengite, *n.* *fen*-jite, muscovite [Min.].
phenic, *a.* *fee*-nik, obtained from coal-tar; carbolic.
phenocryst, *n.* *fee*-no-krist, one of the larger crystals embedded in porphyritic rocks.
phenogam, *n.* *fen*-o-gam, phanerogam.
phenol, *n.* *fee*-nol, carbolic acid. **the phenols,** the group of organic compounds of the aromatic or benzene series [Chem.]. (Fr.)
phenolate, *n.* *fee*-no-late, a salt of phenol or of any of the phenols.
phenology, *n.* fe-*nol*-o-je, the study of the influence of climate on the life, habits, etc., of animals and plants. (*phenomenology.*)
phenomenal, *a.* fe-*nom*-e-nal, pertaining to phenomena; of the nature of a phenomenon; extraordinary.
phenomenalism, *n.* fe-*nom*-e-na-lizm, the philosophical doctrine that phenomena may be known and understood, but not their causes; the theory that phenomena only have true existence.
phenomenalist, *n.* fe-*nom*-e-na-list, an adherent of a doctrine of phenomenalism.
phenomenally, *ad.* fe-*nom*-e-na-le, in the manner of a phenomenon.
phenomenist, *n.* fe-*nom*-en-ist, a phenomenalist.
phenomenology, *n.* fe-*nom*-e-*nol*-o-je, the scientific investigation and classification of phenomena. (Gr. *phainomena* and *logos.*)
phenomenon, *n.* fe-*nom*-e-non (*pl.* **phenomena**), an appearance, or anything which appears; anything perceived by observation or experiment; that which is mentally perceived of a thing as distinct from the reality of the thing itself [Phil.]; a remarkable or unusual appearance [Coll.]. (Gr. *phainomenon.*)
phenotype, *n.* *fee*-no-tipe, an individual or group of individuals classified according to visible, as distinct from genetic, characters [Biol.]. (Gr. *phainein*, to show, and *type.*)
phenyl, *n.* *fee*-nil, an organic radical, present in carbolic acid and benzole, of which benzene is the hydride. (Fr.)
phenylic, *a.* fe-*nil*-ik, pertaining to or derived from phenyl.
pheon, *n.* *fee*-on, a charge representing the barbed head of a dart [Her.]; the broad-arrow.
phew, *int.* few, an exclamation of impatience, dislike, surprise, etc.
phial, *n.* *fy*-al, a small glass vessel or bottle; a vial: *v.t.* to put or keep in a phial. (Gr. *phialē.*)
philander, *v.i.* fe-*lan*-der, to make love or flirt. (Gr. *philos*, loving, *andros*, man.)
philanderer, *n.* fe-*lan*-der-rer, a male flirt; a trifler.
philanthrope, *n.* *fil*-an-thrope, a lover of mankind at large; a philanthropist.
philanthropic, *a.* fil-an-*throp*-ik, characterized by philanthropy; possessing general benevolence.
philanthropism, *n.* fil-*an*-thro-pizm, the practice or theory of philanthropy.
philanthropist, *n.* fe-*lan*-thro-pist, one who exercises philanthropy; a generous giver or benefactor.
philanthropy, *n.* fe-*lan*-thro-pe, the love of mankind; universal goodwill. (L. *philanthropia.*)
philatelic, *a.* fil-a-*tel*-ik, pertaining to philately.
philatelist, *n.* fe-*lat*-e-list, a postage-stamp collector.
philately, *n.* fe-*lat*-e-le, the study and collection of postage stamps. (Fr. *philatélie.*)
philharmonic, *a.* fil-har-*mon*-ik, devoted to music. (Gr. *philos*, and *harmonia*, harmony.)
Philhellenist, *n.* fil-*hel*-en-ist, a friend of the Greeks. (Gr. *philos*, and *Hellen*, a Greek.)
philibeg, *n.* *fil*-e-beg, a filibeg. (Scots.)
philippic, *n.* fe-*lip*-ik, one of three orations of

Demosthenes against Philip of Macedon; hence, any acrimonious discourse or declamation.
philippina, *n.* fil-e-*pee*-na, the half of a nut with a double kernel given to a companion who is expected to reciprocate with a small present.
Philippine, *a. fil*-e-peen, pertaining to or of the Philippine Islands. (From *Philip* II of Spain.)
Philippino, *n.* fil-e-*pee*-no, a Filipino.
philippize, *v.i. fil*-e-pize, to write or utter invective in the manner of a philippic.
Philistine, *n. fil*-is-tine, an inhabitant of Philistia, now part of Syria; a non-university man of the middle class in a university town, esp. in Germany (Ger. *philister*); one without liberal culture; a narrow-minded person: *a.* characteristic of Philistines; prosaic; uncultured.
philistinism, *n. fil*-is-tin-izm, the characteristics or mode of thinking of the modern Philistine.
phillipsite, *n. fil*-ip-site, a hydrated silicate of potassium, calcium, and aluminium, one of the zeolites.
philogyny, *n.* fe-*loj*-e-ne, fondness for women. (Gr. *philos*, and *gyne*, a woman.)
philologer, *n.* fe-*lol*-o-jer, a philologist.
philological, *a.* fil-o-*loj*-e-kal, pertaining to philology.
philologist, *n.* fe-*lol*-o-jist, a student of language.
philology, *n.* fe-*lol*-o-je, the science of language; the study of languages, their structure, history, relations, etc.; linguistics. (L. *philologia.*)
philomath, *n. fil*-o-math, a lover of learning. (Gr. *philos*, and *manthano*, learn.)
philomathic, *a.* fil-o-*math*-ik, pertaining to or having a love of learning.
philomathy, *n.* fe-*lom*-a-the *or fil*-o-math-e, the love of learning.
philomel, *n. fil*-o-mel, the nightingale. (*Philomela*, changed into a nightingale [Myth.].)
philopena, *n.* fil-o-*pee*-na, philippina.
philoprogenitive, *a.* fil-o-pro-*jen*-e-tiv, characterized by philoprogenitiveness; prolific. (Gr. *philos*, and L. *progenies*, offspring.)
philoprogenitiveness, *n.* fil-o-pro-*jen*-e-tiv-ness, the love of offspring.
philosophaster, *n.* fi-*los*-o-*fas*-ter, a pretender to philosophy.
philosophe, *n. fil*-lo-sof, a pretended philosopher, a philosophist. (Fr.)
philosopher, *n.* fe-*los*-o-fer, one devoted to or versed in philosophy; one of a philosophic spirit; a wise man. **philosopher's stone,** an imaginary substance sought by alchemists as the instrument of converting base metals into gold.
philosophic, *a.* fil-o-*sof*-ik, philosophical.
philosophical, *a.* fil-o-*sof*-e-kal, pertaining to philosophy; according to, regulated by, or based on philosophy; like a philosopher or wise man.
philosophically, *ad.* in a philosophical manner.
philosophism, *n.* fe-*los*-o-fizm, would-be or shallow philosophy. (Fr. *philosophisme.*)
philosophist, *n.* fe-*los*-o-fist, a would-be philosopher.
philosophistical, *a.* fe-*los*-o-*fis*-te-kal, pertaining to the love or practice of sophistry.
philosophize, *v.i.* fe-*los*-o-fize, to reason like a philosopher: *v.t.* to explain philosophically.
philosophizer, *n.*, one who philosophizes.
philosophy, *n.* fe-*los*-o-fe, the study and investigation of the phenomena of mind and matter; a particular philosophic system; a scientific explanation; reasoning; practical wisdom; level-headedness; serenity of temper. (Gr. *philosophia*, love of wisdom, from *philos*, loving, *sophia*, wisdom.)
philotechnic, *a.* fil-o-*tek*-nik, having attachment to the arts, esp. industrial arts.
philter, *n. fil*-ter, a love potion: *v.t.* to fascinate or excite with this. (Fr. *philtre.*)
phimosis, *n.* fy-*moh*-sis, constriction of the orifice of the foreskin, making it non-retractile. (Gr. *phimosis*, muzzling.)
phiz, *n.* fiz, the face or visage [Slang]. (*physiognomy.*)
phlebitis, *n.* fle-*by*-tis, inflammation of the inner membrane of a vein. (Gr. *phleps*, vein.)
phlebogram, *n. fleb*-o-gram, a sphygmographic drawing of the movements of a vein. (Gr. *phleps*, a vein, *gramma*, a drawing.)
phlebolite, *n. fleb*-o-lite, a small calculus, occasionally found in a vein. (Gr. *phleps*, and *lithos*, stone.)
phlebology, *n.* fle-*bol*-o-je, the anatomy of the veins; a treatise on the veins.
phlebotomist, *n.* fle-*bot*-o-mist, one who opens a vein to let blood.
phlebotomize, *v.t.* fle-*bot*-o-mize, to let blood from a vein: *v.i.* to practise phlebotomy.
phlebotomy, *n.* fle-*bot*-o-me, the act or practice of blood-letting; venesection. (Gr. *phleps*, a vein, *tome*, cutting.)
phlegm, *n.* flem, tenacious mucus, esp. that discharged in coughing; coolness; sluggishness; indifference. (Fr. *phlegme.*)
phlegmasia, *n.* fleg-*may*-ze-a, an inflammation. **phlegmasia dolens,** milk-leg [Med.]. (Gr.)
phlegmatic, *a.* fleg-*mat*-ik, abounding in phlegm; viscous; dull; sluggish; not easily stirred up.
phlegmatically, *ad.* fleg-*mat*-e-ka-le, in a phlegmatic or apathetic manner.
phlegmon, *n. fleg*-mon, suppurating inflammation of connective tissue [Med.]. (Fr.)
phlegmy, *a. flem*-me, pertaining to phlegm.
phleme, *n.* fleem, a fleam.
phloem, *n. floh*-em, the bast between the bark and the cambium [Bot.]. (Gr. *phloios*, bark.)
phlogistic, *a.* flo-*jis*-tik, resembling or consisting of phlogiston [Chem.]; inflammatory [Med.].
phlogisticate, *v.t.* flo-*jis*-te-kate, to combine phlogiston with [Old Chem.].
phlogiston, *n.* flo-*jis*-ton, a name formerly given to the supposed principle of inflammability. (Gr. *phlogistos*, burnt.)
phlogopite, *n. floh*-go-pite, an amber-coloured magnesia mica. (Gr. *phlogops*, flame-like.)
phlogosis, *n.* flo-*goh*-sis, inflammation [Med.]. (Gr.)
phlorizin, *n.* flo-*ry*-zin, a crystalline glucoside present in the root-bark of certain fruit-trees, as apple, pear, cherry, etc. (Gr. *phloos*, bark, *rhiza*, root.)
phlox, *n.* floks, any of a North American genus of plants, *Phlox*, of the family Polemoniaceæ. (Gr., flame.)
-phobe, fobe, a Greek suffix forming adjectives and nouns denoting fear or hatred, as *Anglophobe.*
-phobia, *foh*-be-ah, a Greek suffix (used also as a noun) forming nouns denoting fear, hate, or morbid dread, as *Anglophobia, claustrophobia.*
Phoca, *n. foh*-ka, the genus of mammals containing most of the seals. (L.)
phocal, *a. foh*-kal, pertaining to the seal tribe.
phocid, *n. foh*-sid, any member of the family Phocidæ, comprising the true seals.
phocine, *a. foh*-sin, phocal.
Phœbus, *n. fee*-bus, the sun-god, Apollo; hence, the sun. (Gr. *phoibus*, brilliant.)
phœnix, *n. fee*-niks, an Arabian bird fabled to immolate itself at very long intervals on a funeral pile, and to rise again in renewed youth [Myth.]; a person of rare distinction, a "rara avis"; a paragon; (*cap.*) a genus of tropical palms including *P. dactylifera*, the date-palm. (Gr. *phoinix.*)
pholad, *n. foh*-lad, any of the piddocks.
Pholas, *n. foh*-las (*pl.* **pholades,** *foh*-la-deez), genus of lamellibranchiate molluscs comprising the piddocks.
phonate, *v.i. foh*-nate, to make vocal sounds: *v.t.* to utter vocally. (Gr. *phone*, sound.)
phonation, *n.* foh-*nay*-shon, the act or process of phonating; the production of phones or speech-sounds.
phonatory, *a. foh*-na-to-re, relating to phonation.
phonautograph, *n.* foh-*naw*-to-graf, an apparatus for producing a visible record of sound-vibrations, a fore-runner of the phonograph. (Gr. *phone*, and *autos*, self, *grapho*, write.)
phone, *n.* fone, a telephone; an earphone: *v.i.* and *t.* to telephone [Coll.].
phone, *n.* fone, the sound of any simple consonant or vowel [Phon.].
phoneme, *n.* foh-*neem*, a phone, or speech sound; a variant of a phone in which the variation is due to phonetic environment [Phon.].
phonendoscope, *n.* fo-*nen*-do-skope, a stethoscope fitted with a sound amplifier.
phonetic, *a.* fo-*net*-ik, pertaining to or representing vocal sounds: *n.pl.* fo-*net*-iks, the science and study of vocal sounds. **phonetic spelling,** a system of spelling in which each character invariably represents a single sound.
phonetician, *n.* foh-ne-*tish*-an, one versed in phonetics.
phoneticize, *v.t.* foh-*net*-e-size, to render phonetic; to spell phonetically.

phoney, *a.* *foh*-ne, phony [Slang].

phoniatrics, *n.* foh-ne-*at*-riks, the study and treatment of defective voice production.

phonic, *a.* *fon*-ik, pertaining to sound of any kind: *n.pl.* acoustics; phonetics.

phonocamptic, *a.* fo-no-*kamp*-tik, having the power to deflect sound. (Gr. *phone*, and *kampto*, bend.)

phonogenic, *n.* *foh*-no-*jen*-ik, possessed of a speaking voice that reveals a pleasant personality [Coll.].

phonogram, *n.* *foh*-no-gram, the record of a phonograph or gramophone; a symbol representing a sound; a telephone message delivered as a telegram. (Gr. *phone*, and *gramma*, a letter or character.)

phonograph, *n.* *foh*-no-graf, an instrument which records and repeats sounds; a character used in phonography: *v.t.* to record and reproduce sounds with a phonograph. (Gr. *phone*, and *grapho*, write.)

phonographic, *a.* foh-no-*graf*-ik, pertaining to phonography.

phonographist, *n.* fo-*nog*-ra-fist, one versed in phonography; a shorthand writer.

phonography, *n.* fo-*nog*-ra-fe, a description of speech-sounds; representation of sounds as pronounced by distinct characters, esp. by the Pitman system of shorthand; the use of the phonograph (Gr. *phone*, and *grapho*, write.)

phonolite, *n.* *foh*-no-lite, clinkstone, a volcanic rock consisting mainly of nepheline and orthoclase. (Gr. *phone*, and *lithos*, stone.)

phonological, *a.* foh-no-*loj*-e-kal, pertaining to phonology.

phonology, *n.* foh-*nol*-o-je, the science or study of vocal sound. (Gr. *phone*, and *logos*, science.)

phonometer, *n.* foh-*nom*-e-ter, an instrument for measuring the intensity of sound.

phonopathy, *n.* foh-*nop*-a-the, any disorder of the vocal organs.

phonophore, *n.* *foh*-no-for, an instrument for telegraphing and telephoning simultaneously along the same wire. (Gr. *phone*, and *phoros*, carrying.)

phonophorous, *a.* fo-*nof*-o-rus, capable of transmitting sound vibrations.

phonoscope, *n.* *foh*-no-skope, an apparatus for testing musical strings; an electrical instrument which transmits sound vibrations in visible form. (Gr. *phone*, and *skopeo*, view.)

phonotype, *n.* *foh*-no-tipe, a printing type used in phonotypy.

phonotypy, *n.* fo-*not*-e-pe, any method of printing in which each speech-sound is represented by a distinct character.

phony, *a.* *foh*-ne, counterfeit; bogus; open to suspicion [Slang].

phoresy, *n.* fo-*ree*-se, transport or dispersal of animals (esp. insects) by self-attachment to some other animal [Zool.].

phormium, *n.* *fore*-me-um, New Zealand flax, *Phormium tenax*. (Gr. *phormos*, a basket.)

phosgene, *n.* *fos*-jeen, a colourless and very poisonous gas prepared from chlorine and carbon monoxide, used in dye manufacture and as a powerful non-persistent irritant in gas-warfare. (Gr. *phos*, light, *gennao*, produce.)

phosgenite, *n.* *fos*-je-nite, a rare crystalline mineral composed of chloro-carbonate of lead.

phosphate, *n.* *fos*-fate, any salt of phosphoric acid.

phosphatic, *a.* fos-*fat*-ik, containing or of the nature of phosphates.

phosphatize, *v.t.* *fos*-fa-tize, to render phosphatic.

phosphene, *n.* *fos*-feen, the luminous impression caused by pressure on the eyeball.

phosphide, *n.* *fos*-fide, a combination of phosphorus with an element or radical.

phosphine, *n.* *fos*-feen, phosphuretted hydrogen.

phosphite, *n.* *fos*-fite, any salt of phosphorous acid.

phosphonium, *n.* fos-*foh*-ne-um, the univalent phosphorus radical (PH_4) analogous to ammonium.

Phosphor, *n.* *fos*-for, Venus, the morning star. (L).

phosphorate, *v.t.* *fos*-fo-rate, to combine or impregnate with phosphorus.

phosphor-bronze, *n.* trade-name of a bronze alloy containing a very small amount of phosphorus.

phosphoresce, *v.i.* fos-fo-*ress*, to shine with, or as with phosphorescence.

phosphorescence, *n.* fos-fo-*res*-sence, the property or process of giving out light without combustion or emission of sensible heat; light so given out.

phosphorescent, *a.* fos-fo-*res*-sent, exhibiting phosphorescence; faintly shining.

phosphoric, *a.* fos-*fo*-rik, pertaining to phosphorus in its higher valency; resembling or obtained from phosphorus. **phosphoric acid,** an acid formed by the oxidation of phosphorus or the decomposition of phosphates.

phosphorism, *n.* *fos*-fo-rizm, chronic poisoning due to phosphorus [Med.].

phosphorite, *n.* *fos*-fo-rite, a concretionary variety of apatite.

phosphorize, *v.t.* *fos*-fo-rize, to phosphorate.

phosphorogenic, *a.* *fos*-fo-ro-*jen*-ik, generating phosphorescence.

phosphorous, *a.* *fos*-fo-rus, pertaining to phosphorus in its lower valency; phosphoric. **phosphorous acid,** a white soluble solid formed by the reaction of various oxides of phosphorus and water, used as a reducing agent.

phosphorus, *n.* *fos*-fo-rus, a non-metallic element of the nitrogen group, which, being combustible at low heat, is luminous in the dark. (Gr.)

phosphuretted, *a.* *fos*-fewr-ret-ed, combined or impregnated with phosphorus. **phosphuretted hydrogen,** an evil-smelling gaseous compound of phosphorus and hydrogen.

phossy-jaw, *n.* *fos*-se-jaw, necrosis of the jaw due to phosphorus.

photalgia, *n.* foh-*tal*-je-a, pain produced by light [Path.]. (Gr. *phos*, *photos*, light, *algos*, pain.)

photic, *a.* *foh*-tik, pertaining to or penetrated by light.

photism, *n.* *foh*-tizm, an illusory sensation of colour accompanying some other (esp. acoustic) sensation. (Gr. *phos*, light.)

photo, *n.* *foh*-toh, a photograph. (Gr. *phos*, light.)

photochemistry, *n.* *foh*-to-*kem*-is-tre, the science or study of chemical changes produced by the action of light.

photochromatic, *a.* *foh*-to-kroh-*mat*-ik, pertaining to or produced by photochromy.

photochrome, *n.* *foh*-to-krome, a photograph in colours.

photochromotype, *n.* *foh*-to-*kroh*-mo-tipe, a coloured print made from photographic process blocks: *v.t.* to manufacture pictures thus.

photochromy, *n.* *foh*-to-kroh-me, the art of photographing in colours.

photodynamics, *n.* *foh*-to-dy-*nam*-iks, the science treating of the effect of light on plants and other organisms.

photoelectric, *a.* *foh*-to-e-*lek*-trik, pertaining to the emission of electrons from, or to the change in electrical resistance in, substances exposed to light of certain wave-lengths.

photo-engraving, *n.* any photographic process for the production of printing blocks.

photo-finish, *n.* a method of accurately recording the result of a race by means of photography.

photogen, *n.* *foh*-to-jen, a light-producing organ or organism [Zool.].

photogene, *n.* *foh*-to-jeen, a retinal impression; an after-image.

photogenic, *a.* foh-to-*jen*-ik, producing light; produced by the action of light; having features that look well in a photograph [Coll.].

photoglyphic, *a.* *foh*-to-*glif*-ik, pertaining to or effected by photoglyphy.

photoglyphy, *n.* *foh*-to-glif-e, an obsolete process of photo-engraving. (*photo*, and Gr. *glyphe*, carving.)

photogram, *n.* *foh*-to-gram, a pictorial photograph; a photomicrograph.

photograph, *n.* *foh*-to-graf, a photographic picture: *v.t.* to take a picture by photography. (Gr. *phos*, and *grapho*, write.)

photographer, *n.* fo-*tog*-ra-fer, one who takes photographs.

photographic, *a.* foh-to-*graf*-ik, pertaining to or obtained by photography.

photographically, *ad.* foh-to-*graf*-e-ka-le, in a photographic manner; by means of photography.

photography, *n.* fo-*tog*-ra-fe, the process or art of producing pictures of objects on a chemically prepared ground on glass, paper, metal, etc., by the action of light.

photogravure, *n.* *foh*-to-gra-*vewr*, a photographic process for the reproduction of pictures and drawings; a reproduction made by this.

photo-lithography, *n.* the art of printing from photographs transferred to stone.

photological, *a.* foh-to-*loj*-e-kal, optical; pertaining to photology.
photology, *n.* fo-*tol*-o-je, the science of light; optics. (Gr. *phos*, and *logos*, science.)
photolysis, *n.* foh-*tol*-e-sis, chemical decomposition by the action of light; the movements of protoplasm under the influence of light. (*photo*, and Gr. *lysis*, a loosening.)
photolytic, *a.* foh-to-*lit*-ik, pertaining to photolysis.
photomechanical, *a.* *foh*-to-me-*kan*-e-kal, pertaining to the mechanical reproduction of pictures, etc., esp. by means of process blocks.
photometer, *n.* fo-*tom*-e-ter, an instrument for measuring the intensity of light.
photometric, *a.* foh-to-*met*-rik, pertaining to a photometer or to photometry. **photometric integrator,** an instrument for measuring the quality of light reaching a given point.
photometry, *n.* fo-*tom*-e-tre, the measurement of the intensity of light.
photomicrograph, *n.* *foh*-to-*my*-kro-graf, an enlarged photograph of a microscopic object taken by photomicrography.
photomicrography, *n.* *foh*-to-my-*krog*-ra-fe, the art of photographing direct from the microscope.
photon, *n.* *foh*-ton, a unit of intensity of light [Opt.]; a light quantum [Physics].
photophobia, *n.* foh-toh-*foh*-be-a, a morbid intolerance of, or excessive sensitiveness to, light. (Gr. *phos*, and *phobos*, fear.)
photophone, *n.* *foh*-toh-fone, a radiophone in which the mutation of light to sound is effected by means of a selenium cell.
photophore, *n.* *foh*-to-for, an electrically lighted apparatus used in internal examinations [Med.]; an organ emitting light [Zool.].
photo-play, *n.* a drama for the cinematograph.
photopsy, *n.* fo-*top*-se, a disease of the retina characterized by the appearance of sparks, etc. (Gr. *phos*, and *opsis*, vision.)
photoscope, *n.* *foh*-to-skope, an apparatus for observing the effects of light or luminosity; a lens for viewing photographs; a form of fluoroscope. (Gr.)
photosculpture, *n.* foh-to-*skulp*-tewr, a photographic process for the mechanical reproduction of objects in relief.
photosphere, *n.* *foh*-to-sfeer, the luminous envelope of the sun. (Gr. *phos*, and *sphere*.)
photostat, *n.* *foh*-to-stat, proprietary name of an apparatus for making facsimiles of documents, drawings, etc.: a facsimile made with this: *v.t.* to make a facsimile by photostatic process.
photostatic, *a.* foh-to-*stat*-ik, pertaining to reproduction by means of the photostat.
photosyntax, *n.* foh-to-*sin*-taks, photosynthesis.
photosynthesis, *n.* *foh*-to-*sin*-the-sis, the means by which plants exposed to light form carbohydrates from water and the carbon dioxide of the air [Bot.].
phototelegraphy, *n.* *foh*-to-te-*leg*-ra-fe, telegraphic transmission of photographs and drawings.
phototherapeutics, *n.* *foh*-to-*the*-ra-*pew*-tiks, phototherapy.
phototherapy, *n.* *foh*-to-*the*-ra-pe, treatment, esp. of skin diseases, by light rays [Path.].
phototrope, *n.* *foh*-to-trope, a phototropic plant or organ [Biol.]; any substance that changes colour on exposure to light [Chem.].
phototropic, *a.* foh-to-*trop*-ik, heliotropic; turning towards, or under the influence of light. (Gr.)
phototype, *n.* *foh*-to-tipe, a process block obtained by photo-engraving; a print from this: *v.t.* to make a phototype of.
phototypy, *n.* *foh*-to-ty-pe, the art or process of making phototypes.
photoxylography, *n.* *foh*-to-zy-*log*-ra-fe, the art or process of engraving on wood a design that has been photographically printed on it.
photozincograph, *n.* *foh*-to-*zing*-ko-graf, a print made by photozincography.
photozincography, *n.* *foh*-to-zing-*kog*-ra-fe, the art or process of engraving on zinc by photomechanical means.
phragmacone, *n.* *frag*-ma-kone, the chambered internal shell of a belemnite or other fossil cephalopod. (Gr. *phragmos*, an enclosure, and *cone*.)
phrase, *n.* fraze, a short expression; a self-contained part of a sentence; an idiomatic mode of speech; style of diction: *v.t.* to express in words or in peculiar words. **phrase book,** a book of idioms. (Fr.)
phraseogram, *n.* *fray*-ze-o-gram, a symbol representing a phrase. (Gr. *phrasis*, and *gramma*.)
phraseological, *a.* fray-ze-o-*loj*-e-kal, pertaining to phraseology; composed of phrases.
phraseology, *n.* fray-ze-*ol*-o-je, a manner of expressing a thought; diction; choice of words. (Gr. *phrasis*, and *logos*, science.)
phratry, *n.* *fray*-tre, a clan; a tribal division. (Gr.)
phrenetic, *a.* fre-*net*-ik, wild and erratic; frantic: *n.* a frenzied person. (O.Fr. *frenetique*.)
phrenic, *a.* *fren*-ik, belonging to the diaphragm: *n.* the phrenic nerve. (Gr. *phren*, the diaphragm.)
phrenitis, *n.* fre-*ny*-tis, brain-fever; inflammation of the brain attended with delirium. (Gr., delirium.)
phrenological, *a.* fren-o-*loj*-e-kal, pertaining to phrenology.
phrenologically, *ad.*, according to phrenology.
phrenologist, *n.* fre-*nol*-o-jist, one versed in phrenology.
phrenology, *n.* fre-*nol*-o-je, the study of the external undulations of the cranium in the belief that these provide indications of the mental faculties and powers; the theory underlying this. (Gr. *phren*, the mind, *logos*, science.)
phrenoplegia, *n.* fren-o-*plee*-je-a, sudden loss of mental power. (Gr. *phren*, and *plege*, stroke.)
Phrygian, *a.* *frij*-e-an, pertaining to Phrygia, an ancient kingdom of Asia Minor, its people, or its language: *n.* the language of the Phrygians. **Phrygian cap,** a close-fitting conical cap adopted as the emblem of enfranchisement and liberty. **Phrygian mode,** the second of the ancient Greek modes, animated and warlike [Mus.]. **Phrygian stone,** a kind of pumice stone, anciently used in dyeing.
phthalein, *n.* *thal*-e-in, any organic dye produced by the combination of phthalic anhydride with the phenols.
phthalic, *a.* *thal*-ik, of, pertaining to, or obtained from naphthaline [Chem.].
phthanite, *n.* *tan*-ite, a variety of chert.
phthiriasis, *n.* the-*ry*-a-sis, pediculosis. (Gr. *phtheir*, a louse.)
phthisic, *a.* *tiz*-ik, phthisical: *n.* phthisis; one suffering from this.
phthisical, *a.* *tiz*-e-kal, pertaining to or of the nature of phthisis; debilitated.
phthisiology, *n.* tiz-e-*ol*-o-je, the study of phthisis. (Gr. *phthisis*, and *logos*, account.)
phthisis, *n.* *thy*-sis, *ty*-sis, *or* *fthy*-sis, pulmonary consumption; tuberculosis of the lungs. (L.)
phugoid, *a.* *few*-goyd, pertaining to the longitudinal stability of an aircraft in flight. **phugoid curve,** a curve of flight [Av.]. (Gr. *phugē*, flight, *eidos*, like.)
phut, *int.* fut *or* foot, an exclamation sounding like a bladder bursting, etc. **to go phut,** to fall; to collapse. (Imit.)
phycography, *n.* fy-*kog*-ra-fe, a treatise on seaweeds. (Gr. *phykos*, and *grapho*, write.)
phycology, *n.* fy-*kol*-o-je, the botany of the algæ. (Gr. *phykos*, a sea-weed, *logos*, science.)
phylacteric, *a.* fe-*lak*-te-rik, pertaining to phylacteries.
phylactery, *n.* fe-*lak*-te-re, an amulet worn as a charm preservative against danger or disease; among the Jews, a strip of parchment inscribed with certain texts of Scripture, enclosed in small cases, and attached to the forehead or left arm. (Gr. *phulakter*, a guard.)
phylarchy, *n.* *fy*-lar-ke, government by a tribe or class. (Gr. *phyle*, a tribe, *arche*, rule.)
phyletic, *a.* fy-*let*-ik, pertaining to a tribe or phylum; racial.
phyllite, *n.* *fil*-ite, a slaty schist containing mica. (Gr. *phyllon*, a leaf, *lithos*, a stone.)
phyllode, *n.* *fil*-ode, a petiole which looks like and functions as a leaf [Bot.]. (Gr. *phyllon*, and *eidos*, like.)
phylloid, *a.* *fil*-oyd, like a leaf.
phyllomania, *n.* fil-o-*may*-ne-a, excessive production of leaves [Bot.].
phyllophagan, *n.* fe-*lof*-a-gan, an animal, esp. an insect, that feeds on leaves. (Gr. *phyllon*, and *phago*, eat.)
phyllophagous, *a.* fe-*lof*-a-gus, leaf-eating.
phyllopod, *n.* *fil*-o-pod, any of a tribe of crustaceans with four or more pairs of leaf-like feet. (Gr. *phyllon*, and *pous*, a foot.)

phyllostome, *n. fil*-os-tohm, a leaf-nosed bat. (Gr. *phyllon*, and *stoma*, a mouth.)
phyllotaxis, *n.* fil-o-*tak*-sis, the arrangement of leaves on the stem [Bot.]. (Gr. *phyllon*, and *taxis*, order.)
Phylloxera, *n.pl.* fil-ok-*seer*-ra, a genus of aphides which form galls on leaves and are very destructive, esp. to the vine. (Gr. *phyllon*, and *xeros*, dry.)
phylogenesis, *n.* fy-lo-*jen*-e-sis, phylogeny.
phylogenetic, *a.* fy-lo-je-*net*-ik, pertaining to phylogenesis, or to the racial history of organisms.
phylogeny, *n.* fy-*loj*-en-e, the evolution of racial or typical forms in the animal or vegetable kingdom. (Gr. *phyle*, and *gennao*, produce.)
phylum, *n. fy*-lum, a sub-division of the animal or vegetable kingdom, the number of which have a common ancestry. (Gr. *phylon*, race.)
phyma, *n. fy*-ma (*pl.* **phymata,** *fy*-ma-ta), an external tubercle; a suppurative tumour larger than a boil [Med.]. (Gr.)
phymatoid, *a. fy*-ma-toyd, resembling a tubercle or a phyma [Med.].
Physalia, *n.* fy-*say*-le-a, a genus of marine hydrozoa including the Portuguese man-o'-war. (Gr. *physalis* bladder.)
Physalis, *n. fy*-sa-lis, an American genus of plants including the winter-cherry and Cape gooseberry. (Gr.)
physalite, *n. fis*-a-lite, a coarse variety of topaz. (Gr. *physalis*, and *lithos*, stone.)
Physeter, *n. fiz*-e-ter, the genus of cetaceans containing the sperm whales. (Gr.)
physiatrics, *n.* fiz-e-*at*-riks, the science of nature-cure; naturopathy.
physic, *n. fiz*-ik, the science or the art of healing diseases; medicine; a medicine that purges; a cathartic: *v.t.* to treat with physic; to purge. **physic garden,** a botanical garden. *p.* and *pp.* **physicked.** *ppr.* **physicking.** (O.Fr. *phisique*.)
★**physical,** *a. fiz*-e-kal, pertaining to material things, also to physics; perceptible by the senses. **physical geography,** that branch of geography treating of natural features. **physical jerks,** physical training, gymnastics [Slang].
physicalist, *n. fiz*-e-ka-list, one holding the theory that human actions and thoughts are governed by physical conditions and relations; a materialist.
physicality, *n.* fiz-e-*kal*-e-te, physical state or condition.
physically, *ad. fiz*-e-ka-le, materially; virtually.
physician, *n.* fe-*zish*-an, a doctor of medicine, esp. one qualified to prescribe remedies but not to perform surgical operations. (O.Fr. *physicien*.)
physicism, *n. fiz*-e-sizm, the theory that attributes the universe to purely physical causes; materialism.
physicist, *n. fiz*-e-sist, a student of, or specialist in, physics; a believer in physicism.
physico-, *comb.f. fiz*-e-ko, expressing physical or physically, or some relationship with physics, as in *physico-chemical*, *physico-logic*. (Gr. *physikos*, natural.)
physico-therapy, *n.* the treatment of disease by physical methods, etc.
physics, *n. fiz*-iks, the group of sciences treating of the non-chemical properties and changes of inanimate matter, esp. as affected by energy; formerly, natural philosophy.
physio-, *comb.f. fiz*-e-o, denoting nature, natural; or as an abbreviation of *physiology*. (Gr. *physis*, nature.)
physiocrat, *n. fiz*-e-o-krat, an economist of the school of the 18th-cent. French philosopher Quesnay, who taught that land is the source of all wealth and agriculture the only industry that increases wealth. (Gr. *physis*, and *kratos*, force.)
physiogeny, *n. fiz*-e-*oj*-en-e, the development of vital functions [Biol.]. (Gr. *physis*, and *gennao*, produce.)
physiognomic, *a.* fiz-e-o-*nom*-ik *or* fiz-e-og-*nom*-ik, pertaining to physiognomy; significative.
physiognomist, *n.* fiz-e-*on*-o-mist *or* fiz-e-*og*-no-mist, one who is skilled in physiognomy.
physiognomy, *n.* fiz-e-*on*-o-me *or* fiz-e-*og*-no-me, the face; the art of discerning the character of the mind from the facial or bodily features; facial expression. (O.Fr. *phisonomie*.)
physiographer, *n.* fiz-e-*og*-ra-fer, a student of, or expert in, physical geography.
physiography, *n.* fiz-e-*og*-ra-fe, physical geography.
physiolatry, *n.* fiz-e-*ol*-a-tre, nature worship. (Gr. *physis*, and *latreia*, worship.)
physiological, *a.* fiz-e-o-*loj*-e-kal, pertaining to physiology.
physiologically, *ad.*, according to physiology.
physiologist, *n.* fiz-e-*ol*-o-jist, one who is versed in physiology.
physiology, *n.* fiz-e-*ol*-o-je, the science treating of the organs of plants and animals, their phenomena and functions. (Gr. *physis*, and *logos*, science.)
physiolysis, *n.* fiz-e-*ol*-e-sis, the disintegration of dead tissue [Path.]. (*physio-*, and Gr. *lysis*, a loosening.)
physiotherapist, *n. fiz*-e-o-*the*-ra-pist, a practitioner of physiotherapy.
physiotherapy, *n. fiz*-e-o-*the*-ra-pe, medical treatment or rehabilitation by massage, gymnastics, and other physical means; physicotherapy.
physique, *n.* fe-*zeek*, bodily structure. (Fr.)
physitheism, *n. fiz*-e-*thee*-izm, deification of natural phenomena; also, anthropomorphism.
physograde, *a. fiz*-o-grade, swimming by means of air-bladders: *n.* a member of the Physograda, a group of oceanic hydrozoa. (Gr. *physa*, an air-bubble, L. *gradior*, walk.)
phytochemistry, *n.* fy-to-*kem*-is-tre, the chemistry of plants.
phytogenesis, *n.* fy-to-*jen*-e-sis, the development of plants. (Gr. *phyton*, and *gennao*, produce.)
phytogenous, *a.* fy-*toj*-en-us, of vegetable origin.
phytogeny, *n.* fy-*toj*-en-e, the study of phytogenesis.
phytogeography, *n.* fy-to-je-*og*-ra-fe, the geographical distribution of plants.
phytography, *n.* fy-*tog*-ra-fe, descriptive or systematic botany. (Gr. *phyton*, and *grapho*, write.)
phytoid, *a. fy*-toyd, plant-like.
phytologist, *n.* fy-*tol*-o-jist, a scientific botanist; a student of phytology.
phytology, *n.* fy-*tol*-o-je, botany; a treatise on plants. (Gr. *phyton*, and *logos*, science.)
phytomer, *n. fy*-to-mer (*pl.* **phytomera,** fy-*tom*-er-ra), a plant unit; any part of a plant which when severed may develop into a new plant. (Gr. *phyton*, plant, *meros*, share.)
phyton, *n. fy*-ton, a phytomer or plant unit; a potential cutting [Hort.]. (Gr. *phyton*, plant.)
phytonomy, *n.* fy-*ton*-o-me, the science of the laws of plant growth. (Gr. *phyton*, and *nomos*, a law.)
phytopathogenic, *a. fy*-to-*path*-o-*jen*-ik, pertaining to or caused by an organism parasitic on plants.
phytopathology, *n. fy*-to-pa-*thol*-o-je, plant pathology [Bot.]; morbid condition due to vegetable organisms or parasites [Med.].
phytophagous, *a.* fy-*tof*-a-gus, subsisting on plants. (Gr. *phyton*, and *phago*, eat.)
phytosis, *n.* fy-*toh*-sis, infestation by vegetable parasites; any disease caused by such.
phytotomy, *n.* fy-*tot*-o-me, the dissection of plants. (Gr. *phyton*, and *tome*, cutting.)
pi, *n.* py, the Greek letter π, *p*; the symbol representing the ratio of the circumference to the diameter [Math.].
pi, *n.* py, a confused mixture of printing types.
pia, *n. py*-a, the pia mater [Anat.]. **pia mater,** *see* **mater.**
piacular, *a.* py-*ak*-yew-lar, expiatory; requiring expiation; atrociously bad. (L. *piacularis*.)
piaffe, *n.* pe-*af*, a slow trotting gait: *v.i.* to move with this gait (of horses). (Fr. *piaffer*, to show off, to piaffe.)
pian, *n.* pe-*an*, frambœsia, the yaws [Braz.].
pianette, *n.* pe-a-*net*, a small piano. (It.)
pianino, *n.* pe-a-*nee*-noh, a pianette.
pianissimo, *ad.* pe-a-*nis*-e-moh, very softly [Mus.]. (It.)
pianist, *n. pee*-a-nist, a performer on the pianoforte.
piano, *ad.* pe-*ah*-noh, softly [Mus.]. (It.)
piano, *n.* pe-*ah*-noh *or* pe-*an*-oh, a pianoforte. (It.)
pianoforte, *n.* pe-*an*-noh-for-tay *or* pe-*an*-noh-fort, a keyed musical instrument in which the notes are produced by the action of hammers striking on wires. (It. *piano*, and *forte*, strong.)
pianola, *n.* pe-a-*noh*-la, the proprietary name of a certain form of piano-player.
piano-organ, *n.*, a hand-operated mechanical organ; a street organ.
piano-player, *n.*, one who plays the piano; a mechanical device for playing the piano.
piassava, *n.* pee-a-*sah*-va, a strong vegetable fibre used in making brooms and brushes, esp. that from the African palm *Raphia vinifera*, or from the

Brazilian palms *Leopoldinia piassaba* and *Attalea funifera*.
piastre, *n.* pe-*as*-ter, a silver coin of varying value in use at various times in Turkey, Egypt, the Balkans, etc. (Fr.)
piazza, *n.* pe-*at*-za, an open square surrounded by buildings, the upper stories of which are generally supported over an arched promenade by pillars; the colonnaded walk itself. (It.)
pibroch, *n.* *pee*-brokh, a martial or elegiac kind of music played on the bagpipe; the bagpipe itself. (Gael. *piobaireachd.*)
pica, *n.* *py*-ka, a depraved craving for substances unfit for human food, such as sand, chalk, etc. [Med.]. (L., magpie, this bird being supposed to have such habits.)
pica, *n.* *py*-ka, a large printing-type, the standard of printing measurements, 12-point, or ⅙ inch; a pre-Reformation tabulated list giving dates of the movable feasts [Eccles.]; the pika.
picador, *n.* *pik*-a-dor, a horseman who, in bull-fighting, rouses the bull with a lance. (Sp.)
picamar, *n.* *pik*-a-mar, a bitter oil extracted from wood-tar. (L. *pix*, pitch, *amarus*, bitter.)
picaresque, *a.* *pik*-a-resk, concerned with the exploits of picaroons, rogues, or criminals. (Fr.)
picarian, *a.* pi-*kare*-re-an, pertaining to the woodpeckers. (L. *picus*, a woodpecker.)
picaroon, *n.* *pik*-a-roon, a rascally vagabond; a plunderer, esp. of wrecks; a pirate: *v.i.* to engage in piracy or brigandage. (Sp., a rogue.)
picayune, *n.* pik-a-*yewn*, a former small silver coin of the southern United States, the half-real, or 5-cent piece. (Fr. *picaillon*, a farthing.)
picayunish, *a.* pik-a-*yew*-nish, of trifling value; paltry; pernickety [U.S.A.].
piccadil, *n.* *pik*-a-dil, a piccadilly.
piccadilly, *n.* *pik*-a-*dil*-le, a high collar, or kind of ruff, of the 17th century. (O.Fr. *piccadille.*)
piccage, *n.* *pik*-aj, money paid at fairs for breaking ground for booths [Law]. (*pitch.*)
piccalilli, *n.* *pik*-a-*lil*-le, a kind of mixed pickles in which mustard is used.
piccaninny, *n.* *pik*-a-nin-ne, pickaninny.
piccolo, *n.* *pik*-o-loh, a small flute, with the notes an octave higher than the ordinary flute. (It.)
pice, *n.* pice, an Indian bronze coin, ¼ of an anna, also a weight slightly over ½ ounce.
piceous, *a.* *pis*-e-us, pertaining to or resembling pitch. (L. *pix*, pitch.)
pichiciago, *n.* *pitsh*-e-se-*ah*-go, a small edentate of S. America, the burrowing armadillo *Chlamyphorus truncatus*. (Native.)
pichurim-bean, *n.* *pich*-yew-rim-*been*, the aromatic seed-lobe of the S. American tree *Nectandra puchury* used as a flavouring.
pick, *n.* pik, a sharp-pointed tool for digging; choice; right of selection; that which is picked: *v.t.* to pluck with the fingers something that grows or adheres to another thing; to pull off or clean with the teeth or fingers; to separate so as to loosen; to steal by taking out with the fingers; to choose or select; to strike with a pick; to peck, as a bird; to puncture; to open by a pointed instrument, as a lock: *v.i.* to strike at with, or as with, a pick; to make careful selection; to eat slowly; to nibble at. **pick up,** to take up; acquire; to regain health; to become acquainted with casually. **pick holes,** to find fault. **pick to pieces,** to criticize unmercifully. **the pick of the bunch,** the best of the lot. (A.S. *pycan.*)
pickaback, *ad.* *pik*-a-bak, in the manner of a pack carried on the shoulders.
pickage, *n.* *pik*-aj, piccage.
pickaninny, *n.* *pik*-a-nin-ne, a negro baby; a small child. (From Sp. *pequeño*, little.)
pickaxe, *n.* *pik*-aks, a curved pick with a handle in the middle and, usually, one end pointed and the other shaped like a chisel: *v.t.* and *i.* to strike with or use a pickaxe. (O.Fr. *picois.*)
picked, *a.* pikt, selected; culled; pointed like a pick.
pickeer, *v.t.* pik-*eer*, to pillage; to skirmish.
Pickelhaube, *n.* *pik*-el-hou-ber, the German spiked military helmet. (Ger.)
picker, *n.* *pik*-er, one who picks or culls; an instrument for picking or separating; a picklock.
pickerel, *n.* *pik*-er-rel, a young or small freshwater pike. **pickerel weed,** various pondweeds, esp. *Pontederia cordata*. (*pike.*)
pickerel, *n.* *pik*-er-rel, the dunlin *Tringa alpina* (in Scotland).
pickeringite, *n.* *pik*-er-ring-ite, a native hydrous sulphate of magnesium and aluminium.
picket, *n.* *pik*-et, a sharp stake or post; a narrow board pointed for a fence; a pointed peg for tethering a horse, fastening a guy, etc.; a guard posted in front of a camp or army; a small body of men selected for a purpose [Mil.]; the punishment of standing on a pointed stake; a guard posted by workers during a strike or lock-out to prevent infringement of trade union rules; one so posted: *v.t.* to supply or fortify with pickets; to enclose with pickets; to fasten to a picket; to post as a picket. (Fr. *piquet.*)
picketeer, *n.* pik-e-*teer*, a member of a picket in a labour dispute.
pickings, *n.pl.* *pik*-ingz, a thing or things picked; amount gained; scraps left over; pilferings; perquisites; choice morsels.
pickle, *n.* *pik*-kl, brine; a solution of salt and water; any liquid in which substances are seasoned and preserved; a vegetable or fruit preserved in pickle; a state of difficulty; a high-spirited child [Coll.]: *v.t.* to preserve in pickle; to treat with pickle. (Dut. *pekel*, brine.)
pickle-herring, *n.*, a buffoon or merry-andrew.
picklock, *n.* *pik*-lok, a tool for opening locks without the key; a person who picks locks.
pick-me-up, *n.*, a medicine or drink with tonic qualities; anything which gives a bracing effect.
pickpocket, *n.* *pik*-pok-et, one who steals from the pocket of another.
picksome, *a.* *pik*-sum, choosey; pernickety; fastidious. [Coll.].
pickthank, *n.* *pik*-thank, a flatterer; a parasite.
pick-up, *n.*, act of picking up; that which is picked up; a bargain; apparatus for picking up; a device replacing the sound-box of a gramophone, etc., enabling records to be heard through a loud-speaker; acceleration, or power to put on speed (of motor-cars).
picnic, *n.* *pik*-nik, an outing with an outdoor meal; a pleasure-party making an excursion into the country and carrying their provisions with them: *v.i.* to take part in a picnic; *ppr.* **picnicking.** *pp.* **picnicked.** (Fr. *piquenique.*)
picnicker, *n.* *pic*-nik-er, one taking part in a picnic.
picot, *n.* *pik*-o, a small loop of thread in embroidery, lace edging, etc. (Fr., a point.)
picotee, *n.* pik-o-*tee*, a variety of parti-coloured carnation. (Fr. *picoté.*)
picotite, *n.* *pik*-o-tite, a variety of spinel containing chromium and iron. (*Picot*, Fr. mineralogist, *d.* 1818.)
picrate, *n.* *pik*-rate, a salt of picric acid.
picric, *a.* *pik*-rik, pertaining to or designating a bitter yellow acid, one of the phenols, used in making explosives, dyes, and antiseptics. (Gr. *pikros*, bitter.)
picrite, *n.* *pik*-rite, any of several igneous rocks consisting largely of olivine and similar minerals.
picrolite, *n.* *pik*-ro-lite, a fibrous variety of serpentine.
picrotoxin, *n.* pik-ro-*toks*-in, a very poisonous substance present in the seeds of *Cocculus indicus*, used medically as an antispasmodic and to destroy parasites. (Gr. *pikros*, and *toxikon*, poison.)
Pict, *n.* pikt, one of a mixed aboriginal and Aryan race formerly occupying the northern parts of Britain. (Late L. *Picti.*)
Pictish, *a.* *pik*-tish, pertaining to or resembling the Picts: *n.* the language of the Picts.
pictograph, *n.* *pik*-to-graf, a hieroglyph, or other pictorial symbol, a record consisting of such. (L.)
pictography, *n.* pik-*tog*-ra-fe, the use of pictographs; picture writing.
pictorial, *a.* pik-*taw*-re-al, pertaining to, containing, or illustrated by, pictures.
pictorially, *ad.*, in a pictorial manner.
***picture,** *n.* *pik*-tewr, a painting or drawing exhibiting the resemblance of anything; a photograph, engraving, or other representation; description; a subject adapted to pictorial treatment; a cinematograph picture: *pl.* an exhibition of films [Coll.]: *v.t.* to paint or draw resemblances; to represent; to describe vividly. **in the picture,** taking part; of importance; congruous [Coll.].
picture gallery, an apartment for the exhibition

of pictures. **picture hat,** a lady's hat with a wide flexible brim. **picture house,** or **palace,** a cinema. **picture rail,** a moulding high on the walls of a room for the support of hanging pictures. **picture writing,** the art of using hieroglyphs, ideograms, etc., for the purposes of language: pictography. (O.Fr.)

picturesque, *a.* pik-tewr-*resk*, expressing that kind of beauty which is agreeable in a picture, natural or artificial; suitable for a picture; vivid (of writing, etc.). (It. *pittoresco.*)

picturesquely, *ad.* in a picturesque manner.

picturesqueness, *n.* state of being picturesque.

picul, *a.* *pik*-ul, *n.* a weight of the Far East, varying between about 132 and 142 pounds. (Malay.)

piddle, *v.i.* *pid*-dl, to trifle; to urinate or make water [Coll.].

piddling, *a.* pidl-ling, trifling; insignificant.

piddock, *n.* *pid*-dok, a burrowing bivalve mollusc of the genus *Pholas*. (Origin unknown.)

pidgin-English, *n.* *pij*-in-*ing*-glish, a mixed dialect used in ports of the Far East. (*business, English.*)

pie, *n.* py, a crust baked with meat or fruit in it or under it. **finger in the pie,** *see* **finger.** (M.E.)

pie, *n.* py, the magpie, or other pied bird. **pie finch,** the chaffinch. (O.Fr., L. *pica.*)

pie, *n.* py, the service book of pre-Reformation times. (Perhaps from *pica.*)

pie, *n.* py, type confusedly mixed, a medley or jumble: *v.t.* to mix type haphazardly. (Perhaps from the first *pie.*)

piebald, *a.* *py*-bawld, with patches of two different colours; mottled. (*pie,* the magpie, *bald,* streaked.)

piece, *n.* peece, a part of anything; a portion; a definite quantity; roll of cloth; a short literary or artistic composition; a gun; a coin; a person; any chessman other than a pawn: *v.t.* to mend; to patch; to add to; to unite: *v.i.* to fit together well. **of a piece,** of the same sort. **piece of eight,** the Spanish-American dollar, containing eight reals. **piece out,** to extend by addition of one or more pieces. (O.Fr.)

piece-goods, *n.pl.*, textiles woven in and sold by recognized lengths.

piecemeal, *a.* *peece*-meel, separately, piece by piece; done by, or made up of, pieces: *ad.* in pieces; by pieces; little by little.

piecer, *n.* *peece*-er, one who pieces; a patcher.

piece-work, *n.* work paid for by the job or piece and not by the day or hour.

pied, *a.* pide, variegated with spots; spotted black and white. (*pie,* the magpie.)

Piedmontese, *a.* *peed*-mon-*teez*, of or pertaining to Piedmont, Italy: *n.* a native of Piedmont.

piedmontite, *n.* *peed*-mon-tite, a variety of epidote containing manganese.

piedness, *n.* *pide*-ness, the condition or quality of being pied.

piedog, *n.* *py*-dog, a pyedog.

pieman, *n.* *py*-man, a maker or seller of pies.

piepowder, *n.* *py*-pou-der, a wayfarer; a pedlar. **Court of Piepowder,** a summary court formerly held at fairs and markets for the hearing of minor charges. (O.Fr. *pie poudreux,* dusty foot.)

pier, *n.* peer, a solid mass of stone or brick for supporting an arch, bridge, or other building; the supporting wall between windows and doors; a pillar, esp. one for a door or a gate; a projecting wharf or landing-place; a jetty or promenade projecting into the sea. (Fr. *pierre,* a stone.)

pierage, *n.* *peer*-aj, toll for using a pier.

pierce, *v.t.* peerce, to thrust into with a pointed instrument; to penetrate; to affect deeply; to dive into: *v.i.* to enter; to penetrate. (Fr. *percer.*)

pierceable, *a.* *peerce*-a-bl, that may be pierced.

piercer, *n.* *peerce*-er, a perforating tool; a stiletto; one who pierces.

piercing, *a.* *peerce*-ing, penetrating with force; sharp; affecting keenly.

piercingly, *ad.* in a piercing manner.

piercingness, *n.* piercing quality.

pier-glass, *n.* a mirror placed or for placing between windows.

Pierian, *a.* py-*eer*-re-an, pertaining to the Muses. (*Pieria,* in Thrace, where they were worshipped.)

pierrette, *n.* pe-a-*ret*, a female pierrot.

pierrot, *n.* *pee*-a-roh, a costumed buffoon or entertainer, properly with whitened face and clad in white and black. (Fr. dim. of *Pierre.*)

pier-table, *n.* a table between windows.

piet, *n.* *py*-et, the magpie; the dipper or water-ouzel.

pieta, *n.* pe-*ay*-ta, a representation of the Virgin Mary lamenting over the dead Christ. (It.)

Pietism, *n.* *py*-et-izm, the principles and practices of the Pietists.

Pietist, *n.* *py*-et-ist, one of a 17th-cent. sect of Lutheran revivalists who attached supreme importance to personal godliness as compared with dogma and the services of the church.

pietistic, *a.* py-e-*tis*-tik, partaking of pietism.

piety, *n.* *py*-e-te, quality of being pious; religious devotion; formerly, affectionate reverence. (Fr. *piété.*)

piewipe, *n.* *py*-wipe, the lapwing. (From its cry.)

piezochemistry, *n.* py-*ee*-zo-*kem*-is-tre, the science treating of the chemical effects of pressure.

piezo-electric, *a.* py-*ee*-zo-e-*lek*-trik, pertaining to the expansion along one axis and contraction along another of certain crystals when subjected to an electric field.

piezo-electricity, *n.* py-*ee*-zo-e-lek-*tris*-e-te, electricity generated by subjecting crystals of Rochelle salt, quartz, tourmaline, etc. to an electric field.

piezometer, *n.* py-ee-*zom*-e-ter, an instrument for measuring pressure, esp. the compressibility of fluids. (Gr. *piezo,* press, *metron,* measure.)

piffero, *n.* *pif*-e-roh, an old form of oboe; a fife; an organ-stop of similar tone. (It.)

piffle, *n.* *pif*-fl, silly chatter; twaddle; futility: *v.i.* to talk nonsense or triflingly.

★**pig,** *n.* pig, the domestic swine; a greedy, obstinate, or dirty person [Coll., in contempt]; an oblong mass of unforged iron, lead, or other metal: *v.t.* to bring forth pigs: *v.i.* to act like pigs; to lie together like pigs. **to pig in,** to share in rough-and-ready fashion. **to pig it,** to live in a piggish way. (M.E. *pigge*; of doubtful origin.)

pig, *n.* pig, a crock, or earthenware jar, pitcher, etc. (Origin uncertain.)

pigeon, *n.* *pij*-en, any species of the dove family; the dove; a person easily imposed on and swindled: *v.t.* to fleece in gambling. **pigeon English,** pidgin-English. **pigeon post,** a system of letter-carrying in which a microphotographic reproduction of the missive is attached to a strong feather in the tail of a trained pigeon. **pigeon's foot,** the long-stalked geranium, *G. columbinum*. (O.Fr.)

pigeon-breasted, *a.* having a constricted breast with sharply projecting sternum.

pigeon-hole, *n.* an entrance for pigeons to a loft, etc.; a small compartment in a desk, cabinet, etc., for papers, etc.: *v.t.* to classify; to put aside for later consideration.

pigeon-livered, *a.* timid or mild in temper; easily frightened.

pigeon-pea, *n.* a kind of pulse; dholl, a species of *Cajanus*.

pigeon-toed, *a.* with turned-in toes.

pig-eyed, *a.* having small deeply sunk eyes.

piggery, *n.* *pig*-er-re, a pigsty, or a range of these; a farm for pigs; a squalid dwelling-place.

piggin, *n.* *pig*-in, a small wooden tub or dish. (Gael. *pigean.*)

piggish, *a.* *pig*-ish, swinish; pertaining to or characteristic of pigs.

pigheaded, *a.* pig-*hed*-ed, stupidly obstinate.

pigheadedness, *n.* quality of being pig-headed.

pig-iron, *n.* *pig*-i-urn, iron cast in pigs or oblong masses.

piglet, *n.* *pig*-let, an immature or diminutive pig.

pigmean, *a.* pig-*mee*-an, pygmean.

pigment, *n.* *pig*-ment, a dry colour powder for paint or dyes; paint; colouring matter. (Fr.)

pigmental, *a.* pig-*men*-tal, pertaining to pigments.

pigmentary, *a.* *pig*-men-ta-re, pertaining to, containing, or characterized by, pigment.

pigmentation, *n.* pig-men-*tay*-shon, coloration as the effect of a pigment, esp. in the tissue of an animal or plant.

pigmy, *n.* *pig*-me, pygmy.

pignorate, *v.t.* *pig*-no-rate, to pawn; to mortgage (L. *pignerare,* to pledge.)

pignoration, *n.* pig-no-*ray*-shon, act of pledging.

pignut, *n.* *pig*-nut, an earth-nut.

pigskin, *n.* *pig*-skin, the skin of the pig; leather made of this; a saddle [Slang].

pigsticking, *n.* *pig*-stik-ing, the sport of hunting the wild boar with a spear, esp. on horseback.

pigsty, *n. pig*-sty, a sty or pen for pigs.
pigtail, *n. pig*-tale, the tail of a pig; the hair of the head grown long and tied in the form of a pig's tail; a small roll of twisted tobacco.
pigwash, *n. pig*-wosh, swill; hogwash.
pigweed, *n. pig*-weed, any herb commonly eaten by pigs, esp. goosefoot and purslane.
pigwidgeon, *n. pig*-wij-on, a fairy; a ninny; anything very small.
pika, *n. py*-ka, any small rodent of the family Ochotonidæ, including the tailless and piping hares of the Rocky Mountains and the deserts of Central Asia.
pike, *n.* pike, a weapon consisting of a long wooden shaft with a pointed flat steel head; a spike; a peak (esp. in the Lake District); the voracious freshwater fish, *Esox lucius.* **pike perch,** the zander, or other fish of the perch family resembling the pike. (Fr. *pique.*)
pike, *n.* pike, a turnpike; a toll-gate. (*turnpike.*)
piked, *a.* pykt, ending in a point or peak.
pikelet, *n. pike*-let, a crumpet or round tea-cake. (W. *pyglyd,* like pitch.)
pikeman, *n. pike*-man, a soldier armed with a pike; a miner who uses a pick.
piker, *n. py*-ker, a tramp frequenting turnpikes; one lacking self-confidence or fearful of risks; or an over-timid gambler [Amer. slang].
pikestaff, *n. pike*-stahf, the shaft of a pike.
pilary, *a. py*-la-re, pertaining to the hair. (L. *pilus, pilaris,* hair.)
pilaster, *n.* pe-*las*-ter, a square pillar, usually set attached to a wall (or piece of furniture) and having a capital and base. (Fr. *pilastre.*)
pilau *or* **pilaw,** *n.* pe-*law,* an Oriental dish of boiled rice and fowl, meat, or fish stewed with almonds and raisins, spices, onions, etc. (Per.)
pilch, *n.* pilch, a flannel cloth worn by infants over the napkin; a light saddle. (A.S. *pylce.*)
pilchard, *n. pil*-chard, a fish of the herring family, *Clupea pilchardus,* the adult sardine. (Origin unknown.)
pile, *n.* pile, a heap; a mass or collection of things piled up, or of combustibles for burning a dead body; a large building; a mass of buildings; a series of plates of different metals so arranged as to produce a current [Elect.]: *v.t.* to lay in a heap or pile; to collect together; to amass; to stack in an orderly manner, muzzles upward (of rifles) [Mil.]. (Fr.)
pile, *n.* pile, a large post or heavy timber, etc., driven into the earth to support a building; the pointed head of an arrow, dart, or lance; an isosceles triangle issuing from the chief and pointing downwards [Her.]: *v.t.* to drive piles into; to furnish with piles. (A.S. *pil,* from L. *pilum,* sharp stake.)
pile, *n.* pile, the nap or fine hairy substance on the surface of woven fabrics. (L. *pilus,* hair.)
pile, *n.* pile, a tumour formed in piles [Med.].
pileate, *a pil*-e-at, having the form of a cap; crested [Zool.]. (L. *pileus,* cap.)
pile-driver, *n.* a machine for driving down piles.
pile-dwelling, *n.* a lake dwelling.
pileous, *a. py*-le-us, hairy. (L. *pilus,* hair.)
piler, *n. pile*-er, one who piles or forms a heap.
piles, *n.pl.* pylz, the hæmorrhoids, or tumours formed by the dilatation of the veins about the verge of the anus. (L. *pila,* ball.)
pileus, *n. py*-le-us (*pl.* **pilei,** *py*-le-eye), the close-fitting brimless cap of the ancient Romans; the cap-like top of certain fungi; the top of a bird's head from the bill to the nape; the umbrella of a jelly-fish (L.).
pileworm, *n. pile*-wurm, the shipworm.
pilewort, *n. pile*-wurt, the lesser celandine, *Ranunculus ficaria,* the roots of which were used formerly in poultices as a specific against hæmorrhoids.
pilfer, *v.i.* and *t. pil*-fer, to steal in small quantities; to practise petty theft. (O.Fr. *pelfrer,* rob.)
pilferage, *n. pil*-fer-raj, the act of pilfering; that which is pilfered.
pilferer, *n. pil*-fer-rer, one who pilfers.
pilfering, *n. pil*-fer-ring, petty theft.
pilferingly, *ad.* in a pilfering manner.
pilgarlic, *n.* pil-*gar*-lik, a bald head, or bald-headed man; a poor, forsaken wretch. (*pilled,* or pealed, *garlic.*)
pilgrim, *n. pil*-grim, a wanderer; one who travels to a distance to visit a holy place: *v.i.* to go on a pilgrimage. **Pilgrim Fathers,** the puritans who sailed in the Mayflower to found a colony in New England in 1620. **pilgrim shell,** a scallop shell. (O.Fr. *pellegrin.*)
pilgrimage, *n. pil*-grim-aj, a reverential journey; a journey to some holy place; the journey of human life.
piliferous, *a.* py-*lif*-er-rus, bearing hairs [Bot.]; covered with hair. (L. *pilus,* hair, *tero,* bear.)
piligerous, *a.* py-*lij*-er-rus, piliferous.
pill, *n.* pil, a medicine in the form of a little ball to be swallowed whole; anything nauseous to be accepted or, as it were, swallowed; a ball [Slang]: *v.t.* to blackball [Slang]. (L. *pilula,* dim. of *pila,* ball.)
pill, *v.t.* pil, to rob; to plunder; to peel: *v.i.* to strip; to be peeled. (O.Fr. *piller.*)
pillage, *n. pil*-aj, plunder; spoil, esp. that taken in war; act of plundering; *v.t.* to strip of money or goods by open violence; to plunder. (*pill.*)
pillager, *n. pil*-a-jer, one who pillages.
pillar, *n. pil*-ar, an upright column, tall in proportion to its breadth, for support, decoration, or commemoration; any detached column; something resembling a pillar; foundation or support; a supporter: *v.t.* to buttress or strengthen with or as with pillars. (O.Fr. *piler.*)
pillar-box, *n.* a letter-box, detached like a pillar, for receiving outgoing mail.
pillared, *a. pil*-ard, having or supported by pillars; like a pillar.
pillarist, *n. pil*-a-rist, a stylite.
pillau, *n.* pe-*law,* pilau.
pillbox, *n. pil*-boks, a small round box for pills; a flat round cap [Mil.]; a small dwelling, carriage, etc. [Coll.]; a concrete blockhouse.
pillion, *n. pil*-yon, a cushion for one to ride on behind another on horseback; a pad behind a saddle for a second rider; a low saddle; a luggage-carrier or extra riding seat of a motor-cycle. (Ir. *pilliun,* pack-saddle.)
pilliwinks, *n. pil*-e-winks, a thumb-screw.
pillory, *n. pil*-o-re, a wooden frame on posts, with movable boards and holes in which the head and hands of a criminal were held by way of punishment and public exposure: *v.t.* to punish with the pillory; to expose to general abuse or ridicule. (O.Fr. *pellori.*)
pillow, *n. pil*-oh, a cushion filled with feathers, or other soft material, to support the head of a person reposing; a block used for the same purpose; a bearing [Mech.]; the block on which the inner end of a bowsprit is supported [Naut.]: *v.t.* to rest or lay on for support; to prop with a pillow. **pillow lace,** bobbin-lace made by hand on a pillow. (A.S. *pylu.*)
pillow-block, *n.* a plummer-block [Mech.].
pillow-case *or* **pillow-slip,** *n.* a removable and washable case for drawing over a pillow.
pillowy, *a. pil*-oh-e, like a pillow; soft.
pillwort, *n. pil*-wurt, any aquatic plant of the genus *Pilularia,* esp. *P. globulifera.*
pilocarpine, *n.* py-loh-*kar*-pin, an alkaloid prepared from the jaborandi or other shrub of the genus *Pilocarpus.* (Gr. *pilos,* cap, *karpos,* fruit.)
pilose, *py*-lohs, hairy; covered with or consisting of hair. (L. *pilosus.*)
pilosity, *n.* pe-*los*-e-te, the condition of being pilose; hairiness.
pilot, *n. py*-lot, a steersman; one qualified and licensed to take charge of the navigation of ships in harbour approaches, or in channels, difficult waters, etc., as specified; an aviator qualified to navigate aircraft; a guide; a director of one's course: *v.t.* to direct the course of, as a ship where navigation is dangerous; to guide through dangers; to lead the way. **pilot officer,** a junior officer in the R.A.F., equivalent in rank to a 2nd lieutenant in the army. **pilot whale,** the blackfish, a species of the dolphin family, *Globicephalus melas.* (O.Fr.)
pilotage, *n. py*-lot-aj, the act or business of piloting; a pilot's fee; the art of piloting (esp. of aircraft).
pilot-balloon, *n.* an unmanned balloon sent up to discover the direction of the wind.
pilot-boat, *n.* a boat used by pilots in meeting incoming vessels.
pilot-cloth, *n.* a stout blue cloth for greatcoats, as worn by pilots.

pilot-engine, *n.* the leading locomotive when two draw a train ; a locomotive sent on ahead of a train to ensure that the road is clear.
pilot-fish, *n.* the marine fish *Naucrates ductor,* so called because it is most often seen with sharks.
pilot-jacket, *n.* a jacket made of pilot-cloth.
pilous, *a. py*-lus, pilose.
pilsener, *n. pil*-sen-er, a brand of lager beer brewed at Pilzen (Ger. *Pilsen*), Czechoslovakia.
pilular, *a. pil*-yew-lar, pertaining to pills.
pilularia, *n.* pil-yew-*lare*-re-a, pillwort.
pilule, *n. pil*-yewl, a small pill.
pimelic, *a.* pi-*mel*-ik, designating a crystalline dibasic acid obtained by the oxidation of fats. (Gr. *pimele,* fat.)
pimelitis, *n.* pim-e-*ly*-tis, inflammation of adipose tissue [Path.].
pimelosis, *n.* pim-e-*loh*-sis, a conversion into fat [Path.].
pimento, *n.* pi-*men*-to, Jamaica-pepper, the berry of *Pimenta officinalis.* (Sp. *pimiento.*)
pimp, *n.* pimp, a procurer ; a pander : *v.i.* to pander ; to procure lewd women.
pimpernel, *n. pim*-per-nel, any plant of the genus *Anagallis,* esp. *A. arvensis,* the scarlet pimpernel. (O.Fr. *pimpernelle.*)
pimple, *n. pim*-pl, a small pustule or inflamed swelling on the skin. (A.S. *piplian,* blister.)
pimpled, *a. pim*-pld, pimply.
pimply, *a. pim*-ple, having pimples.
★pin, *n.* pin, anything thin and pointed used for fastening clothes ; a piece of wood or metal sharpened to fasten together ; anything like a pin ; a thing of little value ; a peg ; a bolt ; a skittle ; a cask holding half a firkin, or 4½ gallons ; the state of being pinned [Chess] : *v.t.* to fasten with a pin ; to make fast ; to enclose ; to make impossible the movement of an opponent's man without his opening check or leaving a more valuable piece to be taken [Chess]. **pins and needles,** the tingling sensation felt in a limb recovering from being numbed. **pin and web,** obsolete name of some eye-disease. **pin-striped,** marked with lines of about a pin's breadth. **pin-up girl,** an attractive woman whose photograph is valued by men as a decoration. (A.S. *pinn.*)
piña-cloth, *n. pee*-nya-kloth, a fine yellowish fabric, made in the Philippines, of the fibres of the leaf of the pine-apple. (Sp. *piña,* a pine-apple.)
pinacoid, *n. pin*-a-koyd, a crystal form in which any two faces are parallel to two axes. (Gr. *pinax,* board, and *-oid.*)
pinafore, *n. pin*-a-for, a long apron to protect the front of the dress.
pinang, *n.* pe-*nang,* the betel palm or nut. (Malay, *pinang,* areca.)
pinaster, *n.* pe-*nas*-ter, the cluster pine of the south of Europe, *Pinus pinaster.* (L. *pinus,* pine.)
pin-case, *n.* a case for holding pins.
pince-nez, *n.* (App.), a pair of eyeglasses that fit on the nose with a spring. (Fr.)
pincers, *n.pl. pin*-serz, an instrument for drawing out nails or gripping things ; the chela of crustacea [Zool.]. (Fr. *pincer,* to pinch.)
pincette, *n.* (App.), a pair of tweezers, forceps, or small pincers. (Fr.)
pinch, *n.* pinch, a painful compression with the ends of the fingers ; that which is taken between the finger and thumb ; a gripe ; distress inflicted or suffered ; straits : *v.t.* to press hard or squeeze ; to nip ; to grip ; to straiten ; to oppress with want ; to distress ; to press ; to press hard ; to steal [Slang] : *v.i.* to act with pressing force ; to bear hard ; to be frugal. **at a pinch,** in a case of urgency or necessity. (Fr. *pincer.*)
pinchbeck, *a. pinch*-bek, inferior ; imitation ; of lower than the purported quality : *n.* an imitation gold consisting of copper with 15 to 20 per cent. zinc. (Name of its inventor.)
pincher, *n. pinch*-er, he who or that which pinches ; a miser ; a petty thief : *pl.* pincers.
pinchfist, *n. pinch*-fist, a miser ; a niggard.
pinchingly, *ad.* in a pinching manner ; stingily.
pincushion, *n. pin*-koosh-on, a cushion in which to stick pins to be ready for use.
Pindaric, *a.* pin-*da*-rik, in the style of Pindar : *n.* an irregular ode after Pindar, a Greek lyric poet.
Pindarism, *n. pin*-da-rizm, style or expression in imitation of Pindar.
pinder, *n. pin*-der, one who puts stray animals into the pound ; a pound-keeper.
pine, *n.* pine, a cone-bearing evergreen tree ; the timber of various coniferous trees ; a pine-apple. (A.S. *pin,* L. *pinus,* a pine.)
pine, *v.i.* pine, to waste away from distress, anxiety, or longing. (A.S. *pin,* pain.)
pineal, *a. py*-ne-al, like a pine cone. **pineal gland,** a small cone-shaped body in front of the cerebellum and, in certain lower vertebrates, of eye-like structure ; formerly supposed to be the seat of the soul, its function is unknown. (L. *pinea,* pine-cone.)
pine-apple, *n.* a tropical plant of the genus *Ananas* and its fruit, in shape resembling a pine-cone.
pine-barren, *n.* arid land producing pines. [Amer.]
pinechafer, *n. pine*-chay-fer, any beetle destructive to pine-trees.
pine-kernel, *n.* the edible seed of the pines.
pine-marten, *n.* the European marten, *Mustela martes,* occasionally found in the mountainous parts of Britain.
pinery, *n. py*-ner-re, a hothouse where pine-apples are grown ; a pine grove or plantation.
pinetum, *n.* py-*nee*-tum, a plantation or collection of pine trees ; a book about conifers.
piney, *a. py*-ne, abounding with pines ; characteristic of pines or pine-trees.
pin-feather, *n.* a small incipient feather.
pin-feathered, *a.* not fully fledged.
pin-fire, *n.* a mechanism which, by driving a pin into the fulminate of a cartridge, discharges firearms.
pinfold, *n. pin*-fohld, a pound, the place in which stray cattle are confined. (M.E. *pindfold.*)
ping, *n.* ping, the whistle of a bullet : *v.i.* to whistle, as a bullet in flight. (From the sound.)
pingpong, *n. ping*-pong, table-tennis. (From the sound made when the bat strikes the ball.)
pinguid, *a. ping*-gwid, fat ; greasy ; unctuous. (L. *pinguis,* fat.)
pinguin, *n. ping*-gwin, a West Indian plant, *Bromelia Pinguin,* with a fleshy plum-like fruit.
pin-hole, *n.* a very small aperture ; a transparent spot on a developed plate [Phot.].
pinic, *a. py*-nik, obtained from or pertaining to the pine-tree.
pinicoline, *a.* py-*nik*-o-line, inhabiting or growing in pine-forests [Zool. and Bot.]. (L. *pinus,* and *-cola,* inhabiting.)
piniform, *a. py*-ne-form, conical ; of the shape of a pine-cone.
piningly, *ad. py*-ning-le, in a languishing manner.
pinion, *n. pin*-yon, the joint of a bird's wing remotest from the body ; a flight-feather ; a wing ; a small wheel working in the teeth of a larger one : *v.t.* to cut off the first joint of the wing of ; to confine by binding the arms or wings of ; to shackle. (O.Fr. *pignon,* the end of a gable.)
pinite, *n. pin*-ite, a hydrous silicate of aluminium and potassium, an altered form of iolite and other minerals.
pink, *n.* pink, a plant or flower of the genus *Dianthus* ; a light-red colour, like that of the garden pink ; the red of a fox-hunter's coat ; something superlatively excellent : *a.* like the pink in colour. **in the pink,** in fox-hunting kit, hence, sprucely turned out, smartly dressed, or in good condition. (Origin unknown.)
pink, *n.* pink, a vessel with a narrow stern. (O. Dut. *pincke,* a small fishing-boat.)
pink, *n.* pink, a parr, or salmon before reaching the smolt stage. (Origin unknown.)
pink, *v.t.* pink, to pierce with small holes ; to prick ; to stab. (M.E. *pinken,* perhaps from *pick.*)
pink-eye, *n.* an influenza among horses characterized by inflammation of the conjunctiva ; a form of ophthalmia in man.
pink-eyed, *a. pink*-ide, having small eyes. (O.Dut. *pincken,* to half-close the eyes, and *eyed.*)
pinkiness, *n. ping*-ke-ness, the state or quality of being pinky.
pinking, *n. ping*-king, knocking, or abnormal detonation in an internal combustion engine [Mech.].
pinkish, *a. ping*-kish, of a somewhat pink colour.
pinkroot, *n. pink*-root, the root of certain herbs of the genus *Spigelia,* used as a purgative and anthelmintic.
Pinkster, *n. pink*-ster, Whitsuntide [U.S.A.]. **pinkster flower,** the N. American azalea, *A. nudiflora.* (Dut., Pentecost.)

pinky, *a. pink*-e, tinged with pink; pinkish.
pin-money, *n.* money allowed by a husband to his wife for dress and her private expenses.
pinna, *n. pin*-na (*pl.* **pinnæ**), upper part of external ear; a single leaflet of a pinnate leaf; a wing, fin, or fin-like structure. (L.)
pinnace, *n. pin*-as, a small oared sailing vessel; a warship's boat next in size to the launch; a ship's boat of various sizes. (Fr. *pinasse*, probably from L. *pinus*, pine.)
pinnacle, *n. pin*-a-kl, a slender turret on the top of a building; a sharp pointed top: *v.t.* to furnish with pinnacles; to place on a pinnacle. (Fr. *pinacle.*)
pinnate, *a. pin*-nat, branching or cleft like a feather; having leaflets arranged on either side of a common petiole [Bot.]; having lateral processes along an axis [Zool.]. (L. *pinnatus*, feathered.)
pinnately, *ad. pin*-at-le, in a pinnate form, esp. of veins in leaves.
pinnatifid, *a.* pe-*nat*-e-fid, feather-cleft; lobed after the manner of a pinnate leaf [Bot.]. (L. *pinna*, a feather, wing, or fin, *findo*, cleave.)
pinnatiped, *a.* pe-*nat*-e-ped, fin-footed; having the toes bordered by membranes [Zool.]. (L. *pinna*, and *pes*, the foot.)
pinner, *n. pin*-ner, one who pins; a pin-maker; a woman's cap with long lappets; a pinafore.
pinniped, *a. pin*-ne-ped, having fin-like feet or flippers: *n.* any member of the Pinnipedia, the group containing the seals and walruses. (L. *pinna*, and *pes*, foot.)
pinnock, *n. pin*-uk, a local name for various birds, esp. the hedge-sparrow. (Dial. Eng.)
pinnulate, *a. pin*-yew-lat, having or resembling pinnules [Bot. and Zool.]. (L. *pinnula*, a tiny feather.)
pinnule, *n. pin*-yewl, a branchlet of a pinnate leaf [Bot.]; the lateral process of a crinoid's arms [Zool.]; a detached finlet [Ichth.].
pinny, *n. pin*-e, a pinafore.
pinochle, *n. pee*-nuk-l *or pin*-o-kl, an American two-handed card-game somewhat resembling bezique; a score at this. (Origin unknown.)
pinole, *n. pee*-nole, meal made from parched corn and usually eaten with sugar and milk [Sp.-Amer.]. (Aztec *pinolli.*)
pinpatch, *n. pin*-patch, the periwinkle, *Littorina littorea.* (Dial. Eng.)
pinpoint, *v.t. pin*-poynt, to mark the exact position; to locate or determine precisely.
pinprick, *n. pin*-prik, a prick or puncture with a pin; a petty annoyance or irritation: *v.t.* to make, or to annoy with, pinpricks.
pint, *n.* pynt, a measure of capacity, the eighth part of a gallon, containing 34·659 cubic inches, equal to ·568 litre; 20 fluid ounces [Med.]. (Fr. *pinte*, perhaps from L. *picta*, *pincta*, painted or marked, like the measuring vessel.)
pin-table, *n.* a board studded with pins among which balls are rolled in a game, usually for small stakes.
pintado, *n.* pin-*tah*-do, the guinea-fowl. **pintado bird,** the Cape pigeon. (Sp.)
pintail, *n. pin*-tale, the sea-duck *Dafila actua*; a variety of grouse distinguished by its pointed tail.
pintle, *n. pin*-tl, a vertical projecting pin; a bolt serving as a pivot; the pin on which the rudder turns [Naut.]; (formerly) the penis. (*pin.*)
piny, *a. py*-ne, piny; characteristic of pine-trees.
piolet, *n. pee*-o-lay, an ice-axe used by mountaineers; also, a skier's spiked staff. (Fr.)
pioneer, *n. py*-o-*neer*, a soldier whose business is to go before an army to clear obstructions [Mil.]; one who goes before to prepare the way; an explorer; a member of a Pioneer Corps: *v.t.* to act as pioneer to. **Pioneer Corps,** a combatant military body with special duties of road repair, demolition, etc. (Fr. *pionnier.*)
pioupiou, *n. pyoo*-pyoo, a French infantryman [Slang]. (Fr.)
pious, *a. py*-us, devout; showing or proceeding from piety; having due respect and affection for parents and relatives; reverential; devout. **pious fraud,** cozenry under the cloak of charity or religion. (L. *pius.*)
piously, *ad.* in a pious manner.
piousness, *n.* state or quality of being pious.
pip, *n.* pip, a disease of fowls in which a horny scale develops on the tongue; a fit of depression. (**O.Fr.** *pepie.*)
pip, *n.* pip, the seed of an apple, orange, or other fruit. (O.Fr. *pepin*, a pip.)
pip, *n.* pip, a suit-mark on a playing card; a star denoting army commissioned rank (3 for captain, 2 for lieutenant, 1 for 2nd lieutenant) [Mil.].
pip, *n.* pip, military signallers' code-name for the letter P. **pip-emma** (pip-*em*-ma), p.m., post meridian; afternoon [Slang].
pip, *v.i.* pip, to cry or cheep (from the sound); to beat or defeat; to blackball.
pipal, *n. pee*-pal, the bo-tree, or sacred fig, of India.
★**pipe,** *n.* pipe, a musical wind instrument; a boatswain's whistle; a long tube; a pipe-line; a tubular organ or vessel [Anat.]; a tube with a bowl at the end for smoking, also, a fill of tobacco for this; the sound of the voice; the small or shrill cry of a bird; a cask of about 105 imperial gallons; a pipe-roll, also (*cap.*) the Pipe-Office: *pl.* the bagpipe; the Pandean pipes: *v.i.* to play on a pipe; to whistle: *v.t.* to play on a pipe; to utter sharply; to call with a boatswain's whistle [Naut.]. **to pipe down,** to cease talking or singing [Slang]. **to pipe the eye,** to weep [Slang]. **to pipe up,** to start talking, singing, etc.; to increase the volume of vocal sound [Slang]. (A.S.)
pipeclay, *n. pipe*-klay, a fine, white, plastic clay used in making tobacco pipes and for whitening leather: *v.t.* to whiten with this.
pipefish, *n. pipe*-fish, a fish of the sea-horse family, so called from its long, slender body.
pipe-light, *n.* anything to light tobacco with.
pipe-line, *n.* a line of pipes, with pumps and other equipment, for conveying oil, etc; any channel of distribution [Fig.].
pipe-major, *n.* the leading player in a band of bagpipe performers.
Pipe-Office, *n.* a former department of the Exchequer (abolished 1832) dealing with the accounts of sheriffs and certain other officers.
piper, *n. pipe*-er, one who plays on a pipe or the bagpipes, esp. as a vagrant; the gurnard, or other fish, which whistles when caught. **pay the piper,** *see* pay.
piperic, *a.* pe-*pe*-rik, pertaining to or obtained from pepper. (L. *piper*, pepper.)
piperidge, *n. pip*-er-ridj, the pipperidge or barberry.
piperine, *n. pip*-er-rin, a crystalline alkaloid extracted from black pepper.
pipe-roll, *n.* the Great Roll of the Exchequer containing the accounts of the sheriffs, etc., formerly drawn up in and kept by the Pipe-Office.
pipestone, *n. pipe*-stone, a variety of clay slate used by the American Indians for pipe-bowls.
pipette, *n.* pe-*pet*, a glass tube for transferring liquids in small quantities. (Fr.)
pipewort, *n. pipe*-wurt, water-pepper, or any marsh-plant of the genus *Eriocaulon.*
piping, *a. py*-ping, weak; shrill; boiling: *n.* a dress embellishment formed by sewing the material over a cord so as to enclose it in a sort of tube.
piping-crow, *n.* an Australian bird of the genus *Gymnorrhina.*
pipistrelle, *n.* pip-e-*strel*, the commonest of the British bats, *Vesperugo pipistrellus.*
pipit, *n. pip*-it, a passerine bird of the genus *Anthus*, resembling the larks. (From its cry.)
pipkin, *n. pip*-kin, an earthen pot with a lid.
pipperidge, *n. pip*-er-ridj, the barberry.
pippin, *n. pip*-pin, a variety of apple, esp. one grown from seed, not from a graft. (O.Fr. *pepin.*)
pipy, *a. py*-pe, tubular; shrill.
piquancy, *n. pee*-kan-se, the quality of being piquant; sharpness; pungency.
piquant, *a. pee*-kant, stimulating to the taste; sharp; pungent; lively; smart. (Fr., pricking.)
piquantly, *ad.* in a piquant manner.
pique, *n.* peek, slight anger; resentment or irritation from wounded feelings: *v.t.* to offend or irritate; to stimulate; to pride or value oneself. (Fr. *piquer*, to prick.)
pique, *n.* peek, the score of 30 points (gaining 30 additional) made in piquet before the opponent has scored: *v.t.* and *i.* to score this. (Fr. *pic.*)
piqué, *n. pee*-kay, a cotton material patterned in the weaving. (Fr.)
piquet, *n.* pi-*ket*, a two-handed card-game played with a pack of 32 cards (8 to ace). (Fr.)

piracy, *n.* *pyr*-ra-se, the act or crime of robbing on the high seas ; an infringement of copyright.
piragua, *n.* pe-*rag*-wah, a pirogue. (Sp.)
pirate, *n.* *pyr*-rat, a robber on the high seas ; a ship engaged in piracy ; one who infringes any right, esp. the law of copyright : *v.i.* to rob on the high seas : *v.t.* to take by theft or without lawful authority. (Fr.)
piratical, *a.* py-*rat*-e-kal, pertaining to piracy; addicted to piracy ; practising literary theft.
piratically, *ad.* in a piratical manner.
pirn, *n.* pern, a bobbin ; the length of thread taken by a bobbin, spool, or reel.
pirogue, *n.* pi-*rohg*, a canoe formed out of the trunk of a tree ; a dugout ; a two-masted, flat-bottomed boat. (Fr.)
pirouette, *n.* pi-roo-*et*, a whirling on the toes in the same spot ; a similar whirling round of a horse : *v.i.* to perform a pirouette. (Fr.)
pisang, *n.* *pee*-sang, the tropical plantain *Musa paradisiaca*, allied to the banana. (Malay.)
piscary, *n.* *pis*-ka-re, the right of fishing in another man's waters [Law]. (L. *piscis*, a fish.)
piscator, *n.* pis-*kay*-tor, an angler.
piscatorial, *a.* *pis*-ka-*taw*-re-al, relating to anglers, angling, or fishing.
piscatory, *a.* *pis*-ka-to-re, piscatorial.
Pisces, *n.pl.* *pis*-eez, the twelfth sign of the Zodiac, the Fishes. (L.)
piscicultural, *a.* pis-e-*kul*-tewr-ral, pertaining to pisciculture.
pisciculture, *n.* pis-e-*kul*-tewr, the artificial breeding and rearing of fish. (L. *piscis*, and *culture*.)
pisciculturist, *n.* *pis*-e-*kul*-tewr-rist, one engaged in, or expert in, the breeding of fish.
piscina, *n.* pe-*sy*-na, a fish-pond ; a basin near the altar into which the priest empties the water used in ceremonial ablutions [Eccles.]. (L., fish-pond.)
piscine, *a.* *pis*-een, pertaining to fish.
piscivorous, *a.* pi-*siv*-o-rus, living or feeding on fish. (L. *piscis*, and *voro*, devour.)
pisé, *n.* *pee*-zay, stiff earth or clay rammed between boards to make walls. (Fr.)
pish, *int.* pish, an expression of disgust, contempt, etc. : *v.i.* to exclaim " pish ! "
pishogue, *n.* pi-*shohg*, witchcraft ; sorcery ; a spell [Irish].
pisiform, *a.* *py*-se-form, pea-shaped. (L. *pisum*, a pea.)
pismire, *n.* *piz*-mire, an ant. (*piss* and *mire*.)
pisolite, *n.* *py*-so-lite, a calcareous stone formed in pea-like concretions. (L. *pisum*, and Gr. *lithos*, a stone.)
pisolitic, *a.* *py*-so-*lit*-ik, of the nature of pisolite.
piss, *n.* pis, urine : *v.i.* to discharge urine : *v.t.* to wet with urine [Vulg.]. (O.F. *pissier*.)
pissasphalt, *n.* *pis*-as-falt, a variety of bitumen of a semi-liquid consistency. (Gr. *pissa*, turpentine, and *asphalt*.)
pistachio, *n.* pis-*tah*-she-o, the nut of *Pistacia vera*, a small tree of the Near East ; the tree itself ; the flavour of the nut. (Sp.)
pistacite, *n.* *pis*-ta-site, epidote. (Named from its resemblance in colour to the *pistachio*.)
pistareen, *n.* *pis*-ta-reen, a former Spanish silver coin worth about 9*d.* : *a.* practically worthless. (Sp.)
piste, *n.* peest, the spoor or trail of an animal ; a race-course or racing track. (Fr.)
pistil, *n.* *pis*-til, the female or seed-bearing part of the flower, comprising the ovary, stigma, and style [Bot.]. (L. *pistillum*, a pestle.)
pistillar, *a.* *pis*-te-lar, shaped like a club [Bot.].
pistillary, *a.* pis-*til*-a-re, growing on the pistil ; of the nature of a pistil [Bot.].
pistillate, *a.* *pis*-til-at, having a pistil ; pistillary.
pistillidium, *n.* pis-te-*lid*-e-um, an archegonium [Bot.].
pistilliferous, *a.* pis-te-*lif*-er-rus, pistillate.
pistol, *n.* *pis*-tol, a small fire-arm or hand-gun : *v.t.* to shoot with this. (Fr. *pistole*, of disputed origin.)
pistole, *n.* pis-*tole*, a former gold coin of Spain and other countries, worth about 16*s.* (Fr.)
pistoleer, *n.* pis-to-*leer*, one armed with, or one skilled in the use of, a pistol.
pistolet, *n.* *pis*-to-let, former term for a pistol, and for a pistole.
piston, *n.* *pis*-ton, a solid disk fitting into a hollow cylinder, and working up and down in it ; a valve in a wind-instrument [Mus.]. **piston ring,** a loose ring on a piston to give gas-tightness. **piston rod,** the rod attaching the piston to its activating machinery. (Fr.)
pit, *n.* pit, a deep hole in the earth, natural or artificial ; a mine ; a quarry ; a trap for wild animals ; an abyss ; the grave ; hell ; the area used for cock-fighting ; the ground-floor of the auditorium of a theatre, also its occupants ; a hollow ; the hollow under the shoulder ; a small scar caused by small-pox ; part of an exchange in which dealings in a specified commodity are transacted [Comm.] ; a noisy round-game at cards : *v.t.* to put into a pit ; to press into or mark with hollows ; to set in competition. (A.S. *pyt*.)
pitapat, *ad.* *pit*-a-pat, in a flutter : *n.* a light, quick step. (*pat*.)
pitch, *n.* pich, a viscous black substance obtained by boiling down tar or distilling turpentine, petroleum, etc. : *v.t.* to smear or soil with or as with pitch. (A.S. *pic*.)
pitch, *n.* pich, the act or manner of pitching ; any point or degree of elevation ; highest rise ; stature ; degree ; intensity ; rate ; amount or degree of steepness or slope ; space between and about wickets at cricket ; site or station, as of a street salesman ; degree of highness or lowness of a tone [Mus.] ; the length of a complete turn of a screw measured along its axis [Mech.] ; the distance between the centres of two teeth in a saw or two teeth in a wheel : *v.t.* to throw, hurl, or fling, esp. at a point or object ; to fix ; to plant ; to bowl ; to throw headlong ; to throw (as hay) with a fork ; to set the key-note [Mus.] : *v.i.* to settle ; to fall headlong ; to plunge ; to fall ; to encamp ; to rise and fall, as the head and stern of a ship or the nose and tail of aircraft. **pitch-and-toss,** the game of pitching coins at a mark, player throwing nearest tossing them and taking all falling heads up. **pitch into,** to attack ; to assail. **pitch upon,** to choose ; to pick out. **pitched battle,** one for which the contestants have made full preparations. **to queer the pitch,** to upset the plans. (Origin uncertain.)
pitch-black, *a.* brownish-black ; as black as pitch.
pitchblende, *n.* *pich*-blend, uraninite, the earliest source of radium.
pitcher, *n.* *pich*-er, a large earthen jug with ears ; a ewer. (O.Fr. *picher*.)
pitcher, *n.* *pich*-er, one who or that which pitches ; that which is pitched ; a feeder at baseball ; the occupant (esp. as street vendor) of a pitch ; a tool for making holes in the ground for stakes ; a small stone paving block.
pitcher-plant, *n.* any of various insectivorous plants with pitcher-shaped leaves.
pitch-farthing, *n.* the game of chuck-farthing.
pitchfork, *n.* *pich*-fork, a long-handled fork used in lifting and pitching hay or sheaves of grain : *v.t.* to throw with or as with a pitchfork ; to place hurriedly or without preparation.
pitchiness, *n.* *pich*-e-ness, state or quality of being pitchy ; darkness.
pitchometer, *n.* pich-*om*-e-ter, an instrument for measuring the pitch of a propeller [Mech.].
pitch-pine, *n.* *pich*-pine, any highly resinous pine, as the Norway spruce, *Picea excelsa*, the American *Pinus palustris*.
pitch-pipe, *n.* a tuning pipe for giving the note in singing or for instruments [Mus.].
pitchstone, *n.* *pich*-stone, obsidian having a resinous lustre, a volcanic rock resembling indurated pitch.
pitchy, *a.* *pich*-e, partaking of the qualities of pitch ; black ; dark.
pit-coal, *n.* mineral coal as opposed to charcoal.
piteous, *a.* *pit*-e-us, that may excite pity ; deserving compassion ; wretched ; lamentable ; paltry. (O.Fr.)
piteously, *ad.* in a piteous manner ; sorrowfully.
piteousness, *n.* the state of being piteous.
pitfall, *n.* *pit*-fawl, a slightly covered pit for use as a trap ; a snare ; an unseen danger.
pith, *n.* pith, the soft, spongy substance in the centre of plant-stems ; the marrow of animals ; the medulla of hairs ; strength or force ; energy ; cogency ; essential part ; weight ; importance : *v.t.* to sever the spinal cord of. (A.S. *pitha*.)
pithead, *n.* *pit*-hed, the surface entry to a mine with the buildings, etc. immediately surrounding it.
pithecanthrope, *n.* *pith*-e-*kan*-throhp, an extinct

primate, remains of which were discovered in Java (1891), forming a hypothetical link between the apes and man. (Gr. *pithekos*, ape, *anthropos*, man.)
pithecoid, *a.* *pith*-e-koyd, ape-like.
pithily, *ad.* *pith*-e-le, in a pithy manner.
pithiness, *n.* quality of being pithy; concentrated force.
pithless, *a.* *pith*-less, destitute of pith; wanting strength or vigour.
pithy, *a.* *pith*-e, containing or abounding with pith; concise; sententious; forcible; energetic.
pitiable, *a.* *pit*-e-a-bl, deserving pity; miserable; rueful.
pitiableness, *n.* state of being pitiable.
pitiably, *ad.* *pit*-e-a-ble, in a pitiable manner.
pitiful, *a.* *pit*-e-ful, full of pity; compassionate; miserable.
pitifully, *ad.* in a pitiful manner.
pitifulness, *n.* the quality of being pitiful.
pitiless, *a.* feeling no pity; merciless; hard-hearted.
pitilessly, *ad.* in a pitiless manner.
pitilessness, *n.* the quality of being pitiless.
pitman, *n.* *pit*-man, one who works in a pit.
pitpan, *n.* *pit*-pan, a long, flat-bottomed dug-out canoe used in Central America. (Native word.)
pitprop, *n.* *pit*-prop, a strong wooden beam used for supporting temporarily the roof in colliery workings.
pit-saw, *n.* *pit*-saw, a long saw worked by the top-sawyer above and **pit-sawyer** in the pit below.
pittacal, *n.* *pit*-a-kal, a carbohydrate obtained from wood-tar, used as a blue dye-stuff. (Gr. *pitta*, pitch, *kalos*, beautiful.)
pittance, *n.* *pit*-ance, a small dole or allowance; a small portion. (Fr. *pitance*.)
pitted, *a.* *pit*-ed, marked with little hollows.
pitter-patter, *n.* *pit*-er-*pat*-er, a rapid pulsation; the rhythmical sound of light successive taps: *ad.* with such a sound: *v.t.* and *i.* to sound, go, or beat etc., with a pitter-patter. (Imit.)
pitticite, *n.* *pit*-e-site, a hydrous arsenic sulphate of iron [Min.].
pittite, *n.* *pit*-ite, a frequenter of the pit in theatres.
pituitary, *a.* pi-*tew*-e-ta-re, containing or secreting mucus. **pituitary gland** or **body,** a ductless gland situated at the base of the brain and considered to affect the growth of the body. (L. *pituita*, mucus.)
pituite, *n.* *pit*-yew-ite, mucus; frothy sputum [Med.].
pituitous, *a.* pi-*tew*-e-tus, consisting of, discharging, or due to mucus.
pit-viper, *n.* any member of the *Crotalidæ*, a family of venomous snakes (mainly of America), characterized by a small hollow between eye and nostril.
pity, *n.* *pit*-e, sympathy with distress; compassion; subject of pity; matter of regret: *v.t.* to have sympathy for; to commiserate: *v.i.* to be compassionate. (O.Fr. *pitet*.)
pityingly, *ad.* *pit*-e-ing-le, compassionately.
pityriasis, *n.* pit-e-*ry*-a-sis, a chronic squamous inflammation of the skin. (Gr. *pityron*, bran.)
pityroid, *a.* *pit*-e-royd, resembling bran. (Gr. *pityron*, bran, *eidos*, like.)
più, *ad.* pew, more [Mus.]. (It.)
pivot, *n.* *piv*-ot, a point on which anything turns; the soldier at the flank upon whom a company wheels; a centre half-back [Football]: *v.i.* to turn on a pivot. (Fr.)
pivotal, *a.* *piv*-ot-al, pertaining to a pivot; of prime importance.
pix, *n.* piks, pyx.
pixy, *n.* *piks*-e, a fairy. (Origin unknown.)
pizzicato, *ad.* *pits*-e-*kah*-toh, played by plucking with the finger-tips (of violins, etc.). (It., pinched.)
pizzle, *n.* *piz*-l, the penis of an animal, esp. a bull.
placability, *n.* plak-a-*bil*-e-te, placableness.
placable, *a.* *plak*-a-bl, that may be appeased; willing to forgive. (L. *placabilis*, appeasable.)
placableness, *n.* quality of being appeasable.
placard, *n.* *plak*-ard, a written or printed paper containing a notice or advertisement displayed publicly; a newspaper contents bill; a poster: *v.t.* to place placards on; to notify by placard. (Fr.)
placate, *v.t.* pla-*kate*, to appease; to pacify. (L. *placatus*, pleased.)
★**place,** *n.* place, any portion of space; position in a series, etc.; locality; residence; town; an open space in a town; passage of a writing or book; rank; official station; room; station in life; sphere, or province; occupation; condition; the position of any of the first three horses in a race: *v.t.* to put or set in a particular place; to locate; to assign a position to; to identify; to obtain an appointment, etc., for one; to fix; to invest; to put out at interest; to lend; to score a goal from a place-kick. **give place,** to give room; to give way. **take place,** to happen. (Fr.)
placebo, *n.* pla-*see*-bo, the vespers in the office for the dead [Rom. Cath. Church]; an inert drug given merely to satisfy a patient [Med.]. (L., he, or it, will please—the opening words of the antiphon.)
place-hunter, *n.* one who seeks a situation under government or public body.
place-kick, *n.* a kick at goal from a placed ball [Rugby Football].
placeman, *n.* *place*-man, a holder of any office under government, esp. of one obtained by influence.
placement, *n.* *place*-ment, the act of placing, esp. in employment or in accordance with qualifications.
place-name, *n.* the name of a geographical place.
placenta, *n.* pla-*sen*-ta, the organ by means of which a fœtus obtains air and nourishment [Zool. and Anat.]; the afterbirth; the part of the ovary to which the ovules are attached [Bot.]. (L., a flat cake.)
placental, *a.* pla-*sen*-tal, pertaining to or characterized by the placenta: *n.* any of the Placentalia.
Placentalia, *n.pl.* plas-en-*tay*-le-a, the division of placental mammals, *i.e.* all except the marsupials and monotremes.
placentation, *n.* plas-en-*tay*-shon, the arrangement or mode of attachment of the placenta in plants and animals.
placentiform, *a.* pla-*sen*-te-form, shaped like a placenta; resembling a flat cake [Bot.].
placentitis, *n.* plas-en-*ty*-tis, inflammation of the placenta. (L. *placenta*.)
placer, *n.* *play*-ser, one who places or locates.
placer, *n.* *play*-ser, a site on which gold is washed from the deposited gravel; an alluvial or glacial deposit of gravel containing gold or other valuable mineral. (Sp., a shoal.)
placet, *n.* *plas*-et, an affirmative vote given on a motion. **non placet,** a negative vote. (L., it pleases.)
placid, *a.* *plas*-id, gentle; quiet; serene; calm; unruffled. (Fr. *placide*.)
placidity, *n.* pla-*sid*-e-te, calmness; content.
placidly, *ad.* *plas*-id-le, in a placid manner.
placidness, *n.* the state of being placid.
plack, *n.* plak, an old Scottish copper farthing. **not worth a plack,** worthless.
placket, *n.* *plak*-et, the slit where a skirt or petticoat is fastened; a woman's pocket. (Origin uncertain.)
placoderm, *n.* *plak*-o-derm, any placoid fish: *a.* with the cell wall consisting of more than one piece; as some algæ [Bot.].
placoid, *a.* *plak*-oyd, plate-shaped [Zool.]; having the skin covered with plate-like scales, as in the elasmobranchs. [Ichth.]. (Gr. *plax*, a plate, *eidos*, like.)
plafond, *n.* pla-*fond* the ceiling of a room; any soffit [Arch.]; a variety of contract bridge. (Fr.)
plagal, *a.* *play*-gal, having the principal notes between the fifth of the key and its octave (in Gregorian modes) [Mus.]. (Gr. *plagios*, oblique.)
plagate, *a.* *play*-gat, having stripes or streaks of colour [Zool.]. (L. *plaga*, a stripe.)
plage, *n.* plahzh, a beach, esp. at a fashionable seaside resort. (Fr.)
plagiarism, *n.* *play*-je-a-rizm, the act of plagiarizing; matter plagiarized.
plagiarist, *n.* *play*-je-a-rist, one who habitually plagiarizes.
plagiarize, *v.t.* *play*-je-a-rize, to purloin from, or surreptitiously pass off as one's own, the writings of another. (L. *plagiare*, to kidnap.)
plagiary, *n.* *play*-je-a-re, a plagiarist; literary theft.
plagiocephalic, *a.* *play*-je-o-se-*fal*-ik, having a skull unequally developed on either side. (Gr. *plagios*, oblique, and *cephalic*.)
plagioclase, *n.* *play*-je-o-klase, any triclinic felspar having an oblique cleavage. (Gr. *plagios*, oblique, *klasis*, fracture.)
plagionite, *n.* *play*-je-o-nite, a blackish crystalline sulphide of lead and antimony [Min.].

plagiostome, *n.* *play*-je-o-stome, any plagiostomous fish.
plagiostomous, *a.* *play*-je-*os*-to-mus, pertaining to that order of fishes which includes the sharks and rays. (Gr. *plagios*, oblique, *stoma*, mouth.)
plague, *n.* playg, anything troublesome or vexatious; any virulently contagious disease, esp. one of a bubonic or pulmonary order; a state of misery; any great natural evil: *v.t.* to infest with calamity or any natural evil; to afflict with the plague; to vex; to tease; to trouble. **plague spot,** a pit or mark on the skin caused by plague; an infected or polluted place or locality. (O.Fr.)
plaguesome, *a.* *playg*-sum, plaguy; pestilential [Coll.].
plaguily, *ad.* *play*-ge-le, in a plaguy manner.
plaguy, *a.* *play*-ge, vexatious; troublesome.
plaice, *n.* place, the edible flat-fish, *Pleuronectes platessa*, allied to the flounder. (O.Fr. *plaiz.*)
plaid, *n.* plad *or* (Scot.) plade, a woollen garment, generally of a checked fabric, to wrap round the body; a maud; a fabric of tartan or similar pattern. (Gael.)
plaided, *a.* *plad*-ed, wearing a plaid.
plain, *a.* plane, smooth; level; open; void of ornament; ugly; ordinary; artless; simple; unaffected; undisguised; sincere; clear; easily seen or discovered; not difficult; not rich or highly seasoned; uncoloured: *ad.* plainly: *n.* level land or open field. **plain chant,** plainsong. **plain clothes,** mufti. **plain sailing,** free from difficulty (cf. *plane sailing*). **plain suit,** any suit other than that of trumps [Cards]. **plain work,** plain needlework. (O.Fr. from L. *planus*, flat.)
plain-dealing, *a.* dealing or communicating with frankness and sincerity; honest; *n.* sincerity of speech or action.
plainly, *ad.* *plane*-le, in a plain manner; not obscurely; artlessly.
plainness, *n.* *plane*-ness, the quality of being plain.
plainsman, *n.* *playnz*-man, a man who lives on the plains.
plainsong, *n.* *plane*-song, Gregorian chant; a mediæval ecclesiastical mode in which the melody is accentual and non-rhythmical [Mus.].
plain-spoken, *a.* speaking with frank sincerity or without reserve; downright.
plaint, *n.* playnt, lamentation; a sad song; an accusation or complaint [Law]. (O.Fr. *pleinte.*)
plaintiff, *n.* *playn*-tif, the prosecutor, or person who sees another [Law]. (Fr.)
plaintive, *a.* *playn*-tiv, expressive of sorrow or sadness.
plaintively, *ad.* in a plaintive manner.
plaintiveness, *n.* quality of being plaintive.
plaintless, *a.* *playnt*-less, without complaint.
plaister, *n.* *plah*-ster *or* *plas*-ter, a plaster [Med.].
plait, *n.* plat, a fold; a pleat; a braid, as of hair, straw, or string: *v.t.* to fold; to pleat; to braid; to interlace three or more strands. (O.Fr. *pleit.*)
plaiter, *n.* *plat*-er, one who or that which plaits.
plan, *n.* plan, a draught or delineation on a plane surface and in horizontal section of a building, machine, etc., or any projected work; a scheme devised; method: *v.t.* to form a draught of any intended work; to scheme or devise; to work according to a drawing or design: *ppr.* **planning.** *pp.* **planned.** (Fr.)
planar, *a.* *play*-nar, pertaining to a plane.
planarian, *a.* pla-*nare*-re-an, belonging to the genus *Planaria*: *n.* a flat-worm. (L. *planarius*, flat.)
planched, *a.* planchd, covered with planks or boards; boarded.
planchet, *n.* *plan*-chet, a flat piece of metal for a coin; a blank.
planchette, *n.* plan-*shet*, a small thin heart-shaped piece of board mounted on two casters and a pencil, used at seances, etc., as a means of receiving communications from disembodied spirits. (Fr.)
★**plane,** *a.* plane, without elevations or depressions; even; flat: *n.* an even or level surface; a stage or level of development, etc.; a sphere of existence; one of the faces of a crystal; one of the wings or supporting surfaces of an aeroplane; an aeroplane [Coll.]: *v.i.* to travel in an aeroplane [Coll.]; to soar on or as on wings. **plane chart,** a chart constructed on the supposition of the earth and sea being an extended plane. **plane geometry,** the geometry of figures on a plane surface. **plane sailing,** the art of determining the ship's place on the supposition that she is moving on a plane; plain sailing. **plane table,** surveying instrument or board marked off into degrees from the centre. (Fr.)
plane, *n.* plane, a tool used in smoothing: *v.t.* to make smooth.
plane, *n.* plane, any tree of the genus *Platanus.*
plane-iron, *n.* the steel cutter of a plane.
planer, *n.* *plane*-er, a tool, esp. a machine-tool, to smooth or plane; one who planes.
planet, *n.* *plan*-et, any celestial body other than a comet or meteor which revolves in an orbit around the sun. **minor planet,** any of the many asteroids between the orbits of Mars and Jupiter. (O.Fr. from L. *planeta*, wandering.)
planetarium, *n.* plan-e-*tare*-re-um, an astronomical machine which represents the motions of the planets; a hall or building for such; an orrery.
planetary, *a.* *plan*-e-ta-re, pertaining to, consisting of, or produced by planets; erratic or wandering; pertaining to an epicyclic train of gear-wheels [Mech.]; having planet-like motion.
planetesimal, *n.* plan-e-*tes*-e-mal, one of countless supposititious meteorite-like bodies revolving round a gaseous nucleus, an aggregation of which formed each of the planets: *a.* pertaining to this theory.
planetoid, *n.* *plan*-e-toyd, an asteroid or minor planet.
plangency, *n.* *plan*-jen-se, the state or quality of being plangent.
plangent, *a.* *plan*-jent, beating with noise, as of a wave. (L. *plangens*, striking.)
planigraph, *n.* *plan*-e-graf, a pivoted drawing instrument used for enlarging and reducing plans, etc.
planimeter, *n.* pla-*nim*-e-ter, an instrument to measure the area of an irregular plane figure. (Gr. *planetes*, wanderer, *metron*, measure.)
planimetrical, *a.* plan-e-*met*-re-kal, pertaining to planimetry.
planimetry, *n.* pla-*nim*-e-tre, the mensuration of plane surfaces.
planipennate, *a.* plan-e-*pen*-at, having broad flat wings [Zool.].
planipetalous, *a.* plan-e-*pet*-a-lus, having flat petals.
planish, *v.t.* *plan*-ish, to polish; to smooth by rolling or hammering.
planisher, *n.* *plan*-ish-er, one who planishes; a tool or machine for planishing.
planisphere, *n.* *plan*-is-feer, a sphere projected on a plane; an adjustable polar projection of the celestial sphere. (L. *planus*, flat, and *sphere.*)
plank, *n.* plank, a broad piece of sawn timber from an inch and a half to four inches thick; a major principle of a political party [Fig.]: *v.t.* to cover or lay with planks; to lay down (esp. money) on or as on a table. (O.Fr.)
plank-bed, *n.* a bed of boards with no mattress, as used in prisons.
planking, *n.* *plang*-king, planks collectively.
planktology, *n.* plank-*tol*-o-je, the scientific study of plankton.
plankton, *n.pl.* *plank*-ton, the minute organisms drifting on or near the surface of seas and rivers. (Gr. *planktos*, roving.)
planless, *a.* *plan*-less, having no plan.
planner, *n.* *plan*-ner, one who forms a plan; a projector; one engaged in town- or country-planning.
planning, *n.* *plan*-ing, the act of one who plans; economical management; the laying-out of towns or the countryside.
plano-, *play*-noh, a prefix to many terms in the arts, signifying plane and, as **plano-concave,** flat on one side and concave on the other; **plano-conical,** one side level the other conical; **plano-convex,** one side flat the other convex; **plano-horizontal,** having a level, horizontal surface or position; **plano-subulate,** smooth and awl-shaped. (L. *planus*, level, flat.)
planography, *n.* pla-*nog*-ra-fe, the art of drawing plans or maps.
planometer, *n.* pla-*nom*-e-ter, a surface plate for gauging a plane surface.
★**plant,** *n.* plahnt, a vegetable organism; a sapling; the fixtures, machinery, tools, etc., necessary to carry on any business; a swindle; a put-up job [Slang]: *v.t.* to set or put in the ground for growth; to furnish with plants; to set firmly; to fix; to

settle; to direct and deliver (a blow); to deposit or conceal, esp. with intent to deceive [Slang]: *v.i.* to perform the act of planting. (A.S. *plante.*)
plantable, *a. plahn*-ta-bl, capable of being planted or of receiving and developing plants from seed.
Plantagenet, *n.* plan-*taj*-e-net, any Angevin king (or member of this family) reigning in England 1154–1399, viz., from Henry II to Richard II. (L. *planta genistæ*, sprig of broom, the emblem of Geoffrey, Count of Anjou.)
plantain, *n. plan*-tan, any plant of the genus *Plantago*, esp. the common weed, *P. major*, with broad acaulescent leaves. (O.Fr., from L. *planta*, sole of the foot.)
plantain, *n. plan*-tan, the tropical plant *Musa paradisiaca*; its fruit, the cooking banana, used as food. **plantain eater,** the touraco, or other bird of the family Musophagidæ. (Sp. *plantano*, from L. *platanus*, plane-tree.)
plantar, *a. plan*-tar, pertaining to the sole of the foot. (L. *planta*, the sole of the foot.)
plantation, *n.* plan-*tay*-shon, the act of planting; the place planted; a group of planted trees; a large estate, esp. one cultivated by slaves; a new settlement; a colony. (L. *plantatio.*)
plant-cane, *n.* sugar cane of the first year's growth.
planter, *n. plahn*-ter, one who plants; one who owns a plantation; a settler; one who founds.
plantership, *n. plahn*-ter-ship, the business of a planter; the management of a plantation.
plantigrade, *a. plan*-te-grade, walking on the sole of the foot: *n.* any plantigrade mammal, as the bear. (L. *planta*, sole, *gradus*, step.)
planting, *n. plahn*-ting, the act of setting in the ground for propagation; the forming of plantations; a plantation.
plantlet, *n. plahnt*-let, a little plant.
plant-louse, *n.* an aphis infesting plants.
planxty, *n. planks*-te, a jig-like Irish or Welsh melody played on the harp. (Origin unknown.)
plaque, *n.* plak, a decorative or commemorative plate of metal, pottery, ivory, etc., for affixing to a wall, door, or furniture, etc.; a small four-sided medallion or dress ornament. (Fr.)
plaquette, *n.* pla-*ket*, a small plaque; a small area of eruption [Path.]; a colourless disk occurring in mammalian blood [Anat.].
plash, *n.* plash, a puddle; a splash: *v.t.* to dabble in water; to sprinkle with colour; to splash. (Imit.)
plash, *n.* plash, a branch partly lopped and interwoven with others: *v.t.* to pleach. (O.Fr. *plessier.*)
plashy, *a. plash*-e, abounding with puddles; splashed with or as with colour.
plasm, *n.* plazm, plasma; the living matter of a cell. (Gr. *plasma*, from *plassein*, mould.)
plasma, *n. plaz*-ma, a green variety of chalcedony; elementary matter, specially that out of which organized tissues develop; the fluid in which the solid matter of the blood floats. (Gr., something formed.)
plasmatic, *a.* plaz-*mat*-ik, plasmic.
plasmic, *a. plaz*-mik, pertaining to plasma; protoplasmic.
plasmin, *n. plaz*-min, a protein present in the plasma of the blood.
plasmocyte, *n. plaz*-mo-site, a leucocyte.
plasmodium, *n.* plaz-*moh*-de-um, a mass of mobile protoplasm formed by the aggregation of single-celled organisms. (Gr. *plasma.*)
plasmogen, *n. plaz*-mo-jen, formative or essential protoplasm; bioplasm. (Gr. *plasma*, and *gennao*, produce.)
plasmogeny, *n.* plaz-*moj*-e-ne, autogeny; the theoretical development of plasm from inorganic matter.
plasmogony, *n.* plaz-*mog*-o-ne, plasmogeny.
plasmology, *n.* plaz-*mol*-o-je, the branch of biology dealing with the ultimate corpuscles of living matter.
plasmolyse, *v.t. plaz*-mo-lize, to subject to plasmolysis.
plasmolysis, *n.* plaz-*mol*-e-sis, the act or process of cell shrinkage due to removal of water by exosmosis [Bot.].
plasmosome, *n. plaz*-mo-sohm, a nucleolus.
plaster, *n. plahs*-ter, a composition of lime, water, and sand, for coating walls; calcined gypsum, or other material, for casts; an irritant or other medicinal preparation for spreading on linen, etc., and applying to the body; sticking-plaster [Med.]: *v.t.* to overlay walls with plaster; to cover a wound with a plaster. **plaster of Paris,** a composition of gypsum, used in casting busts, etc., and as a cement. **plaster stone,** gypsum. (A.S.)
plasterer, *n. plah*-ster-rer, one who overlays with plaster; one who makes figures in plaster.
plastering, *n. plah*-ster-ring, act of overlaying with plaster; a covering of plaster.
plastic, *a. plas*-tik, giving form; capable of being moulded; formative, esp. by modelling in the round, as distinct from graphic or delineative; able to form living tissue; supple; impressionable: *n.* a substance, esp. a synthetic product, that is plastic under certain conditions: *n.pl.* plastic surgery. **plastic surgery,** restoration of lost, damaged, or deformed parts by tissue transference. (Gr. *plastikos.*)
plastically, *ad. plas*-te-ka-le, in a plastic manner; according to plastic art or to plastics.
plasticine, *n. plas*-te-seen, a registered trade-name for a proprietary modelling material.
plasticity, *n.* plas-*tis*-e-te, the state or quality of being plastic. (Fr. *plasticité.*)
plasticize, *v.t. plas*-te-size, to render plastic.
plasticizer, *n. plas*-te-sy-zer, any non-evaporating agent added to lacquers, etc., to preserve their adhesiveness and flexibility.
plastid, *n. plas*-tid, a cell or protoplasmic unit [Biol. and Bot.]
plastin, *n. plas*-tin, a viscous substance present in the nuclei of cells [Biol.].
plastral, *a. plas*-tral, pertaining to a plastron [Zool.].
plastron, *n. plas*-tron, a breastplate, esp. one of padded leather worn by fencers; the ventral portion of the bony case of the chelonians [Zool.]; an ornamental trimming on the front of a woman's dress; a starched shirt-front. (Fr., a breastplate.)
plat, *n.* and *v.t.* plat, plait.
plat, *n.* plat, a small plot of ground; a flower-bed: *v.t.* to make a plan of; to lay out in plots. (*plot.*)
platan, *n. plat*-an, the common plane-tree, *Platanus orientalis.* (L. *platanus.*)
platband, *n. plat*-band, a border of flowers; a border; a flat square moulding; the lintel of a door or window; a fillet between the flutings of a column [Arch.].
★**plate,** *n.* plate, a flat piece of wrought metal, glass, or crockery; a shallow vessel for eating from, also its contents; household utensils of gold and silver; articles coated with gold or silver; a race for a piece of plate; a solid page of metal to print from; a flat piece of engraved copper, steel, or zinc, also a print taken from such plate; a sheet of glass, etc., on which a negative is obtained [Phot.]; a cylinder of nickel forming the anode of a thermionic valve [Wire.]: *v.t.* to overlay with metal; to adorn with plate; to beat into thin plates; to make (set type) into a plate for printing from. (O.Fr.)
plate-armour, *n.* armour of metal plates.
plateau, *n.* pla-*toh* (*pl.* **plateaux,** pla-*tohz*), a broad space of elevated land; a large ornamental dish for the centre of a table; a flat-topped woman's hat. (Fr.)
plate-basket, *n.* a basket or tray for holding forks, spoons, etc., in daily use.
plate-culture, *n.* a culture of bacteria, etc., on glass plates; the cultivation of such.
plateful, *n. plate*-ful, as much as a plate will hold.
plate-glass, *n.* a superior sheet of glass made in thick plates and used for shop-windows, mirrors, shelving, etc.
platelayer, *n. plate*-lay-er, a railway workman employed to lay and repair the rails (these being originally named "plates").
plate-mark, *n.* a legal mark indicating the quality of a metal; the mark on postage-stamps noting the plate from which they were printed.
platen, *n. plat*-en, the part of a printing-press by which the impression is made; the roller of a typewriter. (O.Fr. *platin.*).
plate-powder, *n.* a preparation of precipitated chalk used for polishing table silver.
plater, *n. plate*-er, one who plates; one who fixes plating, esp. on ships; a horse, usually of inferior quality, competing in a race for a cup or plate.
plate-rack, *n.* a fixture for the reception of plates and dishes when drying.
platform, *n. plat*-form, a level place raised above the general level, as in a hall to speak from, or at a

railway station; a solid base for a heavy gun; a political programme; a declared scheme of action or policy. (Fr. *plateforme.*)
platiculture, *n.* *plat*-e-kul-tewr, the cultivation of bacteria on plates [Path.].
platinate, *n.* *plat*-e-nate, a salt of platinic acid.
plating, *n.* *plate*-ing, a coating of metal; the art of covering anything with such a coating; plates (esp. armour-plates) collectively.
platinic, *a.* pla-*tin*-ik, pertaining to or containing platinum.
platiniferous, *a.* pla-te-*nif*-er-us, yielding platinum. (L. *platinum*, and *fero*, bear.)
platinite, *n.* *plat*-e-nite, an iron and nickel alloy having the same coefficient of expansion as platinum.
platinize, *v.t.* *plat*-e-nize, to coat with platinum.
platinoid, *a.* *plat*-e-noyd, of the nature of platinum: *n.* an alloy of copper, zinc, and nickel with a little tungsten; any one of a number of metals found associated with platinum.
platinotype, *n.* *plat*-e-no-tipe, a photographic printing process in which a positive is obtained in platinum-black.
platinous, *a.* *plat*-e-nus, platinic.
platinum, *n.* *plat*-e-num, a malleable, heavy, and ductile metallic element of a silver colour, not affected by any simple acids, used in dental and electrical work, in chemical apparatus, and for jewellery. (Sp. *platina*, from *plata*, silver.)
platinum-black, *n.* a fine black powdered form of platinum obtained from solutions of its salts.
platinum-blonde, *n.* a woman having hair of a natural or artificial golden-silver shade.
platitude, *n.* *plat*-e-tewd, vapidness; flatness; dullness; a commonplace or futile remark. (Fr.)
platitudinarian, *n.* *plat*-e-tew-de-*nare*-re-an, one who utters, or has a reputation for, platitudes.
platitudinize, *v.i.* plat-e-*tew*-de-nize, to utter platitudes.
platitudinous, *a.* plat-e-*tew*-de-nus, of the nature of platitudes; given to platitudinizing.
Platonic, *a.* pla-*ton*-ik, pertaining to Plato or his philosophy or school; untainted with sexuality. **platonic love,** pure spiritual affection, esp. between those of like sex, grounded on intellectual affinities. **platonic year,** the period of the revolution of the equinoxes, being about 26,000 years.
Platonically, *ad.* pla-*ton*-e-ka-le, in the manner of Plato; in Platonic fashion.
Platonism, *n.* *play*-ton-izm, the philosophy or doctrines of Plato and his followers.
Platonist, *n.* *play*-ton-ist, a follower of Plato.
Platonize, *v.t.* *play*-ton-ize, to explain Platonically: *v.i.* to adopt the principles of the Platonic school.
platoon, *n.* pla-*toon*, a small subdivision of a military force commanded by a lieutenant. (Fr. *peloton.*)
platter, *n.* *plat*-ter, a large shallow dish; a wooden plate for bread. (O.Fr. *platel.*)
platting, *n.* *plat*-ting, work done by plaiting; slips of cane or straw braided for making into hats.
platy, *a.* *play*-te, like a plate; laminated; flaky [Geol.].
platycephalic, *a.* *plat*-e-se-*fal*-ik, having a skull flat and broad relatively to its length. (Gr.)
platyhelminth, *n.* *plat*-e-*hel*-minth, any one of the flat-worms [Zool.]. (Gr. *platys*, broad, and *helminth.*)
platypod, *a.* *plat*-e-pod, broad-footed [Zool.].
platypodia, *n.* plat-e-*poh*-de-a, the condition of being flat-footed [Path.].
platypus, *n.* *plat*-e-pus, the duckbill, an Australian egg-laying mammal. (Gr. *platys*, broad, *pous*, foot.)
platyrrhine, *a.* *plat*-e-rine, having a broad nose (of monkeys). (Gr. *platys*, and *rhinos*, nose.)
plaudit, *n.* *plaw*-dit, praise bestowed; an expression of applause. (L. *plaudite*, praise ye.)
plauditory, *a.* *plaw*-de-to-re, applauding.
plausibility, *n.* plaw-ze-*bil*-e-te, the quality of being plausible; speciousness.
plausible, *a.* *plaw*-ze-bl, that may gain favour or approbation; apparently right; specious; using specious arguments. (L. *plausibilis.*)
plausibleness, *n.* plaw-ze-bl-ness, plausibility.
plausibly, *ad.* *plaw*-ze-ble, in a plausible manner.
plausive, *a.* *plaw*-ziv, applauding; plausible.
play, *v.i.* play, to do something for amusement, not as a task or for profit; to sport; to gamble; to frolic; to toy; to trifle; to contend in a game; to give line to [Angling]; to perform on a musical instrument; to behave; to act, esp. on the stage; to move freely in working [Mech.]: *v.t.* to put in action or motion (as a fire-hose, artillery, etc.); to use a musical instrument; to act a part; to perform in character or in a contest. **play off,** to display. **play on,** to let the cricket-ball glance from the bat on to the wicket. **play on words,** a pun; an equivocation. **play the game,** observe the rules; act fairly and squarely. **play truant,** *see* **truant.** **play up to,** to humour. **play upon,** to deceive. **played out,** exhausted; out-worn, stale. (A.S. *plega*, a game.)
***play,** *n.* play, any exercise or series of actions intended for pleasure or diversion; amusement; game; practice in any contest; action; a dramatic composition; dramatic performance; performance on a musical instrument; motion; room for motion; liberty of action; scope.
playable, *a.* *play*-a-bl, capable of being played.
play-acting, *n.* mere pretence; deceptive or insincere behaviour.
play-actor, *n.* a theatrical peformer.
playbill, *n.* *play*-bil, the programme of a theatrical performance; a printed advertisement of a play.
play-book, *n.* a book of dramatic compositions.
playboy, *n.* *play*-boy, a boy actor; a thriftless, irresponsible young man-about-town.
play-day, *n.* a day given to play; a holiday.
play-debt, *n.* a debt contracted in gaming.
player, *n.* *play*-er, one who plays; an actor of dramatic scenes; a musician; a professional, as distinct from amateur, in any game; an idler; a gambler.
player-piano, *n.* a piano played automatically by means of a mechanical apparatus.
playfellow, *n.* *play*-fel-loh, a playmate.
playful, *a.* *play*-ful, sportive; given to play; indulging a sportive fancy; full of playfulness.
playfully, *ad.* in a playful or sportive manner.
playfulness, *n.* state of being playful; sportiveness.
playgoer, *n.* *play*-goh-er, one who frequents the theatre.
playgoing, *a.* and *n.* *play*-goh-ing, frequenting the theatre.
playground, *n.* *play*-ground, a piece of ground on which games are played.
playhouse, *n.* *play*-house, a theatre.
playing, *n.* *play*-ing, the act of playing: *a.* used in playing. **playing cards,** cards used for card games.
playing-field, *n.* a field laid out and tended for games, esp. cricket or football.
playlet, *n.* *play*-let, a short play or dramatic piece.
playmate, *n.* *play*-mate, a companion in amusements.
play-off, *n.* a subsequent game played to obtain a decisive result after a draw.
playpen, *n.* *play*-pen, a light movable enclosure for a small child to play in safely.
play-right, *n.* the exclusive right of public representation of a play, etc.
playsome, *a.* *play*-sum, playful; wanton.
playsomeness, *n.* playfulness; wantonness.
plaything, *n.* *play*-thing, a toy; a person or thing that is merely played with.
playtime, *n.* *play*-time, time given up to recreation.
playwright, *n.* *play*-rite, a writer of plays.
plaza, *n.* *plah*-za, a public square, esp. in Spain. (Sp.)
plea, *n.* plee, an excuse; an apology; entreaty; that which is alleged by a defendant in answer to the plaintiff's declaration [Law]; a law-suit; a case in court. (O.Fr. *plai.*)
pleach, *v.t.* pleech, to interweave branches of trees or shrubs. (O.Fr. *plessier.*)
plead, *v.i.* pleed, to argue in support of a claim, or in defence against the claim of another; to urge reasons for or against; to supplicate with earnestness; to urge; to present an answer to the declaration of a plaintiff [Law]: *v.t.* to argue, as a cause; to allege or adduce in proof or vindication; to offer in excuse; to allege in defence. **to plead guilty,** to acknowledge guilt or liability. (O.Fr. *plaider.*)
pleadable, *a.* *pleed*-a-bl, that may be alleged in proof or vindication.
pleader, *n.* *pleed*-er, one who forms pleas or pleadings; one who argues in a court of justice; one who offers reasons for or against.
pleading, *n.* *pleed*-ing, act of making a plea or supporting by argument; a written statement setting

forth a cause, claim, or defence, or formal allegation [Law]: *a.* imploring; appealing. **special pleading,** *see* **special.**
pleadingly, *ad.* in a pleading manner.
pleasable, *a.* *pleez*-a-bl, that can be pleased.
pleasance, *n.* *plez*-ance, pleasure; pleasantry; a secluded pleasure garden.
pleasant, *a.* *plez*-ant, pleasing; grateful to the mind or senses; cheerful; enlivening; gay; lively. (O.Fr. *plaisant.*)
pleasantly, *ad.* *plez*-ant-le, in a pleasant manner.
pleasantness, *n.* the quality of being pleasant.
pleasantry, *n.* *plez*-ant-re, gaiety; merriment; a sprightly saying; lively talk; a joke; humorous effusion.
★please, *v.t.* pleez, to excite agreeable sensations in; to gratify; to have satisfaction in: *v.i.* to like; to choose; to prefer; to be pleased; to think fit. (O.Fr. *plaisir.*)
pleased, *pp.* and *a.* pleezd, gratified.
pleasedness, *n.* *plee*-zed-ness, state of being pleased.
pleaser, *n.* *pleez*-er, one who pleases or gratifies.
pleasing, *a.* *pleez*-ing, gratifying to the senses or the mind; agreeable; giving satisfaction.
pleasingly, *ad.* *pleez*-ing-le, in a pleasing manner.
pleasingness, *n.* quality of giving pleasure.
pleasurable, *a.* *plez*-zhur-a-bl, pleasing; affording gratification.
pleasurableness, *n.* quality of being pleasurable.
pleasurably, *ad.* in a pleasurable manner.
★pleasure, *n.* *plez*-zhur, the gratification of the mind or senses; agreeable sensations or emotions; enjoyment; delight; sensual gratification; choice, that which the will dictates or desires; a favour: *v.t.* to please; to gratify. (Fr. *plaisir.*)
pleasure-boat, *n.* a boat for pleasure.
pleasure-ground, *n.* a ground laid out for pleasure; a recreation ground.
pleasure-trip, *n.* an excursion for pleasure.
pleat, *n.* pleet, a flat fold: *v.t.* to fold flatly; to double over. (*plait.*)
plebeian, *n.* ple-*bee*-an, one of the lower ranks of society: *a.* pertaining to the populace; vulgar; ill-bred. (O.Fr., from L. *plebs*, the common people.)
plebeianism, *n.* ple-*bee*-a-nizm, plebeian character, quality, or manners; vulgarity.
plebeianize, *v.t.* ple-*bee*-a-nize, to make plebeian.
plebiscitary, *a.* ple-*bis*-e-ta-re, pertaining to or resembling a plebiscite.
plebiscite, *n.* *pleb*-e-sit, the vote of a whole community or a decree founded on it. (Fr.)
plebs, *n.* plebz, the non-privileged commonalty of ancient Rome; hence, the mob, the proletariat. (L.)
plectognath, *a.* *plek*-tog-nath, pertaining or belonging to the Plectognathi, an order of fishes with the cheek-bones united with the jaws, as in the file-fish: *n.* any fish of this order. (Gr. *plektos*, twisted, *gnathos*, a jaw.)
plectrum, *n.* *plek*-trum (*pl.* **plectra** *or* **plectrums**), a small stick or quill with which the ancients plucked the lyre; a similar contrivance used in playing any stringed instrument. (L.)
pled, pled, former *p.* and *pp.* of *plead.*
pledge, *n.* plej, something put in pawn as security; a surety; a security, esp. one given for the repayment of money or as guarantee of good faith; a promise; a drinking to the health of another: *v.t.* to deposit in pawn or as security; to engage by promise; to drink health to. **to take the pledge,** solemnly to engage to abstain from intoxicants. (O.Fr. *plege.*)
pledgeable, *a.* *plej*-a-bl, that may be pledged.
pledgee, *n.* plej-*ee*, one to whom anything is pledged.
pledger, *n.* *plej*-er, one who pledges or pawns anything; one who drinks to the health of another.
pledget, *n.* *plej*-et, a compress or small wad of lint laid over a wound [Surg.].
Pleiad, *n.* *ply*-ad, a brilliant group of notabilities, esp. seven French 16th-cent. poets headed by Ronsard; any one of the Pleiades.
Pleiades, *n.pl.* *ply*-a-deez, the collective name of the seven daughters of the mythological Atlas, who were transformed into the group of stars in the constellation Taurus; hence, these stars. [L.)
pleistocene, *a.* *plice*-to-seen, pertaining to or designating the series of rocks above the Pliocene: *n.* (*cap.*) this formation; the glacial series [Geol.]. (Gr. *pleistos*, most, *kainos*, new.)
plenarily, *ad.* *pleen*-a-re-le, fully; completely.
plenariness, *n.* *pleen*-a-re-ness, the state or quality of being plenary.
plenarty, *n.* *plee*-nar-te, the state of being occupied (used only of ecclesiastical benefices).
plenary, *a.* *plee*-na-re, full; entire; absolute; complete. (Late L. *plenarius*, whole.)
plenilunar, *a.* plen-e-*lew*-nar, pertaining to the full moon. (L. *plenus*, full, *luna*, the moon.)
plenilunary, *a.* plen-e-*lew*-na-re, plenilunar.
plenilune, *n.* *plen*-e-lewn, the full moon; the period of full moon.
plenipotence, *n.* ple-*nip*-o-tence, fullness of power.
plenipotent, *a.* ple-*nip*-o-tent, possessing full powers. (L. *plenus*, and *potens*, powerful.)
plenipotentiary, *n.* plen-e-po-*ten*-sha-re, an envoy or ambassador to a foreign court furnished with full diplomatic powers: *a.* with full powers. (Late L. *plenipotentiarius.*)
plenish, *v.t.* *plen*-ish, to furnish; to provide with implements and utensils; to fit out. (O.Fr., from L. *plenus.*)
plenist, *n.* *pleen*-ist, one who maintains that all space is full of matter. (L. *plenus*, full.)
plenitude, *n.* *plen*-e-tewd, fullness; repletion; abundance; completeness. (O.Fr., from L.)
plenteous, *a.* *plen*-te-us, plentiful; sufficient for every purpose; yielding abundance; having abundance.
plenteously, *ad.* in a plenteous manner.
plenteousness, *n.* the state of being plenteous; abundance, plenty.
plentiful, *a.* *plen*-te-ful, existing in or yielding abundance; copious; fruitful.
plentifully, *ad.* in a plentiful manner.
plentifulness, *n.* the state of being plentiful; plenteousness.
plenty, *n.* *plen*-te, full supply; abundance; fruitfulness: *a.* being in abundance: *ad.* abundantly [Coll.]. (O.Fr. *plenté*, from L. *plenitas*)
plenum, *n.* *pleen*-um, fullness of matter in space; space as filled with matter; a full assembly; a joint meeting of all parts of a legislative body. (L.)
pleochroism, *n.* ple-*ok*-ro-izm, the quality of showing different colours when viewed from different directions [Cryst.], or of being coloured differently under different conditions [Path.]. (Gr. *pleon*, more, *chroas*, colour.)
pleomorphic, *a.* plee-o-*mor*-fik, having several distinct forms.
pleonasm, *n.* *plee*-o-nazm, redundancy in speech or writing. (Gr. *pleonasmos*, abundance.)
pleonaste, *n.* *plee*-o-nast, ceylonite, a dark variety of spinel [Min.].
pleonastic, *a.* ple-o-*nas*-tik characterized by, or pertaining to, pleonasm.
pleonastically, *ad.* with redundancy of words.
pleroma, ple-*roh*-ma, fullness; abundance; (*cap.*) among certain Gnostics, the Æons collectively, the sum-total of the emanations from, or essential attributes of, the Supreme Being. (Gr., fullness.)
plesiomorphism, *n.* *plee*-se-o-*morf*-izm, resemblance in form but difference in chemical composition [Cryst.]. (Gr. *plesios*, near, *morphe*, form.)
plesiomorphous, *a.* *plee*-se-o-*morf*-us, characterized by plesiomorphism.
Plesiosaurus, *n.* *plee*-se-o-*saw*-rus, a genus of extinct long-necked, four-paddled marine reptiles of the Mesozoic formations; (*l.c.*) a reptile of this genus. (Gr. *plesios*, near, *sauros*, lizard.)
plessimeter, *n.* ples-*sim*-e-ter, a pleximeter.
plethora, *n.* *pleth*-o-ra, excessive fullness of blood; repletion; superabundance. (L.)
plethoric, *a.* ple-*tho*-rik, having a full habit of body; over full.
pleura ,*n.* *ploor*-ra (*pl.* **pleuræ**), a thin membrane which covers the interior of the thorax, and invests the lungs [Anat.]; a lateral part, esp. of the radula of a mollusc [Zool.]; a pleuron. (Gr., a rib, a side.)
pleural, *a.* *ploor*-ral, pertaining to the pleura: *n.* a bony process in some chelonians and fishes.
pleurenchyma, *n.* ploor-*eng*-ke-ma, woody tissue [Bot.].
pleurisy, *n.* *ploor*-re-se, inflammation of the pleura, usually accompanied by fever and difficult breathing. (Fr. *pleuresie.*)
pleuritic, *a.* ploor-*rit*-ik, pertaining to, or affected with, pleurisy.
pleurocarpous, *a.* ploor-ro-*kar*-pus, bearing the

fructifying organs on short lateral stems (of mosses, etc.): not acrocarpous [Bot.].

pleurodynia, *n.* ploor-ro-*din*-e-a, a painful rheumatic affection of the walls or muscles of the chest [Med.]. (Gr. *pleura*, and *odyne*, pain.)

pleuron, *n.* *ploor*-ron, a lateral part or process of certain insects and crustaceans [Zool.]. (Gr. *pleura*, a rib.)

pleuro-pneumonia, *n.* simultaneous inflammation of the pleura and the lungs, esp. a disease in cattle.

plexiform, *a.* *plek*-se-form, in the form of network; complicated; resembling a plexus [Anat.]. (L. *plexus*, a twisting, and *form*.)

pleximeter, *n.* plek-*sim*-e-ter, an ivory or other plate used in examination of the chest, etc., by percussion [Med.]. (Gr. *plexis*, percussion, *metron*, measure.)

plexor, *n.* *plek*-sor, the small mallet used with the pleximeter.

plexus, *n.* *plek*-sus, a network of interlacing blood vessels, nerves, or fibres; a complication. **solar plexus,** *see* **solar.** (L.)

pliability, *n.* ply-a-*bil*-e-te, pliableness; flexibility.

pliable, *a.* *ply*-a-bl, easy to be bent; flexible; flexible in disposition; easily persuaded or influenced. (Fr.)

pliableness, *n.* the quality of being pliable.

pliably, *ad.* *ply*-a-ble, in a pliable manner.

pliancy, *n.* *ply*-an-se, easiness to be bent; readiness to be influenced.

pliant, *a.* *ply*-ant, easily bent; flexible; limber; easily moulded; easily influenced; tractable. (Fr.)

pliantly, *ad.* *ply*-ant-le, in a pliant manner.

pliantness, *n.* the quality of being pliant.

plica, *n.* *ply*-ka, a skin-disease causing the hair to become matted and the scalp tender [Med.]; a filthy condition of the hair. (L. *plicare*, fold.)

plicate, *a.* *ply*-kat, plicated.

plicated, *a.* *ply*-ka-ted, plaited; folded like a fan.

plicatile, *a.* *plik*-a-tile, capable of being folded [Zool.].

plication, *n.* ple-*kay*-shon, a folding or fold.

plicature, *n.* *plik*-a-tewr, a fold; a doubling.

pliers, *n.pl.* *ply*-erz, a pair of small pincers for seizing and bending, etc. (*ply*.)

plight, *n.* plite, condition; state; predicament. (O.Fr. *ploit*, plait.)

plight, *n.* plite, an engagement; a pledge: *v.t.* to promise; to engage oneself to marry; to pledge. (A.S. *plihtan*, to pledge.)

plighter, *n.* *plite*-er, one who pledges.

plim, *v.i.* plim, to swell up; to become plump.

plimsoll, *n.* *plim*-sol, a light canvas shoe with a rubber sole.

Plimsoll-mark, *n.* the line placed on the sides of a vessel to indicate the loading capacity. (Samuel *Plimsoll*, M.P., through whom its use was made obligatory in British ships in 1876.)

plinth, *n.* plinth, the lowermost, square-shaped, projecting part or base of a column, a pedestal or a wall, hence, in general, a sub-base or block for statuettes, etc. (Gr. *plinthos*, a brick.)

pliocene, *a.* *ply*-o-seen, pertaining to or designating the most recent of the Tertiary rocks: *n.* (*cap.*) this formation, lying above the Miocene and below the Pleistocene [Geol.]. (Gr. *pleion*, more, *kainos*, new.)

pliosaurus, *n.* ply-o-*saw*-rus, an extinct marine reptile allied to the plesiosaurus, but having a shorter neck. (Gr. *pleion*, more, *sauros*, a lizard.)

plod, *v.i.* plod, to travel or work slowly, but steadily and laboriously; to study heavily with diligence; to toil; to drudge. (Perhaps imit.)

plodder, *n.* *plod*-der, a steady worker.

plodding, *a.* *plod*-ding, steadily laborious, but slow.

ploddingly, *ad.* in a plodding manner.

plonk, *n.* plonk, a dull heavy sound, as that of drawing one's foot from heavy clay; a plunk. (Imit.)

plop, *n.* plop, the sound of something falling into water without splashing: *ad.* sounding thus; heavily: *v.i.* to fall with this sound. (Imit.)

plosive, *n.* *ploh*-siv, an explosive consonant [Phonetics.].

plot, *n.* plot, a small extent of ground; a plat. (A.S.)

plot, *n.* plot, any scheme or plan of a complicated nature; a secret conspiracy; intrigue; stratagem; the story of a play or book, as gradually developed; a plan draughted out: *v.i.* to form a scheme of mischief against another; to contrive a plan; to scheme: *v.t.* to plan; to contrive; to make a plan of. (Perhaps Fr. *complot*.)

plotter, *n.* *plot*-er, one who plots or contrives; a conspirator.

plotting, *n.* *plot*-ing, the action of the verb *to plot*; the recording of data obtained from a survey of land, etc.

★**plough,** *n.* plou, an implement for turning up the soil; tillage; ploughed land; a team of horses for ploughing; a tool for grooving; a failure in an examination: *v.t.* to turn up the soil with a plough; to furrow; to reject at an examination: *v.i.* to advance with difficulty. **the Plough,** Charles's-wain [Astron.]. **Plough Monday,** the Monday after Twelfth-Day. (A.S. *ploh*, plot of land.)

ploughable, *a.* *plou*-a-bl, that may be ploughed; arable.

ploughboy, *n.* *plou*-boy, a boy who drives the plough; a rustic.

plougher, *n.* *plou*-er, one who ploughs land.

plough-iron, *n.* the coulter that cuts the soil at the top of the furrow.

ploughland, *n.* *plou*-land, a hide or carucate of land; land that is suitable for tilling.

ploughman, *n.* *plou*-man, one who ploughs or holds a plough.

ploughshare, *n.* *plou*-share, the pointed shoe which cuts the soil at the bottom of the furrow.

plough-staff, *n.* a spade-shaped implement for cleaning the coulter of a plough from roots, weeds, etc.

ploughtail, *n.* *plou*-tale, the part of a plough which the ploughman holds.

ploughwright, *n.* *plou*-rite, a maker or repairer of ploughs.

plover, *n.* *pluv*-er, the popular name for several species of *Charadrius* and other grallatorial birds frequenting low, moist ground. **green plover,** the lapwing (esp. in Ireland). (O.Fr. *pluvier*.)

plow, *n.* plou, a plough (U.S.A. spelling).

pluck, *n.* pluk, the act or process of plucking; a twitching tug; the heart, liver, and lungs of an animal; courage; spirit: *v.t.* to pull with sudden force, or with a twitch; to strip by plucking; to reject, after examination; to swindle [Coll.]. **a plucked 'un,** one possessing pluck or spirits [Slang]. (A.S. *pluccian*.)

plucker, *n.* *pluk*-er, one who plucks.

pluckily, *ad.* *pluk*-e-le, in a plucky manner.

pluckiness, *n.* *pluk*-e-ness, pluck; the quality of being plucky.

plucky, *a.* *pluk*-e, having pluck or spirit; courageous; daredevil.

plug, *n.* plug, anything used to stop a hole; a stopple; a large peg; tobacco compressed into a cake, also a cake of this; a device with metal contacts for completing a circuit by insertion in a socket [Elect.]: *v.t.* to stop with a plug; to shoot; to plod [Slang]; to attempt to popularize, esp. a song, by constant public performance [Coll.]. **to plug in,** to make connexion with a circuit [Elect.]. (O.Dut. *plugge*.)

plugboard, *n.* *plug*-bord, a switchboard [Elect.].

plugging, *n.* *plug*-ging, the act of stopping with a plug; the material employed.

plug-ugly, *n.* a street rough; a hooligan [Amer. Slang].

plum, *n.* plum, a tree of the genus *Prunus* or its fruit; a raisin; the sum of £100,000 [Slang]; a fortune; anything good or choice of its kind. (A.S. *plume*.)

plumage, *n.* *ploo*-maj, the feathers of a bird; feathers collectively. (O.Fr.)

plumassier, *n.* ploo-ma-*seer*, one who prepares or deals in ornamental feathers. (Fr.)

plumb, *n.* plum, a weight attached to a line, used to ascertain whether a wall, etc., is perpendicular; a plummet: *a.* perpendicular: *ad.* perpendicularly: *v.t.* to adjust by a plumb-line; to set in a perpendicular direction; to sound the depth of water with a plummet. (Fr. *plomb*; L. *plumbum*, lead.)

plumbaginous, *a.* plum-*baj*-e-nus, resembling, consisting of, or of the nature of, plumbago.

plumbago, *n.* plum-*bay*-go, graphite, nearly pure carbon; when used for pencils called blacklead; (*cap.*) a small genus of flowering herbs, including the leadworts [Bot.]. (L.)

plumbean, *a.* *plum*-be-an, consisting of, resembling, or treated with lead; dull; heavy; stupid.
plumbeous, *a.* *plum*-be-us. plumbean.
plumber, *n.* *plum*-mer, one who works in lead, esp. one who fits and repairs pipes, cisterns, etc.
plumbery, *n.* *plum*-mer-re, plumbing; the business of a plumber; articles in lead.
plumbic, *a.* *plum*-bik, pertaining to, derived from, or containing, lead.
plumbiferous, *a.* plum-*bif*-er-rus, containing lead.
plumbing, *n.* *plum*-ming, the action of the verb *to plumb*; the art of working in lead.
plumbism, *n.* *plum*-bizm, lead poisoning [Med.]
plumb-line, *n.* a cord with a plumb attached to it; a perpendicular line.
plumb-rule, *n.* a straight-edge fitted with a plumb-line used by carpenters, bricklayers, etc.
plum-cake, *n.* a cake containing raisins.
plumcot, *n.* *plum*-kot, a cross between a plum and an apricot.
plume, *n.* ploom, a feather, particularly when large; a feather, or such like, worn as an ornament; a feathery appendage [Bot.]; a token of honour: *v.t.* to pick and adjust the feathers of; to strip of feathers; to adorn with or as with feathers; to pride (oneself). **borrowed plumes,** credit, dignity, etc., improperly assumed and paraded. **plume alum,** a fibrous double sulphate of aluminium [Chem.]. **plume grass,** any grass of the genus *Erianthus*. (Fr.)
plumelet, *n.* *ploom*-let, a small plume.
plumicorn, *n.* *ploom*-e-kawrn, one of the pair of ear-like tufts of feathers present on the head of many owls. (L. *pluma*, feather, *cornu*, horn.)
plumiform, *a.* *ploom*-e-form, plume-shaped.
plummer-block, *n.* *plum*-mer-blok, the bearing on which a shaft revolves [Mech.].
plummet, *n.* *plum*-met, a weight attached to a line, esp. to sound the depth of water or adjust erections to a perpendicular line; a sinker [Angling]. (O.Fr. *plommet.*)
plummy, *a.* *plum*-e, abounding in or resembling plums; [Slang] first-rate, most desirable.
plumose, *a.* *ploo*-mohs, feathery. (L. *plumosus.*)
plumosity, *n.* ploo-*mos*-e-te, state of being plumose.
plumous, *a.* *ploo*-mus, resembling feathers; feathery.
plump, *a.* plump, filled out; full; fat and rounded: *v.t.* to extend to fullness; to dilate: *v.i.* to grow plump. (M.E., perhaps from Dut. *plomp*, rude.)
plump, *n.* plump, a sudden plunge; the sound of a heavy fall: *a.* blunt; downright: *ad.* suddenly; heavily; bluntly: *v.i.* to fall suddenly; to vote for only one candidate when qualified to vote for more; also, to give all one's votes to a single candidate or cause: *v.t.* to cause to sink suddenly. (Imit.)
plumper, *n.* *plump*-er, the act of plumping; a vote given to one candidate only; one who gives a plumper; an unqualified lie; a pad or other device for swelling something out.
plumply, *ad.* *plump*-le, fully; roundly.
plumpness, *n.* state of being plump; fullness of skin.
plum-pudding, *n.* pudding containing raisins and currants; a pudding containing plums.
plumpy, *a.* *plump*-e, plump; fat.
plumular, *n.* *ploom*-yew-lar, pertaining to, or resembling, a plumule.
plumule, *n.* *ploom*-yewl, the first bud from a germinating seed [Bot.]; a plumelet; a down feather; a downy scale on butterflies' wings.
plumy, *a.* *ploo*-me, feathery; covered with feathers; adorned with plumes.
plunder, *n.* *plun*-der, pillage; booty; systematic robbery; illicit gain [Slang]: *v.t.* to pillage; to spoil; to take by pillage or open force; to rob. (Ger. *plündern.*)
plunderage, *n.* *plun*-der-raj, embezzlement of goods on board a ship; goods so obtained.
plunderer, *n.* *plun*-der-rer, one who plunders; a hostile pillager; a robber.
plunderous, *a.* *plun*-der-rus, characterized by or addicted to plundering.
plunge, *n.* plunj, the act of plunging; a dive; a place for diving into; a difficulty; distress; a hazardous venture: *v.t.* to thrust suddenly into water or other fluid; to immerse: *v.i.* to rush and dive into; to rush or throw oneself into; to throw the body forward and the hind legs up (of horses); to pitch (of ships); to gamble or take risks recklessly [Slang]. **plunging fire,** direct fire on a target from a superior height. (O.Fr. *plunger.*)
plunger, *n.* *plunj*-er, one who or that which plunges; a diver; one who bets heavily, a rash speculator [Slang]; a piston, or a piece having similar action, *e.g.* a cylinder used as a forcer in force-pumps [Mech.].
plunk, *n.* plunk, a quick or metallic sound, as of twanging a string, dropping a coin, etc.; an act of plunking; a plonk: *v.t.* to pluck the string of (a banjo, etc.); to plump down heavily.
pluperfect, *a.* ploo-*per*-fekt *or* *ploo*-per-fekt, denoting an event that took place previous to another past event [Gram.]. (L. *plus quam perfectum*, more than perfect.)
plural, *a.* *ploor*-ral, consisting of, or denoting, two or more: *n.* the form which expresses more than one [Gram.]. **plural marriage,** polygamy. (O.Fr. *plurel.*)
pluralism, *n.* *ploor*-ra-lizm, the state of being plural; the simultaneous holding of more offices, esp. benefices, than one.
pluralist, *n.* *ploor*-ra-list, one, esp. a clergyman, who practises pluralism.
pluralistic, *a.* ploor-ra-*lis*-tik, characterized by, or pertaining to, pluralism.
plurality, *n.* ploor-*ral*-e-te, the state of being plural; a number of more than one; a majority; pluralism; an office held by a pluralist. (Fr. *pluralité.*)
pluralize, *v.t.* *ploor*-ra-lize, to make plural.
plurally, *ad.* *ploor*-ra-le, in a plural manner.
plurilateral, *a.* ploor-re-*lat*-er-ral, consisting of more than two sides or parties.
pluriliteral, *a.* ploor-re-*lit*-er-ral, having more than three letters (of Hebrew words). (*plus* and *literal.*)
pluriparous, *a.* ploor-*rip*-a-rus, multiparous.
plus, *n.* plus, the symbol +, used as the sign of addition; a positive quantity: *a.* additional; denoting a greater value than usual, or an age exceeding by less than 12 months that mentioned; positive [Elect.]. (L., more.)
plus-fours, *n.pl.* roomy knickerbockers. (So called because originally cut some 4 in. longer in the leg than the ordinary garment.)
plush, *n.* plush, a species of napped cloth with a velvety pile. (Fr. *peluche*, from L. *pilus*, hair.)
plushette, *n.* plush-*et*, an inferior kind of plush.
plutarchy, *n.* *ploo*-tar-ke, plutocracy.
Pluto, *n.* *ploo*-toh, the god of the nether world [Myth.]; a small planet, the outermost known member of the solar system, discovered in 1930.
plutocracy, *n.* ploo-*tok*-ra-se, government by the wealthy. (Gr. *plutos*, wealth, *kratos*, power.)
plutocrat, *n.* *ploo*-to-krat, a member of a plutocracy; one who is powerful or influential on account of his wealth.
plutocratic, *a.* ploo-to-*krat*-ik, pertaining to, or of the nature of, plutocracy or a plutocrat.
plutolatry, *n.* ploo-*tol*-a-tre, the worship of wealth.
plutomania, *n.* ploo-to-*may*-ne-a, insanity causing the patient to think himself immensely wealthy.
Plutonian, *a.* ploo-*toh*-ne-an, Plutonic: *n.* a Plutonist.
Plutonic, *a.* ploo-*ton*-ik, pertaining to Pluto or his kingdom; infernal; dark; igneous [Geol.]. **Plutonic rocks,** unstratified rocks such as granite, supposed, according to the **Plutonic theory,** to have been consolidated from a molten state deep below the surface of the earth. (*Pluto.*)
Plutonism, *n.* *ploo*-ton-izm, the Plutonic theory.
Plutonist, *n.* *ploo*-ton-ist, one who holds the Plutonic theory in regard to the igneous rocks.
plutonium, *n.* ploo-*toh*-ne-um, the unstable trans-uranium element (No. 94) produced by the forced emission of one electron from the nucleus of the uranium radioactive derivative neptunium [Chem.].
plutonomist, *n.* ploo-*ton*-o-mist, a political economist.
plutonomy, *n.* ploo-*ton*-o-me, political economy; the science dealing with the production and distribution of wealth. (Gr.)
pluvial, *a.* *ploo*-ve-al, pertaining or due to rain; rainy; humid. (Fr., from L. *pluvis*, rain.)
pluviograph, *n.* *ploo*-ve-o-graf, an automatically recording rain-gauge. (L. *pluvia*, and Gr. *grapho* write.)
pluviometer, *n.* ploo-ve-*om*-e-ter, a rain-gauge.

pluviometrical, *a.* *ploo*-ve-o-*met*-re-kal, pertaining to or made by a pluviometer.

ply, *n.* ply, a fold; a plait; a layer of wood in ply-wood; a strand; a bent; bias: *v.t.* to fold; to plait. (O.Fr. *ploy*, fold.)

ply, *v.t.* ply, to employ with diligence; to keep busy; to work at; to solicit; to urge: *v.i.* to be employed; to work steadily; to come and go regularly; to go in haste; to endeavour to make way against the wind [Naut.]. (*apply.*)

plyer, *n.* *ply*-er, one who or that which plies.

Plymouth Brethren, *n.* a religious sect, having no definite creed and no ministers, founded at Plymouth about 1830 by John Nelson Darby, a former curate. **Plymouth rock,** a breed of fowls.

Plymouthism, *n.* *plim*-oth-izm, the principles or system of the Plymouth Brethren.

plywood, *n.* *ply*-wood, a thin board formed by gluing layers of wood together with the grains crosswise.

pneumatic, *a.* new-*mat*-ik, consisting of, like, or pertaining to air or gases; moved by air; inflated with air: *n.* a cycle fitted with pneumatic tires; *pl.* the science treating of the physical properties of gases, esp. air. **pneumatic dispatch,** a system of conveying written messages, small parcels, etc., through pipes by air pressure or exhaustion. **pneumatic trough,** a vessel used for the collection of gases above a liquid. (Gr. *pneumatikos*, relating to the air.)

pneumaticity, *n.* new-ma-*tis*-e-te, state of being pneumatic, esp. [Anat.] of having air-cavities.

pneumatocyst, *n.* new-*mat*-o-sist, the air-sac of a bird, and of certain Hydrozoa [Zool.].

pneumatological, *a.* new-ma-to-*loj*-e-kal, pertaining to pneumatology.

pneumatologist, *n.* new-ma-*tol*-o-jist, one versed in pneumatology.

pneumatology, *n.* new-ma-*tol*-o-je, pneumatics; the doctrine of spiritual essences or existences [Phil.]; the science of respiration [Med.]. (Gr. *pneumatikos*, and *logos*, science.)

pneumatometer, *n.* new-ma-*tom*-e-ter, an instrument for measuring the air which the lungs can inhale at a time. (Gr. *pneumatikos*, and *metron*, measure.)

pneumatophore, *n.* new-*mat*-o-for, a part in which an air-sac or -cavity is contained; an air-cavity [Bot. and Zool.].

pneumatosis, *n.* new-ma-*toh*-sis, the condition of having an excessive amount of gas in the body; flatulence [Med.].

pneumococcus, *n.* new-mo-*kok*-us, any micrococcus of the lung, esp. that causing pneumonia [Path.].

pneumoconiosis, *n.* *new*-mo-kon-e-*oh*-sis, a lung-disease caused by the inhalation of minute gritty particles; lithosis.

pneumogastric, *a.* new-mo-*gas*-trik, pertaining to the lungs and stomach. (Gr. *pneumon*, lung, *gaster*, stomach.)

pneumology, *n.* new-*mol*-o-je, the study of the respiratory organs.

pneumonemia, *n.* new-mo-*nee*-me-a, congestion of the lungs.

pneumonia, *n.* new-*moh*-ne-a, acute inflammation of the lungs; pertaining to the lungs. (Gr.)

pneumonic, *a.* new-*mon*-ik, pertaining to the lungs or to pneumonia: *n.* a medicine for, also one suffering from, disease of the lungs.

pneumothorax, *n.* new-mo-*thaw*-raks, the presence of air in the pleural cavity. (Gr. *pneumon*, *thorax.*)

po, *n.* poh (*pl.* **pos**, pohz), a chamber-pot [Coll.]. (Fr. *pot*, pot.)

poa, *n.* *poh*-ah, a large and widely distributed genus of meadow grasses. (Gr., grass.)

poach, *v.t.* poach, to cook shelled eggs in boiling water in which there is a ring or pocket to keep them round in shape. (Fr. *poche.*)

poach, *v.t.* poach, to steal game from another's preserves: *v.i.* to trespass on land in pursuit of game; to secure game or fish illegally; to take an advantage unfairly; to encroach on another's territory or privileges; to hit the ball when it should be returned by one's partner [Tennis]. (Fr. *pocher.*)

poacher, *n.* *poach*-er, one who poaches, esp. who steals game; a vessel in which to poach eggs.

poachiness, *n.* the state of being poachy.

poaching, *n.* *poach*-ing, the act of one who poaches; the illegal taking of game, or trespass in pursuit thereof.

poachy, *a.* *poach*-e, wet and soft, so as to be easily penetrated to some depth by the feet of cattle.

pochard, *n.* *poh*-chard, any of several sea-ducks, esp. of the genus *Nyroca ferina*. (Origin uncertain.)

pochette, *n.* po-*shet*, a wallet; a small flat hand-bag used by women. (Fr.)

pock, *n.* pok, a pustule of the small-pox. (A.S. *poc.*)

***pocket,** *n.* *pok*-et, a small bag in or attached to a garment for carrying small articles; any small bag or the like; a small bag or net to receive the balls at billiards; a small cavity containing ore or foreign matter [Mining and Geol.]; a certain quantity of hops; a patch of rarefied air which causes an aeroplane to drop when in flight; the position of being hemmed in during a race: *v.t.* to conceal in the pocket; to take clandestinely; to hem in during a race; to drive into a pocket (of billiard balls): *a.* suitable for a pocket; of reduced size. **pocket borough,** *see* **borough. in pocket,** in funds; having made a profit. **pocket an insult,** to receive it without resenting it. (O. Norman *poque*, a pouch.)

pocket-book, *n.* a small wallet for carrying papers, note-book, etc., in the pocket.

pocket-hole, *n.* the opening into a pocket.

pocket-knife, *n.* a knife with blades folding into the handle so that it can be carried in the pocket.

pocket-money, *n.* money for occasional expenses.

pock-mark, *n.* a scar made by small-pox.

pockwood, *n.* *pok*-wood, an old name of lignum-vitæ (formerly used as a specific for pox).

pocky, *a.* *pok*-e, infected with the small-pox; full of pocks; syphilitic.

poco, *ad.* *poh*-ko, a little; rather [Mus.]. (It.)

pococurante, *a.* *poh*-ko-koo-*ran*-te, caring little: *n.* an indifferent or non-interested person. (It.)

pococurantism, *n.* *poh*-ko-koo-*ran*-tizm, indifferentism; carelessness. (It. *poco*, little, *curante*, caring.)

poculiform, *a.* po-*kew*-le-form, cup-shaped [Bot.]. (L. *poculum*, a cup.)

pod, *n.* pod, the shell of a pea and other leguminous plant; the envelope of a cocoon, etc.: *v.i.* to swell; to swell; to produce pods. (Origin unknown.)

pod, *n.* pod, a shoal of whales or seals.

pod, *n.* pod, the pod or socket of a brace-and-bit.

podagra, *n.* po-*dag*-ra, gout in the feet. (Gr.)

podagral, *a.* po-*dag*-ral, pertaining to or afflicted with gout.

podagric, *a.* po-*dag*-rik, podagral.

podal, *a.* *poh*-dal, pertaining to the feet [Zool.]. (Gr. *pous*, *podos*, a foot.)

podalgia, *n.* po-*dal*-je-a, pain in the feet.

podded, *a.* *pod*-ded, furnished with pods; leguminous.

podesta, *n.* po-*des*-ta, the title of a magistrate in certain Italian towns, and of the mayor of some former Fascist communes. (It.)

podex, *n.* *poh*-deks, the anal region [Zool.]. (L.)

podge, *n.* poj, a podgy person.

podgy, *a.* *poj*-e, short and fat. (Origin unknown.)

podical, *a.* *poh*-de-kal, pertaining to the podex; anal.

podium, *n.* *poh*-de-um (*pl.* **podia**), a pedestal, with plinth and cornice continued horizontally to support pillars; the part of an amphitheatre projecting over the arena; a balcony [Arch.]. (L.)

podocarp, *n.* *poh*-do-karp, a fruit stalk [Bot.]. (Gr. *pous*, and *karpos*, fruit.)

podophthalmate, *a.* poh-dof-*thal*-mat, having the eyes on stalks (of certain crustacea) [Zool.].

podophyllin, *n.* pod-o-*fil*-in, a purgative drug obtained from the rhizome of the May-apple, *Podophyllum peltatum.*

Podophyllum, *n.* pod-o-*fil*-um, the genus of the May-apple. (Gr. *pous*, and *phyllon*, a leaf.)

podoscaph, *n.* *poh*-do-skaf, a boat propelled by the feet. (Gr. *pous*, and *scaphos*, a boat.)

podosperm, *n.* *pod*-o-sperm, a funiculus [Bot.].

podsol, *n.* *pod*-zol, an ash-coloured soil occurring extensively in Russia. (Russ., salty.)

poe-bird, *n.* *poh*-e-burd, the tui or parson bird.

poem, *n.* *poh*-em, a poetic composition; a piece of poetry; applied also to any thing, action, etc., having poetic qualities. (Fr. *poème.*)

poephagous, *a.* po-*ef*-a-gus, feeding on grass [Zool.]. (Gr. *poe*, grass, *phago*, eat.)

poesy, *n.* *poh*-e-ze, the art of composing poems; poetry; metrical composition. (Gr. *poiesis.*)

poet, *n.* *poh*-et, the author of a poem; one skilled in the composition of poetry; one distinguished for poetic talents or imaginative power. **Poet**

Laureate, a member of the British Royal Household, appointed by the Prime Minister, formerly charged with the duty of producing odes in celebration of royal birthdays and state and public occasions. (Fr. *poete.*)

poetaster, *n.* po-e-*tas*-ter, a petty poet; a pitiful rhymester. (O.Fr. *poetastre,* an indifferent versifier.)

poetess, *n. poh*-e-tes, a female poet.

poetic, *a.* po-*et*-ik, poetical. **poetic justice,** the ideal punishment of vice and reward of virtue. **poetic licence,** that freedom of expression or statement allowed to a poet for the sake of his poetry.

poetic, *a.* po-*et*-ik, poetical.

poetical, *a.* po-*et*-e-kal, pertaining to poetry; suitable to poetry; expressed in poetry; possessing the peculiar beauties of poetry; sublime.

poetically, *ad.* in a poetical manner.

poeticize, *v.t.* po-*et*-e-size, to make poetical: *v.i.* to write poetry; to speak as a poet.

poetics, *n.* po-*et*-iks, the study of poetry as a literary form; a treatise on, or criticism of, poetry; versification.

poetize, *v.i. poh*-et-ize, to write as a poet; to versify.

poetry, *n. poh*-et-re, the art of giving rhythmic expression to imaginative feelings, aspirations, etc., which have been conceived with more or less of passion, knowledge, and insight; any composition, whether in verse or prose, at once nobly fervid and vividly imaginative; any poetical quality, spirit, etc.; metrical composition. (O.Fr. *poetrie.*)

pogrom, *n.* po-*grom,* officially or semi-officially organized plunder and slaughter. (Russ.)

poignancy, *n. poyn*-an-se, the state of being poignant.

poignant, *a. poyn*-ant, sharp; stimulating to taste; keen; pungent; acutely painful. (Fr.)

poignantly, *ad. poyn*-ant-le, to a poignant degree.

poignard, *n. pon*-yerd, a poniard.

poilu, *n. pwah*-loo, a French infantryman, esp. of the front line in the 1914–18 War. (Fr.)

poind, *v.t.* poynd, to put in the pound; to distrain upon; to impound. (Scots.)

Poinsettia, *n.* poyn-*set*-e-a, a genus of Mexican plants with large red bracts, of the family *Euphorbiaceæ.* (From their discoverer J. R. *Poinsette, d.* 1851, Amer. statesman.)

★**point,** *n.* poynt, a sharp end; the mark made by it; a piercing implement; a dot; a stop in punctuation; a spot; verge; exact place; stage or degree; quality; peculiarity; subject; aim; the switch of a railway; a small cape or promontory; the gist of an argument, epigram, etc.; a lively turn of thought; point-lace; tag of a lace; that which has position but no magnitude [Geom.]; the twelfth of a pica [Print.]; a diacritic indicating a vowel [Semitic languages]; any division of the compass [Naut.]; a fielder (or his position) on the off-side of the batsman [Cricket]; a unit in scoring games, comparing qualities or excellencies, reckoning odds in betting, etc.; a unit (value or quantity) in a rationing scheme designed to restrict consumption and secure equable distribution of specified goods in short supply. **point duty,** duty of a constable at a stationary point, not on a beat or patrol. **point lace,** lace made with a needle over a paper pattern. **point of honour,** a matter seriously affecting personal honour. **point of order,** a question (in debates, etc.) relating to procedure, propriety, or observance of customary rule. **point of view,** way of regarding anything; the angle from which a matter is considered. **point-to-point,** from one place direct to another; a cross-country race. **to make a point of,** to regard as of special importance. **to stretch a point,** *see* **stretch. visual point,** *see* **visual.** (O.Fr.)

★**point,** *v.t.* poynt, to sharpen; to direct; to show or indicate; to aim; to punctuate; to mark with vowel points; to fill joints with mortar [Masonry]; to give pungency to: *v.i.* to direct the finger for designating an object; to draw attention to; to be directed towards. **to point at,** to treat with scorn.

pointage, *n. poyn*-taj, the amount represented by a rationing point, or such points collectively.

point-blank, *a.* and *ad.* horizontal; direct; with no elevation for range. (*point,* and Fr. *blanc,* the mark in the centre of a target.)

point-device, *a.* perfectly correct; specially scrupulous: *ad.* completely; to perfection.

pointed, *a. poynt*-ed, sharpened; having a point; aimed at someone or something; epigrammatic; abounding in conceits or lively turns. **pointed style,** Gothic (its characteristic arches being pointed) [Arch.].

pointedly, *ad. poynt*-ed-le, in a pointed manner.

pointedness, *n.* state or quality of being pointed.

pointer, *n. poynt*-er, anything that points; a breed of sporting dog, so called from its habit of indicating the position of game; a stick for pointing.

pointillage, *n.* (App.) massage by means of the finger-tips.

pointillism, *n. pwahn*-til-izm, a method of impressionist painting in which the effect is produced by the application of dots of different colours. (Fr. *pointillé,* having many points.)

pointillist, *n. pwahn*-til-ist, an artist who paints in pointillism: *a.* characterized by pointillism.

pointing, *n. poynt*-ing, punctuation; the act of trimming the lines of mortar in a wall with a mixture of Portland cement and sand; the protective facing thus obtained [Build.].

pointless, *a. poynt*-less, having no point; having no keenness or appositeness; meaningless.

pointlessly, *ad.* without point or effectiveness; irrelevantly.

pointlessness, *n.* the condition or quality of being pointless.

pointsman, *n. poynts*-man, one who looks after the points on a railway; a constable on point duty.

point-to-point, a horse-race or steeplechase over a course defined by landmarks.

poise, *n.* poyz, weight; balance; equipoise; that which balances; a regulating power; way of carrying oneself; dignified deportment: *v.t.* to balance in weight; to hover; to examine or ponder. (O.Fr. *poise.*)

★**poison,** *n. poyz*-on, that which, when absorbed into the system, is destructive or injurious to life; that which taints or destroys moral purity or health: *v.t.* to infect with anything fatal to life; to kill by poison; to taint or corrupt. **poisoned pen,** anonymous letters [Coll.]. (Fr.)

poisoner, *n. poyz*-on-er, one who poisons or corrupts.

poison-gas, *n.* any chemical substance, gaseous, liquid, or solid, used to produce a poisonous, irritant, or blistering effect, esp. in warfare.

poisonous, *a. poyz*-on-us, having the qualities of poison; corrupting.

poisonously, *ad.* in a poisonous manner.

poisonousness, *n.* quality of being poisonous.

poitrel, *n. poy*-trel, armour for the breast of a horse. (Fr.)

poke, *n.* poke, a pocket or small bag. **pig in a poke,** something acquired unseen, its value being unknown. (Probably Scand.)

poke, *n.* poke, a push; a thrust: *v.t.* to push against with anything pointed; to feel or search for with anything pointed; to thrust at with the horns: *v.i.* to feel about in the dark; to pry (about). **poke bonnet,** a bonnet projecting over the forehead. **poke fun at,** make fun of. (Ir. *poc,* a blow.)

poker, *n. poke*-er, one who pokes; an iron bar used in stirring a fire; a tool used in poker-work; the pochard duck.

poker, *n. poke*-er, a card game (originally American) in which the players bet and bluff on the value of the cards held. **poker face,** a face having an inscrutable expression; a person giving no visible clue to his thoughts [Coll.]. (Origin uncertain.)

poker-work, *n.* the decoration of wood by burning patterns into it with a heated poker.

pokeweed, *n. poke*-weed, the poisonous N. American perennial herb, *Phytolacca decandra.*

poking-stick, *n.* a rod formerly used in adjusting the plaits of ruffs.

poky, *a. poke*-e, cramped; small in size; mean.

polacca, *n.* po-*lak*-a, a vessel with three masts, used in the Mediterranean. (It., Polish.)

polacca, *n.* po-*lak*-a, a polonaise or other Polish dance; music for this. (Pol.)

polar, *a. poh*-lar, pertaining to, or situated near, or proceeding from the poles of the earth; pertaining to the magnetic pole. **Polar angle,** an angle formed by two meridians at the pole. **Polar bear,** the large Arctic bear, *Ursus maritimus.* **Polar circles,** two parallels of latitude round the poles at a distance of 23½ degrees. **Polar distance,** the angular distance from one of the poles, especially a celestial pole. (Fr. *polaire.*)

polarimeter, *n.* poh-la-*rim*-e-ter, an instrument for the measurement of the amount of polarization of light.
polarimetry, *n.* poh-la-*rim*-e-tre, the art of using a polarimeter; the measurement of optical activity.
polariscope, *n.* po-*la*-re-skope, an apparatus for showing the phenomena of polarized light. (Late L. *polaris*, and Gr. *skopeo*, view.)
polarity, *n.* pole-*ar*-re-te, condition of being, or disposition to be, attracted and repulsed in opposite directions, esp. that of the magnetic needle in pointing to the poles of the earth; action by, or susceptibility to, polar or magnetic influences.
polarizable, *a.* poh-la-*ry*-za-bl, susceptible of polarization.
polarization, *n.* poh-la-ry-*zay*-shon, the act of giving polarity to a body; the state of being polarized. **polarization of light,** a change produced upon light under the action of certain media, by which it exhibits the appearance of having polarity, or poles possessing different properties.
polarize, *v.t.* *poh*-la-rize, to communicate polarity to.
polarizer, *n.* *poh*-la-ry-zer, that which polarizes light.
polatouche, *n.* *pol*-a-toosh, a small Siberian flying-squirrel. (Russ.)
polder, *n.* *pol*-der, a tract of low land below sea-level that has been drained and cultivated, and is protected by dykes. (Dut.)
pole, *n.* pole, a long slender piece of wood; a mast; a flagstaff; the single shaft of a coach or wagon; a rod or perch, a measure of 5½ yards; a square measure of 30¼ sq. yd.; an instrument for measuring: *v.t.* to furnish with poles; to bear or convey on poles; to impel by poles, as a boat. **poles asunder,** in irreconcilable opposition. **under bare poles,** with all sails furled [Naut.]. (A.S. *pal*, a stake.)
pole, *n.* pole, one of the extremities of the axis on which the sphere of the heavens or the earth revolves; either of the polar regions; the pole-star; one of the two points in a magnetic body where the attractive or the repellent force is concentrated; the terminal of an electric battery or magnet; a point from which rays radiate; either of two opposing principles. **magnetic pole,** either pole of a magnet; the place on the surface of the earth where the needle points vertically. (O.Fr. *pol*, from Gr. *polos*, a pivot.)
Pole, *n.* pole, a native of Poland; one of Polish race.
poleaxe, *n.* *pole*-aks, a long-shafted battle-axe; a slaughterer's axe. (M.E. *pollax*.)
polecat, *n.* *pole*-kat, a small weasel-like carnivore, *Putorius fœtidus*, with glands secreting a fetid liquor. (Perhaps Fr. *poule*, a hen, or O.Fr. *pulent*, stinking, from L. *purulentus*, and *cat*.)
polemarch, *n.* *pol*-e-mark, a military commander, also, a civil magistrate, in ancient Greece. (Gr.)
polemic, *a.* po-*lem*-ik, polemical: *n.* an acrimonious discussion; controversy; a disputant: *pl.* the art of controversy, esp. on religious subjects; a history of such. (Gr. *polemikos*, belligerent.)
polemical, *a.* po-*lem*-e-kal, controversial; disputative.
polemically, *ad.* in a polemic manner.
polemize, *v.i.* *pol*-e-mize, to engage in controversial dispute.
polemoscope, *n.* po-*lem*-o-skope, a telescope affording view of objects not directly in the line of sight.
polenta, *n.* po-*len*-ta, a preparation of semolina or the like; porridge of various ingredients. (It.)
pole-star, *n.* Polaris, the bright star in the Great Bear situated nearly vertical to the pole of the earth; a lode-star; a guide.
polianite, *n.* *poh*-le-an-ite, a grey variety of manganese dioxide. (Gr. *poliaino*, make grey.)
Polianthes, *n.* pol-e-*an*-theez, the genus of plant containing the tuberose. (Gr. *polios*, grey, and *anthos*, a flower.)
police, *n.* po-*leece*, a civil force for the detection and prevention of crime, the preservation of law and order, etc.; the organization or department responsible for this; police constables collectively: *v.t.* to maintain law and order by means of a police force; to supply with police; to discipline. **police constable,** see **constable.** **police court,** a court of summary jurisdiction trying minor charges, esp. those submitted by the police. **police state,** a state under authoritarian rule, all private enterprise and personal activities being strictly subject to governmental control. **police station,** the headquarters of a local police force. (Fr.)
policeman, *n.* po-*leece*-man, a police constable.
policewoman, *n.* po-*leece*-woom-an, a female member of a police force.
policlinic, *n.* pol-e-*klin*-ik, the out-patient department of a hospital; a clinic in a private house. (Gr. *polis*, a city, *klinikos*, relating to a sick-bed.)
policy, *n.* *pol*-e-se, art or manner of governing a nation; the system of state administration; management adopted and pursued by a government; system of regulative measures; a line of conduct; prudence; cunning or dexterity of management; in Scotland (usually *pl.*), the pleasure grounds round a mansion. (O.Fr. *policie*, from Gr. *polites*, a citizen.)
policy, *n.* *pol*-e-se, a writing or instrument by which a contract or indemnity is effected. (Fr. *police*.)
Poligar, *n.* *pol*-e-gar, a minor feudal chief of southern India; (*l.c.*) a tribesman under a Poligar. (Tamil.)
poling, *n.* *pole*-ing, poles erected for scaffolding, etc.
polioencephalitis, *n.* *pol*-e-o-*en*-sef-a-*ly*-tis, inflammation of the grey matter of the brain. (Gr. *polios*, grey, and *encephalitis*.)
poliomyelitis, *n.* *pol*-e-o-*my*-e-*ly*-tis, inflammation of the grey matter in the spinal cord. **acute anterior poliomyelitis,** infantile paralysis. (Gr. *polios*, grey, *myelon*, marrow.)
poliosis, *n.* pol-e-*oh*-sis, greyness of the hair. (Gr. *polios*, grey.)
★polish, *n.* *pol*-ish, a smooth glossy surface; a substance to impart a polish; refinement; elegance of manners: *v.t.* to make smooth and glossy, usually by rubbing; to refine; to make elegant and polite: *v.i.* to become smooth, or glossy. (Fr. *polir*, polish.)
Polish, *a.* *poh*-lish, relating to Poland or its people: *n.* the language of Poland; the Poles collectively.
polishable, *a.* *pol*-ish-a-bl, capable of being polished.
polisher, *n.* *pol*-ish-er, the person or instrument that polishes.
polite, *a.* po-*lite*, well-mannered; well-bred; courteous; refined. (L. *politus*, polished.)
politely, *ad.* po-*lite*-le, in a polite manner.
politeness, *n.* po-*lite*-ness, polish of manners; refinement; courtesy.
politesse, *n.* pol-e-*tess*, tactful politeness; politeness; overacted politeness. (Fr.)
politic, *a.* *pol*-e-tik, constituting the state; sagacious, esp. in policy; scheming and astute; wary; well devised and adapted to the purpose. **body politic,** the whole people; the state. (L. *politicus*, from Gr. *polis*, city.)
★political, *a.* po-*lit*-e-kal, pertaining to politics, or to civil government and its administration; pertaining to a nation or state; possessing a settled system of government; treating of politics. **political economy,** the science or study of wealth, its production, distribution, etc.; economics. **political geography,** that part of geography dealing with frontiers and the political divisions of the earth.
politically, *ad.* in a political or politic manner.
politicaster, *n.* po-lit-e-*kas*-ter, a petty, trivial, or insignificant politician.
politician *n.* pol-e-*tish*-an, one versed in the art of governing, or devoted to politics; a statesman; one who makes a trade of politics.
politicize, *v.t.* po-*lit*-e-size, to talk politics; to make political; to act the politician.
politics, *n.pl.* *pol*-e-tiks, the science or art of governing; political affairs; political views; the management of party affairs.
polity, *n.* *pol*-e-te, the form or constitution of civil government; the constitution; the body politic.
polk, *v.i.* pohlk, to dance the polka [Coll.].
polka, *n.* *pol*-ka, a light, quick, Bohemian dance; its appropriate music. (Possibly from Czech, *pulka*, a half, from the sort of step taken in it.)
poll, *n.* pole, the head, or the back part of it; a register of voters; the voting at or the place of an election, also the number of votes: *v.t.* to lop the tops off trees; to remove the horns of cattle; to shear; to enter names on a list for voting; to bring to the poll: *v.i.* to vote at a poll. (O.Dut. *polle*.)
poll, *n.* pol, a parrot.
pollack, *n.* *pol*-lak, a sea-fish, *Gadus pollachius*, allied to the whiting. (Origin unknown.)

pollan, *n.* *pol*-lan, a freshwater salmonoid fish, *Coregonus pollan*, of the Irish lakes.
pollard, *n.* *pol*-lard, a tree that has been polled; a stag that has cast his horns; a mixture of bran and meal; the chub: *v.t.* to lop trees. (*poll.*)
poll-axe, *n.* *pole*-aks, a poleaxe.
poll-beast, *n.* a hornless ox.
pollen, *n.* *pol*-en, the fertilizing granules shed by the anther of a flower. (L., fine flour.)
pollent, *a.* *pol*-ent, strong; mighty. (L. *pollens*, being strong.)
poller, *n.* *pole*-er, one who polls trees; one who registers voters; a voter.
pollex, *n.* *pol*-eks (*pl.* **pollices**, *pol*-e-seez), the thumb; a thumb-like organ or process [Zool.]. (L.)
pollicitation, *n.* po-lis-e-*tay*-shon, the act of promising; a voluntary engagement or a writing containing it; a promise not yet formally accepted [Law]. (L. *pollicitatus*, promised.)
pollinar, *a.* *pol*-e-nar, covered with fine dust like pollen. [Entom.]
pollinate, *v.t.* *pol*-e-nate, to fertilize with pollen.
pollination, *n.* pol-e-*nay*-shon, action of pollinating; conveyance of pollen from anther to stigma.
polling-booth, *n.* *see* **booth.**
pollinic, *a.* po-*lin*-ik, of or containing pollen [Bot.].
polliniferous, *a.* pol-e-*nif*-er-rus, producing pollen.
pollinose, *a.* *pol*-e-nohs, pollinar.
pollinosis, *n.* pol-e-*noh*-sis, hay-fever [Med.].
polliwog, *n.* *pol*-e-wog, a tadpole. (*poll.*)
poll-man, *n.* *pol*-man, one taking his degree without honours; a passman [Camb. Univ.].
pollock, *n.* *pol*-lok, the pollack.
polloi, *n.* po-*loy*, the rabble, the riff-raff. (Gr. *hoi polloi*, the many.)
pollster, *n.* *pole*-ster, one who, by means of unofficial polls of sample voters, makes forecasts of election results [U.S.A.].
poll-tax, *n.* *pole*-taks, a capitation tax.
pollucite, *n.* po-*lew*-site, a rare hydrated silicate of aluminium and cæsium. (L. *Pollux.*)
pollute, *v.t.* po-*lewt*, to defile or to make unclean; to taint with guilt; to profane; to corrupt; to violate. (L. *pollutus*, defiled.)
pollutedly, *ad.* po-*lew*-ted-le, with pollution.
pollutedness, *n.* state of being polluted.
polluter, *n.* po-*lew*-ter, a defiler; a corrupter.
pollution, *n.* po-*lew*-shon, the act of polluting, or state of being polluted; defilement; among the Jews, legal or ceremonial uncleanness; emission of semen otherwise than in coition [Med.].
polo, *n.* *poh*-lo, a game like hockey, played on horseback with long mallets. (Persian.)
polonaise, *n.* pol-o-*naze*, a robe after a Polish fashion; a Polish air and dance. (Fr. *polonais*, Polish.)
polonium, *n.* po-*loh*-ne-um, a radioactive element found in pitchblende. (L. *Polonia*, Poland, the country of Mme Curie who discovered it, 1898.)
polony, *n.* po-*loh*-ne, a dry sausage of partly cooked meat. (*Bologna.*)
poltergeist, *n.* *pol*-ter-gyst, a spirit that makes its presence known by rapping or other noises; a mysterious agency said to throw objects about. (Ger. *Polter*, noise, *Geist*, ghost.)
poltroon, *n.* pol-*troon*, an arrant coward; a dastard: *a.* base; vile; contemptible. (Fr. *poltron*, a sluggard. It. *poltro*, a bed.)
poltroonery, *n.* pol-*troo*-ner-re, cowardice; baseness of mind; want of spirit.
poly-, *comb.f.* *pol*-e, much; many. (Gr. *polys.*)
polyacoustic, *a.* pol-e-a-*kous*-tik, that multiplies or magnifies sound: *n.* an instrument which does so. (Gr. *polys*, many, *akoustikos*, pertaining to sound.)
polyadelphous, *a.* pol-e-a-*del*-fus, having stamens in three or more bundles [Bot.].
polyandrian, *a.* pol-e-*an*-dre-an, pertaining to polyandry; having many stamens [Bot.].
polyandrist, *n.* pol-e-*an*-drist, a woman practising polyandry.
polyandrous, *a.* pol-e-*an*-drus, polyandrian.
polyandry, *n.* pol-e-*an*-dre, the state or practice of a woman having more living husbands than one. (Gr. *polys*, and *andros*, man.)
polyanthus, *n.* pol-e-*an*-thus, a primulaceous plant, apparently a cross between the primrose and oxlip. (Gr. *polys*, and *anthos*, flower.)
polyarchy, *n.* *pol*-e-ar-ke, a government of many; mob rule. (Gr. *polys*, and *archo*, rule.)
polyatomic, *a.* pol-e-a-*tom*-ik, having an equivalent of more than one [Chem.].
polyautography, *n.* pol-e-aw-*tog*-ra-fe, act or process of multiplying copies of handwriting, etc. (a former name for lithography). (Gr. *polys*, and *autos*, self, *grapho*, write.)
polybasic, *a.* pol-e-*bay*-sik, having two or more equivalents of a base [Chem.].
polybasite, *n.* po-*lib*-a-site, an iron-black silver ore containing sulphur and antimony.
polycarpic, *a.* pol-e-*kar*-pik, capable of fruiting several times [Bot.]. (Gr. *polys*, and *karpos*, fruit.)
polychæte, *n.* *pol*-e-keet, any member of the Polychæta, a large class of marine worms.
polychord, *a.* *pol*-e-kord, having many chords: *n.* a ten-stringed violin-like instrument; an apparatus coupling two octave notes [Organ]. (Gr. *polys*, and *chord.*)
polychroite, *n.* pol-e-*kroh*-ite, the colouring matter of saffron. (Gr. *polys*, and *chroos*, coloured.)
polychromatic, *a.* pol-e-kro-*mat*-ik, exhibiting a play of colours [Min.]. (Gr. *polys*, and *chromatic.*)
polychrome, *a.* *pol*-e-krome, having many colours; in the manner of polychromy: *n.* a statue or other work of art in many colours; esculin [Med.].
polychromy, *n.* *pol*-e-kroh-me, the ancient art of colouring statuary, buildings, pottery, etc.
polycladous, *a.* po-*lik*-la-dus, having many, or over-many, branches [Bot.].
polyclinic, *n.* pol-e-*klin*-ik, a clinic treating all kinds of diseases; a general hospital. (Gr. *polys*, and *clinic.*)
polycotyledon, *n.* *pol*-e-kot-e-*lee*-don, a plant that has more than two cotyledons.
polycotyledonous, *a.* *pol*-e-kot-e-*lee*-do-nus, having more than two cotyledons.
polydactylous, *a.* pol-e-*dak*-te-lus, having supernumary fingers or toes.
polydipsia, *n.* pol-e-*dip*-se-a, morbidly insatiable thirst [Med.]. (Gr. *polys*, and *dipsa*, thirst.)
polyfoil, *n.* *pol*-e-foyl, a circle with many arches on the inner side of its circumference.
polygamian, *a.* pol-e-*gay*-me-an, belonging to the group having hermaphrodite flowers [Bot.].
polygamist, *n.* po-*lig*-a-mist, one who practises or upholds polygamy.
polygamous, *a.* po-*lig*-a-mus, characterized by or practising polygamy; polygamian [Bot.].
polygamy, *n.* po-*lig*-a-me, the state or practice of having a plurality of wives (or husbands) at the same time. (Gr. *polys*, and *gamos*, marriage. Fr. *polygamie*)
polygastric, *a.* pol-e-*gas*-trik, having many stomachs [Zool.]. (Gr. *polys*, and *gastric.*)
polygenesis, *n.* pol-e-*jen*-e-sis, the theory that living organisms derive not from one cell or embryo only but several. (Gr. *polys*, and *genesis.*)
polygenetic, *a.* pol-e-je-*net*-ik, pertaining to or characterized by polygenesis; yielding two or more shades with different mordants (of dye-stuffs).
polygenic, *a.* pol-e-*jen*-ik, pertaining to polygeny; polygenetic.
polygenous, *a.* po-*lij*-e-nus, consisting of many kinds. (Gr. *polys*, and *genos*, kind.)
polygeny, *n.* po-*lij*-e-ne, the theory that the races of mankind are descended not from one original ancestor but from several independent pairs; polygenesis.
polyglot, *a.* *pol*-e-glot, of several languages: *n.* a Bible in several languages; one who can speak or read many languages. (Gr. *polyglottos*, many-tongued.)
polyglottic, *a.* pol-e-*glot*-ik, polyglot; speaking many languages.
polygon, *n.* *pol*-e-gon, a closed figure of many angles [Geom.]. (L. *polygonum.*)
polygonal, *a.* po-*lig*-o-nal, having many angles.
Polygonum, *n.* po-*lig*-o-num, the genus of plants which comprises the knotgrasses. (L.)
polygram, *n.* *pol*-e-gram, a figure consisting of many lines. (Gr. *polys*, and *gramma*, a letter.)
polygraph, *n.* *pol*-e-graf, an apparatus for multiplying copies of a writing; a writer of various kinds of works. (Gr. *polys*, and *grapho*, write.)
polygraphic, *a.* pol-e-*graf*-ik, pertaining to polygraphy; done by a polygraph.
polygraphy, *n.* po-*lig*-ra-fe, the use of the polygraph; copious or versatile literary productivity; ciphering and deciphering.

polygynian, *a.* pol-e-*jin*-e-an, belonging to the group having more than twelve styles or stigmas [Bot.].
polygyny, *n.* po-*lij*-e-ne, plurality of wives; polygamy. (Gr. *polys*, and *gyne*, a female.)
polyhedral, *a.* pol-e-*heed*-ral, having many sides.
polyhedron, *n.* pol-e-*heed*-ron, a solid bounded by many sides or planes [Geom.]. (Gr. *polys*, and *hedra*, a side.)
polyhistor, *n.* pol-e-*his*-tor, a man of vast learning. (Gr. *polys*, and *histor*, the knowing.)
polymath, *n.* *pol*-e-math, one of great and varied learning.
polymathy, *n.* po-*lim*-a-the, knowledge of many arts and sciences. (Gr. *polys*, and *mathesis*, learning.)
polymer, *n.* *pol*-e-mer, any polymeric compound, esp. one of higher molecular weight than the original compound [Chem.].
polymeric, *a.* pol-e-*me*-rik, pertaining to polymerism; subject to polymerism (of compounds) [Chem.].
polymerism, *n.* po-*lim*-er-rizm, such combination of elements that the molecular weights are simple multiples of that of the lowest member of the group [Chem.]. (Gr. *polys*, and *meros*, part.)
polymignite, *n.* pol-e-*mig*-nite, a black crystalline mineral consisting of a niobate and titanate of one of the rare earth metals with iron and calcium. (Gr. *polys*, and *mignynai*, to mix.)
polymorph, *n.* *pol*-e-morf, any polymorphous object or organism. (Gr. *polys*, and *morphe*, shape.)
polymorphic, *a.* *pol*-e-*morf*-ik, polymorphous.
polymorphism, *n.* pol-e-*morf*-izm, the quality or condition of being polymorphous; the condition in which either or both sexes occur in many different forms [Zool.].
polymorphous, *a.* pol-e-*morf*-us, having many forms, shapes, or characters; occurring in several distinct forms.
Polynesian, *n.* pol-e-*nee*-ze-an, a native of Polynesia: *a.* pertaining to Polynesia, a scattered group of archipelagoes in the Pacific. (Gr. *polys*, *nesos*, island.)
polynomial, *a.* pol-e-*noh*-me-al, containing many terms or names: *n.* a multinomial [Alg.]. (Gr. *polys*, and *onoma*, a name.)
polyonymous, *a.* pol-e-*on*-e-mus, having many titles.
polyopia, *n.* *pol*-e-*oh*-pe-a, double or multiple vision. (Gr. *polys* and *opia*, from *ops*, eye.)
polyp, *n.* *pol*-ip, any invertebrate of the genus *Hydra*; a sea-anemone or similar cœlenterate; an individual member of a compound organism [Zool.]. (L. *polypus*.)
polypary, *n.* *pol*-e-pa-re, the hard chitinous covering secreted by many corals, etc. (L. *polypus*.)
polypetalous, *a.* pol-e-*pet*-a-lus, having many petals [Bot.]. (Gr. *polys*, and *petal*, leaf.)
polyphagia, *n.* pol-e-fay-*je*-a, abnormal appetite; bulimia [Med.].
polyphagous, *a.* po-*lif*-a-gus, subsisting on many kinds of food [Zool.]; eating ravenously or to excess [Path.]. (Gr. *polys*, and *phago*, eat.)
polypharmacy, *n.* pol-e-*far*-ma-se, medicine of many ingredients; the prescription of many drugs at one time.
polyphase, *a.* *pol*-e-faze, multiphase; having or producing three or more phases [Elect.].
polyphone, *n.* *pol*-e-fone, a symbol representing more than one sound (as "ough"—*enough*, *bough*, *cough*, etc.).
polyphonic, *a.* pol-e-*fon*-ik, consisting of many voices; consisting of two or more parts, each of which has an independent melody [Mus.]; having the characteristics of poetry (of prose). (Gr. *polys*, and *phone*, sound.)
polyphonism, *n.* po-*lif*-o-nizm, the state or quality of being polyphonic; counterpoint.
polyphonist, *n.* po-*lif*-o-nist, a contrapuntist.
polyphony, *n.* po-*lif*-o-ne, polyphonism; representation of more than one sound by the same character or symbol [Phonetics].
polyphyletic, *a.* pol-e-fy-*let*-ik, polygenetic; belonging to or descended from several types [Biol.].
polyphyllous, *a.* pol-e-*fil*-lus, having many leaves [Bot.]. (Gr. *polys*, and *phyllon*, leaf.)
polypite, *n.* *pol*-e-pite, an individual polyp in coral.
polyplastic, *a.* pol-e-*plas*-tik, having, assuming, or able to assume many forms.
polypod, *a.* *pol*-e-pod, having many feet: *n.* a millipede. (Gr. *polys*, and *pous*, foot.)
polypody, *n.* *pol*-e-pod-e, a fern of the genus *Polypodium*. (Gr. *polypous*, many-footed.)
polypoid, *a.* *pol*-e-poyd, resembling a polyp or a polypus.
polyporus, *a.* po-*lip*-o-rus, having many pores.
polypous, *a.* *pol*-e-pus, of the nature of a polyp or of a polypus; characterized by polypi [Med.].
polypus, *n.* *pol*-e-pus (*pl.* **polypi**), a polyp [Zool.]; a soft tumour growing from mucous membrane, so named because of its numerous foot-like ramifications [Med.]. (Gr. *polys*, and *pous*, foot.)
polyscope, *n.* *pol*-e-skope, a multiplying lens or optical appliance; a diaphanoscope [Surg.]. (Gr. *polys*, and *skopeo*, view.)
polysepalous, *a.* pol-e-*sep*-a-lus, having separate sepals. (Gr. *polys*, and *sepal*.)
polyspermous, *a.* pol-e-*sper*-mus, containing or producing many seeds [Bot.]. (Gr. *polys*, and *sperma*, seed.)
polyspermy, *n.* *pol*-e-sper-me, the impregnation of an ovum by several spermatozoa [Biol.].
polysporous, *a.* pol-e-*spaw*-rus, having or producing many spores [Bot.].
polystome, *n.* *pol*-e-stome, an animal having many mouths. (Gr. *polys*, and *stoma*, a mouth.)
polystyle, *a.* *pol*-e-stile, having numerous columns [Arch.]: *n.* a polystyle edifice. (Gr. *polys*, and *stylos*, pillar.)
polysyllabic, *a.* pol-e-sil-*lab*-ik, consisting of many syllables.
polysyllable, *n.* pol-e-*sil*-a-bl, a word of many syllables. (Gr. *polys*, and *syllable*.)
polysyndeton, *n* pol-e-*sin*-de-ton, repetition of the conjunction in speech for sake of emphasis. (Gr. *polys*, and *syndetos*, bound together.)
polysynthetic, *a.* pol-e-sin-*thet*-ik, composed of several elements (esp. of words formed by agglutination).
polytechnic, *n.* pol-e-*tek*-nik, a school for instruction in the sciences and practical arts: *a.* comprehending, or giving instruction in, many arts and sciences. (Gr. *polys*, and *techne*, an art.)
polythalamous, *a.* pol-e-*thal*-a-mus, many-chambered. (Gr. *polys*, and *thalamos*, a chamber.)
polytheism, *n.* pol-e-*thee*-izm, the worship or doctrine of many gods. (Gr. *polys*, and *theos*, a god.)
polytheist, *n.* pol-e-*thee*-ist, one who believes in a plurality of gods.
polytheistic, *a.* pol-e-the-*is*-tik, pertaining to or embracing polytheism.
polyvalent, *a.* po-*liv*-a-lent, multivalent; having a combining value greater than two atoms of a univalent element [Chem.].
Polyzoa, *n.pl.* pol-e-*zoh*-a, a class of invertebrates living in coral- or tree-like colonies, often resembling seaweeds or forming incrustations on stones, etc.; (*l.c.*) individual members of this class; the bryozoa. (Gr. *polys*, and *zoon*, a living entity.)
polyzoan, *n.* pol-e-*zoh*-an, an individual of a colony of polyzoa: *a.* pertaining to the Polyzoa.
polyzoarium, *n.* pol-e-zo-*ayr*-re-um, a polyzoan colony; the supporting structure of this.
polyzonal, *a.* pol-e-*zoh*-nal, composed of many zones or belts [Opt.]. (Gr. *polys*, and *zone*.)
pom, *n.* pom, a Pomeranian dog.
pomace, *n.* *pom*-as, the refuse pulp of apples crushed in cider-making. (Late L. *pomacium*, cider.)
pomaceous, *a.* po-*may*-shus, pertaining to, or of the nature of, pomes or trees bearing them; pertaining to apples; resembling pomace.
pomade, *n.* po-*mahd*, perfumed ointment for the hair. (Fr. *pommade*.)
pomander, *n.* po-*man*-der a perfumed ball or powder used as preventive of infection.
pomatum, *n.* po-*may*-tum, pomade.
pome, *n.* pome, any compound fleshy fruit with enclosed seeds, as the apple. (O.Fr.)
pomegranate, *n.* *pom*-gran-at, an edible fruit with a thick rind and crimson acid-flavoured pulp containing many seeds; the tree, *Punica granatum*, bearing this. (O.Fr. *pome grenate*, seeded pome.)
pomelo, *n.* *pom*-el-oh, the grapefruit.
Pomeranian, *n.* pom-er-*ray*-ne-an, a native of the German province of Pomerania; a Pomeranian dog, a small dog having long silky hair, bushy tail, and a sharp muzzle: *a.* pertaining to Pomerania.
pomfret, *n.* *pom*-fret, an edible fish of the genus *Stromateus*, of Indian and Pacific waters.

Pomfret-cake, *n. pum*-fret-kake, a cake of liquorice made at Pontefract in Yorkshire.
pomiculture, *n. poh*-me-*kul*-tewr, the cultivation of fruit-trees. (L. *pomum*, and *cultura*.)
pomiferous, *a.* po-*mif*-er-rus, apple-bearing; pome-bearing. (L. *pomum*, and *fero*, bear.)
pomiform, *a. poh*-me-form, like a pome or an apple.
Pommard, *n.* pom-*mard*, a superior red Burgundy wine, from a place of that name in Côte d'Or, France.
pommel, *n. pum*-mel, a knob; the high part of a saddle; a knob on a sword-hilt: *v.t.* to beat with the fists, or with or as with something thick or bulky. (O.Fr. *pomel*.)
pommelling, *n. pum*-mel-ling, a beating or bruising.
pomology, *n.* po-*mol*-o-je, the science or art of growing fruits. (L. *pomum*, and Gr. *logos*, science.)
pomp, *n.* pomp, display of grandeur and splendour; pageantry; ostentation. (Fr. *pompe*.)
pompadour, *n.* and *a. pom*-pa-door, applied to certain styles in dress, furnishings, etc., esp. to a method of hairdressing in which the hair is brushed back and upwards from the forehead. (Madame de *Pompadour*.)
pompano, *n. pom*-pa-no, a food-fish, *Trachinotus carolinus*, of the Atlantic coast of N. America. (Sp.)
pompholyx, *n. pom*-fo-liks, an eruptive disease characterized by vesicles on the palms and soles [Med.]. (Gr., a blister.)
pompier, *n. pom*-pyer, a fireman. **pompier ladder,** a single-poled fireman's scaling ladder, with cross rungs and a strong hook at the top. (Fr.)
pompion, *n. pump*-e-on, a pumpkin, *Cucurbita pepo.*
pompom, *n. pom*-pom, a quick-firing automatic gun, esp. a one-pounder. (From the sound.)
pompon, *n. pom*-pon, a globular tuft ornament; a round tuft on a soldier's headgear [Mil.]. (Fr.)
pomposity, *n.* pom-*pos*-e-te, pompousness; ostentation; boasting.
pomposo, *ad.* pom-*poh*-zo, majestically [Mus.]. (It.)
pompous, *a. pom*-pus, displaying pomp or grandeur; ostentatious; self-important. (Fr. *pompeux*.)
pompously, *ad. pom*-pus-le, in a pompous manner.
pompousness, *n.* the state of being pompous.
ponce, *n.* ponce, a man living on a prostitute's earnings [Slang].
ponceau, *n.* pon(g)-*soh*, the colour of the corn poppy, a brilliant red. (Fr.)
poncho, *n. pon*-choh, a woollen cloak worn in South America, with a slit in the middle for the head and hanging down before and behind; a waterproof cape of similar design. (Sp.)
pond, *n.* pond, a small body of stagnant water; a small lake: *v.t.* and *i.* to make or collect into a pond. (*pound*, an enclosure.)
ponder, *v.t. pon*-der, to weigh in the mind; to consider: *v.i.* to cogitate; to deliberate. (L. *pondero*, weigh.)
ponderability, *n. pon*-der-ra-*bil*-e-te, ponderableness.
ponderable, *a. pon*-der-ra-bl, that may be weighed.
ponderableness, *n.* state of being ponderable.
ponderal, *a. pon*-der-ral, pertaining to weight; estimated by weight.
ponderance, *n. pon*-der-rance, weight; importance.
ponderer, *n. pon*-der-rer, one who ponders.
ponderingly, *ad. pon*-der-ring-le, with consideration.
ponderosity, *n.* pon-der-*ros*-e-te, ponderousness.
ponderous, *a. pon*-der-rus, very heavy; weighty; forcible. (Fr. *pondereux*.)
ponderously, *ad.* with great weight.
ponderousness, *n.* state of being ponderous.
pond-weed, *n.* any plant growing in stagnant water, esp. species of *Potamogeton.*
pondwort, *n. pond*-wurt, the plant water-soldier.
pone, *n. poh*-ne, the card-player to the right of the dealer. (L., place.)
pone, *n.* pone, a kind of bread made of maize flour; Johnny cake. (Algonquian.)
ponent, *a. poh*-nent, western; occidental. (L. *ponere*, to lay, hence to set, as the sun.)
pongee, *n. pon*-jee *or pun*-jee, a soft unbleached silk from undomesticated silkworms; a fine mercerized cotton cloth.
pongo, *n. pong*-go, the orang-outang, or other large African anthropoid ape. (Native African.)
poniard, *n. pon*-yerd, a small dagger: *v.t.* to pierce with a poniard; to stab. (Fr. *poignard*.)
Pontac, *n. pon*-tak, a kind of claret from Pontac in the south of France.

Pontic, *a. pon*-tik, pertaining to the Black Sea. (L. *Pontus*, the Black Sea.)
pontifex, *n. pon*-te-feks, a member of the college of priests of ancient Rome; a pontiff. **pontifex maximus,** the chief of the pontiffs; the Pope. (L., a builder of bridges.)
pontiff, *n. pon*-tif, a high priest; the Pope. (Fr. *pontife*, from L. *pontifex*.)
pontific, *a.* pon-*tif*-ik, pontifical.
pontifical, *a.* pon-*tif*-e-kal, characteristic of or belonging to a pontiff, priest, or Pope; papal; oracular: *n.* a book of rites and ceremonies: *pl.* episcopal vestments.
pontifically, *ad.* in a pontifical manner.
pontificate, *n.* pon-*tif*-e-kate, the dignity of a pontiff; the reign of a Pope: *v.t.* and *i.* to celebrate or officiate pontifically; to play the pontiff. (L. *pontificatus*.)
pontlevis, *n.* pont-*lev*-is, a drawbridge; the rearing of a horse on his hind legs. (Fr.)
pontonier, *n.* pon-to-*neer*, one in charge of pontoons or engaged in constructing a pontoon-bridge [Mil.]. (Fr.)
pontoon, *n.* pon-*toon*, a flat-bottomed boat or structure used for constructing temporary bridges; a large lighter fitted with cranes. **pontoon bridge,** a bridge constructed on pontoons; a bridge of boats. (Fr. *ponton*.)
pontoon, *n.* pon-*toon*, vingt-un, or some similar card-game. (Corruption of Fr. *vingt*, twenty, *un*, one.)
ponty, *n. pon*-te, a punty.
pony, *n. poh*-ne (*pl.* **ponies**), a small horse; a small specimen of its kind, esp. a small glass of liquor; £25 [Slang]; a key or crib used for translations [Amer. slang]: *a.* secondary, auxiliary (esp. of machinery, etc.). **pony motor,** a small motor for bringing synchronous machinery to the necessary speed before synchronizing. (O.Fr. *poulenet*, a little colt.)
pood, *n.* pood, a Russian weight, equal to slightly over 36 lb. av. (Russ.)
poodle, *n. poo*-dl, a breed of small pet dog with long curly hair. (Ger. *Pudel*, from *pudeln*, to waddle.)
pooh, *int.* poo, an exclamation of dislike or contempt.
Pooh-bah, *n. poo*-bah, a holder of many offices simultaneously. (Name of a character in W. S. Gilbert's *Mikado*.)
pooh-pooh, *v.t.* poo-*poo*, to make light of anything; to treat in a sneering way.
pooka, *n. poo*-kah, a malevolent sprite of Irish folk-tales. (Ir.)
pool, *n.* pool, a comparatively deep and still place in a river; a small sheet of water; a puddle; an area of spilled liquid. (A.S. *pol*.)
pool, *n.* pool, the stakes played for in certain games of cards, or the receptacle for them; a game played on the billiard table in which each player has a different coloured cue ball; a combination for gambling or speculating; a trust or cartel [Comm.]; an amalgamation (esp. of revenue) into one general fund: *v.t.* to put in a pool or common fund. **football pool,** a form of gambling (through the post) on the weekly results of League Association football matches. (From Fr. *poule*, a hen, but the connexion is obscure.)
pool-snipe, *n.* the redshank, *Totanus calidris.*
poon, *n.* poon, the East Indian timber-tree *Calophyllum inophyllum*, formerly much used for masts, spars, etc. (Tamil, *punnai*.)
poonac, *n. poon*-ak, crushed seeds after the oil has been extracted. (Singhalese.)
poop, *n.* poop, the raised deck in the stern of a ship: *v.t.* to strike or break over the stern of a vessel, as a wave. (Fr. *poupe*.)
pooped, *a.* poopt, having a poop; struck on the poop.
***poor,** *a.* poor, having little or no means; indigent; necessitous; destitute of strength, beauty, spirit, dignity, etc.; barren; mean; jejune; having little or no worth or weight; dejected; lean; meagre; small; wanting in good qualities; an expression of tenderness, pity, or contempt. **the poor,** necessitous persons, esp. those dependent on charity. **poor white,** *see* **white** (O.Fr. *poure*.)
poor-box, *n.* a collecting-box for alms, esp. one in a church or police-court.
poor-house, *n.* a workhouse.
poor-john, *n. poor*-jon, hake, or similar fish, dried and salted.

poor-law, *n.* the body of regulations dealing with the public support of the poor.
poorliness, *n. poor*-le-ness, the state of being indisposed or poorly.
poorly, *a. poor*-le, somewhat ill; indisposed: *ad.* without wealth; in indigence; inadequately; with little or no success; meanly.
poorness, *n. poor*-ness, quality or state of being poor.
poor-rate, *n.* a rate for the support of paupers.
poor-spirited, *a.* of a mean spirit; cowardly; base.
poor-spiritedness, *n.* the quality of being poor-spirited.
pop, *n.* pop, a small, smart, quick sound or report; ginger beer, or other effervescing drink: *ad.* suddenly: *v.i.* to enter or issue forth with a quick sudden motion; to dart; to move quickly: *v.t.* to push suddenly; to pawn. **pop the question,** propose marriage [Coll.]. (Imit.)
pop, *n.* pop, a popular concert [Coll.].
popcorn, *n. pop*-kawrn, parched maize.
Pope, *n.* pope, the Bishop of Rome; the head of the Roman Catholic church; a priest of the Greek church. **pope's eye,** a gland embedded in fat in the middle of the thigh of an ox or sheep. **pope's nose,** the fleshy prominence supporting the tail feathers of a fowl, turkey, or other bird. **Pope Joan,** a game of cards named after the legendary female Pope, Joan. (A.S. *papa.*)
pope, *n.* pope, the freshwater fish, the ruff.
popedom, *n. pope*-dom, the office, dignity, tenure of office, or jurisdiction of the Pope.
popery, *n. pope*-er-re, Roman Catholicism (in depreciatory use only).
pop-eyed, *a. pop*-ide, having protruding eyes; daft, easily fooled [Amer. slang].
popgun, *n. pop*-gun, a toy gun ejecting pellets by compressed air, used by children.
popinjay, *n. pop*-in-jay, a parrot; the green woodpecker; a mark for shooting at; a fop or coxcomb. (O.Fr. *papegai,* a parrot.)
popish, *a. pope*-ish, relating or pertaining to the Pope or to popery.
popishly, *ad. pope*-ish-le, in a popish direction.
poplar, *n. pop*-lar, a tree of the genus *Populus,* with a white, soft, light wood. (O.Fr. *poplier.*)
poplin, *n. pop*-lin, a ribbed or corded fabric made of silk and worsted. (Fr. *popeline.*)
popliteal, *a.* pop-le-*tee*-al, poplitic.
popliteus, *n.* pop-le-*tee*-us, the hinder part of the knee-joint; the ham [Anat.]. (L.)
poplitic, *a.* pop-*lit*-ik pertaining to the knee-joint or ham. (Gr. *poplitis,* of the ham.)
poppable, *a. pop*-a-bl, capable of being popped (of corn), or [Slang] of being pawned.
poppet, *n. pop*-et, a timber used to support a ship in launching; the head of a lathe; a term of endearment. (*puppet.*)
poppet-valve, *n.* a valve rising perpendicularly to or from its seat.
popping-crease, *n.* the line 4 ft. from and parallel to the stumps within which is the batsman's ground [Cricket].
popple, *v.t. pop*-l, to bubble; to bob up and down. (*pop.*)
poppy, *n. pop*-e, a plant with large scarlet, white, or yellow flowers and narcotic properties, of the genus *Papaver.* **poppy oil,** oil from the seeds of the opium poppy, *Papaver somniferum.* **Welsh poppy,** a species of *Meconopsis, M. cambria,* with yellow flowers. **Flanders poppy,** *see* **Flanders.** (A.S. *popig.*)
poppycock, *n. pop*-e-kok, blather; utter nonsense [Slang].
poppy-head, *n.* a poppy's seed capsule; a finial of foliage or other ornament in woodwork.
populace, *n. pop*-yew-las, the common people. (Fr.)
popular, *a. pop*-yew-lar, pertaining to the people; suitable to common people; easily comprehensible; plain; familiar; pleasing to the people; extensively prevalent. **Popular front,** an alliance between non-Communist and Communist groups for united political action. (Fr. *populaire.*)
popularity, *n. pop*-yew-*la*-re-te, the state of being popular or in favour with the people.
popularize, *v.t. pop*-yew-la-rize, to render popular or common; to spread among the people.
popularly, *ad.* in a popular manner.
populate, *v.t. pop*-yew-late, to furnish with inhabitants; to people. (Late L. *populatus.*)
population, *n.* pop-yew-*lay*-shon, the whole people or the number of people or inhabitants in a country; state of a country as regards population. (Late L. *populatio.*)
populin, *n. pop*-yew-lin, a crystalline glucoside obtained from the bark of the aspen, used as an antipyretic. (L. *populus,* poplar.)
populist, *n. pop*-yew-list, a member of a "popular," or advanced, political party, esp. in the U.S.A.
populous, *a. pop*-yew-lus, full of inhabitants; abounding with people.
populously, *ad.* with many inhabitants.
populousness, *n.* the state of being populous.
porbeagle, *n.* pawr-*bee*-gl, the voracious shark, *Lamna cornubica,* of the Atlantic and Pacific. (Possibly Cornish.)
porcate, *a. pawr*-kate, formed in ridges [Zool.]. (L. *porca,* a ridge.)
porcelain, *n. pawrs*-len, a fine white semi-translucent, earthenware; china: *a.* of or pertaining to porcelain. (Fr. *porcelaine,* It. *porcellana,* the cowry shell, from L. *porcus,* pig, as shaped like a hog's back.)
porcelainized, *a. pawr*-sel-a-nyzd, hardened into a porcelain-like substance [Geol.].
porcellanic, *a.* pawr-se-*lan*-ik, porcellanous.
porcellanite, *n. pawr*-se-la-nite, a light semi-vitrified shale; porcelain-jasper.
porcellanous, *a.* pawr-*sel*-a-nus, resembling or pertaining to porcelain, or having its texture.
porch, *n.* pawrch, a projecting vestibule or entrance to a building; a covered approach to an entrance; a portico; anciently, a covered walk. **the Porch,** the public portico in Athens where Zeno taught, hence, the school of the Stoics. (Fr. *porche.*)
porcine, *a. pawr*-sine, pertaining to or resembling swine. (L. *porcus,* a pig.)
porcupine, *n. pawr*-kew-pine, a rodent of the genus *Hystrix,* furnished with erectile quills; applied to various machines having teeth for heckling, tearing, etc. **Canadian porcupine, tree porcupine,** New World rodents of the genus *Erethizon.* **porcupine disease,** ichthyosis, fish-skin disease. (O.Fr. *porc espin,* from L. *porc,* pig, and *espin,* spine.)
porcupine-fish, *n.* any tropical globe-fish of the genus *Diodon,* covered with spines.
porcupine-grass, *n.* any Australian grass of the genus *Triodia*; the fodder grass *Stipa spartia,* of the western U.S.A.
porcupine-wood, *n.* the outer wood of the coconut palm.
pore, *n.* pawr, a minute orifice in the membranous surfaces of plants or animals by which fluids are exhaled or absorbed; a small interstice between the molecules of bodies. (Fr., from L. *porus,* passage.)
pore, *v.i.* pawr, to study with steady, continued attention or application. (Origin unknown.)
porer, *n. paw*-rer, one who pores or studies diligently.
porge, *v.t.* pawrj, to make ceremonially clean according to Jewish law (of slaughtered beasts). (Connected with *purge.*)
porgy, *n. pawr*-je, any of many marine food-fish, esp. of the genus *Pagrus.*
Porifera, *n.pl.* po-*rif*-er-ra, the sponges. (L. *porus,* a pore, *fero,* bear.)
poriform, *a. paw*-re-form, resembling a pore.
porism, *n. paw*-rizm, a proposition affirming the possibility of finding such conditions as will render a certain problem indeterminate or capable of innumerable solutions; a kind of corollary [Geom.]. (Gr. *porisma,* a deduction.)
porismatic, *a.* paw-riz-*mat*-ik, poristic.
poristic, *a.* paw-*ris*-tik, pertaining to a porism.
porite, *n. poh*-rite, a reef-building coral the surface of which is covered with minute pores.
pork, *n. pawrk,* the flesh of a pig, fresh or salted. (Fr. *porc.*)
porker, *n. pawrk*-er, a young pig; a pig.
porket, *n. pawrk*-et, a porker.
porkling, *n. pawrk*-ling, a porker.
pork-pie, *n.* minced jellied pork enclosed in pastry and eaten cold. **pork-pie hat,** a felt hat with flat crown and turned-up brim.
pornographer, *n.* pawr-*nog*-ra-fer, a writer, creator, or purveyor of obscenities.

pornographic, *a.* pawr-no-*graf*-ik, characterized by or pertaining to pornography.
pornography, *n.* pawr-*nog*-ra-fe, licentious or obscene writing ; literature treating of harlots and harlotry. (Gr. *porne*, a harlot, and *grapho.*)
poroscope, *n.* *paw*-ro-skope, an instrument for determining the porosity of a substance, or [Zool. and Bot.] for examining pores.
porose, *a.* po-*rohs*, abounding in pores (esp. of corals).
porosis, *n.* po-*roh*-sis, the formation of callus [Med.]. (Gr. *poros*, callus.)
porosity, *n.* po-*ros*-e-te, porousness.
porotic, *a.* po-*rot*-ik, pertaining to or promoting porosis [Med.].
porous, *a.* *paw*-rus, having pores, or full of pores or interstices.
porousness, *n.* the state or quality of being porous.
porpentine, *n.* *pawr*-pen-tine, obsolete form of *porcupine.*
porphyrite, *n.* *pawr*-fe-rite, porphyry, esp. that containing no quartz ; any porphyritic rock.
porphyritic, *a.* pawr-fe-*rit*-ik, pertaining to, resembling, or containing porphyry.
porphyrize, *v.t.* *pawr*-fe-rize, to grind to powder, to triturate [Pharm.]. (Originally done on a slab of porphyry.)
porphyrogenitism, *n.* *pawr*-fe-ro-*jen*-e-tizm, royal succession by a son born during the reign of his father to the exclusion of elder brothers not so born. (Late L. *porphyro genitus*, born in the purple.)
porphyroid, *a.* *pawr*-fe-royd, containing or of the nature of porphyry ; any porphyritic rock.
porphyry, *n.* *pawr*-fe-re, a rock, consisting of a compact felspathic base, through which crystals of a different colour are disseminated ; applied also to various igneous rocks. (Gr. *porphyra*, purple.)
porphyry-shell, *n.* the shell of a univalve marine mollusc of the genus *Murex.*
porpoise, *n.* *pawr*-pus, a small gregarious cetaceous mammal of the genus *Phocæna*, allied to the dolphins (O.Fr. *porpeis*, from L. *porcus*, pig, and *piscis*, fish.)
porraceous, *a.* po-*ray*-shus, leek-green. (L. *porraceous*, resembling the leek.)
porrect, *a.* po-*rekt*, extending forth horizontally : *v.t.* to extend ; to stretchout ; to submit [Eccles. Law]. (L. *porrectus*, extended.)
porrection, *n.* po-*rek*-shon, the act of tendering for acceptance [Eccles.].
porret, *n.* *po*-ret, a leek or small onion.
porridge, *n.* *po*-rij, a dish of oatmeal or other meal boiled till it swells. (*pottage.*)
porriginous, *a.* po-*rij*-e-nus, pertaining to or affected with porrigo [Med.].
porrigo, *n.* po-*ry*-go, any skin-disease affecting the scalp ; favus. (L., dandruff.)
porringer, *n.* *po*-rin-jer, a small dish out of which children eat porridge ; a small shallow cooking utensil. (*porridge.*)
port, *n.* pawrt, any harbour which vessels can enter and where they can remain in safety ; any place at which such is situated. **Port Admiral,** the officer commanding a naval port. **port of entry,** a port where there is a custom-house. (A.S., from L. *portus.*)
port, *n.* pawrt, a gate ; a port-hole ; the lid of a port-hole ; a hole for a gun to shoot through ; a hole for light and air ; the inlet or outlet (exhaust) to the cylinder of a steam engine. (Fr. *porte*, from L. *porta.*)
port, *n.* pawrt, mien or external appearance ; the larboard or left side of a ship looking towards the bow : *a.* towards or on the larboard : *v.t.* to turn or put (the helm) to the left, or larboard side, of a ship ; to carry a rifle across the body : *v.i.* to turn to port (of a ship). (Fr.)
port, *n.* pawrt, a red wine made in Portugal, and shipped at Oporto. **port-wine mark,** a birthmark, esp. a congenital discoloration of the skin involving part of the face.
porta, *n.* *pawr*-ta, the opening in a gland, etc., at which blood-vessels and nerves enter [Anat.]. (L., a gate.)
portability, *n.* pawr-ta-*bil*-e-te, the quality of being portable.
portable. *a.* *pawr*-ta-bl, that may be carried about ; not bulky. **portable engine,** a mobile, but not self-propelling, steam or internal combustion engine. (Late L. *portabilis.*)
portage, *n.* *pawr*-taj, the act of carrying goods overland, esp. between terminals in a waterway : a place where this is necessary ; porterage ; freight ; *v.t.* to convey over a portage.
portal, *n.* *pawr*-tal, a gate ; an opening for entrance ; the smaller door where there are two ; an arch over a door or gateway : the portal vein : *a.* pertaining to a porta [Anat.]. **portal vein,** the vein leading to the liver from the junction of the splenic and superior mesenteric veins. (O.Fr.)
portamento, *n.* *pawr*-tah-*men*-toh, appoggiatura; a glide or slur between notes [Mus.]. (It., a carrying.)
portative, *a.* *pawr*-ta-tiv, pertaining to carrying or supporting ; serving to carry. (Fr. *portatif.*)
port-bar, *n.* a boom or other obstacle barring a harbour.
portcrayon, *n.* *pawrt*-kray-on, a small handle for holding a crayon ; a pencil-case.
portcullis, *n.* pawrt-*kul*-is, a strong grated framing resembling a harrow, hung over the gateway of a fortified place to let down in a groove in case of surprise. (O.Fr. *porte coulisse*, a door that slides.)
Porte, *n.* pawrt, the court and government of the former Turkish Empire, so called from the high gate of the imperial palace, where justice was anciently administered.
portend, *v.t.* pawr-*tend*, to indicate something future by signs ; to foreshadow. (L. *portendo*, stretch forth.)
portent, *n.* *pawr*-tent, an omen, esp. of evil. (Fr. *portente.*)
portentous, *a.* pawr-*ten*-tus, ominous ; foreshadowing ill ; monstrous.
portentously, *ad.* in a portentous manner.
porter. *n.* *pawr*-ter, a doorkeeper or gatekeeper ; a janitor. (Fr. *portier*, from L. *porta*, gate.)
★**porter,** *n.* *pawr*-ter, a carrier of luggage, parcels, etc., esp. at stations ; dark brown beer (originally a favourite drink of London porters). **porters' knot,** a pad to support a load carried on the head. (O.Fr. *portour*, from *porter* to carry.)
porterage, *n.* *pawr*-ter-raj, the business of a porter ; money paid for carriage by a porter.
porteress, *n.* *pawr*-ter-ress, a female gatekeeper
porterhouse, *n.* *pawr*-ter-house, a house at which porter was retailed ; a chop-house. **porterhouse steak,** a steak from between the sirloin and tenderloin.
porterly, *a.* *pawr*-ter-le, coarse ; vulgar.
portfire, *n.* *pawrt*-fire, a fuse or slow match used for igniting purposes.
portfolio, *n.* pawrt-*foh*-le-oh, a large flat portable case for keeping papers, maps and drawings ; the office and functions of a cabinet minister as head of a department. (L. *portare*, to carry, *folia*, leaves.)
port-hole, *n.* an opening in the side of a ship for ventilation and admission of light; a passage in a cylinder for steam [Mech.].
portico, *n.* *pawr*-te-ko, a covered walk ; an entrance enclosed by columns ; a colonnade. (It.)
portière, *n.* pawr-te-*ayr*, a curtain over a doorway. (Fr.)
portion, *n.* *pawr*-shon, a part, division, or share ; a helping ; one's lot ; the share of an estate legally passing to an heir ; a wife's fortune : *v.t.* to divide ; to parcel ; to endow. (Fr.)
portioner, *n.* *pawr*-shon-er, one who assigns in shares ; a portionist [Eccles.].
portionist, *n.* *pawr*-shon-ist, one who has a certain academical allowance ; the joint incumbent of a benefice.
portionless, *a.* *pawr*-shon-less, having no portion ; not having a dower or dowry.
Portland, *a.* *pawrt*-land, pertaining to Portland in England. **Portland cement,** an hydraulic cement composed of a mixture of pure limestone and clay or other aluminous material. **Portland stone,** a yellowish white oolitic freestone from Portland, used for building.
Portlandian, *a.* pawrt-*lan*-de-an, designating the middle series of Portland oolites [Geol.].
portliness, *n.* the state of being portly.
portly, *a.* *pawrt*-le, dignified in mien ; of a noble appearance and carriage ; tall and corpulent.
portmanteau, *n.* pawrt-*man*-toh, a framed leather bag for carrying clothes, etc. in travelling. **portmanteau word,** a word composed of elements of two separate words, as *squarson*, from *squire* and *parson.* (Fr.)

portolano, *n.* pawr-to-*lah*-no, a late mediæval Guide for Mariners, containing sea-charts, sailing directions, etc. (It.)
portrait, *n.* *pawr*-trat, a picture or representation of a person, especially of a face drawn from life; a vivid graphic description. **composite portrait,** a picture obtained by superimposing several photographic portraits on the same sensitive plate. **portrait painter,** one who paints portraits. (Fr.)
portraitist, *n.* *pawr*-tra-tist, a maker of portraits, photographic or otherwise.
portraiture, *n.* *pawr*-tra-tewr, a portrait or painted resemblance; portrait-painting; portraits collectively; vivid delineation.
portray, *v.t.* pawr-*tray*, to paint or draw a likeness of; to describe in words; to adorn with pictures. (Fr. *portraire.*)
portrayal, *n.* pawr-*tray*-al, the act or result of portraying; delineation.
portrayer, *n.* pawr-*tray*-er, one who portrays.
portreeve, *n.* *pawrt*-reeve, former title of the mayor or chief magistrate of a town or borough. (A.S. *portgerefa.*)
portress, *n.* *pawr*-tress, a female gatekeeper.
Portuguese, *a.* pawr-tew-*geez*, pertaining to Portugal or its inhabitants: *n.* a native, the people, or the language of Portugal. **Portuguese man-of-war,** any of several large stinging jelly-fish.
pose, *n.* poze, position, posture; attitude: *v.t.* to place in a pose: *v.i.* to assume an attitude. (Fr.)
pose, *v.t.* poze, to puzzle; to nonplus; to bring to a stand. (*oppose.*)
posé, *a.* *poh*-zay, standing still with all feet on the ground (of a lion or other quadruped) [Her.].
poser, *n.* *poh*-zer, one who puzzles by asking difficult questions; a question or proposition that puzzles.
poser, *n.* *poh*-zer, one who attitudinizes; a poseur.
poseur, *n.* po-*zoor*, one noticeable for affectation in his attitudes and demeanour. (Fr.)
posh, *a.* posh, good, smart. **to posh oneself up,** to dress in one's best [Slang].
posingly, *ad.* *poh*-zing-le, so as to puzzle.
posit, *v.t.* *poz*-it, to postulate; to lay down, affirm, or assume as a fact. (L. *positus*, placed.)
★**position,** *n.* po-*zish*-on, state of being placed; situation; attitude; social standing; principle laid down; disposition; state or condition: *v.t.* to place, esp. in some particular position; to locate. (Fr.)
positional, *a.* po-*zish*-o-nal, pertaining to or determined by position.
positive, *a.* *poz*-it-iv, expressed; explicit; absolute; express; real or existing in fact; direct; confident; dogmatic; over-confident; settled or laid down authoritatively; not negative; having power to act directly; dextrorotatory [Opt.]: *n.* what is capable of being affirmed; reality; the positive degree [Gram.]; a picture in its natural lights and shades, a print from a negative [Phot.]. **positive degree,** the simple state of an adjective. **positive electricity,** the electricity excited on glass by rubbing it with silk. **positive philosophy,** positivism. **positive quantity,** an affirmative quantity, or one to be added. (Fr. *positif.*)
positively, *ad.* *poz*-it-iv-le, in a positive manner.
positiveness, *n.* state or quality of being positive.
positivism, *n.* *poz*-it-iv-izm, a system of philosophy which, discarding both the theological and metaphysical account of things, limits itself to the study of phenomena and the laws that regulate them; the system of religion based on this; Comtism.
positivist, *n.* *poz*-it-iv-ist, an upholder of positivism.
positivistic, *a.* poz-it-e-*vis*-tik, pertaining to or of the nature of positivism.
positivity, *n.* poz-e-*tiv*-e-te, positiveness.
positron, *n.* *poz*-e-tron, an elementary positively charged particle, similar in mass to an electron; the positive electron [Physics].
posnet, *n.* *poz*-net, a small basin; a saucepan or cooking-pot. (O.Fr. *pocenet*, a bowl.)
posological, *a.* poh-so-*loj*-e-kal, pertaining to posology.
posology, *n.* po-*sol*-o-je, that branch of medicine which treats of doses; the science of pure quantity [Math.]. (Gr. *posos*, how much, *logos*, science.)
posse, *n.* *pos*-e, a number or body of men having legal authority. **posse comitatus,** the body of men liable to be called out by the sheriff to enforce the law, resist invasion, etc. (L.)

possess, *v.t.* po-*zes*, to hold; to own as property; to seize; to have the power over; to actuate; to imbue. (L. *possessus*, possessed.)
possessed, *a.* po-*zest*, owned; occupied; self-possessed; controlled or dominated by a demon or by evil, insane.
possession, *n.* po-*zesh*-on, the having, holding, or detention of property; estate, or goods owned; anything valuable, possessed, or enjoyed; the state of being under evil influence. **give possession,** to put in another's power. **to take possession,** to enter on. **writ of possession,** a sheriff's precept giving possession of property. (Fr.)
possessional, *a.* po-*zesh*-on-al, pertaining to possession or possessions; characterized by ownership of property; propertied.
possessionalism, po-*zesh*-on-a-lizm, the theory or practice of private ownership of property.
possessive, *a.* po-*zes*-iv, pertaining to possession. **possessive case,** the case denoting possession [Gram.].
possessively, *ad.* in a way showing possession.
possessor, *n.* po-*zes*-or, one who has possession; owner.
possessory, *a.* po-*zes*-o-re, pertaining to possession; having possession.
posset, *n.* *pos*-et, milk curdled with wine and spices (esp. as a night-cap): *v.i.* to curdle. (Origin unknown.)
possibilist, *n.* po-*sib*-e-list, one who, esp. in matters of reform, aims only at what is immediately practicable.
possibility, *n.* pos-e-*bil*-e-te, the power of existing or of happening; state of being possible; a possible thing; a chance.
★**possible,** *a.* *pos*-e-bl, that can be; that can be done; that may be or happen; practicable: *n.* that which is possible; the highest score that can be made. **to do one's possible,** to do all one can. (Fr., from L. *posse*, to be able.)
possibly, *ad.* *pos*-e-ble, perhaps; may be.
possum, *n.* *pos*-sum, opossum.
post, *n.* pohst, a piece of timber, metal, or other solid material set upright, usually as a support for something; a stout pole or stake; a starting or finishing place: *v.t.* to fix to a post; to stick up, as a bill; to expose to public reproach. (A.S. *post*, from L. *postis.*)
post, *n.* pohst, a fixed place or station; a military station; a small fort; a stage; a trading station; an office or employment; a messenger, courier, or letter-carrier; an established system of letter-carrying; a post-office, or mail-box; the mail; a single collection or delivery of postal matter; a relay of horses; a printing paper size, 19¼ by 15½ in.: *ad.* swiftly; with post-horses; with dispatch: *v.t.* to station; to send by mail through the post; to transmit with speed; to carry accounts to the ledger: *v.i.* to travel with speed. **first** and **last post,** bugle-calls sounded at night as a preliminary and final warning of "Lights out" [Mil.]. **to travel post,** to travel rapidly, esp. with post-horses. (Fr. *poste*, from L. *positum*, place.)
post-, pohst, Latin prefix signifying after, behind.
postable, *a.* *pohs*-ta-bl, that may be transmitted by post.
postage, *n.* *pohs*-taj, the charge for conveyance by post. **postage stamp,** an adhesive label (also, on postal stationery, an embossed or printed stamp) showing that postage on the letter, etc. on which it appears has been prepaid.
postal, *a.* *pohs*-tal, connected with the post or the mail service. **postal order,** a draft for money purchasable at any post-office and payable at any other. **Postal Union,** an association of governments for the regulation of inter-nation mails. (Fr.)
post-bag, *n.* a mail bag.
post-bill, *n.* a way-bill of letters transmitted by mail.
postboy, *n.* *pohst*-boy, a postilion; a rider of post-horses; the driver of a post-chaise.
post-captain, *n.* a former naval rank comprising the senior captains, esp. those in command of vessels of 20 or more guns.
post-card, *n.* a stamped card for sending by post.
post-chaise, *n.* a carriage for the conveyance of travellers worked by a change of horses at each stage.
post-communion, *a.* the part of the Communion

Service that follows the act of communion: *a.* used after Holy Communion.
post-costal, *a.* situated behind a rib [Anat.].
post-date, *v.t.* to date after the day of writing.
post-day, *n.* a day on which the mail arrives or departs.
post-diluvian, *a.* after the Flood; *n.* a person living after the Flood.
postea, *n.* *poh*-ste-a, the record of the proceedings and verdict of a civil trial [Law]. (L.)
post-entry, *n.* a subsequent entry.
poster, *n.* *pohs*-ter, a large advertisement, usually in colours, pasted on walls and hoardings.
poste-restante, *n.* pohst-res-*tahnt*, the department of a post-office where letters remain till called for. (Fr.)
posterior, *a.* pos-*teer*-re-or, subsequent in time; coming after; hinder: *n.pl.* the hinder parts of an animal; the buttocks. (L.)
posteriority, *n.* pos-*teer*-re-*o*-re-te, the state or quality of being subsequent.
posteriorly, *ad.* pos-*teer*-re-or-le, subsequently.
posterity, *n.* pos-*te*-re-te, descendants; succeeding generations.
postern, *n.* *pohs*-tern, a back gate; any small door or gate. (Fr. *posterne.*)
post-exilic, *a.* subsequent to the Babylonian captivity of the Jews. (L. *post-*, after, and *exile.*)
post-fact, *n.* a fact occurring after another.
postfix, *v.t.* *pohst*-fiks, to append as a suffix: *n.* a suffix.
post-free, *a.* delivered by mail without extra charge, or without charge to the actual sender.
post-glacial, *a.* since the last glacial period; recent [Geol.].
post-graduate, *a.* pertaining to studies pursued after a degree has been taken.
post-haste, *ad.* with speed in travelling.
post-horn, *n.* the horn formerly blown by the guard of a mail-coach.
post-horse, *n.* one of several horses available at certain stages as relays for travellers.
posthumous, *a.* *pos*-tew-mus, born after the father's death; published after the death of the author; occurring after one's decease. (L. *postumus,* superlative of *posterus,* coming after.)
posthumously, *ad.* after death.
postiche, *n.* pos-*teesh*, an imitation substituted; a sham; additional or incongruous ornamentation: *a.* added subsequent to the work being finished; counterfeit. (Fr.)
posticous, *a.* *pos*-te-kus, situated on the posterior side [Bot.]. (L. *posticus,* hinder.)
postil, *n.* *pos*-til, a marginal note (originally in the Bible); a commentary; a homily delivered after reading the Gospel. (O.Fr. *postille.*)
postilion, *n.* pos-*til*-yon, one who drives the horses in a carriage, riding one of them. (Fr.)
postillate, *v.i.* and *t.* *pos*-til-late, to make or write comments or marginal notes.
postillation, *n.* pos-til-*lay*-shon, the composition of postils.
post-impressionism, *n.* the aims and methods of a school of painting that arose in reaction to impressionism, aiming at the expression of the artist's conception of the things depicted rather than the observer's impression of them.
post-impressionist, *a.* pertaining to post-impressionism: *n.* a painter of this school.
posting, *n.* *pohs*-ting, the transferring of accounts to a ledger; the travelling with post-horses.
postliminy, *n.* pohst-*lim*-in-e, the right of restoration to one's own country, or to lost rights. (L. *post-*, and *limen,* the threshold.)
postlude, *n.* *pohst*-lewd, a closing piece; an organ voluntary [Mus.].
postman, *n.* *pohst*-man, one employed by the post-office to collect and deliver mails; a courier.
post-marital, *a.* subsequent to marriage.
postmark, *n.* *pohst*-mark, the official cancelling mark on the stamp of a letter: *v.t.* to put a postmark on.
postmaster, *n.* *pohst*-mahs-ter, the superintendent of a post-office; a foundation scholar at Merton College, Oxford. **Postmaster-General,** the Minister responsible to Parliament for the post-office department.
postmeridian, *a.* pohst-me-*rid*-e-an, belonging to the afternoon. (L. *postmeridianus,* the afternoon.)
post-millennial, *a.* pertaining to the period after the millennium.
post-millennialism, *n.* the belief that Christ's second coming will follow the millennium.
post-millennialist, *n.* one who believes in post-millennialism.
postmistress, *n.* *pohst*-mis-tres, a woman in charge of a post-office.
post-mortem, *a.* after death: *n.* the medical examination of a body to find the cause of death; an inquiry into a scheme or incident after its completion. (L.)
postnuptial, *a.* pohst-*nup*-shal, happening after marriage.
post-obit, *n.* a bond in which the borrower binds himself to repay a loan on the death of one from whom he has expectations: *a.* effective after the death of someone and not before; post-mortem. (L. *post-*, and *obitum,* death.)
post-office, *n.* a place for the receipt and delivery of letters and parcels; the public department for postal, telegraphic, and telephonic business.
post-paid, *a.* having the postage prepaid.
postponable, *a.* post-*poh*-na-bl, that may be postponed.
postpone, *v.t.* post-*pone*, to put off; to defer; to delay or hold up. (L. *postpono.*)
postponement, *n.* post-*pone*-ment, act of deferring.
postponer, *n.* post-*poh*-ner, one who postpones.
postposition, *n.* pohst-po-*zish*-on, state of being placed after the act of placing after; an affix indicative of relation [Gram.]. (Fr.)
postpositive, *a.* pohst-*poz*-it-iv, placed after something else [Gram.]: *n.* a postpositive enclitic.
postprandial, *a.* pohst-*pran*-de-al, after dinner. (L. *post-*, and *prandium,* dinner.)
postrorse, *a.* pohst-*rawse*, bending backward or downward (the reverse of antrorse); retrorse [Bot.].
postscenium, *n.* pohst-*see*-ne-um, the part of a theatre behind the scenes. (L. *post-*, and *scena,* a scene.)
postscript, *n.* *pohst*-skript, a paragraph or note added to a letter after the signature of the writer; an appendix, or matter appended. (L. *postscriptum,* that which is written subsequently.)
Post-Tertiary, *a.* later than the Tertiary: *n.* the Quaternary series of rocks.
post-town, *n.* a town having a central, or head, post-office.
postulant, *n.* *pos*-tew-lant, one who makes a demand; a candidate [Eccles.]. (Fr.)
postulate, *n.* *pos*-tew-late, a position assumed without proof; an assumption underlying an argument; a self-evident problem [Math.]: *v.t.* to assume without proof; to demand; to stipulate; to nominate to a higher authority a person for promotion [Eccles.]. (L. *postulatus,* demanded.)
postulation, *n.* pos-tew-*lay*-shon, the act of postulating; that which is postulated; necessary assumption.
postulatory, *a.* *pos*-tew-la-to-re, hypothetical.
postural, *a.* *pos*-tew-ral, relating to posture.
posture, *n.* *pos*-tewr, attitude; position; pose of the body; state; condition; disposition: *v.t.* to place the parts of a body for a particular purpose: *v.i.* to pose; to assume an attitude. (Fr.)
posture-master, *n.* one who teaches or practises artificial postures of the body; a contortionist.
posturist, *n.* *pos*-tewr-rist, a posture-master; one who poses.
post-war, *a.* after or since the (specified or understood) war.
posy, *n.* *poh*-ze, a bunch of flowers; a motto engraved on a ring or sent with a nosegay. (*poesy.*)
***pot,** *n.* pot, a cylindrical metal or earthenware vessel for holding or heating liquids and for other domestic and industrial uses; a tankard, also the quantity it contains; a quart; a chamber-, chimney-, coffee-, flower-, or other specified pot; a wicker-work trap for lobsters, etc.; a prize for sporting events; a large sum of money [Slang]; an important person [Slang]; pottery; a small size of printing paper (about 12½ by 16½ in.): *v.t.* to put in pots; to preserve in pots; to plant in a pot; to shoot, or bring down by shooting [Slang]; to drive (a ball) into a pocket [Billiards]. **go to pot,** to go to ruin, as it were back to the melting-pot. **keep the pot boiling,** *see* **boiling.** (A.S. *pott.*)

potability, *n.* poh-ta-*bil*-e-te, suitableness for drinking.
potable, *a.* *poh*-ta-bl, drinkable: *n.* something that may be drunk. (Fr.)
potamic, *a.* po-*tam*-ik, pertaining to rivers, or to river navigation.
potamology, *n.* pot-a-*mol*-o-je, the science of rivers. (Gr. *potamos*, a river, *logos*, science.)
potash, *n.* *pot*-ash, potassium carbonate, a crude fixed alkali obtained from the ashes of plants; pearl-ash. **caustic potash,** potassium hydroxide. **potash alum,** a hydrous sulphate of aluminium and potash. (*pot* and *ash.*)
potassa, *n.* po-*tas*-sa, potash.
potassic, *a.* po-*tas*-ik, pertaining to or containing potassium [Chem.].
potassium, *n.* po-*tas*-se-um, a soft silvery or pinkish white metallic element of the alkali group, the basis of potash. **potassium permanganate,** a deep purple crystalline oxide of manganese and potassium, used as a disinfectant and deodorant. (*potash.*)
potation, *n.* po-*tay*-shon, the act of drinking; a drinking bout; a draught. (L. *potatio.*)
★**potato,** *n.* po-*tay*-to, the tuber of a South American plant, *Solanum tuberosum*, extensively cultivated for food; the plant itself. **potato bug,** the Colorado-beetle. **potato chips,** sliced potatoes fried in oil or deep fat. **potato wart,** *see* **wart-disease. sweet potato,** a tropical vine, *Ipomæa batatas*, with a sweet and farinaceous tuberous root which is cooked for food. (Sp. *patata.*)
potatory, *a.* *poh*-ta-to-re, pertaining to tippling.
pot-bellied, *a.* having a prominent belly.
potboiler, *n.* *pot*-boyl-er, a work of art or literature done as a mere means of livelihood.
pot-bound, *a.* denoting the condition of a plant growing in a pot not large enough for its roots.
pot-boy, *n.* a boy potman in a public house.
pot-companion, *n.* a companion in drinking.
poteen, *n.* po-*teen*, Irish whisky illicitly distilled in a small pot-still. (Ir. *poitín*, a small pot.)
potence, *n.* *poh*-tence, potency; degree of power; efficacy; sexual ability. (L. *potens*, being able.)
potence, *n.* *poh*-tence, the stud in which the lower pivot of the verge is placed [Watchmaking]; a gallows-like framework or object; a T-shaped cross [Her.]. (Fr., a crutch.)
potency, *n.* *poh*-ten-se, inherent physical or mental power; general capability; specific ability; sexual vigour. (L. *potens*, being able.)
potent, *a.* *poh*-tent, powerful; mighty; having great influence or authority. **cross potent,** a potence, or cross with the ends of the arms resembling the head of a crutch [Her.]. (L. *potens*, being able.)
potentate, *n.* *poh*-ten-tate, one possessing great power; a sovereign or ruler.
potential, *a.* po-*ten*-shal, existing in possibility, not in act; latent; expressing power, possibility, obligation, or necessity [Gram.]: *n.* anything that may be possible; the power to do work; a quantity in the mathematical theory of attractions [Maths.]; the power of a charge of electricity on a body or at a point [Elect.]. **atmospheric potential,** the difference between the electrical potential at a point in the atmosphere and at the ground. **potential gradient,** the change of potential with distance; the rate of change with height of atmospheric potential; the change of potential with the first metre from the ground. **potential mood,** the subjunctive mood. (O.Fr., from L. *potens.*)
potentiality, *n.* po-*ten*-she-*al*-e-te, possibility, not actuality; capability.
potentialize, *v.t.* po-*ten*-shal-ize, to render potential.
potentially, *ad.* in possibility; in efficacy.
potentiate, *v.t.* po-*ten*-she-ate, to make possible; to endow with potency.
Potentilla, *n.* poh-ten-*til*-a, a genus of rosaceous plants including the cinquefoil, *P. reptans*, the silverweed, *P. anserina*, and the tormentil, *P. tormentilla*. (L. *potens.*)
potentiometer, *n.* po-*ten*-she-*om*-e-ter, an instrument for measuring differences of potential [Elect.].
potently, *ad.* *poh*-tent-le, powerfully.
potentness, *n.* *poh*-tent-ness, the quality of being potent.
pot-hanger, *n.* *pot*-hang-er, a pot-hook.
potheen, *n.* po-*theen*, poteen.
pother, *n.* *poth*-er, bustle; fuss: *v.i.* to make a stir or a pother: *v.t.* to harass; to puzzle.
pot-herb, *n.* a vegetable for the pot or for cookery.
pot-hole, *n.* a cavity in a river-bed eroded by an eddy in which gravel is kept in gyration.
pot-hook, *n.* a hook on which pots, etc. are hung over the fire; a letter like a pot-hook, clumsily scrawled.
pothouse, *n.* *pot*-house, a low drinking-house.
pot-hunter, *n.* one competing in sporting events merely for a prize or some advantage.
potichomania, *n.* *pot*-e-sho-*may*-ne-a, the craze of sticking painted papers to the interior of glass-ware as an imitation of porcelain. (Fr. *potiche*, a porcelain vessel, and *mania.*)
potin, *n.* *poh*-tin, a composition of copper, lead, tin, and silver, of which Roman coins were made. (Fr.)
potion, *n.* *poh*-shon, a drink; a medicinal draught; a dose: *v.t.* to treat with potions. (Fr.)
pot-luck, *n.* what may chance to be in the pot, hence be provided for dinner.
potman, *n.* *pot*-man, a man employed at a public-house to clean the pots and perform other duties.
pot-metal, *n.* an alloy of lead and copper; stained glass the colour of which is incorporated while the glass is molten.
potomania, *n.* poh-to-*may*-ne-a, dipsomania; delirium tremens [Med.]. (Gr. *poton*, drink, and *mania*).
potoroo, *n.* *pot*-o-roo, the rat kangaroo, an Australian marsupial of the genus *Potorous*. (Native.)
potpourri, *n.* po-*poo*-ree, a medley, as of rose leaves, dried flowers, musical airs, or literary pieces. (Fr. *pot*, pot, *pourrir*, to rot.)
potsherd, *n.* *pot*-sherd, a fragment of a broken pot; a shard. (*pot* and *shard.*)
pot-shot, *n.* an unsportsmanlike shot; a shot requiring no special skill; a lucky shot.
pot-still, *n.* a primitive still in which the heat is applied directly.
potstone, *n.* *pot*-stone, an impure variety of steatite used for culinary vessels; a large flint with a chalk centre.
pott, *n.* pot, pot (size of paper).
pottage, *n.* *pot*-aj, a thick soup or stew. (Fr. *potage.*)
potted, *pp.* and *a.* *pot*-ed, preserved in a pot or cask; hence, condensed or epitomized.
potter, *n.* *pot*-er, a maker of earthenware pots or pottery; one who pots. **potter's clay,** a variety of clay used by potters. **potter's wheel,** the round table revolving horizontally used by potters. (Fr. *potier.*)
potter, *v.i.* *pot*-er, to loiter about; to work leisurely and do little; to busy oneself fussily about trifles. (Origin unknown.)
potterer, *n.* *pot*-er-rer, one who potters; a dallier.
pottery, *n.* *pot*-er-re, earthenware; the manufacture of this; a potter's workshop.
pottinger, *n.* *pot*-tin-jer, a maker of pottage; a cook; a porringer. (Dial.)
pottle, *n.* *pot*-tl, a liquid measure of four pints; a half-gallon tankard; a small conical basket for holding fruit. (O. Fr. *potel*, a small pot.)
potto, *n.* *pot*-toh, the slow lemur of W. Africa, *Perodicticus potto*, in which the index finger and tail are rudimentary; applied also to the kinkajou. (Native word.)
potty, *a.* *pot*-e, petty; small; easy; crazy; foolish; doting [Slang].
pot-valiant, *a.* heated to valour by strong drink.
pot-walloper, *n.* one qualified as a parliamentary voter in certain English boroughs prior to 1832 because he could boil his own pot at his own fire, thus proving he was a householder. (*pot*, and M.E. *wallop*, to boil.)
pouch, *n.* pouch, a small bag; a detachable pocket; a stout leather cartridge-box [Mil.]; a pocket-like cavity [Anat.]; the marsupium of kangaroos, etc.: *v.t.* to pocket; to swallow; to cause to hang loosely or like a pouch: *v.i.* to hang like a pouch. (Fr. *poche.*)
pouched, *a.* poucht, provided with a pouch.
poudrette, *n.* poo-*dret*, a powerful manure of dried excrements, charcoal, and gypsum. (Fr.)
pouffe, *n.* poof, a soft cushion, esp. for use as a seat; a small circular ottoman; a puffed style in hair-dressing. (Fr.)

poulard, *n.* poo-*lard*, a specially fattened pullet. (Fr. *poularde.*)
pouip, *n.* poolp, the octopus. (Fr. *poulpe.*)
poult, *n.* poalt, a young chicken, turkey, or game-bird. (Fr. *poulet*, a chicken.)
poult-de-soie, *n.* (App.), paduasoy; a grained taffeta. (Fr.)
poulterer, *n. poal*-ter-er, one who deals in poultry.
poultice, *n. poal*-tis, a mollifying composition of meal or bread, etc. for applying hot to a sore or inflamed part of the body; a cataplasm: *v.t.* to apply a poultice to. (L. *puls, pultis*, porridge.)
poultry, *n. poal*-tre, domestic fowls in general. (O.Fr. *poletrie.*)
pounce, *n.* pounce, a fine powder formerly sprinkled over freshly written paper to prevent blotting, also into holes in paper in pattern-making; a stencil with the pattern outlined by fine holes: *v.t.* to sprinkle with pounce; to perforate for use as a stencil. (Fr. *ponce*, from L. *pumex*, pumice.)
pounce, *n.* pounce, the claw of a bird of prey; a swoop or pouncing: *v.i.* to fall on suddenly: *v.t.* to fall on and seize with claws. (Origin unknown.)
pounce-box, *n.* a box for sprinkling pounce.
pounced, *a.* pounst, furnished with claws [Her.].
pouncet-box, *n. poun*-set-boks, a pounce-box.
pound, *n.* pound, a standard weight consisting of 7,000 grains or 16 oz. avoirdupois; a money of account consisting of twenty shillings. **pound foolish,** negligent of large sums but niggardly with small. **pound Scots,** a former Scottish money of account equivalent to 20*s.* in 1603 but 20*d.* when abolished in 1707. (A.S. *pund.*)
pound, *n.* pound, a public pinfold for confining stray cattle; a prison; a level between locks on a canal: *v.t.* to confine in or as in a pound. (A.S. *pund*, an enclosure.)
pound, *v.t.* pound, to beat; to reduce to a powder by beating; to pommel; to buffet: *v.i.* to strike sturdy blows; to plod heavily along. (A.S. *punian.*)
poundage, *n. pound*-aj, a charge per pound weight; an allowance of so much in the pound; a former royal levy on imports and exports.
poundage, *n. pound*-aj, confinement in a pound; a charge for pounding cattle.
poundal, *n. pound*-al, the foot-pound unit of force, the force that can give one pound a velocity of one foot per second.
pound-cake, *n.* a rich cake containing pound for pound of each chief ingredient.
pounder, *n. pound*-er, a gun, as carrying so many pounds' weight; anything (as a fish) weighing the specified poundage; formerly an elector, as paying so many pounds' rent.
pounder, *n. pound*-er, one who or that which pounds; a pestle.
pound-keeper, *n.* one in charge of a cattle-pound.
pour, *v.t.* pawr, to empty, as liquids, out of any vessel; to send forth in a stream; to send forth, or utter, with a gush or in profusion: *v.i.* to flow rapidly; to issue forth in a stream; to fall copiously (of rain); to rush in a crowd. (Origin unknown.)
pourboire, *n.* (App.), a tip; a gratuity. (Fr.)
pourer, *n. paw*-rer, one who or that which pours.
pourparler, *n.* (App.), a preliminary discussion or conference. (Fr.)
pourpoint, *n. poor*-poynt, a quilted doublet. (Fr.)
poussette, *n.* poo-*set*, a certain circling figure in a country dance: *v.i.* to swing partners in this figure. (Fr., push-pin.)
poussin, *n.* (App.), a spring chicken. (Fr.)
pout, *n.* pout, various sea-fish with a pouting appearance, esp. the whiting pout.
pout, *n.* pout, a protruding of the lips; a fit of sullenness: *v.i.* to thrust out the lips in sullenness, contempt, displeasure, etc.; to protrude, or be prominent. (Origin unknown.)
pouter, *n. pout*-er, one who pouts; a variety of pigeon having a dilatable crop.
poverty, *n. pov*-er-te, state of being poor; indigence; sterility; barrenness of sentiment or ornament; deficiency; defect (as of words, ideas, etc.). (O.Fr. *poverte.*)
poverty-stricken, *a.* suffering from poverty.
powan, *n. pou*-an, the gwyniad, a freshwater fish.
***powder,** *n. pou*-der, any dry substance composed of minute particles; gunpowder; powder for the face, teeth, hair, etc.; a medicine in powder form: *v.t.* to reduce to powder; to sprinkle with powder; to apply powder to: *v.i.* to become powdery or like powder; to use powder. **powder blue,** powdered smalt, esp. as used in laundries; the greenish-blue colour of this. (Fr. *poudre.*)
powder-box, *n.* a box for toilet powder.
powder-closet, *n.* a small dressing-room in which hair was powdered.
powdered, *a. pow*-derd, reduced to powder; dressed with powder (of the hair, etc.); preserved, pickled (of meat).
powder-flask, *n.* a metal container in which gunpowder was carried for present use.
powder-horn, *n.* a powder-flask of horn.
powder-magazine, *n.* a store for gunpowder.
powder-mill, *n.* a gunpowder factory.
powder-monkey, *n.* a boy who carried charges of powder from the ship's magazine to the guns.
powder-puff, *n.* a pad, usually of down, for applying powder to the face or body.
powdery, *a. pou*-der-re, sprinkled with or resembling powder; friable.
***power,** *n. pou*-er, the faculty of doing or performing anything; force; strength; energy; ability; influence; dominion; authority; a ruler; one who or that which has power; a supposed entity credited with dominion over some part of creation; military force; legal authority; that which produces motion or force [Mech.]; the product arising from the multiplication of a number or quantity into itself [Arith., Alg.]; the capacity of magnification of a lens [Opt.]. **balance of power,** *see* **balance. power boat,** a motor boat. **power house,** a building in which electricity is generated. **power loom,** a loom actuated by mechanical power. **power of attorney,** a written authority to act for another. **power of the keys,** *see* **key. power politics,** political theory or action based solely on the principle that might is right. **power station,** a central building in which power, esp. electrical, is generated for transmission to subsidiary distributing stations. (O.Fr. *poër.*)
powerful, *a. pou*-er-ful, having great power of any kind; potent; efficacious; productive of great effects; intense.
powerfully, *ad.* in a powerful manner.
powerfulness, *n.* quality of being powerful.
powerless, *a.* destitute of power; impotent.
powerlessly, *ad.* in a powerless manner.
powerlessness, *n.* quality of being powerless.
pow-wow, *n. pou*-wou, a North American Indian medicine-man; a conference held by these; any conference or confabulation; an incantation accompanied by noise and dancing: *v.i.* to hold a pow-wow; to practise sorcery: *v.t.* to doctor by the use of magic. (Algonquian.)
pox, *n.* poks, syphilis; any disease characterized by pustules or eruptions; variola [Vet.]. (*pock.*)
poyou, *n. poy*-oo, the weasel-headed armadillo, *Dasypus sexcinctus.* (S. Amer. native word.)
pozzuolana, *n.* pot-swoh-*lah*-na, volcanic ashes used as a component of cement or mortar. (*Pozzuoli*, near Naples.)
pozzy, *n. poz*-ze, jam [Mil. slang].
praam, *n.* prahm, a flat-bottomed boat used in the Baltic and in Holland. (Dut.)
practicability, *n. prak*-te-ka-*bil*-e-te, the state or quality of being practicable.
practicable, *a. prak*-te-ka-bl, that can be done; possible. (Fr.)
practicableness, *n.* practicability.
practicably, *ad.* so as to be practicable.
practical, *a. prak*-te-kal, pertaining to or derived from practice of action; that may be used; that reduces knowledge or theory to use; trained by practice; inclined to action; matter of fact; virtual. **practical joke,** a mischievous trick; a hoax.
practicality, *n.* prak-te-*kal*-e-te, the quality or state of being practical; an instance of this.
practically, *ad.* in a practical manner; to all intents and purposes.
practicalness, *n. prak*-te-kal-ness, practicality.
practice, *n. prak*-tis, action; frequent or customary action; habit; use; actual performance; medical treatment; exercise of a profession; a professional connexion; a rule by which certain arithmetical calculations are abridged. **sharp practice,** unscrupulous taking of advantage; mean trickery.

practician, *n.* prak-*tish*-an, a practitioner.
practise, *v.t.* *prak*-tis, to do or perform frequently or habitually; to exercise, as a profession or art; to accustom: *v.i.* to perform certain acts frequently or customarily; to exercise any profession; to try artifices. (O.Fr. *practiser*.)
practised, *a.* *prak*-tist, having had much practice; skilled from practice.
practiser, *n.* *prak*-tis-er, one who practises; one who exercises a profession.
practising, *a.* *prak*-tis-ing, actively engaged in.
practitioner, *n.* prak-*tish*-on-er, one actually engaged in any art or profession, specially medicine or law. **general practitioner,** a medical man who treats both medical and surgical cases; a doctor who does not limit himself as a specialist; a family doctor.
præ-, *prefix,* pree, before or prior to; pre- [L.].
præcipe, *n.* *pree*-sip-e, a writ requiring something to be done or a reason why it is not done [Law]. (L., instruct.)
præcocial, *a.* pree-*koh*-she-al, able to run about and feed themselves as soon as hatched (of fledgings) [Ornith.]. (L. *præcox*, early mature.)
præcognita, *n.pl.* pre-*kog*-ne-ta, matters of knowledge required for the knowledge of something else. (L. *præcognitus*, known before.)
præcordia, *n.* pre-*kawr*-de-a, the diaphragm; the thoracic viscera [Anat.]. (L.)
præmorse, *a.* pree-*morse*, premorse [Bot.].
præmunire, *n.* pree-mew-*nyr*-re, an act in contempt of the royal prerogative (esp. recognition of papal authority in England), involving forfeiture; a writ founded on it or incurred by it [Law]. (L. *præmonere*, forewarn.)
prænomen, *n.* pree-*noh*-men, a prenomen.
præpostor, *n.* pree-*pos*-tor, a prefect (in certain public schools). (L. *præpositus*, an overseer.)
prætexta, *n.* pree-*teks*-ta, a toga, or Roman's outer garment, bordered with scarlet or purple. (L.)
prætor, *n.* *pree*-tor, a senior magistrate in ancient Rome. (L.)
prætorial, *a.* pre-*taw*-re-al, prætorian.
prætorian, *a.* pre-*taw*-re-an, of or pertaining to a prætor; judicial; exercised by a prætor; pertaining to the Prætorian Guard, a powerful military body of the Roman Empire: *n.* a member of this Guard; one of prætorian rank. **prætorian gate,** the gate in a Roman camp in front of the general's tent and directly facing the enemy.
prætorium, *n.* pre-*taw*-re-um, a Roman general's camp; a Roman governor's residence.
prætorship, *n.* *pree*-tor-ship, the office, or term of office, of a Roman prætor.
pragmatic, *a.* prag-*mat*-ik, pragmatical; relating to state affairs; a sovereign decree; a meddlesome person. **pragmatic sanction,** an imperial decree issued as fundamental law, esp. that by which Charles VI settled the Austrian succession in 1724. (Fr. *pragmatique*, from Gr. *pragma*, to do.)
pragmatical, *a.* prag-*mat*-e-kal, forward to intermeddle; impertinently officious in the concerns of others; dogmatic; pertaining to pragmatism.
pragmatically, *ad.* in a pragmatical manner.
pragmaticalness, *n.* quality of being pragmatical.
pragmatism, *n.* *prag*-ma-tizm, pragmaticalness; the doctrine that it is only by their actual consequences that the truth or otherwise of beliefs or philosophical theories can be demonstrated [Phil.].
pragmatist, *n.* *prag*-ma-tist, an impertinently officious person; an adherent of pragmatism.
pragmatistic, *a.* prag-ma-*tis*-tik, pertaining to, or of the nature of, pragmatism.
pragmatize, *v.i.* *prag*-ma-tize, to consider or represent as real that which is not; to rationalize.
prairie, *n.* *prare*-re, an extensive tract of flat or rolling grassland destitute of trees. (Fr., from L. *pratum*, a meadow.)
prairie-chicken, *n.* popular name of various N. American grouse, esp. *Tympanuchus cupido* and *Pediœcetes phasianellus*.
prairie-dog, *n.* a N. American burrowing rodent of the genus *Cynomys*, allied to the marmots.
prairie-hen, *n.* prairie-chicken.
prairie-oyster, *n.* a pick-me-up consisting of egg beaten up in Worcester sauce with pepper and salt [Slang].
prairie-schooner, *n.* a long canvas-covered emigrant's wagon.
prairie-squirrel, *n.* the gopher, or other N. American ground-squirrel.
prairie-turnip, *n.* breadroot, the edible tuberous root of *Psoralea esculenta*, of the Western U.S.A.
prairie-wolf, *n.* the coyote.
praisable, *a.* *praze*-a-bl, that deserves to be praised.
praise, *n.* praze, commendation; approbation; the expression of gratitude for favours; a glorifying or extolling: *v.t.* to bestow commendation on; to extol; to applaud. (O.Fr. *preis*, merit.)
praiser, *n.* *praze*-er, one who praises or extols.
praiseless, *a.* *praze*-less, without praise; unworthy of praise.
praiseworthily, *ad.* in a praiseworthy manner.
praiseworthiness, *n.* state of being praiseworthy.
praiseworthy, *a.* *praze*-wur-the, deserving of praise; commendable; laudable.
Prakrit, *n.* *prah*-krit, any Hindu dialect derived from Sanskrit or of the same origin. (Sans.)
praline, *n.* *prah*-leen, a sweetmeat of nut kernels roasted in boiling sugar. (Fr.)
pram, *n.* pram, a praam; a perambulator [Coll.].
prance, *v.i.* prahnce, to spring or bound, as a horse in high mettle; to ride with bounding movements or ostentatiously; to walk or strut about in a showy or warlike manner. (Perhaps from *prank*.)
prandial, *a.* *pran*-de-al, relating to a repast or dinner. (L. *prandium*, a meal.)
prang, *v.t.* and *i.* prang, to smash; to wreck [R.A.F. Slang].
prank, *v.t.* prank, to adorn in a showy manner: *v.i.* to make a display. (Perhaps Dut. *pronken*, to show off.)
prank, *n.* prank, a capering; a freak or gambol; merry mischievous trick. (Origin unknown.)
prankish, *a.* *prang*-kish, full of pranks; pranky.
pranky, *a.* *prang*-ke, given to pranks; prankish.
prase, *n.* praze, a translucent leek-green variety of quartz. (Gr. *prasinos*, leek-green.)
praseodymium, *n.* *pray*-ze-o-*dim*-e-um, a metallic element of the rare earth group, discovered in 1885. (Gr. *prasinos*, leek-green, and *didymium*.)
prasine, *n.* *pray*-zin, pseudomalakite, a green-coloured mineral. (Gr.)
pratal, *a.* *pray*-tal, growing in, or pertaining to, meadows. (L. *pratum*, meadow.)
prate, *n.* prate, trifling talk; unmeaning loquacity: *v.i.* to talk much and to little purpose; to babble: *v.t.* to utter foolishly. (M.E. *praten*.)
prater, *n.* *prate*-er, one who prates.
praties, *n.pl.* *pray*-tiz, potatoes [Ir. Coll.].
pratincole, *n.* *prat*-in-kole, any grallatorial bird of the genus *Glareola*, esp. *G. pratincola*, allied to the plovers. (L. *pratum*, meadow, *incola*, inhabitant.)
prating, *a.* *prate*-ing, talking idly; loquacious: *n.* idle and trifling talk.
pratingly, *ad.* *prate*-ing-le, in a prating manner.
pratique, *n.* pra-*teek*, licence to a ship to trade with a place after quarantine, or upon certification that she has not come from an infected place. (Fr.)
prattle, *v.i.* *prat*-tl, to talk much and idly, as a child: *n.* empty and idle chatter. (*prate*.)
prattler, *n.* *prat*-tler, one who prattles; a child.
pravity, *n.* *prav*-e-te, moral perversion; depravity.
prawn, *n.* prawn, an edible crustacean, *Palæmon serratus*, resembling a large shrimp. (Unknown.)
praxinoscope, *n.* prak-*sin*-o-skope, an obsolete zoetrope-like instrument. (Gr. *praxis*, and *skopeo*, view.)
praxis, *n.* *prak*-sis, use; practice; an example, or a set of examples, for practice. (Gr.)
pray, *v.i.* pray, to ask with earnestness, as for a favour; to petition; to address the Supreme Being with adoration: *v.t.* to supplicate; to entreat; to ask with reverence and urgency; to petition. (O.Fr. *preier*.)
prayer, *n.* prare, the earnest asking for a favour; a solemn address to the Supreme Being; a turning of one's soul in reverence, infinite desire, and endeavour to what is highest and best; a formula of church service or worship; practice of supplication; that part of a petition which specifies the request. **prayer meeting,** a meeting for prayer. **prayer shawl,** a tallith. **prayer wheel,** a praying machine. (O.Fr. *preiere*.)
prayer, *n.* *pray*-er, one who prays.
prayer-book, *n.* *prare*-book, a book containing prayers or forms of devotion.

prayerful, *a.* *prare*-ful, devotional; given to prayer; using much prayer.
prayerfully, *ad.* in a prayerful manner.
prayerfulness, *n.* the state of being prayerful.
prayerless, *a.* *prare*-less, not using, or neglecting, prayer.
prayerlessly, *ad.* in a prayerless manner.
prayerlessness, *n.* the state of being prayerless.
praying, *n.* *pray*-ing, the act of praying. **praying machine,** a revolving wheel carrying written prayers, used in Tibet. **praying mantis,** *see* **mantis.**
prayingly, *ad.* *pray*-ing-le, with supplication.
pre-, pre, a Latin prefix signifying before or prior in space, time, or degree (can be attached to almost any noun or verb).
preach, *v.i.* preech, to discourse on a religious subject; to discourse earnestly; to exhort to repentance: *v.t.* to proclaim; to inculcate in religious discourses; to deliver. **preaching friars,** the Dominicans. (O.Fr. *prechier.*)
preacher, *n.* *preech*-er, one who discourses on religious subjects; one who preaches; one licensed to preach.
preachership, *n.* *preech*-er-ship, the status or office of a preacher.
preachify, *v.i.* *preech*-e-fy, to preach unseasonably or tediously; to sermonize.
preachment, *n.* *preech*-ment, a discourse or sermon, in contempt. (O.Fr. *prechement.*)
preachy, *a.* *preech*-e, talking long and tediously; fond of preaching [Coll.].
preacquainted, *a.* pree-a-*kwayn*-ted, previously acquainted.
pre-Adamite, *a.* previous to or existing before Adam; pertaining to the pre-Adamites: *n.* one living in the world prior to Adam; one believing in the existence of such persons.
preadaptation, *n.* *pree*-ad-ap-*tay*-shon, adjustment in advance to some change in circumstances; structural change occurring before the change of habit requiring it [Zool.].
preadmonish, *v.t.* pree-ad-*mon*-ish, to admonish previously.
preadolescent, *n.* *pree*-ad-o-*les*-ent, a juvenile who has not quite reached adolescence.
preamble, *n.* pre-*am*-bl, an introduction; a preliminary statement; the introductory part of a statute, stating the reason and intent of the law: *v.t.* to preface. (L. *præambulo*, walk before.)
preambulatory, *a.* pre-*am*-bew-la-to-re, of the nature of a preamble; going before; preceding.
preappoint, *v.t.* pree-a-*poynt*, to appoint previously.
preappointment, *n.* pree-a-*poynt*-ment, previous appointment.
preapprehension, *n.* pree-ap-re-*hen*-shon, an opinion formed before examination.
prearranged, *a.* pree-a-*raynjd*, arranged in advance or beforehand.
preaudience, *n.* pree-*aw*-de-ence, right of previous audience; precedence at the bar among lawyers.
prebend, *n.* *preb*-end, the stipend granted to a canon out of the estate of a cathedral or a collegiate church; a prebendary or prebendaryship. (O.Fr. *prebende.*)
prebendal, *a.* pre-*ben*-dal, pertaining to a prebend.
prebendary, *n.* *preb*-en-da-re, an ecclesiastic who enjoys a prebend; a stipendiary of a cathedral. (Late L. *prebendarius.*)
prebendaryship, *n.* *preb*-en-da-re-ship, the office of a prebendary.
precarious, *a.* pre-*kare*-re-us, depending on the will or pleasure of another; uncertain; held by a doubtful tenure. (L. *precarius*, attained by prayer, from *precor*, pray.)
precariously, *ad.* in a precarious manner.
precariousness, *n.* state of being precarious.
precatory, *a.* *prek*-a-to-re, suppliant; beseeching; expressing entreaty [Gram.].
precaution, *n.* pre-*kaw*-shon, preventive measure; caution previously employed: *v.t.* to warn or advise beforehand.
precautionary, *a.* pre-*kaw*-shon-a-re, of the nature of a precaution; suggesting caution beforehand; adapted to prevent mischief or secure good.
precautious, *a.* pre-*kaw*-shus, using forethought; taking precautions.
precede, *v.t.* pre-*seed*, to go before in time, place, rank, or importance; to walk in front; to preface. (O.Fr. *preceder.*)
precedence, *n.* pre-*see*-dence *or* *pres*-e-dence, the act of going before in time, rank, dignity, or the place of honour; right of superiority in this sense. **take precedence,** have the right of precedence.
precedency, *n.* pre-*see*-den-se *or* *pres*-e-den-se, precedence.
precedent, *a.* pre-*see*-dent, going before; anterior. (O.Fr.)
precedent, *n.* *pres*-e-dent, something said or done before, as an example to follow in a similar case.
precedented, *a.* *pres*-e-den-ted, having a precedent.
precedential, *a.* pres-e-*den*-shal, of the nature of, or serving as, a precedent.
precedently, *ad.* pre-*see*-dent-le, beforehand.
preceding, *a.* pre-*see*-ding, going before; antecedent.
precent, *v.t.* and *i.* pre-*sent*, to lead in singing; to act as precentor.
precentor, *n.* pre-*sen*-tor, the leader of a choir in a cathedral or church; the leader of the singing in presbyterian churches. (L. *præcentor.*)
precentorship, *n.* pre-*sen*-tor-ship, the office, status, or tenure of a precentor.
precept, *n.* *pree*-sept, an authoritative rule respecting moral conduct; a maxim; a writ, warrant, or other mandate in writing [Law]; an order for the levying of a rate. (O.Fr.)
preceptive, *a.* pre-*sep*-tiv, giving or containing precepts; of the nature of a precept.
preceptor, *n.* pre-*sep*-tor, a teacher; an instructor; a headmaster; the head of a preceptory.
preceptorial, *a.* pree-sep-*taw*-re-al, pertaining to a preceptor.
preceptory, *n.* pre-*sep*-to-re, an outlying establishment of the Knights Templar.
preceptress, *n.* pre-*sep*-tres, a female teacher.
precession, *n.* pre-*sesh*-on, a going onward; precedence; a change in the direction of a spinning body [Mech.]. **precession of the equinoxes,** a slow continuous movement of the equinoctial points from east to west [Astron.]. (O.Fr.)
precessional, *a.* pre-*sesh*-on-al, pertaining to precession.
pre-Christian, *a.* pree-*kris*-tyan, pertaining to the times before the Christian era.
precinct, *n.* *pree*-sinkt, an outward limit or boundary; the enclosed surroundings of a cathedral, church, or other building; a small territorial district: *pl.* environs. (Late L. *præcinctum*, a boundary.)
preciosity, *n.* presh-e-*os*-e-te, fastidious or affected refinement; excessive elegance (esp. literary).
precious, *a.* *presh*-us, of great price; costly; of great value; highly valued; affectedly refined in language, etc.; considerable, great (in irony). **precious metals,** gold, silver, and platinum. **precious stones,** gems of value, esp. diamond, ruby, sapphire, and emerald. (O.Fr. *precieus.*)
preciously, *ad.* *presh*-us-le, in a precious manner.
preciousness, *n.* the quality of being precious; preciosity.
precipe, *n.* *pree*-se-pe, præcipe. (L.)
precipice, *n.* *pres*-e-pis, a steep descent, esp. one nearly or quite perpendicular; an overhanging cliff; an extremely dangerous situation. (Fr. *précipice.*)
precipitability, *n.* pre-*sip*-e-ta-*bil*-e-te, the state or quality of being precipitable.
precipitable, *a.* pre-*sip*-e-ta-bl, that may be precipitated, as a substance in solution.
precipitance, *n.* pre-*sip*-e-tance, precipitancy.
precipitancy, *n.* pre-*sip*-e-tan-se, the quality of being precipitate; rash haste; haste in resolving, forming an opinion, or executing a purpose.
precipitant, *a.* pre-*sip*-e-tant, falling or rushing headlong; hasty; rashly hurried: *n.* a liquor, which, when poured on a solution, separates what is dissolved, and precipitates it [Chem.]. (O.Fr.)
precipitantly, *ad.* in a precipitant or hasty manner.
precipitate, *n.* pre-*sip*-e-tate, a solid substance precipitated [Chem.]: *a.* falling, flowing, or rushing with steep descent; headlong; overhasty; adopted without due deliberation; violent and speedily terminating: *v.t.* to throw headlong, to urge with eagerness or undue haste; to hurry rashly; to throw to the bottom of a vessel, as a solid substance in solution [Chem.]; to cause deposition through

condensation: *v.i.* to fall headlong; to fall to the bottom of a vessel, as a sediment; to be deposited in drops through condensation. **red precipitate**, mercuric oxide obtained through heat. **white precipitate**, ammoniated mercury. **yellow precipitate**, mercuric oxide obtained by precipitation, or peroxide of mercury. (L. *præcipitatus*, cast headlong.)
precipitately, *ad.* in a precipitate manner.
precipitation, *n.* pre-*sip*-e-*tay*-shon, the act of precipitating; great or rash haste; rapid movement; deposition of solid matter from solution [Chem.]; deposit of rain, snow, mist, etc., or the quantity deposited [Meteor.].
precipitator, *n.* pre-*sip*-e-tay-tor, a precipitant [Chem.]; a vessel in which precipitation occurs.
precipitous, *a.* pre-*sip*-e-tus, very steep; headlong; hasty.
precipitously, *ad.* in a precipitous manner.
precipitousness, *n.* the state of being precipitous; rash haste.
précis, *n.* *pray*-se, an abridged statement; a summary: *v.t.* to make a précis of; to summarize. (Fr.)
precise, *a.* pre-*sice*, exact; definite; formal; punctilious; finical. (O.Fr. *precis*, strict.)
precisely, *ad.* in a precise manner.
preciseness, *n.* the quality of being precise.
precisian, *n.* pre-*sizh*-an, a strict observer of rules; a formalist: *a.* formal; punctilious.
precisianism, *n.* pre-*sizh*-a-nizm, the practice of a precisian; excessive exactness.
precision, *n.* pre-*sizh*-on, exactness; accuracy: *a.* adapted for extreme accuracy. (L. *præcisio*, a cutting off.)
precisive, *a.* pre-*sy*-siv, characterized by exactitude; exactly limiting.
preclude, *v.t.* pre-*klood*, to hinder from access or possession; to shut out; to make impossible; to debar. (L. *præcludo*, shut off.)
preclusion, *n.* pre-*kloo*-zhon, the act of precluding; the state of being precluded.
preclusive, *a.* pre-*kloo*-ziv, precluding or tending to preclude.
preclusively, *ad.* in a preclusive manner.
precocious, *a.* pre-*koh*-shus, ripe or developed before the natural time; premature in development; showing precocity; præcocial [Ornith.]. (Fr. *précoce*.)
precociously, *ad.* in a precocious manner.
precociousness, *n.* precocity.
precocity, *n.* pre-*kos*-e-te, the state of being precocious; forwardness, esp. in mental development.
precogitation, *n.* pree-koj-e-*tay*-shon, previous consideration or thought.
precognition, *n.* pree-kog-*nish*-on, previous knowledge; antecedent examination; examination prior to prosecution [Scots Law]. (L. *præcognitio*.)
precognize, *v.t.* pree-kog-*nize*, to know beforehand.
precompose, *v.t.* pree-kom-*poze*, to compose beforehand.
preconceit, *n.* pree-kon-*seet*, a notion previously formed.
preconceive, *v.t.* pree-kon-*seev*, to form a conception, idea, or opinion of beforehand.
preconception, *n.* pree-kon-*sep*-shon, opinion previously formed.
preconcert, *n.* pree-*kon*-sert, a previous agreement.
preconcert, *v.t.* pree-kon-*sert*, to concert beforehand.
preconcertedly, *ad.* pree-kon-*ser*-ted-le, by preconcert.
precondemn, *v.t.* pree-kon-*dem*, to condemn beforehand.
precondemnation, *n.* *pree*-kon-dem-*nay*-shon, condemning beforehand.
precondition, *n.* pree-kon-*dish*-un, a necessary preliminary condition.
preconization, *n.* *pree*-kon-e-*zay*-shon, the formal announcement of the Pope of new appointments to office; publishing by proclamation. (L. *præconizo*, announce.)
preconize, *v.t.* *pree*-ko-nize, to make a public announcement or commendation; to summon by name; publicly to approve the appointment of a bishop (of the Pope).
pre-Conquest, *a.* pertaining to or preceding the time before the Norman Conquest (1066) [Engl. Hist.].
preconsider, *v.t.* pree-kon-*sid*-er, to consider previously.
preconsignment, *n.* *pree*-kon-*sine*-ment, a previous consignment.
preconsolidated, *a.* pree-kon-*sol*-e-day-ted, consolidated beforehand.
preconstitute, *v.t.* pree-*kon*-ste-tewt, to constitute beforehand.
precontract, *n.* pree-*kon*-trakt, a contract previous to another.
precontract, *v.t.* and *i.* pree-kon-*trakt*, to stipulate beforehand; to make a previous contract.
precordia, *n.* pree-*kor*-de-a, the præcordia.
precostal, *a.* pree-*kos*-tal, situated in front of the ribs [Anat.].
precursor, *n.* pree-*kur*-sor, a forerunner; a harbinger; one who or that which precedes and intimates approach. (L. *præcursor*.)
precursory, *a.* pree-*kur*-so-re, preceding as the harbinger; indicating something to follow.
predacious, *a.* pre-*day*-shus, living by prey; predatory. (L. *præda*, prey.)
predacity, *n.* pre-*das*-e-te, the quality or state of being predacious.
predate, *v.t.* pree-*date*, to antedate.
predatory, *a.* *pred*-a-to-re, characterized by or given to plundering; predacious. (L. *prædatorius*.)
predazzite, *n.* *pred*-a-zite, a crystalline metamorphic rock formed by the action of intense heat on magnesian limestone. (First found at *Predazzo*, N. Italy.)
predecease, *n.* pree-de-*seece*, decease before another: *v.i.* to die before (some person or event, etc.).
predecessor, *n.* pree-de-*ses*-sor, one who preceded another in an office, etc.; an ancestor; anything preceding another.
predefinition, *n.* pree-def-e-*nish*-on, predetermination.
predella, *n.* pre-*del*-la, the platform on which an altar stands; a picture or ornamental work on this; the ledge at the back of the altar. (It.)
predesignate, *v.t.* pree-*dez*-ig-nate, to indicate or designate beforehand.
predestinarian, *a.* *pree*-des-te-*nare*-re-an, pertaining to predestination: *n.* one who believes in predestination [Theol.].
predestinate, *a.* pree-*des*-te-nate, appointed or ordained beforehand: *v.t.* to preordain by an unchangeable purpose; to predetermine; to foreordain. (L.)
predestination, *n.* pree-*des*-te-*nay*-shon, the act of decreeing or foreordaining events; foreordination by God of whatever comes to pass, esp. of some to eternal life, and others to eternal death [Theol.].
predestinator, *n.* pre-*des*-te-nay-tor, one who foreordains; one who holds to predestination.
predestine, *v.t.* pre-*des*-tin, to decree beforehand; to foreordain.
predeterminable, *a.* pree-de-*ter*-me-na-bl, capable of being predetermined.
predeterminate, *a.* pree-de-*ter*-me-nat, determined beforehand.
predetermination, *n.* pree-de-*ter*-me-*nay*-shon, previous determination; predestination [Theol.].
predetermine, *v.t.* pree-de-*ter*-min, to determine beforehand; to predestine.
predeterminism, pree-de-*ter*-me-nizm, determinism; the theory that heredity determines individual development [Biol.].
predial, *a.* *pree*-de-al, consisting of or attached to land or farms; accruing from land. (Late L. *prædialia*, from *prædium*, farm, estate.)
predicability, *n.* pred-e-ka-*bil*-e-te, the quality of being assertable.
predicable, *a.* *pred*-e-ka-bl, that may be affirmed or predicated of something: *n.* a term denoting genus, species, differentia, property, or accident that can be predicated of others [Logic].
predicament, *n.* pre-*dik*-a-ment, condition; particular situation; critical state; plight: *pl.* the ten categories of Aristotle [Logic]. (O.Fr.)
predicamental, *a.* pre-*dik*-a-*men*-tal, pertaining to a predicament.
predicant, *a.* *pred*-e-kant, occupied in preaching: *n.* a preacher; a preaching friar; a Dominican; a predikant. (O.Fr.)
predicate, *n.* *pred*-e-kat, that which is affirmed or denied; an attribute; the statement made

about anything [Gram.]: *v.t.* *pred*-e-kate, to affirm one thing of another: *v.i.* to comprise or make an affirmation. (L. *prædicatus*, proclaimed.)
predication, *n.* pred-e-*kay*-shon, the act of asserting; affirmation of something.
predicative, *a.* pre-*dik*-a-tiv, expressing affirmation.
predicatively, *ad.* pre-*dik*-a-tiv-le, as a predicate [Gram.].
predicatory, *a.* *pred*-e-ka-to-re, pertaining to preaching.
predict, *v.t.* pre-*dikt*, to foretell; to prophesy; to divine or estimate correctly. (L. *prædictus*, foretold.)
prediction, *n.* pre-*dik*-shon, a prophecy; the art of foretelling.
predictive, *a.* pre-*dik*-tiv, foretelling; prophetic.
predictor, *n.* pre-*dik*-tor, one who or that which predicts, esp. a device by which the location, speed, direction, etc., of aircraft are plotted and automatically given to anti-aircraft gunners [Mil.].
predictory, *a.* pre-*dik*-to-re, prophetic.
predigestion, *n.* pree-de-*jes*-tyon, artificial digestion of a food before it is taken into the body.
predikant, *n.* *pred*-e-kant, a Dutch Protestant minister, esp. in S. Africa. (Dut.)
predilection, *n.* pree-de-*lek*-shon, a prepossession in favour of something; partiality for. (L. *præ-*, and *dilectum*, love.)
prediscovery, *n.* *pree*-dis-*kuv*-er-re, prior discovery.
predisponent, *n.* pree-dis-*poh*-nent, that which predisposes.
predispose, *v.t.* pree-dis-*poze*, to incline beforehand; to give a disposition to; to bequeath previously.
predisposition, *n.* pree-dis-po-*zish*-on, previous inclination or propensity to anything.
predominance, *n.* pre-*dom*-e-nance, prevalence over others; superiority in strength, power, influence, or authority; ascendancy; superior influence, esp. of a planet [Astrol.].
predominant, *a.* pre-*dom*-e-nant, prevalent over others; superior; ascendant; ruling.
predominantly, *ad.* in a predominant manner.
predominate, *v.i.* pre-*dom*-e-nate, to prevail; to surpass in strength, influence, or authority; to be superior: *v.t.* to rule over. (Late L. *prædominatus*, prevailed.)
predomination, *n.* pree-dom-e-*nay*-shon, the act, condition, or power of predominating; superiority.
predoom, *v.t.* pree-*doom*, to doom beforehand.
predorsal, *a.* pree-*dawr*-sal, situated in front of the dorsal region [Anat.].
pre-elect, *v.t.* pree-e-*lekt*, to choose beforehand.
pre-election, *n.* election by previous determination.
pre-eminence, *n.* pre-*em*-e-nence, superiority in excellence; superiority; precedence.
pre-eminent, *a.* pre-*em*-e-nent, superior in excellence; distinguished; surpassing others.
pre-eminently, *ad.* to a pre-eminent degree.
pre-empt, *v.t.* pre-*empt*, to acquire or appropriate beforehand: *v.i.* to make a pre-emptive bid [Contract].
pre-emption, *n.* pre-*emp*-shon, the act or right of purchasing before others. (L. *præ-*, and *emptio*, a purchasing.)
pre-emptive, *a.* pre-*emp*-tiv, pertaining to, or of the nature of, pre-emption; pre-empting. **pre-emptive bid,** a declaration intended to stop further bidding; an initial bid of three or more [Contract].
preen, *n.* preen, a pin; a trifle [Scots.].
preen, *v.t.* preen, to clean, compose, and dress the feathers with the beak; to plume (oneself). (Perhaps M.E. *proin*, from O.Fr. *proigner*, to prune.)
pre-engage, *v.t.* to engage by previous contract; to attach by previous influence; to engage beforehand.
pre-engagement, *n.* prior engagement; previous attachment.
pre-established, *a.* established beforehand. **pre-established harmony,** a theory by which Leibnitz sought to explain the connexion between mind and body.
pre-examine, *v.t.* to examine beforehand.
pre-exilic, *a.* *pree*-ek-*sil*-ik, before the Babylonian captivity of the Jews.
pre-exist, *v.i.* pree-eg-*zist*, to exist beforehand.
pre-existence, *n.* previous existence; the presumed existence of the soul before its union with the body.
pre-existent, *a.* pree-eg-*zis*-tent, pre-existing.

prefabricated, *a.* pree-*fab*-re-kay-ted, made or prepared in advance (esp. for use in building construction).
preface, *n.* *pref*-as, something spoken or written as introductory to a discourse or book; an introduction or preamble: *v.t.* to introduce by preliminary remarks; to supply with a preface: *v.i.* to say something introductory. (O.Fr.)
prefacer, *n.* *pref*-as-ser, the writer of a preface.
prefatorial, *a.* pref-a-*taw*-re-al, prefatory; pertaining to a preface.
prefatorily, *ad.* in a prefatory manner.
prefatory, *a.* *pref*-a-to-re, introductory, esp. to a book or discourse. (L. *præfatus*, said before.)
prefect, *n.* *pree*-fekt, a governor or civil magistrate, esp. in ancient Rome; in France, the superintendent of a department; in many schools, a monitor or senior pupil with power of discipline. (L. *præfectus*, an overseer.)
prefectorial, *a.* pree-fek-*taw*-re-al, pertaining to prefects or the system of prefecture.
prefecture, *n.* *pree*-fek-tewr, the office, term of office, or jurisdiction of a prefect.
prefer, *v.t.* pre-*fer*, to regard more than another; to like better; to promote; to exalt; to offer; to present. (O.Fr. *preferer*.)
preferability, *n.* *pref*-er-ra-*bil*-e-te, the state or quality of being preferable.
preferable, *a.* *pref*-er-ra-bl, worthy to be preferred; more desirable; more excellent.
preferableness, *n.* *pref*-er-ra-bl-ness, preferability; greater desirableness.
preferably, *ad.* *pref*-er-ra-ble, in preference.
preference, *n.* *pref*-er-rence, the act of preferring of one thing before another; predilection; choice of one thing rather than another; liberty of choice; the thing preferred. **preference shares,** shares the holders of which are entitled to a dividend before the ordinary shareholders [Comm.]. (O.Fr.)
preferential, *a.* *pref*-er-*ren*-shal, constituting, giving, or having a preference. **preferential tariff,** a tariff giving to certain countries advantages over others in import duties [Econ.]. **preferential voting,** a method enabling the voter to indicate his second as well as his first choice.
preferentialism, *n.* pref-er-*ren*-sha-lizm, the system of granting preferences, esp. in international or inter-Dominion trade.
preferentially, *ad.* in a preferential manner.
preferment, *n.* pre-*fer*-ment, advancement to a higher office, dignity, or station; superior office or post.
preferrer, *n.* pre-*fer*-rer, one who prefers.
prefiguration, *n.* pree-fig-yew-*ray*-shon, act of prefiguring; antecedent representation.
prefigurative, *a.* pree-*fig*-yew-ra-tiv, showing by previous figures, types, or similitude.
prefigure, *v.t.* pree-*fig*-ur, to represent by antecedent types or figures; to foretell by similitudes.
prefigurement, *n.* pree-*fig*-ur-ment, act of prefiguring; prefiguration.
prefix, *v.t.* pre-*fiks*, to put or fix in front of or before; to settle or appoint beforehand.
prefix, *n.* *pree*-fiks, a letter, syllable, or word affixed to the beginning of a word.
prefixion, *n.* pre-*fik*-shon, the act of prefixing; the employment of a prefix.
prefixture, *n.* pree-*fiks*-tewr, prefixion; a prefix.
prefloration, *n.* pree-flo-*ray*-shon, the arrangement of petals before expansion; æstivation [Bot.].
prefoliation, *n.* pree-foh-le-*ay*-shon, the disposition of leaves in the bud, vernation [Bot.].
preform, *v.t.* pre-*form*, to form beforehand.
preformation, *n.* pree-for-*may*-shon, previous formation; the obsolete theory that all germs comprise the complete and final organism which attains full development by the mere process of growth [Biol.].
preformative, *n.* pre-*for*-ma-tiv, a formative letter in the beginning of a word; a prefix.
pre-glacial, *a.* before the glacial period [Geol.].
pregnable, *a.* *preg*-na-bl, capable of being taken or won by force. (O.Fr. *prenable*.)
pregnancy, *n.* *preg*-nan-se, the state of being pregnant; fertility; inventive power; significance.
pregnant, *a.* *preg*-nant, being with young; fruitful; full of important matter or significance. (O.Fr.)
pregnantly, *ad.* *preg*-nant-le, in a pregnant manner.

prehallux, *n.* pree-*hal*-luks, a spur or rudimentary digit present on the inner side of the foot in certain amphibians and mammals.
prehensile, *a.* pre-*hen*-sile, seizing; fitted for seizing, as the tails of American monkeys. (L. *prehensus*, laid hold of.)
prehensility, *n.* *pree*-hen-*sil*-e-te, the quality of being prehensile.
prehension, *n.* pre-*hen*-shon, the act of taking hold of or seizing.
prehensory, *a.* pre-*hen*-so-re, adapted for or capable of seizing.
prehistoric, *a.* *pre*-his-*to*-rik, before written records; pertaining to the period embracing the Eolithic, Palæolithic, Neolithic, Bronze, and Iron Ages.
prehistory, *n.* pre-*his*-to-re, facts concerning prehistoric times; an account of such knowledge; the story of the earth and human evolution prior to the existence of written records; a history of the antecedents of any event.
prehnite, *n.* *pray*-nite *or* *pree*-nite, a greenish crystalline silicate of calcium and aluminium occurring in igneous rocks. (Col. van *Prehn*, who introduced it, 1774.)
pre-human, *a.* occurring in, or relating to, times before the existence of man.
pre-ignition, *n.* ignition in an internal combustion engine before compression is complete [Mech.].
preinstruct, *v.t.* pree-in-*strukt*, to instruct previously.
preintimation, *n.* pree-in-te-*may*-shon, previous intimation or suggestion.
prejudge, *v.t.* pree-*judj*, to judge in a cause before it is heard; to condemn beforehand or unheard.
prejudgment, *n.* pree-*judj*-ment, condemnation before trial.
prejudication, *n.* pre-*joo*-de-*kay*-shon, act of judging without examination; a previously formed opinion or judgment.
prejudicative, *a.* pre-*joo*-de-ka-tiv, forming a judgment or opinion without examination.
prejudice, *n.* *prej*-yew-dis, an opinion or decision formed beforehand, and more or less unwarranted or unreasonable; an unreasonable prepossession; hurt; damage; injury: *v.t.* to prepossess with unexamined opinions; to bias the mind; to damage. **without prejudice,** without detriment to existing rights or to pending litigation or negotiations. (O.Fr.)
prejudiced, *a.* *prej*-yew-dist, prepossessed; biased.
prejudicial, *a.* prej-yew-*dish*-al, detrimental; mischievous; injurious.
prejudicially, *ad.* injuriously.
preknowledge, *n.* pree-*nol*-ej, prior knowledge.
prelacy, *n.* *prel*-a-se, the office of prelate; episcopacy; bishops collectively. (O.Fr. *prelacie*.)
prelate, *n.* *prel*-at, a dignitary of the Church, as an archbishop, bishop, abbot, prior, metropolitan, or patriarch. (O.Fr. *prelat*.)
prelatess, *n.* *prel*-at-ess, an abbess or prioress.
prelatical, *a.* pre-*lat*-e-kal, pertaining to prelates or prelacy.
prelatism, *n.* *prel*-at-izm, prelacy (in a hostile sense).
prelatist, *n.* *prel*-at-ist, an advocate of prelacy.
prelatize, *v.i.* and *v.t.* *prel*-at-ize, to make a church episcopal.
prelature, *n.* *prel*-at-yewr, the office of a prelate.
prelect, *v.i.* pre-*lekt*, to discourse; to read a lecture aloud. (L. *prælectus*, read before an audience.)
prelection, *n.* pre-*lek*-shon, a discourse read to an audience. (L. *prælectio*.)
prelector, *n.* pre-*lek*-tor, a lecturer.
prelibation, *n.* pree-ly-*bay*-shon, foretaste; a pouring out previous to tasting. (Late L. *prælibatio*.)
preliminarily, *ad.* in a preliminary manner.
preliminary, *a.* pre-*lim*-e-na-re, coming first; preceding the main discourse or business; introductory: *n.* that which precedes the main business introduction. (L. *præ-*, and *limen*, the threshold.)
prelingual, *a.* pree-*ling*-gwal, before the use of language.
prelude, *n.* *prel*-yewd, something introductory or preparatory, as indicative of what is to follow; a forerunner; a short strain of music before a regular piece or concert: *v.t.* to precede; to introduce; to play before: *v.i.* to serve as an introduction. (L. *præludo*, play beforehand.)
preludial, *a.* pre-*lew*-de-al, introductory.
prelusive, *a.* pre-*lew*-siv, introductory, and indicative of what is to follow.
prelusively, *ad.* by way of prelude.
prelusory, *a.* pre-*lew*-so-re, prelusive.
premandibular, *a.* pree-man-*dib*-yew-lar, situated in front of the mandible or upper jaw [Anat.].
prematernity, *a.* pree-ma-*ter*-ne-te, pertaining to the conditions, etc., of expectant motherhood.
premature, *a.* *prem*-a-tewr, *pree*-ma-teur, *or* prem-a-*tewr*, ripe before the natural time; happening or done before the proper time. (L. *præmaturus*.)
prematurely, *ad.* too soon; too hastily.
prematureness, *n.* prematurity.
prematurity, *n.* prem-a-*tewr*-re-te, the state or condition of being premature; early ripeness; haste.
premaxillary, *a.* pree-mak-*sil*-a-re, situated in front of the jawbone: *n.* either of the bones between the two superior maxillæ in vertebrates.
premeditate, *v.t.* pree-*med*-e-tate, to meditate, or contrive and design beforehand: *v.i.* to deliberate beforehand.
premeditation, *n.* pree-med-e-*tay*-shon, previous deliberation, contrivance, and design.
premier, *a.* *preem*-e-er *or* *prem*-e-er, first; principal; most ancient [Her.]: *n.* (*cap.*) the Prime Minister of Gt. Britain, certain British Dominions, and some other states. (Fr.)
première, *n.* prem-*yare*, the first performance of a stage play, or exhibition of a film, in public.
premiership, *n.* the office of Premier.
premillenarian, *n.* *pree*-mil-e-*nare*-re-an, an adherent of premillennialism; pertaining to this doctrine or to its adherents.
premillennial, *a.* *pree*-mil-*len*-e-al, pertaining to the world of to-day; occurring before the millennium (esp. of the Second Advent).
premillennialism, *n.* *pree*-mil-*len*-e-a-lizm, the belief that the Second Advent of Christ will precede the millennium.
premillennialist, *n.* *pree*-mil-*len*-e-a-list, a premillenarian.
premise, *v.t.* pre-*mize*, to speak or write previously, or as introductory to the main subject; to lay down as propositions to reason from: *v.i.* to state antecedent propositions. (L. *præmissus*, sent forward.)
premise, *n.* *prem*-is, a proposition antecedently assumed or laid down: *pl.* the two propositions of a syllogism, called respectively major and minor, from which the conclusion is deduced [Logic]; subject matter of a conveyance or deed as set forth in the beginning [Law]; *pl.* a building with its land and adjuncts.
premiss, *n.* *prem*-is, a premise [Logic].
premium, *n.* *pree*-me-um, a reward or recompense; a prize; a bounty; something offered or given for an advantage, as a loan of money; amount above par; payment for insurance; fee for apprenticeship. **at a premium,** at an increased value; highly esteemed [Fig.]. **to put a premium on,** to add an incentive. (L. from *præ-*, and *emo*, buy.)
premolar, *a.* pree-*moh*-lar, situated between the molars and canines: *n.* a premolar tooth; a bicuspid.
premonish, *v.t.* pre-*mon*-ish, to forewarn. (L. *præmonitus*, forewarned.)
premonition, *n.* pree-mo-*nish*-on, previous warning, notice, or information; presentiment.
premonitor, *n.* pre-*mon*-e-tor, a warner; a premonitory sign.
premonitory, *a.* pre-*mon*-e-to-re, giving previous warning or notice.
Premonstrant, *n.* pree-*mon*-strant, one of an order of regular canons, called also white canons, founded by St. Norbert at Prémontré, near Laon, in 1120.
Premonstratensian, *a.* *pree*-mon-stra-*ten*-she-an, pertaining to the Premonstrants: *n.* a member of this order, a Norbertine.
premorse, *a.* pre-*morse*, with ends abruptly truncated, as if bitten off [Bot. and Entom.]. (L. *præmorsus*, bitten off in front.)
premotion, *n.* pre-*moh*-shon, previous motion or excitement to action.
premundane, *a.* pree-*mun*-dane, antemundane.
premunire, *n.* pree-mew-*nyr*-re, præmunire.
prenatal, *a.* pre-*nay*-tal, before birth; pertaining to the period of expectant motherhood.
prender, *n.* *prend*-er, the right of taking something

before it is offered [Old Law]. (O.Fr. *prendre*, seize.)
prenomen, *n.* pree-*noh*-men, the personal name, that preceding the family name; the Christian name. (L.)
prenominal, *a.* pree-*nom*-e-nal, pertaining to a first or personal name. (*prenomen.*)
prenominate, *v.t.* pree-*nom*-e-nate, to name beforehand.
prenotify, *v.t.* pree-*noh*-te-fy, to notify in advance.
prenotion, *n.* pree-*noh*-shon, prescience; foreknowledge.
prentice, *n.* *pren*-tis, an apprentice: *a.* characteristic of an apprentice.
preoccupancy, *n.* pre-*ok*-yew-pan-se, the act or right of taking possession before others.
preoccupation, *n.* pree-ok-yew-*pay*-shon, prior occupation; anticipation; prepossession; anticipation of objections.
preoccupied, *a.* pree-*ok*-yew-pide, absorbed in thought or other affairs; already, or previously occupied.
preoccupy, *v.t.* pree-*ok*-yew-py, to take possession of before another; to occupy by anticipation, or with prejudices; to absorb the attention.
preoperative, *a.* pree-*op*-er-ra-tiv, occurring before an operation [Surg.].
preopinion, *n.* pree-o-*pin*-yon, opinion previously formed.
preoption, *n.* pree-*op*-shon, previous choice; right of first choice.
pre-oral, *a.* situated in front of the mouth.
preordain, *v.t.* pree-or-*dane*, to predetermine.
preordinate, *a.* pree-*or*-de-nat, foreordained.
preordination, *n.* pree-or-de-*nay*-shon, act of foreordaining; predestination.
preorganic, *a.* pree-or-*gan*-ik, formed before the first appearance of life [Geol.].
prep, *n.* prep, preparation of lessons; homework.
prepaid, *a.* pree-*pade*, paid beforehand.
preparable, *a.* pre-*pare*-ra-bl, that can be prepared.
preparation, *n.* prep-a-*ray*-shon, act of preparing or fitting for a particular purpose; prior arrangement; state of being prepared; that which is prepared for some special purpose (as medicine, a part of a body for anatomical uses, etc.); the time for the learning of lessons [School]. (O.Fr.)
preparationist, *n.* prep-a-*ray*-shon-ist, one who upholds preparedness, esp. for war.
preparative, *a.* pre-*pa*-ra-tiv, tending to prepare; preparatory: *n.* that which prepares or makes ready.
preparatively, *ad.* by way of preparation.
preparator, *n.* pre-*pa*-ra-tor, a preparer, esp. of museum specimens.
preparatory, *a.* pre-*pa*-ra-to-re, preparing for something; introductory; preliminary; elementary. **preparatory school**, a school for preparing pupils for a public school.
prepare, *v.t.* pre-*pare*, to make ready; to provide: to procure as suitable; to appoint; to establish; *v.i.* to get ready; to take the necessary previous steps; to make oneself ready. (O.Fr. *preparer.*)
preparedly, *ad.* pre-*pare*-red-le, with suitable previous measures.
preparedness, *n.* pre-*pare*-red-ness, state of being in readiness.
preparer, *n.* pre-*pare*-rer, one who prepares.
prepay, *v.t.* pree-*pay*, to pay in advance. *p.* and *pp.* **prepaid.**
prepayable, *a.* payable in advance.
prepayment, *n.* pre-*pay*-ment, payment in advance.
prepense, *a.* pre-*pense*, premeditated; planned in advance. (O.Fr.)
prepensely, *ad.* after deliberation; with premeditation.
preperception, *n.* pree-per-*sep*-shon, previous perception; anticipation of a perception [Psych.].
prepollent, *a.* pre-*pol*-ent, superior in power; prevailing. (L. *præ-*, and *pollens*, being strong.)
preponderance, *n.* pre-*pon*-der-ance, superiority of weight, power, or force. (L. *præponderare*, to outweigh.)
preponderant, *a.* pre-*pon*-der-rant, outweighing; surpassing in influence, force, etc.
preponderantly, *ad.* so as to preponderate.
preponderate, *v.t.* pre-*pon*-der-rate, to outweigh; to overpower by greater weight or influence; *v.i.* to exceed in weight; to incline to one side.
preposition, *n.* prep-o-*zish*-on, a word expressing some relation or quality; a word usually put before a noun or a pronoun to show its relation to another word in the sentence [Gram.]. (L.)
prepositional, *a.* pertaining to a preposition.
prepositionally, *ad.* in the manner of a preposition.
prepositive, *a.* pree-*poz*-e-tiv, put before: *n.* a word or particle put before another word. (Late L.)
prepositor, *n.* pre-*poz*-e-tor, a præpostor, a monitor. (Late L.)
prepossess, *v.t.* pree-po-*zes*, to preoccupy; to take previous possession of; to bias or prejudice, usually in a good sense: *v.i.* to make a favourable impression.
prepossessing, *a.* pree-po-*zes*-ing, attractive; tending to win favour; producing a favourable impression.
prepossession, *n.* pree-po-*zesh*-on, prior possession; preconceived opinion; previous impression; prejudice, generally in a favourable sense.
preposterous, *a.* pre-*pos*-ter-rus, contrary to nature or reason; irrational; absurd. (Literally "last first," from L. *præposterus*, inverted.)
preposterously, *ad.* in a preposterous manner.
preposterousness, *n.* the quality of being preposterous.
prepotency, *n.* pre-*poh*-ten-se, the quality of being prepotent.
prepotent, *a.* pre-*poh*-tent, very powerful; superiorly powerful or potent. (O.Fr.)
pre-preference, *a.* pre-*pref*-er-rence, ranking before a preference share.
prepuce, *n.* *pree*-pewce, the foreskin. (L. *præputium.*)
preputial, *a.* pre-*pew*-shal, pertaining to the prepuce.
pre-Raphaelite, *a.* pre-*raf*-el-ite, realistic in art; peculiar to Pre-Raphaelitism: *n.* (*cap.*) one who practised or upheld Pre-Raphaelitism; a painter who lived before Raphael.
Pre-Raphaelitism, *n.* pre-*raf*-el-ite-izm, a mid-Victorian art-movement, fostered by Holman Hunt, Rossetti, Millais, etc., aiming at the cultivation of the realistic spirit and detailed methods attributed by its promoters to the earlier Italian painters.
pre-release, *n.* *pree*-re-*leece*, a release beforehand; a showing of a picture before its release [Cine.].
preremote, *a.* pre-re-*mote*, further remote; occurring at a more remote period.
prerequisite, *a.* pre-*rek*-we-zit, previously required: *n.* something previously necessary.
preresolve, *v.t.* pre-re-*zolv*, to resolve previously.
prerogative, *n.* pre-*rog*-a-tiv, an exclusive or peculiar privilege attached to a particular person, dignity, etc., esp. to the sovereign. **prerogative court**, a former archiepiscopal court for the trial of testamentary causes, etc., now undertaken by the Court of Probate. **royal prerogative**, the rights of a monarch by virtue of his office. (L. *prærogativa.*)
presage, *n.* *pres*-aj, something which foreshows a future event: *v.t.* pre-*saje*, to forebode; to foretell: *v.i.* to form or utter a prediction. (O.Fr.)
presageful, *a.* pre-*saje*-ful, full of foreboding; ominous.
presanctify, *v.t.* pre-*sank*-te-fy, to sanctify beforehand.
presbyope, *n.* *pres*-be-ohp, one affected with presbyopia.
presbyopia, *n.* pres-be-*oh*-pe-a, an eye defect, due to advancing age, in which longsightedness is combined with indistinct vision of near objects. (Gr. *presbys*, old, *ops*, the eye.)
presbyter, *n.* *pres*-be-ter, an elder with authority to teach and rule in the primitive church; a priest; one having charge of a presbytery. (Gr. *presbyteros*, the comparative of *presbys*, old.)
presbyteral, *a.* pres-*bit*-er-ral, pertaining to a presbyter or a presbytery.
presbyterate, *n.* pres-*bit*-er-rat, the office of presbyter; a body of presbyters; a presbytery.
presbyterial, *a.* pres-be-*teer*-re-al, presbyterian.
presbyterian, *a.* pres-be-*teer*-re-an, pertaining to a presbyter, or church government by presbyters; consisting of presbyters: *n.* (*usually with cap.*) one who belongs to a church governed by presbyters; an upholder of Presbyterianism. (Late L. *presbyterium*, a presbytery.)
Presbyterianism, *n.* pres-be-*teer*-re-a-nizm, that form of a church government which, discarding

prelacy, regards all ministers in conclave as on the same level in rank and function.

presbytery, *n.* *pres*-be-ter-re, a body of elders; a court, consisting of ministers, each with a ruling elder, of the churches within a particular district; the district represented in a presbytery; the east end of a chancel; the sanctuary.

prescience, *n.* *pree*-she-ence, foreknowledge. (Fr.)

prescient, *a.* *pree*-she-ent, knowing what is to come.

prescientific, *a* *pree*-sy-en-*tif*-ik, pertaining to the period prior to the age of science.

prescind, *v.t.* pre-*sind*, to cut off; to abstract. (L. *præscindo*, cut.)

prescribe, *v.t.* pre-*skribe*, to direct; to give as a rule of conduct; to direct medically: *v.i.* to claim by prescript [Law]; to give medical directions. (L. *præscribo*, write.)

prescriber, *n.* pre-*skribe*-er, one who prescribes medically.

prescript, *a.* *pre*-skript, directed; prescribed: *n.* a decree; an order.

prescriptible, *a.* pre-*skrip*-te-bl, liable to or derived from prescription [Law].

prescription, *n.* pre-*skrip*-shon, the act of prescribing or directing by rules; that which is prescribed; a medical recipe; the claim or title to anything by virtue of long use [Law]. (Fr.)

prescriptive, *a.* pre-*skrip*-tiv, giving rules or directions; acquired by immemorial use; pleading long customary use [Law].

presence, *n.* *prez*-ence, the existence of a person or thing in a certain place near or in company; approach face to face; state of being in view; sight; the person of a superior; a presence chamber; mien; personal appearance; demeanour; an influence deemed to be present. **presence chamber,** the room in which a great personage receives company. **presence of mind,** quick and effective decision, or self-control, in an emergency. (O.Fr.)

presensation, *n.* *pree*-sen-*say*-shon, presentiment; previous notion or idea.

presension, *n.* pre-*sen*-shon, previous perception; presensation. (L. *præsensio.*)

***present,** *a.* *prez*-ent, being in a certain place; being before the face or near; being now in view or under consideration; being at this time; ready at hand; not absent in mind: *n.* the present time, now; the present tense [Gram.]; a donation or gift: *pl.* what is written in a deed of conveyance or other instrument [Law]. **at present,** now. **by these presents,** by this document. **present tense,** the form of a verb which expresses action or being in the present time [Gram.]. (O.Fr.)

present, *v.t.* pre-*zent*, to introduce into the presence of a superior; to exhibit; to give; to offer; to deliver; to point, as a gun, at another; to nominate to an ecclesiastical benefice; to lay before a public body or a court; to indict [U.S.A.]. **to present arms,** to hold the rifle vertical, muzzle up, close to and in front of the body, as a salute. (O.Fr. *presenter.*)

presentability, *n.* pre-*zen*-ta-*bil*-e-te, quality of being presentable; fitness for presentation.

presentable, *a.* pre-*zen*-ta-bl, fit for presentation; suitable for introduction to company; clean and tidy.

presentation, *n.* prez-en-*tay*-shon, the act of presenting; a formal gift; theatrical or other representation; the act or right of presenting to a church living; the modification of consciousness involved in instantaneous perception [Met.]; the particular position in which an infant is presented at birth [Med.]. **Feast of the Presentation,** Candlemas. **presentation at court,** a formal introduction to the sovereign. (O.Fr.)

presentative, *a.* pre-*zen*-ta-tiv, having the right of presentation; admitting the presentation of a clerk [Eccles.]; of the nature or or pertaining to a presentation [Met.]; apprehending or apprehended directly [Psych.].

presentee, *n.* prez-en-*tee*, one presented to a benefice; one recommended to an office; a person presented at court; the receiver of a present.

presenter, *n.* pre-*zen*-ter, one who presents.

presentient, *a.* pre-*sen*-she-ent, apprehending; conscious of what will happen. (L. *præsentiens.*)

presentiment, *n.* pre-*zen*-te-ment, an apprehension of something, usually unpleasant, about to happen; a foreboding. (Fr. *pressentiment.*)

presentive, *a.* pre-*zen*-tiv, expressing an intuitive idea; presentative.

presentiveness, *n.* pre-*zen*-tiv-ness, the quality of being presentive.

presently, *ad.* *prez*-ent-le, in a short time; soon; immediately.

presentment, *n.* pre-*zent*-ment, the act of presenting; theatrical or other representation; a likeness; a formal complaint officially made at a parochial visitation [Eccles.]; the notice taken from their own knowledge by a grand jury of any offence; an indictment presented by a grand jury [Law].

preservable, *a.* pre-*zer*-va-bl, that may be preserved.

preservation, *n.* prez-er-*vay*-shon, the act of preserving or keeping safe; the state of being preserved from injury or decay. (O.Fr.)

preservative, *a.* pre-*zer*-va-tiv, tending to preserve; having power to preserve from decay, etc.: *n.* that which preserves, esp. a substance added to foodstuffs to prevent deterioration.

preservatory, *a.* pre-*zer*-va-to-re, tending or serving to preserve; preservative: *n.* a place equipped for the preserving of foods.

preserve, *n.* pre-*zerv*, fruit or vegetable seasoned and kept in sugar; a place for the preservation of game: *v.t.* to keep from injury; to uphold; to keep in a sound state; to season or treat (food stuffs) for preservation; to keep from corruption; to sustain; to protect game within boundaries; to keep private. (O.Fr. *preserver.*)

preserver, *n.* pre-*zer*-ver, the person or thing that preserves; a rescuer; one who makes preserves.

preses, *n.* *pree*-ses, a president or chairman of a meeting [Scot.]. (L. *præ-*, before, *sedeo*, sit.)

preside, *v.i.* pre-*zide*, to be set over for the exercise of authority; to direct, control, or govern; to exercise superintendence; to act as chairman.

presidency, *n.* *prez*-e-den-se, superintendence; the office, jurisdiction, or residence of president; the term during which a president holds office; any one of the large administrative divisions of former British India, Bengal, Bombay, or Madras. (Fr. *présidence.*)

president, *n.* *prez*-e-dent, one who presides; the chief of a republic; the chief of certain colleges and universities. **Lord President,** the presiding judge of the Court of Session. **Lord President of the Council,** the president of the Privy Council.

presidential, *a.* prez-e-*den*-shal, pertaining to a president or his office, or to a presidency; presiding over.

presidentship, *n.* *prez*-e-dent-ship, the office and place of president; his term of office.

presidial, *a.* pre-*sid*-e-al, presidential; presidiary.

presidiary, *a.* pre-*sid*-e-a-re, pertaining to or having a garrison; serving as a garrison. (L. *præsidium*, a garrison, from *præ-*, and *sedeo*, sit.)

presidium, *n.* pre-*sid*-e-um, in the U.S.S.R. a supreme permanent administrative committee, either of the Union or of each constituent Republic.

presignify, *v.t.* pree-*sig*-ne-fy, to intimate or signify beforehand; to show previously.

press, *v.t.* pres, formerly, to engage men for naval or military service by giving them prest-money, hence, to force men into service; to impress or commandeer: *n.* compulsory enlistment; a forced requisition. (*prest.*)

press, *v.t.* pres, to urge with force or weight; to squeeze; to crush; to hurry; to enforce; to hug; to straiten; to constrain; to urge; to make smooth, as paper or cloth: *v.i.* to urge forward with force; to encroach; to crowd; to push with force. (Fr. *presser*, to press.)

press, *n.* pres, a crowd; the act of urging or pushing forward; urgency; a closet for the safe keeping of things; a bookcase; an instrument or machine by which any body is squeezed or forced into a more compact form; a printing-machine; the art or business of printing and publishing; literature, more esp. journalism. **in the press,** being printed. **liberty of the press,** *see* **freedom of the press. press agent,** one who engages to obtain publicity in the press. **press of sail,** as much sail as the state of the wind will permit [Naut.]. **press proof,** *see* **proof.**

press-box, *n.* the place occupied by reporters at a public show, ceremony, or outdoor gathering.

press-cutting, *n.* an extract cut from a newspaper or other periodical. (Fr. *presse.*)

presser, *n.* *pres*-er, one who or that which presses.
press-gallery, *n.* a place for reporters, esp. a legislative chamber.
press-gang, *n.* a detachment of men empowered to impress men for the navy. (*prest-gang.*)
pressing, *a.* *pres*-sing, urgent; importunate.
pression, *n.* *presh*-on, the act of pressing; pressure.
pressirostral, *a.* pres-e-*ros*-tral, having a compressed or flattened beak. (L. *pressum,* and *rostrum,* beak.)
pressman, *n.* *press*-man, one in charge of a printing or other press; a machine-minder [Print.]; a journalist.
pressmark, *n.* *press*-mark, the librarian's mark in a book indicating to which press, bookcase, or shelf it belongs.
press-room, *n.* the room containing the presses in a printing establishment.
press-stud, *n.* a form of fastener for clothing, papers, etc. in which a button clips on to the head of a stud.
pressural, *a.* *presh*-ur-al, pertaining to or of the nature of pressure.
pressure, *n.* *presh*-ur, the act of pressing; the state of being pressed; force of one body acting on another; a constraining force or impulse; anything which oppresses; straits, or the distress accruing; urgency; impression. **pressure gauge,** an instrument indicating pressure. **pressure gradient,** the rate of fall of pressure normal to the isobar [Meteor.]. (O.Fr.)
pressurized, *a.* presh-ur-rized, compressed; rendered capable of withstanding a certain pressure.
presswork, *n.* *press*-wurk, work done by a press [esp. Print.]; press agent's work.
prest, *n.* prest, prest-money; a loan. (O.Fr.).
prestation, *n.* pres-*tay*-shon, the action of paying, esp. as a toll or due; such payment; purveyance. **prestation money,** money formerly paid yearly by archdeacons and other dignitaries to their bishop. (Fr.)
Prester John, *n.* *pres*-ter-*jon,* a mythical mediæval Christian king of some region in Asia or Abyssinia. (O.Fr. *prestre,* a priest.)
prestidigitation, *n.* *pres*-te-dij-e-*tay*-shon, legerdemain; sleight of hand. (*presto,* and L. *digitus,* finger.)
prestidigitator, *n.* *pres*-te-*dij*-e-tay-tor, a conjurer; a juggler.
prestige, *n.* pres-*teezh,* ability to excite admiration; ascendancy or influence due to past achievements, etc.
prestigiation, *n.* pres-tij-e-*ay*-shon, prestidigitation; juggling.
prestissimo, *ad.* pres-*tis*-e-moh, very quickly [Mus.]. (It.)
prest-money, *n.* imprest money, money formerly paid to men on enlistment [Nav. and Mil.].
presto, *ad.* *pres*-toh, quickly [Mus.]: *int., n., ad.* a conjurer's call in disappearing tricks, etc. (It.)
presumable, *a.* pre-*zew*-ma-bl, that may be presumed, or supposed to be true.
presumably, *ad.* by presumption.
presume, *v.t.* pre-*zewm,* to suppose to be true or entitled to belief on probable grounds: *v.i.* to venture without positive permission; to form confident or arrogant opinions; to take a liberty. (O.Fr., from L. *præ-,* and *sumare,* to take.)
presumer, *n.* pre-*zew*-mer, one who presumes.
presuming, *a.* too confident; presumptuous.
presumption, *n.* pre-*zump*-shon, the act of presuming; supposition of the truth or real existence of something, without positive proof; strong probability; presumptuousness; arrogance. (O.Fr.)
presumptive, *a.* pre-*zump*-tiv, grounded on probable evidence; that may be presumed; presumptuous; arrogant. **heir presumptive,** an heir whose succession may be precluded by the birth of an heir apparent. **presumptive evidence,** evidence derived from circumstances which necessarily or usually attend a fact [Law].
presumptively, *ad.* in a presumptive manner.
presumptuous, *a.* pre-*zump*-tew-us, full of presumption; bold and confident to excess; over-confident; arrogant; irreverent with regard to sacred things; wilful. (L. *præsumptiosus.*)
presumptuously, *ad.* in a presumptuous manner.
presumptuousness, *n.* the quality of being presumptuous.
presupposal, *n.* pree-su-*poh*-zal, a presupposition.
presuppose, *v.t.* pree-su-*poze,* to take for granted; to imply as antecedent.
presupposition, *n.* *pree*-sup-o-*zish*-on, a supposition formed in advance; a taking for granted; the act of presupposing.
presurmise, *n.* pree-*sur*-mize, a surmise previously formed.
pretence, *n.* pre-*tence,* excuse; the act of pretending; false or hypocritical profession; pretext; assumption; claim to notice; claim (true or false). **escutcheon of pretence,** *see* **escutcheon.**
pretend, *v.t.* pre-*tend,* to hold out, as a false appearance; to show hypocritically; to counterfeit; to affect; to claim: *v.i.* to act in simulation; to feign; to put in a claim. (O.Fr. *pretendre.*)
pretendedly, *ad.* pre-*ten*-ded-le, by false appearances; hypocritically; feignedly.
pretender, *n.* pre-*ten*-der, one who pretends; one who makes a show of something not real; one who lays claim to anything, esp. a throne. **the Pretender,** the Stuart claimant of the English throne after 1688.
pretendership, *n.* pre-*ten*-der-ship, the attitude, character, or claim of a pretender.
pretendingly, *ad.* pre-*ten*-ding-le, arrogantly.
pretension, *n.* pre-*ten*-shon, claim (true or false); claim to something to be obtained; pretext. (O.Fr. *pretention.*)
pretentious, *a.* pre-*ten*-shus, making great pretensions; assuming an air of unjustified ostentatious superiority.
pretentiously, *ad.* in a pretentious manner.
pretentiousness, *n.* quality of being pretentious.
preter-, *pree*-ter, Latin prefix signifying beyond, beside, or more.
preterhuman, *a.* pree-ter-*hew*-man, more than human.
preterimperfect, *n.* pree-ter-im-*per*-fekt, the tense which expresses action or being not perfectly past [Gram.].
preterist, *n.* *pree*-ter-rist, one chiefly interested in the past; one who holds that the Apocalyptic prophecies are already fulfilled [Theol.].
preterit (*or* **preterite**), *n.* *pret*-er-rit, the past tense: *a.* past; designating the tense which expresses action or being perfectly past or finished [Gram.]. (O.Fr. *preterit.*)
preterition, *n.* pree-ter-*rish*-on, the act of going past or passing over; the state of being past; the summary mention of a thing, on pretence of passing over it [Rhet.]. (L. *præterito.*)
pretermission, *n.* pree-ter-*mish*-on, a passing by; omission; preterition [Rhet.].
pretermit, *v.t.* pree-ter-*mit,* to pass by; to omit; to neglect. (L. *prætermissio.*)
preternatural, *a.* pree-ter-*nat*-yew-ral, beyond or different from what is natural; out of the usual order of things.
preternaturally, *ad.* in a preternatural manner.
preternaturalness, *n.* the state of being preternatural.
preterperfect, *a.* pree-ter-*per*-fekt, perfect: *n.* the perfect tense [Gram.].
preterpluperfect, *a.* *pree*-ter-ploo-*per*-fekt, pluperfect: *n.* the pluperfect tense [Gram.].
pretersensual, *a.* pree-ter-*sen*-sew-al, not within the domain of the senses.
pretext, *n.* *pree*-tekst, pretence: reason or motive assigned to conceal the real one. (Fr. *pretexte.*)
pretext, *v.t.* pre-*tekst,* to allege as pretext.
pretibial, *a.* pree-*tib*-e-al, situated in the front of the tibia [Anat.]. (L. *præ-,* and *tibia.*)
pretone, *n.* *pree*-tone, the syllable or vowel which precedes the accented syllable.
pretor, *n.* *pree*-tor, a prætor.
prettification, *n.* *prit*-e-fe-*kay*-shon, the action or the result of prettifying; the process of making pretty.
prettify, *v.i.* *prit*-e-fy, to make pretty; to embellish with finnicking additions.
prettily, *ad.* *prit*-e-le, in a pretty manner; pleasingly; with neatness and taste.
prettiness, *n.* *prit*-e-ness, a pleasing appearance without stateliness; delicate beauty; neatness and taste; pleasing propriety of manners.
pretty, *a.* *prit*-e, pleasing in appearance; of pleasing colour; neat and appropriate; neatly arranged; crafty; small; affected: *ad.* somewhat; toler-

ably; moderately: *n.* the ornamental band on a drinking glass [Coll.]; the fairway [Golf]. **pretty-pretty,** affectedly or nigglingly pretty. (A.S. *prætig*, tricky, clever.)
prettyish, *a. prit*-e-ish, rather pretty.
pretty-spoken, *a.* spoken or speaking prettily.
pretypify, *v.t.* pree-*tip*-e-fy, to prefigure.
pretzel, *n. pret*-sel, a brittle salted biscuit. (Ger.)
prevail, *v.i.* pre-*vale*, to overcome; to gain the advantage; to be in force; to occur; to extend over with effect; to operate with effect; to persuade; to succeed. (O.Fr.)
prevailing, *a.* pre-*vale*-ing, that prevails; predominant; most usually or widely prevalent; habitual.
prevailingly, *ad.* pre-*vale*-ing-le, in a prevailing, prevalent, or predominating manner.
prevalence, *n. prev*-a-lence, superior strength, influence, or efficacy; predominance; general diffusion; success.
prevalency, *n. prev*-a-len-se, prevalence.
prevalent, *a. prev*-a-lent, gaining advantage or superiority; efficacious; successful; predominant; general. (L. *prævalens*, having great strength.)
prevalently, *ad.* in a prevalent manner.
prevaricate, *v.i.* pre-*va*-re-kate, to shuffle; to quibble; to shift this way or the other from the direct course or from truth; to evade the truth; to collude in a false accusation [Law].
prevarication, *n.* pre-va-re-*kay*-shon, a shuffling or quibbling; deviation from truth or fair dealing.
prevaricator, *n.* pre-*va*-re-kay-tor, one who prevaricates; a shuffler; a quibbler.
prevenance, *n. prev*-e-nance, complaisance; obligingness; attentiveness to the wants or wishes of others. (Fr., from L. *prævenire*, to anticipate.)
prevenient, *a.* pre-*vee*-ne-ent, previous; coming before; anticipatory. (L. *præveniens*, coming before.)
prevent, *v.t.* pre-*vent*, to hinder, impede or obstruct; to stop; to go before. (L. *præventus*.)
preventable, *a.* pre-*ven*-ta-bl, that may be prevented.
preventative, *a.* and *n.* pre-*ven*-ta-tiv, preventive.
preventer, *n.* pre-*ven*-ter, one who or that which prevents; a rope, bolt, etc., supplementing another. [Naut.].
preventible, *a.* pre-*ven*-te-bl, preventable.
preventingly, *ad.* so as to prevent.
prevention, *n.* pre-*ven*-shon, the act of preventing; obstruction; the act of going before.
preventional, *a.* pre-*ven*-shon-al, preventive.
preventionist, *n.* one advocating or employing preventive methods, esp. in relation to disease or war.
preventive, *a.* pre-*ven*-tiv, tending to prevent: *n.* that which prevents; an antidote previously taken; medicine or treatment to avoid anticipated illness. **preventive medicine,** the science of the prevention of disease, prophylaxis. **preventive service,** the coastguard, or service for the prevention of smuggling.
preventively, *ad.* in a preventive manner.
prevertebral, *a.* pree-*ver*-te-bral, in front of the backbone.
preview, *n.* pree-*vew*, a view or showing of a performance, picture, etc. before its public exhibition.
previous, *a. pree*-ve-us, going before in time; antecedent; hasty, premature [Slang]: *ad.* before [Coll.]. **previous question,** *see* **question.** (L. *prævius*, going in front.)
previously, *ad.* in time preceding.
previousness, *n. pree*-ve-us-ness, antecedence.
previse, *v.t.* pre-*vize*, to foresee; to forewarn; to have previous knowledge. (L. *prævisus*, foreseen.)
prevision, *n.* pre-*vizh*-on, foresight; prescience; the faculty of foreseeing.
previshional, *a.* pre-*vizh*-on-al, relating to or characterized by prevision.
pre-war, *a. pree*-wawr, before the outbreak of the (specified or understood) war.
prewarn, *v.t.* pree-*wawrn*, to give notice of; to forewarn.
prey, *n.* pray, spoil; plunder; that which is or may be seized by violence in order to be devoured: *v.i.* to plunder; to seize and devour; to waste gradually; to cause to pine away. (O.Fr. *preie*.)
preyer, *n. pray*-er, a plunderer; a waster.
Priapean, *a.* pry-a-*pee*-an, pertaining to Priapus; grossly sensual; obscene: *n.* a form of mixed dactylic and trochaic verse [Classical Pros.].
priapism, *n. pry*-a-pizm, lewdness; indecency; abnormal or persistent erection of the penis [Med.].
Priapus, *n.* pry-*ay*-pus, the god of procreation; the personification of the male generative power [Myth.].
***price,** *n.* price, the sum of money at which a thing is valued; cost of an article or of services, etc.; value; terms: *v.t.* to set a price on; to appraise; to ask the price of [Coll.]. **price current** or **price list,** a table of current prices. (O.Fr. *pris*.)
priceless, *a. price*-less, too valuable to admit of a price; invaluable; super-excellent (in wit, absurdity, etc.) [Slang].
prick, *n.* prik, the act of pricking; a slender pointed instrument; a goad; a spur; a sharp, stringing pain; remorse; a point; a puncture; a small roll (of tobacco) [Naut.]: *v.t.* to pierce with a sharp-pointed instrument; to erect a pointed thing; to fix by a point; to designate by a puncture; to spur; to incite; to affect with pain or remorse, etc.: *v.i.* to feel as though pricked; to spur on; to point upward. **to prick a chart,** to trace a ship's course on a chart [Naut.]. (A.S. *prica*.)
prick-eared, *a.* with erect pointed ears.
pricker, *n. prik*-er, a sharp-pointed instrument; one who or that which pricks.
pricket, *n. prik*-et, a buck in his second year; a spike for a candle.
pricking, *n. prik*-ing, the act of the verb *to prick*; a sensation as of being pricked.
prickle, *n. prik*-kl, a little prick; a small sharp process or spine [Bot. and Zool.]; a thorn; a wickerwork basket: *v.t.* to prick slightly: *v.i.* to have a prickling or tickling sensation. (A.S. *pricel*.)
prickle-back, *n.* the stickleback or similar small fish.
prickliness, *n. prik*-kle-ness, the state of having prickles or of being prickly.
prickly, *a. prik*-kle, full of sharp points; vexatious; over-sensitive, easily nettled [Coll.]. **prickly ash,** the toothache tree. **prickly heat,** a skin disease *Lichen tropicus*, attended with an aggravating stinging and itch; miliaria. **prickly pear,** the fleshy stemmed plant, *Opuntia vulgaris*.
prickmadam, *n. prik*-mad-am, an old name for various stonecrops, esp. *Sedum reflexum*.
pricksong, *n. prik*-song, contrapuntal music in general; music written to be sung.
prickwood, *n. prik*-wood, the dogwood, also the spindle tree.
pride, *n.* pride, inordinate self-esteem; haughtiness; insolence; noble self-esteem or elation of heart; elevation; splendid show; that of which one is proud; the highest point or acme: *v.t.* to take pride in; to value. **in his pride,** with tail fully expanded and wings dropped (of the peacock, turkey, etc.) [Her.]. (A.S. *pryte*.)
prideful, *a. pride*-ful, full of pride; scornful.
pridefully, *ad.* in a prideful manner.
pridefulness, *n.* the quality of being prideful.
prideless, *a. pride*-less, destitute of pride.
pridian, *a. prid*-e-an, pertaining to the day before. (L. *pridianus*.)
prie-dieu, *n.* pree-dew, a desk at which to kneel in prayer. (Fr.)
prier, *n. pry*-er, one who searches and scrutinizes; an inquisitive person.
priest, *n.* preest, a clergyman, esp. one in the Roman, Eastern, or Anglican Church qualified to administer the sacraments and ranking between bishop and deacon; one who officiates at an altar; a presbyter. (A.S. *preost*.)
priestcraft, *n. preest*-krahft, the knowledge and skill necessary to priests; priestly intrigue for professional aggrandizement.
priestess, *n. prees*-tess, a female priest.
priesthood, *n. preest*-hood, the office of a priest; priests, or the priestly order.
priestliness, *n.* appearance and manner of a priest.
priestly, *a.* sacerdotal; pertaining to a priest.
priest-ridden, *a.* managed or governed by priests.
prig, *n.* prig, a superior person in his own estimation; a pert, conceited fellow; a petty thief: *v.t.* to filch or steal [Slang]. (Perhaps from *prick*.)
priggery, *n. prig*-er-re, the conduct of prigs; priggishness.

priggish, *a. prig*-ish, conceited; affected.
priggishly, *ad.* in a priggish manner.
priggishness, *n.* the quality of being priggish.
priggism, *n. prig*-izm, the quality or manner of a prig.
prim, *a.* prim, formal; precise; affectedly nice; *v.t.* to deck with great nicety; to form with affected preciseness: *v.i.* to pout. (Origin uncertain.)
prima, *a. pree*-mah, first; principal. **prima donna,** the chief female singer in an opera (*pl.* **prima donnas**). (It., first lady.)
primacy, *n. pry*-ma-se, dignity or office of a primate; pre-eminence. (O.Fr. *primacie.*)
primæval, *a.* pry-*mee*-val, primeval.
primage, *n. pry*-maj, a charge in addition to freight for loading or unloading cargo; water carried into the cylinder by priming (of steam-engines). (Fr.)
primal, *a. pry*-mal, first; primary. (L. *primalis.*)
primality, *n.* pry-*mal*-e-te, state of being primal.
primarily, *ad. pry*-ma-re-le, in a primary manner.
primariness, *n.* the state of being primary.
primary, *a. pry*-ma-re, first in order; original; chief; principal; elementary (of education); radical; palæozoic, pertaining to the earliest sedimentary rocks [Geol.]: *n.* that which stands highest in rank or importance; any one of the large feathers on the last joint of a bird's wing; the winding to which current is applied to produce effect in a secondary winding, as in a transformer [Elect.]. **primary battery,** a battery in which electric current is produced [Elect.]. **primary planet,** a planet revolving directly round the sun (as distinct from a satellite). **primary school,** an elementary school. (L. *primarius.*)
primate, *n. pry*-mat, the chief ecclesiastic in a national episcopal church; an archbishop; any member of the order Primates [Zool.]. **Primate of All England** the Archbishop of Canterbury. **Primate of England,** the Archbishop of York. (Fr. *primat.*)
Primates, *n.pl.* pry-*may*-teez, the highest order of mammals, including man, the anthropoid apes, the monkeys, and the lemurs.
primateship, *n. pry*-mat-ship, the office or dignity of a primate.
primatial, *a.* pry-*may*-shal, pertaining to a primate [Eccles.]; possessing primacy.
prime, *a.* prime, first in order of time, rank, importance, excellence, etc.; early; blooming: *n.* the dawn, the first hour after sunrise; the first canonical hour of the day, or the office for this [Eccles.]; the beginning; a prime number; a prime tone; the spring of the year or of life; youth; the best part; the utmost perfection. **prime divisor,** a divisor having no factors. **prime factor,** a factor that is a prime number. **prime meridan,** the meridian from which longitude is reckoned. **Prime Minister,** the responsible head of a ministry. **prime mover,** any natural agency used in the production of power; any mechanical device by which such energy is converted into power. **prime number,** a number divisible only by unity [Arith.]. **prime tone,** the fundamental of a compound tone [Mus.]. **prime vertical,** a great circle passing from east to west through the zenith at right angles to the celestial meridian. (L. *primus,* first.)
prime, *v.t.* prime, to charge the pan of a gun with powder; to lay a train of powder for communicating fire to a charge; to prepare; to lay on the first colour in painting; to fill (esp. with liquor): *v.i.* to serve for the charge of a gun; to carry water into the cylinder with the steam; to come at shorter intervals (of the tide).
primely, *ad. prime*-le, originally; most excellently.
primeness, *n. prime*-ness, supreme excellence.
primer, *n. prime*-er *or prim*-er, a first book; a work of elementary instruction; a small prayer-book (*prim*-er); one of two sizes of type, **great primer,** 18-point, and **long primer,** 10-point.
primer, *n. prime*-er, one who primes; a priming wire; a tube, cap, or wafer serving as a detonator.
primero, *n.* pre-*meer*-ro, an obsolete card game. (Sp.)
primeval, *a.* pry-*mee*-val, original; primitive. (L. *primus,* and *ævum,* an age.)
primevally, *ad.* in primeval times or fashion.
primigenial, *a.* pry-me-*jee*-ne-al, first formed or generated; original; belonging to a primitive type [Zool.]. (L. *primigenius.*)
primine, *n. pry*-min, the outermost integument or sac of an ovule [Bot.]. (L. *primus.*)
priming, *n. prime*-ing, the act of one who primes; material with which anything is primed, as powder or any device for igniting and exploding a charge, the first coat of paint, etc. **priming wire,** a pointed wire used to penetrate the vent of a piece, or for piercing the cartridge, etc.
primipara, *n.* pry-*mip*-a-ra, a woman bearing, or having given birth to, her first child.
primiparous, *a.* pry-*mip*-a-rus, producing young for the first time. (L. *primus,* and *parere,* to bring forth.)
primitiæ, *n.pl.* pri-*mish*-e-ee, first-fruits; the first year's profits of a church living [Eccles. Law]. (L.)
primitive, *a. prim*-e-tiv, pertaining to the beginning or origin, or to an early stage of development; original; primary; belonging to the lowest or earliest strata [Geol.]; radical; formal; simple; old-fashioned: *n.* that which is primitive; a Primitive Methodist; an early Italian painter, or an example of his work; a word not derived from another [Gram.]. **primitive colours,** red, yellow and blue. **Primitive Methodist,** a member of a body of Methodists which seceded from the main sect in 1810. (L. *primitivus.*)
primitively, *ad. prim*-e-tiv-le, originally; primarily.
primitiveness, *n.* quality of being primitive.
primitivism, *n. prim*-e-tiv-izm, the practice of, or belief in the superiority of, primitive life; reaction, esp. in art, to primitive method.
primly, *ad. prim*-le, in a prim, or formal, manner.
primness, *n. prim*-ness, affected formality.
primo, *n. pree*-mo, the first or leading part [Mus.]. (It.)
primogenital, *a.* pry-mo-*jen*-e-tal, pertaining to primogeniture or to the first-born.
primogenitary, *a.* pry-mo-*jen*-e-ta-re, primogenitive.
primogenitive, *a.* pry-mo-*jen*-e-tiv, pertaining to primogeniture.
primogenitor, *n.* pry-mo-*jen*-e-tor, the first forefather; an ancestor.
primogeniture, *n.* pry-mo-*jen*-e-tewr, seniority by birth among children of the same parents; the right to real property which belongs to the eldest son [Law]. (O.Fr.)
primordial, *a.* pry-*mor*-de-al, first in order; original; existing from the beginning; rudimentary; first formed: *n.* first principle or element. (Fr.)
primordiality, *n. pry*-mor-de-*al*-e-te, the quality of being primordial.
primordially, *ad.* originally; in relation to the beginning.
primordium, *n.* pry-*mor*-de-um, a primitive source; an organ or structure in its primitive state [Anat.].
primrose, *n. prim*-roze, the common wild plant *Primula acaulis,* or its pale yellow flower: *a.* of the colour of a primrose; gay or flowery. **evening primrose,** *see* **evening. Primrose League,** a society for the advancement of conservative imperialism formed in memory of the Earl of Beaconsfield, the anniversary of whose death, 19 Apr. 1881, is known as **Primrose Day.** (O.Fr. *prime rose,* from L. *primula.*)
Primula, *n. prim*-yew-la, the genus including the primrose, cowslip, etc.; (*l.c.*) a plant or flower of this genus. (L.)
primulaceous, *a.* prim-yew-*lay*-shus, belonging to the same order as the genus *Primula* [Bot.].
primum-mobile, *n. pry*-mum-*moh*-be-le, first cause of motion; the outermost of the revolving spheres in the Ptolemaic system [Astron.]. (L.)
primus, *n. pry*-mus, first; the eldest; the principal bishop of the Scottish Episcopal Church. **primus stove,** trade name of a make of portable oil-burning cooking-stove. (L.)
prince, *n.* prince, a sovereign; a ruler, esp. of a principality; a man of the highest rank; a king's son; the chief of any body of men. **Prince-Bishop,** a bishop whose diocese is a principality. **Prince Consort,** the husband of a queen regnant. **Prince Imperial,** the eldest son of an emperor. **Prince of the Church,** a cardinal. **Prince of Wales,** the title appertaining to the male heir apparent of the English sovereign. **Prince Regent,** a prince acting as regent. **prince's feather,** popular name of various plants, esp. of the genus *Amaranthus.* (Fr.)

princedom, *n.* *prince*-dum, the jurisdiction, rank, or estate of a prince; a principality.
princeliness, *n.* the quality of being princely.
princeling, *n.* *prince*-ling, a petty prince; a prince of little importance.
princely, *a.* *prince*-le, resembling a prince; having the rank of a prince; befitting a prince; stately; royal; munificent; magnificent.
prince's-metal, *n.* a brass-like alloy of uncertain composition said to have been first made by Prince Rupert (*d.* 1682).
princess, *n.* prin-*sess*, the daughter of a king; the consort of a prince; formerly, a female sovereign. **Princess Royal,** a sovereign's eldest daughter. (Fr. *princesse.*)
princesse, *a.* prin-*sess*, designating a woman's close-fitting gown or slip. (Fr.)
principal, *a.* *prin*-se-pal, chief; leading; first or highest in rank, character, importance, etc.: *n.* a chief or head; one who takes the lead; the president, governor, or chief in authority; the employer of an agent; a chief party, actor, or agent; a capital sum lent on interest; a main member in a structure [Eng.] or building [Arch.]. **principal section,** a plane passing through the optical axis of a crystal. (Fr.)
principality, *n.* prin-se-*pal*-e-te, sovereignty; the territory or jurisdiction of a prince; the country giving title to a prince. **the Principality,** the twelve counties of Wales.
principally, *ad.* *prin*-se-pa-le, chiefly.
principate, *n.* *prin*-se-pat, the jurisdiction, power, or term of office of the early Roman emperors; their form of government; a principality. (L. *princeps*, a chief.)
principia, *n.pl.* prin-*sip*-e-a, first principles. (L.)
principle, *n.* *prin*-se-pl, the source of origin of anything; element; constituent or component part; an axiom or accepted truth; ground or reason; a general truth or law comprehending many subordinate ones; fundamental means of attaining an object, performing an operation, or effecting a process, etc. [Mech.]; the constituent giving a drug, etc., its essential character [Chem.]; tenet or doctrine; a settled law or rule of action; a rule of conduct: *v.t.* to impress with any tenet; to establish firmly in the mind. (Fr. *principe.*)
prink, *v.i.* prink, to prank; to dress for show; to strut: *v.t.* to dress showily. (*prank.*)
prinker, *n.* *pring*-ker, one who prinks.
***print,** *n.* print, a mark made by impression; the impression of types in general; printed matter; a fabric printed in colours; an engraving, picture produced from a negative [Phot.], or anything produced by printing: *v.t.* to mark by pressing one thing on another; to impress; to form by impression; to impress, as letters, on paper; to form a positive from a negative [Phot.]; to reproduce or cause to be reproduced by printing; to publish: *v.i.* to practise the art of printing; to publish a book; to imitate print in writing. **out of print,** sold out (of books). (O.Fr. *preinte*, from *empreinte*, a stamp.)
printable, *a.* *print*-a-bl, capable of being printed or printed from; fit, or lawful, for printing.
printer, *n.* *print*-er, one who prints books, pamphlets, or papers; one who prints on textiles and other materials. **printer's devil,** a messenger-boy or odd-job lad in a printing-office.
printery, *n.* *print*-er-re, a print-works; a textile-printing factory.
printing, *n.* *print*-ing, the art or practice of impressing letters, characters, or figures on paper, cloth, or other material; the business of a printer; typography. **letterpress printing,** printing directly or indirectly from movable types.
printing-machine, *n.* a printing press, in which the work is performed by machinery.
printing-office, *n.* an establishment where printing is carried on.
printing-paper, *n.* paper used for printing on. **printing-out paper,** photographic paper on which the image is brought out by the direct action of light without development by chemicals.
printing-press, *n.* a press for printing.
printless, *a.* *print*-less, that leaves, receives, or retains no impression.
print-shop, *n.* a shop where engravings or other printed pictures are sold.
print-works, *n.* an establishment in which the printing of fabrics, wall-paper, etc. is carried on.
prior, *n.* *pry*-or, the superior of a monastic community, or the next in rank to an abbot. **Grand Prior,** the chief of the Templars; the chief of the Knights Hospitallers. (O.Fr. *priour.*)
prior, *a.* *pry*-or, former; previous; antecedent: *ad.* previously. (L., former.)
priorate, *n.* *pry*-o-rat, dignity, office, or term of office of a prior; government by a prior.
prioress, *n.* *pri*-o-ress, a woman superior of a nunnery.
priority, *n.* pry-*o*-re-te, the state of being prior in time, place, or rank; precedence; an order, etc. taking or giving precedence over all others. (Fr. *priorité.*)
priorship, *n.* *pry*-or-ship, the state or office of a prior.
priory, *n.* *pry*-o-re, a conventual establishment ruled by a prior or prioress. (O.Fr. *priorie.*)
prisage, *n.* *pry*-zaj, an ancient customs duty on wine. (Fr.)
prise, *n.* prize, a lever: *v.t.* to raise with a lever.
prism, *n.* *priz*-'m, a solid whose bases or ends are similar, equal, and parallel plane figures, and whose sides are parallelograms; a solid transparent body with three oblong sides [Opt.]; any substance refracting light. **Nicol prism,** a device, constructed of cut and cemented Iceland spar, used in the polarization of light (named from inventor). (Gr. *prisma*, from *prizo*, saw.)
prismatic, *a.* priz-*mat*-ik, resembling or pertaining to a prism; separated and formed by a prism; columnar. **prismatic colours,** *see* **colour. prismatic compass,** an instrument for taking horizontal angles.
prismatically, *ad.* as or by means of a prism.
prismatoid, *n.* *priz*-ma-toyd, a solid having parallel polygonal bases connected by triangular faces.
prismatoidal, *a.* *priz*-ma-*toy*-dal, prismoidal; resembling a prism.
prismoid, *n.* *priz*-moyd, a prism-like solid, esp. one having unequal ends or bases. (Gr. *prisma*, and *eidos*, like.)
prismoidal, *a.* priz-*moy*-dal, approaching the form of a prism.
prismy, *a.* *priz*-'me, of or like a prism; prismatic.
***prison,** *n.* *priz*-on, a gaol; a public building for the confinement of criminals; any place of confinement: *v.t.* to imprison; to confine; to enchain. **prison breaker,** an escaped prisoner. **prison fever,** typhus fever.
prisoner, *n.* *priz*-on-er, one confined in a prison; a person under arrest; a captive in war. **prisoners' base,** an outdoor game between sides each having a base, the players' object being to transfer opponents from the one to the other.
prison-house, *n.* a prison; figuratively, any restraint or confinement.
pristine, *a.* *pris*-tine, pertaining to an early period; primitive; original. (L. *pristinus*, old.)
prithee, *int.* *prith*-e, corruption of "(I) pray thee."
prittle-prattle, *n.* *prit*-tl-*prat*-tl, twaddle; trifling loquacity.
privacy, *n.* *pry*-va-se *or* *priv*-a-se, a state of retirement; a place of seclusion; retreat; secrecy.
privat-docent, *n.* priv-*aht*-dot-*sent*, a University lecturer recognized, but not paid, by the University, esp. in Germany. (Ger., private teacher.)
***private,** *a.* *pry*-vat, peculiar to oneself; personal; secret; confidential; secluded; not open; not invested with public office or employment: *n.* a soldier of below non-commissioned rank: *pl.* the genitals. **private bill,** a parliamentary bill dealing with matters affecting companies, individuals, or particular localities and not the whole nation. **private parts,** the genitals. (L. *privatus*, separated.)
privateer, *n.* *pry*-va-teer, an armed privately owned and officered ship licensed by government to war against and capture enemy shipping; one engaged in privateering: *v.i.* to cruise in or as a privateer.
privateersman, *n.* pry-va-*teerz*-man, an officer or seaman of a privateer
privately, *ad.* *pry*-vat-le, in a private manner.
privateness, *n.* private state; secrecy; privacy; seclusion.

privation, *n.* pry-*vay*-shon, state of being deprived; deprivation or absence of what is necessary for comfort; absence; destitution; hardship.
privative, *a.* *priv*-a-tiv, causing privation; consisting in the absence or defect of something; negative [Gram.]: *n.* the absence of something; a prefix or suffix (as *un-*, *dis-*, *-less*) which reverses the meaning of a word [Gram.].
privatively, *ad.* *priv*-a-tiv-le, in a privative manner.
privet, *n.* *priv*-et, the evergreen shrub, *Ligustrum vulgare*, used for making garden hedges. **mock privet,** an evergreen of the genus *Phillyrea*. (Origin unknown.)
privilege, *n.* *priv*-e-lej, a benefit or advantage peculiar to a person, company, society, etc.; peculiar advantage, right or immunity; prerogative: *v.t.* to invest with a pecular right or immunity; to exempt from censure. **bill of privilege,** a peer's petition to be tried by his peers. **privilege of clergy,** benefit of clergy. **writ of privilege,** a writ to deliver a privileged person from custody when arrested in a civil suit. (O.Fr.)
privileged, *a.* *priv*-e-lejd, invested with a privilege; enjoying a pecular right or immunity; in easy circumstances.
privily, *ad.* *priv*-e-le, privately; secretly.
privity, *n.* *priv*-e-te, private concurrence; joint knowledge; secrecy. (O.Fr. *privété*.)
privy, *a.* *priv*-e, private; pertaining to some one exclusively; assigned to private uses; clandestine; appropriated to retirement; admitted to the knowledge of what is secret: *n.* a person having an interest in any action at law; a latrine or water-closet. **privy chamber,** the private apartment in a royal residence. **Privy Council,** a body of counsellors originally appointed by the crown to advise on occasions of state emergency, now largely superseded by the Cabinet. **Privy Counsellor,** a member of the Privy Council. **privy purse,** money for the personal use of the sovereign. **Privy Seal,** the seal which the sovereign uses on documents that are not to pass the Great Seal. **Lord Privy Seal,** the keeper of the Privy Seal, a high officer of State now usually a cabinet minister. (Fr.)
prize, *n.* prize, that which is taken from an enemy in war, esp. a vessel captured at sea: *v.t.* to make a prize of. **prize court,** a court which adjudicates on prizes taken at sea. **prize money,** share of the proceeds from a captured vessel, or of spoils taken in war. (Fr. *pris*, taken.)
prize, *v.t.* prize, to prise.
prize, *n.* prize, a reward offered for competition; the reward gained by any performance; what is won in a lottery; any much desired object: *v.t.* to estimate the value of; to value highly; to esteem. (Fr. *prix*, from L. *pretium*, price.)
prize-fight, *n.* a boxing match; a pugilistic contest for a money prize or stake.
prizeman, *n.* *prize*-man, the winner of a prize, esp. as an academic award.
prize-ring, *n.* the enclosure for a prize-fight; prize-fighting.
pro-, proh, a Latin prefix, signifying for, fore, before, forward, forth, or provisional. **pro and con,** for and against (anything).
pro, *n.* proh, a professional player, either on the stage or at certain outdoor sports. (Abbreviation for *professional*.)
proa, *n.* *proh*-a, a Malay sailing canoe, esp. one fitted with an outrigger. (Malay, *prau*.)
proactinium, *n.* pro-ak-*tin*-e-um, protoactinium.
probabiliorism, *n.* prob-a-*bil*-e-o-rizm, the doctrine, in opposition to that of the probabilists, that the side having the stronger evidence in its favour should be supported [Theol.].
probabiliorist, *n.* prob-a-*bil*-e-o-rist, an adherent of probabiliorism.
probabilism, *n.* *prob*-a-bil-izm, the doctrine that in the matters of conscience concerning which there is disagreement, it is lawful to follow any course supported by recognized authority [Theol.]: the theory that though knowledge may not connote certainty it may do so sufficiently for all practical purposes [Phil.].
probabilist, *n.* *prob*-a-bil-ist, one who maintains the doctrine of probabilism; one who maintains that in spiritual matters we have no surer guide than probability.
probability, *n.* prob-a-*bil*-e-te, the quality of being probable; appearance of truth; anything probable; chance; the likelihood of an occurrence, etc. estimated by the ratio between the favourable chances and the total number of chances [Math.]; the presumption in favour of a conclusion for which there is not enough evidence for certainty. (Fr. *probabilité*.)
***probable,** *a.* *prob*-a-bl, likely to be true; having more evidence than the contrary. (Fr.)
probably, *ad.* *prob*-a-ble, more likely than not.
probang, *n.* *proh*-bang, a piece of whalebone with a sponge or the like at the end, for removing obstructions in the throat [Surg.]. (Invented word.)
probate, *n.* *proh*-bate, the official proof of wills; a certified copy of a will proved; the right or jurisdiction of proving wills. (L. *probatus*, proved.)
probation, *n.* pro-*bay*-shon, the act of proving, esp. by trial; a moral trial; novitiate; the suspending of sentence on a delinquent for a specified period of good behaviour. **probation officer,** a police-court official supervising those whose sentence is suspended during probation. (L. *probatio*, a proving.)
probational, *a.* pro-*bay*-shon-al, probationary.
probationary, *a.* pro-*bay*-shon-a-re, pertaining to or serving for probation.
probationer, *n.* pro-*bay*-shon-er, one on trial; a novice; a student licensed to preach and eligible for a charge; a delinquent while on probation.
probative, *a.* *proh*-ba-tiv, serving for trial or proof; tending to prove.
probe, *n.* probe, a surgical instrument for thrusting into a wound: *v.t.* to examine a wound, ulcer, or some cavity of the body by the use of an instrument; to scrutinize; to examine thoroughly. **probe scissors,** scissors used in examining wounds [Surg.]. (L. *probo*, prove.)
probity, *n.* *prob*-e-te *or* *proh*-be-te, tried virtue or integrity; honesty; sincerity. (Fr. *probité*.)
problem, *n.* *prob*-lem, a question proposed for solution; any question involving doubt or uncertainty; a proposition requiring something to be done [Geom.]; a position from which mate (or some other conclusion) is to be reached, generally within a specified number of moves [Chess]. **problem child,** one difficult to manage owing to maladjustment, mental or emotional deficiency, etc. **problem play,** a play treating seriously some socialogical problem. (O.Fr. *problème*.)
problematical, *a.* prob-le-*mat*-e-kal, questionable; disputable; doubtful.
problematically, *ad.* doubtfully.
problemist, *n.* *prob*-lem-ist, a planner of problems; a composer or student of chess problems.
proboscidean, *a.* prob-os-*sid*-e-an, having a proboscis; belong to the Proboscidea, the order of mammals containing the elephant, etc.: *n.* any member of the Proboscidea.
proboscis, *n.* pro-*bos*-sis, a prolongation of the nose and upper lip; the trunk, as of an elephant, to take and convey food to the mouth; the suctorial organ of certain insects, worms, etc. (L.)
procacious, *a.* pro-*kay*-shus, petulant; saucy. (L. *procax*, forward.)
procatarctic, *a.* proh-ka-*tark*-tik, antecedent; being the immediate cause [Med.]. (Gr. *prokatarchein*, to begin beforehand.)
pro-cathedral, *n.* a church used temporarily as, or in place of, a cathedral.
procedural, *a.* pro-*see*-dewr-ral, pertaining to procedure [Law].
procedure, *n.* pro-*see*-dewr, manner of proceeding; course of action; process; operation.
proceed, *v.t.* pro-*seed*, to move or go on from one point to another; to issue; to come from; to prosecute and design; to make progress; to begin and carry on; to act; to take a degree. (O.Fr. *procéder*.)
proceeder, *n.* pro-*seed*-er, one who proceeds.
proceeding, *n.* pro-*seed*-ing, course of conduct; process or movement from one thing to another; measure; transaction: *pl.* course of measures or dealing; steps taken in the prosecution of an action; records of a learned society. (L.)
proceeds, *n.pl.* *proh*-seedz, results; money gained by trade.
proceleusmatic, *a.* *pros*-e-lewce-*mat*-ik, inciting; animating; designating a metrical foot of four short syllables [Pros.]. (Gr. *prokeleusmatikos*, inciting.)

procellarian, *a.* pro-se-*lare*-re-an, belong to the *Procellaria,* the genus of birds containing the petrels. (L. *procella,* a storm.)
procephalic, *a.* *pro*-se-*fal*-ik, pertaining to the front of the head.
procerity, *n.* pro-*se*-re-te, tallness, height. (L. *procerus,* high.)
*__process,__ *n.* *proh*-ses, a proceeding or moving forward; progress; operation; course; a series of changes or measures; the whole course of proceedings in a civil or criminal suit [Law]; any protuberance or projecting part, esp. of a bone [Anat.]; any method of making printing-blocks photographically: *v.t.* to take legal proceedings against; to subject to some technical treatment; to produce a printing block by means of photography. **process block,** a printing-block produced by photography. **process server,** a sheriff's officer, (O.Fr. *proces.*)
process, *v.i.* pro-*sess,* to walk in procession; to promenade [Coll.].
procession, *n.* pro-*sesh*-on, the act of proceeding or of issuing forth; emanation; a number of people in a formal march: *v.t.* and *i.* to go in procession; to be carried in a procession.
processional, *a.* pro-*sesh*-on-al, pertaining to or consisting in a procession: *n.* a book of the ritual of religious processions; a processional hymn.
processionary, *a.* pro-*sesh*-on-a-re, processional; going in procession (esp. of certain caterpillars).
processionist, *n.* pro-*sesh*-on-ist, one who goes in procession.
processive, *a.* pro-*ses*-iv, processional; of the nature of a procession.
prochain, *a.* *proh*-shan, next; nearest [Law). (Fr.)
prochronism, *n.* *proh*-kron-izm, an error in chronology in assigning an event to too early a date. (Gr. *prochronos,* previous.)
procidence, *n.* *proh*-se-dence, a falling down; a prolapsus [Med.]. (L. *procidentia.*)
proclaim, *v.t.* pro-*klame,* to announce or declare publicly; to promulgate; to declare with honour; to outlaw by proclamation. (Fr. *proclamer.*)
proclaimer, *n.* pro-*klay*-mer, one who proclaims.
proclamation, *n.* prok-la-*may*-shon, the act of proclaiming; that which is proclaimed; official notification, esp. by or on behalf of the sovereign. (Fr.)
proclamatory, *a.* pro-*klam*-a-to-re, pertaining to or in the manner of proclaiming.
proclitic, *a.* pro-*klit*-ik, dependent upon [Gram.] (used only of monosyllabic words which depend for accent on the word following): *n.* a proclitic word. (Gr. *proklino,* lean forward.)
proclivity, *n.* pro-*kliv*-e-te, tendency; propensity. (L. *pro-,* and *clivus,* a slope.)
proclivous, *a.* pro-*kly*-vus, inclined; sloping forward (of teeth). (L. *proclivus,* sloping.)
procœlous, *a.* pro-*see*-lus, concave in front (of vertebræ) [Zool.]. (L. *pro-,* and Gr. *koilia,* a cavity.)
proconsul, *n.* pro-*kon*-sul, a Roman magistrate who discharged the duties of a consul; the governor of a province or dependency. (L.)
proconsular, *a.* pro-*kon*-sew-lar, pertaining to the office or duties of a proconsul.
proconsulate, *n.* pro-*kon-sew*-lat, the office, term of office, or jurisdiction of a proconsul.
proconsulship, *n.* pro-*kon*-sul-ship, the term of a proconsul's service.
procrastinate, *v.t.* pro-*kras*-te-nate, to put off; to defer: *v.i.* to dilly-dally. (L. *pro-,* and *crastinatus,* pertaining to to-morrow.)
procrastination, *n.* pro-kras-te-*nay*-shon, a putting off; delay; hesitancy to act.
procrastinative, *a.* pro-*kras*-te-na-tiv, given to procrastination.
procrastinator, *n.* pro-*kras*-te-nay-tor, one who procrastinates.
procrastinatory, *a.* pro-*kras*-te-*nay*-to-re, dilatory.
procreant, *a.* *proh*-kre-ant, pertaining to procreation; generating; producing.
procreate, *v.t.* *proh*-kre-ate, to generate; to beget. (L. *procreatus.*)
procreation, *n.* pro-kre-*ay*-shon, the act of procreating; an engendering; reproduction; offspring.
procreative, *a.* *proh*-kre-ay-tiv, having power to beget; procreant.
procreativeness, *n.* *proh*-kre-*ay*-tiv-ness, the quality of being procreative.
procreator, *n.* *proh*-kre-ay-tor, one who begets; a father.
Procrustean, *a.* pro-*krus*-te-an, reducing by violence to conformity to some standard (*Procrustes,* a robber of Greek myth, was fabled to torture his victims by stretching or mutilation till their bodies were of the length of an iron bed.)
procrypsis, *n.* pro-*krip*-sis, natural protective coloration in insects [Zool.].
procryptic, *a.* pro-*krip*-tik, able to use procrypsis as a means of protection [Entom.].
proctalgia, *n.* prok-*tal*-je-a, pain in the anus. (Gr. *proktos,* anus, *algia,* pain.)
proctitis, *n.* prok-*ty*-tis, inflammation of the rectum.
proctology, *n,* prok-*tol*-o-je, the science treating of the diseases, etc. of the anus and rectum [Med.].
proctor, *n.* *prok*-tor, one employed to manage the affairs of another, esp., formerly, in the Ecclesiastical Courts; a representative of the clergy in Convocation; a university official in charge of discipline. **King's (Queen's) Proctor,** an official representing the Crown, intervening in divorce cases where there is a charge of collusion. (L. *procurator,* from *pro-,* and *cura,* care.)
proctorage, *n.* *prok*-to-raj, management, esp. by a proctor.
proctorial, *a.* prok-*taw*-re-al, pertaining to the duties of, or characteristic of, a proctor.
proctorize, *v.i.* *prok*-to-rize, to exercise a proctor's authority.
proctorship, *n.* *prok*-tor-ship, the office or dignity of a proctor.
procumbent, *a.* pro-*kum*-bent, lying face downwards; prone; leaning forward; trailing [Bot.]. (L. *procumbens,* falling forward.)
procurable, *a.* pro-*kewr*-ra-bl, obtainable.
procurance, *n.* pro-*kewr*-rance, procurement; agency.
procuration, *n.* prok-yew-*ray*-shon, the act of procuring; management of another's affairs; a document conferring the powers of a proctor; a fee paid by incumbents to the bishop or archdeacon for visitations. (L. *procurare,* to procure.)
procurator, *n.* *prok*-yew-ray-tor, the manager of another's affairs, esp. his legal interests. **Procurator-fiscal,** the public prosecutor in the Scottish sheriff courts. (O.Fr.)
procuratorial, *a.* *prok*-yew-ra-*taw*-re-al, pertaining to or characteristic of a procurator.
procuratorship, *n.* *prok*-yew-*ray*-tor-ship, the office of procurator.
procuratory, *a.* *prok*-yew-ra-to-re, tending to or authorizing procuration: *n.* a mandate appointing a procurator.
procuratrix, *n.* prok-yew-*ray*-triks, a female procurator, esp. one who manages the business affairs of an institution (originally of a nunnery).
procure, *v.t.* pro-*kewr,* to obtain: to bring about; to win: *v.i.* to pimp. (Fr., from L. *pro-,* and *curare,* to attend to.)
procurement, *n.* pro-*kewr*-ment, the act of procuring, or of causing; obtainment; acquisition.
procurer, *n.* pro-*kewr*-rer, one who procures or obtains; a pimp.
procuress, *n.* *prok*-yewr-ress, a female pimp; a bawd.
procursive, *a.* pro-*kur*-siv, marked by running forward, esp. of a form of epilepsy [Med.].
Procyon, *n.* *proh*-se-on, the Lesser Dog-star, a star in the constellation Canis Minor; the genus of mammals containing the racoons. (L.)
prod, *n.* prod, a goad or pointed instrument; a dig with such; an incitement: *v.t.* to goad; to thrust at or prick with an awl or point; to urge on.
prodder, *n.* *prod*-er, one who or that which prods.
prodelision, *n.* proh-de-*lizh*-on, elision of an initial vowel (as in you'*re*).
prodigal, *a.* *prod*-e-gal, given to extravagant expenditure; profuse; wasteful: *n.* a wasteful person; a spendthrift. (Fr.)
prodigalism, *prod*-e-ga-lizm, ways characteristic of a prodigal; extravagant living.
prodigality, *n.* prod-e-*gal*-e-te, extravagance; profusion; waste.
prodigalize, *v.t.* and *v.i.* *prod*-e-ga-lize, to spend lavishly; to waste.
prodigally, *ad.* *prod*-e-ga-le, in a prodigal manner.

prodigious, *a.* pro-*dij*-us, very great in size; enormous; monstrous; amazing.
prodigiously, *ad.* to a prodigious extent.
prodigiousness, *n.* quality of being prodigious.
prodigy, *n. prod*-e-je, anything wonderful or extraordinary; an exceptionally gifted person (esp. child); a miracle; a portent; a monstrosity. (L. *prodigium*, a portent.) (Fr. *prodige.*)
prodition, *n.* pro-*dish*-on, treachery; treason. (L.)
prodrome, *n. proh*-drohm, a prelude; an introduction; a warning symptom [Med.] or event. (L. *prodromus.*)
prodromus, *n. proh*-dro-mus (*pl.* **prodromi**), a preliminary treatise. (L., from Gr. *prodromos*, running before.)
produce, *v.t.* pro-*dewce*, to bring forth; to bring to view; to give form to; to generate; to cause; to raise; to make; to exhibit or introduce to the public (of plays, pageants, etc.); to extend [Geom.]. (L. *produco*, lead.)
★**produce,** *n. prod*-yewce, that which is produced; product; raw products.
producer, *n.* pro-*dewce*-er, one who or that which produces or generates; a furnace for the manufacture of producer gas; one responsible for the presentation of a play, etc. **producer gas,** a power gas used in gas-engines, etc., consisting of carbon monoxide with air and steam. **producers' goods,** manufactures (as tools, etc.) used not for consumption but in the production of other goods [Econ.].
producibility, *n.* pro-*dew*-se-*bil*-e-te, power or quality of being producible.
producible, *a.* pro-*dew*-se-bl, that may be brought into being or generated; that may be exhibited.
product, *n. prod*-ukt, that which is produced by nature or by labour; effect; production; result; the result of multiplying two or more numbers [Arith.]. (L. *productum*, brought out.)
productile, *a.* pro-*duk*-til, that may be extended.
production, *n.* pro-*duk*-shon, the act or process of producing; that which is produced; an artistic, theatrical, or similar presentation; a product. **production goods,** producers' goods.
productional, *a.* pro-*duk*-shon-al, pertaining to production.
productive, *a.* pro-*duk*-tiv, having the power of producing; fertile; generative. (L. *productivus.*)
productively, *ad.* in a productive manner.
productiveness, *n.* productivity.
productivity, *n.* proh-duk-*tiv*-e-te, the quality or condition of being productive.
proem, *n. proh*-em, a preface or introduction. (O.Fr. *proeme.*)
proemial, *a.* pro-*ee*-me-al, introductory.
proemptosis, *n.* pro-emp-*toh*-sis, the lunar equation or addition of a day [Chron.]; the addition of a day in correction of an error. (*pro-*, *em-*, in, and Gr. *ptosis*, a falling.)
profanation, *n.* prof-a-*nay*-shon, the violation of sacred things; desecration.
profane, *a.* pro-*fane*, not sacred; secular; polluted or not purified; unholy; heathenish; irreverent; given to swearing: *v.t.* to violate or abuse anything sacred; to treat with irreverence; to pollute; to defile. (Fr. *profaner.*)
profanely, *ad.* pro-*fane*-le, in a profane manner.
profaneness, *n.* pro-*fane*-ness, irreverence of sacred things.
profaner, *n.* pro-*fane*-er, one who treats sacred things with irreverence; a polluter.
profanity, *n.* pro-*fan*-e-te, profaneness; anything profane; profane language; blasphemy.
profess, *v.t.* pro-*fess*, to avow or acknowledge; to declare in strong terms; to declare one's skill in any art or science; to teach as a professor; to pretend. (Fr. *professer.*)
professed, *a.* pro-*fest*, openly declared or avowed.
professedly, *ad.* pro-*fes*-ed-le, by open declaration or avowal.
profession, *n.* pro-*fesh*-on, open declaration of one's sentiments or belief; open declaration; a vocation, occupation, or calling distinct from trade and implying a measure of learning or technical qualification; the collective body of persons engaged in a profession; entrance under a sacred vow into a religious order. **learned professions,** *see* **learned. the profession,** acting, or actors collectively [Slang].
professional, *a.* pro-*fesh*-o-nal, pertaining to a profession: *n.* one practising a profession; one who makes his living by an art, sport, etc., which to others is a hobby or pastime.
professionalism, *n.* pro-*fesh*-o-na-lizm, professional quality, characteristics, or aims; the custom of engaging in sport, etc., professionally.
professionally, *ad.* in a professional way.
professor, *n.* pro-*fes*-sor, one who professes or who makes a religious profession; a teacher appointed under that designation by a college or university; a title self-assumed by public entertainers, etc.
professorial, *a.* pro-fes-*saw*-re-al, pertaining to or characteristic of professors.
professoriate, *n.* pro-fes-*saw*-re-at, the professors of a university, etc., collectively; professorship.
professorship, *n.* pro-*fes*-or-ship, the office of a professor.
proffer, *n. prof*-er, something proposed for acceptance; a tender: *v.t.* to offer for acceptance; to tender. (O.Fr. *proferer.*)
profferer, *n. prof*-fer-rer, one who proffers anything.
proficiency, *n.* pro-*fish*-en-se, the state of being proficient; progress or advancement in any art, science, or knowledge. (L. *proficiens*, advancing.)
proficient, *a.* pro-*fish*-ent, well advanced or versed in any art, science, or branch of learning; competent: *n.* one who is so; an expert.
proficiently, *ad.* to a proficient extent.
profile, *n. proh*-file *or proh*-feel, a head or portrait represented in a side view; the contour or outline of a figure or [Arch.] of a building in vertical section: *v.t.* to draw in profile. (Fr. *profil.*)
profilist, *n. proh*-fil-ist, one who draws profiles or silhouettes.
★**profit,** *n. prof*-it, any pecuniary gain or advantage; any advantage; benefit; excess of return over outlay; that portion of the product of labour accruing to investors or capitalists [Econ.]: *v.t.* to benefit; to improve; to advance: *v.i.* to gain advantage; to improve. **gross profit,** the difference between buying price and selling price. **net profit** the return obtained from a business, etc. after the deduction of expenses. **profit sharing,** co-operation in which the workman receives a share of the profits. (Fr.)
profitable, *a. prof*-it-a-bl, yielding or bringing profit or gain; lucrative; useful; advantageous; beneficial.
profitableness, *n.* quality of being profitable.
profitably, *ad.* with gain; usefully.
profiteer, *n.* prof-e-*teer*, a maker of exorbitant or unreasonable profits, esp. in a time of national emergency: *v.i.* to profit thus.
profitless, *a. prof*-it-less, void of profit or advantage.
profitlessly, *ad.* in a profitless manner.
profligacy, *n. prof*-le-ga-se, dissolute character; a profligate course of life.
profligate, *a. prof*-le-gat, abandoned to vice; lost to principle, virtue, or decency; abandoned; dissolute: *n.* one who has lost all regard for principle or decency. (L. *profligatus*, ruined.)
profligately, *ad.* in a profligate manner.
profligateness, *n.* the quality of being profligate; profligacy.
profluent, *a. proh*-floo-ent, flowing forward copiously. (L. *pro-*, and *fluens*, flowing.)
profound, *a.* pro-*found*, deep; intellectually deep; penetrating deeply; extending to or coming from a great depth; deep in skill; submissive; having hidden qualities: *n.* the deep; the ocean; the abyss. (Fr. *profond.*)
profoundly, *ad.* in a profound manner.
profoundness, *n.* the state or quality of being profound; profundity.
profundity, *n.* pro-*fun*-de-te, profoundless; depth of learning. (Fr. *profondité.*)
profuse, *a.* pro-*fewce*, lavish; liberal to excess; extravagant; exuberant. (L. *profusus*, poured out).
profusely, *ad.* in a profuse manner.
profuseness, *n.* lavishness; prodigality; extravagance.
profusion, *n.* pro-*few*-zhon, profuseness; plentiful supply. (L. *profusio.*)
profusive, *a.* pro-*few*-siv, lavish.
prog, *n.* prog, victuals or provisions sought by begging; victuals: *v.i.* to shift meanly for provisions; to live by beggarly tricks.

prog, *n.* prog, a prod; a goad: *v.t.* to poke; to prod; to stab. (Scots.)
prog, *n.* prog, a proctor: *v.i.* to proctorize [University slang].
progenitive, *a.* pro-*jen*-e-tiv, reproductive.
progenitor, *n.* pro-*jen*-e-tor, an ancestor in the direct line; a forefather. (L.)
progenitorial, *a.* *proh*-jen-e-*taw*-re-al, pertaining to or of the nature of progenitors; ancestral.
progenitress, *n.* pro-*jen*-e-tress, a female progenitor.
progeniture, *n.* pro-*jen*-e-tewr, a begetting or birth; offspring.
progeny, *n.* *proj*-en-e, offspring; descendants; successors collectively; results. (O.Fr. *progenie.*)
progeria, *n.* proh-*jeer*-re-a, a condition combining retarded development and premature senility [Med.]. (*pro-*, and Gr. *geras*, old age.)
proglottis, *n.* pro-*glot*-tis, any segment of a tapeworm capable of breeding.
prognathic, *a.* prog-*nath*-ik, prognathous.
prognathism, *n.* *prog*-na-thizm, the condition of being prognathic.
prognathous, *a.* *prog*-na-thus, having projecting jaws; projecting. (*pro-*, and Gr. *gnathos*, the jaw.)
prognose, *v.t.* prog-*nohz*, to make or give a prognosis of [Med.].
prognosis, *n.* prog-*noh*-sis, prognistication; the art of foretelling the course of a disease; an opinion or judgment formed from this. (Gr.)
prognostic, *a.* prog-*nos*-tik, pertaining to prognosis; foretelling; indicative of something future: *n.* something which foreshows; a prognostication; an omen; a symptom indicating the course of a disease. (Fr. *prognostique.*)
prognosticable, *a.* prog-*nos*-te-ka-bl, that may be foreknown.
prognosticate, *v.t.* prog-*nos*-te-kate, to foreshow, foretell, or prophesy; to betoken. (Late L.).
prognostication, *n.* prog-*nos*-te-*kay*-shon, act of foretelling a course or event by present signs; a forecast; a premonition; prognosis [Med.].
prognosticative, *a.* prog-*nos*-te-ka-tiv, relating to prognostication; predictive.
prognosticator, *n.* prog-*nos*-te-kay-tor, a foreteller of future events by present signs.
program, *n.* *proh*-gram, programme.
programmatic, *a.* proh-gra-*mat*-ik, of the nature of a programme or of programme-music.
programme, *n.* *proh*-gram, an outline of the order to be pursued in any exercise, performance, or entertainment; a bill of the play; the actual performance, entertainment, etc.; agenda; a plan of proceedings; a statement of policy of a political party: *v.t.* to draw up a programme for; to plan. **programme-music,** music suggestive of some event or subject; descriptive music. (Fr.)
progress, *n.* *proh*-gres, a moving or going forward; advancement; advance in knowledge; improvement; passage; a royal tour or journey; a circuit, as of a judge. (L. *progressus.*)
progress, *v.i.* pro-*gres*, to move forward; to proceed; to advance; to make improvement.
progression, *n.* pro-*gresh*-on, motion onward; intellectual advance; course; passage; regular or proportional advance in increase or decrease of numbers [Math.]; a regular succession of chords, or movement of the parts of a musical composition in harmony [Mus.]. **arithmetical, geometrical, harmonic progression,** *see these words.*
progressional, *a.* pro-*gresh*-on-al, relating to progression.
progressionist, *n.* pro-*gresh*-on-ist, one who believes that the human race is in a state of continuous development; an evolutionist; an advocate of social and political progress.
progressist, *a.* pro-*gres*-ist, advocating advance: *n.* a progressive; a progressionist.
progressive, *a.* pro-*gres*-iv, moving forward; advancing; improving: *n.* one in favour of political or social progress, esp. in municipal affairs; a member of a reforming but non-revolutionary political party. **progressive whist,** a series of rounds of hands at whist at a number of tables in which partners are changed after each hand or stated number of hands.
progressively, *ad.* in a progressive manner.
progressiveness, *n.* state or quality of being progressive.
progressivism, *n.* pro-*gres*-iv-izm, the principles of a progressive or progressionist.
prohibit, *v.t.* pro-*hib*-it, to forbid; to interdict by authority; to prevent. (L. *prohibitus*, held.)
prohibiter, *n.* pro-*hib*-it-er, one who prohibits.
prohibition, *n.* pro-he-*bish*-on, the act of prohibiting; a prohibitive order; enforced total abstinence from intoxicants.
prohibitionary, *a.* pro-he-*bish*-o-na-re, pertaining to or involving prohibition; prohibitory.
prohibitionism, *n.* pro-he-*bish*-o-nizm, the system, principles, or policy of the prohibitionists.
prohibitionist, *n.* pro-he-*bish*-on-ist, one in favour of prohibition, esp. of intoxicating drinks: *a.* advocating, characteristic of, or dependent on prohibition.
prohibitive, *a.* pro-*hib*-e-tiv, forbidding; implying prohibition.
prohibitory, *a.* pro-*hib*-e-to-re, prohibitive; excessive; tending to prohibit.
project, *v.t.* pro-*jekt*, to cast or shoot forward; to cause to jut out; to contrive; to scheme; to delineate: *v.i.* to jut out. (O.Fr. *projecter.*)
project, *n.* *proj*-ekt, a scheme; a design; a contrivance; a design not practicable.
projectile, *a.* pro-*jek*-tile, impelling or impelled forward; capable of being projected or [Zool.] thrust outward: *n.* a body projected or impelled forward, esp. through the air; a bullet or shell, etc.; a missile.
projection, *n.* pro-*jek*-shon, the act or state of projecting; a projecting part; the act of scheming; scheme; plan; the act or process of perceiving an idea as an objective reality, also the idea so projected; delineation of an object on a plane. **Mercator's projection,** the method of drawing maps by showing the parallels and meridians as straight lines intersecting at right angles, the distance between the former increasing with the distance from the equator (named from the 16th-cent. Flemish geographer).
projectional, pro-*jek*-shon-al, pertaining to projection or to projections.
projective, *a.* pro-*jek*-tiv, projecting; pertaining to or produced by projection; capable of projection; making ideas, etc. objective.
projectively, *ad.* in a projective way; by projection.
projector, *n.* pro-*jek*-tor, one who forms projects; that which projects something; a company promoter; a parabolic reflector for projecting rays of light.
projecture, *n.* pro-*jek*-tewr, a jutting or standing out; a projecting part.
projet, *n.* *proh*-zhay, the draft of a proposed measure, treaty, etc. (Fr.)
prolabium, *n.* proh-*lay*-be-um, the red or exposed part of the lip. [Anat.]
prolapse, *n.* pro-*laps*, a falling down or out of place, esp. of some organ of the body [Path.]: *v.i.* to fall down or out, esp. to project too much [Path.] as in a prolapse. (L. *prolapsus*, fallen forward.)
prolapsus, *n.* pro-*lap*-sus, a prolapse.
prolate, *a.* *proh*-late, extended beyond the line of an exact sphere; extended towards the poles (opposed to oblate). (L. *prolatus*, carried.)
prolative, *a.* pro-*lay*-tiv, serving to extend the predicate [Gram.].
proleg, *n.* *proh*-leg, one of the fleshy foot-like organs situated behind the true legs in certain larvæ; an abdominal limb [Entom.].
prolegomena, *n.pl.* pro-le-*gom*-en-a (*sing.* **prolegomenon**), preliminary observations; introductory remarks or discourses prefixed to a book or treatise. (Gr. *prolegomenon*, a preface.)
prolegomenary, *a.* pro-le-*gom*-e-na-re, preliminary; of the nature of a prolegomenon.
prolegomenous, *a.* pro-le-*gom*-e-nus, prolegomenary.
prolepsis, *n.* pro-*lep*-sis, anticipation; a figure of speech which anticipates an effect; a figure by which objections are anticipated and presented; the dating of an event before the proper time. (L.)
proleptic, *a.* pro-*lep*-tik, pertaining to prolepsis or anticipation; antecedent; anticipating the usual time [Path.].
proleptically, *ad.* pro-*lep*-te-ka-le, by prolepsis.
proletarian, *a.* pro-le-*tare*-re-an, belonging to the poorest labouring class; low; common; vulgar: *n.* one of the common people. (L. *proletarius*, one who served the state only by keeping it supplied with his children, from *proles*, offspring.)

proletarianism, *n.* pro-le-*tare*-re-a-nizm, the principles and practice, or the social and political system, of proletarians; proletarians collectively.
proletariat, *n.* pro-le-*tare*-re-at, the poorest or lowest class of the community; the propertyless class; the populace. (Fr. *prolétariat.*)
proletary, *a.* *proh*-le-ta-re, proletarian: *n.* a member of the proletariat.
prolicide, *n.* *prol*-e-side, destruction of one's offspring, esp. before or soon after birth. (L. *proles*, offspring, *cædo*, kill.)
proliferate, *v.i.* pro-*lif*-er-rat, to reproduce itself by multiplication of parts or by repeated division of cells.
proliferation, *n.* pro-lif-er-*ray*-shon, the act or process of proliferating; reproduction by budding or division; the result of proliferating.
proliferative, *a.* pro-*lif*-er-ra-tiv, proliferating; tending to proliferate.
proliferous, *a.* pro-*lif*-er-rus, reproducing by buds or other vegetative means [Bot.] or by proliferation [Zool.]. (L. *proles*, and *fero*, I bear.)
proliferously, *ad.* in a proliferous manner.
prolific, *a.* pro-*lif*-ik, fruitful; generative; abundantly productive; proliferous [Bot.].
prolificacy, *n.* pro-*lif*-e-ka-se, the quality of being prolific; fruitfulness.
prolifically, *ad.* in a prolific manner.
prolification, *n.* pro-lif-e-*kay*-shon, the generation of young; the formation of buds in the axils of floral leaves [Bot.].
prolificity, *n.* proh-le-*fis*-e-te, prolificacy.
prolificness, *n.* state of being prolific; prolificacy.
proligerous, *a.* pro-*lij*-er-rus, bearing offspring; proliferous [Bot.]. (L. *proles*, and *gero*, bear.)
prolix, *a.* *proh*-liks, extending or expatiating to a great length; tedious; long-winded. (Fr. *prolixe.*)
prolixity, *n.* pro-*lik*-se-te, quality or state of being prolix; verbosity.
prolixly, *ad.* pro-*liks*-le, to a great length.
prolixness, *n.* the quality of being prolix.
prolocutor, *n.* pro-*lok*-yew-tor *or* *proh*-lo-kew-tor, the chairman of a convocation. (L.)
prolocutorship, *n.* office or status of prolocutor.
prologize, *v.i.* *proh*-lo-jize, to deliver a prologue.
prologue, *n.* *proh*-log, an introduction, esp. one in verse spoken before a dramatic performance; the speaker of a prologue: *v.t.* to introduce with a prologue. (Fr.)
prolong, *v.t.* pro-*long*, to lengthen; to extend the duration of; to protract. (Fr. *prolonger.*)
prolongable, *a.* pro-*long*-a-bl, capable of being lengthened.
prolongate, *v.t.* *proh*-long-gate, to prolong.
prolongation, *n.* proh-long-*gay*-shon, lengthening in time or space; extension; extension of time by delay or postponement.
prolonger, *n.* pro-*long*-er, one who or that which prolongs.
prolusion, *n.* pro-*lew*-zhon, a prelude; an exercise; as essay. (L. *prolusio.*)
prolusory, *a.* pro-*lew*-so-re, pertaining to or of the nature of a prolusion.
prom, *n.* prom, a promenade concert [Coll.].
promenade, *n.* prom-e-*nahd*, a walk for pleasure, parade, or exercise; a place for promenading; an esplanade: *v.i.* to walk for pleasure or parade. **promenade concert,** a concert at which the audience can walk about. (Fr.)
promenader, *n.* prom-e-*nah*-der, one who promenades; a regular attender of promenade concerts [Coll.].
Promethean, *a.* pro-*mee*-the-an, pertaining to Prometheus; instinct with the quickening fire of Prometheus: *n.* an early form of match consisting of a small tube containing an inflammable mixture. (*Prometheus*, the Titan of Gr. myth, who stole the fire of the gods and taught mankind how to use it.)
prominence, *n.* *prom*-e-nence, a standing out from the surface of something; that which juts out; protuberance; conspicuousness; distinction. (L. *prominens*, projecting.)
prominency, *n.* *prom*-e-nen-se, prominence.
prominent, *a.* *prom*-e-nent, standing out; jutting; distinguished among others; principal; conspicuous.
prominently, *ad.* in a prominent manner.
promiscuity, *n.* prom-is-*kew*-e-te, promiscuousness, esp. in sexual relations; communal marriage.
promiscuous, *a.* pro-*mis*-kew-us, collected in a body or mass without order; mingled; indiscriminate; not restricted to one. (L. *pro-*, and *miscere*, to mix.)
promiscuously, *ad.* in a promiscuous manner.
promiscuousness, *n.* state of being promiscuous.
promise, *n.* *prom*-is, an engagement to do or not to do something, usually at another's request or for his benefit; that which affords ground of expectation; that which is promised: *v.t.* to engage to do something; to afford reason to expect: *v.i.* to assure by promise; to afford expectations; to assure. **breach of promise,** *see* **breach.** (Fr. *promesse.*)
promisee, *n.* prom-is-*ee*, the person to whom a promise is made.
promiser, *n.* *prom*-is-er, one who promises.
promising, *a.* *prom*-is-ing, affording just expectations of good or reasonable grounds of hope; favourable.
promisingly, *ad.* in a promising manner.
promisor, *n.* *prom*-is-or, one who promises; one who enters into a covenant [Law].
promissive, *a.* pro-*mis*-iv, promissory.
promissor, *n.* *prom*-is-or, a promisor.
promissory, *a.* pro-*mis*-o-re, containing a written promise or declaration of something to be done or foreborne. **promissory note,** a written promise to pay a stated sum of money to the named person on the specified date.
promnesia, *n.* prom-*nee*-se-a, paramnesia.
promontory, *n.* *prom*-on-to-re, a high point of land or rock projecting into the sea; a headland. (Late L. *promontorium.*)
promote, *v.t.* pro-*mote*, to contribute to the growth, advancement, or increase of; to forward; to excite; to raise to honour; to raise in rank; to float a joint-stock company. (L. *promotus*, moved.)
promoter, *n.* pro-*moh*-ter, he who or that which forwards or promotes; an encourager; one who organizes the formation and launching of a business enterprise, joint-stock company, etc.
promotion, *n.* pro-*moh*-shon, the act of promoting; advancement; encouragement; the state of being promoted; preferment.
promotional, *a.* pro-*moh*-shon-al, pertaining to promotion.
promotive, *a.* pro-*moh*-tiv, tending to promote.
prompt, *a.* prompt, ready and quick to act as occasion demands; acting with alacrity; quick; ready; without delay: *v.t.* to incite; to move to action; to assist a speaker when at a standstill; to suggest to the mind: *n.* an act of prompting, esp. by a stage prompter; instigation; a limit of time for payment [Comm.]. **prompt book,** the book used by the prompter at a theatre. **prompt note,** a written reminder that payment is due by a certain date [Comm.]. **prompt side,** right as seen from the front in England, the side of the stage at which the prompter stands (in America). (Fr.)
prompter, *n.* *promp*-ter, one who prompts; one whose business is to aid an actor or speaker when at a loss for the next words.
promptitude, *n.* *promp*-te-tewd, readiness; quickness of decision and action when occasion demands; readiness of will. (Fr.)
promptly, *ad.* readily; quickly.
promptness, *n.* the quality of being prompt; promptitude.
promptuary, *n.* *promp*-tew-a-re, a note-book; a small reference-book; formerly, a storehouse or repository.
prompture, *n.* *promp*-tewr, suggestion; incitement.
promulgate, *v.t.* *prom*-ul-gate *or* *proh*-mul-gate, to publish; to proclaim. (L. *promulgatus*, made known.)
promulgation, *n.* proh-mul-*gay*-shon, publication; open declaration.
promulgator, *n.* *prom*-ul-gay-tor, one who promulgates.
promulge, *v.t.* pro-*mulj*, to promulgate; to publish esp. officially.
pronaos, *n.* pro-*nay*-os, the porch or vestibule of a temple. (Gr.)
pronate, *v.t.* pro-*nate*, to turn the palm of the hand downwards. (Late L. *pronatus*, bent forward.)
pronation, *n.* pro-*nay*-shon, the act of pronating; position of the hand when the palm is turned downwards.

pronator, *n.* pro-*nay*-tor, a muscle of the forearm which, by its contraction, serves to turn the palm downward. (L.)
prone, *a.* prone, bending forward; inclined; not erect; lying with the face downward; falling headlong; sloping; inclined; disposed. (Fr.)
pronely, *ad.* *prone*-le, in a prone manner.
proneness, *n.* the state of being prone.
prong, *n.* prong, a sharp-pointed projection or implement; a forked instrument; the tine of a fork: *v.t.* to pierce or stab with a prong; to fork. (Origin unknown.)
prongbuck, *n.* *prong*-buk, the pronghorn.
pronged, *a.* prongd, having prongs.
pronghorn, *n.* *prong*-horn, the N. American ruminant *Antilocapra americana*, allied to the antelopes.
pronograde, *a.* *proh*-no-grade, walking with the body horizontal (as quadrupeds) [Zool.].
pronominal *a.* pro-*nom*-e-nal, belonging to or of the nature of a pronoun. (L. *pronominalis*.)
pronominally, *ad.* pro-*nom*-e-na-le, as a pronoun.
pronoun, *n.* *proh*-noun, a word used instead of a noun [Gram.]. (Fr. *pronom*.)
pronounce, *v.t.* pro-*nounce*, to speak; to utter articulately; to utter formally; to utter rhetorically; to declare or affirm: *v.i.* to articulate; to make declaration; to utter an opinion. (Fr. *prononcer*.)
pronounceable, *a.* pro-*nounce*-a-bl, that may be pronounced.
pronounced, *a.* pro-*nounst*, decided; strongly marked.
pronouncedly, *ad.* pro-*noun*-sed-le, in a marked or emphatic manner.
pronouncement, *n.* pro-*nounce*-ment, the act of pronouncing; a statement.
pronouncer, *n.* pro-*nounce*-er, one who can articulate; one who utters or declares.
pronouncing, *a.* pro-*nounce*-ing, pertaining to, indicating, or teaching pronunciation.
pronto, *ad.* *pron*-to, quickly; promptly [Slang]. (Sp.)
pronuncial, *a.* pro-*nun*-she-al, pertaining to pronunciation.
pronunciamento, *n.* pro-*nun*-se-a-*men*-to, a proclamation; a manifesto. (Sp.)
pronunciation, *n.* pro-*nun*-se-*ay*-shon, the mode of pronouncing; utterance; the art, mode, or act of uttering a discourse publicly with propriety and gracefulness; delivery.
pronunciative, *a.* pro-*nun*-se-a-tiv, pertaining to or characterized by pronouncement.
pro-nymph, *n.* *proh*-nimf, an insect in a stage of development between the larval and pupal stages [Entom.].
pro-nymphal, *n.* proh-*nim*-fal, of or pertaining to the stage of a pro-nymph.
proof, *n.* proof, trial or test; experiment; demonstration; that which convinces; hardness or firmness to resist; proved impenetrability; firmness of mind; a standard or degree of strength, esp. of spirit; a printed impression taken for correction; an early impression of an engraving; a printed statement of evidence to be given by a witness: *a.* strong to resist impression or penetration; of standard strength, assay, or quality: *v.i.* to render proof; to make impervious; to take a proof of. **proof mark,** the mark on a gun showing that it has passed the test. **proof spirit,** liquor consisting, by volume, of 57·1 per cent pure alcohol and 42·9 per cent water. **press proof,** the final proof as passed by the author, editor, or publisher for the press. (Fr. *preuve*.)
proof-house, *n.* a building in which gun-barrels are tested.
proofing, *n.* *proof*-ing, the act of making proof; material applied to a fabric to render it gas-tight, protect it against weather, etc.
proofless, *a.* *proof*-less, not established as true.
proof-reader, *n.* one who corrects printers' proofs.
prootic, *a.* pro-*ot*-ik, situated in front of the ear [Anat.].
prop, *n.* prop, a support; a stay sustaining a superincumbent weight; one, or that, on which one may depend: *v.t.* to support by something under or against; to sustain. (M.E. *proppe*.)
propædeutic, *a.* pro-pe-*dew*-tik, pertaining to propædeutics; preliminary: *n.pl.* preliminary learning connected with any art or science. (Gr. *propaideuo*, instruct, from *pais*, a child.)
propagable, *a.* *prop*-a-ga-bl, that may be propagated.
propaganda, *n.* prop-a-*gan*-da, the dissemination of information, opinions, etc. with intent to influence public opinion; information, etc. so disseminated; any organization or movement having this object. **College of the Propaganda,** an institution in Rome charged with the education of priests for missions. **Congregation of Propaganda,** the committee of cardinals responsible for the management of Roman Catholic missions. (L.)
propagandism, *n.* prop-a-*gan*-dizm, the practice or art of propagating tenets or principles; propaganda.
propagandist, *a.* prop-a-*gan*-dist, pertaining to or of the nature of propaganda: *n.* an agent in propaganda.
propagandize, *v.i.* and *t.* prop-a-*gan*-dize, to organize or carry on propaganda.
propagate, *v.t.* *prop*-a-gate, to cause to multiply by generation or successive production; to generate; to extend or disseminate; to impel forward in space; to spread from person to person: *v.i.* to have young; to be multiplied by generation, or by new shoots or plants. (L. *propagatus*, fastened down.)
propagation, *n.* prop-a-*gay*-shon, the act of propagating; the spreading or extension of anything; dissemination.
propagative, *a.* *prop*-a-gay-tiv, pertaining to propagation; tending to propagate.
propagator, *n.* *prop*-a-gay-tor, a propagandist; a gardener who propagates plants by cross-fertilizing.
proparoxytone, *n.* proh-pa-*rok*-se-tone, a word accented on the last syllable but two: *a.* having an acute accent, or a stress, so placed. (Gr.)
propel, *v.t.* pro-*pel*, to drive forward; to urge or press onward; to supply with motive power. (L. *propello*, drive.)
propellant, *n.* pro-*pel*-lant, a propelling agent, esp. an explosive.
propellent, *a.* pro-*pel*-lent, propelling; able or tending to drive forward.
propeller, *n.* pro-*pel*-ler, one who or that which propels; a screw-propeller. **propeller shaft,** the shaft in a motor vehicle connecting the transmission with the rear axle drive.
propense, *a.* pro-*pense*, leaning towards in a moral sense; disposed. (L. *propensus*, hung down.)
propension, *n.* pro-*pen*-shon, tendency to move in one direction; inclination; propensity.
propensity, *n.* pro-*pen*-se-te, bent of mind; natural tendency; disposition.
proper, *a.* *prop*-er, distinctive of one individual; his or her own; peculiar; particularly suited to; fit; correct; decent; in natural colours [Her.]; well-formed: *n.* a special office or mass for an occasion, saint's day, etc. [Eccles.]: *ad.* properly [Coll.]. (Fr. *propre*.)
properispome, *n.* pro-*pe*-re-spome, a word having a circumflex accent on the last syllable but one: *a.* having a circumflex so placed. (Gr.)
properly, *ad.* in a proper way; correctly; suitably.
propertied, *a.* *prop*-er-ted, possessed of property.
***property,** *n.* *prop*-er-te, a peculiar or inherent quality of anything; quality; nature; attribute common to a class, which may or may not be distinctive of it [Logic]; ownership; the thing owned; exclusive right of possession; real estate; an estate: *pl.* articles required on the stage other than scenery and costumes. **property man,** the man in a theatre who has charge of the properties. **property tax,** a direct tax on property. (O.Fr. *properte*.)
prophasis, *n.* *prof*-a-sis, prognosis [Med.]. (Gr.)
prophecy, *n.* *prof*-e-se, a declaration of something to come; a forecast; a book of prophecies [Bible]; public preaching. (O.Fr. *prophecie*.)
prophesier, *n.* *prof*-e-sy-er, one who prophesies.
prophesy, *v.t.* *prof*-e-se, to foretell future events; to foreshow; to instruct in the sacred writings.
prophet, *n.* *prof*-et, one who foretells future events; a preacher; an interpreter; an inspired interpreter of the will of God; the author of any of the prophetical books in the Old Testament (**Major Prophets,** Isaiah, Jeremiah, Ezekiel, and Daniel; **Minor Prophets,** the remaining twelve). **school of the prophets,** an association of prophets among

the ancient Jews. **the Prophet** (among Moslems) Mohammed. (O.Fr. *prophete.*)
prophetess, *n.* *prof*-e-tes, a female prophet.
prophetic, *a.* pro-*fet*-ik, containing prophecy; foretelling future events; predictive.
prophetical, *a.* pro-*fet*-e-kal, prophetic.
prophetically, *ad.* in a prophetic manner.
prophetism, *n.* *prof*-e-tizm, the art or practice of prophesying; the system of the Hebrew prophets.
prophylactic, *a.* prof-e-*lak*-tik, preventive; protecting against disease: *n.* a preventive medicine. (Gr. *prophylaktikos*, guarding against.)
prophylaxis, *n.* prof-e-*lak*-sis, the preventive treatment of disease.
propination, *n.* prop-e-*nay*-shon, ceremony of pledging, or drinking first, and then offering the cup to another. (L. *propinatus*, drank.)
propinquity, *n.* pro-*ping*-kwe-te, nearness in place or time; proximity; nearness of blood. (L. *propinquitas*, from *propinquus*, near.)
propitiable, *a.* pro-*pish*-e-a-bl, that may be propitiated, or made propitious.
propitiate, *v.t.* pro-*pish*-e-ate, to conciliate; to reconcile; to appease. (L. *propitiatus*, conciliated.)
propitiation, *n.* pro-pish-e-*ay*-shon, the act of propitiating or making propitious; that which propitiates, esp. God to man, or the making atonement. (Fr.)
propitiator, *n.* pro-*pish*-e-ay-tor, one who propitiates.
propitiatory, *a.* pro-*pish*-e-a-to-re, serving to propitiate; having the power to make propitious: *n.* among the ancient Jews, the mercy-seat.
propitious, *a.* pro-*pish*-us, disposed to be gracious or merciful; kind; favourable. (L. *propitius.*)
propitiously, *ad.* in a propitious manner.
propitiousness, *n.* the quality or state of being propitious.
proplasm, *n.* *proh*-plazm, a mould; a matrix. (Gr. *proplasma*, a model.)
propodium, *n.* pro-*poh*-de-um, the forepart of the foot in certain mollusca. (*pro-*, and Gr. *pous*, *podis*, foot.)
propolis, *n.* *prop*-o-lis, bee-glue, a waxy substance used by bees to stop crevices in their hives, etc. (Gr.)
proponent, *n.* pro-*poh*-nent, one who makes a proposal, or lays down a proposition: *a.* making a proposal; bringing forward. (L. *proponens*, placing before.)
proportion, *n.* pro-*por*-shon, the comparative relation of any one thing to another; symmetry; a suitable adaptation of one part or thing to another; the identity or similitude of two ratios; equal or just share; a rule by which, when three numbers are given, a fourth number is found; an equality of arithmetical ratios [Arith.]: *v.t.* to adjust the comparative relation of one thing to another: to apportion; to form symmetrically. **harmonic proportion,** the relation of three consecutive terms of a harmonic progression. **inverse proportion,** *see* **inverse. simple proportion,** the rule of three. **in proportion,** according as. (Fr.)
proportionable, *a.* pro-*por*-shon-a-bl, that may be proportioned or made proportional; proportional; being in proportion.
proportionableness, *n.* the quality of being proportionable.
proportionably, *ad.* according to proportion.
proportional, *a.* pro-*por*-shon-al, having a due comparative relation; being in suitable proportion; having the same ratio [Math.]: *n.* a proportional quantity; one of the terms of a ratio. **proportional compasses,** dividers with two pairs of legs working on one adjustable hinge so that the distances between each pair is always proportionate. **proportional representation,** a method of voting and ballot counting designed to ensure that the representatives elected are in proportion to the votes cast for them and that no vote is wasted.
proportionality, *n.* pro-*por*-sho-*nal*-e-te, the quality of being proportional.
proportionally, *ad.* in proportion.
proportionate, *a.* pro-*por*-shon-ate, adjusted to something else according to a certain ratio: *v.t.* to make proportional; to adjust.
proportionately, *ad.* to a proportionate degree.
proportionateness, *n.* the quality of being proportionate.
proportionless, *a.* pro-*por*-shon-less, without proportion or symmetry; shapeless.
proposal, *n.* pro-*poh*-zal, a proposition for consideration; a scheme or design; terms or conditions proposed; an offer; a tender.
propose, *v.t.* pro-*poze*, to bring forward or offer for consideration; to nominate as a candidate; to intend: *v.i.* to offer oneself in marriage. (Fr. *proposer.*)
proposer, *n.* pro-*poh*-zer, one who proposes.
proposition, *n.* prop-o-*zish*-on, that which is proposed or offered for consideration or adoption; a proposal; a statement; a sentence in which something is affirmed or denied [Logic]; a theorem or problem.
propositional, *a.* prop-o-*zish*-on-al, pertaining to a proposition; considered as a proposition.
propound, *v.t.* pro-*pound*, to propose; to offer for consideration; to produce a will for probate [Law]. (L. *propono*, set before.)
propounder, *n.* pro-*poun*-der, one who propounds.
propper, *n.* *prop*-er, one who props; a supporter.
propraetor, *n.* proh-*pree*-tor, the governor of a province who had previously been a praetor in the city of Rome. (L.)
proprietariat, *n.* pro-pry-e-*tare*-re-at, the propertied class.
proprietary, *n.* pro-*pry*-e-ta-re, a body of proprietors or owners; the proprietors of a district: *a.* pertaining to a proprietor or to ownership; holding, or of the nature of, property. **proprietary medicine,** one the manufacture of which is limited or controlled by an owner. **proprietary name,** a distinctive word or phrase used exclusively as a trade-mark. (L. *proprietarius*, an owner.)
proprietor, *n.* pro-*pry*-e-tor, an owner; a possessor in his own right.
proprietorial, *a.* pro-*pry*-e-*taw*-re-al, pertaining to ownership.
proprietorship, *n.* pro-*pry*-e-tor-ship, the state of being proprietor.
proprietress, *n.* pro-*pry*-e-tres, a woman proprietor.
propriety, *n.* pro-*pry*-e-te, decorum; fitness; suitableness; consonance with established principles, rules, or customs; justness; accuracy; originally, property or ownership. **the proprieties,** the conventions of society. (Fr. *propriété.*)
pro-proctor, *n.* an assistant proctor [University].
props, *n.pl.* props, theatrical properties, also, the man in charge of them [Slang].
proptosis, *n.* prop-*toh*-sis, protrusion, a prolapse (esp. of the eye) [Path.]. (Gr.)
propugnation, *n.* proh-pug-*nay*-shon, defence; vindication. (L. *propugno*, to contend for.)
propulsion, *n.* pro-*pul*-shon, the act of propelling or driving forward. (Fr.)
propulsive, *a.* pro-*pul*-siv, propelling; able to propel.
propylaeum, *n.* prop-e-*lee*-um (*pl.* **propylaea**), an open court in front of a temple; the vestibule of a house; a gateway. (L.)
propylene, *n.* *prop*-e-leen, a gaseous hydrocarbon of the olefine class.
propylite, *n.* *prop*-e-lite, a volcanic rock consisting of an altered form of andesite. (Gr. *propylon.*)
propylon, *n.* *prop*-e-lon, a gateway, esp. one before an Egyptian temple. (L.)
pro-rate, *v.i.* pro-*rate*, to divide or assess in proportion [Amer.].
prore, *n.* pror, the prow of a ship. (L. *prora.*)
pro-rector, *n.* an assistant rector; the president in a German university court.
prorogate, *v.t.* *proh*-ro-gate, to prorogue.
prorogation, *n.* proh-ro-*gay*-shon, the act of proroguing; compulsory adjournment.
prorogue, *v.t.* pro-*rohg*, to adjourn without dissolving (esp. of Parliament). (O.Fr. *proroguer.*)
prosaic, *a.* proh-*zay*-ik, pertaining to prose; resembling prose; dull; uninteresting. (L. *prosaicus.*)
prosaically, *ad.* proh-*zay*-e-ka-le, in a prosaic manner.
prosaism, *n.* *proh*-zay-izm, prose character; mere prose; a prosaic expression.
prosaist, *n.* *proh*-zay-ist, a prose writer; one who cannot rise above prose; a prosaic person.
proscenium, *n.* pro-*see*-ne-um, the front part of the stage of a theatre between the curtain and the footlights. (L.)

proscribe, *v.t.* pro-*skribe*, to proclaim as having forfeited life and property; to outlaw; to banish; to denounce or to censure and condemn; to prohibit.
proscriber, *n.* pro-*skribe*-er, one who proscribes.
proscription, *n.* pro-*skrip*-shon, the act of proscribing or dooming to death; condemning to exile; utter rejection; an interdiction.
proscriptive, *a.* pro-*skrip*-tiv, pertaining to or consisting in proscription; apt to proscribe; proscribing.
proscriptively, *ad.* in a proscriptive manner.
★prose, *n.* proze, the ordinary spoken or written language of mankind; unmetrical or unrhymed composition; a prosy discourse: *v.t.* to write in prose; to turn a poem into prose: *v.i.* to talk or write tediously; to make a tedious relation. **prose poem,** prose writing having many of the characteristics of poetry. (Fr.)
prosector, *n.* pro-*sek*-tor, an anatomical dissector; one who prepares dissections for demonstration. (L.)
prosecutable, *a.* *pros*-e-*kew*-ta-bl, that can be prosecuted.
prosecute, *v.t.* *pros*-e-kewt, to follow, carry on, or pursue with a view to reach or accomplish: to seek to obtain by legal process; to accuse before a legal tribunal: *v.i.* to carry on a legal prosecution. (O.Fr. *prosecuter.*)
prosecution, *n.* pros-e-*kew*-shon, the act of prosecuting; the institution and carrying on of a civil or criminal suit [Law]; the party prosecuting.
prosecutor, *n.* *pros*-e-kew-tor, one who pursues any purpose or business; one who institutes and carries on a suit [Law]. **Public Prosecutor,** a law officer who conducts criminal prosecutions in the interest of the community.
prosecutrix, *n.* *pros*-e-kew-triks, a woman prosecutor.
proselyte, *n.* *pros*-e-lite, a convert to some religion, system, opinion, or party, esp. a heathen converted to Judaism: *v.t.* to make a convert to some religion or opinion. **proselyte of the gate,** a convert to Judaism who remained uncircumcised. (Gr. *proselytos*, a newcomer.)
proselytism, *n.* *pros*-e-le-tizm, the act of proselytizing; conversion to a system or creed.
proselytize, *v.t.* *pros*-e-le-tize, to convert: *v.i.* to make converts.
proselytizer, *n.* *pros*-e-le-*ty*-zer, one bent on making proselytes.
proseman, *n.* *proze*-man, a writer of prose as distinct from poetry.
prosencephalon, *n.* *pros*-en-*sef*-a-lon, the anterior part of the brain [Anat.].
prosenchyma, *n.* pro-*seng*-ke-ma, fibrous tissue consisting of fusiform or slender cells and forming wood or bark [Bot.]. (Gr. *pros*, near, *enchyma*, an infusion.)
prosenchymatous, *a.* *pros*-eng-*kim*-a-tus, pertaining to or resembling prosenchyma.
proser, *n.* *proh*-zer, a tedious speaker or writer.
prosify, *v.t.* *proh*-ze-fy, to turn into prose; to make prosaic: *v.i.* to write prose.
prosily, *ad.* *proh*-ze-le, in a prosy manner.
prosiness, *n.* *proh*-ze-ness, the quality of being prosy.
prosit, *int.* *proh*-zit, good luck to you (used as a drinking toast, originally in Germany). (L.)
pro-slavery, *a.* in favour of slavery.
prosodiacal, *a.* pros-o-*dy*-a-kal, pertaining to prosody; prosodial.
prosodial, *a.* pro-*soh*-de-al, pertaining to or according to the rules of prosody.
prosodian, *n.* pro-*soh*-de-an, a prosodist.
prosodic, *a.* pro-*sod*-ik, prosodial.
prosodically, *ad.* pro-*soh*-de-ka-le, in relation to prosody.
prosodist, *n.* *pros*-o-dist, one skilled in prosody.
prosody, *n.* *pros*-o-de, that part of grammar which treats of the quantity of syllables, of accent, and of the laws of versification. (Fr. *prosodie.*)
prosoma, *n.* pro-*soh*-ma, the forward or cephalic segment of the body of certain molluscs, the cuttle-fish, etc. (*pro-*, and Gr. *soma*, body.)
prosopopœia, *n.* pros-o-poh-*pee*-ya, a figure by which things are represented as persons, or the absent or dead as alive and present [Rhet.]. (Gr. from *prosopon*, a person, *poieo*, make.)
prospect, *n.* *pros*-pekt, view of things within the range of the eye; expectation; ground of expectation; the place and the objects seen; object of view; view delineated; aspect; outlook. (L. *prospectus*, a far-distant view.)
prospect, *v.i.* pros-*pekt*, to search, as for minerals.
prospection, *n.* pro-*spek*-shon, the act of looking forward or of providing against the future; the act of prospecting.
prospective, *a.* pro-*spek*-tiv, looking forward in time; regarding the future; acting with foresight; in prospect: *n.* the scene before or around us; the outlook.
prospectively, *ad.* with reference to the future.
prospectiveness, *n.* the quality of being prospective; regard for the future.
prospector, *n.* pros-*pek*-tor, a searcher for minerals.
prospectus, *n.* pro-*spek*-tus, the plan of some projected work; the official statement of the objects of a public company, its capital, and officers; a programme. (L., as *prospect.*)
prosper, *v.t.* *pros*-per, to favour; to render successful: *v.i.* to succeed; to thrive. (O.Fr. *prosperer.*)
prosperity, *n.* pros-*pe*-re-te, successful progress in any business or enterprise; success; good fortune.
prosperous, *a.* *pros*-per-rus, advancing in the pursuit of anything desirable; successful; thriving; favouring success. (L. *prosperus.*)
prosperously, *ad.* successfully.
prosperousness, *n.* the state or quality of being prosperous.
prospicience, *n.* pro-*spish*-e-ence, the act of looking forward; foresight.
prostate, *n.* *pros*-tate, the prostate gland. **prostate gland,** a muscular glandular body situated before the neck of the bladder in male mammals [Anat.]. (Gr. *prostates*, one standing before.)
prostatic, *a.* pros-*tat*-ik, pertaining to the prostate gland.
prostatitis, *n.* *pros*-ta-*ty*-tis, inflammation of the prostate gland.
prosthesis, *n.* *pros*-the-sis, the addition of an artificial part to supply a bodily defect or lost limb, etc. [Surg.]; the prefixing of one or more letters to the beginning of a word [Gram.]. (Gr.)
prosthetic, *a.* pros-*thet*-ik, pertaining to prosthesis; prefixed, as a letter to a word: *n.pl.* the branch of surgery employing prosthesis.
prostitute, *a.* *pros*-te-tewt, prostituted; devoted to base or infamous purposes: *n.* a woman who, for hire, offers her body for promiscuous sexual intercourse; a harlot; a base hireling: *v.t.* to offer for lewd purposes for hire; to devote to base uses; to offer, on vile terms, to unworthy people. (L. *prostitutus*, placed in front.)
prostitution, *n.* pros-te-*tew*-shon, the act or practice of prostituting the body to lewd purposes for hire; devotion to base uses for mercenary ends.
prostitutor, *n.* *pros*-te-tew-tor, one who prostitutes.
prostrate, *a.* *pros*-trate, lying at full length; lying at mercy; lying in the posture of humility, face to the ground. (L. *prostratum*, thrown down.)
prostrate, *v.t.* pros-*trate*, to lay flat; to throw down; to overthrow; to demolish; to cause to sink totally; to bow in humble reverence.
prostration, *n.* pros-*tray*-shon, the act of throwing down or lying flat; the act of falling down or bowing in adoration; great depression; great loss of strength due to disease, exhaustion, etc.
prostyle, *n.* *proh*-stile, a portico in which the columns stand in advance of the building: *a.* having a prostyle [Arch.]. (Gr. *prostylos*, a pillar.)
prosy, *a.* *proh*-ze, prosaic; commonplace; dull and tedious. (*prose.*)
prosyllogism, *n.* pro-*sil*-o-jizm, a syllogism the conclusion of which constitutes the major or the minor premise of another.
protactinium, *n.* pro-tak-*tin*-e-um, protoactinium.
protagonist, *n.* pro-*tag*-on-ist, the leading character in a drama: a chief actor or figure, esp. as a champion. (Gr. *protos*, first, *agonistes*, contender.)
protandrous, *a.* pro-*tan*-drus, proterandrous.
protasis, *n.* *prot*-a-sis (*pl.* **protases,** *prot*-a-seez), the antecedent clause of a conditional proposition; the first part of an ancient drama, in which the audience were introduced to the characters and the plot. (Gr.)
protatic, *a.* pro-*tat*-ik, pertaining to the protasis; placed in the beginning; introductory.

protean, *a.* pro-*tee*-an *or proh*-te-an, readily assuming different shapes; highly variable: *n.* an exceptionally versatile actor (Theat. slang]. (*Proteus.*)
protean, *n.* *proh*-te-an, any primary hydrolytic derivative of a protein [Biochemistry.].
protect, *v.t.* pro-*tekt*, to cover from danger or injury; to shield or defend; to keep safe; to support home industries by imposing duties on imported goods [Econ.]. (L. *protectus*, covered.)
protectingly, *ad.* in the way of protection.
protection, *n.* pro-*tek*-shon, the act of protecting; the state of being protected; that which protects; defence; a writing that protects; a passport; exemption, as from arrest; the encouragement of home industries by imposing duties upon imports [Econ.]. (Fr.)
protectionism, *n.* pro-*tek*-shon-izm, the doctrine of the economic protection of home industries.
protectionist, *n.* pro-*tek*-shon-ist, one who favours protectionism.
protective, *a.* pro-*tek*-tiv, serving to protect; affording or intending to afford protection.
protector, *n.* pro-*tek*-tor, one who protects from injury, evil, or oppression; a defender; a guardian; one who formerly had the care of the kingdom during the king's minority. **Lord Protector,** the title of Oliver Cromwell and his son Richard as heads of the English Commonwealth, 1653-59.
protectoral, *a.* pro-*tek*-to-ral, pertaining to a protector or protectorate.
protectorate, *n.* pro-*tek*-to-rat, government by, office, or term of office of, a protector; the protection of a country by another, usually with control of its foreign relations; a country or territory under such protection.
protectorial, *a.* pro-tek-*taw*-re-al, protectoral.
protectorship, *n.* the office of protector.
protectory, *n.* pro-*tek*-to-re, an institution for the care of persons, esp. homeless or delinquent children: *a.* able to protect; protective.
protectress, *n.* pro-*tek*-tress, a female protector.
protégé, *n.* pro-tay-*zhay* (*fem.* **protégée**), one under protection or patronage; a ward. (Fr.)
proteid, *n.* *proh*-te-id, a protein.
proteiform, *a.* *proh*-te-e-form, protean; changeable in form; having many forms.
protein, *n.* *proh*-te-in *or proh*-teen, an organic compound composed of carbon, hydrogen, oxygen, and nitrogen, with sometimes sulphur and phosphorus, essential as a constituent of the living cell and to animal and vegetable growth. (Gr. *protos*, first.)
proteinaceous, *a.* proh-te-e-*nay*-shus, proteinic; consisting of protein.
proteinic, *a.* proh-te-*in*-ik, pertaining to or of the nature of protein.
proteinous, *a.* pro-*tee*-e-nus, proteinaceous.
protend, *v.t.* pro-*tend*, to hold out; to stretch forth. (L. *protendo*, stretch forward.)
protensity, *n.* pro-*ten*-se-te, the faculty or character of being protensive.
protensive, *a.* pro-*ten*-siv, continuing in time; extending lengthwise.
proteolysis, *n.* *proh*-te-*ol*-e-sis, the splitting up of proteins by or as by digestion [Chem.]. (*protein*, and Gr. *lysis*, loosening.)
proterandrous, *a.* prot-er-*an*-drus, having the stamens ripe before the stigma. (Gr. *protos*, first, *anerandros*, a man.)
proteranthous, *a.* prot-er-*an*-thus, having the flowers appearing before the leaves. (Gr. *protos*, and *anthos*, a flower.)
proterogynous, *a.* *prot*-er-*oj*-en-us, having the stigma ripe before the stamens [Bot.]. (Gr. *proteros*, former, *gyne*, a woman.)
proterozoic, *a.* *proh*-ter-o-*zoh*-ik, designating or pertaining to the period immediately preceding, and including, the first appearance of animal life [Geol.].
protervity, *n.* pro-*ter*-ve-te, pertness; petulance; peevishness. (L. *protervus*, wayward.)
protest, *v.i.* pro-*test*, to affirm with solemnity; to aver; to make a formal declaration against some act or measure: *v.t.* to make a solemn or formal declaration or affirmation of. **to protest a bill of exchange,** to make a formal declaration against the drawer on account of non-payment. (Fr. *protester.*)
***protest,** *n.* *proh*-test, a solemn declaration of opinion, usually in writing, commonly against some public act; a formal declaration made by a notary public of the non-payment of a bill; formal declaration concerning loss of or damage sustained by a vessel in transit [Naut.].
protestant, *n.* *prot*-es-tant, one who makes a protest; (*cap.*) one who protests, in the name of the rights of conscience, against the spiritual authority claimed by the Church of Rome; one of the party who adhered to Luther at the Reformation, and in 1529 protested, at the Diet of Spires, against a decree of the Emperor Charles V: *a.* making a protest; pertaining to Protestants or to Protestantism.
Protestantism, *n.* *prot*-es-tan-tizm, the Protestant religion, or the principles of the Protestants.
Protestantize, *v.t.* *prot*-es-tan-tize, to convert to Protestantism.
protestation, *n.* prot-es-*tay*-shon, a solemn declaration; a solemn declaration of dissent; a protest; an avowal; a declaration in pleading. (Fr.)
protester, *n.* pro-*tes*-ter, one who utters a solemn declaration; one who protests, esp. a bill.
protestingly, *ad.* pro-*tes*-ting-le, by way of protesting.
Proteus, *n.* *proh*-te-us, a marine deity able to assume different shapes at will and thus to elude those who would seize him [Myth.]; one who easily changes his principles; an unreliable person; (*cap*). a genus of salamander-like amphibians, also a genus of bacteria. (Gr.)
prothalamium, *n.* pro-tha-*lay*-me-um, a nuptial song in honour of bride and bridegroom, sung just before the marriage ceremony. (L.)
prothallium, *n.* pro-*thal*-e-um, the minute cellular structure bearing the sex organs in certain ferns and cryptogams [Bot.]. (*pro-*, and Gr. *thallion*, a small shoot.)
prothallus, *n.* pro-*thal*-us, a prothallium [Bot.].
prothesis, *n.* *proh*-the-sis, in the Greek Church, the preparation of the eucharistic elements prior to use; the place where this is done. (Gr.)
prothesis, *n.* *proth*-e-sis, prosthesis [Surg.].
Prothonotariat, *n.* *proh*-thon-no-*tare*-re-at, the College of the seven Apostolic Prothonotaries in charge of certain records of the Roman Catholic Church.
prothonotary, *n.* proh-thoh-*noh*-ta-re, a chief notary; a chief clerk or secretary; the clerk of a court [U.S.A.]; a member of the Prothonotariat (O.Fr., from *proto-*, and *notary.*)
prothorax, *n.* proh-*thaw*-raks, the first or anterior segment of the thorax in insects.
protist, *n.* *proh*-tist, any member of the *Protista.*
Protista, *n.pl.* pro-*tis*-ta, the group of unicellular organisms partaking of the characteristics of both plants and animals. (Gr., first of all.)
protistan, *a.* pro-*tis*-tan, belonging to the *Protista*: *n.* a protist.
protistology, *n.* *proh*-tis-*tol*-o-je, the biology, or the, scientific study, of the *Protista.*
proto-, *proh*-toh, prefix signifying primitive, earliest or chief. (Gr., first.)
protoactinium, *n.* pro-to-ak-*tin*-e-um, a radioactive element yielding actinium on disintegration.
protochordate, *a.* pro-to-*kor*-dat, pertaining to the class containing the lowest vertebrates including the lancelet and sea-squirts: *n.* any member of this class [Zool.].
protococcus, *n.* *proh*-to-*kok*-us, one of the unicellular algæ appearing as scum on stagnant water, as a green coating on damp tiles, etc.
protocol, *n.* *proh*-to-kol, the original copy, draft, or record of an official document or transaction, esp. of a treaty; an official description or account; the formulas used in diplomatic documents: *v.t.* and *i.* to draw up, or record in, a protocol. (Fr. *protocole.*)
protocolist, *n.* *proh*-to-kol-ist, one who drafts protocols; a registrar.
protogenetic, *a.* *proh*-to-je-*net*-ik, protogenic.
protogenic, *a.* proh-to-*jen*-ik, primitive; first-formed [Bot. and Geol.].
protogine, *n.* *proh*-to-jin, a kind of talcose granite occurring in the Alps, in which dynamic action has produced foliation. (*proto-*, and Gr. *gignomai*, be formed.)
protogynous, *a.* pro-*toj*-e-nus, proterogynous.
Protohippus, *n.* a genus of small extinct quadrupeds from which the horse probably derives.
proto-historic, *a.* pertaining to the period of history immediately following the prehistoric.

protomartyr, *n.* *proh*-to-*mar*-ter, the first martyr (St. Stephen); the first to suffer in any cause.
proton, *n.* *proh*-ton, the positively charged particle of the atom, having a charge equal and opposite to that of the electron of which it is some 1,843 times as massive [Physics]; the primary constituent or accumulation of cells of an organism or part [Biol.]. (Gr. *protos*, first.)
protonema, *n.* proh-to-*nee*-ma, the thread-like primary stage of development in the mosses and certain liverworts [Bot.]. (Gr. *proto-*, and *nema*, thread.)
protonotary, *n.* *proh*-to-*noh*-ta-re, a prothonotary.
protophyte, *n.* *proh*-to-fite, any member of the lowest and simplest division of the vegetable kingdom, which comprises the unicellular microscopic plants. (Gr. *proto-*, and *phyton*, plant.)
protophytic, *a.* proh-to-*fit*-ik, pertaining to or derived from the protophytes; resembling a protophyte.
protoplasm, *n.* *proh*-to-plazm, the semifluid, colourless substance, composed of oxygen, hydrogen, carbon, and nitrogen, which forms the physical basis of life. (Gr. *proto-*, and *plasma*, something fashioned.)
protoplasmatic, *a.* *proh*-to-plaz-*mat*-ik, protoplasmic.
protoplasmic, *a.* proh-to-*plaz*-mik, of the nature of or pertaining to protoplasm.
protoplast, *n.* *proh*-to-plast, the first created man; a creator; the unit of protoplasm; an embryonic cell.
protoplastic *a.* proh-to-*plas*-tik, pertaining to a protoplast; constituting an archetype; creative.
protosalt, *n.* *proh*-to-sawlt, a salt containing a metallic protoxide.
protosulphate, *n.* proh-to-*sul*-fate, a compound of sulphuric acid with a protoxide.
Prototheria, *n.pl.* proh-to-*theer*-re-a, a former name of the class of mammals comprising the monotremes. (Gr. *proto-*, and *theria*, beasts.)
prototypal, *a.* *proh*-to-ty-pal, pertaining to, constituting, or serving as a prototype.
prototype, *n.* *proh*-to-tipe, an original model or pattern after which anything is formed; archetype.
prototypic, *a.* proh-to-*tip*-ik, of the nature of, or serving as, a prototype.
protoxide, *n.* proh-*toks*-ide, the member of a series of oxides of a base containing the lowest proportion of oxygen.
Protozoa, *n.pl.* proh-to-*zoh*-a, the lowest division of the animal kingdom, comprising organisms of the simplest type. (Gr. *proto-*, and *zoon*, an animal.)
protozoal, *a.* proh-to-*zoh*-al, pertaining or relating to Protozoa; due to parasitic Protozoa (of disease) [Path.].
protozoan, *a.* proh-to-*zoh*-an, pertaining to the Protozoa: *n.* one of the Protozoa.
protozoic, *a.* proh-to-*zoh*-ik, protozoan [Zool.]; of the period disclosing the first traces of animal life; (of strata) containing remains of the earliest forms of life [Geol.].
protract, *v.t.* pro-*trakt*, to draw out or lengthen in time; to prolong; to put off or defer. (L. *protractus*, drawn forward.)
protractedly, *ad.* pro-*trak*-ted-le, in a protracted manner.
protractible, *a.* pro-*trak*-te-bl, protractile.
protractile, *a.* pro-*trak*-tile, capable of being extended; protrusile.
protractility, *n.* proh-trak-*til*-e-te, the quality of being protractile.
protraction, *n.* pro-*trak*-shon, the act of protracting; the act of delaying the termination of a thing; the making of a plot on paper, also the plot so laid down [Surv.].
protractive, *a.* pro-*trak*-tiv, drawing out; delaying.
protractor, *n.* pro-*trak*-tor, an instrument used in laying down and measuring angles on paper, etc.; a muscle that extends a part or limb [Anat.]; an instrument formerly used for drawing extraneous bodies from a wound [Surg.].
protreptical, *a.* instructive; hortatory. (*pro-*, and Gr. *trepo*, turn.)
protrude, *v.t.* pro-*trood*, to thrust forward; to thrust out as through a hole: *v.i.* to project; to shoot forward. (L. *protrudo*, thrust.)
protrusible, *a.* pro-*troo*-se-bl, protrusile.
protrusile, *a.* pro-*troo*-sil, capable of being protruded and withdrawn. (L. *protrusus*, thrust.)
protrusion, *n.* pro-*troo*-zhon, the act of protruding; the state of being protruded; that which protrudes or is protruded.
protrusive, *a.* pro-*troo*-siv, thrusting forward.
protrusively, *ad.* in a protrusive manner.
protuberance, *n.* pro-*tew*-ber-rance, a swelling or tumour; a prominence; a bump.
protuberant, *a.* pro-*tew*-ber-rant, swelling; prominent. (L. *protuberans*, bulging out.)
protuberantly, *ad.* in a protuberant manner.
protuberate, *v.i.* pro-*tew*-ber-rate, to swell or be prominent: to bulge out.
protyle, *n.* *proh*-tile, the hypothetical original matter from which the elements are supposedly derived [Chem.]. (Gr. *protos*.)
proud, *a.* proud, having inordinate self-esteem; arrogant; haughty; presumptuous; gratified; lofty; of lofty mien; ostentatious; exciting pride. **proud flesh,** a profuse growth of flesh about a wound or ulcer. **to do one proud,** to treat him handsomely, to honour him [Coll.]. (A.S. *prut.*)
proudly, *ad.* *proud*-le, in a proud manner.
proudness, *n.* *proud*-ness, pride.
proustite, *n.* *proos*-tite, sulphide of silver and arsenic, a crystalline mineral. (J. L. *Proust*, Fr. chemist, *d.* 1826.)
provable, *a.* *proov*-a-bl, that may be proved.
provableness, *n.* the quality of being provable.
provably, *ad.* *proov*-a-ble, in a provable manner.
provand, *n.* *prov*-and, provender.
prove, *v.t.* proov, to ascertain or try by an experiment or a test; to try; to evince by testimony or argument; to ascertain the correctness of; to establish the genuineness and validity of (esp. a will); to establish as true: *v.i.* to be found on trial; to be ascertained by the event; to be found true. *pp.* **proved,** proovd, and **proven,** *proo*-ven *or* *proh*-ven. (O.Fr. *prover.*)
provection, *n.* pro-*vek*-shon, the carrying forward of a terminal letter to the first syllable of the next word [Gram.]. (Late L. *provectio.*)
proveditor, *n.* pro-*ved*-e-tor, a governor or civil official of the former Venetian Republic; a provedore. (It.)
provedore, *n.* prov-e-*dore*, a purveyor; one who procures provisions for an army. (Sp. *provedor.*)
proven, *a.* *proo*-ven *or* *proh*-ven, proved. **not proven,** a legal finding based on evidence sufficient to arouse suspicion but not strong enough to justify conviction.
provenance, *n.* *prov*-e-nance, source; origin. (Fr.)
Provençal, *a.* pro-*ven*-shal, pertaining to Provence, a former province of S.E. France, or to its people or language: *n.* the language or a native of Provence.
provender, *n.* *prov*-en-der, dry food for cattle; provisions. (O.Fr. *provendre*, a ration of food.)
provenience, *n.* pro-*vee*-ne-ence, provenance. (L. *provenio*, come forth.)
prover, *n.* *proo*-ver, one who proves or tries; an approver [Law].
proverb, *n.* *prov*-erb, a short sentence expressing a well-known truth, or common fact familiar to experience; a popular saying; a maxim; a by-word: *pl.* a children's mumming demonstrating a proverb; (*cap.*) a book of the Old Testament abounding in wise maxims. (Fr. *proverbe.*)
proverbial, *a.* pro-*ver*-be-al, pertaining to proverbs; of the nature of or comprised in a proverb; generally accepted.
proverbialism, *n.* pro-*ver*-be-a-lizm, a proverbial phrase.
proverbialist, *n.* pro-*ver*-be-a-list, a writer or collector of proverbs.
proverbialize, *v.t.* pro-*ver*-be-a-lize, to make into a proverb; to use proverbially.
proverbially, *ad.* commonly; as a proverb.
proviant, *n.* *proh*-ve-ant, provisions [esp. Mil.]; commissariat.
provide, *v.t.* pro-*vide*, to procure beforehand; to prepare; to furnish; to stipulate previously; to appoint to a benefice: *v.i.* to procure supplies or means of defence; to take precautionary measures. (L. *provideo.*)
provided, *a.* pro-*vy*-ded, supplied; furnished; stipulated: *conj.* on condition; on the understanding. **provided school,** a school provided by a local educational authority; a county school.

providence, *n.* *prov*-e-dence, foresight; timely care or preparation; prudence in managing one's affairs; the care and superintendence which God exercises over His creatures; (*cap.*) God regarded as exercising this care and superintendence. (Fr.)
provident, *a.* *prov*-e-dent, providing for the future; forecasting; prudent; economical. **provident society,** a friendly society.
providential, *a.* prov-e-*den*-shal, effected by or proceeding from divine providence.
providentially, *ad.* in a providential manner.
providently, *ad.* with prudent foresight.
provider, *n.* pro-*vy*-der, one who provides or supplies.
providing, *conj.* pro-*vy*-ding, on condition, or in case (that).
province, *n.* *prov*-ince, among the Romans a territory outside Italy acquired chiefly by conquest and under Roman government; a country, usually at a distance, belonging to a kingdom or state either by conquest or colonization, and more or less dependent on it; a large division of a country or state; the area subject to an archbishop or metropolitan; a district; a country district; a department of knowledge; proper office or business. **the provinces,** those parts of a country at a distance from the metropolis. (Fr.)
provincial, *a.* pro-*vin*-shal, pertaining to or characteristic of a province or the provinces; appendent to a kingdom or state; countrified; rustic: *n.* a native or inhabitant of a province; the local head of an order in a province [Eccles.].
provincialism, *n.* pro-*vin*-shal-izm, a word, mode of speaking, etc. peculiar to a province or the provinces.
provinciality, *n.* pro-*vin*-she-*al*-e-te, a being provincial; peculiarity of language in a province.
provincialize, *v.t.* and *i.* pro-*vin*-shal-ize, to make or to become provincial.
provincially, *ad.* in a provincial manner.
provine, *v.i.* pro-*vine*, to lay a stock or branch of a vine in the ground for propagation. (Fr.)
provision, *n.* pro-*vizh*-on, the act of providing or making previous preparation; previous stipulation or agreement; preparation; measures beforehand; stores, a supply of food, etc., provided; formerly, the appointment (esp. by the Pope) to a see or benefice not yet vacant [Eccles.]: *pl.* food; fare; provender: *v.t.* to supply with a stock of food or other stores. (Fr.)
provisional, *a.* pro-*vizh*-on-al, provided for present need or for the occasion; temporarily established; temporary.
provisionality, *n.* pro-vizh-o-*nal*-e-te, the condition or quality of being provisional.
provisionally, *ad.* in a provisional way.
provisionalness, *n.* provisionality.
provisionary, *a.* pro-*vizh*-o-na-re, temporary, provisional; pertaining to an ecclesiastical provision, or to a proviso.
provisionment, *n.* pro-*vizh*-on-ment, provisioning; supply of provisions.
proviso, *n.* pro-*vy*-zoh, a clause in statute or contract by which a condition is introduced; a conditional stipulation. (L.)
provisor, *n.* pro-*vy*-zor, the purveyor, steward, or treasurer of a religious house; a Pope's presentee to a benefice before the death of the incumbent; a vicar-general. (O.Fr. *provisour.*)
provisorily, *ad.* in a provisory manner.
provisory, *a.* pro-*vy*-zo-re, provisional; conditional; temporary.
provocation, *n.* prov-o-*kay*-shon, the act of provoking; anything that excites anger; incitement. (Fr.)
provocative, *a.* pro-*vok*-a-tiv, annoying; serving or tending to provoke or incite: *n.* that which provokes. (Late L. *provocativus.*)
provocativeness, *n.* pro-*vok*-a-tiv-ness, the quality of being provocative.
provokable, *a.* pro-*voh*-ka-bl, capable of being provoked.
provoke, *v.t.* pro-*voke*, to call into action; to incite or excite; to make angry; to offend; to stir up. (O.Fr. *provoquer.*)
provoker, *n.* pro-*voh*-ker, one who or that which provokes.
provoking, *a.* pro-*voh*-king, tending to provoke; irritating; annoying.
provokingly, *ad.* in a provoking manner.
provost, *n.* *prov*-ost, one appointed to superintend or preside; the official head, esp. of certain colleges; in Scotland, a mayor or chief magistrate. **Lord Provost,** title of the Lord Mayor of Edinburgh, Glasgow, Aberdeen, Perth, and Dundee. (A.S. *prafost*, from L. *præpositus*, a prefect.)
provost-marshal, *n.* *prov*-o-*mar*-shal, an officer appointed to preserve order and discipline in a garrison, camp, or the field [Mil.]; one who has charge of prisoners [Navy].
provostship, *n.* *prov*-ost-ship, the office of provost.
prow, *n.* prou, the beak or fore-part of a ship including the cutwater [Naut.]. (Fr. *proue.*)
prowess, *n.* *prou*-ess, bravery or valour, particularly military; superiority in skill. (Fr. *prouesse.*)
prowl, *n.* proul, a roving for prey; a ramble [Coll.]: *v.t.* to rove over; to search about: *v.i.* to rove for prey; to prey or plunder. **on the prowl,** prowling, esp. with evil intent. (M.E. *prollen*, of uncertain origin.)
prowler, *n.* *proul*-er, one who roves about for prey.
prowling, *a.* *proul*-ing, wandering about for prey.
prowlingly, *ad.* in a prowling manner.
proximad, *ad.* *prok*-se-mad, in the direction of the proximal end (of a bone) [Anat.].
proximal, *a.* *prok*-se-mal, proximate; nearest the centre or axis.
proximally, *ad.* in a proximal situation.
proximate, *a.* *prok*-se-mate, nearest or next; having most intimate connexion; immediate. **proximate cause,** that which immediately and of itself produces the effect. **proximate principles,** constituent organic compounds formed naturally [Chem.]. (L.)
proximately, *ad.* in a proximate manner.
proximity, *n.* prok-*sim*-e-te, immediate nearness in place, time, or blood. (Fr. *proximité.*)
proximo, *a.* *prok*-se-moh, in or of the next succeeding month. (L.)
proxy, *n.* *prok*-se, the agency of another who acts as a substitute; one deputed to act for another, esp. as a voter; a writing granting this power; a substitute. (*procuracy.*)
proxyship, *n.* the office or agency of a proxy.
prude, *n.* prood, a woman of affected propriety or modesty. (Fr.)
prudence, *n.* *prood*-ence, quality of being prudent; wisdom applied to practice; discretion.
prudent, *a.* *prood*-ent, cautious; practically wise; circumspect; careful of consequences; dictated by prudence; foreseeing by instinct; frugal. (Fr.)
prudential, *a.* proo-*den*-shal, proceeding from or actuated by prudence; exercising discretion: *pl.* matters of prudence or practical wisdom; subordinate discretionary concerns. (L. *prudentia.*)
prudentialism, *n.* proo-*den*-sha-lizm, a prudential doctrine or philosophy.
prudentiality, *n.* proo-den-she-*al*-e-te, the quality of being prudential.
prudentially, *ad.* in a prudential manner.
prudently, *ad.* in a prudent manner.
prudery, *n.* *prood*-er-re, affected scrupulousness; excessive propriety in conduct. (Fr. *pruderie.*)
prud'homme, *n.* prood-*om*, a member of a French tribunal which decides between masters and men in labour disputes. (Fr., prudent man.)
prudish, *a.* *prood*-ish, affectedly virtuous or modest; very formal; precise or reserved.
prudishly, *ad.* in a prudish manner.
prudishness, *n.* the quality of being prudish.
pruinose, *a.* *proo*-e-nohs, covered with bloom or minute dust, as if frosted [Bot.]. (L. *pruinosus.*)
prunable, *a.* *proo*-na-bl, capable of being pruned.
prune, *v.i.* proon, to cut off superfluous branches, etc.; to clear from anything superfluous; to trim. (O.Fr. *proigner.*)
prune, *n.* proon, a dried plum; the dark purplish colour of its juice. (L. *prunum.*)
prunella, *n.* proo-*nel*-a, any of a genus of labiate plants, including self-heal, *P. vulgaris*; quinsy, or other throat complaint, which self-heal was used to cure. (L. *Brunella*, lit. brownness.)
prunella, *n.* proo-*nel*-a, a smooth woollen stuff, of which clergymen's gowns were once made, now used for making the uppers of boots and shoes. (Fr. *prunelle*, from its prune-like colour.)
prunello, *n.* proo-*nel*-oh, a superior kind of prune.
pruner, *n.* *proon*-er, one who prunes.

pruniferous, *a.* proo-*nif*-er-us, bearing plums. (L.)
pruning, *n.* *proon*-ing, the lopping of the superfluous branches of trees. **pruning hook, knife,** implements for pruning.
prunt, *n.* prunt, a small ornamental glass piece attached to a vase or the like; a tool for shaping or fixing prunts.
prurience, *n.* *proor*-re-ence, the quality of being prurient; liking for or tendency towards lewdness.
pruriency, *n.* *proor*-re-en-se, prurience.
prurient, *a.* *proor*-re-ent, characterized by lewdness or lecherous desire; given to unclean thoughts. (L. *pruriens*, itching or longing for.)
pruriently, *ad.* *proor*-re-ent-le, with prurience.
pruriginous, *a.* proo-*rij*-e-nus, of the nature of prurigo; affected by or tending to prurigo.
prurigo, *n.* proor-*ry*-go, a papular eruption of the skin, attended with intolerable itching. (L.)
pruritus, *n.* proo-*ry*-tus, intense itching [Med.].
Prussian, *a.* *prush*-an, pertaining to Prussia, its people, or language: *n.* a native of Prussia. **prussian blue,** a deep blue colour or colouring matter derived from ferric ferrocyanide. **prussian carp,** the fresh-water fish *Carassius gibelio*, the crucian or goldfish.
Prussianism, *n.* *prush*-a-nizm, the characteristics, practices, or behaviour of the Prussians; militarism; hectoring autocracy.
Prussianize, *v.t.* *prush*-a-nize, to cause to resemble the Prussians, esp. in their militarism.
prussiate, *n.* *prus*-e-ate, a salt of prussic acid; a cyanide, also a ferro- or ferri-cyanide.
prussic, *a.* *prus*-ik, obtained from Prussian blue. **prussic acid,** hydrocyanic acid, a virulent poison.
pry, *n.* pry, the act of prying; a narrow inspection: *v.i.* to peep into; to inspect closely or scrutinizingly. (O.Fr. *prier*, to pillage.)
pry, *v.t.* pry, to prise; to force up or open with a lever [Coll.]. (Abbrev. of *prise*.)
pryingly, *ad.* with impertinent curiosity.
prytaneum, *n.* prit-a-*nee*-um, in Greek States, a public building in which ambassadors and citizens deserving well of their country were entertained. (Gr.)
prythee, *int.* *prith*-e, prithee; pray thee!
psalm, *n.* sahm, a sacred song. **the Psalms,** a canonical book of the Old Testament consisting of psalms, many of which are ascribed to David. (L. *psalmus*.)
psalmist, *n.* *sahm*-ist, a writer of psalms, esp. David; an inspired singer; a leading chorister.
psalmodic, *a.* sal-*mod*-ik, relating to psalmody.
psalmodist, *n.* *sah*- or *sal*-mo-dist, one practised in psalmody; a psalmist.
psalmody, *n.* *sah*- or *sal*-mo-de, the practice or art of singing psalms; psalms collectively. (Fr. *psalmodie*.)
psalter, *n.* *sawl*-ter, a book consisting of psalms; a collection of psalms for divine service. **the Psaltery,** the Book of Psalms. (O.Fr. *psaltier*.)
psaltery, *n.* *sawl*-ter-re, an ancient zither-like musical stringed instrument.
psammite, *n.* *sam*-ite, any sandstone composed of fine rounded grains. (Gr. *psammos*, sand.)
psammitic, *a.* sa-*mit*-ik, pertaining to or of the nature of psammite.
pschent, *n.* shent, the double crown of the united ancient kingdoms of Upper and Lower Egypt. (Egyptian.)
psellism, *n.* *sel*-izm, imperfect enunciation; any speech defect. (Gr. *psellismos*, a stammering.)
psephite, *n.* *sef*-ite, a conglomerate composed of rounded pebbles. (Gr. *psephos*, a pebble.)
pseudæsthesia, *n.* sew-des-*thee*-ze-a, an imagined sense of feeling in an organ that has been amputated. (Gr. *pseudo*, false, *aisthesis*, sensation.)
pseudepigrapha, *n.pl.* sew-de-*pig*-ra-fa, spurious writings, esp. those attributed to Scriptual characters. (Gr. *pseudo*, *epi*, upon, *grapho*, write.)
pseudepigraphy, *n.* sew-de-*pig*-ra-fe, ascription of false names of authors to works.
pseudo-, *sew*-do, a Greek prefix signifying false, counterfeit, or spurious. (Gr. *pseudos*, falsehood.)
pseudoblepsia, *n.* sew-do-*blep*-se-a, false and misleading vision. (Gr. *pseudo*-, and *blepsis*, vision.)
pseudoblepsis, *n.* sew-do-*blep*-sis, a visual hallucination.
pseudobulb, *n.* *sew*-do-bulb, a stem of bulbous formation, as in certain orchids.
pseudocarp, *n.* *sew*-do-karp, a fruit not consisting solely of the ripened ovary, as the strawberry [Bot.].
pseudograph, *n.* *sew*-do-graf, a spurious writing; literary forgery. (Gr. *pseudo*-, and *grapho*, write.)
pseudologue, *n.* *sew*-do-log, a pseudomaniac.
pseudology, *n.* sew-*dol*-o-je, lying; the art of lying. (Gr. *pseudo*-, and *logos*, speech.)
pseudomalachite, *n.* *sew*-do-*mal*-a-kite, a phosphate and hydroxide of copper resembling malachite.
pseudomania, *n.* sew-do-*may*-ne-a, an insane or morbid tendency to lie; condition of one who accuses himself of uncommitted crime [Path.].
pseudomaniac, *n.* sew-do-*may*-ne-ak, one afflicted with pseudomania; a pathological liar.
pseudomorph, *n.* *sew*-do-morf, a mineral having the crystalline form of one it has replaced.
pseudomorphosis, *n.* *sew*-do-mor-*foh*-sis, transformation into a pseudomorph.
pseudomorphous, *a.* sew-do-*mor*-fus, not having the true form [Cryst.].
pseudonym, *n.* *sew*-do-nim, an assumed or fictitious name; a pen-name. (Gr. *pseudo*-, and *onoma*, a name.)
pseudonymity, *n.* sew-do-*nim*-e-te, the condition of being pseudonymous; the use of a pseudonym.
pseudonymous, *a.* sew-*don*-e-mus, bearing an assumed or fictitious name.
pseudopod, *n.* *sew*-do-pod, a pseudopodium.
pseudopodium, *n.* sew-do-*poh*-de-um (*pl.* **pseudopodia**), the retractile organ of a protoplasmic cell, serving for locomotion and the absorption of food; the foot of a rotifer.
pseudoscope, *n.* *sew*-do-skope, a stereoscopic instrument which shows objects with their true relief reversed.
pshaw, *int.* shaw, an expression of contempt, disdain or dislike. (Imit.)
psilanthropism, *n.* si-*lan*-thro-pizm, the doctrine of the psilanthropists.
psilanthropist, *n.* si-*lan*-thro-pist, one who believes that Christ was a mere man. (Gr. *psilos*, bare, mere, *anthropos*, a man.)
psilanthropy, *n.* si-*lan*-thro-pe, psilanthropism.
psilomelane, *n.* si-*lom*-e-lane, an oxide of manganese containing oxides of barium, sodium, and potassium. (Gr. *psilos*, and *melas*, black.)
psilosis, *n.* sy-*loh*-sis, removal of hair or flesh; depilation [Path.]. (Gr., a stripping bare.)
psittaceous, *a.* sit-*tay*-she-us, belonging or allied to the parrots; psittacine. (L. *psittacus*, parrot.)
psittacine, *a.* *sit*-ta-sin, parrot-like; pertaining to parrots: *n.* a parrot.
psittacosis, *n.* sit-a-*koh*-sis, a disease of parrots communicable to man and other animals as a form of influenza or pneumonia.
psoas, *n.* *soh*-as, either of the two large lumbar muscles. (Gr.)
psora, *n.* *saw*-ra, scabies; the itch [Path.]. (Gr.)
psoriasis, *n.* so-*ry*-a-sis, a chronic skin disease evinced by a dry, scaly non-contagious and non-infectious eruption. (*psora*.)
psoric, *a.* *saw*-rik, pertaining to the psora: *n.* an ointment or medicine for psora.
psorous, *a.* *saw*-rus, affected with the itch [Path.].
psychasthenia, *n.* sy-kas-*thee*-ne-a, mental fatigue, esp. characterized by phobias, lack of decision, etc. [Path.].
Psyche, *n.* *sy*-ke, a beautiful maiden, emblematic of the soul, who excited the jealousy of Venus but won the heart of her son Cupid [Myth.]; (*l.c.*) the mind; the soul; the self. (Gr., the soul.)
psychiatric, *a.* *sy*-ke-*at*-rik, pertaining to or proceeding from psychiatry.
psychiatrist, *n.* sy-*ky*-a-trist, a specialist in mental diseases; one who practises psychiatry.
psychiatrize, *v.t.* sy-*ky*-a-trize, to treat by psychiatry [Med.].
psychiatry, *n.* sy-*ky*-a-tre, medical treatment of mental disorder, also of physical disease through the mind. (Gr. *psyche*, and *iatros*, a healer.)
psychic, *a.* *sy*-kik, psychical; non-physical; activated by or sensitive to non-physical forces: *n.* one apparently having psychic power; [Coll.] a spiritualist medium: *pl.* psychology; psychical research or study.
psychical, *a.* *sy*-ke-kal, pertaining to the mind or soul; psychological; psychic; outside physical law. **psychical research,** the investigation of

thought transference and other phenomena apparently contravening physical laws.
psychically, *ad.* *sy*-ke-ka-le, in a psychic or psychical way.
psychicism, *n.* *sy*-ki-sizm, psychical research.
psychist, *n.* *sy*-kist, a student of psychology; one who engages in psychical research.
psycho-, *comb.f.* *sy*-ko, denoting mind, mental activity, psychological method, or spiritualistic manifestations. (Gr. *psyche*, soul.)
psycho-analyse, *v.t.* *sy*-ko-*an*-a-lize, to subject to the treatment of psycho-analysis.
psycho-analysis, *n.* investigation of the interacting conscious and unconscious elements of the mind for the purpose of treating psychopathic disorders, a method first scientifically used by Sigmund Freud about 1896; the psychology of the unconscious mind.
psycho-analyst, *n.* one who practises psycho-analysis.
psycho-analytic, *a.* pertaining to or effected by psycho-analysis.
psychodynamic, *a.* sy-ko-dy-*nam*-ik, pertaining to mental action.
psychogenesis, *n.* sy-ko-*jen*-e-sis, psychogony; mental origination of disease, etc.
psychogony, *n.* sy-*kog*-o-ne, the origin and development of the soul or mind.
psychogram, *n.* *sy*-ko-gram, a message supposed to have been given by a spirit.
psychograph, *n.* *sy*-ko-graf, any appliance used in spirit-writing; a spirit-photograph.
psychography, *n.* sy-*kog*-ra-fe, descriptive psychology; automatic writing [spiritualism]; the production of spirit-photographs.
psychological, *a.* sy-ko-*loj*-e-kal, pertaining to psychology. **psychological moment,** the instant when the mind is most alert or accessible, hence the critical or exactly right moment.
psychologically, *ad.* in a psychological manner.
psychologist, *n.* sy-*kol*-o-jist, one versed in psychology.
psychology, *n.* sy-*kol*-o-je, the science of the soul or mind; scientific study of the phenomena of consciousness; mental attributes or equipment. (Gr. *psyche*, and *logos*, science.)
psychomancy, *n.* *sy*-ko-man-se, necromancy; a mystic intercommunication of souls; spiritualism.
psychometric, *a.* sy-ko-*met*-rik, pertaining to psychometry.
psychometry, *n.* sy-*kom*-e-tre, the measurement of the duration of mental processes; the occult power of detecting the qualities, character, etc., of an object by the touch or proximity of anything with which it has been in contact. (Gr. *psyche*, and *metron*, measure.)
psycho-motor, *a.* *sy*-ko-moh-tor, inducing muscular action by impulse from the brain; pertaining to such voluntary movement [Anat.].
psycho-neurosis, *n.* sy-ko-new-*roh*-sis, mental disorder characterized by lack of balance between the instincts and power of control.
psychonosology, *n.* *sy*-ko-no-*sol*-o-je, the science of mental derangement.
psychopath, *n.* *sy*-ko-path, one mentally deranged; also, a psychopathist.
psychopathic, *a.* sy-ko-*path*-ik, pertaining to or of the nature of psychopathy; characterized by abnormal sensitiveness.
psychopathist, *n.* sy-*kop*-a-thist, one who treats psychopathy; an alienist.
psychopathology, *n.* *sy*-ko-pa-*thol*-o-je, the pathology of the mind; the science of the psychological features of mental diseases.
psychopathy, *n.* sy-*kop*-a-the, mental disease or disorder, esp. below the stage of insanity.
psychophysical, *a.* sy-ko-*fiz*-e-kal, pertaining to psychophysics.
psychophysics, *n.* sy-ko-*fiz*-iks, the science of the relation of mental to physical or bodily processes.
psychophysicist, *n.* sy-ko-*fiz*-e-sist, a practitioner or student of psychophysics.
psychophysiology, *n.* sy-ko-*fiz*-e-*ol*-o-je, the branch of medicine treating of the involuntary reactions of the body to mental impulses.
psychoplasm, *n.* *sy*-ko-plazm, the assumed primordial substance from which the psychical organism is evolved.
psychosis, *n.* sy-*koh*-sis (*pl.* **psychoses,** sy-*koh*-seez), serious mental disorder or derangement. (Gr., animation.)
psychosomatic, *a.* *sy*-ko-so-*mat*-ik, pertaining to mind and body as a unit. (Gr. *psycho-*, and *soma*, body.)
psychotherapeutics, *n.* *sy*-ko-*the*-ra-*pew*-tiks, the mental treatment of nervous disorders or diseases.
psychotherapist, *n.* *sy*-ko-*the*-ra-pist, one who practises psychotherapy.
psychotherapy, *n.* *sy*-ko-*the*-ra-pe, psychotherapeutics.
psychrometer, *n.* sy-*krom*-e-ter, a wet- and dry-bulb thermometer for measuring the aqueous vapour in the atmosphere; an hygrometer. (Gr. *psychros*, cold, and *metron*.)
ptarmic, *a.* *tar*-mik, sternutative: *n.* a medicine which causes sneezing. (Gr. *ptarmikos*, from *ptairo*, sneeze.)
ptarmigan, *n.* *tar*-me-gan, a bird of the grouse family, *Lagopus mutus*, having white plumage in the winter. (Gael. *tarmachan*.)
Pterichthys, *n.* ter-*rik*-this, an extinct genus of ganoid fish from the Devonian strata of Scotland. (Gr. *pteron*, a wing, *ichthys*, a fish.)
pteridologist, *n.* te-re-*dol*-o-jist, a student of pteridology.
pteridology, *n.* te-re-*dol*-o-je, the science of ferns. (Gr. *pteris*, a fern, *logos*, science.)
pteridophyte, *n.* *te*-re-do-fite, any member of the Pteridophyta, the group of plants including the ferns.
pterocarpous, *a.* te-ro-*kar*-pus, having winged seeds or fruit [Bot.].
pterodactyl, *n.* te-ro-*dak*-til, an extinct flying reptile of the Mesozoic period. (Gr. *pteron*, wing, *dactylos*, finger.)
pterography, *n.* te-*rog*-ra-fe, the description of plumage; pterylography.
pterology, *n.* te-*rol*-o-je, the branch of entomology which deals with the study of insects' wings.
pteromys, *n.* *te*-ro-mis, the flying squirrel. (Gr. *pteron*, and *mys*, a mouse.)
pteropod, *n.* *te*-ro-pod, any member of the Pteropoda, a class of molluscs having two wing-like flippers which are used in swimming. (Gr. *pteron*, and *pous*, a foot.)
pterygium, *n.* te-*rij*-e-um, a growth of skin over the base of a nail; any wing-shaped petal or other part [Bot.]; a chronic thickening of the conjunctiva [Path.]; a generalized limb [Zool.]. (Gr. *pterygion*, a small wing.)
pterygoid, *a.* *te*-re-goyd, wing-like [Anat.]. (Gr. *pteron*, and *eidos*, like.)
pterylography, *n.* *te*-re-*log*-ra-fe, the branch of ornithology which deals with the character and distribution of the bird's plumage.
pterylosis, *n.* *te*-re-*loh*-sis, the arrangement of the feather tracts on a bird's body. (Gr. *pteron*, and *hyle*, cord.)
ptilosis, *n.* ti-*loh*-sis, plumage; pterylosis; (formerly) madarosis [Path.].
ptisan, *n.* *tiz*-an, barley-water or other mucilaginous decoction. (Gr. *ptisane*, peeled barley.)
ptochocracy, *n.* toh-*kok*-ra-se, government by paupers; the poor as a ruling body, or as a class. (Gr. *ptochos*, a beggar, *kratos*, power.)
Ptolemaic, *a.* tol-e-*may*-ik, pertaining to the Greek astronomer Ptolemy (2nd cent. A.D.), or to his system, which taught that the earth was fixed in the centre of the universe and that the heavens revolved around it; pertaining to any of the Greco-Egyptian Ptolemies, rulers of Egypt 323–30 B.C.: *n.* one supporting the Ptolemaic theory of astronomy.
ptomaine, *n.* *toh*-mane, any alkaloid poisonous matter produced by putrefaction of animal tissues. (Gr. *ptoma*, a corpse.)
ptosis, *n.* *toh*-sis, a prolapse of any organ [Med.], esp. inability to raise the upper eyelid due to paralysis of the third nerve. (Gr., a falling.)
ptyalin, *n.* *ty*-a-lin, a ferment, present in saliva, able to convert starch into dextrose. (Gr. *ptualon*, spittle.)
ptyalism, *n.* *ty*-a-lizm, salivation; a morbid or excessive excretion of saliva.
ptyalogogue, *n.* ty-*al*-o-gog, a medicine that promotes discharges of saliva.
ptyalose, *n.* *ty*-a-lohs, maltose.
pub, *n.* pub, a public-house [Slang].
puberal, *a.* *pew*-ber-ral, pertaining to puberty.

puberty, *n.* *pew*-ber-te, the age of sexual maturity; the period at which the reproductive organs are first able to function. (Fr. *puberté*.)
pubes, *n.* *pew*-beez, the pubic hair; the hairy region over the pubic bone [Anat.]; pubescence [Bot. and Zool.]. (L.)
pubescence, *n.* pew-*bes*-ence, the state of puberty; a downy substance on plants, insects, etc.
pubescent, *a.* pew-*bes*-ent, arriving at puberty; covered with pubescence. (L. *pubescens*, growing hairy.)
pubic, *a.* *pew*-bik, pertaining to or designating the lower part of the hypogastric region [Anat.]. **pubic bone,** the pubis. **pubic hair,** the hair on the hypogastric region of adult humans. (L.)
pubis, *n.* *pew*-bis, one of the three bones which together form the innominate bone, or hip-bone [Anat.].
***public,** *a.* *pub*-lik, pertaining to a nation, state, or community; extending to a whole people; circulating among all classes; open to all; notorious; regarding the good of the community; open to common use: *n.* the general body of a nation; the people generally; a public-house [Coll.]. **public library,** a library controlled and maintained by a local authority for the benefit of its public and not for profit. **public school,** a large endowed boarding-school preparing pupils for the universities and the public services; a school maintained by an education authority under state control (esp. Scotland and U.S.A.). **public servant,** an officer or employee of a central or local government authority or of a public utility service. **public utility,** denoting necessary services (as supply of water, light, power, transport, etc.) rendered by a board or company directly or indirectly under government control. (Fr. *publique*, from L. *publicus*, from *populus*, people.)
publican, *n.* *pub*-le-kan, the keeper of an inn, tavern, or public-house; among the Romans, a farmer of public revenues; a collector of tolls or tribute. (L. *publicanus*.)
publication, *n.* pub-le-*kay*-shon, the act of publishing or making public; promulgation; the act of publishing a book or the like, and offering it for sale; a work printed and published. (Fr.)
public-house, *n.* an inn or tavern; a house licensed for the sale of alcoholic liquors for consumption on the premises.
publicist, *n.* *pub*-le-sist, a writer on international law; a political journalist.
publicity, *n.* pub-*lis*-e-te, the quality or state of being public; advertising; published propaganda for the advancement of some object.
publicize, *v.t.* *pub*-le-size, to give publicity to.
publicly, *ad.* *pub*-lik-le, in a public manner.
publicness, *n.* *pub*-lik-ness, state of being public, or belonging to the public.
public-spirited, *a.* having a disposition to advance the interests of the community.
public-spiritedly, *ad.* with public spirit.
public-spiritedness, *n.* the quality of being public-spirited.
publish, *v.t.* *pub*-lish, to make known; to proclaim; to announce; to print and offer for sale; to put into circulation. (Fr. *publier*.)
publishable, *a.* *pub*-lish-a-bl, fit for publication; worth publishing.
publisher, *n.* *pub*-lish-er, one who publishes, esp. literary, artistic, or musical works.
publishment, *n.* *pub*-lish-ment, the act of publishing notice of marriage [U.S.A.].
puce, *a.* pewce, of a brownish-purple colour; flea-colour. (Fr. *puce*, a flea, from L. *pulex*.)
pucelage, *n.* *pew*-se-laj, a state of virginity. (Fr. *pucelle*, a virgin.)
Puck, *n.* puk, the fairy, Robin Goodfellow, the "merry wanderer of the night"; (*l.c.*) the rubber disk used as a ball in ice-hockey; puckeridge. (Ir. *puca*, an elf.)
pucka, *a.* *puk*-a, pukka. (Anglo-Ind.)
puck-bird, *n.* the puckeridge or nightjar.
pucker, *n.* *puk*-er, a fold or wrinkle: *v.t.* to gather into small folds or wrinkles; to wrinkle: *v.i.* to become wrinkled. (Origin unknown.)
puckeridge, *n.* *puk*-er-rij, the nightjar, also a cattle-disease said to be caused by this.
puckish, *a.* *puk*-ish, characteristic of Puck; impish; mischievous.
puddening, *n.* *pood*-en-ing, a fender of rope and yarn to prevent chafing, etc. [Naut.].
pudding, *n.* *pood*-ing, a form of food partly or entirely farinaceous; fruit or meat boiled or steamed in a covering of flour; an intestine; a large sausage; puddening [Naut.]. **pudding face,** a full, round, fat face. **pudding sleeve,** a sleeve of the full-dress clerical gown. (M.E. *poding*.)
puddingstone, *n.* *pood*-ing-stone, a conglomerate composed of rounded and waterworn flint pebbles.
puddle, *n.* *pud*-dl, a small pool of dirty water; a mixture of clay and sand worked together: *v.t.* to make muddy; to make puddle, or make watertight with this; to convert pig-iron into wrought iron: *v.i.* to dabble; to make a dirty stir. (A.S. *pudd*, a ditch.)
puddler, *n.* *pud*-dler, one who puddles; one who converts pig iron into wrought-iron.
puddly, *a.* *pud*-dle, muddy; foul; dirty; abounding in puddles.
puddock, *n.* *pud*-dok, a frog or paddock.
pudency, *n.* *pew*-den-se, modesty; bashfulness. (L. *pudens*, modest.)
pudenda, *n.pl.* pew-*den*-da, the external genital organs, esp. those of the female. (L. *pudendus*, that of which one is ashamed.)
pudendal, *a.* pew-*den*-dal, pertaining to the pudenda.
pudge, *n.* puj, a thickset, stocky person [Coll.].
pudgy, *a.* *puj*-e, podgy; short and thickset.
pudic, *a.* *pew*-dik, pertaining to the pudenda: *n.* the artery supplying the genital organs [Anat.].
pudicity, *n.* pew-*dis*-e-te, modesty; chastity.
pudu, *n.* *poo*-doo, the small deer of the Andes, *Pudua humilis*. (Sp., from native Chilean.)
pueblo, *n.* *pweb*-loh, an Indian settlement of New Mexico and surrounding parts; an inhabitant of a pueblo. (Sp., village.)
puericulture, *n.* *pewr*-re-kul-tewr, the care of women during pregnancy; the training of children. (L. *puer*, a child, and *culture*.)
puerile, *a.* *pew*-e-rile, boyish; childish; trifling. (L. *puerilis*, from *puer*, a boy.)
puerilely, *ad.* in a puerile manner.
puerileness, *n.* the quality of being puerile.
puerilism, *n.* *pewr*-ril-izm, childish behaviour.
puerility, *n.* pew-er-*ril*-e-te, childishness; that which is puerile.
puerperal, *a.* pew-*er*-pe-ral, pertaining to childbirth. (L. *puerpera*, a lying-in woman.)
puff, *n.* puf, a quick forcible breath; a sudden and short blast of wind; a whiff; a light puffy thing; light pastry; an inflated protuberance; a pad to powder with; exaggerated commendatory notice or advertisement: *v.i.* to drive air from the mouth in a single and quick blast; to swell the cheeks with air; to blow in scorn; to breathe with vehemence to move about with hurry; to become inflated; to praise with exaggeration; to flatter in advertising. (Imit.)
puff-adder, *n.* a venomous African viper, *Bitis arietans*, which can puff out its body when irritated.
puff-ball, *n.* a fungus of the genus *Lycoperdon*, emitting spores as powder when broken.
puff-bird, *n.* *puf*-berd, any member of the Cent. and S. American family of picarian birds Bucconidæ, remarkable for erecting their plumage so as to resemble a ball.
puffer, *n.* *puf*-fer, one who or that which puffs; a locomotive [Childish]; one who praises with noisy commendation; one hired to raise prices at sales.
puffery, *n.* *puf*-fer-re, puffing advertisement; extravagant praise.
puffin, *n.* *puf*-fin, a sea-bird of the auk family, *Fratercula arctica*, the sea-parrot. (From its puffed-out appearance.)
puffiness, *n.* *puf*-fe-ness, the state of being puffy.
puffingly, *ad.* *puf*-fing-le, in a puffing manner.
puff-paste, *n.* a rich light pastry or crust.
puffy, *a.* *puf*-fe, swollen with air or any soft matter; gusty; tumid; turgid; bombastic.
pug, *n.* pug, any little domesticated animal, as a dog or monkey; a pug-dog. (Perhaps from *Puck*.)
pug, *n.* pug, worked clay: *v.t.* to make into, or to puddle or pack with, this.
pug, *n.* pug, footprint of a beast: *v.t.* to track a beast by footprints [Anglo-Indian]. (Hind. *pag*, footprint.)
pug, *n.* pug, a pugilist [Slang].

pugaree, *n.* *pug*-a-ree, a light scarf worn round the hat or helmet (Hind.)
pug-dog, *n.* a small close-haired dog resembling a dwarf bulldog.
pugging, *n.* *pug*-ging, worked clay, etc. filling spaces between walls or under floors to intercept sound.
puggree, *n.* *pug*-gree, a pugaree.
pugh, *int.* poo, a word used in contempt or disdain.
pugil, *n.* *pew*-jil, as much as can be taken up between the thumb and two first fingers; a pinch. (L. *pugillus*, a handful.)
pugilism, *n.* *pew*-je-lizm, the practice of boxing or fighting with the fists. (L. *pugil*, boxer, from *pugnus*, fist.)
pugilist, *n.* *pew*-je-list, a boxer.
pugilistic, *a.* *pew*-je-*lis*-tik, pertaining to boxing.
pug-mill, *n.* a mill for working clay.
pugnacious, *a.* pug-*nay*-shus, disposed to fight; quarrelsome. (L. *pugnax*.)
pugnaciously, *ad.* in a pugnacious manner.
pugnaciousness, *n.* the quality of being pugnacious; pugnacity.
pugnacity, *n.* pug-*nas*-e-te, inclination to fight; quarrelsomeness.
pug-nose, *n.* a short and thick nose.
puisne, *a.* *pew*-ne, younger or inferior in rank, applied to judges: *n.* an inferior judge. (O.Fr.)
puissance, *n.* *pew*-is-ance, power; strength.
puissant, *a.* *pew*-is-ant, mighty; forcible. (Fr.)
puissantly, *ad.* *pew*-is-ant-le, in a puissant manner.
puke, *n.* pewk, an act of vomiting; an emetic; *v.i.* to vomit. (Origin unknown.)
puker, *n.* *pewk*-er, one who pukes.
pukka, *a.* *puk*-ka first rate; genuine [Anglo-Ind.]. (Hind. *pakka*, ripe.)
pulchritude, *n.* *pul*-kre-tewd, beauty; loveliness; grace. (L. *pulchritudo*.)
pule, *v.i.* pewl, to cry plaintively; to whine; to chirp. (Imit.)
Pulex, *n.* *pew*-leks, a genus of insects including several of the fleas. (L., a flea.)
pulicide, *n.* *pew*-le-side, any insecticide destructive of fleas.
pulicine, *a.* *pew*-le-sine, pertaining to fleas.
pulicose, *a.* *pew*-le-kohs, infested with fleas.
puling, *a.* *pewl*-ing, whining; crying in a childish manner or like a chicken: *n.* such a cry.
pulingly, *ad.* in a puling manner.
pulka, *n.* *pul*-ka, a Laplander's travelling sledge. (Finnish, *pulkka*.)
pull, *v.t.* pool, to draw towards one; to pluck; to tear; to rend; to propel by rowing; to use influence for a person; to attract custom; to print in a hand-press; to hit a ball round to leg [Cricket]; to strike the ball to the left [Golf]; to slow down a horse that has a chance [Racing]; to take into custody [Slang]: *v.i.* to give a pull; to tug; to haul. **pull a face,** make a grimace. **pull down,** to demolish; to humble. **pull one's leg,** *see* **leg. pull one's weight,** do one's share of work. **pull off,** to separate by pulling; to carry out successfully [Coll.]. **pull out,** to extract; to row out; to emerge. **pull through,** get through. **pull up,** to tear up by the roots; to eradicate; to stop short or suddenly.
★**pull,** *n.* pool, the act of pulling; that which is pulled; a pulling stroke [Cricket, etc.]; the handle of a beer-engine; a bell rope; a struggle; an advantage; a draught or drink.
puller, *n.* *pool*-er, one who or that which pulls.
pullet, *n.* *pool*-et, a young hen. (Fr. *poulette*.)
pulley, *n.* *pool*-le, one of the great mechanical powers; a wheel with grooved rim, turning on a pin in a block for a running rope; a train of such; a rope for lowering or hauling up casks; a wheel for driving with a belt: *v.t.* to hoist with a pulley. (Fr. *poulie*.)
pullman, *n.* *pool*-man, a long railway car comprising sitting and sleeping apartments; a sleeping car mounted on two bogies. (Named from designer.)
pullover, *n.* *pool*-oh-ver, a jersey that is pulled over the head; a sweater.
pull-through, *n.* a cord with weight and rag attached used for cleaning the barrel of a rifle.
pullulant, *a.* *pool*-ew-lant, budding; sprouting.
pullulate, *v.i.* *pool*-ew-late, to germinate; to bud; to spring up. (L. *pullulatus*, sprouted.)
pullulation, *n.* pool-ew-*lay*-shon, act of pullulating; germination.
pull-up, *n.* a tavern, eating-house, or coffee-stall intended primarily for carmen and lorry-drivers.
pulmobranchiate, *a.* pul-mo-*brang*-ke-at, having the branchiæ formed for breathing air, as certain molluscs. (L. *pulmo*, a lung, Gr. *branchia*, gills.)
pulmometer, *n.* pul-*mom*-e-ter, a device for measuring lung capacity.
pulmonary, *a.* *pul*-mo-na-re, pertaining to or affecting the lungs. (L. *pulmonarius*.)
pulmonate, *a.* *pul*-mo-nat, having lungs: *n.* any pulmonate mollusc.
pulmonic, *a.* pul-*mon*-ik, affecting the lungs; subject to lung disease; pulmonary: *n.* a medicine for diseases of the lungs; one whose lungs are affected.
pulmoniferous, *a.* pul-mo-*nif*-er-rus, possessing lungs. (L. *pulmo*, and *fero*, bear.)
pulmotor, *n.* *pul*-moh-tor, an apparatus for restoration of the breathing of one apparently drowned or asphyxiated.
pulp, *n.* pulp, any soft uniform mass; the soft, succulent part of fruit consisting of cellular tissue and juice; marrow: *v.t.* to reduce to pulp; to separate the pulp from. **wood-pulp,** wood, reduced chemically or mechanically to pulp, used in the manufacture of paper. (Fr. *pulpe*.)
pulpiness, *n.* *pul*-pe-ness, the state of being pulpy.
pulpit, *n.* *pool*-pit, an elevated enclosed place in which a preacher stands; a movable desk: *a* pertaining to preaching or the pulpit. **the pulpit,** preachers collectively or preaching. (O.Fr. *pulpite*.)
pulpiteer, *n.* pool-pe-*teer*, a fanatical or denunciatory preacher: *v.t.* to preach (used esp. sneeringly).
pulpous, *a.* *pul*-pus, consisting of or resembling pulp.
pulpy, *a.* *pul*-pe, pulpous; soft; succulent.
pulque, *n.* *pool*-kay, a fermented beverage prepared in Mexico and Central America from the juice of the agave. (Sp. *pulqueria*.)
pulsate, *v.i.* *pul*-sate, to beat or throb; to move rhythmically. (L. *pulsatus*, struck.)
pulsatile, *a.* *pul*-sa-tile, throbbing; pulsatory.
pulsatilla, *n.* pul-sa-*til*-a, the pasque-flower; an alterative and depressant prepared from this [Pharm.].
pulsation, *n.* pul-*say*-shon, the act of beating or throbbing; a movement of the pulse.
pulsative, *a.* *pul*-sa-tiv, pulsatory.
pulsator, *n.* pul-*say*-tor, a striker; a machine used to shake earth from diamonds; any machine that throbs in working. (L.)
pulsatory, *a.* *pul*-sa-to-re, throbbing; capable of or pertaining to pulsation.
pulse, *n.* pulse, the beating or throbbing of the heart and blood-vessels; a regular beat or stroke; *v.i.* to beat, as the pulse. **feel one's pulse** (figuratively), to sound one's opinion. (L. *pulsus*, beating.)
pulse, *n.* pulse, the edible seeds of leguminous plants; plants yielding these. (L. *puls*, pottage.)
pulseless, *a.* *pulse*-less, having no pulsation.
pulselessness, *n.* *pulse*-les-ness, want of pulse.
pulsimeter, *n.* pul-*sim*-e-ter, an instrument to test the strength, rate, or regularity of the pulse; a sphygmometer [Med.]. (L. *puls*, and Gr. *metron*, measure.)
pulsometer, *n.* pul-*som*-e-ter, a vacuum pump having two chambers in which steam is condensed alternately; a pulsimeter.
pultaceous, *a.* pul-*tay*-shus, macerated; softened. (L. *puls*, *pultis*, pottage.)
pulu, *n.* *pew*-loo, a fine silky substance prepared from the fibres of a Hawaiian tree-fern, used for stuffing pillows, etc. (Native.)
pulverable, *a.* *pul*-ver-ra-bl, pulverizable.
pulverine, *n.* *pul*-ver-rin, ashes of barilla. (L.)
pulverizable, *a.* *pul*-ver-riz-a-bl, capable of being crushed or pulverized.
pulverization, *n.* pul-ver-ri-*zay*-shon, the act of reducing to powder; separation into spray (of liquids).
pulverize, *v.t.* *pul*-ver-rize, to reduce to fine powder; to destroy by or as by smashing. (Fr. *pulveriser*, from L. *pluvis*, powder.)
pulverizer, *n.* *pul*-ver-ry-zer, one who or that which pulverizes.
pulverous, *a.* *pul*-ver-rus, powdery; like powder.
pulverulence, *n.* pul-*ve*-rew-lence, dustiness; abundance of dust or powder.
pulverulent, *a.* pul-*ve*-rew-lent, dusty; consisting

of or reducible to fine powder; addicted to lying or rolling in the dust (of birds).
pulvil, *n. pul*-vil, an obsolete scented powder.
pulvinar, *a.* pul-*vee*-nar, of cushion shape: *n.* a prominence on the back of the optic thalamus [Anat.]. (L. *pulvinus*, a cushion.)
pulvinate, *a. pul*-ve-nat, pulvinar [Bot. and Zool.]; bulged out [Arch.].
puma, *n. pew*-ma, the feline American carnivore *Felis concolor*, the cougar. (Peruvian.)
pumice, *n. pum*-is, a hard, porous lava used as a cleaning and polishing agent, light enough to float on water so long as its pores are filled with air: *v.t.* to scrub, smooth, or polish with pumice. (L. *pumex.*)
pumiceous, *a.* pew-*mish*-us, pertaining to, consisting of, or resembling pumice.
pumice-stone, *n.* pumice.
pumiciform, *a.* pew-*mis*-e-form, having the appearance, texture, or form of pumice.
pumicose, *a. pew*-me-kohs, pumiceous.
pummace, *n. pum*-as, pomace.
pummel, *n.* and *v.t. pum*-el, pommel.
★**pump,** *n.* pump, a machine for raising water or other fluid; an air-pump; the act of pumping; one who tries to extract secrets, etc.: *v.i.* to raise water, etc. with a pump; to work a pump: *v.t.* to raise with a pump; to free from water with a pump; to put out of breath; to extract secrets by artful questions. (M.E. *pumpe*, probably Ger. in origin.)
pump, *n.* pump, a light single-soled shoe. (Perhaps connected with *pomp.*)
pumpage, *n. pum*-paj, work done with a pump; amount of water lifted by a pump.
pump-barrel, *n.* the cylinder of a pump.
pump-brake, *n.* the handle of a ship's pump.
pumper, *n. pum*-per, one who pumps; a pump; a pumpman; a well from which oil is pumped.
pumpernickel, *n. pum*-per-nik-el, a species of rye bread formerly peculiar to Westphalia. (Ger.)
pump-handle, *n.* the working arm of a pump: *v.t.* to shake hands effusively or protractedly [Coll.].
pumping-station, *n.* a building housing the pumps of an irrigation system or of a pipe-line.
pumpion, *n. pum*-pyun, a pumpkin.
pumpkin, *n. pump*-kin, any of the varieties of the trailing vine *Cucurbita pepo*; its gourd-like fruit. (O.Fr. *pompon.*)
pumpman, *n. pump*-man, one in charge of a pump, esp. at a mine; one who works a pump.
pump-room, *n.* the location of the pumps at a pumping-station; the main hall of assembly at a spa.
pun, *n.* pun, a play upon words that are similar in sound but different in meaning; a form of paronomasia: *v.i.* to play upon words.
pun, *v.t.* pun, to pound; to ram or work with a punner.
Puna, *n. poo*-na, the high plateau of the Andes; (*l.c.*) its prevalent cold wind; mountain sickness. (Native.)
punch, *n.* punch, a beverage of Indian origin, properly consisting of five ingredients, spirit, water, sugar, lemon-juice, and spice; any spirit drunk with water, sugar, and lemon; toddy. (Perhaps Hind. *panch*, five.)
punch, *n.* punch, a tool for used stamping, embossing, coining, etc. and for piercing or perforating holes; an upper die [Coining]: *v.t.* to perforate, puncture, or stamp with a punch; to drive or herd cattle. (O.Fr. *poinchon.*)
punch, *n.* punch, a quick blow with or as with the fist; forceful quality; effective vigour: *v.t.* to give a punch to. **punching bag,** a stuffed or inflated tethered leather bag used in training boxers or for exercise. (*punch*—the tool.)
punch, *n.* punch, a short fat fellow; a thick-set horse, esp. a **Suffolk punch,** one of a breed of heavy draught-horses. (Perhaps *bunch*, or *punchinello.*)
Punch, *n.* punch, the chief character in a puppet-show; an English humorous illustrated journal satirizing contemporary follies and weaknesses. **pleased as Punch,** very well pleased; beaming with satisfaction. **Punch and Judy,** a puppet-show introducing esp. these two and dog Toby. (It. *pulcinello.*)
punch-bowl, *n.* a bowl in which punch is made; a deep bowl-shaped hollow among hills.
punch-drunk, *a.* suffering from nervous debility and incapacity as a result of repeated blows over a considerable period (esp. of pugilists).
puncheon, *n. punch*-on, a punch for piercing or stamping, etc.; a short upright supporting timber. (O.Fr. *poinchon.*)
puncheon, *n. punch*-on a large cask of varying capacity (72 gallons in cask of beer). (O.Fr. *ponçon.*)
puncher, *n. punch*-er, one who or that which punches; a punching tool; a cowpuncher.
punchinello, *n.* punch-e-*nel*-loh, a clown; a buffoon. (It. *Pulcinello*, a character in comedy.)
punchy, *a. punch*-e, short and thick, or fat.
punctate, *a. punk*-tat, spotted; covered with points; having the surface dotted [Bot.]. (L. *punctatus*, pricked.)
punctiform, *a. punk*-te-form, point-shaped.
punctilio, *n.* punk-*til*-e-oh, a nice point in conduct or ceremony; exactness in forms. (Sp. *puntillo.*)
punctilious, *a.* punk-*til*-e-us, very exact in behaviour; exact to excess.
punctiliously, *ad.* in a punctilious manner.
punctiliousness, *n.* exactness in the observance of forms.
punctual, *a. punk*-tew-al, exact to time; done at the exact time; pertaining to a point [Geom.]. (Fr. *ponctuel.*)
punctualist, *n. punk*-tew-a-list, one who is very observant of forms and ceremonies.
punctuality, *n. punk*-tew-*al*-e-te, quality of being punctual; exactness as regards appointments to time.
punctually, *ad.* in a punctual manner.
punctuate, *v.t. punk*-tew-ate, to mark with points; to divide a sentence by stops; to greet a speech, etc., with short and repeated interruptions; to accentuate. (Late L. *punctuatus.*)
punctuation, *n. punk*-tew-*ay*-shon, the act or art of dividing sentences by points.
punctuative, *a. punk*-tew-a-tiv, pertaining to or serving for punctuation.
punctum, *n. punk*-tum, a dot; a speck [Zool., Bot., and Med.]. (L.)
puncture, *n. punk*-tewr, a perforation; the act of perforating: *v.t.* to prick; to pierce with anything sharp or pointed: *v.i.* to be susceptible of receiving punctures.
pundit, *n. pun*-dit, a Hindu versed in Sanscrit language and in the learning, laws, and religion of India; a learned or would-be learned man. (Sans. *pandita*, learned.)
pungency, *n. pun*-jen-se, the quality of being pungent; sharpness; acridness; acrimony; keenness.
pungent, *a. pun*-jent, affecting the organs of smell or taste with a pricking sensation; piquant; acrid; sarcastic; biting. (L. *pungens*, pricking.)
pungently, *ad.* in a pungent manner.
Punic, *a. pew*-nik, pertaining to the Carthaginians; faithless; treacherous: *n.* the language of the Carthaginians. (L. *Punicus*, from *Pœnus*, Phœnician.)
puniceous, *a.* pew-*nish*-us, purple. (L., purple.)
punily, *ad. pew*-ne-le, in a puny manner; weakly.
puniness, *n. pew*-ne-ness, state of being puny; pettiness; smallness with feebleness.
punish, *v.i. pun*-ish, to afflict with pain, loss, or calamity for an offence, fault, etc.; to chastise; to chasten; to inflict a penalty; to subject to injury or pain; to defeat severely [Coll.]. (Fr. *punissant*, punishing.)
punishability, *n. pun*-ish-a-*bil*-e-te, the quality of being punishable.
punishable, *a. pun*-ish-a-bl, deserving of or liable to punishment.
punisher, *n. pun*-ish-er, one who punishes.
★**punishment,** *n. pun*-ish-ment, the act of punishing; pain or suffering inflicted by authority on a person for an offence, etc.; severe treatment [Slang].
punitive, *a. pew*-ne-tiv, awarding or inflicting punishment. (O.Fr. *punitif.*)
punitory, *a. pew*-ne-to-re, punitive; tending to punishment.
punk, *n.* punk, tinder from a fungus or decayed wood; amadou. (Algonquian.)
punk, *n.* punk, anything worthless; flapdoodle; tosh: *a.* worthless [Slang].
punk, *n.* punk, a prostitute [Old Slang].
punkah, *n. pung*-ka, a large fan hanging from the ceiling and swung by a rope or mechanically. (Hind. *pankha.*)

punner, *n. pun*-er, a heavy tool for ramming down; a beetle (the implement).

punnet, *n. pun*-et, a small shallow chip basket in which fruit, etc. is packed.

punster, *n. pun*-ster, one given to punning.

punt, *v.i.* punt, to play at certain games of cards; to play against the bank; to bet, esp. in a reckless or heavy way. (Fr. *ponter.*)

punt, *n.* punt, a flat-bottomed square-ended craft without stem or sternpost, propelled by means of a pole: *v.t.* to push a punt along thus; to convey in a punt. **punt gun,** a large-bored swivel-gun carried in a punt for wildfowling. **punt pole,** a quant. (A.S.)

punt, *n.* punt, a kick before the ball reaches the ground after dropping from the hands: *v.t.* to kick a ball in this manner [Football].

punt, *n.* punt, the hollow base of a glass bottle.

punter, *n. punt*-er, one who punts; one who gambles or bets recklessly.

punty, *n. pun*-te, an iron rod used by glass-blowers to hold material being worked. (Fr. *pontil.*)

puny, *a. pew*-ne, inferior; petty; undersized; tiny: *n.* a junior; a novice. (O.Fr. *puisné.*)

pup, *n.* pup, a puppy; a young seal: *v.i.* to bring forth whelps. **in pup,** pregnant (of bitches). **to sell one a pup,** to swindle, or perpetrate a hoax upon, one.

pupa, *n. pew*-pa (*pl.* **pupæ**), an insect in the chrysalis state. (L., a girl.)

pupal, *a. pew*-pal, pertaining to a pupa.

pupate, *v.i. pew*-pate, to turn into a pupa.

pupil, *n. pew*-pil, a student (youth or girl) under the care of a tutor or teacher; a ward (boy or girl) under the age of puberty [Law]. (L. *pupillus,* a little boy.)

pupil, *n. pew*-pil, the circular aperture in the iris through which the rays pass to the retina, so called from the little figure seen in it when looked into.

pupilage, *n. pew*-pil-laj, the state of being a pupil; wardship; minority.

pupilarity, *n.* pew-pil-*la*-re-te, the period before puberty, or state of being in this. [Scots. Law.]

pupilate, *a. pew*-pil-lat, marked with a central spot like a pupil [Zool.].

pupillary, *a. pew*-pil-la-re, pertaining to a pupil or ward, or to the pupil of the eye.

pupil-teacher, *n.* a young student who is both being taught and trained to teach others.

Pupipara, *n.pl.* pew-*pip*-a-ra, a division of insects whose eggs are hatched in the matrix of the mother. (L. *pupa,* and *pario,* bring forth.)

pupiparous, *a.* pew-*pip*-a-rus, pertaining to the Pupipara; producing pupæ [Entom.].

pupivorous, *a.* pew-*piv*-o-rus, feeding on pupæ. (L. *pupa,* and *voro,* devour.)

pupoid, *a. pew*-poyd, resembling a pupa.

puppet, *n. pup*-et, a marionette; a small image or doll moved by wires or by the hand in a mock drama; a doll; one who is under the control and is the tool of another. **puppet state,** a state officially independent but actually under the control of another. (Fr. *poupette,* a tiny doll.)

puppet-player, *n.* one who manages the motions of puppets.

puppetry, *n. pup*-et-re, puppets or puppet-shows in general; the art of a puppet-player; mummery; make-believe.

puppet-show, *n.* a mock drama performed by puppets; a marionette performance.

puppet-valve, *n.* a poppet-valve.

puppy, *n. pup*-e, a whelp, esp. a young dog; [Fig.] a conceited or impertinent young fellow. (Fr. *poupée,* from L. *pupa.*)

puppyhood, *n. pup*-e-hood, the state of being a puppy.

puppyism, *n. pup*-e-izm, the empty offensiveness of a conceited young fellow.

purâna, *n.* poo-*rah*-na, any of a class of ancient poems treating of the mythology, theology, cosmogony, etc., of Hinduism, of which they form the Scriptures. (Sans., ancient.)

puranic, *a.* poo-*ran*-ik, pertaining to the purânas.

Purbeckian, *a.* pur-*bek*-e-an, pertaining to the upper group of the Portland Oolites, of the Jurassic [Geol.]. (Isle of *Purbeck.*)

purblind, *a. pur*-blynd, dim-sighted; seeing obscurely; dull-witted, slow to understand or discern. (*pure-blind*).

purblindly, *ad.* in a purblind manner.

purblindness, *n.* dimness of vision.

purchasable, *a. pur*-chas-a-bl, that may be bought; venal.

purchase, *n. pur*-chas, the act of purchasing; acquisition by purchasing; that which is purchased; any mechanical power of advantage in raising or moving heavy bodies: *v.t.* to acquire by any means; to buy; to obtain by paying an equivalent; to obtain by expense of labour, danger, sacrifice, etc.; to raise or draw in by a purchase. **purchase money,** money paid, or contracted to be paid, for anything bought. (O.Fr. *purchacer,* to acquire.)

purchaser, *n. pur*-chas-er, one who purchases.

purdah, *n. pur*-dah, a curtain shutting off the women's apartments; material for such; the custom of secluding women. (Hind.)

pure, *a.* pewr, free from moral defilement; chaste; unsullied; unmixed; free from mixture; unpolluted; unadulterated; mere; that and that only; purely theoretical (of sciences). (O.Fr. *pur.*)

purée, *n.* poo-ray, a thick soup the ingredients of which are passed through a sieve. (Fr.)

purely, *ad. pewr*-le, in a pure manner; innocently; absolutely.

pureness, *n. pewr*-ness, state or quality of being pure; freedom from mixture, defilement, or impropriety.

purfle, *n. pur*-fl, a border of embroidered work: *v.t.* to decorate with a wrought border. (O.Fr. *porfiler.*)

purfling, *n. purf*-ling, an ornamental border; the border on the back and front of stringed instruments.

purgation, *n.* pur-*gay*-shon, cleansing; the act of purging, as by purgatives; physical, moral, or spiritual purification; the act of clearing from the imputation of guilt. (Fr.)

purgative, *a. pur*-ga-tiv, having the power of cleansing, esp. of evacuating the bowels: *n.* a medicine that effects this. (Fr. *purgatif.*)

purgatorial, *a.* pur-ga-*taw*-re-al, cleansing of sin; purifying; pertaining to purgatory.

purgatorian, *a.* pur-ga-*taw*-re-an, purgatorial: *n.* one who believes in purgatory.

purgatory, *a. pur*-ga-to-re, tending to cleanse; purifying: *n.* in the Rom. Cath. Church, a place or state after death, in which souls of the faithful are, through suffering, purified from venial sins; any condition of painful purgation or temporary punishment. (Late L. *purgatorius.*)

purge, *n.* purj, the act of purging; a purgative: *v.t.* to cleanse or purify; to clear from guilt, moral defilement, or accusation, etc.; to sweep away impurities; to evacuate the bowels by means of a purge; to remove, esp. by violent or unconstitutional means, unwanted or obnoxious elements in a state, community, etc.: *v.i.* to become pure by clarification. (Fr. *purger.*)

purger, *n. pur*-jer, one who or that which purges.

purging, *n. pur*-jing, purgation; assisted evacuation of the bowels; clearing from suspicion or accusation: *a.* having a cleaning effect; purifying; purgative.

purification, *n. pewr*-re-fe-*kay*-shon, the act of purifying; the act or operation of cleansing ceremonially; a cleansing from the guilt or pollution of sin. **purification flower,** the snowdrop.

purificatory, *a. pewr*-re-fe-*kay*-to-re, having power to purify; tending to cleanse.

purifier, *n. pewr*-re-fy-er, one who or that which purifies or cleanses.

puriform, *a. pew*-re-form, like pus; in the form of pus [Med.]. (L. *pus,* and *form.*)

purify, *v.t. pewr*-re-fy, to make pure; to free from guilt or pollution; to free from improprieties or barbarisms: *v.i.* to grow or become pure.

Purim, *n. pew*-rim, among the Jews, the feast of lots, in commemoration of their deliverance from the machinations of Haman. (Heb., lots.)

purine, *n. pewr*-rine, a colourless crystalline basic compound prepared from uric acid.

purism, *n. pewr*-rizm, the practice or profession of purity, esp. in literary style.

purist, *n. pewr*-rist, one scrupulously careful of purity of style; a critic who is severe in matters of style.

puristic, *a.* pewr-*ris*-tik, pertaining to, characterized by, or affecting purism.

puritan, *n.* *pewr*-re-tan, an advocate for purity of religious doctrine and practice, esp. an English Protestant nonconformist of the 16th and 17th cents. : *a.* pertaining to the puritans. (Late L. *puritas.*)
puritanic, *a.* pewr-re-*tan*-ik, puritanical.
puritanical, *a.* pewr-re-*tan*-e-kal, pertaining to or characteristic of the puritans, their doctrines, or practice ; exact or rigid in religious practice, profession, or requirement.
puritanically, *ad.* after the manner of the puritans.
puritanism, *n.* *pewr*-re-ta-nizm, the doctrines, ideas, or practice of the puritans.
puritanize, *v.t.* *pewr*-re-ta-nize, to convert to puritanism ; to give a puritan character to : *v.i.* to practise or teach the puritan doctrine.
puritic, *a.* pewr-*rit*-ik, pertaining to pus [Med.].
purity, *n.* *pewr*-re-te, the condition of being pure ; cleanness ; innocence ; chastity ; freedom from foreign idioms or barbarisms. (O.Fr. *purte.*)
purl, *n.* purl, a gentle murmur as of rippling water ; an eddy : *v.i.* to flow or run with a murmuring sound.
purl, *n.* purl, an embroidered and puckered border ; a minute looped edging on ribbon and lace ; inverted stitches giving a ribbed appearance to knitting : *v.t.* to decorate with a fringe or embroidery ; to invert stitches in knitting. (Origin doubtful.)
purl, *n.* purl, an act of whirling ; a capsize ; a purler : *v.i.* to capsize ; to whirl round rapidly ; to throw a somersault.
purl, *n.* purl, a hot drink of beer, gin, ginger, and sugar ; mixed gin and stout. (Origin unknown.)
purler, *n.* *purl*-er, a fall head-foremost from a horse ; a heavy blow ; a cropper [Slang].
purlieu, *n.* *pur*-lew, an adjacent piece of land, originally of a forest, determined by perambulation ; an outlying district ; a slum or depressed area. (O.Fr. *pouralee,* a going through.)
purlin, *n.* *pur*-lin, a horizontal timber supporting the rafters of a roof [Arch.] (Probably O.Fr.)
purloin, *v.t.* pur-*loyn,* to steal ; to take by theft, or by plagiarism : *v.i.* to practise theft. (O.Fr. *purloignier.*)
purloiner, *n.* pur-*loyn*-er, a thief ; a plagiarist.
purparty, *n.* pur-*par*-te, a share, part, or portion of an estate allotted to a coparcerner by partition [Old Law]. (O.Fr. *porpartie.*)
purple, *a.* *pur*-pl, of the colour of red and blue blended ; livid ; dyed with or as with blood : *n.* a purple colour ; a purple robe, esp. as token of office ; the imperial government or power ; the cardinalate : *pl.* swine fever ; livid spots occurring in certain morbid conditions : *v.t.* to make or dye purple : *v.i.* to become purple. **born in the purple,** of royal or imperial birth, esp. born during the reign of the father. **purple of cassius,** a colloidal gold and stannic oxide forming the colouring constituent of ruby glass, etc. **purple emperor,** the emperor butterfly. **the Purple Heart,** United States military decoration awarded to those killed or wounded by enemy action. (L. *purpura,* Gr. *porphyra.*)
purplewort, *n.* *pur*-pl-wurt, the marsh cinquefoil, *Potentilla palustris,* also the white clover, *Trifolium repens,* and other plants with purplish leaf or flower.
purplish, *a.* *pur*-plish, somewhat purple.
purport, *n.* *pur*-port, design ; meaning ; import.
purport, *v.t.* pur-*port,* to intend ; to signify. (O.Fr. *purporter,* intend.)
purportless, *a.* *pur*-port-less, meaningless ; without object.
***purpose,** *n.* *pur*-pus, end or aim in view ; intention ; design ; effect : *v.t.* to intend ; to resolve : *v.i.* to have an intention or design. **on purpose,** with intent ; not accidentally. (O.Fr. *purposer.*)
purposeful, *a.* *pur*-pus-ful, expressly intended.
purposefully, *ad.* *pur*-pus-ful-le, intentionally.
purposeless, *a.* *pur*-pus-less, having no effect or purpose.
purposely, *ad.* *pur*-pus-le, by design ; intentionally.
purposive, *a.* *pur*-pus-iv, having a purpose.
purpresture, *n.* per-*pres*-tewr, an illegal encroachment [Law]. (Fr.)
Purpura, *n.* *pur*-pewr-ra, a genus of univalve molluscs, some of which yielded the Tyrian purple; (*l.c.*) a disease characterized by livid patches on the skin and mucous membranes, due to subcutaneous extravasation of blood [Med.]. (L., purple.)
purpure, *n.* *pur*-pewr, purple, represented in engraving by diagonal lines from left to right [Her.].
purpureal, *a.* pur-*pewr*-re-al, purple.
purpuric, *a.* pur-*pewr*-rik, pertaining to purpura, or to the colour purple. **purpuric acid,** a purplish nitrogenous acid of the nature of uric acid.
purpurin, *n.* *pur*-pewr-rin, an orange-red dye-stuff originally obtained from madder.
purr, *n.* pur, the low, murmuring, continued sound of a cat : *v.i.* to murmur, as a cat when pleased ; to utter a purr : *v.t.* to signify by purring. (Imit.)
purree, *n.* *poo*-ree, a yellow colouring matter, Indian yellow, used in India and the Far East in out-door paint-work. (Hind. *piuri.*)
purse, *n.* purse, a small bag for money, esp. for the pocket ; a pouch ; a sum of money, esp. as prize-money or a gift ; formerly, a definite (but varying) sum of money in the Moslem Near East : *v.t.* to put in a purse ; to contract into folds or wrinkles. **light purse,** poverty. **long purse,** wealth. **privy purse,** *see* **privy. public purse,** the national treasury. (O.Fr. *borse.*)
purse-crab, *n.* a large land-crab, *Birgus latro,* of certain tropical islands, having a purse-like abdomen.
purse-net, *n.* a large fishing-net, the mouth of which may be drawn together like an old-fashioned purse ; a similar net for catching rabbits.
purse-proud, *a.* proud of possessing wealth.
purser, *n.* *purse*-er, a ship's officer who has charge of the stores, accounts, etc. ; a paymaster.
pursership, *n.* *purse*-er-ship, the office of purser.
purse-seine, *n.* *purse*-sane, a purse-net for catching shoal fish.
pursiness, *n.* *pur*-se-ness, the state of being pursy; shortness of breath.
purslane, *n.* *purse*-lan, the succulent plant *Portulaca oleracea,* used in salads and as a pot-herb. **sea purslane,** the plant *Arenaria peploides.* (O.Fr. *porcelaine.*)
pursuable, *a.* pur-*sew*-a-bl, that may be pursued.
pursuance, *n.* pur-*sew*-ance, the act of pursuing ; that which is pursuant ; consequence.
pursuant, *a.* pur-*sew*-ant, done in consequence of ; agreeable ; conformable. (O.Fr. *pursuivant.*)
pursuantly, *ad.* agreeably.
pursue, *v.t.* pur-*sew,* to follow ; to follow with a view to overtake ; to chase ; to seek ; to take and proceed in ; to prosecute ; to follow as an example ; to endeavour to reach ; to follow with enmity : *v.i.* to go on ; to continue. (O.Fr. *pursuir.*)
pursuer, *n.* pur-*sew*-er, one who pursues ; the plaintiff [Scots. Law].
pursuit, *n.* pur-*sewt,* the act of pursuing ; prosecution ; continuance of endeavour ; that which is pursuit ; a business, sport, etc., that one regularly follows. **pursuit plane,** a fast aeroplane for attacking enemy aircraft. (Fr. *poursuite.*)
pursuivant, *n.* *pur*-swe-vant, a state-messenger ; a junior official of the Heralds' College ; an attendant. (O.Fr. *poursuivant,* pursuing.)
pursy, *a.* *pur*-se, fat, short and thick ; short-breathed. (O.Fr. *pourcif,* from *polser,* to pant.)
purtenance, *n.* *pur*-te-nance, appurtenance ; a beast's intestines.
purulence, *n.* *pewr*-roo-lence, state or quality of being purulent ; generation of pus [Med.].
purulent, *a.* *pewr*-roo-lent, pertaining to, consisting of, or containing pus ; putrid. (L. *purulentus.*)
puruloid, *a.* *pewr*-roo-loyd, resembling or pertaining to pus.
purvey, *v.t.* pur-*vay,* to provide with ; to procure : *v.i.* to purchase provisions ; to provide. (O.Fr. *porvoir.*)
purveyance, *n.* pur-*vay*-ance, procurement of provisions ; victuals provided ; the right of pre-emption according to the Crown.
purveyor, *n.* pur-*vay*-or, one who provides victuals ; a caterer.
purview, *n.* *pur*-vew, scope ; extent ; the body or provisions of a statute [Law]. (O.Fr. *purveu.*)
pus, *n.* pus, purulent matter from a wound or sore, the product of suppuration. (L.)
Puseyism, *n.* *pew*-ze-izm, high-church principles ; tractarianism. (Dr. *Pusey,* 1800–82, its leading advocate.)
Puseyite, *n.* *pew*-ze-ite, an upholder of Puseyism.

★**push,** *v.t.* poosh, to press against with force; to urge or drive forward; to press: *v.i.* to make a thrust; to butt; to make an effort: *n.* a thrust; a force applied; an assault or attack; exigence; extremity; a stroke in billiards by which the ball is pushed; a push-stroke; vigour, "go," energetic effort to succeed; a crowd, set, or gang of people [Slang]. **push on,** to hasten. (O.Fr. *pousser,* from L. *pulsare,* drive.)
pushable, *a. poosh*-a-bl, capable of being pushed.
pushball, *n. poosh*-bawl, a game in which a very large inflated leather ball is pushed by opposing sides towards goals; the ball used.
push-bike, *n.* a bicycle worked by the feet [Coll.].
pushbutton, *a. poosh*-but-tn, denoting remote and immediate control, as "pushbutton warfare."
push-cart, *n.* a hand-cart or hand-barrow.
push-chair, *n.* a small wheeled chair for the use of a child.
pusher, *n. poosh*-er, one who or that which pushes or drives forward; an implement with which to push; a man of energy; an aeroplane with the propeller at the rear of the wings.
pushful, *a. poosh*-ful, enterprising; self-assertive.
push-halfpenny, *n.* shove-halfpenny.
pushing, *a. poosh*-ing, pressing forward in business; energetic; enterprising.
pushingly, *ad.* in a pushing manner.
push-pin, *n.* a child's game in which pins are pushed by pins.
push-stroke, *n.* a stroke in which the ball is pushed instead of being struck [Cricket, Golf, Billiards, etc.].
Pushtu, *n. push*-too, the principal language, of Iranian stock, of the Afghans.
pusillanimity, *n. pew*-se-la-*nim*-e-te, cowardice; want of courage; pusillanimousness.
pusillanimous, *a. pew*-se-*lan*-e-mus, destitute of strength and firmness of mind; cowardly; mean-spirited; feeble. (L. *pusillanimis,* weak-hearted.)
pusillanimously, *ad.* in a pusillanimous spirit.
pusillanimousness, *n.* the quality or state of being pusillanimous.
puss, *n.* poos, a pet name for a cat; a hare. **puss in the corner,** a children's romping game.
puss-moth, *n.* the large moth *Cerura vinula.*
puss-tail, *n.* the bristle grass *Panicum glaucum.*
pussy, *n. poos*-e, a small puss; a kitten. **pussy cat,** a child's name for a cat; a willow catkin.
pussyfoot, *n. poos*-e-foot, an excessively cautious person; an advocate of prohibition or teetotalism: *v.i.* to be chary of taking decisive steps; to hedge. (W. E. Johnson, *d.* 1943, Amer. prohibitionist, had this nickname.)
pussy-willow, *n.* the American willow *Salix discolor.*
pustular, *a. pus*-tew-lar, pustulate.
pustulate, *a. pus*-tew-lat, covered with glandular excrescences like pustules: *v.i.* to form into pustules or blisters [Bot.]. (L. *pustula,* a pimple.)
pustulation, *n.* pus-tew-*lay*-shon, the formation of, or the act of forming, pustules.
pustule, *n. pus*-tewl, a little pimple containing pus.
pustulous, *a. pus*-tew-lus, resembling, characterized by, or full of pustules.
★**put,** *v.t.* poot, to set, lay, or place; to bring to; to apply; to throw in; to present or produce; to express; to force or constrain; to dispose; to incite; to propose, as a question; to offer; to cause: *v.i.* to steer, to proceed [Naut.]: *n.* a throw; a thrust; an agreement to deliver a certain amount of something at a stipulated price within a specified time; an obsolete card-game. **put about,** to change the course [Naut.]; to disseminate. **put and take,** a gambling game played with a teetotum. **put by,** to thrust aside; to evade; to save or store. **put down,** to repress; to degrade; to silence. **put forth,** to propose or offer to notice; to extend; to shoot out; to germinate; to bud; to exert; to publish. **put in,** to enter a harbour. **put in mind,** to remind. **put off,** to lay aside; to delay. **put on,** to superpose; to assume; to clothe oneself with; to advance (as speed or the hand of a clock); to deceive or impose upon. **put out,** to place at interest; to make public; to disconcert. **put up,** to lodge. **put up with,** to tolerate; to endure. **putting the shot,** a field-sport in which a weight is hurled from the shoulder. **to stay put,** to remain in position; to continue as at present. (A.S. *potian.*)
put, *n.* put, putt [Golf].
put, *n.* put, a rustic; a clown [Slang].
putamen, *n.* pew-*tay*-men, the stone of a drupe or shell of a nut [Bot.]; the membrane of an egg; the outer layer of the lenticular nucleus of the brain [Anat.]. (L., a husk.)
putative, *a. pew*-ta-tiv, reputed; commonly supposed. (Fr. *putatif.*)
putatively, *ad. pew*-ta-tiv-le, in a putative way; supposedly.
putchuk, *n.* put-*chuk,* the root of the Kashmir plant, *Saussurea lappa,* used in the East in medicine and perfumery. (Hind.)
puteal, *n. pew*-te-al, the stone curb or enclosure round the mouth of a well. (L. *puteus,* a well.)
putid, *a. pew*-tid, mean; worthless. (L. *pus.*)
putidity, pew-*tid*-e-te, putidness.
putidness, *n. pew*-tid-ness, meanness; vileness.
putlog, *n. put*-log, a short piece of timber for the floor of a scaffold to rest on in building.
putrefacient, *a.* pew-tre-*fay*-she-ent, putrefactive: *n.* any putrefactive agent.
putrefaction, *n.* pew-tre-*fak*-shon, a natural process by which animal and vegetable bodies are decomposed; that which is putrified; decay.
putrefactive, *a.* pew-tre-*fak*-tiv, pertaining to or causing putrefaction.
putrefy, *v.t. pew*-tre-fy, to render putrid, or cause to rot; to make carious or gangrenous: *v.i.* to become putrid; to rot. (O.Fr., from L. *putrere,* to be rotten, and *facere,* to make.)
putrescence, *n.* pew-*tres*-ence, the state of being putrescent; a putrid state.
putrescent, *a.* pew-*tres*-ent, becoming putrid; pertaining to or due to putrefaction. (L.)
putrescible, *a.* pew-*tres*-e-bl, that may be putrefied.
putrid, *a. pew*-trid, in a state of decay (of organic matter); rotten; indicating or due to putrefaction; rotten, contemptible [Slang]. (Fr. *putride.*)
putridity, *n.* pew-*trid*-e-te, putridness; something putrid.
putridness, *n. pew*-trid-ness, the quality or state of being putrid.
putrilage, *pew*-tril-aj, putrescent matter; the product of putrefaction.
putsch, *n.* pooch, a popular rising; a local revolutionary movement. (Ger.)
putt, *n.* putt, a stroke intended to hole the ball: *v.t.* to play the ball towards or into the hole when on the putting green [Golf]. **putting green,** the mown and tended area surrounding each hole on a golf-course.
puttee, *n. put*-e, a spiral cloth legging; a leather gaiter with an encircling strap from bottom to top. (Hind.)
putter, *n. put*-er, a short club used for putting [Golf].
puttock, *n. put*-ok, old local name for birds of prey as the kite, buzzard, and marsh-harrier.
putty, *n. put*-e, cement composed of whiting and linseed oil used in glazing: *v.t.* to cement with putty. **plasterer's putty,** fine white lime held in solution by slaking. **putty powder,** a powder of calcined tin or lead used in polishing glass, steel, etc. (O.Fr. *potée.*)
puy, *n.* pwee, a conical hill of volcanic origin, esp. in Auvergne, France. (Fr.)
puzzle, *n. puz*-zl, perplexity; embarrassment; something that puzzles: *v.t.* to perplex; to embarrass; to make intricate; to resolve laboriously: *v.i.* to be bewildered. (Origin unknown.)
puzzledom, *n. puz*-zl-dom, bewilderment.
puzzle-headed, *a.* having the head full of confused notions.
puzzlement, *n. puz*-zl-ment, puzzled state.
puzzler, *n. puz*-zler, one who or that which perplexes.
puzzling, *a. puz*-zling, perplexing; bewildering.
puzzolana, *n. put*-zo-*lah*-na, pozzuolana.
pyæmia, *n.* py-*ee*-me-a, blood-poisoning, due to the absorption into the system of putrid matter. (Gr. *pyon,* pus, *haima,* blood.)
pyæmic, *a.* py-*ee*-mik, pertaining to pyæmia.
pycnite, *n. pik*-nite, a massive variety of topaz. (Gr. *pyknos,* dense.)
pycnodont, *n. pik*-no-dont, any member of an extinct family of fishes abundant esp. in the Oolite: *a.* pertaining to or resembling this family. (Gr. *pyknos,* and *odous,* a tooth.)
Pycnogonid, *n. pik*-no-*gon*-id, a sea-spider.

pycnometer, *n.* pik-*nom*-e-ter, a vessel for measuring the density or specific gravity of fluids.
pycnostyle, *n.* *pik*-no-stile, a colonnade in which the columns stand very close [Arch.]. (Gr. *pychnos*, and *stylos*, a pillar.)
pye, *n.* py, the pie (magpie).
pyedog, *n.* *py*-dog, a pariah dog [Anglo-Ind.]. (Hind. *pahi*, outsider, and *dog*.)
pyelitis, *n.* py-el-*ly*-tis, inflammation of the pelvis of the kidney. (Gr. *pyelos*, trough, pelvis.)
pygal, *a.* *py*-gal, pertaining to the posteriors. (Gr. *pygē*, rump.)
pygmean, *a.* pig-*mee*-an, pertaining to a pigmy or dwarf; very small; dwarfish.
pygmoid, *a.* *pig*-moyd, resembling or of the nature of the Pygmies of Central Africa.
pygmy, *n.* *pig*-me, a dwarf; one of a race of dwarfs of Greek myth who waged war with the cranes; (*cap.*) one of a dwarfish negroid people of Central Africa: *a.* dwarfish; of diminutive size. (Gr. *pygmaioi*, the dwarfs.)
pyjamas, *n.pl.* pi-*jah*-maz, a sleeping suit of jacket and trousers; a pair of loose trousers. (Per.)
pyknometer, *n.* pik-*nom*-e-ter, a pycnometer.
pylon, *n.* *py*-lon, a gateway; a landmark for aircraft; a pyramidal supporting or protective structure in an aircraft; a skeleton tower on which overhead cables are supported. (Gr.)
pyloric, *a.* py-*lo*-rik, pertaining to the pylorus.
pylorus, *n.* py-*law*-rus, the lower and right orifice of the stomach, leading into the intestines. (Gr., from *pyle*, a gate, *ouros*, a watcher.)
pyogenic, *a.* py-o-*jen*-ik, pertaining to the formation of pus; secreting pus.
pyogenesis, *n.* py-o-*jen*-e-sis, the formation of pus. (Gr. *pyon*, pus, *genesis*, creation.)
pyoid, *a.* *py*-oyd, of the nature of pus. (Gr. *pyon*, pus, *eidos*, like.)
pyophthalmitis, *n.* *py*-of-thal-*my*-tis, purulent ophthalmia [Path.].
pyorrhœa, *n.* py-o-*ree*-a, a discharge of pus. **pyorrhœa alveolaris,** inflammation of, with suppuration in, the sockets of the teeth. (Gr. *pyon*, pus, *rhein*, flow.)
pyosis, *n.* py-*oh*-sis, suppuration [Med.].
pyracanth, *n.* *pyr*-ra-kanth, an evergreen species of thorn with white flowers and red berries. (Gr. *pyr*, fire, *akantha*, a thorn.)
pyrallolite, *n.* py-*ral*-o-lite, an altered form of augite, a greenish mineral found in Finland. (Gr. *pyr*, and *lithos*, a stone.)
pyramid, *n.* *pi*-ra-mid, a solid body standing on a triangular, square, or polygonal base, and terminating in a point at the top; a sepulchral, square-based stone structure of this form, esp. of ancient Egypt; any pyramidal structure or part: *pl.* a variety of pool, played on the billiard-table. (Gr. *pyramis*.)
pyramidal, *a.* pi-*ram*-id-al, relating to a pyramid or the Egyptian pyramids; of the form of a pyramid.
pyramidally, *ad.* in a pyramidal manner.
pyramidical, *a.* pi-ra-*mid*-e-kal, pyramidal; having the form of a pyramid.
pyramidoid, *n.* pi-*ram*-id-oyd, a solid resembling a pyramid. (*pyramid*, and Gr. *eidos*, like.)
pyramidoidal, *a.* pi-ra-me-*doy*-dal, like a pyramid.
pyrargillite, *n.* pi-*rar*-je-lite, an altered form of iolite having a clayey odour when heated. (Gr. *pyro-*, and *argillos*, clay.)
pyrargyrite, *n.* pi-*rar*-je-rite, a sulphide of silver and antimony forming a valuable ore of silver. (Gr. *pyro-*, and *argyros*, silver.)
pyre, *n.* pire, a funeral pile. (Gr.)
pyrene, *n.* *pyr*-reen, a putamen; the stone of a drupe [Bot.]. (Gr. *purēn*.)
pyrene, *n.* *pyr*-reen, a white crystalline hydrocarbon present in coal-tar [Chem.]. (Gr. *pyr*, fire.)
pyreneite, *n.* py-*ree*-ne-ite, a greyish variety of garnet [Min.].
pyrethrum, *n.* py-*ree*-thrum, any plant of the chrysanthemum family, esp. the feverfew; an insect-powder made from the flower-heads of certain of these.
pyretic, *a.* py-*ret*-ik, relating to, allaying, or curing fever: *n.* a medicine for curing fever. (Gr. *pyretos*, from *pyr*, fire.)
pyretogenous, *a.* pyr-re-*toj*-e-nus, producing fever [Med.].
pyretology, *n.* py-re-*tol*-o-je, that branch of medicine which treats of fevers.
pyrex, *n.* *pyr*-reks, proprietary name of a make of glassware that withstands high temperatures without breaking.
pyrexia, *n.* py-*rek*-se-a, the febrile state; feverish condition. (Gr. *pyrexis*.)
pyrexial, *a.* pir-*rek*-se-al, feverish.
pyrheliometer, *n.* per-hee-le-*om*-e-ter, an instrument for measuring the intensity of the sun's heat. (Gr. *pyr*, fire, *helios*, the sun, *metron*, measure.)
pyridine, *n.* *pyr*-re-dine, a colourless nitrogenous liquid obtained from coal-tar, etc., used as an antiseptic and antispasmodic, as a germicide and a denaturant of alcohol.
pyriform, *a.* *pyr*-re-form, pear-shaped. (L. *pyrum*, a pear, and *form*.)
pyritaceous, *a.* pyr-re-*tay*-shus, pyritic.
pyrite, *n.* *pyr*-rite, iron disulphide, a native crystalline brass-like mineral used as a source of sulphuric acid.
pyrites, *n.* pe-*ry*-teez, pyrite, or any other native combination of sulphur with a metal (copper, cobalt, tin, etc.), so called because it strikes fire with steel. (L., flint.)
pyritic, *a.* pe-*rit*-ik, pertaining to, or resembling, or characteristic of, pyrites.
pyritiferous, *a.* pyr-re-*tif*-er-rus, producing pyrites.
pyritize, *v.t.* *pyr*-re-tize, to convert into pyrites.
pyritology, *n.* pyr-re-*tol*-o-je, the study of pyrites.
pyritous, *a.* *pyr*-re-tus, pyritic.
pyro, *n.* *pyr*-ro, pyrogallic acid [Coll.].
pyro-, *pyr*-ro *or* *pi*-ro, Greek prefix denoting produced or modified by heat, as **pyro-acid,** an acid obtained from the ordinary acid by subjection to heat [Chem.]. (Gr. *pyr*, fire.)
pyro-cellulose, *n.* a variety of pyroxylin used in smokeless powders.
pyrochlore, *n.* *pyr*-ro-klore, a mineral consisting mainly of columbate and titanate of calcium, occurring in brownish octahedrons. (Gr. *pyro-*, and *chloros*, green.)
pyroclastic, *n.* pyr-ro-*klas*-tik, formed by fragmentation of rock, etc., by volcanic action [Geol.].
pyro-electric, *a.* becoming in a state of electric polarity under heat: *n.* a body which does so.
pyrogallic, *a.* pyr-ro-*gal*-lik, obtained from gallic acid by heating it. **pyrogallic acid,** a poisonous crystalline phenol, an alkaline solution of which is used as a developing agent [Phot.].
pyrogallol, *n.* pyr-ro-*gal*-ol, pyrogallic acid [Chem.].
pyrogenic, *a.* py-ro-*jen*-ik, producing heat, or [Med.] feverishness; pyretogenous. (Gr. *pyro-*, and *gennao*, produce.)
pyrogenetic, *a.* pyr-ro-je-*net*-ik, pyrogenic.
pyrogenous, *a.* py-*roj*-en-us, produced by fire; igneous [Geol.].
pyrognomic, pyr-rog-*nom*-ik, readily becoming incandescent when heated.
pyrographist, *n.* pyr-*rog*-ra-fist, a craftsman in pyrography.
pyrography, *n.* py-*rog*-ra-fe, poker-work; the art of drawing on wood with a red-hot point.
pyrogravure, *n.* *pyr*-ro-gra-*vewr*, a piece of poker-work; pyrography.
pyrolatry, *n.* py-*rol*-a-tre, worship of fire. (Gr. *pyro-*, and *latreia*, worship.)
pyroligneous, *a.* pyr-ro-*lig*-ne-us, generated by the distillation of wood. **pyroligneous acid,** impure acetic acid. (Gr. *pyro-*, and L. *lignum*, wood.)
pyrolignic, *a.* pyr-ro-*lig*-nik, pyroligneous.
pyrolignite, *n.* pyr-ro-*lig*-nite, a salt of pyroligneous acid.
pyrologist, *n.* py-*rol*-o-jist, one versed in the science of heat; one who uses the blowpipe [Chem.].
pyrology, *n.* py-*rol*-o-je, the science of heat; blowpipe analysis; a treatise on the blowpipe. (Gr. *pyro-*, and *logos*, science.)
pyrolusite, *n.* pyr-ro-*lew*-site, manganese dioxide, the chief ore of manganese. (Gr. *pyro-*, and *lyo*, wash.)
pyrolysis, *n.* py-*ro* -e-sis, chemical decomposition of a substance by the action of heat.
pyromagnetic. *a.* *pyr*-ro-mag-*net*-ik, pertaining to magnetism as affected by changes in temperature.
pyromancy, *n.* *pyr*-ro-man-se, divination by fire. (Gr. *pyro-*, and *manteia*, divination.)
pyromania, *n.* pyr-ro-*may*-ne-a, an insane passion

to destroy by fire; maniacal incendiarism. (Gr. *pyro-*, and *mania*).

pyrometamorphism, *n.* *pyr*-ro-met-a-*mor*-fizm, metamorphism, esp. in rocks, due to the action of heat.

pyrometer, *n.* py-*rom*-e-ter, an instrument for measuring the expansion of bodies by heat; an instrument for measuring high degrees of temperature. (Gr. *pyro-*, and *metron*, measure.)

pyrometrical, *a.* pyr-ro-*met*-re-kal, pertaining to the pyrometer or pyrometry.

pyrometry, *n.* py-*rom*-e-tre, the measurement of heat by expansion; the measurement of high degrees of heat.

pyromorphite, *n.* pyr-ro-*mor*-fite, a native crystalline lead chloride and phosphate.

pyromorphosis, *n.* pyr-ro-mor-*foh*-sis, pyrometamorphism.

pyromorphous, *a.* pyr-ro-*mor*-fus, having the property of crystallization after fusion by heat [Min.]. (Gr. *pyro-*, and *morphe*, shape.)

pyrope, *n.* *pyr*-rope, a brilliant red garnet, Bohemian garnet. (Gr. *pyr*, fire, *ops*, the face.)

pyrophanous, *a.* py-*rof*-an-us, rendered transparent or translucent by heat. (Gr. *pyro-*, and *phaino*, show.)

pyrophobia, *n.* pyr-ro-*foh*-be-a, morbid dread of fire.

pyrophoric, *a.* pyr-ro-*fo*-rik, pertaining to or of the nature of a pyrophorus.

pyrophorous, *a.* pyr-*rof*-o-rus, pyrophoric; consisting of a pyrophorus.

pyrophorus, *n.* pyr-*rof*-o-rus, any substance which spontaneously takes fire on exposure to air. (Gr. *pyro-*, and *phoros*, bearing.)

pyroscope, *n.* *pyr*-ro-skope, an instrument for measuring the intensity of radiant heat or cold. (Gr. *pyro-*, and *skopeo*, view.)

pyroscopy, *n.* pyr-*ros*-ko-pe, pyromancy.

pyrosis, *n.* pyr-*roh*-sis, water-brash, a form of indigestion accompanied by heartburn and eructation of an acid or tasteless fluid. (Gr., burning.)

pyrosmalite, *n.* pyr-ro-*zmal*-ite, a hydrous iron and manganese silicate emitting an odour of chlorine when heated.

pyrosome, *n.* *pyr*-ro-sohm, a tropical pelagic ascidian remarkable for its phosphorescence. (Gr. *pyro-*, and *soma*, a body.)

pyrostat, *n.* *pyr*-ro-stat, a thermostat.

pyrotechnic, *a.* py-ro-*tek*-nik, pertaining to fireworks or to pyrotechnics.

pyrotechnics, *n.* pyr-ro-*tek*-niks, the art or science of making fireworks. (Gr. *pyro-*, and *techne*, art.)

pyrotechnist, *n.* pyr-ro-*tek*-nist, a maker of fireworks.

pyrotechny, *n.* pyr-ro-*tek*-ne, pyrotechnics.

pyrotherapy, *n.* pyr-ro-*the*-ra-pe, thermotherapy; cauterization [Med.].

pyrothere, *n.* *pyr*-ro-theer, a member of the Pyrotheria, a group of extinct rhinoceros-like ungulates of the South American Eocene.

pyrotoxin, *n.* pyr-ro-*tok*-sin, a toxin produced by fever [Path.].

pyroxene, *n.* py-*rok*-seen, name of a group of silicates of calcium and magnesium, including diopside, augite, and many similar minerals. (Gr. *pyro-*, and *xenos*, a stranger.)

pyroxenic, *a.* py-rok-*sen*-ik, pertaining or composed of pyroxene.

pyroxyle, *n.* py-*rok*-sil, pyroxylin.

pyroxylic, *a.* pi-rok-*sil*-ik, obtained by the destructive distillation of wood (of crude spirit).

pyroxylin, *n.* pi-*rok*-se-lin, gun-cotton, or other explosive substance, obtained by treating cellulose with nitric or nitro-sulphuric acid. (Gr. *pyro-*, and *xylon*, wood.)

Pyrrhic, *a.* *pi*-rik, pertaining to Pyrrhus. **Pyrrhic victory,** a victory gained at a ruinous cost. (*Pyrrhus*, who defeated the Romans at Asculum, 279 B.C., but suffered grievous losses.)

pyrrhic, *n.* *pi*-rik, a metrical foot, consisting of two short syllables; an ancient military dance of the Greeks: *a.* pertaining to either of these. (Gr., from *Purrhichos*, the inventor.)

Pyrrhonism, *n.* *pi*-ron-izm, scepticism, or universal doubt. (*Pyrrho*, the founder of a school of Greek sceptics, 4th cent. B.C.)

Pyrrhonist, *n.* *pi*-ron-ist, an adherent of Pyrrhonism; a sceptic.

pyrrhotite, *n.* *pi*-ro-tite, magnetic iron sulphide; magnetic pyrites. (Gr. *pyrrhos*, ruddy.)

Pyrus, *n.* *pyr*-rus, a large genus of rosaceous trees, including the pears, apples, medlars, and mountain-ashes. (L., a pear-tree.)

Pythagorean, *n.* py-thag-o-*ree*-an, a follower of the Greek philosopher and mathematician Pythagoras (6th cent. B.C.): *a.* pertaining to him or his philosophy.

Pythagoreanism, *n.* py-thag-o-*ree*-a-nizm, the doctrines of Pythagoras.

Pythiad, *n.* *pith*-e-ad, the period (4 years) between two celebrations of the Pythian games. (Gr.)

Pythian, *a.* *pith*-e-an, pertaining to the Pythoness, the priestess of Apollo. **Pythian games,** one of the four great Panhellenic festivals, anciently held every fourth year at Delphi. (*Pytho*, earlier name of Delphi.)

pythogenic, *a.* py-tho-*jen*-ik, produced by dirt, filth, or putrefaction. (Gr. *pythein*, to rot, *gennao*, produce.)

Python, *n.* *py*-thon, the serpent slain by Apollo [Gr. Myth.]; a genus of large non-venomous snakes allied to the boa constrictors.

Pythoness, *n.* *py*-thon-ess, the priestess who gave oracular answers at Delphi, Greece; a sort of witch. (Gr. *Pytho*, Delphi.)

pythonic, *a.* py-*thon*-ik, pertaining to prophecy; prophetic; oracular; huge, python-like.

pythonism, *n.* *py*-thon-izm, divination after the manner of the Delphic oracle.

pyuria, *n.* py-*ewr*-re-a, the presence of pus in the urine.

pyx, *n.* piks, a small enclosed case or vessel in which the consecrated host is kept [Eccles.]; a box at the Royal Mint to hold sample coins for testing: *v.t.* to test the weight and fineness of coins. **trial of the pyx,** the assaying of gold and silver coins before issue. (L. *pyxis*, a box.)

pyxidium, *n.* pik-*sid*-e-um (*pl.* **pyxidia**), a capsule which divides circularly into an upper and lower half, as in the pimpernels [Bot.]. (Gr. *pyxidion*, a little box.)

pyxis, *n.* *pik*-sis, a small covered vase; a casket, esp. for jewels; a pyxidium [Bot.]; the acetabulum of the hip-bone [Anat.]. (L.)

Q

Q, kew, seventeenth letter of the English alphabet. With the vowel *u*, by which it is always followed (except in some transliterations from Oriental languages), it usually has the sound of *kw* when used initially (*quaint*, *queen*, but not in *quoit*), and that of *k* when in the final position (*clique*, *burlesque*). Q is never used to end a word (the names *Iraq* and *du Parcq* being exceptions). In Old English its sound was usually represented by *cw*.
Q-boat, *n.* *kew*-bote, a warship disguised as a merchantman; a mystery ship. (A "query" boat.)
qua, *ad.* kway, as being; in the capacity of. (L.
qua-bird, *n.* *kwah*- or *kwaw*-bird, the American night-heron, *Nycticorax nævius*. (From its call.)
quack, *n.* kwak, the cry of a duck; a quacksalver; one who pretends to knowledge or skill which he does not possess: *a.* pertaining to quacks; characterized by quackery; prescribed by a quack: *v.i.* to cry like a duck; to boast. (From the sound.)
quackery, *n.* *kwak*-er-re, the methods or practices of a quack; charlatanry; empiricism.
quackish, *a.* *kwak*-ish, like a quack; boasting of skill not possessed.
quackism, *n.* *kwak*-izm, quack practice or pretence.
quacksalver, *n.* *kwak*-sal-ver, one who boasts of his skill in medicines and salves; a pretender to medical skill; a quack. (Dut. *kwakzalver*, to boast of one's salves.)
quad, *n.* kwod, a quadrangle, esp. of a college; a quadrat [Print.]; quod, prison [Slang].
quadra, *n.* *kwod*-ra, a square border or frame; the plinth of a pedestal, etc. [Arch.]. (L., a square.)
quadrable, *a.* *kwod*-ra-bl, capable of being squared; that can be expressed in a finite number of terms [Math.].
quadragenarian, *a.* and *n.* *kwod*-ra-je-*nare*-re-an, (of) a person who has attained the age of forty, and is not yet fifty. (L. *quadragenius*.)
quadragene, *n.* *kwod*-ra-jeen, a formerly granted papal indulgence for forty days.
Quadragesima, *n.* kwod-ra-*jes*-e-ma, Lent, so called because it consists of forty days. **Quadragesima Sunday,** the first Sunday in Lent. (L., fortieth.)
quadragesimal, *a.* kwod-ra-*jes*-e-mal, lasting forty days; pertaining to or used in Lent: *n.pl.* offerings formerly made to the mother-church of a diocese on Mid-Lent Sunday.
quadrangle, *n.* kwod-*rang*-gl, a plane figure with four angles and four sides [Geom.]; a rectangular court surrounded by buildings. (Fr.)
quadrangular, *a.* kwod-*rang*-gew-lar, having four angles and four sides.
quadrangularly, *ad.* in quadrangular form.
quadrant, *n.* *kwod*-rant, the quarter of a circle (an arc of 90°) or of a sphere; a graduated instrument for making angular measurements, esp. one formerly used for taking altitudes at sea. **quadrant of altitude,** a thin pliable strip of brass used to measure distances on an artificial globe. (O.Fr.)
quadrantal, *a.* kwod-*ran*-tal, pertaining to, resembling, or included in a quadrant.
quadrat, *n.* *kwod*-rat, a piece of metal of less than type-high used for spacing type [Print.]; an instrument formerly used in taking altitudes. (O.Fr.)
quadrate, *a.* *kwod*-rate, having four equal and parallel sides; square: *n.* a square; quadrature [Astron.]: *v.i.* to square; to suit; to correspond; to agree: *v.t.* to make square, corresponding, or conformable. (L. *quadratus*, square, from *quatuor*, four.)
quadratic, *a.* kwa-*drat*-ik, involving a square; *n.* a quadratic equation: *pl.* the algebra of quadratic equations. **quadratic equation,** an equation in which the unknown quantity is a square and of no higher power [Alg.].
quadratrix, *n.* kwa-*dray*-triks, a curve, by means of which straight lines equal to the circumference of circles or other curves and the several parts can be found [Geom.]. (L., fem. of *quadrator*.)
quadrature, *n.* *kwod*-ra-tewr, the act of squaring; the reducing of the area of a circle or any enclosed figure to that of a square; a quadrate distance of 90° of a heavenly body from another, esp. of the moon from the sun [Astron.]. (Late L. *quadratura*.)
quadrel, *n.* *kwod*-rel, a kind of artificial stone in square blocks; a square tile. (Late L. *quadrellus*.)
quadrennial, *a.* kwod-*ren*-e-al, comprising or lasting four years; happening once in four years. (L. *quadriennium*, a period of four years.)
quadrennially, *ad.* once in four years.
quadri-, *kwod*-re, prefix signifying having or consisting of four, or fourth. (L., from *quatuor*, four.)
quadribasic, *a.* kwod-re-*bay*-sik, with four of base for one of acid [Chem.]. (L. *quadri-*, and *basic*.)
quadricapsular, *a.* kwod-re-*kap*-sew-lar, having four capsules [Bot.].
quadricentennial, *n.* kwod-re-sen-*ten*-e-al, a four-hundredth anniversary; its celebration; pertaining to this.
quadriceps, *n.* *kwod*-re-seps, the four-headed extensor muscle of the front of the thigh [Anat.].
quadricorn, *n.* *kwod*-re-kawrn, any animal with four horns or antennæ: *a.* having four horns or antennæ [Zool.].
quadricostate, *a.* kwod-re-*kos*-tate, having four ribs.
quadricycle, *n.* *kwod*-re-sy-kl, a four-wheeled velocipede; a motor carrier with four wheels and a bicycle seat for driver.
quadridentate, *a.* kwod-re-*den*-tat, having four indentations or tooth-like projections [Bot.].
quadridigitate, *a.* kwod-re-*dij*-e-tat, with four digits.
quadrifid, *a.* *kwod*-re-fid, having four lobes or segments; four-cleft [Bot.].
quadrifoliate, *a.* kwod-re-*foh*-le-at, four-leaved [Bot.].
quadriga, *n.* kwod-*ry*-ga, a two-wheeled chariot drawn by four horses abreast. (L. *quadrijuga*, four together.)
quadrigeminal, *a.* *kwod*-re-*jem*-e-nal, having four similar parts [Anat.].
quadrigenarious, *a.* *kwod*-re-je-*nare*-re-us, consisting of four hundred. (L.)
quadrijugate, *a.* kwod-re-*joo*-gat, pinnate, with four pairs of leaflets [Bot.].
quadrilingual, *a.* kwod-re-*ling*-gwal, using or composed of four languages.
quadrilateral, *a.* kwod-re-*lat*-er-ral, having four sides: *n.* a plane figure with four sides and four angles; a quadrangular figure. **the Quadrilateral,** the four fortresses of N. Italy, Mantua, Verona, Peschiera and Legnago. (L. *quadrilaterus*, four-sided.)
quadriliteral, *a.* kwod-re-*lit*-er-ral, consisting of four letters: *n.* a quadriliteral word.
quadrille, *n.* kwa-*dril* or ka-*dril*, a square dance in which no fewer than four couples can take part; the music for this; an obsolete four-handed card-game played with 40 cards. (Fr., from Sp.)
quadrillé, *a.* kwo-*dril*-ay, marked off in squares; ruled with equidistant horizontal and vertical lines (of paper). (Fr.)
quadrillion, *n.* kwo-*dril*-yon, in Gt. Britain, a million trillions (a million to the fourth power); in U.S.A. and France, a thousand billions.
quadrilobate, *a.* kwod-re-*loh*-bat, having four lobes [Bot.].
quadrilocular, *a.* kwod-re-*lok*-yew-lar, four-celled [Bot.].
quadrinomial, *a.* kwod-re-*noh*-me-al, consisting of four terms: *n.* a quantity consisting of four terms [Alg.]. (L. *quadri-*, and *nomen*, a name.)
quadripartite, *a.* kwod-re-*par*-tite, divided into four parts. (L. *quadripartitus*.)
quadripartition, *n.* kwod-re-par-*tish*-on, a division by four or into four equal parts.

quadripennate, *a.* kwod-re-*pen*-at, four-winged [Entom.]: *n.* a four-winged insect.
quadriphyllous, *a.* kwod-re-*fil*-us, four-leaved [Bot.]. (L. *quadri-*, and *phyllon*, a leaf.)
quadrireme, *n.* *kwod*-re-reem, a galley with four benches of oars. (L. *quadriremis.*)
quadrisection, *n.* kwod-re-*sek*-shon, division into four equal parts.
quadrisyllabic, *a.* *kwod*-re-se-*lab*-ik, consisting of four syllables.
quadrisyllable, *n.* kwod-re-*sil*-a-bl, a word consisting of four syllables.
quadrivalent, *a.* *kwod*-re-*vay*-lent, tetravalent.
quadrivalvular, *a.* kwod-re-*val*-vew-lar, four-valved [Bot.].
quadrivial, *a.* kwod-*riv*-e-al, having four ways meeting in a point. (L. *quadrivius.*)
quadrivium, *n.* kwod-*riv*-e-um, the mediæval four-branched course of higher study, consisting of arithmetic, music, geometry, and astronomy. (L.)
quadroon, *n.* kwo-*droon*, the offspring of a mulatto and a white; a person quarter negro and three-fourths white-blooded; any analogous hybrid. (Sp. *cuarteron.*)
quadrumanous, *a.* kwo-*droo*-ma-nus, four-handed; pertaining to the Quadrumana, or primates the feet of which have the form of hands [Zool].
quadruped, *a.* *kwod*-roo-ped, four-legged and four-footed: *n.* a quadruped mammal. (L. *quadrupedus*, four-footed.)
quadrupedal, *a.* kwod-*roo*-pe-dal, having or using four limbs; pertaining to a quadruped.
quadruple, *a.* *kwod*-roo-pl, fourfold: *v.t.* to multiply by four.
quadruplet, *n.* *kwod*-roo-plet, a set or combination of four similar things; a cycle for four riders: *pl.* four children born at one birth.
quadruplex, *a.* *kwod*-roo-pleks, fourfold; designating a telegraphic system by which two messages can be sent simultaneously in each direction on one wire.
quadruplicate, *a.* kwod-*roo*-ple-kat, fourfold: *n.* one of a set of four, or of four copies; quadruplicity: *v.t.* to make fourfold. (L. *quadruplicatus.*)
quadruplication, *n.* kwod-roo-ple-*kay*-shon, act of making fourfold.
quadruplicity, *n.* *kwod*-roo-*plis*-e-te, the state of being quadruplex.
quære, *n.* *kweer*-re, a query: *v.t.* to question; to inquire. (L., imperative of *quærere*, to ask.)
quæstor, *n.* *kwees*-tor, an official in ancient Rome having charge of public funds. (L.)
quæstorial, *a.* kwee-*staw*-re-al, pertaining to a quæstor or his office.
quæstorship, *n.* *kwees*-tor-ship, the position or term of office of a quæstor.
quæstuary, *a.* *kwees*-tew-a-re, profit-seeking; money-making; relating to gain.
quaff, *n.* kwahf *or* kwof, a draught: *v.t.* to drink; to swallow in large draughts; *v.i.* to drink largely. (Origin unknown.)
quaffer, *n.* *kwah*-fer *or* *kwof*-er, one who quaffs or drinks largely.
quag, *n.* kwag *or* kwog, a boggy area; a quagmire (Imit.)
quagga, *n.* *kwag*-a, a species of the genus *Equus*, striped only on the fore-parts, and intermediate between the zebras and asses, formerly abundant in S. Africa but now extinct. (Native; from its cry.)
quaggy, *a.* *kwag*-(*kwog*-)e, yielding to or trembling under the feet, as soft, wet earth; boggy. (*quagmire.*)
quagmire, *n.* *kwag*-(*kwog*-)mire, a quag; a piece of soft, wet ground that yields under the foot.
quahog, *n.* *kwaw*-hog *or* kwa-*hog*, the thick-shelled round clam, *Venus mercenaria*, of the N. American Atlantic coast. (Amerind. *poquanhoc.*)
quaich, *n.* quaych, a shallow drinking-cup. (Celt. *cuach.*)
quail, *v.i.* kwale, to lose heart; to flinch; to be afraid; to cower. (Perhaps A.S. *cwelan*, to die.)
quail, *n.* kwale, a small game-bird of the genus *Coturnix.* **bush quail,** a small partridge of S. Europe and Asia; the turnix. **painted quail,** an Asiatic bird of the genus *Excalphatoria.* **swamp quail,** an Australian bird of the genus *Synoicus.* (O.Fr. *quaille.*)
quail-call, *n.* a quail-pipe.
quail-pipe, *n.* a pipe or call for alluring quails into a net.
quaint, *a.* kwaynt, odd; fanciful; old-fashioned; antique. (O.Fr. *coint.*)
quaintly, *ad.* in a quaint manner.
quaintness, *n.* the quality of being quaint.
quake, *n.* kwake, a trembling; a shudder; an earthquake [Coll.]: *v.i.* to shake with emotion; to tremble; to shudder. (A.S. *cwacian*, to quake.)
quaker, *n.* *kwake*-er, one who quakes; (*cap.*) a member of the Society of Friends, a religious body founded by George Fox (*d.* 1691), so first called (originally in derision) *c.* 1650. **quaker gun,** a dummy gun mounted to deceive an enemy.
quaker-bird, *n.* the sooty albatross.
Quakeress, *n.* *kwake*-er-ess, a female Quaker.
Quakerish, *a.* *kwake*-er-ish, like a Quaker.
Quakerism, *n.* *kwake*-er-izm, the tenets, manners, and characteristics of the Quakers.
Quakerly, *a.* *kwake*-er-le, resembling Quakers.
quakiness, *n.* *kwake*-e-ness, condition of being quaky.
quaking-grass, *n.* any grass of the genus *Briza*, whose spikelets have a tremulous motion.
quaky, *a.* *kwake*-e, apt to quake; tremulous; shaky.
qualifiable, *a.* *kwol*-e-fy-a-bl, that may be qualified, abated, or modified.
qualification, *n.* *kwol*-e-fe-*kay*-shon, suitable acquirement and ability; act of qualifying; state or fact of being qualified; legal or requisite power; modification; limitation; restriction.
qualificative, *a.* *kwol*-e-fe-kay-tiv, serving to qualify: *n.* that which serves to qualify.
qualificatory, *a.* *kwol*-e-fe-*kay*-to-re, relating to qualification.
qualified, *a.* *kwol*-e-fide, competent; fitted with the requisite qualifications; modified.
qualifiedly, *ad.* with qualification.
qualifiedness, *n.* state of being qualified.
qualifier, *n.* *kwol*-e-fy-er, he who or that which qualifies or modifies.
qualify, *v.t.* *kwol*-e-fy, to make fit; to make capable of any employment or privilege; to abate; to soften; to ease; to modify; to limit; to dilute; to regulate; to vary. (Fr. *qualifier.*)
qualitative, *a.* *kwol*-e-tay-tiv, relating to quality. **qualitative analysis,** determination only of the nature, and not the amounts, of the constituents of a substance [Chem.].
★**quality,** *n.* *kwol*-e-te, an attribute, characteristic, or property; nature, relatively considered; relative virtue or particular power; disposition; temper; acquirement; accomplishment; character; comparative rank; superior rank; the upper classes collectively. (Fr. *qualité.*)
qualm, *n.* kwahm, faintness; a fit or a sensation of nausea; a scruple of conscience. (A.S. *cwealm.*)
qualmish, *a.* *kwah*-mish, squeamish; inclined to vomit; affected with nausea.
qualmishly, *ad.* in a qualmish manner.
qualmishness, *n.* state or condition of being qualmish; nausea.
qualmy, *a.* *kwah*-me, qualmish.
quamash, *n.* *kwah*-mash, any plant of the N. American genus *Camassia*; the edible bulb of these.
quamoclit, *n.* *kwam*-o-klit, a tropical climbing plant of the genus *Ipomœa.* (Mex.)
quandary, *n.* *kwon*-da-re *or* kwon-*dare*-re, state of difficulty or perplexity. (Origin unknown.)
quandong, *n.* *kwon*-dong, the Australian tree, *Fusianus acuminatus*; its edible peach-like fruit, or nut. (Austral.)
quannet, *n.* *kwon*-et, a flat file used by comb-makers.
quant, *n.* kwont, a long pole with a flanged end for use in punting: *v.t.* to propel with this. (Dial.)
quantic, *n.* *kwon*-tik, a rational function of variables [Algebra]. (L. *quantus.*)
quantification, *n.* *kwon*-te-fe-*kay*-shon, the act of quantifying; modification by reference to quantity.
quantify, *v.t.* *kwon*-te-fy, to express or determine the quantity of; to indicate the quantity or extent of, as the predicate [Logic]. (L. *quantus*, how much, and *facio*, make.)
quantimeter, *n.* kwon-*tim*-e-ter, an instrument for measuring the amount of X-rays to which a patient is exposed [Med.].
quantitative, *a.* *kwon*-te-ta-tiv, relating to quantity; estimable according to quantity (opposed to

qualitative). **quantitative analysis,** determination of the amount of each element constituting a compound or substance [Chem.].
quantitatively, *ad.* in a quantitive manner.
quantitive, *a. kwon*-te-tiv, quantitative.
quantity, *n. kwon*-te-te, that property of anything which may be increased or diminished; extent, bulk, weight, or measure; amount; anything which can be multiplied, divided, or measured [Math.]; the measure or duration of a syllable [Pros.]; the extent of an assertion [Logic]; the relative duration of a tone [Mus.]. **quantity surveyor,** an expert who estimates the dimensions, area, prices, etc. of builders' work. (Fr. *quantité.*)
quantivalence, *n.* kwon-*tiv*-a-lence, valence [Chem.].
quantum, *n. kwon*-tum (*pl.* **quanta,** *kwon*-ta), the quantity; the amount; a sufficiency; the fundamental unit of radiant energy as postulated by the quantum theory [Physics]. **quantum theory,** the theory that the process involved in radiation are not continuous but take place in successive acts of emission and absorption, each being a separate quantum. (L., how much.)
quaquaversal, *a.* kway-kwa-*vers*-al, inclined downward in every direction [Geol.]; pointing in all directions. (L. *quaqua*, every way, *versus*, turned.)
quarantine, *n. kwo*-ran-teen, the prescribed time of isolation (originally 40 days) imposed on a ship suspected of being infected with a contagious disease; the isolation of any place or person on account of infectious or contagious disease: *v.t.* to isolate for fear of infection. **quarantine flag,** a yellow flag indicating the presence of infection. (O.Fr.)
quarender, *n. kwo*-ren-der, a red-skinned variety of apple. (Origin unknown)
quarrel, *n. kwo*-rel, a petty fight or scuffle; a contest; a breach of friendship; a ground of dispute: *v.i.* to wrangle; to squabble; to fall out; to find fault; to disagree. (O.Fr. *querele.*)
quarrel, *n. kwo*-rel, an arrow with a square head; a diamond-shaped pane of glass, or a square pane placed diagonally in a lead frame. (O.Fr. *quarel.*)
quarreller, *n. kwo*-rel-er, one who wrangles or fights.
quarrelling, *n. kwo*-rel-ing, a disputing with angry words; breach of concord; cavilling or finding fault.
quarrellous, *a. kwo*-rel-us, apt to quarrel; querulous; contentious.
quarrelsome, *a. kwo*-rel-sum, apt to quarrel; easily irritated, or provoked to contest; irascible.
quarrelsomely, *ad.* in a quarrelsome manner.
quarrelsomeness, *n.* state of being quarrelsome.
quarried, *a. kwo*-rid, dug or taken from a quarry; cut into (as a hill) for a quarry; (Fig.) obtained laboriously.
quarrier, *n. kwo*-re-er, a quarryman.
quarry, *n. kwo*-re, prey, esp. an animal pursued by hawk or hound; any object of pursuit; formerly, part of entrails of game given to the hounds: *v.i.* to prey upon, as a vulture. (O.Fr. *cuiree*, skin.)
quarry, *n. kwo*-re, a quarrel, or square-headed arrow; a square pane or tile: *v.t.* to set or pave with quarries. (Fr. *carré*, squared.)
quarry, *n. kwo*-re, an open working from which building-stone, slate, etc., is obtained; any source from which material, information, etc., is extracted: *v.t.* and *i.* to dig or take from or as from a quarry. (O.Fr. *quarriere.*)
quarryman, *n. kwo*-re-man, a worker at a quarry.
quart, *n.* kwort, two pints, a quarter of a gallon; a vessel of this content. (Fr. *quarte.*)
quart, *n.* kahrt, four successive cards of the same suit in the game of piquet.
quartan, *a. kwor*-tan, occurring every fourth day, esp. of fevers: *n.* a quartan ague; a measure containing the fourth part of some other measure; a quartern.
quartation, *n.* kwor-*tay*-shon, the alloying of one part of gold with three parts of silver.
quarte, *n.* kahrt, a carte [Fencing].
quarter, *n. kwor*-ter, the fourth part; the fourth of a cwt. (28 lb.); 8 bushels (480 lb.), the measurement unit for wheat; the first and third of the moon's phases; the instant 15 mins. before or after the hour; one of the large divisions of the globe; one of the four points of the compass; any indicated direction; a particular region of a city or country; the fourth of a dollar [U.S.A.]; a haunch; **exemption** from death of a captive or enemy in one's power; clemency; one of the divisions of a shield divided cross-wise [Her.]; the part of a ship's hull between the stern and the main chains; the part of a boot behind the ankle seams; the heel portion of a horseshoe: *pl.* lodging-place; allotted station, encampment, etc. [Mil.]; posts in action [Naut.]: *v.t.* to divide into four equal parts; to separate; to station soldiers [Mil.]; to divide a shield by vertical and horizontal lines into quarters, to arrange charges, etc., quarterly, or to add other arms to one's coat-of-arms [Her.]: *v.i.* to have a temporary residence. **Quarter Sessions,** *see* **sessions.** (O.Fr.)
quarterage, *n. kwor*-ter-raj, a quarterly allowance; a subscription, etc., paid or due quarterly.
quarter-back, *n.* in American football a player in the line between forwards and half-backs (in Rugby called **three-quarter-back**).
quarter-day, *n.* the day when quarterly payments are due (in England, March 25, June 24, Sept. 29, Dec. 25).
quarter-deck, *n.* that part of the upper deck abaft the main-mast; the after part of the promenade deck.
quartered, *a. kwor*-terd, divided into four equal parts; arranged in quarters [Her.]; furnished with lodging.
quartering, *n. kwor*-ter-ring, the act of dividing into quarters, of assigning soldiers to quarters, or of arranging several coats on a shield [Her.]; a compartment of a shield containing a single coat; the passing of the moon from one quarter to the next; sailing with the wind on the quarter [Naut.].
quarterly, *a. kwor*-ter-le, consisting of a fourth part; recurring at the end of each quarter of the year: *ad.* once in a quarter of a year; arranged in quarters [Her.]: *n.* a periodical published at three months' intervals.
quartermaster, *n.* a commissioned officer whose duty is to provide quarters, provisions, forage, and ammunition for the regiment [Mil.]; a petty officer who attends to the helm, signals, stowage, etc. [Naut.]. **Quartermaster-General,** the 3rd Military Member of the British Army Council, responsible for transport, forage, and supply other than clothing and military stores; **quarter-master-sergeant,** a warrant-officer assisting the quartermaster.
quartern, *n. kwor*-tern, the fourth part of a pint, of a peck, and of certain other measures; a gill; a 4-lb. loaf of bread. (O.Fr. *quarteron.*)
quarter-plate, *n.* a plate, or a print, of about 4¼ by 3¼ in. [Phot.].
quarterstaff, *n. kwor*-ter-stahf, an iron-shod pole 6½ feet long, wielded in offence or defence at the middle and a quarter from the end by both hands.
quartet, *n.* kwor-*tet*, anything in a group of fours; a composition in four parts [Mus.]; a stanza in four lines [Poetry]. (It. *quartetto.*)
quartette, *n.* kwor-*tet*, a quartet.
quartile, *n. kwor*-til, an aspect of the planets when distant from each other a quarter of a circle [Astrol.]; the statistical position midway between the median, or average, and either extreme.
quarto, *n. kwor*-toh, a size resulting from folding a sheet twice (4to.); a book with eight pages to each sheet: *a.* having the sheet folded into four leaves. (L. *in quarto*, in a fourth part.)
quartz, *n.* kworts, pure silica occurring either in hexagonal crystals or in massive form. (Ger. *Quarz.*)
quartziferous, *a.* kwort-*sif*-er-rus, consisting of or containing quartz. (*quartz*, and L. *fero*, bear.)
quartzite, *n. kwort*-site, a compact granular metamorphosed sandstone containing much quartz.
quartzitic, *a.* kwort-*sit*-ik, of the nature of quartzite.
quartzoid, *n. kwort*-soyd, a crystal consisting of two six-sided pyramids, base to base [Min.].
quartzose, *a. kwort*-sohz, containing, composed of, or resembling quartz.
quartzy, *a. kwort*-se, quartzose.
quash, *v.t.* kwosh, to crush; to subdue; to annul or make void. (O.Fr. *quasser.*)
quash, *n.* kwosh, the squash or pumpkin.
quashy, *a. kwosh*-e, wet; boggy. (*squashy.*)
quasi, *ad. kway*-sy, as it were; in a sort. (L.)
Quasimodo, *n.* kway-se-*moh*-do, the first Sunday

after Easter. (From the opening words, 1 Pet. ii, 2, of the introit of the mass for this day.) (L.)

quass, *n.* kwahs, kvass (a Russian beer).

quassation, *n.* kwos-*say*-shon, a shaking; a pounding; the act of pulverizing barks, roots, etc. [Pharm.]. (L. *quassare*, to shake.)

Quassia, *n.* *kwosh*-a *or* *kwosh*-e-a, a genus of shrubby tropical American trees; (*l.c.*) a drug extracted from certain of these, esp. *Q. amara* and *Picrasma excelsum*, used in brewing, as a bitter tonic, as an insecticide, etc. (*Quassi*, the Negro who first discovered its virtues.)

quassin, *n.* *kwos*-in *or* *kwas*-in, the bitter principle of quassia.

quat, *n.* kwot, a pustule or pimple. (Dial.)

quater-centenary, *n.* *kway*-ter- *or* *kwot*-er-, a four-hundredth anniversary.

quater-cousin, *n.* *kway*-ter-, a cater-cousin.

quaternary, *n.* kwo-*ter*-na-re, a set of four; the number four: *a.* consisting of four; by fours; the fourth in order; (*cap.*) designating the rocks above the Pliocene and the period from the Tertiary to the present time [Geol.]. (L. *quarternarius*.)

quaternate, *a.* kwo-*ter*-nate, composed of four parts; consisting of four, as of leaflets [Bot.].

quaternion, *n.* kwo-*ter*-ne-on, a set of four; a quire of four sheets folded into 16 pages; a factor, multiplication by which turns one vector into another vector [Math.]: *pl.* the calculus of the quaternion [Math.]: *v.t.* to arrange or divide into sets of four. (L. *quaternio*.)

quaternity, *n.* kwo-*ter*-ne-te, a set or combination of four.

quatorzain, *n.* *kat*-or-zane, a sonnet containing fourteen lines. (O.Fr., fourteen.)

quatorze, *n.* ka-*torz*, the four aces, kings, queens and jacks or tens at piquet. (Fr., fourteen.)

quatrain, *n.* *kwot*-rane, a stanza of four lines, esp. when rhyming alternately. (Fr.)

quatrefoil, *n.* *kat*-re-foyl *or* *kat*-er-foyl, a leaf with four leaflets; a conventional representation of this [Her.]; an ornamental opening in tracery divided by cusps into four leaves [Arch]. (Fr.)

quattrocentist, *n.* *kwah*- or *kah*-tro-*chen*-tist, an Italian painter or writer of the Quattrocento.

Quattrocento, *n.* *kwah*- or *kah*-tro-*chen*-to, the 15th century in Italian art, a period of revival opening the Renaissance. (It., literally, four hundred.)

quaver, *n.* *kway*-ver, a shake or rapid vibration of the voice or on a musical instrument; a note, half the length of a crotchet: *v.i.* to shake the voice; to sing or play with trills or tremulous modulations; to vibrate: *v.t.* to utter with a tremulous sound. (M.E. *quaven*, to shake.)

quaverer, *n.* *kway*-ver-rer, one who quavers.

quavery, *a.* *kway*-ver-re, tremulous; shaky.

quay, *n.* kee, a mole or wharf for loading and unloading vessels; a landing-place: *v.t.* to furnish with a quay or quays. (Fr.)

quayage, *n.* *kee*-aj, quay dues; wharfage; quays collectively.

queachy, *a.* *kwee*-che, shaking; yielding under feet; boggy. (A.S. *cweccan*, shake or move.)

quean, *n.* kween, a worthless woman; a saucy girl; a young or unmarried woman [Scot.]. **quean cat,** a she-cat. (A.S. *cwen*, a woman.)

queasily, *n.* *kwee*-ze-le, in a queasy manner.

queasiness, *n.* nausea; qualmishness.

queasy *a.* *kwee*-ze, affected with nausea; inclined to vomit; fastidious; squeamish; causing nausea. (Origin doubtful.)

quebracho, *n.* ke-*brah*-cho, any of several Cent. and S. American trees the bark of which is used in medicine (as a tonic, antispasmodic, etc.) and in tanning and dyeing.

queen, *n.* kween, the consort of a king; a female sovereign of a kingdom; a queen bee; the chief of her class; a court-card; the most powerful piece in chess; a queen cat; *v.i.* to play the queen: *v.t.* to make a queen of [Chess]. **queen bee,** the fertile female bee of a hive; a pilotless aircraft controlled by wireless. **Queen Consort,** the wife of a king. **Queen Dowager,** the widow of a king. **Queen Mother,** the mother of a reigning king or queen. **Queen Regnant,** a queen in her own right. **Queen's Bench, Counsel, English, Messenger, Proctor, Remembrancer,** *see* these words. (A.S. *cwen*, a woman.)

queen-cake, *n.* a small currant cake.

queendom, *n.* *kween*-dom, a country ruled by a queen; the rank or dignity of a queen.

queenhood, *n.* *kween*-hood, queenly character.

queening, *n.* *kween*-ing, a variety of apple.

queenliness, *n.* *kween*-le-ness, conduct or appearance worthy of a queen.

queenly, *a.* *kween*-le, like or worthy of a queen.

queen-post, *n.* one of two upright posts between the tie-beam and rafters in a roof [Arch.].

queenship, *n.* *kween*-ship, the office, also the personality, of a queen.

queen's-metal, *n.* a pewter-like alloy composed of tin, with zinc, antimony, and lead.

queen's-ware, *n.* cream-coloured glazed earthenware.

queer, *a.* kweer, odd; singular; eccentric; unwell; droll: *v.t.* to spoil or disarrange [Slang]. **in queer street,** in difficulties; in a bad way; very hard up. **to queer the pitch,** *see* **pitch.** (Perhaps Low Ger. *queer*, across.)

queerish, *a.* *kweer*-ish, somewhat queer or singular.

queerly, *ad.* *kweer*-le, in a queer manner.

queerness, *n.* *kweer*-ness, oddity; singularity.

queest, *n.* kweest, the ringdove. (Dial.)

quell, *v.t.* kwel, to crush; to subdue; to allay. (A.S. *cwellan*, kill.)

queller, *n.* *kwel*-ler, one who crushes or subdues.

quench, *v.t.* kwench, to extinguish; to still or repress; to allay; to destroy: *v.i.* to be extinguished; to become cool. (A.S. *cwencan*.)

quenchable, *a.* *kwench*-a-bl, that may be quenched.

quencher, *n.* *kwench*-er, he who or that which extinguishes; a drink (thirst-quencher) [Coll.].

quenchless, *a.* *kwench*-less, that cannot be quenched; inextinguishable; unquenchable.

quenchlessly, *ad.* in a quenchless manner.

quenchlessness, *n.* state of being quenchless.

quenelle, *n.* ke-*nel*, a forcemeat ball of seasoned fowl, meat, or fish. (Fr.)

quercetin, *n.* *kwer*-se-tin, a yellow crystalline dye obtained from quercitrin.

quercetum, *n.* kwer-*see*-tum, a plantation of oaks.

quercitrin, *n.* *kwer*-se-trin, the colouring principle of quercitron bark, a crystalline glucoside used for dyeing yellow.

quercitron, *n.* *kwer*-se-tron, the American oak *Quercus tinctoria*; the bark of this, used in dyeing and tanning. (L. *quercus*, an oak, and *citron*.)

Quercus, *n.* *kwer*-kus, a widely distributed genus of timber trees including the oaks. (L.)

querent, *n.* *kwe*-rent, one who inquires, esp. of an astrologer; a plaintiff [Law].

querimonius, *a.* kwe-re-*moh*-ne-us, complaining; querulous. (L. *querimonia*, a complaint.)

querimoniously, *ad.* in a querimonious way.

querimoniousness, *n.* disposition to complain.

querist, *n.* *kweer*-rist, one who asks questions.

querl, *n.* kwerl, a twist, curl, or coil: *v.t.* to wind round; to coil [U.S.A.]. (*twirl*.)

quern, *n.* kwern, a primitive stone handmill for grinding corn. (A.S. *cweorn*.)

Querquedula, *n.* kwer-*kwed*-ew-la, a genus of ducks including the teal and the garganey. (L.)

querulous, *a.* *kwe*-roo-lus, disposed to murmur; discontented; peevish; expressing complaint. (L. *querulus*.)

querulously, *ad.* in a querulous manner.

querulousness, *n.* disposition to complain.

query, *n.* *kweer*-re, a question; an objection to be considered; a mark of interrogation; *v.i.* to question; to express a doubt: *v.t.* to examine by questions; to doubt of; to mark with a query. (L. *quære*.)

quest, *n.* kwest, the act of seeking; search; the object of search: *v.t.* to search or seek for. (O.Fr. *queste*.)

***question,** *n.* *kwest*-yun, the act of asking; an interrogatory; that which is asked; inquiry; dispute; doubt; subject under discussion; a proposition stated by way of interrogation [Logic]: *v.i.* to ask a question or questions; to doubt: *v.t.* to interrogate; to examine by means of questions; to call in question; to doubt of; to treat as doubtful. **begging the question,** *see* **beg.** **in question,** in debate. **out of the question,** not to be thought of. **popping the question,** proposing marriage [Coll.]. **previous question,** a motion to pass to other business. **question mark,** the sign of

interrogation (?) [Print.]; anything unknown or uncertain. (O.Fr., from L. *quæsita*, sought.)
questionability, *n.* *kwest*-yun-a-bil-e-te, questionableness; a questionable thing.
questionable, *a.* *kwest*-yun-a-bl, that may be questioned; doubtful; suspicious; liable to suspicion.
questionableness, *n.* quality or state of being questionable.
questionably, *ad.* in a questionable manner.
questionary, *a.* *kwest*-yun-a-re, asking questions; in the form of a question: *n.* a questionnaire; formerly, a hawker of relics.
questioner, *n.* *kwest*-yun-er, one who asks questions; an inquirer.
questionist, *n.* *kwest*-yun-ist, a questioner.
questionless, *a.* and *ad.* *kwest*-yun-less, beyond a question or doubt; undoubtedly.
questionnaire, *n.* kwest-yo-*nair*, a series of questions on a specific subject submitted in the form of a memorandum. (Fr.)
questman, *n.* *kwest*-man, one officially empowered to inquire into certain matters; a churchwarden's assistant.
questor, *n.* *kwes*-tor, a pardoner; a treasurer. (L.)
questuary, *a.* *kwes*-tew-a-re, quæstuary.
quetzal, *n.* *ket*-zal, a brilliantly plumaged Cent. American bird of the trogon family (*T. resplendens*), adopted as the national emblem of Guatemala; the unit of currency (*pl.* **quetzales**) of Guatemala, equal to the U.S.A. dollar. (Sp., from Aztec.)
queue, *n.* kew, the tie of a wig; a pigtail; a tail-piece of a stringed instrument; a file of persons or vehicles drawn up behind each other in order of arrival: *v.t.* to dress in a queue (of the hair): *v.i.* to join in or form one of a queue. **to queue up,** to stand and wait in a queue. (Fr., tail.)
quey, *n.* kway, a young cow or heifer. (Scand. *kviga.*)
quibble, *n.* *kwib*-bl, a start or turn from the point in question or the plain truth; an evasion; a play upon words: *v.t.* to evade the question at issue, esp. by artifice; to play upon words; to trifle in argument or discourse. (*quip.*)
quibbler, *n.* *kwib*-bler, one who quibbles.
quibblingly, *ad.* *kwib*-bling-le, evasively; triflingly.
★**quick,** *a.* kwik, speedy; sprightly; characterized by activity or readiness; done with celerity; sharp in discerning; sharp; living; pregnant with child: *ad.* nimbly; with celerity: *n.* living persons; living flesh, esp. that under the finger-nails; sensitive parts. (A.S. *cwic.*)
quickbeam, *n.* *kwik*-beem, the quicken.
quick-change, *a.* changing costumes or appearance rapidly [esp. Theat.].
quicken, *v.t.* *kwik*-en, to vivify; to revive or resuscitate; to make alive spiritually; to accelerate; to sharpen; to stimulate; to cheer; to reinvigorate: *v.i.* to become alive; to show signs of life (esp. of a fœtus); to move with rapidity or activity.
quicken, *n.* *kwik*-en, the mountain-ash or rowan; also, the service-tree.
quickener, *n.* *kwik*-en-er, one who or that which quickens, reinvigorates, or accelerates.
quickening, *a.* *kwik*-en-ing, giving life; reviving: *n.* the earliest recognized movement of a fœtus in the uterus [Med.].
quick-eyed, *a.* *kwik*-ide, having acute sight.
quickfirer, *n.* *kwik*-fire-er, a gun for rapid firing.
quick-firing, *a.* shooting in rapid succession.
quick-hedge, *n.* a hedge or fence formed of growing plants.
quicklime, *n.* *kwik*-lime, lime unslaked; carbonate of lime deprived of its carbonic acid.
quickly, *ad.* *kwik*-le, speedily; without delay.
quickmatch, *n.* *kwik*-match, a fuse or wick impregnated with inflammable material.
quickness, *n.* *kwik*-ness, speed; activity or readiness of intellect.
quicksand, *n.* *kwik*-sand, watery sand readily yielding to pressure; a bed of such sand.
quickset, *n.* *kwik*-set, a living plant or slip, esp. of hawthorn, set to grow for a hedge. **quickset hedge,** a hedge composed of living shrubs.
quick-sighted, *a.* *kwik*-*sy*-ted, having acute sight.
quicksilver, *n.* *kwik*-sil-ver, the metallic element mercury; a slippery or elusive person or thing: *v.t.* to coat or overlay with an amalgam of quicksilver and tin or the like. (A.S. *cwicseolfor*, living silver.)
quick-step, *n.* the step used in marching at quick-time [Mil.]; a dance in quick-time.
quick-time, *n.* *kwik*-time, the customary rate of marching, *i.e.* 128 steps a minute or 4 miles an hour [Mil.]; a similar rate of motion adapted to dancing; a fast fox-trot.
quick-witted, *a.* having ready wit.
quid, *n.* kwid, a piece to chew, esp. of tobacco. (*cud.*)
quid, *n.* kwid, a sovereign, twenty shillings [Slang].
quidam, *n.* *kwy*-dam, somebody; one unknown. (L.)
quiddative, *a.* *kwid*-a-tiv, constituting the essence of a thing.
quiddity, *n.* *kwid*-e-te, the essence of a thing; a trifling nicety; a quibble; a captious question. (Late L. *quidditas.*)
quiddle, *v.i.* *kwid*-dl, to waste time in trifling or useless employments; to dawdle. (Origin unknown.)
quiddler, *n.* *kwid*-dler, a trifler; a potterer.
quidnunc, *n.* *kwid*-nungk, one curious to know everything; a newsmonger; one who pretends to know everything. (L., what now?)
quiesce, *v.i.* kwy-*ess*, to become quiescent; to become silent. (L. *quiesco*, be still.)
quiescence, *n.* kwy-*ess*-ence, the state of being quiescent; rest of the mind; silence.
quiescency, *n.* kwy-*ess*-en-se, quiescence.
quiescent, *a.* kwy-*ess*-ent, at rest; in a state of repose; unagitated; tranquil; not sounded [Phon.]: *n.* a silent letter [Phon.]. (L. *quiescens*, being quiet.)
quiescently, *ad.* in a quiescent manner.
★**quiet,** *a.* *kwy*-et, in a state of rest; not moving; still; making no noise; silent; free from alarm or disturbances; peaceable; calm; not showy; unruffled: *n.* a state of rest; repose; tranquillity; silence; peace: *v.t.* to reduce to a state of rest; to calm; to allay; to appease: *v.i.* to become quiet. (L. *quietus.*)
quieten, *v.t.* *kwy*-et-en, to make quiet: *v.i.* to become quiet.
quieter, *n.* *kwy*-et-er, one who or that which makes quiet.
quietism, *n.* *kwy*-et-izm, tranquillity or dispassion of mind; (*cap.*) the doctrine of the Quietists.
Quietist, *n.* *kwy*-et-ist, an adherent of the mystical religious doctrine that spiritual illumination and perfection depend on maintaining a purely passive, contemplative, and susceptive attitude to Divine communication and revelation: *a.* characteristic of Quietism; quietistic.
quietistic, *a.* *kwy*-e-*tis*-tik, pertaining to or of the nature of Quietism.
quietly, *ad.* *kwy*-et-le, in a quiet manner.
quietness, *n.* *kwy*-et-ness, the state of being quiet.
quietude, *n.* *kwy*-e-tewd, a state of rest; tranquillity; repose. (Fr. *quiétude.*)
quietus, *n.* kwy-*ee*-tus, death; final discharge or acquittance. (L.)
quiff, *n.* kwif, a lock of hair oiled and plastered down on the forehead [Slang].
quill, *n.* kwil, the large strong feather of a bird's wing; the hollow stem of a feather; a pen made from this; a plectrum, tooth-pick, etc., made of a quill; a spine of a porcupine; a piece of small reed on which weavers wind their thread; a tube of cane or reed used as a musical pipe: *v.t.* to pleat; to goffer; to crimp.
quill-driver, *n.* a clerk; one who makes a living by use of the pen.
quillet, *n.* *kwil*-let, quibble. (Probably *quiddity.*)
quilling, *n.* *kwil*-ling, a ruffle, or any fluted material.
quillwork, *n.* *kwil*-wurk, decoration consisting of an overlay of natural or coloured porcupine quills.
quill-wort, *n.* the water plant *Isoëtes lacustris.*
quilt, *n.* kwilt, a counterpane of two cloths stitched together, with wool or down between: *v.t.* to stitch together or sew in the manner of a quilt; to cover with a quilt or padded material. (O.Fr. *cuilte.*)
quilting, *n.* *kwilt*-ing, the act of forming a quilt; the material employed; quilted work.
quin, *n.* kwin, one of a quintuplet [Coll.].
quina, *n.* *kee*-na, quinine. (Sp.)
quinary, *a.* *kwy*-na-re, consisting of or arranged by fives. (L. *quinarius*, arranged in fives.)
quinate, *a.* *kwy*-nat, digitate with five leaflets on a petiole; growing in sets of five [Bot.].

quinate, *n.* *kwin*-ate *or* *kwy*-nate, a salt of quinic acid.
quince, *n.* kwince, the bitter, apple-like fruit of *Pyrus cydonia*; the tree itself. (O.Fr. *coin.*)
quincentenary, *n.* kwin-*sen*-te-na-re, a five-hundredth anniversary: *a.* relating to or attaining five hundred years. (L. *quinque*, five, and *centenary.*)
quincuncial, *a.* kwin-*kun*-shal, having the form of a quincunx.
quincunx, *n.* *kwin*-kunks, the disposition of any five objects, as of trees, in a square, with one at each corner and one in the centre; an arrangement of five leaves or petals [Bot.]. (L. *quinque*, five, *uncia*, a spot on a die.)
quindecagon, *n.* kwin-*dek*-a-gon, a plane figure with fifteen angles [Geom.]. (L. *quinque*, and *decagon.*)
quindecemvir, *n.* kwin-de-*sem*-ver, one of the fifteen priests in Rome who had charge of the books of the Sibyl. (L. *quindecemvir.*)
quingentenary, *n.* and *a.* kwin-*jen*-te-na-re, quincentenary. (L. *quingenti*, five hundred.)
quinia, *n.* *kwin*-e-a, a white, bitter, tonic alkaloid prepared from cinchona [Pharm.].
quinic, *a.* *kwin*-ik, pertaining to or obtained from quinine or cinchona bark.
quinicine, *n.* *kwin*-is-in, an alkaloid produced from quinine.
quinidine, *n.* *kwin*-id-in, an alkaloid found in certain cinchona barks.
quinine, *n.* kwin-*een*, an alkaloid obtained from various species of *Cinchona*; sulphate of quinine, a bitter tonic and febrifuge [Med.]. (Fr.)
quininism, *n.* *kwin*-e-nizm, cinchonism, the condition induced by overdoses of quinine [Path.].
quinize, *v.t.* and *i.* *kwin*-ize, to overdose or saturate with quinine.
quink, *n.* kwink, the brent goose, *Bernicia brenta.*
quinnat, *n.* *kwin*-at, the Pacific salmon, a valuable food-fish of the genus *Oncorhynchus*, common on the N. American Pacific coasts.
quinoa, *n.* kwi-*noh*-a, a plant, *Chenopodium quinoa*, of the Andes, S. America; its seeds, which yield a meal used as a cereal. (Peruvian.)
quinology, *n.* kwi-*nol*-o-je, the scientific study of quinine.
quinone, *n.* kwi-*nohn*, an oxidizing agent prepared from quinic acid and by other methods, used in dyeing and tanning.
quinquagenarian, *a.* *kwin*-kwa-je-*nare*-re-an, fifty years old: *n.* a person fifty years old.
quinquagenary, *a.* kwin-kwa-*jen*-a-re, quinquagenarian: *n.* a fiftieth anniversary. (L. *quinquagenarius*)
Quinquagesima, *n.* kwin-kwa-*jes*-e-ma, or **Quinquagesima Sunday,** the Sunday next before Lent, the fiftieth day (inclusive) before Easter. (L., the fiftieth day.)
quinquangular, *a.* kwin-*kwang*-gew-lar, having five angles. (L. *quinque*, and *angular.*)
quinquarticular, *a.* kwin-kwar-*tik*-yew-lar, relating to five of the articles of religion. (L. *quinque*, and *articular.*)
quinquecapsular, *a.* kwin-kwe-*kap*-sew-lar, having five capsules [Bot.].
quinquecostate, *a.* kwin-kwe-*kos*-tat, having five ribs [Bot.]. (L. *quinque*, and *costa*, a rib.)
quinquedentate, *a.* kwin-kwe-*den*-tat, five-toothed. (L. *quinque*, and *dens*, a tooth.)
quinquefarious, *a.* kwin-kwe-*fare*-re-us, opening into five parts [Bot.]. (L. *quinque*, and *farius.*)
quinquefid, *a.* *kwin*-kwe-fid, five-cleft [Bot.]. (L. *quinque*, and *findo*, cleave.)
quinquefoliate, *a.* kwin-kwe-*foh*-le-at, having five leaves [Bot.].
quinqueliteral, *a.* kwin-kwe-*lit*-er-ral, consisting of five letters. (L. *quinque*, and *literal.*)
quinquelobate, *a.* kwin-kwe-*loh*-bat, five-lobed [Bot.]. (L. *quinque*, and *lobe.*)
quinquelocular, *a.* kwin-kwe-*lok*-yew-lar, five-celled [Bot.]. (L. *quinque*, and *locular.*)
quinquenniad, *n.* kwin-*kwen*-ne-ad, a quinquennium.
quinquennial, *a.* kwin-*kwen*-ne-al, occurring once in, or lasting, five years. (L. *quinquennalis.*)
quinquennium, *n.* kwin-*kwen*-ne-um, a period of five years.
quinquepartite, *a.* kwin-kwe-*par*-tite, divided into five parts. (L. *quinque*, and *pars*, a part.)
quinquereme, *n.* *kwin*-kwe-reem, a galley with five rows of oars. (L. *quinque*, and *remus*, an oar.)
quinquevalent, *a.* kwin-kwe-*vay*-lent, having a combining power of five [Chem.].
quinquevalvular, *a.* kwin-kwe-*val*-vew-lar, having five valves, as a pericarp [Bot.].
quinquina, *n.* kin-*kee*-na, Peruvian bark; quinine.
quinquino, *n.* kin-*kee*-noh, a tropical American tree of the genus *Myroxyton*, yielding Peruvian balsam.
quinsy, *n.* *kwin*-ze, inflammation of the throat, esp. acute suppurative tonsilitis. (Gr. *kynanche*, from *kyon*, a dog, and *anchein*, to throttle.)
quint, *n.* kwint *or* kint, a set of sequence of five cards [Piquet]; an interval of a fifth [Mus.]. (L. *quintus*, fifth.)
quintain, *n.* *kwin*-tan, a pivoted object to be tilted at, so constructed that when one end is struck the other may swing round and strike the tilter; the sport of tilting at this. (O.Fr. *quintaine.*)
quintal, *n.* *kwin*-tal, a weight of either 100 or 112 pounds, or of 100 kilograms (220·46 lb.). (Fr.)
quintan, *a.* *kwin*-tan, recurring every fifth day [Med.]: *n.* an ague which does so. (L. *quintanus.*)
quintessence, *n.* kwin-*tes*-ence, the fifth or highest essence, the "ether" of the ancient philosophers; an extract from anything containing its virtues or most essential part in small quantity; any refined extract; the essential part of anything. (Fr.)
quintessential, *a.* kwin-te-*sen*-shal, of the nature of a quintessence; most typical.
quintet, *n.* kwin-*tet*, a musical composition for five performers; a group or set of five. (It. *quintetto.*)
quintette, *n.* kwin-*tet*, a quintet.
quintic, *a.* *kwin*-tik, of the fifth degree [Math.]: *n.* a quantic of the fifth degree.
quintile, *n.* *kwin*-tile, the aspect of planets when distant from each other one-fifth of a circle. (L. *quintus.*)
quintillion, *n.* kwin-*til*-yun, the number produced by raising a million to the fifth power; in America and France, the sixth power of a thousand. (L. *quintus*, and *million.*)
quintroon, *n.* *kwin*-troon, the offspring of an octoroon and a white person; one having one-sixteenth negro blood.
quintuple, *a.* *kwin*-tew-pl, fivefold: *v.t.* and *i.* to make or increase fivefold.
quintuplet, *n.* *kwin*-tew-plet, a set or combination of five; a cycle for five riders; one of quintuplets: *pl.* five children born at a birth.
quintuplicate, *v.t.* kwin-*tew*-ple-kate, to multiply by five; to make fivefold; to make five copies of: *a.* fivefold.
quintuplication, *n.* kwin-tew-ple-*kay*-shon, the act, or the result, of multiplying by five.
quinzaine, *n.* *kwin*-zane, a period of fifteen days, esp. [Eccles.] one including a feast day.
quinze, *n.* (App.), a game at cards, resembling vingt-un, in which the count is fifteen and no more. (Fr.)
quip, *n.* kwip, a witty remark, a smart reply; a sarcastic jest: *v.t.* to taunt: *v.i.* to scoff. (Probably L. *quippe*, forsooth.)
quipu, *n.* *kee*-poo *or* *kwip*-oo, a cord of various coloured threads and knots, arithmetically used by the ancient Peruvians for recording, message-sending, etc. (Native, a knot.)
quire, *n.* kwire, the twentieth of a ream, twenty-four sheets (of paper, or twenty-five with outside sheet); twenty-six copies of a newspaper or periodical. **in quire,** in sheets before binding (of books). (O.Fr. *quayer.*)
quire, *n.* kwire, a body of singers; a choir: *v.i.* to sing in concert. (*choir.*)
Quirinal, *n.* *kwi*-rin-al, the Italian monarchical, as distinguished from the Papal or Vatican, Government and Court. (*Quirinus*, ancient god of war, from whom one of the seven hills of Rome, and hence the modern palace, was named.)
quirister, *n.* *kwi*-ris-ter, a chorister.
quirk, *n.* kwerk, an evasion or subterfuge; a shift; a quibble; a smart retort; a flourish in drawing or music; a deep groove in a moulding [Arch.]. (Origin unknown.)
quirkish, *a.* *kwerk*-ish, consisting of quirks or artful evasions; resembling a quirk.
quirky, *a.* *kwerk*-e, full of quirks.
quirt, *n.* kwert, a short-handled long-lashed riding-whip [Amer.]. (Mex. Sp. *cuarta.*)
quisling, *n.* *kwiz*-ling, a traitor, esp. one who goes

over to and actively assists an invading enemy; a leader of a fifth column. (Major V. *Quisling*, *b.* 1887, notorious Norwegian Nazi renegade, executed 1945.)
quit, *v.t.* and *i. kwit*, to leave; to depart from; to liberate; to release; to requite; to abandon; to desist from: *a.* free; clear; discharged from: *pl.*, *a.* and *n.*, even; on even terms, neither having any advantage. **double or quits,** a toss or lob to decide whether one should be discharged from, or pay double of, a debt. **to be quits,** to have arrived at a stage at which matters are on equal terms. (O.Fr. *quite*, at rest.)
quitch, *n.* kwitch, couch-grass. (*quick*, from its rapid growth.)
quit-claim, *n.* a renunciation of right: *v.t.* to renounce claim or title to [Law].
★**quite,** *ad.* kwite, completely; entirely; very; certainly, "just so." (Fr. *quitte.*)
quit-rent, *n.* a nominal rent paid by a freeholder to relieve him from certain feudal liabilities.
quits, *a.* and *n.* kwits, *see* **quit.**
quittable, *a. kwit*-a-bl, that may be vacated.
quittal, *n. kwit*-al, requital; repayment.
quittance, *n. kwit*-ance, discharge from a debt or obligation; an acquittance; recompense. (Fr.)
quitter, *n. kwit*-er, one who quits; a work-shy person; one who deserts his post.
quitter, *n. kwit*-er, a suppurating sore or ulcer on the inside quarter of a horse's foot. (Origin unknown.)
quiver, *n. kwiv*-er, a case for carrying arrows in use. (O.Fr. *cuivre.*)
quiver, *v.i. kwiv-er*, to shake or tremble: to quake: *v.t.* to cause to quiver (as wings). (*quake.*)
quivered, *a. kwiv*-erd, furnished with a quiver; kept in or as in a quiver.
quiverful, *n. kwiv*-er-ful, enough arrows to fill a quiver; a large family [Ps. cxxvii, 5].
quiveringly, *ad. kwiv*-er-ring-le, with quivering.
quiverish, *a. kwiv*-er-rish, inclined to quiver.
quixotic, *a.* kwik-*sot*-ik, like Don Quixote; romantic to extravagance; lofty but impracticable.
quixotically, *ad.* in a quixotic manner.
quixotism, *n. kwiks*-ot-izm, quixotry.
quixotry, *n. kwiks*-ot-re, romantic and absurd notions; actions, etc., like those of Don Quixote.
quiz, *n.* kwiz, an enigma; a riddle or obscure question intended to puzzle; a connected series of perplexing questions with their answers; a quizzer; one to be quizzed: *v.t.* to puzzle; to banter; to examine narrowly and mockingly.
quiz-master, *n.* the questioner in a quizzing competition.
quizzer, *n. kwiz*-er, one addicted to quizzing.
quizzical, *a. kwiz*-e-kal, given to quizzing; of the nature of a quiz; comical.
quizzing, *n. kwiz*-ing, the act of the verb *to quiz*, esp. ridiculing or examining another through a quizzing glass. **quizzing glass,** a monocle; a lorgnette.
quoad, *prep. kwoh*-ad, with respect to; so far as. (L.)
quod, *n.* kwod, a quad; a prison [Slang].
quodlibet, *n. kwod*-le-bet a nice point; a subtlety; a medley [Mus.]. (L., what you please.)
quodlibetarian, *n.* kwod-lib-e-*tare*-re-an, one who is given to discussing quodlibets.
quodlibetical, *a.* kwod-le-*bet*-e-kal, of the nature of a quodlibet; purely academic.
quoif, *n.* koyf, a coif.
quoin, *n.* koyn, the external angle of a wall [Arch.]; an internal angle or corner; a keystone; a small wooden wedge to fasten pages of type [Print.]. (*coin.*)
quoit, *n.* koyt, a flattish ring or disk of iron pitched at a pin, or hob, in play, so as to encircle it: *pl.* the game of throwing these. (Origin unknown.)
quondam, *a. kwon*-dam, former: *ad.* formerly. (L.)
quorum, *n. kwaw*-rum, the number of a body competent by law or constitution to transact business. (L., of whom.)
quota, *n. kwoh*-ta, a proportional part or share; that which, or the number that, is allotted. (L., what in number?)
quotability, *n. kwoh*-ta-*bil*-e-te, fitness for quotation.
quotable, *a. kwoh*-ta-bl, that may be quoted.
quotation, *n.* kwo-*tay*-shon, the act of quoting; a passage quoted; the current price of anything; a large quadrat [Print.]. **quotation marks,** inverted commas distinguishing the beginning and end of a quotation.
quote, *v.t.* kwoht, to cite; to repeat or adduce a passage from some author or speaker; to give the current price of; to enclose within quotation marks [Print.]: *n.pl.* quotation marks. (O.Fr. *quoter*, from L. *quotare.*)
quoter, *n. kwoh*-ter, one who cites the words of an author, etc.; one who makes a quotation.
quoth, *v. defective*, kwohth, say, says, or said. (A.S. *cwethan*, to say.)
quotha, *int. kwoh*-thah, indeed!
quotidian, *a.* kwo-*tid*-e-an, recurring daily [Med.]: *n.* a fever whose paroxysms return every day; anything returning daily. (L. *quotidiē*, daily.)
quotient, *n. kwoh*-shent, the number resulting from the division of one number by another. (Fr.)
quotiety, *n.* kwo-*ty*-e-te, the relation between an object and a number; relative frequency. (L. *quoties*, how often?)
quotum, *n. kwoh*-tum, share; a proportion; a quota.
qu'ran, *n.* ko-*rahn*, the Koran.

R

R, ahr, eighteenth letter of the English alphabet, has two sounds: (1) that heard when it precedes a vowel, as in *rat, greed, heron*, and (2) that when it is at the end of a word (*clear, canter, flour*) or is followed by a consonant (*curb, form*). A following *h*, as in *rhomb, unrhymed*, does not affect the sound. **the three R's,** reading (w)riting, and (a)rithmetic.
rabat, *n.* rah-*bah*, a rebato.
rabbet, *n.* *rab*-et, a joint; a groove cut longitudinally in a piece of timber to receive the edge of a plank: *v.t.* to cut a groove thus for receiving the edge of another piece. **rabbet plane,** a plane used for the purpose. (O.Fr. *rabat*, a recess.)
rabbi, *n.* *rab*-by (*pl.* **rabbis**), a Jewish doctor, teacher, or interpreter of the law; a courtesy title of Jewish priests. (Heb., my master.)
rabbin, *n.* *rab*-in, a rabbi. (Fr.)
rabbinate, *n.* *rab*-in-ate, the office or term of office of a rabbi; the rabbis collectively.
rabbinic, *n.* ra-*bin*-ik, the language or dialect of the mediæval rabbis; the later Hebrew: *a.* rabbinical.
rabbinical, *a.* ra-*bin*-e-kal, pertaining to the rabbis, or to their opinions, learning, or language.
rabbinism, *n.* *rab*-in-izm, a rabbinical idiom or linguistic peculiarity.
rabbinist, *n.* *rab*-in-ist, one who adheres to the Talmud and the traditions of the rabbis.
rabbinite, *n.* *rab*-in-ite, a rabbinist.
rabbit, *n.* *rab*-it, the burrowing rodent *Lepus cuniculus*; a useless player, or a coward [Slang]. **rabbit fish,** the king of the herrings, *Chimæra monstrosa*, and other fish with fancied rabbit resemblances. (Origin uncertain.)
rabbiting, *n.* *rab*-it-ing, rabbit-catching.
rabbitry, *n.* *rab*-it-re, an establishment for the breeding of rabbits.
rabbit-warren, *n.* a place where rabbits burrow and breed; an overcrowded house or slum.
rabble, *n.* *rab*-bl, a tumultuous, noisy crowd; the mob; the lower class of the people. (Perhaps from O.Dut. *rabbelen*, chatter.)
rabble, *n.* *rab*-bl, an iron tool like a rake used for skimming the slag off molten iron.
rabblement, *n.* *rab*-bl-ment, a tumultuous crowd of low people; a rabble.
rabdology, *n.* rab-*dol*-o-je, rhabdology.
Rabelaisian, *a.* rab-e-*lay*-ze-an, relating to, or after the manner of, the French writer François Rabelais (*d.* 1553); coarsely humorous or satirical: *n.* an imitator or student of Rabelais.
rabid, *a.* *rab*-id, pertaining to rabies; furious; raging; mad; fanatical. (L. *rabidus*, mad.)
rabidity, *n.* ra-*bid*-e-te, the state of being rabid.
rabidly, *ad.* in a rabid manner.
rabidness, *n.* furiousness; madness.
rabies, *n.* *ray*-be-eez *or* *rab*-e-eez, hydrophobia; madness arising from the bite of a rabid animal; canine madness. (L., madness, primarily of dogs.)
rabinet, *n.* *rab*-in-et, a small obsolete cannon with a bore of about an inch and a half.
raca, *a.* *rah*-ka, worthless; good-for-nothing; depraved (a term of extreme contempt). (Aramaic.)
raccahout, *n.* *rak*-a-hoot, a food prepared from the acorn of the Barbary oak. (Fr., from Arab.)
raccoon, *n.* ra-*koon*, the racoon.
race, *n.* race, a series of descendants from the same stock; a division of mankind forming a distinct human type; a people, nation, tribe, or family; a particular breed; lineage; any class of persons having characteristics or interests, etc., in common; a distinctive flavour, as of wine. **race suicide,** limitation of human fertility with intent to decrease the birth-rate. (Fr., ultimate origin unknown.)
race, *n.* race, a running; a rapid course; a contest in speed; course; career; a strong or rapid current, or its channel; a slipstream [Av.]; a groove or track for a sliding or rolling part [Mech.]; *pl.* a meeting for contests (esp. of horses) in running: *v.i.* to run swiftly; to run in competition; to run wildly, as an engine under diminished load or a propeller out of the water; to contend in running: *v.t.* to set a-running in a race; to run a race with. (Scand.)
race, *n.* race, a root (of ginger). (O.Fr. *rais*, from L. *radix*, root.)
race-card, *n.* the card on which is printed the day's programme at a race-meeting.
racecourse, *n.* *race*-koarse, the track on which a horse-race is run.
race-ginger, *n.* ginger in the root, or not pulverized.
racegoer, *n.* *race*-goh-er, one who frequents racecourses; a patron of the Turf.
racehorse, *n.* *race*-horse, a horse bred for racing.
raceme, *n.* ra-*seem*, a form of inflorescence with equal pedicels. (L. *racemus*, a cluster of grapes.)
race-meeting, *n.* a public gathering for the purposes of horse-racing.
racemic, *a.* ra-*sem*-ik, pertaining to or derived from grapes or grape-juice. **racemic acid,** an acid, isomeric with tartaric, obtained from certain vines.
racemiferous, *a.* ras-e-*mif*-er-rus, bearing racemes. (L. *racemus*, and *fero*, bear.)
racemose, *a.* *ras*-e-mohs, growing in racemes; ordered in clusters; resembling a bunch of grapes [Med.]. (L. *racemosus*.)
racemule, *n.* *ras*-e-mewl, a small raceme.
racer, *n.* *race*-er, a competitor in a race; a racehorse; any animal, vessel, machine, etc., kept for racing purposes; any specially fast moving part of a machine; part of the traverse or turn-table of a heavy gun.
raceway, *n.* *race*-way, a millrace or similar channel.
rach, *n.* ratsh, a setting dog or pointer. (A.S.)
rachialgia, *n.* ray-ke-*al*-je-a, pain in the spine.
rachidian, *a.* ra-*kid*-e-an, spinal; pertaining to the rachis [Anat.]; vertebral.
rachilla, *n.* ra-*kil*-a, a species of inflorescence, as in the spikelets of grasses. (Gr. *rachis*.)
rachis, *n.* *ray*-kis (*pl.* **rachides** ra-*ky*-deez), a peduncle; the petiole of a compound leaf [Bot.]; the vertebral column [Anat.]; the shaft of a feather [Ornith.]. (Gr., spine.)
rachitic, *a.* ra-*kit*-ik, pertaining to rachitis; rickety.
rachitis, *n.* ra-*ky*-tis, rickets. (Gr., inflammation of the spine.)
rachitism, *n.* *rak*-e-tizm, tendency to rickets.
racial, *a.* *ray*-she-al, pertaining to race or breed.
racialism, *n.* *ray*-she-al-izm, the distinctive characteristics of a race; race sentiments and principles; antagonism on account of race.
racily, *ad.* *race*-e-le, in a racy manner.
raciness, *n.* the state of being racy; piquancy.
racing, *n.* *race*-ing, the sport or business of setting horses at competitive running; horse races collectively.
rack, *n.* rak, an instrument of torture for forcibly stretching the human body; torture; an open frame in which articles may be arranged; a wooden frame for the feeding of horses; a grate or grating adapted for various uses; a straight bar, with teeth to fit into those of a wheel [Mech.]; a rack-rail: *v.t.* to stretch or strain on or as on the rack; to torture; to harass by exaction; to wrest; to extend. (M.E. *rekke*, a rack for hay, and O.Dut. *racken*, to torture.)
rack, *n.* rak, the neck and spine of a fore-quarter of veal or mutton. (Origin unknown.)
rack, *n.* rak, light floating vapour in the sky; cloud-drift; ruin; wreck: *v.i.* to fly, as vapour or broken clouds. (*wrack*, or perhaps Scand. *rek*, drift.)
rack, *n.* rak, arrack.
rack, *n.* rak, a horse's rapid gait in which all the legs are sometimes simultaneously off the ground; *v.i.* to use this gait, as a horse.
rack, *v.t.* rak, to draw off from the lees; to decant. (O.Fr. *raquer*.)
rackarock, *n.* *rak*-a-rok, a powerful explosive formerly used in blasting, etc.
racker, *n.* *rak*-er, one who tortures or harasses; a horse that moves with a racking pace.

racket, *n.* *rak*-et, a confused, clattering noise; clamour; bootlegging, or other nefarious undertaking [Amer.]: *v.i.* to make a confused noise; to frolic. **to stand the racket,** to bear the consequences; to pay the bill. (Probably imit.)
racket, *n.* *rak*-et, the stringed bat with which players of tennis, rackets, etc., strike the ball; a snow-shoe: *pl.* a game of the tennis group in which a small hard ball is played against the wall of an enclosed court with rackets. (Fr.)
racketeer, *n.* rak-e-*teer*, one making large profits by means of a racket or any violent or nefarious undertaking: *v.i.* to work a racket; to practise racketeering. (Amer.)
racketeering, *n.* rak-e-*teer*-ing, organized crime which, by use of illegal methods, extorts money or business advantage.
racketing, *n.* *rak*-e-ting, confused and noisy mirth.
rackety, *a.* *rak*-e-te, making a tumultuous noise; dissipated.
rack-rail, *n.* a toothed rail used on inclined railways, placed between or alongside the bearing rails.
rack-rent, *n.* an extortionate rent, one stretched or raised to the utmost value.
rack-renter, *n.* a rapacious landlord, one who extorts an exorbitant rent.
rackwork, *n.* *rak*-wurk, a mechanical device in which motion is communicated by means of a toothed wheel and a toothed bar; a rack and pinion.
râcloir, *n.* ra-klwahr, a small stone palæolithic scraping tool worked on one face only. (Fr., scraper.)
raconteur, *n.* (App.), a teller of stories, especially one who is practised or gifted at so doing. (Fr.)
raconteuse, *n.* (App.), a female raconteur. (Fr.)
racoon, *n.* ra-*koon*, a N. American nocturnal climbing carnivore allied to the bears, *Procyon lotor*, valuable for its thick fur. **racoon berry,** the May-apple. **racoon dog,** a small wild dog of Eastern Asia, *Hyctereutes procyoniodes*, much resembling the racoon. (Algonquian.)
racquet, *n.* *rak*-et, racket (the stringed bat).
racy, *a.* *race*-e, having distinctive or strongly marked characteristics or qualities; tasting of the soil; exciting to mental taste; piquant; spirited. (*race.*)
radar, *n.* *ray*-dar, the science and practice of radiolocation. (Shortened form of "radio detection and ranging.")
raddle, *n.* *rad*-dl, ruddle.
raddle, *n.* *rad*-dl, a long stick used in hedging; a hedge of interwoven branches: *v.t.* to interweave: to twist together. (O.Fr. *reddalle.*)
radial, *a.* *ray*-de-al, pertaining to or resembling a ray or radii; issuing like or from a ray; radiating; moving as from a centre; pertaining to the radius, or small bone of the forearm [Anat.]. (Fr.)
radiality, *n.* ray-de-*al*-e-te, the condition or state of being radial: radiate order.
radialization, *n.* *ray*-de-a-ly-*zay*-shon, the state of being radialized; the act of radializing.
radialize, *v.t.* *ray*-de-a-lize, to cause to radiate; to arrange radially.
radially, *ad.* *ray*-de-a-le, in a radial manner.
radian, *n.* *ray*-de-an, an angle at the centre of a circle subtending an arc equal in length to the radius of the circle, 57·2958° [Math.].
radiance, *n.* *ray*-de-ance, brightness shooting in rays; brilliant or sparkling lustre; vivid brightness.
radiancy, *n.* *ray*-de-an-se, the quality of being radiant; radiance.
radiant, *a.* *ray*-de-ant, radiating; emitting rays of light or heat; beaming with brightness; radiate [Bot.]: *n.* the luminous point or object from which light emanates; a straight line proceeding from a given point about which it revolves [Geom.]; the point from which a star-shower appears to proceed [Astron.]. (Fr.)
radiantly, *ad.* *ray*-de-ant-le, in a radiant manner.
radiantness, *n.* *ray*-de-ant-ness, radiance.
radiate, *a.* *ray*-de-at, having rays; having crystals diverging from a centre: arranged in a radial manner [Min.]: *v.i.* to emit rays; to issue in rays; to shine; to proceed as rays from a point: *v.t.* to emit as rays; to irradiate; to issue or distribute by means of radio. **radiate flower,** a composite flower consisting of a disk in which the florets are tubular. (L. *radiatus*, shone.)
radiation, *n.* ray-de-*ay*-shon, the act of emitting rays; diffusion of rays or in the manner of rays; the emission of wave motion or of electrically charged particles from a source; the condition of diverging from a centre; that which is radiated.
radiative, *a.* *ray*-de-ay-tiv, having the power of radiating; pertaining to or exhibiting radiation.
radiator, *n.* *ray*-de-ay-tor, that which radiates; an apparatus for either heating or cooling by means of radiation; a device by which water circulating round the cylinders of a motor-engine is kept cool.
radical, *a.* *rad*-e-kal, pertaining to the root or origin; growing from the root; original; fundamental; implanted by nature; primitive; underived; proceeding immediately from the root [Bot.]; pertaining to radicalism or the Radical Party [Politics]: *n.* a radix or simple underived uncompounded word; a sound or letter that belongs to the root; the base of a compound, esp. a group of atoms replaceable by a single atom or passing without change through a series of reactions [Chem.]; a quantity expressed as the root of another quantity [Math.]; an advanced Liberal or a member of the Radical Party [Politics]. **Radical Party,** a faction of political reformers advocating fundamental and immediate changes in laws, governmental method, etc., with a view to the extension of the democratic principle. (Fr., from L. *radix*, root.)
radicalism, *n.* *rad*-e-ka-lizm, the spirit or principles of the Radical Party.
radicality, *n.* rad-e-*kal*-e-te, radicalness.
radicalize, *v.t.* *rad*-e-ka-lize, to cause to become radical: *v.i.* to put radical ideas into practice.
radically, *ad.* in a radical manner; fundamentally: essentially.
radicalness, *n.* the quality or condition of being radical or fundamental.
radicant, *a.* *rad*-e-kant, producing roots (as ivy, etc.), from the stem [Bot.].
radicate, *v.t.* *rad*-e-kate, to root; to plant deeply and firmly: *v.i.* to take root: *a.* having a root; rooted [Bot.]; having root-like organs [Zool.]. (L. *radicatus*, rooted.)
radication, *n.* rad-e-*kay*-shon, process of radicating.
radicel, *n.* *rad*-e-sel, a small root; a rootlet.
radiciform, *a.* ra-*dis*-e-form, root-shaped.
radicivorous, *a.* rad-e-*siv*-o-rus, feeding on roots.
radicle, *n.* *rad*-ikl, that part of a seed which, upon vegetating, becomes the root; the root-like part of a vessel, nerve, etc. [Anat.]; a radical [Chem.]. (L. *radicula*, a little root.)
radicular, *a.* ra-*dik*-yew-lar, pertaining to a radicle [Bot.], or [Anat.] to roots (of nerves, etc.); affecting such roots [Path.].
radiculose, *a.* ra-*dik*-yew-lohs, producing many rootlets.
radiferous, *a.* ra-*dif*-er-rus, containing radium.
radio-, *ray*-de-o, combining form from L. *radius*, ray.
radio, *n.* *ray*-de-o, wireless telegraphy or telephony; a message transmitted by these; broadcasting; a wireless receiving set: *v.t.* and *i.* to broadcast or send messages by wireless telegraphy or telephony; to take an X-ray photograph.
radioactivate, *v.t.* *ray*-de-o-*ak*-te-vate, to make radioactive.
radioactive, *a.* *ray*-de-o-*ak*-tiv, pertaining to or having the property of radioactivity.
radioactivity, *n.* *ray*-de-o-ak-*tiv*-e-te, the spontaneous emission by certain elements, through disintegration of the nuclei of their atoms, of invisible rays able to penetrate bodies impervious to ordinary light.
radiochemistry, *n.* *ray*-de-o-*kem*-is-tre, the chemistry of the radioactive elements.
radiogoniometer, *n.* *ray*-de-o-gon-e-*om*-e-ter, a direction-finder used in wireless and in the navigation of aircraft and ships.
radiogram, *n.* *ray*-de-o-gram, a radio-telegram; also [Coll.] a radio-gramophone.
radio-gramophone, *n.* a combination of wireless receiving set and gramophone.
radiograph, *n.* *ray*-de-o-graf, an actinograph; an X-ray photograph: *v.t.* to take such a photograph. (L. *radius*, a ray, Gr. *grapho*, write.)
radiographer, *n.* ray-de-*og*-ra-fer, a practitioner of radiography.
radiography, *n.* ray-de-*og*-ra-fe, the study of X-rays; the act or process of making radiographs.

radiolarian, *a.* ray-de-o-*lare*-re-an, pertaining to or resembling the Radiolaria, a class of marine protozoans having in the centre of the protoplasmic body a membranous capsule surrounding the nucleus: *n.* any member of the Radiolaria.

radiolocation, *n.* *ray*-de-o-lo-*kay*-shun, the science of detecting the presence, position, direction, etc., of rapidly moving objects, esp. aircraft and self-propelled missiles, by means of wireless rays.

radiologist, *n.* ray-de-*ol*-o-jist, a practitioner of radiology or radiotherapy.

radiology, *n.* ray-de-*ol*-o-je, that branch of science that deals with radioactivity, esp. in its therapeutic use; the study, or application, of X-rays in medicine and surgery. (L. *radius*, and Gr. *logos*, science.)

radiometer, *n.* ray-de-*om*-e-ter, an instrument for measuring the intensity of radiant energy.

radiometry, *n.* ray-de-*om*-e-tre, measurement of radiant energy; the use of the radiometer.

radiophone, *n.* *ray*-de-o-fone, an instrument which by means of radiant energy produces sound.

radioscope, *n.* *ray*-de-o-skope, a device by which the presence of radioactivity can be ascertained.

radioscopy, *n.* ray-de-*os*-ko-pe, examination by means of the radioscope [Med.].

radio-telegram, *n.* a telegram transmitted by wireless.

radio-telegraphy, *n.* wireless telegraphy.

radio-telephony, *n.* telephony by means of radio waves.

radiotheraphy, *n.* *ray*-de-o-*the*-ra-pe, treatment involving the use of X-rays or other radioactivity [Med.].

radiothorium, *n.* *ray*-de-o-*thaw*-re-um, a radioactive disintegration product and isotope of thorium.

radish, *n.* *rad*-ish, a plant of the genus *Raphanus*, with a slightly acrid fleshy root, used as a salad. (Fr. *radis*.)

radium, *n.* *ray*-de-um, a very rare radioactive metallic element, chemically related to barium, discovered in pitchblende, 1898. **radium emanation,** radon. (L. *radius*, ray.)

radius, *n.* *ray*-de-us (*pl.* **radii**), the semi-diameter of a circle, any straight line drawn from its centre to the circumference; the exterior bone of the fore-arm [Anat.]; the ray of a flower [Bot.]. **radius of curvature,** the radius of that circle which would have the same tangent as a given curve at a particular point [Geom.]. **radius vector,** a straight line drawn from the centre of an attracting to that of the attracted body [Astron.]. (L., a rod, a spoke, a ray.)

radix, *n.* *ray*-diks, a root, esp. of words; the base of a system of logarithms or of numbers; any one of the spinal nerve-roots [Anat.]. (L., root.)

radon, *n.* *ray*-don, radium emanation, a radioactive gaseous element produced by the disintegration of radium.

radula, *n.* *rad*-yew-la, the lingual ribbon of certain molluscs.

raduliform, *a.* ra-*dew*-le-form, resembling a rasp.

raff, *n.* raf, the rabble; the riff-raff.

raffia, *n.* *raf*-e-a, the Madagascar palm, *Raphia ruffia*, or the Japanese *R. tædigera*; the fibre of either of these, used for tying up plants, etc., and in mat-making, coarse embroidery, etc.

raffish, *a.* *raf*-ish, rakish; dissipated.

raffle, *n.* *raf*-l, a lottery, in which each person pays an equal share of the amount at which the prize is valued: *v.i.* and *t.* to engage in or dispose of by a raffle. (O.Fr.)

Rafflesia, *n.* raf-*flee*-ze-a, a genus of stemless and leafless parasitic plants, having flowers a yard or more across. (Discovered in Sumatra by Sir Stamford *Raffles*, 1818.)

raft, *n.* rahft, a floating floor on a framework; logs fastened together for transport by floating: *v.t.* to carry on a raft: *v.i.* to use a raft. **raft duck,** the scaup. (Ice. *raptr*, a beam.)

rafter, *n.* *rahf*-ter, a roof timber; a man employed on a raft; a lumberman: *v.t.* to furnish with rafters. (A.S.)

raftsman, *n.* *rahfts*-man, one who manages a raft.

rafty, *a.* *rahf*-te, damp; musty.

rag, *n.* rag, a tattered piece of cloth; a fragment of dress: *pl.* garments worn out; mean dress. (Scand. *ragg*, rough hair.)

rag, *n.* rag, a hard coarse limestone; a large roofing slate smoothed on one side only. (Origin unknown.)

rag, *n.* rag, a row; a lark: *v.t.* and *i.* to torment, tease, or play practical jokes upon; to disorder a person's room or clothing; to riot [Slang].

ragamuffin, *n.* *rag*-a-muf-in, a beggarly, disreputable fellow; a ragged boy.

rag-bolt, *n.* an iron pin with barbs on its shank to retain it in its place.

rage, *n.* raje, violent anger; fury; vehemence; extreme violence; enthusiasm; any object pursued with transitory enthusiasm or eagerness: *v.i.* to be furious with anger; to storm; to ravage; to act or move furiously. (Fr.)

rageful, *a.* *raje*-ful, full of rage; violent.

rag-fair, *n.* a sale, or market for the sale, of second-hand wearing apparel.

ragg, *n.* rag, rag (the stone).

ragged, *a.* *rag*-ed, rent or worn into tatters; wearing tattered clothes; rough or jagged; dressed in rags. **ragged robin,** the plant *Lychnis floscuculi*. **ragged school,** a former free charity-school for destitute children.

raggedly, *ad.* in a ragged manner.

raggedness, *n.* the state of being ragged.

ragi, *n.* *rah*-ge, an Indian millet, *Eleusine coracana*, used for food in the East. (Hindi.)

raging, *a.* *raje*-ing, acting with fury; violent; frantic: *n.* fury; violence.

ragingly, *ad.* in a raging manner.

raglan, *n.* *rag*-lan, a style of overcoat leaving sleeves that run straight to the neck with no shoulder-seams: *a.* in or of this style. (Lord *Raglan*, d. 1855.)

ragman, *n.* *rag*-man, a collector of or dealer in rags. **Ragman Roll,** the record, contained on parchment rolls, of those instruments in which the Scottish nobility pledged allegiance to Edward I.

ragoût, *n.* ra-*goo*, a highly seasoned stew. (Fr., from L. *re-*, again, *gustare*, taste.)

ragstone, *n.* *rag*-stone, rag (the stone).

ragtag, *n.* *rag*-tag (*also* **ragtag and bobtail**), the lowest orders in society; the riff-raff.

ragtime, *n.* *rag*-time, a syncopated form of musical composition adopted from negro folk-melodies.

raguly, *a.* *rag*-ew-le, jagged or notched [Her.].

ragweed, *n.* *rag*-weed, any of several plants of the *Compositæ* family.

rag-wheel, *n.* a sprocket-wheel.

ragwort, *n.* *rag*-wurt, a yellow-flowered wayside plant of the genus *Senecio*.

raid, *n.* rade, a predatory incursion; a sudden invasion and retreat; an air-raid; an unexpected visit: *v.t.* to make a raid. (A.S. *rād*, road.)

raider, *n.* *rade*-er, one who takes part in a raid.

***rail,** *n.* rale, a wooden or metal bar, a series of such forming a railing, fence, or balustrade, etc.; one of the crossbars of a panelled door; a steel bar forming a tramway or railway track; a continuous line of such rails, a railway: *v.t.* to fence with or furnish with rails; to send by railway. (O.Fr. *reille*.)

rail, *v.i.* rale, to utter reproaches; to scoff. (Fr. *railler*.)

rail, *n.* rale, any of several small wading birds of the family Rallidæ, esp. the water-rail, *Rallus aquaticus*, and the land-rail. (O.Fr. *raalle*.)

rail-car, *n.* a railway motor-car; [U.S.A.] a railway coach.

railer, *n.* *rale*-er, one who scoffs or rails.

railer, *n.* *rale*-er, one who fits or makes rails.

rail-fence, *n.* a fence made of wooden rails.

railhead, *n.* *rale*-hed, the farthest point reached by a railway under construction; the point on a railway from which supplies, reinforcements, etc., are distributed [Mil.].

railing, *n.* *rale*-ing, a fence, balustrade, etc., of rails; iron fencing; rails in general; materials for rails.

railing, *a.* *rale*-ing, expressing reproach; insulting: *n.* vociferous abuse or reproach.

railingly, *ad.* in a railing, or a bantering, manner.

raillery, *n.* *rale*-er-re, banter; jesting language; good-humoured pleasantry or light satire. (Fr.)

railroad, *n.* *rale*-rode, a railway.

railway, *n.* *rale*-way, a road along steel rails on which trains are run; a track laid with rails; a unified system of such tracks with its stations, sidings, rolling-stock, staff, etc.

raiment, *n.* *ray*-ment, clothing in general; vesture; apparel. (*array* and *-ment*.)

***rain,** *n.* rane, water falling in drops from the

atmosphere; a fall of these: *pl.* the rainy season (esp. in the tropics): *v.i.* to fall in drops from the clouds; to fall like rain: *v.t.* to pour or shower down. **rain goose,** the red-throated diver. (A.S. *regn.*)

rain-band, *n.* a dark band in the solar spectrum caused by the presence of aqueous vapour in the atmosphere.

rainbird, *n. rane*-bird, any of several birds of the genus *Cuculus*, esp. the Jamaican ground cuckoo.

rainbow, *n. rane*-boh, the arched spectrum appearing opposite the sun during rain, produced by the refraction and reflection of the sun's light from the drops. **lunar rainbow,** a phenomenon analogous to the rainbow but produced by the moon. **secondary rainbow,** an additional arch to the rainbow with the prismatic colours in the reverse order. **rainbow trout,** the anadromous Californian trout, *Salmo irideus*. **rainbow wrasse,** the sea-fish, *Labris vulgaris*. (A.S. *regn*, rain, *boga*, a bow.)

raincoat, *n. rane*-koat, a light overcoat suitable for wearing in the rain.

raindrop, *n. rane*-drop, a single drop of rain.

rainfall, *n. rane*-fawl, the amount of rain that falls in any particular place.

rain-gauge, *n.* an instrument for measuring the quantity of rain that falls.

raininess, *n. rane*-e-ness, state of being rainy.

rainless, *a. rane*-less, without rain.

rainproof, *a. rane*-proof, impervious to rain: *n.* a rain-resisting cape.

raintree, *n. rane*-tree, the tropical American tree *Pithecolobium saman*, so called because its leaflets appear to exude water.

rain-water, *n.* water that has fallen as rain.

rainy, *a. rane*-e, abounding with rain; showery. **rainy day,** a time of misfortune or need.

Rais, *n.* race, a Reis, or Moslem chief.

raise, *v.t.* raze, to cause to rise; to lift; to set upright; to erect; to build; to exalt; to produce; to increase; to excite; to stir up; to bring into being; to bring into life; to call up; to originate; to collect; to levy; to cause to grow; to cause to swell. **raise a siege,** to remove a besieging army and abandon the attempt. **raise Cain,** to riot or behave riotously [Slang]. **raise the wind,** to borrow money. (Ice. *reisa.*)

raiser, *n. raze*-er, one who or that which raises.

raisin, *n. raze*-in, a dried grape. (O.Fr.)

raisonné, *a.* ray-zon-*ay*, systematically arranged and described (esp. of entries in a catalogue). (Fr., logical.)

raj, *n.* rahj, rule; dominion [Anglo-Ind.]. (Sans.)

Raja or **Rajah,** *n. rah*-jah, in India, a native prince, king, or tribal chief. (Sans.)

Rajahship, *n. rah*-jah-ship, the rank or dominion of a rajah.

Rajput, *n. rahj*-poot, a Hindu of a dominant and military caste. (Sans. *raja*, and *putra*, son.)

rake, *n.* rake, a long-handled tined implement used for collecting light things, smoothing the soil, etc.: *v.t.* to scrape or gather with a rake; to clear or smooth with a rake; to collect; to search; to enfilade; to fire in the direction of the length [Mil.]: *v.i.* to scrape; to search minutely and meanly. (A.S. *raca.*)

rake, *n.* rake, a loose, dissolute man: *v.i.* to lead a dissolute, debauched life. (*rakehell.*)

rake, *n.* rake, the projection of the upper parts of a ship, at the stern and stem beyond the keel; slope; the inclination, generally aft, of a mast from the perpendicular [Naut.]. (Origin uncertain.)

rakehell, *n. rake*-hell, a lewd, dissolute fellow; a rake.

rake-off, *n.* a commission (esp. when hidden); clandestine profit.

raker, *n. rake*-er, one who rakes.

raking, *a. rake*-ing, enfilading; inclining; speedy.

raking, *n. rake*-ing, the working with a rake: *pl.* matter so collected.

rakish, *a. rake*-ish, given to a dissolute life; debauched; sloping backwards; set at an angle.

rakishly, *ad.* in a rakish manner.

rakishness, *n.* dissolute practices; debauchery.

râle, *n.* rahl, a rattling sound in morbidly affected lungs [Med.]. (Fr., rattle.)

rallentando, *a.* and *ad.* ral-en-*tan*-doh, gradually decreasing in pace [Mus.]. (It.)

ralline, *a. ral*-ine, pertaining to the Rallidæ, the family of birds comprising the rails.

rally, *n. ral*-e, the act of bringing disordered troops to their ranks; the act of recovering strength; a rapid interchange of strokes at tennis or similar game; a prearranged gathering (of persons): *v.t.* to reunite; to collect, as disordered troops: *v.i.* to come back to order; to recover strength. (Fr. *rallier.*)

rally, *n. ral*-le, exercise of good humour or satirical merriment: *v.t.* to attack with raillery; to banter; to indulge in satirical humour. (Fr. *railler.*)

ram, *n.* ram, the male of the sheep; a battering-ram; a steel beak at the bow of a warship; a warship with such a beak; a rammer; a drop-hammer or pile-driver, or the weight used; a hydraulic engine for raising weights: *v.t.* to drive with violence; to force in; to cram; to butt like a ram. **the Ram,** Aries, a constellation of the zodiac. (A.S.)

Ramadan, *n. ram*-a-dan, the ninth month of the Mohammedan year, the Mohammedan Lent. (Ar.)

ramal, *a. ray*-mal, pertaining to branches; branching.

ramble, *n. ram*-bl, a roving; a stroll; a random excursion: *v.i.* to wander about; to rove at large; to be desultory. (Origin uncertain.)

rambler, *n. ram*-bler, one who rambles about; a rover; a climbing rose.

rambling, *ppr.* and *a. ram*-bling, moving about irregularly; desultory; disjointed.

ramblingly, *ad.* in a rambling manner.

rambutan, *n.* ram-*boo*-tan, the Malayan tree *Nephelium lappaceum*, or its pulpy fruit.

ramekin, *n. ram*-e-kin, baked bread-crumbs with cheese and eggs. (Fr. *ramequin.*)

ramentaceous, *a.* ram-en-*tay*-shus, covered with or resembling ramenta.

ramentum, *n.* ra-*men*-tum (*pl.* **ramenta**), a thin brown scale, a number of which form patches on certain ferns, etc. [Bot.]. (L.)

rameous, *a. ray*-me-us, belonging to a branch or branches [Bot.].

ramicorn, *a. ram*-e-kawrn, having branching antennæ [Entom.]: *n.* the horny sheath on the lower mandible (of birds).

ramie, *n. ram*-e, China grass, a species of *Boehmeria*, or its tough cotton-like fibre.

ramification, *n.* ram-e-fe-*kay*-shon, division or separation into branches; a subdivision; manner of branching; production of figures or arrangement like branches. (L. *ramus*, branch, *facio*, make.)

ramify, *v.t. ram*-e-fy, to cause to divide into branches: *v.i.* to shoot into branches; to be divided or subdivided. (Fr. *ramifier.*)

ramline, *n. ram*-line, the rope used to mark the middle line of a ship under construction.

rammer, *n. ram*-er, one who rams or drives; a tool for pounding or for driving anything with force; a ramrod.

rammish, *a. ram*-mish, characteristic of a ram; strong-scented; untamed.

rammishness, *n.* state of being rammish.

rammy, *a. ram*-e, like a ram; strong-scented.

ramollissement, *n.* (App.), a morbid softening of an organ or tissue. (Fr.)

ramose, *a.* ra-*mohs*, branchy; consisting of or full of branches; branched. (L. *ramosus.*)

ramous, *a. ray*-mus, branching; branchy; ramose.

ramp, *n.* ramp, a leap; a bound; a sloping part or passage-way connecting different levels; the slope between the levels of the abutment of a rampant arch [Arch.]: *v.i.* to spring; to bound; to rear; to storm or rampage: *v.t.* to provide with ramps. (Fr. *ramper*, to creep.)

ramp, *n.* ramp, a swindle; financial or commercial trickery [Slang].

rampage, *n.* ram-*paje*, an excited state; violent behaviour: *v.i.* to romp or prance riotously about; to storm unrestrainedly.

rampageous, *a.* ram-*pay*-jus, rowdy; noisy.

rampageously, *ad.* in a rowdy manner.

rampancy, *n. ram*-pan-se, state of being rampant; excessive prevalence or luxuriance.

rampant, *a. ram*-pant, rank in growth; exuberant; widespread; overleaping restraint; aggressive; standing on the hind legs [Her.].

rampantly, *ad.* in a rampant manner.

rampart, *n. ram*-part, a defensive wall or embankment; the mound of earth carrying the parapet [Fort.]: *v.t.* to fortify with ramparts. (Fr. *rempart.*)

rampike, *n. ram*-pike, a dead tree, or one decayed at the top; the stump of a tree [Dial.].
rampion, *n. ram*-pe-on, a bell-flower, *Campanula rapunculus*, with a panicle of red, purple, or blue flowers. (It. *ramponzolo.*)
ramrod, *n. ram*-rod, the rod for ramming home the charge in a muzzle-loading gun.
ramshackle, *a. ram*-shak-kl, makeshift; badly built; falling to bits. (Perhaps *ransack.*)
ramson, *n. ram*-zon, the hedgerow garlic, *Allium ursinum*; its bulbous root (used in salads). (A.S. *hramsan.*)
ramulose, *a. ram*-yew-lohs, ramulous.
ramulous, *a. ram*-yew-lus, having many small branches. (L. *ramulosus.*)
ramus, *n. ray*-mus (*pl.* **rami,** *ray*-my), a process of certain bones; a branch of an artery, vein, or nerve [Anat.]. (L., branch.)
ran, ran, *p.* of *run.*
Rana, *n. rah*-na, the genus of amphibians comprising the frogs and toads. (L., a frog.)
rance, *n.* rahns, a dull red marble with blue and white veining. (Fr.)
ranch, *n.* rahnch, a large farm for grazing cattle and horses [Amer.]: *v.i.* to work a ranch. (Sp. *rancho,* a mess-room.)
rancher, *n. rahn*-cher, one who owns and works a ranch; a ranchman.
ranchero, *n.* rahn-*chare*-ro, one employed on a ranch; a herdsman. (Sp.)
ranchman, *n. rahnch*-man, one engaged on a ranch; a stockbreeder.
rancho, *n. rahn*-cho, a hut or group of huts for herdsmen or farm-labourers; a ranch. (Sp., a mess.)
rancid, *a. ran*-sid, having a rank smell; sour; musty. (L. *rancidus,* rank.)
rancidity, *n.* ran-*sid*-e-te, rancidness.
rancidly, *ad.* in a rancid manner.
rancidness, *n.* the quality of being rancid.
rancorous, *a. rank*-or-us, deeply malignant; intensely spiteful.
rancorously, *ad.* with rancour.
rancour, *n. rank*-or, deep-seated, implacable enmity; spite; virulence; malignity. (O.Fr.)
rand, *n.* rand, a border, edge, or margin; the untilled margin of a field; a thin inner sole, as of cork. **the Rand,** a gold-bearing reef near Johannesburg, Transvaal. (A.S.)
randan, *n.* ran-*dan*, a rowing crew of three, one using sculls, the others oars, the sculler occupying the middle thwart; this method of rowing. **on the randan,** on the spree [Slang].
randem, *ad. ran*-dem, with three (horses) placed one before the other: *n.* a vehicle with horses so harnessed.
random, *a. ran*-dom, done at hazard; left to chance; done or uttered without premeditation. **at random,** without consideration or definite aim. **random shot,** a shot discharged without any direct aim. (O.Fr. *à randon,* in great haste.)
randy, *a. ran*-de, noisy or loud-voiced [Scot.]; lustful.
ranee, *n. rah*-nee, a woman ruling as a rajah; the consort of a rajah. (Hind.)
rang, rang, *p.* of *ring.*
★**range,** *n.* raynj, a row; a class; sphere of power; a wide tract, esp. of grazing land; mountains, or mountainous country; a kitchen-grate or cooking-stove; a line of direction; the length of this, esp. the extreme horizontal distance to which a projectile may be thrown; a place for the practice of shooting: *v.t.* to set in a row; to dispose in proper order; to rove over; to sail along: *v.i.* to rove at large; to be placed in order; to lie in a particular direction; to sail or pass near. (Fr. *ranger.*)
range-finder, *n.* an optical instrument used, esp. in conjunction with a firearm, for determining the distance of an object from the point of observation; a telemeter.
ranger, *n. raynj*-er, one who ranges; a forest or park officer; one who works on a range; a dog trained to search for game; a mounted rifleman trained to fight on foot [Mil.]: *pl.* infantry trained for scouting purposes [Mil.].
rangership, *n. raynj*-er-ship, the post or rank of the ranger of a forest or park.
rangy, *a. rayn*-je, having mountain ranges; long-limbed and slender [U.S.A.].
rani, *n. rah*-nee, a ranee. (Hind.)
ranine, *a. ran*-ine, pertaining to or like frogs [Zool.]; pertaining to the under surface of the tip of the tongue [Anat.]. (L. *rana,* a frog.)
rank, *n.* rank, a row; a line of men placed abreast; relative grade; dignity; eminence; high station; class: *v.t.* to place abreast or in a line; to dispose methodically; to classify: *v.i.* to be placed in a rank; to have a certain grade in society. **other ranks,** those men in the army not bearing commissioned rank [Mil.]. **take rank,** to enjoy precedence. **rank and file,** the whole body, esp. of common soldiers; the common herd. (Fr. *rang.*)
rank, *a.* rank, luxuriant in growth; causing vigorous growth; rancid; rampant; excessive; coarse; high-grown; strong. (A.S. *ranc.*)
ranker, *n. rang*-ker, one who disposes in ranks; one who arranges; a commissioned officer who has been promoted from the other ranks [Mil.].
rankle, *v.i. rang*-kl, to grow more rank or strong; to fester; to be inflamed; to irritate or cause irritation. (O.Fr. *rancler.*)
rankly, *ad.* in a rank manner.
rankness, *n.* the quality of being rank.
ransack, *v.t. ran*-sak, to search thoroughly; to pillage. (Ice. *rann,* house, *saka,* to seek.)
ransom, *n. ran*-sum, the price paid for the redemption of a prisoner or slave, or for goods captured by an enemy; release from captivity, bondage, or possession of an enemy; formerly, a sum paid for a pardon [Law]: *v.t.* to redeem from captivity or bondage; to redeem from the bondage of sin [Theol.]. (Fr. *rançon.*)
ransomer, *n. ran*-sum-er, one who redeems.
rant, *n.* rant, a boisterous and idle declamation: *v.i.* to rave in violent, futile, or bombastic declamation. (Old Dut. *randten,* to rave.)
ranter, *n. rant*-er, a noisy talker; a boisterous preacher. **the Ranters,** a former name of the Primitive Methodists.
rantingly, *ad. rant*-ing-le, in a ranting manner.
rantipole, *a. ran*-te-pole, wild; rakish: *n.* a termagant: *v.i.* to run about wildly. (*rant* and *poll.*)
ranula, *n. ran*-yew-la, a glandular swelling under the tip of the tongue [Med.]. (L., a little frog.)
Ranunculus, *n.* ra-*nun*-kew-lus, a large genus of plants including the buttercups. (L.)
ranz-des-vaches, *n.* (App.), a melody played on the horn by Alpine herdsmen when driving cattle to or from the pastures. (Fr.)
rap, *n.* rap, a quick, smart blow: *v.i.* and *t.* to strike with a quick, sharp blow; to knock. (Scand.)
rap, *n.* rap, a counterfeit Irish halfpenny of the early 18th cent. **not worth a rap,** worthless.
rap, *n.* rap, a yarn measure of 120 yards.
rap, *v.t.* rap, to transport out of oneself; to snatch or hurry away; to seize by violence. (*rape.*)
rapacious, *a.* ra-*pay*-shus, given to plunder; seizing by force; subsisting on prey; greedy; voracious. (L. *rapax,* grasping.)
rapaciously, *ad.* in a rapacious manner.
rapaciousness, *n.* quality of being rapacious.
rapacity, *n.* ra-*pas*-e-te, rapaciousness; addictedness to plunder; ravenousness; greediness of gain.
rape, *n.* rape, a seizing and carrying away by force; the carnal knowledge of a woman against her will [Law]: *v.t.* to commit the act of rape [Law]. (L. *raptum,* seized.)
rape, *n.* rape, any of the six territorial divisions of the county of Sussex. (A.S.; origin unknown.)
rape, *n.* rape, a turnip-like plant of the genus *Brassica,* esp. *B. napus,* from the seeds of which colza oil is expressed. **wild rape,** charlock. (L. *rapa,* a turnip.)
rape, *n.* rape, the refuse of grapes after expression of the juice in wine-making; rape-wine. (Fr. *râpe,* as *rappee.*)
rape-cake, *n. rape*-kake, compressed refuse after the oil has been expressed from rape-seed, used as cattle-food and fertilizer.
rape-wine, *n.* a thin wine made from rape (the refuse of grapes).
Raphaelesque, *a. raf*-ay-el-*esk*, in the style of Raphael Sanzio (1483–1520), the Italian painter.
Raphaelism, *n. raf*-ay-el-izm, the ideal style of art introduced by Raphael.
Raphaelite, *n. raf*-ay-el-ite, a follower of Raphael.
raphania, *n.* ra-*fay*-ne-a, a form of ergotism said to be due to eating seeds of a plant of the genus *Raphanus* (radish).

raphe, *n.* *ray*-fe, a seam-like suture [Anat.]; the process uniting the base of the nucleus with the base of the ovule [Bot.]. (Gr., a seam.)
raphia, *n.* *ray*-fe-ah, raffia.
raphides, *n.pl.* *raf*-e-deez, minute needle-shaped transparent crystals present in the tissues of plants. (Gr. *raphis*, a needle.)
raphilite, *n.* *raf*-il-ite, an asbestiform variety of tremolite. (Gr. *raphis*, needle, *lithos*, stone.)
rapid, *a.* *rap*-id, very quick or swift; speedy: *n.pl.* a considerable descent and swift flow of water. (L. *rapidus*.)
rapidity, *n.* ra-*pid*-e-te, swiftness.
rapidly, *ad.* *rap*-id-le, in a rapid manner.
rapidness, *n.* the quality of being rapid.
rapier, *n.* *ray*-pe-er, a long thin-bladed sword used only in thrusting. (Fr. *rapière*.)
rapier-fish, *n.* the swordfish.
rapine, *n.* *rap*-ine, act of plundering; the seizing and carrying away of things by force; pillage; violence.
rapparee, *n.* rap-a-*ree*, an Irish freebooter or highwayman of the 17th century. (Ir. *rapaire*, a thief.)
rappee, *n.* ra-*pee*, a strong snuff. (Fr. *râpé*, rasped.)
rappel, *n.* ra-*pel*, the beat of drums to arms. (Fr.)
rapper, *n.* *rap*-per, one who raps; a spirit-rapper.
rapport, *n.* ra-*por*, intimate relation; harmony. (Fr.)
rapprochement, *n.* (App.) reconciliation; the act of reconciling or bringing together; restoration of friendly relations between two states. (Fr.)
rapscallion *n.* rap-*skal*-e-on, a scamp; a rascally vagabond. (*rascal*.)
rapt, *a.* rapt, absorbed; carried away by one's thoughts, etc.; in an ecstasy. (L. *raptus*, seized.)
Raptores, *n.pl.* rap-*taw*-reez, a large order of birds of prey (L. *raptor*, a robber.)
raptorial, *a.* rap-*taw*-re-al, pertaining to or characteristic of the birds of prey; predatory.
raptorious, *a.* rap-*taw*-re-us, raptorial [Zool.].
rapture, *n.* *rap*-tewr, enthusiasm; ecstasy; heavenly joy; extreme pleasure. (L. *rapio*, seize.)
raptured, *a.* *rap*-tewrd, enraptured; transported.
rapturist, *n.* *rap*-tewr-rist, an enthusiast.
rapturous, *a.* *rap*-tewr-rus, ecstatic; ravishing.
rapturously, *ad.* in a rapturous manner.
rare, *a.* rare, not frequent; scarce; thinly scattered; not dense; porous; unusually excellent. **rare earth,** any of several oxides of a group of scarce chemically related metallic elements, including lanthanum, cerium, terbium, erbium, yttrium, etc. (L. *rarus*.)
rare, *a.* rare, nearly raw; underdone. (A.S. *hrer*.)
rarebit, *n.* *rare*-bit, a dish of melted or toasted cheese on toast, a Welsh rabbit.
raree-show, *n.* *rare*-re-shoh, a peep-show.
rarefaction, *n.* rare-re-*fak*-shon, the act or process of rarefying; the act of decreasing the density (esp. of air); state of being rarefied. (Fr.)
rarefactive, *a.* rare-re-*fak*-tiv, capable of rarefying; characterized by rarefaction.
rarefiable, *a.* *rare*-re-fy-a-bl, capable of being rarefied.
rarefy, *v.t.* *rare*-re-fy, to make thin and porous or less dense; to expand a body: *v.i.* to become thin and porous. (Fr. *raréfier*.)
rarely, *ad.* *rare*-le, seldom; not often.
rareness, *n.* *rare*-ness, the state of being rare.
rareripe, *a.* *rare*-ripe, ripe before others, or before the usual season: *n.* an early fruit, esp. a variety of early-ripening peach.
rarity, *n.* *rare*-re-te, infrequency; tenuity; anything rare. (L. *raritas*.)
rascal, *n.* *rahs*-kal, a mean fellow; a scoundrel; a rogue (esp. of men guilty of petty offences): *a.* mean; low. (O.Fr. *rascaille*.)
rascaldom, *n.* *rahs*-kal-dom, rascals collectively.
rascalism, *n.* *rahs*-kal-izm, the practices of rascals; rascality.
rascality, *n.* rahs-*kal*-e-te, villainy; mean trickishness or dishonesty; base fraud.
rascally, *a.* *rahs*-kal-e, meanly trickish or dishonest; knavish; vile; worthless.
rase, *v.t.* raze, to raze.
rash, *a.* rash, hasty in counsel or action; precipitate; headstrong; uttered or undertaken with too much haste. (M.E. *rasch*.)
rash, *n.* rash, an eruption on the skin. (O.Fr. *rasche*.)
rasher, *n.* *rash*-er, a thin slice (of ham or bacon for frying). (Origin unknown.)
rashling, *n.* *rash*-ling, one who acts rashly.
rashly, *ad.* *rash*-le, with precipitation; hastily.
rashness, *n.* the quality of being rash; temerity; foolhardiness; a rash act.
rasorial, *a.* ra-*zaw*-re-al, pertaining to the Rasores, an order of birds that scratch the ground for food; gallinaceous. (L. *rasor*, a scraper.)
rasp, *n.* rahsp, a coarse file; the radula of a mollusc: *v.t.* to file with a rasp; to irritate. **rasp palm,** the paxiuba (*Irartea exorrhiza*), a Brazilian palm the rough-surfaced roots of which are used by the natives as graters. (O.Fr. *rasper*.)
raspatory, *n.* *rahs*-pa-to-re, a surgeon's rasp for trimming bone surfaces.
raspberry, *n.* *rahz*-ber-re, the plant *Rubus idæus*, or its fruit; a hiss, or other noise of disapproval [Slang]. **raspberry cane,** the stem or one of the woody shoots of the raspberry. **raspberry jam tree,** the Australian tree *Acacia acuminata* (from the scent of its wood). **raspberry vinegar,** a preparation of raspberry-juice and vinegar. (Origin uncertain.)
rasper, *n.* *rahs*-per, a rasping tool or machine; a difficult fence to jump, also, an unpleasant person or thing [Slang].
raspy, *a.* *rahs*-pe, harsh; grating.
rasse, *n.* rass, a small civet, *Viverra malaccensis*, of China and the East Indies. (Javanese.)
rasure, *n.* *raze*-yewr, the act of scraping or erasing; an erasure. (Fr.)
***rat,** *n.* rat, a rodent of the genus *Mus*; a black-leg, also one who works for less than the trade-union rate; one who deserts his party [Politics]: *v.i.* to hunt rats, esp. with a dog; to play the rat (as a worker or in politics). **rats!** a cry of derision or unbelief. **sea rat,** a pirate [Slang]. **smell a rat,** to be suspicious. **water rat,** the water vole *Microtus amphibius*. (A.S. *ræt*.)
rata, *n.* *rah*-ta, the New Zealand tree *Metrosideros robusta*, of the myrtle family. (Maori.)
ratable, *a.* *rate*-a-bl, rateable.
ratafia, *n.* rat-a-*fee*-ah, a liqueur flavoured with almond or similar kernels; a biscuit thus flavoured. (Fr.)
ratal, *n.* *rate*-al, the value at which property is rated.
ratany, *n.* *rat*-an-e, rhatany.
rataplan, *n.* rat-a-*plan*, the drum-beat. (Fr.)
ratcatcher, *n.* *rat*-katch-er, one whose business it is to catch rats.
ratch, *n.* ratch, ratchet: *v.i.* to sail with the wind abeam, to reach [Naut.].
ratchel, *n.* *ratch*-el, loose stones lying on bed-rock.
ratchet, *n.* *ratch*-et, the bar which stops a ratchet-wheel; a bar furnished with angular teeth, into which a pawl or catch drops, to prevent machines from running back; a detent; a pawl.
ratchet-wheel, *n.* a wheel having angular teeth, into which a ratchet drops, to prevent it from turning backwards.
***rate,** *n.* rate, the proportion or standard by which quantity or value is adjusted; price fixed or stated; settled allowance; degree; degree of value; a municipal tax for local purposes; the order or class of a ship [Navy]: *v.t.* to value; to estimate; to fix the grade of; to find the amount by which a clock gains or loses [Astron.]; to find the horse-power of an engine: *v.i.* to be considered in a class; to be rated as. (O.Fr.)
rate, *v.t.* rate, to scold vehemently; to reprove: *v.i.* to storm. (Origin uncertain.)
rateable, *a.* *rate*-a-bl, that may be set at a certain value; liable for rating; subject to local taxation.
rateably, *ad.* *rate*-a-ble, by rate.
ratel, *n.* *ray*-tel, a badger-like mammal of the genus *Mellivora*, of India and S. Africa. (Taal.)
ratepayer, *n.* *rate*-pay-er, one who pays or is liable for rates.
rater, *n.* *rate*-er, an assessor or person fixing a rate; (as a suffix) a type or class of racing yacht.
rath, *n.* rahth *or* rah, a prehistoric Irish fortification. (Ir.)
rathe, *a.* raythe, coming into flower early; pertaining to the early hours: *ad.* early. (A.S. *hraeth*.)
rather, *ad.* *rah*-ther, more readily or willingly; in preference; sooner than otherwise; more properly;

slightly; especially; assuredly (as an answer). **had** or **would rather,** desire in preference. **the rather,** for better reason. (A.S. *hrathor,* sooner.)
raticide, *n.* *rat*-e-side, any poisonous preparation for the destruction of rats. (*rat,* and L. *cædere,* to kill.)
ratification, *n.* *rat*-e-fe-*kay*-shon, the act of ratifying; confirmation. (Fr.)
ratifier, *n.* *rat*-e-fy-er, one who ratifies.
ratify, *v.t.* *rat*-e-fy, to confirm; to establish; to approve and sanction. (Fr. *ratifier.*)
ratine, *n.* ra-*teen,* a loose-textured fabric resembling petersham; ratteen. (Fr. *ratiné,* frizzed.)
rating, *n.* *rate*-ing, the act of determining a rate; the amount (of rate) determined; the measurement tonnage class of a vessel [Naut.]; the position in the ship's crew of an individual sailor, hence, an enlisted man in the Royal Navy; rank; grade; the power of an engine; the amount by which a nominal watch or clock gains or loses [Astron.].
ratio, *n.* *ray*-she-oh, the relation or proportion of one thing to another. (L.)
ratiocinate, *v.i.* rash-e-*os*-e-nate, to reason in logical sequence; to argue discursively. (L. *ratiocinatus,* reasoned.)
ratiocination, *n.* rash-e-*os*-e-*nay*-shon, the act or process of reasoning or of deducing consequences from premises. (L. *ratiocinatus,* reasoned.)
ratiocinative, *a.* rash-e-*os*-e-na-tiv, argumentative; consisting in the comparison of things and the deduction of inferences from the comparison.
ration, *n.* *rash*-on, a certain allowance of provisions; allowance: *v.t.* to supply with rations; to subject (provisions, etc.) to a rationing scheme. **ration book,** a book of coupons, issued officially to individuals, entitling its legal holder to certain rations. **short rations,** restricted or insufficient supply. (Fr., from L. *ratio.*)
rational, *a.* *rash*-on-al, endowed with reason; agreeable to reason; not absurd or not extravagant; acting in conformity to reason; intelligent; judicious; expressible in, or involving only, finite terms [Math.]. **rational dress,** the knickerbocker costume formerly worn by women cyclists. (*ration.*)
rationale, *n.* rash-o-*nah*-le, a series of reasons assigned; a rational explanation; the principle of the matter. (L. *rationalis.*)
rationalism, *n.* *rash*-on-al-izm, the doctrine which finds in all knowledge a certain contribution of the pure reason; the derivation of all, esp. religious truth, from reason unaided by supernatural revelation; reliance on reason.
rationalist, *n.* *rash*-on-al-ist, one who is guided by reason; an adherent of rationalism; one who resolves the supernatural into the natural, inspiration into insight, or revelation into reason: *a.* pertaining to rationalists; rationalistic.
rationalistic, *a.* *rash*-on-al-*is*-tik, belonging to or in accordance with rationalism.
rationalistically, *ad.* in a rationalistic manner.
rationality, *n.* rash-on-*al*-e-te, the power of reasoning; reasonableness.
rationalization, *n.* *rash*-on-a-ly-*zay*-shon, the act or process of rationalizing; the policy or action of planning and regulating production and ensuring harmonious co-operation between workers and management and in all the internal and external relations of an industry [Econ.].
rationalize, *v.t.* *rash*-on-a-lize, to convert to rationalism; to explain by reason; to apprehend rationally; to effect rationalization [Econ.]: *v.i.* to rely solely or unduly on reason.
rationally, *ad.* in a rational manner; in consistency with reason.
ratite, *a.* *ray*-tite, belonging to the *Ratitæ,* a genus of birds (including the ostrich, emu, etc.), having a keel-less breastbone. (L. *ratis,* a raft.)
ratline, *n.* *rat*-lin, one of the horizontal pieces of rope crossing the shrouds of a ship to form the steps up the rigging. (Origin unknown.)
ratling, *n.* *rat*-ling, ratline.
ratoon, *n.* ra-*toon,* a sprout from the root of a sugar cane which has been cut down. (Sp. *retoño,* a sprout.)
ratsbane, *n.* *rats*-bane, any poison for rats.
rat-snake, *n.* a rat-killing snake of the family *Ptyas,* domesticated in Ceylon.
rat's-tail, *n.* *rats*-tale, a narrow and tapering file or other object; an excrescence growing from the pastern to the middle of the shank of a horse.
rat-tailed, *a.* *rat*-tayld, having a tail with little or no hair (esp. of horses); having a tapered extension of the handle beneath the bowl (of silver spoons and ladles).
rattan, *n.* ra-*tan,* the beat of a drum. (Imit.)
rattan, *n.* ra-*tan,* the stem of various climbing palms esp. *Calamus rotang*; a cane made of this. (Malay.)
rat-tat, *n.* rat-*tat,* a sound as of the postman's knock upon a door.
ratteen, *n.* ra-*teen,* a thick woollen stuff quilted or twilled. (Fr. *ratine.*)
ratten, *v.t.* *rat*-ten, to intimidate or persecute by destroying or removing away the property or tools of non-unionists in a union dispute.
ratter, *n.* *rat*-ter, a man or an animal that catches rats; one who rats, either from a party or as a workman.
rattinet, *n.* *rat*-e-net, a thin kind of ratteen.
ratting, *n.* *rat*-ing, the catching and killing of rats esp. as a sport; the desertion of a party, cause, etc.
rattish, *a.* *rat*-ish, somewhat resembling a rat in appearance or habits; inclined to play the rat (politically).
rattle, *n.* *rat*-tl, a rapid succession of sharp, clattering sounds; an instrument with which a clattering sound is made; loud, rapid talk; a noisy and empty talker; a rattling sound in the throat; a rattlebox: *v.i.* to make a quick, sharp noise rapidly repeated; to speak eagerly and noisily: *v.t.* to cause to make a rattling sound; to rail at clamorously; to fluster or disconcert. **red rattle** the common lousewort. (Low Ger. *ratelen.*)
rattlebox, *n.* *rat*-tl-boks, any plant, the ripe seeds of which rattle in their cases, esp. the **yellow rattle** the hardy annual, *Rhinanthus crista-galli.*
rattler, *n.* *rat*-tler, a noisy person; anything noisy a rattlesnake; a lie; a first-class thing of its sort [Slang].
rattleroot, *n.* *rat*-tl-root, the N. American plant *Cimicifuga racemosa.*
rattlesnake, *n.* *rat*-tl-snake, any venomous snake of the family Crotalidæ, the tails of which end in a rattle.
rattletrap, *a.* *rat*-tl-trap, rubbishly; rickety: *n.* a shaky vehicle.
rattlewing, *n.* *rat*-tl-wing, the golden-eye duck *Clangula glaucion.*
rattling, *a.* *rat*-ling, making a rapid succession of sharp sounds; quick; lively; very [Slang]: *ad.* extremely [Slang].
rat-trap, *n.* *rat*-trap, a trap for catching rats; also a toothed pedal for a bicycle.
ratty, *a.* *rat*-te, angry; irritated; bad-tempered infested with rats.
raucity, *n.* *raw*-se-te, hoarseness.
raucous, *a.* *raw*-kus, hoarse; harsh. (L. *raucus.*)
raughty, *a.* *raw*-te, excellent; tip-top; sprightly [Slang].
ravage, *n.* *rav*-aj, destruction by violence or by decay; devastation; waste: *v.t.* to lay waste; to despoil or plunder; to destroy. (Fr., as *ravish.*)
ravager, *n.* *rav*-aj-er, a plunderer; a spoiler.
rave, *v.i.* rave, to wander in mind or intellect; to be delirious; to talk irrationally; to rage like a madman; to dote. (Fr. *raver.*)
ravel, *v.t.* *rav*-el, to entangle; to entwist; to untwist: *v.i.* to become entangled; to become unravelled; to fray out: *n.* entanglement; the act of entangling; an entangled mass; a frayed end. (Mid. Dut. *ravelen.*)
ravelin, *n.* *rav*-lin, a detached work forming a salient angle to protect a curtain wall [Fort.]. (Fr.)
ravelling, *n.* *rav*-el-ing, the act of entangling or of disentangling; a thread detached by untwisting.
ravelment, *n.* *rav*-el-ment, entanglement; perplexity.
raven, *n.* *ray*-ven, the largest bird of the crow family *Corvus corax*: *a.* black as a raven. (A.S. *hræfn.*)
raven, *n.* *rav*-en, prey; plunder; rapine: *v.t.* to devour with eagerness; to obtain by violence: *v.i.* to go about ravaging; to be rapacious; to be ravenous. (O.Fr. *ravine,* plunder.)
ravener, *n.* *rav*-en-er, one who ravens or plunders.
ravening, *n.* *rav*-en-ing, eagerness for plunder.
ravenous, *a.* *rav*-en-us, famished; furiously voracious; eager for gratification. (Fr. *ravineux.*)
ravenously, *ad.* in a ravenous manner.

ravenousness, *n.* extreme voracity.
raver, *n.* *rave*-er, one who raves or is furious.
ravin, *n.* *rav*-in, plunder; rapine. **beast of ravin,** beast of prey.
ravine, *n.* ra-*veen*, a long, deep gully. (Fr.)
ravingly, *ad.* *rave*-ing-le, with furious wildness.
ravioli, *n.pl.* rah-ve-*oh*-le, pasties containing highly seasoned minced meat. (It.)
ravish, *v.t.* *rav*-ish, to seize and carry away by violence; to violate; to rape; to delight to ecstasy. (Fr., from L. *rapio*, seize and carry off.)
ravisher, *n.* *rav*-ish-er, one who ravishes.
ravishing, *a.* *rav*-ish-ing, delightful; entrancing.
ravishingly, *ad.* in a ravishing manner.
ravishment, *n.* *rav*-ish-ment, rape; forcible violation; abduction; rapture.
raw, *a.* raw, uncooked; not covered with skin; sore; crude; inexperienced; unripe; not matured; not completely manufactured; not trained; cold and damp: *n.* a sore place. **in the raw,** in the natural state. **on the raw,** on a very sensitive spot. **raw deal,** rough treatment; a bad bargain [Coll.]. (A.S. *hræaw.*)
raw-boned, *a.* having little flesh on the bones.
rawhead, *n.* *raw*-hed, a spectre to frighten children.
rawhide, *n.* *raw*-hide, untanned cattle-skin; a rawhide whip: *a.* made of rawhide.
rawish, *a.* *raw*-ish, somewhat raw.
rawly, *ad.* in a raw manner; unskilfully.
rawness, *n.* state of being raw; unskilfulness.
★**ray,** *n.* ray, a beam of light; a glimmering; a beam of intellectual light; a radius; a diverging line like a ray; a beam of any radiant energy (as heat, etc.); a stream of particles from a radio-active substance; the outer part of a compound radiate flower [Bot.]; a spine in a fin [Ichth.]; a longitudinal vein of an insect's wing [Entom.]: *v.t.* to shoot forth: *v.i.* to shine forth. (O.Fr.)
ray, *n.* ray, any species of cartilaginous fishes of the family Raiæ, allied to the skate. (O.Fr. *raye.*)
Rayah, *n.* *rah*-yah, in Turkey, a non-Mohammedan subject. (Ar., peasant.)
rayed, *a.* rayd, having rays.
rayless, *a.* *ray*-less, destitute of light; dark; not illuminated.
rayon, *n.* *ray*-yon, artificial silk, a glossy manufactured cellulose fibre; fabric made of this. (Trade name.)
ray-therapy, *n.* radiotherapy.
raze, *v.t.* raze, to lay level with the ground; to efface or destroy; to demolish. (Fr. *raser.*)
razee, *n.* ra-*zee*, a ship the upper deck of which has been cut away: *v.t.* to lower the rating of a ship thus. (Fr. *raser.*)
razor, *n.* *ray*-zor, an instrument for shaving off the hair: *v.t.* to trim close; to shave. (Fr. *rasoir.*)
razorback, *n.* *ray*-zor-bak, a finback or rorqual.
razorbill, *n.* *ray*-zor-bil, the sea-bird *Alca torda.*
razor-edge, *n.* a very keen edge, as of a razor; a sharp ridge of mountains; a crisis, a narrow line of demarcation [Fig.].
razor-fish, *n.* a small sea-fish of the genus *Xyrichthys*, with a compressed body; a razor-shell.
razor-shell, *n.* a bivalve mollusc of the genus *Solen.*
razz, *n.* raz, a hiss, boo, or other sound of disapproval: *v.t.* to hiss or boo at; to deride [U.S.A. Slang]. (*raspberry.*)
razzia, *n.* *raz*-e-ah, a pillaging or devastating incursion. (Fr., from Algerian.)
razzle, *n.* *raz*-zl, *or* **razzle-dazzle,** a spree; boisterous jollification [Slang].
re- ree, a Latin prefix, signifying back or again.
re, *prep.* ree, as regards. (L. *res*, a thing.)
re, *n.* ray, the second note of the diatonic scale [Mus.]. (It.)
re-absorb, *v.t.* to absorb again.
re-absorption, *n.* the act of re-absorbing.
reaccustom, *v.t.* re-a-*kus*-tom, to habituate again.
reach, *n.* reech, power of reaching or attaining range; limit of power; scheme; expanse; stretch of water: *v.t.* to stretch out; to touch by extending the hand; to arrive at; to extend to; to penetrate to: *v.i.* to be extended so as to touch; to try to obtain; to sail with the wind abeam [Naut.]. (A.S. *ræcan.*)
reach, *v.i.* reech, to retch [Dial.].
reachable, *a.* *reech*-a-bl, within reach.
reacher, *n.* *reech*-er, one who reaches or extends.
reach-me-down, *a.* ready-made, of goods, esp. clothes: *n.pl.* ready-made clothes.
react, *v.t.* re-*akt*, to act over again: *v.i.* to act in response to; to return an impulse; to resist by an opposite force; to act in the reverse way; to act reciprocally; to exert chemical action upon.
reactance, *n.* re-*ak*-tance, the amount of reaction; the resistance to a current in an alternating circuit, inductive resistance [Elect.].
reactant, *n.* re-*ak*-tant, a reacting substance [Chem.].
★**reaction,** *n.* re-*ak*-shon, counteraction; reciprocal action; response to stimulation, etc.; action in the contrary, esp. backward, direction; opposition to change or reform [Politics, etc.]; the magnification of signal strength obtained by passing back a portion of the output from one valve of a wireless apparatus to its grid; regeneration [Wire.].
reactionary, *a.* re-*ak*-shon-a-re, implying or favouring reaction, esp. in politics; retrograde: *n.* one who favours reaction or retrocession from progress.
reactionist, *a.* and *n.* re-*ak*-shon-ist, reactionary.
reactivate, *v.t.* ree-*ak*-te-vate, to render active again.
reactive, *a.* re-*ak*-tiv, pertaining or tending to reaction; having power to react.
reactively, *ad.* by reaction.
reactivity, *n.* ree-ak-*tiv*-e-te, the state or quality of being reactive; power to react.
reactor, *n.* re-*ak*-tor, one who, or an organ or organism that, reacts; a reagent; an apparatus which has electrical reactance.
read, *v.t.* reed, to utter aloud what is written or printed; to peruse; to discover and understand by signs; to study; to learn by observation; to see through: *v.i.* to perform the act of reading; to be studious; to learn by reading; to stand written. *p.* and *pp.* **read,** red. (A.S. *rædan.*)
readability, *n.* reed-a-*bil*-e-te, readableness.
readable, *a.* *reed*-a-bl, legible; easily read; worth reading.
readableness, *n.* the state of being readable.
readably, *ad.* *reed*-a-ble, in a readable manner.
readdress, *v.t.* ree-ad-*dress*, to direct (a letter, etc.) to an address different from that given.
reader, *n.* *reed*-er, one who reads; one whose office is to read prayers; a university lecturer on certain subjects; one studious in books; a corrector of the press; a reading-book; one employed to report on MSS. submitted to a publisher. **readers' cramp,** cramp of the muscles of the eye after much reading. (A.S. *rædere.*)
readership, *n.* *reed*-er-ship, the office, or period of office, of a reader, esp. at a university.
readily, *ad.* *red*-e-le, in a ready manner; promptly; easily; cheerfully.
readiness, *n.* *red*-e-ness, preparedness; promptitude; willingness.
★**reading,** *a.* *reed*-ing, addicted to or devoted to reading: *n.* the act of reading; time spent in reading; study of books; a lecture; a public recital; the way in which a passage reads; interpretation and rendering; the formal presentation of a bill to the legislative body which is to consider it; an observation made from an instrument, as a thermometer, pressure-gauge, etc. (A.S. *ræding.*)
reading-book, *n.* a book with selections for practice in reading.
reading-desk, *n.* a slope, usually adjustable, to support a book being read; a lectern.
reading-glass, *n.* a magnifying glass for use in reading.
reading-room, *n.* a room in a library, club, etc., set aside for the reading of books and periodicals.
readjourn, *v.t.* ree-ad-*jurn*, to adjourn a second time.
readjust, *v.t.* ree-ad-*just*, to adjust or put in order again.
readjustment, *n.* ree-ad-*just*-ment, the act or result of readjusting; reconstruction [Econ.].
readmission, *n.* ree-ad-*mish*-on, act of readmitting; re-entry.
readmit, *v.t.* re-ad-*mit*, to admit again.
readmittance, *n.* re-ad-*mit*-ance, readmission.
readopt, *v.t.* ree-a-*dopt*, to adopt again.
★**ready,** *a.* *red*-e, prepared; willing; disposed; quick; prompt; dexterous; present in hand; near; at hand; easy; *ad.* in a state of preparation;

n. ready money [Slang]; the position in which a firearm is held or gun laid in readiness for immediate firing [Mil.]: *v.t.* to prepare. **make ready,** to provide and put in order. **ready money,** actual and immediate cash payment; done for immediate payment. **ready reckoner,** a book of tables giving money multiplications, rates of interest, etc., for facilitating calculations. (Perhaps A.S. *geræde,* prepared, *i.e.* prepared to ride.)

ready-made, *a.* ready for immediate use; not made to order, esp. of clothes.

reaffirm, *v.t.* ree-af-*ferm,* to affirm again.

reafforest, *v.t.* ree-af-*fo*-rest, to convert again into forest, esp. to plant new trees in place of those cut down.

reafforestation, *n.* ree-af-*fo*-re-*stay*-shun, the methodical planting and tending of trees in place of others decayed or destroyed.

reagency, *n.* ree-*ay*-jen-se, action of, or resembling that of, a reagent; reactive power.

reagent, *n.* ree-*ay*-jent, a reactive force or agent; a substance employed to detect the presence of other bodies by their reaction [Chem.].

reaggravation, *n.* ree-ag-gra-*vay*-shon, the last monitory published after three admonitions and before excommunication [Rom. Cath. Church].

real, *a.* *ree*-al, actually being or existing; not fictitious; true; genuine; authentic; not affected; not personal; pertaining to things fixed, permanent, or immovable, as to lands and tenements [Law]: *n.* a real thing; that which has actual existence. **real action,** an action which concerns real property. **real estate,** landed property. **real presence,** the actual presence in the bread and wine of the Eucharist of the body and blood of Christ. (O.Fr.)

real, *n.* ray-*ahl,* a former silver coin of Spain, one-eighth of a dollar (about 6½*d.*); also, the *sing.* of Port. reis (*which see*). (Sp., from L. *regalis,* royal.)

realgar, *n.* ree-*al*-gar, native disulphide of arsenic, or red arsenic. (Sp. *rejalgar,* from Ar.)

realign, *v.t.* ree-a-*line,* to align afresh; to arrange in new grouping.

realism, *n.* *ree*-a-lizm, the doctrine that general terms or ideas represent or have real existence; the doctrine that immediate perception of external things is possible, and that they are as they seem; the tendency to apprehend and represent objects in their true forms and as they actually appear to the perception and imagination [Art]; fidelity to nature in literature or art, esp. in details.

realist, *n.* *ree*-a-list, one who maintains any doctrine of realism; one who seeks to apprehend and represent life and things just as they present themselves to him.

realistic, *a.* ree-a-*lis*-tik, actual; as though natural; pertaining to the realists or realism.

realistically, *ad.* ree-a-*lis*-te-ka-le, in a realistic manner.

reality, *n.* ree-*al*-e-te, the quality of being real; actual existence; fact; a real thing; the fixed, permanent nature of property called real [Law]. **in reality,** in fact; actually; truly.

realizable, *a.* ree-a-*ly*-za-bl, that may be realized.

realization, *n.* ree-a-ly-*zay*-shon, act of realizing or state of being realized; the considering as real; the bringing into being.

realize, *v.t.* *re*-a-lize, to accomplish; to convert into money; to sell; to bring by sale; to acquire; to consider or treat as real; to bring home to oneself; to bring into actual existence. (Fr. *réaliser.*)

reallege, *v.t.* ree-a-*lej,* to allege again.

realliance, *n.* ree-a-*ly*-ance, a renewed alliance.

really, *ad.* *ree*-al-e, actually; truthfully; in reality.

realm, *n.* relm, a royal jurisdiction; a kingdom; a domain or sphere. (O.Fr. *realme.*)

realness, *n.* *ree*-al-ness, the quality or state of being real; actuality.

realpolitik, *n.* ray-*ahl*-pol-e-*teek,* the doctrine that policy should be determined solely in accordance with material interests; reliance upon force for gaining national aims. (Ger., practical politics.)

realtor, *n.* *ree*-al-tor, a qualified real estate agent or broker [U.S.A.].

realty, *n.* *ree*-al-te, real property (as opposed to personalty) [Law].

ream, *n.* reem, a measure of paper, 20 quires or 480 sheets; *pl.* a large quantity, esp. a great mass of writing [Coll.]. **printer's ream,** 516 sheets. (O.Fr. *raime.*)

ream, *v.t.* reem, to bevel out; to enlarge (esp. a hole in metal); to open for caulking (of seams) [Naut.]. (A.S. *ryman.*)

reamer, *n.* *reem*-er, a tool for reaming.

reanimate, *v.t.* ree-*an*-e-mate, to revive; to resuscitate; to invigorate.

reanimation, *n.* ree-an-e-*may*-shon, act or process of reanimating; state of being reanimated.

reannex, *v.t.* ree-an-*neks,* to annex again; to reunite.

reap, *v.t.* reep, to cut as grain; to clear off a crop by reaping; to gather; to receive as a reward or the fruit of labour, etc.: *v.i.* to perform the act of reaping; to receive the fruit of labour. (A.S. *ripan,* to pluck.)

reaper, *n.* *reep*-er, one who reaps; a reaping-machine.

reaping-hook, *n.* a sickle; a tool used in reaping.

reaping-machine, *n.* a machine for reaping grain.

reapparel, *v.t.* *ree-a-pa*-rel, to clothe again.

reappear, *v.i.* ree-a-*peer,* to appear again.

reappearance, *n.* ree-a-*peer*-rance, a new appearance

reapply, *v.t.* and *v.i.* ree-a-*ply,* to apply again.

reappoint, *v.t.* *ree-a-poynt,* to appoint a person again to the post he has already held.

reappointment, *n.* ree-a-*poynt*-ment, a renewed appointment.

reapportion, *v.t.* ree-a-*por*-shon, to apportion again.

rear, *n.* reer, that which is behind; the hindmost part or position; the last in order; the part of an army or fleet which is behind the other. **in the rear,** at the back. (*arrear.*)

rear, *v.t.* reer, to raise; to lift after a fall; to erect; to bring up; to educate; to cultivate: *v.i.* to rise on the hind legs. (A.S. *ræran,* to raise.)

rear-admiral, *n.* a rank in the British navy intermediate between those of commodore and vice-admiral.

rear-arch, *n.* the rear or inner arch of a single opening when of different design from that in front [Arch.].

rear-guard, *n.* the body of an army that protects the rear. **rear-guard action,** an engagement fought to assist and protect the retreat of the main body of troops.

reargue, *v.t.* and *v.i.* ree-*ar*-gew, to argue a subject over again.

rearise, *v.i.* ree-a-*rize,* to arise or get up again.

rear-line, *n.* the line or body of troops in the rear of an army.

rearm, *v.t.* ree-*arm,* to furnish with fresh arms and military munitions: *v.i.* to return to a state of military preparedness.

rearmament, *n.* ree-*arm*-a-ment, act of furnishing with new armaments; a fresh supply of arms and war materials.

rearmost, *a.* *reer*-mohst, last in position; coming at the end.

rearmouse, *n.* *reer*-mous, a reremouse.

rearrange, *v.t.* ree-a-*raynj,* to arrange afresh; to put into a new order.

rearrangement, *n.* ree-a-*raynj*-ment, the act or result of rearranging.

rear-rank, *n.* the second rank or line of men on parade.

re-arrest, *v.t.* ree-a-*rest,* to arrest again.

rearward, *n.* *reer*-ward, the last troop; the rear-guard; the rear: *a.* in or towards the rear: *ad.* towards the rear.

reascend, *v.t.* and *v.i.* ree-a-*send,* to ascend or mount again.

reascension, *n.* ree-a-*sen*-shun, the act of ascending again.

⋆**reason,** *n.* *ree*-zon, the cause, ground, principle, or motive of anything said or done; efficient cause; final cause; the faculty of judging from observation and information and of distinguishing between right and wrong; the exercise of reason; the premise, esp. the minor, of an argument [Logic]; what is according to reason; right; justice; moderation: *v.i.* to exercise the faculty of reason; to infer conclusions from premises; to argue; to debate: *v.t.* to examine or discuss; to persuade or dissuade by reasoning. **in reason,** according to good sense; in justice. (Fr. *raison,* from L. *ratio,* calculation.)

reasonable, *a.* *ree*-zon-a-bl, endowed with reason; governed by reason; conformable to reason; not excessive; not immoderate; not unjust; tolerable; considerable. (Fr. *raisonnable.*)
reasonableness, *n.* agreeableness to reason; moderation.
reasonably, *ad.* in a reasonable manner.
reasoner, *n.* *ree*-zon-er, one who reasons or argues.
reasoning, *n.* *ree*-zon-ing, exercise of the faculty of reason; argumentation; the arguments adduced: *a.* able to, or exercising, reason; endowed with reason; that reasons.
reasonless, *a.* *ree*-zon-less, void of reason; irrational.
reassemble, *v.t.* and *i.* ree-a-*sem*-bl, to collect together again.
reassert, *v.t.* ree-a-*sert,* to assert again; to maintain after suspension or cessation.
reassess, *v.t.* ree-a-*sess,* to assess anew.
reassessment, *n.* ree-a-*sess*-ment, the act of assessing anew.
reassign, *v.t.* ree-a-*sine,* to assign back; to transfer to another what has been assigned.
reassurance, *n.* ree-a-*shoor*-rance, assurance or confirmation repeated; a second insurance against loss; fortified or restored confidence.
reassure, *v.t.* ree-a-*shoor,* to assure anew; to restore courage or confidence to; to insure a second time against loss.
reassuring, *a.* ree-a-*shoor*-ring, restoring hope or courage; enheartening; comforting.
reasty, *a.* *rees*-te, rancid. (Dial. Eng.)
reata, *n.* re-*ah*-ta, a riata.
reattach, *v.t.* ree-a-*tatch,* to attach anew.
Réaumur, *a.* *ray*-oh-mer, relating to Réaumur, or the thermometric scale he invented. **Réaumur thermometer,** a thermometer in which freezing-point of water is at zero and the boiling-point at 80 deg.
reave, *v.t.* reev, to ravage; to take away by force. (A.S. *reafian.*)
reaver, *n.* *reev*-er, a robber; a pillager.
reavow, *v.t.* ree-a-*vou,* to avow again.
reback, *v.t.* ree-*bak,* to give (esp. a book) a new back.
rebaptize, *v.t.* ree-bap-*tize,* to baptize, a second time.
rebarbative, *a.* re-*bar*-ba-tiv, unprepossessing; grim; repulsive; crabbed. (Fr.)
rebate, *n.* *ree*-bate, diminution; discount; abatement [Comm. and Her.]: *v.t.* re-*bate,* to blunt; to diminish; to deduct from. (Fr. *rebattre,* beat.)
rebate, *n.* *ree*-bate, a rabbet.
rebate, *n.* ree-*bate,* a kind of hard freestone.
rebato, *n.* re-*bah*-to, a sort of ruff or starched collar, worn *temp.* 1600. (Fr.)
rebec, *n.* *ree*-bek, an ancient Moorish three-stringed fiddle played with a bow. (Fr.)
rebel, *n.* *reb*-el, one who revolts from his allegiance or defies authority: *a.* acting in revolt: *v.i.* re-*bel,* to revolt; to renounce and rise against authority. (Fr.)
rebellion, *n.* re-*bel*-yun, insurrection against or open resistance to lawful authority; revolt. (O.Fr.)
rebellious, *a.* re-*bel*-yus, renouncing and resisting lawful authority; engaged in rebellion.
rebelliously, *ad.* in a rebellious spirit.
rebelliousness, *n.* the quality or condition of being rebellious.
rebellow, *v.i.* ree-*bel*-lo, to bellow in return; to echo back.
rebid, *n.* ree-*bid,* a second or later bid in the same suit by the same bidder: *v.i.* to make such a bid [Contract, etc.].
rebind, *v.t.* ree-*bynd,* to bind anew: *n.* *ree*-bynd, a rebound book.
rebirth, *n.* ree-*berth,* a second birth; a renascence.
rebite, *v.t.* ree-*bite,* to sharpen the lines of an engraved plate by biting in again.
reboant, *a.* re-*boh*-ant, rebellowing; responding or re-echoing loudly. (L. *reboans.*)
reboil, *v.t.* ree-*boyl,* to boil again.
rebore, *v.t.* ree-*bore,* to provide (a cylinder, rifle, etc.) with a fresh bore; to bore anew: *n.* *ree*-bore, that which has been rebored [Coll.].
rebound, *ree*-bound, *p.* and *pp.* of *rebind.*
rebound, *n.* re-*bound,* the act of flying back; reaction: *v.i.* to spring back; to recoil: *v.t.* to drive back. **to take one on the rebound,** to persuade or dissuade him by making use of his reactions. (Fr. *rebondir.*)
rebreathe, *v.t.* ree-*breethe,* to breathe again.
rebroadcast, *n.* ree-*brawd*-kahst, a broadcast of matter at the time of its reception from another station; a later transmission of matter already broadcast: *v.t.* and *i.* to broadcast thus [Wire.].
rebuff, *n.* re-*buf,* a beating back; a quick and sudden resistance; sudden check; repulse; refusal: *v.t.* to beat back; to check. (It. *rebuffo.*)
rebuild, *v.t.* ree-*bild,* to build again; to build or construct what has been demolished; to renew.
rebukable, *a.* re-*bewk*-a-bl, worthy of reprehension.
rebuke, *n.* re-*bewk,* act of rebuking; a chiding; a reproof: *v.t.* to chide; to reprove; to check. (O.Fr. *rebuker.*)
rebukeful, *a.* re-*bewk*-ful, abounding in rebuke.
rebuker, *n.* re-*bewk*-er, one who rebukes.
rebukingly, *ad.* re-*bewk*-ing-le, by way of rebuke.
rebury, *v.t.* ree-*be*-re, to inter again.
rebus, *n.* *ree*-bus (*pl.* **rebuses**), a punning representation of a name by picture; a pictorial riddle; a coat of arms conveying pictorially a suggestion of the name of its bearer [Her.]. (L., by things, from *res,* a thing.)
rebut, *v.t.* re-*but,* to repel; to opposed or refute by argument, plea, or countervailing proof [Law]: *v.i.* to answer, as by surrejoinder [Law]. (O.Fr. *rebouter,* repulse.)
rebuttable, *a.* re-*but*-a-bl, that may be rebutted.
rebuttal, *n.* re-*but*-al, the act of refuting; the production of evidence in refutation of a previous statement made in a legal trial.
rebutter, *n.* re-*but*-er, the answer of a defendant to a surrejoinder [Law]; a refutation.
recalcitrance, *n.* re-*kal*-se-trance, the state of being recalcitrant; obstinate refusal to comply.
recalcitrant, *a.* re-*kal*-se-trant, unsubmissive; refractory: *n.* one who is recalcitrant. (L. *recalcitrans.*)
recalcitrate, *v.i.* re-*kal*-se-trate, to protest vigorously against; to be unsubmissive or refractory. (L. *recalcitrare,* to kick out.)
recalcitration, *n.* re-kal-se-*tray*-shon, the act of recalcitrating.
recalesce, *v.i.* ree-ka-*less,* to grow hot anew.
recalescence, *n.* ree-ka-*les*-ence, act of growing hot again (esp. of molten metal).
recall, *n.* re-*kawl,* a calling back; revocation; power of calling back or revoking: *v.t.* to call back; to summon to return.
recallable, *a.* re-*kawl*-a-bl, that may be recalled.
recant, *v.t.* and *i.* re-*kant,* to retract; to abjure; to disavow. (L. *recantare.*)
recantation, *n.* ree-kan-*tay*-shon, the act of recanting; a declaration contradicting a former one.
recapitulate, *v.t.* re-ka-*pit*-yew-late, to go over, by way of summary, the principal facts, points, or arguments, again. (Late L. *recapitulatus.*)
recapitulation, *n.* ree-ka-pit-yew-*lay*-shon, the act of recapitulating; a summary.
recapitulatory, *a.* re-ka-*pit*-yew-la-to-re, repeating in a condensed form; summarizing.
recaption, *n.* ree-*kap*-shon, the act of retaking, esp. persons or goods wrongfully seized [Law].
recaptor, *n.* ree-*kap*-tor, one who retakes, as a prize which had been previously taken; one recovering by recaption [Law].
recapture, *n.* ree-*kap*-tyur, act of retaking; a prize retaken: *v.t.* to retake that which has been taken.
recast, *v.t.* ree-*kahst,* to cast, mould, or fashion again; to plan again; to compute anew: *n.* a product of recasting; the act of recasting.
recede, *v.i.* re-*seed,* to move back; to retreat; to depart from. (L. *recedere,* go back.)
re-cede, *v.t.* ree-*seed,* to retrocede; to grant or yield to a former possessor.
***receipt,** *n.* re-*seet,* the act of receiving; reception; that which is received; prescription or recipe; a signed acknowledgment of money or goods received; formerly, an official place of receiving: *v.t.* to give a receipt for; to discharge. (Fr. *recette.*)
receivable, *a.* re-*seev*-a-bl, that may be received.
receive, *v.t.* re-*seev,* to take as offered, sent, gained, due, or communicated; to accept; to obtain; to embrace; to allow; to admit; to welcome; to accept stolen goods from a thief: *v.i.* to take, accept, acquire, etc.; to partake of the eucharist

[Eccles.]; to act as non-server in tennis, etc.; to hold receptions. (Fr. *recevoir.*)
received, *a.* re-*seevd*, generally accepted as good, true, or correct; standard.
receiver, *n.* re-*seev*-er, one who receives in any sense; a recipient; a vessel for receiving and condensing the product of distillation; a receiving vessel, as one for containing gases or the bell-glass of an air-pump; the earpiece of a telephone; a wireless receiving-set; one appointed by a court to administer property [Law]. **Official Receiver,** an officer of the Bankruptcy Court who takes possession of the debtor's assets when the receiving order is made.
receivership, *n.* re-*seev*-er-ship, the office of receiver or of an Official Receiver.
receiving, *n.* re-*seev*-ing, act of receiving: *a.* intended to receive. **receiving order,** an order to administer an estate in bankruptcy.
receiving-set, *n.* the apparatus used to receive wireless signals; the part of a receiving-station fitted up to receive wireless waves by the use of a tuner, detector, etc.
receiving-station, *n.* a room or building equipped for the reception of radio waves.
recency, *n.* *ree*-sen-se, newness; late origin; lateness. (Late L. *recentia.*)
recension, *n.* re-*sen*-shon, critical revision of a standard text; the text so revised. (Fr.)
recent, *a.* *ree*-sent, of or pertaining to time relatively near; of late origin or occurrence; modern; lately received; fresh; pertaining to the post-glacial or present epoch [Geol.]. (O.Fr.)
recently, *ad.* at a recent date; not long ago.
recentness, *n.* quality of being recent; recency.
recept, *n.* *ree*-sept, a mental image formed by a succession of percepts of similar objects [Phil.].
receptacle, *n.* re-*sep*-ta-kl, a place or vessel into which something is received, and in which it is contained; the support of a head of flowers [Bot.].
receptacular, *a.* ree-sep-*tak*-yew-lar, pertaining to or growing on the receptacle [Bot.].
receptibility, *n.* re-sep-te-*bil*-e-te, the quality or state of being receivable; the possibility of being received.
reception, *n.* re-*sep*-shon, the act of receiving; the state of being received; admission; the official or ceremonious entertainment or receiving of visitors; the act or process of converting radio waves into sound. **reception order,** the order for the detention of a lunatic in an asylum. **reception room,** a living-room as distinct from a bedroom, kitchen, etc.
receptionist, *n.* re-*sep*-shon-ist, one employed (esp. by an hotel or professional worker) to receive and interview callers.
receptive, *a.* re-*sep*-tiv, having the quality of receiving; quick to receive impressions, etc.
receptively, *ad.* in a receptive way.
receptivity, *n.* ree-sep-*tiv*-e-te, the state or quality of being receptive.
recess, *n.* re-*sess*, a vacation, esp. the parliamentary vacation; part of a room formed by the receding of the wall; a place or state of retirement; suspension of business; seclusion; a depression or cavity [Anat., etc.]: *v.t.* to set back; to place in a recess; to form a recess in: *v.i.* to go into a vacation [U.S.A.].
recession, *n.* re-*sesh*-on, the act of withdrawing; withdrawal.
re-cession, *n.* re-*sesh*-on, the act of ceding back.
recessional, *a.* re-*sesh*-on-al, of or relating to recession: *n.* a hymn sung as the choir and clergy leave the chancel in procession.
recessive, *a.* re-*ses*-siv, receding; retiring; tending in a backward direction; having a tendency to disappear [esp. Biol.].
Rechabite, *n.* *rek*-a-bite, a member of a teetotal society named from the descendants of Jonadab, son of Rechab (Jer. xxxv), who bound themselves to abstain from wine.
recharge, *v.t.* ree-*chahrj*, to charge again; to make a new charge against; to attack anew: *n.* a second or new charge.
réchauffé, *n.* re-shoh-fay, a warmed-up dish; a rehash. (Fr.)
recheat, *n.* re-*cheet*, the huntsman's call upon the horn when the hounds have lost the scent: *v.i.* to blow the recheat. (O.Fr. *recet*, a retreat.)
recherché, *a.* re-*share*-shay, choice; rare; much sought after. (Fr.)
recidivation, *n.* res-e-de-*vay*-shun, the relapsing of a disease [Path.]. (Fr. *récidire*, relapse.)
recidivism, *n.* re-*sid*-e-vizm, habitual relapsing into crime after punishment. (Fr. *récidire*, relapse.)
recidivist, *n.* re-*sid*-e-vist, one who is repeatedly sentenced as a law-breaker; an incorrigible criminal.
recidivous, *a.* re-*sid*-e-vus, relapsing; characterized by recidivism.
recipe, *n.* *res*-e-pe, the formula for making any dish in cookery; any written or printed instructions in which the quantities are given for the preparation of the compound. (L., take.)
recipiency, *n.* re-*sip*-e-en-se, a receiving; the state of being a recipient; receptiveness.
recipient, *n.* re-*sip*-e-ent, one who receives: *a.* receiving; receptive. (L. *recipiens*, receiving.)
reciprocal, *a.* re-*sip*-ro-kal, alternate; mutual; reflexive [Gram.]: *n.* that which is reciprocal; the quotient obtained by dividing unity by a given number [Math.]. **reciprocal ratio,** the ratio between reciprocals of two quantities. **reciprocal terms,** terms of the same signification and therefore mutually convertible [Logic]. (L. *reciprocare*, to come and go.)
reciprocality, *n.* re-*sip*-ro-kal-e-te, reciprocalness; reciprocity.
reciprocally, *ad.* interchangeably; mutually.
reciprocalness, *n.* the quality or state of being reciprocal.
reciprocate, *v.i.* re-*sip*-ro-kate, to alternate; to make a similar or equivalent return: *v.t.* to give and take; to interchange; to impart reciprocating motion to.
reciprocating, *a.* re-*sip*-ro-kay-ting, moving backwards and forwards alternately. **reciprocating motion,** motion like that of the piston of a steam engine.
reciprocation, *n.* re-sip-ro-*kay*-shon, the act of reciprocating; mutual interchange; alternation.
reciprocator, *n.* re-*sip*-ro-kay-tor, one who or that which reciprocates.
reciprocity, *n.* res-e-*pros*-e-te, reciprocal obligation or right; equal rights or benefits to be mutually yielded or enjoyed; equality internationally in trade and commercial rights and privileges. (Fr. *réciprocité.*)
recision, *n.* re-*sizh*-on, the act of rescinding.
recital, *n.* re-*sy*-tal, the act of reciting; a detailed list of claims, events, etc.; a narration; a musical performance.
recitation, *n.* res-e-*tay*-shon, the act of reciting; a composition committed or designed to be committed to memory; the oral delivery of such a composition.
recitative, *a.* res-e-ta-*teev*, reciting; narrative; pertaining to or resembling recitative: *n.* a style of declamatory singing employed in opera and oratorio; a passage or piece so sung.
recite, *v.t.* re-*site*, to repeat what has been committed to memory; to relate; to rehearse; to enumerate: *v.i.* to give recitations. (Fr. *réciter.*)
reciter, *n.* re-*sy*-ter, one who recites; a narrator; a book containing pieces for recitation.
reck, *v.t.* and *i.* rek, to care; to mind. (A.S. *reccan.*)
reckless, *a.* *rek*-less, careless; heedless.
recklessly, *ad.* *rek*-less-le, heedlessly.
recklessness, *n.* heedlessness; carelessness.
reckon, *v.t.* *rek*-on, to count; to account or esteem; to set in the number or rank of; to suppose or think [Coll.]: *v.i.* to calculate; to reason with oneself, and conclude from arguments; to charge to account; to rely upon; to suppose [Coll.]. (A.S. *ge-recenian.*)
reckoner, *n.* *rek*-on-er, one who reckons or computes; that which assists in reckoning; a ready reckoner or book of calculations.
reckoning, *n.* *rek*-on-ing, the act of counting or computing; an account of time; settlement of accounts; charges for entertainment; estimation; a ship's position as calculated from the log-book [Naut.]. **day of reckoning,** a day on which accounts are settled; the Day of Judgment.
reclaim, *n.* re-*klame*, the act of reclaiming; reclamation, esp. of land: *v.t.* to claim back; to call back from error, to reform; to restrain; to tame; to bring under cultivation; to make use of, or recover from, a waste product: *v.i.* to protest;

to exclaim; to appeal to the Inner House of the Court of Session from a judgment of a Lord Ordinary [Scots. Law]. (Fr. *réclamer.*)
reclaimable, *a.* re-*klame*-a-bl, that may be reclaimed.
reclaiming, *a.* re-*klame*-ing, appealing [Scots. Law].
reclaimless, *a.* re-*klame*-less, that cannot be reclaimed.
reclamation, *n.* rek-la-*may*-shon, act of reclaiming; demand; restoration to a useful condition; recovery; remonstrance. (L. *reclamatio.*)
réclame, *n.* ray-*klahm*, notoriety; the art of publicity, esp. self-advertisement. (Fr.)
reclinate, *a.* *rek*-le-nat, bending downwards, as a leaf [Bot.]. (L. *reclinatus.*)
reclination, *n.* rek-le-*nay*-shon, the act of reclining or lying down; the state of being reclined.
recline, *a.* re-*kline*, in a leaning posture: *v.t.* to lean back; to lean to one side or sideways: *v.i.* to rest or repose on a couch. (L. *reclino*, bend.)
recliner, *n.* re-*kline*-er, one who or that which reclines.
reclose, *v.t.* ree-*kloze*, to close or shut again.
reclothe, *v.t.* ree-*klohthe*, to dress in new garments; to put garments on again.
recluse, *a.* re-*kloos*, secluded; sequestered; retired from the world; solitary: *n.* one who lives in seclusion, esp. a monk, hermit, or anchorite. (O.Fr.)
reclusion, *n.* re-*kloo*-zhon, the act of retiring, or state of retirement, from society; seclusion.
reclusive, *a.* re-*kloo*-siv, marked by or affording retirement from society.
reclusory, *n.* re-*kloo*-so-re, a hermitage.
recoal, *v.t.* and *i.* ree-*koal*, to refill (esp. the bunkers of a ship) with coal.
recognition, *n.* rek-og-*nish*-on, the act of recognizing; state of being recognized; formal avowal or acknowledgment (as of an ambassador, or of a ruler by his people); favourable notice or appreciation. (O.Fr.)
recognitive, re-*kog*-ne-tiv, pertaining to or marked by recognition.
recognitor, *n.* re-*kog*-ne-tor, formerly a member of a jury upon assize [Law].
recognitory, *a.* re-*kog*-ne-to-re, pertaining to or connected with recognition.
recognizable, *a.* rek-og-*ny*-za-bl, that may be recognized or acknowledged.
recognizably, *ad.* rek-og-*ny*-za-ble, so as to be recognized.
recognizance, *n.* re-*kog*-ne-zance *or* re-*kon*-e-zance, a legal obligation under surety, also, the surety deposited [Law]. (O.Fr. *recognisance.*)
recognizant, *a.* re-*kog*-ne-zant, displaying recognition; acknowledging; perceptive.
recognize, *v.t.* *rek*-og-nize, to know again as something formerly known; to acknowledge; to take notice of one, as by greeting or salutation in passing; to admit the validity, etc., of; to appreciate favourably.
recoil, *n.* re-*koyl*, a starting, falling, or flowing back; rebound; the backward kick of a gun, etc., when fired: *v.i.* to start, fall, roll, or flow back; to rebound; to shrink. (Fr. *reculer.*)
recoiler, *n.* re-*koyl*-er, one who or that which recoils.
recoilingly, *ad.* re-*koyl*-ing-le, with a recoil.
recoilment, *n.* re-*koyl*-ment, the act of recoiling.
recoin, *v.t.* ree-*koyn*, to coin again.
recoinage, *n.* *ree*-koyn-aj, the act of coining anew; a second or later coinage.
re-collect, *v.t.* ree-ko-*lekt*, to collect together again; to rally; to compose (oneself); to recover resolution: *v.i.* to reassemble.
recollect, *v.t.* rek-o-*lekt*, to recover or recall the knowledge of; to remember: *v.i.* to succeed in calling to mind. (L. *recollectus.*)
Recollect, *n.* rek-o-*lekt*, a Recollet.
recollection, *n.* rek-o-*lek*-shon, the act of recalling to memory; the power of recollecting; that which is recollected.
recollective, *a.* rek-o-*lek*-tiv, pertaining to or having the power of recollecting.
Recollet, *n.* rek-o-*lay*, a member of a former very strict order of Franciscans now known (with others) as Friars Minor. (Fr.)
recolonization, *n.* *ree*-kol-o-ny-*zay*-shon, a second colonization.
recolonize, *v.t.* ree-*kol*-o-nize, to colonize a second time.
recolour, *v.t.* ree-*kul*-or, to paint over again with the same or another colour.
recombination, *n.* ree-kom-be-*nay*-shon, combination a second time.
recombine, *v.t.* ree-kom-*bine*, to combine again.
recomfort, *v.t.* ree-*kum*-fort, to comfort again; to give new strength to.
recomforture, *n.* ree-*kum*-for-tewr, consolation.
recommence, *v.t.* and *i.* ree-ko-*mence*, to begin again.
recommencement, *n.* a new beginning.
recommend, *v.t.* rek-o-*mend*, to commend to favour; to make acceptable; to counsel; to advise. (Fr. *recommander.*)
recommendable, *a.* rek-o-*men*-da-bl, that may be recommended; worthy of commendation.
recommendableness, *n.* quality of being recommendable.
recommendably, *ad.* in a recommendable manner.
recommendation, *n.* *rek*-o-men-*day*-shon, act of recommending; that which procures a kind or favourable reception, esp. a letter, testimonial, or other document.
recommendatory, *a.* rek-o-*men*-da-to-re, that recommends.
recommender, *n.* rek-o-*men*-der, one who recommends.
recommission, *v.t.* ree-ko-*mish*-on, to commission again.
recommit, *v.t.* ree-ko-*mit*, to commit again; in parliament, to refer again to committee.
recommitment, *n.* ree-ko-*mit*-ment, recommittal.
recommittal, *n.* ree-*ko-mit*-al, a second commitment; a renewed reference to a committee.
recommunicate, *v.i.* and *t.* ree-ko-*mew*-ne-kate, to communicate again.
recompact, *v.t.* ree-kom-*pakt*, to join anew.
recompense, *n.* *rek*-om-pence, an equivalent returned for anything; requital: *v.t.* to make return of an equivalent; to make amends for; to requite. (Fr. *récompenser.*)
recompenser, *n.* *rek*-om-pen-ser, one who recompenses.
recompile, *v.t.* ree-kom-*pile*, to compile again.
recompose, *v.t.* ree-kom-*poze*, to quiet anew; to compose anew; to adjust anew.
recomposition, *n.* ree-kom-po-*zish*-on, composition renewed; state of being recomposed.
recompound, *v.t.* ree-kom-*pound*, to compound again, or remix.
reconcilable, *a.* rek-on-*sile*-a-bl, capable of being reconciled.
reconcilably, *ad.* rek-on-*sile*-a-ble, in a reconcilable manner.
reconcile, *v.t.* *rek*-on-sile, to restore to friendship; to bring to acquiescence; to bring to agreement; to harmonize; to settle or adjust. (O.Fr. *reconcilier.*)
reconcilement, *n.* rek-on-*sile*-ment, reconciliation.
reconciler, *n.* rek-on-*sile*-er, one who reconciles.
reconciliation, *n.* *rek*-on-sil-e-*ay*-shon, the act of reconciling; the state of being reconciled or brought to agreement.
reconciliatory, *a.* rek-on-*sil*-e-a-to-re, tending to reconciliation.
recondensation, *n.* *ree*-kon-den-*say*-shon, the act of recondensing; that which is recondensed.
recondense, *v.t.* and *i.* ree-kon-*dence*, to condense again.
recondite, *a.* *rek*-on-dite, concealed; out of the way; abstruse; profound; dealing in abstruse matters. (L. *reconditus*, hidden.)
recondition, *v.t.* ree-kon-*dish*-on, to bring again into good condition; to restore to a state fit for use; to renovate.
reconduct, *v.t.* ree-kon-*dukt*, to lead back again.
reconfirm, *v.t.* ree-kon-*ferm*, to confirm anew.
reconnaissance, *n.* re-*kon*-a-sance, the act of reconnoitring; examination or survey preliminary to operations [Mil., Mining, Surveying, etc.]; a body engaged in reconnaissance (esp. Mil.). (Fr.)
reconnoitre, *v.t.* rek-o-*noy*-ter, to view; to survey; to examine by the eye prior to operations; an act of reconnoitring. (Fr.)
reconquer, *v.t.* ree-*kong*-ker, to conquer again; to recover by conquest; to recover.
reconquest, *n.* ree-*kong*-kwest, conquest back or anew.

reconsecrate, *v.t.* ree-*kon*-se-krate, to consecrate anew.
reconsecration, *n.* ree-kon-se-*kray*-shon, a renewed consecration.
reconsider, *v.t.* ree-kon-*sid*-er, to consider again, esp. with a view to rescinding. (O.Fr.)
reconsideration, *n.* ree-kon-*sid*-er-*ray*-shon, the act of reconsidering; a second or renewed consideration or review.
reconstituent, *a.* ree-kon-*stit*-yew-ent, building up afresh: *n.* any remedy restoring health and strength after sickness [Med.].
reconstitute, *v.t.* ree-*kon*-ste-tewt, to reconstruct; to restore to the original or former constitution.
reconstitution, *n.* ree-*kon*-ste-*tew*-shon, the act of constituting anew.
reconstruct, *v.t.* ree-kon-*strukt*, to construct again; to rebuild.
reconstruction, *n.* ree-kon-*struk*-shon, the act of reconstructing; that which is reconstructed.
reconstructive, *a.* ree-kon-*struk*-tiv, reconstructing; tending to reconstruct.
reconvene, *v.t.* ree-kon-*veen*, to call together again: *v.i.* to assemble again.
reconversion, *n.* ree-kon-*ver*-shon, a subsequent conversion; the act of reconverting.
reconvert, *v.t.* ree-kon-*vert*, to convert again: *n.* ree-*kon*-vert, one who has relapsed and is again converted.
reconvey, *v.t.* ree-kon-*vay*, to convey back: to transfer back to a former owner.
reconveyance, *n.* ree-kon-*vay*-ance, conveyance again; restoration to a former owner [Law].
record, *v.t.* re-*kord*, to register; to enrol; to imprint deeply on the mind.
⋆**record,** *n.* *rek*-ord, a register; a recording; the state of being recorded; attestation; an authentic or official copy of any writing or account; an account of a person's (esp. suspect's) career; the formal report of proceedings, pleadings, judgment, etc., of parties in a litigation [Law]; the best performance of the kind hitherto publicly accomplished and recorded; a recording device, esp. for the mechanical reproduction of sound; the disk or cylinder on which phonographic sounds are recorded; the series of marks or perforations made by a recording instrument; the perforated roll or ribbon, etc., from which recorded sounds are audibly reproduced. **off the record,** not intended to be official or authoritative (of public utterances, etc.). **on record,** recorded; available for use as evidence. **the Record Office,** the office in which the state papers are preserved. **to break the record,** to surpass the best performance, etc., yet officially recorded. (O.Fr.)
recorder, *n.* re-*kord*-er, one who enrols or records; a judge of the quarter sessions of a borough; an obsolete kind of flute; an instrument for recording.
recordership, *n.* re-*kord*-er-ship, the office of a recorder.
recording, *n.* re-*kord*-ing, a record; the act of putting on record: *a.* that records; registering.
recount, *n.* ree-*kount*, a second count: *v.t.* to go over in detail; to narrate; to count a second time.
recountal, *n.* re-*kount*-al, a narration or recital.
recoup, *v.t.* re-*koop*, to indemnify; to make good; to compensate; to diminish by keeping back a part [Law]. (Fr. *recouper*, cut.)
recoupment, *n.* re-*koop*-ment, the act of recouping; that which is recouped.
recourse, *n.* re-*koarse*, resorting to a person with a request for aid or protection; a source of aid. (Fr. *recours.*)
re-cover, *v.t.* ree-*kuv*-er, to fit with a new cover.
recover, *v.t.* re-*kuv*-er, to get or obtain that which was lost; to restore from sickness; to repair the loss of; to gain as compensation; to obtain title to by judgment in a law court: *v.i.* to regain health after sickness; to grow well; to regain a former condition; to succeed in a lawsuit.
recoverable, *a.* re-*kuv*-er-ra-bl, that may be recovered or restored.
recoverableness, *n.* re-*kuv*-er-ra-bl-ness, the state of being recoverable.
recoveree, *n.* re-kuv-er-*ree*, the person against whom a judgment is obtained in common recovery [Law].
recoveror, *n.* re-*kuv*-er-ror, the demandant or person who obtains a judgment in an action of common recovery [Law].
recovery, *n.* re-*kuv*-er-re, the act of recovering, or of regaining that which has been taken away or lost; restoration from sickness; restoration to health; the obtaining judgment in one's favour in a lawsuit.
recreancy, *n.* *rek*-re-an-se, the quality of being recreant; a cowardly yielding.
recreant, *a.* *rek*-re-ant, cowardly; mean-spirited; apostate; crying for mercy: *n.* one who yields in combat and cries craven; a mean-spirited, cowardly wretch. (O.Fr.)
recreantly, *ad.* *rek*-re-ant-le, in a recreant manner.
recreate, *v.t.* *rek*-re-ate, to revive from weariness or after toil; to refresh; to gratify; to delight: *v.i.* to take recreation. (L. *recreatus.*)
re-create, *v.t.* ree-kre-*ate*, to create or form anew.
recreation, *n.* rek-re-*ay*-shon, refreshment of the strength and spirits after toil; amusement; diversion. **recreation ground,** a publicly owned place for outdoor games.
re-creation, *n.* ree-kre-*ay*-shon, a forming anew; a new creation.
recreational, *a.* rek-re-*ay*-sho-nal, pertaining to recreation.
recreative, *a.* *rek*-re-ay-tiv, tending to amuse and refresh; giving new vigour or animation.
recreativeness, *n.* quality of being recreative.
recrement, *n.* *rek*-re-ment, superfluous matter separated from what is useful; dross; a secretion (as saliva) that is re-absorbed [Anat.]. (O.Fr.)
recremental, *a.* rek-re-*men*-tal, consisting of recrement or refuse.
recrementitial, *a.* rek-re-men-*tish*-al, pertaining to or of the nature of recrement; recremental.
recrementitious, *a.* rek-re-men-*tish*-us, recremental; pertaining to a recrement.
recriminate, *v.i.* ree-*krim*-e-nate, to return one accusation with another; to charge an accuser with the like crime: *v.t.* to accuse in return.
recrimination, *n.* re-*krim*-e-*nay*-shon, the replying to one accusation with another.
recriminative, *a.* re-*krim*-e-na-tiv, retorting with counter accusation.
recriminator, *n.* re-*krim*-e-nay-tor, one who accuses an accuser with a like crime.
recriminatory, *a.* re-*krim*-e-na-to-re, of the nature of, or given to, recrimination; recriminative.
recross, *v.t.* ree-*kross*, to cross a second time.
recrudesce, *v.i.* ree-kroo-*des*, to become recrudescent.
recrudescence, *n.* ree-kroo-*des*-ence, the state of again becoming sore or active; a fresh outbreak; a severe relapse [Med.]. (L. *recrudescens.*)
recrudescent, *a.* ree-kroo-*des*-ent, growing raw, sore, painful, or active again; breaking out anew.
recruit, *n.* re-*kroot*, one newly enlisted; a replenishment: *v.t.* to make up fresh supplies; to supply with new men; to enlist; to repair; to retrieve: *v.i.* to gain new supplies, esp. of health. (O.Fr. *recruter* to raise troops.)
recruiter, *n.* re-*kroot*-er, one who recruits.
recruitment, *n.* re-*kroot*-ment, the act or business of raising new supplies of men for an army; reinforcement.
recrystallization, *n.* re-*kris*-ta-ly-*zay*-shon, the formation of crystals a second time.
recrystallize, *v.t.* and *i.* ree-*kris*-ta-lize, to crystallize, or become crystallized, again.
rectal, *a.* *rek*-tal, in the region of, or pertaining to, the rectum.
rectangle, *n.* *rek*-tang-gl, a right-angled parallelogram. (Fr.)
rectangled, *a.* rek-*tang*-gld, having one or more angles of ninety degrees.
rectangular, *a.* rek-*tang*-gew-lar, right-angled; having the shape of a rectangle. (L. *rectangulus.*)
rectangularity, *n.* rek-tang-gew-*la*-re-te, the quality of being rectangular.
rectangularly, *ad.* in a rectangular manner.
rectifiable, *a.* *rek*-te-fy-a-bl, that may be rectified.
rectification, *n.* rek-te-fe-*kay*-shon, the act or operation of rectifying; the process of refining; the reduction of a curve to a right line [Geom.]; the conversion of the input from alternating current to direct current in wireless apparatus [Wire.].
rectified, *a.* *rek*-te-fide, put right; re-distilled.
rectifier, *n.* *rek*-te-fy-er, one who or that which rectifies; one who refines a liquid by repeated distillation; an instrument formerly used to show and rectify the variations of the compass [Naut.];

an apparatus that converts an alternating into a direct current [Wire.].
rectify, *v.t.* *rek*-te-fy, to correct; to refine by repeated distillation or sublimation; to adjust (a globe) for the solution of a proposed problem; to find a straight line equal to (a curve) [Geom.]. (Fr. *rectifier.*)
rectigrade, *a.* *rek*-te-grade, walking straight forwards (esp. of certain spiders).
rectilineal, *a.* rek-re-*lin*-e-al, rectilinear.
rectilineally, *ad.* in a right line.
rectilinear, *a.* rek-te-*lin*-e-ar, right-lined; bounded by right lines; straight. **rectilinear lens,** a lens corrected for distortion [Phot.]. (L. *rectilinearis,* composed of straight lines.)
rectilinearly, *ad.* rectilineally.
rectirostral, *a.* *rek*-te-*ros*-tral, having a straight beak [Ornith.].
rectitis, *n.* rek-*ty*-tis, inflammation of the rectum.
rectitude, *n.* *rek*-te-tewd, rightness of principle or practice; uprightness; integrity. (Fr.)
recto, *n.* *rek*-toh, the right-hand page of an open book; the front, as opposed to the back, of a leaf: *ad.* to the right-hand side. (L.)
rector, *n.* *rek*-tor, the incumbent of a parish the tithes of which are not diverted or vested in lay hands; the head of certain schools, colleges, and institutions; the chief elective officer in some universities. **Lord Rector,** *see* **Lord.** (L.)
rectorate, *n.* *rek*-to-rat, the office, term of office, or position of rector.
rectorial, *a.* rek-*taw*-re-al, pertaining to a rector or his office.
rectorship, *n.* *rek*-tor-ship, the office or rank of a rector.
rectory, *n.* *rek*-to-re, the living or benefice of a rector; the parsonage or house appertaining to this. (O.Fr. *rectorie.*)
rectoscope, *n.* *rek*-to-skope, a speculum for inspecting the rectum.
rectotomy, *n.* rek-*tot*-o-me, the operation of cutting or making an incision in the rectum [Surg.].
rectrices, *n.pl.* rek-*try*-seez (*sing.* **rectrix**), the tail feathers of a bird, which act as a rudder. (L.)
rectum, *n.* *rek*-tum, the lowermost part of the large intestine extending from the pelvic colon to the anus [Anat.]. (L., straight.)
rectus, *n.* *rek*-tus, any of certain straight muscles in various parts of the body. (L., straight.)
recumbency, *n.* re-*kum*-ben-se, the act or state of lying down; a recumbent posture. (L. *recumbo,* lie down.)
recumbent, *a.* re-*kum*-bent, leaning; reclining; reposing. (L. *recumbens.*)
recumbently, *ad.* in a recumbent manner.
recuperability, *n.* re-kew-per-ra-*bil*-e-te, power of recovery.
recuperate, *v.i.* and *t.* re-*kew*-per-rate, to be restored to or to recover health. (L. *recuperatus,* recovered.)
recuperation, *n.* re-kew-per-*ray*-shon, restoration to health; convalescence.
recuperative, *a.* re-*kew*-per-ra-tiv, pertaining to recovery; having the power of recuperation.
recur, *v.i.* re-*kur,* to occur again or at intervals; to return to the mind; to have recourse. (L. *recurro,* run.)
recurrence, *n.* re-*ku*-rence, the act of recurring or state of being recurrent; a return or periodical returning; recourse.
recurrent, *a.* re-*ku*-rent, returning from time to time; turning in a direction opposite to its former course [Anat.]: *n.* a recurrent nerve or artery.
recurring, *a.* re-*kur*-ring, recurrent; occurring again; being repeated. **recurring decimal,** a circulating decimal.
recurvate, *a.* re-*kur*-vat, bent back; reflexed; curved downward [Bot.].
recurvature, *n.* re-*kur*-va-tewr, a backward curvature.
recurve, *v.t.* re-*kurv,* to bend backwards: *v.i.* to curve outwards.
recurviroster, *n.* re-*kur*-ve-*ros*-ter, a bird whose beak bends upwards, esp. the avocet. (L. *recurvus,* bent back, *rostrum,* a beak.)
recurvous, *a.* re-*ker*-vus, bent backward [Zool.].
recusancy, *n.* *rek*-yew-zan-se, the state of being recusant; nonconformity, esp., formerly, on the part of Roman Catholics.
recusant, *a.* *rek*-yew-zant, refusing to conform, esp. to the authority of an Established Church: *n.* one who is recusant; a Roman Catholic nonconformist; a dissenter. (Fr. *récusant.*)
recusation, *n.* rek-yew-*zay*-shon, the act of challenging a judge on account of alleged interest or prejudice, etc. [Law].
recuse, *v.t.* re-*kewz,* to reject; to renounce; to object to a judge as prejudiced or incompetent [Law].
***red,** *a.* red, of the colour, hue, or tint red; inflamed; lurid; revolutionary; communistic: *n.* the colour seen at the end of the spectrum dispersing light on the longest wave-lengths, typified by blood, port wine, certain roses, etc., and including scarlet, crimson, vermilion, etc.; the red ball [Billiards]; a revolutionary; a communist; a member of the Red Army. **Admiral of the Red,** the highest class of admiral when there were three classes, Red, White, and Blue. **red admiral,** the butterfly *Vanessa atalanta.* **Red Army,** the army of the Soviet Union. **red biddy,** *see* **biddy. red book,** a former official list of civil servants, state pensioners, etc.; a Court Directory. **red cedar,** the American juniper, *Juniperus Virginiana.* **Red Cross,** the cross of St. George, the national emblem of England; the Geneva cross, the flag of the military hospital service. **red deer,** the largest British deer, *Cervus elaphus.* **red ensign,** the flag of the British Merchant Navy. **red flag,** the signal of danger; the symbol of revolution, used also as the emblem of Communism. **red hat,** a cardinal (from his official head-dress) [Coll.]. **red herring,** a herring cured with saltpetre and smoked; anything intended to divert attention from the matter at issue [Fig.]. **Red Indian,** an American Indian, esp. a copper-coloured Indian of N. America. **red lead,** minium, red oxide of lead. **red light,** a danger signal; any warning indication. **red ochre,** ruddle. **red pepper,** Cayenne pepper. **red rag,** anything that causes anger (red being supposed to enrage a bull) [Slang]. **red rot,** the sundew *Drosera rotundifolia*; a fungous disease of plants. **red spider,** any of several harvest mites. **red tape,** the pink tape used in tying up legal documents, etc.; hence, dilatory formality in official routine: *a.* pertaining to this formality. **red tapery** or **tapism,** government by strict routine; adherence to official routine. **red water,** hæmaturia [Med. and Vet.]; Texas fever. **Royal Red Cross,** a British decoration for ladies (esp. nurses) founded in 1883. **to paint the town red,** *see* **paint. to see red,** to be furious; to fly into a rage. (A.S. *read.*)
redact, *v.t.* re-*dakt,* to reduce to form, esp. literary; to edit. (O.Fr. *redacter.*)
redacteur, *n.* re-dak-ter, an editor. (Fr. *rédacteur.*)
redaction, *n.* re-*dak*-shon, editing; the act of digesting or reducing to order; the digest so made.
redactor, *n.* re-*dak*-tor, one who makes a redaction; an editor.
redan, *n.* re-*dan,* a field-work with a salient angle directed towards the attack [Fort.]. (Fr.)
redargue, *v.t.* re-*dar*-gew, to refute. (Fr. *rédaguer.*)
redbreast, *n.* *red*-brest, the robin, so called from the colour of its breast.
redbud, *n.* *red*-bud, the Judas tree, a species of *Cercis.*
redcap, *n.* *red*-kap, the goldfinch; a military policeman [Slang].
redcoat, *n.* *red*-koat, a British soldier, from the colour of the tunic formerly worn by line regiments.
redd, *v.t.* red, to make tidy; to arrange; to free from; to put an end to. (Scots. and Dial.)
redden, *v.t.* *red*-en, to make red: *v.i.* to grow or become red; to blush.
redding, *n.* *red*-ing, ruddle, or any material for reddening.
reddish, *a.* *red*-ish, somewhat red.
reddishness, *n.* *red*-ish-ness, a moderate redness.
reddition, *n.* re-*dish*-on, restitution; restoration (as to a former owner); surrender. (L. *reddere,* to render.)
reddle, *n.* *red*-dl, ruddle.
rede, *n.* reed, counsel; advice; a scheme or decision adopted; story; proverb: *v.t.* to advise; to interpret (a riddle, etc.): *v.i.* to deliberate. (A.S. *rædan.*)
redeem, *v.t.* re-*deem,* to purchase back; to ransom;

to rescue; to free by making atonement; to make good; to fulfil (a promise); to deliver from sin and its penalties [Theol.]. (Fr. *rédimer.*)
redeemability, *n.* re-deem-a-*bil*-e-te, the state of being redeemable.
redeemable, *a.* re-*deem*-a-bl, capable of redemption; that will be redeemed (esp. of bonds, etc.).
redeemer, *n.* re-*deem*-er, one who redeems or ransoms. **the Redeemer,** the Saviour, Jesus Christ.
redeless, *a.* *reed*-less, without advice; unwise.
redeliver, *v.t.* ree-de-*liv*-er, to deliver back; to deliver again; to liberate a second time.
redeliverance, *n.* ree-de-*liv*-er-rance, a second deliverance.
redelivery, *n.* ree-de-*liv*-er-re, a delivering back; a second liberation; a second delivery.
redemand, *v.t.* ree-de-*mahnd*, to demand back; to demand again.
redemise, *n.* ree-de-*mize*, reconveyance; a regranting, or a transference back, of lands: *v.t.* to transfer back, as an estate.
redemption, *n.* re-*demp*-shon, the act of redeeming or state of being redeemed; ransom; deliverance; repurchase, as of lands alienated; the liberation of an estate from a mortgage; the deliverance of sinners from sin and its penalty by the Atonement [Theol.]. (L. *redemptio.*)
redemptioner, *n.* re-*demp*-shon-er, one who redeems himself from an obligation.
Redemptionist, *n.* re-*demp*-shon-ist, a member of a Roman Catholic order founded, about 1200, originally to redeem Christian slaves and now devoted to missionary work.
redemptive, *a.* re-*demp*-tiv, pertaining to redemption; tending to redeem.
Redemptorist, *n.* re-*demp*-to-rist, a member of a Roman Catholic order founded in 1732 for work among the poor.
Redemptoristine, *n.* re-*demp*-to-*ris*-teen, a member of an order of nuns associated with the Redemptorists.
redemptory, *a.* re-*demp*-to-re, pertaining to redemption; serving to redeem.
redeploy, *v.t.* ree-de-*ploy*, to move (troops) from one area or front to another [Mil.].
redevelop, *v.t.* ree-de-*vel*-op, to develop again; to intensify (a developed picture) [Phot.].
red-eye, *n.* the rudd, and some other fish having a reddish iris.
red-eyed, *a.* having inflamed rims to the eyes; bloodshot.
redfish, *n.* *red*-fish, the Pacific salmon, a species of *Oncorhynchus*; the red gurnard; the male salmon in the spawning season.
red-gum, *n.* an eruption of red pimples in early infancy, associated with teething; one of several species of eucalyptus, also a drug obtained from its bark.
red-handed, *a.* with the hands dyed in blood; hence, in the very act (originally of bloodshedding).
redhead, *n.* *red*-hed, the pochard; the red-headed woodpecker; any person with red hair [Coll.].
red-heat, *n.* the state of being, or the temperature at which, a substance is red-hot.
red-hot, *a.* red-hot, heated to redness, hence, greatly excited, violent, of a sensational character; highly syncopated (of music). **red-hot poker,** the torch lily, *Kniphofia aloides.*
redif, *n.* re-*dif*, a soldier in the reserve of the former Imperial Turkish army. (Turk.)
redingote, *n.* *red*-ing-gote, a long, double-breasted coat. (*riding coat.*)
redintegrate, *v.t.* re-*din*-te-grate, to make whole again; to renew: *a.* restored to wholeness or to a perfect state. (L. *redintegratus.*)
redintegration, *n.* re-*din*-te-*gray*-shon, renovation; restoration to a whole or sound state.
redirect, *v.t.* ree-dy-*rekt*, to re-address; to send on to a new address.
rediscount, *v.t.* ree-*dis*-kount, to sell (a promissory note, bill of exchange, etc.) that has been bought: *n.* a note, etc., so sold; a rediscounting [Comm.].
rediscover, *v.t.* ree-dis-*kuv*-er, to discover anew.
redisseizin, *n.* re-dis-*seez*-in, a writ to recover seizin of lands or tenements [Law].
redisseizor, *n.* re-dis-*seez*-or, a person who disseizes lands or tenements a second time.
redistribute, *v.t.* re-*dis*-tre-bewt, to distribute anew.
redistribution, *n.* re-dis-tre-*bew*-shon, a fresh distribution; rearrangement.
red-legs, *n.* the redshank, purple sandpiper, or other red-legged bird.
red-letter, *a.* lettered in red; auspicious, saints' days being marked with red letters in old calendars; memorable.
redly, *ad.* *red*-le, with redness.
redness, *n.* *red*-ness, the state of being red; the shade of red; the degree of red.
re-do, *v.t.* ree-*doo*, to do over again: *p.* **re-did**; *pp.* **re-done.**
redolence, *n.* *red*-o-lence, sweetness of scent.
redolent, *a.* *red*-o-lent, diffusing a scent; smelling sweetly; strongly suggestive of. (O.Fr.)
redondilla, *n.* *red*-on-*deel*-yah, a form of stanza in which the first and fourth and second and third lines rhyme together. (Sp.)
redouble, *v.t.* ree-*dub*-bl, to repeat often; to increase by repeated additions: *v.i.* to become twice as much; to double an adversary's call of double [Contract, etc.].
redoubt, *n.* re-*dout*, a small detached fort without flanking defences and usually temporary [Fort.]. (Fr. *redoute.*)
redoubtable, *a.* re-*dout*-a-bl, formidable; terrible to foes. (O.Fr.)
redoubted, *a.* re-*dout*-ed, dreaded; celebrated.
redound, *v.i.* re-*dound*, to conduce; to contribute to a result; to be redundant. (Fr. *redonder.*)
redowa, *n.* *red*-o-ah *or* *red*-o-vah, a Bohemian round dance. (Czech *rejdovák.*)
redpoll, *n.* *red*-pole, any of several small finches with reddish heads.
redraft, *n.* ree-*drahft*, a second draft or copy: *v.t.* to draw or draft anew.
redraw, *v.t.* ree-*draw*, to draw a second draft or copy; to draw a new bill of exchange [Comm.].
redress, *n.* re-*dres*, deliverance from wrong or oppression; reparation; indemnification: *v.t.* to set right; to remedy; to indemnify; to relieve. **redress the balance,** to restore equipoise. (Fr. *redresser.*)
redresser, *n.* re-*dres*-er, one who gives redress.
redressable, *a.* re-*dres*-a-bl, that may be redressed.
redressive, *a.* re-*dres*-iv, affording redress.
redressment, *n.* re-*dres*-ment, the act of redressing; correction of deformity [Surg.].
redruthite, *n.* *red*-rooth-ite, copper-glance.
redshank, *n.* *red*-shank, the red-legged sandpiper, *Totanus calidris*; (in contempt) any bare-legged person.
redshirt, *n.* *red*-shirt, a revolutionary [Coll.].
red-short, *a.* *red*-short, brittle, or breaking short, when red-hot, as a metal; hot-short.
redskin, *n.* *red*-skin, a North American Indian (from the coppery colour of his skin).
redstart, *n.* *red*-start, the migratory warbler *Ruticilla phœnicurus*, allied to the redbreast and having a red tail. (*red*, and A.S. *steort*, tail.)
redstreak, *n.* *red*-streek, a kind of cider-producing apple with a streaky red skin.
reduce, *v.t.* re-*dewce*, to bring to a former state; to bring to any state or condition; to diminish; to lower; to subdue; to make thin; to bring into subjection; to bring into classes or under rules; to change from one denomination to another [Arith.]; to decrease the density of a negative [Phot.]; to reset or replace a dislocated or displaced part, organ, etc. [Surg.]; to remove oxygen from, to lower the valency of the positive element of a compound, to bring back to a metallic form [Chem.]; to smelt [Metal.]: *v.i.* to slim. **reduce to the ranks,** to degrade (a non-commissioned officer) to the rank of private [Mil.]. **reducing agent,** any substance that removes the oxygen from a compound [Chem.]. (L. *reduco*, bring back.)
reducent, *a.* re-*dewce*-ent, tending to reduce: *n.* that which reduces.
reducer, *n.* re-*dewce*-er, one who or that which reduces; a chemical agent for reducing negatives [Phot.].
reducibility, *n.* re-*dewce*-e-*bil*-e-te, the quality of being reducible.
reducible, *a.* re-*dewce*-e-bl, that may be reduced.
reducibleness, *n.* re-*dewce*-e-bl-ness, reducibility.
reduction, *n.* re-*duk*-shon, the act of reducing, or state of being reduced; diminution; subjugation; a reduced copy; metallurgical separation; the

bringing of numbers of different denominations into one [Arith.].
reductive, *a.* re-*duk*-tiv, tending to reduce: *n.* that which has the power of reducing.
redundance, *n.* re-*dun*-dans, excess or superfluity; anything redundant. (Fr. *redondance.*)
redundancy, *n.* re-*dun*-dan-se, redundance.
redundant, *a.* re-*dun*-dant, superfluous; superabundant; tautological, using more words than are necessary. (L. *redundans*, redounding.)
redundantly, *ad.* in a redundant manner.
reduplicate, *a.* re-*dew*-ple-kat, doubled; redoubled: *v.t.* to double; to repeat; to repeat a syllable or letter, esp. in tense-formation [Gram.]: *v.i.* to undergo reduplication. (L. *reduplicatus.*)
reduplication, *n.* re-*dew*-ple-*kay*-shon, the act of, or the product of, doubling or redoubling; repetition of the first syllable, esp. in tense-formation [Gram.].
reduplicative, *a.* re-*dew*-pli-ka-tiv, formed by reduplication; reduplicate [Bot.].
redwing, *n.* *red*-wing, the thrush, *Turdus iliacus*, which has a bright scarlet patch on its wings.
redwood, *n.* *red*-wood, any tree the timber of which yields a red dye; the Californian conifer *Sequoia sempevirens*, which attains an immense height.
re-dye, *v.t.* to dye anew.
ree, *n.* ree, the reeve, or female ruff.
reebok, *n.* *ree*-bok, the small, sharp-horned South African antelope, *Pelea capreola.* (Dut., roebuck.)
re-echo, *n.* the echo of an echo: *v.i.* and *i.* to echo back; to reverberate.
reechy, *a.* *ree*-che, dirty, smoky, rancid [Dial.]. (*reek.*)
reed, *n.* reed, an aquatic grass with a long jointed stem; a musical pipe; the sounding part of an organ; a thin slip of reed or metal vibrated by a current of air; a reed instrument; that part of a loom by which the threads of the warp are separated [Weaving]; one of a number of parallel circular mouldings [Arch.]. **reed bunting,** the water-side bird *Emberiza schœniclus.* **reed instrument,** a musical instrument in which the sound is generated by the vibration of a reed. **reed mace,** the cat's-tail, *Typha latifolia*, sometimes called the bulrush. **reed pheasant,** the reedling. **reed pipe,** an organ pipe in which a reed vibrates to produce the tone [Mus.]; a shepherd's pipe. **reed stop,** a set of organ reed pipes controlled by a single stop. **reed warbler** or **wren,** the small warbler *Acrocephalus scirpaceus.* (A.S. *hreod.*)
reedbird, *n.* *reed*-bird, the bobolink.
reedbuck, *n.* *reed*-buk, any of several medium-sized S. African antelopes allied to the waterbuck.
reeded, *a.* *reed*-ed, covered with reeds; formed with reeding or reed mouldings.
re-edification, *n.* operation of rebuilding, reviving, or restoring.
re-edify, *v.t.* to build again after destruction; to establish or build up again.
reeding, *n.* *reed*-ing, moulding like parallel reeds [Arch.].
re-edit, *v.t.* ree-*ed*-it, to edit afresh.
reedless, *a.* *reed*-less, destitute of reeds.
reedling, *n.* *reed*-ling, the bearded titmouse, *Panurus biarmicus.*
re-educate, *v.t.* to educate afresh, esp. to restore faculties impaired by disease or accident.
reedy, *a.* *reed*-e, abounding with reeds; in tone like a reed instrument.
reef, *n.* reef, a portion of a sail, folded or rolled up in high wind: *v.t.* to reduce the area of a sail by folding or rolling; to shorten a spar or bowsprit by removing part of it. **reef band,** the canvas strip stitched across a sail in which are pierced the holes for the reef points. **reef point,** a short length of cord used for tying up reefs [Naut.]. (Dut., from O. Scand. *rif.*)
reef, *n.* reef, a submarine elevation of rock, coral, etc., near enough to the surface to be a danger to shipping; a mineral lode or vein. (Dut. *rif.*)
reefer, *n.* *reef*-er, a short, stout, double-breasted coat as worn by sailors; one who reefs; a midshipmen.
reef-knot, *n.* a knot made by passing the end of the cord through a simple loop, bringing it back over the loop and passing it out under the loop on the same face of the loop as that by which it entered.
reefy, *a.* *reef*-e, full of reefs or submerged rocks.
reek, *n.* reek, smoke; vapour; stink: *v.i.* to emit smoke or vapour; to steam. (A.S. *rec*, smoke or vapour.)
reeky, *a.* *reek*-e, smoky; emitting reek or fumes.
reel, *n.* reel, a frame on which yarn or lines are wound; a bobbin; an angler's winch; a strip of 1,000 ft. of cinema film: *v.t.* to wind upon a reel. **off the reel,** without premeditation or hesitation; in quick succession. **to reel off,** to utter rapidly or fluently. (A.S. *hreol.*)
reel, *n.* reel, a lively Scottish dance; the music for this. (Perhaps Gael. *righil.*)
reel, *v.i.* reel, to stagger; to sway unsteadily from side to side in walking. (Origin uncertain.)
re-elect, *v.t.* to elect again.
re-election, *n.* election a second time.
reeler, *n.* *reel*-er, one who reels; one employed in reeling yarn, etc.; the grasshopper warbler, *Locustella nævea.*
re-eligibility, *n.* the capacity of being re-elected to the same office.
re-eligible, *a.* capable of being elected again to the same office.
reem, *v.t.* reem, to ream (open seams for caulking).
re-embark, *v.t.* and *i.* to put or go on board again.
re-embarkation, *n.* act of embarking again.
re-embody, *v.t.* to embody again.
re-emerge, *v.t.* to emerge after being plunged, obscured, or overwhelmed.
re-enact, *v.t.* to enact again.
re-enforce, *v.t.* ree-en-*force*, to reinforce: *n.* a reinforcement.
re-enlist, *v.t.* and *i.* to take service in or to engage for another period.
re-enlistment, *n.* the act of re-enlisting.
re-enter, *v.t.* and *i.* to enter again; to enter again upon possession [Law]; to point inwards (esp. of angles). **re-entering angle,** an angle, as in a line of troops or fortifications, the apex of which points away from the front.
re-entrance, *n.* act of entering again, or [Law] of resuming possession; re-entry.
re-entrant, *n.* one who or that which re-enters; an inwardly entering angle: *a.* re-entering; directed inwards.
re-entry, *n.* re-entrance. **card of re-entry,** a card that will enable the player to regain the lead [Contract, etc.].
reest, *v.i.* reest, to balk; to come to a sudden stop and refuse to budge (esp. of horses) [Scots.].
re-establish, *v.t.* to establish anew; to confirm; to restore.
re-establishment, *n.* the act of re-establishing; the state of being re-established; renewed confirmation.
reeve, *n.* reev, a steward; formerly, a chief magistrate or high administrative official; in Canada, the mayor of certain municipalities. (A.S. *gerefa.*)
reeve, *n.* reeve, the female ruff, *Machetes pugnax.*
reeve, *v.t.* reev, to pass the end of a rope through a hole [Naut.]: *p.* and *pp.* **rove** or **reeved** (*pp.* also **roven**). (Dut. *reven.*)
re-examination, *n.* renewed examination.
re-examine, *v.t.* to examine anew.
re-exchange, *n.* a renewed exchange; the exchange chargeable on the re-draft of a bill of exchange [Comm.].
re-export, *v.t.* ree-eks-*port*, to export again; to export what has been imported: *n.* re-*eks*-port, re-exportation; a commodity re-exported.
re-exportation, *n.* the act of exporting goods previously imported.
refashion, *v.t.* ree-*fash*-on, to change the form of.
refection, *n.* re-*fek*-shon, refreshment after hunger or fatigue; a light meal. (O.Fr.)
refective, *a.* re-*fek*-tiv, refreshing; restoring: *n.* a restorative; that which refreshes.
refectory, *n.* re-*fek*-to-re, a hall or appartment (originally in a monastery) for taking meals. (Late L. *refectorium.*)
refer, *v.t.* re-*fer*, to send back; to submit to another or to some recognized source, for information or decision; to assign: *v.i.* to have relation to; to allude; to have recourse; to appeal to. (O.Fr. *referer.*)
referable, *a.* *ref*-er-ra-bl, that may be referred.
referee, *n.* ref-er-*ree*, one to whom a thing is referred; one appointed by a court to hear a cause between parties, and report [Law]; an umpire at football,

etc. : *v.i.* to act as referee or umpire. (Fr. *référé*, referred.)

reference, *n. ref*-er-rence, act of referring ; submission to another for information ; assignment ; allusion ; that which is referred to ; relation ; respect ; a person nominated by another as being willing to testify to his character or ability, also, his written testimony ; a note or direction referring a reader to some other passage. **book of reference,** a book for consultation (as an encyclopædia, directory, atlas, etc.) rather than actual reading. **reference Bible,** a Bible annotated with references to corresponding passages. **reference library,** a library the books in which may be consulted but not borrowed. (Fr. *référence.*)

referendary, *n.* ref-er-*ren*-da-re, a former official examiner of petitions to the papal and certain royal courts. (Fr. *référendaire.*)

referendum, *n.* ref-er-*ren*-dum, the referring of parliamentary or constitutional issues to the general decision of the electorate by a direct vote ; the holding of a plebiscite. (L.)

referent, *ref*-er-rent, *n.* one to whom reference is made ; one who may be consulted : *a.* referential ; containing a reference.

referential, *a.* ref-er-*ren*-shal, of the nature of reference ; having reference to something.

referrible, *a.* re-*fer*-re-bl, referable.

refill, *v.t.* ree-*fil*, to fill again : *n. ree*-fil, something to take the place of a similar article.

refinable, *a.* re-*fyn*-a-bl, capable of being refined.

refind, *v.t.* ree-*fynd*, to find again.

refine, *v.t.* re-*fyn*, to purify, as liquors, metals, manners, language, taste, morals : *v.i.* to become pure ; to improve ; to affect nicety or subtlety.

refined, *a.* re-*fynd*, separated from extraneous matter ; polished ; elegant ; affected.

refinedly, *ad.* re-*fyn*-ed-le, in a refined manner.

refinedness, *n.* re-*fynd*-ness, the state of being refined.

refinement, *n.* re-*fyn*-ment, the act of refining ; the state of being refined ; polish of language ; elegance ; purity ; polish of manners ; purity of taste, mind, morals, or heart ; a subtlety in reasoning, etc. ; affectation of nicety.

refiner, *n.* re-*fy*-ner, one who refines ; an inventor of superfluous subtleties.

refinery, *n.* re-*fy*-ner-re, a place or apparatus for refining.

refit, *v.t.* ree-*fit*, to fit or prepare again ; to repair : *v.i.* to be made ready for fresh use (esp. of ships) : *n.* a new or fresh equipment ; an act of refitting.

refitment, *n.* ree-*fit*-ment, the act of refitting ; a fitting out again, esp. of a ship.

reflate, *v.t.* and *i.* ree-*flate*, to bring to or arrive at a state of inflation after a period of deflation [Econ.].

reflation, *n.* ree-*flay*-shon, the act or process of reflating ; inflation of currency after deflation.

reflect, *v.t.* re-*flekt*, to throw back, esp. after being struck ; to mirror : *v.i.* to throw back, as light, heat, or other rays ; to consider mentally ; to bring reproach or discredit on ; to cast censure on. **reflecting telescope,** an astronomical telescope in which the image is seen from a concave reflector instead of through a lens or object glass. (L. *reflecto*, bend.)

reflectible, *a.* re-*flek*-te-bl, that may be reflected.

reflectingly, *ad.* re-*flek*-ting-le, with reflection ; with censure or serious consideration ; thoughtfully.

reflection, *n.* re-*flek*-shon, act of reflecting ; the state of being reflected ; that which is reflected ; thoughtful consideration ; attention to states of self-consciousness or one's mental operations ; the expression of thought ; censure ; reproach.

reflectional, *a.* re-*flek*-shon-al, pertaining to, or due to, reflection.

reflective, *a.* re-*flek*-tiv, reflecting ; considering the operations of the mind or things past ; given to reflection ; reflexive [Gram.].

reflectively, *ad.* in a reflective manner.

reflectiveness, *n.* power of reflection.

reflectivity, *n.* ree-flek-*tiv*-e-te, the state or quality of being reflective.

reflector, *n.* re-*flek*-tor, that which reflects ; a polished surface reflecting light or heat ; a mirror ; a reflecting telescope.

reflex, *a. ree*-fleks, directed back ; introspective ; illuminated by light reflected from another part of the same picture [Painting] ; bent or turned back [Bot.] ; produced in reaction, said of the motor nerves acting independently of the will under a stimulus from impressions made on the sensory nerves [Phys.] : *n.* reflexion ; reflected light ; a reflected image ; a reflex action [Phys.]. (L. *reflexus*, a turning back again.)

reflexibility, *n.* re-*flek*-se-*bil*-e-te, quality of being reflexible.

reflexible, *a.* re-*flek*-se-bl, capable of being reflected.

reflexion, *n.* re-*flek*-shon, reflection ; the act or state of being reflected.

reflexive, *a.* re-*flek*-siv, having respect to something past ; referring back to the subject [Gram.] ; implying action upon the subject by the subject ; reflective : *n.* a reflexive verb or pronoun [Gram.]. (Fr. *réflexif.*)

reflexively, *ad.* in a reflexive manner ; by means of a reflexive [Gram.].

reflexly, *ad.* in a reflex manner.

refloat, *v.t.* and *i.* ree-*flote*, to float again after sinking or running aground ; to float anew.

reflow, *v.i.* ree-*floh*, to flow back : *n.* the ebb.

reflower, *v.i.* ree-*flou*-er, to come into flower again.

refluence, *n. ref*-loo-ence, reflux ; refluent action.

refluent, *a. ref*-loo-ent, flowing back ; ebbing. (L. *refluens.*)

reflux, *n. ree*-fluks, a flowing back ; backward course ; an ebb. (L.)

refold, *v.t.* ree-*fohld*, to fold again.

refoot, *v.t.* ree-*foot*, to provide (a sock, stocking, etc.) with a new foot.

reforest, *v.t.* ree-*fo*-rest, to reafforest.

reforge, *v.t.* ree-*forj*, to forge again.

reform, *n.* re-*form*, a changing for the better ; amendment ; a removal of abuses ; an extension and more equable distribution of the franchise : *v.t.* to change for the better ; to amend ; to correct : *v.i.* to abandon that which is evil or corrupt ; to be amended. (Fr. *réformer.*)

re-form, *v.t.* and *i. ree*-form, to form or arrange again.

reformation, *n.* ref-or-*may*-shon, the act of reforming ; the state of being reformed ; the act of forming anew ; correction or amendment ; the redress of abuses. **the Reformation,** the great religious revolt of the 16th century, headed by Luther, which resulted in the establishment, over a large section of Europe, of the Protestant Churches. (O.Fr.)

re-formation, *n.* ree-for-*may*-shon, the forming or arranging again.

reformative, *a.* re-*for*-ma-tiv, forming again ; improving ; tending to reform.

reformatory, *a.* re-*for*-ma-to-re, tending to produce improvement : *n.* an approved school, or institution for the reform of juvenile delinquents.

reformed, *pp.* and *a.* re-*formd*, restored to a good state. **Reformed Church,** any of the Churches which, after the Reformation, disagreed with certain Lutheran doctrines and adopted the theological system and ecclesiastical polity of Calvin, Zwingli, etc. ; also, any Protestant Church.

reformer, *n.* re-*form*-er, one who effects a reformation ; an active participator in the Reformation ; an advocate of political reform ; a supporter of a Reform Bill, esp. that of 1832.

reformist, *a.* re-*form*-ist, pertaining to reform : *n.* one advocating reform, esp. in religious or political spheres.

refortify, *v.t.* ree-*for*-te-fy, to fortify anew.

re-found, *v.t.* ree-*found*, to establish again.

refract, *v.t.* re-*frakt*, to bend at an angle ; to deflect (esp. a ray) from its correct course. **refracting telescope,** a telescope having an object glass (as opposed to the mirror of a reflecting telescope) to collect the beams of light. (L. *refractus*, bent back.)

refracted, *pp.* and *a.* re-*frak*-ted, turned from a direct course ; bent back at an acute angle [Bot. and Zool.].

refractile, *a.* re-*frak*-tile, capable of refracting.

refraction, *n.* re-*frak*-shon, bending at an angle, esp. of a ray of light or heat passing through the surface of one medium into that of another of different density or through a lens. **angle of refraction,** the angle made by a ray of light and a line perpendicular to the surface of the medium

through which it is passing. **astronomical refraction,** the apparent angular elevation of the celestial bodies above their true places, due to the refracting power of the air. **double refraction,** the refracting of light in two directions. **index of refraction,** *see* **index.**
refractional, *a.* re-*frak*-shon-al, pertaining to refraction.
refractionist, *n.* re-*frak*-shon-ist, an ophthalmologist who specializes in the correction of abnormal refraction of the eye.
refractive, *a.* re-*frak*-tiv, refracting; pertaining to refraction; refractile; capable of repelling infective germs [Path.].
refractiveness, *n.* the quality of refracting.
refractivity, *n.* *ree*-frak-*tiv*-e-te, refractive power; refractiveness.
refractometer, *n.* *ree*-frak-*tom*-e-ter, an instrument for measuring refraction.
refractor, *n.* re-*frak*-tor, a refracting medium; a refracting telescope, in which the object is seen direct through a lens instead of by reflection from a mirror.
refractorily, *ad.* in a refractory manner.
refractoriness, *n.* quality or state of being refractory.
refractory, *a.* re-*frak*-to-re, sullen or perverse in opposition or disobedience; contumacious; difficult of fusion; difficult to deal with; not susceptible (to a disease); not amenable to ordinary treatment [Med.]: *n.* a refractory composition or material; one who is refractory. (L. *refractarius.*)
refracture, *n.* ree-*frak*-tewr, the breaking again of a fractured bone to correct a faulty union [Surg.]: *v.t.* to perform this operation.
refragable, *a.* *ref*-ra-ga-bl, that may be refuted.
refrain, *v.t.* re-*frane*, to forbear; to abstain; to restrain: *v.i.* to keep oneself from action; to forbear. (O.Fr. *refrener.*)
refrain, *n.* re-*frane*, the burden of a song or that which is repeated at the end of each stanza; a kind of musical repetition. (O.Fr.)
reframe, *v.t.* ree-*frame*, to frame or fashion again.
refrangibility, *n.* re-*fran*-je-*bil*-e-te, the quality of being refrangible.
refrangible, *a.* re-*fran*-je-bl, capable of being refracted.
refresh, *v.t.* re-*fresh*, to make fresh again; to give new strength to; to relieve after fatigue, depression, etc.; to revive what is drooping; to supply refreshment to [Coll.]: *v.i.* to take refreshment, esp. a drink. (O.Fr. *refreschir.*)
refresher, *n.* re-*fresh*-er, he who or that which refreshes; an additional fee paid to a barrister in a protracted case; a cooling drink. **refresher course,** a periodical course of training, lectures, etc., to promote continued efficiency.
refreshing, *ppr.* and *a.* re-*fresh*-ing, cooling; invigorating; reanimating.
refreshingly, *ad.* so as to refresh.
refreshingness, *n.* the quality of being refreshed.
refreshment, *n.* re-*fresh*-ment, act of refreshing; the state of being refreshed; new life or animation after depression; that which refreshes, esp. food or drink. (O.Fr. *refreschissement.*)
refrigerant, *a.* re-*frij*-er-rant, cooling; allaying heat: *n.* that which cools; a medicine which allays fever or otherwise refreshes the patient.
refrigerate, *v.t.* re-*frij*-er-rate, to cool; to freeze; to preserve by chilling or freezing in a refrigerator. (L. *refrigeratus*, made cool again.)
refrigeration, *n.* re-*frij*-er-*ray*-shon, the act or process of refrigerating; reduction of temperature, esp. below that of the air; the state of being cooled.
refrigerative, *a.* re-*frij*-er-ra-tiv, refrigerant; tending to cool.
refrigerator, *n.* re-*frij*-er-ray-tor, a machine for extracting heat from a substance; an air-tight box or room supplied with this for use for cold storage; an ice-box.
refrigeratory, *a.* re-*frij*-er-ra-to-re, cooling: *n.* a cooling medium, chamber, or appliance; the part of a still in which the worm is immersed in the cold water that condenses the vapour therein.
refringent, *a.* re-*frin*-jent, refracting.
reft, reft, *pp.* of the verb *to reave*; bereft; deprived.
refuel, *v.t.* and *i.* ree-*few*-el, to supply with or obtain fresh fuel.
refuge, *n.* *ref*-yewj, protection from danger or distress; any place which affords such protection; a temporary retreat or shelter; a place of safety from traffic for pedestrians crossing a street; an asylum; an expedient: *v.t.* and *i.* to give or take refuge. **house of refuge,** a charitable institution for the homeless or destitute. (Fr., from L. *re-* and *fugere*, to flee.)
refugee, *n.* ref-yew-*jee*, one who flees for shelter to a place of refuge, esp. to a foreign country for political reasons, or in times of war or persecution.
refugeeism, *n.* ref-yew-*jee*-izm, the state of being a refugee.
refulgence, *n.* re-*ful*-jence, a flood of light; splendour.
refulgent, *a.* re-*ful*-jent, casting a bright light; shining; radiant. (L. *refulgens*, shining back.)
refulgently, *ad.* in a refulgent manner.
refund, *v.t.* re-*fund*, to repay or pay back; to restore: *n.* *ree*-fund, that which is paid back; refundment. (L. *refundo*, restore.)
refunder, *n.* re-*fund*-er, one who repays.
refundment, *n.* re-*fund*-ment, the act of refunding.
refurbish, *v.t.* re-*fur*-bish, to furbish up again.
refurnish, *v.t.* re-*fur*-nish, to furnish again.
refusable, *a.* re-*fewz*-a-bl, that may be refused.
refusal, *n.* re-*fewz*-al, the act of refusing; denial of anything demanded or offered for acceptance; the choice of taking or refusing.
refuse, *v.t.* re-*fewz*, to deny a request or command; to decline; to reject: *v.i.* to decline to accept; not to comply; to be unable to follow suit [Card-playing]. (Fr. *refuser.*)
refuse, *a.* *ref*-yewce, refused; rejected; worthless: *n.* that which is refused or rejected as useless; waste matter; dross.
re-fuse, *v.t.* and *i.* ree-*fewz*, to fuse again.
refuser, *n.* re-*fewz*-er, one who refuses; a recusant; a horse that declines to jump a ditch, etc.
refutability, *n.* re-*few*-ta-*bil*-e-te, capability of being refuted.
refutable, *a.* re-*few*-ta-bl, that may be refuted; that may be proved false or erroneous.
refutal, *n.* re-*few*-tal, refutation.
refutation, *n.* ref-yew-*tay*-shon, the act of refuting; proof of error, etc.
refutatory, *a.* re-*few*-ta-to-re, tending to refute.
refute, *v.t.* re-*fewt*, to prove to be false or wrong. (Fr., from L. *refutare.*)
refuter, *n.* re-*few*-ter, one who refutes.
regain, *v.t.* re-*gane*, to gain anew; to recover possession of; to reach again. (Fr. *regagner.*)
regal, *a.* *ree*-gal, pertaining to a king; royal; kingly. (Fr. *régale*, from L. *regalis.*)
regal, *n.* *ree*-gal, a small portable organ in use in the 16th and 17th centuries. (Fr.)
regale, *v.t.* re-*gale*, to entertain sumptuously; to entertain with something that delights; to gratify: *v.i.* to feast; to fare sumptuously. (Fr. *régaler.*)
regalement, *n.* re-*gale*-ment, the act of regaling; anything which regales; entertainment.
regalia, *n.pl.* re-*gay*-le-a, the insignia of sovereignty; the symbols of a society; the badge and other decorations pertaining to any order (as of knighthood, masonry, etc.); the rights and prerogatives of a king [Law]. (L.)
regalism, *n.* *ree*-gal-izm, the doctrine of royal supremacy in church matters.
regality, *n.* re-*gal*-e-te, royalty; sovereignty; sovereign jurisdiction; in Scotland, a certain territorial jurisdiction formerly conferred on a noble by the king.
regally, *ad.* *ree*-ga-le, in a royal manner.
regard, *n.* re-*gard*, a meaning look; attention of the mind; consideration; respect; repute: *v.t.* to notice particularly; to heed; to value; to esteem; to respect: *v.i.* to gaze; to pay attention. **as regards,** with respect to; regarding. (Fr. *regarder.*)
regardant, *a.* re-*gar*-dant, looking behind or backwards [Her.]; vigilant. (O.Fr.)
regardful, *a.* re-*gard*-ful, taking notice; heedful; respectful.
regardfully, *ad.* attentively; with regard.
regardfulness, *n.* the quality of being regardful.
regarding, *prep.* re-*gar*-ding, respecting; concerning; related to.
regardless, *a.* re-*gard*-less, heedless; unobservant; neglectful; without regard.
regardlessly, *ad.* heedlessly.

regardlessness, *n.* heedlessness.
regather, *v.t.* ree-*gath*-er, to collect or gather again.
regatta, *n.* re-*gat*-ta, a race-meeting for water craft (originally a gondola race at Venice). (It.)
regelation, *n.* ree-je-*lay*-shon, the phenomenon exhibited by the union into one of two pieces of ice brought into contact above the freezing-point; freezing again after a thaw. (L. *re-*, and *gelatus*, frozen.)
regency, *n.* *ree*-jen-se, government by a regent; jurisdiction of a regent; a body entrusted with vicarious government; the period of rule of a regent. **the Regency,** the period of English history from 1810 to 1820 when the Prince of Wales ruled in place of George III.
regeneracy, *n.* re-*jen*-er-ra-se, the state of being regenerated.
regenerate, *a.* re-*jen*-er-rat, reformed; regenerated: *v.t.* to generate or produce anew; to change fundamentally; to renew the heart by a change from a carnal to a spiritual life. (L. *regeneratus*, produced anew.)
regeneration, *n.* re-*jen*-er-*ray*-shon, the act of regenerating; forming or creating afresh; renascence; repair or renewal of injured tissue [Med.]. **baptismal regeneration,** the doctrine that a spiritual character is bestowed on the soul by the sacrament of baptism.
regenerative, *a.* re-*jen*-er-ra-tiv, pertaining to regeneration; tending to regenerate; renewing.
regenerator, *n.* re-*jen*-er-ray-tor, one who or that which regenerates; a device for obtaining a high temperature in furnaces.
regeneratory, *a.* re-*jen*-er-ra-to-re, regenerative; of the nature of regeneration.
regenesis, *n.* re-*jen*-e-sis, re-birth; the state of being reproduced.
regent, *a.* *ree*-gent, ruling; exercising vicarious authority: *n.* one who governs in the minority, absence, or disability of a monarch; formerly, one of a certain class of university professors; one of a board of superintendents of certain universities [U.S.A.]. (O.Fr.)
regent-bird, *n.* an Australian bower-bird, *Sericulus chrysocephalus*, named after the Prince Regent, later George IV.
regentship, *n.* *ree*-jent-ship, the office of a regent.
regerminate, *v.i.* ree-*jer*-me-nate, to bud again.
regermination, *n.* re-*jer*-me-*nay*-shon, a sprouting or germination anew.
regicidal, *a.* rej-e-*sy*-dal, pertaining to regicide.
regicide, *n.* *rej*-e-side, the killer or the killing of a king. (L. *rex*, *regis*, a king, *cædo*, kill.)
Régie, *n.* ray-*zhee*, a monopoly (*e.g.* of tobacco) by which revenue accrues to a government. (Fr., management of taxation, etc., by the govt.)
regild, *v.t.* ree-*gild*, to gild again.
régime, *n.* ray-*zheem*, mode of governing or managing; administration, social or political; the prevailing social system. (Fr.)
regimen, *n.* *rej*-e-men, administration; orderly government; system of order; regulation of diet or habits with a view to health [Med.]; government, or relation between words [Gram.]. (L.)
regiment, *n.* *rej*-e-ment, a military unit of one or more battalions; a body consisting of a number of companies, troops, or batteries: *v.t.* to form into a regiment or regiments; to organize as a regiment; to subject to control or discipline.
regimental, *a.* rej-e-*men*-tal, pertaining to a regiment: *n.pl.* the uniform worn by the soldiers of a regiment; military uniform.
regimentation, *n.* rej-e-men-*tay*-shon, the act of regimenting; organization into or arrangement by regiments.
regina, *n.* re-*jy*-na, a reigning queen. (L., queen.)
reginal, *a.* re-*jy*-nal, pertaining to a queen; queenly. (L. *regina*, a queen.)
region, *n.* *ree*-jun, a tract of land or space of indefinite, but usually considerable, extent; an administrative or self-contained area; a country; a district; a part or division of the body. (O.Fr.)
regional, *a.* *ree*-jun-al, relating to a region; topographical; sectional.
regionalism, *n.* *ree*-jun-a-lizm, decentralization, esp. of a country into separate administrative areas.
regionally, *ad.* from a regional point of view.
register, *n.* *rej*-is-ter, written official record; the book in which such a register or record is kept; a list; an entry in a list; registration; a recording indicator or any device which registers; an apparatus for regulating the admission of air or heat; a regulator; a stop in an organ; musical compass: exact alignment of type, esp. between the two sides of a sheet [Print.]; exact overlaying of colours [Colour Print.]: *v.t.* to record; to enter or cause to be entered in a register; to indicate; to have postal matter recorded to enable its transit to be traced; to cause to correspond in relative position; to fit; to express some emotion in the face; to reveal in any way: *v.i.* to enrol one's name in a register; to be in exact correspondence or correct alignment; to make an impression [Slang]. **make register,** to make the pages and lines fall exactly on one another [Print.]. **parish register,** a book in which are recorded the baptisms, marriages, and deaths within the parish. **register office,** a place for registry; a record office. **register ton,** *see* **ton.** (O.Fr. *registre.*)
registrable, *a.* *rej*-is-tra-bl, suitable for registration.
registrant, *n.* *rej*-is-trant, one who has registered (himself, or a trade-mark, etc.).
registrar, *n.* *rej*-is-trahr, an official who has the keeping of records; one who registers. **Registrar General,** one appointed to superintend the registration of births, deaths, and marriages. (Late L. *registrarius.*)
registrarship, *n.* *rej*-is-trahr-ship, the office of registrar.
registration, *n.* rej-is-*tray*-shon, the act of registering or enrolling in a register; an entry in a register; the persons registered, collectively; adjustment to secure alignment or prevent overlapping of colour [Print.]; the combination of, or the act of selecting, organ stops in playing [Mus.].
registry, *n.* *rej*-is-tre, the act of recording in a register; the place where a register is kept; a set of facts recorded. **registry office,** the office at which a registrar performs civil marriages and records all births, deaths, and marriages within his district; an employment agency for domestic servants.
regius, *a.* *ree*-je-us, royal. **regius professor,** the incumbent of a university professorship founded by royal bounty, esp. that of Henry VIII. (L.)
reglet, *n.* *reg*-let, a flat, narrow moulding [Arch.]; a slip of wood for separating lines [Print.]. (Fr., from L. *regula*, a rule.)
regma, *n.* *reg*-ma, a dry fruit consisting of several cells which when ripe burst open. (Gr. *rhēgma*, a fracture.)
regnal, *a.* *reg*-nal, pertaining to a reign. **regnal year,** a period of a year commencing from the moment of a sovereign's accession or an anniversary thereof.
regnant, *reg*-nant, reigning; exercising regal authority; ruling; predominant; prevalent. (L. *regnans*, ruling.)
regorge, *v.t.* ree-*gorj*, to vomit; to swallow back again; to swallow eagerly. (Fr. *regorger.*)
regrant, *n.* ree-*grahnt*, a renewed grant: *v.t.* to grant again.
regrate, *v.t.* re-*grate*, to buy (esp. provisions, etc.) in large quantities for resale in the same market or fair at an enhanced price, formerly a punishable offence. (Fr. *regratter*, to scrape.)
re-grate, *v.t.* to grate or scrape the surface of a wall to give it a freshened appearance.
regrater, *n.* re-*grate*-er, one who regrates.
regreet, *n.* ree-*greet*, a return or exchange of salutation: *v.t.* to greet again.
regress, *n.* *ree*-gress, passage back; return: *v.i.* re-*gress*, to go backward; to retrograde. (L. *regressus*, gone back.)
regression, *n.* re-*gresh*-on, the act of passing back or returning; retrogression; reversion to type.
regressive, *a.* re-*gres*-siv, characterized by regression; retrogressive.
regressively, *ad.* in a regressive manner.
★**regret,** *n.* re-*gret*, pain of mind due to reflection on some lost or past action or negligence; sorrow; concern; dissatisfaction: *v.t.* to remember with sorrow; to grieve at; to lament. (O.Fr. *regreter*, perhaps connected with A.S. *grætan*, to weep.)
regretful, *a.* re-*gret*-ful, full of regret.
regretfully, *ad.* re-*gret*-ful-le, with regret.

regrettable, *a.* re-*gret*-a-bl, to be regretted; unwelcome; worthy of reproof.
regrettably, *ad.* in a regrettable way; to a regrettable degree.
regulable, *a.* *reg*-yew-la-bl, capable of being regulated.
★**regular,** *a.* *reg*-yew-lar, agreeable to rule, law, or principle; governed by rule; conforming to type; symmetrical; having equal sides and angles [Geom.]; fully qualified; methodical; orderly; periodical; pursued with uniformity; belonging to a monastic order; unmistakable [Coll.]: *n.* a member of any religious order who has taken the vows of poverty, chastity, and obedience; a soldier belonging to a permanent army; one who, as a customer, etc., is regular [Coll.]. **regular troops,** the troops of a permanent or standing army. (L. *regularis*, according to rule.)
regularity, *n.* reg-yew-*la*-re-te, state or quality of being regular; uniformity or steadiness in a course.
regularization, *n.* *reg*-yew-la-ry-*zay*-shon, the act of making regular.
regularize, *v.t.* *reg*-yew-la-rize, to make regular.
regularly, *ad.* in a regular manner.
regulate, *v.t.* *reg*-yew-late, to adjust by rule; to subject to rule; to put in order. (L. *regulatus*.)
regulation, *n.* reg-yew-*lay*-shon, the act of regulating; the state of being regulated; a prescribed rule or order: *a.* fixed by regulation; in accordance with regulation.
regulative, *a.* *reg*-yew-la-tiv, tending to regulate.
regulator, *n.* *reg*-yew-lay-tor, one who or that which regulates; any part of a watch, machine, etc., which regulates its movements. (L.)
regulatory, *a.* *reg*-yew-la-to-re, pertaining to or making regulations.
regulus, *n.* *reg*-yew-lus, a mineral reduced from its compound by fusion with a reducing agent; a still impure product of smelting; a former name of antimony; the golden-crested wren, *Regulus cristatus*; (*cap.*) a star of the first magnitude in the constellation Leo. (L., a petty king.)
regurgitate, *v.t.* re-*ger*-je-tate, to throw or pour back: *v.i.* to be thrown or poured back. (Late L.)
regurgitation, *n.* re-ger-je-*tay*-shon, the act of pouring back; reabsorption; eructation.
rehabilitate, *v.t.* ree-ha-*bil*-e-tate, to restore to a former capacity; to reinstate.
rehabilitation, *n.* ree-ha-bil-e-*tay*-shon, act of reinstating in a former rank or capacity; restoration to former rights.
rehandle, *v.t.* ree-*han*-dl, to handle anew.
rehang, *v.t.* ree-*hang*, to hang again.
rehash, *v.t.* ree-*hash*, to hash anew; to go over an old argument: *n.* that which has been rehashed; a reiterated presentation.
rehear, *v.t.* ree-*heer*, to hear or try a second time.
rehearing, *n.* ree-*heer*-ing, a retrial or second hearing.
rehearsal, *n.* re-*her*-sal, repetition of the words of another; narration; a trial performance in private.
rehearse, *v.t.* re-*herse*, to repeat the words of another; to narrate; to go through in private preparatory to performance in public. (Fr. *reherser*, harrow over again.)
rehearser, *n.* re-*herse*-er, one who rehearses; one who conducts rehearsals.
re-heat, *v.t.* to heat again.
rehouse, *v.t.* ree-*houz*, to give a new dwelling to; to accommodate in fresh quarters.
rei, *n.* ray, an erroneous singular of *reis*.
Reich, *n.* rykh, Germany; the German State; the former German Empire. (Ger., empire).
Reichsmark, *n.* *rykhs*-mark, the monetary unit of the pre-1945 German state, nominally equivalent to nearly 11¾*d*.
Reichsrath, *n.* *rykhs*-raht, the parliament of the former Austrian Empire; the German State Council or upper house under the Weimar Constitution, 1919. (Ger. *Reich*, and *Rath*, counsel.)
Reichstag, *n.* *rykh*-shtahkh, the lower house of the German parliament which, after the Nazi accession to power (1933), possessed only advisory functions. (Ger. *Reich*, and *Tag*, a day.)
Reichswehr, *n.* *rykhs*-vayr, the standing army of the German republican and Nazi régimes.
reification, *n.* re-e-fe-*kay*-shun, the act, process, or result of reifying; materialization.
reify, *v.i.* *ree*-e-fy, to materialize; to convert mentally an abstraction into a thing.
reign, *n.* rane, royal authority; supreme power; sovereignty; the time during which a monarch reigns; dominion; influence: *v.i.* to rule as a monarch; to prevail; to govern. **reign of terror,** *see* **terror.** (O.Fr. *regne*.)
re-ignite, *v.t.* to set fire to once more.
reillumine, *v.t.* ree-il-*loo*-min, to enlighten again.
reim, *n.* reem, a riem.
reimburse, *v.t.* ree-im-*berse*, to refund; to repay.
reimbursement, *n.* ree-im-*berse*-ment, repayment.
reimport, *v.t.* re-im-*pawrt*, to import back what has been exported: *n.* ree-*im*-pawrt, that which is reimported.
reimportation, *n.* ree-im-por-*tay*-shon, the act of reimporting.
reimpose, *v.t.* ree-im-*poze*, to impose again (esp. of taxes).
re-impression, *n.* a reprint or second impression.
rein, *n.* rane, the strap of a bridle leading from each side of the bit; any means of curbing, restraining, or governing: *v.t.* to govern by a bridle; to restrain. **give rein,** to give licence. **take the reins,** to take the guidance. (O.Fr. *rene*.)
re-incarnation, *n.* re-embodiment; metempsychosis; the return again and again of the soul to earth.
re-incarnationist, *n.* *ree*-in-kar-*nay*-shon-ist, a believer in the theory of re-incarnation.
re-incorporate, *v.t.* to incorporate anew that which has previously been incorporated.
reindeer, *n.* *rane*-deer, any of several species of deer of the genus *Rangifer*, the European species of which, *R. tarandus*, has been semi-domesticated; the N. American caribou. **reindeer moss,** the lichen, *Cladonia rangiferina*, eaten by reindeer. (Ice. *hreinn*, reindeer, and *deer*.)
reinforce, *n.* ree-in-*force*, that which reinforces, esp. the thick part of the breech of a gun: *v.t.* to strengthen by additional men or material; to add to the strength of. **reinforced concrete,** *see* **concrete.**
reinforcement, *n.* ree-in-*force*-ment, the act of reinforcing; an increase of strength; an additional supply of troops, etc. [Mil.].
re-ink, *v.t.* ree-*ink*, to ink again.
reinoculation, *n.* *ree*-in-ok-yew-*lay*-shon, inoculation a second time.
reinless, *a.* *rane*-less, without restraint; unchecked.
reins, *n.pl.* raynz, the kidneys; the loins; the lower part of the back. (O.Fr., from L. *renes*, kidneys.)
reinstall, *v.t.* ree-in-*stawl*, to put in possession again.
reinstate, *v.i.* ree-in-*state*, to restore to a previous state; to replace.
reinstatement, *n.* ree-in-*state*-ment, re-establishment; the act of reinstating.
reinsurance, *n.* ree-in-*shoor*-rance, the act of re-insuring; a transfer of the risks of insurance.
reinsure, *v.t.* ree-in-*shoor*, to insure again; to insure against loss by the grantor of a policy of insurance.
reinsurer, *n.* ree-in-*shoor*-rer, one who reinsures.
reintegration, *n.* ree-in-te-*gray*-shon, redintegration.
reinter, *v.t.* ree-in-*ter*, to bury again.
reinvestment, *n.* ree-in-*vest*-ment, act of investing anew.
reinvigorate, *v.t.* ree-in-*vig*-o-rate, to reanimate; to revive in vigour.
reis, *n.* race, the *pl.* of the *real*, until 1911 a Portuguese money of account of which 1,000 (the milreis) equalled about 4*s*.
Reis, *n.* race, a chief or chieftain in certain Moslem countries. **Reis-effendi,** title of one of the chief ministers of state in the former Ottoman Empire. (Ar.)
reissue, *n.* ree-*ish*-yew, a second or repeated issue; a fresh printing of a book, etc., from the same setting: *v.t.* to issue a second time.
reiterance, *n.* ree-*it*-er-rance, repetition; reiteration.
reiterant, *a.* ree-*it*-er-rant, reiterating.
reiterate, *v.t.* re-*it*-er-rate, to repeat again and again. (Late L. *reiteratus*.)
reiteratedly, *ad.* re-*it*-er-ray-ted-le, repeatedly.
reiteration, *n.* re-it-er-*ray*-shon, repetition.
reiterative, *a.* re-*it*-er-ra-tiv, characterized by reiteration: *n.* a reduplicated word or part of a word; a verb denoting repetition or intensification of the act [Gram.].

reiver, *n. reev*-er, a reaver.
reject, *v.t.* re-*jekt*, to throw away; to discard; to refuse to receive; to refuse to grant; *n. ree*-jekt, a discarded person or thing. (O.Fr. *rejecter.*)
rejectable, *a.* re-*jek*-ta-bl, that may be rejected.
rejectamenta, *n.pl.* re-*jek*-ta-*men*-ta, refuse; matter thrown away. (L.)
rejecter, *n.* re-*jek*-ter, one who rejects or refuses.
rejection, *n.* re-*jek*-shon, act of rejecting; refusal to accept or grant.
rejective, *a.* re-*jek*-tiv, tending to reject.
rejectment, *n.* re-*jekt*-ment, that which is rejected; excrement.
rejector, *n.* re-*jek*-tor, a rejecter.
rejoice, *v.i.* re-*joyce*, to experience joy: *v.t.* to make joyful; to gladden. (O.Fr. *resjouir.*)
rejoicer, *n.* re-*joyce*-er, one who rejoices.
rejoicing, *n.* re-*joyce*-ing, an expression or ebullition of joy; subject of joy or gladness; experience of joy.
rejoicingly, *ad.* with joy or exultation.
rejoin, *v.t.* re-*joyn*, to join again after separation or parting; to meet again; to reunite: *v.i.* to answer to a reply; to answer, as the defendant, to the plaintiff's replication [Law]. (Fr. *rejoindre.*)
rejoinder, *n.* re-*joyn*-der, an answer, esp. to a reply; a retort; the defendant's answer to the plaintiff's replication [Law].
rejoint, *v.t.* ree-*joynt*, to reunite joints; to fill up old joints of walls with fresh mortar.
rejudge, *v.t.* ree-*juj*, to judge again; to re-examine; to call to a new trial and decision.
rejuvenate, *v.t.* ree-*joo*-ve-nate, to render young again; to impart new vigour or vitality to. (L. *re-*, and *juvenis*, young.)
rejuvenation, *n.* ree-joo-ve-*nay*-shon, the act of rejuvenating; the state of being rejuvenated.
rejuvenator, *n.* ree-*joo*-ve-nay-tor, any rejuvenating agent.
rejuvenesce, *v.t.* and *i.* ree-joo-ve-*ness*, to cause to become, or to become, young again; to acquire fresh vitality.
rejuvenescence, *n.* ree-joo-ve-*nes*-ence, renewal of youth or vitality; state of being rejuvenated.
rejuvenescent, *a.* ree-joo-ve-*nes*-ent, rejuvenating; growing young again.
rejuvenize, *v.t.* and *i.* ree-*joo*-ve-nize, to render or become young again.
rekindle, *v.t.* ree-*kin*-dl, to kindle again; to inflame or rouse anew.
relabel, *v.t.* ree-*lay*-bl, to put a fresh label on.
relaid, *ree*-lade, *p.* and *pp.* of the verb *to relay.*
relais, *n.* re-*lay*, a narrow walk outside the rampart to prevent the soil being washed down into the ditch [Fort.]. (Fr.)
reland, *v.t.* ree-*land*, to land again: *v.i.* to go on shore after having embarked.
relapse, *n.* re-*laps*, a sliding or falling back, esp. to a former bad state: *v.i.* to fall back; to return to a former state or practice. (L. *relapsus*, slipped back.)
relapser, *n.* re-*lap*-ser, one who relapses, esp. into vice or error.
relate, *v.t.* re-*late*, to narrate the particulars of an event; to ally by connexion or kindred: *v.i.* to have reference; to refer. (Fr. *relater.*)
related, *a.* re-*late*-ed, allied by kindred; connected by blood or alliance, esp. by consanguinity.
relatedness, *n.* the state of being related.
relater, *n.* re-*late*-er, one who tells, or narrates: an informant; a relator.
relating, *a.* re-*late*-ing, having relation or reference; concerning.
***relation,** *n.* re-*lay*-shon, the act of relating or telling; that which is related; reference; connexion between things; connexion by birth or marriage; a kinsman or kinswoman; resemblance of phenomena; analogy; ratio; proportion; the act of a relator in laying an information before the Attorney-General [Law]. (Fr.)
relational, *a.* re-*lay*-shon-al, having relation or kindred.
relationship, *n.* re-*lay*-shon-ship, the state of being related by kindred, affinity, or other alliance; pertaining to kinship or to relation.
relatival, *a.* rel-a-*ty*-val, pertaining to a relative [Gram.].
relative, *a. rel*-a-tiv, having, or implying, relation; having relation to something else; relating to a word, sentence, or clause [Gram.]; respecting; pertinent: *n.* a person connected by blood or affinity; a kinsman or kinswoman; that which has relation to something else; a word which relates to or represents another word, called its antecedent [Gram.]. (Fr. *relatif.*)
relatively, *ad.* with or in relation; not absolutely.
relativeness, *n.* the state of having relation.
relativism, *n. rel*-a-tiv-izm, the theory that knowledge is relative only, never absolute [Phil.].
relativity, *n.* rel-a-*tiv*-e-te, the state of being relative. **theory of relativity,** the theory propounded by Einstein (Ger.-Swiss physicist, *b.* 1879) demonstrating the impossibility of an observer in a moving system (such as the earth) having any accurate knowledge concerning the relative motion of a moving body in another moving system, with the mathematical and other deductions made from this applying to space-time, etc.
relator, *n.* re-*late*-or, a relater; an informer; one who lays information, or a relation, before the Attorney-General [Law].
relax, *v.t.* re-*laks*, to slacken; to make less tense or rigid; to loosen; to make less strict or severe; to relieve from a state of strain or effort; to relieve from constipation; to make languid: *v.i.* to abate in severity or tension; to remit in close attention. (Fr. *relaxer.*)
relaxable, *a.* re-*lak*-sa-bl, that may be relaxed.
relaxant, *n.* re-*lak*-sant, a medicine that relaxes.
relaxation, *n.* ree-lak-*say*-shon, the act of relaxing; the state of being relaxed; remission of tension or rigour; remission of attention or application; recreation or diversion.
relaxative, *a.* re-*lak*-sa-tiv, having the quality of relaxing; laxative.
relaxing, *a.* re-*lak*-sing, tending to relax; enervating.
relay, *n. ree*-lay, a supply of anything kept for relief; one of a team working in stages; an instrument for strengthening an enfeebled current [Elect.]; a relaid broadcast [Wire.]. **relay race,** a race between teams in which different runners or groups cover successive parts of the course. (Fr. *relais.*)
relay, *v.t.* ree-*lay*, to lay a second time; to pass on, as a message received; to rebroadcast, or broadcast from one station a programme, etc., received from another [Wire.].
releasable, *a.* re-*leece*-a-bl, that may be released.
release, *n.* re-*leece*, liberation from restraint or pain; discharge from an obligation; permission for publication or public exhibition or performance: *v.t.* to set free from restraint; to free from pain, care, trouble, or grief; to free from obligation or claim; to permit the publication, exhibition, etc., of. **deed of release,** a conveyance of property or right in lands or tenements to another, a quitclaim [Law]. (Fr. *relaisser.*)
re-lease, *v.t.* to give a new lease to; to lease again.
releasee, *n.* ree-lee-*see*, one to whom an estate, etc., is released [Law].
releasement, *n.* re-*leece*-ment, the act of releasing.
releaser, *n.* re-*leece*-er, one who releases.
releasor, *n.* re-*leece*-or, one who releases an estate claim, etc., to another [Law].
relegate, *v.t. rel*-e-gate, to banish; to send into exile; to transfer; to place in a lower position. (L. *relegatus*, sent.)
relegation, *n.* rel-e-*gay*-shon, act of relegating; state of being relegated; banishment.
relent, *v.i.* re-*lent*, to soften in temper; to become less severe; to yield. (Fr. *ralentir*, to slacken.)
relentingly, *ad.* re-*lent*-ing-le, in a relenting, forgiving, or mollifying manner.
relentless, *a.* re-*lent*-less, unmoved by pity; unrelenting; merciless.
relentlessly, *ad.* in a relentless manner.
relentlessness, *n.* the being relentless.
re-let, *v.t.* ree-*let*, to let anew, as a house; to sub-let.
relevance, *n. rel*-e-vance, relevancy.
relevancy, *n. rel*-e-van-se, state of being relevant; pertinence; appositeness; sufficiency to warrant the conclusion.
relevant, *a. rel*-e-vant, pertinent; applicable. (Fr. raising.)
relevantly, *ad.* pertinently.
reliability, *n.* re-ly-a-*bil*-e-te, reliableness.
reliable, *a.* re-*ly*-a-bl, that may be relied on or trusted; trustworthy.
reliableness, *n.* the state of being reliable.

reliably, *ad.* so as to be relied on.
reliance, *n.* re-*ly*-ance, rest or repose of mind due to confidence; trust; a ground of confidence.
reliant, *a.* re-*ly*-ant, having reliance.
relic, *n.* *rel*-ik, that which remains after loss or decay of the rest; the remains of a deceased person; a memento of the dead; an object religiously cherished through its association with a saint. (Fr. *relique.*)
relict, *n.* *rel*-ikt, a widow. (L. *relicta*, left behind.)
relief, *n.* re-*leef*, alleviation of pain or grief; that which alleviates; release, as a sentry, from his post, also he who takes his place; a body of men relieving another or a besieged town, post of danger, etc.; aid; redress; prominence beyond the plane on which a carving or embossing, etc., is made; the representation of any prominence by shading of different intensities. **relief map,** a model in which the elevations and depressions are moulded in relief. (Fr.)
relier, *n.* re-*ly*-er, one who relies.
relievable, *a.* re-*leev*-a-bl, capable of being relieved.
relieve, *v.t.* re-*leev*, to set free from; to ease; to alleviate; to release from a post of duty or from a state of siege; to succour; to mitigate; to assist. **relieving officer,** an official in a parish or poor law union entrusted with the relief of the poor. (Fr. *relever.*)
reliever, *n.* re-*leev*-er, one who relieves.
relievo, *n.* re-*lee*-voh *or* rel-e-*ay*-voh, raised or embossed work; prominence of figures in statuary, carving, etc. (It.)
relight, *v.t.* and *i.* ree-*lite*, to light anew; to rekindle.
religieuse, *n.* (App.), a nun. (Fr.)
religieux, *n.* (App.), a monk or friar. (Fr.)
★**religion,** *n.* re-*lij*-on, an habitual sense of dependence on, reverence for, and responsibility to, a higher power; belief in a God or gods, esp. who made the universe and all in it and to whom the worship, homage, and obedience of man is due; a mode of thinking, feeling, and acting which respects, trusts in, and strives after, the Divine; any system of faith and worship. (Fr.)
religionary, *a.* re-*lij*-on-a-re, pertaining to religion.
religioner, *n.* re-*lij*-on-er, a religionist.
religionism, *n.* re-*lij*-on-izm, strict or exaggerated devotion to religion; affectation of religion.
religionist, *n.* re-*lij*-on-ist, one zealously devoted to a particular religion; one who affects religion.
religionize, *v.t.* re-*lij*-on-ize, to make religious: *v.i.* to affect religion.
religionless, *a.* re-*lij*-on-less, without religion.
religiose, *a.* re-*lij*-e-ohs, religious to excess; morbidly religious.
religiosity, *n.* re-*lij*-e-*os*-e-te, excessive, affected, or sentimental religiousness.
religious, *a.* re-*lij*-us, pertaining or relating to religion; pious; godly; devoted to the practice of religion; teaching religion; set apart for religious purposes; scrupulously exact; bound by monastic vows: *n.* one bound thus. (Fr. *religieux.*)
religiously, *ad.* in a religious manner.
religiousness, *n.* quality or state of being religious.
reline, *v.t.* ree-*line*, to provide with a fresh lining; to mark with fresh lines.
relinquent, *a.* re-*ling*-kwent, relinquishing: *n.* one who relinquishes.
relinquish, *v.t.* re-*ling*-kwish, to withdraw from; to quit; to renounce a claim to; to give up. (O.Fr. *relinquir.*)
relinquisher, *n.* one who relinquishes.
relinquishment, *n.* re-*ling*-kwish-ment, the act of relinquishing or giving up; surrender.
reliquary, *n.* *rel*-e-kwa-re, a case for relics; a casket in which relics are kept. (Fr. *reliquaire.*)
relique, *n.* *rel*-ik *or* re-*leek*, a relic. (Fr.)
reliquiæ, *n.pl.* re-*lik*-we-ee, remains, esp. fossil remains of plants and animals. (L.)
relish, *n.* *rel*-ish, sensation of flavour; taste; taste which pleases; appreciation; liking; delight; power of appreciation, or of pleasing; a sauce; an appetizer; a trace of: *v.t.* to give an agreeable taste to; to like the taste of; to be gratified with the enjoyment of: *v.i.* to have a pleasing taste; to give pleasure; to have a flavour. (O.Fr. *relais*, an after-taste.)
relishable, *a.* *rel*-ish-a-bl, having an agreeable taste.
relive, *v.i.* ree-*liv*, to live again; to revive.
reload, *v.t.* ree-*lode*, to load again.
relucence, *n.* re-*lew*-sence, the quality of being relucent.
relucent, *a.* re-*lew*-sent, shining; radiant; refulgent. (L. *relucere*, to shine back.)
reluct, *v.i.* re-*lukt*, to strive against; to express reluctance. (L. *re-*, and *luctari*, to struggle.)
reluctance, *n.* re-*luk*-tance, the state of being reluctant; unwillingness; repugnance; the quality of opposing the passage of magnetic lines of force in a magnetic circuit [Elect.].
reluctancy, *n.* re-*luk*-tan-se, disinclination; repugnance.
reluctant, *a.* re-*luk*-tant, striving against; much opposed in heart; disinclined; done or granted unwillingly. (L. *reluctans*, struggling.)
reluctantly, *ad.* with reluctance.
reluctate, *v.i.* re-*luk*-tate, to reluct; to offer resistance.
reluctation, *n.* ree-luk-*tay*-shon, resistance; reluctancy; opposition.
reluctivity, *n.* ree-luk-*tiv*-e-te, the degree of resistance in a magnetic circuit [Elect.].
relume, *v.t.* re-*lewm*, to light anew; to rekindle. (L. *re-*, and *luminare*, to light.)
rely, *v.i.* re-*ly*, to depend upon; to have confidence in; to trust. (Fr. *relier.*)
remain, *v.i.* re-*mane*, to continue in a place or state; to stay; to be left existing or left over; not to be lost; to be left. (O.Fr. *remaindre.*)
remainder, *n.* re-*mane*-der, anything left after the removal of a part; the quantity left after division [Arith.]; an estate limited to take effect and be enjoyed after another estate is determined [Law]; an unsold copy of a book issued at a reduced price: *v.t.* to sell or offer for sale unsold copies as remainders. **remainder man,** he who has an estate after a particular estate is determined [Law].
remaindership, *n.* re-*mane*-der-ship, the tenure of a remainder [Law].
remains, *n.pl.* re-*maynz*, that which is left; leavings; a corpse; ruins; literary productions left by one deceased.
remake, *v.t.* ree-*make*, to make anew.
reman, *v.t.* ree-*man*, to furnish with fresh men; to infuse courage into.
remand, *v.t.* re-*mahnd*, to call or send back; to remit in custody or on bail: *n.* the act of remanding; the state of being remanded. (Fr. *remander.*)
remanent, *a.* *rem*-a-nent, remaining; residual. (L. *remanens*, remaining.)
remanet, *n.* *rem*-a-net, a remainder; a suit standing over for hearing [Law]; a parliamentary bill left over for the next session. (L.)
re-mark, *v.t.* to mark again.
remark, *n.* re-*mark*, notice or observation, particularly in words or writing; a comment; a remarque: *v.t.* to take notice of; to express by way of remark. (Fr. *remarquer*, mark.)
remarkable, *a.* re-*mark*-a-bl, worthy of notice; extraordinary.
remarkableness, *n.* the quality of being remarkable.
remarkably, *ad.* in a remarkable manner.
remarker, *n.* re-*mark*-er, one who makes remarks.
remarque, *n.* re-*mark*, a small distinguishing design etched on the margin of an engraving; a **remarque proof,** or proof bearing such a design.
remarriage, *n.* ree-*ma*-raj, a subsequent marriage; the act of marrying again.
remarry, *v.t.* and *i.* ree-*ma*-re, to marry again.
remast, *v.t.* re-*mahst*, to provide with a new or different mast or masts.
remasticate, *v.t.* ree-*mas*-te-kate, to chew or masticate again, as in chewing the cud.
remastication, *n.* ree-mas-te-*kay*-shon, the act of remasticating; chewing the cud.
remblai, *n.* (App.), the material used or thrown up to form a rampart or embankment. (Fr.)
remediable, *a.* re-*mee*-de-a-bl, that may be remedied; curable. (L. *remediabilis.*)
remediableness, *n.* state of being remediable.
remediably, *ad.* in a way that may be remedied.
remedial, *a.* re-*mee*-de-al, affording a remedy; intended for a remedy.
remedially, *ad.* by way of remedy.
remediless, *a.* *rem*-e-de-less, not admitting of remedy; incurable; irreparable; irreversible.
remedy, *n.* *rem*-e-de, that which cures a disease;

that which counteracts an evil of any kind; that which cures uneasiness; that which repairs loss or disaster; the allowance in coining of deviation from the standard of weight or fineness: *v.t.* to cure; to heal; to repair. (O.Fr. *remede.*)
remelt, *v.t.* and *i.* ree-*melt*, to melt again.
remember, *v.t.* re-*mem*-ber, to keep or bear in mind; to recall to mind; to recollect; to think of and consider; to bear in mind with gratitude, regard, or reverence. (O.Fr. *remembrer.*)
rememberable, *a.* re-*mem*-ber-a-bl, capable of being remembered; worthy of remembrance.
rememberer, *n.* re-*mem*-ber-er, one who remembers.
remembrance, *n.* re-*mem*-brance, retention in mind; memory; that which assists memory; a memento; power of remembering; the time within which a thing can be remembered; memorandum. (Fr.)
remembrancer, *n.* re-*mem*-brance-er, one who or that which reminds, or revives the remembrance of anything; a reminder; title of certain members of the former Court of Exchequer. **King's (Queen's) Remembrancer,** the officer of the Supreme Court who acts in cases of debts due to the Sovereign. **the City Remembrancer,** the officer of the City of London Corporation who represents it before Parliamentary committees, etc.
remiform, *a.* *rem*-e-form, oar-shaped.
remiges, *n.pl.* *rem*-e-jeez, the flight-feathers of a bird. (L., rowers.)
remigrate, *v.i.* ree-*my*-grate, to return from migration; to return to a former state.
remigration, *n.* ree-my-*gray*-shon, the act of remigrating.
remind, *v.t.* re-*mynd*, to bring to remembrance; to bring to notice or consideration.
reminder, *n.* re-*myn*-der, one who or that which reminds.
remindful, *a.* re-*mynd*-ful, tending to remind.
reminisce, *v.i.* rem-e-*nis*, to indulge in reminiscences [Coll.].
reminiscence, *n.* rem-e-*nis*-ence, the power of recollecting; a recollection or remembrance; a narration or relation of recollections; memory of an earlier state of existence [Theos.]; the theory that knowledge is not newly acquired but is derived from experience in some previous life [Platonic phil.]. (Fr., from L. *reminiscentia*, remembrance.)
reminiscent, *a.* rem-e-*nis*-ent, pertaining to or resembling reminiscence; calling to mind; having recollection: *n.* one who records or narrates past events. (L. *re-*, and *mens*, the mind.)
reminiscential, *a.* rem-e-ne-*sen*-shal, pertaining to reminiscence.
remiped, *a.* *rem*-e-ped, with oar-shaped feet: *n.* a decapod crustacean of the genus *Remipes*, having oar-like feet. (L. *remus*, oar, *pes*, foot.)
remise, *v.t.* re-*meez*, to give or grant back; to release a claim: *v.i.* to deliver a remise [Fencing]: *n.* a granting back or release [Law]; the second of two swift thrusts, the first of which was not returned [Fencing]. (L. *remissus*, sent back.)
remiss, *a.* re-*miss*, careless in performance of duty or business; dilatory; slack; languid. (L. *remissus.*)
remissibility, *n.* re-mis-e-*bil*-e-te, the condition of being remissible.
remissible, *a.* re-*mis*-e-bl, that may be remitted; capable of remission.
remission, *n.* re-*mish*-on, the act of remitting; a remitting; abatement; forgiveness; pardon; relinquishment.
remissive, *a.* re-*mis*-iv, permitting, causing, or marked by remission; forgiving.
remissly, *ad.* in a remiss manner.
remissness, *n.* slackness; carelessness; negligence; want of punctuality.
remit, *v.t.* re-*mit*, to send back; to relax; to forgive to pardon; to give up; to refer; to transmit money or bills: *v.i.* to abate in force or violence. (L. *remitto*, send back.)
remitment, *n.* re-*mit*-ment, the act of remitting money.
remittal, *n.* re-*mit*-al, a giving up; surrender.
remittance, *n.* re-*mit*-ance, the act of transmitting money or bills, in payment; money transmitted. **remittance man,** an emigrant who depends upon remittances from home.
remittee, *n.* rem-e-*tee*, the receiver of a remittance.
remittent, *a.* re-*mit*-ent, having alternate increase and remission or abatement. **remittent fever,** a fever in which the temperature rises but does not become normal.
remitter, *n.* re-*mit*-er, one who remits; one who pardons.
remnant, *n.* *rem*-nant, that which is left after the separation, removal, or destruction of a part; a fragment; a remainder. (O.Fr. *remanant.*)
remodel, *v.t.* ree-*mod*-el, to model or fashion anew.
remolten, *pp.* and *a.* ree-*mohl*-ten, melted again.
re-monetize, *v.t.* to restore as legal tender.
remonstrance, *n.* re-*mon*-strance, expostulation; earnest reproof; strong representation of reasons against a measure; pressing suggestions in opposition to a measure or act. (Fr.)
remonstrant, *a.* re-*mon*-strant, expostulatory; urging strong reasons against: *n.* one who remonstrates: *pl.* the Dutch Arminians who, in 1610, broke away from the strict Calvinists. (Late L. *remonstrans*, remonstrating.)
remonstrate, *v.i.* re-*mon*-strate *or* *rem*-on-strate, to urge strong reasons against; to expostulate. (Late L. *remonstratus.*)
remonstration, *n.* rem-on-*stray*-shon, the act of remonstrating; a strong protest.
remonstrative, *a.* re-*mon*-stra-tiv, expressing or of the nature of a remonstrance.
remonstrator, *n.* re-*mon*-stray-tor, a remonstrant; one who remonstrates.
remontant, *a.* re-*mon*-tant, flowering more than once a year: *n.* a remontant rose.
remontoir, *n.* re-mon-*twah*, the mechanism in a clock giving an even movement to the escapement. (Fr.)
remora, *n.* *rem*-o-ra, the sucking-fish, *Echeneis remora*, provided with a suctorial disk by which it attaches itself to fishes and other objects. (L. *re-*, and *mora*, delay, as fabled to delay ships it adhered to.)
remorse, *n.* re-*mawrs*, the keen pain or anguish excited by a sense of guilt; compunction of conscience; poignant regret. (O.Fr. *remors.*)
remorseful, *a.* re-*mawrs*-ful, full of remorse.
remorsefully, *ad.* in a remorseful manner.
remorsefulness, *n.* state of being remorseful.
remorseless, *a.* re-*mawrs*-less, having no pity; unpitying; relentless.
remorselessly, *ad.* in a remorseless manner.
remorselessness, *n.* quality of being remorseless.
remote, *a.* re-*moht*, distant in place or time; not immediate or proximate; alien; distant in consanguinity or affinity; slight; inconsiderable. **remote control,** control, esp. of moving or movable bodies, operated electrically from a distance. (L. *remotus*, removed.)
remotely, *ad.* in a remote degree.
remoteness, *n.* state of being remote.
remould, *v.t.* ree-*mohld*, to shape anew.
remount, *n.* ree-*mount*, a fresh horse, esp. [Mil.] one bought in replacement of another; a horse bought into the army: *v.t.* and *i.* to mount again; to reascend.
removability, *n.* re-moo-va-*bil*-e-te, the capacity of being removed.
removable, *a.* re-*moo*-va-bl, that may be removed.
removal, *n.* re-*moo*-val, the act of removing or displacing; the state of being removed; change of place; the act of dismissing.
remove, *n.* re-*moov*, removal; change of place; state of being removed; departure; an indefinite distance; a step in a scale of gradation; a dish or course replaced by or replacing another; in certain schools, an intermediate form, usually between the fourth and fifth: *v.t.* to cause to change place; to displace from an office; to banish; to take away: *v.i.* to change place in any manner. (O.Fr. *remouvoir.*)
removed, *a.* re-*moovd*, remote; separate from others; of a following generation in relationship. **cousin once removed,** one's parent's cousin or cousin's child. **cousin twice removed,** one's grandparent's cousin or cousin's grandchild.
remover, *n.* re-*moo*-ver, one who removes; one who contracts to remove furniture, etc.
remplissage, *n.* (App.), padding, or useless matter inserted (in a literary work) merely to lengthen; overloading (in painting). (Fr.)
remunerability, *n.* re-*mew*-ner-ra-*bil*-e-te, capacity of being rewarded.

remunerable, *a.* re-*mew*-ner-ra-bl, that may be rewarded; fit or proper to be rewarded.
remunerate, *v.t.* re-*mew*-ner-rate, to render an equivalent for a service, to pay; to recompense. (L. *remuneratus*, rewarded.)
remuneration, *n.* re-*mew*-ner-*ray*-shon, act of remunerating; equivalent given for service; recompense.
remunerative, *a.* re-*mew*-ner-ra-tiv, yielding a due return; lucrative; profitable.
remuneratively, *ad.* profitably.
remunerator, *n.* re-*mew*-ner-ray-tor, one who remunerates.
remurmur, *v.t.* ree-*mer*-mer, to repeat in low hoarse sounds: *v.i.* to murmur again.
remutation, *n.* *ree*-mew-*tay*-shon, change to an earlier form.
Renaissance, *n.* re-*nay*-sance, the revival of the arts and letters that commenced in W. Europe in the 15th century; a style of art, esp. architecture, which succeeded the Gothic; (*l.c.*) renascence. (O.Fr.)
renal, *a.* *ree*-nal, pertaining to the kidneys. (O.Fr.)
rename, *v.t.* ree-*name*, to name afresh.
renard, *n.* *ren*-ard, reynard, a fox.
renascence, *n.* re-*nas*-sence, the state of being renascent; revival; a rebirth; (*cap.*) the Renaissance. (L. *renascens.*)
renascent, *a.* re-*nas*-sent, renewing; rejuvenating; reviving; pertaining to the Renaissance.
renature, *v.t.* ree-*nay*-tewr, to restore to its original nature (esp. of denatured alcohol).
rencontre, *n.* (App.), *or* ren-*kon*-ter, a meeting; a rencounter. (Fr.)
rencounter, *n.* ren-*koun*-ter, a meeting in opposition; a casual sudden contest; a combat: *v.i.* to meet unexpectedly; to clash; to fight hand to hand. (O.Fr. *rencontrer.*)
rend, *v.t.* rend, to tear asunder; to split; to tear asunder or away with violence: *v.i.* to be rent. *p.* and *pp.* **rent.** (A.S. *rendan.*)
render, *n.* *ren*-der, one that rends.
render, *n.* *ren*-der, a payment or requital in return; a coat of plaster applied directly on a wall: *v.t.* to return; to pay back; to inflict; to give; to deliver; to extract; to boil down; to perform; to cause to be; to reproduce or translate; to surrender; to ease up or slacken; to plaster on a lathless surface. (Fr. *rendre.*)
renderable, *a.* *ren*-der-ra-bl, that may be rendered.
renderer, *n.* *ren*-der-rer, one who renders; a vessel in which lard, etc., is rendered.
rendering, *n.* *ren*-der-ring, version; translation; delineation; reproduction; representation; the laying on of the first coat of plaster.
rendezvous, *n.* *ron-* or *ren*-de-voo, a place of meeting; a place for assembling, esp. of troops or ships: *v.i.* and *t.* to assemble; to meet. (Fr., render yourselves, repair.)
rendition, *n.* ren-*dish*-on, surrender; translation; rendering (of music, etc.). (Fr.)
renegade, *n.* *ren*-e-gade, an apostate; a deserter: *v.i.* to turn deserter. (Sp. *renegado.*)
renegado, *n.* ren-e-*gah*-do, a renegade.
renegation, *n.* ren-e-*gay*-shon, the act of renouncing or turning renegade.
renege, *v.i.* re-*neeg*, to revoke [Card-playing]: *n.* a revoke. (Late L. *renego*, deny.)
renegue, *v.i.* and *n.* re-*neeg*, renege.
renew, *v.t.* re-*new*, to renovate; to continue; to make again; to grant again; to repeat; to revive; to make new; to make fresh or vigorous; to regenerate: *v.i.* to begin again; to become rejuvenated.
renewability, *n.* re-new-a-*bil*-e-te, the state of being renewable.
renewable, *a.* re-*new*-a-bl, that may be renewed.
renewal, *n.* re-*new*-al, the act of renewing; renovation; regeneration; revival; restoration to a former or to a good state. **renewal shoot,** a shoot in a leaf-axil which lasts over the winter [Bot.].
renewer, *n.* re-*new*-er, one who renews.
renidification, *n.* re-*nid*-e-fe-*kay*-shon, the act of building a new nest.
renidify, *v.i.* re-*nid*-e-fy, to build a fresh nest. (L. *re-*, *nidus*, nest, and *facio*, make.)
reniform, *a.* *ren*-e-form, having the form or shape of a kidney [Bot.]. (L. *renes*, kidneys, *forma*, shape.)
renitent, *a.* *ren*-e-tent, resisting pressure; recalcitrant. (L. *renitens*, striving.)
rennet, *n.* *ren*-et, the inner membrane of a calf's stomach prepared so as to coagulate milk; an artificial substitute for this. (Perhaps A.S. *rennan*, to cause to run.)
rennet, *n.* *ren*-et, any of several varieties of apple. (Fr. *reinette*, little queen.)
rennin, *n.* *ren*-in, a natural enzyme, present in gastric juice, etc., that clots milk. (*rennet.*)
renominate, *v.t.* ree-*nom*-e-nate, to nominate anew.
renomination, *n.* ree-nom-e-*nay*-shon, the act of renominating; renewed nomination.
renounce, *n.* re-*nounce*, a revoke [Card-playing]: *v.t.* to disown; to disclaim; to reject; to cast off; to forsake: *v.i.* not to follow suit at cards. (Fr. *renoncer.*)
renouncement, *n.* re-*nounce*-ment, renunciation.
renouncer, *n.* re-*nounce*-er, one who renounces.
renovate, *v.t.* *ren*-o-vate, to renew; to restore to the first state, or to a good state, after decay. (L. *renovatus*, renewed.)
renovation, *n.* ren-o-*vay*-shon, the act of renewing; a state of being renewed.
renovator, *n.* *ren*-o-vay-tor, one who or that which renovates.
renown, *n.* re-*noun*, fame; celebrity; exalted reputation. (O.Fr. *renon.*)
renowned, *a.* re-*nound*, having renown; eminent.
renownedly, *ad.* re-*noun*-ed-le, with renown.
rensselaerite, *n.* *rens*-la-rite, a variety of talc with a fine, compact texture and greasy to the touch. (Named after S. van *Rensselaer*, Amer. politician, *d.* 1839.)
rent, rent, *p.* and *pp.* of *rend.*
rent, *n.* rent, an opening produced by rending or violent separation; a schism; a separation. (*rend.*)
rent, *n.* rent, an amount in money or value receivable periodically as payment for use of lands or tenements; similar payment in respect of any property: *v.t.* to lease or hold in tenancy lands or tenements for a certain consideration: *v.i.* to be leased or let for rent. (Fr. *rente.*)
rentable, *a.* *rent*-a-bl, that may be rented.
rental, *n.* *rent*-al, a schedule or account of rents; rent-roll; amount of rent.
rent-charge, *n.* a rent from land that goes to another than the landlord.
rent-day, *n.* the day for paying rent.
rente, *n.* (App.) an annuity derivable from French state funds. (Fr.)
renter, *n.* *rent*-er, one who leases an estate or holds premises on the payment of rent; one who rents property of any kind.
renter, *v.t.* *rent*-er, to fine-draw; to sew together the edges of two pieces of cloth without doubling them, so that the seam is scarcely visible; to restore or sew up skilfully. (Fr. *rentraire.*)
rent-free, *a.* without payment of rent.
rentier, *n.* (App.) one whose income is derived from holdings in *rentes* or public funds; one in receipt of a fixed income. (Fr.)
rent-roll, *n.* an account of rents or income; total income derived from rents.
renuent, *a.* *ren*-yew-ent, throwing the head back (of certain muscles) [Anat.]. (L. *renuens*, nodding.)
renule, *n.* *ren*-yewl, a small kidney. (L.)
renumber, *v.t.* ree-*num*-ber, to number again; to place a new number upon.
renunciant, *a.* re-*nun*-se-ant, renunciative: *n.* one who renounces the world.
renunciation, *n.* re-nun-se-*ay*-shon, the act of renouncing; disownment. (O.Fr. *renonciation.*)
renunciative, *a.* re-*nun*-se-a-tiv, pertaining to a renunciation; expressing renunciation.
renunciatory, *a.* re-*nun*-se-a-to-re, relating to a renunciation.
renversé, *a.* (App.), inverted; with the head downward [Her.]. (O.Fr. *renverser.*)
reobtain, *v.t.* ree-ob-*tane*, to get again.
reoccupation, *n.* ree-ok-yew-*pay*-shon, the act of reoccupying; a second occupation.
reoccupy, *v.t.* re-*ok*-yew-py, to occupy again.
re-oil, *v.t.* ree-*oyl*, to oil again; to refuel with oil.
reopen, *v.t.* ree-*oh*-pen, to open again: *v.i.* to be or become opened again.
reorganization, *n.* re-*awr*-ga-ny-*zay*-shon, act of organizing anew.

reorganize, *v.t.* re-*awr*-ga-nize, to organize anew.
reorder, *v.t.* ree-*awr*-der, to order anew: *n.* a subsequent order on the same dealer.
reorient, *a.* ree-*aw*-re-ent, rising again.
reorientation, *n.* ree-aw-re-en-*tay*-shon, a changed adjustment to surroundings.
rep, *n.* rep, a fabric with a ribbed or corded surface. (Fr. *reps*; origin doubtful.)
rep, *n.* rep, a debauchee [Slang]. (*reprobate.*)
rep, *n.* rep, recitation [Slang]. (*repetition.*)
repacify, *v.t.* ree-*pas*-e-fy, to pacify again.
repack, *v.t.* ree-*pak*, to pack anew or a second time.
repaid, re-*payd*, *p.* and *pp.* of *repay*.
repaint, *v.t.* ree-*paynt*, to paint afresh.
repair, *n.* re-*pare*, restoration to a sound state; good condition: *v.t.* to restore to a sound or good state after decay; to rebuild a part decayed; to make amends or indemnify for. (O.Fr. *reparer.*)
repair, *n.* re-*pare*, the act of betaking oneself to any place; a haunt: *v.i.* to betake oneself; to resort. (O.Fr. *repairer.*)
repairable, *a.* re-*pare*-ra-bl, reparable; mendable.
repairer, *n.* re-*pare*-rer, one who or that which repairs or makes amends.
repand, *a.* re-*pand*, having an uneven, sinuous margin [Bot.]. (L. *repando*, spread.)
repaper, *v.t.* ree-*pay*-per, to put fresh paper on (a wall).
reparable, *a.* *rep*-a-ra-bl, that may be repaired or recovered; repairable. (O.Fr.)
reparably, *ad.* *rep*-a-ra-ble, in a reparable manner.
reparation, *n.* rep-a-*ray*-shon, act of repairing or restoring to soundness; supply of what is wasted; amends; indemnification, esp. on account of war damage; satisfaction. (O.Fr.)
reparative, *a.* re-*pa*-ra-tiv, repairing; restoring to a sound state; indemnifying.
reparatory, *a.* re-*pa*-ra-to-re, reparative.
repartee, *n.* rep-ar-*tee*, a ready and witty reply; a clever retort. (Fr. *repartie.*)
repartition, *v.t.* ree-par-*tish*-on, to make a new partition or allotment: *n.* a second or subsequent dividing-up.
repass, *v.t.* ree-*pahss*, to pass again; to travel back: *v.i.* to go or move back.
repassage, *n.* ree-*pas*-aj, the act of repassing; passage back.
repast, *n.* re-*pahst*, the act of taking food; the food taken; a meal; victuals: *v.i.* to feed. (O.Fr.)
repatriate, *v.t.* and *i.* re-*pay*-tre-ate, to send back or return to the native country. (Late L. *repatriatus.*)
repatriation, *n.* re-*pat*-re-*ay*-shon, restoration to one's native country.
repay, *v.t.* ree-*pay*, to pay back; to refund; to make return for; to recompense as for a loss; to compensate: *v.i.* to make requital. (O.Fr. *repaier.*)
repayable, *a.* ree-*pay*-a-bl, that which can or must be repaid.
repayment, *n.* ree-*pay*-ment, the act of paying back; reimbursement; the money repaid.
repeal, *n.* re-*peel*, revocation; abrogation: *v.t.* to recall; to revoke; to abrogate. (Fr. *rappeler.*)
repealability, *n.* re-*peel*-a-*bil*-e-te, the quality or state of being repealable.
repealable, *a.* re-*peel*-a-bl, capable of being repealed or revoked; revocable.
repealer, *n.* re-*peel*-er, one who seeks a repeal; one in favour of a repeal, as of the Corn Laws or of the union between Great Britain and Ireland.
repeat, *n.* re-*peet*, repetition; a passage to be repeated, or a mark directing this [Mus.]: *v.t.* to do or try again; to say again; to reiterate; to recite: *v.i.* to recur; to happen again; to taste of again. (Fr. *répéter.*)
repeatable, *a.* re-*peet*-a-bl, fit for repetition.
repeatedly, *ad.* re-*peet*-ed-le, with repetition; again and again; frequently.
repeater, *n.* re-*peet*-er, one who repeats; a watch that strikes the hours and parts of hours at will; a repeating rifle or other fire-arm; a relay or automatic retransmitter in telegraphy; a vacuum tube amplifier in telephony; a repeating decimal.
repeating, *a.* re-*peet*-ing, reproducing; saying or doing anything again; regurgitating. **repeating circle,** a mathematical instrument for diminishing the effects of errors of graduation. **repeating decimal,** a decimal in which the same figures regularly recur in the same order [Arith.]. **repeating rifle,** a rifle provided with a magazine for rapid fire without reloading.
repel, *v.t.* re-*pel*, to drive back; to check advance; to repulse; to resist; to ward off. (L. *repello*, drive.)
repellency, *n.* re-*pel*-en-se, the principle of repulsion; the quality of being repellent.
repellent, *a.* re-*pel*-ent, driving back; tending to repel; repulsive: *n.* a repelling influence; a medicine which repels morbid humours [Med.].
repeller, *n.* re-*pel*-ler, he who or that which repels.
repent, *a.* *ree*-pent, creeping [Bot. and Zool.]. (L. *repens*, creeping.)
repent, *v.i.* re-*pent*, to feel pain, sorrow, or regret for something done or spoken; to sorrow for sin and amend one's ways; to change one's mind and amend one's ways: *v.i.* to remember with sorrow. (Fr. *repentir.*)
repentance, *n.* re-*pent*-ance, sorrow, pain, or grief for anything done or said with a consequent change of conduct; penitence; contrition. (Fr.)
repentant, *a.* re-*pent*-ant, expressing repentance; sorrowful for past conduct, or for sin.
repentantly, *ad.* in a penitent manner.
repentingly, *ad.* with repentance.
repeople, *v.t.* ree-*pee*-pl, to people anew.
repercussion, *n.* ree-per-*kush*-on, the act of driving back; reverberation; echo; frequent repetition of the same sound [Mus.]. (O.Fr.)
repercussive, *a.* ree-per-*kus*-iv, driving back; causing to reverberate; reverberated. (L. *repercussus*, struck back.)
repertoire, *n.* rep-er-*twahr*, a repertory; stock of pieces readily at command. (Fr. *répertoire.*)
repertorial, *a.* rep-er-*taw*-re-al, pertaining to a repertory.
repertory, *n.* *rep*-er-to-re, a place in which things are so arranged that they can be easily found; a treasury; storehouse; a repertoire. **repertory theatre,** a theatre in which a succession of plays are performed for short runs rather than a single play for a long run. (Fr. *répertoire.*)
reperusal, *n.* ree-per-*roo*-zal, a second perusal.
reperuse, *v.t.* ree-per-*rooz*, to peruse again.
repetend, *n.* rep-e-*tend*, that part of a repeating decimal which recurs [Arith.]. (L. *repeto.*)
repetition, *n.* rep-e-*tish*-on, the act of doing or uttering a second time; act of reciting or rehearsing; recital; reiteration.
repetitional, *a.* rep-e-*tish*-on-al, repetitionary.
repetitionary, *a.* rep-e-*tish*-on-a-re, containing repetition.
repetitious, *a.* rep-e-*tish*-us, characterized by repetition; tediously reiterating.
repetitive, *a.* re-*pet*-e-tiv, of the nature of repetition; repetitious.
rephrase, *v.t.* ree-*fraze*, to phrase afresh, to repeat in other words.
repine, *v.i.* re-*pine*, to fret oneself; to be discontented; to feel an inward discontent that preys upon the spirits; to complain discontentedly; to murmur. (L. *re-*, and *pine.*)
repiner, *n.* re-*pine*-er, one who repines or murmurs.
repiningly, *ad.* re-*pine*-ing-le, with repining.
repique, *n.* re-*peek*, the scoring of 30 points before leading a card and before the opponent has scored: *v.t.* and *i.* to make a repique [Picquet].
replace, *v.t.* re-*place*, to put again in the former place; to put in a new place; to repay; to refund; to supply with a proper substitute; to take the place of. (L. *re-*, and *place.*)
replaceable, *a.* re-*place*-a-bl, capable of replacement.
replacement, *n.* re-*place*-ment, the act of replacing; that which replaces; the removal of an angle or an edge of a crystal.
replacer, *n.* re-*place*-er, one who replaces; a substitute for anything.
replacing-switch, *n.* a device enabling a derailed locomotive to be set again upon the rails.
replant, *v.t.* *ree*-plahnt, to plant anew; to resettle.
replay, *v.t.* ree-*play*, to play over again [Mus., Cards, etc.]; to play a drawn match again to ensure a result [Football, etc.]: *n.* *ree*-play, a match replayed following a draw.
repleader, *n.* ree-*pleed*-er, a second pleading; the power or right of pleading again [Law].
repledge, *v.t.* ree-*pledj*, to pledge a second time.
replenish, *v.t.* re-*plen*-ish, to fill again; to fill full;

to stock with abundance; *v.i.* to recover former fullness. (O.Fr. *replenir.*)
replenisher, *n.* re-*plen*-ish-er, one who or that which replenishes; a device used to maintain the charge of an electrometer [Elect.].
replenishment, *n.* re-*plen*-ish-ment, the act of filling up again; a further supply.
replete, *a.* re-*pleet,* completely filled; full up. (O.Fr.)
repleteness, *n.* the state of being replete.
repletion, *n.* re-*plee*-shon, state of being completely filled; overcrowding; fullness of blood [Med.].
repleviable, *a.* re-*plev*-e-a-bl, that may be bailed, or recovered by replevin [Law].
replevin, *n.* re-*plev*-in, an action for replevying [Law]. (O.Fr.)
replevisable, *a.* re-*plev*-is-a-bl, repleviable.
replevisor, *n.* re-*plev*-is-or, one who replevies.
replevy, *v.t.* re-*plev*-e, to take back what has been distrained upon giving security to try the right at law; to bail [Law]. (O.Fr. *replevir.*)
replica, *n.* *rep*-le-ka, a facsimile; an exact copy of a work of art by its original author. (It.)
replicate, *a.* *rep*-le-kat, repeated; doubled back or down [Bot.]: *n.* a tone separated by one or more octaves from a given tone [Mus.]. (L. *replicatus* refolded.)
replication, *n.* rep-le-*kay*-shon, a reply; an echo; the plaintiff's reply to the defendant's plea [Law]; the refolding or duplication of a part [Med.]; a replicate [Mus.].
replicative, *a.* *rep*-le-ka-tiv, replicate [esp. Bot.].
replier, *n.* re-*ply*-er, one who replies.
replum, *n.* *rep*-lum *or* *ree*-plum, the framework of a pod or legume.
reply, *n.* re-*ply,* that which is said, written, or done, in answer; a response: *v.i.* to make answer in words or writing; to answer in any way; to answer a defendant's plea [Law]: *v.t.* to return as an answer. **reply paid,** denoting a telegram for the telegraphic answer of which prepayment has been made. (O.Fr. *replier.*)
repoint, *v.t.* ree-*poynt,* to supply with a fresh point; to renew the edges of mortar in brickwork, etc.
repolish, *v.t.* ree-*pol*-ish, to polish again.
repone, *v.t.* re-*pohn,* to replace or reply; to restore to a former office or position [Scots. Law]. (L. *repono.*)
repopulate, *v.t.* ree-*pop*-yew-late, to populate anew.
report, *n.* re-*pawrt,* rumour; common fame; repute; a statement of facts given in reply to inquiry; relation; statement of a judicial decision; an official statement of facts; a sudden noise, esp. that of an explosion: *v.t.* to bring back, as an answer; to give an account of; to relate or recite; *v.i.* to make a statement of facts. **report progress,** to state the exact position of a matter at a given moment. **report stage,** the period in the passage of a bill through the House of Commons after it has been considered in committee and before its third reading. (Fr. *reporter.*)
reportable, *a.* re-*pawrt*-a-bl, suitable for publication.
reportage, *n.* re-*pawrt*-aj, mere rumour; a journalistic report or piece of reporting.
reporter, *n.* re-*pawrt*-er, one who reports; one who makes official statements of law proceedings, legislative decisions, etc.; one who reports proceedings or occurrences for the press; a journalist.
reporterism, *n.* re-*pawrt*-er-rizm, the occupation of a reporter; his manner of working.
reportorial, *a.* re-por-*taw*-re-al, connected with newspaper reporting; characteristic of reporters.
reposal, *n.* re-*poh*-zal, the act of reposing confidence or trust in.
repose, *v.t.* re-*poze,* to place or set (confidence, etc.) in. (L. *re-*, and *positum,* placed.)
repose, *n.* re-*poze,* a lying at rest; state of sleep; rest of mind; cause of rest; a rest or pause; quietude of colour and treatment in a work of art; *v.t.* to lay at rest; to cause to rest: *v.t.* to rest; to lie at rest; to recline. (Fr. *reposer,* from L. *re-* and *pausare,* to pause.)
reposedly, *ad.* re-*poh*-zed-le, in a reposeful manner.
reposedness, *n.* state of being at rest.
reposeful, *a.* re-*poze*-ful, inducing repose.
reposit, *v.t.* re-*poz*-it, to lay up; to deposit, as for safety or preservation. (L. *repositus,* replaced.)
reposition, *n.* ree-po-*zish*-on, the act of repositing or replacing; reinstatement; the operation of replacing a part [Surg.].
repositor, *n.* re-*poz*-e-tor, an instrument used in reposition [Surg.].
repository, *n.* re-*poz*-e-to-re, a place where things are deposited for safety or preservation; a depository; a store, esp. for furniture. (O.Fr. *repositoire.*)
repossess, *v.t.* re-po-*zess,* to possess again.
repossession, *n.* re-po-*zesh*-on, the act of repossessing.
repot, *v.t.* ree-*pot,* to transfer a plant from one pot to another, usually larger.
repoussage, *n.* re-*poo*-sahzh, the act of embossing by hammering on the back; repoussé work. (Fr.)
repoussé, *a.* re-*poo*-say, embossed by hammering or punching from behind, and afterwards by chasing: *n.* repoussé work. (Fr.)
repped, *a.* rept, corded or ribbed transversely. (*rep.*)
reprehend, *v.t.* rep-re-*hend,* to censure; to reprove; to find fault with. (L. *reprehendo,* seize.)
reprehender, *n.* rep-re-*hen*-der, one who reprehends.
reprehensible, *a.* re-pre-*hen*-se-bl, deserving reproof; blamable. (O.Fr.)
reprehensibleness, *n.* the quality of being reprehensible.
reprehensibly, *ad.* in a reprehensible manner.
reprehension, *n.* rep-re-*hen*-shon, reproof; censure; open blame.
reprehensive, *a.* rep-re-*hen*-siv, containing reproof.
reprehensory, *a.* re-pre-*hen*-so-re, reprehensive.
represent, *v.t.* rep-re-*zent,* to delineate; to show or exhibit by resemblance; to describe; to exhibit; to personate; to stand and act for; to show by arguments, reasoning, or statements; to stand in the place of; to act as delegate or spokesman for. (Fr. *représenter.*)
re-present, *v.t.* ree-pre-*zent,* to present anew.
representability, *n.* *rep*-re-*zen*-ta-*bil*-e-te, the quality or state of being representable.
representable, *a.* rep-re-*zen*-ta-bl, that may be represented.
representamen, *n.* re-pre-zen-*tay*-men, the product of representation, esp. of an object that illustrates an act [Phil.]. (L. *represento,* represent.)
representation, *n.* *rep*-re-zen-*tay*-shon, the act of representing; that which represents something; likeness; exhibition, as of a play or of a character in a play; statement or account; a standing in the place of another; appearance for another; the business or function of a representative; representatives collectively. **proportional representation,** *see* **proportional.** (O.Fr.)
representational, *a.* rep-re-zen-*tay*-shon-al, pertaining to or of the nature of representation.
representationism, *n.* re-pre-zen-*tay*-shon-izm, Descartes's theory that the object immediately perceived is not the entity itself but simply a mental conception of it.
★**representative,** *a.* re-pre-*zen*-ta-tiv, representing; acting for others; bearing the character or power of another; conducted by delegates: *n.* one who or that which exhibits the likeness of another; a specimen; an agent, deputy, or substitute; one who stands in the place of another as heir [Law]; (*cap.*) a member of a House of Representatives. **representative government,** government by elected representatives. **representative peers,** the Scottish and Irish peers elected to sit in the House of Lords. **House of Representatives,** the Lower House in the legislatures of the United States, Australia, and Japan.
representatively, *ad.* in a representative manner.
representativeness, *n.* the quality of being representative.
representer, *n.* rep-re-*zen*-ter, one who exhibits; a representative.
representment, *n.* rep-re-*zent*-ment, representation; an image.
re-presentment, *n.* ree-pre-*zent*-ment, presentment anew.
repress, *v.t.* re-*press,* to put down; to crush; to check; to restrain; to exercise repression [Psychan.]. (L. *repressus,* pressed back.)
re-press, *v.t.* ree-*press,* to press anew.
represser, *n.* re-*pres*-er, one who crushes or checks.
repressible, *a.* re-*pres*-e-bl, capable of repression.
repression, *n.* re-*presh*-on, the act of repressing;

check; restraint; the state of being repressed; the involuntary exclusion of unwelcome desires or impulses whereby such desires, etc., are apt to operate in the unconscious mind [Psychan.].

repressive, *a.* re-*pres*-iv, tending to subdue or restrain.

repressively, *ad.* in a repressive manner.

reprieval, *n.* re-*preev*-al, respite; reprieve.

reprieve, *n.* re-*preev*, the temporary suspension of the execution of a criminal's sentence; respite: *v.t.* to respite after sentence of death; to suspend the execution of for a time; to grant a respite to. (O.Fr. *repreuve.*)

reprimand, *n. rep*-re-mahnd, severe reproof: *v.t.* to reprove severely; to reprove publicly and officially by way of sentence. (Fr. *réprimande.*)

re-primer, *n.* ree-*prime*-er, a device by which a percussion cap can be fixed to a cartridge-case so that it can be used a second time.

reprint, *n. ree*-print, a new impression; a subsequent edition without alterations; an off-print: *v.t.* ree-*print*, to print again.

reprisal, *n.* re-*prize*-al, seizure by way of retaliation or indemnification; that which is taken from an enemy by way of retaliation or indemnity; recaption. (Fr. *représaille.*)

reprise, *n.* re-*prize*, reprisal; the recapture of a ship, or a ship recaptured; a yearly deduction or payment (*e.g.* rent-charge) out of the value of lands [Law]; a refrain or repetition [Mus.]. (Fr.)

reproach, *n.* re-*proach*, censure mingled with contempt; shame or disgrace; an object of scorn or contempt: *v.t.* to censure in terms of opprobrium; to charge severely with a fault; to upbraid. (Fr. *reprocher.*)

reproachable, *a.* re-*proach*-a-bl, deserving reproach.

reproachableness, *n.* the quality or state of being reproachable.

reproachably, *ad.* with reproaches.

reproacher, *n.* re-*proach*-er, one who reproaches.

reproachful, *a.* re-*proach*-ful, expressing reproach; bringing a lasting reproach; shameful; base.

reproachfully, *ad.* in a reproachful manner.

reproachfulness, *n.* the quality of being reproachful.

reprobacy, *n. rep*-ro-ba-se, the state or character of being reprobate.

reprobate, *a. rep*-ro-bate, depraved; wholly given up to sin; abandoned to error: *n.* a person abandoned to sin; a dissolute scamp: *v.t.* to disapprove with detestation; to condemn; to disown; to abandon to wickedness or fate. (L. *reprobatus*, rejected.)

reprobation, *n.* rep-ro-*bay*-shon, act of reprobating; the state of being reprobated; the state of being rejected by God.

reprobationer, *n.* rep-ro-*bay*-shon-er, one who believes in the abandonment, by Divine decree, of the non-elect to eternal destruction.

reprobator, *n. rep*-ro-bay-tor, an action by which it was formerly sought to prove that a witness was prejudiced or perjured [Scots. Law].

reproduce, *v.t.* ree-pro-*dewce*, to produce again; to bring forth offspring; to propagate; to copy; to exhibit again.

reproducer, *n.* ree-pro-*dewce*-er, one who or that which reproduces; the sound-box of a radio, etc.

reproducible, *a.* ree-pro-*dew*-se-bl, that can be reproduced; capable of reproduction.

reproduction, *n.* ree-pro-*duk*-shon, the act or process of reproducing; the process, or the power, of producing new individuals of a species by generation [Zool. and Bot.]; that which is reproduced; a copy.

reproductive, *a.* ree-pro-*duk*-tiv, pertaining to, of the nature of, or contributing to reproduction. **reproductive faculty,** the power to call to mind objects once apprehended.

reproductively, *ad.* by reproduction.

reproductiveness, *n.* reproductivity.

reproductivity, *n.* ree-pro-duk-*tiv*-e-te, the state or quality of being reproductive.

reproof, *n.* re-*proof*, censure; blame; indication of blame; a chiding; reprehension.

re-proof, *v.t.* ree-*proof*, to render waterproof once more.

reprovable, *a.* re-*proov*-a-bl, worthy of reproof; deserving censure; blamable.

reprovableness, *n.* the state or quality of being reprovable.

reprovably, *ad.* in a reprovable manner.

reproval, *n.* re-*proov*-al, the act of reproving; admonition.

reprove, *v.t.* re-*proov*, to blame or censure; to charge with a fault, esp. to the face; to reprehend or rebuke; to scold. (O.Fr. *reprover.*)

re-prove, *v.t. ree*-proov, to prove again.

reprover, *n.* re-*proov*-er, one who reproves.

reprovingly, *ad.* re-*proov*-ing-le, in a reproving manner.

reprune, *v.t.* ree-*proon*, to prune a second time.

reptant, *a. rep*-tant, creeping [Zool.]; creeping and rooting [Bot.]. (L. *reptare*, to creep.)

reptation, *n.* rep-*tay*-shon, the action of creeping.

reptatorial, *a.* rep-ta-*taw*-re-al, reptatory.

reptatory, *a. rep*-ta-to-re, creeping [Zool.].

reptile, *a. rep*-tile, creeping; moving on the belly or with very short legs; grovelling; base: *n.* any of the Reptilia; a grovelling or mean person. (Fr. from L. *reptilis*, creeping.)

Reptilia, *n.pl.* rep-*til*-e-a, a class of cold-blooded vertebrates, embracing the snakes, lizards, crocodiles, tortoises, and turtles, etc. (L.)

reptilian, *a.* rep-*til*-e-an, pertaining to reptiles: *n.* a reptile.

reptiliferous, *a.* rep-te-*lif*-er-us, containing fossil reptiles as certain strata [Geol.]. (L. *reptilis*, and *fero*, bear.)

reptiliform, *a.* rep-*til*-e-form, of the form of a reptile. (L. *reptilis*, and *forma*, shape.)

reptilious, *a.* rep-*til*-e-us, resembling a reptile.

reptilivorous, *a.* rep-te-*liv*-o-rus, devouring or living upon reptiles. (L. *voro*, devour.)

republic, *n.* re-*pub*-lik, a state in which the exercise of the sovereign power is lodged in representatives elected by the people; a commonwealth. **republic of letters,** the collective body of literary or learned men. (L. *respublica*, from *res*, affair, and *publica*, public.)

republican, *a.* re-*pub*-le-kan, pertaining to or according to the spirit or manner of a republic; advocating republican principles or policy: *n.* one who favours or prefers a republican form of government; one of a party in the U.S.A. in favour of a liberal construction of the Constitution and who advocate the extension of central, as opposed to State, government.

republicanism, *n.* re-*pub*-le-ka-nizm, a republican form or system of government; attachment to this.

republicanize, *v.t.* re-*pub*-le-ka-nize, to convert to republican principles or the republican form of government.

republication, *n. ree*-pub-le-*kay*-shon, a new publication of something before published; renewal.

republish, *v.t.* ree-*pub*-lish, to issue a reprint of a book; to publish anew.

repudiable, *a.* re-*pew*-de-a-bl, that may be repudiated; fit or proper to be repudiated.

repudiate, *v.t.* re-*pew*-de-ate, to cast away; to reject; to discard; to put away; to divorce; to disclaim a debt or a liability. (L. *repudiatus*, rejected.)

repudiation, *n.* re-pew-de-*ay*-shon, the act of repudiating; rejection of responsibility.

repudiationist, *n.* re-pew-de-*ay*-shon-ist, an advocate of the disclaiming of a public debt or other obligation.

repudiator, *n.* re-*pew*-de-ay-tor, one who repudiates.

repugn, *v.t.* and *i.* re-*pewn*, to oppose; to resist.

repugnance, *n.* re-*pug*-nance, opposition of mind; strong dislike; reluctance; inconsistency.

repugnancy, *n.* re-*pug*-nan-se, repugnance.

repugnant, *a.* re-*pug*-nant, contrary; antagonistic; adverse; distasteful. (O.Fr.)

repugnantly, *ad.* in a repugnant manner.

repugnatorial, *a.* re-pug-na-*taw*-re-al, serving for self-defence (as certain glands, etc.) [Zool.].

repullulate, *v.i.* ree-*pul*-yew-late, to bud or shoot again [Bot.]; to break out again, to recur [Med.].

repullulation, *n.* ree-pul-yew-*lay*-shon, the act of budding again; recurrence [Med.].

repulse, *n.* re-*pulse*, the act of repulsing or state of being repulsed; refusal; rebuff: *v.t.* to repel; to beat back; to rebuff. (L. *repulsa.*)

repulser, *n.* re-*pulse*-er, one who drives back.

repulsion, *n.* re-*pul*-shon, the act of repelling; the

state of being repelled; power or tendency to repel; extreme aversion.
repulsive, *a.* re-*pul*-siv, causing or arousing repulsion; repelling; forbidding; loathsome; disgusting.
repulsively, *ad.* in a repulsive manner.
repulsiveness, *n.* quality of being repulsive.
repulsory, *a.* re-*pul*-so-re, repulsive; driving back; acting by repulsion.
repurchase, *n.* ree-*per*-chas, the act of buying again; that which is repurchased: *v.t.* to buy back or again.
reputability, *n.* rep-yew-ta-*bil*-e-te, the quality or condition of being reputable.
reputable, *a.* *rep*-yew-ta-bl, being in good repute; held in esteem; honourable.
reputableness, *n.* the quality of being reputable.
reputably, *ad.* in a reputable manner.
reputation, *n.* rep-yew-*tay*-shon, good name; the credit, honour, or character which is derived from a favourable public opinion or esteem; character by report; repute.
reputative, *a.* re-*pew*-ta-tiv, putative.
repute, *n.* re-*pewt*, reputation; character by report; good character; established opinion: *v.t.* to reckon or think; to account; to esteem. (Fr. *réputer.*)
reputed, *a.* re-*pew*-ted, generally regarded; customary; not guaranteed (esp. of measures of capacity other than imperial).
reputedly, *ad.* in the general regard; by repute.
⋆**request**, *n.* re-*kwest*, the expression of desire for something to be granted or done; prayer; petition; the thing asked for or requested: *v.t.* to express desire for; to ask. **in request**, much desired or esteemed. (O.Fr. *requeste.*)
requester, *n.* re-*kwes*-ter, one who requests.
requicken, *v.t.* ree-*kwik*-en, to reanimate.
requiem, *n.* *rek*-we-em *or* *ree*-kwe-em, a service for the dead, beginning with this word; a setting for this or composition in honour of some dead person [Mus.]; a dirge. (L.)
requiescence, *n.* rek-we-*es*-ence, a state of quiescence; rest.
requirable, *a.* re-*kwire*-ra-bl, that may be required; fit or proper to be demanded.
require, *v.t.* re-*kwire*, to want, to ask, as of right or by authority; to claim; to request; to call to account for; to make necessary. (O.Fr. *requerre.*)
requirement, *n.* re-*kwire*-ment, demand; that which is required.
requisite, *a.* *rek*-we-zit, required by the nature of things; necessary: *n.* that which is necessary; something indispensable. (L. *requisitus*, asked back.)
requisiteness, *n.* the state of being requisite; necessity.
requisition, *n.* rek-we-*zish*-on, the act of demanding; application made as of right; an authoritative demand or order for; that which is requisitioned: *v.t.* to request; to demand as a right; to make an authoritative demand on, esp. for military purposes. (O.Fr.)
requisitory, *a.* re-*kwiz*-e-to-re, of the nature of or conveying a requisition.
requital, *a.* re-*kwite*-al, return for any action, good or bad; compensation; recompense; retaliation; punishment.
requite, *v.t.* re-*kwite*, to repay either good or evil; to recompense; to retaliate; to punish; to do or give in return. (*re-* and *quit.*)
requiter, *n.* re-*kwite*-er, one who requites.
re-rail, *v.t.* to place on rails again; to equip with a fresh set of rails.
re-read, *v.t.* to read a second or subsequent time.
rere-arch, *n.* a rear-arch.
rerebrace, *n.* *reer*-brace, plate armour for the upper part of the arm.
re-record, *v.t.* ree-re-*kord*, to record again; to prepare a new record from an existing disk or sound track [Cine.].
reredos, *n.* *reer*-dos, the decorated screen or wall at the back of the altar; an ornamental screen at the back of a fireplace. (O.Fr.)
rerefief, *n.* *reer*-feef, an arrière fee.
reremouse, *n.* *reer*-mouse, a bat [Zool.]. (A.S. *hreremūs.*)
re-route, *v.t.* ree-*root*, to designate a different route for; to send by a new route.
re-run, *v.t.* ree-*run*, to run (a race, etc.) over again.
resail, *v.t.* and *i.* ree-*sale*, to sail over or back again.
resale, *n.* ree-*sale*, a sale at second hand; the act of selling again.
resalute, *v.t.* ree-sa-*lewt*, to salute anew or in return.
rescind, *v.t.* re-*sind*, to annul; to revoke; to abrogate. (Fr. *rescinder.*)
rescission, *n.* re-*sizh*-on, the act of rescinding or annulling. (L. *rescissus*, rescinded.)
rescissory, *a.* re-*sis*-o-re, tending to rescind; having the effect of rescission.
re-score, *v.t.* ree-*skore*, to score anew; to rearrange a score for a different set of instruments [Mus.].
rescript, *n.* *ree*-skript, an edict or decree, esp. of an emperor or pope, given in answer to some question in law, etc., officially submitted to him. (O.Fr., from L. *re-* and *scriptum*, written.)
rescuable, *a.* *res*-kew-a-bl, that may be rescued.
rescue, *n.* *res*-kew, deliverance from restraint, violence, or danger; forcible seizure or release from the custody of the law [Law]: *v.t.* to deliver from the power of another; to free from any confinement, danger, or evil. (O.Fr. *rescoure.*)
rescuer, *n.* *res*-kew-er, one who rescues.
research, *n.* re-*serch*, scientific inquiry; original study; diligent, careful search, or investigation: *v.t.* to search or examine with care; to search again: *v.i.* to make researches. (Fr. *recherche.*)
researcher, *n.* re-*serch*-er, one who diligently examines or devotes himself to research.
reseat, *v.t.* ree-*seet*, to seat or set again; to put a new seat into.
reseau, *n.* ray-*zoh*, a network ground for lace; a graticule used in astro-photography for facilitating measurements. (Fr., net.)
resect, *v.t.* re-*sekt*, to remove a portion of, to pare down (esp. of bone) [Surg.].
resection, *n.* re-*sek*-shon, the act of cutting or paring off; the excision of a part of an organ, esp. of the ends of bones and other structures forming a joint [Surg.]. (L. *resectio.*)
Reseda, *n.* res-*ee*-da, a genus of plants including the mignonette, *R. odorata*; a greyish-green tint. (L.)
reseize, *v.t.* ree-*seez*, to seize again; to take possession of disseized lands and tenements [Law].
reseizure, *n.* ree-*seez*-yewr, a second seizure.
resell, *v.t.* ree-*sel*, to sell again; to sell soon after buying.
resemblance, *n.* re-*zem*-blance, state of being like; likeness; similitude; a point of likeness; something similar; similarity.
resemblant, *a.* re-*zem*-blant, similar; characterized by resemblance.
resemble, *v.t.* re-*zem*-bl, to have the likeness of; to be like; to have similar features or characteristics. (Fr. *resembler.*)
resend, *v.t.* ree-*send*, to send back or onward; to repeat (as a telegram).
resent, *v.t.* re-*zent*, to take ill; to consider as an injury or affront; to feel or express anger at. (Fr. *ressentir.*)
resenter, *n.* re-*zen*-ter, one who resents.
resentful, *a.* re-*zent*-ful, easily provoked to anger; irritable; full of resentment.
resentfully, *ad.* with resentment.
resentingly, *ad.* with a degree of anger.
resentive, *a.* re-*zen*-tiv, inclined to resent.
resentment, *n.* re-*zent*-ment, a deep sense of injury, or umbrage excited by it; anger. (Fr. *ressentiment.*)
reservable, *a.* re-*zer*-va-bl, that may be reserved.
reservation, *n.* rez-er-*vay*-shon, the act of reserving or keeping back; reserve; that which is kept back; a limitation; a clause by which something is reserved [Law]; a tract of land reserved for a definite purpose, as a tribal location, place for nature study, etc.; the holding back of the consecrated elements for adoration after the eucharist. **mental reservation**, the withholding or failing to disclose something which, if stated, would materially alter an asseveration, etc.
reserve, *n.* re-*zerv*, that which is reserved or kept for other or future use; a fund or sum of money set aside for an emergency or some specific purpose; self-restraint; reservedness; an exception; that branch of the defensive forces whose services are only required in time of war or national emergency; one nominated to substitute another in a team, etc., in case of need [Sport]; a stretch of country set aside as a reservation; *pl.* troops kept back in

action, to give support when needed; the second best team of a club [Sport]: *v.t.* to keep in store; to withhold from present use for another purpose; to retain; to destine. **in reserve,** available for use if required. **without reserve,** with no limit imposed; unrestrictedly. (O.Fr. *reserver.*)
reserved, *a.* re-*zervd,* set aside; destined for special use; restrained; not free or frank in words, actions, or social intercourse; shy. **reserved list,** a roll of officers, retired or on half-pay, who can be recalled on an emergency.
reservedly, *ad.* re-*zer*-ved-le, in a reserved manner.
reservedness, *n.* re-*zer*-ved-ness, the quality of being reserved; modest diffidence; coldness.
reservist, *n.* re-*zer*-vist *or* *rez*-er-vist, a member of the reserve [Mil.].
reservoir, *n.* *rez*-er-vwar, a place or receptacle in which anything, esp. a fluid, may be kept in store; a construction for the storage of water in bulk; the container of a fountain-pen; a reserve supply. (Fr.)
reset, *n.* ree-*set,* the receiving and harbouring of an outlaw or criminal [Scots. Law]; the receiving of stolen goods: *v.t.* to receive an outlaw or stolen goods. (O.Fr. *recet,* from L. *receptum,* received.)
reset, *v.t.* ree-*set,* to set again (as type, jewellery, a saw, etc.): *n.* that which is reset. (*re-* and *set.*)
resetter, *n.* ree-*set*-er, a receiver of stolen goods.
resettle, *v.i.* and *t.* ree-*set*-tl, to settle again; to install again.
resettlement, *n.* ree-*setl*-ment, the act of resettling; the act of settling or composing again; state of settling or subsiding again.
reshape, *v.t.* ree-*shape,* to shape or model afresh.
reship, *v.t.* ree-*ship,* to ship again; to ship what has been imported.
reshipment, *n.* ree-*ship*-ment, the act of shipping a second time; the shipping for exportation what has ben imported; that which is reshipped.
reshuffle, *v.t.* ree-*shufl,* to shuffle again (esp. at cards): *n.* an act of reshuffling; an arrangement in a different order or sequence.
reside, *v.i.* re-*zide,* to dwell permanently or for a length of time; to inhere. (O.Fr. *resider.*)
residence, *n.* *rez*-e-dence, the act of residing or dwelling in a place; place where one dwells; residing where one's duties are; domicile. (O.Fr.)
residency, *n.* *rez*-e-den-se, the official residence of the former representative of the British government at the court of an Indian prince.
resident, *a.* *rez*-e-dent, dwelling in a place for a length of time; dwelling where one's duties are: *n.* one who resides in a place for some time; a former political agent of the British government at the court of an Indian ruler. (O.Fr.)
residenter, *n.* rez-e-*dent*-er, a resident [Scots.].
residential, *a.* rez-e-*den*-shal, pertaining to residents or residence.
residentiary, *a.* rez-e-*den*-sha-re, having residence; bound by the terms of office to a certain residence: *n.* a resident; one, esp. an ecclesiastic, who is residentiary.
residentship, *n.* *rez*-e-dent-ship, the office or period of office of a political resident.
resider, *n.* re-*zide*-er, one who resides in a particular place.
residual, *a.* re-*zid*-yew-al, pertaining to or of the nature of a residue; remaining after a part is taken, or as residue. **residual air,** the air still staying in the lungs after the utmost effort of expiration. (L. *residuus,* a remainder.)
residuary, *a.* re-*zid*-yew-a-re, pertaining to the residue or part remaining. **residuary clause,** the clause in a will by which all that is left over from the dispositions in the previous clauses is disposed of. **residuary legatee,** the legatee to whom is bequeathed the part of the goods or estate which remains after deducting all debts and specific legacies [Law].
residue, *n.* *rez*-e-dew, the remaining part; that which is left; the remainder. (O.Fr. *residu.*)
residuent, *n.* re-*zid*-yew-ent, a by-product of a process of manufacture; a waste product.
residuous, *a.* re-*zid*-yew-us, residual; remaining.
residuum, *n.* re-*zid*-yew-um (*pl.* **residua**), residue; what is left after any process of separation or purification; leavings; dregs. (L.)
resign, *v.t.* re-*zine,* to give up or back, as an office or commission; to withdraw, as a claim; to yield; to relinquish; to submit: *v.i.* to give up (one's office, etc.); to yield; to retire. (O.Fr. *resigner.*)
re-sign, *v.t.* ree-*sine,* to sign again.
resignation, *n.* rez-ig-*nay*-shon, the act of resigning; the state of being resigned; submission; submission with acquiescence or reconciled submission, esp. to the dispensations or will of Providence. (O.Fr.)
resigned, *a.* re-*zynd,* submissive; patient.
resignedly, *ad.* re-*zy*-ned-le, with resignation.
resignee, *n.* rez-e-*nee,* the person or party to whom a thing is resigned [Law].
resigner, *n.* re-*zy*-ner, one who resigns.
resile, *v.i.* re-*zile,* to start back; to recede or withdraw from an engagement, etc.; to exhibit elasticity. (L. *resilio,* leap.)
resilience, *n.* re-*zil*-e-ence, the act of springing back or rebounding; recoil; elasticity; healthy reaction [Med.].
resiliency, *n.* re-*zil*-e-en-se, resilience.
resilient, *a.* re-*zil*-e-ent, leaping or starting back; rebounding; having or exhibiting elasticity; buoyant. (L. *resiliens.*)
resin, *n.* *rez*-in, a vitreous solid insoluble in water, exuding from trees and containing carbon, hydrogen, and oxygen; a synthetic or otherwise artificially produced substitute for this; rosin: *v.t.* to treat with resin; to apply resin to. (L. *resina.*)
resinaceous, *a.* *rez*-e-*nay*-shus, resinous.
resinate, *n.* *rez*-e-nate, a salt or ester of a resin acid: *v.t.* to flavour or treat with resin.
resinic, *a.* rez-*in*-ik, pertaining to or derived from resin.
resiniferous, *a.* rez-e-*nif*-er-rus, yielding resin.
resinification, *n.* rez-*in*-e-fe-*kay*-shon, the act or process of resinifying; treatment with resin.
resiniform, *a.* rez-*in*-e-form, of a resinous character.
resinify, *v.i.* rez-*in*-e-fy, to become resinous: *v.t.* to convert into or treat with resin.
resinoid, *a.* *rez*-e-noyd, like resin; somewhat resinous: *n.* any synthetic or artificial resin.
resinous, *a.* *rez*-e-nus, characteristic of or of the nature of resin.
resinously, *ad.* by the agency of resin.
resinousness, *n.* resinous quality.
resiny, *a.* *rez*-e-ne, like resin; resinous.
resipiscence, *n.* res-e-*pis*-sence, wisdom derived from experience; acknowledgment of error; repentance. (L. *resipiscens,* being wise.)
resipiscent, *a.* res-e-*pis*-ent, restored to a sane or sensible condition; rendered wise by experience.
resist, *v.t.* re-*zist,* to withstand; to act in opposition to; to strive against; to baffle: *v.i.* to make opposition: *n.* a resistant, esp. a substance to preserve the parts white in calico-printing. (O.Fr. *resister.*)
resistance, *n.* re-*zis*-tance, the act of resisting; opposition; hindrance; hostility; the opposition of an electric circuit to the passage of the current; that power of a body which acts in opposition to the impulse or pressure of another, or which prevents the effect of another power [Mech.]; the retardation imposed by a medium on a body (bullet, ship, aircraft, etc.) moving through it; the opposition to its passage met by an electric current, whereby the electricity is converted into heat; a resistance-coil or other source of resistance [Elect.]. **passive resistance,** *see* **passive.**
resistance-box, *n.* the container of a number of resistance-coils.
resistance-coil, *n.* a length of wire coiled to increase resistance [Elect.].
resistant, *n.* re-*zis*-tant, one who or that which resists; *a.* resisting.
resister, *n.* re-*zis*-ter, one who resists.
resistibility, *n.* re-*zis*-te-*bil*-e-te, the quality of being resistible.
resistible, *a.* re-*zis*-te-bl, that may be resisted.
resistibly, *ad.* in a resistible manner.
resistive, *a.* re-*zis*-tiv, having the power to resist; pertaining to resistance [Elect.].
resistivity, *n.* rez-is-*tiv*-e-te, capacity for resisting; capacity for resistance (as opposed to conductivity) [Elect.].
resistless, *a.* re-*zist*-less, irresistible; that cannot be opposed.
resistlessly, *ad.* in a resistless manner.

resistlessness, *n.* the quality of being resistless.
resistor, *n.* re-*zis*-tor, any device offering resistance to a current [Elect.].
resolder, *v.t.* ree-*sol*-der, to solder anew.
resole, *v.t.* re-*sole*, to provide with a new sole.
resolubility, *n.* *ree*-sol-yew-*bil*-e-te, the quality of being resoluble.
resoluble, *a.* *rez*-o-lew-bl, capable of being resolved; analysable.
re-soluble, *a.* ree-*sol*-yew-bl, capable of being again dissolved.
resolute, *a.* *rez*-o-loot *or* -lewt, having fixedness of purpose; determined; constant in pursuing a purpose. (L *resolutus*, decided.)
resolutely, *ad.* in a resolute manner.
resoluteness, *n.* the quality of being resolute.
resolution, *n.* rez-o-*lew*-shon, the act or process of resolving or of separating the parts of anything; analysis; dissolution; firmness of purpose; fixed determination; constancy; a declaration or proposal passed by any public assembly or formal meeting; solution [Math.]; the changing from a dissonant chord to a consonant chord [Mus.]. **resolution of an equation,** its reduction, to ascertain the value of the unknown quantity [Alg.]. **resolution of forces,** the dividing of a force into two or more, which would have the same effect [Mech.]. (O.Fr.)
resolutioner, *n.* rez-o-*lew*-shon-er, one who joins with others in a resolution or declaration.
resolutive, *a.* *rez*-o-lew-tiv, having the power to dissolve or relax: *n.* any resolvent drug or application [Med.].
resolvability, *n.* re-*zol*-va-*bil*-e-te, the quality of being resolvable.
resolvable, *a.* re-*zol*-va-bl, that may be resolved.
resolve, *n.* re-*zolve*, a resolution, or fixed purpose of mind; settled determination; a resolution of a deliberative body, association, etc.: *v.t.* to separate a complex body or idea into simple parts or elements; to analyse; to unravel; to solve; to explain; to determine; to settle in an opinion; to make certain; to melt; to form or constitute by resolution; to determine on; to disperse, as an inflammation or tumour [Med.]: *v.i.* to determine; to determine by vote; to dissolve; to separate into its elements; to be settled in opinion. (L. *resolvo*, loose.)
resolved, *a.* re-*zolvd*, determined in purpose.
resolvedly, *ad.* re-*zol*-ved-le, in a resolved manner.
resolvedness, *n.* re-*zol*-ved-ness, the quality of being resolute; fixity of purpose.
resolvent, *a.* re-*zol*-vent, having the power of resolving; causing solution: *n.* that which has the power of resolving or dispersing, as an inflammation or tumour [Med.]; a solvent. (L. *resolvens*.)
resolver, *n.* re-*zol*-ver, one who or that which resolves.
resonance, *n.* *rez*-o-nance, a resounding; an echoing; reverberation of sound; sonority; the condition when two oscillatory circuits have the same natural frequency, also when the frequency of the electromotive force impressed upon a circuit is equal to the natural frequency of a circuit [Elect. and Wire.]; the sound elicited by percussing the chest [Med.].
resonant, *a.* *rez*-o-nant, resounding; returning sound; echoing back. (L. *resonans*, resounding.)
resonate, *v.t.* *rez*-o-nate, to resound; to re-echo; to produce or possess resonance.
resonator, *n.* *rez*-o-nay-tor, a sounding board or box; a metallic device for detecting a tone amidst a number of sounds; any device to intensify a musical tone or to increase its power by sympathetic vibration.
resorb, *v.t.* re-*sawrb*, to absorb again; to swallow up. (L. *resorbeo*, suck in.)
resorbent, *a.* re-*sawr*-bent, absorbing anew.
resorcin, *n.* ree-*sawr*-sin, a crystalline substance originally obtained by the fusion of resins with caustic alkalies, used in dyeing, medicine, etc. (*resin* and *orcin*.)
resorption, *n.* re-*sawrp*-shon, re-absorption.
resorptive, *a.* re-*sawrp*-tiv, relating to, or apt to cause, resorption.
resort, *n.* re-*zawrt*, a betaking oneself; assembly; meeting; concourse; the place frequented; an expedient: *v.i.* to have recourse; to betake; to repair. (O.Fr. *resortir*.)
re-sort, *v.t.* *ree*-sawrt, to sort again.
resorter, *n.* re-*zawr*-ter, one who resorts or frequents.
resound, *v.t.* re-*zound*, to send back sound; to echo; to sound loudly; to spread the fame of: *v.i.* to be sent back, as sound; to reverberate. (O.Fr. *resoner*.)
re-sound, *v.t.* ree-*sound*, to sound again.
resounding, *a.* re-*zoun*-ding, re-echoing; ringing; sonorous.
resource, *n.* re-*sawrce*, any source of aid or support; an expedient to which one may resort; means yet untried: *pl.* money or any property convertible into supplies; means of raising money; quickness in use of expedients. (O.Fr. *resource*.)
resourceful, *a.* re-*sawrce*-ful, clever at devising ways and means.
resourcefully, *ad.* in a resourceful manner.
resourcefulness, *n.* the quality of being resourceful.
resourceless, *a.* destitute of resources.
resow, *v.t.* ree-*soh*, to sow over again.
resp, *n.* resp, red water or similar disease affecting sheep [Vet.].
respeak, *v.i.* and *v.t.* ree-*speek*, to re-echo; to reply.
★**respect,** *n.* re-*spekt*, relation; regard; attention; esteem, or its expression; respectful demeanour; due attention; favour; partiality; respected character; relation: *v.t.* to regard; to relate to; to honour or esteem. (Fr., from L. *respectus*, looked.)
respectability, *n.* re-*spek*-ta-*bil*-e-te, respectableness; a respectable person.
respectable, *a.* re-*spek*-ta-bl, possessing the qualities which command respect; held in respect; moderate in excellence or number, etc., but not negligible. (Fr.)
respectableness, *n.* re-*spek*-ta-bl-ness, the state or quality of being respectable.
respectably, *ad.* in a respectable manner.
respectant, *a.* re-*spek*-tant, looking towards each other (of animals) [Her.].
respecter, *n.* res-*pek*-ter, one who respects. **respecter of persons,** one who favours, or is likely to favour, another to the prejudice of justice and equity.
respectful, *a.* re-*spekt*-ful, characterized by respect.
respectfully, *ad.* in a respectful manner.
respectfulness, *n.* quality of being respectful.
respecting, *prep.* re-*spek*-ting, in regard to; concerning.
respective, *a.* re-*spek*-tiv, relative; not absolute; relating to a particular person or thing; several.
respectively, *ad.* as each belongs to each; as relating to each; relatively.
respectless, *a.* re-*spekt*-less, having no respect; without regard.
re-spell, *v.t.* to spell again in a different way (as by some phonetic method).
respirability, *n.* re-*spyr*-ra-*bil*-e-te, the quality of being respirable.
respirable, *a.* re-*spyr*-ra-bl, that may be breathed; fit for respiration.
respiration, *n.* res-per-*ray*-shon, the act or function of breathing. (Fr.)
respirational, *a.* res-per-*ray*-shon-al, relating to respiration.
respirator, *n.* *res*-per-ray-tor, a contrivance worn to protect the lungs from the inspiration of smoke, gases, etc.; a gas-mask; an apparatus for maintaining respiration artificially.
respiratorium, *n.* *res*-per-ra-*taw*-re-um, one of the gill-like organs of certain aquatic larvæ [Entom.].
respiratory, *a.* res-*pyr*-ra-to-re *or* *res*-per-ra-to-re, serving for or connected with respiration.
respire, *v.i.* res-*pyr*, to breathe; to inhale air into the lungs and exhale it: *v.t.* to exhale; to breathe out. (Fr. *respirer*.)
respirometer, *n.* res-per-*rom*-e-ter, a device for measuring respirations.
respite, *n.* *res*-pit, temporary intermission of labour, process, or operation; interval of rest; pause; suspension of the execution of a criminal; the prolongation of time for the payment of a debt: *v.t.* to relieve by an interval of rest; to suspend the execution of; to postpone. (O.Fr. *respit*.)
resplendence, *n.* re-*splen*-dence, brilliant lustre; vivid brightness.
resplendency, *n.* re-*splen*-den-se, resplendence.
resplendent, *a.* re-*splen*-dent, very bright; shining with brilliant lustre. (L. *resplendens*, glittering.)
resplendently, *ad.* in a resplendent manner.
resplit, *v.t.* *ree*-split, to split again.

respond, *n.* re-*spond*, a short anthem chanted in the interval of reading a chapter in a religious service; a responsory [Eccles.]: *v.i.* to reply; to correspond to or suit: *v.t.* to answer; to satisfy by payment [U.S.A.]. (O.Fr. *respondre*, from L. *respondere.*)

respondent, *a.* re-*spon*-dent, that answers to demand or expectation: *n.* one who answers to a suit at law, esp. for divorce; a defendant; in the schools, one who maintains a thesis in reply.

respondentia, *n.* *res*-pon-*den*-she-a, a loan upon a ship's cargo [Comm.].

responsal, *n.* re-*spon*-sal, a response; a responsory. (Late L. *responsalis.*)

response, *n.* re-*spons*, the act of answering; a reply; a versicle, etc., as answer of the congregation to the priest; a responsory. (O.Fr. *respons.*)

responsibility, *n.* re-*spon*-se-*bil*-e-te, the state of being responsible for a trust, office, debt, etc.; accountability; what one is responsible for; ability to answer in payment.

★**responsible,** *a.* re-*spon*-se-bl, answerable; liable to account; able to discharge an obligation. (Late L. *responsabilis.*)

responsibleness, *n.* re-*spon*-se-bl-ness, the quality of being responsible; responsibility.

responsibly, *ad.* in a responsible manner.

responsions, *n.* re-*spon*-shonz, the first of three examinations at Oxford for the degree of B.A.

responsive, *a.* re-*spon*-siv, answering; making reply; readily reacting to stimulus.

responsively, *ad.* in a responsive manner.

responsiveness, *n.* the quality of being responsive.

responsory, *a.* re-*spon*-so-re, pertaining to or containing an answer: *n.* a response; the answer of the congregation to the priest [Eccles.]. (Late L. *responsorium.*)

ressaldar, *n.* res-al-*dar*, a native captain in an Indian cavalry regiment. (Urdu.)

★**rest,** *n.* rest, cessation from motion or action of any kind; repose; quiet; sleep; peace; place of quiet or repose; that on which anything rests; a short pause; a pause or interval of time, during which there is an intermission of the voice or sound; a prop or stand for a gun, etc.; a support for a tool in a lathe; a long cue with a bridge [Billiards]; a rally [Tennis]: *v.i.* to cease from action or motion; to be quiet; to repose; to sleep; to be dead; to lean; to stand on; to acquiesce; to rely; to abide: *v.t.* to cause to cease from action, etc.; to place at rest or for support; to quiet; to lay in rest. (A.S.)

rest, *n.* rest, that which is left; the remainder; the others; the undivided profits remaining at the time of balancing; a reserve, esp. the Bank of England reserve fund: *v.i.* to remain. (Fr. *rester.*)

rest, *n.* rest, a projection welded to a mediæval breast-plate to support the butt of a lance. (*arrest.*)

restamp, *v.t.* ree-*stamp*, to stamp again.

restant, *a.* *res*-tant, persistent [Bot.].

restate, *v.t.* ree-*state*, to state a second time.

restatement, *n.* ree-*state*-ment, the act of restating; that which is restated.

restaurant, *n.* *res*-te-rong (*or* App.), an establishment for refreshments; a public dining-room; a better class eating-house. (Fr.)

restaurateur, *n.* (App.), a restaurant-keeper. (Fr.)

restauration, *n.* res-taw-*ray*-shon, restoration; reinstatement.

rest-cure, *n.* a treatment for nervous disorders consisting essentially of rest, seclusion, and massage.

rest-day, *n.* a day of cessation from work; the Sabbath.

restful, *a.* *rest*-ful, of the nature of rest; affording rest; being at rest.

restfully, *ad.* in a restful manner.

restfulness, *n.* the state of being restful.

restharrow, *n.* *rest*-ha-ro, any plant of the genus *Ononis*, esp. *O. arvensis*, the pink-flowered cammock. (So called because their thick roots arrest a harrow in its course.)

rest-house, *n.* a hostel for travellers (originally a dak bungalow in India).

restiform, *a.* *res*-te-form, cord-like [Anat.]. (L. *restis*, rope, and *forma.*)

resting-place, *n.* a place for rest; a staircase landing; the grave.

restitution, *n.* res-te-*tew*-shon, the act of restoring esp. some right or thing of which a person has been deprived; indemnification; compensation; state of restoration. (Fr.)

restitutive, *a.* *res*-te-tew-tiv, tending to restore relating to restitution.

restitutory, *a.* re-*stit*-ew-to-re, pertaining to or o the nature of restitution.

restive, *a.* *res*-tiv, unwilling to go or move forward obstinate; stubborn; restless or impatient unde restraint; inclined to jib. (Fr. *restif.*)

restively, *ad.* in a restive manner.

restiveness, *n.* the quality of being restive.

restless, *a.* *rest*-less, continually moving; sleepless uneasy; not satisfied to remain at rest; turbulent unsettled.

restlessly, *ad.* in a restless manner.

restlessness, *n.* the state of being restless.

restock, *v.t.* ree-*stok*, to stock anew.

restorable, *a.* re-*staw*-ra-bl, that may be restored.

restorableness, *n.* state of being restorable.

restoration, *n.* res-taw-*ray*-shon, act of restoring renewal; recovery; the final recovery of all men from sin to a state of salvation; that which is restored; a model of an extinct animal, etc. **the Restoration,** the return of Charles II and re establishment of the monarchy in 1660. (O.Fr.)

restorationism, *res*-taw-*ray*-shon-izm, the doctrin of the restorationists.

restorationist, *n.* res-taw-*ray*-shon-ist, one who believes in the final salvation or restoration of all men

restorative, *a.* res-*taw*-ra-tiv, that has power to renew strength: *n.* a medicine for restoring strength and vigour; a tonic.

restoratively, *ad.* so as to restore strength.

restore, *v.t.* re-*store*, to bring back to a forme state; to repair; to heal; to rebuild; to renew to revive; to recover; to give back; to return to replace. (O.Fr. *restorer*, from L. *restauro*, stand.

re-store, *v.t.* ree-*store*, to store again.

restorer, *n.* re-*staw*-rer, one who or that which restores.

restrain, *v.t.* re-*strane*, to hold back or check to repress; to hinder; to keep under control o restraint. (O.Fr. *restraindre.*)

restrainable, *a.* re-*stray*-na-bl, capable of bein restrained.

restrainedly, *ad.* re-*stray*-ned-le, with restraint; i a restrained manner.

restrainer, *n.* re-*stray*-ner, he who or that whic restrains.

restraint, *n.* re-*straynt*, the act of restraining abridgment of liberty; confinement (as in a asylum); that which restrains; a check; avoid ance of excess; self-control. **restraint of trade** prevention or limitation of free competition i trading. (O.Fr.)

restrict, *v.t.* re-*strikt*, to limit; to confine; t restrain within bounds. (L. *restrictus*, bound back

restrictedly, *ad.* re-*strik*-ted-le, in a restricte manner.

restriction, *n.* re-*strik*-shon, limitation; restraint.

restrictionist, *n.* re-*strik*-shon-ist, an advocate c restriction (of imports, the liquor traffic, etc.).

restrictive, *a.* re-*strik*-tiv, having the quality (limiting; imposing restraint.

restrictively, *ad.* in a restrictive manner.

restrike, *v.t.* ree-*strike*, to strike again: *n.* a coi struck from a disused die.

restringent, *a.* re-*strin*-jent, astringent; styptic *n.* an astringent medicine. (L. *restringens.*)

resty, *a.* *res*-te, restive; (formerly) inactive.

restyle, *v.t.* ree-*style*, to refashion.

resublimation, *n.* *ree*-sub-le-*may*-shon, a secon subliming.

result, *n.* re-*zult*, consequence; conclusion; effect the outcome of a calculation; the answer to problem: *v.i.* to follow as a consequence; to hav an issue. (O.Fr. *resulter.*)

resultance, *n.* re-*zul*-tance, the fact of resulting; result.

resultant, *a.* re-*zul*-tant, following as a result resulting from the combination of two or mor forces: *n.* that which results; the force resultin from the combination of two or more forces actin in different directions [Dynamics]. **resultan tones,** secondary sounds audible when tw differently pitched tones are sounded together an sustained.

resulting, *a.* re-*zul*-ting, following as a consequence.
resultless, *a.* re-*zult*-less, without result.
resumable, *a.* re-*zew*-ma-bl, that may be resumed.
resume, *v.t.* re-*zewm*, to take back; to take again what has been given; to begin again. (Fr. *résumer.*)
resumé, *n.* *rez*-oo-may, a summing up; a condensed statement. (Fr.)
resummon, *v.t.* ree-*sum*-on, to summon or call again.
resumption, *n.* re-*zump*-shon, the act of resuming. (L. *resumptus*, taken up anew.)
resumptive, *a.* re-*zump*-tiv, taking back or again.
resupinate, *a.* re-*sew*-pe-nat, inverted; as though upside down [Bot.].
resupination, *n.* re-sew-pe-*nay*-shon, a twisting to an apparently upside down position [Bot.].
resupine, *a.* re-sew-*pine*, lying on the back; supine. (L. *resupinus.*)
resurface, *v.t.* ree-*sur*-face, to provide with a new surface: *v.i.* to come to the surface again.
resurge, *v.i.* re-*surj*, to rise again; to be resurrected.
resurgence, *n.* re-*sur*-jence, a return to life or activity; renascence.
resurgent, *a.* re-*sur*-jent, rising again, esp. from death: *n.* one risen from the dead. (L. *resurgens*, rising.)
resurrect, *v.t.* rez-er-*rekt*, to restore to life; to raise again from the dead; to reanimate.
resurrection, *n.* rez-er-*rek*-shon, a rising again, esp. (*cap.*) the rising of Christ from the dead; the risen life; a return to animation; exhumation. **resurrection man,** a resurrectionist. (O.Fr.)
resurrectional, *a.* rez-er-*rek*-shon-al, pertaining to resurrection.
resurrectionist, *n.* rez-er-*rek*-shon-ist, one who stealthily exhumes dead bodies for dissection; a body-snatcher.
resurvey, *n.* ree-*ser*-vay, a second survey: *v.t.* ree-ser-*vay*, to review; to survey again.
resuscitate, *v.t.* re-*sus*-e-tate, to revivify; to revive; to recover from apparent death: *v.i.* to revive. (L. *resuscitatus*, revived.)
resuscitation, *n.* re-sus-e-*tay*-shon, act of reviving from a state of apparent death; the state of being resuscitated.
resuscitative, *a.* re-*sus*-e-ta-tiv, revivifying; raising from apparent death.
resuscitator, *n.* re-*sus*-e-tay-tor, one who resuscitates.
ret, *v.t.* ret, to destroy cohesion among the fibres of flax by steeping it. (Origin uncertain.)
retable, *n.* re-*tay*-bl, a ledge above the back of an altar on which candelabra and other objects may be set; a carving or decorative panel forming the back piece of an altar. (Fr.)
retail, *v.t.* re-*tale*, to sell in small quantities; to tell in detail, esp. to many; to recount. (O.Fr., literally, a paring.)
retail, *a.* *ree*-tale, pertaining to dealing in small quantities: *n.* the sale of commodities in small quantities.
retailer, *n.* re-*tale*-er, one who retails; one who sells goods in small quantities or by retail.
retailment, *n.* re-*tale*-ment, act of retailing.
retain, *v.t.* re-*tane*, to hold or keep in possession; to detain; to keep back; to keep in pay; to engage by prepayment. (Fr. *retenir.*)
retainable, *a.* re-*tane*-a-bl, that may be retained.
retainer, *n.* re-*tane*-er, one who or that which retains; an attendant; a dependant; a retaining fee (esp. among lawyers); retention by legal right.
retaining, *a.* re-*tane*-ing, keeping in possession; engaging by a fee. **retaining fee,** a fee paid in advance to engage a barrister; a fee paid periodically to an adviser. **retaining wall,** a wall to prevent a bank of earth from slipping.
retake, *v.t.* ree-*take*, to take again; to recapture.
retaliate, *v.t.* re-*tal*-e-ate, to return like for like; to repay (esp. an injury) in kind. (L. *retaliatus*, requited.)
retaliation, *n.* re-tal-e-*ay*-shon, the return of like for like; requital, esp. of evil.
retaliative, *a.* re-*tal*-e-a-tiv, retaliatory.
retaliator, *n.* re-*tal*-e-ay-tor, one who retaliates.
retaliatory, *a.* re-*tal*-e-a-to-re, returning like for like.
retard, *n.* re-*tard*, retardation; delay: *v.t.* to diminish the velocity of; to render more late; to hinder. (Fr. *retarder.*)
retardation, *n.* ree-tar-*day*-shon, the act of retarding; an instance of this; hindrance; delay; rate of loss of velocity [Dynamics].
retardative, *a.* re-*tar*-da-tiv, tending to retard.
retardatory, *a.* re-*tar*-da-to-re, having a retarding effect; retardative.
retarder, *n.* re-*tar*-der, one who or that which retards or delays.
retardment, *n.* re-*tard*-ment, the act of checking or delaying; retardation.
retch, *v.i.* retch *or* reech, to make an effort to vomit; to strain, as in vomiting. (A.S. *hræcan.*)
retching, *n.* *retch*- or *reech*-ing, an unsuccessful attempt to vomit.
rete, *n.* *ree*-te, a plexus of blood-vessels or nerves; a part resembling network [Anat.]. (L. *rete*, a net.)
retell, *v.t.* ree-*tel*, to tell over again or in another form. *p.* and *pp.* **retold.**
retent, *n.* re-*tent*, that which is retained.
retention, *n.* re-*ten*-shon, the act of retaining; the power of retaining, esp. ideas in the mind; a keeping possession or control of; restraint; a stoppage of normal evacuation [Med.]. (L. *retentus*, held back.)
retentive, *a.* re-*ten*-tiv, having the power to retain; having a good memory.
retentively, *ad.* with retentiveness.
retentiveness, *n.* the quality of being retentive.
retentivity, *n.* ree-ten-*tiv*-e-te, the power of retaining; the power of resisting magnetization or demagnetization.
retentor, *n.* re-*ten*-tor, a retaining muscle [Anat.].
retexture, *n.* ree-*teks*-tewr, a second weaving.
retial, *a.* *ree*-te-al, of the nature of a rete [Anat.].
retiary, *a.* *ree*-she-a-re, net-like; pertaining to or using nets: *n.* a gladiator armed with net and trident; any net-weaving spider. (L. *retiarius*, relating to a net.)
reticence, *n.* *ret*-e-sence, reserve in speech, esp. about one's own affairs.
reticency, *n.* *ret*-e-sen-se, reticence.
reticent, *a.* *ret*-e-sent, reserved in speech; taciturn. (L. *reticens*, being silent.)
reticle, *n.* *ret*-e-kl, a graticule for the eyepiece of a telescope; a reticule.
reticular, *a.* re-*tik*-yew-lar, having the form of network; formed with interstices.
reticularly, *ad.* in a reticular manner.
reticulate, *a.* re-*tik*-yew-lat, reticulated; formed of or resembling network: *v.t.* to mark with intersecting lines; to arrange in or divide into a network. **reticulated work,** a species of masonry formed of small square stones or bricks placed lozenge-wise. (L. *reticulatus.*)
reticulately, *ad.* re-*tik*-yew-lat-le, in a reticulate form or manner.
reticulation, *n.* re-tik-yew-*lay*-shon, the state of being reticulated; network.
reticule, *n.* *ret*-e-kewl, a little hand-bag, originally of network; a ladies' work-bag; a graticule, or contrivance of very fine network dividing the field of view in telescopes to measure small distances. (Fr. *réticule.*)
reticulose, *a.* re-*tik*-yew-lohs, resembling or of the nature of network.
reticulum, *n.* re-*tik*-yew-lum, a network or net-like structure; the second stomach of ruminants.
retiform, *a.* *ret*-e-form, composed of intersecting lines; reticulate; resembling network.
retina, *n.* *ret*-e-na, a retiform expansion of the optic nerve by which the impressions that give rise to vision are received. (L.)
retinacular, *a.* ret-e-*nak*-yew-lar, pertaining to or of the nature of a retinaculum.
retinaculum, *n.* ret-e-*nak*-yew-lum, a restraining or connecting band or gland [Zool. and Bot.]. (L.)
retinal, *a.* *ret*-e-nal, pertaining to the retina.
retinalite, *n.* re-*tin*-a-lite, a massive variety of serpentine. (Gr. *retine*, resin, *lithos*, a stone.)
retinerved, *a.* *ret*-e-nervd, retiform; cross-veined [Bot.].
retinite, *n.* *ret*-e-nite, pitchstone, a mineral resin.
retinitis, *n.* ret-e-*ny*-tis, inflammation of the retina.
retinoid, *a.* *ret*-e-noyd, resin-like. (Gr. *retine*, resin, *eidos*, like.)
retinol, *n.* *ret*-e-nol, an oily hydrocarbon obtained from certain resins, used as a lubricant and solvent and as an antiseptic.
retinoscopy, *n.* *ret*-e-*nos*-ko-pe, a method of deter-

mining the refraction of the eye by use of the ophthalmoscope. (L. *retina*, and Gr. *skopeo*, view.)
retinue, *n.* *ret*-e-new, the staff or attendants of a distinguished personage; suite. (O.Fr. *retenue.*)
retiracy, *n.* re-*tyr*-ra-se, retirement; retirement from business; a fortune sufficient to retire on.
retiral, *n.* re-*tyr*-ral, the act of retiring or retreating: the withdrawing of a bill or note from circulation.
retire, *v.i.* re-*tire*, to go from company or from a public place into privacy; to withdraw; to break up; to retreat; to recede: *v.t.* to cause to withdraw or resign; to take up and pay, as a bill, when due. (Fr. *retirer*).
retired, *a.* re-*tyrd*, secluded from society; private; gone into retirement. **retired list,** a list of officers who have retired from service; hence, a roll of any who have passed into retirement.
retiredness, *n.* re-*tyrd*-ness, the state or quality of being retired; reserve.
retirement, *n.* re-*tyr*-ment, the act of retiring; the withdrawing from society or public life; the state of being retired; retired abode; privacy.
retiring, *a.* re-*tyr*-ring, reserved; not forward or obtrusive.
retold, *ree*-tohld, *p.* and *pp.* of *retell.*
retort, *n.* re-*tort*, a ready reply: *v.t.* to throw back; to return, as an argument or a charge: *v.i.* to make a severe reply. (O.Fr.)
retort, *n.* re-*tort*, a bulbous, long-necked vessel in which distillation is effected; a large similarly shaped receptacle of cast iron or fireclay for the manufacture of coal-gas: *v.t.* to treat by heating in a retort.
retorter, *n.* re-*tort*-er, one who retorts.
retortion, *n.* re-*tor*-shon, the act of retorting; a turning or twisting back; reflection; retaliation [International law]. (Late L.)
retoss, *v.t.* ree-*toss*, to toss or throw back again.
retouch, *n.* ree-*tuch*, the act of retouching: *v.t.* to touch again; to improve by new touches, as a picture; to revise. (Fr. *retoucher.*)
retrace, *v.t.* re-*trace*, to trace back; to renew the outline of, as a drawing; to return by the same way.
retraceable, *a.* re-*trace*-a-bl, capable of being retraced.
retract, *v.t.* re-*trakt*, to draw back; to take back; to recall; to recant: *v.i.* to withdraw. (L. *retractus*, drawn back.)
retractability, *n.* re-trak-ta-*bil*-e-te, the capability of being retracted.
retractable, *a.* re-*trak*-ta-bl, that may be retracted.
retractation, *n.* ree-trak-*tay*-shon, the act of retracting; recantation. (O.Fr.)
retractile, *a.* re-*trak*-tile, admitting of retraction; retractable.
retractility, *n.* ree-trak-*til*-e-te, the fact or condition of being retractile.
retraction, *n.* re-*trak*-shon, act of drawing back; act of retracting; recantation; disavowal.
retractive, *a.* re-*trak*-tiv, serving to, or inclined to, retract.
retractor, *n.* re-*trak*-tor, a retractive muscle; an instrument or appliance for drawing back a part during amputation, etc. [Surg.]; a device for extracting spent cartridges from a gun. (L. *retractus.*)
retrad, *ad.* *ret*-rad, backward [Anat.]. (L. *retro*, behind.)
retrahent, *a.* *ree*-tra-hent, retractive, esp. [Anat.] of muscles. (L. *retrahens*, drawing back.)
retral, *a.* *ret*-ral, located at the rear; retrorse; posterior. (L. *retro.*)
retransfer, *v.t.* ree-trans-*fer*, to transfer again: *n.* ree-*trans*-fer, the act of retransferring.
retransform, *v.t.* ree-trans-*form*, to transform anew.
retranslate, *v.t.* ree-trans-*late*, to translate anew; to translate back into the original language.
retransmission, *n.* ree-trans-*mish*-on, transmission anew.
retraverse, *v.t.* ree-*trav*-ers, to traverse again; to go over repeatedly.
retraxit, *n.* re-*trak*-sit, the withdrawing of a suit and consequent loss of the action [Obsolete law term]. (L., he has withdrawn.)
retread, *v.t.* ree-*tred*, to retrace; to tread a second time; to furnish (a tire) with a new tread.
retreat, *n.* re-*treet*, the act of retiring; retirement or seclusion; place of retirement, esp. [Eccles.] for meditation and prayer; place of safety or security; a lair; the retiring of an army from before an enemy or an advanced position; a signal for retiring to quarters or from an engagement: *v.i* to retire from any position or place; to withdraw to seclusion or safety; to retire into a retreat; to retire from an enemy: *v.i.* to cause to retire (O.Fr. *retrete.*)
retree, *n.* re-*tree*, paper damaged or left imperfect in course of manufacture. (Fr. *retrait*, withdrawal.)
retrench, *v.t.* re-*trench*, to cut off; to pare away; to lessen; to curtail; to furnish with a retrenchment [Mil.]: *v.i.* to cut down expenses. (Fr. *retrancher.*)
retrenchment, *n.* re-*trench*-ment, the act of lopping off or removing what is superfluous; curtailment; reduction of expenditure; a work constructed within another to prolong the defence [Mil.].
retrial, *n.* ree-*try*-al, a fresh trial.
retribute, *v.t.* re-*trib*-yewt, to make return for; to retaliate; to compensate.
retribution, *n.* ret-re-*bew*-shon, suitable requital, esp. for evil; recompense; punishment; the distribution of rewards and punishments at the judgment day. (O.Fr.)
retributive, *a.* re-*trib*-yew-tiv, retributory.
retributor, *n.* re-*trib*-yew-tor, one who makes retribution.
retributory, *a.* re-*trib*-yew-to-re, rewarding for good deeds and punishing for offences; pertaining to retribution.
retrievable, *a.* re-*tree*-va-bl, that may be retrieved or recovered.
retrievably, *ad.* in a retrievable manner.
retrieval, *n.* re-*tree*-val, the act of retrieving.
retrieve, *v.t.* re-*treev*, to restore; to recover; to repair; to regain. (O.Fr. *retrover.*)
retrievement, *n.* re-*treev*-ment, retrieval.
retriever, *n.* re-*tree*-ver, a dog trained to fetch game that has been shot; the breed of dog, either black or golden and smooth- or curly-coated, probably in part derived from the Labrador, commonly used for this purpose.
retrim, *v.t.* ree-*trim*, to trim anew.
retro-, a Latin prefix, signifying back or backward.
retroact, *v.i.* ree-tro-*akt*, to act in return or opposition; to react.
retroaction, *n.* ree-tro-*ak*-shon, action returned or action backwards; operation on something past or preceding; reaction [Wire.].
retroactive, *a.* ree-tro-*ak*-tiv, operating backwards; having had effect in the past; affecting what is past; retrospective.
retroactively, *ad.* in a retroactive manner.
retroactivity, *n.* ree-tro-ak-*tiv*-e-te, the quality or condition of being retroactive.
retrobulbar, *a.* ret-ro-*bul*-bar, situated at the rear of the eyeball [Anat.].
retrocede, *v.t.* *ret*-ro-seed, to cede or grant back: *v.i.* to go back. (L. *retro-*, and *cedo*, yield, go.)
retrocedence, *n.* ret-ro-*see*-dence, retrocession; retrogression.
retrocedent, *a.* ret-ro-*see*-dent, disposed to retrocede; moving about from the surface to the interior of the body [Med.].
retrocession, *n.* ret-ro-*sesh*-on, a ceding or granting back; the act of giving back. (Fr. *retrocession.*)
retrocessive, *a.* ret-ro-*ses*-iv, characterized by retrocession; retrograde.
retrochoir, *n.* *ree*-tro-kwire, a chapel or other space behind the high altar. (L. *retro-*, and *choir.*)
retrocollic, *a.* ret-ro-*kol*-ik, pertaining to the muscles at the back of the neck. (L. *retro-*, and *collum*, neck.)
retrodate, *v.t.* *ret*-ro-date, to antedate.
retroduction, *n.* ret-ro-*duk*-shon, a bringing back.
retroflex, *a.* *ret*-ro-fleks, bent or turned sharply backwards [Bot.]. (L. *retro-*, and *flexus*, bent.)
retroflexion, *n.* *ree*-tro-*flek*-shon, the act of bending back; the state of being bent back.
retrofract, *a.* *ret*-ro-frakt, retrofracted.
retrofracted, *a.* *ret*-ro-frak-ted, bent back, so as to appear broken [Bot.]. (L. *retro-*, and *fractus*, broken.)
retrogradation, *n.* ret-ro-gra-*day*-shon, retrogression; decline in excellence.
retrograde, *a.* *ret*-ro-grade, going or moving backward; apparently moving backwards, and contrary to the succession of the signs [Astron.]: declining

from a better to a worse state; deteriorating: *v.i.* to go or move backward: *v.t.* to cause to go backward. (L. *retro-*, and *gradi*, to step.)
retrogress, *v.i.* ret-ro-*gres*, to retrograde; to degenerate.
retrogression, *n.* ret-ro-*gresh*-on, the act of going backward; the backward or apparent motion backward in the zodiac of a heavenly body [Astron.]. (L. *retrogressus*, stepped backwards.)
retrogressive, *a.* ret-ro-*gres*-iv, going or moving backward; declining in excellence: *n.* one inclined to retrogress; one in favour of retrogression.
retrogressively, *ad.* in a retrogressive manner.
retrogressiveness, *n.* the state of being retrogressive.
retroject, *v.t.* *ree*-tro-jekt, to throw backwards.
retromingent, *a.* ret-ro-*min*-jent, discharging the urine backwards: *n.* an animal that discharges its urine backwards. (L. *retro-*, and *mingo*, make water.)
retroposition, *n.* ret-ro-po-*zish*-on, displacement rearwards.
retropulsion, *n.* ret-ro-*pul*-shon, the tendency shown in certain locomotory disorders to walk backwards [Path.].
retropulsive, *a.* ret-ro-*pul*-siv, repelling.
retrorse, *a.* re-*trorse*, turned or bent backwards or downwards. (L. *retrorsus*, contracted from *retroversus.*)
retrorsely, *ad.* in a backward direction.
retrorsion, *n.* re-*tror*-shon, direction backwards or downwards.
retroserrate, *a.* ret-ro-*se*-rate, having serrations or barbs pointing towards the base [Bot.].
retrospect, *n.* *ret*-ro-spekt, a looking back on things past; review. (L. *retrospectus*, looked back.)
retrospection, *n.* ret-ro-*spek*-shon, the act, faculty, or mood of looking back on things past.
retrospective, *a.* ret-ro-*spek*-tiv, looking back on past events; affecting things past; tending to look back.
retrospectively, *ad.* by way of retrospection.
retrospectiveness, *n.* the quality of being retrospective.
retroussage, *n.* re-*troo*-sahzh, a method by which a soft tone can be given to etchings through wiping off the ink from portions of the plates. (Fr.)
retroussé, *a.* re-*troo*-say, upturned, as a nose. (Fr.)
retrovaccination, *n.* *ret*-ro-*vak*-se-*nay*-shon, the vaccination of a cow with human virus.
retrovaccine, *n.* *ret*-ro-*vak*-seen, the humanized lymph yielded by a cow subjected to retrovaccination.
retroversion, *n.* ree-tro-*ver*-shon, a turning or falling backward; the state of being turned backward.
retrovert, *v.t.* *ree*-tro-vert, to turn back; to revert: *n.* a convert who has relapsed to his former faith. (L. *retro-*, and *verto*, turn.)
retrovision, *n.* ret-ro-*vizh*-on, the alleged power of second sight in relation to past events (opposed to *prevision*).
retry, *v.t.* ree-*try*, to try a second time.
rettery, *n.* *ret*-er-re, a place where retting is done.
retting, *n.* *ret*-ing, the steeping of flax to separate the fibre. (*ret.*)
retund, *v.t.* re-*tund*, to repress; to refute; to blunt; to dull. (L. *re-*, and *tundo*, beat.)
return, *n.* re-*turn*, the act of going back; the act of giving back; that which is given back; periodical coming back; periodical renewal; an official report; the act of electing or state of being elected; profit of business; repayment; restitution; a return match, or ticket; the rendering back or delivery of a writ, precept, or execution [Law]; *v.i.* to come back or go back to the same place or state; to answer; to revert; to recur: *v.t.* to bring or send back; to repay; to give back in requital or in reply; to relate; to retort; to report officially; to transmit; to elect; to lead from the same suit as one's partner [Card playing]. **return match,** a second match played between the same clubs or players. **return ticket,** a ticket available for a journey there and back; the return half of this. **to return thanks,** to thank; to reply to a toast; to say grace. (Fr. *retourner.*)
re-turn, *v.t.* and *v.i.* re-*turn*, to turn again.
returnable, *a.* re-*turn*-a-bl, required to be returned, or restored; that is to be returned or rendered [Law].
return-day, *n.* the day when the defendant is to appear in court, and the sheriff has to make his return [Law].
returner, *n.* re-*turn*-er, one who returns; one who repays or remits money.
returning-officer, *n.* the presiding official at a election.
returnless, *a.* re-*turn*-less, admitting no return.
retuse, *a.* re-*tewce*, blunt; having a round end the centre of which is depressed [Bot. and Zool.].
reunification, *n.* *ree*-yew-ne-fe-*kay*-shon, the act of reunifying; state of reunion.
reunify, *v.t.* re-*yew*-ne-fy, to unify again.
reunion, *n.* re-*yew*-nyon, union formed anew after separation; a meeting or an assembly of friends or associates; the joining of severed parts [Surg.]. (O.Fr.)
reunite, *v.t.* ree-yew-*nite*, to join after a separation; to reconcile after variance: *v.i.* to be or become united again.
re-urge, *v.t.* ree-*urj*, to urge again.
reus, *n.* *ree*-us, a defendant in an action at civil law; a debtor. (L.)
re-use, *v.t.* ree-*yewz*, to use again.
reussite, *n.* *roy*-site, mirabilite, an impure native Glauber salt. (A. E. von *Reuss*, *d.* 1873, Austrian mineralogist.)
rev, *n.* rev, a revolution [Mech., Coll.]: *v.t.* to make an internal combustion engine go quickly: *v.i.* to make revolutions [Mech.].
revaccinate, *v.t.* ree-*vak*-se-nate, to vaccinate again.
revalenta, *n.* rev-a-*len*-ta, a preparation of lentil meal for the use of invalids.
revalorization, *n.* *ree*-val-o-ry-*zay*-shon, the restoration or the process of restoring the value of a national currency.
revaluation, *n.* *ree*-val-yew-*ay*-shon, a further valuation; the act of revaluing.
revalue, *v.t.* ree-*val*-yew, to value anew.
revamp, *v.t.* *ree*-vamp, to patch up again.
reveal, *v.t.* re-*veel*, to make known something before unknown or kept secret; to make known supernaturally; to disclose; to divulge. **revealed religion,** a religion held by its adherents to have been communicated directly by God to man, esp. Christianity through the medium of the Bible. (Fr. *révéler*, from L. *revelare*, to uncover.)
reveal, *n.* re-*veel*, the vertical side of an opening for a window or doorway. (O.Fr. *revaler*, from *re-* and *avaler*, to descend.)
revealable, *a.* re-*veel*-a-bl, that can be revealed.
revealableness, *n.* quality of being revealable.
revealer, *n.* re-*veel*-er, one who reveals.
revealment, *n.* re-*veel*-ment, act of revealing.
reveille, *n.* re-*vel*-e *or* re-*val*-e, the call (by bugle, trumpet, or drum) that it is time for the troops to rise and for the sentries to cease challenging [Mil.]. (Fr. *réveil.*)
revel, *n.* *rev*-el, a merrymaking; a carousal: *v.i.* to feast with loose and clamorous merriment; to carouse; to make merry. **to revel in,** to enjoy immensely. (O.Fr.)
revelation, *n.* rev-e-*lay*-shon, the act of revealing; that which is revealed; that which is divinely revealed to man; (*cap.*) the Apocalypse. (O.Fr.)
revelational, *a.* rev-e-*lay*-shon-al, pertaining to revelation.
revelative, *a.* rev-e-*lay*-tiv, conveying revelation; revealing.
revelatory, *a.* *rev*-el-a-to-re, pertaining to or of the nature of revelation.
revellent, *a.* re-*vel*-ent, revulsive: *n.* a counter-irritant or other revulsive agent [Med.].
reveller, *n.* *rev*-el-er, one who indulges in revelry.
revelment, *n.* *rev*-el-ment, act of revelling; revelry.
revel-rout, *n.* tumultuous festivity; an unruly or unlawful assembly.
revelry, *n.* *rev*-el-re, noisy festivity; merrymaking; carousal.
revenant, *n.* (App.) one who comes back, esp. after long absence, or one who returns from the dead; a ghost. (Fr.)
revendicate, *v.t.* re-*ven*-de-kate, to reclaim or recover by revendication. (Fr., from late L. *revindicatus.*)
revendication, *n.* re-*ven*-de-*kay*-shon, a formal claim for the restoration of property or territory that has been illegally seized [Law].

revenge, *n.* re-*venj*, the act of revenging; retaliation; a malicious or spiteful infliction of pain or injury in return for injury; the urge to inflict revenge: *v.t.* to inflict pain or injury in return for injury; to inflict injury from feelings of malice for a wrong; to retaliate. (O.Fr. *revengier.*)
revengeful, *a.* re-*venj*-ful, full of desire to inflict pain for injury received; vindictive.
revengefully, *ad.* in a revengeful manner.
revengefulness, *n.* quality of being revengeful.
revengement, *n.* re-*venj*-ment, revenge.
revenger, *n.* re-*venj*-er, one who revenges.
revengingly, *ad.* re-*venj*-ing-le, with revenge.
revenue, *n.* *rev*-e-new, income; the general income of the state; the state department charged with the collection of this. **Inland Revenue,** *see* **inland. revenue cutter,** a small vessel employed in the service of the Customs. **revenue officer,** an officer of the Customs or Excise. **revenue stamp,** a stamp indicating that a government due or fee has been paid. (O.Fr. *revenu.*)
reverberant, *a.* re-*ver*-ber-rant, tending to reverberate; reverberating; resounding.
reverberate, *v.t.* re-*ver*-ber-rate, to send back, as sound; to echo; to send, or strike back, or reflect, as light, heat, or flame: *v.i.* to be driven back, as light or sound; to resound; to recoil. (L. *reverberatus,* beaten back.)
reverberation, *n.* re-ver-ber-*ray*-shon, the act of reverberating, as light, heat, or sound; the sound, etc., echoed back.
reverberative, *a.* re-*ver*-ber-ra-tiv, reverberating.
reverberatory, *a.* re-*ver*-ber-ra-to-re, reverberating: *n.* a furnace with a low arched roof that reflects the flame downwards.
revere, *v.t.* re-*veer,* to regard with veneration or great respect; to reverence. (O.Fr. *reverer.*)
revere, *n.* re-*veer,* a revers.
reverence, *n.* *rev*-er-rence, fear mingled with respect and esteem; veneration; an act of respect or obeisance; a title of the clergy: *v.t.* to regard with reverence; to pay reverence to.
reverencer, *n.* *rev*-er-ren-ser, one who reverences.
reverend, *a.* *rev*-er-rend, worthy of or entitled to reverence or respect; (*cap.*) a title of respect given to the clergy generally—**Most Reverend** to an archbishop, **Right Reverend** to a bishop, **Very Reverend** to a dean. (L. *reverendus,* to be revered.)
reverent, *a.* *rev*-er-rent, expressing reverence or submission; submissive.
reverential, *a.* rev-er-*ren*-shal, proceeding from reverence, or expressing it.
reverentially, *ad.* in a reverential manner.
reverently, *ad.* in a reverent manner.
reverer, *n.* re-*veer*-rer, one who reveres or venerates.
reverie, *n.* *rev*-er-re, a state of waking dreaminess; a loose irregular train of thoughts occurring in musing or meditation; an extravagant conceit of the fancy. (Fr.)
revers, *n.* re-*vare,* a lapel or similar part of a garment that turns back to show the inner surface. (Fr.)
reversal, *n.* re-*ver*-sal, the act of reversing; a change or overthrowing. (Fr.)
reverse, *n.* re-*verse,* change or turn of affairs for the better or for the worse; a misfortune; a reversing gear; the opposite; the back surface, esp. of a coin; a thing reversed; a partial defeat: *a.* turned backward; inverted; having an opposite direction: *v.t.* to turn in a contrary direction; to turn upside down; to subvert; to revoke; to make void, as a sentence. (O.Fr. *revers.*)
reversed, *pp.* re-*verst,* turned side for side; changed to the contrary; overthrown or annulled; *a.* resupinate [Bot.]; with volutions like a left-handed screw [Malac.].
reversedly, *ad.* re-*ver*-sed-le, in a reversed manner.
reversely, *ad.* in a reverse manner.
reverser, *n.* re-*ver*-ser, one who or that which reverses; a device for reversing current [Elect.].
reversi, *n.* re-*ver*-se, a parlour game played with a chequered board and circular counters of a different colour on their upper and under surfaces. (Fr.)
reversibility, *n.* re-*ver*-se-*bil*-e-te, the capacity of being reversed.
reversible, *a.* re-*ver*-se-bl, that can be reversed.
reversing-gear, *n.* the gear by which the direction of an engine's motion is reversed.
reversion, *n.* re-*ver*-shon, a reverting to a former condition, etc.; atavism, tendency towards the reproduction of remote ancestral characters [Zool.]; the right of succession to a present holder; the right of property which remains after some particular estate has ceased.
reversionary, *a.* re-*ver*-shon-a-re, pertaining to or involving reversion; connected with or of the nature of a reversion [Law].
reversioner, *n.* re-*ver*-shon-er, one having or entitled to a reversion [Law].
revert, *v.t.* re-*vert,* to turn back; to reverse: *v.i.* to return; to fall back; to recur; to return to the former proprietor by reversion [Law]: *n.* one who or that which reverts; one who returns to a faith formerly held, a retrovert. (O.Fr. *revertir.*)
revertible, *a.* re-*ver*-te-bl, that may revert or return.
revertive, *a.* re-*ver*-tiv, changing back; reverting.
revest, *v.t.* ree-*vest,* to clothe again; to reinvest: *v.i.* to take effect again; to return to a former owner. (O.Fr. *revestir.*)
revestiary, *n.* re-*ves*-te-a-re, the vestry of a church.
revet, *v.t.* re-*vet,* to furnish with a revetment.
revetment, *n.* re-*vet*-ment, a strong wall on the outside of a rampart; a retaining wall; a facing of steel, stone, or other material [Fort.]. (Fr.)
revictual, *v.t.* ree-*vit*-tl, to provision again.
review, *n.* re-*vew,* a second examination; revision, with a view to improvement; a formal or official inspection of troops, ships of war, etc. [Mil.]; a periodical publication containing essays, etc., on literature and other subjects; a critical examination; a retrospect: *v.t.* to look back on; to see again; to view and examine again; to examine critically; to revise; to inspect; to write a press notice of. (L. *re-*, and *view.*)
reviewable, *a.* re-*vew*-a-bl, that may be reviewed.
reviewal, *n.* re-*vew*-al, the act of reviewing; review.
reviewer, *n.* re-*vew*-er, one who reviews; the writer of a review.
revigorate, *v.t.* re-*vig*-o-rate, to give new vigour to. (L. *revigoratus.*)
revile, *v.t.* re-*vile,* to treat with opprobrium; to vilify; to reproach. (O.Fr. *reviler.*)
revilement, *n.* re-*vile*-ment, the act of reviling; contemptuous language; reproach.
reviler, *n.* re-*vile*-er, one who reviles another.
revilingly, *ad.* re-*vile*-ing-le, with reviling.
revindicate, *v.t.* ree-*vin*-de-kate, to vindicate again; to revendicate. (Late L. *revindicatus.*)
revisal, *n.* re-*vy*-zal, revision.
revise, *n.* re-*vize,* a revision; that which has been revised; a proof-sheet taken after the first correction: *v.t.* to correct; to look over for correction. **Revised Version,** the revision of the English Authorized Version of the Bible prepared by authority and published 1881–85. **revising barrister,** a barrister appointed to revise the list of parliamentary voters in a constituency. (O.Fr. *reviser.*)
reviser, *n.* re-*vy*-zer, one who revises for correction.
revision, *n.* re-*vizh*-on, the act of correcting or of examining for correction; that which is revised. (O.Fr.)
revisional, *a.* re-*vizh*-on-al, pertaining to revision.
revisionary, *a.* re-*vizh*-on-a-re, revisional.
revisionism, *n.* re-*vizh*-on-izm, advocacy of revision.
revisionist, *n.* re-*vizh*-on-ist, a supporter of revision.
revisit, *v.t.* ree-*viz*-it, to visit again.
revisitation, *n.* ree-viz-e-*tay*-shon, act of revisiting.
revisory, *a.* re-*vy*-zo-re, revising; having power to revise.
revitalize, *v.t.* ree-*vy*-ta-lize, to bring back vitality to.
revivable, *a.* re-*vy*-va-bl, that may be revived.
revival, *n.* re-*vy*-val, return or recovery to life; returning into fashion; recall or return to activity from a state of languor, neglect, etc.; a religious awakening. **the Revival of Learning,** the Renaissance.
revivalism, *n.* re-*vy*-va-lizm, the methods or characteristic quality of religious revivals.
revivalist, *n.* re-*vy*-va-list, one who promotes or is concerned in religious revivals: *a.* revivalistic.
revivalistic, *a.* re-*vy*-va-*lis*-tik, pertaining to or characteristic of religious revivals.
revive, *v.i.* re-*vive,* to recover life; to recover new life; to recover from a state of neglect or depression; to return to its natural state, as a metal

[Chem.]: *v.t.* to bring to life again; to raise from languor, depression, or discouragement; to rouse; to renew; to refresh; to recall; to resuscitate; to quicken; to restore to its natural or metallic state [Chem.]. (Fr. *revivre.*)
reviver, *n.* re-*vy*-ver, one who or that which revives.
revivification, *n.* ree-viv-e-fe-*kay*-shon, restoration of life. (Late L. *revivificatio.*)
revivify, *v.t.* ree-*viv*-e-fy, to recall to life; to re-animate; to give new life or vigour to.
revivingly, *ad.* re-*vy*-ving-le, in a reviving manner.
reviviscence, *n.* rev-e-*vis*-ence, renewal of life; return to animation. (L. *revivescens.*)
reviviscent, *a.* rev-e-*vis*-ent, restoring to life; reviving. (L. *reviviscens.*)
revivor, *n.* re-*vy*-vor, the reviving of a suit which has been abated by death [Law].
revocable, *a.* re-*voh*-ka-bl *or* *rev*-o-ka-bl, that may be revoked. (O.Fr.)
revocableness, *n.* the quality of being revocable.
revocably, *ad.* *rev*-o-ka-ble, in a revocable manner.
revocation, *n.* rev-o-*kay*-shon, the act of revoking; repeal; reversal of a decree, edict, or deed. (O.Fr.)
revocatory, *a.* *rev*-o-ka-to-re, revoking; recalling.
revokable, *a.* re-*voh*-ka-bl, revocable.
revoke, *n.* re-*voke*, act of revoking at cards: *v.t.* to recall; to repeal; to declare void: *v.i.* to fail to follow suit when able to do so [Card playing]. (O.Fr. *revocquer.*)
revokement, *n.* re-*voke*-ment, revocation; reversal.
revolt, *n.* re-*vohlt* *or* re-*volt*, desertion; renunciation of allegiance; rebellion; insurrection: *v.i.* to renounce allegiance; to feel disgust: *v.t.* to shock; to do violence to. (Fr. *revolte.*)
revolter, *n.* re-*vohl*-ter, one who renounces allegiance.
revolting, *a.* re-*vohl*-ting, doing violence to the feelings; exciting abhorrence; offensive; disgusting.
revoltingly, *ad.* offensively.
revolute, *a.* *rev*-o-loot, rolled or curled back from the edge [Bot. and Zool.]. (L. *revolutus.*)
revolute, *v.i.* *rev*-o-loot, to make or participate in a revolution [Coll.].
revolution, *n.* rev-o-*loo*-shon, rotation; period of rotation; circular motion of a body on its axis; the motion of a body round a centre; motion returning to the same point or state; continued course; marked regular return; space marked by some revolution; fundamental and (usually) violent change, esp. in the constitution of a government. **the Glorious Revolution,** the expulsion of the Stuarts from the English throne in 1688. (O.Fr.)
revolutionary, *a.* rev-o-*loo*-shon-a-re, pertaining to or tending to produce a revolution in government: *n.* a revolutionist; one who advocates revolution. **the Revolutionary War,** the War of American Independence, 1775–83.
revolutionism, *n.* rev-o-*loo*-shon-izm, revolutionary principles; the advocacy of these.
revolutionist, *n.* rev-o-*loo*-shon-ist, an abettor of a revolution.
revolutionize, *v.t.* rev-o-*loo*-shon-ize, to effect a thorough change in anything, esp. in the constitution or government of a country.
revolve, *v.i.* re-*volv*, to turn or roll round; to rotate; to move round a centre: *v.t.* to turn over and over in the mind; to consider attentively. (L. *revolvo*, roll.)
revolvency, *n.* re-*vol*-ven-se, state, act, or principle of revolving.
revolver, *n.* re-*vol*-ver, that which revolves, esp. a pistol which, by means of revolving barrels or a revolving breech, can be fired several times without reloading.
revue, *n.* re-*voo* *or* re-*vew*, a spectacular and usually topical musical variety entertainment. (Fr.)
revulsant, *n.* re-*vul*-sant, a revulsive; an agent drawing blood from a distant part of the body [Med.].
revulsion, *n.* re-*vul*-shon, a holding or drawing back; recoil; diversion of a disease, or of blood, from one part of the body to another, esp. by counter-irritation [Med.]. (O.Fr.)
revulsionary, *a.* re-*vul*-shon-a-re, pertaining to or of the nature of revulsion.
revulsive, *a.* re-*vul*-siv, causing or tending to cause revulsion: *n.* a counter-irritant or other agent for producing revulsion [Med.].

***reward,** *n.* re-*wawrd*, that which is given or offered in return for good or evil done or some service rendered; recompense; a sum offered for the return of lost property, capture of a fugitive, etc.: *v.t.* to give a reward; to recompense: to distinguish for merit. (O.Fr. *rewarder.*)
rewardable, *a.* re-*wawrd*-a-bl, worthy of reward.
rewardableness, *n.* the quality of being rewardable.
rewardably, *ad.* in a rewardable manner.
rewarder, *n.* re-*wawrd*-er, one who rewards.
rewardless, *a.* re-*wawrd*-less, having no reward.
rewire, *v.t.* ree-*wire*, to fit with new wires: *v.i.* to telegraph again.
reword, *v.t.* ree-*wurd*, to state anew in other words.
rewrite, *v.t.* ree-*rite*, to write over again.
rex, *n.* reks, a king. (L.)
rexine, *n.* *rek*-seen, proprietary name of an artificial leather used chiefly in upholstery and book-binding.
Rexist, *a.* *rek*-sist, designating the Belgian Fascist party of about 1935–40: *n.* a member of this party.
reynard, *n.* *ray*-nard, a fox. (O.Fr. *renard.*)
rhabarbarate, *n.* ra-*bahr*-ba-rate, a salt of rhabarbaric acid. (Late L. *rhabarbar*, rhubarb.)
rhabarbaric, *a.* rab-ar-*ba*-rik, pertaining to or derived from rhubarb. **rhabarbaric acid,** rhabarbarin.
rhabarbarin, *n.* re-*bahr*-ba-rin, a yellow crystalline compound obtained from rhubarb and other plants.
rhabdoidal, *a.* rab-*doy*-dal, like a rod. (Gr. *rhabdos*, a rod, *eidos*, like.)
rhabdology, *n.* rab-*dol*-o-je, the art of computing by means of Napier's rods; rhabdomancy. (Gr. *rhabdos*, and *logos*, science.)
rhabdomancy, *n.* *rab*-do-man-se, dowsing; the use of the divining-rod; water-divining. (Gr. *rhabdos*, and *manteia*, divination.)
rhabdophane, *n.* *rab*-do-fane, a massive hydrous phosphate of cerium, lanthanum, yttrium, etc.
Rhadamanthine, *a.* rad-a-*man*-thin, rigorous; inflexible. (*Rhadamanthus*, one of the three judges of the souls of the dead in the nether world.)
Rhætic, *n.* *ree*-tik, the uppermost group of the Triassic rocks, characteristic of the Rhætian Alps in Switzerland.
Rhæto-Romanic, *a.* *ree*-to-ro-*man*-ik, belonging to the group of Romance dialects spoken in S.E. Switzerland and the Tyrol: *n.* any of these dialects.
rhamphoid, *a.* *ram*-foyd, beak-shaped. (Gr. *ramphos*, beak.)
rhapontic, *n.* ra-*pon*-tik, a variety of rhubarb used in pharmacy. (Late L. *rha Ponticum*, Pontic rhubarb.)
rhapsode, *n.* *rap*-sode, an itinerant reciter of epic, and esp. Homeric, poems in ancient Greece.
rhapsodic, *a.* rap-*sod*-ik, relating to rhapsody.
rhapsodical, *a.* rap-*sod*-e-kal, pertaining to or of the nature of rhapsody; disconnected.
rhapsodist, *n.* *rap*-so-dist, one who recites or sings rhapsodies; a professional reciter of the verses of Homer and other poets; one who rhapsodizes.
rhapsodize, *v.i.* *rap*-so-dize, to utter rhapsodies; to speak or write in a confused, incoherent, and excited manner.
rhapsody, *n.* *rap*-so-de, recitation or chanting of poems, esp. from Homer; a rambling composition conceived in a confused and excited state of mind. (Gr. *rhapsodos*, from *rhaptein*, to stitch together).
rhatany, *n.* *rat*-a-ne, the astringent and tonic root of the Peruvian shrub, *Krameria triandra.*
rhea, *n.* *ree*-a, any of a genus of flightless birds including the South American ostriches; the nandu. (Gr. *Rhea*, the Mother of the Gods.)
rhea, *n.* *ree*-a, ramie or China grass, or its fibre. (Assamese, *riha.*)
rheic, *a.* *ree*-ik, pertaining to or obtained from rhubarb. (Fr. *rhéique*, as *rhubarb.*)
rhein, *n.* *ree*-in, rheic acid; rhabarbarin.
rhematic, *a.* re-*mat*-ik, pertaining to word formation; derived from a verb. (Gr. *rhema*, word.)
Rhemish, *a.* *reem*-ish, pertaining to Rheims. **Rhemish Testament,** the New Testament of the Douay Bible.
Rhenish, *a.* *ren*-ish, pertaining to the Rhine or the Rhineland: *n.* wine from the Rhineland or Rhine valley.
rhenium, *n.* *ree*-ne-um, a very hard rare metallic element, chemically resembling manganese, discovered in tantalite, 1925. (L. *Rhenus*, the Rhine.)

rheochord, *n.* *ree*-o-kord, a wire used to measure the resistance or diminish the strength of an electric current. (Gr.)
rheocrat, *n.* *ree*-o-krat, a form of motor speed controller. (Gr. *rheo*, to flow, *kratein*, to rule.)
rheology, *n.* ree-*ol*-o-je, the branch of dynamics treating of the flow of matter.
rheometer, *n.* re-*om*-e-ter, an instrument for measuring the strength of an electric current; a form of sphygmometer. (Gr. *rheo*, flow, *metron*, a measure.)
rheometry, *n.* re-*om*-e-tre, the art of using the rheometer.
rheomotor, *n.* re-o-*moh*-tor, former name of any apparatus by which electricity is originated.
rheophore, *n.* *ree*-o-for, a connecting electric wire; an electrode. (Gr. *rheo*, and *phero*, bear.)
rheoscope, *n.* *ree*-os-kope, a galvanoscope; an electroscope. (Gr. *rheo*, and *skopeo*, view.)
rheostat, *n.* *ree*-o-stat, an instrument for regulating current [Elect.]; a rheochord. (Gr. *rheo*, and *statos*, standing.)
rheotome, *n.* *ree*-o-tome, a device for breaking an electric current. (Gr. *rheo*, and *tome*, cutting.)
rheotrope, *n.* *ree*-o-trope, a commutator [Elect.]. (Gr. *rheo*, and *tropos*, turning.)
rhesus, *n.* *ree*-sus, the bandar, *Macacus rhesus*, a macaque of Bengal. (L.)
rhetor, *n.* *ree*-tor, a teacher of rhetoric, esp. in ancient Greece; an empty orator.
rhetoric, *n.* *ret*-o-rik, the art of persuasive or effective speech; the art of speaking with propriety, elegance, and force; florid oratory; pompous declamation. (O.Fr. *rhetorique*, from Gr.)
rhetorical, *a.* re-*to*-re-kal, pertaining to rhetoric; oratorical; declamatory.
rhetorically, *ad.* in a rhetorical manner.
rhetorician, *n.* ret-o-*rish*-an, one who teaches rhetoric; an expert in rhetoric or oratory; an empty or declamatory orator.
rhetorize, *v.i.* *ret*-o-rize, to play the orator; to write rhetorically.
rheum, *n.* room, a thin serious fluid secreted by the mucous glands; a discharge of this; catarrh. (O.Fr. *rheume*.)
Rheum, *n.* *ree*-um, a genus of plants including rhubarb. (Gr. *rheon*.)
rheumarthrosis, *n.* room-ar-*throh*-sis, rheumatism of the joints.
rheumatic, *a.* roo-*mat*-ik, pertaining to, due to, or suffering from, rheumatism: *n.* a person subject to or afflicted with rheumatism.
rheumatically, *ad.* in a rheumatic manner.
rheumaticky, *a.* roo-*mat*-e-ke, having rheumatism; resembling rheumatism [Coll.].
rheumatism, *n.* *roo*-ma-tizm, a constitutional disease marked by a painful affection of the muscles and joints. (L. *rheumatismus*, rheum.)
rheumatismal, *a.* roo-ma-*tiz*-mal, pertaining to or characterized by rheumatism.
rheumatiz, *n.* *roo*-mat-iz, rheumatism [Coll.].
rheumatoid, *a.* *roo*-ma-toyd, pertaining to or resembling rheumatism. **rheumatoid arthritis,** a painful disorder characterized by wasting of the joint-surfaces, thickening of the parts around the joint, and distortion due to muscular contraction.
rheumy, *a.* *roo*-me, full of rheum or watery matter; consisting of rheum; causing rheumatism.
rhinal, *a.* *ry*-nal, pertaining to the nose.
rhinalgia, *n.* ry-*nal*-je-a, neuralgia in the nose.
Rhinanthus, *n.* ry-*nan*-thus, a genus of plants, of which the yellow-rattle is the type.
rhine, *n.* ryne, a large ditch or runnel; an open drain. (A.S. *ryne*.)
rhinencephalic, *a.* *ry*-nen-se-*fal*-ik, pertaining to the olfactory part of the brain. (Gr. *rhis*, *rhinos*, nose, *engkephalos*, brain.)
rhinitis, *n.* re-*ny*-tis, inflammation of the mucous membrane of the nose.
rhino, *n.* *ry*-no, a rhinoceros.
rhino, *n.* *ry*-no, a cant word for money.
rhino-, *pref.* *ry*-no, connected with the nose. (Gr. *rhis*, *rhinos*, the nose.)
rhinocerical, *a.* ry-no-*se*-re-kal, pertaining to, characteristic of, or resembling a rhinoceros.
rhinoceros, *n.* ry-*nos*-er-ros, a large pachydermatous ungulate with either one or two horns on the nose. (L., from Gr. *rhinos*, the nose, *keras*, a horn.)
rhinocerotic, *a.* *ry*-no-se-*rot*-ik, rhinocerical.
rhinolith, *n.* *ry*-no-lith, a calculous formation in the nose [Med.].
rhinology, *n.* ry-*nol*-o-je, the scientific study of the nose and nasal diseases.
rhinoplastic, *a.* ry-no-*plas*-tik, pertaining to rhinoplasty.
rhinoplasty, *n.* ry-no-*plas*-te, the operation of forming an artificial nose [Surg.]. (Gr. *rhinos*, and *plasso*, fashion.)
rhinoscope, *n.* *ry*-no-skope, an instrument by which the interior of the nasal passages can be seen by reflection. (Gr. *rhinos*, and *skopeo*, view.)
rhinoscopy, *n.* ry-*nos*-ko-pe, inspection of the nasal passages by means of the rhynoscope.
rhizic, *a.* *ry*-zik, pertaining to the root of an equation [Math.]. (Gr. *rhiza*, a root.)
rhizocarpic, *a.* *ry*-zo-*kar*-pik, rhizocarpous [Bot.].
rhizocarpous, *a.* *ry*-zo-*kar*-pus, having perennial roots but annual stems and foliage [Bot.]. (Gr. *rhiza*, root, *karpos*, fruit.)
rhizogen, *n.* *ry*-zo-jen, a plant parasitic on the roots of another. (Gr.)
rhizogenic, *a.* ry-zo-*jen*-ik, root-producing [Bot.].
rhizoid, *a.* *ry*-zoyd, root-like: *n.* a filamentous root-like organ of attachment in mosses, etc.
rhizomatic, *a.* ry-zo-*mat*-ik, rhizomatous.
rhizomatous, *a.* ry-*zoh*-ma-tus, resembling or of the nature of rhizomes.
rhizome, *n.* *ry*-zome, an underground creeping stem which sends out shoots above and roots below [Bot.]. (Gr. *rhizoma*, from *rhiza*, a root.)
rhizophagous, *a.* ry-*zof*-a-gus, feeding on roots. (Gr. *rhiza*, and *phago*, eat.)
rhizophorous, *a.* ry-*zof*-o-rus, root-bearing. (Gr. *rhiza*, and *phero*, bear.)
rhizopod, *n.* *ry*-zo-pod, any of the Rhizopoda, a group of animalcules forming the lowest class of the Protozoa. (Gr. *rhiza*, and *pous*, a foot.)
rho, *n.* roh, the seventeenth letter of the Greek alphabet (P, ρ).
rhodanic, *a.* ro-*dan*-ik, producing a red colour with salts of iron. (Gr. *rhodon*, a rose.)
Rhodesian, *a.* roh-*dee*-ze-an, of or pertaining to Rhodesia in S. Africa: *n.* an inhabitant of Rhodesia.
Rhodian, *a.* *roh*-de-an, pertaining to or issuing from Rhodes: *n.* a native of Rhodes.
rhodic, *a.* *roh*-dik, containing or pertaining to rhodium.
rhodium, *n.* *roh*-de-um, a rare whitish metallic element of the platinum group, used with platinum to make alloys. (Gr. *rhodeos*, rosy.)
rhodium, *n.* *roh*-de-um, the scented wood of two species of convolvulus growing in the Canary Islands; oil obtained from this wood. (L. *rodius*, rose-like.)
rhodochrome, *n.* *roh*-do-krome, a rose-coloured silicate of magnesium and aluminium, a variety of penninite [Min.].
rhodochrosite, *n.* roh-do-*kroh*-site, a mineral closely related to dialogite.
rhododendron, *n.* roh-do-*den*-dron, a large ericaceous genus of evergreen shrubs and trees with ornately handsome flowers. (Gr. *rhodon*, rose, *dendron*, tree.)
rhodonite, *n.* *roh*-do-nite, a rose-pink variety of manganese spar. (Gr. *rhodon*.)
rhodophyll, *n.* *roh*-do-fil, the compound essential pigment of the red algæ.
rhodora, roh-*daw*-ra, a pink-flowered shrub of Canada and New England, *Rhodora canadensis*, resembling the rhododendron.
rhomb, *n.* romb, a rhombus; a rhombohedron.
rhombic, *a.* *rom*-bik, having the figure of a rhombus.
rhombohedral, *a.* rom-bo-*hee*-dral, related to, or of the form of, the rhombohedron.
rhombohedron, *n.* rom-bo-*hee*-dron, a solid contained by six equal rhombic planes. (Gr. *rhombos*, rhomb, *hedra*, a side.)
rhomboid, *n.* *rom*-boyd, a rhombus with its opposite sides equal and adjoining sides unequal: *a.* rhomboidal. (Gr. *rhombos*, and *eidos*, like.)
rhomboidal, *a.* rom-*boy*-dal, shaped like a rhomboid.
rhombspar, *n.* *romb*-spar, a crystallized form of dolomite; bitter-spar.
rhombus, *n.* *rom*-bus (*pl.* **rhombi** or **rhombuses**), an oblique-angled equilateral parallelogram; a rhombohedron. (Fr. *rhombe*.)
rhonchus, *n.* *ron*-kus, a form of râle, a wheezy

sound heard by auscultation, esp. in cases of bronchitis and asthma.
hopalic, *a.* roh-*pal*-ik, describing a line in which each word has one more syllable than that preceding it (as "Youth worships physical ability pre-eminently") [Pros.]. (Gr. *rhopalikos*, club-shaped, *i.e.* becoming thicker.)
hopalism, *n.* *roh*-pa-lizm, an instance of, or the composition of, rhopalic verse.
hotacism, *n.* *roh*-ta-sizm, over-sounding of the letter *r*; burning; the changing of *s* or *z* to *r*. (Gr. *rhō*, the letter *r*.)
hubarb, *n.* *roo*-bahrb, any herbaceous plant of the twenty species of the genus *Rheum*, esp. the garden rhubarb, *R. rhaponticum*, whose acidulous leaf-stalks are used for making tarts, etc., and *R. officinale*; a purgative medicine prepared from the latter. (O.Fr. *reubarbe*, from Late L. *rheubarbarum*.)
hubarby, *a.* *roo*-bahr-be, like rhubarb.
humb, *n.* rum, a rhumb-line; any one of the 32 points of the compass. (O.Fr. *rumb*, from L. *rhombus*.)
humba, *n.* *rum*-ba, the rumba, a negro dance.
humb-line, *n.* a line on a sphere or the earth cutting each meridian at the same oblique angle; the path of a ship sailing a direct course at an angle to the meridian.
hyacolite, *n.* ry-*ak*-o-lite, a variety of orthoclase occurring in lava; ice-spar. (Gr. *rhyax*, a stream of lava, *lithos*, stone.)
hyme, *n.* rime, correspondence of sounds in the terminating words or syllables of two or more lines in poetry; a word answering in sound to another; a harmonical succession of sounds; poetry; a poem: *v.i.* to accord in sound; to make verses: *v.t.* to put into rhyme. **feminine rhyme,** one in which the two final syllables agree, the accent being on the first. **masculine** or **male rhyme,** one in which only the final syllables agree. **without rhyme or reason,** bad both in sound and sense; without sense or consideration. (Fr. *rime*, as *rhythm*.)
hymeless, *a.* *rime*-less, not rhyming.
hymer, *n.* *rime*-er, one who makes rhymes; a versifier; a poor poet.
hymester, *n.* *rime*-ster, a rhymer; a poetaster.
hymist, *n.* *rime*-ist, a rhymester.
hyncho-, *prefix*, *ring*-ko, having a snout. (Gr. *rhynchos*, snout.)
hyncholite, *n.* *ring*-ko-lite, the fossilized jaw-tip of a Triassic nautiloid cephalopod. (Gr. *rhyncho-*, and *lithos*, stone.)
hynchophore, *n.* *ring*-ko-for, a member of the Rhynchophora, the sub-order of the Coleoptera which comprises the weevils.
hyolite, *n.* *ry*-o-lite, an acidic trachyte-like rock of volcanic origin containing much quartz.
hyparography, *n.* *ry*-pa-*rog*-ra-fe, the painting or description of sordid subjects; still-life painting. (Gr. *rhyparos*, mean, dirty, *graphē*, writing.)
hythm, *n.* rithm, measured or timed movement in the succession of sound; harmonious recurrence of accent; metre; verse; number; disposition of notes as regards time or measure [Mus.]. (O.Fr. *rithme*, from Gr. *rhythmos*.)
hythmic, *a.* *rith*-mik, rhythmical.
hythmical, *a.* *rith*-me-kal, pertaining to rhythm; agreeable to rhythm.
hythmically, *ad.* in a rhythmical manner.
hythmist, *n.* *rith*-mist, one versed in, or who has a natural gift for, rhythm.
al, *n.* *ry*-al, a Persian money of account nominally equivalent to 3*d*.
alto, *n.* re-*al*-to, an exchange; a market-place. (It., name of site of former Exchange in Venice.)
ant, *a.* *ry*-ant, gay; smiling; cheerful. (Fr.)
ata, *n.* re-*ah*-ta, a raw-hide lassoo. (Sp.)
b, *n.* rib, any one of the series of bones extending forwards from each side of the spine; anything like a rib; something long, thin, and narrow; a strip; a frame or timber of a ship; a fore-and-aft member of the framework of the wing of an aeroplane; the continuation of the petiole along the middle of a leaf; a vein of an insect's wing; a moulding of the interior of a vaulted roof; a narrow ridge in textiles; one of the hinged rods of an umbrella-frame; a batten [Naut.]; a wife [Coll.]: *v.t.* to furnish or mark with ribs; to enclose with ribs. **false rib,** one of the five lower ribs not attached directly to the sternum [Anat.]. (A.S. *ribb*.)
ribald, *n.* *rib*-ald, a low, vulgar, lewd fellow: *a.* scurrilous; base; obscene. (O.Fr.)
ribaldrous, *a.* *rib*-al-drus, containing ribaldry.
ribaldry, *n.* *rib*-al-dre, low, vulgar, or obscene language; irreverent jesting.
riband, *n.* *rib*-and, a ribbon. (Fr.)
ribband, *n.* *rib*-and, one of the harpings used in shipbuilding; any plank, scantling, etc., used in constructional work.
ribbed, *a.* ribd, furnished with ribs; narrowly ridged; marked with rising lines and channels.
ribbing, *n.* *rib*-bing, an assemblage of ribs, as for a vault or coved ceiling; a method of ploughing in which strips are left between furrows.
ribbon, *n.* *rib*-bon, a narrow band worn by way of ornament or as a distinction; the short strip of silk by which a medal, etc., is suspended; a narrow strip of anything; the inked tape-like strip used in typewriters: *pl.* driving-reins [Slang]. **blue ribbon,** *see* **blue. ribbon of the Atlantic,** the distinction accorded to the liner making the fastest Atlantic crossing. **ribbon development,** the building of houses on a highway designed for fast through traffic. (O.Fr. *riban*.)
ribbon-fish, *n.* any fish with an elongated much-compressed body, as the bandfish, oarfish, etc.
ribbon-grass, *n.* canary grass, *Phalaris canariensis*, or other ornamental grass.
ribbonism, *n.* *rib*-bon-izm, the principles of a secret Irish Roman Catholic association opposed to the Orange confederation and very active in the early 19th century.
ribbon-saw, *n.* a long bandsaw.
Ribes, *n.* *ry*-beez, a genus of the saxifrage order including the red currant, black currant, and gooseberry.
rib-grass, *n.* the rib-leaved or narrow-leaved plantain, *Plantago lanceolata*.
ribless, *a.* *rib*-less, having no ribs.
ribston, *n.* *rib*-ston, a variety of apple also known as the ribston-pippin. (*Ribston* Park, Yorks.)
ribwort, *n.* *rib*-wurt, rib-grass.
***rice,** *n.* rice, the cereal plant *Oryza sativa*, extensively cultivated and used as food. (Fr. *riz*, from Gr. *oryza*—of Oriental origin.)
ricebird, *n.* *rice*-bird, the bobolink; also the Java sparrow and other birds.
rice-flower, *n.* any of the *Pimelea*, a genus of Australian evergreen shrubs, the unopened buds of which resemble rice-grains.
rice-milk, *n.* milk boiled up and thickened with rice.
rice-paper, *n.* a material prepared from the pith of *Fatsia papyrifera*, used by Chinese artists and for manufacturing fancy articles.
rice-weevil, *n.* the beetle, *Sitophilus oryzæ*, resembling the common wheat-weevil.
rich, *a.* ritch, wealthy; abounding in money or possessions; splendid; costly; abundant; abundant in valuable materials or qualities; full of beauty; fertile; vivid; sumptuous; abounding with a variety of delicious food; containing much fat or flavouring; luscious; full of sweet or harmonious sounds: *n.* wealthy persons collectively. (A.S. *rice*.)
riches, *n.* *ritch*-ez, possession of land, goods, or money in abundance; wealth; abundance. (Fr. *richesse*, wealth.)
richly, *ad.* *ritch*-le, in a rich manner.
richness, *n.* *ritch*-ness, the quality of being rich; opulence; wealth; splendour; fertility; abundance of anything.
rick, *n.* rik, a built stack of grain or hay: *v.t.* to pile in a rick. (A.S. *hrēac*.)
rick, *n.* rik, a wrick or sprain: *v.t.* to wrench. (*wrick*.)
rickets, *n.pl.* *rik*-ets, a disease of children, characterized by bodily distortion, due to a weakness in the bones. (Perhaps a corruption of Gr. *rachitis*, because thought to be due to inflammation of the spine.)
rickety, *a.* *rik*-e-te, affected with rickets; feeble in the joints; tottering; shaky.
rickshaw, *n.* *rik*-shaw, a jinricksha.
rick-stand, *n.* a raised stage on which a rick is built; a staddle.
ricochet, *n.* *rik*-o-shay, a rebounding as of a projectile that strikes the ground like a stone thrown from

the hand to skim over the water: *v.t.* to hit or aim at by this method: *v.i.* to skim or skip thus. *p.* and *pp.* **ricochetted,** *rik*-o-shade. (Fr.)
rictus, *n.* *rik*-tus, the vertical width of an open mouth; the gape of a bird's beak; the opening of a two-lipped corolla [Bot.]. (L.)
rid, *a.* rid, free; clear: *v.t.* to free; to drive away; to clear from; to disencumber; to destroy. (O. Scand. *hrythja*).
riddance, *n.* *rid*-ance, the act of ridding; deliverance; disencumbrance.
ridden, *rid*-en, *pp.* of the verb *to ride.*
riddle, *n.* *rid*-l, a large sieve with meshes for separating grosser materials from finer: *v.t.* to separate with a riddle, as grain from the chaff; to perforate with or as with shot. **riddle cake,** a bannock. (A.S. *hridder,* a sieve.)
riddle, *n.* *rid*-l, an enigmatic proposition or puzzle; anything ambiguous or puzzling: *v.t.* to solve; to explain: *v.i.* to speak ambiguously, obscurely, or enigmatically. (A.S. *rædan,* to read, to guess.)
riddler, *n.* *rid*-dler, one who speaks ambiguously or propounds riddles; one who works with a riddle.
riddlings, *n.pl.* *rid*-dlingz, that which is deposited by sifting; siftings.
riddingly, *ad.* *rid*-dling-le, in the manner of a riddle; enigmatically.
ride, *n.* ride, act of riding; an excursion on horseback or in a vehicle; a road for riding on, esp. one through a wood; a district under an excise officer: *v.i.* to be borne along as on horseback or on a cycle or in a carriage or car; to practise riding; to float; to lie at anchor: *v.t.* to sit on and be carried by; to traverse by riding; to follow (a hobby, etc.) exclusively or assiduously; to domineer over; to manage autocratically. **ride easy,** lying at anchor with no great strain on the cables [Naut.]. **ride hard,** to pitch violently at anchor [Naut.]. **ride out a gale,** to keep safely afloat when hove to or at anchor in a storm [Naut.]. **to ride for a fall,** to take great risks; to proceed recklessly. **to take one for a ride,** to take him away in a car in order to kill or maltreat him [Slang]. *p.* **rode.** *pp.* **ridden.** (A.S. *ridan.*)
rideau, *n.* ri-*doh,* a small mound of earth to cover an approach [Fort.]. (Fr., a curtain.)
rident, *a.* *ry*-dent, riant; bubbling over with joy or merriment. (L. *ridens,* laughing.)
rider, *n.* *ride*-er, one who rides on a horse or cycle, or in a carriage or car; an addition made to a verdict; an additional clause; a further development of a geometrical proposition; a stone that dislodges another [Curling]; a mass of rock enclosed in a lode [Mining]; a supplementary timber to strengthen the frame [Shipbuilding]; an upper row of casks; any top row.
riderless, *a.* *ride*-er-less, having no rider; having lost the rider.
ridge, *n.* rij, a long continuous range of hills or mountains, or the back of such; a long crest; the crest of a roof; a raised line; a raised hot-bed for growing cucumbers, etc.; a raised strip of land in a ploughed field formed by furrows on each side [Agr.]; a band of high pressure between two cyclonic areas [Meteor.]; the highest part of a glacis [Mil.]: *v.t.* to form a ridge; to wrinkle: *v.i.* to form into ridges; to extend in ridges. (A.S. *hrycg.*)
ridge-band, *n.* the part of a horse's harness which crosses the saddle and supports the shafts.
ridged, *a.* rijd, having a ridge.
ridge-fillet, *n.* a fillet between flutes of a column [Arch.].
ridgel, *n.* *rij*-el, a half-castrated male animal, or one having only one testicle.
ridge-plough, *n.* a plough with a double mouldboard to turn up ridges.
ridge-pole, *n.* an upright piece of timber supporting the rafter of a roof.
ridge-rope, *n.* a rope supporting the ridge of an awning.
ridgeway, *n.* *rij*-way, a road along the top of a ridge.
ridgling, *n.* *rij*-ling, a male having only one testicle [Path.]; a ridgel.
ridgy, *a.* *rij*-e, rising in a ridge or ridges.
ridicule, *n.* *rid*-e-kewl, contemptuous laughter, or that which provokes it; writing, words, or action which excites contempt with laughter: *v.t.* to treat with ridicule; to deride; to expose to contempt o derision. (L. *ridiculum,* absurd.)
ridiculer, *n.* *rid*-e-kew-ler, one who ridicules.
ridiculous, *a.* re-*dik*-yew-lus, fitted to excit ridicule or contemptuous laughter.
ridiculously, *ad.* in a ridiculous manner.
ridiculousness, *n.* the quality of being ridiculous.
riding, *n.* *ride*-ing, one of the three divisions c Yorkshire administered as a separate county; sub-division of a county in New Zealand. (Origin ally *thriding,* a third part.)
riding, *a.* *ride*-ing, employed to travel on business employed to ride on: *n.* a road cut through a woo or ground for riding in.
riding-boot, *n.* a boot worn when riding.
riding-crop, *n.* a whip with a short stock terminatin in a leather loop in place of a lash.
riding-glove, *n.* a gauntlet; any strong glove use in riding.
riding-habit, *n.* a skirted costume sometimes wor by women when riding.
riding-hood, *n.* a hood formerly used by wome when they rode.
riding-light, *n.* the white light hung in the riggin when a ship is at anchor.
riding-master, *n.* a teacher of horsemanship; a officer who instructs officers and men in riding an managing their horses [Mil.].
riding-rhyme, *n.* *ride*-ing-rime, the decasyllabi couplet as used by Chaucer in the "Canterbur Tales."
riding-school, *n.* an institution or place wher the art of riding is taught.
riding-whip, *n.* a whip used on horseback.
ridotto, *n.* re-*dot*-toh, a public entertainment co sisting of music and dancing, in the latter of whic the whole company join. (It.)
riem, *n.* reem, a pliable ox-hide thong or strap. (Dut
rifacimento, *n.* re-*fah*-che-*men*-toh, the recastin of a literary composition. (It., from L. *re-,* a *facio,* make.)
rife, *a.* rife, prevalent; abundant. (A.S. *ryfe.*)
rifeness, *n.* the state of being rife.
Riff, *n.* rif, a Berber of the Riff district in Morocc *a.* of or pertaining to the Riffs.
Riffian, *n.* *rif*-e-an, a Riff: *a.* (*l.c.*) of or belonging the Riffs.
riffle, *n.* *rif*-fl, a crossbar in the bed of a trough cradle [Mining]; an obstruction or rapid in a riv or stream.
riffler, *n.* *rif*-fler, a curved file for use in shallo depressions. [Carp. and Mech.].
riffraff, *n.* *rif*-raf, sweepings; refuse; the rabbl (O.Fr. *rif et raf,* every tiny bit.)
rifle, *v.t.* ryfl, to seize and bear away by forc to strip; to plunder; to ransack. (O.Fr. *rifler.*)
rifle, *n.* ryfl, a hand fire-arm the barrel of which spirally grooved to give a rotary motion to t projectile: *pl.* troops armed with rifles: *v.t.* groove, as a rifle. (Fr. *rifler,* to file.)
rifle-bird, *n.* a beautifully plumaged Australasi bird of paradise, *Ptilorhis paradisea.*
rifleman, *n.* *ryfl*-man, a man armed with a rifl one of a rifle-corps.
rifler, *n.* *ryfl*-ler, one who rifles; a robber.
rifle-range, *n.* a place with butts or targets for t practice of shooting with the rifle.
rifling, *n.* *ryfl*-ling, the process of making the groov in a gun; the sequence of these grooves.
rift, *n.* rift, a cleft; a fissure; an opening made riving: *v.t.* to cleave; to rive: *v.i.* to burst ope to split. (Scand.)
rig, *v.t.* rig, to dress; to put on; to furnish wi apparatus; to fit with tackle; to fit the ropes their respective masts and yards; to set a spar or out; to assemble and align aircraft: *n.* dre esp. gay and flaunting, or the style of this; sty and number of masts and sails [Naut.]. (Perha Scand.)
rig, *n.* rig, a frolic; a prank; a trick or swindli dodge: *v.t.* to befool; to swindle; to manipula illegally. **to rig the market,** to engineer a ri or fall in prices so as to secure illicit profi (Origin unknown.)
rig, *n.* rig, a ridge. (Dial. Eng.)
rigadoon, *n.* rig-a-*doon,* a sort of jig, performed one couple; music for this. (Fr. *rigadon.*)
rigescence, *n.* ri-*jes*-ence, a becoming stiff or rigid numbness.

rigescent, *a.* ri-*jes*-ent, growing or tending to become rigid.
rigged, *a.* rigd, carrying a certain type of rigging, as square-rigged.
rigger, *n.* *rig*-er, one whose occupation is to fit the rigging of a ship or to rig aircraft; a cylindrical pulley or drum.
rigging, *n.* *rig*-ing, tackle; the ropes which support the masts and set and work the sails of a ship. **running rigging,** halyards, braces, sheets, etc. **standing rigging,** fixtures such as shrouds and stays.
riggish, *a.* *rig*-ish, wanton; lewd.
right, *a.* rite, straight; just; according to truth and justice; fit; proper; lawful; genuine; correct; not mistaken; most convenient or dexterous; well, sound, or sane; well-performed; straight; most direct; upright, not oblique; having the base perpendicular to the axis; on or pertaining to the side of the body opposite that in which the heart is situated; on the right hand: *ad.* in a right or straight line; rightly; justly; correctly; very: *int.* well done! **right angle,** an angle of 90 degrees or one-fourth of a circle [Geom.]. **right ascension,** *see* **ascension. right hand,** the hand at one's right side, the more useful hand; the position of this; the place of honour; an indispensable friend or assistant; a warm welcome. **Right Honourable,** *see* **honourable. right line,** a straight line. **right of search,** *see* **search. right side,** the side to the right; the correct side for the purpose; the surface exposed when material is made up. **right side up,** the top being kept above. **right whale,** the whalebone whale, *Balæna mysticetus.* (A.S. *riht.*)
***right,** *n.* rite, conformity to truth and justice; rectitude; justice; propriety; freedom from error; just claim; that to which one has a just claim; legal title; prerogative; privilege; authority; property; the side opposed to the left; the ministerial side in a legislative assembly; the more conservative or anti-socialist party. **bill of rights,** a declaration of rights, specially as granted by William III in 1689. **put to rights,** to put in good order; to adjust. **right and left,** in every direction. **right of way,** a customary right of transit over property belonging to another. **writ of right,** a writ formerly protecting feudal tenants in the enjoyment of their freeholds.
right, *v.t.* rite, to do justice to; to relieve from wrong; to put in a proper position; to set upright: *v.i.* to resume the natural state or position. **to right the helm,** to put the helm in line with the keel.
right-about, *n.* *rite*-a-bout, the opposite direction; the reverse: *ad.* in the reverse direction. **to send to the right-about,** to dismiss curtly, to send packing, to cause to retreat.
right-angled, *a.* *rite*-ang-gld, having a right angle.
righten, *v.t.* rytn, to set right.
righteous, *a.* *ry*-chus, holy; upright; just; equitable; merited. (A.S. *riht,* and *wis,* way or wise.)
righteously, *ad.* in a righteous manner.
righteousness, *n.* quality of being righteous; holiness; purity of heart and rectitude of life; uprightness; justice; perfection of moral character [Theol.]; justification [Theol.]; integrity.
righter, *n.* *rite*-er, one who sets to rights; a redresser of wrongs.
rightful, *a.* *rite*-ful, having a just claim; being by right; just; consonant to justice.
rightfully, *ad.* in a rightful manner.
rightfulness, *n.* justice; moral rectitude.
right-hand, *a.* on or to the right hand; clockwise: *n.* a person indispensable to one [Coll.]. **right-hand screw,** a screw which when driven is turned clockwise. **right-hand thread,** the thread of a right-hand screw.
right-handed, *a.* using the right hand more easily than the left; to the right.
right-handedness, *n.* the quality of being right-handed; dexterity.
right-hearted, *a.* having right disposition.
rightist, *a.* *rite*-ist, having a bias towards the conservative side in politics: *n.* one favouring a conservative or reactionary policy [Coll.].
rightless, *a.* *rite*-less, destitute of right; having no rights; deprived of rights.
rightly, *ad.* *rite*-le, in a right manner.

right-minded, *a.* having a right mind; well disposed.
right-mindedness, *n.* the quality of being right-minded.
rightness, *n.* *rite*-ness, the state or quality of being right; conformity to truth.
rightwards, *ad.* *rite*-wardz, towards the right.
rigid, *a.* *rij*-id, stiff; not pliant; not easily bent; strict; inflexible; severely just. (L. *rigidus.*)
rigidity, *n.* ri-*jid*-e-te, stiffness; want of pliability; resistance to change of form [Mech.]; stiffness of manner.
rigidly, *ad.* *rij*-id-le, in a rigid manner.
rigidness, *n.* the quality of being rigid; rigidity.
riglet, *n.* *rig*-let, a reglet.
rigmarole, *n.* *rig*-ma-role, a long confused rambling silly story; gibberish: *a.* consisting of rigmarole; unintelligible. (*ragman's roll.*)
rigor, *n.* *rig*-or *or* *ry*-gor, stiffness, as in death; a sudden chill, or shivering [Med.]. **rigor mortis,** the rigidity of the body following death. (L.)
rigorism, *n.* *rig*-o-rizm, strictness; austerity; severity in style. (Fr. *rigorisme.*)
rigorist, *n.* *rig*-o-rist, one very strict or rigorous.
rigorous, *a.* *rig*-o-rus, strict; severe; exact; inflexible; scrupulously accurate. (Fr. *rigoreux.*)
rigorously, *ad.* in a rigorous manner.
rigorousness, *n.* the quality of being rigorous; exactness; severity.
rigour, *n.* *rig*-or, rigidness; stiffness; strictness; severity; austerity; asperity; a sense of chilliness with shivering [Med.]. (Fr. *rigueur*).
Rigsdag, *n.* *rigs*-dag, the two-chambered parliament of Denmark. (Dan. *rige,* a kingdom, *dag,* day.)
Rig-Veda, *n.* rig-*vay*-da, the most ancient and important of the Vedas, including the body of the sacred hymns of the Hindus. (Sans. *ric,* praise, *vid,* to know.)
Riksdag, *n.* *riks*-dag, the Swedish two-chambered parliament. (*Rigsdag.*)
rile, *v.t.* rile, to make angry.
rill, *n.* ril, a small brook; a rivulet: *v.i.* to run in a small stream. (Ger. *Rille.*)
rille, *n.* ril, a lunar valley. (Ger., furrow.)
rillet, *n.* *ril*-et, a small stream; a rivulet.
rim, *n.* rim, a border or margin; a brim; the circular part of a wheel between the spokes and tire: *v.t.* to put on a rim; to form a rim round. (A.S. *rima.*)
rime, *n.* rime, hoar frost: *v.t.* to cover with or as with rime: *v.i.* to congeal into hoar frost. (A.S. *hrim.*)
rime, *n.* and *v.* rime, rhyme. (Fr.)
rimer, *n.* *rime*-er, a reamer for use on metal: *v.t.* to ream. (*ream.*)
rimless, *a.* *rim*-less, having no rim.
rimmed, *a.* rimd, having a rim.
rimmer, *n.* *rim*-er, a mould for marking the edges of pastry; a reamer.
rimose, *a.* *ry*-mohs, rimous.
rimous, *a.* *ry*-mus, chinky; abounding with clefts, cracks, or chinks, as the bark of trees. (L. *rimosus,* from *rima,* a cleft.)
rimple, *n.* *rim*-pl, a fold or wrinkle; a rumple: *v.t.* to pucker; to wrinkle; to ripple. (A.S. *hrympel.*)
rimy, *a.* *rime*-e, abounding with rime; frosty.
rind, *n.* rynd, the outer coating of fruit, that may be peeled off; skin; bark: *v.t.* to strip the rind from. (A.S. *rinde.*)
rinderpest, *n.* *rin*-der-pest, a malignant and very infectious cattle plague. (Ger. *Rinder,* cattle, and *Pest,* plague.
rindle, *n.* *rin*-dl, a small watercourse or gutter; a runnel.
rine, *n.* ryn, a ditch or rhine.
***ring,** *n.* ring, a circle, or anything in the form of a circular line or hoop; a finger-ring; a circular course or area; a surrounding group; a combination of persons for selfish ends; a betting enclosure; an enclosed space for boxing; prize-fighting; the pugilistic class: *v.t.* to encircle; to hem in; to fit with a ring or rings; to cut the bark of a tree in circles, so as to kill it: *v.i.* to form a ring; to move in a ring or rings. **ring fence,** *see* **fence. ring money,** a wife's allotment from her soldier-husband's pay [Mil. coll.]. **ring wall,** a ring fence. (A.S. *hring.*)
ring, *n.* ring, the sound of vibrating metal; any loud sound, or sound continued, repeated, or

reverberated; the act of ringing a bell; a peal of bells harmonically tuned; resonant quality: *v.t.* to cause a metallic body to sound; to sound aloud; to notify, summon, etc., by ringing: *v.i.* to sound as a bell or other sonorous body; to resound; to practise the art of ringing bells; to tinkle; to tingle. **ring off,** to put an end to a telephonic conversation; to cease [Coll.]. **ring up,** to attempt to get into telephonic communication with anyone; to raise the curtain [Theat.]. *p.* **rang.** *pp.* **rung.** (A.S. *hringan.*)
ring-bark, *v.t.* to ring (a tree).
ring-bolt, *n.* a bolt having a ring or eye at one end.
ring-bone, *n.* a callus on the pastern of a horse.
ringcraft, *n.* *ring*-krahft, boxing; the pugilistic art.
ring-dial, *n.* a pocket sundial in the form of a ring.
ring-dove, *n.* *ring*-duv, the wood-pigeon, so called from the white ring round the neck.
ringed, *a.* ringd, marked with, wearing, or encircled by a ring or rings.
ringent, *a.* *rin*-jent, irregular and gaping; having the lips separated and the upper one arched [Bot.]. (L., gaping.)
ringer, *n.* *ring*-er, one who or that which rings; a quoit thrown on to the peg; a certain game at marbles; an expert (esp. in sport); a hunted fox running in a circle.
ring-finger, *n.* the third finger of the left hand, on which the engagement and wedding rings are placed.
ringhals, *n.* *ring*-hals, the spitting cobra, *Sepedon hæmachates*, a venomous S. African snake. (Dut. *ring*, and *hals*, neck.)
ringing, *a.* *ring*-ing, sounding like metal when struck: *n.* the act of sounding as a bell; a sound as of a bell ringing; tinnitus [Med.].
ringleader, *n.* *ring*-leed-er, the leader of an association, esp. of lawbreakers, rioters, etc.
ringlestone, *n.* *ring*-gl-stone, a local name of the ring-plover.
ringlet, *n.* *ring*-let, a small ring; a little curl; a circlet; a dancing ring formed by fairy feet; any of several butterflies of the wall-brown family, such as *Hipparchia hyperanthus*.
ringleted, *a.* *ring*-let-ed, having ringlets.
ringlety, *a.* *ring*-let-e, adorned with ringlets.
ring-mail, *n.* armour of metal rings sewn on leather or cloth.
ringmaster, *n.* *ring*-mahs-ter, the manager of a circus arena.
ring-neck, *n.* a name given to birds, as plover or duck, etc., having a collar of coloured feathers.
ring-ouzel, *n.* a migratory bird of the thrush family, with a white collar on the throat, *Turdus torquatus*.
ring-plover, *n.* one of several small plovers having a black collar of feathers, esp. *Ægialitis hiaticulus*.
ringside, *n.* *ring*-side, the row of spectators; seats immediately outside a prize-ring.
ring-streaked, *a.* having circular streaks or lines on the body.
ringtail, *n.* *ring*-tale, the female of the hen-harrier; a narrow sail set on the gaff abaft the spanker as a fore-and-aft studding-sail [Naut.].
ring-tailed, *a.* having the tail striped as if surrounded by a ring. **ring-tailed eagle,** the immature golden eagle.
ring-velvet, *n.* an extremely fine variety of velvet.
ringworm, *n.* *ring*-wurm, a fungoid contagious disease, commonly on the scalp, characterized by a circular eruption in small vesicles with a reddish base.
rink, *n.* rink, a space on the ice measured off for curling; a sheet of artificial ice for skaters, or area for roller-skating; a team of players [Curling, Quoits]; a lengthwise division of a bowling-green: *v.t.* to skate on a rink. (*ring.*)
rinse, *n.* rince, a wash-through, or rinsing: *v.t.* to cleanse with clean water; to cleanse, with a second or repeated application of water after washing. (O.Fr. *rinser.*)
rinser, *n.* *rince*-er, one who or that which rinses.
riot, *n.* *ry*-ot, uproar; tumult by more than three people; violent or tumultuous disturbance of the peace; noisy festivity; excessive indulgence; luxuriance: *v.i.* to revel; to run to excess in sensual indulgence; to luxuriate; to raise an uproar. **to read the Riot Act,** officially to warn against participation in impending riot. **to run riot,** to act without restraint; to grow or spread in profusion (esp. of weeds). (O.Fr. *riote.*)
rioter, *n.* *ry*-ot-er, a participator in or promoter of a riot.
riotous, *a.* *ry*-ot-us, indulging in riot or excess; tumultuous; seditious; guilty of riot.
riotously, *ad.* in a riotous manner.
riotousness, *n.* the state of being riotous.
rip, *n.* rip, a rent made by tearing; a laceration: *v.t.* to cut or tear asunder; to unstitch; to saw timber along the direction of the grain [Carp.]; to tear up for search, disclosure, or alteration; to rush violently along. (Scand.)
rip, *n.* rip, a rake or debauchee; a worn-out horse; any worthless beast. (*reprobate.*)
rip, *n.* rip, an eddy; a reach of broken water. (*ripple.*)
rip, *n.* rip, a wicker basket, esp. for fish. (Scand.)
riparian, *a.* ry-*pare*-re-an, pertaining to or frequenting the banks of rivers: *n.* one who dwells or owns property on a river-bank. **riparian rights,** the fishing and other rights held by the owner of the land through which a stream runs. (L. *riparius*, from *ripa*, a bank.)
rip-cord, *n.* the cord by which a ripping-valve is actuated.
ripe, *a.* ripe, brought to perfection in growth; fit for use; matured; finished; ready; prepared; fully qualified; resembling ripe fruit; suppurated [Med.]; intoxicated [Slang]: *v.i.* to grow ripe: *v.t.* to mature; to ripen. (A.S. *ripe.*)
ripely, *ad.* as in a ripe manner.
ripen, *v.i.* *ripe*-en, to grow ripe: *v.t.* to mature; to make ripe; to bring to maturity or perfection.
ripeness, *n.* *ripe*-ness, the state of being ripe; full growth; completeness.
ripidolite, *n.* ry-*pid*-o-lite, a hydrated silicate of aluminium and magnesium with iron; clinochlore. (Gr. *rhipidos*, a fan.)
riposte, *n.* re-*pohst*, a lightning-like return lunge [Fencing]; a counterstroke; a smart repartee. (Fr.)
ripper, *n.* *rip*-er, one who tears or cuts open; metaphorically, a splendid affair or person.
ripping, *a.* *rip*-ing, first-rate, "topping" [Slang].
ripping-valve, *n.* a gore in the envelope of an airship, etc., that can readily be torn off for rapid deflation.
ripple, *n.* *rip*-l, the fretting of the surface of water; a little curling wave: *v.i.* to curl in ripples; to sound as ripples in water: *v.t.* to raise as in ripples; to curl. (Origin uncertain.)
ripple, *n.* *rip*-l, a large comb for cleaning flax: *v.t.* to clean away seed from flax. (Dut. *repel.*)
ripple-cloth, *n.* a woollen dress material with long silky hairs on the outer surface.
ripple-grass, *n.* rib-grass, the rib-leaved plantain.
ripple-mark, *n.* small undulations on the surface of a sea-beach, left by the receding waves; similar undulations on the surface of rocks [Geol.].
rippler, *n.* *rip*-pler, one who ripples flax; a tool for rippling.
ripplet, *n.* *rip*-plet, a tiny ripple.
ripplingly, *ad.* *rip*-pling-le, in a rippling manner.
ripply, *a.* *rip*-ple, having ripples.
riprap, *n.* *rip*-rap, a loose foundation of stones in deep water on a soft bottom; a firework exploding in successive detonations. (*rap.*)
ripsaw, *n.* *rip*-saw, a saw for sawing wood in the direction of the grain.
Ripuarian, *a.* rip-yew-*ayr*-re-an, designating that branch of the ancient Franks established on both banks of the Rhine and between Meuse and Moselle.
rise, *n.* rize, the act of rising; ascent; elevation; origin; appearance above; increase; advance in rank, fame, prosperity, income, etc.; advancement; promotion; the vertical part of a step or arch; the attempt of a fish to take a fly: *v.i.* to ascend; to get up; to grow; to swell; to appear above; to come into being; to spring; to slope upwards; to begin to stir; to increase; to be promoted; to be roused; to be raised; to amount; to close or adjourn a session. **to give rise to,** to be the cause of. **to rise to the occasion,** to be equal to an emergency. **to take a rise out of one,** to befool him. *p.* **rose**; *pp.* **risen.** (A.S. *risan.*)
risen, *riz*-en, *pp.* of *rise*.
riser, *n.* *rize*-er, one who rises; the upright part of a step or stair.
rishi, *n.* *rish*-e, a poet or inspired singer in the Vedic hymns; a person inspired; a seer. **the Seven**

Rishis, the " mind-born " sons of Brahma, reputed authors of some of the Vedic hymns, fabled to have become the principal stars of the Great Bear. (Sans.)
risibility, *n.* riz-e-*bil*-e-te, inclination to laugh; the quality of being risible. (L. *risor,* laughter.)
risible, *a.* *riz*-e-bl, having the faculty of laughing; capable of exhibiting laughter; laughable. (Fr.)
risibly, *ad.* *riz*-e-ble, in a risible manner.
rising, *a.* *rize*-ing, increasing in wealth, power, or distinction; approaching any given age, amount, size or the like; growing to manhood: *n.* a mounting up; the act of getting up or ascending; an insurrection; a tumour; act of closing a session; resurrection.
risk, *n.* risk, exposure to injury; hazard; danger; the chances of loss [Comm.]; the insured person or object [Insurance]: *v.t.* to expose to injury or loss; to dare to undertake. **run a risk,** incur or to encounter danger. (Fr. *risque,* It. *risco.*)
risky, *a.* *ris*-ke, full of risk; hazardous.
risorgimento, *n.* ree-*sor*-je-*men*-toh, a renaissance or revival, esp. (*cap.*) the Italian movement towards political unity and freedom from Austria in the mid-19th century.
risorial, *a.* ri-*zaw*-re-al, connected with laughter. (L. *risor,* laughter.)
risotto, *n.* ri-*zot*-toh, an Italian dish, consisting of rice cooked with meat or cheese, etc., and onions. (It.)
risp, *n.* risp, the stalks of growing peas or potatoes; a bush; a twig: *v.i.* to rasp [Scots.].
risqué, *a.* *ris*-kay, bordering on indecency or obscenity; indecorous. (Fr.)
rissaldar, *n.* ris-al-*dar,* a ressaldar.
rissole, *n.* *ris*-ole, meat or fish minced and mixed with bread crumbs and eggs. (Fr.)
rite, *n.* rite, a ceremonious usage. (L. *ritus.*)
ritornello, *n.* ree-tor-*nel*-loh, a repetition; the burden of a song; a short introduction [Mus.]. (It.)
ritual, *a.* *rit*-yew-al, pertaining to or consisting of rites; prescribing rites: *n.* a book of rites; the manner of performing divine service; ritual observances generally. (L. *ritualis.*)
ritualism, *n.* *rit*-yew-a-lizm, the system of ritual or prescribed forms of religious worship; the observance of these; an exaggerated respect for and observance of ritual or religious forms.
ritualist, *n.* *rit*-yew-a-list, one skilled in ritual; one who attaches great importance to ritual.
ritualistic, *a.* *rit*-yew-a-*lis*-tik, pertaining to or agreeable to ritual; specially observant of ritual.
ritually, *ad.* in a ritual manner.
rivage, *n.* *ry*-vaj *or* *riv*-aj, a bank, shore, or coast. (Fr.)
rival, *n.* *ry*-val, one who competes with another in any pursuit or strife; a competitor or antagonist: *a.* having the same pretensions or claims; standing in competition for superiority: *v.t.* to stand in competition with; to strive to equal or excel; to emulate. (Fr.)
rivalry, *n.* *ry*-val-re, a striving or strife for the same object or for superiority; competition; emulation.
rivalship, *n.* *ry*-val-ship, state of a rival; rivalry.
rive, *n.* rive, a rent or tear: *v.t.* to rend asunder by force; to split: *v.i.* to be rent. *p.* **rove.** *pp.* **riven.** (Scand.)
rivelled, *a.* *riv*-eld, shrunken by heat (A.S.)
riven, *a.* *riv*-en, split; rent or burst asunder (*pp.* of *rive.*)
***river,** *n.* *riv*-er, a large stream of water flowing in a natural channel towards the ocean, a lake, or another river; a large stream; copious flow; abundance. (Fr. *rivière.*)
river, *n.* *ry*-ver, one who rives or splits.
riverain, *a.* *riv*-er-rane, riparian: *n.* one living on or near a river bank. (Fr.)
river-basin, *n.* the tract of country drained by a river.
river-bed, *n.* the bed or bottom of a river.
river-crab, *n.* a freshwater crab.
river-craft, *n.* small vessels or boats.
river-god, *n.* a god presiding over or personifying a river.
river-head, *n.* the source of a river.
river-horse, *n.* the hippopotamus.
riverine, *a.* *riv*-er-rine, pertaining to a river; riparian.
riverside, *n.* *riv*-er-side, the ground adjacent to either bank of a river: *a.* pertaining to or built on this.
rivet, *n.* *riv*-et, a metal bolt fastened by clinching: *v.t.* to fasten with rivets; to clinch; to make firm; to engross (the attention, etc.). (Fr.)
riveter, *n.* *riv*-et-er, one who or that which rivets; a riveting machine.
rivière, *n.* riv-ee-*ayr,* a necklace of precious stones, esp. one of more than one row. (Fr.)
rivose, *a.* re-*vohs* *or* *ry*-vohs marked with sinuate furrows [Entom.]. (L. *rivus,* a stream.)
rivulet, *n.* *riv*-yew-let, a small stream or brook. (L. *rivulus,* a tiny brook.)
rivulose, *a.* *riv*-yew-lohs, marked with thin wavy lines [Bot.].
rix-dollar, *n.* *riks*-dol-lar, a former silver coin of Germany, Holland, and Scandinavia. (Ger. *Reich,* realm, *Thaler,* a dollar.)
riziform, *a.* *riz*-e-form, resembling grains of rice. (Fr. *riz,* rice, and *form.*)
rizzared, *a.* *riz*-ard, salted and dried in the sun (esp. of fish).
roach, *n.* roach, the small freshwater fish *Leuciscus rutilus,* allied to the carp. (O.Fr. *roche.*)
roach, *n.* roach, the curve in the foot of a square-sail [Naut.]. (Origin unknown.)
***road,** *n.* rode, a highway; a public way for travelling; a way; a roadstead. **on the road,** travelling; working as a commercial traveller. **rule of the road,** *see* **rule.** (A.S. *rad.*)
roadability, *n.* rode-a-*bil*-e-te, the qualities collectively to be sought for in a car for use on the roads.
road-book, *n.* a traveller's guide-book of roads and distances; a book of itineraries.
road-hog, *n.* one who drives a vehicle regardless of the comfort or safety of others on the road.
road-house, *n.* a place (licensed or unlicensed) at which travellers by road are catered for.
roadman, *n.* *rode*-man, one who keeps a road in repair.
road-map, *n.* a map in which roads are shown usually with their classification, gradients, distances between points, etc., indicated.
road-metal, *n.* broken stone used for macadamizing.
roadside, *n.* *rode*-side, the side of a road: *a.* pertaining to or situated by this.
roadstead, *n.* *rode*-sted, a place where ships may ride at anchor.
roadster, *n.* *rode*-ster, a hackney horse; one accustomed to driving; a cycle or car for use on roads as opposed to a racing machine; one who keeps to roads instead of following hounds [Hunting slang]; a vessel riding at anchor in a roadstead [Naut.].
roadway, *n.* *rode*-way, a highway; the part of a road travelled by vehicles.
roadworthy, *a.* *rode*-wur-the, fit to be used on the road (of vehicles).
roam, *v.i.* rome, to move about from place to place without any certain purpose or direction; to ramble about; to rove: *v.t.* to range; to wander over. (Origin unknown.)
roamer, *n.* *rome*-er, a wanderer; a rover.
roaming, *n.* *rome*-ing, the act or habit of wandering.
roan, *a.* rone, of a bay or dark colour, with grey or white spots; of a mixed colour, with a decided shade of red: *n.* roan colour; a roan-coloured horse. (O.Fr.)
roan, *n.* rone, a soft leather of sheepskin stained and used in binding books. (Probably *Rouen,* the French town.)
roar, *n.* rawr, any loud continuous sound; the cry of a beast; the loud cry of one in distress; outcry of mirth; a continued or tempestuous sound: *v.i.* to cry with a full, loud, continued sound; to bellow; to cry aloud; to make a loud noise: *v.i.* to shout out. (A.S. *rarian,* to bellow.)
roarer, *n.* *raw*-rer, one who or that which roars; a horse broken in wind.
roaring, *a.* *raw*-ring, noisy; disorderly; brisk: *n.* the loud cry of a lion or other beast; outcry of distress; continued sound, as of the billows of the sea; a disease in the air-passages (esp. of horses) occasioning a grating sound. **the roaring forties,** *see* **forty.** **the roaring game,** curling.
roaringly, *ad.* in a roaring manner.
roast, *n.* rohst, that which is roasted, esp. a large joint of meat: *a.* roasted: *v.t.* to cook by exposure

in front of a fire; to heat to excess; to parch by exposure to heat; to banter or to criticize severely; to dissipate the volatile parts of ore by heat [Metal.]. **to rule the roast**, to be the chief. (O.Fr. *rostir*.)
roaster, *n.* *rohs*-ter, one who roasts meat; a furnace or other contrivance for roasting; an animal, bird, potato, etc., suitable for roasting.
roasting-jack, *n.* *rohs*-ting-jak, a contrivance for turning a spit; a clockwork machine for roasting a suspended joint.
rob, *v.t.* rob, to seize and carry from by violence and with felonious intent; to plunder or strip unlawfully; to withhold what is due; to take from the person of another feloniously, forcibly, and by putting him in fear [Law]. (O.Fr. *rober*, spoil.)
rob, *n.* rob, a conserve formerly made of the juice of ripe fruit mixed with honey or sugar. (Ar.)
robalo, *n.* *rob*-a-loh, a pike-like food-fish, *Centropromus undecimalis*, of tropical American seas. (Sp.)
roband, *n.* *roh*-band, a robbin [Naut.].
robber, *n.* *rob*-er, one who takes goods or money by force; one who steals, plunders, or strips by violence.
robbery, *n.* *rob*-er-re, the act of robbing; a plundering or pillaging; a taking away by violence, wrong, or oppression.
robbin, *n.* *rob*-in, a rope-band for the head of a sail.
robe, *n.* robe, a long, loose outer garment as a dress of state or dignity; ladies' dress in one piece; an infant's long outer garment: *pl.* official or academic costume: *v.i.* to put on a robe: *v.t.* to dress with a robe; to array. (Fr.)
Robert, *n.* *rob*-ert, herb Robert (*see* **herb**); a policeman [Slang]. (Personal name.)
robin, *n.* *rob*-in, the warbler *Erithacus rubecula*, a small bird with a red breast. **Robin Goodfellow**, a roguish merry-making domestic sprite or fairy. **robin redbreast**, the robin. **round robin**, *see* **round.** (Fr., a pet name for *Robert*.)
Robinia, *n.* ro-*bin*-e-a, a North American genus of plants, including the locust tree, popularly known as the acacia. (Jean *Robin*, Fr. botanist, *d.* 1629.)
roble, *n.* *roh*-blay, various species of oak, esp. *Quercus lobata*, the Californian white oak. (Sp., from L. *robur*, oak-tree.)
roborant, *a.* *roh*-bo-rant, strengthening: *n.* a medicine that strengthens; a tonic. (L. *roborans*, strengthening.)
robot, *n.* *roh*-bot, an automaton simulating human movements; a person whose acts are purely mechanical. (Czech.)
robotization, *n.* *roh*-bo-ty-*zay*-shon, the process of making mechanical; mechanical behaviour.
robotize, *v.t.* *roh*-bo-tize, to make mechanical; to permit to be done mechanically or by an automaton.
rob-roy, *n.* rob-*roy*, a form of canoe propelled by a double-bladed paddle. (*Rob Roy*, the pseudonym of the writer John MacGregor, *d.* 1892.)
roburite, *n.* *roh*-ber-ite, a flameless explosive of varying composition used for blasting. (L. *robur*, force.)
robust, *a.* ro-*bust*, possessing great strength and vigour; muscular; vigorous; hearty; rough; requiring strength (of sports, etc.). (Fr. *robuste*.)
robustious, *a.* ro-*bus*-tyus, robust; sinewy; boisterous.
robustly, *ad.* ro-*bust*-le, in a robust manner.
robustness, *n.* the quality of being robust.
roc, *n.* rok, a fabulous bird of immense size and strength. (Per. *rukh*.)
rocambole, *n.* *rok*-am-bole, Spanish garlic, *Allium scorodoprasum*, a species of leek. (Fr.)
Roccella, *n.* rok-*sel*-a, the genus of lichens containing the archil. (Port. *roccha*, a rock.)
roccellic, *a.* rok-*sel*-lik, obtained from archil.
Rochelle-salt, *n.* ro-*shel-sawlt*, a tartrate of potash and soda. (*Rochelle*, in France.)
rochet, *n.* *rotch*-et, a linen vestment resembling the surplice, worn by bishops and other dignitaries. (Fr.)
rochet, *n.* *rotch*-et, the red gurnard.
rock, *n.* rok, a natural deposit of mineral matter occurring in large quantities as part of the earth's crust; a piece or mass of this; a cliff; a firm or immovable foundation; a hard kind of sweetmeat. **the Rock**, Gibraltar. **on the rocks**, destitute, down-and-out [Coll.]. (O.Fr. *roke*.)
rock, *n.* rok, a distaff used in spinning. (Scand.)
rock, *v.t.* rok, to move backwards and forwards; to lull to quiet: *v.i.* to move backwards and forwards; to reel: *n.* the action of rocking; a rocking motion. (A.S. *roccian*.)
rock-alum, *n.* the purest kind of alum.
rockaway, *n.* *rok*-a-way, a four-wheeled two-seated covered carriage [U.S.A.].
rock-basin, *n.* a cavity or artificial basin worn in rock.
rock-bottom, *a.* the very lowest (of prices): *n.* the lowest stratum; the ultimate point [Fig.].
rock-bound, *a.* hemmed in by rocks.
rock-butter, *n.* an impure butter-like efflorescence occurring in alum shales.
rock-cake, *n.* a small cake with a rough, hard exterior.
rock-cook, *n.* a species of wrasse.
rock-cork, *n.* a variety of asbestos resembling cork.
rock-cress, *n.* any plant of the genus *Arabis*.
rock-crystal, *n.* a clear transparent quartz.
rock-dove, *n.* the pigeon *Columba livia*.
rocker, *n.* *rok*-er, one who rocks a cradle; the curving piece of wood on which a cradle rocks; the curve on which anything rocks; a skate with a curved blade. **off one's rocker**, very eccentric; daft. [Slang.]
rockery, *n.* *rok*-er-re, a bank of earth with rocks, stones, etc., for plants to grow on.
rocket, *n.* *rok*-et, a firework that is tied to a stick and projected through the air by its explosion, used for display, signalling, life-saving, etc.; one of a series of tubes containing material generating gas, the regulated escape of which propels a projectile, aeroplane, etc.: *v.t.* to bombard with rockets: *v.i.* to fly upwards as a startled pheasant; to rise suddenly and severely (of prices). **rocket gun**, a gun for the firing of rockets. **rocket tester**, a rocket generating dense smoke used for testing drains for leaks. (It. *rocchetta*, a little distaff.)
rocket, *n.* *rok*-et, a popular name of some species of *Sisymbrium*, *Diplotaxis*, and other cruciferæ. **dyer's rocket**, a species of *Reseda*.
rocketer, *n.* *rok*-et-er, a bird that rockets.
rock-fish, *n.* a species of goby, also of wrasse.
rock-garden, *n.* a large rockery; a garden in which Alpine and rock plants are grown.
rock-goat, *n.* the ibex.
rockily, *ad.* *rok*-e-le, in a shaky manner.
rockiness, *n.* *rok*-e-ness, the state of being rocky.
rocking-chair, *n.* a chair mounted on rockers.
rocking-horse, *n.* a wooden horse on rockers.
rocking-stone, *n.* *rok*-ing-stone, a great stone so exactly poised by nature upon another stone as to rock to and fro, a logan-stone.
rockling, *n.* *rok*-ling, a fish of the genus *Motella*, of the cod and haddock family.
rock-oil, *n.* petroleum.
rock-pigeon, *n.* a rock-dove; a pigeon inhabiting rocks and caves.
rock-pipit, *n.* the small shore-bird, *Anthus obscurus*.
rock-rabbit, *n.* the cony of Syria and South Africa, one of the hyraxes.
rock-rose, *n.* any plant of the genus *Cistus*; a species of *Helianthemum*.
rock-ruby, *n.* a fine bluish-red variety of garnet.
rock-salmon, *n.* *see* **salmon.**
rock-salt, *n.* common salt or chloride of sodium.
rock-soap, *n.* a soft greasy mineral, aluminium silicate, used for crayons.
rock-tar, *n.* petroleum.
rock-temple, *n.* a temple hewn out of solid rock.
rock-wood, *n.* ligniform asbestos; rock-cork.
rock-work, *n.* stone fixed in mortar in imitation of the asperities of rock; a rockery; a natural wall of rock.
rocky, *a.* *rok*-e, full of rocks; resembling a rock; very hard; stony; unfeeling; shaky [Slang]. **the Rockies**, the Rocky Mountains of N. America.
rococo, *n.* ro-*koh*-ko, a florid architectural ornamentation; the style in furniture and decoration fashionable in the reigns of Louis XIV and Louis XV; antiquated; debased. (Fr., from *rocaille*, rock-work.)
***rod**, *n.* rod, a long twig; a wand; instrument of correction or punishment; a slender, tapering cane or stick used by anglers and generally jointed; a slender metal bar; a measure of 5½ yards, a pole or perch; power; a tribe. **to kiss the rod**, *see* **kiss.** (A.S.)

rode, rode, *p.* of *ride.*

rode, *v.i.* rode, to make a regular inland flight in the evening (of certain wildfowl). (Origin unknown.)

rodent, *a.* *roh*-dent, gnawing: *n.* any member of the Rodentia. **rodent ulcer,** a locally malignant ulcer, usually on the face, which gradually eats away the soft tissues and underlying bone. (L. *rodens*, gnawing.)

Rodentia, *n.pl.* ro-*den*-she-a, an order of mammals with two large chisel-edged incisor teeth in each jaw, adapted for gnawing. (L.)

rodential, *a.* ro-*den*-shal, pertaining to the Rodentia or to rodents.

rodeo, *n.* roh-*day*-oh, a round-up of cattle on a ranch; the enclosure in which they are confined; a public entertainment presenting a round-up. (Sp.)

rodlike, *a.* *rod*-like, resembling a rod.

rodomontade, *n.* rod-o-mon-*tade*, vain boasting; empty bluster or vaunting; rant: *v.i.* to boast; to brag; to bluster. (It. *Rodomonte*, a boastful personage in Ariosto's "Orlando Furioso.")

rodster, *n.* *rod*-ster, an angler.

roe, *n.* roh, a small species of deer, *Capreolus capræa.* (A.S. *ra.*)

roe, *n.* roh, the eggs of fish. **hard roe,** the spawn of the female. **soft roe,** the milt or sperm of the male fish. (Scand.)

roebuck, *n.* *roh*-buk, the male of the roe (deer).

roentgen, roentgen ray, etc., *see* **röntgen.**

roe-stone, *n.* *roh*-stone, oolite, so called as formed of small globules like the hard roe of fish [Geol.]

rogation, *n.* ro-*gay*-shon, litany; supplication. **rogation flower,** the milkwort. **Rogation Week,** the week containing the **Rogation Days,** the Monday, Tuesday, and Wednesday before Ascension-day. (L. *rogare*, to ask.)

Roger, *n.* *roj*-er, a masculine personal name. **Sir Roger de Coverley,** an English rustic dance. **the Jolly,** or **Black, Roger,** the black flag with a device of skull and cross-bones flown by pirates.

rogue, *n.* rohg, a knave; a dishonest person; a term of endearment; a wag; a vagrant; a sport or variation from type [Bot.]; a vicious or jibbing horse; an animal (esp. elephant or badger) turned particularly dangerous. **rogue's march,** music formerly played when a disgraced soldier was drummed out of the regiment. **rogue's twist,** a yarn of different twist and colour from the rest. (Fr. *rogue*, proud.)

roguery, *n.* *roh*-ger-re, knavish tricks; cheating; fraud; arch tricks; waggery; mischievousness.

roguish, *a.* *roh*-gish, knavish; fraudulent; dishonest; waggish.

roguishly, *ad.* in a roguish manner.

roguishness, *n.* the quality of being roguish.

rohan, *n.* *roh*-han, a large E. Indian tree, *Soymida febrifuga*, yielding a hard reddish timber; a tonic prepared from the bark of this [Med.]. (Hind. *rohun.*)

roil, *v.t.* royl, to render turbid by stirring up dregs; to excite to anger; to rile. (Perhaps Fr.)

roister, *v.i.* *roy*-ster, to bluster; to swagger; to bully. (O.Fr. *rustre*, a ruffian.).

roisterer, *n.* *roy*-ster-rer, a bold, blustering, turbulent fellow.

rokelay, *n.* *rok*-e-lay, a roquelaure, or short cloak.

roker, *n.* *roke*-er, a skate, ray, or thornback.

Roland, *n.* *roh*-land, a masculine personal name. **a Roland for an Oliver,** a smart repartee; any effective counter-thrust. (Names of two of Charlemagne's paladins.)

role, *n.* role, the part an actor performs; the part one acts in life. (Fr. *rôle*, a roll or list.)

roll, *n.* role, the act of rolling, or state of being rolled; a mass rolled or formed by rolling; a roller; the corkscrew revolution of an aeroplane about its longitudinal axis [Av.]; an official writing; a register; a chronicle; the beating of a drum with rapid strokes; a small loaf; a volute or convex moulding; *v.t.* to revolve along; to turn on an axis or move in a circular direction; to wrap round on itself; to drive forward with a circular motion; to spread or level with a roller: *v.i.* to move on by turning; to revolve; to move circularly; to move as waves; to form into a roll or ball; to spread under a roller; to rock or move from side to side; to beat a drum with rapid strokes. **Master of the Rolls,** the judge ranking after the Lord Chancellor and Lord Chief Justice into whose charge the public records are committed. **Roll of Honour,** a list of the names of those fallen in war. **rolls of court, parliament,** etc., the parchments on which are engrossed the acts and proceedings of the body. **roll up,** to form into a roll; to congregate, to appear on the scene [Slang]. **to strike off the roll,** to expel; to remove from membership. (O.Fr. *roler.*)

roll-call, *n.* the calling over of a list of names on parade, at school, etc.; the signal for this.

rolled, *a.* roald, plated by rolling. **rolled gold,** base metal coated with a thin film of gold. **rolled oats,** milled oats flattened between rollers.

roller, *n.* *role*-er, that which rolls or turns on its own axis; a cylinder used for smoothing or rolling; a long, heavy-wave [Naut.]; a long broad bandage [Surg.]; the picarian bird *Coracias garrulus*, so called from its curious flight; a tumbler pigeon; a breed of canary with a rolling or recurrent song. **roller towel,** an endless towel suspended round a roller. **roller skate,** a skate to which four wheels have been fitted in place of a runner. **roller skating,** the amusement of skating on roller skates.

rollick, *v.i.* *rol*-ik, to frolic in a boisterous way; to move in a careless, swaggering manner. (Probably *roll* and *frolic.*)

rollicking, *a.* *rol*-e-king, careless; swaggering.

rolling, *a.* *role*-ing, moving on wheels; undulating; used for rolling: *n.* the motion of a ship from side to side. **rolling stone,** a person unable to remain in constant employment; one with a thirst for travel.

rolling-mill, *n.* a workshop or factory containing machinery for rolling out heated metal.

rolling-pin, *n.* a short round bar with which dough is flattened for cooking.

rolling-press, *n.* a press for calendering; a copper-plate printer's press.

rolling-stock, *n.* the locomotives, carriages, wagons, and all wheeled vehicles of a railway.

roll-top, *a.* having a flexible cover which may be rolled back (of desks).

roly-poly, *n.* *roh*-le-*poh*-le, a game in which a ball wins by rolling into a certain place; a pudding made of paste covered with jam and rolled up. (*roll.*)

rom, *n.* rom (*pl.* **roma**), a male gipsy or Romany, esp. married. (Romany, man, husband.)

Romaic, *n.* ro-h*may*-ik, modern vernacular Greek: *a.* pertaining to modern Greece or to Romaic. (Late L. *romaicus.*)

romaika, *n.* roh-*may*-e-ka, a folk-dance of the modern Greeks.

romal, *n.* *roh*-mal, an East Indian silk handkerchief. (Hind. *rumal.*)

romal, *n.* roh-*mahl*, a plaited whip of rawhide [Mex.]. (Sp. *ramal*, a rope-end.)

Roman, *a.* *roh*-man, pertaining to Rome, the Roman people, or the Roman Catholic religion; plain and upright as distinct from Gothic, italic, etc.; denoting numerals in letters, not in figures: *n.* a native or citizen of Rome. **Roman alphabet,** the alphabet formerly used by the Romans and still commonly in use in western Europe and America. **Roman candle,** a firework throwing up jets of sparks and stars at intervals. **Roman Catholic,** a member of that part of the Catholic Church acknowledging the supremacy of the Pope; pertaining to this body of Christians. **Roman Catholicism,** the doctrine, practice, etc., of the Roman Catholics. **Roman cement,** a strong hydraulic cement formerly used for under-water purposes. **Roman Empire,** the empire founded by Augustus Cæsar (A.D. 27) and partitioned in 395 into the Western or Latin and Eastern or Greek Empires, the former being represented, 800–1806, by the **Holy Roman Empire,** and the latter being extinguished with the fall of Constantinople, 1453. **Roman fever,** malaria. **Roman indiction,** the indiction, or cycle of fifteen years instituted A.D. 312. **Roman nose,** an aquiline, high-bridged nose characteristic of patrician Romans. **Roman numerals,** capital letters used in the Roman system of notation to denote numerals (*see* Appendix), and still in use in place of figures for certain purposes. **Roman pace,** the *passus* of the ancient Romans, 4 ft. 10$\frac{1}{5}$ in. **Roman step,** the goose-step of the Fascists. **Roman type,** the

ordinary type as distinct from *italic*, fancy types, etc. [Print.].
romance, *n.* ro-*mance*, a fabulous relation or story of wonderful adventures, usually connected with war or love; a fiction full of extravagant fancies and situations; a romantic narrative; a fiction; a falsehood; a picturesque fabrication; the character or quality of that which is romantic; a mental tendency to and sympathy with chivalry; the atmosphere of the old tales of chivalry; a romantic event; any melody suggestive of a love song [Mus.]; (*cap.*) any of several dialects sprung from Latin of the districts of southern Europe that had been provinces of Rome: *a.* belonging to these dialects: *v.i.* to write or tell fictitious stories; to indulge in romantic fancies. (O.Fr. *romanz.*)
romancer, *n.* ro-*man*-ser, one who romances; a writer of romance; a liar.
romancist, *n.* ro-*man*-sist, a writer of romances.
Romanes, *n.* *rom*-a-nez, the gipsy tongue or language, Romany.
Romanese, *n.* rom-a-*neez*, Romansh.
romanesque, *n.* roh-ma-*nesk*, any Romance language or dialect; the debased style adopted in architecture imitative of the Roman: *a.* pertaining to such dialect or architecture. (Fr.)
Romanic, *a.* ro-*man*-ik, pertaining to the Romance dialects, or those speaking Romance; derived from Latin: *n.* any Romance language.
Romanish, *a.* *roh*-ma-nish, pertaining to or characteristic of the Roman Catholic Church.
Romanism, *n.* *roh*-ma-nizm, the tenets of the Church of Rome; Romanity.
Romanist, *n.* *roh*-ma-nist, a Roman Catholic.
Romanistic, *a.* roh-ma-*nis*-tik, Romanish.
Romanity, *n.* roh-*man*-e-te, the system, institutions, etc., or the influence, of the ancient Romans.
romanization, *n.* roh-ma-ny-*zay*-shon, the act of making Roman or of converting to Roman Catholicism.
romanize, *v.t.* *roh*-ma-nize, to Latinize; to convert to the Roman Catholic faith: *v.i.* to use Latin words; to conform to Roman Catholicism.
romanizer, *n.* *roh*-ma-ny-zer, one who romanizes.
Romansh, *n.* ro-*mansh*, the language, derived from Latin, of the Grisons in Switzerland.
romantic, *a.* ro-*man*-tik, pertaining to, characteristic of, or resembling romance; wild; fanciful; chimerical; full of wild scenery; anti-classical: *n.* a person having romantic ideas, disposition, etc.; an artist or litterateur of the romantic school; a romanticist. **the Romantic Revival,** in English literature, the early 19th-cent. revolt against the classicism of the 18th century.
romantically, *ad.* in a romantic manner.
romanticism, *n.* ro-*man*-te-sizm, romanticness; a romantic notion or feeling; a movement in literature (and in music, etc.), originating in Germany about the end of the 18th century, directed against the prevailing formalism based on the ancient classical style; romantic character; disposition towards romance.
romanticist, *n.* ro-*man*-te-sist, one who advocates, or writes in the vein of, romanticism.
romanticize, *v.t.* ro-*man*-te-size, to impregnate with romance; to put in an aura of romance: *v.i.* to give way to romance.
romanticness, *n.* ro-*man*-tik-ness, the quality or state of being romantic; wildness; extravagance; wildness of scenery.
Romany, *n.* *rom*-a-ne, a gipsy; the gipsy language. (Gipsy word *Romani*, a gipsy.)
romaunt, *n.* ro-*mawnt*, a romance; a versified tale of chivalry. (O.Fr. *romant.*)
Rome, *n.* rome, the Eternal City, once capital of the Roman Empire and now of Italy; the Roman Empire; the Roman Church. **Rome penny,** or **Rome scot,** Peter's pence. (L. *Roma.*)
romeite, *n.* *roh*-me-ite, antinomite of calcium. (*Romé* de Lisle, Fr. mineralogist, *d.* 1790.)
Romewards, *ad.* *rome*-wardz, in the direction of Rome, esp. of the Roman Catholic Church.
Romish, *a.* *rome*-ish, Romanish (in derogation).
romp, *n.* romp, a girl or child given to romping; rough play or frolic: *v.i.* to play actively and boisterously; to leap and frisk about in play. (*ramp.*)
romper, *n.* *romp*-er, one who romps: *pl.* a combination overall for a child.
rompish, *a.* *romp*-ish, given or inclined to romp.
rompishly, *ad.* in a rompish manner.
rompishness, *n.* the quality of being rompish.
rompu, *a.* *rom*-pew (or App.), broken, esp. of a chevron or bend [Her.]. (Fr.)
rompy, *a.* *rom*-pe, disposed to romp; frolicsome.
ronde, *n.* rond, round-hand; a form of type imitating script [Print.]. (Fr.)
rondeau, *n.* *ron*-doh, a verse consisting of thirteen lines in three unequal strophes, having two rhymes only, and a refrain; a rondo; a kind of jig, which ends with the first strain repeated. (Fr.)
rondel, *n.* *ron*-del, an early form of rondeau; a short poem with a recurrent refrain. (Fr.)
rondo, *n.* *ron*-doh, a piece of music, vocal or instrumental, having a principal theme to which a return is made. (It.)
rondure, *n.* *ron*-dewr, a ring; a circle; roundness.
Roneo, *n.* *roh*-ne-o, proprietary name of a machine for reproducing typescript: *v.t.* (*l.c.*) to reproduce with this.
röntgenism, *n.* *runt*-yen-izm, the use of X-rays; morbid condition induced by X-rays [Med.].
röntgenize, *v.t.* *runt*-yen-ize, to apply or subject to the action of X-rays.
röntgenogram, *n.* *runt*-yen-o-gram, a photograph taken by X-rays.
röntgenography, *n.* *runt*-yen-*og*-ra-fe, the process of taking photographs by X-rays.
röntgenology, *n.* *runt*-yen-*ol*-o-je, the scientific study of X-rays, esp. in the therapeutic field.
röntgenoscopy, *n.* *runt*-yen-*os*-ko-pe, the use of X-rays in surgical examinations.
röntgenotherapy, *n.* *runt*-yen-o-*the*-ra-pe, the treatment of disease by X-rays.
röntgen-ray, *n.* *runt*-yen-*ray*, an X-ray, an invisible ray capable of penetrating many solids, affecting photographic plates, etc. (von *Röntgen*, Ger. physicist, discoverer, 1895.)
röntography, *n.* run-*tog*-ra-fe, the art of making X-ray photographs.
ronyon, *n.* *ron*-yon, runnion.
rood, *n.* rood, a figure of the Cross, and generally of the crucifix; the fourth part of an acre; a measure of 1,210 square yards. (*rod.*)
rood-loft, *n.* a gallery over the rood-screen in which the rood was fixed.
rood-screen, *n.* a stone or wooden screen, usually carved or decorated, between the nave and choir in a church.
⋆**roof,** *n.* roof, the covering of a house or building; a vault or arch in the interior; something serving as a roof; a house or dwelling [Fig.]; the palate: *v.t.* to cover with a roof, to shelter. (A.S. *hrof.*)
roofage, *n.* *roof*-aj, material for or used for roofs; roofing.
roofer, *n.* *roof*-er, one who repairs or fixes roofs.
roof-garden, *n.* a garden on a flat roof, usually formed by plants in tubs, etc.
roofing, *n.* *roof*-ing, covering with a roof; materials for a roof; a roof.
roofless, *a.* *roof*-less, having no roof; unsheltered; houseless.
roof-tree, *n.* the beam in the angle of the roof.
roofy, *a.* *roof*-e, having a roof; abounding in roofs.
rooinek, *n.* *roh*-e-nek, a Boer nickname for an Englishman. (Dut. *rood nek*, red neck.)
rook, *n.* rook, a gregarious bird distinguishable from the crow by its colour and habits, and esp. by a naked, warty skin at the base of the bill, *Corvus frugilegus*; a cheat; a trickish, rapacious fellow: *v.i.* and *t.* to cheat; to defraud; to overcharge. (A.S. *hroc.*)
rook, *n.* rook, a piece at chess, the castle. (Fr. *roc*, from Per. *rukh.*)
rookery, *n.* *rook*-er-re, a group of nests on trees occupied by rooks; the rooks forming the colony; a breeding-place, or a colony, of other gregarious birds, or of seals; a group of mean houses; a slum; a resort of thieves.
rookie, *n.* *rook*-e, a raw recruit [Slang].
rooky, *a.* *rook*-e, abounding in rooks.
⋆**room,** *n.* room, space,; space unoccupied; place of another; opportunity; scope; an apartment: *v.i.* to occupy an apartment; to lodge [U.S.A.]. **give room,** to withdraw. **make room,** to open a way or passage. (A.S. *rūm.*)
roomage, *n.* *room*-aj, space for stowage; the number of rooms.

roomful, *n. room*-ful, as many or as much as a room will contain.
roomily, *ad. room*-e-le, spaciously.
roominess, *n.* spaciousness ; large extent of space.
roomy, *a. room*-e, having ample room ; spacious.
roop, *n.* roop, roup ; hoarseness.
roopy, *a. roop*-e, roupy ; hoarse.
roosa, *n. rooz*-a, the Indian grass, *Andropogon schœnanthus*, a source of geranium oil.
roost, *n.* roost, the pole or other support on which fowls rest at night ; a number of fowls roosting together ; a lodging [Coll.] : *v.i.* to sit, rest, or sleep, as birds on a pole ; to lodge. **at roost,** in a state for rest and sleep. (A.S. *hrost.*)
roost, *n.* roost, a strong tidal race in the narrow channels of the Orkneys and Shetlands. (Old N.)
rooster, *n. roos*-ter, the male of the domestic fowl.
★**root,** *n.* root, the descending, usually subterranean, part of a plant through which nourishment is drawn ; a young plant for transplanting ; an edible root ; what resembles a root ; the lower or embedded part of a structure, etc. ; the original or cause of anything ; the primitive of a derivative word ; the quantity which, multiplied by itself, produces a given quantity [Math.] ; the fundamental note of any chord [Mus.] : *pl.* a root with all the parts into which it divides : *v.i.* to fix the root ; to be firmly fixed ; to support vociferously a side at any game [U.S.A. slang] : *v.t.* to fix by the root ; to plant deeply. **root and branch,** the whole lot ; completely. **to take root,** to become planted or fixed. (Ice. *rot.*)
root, *v.i.* and *t.* root, to turn up the earth with the snout, as swine ; to rummage about. **root out,** to eradicate. (A.S. *wrot*, a snout.)
rootage, *n. root*-aj, manner of rooting (of plants) ; a taking root ; firm establishment.
root-crop, *n.* a crop of esculent roots.
rooted, *a. root*-ed, having a root ; having the root fixed in the earth ; deep.
rootedly, *ad.* in a rooted manner ; deeply.
rootedness, *n.* the quality of being rooted.
rooter, *n. root*-er, one who or an animal which tears up by the roots ; one who roots or cheers [U.S.A. slang].
rootery, *n. root*-er-re, a pile of roots and stumps of trees for plants to be grown on as on a rockery.
rootle, *v.i.* rootl, to root or grub about ; to burrow.
root-leaf, *n.* a leaf growing immediately from the root.
rootless, *a. root*-less, without root.
rootlet, *n. root*-let, a small root ; a radicle ; the fibrous part of a root.
rootstock, *n. root*-stok, a rhizome, a prostrate rooting stem annually producing young branches or plants [Bot.] ; a source [Fig.].
rooty, *a. root*-e, full of roots ; of root-like quality.
rooty, *n. root*-e, bread [Mil. slang). (Hind. *roti.*)
rope, *n.* rope, a stout cord (esp. over 1 in. circumference) formed of twisted strands ; a row of things strung together ; a halter ; the viscous formation in a ropy fluid : *pl.* a barrier formed of ropes : *v.i.* to draw out in a filament, as any viscous matter : *v.t.* to fasten with, or together with, a rope ; to bridle in. **give plenty of rope,** to allow full liberty or chances. **know the ropes,** to be conversant with. **pull the ropes,** to control, usually indirectly. **rope of sand,** a tie or union easily broken ; something of no cohesion. **rope's end,** a short piece of rope for flogging with. **to rope in,** to get in ; to induce to join (esp. by trickery). (A.S. *rap.*)
rope-dancer, *n.* one who performs feats on a rope extended above the ground.
rope-ladder, *n.* a flexible ladder made of two ropes connected by rings of wood, metal, or rope.
ropemaking, *n. rope*-make-ing, the business of making ropes.
ropery, *n. rope*-er-re, a place where ropes are made.
rope-walk, *n.* a long covered walk where ropes are made.
rope-walker, *n.* a rope-dancer.
ropeway, *n. rope*-way, an aerial rope used as a means of transport ; a cableway.
ropeyarn, *n. rope*-yarn, yarn for ropes, consisting of a single thread.
ropiness, *n. rope*-e-ness, quality of being ropy.
ropy, *a. rope*-e, adhesive ; viscous ; capable of being drawn into strings.
roque, *n.* roke, a form of croquet played on a ground with a raised border.
roquefort, *n. rok*-fawr, a cheese of the milk of goats and sheep, made at Roquefort in Aveyron, France.
roquelaure, *n. rok*-el-awr, a cloak for men buttoning all the way down. (Duc de *Roquelaure.*)
roquet, *n. roh*-kay, in croquet, the hitting of another's ball with one's own in play : *v.t.* to strike another ball thus. (*croquet.*)
roral, *a. raw*-ral, pertaining to or resembling dew ; dewy. (L. *ros, roris*, dew.)
roric, *a. raw*-rik, roral ; like dew in appearance.
rorqual, *n. rawr*-kwal, a fin-whale of the genus *Balænoptera.* (Scand.)
rorty, *a. raw*-te, raughty ; full of good spirits.
rosaceous, *a.* ro-*zay*-shus, pertaining to the Rosaceæ or rose family ; rose-like ; composed of several petals arranged in a circular form. (L. *rosa*, a rose.)
rosanilin, *n.* ros-*an*-e-lin, a red aniline dye.
rosarian, *n.* ro-*zare*-re-an, a specialist in roses ; an amateur rose-grower ; (*cap.*) a member of a Confraternity of the Rosary [Eccles.].
rosary, *n. roze*-a-re, a rose garden ; a string of beads used by Roman Catholics, to count prayers ; the series of prayers repeated ; an anthology. **rosary plant,** the Indian twining herb, *Abrus precatorius*, so called from its black-tipped red seeds used in rosaries. (O.Fr. *rosarie.*)
rose, roze, *p.* of *rise.*
rose, *n.* roze, a plant, bush, or flower of the genus *Rosa*, of many species and varieties ; a light pink or crimson colour ; a knot of ribbons ; a rosette ; a rose-window ; a perforated nozzle ; erysipelas ; a circular card marked with the points of the compass. **rose of Jericho,** the cruciferous plant *Anastatica hierochantina.* **rose of Sharon,** the large-flowered St. John's Wart, *Hypericum calycinum.* **under the rose,** in secret ; in a manner that forbids disclosure. **Wars of the Roses,** the civil war in England, 1455–85, between the Yorkists (white rose) and Lancastrians (red rose). (A.S.)
rose-acacia, *n.* the tree *Robinia hispida.*
roseal, *a. roze*-e-al, roseate.
rose-apple, *n. roze*-ap-pl, the Malay apple, or other of the many tropical species of *Eugenia.*
roseate, *a. roze*-e-at, rosy ; blooming ; of a rose colour ; optimistic. **roseate tern,** the pink sea-swallow, *Sterna dougalli.* (L. *roseus.*)
rose-bay, *n.* a species of willow-herb, *Epilobium angustifolium* ; also *Nerium oleander.*
rose-box, *n.* the plant *Cotoneaster microphylla.*
rosebud, *n. roze*-bud, the unopened flower of the rose ; a young girl [Fig.].
rose-bug, *n.* a diurnal beetle which feeds on rose blossoms ; the rose-chafer.
rose-chafer, *n.* the beetle *Cetonia aurata.*
rose-colour, *n.* colour of the pink or red rose ; attractive or deceptive beauty.
rose-coloured, *a.* having a rose colour ; attractive ; deceptively fine ; optimistic.
rose-diamond, *n.* a diamond cut with a flat base and from 12 to 36 facets rising pyramidally.
rose-drop, *n.* an ear-ring ; a lozenge flavoured with essence of roses ; a pimple due to drinking.
rose-gall, *n.* an excrescence on rose-leaves, due to the insect *Rhodites rosea.*
rose-hip, *n.* the fruit of the rose.
rose-knot, *n.* a rosette.
roselite, *n. roh*-ze-lite, a native arseniate of cobalt and calcium. (Gustav *Rose*, Ger. mineralogist, *d.* 1873.)
rosella, *n.* ro-*zel*-la, the brilliantly plumaged parrakeet, *Platycercus eximius.* (*Rose-hill*, near Parramatta, New South Wales.)
roselle, *n.* ro-*sel*, rozelle.
rose-mallow, *n.* the hollyhock ; any of several pink-flowered hibiscus, esp. *H. moscheutos.*
rosemary, *n. roze*-ma-re, the evergreen aromatic labiate plant *Rosmarinus officinalis*, of the mint family. (O.Fr. *rosmarin*, from L. *rosmarinus*, dew of the sea.)
rose-noble, *n.* an English gold coin of the 15th-16th cents. originally current at 6*s.* 8*d.*
roseola, *n.* roh-*zee*-o-la, a sort of rash ; a non-contagious inflammatory affection of the skin ; German measles. (L. *roseus*, rosy.)
rose-quartz, *n.* a rose-red variety of quartz.
rose-rash, *n.* roseola.
roset, *n.* ro-*zet*, a red colour used by painters.

Rosetta stone, ro-*zet*-ta, an inscribed slab of basalt discovered near Rosetta, Egypt, by which the key to Egyptian hieroglyphics was found. **rosetta wood,** an Indian wood of a bright orange-red colour with dark veins.

rosette, *n.* ro-*zet*, an ornament or imitation of a rose made of ribbons, coloured leather, or rubber strips, etc.; a rose-shaped ornament [Arch.]; a disease of plants causing the leaves to bunch in clusters. (Fr.)

rose-water, *n.* water tinctured with roses by distillation: *a.* merely sentimental; affectedly delicate.

rose-window, *n.* a circular window, with compartments branching from the centre [Arch.].

rosewood, *n.* *roze*-wood, the fragrant wood of a species of *Dalbergia* and of other tropical trees. **rosewood oil,** rhodium oil.

Rosicrucian, *n.* roz-e-*kroo*-shan, a member of a secret society of the 16th and 17th cents. given to the study and practice of occultism, alchemy, and the secrets of nature: *a.* pertaining to or characteristic of the Rosicrucians. (From name of alleged Ger. founder, Christian *Rosenkreuz*, about 1430.)

Rosicrucianism, *n.* roz-e-*kroo*-shan-izm, the principles and practices of the Rosicrucians.

rosily, *a.* *roh*-ze-le, in a rosy manner.

rosin, *n.* *roz*-in, the residue after oil of turpentine has been distilled from crude turpentine; resin: *v.t.* to rub or smear with rosin, as a violin bow.

Rosinante, *n.* *roz*-e-*nan*-te a broken-down or worn-out horse; a jade. (Don Quixote's horse.)

rosiness, *n.* *roh*-ze-ness, the quality of being rosy.

rosinweed, *n.* *roz*-in-weed, the American compass plant, *Silphium laciniatum*, giving a resinous odour.

rosiny, *a.* *roz*-e-ne, resembling rosin; resinous.

rosland, *n.* *ros*-land, a heath-covered district; moorland. (W. *rhos*, a moor.)

rosmarine, *n.* *roze*-ma-reen, rosemary.

rosolio, *n.* ro-*zoh*-le-oh, a liqueur made from raisins.

ross, *n.* ros, the rough scaly surface of the barks of trees; bark chips: *v.t.* to remove ross from bark; to divest a log of bark; to cut up bark for tanning. (Norw. *ros*, peel.)

rosser, *n.* *ros*-er, a workman employed on rossing; a tool or machine that strips bark from logs.

rossignol, *n.* (App.), the nightingale. (Fr.)

rostellate, *a.* *ros*-te-lat, having a rostellum.

rostellum, *n.* ros-*tel*-um, a small projection on the stigma of orchids; the radicle of a plant [Bot.]; a beak-shaped process [Entom.]. (L. from *rostrum*.)

roster, *n.* *ros*-ter, a prescribed order regulating the rotation in which individuals, companies, regiments, etc., are to be called on duty [Mil.]. (Dut. *rooster*, a grid, a list.)

rostral, *a.* *ros*-tral, resembling or pertaining to a rostrum or beak.

rostrate, *a.* *ros*-trat, beaked; having a process resembling a bird's beak [Bot. and Malac.]. (L. *rostratus*.)

rostriform, *a.* *ros*-tre-form, having the form of a beak.

rostroid, *a.* *ros*-troyd, like a beak [Zool.].

rostrum, *n.* *ros*-trum, the beak or head of a ship; in ancient Rome, a stage in the Forum for orators to speak from (because adorned with beaks of ships taken in battle), hence, a pulpit or platform from which a speaker addresses his audience; a beak-like snout or process [Zool. and Bot.]; a pipe for conveying distilled liquor into its receiver [Chem.]. (L.)

rosulate, *a.* *roz*-yew-lat, having the leaves arranged in rose-like clusters [Bot.].

rosy, *a.* *roh*-ze, resembling a rose; blooming with health; favourable [Fig.]. **the Rosy Cross,** Rosicrucianism.

rot, *n.* rot, putrefaction; dry-rot; a fatal distemper incident to sheep; a disease of the potato; rubbish: *v.i.* to putrefy; to become decomposed; to go to corruption; to be affected with rot: *v.t.* to affect with decay or rot; to make rotten; [Slang] to rally or banter; to chaff unmercifully. (A.S. *rotian*.)

rota, *n.* *roh*-ta, a list regulating the order of service; a roster; the supreme ecclesiastical court of the Roman Curia, consisting of 10 judges; a short-lived club of English politicians, founded 1659, advocating the retirement of ministers, etc., in rotation. (L., a wheel.)

rotameter, *n.* ro-*tam*-e-ter, a device for measuring curved lines; an opisometer; a curvometer. (L. *rota*, wheel, *metron*, measure.)

rotaplane, *n.* *roh*-ta-plane, a flying machine supported in flight by the action of a number of freely rotating wings or rotors attached to a common shaft; an autogyro.

Rotarian, *n.* ro-*tare*-re-an a member of a Rotary Club: *a.* pertaining to or characteristic of rotarianism.

rotarianism, *n.* ro-*tare*-re-a-nizm, the system, principles, etc., of Rotarians.

rotary, *a.* *roh*-ta-re, turning on an axis like a wheel: *n.* a rotary engine or other machine. **Rotary Club,** a local business man's club affiliated to an international organization for promotion of business, service, and social relationships. **rotary engine,** an engine in which the motive power is derived from revolving as opposed to reciprocating motion. (L. *rota*, a wheel.)

rotatable, *a.* roh-*tay*-ta-bl, capable of being rotated or of rotating.

rotate, *a.* *roh*-tate, wheel-shaped, spreading flat (of a corolla) [Bot.]: *v.i.* roh-*tate*, to revolve round a centre; to go by rotation: *v.t.* to cause to revolve like a wheel. (L. *rotatus*.)

rotation, *n.* roh-*tay*-shon, act of turning, as a wheel; regular succession. **rotation of crops,** regular succession of different crops in the same field to maintain fertility of soil.

rotational, *a.* roh-*tay*-shon-al, relating to rotation.

rotationally, *ad.* in a rotative manner.

rotative, *a.* *roh*-ta-tiv, turning, as a wheel.

rotator, *n.* roh-*tay*-tor, that which gives a circular motion; a muscle which does so.

rotatory, *a.* *roh*-ta-to-re, turning on an axis, like a wheel; going in a circle; following in succession.

rotche, *n.* rotch, the little auk, *Mergulus alle*.

rote, *n.* rote, frequent or mechanical repetition of words without understanding; mere repetition of memorized matter. (O.Fr.)

rotge, *n.* *rot*-ge, the rotche or little auk. (Dut.)

rotifer, *n.* *roh*-te-fer, one of the Rotifera.

Rotifera, *n.pl.* ro-*tif*-er-ra, a class of minute aquatic animals, the wheel animalcules, so called from their apparently rotary movement. (L. *rota*, and *fero*, bear.)

rotiform, *a.* *roh*-te-form, wheel-shaped [Zool., etc.].

rotograph, *n.* *roh*-to-graf, a photograph printed by a special automatic process, esp. of a printed or written page; the photographic apparatus. (L. *rota*, and Gr. *grapho*, write.)

rotogravure, *n.* *roh*-to-gra-*vewr*, photogravure produced from an etched cylindrical plate on a rotary press; a print so produced [Print.].

rotor, *n.* *roh*-tor, a vector having definite position in space, e.g. rotation about a given axis; a revolving or rotating part, esp. the rotating part of an electrical machine or of a steam turbine.

rotten, *a.* *rot*-en, decaying; decomposed; putrid; unsound; treacherous; fetid. **rotten borough,** a pre-1832 parliamentary division containing very few voters. (Ice. *rotinn*.)

rottenly, *ad.* in a rotten manner.

rottenness, *n.* *rot*-en-ness, state of being rotten.

rottenstone, *n.* *rot*-en-stone, a soft stone, derived from the decomposition of shale or siliceous limestone, used in polishing metal.

rotter, *n.* *rot*-er, a slacker; a low, objectionable, or despicable fellow [Coll.].

rotula, *n.* *rot*-yew-la, the patella [Anat.].

rotund, *a.* ro-*tund*, round; rounded; orotund; grandiloquent; sonorous. (L. *rotundus*, from *rota*, a wheel.)

rotunda, *n.* ro-*tun*-da, a building circular in plan and usually having a dome. (It.)

rotundifolious, *a.* ro-*tun*-de-*foh*-le-us, having round leaves. (L. *rotundus*, and *folium*, a leaf.)

rotundity, *n.* ro-*tun*-de-te, roundness; sphericity.

rouble, *n.* *roo*-bl, a Russian coin, and money of account, after 1936 equivalent to about 9·64*d*. (Russ. *ruble*.)

roucou, *n.* roo-*koo*, the W. Indian and S. American tree *Bixa orellana*; annatto, a dyestuff obtained from this. (Brazilian.)

roué, *n.* roo-*ay*, one devoted to a life of sensual pleasure; a fashionable rake; a debauchee (Fr., broken on the wheel.)

rouge, *n.* roozh, colcothar, a red powder used for polishing glass and metals; a red cosmetic made from safflower, carmine, etc.; a bet on the red [Roulette]: *v.i.* and *t.* to paint or tinge with rouge. (Fr., from L. *rubeus*, red.)

rouge, *n.* roozh, a touchdown in the Eton game of football. (Origin unknown.)

rouge-et-noir, *n.* roozh-ay-*nwahr*, a game of chance played with cards. (Fr., red and black.)

★**rough,** *a.* ruf, not smooth or even; not polished; having excrescences or irregularities; abounding with stones or stumps; stormy; harsh to the taste; grating; inharmonious; coarse in manners; violent; hard-featured; rugged; shaggy: *ad.* roughly: *n.* unfinished state; a rowdy or ruffian; a spike for a horseshoe; broken or over-grown ground (esp. on a golf course, as opposed to the fairway): *v.t.* to roughen; to break in; to do roughly. **rough-and-ready,** makeshift; provisional; unpolished in manner, etc., but effective. **rough-and-tumble,** boisterous; haphazard; a scuffle or scrimmage. **rough diamond,** *see* **diamond. rough draft,** a draft not perfected; a sketch. **rough it,** to submit to hardships. **rough luck,** misfortune greater than is deserved. **rough out.** to sketch or prepare an outline of. **rough passage,** a stormy sea-voyage; hence, any trying experience. (A.S. *ruh.*)

roughage, *n. ruf*-aj, coarse food or fodder; the bran of cereals, useful as promoting action in the alimentary canal.

rough-cast, *n.* the form of a thing in its first rudiments; plaster mixed with pebbles or shells: *v.t.* to fashion or mould roughly; to plaster roughly.

rough-draw, *v.t.* to draw roughly or coarsely.

rough-dry, *v.t.* to dry without smoothing or ironing [Laundry]: *a.* not ironed.

roughen, *v.t. ruf*-en, to make rough: *v.i.* to become rough.

rougher, *n. ruf*-er, one who roughs out anything; a tool for roughing out.

rough-hew, *v.t.* to hew coarsely; to give the first form or shape to.

rough-hewn, *a.* rugged; unpolished.

rough-hound, *n.* the dogfish *Scyllium canicula.*

rough-house, *n.* quarrelsomely boisterous conduct; horseplay; a place where this occurs [Slang].

roughish, *a. ruf*-ish, in some degree rough.

roughly, *ad. ruf*-le, in a rough manner.

roughness, *n. ruf*-ness, the state of being rough.

rough-rider, *n.* one who breaks horses, esp. for cavalry use; one who can ride unbroken horses; a mounted auxiliary [Mil.].

rough-shod, *a.* shod with shoes armed with points or roughs: *ad.* regardless of consequences; in a domineering manner.

rough-wrought, *a. ruf*-rawt, done coarsely, or in the preliminary stages only.

roulade, *n.* roo-*lahd*, a quavering or rapid run of notes [Mus.]. (Fr.)

rouleau, *n.* (*pl.* **rouleaux**), roo-*loh*, a little roll, esp. of coins in paper: *pl.* round bundles of fascines to serve as cover [Mil.]. (Fr.)

roulette, *n.* roo-*let*, a game of chance played with a revolving disk and ball; a wheeled instrument for making dotted lines or perforations; a roller used in massage. (Fr.)

Roumanian, *a.* roo-*may*-ne-an, pertaining to Roumania; *n.* a native or the language of Roumania.

Roumansh, *n.* roo-*mansh*, Romansh.

rounce, *n.* rounce, the handle with which the bed of a hand printing-press is worked. (Dut. *rons.*)

rouncival, *n. roun*-se-val, the marrowfat pea.

round, *a.* round, having the form of a circle, arch, sphere, or cylinder; full; large; smooth; flowing; not cramped; rounded; plain; candid; brisk; plump; positive; in even numbers, esp. divisible by ten: *ad.* on all sides; circularly; from one side or party to another; not in a direct line: *prep.* on every side of; about. **bring round,** to restore to consciousness. **come round,** to regain consciousness; to be persuaded to a point of view. **get round one,** to gain advantage by flattery or deception. **round number,** the nearest multiple of tens (or hundreds, etc.) to the actual number; a rough total. **round robin,** a written petition or memorial signed by names in a ring so that it may not be known who originated it. **Round Table,** *see* **table. round table conference,** a conference at which those present are all on an equal footing. **round tower,** one of numerous narrow stone towers, tapering upwards and with a conical cap, built in Ireland as detached campaniles of churches and often used for defence against Scandinavian raiders. **round trip,** a journey to a destination and back to the starting-place.

★**round,** *n.* round, that which is round; a circle or a sphere; circumference; that which goes or passes round or the passage round; a recurring series; rotation; a heat or cycle; a step of a ladder; a daily series of visits; walk round of an officer or guard [Mil.]; beat; a short composition in three or more parts [Mus.]; a returning dance; a general discharge of fire-arms, in which each soldier fires once. **in the round,** carved as a complete figure ((opposed to relief) [Sculp.]. **round of beef,** a cut off the thigh through and across the bone. **round of cartridges,** one cartridge to each man.

round, *v.t.* round, to make round; to make circular, spherical, or cylindrical; to encircle; to move round or about; to make full, smooth, and flowing: *v.i.* to grow or become round; to go round. **round to,** to turn to the wind [Naut.]. **round upon,** to oppose unexpectedly; to inform against.

roundabout, *a. round*-a-bout, indirect; loose; ample; encompassing: *n.* a merry-go-round; part of a traffic control system where vehicles must proceed in a circular direction; anything that is or goes round.

round-arm, *n.* a style of bowling in cricket in which the hand is not lifted above the shoulder.

round-backed, *a.* having a curved back.

roundel, *n. roun*-del, a round disk; a Norman shield; a semi-circular bastion; a roundelay; a rondel. (O.Fr. *rondel.*)

roundelay, *n. roun*-de-lay, a lively song with a refrain; a mediæval verse-form resembling the rondeau. (O.Fr. *rondelet*, a little ballad.)

rounder, *n. roun*-der, one who goes on rounds; one who or an implement which rounds; a complete circuit of the bases in rounders: *pl.* an early form of baseball played with a ball and a short stick in which the players try to make a round of a number of bases after the ball is struck.

round-hand, *n.* handwriting in well-rounded letters.

roundhead, *n. round*-hed, a name given in derision to the Puritans by the Cavaliers from their close-cropped hair.

roundhouse, *n. round*-house, a constable's prison; in a ship of war, a certain accommodation for the use of particular officers; a cabin under the poop.

rounding, *a. roun*-ding, roundish; nearly round: *n.* act of making, becoming, or going round; material wound round a rope to prevent chafing [Naut.].

roundish, *a. roun*-dish, somewhat round.

roundishness, *n.* the state of being roundish.

roundlet, *n. round*-let, a little circle; a roundel.

roundly, *ad.* in a round manner; plainly; boldly.

roundness, *n.* the quality of being round.

roundridge, *v.t. round*-rij, to form round ridges in ploughing. (Agric.)

round-shouldered, *a.* round-backed.

roundsman, *n. roundz*-man, a tradesman's assistant delivering goods out of doors; a farm labourer who worked part-time for several farmers and was paid in part from parish funds.

round-up, *n. round*-up, the herding of cattle, horses, etc., into large groups for branding, picking out the young, etc.: *v.t.* to gather cattle or other animals into herds.

round-worm, *n.* the nematode parasitic worm *Ascaris lumbricoides* [Path.]; any nematode, as distinguished from the tapeworm.

roup, *n.* roop, a contagious disease in poultry.

roup, *n.* roup, hoarseness; an auction [Scots.]: *v.t.* to sell by auction: *v.i.* to shout; to cry hoarsely. (A.S. *hrop.*)

roupy, *a. roop*-e, pertaining to or affected with roup.

rouse, *n.* rouz, a drinking bout or carouse.

rouse, *v.t.* rouz, to wake up; to stir up: *v.i.* to awake. (Origin uncertain.)

rouseabout, *n. rouz*-a-bout, a roustabout; a man of all work, esp. on a sheep-farm [Austral. slang.].

rouser, *n. rouz*-er, one who or that which rouses.

rousing, *a. rouz*-ing, having power to awaken or excite; stimulating; great; violent.

rousingly, *ad.* *rouz*-ing-le, in a rousing manner.
roust, *v.t.* roust, to drive out or away.
roustabout, *n.* *roust*-a-bout, a hand on a barge or other river boat; a deck-hand [U.S.A. slang].
rout, *n.* rout, a clamorous multitude; a tumultuous crowd; uproar; a large evening party; the assembly of three or more people intent on committing an unlawful act [Law]; the defeat and flight of an army, or the resulting disorder or confusion; *v.t.* to defeat and put to disorderly flight. (Fr. *route,* a defeat.)
rout, *v.t.* rout, to root up; to scoop or gouge out.
route, *n.* root, a way travelled or to be travelled; a march, also the order to march [Mil.]: *v.t.* to send or transport by a certain route; to direct or arrange the course of. **en route,** on the way; in transit. **route march,** a march for practice or exercise [Mil.]. (Fr., a road.)
router, *n.* *rout*-er, a plane resembling a spokeshave; a plane or tool for routing, cutting grooves, etc.
routine, *n.* roo-*teen,* a round or course of duties regularly or frequently returning; rigid habit of proceeding, acquired and grown familiar by mere force of repetition: *a.* done by rule or mechanically. (Fr.)
routinism, *n.* roo-*teen*-izm, the system of routine; adherence to, or the prevalence of, this.
routinist, *n.* roo-*teen*-ist, one adhering strictly to routine.
roux, *n.* roo, a preparation of butter and flour melted together, used to thicken soups and gravies. (Fr., red.)
rove, *v.i.* rove, to wander, range, or stray about at large; to troll with live bait; to aim at a chance mark [Archery]: *v.t.* to wander over. **roving commission,** a commission the method of execution of which is left to the discretion of its holder. (Perhaps Dut. *rooven,* to rob.)
rove, *n.* rove, a slightly twisted sliver of cotton, wool, etc.: a ring or washer for a rivet, etc.: *v.t.* to draw, as a thread or cord through an eye or aperture. (Origin unknown.)
rove-beetle, *n.* any member of the family Staphylinidæ, having long bodies and short elytra; the devil's coach-horse; a cocktail.
roven, *v.t.* *roh*-ven, alternative *pp.* of *reeve.*
rover, *n.* *rove*-er, a wanderer; a fickle person; a robber or pirate; a freebooter; a senior grade of Boy Scouts; a mark chosen casually [Archery]; a ball which has passed through all the hoops but is still in play [Croquet]. **at rovers,** at random. (*rove,* to wander.)
rover, *n.* *rove*-er, one who or a machine which roves thread, etc.
rovingly, *ad.* *rove*-ing-le, in a roving manner.
rovingness, *n.* *rove*-ing-ness, the state of roving.
row, *n.* roh, a series of persons or things arranged in line; a line; a rank; a file. **a hard row to hoe,** a difficult, laborious, or lengthy task. (A.S. *raw.*)
row, *n.* roh, the act, or a spell, of rowing; an excursion by rowing boat: *v.t.* to propel by oars or sculls; to transport by rowing: *v.i.* to work with the oar. (A.S. *rowan.*)
row, *v.t.* rou, to upbraid or reprimand: *v.i.* to make a row: *n.* a noisy disturbance; tumult. (Origin unknown.)
rowan, *n.* *roh*-an, the hardy deciduous red-berried tree, *Pyrus aucuparia*; the mountain-ash. (Scand. *rönn.*)
rowdily, *ad.* *rou*-de-le, in a noisy manner.
rowdiness, *n.* an uproar or disturbance.
rowdy, *a.* *rou*-de, boisterously noisy; rough; blackguardly: *n.* a riotous, turbulent fellow.
rowdyism, *n.* *rou*-de-izm, rude turbulent conduct.
rowel, *n.* *rou*-el, the small sharp-pointed wheel of a spur; a flat ring on horses' bits; a seton made of hair or silk to pass through a horse's flesh: *v.t.* to insert a rowel in the skin as a seton. (O.Fr. *rouelle.*)
rowen, *n.* *rou*-en, a second growth of grass; a stubble field left unploughed till after Michaelmas for grazing. (O.Fr. *regain.*)
rower, *n.* *roh*-er, one who rows in a boat.
rowing, *n.* *rou*-ing, a scolding or reprimand.
rowlock, *n.* *rul*-ok, the crutch or other device on a boat's gunwale in which an oar works. (*oarlock.*)
rowport, *n.* *roh*-pawrt, a port-hole on a small vessel for working an oar or sweep.
roxburghe, *n.* *roks*-bu-ra, a style of binding for books comprising leather back, cloth or board sides, top edge gilt and others untrimmed. (3rd Duke of *Roxburghe.*)
royal, *a.* *roy*-al, pertaining to a king or the crown; becoming a king or queen; regal; magnificent; noble; patronized by royalty: *n.* a size of paper (writing, 19 by 24 in., printing, 20 by 25); the sail immediately above the topgallant sail; a stag with twelve or more tines; a ryal (coin); an ace with court-card of same suit (in certain card games). **royal fern,** the osmund. **royal mast,** the mast above the top-gallant mast. (O.Fr. *roial*).
royalism, *n.* *roy*-a-lizm, attachment to the principles or cause of royalty or monarchical government.
royalist, *a.* *roy*-a-list, supporting monarchical government; pertaining to a royalist party: *n.* a supporter of a king, line of kings, or monarchical government.
royalize, *v.t.* *roy*-a-lize, to make royal.
royally, *ad.* *roy*-a-le, in a royal manner.
royalty, *n.* *roy*-al-te, the character, state, office, or person of a king; royal domains; a member of the royal family; a right or prerogative of a king or superior; an emblem of royalty; an agreed sum or percentage to be paid to the owner of a copyright or patent for each copy or article sold, or for its use, etc.; a share of the profits paid to the landowner for the right to work a mine. (O.Fr. *roialte.*)
rozelle, *n.* ro-*zel,* the East Indian plant *Hibiscus sabdariffa,* or its fruit.
rub, *v.t.* rub, to move something along a surface with pressure; to wipe; to clean; to scour; to spread over; to polish; to chafe; to remove by rubbing; to take a rubbing: *v.i.* to move along with pressure; to fret; to chafe; to move or pass with difficulty. **rub down,** to clean, or to reduce the size of, by rubbing. **rub off,** to obliterate. **rub out,** to erase. **rub shoulders,** to be in friendly association with. **rub the wrong way,** to arouse displeasure or opposition; to irritate. **rub up,** to burnish; to refresh (one's memory, etc.). (Dan. *rubbe.*)
***rub,** *n.* rub, act of rubbing; friction; that which rubs and renders motion difficult; obstruction; difficulty; a jibe.
rub, *n.* rub, a rubber at cards [Coll.]. (*rubber.*)
rub-a-dub, *n.* *rub*-a-*dub,* the noise made by the swift beating of a drum.
rubasse, *n.* roo-*bass,* a ruby-red variety of quartz. (Fr. *rubace.*)
rubato, *a.* roo-*bah*-to, tempo rubato [Mus.]. (It., robbed.)
rubber, *n.* *rub*-er, one who or that which rubs; the instrument or thing used in rubbing or cleaning; caoutchouc or india-rubber; an eraser; a whetstone; a coarse file. **rubber latex,** crude india-rubber as exuded from the tree. **rubber plantation,** an area occupied by cultivated rubber trees. **rubber stamp,** a stamp of rubber for making inked impressions; one who merely echoes another or acts not on his own authority [Fig.]. **rubber tree,** any plant or tree yielding rubber, esp. *Ficus elastica* of India and Malaya and *Hevea brasiliensis* of the Amazon basin. (From *rub,* the verb.)
rubber, *n.* *rub*-er, a series of three games, won by two out of three [Whist, Contract, etc.]. (Origin unknown.)
rubberize, *v.t.* *rub*-er-rize, to impregnate or treat with rubber or a rubber solution.
rubberneck, *n.* *rub*-er-nek, a tourist or sightseer; one who seeks to pry into anything [U.S.A. slang.].
rubbery, *a.* *rub*-er-re, of the nature of or resembling india-rubber.
rubbing, *n.* *rub*-ing, an impression of a design taken by rubbing paper laid on it with graphite or chalk.
rubbish, *n.* *rub*-ish, waste, broken, or discarded matter; debris; anything worthless. (O.Fr. *robeux.*)
rubbishing, *a.* *rub*-ish-ing, rubbishy.
rubbishy, *a.* *rub*-ish-e, composed of rubbish; trashy.
rubble, *n.* *rub*-l, rough undressed stones; old building materials used again; a mass of fragments of rock [Geol.]. (Origin unknown.)
rubble-stone, *n.* the upper fragmentary and decomposed portions of a mass of stone.

rubble-work, *n.* coarse walling constructed of rough stones.
rubbly, *a. rub*-ble, pertaining to or containing rubble.
rubefacient, *a.* roo-be-*fay*-she-ent, making red: *n.* a substance or application which produces redness of the skin [Med.]. (L. *rubefaciens.*)
rubefaction, *n.* roo-be-*fak*-shon, the action or effect of a rubefacient.
rubella, *n.* roo-*bel*-a, rubeola.
rubellite, *n.* roo-*bel*-lite, a pink variety of tourmaline. (L. *rubellus.*)
rubeola, *n.* roo-*bee*-o-la, measles; German measles [Med.]. (L. *ruber.*)
rubescence, *n.* roo-*bes*-ence, state or quality of being rubescent; a flush.
rubescent, *a.* roo-*bes*-ent, growing or becoming red. (L. *rubescens,* growing red.)
Rubia, *n. roo*-be-a, the genus of plants, which includes madder, cleavers, and woodruff. (L.)
rubiaceous, *a.* roo-be-*ay*-shus, pertaining to, or of, the genus *Rubia* [Bot.].
rubicelle, *n. roo*-be-sel, a yellow or yellowish variety of ruby. (Fr.)
Rubicon, *n. roo*-be-kon, a river in Italy, the crossing of which by Cæsar in 49 B.C. amounted to a declaration of war against the Republic; hence, **to cross the Rubicon,** to take an irrevocable step.
rubicund, *a. roo*-be-kund, inclining to redness; ruddy. (Fr. *rubicond.*)
rubicundity, *n.* roo-be-*kun*-de-te, ruddiness; inclination to redness.
rubidic, *a.* roo-*bid*-ik, of or pertaining to rubidium.
rubidium, *n.* roo-*bid*-e-um, a very rare, slightly radioactive, silvery white metallic element of the potassium group. (L. *rubidus,* red.)
rubied, *a. roo*-bid, red as a ruby.
rubific, *a.* roo-*bif*-ik, making red; rubefacient.
rubification, *n.* roo-be-fe-*kay*-shon, the act or process of making red.
rubify, *v.t. roo*-be-fy, to make red.
rubiginous, *a.* roo-*bij*-e-nus, brownish-red; ferruginous. (Late L. *rubiginosus.*)
rubious, *a. roo*-be-us, ruby-coloured.
ruble, *n. roo*-bl, a rouble. (Russ.)
rubric, *n. roo*-brik, the title or heading of a statute, etc., written in red; directions for the conduct of divine service formerly printed in red: *v.t.* to rubricate. (Fr. *rubrique.*)
rubrical, *a. roo*-bre-kal, pertaining to or placed in liturgical rubrics.
rubricate, *v.t. roo*-bre-kate, to write, print, or illuminate in red; to furnish with a rubric: *a.* marked in red. (L. *rubricatus.*)
rubrication, *n.* roo-bre-*kay*-shon, the act or process of rubricating; a rubricated letter, etc.
rubricator, *n. roo*-bre-kay-tor, one who rubricates; a mediæval illuminator of manuscripts.
rubrician, *n.* roo-*brish*-an, one versed in rubrics; an advocate of rubrics.
rubstone, *n. rub*-stone, a whetstone, or any stone used for sharpening instruments, tools, etc.
Rubus, *n. roo*-bus, the genus of plants including the blackberry and raspberry. (L.)
ruby, *n. roo*-be, a precious stone, a variety of corundum of a carmine-red colour; this colour; red wine, esp. port; a carbuncle; a small-sized type (now 5½-point): *a.* of the colour of a ruby: *v.t.* to make red. **rock ruby,** a fine red variety of garnet. **ruby copper,** cuprite. **ruby of zinc,** red blende. (O.Fr. *rubi.*)
ruche, *n.* roosh, a pleated frilling; a ruffle. (Fr.)
ruching, *n. roosh*-ing, dress trimming composed of ruches.
ruck, *n.* ruk, a wrinkle or plait: *v.t.* to wrinkle; to crease. (Ice. *hrukka.*)
ruck, *n.* ruk, a heap; a pile; the ordinary crowd; the horses coming in a crowd at the end of a race. (Perhaps *rick.*)
ruckle, *v.t. ruk*-kl, to wrinkle; to crease.
ruckle, *n. ruk*-kl, the death-rattle: *v.i.* to make this sound. (Scand.)
rucksack, *n. rook*-sak, a knapsack carried on the back by straps round the shoulders. (Ger.)
ruction, *n. ruk*-shon, an uproar; a row [Slang].
Rudbeckia, *n.* rud-*bek*-e-a, a group of composite plants from N. America with yellow aster-like flowers. (Glaus *Rudbeck,* Swed. botanist, *d.* 1702.
rudd, *n.* rud, a freshwater fish, the red-eye, a species of *Leuciscus.* (A.S. *rudu,* redness.)
rudder, *n. rud*-er, the appendage at the stern of a ship by which it is steered; an analogous contrivance on an aircraft; that which guides or governs the course of anything. (A.S. *rother.*)
rudder-bar, *n.* the foot rod by means of which the pilot of an aeroplane operates the rudder.
rudderfish, *n.* the pilot-fish, the marine fish *Pammelas perciformis,* and others.
rudderless, *a. rud*-er-less, having no rudder.
ruddied, *a. rud*-id, made red.
ruddiness, *n. rud*-e-ness, the state of being ruddy.
ruddle, *n. rud*-l, red ochre for marking sheep: *v.t.* to mark with ruddle. (A.S. *rudu.*)
ruddle-man, *n.* one who digs or sells ruddle.
ruddock, *n. rud*-ok, the robin. (A.S. *rudduc.*)
ruddy, *a. rud*-e, of a red colour; florid; of a lively flesh colour: *v.t.* and *i.* to make or become ruddy. (A.S. *rudig.*)
rude, *a.* rood, rough; rugged; untaught; savage; unformed by art; unsophisticated; of coarse manners; clownish; uncivil; robust; violent; tumultuous. (Fr.)
rudely, *ad. rood*-le, in a rude manner.
rudeness, *n.* the quality of being rude; coarseness of manners; ignorance; unskilfulness; violence.
ruderal, *a. roo*-der-al, growing on waste heaps [Bot.].
Rudesheimer, *n. roo*-des-*hy*-mer, a white wine made at Rüdesheim, on the Rhine.
rudiment, *n. roo*-de-ment, a thing in its rude or unformed state; a first principle, element, or step; a beginning. (Fr.)
rudimental, *a.* roo-de-*men*-tal, rudimentary.
rudimentary, *a.* roo-de-*men*-ta-re, pertaining to, containing, or consisting of first principles: in an unformed or undeveloped state.
rudish, *a. roo*-dish, somewhat rude.
Rudolphine, *a.* roo-*dol*-fin, designating a set of astronomical tables computed by Tycho Brahe and Kepler and dedicated to the Emperor Rudolf II in 1602.
rue, *v.t.* roo, to lament; to regret sorrowfully; to repent of. (A.S. *hreowan,* grieve.)
rue, *n.* roo, a strong-smelling plant, *Ruta graveolens,* formerly used as a charm and as a stimulant. (Fr.)
rueful, *a. roo*-ful, expressing sorrow; mournful.
ruefully, *ad.* in a rueful manner.
ruefulness, *n.* the state of being rueful.
ruelle, *n.* roo-*el,* the space between bed and wall; the part of a bed next the wall; a morning reception formerly held by the French in bedrooms; a clique. (Fr., alley.)
rufescent, *a.* roo-*fes*-sent, reddish; tinged with red. (L. *rufescens,* becoming reddish.)
ruff, *n.* ruf, a pleated linen collar worn round the neck; something puckered or pleated; a bird allied to the sandpipers, a species of *Machetes,* with its feathers raised in a ruff round its neck; a species of pigeon, with a ruff of feathers: *v.t.* to ruffle; to disorder; to heckle flax. (*ruffle.*)
ruff, *n.* ruf, the act of trumping at cards; a rudimentary and obsolete form of whist: *v.t.* and *i.* to trump at cards when one cannot follow suit. (O.Fr. *roffle,* a card-game.)
ruff, *n.* ruf, a small freshwater fish of the perch family, *Acerina vulgaris.* (Probably from *rough.*)
ruffed, *a.* ruft, having a ruff.
ruffian, *n. ruf*-e-an *or ruf*-yan, a boisterous brutal fellow; one ready for any desperate crime; a robber; a murderer: *a.* brutal; savagely boisterous: *v.i.* to play the ruffian. (O.Fr. *ruffien.*)
ruffianage, *n. ruf*-e-a-naj, ruffians collectively.
ruffianish, *a, ruf*-e-a-nish, ruffianly.
ruffianism, *n. ruf*-e-a-nizm, ruffianly conduct.
ruffianly, *a.* like a ruffian; violent.
ruffle, *n. ruf*-l, a strip of fine cloth, lace, etc., pleated and attached to some part of a garment; small ruffs for the wrist; disturbance; agitation; a ripple on calm water; a subdued roll on the drum: *v.t.* to disorder by disturbing a smooth or a calm state; to vex; to discompose; to throw into disorder; to furnish with ruffles: *v.i.* to grow rough or turbulent; to flutter; to swagger; to beat the ruffle on a drum. (Perhaps Dut. *rufelen,* to rumple.)
ruffler, *n. ruf*-ler, a bully; a swaggerer.
ruffling, *n. ruf*-ling, commotion; disturbance; a low rolling of the drum.

rufous, *a.* *roo*-fus, of a brownish or yellowish red colour. (L. *rufus*, red.)
rug, *n.* rug, a thick woollen cloth, used for a wrap or coverlet ; a mat for the floor ; a rough, woolly, or shaggy dog. (Scand. *rugg*, coarse matted hair.)
rugate, *a.* *roo*-gate, wrinkled ; having ridges. (L. *ruga*, a wrinkle.)
Rugbeian, *n.* rug-*bee*-yan, a past or present pupil of Rugby school.
Rugby, *n.* *rug*-be, a town in Warwickshire, England, where is the public school at which the game of Rugby football was evolved ; the game itself.
rugged, *a.* *rug*-ed, rough ; having asperities on the surface ; jagged ; shaggy ; rough in temper ; uncouth ; harsh ; surly ; tempestuous ; boisterous. (Scand. *ruggia*, hairy.)
ruggedly, *ad.* in a rugged manner.
ruggedness, *n.* the quality of being rugged ; roughness ; coarseness ; boisterousness.
rugger, *n.* *rug*-er, Rugby football [Coll.].
rugose, *a.* roo-*gose* or *roo*-gose, wrinkled ; full of wrinkles [Bot. and Zool.]. (L. *rugosus*, for *ruga*, a wrinkle.)
rugosity, *n.* roo-*gos*-e-te, a state of being wrinkled ; a wrinkle.
rugous, *a.* *roo*-gus, rugose.
rugulose, *a.* *roo*-gew-lohs, finely wrinkled.
ruin, *n.* *roo*-in, destruction (physical or moral) ; overthrow ; that which destroys ; cause of destruction ; ruined state ; a ruined structure or [Fig.] person : *pl.* the remains of anything demolished or decayed : *v.t.* to pull down, destroy, subvert, or defeat ; to impoverish ; to bring to everlasting misery ; to destroy morally : *v.i.* to fall into ruins or ruin. (L. *ruina*, from *ruo*, fall or tumble down.)
ruinate, *v.t.* *roo*-e-nate, to bring to destruction ; to reduce to ruins : *v.i.* to go to ruin : *a.* ruined. (Late L. *ruinatus*, spoiled.)
ruination, *n.* roo-e-*nay*-shon, the state or fact of being ruined ; overthrow.
ruiner, *n.* *roo*-e-ner, one who ruins or destroys.
ruinous, *a.* *roo*-e-nus, fallen to ruin ; dilapidated ; bringing to or causing ruin.
ruinously, *ad.* in a ruinous manner.
ruinousness, *n.* state or quality of being ruinous.
rulable, *a.* *rool*-a-bl, subject or amenable to rule ; conformable to rule.
★**rule,** *n.* rool, the act of ruling ; government ; sway ; established principle, standard, or directory ; established or regular mode of proceeding ; a maxim or canon ; an instrument for drawing straight lines and, when graduated, as a measure ; a thin strip of brass used to print a line or lines ; in a monastery, etc., that which is established for its direction ; a determinate mode prescribed for performing any operation and producing certain results [Math.] ; an established form of construction in a particular class of words [Gram.] ; an order made to regulate either court practice or the action of parties to a suit [Law]. **as a rule,** in the ordinary way ; usually. **rule absolute, nisi,** *see these words*. **rule of the road,** the body of regulations controlling land, sea, or air traffic. **rule of three,** the rule for finding the fourth proportional number of three given numbers. **rule of thumb,** any system that has become purely mechanical as a matter of personal experience. (O.Fr. *reule*, from L. *rigula*, a ruler or measuring strip.)
rule, *v.t.* rool, to govern ; to manage ; to settle as by rule ; to determine, as a court ; to decide ; to mark lines by a ruler : *v.i.* to have power or command ; to stand or maintain a level [Comm.]. (O.Fr. *riule*.)
ruler, *n.* *rool*-er, one who rules ; one who makes laws or governs ; an instrument of wood or metal, etc., by which straight lines are drawn, a straightedge ; a man who or machine which rules paper.
ruling, *a.* *rool*-ing, governing ; determining ; marking by a ruler ; predominant : *n.* an authoritative decision.
rulingly, *ad.* by way of rule.
rulley, *n.* *rul*-e, a dray.
rum, *n.* rum, spirit distilled from fermented molasses or the juice of the sugar-cane. (Contraction of the earlier *rumbullion*, a word of doubtful origin.)
rum, *a.* rum, old-fashioned ; odd ; queer [Slang].
Rumanian, *a.* and *n.* roo-*may*-ne-an, Roumanian.
rumba, *n.* *rum*-ba, a popular American dance originated by Cuban Negroes ; music suitable for this. (Sp.)
rumble, *n.* *rum*-bl, a rumbling sound ; a seat or compartment for luggage at the back of a carriage ; an uncovered folding seat in the rear of a motor-car : *v.i.* to make a low, continued sound, as by rolling heavily : *v.t.* and *i.* to fathom or detect to see through [Slang]. (M.E. *rombelen*.)
rumbler, *n.* *rum*-bler, a person or thing that rumbles.
rumble-tumble, *n.* jerking motion, as of a country cart.
rumbling, *a.* *rum*-bling, making a low, heavy continuous sound : *n.* a sound of this sort.
rumblingly, *ad.* with a rumbling sound or motion.
rum-bud, or **-blossom,** *n.* a red pimple or blotch due to alcoholic excess, a grog-blossom [Coll.].
rumbustical, *a.* rum-*bus*-te-kal, boisterous. (Dial.)
rumbustious, *a.* rum-*bus*-chus, heartily hilarious ; rumbustical.
rumen, *n.* *roo*-men, the first stomach of a ruminant, the receptacle of the cud. (L., a throat.)
rumgumption, *n.* rum-*gump*-shon, shrewdness ; common sense [Scots.].
ruminant, *a.* *roo*-me-nant, chewing the cud ; meditative : *n.* any member of the Ruminantia, an order of hoofed herbivorous mammals that chew the cud, including the oxen, sheep, deer, camels, etc. (L. *ruminans*, ruminating.)
ruminantly, *ad.* in a ruminant manner.
ruminate, *v.i.* *roo*-me-nate, to chew the cud ; to meditate ; to ponder : *v.t.* to chew again ; to muse on. (L. *ruminatus*, ruminated.)
rumination, *n.* roo-me-*nay*-shon, the act of ruminating ; remastication of swallowed food ; meditation.
ruminative, *a.* *roo*-me-na-tiv, given to pondering ; engaged in rumination.
ruminatively, *ad.* in a ruminative manner.
ruminator, *n.* *roo*-me-nay-tor, one who muses deliberately on any subject.
rummage, *n.* *rum*-aj, a careful searching ; a clearing out : *v.t.* and *i.* to clear a ship's hold ; to search closely by looking into every corner and tumbling things about. **rummage sale,** a sale of old clothes, odds and ends, etc., usually for some social service. (O.Fr. *arrumage*.)
rummager, *n.* *rum*-a-jer, one who rummages.
rummer, *n.* *rum*-er, a deep wine-glass or drinking cup. (Low Ger. *römer*.)
rummily, *ad.* *rum*-e-le, in a queer manner.
rummy, *a.* *rum*-e, characteristic of rum ; queer : *n.* a simple round card game for from 3 to 6 players.
rumness, *n.* *rum*-ness, queerness.
rumorous, *a.* *roo*-mo-rus, of the nature of rumour ; pertaining to a rumour.
rumour, *n.* *roo*-mur, hearsay ; popular report ; a current but unauthenticated story ; report of a fact ; fame : *v.t.* to circulate as a report. (L. *rumour*.)
rumour-monger, *n.* one who spreads rumours.
rump, *n.* rump, the end of the backbone with the parts adjacent ; the buttocks ; the fag-end. **the Rump,** a name of contempt given to the remnant of the Long Parliament in 1659. (Ice. *rumpr*.)
rumple, *n.* *rum*-pl, a fold or plait : *v.t.* to wrinkle ; to make uneven, or untidy. (*rimple*.)
rumpless, *a.* *rump*-less, destitute of a rump or tail.
rump-steak, *n.* a steak cut from near the rump of beef.
rumpus, *n.* *rum*-pus, a disturbance ; a quarrel [Slang].
rumpy, *n.* *rum*-pe, a Manx tailless cat. (*rump*.)
rum-runner, *n.* one engaged in the illicit introduction of alcoholic liquor into a prohibited area ; a bootlegger.
rum-shrub, *n.* a flavoured cordial of which the alcoholic base is rum.
rum-tum, *n.* a sculling boat on the tidal Thames.
run, *v.i.* run, to move or pass swiftly on the ground with the legs ; to use the legs in moving ; to move in a hurry ; to spread ; to extend ; to rush violently ; to sail ; to slide ; to move on or as on wheels, or as a fluid ; to revolve as a wheel ; to contend in a race, competition, or election, etc. ; to flee for escape ; to flow in any manner ; to drip ; to melt ; to turn ; to go ; to pass ; to fall ; to have a course ; to be carried ; to ravel lengthwise (of stockings, etc.) ; to discharge matter ; to continue in opera-

tion; to be current. **run away,** to flee; to escape; to run uncontrolled. **run down,** to stop, as an unwound clock; to become weak in health; to be discharged, as an electric cell. **run on,** to talk incessantly. **run out,** to come to an end; to be wasted or exhausted. **run over,** to overflow. **run riot,** *see* **riot. run short,** to come to an end of; to become insufficient. **run true,** to function as naturally expected. **run wild,** to live, go, or become untamed or without culture. *p.* **ran.** *pp.* **run.** (A.S. *rinnan.*)

run, *v.t.* run, to drive; to force; to cause to be driven; to fuse; to cast; to incur; to manage or carry through; to operate; to smuggle; to break through; to pursue in thought; to thrust; to draw; to cause to ply; to cause to pass; to discharge; to pursue; to sew by taking several stitches on the needle simultaneously; to arrest [Slang]. **run against,** to encounter; to work in opposition. **run down,** to pursue until taken; out of condition [Med.]; having become unwound (of clocks, etc.); to collide with and sink (a vessel) or put out of action (a car, etc.); to disparage. **run in,** to operate (a new machine) in such a way that the moving parts become fully adjusted to their bearings [Mech.]; to insert as an addition without leaving a break [esp. Print.]; to arrest [Slang]. **run on,** to continue without a break [esp. Print.]; to go on (talking, etc.) endlessly. **run over,** to narrate; to run the eye over hastily; to ride or drive over. **run through,** to examine hastily; to squander. **run up,** to increase; to accumulate; to force (prices) up. **run up against,** to meet casually or by accident; to collide with.

★**run,** *n.* run, act of running; course; flow; a successful running of batsmen from one popping-crease to the other [Cricket]; a complete circuit of the bases [Baseball]; sudden and sustained demands on a bank for withdrawals, on a dealer for goods, etc.; habitual course; distance sailed over; a voyage; a trip; a continuous period (of office, etc.), series, or succession; a ladder or lengthwise ravel (in stockings, etc.); a roulade [Mus.]; a burrow; an enclosure for fowls, etc.; a large grazing ground. **in the long run,** in the final result. **on the run,** hurrying; in retreat; evading arrest. **the run of mankind,** the generality of people.

runabout, *n. run*-a-bout, a light motor-car, motor-boat, or aeroplane; a small open wagon.

runagate, *n. run*-a-gate, a fugitive; a vagabond. (O.Fr. *renegat,* a renegade.)

runaway, *n. run*-a-way, one who flees from danger or restraint; a deserter; a bolting horse; a fugitive: *a.* fleeing; won by a long lead [Racing]. **runaway marriage,** marriage clandestinely after elopement.

runcible spoon, *n. run*-se-bl, a fork with three broad tines, an outer one of which has a cutting edge. (Origin uncertain.)

runcinate, *a. run*-se-nate, coarsely toothed; with lobes or indentations pointed backwards [Bot.]. (L. *runcinatus.*)

rundle, *n. run*-dl, a round; a step of a ladder; anything revolving round an axis. (*roundel.*)

rundlet, *n. rund*-let, a small barrel, a runlet.

rune, *n.* roon, a character of the earliest alphabet in use in Northern Europe; a canto in Finnish poetry: *pl.* poetry in runes. (A.S. *run,* a mysterious communication.)

runer, *n. roo*-ner, one who composed in or wrote runes; a Gothic bard.

rung, rung, *p.* and *pp.* of *ring.*

rung, *n.* rung, a step or round of a ladder; a spoke; a floor-timber in a ship. (A.S. *hrung,* pole.)

runic, *a. roo*-nik, pertaining to the Norse alphabet; cut in runes. **runic-knot,** a Scandinavian twisted ornamentation.

runlet, *n. run*-let, a small barrel of varying capacity but not more than about 18 gallons. (O.Fr. *rondelet.*)

runlet, *n. run*-let, a little stream; a runnel.

runnable, *a. run*-a-bl, warrantable, capable of being hunted (of a stag).

runnel, *n. run*-el, a rivulet or small brook; a gutter. (A.S. *rynel.*)

runner, *n. run*-er, one that runs; a racer; a messenger; formerly, a constable; that part on which a sledge, etc., slides; the blade of a skate; any device to assist gliding motion [Mech.]; the revolving stone of a mill; a sliding part; a slender creeping branch forming roots [Bot.]. **runner bean,** the scarlet runner. **runner tackle,** a kind of tackle with a movable block running on a fall fastened at one end.

runner-up, *n.* the second in a race, etc.; one who raises the bids at an auction.

running, *a. run*-ing, kept for a race; in succession; flowing; discharging pus: *n.* act of passing with speed; that which runs or flows; discharge from a sore: *ad.* in succession. **running commentary,** a report of a contemporaneous event, race, etc., made or broadcast by a spectator. **running fight,** a battle in which one party flees and the other pursues. **running fire,** a constant firing of arms. **running rigging,** the rigging or rope passing through blocks [Naut.]. **running title,** the title printed at the head of every, or every left-hand, page of a book. **in the running,** having a fair chance of success. **to make the running,** to lead; to set the pace.

running-board, *n.* the footboard at either side of some motor-cars.

runnion, *n. run*-yun, a mangy or scabby creature; a drab.

runny, *a. run*-e, semi-liquid; having a tendency to run.

runologist, *n.* roo-*nol*-o-jist, one skilled on runology; a collector of runes.

runology, *n.* roo-*nol*-o-je, the study of runes.

runt, *a.* runt, stunted in growth, especially of cattle: *n.* any stunted animal; one of a small breed of oxen; a dwarf; a large variety of pigeon. (Origin unknown.)

runty, *a. run*-te, stunted; dwarfish.

runway, *n. run*-way, a trail; a passage-way for fowls, etc.; a prepared strip for the take-off and landing of aeroplanes.

rupee, *n.* roo-*pee,* the Indian standard coin, worth, at parity, 1*s.* 6*d.* (Hind. *rūpiya.*)

rupestral, *a.* ru-*pes*-tral, growing on or inhabiting rocks.

rupestrine, *a.* ru-*pes*-trine, rupestral.

rupia, *n. roop*-ya, a severe non-contagious skin disease of syphilitic origin. (Gr. *ryppos,* filth.)

ruptive, *a. rup*-tiv, tending to break or rupture.

rupturable, *a. rup*-tewr-ra-bl, capable of being ruptured.

rupture, *n. rup*-tewr, the act of breaking or bursting; the state of being broken or violently parted; breach or interruption of peace; hernia [Med.]: *v.t.* to burst: *v.i.* to suffer a breach or disruption. (Fr.)

ruptured, *a. rup*-tewrd, broken; having a hernia [Med.].

rupturewort, *n. rup*-tewr-wurt, the plant, *Herniaria glabra.*

rural, *a. roor*-ral, pertaining to the country, as distinguished from the town; rustic; agricultural; suiting or resembling the country. **rural dean,** a clergyman, ranking next below archdeacon, having supervision of the churches and church property in a district called a **rural deanery. rural district,** an administrative division of a county. (Fr., from L. *ruralis.*)

ruralist, *n. roor*-ra-list, one who leads a rural life.

rurality, *n.* roor-*ral*-e-te, ruralness; a country property. (Fr. *ruralité.*)

ruralize, *v.t. roor*-ra-lize, to render rural: *v.i.* to rusticate.

rurally, *ad. roor*-ra-le, as in the country.

ruralness, *n.* quality or state of being rural.

ruridecanal, *a.* roor-re-*dek*-a-nal *or* -de-*kay*-nal, relating to a rural dean or his office.

Ruritanian, *a.* roor-re-*tay*-ne-an, romantic, imaginative, and concerned with court intrigue. (*Ruritania,* east European kingdom of Anthony Hope's "Prisoner of Zenda," 1894).

Rusa, *n. rooz*-ah, a genus of large-sized Indian deer, including the sambar. (Malay.)

Ruscus, *n. rus*-kus, the genus of plants which includes the butcher's-broom, *R. aculeatus.* (L.)

ruse, *n.* rooz, a trick; artifice; stratagem. **ruse de guerre,** a stratagem of war. (Fr.)

rush, *n.* rush, a plant of the genus *Juncus,* growing mostly in wet ground; anything of little or no value. (A.S. *risc.*)

rush, *n.* rush, a driving forward with eagerness and haste; a sudden run; a stampede; a thronging to a new goldfield, etc.; insistent demand; a swindle, an extortionate charge [Slang]; an attempt to get the ball to the goal of the opposite side [Football]: *v.i.* to press forward with impetuosity; to enter with undue eagerness: *v.t.* to make an assault on; to repulse; to defraud or cheat [Slang]. (A.S. *hriscan*, to create an uproar.)

rush-bottomed, *a.* seated with rushes.

rush-candle, *n.* a narrow taper made of the pith of a rush dipped in melted tallow.

rushen, *a. rush*-en, made of rushes.

rusher, *n. rush*-er, one who rushes forward.

rush-hour, *n.* a peak period, esp. a time when traffic is most busy and congested.

rush-light, *n.* the light of a rush-candle; a small feeble light; a rush-candle.

rush-mat, *n.* a mat made of rushes.

rushy, *a. rush*-e, abounding in or made of rushes.

rusk, *n.* rusk, a kind of light crusty cake or crisp bread. (Sp. *rosca*, a twist of bread.)

Russ, *a.* rus, pertaining to Russia or the Russians: *n.* the language of the Russians; a Russian. (Russ. *Rūsi*, Russia.)

russet, *a. rus*-et, reddish-brown; coarse; homespun: *n.* a coarse homespun dress; a rough-skinned kind of apple of russet colour. (O.F. *rousset.*)

russety, *a. rus*-e-te, of a russet colour.

russia, *n. rush*-a, or **russia leather,** a soft, specially tanned leather dressed with birch oil, originally made in Russia and used for book-binding.

Russian, *a. rush*-an, pertaining to Russia: *n.* a native or the language of Russia.

Russianize, *v.t. rush*-an-ize, to make Russian.

Russification, *n.* rus-e-fe-*kay*-shon, the act of making Russian or impregnating with Russian ideals.

Russify, *v.t. rus*-e-fy, to Russianize.

Russophil, *a. rus*-o-fil, favouring Russia (esp. tsarist Russia) and its civilization: *n.* an uncritical admirer of Russia (esp. tsarist Russia). (*Russo*, and Gr. *philos*, love.)

Russophilism, *n. rus*-o-fil-izm, uncritical admiration of Russia (esp. tsarist Russia) and its civilization.

Russophobe, *a. rus*-o-fohb, disliking Russia: *n.* one who dislikes Russia.

Russophobia, *n.* rus-o-*foh*-be-a, dread or hatred or Russia, her political or military power and ambition.

rust, *n.* rust, the red incrustation on iron, caused by its oxygenation under exposure to air and moisture; anything like rust; a disease on grasses, due to fungi, characterized by brown orange-coloured spots; any fungus causing rust; deterioration due to inactivity [Fig.]: *v.i.* to contract rust; to degenerate in idleness: *v.t.* to cause to contract rust. (A.S.)

rustic, *n. rus*-tik, a peasant; countryman; a boor: *a.* pertaining to the country; rural; rude; unpolished; uncouth; awkward; artless; hacked and pecked to imitate rough work (of exterior building-stone); in, or in imitation of, its rough, natural state (of timber, etc.). (Fr. *rustique.*)

rustically, *ad. rus*-te-ka-le, in a rustic or unpolished manner.

rusticate, *v.i. rus*-te-kate, to dwell in or withdraw to the country: *v.t.* to compel to reside in the country; to suspend for a time from a University; to give a rustic appearance to (masonry, woodwork, etc.). (L. *rusticatus*, banished to the land.)

rustication, *n.* rus-te-*kay*-shon, residence in the country; temporary exclusion from a University; to make rustic (of masonry, woodwork, etc.).

rusticity, *n.* rus-*tis*-e-te, rustic manners; absence of refinement; clownishness. (Fr. *rusticité.*)

rustily, *ad. rus*-te-le, in a rusty manner.

rustiness, *n.* the state of being rusty.

rustle, *n. rus*-l, a rustling: *v.i.* to make a quick succession of gentle sounds, like the rubbing of silk cloth or dry leaves; to hustle [Amer. slang]. (Imit.)

rustler, *n. rus*-ler, one who rustles; a hustler.

rustless, *a. rust*-less, not susceptible of becoming rusty; without rust.

rusty, *a. rus*-te, covered or affected with rust; as if covered with rust; inexpert from inactivity; harsh; husky. (A.S. *rustig.*)

rut, *n.* rut, the periodic œstrual excitement of animals, esp. deer; the period of this: *v.i.* to have this excitement or impulse: *v.t.* to cover in copulation (of deer). (O.Fr.)

rut, *n.* rut, a wheel-track; a well-worn groove; a settled habit; a monotonous manner of living: *v.t.* to cut ruts in.

rutabaga, *n.* roo-ta-*bay*-ga, the swede or Swedish turnip. (Swed.)

ruth, *n.* rooth, mercy; pity; tenderness; sorrow for another. (A.S. *hreow*, pity.)

Ruthene, *n.* roo-*theen*, a Ruthenian.

Ruthenian, *a.* roo-*thee*-ne-an, pertaining to the Ruthenians or their language: *n.* a member of a Little Russian race of Eastern Czechoslovakia; the Little Russian or Ukrainian language. (Late L. *Rutheni*, Russians.)

ruthenic, *a.* roo-*thee*-nik, pertaining to or derived from ruthenium.

ruthenium, *n.* roo-*thee*-ne-um, a hard, brittle and malleable metallic element of the platinum group. (*Ruthenia.*)

ruthful, *a. rooth*-ful, rueful; compassionate.

ruthless, *a. rooth*-less, without ruth; cruel; pitiless; barbarous.

ruthlessly, *ad.* in a ruthless manner.

ruthlessness, *n.* the quality of being ruthless.

rutilant, *a. roo*-te-lant, shining. (L. *rutilans*, shining.)

rutile, *n. roo*-til, titanium dioxide, a red crystalline mineral and gem-stone. (L. *rutilus*, red.)

rutin, *n. roo*-tin, a glucoside present in rue and other plants.

ruttish, *a. rut*-ish, lustful; libidinous.

rutty, *a. rut*-e, abounding in ruts.

ryal, *n. ry*-al, an English gold coin, of varying value, current from about 1465 to 1630. (*royal.*)

rye, *n.* ry, the cereal plant *Secale cereale*, or its seeds; whisky made from rye [Amer.]. (A.S. *ryge.*)

rye, *n.* ry, a young man; a gentleman. (Romany.)

rye-grass, *n.* a grass of the genus *Lolium*, extensively cultivated for fodder for cattle.

ryepeck, *n. ry*-pek, a pole to which to moor a punt, etc., serving also or as a mark in aquatic sports.

rynd, *n.* rynd, a mill-rind.

ryot, *n. ry*-ot, a Hindu cultivator of the soil; an Indian peasant. (Hind. *raiyat.*)

S

S, es, the nineteenth letter in the English alphabet is generally sounded as in *sand*, *basic*, often as *z* (*rose*, *physic*), *sh* (*sugar*, *pressure*), or *zh* (*treasure*, *invasion*), and is sometimes silent (*island*, *tapis*). As a suffix it forms the plural of many nouns, and the third pers. pres. indicative of verbs.
sabadilla, *n.* *sab*-a-*dil*-a, the Mexican plant *Schœnocaulon officinale*, yielding an alkaloid used as an insecticide, in cases of rheumatism and neuralgia, and in the manufacture of tear-gas.
Sabæan, *n.* sa-*bee*-an, one of an ancient people of Saba, or southern Arabia, the biblical Sheba: *a.* pertaining to this people or to its Semitic language.
Sabaism, *n.* *say*-ba-izm, the worship of the heavenly hosts, as at once embodiments and symbols of the deity. (Heb. *tsabha*, host.)
Sabaoth, *n.pl.* sa-*bay*-oth, armies. (Heb.)
Sabbatarian, *n.* sab-a-*tare*-re-an, a Jew who observes the seventh day of the week as the Sabbath; a strict observer of the Christian Sabbath: *a.* pertaining to the Sabbatarians or Sabbatarianism.
Sabbatarianism, *n.* sab-a-*tare*-re-a-nizm, the doctrine or practice of the Sabbatarians.
Sabbath, *n.* *sab*-ath, a day of the week set apart for rest and divine worship (Saturday among the Jews, Sunday the Christians, and Friday the Mohammedans); a time of rest; a sabbatical year. **witches' Sabbath**, *see* **witch.** (Heb. *shabbath*, rest.)
Sabbath-breaker, *n.* one who profanes the Sabbath.
Sabbath-breaking, *n.* profanation of the Sabbath.
Sabbathless, *a.* *sab*-ath-less, having no sabbath; without intermission of daily labour.
Sabbatic, *a.* sa-*bat*-ik, sabbatical.
Sabbatical, *a.* sa-*bat*-e-kal, pertaining to or resembling the Sabbath. **Sabbatical year**, in the Jewish economy, every seventh year, during which the lands were to rest or lie without tillage—hence, the one year's vacation in every seven awarded to professors in certain American universities.
Sabbatism, *n.* *sab*-a-tizm, strict observance of the Sabbath; intermission of labour.
Sabellian, *a.* sa-*bel*-e-an, pertaining to Sabellianism: *n.* a follower of Sabellius, a 3rd-cent. Libyan theologian, who maintained that the Trinity was a trinity of function and manifestation only, not of Persons.
Sabellianism, *n.* sa-*bel*-e-a-nizm, the doctrine of Sabellius.
sabelline, *a.* *say*-bel-ine, pertaining to, or of the colour of the fur of, the sable.
Sabianism, *n.* *say*-be-a-nizm, the religion of the Sabæans; (erroneously) Sabaism.
sabicu, *n.* *sab*-e-kew, the hard wood of either of the W. Indian trees *Lysiloma sabicu* or *Peltophorum adnatum*, used for furniture, etc.
Sabine, *n.* *sab*-ine, one of an ancient Italian race merged in the Roman: *a.* pertaining to this people.
sable, *n.* *say*-bl, a small carnivore of the weasel family, *Mustela zibellina*, whose fur is highly valued; its fur; an artist's brush made from its hair; black colour [Her.]: *pl.* sable furs for wear; black or mourning garments: *a.* black; dark: *v.t.* to make sable. (Russ. *sobole*, sable.)
sabot, *n.* *sab*-oh, a wooden shoe, esp. as used by the French and Belgian peasantry. (Fr.)
sabotage, *n.* *sab*-o-tahzh, deliberate damage, esp. by strikers or people of enemy-occupied countries, to machinery, tools, property, etc. (Fr.)
saboteur, *n.* sab-o-toor, one who practises sabotage; a partisan [Mil.].
sabre, *n.* *say*-ber, a sword with a thick back and slightly curved blade for use of cavalry: *v.t.* to strike, cut, or kill with a sabre. (Fr.)
sabretache, *n.* *sab*-er-tash, a leather case suspended from the sword-belt of a cavalry officer. (Fr.)
sabre-toothed, *a.* having long curved canine teeth like the extinct sabre-toothed tiger, *Felis machairodus.*
sabreur, *n.* sa-*brur*, one who carries **a sabre**; a cavalryman. (Fr.)
sabulite, *n.* *sab*-yew-lite, a high explosive consisting of ammonium nitrate, calcium silicide, and T.N.T.
sabulous, *a.* *sab*-yew-lus, sandy; gritty; arenaceous (L. *sabulum*, sand.)
saburra, *n.* sa-*bu*-ra, foulness of the mouth or stomach; sordes. (L., sand.)
saburral, *a.* sa-*bu*-ral, pertaining to foulness of the stomach, tongue, or teeth; affected with sordes [Path.].
saburration, *n.* *sab*-ur-*ray*-shon, sand-bathing; the application of hot sand to the body [Med.].
sac, *n.* sak, any cavity or bag-like part [Anat. and Bot.]; the outer wall of a tumour or cyst. (Fr., from L. *saccus*, a bag.).
sac, *n.* sak, a jurisdictional right belonging to the lord of a manor among the Anglo-Saxons [Old law].
saccade, *n.* sa-*kade*, a sudden check of a horse with the reins; a strong pressure of the bow against the strings [Mus.]. (Fr.)
saccate, *a.* *sak*-at, having the form of a bag; encysted [Med.]; dilated [Bot.].
saccharate, *n.* *sak*-a-rate, a salt or ester of saccharic acid.
saccharic, *a.* sa-*ka*-rik, pertaining to or obtained from sugar. (L. *saccharum*, sugar.)
sacchariferous, *a.* *sak*-a-*rif*-er-rus, producing sugar. (L. *saccharum*, and *fero*, yield.)
saccharification, *n.* sa-*ka*-re-fe-*kay*-shon, conversion into sugar.
saccharify, *v.t.* sa-*ka*-re-fy, to convert into sugar. (L. *saccharum*, and *facio*, make.)
saccharimeter, *n.* *sak*-a-*rim*-e-ter, an instrument for testing sugars by polarized light.
saccharin, *n.* *sak*-a-rin, a crystalline compound of extreme sweetness derived from coal-tar. (Fr.)
saccharine, *a.* *sak*-a-rine, sweet; sweetening; pertaining to or having the qualities of sugar. (Fr. *saccharin.*)
saccharinity, *n.* sak-a-*rin*-e-te, sweetness.
saccharite, *n.* *sak*-a-rite, a white or greenish-white variety of felspar.
saccharize, *v.t.* *sak*-a-rize, to form into sugar.
saccharoid, *a.* *sak*-a-royd, resembling cube sugar in texture; of granular structure: *n.* a sugar-like or saccharoid substance.
saccharometer, *n.* *sak*-a-*rom*-e-ter, a saccharimeter; a form of hydrometer for determining the quantity of saccharine matter in liquids. (L. *saccharum*, sugar, Gr. *metron*, measure.)
saccharometry, *n.* *sak*-a-*rom*-e-tre, the process of determining the amount of sugar in a solution.
saccharon, *n.* *sak*-a-ron, sucrose. (L.)
saccharose, *n.* *sak*-a-rohs, sucrose; also any compound sugar.
Saccharum, *n.* *sak*-a-rum, a genus of tropical grasses of which *S. officinarum* is the sugar-cane; (*l.c.*) invert sugar. (Late L.)
sacciform, *a.* *sak*-se-form, saccate; baggy.
saccular, *a.* *sak*-yew-lar, like a small sac.
sacculate, *a.* *sak*-yew-lat, having a sac or sacs; encysted.
sacculated, *a.* *sak*-yew-lay-ted, divided into sacs.
sacculation, *n.* sak-yew-*lay*-shon, state of being sacculate; a part resembling a sac.
saccule, *n.* *sak*-yewl, a small sac. (L. *sacculus.*)
sacellum, *n.* sa-*sel*-um, an unroofed enclosure with an altar; a canopied tomb used as an altar. (L.)
sacerdotal, *a.* sas-er-*doh*-tal, pertaining to priests or the priesthood; priestly. (Fr.)
sacerdotalism, *n.* sas-er-*doh*-ta-lizm, a priestly system, esp. one professing to mediate divine benefit by the ministry of priests.
sacerdotalist, *n.* sas-er-*doh*-ta-list, a supporter of priesthood; a high churchman.
sacerdotalize, *v.t.* sas-er-*doh*-ta-lize, to make conformable or subservient to sacerdotalism.
sacerdotally, *ad.* in a sacerdotal manner.
sachem, *n.* *say*-chem, a sagamore, a chief among the

North American Indians; a chief of a political group, esp. of the Tammany Society [U.S.A.]. (Algonquian.)
sachemship, *n.* *say*-chem-ship, the office or jurisdiction of a sachem.
sachet, *n.* *sash*-ay, a scent-bag. (Fr.)
sack, *n.* sak, a long coarse bag used for holding grain, flour, potatoes, etc.; the quantity a sack contains; a sacque or other loose gown: *v.t.* to put in a sack or sacks; to discharge from employment. **to hold the sack,** to get nothing; to be left empty-handed [Coll.]. (A.S. *sacc.*)
sack, *n.* sak, a dry white wine from Spain or the Canaries. (Fr. *sec*, from L. *siccus*, dry.)
sack, *n.* sak, the plundering or pillage of a captured town or place: *v.t.* to plunder a town when taken by storm. (Fr. *sac.*)
sackage, *n.* *sak*-aj, the act of taking by storm; pillaging.
sackbut, *n.* *sak*-but, a primitive form of trombone; a Babylonian harp. (Fr. *saquebute*—origin doubtful.)
sackcloth, *n.* *sak*-kloth, cloth of which sacks are made; coarse cloth anciently worn as a sign of mourning, distress, or penitence.
sacker, *n.* *sak*-er, one who sacks a town; one who makes or fills sacks.
sackful, *n.* a full sack; as much as a sack will hold.
sacking, *n.* *sak*-ing, cloth of which sacks or bags are made; the coarse canvas that supports a bed.
sackless, *a.* *sak*-less, free of crime; innocent; feeble-minded [Scots.]. (A.S. *sac leas*, without guilt.)
sacque, *n.* sak, a woman's loose-fitting gown or cloak; a short loose-bodied coat. (Pseudo-Fr.)
sacral, *a.* *say*-kral, pertaining to the sacrum.
sacrament, *n.* *sak*-ra-ment, any one of the religious rites in the Christian Church instituted as an outward and visible sign of an inward and spiritual grace, esp. (among Protestants) the eucharist or Lord's Supper and baptism; the consecrated elements of the eucharist. (O.Fr.)
sacramental, *a.* sak-ra-*men*-tal, pertaining to or constituting a sacrament; bound by oath.
sacramentalism, *n.* sak-ra-*men*-ta-lizm, excessive appreciation of the value of sacraments.
sacramentally, *ad.* in a sacramental manner.
sacramentarian, *a.* *sak*-ra-men-*tare*-re-an, pertaining to the sacraments or the Sacramentarians: *n.* one given to sacramentalism; (*cap.*) one of the early German Reformers who rejected the doctrine of the real presence held by Luther.
Sacramentary, *n.* sak-ra-*men*-ta-re, an ancient service-book of the Roman Church used in the celebration of the sacraments; a Sacramentarian. (Late L. *sacramentarium.*)
sacrarium, *n.* sa-*krare*-re-um, a shrine; the space between the altar and the altar-rails. (L.)
sacred, *a.* *say*-kred, consecrated to a religious purpose; connected with religion or a religious service; consecrated; holy; venerable; inviolable. **sacred beetle,** the scarabæus. **Sacred College,** the College of Cardinals. **sacred music,** music suitable for performance at religious services. (Fr. *sacrer*, to consecrate.)
sacredly, *ad.* in a sacred manner.
sacredness, *n.* state of being sacred; sanctity; inviolableness.
sacrificant, *n.* sa-*krif*-e-kant, one who offers a sacrifice.
sacrifice, *n.* *sak*-re-fice, the act of sacrificing; that which is sacrificed; the giving up of one thing for another; that which is so given up; a holocaust; a sale at a loss: *v.t.* to offer to a divinity upon an altar; to give up for something else; to devote with loss; to destroy. (Fr.)
sacrificer, *n.* *sak*-re-fy-ser, one who sacrifices.
sacrificial, *a.* sak-re-*fish*-al, connected with sacrifice; performing or consisting in sacrifices.
sacrilege, *n.* *sak*-re-lij, the crime of profaning sacred things; alienation of consecrated property, etc., to lay use; breaking into and stealing from a church. (O.Fr.)
sacrilegious, *a.* sak-re-*lij*-us, violating sacred things; committing or involving sacrilege.
sacrilegiously, *ad.* in a sacrilegious manner.
sacrilegiousness, *n.* the quality of being sacrilegious; disposition to sacrifice.
sacrilegist, *n.* *sak*-re-le-jist, one guilty of sacrilege.
sacring, *n.* *say*-kring, consecration, esp. of the eucharistic elements, and of bishops and sovereigns. **sacring bell,** the sanctus bell.
sacrist, *n.* *say*-krist, a sacristan; a cathedral official who copies out music for the choir and has charge of the books. (Late L. *sacrista.*)
sacristan, *n.* *sak*-ris-tan, one who has charge of the sacristry and the sacred vessels and movables of a church; a sexton. (Fr. *sacristan.*)
sacristy, *n.* *sak*-ris-te, a room in a church where the sacred utensils and vestments are kept; the vestry.
sacro-iliac, *a.* *say*-kro-*il*-e-ak, pertaining to the sacrum and ilium. [Anat.].
sacrosanct, *a.* *sak*-ro- *or* *say*-kro-sankt, most sacred; inviolable. (L. *sacrosanctus.*)
sacrosanctity, *n.* sak-ro- *or* *say*-kro-*sank*-te-te, the quality or condition of being sacrosanct.
sacrum, *n.* *say*-krum (*pl.* **sacra**), a compound triangular bone at the base of the vertebral column uniting with the haunch bones to form the pelvis. (L.)
★**sad,** *a.* sad, weighed or cast down with grief; melancholy; downcast; serious or grave; calamitous; bad; dark or dingy (of colour); heavy (of bread). (A.S. *sæd*, sated.)
sadden, *v.t.* *sad*-en, to make sad or sorrowful; to tone down, as a colour: *v.i.* to grow sad.
saddish, *a.* *sad*-ish, somewhat sad.
saddle, *n.* *sad*-dl, a seat on a horse's back or on a cycle or similar machine for the rider to sit on; something like a saddle; a joint (esp. mutton) consisting of upper back with both loins; a support or connecting piece [Mech.]; a col [Geog.]: *v.t.* to put a saddle on; to load. (A.S. *sadol.*)
saddleback, *n.* *sad*-dl-bak, a long ridge with a similar slope on each side; a roof with two gables and one ridge; a name for various animals, as the great black-backed gull, *Larus marinus*, and the harp seal, *Phoca grænlandica*.
saddlebacked, *a.* *sad*-dl-bakt, having a low back and elevated neck and head, as a horse; having saddle-like markings [Zool.]; having upward curving ends.
saddle-bag, *n.* one of a pair of pouches united by straps for carriage on horseback.
saddle-bar, *n.* a longitudinal strut in the framework of a saddle; a strengthening bar of a stained-glass window.
saddlebow, *n.* *sad*-dl-boh, the front part of a saddle, or the pieces forming this.
saddle-cloth, *n.* a cloth under a saddle.
saddle-horse, *n.* a horse for riding.
saddle-joint, *n.* a concavo-convex articulation [Anat.].
saddler, *n.* *sad*-ler, a maker of saddles.
saddle-roof, *n.* a roof with two gables.
saddlery, *n.* *sad*-ler-re, the trade of a saddler; the articles he deals in; a saddler's shop.
saddle-tree, *n.* the frame of a saddle; the tulip tree.
Sadducean, *a.* *sad*-yew-*see*-an, pertaining to the Sadducees.
Sadducee, *n.* *sad*-yew-see, a member of a Jewish anti-ritualistic party of about 160 B.C. to A.D. 60 which, opposing the Pharisees, held by the written word to the exclusion of tradition and denied the doctrine of immortality or the existence of spirits. (Late L., probably from Heb. *Zadok*, the reputed founder.)
Sadduceeism, *n.* *sad*-yew-*see*-izm, the doctrines of the Sadducees.
Sadhu, *n.* *sah*-doo, a Hindu holy man or ascetic. (Sans., pious.)
sad-iron, *n.* a smoothing iron, or box-iron.
sadism, *n.* *sah*-dizm, sexual perversion in which cruelty is a characteristic feature. (Marquis de *Sade*, French novelist, *d.* 1814.)
sadist, *n.* *sah*-dist, one addicted to sadism; one exulting in cruelty to others for its own sake.
sadistic, *a.* sa-*dis*-tik, pertaining to sadism; revoltingly cruel, esp. from pathological causes.
sadly, *ad.* *sad*-le, in a sad manner.
sadness, *n.* the state of being sad; seriousness.
safari, *n.* sa-*fah*-re, a big-game hunting expedition, esp. in E. Africa; a big-game hunter's retinue or caravan. (Swahili.)
★**safe,** *a.* safe, free from danger of any kind; free from hurt, injury, or damage; secure or securing from harm; no longer dangerous; prudent; reliable;

trustworthy: *n.* a chest or strong-room secure against thieves or fire; a ventilated cupboard for meat and provisions. **safe deposit,** a series of safes and strong rooms for the storage of valuables. (O.Fr. *sauf.*)
safe-conduct, *n.* a convoy, guard, warrant, or passport ensuring a safe passage.
safeguard, *n. safe*-gard, one who or that which guards safely; defence; a protection; a protective convoy; protective warrant granted to a foreigner: *v.t.* to put watch over; to guard in safety. **safeguarding,** *n* the protection of home industries by means of duties on imports [Econ.].
safe-keeping, *n.* act of preserving in safety from injury or escape; secure custody.
safely, *ad. safe*-le, in a safe manner.
safeness, *n.* state of being safe, or conferring safety.
safety, *n. safe*-te, freedom from danger, hurt, injury, or loss; close custody; a safety-bicycle. **safety curtain,** an asbestos curtain for lowering between stage and auditorium in event of fire [Theat.]. **safety glass,** transparent glass so treated as to resist shattering. (Fr. *sauveté.*)
safety-bicycle, *n.* a geared bicycle with both wheels of approximately 28 in. in diameter.
safety-lamp, *n.* a lamp covered with wire gauze, to give light in mines without danger.
safety-match, *n.* a match that ignites only on the box.
safety-pin, *n.* a pin with a guarded point; a pin for fastening, locking, or securing some part of a machine.
safety-razor, *n.* a razor with a guard and a detachable blade.
safety-valve, *n.* a valve fitted to the boiler of a steam-engine automatically allowing escape of surplus steam; any valve designed to prevent damage; an outlet or vent for over-wrought emotion, etc. [Fig.].
saffian, *n. saf*-e-an, a bright-coloured leather of goat- or sheep-skin tanned with sumac. (Russ., from Per. *sakhtiyan,* goat leather.)
safflower, *n. saf*-flou-er, a composite plant, *Carthamus tinctorius,* allied to the thistle, yielding a red dye. (O.Fr. *saflor.*)
saffron, *n. saf*-ron, the bulbous plant *Crocus sativus*; a colouring and flavouring material from its flower: *a.* saffron-coloured; deep yellow: *v.t.* to tinge with saffron; to make yellow. **meadow saffron,** a bulbous plant of the genus *Colchicum.* (Ar.)
saffrony, *a. saf*-ron-e, having the colour of saffron.
safranin, *n. saf*-ra-nin, the colouring matter of saffron; a saffron-coloured coal-tar dye. (Fr. *safran.*)
sag, *v.i.* sag, to yield; to incline from an upright or a horizontal position owing to want of support; to sink down; to incline to leeward [Naut.]: *v.t.* to cause to bend or give way: *n.* the action, fact, or dip of sagging. (Scand.)
saga, *n. sah*-ga, a mediæval Scandinavian tale in prose; a general name of those ancient compositions which comprise the history and mythology of the northern European races; a story of heroic feats. (Ice., a tale.)
sagacious, *a.* sa-*gay*-shus, quick or acute in discernment; judicious; wise; quick of scent (of animals). (L. *sagax,* of quick perception.)
sagaciously, *ad.* in a sagacious manner.
sagaciousness, *n.* the quality of being sagacious.
sagacity, *n.* sa-*gas*-e-te, sagaciousness; quickness of discernment; readiness of apprehension; discriminative intelligence.
sagamore, *n. sag*-a-more, an American Indian chief; a sachem. (Algonquian.)
sagan, *n. say*-gan, the suffragan or deputy of the Jewish high priest. (Heb.)
sagapenum, *n.* sag-a-*pee*-num, a medicinal gum-resin from a species of *Ferula* growing in Persia. (L.)
sage, *a.* saje, wise, sagacious; grave; proceeding from wisdom: *n.* a wise man; a venerable man of gravity and proven wisdom. (Fr.)
sage, *n.* saje, the savoury herb *Salvia verbenaca,* or the garden sage, *S. officinalis.* **scarlet sage,** the garden plant, *S. splendens.* (O.Fr. *sauge.*)
sage-brush, *n.* an American species of *Artemisia.*
sage-cock or **-grouse,** *n.* an American grouse of the genus *Centrocerus.*
sage-green, *a.* and *n.* greyish-green.
sagely, *ad. saje*-le, in a sage manner.
sagene, *n.* sa-*jeen,* a seine or fishing-net; a network [Fig.]. (L. *sagena.*)
sagene, *n.* sa-*zheen,* a former Russian measure of length equal to 7 ft. (2·134 metres). (Russ.)
sageness, *n.* the quality of being sage; sagacity; wisdom.
saggar, *n. sag*-er, a cylindrical case of fire-clay, in which fine stoneware is enclosed while baking. (Perhaps abbrev. of *safeguard.*)
sagittal, *a. saj*-e-tal, pertaining to or resembling an arrow. (L. *sagitta,* an arrow.)
Sagittarius, *n.* saj-e-*tare*-re-us, the ninth sign of the zodiac, the Archer. (L., an archer.)
sagittary, *n. saj*-e-ta-re, a centaur armed with a bow and quiver: *a.* pertaining to an arrow.
sagittate, *a. saj*-e-tat, shaped like the head of an arrow; elongated triangular [Bot.].
sago, *n. say*-goh, a starchy foodstuff obtained from the pith of several palms. (Malay, *sagu.*)
sagouin, *n.* sa-*goyn,* a small S. American marmoset. esp. of the genus *Callithrix.* (Fr.)
sagum, *n. say*-gum, a military cloak of the ancient Romans. (L.)
sagy, *a. say*-je, full of sage; seasoned with sage.
sahib, *n. sah*-ib, an Indian term of address to a European gentleman. (Urdu, from Ar. *cahib,* friend.)
sahlite, *n. sah*-lite, a green variety of pyroxene.
sai, *n. sah*-e, the capuchin, or any other monkey of the genus *Cebus.* (Port., from Brazilian native.)
saic, *n. say*-ik, a Turkish or Greek ketch. (Turk.)
said, sed, *p.* and *pp.* of *say,* declared; reported. **the said . . .,** the before-mentioned.
saiga, *n. sy*-ga *or say*-ga, the puff-nosed antelope of Eastern Europe and Western Asia. (Russ., an antelope.)
★**sail,** *n.* sale, a spread of canvas or similar fabric for receiving the impulse of the wind by which a ship is driven; sails collectively; a sailing ship or other vessel; the arm of a windmill; a passage or excursion by water: *v.i.* to be impelled by the action of wind upon sails; to go by water; to set sail; to glide through the air; to pass smoothly along: *v.t.* to pass over in a ship; to navigate. **make sail,** to hoist an additional quantity of sail. **set sail,** to hoist the sails; to begin a voyage. **shorten sail,** to reduce the extent of sail. **strike sail,** to lower the sails suddenly. **under sail,** *see* **under.** (A.S. *segel.*)
sailable, *a. sale*-a-bl, navigable; that may be passed by ships; that can be sailed.
sailcloth, *n. sale*-kloth, duck or canvas for sails; a similar, but lighter, dress material.
sailer, *n. sale*-er, a vessel, with reference to her speed or manner of sailing.
sail-fish, *n.* a large deep-sea fish allied to the sword-fish, having a very large dorsal fin.
sailing-master, *n.* an officer in charge of the navigation of a ship.
sailless, *a. sale*-less, destitute of sails.
sail-loft, *n.* an apartment where sails are cut out and made.
sailmaker, *n. sale*-make-er, one whose occupation is to make or repair sails.
sail-needle, *n.* a large needle with a triangular tapering point.
sailor, *n. sale*-or, a mariner; a seaman; one of the crew of a ship, esp. as distinct from an officer. **sailor's knot,** a simple knot such as is tied in a necktie; the wild geranium.
sailoring, *n. sale*-or-ring, the life, occupation, etc., of a sailor.
sailplane, *n. sale*-plane, a glider [Av.].
sail-room, *n.* an apartment in a vessel where the sails are stowed.
sain, *v.t.* sane, to make the sign of the cross on; to bless. (A.S. *segnian.*)
sainfoin, *n. sane*-foyn, the leguminous clover-like plant *Onobrychis sativa,* extensively cultivated for fodder. (Fr. *sain,* wholesome, *foin,* hay.)
saint, *a.* saynt, holy; sacred (as title of canonized persons usually abbreviated to **St.**): *n.* a person eminent for piety and virtue; a beatified holy person; one canonized by the Church; one of the blessed departed: *v.t.* to canonize; to regard as a saint: *v.i.* to act as a saint or with a show of piety. **St. Bernard,** a large rough-coated variety of dog

originally bred at the monastery of St. Bernard, Switzerland, for rescuing snow-bound travellers. **St. Elmo's fire,** the corposant. **St. John's evil,** epilepsy. **St. Leger,** s'nt-*ledj*-er *or* *sil*-en-jer, a horse-race (1 m. 6 fur. 132 yds.) for 3-yr.-olds run at Doncaster in September. **St. Luke's summer,** Indian summer. **St. Peter's fish,** the dory; the haddock. **St. Peter's pence,** *see* **Peter. saint's day,** a festival in commemoration of a particular saint. **St. Swithin's Day,** July 15, the weather prevailing on which is said to govern that of the succeeding forty days. **St. Vitus's dance,** chorea [Path.]. (Fr., from L. *sanctus*, holy, sacred.)

sainted, *pp.* *saynt*-ed, canonized: *a.* holy; pious among the saints in heaven.

saintliness, *n.* the quality of being saintly.

saintly, *a.* *saynt*-le, like a saint; befitting a saint.

saint-name, *n.* *saynt*-name, the name of a saint as distinctive. Numerous plants, including the following, bear saint-names:—**St. Agnes flower,** the snowflake; **St. Anthony's nut,** the pig-nut; **St. Barbara's cress,** yellow rocket; **St. Barnaby's thistle,** the yellow star-thistle, *Centaurea solstitialis*; **St. Bernard's lily,** *Anthericum liliago*; **St. Bruno's lily,** *Anthericum liliastrum*; **St. Catherine's flower,** love-in-a-mist; **St. Dabeoc's heath,** Irish heath, *Menziesia polifolia*; **St. George's herb,** valerian; **St. Jacob's dipper,** the pitcher-plant; **St. James's wort,** ragwort; **St. John's bread,** the carob; **St. John's wort,** any species of *Hypericum*; **St. Mary's flower,** the rose of Jericho; **St. Patrick's cabbage,** London pride; **St. Peter's wort,** samphire (and others).

saintship, *n.* *saynt*-ship, the character or qualities of a saint.

Saint-Simonian, *n.* *saynt*-se-*moh*-ne-an, a follower of the Count de St. Simon, French socialist (*d.* 1825), who recommended state ownership and the just division of the fruits of common labour as a solution of the social problem.

saith, seth, *pres. ind.* of the verb *to say*, says.

saithe, *n.* sayth, the coalfish [Scots.]. (Ice. *seythr.*)

Saiva, *n.* *sy*-va, a votary of Siva. (Hind.)

sajene, *n.* sa-*jene*, sagene (Russ. measure of length).

sajou, *n.* sa-*zhoo*, a sapajou. (Fr., from Brazilian.)

sake, *n.* sake, final cause; end; purpose; account; regard. (A.S. *sacu*, strife.)

saké, *n.* *sah*-ke, an alcoholic drink made from fermented rice. (Japanese.)

saker, *n.* *say*-ker, the hawk *Falco sacer*; a small obsolete piece of artillery. (Fr. *sacre.*)

saki, *n.* *sah*-ke, a long-haired S. American monkey of the genus *Pithecia*, with a bushy non-prehensile tail. (Brazilian.)

sakia, *n.* *sah*-ke-a, a water-wheel with earthen pots as buckets, used in N. Africa for irrigation. (Ar.)

sal, *n.* sawl, the Indian timber tree, *Shorea robusta*, a source of dammar. (Hind.)

sal, *n.* sal, salt [Chem.]. **sal alembroth,** alembroth. **sal ammoniac,** ammonium chloride. **sal prunella,** saltpetre fused and cast into cakes or balls. **sal seignette,** Rochelle-salt. **sal volatile** (vo-*lat*-e-le), an aromatic solution of carbonate of ammonia. (L.)

salaam, *n.* sa-*lahm*, a ceremonious Oriental salutation; an obeisance. (Ar., peace.)

salable, *a.* *sale*-a-bl, saleable.

salacious, *a.* sa-*lay*-shus, lustful; lecherous; obscene. (L. *salax*, lustful.)

salaciously, *ad.* in a salacious manner.

salaciousness, *n.* quality of being salacious.

salacity, *n.* sa-*las*-e-te, salaciousness; obscenity; strong propensity to venery.

salad, *n.* *sal*-ad, a dish of cold or uncooked vegetables with oil, salt, and vinegar, etc., often with egg or crab, etc. **salad days,** days of youthful inexperience. **salad cream** or **dressing,** a mayonnaise or other piquant sauce for salads. **salad oil,** refined olive oil or nut-oil. **small salad,** mustard and cress. (O.Fr.)

salade, *n.* sa-*lahd*, a sallet. (Fr.)

salading, *n.* *sal*-ad-ing, vegetables for salad.

salal, *n.* *sal*-al, a small shrub, *Gaultheria shallon*, of the western U.S.A.; its edible berry.

salamander, *n.* sal-a-*man*-der, a tailed amphibian of the genus *Salamandra*, formerly fabled to be able to live in fire; a spirit inhabiting fire; a cooking utensil for use in great heat, esp. one for browning. **salamander's hair** or **wool,** a species of asbestos. (Fr. *salamandre.*)

salamandrian, *a.* and *n.* salamandrine [Zool.].

salamandrine, *a.* sal-a-*man*-drine, resembling a salamander; enduring fire or great heat: *n.* a spirit said to inhabit fire.

salamandroid, *a.* sal-a-*man*-droyd, having the form of a salamander; salamandrine.

salami, *n.* sa-*lah*-me, a highly seasoned Italian sausage. (It.)

salangane, *n.* *sal*-ang-gain, a Far Eastern swift of the genus *Collocalia*, the nests of which are edible. (Tagalog, *salangan.*)

salariat, *n.* sa-*lare*-re-at, the salaried class, esp. as opposed to the proletariate.

salaried, *a.* *sal*-a-rid, paid by salary.

salary, *n.* *sal*-a-re, a fixed wage paid at regular intervals (usually per quarter or month), esp. to officials and professional or clerical workers; a stipend. (O.Fr. *salarie.*)

sale, *n.* sale, the act of selling; the exchange of a commodity for money of equivalent value; an auction; a demand (for); a disposal (of surplus stock, etc.) at reduced prices. **sale of work,** a bazaar for raising funds at which most of the articles on sale are the handiwork of those interested in its object. **sale price,** the reduced price at which an article is offered at a seasonal of surplus sale. (A.S. *sala.*)

saleability, *n.* sale-a-*bil*-e-te, saleableness.

saleable, *a.* *sale*-a-bl, that may be sold; in good demand; marketable.

saleableness, *n.* quality of being saleable.

salebrosity, *n.* sal-e-*bros*-e-te, ruggedness.

salebrous, *a.* *sal*-e-brus, rough; rugged. (L. *salebra*, an uneven road.)

salep, *n.* *sal*-ep, a farinaceous meal prepared from the dried tubers of various species of *Orchis*. (Ar.)

saleratus, *n.* sal-er-*ray*-tus, impure bicarbonate of potash or soda, used as a baking powder. (L. *sal aeratus*, aerated salt.)

sale-room, *n.* a room in which goods are sold, esp. by auction.

salesman, *n.* *saylz*-man, one whose business is to sell, esp. merchandise transport service, securities, etc.; a commercial traveller; a shop-assistant.

salesmanship, *n.* *saylz*-man-ship, the art of, or skill in, selling.

saleswoman, *n.* *saylz*-woom-an, a female shop-assistant; a woman who sells in a warehouse.

sale-work, *n.* work perfunctorily performed; things made just good enough to sell.

Salian, *a.* *say*-le-an, Salic: *n.* a member of the Salic tribe.

Salian, *a.* *say*-le-an, in honour of, or pertaining to the priests of, Mars. (L. *Salii*, priests of Mars.)

Salic, *a.* *sal*-ik, relating to a tribe of Franks who settled on the R. Sala (now Yssel) and later on the lower Rhine, ancestors of the Merovingian kings. **Salic law,** a late 5th-cent. code of Frankish law, esp. its provision excluding females from the inheritance of lands and hence from succession to the throne.

salicaceous, *a.* sal-e-*kay*-shus, of or pertaining to the willow family [Bot.]. (L. *salix*, willow.)

salicet, *n.* *sal*-e-set, a salicional [Mus.].

salicilate, *n.* sa-*lis*-e-late, a salt of salicylic acid: *v.t.* to treat or impregnate with this.

salicin, *n.* *sal*-e-sin, the bitter principle of certain species of *Salix*. (L. *salix*, willow.)

salicional, *n.* sa-*lish*-on-al, an 8-ft. open organ stop producing a tone like that of a willow pipe [Mus.]. (L. *salix.*)

salicylic, *a.* sal-e-*sil*-ik, pertaining to or designating **salicylic acid,** an antiseptic and preservative acid, formerly obtained from salicin but now from sodium phenolate. (L. *salix*, and Gr. *hyle*, matter.)

salience, *n.* *say*-le-ence, the state or quality of being salient; a prominent feature.

salient, *a.* *say*-le-ent, leaping; springing; in a leaping posture [Her.]; projecting outward; prominent: *n.* a prominent angle; an outwardly projecting part of a defensive system [Mil.]. (L. *saliens*, leaping.)

saliently, *ad.* in a salient manner.

saliferous, *a.* sa-*lif*-er-us, producing salt; containing rock-salt. **saliferous system,** the Triassic formation [Geol.]. (L. *sal*, and *fero*, bear.)

salifiable, *a.* sal-e-*fy*-a-bl, capable of combining with an acid to form a salt.
salification, *n.* sal-e-fe-*kay*-shon, the act or result of changing into salt.
salify, *v.t.* *sal*-e-fy, to form into a salt by combining an acid with a base. (L. *sal*, and *facio*, make.)
salimeter, *n.* sa-*lim*-e-ter, a salinometer.
salina, *n.* sa-*ly*-na, a salt-marsh: a salt-works. (Sp.)
saline, *a.* sa-*line* or *say*-line, consisting of, resembling, or containing salt: *n.* a deposit of salt; a salt-spring; an effervescing aperient. (Fr. *salin.*)
salineness, *n.* *say*-line-ness, salinity.
saliniferous, *a.* sal-e-*nif*-er-rus, producing salt.
salinity, *n.* sa-*lin*-e-te, saltness; the state of being saline.
salinometer, *n.* sal-e-*nom*-e-ter, an instrument for measuring saltness, esp. one for testing the density of sea-water in marine steam-boilers. (L. *saline*, and Gr. *metron.*)
Salique, *a.* sa-*leek*, Salic.
saliva, *n.* sa-*ly*-va, spittle; the fluid secreted by the salivary glands, serving to moisten the mouth and as an aid to digestion. (L.)
salivant, *a.* *sal*-e-vant, stimulating saliva: *n.* a medicament to produce salivation.
salivary, *a.* *sal*-e-va-re, pertaining to saliva or to the salivary glands; secreting saliva. **salivary gland,** any of the glands which secrete saliva.
salivate, *v.t.* *sal*-e-vate, to produce an unusual secretion and discharge of saliva, esp. by treatment with mercury: *v.i.* to have an excessive flow of saliva.
salivation, *n.* sal-e-*vay*-shon, an abnormally abundant flow of saliva, or the act of producing this; ptyalism.
salivator, *n.* *sal*-e-vay-tor, an agent causing salivation [Med.].
Salix, *n.* *say*-liks, the genus of trees containing the willows. (L.)
salle, *n.* sal, a large room; a hall. (Fr.)
Salleeman, *n.* *sal*-e-man, a pirate, or pirate ship, from Sallee on the coast of Morocco.
sallenders, *n.* *sal*-en-derz, an eczematous sore occurring at the bend of the knee and on the hock of a horse's hind leg (*cp.* **mallenders**) [Vet.].
sallet, *n.* *sal*-let, a mediæval bowl-shaped military helmet. (O.Fr. *salade.*)
sallow, *n.* *sal*-lo, a willow, particularly the goat willow, *Salix caprea.* **sallow thorn,** the sea-buckthorn, *Hippophaë rhamnoides.* (A.S. *sealh.*)
sallow, *a.* *sal*-loh, of a pale, sickly, yellow colour. (A.S. *salu.*)
sallowish, *a.* *sal*-lo-ish, somewhat sallow.
sallowness, *n.* the quality of being sallow.
sallowy, *a.* *sal*-lo-e, abounding in sallows.
sally, *n.* *sal*-le, a sortie; a rushing forth of besieged troops to attack the besiegers; a sprightly outburst; flight; excursion; act of levity; frolic: *v.i.* to issue or rush out suddenly. **Sally Lunn,** a sweet light tea-cake served hot. (Fr. *saillie.*)
sally-port, *n.* a postern gate or other passage for the troops to sally out by [Fort.].
salmagundi, *n.* *sal*-ma-*gun*-de, a mixture of chopped meat, pickled herring or anchovy, etc., with seasoning; a miscellaneous mixture; a medley. (Fr. *salmigondis.*)
salmi, *n.* *sal*-mee, a ragoût, esp. of game stewed in wine sauce. (Fr.)
salmon, *n.* *sam*-on, the valuable food-fish *Salmo salar*, found in northern seas, whence it ascends the rivers in the spring to spawn (it is known at successive stages of its development as an alevin, a parr, smolt, and grilse). **Pacific salmon,** the quinnat. **rock-salmon,** a fishmonger's name for certain food-fish of the salt-water blenny, pilchard, and other families. (Fr. *saumon.*)
salmonet, *n.* *sam*-on-et, a samlet.
salmonoid, *a.* *sam*-on- *or* *sal*-mon-oyd, like or typical of the salmons: *n.* any member of the family Salmonidæ. (L. *salmonis*, and Gr. *eidos*, like.)
salmon-trout, *n.* the European sea-trout.
salon, *n.* (App.), a saloon; a drawing-room; a reception of literary or other celebrities; an exhibition of pictures. (Fr.)
saloon, *n.* sa-*loon*, a spacious apartment for the reception of company; a ship's dining-room; a railway dining-car; a first-class furnished railway coach not divided into compartments; a closed motor-car with no internal partition; a drinking bar. **saloon rifle,** a rifle for use in a shooting gallery. (Fr.)
saloop, *n.* sa-*loop*, an infusion of sassafras bark; salep.
Salopian, *a.* sa-*loh*-pe-an, pertaining to Shropshire: *n.* a native of Shropshire. (*Sloppesberie*, Anglo-Fr. form of *Shrewsbury.*)
salpicon, *n.* *sal*-pe-kon, a savoury dish of minced meat or fish with bread, etc.; a stuffing of minced meat and herbs. (Sp.)
Salpiglossis, *n.* *sal*-pe-*glos*-is, a genus of solanaceous South American plants with showy flowers. (Gr. *salpinx*, trumpet, *glossis*, tongue.)
salpingian, *a.* sal-*pin*-je-an, pertaining to a salpinx.
salpingitis, *n.* sal-pin-*jy*-tis, inflammation of a salpinx.
salpinx, *n.* sal-*pinks*, a Eustachian tube, or one of the Fallopian tubes [Anat.]. (Gr., a trumpet.)
salse, *n.* sahls *or* sals, a mud volcano. (Fr.)
salsify, *n.* *sal*-se-fe, the composite plant *Tragopogan porrifolius*, or purple goatsbeard, cultivated for its edible root. **black salsify,** *Scorzonera hispanica*, eaten as winter greens. (Fr. *salsifis.*)
salsilla, *n.* sal-*sil*-la, the South American plant *Bomarea edulis*, with tuberous edible root. (Sp.)
***salt,** *n.* sawlt, chloride of sodium, used for the seasoning and preservation of food; a body composed of an acid and a base [Chem.]; taste; anything like salt; piquancy; wit; a salt-cellar; a sailor: *a.* having the taste of salt; impregnated or abounding with salt; overflowed with or growing among salt; salacious; pungent or bitter; costly [Slang]: *pl.* smelling salts; any mineral saline compound used as an aperient [Med.]: salt-marshes: *v.t.* to sprinkle, impregnate, or season with salt; to fill with salt: *v.i.* to deposit salt from a saline substance. **below the salt,** in an inferior position or class. **spirits of salt,** hydrochloride acid. **the salt of the earth** (Matt. v, 13), that part of a community having the best influence on it. **to eat one's salt,** to accept his hospitality. **to salt a mine,** to sprinkle a poor mine with bits of ore with intent to deceive. **with a grain of salt,** with reservation. **worth one's salt,** worth one's keep; hence, of value, useful. (A.S. *sealt.*)
saltant, *a.* *sal*-tant, leaping [Her.]. (L. *saltans*, dancing.)
saltarello, *n.* sal-ta-*rel*-lo, a lively Italian dance or jig; music for this. (It.)
saltation, *n.* sal-*tay*-shon, a leaping or jumping; a beating or palpitation [Path.]. (Fr.)
saltatorial, *a.* sal-ta-*taw*-re-al, characterized by, pertaining to, or adapted for leaping or dancing. (L. *saltare*, to dance, from *salire*, to leap.)
saltative, *a.* *sal*-ta-tiv, designating an abrupt variation of species [Biol.].
saltatory, *a.* *sal*-ta-to-re, saltatorial; characterized by saltations or [Fig.] abrupt changes.
salt-box, *n.* a box with a lid, used for holding a supply of salt.
saltbush, *n.* *sawlt*-bush, an Australian species of *Atriplex*, and other fodder plants.
salt-cake, *n.* crude sulphate of soda.
salt-cat, *n.* a mixture of gravel, seed, and salt, etc., given to pigeons.
salt-cellar, *n.* a small vessel for holding salt for use at the table. (Fr. *salière*, a salt-cellar.)
salter, *n.* *sawl*-ter, one who salts; one who makes or sells salt; a workman at a salt-works.
saltern, *n.* *sawl*-tern, a place where salt is extracted from sea-water; a salt factory.
saltigrade, *a.* *sal*-te-grade, leaping; formed for leaping: *n.* one of the Saltigrada, a family of spiders that leap to seize their prey. (L. *saltus*, and *gradior*, walk.)
saltine, *n.* *sawl*-tine, a thin crisp biscuit sprinkled with salt [U.S.A.].
saltiness, *n.* *sawl*-te-ness, quality of being salty.
salting, *n.* *sawl*-ting, a salt-water marsh; the process of applying salt to the preservation of food-stuffs.
saltire, *n.* *sal*-tire, an ordinary, representing a bend sinister conjoined with a bend dexter, in the form of an X [Her.]; a St. Andrew's cross. (O.Fr. *saultoir.*)
saltish, *a.* *sawl*-tish, somewhat salt.
saltishly, *ad.* with saltishness.
saltishness, *n.* a moderate degree of saltness.
salt-junk, *n.* dry salt beef, esp. for use at sea.

saltless, *a.* *sawlt*-less, destitute of salt; insipid.
salt-lick, *n.* a place where the ground is impregnated with salt to which wild animals come to lick it up; an artificial preparation of salt placed where sheep and cattle can lick it.
saltly, *a.* *sawlt*-le, with taste of salt.
salt-marsh, *n.* grassy land subject to the overflow of salt-water.
salt-mine, *n.* a mine where rock-salt is worked.
saltness, *n.* *sawlt*-ness, the quality of being salt; the taste of salt.
salt-pan, *n.* a pan, basin, or pit where salt is obtained from brine by evaporation.
saltpetre, *n.* sawlt-*pee*-ter, nitre; nitrate of potash. (Fr. *saltpêtre.*)
saltpetrous, *a.* sawlt-*pee*-trus, pertaining to, impregnated with, or of the nature of saltpetre.
salt-pit, *n.* a place where salt is obtained.
salt-rheum, *n.* *sawlt*-room, eczema, or other cutaneous eruption [U.S.A.]; herpes.
salts, *n.pl.* sawlts, *see* **salt.**
salt-water, *n.* sea-water; water impregnated with salt: *a.* living in or pertaining to the sea.
salt-works, *n.* a place where salt is made or whence it is obtained.
saltwort, *n.* *sawlt*-wurt, applied to many plants growing beside the sea, esp. *Salsola kali* and *Glaux maritima.*
salty, *a.* *sawl*-te, somewhat salt; containing or tasting of salt.
salubrious, *a.* sa-*lew*-bre-us, favourable to health; healthful. (L. *salubris.*)
salubriously, *ad.* so as to promote health.
salubriousness, *n.* the quality of being salubrious.
salubrity, *n* sa-*lew*-bre-te, salubriousness.
saluki, *n.* sa-*loo*-ke, a swift and graceful hunting-dog of the Middle East, with long silky hair. (Ar. *salūqi.*)
salutarily, *ad.* *sal*-yew-ta-re-le, in a salutary manner.
salutariness, *n.* the quality of being salutary or contributing to health or prosperity.
salutary, *a.* *sal*-yew-ta-re, wholesome; promoting health; contributing to some beneficial purpose. (L. *salutaris.*)
salutation, *n.* *sal*-yew-*tay*-shon, the act or style of saluting or paying respect; a greeting. (Fr.)
salutatorily, *ad.* sa-*lew*-ta-to-re-le, by way of salutation.
salutatory, *a.* sa-*lew*-ta-to-re, greeting: *n.* an address of greeting, esp. at a University [U.S.A.].
salute, *n.* sa-*loot*, an expression of kind wishes or respect; a kiss; a discharge of guns or other mark of respect in honour of a notability; the formal act of deference accorded by other ranks and juniors to officers [Mil., etc.] or by any subordinate to his superior: *v.t.* to address with expressions of kind wishes; to greet with a kiss, bow or gesture; to honour by a discharge of guns, by dipping colours, by the prescribed movement of hand, rifle, or sword, etc., and in other ways. (L. *saluto.*)
saluter, *n.* sa-*loo*-ter, one who salutes.
salutiferous, *a.* *sal*-yew-*tif*-er-rus, bringing or conducive to health.
salvability, *n.* *sal*-va-*bil*-e-te, the quality or state of being salvable.
salvable, *a.* *sal*-va-bl, admitting of being saved.
salvage, *n.* *sal*-vaj, compensation allowed by law for the saving of a ship or goods from loss at sea; the act of saving; that which is saved from wreck, fire, destroyed or demolished premises, etc.: *v.t.* to reclaim from wreckage, fire, ruins, etc. (O.Fr.)
salvarsan, *n.* *sal*-var-san, proprietary name of a synthetic arsenical compound used in the treatment of syphilis.
salvation, *n.* sal-*vay*-shon, the act of saving; preservation from destruction, danger, or great calamity; the redemption of man from sin and death [Theol.]; deliverance. **Salvation Army,** an organization founded in London in the 1870's on quasi-military lines for the revival of religion among the masses and later extended to social and philanthropic work. (Fr.)
Salvationism, *n.* sal-*vay*-shon-izm the tenets, practices, etc., of the Salvation Army.
Salvationist, *n.* sal-*vay*-shon-ist, a member of the Salvation Army.
salve, *v.t.* sahv *or* salv, to save; to salvage.
salve, *n.* sahv *or* salv, an adhesive composition, or an ointment, applied to wounds or sores; help; remedy: *v.t.* to soothe; to heal. (A.S. *sealf.*)
salver, *n.* *sal*-ver, a tray or waiter on which cards, etc., are presented by servants. (Sp. *salva.*)
Salvia, *n.* *sal*-ve-a, a large genus of herbaceous perennials including the sage.
salvo, *n.* *sal*-voh, an exception; a proviso; a mental reservation. (L. *salvo jure*, right reserved.)
salvo, *n.* *sal*-voh, a simultaneous discharge of a number of guns concentrated on one spot as a salute; a simultaneous discharge of all guns; a volley; a double broadside. (It. *salva.*)
salvor, *n.* *sal*-vor, one who saves a ship or goods from destruction at sea or by fire; one who effects salvage.
samaj, *n.* sa-*mahj*, a congregation; a Church; a society. (Hind.)
samara, *n.* sa-*mah*-ra, a winged fruit, as of the maple or sycamore, or the key of the ash. (L.)
Samaritan, *a.* sa-*ma*-re-tan, pertaining to Samaria; in use among the Samaritans (esp. of certain characters used by the Hebrews before the Babylonish captivity): *n.* the language of Samaria; an inhabitant of Samaria; a charitable person.
samarium, *n.* sa-*mare*-re-um, a rare, slightly radio-active, metallic element of the cerium group. (*Samarskite.*)
samarskite, *n.* sa-*mar*-skite, an ore containing tantalates and columbates of iron, calcium, thorium, etc., with traces of samarium. (Col. *Samarski*, Russ. mineralogist.)
Sama-Veda, *n.* *sah*-ma-*vay*-da, the Veda containing the chants, the texts of which are mainly verses from the Rig-veda. (Sans.)
sambar, *n.* *sam*-bar, the sambur.
sambo, *n.* *sam*-boh, a Negro; the offspring of negro and mulatto parents. (Sp. *zambo*, bandy-legged.)
sambuca, *n.* sam-*bew*-ka, an ancient instrument of music resembling a large harp. (L.)
sambur, *n.* *sam*-ber, the woodland deer of South Eastern Asia, *Rusa unicolor.* (Hind. *sabar.*)
★**same,** *a.* same, identical; not different; of the identical kind, sort of degree; exactly similar; mentioned before. (A.S.)
sameness, *n.* *same*-ness, state of being the same; identity; resemblance; monotony.
Samian, *a.* *say*-me-an, pertaining to the Grecian island of Samos: *n.* a native of Samos. **Samian earth,** a kind of marl found in Samos, formerly used as an astringent, and for pottery. **Samian ware,** ancient red or black glazed pottery, usually decorated in relief.
samiel, *n.* *say*-me-el, the simoom. (Turk.)
samisen, *n.* *sam*-e-sen, a three-stringed Japanese instrument of the banjo family, played with a plectrum.
samite, *n.* *say*-mite, a rich silk usually interwoven with gold or silver thread. (O.Fr. *samit.*)
samlet, *n.* *sam*-let, a parr or young salmon. (*salmonet.*)
samovar, *n.* *sam*-o-var, a Russian copper tea-urn with an internal heater.
Samoyed, *a.* *sam*-oh-yed, pertaining to the Samoyeds or their language: *n.* one of a Mongolian race of northern Siberia; a long-haired domesticated Arctic dog with cream or white coat.
samp, *n.* samp, a dish of boiled crushed maize and milk. (Algonquian.)
sampan, *n.* *sam*-pan, a Chinese river boat, often used for habitation. (Chin.)
samphire, *n.* *sam*-fire, a fleshy umbelliferous plant of the genus *Crithmum*, growing usually on cliffs by the sea. (Fr. *Saint Pierre*, St. Peter.)
sample, *n.* *sahm*-pl, a part shown as evidence of the quality of the whole; an example; a specimen: *v.t.* to take or make a sample; to test by sampling. (O.Fr. *essample.*)
sampler, *n.* *sahm*-pler, a piece of embroidery worked for practice; one who samples. (O.Fr. *examplaire.*)
samplery, *n.* *sahm*-pler-re, the art of making samplers.
samshu, *n.* *sam*-shoo, a spirit distilled from rice. (Chin.)
Samson-post, *n.* *sam*-sun-pohst, a strong post resting on the kelson, and supporting a beam of the deck over the hold; in whalers, the upright to which the harpoon rope is fastened [Naut.].
samurai, *n.pl.* *sam*-oo-ry, one of the military class in feudal Japan; this class. (Jap.)

sanable, *a.* *san*-a-bl, that may be healed; curable. (L. *sanabilis.*)
sanative, *a.* *san*-a-tiv, sanatory; having the power to heal; tending to heal. (Late L. *sanativus.*)
sanatorium, *n.* san-a-*taw*-re-um (*pl.* **sanatoria**), a health station; a resort for invalids; an establishment for the provision of medical treatment. (Late L. *sanatorius*, health-giving.)
sanatory, *a.* *san*-a-to-re, curative; conducive to or pertaining to healing.
sanbenito, *n.* *san*-be-*nee*-to, a penitential garment, esp. a robe painted with flames, devils, etc., worn on their way to execution by persons condemned to death by the Inquisition. (Sp. *sambenito.*)
sancho, *n.* *sang*-koh, a primitive guitar used by American Negroes.
sanctification, *n.* sank-te-fe-*kay*-shon, act or process of sanctifying; sanctified state; consecration. (Late L. *sanctificatio.*)
sanctifier, *n.* *sank*-te-fy-er, he who sanctifies; (*cap.*) the Holy Spirit.
sanctify, *v.t.* *sank*-te-fy, to make holy; to consecrate; to purify for divine service; to purify from sin; to make the means of holiness; to own or to vindicate as holy; to sanction. (Fr. *sanctifier.*)
sanctimonious, *a.* *sank*-te-*moh*-ne-us, having the appearance of sanctity; hypocritically pious. (L. *sanctimonia*, holiness.)
sanctimoniously, *ad.* with sanctimony.
sanctimoniousness, *n.* the state of being sanctimonious; sanctity, or the show of it.
sanctimony, *n.* *sank*-te-mo-ne, the affectation of devoutness; hypocritical piety.
sanction, *n.* *sank*-shon, ratification on the part of a superior; authorization; support; a provision for enforcing obedience; a reward or penalty for observance or non-observance of a treaty or legal decision: *v.t.* to give validity or authority to; to enforce by penalty; to ratify; to confirm. (Fr.)
sanctionary, *a.* *sank*-shon-a-re, relating to or implying a sanction.
sanctitude, *n.* *sank*-te-tewd, holiness; devoutness.
sanctity, *n.* *sank*-te-te, state of being sacred or holy; godliness; saintliness; sacredness; solemnity: *pl.* sacred or holy persons or objects (Fr. *sainteté.*)
sanctuary, *n.* *sank*-tew-a-re, a sacred place; a building consecrated for worship; the Jewish temple, or its Holy of Holies; that part of a church where the altar is situated; (till 1623) a place where legal process could not be executed, hence, a place of refuge or protection; an area set apart for the preservation of animals in their wild state. (O.Fr. *saintuarie.*)
sanctum, *n.* *sank*-tum, a sacred place; a private study. **sanctum sanctorum,** the Holy of Holies; a den or private retreat [Coll.]. (L.)
Sanctus, *n.* *sank*-tus, the hymn " Holy, Holy, Holy," sung in the communion service; a setting of this. **sanctus bell,** a bell, usually in a turret at the junction of nave and chancel, rung when the sanctus is sung. (L.)
★**sand,** *n.* sand, a mass of separate grains of quartz with or without those of other minerals: *pl.* tracts of sand, as of the sea-shore, submarine banks, or deserts; moments or hours [Fig.]: *v.t.* to sprinkle or adulterate with sand; to drive upon the sand. (A.S.)
sandal, *n.* *san*-dal, a kind of shoe consisting of a sole fastened to the foot by straps. (Fr. *sandale.*)
sandalled, *a.* *san*-dald, wearing sandals.
sandalwood, *n.* *san*-dal-wood, the fragrant wood of the East Indian tree *Santalum album*, much used for cabinet-work. (Sans. *chandana*, and *wood.*)
sandarac, *n.* *san*-da-rak, a gum-resin from the North African coniferous tree *Callitris quadrivalvis*; realgar [Min.]. (L. *sandaraca.*).
sand-badger, *n.* the hog-badger, an Indian species of *Arctonyx.*
sandbag, *n.* *sand*-bag, a bag filled with sand, used as protection against blast, as ballast, as a weapon, etc.: *v.t.* to protect with sand-bags; to hit or stun with a sandbag.
sandbagger, *n.* *sand*-bag-ger, a footpad, etc., who stuns his victim from behind with a sandbag.
sandbank, *n.* *sand*-bank, a sandy shoal.
sandbath, *n.* *sand*-bahth, a bath of hot sand for therapeutic purposes; a vessel containing hot sand for equable heating in chemical work.
sand-blast, *n.* a jet of forcibly driven sand for cleansing or cutting or engraving glass, stone, or metal; the apparatus for this purpose: *v.t.* to cut or engrave, etc., by this means.
sand-blind, *a.* weak sighted; having a defect of sight due to specks floating before the eye.
sand-blindness, *n.* state of being sand-blind.
sandbox, *n.* *sand*-boks, the tropical American tree *Hura crepitans*, the seeds of which, when the pericarp bursts, are scattered with a loud report.
sand-box, *n.* a box for holding sand, esp. one with a perforated top for sprinkling; the box on a locomotive from which sand runs on to the rails when slippery.
sandboy, *n.* *sand*-boy, a sand-flea; a lad who hawked sand at seaside resorts.
sand-crack, *n.* a fracture of the horny fibres of a horse's hoof, usually in a downward direction.
sand-dune, *n.* a ridge of drifted sand.
sanded, *a.* *san*-ded, sprinkled or covered with sand; of a sandy colour.
sand-eel, *n.* a small marine fish of the genus *Ammodytes*, which buries itself in the sand between tide-marks.
Sandemanian, *n.* *san*-de-*may*-ne-an, a follower of Robert Sandeman (*d.* 1771), a secessionist from the Glassites.
sander, *n.* *san*-der, the zander [Ichth.].
sanderling, *n.* *san*-der-ling, a small wading bird, *Calidris arenaria*, allied to the sandpipers.
sanders, *n.* *san*-derz, red sandalwood.
sand-flea, *n.* a sand-hopper.
sand-fly, *n.* a small dipterous biting midge; an angler's fly.
sand-glass, *n.* an hour-glass; any similar apparatus for measuring time.
sand-grouse, *n.* any of the Pteroclidæ, a family of desert-dwelling birds structurally allied to the pigeons.
sand-hill, *n.* a natural hill of sand; a dune.
sand-hopper, *n.* the small leaping amphipodous crustacean *Talitrus saltator.*
sandiness, *n.* *san*-de-ness, state of being sandy.
sand-iron, *n.* a golf club for lifting a ball from sand.
sandiver, *n.* *san*-de-ver, a whitish salt scum cast up from glass in a state of fusion; glass-gall. (Fr. *suint de verre*, sweating of glass.)
sandix, *n.* *san*-diks, a kind of minium or red-lead. (L.)
sand-lark, *n.* the sanderling; the sandpiper.
sand-launce, *n.* *sand*-lahnce, a sand-eel.
sandman, *n.* *sand*-man, the fairy-tale gnome said to make sleepy children rub their eyes.
sand-martin, *n.* the bank swallow, *Hirundo riparia*, nesting in sandpits, etc.
sandpaper, *n.* *sand*-pay-per, paper covered with a gritty substance for polishing, intermediate in fineness between glass-paper and emery-paper: *v.t.* to polish or smooth with sandpaper.
sandpipe, *n.* *sand*-pipe, a cylindrical hollow tapering into the chalk, filled with sand, clay, gravel, etc. [Geol.].
sandpiper, *n.* *sand*-py-per, the popular name of several small plovers allied to the ruff and dunlin.
sandpit, *n.* *sand*-pit, a pit sunk in sandy soil for the extraction of sand.
sand-poker, *n.* the pochard.
sand-shoe, *n.* a light canvas rubber-soled shoe for use on the sands; a plimsoll.
sandstone, *n.* *sand*-stone, a sedimentary rock composed chiefly of grains of quartz.
sandstorm, *n.* *sand*-storm, a violent storm of wind carrying quantities of sand, esp. over a desert.
sandwich, *n.* *sand*-widj *or* -witch, two pieces of bread (usually buttered) with a thin slice of meat, fish, cheese, etc., between them; anything of similar arrangement; two thin pieces of spongecake having a layer of jam between: *v.t.* to interpose; to place between. (4th Earl of *Sandwich*, *d.* 1792.)
sandwichman, *n.* *sand*-widj-man, a man who walks between two advertisement-boards hanging over his shoulders.
sand-widgeon, *n.* the gadwall.
sandwort, *n.* *sand*-wurt, any plant of the genus *Arenaria.*
sandy, *a.* *san*-de, abounding with or full of sand; covered or sprinkled with sand; like sand; not firm or solid; of the colour of sand, yellowish red.

Sandy, *n.* *san*-de, a Scotsman [Coll.]. (For *Alexander.*)
sandy-head, *n.* the pochard.
sandyish, *a.* *san*-de-ish, somewhat sandy.
sane, *a.* sane, sound in mind; sound in opinion; reasonable. (L. *sanus*, sound.)
sanely, *ad.* *sane*-ly, in a sane manner; intelligently.
saneness, *n.* *sane*-ness, the quality or condition of being sane.
sang, sang, *p.* of *sing.*
sangar, *n.* *sang*-gar, a temporary defensive breastwork [Fort.]. (Hind.)
sangaree, *n.* *sang*-ga-ree, a drink of cold wine and water, sweetened and spiced, taken in the tropics. (Sp. *sangria*, bleeding.)
sangfroid, *n.* (App.) coolness; freedom from excitement or nervousness; presence of mind. (Fr. literally, cold blood.)
Sangha, *n.* *sang*-ha, the monastic order or society of Buddhist mendicants; a similar organization among the Jains. (Sans.)
sangraal, *n.* sang-*grahl*, the holy grail. (O.Fr.)
sanguiferous, *a.* sang-*gwif*-er-rus, conveying blood. (L. *sanguis*, blood, *fero*, bear.)
sanguification, *n.* *sang*-gwif-e-*kay*-shon, the formation of blood, esp. the conversion of chyle into blood. (L. *sanguis*, and *facio*, make.)
sanguifier, *n.* *sang*-gwe-fy-er, any substance that promotes the production of blood.
sanguifluous, *a.* sang-*gwif*-loo-us, running with blood. (L. *sanguis*, and *fluo*, flow.)
sanguinarily, *ad.* in a sanguinary manner.
sanguinariness, *n.* quality of being sanguinary.
sanguinary, *a.* *sang*-gwin-a-re, attended with much bloodshed; bloodthirsty. (L. *sanguinarius.*)
sanguine, *a.* *sang*-gwin, having the colour of blood; abounding with blood; ardent; confident; hopeful: *n.* blood colour; a red crayon, or a drawing with this: *v.t.* to ensanguine; to stain or varnish with a blood colour. (Fr. *sanguin.*)
sanguinely, *ad.* in a sanguine manner.
sanguineness, *n.* the state or quality of being sanguine.
sanguineous, *a.* sang-*gwin*-e-us, pertaining to or of the nature of blood; abounding with blood; sanguine, blood-red. (L. *sanguineus.*)
sanguinivorous, *a.* sang-gwe-*niv*-o-rus, subsisting on blood. (L. *sanguis*, and *voro*, devour.)
sanguinolent, *a.* sang-*gwin*-o-lent, tinged with blood.
sanguisorb, *n.* *sang*-gwe-sorb, burnet, or any plant of the rosaceous genus *Sanguisorba.*
Sanhedrin, *n.* *san*-he-drin the former great council of the Jews, consisting of an equal number (about 72) of priests, scribes, and elders, generally presided over by the high priest. (Heb.)
sanicle, *n.* *san*-e-kl, the umbelliferous plant *Sanicula europæa*, allied to the parsley. (Fr.)
sanidine, *n,* *san*-e-deen, a glassy-fissured orthoclase felspar.
sanies, *n.* *say*-ne-eez, a serous matter, or thin blood-stained discharge, from wounds or sores. (L.)
sanify, *v.t.* *san*-e-fy, to make healthy; to provide with sanitary surroundings.
sanious, *a.* *say*-ne-us, pertaining to or of the nature of sanies; running with sanies.
sanitarian, *a.* san-e-*tare*-re-an, sanitary; pertaining to sanitary matters: *n.* a student of sanitation; an advocate of sanitary reforms.
sanitarily, *ad.* *san*-e-ta-re-le, having regard to sanitary condition.
sanitarium, *n.* san-e-*tare*-re-um, a sanatorium.
sanitary, *a.* *san*-e-ta-re, pertaining to or designed to secure health; hygienic; pertaining to plumber's work.
sanitation, *n.* san-e-*tay*-shon, sanitary science, or its application.
sanity, *n.* *san*-e-te, condition or quality of being sane; mental healthiness. (L. *sanitas.*)
sanjak, *n.* *san*-jak, an administrative sub-division of a Turkish province. (Turk.)
sank, sank, *p.* of *sink.*
sannup, *n.* *san*-up, a Red Indian warrior other than a chief; the husband of a squaw [U.S.A.].
sannyasi, *n.* sun-*yah*-see, a peripatetic religious mendicant of India. (Hind.)
sans, *prep.* sanz, without. (Fr.)
sansculotte, *n.* sahn-koo-*lot*, a violent revolutionary; an anarchical fellow (originally applied in contempt by the aristocratic to the extreme democratic party of the French Revolution, and adopted by the latter as a title of honour). (Fr., without breeches.)
sansculottic, *a.* sahn-koo-*lot*-ik, pertaining to or proceeding from sansculottism.
sansculottism, *n.* sahn-koo-*lot*-izm, the doctrine or practice of the sansculottes; extreme republicanism.
Sanskrit, *n.* *sans*-krit, the ancient language of the Hindus, as preserved in their literature, and the oldest known member of the Indo-European family of languages: *a.* pertaining to or written in Sanskrit. (Sans., well made.)
Sanskritic, *a.* sans-*krit*-ik, Sanskrit; using, derived from, or resembling Sanskrit.
Sanskritist, *n.* *sans*-krit-ist, a Sanskrit scholar.
sans-serif, *n.* sanz-*se*-rif, a printing-type the characters of which have no serifs. (Fr. *sans*, without, and *serif.*)
santal, *n.* *san*-tal, red sandalwood.
santalin, *n.* *san*-ta-lin, the colouring matter of red sandalwood. (Late L. *santalum*, sandalwood.)
santon, *n.* *san*-ton, a marabout; a dervish. (Sp.)
santonica, *n.* san-*ton*-e-ka, wormwood; the unexpanded flower-heads of this, used as an anthelmintic. (L., wormwood.)
santonin, *n.* *san*-to-nin, a crystalline bitter principle of santonica, obtained from *Artemisia maritima.*
sap, *n.* sap, the circulating juice of plants; sapwood; vital fluid, vigour [Fig.]. (A.S. *sæp.*)
sap, *n.* sap, the act of sapping; a deep trench for undermining; a studious or plodding worker [Slang]: *v.t.* to undermine; to subvert by digging or wearing away, or by removing the foundation of: *v.i.* to proceed by secretly undermining; to work hard, to grind [Slang]. (Fr. *sape.*)
sapajou, *n.* *sap*-a-joo, the capuchin monkey, a S. American monkey of the genus *Cebus.* (Fr.)
sapan, *n.* sa-*pan*, an Asiatic dye-wood, *Cæsalpinia sappan*, yielding a red colour. (Malay.)
sap-colour, *n.* an expressed vegetable juice, inspissated by evaporation, used as paint.
sap-green, *n.* a light green pigment from inspissated juice.
sap-head, *n.* the point to which a sap has been constructed; a daft person, a softy [Slang].
sapid, *a.* *sap*-id, affecting the taste; savoury; not insipid. (L. *sapidus*, savoury.)
sapidity, *n.* sa-*pid*-e-te, sapidness.
sapidness, *n.* *sap*-id-ness, the quality of being sapid.
sapience, *n.* *say*-pe-ence, wisdom (generally used ironically). (Fr.)
sapient, *a.* *say*-pe-ent, wise; would-be wise. (L. *sapiens*, being wise.)
sapiential, *a.* *say*-pe-*en*-shal, pertaining to wisdom
sapiential books, certain of the scriptural books—Proverbs, Ecclesiastes, and others.
sapiently, *ad.* *say*-pe-ent-le, in a sapient manner.
sapindaceous, *a.* sap-in-*day*-shus, belonging to, or resembling plants of, the soapberry or *Sapindus* family. (L. *sapo*, soap, *Indus*, Indian.)
sapless, *a.* *sap*-less, destitute of sap; dry.
sapling, *n.* *sap*-ling, a young tree; a young greyhound; a youth [Fig.].
sapodilla, *n.* sap-o-*dil*-a, a large West Indian tree, *Achras sapota*, its edible fruit, or its timber. (Sp. *zapotilla.*)
saponaceous, *a.* sap-o-*nay*-shus, soapy; resembling or having the qualities of soap. (L. *sapo*, soap.)
saponifiable, *a.* sa-*pon*-e-*fy*-a-bl, capable of being saponified.
saponification, *n.* sa-*pon*-e-fe-*kay*-shon, conversion into soap.
saponify, *v.t.* and *i.* sa-*pon*-e-fy, to convert or be converted into soap. (L. *sapo*, and *facio*, make.)
saponin, *n.* *sap*-o-nin, a glucoside obtained from the soapwort and other plants.
sapor, *n.* *say*-por, the distinctive flavour of anything. (L.)
saporific, *a.* sap-o-*rif*-ik, producing taste.
saporosity, *n.* sap-o-*ros*-e-te, the quality in a body that excites the sensation of taste. (L. *sapor.*)
sappan, *n.* sap-*pan*, sapan.
sapper, *n.* *sap*-er, one who saps; a private in the Royal Engineers (originally the Sappers and Miners.)
sapphic, *a.* *saf*-ik, pertaining to Sappho, a Greek poetess, from whom was derived the Sapphic verse, of five feet, and the Sapphic strophe of three verses,

followed by an adonic: *n.* a stanza or poem in the Sapphic metre.
sapphire, *n.* *saf*-fire, a transparent, brightly coloured variety of corundum of a blue colour, one of the more valuable precious stones; the light blue colour of the sapphire; a blue-breasted S. American humming-bird of the genus *Hylocharis*: *a.* sapphirine; of a sapphire-blue colour. (Fr. *saphir.*)
sapphirine, *a.* *saf*-e-rine, resembling, having the qualities of, or made of sapphire: *n.* a pale-blue silicate of aluminium and magnesium. **sapphirine gurnard,** the tub-fish.
Sapphism, *n.* *saf*-izm, unnatural vice practised among women; a sexual perversion in which the male element does not participate. (*Sappho*, Greek poetess.)
Sapphist, *n.* *saf*-ist, a woman addicted to Sapphism.
sappiness, *n.* *sap*-e-ness, succulence; juiciness.
sapping, *n.* *sap*-ing, the work of a sapper, the art of constructing fortifications, trenches, etc.: *a.* undermining.
sappy, *a.* *sap*-e, abounding with sap; juicy; weak.
sapræmia, *n.* sa-*pree*-me-a, septic poisoning occasioned by bacteria in the blood [Med.]
saprodontia, *n.* sap-ro-*don*-she-a, caries or decay of the teeth.
saprogenic, *a.* sap-ro-*jen*-ik, producing or produced by decay. (Gr. *sapros*, putrid, *genesis*, creating.)
saprophagan, *n.* sa-*prof*-a-gan, a saprophagous lamellicorn beetle: *a.* saprophagous.
saprophagous, *a.* sa-*prof*-a-gus, feeding on putrid animal and vegetable substances. (Gr. *sapros*, putrid, *phago*, eat.)
saprophilous, *a.* sa-*prof*-e-lus, infesting decaying matter.
saprophyte, *n.* *sap*-ro-fite, a vegetable organism that lives on decaying organic matter. (Gr. *sapros*, and *phyton*, a plant.)
saprophytic, *a.* sap-ro-*fit*-ik, pertaining to or living as a saprophyte.
saprostomous, *a.* sa-*pros*-to-mus, having foul breath [Path.].
sap-rot, *n.* dry-rot.
sapsago, *n.* *sap*-sa-go, a sweet greenish Swiss cheese used chiefly in cookery. (Ger. *Schabzieger.*)
sapsucker, *n.* *sap*-suk-er, a small North American woodpecker.
sapucaia, *n.* *sap*-oo-*ky*-a, a tropical S. American tree of the genus *Lecythis*, bearing edible nuts. (Brazilian.)
sapwood, *n.* *sap*-wood, the external part of wood, newly formed under the bark; alburnum.
saraband, *n.* *sa*-ra-band, a slow Spanish dance; a short piece of music for this. (Sp. *zarabanda.*)
Saracen, *n.* *sa*-ra-sen, originally, a nomad Arab of the Syro-Arabian deserts; later, a Moslem opponent of the crusaders. (L. *Saracenus.*)
saracenic, *a.* sa-ra-*sen*-ik, pertaining to the Saracens.
Saratoga, *n.* sa-ra-*toh*-ga, a large travelling trunk; in full, **Saratoga trunk.** (U.S.A. town.)
sarcasm, *n.* *sar*-kazm, a keen derisive or wounding expression; a taunting or satirical remark uttered with scorn or contempt. (Fr. *sarcasme.*)
sarcast, *n.* *sar*-kast, a sarcastic writer or orator.
sarcastic, *a.* sar-*kas*-tik, using or characterized by sarcasm; bitterly ironical. (Fr. *sarcastique*, from Gr. *sarkastikos*, flesh-tearing.)
sarcastically, *ad.* in a sarcastic vein.
sarcenet, *n.* *sars*-net, sarsenet. (O.Fr.)
sarcin, *n.* *sar*-sin, a nitrogenous toxic alkaloid produced in the living tissue [Biochemistry]. (Gr. *sarkinos*, fleshy.)
Sarcina, *n.* *sar*-se-na, a genus of bacteria the cocci of which form into cubical masses. (L., a bundle.)
sarcocarp, *n.* *sar*-ko-karp, the fleshy part of some fruit. (Gr. *sarx*, flesh, *karpos*, fruit.)
sarcocele, *n.* *sar*-ko-seel, a fleshy tumour of a testicle. (Gr. *sarx*, and *kele*, a tumour.)
sarcocol, *n.* *sar*-ko-kol, a gummy resin from certain Arabian trees, formerly used as an antiseptic. (Gr. *sarx*, and *kolla*, glue.)
sarcode, *n.* *sar*-kode, animal protoplasm. (Gr. *sarkodes*, flesh-like.)
sarcodic, *a.* sar-*kod*-ik, pertaining to, resembling, or consisting of sarcode.
sarcoid, *a.* *sar*-koyd, flesh-like: *n.* a skin-complaint giving rise to scars, also, one of these scars [Path.]; a sarcomatous growth.
sarcolemma, *n.* *sar*-ko-*lem*-ma, a membrane coating striped muscular tissue.
sarcoline, *a.* *sar*-ko-lin, flesh-coloured [Min.].
sarcolite, *n.* *sar*-ko-lite, a flesh-coloured silicate of calcium and aluminium with iron, magnesium, and sodium. (Gr. *sarx*, and *lithos*, a stone.)
sarcology, *n.* sar-*kol*-o-je, that part of anatomy which treats of the fleshy parts of the body. (Gr. *sarx*, and *logos*, science.)
sarcoma, *n.* sar-*koh*-ma (*pl.* **sarcomata,** sar-*koh*-ma-ta), any malignant tumour derived from connective tissue, usually invading adjacent tissue and organs. (Gr.)
sarcomatosis, *n.* *sar*-koh-ma-*toh*-sis, morbid condition due to the presence of a sarcoma; sarcomatous degeneration.
sarcomatous, *a.* sar-*koh*-ma-tus, pertaining to or resembling sarcoma [Path.].
sarcophagous, *a.* sar-*kof*-a-gus, feeding on flesh. (Gr. *sarx*, and *phago*, eat.)
sarcophagus, *a.* sar-*kof*-a-gus (*pl.* **sarcophagi**), a variety of stone used for coffins alleged to consume bodies deposited in it within a few weeks; a stone coffin, esp. one of elaborate design. (Gr., flesh-eater.)
sarcoplasm, *n.* *sar*-ko-plazm, the semi-fluid substance in which the muscles are embedded [Anat.].
sarcosis, *n.* sar-*koh*-sis, the condition of one affected with sarcoma; abnormal formation of flesh. (Gr.)
sarcotic, *a.* sar-*kot*-ik, promoting the growth of flesh: *n.* a sarcotic medicine.
sarcous, *a.* *sar*-kus, fleshy; pertaining to flesh or muscle.
sard, *n.* sard, a precious stone, a variety of quartz of a deep blood-red colour. (*Sardis.*)
sardachate, *n.* *sar*-da-kat, a variety of agate containing layers of sard. (L. *sardachates.*)
sardine, *n.* sar-*deen*, the young of the pilchard, *Clupea pilchardus*, abundant in the Mediterranean and Bay of Biscay, and exported preserved in oil. (Fr. *sardine*, because originally from the Sardinian coasts.)
Sardinian, *a.* sar-*din*-e-an, pertaining to the Mediterranean island, Sardinia: *n.* a native of Sardinia.
sardius, *n.* *sar*-de-us, sard, or sardonyx.
sardonic, *a.* sar-*don*-ik, forced; sneering; expressing bitter irony and contempt. **sardonic grin** or **smile,** a convulsive affection of the face muscles [Path.]. (Fr. *sardonique.*)
sardonically, *ad.* in a sardonic manner.
sardonyx, *n.* *sar*-do-niks, onyx variegated with alternate layers of sard. (L.)
sargasso, *n.* sar-*gas*-oh, the floating gulf weed, *Sargassum bacciferum.* (Port.)
sari, *n.* *sah*-ree, the principal outer garment of a Hindu woman. (Hind.)
sark, *n.* sark, a shirt or chemise. (Scand. *serkr.*)
sarking, *n.* *sark*-ing, the sheathing of a roof above the rafters.
sarlac, *n.* *sar*-lak, the yak. (Mongolian.)
Sarmatian, *a.* sar-*may*-shan, pertaining to Sarmatia, an ancient territory extending from the Vistula to the Volga: *n.* one of a tribe inhabiting this; their language; a Pole.
sarmentous, *a.* sar-*men*-tus, having runners [Bot.].
sarmentum, *n.* sar-*men*-tum, a runner [Bot.]. (L.)
sarong, *n.* sa-*rong*, a strip of cloth worn as a petticoat by both sexes in Malaya. (Malay.)
saros, *n.* *sare*-ros, a cycle of 18 years 11 days, in which there are 19 returns of the sun and 242 of the moon to the same node and the eclipses recur as before [Astron.].
sarplier, *n.* *sar*-pleer, a sack of wool containing 80 tods; packing canvas. (Fr.)
Sarracenia, *n.* *sa*-ra-*see*-ne-a, a genus of N. American pitcher-plants. (Dr. *Sarrazin*, Fr.-Canad. botanist.)
sarrusophone, *n.* sa-*rus*-o-fone, a brass, double-reeded bassoon-like wind instrument sometimes used in military and jazz bands. (Invented 1863, by *Sarrus*, a French bandmaster.)
sarsaparilla, *n.* *sar*-sa-pa-*ril*-a, the dried root of certain species of *Smilax*, used as a tonic, etc. (Sp. *zarzaparrilla.*)
sarsen, *n.* *sar*-sen, a large block of eroded sandstone such as those found scattered over the Wiltshire chalk downs. (Probably *Saracen.*)

sarsenet, *n.* *sars*-net, a fine woven silk material used for linings. (Probably *Saracen.*)
sartorial, *a.* sar-*taw*-re-al, pertaining to tailors or tailoring, or to the sartorius. (L. *sartor*, a tailor.)
sartorius, *n.* sar-*taw*-re-us, the muscle which throws one leg across the other, the "tailor's muscle" [Anat.].
sash, *n.* sash, a scarf worn for ornament round the waist or (as a badge of office, etc.) over the shoulder. (Ar. *shash*, muslin.)
sash, *n.* sash, the framing of the glass of a window, esp. a sliding frame: *v.t.* to provide with sashes. (Fr. *chassis.*)
sasin, *n.* *sah*-seen, the black-buck, the common Indian antelope, *Antilope cervicapra.* (Nepalese.)
sassaby, *n.* *sas*-a-be, a large antelope, *Damaliscus lunatus*, of S.E. Africa, allied to the hartebeests. (Sechuana, *tsesebe.*)
sassafras, *n.* *sas*-sa-fras, a N. American tree, *S. officinale*, of the laurel family, from the bark of which a medicinal oil is obtained. (Sp.)
Sassenach, *n.* *sas*-en-akh, a Saxon or Englishman; a Scottish lowlander. (Gael.)
sassolite, *n.* *sas*-o-lite, native boracic acid. (*Sasso*, in Italy.)
Sastra, *n.* *sas*-tra, the Shastra.
sat, sat, *p.* of *sit.*
Satan, *n.* *say*-tn, the devil or prince of darkness, the spiritual enemy of mankind. (Heb., adversary.)
satanic, *a.* sa-*tan*-ik, having the qualities of Satan; infernal; extremely malicious.
satanically, *ad.* sa-*tan*-e-ka-le, in a satanic manner.
Satanism, *n.* *say*-tan-izm, devil worship; deliberate wickedness; the evil and malicious disposition of Satan.
Satanology, *n.* *say*-tan-*ol*-o-je, the study of or literature about Satan or the devil.
satara, *n.* sa-*tah*-ra, a highly finished ribbed woollen fabric. (Town in Bombay.)
satchel, *n.* *satch*-el, a small bag slung from the shoulder, for books, papers, or money. (O.Fr. *sachel.*)
sate, *v.t.* sate, to satiate; to satisfy the appetite of; to glut. (L. *satis*, enough.)
sate, sat, *former p.* of *sit.*
sateen, *n.* sa-*teen*, a cotton imitation of satin.
sateless, *a.* *sate*-less, insatiable.
satellite, *n.* *sat*-e-lite, a moon; a companion to a planet; an obsequious attendant. **satellite state,** a nominally autonomous state in servile relationship with another. (Fr.)
satellitism, *n.* *sat*-e-lite-izm, mutualism, symbiosis [Biol.].
sati, *n.* *sah*-te, suttee.
satiable, *a.* *say*-she-a-bl, that can be satiated.
satiate, *v.t.* *say*-she-ate, to fill or fully gratify; to glut; to surfeit: *a.* satiated; glutted. (L. *satiatus*, glutted.)
satiation, *n.* *say*-she-*ay*-shon, the action of satiating, or state of being glutted.
satiety, *n.* sa-*ty*-e-te, fulness of gratification beyond desire; an excess of gratification which excites loathing; satiation. (Fr. *satiété.*)
satin, *n.* *sat*-in, a species of glossy silk fabric of a thick close texture: *a.* made of satin: *v.t.* to give a satiny appearance to (esp. of paper). **patent satin,** mitcheline.
satin-bird, *n.* one of the Australian bower-birds.
satinet, *n.* sat-e-*net*, a thin kind of satin; a glossy cloth woven with cotton and wool. (Fr.)
satinette, *n.* sat-e-*net*, a variety of domestic pigeon.
satin-flower, *n.* the stitchwort *Stellaria holostea.*
satin-paper, *n.* a glossy writing-paper.
satin-spar, *n.* a fine fibrous variety of gypsum, or aragonite, etc., having a pearly lustre.
satin-wood, *n.* a hard ornamental wood used in cabinet-work, esp. that of the East Indian tree *Chloroxylon swietenia.*
satiny, *a.* *sat*-e-ne, like satin.
satire, *n.* *sat*-ire, a composition, in verse or prose, in which contemporary vices or follies are held up to reprobation or ridicule; trenchant wit; irony; sarcasm. (Fr.)
satirical, *a.* sa-*ti*-re-kal, pertaining to or conveying satire; given to satire; censorious; severe.
satirically, *ad.* in a satirical manner.
satirist, *n.* *sat*-i-rist, one who satirizes or writes satire.
satirise, *v.t.* *sat*-i-rize, to attack with satire; to censure or ridicule with severity.
satisfaction, *n.* sat-is-*fak*-shon, state of being satisfied; the act of satisfying; that which satisfies; content; gratification; amends; payment. (Fr.)
satisfactorily, *ad.* in a satisfactory manner.
satisfactoriness, *n.* the quality of being satisfactory or of giving content.
satisfactory, *a.* sat-is-*fak*-to-re, giving or producing satisfaction; yielding content; relieving the mind from doubt or uncertainty; making amends; atoning. (Fr. *satisfactoire.*)
satisfiable, *a.* sat-is-*fy*-a-bl, that may be satisfied.
satisfier, *n.* *sat*-is-fy-er, one who or that which gives satisfaction.
satisfy, *v.t.* *sat*-is-fy, to gratify fully; to supply fully; to free from doubt; to convince; to pay to the full extent of claims; to discharge: *v.i.* to give content; to supply fully; to make payment. (Fr. *satisfaire.*)
satrap, *n.* *sat*-rap, the governor or viceroy of an ancient Persian province; a despot [Fig.]. (Gr., from Old Per.)
satrapal, *a.* *sat*-ra-pal, pertaining to a satrap.
satrapy, *n.* *sat*-ra-pe, government, authority, or province of a satrap.
Satsuma, *n.* sat-*soo*-ma, hard, glazed, pale yellow pottery made in Satsuma, Japan.
saturable, *a.* *sat*-yew-ra-bl, that may be saturated.
saturant, *a.* *sat*-yew-rant, saturating: *n.* a substance which neutralizes acidity or alkalinity [Med.].
saturate, *v.t.* *sat*-yew-rate, to soak; to impregnate to the full; to add as much as can be dissolved [Chem.]; to imbue with: *a.* filled to repletion. (L. *saturatus*, filled.)
saturation, *n.* sat-yew-*ray*-shon, the act of saturating; state of being saturated; impregnation of one body with another till the latter can contain no more; a magnetic condition in which a substance cannot be further magnetized.
saturator, *n.* *sat*-yew-ray-tor, an apparatus or device for saturating.
Saturday, *n.* *sat*-ur-day, the seventh day of the week. (A.S. *Sæter-dæg*, Saturn's day.)
Saturn, *n.* *sat*-urn, an ancient Italian god of field husbandry, later identified with the Greek Kronos [Myth.]; the sixth major planet in distance from the sun, distinguished by its three rings and ten satellites. (L. *Saturnus.*)
Saturnalia, *n.pl.* *sat*-ur-*nay*-le-a, a Roman festival in honour of Saturn, notorious for its revels (possibly the origin of Christmas festivities), in which all classes gave themselves up to unrestrained mirthful and licentious indulgence; a season of revelry. (L.)
saturnalian, *a.* *sat*-ur-*nay*-le-an, pertaining to the saturnalia; loose; dissolute; sportive.
saturnian, *a.* sa-*tur*-ne-an, pertaining to Saturn whose reign is called the golden age; happy; distinguished for purity, integrity, and simplicity; pertaining to the metre of early Latin verse; *n.* one born under the influence of Saturn.
saturnine, *a.* *sat*-ur-nine, dull; heavy; phlegmatic; not easily susceptible of excitement (because under the influence of the planet Saturn).
saturnism, *n.* *sat*-ur-nizm, lead-poisoning [Med.].
saturnist, *n.* *sat*-ur-nist, a saturnine person.
satyagraha, *sut*-yah-*grah*-hah, the policy of non-co-operation and non-violent civil disobedience inaugurated in India by Mahatma Gandhi, 1919. (Hind., truth-grasping.)
satyr, *n.* *sat*-er, a sylvan deity represented as part man and part goat, with pointed ears and budding horns [Myth.]; an inordinately lecherous man. (Gr.)
satyriasis, *n.* sat-e-*ry*-a-sis, lascivious madness; immoderate venereal appetite in a male [Path.].
satyric, *a.* sa-*ti*-rik, pertaining to satyrs.
satyrism, *n.* *sat*-e-rizm, unrestrained lecherousness.
satyromaniac, *n.* *sat*-e-ro-*may*-ne-ak, one having satyriasis.
sauce, *n.* sawce, a liquid mixture of condiments, etc., used as a relish; cheek, impudence [Fig.]: *v.t.* to put sauce into; to gratify with rich tastes; to render pungent; to treat with impudence. (Fr.)
sauce-alone, *n.* the weed hedge-garlic, formerly used as a flavouring.
sauce-boat, *n.* a small deep dish for sauce at table.
sauce-box, *n.* a saucy impudent child.
saucepan, *n.* *sawce*-pan, a handled cooking pot used for boiling; a stewpan.

saucer, *n.* *saw*-ser, a piece of ware in which a cup is set; any similar vessel. (Fr. *saucière.*)
saucily, *ad.* *saw*-se-le, impudently; petulantly.
sauciness, *n.* *saw*-se-ness, the quality of being saucy; impertinent boldness; contempt for superiors.
saucisson, *n.* (App.), a long pipe filled with powder for use as a fuse; a bundle of large fascines [Fort.] (Fr. *saucisse*, a sausage.)
saucy, *a.* *saw*-se, impudent; rude; contemptuous towards superiors; smart (esp. of ships). (*sauce.*)
sauerkraut, *n.* *sour*-krout, chopped cabbage pressed in layers with salt between till it ferments. (Ger., sour cabbage.)
sault, *n.* soo, a rapid in a Canadian river. (O.Fr., a leap.)
Saumur, *n.* so-*moor*, a still or sparkling white wine. (From *Saumur*, on the Loire, France.)
saunders, *n.* *sawn*-derz, sanders, red sandalwood.
saunter, *n.* *sawn*-ter, a sauntering; a pace suited for sauntering: *v.i.* to wander or stroll about idly; to loiter. (Late L. *exadventurare*, through Fr. *s'aventurer*, to go adventuring.)
saunterer, *n.* *sawn*-ter-er, one who saunters.
saurian, *a.* *saw*-re-an, pertaining to or resembling the Sauria, a group of reptiles including the lizards: *n.* a lizard; a lizard-like reptile. (Gr. *sauros*, lizard.)
sauroid, *a.* *saw*-royd, like a saurian: *n.* a sauroid fish.
Sauropsida, *n.pl.* saw-*rop*-se-da, the group of animals consisting of the reptiles and the birds.
saury, *n.* *saw*-re, a pike-like marine fish of the N. Atlantic, *Scombresox saurus*, allied to the flying-fishes.
sausage, *n.* *sos*-aj, a roll of seasoned, finely chopped meat packed in a skin; a kite-balloon [Mil. slang]. (Fr. *saucisse.*)
sausage-poisoning, *n.* botulism.
sausage-roll, *n.* a roll of sausage-meat baked in a wrapping of flour paste.
saussurite, *n.* *saw*-sew-rite, a mineral of a greenish-grey colour produced by the decomposition of feldspar. (H. B. de *Saussure*, *d.* 1799, discoverer.)
sauté, *a.* *soh*-tay, fried quickly in a little fat. (Fr.)
Sauterne, *n.* soh-*tern*, white claret. (Commune in the Bordeaux country, France.)
savable, *a.* *save*-a-bl, capable of being saved.
savableness, *n.* state of being savable.
savage, *a.* *sav*-aj, wild; uncultivated; untamed; uncivilized; unpolished; cruel; barbarous: *n.* an uncivilized human being; a barbarian; one of a brutal unfeeling disposition: *v.t.* to treat with savagery; to make savage; to attack or tear violently (of animals).
savagedom, *n.* *sav*-aj-dom, savages collectively; the state of being a savage.
savagely, *ad.* in a savage manner.
savageness, *n.* condition of being savage; cruelty.
savagery, *n.* *sav*-aj-re, the savage or wild state; savageness; barbarism; barbarity.
savagism, *n.* *sav*-aj-izm, the state or characteristics of savages; savagery.
savanna, *n.* sa-*van*-a, a large grass-covered treeless plain. (Sp. *sabana*—probably from Carib.)
savant, *n.* (App.) a man of learning; a scientist. (Fr., knowing.)
savate, *n.* sa-*vaht*, boxing in the French way, in which both hands and feet are used. (Fr.)
save, *v.t.* save, to bring out of danger, sickness, or any harm; to rescue from spiritual ruin and death; to hinder from being spent or lost; to prevent; to maintain intact: to keep safely; to preserve from; to lay by; to spare: *v.i.* to be economical; to hoard: *prep.* except: *conj.* unless: *n.* the act of preventing a score [Sports]. (Fr. *sauver.*)
save-all, *n.* anything to prevent waste, esp. a small spike in a candlestick to save candle-ends; a strip of canvas along the roach of a sail [Naut.].
saveloy, *n.* *sav*-e-loy, a dry highly seasoned sausage of salted young pork, originally of brains. (O.Fr. *cervelat*, brains.)
saver, *n.* *save*-er, one who saves or economizes; that which prevents waste, loss, or damage.
savin, *n.* *sav*-in, the small evergreen conifer, *Juniperus sabina*, yielding a volatile medicinal oil. (Fr.)
saving, *a.* *save*-ing, frugal; thrifty; incurring no loss, though yielding no gain; excepting; effecting salvation [Theol.]: *n.* something kept from being expended; reservation; *pl.* unexpended money put aside to accrue: *prep.* excepting. **saving grace,** a redeeming feature. **savings bank,** a bank in which small savings are deposited and placed at interest for the benefit of the depositors. **savings stamp,** a stamp (6*d.*, 2*s.* 6*d.*, or 5*s.*) issued as a receipt for small deposits in National Savings.
savingly, *ad.* in a saving manner.
saviour, *n.* *save*-yur, one who saves or delivers from danger; a rescuer. **the Saviour,** Jesus Christ, as the Redeemer.
savonette, *n.* sav-o-net, a ball of toilet soap. **savonette tree,** the shagbark of the W. Indies, the bark of which has been used as soap. (Fr.)
savory, *n.* *say*-vo-re, an aromatic pot-herb of the genus *Satureia.* (Fr. *savorie.*)
savour, *n.* *say*-vor, taste; flavour; scent; odour; distinctive quality; character [Fig.]: *v.i.* to have a particular smell or taste; to exhibit tokens of: *v.t.* to taste or smell, esp. with pleasure; to appreciate; to delight in. (O.Fr. *savor.*)
savourily, *ad.* *say*-vo-re-le, in a savoury manner.
savouriness, *n.* the quality of being savoury.
savourless, *a.* *say*-vor-less, destitute of savour.
savoury, *a.* *say*-vo-re, pleasing to the smell or taste; pleasant: *n.* a piquant dish, esp. as served after the sweets at dinner.
savoy, *n.* sa-*voy*, a curly cabbage much cultivated for winter use. (*Savoy*, in France.)
Savoyard, *a.* sa-*voy*-ard (or App.), pertaining to Savoy, Italy: *n.* a native of Savoy; one who took part in the original production of any of the Gilbert and Sullivan comic operas at the Savoy Theatre, London; an enthusiastic admirer of these operas.
savvy, *n.* *sav*-e, rapid comprehension; nous; cleverness: *v.i.* and *t.* to understand [Slang]. (Sp. *sabe*, know.)
saw, saw, *p.* of *see.*
saw, *n.* saw, a steel cutting tool with toothed edge: *v.t.* to cut or separate with a saw; to form by cutting with a saw: *v.i.* to do sawing; to be cut with a saw. *p.* **sawed.** *pp.* **sawed** and **sawn.** (A.S. *sage.*)
saw, *n.* saw, a saying or maxim. (*say.*)
saw-bill, *n.* applied to various birds with serrated bill, esp. the goosander and mot-mot.
sawbones, *n.* *saw*-bohnz, a surgeon [Slang].
sawder, *n.* *saw*-der, solder. **soft sawder,** flattery.
sawdust, *n.* *saw*-dust, the dust or small fragments produced in sawing wood.
saw-fish, *n.* any of several shark-like fish of the genus *Pristis* having an elongated and flattened snout serrated along each edge.
saw-fly, *n.* one of the Tenthredinidæ, a genus of insects of which the female has a saw-like ovipositor for boring holes for the deposition of eggs.
sawmill, *n.* *saw*-mil, a mill for sawing timber.
Sawney, *n.* *saw*-ne, a Scotsman [Coll.]; (*l.c.*) a simpleton. (*Sandy*, for Alexander.)
saw-pit, *n.* a pit over which timber is sawn by two men, one standing below the log, the other above.
saw-set, *n.* a tool used to set the teeth of saws.
saw-wort, *n.* any plant of the genus *Serratula*, having its leaves edged with cutting teeth.
saw-wrack, *n.* black wrack, the common seaweed *Fucus serratus.*
saw-wrest, *n.* a saw-set.
sawyer, *n.* *saw*-yer, one who saws timber into planks; any of several boring beetles; a tree in a river, whose branches sway up and down with the current [U.S.A.].
sax, *n.* saks, a slater's hammer with a point or peen for making holes for the nails. (A.S. *seax*, knife.)
saxatile, *a.* *saks*-a-tile, pertaining to or living among rocks. (L. *saxatilis.*)
saxe, *a.* saks, from or as from Saxony. **saxe-blue,** a dye prepared from indigo. **saxe-green,** cobalt-green. **saxe-paper,** an albumenized photographic paper.
saxhorn, *n.* *saks*-hawrn, a brass musical instrument with its pistons. (A. J. Adolphe *Sax*, 1814–94, its inventor, and *horn.*)
saxicavous, *a.* *saks*-e-*kay*-vus, rock-boring (esp. of certain molluscs). (L. *saxum*, a rock, *cavo*, hollow.)
saxicolous, *a.* sak-*sik*-o-lus, growing on rocks [Bot.]. (L. *saxum*, a rock, *colere*, to inhabit.)
saxifrage, *n.* *saks*-e-fraj, any of the *Saxifraga*, a

genus of plants (including London pride) formerly thought good for stone in the bladder. (L. *saxifraga*, a rock-breaker.)

Saxon, *n. sak*-son, a native of Saxony or of the Saxe duchies; one (or a descendant) of a people formerly settled on the coast of N. Germany, and who, with the Angles, invaded and conquered England in the 5th and 6th centuries; (in Ireland) an Englishman, (in Scotland) a lowlander: *a.* pertaining to the Saxons, their country or language. **Saxon-blue,** saxe-blue. **Saxon Shore,** in Roman Britain, the English coast from the Wash to Beachy Head. (A.S. *Seaxan*, the Saxons.)

Saxonism, *n. sak*-son-izm, a Saxon idiom.

Saxonist, *n. sak*-son-ist, one versed in Saxon.

saxophone, *n. sak*-so-fone, a brass musical instrument with a clarinet mouthpiece invented by the inventor of the saxhorn. (Gr. *phoné*, sound.)

saxophonist, *n. sak*-so-foh-nist, a player of the saxophone.

saxtuba, *n. saks*-tew-ba, a large sized saxhorn.

say, *n.* say, a former thin woollen stuff or serge of mixed silk and wool.

★**say,** *n.* say, something said; one's turn to speak: *v.t.* to utter in words; to speak; to declare; to utter; to allege; to repeat; to pronounce; to report; to answer; to suppose: *v.i.* to assert. *p.* and *pp.* **said,** sed. (A.S. *secgan.*)

saying, *n. say*-ing, something said; an expression; a proverb; an apophthegm. **to go without saying,** to be self-evident.

Sayyid, *n. sy*-id *or sah*-yid, a Moslem title accorded to one whose descent from the elder son of Fatima, daughter of the Prophet, is acknowledged.

sbirro, *n. sbi*-ro, an Italian policeman. (It.)

scab, *n.* skab, a rough and dry incrustation formed over a sore in healing; a highly contagious mange affecting sheep, cattle, etc.; a mean, dirty, paltry fellow; a worker refusing to join his trade-union; a black-leg. **scab shop,** a factory, etc., employing only non-union labour. (A.S. *sceabb*, from O.Scand. *skabbr.*)

scabbard, *n. skab*-ard, the sheath of a sword: *v.t.* to put in a scabbard. (Anglo-Fr. *escaubers.*)

scabbard-fish, *n.* the sea-fish *Lepidopus caudatus*, with a long compressed body.

scabbed, *a.* skabd, diseased with the scab, or with scabies; affected with scabs; mean; paltry; worthless.

scabbiness, *n.* the state of being scabby.

scabble, *v.t. skab*-bl, to rough-hew the face of building stone, to scapple.

scabby, *a. skab*-e, affected with scabs; rough; itchy; leprous; mangy.

scabies, *n. skay*-be-eez, the itch, a troublesome contagious skin disease caused by the mite *Ascaris scabiei.* (L.)

scabietic, *a.* skay-be-*et*-ik, pertaining to or affected with scabies.

scabious, *a. skay*-be-us, consisting of scabs; scabby; affected with scabies: *n.* any plant of the herbaceous genus *Scabiosa*, formerly deemed efficacious in scaly eruptions. (L. *scabiosus.*)

scabrescent, *a.* ska-*bres*-ent minutely scabrous [Bot.].

scabrid, *a. skay*-brid, somewhat scabrous.

scabridity, *n.* ska-*brid*-e-te, the condition of being scabrous.

scabrous, *a. skay*-brus, bristly; rough; rugged; having sharp points. (Fr. *scabreux.*)

scabrousness, *n.* quality of being scabrous.

scad, *n.* skad, any of various sea-fish of the genus *Caranx*, esp. the horse-mackerel, *C. trachurus.*

scaffold, *n. skaf*-old, a temporary structure to support workmen in the erection of a building; a temporary stage, raised for shows or spectators; an elevated platform for the execution of a criminal: *v.t.* to furnish with a scaffold; to sustain. (O.Fr. *escafaut.*)

scaffolder, *n. skaf*-ol-der, a workman who erects scaffolds.

scaffolding, *n. skaf*-ol-ding, a scaffold; a framework; materials for scaffolds.

scaglia, *n. skah*-le-a, a whitish or reddish limestone of the Southern Alps. (It.)

scagliola, *n.* skal-*yoh*-la, plaster-work in imitation of stone or marble. (It.)

scalable, *a. skale*-a-bl, that may be scaled.

scalade, *n.* ska-*lahd*, an escalade. (L. *scala*, a ladder.)

scalar, *a. skay*-lar, scalariform; of the nature of a scalar [Math.]: *n.* a quantity having magnitude but not direction [Math.].

scalariform, *a.* ska-*la*-re-form, ladder-shaped [Bot and Zool.]. (L. *scalaria*, a ladder, and *form.*)

scalawag, *n. skal*-a-wag, a scallywag.

scald, *n.* skawld, a burn or injury caused by a boiling liquid or hot vapour; an inflamed part (esp. in sheep) [Vet.]; the parasitic plant dodder (local name): *v.t.* to burn or injure by means of boiling liquid, etc.; to expose to a violent heat over a fire or in a liquid; to bring to nearly boiling-point (of milk). (O.Fr. *escalder.*)

scald, *n.* skawld, scall; scurf: *a.* affected with scall; paltry; poor. (Scand.)

scald, *n.* skawld, an ancient Norse poet, a skald.

scalder, *n. skawl*-der, one who scalds; a vessel or utensil for scalding.

scald-head, *n.* a fungous disease of the scalp.

scaldic, *a. skawl*-dik, skaldic.

★**scale,** *n.* skale, the dish of a balance; (*pl.*) a balance; the thin horn-like covering formed from the skin of a fish or a reptile, also any similar protection, as on the legs of a bird or in plants, etc.; an incrustation: *v.t.* to amount to in weight; to pare off a surface: *v.i.* to come off in thin layers. **scale insect,** any small plant-destroying pest of the family Coccidæ. (O.Fr. *escale.*)

★**scale,** *n.* skale, anything regularly graduated, esp. for use as a measure, standard of reference, etc.; a mathematical instrument on which are marked lines and figures at regular intervals; the proportion which any measurement on a map, etc., bears to the actual distance represented; an allowance; a gamut, or graduated series of ascending or descending tones [Mus.]: *v.t.* to climb by ladders; to mount by or as by steps; to draw or represent in the true proportions. (L. *scala.*)

scale-armour, *n.* armour of steel plates overlapping each other like the scales of a fish.

scaled, *a.* skayld, having scales like a fish, etc.; squamous; with the scales removed; furnished with a graduated scale.

scaleless, *a. skale*-less, destitute of scales.

scalene, *a.* ska-*leen*, having all the sides and angles unequal (of triangles); having the axis inclined to the base (of cones): *n.* a scalene triangle. (Gr. *skalenos*, crooked.)

scalenohedron, *n.* ska-*lee*-no-*hee*-dron, a crystal having twelve faces, each of which is a scalene triangle. (Gr. *skalenos*, uneven, *hedra*, a base.)

scaler, *n. skale*-er, one that scales; a tool for removing scale.

scaliness, *n. skale*-e-ness, the state of being scaly.

scaling-ladder, *n.* a ladder for enabling troops to scale a wall.

scall, *n.* skawl, scab; a scaly eruption. **dry scall,** psoriasis [Path.]. (Scand.)

scallion, *n. skal*-yun, a variety of onion. (O.Fr. *escalogne.*)

scallop, *n. skol*-op, a bivalve mollusc of the genus *Pecten*; a scallop-shell, esp. as the badge of a pilgrim; a decorative undulating edge: *v.t.* to cook in or as in a scallop-shell; to mark or cut an edge or border into wavy segments. (O.Fr. *escalope.*)

scallywag, *n. skal*-e-wag, a scapegrace; a scamp.

scalp, *n.* skalp, the skin of the top of the head; this skin, or part of it, with the hair on, torn off as a trophy: *v.t.* to deprive of the scalp; to castigate or criticize severely [Fig.]. (Scand.)

scalpel, *n. skal*-pel, a thin sharp dissecting knife [Anat., etc.]. (L. *scalpellum*, a small knife.)

scalper, *n. skal*-per, one who scalps; a wood-engraver's tool.

scalpriform, *a. skal*-pre-form, chisel-shaped [Zool.].

scaly, *a. skale*-e, covered or abounding with scales; resembling scales; composed of scales lying over each other [Bot.]; stingy [Slang].

scamble, *n. skam*-bl, a scramble: *v.t.* to mangle; to maul: *v.i.* to muddle along; to scramble.

scambler, *n. skam*-bler; one who scambles; one who sponges on others.

scamillus, *n.* ska-*mil*-us, a small plinth below the base of an Ionic or Corinthian column [Arch.]. (L., a small bench.)

scammony, *n. skam*-o-ne, the plant *Convolvulus*

scammonia; the inspissated sap of this, used as a cathartic [Med.]. (L. *scammonia.*)

scamp, *n.* skamp, a dishonest knave; a mean villain; a rogue. (*scamper.*)

scamp, *v.t.* skamp, to do or execute a work in a careless, superficial style.

scamper, *n. skamp*-er, flight in haste: *v.i.* to run off in flight with haste. (O.Fr. *escamper*, to flee.)

scampish, *a. skamp*-ish, befitting a scamp.

scan, *v.t.* skan, to examine with critical care; to scrutinize; to analyse verse according to the laws of prosody, to count the feet in a line; to reproduce or transmit an image by television by means of the repeated traversing of its surface by a beam of light or electrons projected through a series of apertures, etc., on a rotating disk: *v.i.* to be right for the metre. (L. *scando*, climb.)

scandal, *n. skan*-dal, offence given by the faults of others; something uttered which is false and injurious to reputation; defamation of character [Law]; malicious gossip. (Fr. *scandale.*)

scandalize, *v.t. skan*-da-lize, to offend or shock by impropriety or indecorous conduct; to talk scandal; to defame.

scandal-monger, *n.* a spreader of scandal.

scandalous, *a. skan*-da-lus, involving scandal; disgraceful to reputation; defamatory.

scandalously, *ad.* in a scandalous manner.

scandalousness, *n. skan*-da-lus-ness, quality of being scandalous.

scandent, *a. skan*-dent, climbing [Bot.]. (L. *scandens.*)

Scandinavian, *a. skan*-de-*nay*-ve-an, pertaining to Scandinavia; relating to the ancient language and literature of Scandinavia and Iceland: *n.* a native or the language of Scandinavia.

scandium, *n. skan*-de-um, a metallic element of the cerium group, present in certain rare-earth metals, esp. in Sweden. (L. *Scandia*, Scandinavia.)

scannable, *a. skan*-a-bl, capable of being scanned metrically or for purposes of television.

scansion, *n. skan*-shon, the act or operation of scanning. (Fr.)

Scansores, *n.pl.* skan-*saw*-reez, the order containing the climbing-birds, including the woodpeckers, cuckoos, parrots, etc. (L. *scansus*, climbed.)

scansorial, *a.* skan-*saw*-re-al, pertaining to the Scansores, or to climbing (esp. of the feet): *n.* a climbing-bird.

scant, *a.* skant, not full, large, or plentiful; scarcely sufficient; deficient: *v.t.* to stint; to straiten: *v.i.* to fail or become less. (Ice. *skamt*, short.)

scantily, *ad. skan*-te-le, in a scanty measure.

scantiness, *n.* state of being scanty; want of sufficiency.

scantity, *n. skan*-te-te, scarceness.

scantle, *n. skan*-tl, a gauge for slates; a small slate: *v.t.* to partition: *v.i.* to become less; to be deficient. (O.Fr. *escanteler.*)

scantling, *n. skant*-ling, a pattern; a quantity cut for a particular purpose; a small quantity; a certain proportion; timber cut into quartering under five inches; timber of small section. (O.Fr. *escantillon.*)

scantly, *ad. skant*-le, not fully or sufficiently.

scantness, *n. skant*-ness, narrowness; smallness.

scanty, *a. skan*-te, wanting amplitude or extent; narrow; small; not ample; hardly sufficient; sparing.

scape, *n.* skape, the spring of a column [Arch.]; a leafless flower-stalk rising from the root [Bot.]; the lower part of an antenna [Entom.]; the shaft of a feather. (L. *scapus*, a shaft.)

scapegoat, *n. skape*-goat, a goat on which the Jewish high priest laid the sins of the people, sending it thereafter into the wilderness; hence, one who is made to bear the blame of another's crimes. (*escape* and *goat.*)

scapegrace, *n. skape*-grace, a graceless, good-for-nothing fellow.

scapeless, *a. skape*-less, destitute of a scape.

scapement, *n. skape*-ment, escapement.

scaphism, *n. skaf*-izm, a former capital punishment among the Persians, confinement in the hollow of a tree, the head and limbs being smeared with honey and exposed to the tortures of insect stings. (Gr. *skaphos*, a boat, or anything hollow.)

scaphite, *n. skaf*-ite, a boat-shaped fossil cephalopod.

scaphoid, *a. skaf*-oyd, resembling a boat in form.

scaphoid bone, a bone of the wrist, also the corresponding bone in the ankle.

scaphopod, *n. skaf*-o-pod, any of the Scaphopoda, a class of burrowing marine molluscs with a long tapering shell; a tooth-shell.

scapigerous, *a.* ska-*pij*-er-rus, scape-bearing [Bot.].

scapolite, *n. skap*-o-lite, any of several crystalline minerals consisting chiefly of silicate of aluminium, calcium, and sodium. (Gr. *skapos*, a rod, *lithos*, a stone.)

scapple, *v.t. skap*-pl, to dress stone to a straight or level surface. (O.Fr. *escapeler.*)

scapula, *n. skap*-yew-la, the shoulder-blade. (L.)

scapular, *a. skap*-yew-lar, pertaining to the shoulder or scapula: *n.* a scapulary; a bandage for the shoulder; any of the feathers springing from the shoulder and lying along the side of the back [Ornith.].

scapulary, *n. skap*-yew-la-re, a part of the habit of certain religious orders consisting of a narrow piece of stuff hanging over the shoulders.

scapulated, *a. skap*-yew-lay-ted, having white or otherwise conspicuous shoulder-feathers [Ornith.]

scapulimancy, *a. skap*-yew-le-man-se, divination by the cracks on a shoulder-blade subjected to heat. (L. *scapula*, and Gr. *manteia*, divination.)

scar, *n.* skar, a mark left by a wound or sore; a blemish; a bare patch on a rock: *v.t.* to mark with a scar. (Gr. *eschara*, a hearth.)

scar, *n.* skar, any fish of the genus *Scarus*.

scar, *n.* skar, a steep rock; a crag; an isolated eminence. (Ice. *sker.*)

scarab, *n. ska*-rab, a beetle of the genus *Scarabæus*; a gem with the scarabæus engraved upon it. (L. *scarabæus*, beetle.)

Scarabæus, *n.* ska-ra-*bee*-us, a genus of dung-eating beetles; esp. *S. sacer*, regarded with veneration by the ancient Egyptians; an amulet bearing the engraved form of the scarabæus. (L.)

scaramouch, *n, ska*-ra-moosh, a buffoon in old comedy, representing one who is at once a poltroon and a braggart; a poltroon and braggart. (It.)

scarce, *a.* skarece, not plentiful; rare; deficient: *ad.* hardly; with difficulty. **make oneself scarce,** to get away; to keep out of the way. (O.Fr. *escars*, niggard.)

scarcely, *ad. skarece*-le, hardly; with difficulty.

scarceness, *n.* the state of being scarce.

scarcity, *n. skare*-se-te, scarceness; deficiency; dearth. (O.Fr. *escarsete.*)

scare, *n.* skare, a state of being scared; a panic: *v.t.* to strike with sudden fright; to terrify. **to scare away,** to frighten away. (Ice. *skiarr*, shy.)

scarecrow, *n. skare*-kroh, anything set up to frighten crows, etc., from crops; an imaginary terror; a guy.

scaremonger, *n. skare*-mung-ger, an exciter of panic, esp. by spreading false rumours.

scarf, *n.* skarf, a loose covering for the shoulders; a light neckerchief or necktie. (Origin uncertain.)

scarf, *n.* skarf (*pl.* **scarfs** or **scarves**), a joint uniting two pieces of timber longitudinally by chamfering and bolting to gether; the end of a piece of timber thus prepared: *v.t.* to unite two pieces of timber into one by the ends. (Scand. *skarfva*, to join together.)

scarfskin, *n. skarf*-skin, the cuticle, or the outer layer of skin that may peel off in scales.

scarification, *n.* ska-re-fe-*kay*-shon, the act of scarifying. (Fr.)

scarificator, *n. ska*-re-fe-kay-tor, an instrument used in scarification or cupping [Surg.].

scarifier, *n. ska*-re-fy-er, one who scarifies; a scarificator; an implement for loosening the soil.

scarify, *v.t. ska*-re-fy, to scratch or cut the skin so as to draw blood; to stir the soil; to lacerate the feelings of; to criticize unmercifully; to scare [Coll.]. (Fr. *scarifier.*)

scarious, *a. skare*-re-us, tough, thin, and semi-transparent [Bot.]; shrivelled. (L. *scaria*, a shrub with thorns.)

scarlatina, *n.* skar-la-*tee*-na, scarlet fever. (It.)

scarlatinous, *a.* skar-*lat*-e-nus, of the nature of scarlatina.

scarlet, *n. skar*-let, a bright-red colour; cloth of a scarlet colour: *a.* of scarlet colour. **scarlet fever,** an acute contagious fever, characterized by a scarlet efflorescence of the skin and the mucous membrane of the fauces and the tonsils, and ending with a shedding of the skin. **scarlet lightning,** the garden plant *Lychnis chalcedonica*, also the red valerian. **scarlet runner,** the edible bean *Phaseolus multiflorus*. **the scarlet woman,** pagan Rome (Rev. xvii); applied opprobriously to the Roman Catholic Church and the papacy. (O.Fr. *escarlate*.)

scarp, *n.* skarp, a nearly perpendicular slope; the interior slope of the ditch at the foot of a rampart [Fort.]: *v.t.* to cut to a nearly perpendicular slope. (Fr. *escarpe*.)

scarp, *n.* skarp, a bend sinister of half the regular width [Her.]. (O.Fr. *escarpe*, a scarf.)

scarred, *a.* skard, marked with scars.

scart, *n.* skart, the cormorant or the shag [Scots.].

Scarus, *n. skare*-rus, the genus of sea-fish including the parrot fishes. (L.)

scary, *a.* skare-re, easily scared; alarming [Coll.].

scat, *n.* skat, a tax or tribute [Orkneys and Shetlands]; a wind-driven shower: *int.* clear out! be off!

scatch, *n.* skatsh, an oval bit for a bridle. (Fr.)

scatches, *n.pl. skatsh*-ez, stilts. (Fr.)

scathe, *n.* skaythe, damage; injury: *v.t.* to injure. (Scand.)

scatheful, *a. skaythe*-ful, injurious; harmful.

scatheless, *a. skaythe*-less, without scathe or damage.

scathing, *a. skaythe*-ing, destroying; withering; bitterly severe [Fig.].

scathingly, *ad. skaythe*-ing-le, in a bitterly injurious manner.

scatological, *a. skat*-o-*loj*-e-kal, pertaining to scatology or the cult of filth.

scatology, *n.* ska-*tol*-o-je, the study of excrements, or of coprolites; prurient interest in obscenity or pornography [Fig.]. (Gr. *skor*, *skatos*, dung, *logos*, science.)

scatophagous, *a.* ska-*tof*-a-gus, dung-eating, coprophagous. (Gr. *skor*, *skatos*, dung, *phagein*, to eat.)

scatter, *v.t. skat*-er, to throw loosely about; to disperse; to rout: *v.i.* to be dispersed or dissipated. (Perhaps *shatter*.)

scatter-brained, *a.* thoughtless; flighty.

scattered, *a. skat*-erd, widely or irregularly dispersed; irregular in position [Bot.].

scatteringly, *ad. skat*-er-ing-le, in a scattered manner; intermittently.

scatterings, *n. skat*-er-ing, anything scattered.

scatterling, *n. skat*-er-ling, a vagabond.

scatty, *a. skat*-e, showery; daft, crazy [Slang].

scaup, *n.* skawp, the sea duck *Fuligula marila*. (Ice.)

scauper, *n. skawp*-er, a wood-engraver's gouge. (*scalper*.)

scaur, *n.* skawr, a steep bank of clays and sands; a cliff; a bluff precipice of rock.

scavage, *n. skav*-aj, a former toll on goods offered for sale by strangers in certain markets. (O.Fr. *escavage*.)

scavenge, *v.i.* and *t. skav*-enj, to work or act as a scavenger; automatically to remove products of combustion from the cylinders of internal combustion engines. (*scavenger*.)

scavenger, *n. skav*-en-jer, a street cleaner; a carrion-feeding animal; one willing to do objectionable or dirty work; originally one who took scavage. (O.Fr. *scavager*, customs officer; inspector.)

scazon, *n. skay*-zon, an iambic verse in which the final iambus is replaced by a trochee or spondee. (Gr., limping.)

scelides, *n.pl. sel*-e-deez, the hind limbs of a mammal. (Gr. *skelos*, leg.)

scenario, *n.* sha-*nah*-re-oh *or* se-*nare*-re-oh, the plan of a play, giving the order of the scenes and an outline of the story. (It.)

scenarist, *n.* se-*nare*-rist, a writer of cinematograph scenarios.

scend, *n.* send, the upward motion of a ship before she pitches: *v.i.* to lift or heave upward (of a ship in motion). (*send*.)

scene, *n.* seen, a stage; the place where dramatic pieces, etc., are exhibited; a series of actions and events, or groups of objects exhibited; a spectacle; the division of an act of a play; the place or the picture of the place of action; any remarkable exhibition; a display of feeling. (Gr. *skene*, a tent.)

scene-dock, *n.* the scenery store at a theatre.

scene-painter, *n.* one who paints theatrical scenery.

scenery, *n. seen*-er-re, the appearance of a place or of the various objects presented to view; a picturesque landscape; the painted scenes, back cloth, and other accessories representing the scene of action on the stage. (L. *scenarius*, scenic.)

scene-shifter, *n.* a man who shifts the scenery and prepares the stage at a theatre.

scenic, *a. see*-nik *or sen*-ik, pertaining to the stage; dramatic; theatrical.

scenically, *ad. see*-ne- *or sen*-e-ka-le, in a scenic manner.

scenograph, *n. see*-no-graf, a representation of an object in perspective.

scenographer, *n.* see-*nog*-ra-fer, one skilled in scenography.

scenographic, *a. see*-no-*graf*-ik, pertaining to scenography; drawn in perspective.

scenographically, *ad.* in perspective.

scenography, *n.* see-*nog*-ra-fe, the art of representing an object on a perspective plane. (Gr. *skenographia*.)

scent, *n.* sent, odour; perfume; sense of smell; an animal's trail of odour; course of pursuit; track: *v.t.* to smell; to perfume; to suspect. **on the scent,** on the right track (esp. of animals.) (Fr. *sentir*, to perceive by the senses.)

scentless, *a. sent*-less, inodorous; destitute of smell, or (rarely) of the sense of smell.

sceptic, *n. skep*-tik, one who doubts the truth of any principle or system of principles or doctrines, esp. of the Christian religion; one who denies or doubts the trustworthiness of the senses regarded as media of absolute truth: *a.* sceptical. (Fr. *sceptique*.)

sceptical, *a. skep*-te-kal, doubting; hesitating to admit the certainty of doctrines or principles; denying the truth of revelation.

sceptically, *ad. skep*-te-ka-le, with doubt.

scepticism, *n. skep*-te-sizm, the state of being sceptical; doubt, esp. in regard to revealed religion or to the supersensible or transcendental; a sceptical principle or system.

scepticize, *v.i. skep*-te-size, to adopt a sceptical attitude; to doubt of everything.

sceptre, *n. sep*-ter, a royal mace, the emblem of regal authority; royal power or authority. (Fr.)

sceptred, *a. sep*-terd, bearing a sceptre.

schadenfreude, *shah*-den-froy-da, malicious satisfaction aroused by other people's troubles. (Ger. *Schaden*, mischief, *Freude*, satisfaction.)

schedule, *n. shed*-yewl, a document containing a list, inventory, or catalogue, esp. as an addendum to another document; a time-table: *v.t.* to place in a list or catalogue; to add as a schedule. (O.Fr.)

scheelite, *n. shee*-lite, native calcium tungstate, a source of tungsten. (K. W. *Scheele*, *d.* 1786, Swedish scientist.)

schema, *n. skee*-ma (*pl.* **schemata,** *skee*-ma-ta), a scheme, plan, outline, or synopsis; a diagram; a figure of a syllogism [Logic]; a figure of speech; a general type, the image by which the intellect determines the form of a particular presentation [Kantian Phil.]. (Gr. *schema*, form.)

schematic, *a.* ske-*mat*-ik, pertaining to or resembling a scheme or schema; conforming to a recognized model or pattern.

schematical, *a.* ske-*mat*-e-kal, pertaining to a schema; schematic.

schematically, *ad.* in a schematic manner.

schematism, *n. skee*-ma-tizm, form or disposition of anything; outline; the combination of the aspects of heavenly bodies [Astrol.].

schematist, *n. skee*-ma-tist, one given to form schemes or schemata.

schematize, *v.t. skee*-ma-tize, to arrange in a schema: *v.i.* to make a schema.

scheme, *n.* skeem, a plan; a system; a project or contrivance; a graphic or diagrammatic representation: *v.t.* to contrive: *v.i.* to form a plan; to plot. (Gr. *schema*.)

schemer, *n. skee*-mer, one who schemes; a contriver; a plotter or intriguer.

scheming, *a. skee*-ming, given to forming schemes or intrigues; calculating; artful.

schemingly, *ad. skee*-ming-le, by scheming.

schemist, *n. skee*-mist, one given to forming schemes.

schene, *n.* skeen, an Egyptian lineal measure of from $3\frac{1}{2}$ to $7\frac{1}{2}$ miles), adopted by the ancient Greeks. (L. *schænus*)
scherzando, *ad.* skayrt-*zan*-doh, in a playful manner [Mus.]. (It.)
scherzo, *n. skayrt*-zoh, a playful passage in a musical composition. (It.)
schesis, *n. skee*-sis, habitude; disposition of one thing with regard to other things. (Gr., habit.)
schetic, *a. sket*-ik, habitual; constitutional.
schiedam, *n.* ske-*dam*, hollands gin; schnapps. (Name of town where first made.)
schieferspar, *n. shee*-fer-spar, shiver-spar [Min.]. (Ger.)
schiller, *n. shil*-er, a bronze-like iridescence characteristic of certain minerals and beetles. (Ger.)
schillerization, *n.* shil-er-ry-*zay*-shon, the process, or result, of schillerizing.
schillerize, *v.t. shil*-er-rize, to impart a schiller to.
schilling, *n. shil*-ing, a former small-value silver coin of Germany, Austria, etc. (Ger.)
schipperke, *n. skip*-er-ke, a small Belgian breed of dog allied to the Pomeranian. (Dut.)
schism, *n.* sizm, a division or separation in a community, esp. in a Church; the sin of causing schism. (Fr. *schisme.*)
schismatic, *a.* siz-*mat*-ik, schismatical: *n.* one who separates from Church or religious faith through diversity of opinion.
schismatical, *a.* siz-*mat*-e-kal, pertaining to, tending to, or implying schism.
schismatically, *ad.* in a schismatic manner.
schismatize, *v.i. siz*-ma-tize, to commit or practise schism: *v.t.* to lead into schism.
schist, *n.* shist, a rock having the constituent minerals crystallized in parallel, lenticular, and wavy layers or folia [Geol.]. (Gr. *schistos*, split.)
schistaceous, *a.* shis-*tay*-shus, of a slate-grey colour.
schistoid, *a. shis*-toyd, schistose.
schistoscope, *n. shis*-to-skope, a polariscope adapted with selenite plates to produce complementary colours.
schistose, *a. shis*-tohs, of the nature of schist; foliated [Geol.].
schistosomiasis, *n. shis*-to-so-*my*-a-sis, the disease bilharziasis, caused by a trematode parasite of the family Schistosomidæ. (Gr. *schistos*, cleft, *soma*, body.)
schistous, *a. shis*-tus, schistose.
schizanthus, *n.* sky-*zan*-thus, the butterfly-flower, an annual garden plant from Chile. (Gr. *schizo*, to cleave, *anthos*, flower.)
schizocarp, *n. sky*-zo-karp, a dry fruit splitting into single-seeded carpels. (Gr. *schizo*, and *karpos*, fruit.)
schizogenesis, *n. sky*-zo-*jen*-e-sis, reproduction by fission [Biol.]. (Gr. *schizo*, and *genesis*, origin.)
schizogenetic, *a. sky*-zo-je-*net*-ik, pertaining to or formed by schizogenesis.
schizognathous, *a.* sky-*zog*-na-thus, having the palate bones separated from each other and from the vomer, as in the penguins, gulls, gallinaceous birds, etc. [Ornith.]. (Gr. *schizo*, and *gnathos*, jaw.)
schizoid, *a. sky*-zoyd *or skiz*-oyd, resembling or afflicted with schizophrenia: *n.* one suffering from this.
schizomycete, *n. sky*-zo-my-seet, any member of the group of bacteria which multiply by fission.
schizophrene, *n. sky*-zo- *or skiz*-o-freen, one affected by schizophrenia.
schizophrenia, *n. sky*-zo *or skiz*-o-*free*-ne-a, a form of insanity characterized by disorganization of personality and intermittent replacement of the conscious by the unconscious; split personality. (Gr. *schizo*, split, *phrēn*, mind.)
schizophrenic, *n. sky*-zo- *or skiz*-o-*fren*-ik, pertaining to or resembling schizophrenia: *n.* one suffering from this.
schnapper, *n. shnap*-er, a valuable food-fish of Australasian waters, allied to the sea-breams.
schnapps, *n.* shnaps, schiedam; Dutch gin. (Ger.)
schnauzer, *n. shnou*-zer, a long-headed wiry-coated German terrier. (Ger., snarler.)
schnitzel, *n. shnit*-sel, a grilled veal cutlet served with gravy and seasoning. (Ger.)
schnorrer, *n. shnor*-rer, a Jewish beggar (Yiddish).
scholar, *n. skol*-ar, a pupil; a disciple; a man of learning; an undergraduate on the foundation of a college. (O.Fr. *escoler.*)
scholarlike, *a. skol*-ar-like, befitting a scholar.
scholarly, *a. skol*-ar-le, scholarlike; learned.
scholarship, *n. skol*-ar-ship, attainments in the humanities or science; erudition; maintenance for a scholar; foundation for the support of a student.
scholastic, *a.* sko-*las*-tik, pertaining to a scholar or to schools, esp. those of the schoolmen; academic; pedantic: *n.* a mediæval schoolman; one who adheres to the subtleties of schoolmen, a pedantic philosopher. (Fr. *scolastique.*)
scholastically, *ad.* in a scholastic manner.
scholasticism, *n.* sko-*las*-te-sizm, the philosophy or learning of the schoolman; adherence to the subtleties of the schools.
scholiast, *n. skoh*-le-ast, an ancient commentator on Greek or Latin classics. (Gr. *scholiastēs.*)
scholiastic, *a.* skoh-le-*as*-tik, that pertains to a scholiast.
scholium, *n. skoh*-le-um (*pl.* **scholia**), a marginal annotation, esp. on a passage in a Greek or Latin classic; an explanatory observation. (Late L.)
***school,** *n.* skool, a place or an establishment for education or instruction, esp. for the young; the pupils of a school; instruction; a period of teaching; a mediæval seminary; the system of a master or his sect; a body of followers; any place of improvement or learning: *v.t.* to instruct; to discipline; to reprove. **school board,** a former body (abolished 1902) elected by ratepayers to provide for and manage the primary education of all children in a district. **school year,** the parts of the year collectively during which a school is in session. (L. *schola.*)
school, *n.* skool, a shoal of fish, porpoises, etc.: *v.i.* to swim together in a school; to form a shoal at or near the surface. (Dut., a shoal.)
schoolable, *a. skool*-a-bl, of an age to attend school.
schoolboy, *n. skool*-boy, a boy attending school.
schoolcraft, *n. skool*-krahft, learning.
school-divinity, *n.* theology as reasoned by the schoolmen; argumentative theology.
schoolfellow, *n. skool*-fel-oh, one taught at the same school at the same time.
schoolgirl, *n. skool*-girl, a girl attending school.
schoolhouse, *n. skool*-house, a house appropriated for the use of a school; the chief of the school buildings.
schooling, *n. skool*-ing, instruction in school; tuition; reproof, reprimand [Coll.].
schoolman, *n. skool*-man, a man versed in the niceties of academical disputation, or of school philosophy or divinity; an academic, esp. monastic, philosopher of about the 9th to 14th centuries.
schoolmarm, *n. skool*-marm, a schoolmistress.
schoolmaster, *n. skool*-mahs-ter, one who presides over or teaches in a school; one who or that which acts as a schoolmaster.
schoolmate, *n. skool*-mate, a schoolfellow.
schoolmistress, *n. skool*-mis-tres, a female teacher; the female head of a school.
schoolmistressy, *a. skool*-mis-tres-e, characteristic of a schoolmistress; prim; pedantic.
school-teacher, *n.* one who teaches in a school (esp. public elementary).
school-treat, *n.* a pleasure outing for the children of a school or Sunday School.
schooner, *n. skoon*-er, a fore-and-aft vessel with two or more masts and usually a square fore-topsail and fore-topgallant-sail; a tall beer-glass [U.S.A.]. (Dial. *scoon*, to skip or skim.)
schorl, *n.* shorl, a black variety of tourmaline. (Ger.)
schottische, *n.* shot-*teesh*, a round polka-like dance; the music for this. (Ger. *schottisch*, Scottish.)
schwa, *n.* shvah, an unaccented neutral vowel sound, as in the first syllable of "away" and the second of "diet." (Heb.)
sciagraph, *n. sy*-a-graf, a skiagraph. (Gr. *skia*, a shadow, *grapho*, write.)
sciagrapher, *n.* sy-*ag*-ra-fer, one skilled in sciagraphy.
sciagraphic, *a.* sy-a-*graf*-ik, pertaining to sciagraphy.
sciagraphy, *n* sy-*ag*-ra-fe, the art or act of projecting or depicting shadows; the study of the representation of light and shade; also, skiagraphy.

sciamachy, *n.* sy-*am*-a-ke, fighting with shadows. (Gr. *skiamachia.*)
sciamancy, *n.* *sy*-a-man-se, sciomancy.
sciatic, *a.* sy-*at*-ik, pertaining to or affecting the hip; suffering from or caused by sciatica. (Fr. *sciatique.*)
sciatica, *n.* sy-*at*-e-ka, neuralgia in the sciatic nerve.
***science,** *n.* *sy*-ence, systematic knowledge of the organic or inorganic; knowledge reduced to system; a department of knowledge so reduced. **applied science,** science as dealing with material phenomena, industrial processes, etc. **natural science,** *see* **natural. pure science,** science in and for itself, as distinguished from applied science. **the dismal science,** *see* **dismal. the gay science,** literary criticism. (Fr., from L. *scienta,* knowledge.)
scienter, *ad.* sy-*en*-ter, with full knowledge; deliberately [Law]. (L.)
sciential, *a.* sy-*en*-shal, pertaining to or producing science; knowledgeable.
scientific, *a.* sy-en-*tif*-ik, pertaining to, employed in, or according to science; well versed in science.
scientifically, *ad.* sy-en-*tif*-e-ka-le, in a scientific manner.
scientism, *n.* *sy*-en-tizm, the views, methods, etc., of men of science.
scientist, *n.* *sy*-en-tist, one versed in science; an authority on scientific matters; a worker in scientific research; (*cap.*) a member of the Christian Science Church [U.S.A.].
scilicet, *sy*-le-set, to wit; namely. (L., contracted from *scire licet,* you may know.)
Scilla, *n.* *sil*-a, a genus of bulbous plants including the squills and the English bluebell. (L.)
scillitin, *n.* *sil*-e-tin, the active principle of the squill.
scimitar, *n.* *sim*-e-tar, a short curved sword broadest at the point. (It. *scimitarra.*)
scincoid, *a.* *sing*-koyd, resembling a skink.
scintilla, *n.* sin-*til*-a, a spark; a trace. (L.)
scintillant, *a.* *sin*-te-lant, emitting sparks.
scintillate, *v.i.* *sin*-te-late, to emit sparks; to sparkle. (L. *scintillatus,* sparkled.)
scintillation, *n.* sin-te-*lay*-shon, the act of sparkling or twinkling; a twinkling, as of stars. (Fr.)
sciolism, *n.* *sy*-o-lizm, superficial knowledge.
sciolist, *n.* *sy*-o-list, a smatterer, or one who knows little or who knows many things superficially. (L. *sciolus,* one of little knowledge.)
sciolistic, *a.* sy-o-*lis*-tik, pertaining to or resembling a sciolist or sciolism.
sciomachy, *n.* sy-*om*-a-ke, sciamachy.
sciomancy, *n.* *sy*-o-man-se, divination by shadows. (Gr. *skia,* a shadow, *manteia,* divination.)
scion, *n.* *sy*-on, a twig for grafting; a young branch or descendant; a child. (O.Fr. *cion.*)
scioptic, *a.* sy-*op*-tik, pertaining to the camera obscura, or to the art of scioptics.
scioptics, *n.* sy-*op*-tiks, the art of exhibiting images of external objects, received through a lens, in a darkened room; the use of the camera obscura. (Gr. *skia,* and *optikos,* of sight.)
scioptric, *a.* sy-*op*-trik, scioptic.
scirocco, *n.* si-*rok*-o, sirocco.
scirrhoid, *a.* *si*-royd, resembling scirrhus.
scirrhoma, *n.* si-*roh*-ma, scirrhus.
scirrhosity, *n.* si-*ros*-e-te *or* ski-*ros*-e-te, morbid induration, esp. of a gland [Med.].
scirrhous, *a.* *si*-rus *or* *ski*-rus, proceeding from or resembling scirrhus; indurated; knotty.
scirrhus, *n.* *si*-rus *or* *ski*-rus, a hard cancer with marked predominance of connective tissue [Med.]. (Gr. *skirrhos,* hard.)
scissel, *n.* *sis*-el, the clippings of metals; the remains of a metal plate after blanks for coins are punched from it. (Fr. *cisaille.*)
scissile, *a.* *sis*-ile, that may be cut or divided.
scission, *n.* *sizh*-un, the act of cutting or dividing, esp. with an edged instrument; separation; a split. (Fr.)
scissor, *v.t.* *siz*-or, to cut with scissors.
scissor-bill, *n.* the skimmer (sea-bird).
scissor-leg, *n.* a deformity causing the legs to cross in walking [Med.].
***scissors,** *n.pl.* *siz*-orz, an implement consisting of two blades pivoted together for cutting material, etc., placed between them; a small pair of shears. **scissors and paste,** literary matter cut from other works. (Fr. *cisoires.*)
scissor-tail, *n.* the tropical American fork-tailed flycatcher, *Muscivora forficata.*
scissure, *n.* *sizh*-yewr, a longitudinal opening in a body made by cutting; a natural cleft in an organ [Anat.].
sciurine, *a.* *sy*-yew-rin, pertaining to or resembling the squirrel family. (Gr. *skiouros,* squirrel.)
Sclav, *n.* and *a.* sklahv, Slav.
Sclavonic, etc., Slavonic, etc.
sclera, *n.* *skleer*-ra, the tough white outer membrane of the eyeball; the sclerotic.
sclerenchyma, *n.* skle-*reng*-ke-ma, the woody cell tissue of nuts, etc. [Bot.]; the scleroderm of corals [Zool.]. (Gr. *skleros,* hard, *enchyma,* infusion.)
scleriasis, *n.* skle-*ry*-a-sis, morbid hardening, esp. of tissues [Path.]. (Gr.)
sclerify, *v.t.* *skleer*-re-fy, to become converted into sclerenchyma [Bot.].
scleroderm, *n.* *skleer*-ro-derm, a hardened integument; skeletal tissue; the exoskeleton of corals [Zool.]. (Gr. *skleros,* hard, *derma,* a skin.)
scleroderma, *n.* skle-ro-*der*-ma, a chronic indurated skin-disease.
sclerodermatous, *a.* *skleer*-ro-*der*-ma-tus, having a hard external covering, or a skeleton of scleroderm [Zool.]; affected with or pertaining to scleroderma [Med.].
sclerogen, *n.* *skleer*-ro-jen, a hard deposit in the cell walls of certain plants. (Gr. *skleros,* and *gennao,* produce.)
scleroma, *n.* skle-*roh*-ma (*pl.* **scleromata**), abnormal hardness of a part [Med.]; sclerosis.
scleroid, *a.* *skleer*-royd, hard in texture [Bot. and Zool.]. (Gr. *skleroeides.*)
sclerometer, *n.* skle-*rom*-e-ter, an instrument for determining the relative hardness of crystals, etc.
sclerosed, *a.* skle-*rohst,* indurated.
sclerosis, *n.* skle-*roh*-sis (*pl.* **scleroses**), a hardening of a cell-wall [Bot.]; thickening or induration of connective tissue [Anat.]. (Gr.)
sclerotic, *a.* skle-*rot*-ik, hard or firm (of tunic of the eye); pertaining to the sclera; pertaining to or affected with sclerosis: *n.* the firm white outer coat of the eye; a hardening application [Med.]. (Gr. *sklerotes.*)
sclerotitis, *n.* skle-ro-*ty*-tis, inflammation of the sclerotic coat of the eye.
sclerous, *a.* *skleer*-rus, hardened; ossified. (Gr. *skleros.*)
scobby, *n.* *skob*-e, the chaffinch. (Dial.)
scobiform, *a.* *skoh*-be-form, resembling sawdust or raspings [Bot.]. (L. *scobs,* sawdust, and *form.*)
scobs, *n.pl.* skobz, raspings of ivory, hartshorn, or other hard substance. (L.)
scoff, *n.* skof, derision; expression of scorn or contempt: *v.i.* to manifest contempt by derision: *v.t.* to treat with derision or scorn; to ridicule; to jeer. (M. E., perhaps from Scand.)
scoff, *n.* skof, food: *v.t.* and *i.* to eat greedily; to seize [Slang]. [S.-Afr. Dut.]
scoffer, *n.* *skof*-er, one who scoffs.
scoffingly, *ad.* *skof*-ing-le, in a scoffing manner; by way of derision.
scold, *n.* skoald, a rude, clamorous woman; a scolding: *v.i.* to find fault; to rail; *v.t.* to chide; to find fault with noisily or with rudeness; to rate. (Perhaps Scand.)
scolder, *n.* *skoal*-der, one who scolds or rails.
scolding, *a.* *skoal*-ding, given to scolding: *n.* a rating; railing language.
scolecite, *n.* *skol*-e-site, hydrated silicate of lime and aluminium, akin to natrolite [Min.]; a vermiform body present in the fructification of certain fungi [Bot.]. (Gr. *skōlex,* worm.)
scolex, *n.* *skoh*-leks (*pl.* **scolices,** *skoh*-le-seez), the embryo of the tape-worm. (Gr.)
scolioma, *n.* skol-e-*oh*-ma, curvature of the spine [Path.]. (Gr.)
scoliosis, *n.* skol-e-*oh*-sis, lateral curvature of the spine [Med.]. (Gr.)
scoliotic, *a.* skol-e-*ot*-ik, pertaining to or characterized by scoliosis.
scollop, *n.* and *v.t.* *skol*-lop, scallop.
scolopaceous, *a.* skol-o-*pay*-shus, resembling a woodcock. (Gr. *scolopax,* a woodcock.)
Scolopendra, *n.* skol-o-*pen*-dra, a genus of millipedes including the larger centipedes. (Gr., a milliped.)

scolopendrine, *a.* skol-o-*pen*-drine, of the centipede family: *n.* a centipede.
Scolopendrium, *n.* skol-o-*pen*-dre-um, the hart's-tongue genus of ferns. (Gr. *scolopendrion.*)
scolytus, *n.* *skol*-e-tus, any of a large group of small bark-boring beetles. (Gr. *skolypto,* nip off.)
Scomber, *n.* *skom*-ber, a genus of fishes including the mackerels. (L.)
sconce, *n.* skonce, a fort or bulwark; the head, hence common sense or discretion [Coll.]; the socket of a candlestick; a hanging or projecting candlestick, esp. with a reflector; a fine for a slight offence (at Universities): *v.t.* to provide with a sconce; to fine. (O.Fr. *esconse,* lantern.)
sconcheon, *n.* *skon*-chun, scuncheon.
scone, *n.* skon *or* skone, a small plain soft cake of flour or barleymeal cooked on a girdle. (Scots.)
scoop, *n.* skoop, a large ladle; an instrument for scooping out; a bucket; a hollow; a swoop; the first publication of an item of news; a stroke of luck: *v.t.* to lade out; to empty by baling; to make hollow; to dig out; to forestall others in publishing important news, etc. (Scand.)
scooper, *n.* *skoop*-er, one who or that which scoops; a scaup; the avocet [Ornith.]
scoop-net, *n.* a hand-net so formed as to sweep the bottom of a river.
scoop-wheel, *n.* a dredging wheel set with buckets.
scoot, *v.i.* skoot, to run away hurriedly. (Perhaps *scuttle.*)
scooter, *n.* *skoot*-er, a child's two-wheeled toy on which he stands with one foot and pushes himself along with the other; a coastal motor-boat; a sailing-vessel adapted for use in water or on ice [U.S.A.].
scope, *n.* skope, aim; intention; drift; room; range of capacity. (Gr. *skopos,* a looker-out.)
scopiform, *a.* *skop*-e-form, broom-like; disposed in bundles, as the hairs of a brush [Zool.]. (L. *scopa,* a broom.)
scopiped, *n.* *skop*-e-ped, a bee having brush-like appendages on the hind legs. (L. *scopa,* and *pes,* foot.)
scopolamine, *n.* sko-*pol*-o-meen, an alkaloid derived from coca used, in combination, as a sedative and narcotic [Med.].
scopophobia, *n.* skoh-poh-*foh*-be-a, a morbid dread of being seen. (Gr. *skopos,* a watcher, and *phobia.*)
scopulate, *a.* *skop*-yew-lat, scopiform [Zool.].
scorbutic, *a.* skor-*bew*-tik, pertaining to, affected with, or resembling scurvy. (Late L. *scorbutus,* scurvy.)
scorch, *n.* skortch, a superficial burn; the result of scorching; a run or ride at high speed: *v.t.* to burn superficially; to affect painfully with heat: *v.i.* to be parched or dried up; to ride at top speed. **scorched earth policy,** devastation and destruction by a force retreating in its own territory to impede the advance of the enemy [Mil.]. (O.Fr. *escorcher.*)
scorcher, *n.* *skortch*-er, one who or that which scorches; one given to extreme courses [Coll.].
score, *n.* skore, a notch or incision; the number twenty (formerly represented on tallies by a notch); a line drawn; an account or reckoning; ground or reason; a copy of an orchestral or other work giving all its component parts [Mus.]; the number of points gained by contestants [Games]; a tit for tat [Coll.]: *pl.* any large but indefinite number: *v.t.* to notch; to cut; to groove; to mark by a line; to set down, as a debt; to set down or take, as an account; to make a score [Games]; to enter the score of; to orchestrate [Mus.]. **score off,** to get the better of. **settle old scores,** to have requital for an injury, etc. (A.S. *scor,* twenty; Ice. *skor,* a cut.)
scorer, *n.* *skaw*-rer, one who scores, or makes points in a game, etc.; one who records a score; one who marks trees, etc., by scoring, also, an implement for this purpose; a block, tablet, etc., on which scores (esp. at cards) are kept.
scoria, *n.* *sko*-re-a (*pl.* **scoriæ,** *sko*-re-ee), dross; slag; the refuse of metals in fusion; *pl.* volcanic ashes. (Gr.)
scoriaceous, *a.* sko-re-*ay*-shus, of the nature of scoria.
scorification, *n.* *sko*-re-fe-*kay*-shon, the act or operation of scorifying.
scorifier, *n.* *sko*-re-fy-er, one who scorifies; an implement or utensil used in scorifying.
scoriform, *a.* *sko*-re-form, like scoria or dross.
scorify, *v.t.* *sko*-re-fy, to reduce to scoria (esp. of metals in assaying). (Gr. *scoria,* and L. *facio,* make.)
scorn, *n.* skorn, extreme contempt; a feeling of disdain due to one's own superiority or sense of the meanness of an object; derision; an object of extreme contempt: *v.t.* to hold in extreme contempt; to disdain; to slight. **laugh to scorn,** to deride. **think scorn of,** to disdain. (O.Fr. *escarne.*)
scorner, *n.* *skorn*-er, one who scorns; a derider.
scornful, *a.* *skorn*-ful, full of scorn; disdainful.
scornfully, *ad.* in a scornful manner.
scornfulness, *n.* the quality of being scornful.
scorodite, *n.* *sko*-ro-dite, a greenish brown native hydrous arseniate of iron. (Gr. *skorodon,* garlic.)
Scorpio, *n.* *skor*-pe-o, one of the zodiacal constellations; the eighth sign of the zodiac, between Libra and Sagittarius. (L. *scorpio.*)
scorpioid, *a.* *skor*-pe-oyd, like a scorpion, or pertaining to the Scorpionida [Zool.]; (of petals) curled up at the ends and opening as development proceeds [Bot.]. (L. *scorpio,* and Gr. *eidos,* like.)
scorpion, *n.* *skor*-pe-on, an arachnid with claws like a lobster and a six-jointed tail ending in a sting; an ancient military catapult for stones; in the Bible, a whip armed with points like a scorpion's tail, hence, a painful scourge. **the Scorpion** [Astron.], Scorpio. **scorpion fish,** a sea-scorpion. (L.)
scorpion-fly, *n.* the black flat-winged fly *Panopus communis,* having a beak with biting parts and the three last body-segments curved like a tail.
scorpion-grass, *n.* the wild forget-me-not.
scorpion-plant, *n.* the large white-flowered Javanese orchid *Renanthera arachnitis.*
scorpion-shell, *n.* the shell of any marine snail, esp. *Pterocera chiragra,* bearing long curved spines.
scortatory, *a.* *skor*-ta-to-re, pertaining to or consisting of lewdness. (L. *scortum,* a prostitute.)
scorza, *n.* *skor*-zah, a variety of epidote. (It., bark.)
scorzonera, *n.* *skor*-zo-neer-ra, the viper's grass, *Scorzonera hispanica,* or black salsify, grown for its edible root. (It.)
scot, *n.* skot, a tax [Law]. **scot and lot,** parish payments; tax according to lot or ability. (A.S.)
Scot, *n.* skot, a native of Scotland; one of the ancient race of Scots; a Scotsman. (A.S.)
Scotch, *a.* skotch, Scottish: *n.* the kind of English spoken by Scotsmen; the Scottish people; Scotch whisky, or a drink of this. **Scotch barley,** barley stripped of the husk, pot barley. **broad Scotch,** the dialect of the Scottish Lowlands. **Scotch broth,** a mutton soup containing chopped vegetables and pearl-barley. **Scotch cap,** a glengarry. **Scotch collops,** scotched collops. **Scotch fir** or **pine,** the common pine, *Pinus sylvestris,* furnishing a hard yellow wood. **Scotch mist,** a dense white mist. **Scotch terrier,** a small short-legged and large-headed dog with a wiry long-haired black or greyish coat. **Scotch thistle,** any of several thistles, esp. *Onopordon acanthium,* the national emblem of Scotland. **Scotch whisky,** whisky distilled in Scotland. **Scotch woodcock,** a dish of eggs served on toast with anchovies or anchovy paste.
scotch, *n.* skotch, a slight cut or shallow incision; a sprag or block to prevent a wheel, etc., slipping: *v.t.* to cut or wound slightly; to disable; to frustrate. **scotched collops,** meat cut into small pieces.
Scotchman, *n.* *skotch*-man, a Scotsman.
scoter, *n.* *skoh*-ter, a large black sea-duck of the genus *Œdemia.* (Origin unknown.)
scot-free, *a.* free from payment; untaxed; unhurt; safe.
Scotia, *n.* *skoh*-she-a, Scotland personified. (L.)
scotia, *n.* *skoh*-she-a, a hollow moulding in the base of a column [Arch.]. (Gr., darkness.)
Scotism, *n.* *skoh*-tizm, the philosophy of Duns Scotus, the 13th-cent. scholastic theologian.
scotograph, *n.* *skoh*-to-grahf, a writing instrument for use in the dark or by the blind. (Gr. *skotos,* darkness, *grapho,* write.)
scotoma, *n.* sko-*toh*-ma, a blind or partially blind area in the visual field [Med.]. (Gr.)

scotophobia, *n.* skoh-to-*foh*-be-a, morbid dread of the dark [Path].
scotoscope, *n.* *skoh*-to-skope, an obsolete optical instrument to assist vision in the dark. (Gr.)
Scots, *a.* skots, Scottish : *n.* the dialect of the lowland Scots, Scotch : *pl.* a Gaelic race from Ireland that invaded and settled in the West of Scotland. **pound Scots,** *see* **pound.**
Scotsman, *n.* *skots*-man, a male native of Scotland.
Scottice, *ad.* *skot*-e-se, in the Scottish manner of dialect.
Scotticism, *n.* *skot*-e-sizm, a Scottish idiom.
Scotticize, *v.t.* *skot*-e-size, to give a Scottish character to.
scottie, *n.* *skot*-e, a Scotch terrier [Coll.].
Scottify, *v.t.* *skot*-e-fy, to render Scottish; to endue with Scottish characteristics.
Scottish, *a.* *skot*-ish, pertaining to Scotland, its people, language, or literature, etc.; Scotch; Scots.
scoundrel, *n.* *skoun*-drel, a low worthless fellow; a rascal; a villain : *a.* low; mean; unprincipled. (A.S. *scunian,* loathe.)
scoundrelism, *n.* *skound*-drel-izm, baseness; rascality.
scoundrelly, *a.* *skoun*-drel-e, like a scoundrel.
scour, *n.* skour, a cleaning or clearing; a cleansing agent; diarrhœa [Vet.]; a swift deep current; a sudden gust of wind and rain.
scour, *v.t.* skour, to clean by rubbing with something rough; to rub clean or bright; to remove by scouring; to purge violently [Vet.]; to range over; to clear; to brush along : *v.i.* to clean; to be purged to excess; to range about; to scamper. (O.Fr. *escurer.*)
scourer, *n.* *skour*-rer, one who scours; a wanderer; a drastic cathartic.
scourge, *n.* skurj, a whip of thongs; an instrument or other means of affliction of punishment; a punishment; any continued evil or calamity : *v.t.* to whip severely; to punish with severity; to chastise; to afflict greatly. (O.Fr. *escorgiee.*)
scourger, *n.* *skur*-jer, one who scourges or punishes; one that afflicts severely.
scout, *n.* skout, one sent to observe the motions of an enemy; an act or the art of scouting; an aeroplane used for reconnaissance; a college servant [Oxford]; a fieldsman [Cricket, etc.]; (*cap.*) a Boy Scout : *v.i.* to act as a scout; to reconnoitre; to field at cricket or rounders. (O.Fr. *escouter,* listen.)
scout, *n.* skout, a Dutch flat-bottomed sailing boat. (Dut. *schuit.*)
scout, *v.t.* skout, to sneer at; to treat with disdain or contempt; to flout. (Scand.)
scouter, *n.* *skou*-ter, one who scouts; a senior Boy Scout.
scoutmaster, *n.* *skout*-mahs-ter, a leader of a body of scouts; one in charge of a troop of Boy Scouts.
scovillite, *n.* *skoh*-vil-ite, rhabdophane [Min.]. (*Scoville* mine, Salisbury, Conn., where found.)
scow, *n.* skou, a large flat-bottomed boat with square ends : *v.t.* to convey in this. (Dut. *schouw.*)
scowl, *n.* skoul, a frowning or sullen look; a look of displeasure or anger : *v.i.* to wrinkle the brows in frowning, etc.; to frown; to look sullen or angry. (Probably Scand.)
scrabble, *v.i.* *skrab*-bl, to make irregular unmeaning marks; to scribble : *v.t.* to mark with irregular lines or letters. (*scrape.*)
scrag, *n.* skrag, anything thin or lean with roughness; a crooked branch; a thing of mere skin and bone; the bony part of a neck : *v.t.* to throttle, or kill by throttling [Slang]. (Swed. *skragg,* a very lean person.)
scragged, *a.* *skrag*-ed, scraggy.
scraggedness, *n.* the state of being scragged.
scraggily, *ad.* *skrag*-e-le, in a scraggy manner.
scragginess, *n.* the state of being scraggy.
scraggy, *a.* *skrag*-e, rugged; lean and bony.
scram, *v.t.* skram, to benumb; to paralyze : *a.* withered; puny. (A.S. *scrimman,* to be shrunk.)
scram, *int.* skram, be off!; clear out! [Slang]. (*scramble.*)
scramble, *n.* *skram*-bl, a rude, eager struggle for something; the act of scrambling : *v.t.* to move or climb by catching hold with the hands; to clutch eagerly among others; to catch eagerly and unceremoniously at anything; to beat up, as egg, and mix with butter, etc. (*scrabble.*)
scrambler, *n.* *skram*-bler, one who scrambles.
scrambling, *a.* *skram*-bling, straggling.
scramblingly, *ad.* in a scrambling manner.
scran, *n.* skran, provisions, esp. for an alfresco meal broken victuals : *v.t.* and *i.* to provide with or t collect scran; to beg [Slang].
scranch, *v.t.* skranch, to grind with the teeth, an with a crackling sound; to crunch. (Imit.)
scranky, *a.* *skrang*-ke, lean; scraggy [Scots.].
scrannel, *a.* *skran*-nel, slight; slender. (Scand.)
scrap, *n.* skrap, a small piece; any broken meta that has been used and can be re-melted; a detache piece; a fight, a scrimmage [Slang] : *v.t.* to discard to clear out as useless : *v.i.* to fight [Slang]. **scrap iron,** old, disused, or broken-up iron for recasting **scrap of paper,** a pledge intended to be broke at the discretion of its giver. **scrap paper,** pieces o inferior paper used for rough notes, etc. (Ice *skrap.*)
scrapbook, *n.* *skrap*-book, a blank book for th preservation of press-cuttings, pictures, etc.
scrape, *v.t.* skrape, to rub with something sharp o rough; to clean by scraping; to remove b scraping; to gather laboriously by small gains o savings : *v.i.* to make a harsh noise; to pla awkwardly on the violin; to make an awkwar bow; to hoard. **to scrape acquaintance,** t contrive to make oneself acquainted. **to scrape through,** to get through with difficulty or wit little to spare. **to bow and scrape,** to be exces sively obsequious. (Scand.)
scrape, *n.* skrape, an act of scraping; a thin layer the sound of the foot drawn over the floor; a awkward bow; a difficulty, perplexity, or awkwar predicament.
scraper, *n.* *skrape*-er, a tool for scraping with; contrivance for scraping the mud off boots; on who scrapes; a miser; an awkward fiddler.
scrap-heap, *n.* a rubbish heap; a place for o collection of discarded things.
scraping, *n.* *skrape*-ing, anything scraped off.
scrappy, *a.* *skrap*-e, fragmentary.
scratch, *n.* skratsh, a mark by scratching; slight wound with the nails; a slight wound; th starting line in a race; a line across the prize ring at which pugilists begin a fight; a scratch-wig the test [Fig.] : *pl.* a cutaneous disease on the foot o horses : *a.* collected at random; allowed no handi cap : *v.t.* and *i.* to mark by drawing somethin sharp over a surface; to scrape with the nails o claws; to erase; to use the nails or claws in tearin or hollowing; to remove from, or retire from, contest before its start [Sport]. **Old Scratch,** th Devil. **scratch race,** a race in which all th entrants start from scratch. (Origin obscure.)
scratcher, *n.* *skratsh*-er, one who or that whic scratches; a bird that scratches for food.
scratchily, *ad.* *skratsh*-e-le, in a scratchy manner with a scratching sound.
scratchiness, *n.* *skratsh*-e-ness, the condition of bein scratchy.
scratch-wig, *n.* a wig covering only part of the head
scratchy, *a.* *skratsh*-e, roughly drawn; producin the sound of scratching; causing irritation. **scratchy team,** one collected haphazard.
scraw, *n.* skraw, a turf or short strip of grass. (Ir.
scrawl, *n.* skrawl, unskilful writing; a piece o hasty bad writing : *v.t.* to draw or mark awkwardl and irregularly; to write badly : *v.i.* to scribble (Origin obscure.)
scrawler, *n.* *skraw*-ler, one who scrawls; a hast or awkward writer.
scrawly, *a.* *skraw*-le, badly written; sprawling.
scrawny, *a.* *skraw*-ne, lean; raw-boned; scranny
scray, *n.* skray, the common tern. (W. *ysgräen.*)
screak, *n.* skreek, a creaking; a screech : *v.t.* t shriek; to scream; to creak. (*screech.*)
scream, *n.* skreem, a sudden harsh or shrill cry o terror or laughter : *v.t.* to shriek from terror o pain; to utter a scream. (Scand.)
screamer, *n.* *skreem*-er, one who or that whic screams; a bird that screams, esp. the large S American **crested screamer,** a species of *Chaun* having two spurs on each wing, and the seriema **horned screamer,** the kamichi, a South America bird.
scree, *n.* skree, a steep slope covered with sma

loose stones; the stones at the foot of a cliff. (Scand.)
screech, *n.* skreech, a short, loud scream: *v.i.* to cry out with a sharp, shrill voice. (Scand.)
screech-hawk, *n.* the nightjar.
screech-owl, *n.* any owl that utters a harsh, disagreeable screech instead of a hoot—regarded as an evil omen.
screech-thrush, *n.* the missel thrush; also the fieldfare.
screed, *n.* skreed, a shred; a piece torn off; a hysterical appeal or scolding; a long tiresome harangue; a diatribe (oral, written, or printed); a plasterer's wooden rule for running mouldings [Arch.]. (*shred.*)
screen, *n.* skreen, that which shelters from danger, observation, etc.; something movable used to intercept heat, cold, or light; a partition, esp. one in a church separating nave from choir; a device protecting apparatus from outside electrical interference [Elect.]; a sheet or prepared surface on which pictures are shown by lantern or cinematograph, and hence, such pictures collectively; a smoke-screen; a riddle or sieve; a reticulated glass plate used in photographic reproduction for the half-tone process [Print.]: *v.t.* to shelter from inconvenience, injury, or danger; to conceal; to isolate from the influence of extraneous electrical disturbances; to project (pictures) upon a screen; to film (a story, etc.) for reproduction thus; to pass through a coarse sieve. (O.Fr. *escren.*)
screenings, *n.pl.* *skreen*-ingz, refuse matter obtained after screening with a sieve.
screeve, *v.t.* *skreev,* to write: *v.i.* to draw pictures on pavements [Slang].
screever, *n.* *skree*-ver, one who screeves; a begging-letter writer; a pavement artist.
screw, *n.* skroo, a spiral groove; a cylinder of wood or metal grooved spirally; one of the six mechanical powers, being a modification of the inclined plane; a screw-propeller; a curved turning motion; a twist; a small twisted-up package (esp. of tobacco); a worn-out horse [Coll.]; a miser [Slang]; a salary [Slang]; a prison warder [Slang]: *v.i.* to turn or apply a screw to; to fasten by a screw; to squeeze; to press; to oppress by exactions; to twist or distort. **put the screw on,** to bring pressure to bear. **the screws,** rheumatism [Slang]. **to have a screw loose,** to be eccentric or crazy [Slang]. **male, female screw,** *see* these words. (O.Fr. *escroue.*)
screwbolt, *n.* *skroo*-bohlt, a screw fitted with a nut.
screw-driver, *n.* a tool for turning screws with; a turnscrew.
screwed, *a.* skrood, fastened with screws; intoxicated [Slang].
screwer, *n.* *skroo*-er, one who or that which screws.
screw-eye, *n.* a screw with a loop at the head.
screw-jack, *n.* a tool in which the principle of the screw is employed to raise heavy weights or exert pressure.
screw-pile, *n.* a pile with a screw at the end.
screw-pine, *n.* any tropical palm of the genera *Pandanus* or *Freycinetia*, in which the stem is twisted so that the leaves form spirals.
screw-propeller, *n.* a modification of the screw for propelling ships and aircraft.
screw-thread, *n.* the ridge on a screw.
screwy, *a.* *scroo*-e, like a screw; winding; slightly drunk [Slang].
scribal, *a.* *skry*-bal, pertaining to or characteristic of a scribe.
scribble, *n.* *skrib*-bl, hasty or careless writing; a writing of no value: *v.t.* to write with haste or without care or regard to correctness; to fill with worthless writing: *v.i.* to scrawl; to card or tease coarsely. (*scribe.*)
scribbler, *n.* *skrib*-bler, one who scribbles; a hack journalist; a carding machine.
scribblingly, *ad.* *skrib*-bling-le, in a scribbling manner.
scribblings, *n.pl.* *skrib*-blingz, scribbled notes, etc.; inferior literary works; the results of doodling.
scribbly, *a.* *skrib*-bly, resembling or composed of scribbles; badly written.
scribe, *n.* skribe, a writer; a notary; a clerk; a secretary; in Scripture, one learned in the law; a pointed tool for scribing: *v.t.* to mark by a rule or compasses; to mark a piece for fitting into another; to inscribe; to cut letters into wood; to adjust [Carp.]. (L. *scriba,* a writer.)
scriber, *n.* *skribe*-er, a pointed tool for marking where metal, etc., is to be cut.
scriggle, *v.i.* *skrig*-gl, to wriggle: *n.* a squirming or wriggling movement. (Dial.)
scrim, *n.* skrim, a thin canvas used as lining in upholstery, etc.
scrimmage, *n.* *skrim*-aj, a close, confused struggle; a scrummage: *v.i.* to engage in such. (*skirmish.*)
scrimmager, *n.* *skrim*-a-jer, one taking part in a scrimmage.
scrimp, *a.* skrimp, scanty; narrow: *n.* a miser [U.S.A.]: *ad.* scarcely: *v.t.* to reduce, shorten, or stint too much. (A.S. *scrimman.*)
scrimpiness, *n.* *skrim*-pe-ness, the state of being scrimpy; scantiness.
scrimpy, *a.* *skrim*-pe, meagre; insufficient; scrimp.
scrimshanker, *n.* *skrim*-shang-ker, a work-shy person; a malingerer [Slang].
scrimshaw, *n.* *skrim*-shaw, an engraved shell, tusk, etc.: *v.t.* and *i.* to decorate shells, ivory, etc., thus.
scrip, *n.* skrip, a small bag or wallet. (Ice.)
scrip, *n.* skrip, a certificate or schedule, esp. a certificate of stock or of shares in a joint-stock company. (*script.*)
script, *n.* skript, a piece of manuscript or typescript; handwriting, also type in imitation of this. (O.Fr. *escript.*)
scriptorium, *n.* skrip-*taw*-re-um, a writing-room, esp. of a monastery. (Late L.)
scriptory, *a.* *skrip*-to-re, pertaining to or expressed in writing; not verbally delivered.
Scriptural, *a.* *skrip*-tewr-ral, contained in, based on, or according to Scripture.
Scripturalism, *n.* *skrip*-tewr-ral-izm, Scripturalness; adherence to the letter of Scripture.
Scripturalist, *n.* *skrip*-tewr-ral-ist. one who adheres literally to the Scriptures.
Scripturally, *ad.* in a Scriptural manner.
Scripturalness, *n.* the quality of being Scriptural.
Scripture, *n.* *skrip*-tewr, the Bible; the Old and New Testaments; what is written in Scripture. (O.Fr. *escripture.*)
Scripturist, *n.* *skrip*-tewr-rist, one versed in the Scriptures.
scrivello, *n.* skri-*vel*-loh, an elephant's tusk less than 20 lb. in weight. (Port.)
scrivener, *n.* *skriv*-en-er, a law stationer; one who drew up contracts or other writings; formerly, a money-broker; one whose business was to place money at interest. **scriveners' palsy,** writers' cramp. (O.Fr. *escrivain.*)
scrobiculate, *a.* skro-*bik*-yew-lat, pitted; having depressions or hollows, foveate [Bot., Entom., etc.]. (L. *scrobiculus,* a groove.)
scrofula, *n.* *skrof*-yew-la, a defect of constitution tending to the formation and deposition of tubercle in the lymphatic glands; king's evil. (L. *scrofula,* a little breeding sow.)
scrofulosis, *n.* skrof-yew-*loh*-sis, a scrofulous condition or disease [Path.].
scrofulous, *a.* *skrof*-yew-lus, pertaining to, of the nature of, or affected with scrofula.
scrofulously, *ad.* in a scrofulous manner.
scrofulousness, *n.* the state of being scrofulous.
scrog, *n.* skrog, a stunted shrub or bush. (Dial.)
scroll, *n.* skrole, a roll of paper or parchment; a writing in the form of a roll; a ribbon for a motto [Her.]; a spiral ornament [Arch., etc.]: *v.t.* and *i.* to roll up like a scroll. (O.Fr. *escroue.*)
scroop, *v.i.* skroop, to crack; to grate: *n.* a grating sound. (Imit.)
scrophularia, *n.* *scrof*-yew-*lare*-re-a, figwort, so called from its supposed virtues in curing scrofula.
scrotal, *a.* *skroh*-tal, pertaining to the scrotum.
scrotiform, *a.* *skroh*-te-form, purse-shaped.
scrotocele, *n.* *skroh*-to-seel, a hernia in the scrotum [Med.]. (L. *scrotum,* and Gr. *kele,* a tumour.)
scrotum, *n.* *skroh*-tum (*pl.* **scrota**), the pouch containing the testicles. (L.)
scrounge, *v.i.* and *t.* skrounj, to cadge; to appropriate; to pilfer [Slang].
scrounger, *n.* *skroun*-jer, one who scrounges.
scroyle, *n.* skroyl, a mean fellow. (Origin obscure.)
scrub, *n.* skrub, one who labours hard and lives meanly; something small and mean; a worn-out brush; underwood; a tract of stunted trees and

scattered bushes: *v.t.* to cleanse, scour, or brighten by rubbing with something hard and coarse: *v.i.* to be diligent and penurious [Fig.]. (Scand.)

scrubber, *n.* *skrub*-er, one who or that which scrubs; an apparatus for cleaning gas; a mean, insignificant person [Fig.].

scrubbiness, *n.* *skrub*-e-ness, the condition of being scrubby.

scrubby, *a.* *skrub*-e, like or abounding in scrub or underwood; small and mean; stunted; bristly.

scruff, *n.* skruf, the back of the neck.

scruffy, *a.* *skruf*-e, scurfy; scaly; unkempt [Fig.].

scrum, *n.* skrum, a scrummage: *v.i.* to form or take part in a scrimmage.

scrum-half, *n.* in Rugby football, the half-back in position immediately behind the scrummage formed by the forwards.

scrummage, *n.* *skrum*-aj, an organized struggle or scrimmage at Rugby football: *v.i.* to scrimmage.

scrumptious, *a.* *skrump*-shus, delightful [Slang].

scruple, *n.* *skroo*-pl, an apothecaries' weight of 20 grains, or $\frac{1}{24}$ oz.; a very small quantity; hesitation, from conscientious motives: *v.t.* to doubt; to hesitate to believe: *v.i.* to hesitate. (Probably L. *scrupulus*, a small sharp stone.)

scrupulosity, *n.* *skroo*-pew-*los*-e-te, scrupulousness; niceness; preciseness. (L. *scrupulositas.*)

scrupulous, *a.* *skroo*-pew-lus, having scruples; cautious; careful; exact; strict. (Fr. *scrupuleux*)

scrupulously, *ad.* in a scrupulous manner.

scrupulousness, *n.* quality of being scrupulous.

scrutable, *a.* *skroo*-ta-bl, discoverable by inquiry or critical examination. (Late L. *scrutabilis.*)

scrutator, *n.* skroo-*tay*-tor, one who scrutinizes or examines closely. (L.)

scrutatory, *a.* *skroo*-ta-to-re, searching.

scrutineer, *n.* skroo-te-*neer*, one who scrutinizes; an official examiner of votes cast.

scrutinize, *v.t.* *skroo*-te-nize, to search closely; to examine into minutely or critically.

scrutinizer, *n.* *skroo*-te-ny-zer, one who scrutinizes.

scrutiny, *n.* *skroo*-te-ne, close search; minute inquiry; critical examination; an official examination of the votes given at an election. (L. *scrutinium*, careful inquiry.)

scruto, *n.* *skroo*-to, a spring trap-door on the stage.

scry, *v.i.* skry, to practise crystal-gazing. (*descry.*)

scud, *n.* skud, a driving along; a rushing with precipitation; loose, vapoury clouds driven along by the wind: *v.i.* to run quickly; to run before the wind: *v.t.* to pass over quickly. (Scand.)

scudo, *n.* *skoo*-doh (*pl.* **scudi,** *skoo*-dee), a former Italian silver (or gold) coin corresponding to the crown, equal to about 4*s.* (It., a shield, from L. *scutum.*)

scuff, *v.t.* skuf, to brush or wipe lightly; to scrape with the feet in walking; to injure (shoes, etc.) by hard wear.

scuffle, *n.* *skuf*-fl, a garden hoe: *v.t.* to hoe up weeds, disturb a gravel surface, etc., with this. (Dial.)

scuffle, *n.* *skuf*-fl, a struggle for mastery with close grappling; a confused contest: *v.i.* to struggle closely; to fight confusedly. (Scand.)

scuffler, *n.* *skuf*-fler, one who scuffles.

sculduddery, *n.* skul-*dud*-er-re, lewdness; fornication: *a.* obscene; bawdy. [Scots.]

scull, *n.* skul, a one-handed oar; an oar to scull with: *v.t.* to propel a boat by moving and working an oar over the stern; to propel a boat by means of sculls in pairs. (Origin doubtful.)

sculler, *n.* *skul*-er, one who sculls; a boat for sculling.

scullery, *n.* *skul*-er-re, the room adjoining the kitchen in which dishes are washed and other rough culinary work done. (O.Fr. *escuelerie.*)

scullion, *n.* *skul*-yon, a washer-up of kitchen utensils. (O.Fr. *escouillon*, a dish-clout.)

scullionly, *a.* *skul*-yon-le, like a scullion; low.

sculp, *v.t.* and *i.* skulp, to sculpture [Coll.].

sculpin, *n.* *skul*-pin, any of several large-headed spiny fish of the N. Atlantic, esp. the dragonet.

sculptor, *n.* *skulp*-tor, one who sculptures.

sculptural, *a.* *skulp*-tewr-ral, pertaining to sculpture.

sculpturally, *ad.* *skulp*-tewr-ral-e, by sculpture.

sculpture, *n.* *skulp*-tewr, the art of representation of natural objects in the solid; the art of carving, cutting, or hewing wood, stone, marble, metal, etc., into any designed form; carved work: *v.t.* to carve; to fashion, as in sculpture. (L. *sculpere*, to carve.)

sculpturesque, *a.* skulp-tewr-*resk*, in the style of sculpture; as in sculpture.

scum, *n.* skum, the impurities which rise to the surface of liquors in boiling or fermentation; the refuse, anything vile [Fig.]. (Dan. *skum*, froth.)

scumble, *v.t.* *skum*-bl, to rub over thinly with a semi-opaque colour to modify or soften the effect. (*scum.*)

scummer, *n.* *skum*-er, a utensil for removing scum.

scummings, *n.pl.* *skum*-ingz, matter skimmed from boiling liquors.

scummy, *a.* *skum*-e, covered with or containing scum; low; worthless.

scuncheon, *n.* *skun*-shon, a small buttress across the angle of a square tower to support one of the alternate sides of the spire [Arch.]. (*sconce.*)

scunner, *n.* *skun*-er, a feeling of dislike, disgust, or loathing: *v.t.* to disgust, to nauseate [Scots.].

scup, *n.* skup, the porgy, a food-fish of the U.S.A. North Atlantic coast.

scupper, *n.* *skup*-er, the channel cut through the waterways and sides of a ship, for carrying off the water [Naut.]: *v.t.* to throw a ship on her scuppers; hence, to disable, to throw into confusion [Slang] (O.Fr. *escope*, a scoop.)

scupper-hose, *n.* the spout of a scupper carrying the water clear of the side of a vessel.

scurf, *n.* skurf, a dry miliary scab formed on the skin; an exfoliation; dandruff; anything adhering to a surface. (Scand.)

scurf, *n.* skurf, the bull-trout, *Salmo eriox.*

scurfiness, *n.* *skurf*-e-ness, the state of being scurfy

scurfy, *a.* *skurf*-e, covered with or resembling scurf.

scurrile, *a.* *sku*-ril, scurrilous; abusive.

scurrility, *n.* sku-*ril*-e-te, scurrilousness; that which is scurrilous; low vulgar abuse.

scurrilous, *a.* *sku*-re-lus, befitting a buffoon indecently jocular; given to, or pertaining to vulgarity or low and indecent language; foul abusive. (L. *scurra*, a buffoon.)

scurrilously, *ad.* in a scurrilous manner.

scurrilousness, *n.* quality of being scurrilous.

scurry, *n.* *sku*-re, a short quick run; a scamper the sound of scurrying: *v.i.* to hurry along with short quick steps. (*scour.*)

scurvily, *ad.* in a scurvy manner; meanly.

scurviness, *n.* state or quality of being scurvy.

scurvy, *n.* *skur*-ve, a deficiency disease due to lack of fruit and vegetables containing vitamin C: *a.* scurfy; scabby; diseased with scurvy; vile shabby; worthless. (Scand.)

scurvy-grass, *n.* a plant of the genus *Cochlearia* with an acrid, bitter taste, formerly used in cases of scurvy.

scut, *n.* skut, the tail of a hare or other short-tailed mammal. (Scand.)

scutage, *n.* *skew*-taj, a tax levied upon those who held lands by knight-service, as a substitute for the personal services of the vassal. (Late L. *scutagium.*

scutate, *a.* *skew*-tate, buckler-shaped [Bot.]; protected by large scales [Zool.]. (L. *scutum*, a shield.

scutation, *n.* skew-*tay*-shon, arrangement of scutes [Zool.].

scutch, *v.t.* skutch, to beat or whip slightly; to comb; to loosen fibres by beating: *n.* a scutcher the coarse tow separated from flax by scutching (O.Fr. *escouche.*)

scutcheon, *n.* *skutch*-on, an escutcheon; a plate for an inscription; the ornamental plate surrounding a keyhole.

scutcher, *n.* *skutch*-er, an appliance or machine for beating and dressing fibres; a swingle.

scute, *n.* skewt, a scale or bony plate, as of a reptile armadillo, etc. (L. *scutum*, a shield.)

scutellar, *a.* skew-*tel*-ar, pertaining to, or having, a scutellum [Bot. and Zool.].

scutellate, *a.* *skew*-tel-lat, scutellated.

scutellated, *a.* *skew*-tel-lay-ted, having a surface composed of scales or small plates [Zool.]. (L. *scutella*, a salver.)

scutellum, *n.* skew-*tel*-um, one of the rounded apothecia in lichens, and a similar small shield shaped organ in other plants; part of the thoracic segment in insects; a transverse horny scale on the toes of certain birds. (Late L., a small shield.)

scutiform, *a.* *skew*-te-form, having the form of a shield. (L. *scutum*, a shield, *forma*, shape.)

scuttle, *n.* *skut*-tl, a broad shallow basket; a receptacle for holding coals; a cowling. (A.S. *scutel.*)

cuttle, *n.* *skut*-tl, a small hatchway in a deck, covered with a lid or hatch [Naut.]; a hole in the side or the bottom of a ship; a similar hole in a roof; the hatch or lid: *v.t.* to cut large holes through the bottom of a ship; to sink by doing so. (O.Fr. *escoutille.*)
cuttle, *n.* *skut*-tl, a quick pace or short run: *v.i.* to run with affected precipitation; to hurry; to abandon a position. (Scand.)
cuttle-cask, *n.* a butt or cask with a withdrawal hole in its bilge [Naut.].
cuttler, *n.* *skut*-tl-er, one who scuttles: one supporting a policy of clearing out.
cutum, *n.* *skew*-tum, a scute; one of the parts of the thoracic segment in insects; a chitinous or bony plate [Zool.]. (L., a shield.)
cyphose, *a.* *sy*-fohs, having scyphi [Bot.].
cyphus, *n.* *sy*-fus (*pl.* **scyphi**), a corona [Bot.]; the cup-shaped organ containing the spore-sacs in certain lichens. (Gr. *skyphos*, a deep cup with handles.)
cythe, *n.* sythe, an implement with a long, curving, sharp-edged blade for mowing grass and cutting grain. (A.S. *sithe.*)
cytheman, *n.* *sythe*-man, one who uses a scythe.
cythian, *a.* *sith*-e-an, belonging to Scythia or to the race anciently inhabiting it: *n.* a native or the language of ancient Scythia. **Scythian disease,** atrophy of the male genitalia [Path.]. **Scythian lamb,** the barometz, Tartarian lamb.
'death, *int.* sdeth, an Elizabethan oath, contracted from "By God's death."
e-, a Latin prefix signifying without, aside, apart, as in *seduce, segregate*, etc.
sea, *n.* see, the expanse of salt water that covers the more depressed portion of the earth's surface: a definite part of this expanse; the ocean; a wave; a surge; the swell of the ocean in a tempest; a large quantity of a fluid substance; a rough or agitated place or element; a large crowd or flood (of people, etc.) [Fig.]. **at sea,** on the ocean; wrong, muddled, uncertain [Fig.]. **go to sea,** to become a sailor. **half-seas over,** half tipsy. **on the high seas,** in the open sea. **put to sea,** start a voyage. **Sea Lord,** any of five service members of the British Board of Admiralty, the First Sea Lord being Chief of the Naval Staff. **the Seven Seas,** the N. and S. Atlantic, the N. and S. Pacific, and the Arctic, Antarctic, and Indian Oceans. **short sea,** *see* **short.**
ea-acorn, *n.* a barnacle.
ea-anchor, *n.* a floating sail stretched on spars, used as an anchor to prevent a ship's drifting.
ea-anemone, *n.* a polyp allied to the corals.
ea-ape, *n.* the sea-otter; the thresher shark.
ea-bank, *n.* the sea-shore; a bank built as a defence against the sea.
ea-bar, *n.* a tern.
ea-bat, *n.* a variety of flying-fish.
ea-bear, *n.* a species of seal; the polar bear.
ea-beet, *n.* the wild beet, *Beta maritima.*
eabird, *n.* *see*-berd, a bird frequenting the sea, as the gulls, albatrosses, etc.; a sea-fowl.
ea-blite, *n.* *see*-blite, the plant *Suæda maritima*, of the goose-foot family.
eaboard, *n.* *see*-bord, the sea-shore; a region adjoining the sea: *a.* adjoining the sea.
ea-boat, *n.* a vessel in reference to its sea-going qualities.
ea-borne, *a.* carried on the, or transported by, sea.
ea-breach, *n.* irruption of the sea by breaking the banks; a breach in the banks.
ea-bream, *n.* a marine fish of the genus *Pagellus.*
ea-breeze, *n.* a breeze blowing, usually in the daytime, from the sea upon the land.
ea-buckthorn, *n.* the sallow thorn *Hippophaë rhamnoides*, a maritime shrub yielding a yellow dye.
ea-calf, *n.* the common seal, a species of *Phoca.*
ea-captain, *n.* a captain of a merchant ship.
ea-card, *n.* the card of the mariner's compass.
ea-change, *n.* a change wrought by the action of the sea; a marked transformation.
ea-coal, *n.* coal, so called to differentiate from charcoal when originally brought to London from Newcastle-on-Tyne by sea.
ea-coast, *n.* the shore of the sea; land near it.
ea-cob, *n.* a sea-gull.
ea-cock, *n.* a valve giving direct access through a ship's hull to the exterior.
sea-cow, *n.* the manatee, or other sirenian; a walrus.
seacraft, *n.* *see*-krahft, seamanship.
sea-crow, *n.* local name of various birds, as the cormorant, black-headed gull, and chough.
sea-cucumber, *n.* a sea-slug of the genus *Holothuria*; the trepang.
sea-dace, *n.* the bass, *Labrax lupus.*
sea-devil, *n.* the angler, *Lophius piscatorius.*
sea-dog, *n.* the common seal *Phoca vitulina*; the dog-fish; an old sailor.
sea-dotterel, *n.* the turnstone, *Strepsilas interpres.*
sea-dragon, *n.* the dragonet; the weever; any pipefish, or other fish resembling the sea-horse.
seadrome, *n.* *see*-drome, a floating aerodrome moored in the sea on trans-oceanic airways.
sea-eagle, *n.* *see*-ee-gl, the osprey, the white-tailed eagle, *Haliaëtus albicilla*, and others.
sea-ear, *n.* the ormer, a mollusc of the genus *Haliotis*, with a shell reminiscent of the human ear.
sea-egg, *n.* a sea-urchin.
sea-elephant, *n.* the large seal family, *Macrorhinus elephantinus*, the male of which has a short proboscis.
sea-fan, *n.* any of the *Gorgonia*, esp. *G. flabellum* of the Caribbean.
seafarer, *n.* *see*-fare-rer, a mariner.
seafaring, *a.* *see*-fare-ring, following the seaman's occupation: *n.* this employment.
sea-fennel, *n.* samphire.
sea-fight, *n.* a naval action.
sea-fish, *n.* any marine fish as distinguished from freshwater fish.
sea-fowl, *n.* a bird living on sea-coasts and procuring its food from the sea; a seabird.
sea-fox, *n.* the thresher, a species of shark.
sea-front, *n.* the part of a watering-place facing the sea; the buildings, etc., on it.
sea-gauge, *n.* the depth that a vessel sinks in water; a gauge for sounding the depths of the sea.
sea-girt, *a.* surrounded by the sea.
sea-god, *n.* a divinity presiding over the sea.
sea-going, *a.* sailing on the deep sea, as opposed to coasting; seafaring.
sea-green, *a.* of a faint bluish green: *n.* this colour.
seagull, *n.* *see*-gull, any of the gull family of birds.
seah, *n.* *see*-a, a Hebrew dry measure of about 12 litres or 1½ pecks.
sea-hare, *n.* a nudibranchiate mollusc of the genus *Aplysia.*
sea-hay, *n.* the plant grass-wrack.
sea-heath, *n.* a maritime shrub of the genus *Frankenia.*
sea-hog, *n.* the porpoise.
sea-holly, *n.* the evergreen herb *Eryngium maritimum.*
sea-horse, *n.* the hippocampus; the walrus; the hippopotamus; a large white-capped breaker.
sea-island, *a.* designating a West Indian cotton having specially long and silky fibre.
sea-kale, *n.* the cruciferous plant *Crambe maritima.*
sea-king, *n.* a Norse chieftain; a viking.
sea-kittie, *n.* the kittiwake.
seal, *n.* seel, a pinniped carnivorous amphibious marine mammal, one of the fur seals or one of the earless seals: *v.t.* to catch seals. (A.S. *seolh.*)
seal, *n.* seel, a stamp or die, engraved with some image or device, or its impression; the wax placed on a deed or other legal docment, and stamped with a seal; any impression on wax or wafer; the wax or gum by which an envelope is closed; any act of confirmation; that which confirms or ratifies; that which makes fast: *v.t.* to fasten with or as with a seal; to set a seal to; to ratify or confirm; to close hermetically; to make fast; to impress. **sealed orders,** secret instructions to be looked at only at a given time or occasion. **the Great Seal,** *see* **great. the seals,** the symbols of public office. (O.Fr. *seel.*)
sea-lark, *n.* the dunlin, ringed plover, or similar shore-bird; the rock-pipit.
sea-lavender, *n.* the plant *Statice limonium.*
sea-lawyer, *n.* a sailor fond of arguing.
sea-legs, *n.* ability to walk on a ship's deck when pitching or rolling.
sea-lemon, *n.* a mollusc of the genus *Doris.*
sea-leopard, *n.* an eared seal with a spotted skin.
sealer, *n.* *seel*-er, one who affixes a seal; a machine for sealing tins, cans, etc.; a ship or man engaged in sealing.

sealery, *n.* *seel*-a-re, a seal-fishing station; the occupation of catching seals or of dressing, etc., sealskin.
sea-letter, *n.* a former type of navicert issued by the Custom House in time of war.
sea-level, *n.* the level of the mean tide.
sea-lily, *n.* any of the crinoids.
sea-line, *n.* the horizon at sea.
sealing, *n.* *seel*-ing, the act of affixing a seal; the business of catching seals and curing their skins.
sealing-tape, *n.* gummed paper in tape form for securing packages, etc.
sealing-wax, *n.* a resinous, easily melted composition for receiving impressions or sealing letters, packages, bottles, etc.
sea-lintie, *n.* the rock-pipit, *Anthus obscurus*.
sea-lion, *n.* an eared seal of the genus *Otaria*; a fabulous animal, half lion and half fish [Her.].
sealskin, *n.* *seel*-skin, the fur, or the prepared skin, of a fur-seal of the genus *Otaria*.
sealyham, *n.* *see*-le-am, a small short-legged long-headed terrier, with a dense, wiry, and usually white coat. (Name of place in Pembrokeshire, Wales, where first bred.)
seam, *n.* seem, the fold where two edges of cloth are sewn together; a suture [Anat.]; a cicatrix or scar; the juncture of planks in a ship's side or deck; a vein or stratum [Min.]; a thin layer separating strata of greater magnitude [Geol.]: *v.t.* to form a seam in; to sew or otherwise unite; to mark with a cicatrix; to scar. (A.S. *seam.*)
seam, *n.* seem, a measure of 8 bushels of corn, tallow, etc.; a cart-load of hay, straw, etc. (Late L. *sauma*, from Gr. *sagma*, pack-saddle.)
seaman, *n.* *see*-man, a mariner; a sailor (esp. below the rank of officer); a navigator.
seamanlike, *a.* *see*-man-like, like a skilful seaman.
seamanly, *a.* *see*-man-le, seamanlike.
seamanship, *n.* *see*-man-ship, the skill of a good seaman; the art of rigging and working a ship.
seamark, *n.* *see*-mark, a lighthouse, beacon, or anything on shore marking the way at sea.
sea-mat, *n.* any species of *Flustra*, a marine polyzoan forming branching colonies.
seamer, *n.* *seem*-er, one who or that which makes or removes seams; a sewing-machine for seaming; a machine for joining sheet-metal.
seamew, *n.* *see*-mew, a seagull, esp. *Larus canus*.
sea-mile, *n.* a geographical or nautical mile, 6,080 feet.
sea-milkwort, *n.* *see*-milk-wurt, a plant of the genus *Glaux*.
seamless, *a.* *seem*-less, having no seam.
sea-moss, *n.* a moss-like species of *Corallina*; carrageen.
sea-mouse, *n.* a marine iridescent annelid of the genus *Aphrodite*.
seamstress, *n.* *sem*-stress, a needlewoman. (A.S.)
seamy, *a.* *seem*-e, containing seams; showing the seams, shabby; disreputable. **the seamy side,** the worse or unpleasant side.
sean, *n.* sean, a seine or drag-net.
Seanad Eirann, *n.* *san*-ad-*ayr*-ran, the Senate or Upper House of the legislature of Eire under the constitutions of 1922 and 1937. (Ir.)
séance, *n.* (App.), a session of a deliberative body; a meeting of spiritualists for the reception of communications from the departed. (Fr., a sitting.)
sea-needle, *n.* the garfish.
sea-nettle, *n.* any stinging jelly-fish.
seannachie, *n.* se-nakh-e, *see* **sennachie.**
sea-onion, *n.* the squill, *Scilla maritima*.
sea-ooze, *n.* the soft mud of the bed of the sea.
sea-otter, *n.* a marine carnivore of the N. Atlantic, *Latrix lutris*.
sea-owl, *n.* the lump-fish.
sea-pad, *n.* any species of starfish.
sea-parrot, *n.* the puffin.
sea-peck, *n.* *see*-pek, the dunlin, *Tringa alpina*.
sea-pen, *n.* any of the *Alcyonaria*, esp. a species of *Pennatula*.
sea-pheasant, *n.* the pintail duck, *Dafila acuta*.
sea-pie, *n.* the oyster-catcher; paste and meat boiled or baked together, formerly common among sailors.
sea-piece, *n.* a picture representing a scene at sea.
sea-pig, *n.* the dugong; a porpoise.
sea-pigeon, *n.* one of the smaller guillemots; the rock-dove.
sea-pike, *n.* garfish, hake, or other pike-like marin fish.
sea-pink, *n.* a species of *Armeria*, thrift.
seaplane, *n.* *see*-plane, an aeroplane capable o taking off from and alighting on water.
sea-plover, *n.* the grey plover, *Squatarola helvetica*
sea-poppy, *n.* the yellow poppy, *Glaucium luteum*.
sea-porcupine, *n.* the porcupine-fish.
seaport, *n.* *see*-port, a port on the coast; a tow with a harbour on or connected with the sea.
seapurse, *n.* *see*-purse, the egg-case of the shark ray, or skate.
sea-purslane, *n.* the plant *Obione portulacoides*, on of the chenopodium family.
seaquake, *n.* *see*-kwake, an earthquake occurrin beneath the ocean bed.
sear, *n.* seer, the catch in a gun-lock. (O.Fr. *serre.*
sear, *a.* seer, dry; withered: *v.t.* to burn (a surface to dryness and hardness; to cauterize; to wither to make callous or insensible. **sear up,** to clos by searing. (A.S. *searian*, dry.)
sea-rat, *n.* the rabbit fish or king-of-the-herrings *Chimæra monstrosa*; a pirate.
search, *n.* sertch, a seeking or looking for something a seeking; inquiry; pursuit for finding: *v.t.* t explore; to examine; to inquire; to probe: *v.* to seek; to look for; to make inquiry. **right o search,** the right claimed by a belligerent nation t board and to examine for contraband the merchar vessels of neutrals on the high seas. (Fr. *chercher.*
searchable, *a.* *sertch*-a-bl, that may be searched c explored.
searcher, *n.* *sertch*-er, one who or that which searche or examines; one employed to search.
searching, *a.* *sertch*-ing, penetrating; trying close: *n.* examination; close inquiry.
searchingly, *ad.* in a searching manner.
searchlight, *n.* *sertch*-lite, an apparatus for prc jecting a powerful light over long distances fc searching, lighting, or signalling.
search-warrant, *n.* a warrant issued by a magistrat authorizing the search of premises for stolen prc perty, etc.
seared, *a.* seerd, cauterized; hardened; callous.
searedness, *n.* *seerd*-ness, the state of being seared hardness; insensibility.
sea-risk, *n.* hazard of injury or loss at sea.
sea-robber, *n.* a pirate.
sea-robin, *n.* the American red gurnard, a species c *Prionotus*.
sea-rocket, *n.* the cruciferous plant, *Cakile maritima*
sea-room, *n.* ample space or distance from lanc rocks, or other ships for a vessel to move in.
sea-rover, *n.* a pirate; a pirate ship.
seascape, *n.* *see*-skape, a sea-piece.
sea-scorpion, *n.* any of several spiny sea-fish; th father-lasher, *Cortus scorpius*.
Sea-Scout, *n.* a member of the branch of the Bo Scouts whose training is carried out at or for th sea.
sea-serpent, *n.* a sea-snake; a large serpent-lik monster reported (on insufficient evidence) to hav been seen at sea from time to time.
sea-shell, *n.* the shell of any marine mollusc.
sea-shore, *n.* the shore of the sea; the groun between the tide-range; land adjacent to the sea.
seasick, *a.* *see*-sik, sick from the motion of the shi
seasickness, *n.* the state of being seasick.
seaside, *n.* *see*-side, land adjacent to the sea; watering-place: *a.* bordering on the sea.
sea-slug, *n.* any marine shell-less gastropod, es the béche-de-mer; a sea-cucumber.
sea-snail, *n.* a small fish of the genus *Liparis*; an spiral-shelled marine gastropod.
sea-snake, *n.* any of several venomous aquati snakes of tropical seas.
sea-snipe, *n.* the dunlin; the trumpet-fish.
season, *n.* *see*-zon, a fit or suitable time; the usu or appointed time; any time; a period of time one of the four divisions of the year (sprin summer, autumn, winter). **in season,** in goc time; obtainable in the best condition; in hea (of animals). **out of season,** too late; inoppo tune. **season ticket,** a ticket for a specified perio irrespective of the number of journeys or visit **silly season,** the Parliamentary autumn reces when there is less important matter for newspape than usual [Coll.]. (Fr. *saison.*)
season, *v.t.* *see*-zon, to fit; to prepare; to mature

to accustom; to prepare for use; to render more agreeable; to give a relish to; to render less severe; to temper; to imbue: *v.i.* to become mature, inured, or seasoned.
easonable, *a.* *see*-zon-a-bl, in season; that comes, happens, or is done, in good time; opportune.
easonableness, *n.* the quality or state of being seasonable.
easonably, *ad.* in a seasonable manner.
easonal, *a.* *see*-zon-al, pertaining to or characteristic of a certain season. **seasonal occupation,** work that is possible only at a particular season.
easonally, *ad.* *see*-zon-a-le, at particular times or seasons.
easoned, *a.* *see*-zond, matured (esp. of timber); acclimatized, accustomed to; treated with seasoning; spiced.
easoner, *n.* *see*-zon-er, that which seasons or gives a relish; seasoning.
easoning, *n.* *see*-zon-ing, a mixture of culinary herbs; condiments; that which is added to give a relish or piquancy to food or to enhance enjoyment.
ea-spider, *n.* any of the Pycnogonida, a group of marine spider-like arthropods; a spider-crab.
ea-squirt, *n.* an ascidian [Zool.]
ea-swallow, *n.* a tern; the stormy petrel.
seat, *n.* seet, something to sit on; a chair, bench, or stool; the buttocks, also the part of a garment covering these; the place of sitting; posture in sitting; throne; tribunal; abode; residence; mansion; situation; a pew in a church; a place, or right to a place, in a legislative body, etc.: *v.t.* to place on a seat; to cause to sit down; to instal; to settle; to fix in a place; to set firm; assign seats to; to provide with a seat or seats. (Scand.)
ater, *n.* *seet*-er, that which seats, as a single-seater; one who seats chairs, etc.
ating, *n.* *seet*-ing, material for seats; seats.
a-toad, *n.* the toadfish, sculpin, father-lasher, or certain other fish.
a-trout, *n.* the salmon-trout, *Salmo trutta.*
at-worm, *n.* a nematode worm of the genus *Oxyurus* infesting the fundament.
ea-unicorn, *n.* the narwhal.
ea-urchin, *n.* an echinus, a globular brittle-shelled echinoderm covered with sharp spines.
eave, *n.* seev, the common rush, *Juncus communis*; a rush-light.
eavy, *a.* *see*-ve, containing, abounding in, or composed of rushes.
ea-wall, *n.* a wall to keep out the sea.
eaward, *a.* *see*-ward, directed or situated toward the sea: *ad.* towards the sea: *n.* the direction toward the sea.
ea-way, *n.* the progress made by a ship at sea; an ocean traffic route; a clear way for navigation; a rough sea.
eaweed, *n.* *see*-weed, any species of marine algæ.
ea-wolf, *n.* the wolf-fish, *Anarrhicas lupus*; the elephant-seal; the sea-lion; a pirate.
ea-woodcock, *n.* the bar-tailed godwit, *Limosa lapponica.*
eaworthiness, *n.* state of being seaworthy.
eaworthy, *a.* *see*-wur-the, fit for a voyage; that may be trusted to transport a cargo with safety.
ebaceous, *a.* se-*bay*-shus, fatty; consisting of, or secreting, fat. **sebaceous glands,** the subcutaneous glands which secrete sebum [Anat.]. (L. *sebaceus*, suet-like.)
ebacic, *a.* se-*bas*-ik, obtained from or pertaining to fat. **sebacic acid,** an acid obtained from fat.
ebate, *n.* *see*-bate, a salt of sebacic acid.
ebesten, *n.* se-*bes*-ten, the dried fruit of trees of the genus *Corda*, used medicinally in the East. (Ar.)
ebiferous, *a.* se-*bif*-er-rus, producing fat or matter like fat. (L. *sebum*, tallow, *fero*, bear.)
ebiparous, *a.* se-*bip*-a-rus, producing sebum; sebaceous.
ebum, *n.* *see*-bum, the fatty matter secreted by the sebaceous glands [Anat.].
ec, *a.* sek, dry, not sweet (of wines). (Fr.)
ecale, *n.* se-*kay*-le, the genus of plants that includes the rye, *S. cereale.* (L.)
ecancy, *n.* *sek*-an-se, the property of being secant.
ecant, *a.* *see*-kant, intersecting: *n.* a line that cuts another [Geom.]; a straight line intersecting an arc of a circle, drawn from the centre through one end of the arc and terminated by a tangent drawn through the other end [Trig.]. (L. *secans*, cutting.)
secateur, *n.* sek-a-*ter*, pruning scissors. (Fr.)
secco, *n.* *sek*-koh, painting on dry plaster; tempera-painting. (It.)
seccotine, *n.* *sek*-o-teen, a liquid glue [Trade name].
secede, *v.i.* se-*seed*, to withdraw from fellowship or association; to separate oneself. (L. *secedo*, withdraw.)
seceder, *n.* se-*seed*-er, one who secedes: *pl.* (*cap.*) a body which seceded from the Established Church of Scotland in 1733.
secern, *v.t.* se-*sern*, to secrete [Phys.]; to discriminate. (L. *secerno*, separate.)
secernent, *a.* se-*sern*-ent, secreting: *n.* an organ that separates matter from the blood [Phys.].
secernment, *n.* se-*sern*-ment, the process of secreting.
secession, *n.* se-*sesh*-on, act of seceding. (O.Fr.)
secessionist, *n.* se-*sesh*-on-ist, a seceder; an advocate of secession, esp. (*cap.*) of that of the Southern States of North America in the Civil War, 1861–65.
seclude, *v.t.* se-*klood*, to separate from society and keep apart for a time; to shut up. (L. *secludere*, shut off.)
secluded, *a.* se-*kloo*-ded, separated from others; living in retirement.
secludedly, *ad.* in a secluded manner.
seclusion, *n.* se-*kloo*-zhon, separation from society; retirement; privacy.
seclusive, *a.* se-*kloo*-siv, that secludes or sequesters.
★**second,** *a.* *sek*-ond, the next following the first in order of place or time; next in value, power, or dignity; inferior; supplementary; of lower pitch [Mus.]: *n.* one or that next the first; one who attends another in a duel or prizefight; a supporter; the sixtieth part of a minute of angular measure and of a minute of time; an instant [Coll.]; the interval between one tone and the next [Mus.]; a lower part, esp. alto [Mus.]: *pl.* coarse flour; any second-rate article [Comm.]: *v.t.* to follow; to support; to encourage; to support, as a motion or the mover; (se-*kond*), temporarily to remove from the active list while on special employment [Mil.]. **Second Advent,** the second coming of Christ, at the final resurrection of the dead. **second chamber,** the upper house of a legislature. **second childhood,** dotage. **second cousin,** the child of a first cousin of one's father or mother. **second nature,** acquired characteristics or habits. **second sight,** the psychic power of seeing things future or distant, esp. as ascribed to some Highlanders. (Fr.)
secondarily, *ad.* in a secondary manner.
secondariness, *n.* state of being secondary.
secondary, *a.* *sek*-on-da-re, succeeding next in order to the first; not primary; not of the first order or rate; revolving around a primary planet; acting by deputation; subordinate; mesozoic [Geol.]: *n.* one who acts in subordination to another; a feather of the second joint of a bird's wing; a subsidiary region of low pressure [Meteor.]; the outer winding of a transformer carrying the output [Wire]. **secondary battery,** a storage battery [Elect.]. **secondary cell,** an accumulator [Elect.]. **secondary coil,** a coil carrying an induced current [Elect.]. **secondary current,** induced current [Elect.]. **secondary rocks,** the formation between the primaries and the tertiaries, the mesozoic rocks [Geol.]. **secondary school,** a school for pupils of 11 to 16 years, including modern, technical, and grammar schools; a high school. **secondary winding,** the output winding from a transformer in which an electro-motive force is induced from the primary winding. (Fr. *secondaire.*)
second-best, *a.* best excepting only the actual best.
seconde, *n.* se-*gond*, one of the parries in fencing.
seconder, *n.* *sek*-on-der, one who supports what another attempts; the supporter of a motion.
second-hand, *a.* not original or primary; not new; that has been used by another; pertaining to or dealing in what is second-hand.
secondhand, *n.* *sek*-ond-hand, the hand that marks the seconds on a clock or watch.
secondly, *ad.* *sek*-ond-le, in the second place.
secondment, *n.* *sek*-ond-ment, the act of seconding (a motion, proposal, etc.).
second-rate, *a.* of second quality; inferior in value.

secrecy, *n.* *see*-kre-se, concealment from the observation of others; privacy; retirement; seclusion; fidelity to a secret; the habit of keeping secrets.

★**secret,** *a.* *see*-kret, concealed from notice; private; unknown; occult; not apparent; *n.* something studiously concealed; a thing not discovered; an inaudible prayer by the celebrant at Mass; the key by which something is explained. **in secret,** in a private place. **secret agent,** an agent of the **secret service,** the governmental detective organization. (O.Fr.)

secretaire, *n.* sek-re-*tare*, an escritoire; a writing cabinet. (Fr.)

secretarial, *a.* *sek*-re-*tare*-re-al, pertaining to a secretary, his office, or duties.

secretariat, *n.* *sek*-re-*tare*-re-at, a secretarial department or its official quarters; a body of secretaries with their assistants. (Fr.)

★**secretary,** *n.* *sek*-re-ta-re, a confidential clerical assistant; the official representative of a company; one who conducts a particular department of Government; an escritoire. **secretary bird,** the long-legged snake-eating S. African bird *Serpentarius secretarius*, with a crest of feathers which, when depressed, resembles pens stuck in the ear. (Fr. *secrétaire.*)

secretaryship, *n.* *sek*-re-ta-re-ship, the occupation of a secretary.

secrete, *v.i.* se-*kreet*, to hide; to conceal; to retire from notice; to abscond; to separate from the blood or sap by secretion [Phys.]. (Fr. *sécréter.*)

secretion, *n.* se-*kree*-shon, the act of secreting or hiding; the process of separating from the blood or sap useful or waste matter [Phys.]; the fluid or other matter secreted. (O.Fr.)

secretional, *a.* se-*kree*-shon-al, secretionary.

secretionary, *a.* se-*kree*-shon-a-re, pertaining to, or adapted for the purposes of, secretion [Phys.].

secretive, *a.* se-*kree*-tiv, given to secrecy; reticent; promoting or connected with secretion.

secretiveness, *n.* the quality of being secretive.

secretly, *ad.* *see*-kret-le, without the knowledge of others; privately.

secretory, *a.* se-*kree*-to-re, able to secrete; pertaining to the process of secretion [Phys.]: *n.* a secretary gland or organ.

sect, *n.* sekt, a body of seceders from a Church, denomination; school of thought, etc., on grounds of difference in opinion; the adherents of a particular school of philosophy. (Fr. *secte.*)

sectarial, *a.* sek-*tare*-re-al, distinctive of a sect (esp. among the natives of India).

sectarian, *a.* sek-*tare*-re-an, pertaining or peculiar to a sect: *n.* a sectary.

sectarianism, *n.* sek-*tare*-re-a-nizm, a sectarian spirit or tendency; sectarian views; adherence or devotion to a sect.

sectarianize, *v.t.* sek-*tare*-re-a-nize, to affect with sectarianism.

sectary, *n.* *sek*-ta-re, one who belongs to a sect, esp. of seceders from a Church; a Protestant dissenter. (Fr. *sectaire.*)

sectile, *a.* *sek*-tile, capable of being cut. (L. *sectilis.*)

section, *n.* *sek*-shon, the act of cutting or separating by cutting; a part separated from the rest; a division; a distinct portion; the subdivision of a chapter; a distinct part of a city, country, people, etc.; a square mile of public land [U.S.A.]; the representation of a building, machine, etc., cut asunder vertically; a representation of the earth's crust on any given line; the intersection of one surface with another or of a surface with a solid [Geom.]; a section-mark; an exposure of geological structure; a thin slice of some substance to be submitted to microscopical examination: *v.t.* to divide, arrange, or represent in sections. (Fr., from L. *sectus*, cut.)

sectional, *a.* *sek*-shon-al, pertaining to a section; made up of sections; incomplete.

sectionalism, *n.* *sek*-shon-a-lizm, party spirit; bigoted devotion to party interests.

sectionalize, *v.t.* *sek*-shon-a-lize, to make sectional; to divide into sections.

sectionally, *ad.* in a sectional manner.

section-house, *n.* a house for the board and lodging of the unmarried policemen of a division.

section-mark, *n.* the fourth reference mark for foot-notes, "§" [Print.].

sector, *n.* *sek*-tor, the part of a circle comprehended between two radii and the intercepted arc [Geom.]; a hinged mathematical instrument, marked with sines, tangents, etc., for determining a fourth proportional; an astronomical instrument for measuring angles; a section or sub-division of a trench, area of operations, etc. [Mil.]. (L.)

sectorial, *a.* sek-*taw*-re-al, pertaining to a sector; adapted to cutting (of teeth) [Zool.].

secular, *a.* *sek*-yew-lar, pertaining to things not sacred; worldly; temporal; lasting; persisting through the ages; not bound by monastic vows or rules; coming or observed once in a century or an age; pertaining to secularism: *n.* an ecclesiastic not bound by monastic vows; a lay official of a church. (Fr. *séculier.*)

secularism, *n.* *sek*-yew-la-rizm, the doctrine that for a moral and ethical way of life any form of religion is unnecessary; (*cap.*) a system of non-theistic social ethics propounded by J. G. Holyoake (1817–1906) about 1854.

Secularist, *n.* *sek*-yew-la-rist, an adherent of Secularism; (*l.c.*) an opponent of the teaching of religion in schools.

secularity, *n.* sek-yew-*la*-re-te, the state or condition of being secular; worldliness; excessive attention to things of the present life.

secularization, *n.* *sek*-yew-la-ry-*zay*-shon, the act of secularizing.

secularize, *v.t.* *sek*-yew-la-rize, to make secular; to convert from religious to secular use; to convert that which is regular or monastic into secular.

secularly, *ad.* in a secular manner.

secund, *a.* *see*-kund, arranged on only one side of the axis (of flowers) [Bot.]. (L. *secundus.*)

secundine, *n.* *sek*-un-din, the second coat of an ovule [Bot.]; the afterbirth. (Fr. *secondine.*)

secure, *a.* se-*kewr*, free from danger of being taken; free from fear or danger; safe; undisturbed; unalarmed; confident; careless; certain: *v.t.* to guard effectually from danger; to make safe; to ensure the payment of a debt, fulfilment of a bond, etc.; to make certain; to confine effectually; to ensure; to make fast. (L. *securus.*)

securely, *ad.* se-*kewr*-le, in a secure manner.

securement, *n.* se-*kewr*-ment, the act of securing.

securiform, *a.* se-*kewr*-re-form axe-shaped [Bot. and Entom.]. (L. *securis*, axe, *forma*, shape.)

security, *n.* se-*kewr*-re-te, state of being or feeling secure; protection; effectual defence or safety from danger of any kind; that which secures; a pledge; a bond; a certificate; one who becomes surety; an evidence of debt or of property; something given or done to secure peace or good behaviour. (Fr. *securité.*)

sedan, *n.* se-*dan*, a covered chair for one person borne on two poles by two men; a motor-car with a body enclosing seats for passengers and chauffeur. (Derivation unknown.)

sedate, *a.* se-*date*, composed; calm; serious. (L. *sedatus*, calmed.)

sedately, *ad.* in a sedate manner.

sedateness, *n.* calmness of mind; composure; tranquillity.

sedation, *n.* se-*day*-shon, the producing of a sedative effect [Med.].

sedative, *a.* *sed*-a-tiv, allaying irritability; assuaging pain: *n.* anything (esp. a medicine) which allays irritability and assuages pain. (Fr. *sédatif.*)

sedentarily, *ad.* in a sedentary manner.

sedentariness, *n.* quality of being sedentary.

sedentary, *a.* *sed*-en-ta-re, accustomed to sit much; requiring much sitting; passed for most part in sitting; inactive; sluggish; not migratory [Zool.]: *n.* one of a group of spiders which remain motionless until their prey is entangled in their web. (Fr. *sédentaire*, from L. *sedere*, to sit.)

sederunt, *n.* se-*deer*-runt, a sitting of a court; an ecclesiastical assembly; a meeting. **act of sederunt,** an ordinance regulating forms of procedure before the Scottish Court of Session. (L. they sat.)

sedge, *n.* sej, a plant of the genus *Carex*, allied to the grasses and common in marsh-land. **sedge warbler** or **sedge wren,** *Acrocephalus schœnobænus*, a reed warbler frequenting the banks of rivers. (A.S. *secg.*)

sedgy, *a.* *sej*-e, overgrown with sedges.

sedilia, *n.pl.* se-*dil*-e-a, three seats within the

altar rails of a church, originally for the celebrant of the mass and his assistants [Arch.]. (L.)
sediment, *n. sed*-e-ment, the matter which subsides to the bottom of liquor; lees; dregs. (L. *sedimentum.*)
sedimentary, *a. sed*-e-*men*-ta-re, pertaining to or formed of sediment.
sedimentation, *n. sed*-e-men-*tay*-shon, act of depositing, or deposition of, sediment.
sedition, *n.* se-*dish*-on, conduct or speech tending to provoke rebellion; incipient insurrection. (O.Fr.)
seditionary, *a.* se-*dish*-o-na-re, seditious; involving sedition: *n.* a seditionist.
seditionist, *n.* se-*dish*-on-ist, one practising or promoting sedition.
seditious, *a.* se-*dish*-us, pertaining to or of the nature of sedition; tending to excite sedition; guilty of sedition. (Fr. *séditieux.*)
seditiously, *ad.* in a seditious manner.
seditiousness, *n.* the state of being seditious.
seduce, *v.t.* se-*dewce*, to draw aside or entice from rectitude and duty; to corrupt; to induce to a surrender of chastity. (L. *seduco*, lead.)
seducement, *n.* se-*dews*-ment, the act of seducing; seduction; an enticement.
seducer, *n.* se-*dew*-ser, one who or that which seduces; one who induces a woman to surrender her chastity.
seducible, *a.* se-*dew*-se-bl, capable of being seduced.
seducingly, *ad.* in a seducing manner.
seduction, *n.* se-*duk*-shon, the act of seducing; the means employed to seduce; the act of inducing a woman to surrender her chastity. (O.Fr.)
seductive, *a.* se-*duk*-tiv, alluring; tending to seduce or lead astray.
seductively, *ad.* in a seductive manner.
seductiveness, *n.* se-*duk*-tiv-ness, seductive quality; the fact of being seductive.
sedulity, *n.* se-*dew*-le-te, sedulousness; careful attention to duty.
sedulous, *a. sed*-yew-lus, assiduous; steadily industrious; steady and persevering in business and endeavour. (L. *sedulus.*)
sedulously, *ad.* in a sedulous manner.
sedulousness, *n.* the state or quality of being sedulous; assiduity.
Sedum, *n. see*-dum, a large genus of widely distributed fleshy herbs including the stonecrops.
see, *n.* see, a diocese; the jurisdiction of a bishop or archbishop. **Holy See,** *see* **holy.** (L. *sedes*, a seat.)
★**see,** *v.t.* see, to perceive by the eye; to observe; to take care; to discover; to converse or have intercourse with; to visit; to attend; to experience; to perceive; to accept a challenge (at poker, etc.): *v.i.* to have the power of sight or of perceiving; to discern; to examine into; to be attentive; to consider with care; to make provision for; to comprehend. **to see one off,** to escort him to the place of departure. **to see red,** to become furious or enraged [Coll.]. **to see through,** to comprehend the hidden purpose, real character, etc.; to go through with to the end; to help through. *p.* **saw.** *pp.* **seen.** (A.S. *seon.*)
seeable, *a. see*-a-bl, visible; able to be seen.
seecatchie, *n.* see-*katch*-e, the mature male fur seal. (Russ.)
★**seed,** *n.* seed, that which nature prepares for the reproduction and conservation of the species; the mature fertilized ovule in flowering plants; the male fertilizing fluid, semen; that from which anything springs; a first principle; an original; principle of production; progeny; offspring; generation: *v.t.* to sow; to sprinkle with seed; to remove seeds from; to conduct a draw so that certain players (usually the best) in a tournament do not meet until the later rounds [Lawn Tennis, etc.]: *v.i.* to produce or shed seed. **to run to seed,** to form seed; to mature, esp. [Fig.] prematurely. (A.S. *sæd.*)
seed-bed, *n.* ground prepared for sowing seed.
seed-bud, *n.* an ovule; the germ of the fruit.
seed-cake, *n.* a sweet cake containing caraway seeds.
seed-corn, *n.* corn reserved for sowing.
seed-eater, *n.* any granivorous bird; a S. African finch of the genus *Serinus.*
seeded, *a. seed*-ed, supplied with seed; matured; the seeds having been extracted; (of tournaments, etc.) drawn in such a way that the better players cannot be eliminated in the early rounds [Sports].
seeder, *n. seed*-er, a utensil for removing seeds from fruit; a machine or apparatus for sowing seed; one who seeds.
seed-fish, *n.* a fish ready to spawn.
seed-grain, *n.* seed-corn.
seedily, *ad. seed*-e-le, shabbily.
seediness, *n. seed*-e-ness, the state of being seedy.
seed-lac, *n.* the resin lac dried.
seed-leaf, *n.* a cotyledon [Bot.].
seedless, *a. seed*-less, without seeds.
seedling, *a. seed*-ling, grown from the seed: *n.* a plant reared from the seed; a young plant for transplanting.
seed-lop, *n.* a vessel in which a sower carries the seed to be sown.
seed-pearl, *n.* a very small seed-like pearl.
seed-plot, *n.* a piece of ground on which seeds are sown to produce plants for transplantation.
seedsman, *n. seedz*-man, a dealer in seeds of plants.
seed-time, *n.* the season proper for sowing.
seed-vessel, *n.* the pericarp [Bot.].
seedy, *a. seed*-e, abounding with seeds; run to seed; poor and miserable-looking; shabby; out of health; of dubious character [Slang].
seeing, *conj. see*-ing, since; it being so; inasmuch as.
seek, *v.t.* seek, to go in search of; to look for; to ask for; to resort to: *v.i.* to make search or inquiry; to endeavour. *p.* and *pp.* **sought,** sawt. (A.S. *secan.*)
seeker, *n. seek*-er, one who seeks; an inquirer; (*cap.*) one of a 17th-cent. English sect which acknowledged no Church and professed to be seeking a true religion.
seel, *v.t.* seel, to close the eyes of (a hawk); to hoodwink. (O.Fr., from L. *cilium*, an eye-lash.)
★**seem,** *v.i.* seem, to appear; to have the appearance of. (A.S. *seman*, to suit.)
seemer, *n. seem*-er, a pretender; one who assumes an appearance or semblance.
seeming, *a. seem*-ing, appearing; having the appearance or semblance, whether real or not; specious: *n.* appearance (esp. false); show; semblance; fair appearance; opinion.
seemingly, *ad. seem*-ing-le, in appearance.
seemingness, *n.* fair appearance; plausibility.
seemliness, *n.* the state of being seemly; comeliness; grace; fitness; propriety.
seemly, *a. seem*-le, becoming; suited to the object, occasion, purpose, or character; suitable. (Ice. *sæmiligr.*)
seen, *seen, pp.* of *see.*
seep, *v.i.* seep, to ooze away; to drain away; to percolate. (A.S. *sipian*, soak away.)
seepage, *n. seep*-aj, that which seeps.
seer, *n. see*-er, one who sees; (*pronounced* seer) one gifted with prophetic vision or insight; a soothsayer.
seer, *n.* seer, an Indian weight, officially 1 kg. (2·2 lb.) but varying from ½ lb. to over 3 lb. (Hind.)
seerfish, *n. seer*-fish, the East Indian marine fish *Cybium guttatum*, allied to the mackerel. (Port. *serra*, saw, and *fish.*)
seership, *n. seer*-ship, the rank, function, or occupation of a seer.
see-saw, *n.* a reciprocating vertical motion at both ends; a game in which two children seated each on one end of a board supported in the centre, move alternately up and down: *a.* moving up and down or to and fro: *v.t.* to cause to move in a see-saw manner: *v.i.* to move with a reciprocating motion; to vacillate.
seethe, *v.t.* seethe, to boil; to decoct or prepare for food in hot liquor; to soak: *v.i.* to be in a state of ebullition; to be much agitated [Fig.]. Former *p.* and *pp.* **sod, sodden.** (A.S. *seothan*, boil.)
seg, *n.* seg, a bullock castrated when fully grown. (Dial.)
segar, *n.* se-*gar*, an obsolete form of *cigar.*
seggar, *n. seg*-ar, a saggar.
segment, *n. seg*-ment, a piece cut off; a separable piece; a part cut off from a figure by a line or plane [Geom.]: *v.t.* and *i.* to divide or be divided into segments. (L. *segmentum.*)
segmental, *a.* seg-*men*-tal, pertaining to, consisting of, or like a segment.
segmentary, *a.* seg-*men*-ta-re, segmental.
segmentate, *a. seg*-men-tate, segmented [Zool.].

segmentation, *n.* seg-men-*tay*-shon, act or process of dividing into segments ; cleavage.
segno, *n.* *say*-nyo, a mark of repetition, thus :𝄋: [Mus.]. (It., sign.)
segregable, *a.* *seg*-re-ga-bl, capable of being segregated.
segregate, *a.* *seg*-re-gate, separated from its kind : *v.t.* to separate from others ; to set apart : *v.i.* to become separated. (L. *segregatus.*)
segregation, *n.* *seg*-re-*gay*-shon, act of segregating ; state of being segregated ; separation from a main body.
segregative, *a.* *seg*-re-ga-tiv, characterized by segregation ; tending to segregate.
seguidilla, *n.* say-ge-*deel*-ya, a Spanish verse form ; a lively dance (or its music) in triple time. (Sp.)
seiche, *n.* saysh, a periodical oscillation or change of level in the surface of certain lakes, esp. in Switzerland. (Swiss Fr.)
Seidlitz, *n.* *sed*-lits, a saline mineral water from Seidlitz, a village in Bohemia. **seidlitz powder,** an aperient composed of a mixture of potassium tartrate and sodium bicarbonate, and tartaric acid, which are dissolved separately and then mixed.
seigneur, *n.* *sane*-yewr, a seignior ; in Canada, one of a class who, till 1854, held land under a feudal tenure. (Fr.)
seigneurial, *a.* sen-*yewr*-re-al, manorial ; pertaining to a seigneur or seigneury.
seigneury, *n.* *sayn*-yewr-re, a seigniory ; an estate in Canada formerly held by a seigneur.
seignior, *n.* *seen*-yor, a feudal lord ; the lord of the manor. **the Grand Seignior,** a title of the former Sultan of Turkey. (Fr. *seigneur.*)
seigniorage, *n.* *seen*-yo-raj, a royal prerogative formerly allotting the sovereign a percentage on all gold and silver minted ; the profit derived from issuing coins at a rate above their intrinsic value [Comm] ; a mining royalty on certain metals, esp. tin.
seigniorial, *a.* sen-*yaw*-re-al, seigneurial.
seigniory, *n.* *seen*-yo-re, a lordship ; a manor ; in mediæval Italy, a signory. (Fr. *seigneurie.*)
Seimas, *n.* *say*-mas, the Diet of the former Lithuanian Republic. (Lith.)
seine, *n.* sane, a draught net for catching fish : *v.t.* and *i.* to catch or trawl with a seine. (Fr.)
seiner, *n.* *sane*-er, one who trawls with a seine ; a boat used in seining.
seise, *v.t.* seez, to put in possession of [Law] ; to have in legal possession.
seised, *a.* seezd, possessed of ; owning by legal right.
seisin, *n.* *see*-zin, seizin. (O.Fr.)
seismal, *a.* *size*-mal, seismic.
seismic, *a.* *size*-mik, pertaining to or produced by an earthquake. (Gr. *seismos*, earthquake.)
seismogram, *n.* *size*-mo-gram, a record obtained from a seismograph.
seismograph, *n.* *size*-mo-graf, a recording seismometer.
seismographic, *a.* *size*-mo-*graf*-ik, pertaining to seismography.
seismography, *n.* size-*mog*-ra-fe, an account of, or the art of measuring and registering, earthquakes.
seismologist, *n.* size-*mol*-o-jist, one versed in seismology.
seismology, *n.* size-*mol*-o-je, the science of earthquakes. (Gr. *seismos*, and *logos*, science.)
seismometer, *n.* size-*mom*-e-ter, an instrument for measuring the intensity and indicating the direction of an earthquake. (Gr. *seismos*, and *metron*, measure.)
seismoscope, *n.* *size*-mo-skope, a simplified form of seismometer.
seity, *n.* *see*-e-te, that which constitutes self [Phil.]. (L. *se*, oneself.)
seizable, *a.* *seez*-a-bl, liable to be seized.
seize, *v.t.* seez, to grasp suddenly ; to take possession of by force, with or without right ; to take hold of ; to apprehend ; to join ropes by binding the ends together with yarn : *v.i.* to stick fast (of machinery, etc.) ; to adhere. (Fr. *saisir.*)
seizer, *n.* *seez*-er, one who seizes.
seizin, *n.* *seez*-in, possession, esp. of land under a freehold ; the act of taking possession ; the thing possessed [Law].
seizing, *n.* *seez*-ing, the binding of two ropes together with yarn ; the yarns used for binding them.
seizor, *n.* *see*-zor, one who takes possession [Law].
seizure, *n.* *seez*-yur, the act of seizing ; taking possession by force ; the act of taking by warrant ; the thing seized ; grasp ; possession ; a fit, or other sudden attack [Med.].
sejant, *a.* *see*-jant, sitting, with the fore-legs erect (of beasts) [Her.]. (O.Fr. *séant*, sitting.)
sejm, *n.* same, the Diet, or lower House, of the Polish Parliament.
sejugous, *a.* *see*-ju-gus, having six pairs of leaflets [Bot.]. (L. *sejugis*, a team of six horses.)
selachian, *a.* se-*lay*-ke-an, pertaining to the Selachii, the group of fish including the sharks and dogfish : *n.* one of the Selachii. (Gr. *selachos*, shark.)
seladang, *n.* se-*lah*-dahng, the gaur, or Indian wild ox. (Malay.)
selah, *n.* *see*-la, in the Psalms, a word supposed to be a direction, probably indicating a pause. (Heb.)
selamlik, *n.* se-*lahm*-lik, the men's apartments in a Turkish house ; the ceremonial visit of the former Turkish Sultans to the mosque each Friday. (Turk.)
seldom, *ad.* *sel*-dom, rarely ; not often. (A.S.)
select, *a.* se-*lekt*, choice ; preferable ; more valuable or excellent than others : *v.t.* to choose ; to take by preference from among others ; to pick out (L. *selectus*, gathered.)
selectedly, *ad.* se-*lek*-ted-le, with care in selection.
***selection,** *n.* se-*lek*-shon, the act, or the right, of selecting ; the thing or things selected ; the land held by a selector [Austral.]. **natural selection** the survival of the animals and plants most fitted to live on under changed conditions [Biol.]. (L *selectio.*)
selective, *a.* se-*lek*-tiv, capable of selecting ; tending to select.
selectively, *ad.* in a selective manner.
selectivity, *n.* se-lek-*tiv*-e-te, condition or state of being selective ; power of excluding from a receiving-set all but the desired wave-length [Wire.].
selectman, *n.* se-*lekt*-man, a popularly elected local government officer [U.S.A.].
selectness, *n.* the state of being select.
selector, *n.* se-*lek*-tor, one who or that which chooses from a number ; one who takes up a portion of public land, paying for the freehold by periodical instalments [Austral.] ; the device by means of which radio or telephonic impulses are transmitted or received by the appropriate wave-lengths or lines.
selenate, *n.* *sel*-e-nate, a salt of selenic acid.
selenian, *a.* se-*lee*-ne-an, pertaining to the moon [Astron.].
selenic, *a.* se-*len*-ik, pertaining to or containing selenium. **selenic acid,** a compound obtained by the oxidization of selenious acid.
selenide, *n.* *sel*-e-nide, a compound of selenium with another element or radical.
seleniferous, *a.* *sel*-e-*nif*-er-rus, containing selenium.
selenious, *a.* se-*lee*-ne-us, selenic. **selenious acid,** an acid obtained by oxidation of selenium.
selenite, *n.* *sel*-e-nite, a salt of selenious acid ; transparent variety of gypsum.
selenitic, *a.* sel-e-*nit*-ik, pertaining to selenite.
selenium, *n.* se-*lee*-ne-um, a non-metallic allotropic element occurring in native sulphur and obtained as a by-product in copper-refining, one form of which has powers of electrical conduction which increase with the intensity of light, making it a valuable factor in various photo-electrical devices (Gr. *selēne*, the moon.)
selenodont, *a.* se-*lee*-no-dont, having teeth with crescent-shaped ridges on the crown. (Gr. *selēne* and *odontos*, tooth.)
selenograph, *n.* se-*lee*-no-graf, a chart of the moon's surface or of a part thereof.
selenographic, *a.* *sel*-e-no-*graf*-ik, pertaining to selenography.
selenography, *n.* *sel*-e-*nog*-ra-fe, a description of the moon. (Gr. *selēne*, the moon, *grapho*, write.)
selenology, *n.* *sel*-e-*nol*-o-je, the branch of astronomy treating of the moon.
selenomancy, *n.* se-*lee*-no-man-se, divination by means of observation of the moon.
selenotropic, *a.* se-*lee*-no-*trop*-ik, turning toward the moon.
selenotropism, *n.* *sel*-e-*not*-ro-pizm, a tendenc

(in a plant) to turn towards the light of the moon [Bot.].

★**self,** *n.* self (*pl.* **selves**), one's own person; individual identity; the ego; personal interest; selfishness: *a.* very; particular; uniform (of colour). [The word is affixed to certain personal pronouns to express emphasis or distinction, as **myself, himself,** etc., and, as a prefix, forms many compounds the meaning of most of which is self-evident.] (A.S.)

self-abandonment, *n.* disregard of self.

self-abasement, *n.* abasement of self.

self-absorbed, *a.* deep in thought; wrapped up in self.

self-abuse, *n.* abuse of one's faculties or powers; masturbation.

self-acting, *a.* acting or capable of acting of itself; automatic.

self-assertion, *n.* presumptuous assertion of oneself or one's claims.

self-binder, *n.* a harvesting machine that automatically binds the sheaves.

self-centred, *a.* egoistic; wrapped in self.

self-coloured, *a.* of the natural, or of a single, colour; not dyed.

self-command, *n.* self-control.

self-complacent, *a.* having an air of satisfaction with oneself.

self-conceit, *n.* a high opinion of oneself.

self-confident, *a.* confident of one's own ability; trusting to one's own judgment.

self-conscious, *a.* conscious of self; conscious of oneself as seen through the eyes of others.

self-consciousness, *n.* the consciousness of an external world and of ourselves as related thereto; the embarrassment of a self-conscious person.

self-contained, *a.* self-possessed; reticent; complete in itself.

self-control, *n.* restraint over self.

self-defence, *n.* defence of oneself. **the art of self-defence,** boxing.

self-denial, *n.* forbearance from gratifying one's own desires.

self-destruction, *n.* suicide.

self-determination, *n.* the principle of free-will, as opposed to fatalism [Phil.]; the right of a people to determine their own policy without external influence or interference.

self-evident, *a.* evident of itself without proof.

self-exciting, *a.* (of a dynamo) energizing its own field magnets by a current produced by itself [Elect.].

self-existent, *a.* existing by itself; not derived from, and independent of, others.

self-explanatory, *a.* readily understandable without an explanation.

self-government, *n.* government of self; the government of a people by themselves.

self-heal, *n.* the labiate plant, *Prunella vulgaris.*

self-help, *n.* unaided effort; the practice of fulfilling one's ambitions without outside assistance.

selfhood, *n.* *self*-hood, that which constitutes self; individuality; the ego.

self-interest, *n.* personal advantage; the pursuit of this.

selfish, *a.* *self*-ish, regardful of one's own interest chiefly or solely; influenced in one's action by regard to private advantage.

selfishly, *ad.* in a selfish manner.

selfishness, *n.* the quality of being selfish; the exclusive regard of a person to his own interest or happiness.

selfless, *a.* *self*-less, having no regard to self.

self-love, *n.* esteem of oneself; regard for the preservation of one's being and well-being.

self-made, *a.* risen from obscurity, etc., by one's own unaided efforts.

self-opinionated, *a.* obstinate in opinion.

self-portrait, *n.* a portrait of oneself made by oneself.

self-possessed, *a.* calm and collected; having presence of mind.

self-possession, *n.* the state of being self-possessed; composure of mind.

self-registering, *a.* registering automatically.

self-reliant, *a.* self-confident.

self-respect, *n.* due regard for one's own character, position, etc.; reasonable esteem of oneself.

self-righteous, *a.* righteous in one's own regard.

self-righting, *a.* righting itself when capsized.

self-rising, *a.* rising of itself (esp. of flour needing no addition of leaven).

self-sacrifice, *n.* sacrifice of self for the sake of others.

selfsame, *a.* *self*-same, the very same.

self-seeking, *a.* seeking one's own advantage regardless of others: *n.* selfishness.

self-starter, *n.* a device for starting an engine (esp. of motor-cars) without the use of man-power; hence, a motor-car fitted with this.

self-styled, *a.* called by oneself, but not officially or authoritatively; soi-disant.

self-sufficient, *a.* having perfect confidence in one's own abilities or resources; sufficient in itself; haughty.

self-willed, *a.* obstinate; unyielding to the advice or wishes of others.

Seljuk, *n.* sel-*jook*, any member of a Turkish dynasty descended from a chieftain of this name ruling in W. Asia from about the 11th to the 13th century.

sell, *v.t.* sel, to transfer property to another for an equivalent in money; to part with for a price; to betray or deliver up for reward; to part with; to hoax, disappoint, or deceive [Slang]: *v.i.* to practise selling; to be sold: *n.* a hoax, disappointment, or swindle [Slang]. **sell the pass,** *see* **pass. selling-race,** a horse-race in which the winner must be sold by auction or at a previously stated price. *pp.* **sold.** (A.S. *sellan*, to deliver.)

sellable, *a.* *sel*-a-bl, saleable; capable of being sold.

sellanders, *n.* *sel*-an-derz, sallenders.

Sellenger's-round, *n.* *sel*-en-jerz-round, an old English country-dance; music for this. (*St. Leger.*)

seller, *n.* *sel*-er, one who sells; a vendor. **best seller,** an article (esp. a book) that is bought very readily. **sellers' market,** the condition in which consumers' goods are scarce and, hence, prices are high [Econ.].

selliform, *a.* *sel*-e-form, saddle-shaped. (L. *sella*, a saddle.)

seltzer, *n.* *selt*-zer, a mildly stimulant effervescing mineral water, natural or artificial, containing carbon dioxide. (Nieder *Selters*, in the Rhineland.)

seltzogene, *n.* *selt*-zo-jeen, a household appliance for making aerated waters from powders; a gazogene. (Fr. *selzogène.*)

selvage, *n.* *sel*-vaj, the selvedge.

selvagee, *n.* *sel*-va-jee, a kind of skein of rope yarns used for stoppers [Naut.].

selvedge, *n.* *sel*-vej, the edge of cloth where it is closed by complicating the threads: a woven border. (O.Dut. *selfegge.*)

selvedged, *a.* sel-vejd, having a selvedge.

selves, selvz, *pl.* of *self.*

semantic, *a.* se-*man*-tik, dealing with the meaning of words. (Gr. *semantikos*, significant.)

semantics, *n.pl.* se-*man*-tiks, that branch of philology which deals with the meanings of words.

semantron, *n.* se-*man*-tron, an iron or wooden bar struck by a mallet, used in place of a bell in the Greek church. (Gr.)

semaphore, *n.* *sem*-a-for, any signalling apparatus, consisting of a movable arm (as on railways) or arms, flags, or lamps: *v.t.* and *i.* to signal with this. (Gr. *sema*, a sign, *phero*, bear.)

semaphoric, *a.* sem-a-*fo*-rik, pertaining to semaphores.

semaphorically, *ad.* sem-a-*fo*-re-ka-le, by means of the semaphore.

semasiological, *a.* see-*may*-se-o-*loj*-e-kal, pertaining to semasiology.

semasiology, *n.* see-*may*-se-*ol*-o-je, semantics. (Gr. *semasia*, signification, and *logos.*)

sematic, *a.* se-*mat*-ik, significant; serving as a warning of danger [Zool.]. (Gr. *sēma*, sign.)

sematography, *n.* sem-a-*tog*-ra-fe, the use of signs or marks instead of letters.

semblable, *a.* *sem*-bla-bl, similar; resembling; ostensible.

semblance, *n.* *sem*-blance, likeness; resemblance; appearance; show. (Fr.)

semblant, *a.* *sem*-blant, only seeming. (Fr. *sembler*, seem.)

semé, *a.* *sem*-ay, strewed with the specified objects (of fields, etc.) [Her.]. (Fr., sown.)

semeiography, *n.* *see*-my-*og*-ra-fe, a description of symptoms [Med.]. (Gr. *semeion*, a sign, *grapho*, write.)

semeiological, *a.* see-my-o-*loj*-e-kal, pertaining to semeiology or symptoms.
semeiology, *n.* see-my-*ol*-o-je, symptomatology [Med.]; sign language. (Gr. *semeion*, and *logos*, science.)
semeiotic, *a.* see-my-*ot*-ik, relating to signs or symptoms: *n.pl.* the art of using symbols; symptomatology [Med.]. (Gr. *semeion*.)
semen, *n.* *see*-men, the fertilizing fluid of the male; seed. (L.)
semester, *n.* se-*mes*-ter, a period of six months; a college half-year in certain European and American Universities. (L. *semestris*.)
semestral, *a.* se-*mes*-tral, half-yearly, occurring once in six months; lasting for six months.
semi-, *pref.* *sem*-e, used with a large number of adjectives and nouns to denote half (exactly or approximately), partly, or imperfectly. (L.)
semi-annual, *a.* half-yearly.
semi-annular, *a.* half round; semicircular.
semi-articulate, *a.* loose-jointed [Zool.].
semi-barbarous, *a.* half-civilized.
semibreve, *n.* *sem*-e-breev, a musical note equal to two minims; a whole note [Mus.]. (It.)
semi-bull. *n.* a bull issued by an elected Pope before his enthronement.
semi-chorus, *n.* a part or half of a choir; a passage to be sung by selected voices of a choir.
semicircle, *n.* *sem*-e-ser-kl, the half of a circle.
semicircular, *a.* *sem*-e-*ser*-kew-lar, having the form of half a circle.
semi-circumference, *n.* half a circumference.
semicolon, *n.* *sem*-e-koh-lon, the mark (;) used in punctuation, intermediate between a comma and a colon.
semi-conscious, *a.* partially conscious.
semi-cylindrical, *a.* of the shape of a cylinder divided longitudinally.
semi-demisemiquaver, *n.* the sixty-fourth of a semibreve [Mus.].
semidetached, *a.* *sem*-e-de-*tatcht*, detached on one side only (of adjoining houses).
semidiameter, *n.* *sem*-e-dy-*am*-e-ter, a radius.
semi-diurnal, *a.* consisting of or lasting half a day; at intervals of half a day.
semifinal, *a.* *sem*-e-*fy*-nal, denoting the last round, match, etc., in a contest before the final [Sport]: *n.* a semifinal match.
semifinalist, *n.* *sem*-e-*fy*-na-list, one taking part in a semifinal round [Sport].
semi-fluid, *a.* imperfectly fluid, as treacle.
semi-independent, *a.* partially independent.
semilunar, *a.* *sem*-e-*lew*-nar, having the shape of a crescent, or half-moon.
semi-metal, *n.* a non-malleable metallic element, such as bismuth; a metalloid.
seminal, *a.* *sem*-e-nal, pertaining to seed or to reproduction; contained in or having the virtue of seed; radical; germinal; original. (*semen*.)
seminar, *n.* *sem*-e-nar, at Universities, a group of advanced students engaged in some special study or research. (Ger., from L. *seminarium*, a seed-plot.)
seminarist, *n.* *sem*-e-na-rist, one educated in a seminary; formerly, a Rom. Cath. priest from the English College at Douai.
seminary, *n.* *sem*-e-na-re, a place of education; an academy; a college esp. for Rom. Cath. priests. (Fr. *séminaire*, from L. *seminarium*, a seed-plot.)
seminate, *v.t.* *sem*-e-nate, to sow; to inseminate; to disseminate [Fig.]. (L.)
semination, *n.* sem-e-*nay*-shon, the act of sowing; impregnation; the natural dispersion of seeds [Bot.].
seminiferous, *a.* sem-e-*nif*-er-rus, producing seed; producing or conveying semen.
seminific, *a.* sem-e-*nif*-ik, forming or producing seed. (L. *semen*, and *facio*, make.)
semi-official, *a.* of official origin but not having official authority.
semiology, *n.* *see*-my-*ol*-o-je, semeiology.
semi-opal, *n.* a non-opalescent variety of opal.
semi-opaque, *a.* partially transparent.
semi-osseous, *a.* of a bony nature; partly ossified.
semi-palmate, *a.* webbed only halfway down the toes [Ornith.]
semiped, *n.* *sem*-e-ped, a verse of half a foot [Pros.]. (L. *semi-*, and *pes*, a foot.)
semi-Pelagianism, *n.* a 5th-cent. modification of Pelagianism teaching that while divine assistance is offered freely to all it is open to each to accept or reject it and that the individual must make his choice.
semi-plantigrade, *a.* partially digitigrade.
semiquaver, *n.* *sem*-e-kway-ver, a note of half the duration of the quaver [Mus.].
semi-rigid, *a,* not completely rigid (esp. of an airship with non-rigid envelope and stiffened keel).
semi-sedentary, *a.* nomadic for part of the year only (of tribes, etc.) [Anthrop.].
semi-sextile, *n.* the aspect of two heavenly bodies when separated by 30° or $\frac{1}{12}$ circle.
semi-solid, *a.* not quite solid; highly viscous.
Semite, *n.* *see*-myt, a supposed descendant of Shem (including the Hebrews and Arabs, with certain ancient peoples).
Semitic, *a.* se-*mit*-ik, pertaining to the family of languages which includes Hebrew, Arabic, and Geez, with many dead oriental tongues; pertaining to or derived from the Semites or their culture; Jewish: *n.* any one of the Semitic family of languages. (*Shem.*)
Semitism, *n.* *sem*-e- *or* *see*-me-tizm, Semitic character or characteristics; a tendency or policy favourable to the Jews.
semitone, *n.* *sem*-e-tone, an interval of half a tone [Mus.]. (Late L. *semitonium*.)
semitonic, *a.* *sem*-e-*ton*-ik, pertaining to or consisting of a semitone or semitones.
semitransparent, *a.* *sem*-e-trans-*pare*-rent, imperfectly transparent; translucent.
semi-tropical, *a.* intermediate between temperate and tropical.
semi-vocal, *a.* pertaining to a semi-vowel; imperfectly sounding.
semi-vowel, *n.* a half-vowel, as *w* and *y*; an articulation accompanied with an imperfect sound, as *l*.
semi-weekly, *a.* appearing or happening twice a week.
semmit, *n.* *sem*-it, a vest worn next the skin [Scots.].
Semnopithecus, *n.* *sem*-no-pe-*thee*-kus, the genus of monkeys comprising the langurs; (*l.c.*) any member of this genus [Zool.]. (Gr. *semnos*, holy *pithekos*, ape.)
semolina, *n.* *sem*-o-*lee*-na, the purified hard grains found in certain wheats too coarse to pass through the sieve in the bolting, used for puddings, macaroni, etc.
sempervirent, *a.* *sem*-per-*vy*-rent, always green or fresh. (L. *semper*, always, *virens*, being green.)
Sempervivum, *n.* *sem*-per-*vy*-vum, the genus of plants including the houseleek. (L., living for ever.)
sempiternal, *a.* *sem*-pe-*ter*-nal, everlasting; eternal. (L. *sempiternus*, eternal.)
sempiternity, *n.* *sem*-pe-*ter*-ne-te, duration without end.
semplice, *ad.* *sem*-ple-chay, with simplicity and chasteness, unaffected [Mus.]. (It.)
sempstress, *n.* *semp*-stres, a seamstress.
sen, *n.* sen, a Japanese bronze coin, the hundredth of a yen or about $\frac{1}{4}$d. (Japanese.)
senarmontite, *n.* sen-ar-*mon*-tite, native antimony trioxide [Min.]. (H. de *Senarmont*, Fr. mineralogist, *d.* 1862.)
senary, *a.* *see*-na-re *or* *sen*-a-re, belonging to or containing six: *a.* using six as a radix or base [Math.]. (L. *senarius*.)
senate, *n.* *sen*-at, an assembly or council of elders; an upper house of legislature; any legislative or deliberative body; the governing body of certain universities. (L. *senatus*.)
senator, *n.* *sen*-a-tor, a member of a senate; a counsellor. (L.)
senatorial, *a.* *sen*-a-*taw*-re-al, pertaining to a senate or senator; becoming a senator; entitled to elect a senator [U.S.A.].
senatorially, *ad.* in a senatorial manner.
senatorship, *n.* *sen*-a-tor-ship, the office or dignity of a senator.
senatus, *n.* se-*nay*-tus, the governing body of a University, esp. in Scotland.
***send,** *v.t.* send, to cause to be conveyed or transmitted; to cause to go; to dispatch; to throw, cast, or impel; to commission: *v.i.* to dispatch a messenger; to cause to come, or to do. **send to Coventry,** to exclude from society; to ostracize. **send down,** to rusticate [Univ.]. **send for,** to require by message to come or be brought. **send forth,** to put forth; to emit. **send packing,** to

get rid of, to dismiss unceremoniously. *p.* and *pp.* **sent.** (A.S. *sendan.*)
sendal, *n. sen*-dal, a kind of thin silk or linen used in the Middle Ages. (O.Fr.)
sender, *n. send*-er, one who or that which sends.
send-off, *n.* a friendly demonstration towards one starting on a journey.
Senecio, *n.* se-*nee*-she-oh, a large cosmopolitan genus of composite plants including the groundsel. (L.)
senega, *n. sen*-e-ga, the dried root of the snake-root *Polygala senega*, used as an expectorant and formerly in cases of snake-bite. (*Seneca*, a N. Amerind. tribe.)
Senegalese, *n.* sen-e-ga-*leez*, a native, or the natives, of Senegal, French W. Africa: *a.* pertaining to Senegal or its people.
senescence, *n.* se-*nes*-ence, the state of growing old. (L. *senescens*, growing old.)
senescent, *a.* se-*nes*-ent, growing old.
seneschal, *n. sen*-e-shal, a steward or officer in the house of a prince or dignitary who arranged matters of ceremony and feasting, and sometimes acted as judge. (O.Fr.)
sengierite, *n. son(g)*-zhe-er-rite, a copper-uranium vanadium mineral found, 1948, in the Belgian Congo. (*Sengier*, personal name.)
sengreen, *n. sen*-green, the houseleek. (A.S. *sin*, ever, *grene*, green.)
senile, *a. see*-nile, pertaining to old age; proceeding from age. (L. *senilus.*)
senilism, *n. see*-ne-lizm, premature senility [Med.].
senility, *n.* se-*nil*-e-te, old age; dotage.
senior, *a. seen*-yor, elder; older in rank, office, etc.: *n.* one older than another; one older in rank, etc.; an aged person. (L., older.)
seniority, *n.* see-ne-*o*-re-te, priority in age or in rank, office, etc.
senna, *n. sen*-na, the dried leaves of various species of *Cassia*, used as a cathartic. **senna-tea,** an infusion of this. (Ar.)
sennachie, *n. sen*-a-khe, a reciter or student of Gaelic traditional romance; a Gaelic bard. (Gael.)
sennet, *n. sen*-et, a trumpet-call. (*signet.*)
sennight, *n. sen*-ite, seven nights and days; a week.
sennit, *n. sen*-it, a flat braided cord of from three to nine strands; a flat plait of five or seven strands [Naut.]. (Perhaps *seven* and *knit.*)
senocular, *a.* se-*nok*-yew-lar, having six eyes. (L. *seni*, six each, *oculus*, an eye.)
señor, *n.* se-*nyor*, the Spanish form of address equivalent to "Mr."; a Spanish gentleman.
señora, *n.* se-*nyor*-rah, the Spanish form of address equivalent to "Mrs."; a Spanish lady.
senorita, *n.* sen-yo-*ree*-tah, the Spanish form of address equivalent to "Miss"; a young Spanish lady.
sensation, *n.* sen-*say*-shon, perception by the senses; an impression on the mind or the brain by means of the senses; a feeling; a state of excited interest or feeling, or that which produces it; a very small amount (as of liquor) [Slang]. (Fr.)
sensational, *a.* sen-*say*-shon-al, due to sensation or sense-perception; producing a sensation or an excited interest by highly coloured description, esp. of horrors and crimes.
sensationalism, *n.* sen-*say*-shon-al-izm, the derivation of all ideas from sense-impressions [Phil.]; the use of sensational events, or methods, in literature.
sensationalist, *n.* sen-*say*-shon-al-ist, an upholder of sensationalism; a sensational writer.
sensationalize, *v.t.* sen-*say*-shon-al-ize, to make sensational; to exaggerate sensationally.
sensationally, *ad.* sen-*say*-shon-a-le, in a sensational manner; in regard to sensation.
***sense,** *n.* sence, the faculty of perceiving what is external by means of impressions on an organ; sensation; perception by the senses; perception by the intellect; apprehension; discernment; sensibility; understanding; reason; conviction; moral perception; meaning: *v.t.* to perceive by the senses; to have awareness of; to comprehend [Coll.]. **the five senses,** sight, sound, touch, taste, smell. **the sixth sense,** an intuitive apperception. **out of one's senses,** crazy. **to make sense,** to be intelligible; to be in accord with probability. (Fr. *sens.*)
senseless, *a. sence*-less, wanting the faculty of perception; unfeeling; unreasonable; foolish; idiotic; contrary to reason; unconscious; wanting sensibility.
senselessly, *ad.* in a senseless manner.
senselessness, *n.* the quality of being senseless; stupidity; absurdity.
sensibility, *n. sen*-se-*bil*-e-te, susceptibility of impressions, of sensation, or of feeling; delicacy of feeling; actual feeling; capacity of being sensitive or easily affected. (Fr. *sensibilité.*)
sensible, *a. sen*-se-bl, perceptible by the senses or by the mind; having sense or perception; having moral perception; easily affected; intelligent; discerning; containing good sense or sound reason.
sensibleness, *n.* the quality of being sensible.
sensibly, *ad. sen*-sib-le, in a sensible manner.
sensigenous, *a.* sen-*sij*-e-nus, producing sensation [Biol.].
sensile, *a. sen*-sile, capable of perception.
sensitive, *a. sen*-se-tiv, having sense or feeling; easily or excessively affected by external circumstances; having feelings easily affected; readily affected by certain agents [Chem. and Phot.]; pertaining to the senses or to sensation; that affects the senses. **sensitive paper,** sensitized paper [Phot.]. **sensitive plant,** a species of *Mimosa*, so called from the shrinking of its leaves on being touched. (Fr. *sensitif.*)
sensitively, *ad.* in a sensitive manner.
sensitiveness, *n.* the state of being sensitive.
sensitivity, *n. sen*-se-*tiv*-e-te, sensitiveness; capacity of an organ of sense to respond to stimulation.
sensitization, *n. sen*-se-ty-*zay*-shon, the act or process of sensitizing.
sensitize, *v.t. sen*-se-tize, to render sensitive to light [Phot.], or (of persons) to the action of a serum, drug, etc. [Med.].
sensitizer, *n. sen*-se-ty-zer, one who or that which sensitizes; a non-catalyst that facilitates catalytic reaction [Chem.]; a sensitizing antibody [Med.].
sensitometer, *n. sen*-se-*tom*-e-ter, an apparatus for testing the sensitiveness of photographic films. (*sensitive*, and Gr. *metron*, measure.)
sensorial, *a.* sen-*saw*-re-al, pertaining to the sensorium.
sensorium, *n.* sen-*saw*-re-um, the brain, or its grey matter; the nervous system as susceptible of sensations. (Late L.)
sensory, *a. sen*-so-re, sensorial; pertaining to sensation: *n.* the sensorium.
sensual, *a. sen*-sew-al, pertaining to the senses; consisting in or depending on sense; affecting or derived from the senses; materialistic; not spiritual; devoted to the gratification of sense; affected by sensuality; lewd; pertaining to sensationalism [Phil.]. (Late L. *sensualis.*)
sensualism, *n. sen*-sew-a-lizm, subjection to sensual feelings or passions; the derivation of the intellect from sense; sensationalism [Phil.].
sensualist, *n. sen*-sew-a-list, one given to the indulgence of appetite; a voluptuary; an upholder of the doctrine of sensualism.
sensualistic, *a. sen*-sew-a-*lis*-tik, pertaining to sensualism.
sensuality, *n. sen*-sew-*al*-e-te, state or quality of being sensual; devoted to the gratification of the appetites. (Fr. *sensualité.*)
sensualize, *v.t. sen*-sew-a-lize, to make sensual; to debase by carnal gratifications.
sensually, *ad. sen*-sew-a-le, in a sensual manner.
sensualness, *n.* the state of being sensual.
sensuism, *n. sen*-sew-izm, sensationalism [Phil.].
sensuous, *a. sen*-sew-us, pertaining to or appealing to the senses; affected and moved by the senses; voluptuous. (L. *sensus.*)
sensuously, *ad. sen*-sew-us-le, in a sensuous manner.
sensuousness, *n.* the quality of being sensuous.
sent, sent, *p.* and *pp.* of *send.*
sentence, *n. sen*-tence, an ordered series of words containing complete sense [Gram.]; an opinion; judgment pronounced; judicial decision; a maxim or short saying: *v.t.* to pronounce judgment on; to doom. (L. *sententia.*)
sentential, *a.* sen-*ten*-shal, sententious.
sententiary, *n.* sen-*ten*-she-a-re, a writer of aphorisms.
sententious, *a.* sen-*ten*-shus, comprised in a sentence; abounding with sentences, axioms, and maxims; terse and pithy in expression; pompously formal. (Fr. *sentencieux.*)
sententiously, *ad.* in a sententious manner.

sententiousness, *n.* the quality of being sententious.
sentience, *n.* *sen*-she-ence, the state or quality of being sentient; consciousness.
sentiency, *n.* *sen*-she-en-se, sentience.
sentient, *a.* *sen*-she-ent, having the faculty of perception; having sensation: *n.* a sentient being. (L. *sentiens.*)
sentiently, *ad.* in a sentient manner.
sentiment, *n.* *sen*-te-ment, thought prompted by emotion; sensibility; feeling; prevailing or pervading feeling; the sense contained in words; an opinion; a maxim; a toast. (Fr.)
sentimental, *a.* *sen*-te-*men*-tal, abounding with sentiment or reflections; swayed by sentiment, esp. to excess; affecting sensibility.
sentimentalism, *n.* *sen*-te-*men*-ta-lizm, quality or state of being sentimental; sentimentality.
sentimentalist, *n.* *sen*-te-*men*-ta-list, one who affects sentiment, fine feeling, or unusual sensibility.
sentimentality, *n.* *sen*-te-men-*tal*-e-te, affectation of fine feeling or acute sensibility.
sentimentalize, *v.i.* *sen*-te-*men*-ta-lize, to affect sensibility: *v.t.* to render sentimental; to infuse with sentiment.
sentimentally, *ad.* in a sentimental manner.
sentinel, *n.* *sen*-te-nel, a soldier on guard: *v.t.* to stand guard over; to furnish with or post as a sentinel. (Fr. *sentinelle.*)
sentry, *n.* *sen*-tre, a sentinel; a watch; guard; duty of a sentinel. (O.Fr. *sentrie.*)
sentry-box, *n.* a hut or temporary shelter for a sentry at his post.
sentry-go, *n.* a turn of duty of a sentry.
senza, *prep.* *sen*-za, without; as *senza rigore,* not in strict time [Mus.]. (It.)
sepal, *n.* *sep*-al *or see*-pal, a leaf of the calyx, the outer whorl of the perianth [Bot.]. (Fr. *sépale.*)
sepaline, *a.* *sep*-a-line, relating to a sepal.
sepalody, *n.* se-*pal*-o-de, the reversion of petals to sepals.
sepaloid, *a.* *sep*-a-loyd, like a sepal.
separability, *n.* *sep*-a-ra-*bil*-e-te, separableness.
separable, *a.* *sep*-a-ra-bl, that can be separated.
separableness, *n.* quality of being separable.
separably, *ad.* in a separable manner.
★**separate,** *a.* *sep*-a-rat, divided from the rest; disconnected; distinct: *v.t.* *sep*-a-rate, to part; to set apart from a number for a particular service; to disunite or disconnect: *v.i.* to part; to be disunited; to withdraw from each other. **separate estate,** any estate in sole ownership, esp. the property of a married woman held independently of her husband [Law]. (L. *separatus.*)
separately, *ad.* *sep*-a-rat-le, in a separate manner.
separateness, *n.* the quality of being separate.
separation, *n.* *sep*-a-*ray*-shon, the act of separating; disjunction; the state of being separate; disunion; partial divorce without right of remarriage. (O.Fr.)
separatism, *n.* *sep*-a-ra-tizm, secession, esp. from a political party or church, etc.; the principles of the separatists.
separatist, *n.* *sep*-a-ra-tist, one who separates himself from others, esp. one who withdraws from a church; an advocate of separation or decentralization: *a.* pertaining to separatism; characteristic of separatists.
separative, *a.* *sep*-a-ra-tiv, indicating or tending to cause separation.
separator, *n.* *sep*-a-ray-tor, one who or that which divides or disjoins; a machine for separating cream from milk for making butter. (Late L.)
separatory, *a.* *sep*-a-ra-to-re, used in, or capable of, separating: *n.* an appliance for separating liquors.
separatrix, *n.* *sep*-a-ra-triks, any mark that separates, as the boundary line of the shadow on an object in the light, or the decimal point.
sepawn, *n.* se-*pawn,* supawn.
Sephardim, *n.pl.* se-*far*-dim, the Spanish and Portuguese branch of the Jews, as distinguished from the Ashkenazim, or Jews of northern Europe. (Heb.)
sepia, *n.* *see*-pe-a, a cuttle-fish, *Sepia officinalis*; a brown pigment prepared from the inky secretion of this. (Gr.)
sepiment, *n.* *sep*-e-ment, a dissepiment.
sepoy, *n.* *see*-poy, a native infantrymen of the Indian army. (Hindu, *sipahi,* a soldier.)
seps, *n.* seps, a sub-tropical serpent-like lizard allied to the skink. (L.)
sepsin, *n.* *sep*-sin, a toxic ptomaine present in blood and yeast.
sepsis, *n.* *sep*-sis, blood-poisoning caused by pathogenic bacteria. (Gr., decaying matter.)
sept, *n.* sept, a clan in ancient Ireland. (*sect.*)
septa, *n.pl.* *sep*-ta plural of *septum.*
septal, *a.* *sep*-tal, pertaining to a septum or a sept.
septan, *a.* *sep*-tan, recurring every seventh day (esp. of intermittent fevers).
septangle, *n.* *sep*-tang-gl, a heptagon. (L. *septem,* seven, and *angular.*)
septangular, *a.* sep-*tang*-gew-lar, heptangular.
septaria, *n.pl.* sep-*tare*-re-a, concretionary masses of argillaceous limestone or clay-ironstone [Geol.]. (L., partitions.)
septate, *a.* *sep*-tat, divided into compartments [Bot.]. (L. *septatus,* as *septum.*)
September, *n.* sep-*tem*-ber, the ninth calendar month (the seventh of the Julian year). (L.)
Septembrist, *n.* sep-*tem*-brist, one of the agents of the massacre in Paris, Sept. 1792.
septempartite, *a.* *sep*-tem-*par*-tite, divided into seven parts. (L. *septem,* seven, *pars,* a part.)
septemvir, *n.* sep-*tem*-vir, one of seven men forming a government. (L.)
septemvirate, *n.* sep-*tem*-ver-rat, the office of, or government by septemvirs; a group of seven men.
septenary, *a.* *sep*-ten-a-re, consisting of or relating to seven; lasting seven years: *n.* a set of seven, esp. years. (L. *septenarius.*)
septenate, *a.* *sep*-ten-at, growing in sevens [Bot.].
septennate, *n.* sep-*ten*-at, a period of seven years. (L. *septennium.*)
septennial, *a.* sep-*ten*-e-al, lasting seven years; occurring every seven years. (L. *septem,* and *annus,* a year.)
septennially, *ad.* once in seven years.
septennium, *n.* sep-*ten*-e-um, a septennate. (L.)
Septentrion, *n.* sep-*ten*-tre-on, the Great Bear [Astron.]; the northern regions. (L. *septentrio,* the north.)
septentrional, *a.* sep-*ten*-tre-o-nal, northern.
septet, septette, *n.* sep-*tet,* a party of seven; a musical composition for seven performers. (L. *septem,* seven.)
septfoil, *n.* *sept*-foyl, *Potentilla tormentilla*; a figure composed of seven equal segments of a circle, used as a symbol of the seven sacraments; the plant tormentil. (Fr. *sept,* seven, *feuille,* leaf.)
septic, *a.* *sep*-tik, producing sepsis; capable of causing putrefaction; putrefying: *n.* a putrefactive substance. **septic tank,** a receptacle in which the solid matter of sewage is retained until disintegrated by bacteria. (Gr. *septos,* putrid.)
septicæmia, *n.* *sep*-te-*see*-me-a, blood-poisoning; sepsis. (Gr. *septos,* and *haima,* blood.)
septicæmic, *a.* *sep*-te-*see*-mik, characteristic of, affected by, or producing septicæmia.
septicidal, *a.* *sep*-te-*sy*-dal, splitting through the partitions [Bot.]. (L. *septum,* and *cædo,* cut.)
septicity, *n.* sep-*tis*-e-te, quality or state of being septic; tendency to promote putrefaction.
septifarious, *a.* *sep*-te-*fare*-re-us, turned seven different ways [Bot.]. (L.)
septiferous, *a.* sep-*tif*-er-rus, bearing septa. (L.)
septiform, *a.* *sep*-te-form, of the nature of a septum; having seven parts. (L. *septum,* and *forma,* shape.)
septilateral, *a.* *sep*-te-*lat*-er-ral, having seven sides. (L. *septem,* and *latus,* a side.)
septillion, *n.* sep-*til*-yon, the seventh power of a million, represented by 1 followed by 42 noughts (English numeration).
septimole, *n.* *sep*-te-mole, a group of seven notes playable in the time of four or six [Mus.].
septinsular, *a.* sep-*tin*-sew-lar, consisting of seven isles (esp. of the Ionian Islands).
septonasal, *a.* *sep*-to-*nay*-zal, pertaining to the septum separating the nostrils [Anat.].
septuagenarian, *n.* *sep*-tew-a-je-*nare*-re-an, a person seventy, or from seventy to seventy-nine, years of age.
septuagenary, *a.* *sep*-tew-*aj*-e-na-re, consisting of seventy or seventy years. (L. *septuagenarius.*)
Septuagesima, *n.* *sep*-tew-a-*jes*-e-ma, the third Sunday before Lent, so called as roundly seventy days before Easter. (L.)
Septuagint, *n.* *sep*-tew-a-jint, a Greek version of the Old Testament, executed at Alexandria by, it is said, seventy translators, about 280-270 B.C. (L. *septuaginta,* seventy.)

septum, *n.* *sep*-tum (*pl.* **septa**), a partition separating the cells of fruit [Bot.], two cavities [Anat.], etc.; a partition in the shell of the nautilus and its allies [Zool.]. (L., an enclosure.)
septuple, *a.* *sep*-tew-pl, seven-fold.
sepulchral, *a.* se-*pul*-kral, pertaining to or suggestive of burial or funeral monuments; funereal; hollow or solemn in sound. (L. *sepulcralis.*)
sepulchre, *n.* *sep*-ul-ker, a grave; a tomb; a burial vault: *v.t.* to entomb. (L. *sepulcrum.*)
sepulture, *n.* *sep*-ul-tewr, burial; interment. (L.)
sequacious, *a.* se-*kway*-shus, inclined to be led; pliant; following; attendant; consistent.
sequaciousness, *n.* se-*kway*-shus-ness, the condition of being sequacious.
sequacity, *n.* se-*kwas*-e-te, a following, or disposition to follow; unresisting compliance. (L. *sequax.*)
sequel, *n.* *see*-kwel, that which follows; a succeeding part; a consequence. (Fr. *séquelle.*)
sequela, *n.* see-*kwee*-la (*pl.* **sequelæ**), any morbid condition following a disease; a supervening disease; a consequence. (L.)
sequence, *n.* *see*-kwence, a following, or that which follows; order of succession; a series; a run of consecutive cards in the same suit; a regular alternate succession of similar chords [Mus.]. (L.) *sequens,* following.)
sequent, *a.* *see*-kwent, following; succeeding.
sequential, *a.* se-*kwen*-shal, in succession.
sequentiality, *n.* se-*kwen*-she-*al*-e-te, the quality of being sequential.
sequentially, *ad.* se-*kwen*-shal-le, in succession.
sequester, *v.t.* se-*kwes*-ter, to put aside; to separate from the owner for a time; to seize possession of property as security for some claim; to withdraw or seclude: *v.i.* to decline, as a widow, any concern with the estate of a deceased husband [Law]. (L. *sequester,* a trustee.)
sequestered, *a.* se-*kwes*-terd, secluded; retired.
sequestrate, *v.t.* and *i.* see-*kwes*-trate, to sequester [Law].
sequestration, *n.* see-kwes-*tray*-shon, the act of sequestering, esp. the seizing of property by the state or by creditors; retirement; seclusion; isolation [Med.].
sequestrator, *n.* *see*-kwes-tray-tor, one who sequesters property; one to whose keeping sequestered property is committed.
sequin, *n.* *see*-kwin, a former Italian gold coin worth about 9s.; a small sparkling spangle. (It. *zecchino,* from *zecca,* the Venetian Mint.)
Sequoia, *n.* see-*kwoy*-a, the genus of coniferous trees, also known as *Wellingtonia,* including the redwood *S. sempervirens,* and the mammoth-tree of California, *S. gigantea.* (Cherokee Indian name.)
sérac, *n.* se-*rak,* a towering mass of ice in a glacier. (Fr., from a cheese of that shape made in Switzerland.)
serafile, *n.* *se*-ra-file, a serrefile.
seraglio, *n.* se-*rah*-le-oh, palace of the former sultans at Constantinople; a harem. (It., an enclosure.)
serai, *n.* se-*rah*-e, an Oriental caravansary or resthouse; a seraglio. (Per., a court.)
seralbumen, *n.* *seer*-al-*bew*-men, albumen contained in the serum of the blood. (*serum* and *albumen.*)
serang, *n.* se-*rang,* a Lascar boatswain. (Per.)
serape, *n.* se-*rah*-pay, a shawl or plaid, usually brightly coloured, worn by Spanish-Americans. (Mex.-Sp.)
seraph, *n.* *se*-raf (*pl.* **seraphs** or **seraphim**), a six-winged angel mentioned in Isaiah vi; a celestial being of highest rank. (Heb.)
seraphic, *a.* se-*raf*-ik, pertaining to or like a seraph; pure; angelic; sublime.
seraphically, *ad.* in a seraphic manner.
seraphim, *n.* *se*-ra-fim: *pl.* of *seraph.* (Heb.)
seraphine, *n.* *se*-ra-feen, an early form of harmonium, patented 1839. (*seraph.*)
seraskier, *n.* se-ras-*keer,* former title of the Turkish commander-in-chief and war minister. (Turk.)
Serb, *n.* serb, a native of Serbia, now part of Yugoslavia: *a.* Serbian.
Serbian, *a.* *ser*-be-an, pertaining to Serbia, its language, or the Serbs: *n.* a Serb, or the Serb language.
Serbocroatian, *n* ser-boh-kroh-*ay*-shan, the language of Yugoslavia.
Serbonian, *a.* ser-*boh*-ne-an, presenting a treacherous surface in which one sinks and is lost; hence, well-nigh inextricable (of difficulties, etc.). (Lake Serbonis, an ancient Egyptian quagmire in which whole armies were fabled to have been engulfed.)
sere, *a.* seer, dry; withered; sear.
serein, *n.* se-*rain,* fine rain from a cloudless sky shortly after sunset, esp. in the tropics. (Fr.)
serenade, *n.* se-re-*nade,* music performed in the open-air, esp. by a lover under his mistress's window, or in honour of someone; a piece of soft music: *v.t.* to entertain thus. (Fr. *sérénade.*)
serenader, *n.* se-re-*nay*-der, one who serenades.
serenata, *n.* se-re-*nah*-ta, a piece of music on an amorous or pastoral subject. (It.)
serendipity, *n.* se-ren-*dip*-e-te, the gift for finding valuable objects of art, etc., by chance. (*Serendib,* old name for Ceylon.)
serene, *a.* se-*reen,* clear and calm; placid; quiet; calm; unruffled; a form of address formerly applied to certain German princes: *n.* the clear expanse of cloudless sky [Poet.]. (L. *serenus,* clear.)
serenely, *ad.* calmly.
sereneness, *n.* se-*reen*-ness, serenity.
serenity, *n.* se-*ren*-e-te, state of being serene; calmness; quietness; stillness; calmness of mind; evenness of temper. (Fr. *sérénité.*)
serf, *n.* serf, a feudal labourer, one either the property of his master or attached to the soil and transferable with it; a bondsman. (Fr.)
serfage, *n.* *serf*-aj, serfdom; serfs collectively.
serfdom, *n.* *serf*-dom, the condition of a serf.
serfhood, *n.* *serf*-hood, serfs collectively; serfdom.
serge, *n.* serj, a kind of twilled woollen cloth dyed in the piece. **silk serge,** a twilled silk fabric. (Fr., from L. *serica,* silk stuff.)
sergeancy, *n.* *sar*-jen-se, the office or commission of a serjeant.
sergeant, *n.* *sar*-jent, a non-commissioned officer in the army, in rank next above a corporal; a grade in the police next above a constable. **sergeant-at-arms, -at-law,** see **serjeant-. sergeant-major,** a senior sergeant (**company s.-m.** is the highest non-commissioned officer in a company, and a **regimental s.-m.,** a warrant officer assisting the adjutant.) (Fr. *sergent.*)
sergeant-fish, *n.* name applied to various marine fish having markings resembling a sergeant's stripes.
sergeantship, *n.* the office of a sergeant.
sergette, *n.* ser-*jet,* a thin kind of serge.
serial, *a.* *seer*-re-al, pertaining to, consisting of, or of the nature of a series: *n.* a periodical; a literary work issued in parts periodically or appearing in instalments in successive issues of a periodical.
serialize, *v.t.* *seer*-re-a-lize, to convert into or publish in serial form.
serially, *ad.* in a series; in serial form.
seriate, *a.* *seer*-re-at, arranged in a series or sequence. (Late L. *seriatus.*)
seriately, *ad.* in a regular series.
seriatim, *ad.* *seer*-re-*ay*-tim, in regular order; point by point. (L.)
seric, *a.* *se*-rik, silken. (Gr. *serikos,* silk.)
sericeous, *a.* se-*rish*-e-us, pertaining to or consisting of silk; silky.
sericite, *n.* *se*-re-site, a talc-like variety of muscovite. (Gr. *sērikos,* silk.)
sericulture, *n.* *se*-re-*kul*-tewr, the breeding of silkworms and production of raw silk.
seriema, *n.* se-re-*ee*-ma, a large S. American bird, *Cariama cristata,* allied to the bustards; also, the crested screamer. (Brazilian.)
series, *n.* *seer*-re-eez *or* *seer*-reez, a connected succession of things having certain properties in common; succession; sequence; order; progression; a number of terms in succession increasing or diminishing in a certain manner. **arithmetical series,** a series changing by addition or subtraction. **geometrical series,** a series changing by multiplication or division [Math.]. **in series,** so arranged that the current flows through them successively (of parts or instruments) [Elect.]. **series motor,** a motor in which armature and field winding are in series [Elect.]. (L. from *sero,* join.)
serif, *n.* *se*-rif, the fine short line at the end of stems and arms of letters [Print.].
serin, *n.* *se*-rin, a small finch, *Serinus hortulanus,* allied to the canary. (Fr.)
serinette, *n.* se-re-*net,* a bird-organ or similar instrument for training song-birds.
seringa, *n.* a Brazilian tree of the species *Hevea,* yielding rubber; the syringa. (Port.)

serio-comic, *a.* *seer*-re-o-*kom*-ik, having a mixture of seriousness and comicality.
★**serious,** *a.* *seer*-re-us, grave in manner or disposition; in earnest; of weight or importance; attended with danger; gravely attentive to religious concerns. (L. *serius*, grave.)
seriously, *ad.* in a serious manner.
seriousness, *n.* quality or state or being serious; gravity of manner, etc.
Serjeant-at-arms, *n.* *sar*-jent-at-*armz*, an officer to preserve order in a legislative assembly.
serjeant-at-law, *n.* *sar*-jent-at-*law*, a former member of the highest order of barristers, having the privilege of exclusive audience in the Court of Common Pleas.
serjeanty, *n.* *sar*-jen-te, a form of feudal tenure. **grand serjeanty,** a particular kind of knight-service, due to the king only. **petit serjeanty,** a tenure by which the tenant rendered to the king annually some small implement of war, as a bow, lance, etc.
sermon, *n.* *ser*-mon, a public religious discourse, usually based on a text. (Fr.)
sermonette, *n.* ser-mo-*net*, a short sermon.
sermonic, *a.* ser-*mon*-ik, of the nature of a sermon; characteristic of a sermonizer.
sermonize, *v.i.* *ser*-mon-ize, to deliver a sermon; to compose sermons: *v.t.* to lecture or admonish.
sermonizer, *n.* *ser*-mon-ize-er, one who sermonizes.
serology, *n.* se-*rol*-o-je, the science treating of the use, preparation, etc., of serum; immunology [Path.].
seroon, *n.* se-*roon*, a bale or package (of varying capacity) for dried fruit, drugs, etc. (Sp. *ceron*, crate.)
seropurulent, *a.* *se*-ro-*pew*-roo-lent, composed of serum and pus [Med.].
serosity, *n.* se-*ros*-e-te, the state of being serous; serum; synovial fluid.
serotherapeutics, *n.* *se*-ro-the-ra-*pew*-tiks, serum therapy, the treatment of disease by the use of blood-serum containing antitoxins [Med.].
serotine, *n.* *se*-ro-teen, a species of European bat, *Vesperugo serotinus*.
serotinous, *a.* se-*rot*-e-nus, appearing late in the season [Bot.]. (L. *serotinus*, from *serus*, late.)
serous, *a.* *seer*-rus, pertaining to or resembling serum; thin; watery. (L. *serum*, fluid.)
serow, *n.* se-*roh*, a species of Asiatic goat-antelope, of the genus *Nemorhædus*. (Tib.)
serpent, *n.* *ser*-pent, a reptile with an elongated scaly body, which moves by means of its ribs and scales; a snake; a subtle or malicious person [Fig.]; an obsolete bass wind instrument of serpentine form made of wood and leather [Mus.]; (*cap.*) a constellation in the northern hemisphere [Astron.]. **serpent grass,** the Alpine bistort. (L. *serpens*, creeping.)
serpentaria, *n.* ser-pen-*tare*-re-a, the dried rhizome of certain snake-roots of the genus *Aristolochia*, used as a tonic and diaphoretic [Pharm.].
serpent-eater, *n.* the secretary-bird.
serpentiform, *a.* ser-*pen*-te-form, having the form of a serpent; serpentine.
serpentine, *a.* *ser*-pen-tine, pertaining to or resembling a serpent; winding like a moving serpent; spiral; having the qualities of a serpent: *n.* a mottled rock capable of a high polish consisting chiefly of hydrated silicate of magnesium: *v.i.* to wind like a serpent; to meander. **serpentine verse,** a verse which begins and ends with the same word. (Fr. *serpentin*.)
serpentinely, *ad.* in a serpentine manner.
serpentry, *n.* *ser*-pen-tre, serpents collectively; a natural or artificial breeding-place of serpents.
serpiginous, *a.* ser-*pij*-e-nus, affected with serpigo; creeping from one part to another. [Med.].
serpigo, *n.* ser-*py*-go, a dry eruption on the skin; ringworm. (L.)
serpolet, *n.* *ser*-po-let, wild thyme. (Fr.)
Serpula, *n.* *ser*-pew-la, a genus of marine worms inhabiting a calcareous tube secreted by themselves and attached to rocks and shells. (L., a tiny serpent.)
serpulite, *n.* *ser*-pew-lite, the fossil tube of a serpula.
serra, *n.* *se*-ra (*pl.* **serræ**), dentation resembling that of saw-teeth; one of such serrations [Bot. and Zool.]; a saw-like organ [Zoo].]; a saw-fish. (L., saw.)
serradilla, *n.* se-ra-*dil*-a, serratella.
serrate, *a.* *se*-rat, notched on the edge like a saw. (L. *serratus*, from *serra*, a saw.)
serratella, *n.* se-ra-*tel*-a, a species of bird's-foot clover, *Ornithopus sativus*, grown for fodder.
serration, *n.* se-*ray*-shon, a formation in the shape of the toothed edge of a saw.
serratirostral, *a.* se-*ray*-te-*ros*-tral, saw-billed.
serrature, *n.* *se*-ra-tewr, a notching in the edge like a saw. (Late L. *serratum*, a cutting with a saw.)
serrefile, *n.* *se*-re-file, a supernumerary officer N.C.O., or man acting as scout, etc., at the rear of a body of troops; a line of these [Mil.]. (Fr. *serre*, to close up the ranks, *file*, file.)
serricorn, *a.* *se*-re-kawrn, having serrated antennæ [Entom.]: *n.* a beetle thus furnished. (L. *serra*, saw *cornu*, a horn.)
serried, *a.* *se*-rid, close together in ranks; crowded compacted. (Fr. *serrer*, press close.)
serriform, *a.* *se*-re-form, saw-shaped; serrated.
serrulate, *a.* *se*-rew-lat, finely serrate; having minute teeth or notches. (L. *serrula*, a little saw.
serrulation, *n.* se-rew-*lay*-shon, a minute serration the state of being serrulate.
Sertularia, *n.pl.* *ser*-tew-*lare*-re-a, a genus of delicately branching hydrozoans. (L. *sertum*, a wreath.
serula, *n.* se-rew-la, a local name of the red-breasted merganser. (It.)
serum, *n.* *seer*-rum, the thin transparent part of the blood; lymph, esp. when treated and used for antitoxic purposes; the thin part of milk; whey (L.)
serval, *n.* *ser*-val, the African spotted wild-cat *Felis serval*. (Port. *cerval*, from L. *cervus*, stag.)
★**servant,** *n.* *ser*-vant, one who is in the service of or attendant on another; one in domestic service one in a state of subjection; a devoted adherent; one giving service; a tool. **civil servant,** *see* **civil.** (Fr.)
servant-girl, *n.* a maidservant; a serving-maid.
serve, *v.t.* serv, to wait on; to work for; to perform official duties to; to submit to; to be sufficient for; to requite; to manage; to assist; to treat to cover, or copulate with (of male animals) to bind with small yarn [Naut.]; to deliver (a summons, etc.): *v.i.* to be a servant; to be employed in labour or other business for another; to be in subjection; to perform domestic offices or public duties; to be in one of the services (Navy, Army, etc.); to suffice; to suit; to conduce; to officiate; to lead off (in tennis, etc.) by striking a ball; to levy an attachment, execution, etc. [Law]: *n.* an act or turn of serving [Tennis, etc.]. **serve an office,** to discharge a public duty. **serve a warrant,** go seize the person against whom it is issued. **serve one right,** to befall as one deserves. **serve one's time,** to fulfil a period of apprenticeship. **serve one's turn,** to avail for one's immediate purpose. **serve one out,** to retaliate upon one. **serve out,** to distribute in portions. **serve time,** to undergo imprisonment. **serve up,** to prepare and present in a dish. (Fr. *servir*.)
server, *n.* *ser*-ver, one who serves; an assistant to a priest officiating at the altar; a salver; a utensil for serving out food at table.
Servian, *a.* and *n.* *ser*-ve-an, Serbian.
service, *n.* *ser*-vis, the act of serving; performance of duty; labour for another; the business of or employment as a servant; the state of being a servant; a branch of public employment (as naval, military, civil, diplomatic, etc.), also, the persons employed in any of these; business; use; useful office; public worship, or office of devotion; a musical composition for church use; order of dishes at table; set of table-ware; act or manner of serving the ball, or a turn at serving [Tennis, etc.]; legal delivery or publication of a writ; the supply of necessities; means of supply (esp. of a public utility, as gas, railway, posts, etc.); maintenance or assistance from an original supplier: *a.* pertaining or belonging to an armed or the civil service, or to domestic service: *v.t.* to be of service to; to furnish maintenance, repairs, etc., in respect of goods supplied. **at your service,** ready to serve your pleasure. **civil, secret service,** *see* these words. **see service,** to come into actual contact with the enemy. **service dress,** ordinary uniform [Mil.]. **take service with,** to enter the service of. (Fr.)

serviceable, *a.* *ser*-vis-a-bl, able or ready for service; beneficial; advantageous; useful.
serviceableness, *n.* quality of being serviceable; usefulness in promoting good of any kind.
serviceably, *ad.* in a serviceable manner.
service-book, *n.* a prayer-book for public worship.
service-flat, *n.* a flat in which certain domestic service is provided as part of the return for rent paid.
service-line, *n.* a line across a tennis court, 21 ft. from the net, between which and the net a ball served must land.
service-pipe, *n.* a pipe from a main into a house.
service-station, *n.* a depot where purchasers of cars, wireless apparatus, etc., may obtain advice, assistance, accessories, and spare parts, etc.
service-tree, *n.* any of several trees of the genus *Sorbus*, some of which have edible fruit. (A.S. *syrf-trēow.*)
serviette, *n.* ser-ve-*et*, a table-napkin. (Fr.)
servile, *a.* *ser*-vile, such as beseems a slave; slavish; meanly submissive; dependent; cringing; fawning; not belonging to the original root [Gram.]; subserving sound but not sounded [Gram.]. (Fr.)
servilely, *ad.* in a servile manner.
servility, *n.* ser-*vil*-e-te, quality of being servile; slavish deference; mean obsequiousness. (Fr. *servilité.*)
serving-maid, *n.* a female servant; a menial.
serving-man, *n.* a male servant; a menial.
servitor, *n.* *ser*-ve-tor, a servant; an attendant; an adherent; formerly, an Oxford undergraduate, partly supported by college funds, who, like the Cambridge sizar, had certain servile duties to perform. (Fr. *serviteur.*)
servitorship, *n.* *ser*-ve-tor-ship, the office or status of a servitor.
servitude, *n.* *ser*-ve-tewd, the condition of a slave; bondage; enforced labour; a state of slavish dependence. **penal servitude,** former judicial sentence (1853–1948) of imprisonment with hard labour for three years or over. (L. *servitudo.*)
servo-motor, *n.* *ser*-vo-*moh*-tor, an auxiliary motor for various purposes in cars, marine engines, etc.
sesame, *n.* *ses*-a-me, an annual herbaceous plant with oily seeds, *Sesamum indicum*, the source of gingili oil or benne. **open sesame!** a ready means of resolving a difficulty (alluding to the formula used as a key by Ali Baba in the Arabian Nights). (Gr. *sesamon.*)
sesamoid, *a.* *ses*-a-moyd, like sesame-seeds, esp. of certain applied small bones present in tendons [Anat.]: *n.* a sesamoid bone. (Gr. *sesamon*, and *eidos*, like.)
sesban, *n.* *ses*-ban, a tropical leguminous marsh plant, *Sesbania aculeata*, with floating roots from the base of the stem. (Ar. *saisaban.*)
Seseli, *n.* *ses*-e-le, a genus of plants including the meadow saxifrage, *Seseli libanotis*, and cicely. (L. *seselis.*)
sesqui-, *ses*-kwe, prefix signifying a whole and a half, used esp. of a compound in which two atoms of one element are combined with three of another [Chem.]. (L.)
sesquialtera, *n.* *ses*-kew-*al*-te-ra, an interval with the ratio 3 to 2 [Mus.]; a compound stop on the organ. (L. *sesqui*, and *alter*, another.)
sesquialteral, *a.* *ses*-kwe-*al*-te-ral, designating a ratio where one quantity or number contains another once and half as much more [Math.].
sesquiduplicate, *a.* *ses*-kwe-*dew*-ple-kate, designating the ratio of two and a half to one.
sesquipedalian, *a.* *ses*-kwe-pe-*day*-le-an, consisting of a foot and a half; containing many syllables (of words); given to using such words. (L. *sesquipedalis.*)
sesquiplicate, *a.* ses-*kwip*-le-kat, designating the ratio of a cube to a square. (L. *sesqui*, and *plico*, fold.)
sesquitertian, *a.* *ses*-kwe-*ter*-she-an, designating the ratio of 4 to 3. (L. *sesqui*, and *tertius*, third.)
sesquitone, *n.* *ses*-kwe-tone, an interval of three semitones, a minor third [Mus.].
sess, *n.* sess, cess.
sessile, *a.* *ses*-ile, attached directly; not having a foot-stalk [Bot. and Zool.]. (L. *sessilis.*)
session, *n.* *sesh*-on, the act of sitting; a sitting or assembly of a court, council, legislative body, etc.; the time or term of a sitting; the time between the first meeting and the prorogation of Parliament. **Court of Session,** *see* **court. Kirk Session,** *see* **kirk. Petty Sessions,** court for the trial of minor offences. **Quarter Sessions,** a court held in counties and boroughs for the trial of minor felonies and misdemeanours and for general administrative purposes. (Fr.)
sessional, *a.* *sesh*-on-al, pertaining to a session.
sesterce, *n.* *ses*-terse, an ancient Roman coin, worth about 2*d.*
sestertium, *n.* ses-*ter*-she-um (*pl.* **sestertia**), ancient Roman money of account, equal to 1,000 sesterces. (L. *sestertius.*)
sestet, *n.* ses-*tet*, a musical composition for six performers [Mus.]. (It.)
sestina, *n.* ses-*tee*-na, a Provençal verse-form of six six-lined stanzas with a final triplet, the last word of each line being repeated as a last line but in different order. (It.)
set, *v.t.* set, to place in any situation; to locate; to put; to fix; to regulate; to adapt; to arrange; to plant; to stud; to point; to replace; to attach or join; to settle; to appoint; to bring to a fine edge; to spread (sail) [Naut.]; to apply (oneself) to; to fit (music) to words; to compose (type) [Print.]: *v.i.* to pass below the horizon; to become fixed; to congeal or concrete; to plant; to flow (of tides, etc.); to point at game (as a setter, etc.); to face one's partner [Dancing]. **set about,** to begin, or apply to; to fall on. **set against,** to oppose. **set agoing,** to cause to begin to move. set apart, to separate from the rest. **set aside,** to omit for the present; to reject. **set at ease,** to tranquillize. **set at nought,** to undervalue. set before, to exhibit; to propose. **set by,** to set apart. **set by the compass,** to observe the bearing or situation of by the compass [Naut.]. **set by the ears,** *see* **ear. set down,** to place upon the ground; to register. **set the eyes on,** *see* **eye. set forth,** to manifest; to exhibit. **set forward,** to advance; to begin to march. **set free,** to release from confinement. **set in,** to begin; to move shoreward (of the tide). **set in order,** to reduce to method. **set off,** to adorn; to eulogize. **set on** or **upon,** to assault; to incite. **set on foot,** *see* **foot. set on fire,** *see* **fire. set the Thames on fire,** to do something wonderful. **set over,** to appoint or constitute. **set out,** to assign; to adorn; to state at large; to begin a journey. **set right,** to put in order. **set sail,** *see* **sail. set the hand to,** *see* **hand. set the teeth on edge,** *see* **edge. set to,** to apply oneself to. **set up,** to erect; to institute; to begin business; to put into type. **set upon,** to incite. (A.S. *settan.*)
set, *a.* set, regular; formal; immovable; established; fixed in opinion; determined; predetermined; prescribed: *n.* a number of things of the same kind, or fitted to be used together; a number of persons associated; a number of particular things united in the formation of a whole; a young plant for growth; descent below the horizon; flow; a permanent twist or bias; trend; drift; a series of games, as in tennis; a clutch of eggs; posture, carriage, or pose; manner of fitting (of coats, etc.); the act of a setter when it discovers the game; the arrangement of the teeth of a saw; a stage scene; the setting of a motion-picture; arrangement and spacing of type [Print.]; a sett [Mining and Road-making]. **dead set,** *see* **dead. set speech,** a speech prepared beforehand.
seta, *n.* *see*-ta (*pl.* **setæ**), a bristle, or bristle-like organ [Bot. and Zool.]; the stalk of the capsule of mosses. (L., a bristle.)
setaceous, *a.* se-*tay*-shus, bristly; set with or consisting of bristles; like a bristle. (L. *seta*, a bristle.)
setback, *n.* *set*-bak, a check in progress; a reverse.
set-down, *n.* a humiliating rebuke; a snub.
set-hammer, *n.* a hammer used by blacksmiths in swaging; a hammer for beating down the edges of rivet heads.
setiferous, *a.* se-*tif*-er-rus, having or bearing bristles. (L. *seta*, and *fero*, bear.)
setiform, *a.* *see*-te-form, bristle-shaped.
setigerous, *a.* se-*tij*-er-rus, furnished with bristles.
set-off, *n.* *set*-off, something which adorns; a mark accidentally transferred from a printed sheet before the ink is dry; a counter demand; the

amount which the defendant is entitled to in reduction of the plaintiff's claim [Law.].

seton, *n. see*-ton, a skein of cotton or silk, or a slip of gutta-percha, inserted in a wound to provoke and maintain an issue [Surg.]. (L. *seta*, a bristle.)

setose, *a. see*-tohs, bristly; resembling, or having the surface set with, bristles. (L. *setosus*.)

set-piece, *n.* a stage scene with supporting framework; a number of fireworks fixed to a frame and forming a design when fired; an elaborate or formal artistic composition.

set-square, *n. set*-skware, a right-angled triangular instrument used by mechanical draughtsmen, etc.

sett, *n.* set, a number of mines taken upon lease; pressure obtained by use of a screw or other power [Shipbuilding]; a piece placed temporarily on the head of a pile when this cannot be reached directly; a paving block of stone or wood.

settee, *n.* se-*tee*, a seat for two or more with a back and end-pieces; a sofa. (*settle*.)

settee, *n.* se-*tee*, a single-decked vessel, with a very long sharp prow and two or three masts with lateen sails, used in the Mediterranean. (It. *saettia*.)

setter, *n. set*-er, one who sets, as types, music to words, etc.; a dog for starting game, setting or crouching when it perceives the scent. **setter on,** an instigator.

setterwort, *n. set*-er-wurt, the stinking hellebore, or bear's-foot, *Helleborus fœtidus*.

setting, *n. set*-ing, the act of setting; the direction of a current; the hardening of plaster, cement, etc.; a jewel mounting; a musical accompaniment; the scenery and scenic environment of a play, film, etc.; the number of eggs set under a hen.

settle, *n. set*-tl, a long bench with a high back. (A.S. *setl*.)

settle, *v.t. set*-tl, to place in a permanent condition; to establish; to establish in business, or in married life; to pay; to determine; to render fixed; to make compact; to fix by gift or grant; to secure property, etc., on; to fix firmly; to cause to sink or subside; to compose; to ordain; to colonize; to adjust; to liquidate: *v.i.* to fall to the bottom of liquor; to subside; to deposit; to fix one's habitation; to marry and establish a domestic state; to become fixed, stationary, or permanent; to become calm; to adjust differences or accounts. (A.S. *setlan*.)

settlement, *n. set*-tl-ment, the act of settling or establishing; a state of being settled; subsidence; the conveyance of property for the benefit of some person or persons; property so conveyed; a jointure; place settled; adjustment; a colony; legal residence; a mission centre in a poor neighbourhood. **Act of Settlement,** the statute of 1701 by which the British crown was limited to the line of the house of Hanover.

settler, *n. set*-tler, one who settles in a colony; something finally decisive.

settling, *n. set*-tling, the act of adjusting; a planting or colonizing; subsidence: *pl.* lees. **settling day,** the fortnightly day for the settlement of accounts on the Stock Exchange.

set-to, *n.* a warm debate or argument: a fight, esp. with fists [Slang].

set-up, *n.* the way anything is set up; arrangement; make-up: material arranged; arrangement of properties, etc., on a set [Cine.]; an organization; a contest purposely made easy [Slang].

set-wall, *n. set*-wawl, the plant valerian; also, zedoary [Pharm.]. (Ar. *zedwar*.)

seven, *a.* and *n. sev*-en *or* sevn, six and one. **the Seven Champions of Christendom,** St. George (for England), St. Andrew (Scotland), St. Patrick (Ireland), St. David (Wales), St. Denis (France), St. James (Spain), and St. Anthony (Italy). **the Seven Churches of Asia,** Ephesus, Smyrna, Pergamos, Thyatira, Sardis, Philadelphia, and Laodicea (Rev. i, 4 and 11). **the Seven Deadly Sins,** *see* **sin. Seven Dolours,** *see* **dolour. the Seven Seas,** *see* **sea. the Seven Sleepers,** seven Christians of Ephesus fabled to have been immured in a cave near the city about A.D. 220, where they fell asleep and awoke some 200 years later. **the Seven Stars,** the Pleiades. **the Seven Wise Men,** seven Greek sages, Periander, Solon, Thales, Pittacus, Bias, Chilon and Cleobulus. **the Seven Wonders of the World,** the Pyramids, the Hanging Gardens of Babylon, the Temple of Diana at Ephesus, the Mausoleum, the Colossus, the Pharos at Alexandria, and the Statue of Jupiter by Phidias. (A.S. *seofon*.)

sevenfold, *a. sevn*-fohld, seven times as much or as many; repeated seven times.

seventeen, *a.* and *n. sevn*-teen, seven and ten.

seventeenth, *a.* sevn-*teenth*, the next after the sixteenth; the ordinal of seventeen: *n.* one of seventeen equal parts.

seventh, *a. sev*-enth *or* sevnth, the ordinal of seven: *n.* the next after the sixth; one part in seven; an interval of seven degrees of the staff [Mus.]. **Seventh day,** Saturday; the Jewish Sabbath. **Seventh-day Baptist,** a dissenting sect recognizing only the seventh day of the week as the Sabbath. **seventh heaven,** the state of extreme bliss.

seventhly, *ad. sevnth*-le, in the seventh place.

seventieth, *a. sevn*-te-eth, the ordinal of seventy *n.* one part in seventy.

seventy, *a. sevn*-te, consisting of or amounting to seven times ten: *n.* seven times ten. **the Seventy,** the translators of the Septuagint; the Jewish Sanhedrin. **seventy-four,** a former line-of-battle ship carrying 74 guns.

seven-up, *n.* an American card-game of the all-fours family, seven points constituting a game.

sever, *v.t. sev*-er, to part or divide by violence; to separate; to disjoin; to disunite: *v.i.* to part; to suffer disjunction. (Fr. *sevrer*.)

severable, *a. sev*-er-ra-bl, separable.

several, *a. sev*-ral *or sev*-er-ral, separate; distinct; sundry; various; single; consisting of a number; privately owned or occupied [Law]: *n.* a few; each particular, or a small number, taken singly. (O.Fr.)

severality, *n. sev*-er-*ral*-e-te, each particular, singly taken.

severalize, *v.t. sev*-er-ra-lize, to separate; to distinguish.

severally, *ad.* separately; apart from others.

severalty, *n. sev*-er-ral-te, a state of separation from the rest or from all others; exclusive ownership or tenure [Law].

severance, *n. sev*-er-rance, separation; partition; the act of separating.

severe, *a.* se-*veer*, rigid; harsh; not mild or indulgent; rigorous; very strict or over-strict; grave; rigidly exact; sharp; biting; concise; critical. (O.Fr.)

severely, *ad.* in a severe manner; sharply; rigorously; painfully.

severeness, *n.* se-*veer*-ness, severity.

severer, *n. sev*-er-rer, one who severs.

severity, *n.* se-*ve*-re-te, the quality of being severe; harshness; rigour; austerity; extreme degree (esp. of weather). (Fr. *sévérité*.)

severy, *n. se*-ve-re, a compartment of a vaulted ceiling [Arch.]. (O.Fr. *civoire*, ciborium.)

Seville, *a. sev*-il, designating a bitter type of orange. (Name of town in Spain.)

Sèvres, *n.* sayvr, a fine porcelain manufactured at Sèvres, France.

sew, *v.t.* soh, to unite or fasten together with thread; to mend, attach, etc., by sewing: *v.i.* to practise sewing; to join things with stitches. *pp.* **sewed** and **sewn.** (A.S. *siwian*.)

sewage, *n. sew*-aj, drainage carried off by sewers: *v.t.* to fertilize with sewage.

sewellel, *n.* se-*wel*-el, a North American rodent of the genus *Hapoldon*. (Chinook.)

sewer, *n. sew*-er, a channel underground for carrying off the water and refuse borne into it by drains. (O.Fr. *sewiere*.)

sewer, *n. soh*-er, one who uses the needle.

sewer, *n. sew*-er, one who placed and removed the dishes at a mediæval feast. (O.Fr. *asseour*.)

sewerage, *n. sew*-er-raj, a system of draining by sewers; sewers collectively.

sewin, *n. sew*-en, the fish *Salmo cambricus*, allied to the sea-trout, distinguished by black crosses above the lateral line. (Origin unknown.)

sewing, *n. soh*-ing, the occupation of using a needle, or that which is sewn by it; needlework.

sewing-machine, *n.* a machine worked by hand, foot, or power for sewing and stitching.

sewing-press, *n.* the frame used by bookbinders in stitching books.

***sex,** *n.* seks, either of the two divisions, of living organisms, also, the distinctive quality of each: *a.* pertaining to sex; appealing to sexual instincts,

male and female. **the sex, the fair, gentle,** or **weaker sex,** women. **sex appeal,** that quality or attribute serving to attract a person of opposite sex. (L. *sexus.*)
sexagenarian, *a.* *seks*-a-je-*nare*-re-an, sixty years old: *n.* a person aged between 60 and 69. (L. *sexagenarius,* from *sexaginta,* sixty.)
sexagenary, *a.* sek-*saj*-e-na-re, pertaining to the number sixty: *n.* something composed of sixty; a sexagenarian.
Sexagesima, *n.* *seks*-a-*jes*-e-ma, the second Sunday before Lent, so called as being about sixty days before Easter. (L.)
sexagesimal, *a.* *seks*-a-*jes*-e-mal, sixtieth; pertaining to sixty; computed by sixties (as with minutes and seconds).
sexangle, *n.* *seks*-ang-gl, a hexagon [Geom.].
sexangular, *a.* seks-*ang*-gew-lar, having six angles; hexagonal.
sexcentenary, *n.* seks-sen-*ten*-a-re, a six-hundredth anniversary.
sexed, *a.* sekst, pertaining to or having sex.
sexennial, *a.* seks-*en*-e-al, lasting six years; happening once in six years. (L. *sexennium.*)
sexennially, *ad.* seks-*en*-e-a-le, every six years.
sexfid, *a.* *seks*-fid, six-cleft [Bot.]. (L. *sex,* six, *findo,* cleave.)
sexisyllabic, *a.* *seks*-e-se-*lab*-ik, having six syllables.
sexivalent, *a.* seks-e-*vay*-lent, having a valency of six [Chem.].
sexless, *a.* *seks*-less, having no sex; asexual.
sexlessness, *n.* *seks*-less-ness, quality or state of being without sex; absence of sexuality.
sexlocular, *a.* seks-*lok*-yew-lar, six-celled [Bot.].
sexological, *a.* seks-o-*loj*-e-kal, pertaining to sexology.
sexologist, *n.* seks-*ol*-o-jist, a student of sexology.
sexology, *n.* seks-*ol*-o-je, the branch of physiology that treats of sex and relations between the sexes.
sexpartite, *a.* seks-*par*-tite, divided into six.
sext, *n.* sekst, in the Roman Church, the office for the sixth hour or noon.
sextain, *n.* *seks*-tayn, a stanza of six lines; a sestina. (L. *sextus,* sixth.)
sextan, *a.* *seks*-tan, recurring every sixth day (of intermittent fevers) [Med.].
sextant, *n.* *seks*-tant, the sixth part of a circle; an instrument for measuring altitudes and other angular distances of which the limb comprehends 60° (one-sixth of a circle).
sextet, *n.* *seks*-tet, a group of six: a sestet [Mus.]. (L. *sextus.*)
sextile, *n.* seks-*tile,* the aspect or position of two planets when 60° distant from each other. (L. *sextilis,* sixth.)
sextillion, *n.* seks-*til*-yon, a million raised to the sixth power, represented by 1 followed by 36 noughts, or, in U.S.A. and France, the seventh power of 1,000 (1 and 21 noughts).
sexto, *n.* *seks*-toh, a book in which each sheet is folded into six leaves. (L. *sextus.*)
sextodecimo, *n.* *seks*-to-*des*-e-moh, a book in which each sheet is folded into sixteen leaves. (L.)
sexton, *n.* *seks*-ton, an official in charge of the fabric, fittings, etc., of a church and the churchyard, sometimes acting also as parish clerk and grave-digger. (*sacristan.*)
sextonship, *n.* *seks*-ton-ship, the office of sexton.
sextuple, *a.* *seks*-tew-pl, six-fold; six times as much or as many: *v.t.* to multiply by six. (L. *sextus.*)
sextuplet, *n.* *seks*-tew-plet, a group of six.
sexual, *a.* *seks*-yew-al, pertaining to sex, the sexes, or to the distinctive organs of sex; distinguishing the sex; founded on sex; pertaining to copulation. (L. *sexualis.*)
sexualism, *n.* *seks*-yew-a-lizm, undue emphasis upon or interest in sex.
sexualist, *n.* *seks*-yew-a-list, one holding the theory that most psychological phenomena are due to sexual causes or influences.
sexuality, *n.* *seks*-yew-*al*-e-te, the state of being distinguished by sex; possession or exercise of sexual functions; sexualism.
sexualize, *v.t.* *seks*-yew-a-lize, to attribute sexual characteristics to; to endow with sex.
sexually, *ad.* in a sexual manner.
sexy, *a.* *seks*-e, lewdly referring to sex; over-sexed [Coll.].

Seym, *n.* same, the Polish Sejm or Lower House.
sforzando, *ad.* sfor-*tsan*-doh, to be played forcibly [Mus.]. (It.)
sgraffito, *n.* sgra-*fee*-toh, a graffito. (It.)
shabbily, *ad.* *shab*-e-le, in a shabby manner.
shabbiness, *n.* *shab*-e-ness, the quality of being shabby; meanness; paltriness.
shabby, *a.* *shab*-e, ragged; worn threadbare; in a threadbare dress; mean; despicable. **shabby-genteel,** poor, but making an effort to keep up appearances. (*scabby.*)
shabbyish, *a.* *shab*-e-ish, somewhat shabby.
shabrack, *n.* *shab*-rak, a saddle-cloth, esp. of goat-skin. (Fr. *shabracque,* from Turk. *chapraq.*)
shack, *n.* shak, fallen grain, etc., used as pig-food; an ancient liberty of winter pasturage of pigs; a roughly built cabin; a log hut: *v.t.* and *i.* to feed, or cause (pigs, etc.) to feed, in stubble or on fallen grain. (*shake.*)
shackle, *n.* *shak*-kl, a U-shaped link; a staple; a gyve, manacle, or fetter: *pl.* obstruction to free action: *v.t.* to chain; to fetter; to confine so as to prevent or embarrass motion. (A.S. *sceacul.*)
shad, *n.* shad, any of several food-fish of the herring family, including the allice, twait, and the American shad, *Clupea sapidissima.* (A.S. *sceadda.*)
shaddock, *n.* *shad*-ok, the fruit of *Citrus decumana,* resembling a large grapefruit. (Capt. *Shaddock,* introducer, about 1697.)
★**shade,** *n.* shade, obscurity, esp. due to interception of light-rays; darkness; that which shades; a shady place; a secluded retreat; gradation of light; something that intercepts light or heat; shelter; the dark part of a picture [Painting]; a spirit or ghost: *pl.* the abode of spirits or ghosts, Hades; twilight, the darkness of evening: *v.t.* to screen from light or heat; to obscure; to shelter; to darken; to paint with gradations of colour. **in the shade,** overshadowed; in comparative obscurity. (A.S. *sceadu.*)
shadily, *ad.* *shade*-e-le, in a shady manner.
shadiness, *n.* *shade*-e-ness, state of being shady; underhandedness.
shading, *n.* *shade*-ing, the representation of light and shade; a qualification or slight variation; protection from the light.
shadoof, *n.* sha-*doof,* a contrivance for raising water by means of a pivoted pole having a bucket at one end. (Ar.)
shadow, *n.* *shad*-oh, shade within defined limits; shade caused by a form which intercepts the rays of light; darkness; obscurity; shelter; the dark part of a picture; an imperfect and faint representation; an inseparable companion; a type; a slight or faint appearance; a reflected image: *v.t.* to shade; to cloud; to darken; to conceal; to screen; to paint in obscure colours; to represent faintly or typically; to keep under observation. **shadow cabinet,** the members of an opposition supposedly ready to take office on their displacing the sitting government [Polit.]. **to shadow forth,** to represent faintly. (*shade.*)
shadow-box, *v.i.* to box against an imaginary opponent (as in training).
shadowgraph, *n.* *shad*-oh-graf, a picture formed by a still or moving shadow thrown upon a screen; an X-ray photograph.
shadowiness, *n.* state of being shadowy.
shadowless, *a.* *shad*-oh-less, having no shadow.
shadowy, *a.* *shad*-oh-e, full of shade; dark; gloomy; poorly lighted; unsubstantial.
shady, *a.* *shade*-e, abounding with shade; overspread with shade; umbrageous; sheltered from light or sultry heat; of doubtful character or bad repute [Fig.]; uncertain. **on the shady side of,** older than [Coll.].
shaft, *n.* shahft, the long slender handle of a spear or other weapon; anything long and straight, as a ray of light; an arrow; a deep narrow entrance to a mine; a perpendicular pit; a high chimney; the body of a column between the base and the capital [Arch.]; the stem of a feather; one of the two bars between which a draught-horse is harnessed, a thill; a cylindrical rotating bar or tube by which the power or motion is transmitted [Mech.]; an axle. (A.S. *sceaft.*)
shafted, *a.* *shahf*-ted, fitted with a shaft.
shafting, *n.* *shahf*-ting, a system or series of shafts for the transmission of power.

shag, *n.* shag, rough woolly hair; a kind of cloth with a long coarse nap; the green or crested cormorant, *Phalacrocorax graculus*; fine-cut Virginia tobacco: *v.t.* to make rough or hairy; to deform. (A.S. *sceacga.*)
shagbark, *n. shag*-bark, the white hickory, *Carya ovata*; the W. Indian savonette tree, *Pithecolobium micradenium.*
shagged, *a. shag*-ed, shaggy.
shagginess, *n.* the quality of being shaggy.
shaggy, *a. shag*-e, rough; with long hair or wool.
shagreen, *n.* sha-*green,* a kind of grained leather prepared from the skins of horses, etc., also of sharks and seals. **shagreen ray,** a fish of the skate family, *Raiia fullonica.* (Turk.)
Shah, *n.* shah, the monarch of Persia. (Per.)
★**shake,** *n.* shake, act or result of shaking; rapid motion one way and another; agitation; a jolt or shock; a motion of hands clasped; a trill: *v.i.* to be agitated; to tremble; to shiver; to totter; to trill: *v.t.* to agitate; to make to totter or tremble; to cause vibration; to drive off or away; to weaken the stability of; to cause to waver or doubt. **shake hands,** to join hands at meeting or parting; to agree or contract with. **no great shakes,** not much good, not up to much [Slang]. *pp.* **shaken.** *p.* **shook.** (A.S. *sceacan.*)
shakeable, *a. shake*-a-bl, capable of being shaken.
shakedown, *n. shake*-doun, a makeshift for a bed; a bringing into working order by trial or practice (esp. of ships).
shaker, *n. shake*-er, one who or that which shakes; (*cap.*) a member of an American religious community which formerly practised a kind of dancing movement in worship.
Shakeress, *n.* shake-er-*ress,* a female Shaker.
Shakerizm, *n. shake*-er-rizm, the tenets and practices of the Shakers.
Shakespearian, *a.* shake-*speer*-re-an, relating to or characteristic of Shakespeare or his works: *n.* a student of or authority on these.
shakily, *ad.* in a shaky manner.
shakiness, *n.* the state of being shaky.
shako, *n. shak*-oh, a tall peaked military head-dress, usually with a plume. (Hungarian *csákó.*)
shaky, *a. shake*-e, in a shaking or weak condition; full of slits or clefts, as timber; dubious; of uncertain capability, solvency, etc.
shale, *n.* shale, laminated or thinly stratified clay. (Ger. *Schale,* a shell.)
shall, *v.aux.* shal (*p.* and *subjunctive* **should**), must; ought; a defective verb denoting promise, obligation, determination, command, etc. (A.S. *sceal,* I must.)
shalloon, *n.* sha-*loon,* a light woollen fabric used chiefly for linings. (*Châlons,* in France.)
shallop, *n. shal*-op, a small open river boat, propelled by oar, sail, or both. (Fr. *chaloupe.*)
shallot, *n.* sha-*lot,* the small species of onion *Allium ascalonicum.* (O.Fr. *eschalote.*)
shallow, *a. shal*-oh, having little depth; not deep; not penetrating deeply; not profound; superficial: *n.* a shoal; a sandbank; a hawker's basket, barrow, or cart; the rudd (freshwater fish): *v.t.* and *i.* to make or become shallow (of water). (M.E. *schalowe.*)
shallowly, *ad.* with little depth; superficially.
shallowness, *n.* the quality of being shallow; superficiality of intellect.
shalt, *v.aux.* shalt, *second person singular* of *shall.*
shaly, *a. shale*-e, partaking of the qualities of shale; breaking into fragile slabs.
sham, *a.* sham, false; counterfeit; pretended: *n.* one who or that which deceives expectation; imposture: *v.t.* to deceive; to trick; to cheat; to feign: *v.i.* to make false pretences. **sham Abraham,** *see* **Abraham.** (*shame.*)
shama, *n. shah*-ma, a family of Indian warblers, one species of which, *Cittocincla macrura,* is a favourite cage-bird; wild rice, a millet-like cereal cultivated in India. (Hind.)
Shaman, *n. sham*-an, a priest or medicine-man among the Eskimos and other races of Northern Asia. (Hind. *shamon,* a heathen.)
Shamanism, *n. sham*-an-izm, the religion of the Shamans, the chief feature of which is a belief in the agency of good and evil spirits and the power of certain magic rites to propitiate them.
shamble, *v.i. sham*-bl, to walk in a shuffling way or with a clumsy gait: *n.* an awkward, clumsy, irregular gait. (See *scamble* and *scamper.*)
shambles, *n.pl. sham*-blz, a slaughter-house; place of slaughter or great carnage; meat stalls in a market. (A.S. *scamel.*)
★**shame,** *n.* shame, a painful sensation due to a sense of guilt, dishonour, humiliation, etc.; the cause of shame; disgrace; reproach: *v.t.* to make ashamed; to cause to blush; to disgrace; to mock at. (A.S. *sceamu.*)
shamefaced, *a. shame*-fayst, bashful; easily put out of countenance.
shamefacedly, *ad.* in a shamefaced manner.
shamefacedness, *n.* bashfulness.
shameful, *a. shame*-ful, that which brings shame; disgraceful; causing shame in others; indecent.
shamefully, *ad.* in a shameful manner.
shamefulness, *n.* the quality of being shameful.
shameless, *a. shame*-less, destitute of shame; wanting modesty; brazen-faced; indicating want of shame.
shamelessly, *ad.* in a shameless manner.
shamelessness, *n.* the quality of being shameless.
shammer, *n. sham*-er, one who shams; an impostor.
shammoy, *v.t. sham*-oy, to prepare leather by impregnating it with oil or grease [Coll.]. (*chamois.*)
shammy, *n. sham*-me, leather prepared from chamois-skin; any leather similarly prepared. (*chamois.*)
shampoo, *v.t.* sham-*poo,* to massage the limbs in a warm bath; to rub; to wash the hair of the head with warm soapy water or a soapy fluid and rinse it with cold water or (**dry shampoo**) with a spirituous preparation: *n.* the act of shampooing; a shampooing preparation. (Hind.)
shamrock, *n. sham*-rok, any of several plants with ternate obcordate leaves, esp. the lesser yellow trefoil, *Trifolium minus,* the national emblem of Ireland. **four-leaved shamrock,** *Trifolium repens purpureum.* (Ir. *seamrog.*)
shandrydan, *n. shan*-dre-*dan,* a light two-wheeled cart; a rickety vehicle. (Ir.)
shandygaff, *n. shan*-de-gaf, a mixture of ale and gingerbeer in about equal quantities. **lemon shandygaff,** a similar mixture of ale and lemonade. (Origin unknown.)
Shanghai, *v.t.* shang-*hy,* to stupefy a man with drink or drugs and then ship him as a sailor; a long-legged breed of domestic fowl. (Name of Chinese port.)
shank, *n.* shank, the leg from the knee to the ankle; the tibia; the shaft of a column [Arch.]; the long part or lever portion of any tool or instrument; the eye of a button: *v.i.* to be affected with decay in the foot-stalks [Bot.]. **on Shanks's mare,** or **pony,** on foot. (A.S. *sceanca.*)
shanked, *a.* shankt, having a shank.
shanker, *n. shank*-er, a chancre.
shank-painter, *n.* a short rope and chain for holding the anchor against a ship's side [Naut.].
shanny, *n. shan*-e, the smooth blenny, *Blennius pholis.*
shantung, *n.* shan-*tung,* a soft, undressed and usually undyed fabric of Chinese silk. (Name of Chinese province.)
shanty, *n. shan*-te, a sea-song with a chorus, sung by sailors when at work. (Fr. *chanter,* to sing.)
shanty, *n. shan*-te, a hut or mean dwelling. (Probably Fr. *chantier de bois,* a timber-yard.)
shape, *n.* shape, form or figure; external appearance; a definite form; a pattern; an untrimmed hat; a mould [Cookery]; a sweet made in a mould: *v.t.* to form; to make into a particular form; to adapt to a purpose; to direct; to conceive: *v.i.* to take shape; to square; to suit. **in good shape,** very fit, in first-rate condition. (A.S. *scieppan.*)
shapeable, *a. shape*-a-bl, capable of being shaped.
shapeless, *a. shape*-less, destitute of regular form; wanting symmetry.
shapelessness, *n.* the quality of being shapeless.
shapeliness, *n. shape*-le-ness, the quality of being shapely; beauty or proportion of form.
shapely, *a. shape*-le, well formed; symmetrical.
shaper, *n. shape*-er, one who or that which shapes; a machine tool for shaping metals.
shard, *n.* shard, a fragment, esp. of earthenware; an egg-shell or snail-shell; a wing-case, esp. of a beetle: *v.t.* and *i.* to break or flake off. (A.S. *sceard.*)
share, *n.* share, a due part; a portion pertaining to one; a part of anything owned by two or more in common; one of the equal portions into which the

capital of a company is divided; allotment; a ploughshare; the blade of a cultivator, etc.: *v.t.* to divide in parts; to partake with others; to distribute; to apportion, or participate in: *v.i.* to have a part; to participate. **go shares,** to be equally concerned. (A.S. *scearu*, a cutting, division.)

share-bone, *n.* the pubic bone, part of the innominate bone or pelvic girdle. (A.S. *scearu*, division, and *bone*.)

sharebroker, *n. share*-broh-ker, one who deals in shares as a broker [Stock Exchange].

shareholder, *n. share*-hohl-der, one who holds a share or shares in a joint property.

share-list, *n.* a price-list of shares.

share-out, *n.* distribution in or of shares.

share-pusher, *n.* a peddler of shares, esp. those of bogus or questionable companies.

sharer, *n. share*-rer, one who participates with another.

shark, *n.* shark, a voracious elasmobranch fish of various species with an unequally lobed tail, lateral gills, and the mouth on the under surface; a greedy artful fellow; a rapacious swindler: *v.t.* to pick up hastily or slily: *v.i.* to play the petty thief; to live by fraud or trickery; to swindle. (Origin uncertain.)

***sharp,** *a.* sharp, having a very thin edge or fine point; terminating in an edge or point; peaked; acute-angled; not obtuse; acute of mind; ready at invention; witty; of quick nice perception; sour; piquant; shrill; severe; harsh; sarcastic; severely rigid; keen; fierce; very painful; very vigilant; piercing; subtle; thin: *ad.* exactly: *n.* an acute sound; a note artificially raised a semitone marked thus ♯; the mark itself [Mus.]; a sharper: *v.t.* to raise the pitch a note, to mark with a sharp [Mus.]: *v.i.* to swindle; to play tricks in bargaining. (A.S. *scearp.*)

sharp-cut, *a.* clearly outlined or defined.

sharpen, *v.t. sharp*-en, to make sharp or keen; to make more eager, pungent, sarcastic, acid, shrill, or distressing: *v.i.* to grow sharp.

sharpener, *n. sharp*-en-er, one who or that which sharpens; a device for sharpening pencils.

sharper, *n. sharp*-er one who lives by his wits; a tricky fellow; a cheat in business or gaming.

sharpish, *a. sharp*-ish, somewhat sharp.

sharply, *ad.* in a sharp manner.

sharpness, *n.* the quality of being sharp.

sharps, *n.pl.* sharps, wheat middlings.

sharp-set, *a.* very hungry; eager of gratification.

sharpshooter, *n. sharp*-shoot-er, a skilled rifleman; a skirmisher; a sniper.

sharpshooting, *n. sharp*-shoot-ing, shooting with accuracy; good marksmanship; sniping.

sharp-sighted, *a.* of quick sight or discernment.

sharp-witted, *a.* having an acute or nicely discerning mind.

Shastra, *n. shas*-tra, the Hindu scriptures collectively, esp. the treatises on law. (Sans., a sacred book.)

shatter, *v.t. shat*-er, to break at once into pieces; to rend; to crack; to rive into splinters; to dissipate; to derange; to overthrow: *v.i.* to be broken into fragments. (*scatter.*)

shatters, *n.pl. shat*-erz, broken fragments.

shattery, *a. shat*-er-re, brittle; not compact.

shave, *n.* shave, a getting shaved; the act of shaving; a slice; a knife for shaving, esp. a spokeshave: *v.t.* to cut or pare off with a razor or other edged instrument (esp. of the hair on the face); to cut in thin slices; to brush past merely grazing; to fleece [Slang]. **close shave,** a narrow escape. (A.S. *sceafan.*)

shavegrass, *n. shave*-grahs, the scouring rush, a plant of the genus *Equisetum.*

shave-hook, *n.* a metal-workers' scraping tool having a triangular blade set transversely to its shank.

shaveling, *n. shave*-ling, a tonsured priest; a stripling.

shaver, *n. shave*-er, a barber; a sharp dealer; one who fleeces; a droll fellow; a youngster.

Shavian, *a. shave*-e-an, pertaining to the works, literary style, theories, or personality of George Bernard Shaw: *n.* a follower of G. B. Shaw.

shaving, *n. shave*-ing, the act of one who shaves; a thin slice pared off with a shave, knife, plane, or other cutting instrument.

shaw, *n.* shaw, a small wood or thicket. (A.S. *scaga.*)

shawl, *n.* shawl, a loose covering for the neck and shoulders. (Per.)

shawm, *n.* shawm, an ancient wind instrument, allied to the clarinet. (Fr. *chalemie*, a pipe.)

shay, *n.* shay, a chaise. (*chaise.*)

she, *pron. third pers. sing. fem.* shee, the female before mentioned: *n.* a woman; a female: *a.* female, as *she-bear.* (A.S. *seo*, feminine of *se*, the definite article.)

shea, *n. shee*-a, a tropical African tree, *Butyrospermum parkii*, yielding an edible fatty substance known as **shea-butter.**

sheading, *n. sheed*-ing, any of the six administrative divisions of the Isle of Man. (A.S. *sceadan*, to divide.)

sheaf, *n.* sheef (*pl.* **sheaves**), a bundle of new-cut corn bound together; any bundle or collection: *v.t.* to sheave; to make sheaves of. (A.S. *sceaf.*)

sheafy, *a. sheef*-e, consisting of sheaves.

shealing, *n. sheel*-ing, a shieling.

shear, *v.t.* sheer, to clip, cut off, or separate as with scissors or shears; to plunder; to strip: *v.i.* to use shears; to become more or less divided through subjection to a shear: *n.* a shearing (as of sheep); a metal-cutting machine; a transverse stress in metal, etc., causing contiguous parts to slide from each other; change of structure due to transverse pressure [Geol.]. *p.* **sheared** (and, formerly, **shore**). *pp.* **shorn** or **sheared.** (A.S. *sceran.*)

shear-bill, *n.* the skimmer or scissors-bill (seabird).

shearer, *n. sheer*-rer, one who or a machine which shears.

shear-hog, *n.* a sheep after the first shearing.

shearing, *n. sheer*-ring, the act of shearing; what is sheared off; dividing with shears.

shear-legs, *n.* sheers.

shearling, *n. sheer*-ling, a sheep that has been shorn but once.

shearman, *n. sheer*-man, one whose occupation is to shear cloth; a workman who shears metal.

shears, *n.pl.* sheerz, a double-bladed instrument for cutting, like scissors, but larger; something in the form of the blades of shears; sheers.

shear-steel, *n.* high-grade steel formed of short bars heated together and welded.

shear-tail, *n.* a name of various birds, including the common tern and certain forked-tail humming-birds.

shearwater, *n. sheer*-waw-ter, a sea-bird of the genus *Puffinus*, allied to the petrels.

sheatfish, *n. sheet*-fish, a large eel-like freshwater catfish of S.E. Europe, *Silurus glanis.* (Ger. *Schaidfisch.*)

sheath, *n.* sheeth, a protective case for a blade, tool, etc.; a scabbard; the wing-case of an insect; connective tissue investing a part or organ [Anat.]; a membrane investing a stem [Bot.]. (A.S. *scæth.*)

sheathe, *v.t.* sheethe, to put into a sheath or scabbard; to cover with a sheath; to cover, line, or case with boards, copper sheets, etc., to conceal; to invest with a sheath [Bot. etc.]. **sheathe the sword,** to make peace.

sheathing, *n. sheeth*-ing, a casing or covering, esp. of a ship's hull below the waterline, and of the tips, etc., of airscrew blades; material used for this.

sheath-knife, *n.* a knife with a fixed blade protected by a sheath.

sheathless, *a. sheeth*-less, without a sheath or covering.

sheave, *v.t.* sheev, to gather into sheaves; to bring together; to collect. (*sheaf.*)

sheave, *n.* sheev, a grooved wheel of a pulley on which the rope works. (*shive.*)

sheave-hole, *n.* a channel in which to fix a sheave.

shebang, *n.* she-*bang*, a concern, business, or outfit; a gaming-house or saloon [U.S.A. slang].

Shebat, *n. shay*-bat, the fifth month of the Jewish civil year and eleventh of the sacred year. (Heb.)

shebeen, *n.* she-*been*, an unlicensed house where excisable liquors are sold; a low or small beer-house. (Ir., a little shop.)

Shechinah, *n.* she-*ky*-na, the Shekinah.

shed, *v.t.* shed, to pour or suffer to flow out; to cast off; to emit; to diffuse: *v.i.* to let fall its seed, covering, etc.: *n.* a parting, as of the hair of the head, the wool of sheep, etc.; the parting of the warp-threads to allow of the passage through

of the shuttle [Weaving]: the elevated ridge of a watershed. (A.S. *sceadan.*)
shed, *n.* shed, a wooden hut; a temporary open-ended building; a hovel. (*shade.*)
shedder, *n. shed*-er, one who sheds or causes to flow out.
shedding, *n. shed*-ing, the act of shedding; that which is cast off; sheds, materials for sheds: *pl.* a group of sheds.
sheen, *n.* sheen, shine; brightness; glitter; gleam. (A.S. *scēne*, bright.)
sheeny, *a. sheen*-e, bright; shining; having sheen.
sheeny, *n. sheen*-e, a Jew [Slang]. (Origin uncertain.)
***sheep,** *n. sing.* and *pl.* sheep, an ovine ungulate of the genus *Ovis*, valuable for its flesh and wool; sheepskin leather; a bashful or silly fellow: *pl.* the elect [Theol.]; the members of a pastor's flock. **black sheep,** a ne'er-do-well, a disgrace to the family. **the sheep and the goats,** *see* **goat. vegetable sheep,** the composite plant *Raoulia eximia*, of New Zealand. (A.S. *sceap.*)
sheepcote, *n. sheep*-kot, a small enclosure for sheep; a sheepfold.
sheep-dip, *n.* sheep-wash.
sheep-dog, *n.* a dog trained to tend sheep; a large tailless or bob-tailed shaggy-coated English dog; a collie.
sheep-faced, *a. sheep*-fayst, bashful; sheepish.
sheep-fly, *n.* any fly the larvæ of which live on sheep.
sheepfold, *n. sheep*-fohld, a place where sheep are collected or confined; [Fig.] a church.
sheep-hook, *n.* a shepherd's crook.
sheepish, *a. sheep*-ish, like a sheep; bashful; timorous.
sheepishly, *ad.* bashfully.
sheepishness, *n.* quality of being sheepish; bashfulness.
sheep-louse, *n. sheep*-louse, a louse infesting sheep, *Trichodectes ovis*; a sheep-tick.
sheepmaster, *n. sheep*-mahs-ter, a sheep farmer.
sheep-run, *n.* an extensive tract of land where sheep may wander and feed.
sheep's-bane, *n.* the marsh pennywort, *Hydrocotyle vulgaris.*
sheep's-bit, *n.* the scabious-like herb, *Jasione montana.*
sheep's-eye, *n.* a modest, diffident look; a wistful look: *pl.* amorous glances.
sheepshank, *n. sheep*-shank, a combination of two hitches by which a rope is shortened [Naut.].
sheep's-head, *n.* the head of a sheep prepared for eating; a name of various food-fish, esp. *Sargus ovis*, of the N. American Atlantic coast, allied to the sea-breams; a dull-witted oaf [Coll.].
sheepshearing, *n. sheep*-sheer-ring, act or time of shearing sheep; a feast held at this time.
sheepskin, *n. sheep*-skin, the skin of a sheep or the leather prepared from it; a rug, coat, etc., made of this.
sheep-sorrel, *n.* the small herb *Rumex acetosella.*
sheep-tick, *n.* the wingless insect, *Melophagus ovinus*, parasitic to and sucking the blood of sheep.
sheepwalk, *n. sheep*-wawk, a small sheep-run.
sheep-wash, *n.* a disinfecting lotion for clearing sheep of vermin, etc.
sheer, *a.* sheer, pure; clear; unmingled; simple; thin; plumb; precipitous. (Ice. *skærr.*)
sheer, *n.* sheer, the upper longitudinal curve of a ship's side; the position in which a ship is kept at single anchor with the anchor ahead [Naut.]; a swerving course: *v.i.* to slip or move aside. **sheer off,** to move to a distance. (Probably *shear.*)
sheer-hulk, *n.* a ship retired from service fitted with sheers to hoist or fix masts, and for general use in harbour.
sheer-legs, *n.* sheers.
sheerly, *ad. sheer*-le, purely; utterly; vertically.
sheers, *n.pl.* sheerz, a three-legged crane, consisting essentially of two long legs and a stay, for raising heavy weights; a hoisting apparatus for masting ships.
sheet, *n.* sheet, a thin flat piece of anything; a wide expanse; anything expanded; a broad rectangular piece of linen or cotton cloth used as part of bedding or for wrapping, etc.; a large broad piece of paper; a pamphlet or newspaper; one complete printing of postage-stamps; a rope for extending or working a sail [Naut.]: *v.t.* to form into sheets; to cover or wrap with a sheet. **between the sheets,** in bed. **clean sheet,** a record free from reproach. **in sheets,** not yet bound (of books). **three sheets in the wind,** quite drunk [Slang]. (A.S. *scete.*)
sheet-anchor, *n.* the largest anchor of a ship; the last refuge for safety; the chief stay.
sheet-copper, *n.* copper in broad thin plates.
sheeted, *a. sheet*-ed, enveloped in a sheet; wrapped in a winding-sheet; in the form of a sheet; sheety.
sheet-glass, *n.* glass made in large sheets.
sheet-ice, *n.* surface ice.
sheeting, *n. sheet*-ing, material for sheets; a covering, esp. of metal, for surface protection.
sheet-iron, *n.* iron in sheets.
sheet-lead, *n.* lead in sheets.
sheet-lightning, *n.* lightning appearing in broad extended flashes through diffusion and reflection by clouds.
sheet-music, music printed on unbound sheets.
sheety, *a. sheet*-e, spreading broadly like a sheet.
Sheffield plate, *n. shef*-eeld-*plate*, plated ware made of copper covered (by a process now disused) with silver. (*Sheffield*, manufacturing city of Yorks, W.R.)
sheikh, *n.* sheek *or* shake, an Arab chief; a prince; in India, a Hindu convert to Islam; a man reputed to possess irresistible fascination in the eyes of women [Slang]. **Sheikh ul Islam,** the chief judge of a Moslem community, esp. the Grand Mufti of Istanbul, formerly head of the Moslem religion in Turkey. (Ar. *shayk.*)
shekarry, *n.* she-*ka*-re, a shikari.
shekel, *n. shek*-el, a weight and coin among the Jews and other Semitic peoples, both of varying values: *pl.* cash, riches [Slang]. (Heb.)
Shekinah, *n.* she-*ky*-na, a radiance of glory issuing from the mercy-seat and reflected from the overshadowing cherubim as a symbol and token of the Divine presence. (Heb.)
sheldrake, *n.masc. shel*-drake (*fem.* **shelduck,** *shel*-duk), a shore-bird of the genus *Tadorna*, the burrow-duck. (A.S. *scild*, shield, and *drake.*)
***shelf,** *n.* shelf (*pl.* **shelves**), a horizontal board placed against a wall, or in a cupboard, bookcase, etc., for supporting things; a sand-bank or ledge of rocks near the surface in the sea; a flat projecting layer of rock. (A.S. *scilfe.*)
shelfy, *a. shelf*-e, abounding with sandbanks or rocks, esp. to the danger of navigation.
shell, *n.* shel, the hard covering or outer coat of a nut, a testaceous animal, or an egg, pupa, etc.; a carapace; a husk; a framework; the outer part of a house unfinished; an inner or a rough kind of coffin; a light racing boat; the outer or superficial parts; a lyre; a hollow projectile containing a bursting charge ignited by a fuse; (in some schools) an intermediate form: *v.t.* to break off the shell; to take out of or divest of the shell; to separate from the ear; to bombard with shells: *v.i.* to fall off, as a shell; to cast the shell. **to come out of one's shell,** to drop one's reserve. (A.S. *scell.*)
shellac, *n.* she-*lak*, lac purified and spread into thin plates: *v.t.* to varnish with this.
shellback, *n. shel*-bak, an old seaman [Slang].
shell-bark, *n.* a species of loose-barked hickory.
shelled, *a.* sheld, having a shell; covered with shells, shelly (of beaches); divested of its shell; bombarded with shells [Mil.].
shell-egg, *n.* the untreated egg of a fowl as distinct from egg dried, tinned, or otherwise processed.
sheller, *n. shel*-er, an implement for use in shelling nuts, etc.
shellfire, *n. shel*-fire, the shooting of shells.
shell-fish, *n.* any aquatic mollusc or crustacean, esp. such as are edible.
shell-jacket, *n.* an undress military jacket.
shell-lime, *n.* lime obtained from burning sea-shells.
shell-out, *n.* a game of the pyramid family played on the billiard-table: *v.i.* and *t.* to pay up [Slang].
shell-proof, *a.* proof against shells, etc. [Mil.].
shell-shock, *n.* a form of neurasthenia or anxiety neurosis among soldiers brought about by the conditions of modern warfare, originally thought to be due to concussion caused by the explosion of a shell close by; hence, **shell-shocked**: *a.* suffering from this.
shell-work, *n.* designs or ornamentation carried out by means of shells of molluscs, etc.

shelly, *a.* *shel*-e, abounding with or consisting of shells; shell-like.
Shelta, *n.* *shel*-ta, tinkers' jargon, consisting mainly of debased Gaelic and Old Irish.
shelter, *n.* *shel*-ter, that which shields or defends from injury; protection; a refuge; a place of safety; a deep or strongly reinforced place giving protection against aerial assault: *v.t.* to shield from injury, etc.; to defend; to harbour; to place under cover; to cover from notice: *v.i.* to take shelter. **sheltered occupation,** one protected from undue competition. (A.S. *scildtruma*, a guard.)
shelterer, *n.* *shel*-ter-rer, one who takes shelter.
shelterless, *a.* *shel*-ter-less, destitute of shelter or protection; without home or refuge.
sheltie, *n.* *shel*-te, a Shetland pony. (Scots.)
shelve, *v.t.* shelv, to place on a shelf or on shelves; to put aside; to defer indefinitely. (*shelf*.)
shelve, *v.i.* shelv, to incline; to slope gently. (Origin uncertain, perhaps Ice. *skelgjask*, to be awry.)
shelving, *a.* *shel*-ving, inclining; sloping: *n.* shelves collectively; materials for shelves.
shelvingly, *ad.* in a shelving manner.
shelvy, *a.* *shel*-ve, shelfy; overhanging like a shelf.
shemozzle, *n.* she-*moz*-zl, a rough-and-tumble; a row: *v.i.* to decamp [Slang].
she-oak, *n.* *shee*-oke, an Australian tree of the genus *Casuarina*.
Sheol, *n.* *shee*-ol, among the Hebrews the place of departed spirits or the dead; hell; the pit. (Heb., a cave.)
shepherd, *n.* *shep*-erd, a man in charge of sheep; a swain; a pastor: *v.t.* to tend as a shepherd; to assemble into safety. **shepherd's club,** the plant *Verbascum thapsus*. **shepherd's cress,** the cruciferous plant *Teesdalia nudicaulis*. **shepherd's knot,** tormentil. **shepherd's myrtle,** the butcher's-broom. **shepherd's needle,** Venus's comb, an annual plant of the genus *Scandix*. **shepherd's pie,** a pie of diced cooked meat with mashed potato crust. **shepherd's plaid,** a pattern of black and white in squares. **shepherd's purse,** the cruciferous plant *Capsella bursa-partoris*. **shepherd's rod,** a plant of the genus *Dipsacus*, a species of teasel. (A.S. *sceaphyrde*.)
shepherdess, *n.* *shep*-erd-ess, a female shepherd.
shepherdly, *a.* *shep*-erd-le, befitting a shepherd; pastoral.
sherardize, *v.t.* *she*-rar-dize, to cover iron, etc., with a coating of zinc by a process invented by Sherard Cowper Coles about 1904.
Sheraton, *a.* *she*-ra-ton, in the style of cabinet work introduced in England by Thomas Sheraton about 1790.
sherbet, *n.* *sher*-bet, a cooling drink composed of water and fruit juices; a sweetened and flavoured effervescing drink. (Ar.)
sherd, *n.* sherd, a fragment. (*shard*.)
Shereef *or* **Sherif,** *n.* she-*reef*, a title of honour given by Moslems to male descendants of Mohammed, through his daughter Fatima. **the Grand Sherif,** the chief magistrate of Mecca. (Ar. *sharif*, noble.)
Shereefian, *a.* she-*ree*-fe-an, pertaining to a Shereef. **the Shereefian Empire,** Morocco.
sheriff, *n.* *she*-rif, a county officer entrusted with the execution of the laws, the conduct of elections, etc.; in Scotland, a sheriff-depute; in the U.S.A., an elective executive county official. **sheriff's officer,** a bailiff. (A.S. *scir*, shire, and *gerefa*, reeve.)
sheriff-clerk, *n.* the registrar of a sheriff's court in Scotland.
sheriff-depute, *n.* *she*-rif-*dep*-yewt, the chief local judge in a Scottish county.
sheriffdom, *n.* *she*-rif-dum, the office or jurisdiction of a sheriff.
sheriff-substitute, *n.* the judge ranking next below the sheriff-depute.
Sherifian, *a.* she-*rif*-e-an, Shereefian.
sherry, *n.* *she*-re, a white wine, exported from Xeres, in Spain, where it is made. **sherry cobbler,** an iced sweetened drink of sherry and water flavoured with lemon, etc., sucked through a straw. (*Xeres*.)
sheth, *n.* sheth, a lath; a bar or cross-bar in a framework; a number of rows intersecting similar rows at right angles. (As *sheath*.)
shew, *v.i.* and *v.t.* shoh, to show. *p.* and *pp.* **shewn.**
shewbread, *n.* *shoh*-bred, showbread.
Shiah, *n.* *shee*-a, a Shiite.
shibboleth, *n.* *shib*-o-leth, a word forming a criterion by which to distinguish the Ephraimites from the Gileadites, the former pronouncing *sh* as *s*; hence, a word used as a test; a criterion or watchword of a party; a discredited doctrine. (Heb., *see* Judges xii.)
shield, *n.* sheeld, a broad piece of defensive armour borne on the left arm; a buckler; a stout screen; defence; protection, or anything used for this; the escutcheon or field of a coat-of-arms [Her.]: *v.t.* to protect, with or as with a shield. (A.S. *scild*.)
shield-fern, *n.* various ferns of the genus *Dryopteris*.
shieldless, *a.* *sheeld*-less, destitute of protection.
shieling, *n.* *sheel*-ing, a Highland cottage; a shelter for sheep; summer pasturage. (Scots.)
shier, *n.* *shy*-er, a horse that habitually shies.
shift, *v.i.* shift, to move; to change places or direction; to give place to other things; to resort to expedients; to practise indirect methods; to change quarters [Mil.]: *v.t.* to change; to alter; to change clothes. **shift about,** to turn quite round. **shift for oneself,** to provide for one's own needs, interests, etc. **make shift with,** to do or manage with; to accept as a usable substitute. (A.S. *sciftan* to divide.)
shift, *n.* shift, a change; a turning from one thing to another; an expedient tried in difficulty; a chemise; a relay of men, working in relays; a last resource; fraud; artifice.
shifter, *n.* *shif*-ter, a scene-shifter; a contrivance for shifting [Mech.]; a shifty person [Slang].
shiftily, *ad.* *shif*-te-le, in a shifty manner.
shiftingly, *ad.* *shif*-ting-le, by shifts and changes; in an unreliable or unstable manner.
shiftless, *a.* *shift*-less, destitute of expedients; wanting means to live.
shiftlessly, *ad.* in a shiftless manner.
shiftlessness, *n.* the quality of being shiftless.
shifty, *a.* *shif*-te, fertile in resources; deceitful; tricky; unreliable.
Shiism, *n.* *shee*-izm, the doctrines and tenets of the Shiites.
Shiite, *a.* *shee*-ite, pertaining to the Shiites; *n.* a member of the large sect of Mohammedans which rejects the Sunna, or body of traditions respecting Mohammed, and does not recognize the first three caliphs, taking Ali, Mohammed's son-in-law, as the first rightful successor of the Prophet. (Ar., sectary.)
shikar, *n.* she-*kar*, big-game hunting (in India).
shikari, *n.* she-*ka*-re, a hunter; a big-game hunt; a guide in a hunting party (all in India). (Hind.)
shillelagh, *n.* she-*lay*-la, an oak sapling; a cudgel of blackthorn or oak; any heavy stick carried by an Irishman. (Ir., a village in Co. Wicklow.)
shilling, *n.* *shil*-ing, a British silver coin (from 1922 to 1946 half silver, thereafter cupro-nickel) equal to 12 pence, the twentieth of a pound. **cut off with a shilling,** deprived of an expected legacy. (A.S. *scilling*.)
shilly-shally, *n.* *shil*-e-*shal*-e, foolish trifling; indecision: *v.i.* to act irresolutely; to vacillate. (*shill I? shall I?*)
shim, *v.t.* shim, to level or wedge up with a shim; to weed with a shim: *n.* a wedge for levelling, tightening joints, preventing wear in bearings, etc.; a knife attached to a harrow for tearing up weeds [Agric.].
shimmer, *n.* *shim*-er, a glimmer; a tremulous gleam: *v.i.* to gleam; to glisten. (A.S. *scymrian*.)
shimmery, *a.* *shim*-er-re, shimmering; glistening softly.
shimmy, *n.* *shim*-me, a chemise [Coll.]; a fox-trot danced with an undulating movement of the body; abnormal vibration, esp. in a motor-car.
shin, *n.* shin, the fore-part of the bone of the leg between ankle and knee: *v.t.* to climb, esp. a tree. (A.S. *scinu*.)
shindy, *n.* *shin*-de, a disturbance; a commotion; a spree [Slang].
shine, *n.* shine, sunshine; fair weather; lustre; a shindy [Slang]: *v.i.* to emit rays of light; to be bright; to glitter; to sparkle; to be lively and animated; to be eminent, conspicuous, or distinguished; to stand out clearly. **to take the shine out of one,** to deprive him of his glory; to

make him look small [Coll.]. *p.* and *pp.* **shone.** (A.S. *scinan.*)

shiner, *n. shine*-er, one who or that which shines; a name of various silver-scaled fish; a new coin, esp. a sovereign [Slang].

shingle, *n. shing*-gl, a thin piece of wood split or sawn for use as a roofing tile; water-worn loose pebbles on shores and coasts; cutting of a woman's hair close to the head at the back; this style of hair-dressing: *v.t.* to cover with shingle; to roof with shingles; to crop a woman's hair close to the head at the back. (L. *scindo*, split.)

shingles, *n.pl. shing*-glz, herpes zoster, an eruptive inflammatory skin disease often spreading round the body like a girdle. (O.Fr. *cengle*, a girth.)

shingly, *a. shing*-gle, abounding with shingle; resembling shingles [Med.].

shining, *ppr. shine*-ing, gleaming; resplendent; illustrious: *n.* effusion of light; brightness.

shinny, *n. shin*-e, shinty.

Shinto, *n. shin*-toh, the chief religious cult of Japan, a combination of ancestor-worship and nature-worship. (Chinese, *chin*, god, *tao*, way.).

Shintoism, *n. shin*-toh-izm, Shinto [an incorrect form].

shinty, *n. shin*-te, a variety of hockey played in Scotland; the club used in this.

shiny, *a. shine*-e, bright; lustrous; glossy.

★**ship,** *n.* ship, a large vessel adapted to navigation; a vessel with not fewer than three masts, each square-rigged and having tops: *v.t.* to put on board ship; to convey by water; to engage to serve in a ship; to receive into a ship; to send by ship; to place, as oars, in their proper place: *v.i.* to go aboard ship; to engage for service on a ship. **ship a sea,** to have a wave break over the side. **ship of the desert,** the camel [Coll.]. **ship of the line,** a battleship, formerly, a seventy-four, or larger warship. **ship's time,** the local mean time on board ship. (A.S. *scip.*)

shipboard, *n. ship*-bord, the side of a ship; a ship.

shipboy, *n. ship*-boy, a boy who serves on board ship; a cabin boy.

ship-breaker, *n.* one who buys outworn or useless ships and breaks them up for materials.

ship-broker, *n.* a broker who procures cargoes for or insurance on ships.

shipbuilder, *n. ship*-bil-der, one who builds ships; a naval architect; a shipwright.

shipbuilding, *n. ship*-bil-ding, the craft, workmanship, or business of a shipbuilder.

ship-canal, *n.* a canal for seagoing vessels.

ship-chandler, *n.* one who deals in cordage, canvas, and other furniture of ships.

ship-chandlery, *n.* the business, stores, or premises of a ship-chandler.

ship-load, *n.* the amount a ship can carry; a cargo.

shipman, *n. ship*-man, a shipmaster; a pilot; a seaman.

shipmaster, *n. ship*-mahs-ter, the captain of a merchant ship.

shipmate, *n. ship*-mate, a sailor who serves with another in the same ship.

shipment, *n. ship*-ment, the act of putting anything on board ship; embarkation; goods shipped or put on board ship.

ship-money, *n.* an impost formerly charged on the ports, towns, cities, boroughs, and counties of England for providing ships for the navy.

shipowner, *n. ship*-oh-ner, one who owns ships.

shippen, *n. ship*-en, a shippon.

shipper, *n. ship*-per, one who sends goods by ship or other form of conveyance; an importer or exporter.

shipping, *a. ship*-ping, relating to ships: *n.* ships of any kind; ships collectively; tonnage; sailing. **shipping articles,** articles of agreement between the captain of a vessel and the seamen on board.

shipping-master, *n.* an official who witnesses the agreement signed between captain and crew, superintends paying-off, etc.

shippon, *n. ship*-on, a cattle-shed; a byre. (A.S. *scypen.*)

ship-rigged, *a.* square-rigged with three or more masts.

shipshape, *a.* and *ad. ship*-shape, in a seamanlike manner; well arranged; in good trim.

ship's-husband, *n.* one who attends to the repairs, provisioning, and requisites of a ship when in port.

shipway, *n. ship*-way, the timbers or ways on which a ship is built.

ship-worm, *n.* a boring mollusc of the genus *Teredo.*

shipwreck, *n. ship*-rek, the destruction of a ship by being cast ashore or otherwise; any similar destruction; ruin: *v.t.* to cause to suffer shipwreck; to cast ashore; to bring to disaster; to destroy.

shipwright, *n. ship*-rite, a skilled craftsman employed in shipbuilding.

shipyard, *n. ship*-yard, a shipbuilding yard.

shire, *n.* shire, a county. **the shires,** the fox-hunting counties of Rutland, Leicester, and Northampton. **shire horse,** a breed of heavy draught horses originally bred in the Midlands. (A.S. *scir.*)

shiremoot, *n. shire*-moot, in Anglo-Saxon England, the judicial assembly of a county, and later, the court of a county. (A.S. *scire*, and *mote*, meeting.)

shirk, *n.* shirk, a shirker: *v.t.* and *v.i.* to evade or slink away from; to scamp. (*shark.*)

shirker, *n. shirk*-er, an evader of responsibility or duty; one who lives by shifts and tricks or will not work.

shirky, *a. shirk*-e, given to shirking; disposed to shirk.

shirr, *n.* shir, elastic tape or thread used for making a gathering in garments, etc.; a gathering; a pucker.

★**shirt,** *n.* shirt, a loose sleeved under-garment for the body worn by men and boys; a blouse worn by women: *v.t.* to cover, as with a shirt. **boiled shirt,** *see* **boil. in shirt sleeves,** informally dressed; prepared for work. **to get one's shirt out,** to rouse oneself, or another, into a temper. **to put one's shirt on . . . ,** to support or back with all one's resources. (A.S. *scyrte.*)

shirt-front, *n.* the front of a shirt; a dickey.

shirting, *n. shirt*-ing, material for shirts.

shirt-waist, *n.* a woman's tailored blouse with collar and cuffs.

shirty, *a. shirt*-e, peevish; ill-tempered; cantankerous [Slang].

shittim, *n. shit*-tim, the hard-grained wood of *Acacia seyal*, a tree of the Dead Sea valley, used in the construction of the Jewish Tabernacle and its furniture; in the U.S.A., the cascara buckthorn and other trees. (Heb.)

shive, *n.* shive, a slice; a thin cut; a small piece or fragment; a wooden bung; a broad flat cork. (Ice.)

shiver, *n. shiv*-er, a fragment broken off; a variety of blue slate; shale: *v.t.* to shatter; to dash to pieces: *v.i.* to fall into shivers. (*sheave.*)

shiver, *v.i. shiv*-er, to quake; to tremble: *v.t.* to cause to shake. (Source uncertain; perhaps *quiver.*)

shiverer, *n. shiv*-er-rer, one who shivers (in either sense).

shiveringly, *ad. shiv*-er-ring-le, with trembling or shaking with cold or fear.

shiver-spar, *n.* a slaty variety of calcite; slate-spar. (Ger. *Schieffer*, slate, and *spar.*)

shivery, *a. shiv*-er-re, causing or characterized by shivering; easily shaking into pieces; incompact.

shoad, *n.* shohd, loose fragments of ore indicating the near-by presence of a lode [Mining]. (Probably A.S. *scadan*, to divide.)

shoal, *n.* shole, a multitude of fishes or other aquatic animals; a crowd; a throng: *v.i.* to form a shoal; to crowd together. (A.S. *scolu*, a crowd.)

shoal, *a.* shole, shallow: *n.* a shallow; a sandbank or bar: *v.i.* to become more shallow. (*shallow.*)

shoaliness, *n. shole*-e-ness, the state of being shoaly; little depth of water.

shoaly, *a. shole*-e, abounding in shallows.

shoat, *n.* shote, a young hog. (Dial.)

★**shock,** *n.* shok, a violent collision or its effect; a sudden depression of the bodily functions or mental agitation; a concussion; a fierce onset; a severe surprise; external violence; offence; prostration; the effect on the animal system of an electric discharge [Elect.]: *v.t.* to shake by sudden collision; to encounter; to offend; to disgust: *v.i.* to give a shock or shocks. (Fr. *choquer, choc.*)

shock, *n.* shok, a pile of sheaves; a stook; a mass of short hair; a shaggy dog: *v.i.* to collect or pile sheaves in shocks. (O.Teut. *scok, schok.*)

shock-absorber, *n.* a device fitted to motor-cars,

aeroplanes, etc., to lessen the shock of jolting, collision, or of landing, etc.
hocker, *n. shok*-er, one who or that which shocks; a sensational novel, generally short and cheap.
shock-headed, *a.* having a full crop of bushy hair.
shocking, *a. shok*-ing, striking, as with horror; disgusting; extremely offensive; of bad quality.
shockingly, *ad.* in a shocking manner.
shockingness, *n.* the state of being shocking.
shock-troops, *n.pl.* troops specially selected and trained for difficult and dangerous attacks.
shod, shod, *p.* and *pp.* of *shoe.*
shoddy, *n. shod*-e, wool obtained from tearing down worn-out fabrics; coarse, inferior cloth made of this: *a.* made of shoddy; of shoddy quality; not genuine; cheap and nasty. (Origin unknown.)
shode, *n.* shohd, shoad.
***shoe,** *n.* shoo, a covering for the foot, usually of leather, of a thick sort for the sole and a thinner for the uppers; a plate or rim of iron nailed to the hoof of a horse to preserve it from injury; the part of a brake which touches the wheel; anything like a shoe in shape or use: *v.t.* to furnish with or put on shoes; to cover at the bottom. **dead men's shoes,** expectation of receiving a legacy or betterment upon a decease. **where the shoe pinches,** where the actual source of the trouble is. *p.* and *pp.* **shod.** (A.S. *sceoh.*)
shoebill, *n. shoo*-bil, the whale-headed heron *Balæniceps rex,* allied to the storks.
shoeblack, *n. shoo*-blak, one who cleans boots or shoes; a preparation for blacking shoes, etc.
shoeflower, *n. shoo*-flou-er, the Asiatic plant *Hibiscus rosa-sinensis,* the sap of which is used as blacking and as a hair-dye.
shoe-horn, *n.* an appliance for easing the foot into a shoe.
shoe-lace, *n. shoo*-lace, a shoe-string.
shoemaker, *n. shoo*-make-er, a maker of shoes and boots; a dealer in leather footwear.
shoer, *n. shoo*-er, one who shoes horses; a farrier.
shoe-string, *n.* a lace or thong for fastening a shoe with.
shoe-tie, *n.* a shoe-string.
shofar, *n. shoh*-far, shophar.
shog, *n.* shog, a jerk; a shock: *v.t.* to shake; to agitate: *v.i.* to move off; to jog. (M.E. *shogge,* a swinging gait.)
Shogun, *n. shoh*-goon, the head of a military dynasty in Japan which, for centuries preceding the revolution of 1868, usurped the power of the Emperors; a Japanese military governor in feudal times. (Jap., generalissimo.)
shogunate, *n. shoh*-goo-nate, the office, period of office, or government of a Shogun.
shole, *n.* shole, a plank or plate placed transversely beneath a post, etc., to support and protect it [Naut.]. (Perhaps from *sole* or *shoe.*)
shone, shon, *p.* and *pp.* of *shine.*
shoo, *n.* shoo, a cry used for scaring away birds, small animals, etc.: *v.i.* to make this cry: *int.* begone! scram!
shook, shook, *p.* of *shake.*
shook, *n.* shook, a set of staves for a cask, also of boards for boxes; a shock of corn. (*shock.*)
shool, *n.* shool, shul.
shoon, *n.pl.* shoon, obsolete form of *shoes.*
shoot, *n.* shoot, the discharge of a fire-arm or bow; a shooting meet or party; a young branch; a quick darting pain; a chute or inclined plane for goods, etc.: *v.t.* to let fly or drive with force; to discharge and let off; to strike with anything shot; to send out; to thrust forth; to propel; to kill by a bullet, arrow, or other missile; to pass through with swiftness; to unload by tipping; to take a motion-picture of: *v.i.* to perform the act of shooting; to engage in shooting; to germinate; to send forth branches; to form by shooting; to be emitted; to project; to pass as an arrow or pointed instrument; to drive the ball at the goal [Football, etc.]; to grow rapidly; to move with velocity. **shoot ahead,** to outstrip, as in running; sailing, etc. **shoot the moon,** to remove one's goods clandestinely by night. **shoot the sun,** to take the sun's altitude [Coll.]. **shoot up,** to grow, esp. rapidly; to intimidate or quell by reckless shooting [Amer. slang]. *p.* and *pp.* **shot.** (A.S. *sceotan.*)
hooter, *n. shoot*-er, one who shoots; a fire-arm; a fast low ball moving level with the pitch [Cricket].
shooting, *n. shoot*-ing, the act of discharging fire-arms or arrows; the act or practice of killing game with the gun; a game-preserve; the right to shoot game over land; sensation of a quick glancing pain. **shooting star,** an incandescent meteor which darts across the sky.
shooting-box, *n.* a house for sportsmen's use during the shooting season.
shooting-gallery, *n.* a long apartment used for practice at shooting.
shooting-range, *n.* a place, open or enclosed, with measured distances for practice at shooting.
shooting-stick, *n.* the stick with which a printer drives up his quoins; a gangster's fire-arm [Slang]; a spiked stick with a handle expanding to form a seat.
shoot-off, *n.* the final heat in a shooting competition.
shop, *n.* shop, a building in which goods are sold by retail; a place where work, esp. engineering, is done: *v.i.* to visit shops, to purchase goods in shops: *v.t.* to arrest and imprison, also to lay information against [Slang]. **all over the shop,** scattered [Slang]. **shut up shop,** to give up one's occupation; to cease work. **talk shop,** to talk about one's own business. (A.S. *sceoppa,* a booth.)
shop-assistant, *n.* a salesman or saleswoman in a retail shop or stores.
shop-board, *n.* a bench on which work is done, esp. by tailors.
shop-boy, -girl, *n.* one employed in a shop.
shophar, *n. shoh*-far, a ram's-horn trumpet, blown ceremoniously in synagogues on the Day of Atonement. (Heb.)
shopkeeper, *n. shop*-keep-er, a retailer of goods in a shop.
shoplifter, *n. shop*-lif-ter, one who enters a shop when it is open to customers and takes occasion to steal.
shoplifting, *n. shop*-lif-ting, practice of a shoplifter.
shopman, *n. shop*-man, a petty trader; one who serves in a shop; a mechanic in a workshop.
shopper, *n. shop*-er, one who shops.
shopping, *n. shop*-ing, act of visiting shops for the purchase of goods; one's purchases while shopping.
shoppy, *a. shop*-e, characteristic of retail trade or tradesmen, or of one who talks shop.
shopsoiled, *a. shop*-soyld, faded or otherwise impaired through being exposed for sale or handled.
shop-steward, *n.* a trade-union official in a factory, etc., elected by his fellow-workers to represent them in negotiations, etc.
shop-walker, *n.* one employed in a shop to direct customers and see that they are attended to.
shore, *n.* shore, the coast or land adjacent to the sea, river, or any piece of water, lake, etc.; the area between high- and low-watermarks [Law]. (A.S. *score*).
shore, *n.* shore, a prop or support for a building or for a ship on the stocks; a temporary buttress: *v.t.* to support by a prop or shore. (Perhaps Dut. *schoor,* prop.)
shore-bird, *n.* any bird that frequents the seashore or estuaries.
shore-lark, *n.* the bird *Otocorys alpestris.*
shoreless, *a. shore*-less, having no shore or coast; of indefinite or unlimited extent.
shore-pipit, *n.* the rock-pipit, *Anthus obscurus.*
shoreward, *a.* and *ad. shore*-ward, toward the shore.
shoring, *n. shore*-ring, the props used as shores.
shorling, *n. shor*-ling, formerly, wool shorn from a live sheep (as opposed to morling).
shorn, shorn, *pp.* of *shear*: *a.* cut off; having the hair or wool sheared off; deprived of.
***short,** *a.* short, not long; not of long duration; not of sufficient length or range; inadequate; less than; deficient; scanty; brief; concise; brittle; friable; abrupt; petulant; unaccented; not having goods, stock, etc., at time of selling: *ad.* abruptly; at once: *n.* the mark (˘) indicating that a vowel is short; a short vowel; a short article or paragraph; a short-circuit [Elect.]: *v.t.* and *i.* to curtail; to short-circuit. **be short,** to be scantily supplied. **be taken short,** to be seized with urgent necessity. **come short,** to fail. **cut short,** to abridge. **fall short,** to fail; to be less. **in short,** briefly. **sell short,** to sell for future delivery [Stock Exchange]. **short commons,** *see* **commons. short cut,** a more direct route or a quicker method of procedure

than the usual. **short head,** a very short distance, esp. between the winner and runner-up in a race. **short sea,** a choppy sea. **short shrift,** *see* **shrift. short suit,** one in which only three cards or less are held [Whist, etc.]. **short ton,** *see* **ton. short waves,** wireless waves of not less than 10 or more than 50 metres. **stop short,** to stop at once, or without reaching the aim. (A.S. *sceort.*)
shortage, *n. short*-aj, deficiency ; the amount short.
shortbread, *n. short*-bred, shortcake.
shortcake, *n. short*-kake, a flat cake of flour, butter, and sugar, short in fracture.
short-circuit, *n.* the shortening of an electric circuit by accidental contact : *v.t.* to form or introduce a short-circuit in.
shortcoat, *n. short*-koat, short clothes for an infant (*usually in pl.*) : *v.t.* short-*koat,* to shorten (an infant).
shortcoming, *n. short*-kum-ing, a failure in produce or in duty ; remissness.
short-dated, *a.* having little time to run.
shorten, *v.t. shor*-tn, to make shorter in measure, extent, or time; to abridge; to contract; to confine; to lop; to put an infant into short clothes: *v.i.* to become short or shorter; to contract.
shortening, *n. shor*-tn-ing, act of becoming short or shorter, or of putting an infant into shortcoats ; fat used in making pastry.
shortfall, *n. short*-fawl, deficit ; adverse balance.
shorthand, *n. short*-hand, an abbreviated method of writing ; stenography.
shorthanded, *a.* short-*hand*-ed, undermanned.
shorthorn, *n. short*-horn, one of a valuable breed of cattle with short horns originating in the north of England.
short-hose, *n.* the stockings worn with a kilt.
short-leg, *n.* one who fields to leg, close in ; this position in the field [Cricket].
short-lived, *a.* being of short continuance ; not living or lasting long.
shortly, *ad.* soon ; in a short way ; curtly.
shortness, *n.* brevity ; state of being short ; scantiness of supply ; deficiency.
short-rib, *n.* one of the lower ribs ; a false rib.
shorts, *n.pl.* shorts, the bran and coarse part of meal in mixture ; loose breeches with open legs ending just above the knees, for outdoor games or tropical wear.
short-sighted, *a.* not able to see far ; near-sighted ; not able to see far into the future ; of limited penetration.
short-sightedness, *n.* myopia, the quality of being short-sighted.
short-slip, *n.* one who fields behind the striker on the off side [Cricket].
short-spoken, *a.* curt.
short-tempered, *a.* of a quick or irritable temper.
short-term, *a.* limited to, intended for, or pertaining to a short period only.
short-waisted, *a.* short from armpits to waist.
short-winded, *a.* affected with shortness of breath.
short-witted, *a.* having little wit ; of scanty judgment or intellect ; mentally deficient.
shot, shot, *p.* and *pp.* of *shoot.*
shot, *n.* shot, discharge of a missile weapon ; act of shooting ; a projectile ; very small bullets (*sing.* used as *pl.*) ; a charge of blasting explosive ; the flight of a missile ; a marksman ; a try ; an aim ; a stroke [Games] ; a photograph taken with a cinematograph camera ; formerly, a tavern reckoning : *v.t.* to load with shot. **a big shot,** an important person [U.S.A.]. **a shot in the dark,** a random attempt. **a shot in the locker,** *see* **locker. like a shot,** instantly, in the twinkling of an eye. **putting the shot,** *see* **put. shot of a cable,** the splicing of two cables together, or the whole length of two thus spliced. **shot silk,** silk so woven with different coloured threads as to present different shades of colour. (A.S. *scot,* a shot.)
shot-belt, *n.* a belt fitted to carry cartridges or shot.
shotgun, *n. shot*-gun, a fowling-piece ; a smooth-bore sporting gun.
shot-proof, *a.* proof against shot.
shott, *n.* shot, a shallow saline lake or swamp of N. Africa. (Arab. *shatt.*)
shotten, *a.* shotn, having ejected the spawn ; dislocated ; curdled and sour. (A.S. *sceōtan,* shoot.)

shough, *n.* shok, a shock, or species of shaggy dog. (*shock.*)
should, shood, *p.* of *shall.*
shoulder, *n. shole*-der, the joint, or parts about the joints, by which the arm (or foreleg of a quadruped) is connected with the body ; the upper joint of the foreleg of an animal cut as meat ; anything resembling a shoulder ; a prominence ; the angle of a bastion ; that which elevates and sustains [Fort] : *pl.* the upper part of the back : *v.t.* to push with the shoulder or with violence ; to take upon the shoulder. **cold shoulder,** *see* **cold-shoulder. rub shoulders,** *see* **rub. shoulder of mutton sail,** a triangular sail. **shoulder to shoulder,** with common action ; in co-operation. (A.S. *sculdor.*)
shoulder-belt, *n.* a belt, bandolier, etc., crossing the shoulder.
shoulder-blade, *n.* the scapula, or broad and triangular blade-bone covering the hind part of the ribs.
shoulder-bone, *n.* the shoulder-blade.
shoulder-knot, *n.* an epaulette or ornamental knot worn on the shoulders.
shoulder-slip, *n.* dislocation of the shoulder.
shoulder-strap, *n.* a narrow strap worn on the shoulders of military uniform, etc. ; a strap crossing one shoulder for supporting a bag, etc. ; either of two ribbons, tapes, etc., supporting a sleeveless garment from the shoulders.
shout, *n.* shout, a loud cry ; a sudden outcry or outburst of joy, triumph, warning, or encouragement; a turn in paying for drinks [Coll.] : *v.i.* to utter a shout : *v.t.* to utter with a shout. **shout down,** to silence (a speaker) by clamour. (M.E. *shouten.*)
shouter, *n. shout*-er, one who shouts.
shove, *n.* shuv, the act of pushing or a push : *v.t.* to push before one ; to press against : *v.i.* to drive forward ; to push. (A.S. *scufan.*)
shove-ha'penny, *n.* the game of shovel-board played with ha'pennies or small metal disks in place of wooden disks.
shovel, *n.* shuvl, a spade-like tool with a broad flat scoop used for lifting or sifting loose objects : *v.t.* to take up and throw with a shovel ; to gather in great quantities. (A.S. *scofl.*)
shovel-board, *n.* a board on which wooden disks are shoved by players at a mark ; the game itself.
shovelful, *n. shuvl*-ful, as much as a shovel will hold.
shovel-hat, *n.* a clerical hat with a broad brim turned up at the sides.
shoveller, *n. shuvl*-er, one who shovels ; the broad-billed river duck *Spatula clypeata.*
shover, *n. shuv*-er, one who or that which shoves ; a pushful person ; a chauffeur [Slang].
show, *n.* shoh, the act of showing ; exhibition to view ; appearance ; ostentatious display ; semblance ; plausibility ; pretence ; a spectacle or other entertainment ; a chance or opportunity [Slang] ; a business [Coll.] : *v.t.* to present to the view ; to enable to see or perceive ; to teach or inform ; to point out ; to prove ; to manifest : *v.i.* to appear ; to be in appearance. **give the show away,** to divulge (intentionally or inadvertently). **run the show,** to act as boss or manager. **show fight,** to resist. **show forth,** to proclaim. **show off,** to exhibit in an ostentatious manner. **show of hands,** a raising of hands as a vote. **show up,** to expose. **steal the show,** to be given most of the applause [Coll.]. *p.* and *pp.* **shown.** (A.S. *sceawian.*)
show-bill, *n.* a placard or broadsheet containing an advertisement ; a contents bill.
show-box, *n.* a box containing some object of curiosity for exhibition ; the box of a peep-show.
showbread, *n. shoh*-bred, among the ancient Jews, the twelve loaves placed by the priest on the golden table in the sanctuary, one for each tribe, in acknowledgment of the Divine bounty.
show-card, *n.* a tradesman's advertisement card ; a display card for samples.
show-case, *n.* a glass or glass-fronted case or box containing articles for exhibition.
showdown, *n. shoh*-doun, the exposure of one's hand face up [Cards] ; a complete disclosure, esp. as between parties at variance.
shower, *n. shou*-er, a short or light fall of rain, snow, etc. ; a copious fall of things in quick succession ; liberal distribution : *v.t.* to wet with a shower ; to

wet copiously with rain; to bestow liberally: *v.i.* to fall in showers. (A.S. *scur.*)
shower, *n.* *shoh*-er, one who shows; an exhibitor.
shower-bath, *n.* a bath in which one may be sprayed from above.
showeriness, *n.* state of being showery.
showery, *a.* *shou*-er-re, raining in showers; abounding in showers.
show-girl, *n.* an actress engaged primarily for her good looks or figure; a mannequin.
showily, *ad.* *shoh*-e-le, in a showy manner.
showiness, *n.* *shoh*-e-ness, ostentation; display; pompousness; great parade.
showman, *n.* *shoh*-man, the exhibitor of a show; one proficient in showing off.
showmanship, *n.* *shoh*-man-ship, the art of a showman; power of showing one's attainments, etc., to the best advantage.
shown, shohn, *pp.* of *show.*
show-place, *n.* a place attractive to tourists.
showroom, *n.* *shoh*-room, a room for the exhibition of wares or samples, esp. at a wholesaler's.
showy, *a.* *shoh*-e, making a show; gaudy; ostentatious.
shram, *v.t.* shram, to benumb with cold. (Dial.)
shrank, shrank, *p.* of *shrink.*
shrapnel, *n.* *shrap*-nel, a projectile containing bullets and a bursting charge; (incorrectly) fragments of burst shell. (Gen. Hy. *Shrapnel*, *d.* 1842.)
shred, *n.* shred, a long narrow piece cut off; a strip; a fragment: *v.t.* to tear or cut into small strips. (A.S. *screade.*)
shredder, *n.* *shred*-er, an implement for shredding.
shreddy, *a.* *shred*-e, consisting of or of the nature of shreds; ragged.
shrew, *n.* shroo, a shrew-mouse; an ill-tempered, nagging, or turbulent woman; a scold. (A.S. *scréawa*, shrew-mouse.)
shrewd, *a.* shrood, of acute judgment; of nice discernment; sagacious; shrewish. **shrewd turn,** a mean trick, a piece of malicious mischief. (M.E. *schrewed*, cursed.)
shrewdly, *ad.* *shrood*-le, in a shrewd manner.
shrewdness, *n.* *shrood*-ness, the quality of being shrewd; sly cunning; sagacity.
shrewish, *a.* *shroo*-ish, having the qualities of a shrew; ill-natured, scolding, and vexatious.
shrewishly, *ad.* *shroo*-ish-le, in a shrewish manner.
shrewishness, *n.* the quality of being shrewish.
shrew-mole, *n.* an insectivore of the genus *Scalops* or *Scapanus*, esp. the web-footed *Scalops aquaticus*, nearly allied to the mole.
shrew-mouse, *n.* a small insectivorous burrowing mammal of the family Soricidæ.
shriek, *n.* shreek, a sharp shrill outcry or scream from sudden surprise, pain, or terror: *v.i.* to utter a shriek; to scream. (*screech.*)
shrieker, *n.* *shreek*-er, one who shrieks; the black-tailed godwit, *Limosa belgica.*
shrievalty, *n.* *shree*-val-te, the office or jurisdiction of a sheriff; a sheriff's term of office.
shrift, *n.* shrift, the act of shriving; confession; absolution. **short shrift,** a very short time (from the short time between the shriving and execution of a criminal). (A.S. *scrift.*)
shrike, *n.* shrike, the butcher-bird, a species of the genus *Lanius* preying on small animals which it impales on thorns to form a larder. (O.N. *skrīkja.*)
shrill, *a.* shril, sharp; piercing in sound: *v.i.* to utter an acute piercing sound: *v.t.* to express shrilly. (M.E. *schrill.*)
shrillness, *n.* *shril*-ness, the quality of being shrill; acuteness of sound.
shrilly, *ad.* *shril*-le, in a shrill manner: *a.* somewhat shrill.
shrimp, *n.* shrimp, a small long-tailed marine crustacean, *Crangon vulgaris*, allied to the prawn and esteemed as an article of food; a dwarf or undersized person: *v.t.* to fish for shrimps. (A.S. *scrimman*, shrink.)
shrimper, *n.* *shrim*-per, one who catches shrimps; a boat so employed.
shrimpish, *a.* *shrim*-pish, dwarfish; diminutive.
shrimp-net, *n.* a net fixed to a frame on a staff, for catching shrimps.
shrine, *n.* shrine, a case; a reliquary; a tomb; a sacred place: *v.t.* to enshrine. (A.S. *scrin.*)
shrink, *v.i.* shrink, to become smaller by contraction; to shrivel; to become wrinkled; to draw back, as from danger; to recoil, as in fear or horror; to express fear or pain by shrugging or contracting the body: *v.t.* to cause to contract: *n.* an act of shrinking. *p.* **shrank.** *pp.* **shrunk, shrunken.** (A.S. *scrincan.*)
shrinkable, *a.* *shring*-ka-bl, capable of being shrunk; liable to shrink.
shrinkage, *n.* *shring*-kaj, reduction in bulk; contraction, also amount of this.
shrinker, *n.* *shring*-ker, one who shrinks; one who withdraws from danger; an appliance for shrinking a heated metal tire.
shrinkingly, *ad.* *shring*-king-le, with shrinking.
shrive, *v.t.* and *i.* shrive, to receive confession and grant absolution. *p.* **shrove.** *pp.* **shriven.** (A.S. *scrifan.*)
shrivel, *v.i.* shrivl, to contract into wrinkles; to shrink: *v.t.* to cause to become wrinkled. (Scand.)
shroff, *n.* shrof, in India and the East, a money-changer or banker; *v.t.* and *i.* to examine coins and part the good from the bad. (Hind. *sarrāf.*)
shroffage, *n.* *shrof*-aj, the art of, or charge for, shroffing.
shroud, *n.* shroud, the burial garment of a corpse, a winding sheet; that which covers, protects, or conceals: *pl.* the ropes in pairs that form the standing rigging and extend from the mast-heads to the sides of a ship [Naut.]: *v.t.* to dress for the grave; to cover; to conceal; to disguise. (A.S. *scrud.*)
shrover, *n.* *shroh*-ver, a lad or girl who went from house to house singing at Shrovetide.
Shrovetide, *n.* *shrohv*-tide, the period immediately before Lent, when the people confessed their sins and afterwards gave themselves up to sports; carnival time. **Shrove Tuesday,** the day before Ash Wednesday. (*shrive.*)
shroving, *n.* *shroh*-ving, the festivities of Shrovetide.
shrub, *n.* shrub, a low dwarf tree; a plant with woody stems branching from the root, and of no great height. (A.S. *scrob.*)
shrub, *n.* shrub, a cordial of lemon or other juice and sugar, with addition of spirit, esp. rum. (Ar.)
shrubbery, *n.* *shrub*-er-re, a plantation of shrubs.
shrubbiness, *n.* the quality of being shrubby.
shrubby, *a.* *shrub*-e, like a shrub; full of or consisting of shrubs.
shruff, *n.* shruf, the refuse of metals; dross; refuse for burning. (Dial.)
shrug, *v.t.* shrug, to draw up or to contract, as the shoulders, in expression of dislike or dissatisfaction: *v.i.* to raise or draw up the shoulders: *n.* act of shrugging. (Origin unknown.)
shrunk, shrunk, *p.* and *pp.* of *shrink.*
shrunken, *shrung*-ken, *pp.* of *shrink*: *a.* shrivelled.
shuck, *n.* shuk, a husk or pod: *v.t.* to remove the husk from. (Origin unknown.)
shucks, *int.* shuks, nonsense! rubbish! [Slang].
shudder, *n.* *shud*-er, a tremor; a sudden shaking with fear or horror: *v.i.* to quake; to tremble; to shiver. (M.E. *shodderen.*)
shudderingly, *ad.* *shud*-er-ring-le, with quaking.
shuffle, *n.* *shuf*-fl, the act of shuffling; an evasion; a trick: *v.t.* to change the relative positions of; to remove or introduce by artificial confusion: *v.i.* to change the relative position of cards in a pack; to shift ground; to evade fair questions; to drag the feet; to move with an irregular gait. **shuffle off,** to push off; to rid oneself of. (*scuffle.*)
shuffle-board, *n.* shovel-board.
shuffle-cap, *n.* a game played by shaking money in a hat or cap.
shuffler, *n.* *shuf*-fler, one who shuffles; a deceitful or prevaricating fellow.
shuffling, *n.* *shuf*-fling, act of dragging the feet along the ground; shifty conduct: *a.* evasive.
shufflingly, *ad.* *shuf*-fling-le, by shuffling; evasively.
shul, *n.* shool, a synagogue. (Yiddish.)
shun, *v.t.* to avoid; to keep clear of; not to mix or associate with. (A.S. *scunian.*)
shunless, *a.* *shun*-less, not to be avoided; ineluctable.
shunt, *n.* shunt, a diversion to another track; a diversion of a circuit from one wire to another, also the conductor effecting this [Elect.]: *v.t.* to turn off to one side; to move as a railway train from one line to another. (A.S. *scunian.*)
shunter, *n.* *shunt*-er, one who shunts.

★**shut,** *a.* shut, closed; barred: *v.t.* to close; to bar; to exclude: *v.i.* to close itself; to be closed. **shut down,** to stop working. **shut in,** to confine. **shut off,** to prevent the flow or passage of; to exclude. **shut out,** to exclude. **shut up,** to close; to confine; to conclude; to stop talking. **shut one's eyes to,** to ignore; to refuse to take into consideration. **to shut one's mouth,** to maintain, or to compel another to maintain, silence. **to be shut of** [Coll.], to be rid of. (A.S. *scyttan*, to bar or lock.)
shutter, *n.* *shut*-ter, one who or that which shuts; a close cover for a window; an appliance allowing light to pass through the lens of a camera and shutting it off when required [Phot.]: *v.t.* to provide or cover with a shutter or shutters.
shuttle, *n.* *shut*-tl, an instrument for shooting the thread of the woof through the warp [Weaving]; a sliding thread-holder. **shuttle service,** a service of trains, aircraft, etc., operating forwards and backwards between fixed points. **shuttle train, bus,** etc., a train, etc., operating such a service. (A.S. *scyttel*, door-bolt.)
shuttle-cock, *n.* a cork stuck with feathers, and struck by a battledore; the game played with it.
shy, *a.* shy, shunning approach; reserved; cautious; timid; suspicious (**shyer, shyest**): *n.* the act of shying: *v.i.* to start suddenly aside from fear (esp. of a horse); to have scruples about. **to fight shy of,** to avoid. (A.S. *sceoh*, Ger. *scheu*, timid.)
shy, *v.t.* shy, to throw, as a ball: *n.* act of shying.
Shylock, *n.* *shy*-lok, a merciless money-lender or extortioner. (Character in Shakespeare's "Merchant of Venice.")
shyly, *ad.* *shy*-le, in a shy manner.
shyness, *n.* *shy*-ness, the quality of being shy.
shyster, *n.* *shy*-ster, a tricky or unprincipled person, esp. a business man or lawyer [Amer. slang].
si, *n.* see, the seventh note in the musical scale.
sialagogue, *n.* sy-*al*-a-gog *or* *sy*-a-la-gohg, a medicine that promotes the flow of saliva. (Gr. *sialon*, spittle, *ago*, lead.)
siamang, *n.* *sy*-a-mang, a large gibbon, *Hylobates syndactylus*, of Malaysia and Sumatra. (Malay.)
Siamese, *a.* sy-a-*meez*, pertaining to Siam (Thailand): *n.* a native, or the people, of Siam; the Siamese language; a domesticated cat peculiar to Siam. **Siamese twins,** a congenitally united pair of human twins; any double monstrosity.
sib, *a.* sib, akin; related to: *n.* a kinsman or kinswoman; kinsfolk; relationship. (A.S. *sibb*, akin.)
Siberian, *a.* and *n.* sy-*beer*-re-an, pertaining to, or a native of, Siberia.
sibilance, *n.* *sib*-e-lance, a hissing sound; sibilancy.
sibilancy, *n.* *sib*-e-lan-se, quality of being sibilant.
sibilant, *a.* *sib*-e-lant, hissing: *n.* a letter uttered with a hissing sound, as *s*. (L. *sibilans*, hissing.)
sibilate, *v.t.* and *i.* *sib*-e-late, to speak, utter, or pronounce with hissing.
sibilation, *n.* sib-e-*lay*-shon, utterance with a hissing sound; hissing.
sibyl, *n.* *sib*-il, one of a number of women anciently held to represent the voice of God in nature; a pagan prophetess; a sorceress. (Gr. *sibylla*.)
sibylline, *a.* *sib*-e-line, pertaining to or uttered, written, or composed by the sibyls; prophetic; oracular. **the Sibylline books**, books brought by the Sibyl of Cumæ to King Tarquin, and alleged to contain oracles respecting the fortunes of Rome.
sic, *ad.* sik, so written or printed. (L., so.)
siccative, *a.* *sik*-a-tiv, drying; causing to dry: *n.* that which promotes drying. (L. *siccatus*, dried.)
siccity, *n.* *sik*-se-te, aridity; absence of moisture.
sice, *n.* sice, the number six at dice [Slang]. (*six*.)
sice, *n.* sice, a syce, an Indian groom.
Siceliot, *n.* se-*sel*-e-ot, an ancient Greek colonizer of Sicily.
Sicilian, *a.* se-*sil*-yan, pertaining to Sicily: *n.* a native of Sicily; the siciliana. **Sicilian Vespers,** a massacre of the French in Sicily on Easter Monday, 1282, commenced at the hour of vespers.
siciliana, *n.* se-*sil*-e-*ah*-na, a graceful peasant dance of the Sicilians [Mus.]. (It.)
sick, *a.* sik, affected with nausea; inclined to vomit; disgusted; not in health; ill; set apart for sick people: *n.* sick persons collectively. **sick bay,** the space in a ship allotted for the hospital [Naut.]. **sick benefit** or **pay,** money received from insurance or club funds by one incapacitated by sickness. **sick as a dog,** vomiting copiously. **sick at heart,** full of sorrow; dispirited. **sick headache,** migraine. (A.S. *seoc*.)
sicken, *v.t.* *sik*-en, to make sick; to make squeamish; to disgust: *v.i.* to become sick; to fall into disease; to be filled to disgust; to languish.
sickener, *n.* *sik*-en-er, a cause of disgust.
sickening, *a.* *sik*-en-ing, becoming or making sick; disgusting; particularly loathsome.
sickish, *a.* *sik*-ish, somewhat sick or diseased; inclined to be sick; queasy.
sickishness, *n.* the quality of exciting disgust.
sickle, *n.* *sik*-l, a reaping-hook. (A.S. *sicol*.)
sick-leave, *n.* leave of absence granted on account of ill health.
sicklied, *a.* *sik*-lid, having a sickly hue
sickliness, *n.* *sik*-le-ness, the state of being sickly.
sick-list, *n.* a list containing the names of the sick.
sickly, *a.* *sik*-le, somewhat affected with sickness or disease; habitually indisposed; marked with sickness; inducing sickness; unhealthy; languid.
sickness, *n.* *sik*-ness, state of being sick; illness; a disease or malady.
sick-room, *n.* an apartment to which a person is confined by illness.
Sida, *n.* *sy*-da, a genus of mallows including *S. aurea*, the Indian mallow. (Gr. *sidē*.)
★**side,** *n.* side, the broad and long part or surface of a thing; margin or edge; a half opposite to another half; the rib part of an animal; the part between the top and bottom, as the slope of a hill; quarter; region; one part, or one aspect or view of a thing; one of two or more opposing bodies or views; a faction or sect; separate line of descent; a spin given to the cue-ball [Billiards]; swagger [Slang]: *a.* lateral; being on or toward the side; oblique; incidental: *v.i.* to embrace the opinions of a party, or engage in its interest. **choose sides,** to select parties for competition. **put on one side,** to lay by for future use or attention; to shelve or defer. **put on side,** to behave in a conceited or swaggering manner. **shake one's sides,** to laugh heartily. **side by side,** alongside each other. **side issue,** a matter subsidiary to or apart from the main point. **take sides,** to attach oneself to the interest of a party. (A.S.)
side-arm, *n.* a weapon, esp. bayonet, carried at the left side.
sideboard, *n.* *side*-bord, a piece of dining-room furniture serving as shelf and cupboard; a board placed at the side of a wagon to widen it.
sidecar, *n.* *side*-kar, a vehicle, usually one-wheeled and one-seated, laterally attached to a motor-cycle.
sided, *a.* *side*-ed, having a side, as, one-sided; flattened on one or two sides.
side-dish, *n.* *side*-dish, an entrée.
side-drum, *n.* the small drum beaten only on the top head.
side-light, *n.* light admitted from the side; a subsidiary light on the side of a ship, car, etc.; incidental information on a subject [Fig.].
side-line, *n.* a line at a side, as on a tennis court, etc.; a line running from a main railway-line; a supplementary line of goods, course of business, etc.
sideling, *a.* *side*-ling, sloping; oblique: *ad.* sideways; in a sidelong direction.
sidelong, *a.* *side*-long, lateral; oblique; not in front: *ad.* laterally; obliquely; on the side.
side-note, *n.* a marginal note.
side-play, *n.* freedom of movement from side to side [Mech.].
sider, *n.* *side*-er, a partisan; one who takes a side.
sidereal, *a.* sy-*deer*-re-al, pertaining to the stars; containing stars; measured by the seeming movements of the stars [Astrol.]. **sidereal clock,** a clock regulated to keep sidereal time. **sidereal time,** time measured by the axial rotation of the earth with reference to a fixed star or the vernal equinox. **sidereal year,** the period in which the earth makes one revolution in its orbit with respect to the stars, *i.e.*, approximately 20 min. longer than the astronomical year (*see* **year**). (L. *sideralis*, relating to the stars.)
siderism, *n.* *sy*-der-rizm, the belief or doctrine that human activities are influenced by the stars.
siderite, *n.* *sid*-er-rite, chalybite, ferrous carbonate; meteoric iron. (O.Fr.)
siderographic, *a.* sid-er-ro-*graf*-ik, pertaining to or done by siderography.

siderographist, *n.* *sid*-er-*rog*-ra-fist, one who engraves steel plates.
siderography, *n.* *sid*-er-*rog*-ra-fe, an art or practice of engraving on steel. (Gr. *sideros*, iron, *grapho*, write.)
siderolite, *n.* *sid*-er-ro-lite, a meteorite containing stone and iron. (Gr. *sideros*, iron, *lithos*, a stone.)
sideroscope, *n.* *sid*-er-ro-skope, an instrument for magnetically detecting small quantities of iron. (Gr. *sideros*, iron, *skopeo*, view.)
siderosis, *n.* sy-der-*roh*-sis, iron-grey colouring of the tissues [Path.].
siderostat, *n.* *sid*-er-ro-stat, an instrument for transmitting a beam of light along a fixed telescope.
Sideroxylon, *n.* *sid*-er-*rok*-se-lon, a large genus of tropical trees remarkable for the hardness and heaviness of their wood. (Gr. *sideros*, *xylon*, wood.)
side-saddle, *n.* a saddle for a woman, the rider sitting with both feet on the same side of the horse; the common pitcher-plant.
side-show, *n.* *side*-shoh, a subsidiary exhibition, entertainment, or affair.
sideslip, *n.* *side*-slip, a slip to one side; a skid; a shoot from a plant: *v.i.* to slip sideways; to skid.
sidesman, *n.* *sydz*-man, an assistant to a churchwarden. (*side* and *man*.)
side-splitting, *a.* extremely laughable.
side-step, *n.* a step or movement to one side: *v.i.* to step to one side.
sidestroke, *n.* *side*-stroke, an overhand stroke in swimming; a stroke made sideways or on the side of something.
sidetrack, *n.* *side*-trak, a siding: *v.t.* to shunt; to divert; to postpone considering.
side-view, *n.* an oblique view.
sidewalk, *n.* *side*-wawk, a raised footway along a road; the pavement [Amer.].
sideways, *ad.* *side*-wayz, toward or on one side; laterally; inclining.
side-wind, *n.* a cross wind; indirect means or attack [Fig.].
siding, *n.* *side*-ing, the attaching of oneself to a party; a short line of railway connected with the main track: *pl.* a group of such lines; a marshalling yard.
sidle, *v.i.* *sy*-dl, to go or move side foremost. (*side*.)
sidy, *a.* *sy*-de, full of swank; swaggering; pretentious [Slang].
siege, *n.* seej, the setting of an army round or before a fortified place to compel surrender; the state of being besieged; a continued endeavour to gain possession. **lay siege to, raise a siege,** *see* these words. **stand siege,** to undergo or resist a siege. (O.Fr.)
siege-gun, *n.* a gun heavier than a field-piece and used for battering fortifications.
siege-piece, *n.* *seej*-peece, a siege-gun; a coin issued in a besieged place [Numis.].
siege-train, *n.* the guns and their equipment used by a besieging army.
sienna, *n.* se-*en*-na, a brownish yellow pigment, consisting of hydrated ferric oxide with manganese dioxide. (*Sienna*, in Italy.)
sierra, *n.* se-*e*-ra, a mountain range with a saw-like ridge; the chromosphere [Astron.]; a fish of the mackerel family.
siesta, *n.* se-*es*-ta, a sleep during the heat of the day. (Sp.)
sieve, *n.* siv, an implement for separating through its meshes the finer particles of any substance from the coarser: *v.t.* to sift. (A.S. *sife*.)
sifaka, *n.* se-*fah*-ka, any of several species of Madagascar lemur of the genus *Propithecus*. (Malagasy.)
siffle, *v.t.* *sif*-fl, to whistle: *n.* sibilant respiration [Med.]. (Fr. *siffler*, whistle.)
siffleur, *n.* (App.), an expert at, or artiste in, whistling; the whistling marmot, *Marmota caligata*, of N. America. (Fr.)
siffleuse, *n.* (App.), a woman whistler. (Fr.)
sift, *v.t.* sift, to separate by a sieve; to separate; to examine critically; to scrutinize. (A.S. *siftan*.)
sifter, *n.* *sif*-ter, a small sieve or caster.
sigh, *n*, sy, a single deep respiration, as in grief; the involuntary and usual emotional inhaling of a quantity of air, and its sudden emission: *v.i.* to utter a sigh; to mourn: *v.t.* to express by sighs. (A.S. *sícan*.)
sigher, *n.* *sy*-er, one who sighs.
sighingly, *ad.* *sy*-ing-le, with sighs.

sight, *n.* site, the act or faculty of seeing; perception; view; visibility; the object seen; the range of view; inspection; aperture to see through, or something directing the vision, esp. on a fire-arm, optical instrument, etc.; that which is beheld; a spectacle; something remarkable or wonderful; [Coll.] a great quantity: *v.t.* to discover by sight; to adjust the sight on fire-arms. **at sight,** on presentation for payment. **take sight,** to take aim. **the sights,** the notable, worth-visiting places (of a town, district, etc.). (A.S. *gesihth*.)
sight-bill, -draft, *n.* a money order or draft payable at sight.
sighted, *a.* *site*-ed, having the power of sight; seeing in a particular manner, as short-sighted.
sighter, *n.* *site*-er, a trial shot; a shot to ascertain the range.
sightless, *a.* *site*-less, wanting sight; blind; offensive to the eye.
sightlessly, *ad.* in a sightless manner.
sightlessness, *n.* the state of being sightless.
sightliness, *n.* agreeableness to the eye.
sightly, *a.* *site*-le, pleasing to the eye; striking to the view; open to the view.
sight-reading, *n.* reading music, languages, or shorthand, etc., easily at first sight.
sightseeing, *n.* *site*-see-ing, the act of going about to view objects of interest or curiosity.
sightseer, *n.* *site*-see-er, a tourist, etc., engaged in seeing the sights.
sigil, *n.* *sij*-il, a seal; a signature. (L. *sigillum*.)
Sigillaria, *n.pl.* *sij*-e-*lare*-re-a, a genus of fossil plants found in the Devonian, Carboniferous, and Permian formations.
sigillary, *a.* *sij*-e-la-re, pertaining to a seal.
sigillate, *a.* *sij*-e-lat, marked as with a seal [Bot.].
sigma, *n.* *sig*-ma, the name of the Greek letter Σ, σ, ς, represented in English, etc., by *s*.
sigmate, *a.* *sig*-mat, shaped like an *s* or sigma: *v.t.* to add *s* or a sigma to.
sigmation, *n.* sig-*may*-shon, the adding of an *s* to a word.
sigmatism, *n.* *sig*-ma-tizm, defective pronunciation of the letter *s*.
sigmoid, *a.* *sig*-moyd, curved like an *s* [Anat.]. **sigmoid curve,** Hogarth's line of beauty. **sigmoid flexure,** the double turn of the colon before it enters the rectum [Anat.]. (Gr. *sigma*, and *eidos*, like.)
sigmoidal, *a.* sig-*moy*-dal, sigmoid.
sigmoiditis, *n.* sig-moy-*dy*-tis, inflammation of the sigmoid flexure.
★**sign,** *n.* sine, that by which anything is shown, indicated, or represented; a token; a nod or gesture indicative of a wish or command; a wonder; a miracle; evidence or proof; a sign-board; a memorial; a visible representation; a spoor; a mark of distinction; a symbol; a constellation dominatng a twelfth of the zodiac [Astron.]; a mark indicating operation [Alg.]; a countersign or password known only among confederates; a signature; a symptom; a character [Mus.]: *v.t.* to mark with characters or write one's name or initials; to subscribe; to signify, order, or make known by a gesture, etc.; to mark. **sign away,** to assign. **sign off,** to stop work; to announce the end of (a message, broadcast, etc.); to withdraw one's name from a club, etc. (O.Fr. *signe*.)
signable, *a.* *sine*-a-bl, that may be signed.
signal, *n.* *sig*-nal, a sign agreed upon; a device for distant communication; notice given: *a.* distinguished from what is ordinary; eminent; remarkable: *v.t.* to announce by signal; to make signals to: *v.i.* to give signals. (Fr.)
signal-book, *n.* a book giving a list of signals.
signal-box or **-cabin,** *n.* a room or hut from which railway signals are worked.
signal-fire, *n.* a fire intended for a signal.
signalize, *v.t.* *sig*-nal-ize, to make signal or eminent; to render distinguished from what is common.
signaller, *n.* *sig*-nal-er, one who signals; a member of the Royal Corps of Signals.
signally, *ad.* *sig*-nal-e, in a signal manner.
signalman, *n.* *sig*-nal-man, a man who works railway signals; a seaman, soldier, etc., who transmits and interprets signals; a private in the Royal Corps of Signals.

signary, *n.* *sig*-na-re, a series of alphabetic, hieroglyphic, or other symbols.
signatory, *a.* *sig*-na-to-re, signing; bound by signature: *n.* the signer of a document, esp. as representing a state. (L. *signatorius.*)
signature, *n.* *sig*-na-tewr, a sign, stamp, or mark impressed; sign-manual; the name of a person written by himself; the sign that shows the key in music; a letter or figure distinguishing the sheets and noting their order as a direction to the binder, or the sheet so distinguished [Printing]. **doctrine of signatures,** the ancient belief that plants and animals indicate by their external characters the diseases for which Nature intends them as remedies. **signature tune,** a special air or tune heralding a certain turn or feature in a broadcast programme. (Fr.)
signboard, *n.* *sine*-bord, a board giving the name and trade of a tradesman, the name of an inn, etc.
signer, *n.* *sine*-er, one who subscribes his name.
signet, *n.* *sig*-net, a small seal; in England, a seal for the authentication of royal grants; the privy seal. **signet-ring,** *n.* a ring containing a seal. (Fr.)
significance, *n.* sig-*nif*-e-kance, meaning; import; force; impressiveness; importance. (O.Fr.)
significancy, *n.* sig-*nif*-e-kan-se, significance.
significant, *a.* sig-*nif*-e-kant, expressive of something; bearing a meaning beyond the external sign; betokening something; noteworthy; indicative of some fact of importance.
significantly, *ad.* sig-*nif*-e-kant-le, in a significant manner; with meaning; with force of expression.
signification, *n.* *sig*-ne-fe-*kay*-shon, the act of signifying; that which is signified; meaning. (Fr.)
significative, *a.* sig-*nif*-e-ka-tiv, betokening or representing by an external sign; having signification or meaning. (Fr. *significatif.*)
significatively, *ad.* sig-*nif*-e-ka-tiv-le, in a significant manner; so as to represent by an external sign.
significativeness, *n.* sig-*nif*-e-ka-tiv-ness, the quality of being significant.
significator, *n.* sig-*nif*-e-kay-tor, he who or that which signifies.
significatory, *a.* sig-*nif*-e-ka-to-re, having meaning: *n.* that which betokens, signifies, or represents.
signify, *v.t.* *sig*-ne-fy, to make known either by signs or words; to declare; to mean; to import; to matter; to make known. (Fr. *signifier.*)
sign-manual, *n.* sine-*man*-yew-al, a signature in autograph, esp. that of a sovereign.
signor, *n.* *seen*-yor, an Italian title of address equal to the English *Mr.*
signora, *n.* seen-*yor*-ra, *Mrs.* in Italian. (It.)
signorina, *n.* *seen*-yo-*reen*-a, Miss in Italian. (It.)
signory, *n.* *seen*-yo-re, seigniory; the chief executive body of certain mediæval Italian cities.
signpainter, *n.* *sine*-paynt-er, one who paints signs, signboards, and facias.
sign-post, *n.* *sine*-pohst, a post on which a sign is exhibited: *v.t.* to furnish with sign-posts.
sike, *n.* sike, a small stream or rill; a ditch. (Ice.)
Sikh, *n.* seek, one of a sect embracing a monotheistic and casteless Hinduism, which eventually became a nation in Northern India with a military organization in defence of its faith. (Sans., disciple.)
silage, *n.* *sy*-laj, ensilage.
silcot, *n.* *sil*-kot, a cotton material with a silk-like finish.
silence, *n.* *sy*-lence, stillness or the entire absence of sound; forbearance of speech or noise; habitual taciturnity; secrecy; quiet; absence of mention; oblivion: *int.* be silent: *v.t.* to restrain from noise or speaking; to stop; to quiet; to cause to cease firing [Mil.]; to restrain from preaching; to put an end to. (Fr.)
silencer, *n.* *sy*-len-ser, an appliance for reducing noise, esp. that produced by internal combustion engines, fire-arms, etc.; a door- or window-stop.
Silene, *n.* sy-*lee*-ne, a large genus of hardy and half-hardy herbaceous plants comprising the pinks and campions. (Gr. *sialon*, salvia.)
silent, *a.* *sy*-lent, not speaking; taciturn; still; noiseless; not mentioning; calm; not acting; having no sound, as a letter. (L. *silens*, being quiet.)
silentiary, *n.* sy-*len*-she-a-re, one appointed to keep silence in court; one sworn not to divulge secrets of state.
silently, *ad.* *sy*-lent-le, in a silent manner; without speech, noise, or mention.
silentness, *n.* *sy*-lent-ness, the state of being silent.
Silenus, *n.* sy-*lee*-nus, a tipsy old reveller. (Name of the oldest of the Satyrs of Gr. myth, attendant and preceptor of Bacchus.)
silesia, *n.* sy-*lee*-shya, a kind of linen cloth, originally made in Silesia; a light fabric of twilled cotton.
silex, *n.* *sy*-leks, flint; silica. (L.)
silhouette, *n.* sil-oo-*et*, a portrait profile filled in with black; a black shadow in profile; a shadowgraph: *v.t.* and *i.* to portray in silhouette; to make a silhouette-like outline. (Name of an 18th-cent. Fr. minister of finance, which became a synonym for cheapness.)
silica, *n.* *sil*-e-ka, silicon dioxide, a substance entering into the composition of most earthy minerals, and forming the chief constituent of the earth's surface. **silica valve,** a transmitting thermionic valve having a bulb of silica instead of glass in order to resist high temperatures [Wire.]. (L. *silex.*)
silicate, *n.* *sil*-e-kate, a salt of silicic acid: *v.t.* to combine or impregnate with silica.
silicated, *a.* *sil*-e-kay-ted, combined or impregnated with silica or silicates [Chem.].
siliceous, *a.* se-*lish*-us, flinty; pertaining to silica or partaking of its nature and qualities. (L. *siliceus.*)
silicic, *a.* se-*lis*-ik, pertaining to or derived from silica.
silicide, *n.* *sil*-i-side, a compound of silicon with a metal or other element [Chem.].
siliciferous, *a.* sil-e-*sif*-er-rus, producing silica.
silicification, *n.* se-*lis*-e-fe-*kay*-shon, the act or process of silicifying; changing into flint.
silicify, *v.t.* se-*lis*-e-fy, to convert into or impregnate with silica; to petrify: *v.i.* to become silica or silicated. (L. *silex*, and *facio*, make.)
silicious, *a.* se-*lish*-us, siliceous.
silicium, *n.* se-*lish*-e-um, silicon.
silicle, *n.* *sil*-e-kl, a short broad pod [Bot.]. (Fr.)
silicolous, *a.* sil-e-*koh*-lus, inhabiting or growing on rocks rich in silica [Zool. and Bot.].
silicon, *n.* *sil*-e-kon, the non-metallic element occurring in silica and, next to oxygen, the most abundant of the elements. (L. *silex*, flint.)
silicosis, *n.* sil-e-*koh*-sis, a disease of the lungs due to the inhalation of particles of sand, etc.; grinder's disease [Med.]. (L. *silex*, flint.)
silicule, *n.* *sil*-e-kewl, a silicle. (Fr. *silicule.*)
siliculose, *a.* se-*lik*-yew-lohs, having or pertaining to silicles.
siliqua, *n.* *sil*-e-kwa, the long seed vessel or pod of a cruciferous plant. (L.)
siliquiform, *a.* si-*lik*-we-form, having the form of a siliqua.
siliquose, *a.* *sil*-e-kwohs, having a pod or capsule of the nature of a siliqua.
siliquous, *a.* *sil*-e-kwus, siliquose.
★**silk,** *n.* silk, the fine lustrous thread produced by the pupa of a moth of the genus *Bombyx*; cloth made of silk; a dress of silk; a King's Counsel [Coll.]: *a.* silken. **artificial silk,** thread or fabric made from collodion or wood-pulp. **to take silk,** to become a King's (or Queen's) Counsel. (A.S. *seolc.*)
silk-cotton, *n.* *silk*-kot-ton, a silky fibre covering the seed-pods of the bombax or silk-cotton tree (*Ceiba pentandra*) of tropical America, and other tropical trees.
silken, *a.* *silk*-en, made of or consisting of silk; like silk; soft to the touch; delicate; effeminate.
silk-grass, *n.* a species of yucca, *Y. filamentosa*; the needle-grass, *Stipa comata*; and other plants.
silkiness, *n.* *silk*-e-ness, the qualities of silk.
silkman, *n.* *silk*-man, a maker of silk; a silk-mercer.
silk-mercer, *n.* a dealer in silks.
silk-mill, *n.* *silk*-mil, a mill for spinning and manufacturing silk.
silk-thrower or **-throwster,** *n.* one who spins and prepares silk for weaving.
silk-weaver, *n.* a weaver of silk fabrics.
silkworm, *n.* *silk*-wurm, the caterpillar of the moth, *Bombyx mori*, which produces silk.
silkworm-gut, *n.* a fine gut for angling drawn from the glands of silkworms.
silky, *a.* *silk*-e, made of silk; consisting of silk; like silk; silken; suave [Fig.].

sill, *n.* sil, the piece of timber on which a structure rests; the timber or stone at the foot of a door or window; an intrusive sheet of igneous rock [Geol.]; the top level of a weir. (A.S. *syll.*)
sillabub, *n. sil*-la-bub, a liquor made by mixing wine or cider with milk and sugar, and thus forming a soft curd. (Dial. Eng. *sillibouk.*)
siller, *n. sil*-er, money; silver [Scots.].
sillily, *ad. sil*-le-le, in a silly manner.
sillimanite, *n. sil*-le-man-ite, fibrolite, a fibrous or massive silicate of alumina. (Benj. *Silliman*, Amer. chemist, d. 1864.)
silliness, *n. sil*-le-ness, the quality of being silly.
sillon, *n. sil*-lon, a mound raised in the middle of a moat for defence when it is too wide [Fort.]. (Fr.)
silly, *a. sil*-le, weak in intellect; witless; foolish; simple; proceeding from want of judgment; characterized by weakness or folly; unwise: *n.* a foolish person. **silly leg, point,** etc., in cricket, the fieldsman's position corresponding to leg, point, etc., but much closer to the wicket. **silly season,** *see* **season.** (A.S. *sælig*, happy, innocent, simple.)
silo, *n. sy*-loh, a pit in which green fodder is placed to make ensilage: *v.t.* to put in this; to convert to ensilage. (Sp.)
Silphium, *n. sil*-fe-um, a genus of hardy border perennials allied to the sunflowers.
silphology, *n.* sil-*fol*-o-je, the study of larval forms. (Gr. *silphe*, beetle, *logos*, science.)
silt, *n.* silt, a deposit in water of mud or sand: *v.t.* to choke or obstruct with silt: *v.i.* to become silted up. (Scand.)
silty, *a. sil*-te, full of, or composed of, silt; resembling silt.
Silurian, *a.* sy-*lewr*-re-an, pertaining to the Silures, an ancient British tribe settled in S. Wales: *n.* a major subdivision of the Palæozoic below the Devonian [Geol.].
silvan, *a. sil*-van, sylvan. (L. *silvanus.*)
★**silver,** *n. sil*-ver, a metallic element and precious metal of a brilliant lustre; coin of silver or a recognized substitute; money; silver domestic utensils; anything like silver: *a.* made of silver; like silver; white like silver; of a pale lustre; bright; soft: *v.t.* to cover with silver; to cover with tinfoil amalgamated with quicksilver; to make smooth and bright; to make hoary. **silver fir,** a species of fir, *Abies pectinata*, with silvery bark and leaves having silvery-white undersides. **silver jubilee,** a twenty-fifth anniversary. **silver lining,** a bright or hopeful prospect [Fig.]. **silver nitrate,** *see* **nitrate of silver. silver paper,** thin tin-foil. **the silver ring,** an enclosure on a race-course in which the smaller bets are made. **silver sand,** a fine light-coloured sand. **silver wedding,** the twenty-fifth anniversary of the wedding-day. (A.S. *seolfor.*)
silver-bath, *n.* a solution of silver nitrate for sensitizing [Phot.].
silver-fish, *n.* a wingless insect, *Lepisma saccharina*, of the bristle-tail family destructive to furs, clothes, paper, etc.
silver-fox, *n. sil*-ver-*foks*, a variety of the common red fox with glossy black hair, many hairs of which have white near the tips; the valuable fur of this.
silver-gilt, *n.* silver or silverware with a coating of gold.
silveriness, *n. sil*-ver-re-ness, the state of being silvery.
silvering, *n. sil*-ver-ring, the art or process of covering the surface of anything with silver; a silver coating.
silverite, *n. sil*-ver-rite, a bimetallist; an opponent of the demonetization of silver.
silverize, *v.t. sil*-ver-rize, to coat with silver.
silver-leaf, *n.* silver beaten into a thin leaf.
silverling, *n. sil*-ver-ling, a silver coin; a shekel.
silverly, *ad. sil*-ver-le, with the appearance of silver; sounding soft and clear.
silvern, *a. sil*-vern, of silver.
silver-point, *n.* a drawing made with a silver pencil on a specially prepared surface; the process of making this.
silver-print, *n.* a print from a negative on paper sensitized with a silver salt [Phot.].
silverside, *n. sil*-ver-side, the upper, and better, part of a round of beef.
silversmith, *n. sil*-ver-smith, a maker of or worker or dealer in silver articles.
silver-tongued, *a.* eloquent; plausible.
silver-tree, *n.* in S. Africa, *Leucadendron argenteum*, with long silky silver-grey leaves; in the W. Indies, a shrub of the genus *Eugenia*; in Australia, the timber tree, *Tarrietia argyrodendron*.
silverware, *n. sil*-ver-ware, domestic articles, table-ware, utensils, etc., of silver.
silver-weed, *n. sil*-ver-weed, the perennial plant *Potentilla anserina*, with silvery leaves.
silvery, *a. sil*-ver-re, like silver; white; of a mild lustre; besprinkled or covered with silver.
silviculture, *n. sil*-ve-kul-tewr, sylviculture.
Simaruba, *n. sim*-a-*roo*-ba, a genus of tropical American trees, one of which, *S. amara*, yields a bark valuable as a tonic and astringent; this bark. (Caribbean.)
Simeonite, *n. sim*-e-on-ite, a Low Churchman, so called from Charles Simeon, of Cambridge, a noted evangelical divine (*d.* 1836).
Simia, *n. sim*-e-a, the genus of anthropoid apes to which the orang, *S. satyrus*, belongs. (L., an ape.)
simian, *a. sim*-e-an, pertaining to anthropoid apes; resembling an ape in appearance or habits, etc.: *n.* an anthropoid ape. (L. *simia*, an ape.)
similar, *a. sim*-e-lar, like; resembling; having a like form or appearance: *n.* that which is like. (Fr. *similaire.*)
similarity, *n. sim*-e-*la*-re-te, state of being similar; likeness; resemblance.
similarly, *ad. sim*-e-lar-le, in a similar manner; with resemblance.
simile, *n. sim*-e-le, a similitude; a comparison which asserts the resemblance of one thing to another in one of its aspects. (L.)
similitude, *n.* se-*mil*-e-tewd, likeness; resemblance; simile; image; counterpart. (Fr.)
similor, *n. sim*-e-lor, an alloy of copper and zinc made to imitate gold. (Fr.)
similize, *v.i.* and *t. sim*-e-lize, to illustrate by simile; to use a simile; to symbolize.
simioid, *a. sim*-e-oyd, simian; simious.
simious, *a. sim*-e-us, pertaining to or like an anthropoid ape. (L. *simia.*)
simmer, *n. sim*-mer, a gentle boil: *v.i.* and *t.* to boil gently; to be about to express rage, laughter, or agitation. (Scand.)
simnel, *n. sim*-nel, a rich raised cake coloured with saffron and boiled first and baked afterwards, customary at certain festivals, esp. Mothering Sunday. (O.Fr. *simenel.*)
simoniac, *n.* se-*moh*-ne-ak, one guilty of simony.
simoniacal, *a.* sim-o-*ny*-a-kal, guilty of simony; involving or obtained by simony.
simoniacally, *ad.* with the guilt of simony.
simony, *n. sy*-mo-ne, the crime of buying or selling holy orders or church preferment. (*Simon* Magus, who sought to purchase the power of conferring spiritual benefit, Acts viii, 18.)
simoom, *n.* sy-*moom*, a hot, dry, suffocating wind, which blows occasionally from the interior deserts of Arabia and N. Africa, etc. (Ar. *samum.*)
simous, *a. sy*-mus, having a flat or snub nose; concave. (L. *simus*, flat-nosed.)
simpai, *n. sim*-py, the crested langur of Sumatra, *Semnopithecus cristatus*. (Native word.)
simper, *n. sim*-per, a silly or affected smile: *v.i.* to smile in a silly or insincere way. (Scand.)
simperer, *n. sim*-per-rer, one who simpers.
simperingly, *ad.* with simpering.
★**simple,** *a. sim*-pl, consisting of one thing; uncompounded; pure; plain; artless; unaffected; unadorned; not complex; silly; weak in intellect; unsuspecting; undivided [Bot.]; not decomposed [Chem.]: *n.* something not mixed or compounded: *pl.* herbs that have a medicinal value: *v.i.* to gather simples or plants. **simple addition,** the addition of numbers or quantities of the same denomination or kind. **simple equation,** an equation containing only the first power of the unknown quantity. **simple interest,** interest on money paid each year and not added to capital as with compound interest. **simple quantity,** a quantity expressible by a single number or sign. **simple sentence,** a sentence without subordinate sentences. (Fr.)
simple-minded, *a.* artless; undesigning; unsuspecting.

simpleness, *n.* *sim*-pl-ness, state or quality of being simple; artlessness; weakness of intellect.
simpler, *n.* *sim*-pler, a collector of medicinal herbs.
simpleton, *n.* *sim*-pl-ton, a simple or gullible person; a person of weak intellect.
simplex, *a.* *sim*-pleks, simple; not duplex or multiple; pertaining to a telegraphic or telephonic system in which one message only can be transmitted at the same time over one line.
simpliciter, *ad.* sim-*plis*-e-ter, without implying anything not actually mentioned. (L.)
simplicity, *n.* sim-*plis*-e-te, the state of being simple; artlessness of mind; sincerity; plainness; innocence; freedom from artificial ornament; freedom from abstruseness; weakness of intellect; silliness. (Fr. *simplicité.*)
simplification, *n.* *sim*-ple-fe-*kay*-shon, the making simple.
simplify, *v.t.* *sim*-ple-fy, to make simple; to reduce what is complex to simplicity; to make plain or easy. (Fr. *simplifier.*)
simplism, *n.* *sim*-plizm, pretended simplicity.
simplist, *n.* *sim*-plist, one skilled in simples or medicinal herbs; a dealer in these.
simply, *ad.* *simp*-le, in a simple manner; by itself; merely; weakly.
simulacrum, *n.* *sim*-yew-*lay*-krum (*pl.* **simulacra** *or* **simulacrums**), a mere resemblance; a representation; a phantom; a sham. (L.)
simulant, *a.* *sim*-yew-lant, simulating.
simulate, *v.t.* *sim*-yew-late, to feign; to counterfeit; to mimic; to assume the mere appearance of something, without the reality. (L. *simulatus,* feigned.)
simulation, *n.* *sim*-yew-*lay*-shon, the act of feigning to be that which is not; the assumption of a deceitful appearance or character.
simulative, *a.* *sim*-yew-la-tiv, characterized by simulation; simulating.
simultaneity, *n.* *sim*-ul-ta-*nee*-e-te, simultaneousness.
simultaneous, *a.* *sim*-ul-*tay*-ne-us, existing or happening at the same time. (Late L. *simultaneus.*)
simultaneously, *ad.* at the same time.
simultaneousness, *n.* the state or quality of being simultaneous.
simurgh, *n.* se-*moorg*, a gigantic and wonder-working bird of Oriental mythology. (Per. *simurgh.*)
sin, *n.* sin, transgression of the divine law; wickedness; iniquity; depravity; an offence: *v.i.* to commit sin; to offend against. **original sin,** an innate sinfulness or depravity attributed by some theologians to the human race as a result of the Fall of Adam. **the Seven Deadly Sins,** pride, coveteousness, lust, gluttony, anger, envy, sloth. (A.S. *synn.*)
Sinaitic, *a.* *sy*-na-*it*-ik, pertaining to Mount Sinai.
sinamine, *n.* *sin*-a-min, a crystalline compound obtained from mustard oil.
Sinanthropus, *n.* *sin*-an-*throh*-pus, one of the earliest known types of primitive man, discovered in the Pleistocene near Pekin, 1926–29. (Gr. *sinai,* Chinese, *anthropos,* man.)
sinapin, *n.* *sin*-a-pin, an alkali from white mustard.
Sinapis, *n.* se-*nay*-pis, a genus of crucifers including the white mustard, charlock, etc. (L.)
sinapisin, *n.* se-*nap*-e-sin, a white crystalline organic base extracted from mustard seed.
sinapism, *n.* *sin*-a-pizm, a mustard plaster.
since, *conj.* sinse, because that; during the time when; inasmuch as: *ad.* before this; ago: *prep.* after; from that time. (A.S. *sith,* after, *than,* that.)
sincere, *a.* sin-*seer*, pure; unmixed; genuine; not simulated; honest; undissembling; true. (L. *sincerus,* pure.)
sincerely, *ad.* in a sincere manner; honestly; unfeignedly.
sincereness, *n.* the quality of being sincere.
sincerity, *n.* sin-*se*-re-te, sincereness; honesty of mind or intention; freedom from false pretence. (L. *sinceritas.*)
sincipital, *a.* sin-*sip*-e-tal, pertaining to the sinciput [Anat.].
sinciput, *n.* *sin*-se-put, the fore-part of the head from the forehead to the coronal suture. (L. *semi,* half, *caput,* the head.)
sindon, *n.* *sin*-don, a wrapper or winding sheet. (L.)
sine-, *sy*-ne, a Latin prefix signifying without.
sine, *n.* sine, a straight line drawn from the end of an arc perpendicular to the diameter drawn through the other end [Geom.]. (L. *sinus,* a bending.)
sin-eating, *n.* *sin*-eet-ing, the taking over the sins of another person for a money payment.
sinecure, *n.* *sy*-ne-kewr, a benefice without cure of souls; an office with a salary but with no, or with very few, duties. (L. *sine,* and *cure,* a cure.)
sinecurism, *n.* *sy*-ne-kewr-rizm, possession of a sinecure.
sinecurist, *n.* *sy*-ne-*kewr*-rist, one who holds or seeks a sinecure.
sinew, *n.* *sin*-yew, that which unites a muscle to a bone; a tendon: *pl.* that which supplies strength: *v.t.* to knit as by sinews; to supply with sinews. **sinews of war,** money. (A.S. *sinu.*)
sinewed, *a.* *sin*-yewd, consisting of sinews; furnished with sinews; strong; vigorous.
sinew-shrunk, *a.* of a horse, gaunt-bellied through shrinkage of belly-sinews due to overwork.
sinewy, *a.* *sin*-yew-e, consisting of sinews; strong; well-braced with sinews; vigorous.
sinfonia, *n.* sin-*foh*-ne-a, symphony [Mus.]. (It.)
sinful, *a.* *sin*-ful, tainted with sin; iniquitous; wicked; involving sin.
sinfully, *ad.* in a sinful manner.
sinfulness, *n.* the quality of being sinful; iniquity; wickedness.
sing, *v.i.* sing, to utter sweet or melodious sounds; to make a small shrill sound; to relate in verse; to write poetry: *v.t.* to utter with musical modulations; to celebrate in song; to relate in poetic numbers. *p.* **sang,** *pp.* **sung.** (A.S. *singan.*)
singable, *a.* *sing*-abl, suitable for singing.
singe, *n.* sinj, a slight burning of the surface: *v.t.* to burn slightly the ends or surface of. (A.S. *sengan.*)
singeing, *n.* *sinj*-ing, a burning off of the tips; a superficial burning.
singer, *n.* *sing*-er, one who sings; one whose occupation is to sing; a bird that sings.
Singhalese, *n.* sing-ga-*leez*, Sinhalese.
singing, *n.* *sing*-ing, the art of vocal music.
singing-bird, *n.* a bird that sings.
singingly, *ad.* in a singing manner; with sounds like singing.
singing-man, *n.* a man employed to sing; a male member of a choir.
singing-master, *n.* one who teaches vocal music.
single, *a.* *sing*-gl, separate; consisting of one only; for one only; individual; unmarried; uncompounded; alone; not double; undivided; pure; simple: *n.* a single round, game, or score, etc.: *pl.* in tennis, golf, etc., a game with one player only on each side; a reeled filament of silk: *v.t.* to separate; to select; to choose one from others. **single engine,** having only one pair of driving wheels. **single flower,** with only one flower on a stem. (L. *singulus.*)
single-breasted, *a.* buttoning on one side only (of coats, etc.).
single-entry, *n.* entry of a transaction into one account only [Comm.].
single-handed, *a.* having one hand or workman only; alone.
single-hearted, *a.* having no duplicity.
single-minded, *a.* having a single purpose.
singleness, *n.* *sing*-gl-ness, the state of being one only; simplicity; sincerity.
single-phase, *a.* denoting a plain alternating electric current, or a machine worked by or producing such current [Elect.].
single-stick, *n.* *sing*-gl-stik, a stick used for sword-exercise; practice for sword-exercise.
singlet, *n.* *sing*-glet, a woollen undervest.
single-tax, *n.* a proposed economic system under which taxation would be levied only on land or land-rents.
singleton, *n.* *sing*-gl-ton, the only one of a suit in a hand at cards. (Fr.)
single-track, *a.* having only one track [Rly.]; able to move or act only in one direction or on one route.
singly, *ad.* *sing*-gle, individually; alone; by oneself; sincerely.
sing-sing, *n.* *sing*-sing, an African antelope, *Kobus defassa,* allied to the water-buck. (Native name.)

singsong, *a.* *sing*-song, drawling: *n.* a convivial concert; bad singing; drawling singing.

singular, *a.* *sing*-gew-lar, not complex or compound; particular; peculiar; unusual; expressing one person or thing [Gram.]; not common; being alone: *n.* the singular number [Gram.]. (L. *singularis.*)

singularism, *n.* *sing*-gew-la-rizm, any philosophy attributing the phenomena of the universe to a single principle.

singularist, *n.* *sing*-gew-la-rist, one who affects singularity; an adherent of singularism; the holder of one benefice only (as opposed to a pluralist).

singularity, *n.* *sing*-gew-*la*-re-te, peculiarity; uncommon character or form; peculiar privilege; oddity. (Fr. *singularité.*)

singularize, *v.i.* *sing*-gew-la-rize, to make singular.

singularly, *ad.* *sing*-gew-lar-le, in a singular manner; peculiarly; strangely.

singultus, *n.* sing-*gul*-tus, hiccough [Med.]. (L.)

Sinhalese, *a.* sin-ha-*leez*, pertaining to Ceylon or its people: *n.* a native, or the natives, of Ceylon, also their language.

Sinic, *a.* *sin*-ik, Chinese. (Late L. *Sinæ*, Ar. *Sin*, China.)

sinical, *a.* *sin*-e-kal, pertaining to a sine.

Sinicism, *n.* *sin*-e-sizm, a Chinese idiom or custom.

Sinicization, *n.* *sin*-e-sy-*zay*-shon, the act or process of Sinicizing.

Sinicize, *v.t.* and *i.* *sin*-e-size, to make or become Chinese in character.

Sinify, *v.t.* *sin*-e-fy, to Sinicize.

Sinism, *n.* *sin*-izm, Sinicism.

sinister, *a.* *sin*-is-ter, on the left side (of an heraldic shield, *i.e.* on the right as seen by the observer); evil; dishonest; unlucky; inauspicious. (L.)

sinisterly, *ad.* *sin*-is-ter-le, in a sinister manner.

sinistrad, *ad.* *sin*-is-trad, toward the left [Anat.].

sinistral, *a.* *sin*-is-tral, pertaining to the left; sinistrous.

sinistrally, *ad.* *sin*-is-tral-le, to the left.

sinistration, *n.* *sin*-is-*tray*-shon, state of inclining or turning to the left.

sinistrorsal, *a.* *sin*-is-*tror*-sal, twining from left to right, as a spiral line.

sinistrorse, *a.* *sin*-is-trorse, twisting spirally from right to left [Zool.]. (L. *sinistrorsus.*)

sinistrous, *a.* *sin*-is-trus, being on or directed towards the left side; inclined to the left; perverse.

sinistrously, *ad.* in a sinistrous manner; with a tendency to use the left as the stronger hand.

sink, *n.* sink, a drain to carry off filthy water; a basin or trough to receive waste or filthy water, slops, etc.; a place of filth; a depression due to mining, or to erosion by underground waters; a swallow-hole: *v.i.* to fall towards the bottom; to subside; to fall gradually; to penetrate; to become lower; to settle to a level; to be overwhelmed; to enter deeply; to decline: *v.t.* to cause to sink; to immerse in a fluid; to make by digging; to depress; to degrade; to reduce; to diminish; to waste. *p.* **sank.** *pp.* **sunk.** (A.S. *sincan.*)

sinker, *n.* *sing*-ker, one who or that which sinks; a plummet; a weight on anything to sink it.

sink-hole, *n.* *sink*-hole, a hole for draining water from a sink; a hole in limestone formations through which water sinks [Geol.].

sinking, *a.* *sing*-king, falling; subsiding: *n.* the excavation of shafts and wells. **sinking fund,** a fund created for the reduction of a public debt; a sum set aside from revenue to pay off capital.

sinless, *a.* *sin*-less, free from sin; pure; perfect; innocent.

sinlessly, *ad.* in a sinless manner.

sinlessness, *n.* the state of being sinless; freedom from sin.

sinner, *n.* *sin*-ner, one who sins or is sinful; one who is still in sin; an offender; a criminal.

sinnet, *n.* *sin*-net, sennit; yarn bound round ropes to prevent galling [Naut.].

Sinn-Fein, *n.* shin-*fane*, the political party in pre-republican Eire in favour of an independent republic and the use of the Irish language as an aid in obtaining it. **Sinn-Feiner,** a member of this.

Sinningia, *n.* se-*nin*-je-a, a genus of tropical American herbs including the gloxinia.

sin-offering, *n.* a sacrifice for sin; something offered as an expiation for sin.

sinogram, *n.* *sin*-o-gram, a Chinese written character. (Gr. *Sinai*, Chinese, *gramma*, letter.)

sinologer, *n.* se-*nol*-o-jer, a sinologue. (Gr. *Sinai*, and *logos*, science.)

sinological, *a.* *sin*-o-*loj*-e-kal, pertaining to sinology.

sinologist, *n.* se-*nol*-o-jist, a sinologue.

sinologue, *n.* *sin*-o-log, one versed in sinology.

sinology, *n.* se-*nol*-o-je, knowledge of Chinese literature, laws, etc. (Gr. *Sinai*, China, *logos*, science.)

sinophil, *a.* *sin*-o-fil, being fond of the Chinese.

Sinophile, *n.* *sin*-o-file, an admirer of the Chinese; a supporter of Chinese national policy.

Sinophobe, *n.* *sin*-o-fohb, one entertaining detestation or fear of the Chinese.

sinopia, *n.* se-*noh*-pe-a, a red pigment prepared from sinopite. (*Sinope*, on the Black Sea.)

Sinopic, *a.* se-*nop*-ik, pertaining to or obtained from Sinope or its neighbourhood. **Sinopic earth,** sinopite.

sinopite, *n.* *sin*-o-pite, a brick-red ferruginous clay formerly used as a paint. (*Sinope*, on the Black Sea, whence originally obtained.)

sinople, *n.* *sin*-o-pl, red ferruginous quartz. (Fr.)

sinter, *n.* *sin*-ter, a siliceous or calcareous deposit made by mineral springs: *v.t.* and *i.* to coalesce through heating without actually melting. (Gr.)

Sintooism, *n.* *sin*-too-izm, Shintoism.

sinuate, *v.t.* *sin*-yew-ate, to wind; to bend in and out: *a.* wavy (of leaves having large curved breaks in the margin) [Bot.]. (L. *sinuatus.*)

sinuated, *a.* *sin*-yew-ay-ted, sinuate.

sinuately, *ad.* *sin*-yew-at-le, in a sinuate manner.

sinuation, *n.* *sin*-yew-*ay*-shon, the act of bending in and out; a sinuosity.

sinuose, *a.* *sin*-yew-ohs, sinuous; waved from side to side [Bot.].

sinuosity, *n.* *sin*-yew-*os*-e-te, the quality of curving in and out; a series of bends and turns in arches or other irregular figures.

sinuous, *a.* *sin*-yew-us, bending in and out; winding; undulating. (L. *sinuosus.*)

sinuously, *ad.* in a sinuous manner.

sinupalliate, *a.* *sin*-yew-*pal*-le-at, with a sinuous pallial margin on the shell.

sinus, *n.* *sy*-nus, an opening; a hollow; a cavity in a bone or other part [Anat.]; a fistula; a groove or cavity [Conch.]; a curve between adjoining lobes of a leaf, etc. [Bot.]. (L., a recess.)

sinusitis, *n.* *sy*-nus-*sy*-tis, inflammation of a sinus, esp. the nasal sinus.

sinusoid, *n.* *sy*-nus-oyd, a curve of sines.

sinusoidal, *a.* *sy*-nus-*soy*-dal, pertaining to or consisting of a sinusoid; undulating.

Siouan, *a.* *soo*-an, pertaining to the Sioux.

Sioux, *n.* soo (*pl.* unchanged, soo *or* sooz), a nation of American Indians of the Dakota group. (Indian name.)

sip, *n.* sip, the taking of liquor with the lips; a very small draught of liquor: *v.t.* and *i.* to take into the mouth, or to drink or imbibe, in small quantities; to drink out of; to take a fluid with the lips. (A.S. *sypian.*)

sipe, *v.i.* sipe, to ooze; to issue slowly: *n.* a small pool, esp. from a spring. (*seep.*)

siphon, *n.* *sy*-fon, a bent tube or pipe, with one end longer than the other, used for drawing off fluids over the edge of the container; a bottle fitted with a siphon for discharging aerated water by means of the pressure of the gas; a tubular organ in certain cephalopods, gastropods, etc.: *v.t.* to draw off by a siphon. (Fr.)

siphonage, *n.* *sy*-fon-aj, the action of a siphon.

siphonal, *a.* sy-*foh*-nal, siphonic; resembling a siphon.

Siphonaptera, *n.pl.* sy-fo-*nap*-te-ra, the order of insects comprising the fleas.

siphonate, *a.* *sy*-fon-at, furnished with a siphon or siphons (esp. of molluscs, etc.): *n.* a liquid drawn by means of a siphon; a siphonate mollusc.

siphon-cup, *n.* a lubricating apparatus in which the oil is led over the edge of the reservoir by a bent wick.

siphon-gauge, *n.* a gauge in the form of a bent tube containing mercury to show variations of pressure in a reservoir.

siphonic, *a.* sy-*fon*-ik, pertaining to a siphon.

siphuncle, *n.* *sy*-fung-kl, the tube which runs through the partitions of nautiloid shells; the honey-dew tube of an aphid [Zool.]. (L. *siphunculus*, diminutive of *siphon*.)
siphuncular, *a.* sy-*fung*-kew-lar, pertaining to a siphuncle.
siphunculated, *a.* sy-*fung*-kew-lay-ted, having a little siphon or spout [Zool.].
sipper, *n.* *sip*-per, one who sips.
sippet, *n.* *sip*-pet, a small piece of bread, fried or toasted, used as a garnish for hashes, etc. (*sip*.)
sir, *n.* ser, a word of respect used in addressing a man; (*cap.*) title prefixed to the Christian name of a knight or baronet. (Fr. *sire*, from L. *senior*, elder.)
sircar, *n.* *ser*-kar, sirkar.
sirdar, *n.* *ser*-dar, the title of the commander-in-chief of the former Anglo-Egyptian army, and of certain native nobles of India. ((Hind.)
sire, *n.* sire, a father; a title in addressing the sovereign; the male parent of a beast; an ancestor: *v.t.* to procreate, as beasts. (O.Fr.)
siren, *n.* *sire*-ren, a mermaid; one of a class of sea-nymphs who were fabled to lure the passing sailor to his ruin by the fascination of their music [Myth.]; an enticing woman; a woman dangerous from her enticing arts; a sirenian; a steam-whistle or fog-horn; a hooting device used in civil defence to give warnings over a wide area; (*cap.*) a genus of tailed amphibians including the mud-eel, *S. lacertina*: *a.* pertaining to a siren; bewitching. (L., a sea-nymph.)
sirenian, *n.* sy-*ree*-ne-an, one of the Sirenia, an order of large herbivorous aquatic mammals including the dugongs, manatees, and sea-cows.
sirenic, *a.* sire-*ren*-ik, siren-like; fascinating; seductive.
sirgang, *n.* *ser*-gang, the long-tailed bright green crested jay, *Cissa chinensis*, of the Far East, the Chinese roller.
siriasis, *n.* se-*ry*-a-sis, an affection due to the excessive heat of the sun; sunstroke. (L.)
Sirius, *n.* *si*-re-us, the Dog Star in the constellation Canis Major, the brightest star in the heavens. (L.)
sirkar, *n.* *ser*-kar, the government or supreme authority (in India); a district under the Mogul Empire; a house steward or accountant (in Bengal). (Hind.)
sirloin, *n.* *ser*-loyn, that part of the loin of beef in which the undercut is largest. (Fr. *surlonge*.)
sirocco, *n.* se-*rok*-koh, an oppressive southerly wind from the Libyan deserts, blowing chiefly in Italy, Malta, and Sicily. (It.)
sirrah, *n.* *si*-rah, a term of reproach and contempt addressed to a man or boy.
sirup, *n.* *si*-rup, syrup. (Fr. *sirop*.)
sirvente, *n.* (App.), a Provençal verse-form used by mediæval troubadours.
sisal, *n.* *sis*-al, the fibre of the West Indian agave (*Agave sisalina*) used for cordage, etc.; the plant yielding this, sisal hemp. (*Sisal*, a former port in Yucatan.)
siscowet, *n.* *sis*-koh-wet, a species of large trout found in Lake Superior.
siskin, *n.* *sis*-kin, a small migratory song-bird of the finch family, *Carduelis spinus* (Dan.)
sissoo, *n.* sis-*soo*, the East Indian tree, *Dalbergia sissoo*; its timber, used in shipbuilding, for railway-sleepers, etc. (Hind. *sisū*.)
sissy, *n.* *sis*-e, a young girl [Coll., U.S.A.]; an effeminate man or boy, an ineffective youth [Slang]: *a.* characteristic of, or like, a sissy [Slang]. (*sister*.)
sist, *v.t.* sist, to stop; to summon: *n.* a stay of proceedings [Scots. Law]. (L. *sisto*, stand.)
★sister, *n.* *sis*-ter, a female of the same parentage; a female of the same society, as a nun; one of the same kind; a fully qualified or senior hospital-nurse, a nurse in charge of a ward: *v.t.* and *i.* to stand in sisterly relationship; to treat as a sister. **the Three Sisters,** the Parcæ or Fates. (A.S. *sweoster*.)
sisterhood, *n.* *sis*-ter-hood, sisters collectively, or a society of sisters; a community of women united in one faith or order; the relationship of sister.
sister-in-law, *n.* the sister of a husband or wife; a brother's wife.
sisterliness, *n.* *sis*-ter-le-ness, the quality of being sisterly; sisterly love or feeling.
sisterly, *a.* *sis*-ter-le, like a sister; becoming a sister; affectionate.
Sistine, *a.* *sis*-tine, pertaining to any of the Popes named Sixtus, esp. the Fourth (1471–84) or Fifth (1585–90). (It. *Sistino*.)
sistrum, *n.* *sis*-trum, a kind of rattle used by the ancient Egyptians in the worship of Isis. (L.)
Sisyphean, *a.* sis-e-*fee*-an, pertaining to Sisyphus, a Titan of Greek myth who was condemned eternally to roll up a hill a stone that eternally rolled back; hence. vainly toilsome.
sit, *v.i.* sit, to rest upon the haunches; to perch; to occupy a seat; to rest; to lie; to hold a session; to exercise authority; to incubate; to be placed; to be suited; to fit (of clothes); to pose (for a portrait): *v.t.* to keep the seat upon; to cause to sit; to seat. **sit down,** to place oneself on a seat; to begin a siege; to fix a permanent abode. **sit-down strike,** a strike in which workers attend the factory, etc., but do no work until agreement is reached. **sit on,** to repress; to snub. **sit out,** to remain to the end; to stay longer than others; to refrain from taking part (in a dance, game, etc.). **sit pretty,** to remain as one is, esp. when in a favourable situation. **sit tight,** to make no move. **sit under,** to be a regular attendant at a certain clergyman's services. **sit up,** not to go to bed; to be on the alert. *p.* and *pp.* **sat.** (A.S. *sittan*.)
sitar, *n.* se-*tahr*, an Indian musical instrument resembling the guitar. (Hind.)
sitatunga, *n.* sit-a-*tung*-ga, an antelope of the species *Limnotragus*, of equatorial Africa.
site, *n.* *site*, situation; local position; ground plot: *v.t.* to locate: *v.i.* to be situated. (Fr.)
sitfast, *a.* *sit*-fahst, stationary: *n.* an ulcer on a horse's back under the saddle.
sith, *conj.* sith, since; seeing that.
sitiology, *n.* *sit*-e-*ol*-o-je, sitology.
sitology, *n.* si-*tol*-o-je, a treatise on food or the regulation of diet; dietetics. (Gr. *sitos*, food, *logos*, account.)
sitomania, *n.* sit-o-*may*-ne-a, sitophobia; periodic bulimia.
sitophobia, *n.* sit-o-*foh*-be-a, repugnance to food or particular kinds of it. (Gr. *sitos*, *phobos*, fear.)
Sitta, *n.* *sit*-ta, a genus of birds which includes the nuthatch *S. cæsia*. (Gr. *sitte*, a nuthatch.)
sitter, *n.* *sit*-ter, one who sits, esp. to an artist, or as a temporary guardian of children, invalids, etc.; a bird that incubates, hence an easy prey, or an easy chance in games [Coll.].
sitting, *a.* *sit*-ting, resting on the haunches; perching; incubating; holding court; sessile [Bot.]: *n.* the posture of being on a seat; the setting oneself on a seat; the time of sitting; a rented seat in a church; a session; incubation; a clutch of eggs for hatching.
sitting-room, *n.* *sit*-ting-room, a room for sitting in; a parlour, or reception room.
situate, *a.* *sit*-yew-at, situated.
situated, *a.* *sit*-yew-ay-ted, seated, placed, or standing with respect to any other object; placed or being in any state or condition with regard to others or other things. (Late L. *situatus*.)
situation, *n.* *sit*-yew-*ay*-shon, position; state; condition; place; berth; job; office.
situs, *n.* *sy*-tus, a position, site, or location, esp. [Anat., Bot.] of an organ. (L.)
sitz-bath, *n.* *sits*-bahth, a bath for bathing in a sitting attitude; a hip-bath; a bath in a sitting posture. (Ger. *sitzen*, to sit, and *bath*.)
Siva, *n.* *see*-va, the Supreme Being in the Hindu trinity in the character of destroyer, killing that he may make alive. (Sans., the propitious.)
Sivan, *n.* *siv*-an, the third month of the Jewish ecclesiastical year and the ninth of the civil, partly in May and partly in June. (Heb.)
sivatherium, *n.* *siv*-a-*theer*-re-um, an extinct ruminant, larger than the rhinoceros, with two pairs of horns and a proboscis, discovered in India (*Siva*, and Gr. *ther*, a wild beast.)
six, *a.* siks, twice three: *n.* the number of twice three; the figure representing it. **at sixes and sevens,** in disorder. (A.S.)
sixfold, *a.* *siks*-fohld, six times repeated; six times as much.
six-footer, *n.* a person six feet or more in height.
sixpence, *n.* *siks*-pence, a silver coin of the value of six pennies; the value of six pennies.

sixpenny, *a.* *siks*-pen-ne, worth or valued at sixpence.
sixpennyworth, *n.* siks-*pen*-ne-wurth *or* siks-*pen*-urth, of the value of sixpence.
six-shooter, *n.* *siks*-shoot-er, a revolver or automatic pistol carrying six cartridges.
sixteen, *a.* and *n.* siks-*teen*, six and ten. (A.S.)
sixteenmo, *n.* siks-*teen*-moh, sextodecimo.
sixteenth, *a.* siks-*teenth*, the ordinal of sixteen: *n.* one of sixteen equal parts.
sixth, *a.* siksth, the ordinal of six: *n.* the sixth part; a hexacord [Mus.]. **the sixth sense,** *see* **sense.**
sixthly, *ad.* *siksth*-le, in the sixth place.
sixtieth, *a.* *siks*-te-eth, the ordinal of sixty: *n.* one of sixty equal parts.
sixty, *a.* *siks*-te, ten times six: *n.* the product of this, or the figure. (A.S. *sixtig.*)
sizar, *n.* *sy*-zar, a student at Cambridge and Dublin of a corresponding grade with the servitor at Oxford. (*size*, a fixed allowance of food.)
sizarship, *n.* the status of, or the position of being, a sizar; the pecuniary assistance attaching to this position.
***size,** *n.* size, bulk; magnitude; dimensions; settled quantity or allowance, specially of food and drink, as to sizars at Cambridge: *v.t.* to adjust or arrange according to size; to bring to a required size: *v.i.* at Cambridge University, to order food or drink from the buttery. **size up,** take the measure of [Coll.]. (Fr. *assize*, a fixed quantity.)
size, *n.* size, a kind of weak glue used for glazing; anything of a gluey nature: *v.t.* to prepare or cover with size. **size-water,** an aqueous solution of size used as an undercoat on walls, or added to plaster to retard its setting. (It. *sisa.*)
sizeable, *a.* *size*-a-bl, of considerable size; of reasonable or suitable size.
sized, *a.* sized, having a particular magnitude (used in compound words).
sizel, *n.* *siz*-el, scissel.
sizer, *n.* *size*-er, a machine or device to grade articles by size; one who applies size.
siziness, *n.* *size*-e-ness, the quality of being sizy.
sizy, *a.* *size*-e, glutinous; having the adhesiveness of size.
sizzle, *v.t.* *siz*-zl, to make the hissing sound of frying. (From the sound.)
sjambok, *n.* *zham*-bok, a whip of rhinoceros hide: *v.t.* to flog with this. (South African Dutch.)
skald, *n.* skawld, an ancient Scandinavian bard who composed poems in honour of heroes and their deeds, and recited or sang them on public occasions. (O.N.)
skaldic, *a.* *skawl*-dik, pertaining to a skald, his occupation, or his works; composed by a skald.
skat, *n.* skaht, a game of cards for three. (Ger.)
skate, *n.* skate, a sort of sandal fitted on the boot, and furnished with a steel runner to glide over ice with: *v.i.* to glide on skates. **roller skate,** *see* **roller. to skate on thin ice,** to go into danger, to take a hazardous chance. (Dut. *schaats.*)
skate, *n.* skate, a cartilaginous fish of the genus *Raia*, esp. the large food-fish *R. batis*. (Ice. *skata.*)
skater, *n.* *skate*-er, one who skates.
skean *or* **skean-dhu,** *n.* skeen-*dhoo*, a Highlander's dirk or knife, usually stuck in the stocking. (Gael. *sgian*, knife, *dubh*, black.)
skedaddle, *v.i.* ske-*dadl*, to scamper off or run away, as in a panic. (Slang.)
skeel, *n.* skeel, a wooden bucket or pail, esp. one for holding milk. (Ice.)
skeen, *n.* skeen, the Himalayan ibex. (Tib. *skyin.*)
skeet, *n.* skeet, a long scoop used to wet the sides of ships to keep them cool, or the sails of small vessels, to make them hold the wind better [Naut.].
skeeter, *n.* *skee*-ter, a mosquito [Slang].
skeg, *n.* skeg, a sort of wild plum: *pl.* a sort of oats. (Dial. Eng.)
skein, *n.* skane, a measure or coil of thread, yarn, or silk; a flock of wild geese in flight. (O.Fr. *escaigne.*)
skeletal, *a.* *skel*-e-tal, pertaining to, or of the nature of, a skeleton.
skeletization, *n.* *skel*-e-ty-*zay*-shon, extreme emaciation [Path.].
skeletogenous, *a.* skel-e-*toj*-e-nus, forming, or taking part in forming, the skeleton.
skeletology, *n.* skel-e-*tol*-o-je, the branch of anatomy treating of the solid or bony parts of the body. (Gr. *skeleton*, and *logos*, science.)
skeleton, *n.* *skel*-e-ton, the bones of an animal body divested of the flesh, etc., and fastened in their natural posture; the supporting parts of an animal whether vertebrate or invertebrate; the general supporting framework of anything; outline; a very lean person. (Gr. *skeletos*, dried up.)
skeletonize, *v.t.* *skel*-e-ton-ize, to make a skeleton of; to reduce to an outline.
skeleton-key, *n.* *skel*-e-ton-*kee*, a thin light key, with the side-webs filed away; a master-key.
skellum, *n.* *skel*-um, a scamp; a ne'er-do-well; a rogue or vicious animal. (Ger. *Schelm*, rascal.)
skelp, *n.* skelp, a blow; a smart stroke: *v.t.* to strike; to smack: *v.i.* to hurry off. (Gael. *sgealp.*)
skene, *n.* skeen, a skean.
skep, *n.* skep, a straw beehive; a wicker basket. (Ice. *skeppa.*)
skeptic, *n.* *skep*-tik, sceptic.
skerry, *n.* *ske*-re, a rocky isle; a reef. (Ice. *sker.*)
sketch, *n.* sketch, an outline or general delineation of anything; a first rough draught; a descriptive essay; a short or light dramatic piece, musical composition, etc.: *v.t.* to draw the outline or general figure of; to make a rough draught of: to plan by giving the principal points or ideas of: *v.i.* to practise sketching. (Dut. *schets.*)
sketchable, *a.* *sketch*-a-bl, that can be sketched.
sketch-book, *n.* *sketch*-book, a book for sketches; a collection of light essays.
sketcher, *n.* *sketch*-er, one who sketches.
sketchily, *ad.* *sketch*-e-le, in a sketchy manner.
sketchiness, *n.* quality of being sketchy.
sketch-map, *n.* a rough or preliminary map.
sketchy, *a.* *sketch*-e, consisting only of an outline; roughly delineated; incomplete.
skew, *a.* skew, oblique; slanting; unsymmetrical: *ad.* awry; obliquely: *n.* an oblique course or movement; a deviation: *v.i.* to move sideways; to swerve; to squint or look askance. (O.F. *eschuer*, to eschew or avoid.)
skew-back, *n.* the sloping stone from which an arch springs.
skewbald, *a.* *skew*-bawld, marked with spots or blotches of white and some colour other than black (of horses): *n.* a skewbald horse.
skew-bridge, *n.* a bridge which crosses a road or river, etc., obliquely.
skewer, *n.* *skew*-er, a pin of wood or metal for keeping a joint of meat in shape: *v.i.* to fasten with skewers.
skew-whiff, *a.* skew-*whif*, awry.
ski, *n.* shee, a long flat wooden runner used for skating on snow: *v.i.* to travel or glide on skis. (Scand.)
skiagraph, *n.* *sky*-a-graf, an X-ray photograph; a vertical section of a building exhibiting its interior [Arch.]. (Gr. *skia*, shadow, *grapho*, write.)
skiagraphical, *a.* pertaining to skiagraphy.
skiagraphy, *n.* sky-*ag*-ra-fe, the art of delineating shadows; a skiagraph; the art of finding the hour by the shadows of the sun or moon; the art of dialling [Astron.].
skiamachy, *n.* sky-*am*-a-ke, sciamachy.
skiametry, *n.* *sky*-am-e-tre, the art of determining the density of shadows in X-ray photographs.
skiascopy, *n.* sky-*as*-ko-pe, examination (esp. of the eye) by use of X-ray photography or by the fluoroscope; retinoscopy.
skid, *n.* skid, a curving timber to preserve a ship's side from injury; a drag to check the wheel of a wagon when descending a hill; part of the landing gear of an aeroplane; a brake; a piece of timber to keep one object from resting on another; a side-slip: *v.t.* to check with a skid: *v.i.* to side-slip. (Ice. *skidh*, a slip of wood.)
skied, *a.* skide, hung high; hit up high.
skier, *n.* *shee*-er, one who glides or travels on skis.
skiff, *n.* skif, a small light boat; a sculling boat. (O.Fr. *esquif.*)
skijoring, *n.* she-*yaw*- *or* she-*jaw*-ring, a winter-sport in which one on skis is drawn over the snow, usually by a horse.
skilful, *a.* *skil*-ful, well versed in any art: dexterous; expert; showing skill.
skilfully, *ad.* *skil*-ful-le, in a skilful manner.

skilfulness, *n.* the quality of being skilful.
skill, *n.* skil, familiar knowledge of any art, united with dexterity in the practice of it; expertness in execution: *v.t.* to understand. (Ice. *skil.*)
skilled, *a.* skild, having skill; skilful; familiarly acquainted with; necessitating skill.
skilless, *a. skil*-less, wanting skill or knowledge.
skillet, *n. skil*-let, a small metal vessel with a long handle, used for boiling or heating. (O.Fr. *escuellette*, a tiny vessel.)
skilling, *n. skil*-ling, a bay of a barn; a lean-to; a slight addition to a cottage.
skilling, *n. skil*-ling, an old North German and Scandinavian coin worth a penny or less. (Scand.)
skill-less, *a.* skil-less, skilless.
skilly, *n. skil*-le, thin gruel.
skim, *n.* skim, scum; the thick matter on the surface of a liquor: *v.t.* to take off the scum; to remove cream from the surface of milk; to take off by skimming; to brush the surface off lightly; to scan superficially: *v.i.* to pass over lightly; to glide over the surface; to hurry over superficially. (*scum.*)
skimble-skamble, *a. skim*-bl-*skam*-bl, confused; wandering; incoherent.
skim-coulter, *n.* a knife-like attachment to a plough for removing the ground surface and turning it into the furrow.
skimmer, *n. skim*-mer, a scoop used for skimming; one who skims over a subject; the scissor-bill, a N. American sea-bird of the genus *Rhynchops.*
Skimmia, *n. skim*-me-a, a genus of hardy evergreen shrubs of E. Asia, with red berries. (Jap.)
skim-milk, *n.* milk from which the cream has been skimmed.
skimmingly, *ad. skim*-ming-le, in a skimming manner.
skimmings, *n.pl. skim*-mingz, that which is skimmed from the surface of liquors.
skimp, *v.t.* skimp, to stint; to scamp; to give poor quantity, as of food: *v.i.* to be stingy. (*scamp.*)
skimpily, *ad. skim*-pe-le, in a skimpy manner.
skimping, *a. skim*-ping, skimpy; miserly.
skimpy, *a. skim*-pe, scanty; meagre.
★skin, *n.* skin, the natural outer covering of an animal; a hide; the bark of a plant; the covering of a fruit: *v.t.* to strip off the skin or hide; to flay; to peel; to cover with skin; to cover the surface of; to fleece or despoil: *v.i.* to become covered with skin; to shed the skin. **by the skin of the teeth,** barely; only just. **keep your eyes skinned,** watch closely; be very wary. **skin effect,** the condition in which current at high frequencies is greater at the surface of the conductor than within [Elect.]. **skin game,** any swindling game; the confidence trick. **to skin a flint,** to be excessively mean and grasping. **under one's skin,** so intimately as to have powerful effect. **with a whole skin,** unharmed; safe and sound. (A.S. *scinn.*)
skin-deep, *a. skin*-deep, superficial.
skinflint, *n. skin*-flint, a very niggardly person.
skinful, *n. skin*-ful, as much drink as will cause intoxication [Slang.].
skink, *n.* skink, a small lizard of the genus *Scincus*, with four short legs, five serrated toes and a short conical tail. (L. *scincus.*)
skinker, *n. sking*-ker, one who draws and serves drink, a tapster. (O.Ger. *schencker.*)
skinner, *n. skin*-ner, one who skins, or who deals in skins; a furrier; an implement used in skinning.
skinniness, *n.* the quality of being skinny.
skinny, *a. skin*-ne, consisting only of skin; wanting flesh; emaciated.
skin-tight, *a.* fitting closely to the skin.
skin-wool, *n.* wool pulled from the dead sheep.
skip, *n.* skip, a leap; a bound; a spring; a college servant (Dublin); the captain or skipper of a bowls team: *v.i.* to leap; to jump with a skipping-rope; to spring lightly; to gambol; to run off hurriedly; to pass without notice: *v.t.* to pass over or by; to omit; to read carelessly; to captain a side at bowls. (Scand.)
skip, *n.* skip, a basket used in textile factories; a basket or bucket used in mines. (*skep.*)
skip-jack, *n. skip*-jak, an upstart; a click-beetle; any of several marine and freshwater fish that play near or jump from the surface of the water, as the bonito and the blue-fish.
skipper, *n. skip*-per, one who or that which skips; a dancer; a young thoughtless person; a skip-jack; any skipping insect; the cheese maggot; a butterfly-like insect of the family Hesperidæ; name given to various fish, esp. the saury pike, *Scombresox saurus.*
skipper, *n. skip*-per, the master of a merchant ship; a sea-captain; the captain of a side: (esp. at bowls): *v.t.* to act as captain; to lead. (Dut. *schipper*, seaman.)
skippet, *n. skip*-pet, the flat round box containing the seal of a document; a small skep or skip.
skipping, *a. skip*-ping, leaping; bounding.
skippingly, *ad. skip*-ping-le, in a skipping manner.
skipping-rope, *n.* a small rope used by children in skipping.
skirl, *n.* skerl, a shrill sound; a snatch of music as played by the bagpipes: *v.i.* to scream out; to play the bagpipes.
skirmish, *n. sker*-mish, an irregular engagement in which small numbers are engaged; a contest: *v.i.* to fight slightly or in small parties; to fight in extended order. (O.Fr. *escarmouche.*)
skirmisher, *n. sker*-mish-er, one who skirmishes; a member of an advance body of troops deployed in extended order [Mil.].
skirret, *n. ski*-ret, a water parsnip; sugar-root, the edible root of *Sium sisarum.* (Scand.)
★skirt, *n.* skert, the lower and loose part of a coat or other garment; the edge of any part of a dress; border; margin; a woman's outer garment, like a petticoat in shape; the diaphragm or midriff in animals: *v.t.* to border; to run along the edge of: *v.i.* to be on the border; to move or lie on or near the confines of. (Ice. *skyrta.*)
skirting, *n. skert*-ing, the lower edge of a dado; material for women's skirts.
skirting-board, *n. skert*-ing-board, the board that runs along the wall at its junction with the floor.
skit, *n.* skit, a lampoon; a caricature; a burlesque; a number or crowd [Coll.]: *pl.* lots: *v.i.* to move or leap rapidly away from; to be skittish: *v.t.* to satirize or ridicule by means of a skit. (Scand.)
skite, *n.* skite, a sudden or a slanting blow; a mean trick; a contemptible person [Coll.]: *v.i.* to slip or glide away; to brag [Slang]. (Scots., from Scand.)
skitter, *v.i. skit*-ter, to glide or pass away rapidly; to move quickly over the surface; in angling, to draw the bait jerkily on the surface: *v.t.* to cause to skitter.
skittish, *a. skit*-tish, shy; easily frightened; volatile; fickle. (Scand.)
skittishly, *ad.* in a skittish manner.
skittishness, *n.* the quality of being skittish.
skittle, *n.* skitl, one of the pins aimed at in the game of ninepins; *pl.* the game itself, also a set of ninepins; a rapid or off-hand game of chess: *v.i.* to play at ninepins; to defeat an opponent quickly, esp. [Cricket] to dismiss batsmen in rapid succession [Coll.]. (Scand.),
skittle-alley, *n.* an enclosed and covered court for the game of skittles.
skittle-pool, *n.* skitl-*pool*, a game of the pyramid family played on the billiard-table.
skive, *v.t.* skive, to pare off; to split (leather).
skiver, *n. sky*-ver, a sheepskin split or divided for bookbinding; inferior leather; the knife used in skiving; a skewer. (Ice. *skifa*, a strip or slice.)
skivvy, *n. skiv*-e, a maid-of-all-work [Slang].
skoal, *int.* skole, good health! Hail! (Scand.)
skua, *n. skew*-a, a pirate gull of the genus *Megalestris.* (Scand.)
skulk, *v.i.* skulk, to lurk; to sneak out of the way; to avoid work: *n.* a skulker. (Scand.)
skulker, *n. skulk*-er, one who skulks; a shirker.
skulkingly, *ad. skulk*-ing-le, in a skulking manner.
skull, *n.* skul, the bony case that encloses the brain; the cranium. **skull and cross-bones,** a representation of a human skull over cross-bones, a symbol of death and of piracy. (Ice. *skal*, shell.)
skull-cap, *n.* a brimless cap fitting closely to the skull; a head-piece; the sinciput; a plant of the genus *Scutellaria.*
skulpin, *n. skul*-pin, the sculpin.
skunk, *n.* skunk, a N. American carnivore of the genus *Mephitis*, which defends itself when pursued by the ejection of offensively fœtid matter; its weasel-like fur; [Coll.] a mean contemptible

fellow: *v.t.* to defeat an opponent (esp. at cards) without his scoring [Amer. slang]. (Amerind. *segonku.*)
skunk-bird, *n.* *skunk*-berd, the bobolink.
skunkish, *a.* *skung*-kish, like a skunk.
Skupshtina, *n.* skoop-*shtee*-na, the parliament of Yugoslavia, and formerly of Serbia. (Serbian.)
skutterudite, *n.* *skut*-ter-ru-dite, a native compound of cobalt and arsenic. (*Skutterud*, in Norway.)
★**sky,** *n.* sky, the aerial region which surrounds the earth; the apparent vault of heaven; the heavens; the weather: *v.t.* to hit or throw high in the air; to hang (a picture) high, or in any unenviable position at an exhibition [Coll.]. (Ice.)
sky-blue, *a.* of the blue colour of the sky.
sky-colour, *n.* the colour of sky; azure.
Skye, *n.* sky, a Skye terrier, a small rough-haired variety of Scotch terrier. (Isle of *Skye.*)
skyey, *a.* *sky*-e, in or pertaining to the sky.
sky-high, *a.* and *ad.* as high as the sky.
skyish, *a.* *sky*-ish, like the sky; ethereal.
skylark, *n.* *sky*-lark, the singing bird *Alauda arvensis*, that mounts and sings as it flies.
skylarking, *n.* *sky*-lark-ing, frolicking about; playing roughly; boisterous amusement.
skylight, *n.* *sky*-lite, a window placed in the roof of a building or room.
sky-line, *n.* *sky*-line, the horizon; the outline of a hill, etc., against the sky.
sky-pilot, *n.* a padre or clergyman [Slang]; an aviator [Coll.].
sky-rocket, *n.* a rocket that rises high in the air, bursting spectacularly at its highest.
skysail, *n.* skysl, a square-sail set next above a royal.
skyscraper, *n.* *sky*-skrape-er, the sail set next above the skysail [Naut.]; a very tall building [Coll.].
skyward, *a.* and *ad.* *sky*-ward, toward the sky.
skyway, *n.* *sky*-way, an aviation route; an airway.
sky-writing, *n.* the formation in the air through smoke-trails emitted by aircraft of words, usually for advertising purposes.
slab, *n.* slab, a flat, thickish piece of anything; a thin, flat piece of marble or other stone; an outside piece taken from timber in sawing it into planks: *v.t.* to cut into slabs; to cut into thick slices; to square (a log). **slab of tin,** a mass into which melted tin is cast. (O.Fr. *esclape.*)
slabber, *n.* *slab*-ber, a saw or machine for slabbing; one who cuts or prepares slabs.
slabber, *n.* *slab*-ber, slaver from the mouth: *v.t.* to slobber: *v.i.* to slaver. (Low Ger. *slabbern.*)
slabberer, *n.* *slab*-ber-rer, a slobberer.
slabbiness, *n.* *slab*-be-ness, the state of being slabby.
slabby, *a.* *slab*-be, thick; viscous; wet; dirty; sloppy. (Ice. *slab*, puddle.)
slabstone, *n.* *slab*-stone, a flagstone.
slack, *a.* slak, not tense; not hard drawn; not holding fast; remiss; careless; not earnest or eager; not violent; not rapid; not brisk: *ad.* in a slack manner; partially; insufficiently: *n.* the part of a rope that hangs loose; a loose part; low tide; a dull season in trade; small-coal: *n.pl.* loose-fitting trousers: *v.t.* and *i.* to slacken; to evade one's work: to become a slacker. **slack in stays,** slow in going about [Naut.]. **slack water,** the interval between the ebb and flow of the tide. (A.S. *sleac.*)
slack-baked, *a.* *slak*-baykt, imperfectly baked.
slacken, *v.i.* *slak*-en, to become less tense; to be remiss; to lose cohesion; to abate; to become slower; to languish: *v.t.* to lessen the tension of; to relax; to mitigate; to cause to become slower; to abate; to withhold; to deprive of cohesion; to repress.
slacker, *n.* *slak*-er, a shirker; a lackadaisical fellow.
slackly, *ad.* *slak*-le, not tightly; negligently.
slackness, *n.* looseness; remissness; slowness; weakness.
slade, *n.* slade, a little dell or valley; a flat piece of low moist ground; the sole of a plough. (A.S. *slæd.*)
slag, *n.* slag, vitrified cinders; the scoria or the dross of a metal; the scoria of a volcano: *v.t.* and *i.* to convert into or to form a slag. (Swed. *slagg.*)
slaggy, *a.* *slag*-ge, pertaining to or like slag.
slain, slane, *pp.* of *slay.*
slainte, *n.* *slawn*-te, good health! (Ir.)

slake, *v.t.* slake, to quench; to extinguish; to mix with water, as lime: *v.i.* to become mixed with water; to die down or go out; to become extinguished; to abate. (A.S. *slacian.*)
slalom, *n.* *slah*-lom, a zigzag downhill race on skis, generally between flags. (Norw.)
slam, *n.* slam, a violent shutting of a door; the noise produced; at whist, contract, etc., the winning of all the tricks: *v.t.* to shut with violence; to bang; to win all the tricks, or all but one, at contract, etc. **grand slam, little slam,** the winning of thirteen, or of twelve, tricks at contract, etc. (Imit.)
slammer, *n.* *slam*-mer, one who slams; one who wins a slam; a violent gust of wind.
slammerkin, *n.* *slam*-mer-kin, a slut; a slatternly woman. (Dial. Eng.)
slander, *n.* *slahn*-der, a malicious report uttered to damage one; a defamation; calumny: *v.t.* to defame; to injure by maliciously uttering a false report. (O.Fr. *esclandre.*)
slanderer, *n.* one who slanders; a defamer.
slanderous, *a.* *slahn*-der-rus, uttering slander; containing slander; defamatory; calumnious.
slanderously, *ad.* with slander.
slanderousness, *n.* the quality of being slanderous or defamatory.
slang, *n.* slang, colloquial language that seldom lasts long; a conversational expression of an irregular, more or less vulgar, type, familiar to and in vogue among a class; the special language, jargon, or technical terms of a class, trade, profession, sport, science, etc.: *v.i.* to scold; to abuse. **back slang,** *see* **back-slang. rhyming slang,** a form of slang in which the word intended is replaced by a word or phrase in rhyme with it, as "plates of meat" for "feet." (Origin doubtful.)
slangily, *ad.* in a slangy nature.
slanginess, *n.* slangy nature.
slangy, *a.* *slang*-e, of the nature of slang; addicted to the use of slang.
slant, *a.* slahnt, sloping; oblique; inclined from the direct line, whether horizontal or perpendicular: *n.* a slope; an inclined plane; an oblique reflection or gibe; a point of view [U.S.A.]: *v.t.* to turn from a direct line; to give an oblique direction to: *v.i.* to slope: *ad.* aslant; in an oblique direction or manner. **slant of wind,** a transitory breeze. (Swed. *slanta.*)
slanting, *a.* *slahnt*-ing, sloping.
slantingly, *ad.* with a slope or inclination.
slantly, *ad.* slantwise.
slantwise, *ad.* *slahnt*-wize, obliquely; in an inclined direction.
slap, *n.* slap, a blow with the open hand or with something flat: *ad.* with a sudden and violent blow: *v.t.* to give a slap to. **to have a slap at,** to start a fight with; to make an attempt at [Slang]. (Imit.)
slap-bang, *ad.* *slap*-bang, violently; slap-dash.
slap-dash, *ad.* *slap*-dash, all at once; carelessly; boldly; rashly; without premeditation.
slapjack, *n.* *slap*-jak, a sort of pancake baked on a griddle; a flap-jack.
slapstick, *n.* *slap*-stik, a wooden wand of two blades looking as one fastened together at the handle so as to make a noisy slap when used: *a.* knockabout (esp. of stage acts).
slap-up, *a.* excellent; of the best quality [Slang].
slash, *n.* slash, a long cut; a cut made at random; an ornamental vertical slit in a garment: *v.t.* to cut by striking violently and at random; to cut in long cuts; to lash: *v.i.* to strike violently and at random with an edged instrument; to lay about one with blows. (O.Fr. *esclachier.*)
slashing, *a.* severely critical; very large [Slang].
slat, *n.* slat, a thin wooden strip like a blind-lath or a bed-lath; a hoop of a covered wagon; a narrow piece or slip of timber, used to fasten together larger pieces; a thin slab of stone used for roofing instead of a slate; the movable or fixed part forming the front of a slot in an aeroplane wing: *v.t.* to cover with slats. (O.Fr. *esclat.*)
slatch, *n.* slatch, the slack of a rope; the period of a transitory breeze; a short interval of fair weather [Naut.]. (*slack.*)
slate, *n.* slate, an argillaceous rock, which readily splits into plates; a piece of such for roofing buildings; a piece for writing on: *v.t.* to cover with

slate; to find fault with; to criticize severely; to reprimand. **slate club,** a group of persons periodically paying into and sharing out from a common fund under predetermined rules. (O.Fr. *esclat.*)
slate-axe, *n.* a slater's tool; a sax.
slate-grey, *n.* and *a.* dull bluish-grey.
slate-pencil, *n.* pencil made of soft slate for use in writing on slates.
slater, *n. slay*-ter, one who fixes slates; a woodlouse.
slatiness, *n. slay*-te-ness, the quality of being slaty.
slating, *n. slay*-ting, the act of covering with slates; a covering of slates; materials for slating; slates; a severe criticism; a reprimand.
slattern, *n. slat*-tern, a woman who is negligent of dress or untidy; a sluttish woman.
slatternliness, *n.* state of being slatternly.
slatternly, *a.* like a slattern; untidy; dirty: *ad.* slovenly; untidily; negligently.
slaty, *a. slay*-te, resembling slate; having the nature or properties of slate.
slaughter, *n. slaw*-ter, killing cattle; wholesale destruction of life by violence; carnage: *v.t.* to kill; to slay; to kill cattle or sheep or pigs for the market. (Ice. *sldir.*)
slaughterer, *n.* one engaged in slaughtering cattle; a slayer.
slaughter-house, *n.* a place where beasts are killed for the market, an abattoir; a scene of slaughter or carnage.
slaughterman, *n.* a slaughterer (of cattle).
slaughterous, *a. slaw*-ter-rus, destructive; murderous.
slaughterously, *ad.* in a slaughterous manner.
slaughtery, *n. slaw*-ter-re, a slaughter-house; slaughter.
Slav, *n.* slahv, one of a race inhabiting Eastern Europe, including among others the Russians and the Poles; a Slavonic language: *a.* Slavonic. (Ger. *Sklave.*)
slave, *n.* slave, a person who is wholly subject to the will of another; a bondservant; one who has lost the power of resisting some passion; one in the lowest condition; one who drudges or labours like a slave: *v.i.* to drudge; to labour as a slave. **slave trade,** the business of procuring and selling slaves; traffic in slaves. **white slave traffic,** *see* **white.** (Fr. *esclave.*)
slave-driver, *n.* one who oversees slaves and keeps them at their work; a hard taskmaster.
slave-grown, *a.* produced by slave labour.
slave-holder, *n.* one who owns slaves.
slave-holding, *a.* holding others in slavery.
slave-hunter, *n.* one who hunts for slaves.
slave-like, *a.* like a slave; fitting a slave.
slaver, *n. slave*-er, a ship employed in the slave trade; one who trades in slaves.
slaver, *n. slav*-er, saliva dribbling from the mouth; rubbishy nonsense; flattery: *v.i.* to let the spittle flow from the mouth: *v.t.* to smear with saliva. (Ice. *slafra,* slaver.)
slaverer, *n. slav*-er-rer, a driveller; an idiot.
slavery, *n. slay*-ver-re, the condition of a slave; entire subjection to the will of another; bondage; slave-holding; drudgery.
slavey, *n. slay*-ve, a low-class servant girl [Slang].
Slavic, *a.* and *n. slah*-vik, Slavonic.
slavish, *a. slay*-vish, pertaining to or like slaves; servile; mean; laborious; consisting in drudging.
slavishly, *ad.* in a slavish manner.
slavishness, *n.* slavish character; the state of being slavish.
Slavism, *n. slav*-izm, the racial character, or the common interests, of Slavs; a Slavic idiom.
Slavonian, *a.* sla-*voh*-ne-an, Slavonic; pertaining to the former Austrian province, Slavonia, later part of Yugoslavia: *n.* Slavonic; a Slav; a native of Slavonia.
Slavonic, *a.* sla-*von*-ik, pertaining to the Slavs or their language: *n.* the Slav language.
Slavophil, *n. slah*-vo-fil, an admirer of the Slavs. (*Slav,* and Gr. *philos,* lover of.)
Slavophobe, *n. slah*-vo-fobe, a hater of the Slavs. (*Slav,* and Gr. *phobos,* hate.)
slaw, *n.* slaw, a salad of shredded cabbage [U.S.]. (Dut. *sla,* salad.)
slay, *v.t.* slay, to put to death with a weapon or by violence; to destroy. *pp.* **slain,** *p.* **slew.** (A.S. *slean,* Ger. *schlagen,* strike.)
slay, *n.* and *v.t.* sley.
slayer, *n. slay*-er, one who slays; a murderer; a destroyer of life.
sleave, *n.* sleev, soft floss or unwrought silk: *v.t.* to separate or divide a collection of threads. (A.S. *slæfan.*)
sleaziness, *n.* state or quality of being sleazy.
sleazy, *a. slee*-ze, thin; flimsy; wanting firmness of texture or substance.
sled, *n.* sled, a carriage or vehicle, moved on runners, for transporting loads over snow; a sledge; a toboggan: *v.t.* to convey or transport on a sled: *v.i.* to travel in a sled. (O.Dut. *sledde.*)
sledded, *a. sled*-ed, conveyed or mounted on a sled.
sledding, *n. sled*-ding, the act of transporting on a sled; the means of conveying on sleds; snow sufficient for the running of sleds.
sledge, *n.* slej, a large, two-handed heavy hammer, used chiefly by blacksmiths. (A.S. *slecge.*)
sledge, *n.* slej, a vehicle moved on runners to slide over snow; a sleigh; an aeroplane's runner: *v.t.* to convey in a sledge: *v.i.* to travel in a sledge. (*sled.*)
sledge-hammer, *n.* a sledge (blacksmiths' tool): *v.t.* to strike with heavy, violent blows; to criticize harshly [Fig.].
sleek, *ad.* sleek, smoothly; with ease: *a.* smooth; glossy; not rough or harsh; fawning: *v.t.* to make even and smooth; to render smooth and glossy; to smooth down. (Ice. *slikr,* sleek.)
sleeker, *n. sleek*-er, a rounded implement for sleeking or smoothing.
sleekly, *ad. sleek*-le, in a sleek manner.
sleekness, *n. sleek*-ness, the quality of being sleek; smoothness of surface.
sleek-stone, *n. sleek*-stone, a smoothing or polishing stone.
sleeky, *a. sleek*-e, of a sleek or smooth appearance.
★**sleep,** *n.* sleep, a temporary suspension of the active powers of mind and body for the refreshment and invigoration of the system; rest from physical action; the period of hibernation or æstivation in animals: *v.i.* to take rest by sleep; to be asleep; to be inactive or motionless; to lie or be still; to slumber; to become numb with pressure; to spin steadily so as to seem to be motionless; to rest in the grave: *v.t.* to provide with sleeping accommodation [Coll.]; to put up. **sleep in,** to lodge on one's employer's premises. **sleep off,** to rid oneself of by sleep. **sleep on,** to have a night's rest before deciding. *p.* and *pp.* **slept.** (A.S. *slæpan.*)
sleeper, *n. sleep*-er, a person who sleeps; a lazy person; an animal that lies dormant in winter or summer; the foundation timber; one of the timbers to which a line or rail is fixed; a sleeping-car [Coll.].
sleepily, *ad. sleep*-e-le, drowsily.
sleepiness, *n. sleep*-e-ness, inclination to sleep.
sleeping, *a. sleep*-ing, reposing in sleep; given to sleeping; for sleeping in; inducing sleep: *n.* the state of resting in sleep, or of being at rest. **sleeping partner,** one who has a share in a business, but takes no part in the practical management. **sleeping sickness,** the tropical disease trypanosomiasis (sometimes used also of *sleepy sickness*).
sleeping-bag *n.* a warmly lined waterproofed canvas sack for sleeping in in a tent or the open.
sleeping-car, *n.* a railway coach fitted with berths and compartments for sleeping in.
sleeping-draught, *n.* any drug or medicine in liquid form to induce sleep; a soporific.
sleepless, *a.* having no sleep; wakeful; having no rest; perpetually agitated or watchful [Fig.].
sleeplessly, *ad.* in a sleepless manner.
sleeplessness, *n.* want or destitution of sleep.
sleep-walker, *n.* a somnambulist.
sleep-walking, *n.* somnambulism.
sleepy, *a. sleep*-e, drowsy; inclined to sleep; tending to induce sleep; dull; lazy; over-ripe. **sleepy sickness,** epidemic encephalitis, encephalitis lethargica; (incorrectly used of) sleeping sickness.
sleepyhead, *n. sleep*-e-hed, a drowsy person, esp. a child who has stayed up too late.
sleet, *n.* sleet, fine snow mingled with rain: *v.i.* to snow or hail with mixture of rain. (Scand.)
sleetiness, *n.* the state of being sleety.
sleety, *a. sleet*-e, bringing or consisting of sleet.

sleeve, *n.* sleev, the part of a garment that covers the arm; a tube in which another tube works: *v.t.* to furnish with sleeves. **hang on the sleeve,** to be or make dependent on others. **laugh in the sleeve,** to laugh to oneself. **up one's sleeve,** hidden as a reserve or surprise. (A.S. *slyf.*)
sleeved, *a.* sleevd, having sleeves.
sleeve-fish, *n.* the squid *Loligo vulgaris*, or any member of the cuttle-fish family.
sleeveless, *a.* having no sleeves; without excuse; uncalled for; fruitless.
sleeve-link, *n.* two studs joined by a link, used as a cuff-holder.
sleeve-target, *n.* a tubular target of some textile material towed by an aeroplane for anti-aircraft firing practice.
sleeve-valve, *n.* a valve in the form of a sleeve round the inside of a cylinder of an internal combustion engine.
sleeve-waistcoat, *n.* a waistcoat with sleeves.
sleigh, *n.* slay, a sled or sledge; a carriage on runners for use on snow: *v.i.* to travel by or to drive a sleigh. (Dut. *sleve.*)
sleighing, *n. slay*-ing, the state of the snow which admits of sledging; the act of sleigh-riding.
sleight, *n.* slite, an artful trick; a trick or feat so dexterously performed that the manner of performance escapes notice; dexterity; quickness of handling. **sleight of hand,** legerdemain. (Ice. *slægdh.*)
slender, *a. slen*-der, thin; small in circumference compared with the length; small in the waist; not strong; small; inconsiderable; slight; weak; insufficient; spare; abstemious. (O.Fr. *esclendre.*)
slenderize, *v.i.* and *t. slen*-der-rize, to slim.
slenderly, *ad.* to a slender degree.
slenderness, *n.* the quality of being slender; thinness; weakness; spareness.
slept, slept, *p.* and *pp.* of *sleep.*
sleuth, *n.* slooth, a bloodhound; a detective (formerly the track of an animal or human): *v.i.* to trail; to act as a detective. (Ice. *sloth*, a trail.)
sleuth-hound, *n. slooth*-hound, a bloodhound; a hound that tracks a man by scent.
slew, sloo, *p.* of *slay.*
slew, *v.t.* sloo, slue.
sley, *n.* slay, a weaver's reed; a guiding comb: *v.t.* to pass the threads of the warp through the sley. (A.S. *slege.*)
slice, *n.* slice, a thin broad piece cut off; a broad piece; a fire-shovel; a spatula; a knife for serving fish: *v.t.* to cut into thin pieces, or cut off a thin broad piece; to cut into parts; to divide: *v.i.* and *v.t.* slice, to strike the ball in cricket, golf, etc., in a way that sends it to the right of the player. (O.Fr. *esclice.*)
slicer, *n. slice*-er, one who or that which slices.
slick, *a.* slik, smart; adroit; quick: *ad.* at once; effectually; easily done. (*sleek.*)
slickensides, *n.pl. slik*-en-sydz, a variety of galena peculiar to Derbyshire; the rubbed and striated surface of fissures or faults in rocks. (*slick* and *side.*)
slid, slid, *p.* and *pp.* of *slide.*
slidder, *v.t. slid*-der, to slide; to make slippery. (A.S. *slidrian.*)
sliddery, *a. slid*-der-re, slippery; fickle.
slide, *n.* slide, a smooth and easy passage; flow; a surface of ice to slide on; a smooth declivity; a shute; a slip of glass for a microscope object, or for a magic-lantern picture; a grace consisting of two small notes moving by degrees [Mus.]; something which slides: *v.i.* to move along smoothly; to pass inadvertently; to pass unobserved; to pass silently and gradually; to glide; to slip; to fall: *v.t.* to cause to slip; to thrust along. (A.S. *slidan.*)
slideable. *a. slide*-a-bl, liable to be moved by sliding; fit or prepared for sliding.
slider, *n. slide*-er, one who slides; the part of an instrument or machine that slides.
slide-rest, *n.* the part of a lathe that carries the cutting tool.
slide-rule, *n.* an instrument for working mathematical calculations on logarithmic principles, and composed of parts sliding or rotating alongside one another.
sliding-keel, *n.* a centreboard let down through the bottom of a small vessel [Naut.].
sliding-scale, *n.* a scale of duties, wages or charges according to fluctuations in price or other conditions.
sliding-seat, *n.* a seat on a rowing-boat thwart that slides on runners with the swing of the oarsman's body.
slight, *a.* slite, weak; inconsiderable; not deep; not violent; trifling; not strong or firm: *n.* a moderate degree of contempt, manifested by neglect; neglect: *v.t.* to neglect; to disregard. (Ger. *schlicht*, plain, smooth.)
slightingly, *ad.* with neglect; with disrespect.
slightly, *ad.* only a little; in a slight manner.
slightness, *n.* slenderness; weakness.
slily, *ad. sly*-le, slyly.
slim, *a.* slim, slender; of small diameter; weak; slight; astute: *v.i.* to take special steps, by dieting or otherwise, to become thinner; to reduce one's weight. (Dut.)
slime, *n.* slime, soft, moist, adhesive earth; viscous mud; bitumen; viscous exudation; any viscous substance: *v.t.* to besmear or besmirch with slime; to rid of slime. (A.S. *slim.*)
slime-pit, *n.* a pit of bitumen or slime.
slimily, *ad.* in a slimy manner.
sliminess, *n.* the state of being slimy.
slimmish, *a. slim*-ish, somewhat slim.
slimness, *n. slim*-ness, the state or quality of being slim; slenderness; cunning.
slimy, *a. sly*-me, resembling slime; consisting of slime; overspread with slime; viscous; unctuously ingratiating [Fig.].
sling, *n.* sling, a weapon for throwing stones consisting of a strap and two strings; a throw; a hanging bandage for a wounded arm; a rope or band by which anything is suspended and swung out or in; a looped support: *v.t.* to throw with a sling; to throw; to hurl; to hang so as to swing; to swing (an object) by a rope which suspends it. *p.* and *pp.* **slung.** (A.S. *slingan.*)
sling, *n.* sling, a drink of gin or other spirit and water sweetened [U.S.A.] (Ger. *schlingen*, to swallow.)
slinger, *n. sling*-er, one who slings or uses a sling.
slingsman, *n. slingz*-man, a slinger.
sling-stone, *n. sling*-stone, a pebble suitable for throwing with a sling.
slink, *v.i.* slink, to sneak away; to miscarry, as a beast: *v.t.* to cast prematurely, as the female of a beast. *p.* **slank** or **slunk.** *pp.* **slunk.** (A.S. *slincan.*)
slinky, *a. sling*-ke, close-fitting (of a garment).
slip, *v.i.* slip, to slide; to glide; to move out of place; to slink; to err through haste or carelessness; to enter by oversight; to escape: *v.t.* to convey secretly; to omit; to part from a branch or stem; to escape from; to leave slily; to let loose; to throw off; to miscarry. **slip a cable,** to veer out and let go the end. **slip on,** to put on in haste. **slip up,** to make a careless mistake or *faux pas.* (M.E. *slippen.*)
★**slip,** *n.* slip, act of slipping; a false step; an unintentional error; a twig from a stock; a leash for a dog; an escape; a long narrow piece; a woman's undergarment, or separate lining, easily slipped on and off; a loose cover for a pillow, etc.; a launching slope; a cutting from a newspaper column; a galley-proof; loss of efficiency in transmitting power; a fielder at cricket on the off-side behind the wicket; a stripling; *pl.* bathing-drawers; the actors' approach-way to the stage. **slip of the tongue,** an inadvertent mistake in speaking. **to give (one) the slip,** to elude, to escape.
slip-board, *n.* a board sliding in grooves.
slip-coach or **-carriage,** *n.* a railway carriage which can be detached from a train while it is running at speed.
slip-dock, *n.* a dock having a sloping floor with the lower end submerged.
slipe, *n.* slipe; a mining skip with runners instead of wheels.
slip-knot, *n. slip*-not, a knot which slips along the rope on which it is made.
slippage, *n. slip*-aj, the act or amount of slipping.
slipper, *n. slip*-er, one who or that which slips or lets slip; one who releases the dogs in coursing; a loose shoe easily slipped on, and worn in undress; a child's apron easily slipped on over the clothes to keep them clean. **slipper-bath,** a bath roughly of slipper shape with one covered end.
slipper-brake or **-drag,** a metal skid placed under

the wheel of a vehicle or against a moving part of machinery to retard or prevent motion ; a tramcar brake acting directly on the rails.

slippered, *a. slip*-erd, wearing slippers.

slipperily, *ad.* in a slippery manner.

slipperiness, *n.* the quality of being slippery; lubricity ; uncertainty ; lubricity of character.

slipperwort, *n. slip*-er-wurt, any plant of the genus *Calceolaria.*

slippery, *a. slip*-er-re, smooth ; apt to slip ; not affording a firm footing ; uncertain ; changeable ; lubricous. **slippery elm,** the N. American red elm, *Ulmas fulva,* or its medicinal bark.

slippiness, *n.* the quality of being slippy.

slippy, *a. slip*-e, slippery ; smooth ; quick.

slipshod, *a. slip*-shod, wearing shoes down at heel ; slovenly and inaccurate.

slipslop, *a. slip*-slop, feeble ; poor ; jejune : *n.* bad liquor ; feeble composition.

slip-stream, *n.* the stream of fluid behind a propeller or an airscrew.

slip-up, *n.* an incidental mistake, a careless, unwelcome error.

slipway, *n. slip*-way, a slope in a graving dock or shipyard ; a launching way.

slit, *n.* slit, a long cut ; a narrow opening : *v.t.* to cut lengthwise ; to cut into long pieces or strips ; to rend ; to split. (A.S. *slitan.*)

slither, *v.t. slith*-ther, to slidder ; to slide about : *n.* the act of slithering or slipping.

slithery, *a. slith*-ther-re, slippery ; untrustworthy ; deceitful.

slitter, *n. slit*-ter, one who or that which slits.

slitting-mill, *n.* a mill where iron plates are slit into strips ; a machine for slitting gems ; a sawing-machine for making laths.

sliver, *n. sliv*-er, a long piece cut or rent off, or a piece cut or rent lengthwise ; a continuous strand of untwisted fibre prepared for spinning : *v.t.* to cut or divide into long thin pieces ; to cut lengthwise : *v.i.* to split away in slivers. (A.S. *slifan,* cleave.)

sloam, *n.* slome, a layer of clay between beds of coal.

sloat, *n.* slote, a timber cross-bar. (O.Fr. *esclat.*)

slob, *n.* slob, muddy ground. (Irish.)

slobber, *v.i. slob*-ber, to run at the mouth with saliva ; to dribble ; to bungle. (*slubber.*)

slobberer, *n.* one who slobbers.

slobbery, *a. slob*-ber-re, fouled with slobber ; moist ; wet.

sloe, *n.* sloh, a small wild plum, the fruit of the blackthorn ; the blackthorn. (A.S. *sla.*)

slog, *v.t.* slog, to hit a ball hard ; to swipe ; to plod.

slogan, *n. sloh*-gan, the war-cry or gathering cry of a Highland clan ; a catch-phrase for party, propaganda, or advertising purposes. (Gael. *sluagh-ghairm.*)

slogger, *n. slog*-ger, a hard hitter ; a hard worker.

sloid, *n.* sloyd, manual training by means of carpentry and other trades. (Swed. *slojd,* skill.)

sloop, *n.* sloop, a cutter-rigged vessel with a standing bowsprit and the forestay leading from the bowsprit's outer-end. **sloop of war,** formerly a small warship rated below a frigate, now a small corvette used principally for convoy work. (Dut. *sloep.*)

slop, *n.* slop, water spilt or carelessly thrown about on a table or floor ; a puddle ; mean liquor ; poor liquid food ; *pl.* dirty water : *v.t.* to soil by spilling a liquid on. (A.S. *sloppe,* cow-droppings.)

slop, *n.* slop, a policeman [Slang].

slop-basin, *n.* a bowl for the dregs of cups.

★**slope,** *n.* slope, an oblique direction ; inclination, or an incline downwards ; a declivity ; an acclivity : *ad.* in a sloping manner : *v.t.* to form with a slope ; to direct obliquely ; to incline : *v.i.* to take an oblique direction. (A.S. *slupan,* slip.)

slopingly, *ad. slope*-ing-le, in a sloping manner.

slop-pail, *n.* bucket for collecting household slops.

sloppily, *ad. slop*-e-le, in a sloppy manner.

sloppiness, *n. slop*-e-ness, the state of being sloppy.

sloppy, *a. slop*-e, wet ; muddy ; slovenly ; maudlin.

slops, *n.pl.* slops, a loose lower garment ; trousers ; ready-made clothes ; overalls. (Ice. *sloppr.*)

slop-seller, *n.* one who sells ready-made clothes.

slop-shop, *n.* a shop where ready-made clothes are sold.

slosh, *n.* slosh, slush ; foolish sentimentality ; a sudden violent blow : *v.t.* to hit violently ; to assault [Slang].

slot, *n.* slot, a slit ; a narrow opening ; a hole in metal ; a groove ; a bar or bolt as a fastening or to hold larger pieces together : *v.t.* to make a slot in. (Origin doubtful.)

slot, *n.* slot, the track of a deer. **slot-hound,** a sleuth-hound. (O.Fr. *esclot.*)

sloth, *n.* slohth, tardiness ; sluggishness ; laziness ; a tropical American edentate, living and feeding on trees, so called from its slow, awkward movement on the ground. **giant** or **ground sloth,** a megatherium. **three-toed sloth,** a species of *Bradypus.* **two-toed sloth,** a species of *Cholœpus.* (A.S. *slaw,* slow.)

sloth-bear, *n.* the Indian long-clawed carnivore, *Melursus labiatus.*

slothful, *a.* inactive ; sluggish : indolent.

slothfully, *ad.* in a slothful manner.

slothfulness, *n.* the indulgence of sloth ; laziness.

sloth-monkey, *n.* the slow loris.

slot-machine, *n.* a machine operating when a coin has been inserted in the slot.

slot-meter, *n.* a container, etc., that allows the supply of a stated quantity of gas, electricity, etc., on the insertion of a coin in attached mechanism.

slotted, *a. slot*-ed, having a slot or slots.

slouch, *n.* slouch, a hanging down, as of the head or other part of the body ; an ungainly, clownish gait ; an awkward clownish fellow : *v.i.* to hang down ; to have a clownish look or gait : *v.t.* to depress ; to cause to hang down ; to do negligently. (O.Fr. *esloucher.*)

slouch-hat, *n.* a hat with a large slouching brim.

slough, *n.* slou, a muddy swamp. **slough of despond,** hopeless dejection. (A.S. *sloh.*)

slough, *n.* sluf, a cast skin ; the dead soft tissue that separates in an ulceration : *v.i.* to separate from the sound flesh ; to come off, as the matter formed over a sore, ulcer, etc. (Origin uncertain.)

sloughy, *a. slou*-e, full of sloughs or swampy areas ; miry.

sloughy, *a. sluf*-e, of the nature of slough or cast-off matter.

Slovak, *n. sloh*-vak *or* slo-*vak,* one of a race of western Slavs inhabiting parts of Moravia and adjacent areas included after the 1914–18 War in Czechoslovakia ; their language : *a.* Slovakian. (Czech.)

Slovakian, *n.* slo-*vak*-e-an, pertaining to the Slovaks : *n.* the language of the Slovaks.

sloven, *n. sluv*-en, one careless of dress or negligent of cleanliness ; one habitually negligent of neatness and order ; a slattern. (O.Dut. *sloef.*)

Slovene, *n.* slo-*veen,* one of the south-western branch of the Slavs, now inhabiting Yugoslavia. (Gr. *sklabenos.*)

Slovenian, *a.* slo-*vee*-ne-an, pertaining to Slovenia or to the Slovenes : *n.* the language of the Slovenes.

slovenliness, *n.* the habit of being slovenly ; negligence of dress ; neglect of order and neatness.

slovenly, *a. sluv*-en-le, negligent of dress or neatness ; untidy ; disorderly : *ad.* negligently ; in a disordered manner.

★**slow,** *a.* sloh, not quick in motion ; not ready ; dull ; inactive ; tardy ; not hasty ; behind time ; not advancing rapidly : *v.t.* to go slow : *v.i.* to become slow : *ad.* slowly. (A.S. *slaw.*)

slowcoach, *n. sloh*-koach ; a dull person ; a laggard.

slowly, *ad. sloh*-le, in a slow manner.

slow-match, *n.* a fuse burning slowly.

slow-motion, *a.* with the rate of movement much decreased [Cine.].

slowness, *n.* the quality or state of being slow ; dullness ; caution in deciding ; tardiness.

slow-worm, *n. sloh*-wurm, the limbless lizard, *Anguis fragilis.* (A.S. *sla-wyrm,* the slaying worm, in the belief that it was venomous.)

sloyd, *n.* sloyd, sloid.

slub, *n.* slub, a slightly twisted strand of fibres : *v.t.* to draw out and twist in preparation for spinning.

slubber, *n. slub*-ber, a slubbing-machine ; one who operates this : *v.t.* to do lazily, imperfectly, or coarsely ; to daub ; to stain ; to cover carelessly ; to slabber.

slubberdegullion, *n. slub*-ber-de-*gul*-yon, a mean, dirty fellow [Slang].

sludge, *n.* sluj, melting snow ; soft mud ; wet refuse ; settlings of lubricating or other oil. (M.E. *sluche.*)

sludger, *n.* *sluj*-er, a vessel for the disposal of sewage refuse out at sea; a tube or other apparatus for extracting mud from bore-holes, shot-holes, etc. [Eng.].
sludgy, *a.* *sluj*-e, slushy; muddy.
slue, *v.t.* sloo, to turn anything about its axis without removing it; to swing askew; to turn round. (Ice.)
slug, *n.* slug, an air-breathing mollusc in which the shell is rudimentary or absent; a slow, heavy, lazy fellow; a piece of metal used as shot; a clump of metal thicker than a lead, but of the same length, cast on to the bodies of type; a line of type cast by a linotype machine [Print.]. (M.E. *slugge.*)
slug, *v.t.* slug, to strike heavily with the fist or a sandbag, etc.: *v.i.* to indulge in such hitting [Slang]. (*slog.*)
slugabed, *n.* *slug*-a-bed, one who indulges in lying abed.
sluggard, *a.* *slug*-ard, sluggish; lazy: *n.* a person habitually lazy.
sluggardize, *v.t.* *slug*-ard-ize, to make lazy.
sluggish, *a.* *slug*-ish, indolent or lazy; slothful; slow; inert; inactive.
sluggishly, *ad.* in a sluggish manner.
sluggishness, *n.* indolence; slowness; inertness.
slug-horn, *n.* a trumpet. (Erroneous formation from *slogan.*)
sluice, *n.* sloose, a vent for water fitted with a door; a floodgate; a stream of water issuing through a floodgate; a long inclined trough for washing auriferous sand, etc.; a reserve store [Fig.]: *v.t.* to wash out; to flush with water; to provide with sluices. (O.Fr. *escluse.*)
sluice-gate, *n.* the sliding gate of a sluice that controls the flow of the water; the upper gate of a lock.
sluicy, *a.* *sloo*-se, falling in streams, as from a sluice.
slum, *n.* slum, a low mean street or district in a large town: *v.t.* to visit slums for social and philanthropic purposes, or merely out of curiosity. (Origin doubtful.)
slumber, *n.* *slum*-ber, light sleep; repose: *v.i.* to sleep, esp. lightly; to doze; to be in a state of sloth, supineness, or inactivity. (A.S. *sluma.*)
slumberer, *n.* *slum*-ber-rer, one who slumbers; a dilatory or lethargic person.
slumberingly, *ad.* in a slumbering manner.
slumberous, *a.* *slum*-ber-rus, inviting or causing sleep; sleepy; not waking.
slumbersome, *a.* *slum*-ber-sum, slumberous.
slumbery, *a.* *slum*-ber-re, slumberous; drowsy.
slumbrous, *a.* *slum*-brus, slumberous.
slummer, *n.* *slum*-mer, one who visits slums with a charitable or philanthropic object.
slummock, *v.i.* *slum*-ok, to slouch; to dawdle; to be awkward or ungainly.
slummocky, *a.* *slum*-o-ke, careless; slovenly; sloppy.
slummy, *a.* *slum*-me, abounding in slums; having the characteristics of a slum.
slump, *n.* slump, a sudden fall; a sinking; a collapse; a sudden fall in demand or prices: *v.i.* to fall in value, demand, esteem, etc.; to sag; to collapse; to sink suddenly when walking on a hard surface, as on semi-frozen ground. (Scand. and Teut., plump, splash.)
slung, slung, *p.* and *pp.* of *sling.*
slung-shot, *n.* *slung*-shot, a weapon consisting of a weight or ball attached to a thong.
slunk, slunk, *p.* and *pp.* of *slink.*
slur, *n.* slur, slight reproach or disgrace; a stigma; a mark connecting notes that are to be played or sung glidingly [Mus.]: *v.t.* to disparage; to pass over lightly; to smudge [Print.]; to sing or perform in a smooth, gliding style [Mus.]. (O.Dut. *sleuren,* drag.)
slurred, *a.* slurd, marked or performed with a slur [Mus.].
slurry, *v.t.* *slu*-re, to dirty; to smear: *n.* a watery paste as of cement, mortar, or mud; a thin loam put on moulds for casting metal.
slush, *n.* slush, sludge; melted snow and mud; a soft greasy mixture; maudlin or worthless talk or writing.
slushy, *a.* consisting of or overspread with slush; rubbishy.
slut, *n.* slut, a dirty, slovenly, untidy woman; a name of contempt for a woman. (M.E. *slutte.*)
slutch, *n.* sluch, mud; mire; sludge.
sluttery, *n.* *slut*-ter-re, neglect of cleanliness and order; disorder; sluttishness.
sluttish, *a.* *slut*-tish, careless of dress or cleanliness; untidy and dirty.
sluttishly, *ad.* in a sluttish manner.
sluttishness, *n.* the quality of being sluttish, dirtiness of person and surroundings.
sly, *a.* sly, artful; meanly cunning; crafty; dexterous in performing things secretly; marked with artful secrecy; quietly humorous; arch. (Scand.)
sly-boots, *n.* a sly, cunning, or waggish person.
sly-goose, *n.* the sheldrake *Tadorna cornuta.*
slyly, *ad.* in a sly manner; with artful secrecy.
slyness, *n.* the quality of being sly; artful secrecy.
slype, *n.* slipe, a passage between two walls; a covered passage from a cathedral to any building within the precincts. (*slip.*)
smack, *n.* smak, a blow from the open hand; a slap; a loud kiss; a quick, sharp noise; a taste; a tincture; pleasing taste; a small quantity: *v.t.* to slap smartly; to kiss with a close compression of the lips and a sharp noise; to make a noise by separation of the lips after tasting: *v.i.* to have a taste; to have a tincture; to make a sharp noise with the hands; to crack. **to have a smack at,** to make an attempt, to have a go [Slang]. (A.S. *smæc.*)
smack, *n.* smak, a small vessel used in the fishing trade; a small coaster; a yawl. (Dut. *smak.*)
smacker, *n.* *smak*-er, one who smacks; a loud kiss.
smacksman, *n.* *smaks*-man, the master of a fishing smack.
***small,** *a.* smawl, relatively little; less than standard; slender; of little moment; of little genius; weak; gentle; mean; petty: *n.* the slender part of a thing; *pl.* small articles for the laundry; small-clothes; responsions (at Oxford Univ.). **small-and-early,** an evening party [Coll.]. **small change,** coin of small denomination; matters, things, etc., of little importance. **small fry,** persons or things of only trifling consequence. **small hours,** those immediately after midnight. **sing small,** to adopt a humble tone. (A.S. *smæl.*)
smallage, *n.* *smawl*-aj, wild celery, *Apium graveolens.* (*small,* and Fr. *ache,* parsley.)
small-arms, *n.pl.* portable fire-arms (rifles, revolvers, etc.) as distinct from artillery.
small-beer, *n.* weak or mild beer; a person or thing of very minor importance [Coll.].
small-clothes, *n.pl.* knee-breeches.
small-coal, *n.* coals not in lumps, but small pieces.
small-craft, *n.* vessels in general of a small size.
small-hand, *n.* ordinary writing.
small-holder, *n.* one who cultivates a small-holding.
small-holding, *n.* a piece of land of not more than 50 acres let conditionally for cultivation by a public authority.
smallish, *a.* *smawl*-ish, somewhat small.
smallness, *n.* the quality of being small.
smallpox, *n.* *smawl*-poks, variola; a contagious and infectious fever, attended with an eruption.
smallsword, *n.* *smawl*-sord, a light sword for fencing or duelling; a rapier.
small-talk, *n.* light or desultory conversation.
small-wares, *n.pl.* *smawl*-warez, small textile articles of various kinds; haberdashery.
smalm, *v.t.* smahm, to smear; to bedaub; to flatter or fawn upon.
smalmy, *a.* *smah*-me, sticky to the touch; wheedling, fawning.
smalt, *n.* smawlt, a dark-blue pigment composed of the silicates of cobalt and potassium; glass tinged of a fine deep blue. (It. *smalto.*)
smaltine, *n.* *smawl*-teen, smaltite.
smaltite, *n.* *smawl*-tite, a tin-white or gray mineral composed of cobalt di-arsenide with nickel admixture.
smaragd, *n.* *sma*-ragd, the emerald. (L. *smaragdus.*)
smaragdine, *a.* sma-*rag*-deen, pertaining to, consisting of, or resembling emerald; of an emerald green.
smaragdite, *n.* sma-*rag*-dite, a grass-green variety of augite.
smarm, *v.t.* smarm, to smalm; to act as a toady or with insincere politeness; to smooth or plaster down, as the hair with grease.

smarmy, *a. smar*-me, smalmy.
smart, *n.* smart, quick pungent pain, either of body or mind : *a.* causing a sharp pain ; pricking ; sharp ; severe ; brisk ; active ; acute and pertinent ; witty ; vivacious ; spruce, in the latest style : *v.i.* to feel a smart ; to feel sharp pain ; to endure punishment. **smart Alec,** a bumptious fellow, a know-all [U.S.A. slang]. (A.S. *smeortan.*)
smarten, *v.t. smar*-ten, to make smart.
smartish, *a. smar*-tish, rather smart.
smartly, *ad.* in a smart manner ; keenly ; briskly ; vigorously ; sprucely.
smart-money, *n.* money paid to buy oneself off from enlistment or an engagement ; money allowed to soldiers or sailors who have been wounded or injured ; excessive damages.
smartness, *n.* the quality of being smart ; poignancy ; quickness ; wittiness.
smart-ticket, *n.* a warrant or certificate entitling one to smart-money.
smartweed, *n. smart*-weed, the water-pepper, *Polygonum hydropiper.*
★**smash,** *n.* smash, the act of smashing : *v.t.* to break in pieces by violence ; to crush ; at tennis, to hit the ball with a hard overhand stroke : *v.i.* to go bankrupt. (Scand.)
smash, *n.* smash, a drink of spiced spirits with broken ice.
smasher, *n.* one who or that which smashes ; something huge or extraordinary ; a clinching argument ; a coiner or passer of bad money [Slang].
smash-up, *n.* a complete smash ; a bad collision ; bankruptcy ; disaster.
smatter, *n. smat*-ter, a smattering : *v.i.* to talk superficially ; to have a slight knowledge of. (Scand.)
smatterer, *n.* one who has only a smattering ; a sciolist ; a dilletante.
smattering, *n.* a slight superficial knowledge.
smear, *n.* smeer, a stain made by smearing : *v.t.* to overspread with anything viscous or oily ; to besmear ; to daub ; to soil ; to contaminate. (A.S. *smerwan.*)
smeariness, *n.* smeary state ; stickiness.
smeary, *a. smeer*-re, that smears or soils ; adhesive.
smectite, *n. smek*-tite, a sort of fuller's earth. (Gr. *smectos*, greasy.)
smee, *n.* smee, the wigeon ; the pochard [Engl.]; the pintail [U.S.A.]. (From *smew.*)
smegma, *n. smeg*-ma, a glandular soapy secretion in the folds of the skin, esp. about the prepuce. (Gr. *smegma*, soap.)
smegmatic, *a.* smeg-*mat*-ik, soapy ; cleansing ; detersive : *n.* a detergent or cleanser.
★**smell,** *v.i.* smel, to affect the nose ; to have an odour ; to smack of ; to exercise the sense of smell : *v.t.* to perceive by the nose. **smell a rat,** to become suspicious. **smell out,** to find out by sagacity. *p.* and *pp.* **smelt** (formerly **smelled**). (Low Ger. *smelen*, smoulder.)
smell, *n.* smel, the power or faculty of smelling ; scent ; odour.
smeller, *n. smel*-ler, one who smells or smells out ; one who exudes odour ; [Slang] the nose.
smelling-bottle, *n.* a bottle or phial for holding smelling-salts.
smelling-salts, *n.pl.* perfumed ammonium carbonate, or other substance calculated to stimulate the olfactory nerves.
smelly, *a. smel*-le, malodorus ; having an odour.
smelt, smelt, *p.* and *pp.* of *smell.*
smelt, *n.* smelt, a small food-fish of the salmon family, *Osmerus eperlanus* ; applied also to other small fish, as the argentine, tomcod, and smolt. (A.S.)
smelt, *v.t.* smelt, to melt ore, so as to separate the metal. (Scand.)
smelter, *n. smelt*-er, one who smelts ore.
smeltery, *n. smelt*-er-re, a house or place for smelting.
smew, *n.* smew, a migratory sea duck, allied to the goosander and mergansers, *Mergus albellus.*
smicker, *v.i. smik*-er, to look amorously or wantonly ; to smirk.
smiddy, *n. smid*-de, a smithy. (Scots.)
smift, *n.* smift, a fuse or slow-match.
Smilax, *n. smy*-laks, a liliaceous genus of plants of many species, the roots of some of which yield sarsaparilla. (Gr.)
★**smile,** *n.* smile, a look of pleasure, or kindness, or slight contempt ; gay or joyous appearance ; favour : *v.i.* to express pleasure, love, or kindness by the countenance ; to laugh gently ; to look happy. **smile at,** to consider with slight contempt. **smile on,** to countenance favourably. (Scand.)
smileless, *a. smile*-less, not having a smile.
smiler, *n. smile*-er, one who smiles.
smilingly, *ad. smile*-ing-le, with a smile of pleasure.
smilingness, *n. smile*-ing-ness, state of smiling.
Smilodon, *n. smy*-lo-don, a genus of New World Pleistocene sabre-toothed tigers.
smirch, *v.t.* smurtsh, to cloud ; to soil ; to smear ; to depreciate : *n.* a smear, stain, or smudge ; that which smirches ; a moral defect. (A.S. *smerwan*, smear.)
smirk, *n.* smurk, a silly smile ; a simper : *v.i.* to look affectedly soft or kind. (A.S. *smearcian*, to smile.)
smit, *n.* smit, the owner's mark on sheep ; formerly, ruddle for marking sheep. (A.S. *smitte.*)
smite, *v.t.* smite, to strike hard ; to kill ; to blast ; to afflict ; to chasten ; to strike or affect with passion. *pp.* **smitten.** *p.* **smote** : *n.* a heavy blow. (A.S. *smitan.*)
smiter, *n. smite*-er, one who smites or strikes ; a hard hitter.
smith, *n.* smith, one who forges with the hammer ; one who works in metals. (A.S.)
smithereens, *n.pl.* smith-er-*reenz*, small fragments.
smithers, *n.pl. smith*-erz, smithereens.
smithery, *n. smith*-er-re, the workshop of a smith ; the occupation of a smith ; work done by a smith.
smithing, *n. smith*-ing, the art or act of working iron into shape.
smithsonite, *n. smith*-son-ite, native carbonate of zinc. (James *Smithson*, English physicist, *d.* 1829.)
smithy, *n. smith*-e, the workshop of a smith.
smitten, *smit*-en, *pp.* of *smite* : *a.* affected with some passion ; very much in love.
smock, *n.* smok, a woman's under-garment ; a chemise ; a smock-frock ; a woman's or child's overall ; [Slang] a female. (A.S. *smoc.*)
smock-faced, *a. smok*-fayst, having a feminine countenance or complexion.
smock-frock, *n.* smok-*frok*, a coarse linen frock worn by farm-labourers over the other clothes.
smocking, *n. smok*-ing, close pleating ; honeycomb work.
smockmill, *n. smok*-mil, a windmill whose top rotates to meet the wind.
smock-race, *n. smok*-race, a race formerly run by women for the prize of a fine smock.
smog, *n.* smog, a mixture in the atmosphere of smoke and fog with acid fumes [Coll.].
smokable, *a. smoke*-a-bl, that can be smoked.
★**smoke** *n.* smoke, the visible exhalation that escapes from burning materials ; vapour ; something to smoke, esp. a cigar [Coll.] ; failure : *v.i.* to emit smoke ; to use tobacco ; to inhale and exhale tobacco-smoke ; to raise dust by rapid motion ; to burn ; to rage : *v.t.* to apply smoke to ; to scent, dry, or medicate by smoke ; to drive out by smoke ; to inhale the smoke of ; to suspect, understand, or get the drift of, also to banter or ridicule [old Coll.]. **to end in smoke,** to come to nothing. (A.S. *smoca.*)
smoke-black, *n.* lampblack.
smoke-board, *n.* a board before the upper part of a fireplace to increase the draught, and prevent the chimney smoking.
smoke-bomb, *n. smoke*-bom, a shell or bomb that emits a dense cloud of smoke on bursting.
smoke-box, *n.* the chamber of a steam boiler in which smoke collects before passing to the chimney or funnel.
smoke-cloud, *n. smoke*-kloud, a cloud of smoke ; a smoke-screen.
smoke-dried, *a.* dried in smoke.
smoke-helmet, *n.* a helmet with self-contained air-supply used by fire-fighters ; a gas-mask.
smoke-jack, *n. smoke*-jak, an apparatus for turning a spit driven by the current of air ascending the chimney.
smokeless, *a. smoke*-less, having or emitting no smoke.
smoker, *n. smoke*-er, one who dries by smoke ; one who smokes tobacco ; an informal concert at which smoking is permitted ; a railway carriage for smokers.

smoke-rocket, *n.* a contrivance for emitting smoke into a drain to discover a leak.
smoke-sail, *n.* *smoke*-sl, a small sail set forward of the funnel of a vessel's galley.
smoke-screen, *n.* a long cloud of smoke raised for concealing warlike operations; any concealing device or manœuvre [Fig.].
smoke-stack, *n.* a tall chimney; the funnel of a steamer.
smoke-tree, *n.* the Venetian sumac, *Rhus cotinus.*
smokily, *ad.* *smoke*-e-le, in a smoky manner.
smokiness, *n.* the state of being smoky.
smoking, *a.* emitting smoke; for the use of smokers: *n.* the act of emitting smoke; the practice of inhaling and emitting tobacco fumes; the process of curing by means of smoke.
smoky, *a.* *smoke*-e, emitting smoke; having the appearance or nature of smoke; filled with smoke; subject to be filled with smoke from a chimney; tarnished with smoke.
smolt, *n.* smohlt, a salmon older than a parr and younger than a grilse.
⋆**smooth,** *a.* smoothe, having an even surface; not rough; glossy; gently flowing; unruffled; bland in manners; mild; flattering: *n.* the smooth part of a thing; the act of smoothing: *v.i.* to become smooth.
smooth-bore, *n.* a gun with a barrel that has not been rifled: *a.* not rifled.
smoothe, *v.t.* smoothe, to make smooth; to make easy; to make flowing; to palliate; to calm; to ease; to flatter. (A.S. *smethe.*)
smoothen, *v.t.* and *i.* *smoothe*-en, to make or become smooth.
smooth-faced, *a.* clean-shaven; brazen; hypocritical.
smooth-hound, *n.* *smoothe*-hound, the small shark or dogfish, *Mustelus vulgaris.*
smoothing-iron, *n.* a polished iron for smoothing clothes.
smoothing-plane, *n.* a carpenter's plane used for smoothing and finishing work.
smoothly, *ad.* *smoothe*-le, in a smooth manner.
smoothness, *n.* *smoothe*-ness, the quality of being smooth; evenness; softness; mildness; blandness.
smooth-spoken or **-tongued,** *a.* hypocritical in speech; plausible; flattering.
smorzato, *ad.* smor-*tsah*-toh, an expression to indicate a gradual diminution of tone to its dying away [Mus.]. (It., dying away.)
smote, smote, *p.* of *smite.*
smother, *n.* *smuthe*-er, smoke; thick dust: *v.t.* to suffocate; to stifle; to suppress; to conceal or hush up; to cover: *v.i.* to be suffocated; to smoulder without vent. (A.S. *smorian.*)
smothery, *a.* *smuthe*-er-re, tending to smother.
smouch, *n.* smouch, a smudge; a smutch.
smoulder, *v.i.* *smole*-der, to burn away slowly; to burn or exist in a stifled state: *n.* a slow-burning fire; the result of slow combustion. (Low Ger. *smolen.*)
smudge, *n.* smuj, a black or dark stain; a smear; a suffocating smoke; a smouldering fire to suffocate mosquitoes [U.S.A.]: *v.t.* to smear or soil: to blur. (M.E. *smogen.*)
smudgy, *a.* *smuj*-e, marked with smudges; smeared.
smug, *a.* smug, neat; affectedly nice in dress; prim; self-satisfied. (Origin uncertain.)
smug, *v.t.* smug, to steal; to crib or copy surreptitiously; to arrest. [Slang]
smuggle, *v.t.* *smug*-gl, secretly to import or export goods without paying customs duties; to convey or introduce clandestinely. (Dan. *smugle.*)
smuggler, *n.* *smug*-ler, one who smuggles; a vessel employed in carrying smuggled goods.
smuggling, *n.* *smug*-ling, the offence of clandestinely importing or exporting prohibited goods or other goods without paying the customs duties.
smugly, *ad.* *smug*-le, in a smug manner; neatly.
smugness, *n.* *smug*-ness, the quality of being smug.
smut, *n.* smut, a spot made with soot or coal, or the foul matter itself; a parasitic fungus on grasses; obscenity: *v.t.* to stain or mark with smut; to taint with mildew; to blacken; to tarnish: *v.i.* to gather smut; to be attacked by smut [Bot.]. (Ger. *Schmutz,* filth.)
smut-ball, *n.* *smut*-bawl, a name given to various fungi; a puff-ball.

smutch, *n.* smutch, smut; a smudge: *v.t.* to blacken with smoke, soot, or coal.
smuttily, *ad.* *smut*-te-le, in a smutty manner.
smuttiness, *n.* the state of being smutty.
smutty, *a.* *smut*-te, soiled with smut; affected with smut [Bot.]; tainted with mildew; obscene, bawdy; given to filthy talk or writing.
snack, *n.* snak, a slight hasty repast. **snack-bar,** a quick-lunch counter. **to go snacks,** to share and share alike.
snaffle, *n.* snafl, a slender bit with a joint in the middle, having no branches but occasionally sidebars: *v.t.* to bridle; to hold or manage with a bridle; [Slang] to appropriate, to pinch. (Dut. *snavel.*)
snafu, *a.* snaf-*foo,* in a complete mess; haywire [Mil. slang]. (Said to be from initials of "Situation normal—all fouled up!")
snag, *n.* snag, a short branch; a shoot; a knot; a stump or branch of a tree, sunk or floating, forming a danger to navigation; a projecting tooth; an obstacle: *v.t.* to lop snags from trees; to damage by snags. (Norw.)
snagged, *a.* snagd, snaggy.
snaggle-toothed, *a.* *snagl*-toothd, having projecting or badly spaced teeth.
snaggy, *a.* *snag*-e, full of snags; abounding with knots.
snail, *n.* snale, a slimy, slow-creeping, air-breathing univalve mollusc; a drone; a slow-moving person; a spiral cam. (A.S. *snægl.*)
snail-clover, *n.* snail-trefoil.
snailery, *n.* *snale*-er-re, a snail farm or place where edible snails are grown for market.
snail-fish, *n.* a fish of the genus *Liparis,* the sea-snail.
snail-flower, *n.* a plant allied to the kidney-bean, *Phaseolus caracalla*; snail-trefoil.
snail-like, *a.* like a snail in motion: *ad.* in the manner of a snail.
snail-trefoil, *n.* any of the varieties of medic, esp. *Medicago scutellata.*
⋆**snake,** *n.* snake, a long reptile without developed limbs; a serpent; a treacherous person: *v.i.* to wind, twist, or move stealthily like a snake: *v.t.* to wind a small rope round a large one spirally [Naut.]. **snake in the grass,** a secret or lurking enemy. (A.S. *snaca.*)
snake-bird, *n.* the darter, a species of *Plotus,* so called from the length of its neck; the wryneck, *Iynx torquilla.*
snake-eel, *n.* a species of eel, with a tail without any fin.
snake-root, *n.* the common name of several plants of different genera reputed to be efficacious against snake-bite.
snake's-head, *n.* popular name of many plants, esp. the fritillary (*F. meliagris*) and *Hermodactylus tiberosis.*
snakestone, *n.* *snake*-stone, an ammonite; a small piece of rounded stone or other hard substance, alleged to be efficacious in curing snake-bites.
snakeweed, *n.* *snake*-weed, the plant *Polygonum bistorta.*
snake-wood, *n.* a wood supposed to be a remedy for the bite of snakes; letterwood.
snakily, *ad.* *snake*-e-le, in a snaky manner.
snakish, *a.* *snake*-ish, having the qualities of a snake; snaky.
snaky, *a.* *snake*-e, pertaining to or resembling a snake; serpentine; winding; sly; insinuating; deceitful; abounding in snakes.
snap, *n.* snap, a sudden breaking or rupture of any substance; a sudden eager bite, or effort to bite; a crack, as of a whip; a catch or small fastening; a sudden turn of cold weather; a small gingerbread cake; a game of cards; a snapshot photograph: *v.t.* to break short or at once; to strike with a sharp sound; to catch at suddenly with the teeth; to crack; to photograph instantaneously: *v.i.* to break short; to part asunder suddenly; to try to bite; to catch. **snap division,** a division taken without warning to the Opposition [Polit.]. **snap off,** to bite off suddenly. **snap one up,** to treat with sharp words. **snap the fingers at,** to make light of. **snap vote,** a vote taken suddenly. (Dut. *snappen,* to snap.)
snapdragon, *n.* *snap*-drag-on, a plant of the genus *Antirrhinum,* having a personate corolla, which shuts with a snap when opened; a pastime in

which raisins are snatched from burning brandy and put into the mouth; the raisins snatched up.
snaphance, *n. snap*-hance, the spring-lock of a 17th-cent. form of musket; the musket itself. (Dut.)
snapper, *n. snap*-per, one who snaps; one who takes snapshots; one of several aquatic turtles of southern N. America, esp. the snapping turtle, *Chelydra serpentina* or the alligator terrapin, *Macrochelys temminckii*; a popular name for various plants, birds, and fishes.
snappily, *ad.* in a snappy or snappish manner.
snappish, *a. snap*-pish, apt to snap; eager to bite; curt in reply; apt to speak angrily or tartly.
snappishly, *ad.* in a snappish manner.
snappishness, *n.* the quality of being snappish.
snappy, *a. snap*-e, snappish; crackling; very much alive, full of "go" [Coll.]; smart [Slang]; having a snap in it (of weather).
snapshot, *n. snap*-shot, a shot without a deliberate aim; an instantaneous photograph.
snapweed, *n. snap*-weed, any species of the genus *Impatiens*, which comprises the balsams.
snare, *n.* snare, a contrivance, esp. a wire noose, for catching animals; that by which one is entangled; the gut across the head of a side-drum: *v.t.* to catch with a snare; to entangle. (A.S. *snear*, a string.)
snarer, *n. snare*-rer, one who lays snares or entangles.
snark, *n.* snark, an illusory quest (from the imaginary animal invented by Lewis Carrol in "The Hunting of the Snark," 1876).
snarky, *a. snark*-e, peevish; bad-tempered [Slang].
snarl, *n.* snarl, an angry contention or quarrel; a surly or savage remark or exclamation: *v.i.* to show the teeth and growl; to gird at; to speak roughly or surlily; to emboss. (O.Dut. *snarren*, to quarrel.)
snarl, *n.* snarl, entanglement; a complication, especially of hair or thread, difficult to disentangle: *v.t.* to entangle; to complicate; to involve in knots. (*snare.*)
snarler, *n. snarl*-er, one who snarls; a surly growling animal; a grumbling, quarrelsome fellow.
snarling, *pp.* and *a. snarl*-ing, growling; grumbling angrily; snappish; embossing; entangling. **snarling iron,** a tool for embossing.
snarly, *a. snarl*-e, given to snarling; bad tempered.
snarly, *a. snarl*-e, full of snarls; tangled.
snary, *a, snare*-re, resembling a snare; ensnaring; insidious.
snatch, *n.* snatch, a hasty catching or seizing; an attempt to seize suddenly; a short fit of exertion; a short spell of singing, talk, etc.; a fragment: *v.t.* to seize hastily or abruptly; to seize without permission or ceremony; to seize and transport away: *v.i.* to catch at. (M.E. *snacchen.*)
snatch-block, *n.* a block with an opening on one side to receive the bight of a rope.
snatcher, *n. snatch*-er, one who snatches or takes abruptly.
snatchingly, *ad. snatch*-ing-le, by snatching; hastily; abruptly.
snatchy, *a. snatch*-e, done in or characterized by snatches; spasmodic.
snathe, *n.* snathe, a snead [U.S.A.].
snead, *n.* sneed, the shaft or handle of a scythe. (A.S. *snæd.*)
sneak, *n.* sneek, a mean fellow; one who sneaks; a tale-bearer; a ball that is bowled along the ground [Cricket]: *v.i.* to creep or steal away privately or meanly, as afraid or ashamed to be seen; to behave with meanness and servility; to crouch; to truckle; to tell tales; to steal. **sneak thief,** a petty thief; a pilferer. (Derivation obscure.)
sneaker, *n.* one who sneaks; a sneak at cricket.
sneaking, *a. sneek*-ing, acting like a sneak; mean; servile; crouching; niggardly.
sneakingly, *ad.* in a sneaking manner.
sneakingness, *n.* the quality of being a sneak; meanness; niggardliness.
sneaky, *a. sneek*-e, like a sneak; sneaking.
sneck, *n.* snek, a door-latch; the catch of a lock: *v.t.* to fasten by a latch [Scots.].
sneer, *n.* sneer, a look of contempt, disdain, derision, or ridicule; an expression of contemptuous scorn: *v.i.* to show contempt by turning up the nose or by a particular cast of countenance; to insinuate contempt by a covert expression; to treat with contempt. (O.Teut.)
sneerer, *n. sneer*-rer, one who sneers.
sneeringly, *ad.* in a sneering manner; with a look of contempt or scorn.
sneeshing, *n. snee*-shing, snuff [Scots.].
★**sneeze,** *n.* sneez, the act of sneezing: *v.t.* to emit air through the nose convulsively, in consequence of irritation in the inner membrane of the nose. (A.S. *fneosan.*)
sneeze-wood, *n.* a South African tree, *Ptæroxylon utile*, yielding a valuable timber, so called from the sternutatory properties of its sawdust.
sneezewort, *n. sneez*-wurt, the wild pellitory, *Achillea ptarmica.*
sneezing, *n.* the act of one who sneezes; snuff.
snell, *a.* snel, active; keen; severe [Scots.].
snell, *n.* snel, a short gut snood for attaching a fish-hook to the line.
snib, *n.* snib, a bolt or other fastener: *v.t.* to fasten with this; to catch.
snick, *n.* snik, a notch; a nick; a glancing hit [Cricket]: *v.t.* to nick; to hit so as to cause merely a deviation in the ball's flight [Cricket].
snicker, *v.i. snik*-er, to snigger.
snickersnee, *n. snik*-er-snee, a large cut-and-thrust knife.
snide, *a.* snide, spurious; bogus; tricky: *n.* sham jewellery; meretricious ornament [Slang].
Snider, *n. sny*-der, an obsolete breech-loading rifle used in the mid-Victorian British army. (Name of inventor.)
sniff, *n.* snif, perception by the nose; what is snuffed in; sound or act of sniffing: *v.i.* to draw air audibly up the nose: *v.t.* to draw in with the breath; to smell. (Scand.)
sniffle, *v.i.* snifl, to sniff repeatedly or continuously: *n.* a sniffling. **the sniffles,** a bout of sniffling.
sniffy, *a. snif*-e, prone to sniff; disdainful.
snift, *v.i.* snift, to snort; to sniff; to snivel.
snifting-valve, *n.* a valve in the cylinder of a steam engine for the escape or entrance of air or the discharge of accumulated water.
snig, *n.* snig, a small eel. (Dial. Eng.)
snigger, *v.i. snig*-ger, to laugh with small audible catches of voice, as when one attempts to suppress loud laughter: *n.* a suppressed laugh of this kind. (Imit.)
sniggle, *v.t. snig*-gl, to snare; to catch; to fish for eels by thrusting bait into their holes.
snip, *n.* snip, a clip; a single cut with scissors; a small shred; a snipper; a patch of white on a horse's muzzle; a tailor [Slang]; a good racing-tip, a stroke of good luck [Slang]: *pl.* small hand shears for cutting sheet metal: *v.t.* to clip; to cut off with shears or scissors. (Dut. *snippen.*)
snipe, *n.* snipe, a bird of the genus *Gallinago*, having a long straight bill: *v.i.* to shoot snipe; to pick off individual enemies from cover [Mil.]: *v.t.* to shoot at from an ambush. (Ice. *snipa.*)
sniper, *n. snipe*-er, one who snipes; a sharpshooter.
snipper, *n. snip*-per, one who snips or clips.
snipper-snapper, *n. snip*-per-*snap*-per, a whipper-snapper.
snippet, *n. snip*-pet, a small part or share; a small piece snipped off.
snippety, *a. snip*-e-te, fragmentary; consisting of snippets.
snippy, *a. snip*-e, snippety; snappish; stingy.
snip-snap, *a. snip*-snap, smart: *n.* a smart sharp dialogue.
snitch, *v.t.* snitch, to catch in a noose; to pilfer: *v.i.* to inform, to peach [Slang]: *n.* the nose [Slang].
snitcher, *n. snitch*-er, a handcuff of cord; an informer or telltale [Slang].
snivel, *n. sniv*-el, mucus, running from the nose; hypocritical or affected weeping; humbug: *v.i.* to run at the nose; to cry as children with snuffling or snivelling; to draw up the snivel; to complain in a whining or abject manner. (A.S. *snofl*, mucus.)
sniveller, *n. sniv*-el-er, one who snivels; one who cries with snivelling; one who weeps for slight causes.
snivelly, *a. sniv*-el-e, running at the nose; whining.
snob, *n.* snob, a shoemaker: a vulgar person who apes gentility; a blackleg during a strike: *v.t.* to cobble. (Scand.)
snobbery, *n. snob*-er-re, snobbishness; the state of being a snob.

snobbish, *a.* *snob*-ish, belonging to, or resembling a snob; given to snobbery.
snobbishly, *ad.* *snob*-ish-le, like a snob.
snobbishness, *n.* *snob*-ish-ness, the quality of being a snob.
snobbism, *n.* *snob*-izm, snobbishness.
snobby, *a.* *snob*-e, snobbish.
snobocracy, *n.* snob-*ok*-ra-se, the body of snobs regarded as wielding some social influence.
snoek, *n.* snook, a mackerel-like food-fish, *Thyrsites atun*, of S. African and Australasian waters. (Dut.)
snood, *n.* snood, a ribbon binding a girl's hair, formerly emblematic of maidenhood; the short length of gut or other material on which a hook is mounted: *v.t.* to bind with or fasten with a snood. (A.S. *snod.*)
snook, *n.* snook, a derisive extension of the fingers with the thumb at the tip of the nose.
snooker, *n.* *snook*-er, a variety of pyramids, played on the billiard-table (also called **snooker-pool**): *v.t.* to frustrate; to baffle.
snoop, *v.i.* snoop, to pry around; to be sneakingly inquisitive.
snooper, *n.* *snoop*-er, one who pries around; an over-officious inspector; a peeping Tom.
snooty, *a.* *snoot*-e, superciliously peevish or unpleasant; snobbish [Slang].
snooze, *n.* snooz, a short sleep or nap: *v.i.* to slumber; to take a nap in the daytime. (Dial. Eng.)
snoozer, *n.* *snooz*-rer, one who snoozes.
snore, *n.* snore, a hoarse breathing in sleep: *v.i.* to breathe noisily in sleep with the mouth open. (Imit.)
snorer, *n.* *snore*-er, one who snores.
snort, *n.* snort, the sound produced by snorting: *v.i.* to force the air with violence through the nostrils like a horse. (Dut. *snorken.*)
snorter, *n.* *snort*-er, one who snorts; the wheatear; a strong wind; anything strikingly violent, noisy, intense, etc.
snot, *n.* snot, mucus from the nose; used also as a term of personal contempt. (A.S. *ge-snot.*)
snotty, *a.* *snot*-te, foul with mucus; mean; dirty; huffed, out of temper [Coll.]: *n.* a midshipman [Slang].
snout, *n.* snout, the long projecting nose of a beast, as of swine; the nose of a man, in contempt; a nozzle; a projecting part. (Dut. *snuit.*)
snouted, *a.* *snout*-ed, having a snout.
snouty, *a.* *snout*-e, resembling a snout; haughty.
★**snow,** *n.* snoh, the watery particles in the atmosphere frozen into small white crystalline flakes and falling to the earth; [Slang] cocaine: *v.i.* to fall in snow: *v.t.* to scatter like snow. **snowed in** or **up,** blockaded or imprisoned by snow. (A.S. *snaw.*)
snow, *n.* snoh, a vessel with two masts like a brig without a spanker, with a jigger-mast abaft the mainmast, carrying a trysail. (Dut. *snauw*, a snout.)
snowball, *n.* *snoh*-bawl, a round mass of snow, pressed or rolled together; anything, esp. a fund, that grows progressively by accretion: *v.t.* to pelt with snowballs: *v.i.* to throw snowballs; to accumulate by degrees.
snowball-tree, *n.* the guelder rose.
snowberry, *n.* *snoh*-be-re, a shrub of the genus *Symphoricarpus*, having snow-white berries.
snow-bird, *n.* the American finch, *Fringilla hiemalis.*
snow-blind, *a.* affected with snow-blindness.
snow-blindness, *n.* partial blindness due to the reflection from snow; niphablepsia.
snow-blink, *n.* the reflection from snow.
snow-bound, *a.* shut in, or impeded in movement by a heavy fall of snow.
snow-broth, *n.* snow and water mixed.
snow-bunting, *n.* an arctic bird of the genus *Plectrophanes.*
snow-capped, *a.* crowned with snow.
snow-cock, *n.* a large gallinaceous bird of the Himalayas.
snow-drift, *n.* a bank of snow driven together by the wind.
snowdrop, *n.* *snoh*-drop, a bulbous plant of the genus *Galanthus*, bearing a white flower in early spring.
snowfall, *n.* *snoh*-fawl, the amount of snow fallen in a given time: a fall of snow.
snow-field, *n.* a permanent expanse of snow.
snow-finch, *n.* the brambling; also a small Alpine bird, *Montefringilla nivalis*, with striking black and white plumage.
snowflake, *n.* *snoh*-flake, a flake of snow; the snow-bunting; a plant of the genus *Leucojum.*
snow-glory, *n.* a plant of the genus *Chionodoxa.*
snow-goose, *n.* any of the Arctic American geese of the genus *Chen.*
snow-grouse, *n.* the ptarmigan, *Tetrao mutus.*
snow-ice, *n.* ice formed from the freezing of melting snow.
snowily, *ad.* *snoh*-e-le, in a snowy manner.
snow-leopard, *n.* the ounce, *Felis uncia*, a leopard-like cat of Tibet.
snowless, *a.* *snoh*-less, destitute of snow.
snowlike, *a.* *snoh*-like, resembling snow.
snow-line, *n.* the limit of perpetual snow.
snow-plough, *n.* a machine for clearing away snow from roadways and railways.
snow-shoe, *n.* a racket-like shoe to prevent the feet from sinking into the snow.
snow-slip, *n.* an avalanche, a large mass of snow which slips down the side of a mountain.
snowstorm, *n.* *snoh*-storm, a storm with a heavy fall of snow.
snow-white, *a.* white as snow.
snow-wreath, *n.* a heap of drifted snow; the half-hardy rosaceous shrub, *Neviusia alabamensis*, with white feathery flowers.
snowy, *a.* *snoh*-e, white like snow; abounding or covered with snow; tending to snow; pure, unblemished [Fig.]. **snowy owl,** the great white owl, *Nyctea scandiaca.*
snub, *n.* snub, a knot or protuberance in wood; a snag; a check or act of snubbing; a rebuff; a snub nose: *v.t.* to clip off; to check; to reprimand; to slight; to check or rebuke with a tart sarcastic remark or reply. **snub a cable,** to check it suddenly in running out [Naut.]. **snub nose,** a nose that is short and broad with the end turned up. (Dan. *snibbe*, to nip.)
snubber, *n.* *snub*-er, a form of motor-car shock-absorber.
snubby, *a.* *snub*-e, stumpy; inclined to snub.
snub-nosed, *a.* *snub*-nohzd, having a snub nose.
snudge, *n.* snuj, a miser or a sneaking fellow.
snuff, *n.* snuf, the charred part of a candlewick; a candle almost burnt out; finely ground tobacco or a medicated substance, inhaled by the nose; resentment; huff, expressed by a snuffing of the nose: *v.t.* to draw in through the nose; to scent; to smell; to take the snuff off: *v.i.* to snort; to inhale the air with violence or with noise; to take offence. **up to snuff,** wideawake; enlightened in the matter. (O.Dut. *snuffen*, to sniff.)
snuff-box, *n.* a box for carrying snuff.
snuffer, *n.* *snuf*-fer, one who takes snuff: *pl.* a tool for cropping the snuff of a candle.
snuffiness, *n.* *snuf*-fe-ness, the state of being snuffy.
snuffle, *v.i.* *snuf*-fl, to breathe hard or speak through the obstructed nose: *n.* the act or sound of snuffling; a snivel: *pl.* obstruction of the nose by mucus; cold in the nose. (Low Ger. *schnuffeln.*)
snuffler, *n.* *snuf*-fler, one who snuffles.
snuff-mull, *n.* a snuff-box, esp. one made from a curled ram's horn [Scots.].
snuffy, *a.* *snuf*-fe, like snuff; soiled with tobacco snuff.
snug, *a.* snug, lying close; closely pressed; close; concealed; in good order; compact, tidy, and comfortable: *v.i.* to snuggle: *v.t.* to make snug: *n.* a snuggery. (Scand.)
snuggery, *n.* *snug*-ger-re, a small, comfortable room; a cosy bar-parlour.
snuggle, *v.i.* *snug*-gl, to lie close for comfort and warmth; to cuddle. (*snug.*)
snugly, *ad.* *snug*-le, in a snug manner.
snugness, *n.* *snug*-ness, state of being snug.
★**so,** *ad.* soh, in like manner; in such manner; to such degree; thus: *conj.* therefore; provided that. **so much,** *see* **much. so much as,** however much. **so much for,** and that's enough of him, or that matter, etc. **so so,** such as it was; indifferently. **so then,** therefore. (A.S. *swa.*)
soak, *v.t.* soke, to steep; to wet thoroughly; to drench; to imbibe by the pores, as the skin; to charge heavily [Slang]: *v.i.* to lie steeped in fluid; to enter into pores or interstices; to drink intemperately: *n.* the act of soaking; the state of

being soaked; a bout of hard drinking, a hard drinker [Slang]. (A.S. *socian*, to suck.)
soakage, *n. soke*-aj, the amount soaked in.
soaker, *n. soke*-er, one who or that which soaks in a liquid; a hard drinker.
soaking, *a. soke*-ing, that wets thoroughly: *n.* a complete or thorough wetting.
so-and-so, *n. soh*-and-soh, a person or thing not named (also used euphemistically of some disrespectful appelation).
⋆**soap,** *n.* sope, an alkaline or unctuous substance used in washing and cleansing: *v.t.* to rub or wash over with soap. (A.S. *sape.*)
soapberry, *n. sope*-be-re, the red saponaceous berry of the tropical evergreen, *Sapindus saponaria*, used as a substitute for soap.
soap-boiler, *n.* a maker of soap; a soap-pan.
soap-bubble, *n.* an inflated filmy sphere of soapy water.
soapily, *ad. sope*-e-le, in a soapy or unctuous manner.
soapiness, *n. sope*-e-ness, the state of being soapy.
soap-pan, *n.* a boiler for the manufacture of soap.
soapstone, *n. sope*-stone, talc or steatite.
soap-suds, *n.pl.* water impregnated with soap.
soap-tree, *n.* the soapberry or other tree yielding a substitute for soap.
soap-works, *n.* a soap factory.
soapwort, *n. sope*-wurt, a trailing herbaceous plant of the genus *Saponaria*.
soapy, *a. sope*-e, like or having the qualities of soap; soft and smooth; covered with soap; unctuous.
soar, *n.* sore, a towering flight: *v.i.* to fly aloft; to rise high; to mount; to tower in imagination; to rise in ambition or heroism; to rise aloft; [Av.] to fly with the engine cut off and without losing height. (Fr. *essorer.*)
soaringly, *ad. sore*-ring-le, upwardly.
soave, *ad.* soh-*ah*-vay, softly; with sweetness [Mus.]. (It.)
sob, *n.* sob, a convulsive sigh with tears, or act of respiration obstructed by sorrow: *v.i.* to sigh or utter deep sobs. (A.S. *seofian*, to bewail.)
sobbing, *n. sob*-bing; a convulsive respiration due to sorrowful emotion.
sober, *a. soh*-ber, not drunk; temperate, specially in the use of spirituous liquors; not excited or heated with passion; calm; grave; serious: *v.t.* to make sober: *v.i.* to become sober. (Fr. *sobre.*)
soberish, *n. soh*-ber-ish, more or less sober.
soberize, *v.t. soh*-ber-rize, to make sober.
soberly, *ad.* in a sober manner.
sober-minded, *a.* having a disposition or temper habitually sober, temperate, and calm.
sober-mindedness, *n.* the quality of being sober-minded.
soberness, *n.* the state of being sober.
sobersides, *n. soh*-ber-sydz, a sedate person.
soboles, *n.* (*sing.* and *pl.*) so-*boh*-leez, a sucker or underground stem [Bot.]. (L., a shoot.)
soboliferous, *a.* soh-boh-*lif*-er-rus, bearing soboles.
Sobranje, *n.* so-*brahn*-ye, the national assembly of Bulgaria. (Bulgarian.)
sobriety, *n.* so-*bry*-e-te, habitual temperance, especially in drinking spirituous liquors; freedom from intoxication; habitual freedom from passion; seriousness; gravity. (Fr. *sobriété.*)
sobriquet, *n. soh*-bre-kay, a nickname; a derisive surname; an assumed name. (Fr.)
sob-sister, *n. sob*-sis-ter, a woman reporter who dresses news-stories in gushing sentimentality [Amer. Slang].
sob-stuff, *n. sob*-stuff, a sentimentalized newspaper report; pathos [Amer. Slang].
soc, *n.* sok, power or privilege of holding a court in a district; a district under such jurisdiction; privilege of tenants secured from customary burdens. (A.S. *socn.*)
socage, *n. sok*-aj, a tenure of lands by certain and determinate service. (A.S. *socn.*)
socager, *n. sok*-a-jer, a tenant by socage.
so-called, *a. soh*-kawld, so named.
soccer, *n. sok*-er, socker.
sociability, *n. soh*-she-a-*bil*-e-te, disposition to associate and converse with others; the practice of familiar intercourse.
sociable, *a. soh*-shabl, companionable; inclined to associate; disposed to converse; free in conversation: *n.* a four-wheeled carriage with two seats facing each other; a tricycle for two abreast; a motor-cycle, aeroplane, etc., for two; an informal party, a social. (Fr.)
sociableness, *n. soh*-shabl-ness, the quality of being sociable; disposition to associate; inclination to company and converse.
sociably, *ad. soh*-sha-ble, in a sociable manner.
social, *a. soh*-shal, pertaining to society or men living in society; inclined to friendly converse; consisting in mutual converse; disposed to unite in society; convivial; gregarious; growing in groups [Bot.]; living in rudimentarily organized communities [Zool.]: *n.* a social gathering. **social contract,** the assumed or existing agreement between members of a state, etc., regulating their relationships between each other and with the government. **social credit,** credit based on the socially created resources of a state [Econ.]. **social evil,** prostitution. **social science,** sociology. **social security,** freedom from want, esp. as attained by means of state insurance. (L. *socialis.*)
socialism, *n. soh*-sha-lizm, the political and economic doctrine that society should be organized on the basis of the collective ownership of the means and sources of production, with the employment of labour directly by the State, democratic control of industry, and the elimination of capitalist and individualist competition.
socialist, *n. soh*-sha-list, an advocate of socialism: *a.* pertaining to socialism; controlled by, or composed of, socialists.
socialistic, *a. soh*-sha-*lis*-tik, pertaining to socialism; characteristic of, or favouring, socialism.
sociality, *n. soh*-she-*al*-e-te, socialness. (L. *socialitas.*)
socialization, *n.* soh-sha-ly-*zay*-shon, the act or process of socializing; state of being socialized.
socialize, *v.t. soh*-sha-lize, to render social; to convert to a social or socialistic state.
socially, *ad. soh*-sha-le, in a social manner.
socialness, *n. soh*-shal-ness, the quality or condition of being social.
societary, *a.* so-*sy*-e-ta-re, pertaining to society or to social conditions.
⋆**society,** *n.* so-*sy*-e-te, people collectively; the world of fashion; a number of persons united in community; an association for the promotion of some common object; a fraternity; companionship; fellowship; partnership: *a.* pertaining to or characteristic of fashionable society. **Society of Friends,** the Quakers. **Society of Jesus,** the Jesuits. **society verse,** light highly polished lyrical verse. (Fr. *société.*)
Socinian, *n.* so-*sin*-e-an, a follower of Lælius Socinius and his nephew, who, in the 16th cent., denied the Trinity, the divinity and atonement of Christ, and the doctrine of original depravity: *a.* pertaining to Socinianism.
Socinianism, *n.* so-*sin*-e-a-nizm, the doctrine of the Socinians.
sociological, *a. soh*-se-o-*loj*-e-kal, pertaining to sociology.
sociologist, *n. soh*-se-*ol*-o-jist, one learned in sociology.
sociology, *n. soh*-se-*ol*-o-je, the science which treats of the nature and development of human society and social conditions and institutions. (L. *socius*, a companion, Gr. *logos*, science.)
⋆**sock,** *n.* sok, a stocking with a short leg; a thin removable inner sole for a boot or shoe; the shoe of the ancient actors of comedy; comedy. **to pull up one's socks,** to prepare for a strenuous effort. (A.S. *socc.*)
sock, *n.* sok, a ploughshare. (Breton, or O.F. *soc.*)
sock, *v.t.* sok, to fling at; to hit: *n.* a blow [Slang].
sockdologer, *n.* sok-*dol*-o-jer, a crusher, a settler (of an argument, etc.); a big one [all Amer. Slang].
socker, *n. sok*-er, Association football [Slang].
socket, *n. sok*-et, a hollow into which something fits. (O.Fr. *soket.*)
socket-chisel, *n.* a strong chisel used by carpenters for mortising.
sockeye, *n. sok*-eye, a species of *Oncorhynchus*, the blueback salmon, an important food-fish of the Pacific coast of the U.S.A.
socle, *n.* sokl, a plain block or plinth, forming a low pedestal or the base of a wall. (Fr.)
socman, *n. sok*-man, a socager.
Socotrine, *a.* so-*koh*-trine *or sok*-o-trine, pertaining to Socotra, an island in the Indian Ocean: *n.* a

native of Socotra; a species of aloe, *A. socotrina*, growing here and yielding a medicinal drug.
Socratic, *a.* so-*krat*-ik, pertaining to Socrates, his philosophy, or his manner of teaching.
Socratically, *ad.* in a Socratic manner.
sod, *n.* sod, earth on the surface held together by the roots of the grass; a cut slab of this; sward: *v.t.* to cover with sod; to turf. (Probably from its usually sodden state.)
sod, sod, *p.* and *pp.* of *seethe*.
sod, *n.* sod, a sodomite (usually as an unmeaning and vulgar term of abuse) [Slang].
soda, *n.* *soh*-da, a compound, esp. a crystalline carbonate or bicarbonate, of sodium; aerated soda-water. (It.)
soda-lime, *n.* a compound of caustic soda and quicklime, used as an absorbent in gas-masks.
sodalite, *n.* *soh*-da-lite, sodium-aluminium silicate with sodium chloride. (Gr. *lithos*, a stone.)
sodality, *n.* so-*dal*-e-te, fellowship or fraternity. (L. *sodalitas*.)
soda-salt, *n.* a salt having soda for base.
soda-water, *n.* a beverage consisting of water highly charged with carbonic acid; aerated water.
sodden, *sod*-den, *pp.* of *seethe*; saturated; soaked; boiled; bloated, esp. with drink; heavy and moist: *v.i.* to become sodden; to settle down: *v.t.* to soak; to saturate with drink.
soddy, *a.* *sod*-e, turfy; abounding in or consisting of sods; covered with sod.
sodic, *a.* *soh*-dik, containing sodium.
sodium, *n.* *soh*-de-um, a soft silver-white metallic element of the alkali group, the base of soda, common salt, etc.
sodoku, *n.* *soh*-do-koo, rat-bite fever [Jap.].
sodomite, *n.* *sod*-o-mite, an inhabitant of Sodom; one given to sodomy.
sodomitical, *a.* sod-o-*mit*-e-kal, pertaining to, of the nature of, or given to the practice of, sodomy.
sodomy, *n.* *sod*-o-me, unnatural vice practised between males; bestiality. (*Sodom*.)
soever, *n.* soh-*ev*-er, a compound affixed to emphasize such words as who, what and where.
sofa, *n.* *soh*-fa, a long stuffed seat with a raised end and back. (Ar. *suffah*.)
soffit, *n.* *sof*-fit, the under part of a cornice or balcony, etc., presenting a flat surface [Arch.]. (Fr. *soffite*.)
Sofi, *n.* *soh*-fe, in Persia, a Sufi; a Sophy. (Ar. *sufiy*, intelligent.)
Sofism, *n.* *soh*-fizm, sufism.
★**soft,** *a.* soft, not hard; easily worked; smooth to the touch; delicate; yielding to touch; impressionable; tender; courteous; gentle; placid; effeminate; credulous; smooth and gently flowing; low-toned; readily forming a lather (of water): not bony or cartilaginous [Anat.]; non-alcoholic (of drink) [U.S.A., Coll.]: *ad.* softly: gently; quietly: *int.* be soft; hold; stop. **soft palate,** the fleshy posterior part of the roof of the mouth. (A.S. *softe*.)
Softa, *n.* *sof*-ta, a Moslem student of theology and sacred law attached to a mosque.
soft-coal, *n.* bituminous coal.
soften, *v.t.* sofn, to make soft or softer; to mollify; to make less harsh, severe, or offensive; to palliate; to alleviate: to make calm and placid; to tone down; to enervate: *v.i.* to become soft or softer; to become less rude; to relent; to become more mild or less harsh; to clear from lime.
softener, *n.* *sofn*-er, one who or that which softens; an apparatus for making hard water soft.
softening, *n.* *sofn*-ing, the act of making or becoming softer; the blending of colours with harmony; a decrease of the consistency of a tissue [Med.].
soft-finned, *a.* *soft*-finned, having fins without spines.
soft-goods, *n.pl.* drapery [Comm.].
soft-grass, *n.* a fodder-grass of the genus *Holcus*.
soft-hearted, *a.* tender-hearted; gentle; meek; susceptible of pity.
softish, *a.* *soft*-ish, somewhat soft.
softling, *n.* *soft*-ling, an effeminate person.
softly, *ad.* *soft*-le, in a soft manner; quietly.
softness, *n.* *soft*-ness, the quality of being soft.
soft-soap, *n.* semi-liquid soap made with potash; flattery: *v.t.* to flatter ingratiatingly.
softy, *n.* *sof*-te, a daft or weak-minded person [Coll.].
soggy, *a.* *sog*-e, wet; filled or soaked with water.
soho, *int.* so-*hoh*, a form of calling to one afar off; a sportsman's halloo.
soi-disant, *a.* (App.), self-styled; pretended. (Fr. *soi*, self, *disant*, saying.)
soil, *n.* soyl, the ground on the surface of the earth which yields nourishment to plants; land; country; cultivated ground. (O.Fr.)
soil, *n.* soyl, dirt; dung; foulness; stain; tarnish; a marshy place in which a hunted animal takes refuge: *v.t.* to make dirty; to stain; to tarnish; to manure. **take soil,** to run into water when pursued, as a deer. (Fr. *souiller*, from L. *sus*, a sow.)
soilless, *a.* *soyl*-less, destitute of soil.
soil-pipe, *n.* the discharge-pipe of a water-closet.
soilure, *n.* *soyl*-yewr, stain; pollution. (Fr.)
soirée, *n.* (App.) an evening party for social intercourse, usually accompanied by an entertainment and refreshments. (Fr.)
sojourn, *n.* *soj*-urn *or* *suj*-urn, a temporary residence, as that of a traveller in a foreign land: *v.i.* to dwell for a time. (Fr. *séjourner*.)
sojourner, *n.* a temporary resident.
sojournment, *n.* sojourning; sojourn.
soke, *n.* soke, soc. (A.S.)
Sokol, *n.* *soh*-kol, a Slav non-political educational association founded in Prague in 1861 to train the Czech nation in physical, mental, and moral fitness, and named from its falcon badge; a member of this. (Czech., a falcon.)
sol, *n.* sol, a colloidal solution or suspension [Chem.].
sol, *n.* sol, the sun; gold. (L.)
sol, *n.* sol, the fifth note in the diatonic scale [Mus.]. (It.)
sol, *n.* sol, a French halfpenny; a sou. (O.Fr.)
sola, *n.* *soh*-lah, the pith of the Indian shrub *Æschynomene aspera*, used for sun helmets. (Hind.)
solace, *n.* *sol*-as, comfort in grief; consolation; compensation: *v.t.* to cheer in grief; to console; to assuage. (O.Fr. *solaz*.)
solacement, *n.* act of solacing; state of being solaced.
solanaceous, *a.* *soh*-la-*nay*-shus, relating to plants of the potato order. (L.)
solan-goose, *n.* *soh*-lan-goos, the gannet. (Ice. *sula*.)
solanine, *n.* *soh*-la-nine, a poisonous alkaloid obtained from several species of *Solanum*.
solano, *n.* so-*lah*-no, a hot oppressive south-east wind in the Mediterranean. (Sp.)
Solanum, *n.* so-*lay*-num, a large genus of plants, comprising the potato, *S. tuberosum*, the egg-fruit, *S. melongena*, and the nightshades. (L.)
solar, *a.* *soh*-lar, pertaining to the sun; proceeding from the sun; measured by the progress of the sun; [Zool.] with branches or filaments radially disposed: *n.* a room built for receiving sunshine. **solar cycle,** a period of twenty-eight years, in any corresponding year of which the days of the week recur on the same days of the month; the period of about 11 yrs. 6 wks. from one sunspot maximum to the next. **solar flowers,** flowers that open and shut at certain determinate hours. **solar microscope,** a microscope in which the object is illuminated by the concentrated light of the sun. **solar myth,** a myth based on the motions and influence of the sun. **solar plexus,** the epigastric plexus, a network of nerves in the pit of the stomach. **solar system,** the group of celestial bodies comprising the planets and comets which revolve round the sun. **solar time,** the time at any given place as determined by its existing position relative to that of the sun; sundial time. (L. *solaris*.)
solarism, *n.* *soh*-la-rizm, the ascription of folk-tales, legends, etc., to an origin in solar myth.
solarist, *n.* *soh*-la-rist, one who indulges in solarism.
solarization, *n.* *soh*-la-ry-*zay*-shon, the effect of solarizing.
solarize, *v.i.* *soh*-la-rize, to be injured by too long exposure in the camera to the sun's light: *v.t.* to expose (a plate) too long in the camera [Phot.].
solatium, *n.* so-*lay*-she-um, compensation for injury, loss, or wounded feelings. (L.)
sold, sohld, *p.* and *pp.* of *sell*.
soldanella, *n.* sol-da-*nel*-la, a purple, bluish, or white flowered hardy herbaceous perennial of the order Primulaceæ; the blue moonwort.
solder, *n.* *sol*-der *or* *sod*-er, an easily fusible metallic cement: *v.t.* to unite metals by metallic cement in fusion. (O.Fr. *soudure*.)

soldering-bolt, *n.* a tool for applying solder.
soldier, *n.* *sohl*-jer, a man engaged in military service; a private soldier as distinct from a commissioned officer; a man of military experience or distinguished valour: *v.i.* to go or serve as a soldier. **soldier-ant,** an asexual fighter member of a community of termites. **soldier-beetle,** a reddish beetle preying on the larvæ of others. **soldier-bird,** the Australian honey-eater. **soldier-crab,** the hermit-crab. **soldier-fish,** the red gurnard, and many brilliantly coloured tropical marine fishes. **soldier-orchis,** the orchid with red spots on a white centre and a slate helmet, *Orchis militaris.* **soldier-wood,** the wood of the West Indian tree *Calliandra purpurea.* **old soldier,** a veteran; a crafty or experienced person; a bottle that has been emptied [Slang]. **soldier of fortune,** a soldier willing to fight in any army for pay. (O.Fr. *soldier*, one who fights for pay.)
soldiering, *n.* *sohl*-jer-ing, military service; the profession of, or act of serving as, a soldier. **old soldiering,** malingering, evading one's duty [Slang].
soldierly, *a.* like or becoming a soldier; brave; martial; heroic; honourable.
soldiership, *n.* military qualities; martial character or state; martial skill; soldierly behaviour.
soldiery, *n.* *sohl*-jer-re, the body of military men; soldiers collectively; military training or knowledge.
soldo, *n.* *sol*-doh (*pl.* **soldi**), an Italian coin, the twentieth of a lira, the equivalent of the French sou. (It.)
sole, *n.* sole, the sea flatfish *Solea vulgaris*, and other flatfishes known locally as lemon soles. (L.)
sole, *n.* sole, the underside of the foot; the foot itself; the bottom of a shoe or boot; the part that forms the bottom of anything: *v.t.* to furnish with a sole. (A.S.)
sole, *a.* sole, alone; single; being or acting without another; unmarried [Law]. (O.Fr. *sol.*)
solecism, *n.* *sol*-e-sizm, impropriety in language in violation of syntax or idiom; any unfitness, absurdity or impropriety. (Gr. *soloikismos*, relating to those who speak incorrectly, as the people of Soloi, a city of Cilicia.)
solecist, *n.* *sol*-e-sist, one who commits solecisms.
solecistical, *a.* sol-e-*sis*-te-kal, incorrect; incongruous.
solecistically, *ad.* in a solecistical manner.
solecize, *v.i.* *sol*-e-size, to commit a solecism.
solely, *ad.* *sole*-le, singly; alone.
solemn, *a.* *sol*-em, marked with religious gravity, pomp, or sanctity; religiously grave or serious; affecting with seriousness; grave; formal; attended with a serious appeal to God; marked with solemnities. (O.Fr. *solemne.*)
solemnity, *n.* so-*lem*-ne-te, a ceremony performed with religious reverence or adapted to impress awe; a religious rite or ceremony; gravity; seriousness; impressiveness; affected gravity.
solemnization, *n.* *sol*-em-ny-*zay*-shon, the act of solemnizing; the act of celebrating a religious service, esp. that of matrimony.
solemnize, *v.t.* *sol*-em-nize, to celebrate; to perform with ritual ceremonies; to make solemn.
solemnizer, *n.* *sol*-em-ny-zer, one who solemnizes.
solemnly, *ad.* *sol*-em-le, in a solemn manner.
solemnness, *n.* *sol*-em-ness, the quality of being solemn.
solen, *n.* *soh*-len, any of the Solenidæ, a group of burrowing lamellibranchs including the razor-fish. (Gr.)
solenacean, *n.* *soh*-le-*nay*-she-an, a member of the solen genus of marine molluscs: *a.* pertaining to this genus.
soleness, *n.* *sole*-ness, singleness.
solenette, *n.* soh-le-*net*, the smallest of the European soles, *Solea minute.* (Fr.)
solenite, *n.* *soh*-len-ite, a fossil solen.
solenodon, *n.* soh-*len*-o-don, an insectivorous mammal of the West Indies allied to the tenrec.
solenoid, *n.* *soh*-le-noyd, a close wire spiral having its diameter shorter than its length; a core-less helix of wire for the passage of a current for the production of a magnetic field [Elect.]. (Gr. *solen*, pipe, *eidos*, like.)
solenostomatous, *a.* *soh*-le-nos-*tom*-a-tus, of or pertaining to the Solenostomi, a family of small fishes of Indian waters having long tubular snouts.
sol-fa, *n.* *sol*-fah, solmization: *v.i.* to sing the notes of the gamut, do, re, mi, fa, sol, la, si. **tonic sol-fa,** *see* **tonic.** (It.)
solfatara, *n.* *sol*-fa-*tah*-ra, a volcanic vent which emits sulphurous and other gases. (It.)
solfeggio, *n.* sol-*fej*-e-oh, an arrangement or an exercise in sol-fa; solmization [Mus.]. (It.)
solferino, *n.* *sol*-fer-*ree*-no, the colour of rosaniline. (After the battle of Solferino, 1859, in which year the colour was first prepared.)
solicit, *v.t.* so-*lis*-it, to ask with earnestness; to seek by petition; to summon or invite; to try to obtain; to importune. (Fr. *solliciter.*)
solicitant, *n.* so-*lis*-e-tant, one who solicits: *a.* making petition; imploring.
solicitation, *n.* so-*lis*-e-*tay*-shon, earnest request; excitement; invitation.
solicitor, *n.* so-*lis*-e-tor, one who asks with earnestness; an attorney; one qualified to act for another in legal matters; one who solicits orders [U.S.A.]. (Fr. *solliciteur.*)
Solicitor-General, *n.* the second in rank of the law officers of the British crown.
solicitorship, *n.* the office of solicitor.
solicitous, *a.* so-*lis*-e-tus, careful; anxious; very desirous; concerned. (L. *sollicitus.*)
solicitously, *ad.* anxiously.
solicitousness, *n.* state of being solicitous.
solicitude, *n.* so-*lis*-e-tewd, solicitousness; concern; anxiety. (Fr. *sollicitude.*)
★**solid,** *a.* *sol*-id, having its particles so close as to resist impression; firm; compact; not hollow; cubic; strong; sound; valid; grave; profound; united; without leads between the lines [Print.]: *n.* a firm compact body; a body with length, breadth, and thickness. **solid geometry,** geometry of the three dimensions—length, breadth, and thickness. (Fr. *solide.*)
Solidago, *n.* sol-e-*day*-goh, a large genus of yellow-flowered hardy herbaceous perennials including the golden-rod. (L.)
solidarity, *n.* sol-e-*da*-re-te, that community of being which binds humanity into one whole so that each affects and is affected by all; consolidation of interests. (Fr. *solidarité*, joint and several liability.)
solidifiable, *a.* so-lid-e-*fy*-a-bl, capable of being solidified.
solidification, *n.* so-*lid*-e-fe-*kay*-shon, the act of solidifying.
solidify, *v.t.* so-*lid*-e-fy, to make solid: *v.i.* to become solid. (Fr. *solidifier.*)
solidism, *n.* *sol*-e-dizm, the doctrine that refers all diseases to condensation or rarefaction of the solid tissues of the body.
solidist, *n.* *sol*-e-dist, one who believes in solidism.
solidity, *n.* so-*lid*-e-te, firmness; compactness; fullness of matter; strength; moral firmness; validity; solid content. (Fr. *solidité.*)
solidly, *ad.* *sol*-id-le, in a solid manner.
solidness, *n.* *sol*-id-ness, solidity; soundness.
solidungulate, *n.* *sol*-e-*dung*-gew-late, a mammal, such as the horse, the foot of which terminates in a single toe encased in a single undivided hoof. (L. *solidus*, *ungula*, a hoof.)
solidungulous, *a.* sol-e-*dung*-gew-lus, having a single undivided hoof.
solidus, *n.* *sol*-e-dus, a Roman coin introduced by Constantine; the oblique line, originally denoting a shilling, separating money denominations, as in £3/6/8 for £3 6*s.* 8*d.*, or in dates, etc. (Late L.)
Solifidian, *n.* *sol*-e-*fid*-e-an, one who holds the doctrine that mere faith is sufficient for salvation. (L. *solus*, alone, *fides*, faith.)
solifidianism, *n.* doctrine of the Solifidians.
soliloquize, *v.i.* so-*lil*-o-kwize, to utter soliloquies; to talk to oneself.
soliloquy, *n.* so-*lil*-o-kwe, a talking or discourse to oneself; a written composition reciting what a person speaks to himself; a monologue. (Late L. *soliloquium.*)
soliped, *n.* *sol*-e-ped, a mammal whose hoof is not cloven; a solidungulate. (L. *solus*, *pedis*, foot.)
solipsism, *n.* *sol*-ip-sizm, the doctrine that knowledge of anything outside oneself is unattainable; the theory that self is the only existent thing; absolute egoism. (L. *solus*, alone, *ipse*, self.)
solipsist, *n.* *sol*-ip-sist, an adherent of the doctrine of solipsism: *a.* characterized by or favouring solipsism.

solisequious, *a.* *sol*-e-*seek*-we-us, following the course of the sun [Bot.]. (L. *sol*, sun, *sequor*, follow.)
solitaire, *n.* *sol*-e-tare, a person who lives in solitude; a recluse; a single jewel, especially a diamond, in its setting, or the setting; any game which a person can play alone, such as patience, or one in which marbles, pegs, etc., are moved on a board all the spaces on which but one are occupied; the flightless pigeon of Rodriguez, *Pezophaps solitaria*, now extinct; a North American thrush. (Fr.)
solitarily, *ad.* *sol*-e-ta-re-le, in a solitary manner.
solitariness, *n.* the state of being solitary.
solitary, *a.* *sol*-e-ta-re, living alone; retired; remote from society; lonely; gloomy; single: *n.* one who lives alone or in solitude; a hermit. **solitary snipe,** the great snipe, *Gallinago major*. (Fr. *solitaire*.)
solitude, *n.* *sol*-e-tewd, state of being alone; loneliness; a solitary place; a desert. (Fr.)
solivagant, *a.* so-*liv*-a-gant, wandering alone. (L. *solus*, and *vagus*, wandering.)
solivagous, *a.* so-*liv*-a-gus, wandering alone.
sollar, *n.* *sol*-ar, a solar; an attic that is open to the sun.
sollecito, *ad.* *sol*-le-*chee*-toh, carefully; pensively; precisely [Mus.]. (It.)
solleret, *n.* *sol*-er-ret, the plate, or series of plates, that covered the foot in a suit of armour. (Fr. *soleret*.)
solmizate, *v.t.* and *i.* *sol*-me-zate, to express by or to employ solmization [Mus.].
solmization, *n.* *sol*-me-*zay*-shon, a recital of the names of the notes of the gamut; sol-fa-ing [Mus.]. (Fr. *solmisation*.)
solo, *n.* *soh*-loh, a tune, air, or strain to be played by a single instrument, or sung by a single voice; a variety of whist; a call at this game; a motor-cycle with no side-car; a solo flight [Av.]: *a.* alone without assistance; by oneself. (It., from L. *solus*.)
soloist, *n.* *soh*-loh-ist, the performer of a solo; a solo flyer [Av.], or motor-cyclist.
Solomon, *n.* *sol*-o-mon, wise man. **Solomon's seal,** a plant of the genus *Polygonatum*; a six-pointed figure formed by the interlacement of two triangles. (After *Solomon*, king of Israel, renowned for wisdom.)
Solon, *n.* *soh*-lon, a wise legislator. (After *Solon*, the great Athenian lawgiver.)
so-long, *int.* soh-*long*, good-bye; au revoir [Slang].
solstice, *n.* *sol*-stis, the point in the ecliptic at which the sun ceases to recede from the equator, either north in summer, or south in winter; the time (about 21 June and 22 Dec.) when it is farthest from the equator. (Fr.)
solstitial, *a.* sol-*stish*-al, pertaining to the solstice; happening at a solstice.
solubility, *n.* *sol*-yew-*bil*-e-te, solubleness.
soluble, *a.* *sol*-yew-bl, capable of being dissolved in a fluid; capable of solution. (Fr.)
solubleness, *n.* quality or state of being soluble.
solus, *a.* *soh*-lus, (*fem.* **sola,** *soh*-lah), alone (esp. as a stage direction), *n.* an advertisement appearing on a page that carries no other. (L.)
solute, *n.* so-*lewt*, any substance, solid or gaseous, held in solution [Chem.]: *a.* dissolved; not adhering [Bot.].
solution, *n.* so-*lew*-shon, the act of separating the parts, specially the connected parts, of any body; the dissolving of a solid in a fluid or the result of this process; semi-liquid rubber for repairing pneumatic tyres, etc.; an explanation; removal of a difficulty or doubt; the resolving of a problem proposed [Math. etc.]; release; deliverance. (Fr.)
solutionist, *n.* so-*lew*-shon-ist, one, esp. a professional who solves newspaper puzzles, problems, etc.
Solutrian, *a.* so-*lew*-tre-an, of or pertaining to the palæolithic age between the Aurignacian and the Magdalenian above it. (After the *Solutré* cavern in Saône-et-Loire, France.)
solvability, *n.* *sol*-va-*bil*-e-te, solubility; solvency.
solvable, *a.* *sol*-va-bl, that may be solved, resolved, or explained; that may be paid.
solvableness, *n.* *sol*-va-bl-ness, quality of being solvable; solvability.
solve, *v.t.* solv, to separate the parts; to explain; to clear up; to resolve; to remove. (O.Fr. *solver*.)
solvency, *n.* *sol*-ven-se, ability to pay all debts.
solvent, *a.* *sol*-vent, having the power of dissolving; able or sufficient to pay all just debts: *n.* a fluid that dissolves any substance; a menstruum.
solver, *n.* *sol*-ver, one who or that which solves.
soma, *n.* *soh*-ma, the inebriating juice of a plant offered in libation in Hindu religious ceremonies and identified with the invigorating and immortalizing principle in nature; the vine, *Sarcostemma acidum*, from which this is prepared. (Sans.)
soma, *n.* *soh*-ma, the body of an animal exclusive of the limbs; also, an entire organism not including germ-cells. (Gr., body.)
somaj, *n.* so-*mahj*, samaj. (Hind.)
somatic, *a.* so-*mat*-ik, corporeal; pertaining to the body: *n.pl.* somatology. **somatic cell,** any cell other than a germ cell [Bot. and Anat.]. (Gr. *soma*, a body.)
somatology, *n.* *soh*-ma-*tol*-o-je, a treatise on the properties of organisms; the science of human physiology and anatomy.
somatome, *n.* *soh*-ma-tohm, a segment of an animal body; a somite.
sombre, *a.* *som*-ber, dark; dull; dusky; gloomy; melancholy. (Fr.)
sombrely, *ad.* *som*-ber-le, in a sombre or depressing manner.
sombreness, *n.* the state of being sombre.
sombrerite, *n.* som-*breer*-rite, a phosphatic leached guano, also a phosphatized limestone, both found on Sombrero, an island of the Caribbean.
sombrero, *n.* som-*brare*-ro, a broad-brimmed soft felt hat. (Sp.; *Sombrero*, in the Antilles.)
sombrous, *a.* *som*-brus, of a sombre character or appearance; gloomy.
★**some,** *a.* sum, an indeterminate quantity, number, person, or thing; more or less; one or other; a considerable quantity of: *ad.* about; approximately; slightly; somewhat: *pron.* a particular but undetermined or unspecified part, etc. **and then some,** and a good deal (or many) more besides [Slang]. (A.S. *sum*.)
somebody, *n.* *sum*-bod-e, a person unknown or uncertain; a person indeterminate; a person of consideration.
somehow, *ad.* *sum*-hou, one way or other; in some way not yet known.
someone, *n.* *sum*-wun, some person; somebody.
somersault, *n.* *sum*-mer-sawlt, a leap in which a person turns heels over head and alights on his feet: *v.i.* to make a somersault. (O.Fr. *sombresault*.)
somerset, *n.* *sum*-mer-set, a somersault.
somerset, *n.* *sum*-mer-set, a saddle for a man who has lost a leg, so padded that it affords support to the stump. (Name of inventor, Lord Fitzroy *Somerset*, 1st Baron Raglan, *d.* 1855.)
somervillite, *n.* *sum*-er-vil-lite, a yellow variety of melilite, a Vesuvian mineral. (After Dr. Wm. *Somerville*, F.R.S., *d.* 1860.)
something, *n.* *sum*-thing, an indeterminate or unknown thing or event; a substance unknown or unspecified; a portion; an indefinite quantity: *ad.* in some degree.
sometime, *ad.* *sum*-time, formerly; at one time or other hereafter; *a.* former; late.
sometimes, *ad.* at times; at intervals; at one time.
somewhat, *n.* *sum*-whot, something, though uncertain what: *a.* more or less; rather: *ad.* in some degree or quantity.
somewhen, *ad.* *sum*-when, sometime.
somewhere, *ad.* *sum*-whare, in some place unknown or not specified; in one place or another.
somewhither, *ad.* *sum*-whith-er, to some indeterminate place.
somite, *n.* *soh*-mite, one of the segments into which the bodies of most articulates and vertebrates are divided; a somatome; a metamere. (Gr. *soma*, body.)
somitic, *a.* soh-*mit*-ik, pertaining to or resembling a somite [Zool.].
somnambulant, *a.* som-*nam*-bew-lant, addicted to walking while asleep: *n.* a somnambulist.
somnambulate, *v.i.* som-*nam*-bew-late, to walk while asleep.
somnambulation, *n.* som-*nam*-bew-*lay*-shon, somnambulism. (L. *somnus*, sleep, *ambulo*, walk.)
somnambulism, *n.* som-*nam*-bew-lizm, the practice

of walking and performing actions of various kinds in sleep or in a sleep-like state.
somnambulist, *n.* som-*nam*-bew-list, a person who walks in sleep.
somnambulistic, *a.* som-*nam*-bew-*lis*-tik, pertaining to somnambulism.
somnifacient, *a.* som-ne-*fay*-she-ent, producing sleep: *n.* any hypnotic or soporific medicine.
somniferous, *a.* som-*nif*-er-rus, causing or inducing sleep. (L. *somnifer*, sleep-bringing.)
somnific, *a.* som-*nif*-ik, tending to induce sleep. (L. *somnus*, and *facio*, make.)
somniloquism, *n.* som-*nil*-o-kwizm, talking in sleep.
somniloquist, *n.* som-*nil*-o-kwist, one who talks in sleep.
somniloquous, *a.* som-*nil*-o-kwus, talking, or inclined to talk, in sleep.
somniloquy, *n.* som-*nil*-o-kwe, a talk during sleep. (L. *somnus*, and *loquor*, speak.)
somnipathist, *n.* som-*nip*-a-thist, one in a hypnotic sleep.
somnipathy, *n.* som-*nip*-a-the, sleep arising from hypnotism. (L. *somnus*, Gr. *pathos*, suffering.)
somnolence, *n.* *som*-no-lence, somnolency.
somnolency, *n.* *som*-no-len-se, drowsiness; inclination to sleep; an intermediate stage between waking and sleeping. (L. *somnolentus*.)
somnolent, *a.* *som*-no-lent, sleepy; drowsy.
somnolently, *ad.* in a somnolent manner.
somnolism, *n.* *som*-no-lizm, hypnotic sleep.
★**son,** *n.* sun, a male child; a male descendant; the style of address of an old man to a young one; a term of affection; the native of a country; the produce of anything; one adopted into a family; a pupil; offspring. **Son of God,** Jesus Christ, esp. as the Second Person of the Trinity. **Son of Heaven,** a title of the former Emperors of China. (A.S. *sunu*.)
sonance, *n.* *soh*-nans, sonancy.
sonancy, *n.* *soh*-nan-se, the quality or state of being sonant.
sonant, *a.* *soh*-nant, sounding; uttered with vocal sound; *n.* a sonant letter. (L. *sonans*, sounding.)
sonantal, *a.* so-*nan*-tal, of a sonant character.
sonata, *n.* so-*nah*-ta, a musical composition in several movements tonally related but rhythmically contrasted, and intended for one or two instruments. (It.)
sonatina, *n.* *son*-a-*tee*-na, a short and simple sonata.
★**song,** *n.* song, vocal music; that which is sung or uttered with musical modulations of the voice; a little poem to be sung; a ballad; a hymn; a strain; poetry in general; the notes of birds. **an old song,** a mere trifle. **Song of Solomon,** the Canticles, a canonical book of the Old Testament. (A.S. *sang*.)
song-bird, *n.* *song*-berd, a bird that sings.
songcraft, *n.* *song*-krahft, the art of song-making.
songful, *a.* *song*-ful, full of song.
songless, *a.* *song*-less, unable to sing; not singing.
songster, *n.* *song*-ster, one skilled in singing; a bird that sings. (A.S. *sangystre*.)
songstress, *n.* *song*-stress, a female singer.
song-thrush, *n.* the common thrush or throstle, *Turdus musicus*.
sonic, *a.* *soh*-nik, pertaining to sound-waves; utilizing reflected sound-waves, as in a depth-finder.
soniferous, *a.* so-*nif*-er-rus, producing or conveying sound. (L. *sonus*, and *fero*, bring.)
son-in-law, *n.* *sun*-in-law, a man married to one's daughter.
sonnet, *n.* *son*-net, a short lyric poem of fourteen iambic pentameter lines only, having a special rhyme sequence and dealing with one idea, generally in two phases. (Fr.)
sonneteer, *n.* son-e-*teer*, a composer of sonnets: *v.i.* to compose sonnets.
Sonnite, *n.* *son*-nite, a Sunnite.
sonny *n.* *sun*-ne, a little son; a term of endearment.
sonometer, *n.* so-*nom*-e-ter, an instrument for demonstrating the nature of sound, for measuring sound, or sound vibrations, or for testing its effects; a phonometer; a monochord (apparatus); an audiometer. (L. *sonus*, and Gr. *metron*, measure.)
sonorescence, *n.* *soh*-no-*ress*-ence, the state of being sonorescent.
sonorescent, *a.* *soh*-no-*ress*-ent, emitting sound when affected by heat or light.
sonorific, *a.* *son*-o-*rif*-ik, producing sound. (L. *sonus*, and *facio*, make.)
sonority, *n.* so-*naw*-re-te *or* so-*no*-re-te, sonorousness.
sonorous, *a.* so-*naw*-rus, giving sound when struck; loud-sounding; yielding sound; high-sounding; melodious. (L. *sonorus*.)
sonorously, *ad.* so-*naw*-rus-le, in a sonorous manner.
sonorousness, *n.* so-*naw*-rus-ness, the quality of being sonorous; having or giving a loud or clear sound.
sonship, *n.* *sun*-ship, state of being a son; filiation; the character of a son.
sonsy, *a.* *son*-se, plump, buxom; tractable (of animals); bringing good luck. (Scots.)
soon, *ad.* soon, in a short time; presently; early; readily; willingly. (A.S. *sona*.)
soosoo, *n.* *soo*-soo, the susu [Zool.].
soot, *n.* soot, a black carbonaceous substance disengaged from fuel during imperfect combustion: *v.t.* to cover, manure, or foul with soot. (A.S. *sot*.)
sooterkin, *n.* *soot*-er-kin, a false birth fabled to be produced by Dutch women from sitting over their stoves; an abortive plan or proposal.
sooth, *n.* sooth, truth; reality. (A.S. *soth*, true.)
soothe, *v.t.* soothe, to please with soft words; to flatter; to calm; to mollify; to gratify. (A.S. *ge-sothian*, to prove to be true.)
soother, *n.* *soothe*-er, a flatterer; he who or that which soothes.
soothfast, *a.* *sooth*-fast, truthful; faithful.
soothingly, *ad.* *soothe*-ing-le, in a soothing manner.
soothsay, *v.i.* *sooth*-say, to foretell. (*sooth*, *say*.)
soothsayer, *n.* *sooth*-say-er, a prognosticator.
soothsaying, *n.* *sooth*-say-ing, the art or practice of predicting the future; prophecy.
sootiness, *n.* *soot*-e-ness, quality of being sooty.
sooty, *a.* *soot*-e, pertaining to or producing soot; foul with soot; black as soot; fuliginous. **sooty albatross,** the large web-footed sea-bird of the S. Pacific, *Phœbetria fulginosa*. **sooty tern,** a gull-like sea-bird of the tropics, *Sterna fuscata*.
sop, *n.* sop, anything steeped or dipped and softened in liquor, esp. soup, in order to be eaten; anything given to pacify, so called from the sop given to Cerberus for the purpose: *v.t.* to steep or dip in a liquid. (A.S. *soppe*.)
soph *n.* sof, a sophister; a sophomore [Amer. Slang].
Sopherim, *n.pl.* *soh*-fer-rim, the ancient Hebrew scribes and interpreters of the Law. (Heb.)
sophiology, *n.* sof-e-*ol*-o-je, the doctrine of ideas; the study of the development of sciences and philosophies.
sophism, *n.* *sof*-izm, a specious but fallacious argument; a fallacy. (Gr. *sophisma*, a skilful device.)
sophist, *n.* *sof*-ist, a captious or fallacious reasoner; in ancient Greece, originally a wise man and later one of a class of philosophers who assailed the conventional on merely subjective grounds.
sophister, *n.* *sof*-is-ter, a university undergraduate of a certain standing; a sophist. (Fr. *sophiste*.)
sophistical, *a.* so-*fis*-te-kal, containing sophistry; fallaciously subtle. (Gr. *sophistikos*.)
sophistically, *ad.* in a sophistical manner.
sophisticalness, *n.* the state of being sophistical.
sophisticate, *v.t.* so-*fis*-te-kate, to adulterate; to corrupt by something spurious or foreign; to render spurious; to spoil the naturalness or innocence of: *v.i.* to make a habit of sophistication: *a.* sophisticated. (Late L. *sophisticatus*.)
sophisticated, *a.* not pure; not genuine; deprived of simplicity; worldly-wise.
sophistication, *n.* so-*fis*-te-*kay*-shon, act of adulterating, or of debasing the purity of anything by foreign admixture; state of being subtle, or without directness or naturalness.
sophisticator, *n.* so-*fis*-te-kay-tor; one who sophisticates or adulterates.
sophistry, *n.* *sof*-is-tre, specious but fallacious reasoning. (O.Fr. *sophisterie*.)
sophomore, *n.* *sof*-o-mor, a student in his second year [U.S.A.]. (Gr. *sophos*, wise, *moros*, foolish.)
sophomoric, *a.* *sof*-o-*mo*-rik, characteristic of or pertaining to a sophomore; bombastic.
Sophora, *n.* so-*faw*-ra, a genus of several species of hard-wooded trees and shrubs of the bean family, including the pagoda tree. (Ar.)
Sophy, *n.* *soh*-fe, a former title of the Persian monarch; a Sufi.

soporiferous, *a.* *soh*-po-*rif*-er-rus, soporific. (L.)
soporiferousness, *n.* quality of causing sleep.
soporific, *a.* *soh*-po-*rif*-ik, causing or tending to produce sleep: *n.* a medicine which induces sleep. (L. *sopor*, sleep, *facio*, make.)
soporose, *a.* *soh*-po-rohs, sleepy.
soporous, *a.* *soh*-po-rus, causing sleep; sleepy.
sopper, *n.* *sop*-per, one who dips in liquor something to be eaten; one who or that which sops.
soppy, *a.* *sop*-pe, soaked; very wet; [Slang] effeminate, weak, silly.
sopranist, *n.* so-*prah*-nist, a treble singer.
soprano, *n.* so-*prah*-noh (*pl.* **sopranos** *or* **soprani,** so-*prah*-nee), the highest kind of female voice; a singer with such a voice. (It.)
sora, *n.* *saw*-ra, the small N. American water-rail *Porzana carolina.*
sorb, *n.* sorb, the service-tree, *Pyrus torminalis*, or its fruit, the **sorb-apple.** (L. *sorbus.*)
sorbate, *n.* *sor*-bate, a salt of sorbic acid.
sorbefacient, *a.* *sor*-be-*fay*-she-ent, promoting absorption: *n.* that which produces absorption [Med.]. (L. *sorbeo*, absorb, *facio*, make.)
sorbet, *n.* *sor*-bet, sherbet; a flavoured water ice. (Fr.)
sorbic, *a.* *sor*-bik, pertaining to or derived from the mountain-ash or the service-tree. **sorbic acid,** an acid extracted from the unripe fruit of the mountain-ash.
sorbine, *n.* *sor*-bin, a saccharine substance from the berries of the mountain-ash. (*sorb.*)
sorbite, *n.* *sor*-bite, a form of pearlite produced in the tempering of steel. (H. C. *Sorby*, Eng. petrologist, *d.* 1908.)
Sorbonist, *n.* *sor*-bon-ist, a doctor or student of the Sorbonne, an ancient theological institution connected with the University of Paris, founded by Robert de *Sorbon* about 1259.)
sorcerer, *n.* *sor*-ser-rer, one who practises sorcery; a magician; a wizard. (O. Fr. *sorcier.*)
sorceress, *n.* *sor*-ser-ress, a female sorcerer.
sorcerous, *a.* *sor*-ser-us, pertaining to sorcery.
sorcery, *n.* *sor*-ser-re, divination by the assistance of evil spirits, or the power of commanding them; magic; witchcraft. (O.Fr. *sorcerie.*)
sordavalite, *n.* *sor*-da-*val*-ite, a black silicate of alumina and magnesia from Sordavala, Finland.
sordes, *n.* *sor*-deez; foul matter; execretions or crusts on the lips and teeth, esp. in fevers; filthy or rejected matter of any kind. (L.)
sordid, *a.* *sor*-did, squalid; filthy; foul; vile; base; niggardly; meanly avaricious; of mean or low ideals. (Fr. *sordide.*)
sordidly, *ad.* *sor*-did-le, in a sordid manner.
sordidness, *n.* *sor*-did-ness, the quality of being sordid; filthiness; meanness.
sordine, *n.* *sor*-deen, a contrivance for muffling the sound of a musical instrument. (O.Fr. *sourdine.*)
sore, *a.* sore, painful in body or mind; severe; distressing; tender and susceptible of pain from pressure; easily pained, grieved, or vexed; affected with inflammation: *n.* a raw, inflamed, or tender part of the body; a chafe; a boil; grief; affliction: *ad.* intensely; grievously. **sore throat,** any morbid affection of the throat. (A.S. *sar*, painful.)
sore, *n.* sore, a hawk of the first year; a buck of the fourth year.
soredia, *n.pl.* so-*ree*-de-a, *see* **soredium.**
soredial, *a.* so-*ree*-de-al, pertaining to or resembling soredia.
sorediate, *a.* so-*ree*-de-at, having soredia.
soredium, *n.* so-*ree*-de-um (*pl.* **soredia**), one of the reproductive buds in lichens.
sorehon, *n.* *sore*-hon, a former Irish tenure binding a tenant to maintain a chief and his retinue gratuitously whenever required to do so. (Ir.)
sorel, *n.* *so*-rel, a buck of the third year.
sorely, *ad.* in a sore manner; severely; greatly.
soreness, *n.* *sore*-ness, the state of being sore; painfulness; tenderness.
Sorex, *n.* *saw*-reks, a genus of insectivorous mammals, including the shrew-mice. (L.)
sorghum, *n.* *sor*-gum, the genus of grasses allied to the sugar-cane and including the Indian millet. (It. *sorgo.*)
sori, *n.* *saw*-ry, *pl.* of *sorus.*
Sorices, *n.* *saw*-re-seez, *pl.* of *Sorex.*
soricine, *a.* *so*-re-sine, pertaining to the shrews; like a mouse. (L. *sorex*, a shrew-mouse.)
soriferous, *a.* so-*rif*-er-rus, bearing sori. (Gr. *soros*, and L. *fero*, bear.)
sorites, *n.* so-*ry*-teez, a syllogistic argument in the premises of which each term occurs twice, except the first and last, which appear in the conclusion as respectively subject and predicate. (Gr. *soreites*, from *soros*, a heap.)
sorn, *v.i.* sorn, to obtrude on friends for the sake of board and lodging. (Scots.)
soroche, *n.* so-*roh*-chay, mountain sickness (esp. in the Andes). (Sp.)
sororal, *a.* so-*raw*-ral, pertaining to or characteristic of sisters.
sororate, *n.* so-*raw*-rate, the primitive custom requiring or allowing a man to marry his wife's younger sisters.
sororicide, *n.* so-*ro*-re-side, the murder, or murderer, of a sister. (L. *soror*, a sister, *cædo*, kill.)
sorority, *n.* so-*ro*-re-te, a sisterhood or other body of women; a club for young women, esp. in an American university. (L. *soror*, sister.)
sorosis, *n.* so-*roh*-sis, a compound fleshy fruit like that of the pine-apple or the mulberry. (Gr. *soros*, a heap.)
sorrel, *a.* *so*-rel, of a yellowish brown colour: *n.* the colour itself; a horse of this colour; (*incorrectly*) a sorel. (O.Fr. *sorel.*)
sorrel, *n.* *so*-rel, a plant so named from its acid taste, *Rumex acetosa.* **sorrel tree,** a tree of the heath order, *Oxydendrum arboreum*, a native of the Alleghanies; the Australian hibiscus, *H. heterophyllus.* (Fr. *surelle.*)
sorrily, *ad.* *so*-re-le, in a sorry manner; meanly; pitiably; in a wretched manner.
sorriness, *n.* *so*-re-ness, the state of being sorry; meanness; despicableness.
sorrow, *n.* *so*-roh, uneasiness or pain of mind due to loss or misfortune; grief; affliction; regret: *v.i.* to feel sorrow or pain of mind; to grieve. (A.S. *sorge*, care, sorrow.)
sorrower, *n.* *so*-roh-er, one who grieves.
sorrowful, *a.* *so*-roh-ful, full of sorrow; producing sorrow; accompanied with sorrow.
sorrowfully, *ad.* in a sorrowful manner.
sorrowfulness, *n.* state of being sorrowful; grief.
sorry, *a.* *so*-re, regretful; feeling pity, grieved at some loss or misfortune; chagrined; poor; mean; vile; worthless; contemptibly pitiful; ludicrously bad. (A.S. *sarig.*)
★**sort,** *n.* sort, a kind or species; class or order; manner; degree of any quality; *pl.* any particular types as distinct from a complete fount [Print.]: *v.t.* to separate into classes; to reduce to order from a state of confusion; to put together in distribution; to select: *v.i.* to be joined with others of the same species; to consort; to suit; to fit. **out of sorts,** in poor health; unwell; deficient in certain types of fount [Print.]. (Fr. *sorte.*)
sortable, *a.* *sor*-ta-bl, that may be sorted; befitting.
sortation, *n.* sor-*tay*-shon, the act of sorting; classification; the work of a letter-sorter.
sorter, *n.* *sor*-ter, one who separates and sorts.
sortes, *n.* *sor*-teez, divination by means of a chance selection of a passage from some author or book, etc.; stichomancy. (L., lots.)
sortie, *n.* *sor*-tee, a sally, esp. of a body of troops from a besieged place to attack the besiegers; a single there-and-back operational flight by one aircraft [Mil. Av.]. (Fr.)
sortilege, *n.* *sor*-te-lej, the act or practice of drawing lots; divination by drawing lots. (Fr.)
sortition, *n.* sor-*tish*-on, the casting of lots; selection or appointment by lot. (L. *sortitio.*)
sortment, *n.* *sort*-ment, the act of sorting; distribution into classes or kinds; an article sorted.
sorus, *n.* *saw*-rus (*pl.* **sori**), a cluster of capsules on the fronds of ferns; a powdery heap of soredia on the thallus of lichens. (Gr. *soros*, a heap.)
S O S, *n.* *ess*-oh-*ess*, the international radio-signal of distress; any cry or indication of despair; a broadcast appeal, especially to the relative of a dangerously ill or dying person.
so-so, *a.* *soh*-soh, indifferent.
sospiro, *n.* sos-*pee*-roh, a crotchet rest [Mus.]. (It.)
sostenuto, *ad.* *sos*-te-*new*-toh, sustainedly; in a steadily prolonged style [Mus.]. (It.)
sot, *n.* sot, a stupid person; an habitual drunkard: *v.i.* to tipple to stupidity. (A.S.)
soteriology, *n.* so-*teer*-re-*ol*-o-je, a discourse on

health; the science of hygiene; the doctrine of salvation. (Gr. *soter*, saviour, *logos*, account.)
sothic, *a.* *soh*-thik, pertaining to the dog-star, by whose heliacal rising the Egyptians calculated their year of 365¼ days. (Gr. *Sothis*, the dog-star.)
sotnia, *n.* *sot*-ne-ah, a Cossack troop. (Russ. *sotnya*, one hundred.)
sottise, *n.* sot-*teese*, foolish or irrational behaviour; a stupid deed. (Fr.)
sottish, *a.* *sot*-tish, stupid; like a sot; given to drinking; besotted with intemperance.
sottishly, *ad.* *sot*-tish-le, in a sottish manner.
sottishness, *n.* *sot*-tish-ness, state of being sottish; dullness; stupidity from intoxication.
sotto voce, *ad.* *sot*-toh-*voh*-chay, in an undertone or whisper: *n.* an aside. (It., under the voice.)
sou, *n.* soo, a French copper coin, in value the twentieth part of a franc, or five centimes. (Fr.)
souari, *n.* soo-*ah*-re, the butternut, a tropical American tree of the genus *Caryocar*. (Native name.)
soubise, *n.* soo-*beeze*, onion sauce. (Fr.)
soubrette, *n.* soo-*bret*, a waiting-maid; an actress in a lively comedy part. (Fr.)
soubriquet, *n.* *soo*-bre-kay, a sobriquet. (Fr.)
souchong, *n.* *soo*-shong, a kind of black tea from China with a tarry flavour. (Fr.)
soufflé, *a.* *soo*-flay, fried in fat so as to be distended with air: *n.* a light dish, consisting chiefly of the white of eggs whisked, spiced, and baked. (Fr.)
souffle, *n.* *soo*-fl, a soft blowing sound [Med.]. (Fr.)
sough, *n.* suf *or* sou, a low, continuous moaning sound as of the wind through an aperture; the whistle of the wind: *v.i.* to sigh as the wind. (A.S. *suogan*.)
sough, *n.* suf, a channel at the foot of an embankment, etc., for draining away surface water; an adit for draining a mine.
sought, sawt, *p.* and *pp.* of *seek*, searched for.
soul, *n.* sole, the spiritual part of man held, theologically, to be immortal and indestructible; the seat of reason and conscience; the intellectual principle or understanding; the vital principle; spirit; essence; a disembodied spirit; life; internal power; an individual person; animal life; active power; courage; heart. **the life and soul of,** the inspirer of "go," enthusiasm, or factor making a success. **upon my soul**! as I hope to be saved! (a strong affirmation); well! well! (A.S. *sawel*.)
soul-bell, *n.* the passing-bell.
souled, *a.* sohld, furnished with a soul.
soulful, *a.* satisfying or appealing to the nobler emotions; emotional.
soulfully, *ad.* in a soulful manner.
soulfulness, *n.* the quality of being soulful.
soulless, *a.* *sole*-less, without a soul; without greatness or nobleness of mind; mean; spiritless.
soullessly, *ad.* *sole*-less-le, in a soulless or perfunctory manner; ignobly; unfeelingly.
soul-sick, *a.* diseased in mind or soul; morally diseased.
sound, *a.* sound, entire; whole; unbroken; undecayed; perfect; healthy; hearty; solid; valid; right; stout; lusty; not deranged. (A.S. *sund*.)
★**sound,** *n.* sound, a sensation produced in the ear by vibrations in the air; that which affects the ear; noise; report; noise without signification; empty noise: *v.t.* to cause to make a noise; to utter audibly; to play on; to signal by a sound; to celebrate or honour by sounds; to proclaim or publish: *v.i.* to make a noise; to utter a voice; to exhibit by sound; to be spread or published. (Fr. *son*.)
sound, *n.* sound, a narrow passage of water; a shallow sea or strait connecting two seas; the air-bladder of a fish. (A.S. *sund*, swimming.)
sound, *n.* sound, a surgical instrument for examining what is beyond the reach of the fingers, a probe: *v.t.* to ascertain the depth of water; to introduce a sound into the bladder of a patient; to try; to examine; to endeavour to discover that which lies concealed in another's breast [Fig.]: *v.i.* to dive deeply (of whales, etc.). (Fr. *sonder*.)
sound-board, *n.* a thin piece of wood so placed in a musical instrument that its sound is reinforced; a sounding-board.
sound-box, *n.* the part of a gramophone, radio receiving-set, etc., which contains the mechanism that converts vibrations into sound.
sound-camera, *n.* the apparatus with which the sound accompanying a motion-picture is photographically recorded [Cine.].
sounder, *n.* *sound*-er, a telegraphic instrument signalling by means of sound; one who takes soundings; an apparatus for taking soundings.
sounder, *n.* *sound*-er, a herd of wild swine; a young boar. (A.S. *sunor*, herd.)
sounding, *a.* *sound*-ing, sonorous; making a noise.
sounding, *n.* *sound*-ing, ascertaining the depth of water; the measurement so obtained; the act of endeavouring to discover opinions or desires: *pl.* any place or part of the sea where a sounding-line will reach the bottom.
sounding-board, *n.* a board or structure over a pulpit to assist the sound of the preacher's voice.
sounding-line, *n.* a line for taking soundings.
sounding-post, *n.* a small post in a violin and violoncello, for transmitting the sound to the body of the instrument.
sounding-rod, *n.* a graduated rod used to ascertain the depth of water in a ship's hold; a dipstick.
sounding-wire, *n.* a wire for taking deep-sea soundings.
soundless, *a.* that cannot be fathomed.
soundless, *a.* having no sound; silent.
soundly, *ad.* heartily; evenly; lustily; truly; firmly.
soundness, *n.* the state of being sound; the state of being healthy.
sound-track, *n.* the part of a cinematograph film on which the sound is photographically recorded.
sound-wave, *n.* each of the progressive longitudinal vibratory disturbances of the air that stimulate the auditory nerves and brain centres thus producing the sensation of sound.
★**soup,** *n.* soop, broth; a decoction for food. **in the soup,** in a quandary or difficulty [Slang.]. (Fr.)
soupçon, *n.* (App.) just a taste. (Fr., a suspicion.)
soup-kitchen, *n.* a former public establishment for supplying soup gratuitously to the poor.
soup-maigre, *n.* soop-*may*-ger, soup made from vegetables without meat. (Fr., thin soup.)
soup-plate, *n.* a deep plate in which soup is served.
soupy, *a.* *soop*-e, like soup.
sour, *a.* sour, acid; sharp to the taste; acid and astringent; harsh of temper; crabbed; peevish; expressing peevishness; harsh to the feelings; rancid; turned, as milk: *v.t.* to make acid; to make harsh, cold, or unkindly; to make cross, peevish, or discontented: *v.i.* to turn acid; to become peevish or crabbed: *n.* that which is sour, or [Fig.] unpleasant; a drink of spirits with lemon- or lime-juice. **sour grapes,** anything one affects to despise because it is unattainable. (A.S. *sur*.)
source, *n.* sorse, the spring or fountain from which a stream of water flows; first cause; original; the first producer. **source book,** a printed collection of original documents forming the basis of an historical study. (O.Fr. *sorse*.)
sourdeline, *n.* *soor*-de-leen, a small bagpipe. (Fr.)
sourdine, *n.* *soor*-deen, a sordine. (Fr.)
sour-dock, *n.* *sour*-dok, sorrel, *Rumex acetosa*.
sourdough, *n.* *sour*-doh, a prospector in Alaska or northern Canada; an old-timer [U.S.A. Coll.].
sour-gourd, *n.* *sour*-goord, the fruit of the Australian tree *Adansonia digitata*; the tree itself.
souring, *n.* *sour*-ring, that which turns to acid; a method of bleaching with acid.
sourish, *a.* somewhat sour; moderately acid.
sourly, *ad.* with acidity; discontentedly.
sourness, *n.* acidity; tartness; asperity.
soursop, *n.* *sour*-sop, a small tropical American evergreen tree, *Annona muricata*; its fruit.
souse, *n.* souse, pickle; something kept or steeped in pickle; sauce; the ears and feet of pigs, pickled; a sudden downpour of rain; an immersion in water: *v.t.* to steep in pickle; to plunge into water; [Slang] to drink heavily. (O.Fr. *souce*.)
souse, *ad.* souse, with sudden violence: *v.t.* to strike with sudden violence: *v.i.* to fall suddenly on. (Teut., or perhaps imit.)
souslik, *n.* *soos*-lik, the suslik [Zool.].
soutache, *n.* soo-*tahsh*, a narrow embroidery braid. (Fr.)
soutane, *n.* soo-*tahn*, a cassock. (Fr.)
souteneur, *n.* (App.) a man who lives on the immoral earnings of women.
souter, *n.* *soo*-ter, a shoemaker; a cobbler. (A.S. *sutere*.)

south, *n.* south, one of the four cardinal points; the part of the heavens, in the northern hemisphere, where the sun is at noon; the southern regions: *a.* being in a southern direction: *ad.* from or toward the south: *v.i.* to move southward or to reach the south. (A.S. *suth.*)

iouthdown, *a. south*-doun, from or pertaining to the English South Downs: *n.* a sheep bred there.

outh-east, *n.* the point equidistant between the south and east: *a.* in or coming from this direction.

outh-easter, *n.* a south-easterly wind.

outh-easterly, *a.* towards or from the south-east generally; situated in the south-east: *ad.* in the direction of the south-east.

outh-eastern, *a.* south-east.

outher, *n. south*-er, a wind or gale from the south.

outherliness, *n. suthe*-er-le-ness, the state of being southerly.

outherly, *a. suthe*-er-le, lying in or proceeding from the south generally: *ad.* in the direction of the south.

outhern, *a. suthe*-ern, belonging to, lying towards, or coming from the south. **Southern Cross,** a group of four bright stars in the constellation *Crux*, used as a pointer to the south celestial pole. (A.S. *sutherne.*)

outherner, *n.* an inhabitant of the south.

outhernly, *ad.* toward the south.

outhernmost, *a.* farthest south.

outhernwood, *n. suthe*-ern-wood, an aromatic plant allied to wormwood, otherwise known as old man, *Artemisia abrotanum.*

outhing, *a. southe*-ing, going towards the south; edging south: *n.* tendency or motion to the south; the time when a heavenly body crosses the meridian; course or distance south.

outhmost, *a.* farthest towards the south.

outhness, *n.* the state of being south or relatively south; a tendency in a magnetic needle to point south.

outhron, *a. suthe*-ron, pertaining to, characteristic of, or dwelling in the south (*i.e.*, of Britain): *n.* (*cap.*) an inhabitant of the south, esp. an Englishman as distinct from a Scot.

outhward, *a.* and *ad.*, towards the south; in a southerly direction.

outh-west, *n.* the point of the compass equidistant between south and west: *a.* lying in the direction or coming from the south-west: *ad.* in a south-westerly direction.

outh-westerly, *a.* and *ad.* towards or from the south-west generally; in the direction of the south-west.

outh-western, *a.* south-west.

ouvenir, *n. soo*-ve-neer, a keepsake. (Fr.)

ou'wester, *n.* sou-*wes*-ter, a strong wind from the south-west; a sailor's waterproof hat with a flap over the back of the neck. (*south-wester*).

overeign, *a. sov*-ran, possessing supreme dominion; superior to all others; supreme; effectual: *n.* a supreme ruler; a monarch; a former British gold coin, nominally equivalent to 20s. (O.Fr. *souverain*)

overeignly, *ad. sov*-ran-le, royally; superbly; in a supreme degree.

overeignty, *n. sov*-ran-te, supreme power; supreme dominion.

oviet, *n. soh*-ve-et, a local council in Russia, esp. one of the councils of workers, soldiers, and peasants elected after the Revolution of 1917, or one of the superior governing bodies formed by nomination or election of delegates from these or from such governing bodies; loosely, the bicameral Supreme Council of the U.S.S.R., and the U.S.S.R. itself: *a.* belonging or pertaining to the U.S.S.R. **the Soviet Union,** the Union of Soviet Socialist Republics, which replaced the Tsarist Russian Empire after the October 1917 Revolution. (Russ., council.)

ovietism, *n. soh*-ve-et-izm, the method of government by Soviets; this class of government; communism.

ovietize, *v.t. soh*-ve-et-ize, to convert to Sovietism.

ovran, *a.* and *n. sov*-ran, sovereign [Poet.].

ow, *n.* sou, a female pig; the furrow in the ground along which molten iron runs to form pigs; the metal cast in this trough. (A.S. *sugu.*)

ow, *v.t.* soh, to scatter seed for growth; to scatter seed over; to propagate; to scatter over: *v.i.* to scatter seed for growth. *pp.* **sown** and **sowed.** (A.S. *sawan.*)

sowar, *n.* so-*wahr*, a native cavalryman of the Indian army. (Hind.)

sowbread, *n. sou*-bred, a tuberous-rooted plant of the genus *Cyclamen.*

sowens, *n.pl. soh*-enz, flummery made from the husk of oats. (Scots.)

sower, *n. soh*-er, one who scatters seed for propagation; a machine or implement for sowing; one who disseminates; a promoter.

sow-thistle, *n. sou*-this-sl, a thistle of the genus *Sonchus.*

sox, *n.pl.* soks, socks (footwear) [U.S.A., and Comm.].

soy, *n.* soy, a sauce prepared in the Far East from the bean of *Soja hispida.* **soy-bean,** the soya-bean. (Jap.)

soya-bean, *n. soy*-ya-, seed of the widely cultivated Far Eastern plant *Soja hispida*, yielding edible oil, flour, and meal, and serving locally as a supplement to rice.

sozzled, *a.* sozld, drunk [Slang].

spa, *n.* spah, a spring of mineral water; the place of such. (*Spa*, town in Belgium.)

★**space,** *n.* space, room; infinite extension; interval between lines; quantity of time; interval between two points of time; a while; a blank piece of type-metal for placing between words, etc. [Print.]: *v.t.* to arrange with intervening spaces; to set (type) with correct intervals between words or lines. (Fr. *espace.*)

space-bar, *n.* a bar on a typewriter by means of which the operator spaces the words, etc.

spacer, *n. spay*-ser, any device for spacing, esp. in a type-setting machine or typewriter; an instrument to reverse current to increase speed of transmission [Elect. teleg.].

space-time, *n.* in the Einstein theory of relativity, the product of welding together into a uniform four-dimensional continuum the scientific conceptions of space and time.

spacial, *a. spay*-shal, spatial.

spacious, *a. spay*-shus, having large or ample room; wide; extensive; vast in extent.

spaciously, *ad.* extensively.

spaciousness, *n.* the quality of being spacious; largeness or vastness of extent.

spadassin, *n.* spa-*das*-sin, a bravo; a bully. (Fr.)

★**spade,** *n.* spade, an implement with a long handle and a broad palm on the top edge of which the foot can be placed in digging; a spade-shaped instrument for various uses: *v.t.* to dig with a spade. **spade guinea,** an English gold guinea of from 1787 to 1799 having on the reverse the coat-of-arms in a shield of pointed spade shape. **to call a spade a spade,** to use the correct term or name, however coarse; to be bluntly outspoken. (A.S. *spadu.*)

spade, *n.* spade, the conventional figure of a pointed spade marking, in black, a suit of playing-cards; a card of this suit. (It., from Sp. *espada*, a sword.)

spade, *n.* spade, a gelded beast. (L. *spado.*)

spade-bone, *n.* the shoulder-blade.

spadeful, *n. spade*-full, as much as a spade will hold.

spade-work, *n.* preparatory work; pioneer research; routine work.

spadiceous, *a.* spa-*dish*-us, of a light-red colour; bay; resembling a spadix [Bot.]. (L. *spadiceus.*)

spadille, *n.* spa-*dil*, the ace of spades at ombre and quadrille. (Fr.)

spadix, *n. spay*-diks, a succulent spike with numerous flowers included in a spathe [Bot.]. (L.)

spado, *n. spay*-doh, a gelding; one who has no generative power [Law]. (L.)

spae, *v.t.* and *i.* spay, to foretell; to predict [Scots.].

spaewife, *n. spay*-wife, a female fortune-teller; a witch [Scots.].

spaghetti, *n.* spa-*get*-te, a sort of slender macaroni in string-like coils. (It.)

Spahi, *n. spah*-e, an Algerian cavalryman in the French army. (Turk. *sipahi.*)

spake, spake, *old p.* of *speak.*

spall, *v.t.* spawl, to break up with a hammer; to split; to chip: *n.* a chip; a splinter of stone. (O.Dut. *spalden.*)

spalpeen, *n.* spal-*peen*, a scamp; a rascal. (Ir.)

spalt, *a.* spawlt, liable to break or split; brittle (esp. of wood).

spam, *n.* spam, proprietary name of a food-stuff,

based upon pork and ham, manufactured in the U.S.A.
span, *n.* span, the space from the end of the thumb to the end of the little finger when extended; nine inches; a short space of time; the full extent; the spread or extent of an arch between its abutments [Arch.] or between the wing-tips of an aeroplane [Av.], etc.; a yoke of animals, specially of horses, like each other, harnessed side by side [U.S.A.]: *v.t.* to measure, as by the fingers extended; to extend from one side to the other: *v.i.* to be a good match [U S.A.]. (A.S. *spann.*)
span, span, *p.* of *spin.*
spanæmia, *n.* spa-*nee*-me-a, thinness or poorness of blood [Med.]. (Gr. *spanos,* rare, *haima,* blood.)
spancel, *n.* *span*-sel, a rope for hobbling a beast or horse: *v.t.* to hobble with this. (O.Dut. *spansel.*)
spandrel, *n.* *span*-drel, the irregular triangular space between the curve of an arch and the rectangle enclosing it [Arch.]. (O.Fr. *espandre,* to spread out.)
spang, *n.* spang, a jerk; a leap or bound: *v.t.* to throw with a jerk: *v.i.* to leap; to spring [Scots.].
spangle, *n.* *spang*-gl, a thin little disk of shining metal; any little thing sparkling and brilliant, esp. as a dress ornament: *v.t.* to set or adorn with spangles. (A.S. *spang,* a metal clasp.)
spangler, *n.* *spang*-gler, one who or that which spangles.
spangly, *a.* *spang*-gle, bestrewn or adorned with spangles; spangled.
Spaniard, *n.* *span*-yerd, a native of Spain.
spaniel, *n.* *span*-yel, a dog of the retriever type formerly much used in field-sports; a toy dog with long drooping ears, silky coat, and a short muzzle; a mean cringing person. (O.Fr. *espagneul,* Spanish.)
Spanish, *a.* *span*-ish, pertaining to Spain: *n.* the Spaniards; the language of Spain. **Spanish Main,** the Caribbean Sea (originally, the coasts of northern South America).
Spanish-bayonet, *n.* a species of *Yucca,* with rigid, sharp-pointed leaves.
Spanish-black, *n.* a soft black from burnt cork.
Spanish-broom, *n.* a Mediterranean leguminous shrub of the genus *Spartium.*
Spanish-brown, *n.* a species of reddish-brown earth used in paints.
Spanish-chalk, *n.* a kind of steatite obtained from Aragon, Spain.
Spanish-chestnut, *n.* the large cultivated tree, *Castanea sativa* (or *C. vesca*); its edible nut.
Spanish-fly, *n.* the beetle, *Cantharis vesicatoria,* used for raising blisters.
Spanish-grass, *n.* esparto grass.
Spanish-juice, *n.* extract of liquorice root.
Spanish-moss, *n.* a perennial herbaceous flowering plant of the genus *Usnea,* growing as an epiphyte.
Spanish-nut, *n.* popular name of various small edible nuts, esp. that of *Corylus avellana barcelo-niensis.*
Spanish-red, *n.* Venetian red.
Spanish-white, *n.* a white pigment obtained from chalk or from bismuth sub-nitrate.
Spanish-yellow, *n.* golden yellow.
spank, *n.* spank, a blow; a slap on the buttocks: *v.t.* to strike with the open hand; to slap: *v.i.* to run briskly or spiritedly. (Low Ger. *spenkern,* move quickly.)
spanker, *n.* one who spanks; one who takes long strides; a fast horse; a fine specimen; the aftermost sail of a ship or barque or the gaff sail on the mizen-mast.
spanking, *a.* *spang*-king, dashing; free-going; large; stout: *n.* a whacking.
span-long, *a.* of the length of a span.
spanner, *n.* *span*-ner, one who or that which spans; a wrench used to tighten the nuts upon screws; a span-worm.
span-new, *a.* quite new. (Ice. *spann,* a chip.)
span-roof, *n.* a common roof with eaves on the two sides.
span-worm, *n.* the larva of a looper moth.
spar, *n.* spar, any easily and regularly frangible non-metallic crystalline mineral. (A.S. *spærstan.*)
spar, *n.* spar, a general term for masts, yards, booms, and gaffs; a main lateral member of an aeroplane wing; a long piece of timber: *v.t.* to fit with spars (A.S. *sparrian,* to shut a door by means of a bar.)
spar, *v.i.* spar, to box, or fling out the arms as in boxing; to dispute; to wrangle. **sparring partner,** a pugilist with whom another practises [Coll.] a foil or stooge. (O.Fr. *esparer.*)
sparable, *n.* *spa*-ra-bl, a nail driven into shoe soles (*sparrow-bill,* from its shape.)
spar-deck, *n.* the upper deck of a vessel.
spare, *a.* spare, scanty; parsimonious; superfluous lean; kept in reserve; extra: *n.* a part kept to b used in replacement: *v.t.* to use frugally; not t waste; to withhold; to do without; to omit; t treat tenderly; to forbear to afflict, punish o destroy; to allow: *v.i.* to live frugally; to forgive **spare room,** a bedroom kept for the use of guests (A.S. *sparian.*)
sparely, *ad.* sparingly.
spareness, *n.* state of being lean or thin; lean ness.
sparer, *n.* *spare*-rer, one who is sparing; one wh avoids unnecessary expense.
sparerib, *n.* *spare*-rib, a cut of pork consisting of th ribs somewhat closely trimmed.
sparge, *v.t.* sparj, to sprinkle. (L. *spargo,* sprinkle.
sparger, *n.* *spar*-jer, a vessel or apparatus used i sprinkling, esp. in brewing.
spargosis, *n.* spar-*goh*-sis, abnormal enlargement o a part [Med.]; elephantiasis. (Gr.)
sparing, *a.* *spare*-ring, the action of economizing o of showing forbearance, etc.; frugal; parsimonious *n.pl.* savings.
sparingly, *ad.* in a sparing manner.
sparingness, *n.* the quality of being sparing.
spark, *n.* spark, a bright, glowing particle throw off in combustion; a small shining body or transien light; the luminous effect of a disruptive electrica discharge; a very small portion or fragment; flash of wit; a brisk showy young fellow; a lover *v.i.* to emit sparks; to produce electric sparks to pay court; to play the spark or gallant. (A.S *spearca,* a spark.)
sparkful, *a.* *spark*-ful, lively; brisk; gay.
sparking-plug, *n.* a device by which an electri spark is introduced into the cylinders of an interna combustion engine for the purpose of igniting th charge.
sparkish, *a.* gay; showy; well-dressed; fine.
sparkle, *n.* sparkl, a spark; a luminous particle *v.i.* to emit sparks; to glitter; to twinkle; t glisten; to exhibit an appearance of animation; t be brilliant; to emit little bubbles, as spirituou liquors. (Dut. *sparkelen,* sparkle.)
sparkler, *n.* he who or that which sparkles; on whose eyes sparkle; a firework that emits smal bright sparks.
sparklet, *n.* *spark*-let, a small sparkle; trade nam for a small capsule containing a charge of carboni acid compressed for the purpose of aerating water.
sparkling, *a.* *spark*-ling, emitting sparks; glitte ing; lively; brilliant; effervescing (of wines).
sparklingly *ad.* in a sparkling manner.
sparks, *n.* sparks, a wireless operator, esp. on boar ship; a torpedo officer [Slang].
sparling, *n.* *spar*-ling, a smelt. (O.Fr. *espealing.*
sparring, *n.* *spar*-ring, the action of the verb *t spar*; preliminary strokes in boxing.
sparrow, *n.* *spa*-roh, a small brownish finch of th genus *Passer.* **Java sparrow,** the paddy-bird (A.S. *spearwa.*)
sparrow-grass, *n.* a corruption of the wor asparagus.
sparrow-hawk, *n.* a small short-winged hawk *Accipiter nisus.*
sparrow's-tongue, *n.* knotgrass, the plant *Poly gonum aviculare.*
sparrow-wort, *n.* the common name of plants c the genus *Passerina.*
sparry, *a.* *spar*-re, resembling or consisting of spa **sparry iron,** siderite.
sparse, *a.* spars, thinly scattered; set or plante here and there. (L. *sparsus,* scattered.)
sparsedly, *ad.* *spars*-ed-le, in a scattered manner.
sparsely, *ad.* *spars*-le, in a sparse manner.
sparseness, *n.* thinness; scattered state.
sparsity, *n.* *spar*-se-te, sparse or scattered con dition; sparseness.
Spartacist, *n.* *spar*-ta-sist, a revolutionary, esp. member of the ultra-socialist Spartacus Party i

Germany in 1918. (L. *Spartacus*, leader of the Servile War against Rome, 73 B.C.)
spartalite, *n.* *spar*-ta-lite, a red oxide of zinc.
spartan, *a.* *spar*-tan, pertaining to Sparta; severe; hardy; undaunted.
sparterie, *n.* *spar*-ter-re, spun or woven work of esparto grass. (Fr.)
spasm, *n.* spazm, a sudden, involuntary, and violent contraction of the muscles; a fit. (Gr. *spasmos.*)
spasmodic, *a.* spaz-*mod*-ik, relating to or consisting in spasm; convulsive; implying great but futile effort: *n.* a medicine good for removing spasm. (Gr. *spasmodes.*)
spasmodically, *ad.* in a spasmodic manner.
spasmology, *n.* spaz-*mol*-o-je, the branch of medical science treating of convulsions.
spastic, *a.* *spas*-tik, resembling spasms; spasmodic; tetanic. (Gr. *spastikos.*)
spasticity, *n.* spas-*tis*-e-te, spastic condition; tendency to spasm.
spat, *v.i.* spat, *p.* of *spit*.
spat, *n.* spat, a short cloth gaiter. (*spatterdash.*)
spat, *n.* spat, the spawn of mollusca, esp. oysters.
spatangus, *n.* spa-*tang*-gus, a genus of heart-shaped echinoderms. (Gr., a sea-urchin.)
spatchcock, *n.* *spatch*-kok, a fowl killed and cooked hurriedly as an emergency meal: *v.t.* to interpolate as an afterthought or furtively. (*dispatch* and *cock.*)
spate, *n.* spate, a flood in a stream after rain. (O.Fr. *espoit*, a spouting forth.)
spathaceous, *a.* spa-*thay*-shus, having a spathe.
spathe, *n.* spaythe, a sheath protecting an inflorescence [Bot.]. (L. *spatha.*)
spathic, *a.* *spath*-ik, cleaving like spar; foliated or lamellar. (Ger. *spath*, spar.)
spathiform, *a.* *spath*-e-form, resembling spar in form. (Ger. *spath*, spar, and *form.*)
spathose, *a.* *spay*-thohs, spathic; abounding in or consisting of spar.
spatial, *a.* *spay*-shal, pertaining to, characterized by, or occupying space. (L. *spatium*, space.)
spatiality, *n.* spay-she-*al*-e-te, the quality or property of being spatial.
spatially, *ad.* *spay*-sha-le, by means of or with reference to space.
spatter, *v.t.* *spat*-ter, to scatter about; to sprinkle with anything wet or dirty; to asperse: *v.i.* to throw out of the mouth in a scattered manner; to sputter: *n.* a sprinkling or spattering, a splash. (*spat.*)
spatterdashes, *n.pl.* *spat*-ter-*dash*-ez, coverings for the legs, to protect them from mud; leather leggings for equestrians; spats.
spatula, *n.* *spat*-yew-la, a broad thin knife for spreading plasters, paints, ointments, etc.; a surgical instrument for depressing the tongue. (L.)
spatulate, *a.* *spat*-yew-lat, shaped like a spatula; elliptical [Bot.].
spatule, *n.* *spat*-yewl, the end of a bird's tail feather when it is broad. (Fr.)
spavin, *n.* *spav*-in, a swelling in some of the joints of a horse, producing lameness. (O.Fr. *esparvin.*)
spavined, *a.* *spav*-ind, affected with spavin.
spawl, *n.* spawl, saliva or spittle thrown out carelessly: *v.i.* to scatter saliva from the mouth.
spawn, *n.* spawn, the eggs of fish, frogs, or molluscs when ejected; the mycelium of fungi; any product or offspring (in contempt); offsets; shoots: *v.t.* to produce or deposit, as fish or amphibians, etc.; to bring forth; to generate (in contempt): *v.i.* to deposit eggs, as fish or frogs; to issue, as offspring (in contempt). (O.Fr. *espaundre.*)
spawner, *n.* *spawn*-er, the female fish.
spay, *v.t.* spay, to render (a female animal) infertile by removing or destroying the ovaries. (L. *spado.*)
speak, *v.i.* speek, to utter words or articulate sounds; to express thought vocally; to utter a speech or discourse; to talk; to dispute; to make mention of; to converse; to express by signs: *v.t.* to utter articulately; to declare; to celebrate; to talk in; to communicate. **speak a ship,** to pass within hail of her; to converse with her by means of signal flags. **speak for,** to speak in favour of; to be an indication or proof of. **to speak volumes,** to be very significant. *p.* **spoke,** and formerly **spake.** *pp.* **spoken.** (A.S. *specan.*)
speakable, *a.* *speek*-a-bl, that can be spoken.
speak-easy, *n.* a saloon where liquor can be obtained in defiance of the law; a dive [Amer. slang].
speaker, *n.* *speek*-er, one who speaks; one who pronounces a discourse; the president of a deliberate assembly, especially of the House of Commons; a loud-speaker.
speakership, *n.* *speek*-er-ship, the office of speaker.
speaking, *a.* *speek*-ing, used for speaking with; lifelike (of portraits). **on speaking terms,** slightly intimate.
speaking-trumpet, *n.* a trumpet-shaped instrument for intensifying the sound of the human voice; a megaphone.
speaking-tube, *n.* *speek*-ing-tewb, a pipe for use in speaking from one part of a building to another.
speal-bone, *n.* *speel*-bone, the shoulder-blade as used in the art of scapulimancy. (Scots.)
spear, *n.* speer, a long pointed weapon for throwing or thrusting; a lance; a large pointed instrument with barbs, used for stabbing fish and other animals; a shoot, as of grass: *v.t.* to pierce or kill with a spear: *v.i.* to shoot into a long stem [Hort.]. (A.S. *spere.*)
spear-foot, *n.* the off hind foot of a horse.
spear-grass, *n.* long stiff grass of various species.
spear-head, *n.* the point of a spear; the leader or leaders of an advance or attack.
spearman, *n.* *speer*-man, one armed with a spear.
spearmint, *n.* *speer*-mint, the garden mint, *Mentha viridis*, with spear-shaped leaves.
spear-thistle, *n.* the common thistle, *Carduus lanceolatus*.
spearwort, *n.* *speer*-wurt, a popular name for various species of *Ranunculus*.
★**special,** *a.* *spesh*-al, distinctive; designating a species or sort; particular; peculiar; designed for a particular purpose, subject, or occasion; extraordinary; limited in range; chief in excellence: *n.* a person or thing specially appointed. **special constable,** a member of a force of civilians sworn in to assist the police in time of war, civil commotion, etc. **special grace,** the renewing and sanctifying influences of the Holy Spirit. **special jury,** a jury selected from among persons of a particular class or calling. **special licence,** a licence to marry without banns at any time or place. **special pleading,** the allegation of special new matter; pleading to gain a special point; biased or unfair argument. **special verdict,** one in which the facts of the case are found by the jury, and the law is submitted to the judges. (Fr. *spécial.*)
specialism, *n.* *spesh*-al-izm, the devotion of a specialist to his particular branch of learning, etc.; the branch specialized in; an instance of specializing.
specialist, *n.* *spesh*-al-ist, one who devotes himself to a special branch of a science or an art; an authority on a special subject.
specialistic, *a.* spesh-al-*lis*-tik, pertaining to specialism or specialists.
speciality, *n.* *spesh*-e-*al*-e-te, specialty; quality peculiar to a species; distinctive skill or experience.
specialization, *n.* *spesh*-al-ly-*zay*-shon, application to a special function or use.
specialize, *v.t.* *spesh*-al-ize, to mention specially; to apply to special use: *v.i.* to study a special branch of learning or practice.
specially, *ad.* *spesh*-al-le, in a special manner; for a particular purpose; especially.
specialty, *n.* *spesh*-al-te, a special contract; an obligation or bond, esp. [Law] one under seal; a particular talent; a distinctive feature; a speciality. **in specialty,** in a particular manner or degree.
specie, *n.* *spee*-shee, coined money as distinct from paper money; gold or silver. (L.)
species, *n.* *spee*-sheez, a group of plants or animals such as has been or may be derived by germination or generation from a common root or stock and resemble each other and are capable of reproducing themselves with the same characteristics; the subdivision of a genus; sort; kind; appearance to the senses or the mind. (L., outward appearance.)
specific, *a.* spe-*sif*-ik, pertaining to species; that specifies, or particularizes, or tends to do so; efficacious for the cure of a particular disease: *n.* a remedy for a particular disease; an unfailing agency or means. **specific gravity,** relative weight density or density of a substance. **specific heat,** the quantity required to raise equal weights of different bodies through equal intervals of temperature. **specific name,** the systematic

name by which one species of a genus is distinguished from another. (Fr. *spécifique.*)
specifically, *ad.* in a specific manner.
specification, *n.* *spes*-e-fe-*kay*-shon, the act of specifying; a detailed statement of particulars; particular mention; an article or thing specified. (Late L. *specificatio.*)
specificity, *n.* spes-e-*fis*-e-te, the state, quality, or fact of being specific.
specificness, *n.* spe-*sif*-ik-ness, specific character; specificity.
specify, *v.t.* *spes*-e-fy, to mention or name particularly; to designate in words, so as to distinguish a thing from every other; to include in a specification. (O.Fr. *specifier.*)
specimen, *n.* *spes*-e-men, a sample; a part of anything intended to exhibit the quality of the whole; a type or example. (L.)
speciology, *n.* spee-she-*ol*-o-je, the branch of biology treating of the origin and development of species.
speciosity, *n.* *spee*-she-*os*-e-te, fair outward show. (O.Fr. *speciosite.*)
specious, *a.* *spee*-shus, apparently right; plausible; merely apparent. (Fr. *spécieux.*)
speciously, *ad.* with a fair or plausible appearance; deceptively.
speciousness, *n.* plausible appearance; speciosity.
speck, *n.* spek, a spot; a stain; a blemish; a very small thing: *v.t.* to spot; to stain in spots or drops. (A.S. *specca.*)
speck, *n.* spek, fat or blubber, as of whales, walruses, etc. (A.S. *spic.*)
speckle, *n.* spekl, a small speck or stain: *v.t.* to cover with small spots of different colour. (*speck.*)
speckledness, *n.* *spek*-ld-ness, the state of being speckled.
speckless, *a.* *spek*-less, spotless.
specksioneer, *n.* spek-sho-*neer*, the chief harpooner [Whaling]. (*speck*, blubber.)
specs, *n.pl.* speks, eyeglasses. [Coll., from *spectacles.*]
spectacle, *n.* *spek*-ta-kl, a show; something exhibited to view; a pageant; a representation; a scenic display; a sight: *pl.* glasses for the two eyes mounted in a light frame that rests on the nose and has side wires or pieces to the ears; something that aids the intellectual sight. (Fr.)
spectacled, *a.* *spek*-ta-kld, wearing spectacles. **spectacled bear,** the South American bear, *Ursus ornatus.* **spectacled goose,** the gannet.
spectacular, *a.* spek-*tak*-yew-lar, pertaining to shows; of the nature of a show. (L. *spectaculum.*)
spectacularism, *n.* spek-*tak*-yew-la-rizm, spectacular quality or condition.
spectacularly, *ad.* from a spectacular view-point.
spectator, *n.* spek-*tay*-tor, a looker-on; an eyewitness. (L.)
spectatorial, *a.* spek-ta-*taw*-re-al, pertaining to a spectator.
spectatress, *n.* spek-*tay*-tress, a female spectator.
spectra, *n.* *spek*-tra, *pl.* of *spectrum.* (L.)
spectral, *a.* *spek*-tral, ghostly; pertaining to or resembling a spectre; by means of or pertaining to the spectrum. (L. *spectrum.*)
spectrality, *n.* spek-*tral*-e-te, the state of being spectral; a phantom.
spectrally, *ad.* *spek*-tra-le, in a spectral manner.
spectre, *n.* *spek*-ter, an apparition; a ghost; a phantom. (Fr.)
spectre-bat, *n.* *spek*-ter-bat, any of the leaf-nosed bats of S. America, esp. *Vampyrus spectrum*; a vampire.
spectrogram, *n.* *spek*-tro-gram, a photographic or other representation of a spectrum.
spectrograph, *n.* *spek*-tro-graf, a camera for photographing spectra. (L. *spectrum*, and Gr. *grapho*, write.)
spectro-heliograph, *n.* *spek*-tro-*hee*-le-o-graf, an instrument for photographing the spectrum of the sun.
spectrological, *a.* *spek*-tro-*loj*-e-kal, pertaining to or by help of spectrology.
spectrology, *n.* spek-*trol*-o-je, the science which determines the constituents of bodies from the analysis of their spectra; demonology. (L. *spectrum*, and Gr. *logos*, science.)
spectrometer, *n.* spek-*trom*-e-ter, an instrument for measuring the angular deviation of the spectral rays. (L. *spectrum*, and Gr. *metron*, measure.)
spectrophone, *n.* *spek*-tro-fohn, a photophon adapted for use in spectrum analysis.
spectrophotometer, *n.* *spek*-tro-fo-*tom*-e-ter, a instrument for determining the amount or intensit of colour in spectrum analysis.
spectroscope, *n.* *spek*-tro-skope, an instrumen for examining the spectra formed by passing th light from a luminous body through a prism. (L *spectrum*, and Gr. *skopeo*, view.)
spectroscopic, *a.* *spek*-tro-*skop*-ik, pertaining t or by means of the spectroscope.
spectroscopically, *ad.* by means of the spectroscope
spectroscopist, *n.* spek-*tros*-ko-pist, a worker wit the spectroscope.
spectroscopy, *n.* spek-*tros*-ko-pe, the use of, or th art of using, the spectroscope.
spectrum, *n.* *spek*-trum (*pl.* **spectra**), an image o something seen, continuing after the eyes are closed the coloured stripe of an analysed beam of light **spectrum analysis,** the chemical analysis c substances through the investigation of thei spectra. (L., something seen.)
specular, *a.* *spek*-yew-lar, having the qualities c a speculum; having a smooth reflecting surface **specular iron,** a crystalline variety of hæmatite (L. *specularis.*)
speculate, *v.i.* *spek*-yew-late, to meditate; to con sider a subject by turning it in the mind and viewin it in its different aspects and relations; to buy u land, goods, or stock, in the expectation of gain fron a rise in the price; to venture. (L. *speculatus.*)
speculation, *n.* spek-yew-*lay*-shon, the act o speculating; consideration of anything in its variou aspects and relations; train of thoughts formed ir this way; mere thinking; making purchases ir expectation of gain from a rise in price; a venture of this kind; a game of cards.
speculatist, *n.* *spek*-yew-la-tist, a speculator; a theorizer.
speculative, *a.* *spek*-yew-la-tiv, given to specula tion; contemplative; formed by speculation theoretical; not verified by fact, experiment, o practice; adventurous in business.
speculatively, *ad.* theoretically; in speculation.
speculativeness, *n.* state of being speculative.
speculator, *n.* *spek*-yew-lay-tor, one who speculates or forms theories; one who conducts financial o commercial speculations, esp. as a business; a venturer.
speculatory, *a.* *spek*-yew-la-to-re, speculative affording facility for observation.
speculum, *n.* *spek*-yew-lum, a mirror; a metallic o other reflector; a surgical instrument for dilating a passage with a speculum attached to reflect the interior; the iridescent patch of colour on the wing of certain ducks. **speculum metal,** an alloy of copper and tin with usually a trace o arsenic, antimony, or zinc. (L.)
sped, sped, *p.* and *pp.* of *speed.*
speech, *n.* speech, the faculty or art of uttering articulate sounds or words; language; that which is spoken; formal discourse in public; an oration (A.S. *spæc.*)
Speech-day, *n.* *speech*-day, the annual prize-giving day at school.
speechful, *a.* loquacious; talkative.
speechification, *n.* *speech*-e-fe-*kay*-shon, oratory; an oration or harangue.
speechifier, *n.* *speech*-e-*fy*-er, one who speechifies.
speechify, *v.i.* *speech*-e-fy, to make a speech fo the sake of speaking; to harangue.
speechless, *a.* deprived of the faculty or power o speech; dumb; silent.
speechlessness, *n.* the state of being speechless; muteness.
speech-maker, *n.* one who speaks much in public.
speech-reader, *n.* a deaf mute, or other person who understands what is said by observing the movement of the lips.
speed, *n.* speed, quickness; celerity; haste dispatch; rapid pace; success; prosperity: *v.i* to move with celerity; to drive at an illegal o dangerous speed [Motor.]; to prosper; to succeed to fare: *v.t.* to dispatch; to send away in haste; to hasten; to hasten to a conclusion; to aid; to cause to succeed. **speed limit,** a legal limit o speed (esp. of traffic). (A.S. *sped.*)
speed-alarm, *n.* a device automatically notifying a motorist when his driving reaches a certain speed

peed-boat, *n.* a fast motor-boat.
peed-cop, *n.* a policeman detailed to report on the speed of motorists and to enforce traffic regulations [Slang].
peeder, *n.* one who or that which speeds; one who exceeds a speed limit; a device for regulating speed [Mech.].
peedful, *a.* serviceable; useful; speedy; hasty.
peedfully, *ad.* with speed; with success.
peedily, *ad.* with speed; quickly.
peediness, *n. speed*-e-ness, the state of being speedy; dispatch.
peedometer, *n.* spe-*dom*-e-ter, a speed indicator.
peedster, *n. speed*-ster, one who habitually drives (or flies) at very high speed; a fast car, motor-boat, etc.
peed-up, *n.* acceleration; the act of accelerating; increase in rate of production, esp. if unreasonable: *v.i.* to accelerate, to put on speed; to increase a rate of production [Manu.].
peedway, *n. speed*-way, motor-cycle racing track.
peedwell, *n. speed*-wel, an herbaceous plant or small shrub of the genus *Veronica*.
peedy, *a. speed*-e, quick; swift; nimble; quick in performance. (A.S. *spedig.*)
peiss, *n.* spice, a solution of impure arsenical compounds produced in the smelting of arsenical ores. (Ger.)
pelæan, *a.* spe-*lee*-an, pertaining to or dwelling in caves. (L. *spelæum*, cave.)
pelæologist, *n.* spel-e-*ol*-o-jist, a student of or authority on caves.
pelæology, *n.* spel-e-*ol*-o-je, the scientific study of caves, their structure, contents, etc.
pelding, *n. speld*-ing, a whiting or other small fish split and dried in the sun. (Scots.)
pelean (etc.), *a.* spe-*lee*-an, spelæan (etc.).
pelk, *n.* spelk, a splinter; a small stick used in thatching. (A.S. *spelc.*)
pell, *n.* spel, a charm consisting of words of some occult power: *v.t.* to charm. (A.S., a saying.)
pell, *n.* spel, a turn at work or duty; a short period.
pell, *v.t.* spel, to tell the letters of a word; to write or print with the proper letters; to read: *v.i.* to form words with the proper letters. *p.* and *pp.* **spelled** and **spelt.** (A.S., *spellian.*)
pell, *n.* spel, the wooden trap used in the game of knurr-and-spell.
pellable, *a. spel*-a-bl, capable of being spelled.
pellbind, *v.t. spel*-bynd, to fascinate; to enchant; to make spell-bound. (Back-formation from *spell-bound.*)
pell-binder, *n.* a speaker whose oratory fascinates his audience.
pell-bound, *a.* fascinated.
peller, *n. spel*-er, one skilled in spelling; a spelling-book.
pellican, *n. spel*-e-kan, spillikin.
pelling, *n. spel*-ling, the act of naming the letters of a word; orthography.
pelling-bee, *n.* a competition in spelling.
pelling-book, *n.* a book for teaching children to spell and read.
pelt, spelt, *p.* and *pp.* of *spell.*
pelt, *n.* spelt, a poor but hardy variety of wheat; German wheat, *Triticum spelta.* **small spelt,** one-grained wheat, *T. monococcum.* (A.S.)
pelter, *n. spel*-ter, a commercial name for zinc in ingot form; an alloy of copper and zinc used for brazing or hard soldering. (Low Ger. *spialter.*)
pence, *n.* spence, a buttery; a larder; a place where provisions are kept. (*dispense.*)
pencer, *n. spen*-ser, one who had care of the spence.
pencer, *n. spen*-ser, a short over-jacket worn by men or women, introduced by the third Earl Spencer.
pencer, *n. spen*-ser, a gaff-sail similar in shape to a spanker and carried on any mast but the aftermost.
pencerian, *a.* spen-*seer*-re-an, pertaining to the philosopher Herbert Spencer or to his philosophy.
pend, *v.t.* spend, to lay out; to dispose of; to part with; to consume; to waste; to pass, as time; to exhaust: *v.i.* to make expense; to waste away; to be dissipated, or consumed. *p.* and *pp.* **spent.** (A.S. *spendan.*)
pender, *n. spen*-der, one who spends; a prodigal; a lavisher.
pendthrift, *n. spend*-thrift, one who spends his means lavishly; a prodigal: *a.* like a spendthrift; wasteful.
Spenserian, *a.* spen-*seer*-re-an, pertaining to the poet Edmund Spenser or his works.
spent, *a.* spent, exhausted; having spawned. (*spend.*)
sperm, *n.* sperm, the fecundating fluid of male animals; semen. (Fr. *sperme.*)
sperm, *n.* sperm, spermaceti; the cachalot or sperm-whale which yields this.
spermaceti, *n. sper*-ma-*see*-te, a brittle waxy substance obtained chiefly from the head of the sperm-whale. (L. *sperma*, seed, *cetus*, whale.)
spermary, *n. sper*-ma-re, an organ for the development of spermatozoa; a testicle.
spermatheca, *n.* sper-ma-*thee*-ka, the sac in certain female insects and other invertebrates for the reception of spermatozoa.
spermatic, *a.* sper-*mat*-ik, consisting of, pertaining to, or conveying sperm; pertaining to the spermary.
spermatism, *n. sper*-ma-tizm, emission of semen; the old doctrine of spermism.
spermatoblast, *n. sper*-ma-to-blast, a cell producing sperm or spermatozoa [Biol.].
spermatocele, *n. sper*-ma-to-*seel*, a cystic affection of the testis.
spermatogenesis, *n. sper*-ma-to-*jen*-e-sis, the formation or development of spermatozoa.
spermatogenous, *a. sper*-ma-*toj*-e-nus, producing spermatozoa. (Gr. *sperma*, and *gennao*, produce.)
spermatology, *n. sper*-ma-*tol*-o-je, the scientific study of sperm. (Gr. *sperma*, and *logos*, science.)
spermatophore, *n. sper*-ma-to-*for*, a capsule containing spermatozoa, as in molluscs, etc.
spermatophyte, *n.* sper-*mat*-o-fite, any member of the Spermatophyta, the large division of plants that produce seeds. (Gr. *sperma*, *spermatos*, seed, *phyton*, plant.)
spermatorrhœa, *n. sper*-ma-to-*ree*-a, involuntary emission of semen. (Gr. *sperma*, and *rheo*, flow.)
spermatozoa, *n.pl. sper*-ma-to-*zoh*-a (*sing.* **spermatozoon**), sperm cells; the male fertilizing cells. (Gr. *sperma*, *zoon*, an animal.)
spermatozoal, *a. sper*-ma-to-*zoh*-al, pertaining to spermatozoa.
spermatozoan, *a. sper*-ma-to-*zoh*-an, spermatozoal: *n.* a spermatozoon.
spermatozoid, *n. sper*-ma-to-*zoyd*, the gamete or male cell of certain ferns, mosses, sea-weeds, etc.
spermatozoon, *n.pl.* sper-ma-to-*zoh*-on, *see* **spermatozoa.**
spermism, *n. sper*-mizm, the obsolete theory that the embryonic germ is contained in the unfecundated spermatozoa.
spermoblast, *n. sper*-mo-blast, a spermatoblast.
spermoderm, *n. sper*-mo-derm, the integument of a seed [Bot.]. (Gr. *sperma*, and *derma*, skin.)
sperm-oil, *n.* oil obtained from the sperm-whale.
spermological, *a.* pertaining to spermology.
spermologist, *n.* sper-*mol*-o-jist, a student or practitioner of spermology.
spermology, *n.* sper-*mol*-o-je, the branch of botany treating of seeds; a treatise on seeds. (Gr. *sperma*, and *logos*, science.)
spermophile, *n. sper*-mo-fil, a burrowing rodent of the northern hemisphere; the gopher or ground-squirrel.
spermophore, *n. sper*-mo-for, the placenta in plants.
sperm-whale, *n. sperm*-whale, the cachalot, *Physeter macrocephalus*, yielding spermaceti.
sperrylite, *n. spe*-re-lite, arsenide of platinum. (Named, 1889, after F. L. *Sperry*, Canadian mineralogist, and Gr. *lithos*, stone.)
spew, *v.t.* spew, to eject from the stomach; to eject; to cast out with abhorrence: *v.i.* to vomit. (A.S. *spiwan.*)
spewiness, *n. spew*-e-ness, the state of being spewy.
spewy, *a. spew*-e, wet (of land); boggy.
sphacelate, *v.i. sfas*-e-late, to mortify; to become gangrenous, as flesh; to become carious, as bone: *v.t.* to affect with gangrene. (Gr. *sphakelos*, gangrene.)
sphacelation, *n.* sfas-e-*lay*-shon, mortification; the process of becoming or making gangrenous.
sphacelism, *n. sfas*-e-lizm, necrosis; inflammation of the brain [Path.].
sphacelus, *n. sfas*-e-lus, gangrene; caries [Med.].
sphærulite, *n. sfeer*-roo-lite, spherulite.

sphagnology, *n.* sfag-*nol*-o-je, the study of the bog-mosses. (Gr. *sphagnos* and *logos.*)
sphagnous, *a. sfag*-nus, pertaining to bog-moss; mossy. (Gr. *sphagnos*, a moss.)
sphagnum, *n. sfag*-num, bog-moss. (Gr. *sphagnos.*)
sphairistike, *n.* sfa-*ris*-te-ke, the name under which lawn tennis was introduced in the 1870's. (Gr. *sphaira*, a ball.)
sphalerite, *n. sfal*-er-rite, native zinc sulphide, an important source of zinc.
sphene, *n.* sfeen, titanite. (Gr. *sphen*, a wedge.)
sphenodon, *n. sfee*-no-don, the generic name of the tuatara, *S. punctatum*, a primitive lizard of New Zealand. (Gr. *sphen*, a wedge, *odous*, a tooth.)
sphenogram, *n. sfee*-no-gram, a cuneiform character. (Gr. *sphen*, and *gramma*, a letter.)
sphenographer, *n.* sfe-*nog*-ra-fer, one skilled in sphenography.
sphenography, *n.* sfe-*nog*-ra-fe, the art of reading, and deciphering cuneiform characters. (Gr. *sphen*, and *grapho*, write.)
sphenoid, *a. sfee*-noyd, resembling a wedge. **sphenoid bone,** the pterygoid bone at the anterior part of the basis of the skull, and wedging the other cranial bones firmly together. (Gr. *sphen*, and *eidos*, like.)
sphenoidal, *a.* sfe-*noy*-dal, sphenoid.
spheral, *a. sfeer*-ral, pertaining to or like a sphere; pertaining to the heavenly spheres.
sphere, *n.* sfeer, a solid body contained under a single surface, each point in which is equidistant from a central point [Geom.]; circuit; orbit; a globe; one of the heavenly bodies; the vault of the sky; circuit of action, knowledge, or influence; compass; province; employment; order of society: *v.t.* to form into roundness; to ensphere. **parallel sphere,** one whose poles are in the zenith and nadir. **right sphere,** a sphere whose poles are in the horizon [Astron. and Geog.]. (Gr. *sphaira*, a ball.)
spheric, *a. sfe*-rik, spheral; spherical.
spherical, *a. sfe*-re-kal, globular; orbicular; relating to a sphere or to the orbs of the planets. **spherical angle,** an angle formed on the surface of a sphere by the arcs of two great circles. **spherical geometry,** that branch of geometry which treats of spherical magnitudes. **spherical triangle,** a figure bounded by the arcs of three great circles which intersect each other. **spherical trigonometry,** the resolution and calculation of the sides and angles of spherical triangles.
spherically, *ad.* in a spherical manner.
sphericalness, *n.* state or quality of being spherical.
sphericity, *n.* sfe-*ris*-e-te, globularity; roundness.
spherics, *n. sfe*-riks, spherical geometry and trigonometry.
spherograph, *n. sfeer*-ro-graf, a contrivance for the mechanical solution of problems in geography and navigation. (Gr. *sphaira*, and *grapho*, write.)
spheroid, *n. sfeer*-royd, a figure approaching to a sphere, but not perfectly sphericai; a solid generated by the rotation of an ellipse round either of its axes. (Gr. *sphaira*, and *eidos*, like.)
spheroidal, *a.* sfe-*roy*-dal, having the form of a spheroid; bounded by several convex faces. [Crystal.].
spheroidic, *a.* sfeer-*roy*-dik, spheroidal.
spheroidicity, *n.* sfeer-roy-*dis*-e-te, the state or quality of being spheroidal.
spherometer, *n.* sfe-*rom*-e-ter, an instrument for measuring curvature, esp. of lenses. (Gr. *sphaira* and *metron.*)
spherosiderite, *n. sfe*-ro-*sid*-er-rite, siderite occurring in spheroidal masses. (Gr. *sphaira*, and *sideros*, iron.)
spherular, *a. sfe*-rew-lar, in the form of a spherule.
spherule, *n. sfe*-rool, a little sphere or globe.
spherulite, *n. sfe*-roo-lite, a fibrous crystalline substance found in pearl-stone and in certain rocks. (Gr. *sphaira*, and *lithos*, a stone.)
spherulitic, *a. sfe*-roo-*lit*-ik, composed of, containing, or resembling spherulites.
sphery, *a. sfeer*-re, pertaining to the spheres or heavenly bodies; spherical; heavenly.
sphincter, *n. sfink*-ter, a muscle that contracts or shuts an orifice or aperture round which it is placed [Anat.]. (Gr.)
Sphinx, *n.* sfinks, a monster of ancient Greek legend who devoured those unable to solve riddles propounded by her, till Œdipus found out her secret when she threw herself into the sea; in Egypt, a representation of the Sphinx, usually a lion with the head of a man, a ram, or a hawk; a hawk-moth; a baboon, *Cynocephalus sphinx*, of Guinea; [Fig.] an enigmatic or taciturn person. (Gr., the strangler.)
sphragistics, *n.* sfra-*jis*-tiks, the study of engraved seals, as bearing upon the age of documents to which they are attached. (Gr. *sphragis*, a seal.)
sphygmic, *a. sfig*-mik, pertaining to the pulse. (Gr. *sphygmos*, the pulse.)
sphygmogram, *n. sfig*-mo-gram, a record of pulse-beats made by a sphygmograph. (Gr. *sphygmos*, the pulse.)
sphygmograph, *n. sfig*-mo-graf, a contrivance for indicating and registering the movements of the pulse. (Gr. *sphygmos*, and *grapho*, write.)
sphygmology, *n.* sfig-*mol*-o-je, the scientific study of the pulse.
sphygmomanometer, *n. sfig*-mo-ma-*nom*-e-ter, an instrument for measuring arterial blood-pressure. (Gr. *sphygmos*, *manometer.*)
sphygmometer, *n.* sfig-*mom*-e-ter, an instrument for measuring the strength of pulsations [Phys.]; a pulsimeter [Med.]. (Gr. *sphygmos*, and *metron*, measure.)
sphygmophone, *n. sfig*-mo-fohn, an instrument for ascertaining the rhythm of the pulse by audition.
sphygmoscope, *n. sfig*-mo-skope, an instrument for showing pulsations and the movements of the heart.
sphygmus, *n. sfig*-mus, the beat of the heart; a pulsation. (Gr. *sphygmos*, the pulse.)
spica, *n. spy*-ka, a spike [Bot.]; a surgical bandage wound from an extremity towards the trunk.
spicate, *a. spy*-kat, having a spike or ear [Bot.].
spiccato, *ad.* spik-*kah*-toh, a term indicating that every note is to have its distinct sound [Mus.]. (It., detached.)
spice, *n.* spice, an aromatic and pungent vegetable product used for seasoning food or as a condiment; a small quantity or tincture: *v.t.* to season with spice; to tincture. (O.Fr. *espice.*)
spicery, *n. spice*-er-re, spices in general; a room or cupboard for spices.
spice-wood, *n.* the gum-benzoin tree, *Styrax benzoin*; the N. American shrub, *Benzoin æstivale.*
spiciform, *a. spy*-se-form, spike-shaped [Bot.].
spicily, *ad. spy*-se-le, in a spicy manner.
spiciness, *n. spy*-se-ness, the quality of being spicy; spicy flavour or odour.
spick-and-span, *a. spik*-and-*span*, quite or altogether new; smart; natty. (*spick*, nail, and Ice. *spann*, chip.)
spicknel, *n. spik*-nel, spignel.
spicula, *n. spik*-yew-la, a small spike [Bot.]; a spike-shaped fragment of bone [Med.]; plural of *spiculum* [Zool.]. (L.)
spicular, *a. spik*-yew-lar, resembling a dart; having sharp points. (L. *spiculum*, a sting, a dart.)
spiculate, *a. spik*-yew-lat, consisting of or covered with spicules. (L. *spiculatus.*)
spicule, *n. spik*-yewl, a slender sharp-pointed granule or point; a spicula [Med.]. (L. *spicula.*)
spiculiform, *a. spik*-yew-le-form, having the form of a spicule; sharp-pointed.
spiculigenous, *a. spik*-yew-*lij*-e-nus, producing or containing spicules. (L. *spicula*, and *gigno*, produce.)
spiculum, *n. spik*-yew-lum (*pl.* **spicula**), a needle-like organ or process; a sharp-pointed concretion of carbonate of lime in certain land snails [Zool.]; a spine or spicula [Bot.]. (L.)
spicy, *a. spy*-se, producing or abounding with spice; having the qualities of spice; fragrant; aromatic; hot; keen, racy, smart, suggestive [Slang].
spider, *n. spy*-der, the popular name for many species of the arachnid order Araneæ, most of which capture their prey in webs; something like a spider; a special rest used at billiards, snooker, etc. (M.E. *spitfire.*)
spider-catcher, *n.* a long-billed East Indian sunbird of the genus *Arachnothera*; the wall-creeper.
spider-crab, *n.* any of several crabs with long thin legs of the group Oxyrhynchus.
spider-fly, *n.* a tick or parasitic dipterous insect; an artificial fly resembling a spider.
spider-line, *n.* a thread of a spider's web, esp. as used in an optical instrument.

spider-monkey, *n.* a small American monkey of the genus *Ateles*, with long slender limbs, and sensitive prehensile tail.
spider-orchis, *n.* a European orchid with yellow-streaked brown lip, *Arachnites aranifera*.
spiderwort, *n.* *spy*-der-wurt, the popular name for several species of *Tradescantia*.
spidery, *a.* *spy*-der-re, like a spider, or a spider's web; infested with spiders.
spiegeleisen, *n.* *spee*-g'l-*ize*-en, a highly carburized and crystalline form of white pig-iron containing manganese. (Ger. *Spiegel*, mirror, *Eisen*, iron.)
spiffing, *a.* *spif*-fing, delightful, excellent [Slang].
spifflcate, *v.t.* *spif*-le-kate, to thrash; to suffocate; to do for [Slang].
spignel, *n.* *spig*-nel, the umbelliferous plant *Meum athamanticum*.
spigot, *n.* *spig*-ot, a pin or peg to stop a small hole in a cask; a faucet, or its turning-plug. **spigot and socket,** designating a type of joint for cast-iron pipes in which the plain end of one length fits into the socket end of the next and is caulked. (*spike*.)
spike, *n.* spike, a large nail or peg; a sharp-pointed metal object; an ear of corn or grain; a species of inflorescence in which the flowers are sessile round an axis; a species of lavender, *Lavandula spica*: *v.t.* to fasten with a spike or spikes; to bring to a sharp point; to stop the vent of a cannon with a spike. **to have the spike,** to be angry or very annoyed [Slang]. **to spike one's guns,** to upset his scheme. (L. *spica*.)
spikelet, *n.* *spike*-let, a small spike; the inflorescence of grasses [Bot.].
spike-nail, *n.* a long nail.
spikenard, *n.* *spike*-nard, perfume from the fragrant Indian plant, *Nardostachys jatamansi*, with a spike inflorescence; also the plant. (O.Fr. *spiquenard*.)
spiky, *a.* *spike*-e, having a sharp point; furnished with spikes.
spile, *n.* spile, a small peg, used to stop a hole with; a stake driven into the ground to protect a bank: *v.t.* to pierce and insert a spile (of casks). (Dut. *spijl*, a bar.)
spill, *v.t.* spil, to suffer to run out of a vessel; to suffer to be shed; to shed; to throw away: *v.i.* to waste; to be shed; to be suffered to fall, be lost, or wasted: *n.* an act of spilling; anything spilt; an accidental throwing off or out, as from a horse, vehicle, or aircraft. **spill the beans,** to lay information; to blab; to divulge a secret [All Slang]. (A.S. *spillan*.)
spill, *n.* spil; a thin strip for lighting a candle or cigarette, etc.; a sliver. (Perhaps *spile*.)
spiller, *n.* *spil*-ler, one who spills or sheds; a kind of fishing-line; a small seine used to remove captured fish from a larger one.
spillikin, *n.* *spil*-le-kin, a peg used in scoring cribbage, etc.; a slender splinter of ivory, wood, etc., used in the game of **spillikins,** in which these are drawn from a heap with a hook. (*spile*, a sliver.)
spilling-lines, *n.pl.* *spil*-ling-linez, ropes for furling the square-sails [Naut.].
spillway, *n.* *spil*-way, an overflow channel from a reservoir, millpond, etc.
spiloma, *n.* spe-*loh*-ma, a birthmark. (Gr.)
spilosite, *n.* *spil*-o-site, any of a group of greenish schistose felspathic rocks with chloritic scales.
spilt, spilt, *p.* and *pp.* of *spill*.
spilth, *n.* spilth, anything spilt.
spin, *n.* spin, the act of revolving; a rapid revolution; a brief spell of exercise; a diving rotatory descent (Av.): *v.t.* to draw out and twist into threads; to draw out tediously; to extend to a great length; to protract; to cause to whirl; to fish with spinning bait: *v.i.* to practise spinning; to twirl; to perform the act of drawing and twisting threads; to move round rapidly; to develop a rotatory movement (esp. of aircraft); to issue in a thread or small current. **spin out,** to lengthen; to protract; to make tedious. **spin a yarn,** to tell a story, esp. in a prolix way. **flat spin,** *see* **flat.** *p.* **span**; *pp.* **spun.** (A.S. *spinnan*.)
spinaceous, *a.* spi-*nay*-shus, pertaining to or resembling spinach.
spinaceous, *a.* spy-*nay*-shus, having spines [Bot. and Zool.].
spinach, *n.* *spin*-aj, a herb of the genus *Spinacia*, esp. *S. oleracea*, the succulent leaves of which are boiled and eaten. (O.Fr. *spinache*.)
spinal, *a.* *spy*-nal, pertaining to the spine. **spinal column,** the vertebral column or backbone. **spinal cord,** an elongated part of the cerebro-spinal axis contained within the spinal column. (Late L. *spinalis*.)
spinate, *a.* *spy*-nat, spiny; spiniform [Bot.].
spindle, *n.* *spin*-dl, a pin used in spinning for twisting the thread, on which when twisted it is wound; an axis of revolution; a slender-pointed rod or pin on which anything turns; any long, slender thing: *v.i.* to grow into a long slender stalk or body. **spindle cousin,** a cousin on the spindle side, *i.e.*, the mother's side, of the family. (A.S.)
spindle-legs, *n.* slender legs; a spindle-shanks.
spindle-shanks, *n.* a tall thin person.
spindle-shaped, *a.* having the shape of a spindle; tapering from the middle to both ends.
spindle-side, *n.* the female side of descent.
spindle-tree, *n.* a shrub of the genus *Euonymus*, the wood of which is good for making spindles.
spindly, *a.* *spind*-le, tall and thin; weak.
spindrift, *n.* *spin*-drift, the spray blown up from the waves by the wind; spoondrift.
spine, *n.* spine, the backbone of an animal; a thorn; a sharp process; the back of a book between the covers. (O.Fr. *espine*.)
spinel, *n.* *spin*-el, anhydrous aluminate of magnesia occurring in crystals, and of various colours. (Fr. *spinelle*.)
spineless, *a.* *spine*-less, without a spine; [Fig.] irresolute; infirm of purpose.
spinescent, *a.* spe-*ness*-ent, more or less spiny; spinous; tapering; becoming hard and thorny.
spinet, *n.* *spin*-et, a musical instrument, resembling a harpsichord in which the wires were plucked by spines or quills. (O.Fr. *espinette*.)
spinicarpous, *a.* spin-e-*kar*-pus, producing spiny fruit.
spiniferous, *a.* spe-*nif*-er-rus, producing spines; bearing thorns. (L. *spina*, a thorn, *fero*, bear.)
spinifex, *n.* *spy*-ne-feks, porcupine grass, *Triodia irritans*, an Australian grass of a spiny nature. (L. *spina*, and *facio*, make.)
spiniform, *a.* *spy*-ne-form, shaped like a thorn.
spinigerous, *a.* spe-*nij*-er-rus, bearing thorns. (L. *spina*, and *gero*, bear.)
spink, *n.* spink, the chaffinch; the cuckoo-flower *Cardamine pratensis*, and other hedge plants. (Dial. Eng.)
spinnaker, *n.* *spin*-a-ker, a subsidiary sail set on the opposite tack to the mainsail in fore-and-aft vessels when running before the wind. (*spin*, or perhaps from *Sphinx*, said to be the name of the yacht on which it was first carried.)
spinner, *n.* *spin*-ner, one who or that which spins; one skilled in spinning; a spider; an artificial bait.
spinneret, *n.* *spin*-er-ret, an organ with which arthropods, such as spiders and insects, form their webs or coverings; the finely perforated plate through which the cellulose solution is passed in the manufacture of rayon filament.
spinnerule, *n.* *spin*-er-rool, one of the many ducts through which a spider emits fluid silk.
spinnery, *n.* *spin*-er-re, a spinning mill.
spinney, *n.* *spin*-ne, a small thicket with undergrowth; a copse. (O.Fr. *espinei*, a thorny place.)
spinning, *n.* *spin*-ning, the operation of drawing out and twisting into threads; the act of forming webs; the act of unduly protracting.
spinning-jenny, *n.* *spin*-ning-*jen*-ne, a machine invented by James Hargreaves about 1766 by which many threads can be spun out at once.
spinning-mill, *n.* a mill or factory at which spinning is carried on.
spinning-wheel, *n.* a wheel for spinning wool, cotton, or flax, by the hand.
spinny, *n.* *spin*-ne, a spinney.
spinose, *a.* *spy*-nohs, spinous. (L. *spinosus*.)
spinosity, *n.* spy-*nos*-e-te, the state of being thorny or crabbed.
spinous, *a.* *spy*-nus, characteristic of, resembling, or full of spines; thorny; pertaining to the spine [Anat.].
Spinozism, *n.* spy-*noh*-zizm, the form of pantheism taught by Benedict Spinoza in the 17th century, who resolved all being into extension and thought, which he regarded as attributes of the one substance, God, in whom all things, as modes of exten-

sion, and all ideas, as modes of thought, are viewed as comprehended and having place, the conception underlying the whole being a mathematical one; a philosophical Calvinism.
Spinozist, *n.* spe-*noh*-zist, an upholder of Spinozism.
spinster, *n.* *spin*-ster, a woman whose occupation is to spin; an unmarried woman [Law]. (*spin.*)
spinsterhood, *n.* *spin*-ster-hood, the condition of being an unmarried women; old maids collectively.
spinstry, *n.* *spin*-stre, the business of spinning.
spinthariscope, *n.* spin-*tha*-ris-kope, an instrument for showing the luminous effects of radium. (Gr. *spinther*, a spark, *skopeo*, view.)
spintherism, *n.* *spin*-ther-rizm, the illusory sensation of seeing sparks. (Gr. *spinther*, a spark.)
spinule, *n.* *spin*-yewl, a minute spine or thorn-like process [Bot. and Zool.]. (L. *spinula.*)
spinulous, *a.* *spin*-yew-lus, covered with or having the form of spinules [Bot. and Zool.].
spiny, *a.* *spy*-ne, full of spines; like a spine; thorny.
spiracle, *n.* *spi*-ra-kl, a breathing orifice; a pore; a vent for lava, etc. (O.Fr.)
spiracular, *a.* spi-*rak*-yew-lar, pertaining to or serving the purpose of spiracles.
spiraculate, *a.* spi-*rak*-yew-lat, having spiracles.
Spiræa, *n.* spi-*ree*-a, a genus of rosaceous plants, including *S. ulmaria*, the meadowsweet. (L.)
spiral, *a.* *spire*-ral, rising or pointed like a spire; tapering.
spiral, *a.* *spire*-ral, winding like the thread of a screw; coiled conically or cylindrically: *n.* a curve which continually recedes from a centre, round which it revolves [Geom.]; a wire coiled spirally; a spiral nebula [Astron.]; a spiral glide [Av.]: *v.i.* to move in or form spirals; to descend spirally [Av.]. (Fr.)
spirality, *n.* spire-*ral*-e-te, the quality of being spiral.
spirally, *ad.* *spire*-ra-le, in a spiral manner; in the manner of a screw.
spirant, *n.* *spire*-rant, a consonant uttered with emission of breath, such as *h*, *f* and *v*; *a.* pronounced as a spirant. (L. *spirans*, breathing.)
spiranthy, *n.* spire-*ranth*-e, spiral distortion [Bot.]. (Gr. *speira*, a spire, *anthos*, a flower.)
spire, *n.* spire, a winding line or structure like the thread of a screw; a curl; a wreath (of smoke, etc.); a single convolution of a series forming a spiral. (Fr., from Gr. *speira*, a coil.)
spire, *n.* spire, a tapering body; the tall tapering roof of a tower; that portion of a steeple which is above the tower; a stalk or blade of grass; top: *v.i.* to shoot up pyramidically; to sprout, as grain in malting: *v.t.* to furnish with a spire. (A.S. *spir*, as *spear.*)
spired, *a.* spyrd, having a spire or spires.
Spirifer, *n.* *spi*-re-fer, an extinct genus of brachiopods with internal spirally coiled lamellæ. (L. *spira*, and *fero*, bear.)
Spirillum, *n.* spi-*ril*-lum, a genus of spirally coiled bacteria. (L. *spira*, a coil.)
spirit, *n.* *spi*-rit, spiritual substance or being, or self-conscious life; a spiritual being; the soul; a disembodied soul or ghost; a spectre; a sprite or elf; animation; ardour; elevation or vehemence of mind; vigour of intellect; enthusiasm; genius; disposition; turn of mind; temper; a person of superior ability; essential quality; active quality or essence of a thing; real meaning; distilled liquor: *pl.* distilled alcoholic liquors: *v.t.* to animate; to inspirit; to encourage. **spirit off** or **away,** to kidnap, or bear away surreptitiously. **the Spirit,** the Holy Ghost; the Divine Being, as animating, especially man, in a spiritual manner. **spirits of wine,** an alcohol, so called from being originally obtained from wine. (Fr. *esprit*, from L. *spiritus*, breath.)
spirited, *a.* *spi*-rit-ed, animated; full of life; lively; full of spirit or fire; vigorous.
spiritedly, *ad.* in a spirited manner.
spiritedness, *n.* state of being spirited; disposition of mind.
spiritism, *n.* *spi*-rit-izm, the philosophic doctrine that spirit is the only reality or that it exists as distinct from matter; idealism; spiritualism [Coll.].
spiritist, *n.* *spi*-rit-ist, an adherent of spiritism.
spirit-lamp, *n.* a lamp in which methylated spirit is burned.
spiritless, *a.* *spi*-rit-less, destitute of spirits; dispirited; wanting animation; depressed.
spiritlessly, *ad.* in a spiritless manner.
spiritlessness, *n.* the state of being spiritless.
spirit-level, *n.* an instrument for obtaining an exact horizontal line, by means of a bubble of air in spirit.
spiritoso, *ad.* spi-re-*toh*-zoh, with spirit [Mus.]. (It.)
spirit-rapper, *n.* a believer in spirit-rapping.
spirit-rapping, *n.* the alleged power of calling up the spirits of deceased persons, who manifest their presence and answer questions by rapping.
spirit-stirring, *a.* animating the spirit.
spiritual, *a.* *spi*-rit-yew-al, consisting of or of the nature of spirit; not material; intellectual; mental; relative to mind only; not sensual; in reference to the spirit; affecting the moral life; determinative of the moral life; not lay or temporal; ecclesiastical: *n.* a religious song crooned or sung by American Negroes. **spiritual court,** an ecclesiastical court. (Fr. *spirituel.*)
spiritualism, *n.* *spi*-rit-yew-a-lizm, the belief in communication with the unseen world of the departed through the impressibility of certain media to so-called spiritual influence; necromancy; the doctrine of the existence of spirit independently of matter, or that all which exists is spirit or soul.
spiritualist, *n.* *spi*-rit-yew-a-list, a believer in spiritualism (in either of its senses).
spiritualistic, *a.* *spi*-rit-yew-a-*lis*-tik, pertaining to spiritualism; due to the presumed agency of spirits.
spirituality, *n.* *spi*-rit-yew-*al*-e-te, immateriality; intellectual nature; spiritual nature; spiritual state of mind; unworldliness; that which belongs to the Church.
spiritualization, *n.* *spi*-rit-yew-a-ly-*zay*-shon, the act of spiritualizing.
spiritualize, *v.t.* *spi*-rit-yew-a-lize, to render spiritual; to infuse spiritual attributes into; to interpret spiritually.
spiritualizer, *n.* one who spiritualizes.
spiritually, *ad.* *spi*-rit-yew-al-le, in a spiritual manner; with spiritual affection; by the spirit.
spiritualness, *n.* *spi*-rit-yew-al-ness, spirituality.
spirituel (or **-elle**), *a.* *spi*-re-tew-*el*, ethereal; of a highly refined nature; sprightly; witty. (Fr.)
spirituosity, *n.* *spi*-rit-yew-*os*-e-te, spirituous nature; state of containing distilled spirit.
spirituous, *a.* *spi*-rit-yew-us, containing spirit; alcoholic; ardent; having the quality of spirit; fine; pure; active.
spirituousness, *n.* quality of being spirituous.
spiritus, *n.* *spi*-re-tus, a breathing. **spiritus asper,** the rough or *h* breathing in Greek, represented by ‘. **spiritus lenis,** the soft breathing represented by ’ [Gr. Gram.]. (L.)
spirivalve, *a.* *spi*-re-valv, having a spiral shell (of certain molluscs).
spirket, *n.* *sper*-ket, a harness-peg, or other strong hooked peg; space between the floor-timbers forward and aft [Naut.].
spirketing, *n.* *sper*-ket-ing, the planks from the waterways to the port-sills in a wooden sailing ship [Naut.].
spirochæte, *n.* *spire*-ro-keet, a parasitic bacterium with undulating spiral rods. (Gr. *speira*, coil, *chaite* bristle.)
spirograph, *n* *spire*-ro-graf, an instrument for recording the movement in breathing. (L. *spiro* breathe, Gr. *grapho*, write.)
spirometer, *n.* spi-*rom*-e-ter, an apparatus for ascertaining the volume of air which the lungs can contain. (L. *spiro*, breathe, Gr. *metron.*)
spirometry, *n.* spi-*rom*-e-tre, the measurement of the breathing capacity.
spirophore, *n.* *spire*-ro-for, an instrument for inducing artificial respiration.
spirt, *n.* spert, a spurt: *v.t.* and *v.i.* to spurt.
spirtle, *v.t.* *sper*-tl, to spurtle.
Spirula, *n.* *spy*-roo-la, a genus of cephalopods, having a discoid, multilocular shell. (L. *spira*, a spire.)
spiry, *a.* *spire*-re, of a spiral form; like a spire pyramidal; having many spires.
spissated, *a.* *spis*-say-ted, inspissated; thickened.
spissitude, *n.* *spis*-se-tewd, density; viscosity state of being thickened. (L. *spissus*, thick.)
spit, *n.* spit, an iron prong or bar pointed, on which meat is roasted; a point of land or long narrow shoal running into the sea: *v.t.* to thrust a spit through; to thrust through; to pierce. (A.S. *spitu.*)

spit, *n.* spit, what is ejected from the mouth; saliva; the exact likeness of [Coll.]: *v.t.* to eject from the mouth, as saliva; to eject with violence: *v.i.* to throw out saliva from the mouth; to make a sound as if spitting. *p.* and *pp.* **spat.** (A.S. *spittan.*)

spit, *n.* spit, a form of spade; a spadeful; the depth of a spade blade. (Dial. Eng.)

spital, *n. spit*-al, spittle.

spitchcock, *n. spitch*-kok, an eel split and broiled: *v.t.* to split an eel and broil it.

spite, *n.* spite, a malicious disposition to thwart another; grudge; malice: *v.t.* to thwart maliciously; to vex. **in spite of,** in defiance of. (*despite.*)

spiteful, *a. spite*-ful, filled with spite; desirous to vex, annoy, or injure; malignant; malicious.

spitefully, *ad.* in a spiteful manner.

spitefulness, *n.* the quality of being spiteful.

spitfire, *n. spit*-fire, a violent or passionate person (usually in contempt).

spitter, *n. spit*-ter, one who puts meat on a spit; one who ejects saliva; a young deer whose horns begin to shoot; a form of spade, or its user.

spittle, *n. spit*-tl, saliva spat out of the mouth. (A.S. *spatl.*)

spittle, *n. spit*-tl, a small spade; a baker's peel.

spittle, *n. spit*-tl, a hospital. **Spittle sermon,** a sermon formerly preached at Eastertide at the former priory Spitalfields, London, and later at Christ Church, Newgate Street.

spittoon, *n.* spit-*toon,* a receptacle for spitting into; a cuspidor.

spitz, *n.* spits, a Pomeranian dog. (Ger.)

spiv, *n.* spiv, a flashy young man living on black-market deals or by similar questionable methods [Slang]. (Origin disputed.)

spivery, *n. spiv*-er-re, the methods or practices of spivs [Slang].

spivish, *a. spiv*-ish, characteristic of or pertaining to spivs [Slang].

splanchnic, *a. splank*-nik, pertaining to the viscera.

splanchnology, *n.* splank-*nol*-o-je, that department of the science of medicine which treats of the viscera. (Gr. *splanghna,* the bowels, *logos,* science.)

splanchnotomy, *n.* splank-*not*-o-me, dissection of the viscera. (Gr. *splanghna,* and *tome,* cutting.)

splash, *n.* splash, water, or water and dirt, thrown upon anything; a pool or running water in a road due to an overflow; a small quantity of soda-water to add to a drink of spirits; [Slang] ostentatious display: *v.t.* to spatter with water or mud: *v.i.* to dash water about; to be ostentatiously extravagant. **to make a splash,** to create a sensation; to make extravagant display. (*plash.*)

splash-board, *n.* a guard in front of a vehicle to protect the occupants from mud; a mudguard.

splasher, *n. splash*-er, one who or that which splashes; a wall protection against splashes from washhand-basins, etc.; a guard over the wheels of locomotives; a mudguard.

splashy, *a. splash*-e, full of dirty water; wet and muddy.

splatter, *v.i. splat*-ter, to splash.

splay, *n.* splay, an outward spread or curve; a slope or bevel, as at the sides of a window, etc. [Arch.]; amount of bevel: *a.* oblique; turned outward: *v.t.* to dislocate or break a horse's shoulder-bone; to slant: *v.i.* to spread out. (*display.*)

splay-foot, *n.* a flat foot turned outward.

splay-footed, *a.* having the foot turned outward; broad-footed.

splay-mouth, *n.* a wide mouth; a mouth stretched or distorted by design.

splay-mouthed, *a.* having a wide mouth.

spleen, *n.* spleen, a soft vascular gland, situated in the left hypochondriac region, and supposed by the ancients to be the seat of vexation, anger, and melancholy; anger; ill-humour; melancholy. (Gr. *splen.*)

spleenful, *a. spleen*-ful, angry; peevish; fretful; melancholy.

spleenish, *a. spleen*-ish, spleeny; affected with spleen.

spleenishly, *ad.* in a spleenish manner.

spleenishness, *n.* the state of being spleenish.

spleenless, *a. spleen*-less, having no spleen; kind; gentle; mild.

spleenwort. *n. spleen*-wurt, a fern of the genus *Asplenium.*

spleeny, *a. spleen*-e, angry; fretful; melancholy; affected with nervous complaints.

splendent, *a. splen*-dent, shining; beaming with light; illustrious. (L. *splendens,* shining.)

splendid, *a. splen*-did, magnificent; sumptuous; pompous; brilliant; illustrious; excellent. (L. *splendidus.*)

splendidly, *ad.* in a splendid manner.

splendidness, *n.* the quality of being splendid.

splendour, *n. splen*-dur, great brightness; magnificence; pomp; parade; brilliancy.

splenectomy, *n.* sple-*nek*-to-me, surgical removal or excision of the spleen.

splenetic, *a.* sple-*net*-ik, affected with spleen; morose; peevish: *n.* one affected with spleen; a medicine for a splenic ailment. (O.Fr. *splenetique.*)

splenetically, *ad.* sple-*net*-e-ka-le, in a splenetic manner.

splenic, *a. splen*-ik, pertaining to the spleen.

splenification, *n. splen*-e-fe-*kay*-shon, splenization [Med.].

splenitis, *n.* sple-*ny*-tis, inflammation of the spleen.

splenitive, *a. splen*-e-tiv, passionate; impetuous; splenetic.

splenius, *n. splee*-ne-us (*pl.* **splenii**), a cervical muscle [Anat.]. (Gr. *splenion,* bandage.)

splenization, *n.* splen-e-*zay*-shon, a change produced in the lungs by inflammation, in which the tissue resembles that of the spleen.

splenocele, *n. splen*-o-seel, hernia of the spleen. (Gr. *splen,* and *kele,* a tumour.)

splenoid, *a. splen*-oyd, resembling the spleen.

splenology, *n.* sple-*nol*-o-je, scientific study of the spleen; a treatise on the spleen.

splenomegaly, *n.* splen-o-*meg*-a-le, abnormal enlargement of the spleen.

splenopathy, *n.* sple-*nop*-a-the, any disease of the spleen.

splenotomy, *n.* sple-*not*-o-me, dissection or incision of the spleen. (Gr. *splen,* and *tome,* cutting.)

spleuchan, *n. sploo*-khan, a pouch. (Gael.)

splice, *n.* splice, the union of ropes by interweaving the strands; the junction of two pieces of wood lengthways: *v.t.* to unite the ends of two ropes by interweaving the strands; to join two pieces of wood lengthways; to marry. **splice the main-brace,** to serve an extra allowance of spirits [Naut.] (Dut. *splitsen.*)

splicer, *n. sply*-ser, one who splices ropes; an implement used in splicing.

spline, *n.* spline, a flexible ruler used in drawing curves; a cotter-pin, also the slot into which it fits: *v.t.* to provide with a slot for a spline.

splint, *n.* splint, a piece of wood split off; an appliance of wood, metal, or plaster, etc., used to hold or confine a broken bone when set, or to keep any part in a fixed position [Surg.]; a hard excrescence growing on the shank-bones of horses: *v.t.* to confine with splints. (Scand.)

splint-bone, *n.* one of two small bones behind a horse's cannon-bone forming the rudiments of the second and fourth metacarpals.

splinter, *n. splin*-ter, a small fragment that has been split off: *v.t.* to split into splinters; to support or confine with splints: *v.i.* to be split into splinters. (*splint.*)

splinter-bar, *n.* a cross-bar in a vehicle, which supports the springs; also one to which the traces are fastened.

splinter-bone, *n.* the splint-bone or fibula.

splinter-proof, *a.* strong enough to resist the splinters of bursting shells.

splintery, *a. splin*-ter-re, consisting of or resembling splinters; liable to splinter; having a surface as though covered with wedge-shaped splinters (of fractured metal).

split, *n.* split, a crack, rent, or longitudinal fissure; a breach or separation; a half-bottle; [Slang] a detective: *a.* divided: *v.t.* to divide lengthwise; to rive; to cleave; to rend; to divide; to break into discord; to strain and pain with laughter: *v.i.* to divulge a secret; to burst; to burst with laughter, to be dashed to pieces. **split on a rock,** to err fatally. **split the difference,** to halve the difference. **split hairs,** to quibble, to make unnecessary or useless distinctions. **split infinitive,** the locution in which an adverb is interpolated between "to" and its verb, as in "to publicly protest." *p.* and *pp.* **split.** (O.Dut. *splitten*; cf. Dan. *splitte.*)

split-pease, *n.* *split-peez,* husked pease split.

split-ring, *n.* a ring consisting of two turns of a spiral pressed together so as to look as if split.

splitter, *n.* *split*-ter, one who or that which splits; [Slang] an informer.

splodge, *n.* splodj, a splotch.

splotch, *n.* splotch, a daub; a patch.

splotchy, *a.* *splotch*-e, having, or covered with, splotches.

splurge, *n.* splurj, an ostentatious display, a showing off: *v.i.* to behave ostentatiously.

splutter, *v.i.* *splut*-ter, to scatter saliva from the mouth when speaking or ink from the pen when writing; to sputter: *n.* a sputtering; a bustle; a stir.

Spode, *n.* spode, a fine porcelain made by Josiah Spode at Stoke, Staffs., about 1770–1830.

spodomancy, *n.* *spod*-o-man-se, divination by ashes. (Gr. *spodos,* ashes, *manteia,* divination.)

spodumene, *n.* *spod*-yew-meen, a mineral of a foliated structure, chiefly composed of silica, alumina, and lithia. (Gr. *spodoumenos,* reduced to ashes.)

spoil, *n.* spoyl, that which is taken by violence or from another without permission; pillage; booty; that which is gained by effort; robbery; corruption; the cast or peeled skin of a serpent or other animal: *v.t.* to plunder; to strip by violence; to seize by violence; to corrupt; to vitiate; to ruin by indulgence; to render useless by injury; to injure fatally: *v.i.* to practise plunder or robbery; to decay; to go bad through keeping; to be eager (for a fight, etc.). **spoils system,** the distribution by a political party of paid public offices to its own, rather than to the public, advantage [U.S.A.]. *p.* and *pp.* **spoilt** and **spoiled.** (Fr. *spolier.*)

spoilage, *n.* *spoyl*-aj, that which is spoiled (esp. of printing-paper).

spoiler, *n.* *spoyl*-er, a plunderer; one who corrupts, mars, or renders useless.

spoil-five, *n.* a game of cards, with the object of winning at least three of the five possible tricks.

spoilsman, *n.* *spoylz*-man, one seeking or holding political office in return for services rendered to a party; a beneficiary of the spoils system [U.S.A.].

spoil-sport, *n.* a killjoy; an intermeddler.

spoke, spoke, *p.* of *speak.*

spoke, *n.* spoke, a radial bar, rod, or wire in a wheel; a handle of a steering wheel; a skid for locking a wheel in descending a hill; the rung of a ladder. **to put a spoke in one's wheel,** to obstruct or thwart him. (A.S. *spaca.*)

spoken, *a.* *spoh*-kn, uttered in speech.

spokeshave, *n.* *spoke*-shave, a sort of plane with a handle at each end used crossways in dressing wheel spokes and other curved work.

spokesman, *n.* *spokes*-man, one who speaks for others.

spoliate, *v.t.* *spoh*-le-ate, to plunder; to pillage: *v.i.* to practise plunder; to rob. (L. *spoliatus,* spoiled.)

spoliation, *n.* spoh-le-*ay*-shon, pillage; the act of plundering, particularly in time of war.

spoliator, *n.* *spoh*-le-ay-tor, one who spoliates.

spoliatory, *a.* *spoh*-le-a-to-re, characterized by spoliation; plundering.

spondaic, *a.* spon-*day*-ik, pertaining to a spondee; consisting of spondees.

spondee, *n.* *spon*-dee, a poetic foot of two long syllables. (Gr. *sponde,* a libation, the melody accompanying which being slow and solemn.)

spondulicks, *n.* spon-*dew*-liks, money; wealth [Amer. slang].

spondyle, *n.* *spon*-dil, a joint of the backbone; a vertebra. (Gr. *spondylos.*)

spondylitis, *n.* *spon*-de-*ly*-tis, inflammation of the spinal vertebræ.

★**sponge,** *n.* spunj, the popular name for the various species of Porifera; their fibrous skeleton; a substance or instrument used for sponging, as a mop for cleaning cannon after a discharge; the extremity or point of a horseshoe; a sponger; something like a sponge, as a mass of bread pulp under fermentation; spongy pastry: *v.t.* to wipe with a sponge; to wipe out or cleanse with a sponge; to wipe out completely: *v.i.* to suck in, as a sponge; to live parasitically on others; cadge. **throw up the sponge,** to acknowledg defeat. (L. *spongia.*)

sponge-cake, *n.* a very light plain sweet cake.

spongelet, *n.* *spunj*-let, a spongiole.

spongeous, *a.* *spun*-jus, spongy.

sponger, *n.* *spun*-jer, one who uses a sponge; incorrigible cadger; a parasitical guest.

spongicolous, *a.* spun-*jik*-o-lus, living in or association with sponges.

spongiform, *a.* *spun*-je-form, resembling a sponge soft and porous.

sponginess, *n.* *spun*-je-ness, state of being spongy

sponging-house, *n.* a bailiff's house, to put debto in before final committal to prison.

spongioblast, *n.* *spun*-je-o-blast, one of the ce that develop into neuroglia [Biol.].

spongiole, *n.* *spun*-je-ole, the absorbent cellul tissue at the extremities of roots [Bot.].

spongiopiline, *n.* *spun*-je-o-*py*-lin, a spongy tissu backed with rubber used as a poultice and fomentations. (Gr. *spongion,* and *pilos,* hair.)

spongiose, *a.* *spun*-je-ohs, having sponge-lik texture.

spongy, *a.* *spun*-je, like a sponge; soft and full cavities; having the quality of imbibing wet drenched.

sponsal, *a.* *spon*-sal, relating to marriage or to spouse; spousal. (L. *sponsus,* a spouse.)

sponsion, *n.* *spon*-shon, the act of becoming suret for another; an engagement pending ratificatio (L. *sponsio.*)

sponson, *n.* *spon*-son, a projection from a ship side as protection, or to carry a gun, etc.; th angular platform on either side of a paddle-bo [Naut.].

sponsor, *n.* *spon*-sor, a surety, one who binds him self to answer for another, and is responsible for h default; a godparent at baptism as representin and engaging for the child; a concern paying for broadcast which shall include an advertisement its products or services: *v.i.* to stand sponsor for to accept responsibility for; to favour or suppo strongly. (L.)

sponsorial, *a.* spon-*saw*-re-al, pertaining to sponsor or to sponsorship.

sponsorship, *n.* *spon*-sor-ship, the state of being sponsor; the office of sponsor.

spontaneity, *n.* *spon*-ta-*nee*-e-te, spontaneousness action, specially muscular, of purely internal su gestion. (Fr. *spontanéité.*)

spontaneous, *a.* spon-*tay*-ne-us, of one's own fre accord; purely self suggested, originated, derived; of itself, without external interference constraint; acting on impulse. **spontaneou combustion,** a taking fire of itself. **spontaneou generation,** abiogenesis, the discredited belief th living can be generated from non-living matte (L. *spontaneus.*)

spontaneously, *ad.* in a spontaneous manner.

spontaneousness, *n.* the quality of being spo taneous.

spontoon, *n.* spon-*toon,* a kind of military half pik formerly carried by non-commissioned office (Fr. *sponton.*)

spoof, *n.* spoof, a sham: *v.t.* to hoax [Slang].

spook, *n.* spook, a ghost. (Dut.)

spooky, *a.* *spook*-e, suggestive of spooks; eri spectral; haunted.

spool, *n.* spool, a reel; a piece of cane or reed use by weavers for winding yarn on: *v.t.* to wind a spool. (O.Dut. *spoele.*)

spoom, *v.i.* spoom, to scud; to be driven befo the wind [Naut.].

★**spoon,** *n.* spoon, a ladle with a handle in the sar curve as the bowl, for dipping in liquids, a stirring with; a golf club: *v.t.* to take up with spoon; to make love to or together [Slang]; hit up an easy catch [Cricket]. **wooden spoo** a spoon made of wood; ironical "honour" a title accorded to the lowest taking honours in t Mathematical Tripos, Cambridge Univ. (A. *spoon,* a chip of wood.)

spoon-bait, *n.* an anglers' artificial bait resembli a bright metal spoon-bowl.

spoonbill, *n.* *spoon*-bil, the bird *Platalea leucorodi* belonging to the same family as the ibis, so call from the shape of its bill; the shoveller duck.

spoondrift, *n.* *spoon*-drift, a showery sprinkling

sea-water, swept from the surface by the wind; spindrift [Naut.].
poonerism, *n.* *spoon*-er-rizm, involuntary or facetious transposition of initials or successive sounds in words. (Dr. *Spooner*, *d.* 1930, Warden of New College, Oxford, who was credited with the habit.)
poonful, *n.* *spoon*-ful, as much as a spoon contains; a small quantity.
poonily, *ad.* *spoon*-e-le, in a spoony manner.
poonmeat, *n.* *spoon*-meet, food to be taken with a spoon; liquid or infant's food.
poony, *a.* *spoon*-e, soft; silly; softly amorous: *n.* a weak-minded person.
poor, *n.* spoor, a trail, esp. of an animal. (Dut.)
poradic, *a.* spo-*rad*-ik, separate; single; scattered irregularly. **sporadic disease,** one occurring locally, not widespread or epidemic. (Gr. *sporadikos*, scattered.)
poradically, *ad.* in a sporadic manner; separately.
porangial, *a.* spo-*ran*-je-al, pertaining to or composed of sporangia.
porangium, *n.* spo-*ran*-je-um (*pl.* **sporangia**), a spore-case. (Gr. *spora*, and *angeion*, a vessel.)
pore, *n.* spore, a reproductive cell; a germ; that part of a flowerless plant which performs the function of the seed [Bot.]. (Gr. *sporos.*)
pore-case, *n.* the covering of spores.
porification, *n.* *spo*-re-fe-*kay*-shon, spore-production.
porigenous, *a.* spo-*rij*-e-nus, producing spores.
poration, *n.* spo-*ray*-shon, spore-production; the formation of spores.
porocarp, *n.* *spo*-ro-karp, a fructification in certain ferns, fungi, and algæ in which spores or sporangia are formed.
porogenesis, *n.* spo-ro-*jen*-e-sis, spore formation; reproduction by means of spores.
porogony, *n.* spo-*rog*-o-ne, reproduction by spores.
porophore, *n.* *spo*-ro-for, a spore-bearing organ [Bot.].
porophyte, *n.* *spo*-ro-fite, the individual or generation, in certain plants, that produces asexual spores (as opposed to gametophytes.)
porozoa, *n.pl.* spo-ro-*zoh*-a, a class of parasitic protozoa reproducing by sporulation.
porran, *n.* *spo*-ran, a pouch worn in front of a kilt. (Gael.)
port, *n.* sport, mirth; diversion; contemptuous mirth; play; outdoor recreation; jest; variation from the normal condition [Bot. and Zool.]; a sportsman; a good fellow [Slang]: *v.t.* to divert; to vary from the normal; to represent by any kind of play; to wear: *v.i.* to play; to trifle. **to sport one's oak,** *see* **oak.** (*disport.*)
porter, *n.* *sport*-er, one who sports.
portful, *a.* *sport*-ful, merry; frolicsome; full of jesting; playful; done in jest.
portfully, *ad.* in a sportful manner.
portfulness, *n.* the quality of being sportful; a playful disposition; playfulness.
porting, *a.* indulging in sports; connected with sport; sportsmanlike; possible but improbable. **sporting chance,** a problematic possibility of success.
portive, *a.* *sport*-iv, merry; playful; frolicsome.
portively, *ad.* in a sportive manner.
portiveness, *n.* the quality of being sportive; playfulness; disposition to mirth.
portless, *a.* *sport*-less, without any element of sport; joyless.
ports-, pref., denoting special suitability for use in sport, as *sports-jacket*, *sports-car.*
portsman, *n.* *sports*-man, one actively interested in outdoor sports; an opponent who behaves with considerate fairness; a good fellow.
portsmanlike, *a.* like a sportsman; fair and considerate; straightforward.
portsmanship, *n.* *sports*-man-ship, practice or skill in field sports; playing the game.
portswoman, *n.* *sports*-woom-an, a female sportsman.
porty, *a.* *sport*-e, sportsmanlike; gay, fast, flashy in dress or appearance.
porular, *a.* *spo*-roo-lar, pertaining to sporules; resembling a sporule.
porulation, *n.* spo-roo-*lay*-shon, the production of spores [Bot.]; multiple gemmation [Zool.].
porule, *n.* *spo*-rool, a small or secondary spore.

sporuliferous, *a.* spo-roo-*lif*-er-rus, bearing sporules (Gr. *sporos*, and L. *fero*, bear.)
spot, *n.* spot, a mark made by foreign matter; a stain; a stain on character or reputation; disgrace; reproach; fault; blemish; small extent of space; a particular place; a place of a different colour from the ground; a dark place on a luminous disk; a marked point on a billiard table; a small quantity of (drink, etc.) [Coll.]; a spot-light [Cine.]: *v.t.* to stain; to discolour; to patch; to blemish; to single out; to locate (esp. an enemy position): *a.* paid, or available for payment upon the spot or immediately (of cash); ready for immediate delivery (of commodities) [Comm.]. **on the spot,** in danger, esp. of murder [U.S.A. slang]. **upon the spot,** immediately. (*spout.*)
spotless, *a.* *spot*-less, free from spots, foul matter, or discoloration; pure; untainted.
spotlessly, *ad.* in a spotless manner.
spotlessness, *n.* freedom from spot, stain, or reproach.
spot-light, *n.* *spot*-lite, an adjustable focused light on a motor-car, etc., for throwing a beam in any direction; a strong light for illuminating a single person, group, etc., on the stage or set [Theatre and Cinema]; the circle of light thrown by this.
spotted, *pp.* and *a.* *spot*-ted, marked with spots or places of different colour from the ground. **spotted fever,** cerebrospinal meningitis, and other eruptive fevers.
spottedness, *n.* *spot*-ted-ness, state or quality of being spotty.
spotter, *n.* *spot*-ter, one who spots or makes spots; an observer [Mil. Av.]; an instrument used in locating an enemy position.
spottiness, *n.* *spot*-e-ness, the state of being spotty.
spotty, *a.* *spot*-e, full of spots; marked with discoloured places.
spousal, *a.* *spou*-zal, pertaining to marriage; nuptial; connubial: *n.pl.* marriage; nuptials. (O.Fr. *espousaille.*)
spouse, *n.* spouz, a husband or wife. (O.Fr. *spus.*)
spouseless, *a.* having no spouse; unwedded.
spout, *n.* spout, the projecting mouth of a vessel from which a liquid issues; a pipe for conducting water, especially from a roof; a waterspout: *v.t.* to throw out, as liquids through a pipe; to mouth; [Coll.] to pawn: *v.i.* to speechify; to issue with violence, as water through an orifice. **up the spout,** in pawn [Slang]. (M.E. *spouten.*)
spouter, *n.* *spout*-er, one who or that which spouts; a whale; a gushing oil-well; a ranter.
spout-hole, *n.* the spiracle of a whale.
sprack, *a.* sprak, vigorous; sprightly; alert. (Origin unknown.)
sprag, *n.* sprag, a young salmon (applied also to cod). (Dial. Eng.)
sprag, *n.* sprag, a stout piece of wood; a bar or block to prevent the wheel of a vehicle turning; a supplementary brake acting on the transmission of a motor-car: *v.t.* to stop or check motion with a sprag.
sprain, *n.* sprane, an excessive strain or twist of the muscles or ligaments of a joint without dislocation: *v.t.* to overstrain or twist the muscles or ligaments of a joint, so as to injure them. (L. *ex-*, and *premo*, press.)
spraints, *n.pl.* spraynts, dung of an otter. (O.Fr.)
sprang, sprang, *p.* of *spring.*
sprat, *n.* sprat, the small sea-fish *Clupea sprattus.* **Sprat day,** the ninth of November. (Dut.)
spratter, *n.* *sprat*-ter, a man or vessel engaged in spratting.
spratting, *n.* *sprat*-ing, fishing for sprats.
sprawl, *v.i.* sprawl, to lie with the limbs stretched out or as struggling; to stretch or toss out the limbs or move awkwardly; to widen or open irregularly, as a body of mounted men. (A.S. *spreāwlian.*)
sprawler, *n.* *spraw*-ler, one who sprawls.
sprawly, *a.* *spraw*-le, of a sprawling character.
spray, *n.* spray, a small shoot or branch of a tree; the extremity of a branch; a small plume or bunch. (A.S. *spræc*, a shoot.)
spray, *n.* spray, minute particles of water from a jet or driven by the wind; an atomizer or implement to spray with; vapour from an atomizer: *v.t.* to squirt in the form of spray; to treat with a spray. (Ger. *sprei*, a drizzle.)

sprayer, *n.* *spray*-er, a spray, an atomizer or other spraying apparatus.
sprayey, *a.* *spray*-e, having or resembling sprays; spreading.
spread, *n.* spred, extent; compass; expansion; a cover; a table spread or furnished with a meal; a feast: *v.t.* to extend in length and breadth; to stretch out; to extend; to pitch; to cover over; to propagate; to diffuse; to prepare; to unfurl: *v.i.* to be extended or stretched; to be propagated. **spread oneself,** to make every effort; also to behave ostentatiously [Slang]. (A.S. *sprædan.*)
spread-eagle, *n.* spred-*ee*-gl, the figure of an eagle with its wings elevated and its legs extended [Her.]; a fowl split open and broiled; the position of a man fastened for flogging; a figure in skating: *a.* pretentious; bombastically patriotic; inflated: *v.t.* to extend and fasten the limbs of a person for flogging.
spread-eagleism, *n.* spread-*ee*-gl-izm, bombastic patriotism [U.S.A.].
spreader, *n.* *spred*-er, one who or that which spreads; one who divulges; a crosstree [Naut.]; the stretcher of chain traces; the appliance separating the wire of multi-wired aerials [Wire.].
spreading, *a.* extending over a large space.
spread-over, *n.* any system by which the working-hours over a given period are arranged in diverse or irregular turns.
spree, *n.* spree, frolic; a drinking bout; a laughable episode. (Perhaps Ir. *spre,* spirit.)
sprent, *v.t.* sprent, to sprinkle; to spatter. (O. Scand. *sprenta.*)
sprig, *n.* sprig, a small shoot or twig; a scion; a brad or nail without a head; a representation of a sprig in embroidery; a forward young fellow: *v.t.* to adorn with sprigs; to drive sprigs into.
spriggy, *a.* *sprig*-e, full of sprigs or small branches.
spright, *n.* sprite, a sprite. (Fr. *esprit.*)
sprightful, *a.* lively; brisk; vivacious; sprightly.
sprightless, *a.* *sprite*-less, destitute of life; dull; sluggish.
sprightliness, *n.* the state of being sprightly; liveliness; briskness; activity.
sprightly, *a.* *sprite*-le, full of life and activity; lively; brisk: *ad.* in a sprightly manner. (*sprite.*)
spring, *v.i.* spring, to originate; to arise; to begin to grow; to proceed; to appear, esp. unexpectedly; to issue forth; to leap; to fly or start back; to start; to rise; to rebound; to warp or split. **spring at,** to leap forward. **spring forth,** to rush out. **spring in,** to rush in. **spring on,** to assault. *p.* **sprang**; *pp.* **sprung.** (A.S. *springan.*)
spring, *v.t.* spring, to start or rouse; to cause to explode; to burst; to crack; to cause to close suddenly. **spring a leak,** to commence leaking. **spring a rattle,** to put a rattle in action. *p.* **sprang**; *pp.* **sprung.**
★**spring,** *n.* spring, a leap; a bound; a recoil or flying back; elastic force; an elastic contrivance, as a coiled metal band; any active power; an issue of water from the earth; a fountain; source; rise; original cause; the vernal season; youth [Fig.]; a crack or fissure in a piece of wood; a flock of teal; certain ropes on sailing-ships [Naut.]. **spring chicken,** a young fowl, esp. one born in the spring and about 8 months old. **spring tide,** *see* **tide.**
springald, *n.* *spring*-ald, a youth.
spring-back, *n.* a binding-case in which the sheets are gripped by a spring instead of being sewn.
spring-balance, *n.* a balance consisting of a coiled spring provided with an index that moves on a graduated plate.
spring-board, *n.* a projecting plank to dive or jump from.
springbok, *n.* *spring*-bok, an African antelope allied to the gazelle, *Antidorcas euchore*; [Slang] a South African. (S. African Dut.)
spring-box, *n.* the barrel containing the mainspring of a watch.
spring-cart, *n.* a cart supported on springs.
springe, *n.* sprinj, a gin; a noose or snare for small game: *v.t.* to catch in a springe; to ensnare. (*spring.*)
springer, *n.* *spring*-er, one who springs; one who or a dog, esp. a spaniel, which rouses game; the springbok; the grampus; the impost, or point at which an arch unites with its support; the rib of a groined roof [Arch.].
spring-gun, *n.* a gun involuntarily discharged b the enemy or intruder by means of a spring.
springhalt, *n.* *spring*-hawlt, stringhalt.
spring-head, *n.* a fountain or source.
springily, *ad.* *spring*-e-le, in a springy manner.
springiness, *n.* *spring*-e-ness, the state of bein springy; elasticity; sponginess.
springing, *a.* *spring*-ing, shooting up; leaping: *n* act or process of leaping; growth; increase; th impost or springer [Arch.].
spring-tail, *n.* an insect of the sub-order Collembol having bristles below the abdomen with which the leap.
springtide, *n.* *spring*-tide, springtime; spring tide
springtime, *n.* *spring*-time, the time of spring the vernal season.
spring-wheat, *n.* wheat sown in spring.
springy, *a.* *spring*-e, elastic; having great elasti power; able to leap far; abounding with springs wet; spongy.
sprinkle, *n.* *spring*-kl, a small quantity scattered a light shower: *v.t.* to scatter in small drops; t besprinkle: *v.i.* to scatter a liquid; to rai moderately. (*spring.*)
sprinkler, *n.* *spring*-kler, one who or that whic sprinkles; a mobile tank for watering roads, etc. an automatic fire-fighting device.
sprinkling, *n.* *spring*-kling, the act of scattering i small drops; a small quantity sprinkled; mottling
sprint, *n.* sprint, a short turn of rapid running; short-distance race: *v.i.* to run or race at full spee for a short distance. (M.E. *sprenten.*)
sprinter, *n.* *sprint*-er, a runner for short distances.
sprit, *n.* sprit, a shoot or sprout; a small boom o spar; a boom which crosses the sail diagonall and elevates and extends it [Naut.]. (A.S. *spreo* a pole.)
sprite, *n.* sprite, an apparition; a fairy. (*spirit.*)
spritsail, *n.* *sprit*-sl, a sail extended by a sprit; on under the bowsprit attached to a horizontal yar [Naut.].
sprocket, *n.* *sprok*-et, one of a number of teet on a wheel to carry an endless chain; a cog.
sprocket-wheel, *n.* a wheel carrying cogs o sprockets and forming part of a transmissio gearing [Mech.].
sprod, *n.* sprod, a salmon in its second year. (Dial
sprout, *n.* sprout, the shoot of a plant; a youn shoot from an old cabbage: *pl.* Brussels-sprouts *v.i.* to germinate; to shoot into ramifications; t grow, like shoots of plants. (A.S. *spreotan.*)
spruce, *a.* sprooce, trim; smart; neat, withou elegance or dignity: *v.t.* and *i.* to dress with affecte neatness; to deceive thus, to swank [Slang].
spruce, *n.* sprooce, a species of fir-tree, of the genu *Picea.* **spruce-beer,** a beer tinctured with a extract obtained from a decoction of the green top of the black spruce.
sprucely, *ad.* *sprooce*-le, in a spruce manner.
spruceness, *n.* the quality of being spruce.
sprue, *n.* sproo, a tropical disease characterized b ulcerated mouth, diarrhœa, and digestive troubles
sprue, *n.* sproo, the small channel used in castin a mould; the waste metal solidifying in this.
sprue, *n.* sproo, asparagus of poor quality.
spruit, *n.* *sproo*-it, a watercourse that is dry excep after rain. (Dut., sprout.)
sprung, sprung, *pp.* of *spring*; tipsy [Slang].
sprunt, *n.* sprunt, a leap: *v.i.* to spring up; t start. (Dial. Eng.)
spry, *a.* spry, alert; active; vigorous. (Perhap from A.S. *spræc,* lively.)
spryly, *ad.* *spry*-le, in a spry manner.
spud, *n.* spud, a narrow spade; a potato; any shor thing or person, in contempt. (Dial. Eng.)
spue, *v.t.* and *i.* spew, to spew.
spume, *n.* spewm, froth; foam; scum: *v.i.* t froth; to foam. (L. *spuma,* from *spuo,* spit out.)
spumescence, *n.* spew-*mes*-ence, frothiness; stat of foaming.
spumescent, *a.* spew-*mes*-ent, foaming.
spumiferous, *a.* spew-*mif*-er-rus, producing foam.
spuminess, *n.* *spew*-me-ness, state of being spum;
spumous, *a.* *spew*-mus, spumy.
spumy, *a.* *spew*-me, consisting of froth or scum foamy.
spun, spun, *pp.* of *spin.*
spunge, *n.* and *v.* spunj, obsolete form of *sponge.*
spunk, *n.* spunk, touchwood; amadou; tinde

pluck, mettle [Coll.]; a match [Scots.]. (Perhaps Ir. *sponc*, tinder, as *sponge*.)
punky, *a.* *spung*-ke, spirited; plucky.
pun-yarn, *n.* a line of two or three rope yarns twisted, but not laid; rope yarns twisted by hand.
pur, *n.* spur, a sharp-pointed appliance worn on a horseman's heel with which to prick the horse's side; incitement; stimulus; the hard projection on a cock's leg; that which projects; a small mountain range projecting laterally or at right angles from a larger; the largest root of a tree; a projection like a cock's spur [Bot.]; a climbing-iron; a morbid excrescence on rye: *v.t.* to prick with spurs; to incite to a more hasty pace; to incite; to instigate; to impel; to put spurs on: *v.i.* to press forward. **on the spur of the moment,** without premeditation or preparation. **to win one's spurs,** to attain knighthood, esp. through valour; to gain distinction for the first time [Fig.]. (A.S. *spura*.)
pur-dog, *n.* the dogfish *Acanthias vulgaris*.
pur-fowl, *n.* a long-tailed Indian partridge, the cock having spurs on each leg.
purgall, *n.* *spur*-gawl, a place galled or excoriated by much using of the spur: *v.t.* to gall or wound with a spur.
purge, *n.* spurj, a plant of the genus *Euphorbia*. **spurge laurel,** the evergreen shrub *Daphne laureola*. (L. *ex-*, and *purgo*, purge.)
pur-gearing, *n.* gearing in which spur-wheels are used.
purious, *a.* *spewr*-re-us, not genuine; not proceeding from the true source or the source pretended; counterfeit; not legitimate; bastard. (L. *spurius*.)
puriously, *ad.* in a spurious manner.
puriousness, *n.* the quality of being spurious.
purling, *n.* *spur*-ling, the sparling or smelt.
purling-line, *n.* *spurl*-ing-line, the line which forms the communication between the steering-wheel and the telltale in the cabin [Naut.].
purn, *n.* spurn, the act of spurning or of rejecting disdainfully; contemptuous treatment: *v.t.* to kick or drive away as with the foot; to reject with disdain; to treat with contempt: *v.i.* to manifest disdain in rejecting anything; to make contemptuous opposition; to kick or toss up the heels. (A.S. *speornan*.)
purner, *n.* *spurn*-er, one who spurns.
purred, *a.* spurd, furnished with spurs; having shoots like spurs. **spurred rye,** rye infested with ergot.
purrer, *n.* *spur*-rer, one who uses spurs or incites.
purrey, *n.* *spu*-re, spurry.
purrier, *n.* *spu*-re-er, a spur-maker.
pur-royal, *n.* spur-*roy*-al, an English gold coin (nominally worth 15*s.*) of the 16th and early 17th cents., with on its reverse a star like the rowel of a spur.
purry, *n.* *spu*-re, any weed of the genus *Spergula*, esp. the white-flowered corn spurry, *S. arvensis*. (O.Fr. *spurrie*.)
purt, *n.* spurt, a sudden or violent ejection or gushing of a liquid substance from a tube; a jet; a short sudden effort: *v.t.* to spirt; to throw out in sudden jets: *v.i.* to gush or issue out in jets; to make a brief sudden effort, esp. in racing. (A.S. *spryttan*, cf. also Ice. *sprettr*.)
purtle, *v.t.* *spur*-tl, to spurt in a scattering manner.
pur-way, *n.* a bridle-road; a narrow path; a short connecting road.
pur-wheel, *n.* a wheel with cogs around the edge pointing from the centre.
putter, *n.* *sput*-ter, moist matter thrown out in particles; sputtering: *v.i.* to spit or to emit saliva from the mouth in small and scattered portions; to throw out moisture in scattered drops; to fly off in small particles with a crackling noise; to utter words hastily and indistinctly; to speak so rapidly as to emit saliva: *v.t.* to throw out with haste and noise; to utter indistinctly. (*spout*.)
putterer, *n.* *sput*-ter-rer, one who sputters.
putum, *n.* *spew*-tum, spittle; that which is expectorated [Med.]. (L.)
py, *n.* spy, a secret agent; a person sent into an enemy's camp to watch and report what is going on; one set to watch or one who watches the conduct of others: *v.t.* to see; to discover at a distance or in a state of concealment; to examine secretly; to explore: *v.i.* to search narrowly; to scrutinize. (O.Fr. *espier*.)
spy-boat, *n.* a boat sent to make discoveries and bring intelligence.
spy-glass, *n.* a small telescope.
spy-hole, *n.* a peep-hole.
spyism, *n.* *spy*-izm, the business or practice of spying; employment of spies.
spy-money, *n.* payment for secret intelligence.
squab, *a.* skwob, short and fat; plump; unfledged: *n.* a young pigeon; a short fat person; a kind of sofa or couch; a stuffed cushion: *ad.* striking at once: with a heavy fall: *v.i.* to fall plump; to strike at one dash or with a heavy sound; to stuff and sew through. (Scand.)
squabbish, *a.* *skwob*-bish, somewhat squabby.
squabble, *n.* *skwob*-bl, a wrangle; a brawl; a petty quarrel: *v.i.* to quarrel in a small way; to wrangle: *v.t.* to throw (type) into disorder [Print.]. (Scand.)
squabbler, *n.* skwob-bler, a noisy contentious person; a brawler. (Scand.)
squabby, *a.* *skwob*-be, thick; fat; heavy.
squab-pie, *n.* skwob-py, a thick-crusted pie of pork or mutton with apples, onions, etc. (Dial. Eng.)
squacco, *n.* *skwak*-oh (*pl.* **squaccos**), the small crested heron, *Ardea ralloides*.
squad, *n.* skwod, a small detachment [Mil.]; any small party: *v.t.* to arrange in squads; to assign to a squad. **awkward squad,** a body of recruits not fit to take their place in the regiment. **flying squad,** a small body, esp. of police, equipped and trained for taking rapid mobile action. (O.Fr. *esquadre*.)
squadron, *n.* *skwod*-ron, a division of a regiment of cavalry containing three or four troops; a fleet of warships; the Royal Air Force unit of aeroplanes with complete equipment and personnel: *v.t.* to form into squadrons. **squadron leader,** an officer in the R.A.F. equivalent in rank to a naval lieut. commander or an army major. (Fr. *esquadron*.)
squails, *n.* squaylz, a game in which disks are flicked from the edge of a table.
squalid, *a.* *skwol*-id, poverty-stricken; filthy; extremely dirty. (L. *squalidus*, stiff with dirt.)
squalidity, *n.* skwo-*lid*-e-te, squalidness.
squalidly, *ad.* *skwol*-id-le, in a squalid manner.
squalidness, *n.* the state of being squalid.
squall, *n.* skwawl, a loud scream; a harsh cry; a sudden, violent gust of wind: *v.i.* and *t.* to cry out violently. **white squall,** a sudden tropical storm unheralded by cloud or otherwise. (Swed. *skvala*.)
squaller, *n.* *skwawl*-er, a loud screamer.
squally, *a.* *skawl*-e, abounding with squalls; disturbed often with sudden, violent gusts of wind; threatening (of the weather).
squaloid, *a.* *skway*-loyd, resembling a shark; belonging to the Squalidæ, or dogfish family. (L. *squalus*, shark, Gr. *eidos*, like.)
squalor, *n.* *skwol*-or, foulness; coarseness; wretched and unkempt condition. (L. *squālor*.)
squalus, *n.* *skway*-lus, a shark. (L.)
squama, *n.* *skway*-ma (*pl.* **squamæ**), a scale or scale-like part [Bot. and Zool.]; a scaly piece of bone [Anat.]. (L.)
squamate, *a.* *skway*-mat, scaly.
squamiform, *a.* *skway*-me-form, having the form of scales.
squamigerous, *a.* skwa-*mij*-er-rus, bearing scales.
squamoid, *a.* *skway*-moyd, resembling a scale; covered with scales. (L. *squama*, and Gr. *eidos*, like.)
squamosal, *a.* skwa-*moh*-sal, pertaining to the squamous bone: *n.* the squamous bone.
squamose, *a.* *skway*-mohs, squamous.
squamous, *a.* *skway*-mus, scaly; formed by, covered with or composed of scales. **squamous bone,** the scaly part of the temporal bone.
squander, *v.t.* *skwon*-der, to spend lavishly and wastefully; to dissipate. (Origin uncertain.)
squanderer, *n.* *skwon*-der-rer, a spendthrift; a prodigal; a waster; a lavisher.
squandermania, *n.* *skwon*-der-*may*-ne-a, an irresistible urge towards reckless expenditure, esp. by a public authority [Coll.].
square, *a.* skware, having four equal sides and four right angles; at right angles to; forming a right angle; rectangular; having a frame formed with straight lines; fair; just; exactly suitable;

leaving no balance; absolute; satisfactory; converted from a unit of length to a unit of area [Math.]: *ad.* squarely. **square deal,** a fair and honest arrangement, bargain, or transaction. **square knot,** *n.* a reef-knot. **square meal,** *see* **meal. square measure,** the square of a lineal measure; the system of measuring areas. **square root,** the quantity which, multiplied by itself, produce the given quantity [Math.]. (O.Fr. *esquarre.*)

★**square,** *n.* skware, a figure having four equal sides and four right angles [Geom.]; an area of four sides, with buildings on each side; a rectangular division of a draught-board, window-pane, etc.; a mathematical instrument having one straight edge at angles to another; rule; regularity; proper proportion; a square body of troops; a hundred square feet; the product of a number multiplied by itself [Arith.]. **on the square,** honestly; fairly; belonging to the fraternity of Freemasons [Coll.].

square, *v.t.* skware, to form with four equal sides and four right angles; to reduce to a square or to right angles; to adjust; to regulate; to make even; to bribe [Slang]; to multiply a number by itself [Arith.]; *v.i.* to be at right angles with; to suit; to fit; to accord or agree. **square the circle,** to determine the exact contents of a circle in square measure; to try to do the impossible [Fig.]. **square the yards,** to place them at right angles with the mast and keel [Naut.]. **square up,** to put straight, or to rights. **square up to,** to adopt a fighting attitude.

squarehead, *n.* *skware*-hed, a Scandinavian or German living in U.S.A. or Canada [U.S.A. slang.].

squarely, *ad.* *skware*-le, in a square form or fashion; so as to form a square; fairly; honestly.

squareness, *n.* *skware*-ness, the state of being square; fairness.

square-rigged, *a.* *skware*-rigd, having the principal sails of a vessel extended by yards and suspended by the middle, and not by stays, gaffs, or boom.

square-sail, *n.* *skware*-sl, a four-sided sail extended to a yard suspended by the middle.

square-toed, *a.* *skware*-tohd, having the toes or ends square; precise; formal.

square-toes, *n.* *skware*-tohz, a precise old-fashioned person [Coll.].

squarish, *a.* *skware*-rish, nearly square.

squarrose, *a.* *skwo*-rohs, rough with hairs or scales projecting at right angles [Bot.]. (L. *squarrosus,* scurfy.)

squarrous, *a.* *skwo*-rus, squarrose; scurfy [Med.].

squarson, *n.* *squar*-son, a parson who is also the squire [Slang]. (*squire* and *parson.*)

squash, *n.* skwosh, something soft and easily crushed; something unripe or soft; a sudden fall of a heavy soft body; a shock of soft bodies; a drink of aerated water with a squashed lemon or other juicy fruit in it: *v.t.* to beat or press into pulp or a flat mass; to confound and humiliate [Coll.]: *v.i.* to compress or squeeze oneself into. (O.Fr. *esquacher.*)

squash, *n.* skwosh, a species of gourd; a pumpkin. **squash beetle, bug,** etc., garden pests infesting squashes, etc. [U.S.A.]. (Amerind. *asquash,* green, raw.)

squash-rackets, *n.* a game very similar to rackets played with a soft rubber ball.

squasher, *n.* *skwosh*-er, one who squashes; an appliance for squashing fruit.

squashy, *a.* *skwosh*-e, like a squash; muddy.

squat, *a.* skwot, sitting in a squatting position or close to the ground; cowering; short and thick: *n.* the posture of one who squats: *v.i.* to sit down upon the heels; to cower, as an animal; to settle on land without title. (O.Fr. *esquatir.*)

squatter, *n.* *skwot*-ter, one who squats; one who settles on land without title to it; in Australia, one who occupies land for sheep pasture under lease from government.

squattiness, *n.* the state of being squatty.

squatty, *a.* *skwot*-e, squat.

squaw, *n.* skwaw, the wife of an American Indian; an Indian woman. (Amerind., woman.)

squawk, *n.* skwawk, a loud harsh squeak: *v.i.* to cry loudly and harshly [Local U.S.A.].

squawman, *n.* *skwaw*-man, a white man with an American-Indian wife.

squeak, *n.* skweek, a sharp shrill sound: *v.i.* to utter a short shrill cry; to break silence or secrecy to speak: *v.t.* to utter with a squeak. **narrov** **squeak,** a narrow escape. (Scand.)

squeaker, *n.* *skweek*-er, one who utters a shar shrill sound; a young bird; a traitor or informe [Slang].

squeal, *n.* skweel, a long, shrill squeak: *v.i.* to cr with a sharp shrill voice; to sneak; to tur informer [Slang]. (Scand.)

squeamish, *a.* *skweem*-ish, nice to excess in taste fastidious or over-nice; easily made sick; sickish apt to be offended at trifling improprieties; over scrupulous. (M.E. *squaimous.*)

squeamishly, *ad.* in a squeamish manner.

squeamishness, *n.* excessive niceness; fastidious ness.

squeegee, *n.* skwee-*jee,* a strip or roller of rubbe used to remove surface wet: *v.t.* to treat with squeegee.

squeezable, *a.* *skweez*-a-bl, that may be squeezed amenable to pressure.

squeeze, *n.* skweez, pressure; compression betwee bodies; a close hug; an impression taken by squeezing with the hand instead of with a press a crush or crowd; pressure used for purposes o extortion; method of play in contract, etc., forcin opponent to discard a valuable card: *v.t.* to pres or crush between two bodies; to embrace closely to force a squeeze (in contract, etc.) by playing suit in which one's opponent is short; to oppres financially; to extort from; to cause to pass: *v.i* to force by pressing; to crowd; to pass by pressing (A.S. *cwiesan,* to crush.)

squeezer, *n.* *skweez*-er, one who or that whic squeezes; a thin playing card with identificatio marks in the opposite corners so that the hand ca be held almost closed.

squelch, *n.* skwelch, a flat heavy fall; a heavy blow *v.t.* to crush with a weight or blow: *v.i.* to make combined splashing and sucking sound in mud o liquid. (Imit.)

squib, *n.* skwib, a paper tube filled with combustib matter which, when ignited, emits a stream o sparks and then explodes with a bang; a lampoon a skit; a contemptible little fellow [Slang]: *v.* to write squibs: *v.t.* to lampoon; to satirize with squib.

squid, *n.* skwid, a cuttlefish; a calamary; a artificial bait for trolling: *v.i.* to troll with this.

squiffy, *skwif*-e, tipsy; slightly drunk [Slang].

squiggle, *v.i.* *skwig*-gl, to shake and wash a flui about the mouth with lips closed; to wriggle.

squill, *n.* skwil, the sea-onion, a bulbous plan *Urginea scilla,* which yields a substance valuable i medicine as a diuretic and expectorant; othe plants of the genus *Scilla*; the mantis shrim (Fr. *squille.*)

squillitic, *a.* squil-*lit*-ik, pertaining to squills.

squinancy-wort, *n.* *skwin*-an-se-wurt, the sma woodruff or quinsy-wort, *Asperula cynanchica.*

squinch, *n.* skwinch, an arch across the angle of square tower to carry the side of an octagon; sconce. (*sconce.*)

squint, *a.* skwint, looking obliquely; not havin the optic axes coincident; looking with suspicion *n.* strabismus; the act or habit of squinting; peep or glance; a hagioscope; an oblique opening *v.i.* to take a glance at or through; to see obliquely to have the axes of the eyes directed to differe objects; to deviate from the true line; to ru obliquely: *v.t.* to turn the eye to an obliqu position. **squint-eyed,** having eyes that squint oblique; indirect; looking obliquely or with sid glances. (Perhaps Dut. *schuinte,* slant.)

squinting, *n.* the act or habit of looking asquint.

squintingly, *ad.* with a squint.

squire, *n.* skwire, a country gentleman; the chi landowner in a country parish; a knight's atten ant; an esquire; a gallant; a justice of th peace [U.S.A.]: *v.t.* to attend as a squire; t escort as a gallant [Coll.]. (*esquire.*)

squirearchy, *n.* *skwire*-ar-ke, landed proprieto collectively, or their power in the state. (*squir* and Gr. *archo,* rule.)

squireen, *n.* skwire-*reen,* a petty squire.

squirehood, *n.* *skwire*-hood, squireship.

squireling, *n.* *skwire*-ling, a petty squire; a sma landowner.

squirely, *a.* *skwire*-le, befitting a squire.

squireship, *n.* the rank and state of a squire.
squirm, *n.* skwurm, the act of squirming : *v.t.* and *i.* to move like a worm or eel, with writhings or contortions ; to clamber
squirrel, *n. skwi*-rel, a bushy-tailed arboreal rodent of the genus *Sciurus*, of which the many species are widely distributed ; the fur of the squirrel. **grey squirrel,** the large N. American variety, *S. carolinensis*, introduced into Great Britain where it has largely exterminated the native species. **ground squirrel,** a chipmunk of the genus *Tamais*. **spiny squirrel,** a squirrel of the genus *Xerus*. (O.Fr. *escurel*.)
squirrel-monkey, *n.* a South American monkey of the genus *Chrysothrix*.
squirrel-tail, *n.* a spiked barley-like grass of the genus *Hordeum*, esp. *H. maritinum*.
squirt, *n.* skwert, an instrument for squirting ; a syringe ; a small jet : *v.t.* to eject from a narrow orifice in a stream : *v.i.* to be ejected so. (Low Ger. *swirtjen*.)
squirter, *n.* one who or that which squirts.
squirting-cucumber, *n.* a cucumber, *Ecballium elaterium*, which falls from its stalk and bursts its capsules when ripe.
stab, *n.* stab, the thrust of a pointed weapon, or the wound ; an injury given furtively or in the dark : *v.t.* to pierce with a pointed weapon ; to wound mortally with a stab ; to injure secretly or by malicious falsehood : *v.i.* to give a stab ; to give a mortal wound. **stab in the back,** an injury inflicted by foul play or treachery. (Swed. *stabbe*, a stump.)
Stabat Mater, *n. stah*-bat *mah*-ter, an old hymn on the Crucifixion beginning with these words ; music for this. (L., the Mother stood.)
stabber, *n. stab*-ber, one who stabs ; an awl : a marline-spike.
stability, *n.* sta-*bil*-e-te, stableness ; firmness ; steadiness, both physical and moral ; the dynamic condition by which a body retains its position, shape, or motion. (Fr. *stabilité*.)
stabilization, *n.* stay-be-ly-*zay*-shon, the act or process of stabilizing ; the fixing of the value of a currency in terms of gold with the object of maintaining purchasing power [Econ.].
stabilize, *v.t. stay*-be-lize, to make stable ; to effect stabilization [Econ.].
stabilizer, *n. stay*-be-ly-zer, a device for obtaining stability, as in ships and aeroplanes ; a substance preventing deterioration or spontaneous combustion in explosives.
stable, *a. stay*-bl, firmly established ; steady of purpose ; having no tendency to change [Chem.] ; fixed ; firm ; durable. (L. *sto*, stand.)
stable, *n. stay*-bl, a building for horses to lodge in ; the racehorses trained at or belonging to a particular stable : *v.t.* to put or keep in a stable : *v.i.* to dwell or lodge in a stable. **stable companion,** a horse of the same stable [Racing] ; a member of the same set, coterie, school, etc. [Fig.]. (O.Fr. *estable*.)
stableboy, *n. stay*-bl-boy, a man or lad who works in a stable.
stableman, *n. stay*-bl-m'n, one who attends to the stable and the animals therein.
stableness, *n.* the state of being stable ; stability.
stabling, *n. stay*-bling, the act of putting into a stable ; stable accommodation.
stablish, *v.t. stab*-lish, to establish.
stably, *ad. stay*-ble, firmly.
staccato, *ad.* stak-*kah*-toh, disconnectedly; with each note distinctly sounded [Mus.]. (It., detached.)
stack, *n.* stak, a large pile of hay, grain, or straw, sometimes thatched ; a conical pile ; a number of funnels or chimneys standing together ; a funnel or chimney ; a towering rock-pillar, esp. near marine cliffs [Geol.] : *v.t.* to lay in a conical or other pile ; to pile rifles. (Ice. *stakkr*.)
stacker, *n. stak*-er, one who or that which stacks ; a machine or device for stacking hay, straw, timber, etc.
stack-stand, *n.* a stage on which to pile a stack.
stackyard, *n. stak*-yard, a yard for stacks of hay.
stacte, *n. stak*-te, an odoriferous spice formerly used by the Jews in the preparation of incense. (Gr. *stazo*, drop.)
stactometer, *n.* stak-*tom*-e-ter, a tube for measuring liquids in drops.

stadda, *n. stad*-dah, a double-bladed saw for cutting tooth-combs.
staddle, *n. stad*-dl, anything which serves for support ; a staff ; a crutch ; a stack-stand ; a small tree left standing : *v.t.* to leave staddles when a wood is cut. (Dial. Eng.)
staddle-roof, *n.* the roof or covering of a stack.
stadium, *n. stay*-de-um, an ancient measure of diverse lengths, in Greece about 606 ft. ; an oblong area or course for foot-races and other athletic or sporting contests ; a running track ; a stage or period in development [Biol.], or in a disease [Med.]. (Gr. *stadion*.)
Stadtholder, *n. stat*-hohl-der, formerly the chief magistrate of the United Provinces of Holland ; the governor or lieutenant-governor of a province. (Dut.)
stadtholderate, *n. stat*-hohl-der-rat, the jurisdiction of a stadtholder.
stadtholdership, *n.* the office of stadtholder.
staff, *n.* stahf (*pl.* **staffs** or **staves**), a stick carried in the hand for support or defence ; a support ; a club ; a stick, pole, or handle ; the five lines and the spaces on which music is written ; an ensign of authority ; a pole, etc., for displaying a flag or for carrying as an emblem of office or authority ; a surveyor's cross-staff ; a body of skilled officers attached to an army or to its commander [Mil.] ; the executive and clerical assistants of a business concern, newspaper, institution, etc., collectively ; a body of officials connected with a department ; the group of persons engaged in the carrying on of any enterprise. **staff work,** the business of organization or management. (A.S. *staef*.)
staff-officer, *n.* an officer on a staff [Mil.].
stag, *n.* stag, the male red deer ; the male of the hind ; a colt ; an animal castrated when mature ; a man attending a function unaccompanied by a woman [Coll.] ; a vendor of new securities quoted at a premium before allotment [Stock Exch.] : *v.i.* to act as a stag [Stock Exch.]. (Ice. *staggr*.)
stag-beetle, *n.* the beetle *Lucanus cervus*, of which the male has mandibles like stag's horns.
★**stage,** *n.* staje, an elevated floor or platform, as for the exhibition of something to public view ; the floor of a theatre on which the actors perform ; a temporary platform for workmen ; the theatre ; theatrical representations ; the theatrical profession ; the small platform on a microscope-stand on which the object to be examined is placed ; place of action ; a place of rest, or a stopping-place, on a journey, also the distance between such places ; a single step ; degree of progression, either in increase or decrease ; a stage-coach : *v.t.* to put on the stage ; to present dramatically. **by easy stages,** with frequent breaks ; little by little. (Fr. *étage*.)
stage-coach, *n.* a coach running regularly and by stages for the conveyance of passengers.
stagecraft, *n. staje*-krahft, practical knowledge of dramatic effect ; the art of writing or of producing plays.
stage-driver, *n.* the driver of a stage-coach.
stage-fright, *n.* nervousness at appearing before an audience.
stage-manage, *v.t.* to supervise the setting, etc. (as distinct from the acting), of a play ; to arrange with an eye to dramatic effect.
stage-play, *n.* a theatrical entertainment.
stager, *n. staje*-er, one who has long acted on the stage of life ; a person of long experience ; a horse used in a stage-coach.
stagery, *n. staje*-er-re, scenic exhibition ; exhibition on the stage ; stage effects, properties, etc.
stage-struck, *a.* smitten with a desire to go on the stage.
stag-evil, *n. stag*-ee-vil, a kind of lockjaw in horses.
stage-whisper, *n.* a whisper meant to be heard by others ; an aside.
staggard, *n. stag*-gard, a stag of four years of age.
stagger, *n. stag*-ger, an act of staggering ; a staggering movement ; the relative displacement in the direction of the chord of the wings of a biplane [Av.] : *pl.* a disease of horses, etc., attended with giddiness and reeling : *v.i.* to reel ; to be unsteady in standing or walking ; to begin to give way ; to hesitate : *v.t.* to cause to reel ; to make to hesitate ; to shock ; to arrange in alternate and equally spaced positions on either side of a median line ; to

arrange so as to overlap or alternate in time, as working hours, holidays, etc. (Ice. *stakra.*)
staggerbush, *n.* *stag*-ger-bush, an American plant with nodding white flowers, poisonous to cattle.
staggered, *a.* *stag*-gerd, of the planes of an aeroplane, when the upper plane is in advance of the lower plane [Av.]; arranged to occur at overlapping times (of working hours, holidays, etc.).
staggeringly, *ad.* *stag*-ger-ring-le, with a reeling gait; with hesitation.
staggerwort, *n.* *stag*-ger-wurt, ragwort.
staggery, *a.* *stag*-ger-re, shaky; apt to stagger.
staghorn, *n.* *stag*-hawrn, the material of stags' horns; a large fern of the genus *Platycerium.*
staghound, *n.* *stag*-hound, the large and powerful dog formerly kept for stag-hunting; the buck-hound.
stagily, *ad.* *stay*-je-le, in a stagy manner.
staginess, *n.* *stay*-je-ness, theatricality.
staging, *n.* *stay*-jing, a structure of posts and boards for support; a temporary scaffolding; the running of, or journeying in, stage-coaches; the art or act of putting on the stage.
Stagirite, *n.* *staj*-e-rite, an appellation given to the Greek philosopher Aristotle (*d.* 322 B.C.) because born at Stagyra, in Macedonia.
stagnancy, *n.* *stag*-nan-se, state of being stagnant.
stagnant, *a.* *stag*-nant, not flowing; not running in a current or stream; motionless; dull; not brisk. (L. *stagnum,* a pool of standing water.)
stagnantly, *ad.* *stag*-nant-le, in a stagnant manner.
stagnate, *v.i.* *stag*-nate, to cease to flow; to be motionless; to cease to move; to cease to be brisk and active; to become dull.
stagnation, *n.* stag-*nay*-shon, the act of stagnating; the state of being stagnant; the cessation of action or of brisk action; the state of being dull.
stagnicolous, *a.* stag-*nik*-o-lus, living in stagnant water [Zool.].
stag-party, *n.* a social gathering for men only [Slang].
stagy, *a.* *stay*-je, conventionally theatrical; melodramatic; unreal.
staid, stade, *p.* and *pp.* of *stay.*
staid, *a.* stade, grave; sober; steady.
staidly, *ad.* *stade*-le, in a staid manner.
staidness, *n.* *stade*-ness, the quality of being staid.
stain, *n.* stane, discoloration; a spot of a colour different from the ground; taint of guilt; reproach; cause of reproach; a dye (esp. for use in microscopy): *v.t.* to discolour or spot with foreign matter; to tinge; to impress with figures of a different colour from the ground; to soil; to mark with guilt or infamy. (M.E. *steinen.*)
stained, *a.* staned, discoloured; tarnished. **stained glass,** glass coloured or stained by certain metallic pigments.
stainer, *n.* *stane*-er, one who stains, blots, or tarnishes; a dyer. **painter-stainer,** former designation of any worker, artistic or decorative, in paint, later restricted to heraldic craftsmen.
stainless, *a.* *stane*-less, that cannot be stained; free from stains; free from sin. **stainless steel,** an alloy of steel rendered immune to rusting and corrosion by the addition of chromium.
stair, *n.* stare, one of a series of steps to ascend by. **flight of stairs,** a series of steps from one landing to another. **below stairs,** in or pertaining to the servants' quarters. (A.S. *stigan,* to ascend.)
stair-carpet, *n.* a carpet to cover a stair.
staircase, *n.* *stare*-kace, a flight of stairs with their framework. **moving staircase,** an escalator.
stair-rod, *n.* *stare*-rod, a rod of metal or wood for keeping a stair-carpet in its place.
stairway, *n.* *stare*-way, a staircase.
staithe, *n.* stathe, a stage for loading or unloading coals. (A.S. *stæth,* shore.)
stake, *n.* stake, a stick sharpened at one end and set, or to be set, in the ground; a palisade; the timber or other post to which a martyr was bound when he was to be burned; martyrdom; an amount wagered for; a deposit held until the completion of a contract; a share; the state of being pledged as a wager; a money prize for a race; a small anvil; (*pl.*) race run for a money prize: *v.t.* to fasten, support, or defend with stakes; to mark the limits by stakes; to wager; to pledge; to pierce with a stake. (A.S. *staca.*)
stake-boat, *n.* a stationary boat serving as starting-point or a mark in boat-races.
stake-holder, *n.* one who holds the stakes or with whom the bets are deposited when a wager is laid.
stake-net, *n.* a fishing-net stretched on stakes in estuaries, etc.
stalactic, *a.* sta-*lak*-tik, of the nature or in the form of a stalactite.
stalactiform, *a.* sta-*lak*-te-form, like a stalactite.
stalactite, *n.* *stal*-ak-tite *or* sta-*lak*-tite, a pendent cone of carbonate of lime, hanging like an icicle from the roof of a cavern, and formed by the percolation of water through the rock above. (Gr. *stalaktos,* dripping.)
stalactitic, *a.* *stal*-ak-*tit*-ik, of the form of a stalactite.
Stalag, *n.* *shtah*-lag, a German prisoner-of-war camp for N.C.O.s and men. (Ger.)
stalagmite, *n.* *stal*-ag-mite *or* sta-*lag*-mite, an erect cone of carbonate of lime formed by water dripping on to the floors of caverns from a stalactite above. (Gr. *stalagmos,* dripping.)
stalagmitic, *a.* *stal*-ag-*mit*-ik, having the form of a stalagmite.
stalder, *n.* *stawl*-der, a frame to set casks on.
stale, *a.* stale, too long kept; vapid or tasteless from age; not new; having lost its spirit or vigour; worn out by use; trite; out of condition, esp. through over-training [Sport]: *n.* urine of horses and cattle: *v.t.* to make vapid or useless; to wear out: *v.i.* to discharge urine, as a horse. (Scand.)
stale, *n.* *stale,* a decoy-bird; a lure [Fig.]. **common stale,** a prostitute. (O.Teut.)
stalely, *ad.* *stale*-le, in a stale manner.
stalemate, *n.* *stale*-mate, in chess, a drawn position in which one side's unchecked king being his only piece able to move cannot do so without placing himself in check; hence, an inconclusive result, a draw: *v.t.* to give stalemate to; to place in a position of deadlock; to bring to a standstill. (*stale* and *mate.*)
staleness, *n.* *stale*-ness, the state of being stale; vapidness; triteness.
stalk, *n.* stawk, the stem or main axis of a plant; the peduncle of a flower; the stem of a quill; a tall chimney; anything similar to a stalk as a seta in mosses or the peduncle in barnacles, etc. (A.S. *stæla.*)
stalk, *n.* stawk, a stately walk; the act of stalking game: *v.i.* to walk with pompous or stately steps; to walk behind a stalking-horse or behind a screen: *v.t.* to approach warily and under cover so as to kill (esp. of deer, etc.). (A.S. *stealcian.*)
stalked, *a.* stawkt, having a stalk.
stalker, *n.* *stawk*-er, one who stalks; one who stalks game; a kind of fishing-net.
stalking, *n.* *stawk*-ing, the act of stealing secretly upon the game, as in deerstalking.
stalking-horse, *n.* *stawk*-ing-horse, a horse, real or factitious, behind which a sportsman conceals himself from the sight of the game which he intends to kill; a mask; a pretence.
stalkless, *a.* *stawk*-less, having no stalk.
stalky, *a.* *stawk*-e, hard as a stalk; resembling a stalk.
stall, *n.* stawl, a stand or division of a stable where a horse or an ox is kept and fed; a stable; a place for cattle; a bench on which anything is exposed for sale; a market shed; a finger-stall; a seat of the clergy or choristers in the choir of a cathedral or collegiate church; a canonry or prebend; a reserved seat in a theatre; the condition obtaining when the speed of an aeroplane is below that at which it can be controlled [Av.]: *v.t.* to put into or keep in a stall; to instal; to fix, as in mire; to put one's machine into a stall [Av.]: *v.i.* to dwell; to kennel; to be fixed, as in mire; to be tired of eating, as cattle; to lose speed; to come to a standstill; to get into a stall [Av.]. (A.S *steall,* a standing-place.)
stallage, *n.* *stawl*-aj, the right of erecting stalls in fairs; the rent for this.
stall-fed, *a.* fattened in a stall on dry fodder.
stallion, *n.* *stal*-yon, a male horse, not castrated (O.Fr. *estalon.*)
stalwart, *a.* *stawl*-wert, brave; bold; redoubted; strong; sturdy: *n.* a stalwart person; a resolute partisan. (A.S. *stælwyrthe.*)

stalwartly, *ad.* *stawl*-wert-le, in a stalwart manner.
stalwartness, *n.* the state of being stalwart.
stamen, *n.* *stay*-men, the male pollen-bearing organ of a flowering plant. (L., the warp in an upright loom.)
stamina, *n.* *stam*-e-na, innate vigour; strength; power of endurance. (L., as *stamen.*)
staminal, *a.* *stam*-e-nal, pertaining to or consisting of stamens; pertaining to a person's stamina.
staminate, *a.* *stam*-e-nat, furnished with stamens but not with pistils.
stamineous, *a.* sta-*min*-e-us, consisting of stamens; attached to the stamen.
staminiferous, *a.* *stam*-e-*nif*-er-rus, bearing stamens. (L. *stamen,* and *fero,* bear.)
staminode, *n.* *stam*-e-node, an aborted stamen.
stammel, *n.* *stam*-mel, a kind of red colour; a rough woollen cloth dyed red. (O.Fr. *estamine.*)
stammer, *n.* *stam*-mer, a stutter: *v.i.* to stutter; to hesitate or falter in speaking: *v.t.* to utter with hesitation. (A.S. *stamor.*)
stammerer, *n.* *stam*-mer-rer, one who stammers.
stammering, *a.* *stam*-mer-ring, apt to stammer; *n.* the act of stopping or hesitating in speaking; impediment in speech.
stammeringly, *ad.* *stam*-mer-ring-le, with stops or hesitation in speaking.
stamp, *v.t.* stamp, to strike with the sole of the foot by thrusting it downward; to impress with some mark; to impress; to imprint; to fix a mark by impressing it; to coin; to crush ore; to form; to affix a stamp to; to pound: *v.i.* to strike the foot forcibly downward. **stamp out,** to crush or pulverize with the feet; to extinguish; to extirpate. (A.S. *stempen.*)
★**stamp,** *n.* stamp, the act of stamping; any instrument for making impressions or cutting out a pattern; a mark imprinted; an impression; a thing stamped; a government mark on dutiable articles showing that the duty is paid; a label affixed to a letter, etc., showing that the postage is paid; current value; make; cast; form; character; a kind of pestle used for pounding or beating [Metal.].
stamp-album, *n.* a book for the keeping and classification of postage-stamp collections.
stamp-collector, *n.* a collector or receiver of stamp duties; a collector of postage stamps, used or unused; a philatelist.
stamp-duty, *n.* a tax imposed on certain legal instruments to give them validity, the evidence of payment being a stamp on the document.
stampede, *n.* stam-*peed,* a sudden panic seizing a herd of animals, under which they take flight; flight due to panic: *v.i.* to start off in a panic: *v.t.* to cause to start off in a panic. (Sp.)
stamper, *n.* *stamp*-er, one who stamps; an instrument for stamping.
stamp-machine, *n.* an automatic slot-machine delivering stamps on the insertion of a coin.
stamp-mill, *n.* a machine for crushing ore.
stance, *n.* stance, station; attitude in standing; position preparatory to making a stroke [Golf].
stanch, *a.* stahnsh, staunch, trustworthy; sound; firm; firm in principle; steady; loyal: *v.t.* to stop the flowing of, as blood: *v.i.* to stop, as blood; to cease to flow. (O.Fr. *estancher,* stanch.)
stancher, *n.* *stahnsh*-er, one who or that which stops the flowing of blood.
stanchion, *n.* *stahn*-shon, a prop or support of wood or metal; a bar or device to prevent the escape of cattle: *v.t.* to provide with or secure by stanchions. (O.Fr. *estanchon.*)
stanchless, *a.* *stahnsh*-less, that cannot be stanched.
stanchness, *n.* *stahnsh*-ness, soundness; firmness in principle; loyalty; closeness of adherence.
stand, *v.i.* stand, to be upon the feet; to be erect; not to be overthrown; to be situated; to remain upright; to become erect; to stop; to continue; to be fixed; to maintain a position; to be placed; to contest; to hold a course at sea; to have a direction; to be a candidate; to persist; to abide; to stagnate: *v.t.* to endure; to sustain; to bear; to abide by; to pay for. **stand a chance,** to have a chance. **stand against,** to oppose. **stand by,** to be present; to defend; to support; to await further orders. **stand fast,** to be fixed. **stand fire,** to receive an enemy's fire without giving way. **stand for,** to offer as a candidate; to side with; to represent; to put up with [Coll.] **stand in,** to cost. **stand off,** to keep at a distance; not to comply; to hold aloof; to put temporarily out of work; to direct the course from land [Naut.]; cessation from work. **stand on,** to sail towards the land [Naut.]. **stand one's ground,** to maintain one's position. **stand out,** to project; to continue to resist. **stand over,** to be left for future treatment or consideration. **stand pat,** to be content with one's hand as dealt [Poker, etc.]; to refuse to change in opinion, policy, etc. [Fig.]. **stand to,** to persevere; to adhere; not to yield; to remain equipped and in readiness [Mil.]. **stand treat,** to bear the expense (of a drink, entertainment, etc.). **stand under,** to undergo. **stand up for,** to defend. **stand upon,** to insist. *p.* and *pp.* **stood.** (A.S. *standan.*)
stand, *n.* stand, a point beyond which one does not proceed; a stop; a halt; a place or post where one stands; a station; a raised station for spectators; the act of opposing; a frame, shelf, etc., on which articles are placed or vessels and utensils are laid; a small table; a platform. **be at a stand,** to stop on account of some doubt or difficulty; to be perplexed; to hesitate. **stand of arms,** a rifle complete with ammunition and accessories for one man [Mil.].
standard, *n.* *stand*-ard, that which is authoritatively established as a rule; that which is established by public opinion or custom; criterion; test; rule; a grade of classification, esp. in elementary schools; a banner; a flag, esp. the colours carried by certain cavalry regiments; the proportion of weight of fine metal or alloy in coinage, established by authority; an upright support; a fruit-tree not trained to a wall but left to grow naturally; a tree or shrub the foliage, etc. of which is grown at the top of a trunk-like stem [Hort.]; a vexillum [Bot.]; an inverted knee placed upon the deck instead of beneath it [Ship-building]: *a.* fixed in value by some standard. **Royal Standard,** the personal banner of the sovereign, used only to indicate his actual presence. **standard of living,** *see* **living. standard time,** *see* **time.** (O.Fr. *estandard.*)
standard-bearer, *n.* one who bears the standard; a leading advocate of some cause.
standardization, *n.* the act of standardizing; reduction to a common standard or pattern.
standardize, *v.t.* *stand*-ard-ize, to make regular; to make conformable to a standard; to bring up to standard.
standard-lamp, *n.* *stand*-ard-lamp, a lamp on a tall movable stand; a lamp whose luminous intensity is known in terms of the international standard.
stand-by, *n.* *stand*-by, one who or that which can be relied upon in an emergency; something kept ready for immediate use.
standel, *n.* *stan*-del, an immature timber tree.
stander, *n.* *stand*-er, one who stands.
stander-by, *n.* *stand*-er-by, one who stands near or is present; a mere spectator; a bystander.
stand-in, *n.* one who takes the place of a leading actor during adjustment of camera, lights, etc. [Cine.].
standing, *a.* *stand*-ing, established; permanent; not liable to fade or vanish; stagnant; fixed; not cut down: *n.* continuance; duration; possession of an office, character, or place; station; power to stand; rank; condition in society. **standing army,** a permanent military force of paid officers and men. **standing orders,** permanent regulations. **standing rigging,** the ropes and chains sustaining the masts and remaining fixed in position [Naut.]. **standing room,** accommodation only for standing spectators, passengers, etc. **standing type,** type kept set in readiness for printing from or stereotyping, etc. [Print.].
standing-stones, *n.pl.* prehistoric unhewn stones, standing singly or in groups.
standish, *n.* *stand*-ish, a tray for pen and ink; an inkstand.
stand-offish, *a.* stand-*off*-ish, reserved; not companionable.
stand-pipe, *n.* a pipe fixed or for fixing vertically, esp. one for connection with a water-main and fitted with a tap or nozzle.
standpoint, *n.* *stand*-poynt, point of view.
standstill, *n.* *stand*-stil, a stop; a standing without

moving either way; a state of rest or inaction. **standstill agreement,** an agreement to maintain temporarily the *status quo.*
stand-up, *a. stand*-up, in an erect position; valiantly contested (of a fight); taken standing (of a meal, etc.).
stang, *n.* stang, a pole; a long bar; a cart shaft. **ride the stang,** to be carried on a pole on men's shoulders, in derision. (A.S. *steng.*)
stanhope, *n. stan*-hope *or stan*-up, a light two-wheeled uncovered carriage, first built for Hon. Fitzroy Stanhope about 1815. **Stanhope lens,** a double-convex lens in which the curves differ. **Stanhope press,** a printing press. (Both invented by 3rd earl Stanhope, *d.* 1816.)
staniel, *n. stan*-yel, the kestrel.
stank, stank, *p.* of *stink.*
stank-hen. *n. stank*-hen, the moorhen.
stannary, *a. stan*-na-re, relating to tin mines or tin works: *n.* a tin mine or works. **stannary courts,** former courts (abolished 1896) for the administration of justice among the miners of Devon and Cornwall. (L. *stannum,* tin.)
stannate, *n. stan*-nat, a salt of stannic acid.
stannic, *a. stan*-nik, pertaining to, containing, or procured from tin.
stanniferous, *a.* stan-*nif*-er-rus, containing or affording tin. (L. *stannum,* and *fero,* bear.)
stannine, *n. stan*-in, native sulphide of tin; a brittle metal composed of tin, sulphur, copper, and iron.
stannous, *a. stan*-us, pertaining to tin; containing tin in combination [Chem.].
stanza, *n. stan*-za, a number of lines or verses connected with each other, and ending in a full point or pause; a part of a poem containing every variation of measure in the poem. (It.)
stanzaic, *a.* stan-*zay*-ik, consisting of stanzas.
stapedial, *a.* sta-*pee*-de-al, pertaining to the stapes.
stapes, *n. stay*-peez, the innermost of the bones of the middle ear, so called from its stirrup-like shape [Anat.]. (L., a stirrup.)
staphyle, *n. staf*-e-le, the uvula [Anat.]. (Gr., a bunch of grapes.)
staphyline, *a. staf*-e-line, having the form of a bunch of grapes [Min.]; pertaining to the uvula [Anat.]. (Gr. *staphyle.*)
staphylitis, *n.* staf-e-*ly*-tis, inflammation of the uvula [Med.].
staphyloma, *n. staf*-e-*loh*-ma, a protrusion on the anterior surface of the eyeball.
staphylorraphy, *n.* staf-e-*lo*-ra-fe, the operation of uniting a cleft palate. (Gr. *staphyle,* and *rapto,* sew.)
staphylotomy, *n.* staf-e-*lot*-o-me, amputation of the staphyle or uvula; the operation of removing a staphyloma.
staple, *n. stay*-pl, a settled mart or market; an emporium; a principal commodity or production of a country or district; the principal element or topic; raw material; the thread or pile of wool, cotton, or flax; quality; a loop of iron to hold a hook, pin, or padlock; a fine bent wire used in wire-stitching: *a.* settled; established in commerce; regularly produced for market; chief: *v.t.* to sort the different staples of, as wool. **staple of land,** the particular nature and quality of land. (A.S. *stapul.*)
stapled, *a. stay*-pld, having a staple or fibre.
stapler, *n. stay*-pler, a dealer in staple commodities; a woolstapler; a machine for stapling or wire-stitching.
★**star,** *n.* star, a celestial body, especially one that is self-luminous and apparently fixed; such a body as affecting one's destiny; the figure or anything with the figure of a star; a radiated mark in printing or writing, an asterisk (*); a badge of an order of knighthood; a person of brilliant abilities, specially in acting; a patch of white on a horse's forehead: *v.t.* to set or adorn with stars; to put an asterisk against; to single out: *v.i.* to shine or attract attention, as a star; to take the leading part. **Star Chamber,** a civil and criminal court of jurisdiction abolished in the reign of Charles the First, notorious for its despotism and injustice, said to be so called from the stars painted on the ceiling of the apartment in which it was held. **Star of Bethlehem,** a bulbous plant of the genus *Ornithogalum.* **Star of Jerusalem,** salsify. **Stars and Stripes,** the national flag of the United States of America. **star turn,** the chief performer, or principal item, in an entertainment, etc. (A.S. *steorra.*)
star-apple, *n. star*-ap-pl, the tropical American tree, *Chrysophyllum cainto,* or its fruit which, when cut across, has a star-like appearance.
star-blind, *a. star*-blynd, partially blind.
starboard, *n. star*-bord, the right-hand side of a ship as one looks forward: *a.* pertaining to, being or lying on the right side [Naut.]. (*steer* and *board,* the steersman formerly standing on the right to steer.)
starch, *n.* starch, a carbohydrate occurring in grains in the cellular tissue of plants, and used to stiffen linen and other cloth: *v.t.* to stiffen with starch: *a.* stiff; precise; rigid. (A.S. *stearc,* strong.)
starchedness, *n. starcht*-ness, stiffness in manners; primness; formality.
starcher, *n. starch*-er, one who starches, or whose occupation is to starch.
starch-hyacinth, *n.* the grape-hyacinth, *Muscari racemosum,* which has a starch-like smell.
starchiness, *n.* the state of being starchy.
starchly, *ad. starch*-le, in a starchy manner.
starchness, *n. starch*-ness, stiffness of manner.
starchy, *a. starch*-e, consisting of starch; stiff; precise.
stardom, *n. star*-dom, the status, or the milieu of a stage or cinema star; such stars collectively.
stare, *n.* stare, the starling. (A.S.)
stare, *n.* stare, a fixed look with eyes wide open: *v.i.* to gaze; to look with fixed eyes wide open, as in wonder, surprise, stupidity, horror, fright, eagerness, or impudence; to stand out; to be prominent: *v.t.* to affect by staring. **stare in the face,** to be undeniably evident. (A.S. *starian.*)
starer, *n. stare*-rer, one who stares or gazes.
starfinch, *n. star*-finch, the redstart.
starfish, *n. star*-fish, a flat echinoderm in the form of a star with five or more rays.
stargazer, *n. star*-gaze-er, an astronomer (in derision); popular name of many marine fishes with eyes on the top of the head.
stargazing, *n. star*-gaze-ing, the act or practice of observing the stars with attention; astrology; occupation with trifling interests to the neglect of serious and urgent ones.
staringly, *ad. stare*-ring-le, in a staring manner; with a fixed look.
star-jelly, *n. star*-jel-le, a cryptogamous plant, the alga *Nostoc commune.*
stark, *a.* stark, stiff; strong; gross; absolute: *ad.* in a stark manner; wholly; entirely; absolutely (esp. in *stark naked*). (A.S. *stearc.*)
starkly, *ad. stark*-le, in a stark manner; firmly.
starkness, *n.* the state of being stark; stiffness; sternness; uncovered condition.
starless, *a. star*-less, with no stars visible.
starlight, *n. star*-lite, the light proceeding from the stars: *a.* lighted by the stars, or by the stars only.
starlike, *a.* resembling a star; bright; shining.
starling, *n. star*-ling, a passerine bird of the genus *Sturnus*; in America, a bird of the family Icteridæ. (A.S. *stærlinc.*)
starling, *n. star*-ling, a defence of piles driven round the piers of a bridge. (Perhaps A.S. *stathol,* base, foundation.)
starlit, *a. star*-lit, lighted by stars.
star-nose, *n. star*-nohz, a North American insectivore of the genus *Condylura,* allied to the mole, with cartilaginous rays on the nose disposed like a star.
starost, *n.* sta-*rost,* in Tsarist Russia, a village headman; in the ancient kingdom of Poland, an ennobled landowner.
starred, *a.* stard, studded with stars; marked with or bearing a star; influenced in fortune by the stars.
starriness, *n.* the quality of being starry.
starry, *a. star*-re, abounding or adorned with stars; consisting of, shining like, or resembling stars.
star-shell, *n. star*-shel, a projectile bursting in flight and shedding a bright light around.
star-spangled, *a. star*-spangld, strewn or covered with stars. **star-spangled banner,** the Stars and Stripes.
starstone, *n. star*-stone, variety of sapphire showing a six-rayed star; any asteriated stone.
★**start,** *n.* start, a sudden motion or twitch from alarm; a spring; excitement; a sally; a sudden fit; a

quick spring; a darting; act of setting out; a beginning; a starting-place; the amount of lead given to a competitor [Sport]: *v.i.* to move suddenly, as if by a twitch or an involuntary shrinking; to move, as with a spring or leap; to shrink; to wince; to move suddenly aside; to move out of place; to warp or become loose; to set out; to commence: *v.t.* to alarm; to startle; to rouse suddenly from concealment; to raise; to invent; to move suddenly from its place; to empty (a cask) [Naut.]. **get the start,** to begin before another. **starting price,** the last state of the odds before the race begins. (M.E. *staerten.*)

startability, *n. start*-a-*bil*-e-te, the capacity, esp. of a motor, to be brought quickly and efficiently into action from a state of rest.

starter, *n. start*-er, one who or that which starts; a dog that rouses game. **self-starter,** *see under* **self-.**

star-thistle, *n. star*-this-sl, a plant of the genus *Centaurea*; knapweed.

starting-post, *n.* a barrier or place from which competitors begin a race.

startish, *a. start*-ish, apt to start or wince; skittish.

startle, *n.* startl, a sudden shock occasioned by unexpected alarm: *v.t.* to alarm; to frighten; to surprise.

startling, *a. start*-ling, suddenly impressing with fear or surprise; very surprising.

startlingly, *ad. start*-ling-le, in a startling manner.

starvation, *n.* star-*vay*-shon, act of starving, or state of being starved; death from hunger.

starve, *v.i.* starv, to perish or die of cold or hunger; to suffer extreme hunger or want: *v.t.* to kill with hunger or cold; to subdue by famine; to keep from food; to destroy by want. (A.S. *steorfan.*)

starveling, *a. starv*-ling, hungry; lean; pining with want: *n.* an animal or plant thin and weak from want of nutriment.

starwort, *n. star*-wurt, popular name of various plants of the genera *Aster* and *Stellaria.* **water starwort,** *Callitriche verna.*

stasis, *n. stay*-sis, stagnation of a fluid, esp. [Med.] of the blood-current. (Gr., standing.)

statable, *a. state*-a-bl, that can be stated.

statant, *a. stay*-tant, standing still with all the feet on the ground [Her.].

state, *a.* state, pertaining to the state; ceremonial: *n.* condition; rank; quality; pomp; dignity; grandeur; a commonwealth or body politic; the whole body of people united under one government; civil community or government; legislative body; an impression from an engraved plate taken at some particular stage: *v.t.* to express the particulars of; to set down in detail and with formality; to narrate explicitly. **State's evidence,** the American equivalent of "King's evidence." (*estate.*)

state-carriage, -coach, *n.* a large and luxurious vehicle for occasions of state.

statecraft, *n. state*-krahft, statesmanship; the art of politics.

state-criminal, *n.* an offender against the state; one guilty of treason.

stated, *a. state*-ed, settled; established; regular; related as a fact.

statedly, *ad. state*-ed-le, at stated times.

statehood, *n. state*-hood, the status of a political state; the condition of being a citizen of a state.

State-house, *n.* the house of legislature of a state, esp. one of the United States of America.

stateless, *a. state*-less, without pomp; without a political community; in a condition of having no nationality; not owned as a citizen by any state.

statelily, *ad. state*-le-le, in a stately manner.

stateliness, *n. state*-le-ness, loftiness of mien or manner; majestic appearance; dignity.

stately, *a. state*-le, characterized by dignity and loftiness; magnificent; elevated in sentiment.

★**statement,** *n. state*-ment, the act of stating; that which is stated; a formal account of or declaration concerning facts [Comm.]; an announcement or recital.

state-monger, *n.* one posing as versed in politics; one who dabbles in state affairs.

state-paper, *n.* a document relating to the political interests or government of a state.

state-prisoner, *n.* one in confinement for political offences.

stater, *n. stay*-ter, an ancient Greek coin in silver and gold, of varying values.

state-room, *n.* a magnificent reception room in a palace or great house; a private cabin on board ship; a separate sleeping apartment in a railway train [U.S.A.].

States-General, *n.pl.* in pre-Revolutionary France, the assembly of the three legislative orders of the kingdom.

statesman, *n. states*-man, a man versed in the arts of government; one skilled in public affairs; a small landholder (esp. in Cumberland and Westmorland).

statesmanlike, *a.* having the qualities of a statesman or good statesmanship.

statesmanship, *n.* the qualification or employments of a statesman.

state-trial, *n.* a trial of persons prosecuted by the state for political offences.

static, *a. stat*-ik, pertaining to bodies at rest or in equilibrium; acting with the effect of mere weight or pressure; not moving; quiescent; stable; caused by statics [Wire.].

statically, *ad. stat*-e-ka-le, in a static manner.

Statice, *n. stat*-e-see, the genus of plants which comprises the sea-lavenders.

statics, *n. stat*-iks, that branch of mechanics which treats of the forces which keep bodies at rest or in equilibrium: *n.pl.* atmospherics; any electrical discharge audible on a receiver [Wire.]. (Gr. *statike,* stopping.)

★**station,** *n. stay*-shon, the spot or place where a person or thing stands; post assigned; office; situation; position; place assigned for the rendezvous of troops; a naval, military, or police headquarters; employment; occupation; rank; condition of life; a regular stopping-place for railway trains, a starting-place for a line of motor-coaches, a landing-ground on an air-route; an Australian stock-farm: *v.t.* to place; to appoint to the occupation of a place, post, or office **Stations of the Cross,** the series of representations of the fourteen incidents of the Passion displayed in or near churches and visited successively for devotional exercises. (Fr. *station.*)

stational, *a. stay*-shon-al, pertaining to a station.

stationariness, *n.* state of being stationary.

stationary, *a. stay*-shon-a-re, fixed; not moving, progressively or regressively; not appearing to move; not advancing; not improving **stationary engine,** a steam-engine in a fixed position.

stationer, *n. stay*-shon-er, one who sells paper, pens, and other articles for writing.

stationery, *n. stay*-shon-er-re, articles sold by stationers; writing materials and accessories.

station-master, *n.* a railway official in charge of a railway station.

statist, *n. stat*-ist, a statistician; formerly denoting also a politician or statesman.

statistical, *a.* sta-*tis*-te-kal, pertaining to or containing statistics; concerned with statistics.

statistically, *ad.* by means of statistics.

statistician, *n. stat*-is-*tish*-an, a person dealing with or versed in statistics.

statistics, *n.* sta-*tis*-tiks, the science of the collection and classification of numerical facts, esp. those respecting the state of a people, its domestic economy, health, longevity, wealth, etc.; such classified facts themselves; the science which treats of these subjects.

statistology, *n.* stat-is-*tol*-o-je, statistics; the science of organizing and making use of statistics.

stator, *n. stay*-tor, the stationary part of a generator, etc., around which the rotor revolves; the case, also the body of stationary blades, of a turbine.

statoscope, *n. stat*-o-skope, an aneroid barometer for indicating minute fluctuations in pressure; an instrument for indicating variations in the altitude of aircraft. (Gr. *statos,* standing, *skopos,* looker-out.)

statuary, *a. stat*-yew-a-re, pertaining to statuary: *n.* the art of sculpture; statues collectively; a sculptor.

statue, *n. stat*-yew, an image carved, or cast in a mould. (L., from *statuo,* to set up.)

statued, *a. stat*-yewd, furnished with statues; represented in statuary.

statuesque, *a. stat*-yew-*esk,* in the style or manner of a statue.

statuette, *n. stat*-yew-*et,* a small statue.

stature, *n. stat*-yewr, the natural height of the body.

status, *n.* *stay*-tus, standing; condition; relative position in society. (L.)
statutable, *a.* *stat*-yew-ta-bl, made or introduced by statute; conformable to statute.
statutably, *ad.* agreeably to statute.
statute, *n.* *stat*-yewt, an enactment by the legislature of a state; written law; an act of parliament; the act of a corporation or of its founder, intended as a permanent rule or law. **statute-barred,** rendered ineffective by the Statute of Limitations (of claims for debt). **statute-book,** the official collection of a nation's statutes. **statute mile,** the land mile, 1,760 yards. (Fr. *statut.*)
statutory, *a.* *stat*-yew-to-re, enacted by statute; depending on statute for its authority.
staunch, *a.* stawnsh *or* stahnsh, stanch; firm; trustworthy: *v.t.* to stanch.
stauncher, staunchless, *etc., see* **stancher,** etc.
staurolite, *n.* *staw*-ro-lite, a mineral composed of silicate of aluminium, magnesium, and iron, crystallized in prisms, often in the shape of a cross. (Gr. *stauros,* a cross, *lithos,* a stone.)
stauroscope, *n.* *staw*-ro-skope, a kind of polariscope used in the examination of crystals.
stave, *n.* stave, one of the curved side timbers of a cask; a rod or bar; the rung of a ladder; a stanza or part of a song; the five lines and spaces on which music is written [Mus.]: *v.t.* to break a hole in; to burst; to push, as with a staff; to furnish with staves. **stave off,** to avert. *p.* and *pp.* **staved** or **stove.** (*staff.*)
stave-rhyme, *n.* alliteration.
staves, *n.* stavez, an old *pl.* of *staff.*
stavesacre, *n.* *stavez*-ay-ker, the plant *Delphinium staphisagria,* a preparation of the seeds of which is destructive to lice. (Gr.)
stay, *n.* stay, continuance in a place; abode for a time; stand; stop; obstruction; fixed state; support; one of the large ropes supporting a mast from above [Naut.]: *pl.* a stiffened bodice, a corset: *v.i.* to remain; to persist without tiring; to continue in a place or a state; to wait; to stand still; to rest; to rely: *v.t.* to stop; to restrain; to delay; to obstruct; to keep from departure; to prop; to support. **in stays,** going from one tack to another [Naut.]. **miss stays,** to fail in attempting to tack [Naut.]. **stay-in-strike,** a strike in which employees are present during the specified hours but remain idle or are obstructive. **stay on,** to remain for a longer period. **stay put,** to remain as placed or indefinitely. *p.* and *pp.* **staid** or **stayed.** (O.Fr. *estayer.*)
stay-at-home, *n.* *stay*-at-home, one who rarely ventures from home; one disliking travel: *a.* untravelled.
stayer, *n.* *stay*-er, one who or that which stays; one that stops or restrains; one that upholds or supports; that which props; one not easily tired out.
stay-lace, *n.* a thin cord for fastening corsets.
stay-maker, *n.* one who makes stays.
staysail, *n.* *stay*-sl, any triangular sail extended on a stay [Naut.].
stead, *n.* sted, place or room which another had or might have; the frame on which a bed is laid. **stand in stead,** to be of use or advantage. (A.S. *stede,* a place.)
steadfast, *a.* *sted*-fast, firm; firmly fixed; constant; not fickle; steady. (A.S. *stedefæst,* firm in its place.)
steadfastly, *ad.* in a steadfast manner.
steadfastness, *n.* the quality of being steadfast; firmness of mind or purpose; firmness of principle; constancy.
steadily, *ad.* *sted*-e-le, in a steady manner.
steadiness, *n.* *sted*-e-ness, the quality of being steady; firmness of purpose; constancy.
steading, *n.* *sted*-ing, the outhouses of a farm.
steady, *a.* *sted*-e, firm in standing or position; firm; fixed; constant in mind, purpose, or pursuit; not fickle, changeable, or wavering; constant; uniform: *v.t.* to make or keep steady: *v.i.* to become steady. (*stead.*)
steak, *n.* stake, a thick slice of meat or fish, broiled or fried. (Scand.)
steal, *v.t.* steel, to take or carry away feloniously, as the personal goods of another; to withdraw or convey clandestinely; to gain or win by address or by gradual imperceptible means: *v.i.* to withdraw or pass privily; to abscond; to practise theft; to take feloniously. *p.* **stole;** *pp.* **stolen.** (A.S. *stelan.*)
stealer, *n.* *steel*-er, one who steals; a thief.
stealingly, *ad.* *steel*-ing-le, stealthily; privately.
stealth, *n.* stelth, clandestine or underhand procedure; furtiveness.
stealthily, *ad.* *stelth*-e-le, in a stealthy manner.
stealthiness, *n.* *stelth*-e-ness, stealth; the state or quality of being stealthy.
stealthy, *a.* *stelth*-e, furtive; done by stealth; clandestine; unperceived.
★**steam,** *n.* steem, the invisible gas obtained by heating water to the boiling-point; the mist formed by vapour when condensing; any exhalation; energy, go [Fig.]: *v.i.* to rise or pass off in steam; to send off visible vapour; to move by steam: *v.t.* to expose to steam; to apply steam to for softening, dressing, cooking, or preparing. **to have** or **get steam up,** to be or become full of energy, enthusiasm, etc. **to let off steam,** to relieve one's feeling. **to steam up,** to become covered with steam. (A.S.)
steamboat, *n.* a vessel propelled through water by steam.
steam-boiler, *n.* a boiler in which water is converted into steam.
steam-chest, *n.* the chamber from which steam is passed into the cylinder of a steam-engine.
steam-crane, *n.* a crane worked by steam.
steam-engine, *n.* an engine in which the motive power is supplied by the expansion of steam.
steamer, *n.* *steem*-er, a vessel propelled by steam; a vessel in which articles are steamed; a fire-engine worked by steam.
steamer-duck, *n.* a large Patagonian sea-duck that loses the power of flight when mature.
steam-gas, *n.* highly superheated steam.
steam-gauge, *n.* an apparatus attached to a boiler to indicate the pressure of the steam.
steam-gun, *n.* an apparatus for ejecting a projectile by means of the elastic force of steam.
steam-hammer, *n.* a forge hammer worked by steam.
steaminess, *n.* *steem*-e-ness, mistiness; the condition of being steamy.
steam-navvy, *n.* *steem*-nav-ve, an excavating machine driven by steam.
steampipe, *n.* *steem*-pipe, a pipe conveying steam, esp., on a steam-engine, one through which the steam passes on its way from the boiler to the cylinder.
steam-roller, *n.* a heavy steam-driven locomotive with broad wheel or wheels for compacting and smoothing road-surfaces; a ruthless or crushing force [Coll.].
steamship, *n.* *steem*-ship, a ship propelled by steam.
steam-trap, *n.* a contrivance for allowing the passage of water while stopping the escape of steam.
steam-whistle, *n.* a pipe attached to the boiler of a steam-engine, through which steam is discharged, producing a loud, shrill whistle.
steamy, *a.* *steem*-e, full of vapour; misty.
steam-yacht, *n.* a yacht propelled by steam.
steaning, *n.* *steen*-ing, steening.
steapsin, *n.* stee-*ap*-sin, a fat-saponifying ferment present in the pancreatic juice. (Gr. *stear,* fat, and *pepsin.*)
stearate, *n.* *stee*-a-rate, a salt of stearic acid.
stearic, *a.* ste-*a*-rik, pertaining to, obtained from, or resembling stearin.
steariform, *a.* *steer*-re-form, resembling fat.
stearin, *n.* *stee*-a-rin, the chief component of solid fats; stearic acid. (Gr. *stear,* fat.)
stearoptene, *n.* *stee*-a-*rop*-teen, the solid crystalline portion of an essential oil as apart from the elæoptine, or liquid component.
steatite, *n.* *stee*-a-tite, soapstone, a massive variety of talc of a soapy feel. (Gr. *steatos,* of fat.)
steatitic, *a.* *stee*-a-*tit*-ik, pertaining to or resembling steatite.
steatocele, *n.* *stee*-a-to-*seel,* a fatty tumour of the scrotum. (Gr. *stear,* fat, *kele,* tumour.)
steatoma, *n.* stee-a-*toh*-ma, a wen or encysted tumour containing matter like suet.
steatomatous, *a.* stee-a-*toh*-ma-tus, of the nature of a steatoma.
steatopygous, *a.* stee-a-*top*-e-gus, having large buttocks. (Gr. *steatos,* and *pyge,* rump.)
steatosis, *n.* stee-a-*toh*-sis, abnormal adiposity; fatty degeneration [Path.].

stechiology, *n* stek-e-*ol*-o-je, stoichiology.
steed, *n.* steed, a horse, esp. a spirited horse for state occasions or war. (A.S. *steda.*)
★**steel,** *n.* steel, iron so treated with carbon that its hardness, elasticity, and capacity for retaining an edge are greatly intensified; any instrument of steel; a sword; a prepared steel rod for sharpening knives; a stiffener of a corset; iron chloride, or other chalybeate [Med.]; extreme hardness [Fig.]: *a.* made of steel; very strong or tight; like steel: *v.t.* to overlay, point, or edge with steel; to sharpen on a steel; to harden; to make insensible or obdurate. **steel blue,** a lustrous dark blue colour. **steel engraving,** engraving on steel plates: an engraving on a steel plate; an impression from such. (A.S. *stel.*)
steeliness, *n. steel*-e-ness, great hardness or obduracy.
steel-plated, *a.* steel-*plate*-ed, plated with steel.
steely, *a. steel*-e, made of steel; hard; firm; obdurate.
steelyard, *n. steel*-yard, a lever balance with arms of unequal length, for ascertaining weights, the weight being slid on the long, and the article to be weighed suspended from the short, arm. (Ger. *Stahlhof,* sample yard.)
steen, *v.t.* steen, to line (a shaft or well) with stone, brick, etc. (A.S. *stænan,* a stone.)
steenbok, *n. steen*-bok, the steinbok.
steening, *n. steen*-ing, the stone or brick lining of a well, etc. (*steen.*)
steep, *a.* steep, ascending or descending at a high gradient; precipitous: *n.* a precipitous place or ascent; a precipice. (A.S. *steap.*)
steep, *n.* steep, the process of steeping; a liquid used in steeping: *v.t.* to soak in a liquid; to imbue. (Ice. *steypa,* pour out, as metal.)
steepen, *v.t.* and *i. steep*-en, to make or become steep.
steeper, *n. steep*-er, one who steeps; a vessel in which things are steeped; a heavy downpour of rain [Coll.].
steeple, *n. stee*-pl, a tower, esp. a church tower, usually with a spire. (A.S. *stypel.*)
steeplechase, *n. stee*-pl-chase, a horse-race across country or on a course obstructed by hedges, ditches, etc. (originally towards a steeple as landmark).
steepled, *a. stee*-pld, furnished or adorned with a steeple or steeples.
steeple-jack, *n.* a man who works on steeples and tall chimneys.
steeply, *ad. steep*-le, in a steep manner.
steepness, *n. steep*-ness, the state of being steep; precipitous declivity.
steepy, *a. steep*-e, having a steep declivity.
steer, *n.* steer, a bullock up to four years. (A.S. *steor*).
steer, *v.t.* steer, to direct the course of a moving ship, car, aeroplane, etc.; to direct; to guide: *v.i.* to direct and govern a ship in its course; to conduct oneself; to take or pursue a course or way. (A.S. *steoran.*)
steerable, *a. steer*-a-bl, that may be steered.
steerage, *n. steer*-aj, accommodation for passengers on board ship paying the lowest fares; formerly, the part of a ship from which it was steered, also, quarters for junior officers on a ship-of-war; the act of steering; the effect of a rudder on a ship, car, or aircraft, etc. **steerage-way,** sufficient speed for effective steering.
steerer, *n. steer*-er, one who steers; a pilot.
steering-wheel, *n.* the wheel by which the rudder is controlled [Naut.], or a motor-car or aircraft is steered.
steerling, *n. steer*-ling, a young steer.
steersman, *n. steerz*-man, a helmsman.
steersmanship, *n. steerz*-man-ship, skill in steering.
steeve, *n.* steeve, a derrick for stowing cargo; the outward slope of an outboard spar: *v.t.* to slope a spar upwards; to pack closely; to stow. [Naut.]. (A.S. *stifian,* as *stiff.*)
steeving, *n. steev*-ing, the angle of elevation which a ship's bowsprit makes with the horizon [Naut.].
steganographist, *n. steg*-a-*nog*-ra-fist, one skilled in steganography.
steganography, *n. steg*-a-*nog*-ra-fe, the art of writing in cipher or secret characters; cryptography. (Gr. *steganos,* covered, concealed, *grapho,* write.)
steganopod, *n.* ste-*gan*-o-pod, one of the Steganopodes, a family of birds with all the toes webbed, as the pelicans, etc. (Gr. *steganos,* and *pous, podos,* the foot.)
steganopodous, *a.* steg-a-*nop*-o-dus, of or pertaining to the Steganopodes; totipalmate.
stegnosis, *n.* steg-*noh*-sis, constriction of pores or ducts; constipation [Med.]. (Gr., constriction.)
stegnotic, *a.* steg-*not*-ik, tending to render costive: *n.* a medicine which does so; an astringent.
stegomyia, *n.* steg-o-*my*-ya, the mosquito, *Aëdes ægypti,* that transmits yellow fever.
Stegosaurus, *n.* steg-o-*saw*-rus, a genus of large dinosaurs of the Upper Jurassic of N. America. (Gr. *stegein,* to cover, *sauros,* lizard.)
stein, *n.* stine, an earthenware beer-mug [U.S.A.]. (Ger., stone.)
steinbock, *n. stine*-bok, the Alpine ibex. (Ger.)
steinbok, *n. stine*-bok, a small South African antelope of the genus *Raphicerus.* (Dut. *steenbok,* stone-buck.)
steining, *n. stayn*-ing, steening.
stela, *n. stee*-la, a small column without base or capital. (Gr. *stele,* a post.)
stelar, *a. stee*-lar, pertaining to or resembling a stele or stela.
stele, *n. stee*-le, an inscribed stela; the central cylinder of the conducting system in the higher plants [Bot.].
stellar, *a. stel*-lar, pertaining to stars; astral; starry; full of or set with stars. (L. *stella,* star.)
Stellaria, *n.* stel-*lare*-re-a, a genus of plants with star-like flowers, including the stitchworts.
stellate, *a. stel*-at, resembling a star; radiated.
stellated, *a. stel*-a-ted, stellate.
stellenbosch, *v.t. stel*-en-bosh, to transfer to a subordinate post on account of incompetence. (Town in S. Africa to which unsuccessful officers were sent during the Kaffir wars.)
stelliferous, *a.* ste-*lif*-er-rus, abounding with stars. (L. *stella,* and *fero,* bear.)
stelliform, *a. stel*-le-form, in the shape of a star; radiated.
stellion, *n. stel*-yon, a small lizard of S.E. Europe and Asia of the genus *Stellio.*
stellite, *n. stel*-lite, trade-name of a cobalt-chromium alloy used for cutlery, machine-tools, etc.
stellular, *a. stel*-yew-lar, resembling little stars. (L. *stellula,* a little star.)
stelography, *n.* ste-*log*-ra-fe, an inscription on a pillar; the art of inscribing characters on pillars. (Gr. *stele,* a pillar, *grapho,* write.)
★**stem,** *n.* stem, the ascending axis of a plant; the peduncle of a flower; the stalk; the slender part of certain things, as a tobacco-pipe, wine-glass, etc.; the main part of a word to which prefixes and suffixes are affixed [Gram.]; the stock of a family; a branch of a family; the curved piece of timber to which the two sides of a ship are united at the fore end; the cutwater: *v.t.* to divest of the stem or stems. **from stem to stern,** from one end of the ship to the other; throughout. (A.S. *stefn.*)
stem, *v.t.* stem, to oppose or resist; to stop; to check; to stanch: *v.i.* to advance against difficulty; to develop like a stem; to derive (from). (Ice. *stemma.*)
stem-leaf, *n.* a leaf growing from the stem.
stemless, *a. stem*-less, having no stem.
stemlet, *n. stem*-let, a small stem.
stemma, *n.* stem-ma (*pl.* **stemmata**), a genealogy, esp. one displayed diagrammatically. (L., from Gr. *stemma,* a garland.)
stemple, *n. stem*-pl, a cross-bar of wood forming a step in a mine-shaft. (Ger. *Stempel.*)
stemson, *n. stem*-son, the strong arched timber strengthening stem and keelson near the bow [Naut.].
stench, *n.* stensh, an offensive odour. (A.S. *stenc.*)
stenchy, *a. stensh*-e, foul-smelling.
stencil, *n. sten*-sil, a piece of thin metal or other substance so cut as to allow a desired pattern, word, etc., to be produced upon a surface on which it is superimposed: *v.t.* to mark or decorate by the use of a stencil. (O.Fr. *estenciler.*)
stenciller, *n. sten*-sil-ler, one who stencils.
sten-gun, *n.,* a light and simple automatic hand fire-arm. (Arbitrary coinage.)
stenocardia, *n. sten*-o-*kar*-de-a, angina pectoris [Med.]. (Gr. *stenos,* narrow, *kardia,* heart.)
stenocephaly, *n.* sten-o-*sef*-a-le, narrowness of the head.

stenochrome, *n.* *sten*-o-krome, a print made by stenochromy.
stenochromy, *n.* *sten*-o-kroh-me, the art of printing in several colours at the same time. (Gr. *stenos*, and *chrome*, colour.)
stenograph, *n.* *sten*-o-graf, a shorthand character: *v.t.* and *i.* to write in shorthand. (Gr. *stenos*, and *grapho*, write.)
stenographer, *n.* ste-*nog*-ra-fer, a shorthand writer.
stenographic, *a.* sten-o-*graf*-ik, pertaining to stenography; expressed in shorthand.
stenographist, *n.* ste-*nog*-ra-fist, a stenographer.
stenography, *n.* ste-*nog*-ra-fe, the art of writing in shorthand by the use of special characters and abbreviations.
stenosed, *a.* *sten*-ohst, contracted; affected with stenosis [Path.].
stenosis, *n.* ste-*noh*-sis, the narrowing of an orifice or duct [Med.]. (Gr. *stenos*.)
stenotype, *n.* *sten*-o-typ, one or more ordinary letters representing a sound in stenotypy.
stenotypy, *n.* *sten*-o-ty-pe, any form of shorthand using only the ordinary characters; abbreviated longhand. (Gr. *stenos*, and *typos*, type.)
Stentor, *n.* *sten*-tor, a person with a powerful voice. (*Stentor*, Greek herald in the Trojan war.)
stentorian, *a.* sten-*taw*-re-an, extremely loud; able to utter a very loud sound.
stentorophonic, *a.* *sten*-to-ro-*fon*-ik, speaking or sounding very loud. (*Stentor*, Gr. *phone*, voice.)
stentorphone, *n.* *sten*-tor-fohn, an electric loud-speaker.
★**step,** *n.* step, a footfall; a pace; the space between the feet in walking, running, or dancing; the tread of a stair; a small space; gradation; degree; progression; footstep; footprint; gait; proceeding; an action; a rung of a ladder; a foot-piece; that on which the foot of a mast rests [Naut.]: *v.i.* to advance or recede by a movement of the foot; to go; to walk gravely or resolutely; to dance sedately: *v.t.* to set, as a foot; to put a mast in its place [Naut.]. **pair of steps,** a folding self-supporting step-ladder. **step on it** or **step on the gas!** hurry up! [U.S.A. slang]. **step out,** lengthen the stride; hurry. **step up,** to accelerate; to increase the rate, or [Elect.] the voltage of. **watch one's step,** to proceed cautiously, to be wary [Slang]. (A.S. *stæpe*.)
step-, *n.* step, a prefix to express the nominal relationship arising in a family by the subsequent marriage of one parent. **stepbrother, stepsister,** a brother or sister related through one parent only. **stepchild, stepdaughter, stepson,** a child of one's spouse through a previous marriage. **stepfather, stepmother,** the later husband of one's mother or wife of one's father.
stepgirl, *n.* *step*-girl, a girl who cleans doorsteps.
stephane, *n.* *stef*-a-ne, an ancient Greek head-dress.
stephanite, *n.* *stef*-a-nite, the iron-black mineral sulph-antimonite of silver. (Named from an Austrian Archduke *Stephan*.)
stephanotis, *n.* *stef*-a-*noh*-tis, a tropical climbing plant with scented waxy flowers. (Gr. *stephanos*, a wreath.)
step-ins, *n.* *step*-inz, an undergarment that can be put on by being stepped into.
step-ladder, *n.* *step*-lad-der, a ladder with flat treads; a pair of steps.
stepney, *n.* *step*-ne, a spare wheel carried on a motor-car ready for fixing. (Place-name.)
steppe, *n.* step, an expanse of uncultivated treeless plains, esp. in Russia and south-west Asia. (Russ.)
stepper, *n.* *step*-per, a horse with high action; he who or that which steps.
stepping-stone, *n.* *step*-ping-stone, a stone to raise the feet above the water or dirt in walking; a means of progress; a means to an end.
stercoraceous, *a.* *ster*-ko-*ray*-shus, pertaining to, composed of, or like fæces. (L. *stercus*, dung.)
stercoral, *a.* *ster*-ko-ral, pertaining to excrement; living in or feeding on dung [Zool.].
stercorary, *n.* *ster*-ko-ra-re, a place secure from the weather for containing manure.
stere, *n.* steer, the metric unit of solid measure, equal to a cubic metre, or 1·308 cu. yd. (Fr., from Gr. *stereos*, solid.)
stereo, *n.* *steer*-re-oh, a stereotype. (Gr. *stereos*, hard.)
stereobate, *n.* *steer*-re-o-bate, the solid substructure of a building, esp. one that is visible. (Gr. *stereos*, solid, *bainos*, stand.)
stereo-chemistry, *n.* *steer*-re-o-*kem*-is-tre, the branch of chemistry concerned with the arrangement of atoms and molecules in space.
stereochromy, *n.* *steer*-re-*ok*-ro-me, a method of painting walls, in which the colours are fixed by fluo-silicic acid and waterglass. (Gr. *stereos*, solid, *chroma*, colour.)
stereograph, *n.* *steer*-re-o-graf, a stereographic picture or diagram; a picture or pair of pictures for use in a stereoscope. (Gr. *stereos*, and *grapho*, write.)
stereographic, *a.* steer-re-o-*graf*-ik, made or done according to the rules of stereography; delineated on a plane.
stereographically, *ad.* in a stereographic manner.
stereography, *n.* *steer*-re-*og*-ra-fe, the delineation of solid bodies on a plane.
stereome, *n.* *ste*-re-ohm, the strengthening tissue of plants.
stereometer, *n.* steer-re-*om*-e-ter, an instrument for determining the specific gravity of bodies, also one for measuring the volume of solid bodies. (Gr. *stereos*, and *metron*.)
stereometrical, *a.* *steer*-re-o-*met*-re-kal, pertaining to or performed by stereometry.
stereometry, *n.* *steer*-re-*om*-e-tre, the art of measuring solid bodies; solid geometry; the measurement of the content of a hollow body.
stereopticon, *n.* *ste*-re-*op*-te-kon, a high-powered magic lantern, usually constructed to produce dissolving views.
stereoscope, *n.* *steer*-re-o-skope, an optical instrument through which two pictures of the same object appear as one and cause it to stand out in solid form as in nature. (Gr. *stereos*, and *skopeo*, view.)
stereoscopic, *a.* *steer*-re-o-*skop*-ik, pertaining to the stereoscope.
stereoscopist, *n.* steer-re-*os*-ko-pist, one skilled in stereoscopy.
stereoscopy, *n.* steer-re-*os*-ko-pe, the stereoscopic science or art.
stereotomical, *a.* *steer*-re-o-*tom*-e-kal, pertaining to or performed by stereotomy.
stereotomy, *n.* steer-re-*ot*-o-me, the art of cutting solids, esp. stone, into figures of desired shape. (Gr. *stereos*, and *tome*, cutting.)
stereotype, *n.* *ste*-re- *or* *steer*-re-o-tipe, a metallic plate cast from a mould taken from a forme of movable types; anything purely conventional or reproduced without variation [Fig.]: *v.t.* to cast in stereotype; to print with stereotype; to fix unchangeably. (Gr. *stereos*, and *type*.)
stereotyper, *n.* *ste*-re- *or* *steer*-re-o-ty-per, one who casts stereotype plates.
stereotypist, *n.* *ste*-re- *or* *steer*-re-o-ty-pist, a stereotyper.
stereotypography, *n.* *ste*-re- *or* *steer*-re-o-ty-*pog*-ra-fe, art or practice of printing from stereotype.
stereotypy, *n.* *ste*-re- *or* *steer*-re-o-*ty*-pe, the art of making or printing from stereos; mechanical repetition.
sterile, *a.* *ste*-rile, barren; unfruitful; producing little or no crop; producing no young; barren of ideas or sentiment; free from living matter, esp. [Path.] septic germs. (O.Fr.)
sterility, *n.* ste-*ril*-e-te, barrenness; unfruitfulness; barrenness of ideas or sentiments; want of fertility.
sterilizable, *a.* *ste*-re-*ly*-za-bl, capable of being sterilized.
sterilization, *n.* *ste*-re-ly-*zay*-shon, act or process of sterilizing; state of being sterile.
sterilize, *v.t.* *ste*-re-lize, to make incapable of bearing offspring; to exhaust of fertility; to destroy bacteria; to treat with an antiseptic.
sterilizer, *n.* *ste*-re-*ly*-zer, a sterilizing agent; an apparatus for sterilizing.
sterlet, *n.* *ster*-let, a species of sturgeon, *Acipenser ruthenus*, found in the Caspian Sea and in Russian rivers, the source of the best caviare. (Russ.)
sterling, *a.* *ster*-ling, of standard worth; genuine; pure; of excellent quality: *n.* English money or currency; sterling silver. **sterling silver,** an alloy containing 92·5 per cent. silver (until 1920 used for British coinage). (Origin doubtful.)
stern, *a.* stern, severe in expression or manner; austere; harsh; rigidly steadfast; immovable; unrelenting. (A.S. *styrne*.)

stern, *n.* stern, the hind part of a ship; the hinder part; the rump. (Ice. *stjorn,* steering.)
sternal, *a. stern*-al, pertaining to the sternum.
sternalgia, *n.* ster-*nal*-je-a, pain in the chest, or sternum; angina pectoris. (Gr. *sternon,* breast, *algos,* pain.)
sternbergite, *n. stern*-berg-ite, a foliated sulphide of silver and iron. (From a Count *Sternberg.*)
sternboard, *n. stern*-bord, the flat board at the stern of a boat, punt, etc.; the backward motion of a vessel; the loss of way in making a tack [Naut.].
stern-chase, *n.* a pursuit at sea in which the one vessel follows directly in the wake of the other.
stern-chaser, *n.* a ship's gun so mounted as to fire astern.
stern-fast, *n.* a rope to moor the stern of a ship.
sternly, *ad. stern*-le, in a stern manner.
sternmost, *a. stern*-mohst, farthest astern.
sternness, *n. stern*-ness, the state of being stern.
sternocostal, *a. ster*-no-*kos*-tal, pertaining to the sternum and ribs.
sternpost, *n. stern*-pohst, the principal vertical, or nearly vertical, member at the after end of a ship, aeroplane, or seaplane; the casting on which a ship's rudder hangs.
stern-sheets, *n.pl.* that part of the boat between the stern and the aftmost thwarts.
sternum, *n. ster*-num (*pl.* **sterna**), the breast-bone in vertebrates, in man forming the front of the chest from the neck to the stomach; the ventral part of a somite in arthropods. (L.)
sternutation, *n.* ster-new-*tay*-shon, the act of sneezing. (L. *sternutatio.*)
sternutative, *a.* ster-*new*-ta-tiv, provocative of sneezing.
sternutatory, *a.* ster-*new*-ta-to-re, provoking sneezing: *n.* a substance whuch has this quality.
sternway, *n. stern*-way, the movement of a ship backward, or stern foremost.
stern-wheeler, *n.* a steamer driven by a paddle-wheel at the stern.
sterol, *n. ste*-rol, any of a class of complex solid organic compounds present in most forms of life and taking part in certain physiological processes. (Back-formation from *cholesterol.*)
stertorous, *a. ster*-to-rus, snoring; loudly breathing. (L. *sterto,* snore.)
stet, *v.i.* stet, it may stand: *v.t.* let it stand, a direction on a proof notifying the printer that a correction made is cancelled. (L.)
stethometer, *n.* ste-*thom*-e-ter, an instrument for measuring the movement of the walls of the chest in breathing. (Gr. *stethos,* the breast, and *metron.*)
stethoscope, *n. steth*-o-skope, an instrument for distinguishing sounds within the thorax and other cavities of the body: *v.t.* to auscultate with this. (Gr. *stethos,* and *skopeo,* view.)
stethoscopic, *a.* steth-o-*skop*-ik, pertaining to the stethoscope.
stethoscopist, *n.* ste-*thos*-ko-pist, one versed in stethoscopy.
stethoscopy, *n.* ste-*thos*-ko-pe, the art of using the stethoscope; stethoscopic examination.
stetson, *n. stet*-son, a soft, broad-brimmed hat. (From name of maker.)
stevedore, *n. stee*-ve-dor, one whose occupation is to stow goods in a ship's hold; a loader or unloader of vessels. (Sp. *estivar,* from L. *stipo,* press together, cram.)
stew, *n.* stew, a fishpond; a tank for keeping fish for eating; an artificial oyster-bed. (O.Fr. *estui,* from *estuier,* to hold in reserve.)
stew, *n.* stew, meat stewed; a state of agitation; *pl.* a brothel: *v.t.* to boil raw meat or fruit, etc., slowly and gently with little moisture: *v.i.* to be boiled in a slow gentle manner. **stew in one's own juice,** to bear the consequences of one's action. (O.Fr. *estuve,* bath, hot-house.)
steward, *n. stew*-ard, one who manages the concerns of a large estate or a great family, superintending the servants, collecting the rents, and keeping the accounts; an officer of state; an officer in a college, club, etc., who superintends the catering and concerns of the kitchen and household staff; the head of the commissariat department in a ship; a waiter, esp. on a ship or other conveyance. (A.S. *stiweard.*)
stewardess, *n. stew*-ard-ess, a female steward, esp. an attendant on women and children on board ship.

stewardship, *n. stew*-ard-ship, the office of a steward; management.
stewartry, *n. stew*-ar-tre, a Scottish stewardship and its territorial extent.
stew-pan, *n.* a pan in which food is stewed.
sthenic, *a. sthen*-ik, active; indicative of vigour; attended with excess of organic action [Path.]. (Gr. *sthenos,* strength.)
stiacciato, *a. stee*-at-*chah*-toh, in very low relief [Art]. (It.)
stibial, *a. stib*-e-al, like or having the qualities of antimony; antimonial. (L. *stibium,* antimony.)
stibialism, *stib*-e-a-lizm, antimony poisoning.
stibiated, *a. stib*-e-ay-ted, combined with or impregnated with antimony.
stibic, *a. stib*-ik, antimonic.
stibine, *n. stib*-ine, the poisonous colourless gas, antimony hydride.
stibium, *n. stib*-e-um, antimony. (L.)
stibnite, *n. stib*-nite, grey antimony, the trisulphide, the commonest antimony ore.
sticcado, *n.* stik-*kah*-doh, a xylophone [Mus.]. (It.)
stich, *n.* stik, a verse; a metrical line [Pros.]. (Gr. *stichos,* a line, a verse.)
stichic, *a. stik*-ik, pertaining to or consisting of lines and verses.
stichomancy, *n. stik*-o-man-se, sortes; divination by haphazard selection of a passage from a book. (Gr. *stichos,* and *mantia,* divination.)
stichometry, *n.* ste-*kom*-e-tre, the measurement of a MS. or book by its number of lines; a list of books of Scripture with the number of verses each contains; the division of a writing into lines according to the sense. (Gr. *stichos,* and *metron,* measure.)
stichomythia, *n. stik*-o-*mith*-e-a, a sharp altercation in alternating lines (esp. in Greek drama). (Gr. *stichos,* and *mythos,* talk.)
★**stick,** *n.* stik, a small shoot or branch cut off a tree; a long slender piece of wood or other material; a slender piece; a staff; a baton, drumstick, fiddlestick, etc.; a walking-stick; a composing stick; a thrust with a pointed instrument that penetrates the body; a stab; a dull unresponsive person. **in a cleft stick,** in a fix or an awkward dilemma. **the wrong end of the stick,** an erroneous conclusion, solution, version, etc. (A.S. *sticca.*)
stick, *v.t.* stik, to pierce; to stab; to thrust in; to fasten; to set; to fix in; to set with something pointed; to fix on something pointed; to cause to adhere to; to furnish with sticks (of growing plants): *v.i.* to be inserted into; to project from; to become fixed; to adhere; to cling fast to; to stop; to be impeded; to hesitate; to be stopped; to be embarrassed. *p.* and *pp.* **stuck. stick in one's throat,** to remain unsaid. **stick out,** to project. **stick out for,** to insist upon maintaining or having. **stick to,** to adhere closely. **stick up,** to hold up (as a highwayman), to rob [U.S.A.]. **stick up for,** to defend. **stick upon,** to dwell upon. (A.S. *stician.*)
sticker, *n. stik*-er, one who or that which sticks; a billsticker; an adhesive; a persistent person.
stickful, *n. stik*-ful, the amount of type that a composing stick will hold [Print.].
stickiness, *n. stik*-e-ness, adhesiveness; viscousness; glutinousness.
sticking-plaster, *n.* an adhesive plaster for wounds, etc.
stick-insect, *n.* one of many of the stick-like insects of the family Phasmidæ whose form and colour resemble twigs of the trees they frequent.
stick-in-the-mud, *n. stick-* . . ., a lethargic, unprogressive fellow; an old fogy: *a.* ultra-conservative; lazily contented.
stickit, *a. stik*-it, stuck; unable to proceed [Scots.]. **stickit minister,** a minister who, through failure, is unable to obtain advancement.
stickjaw, *n. stik*-jaw, any sweetmeat, pudding, etc., awkward to masticate through its stickiness [Slang].
stickle, *n. stik*-kl, a rapid in a stream; a scour: *a.* steep; rapid. (A.S. *sticol,* steep.)
stickle, *v.i. stik*-kl, to insist on every trifle; to contend obstinately. (A.S. *stihtan,* to arrange.)
stickleback, *n. stik*-kl-bak, a small nest-building fish of the genus *Gasterosteus,* with spiny back.
stickler, *n. stik*-ler, an umpire at fencing or wrestling bouts, etc.; one who judges a combat; an obstinate

contender about anything. (M.E., *stihtlen*, settle a dispute.)
stick-up, *n.* *stik*-up, a hold-up with intent to rob; an assault on the highway [U.S.A. slang].
★**sticky,** *a.* *stik*-e, adhesive; gluey; viscous; clammy humid and moist (of the weather); awkward, difficult; like a stick: *v.t.* to make sticky; to smear with something sticky.
★**stiff,** *a.* stif, not easily bent; rigid; not liquid or fluid; inspissated; strong; violent; stubborn; obstinate; constrained; formal; hard to effect; exorbitant: *n.* [Slang] a loafer; a boor; a corpse. **bored, scared** (etc.) **stiff,** excessively bored (etc.) [Coll.]. (A.S.)
stiffen, *v.t.* *stif*-en, to make stiff or rigid; to inspissate: *v.i.* to become stiff; to become thicker; to become less yielding.
stiffener, *n.* *stif*-en-er, that which stiffens; a strong tot of spirits [Slang].
stiffening, *n.* *stif*-en-ing, something to stiffen a substance.
stiffish, *a.* *stif*-ish, rather stiff.
stiffly, *ad.* *stif*-le, in a stiff manner.
stiff-neck, *n.* *stif*-nek, a rheumatic affection of the neck in which a lateral movement of the head causes great pain. **stiff-neck fever,** cerebrospinal meningitis.
stiff-necked, *a.* *stif*-nekt, stubborn; inflexibly obstinate; contumacious.
stiff-neckedness, *n.* *stif*-nekt-ness, the quality of being stiff-necked; stubbornness.
stiffness, *n.* *stif*-ness, the quality of being stiff.
stifle, *v.t.* *sty*-fl, to suffocate; to choke; to stop; to stop the breath temporarily; to extinguish; to deaden; to smother; to suppress. (Ice. *stifla.*)
stifle, *n.* *sty*-fl, the joint in a horse's hind leg corresponding to the human knee; a disease in the knee-pan of a horse or other animal. **stifle-bone,** *n.* the patella or knee-pan of a horse. (Perhaps O.Scand. *stiva*, to stiffen.)
stiflingly, *ad.* *sty*-fling-le, so as to stifle.
stigma, *n.* *stig*-ma, a mark made with a branding-iron; a brand; any mark of infamy; moral spot on or imputation attaching to character; the receptive organ for the pollen grains placed at the top of a pistil [Bot.]. (Gr.)
stigmaria, *n.* stig-*mare*-re-a, the root of species of *Sigillaria* and *Lepidodendron* found fossil in the coal measures.
stigmata, *n.pl.* *stig*-ma-ta, the apertures in the bodies of insects, communicating with the tracheæ or air-vessels; marks alleged to have been supernaturally imprinted on the bodies of certain saints in imitation of the wounds of Christ; visible marks characteristic of a specified disease or morbid condition. (Gr., *pl.* of *stigma.*)
stigmatic, *a.* stig-*mat*-ik, conveying a stigma or reproach; ignominious; pertaining to the stigmata; resembling or constituting a stigma [Bot.]: *n.* a person bearing the stigmata.
stigmatiferous, *a.* stig-ma-*tif*-er-rus, having a stigma or stigmas [Bot.].
stigmatism, *n.* *stig*-ma-tizm, absence of astigmatism; the condition of bearing the stigmata.
stigmatist, *n.* *stig*-ma-tist, one marked with the stigmata.
stigmatization, *n.* *stig*-ma-ty-*zay*-shon, the act of stigmatizing; the alleged impression of the stigmata or wounds of Christ on certain saints.
stigmatize, *v.t.* *stig*-ma-tize, to brand with a stigma; to hold up to disgrace; to disgrace with some mark of reproach or infamy; to cause the stigmata to appear upon.
stigmatose, *a.* *stig*-ma-tohs, stigmatic.
stigmatosis, *n.* *stig*-ma-*toh*-sis, spotted inflammation of the skin.
stilbite, *n.* *stil*-bite, a mineral of the zeolite group, a silicate of sodium, calcium, and aluminium with water. (Gr. *stilbo*, shine.)
stile, *n.* stile, a step or a set of steps or any similar arrangement for ascending and descending over a fence or wall. (A.S. *stigel*, a step.)
stiletto, *n.* sti-*let*-to (*pl.* **stilettos**), a small dagger; a pointed instrument for making eyelet holes: *v.t.* to stab with a stiletto. (It., a little dagger.)
★**still,** *a.* stil, silent; quiet; calm; motionless; not sparkling: *n.* calm; silence; a photograph not implying motion; a single photograph from a film, esp. as an advertisement [Cine.]: *ad.* to this time; nevertheless; always; after that: *v.t.* to quiet; to silence; to render motionless; to appease. (A.S. *stille.*)
still, *n.* stil, an apparatus used in the distillation of spirituous liquors: *v.t.* to distil. (*distil.*)
stillage, *n.* *stil*-aj, a stand for a broached cask; a framework to raise something off the floor.
stillatitious, *a.* *stil*-la-*tish*-us, falling in drops. (L. *stilla*, a drop.)
stillatory, *n.* *stil*-la-to-re, a distillery; a laboratory.
still-birth, *n.* the bringing forth of a dead child; a child born dead; an abortive project.
still-born, *a.* *stil*-born, born lifeless; abortive.
stiller, *n.* *stil*-ler, one who stills or quiets; one who distils.
stilliform, *a.* *stil*-e-form, drop-shaped. (L. *stilla*, a drop, *forma*, shape.)
stilling, *n.* *stil*-ling, a stand for casks.
stillion, *n.* *stil*-yon, a stilling.
still-life, *n.* a picture representing objects without life, as flowers, dead game, porcelain, etc.
stillness, *n.* *stil*-ness, the absence of movement; silence.
still-room, *n.* *stil*-room, a store-room for liquors; a room in which tea and coffee and light meals are prepared; a housekeeper's room.
stilly, *a.* *stil*-e, still; quiet; calm; without sound.
stilly, *ad.* *stil*-le, silently; quietly; calmly.
stilt, *n.* *stilt*, a support of wood with a rest for the foot used in pairs for raising a person in walking; a long-legged plover of the genus *Himantopus*, allied to the avocets: *v.t.* to raise on, or as if on, stilts: *v.i.* to limp. (Scand. *stylta.*)
stilted, *a.* *stil*-ted, raised on or as on stilts; pompous; bombastic; springing from a course of masonry superimposed on the impost (of arches, etc.) [Arch.].
stilton, *n.* *stil*-ton, a rich variety of cheese deriving its name from Stilton in Huntingdonshire.
stimulant, *a.* *stim*-yew-lant, serving to stimulate; producing a transient increase of vital energy: *n.* anything having this effect; an alcoholic drink.
stimulate, *v.t.* *stim*-yew-late, to excite to action or more vigorous exertion; to produce a sudden increase of vital energy in: *v.i.* to act as a stimulus. (L. *stimulatus.*)
stimulation, *n.* *stim*-yew-*lay*-shon, act of goading or exciting; a sudden increase of vital energy.
stimulative, *a.* *stim*-yew-la-tiv, having the power of stimulating.
stimulator, *n.* *stin*-yew-lay-tor, one who or that which stimulates; a device for conveying a stimulus.
stimulus, *n.* *stim*-yew-lus (*pl.* **stimuli,** -ly), something which stimulates; an incitement; a goad; anything giving rise to reaction in a nerve [Phys.]. (L., a pricking instrument, a goad.)
stimy, *n.* and *v.t.* *sty*-me, stymie.
sting, *n.* sting, a sharp organ conveying poison with which certain animals are armed; the act of stinging; the thrust of a sting into the flesh; the pain given; anything that gives acute pain; the point in an epigram, repartee, etc.; that which constitutes the chief terror: *v.t.* to pierce or wound with a sting, like a wasp or scorpion; to pain acutely. *p.* and *pp.* **stung.** (A.S.)
stingaree, *n.* *sting*-ga-ree, the sting-ray.
stinger, *n.* *sting*-er, he who or that which stings, vexes, or gives acute pain; a sharp blow.
sting-fish, *n.* *sting*-fish, a weever, a species of the genus *Trachinus*; the father-lasher, *Cottus scorpius*.
stingily, *ad.* *stin*-je-le, in a stingy manner.
stinginess, *n.* the quality of being stingy.
stingless, *a.* *sting*-less, having no sting.
stingo, *n.* *sting*-goh, strong malt liquor [Slang].
sting-ray, *n.* *sting*-ray, the tropical sea-fish *Trygon pastinaca*, which has a long tail armed with spines.
stingy, *a.* *stin*-je, extremely close and covetous meanly avaricious; niggardly.
stink, *n.* stink, a strong offensive smell; *v.i.* to emit a strong offensive smell; to have an unsavoury reputation. *p.* **stank, stunk.** *pp.* **stunk.** (A.S *stincan.*)
stinkard, *n.* *sting*-kard, a mean, stinking, paltry fellow; the teledu, the skunk, or other animal emitting a foul odour when irritated.
stink-bomb, *n.* a small bomb which diffuses an offensive odour when burst or exploded; a stinkpot.
stinker, *n.* *sting*-ker, something with an offensive smell; a stinkard; anything unpleasant [Slang].

stinkhorn, *n.* *stink*-horn, any of the evil-smelling fungi of the order Phallales, esp. the poisonous *Ithyphallus impudicus.*
stinkingly, *ad.* *sting*-king-le, disgustingly.
stinkpot, *n.* *stink*-pot, an earthern jar, charged with powder, grenades and other materials with an offensive and suffocating smell; a stink-bomb.
stinkstone, *n.* *stink*-stone, a variety of bituminous limestone which emits a fetid odour when struck.
stinktrap, *n.* *stink*-trap, a contrivance to prevent effluvia escaping from a drain or sewer.
stint, *n.* stint, limit; restriction; quantity assigned; proportion allotted; a small bird of the sandpiper group, a species of *Tringa*; a definite task allotted [U.S.A.]: *v.t.* to restrain within certain limits; to bound; to supply grudgingly or in insufficient quantity; to assign a certain task to [U.S.A.]. (A.S. *styntan.*)
stintedness, *n.* *stint*-ed-ness, the quality of being stinted.
stipe, *n.* stipe, a footstalk, as the base of a frond or stem of a fungus [Bot.]; a stipes [Zool.]. (Fr.)
stipel, *n.* *sty*-pel, a secondary stipule at the base of a compound leaf.
stipend, *n.* *sty*-pend, an annual payment for services rendered; a fixed salary, esp. of a clergyman. (L. *stipendium.*)
stipendiary, *a.* sti-*pen*-de-a-re, receiving salary in return for services: *n.* one who receives a salary for his services. **stipendiary magistrate,** a paid magistrate in the service of the crown.
stipes, *n.* *sty*-peez, a specialized stalk [Bot.]; a stalk-like organ, as the basal segment of an insect's maxilla [Zool.]. (L., stalk.)
stipiform, *a.* *sty*-pe-form, resembling a stipe in appearance or character.
stipitate, *a.* *stip*-e-tate, having a stalk; supported by or elevated on a stipe [Bot.].
stipitiform, *a.* sty-*pit*-e-form, of the form of a stipes; stalk-shaped; stipiform.
stipple, *v.t.* and *i.* *stip*-pl, to paint, draw, or engrave by means of dots instead of lines. (Dut.)
stipula, *n.* *stip*-yew-la, a stipule [Bot.].
stipulaceous, *a.* *stip*-yew-*lay*-shus, stipular.
stipular, *a.* *stip*-yew-lar, resembling or consisting of stipules; growing on stipules.
stipulate, *v.i.* *stip*-yew-late, to make an agreement; to contract; to settle terms. (L. *stipulatus.*)
stipulate, *a.* *stip*-yew-lat, having stipules [Bot.].
stipulation, *n.* *stip*-yew-*lay*-shon, the act of stipulating; contract or bargain; the situation and structure of the stipules [Bot.].
stipulator, *n.* *stip*-yew-lay-tor, one who stipulates, contracts, or covenants.
stipule, *n.* *stip*-yewl, a basal appendage of the leaf-stalk. (L. *stipula.*)
stipuled, *a.* *stip*-yewld, furnished with stipules.
stir, *v.t.* stir, to move; to agitate; to incite; to excite. **stir up,** to instigate; to excite; to quicken; to disturb: *v.i.* to move oneself; to go or be carried in any manner; to be in motion; to rise in the morning: *n.* agitation; tumult; bustle; public disturbance; agitation of thoughts; conflicting passions; [Slang] prison. (A.S. *styrian.*)
stirabout, *n.* *stir*-a-bout, hastily made oatmeal porridge; a hustle; a hustler.
stirk, *n.* stirk, a yearling bull or heifer. (A.S. *stirc.*)
stirless, *a.* *stir*-less, still; without stirring.
stirpiculture, *n.* *stir*-pe-kul-tewr, the breeding of special stocks.
stirps, *n.* stirps, a progenitor; a branch of a family [Law]; a group or sub-family [Zool.]. [L., stock.)
stirrer, *n.* *stir*-rer, one who or that which stirs.
stirring, *a.* *stir*-ring, active; animating; rousing; thrilling.
stirrup, *n.* *sti*-rup, a metal loop or ring suspended from a strap, for a horseman's foot, to enable him to mount or sit steadily on horseback; a rope having an eye in one end for reeving a foot-rope [Naut.]. (A.S. *stigan*, mount, *rap*, a rope.)
stirrup-cup, *n.* a parting cup on horseback.
stirrup-leather, *n.* a strap of leather for supporting a stirrup.
stirrup-pump, *n.* a light portable pump for a fire-hose held in place by the foot in its stirrup while being worked by hand.
stitch, *n.* stitch, one complete pass of a needle and thread when sewing; a similar pass of wool or thread in knitting; a link of yarn; a sharp local twinge of pain: *v.t.* to sew in a continuous line; to unite together by sewing: *v.i.* to practise needlework. (A.S. *stice*, a stab, puncture.)
stitcher, *n.* *stitch*-er, one who or a machine that stitches.
stitchery, *n.* *stitch*-er-re, needlework.
stitching, *n.* *stitch*-ing, the act of stitching; work done by sewing, to show a continuous line of stitches.
stitchwort, *n.* *stitch*-wurt, any plant of the genus *Stellaria*, which includes the chickweeds.
stithy, *n.* *stith*-e, an anvil; a smithy. (Ice. *stethi.*)
stive, *v.t.* stive, to stew: *v.i.* to be stewed; to be stifled. (O.Fr. *estuver.*)
stiver, *n.* *sty*-ver, a Dutch halfpenny; any coin of little worth. (Dut. *stuiver.*)
stoa, *n.* *stoh*-a, a porch; a colonnade; the Stoic philosophy. **the Stoa,** the public walk at Athens where Zeno, the stoic philosopher, taught. (Gr.)
stoat, *n.* stoht, the ermine, *Mustela erminea*, allied to the weasel; the ferret. (M.E. *stot.*)
stoccado, *n.* stok-*kah*-doh, a stab; a thrust with a rapier in fencing. (It.)
stock, *n.* stok, the stem of a tree or other plant; a post; a dull, stupid, senseless person; the frame of a rifle; a necktie; the original progenitor; lineage; a family; a distinct group of languages; share of a public debt; a fund; capital; merchandise unsold; goods on hand; the domestic animals or beasts belonging to a farm; a plant, the stock gilly-flower, of the genus *Matthiola*: *pl.* a frame in which the legs of delinquents were confined by way of punishment; the frame on which a ship rests while building; the public funds: *a.* kept in stock; permanent: *v.i.* to store for sale or use; to supply; to fill; to lay up in store; to pack; to supply with domestic animals; to supply with seed. **stock-in-trade,** the goods, tools, and other appliances of a trade or business; resources. **on the stocks,** in course of construction; in preparation. **take stock,** to make an inventory; to estimate a position, etc. (A.S. *stocc.*)
stockade, *n.* stok-*kade*, a palisaded defence; a line of posts or stakes set as a fence or barrier [Fort.]; an enclosure for cattle: *v.t.* to surround or fortify with sharpened posts fixed in the ground. (Sp. *estacada.*)
stockbroker, *n.* *stok*-broh-ker, a member of a stock exchange who deals with a stockjobber in the purchase and sale of stocks or shares on behalf of his clients.
stockbroking, *n.* *stok*-bro-king, the business of a stockbroker.
stock-dove, *n.* the wild pigeon, *Columba œnas.*
stock-exchange, *n.* an official organization, acting as a central market for trading in securities, stocks, and shares; the building in which such securities are bought and sold.
stock-fish, *n.* fish, such as cod or ling, split and dried unsalted in the sun. (Dut. *stokvisch.*)
stockholder, *n.* *stok*-hohl-der, a proprietor of stock in the public funds or a public company.
stockiness, *n.* *stok*-e-ness, the condition of being stocky.
stockinet, or **-nette,** *n.* stok-e-*net*, a knitted fabric used for underwear.
★**stocking,** *n.* *stok*-ing, a close-fitting knitted or woven covering for the leg and foot.
stockinger, *n.* *stok*-ing-er, a stocking weaver.
stocking-frame, *n.* *stok*-ing-frame, a machine for weaving stockings or the fabric of which they are made.
stockish, *a.* *stok*-ish, stupid; blockish.
stockist, *n.* *stok*-ist, a dealer who keeps certain specified goods in stock.
stockjobber, *n.* *stok*-job-ber, one who acts as intermediary between buying and selling stockbrokers; a professional speculator in securities.
stockjobbery, *n.* *stok*-job-er-re, stockjobbing.
stockjobbing, *n.* dealing in stocks or shares.
stock-lock, *n.* a lock fixed in a wooden case or frame.
stockman, *n.* *stok*-man, a herdsman.
stock-market, *n.* a stock exchange; a market for cattle or livestock.
stockpot, *n.* *stok*-pot, a pot in which the basis of soup is prepared or stored.
stockrider, *n.* *stok*-ride-er, a mounted stockman (esp. in Australia).

stock-still, *a.* still as a fixed post; perfectly still.
stocktaker, *n.* *stok*-take-er, one who makes a list of goods or properties on hand.
stocktaking, *n.* *stok*-take-ing, making a list of the stock-in-trade.
stockwhip, *n.* *stok*-whip, a short-handled whip with a thong of great length used in herding cattle.
stocky, *a.* *stok*-e, thick and firm; stumpy.
stockyard, *n.* *stok*-yard, a yard in which cattle and sheep are kept.
stodge, *n.* stodj, heavy, semi-solid food; a heavy feed or meal: *v.t.* and *i.* to stuff full; to gorge with food. (Dial. Eng.)
stodginess, *n.* *stodj*-e-ness, the state of being stodgy.
stodgy, *a.* *stodj*-e, thick and badly mixed; indigestible; dull, uninspired [Slang].
stoep, *n.* stoop, the verandah or roofed platform in houses of Dutch style. (S. African Dut.)
Stoic, *n.* *stoh*-ik, a disciple of the philosopher Zeno, who taught that men should subdue all passion, conform to reason, and accept the inevitable; one actually or professedly indifferent to joy and sorrow or pleasure and pain. (Gr. *Stoa*, the Porch, a promenade on which Zeno taught in Athens.)
stoical, *a.* *stoh*-e-kal, pertaining to the Stoics or their doctrines; not affected by passion; unfeeling; manifesting indifference to pleasure and pain.
stoically, *ad.* *stoh*-e-ka-le, in a stoical manner.
stoicalness, *n.* *stoh*-e-kal-ness, the state of being stoical (real or affected); indifference to pleasure or pain.
stoichiology, *n.* *stoy*-ke-*ol*-o-je, the science or doctrine of elements and elementary principles; the branch of physiology treating of the composition, etc., of animal tissues. (Gr. *stoicheion*, an element, and *logos*, science.)
stoichiometry, *n.* *stoy*-ke-*om*-e-tre, the determination of the proportions in which elements or compounds react with one another; the determination of atomic and molecular weights; the doctrine of chemical equivalents. (Gr. *stoicheion*, and *metron*, measure.)
stoicism, *n.* *stoh*-e-sizm, the opinions and maxims of the Stoics; stoicalness; calm fortitude.
stoke, *v.t.* stoke, to tend a fire as a stoker. **stoke up,** to take a hearty meal [Slang]. (Dut. *stoken*.)
stokehold, *n.* *stoke*-hohld, the part of a ship's hold containing the boilers.
stokehole, *n.* *stoke*-hole, the mouth of a furnace, also the space in front of it accommodating the stokers; a stokehold; the opening in a blast-furnace for use of the stirring tool.
stoker, *n.* *stoke*-er, one who manages a furnace.
stole, stole, *p.* of *steal*.
stole, *n.* stole, the outer robe of ancient Greek or Roman matrons; a long strip or band of silk reaching from the neck to the foot worn over both shoulders by priests and bishops and over the left shoulder only by deacons; a fur or feather neck-wrap for women. (Gr.)
stole, *n.* stole, a close-stool. **Groom of the Stole,** title, till its discontinuance in 1837, of a high official in the British Royal household.
stole, *n.* stole, a stolon.
stolen, *stoh*-len, *pp.* of *steal*.
stolid, *a.* *stol*-id, impassive; foolish; stupid. (L. *stolidus*.)
stolidity, *n.* sto-*lid*-e-te, stolidness; dullness.
stolidly, *ad.* *stol*-id-le, in a stolid manner.
stolidness, *n.* the state of being stolid.
stolon, *n.* *stoh*-lon, a trailing stem which roots and develops a new plant at intervals. (L.)
stolonate, *a.* *stoh*-lo-nat, having a stolon or stolons; springing from a stolon [Bot.].
stoloniferous, *a.* *stoh*-lo-*nif*-er-rus, putting forth stolons. (L. *stolonis*, and *fero*, bear.)
stolzite, *n.* *stol*-zite, tungstate of lead. (After the discoverer, *Stolz*.)
stoma, *n.* *stoh*-ma (*pl.* **stomata**), a breathing pore or orifice, specially in the epidermis of a leaf. (Gr., the mouth.)
★**stomach,** *n.* *stum*-ak, a membranous receptacle below the liver and diaphragm, the principal organ of digestion in which the food is prepared for the nourishment of the body; the desire of food; appetite; inclination; liking; anger; sullenness; resentment; pride: *v.t.* to tolerate; to brook. (Gr. *stomachos*, the gullet, from *stoma*.)
stomache-ache, *n.* pain in the stomach or adjacent parts.
stomachal, *a.* *stum*-a-kal, stomachic.
stomacher, *n.* *stum*-a-ker, a covering for the breast, often ornamented, part of women's 15th to 17th century dress; a blow on the stomach [Pugilism].
stomachic, *a.* sto-*mak*-ik, pertaining to the stomach; strengthening to the stomach; exciting the action of the stomach: *n.* a stomachic medicine.
stomachless, *a.* *stum*-ak-less, being without a stomach; having no appetite.
stomach-pump, *n.* *stum*-ak-pump, a small pump or syringe, with a flexible tube, for drawing liquids from the stomach, or for injecting them.
stomata, *n.* *stoh*-ma-ta *or* *stom*-a-ta, *pl.* of *stoma*.
stomatic, *a.* sto-*mat*-ik, relating to or like a stoma.
stomatitis, *n.* *stoh*-ma-*ty*-tis, inflammation of the mucous lining of the mouth [Med.]. (Gr. *stoma*.)
stomato-gastric, *a.* *stoh*-ma-to-*gas*-trik, pertaining to the mouth and stomach.
stomatology, *n.* stoh-ma-*tol*-o-je, the branch of medicine treating of the mouth and its diseases.
stomato-plastic, *a.* pertaining to stomato-plasty. [Surg.].
stomato-plasty, *a.* plastic surgery of the mouth [Surg.].
Stomatopoda, *n.* *stoh*-ma-*top*-o-da, an order of small marine burrowing crustaceans.
stomatoscope, *n.* stoh-*mat*-o-skope, an instrument for viewing the interior of the mouth.
★**stone,** *n.* stone, a fragment of rock; a gem or precious stone; a millstone, tombstone, monument, or anything made of stone; a calculous concretion in the kidneys or bladder [Path.]; a testicle; the nut of a drupe or stone-fruit; the weight of fourteen pounds; a weight varying in different trades: *a.* made of stone or like stone: *v.t.* to pelt or kill with stones; to free from stones; to wall or face with stones; to line or fortify with stones. **leave no stone unturned,** to spare no exertions. **Stone Age,** the period of stone implements antecedent to the use of bronze, and divided in Europe into the Eolithic, Palæolithic, Megalithic and subsidiary stages. **stone parsley,** the umbelliferous plant, *Sisum amomum*, growing in hedges. (A.S. *stan*.)
stonebiter, *n.* *stone*-bite-er, the cat-fish, *Anarrhichas lupus*; the hawfinch.
stone-blind, *a.* perfectly blind.
stone-bow, *n.* a cross-bow for shooting stones.
stonebrash, *n.* *stone*-brash, a finely broken rock; a subsoil of loose stones.
stonebreak, *n.* *stone*-brake, any plant of the genus *Saxifraga*; the parsley-fern.
stone-breaker, *n.* one who or a machine that breaks or crushes stones.
stone-butter, *n.* a native alum having a greasy surface; rock-butter.
stonechat, *n.* *stone*-chat, the wheatear.
stone-coal, *n.* anthracite.
stone-cold, *a.* quite cold.
stonecrop, *n.* *stone*-krop, a succulent plant of the genus *Sedum*.
stone-curlew, *n.* the thicknee curlew; also, the whimbrel, and stone-plover.
stone-cutter, *n.* one whose occupation is to hew stones, esp. for buildings; a machine or implement for dressing stone.
stone-dead, *a.* stone-*ded*, as lifeless as a stone.
stone-deaf, *a.* stone-*def*, deaf as a stone; quite deaf.
stone-dresser, *n.* one who smoothes and shapes stones for building.
stone-eater, *n.* a mollusc that bores into stone.
stone-falcon, *n.* the stone-hawk.
stone-fly, *n.* a neuropterous insect of the genus *Perla*, used as bait by trout fishers; an artificial imitation of this.
stone-fruit, *n.* fruit whose seeds are covered with a hard shell enveloped in the pulp, as in the plums, peaches, etc.
stone-hammer, *n.* a hammer for breaking stones; a hammer with a stone head.
stone-hatch, *n.* the stone-plover.
stone-hawk, *n.* the merlin, *Falco æsalon*.
stone-horse, *n.* a stallion.
stoneless, *a.* *stone*-less, without stones.
stone-lily, *n.* an encrinite.
stone-marten, *n.* the beech-marten, *Mustela foina*.

a small carnivore with a white patch on the breast; the fur of this.
stonemason, *n. stone*-may-son, a mason who works in or dresses stone.
stone-oil, *n. stone*-oyl, petroleum.
stone-pine, *n.* the coniferous tree, *Pinus pinea*, of southern Europe; the Swiss pine, *Pinus cembra*.
stonepit, *n. stone*-pit, a pit or quarry where stones are dug.
stone-pitch, *n. stone*-pitch, hard inspissated pitch.
stone-plover, *n.* the ringed plover, *Ægialitis hiaticulus*; the stone-curlew.
stoner, *n. stone*-er, one who beats or kills with stones; one who walls with stones; an implement for removing stones from fruit, etc.
stone-snipe, *n. stone*-snipe, the long-legged tattler, *Totanus melanoleucus*.
stone's-throw, *n.* the distance which a stone may be thrown by hand; any short distance.
stone-still, *a.* perfectly still or motionless.
stonewall, *v.i.* and *t.* stone-*wawl*, in cricket, to bat stolidly on the defensive; to block; in politics, to consume time by uselessly protracting debate: *n.* a certain formation of the pawns in chess: *a.* determined; obstinate.
stoneware, *n. stone*-ware, a species of potter's ware of a coarse kind.
stonework, *n. stone*-wurk, masonry; work in stone.
stonily, *ad. stoh*-ne-le, in a stony manner.
stoniness, *n. stoh*-ne-ness, the quality of being stony; hardness of heart.
stony, *a. stoh*-ne, made of stone; consisting of stone; abounding with stones; petrifying; hard; obdurate; unrelenting. **stony broke,** penniless, bankrupt [Slang].
stony-hearted, *a.* hard-hearted; unfeeling.
stood, stood, *p.* and *pp.* of *stand*.
stooge, *n.* stooj, one of a pair, esp. of comedians, forming a butt or foil to the other; a dupe; a person ready to be deceived [Slang].
stook, *n.* stook, a shock of corn; a stand of sheaves piled against each other: *v.t.* to set up sheaves in stooks. (M.E. *stouke*.)
stool, *n.* stool, a seat without a back; a little form with three or four legs as a seat for one person; a seat used in evacuating the bowels, an evacuation; the stump of a tree from which shoots sprout; a sucker [Bot.]: *v.i.* to ramify; to tiller, as grain; to shoot out suckers. **stool of repentance,** in Scotland, a cutty-stool. **fall between two stools,** to fail through hesitating between two choices, or through adopting both. (A.S. *stol*.)
stool-ball, *n.* an early form of cricket in which the wicket was a stool and the bat used one-handed.
stool-pigeon, *n.* a decoy; a dupe; an informer.
stoom, *v.t.* stoom, to stum.
stoop, *n.* stoop, act of stooping; condescension; swoop: *v.i.* to bend down or incline the body; to yield; to submit; to condescend; to be inferior; to swoop down; to sink to a lower place: *v.t.* to cause to incline downward. (A.S. *stupian*.)
stoop, *n.* stoop, a stoup; a tankard. (O.Dut.)
stoop, *n.* stoop, a stoep.
stooper, *n. stoop*-er, one who stoops.
stoopingly, *ad. stoop*-ing-le, in a stooping manner.
stoor, *n.* stoor, dust flying about; a commotion: *v.t.* to stir up; to pour out: *v.i.* to rise in clouds [Scots.].
★**stop,** *n.* stop, cessation of progressive motion; obstruction; repression; interruption; obstacle; a peg or the like for stopping movement; a point or mark in writing for regulating the necessary pauses; that by which the sounds of musical instruments are regulated; a diaphragm in a camera; a temporary lashing for securing a rope [Naut.]; the act of applying the stops [Mus.]; a consonant (*p*, *b*, etc.) formed by stoppage of the breath [Phonetics]: *v.t.* to close by filling or obstructing; to obstruct; to check or arrest; to impede; to repress; to restrain; to intercept; to regulate sounds; to punctuate: *v.i.* to cease to go forward; to cease. (A.S. *stoppian*.)
stopcock, *n. stop*-kok, a valve for regulating flow.
stope, *n.* stope, one of a series of ledges in which ore is excavated: *v.t.* to form stopes. (*stop*.)
stopgap, *n. stop*-gap, a temporary expedient; a substitute.
stoping, *n. stoh*-ping, any method by which ore is stoped.
stoppage, *n. stop*-aj, the act of stopping or arresting progress or motion; the state of being stopped; deduction from pay [Mil.]; a strike or lock-out.
stopper, *n. stop*-per, one who or that which stops; that which closes or fills a vent or hole in a vessel; a plug; a short piece of rope used for making fast [Naut.]: *v.t.* to close or secure with a stopper.
stopping, *n. stop*-ping, something that stops; a filling; punctuation.
stopple, *n. stop*-pl, that which stops or closes the mouth of a vessel; a cork; a plug: *v.t.* to close with a stopple.
stop-press, *n.* late news printed in a newspaper in a special space.
stop-watch, *n. stop*-wotch, a watch with a special hand that can be started or stopped at any fraction of a second for the timing of the duration of events.
storage, *n. staw*-raj, a placing in store; the safe keeping of goods in a warehouse; the price for keeping goods in a store; the system of storing electricity in cells of grids of lead superficially coated with oxide, which are immersed in dilute sulphuric acid and polarized by the passage of the current. **storage battery,** an accumulator [Elect.]. **cold storage,** keeping victuals, or furs, etc., in refrigerating chambers.
storax, *n. staw*-raks, an odoriferous resin obtained from *Styrax officinalis*; an expectorant and stimulant prepared from *liquidambar orientalis*; any tree of the genus *Styrax*.
★**store,** *n.* store, a stock laid up for supply; abundance; plenty; quantity accumulated; a warehouse; a shop, esp. one selling a diversity of goods: *pl.* a shop with many departments; arms, ammunition, provisions, and clothing [Mil. and Naval]: *v.t.* to furnish; to supply; to hoard up; to warehouse. **in store,** in reserve; in a state of readiness. **set store by,** to value highly. (L. *instauro*, renew.)
storehouse, *n. store*-house, a place for storing provisions; a repository; a warehouse; a magazine.
storekeeper, *n. store*-keep-er, one who has the care of stores; a shopkeeper [U.S.A.].
storer, *n. store*-er, one who lays up or forms a store.
storeroom, *n.* a room in which articles are stored.
storeship, *n. store*-ship, a vessel employed to carry military or naval stores.
storey, *n. staw*-re, a story of a house.
storiated, *a. staw*-re-ay-ted, embellished with storiation.
storiation, *n. staw*-re-*ay*-shon, ornamentation with pictures of historical incidents, emblematic interest, etc. (*story*.)
storied, *a. staw*-rid, adorned with historical paintings; related or celebrated in story or history; having stories or floors.
storiette, *n.* staw-re-*et*, a very short story.
storiologist. *n. staw*-re-*ol*-o-jist, a student of folklore.
storiology, *n.* staw-re-*ol*-o-je, the scientific study of folklore, popular legend, etc.
stork, *n.* stork, a large wading-bird of the genus *Ciconia*, allied to the heron. (A.S. *storc*.)
storksbill, *n. storks*-bil, a plant of the genus *Erodium*, the beak of the fruit of which is like a stork's bill.
storm, *n.* storm, a violent commotion in the atmosphere, generally widespread and destructive; a tempest; assault on a fortified place; violent civil commotion; insurrection; clamour; tumult; distress; violence; tumultuous force: *v.t.* to assault; to take by storm: *v.i.* to raise a tempest; to blow with violence; to rage. **take by storm,** to capture by assault or sudden attack; to make an immediate conquest, to have instantaneous success [Fig.]. (A.S.)
storm-beat, *a.* beaten or impaired by storms.
storm-bird, *n.* the stormy petrel, as herald of approaching storms.
storm-centre, *n.* the place of lowest pressure in a cyclonic storm; [Fig.] the focus of a disturbance, etc.
storm-cock, *n.* the mistle-thrush; the fieldfare.
storm-cone, *n.* the cone of a storm-signal.
storm-drum, *n.* the drum of a storm-signal.
stormer, *n. storm*-er, one who storms; one of a storming-party.
stormful, *a. storm*-ful, abounding with storms.
stormfulness, *n.* the state of being stormful.
storm-glass, *n.* a weather-glass.
stormily, *ad. stor*-me-le, in a stormy manner.

storminess, *n.* *stor*-me-ness, tempestuousness; the state of being agitated by violent winds.
storming-party, *n.* a party selected to lead an assault on a fortified place.
stormsail, *n.* *storm*-sl, a small strong sail used in a storm.
storm-signal, *n.* an arrangement of a hollow canvas drum and cone to intimate the approach of a storm, its expected direction, and its intensity.
storm-tossed, *a.* *storm*-tost, beaten by storms; agitated by passion.
storm-trooper, *n.* one of a body of storm-troops; a member of the former Nazi S.A. (*Sturmabteilung*), Hitler's original gangster bodyguard.
storm-troops, *n.pl.* soldiers specially trained and armed for undertaking assaults, etc.
stormy, *a.* *storm*-e, tempestuous; accompanied or agitated with furious winds; boisterous; violent. **stormy petrel,** the small sea-bird Mother Carey's chicken, *Procellaria pelagica*.
Storthing, *n.* *stor*-thing, the parliament of Norway. (Dan. *stor*, great, *thing*, court.)
★**story,** *n.* *staw*-re, a verbal narration or written narrative of a series of facts or events; history; a petty or trifling tale; a fiction; the plot of a play, novel, etc.; an event recorded or to be recorded in a newspaper; a news article; a fib. (*history.*)
story, *n.* *staw*-re, a floor; the space between two floors; a set of rooms on the same floor. **upper story,** brain, intelligence [Coll.]. (*history.*)
story-book, *n.* a book of stories or short tales.
story-post, *n.* a vertical post used to support a floor.
storyteller, *n.* *staw*-re-tel-er, one who tells stories; one who tells fictitious stories; a liar.
storytelling, *n.* the practice of telling stories.
stot, *n.* stot, a young bullock or steer [Scots.].
stoup, *n.* stoop, a flagon; a basin for holy water; a measure for liquids. (O.Dut.)
stour, *a.* stoor, unbending; stubborn; coarse in texture [Scots.]: *n.* stoor [Scots.].
stout, *a.* stout, strong; lusty; bold; intrepid; thickset; corpulent; proud; resolute; stubborn: *n.* a dark brown beer stronger than porter. (O.Fr. *estout.*)
stout-hearted, *a.* brave; resolute.
stoutly, *ad.* *stout*-le, lustily; boldly; obstinately.
stoutness, *n.* *stout*-ness, the quality or state of being stout; boldness; fortitude; stubbornness.
stovaine, *n.* sto-*vay*-ine, a hydrochlorate solution used as an injection to induce local analgesia [Surg.].
stove, *n.* stove, a cooking grate or range; an apparatus enclosing a fire for heating or cooking; a hot-house: *v.t.* to keep warm in a house or room by artificial heat; to force by artificial heat; to heat. (A.S. *stofa*, a bath-house.)
stove, stove, *p.* and *pp.* of *stave*.
stove-pipe, *n.* a pipe to carry off the smoke of a stove.
stove-plant, *n.* a hothouse plant.
stove-plate, *n.* a plate for filling a hole on the top of a stove.
stover, *n.* *stoh*-ver *or* *stuv*-er, fodder for cattle. (Dial. Eng.)
stow, *v.t.* stoh, to place; to put in a suitable place or position; to lay up; to pack. (A.S. *stow*, a place.)
stowage, *n.* *stoh*-aj, the act of stowing; the state of being stowed; room for stowing things; money paid for stowing things.
stowaway, *n.* *stoh*-a-way, one hiding in a ship (or other conveyance) in order to secure a free passage or make an escape.
stower, *n.* *stoh*-er, one who stows.
strabismal, *a.* stra-*biz*-mal, strabismic.
strabismic, *a.* stra-*biz*-mik, pertaining to or affected by strabismus.
strabismus, *n.* stra-*biz*-mus, a non-coincidence of the optic axes of the eyes upon an object; squinting. (Gr. *strabos*, twisted, squinting.)
strabotome, *n.* *strab*-o-tome, the knife used in the operation of strabotomy.
strabotomy, *n.* stra-*bot*-o-me, the surgical removal of strabismus. (Gr. *strabos*, and *tome*, cutting.)
Strad, *n.* strad, a violin (or other stringed instrument) made by Antonio Stradivari (*d.* 1737) the noted Italian craftsman [Coll.].
straddle, *n.* *strad*-dl, the act of straddling; distance between legs astraddle: *v.i.* to part the legs wide; to stand or walk with the legs far apart; to bracket, or place shots short of and beyond a target so tha[t] the true range may be ascertained [Gunnery] *v.t.* to bestride. (*stride.*)
Stradivarius, *n.* strad-e-*vare*-re-us, a Strad.
strafe, *v.t.* straf, to punish, attack, or criticiz[e] savagely; to chastise; to bomb: *n.* a heav[y] bombardment; a strafing. (Ger. *straffen*, t[o] punish; from phrase "Gott strafe England" use[d] by Germans during the War of 1914–18.)
strafing, *n.* *straf*-ing, severe punishment, a goo[d] dressing-down. (*strafe.*)
straggle, *v.i.* *strag*-gl, to wander from the direc[t] course or way; to rove; to wander at large withou[t] any certain direction or object; to ramble; t[o] shoot too far in growth; to be dispersed; to b[e] apart from any main body. (M.E. *straken*, to roam.)
straggler, *n.* *strag*-gler, one who straggles; wanderer; something that grows beyond the res[t] or is left behind; something that stands by itself.
straggling, *a.* wandering; rambling; scattered.
stragglingly, *ad.* in a straggling manner.
straggly, *a.* *strag*-gle, straggling; dispersed.
★**straight,** *a.* strate, right; direct; not deviatin[g] or crooked; not deviating from truth or fairness *n.* a straight part of anything, esp. a straigh[t] stretch of a race-course, river, etc.: *ad.* immediately directly. **a straight face,** an inexpressive o[r] unsmiling look. (A.S. *streht*, stretched.)
straightaway, *a.* *strate*-a-way, at once; straigh[t] forward: *n.* a straight course (for races).
straight-cut, *a.* cut lengthwise (of tobacco leaf).
straight-edge, *n.* a rule of wood or metal havin[g] one edge perfectly straight.
straight-eight, *n.* a motor-car, or engine, havin[g] eight cylinders in line.
straighten, *v.t.* *stray*-tn, to make straight; t[o] reduce from a crooked to a straight form.
straightener, *n.* *stray*-tn-er, he who or that whic[h] straightens.
straightforward, *a.* strate-*for*-ward, proceedin[g] in a straight course; upright; honest; open.
straightforwardly, *ad.* in a straightforward manne[r]
straightforwardness, *n.* the quality of bein[g] straightforward.
straight-grained, *a.* having a grain runnin[g] parallel to the length (of wood).
straightly, *ad.* *strate*-le, in a right line; directly; i[n] a straight manner.
straightness, *n.* state or quality of being straight.
straightway, *ad.* *strate*-way, immediately; with out delay.
straik, *n.* strake, a strake.
strain, *n.* strane, a violent effort; an injury b[y] excessive exertion; drawing or stretching; tension continued manner of speaking or writing; a song a particular part of a tune; turn; tendency manner of speech or action; race; spirit: *v.t* to stretch; to draw with force; to injure b[y] stretching; to stretch violently; to put to th[e] utmost extent; to purify or separate fro[m] extraneous matter by filtration; to filter; t[o] make tighter; to force; to constrain: *v.i.* to mak[e] violent efforts; to be filtered. **strain a point,** to stretch a point. **strain at,** to be over-scrupulous about. (L. *stringo*, draw tight.)
strainer, *n.* *stray*-ner, an instrument for filtration a sieve; a percolator.
strait, *a.* strate, narrow; strict; rigorous; difficult; distressful: *n.* (usually *pl.*) a narrow sea pass, or passage between two portions of land distress; difficulty; distressing necessity. (L. *strictus*, drawn together.)
straiten, *v.t.* *stray*-tn, to make narrow; to contract to confine; to make tense or tight; to distress to perplex; to press with poverty or other necessity to press by want of sufficient room. **in straitened circumstances,** needy; badly off.
strait-jacket, *n.* strate-*jak*-et, a strait-waistcoat.
strait-laced, *a.* *strate*-layst, gripped with stays constrained; strict in manners or morals.
straitly, *ad.* *strate*-le, narrowly; closely; strictly.
straitness, *n.* *strate*-ness, narrowness; strictness distress; want.
strait-waistcoat, *n.* strate-*wayst* (or *wes*)-koat, [a] garment to restrain the arms of a violent lunatic.
strake, *n.* strake, one of the iron plates forming th[e] tire of a wheel; a single breadth of plank or platin[g] along a ship's side; a shallow trough or box fo[r] washing ore [Min.].

stramash, *n.* stra-*mash*, an uproar, a rumpus.
stramineous, *a.* stra-*min*-e-us, consisting of or like straw; chaffy; light. (L. *stramen*, straw.)
stramonium, *n.* stra-*moh*-ne-um, the thorn-apple; a drug, used in asthma, prepared from this. (L.)
strand, *n.* strand, the shore or beach: *v.t.* to drive or run aground; to bring into difficulties, esp. financial: *v.i.* to drift or be driven ashore; to run aground. (A.S.)
strand, *n.* strand, one of the twists of yarn of which a rope is composed: *v.t.* to break one of the strands of a rope. (Old Ger. *streno*, cord.)
stranded, *a.* *stran*-did, without resources [Coll.].
stranded, *a.* *stran*-did, composed of strands; arranged in strands or plaits.
strandlooper, *n.* *strand*-loo-per, a Hottentot beachcomber. (S.Afr.Dut.)
★**strange,** *a.* straynj, foreign; belonging to others; not before known, heard, or seen; wonderful; odd; unusual; reserved; unfamiliar. (O.Fr. *estrange*, from L. *extraneus*, external.)
strangely, *ad.* in a strange manner; wonderfully.
strangeness, *n.* state or quality of being strange.
stranger, *n.* *strayn*-jer, one who belongs to another town or country; one unknown; one unacquainted; a guest; a visitor; one not party or privy to any act [Law].
strangle, *v.t.* *strang*-gl, to destroy life by stopping respiration; to hinder from birth or appearance; to suppress. (O.Fr. *estrangler.*)
strangle-hold, *n.* an illegal choking grip in wrestling; [Fig.] an effectually restraining act, condition, or influence.
strangler, *n.* *strang*-gler, one who or that which strangles.
strangles, *n.* *strang*-glz, an infectious catarrh in horses, in which a tumour is formed under the jaw.
strangulated, *a.* *strang*-gew-lay-ted, having the circulation stopped in any part by compression [Surg.]; irregularly contracted at intervals [Bot.]; choked.
strangulation, *n.* *strang*-gew-*lay*-shon, the act of strangling; hysterical constriction of the throat; compression of the intestines in hernia.
strangurious, *n.* strang-*gewr*-re-us, labouring under strangury; pertaining to strangury.
strangury, *n.* *strang*-gewr-re, painful micturition due to spasmodic contraction of the urethra and bladder [Med.]. (L. *stranguria.*)
strap, *n.* strap, a long narrow strip of cloth or leather with a buckle; a strop; a strip, band, or metal plate for connecting parts or holding them together; a small ring of rope used to retain a block in position [Naut.]; a shoulder-strap; a ligula [Bot.]: *v.t.* to beat or chastise with a strap; to fasten or bind with a strap; to strop. (A.S. *stropp*, L. *struppus.*)
straphanger, *n.* *strap*-hang-er, a standing passenger steadying himself by holding on to a strap.
strappado, *n.* stra-*pah*-doh, an old torture or military punishment of drawing up a person to a height by a rope and letting him fall to its length: *v.t.* to torture so. (It.)
strapper, *n.* a groom; one who secures with straps; a tall, well-set-up man [Coll.].
strapping, *a.* *strap*-ping, tall, lusty, and handsome: *n.* material for straps; adhesive plaster [Med.].
strap-work, *n.* decorative design of crossed or interlaced bands.
strapwort, *n.* *strap*-wurt, the small seashore plant, *Corrigialis littoralis*, with strap-shaped leaves.
strass, *n.* strass, a lead glass or paste used for making artificial gems. (Joseph *Strasser*, the 18th-cent. inventor.)
strass, *n.* strass, silk wasted during its winding into skeins; waxed straw used in millinery. (Fr. *strasse*, as *extract.*)
strata, *n.* *stray*-ta (*pl.* of **stratum**), beds, layers [Geol.]. (L.)
stratagem, *n.* *strat*-a-jem, an artifice, particularly in war; a plan, scheme, or trick for deceiving an enemy or gaining an advantage. (Fr.)
stratal, *a.* *stray*-tal, pertaining to strata or a stratum.
strategetic, *a.* strat-e-*jet*-ik, strategic.
strategic, *a.* stra-*tej*-ik, pertaining to strategy; showing strategy; done by strategy.
strategical, *a.* stra-*tej*-e-kal, strategic.
strategically, *ad.* in a strategical manner.
strategist, *n.* *strat*-e-jist, one skilled in strategy.
strategy, *n.* *strat*-e-je, generalship; the science or art of combining and employing military resources, or of manœuvring an army; direction of the operations of war. (Gr. *strategia.*)
strath, *n.* strath, an open valley through which a river runs. (Gael.)
strathspey, *n.* strath-*spay*, a lively Scottish dance; music adapted to it. (*Strathspey*, in Scotland.)
straticulate, *a.* stra-*tik*-yew-lat, deposited in many thin layers or strata.
stratification, *n.* *strat*-e-fe-*kay*-shon, the process or act of stratifying; the state of being stratified; the arrangement of strata.
stratified, *a.* *strat*-e-fide, ranged in strata or layers.
stratiform, *a.* *strat*-e-form, in layer formation.
stratify, *v.t.* *stra* -e-fy, to form into a layer or layers, as rocks in the earth; to lay in strata. (L. *stratum.*)
stratigraphical, *a.* strat-e-*graf*-e-kal, pertaining to stratigraphy.
stratigraphically, *ad.* in a stratigraphical manner.
stratigraphy, *n.* stra-*tig*-ra-fe, the science of the geological arrangement of strata. (L. *stratum*, and Gr. *grapho.*)
stratocracy, *n.* stra-*tok*-ra-se, a military government; government by military chiefs or a military caste. (Gr. *stratos*, army, *kratos*, dominion.)
stratocruiser, *n.* *strat*-o-*kroo*-zer, proprietary name (Boeing Co.) of a large passenger- and freight-carrying aeroplane designed to cruise at 30,000 feet.
strato-cumulus, *n.* *stray*-toh-*kew*-mew-lus, cumulo-stratus.
stratographical, *a.* strat-o-*graf*-e-kal, relating to stratography.
stratographically, *ad.* in a stratographical manner
stratography, *n.* stra-*tog*-ra-fe, description of armies or what belongs to an army.
stratosphere, *n.* *strat*-o- *or* *stray*-to-sfeer, the upper portion of the atmosphere, commencing about 7 miles above the earth's surface and of unknown thickness, where the temperature ceases to fall as the height increases; the isothermal region.
stratospheric, *a.* strat-o-*sfe*-rik, pertaining to the stratosphere.
stratum, *n.* *stray*-tum (*pl.* **strata**), a bed or layer of rock as arranged in series in the crust of the earth; a bed or layer artificially made; a level region, as of the air or sea; a sociological or cultural grade, group, or rank. (L.)
stratus, *n.* *stray*-tus (*pl.* **strati**), a cloud-form spread over the sky in horizontal layers.
straught, strawt, *former p.* and *pp.* of *stretch.*
stravaig, *v.i.* stra-*vayg*, to wander about aimlessly: *n.* a ramble [Scots.].
straw, *n.* straw, the stalk or stem of certain species of grasses; a mass of such stalks after being cut and thrashed; anything proverbially worthless; a stalk of wheat-straw for sucking up liquids; a narrow strip of pastry, a cheese straw; a straw-hat [Coll.]. **straw vote,** an unofficial ballot taken for an indication of public opinion [U.S.A.]. (A.S. *streaw.*)
strawberry, *n.* *straw*-be-re, the fruit of any of the plants of the genus *Fragaria*; the plant itself a low-growing stemless perennial. **strawberry-leaf,** a leaf of the strawberry, representations of which adorn the ducal coronet; hence, a dukedom. **strawberry-mark,** a soft reddish birthmark. **strawberry-tree,** an evergreen tree of the genus *Arbutus*. **crushed strawberry,** a dull crimson colour. (A.S. *streawberige.*)
straw-board, *n.* a thick paper made of straw.
straw-colour, *n.* a pale yellow.
strawcutter, *n.* *straw*-kut-ter, an instrument or machine for cutting straw for fodder.
straw-hat, *n.* a hat made of plaited straw.
straw-plait, *n.* plaited straw.
straw-rope, *n.* a rope of twisted straw.
strawy, *a.* *straw*-e, made or consisting of straw; like straw.
stray, *n.* stray, any domestic animal that has left an enclosure and wanders at large or is lost; a lost or forlorn child; a waif: *a.* gone astray: *v.i.* to wander, as from a direct course, from company, from the proper limits, or from the path of duty or rectitude; to roam. (O.Fr. *estraier.*)
strayer, *n.* *stray*-er, one who strays.
streak, *n.* streek, a line or stripe of a different colour from the ground; a stripe; the mark on a mineral when streaked for identification; a tendency [Fig.]: *v.t.* to mark or variegate with

streaks; to form streaks on: *v.i.* to become streaky. **like a streak of lightning,** like a flash, very fast. **yellow streak,** *see* **yellow. to streak,** or **make streaks,** to clear off hurriedly [Slang]. (*strike.*)
streaked, *a.* streekt, marked with streaks.
streakiness, *n.* the state of being streaky.
streaky, *a.* *streek*-e, having stripes; streaked; with fat and lean in alternate layers (of bacon).
stream, *n.* streem, a current of water or other fluid; a river, brook, or rivulet; a current of air or of light; current; drift; the act of streaming: *v.i.* to flow; to move or run in a continuous current; to shed in a stream or current; to issue in a stream; to extend in a long line, as a pennant: *v.t.* to cause to flow; to cause to wave in the wind. (A.S.)
streamer, *n.* *streem*-er, a long narrow banner; a pennant; a beam or stream of light shooting up from the horizon.
streamless, *a.* *streem*-less, without streams.
streamlet, *n.* *streem*-let, a small stream; a rivulet.
stream-line, *n.* the direction of a current of air or water on a moving body; the shape of a surface or body, especially of an aeroplane or motor-car, designed to offer minimum resistance to such current: *v.t.* to give a stream-line shape to.
stream-lined, *a.* shaped to offer low resistance to movement in air or water.
stream-tin, *n.* *streem*-tin, tin ore found in beds of streams or the adjoining alluvial ground.
streamy, *a.* *streem*-e, abounding with running water; flowing in a stream or streak.
★**street,** *n.* street, a paved road in a city or town, lined with and including houses; a Roman road. **street arab,** *see* **Arab. not in the same street,** not to be compared with [Coll.]. **on the streets,** homeless; (of a woman) living as a prostitute. **the street,** (in London) Fleet Street; (in New York) Wall Street. (A.S. *stræt.*)
street-orderly, *n.* a scavenger; a receptacle for street sweepings.
street-sweeper, *n.* he who or that which sweeps the streets.
streetwalker, *n.* *street*-waw-ker, a prostitute.
strelitz, *n.* *strel*-its, a soldier of a body of Russian household troops raised in the 16th cent. and disbanded by Peter the Great, 1682. (Russ.)
strength, *n.* strength, quality of being strong; active power or vigour of an animal body; firmness; solidity or toughness; power or vigour of any kind; power of resisting attack; support or stay; robustness; intensity; spirit; vividness; force; legal or intellectual force; amount or proportion of a military or naval force. **on the strength,** on the pay-roll [Mil.]. **on the strength of,** relying on, because of. **up to strength,** having the full complement, esp. of troops. (A.S. *strengthu,* from *strang,* strong.)
strengthen, *v.t.* *streng*-then, to add strength to, either physical, legal, or moral; to make strong or stronger; to cause to increase in power or security: *v.i.* to grow strong or stronger.
strengthener, *n.* that which increases strength; a strengthening medicine.
strengthening, *a.* increasing strength.
strengthless, *a.* *strength*-less, wanting in strength; destitute of power.
strenuosity, *n.* *stren*-yew-*os*-e-te, strenuousness.
strenuous, *a.* *stren*-yew-us, eagerly pressing or urgent; zealous; ardent; bold and vigorous; needing effort; persistent. (L. *strenuus.*)
strenuously, *ad.* in a strenuous manner.
strenuousness, *n.* *stren*-yew-us-ness, the quality of being strenuous; eagerness; active zeal.
strepitant, *a.* *strep*-e-tant, loud; noisy.
strepitoso, *ad.* *strep*-e-*toh*-soh, to be executed in a boisterous, impetuous style [Mus.]. (It.)
streptococcic, *a.* strep-toh-*kok*-sik, pertaining or caused by streptococci.
streptococcus, *n.* strep-toh-*kok*-us (*pl.* **streptococci,** -*kok*-sy), a large group of bacterial organisms of many strains. (Gr. *streptos,* torque, *kokkus,* grain.)
streptomycin, *n.* strep-toh-*my*-sin, a drug prepared from a bacteria-like fungus, useful in cases of tuberculous meningitis and miliary tuberculosis, etc. (Gr. *streptos,* and *mykes,* mushroom.)
stress, *n.* stress, force; urgency; pressure; importance; that which bears most weight; violence; strain; emphasis; accent: *v.t.* to subject to a strain; to emphasize; to draw particular notice to. (O.Fr. *estrecier.*)
★**stretch,** *n.* stretch, the act of stretching; extension in length or breadth; reach; effort; strain; straining; utmost extent of meaning; utmost reach of power; tack; course; direction; a reach (of water); a tract (of land); a term (esp. one year) of imprisonment [Slang]: *v.t.* to draw out to greater length; to extend; to spread; to expand; to widen; to reach; to protrude; to strain; to exaggerate [Coll.]: *v.i.* to be drawn out in length or in breadth; to be extended; to straighten and extend the limbs and body; to spread; to exaggerate [Coll.]; to sail [Naut.]. **to stretch a point,** to exceed what is strictly legal or warranted; to give the benefit of the doubt. (A.S. *streccan.*)
stretcher, *n.* *stretch*-er, one who or that which stretches; a brick or stone laid lengthwise in the surface of the wall; a piece of timber in building; a narrow piece of plank placed across a boat for the rower to set his feet against; a frame or litter for carrying sick or wounded; one of the rods of an umbrella; the frame on which an artist's canvas is stretched.
stretching-course, *n.* *stretch*-ing-koarse, a course or row of stretchers [Masonry].
stretchy, *a.* *stretch*-e, apt to stretch.
stretto, *ad.* *stret*-toh, accelerando: *n.* a finale in quicker time; the part of a fugue in which subject and answer overlap [Mus.]. (It.)
strew, *v.t.* stroo, to scatter; to spread by scattering; to cover by being scattered over; to scatter loosely. *pp.* **strewed** and **strewn.** (A.S. *streowian.*)
striæ, *n.pl.* *stry*-ee, small channels or thread-like lines; the fillets between the flutes of columns. (L.)
striate, *a.* *stry*-at, striated.
striate, *v.t.* *stry*-ate, to mark with striæ; to channel; to streak.
striation, *n.* stry-*ay*-shon, state of being striated; *pl.* the alternating light and dark bands of an electrical discharge.
striature, *n.* *stry*-a-tewr, disposition of striæ.
strick, *n.* strik, a handful of flax ready for slivering; a straight-edge or strickle: *v.t.* to heckle (flax), or prepare for heckling; to level with a strickle.
stricken, *strik*-en, *pp.* of *strike*: *a.* struck; wounded; afflicted. **stricken field,** a pitched battle. **stricken in years,** aged.
strickle, *n.* *strik*-kl, a straight-edge to strike grain to a level with the measure; a hone for whetting scythes. (*strike.*)
strict, *a.* strikt, drawn close; rigorous; exact; accurate; definite; restricted. (L. *stringo, strictum,* draw tight.)
strictly, *ad.* *strikt*-le, exactly; literally.
strictness, *n.* *strikt*-ness, the quality of being strict; rigorous accuracy; rigour; severity.
stricture, *n.* *strik*-tewr, a critical remark; censure; animadversion; a spasmodic or other morbid contraction of any passage of the body [Med.]. (L.)
stride, *n.* stride, a long step; a wide stretch of the legs; the distance thus covered: *v.i.* to walk with long steps; to straddle: *v.t.* to pass over at a step; to bestride. **take in one's stride,** to do or effect without difficulty or extra exertion. *pp.* **stridden** and **strid.** *p.* **strode.** (A.S. *stridan.*)
stridency, *n.* *stry*-den-se, the quality of being strident.
strident, *a.* *stry*-dent, harsh, grating or creaking; loud. (L. *stridens.*)
stridently, *ad.* *stry*-dent-le, in a strident manner.
stridor, *n.* *stry*-dor, a harsh, creaking or grinding noise, esp. through obstruction of respiration [Med.]. (L.)
stridulant, *a.* *strid*-yew-lant, strident; stridulating.
stridulate, *v.i.* *strid*-yew-late, to make a harsh grating noise like a cricket.
stridulation, *n.* *strid*-yew-*lay*-shon, the act of stridulating; the sound produced by this.
stridulator, *n.* *strid*-yew-*lay*-tor, an insect that stridulates; a stridulatory organ.
stridulatory, *a.* *strid*-yew-*lay*-to-re, pertaining to or causing stridulation.
stridulous, *a.* *strid*-yew-lus, making a harsh creaking sound. (L. *stridulus.*)
strife, *n.* strife, contention for superiority; contest of emulation; struggle for victory; discord.

strig, *n.* strig, a footstalk [Bot.].
strigæ, *n.pl.* *stry*-jee, short stiff hairs swollen at their roots [Bot.]. (L. *striga*, a furrow.)
strigil, *n.* *strij*-il, an instrument for scraping the skin at the bath [Classical antiq.]; in certain insects, an organ for cleaning the antennæ. (L. *strigilis.*)
strigose, *a.* *stry*-gohs, having stiff, lanceolate bristles [Bot.]. (L. *striga.*)
strigous, *a.* *stry*-gus, strigose.
strike, *v.t.* strike, to touch or hit with some force; to give a blow to; to hook; to dash; to stamp; to coin; to thrust in; to punish; to cause to sound; to affect sensibly or strongly; to make and ratify; to affect suddenly; to be suddenly reminded; to occur suddenly to the mind; to lower (a sail or tent); to level a measure of grain, salt or the like, by scraping off with a straight instrument what is above the level of the top; to find; to propagate by slips or scions. **strike off,** to erase from an account; to print; to separate by a blow. **strike oil,** *see* **oil.** **strike out,** to produce by collision; to erase; to contrive. **strike sail,** *see* **sail**: *v.i.* to make a quick blow or thrust; to hit; to dash against; to sound by percussion; to make an attack; to sound with blows; to be stranded; to dart; to lower a flag or colours in token of respect or surrender; to take root; to quit work in a body or by combination in order to compel an employer to yield to a demand or as a protest. **strike in,** to enter suddenly; to disappear. **strike in with,** to conform to. **strike out,** to make a sudden excursion. **strike up,** to begin to sound; to begin to sing or play. *p.* **struck.** *pp.* **struck** and **stricken.** (A.S. *strican.*)
strike, *n.* strike, the act of striking; an instrument with a straight edge for levelling a measure of grain by scraping off what is above the level of the top; a strickle; the act of workmen combining in a refusal to work until the end for which they strike is attained; the direction of the outcrop of a stratum [Geol.]; a sudden discovery of rich ore or oil in quantity, etc. **lightning strike,** *see* **lightning.** **lucky strike,** a lucky find.
strike-a-light, *n.* *strike*-a-lite, a piece of flint or other material from which a spark is obtained by striking.
strikebreaker, *n.* *strike*-brake-er, one imported to take the place of a worker on striker.
strike-measure, *n.* a measure of grain levelled off with a strickle.
striker, *n.* *strike*-er, one who or that which strikes; a blacksmith's assistant; a worker on strike; the batsman [Cricket]; the player not serving [Tennis].
striking, *a.* *strike*-ing, affecting with strong emotions; surprising; forcible; impressive.
strikingly, *ad.* *strike*-ing-le, in a striking manner.
strikingness, *n.* *strike*-ing-ness, the quality of being striking, of affecting or surprising.
string, *n.* string, a small rope, line, or cord used for fastening or tying anything; a ribbon; a thread on which a thing is filed; the gut or wire cord of a musical instrument, as of a harp; any wire; a fibre; a nerve or tendon; the line or cord of a bow; a line or series of things; a file of animals, persons, or vehicles; a stud of racehorses; a thin vein or ramification [Min.]; (*pl.*) stringed instruments, also their players: *v.t.* to furnish with strings; to put in tune a stringed instrument; to thread on a string; to file; to make tense; to strip of fibres or strings: *v.i.* to become stringy; at billiards, to decide which player starts by playing a ball from baulk on to the top cushion. **have two strings to one's bow,** to have two expedients in store or objects in view. **on a string,** under control. **pull strings,** to exert influence in the background or clandestinely. *p.* and *pp.* **strung.** (A.S. *streng.*)
string-band, *n.* a band of stringed instruments.
string-board, *n.* a board with its face next the well-hole in a wooden staircase.
string-course, *n.* a projecting horizontal band or line of mouldings in a building.
stringed, *a.* stringd, having strings; produced by strings or stringed instruments.
stringency, *n.* *strin*-jen-se, the state of being stringent; strictness.
stringendo, *ad.* strin-*jen*-doh, in accelerated time [Mus.]. (It.)
stringent, *a.* *strin*-jent, strictly enforceable; strict; severe. (L. *stringo*, draw tight.)
stringently, *ad.* in a stringent manner.
stringentness, *n.* *strin*-jent-ness, stringency.
stringer, *n.* *string*-er, a maker of strings; a horizontal timber or bar serving as a tie; a string-board.
stringhalt, *n.* *string*-hawlt, an affection of the hind leg of a horse causing a twitching or convulsive movement in certain muscles.
stringiness, *n.* *string*-e-ness, the state of being stringy.
stringless, *a.* *string*-less, having no strings.
stringy, *a.* *string*-e, consisting of strings or small threads; filamentous; ropy; viscid; tough.
stringy-bark, *n.* a name for many species of *Eucalyptus*, the bark of which was used by the Australian aborigines to make cordage.
strip, *n.* strip, a long, narrow piece; an act of stripping; a comic strip: *v.t.* to pull or tear off, as a covering; to deprive of covering; to skin; to deprive; to bereave; to divest; to pillage; to press out the milk of; to unrig: *v.i.* to undress. **comic strip,** a series of drawings in a periodical or newspaper depicting connected humorous incidents. **strip-tease act,** a stage performance in which an actress apparently undresses. (A.S. *strypan.*)
stripe, *n.* stripe, a line or long narrow division of anything of a different colour from the ground; a chevron (as mark of non-commissioned rank [Mil.]); a wale or mark of a lash; affliction; punishment: *v.t.* to make stripes on; to form with lines of different colours; to scourge. (Old. Dut. *strijpe.*)
striped, *a.* strypt, marked with a stripe or stripes; having stripes of different colours.
stripling, *n.* *strip*-ling, a youth just passing from boyhood to manhood; a lad.
stripper, *n.* *strip*-per, one who strips.
stripy, *a.* *stry*-pe, striped; suggesting stripes.
strive, *v.i.* strive, to make efforts; to endeavour with earnestness; to labour hard; to struggle; to vie. *pp.* **striven.** *p.* **strove.** (O.Fr. *estriver.*)
striver, *n.* *strive*-er, one who strives; one who makes efforts of body or mind.
strivingly, *ad.* with earnest efforts; with struggles.
strob, *n.* strob, the angular velocity of one radian per second. (Gr. *strobos*, a whirling.)
strobila, *n.* *stroh*-be-la, a stage in the development of certain cœlenterates in which the body divides into segments; the chain of segments of which the tapeworm is composed.
strobilation, *n.* stroh-be-*lay*-shon, a sexual reproduction among certain cœlenterates, etc., by terminal budding; the formation of zooids by fission or gemmation [Biol.].
strobile, *n.* *stroh*-bile, a hardened catkin, the carpels of which are scale-like, as in the pines. (Gr. *strobilos.*)
strobiliform, *a.* stroh-*bil*-e-form, shaped like a strobile; cone-shaped.
strobiline, *a.* *strob*-e-line, pertaining to a strobila or to a strobile; strobiliform.
stroboscope, *n.* *strob*-o-skope, an instrument for noting velocity by the intermittent lighting of the rotating object; a zoetrope. (Gr. *strobos*, a whirling, *skopeo*, view.)
stroke, *n.* stroke, a blow; the striking of one body against another; a hostile blow or attack; a sudden attack of disease (as apoplexy or paralysis) or affliction; calamity; the sound of a clock; the touch of a pencil; a touch; a masterly effort; an effort suddenly or unexpectedly produced; one of a series of recurring operations; a dash in writing or printing; a line; the working length of a piston-rod, etc.; the travel or throw of a valve; the aftermost oarsman, who sets the rate of rowing; the sweep of an oar: *v.t.* and *i.* to pull stroke-oar and so set the rate of rowing. (*strike.*)
stroke, *n.* stroke, the act of stroking; a gentle caress: *v.t.* to rub gently with the hand by way of expressing kindness; to soothe; to rub gently in one direction; to make smooth. **stroke the wrong way,** to vex, to irritate, esp. unintentionally.
stroke-oar, *n.* the aftermost oarsman or oar.
stroker, *n.* *stroke*-er, one who strokes; one who pretends to cure by stroking
stroll, *n.* strole, a saunter; a leisurely walk: *v.i.* to ramble idly or leisurely; to rove. (Scand.)

stroller, *n.* *strole*-er, one who strolls; an itinerant actor; a vagrant.
stroma, *n.* *stroh*-ma, the groundwork of a tissue or organ [Anat.]. (Gr.)
stromatic, *a.* stro-*mat*-ik, pertaining to or resembling a stroma.
stromb, *n.* stromb, a tropical gastropod of the genus *Strombus*, which comprises the wing-shells; one of these shells.
strombuliform, *a.* strom-*bew*-le-form; like a top; spirally twisted [Bot.]. (Gr. *strombos*, a top.)
stromeyerite, *n.* *stroh*-my-er-rite, a steel-grey sulphide of silver and copper. (Fried. *Stromeyer*, Ger. chemist, *d.* 1835.)
★**strong,** *a.* strong, hale; sound; having physical power; vigorous; firm; having ability to bear or endure; fortified; powerful; resourceful; violent; forcible; cogent; zealous; of great strength; evil-smelling; affecting a sense forcibly; full of spirit; intoxicating; having great force; having great force of mind, intellect, or any faculty. **strong water,** alcoholic drinks. (A.S. *strang*.)
strong-box, *n.* a safe for valuables; a cash-box.
stronghold, *n.* *strong*-hohld, a fastness; a fortified place; a place of security.
strongly, *ad.* *strong*-le, in a strong manner.
strong-room, *n.* a burglar-resisting and fire-proof room in which valuables are kept.
strongyle, *n.* *stron*-jile, a round nematoid intestinal worm. (Gr., round.)
strontia, *n.* *stron*-she-a, strontium monoxide.
strontian, *n.* *stron*-she-an, strontium; strontianite: *a.* pertaining to or containing strontium.
strontianite, *n.* *stron*-she-a-nite, native carbonate of strontium.
strontium, *n.* *stron*-she-um, a yellowish metallic element of the alkaline-earth group. (First discovered at *Strontian*, Argyllshire.)
strop, *n.* strop, a strip of leather and textile material for sharpening razors on; a strap for a block [Naut.]: *v.t.* to sharpen by means of a strop. (*strap*.)
Strophanthus, *n.* stro-*fan*-thus, a genus of Old World tropical trees, the seed of most of which are highly poisonous; (*l.c.*) a cardiac stimulant prepared from this poison.
strophe, *n.* *stroh*-fe, in the Greek drama, the part sung by the chorus when moving to the left; in Greek poetry the first part of an ode. (Gr., turning.)
strophic, *a.* *strof*-ik, pertaining to or consisting of strophes.
strophiolate, *a.* *strof*-e-o-late, having a caruncle near the hilum [Bot.]. (Gr.)
strophiole, *n.* *strof*-e-ole, a caruncle, an excrescence at the scar of a seed [Bot.]. (L. *strophiolum*, a chaplet.)
strophulus, *n.* *strof*-yew-lus, tooth-rash or red-gum rash, a papular skin disease peculiar to infants [Med.]. (Gr. *strophos*, a twisted cord.)
strouding, *n.* *stroud*-ing, a coarse kind of cloth.
strove, strove, *p.* of *strive*.
struck, struk, *p.* and *pp.* of *strike*.
structural, *a.* *struk*-tewr-ral, pertaining to structure.
structurally, *ad.* with regard to structure.
★**structure,** *n.* *struk*-tewr, manner of building; form; make; construction; a building of any kind, but chiefly one of some size or magnificence; the arrangement of the elements or parts of a complex whole; texture; manner of organization. (L. *structum*.)
structured, *a.* having organic structure.
structureless, *a.* *struk*-tewr-less, without structure; without organization.
struggle, *n.* *strug*-gl, forcible effort to obtain an object or to avoid an evil; contest; contention; agony; contortions of extreme distress: *v.i.* to use great efforts, esp. against difficulties; to twist and contort the body; to strive; to contend; to labour in pain; to be in agony. (M.E. *strogelen*.)
struggler, *n.* *strug*-gler, one who struggles, strives or contends.
strum, *v.i.* strum, to play badly and noisily on a stringed instrument: *n.* a strumming. (Imit.)
struma, *n.* *stroo*-ma, scrofula; a scrofulous tumour; goitre; (*pl.* **strumæ**) a swelling at the root of a leaf [Bot.]. (L.)
strumitis, *n.* stroo-*my*-tis, inflammation of the thyroid body [Path.].
strumose, *a.* *stroo*-mohs, having a struma or strumæ [Bot. and Path.].
strumous, *a.* *stroo*-mus, scrofulous; having strumæ. **strumous lizard,** the S. American *Lacerta strumosa*, having a protuberance on the breast.
strumousness, *n.* quality of being strumous.
strumpet, *n.* *strum*-pet, a prostitute: *a.* like a strumpet; inconstant. (Origin uncertain.)
strung, strung, *p.* and *pp.* of *string*.
strut, *n.* strut, a lofty proud step or walk, with the head erect; affection of dignity in walking; a structural member for the resistance of pressure in the direction of its length [Eng.]; a support; a prop and brace [Carp.]: *v.i.* to walk with a proud gait and erect head; to walk with affected dignity or pomposity. (A.S. *strutian*.)
'struth, *int.* strooth, an expression of surprise; a mild imprecation. (Short for " God's truth.")
Struthio, *n.* *stroo*-the-oh, the genus of birds containing the ostriches. (L.)
struthious, *a.* *stroo*-the-us, pertaining to or like the ostrich; belonging to the ostrich family.
strutter, *n.* *strut*-ter, one who struts.
struttingly, *ad.* with a proud step; boastingly.
strychnic, *a.* *strik*-nik, pertaining to strychnine.
strychnine, *n.* *strik*-neen, a poisonous alkaloid, valuable as a medicine, usually obtained from the seeds of *Strychnos nux vomica*. (Gr. *strychnos*, nightshade.)
strychninism, *n.* *strik*-ne-nizm, the morbid condition produced by strychnine poisoning.
strychnism, *n.* *strik*-nizm, strychninism.
stub, *n.* stub, the stump of a tree after the tree has been cut down; a short thick end or remaining part of anything; a stub-nail; a short exhaust pipe from the cylinder of an aero-engine: *v.t.* to grub up by the roots; to extirpate; to rid of roots; to strike the toe against a stump or stone [U.S.A.]. (A.S. *stybb*.)
stubbed, *a.* stubd, pollarded; cut or reduced to a stub; divested of stubs; stubby; blunted.
stubbiness, *n.* *stub*-e-ness, the state of being stubby.
stubble, *n.* *stub*-bl, the stumps of cereals left in the ground after reaping; the short bristles on an unshaven face [Coll.]. (*stub*.)
stubbled, *a.* *stub*-bld, covered with stubble.
stubble-goose, *n.* *stub*-bl-goos, a goose fed among stubble; the greylag, *Anser cinereus*.
stubbly, *a.* *stub*-le, stubbled; like stubble.
stubborn, *a.* *stub*-ern, unreasonably obstinate; inflexibly fixed in opinion; persevering; persisting; stiff; not flexible; hardy; refractory; intractable; not easily melted or worked. (*stub*.)
stubbornly, *ad.* in a stubborn manner.
stubbornness, *n.* the quality of being stubborn; contumacy; stiffness; refractoriness.
stubby, *a.* *stub*-e, abounding with stubs; short and thick; short and strong.
stub-nail, *n.* *stub*-nale, a nail broken off; a short thick nail, as that of a horseshoe.
stucco, *n.* *stuk*-oh, a fine plaster of any kind used as a coating for walls or for internal decorations; work made of stucco: *v.t.* to plaster or coat with stucco. (It., from O. Ger. *stucchi*, crust.)
stuccoed, *a.* *stuk*-ode, overlaid with stucco.
stuck, stuk, *p.* and *pp.* of *stick*.
stuck-up, *a.* stuk-*up*, conceited; affecting an air of consequence; erect; not turned down.
stud, *n.* stud, an ornamental knob; a double-headed shirt-button; a small piece of timber or joist to support the main timbers; an intermediate post in a partition: *v.t.* to adorn with shining studs or knobs; to set with detached ornaments or prominent objects. (A.S. *studu*, a post.)
stud, *n.* stud, an establishment of animals, esp. horses, kept for breeding, racing, or any special purpose. **at stud,** in use for breeding. (A.S. *stod*.)
stud-bolt, *n.* a bolt threaded at both ends.
stud-book, *n.* book of pedigrees of prize animals.
studding-sail, *n.* *stud*-ing-sale *or* *stun*-sl, a sail set alongside the leech of a squaresail; a scudding-sail [Naut.].
student, *n.* *stew*-dent, a person engaged in study; a pupil at an advanced or technical school or college; a man devoted to books; a studious person; one receiving a grant for research work, etc. (L. *studens*.)
studenthood, *n.* *stew*-dent-hood, the condition of being a student.

studentry, *n.* *stew*-den-tre, students collectively; students as a group.
studentship, *n.* state of a student; a scholarship.
stud-farm, *n.* a breeding establishment for horses.
stud-groom, *n.* a groom at a stud-farm.
stud-horse, *n.* a stallion kept for breeding purposes.
studied, *pp.* *stud*-id, closely examined; diligently and attentively considered: *a.* well versed in any branch of learning; qualified by study; premeditated.
studiedly, *ad.* *stud*-id-le, in a studied manner.
studio, *n.* *stew*-de-oh, the work-room of a painter, sculptor, photographer, etc.; a room adapted for the making of gramophone records, the staging of motion-pictures, etc.; a room in a radio transmission station for broadcasting or for auditions. (It.)
studious, *a.* *stew*-de-us, devoted to the acquisition of knowledge from books; contemplative; diligent or eager to find or effect something; attentive to; planned with study; favourable to study. (L. *studiosus.*)
studiously, *ad.* *stew*-de-us-le, in a studious manner.
studiousness, *n.* *stew*-de-us-ness, the quality of being studious; the practice or habit of study.
studwork, *n.* *stud*-wurk, brickwork between the intermediate posts of a partition; leather or other work ornamented with studs.
study, *n.* *stud*-e, application of mind to books or to any subject for the purpose of acquiring knowledge or skill in it; thoughtful attention; meditation; any branch of learning that is studied; subject of attention; an apartment devoted to study or literary employment; a work undertaken for improvement in an art; an artist's sketch for aid in the composition of a larger work: *v.i.* to fix the mind closely upon a subject; to apply the mind to books; to endeavour diligently: *v.t.* to apply the mind to for the purpose of learning and understanding; to consider attentively; to con over. **brown study,** a state of deep thoughtfulness; a reverie. (L. *studeo.*)
stufa, *n.* *stoo*-fa, a jet of steam issuing from the earth. (It.)
stuff, *n.* stuf, a mass of matter or collection of substances; the matter of which anything is formed; furniture; textile material; worthless or rubbishy matter; nonsense: *v.t.* to fill; to fill very full; to cram; to thrust in; to cause to bulge by filling; to fill meat with seasoning; to fill the skin of a dead animal for preserving its form: *v.i.* to feed gluttonously. (O.Fr. *estoffe.*)
stuffer, *n.* *stuf*-fer, one who or that which stuffs.
stuffiness, *n.* *stuf*-fe-ness, the state of being stuffy.
stuffing, *n.* *stuf*-fing, that which is used for filling anything; seasoning of savoury herbs used in cooking; taxidermy; guts, pluck [Slang].
stuffing-box, *n.* *stuf*-fing-boks, an air-tight compartment through which the piston works in the top of a cylinder without losing steam; a contrivance for preventing leakage through the action of a moving part.
stuffy, *a.* *stuf*-fe, close; badly ventilated; angry, sulky, or dull [Slang].
stultification, *n.* *stul*-te-fe-*kay*-shon, the act of stultifying; an instance of this.
stultify, *v.t.* *stul*-te-fy, to render worthless or absurd; to spoil what has been done; to allege or prove to be insane [Law]. **stultify oneself,** to act in a way to expose oneself to a charge of inconsistency. (L. *stultifico*, make foolish.)
stultiloquence, *n.* stul-*til*-o-kwence, foolish talk; silly discourse; babbling.
stultiloquent, *a.* stul-*til*-o-kwent, given to stultiloquence. (L. *stultus*, foolish, *loquor*, speak.)
stultiloquy, *n.* stul-*til*-o-kwe, stultiloquence.
stum, *n.* stum, must; grape juice unfermented; wine revived by new fermentation: *v.t.* to renew wine by mixing must with it, and raising a new fermentation. (Dut. *stom.*)
stumble, *n.* *stum*-bl, a trip in walking or running; a blunder; a failure: *v.i.* to trip in walking; to strike the foot against something; to fall into crime or error. **stumble at,** to be dubious about; to hesitate (before an obstacle). **stumble on,** to light on by chance. (Ice. *stumra.*)
stumbler, *n.* one who stumbles or blunders.
stumbling-block, *n.* that which causes or tempts to err; an obstacle; any cause of hesitation or stumbling.
stumblingly, *ad.* in a stumbling manner.
stumer, *n.* *stew*-mer, a counterfeit coin, a forged or "dud" cheque; a fraudulently run or disappointing racehorse; a failure [all Slang].
stump, *n.* stump, the part of a tree remaining in the earth after the trunk is cut down; the part of a limb or other body remaining after the rest is amputated, worn out, or destroyed; a remnant; one of the upright sticks of a wicket [Cricket]; a roll of leather or paper used to smear a crayon or pencil drawing in order to produce a tint: *pl.* legs: *v.t.* to lop; to travel for election purposes; to put out by knocking down the wicket [Cricket]: *v.i.* to walk heavily or clumsily; to go about speechifying. **stump up,** to pay up [Slang]. (Scand.)
stumper, *n.* *stum*-per, a poser, an awkward question; a wicketkeeper [Cricket].
stump-orator, *n.* one who harangues a mob from some improvised place of vantage; one who appeals to the passions of the mob.
stump-oratory, *n.* the art of the stump-orator; mere talk.
stump-speech, *n.* a rambling, incoherent harangue; a second-rate electioneering speech.
stumpy, *a.* *stum*-pe, short and thick; stubby; abounding in stumps.
stun, *v.t.* stun, to make senseless by a blow; to blunt or stupefy the organs of hearing; to confound or make dizzy by loud and mingled sound; to amaze. (A.S. *stunian.*)
stung, stung, *p.* and *pp.* of *sting.*
stunk, stunk, *p.* and *pp.* of *stink.*
stunner, *n.* he who or that which stuns; something specially fine or astonishing; he who or that which excels [Slang].
stunning, *a.* excellent; astonishing [Slang].
stunsail, *n.* *stun*-sl, a studding-sail.
stunt, *n.* stunt, a feat of skill; a performance, esp. for the sake of applause, notoriety, or mere showing-off; a newspaper sensation or agitation: *v.i.* to do a stunt: *v.t.* to make (esp. an aeroplane) do a stunt. (Orig. U.S.A. slang; perhaps from Ger. *stunde*, lesson.)
stunt, *n.* stunt, a check in growth; anything stunted: *v.t.* to hinder from growth.
stuntedness, *n.* *stun*-tid-ness, the state of being stunted.
stupa, *n.* *stew*-pa, filamentous matter; a stupe.
stupa, *n.* *stew*-pa, a Buddhist monument or shrine; a tope; a dagoba. (Sans., a mound.)
stupe, *n.* stewp, a compress of flannel or other soft material dipped and applied as a fomentation [Med.]: *v.t.* to treat or foment with this. (L. *stupa*, tow.)
stupefacient, *a.* *stew*-pe-*fay*-she-ent, having a stupefying power: *n.* a narcotic.
stupefaction, *n.* *stew*-pe-*fak*-shon, the act of rendering stupid; a stupefied state; dullness: stupidity.
stupefactive, *a.* *stew*-pe-*fak*-tiv, deadening the feeling or understanding: *n.* a narcotic.
stupefier, *n.* *stew*-pe-fy-er, that which stupefies.
stupefy, *v.t.* *stew*-pe-fy, to make stupid or dull; to deprive of sensibility. (L. *stupefacio.*)
stupendous, *a.* stew-*pen*-dus, striking dumb by magnitude; astonishing; wonderful; of astonishing magnitude or elevation. (L. *stupendus.*)
stupendously, *ad.* in a manner to excite astonishment.
stupendousness, *n.* the quality of being stupendous or astonishing.
stupeous, *a.* *stew*-pe-us, having long loose scales; covered with matted hair or filaments [Bot. and Zool.]. (L. *stupa*, tow.)
stupid, *a.* *stew*-pid, dull; senseless; wanting in understanding; slow in perception; foolish; heavy: *n.* a stupid fellow; a blockhead. (L. *stupidus.*)
stupidity, *n.* stew-*pid*-e-te, extreme dullness of perception or understanding.
stupidly, *ad.* *stew*-pid-le, in a stupid manner.
stupidness, *n.* *stew*-pid-ness, stupidity.
stupor, *n.* *stew*-por, great diminution or suspension of sensibility; torpor; numbness. (L.)
stuporous, *a.* *stew*-po-rus, characterized by or affected with stupor.
stupose, *a.* *stew*-pohs, stupeous.
stuprate, *v.t.* *stew*-prate, to ravish; to debauch.
stupration, *n.* stew-*pray*-shon, rape; violation of chastity by force. (L. *stupratus*, dishonoured.)

sturdily, *ad.* *stur*-de-le, in a sturdy manner.
sturdiness, *n.* *stur*-de-ness, the state of being sturdy; stoutness; hardiness.
sturdy, *a.* *stur*-de, hardy; stout; strong; lusty; robust; violent; laid on with strength; bold. (O.Fr. *estourdi*, amazed, stunned.)
sturdy, *n.* *stur*-de, gid, a disease in sheep, due to the larva of a tapeworm in the brain causing a staggering, stupid gait and, usually, death.
sturgeon, *n.* *stur*-jon, the ganoid fish *Acipenser sturio*, the roe of which furnishes caviare and the air-bladder isinglass. (O.Fr. *estourgeon*.)
sturnoid, *a.* *stur*-noyd, resembling a starling; belonging to the Sturnidæ, the large family of birds comprising the starlings. (L. *sturnus*, a starling.)
stutter, *n.* *stut*-ter, hesitation in speech: *v.i.* to stammer; to keep hesitating in uttering words. (M.E. *stoten*.)
stutterer, *n.* *stut*-ter-rer, a stammerer.
stuttering, *n.* *stut*-ter-ring, hesitation in speaking: *a.* characterized by stutters.
stutteringly, *ad.* *stut*-ter-ring-le, with stammering.
sty, *n.* sty, a pen or enclosure for swine; a hovel or mean habitation; a place of bestial debauchery: *v.t.* to shut up in a sty. (A.S. *stig*.)
sty, *n.* sty, an inflamed gland on the edge of the eyelid; a hordeolum. (A.S. *stigend*.)
Stygian, *a.* *stij*-e-an, pertaining to the Styx; hellish; infernal; impenetrably dark.
stylar, *a.* *stile*-ar, pertaining to a writing style.
style, *n.* stile, a pointed instrument used by the ancients for writing on wax tablets; a pointed instrument of surgery; something with a sharp point, as a graver; the pin or gnomon of a sundial; the support of the stigma [Bot.]; a bristle-like process on certain insects, crustaceans, etc. [Zool.]; a styloid process on a bone [Anat.]; manner of writing, speaking, painting, or musical composition; the code of a printing-house regulating its spelling, use of italics and capitals, etc.; title; appellation; manner; fashion; form; sort or make; practice; a mode of reckoning time, with regard to the Julian (**Old Style**) and Gregorian (**New Style**) calendar: *v.t.* to entitle in addressing; to call, name, or denominate. (Fr., from Gr. *stylos*, pillar.)
stylet, *n.* *sty*-let, a small poniard or dagger; an instrument for examining wounds [Surg.]; a bristle-like organ [Zool.].
styliform, *a.* *sty*-le-form, like a style or bristle.
stylish, *a.* *sty*-lish, being in fashionable form or in high style; showy.
stylishly, *ad.* *sty*-lish-le, in a stylish manner.
stylishness, *n.* the quality of being stylish.
stylist, *n.* *stile*-list, a writer who devotes great attention to style.
stylistic, *a.* sty-*lis*-tik, pertaining to literary style.
stylistically, *ad.* sty-*lis*-te-ka-le, in a stylized manner; with regard to style.
stylistics, *n.* the science or study of literary style.
stylite, *n.* *sty*-lite, one of a mediæval sect of solitaries who lived an extremely ascetic life on the tops of pillars, chiefly in Syria. (Gr. *stylos*, pillar.)
stylized, *a.* *stile*-lyzd, made conformable to a style; conventionalized.
stylobate, *n.* *sty*-lo-bate, a continuous base below a range of columns. (Gr. *stylos*, and *baino*, stand.)
stylograph, *n.* *sty*-lo-graf, a fountain pen with a spring point instead of a nib.
stylographic, *a.* *sty*-lo-*graf*-ik, pertaining to a stylograph or to stylography.
stylography, *n.* sty-*log*-ra-fe, a mode of tracing lines by means of a style or pointed instrument. (Gr. *stylos*, and *grapho*, write.)
styloid, *a.* *sty*-loyd, having some resemblance to a style or pen, as the temporal bone [Anat.]: *n.* the styloid process, a spine on the base of the temporal bone. (Gr. *stylos*, and *eidos*, like.)
stylolite, *n.* *sty*-lo-lite, a striated columnar structure due to pressure found in certain limestone and calcareous shales. (Gr. *stylos*, and *lithos*, stone.)
stylus, *n.* *sty*-lus, a style or writing implement; a tracing point in various recording or reproducing instruments; a pointer or gnomon. (L.)
stymie, *n.* *sty*-me, the position of a ball played between another ball and the hole: *v.i.* to lay a stymie: *v.t.* to hinder by a stymie [Golf.]
styptic, *a.* *stip*-tik, that stops bleeding; hæmostatic: *n.* a local application to stop bleeding. (Gr. *styptikos*, astringent.)
stypticity, *n.* stip-*tis*-e-te, quality of being styptic.
styracin, *n.* *styr*-ra-sin, a white crystalline substance obtained from storax.
Styrax, *n.* *styr*-raks, a large genus of widely distributed plants comprising *S. officinale*, storax, *S. benzoin*, gum-benjamin, etc.; (*l.c.*) storax. (L. and Gr.)
stythe, *n.* stythe, choke-damp [Mining]. (Dial. Eng.)
Styx, *n.* stiks, the principal river of the infernal regions, over which Charon ferried the dead, and by which the gods pledged their word [Myth.]. (Gr.)
suability, *n.* sew-a-*bil*-e-te, liability to be sued at law.
suable, *a.* *sew*-a-bl, that may be sued at law; subject by law to be called to answer in a court.
suasible, *a.* *sway*-ze-bl, easily persuasible.
suasion, *n.* *sway*-zhon, act of persuading; persuasion as opposed to compulsion. (O.Fr.)
suasive, *a.* *sway*-ziv, having the power to persuade: agreeable; urbane.
suasively, *ad.* persuasively.
suasory, *a.* *sway*-zo-re, tending to persuade; having the quality of convincing.
suave, *a.* swahv *or* swave, pleasant; bland. (Fr.)
suavely, *ad.* in a suave manner; soothingly.
suavity, *n.* *swav*-e-te, sweetness; agreeableness: pleasantness; blandness.
sub-, sub, a Latin prefix signifying under, from below, slightly; extensively used to express a subordinate degree or imperfect state of a quality.
sub, *v.i.* sub, to work as a substitute for; to sub-edit; to obtain in advance part of a payment falling due: *n.* a subscription; a subaltern, substitute, or subordinate, etc.; a sub-editor.
subabdominal, *a.* *sub*-ab-*dom*-e-nal, in or situated below the lower region of the abdomen.
subacid, *a.* sub-*as*-id, moderately acid or sour: *n.* a substance moderately acid. (L. *subacidus*.)
subacidity, *n.* sub-a-*sid*-e-te, quality or state of being subacid.
subacrid, *a.* sub-*ak*-rid, moderately sharp, pungent, or acrid.
subacute, *a.* sub-a-*kewt*, acute in a moderate degree.
subadar, *n.* soo-ba-*dar*, a subahdar.
subaerial, *a.* *sub*-ay-*eer*-re-al, produced or being under the sky or in the open air, as distinct from subterranean or submarine [Geol.].
sub-agency, *n.* sub-*ay*-jen-se, a subordinate agency.
sub-agent, *n.* sub-*ay*-jent, the agent of an agent.
subah, *n.* *soo*-ba, a province or viceroyship of the former Mogul Empire. (Hind.)
subahdar, *n.* soo-ba-*dar*, the governor of a subah; the chief native officer of a company of sepoys in the British Indian army. (Hind.)
subalpine, *a.* sub-*al*-pine, lower than Alpine; pertaining to regions immediately below the timber-line.
subaltern, *n.* *sub*-al-tern, a commissioned officer in the army under the rank of captain: *a.* inferior; subordinate; differing in quantity, but not in quality [Logic]. (Fr. *subalterne*.)
subalternate, *n.* *sub*-awl-*ter*-nat, the particular of a universal, a particular proposition [Logic]: *a.* successive; alternate, but tending to become opposite [Bot.].
subalternation, *n.* *sub*-awl-ter-*nay*-shon, state of subaltern relation [Logic].
subalternity, *n.* sub-awl-*ter*-ne-te, subaltern quality; subordinate position.
subangular, *a.* sub-*ang*-gew-lar, slightly angular.
subapennine, *a.* sub-*ap*-e-nine, under or at the foot of the Apennines; applied to a series of tertiary strata of the Older Pliocene period [Geol.].
subapostolic, *a.* *sub*-ap-os-*tol*-ik, pertaining to the period of Church history next following that of the Apostles.
subaquatic, *a.* sub-a-*kwot*-ik, subaqueous.
subaqueous, *a.* sub-*ay*-kwe-us, being under water; formed under water. (L.)
subarctic, *a.* sub-*ark*-tik, pertaining to regions adjacent to the arctic.
subastral, *a.* sub-*as*-tral, terrestrial.
subastringent, *a.* *sub*-as-*trin*-jent, astringent in a small degree.
subatom, *n.* sub-*at*-om, a component part of an atom [Chem. and Physics].

subatomics, *n.* sub-a-*tom*-iks, scientific study of the phenomena occurring inside atoms.
subaudition, *n.* *sub*-aw-*dish*-on, act of understanding something not expressed; that which is understood. (L. *subauditio.*)
subaxillary, *a.* *sub*-ak-*zil*-a-re, placed under the axil or angle formed by the branch of a plant with the stem, or by a leaf with the branch [Bot.]; under the armpit [Anat.].
sub-base, *n.* a secondary base; a base placed beneath the bottom of a machine, etc.
sub-bass, *n.* the deepest pedal stop, or the lowest notes of an organ [Mus.].
subcalcareous, *a.* sub-kal-*kare*-re-us, rather calcareous.
subcarbonate, *n.* sub-*kar*-bo-nate, a basic carbonate.
subcaudal, *a.* sub-*kaw*-dal, beneath the tail. (L. *sub-*, and *cauda*, the tail.)
subcaulescent, *a.* sub-kaw-*les*-ent, not quite acaulescent [Bot.].
subcelestial, *a.* *sub*-se-*les*-te-al, terrestrial.
subcentral, *a.* *sub*-sen-tral, being under the centre; somewhat central.
subclass, *n.* *sub*-klahs a subdivision of a class.
subclavian, *a.* sub-*klay*-ve-an, situated under the collar-bone. (L. *sub-*, and *clavis*, key.)
sub-committee, *n.* an under-committee.
subconscious, *a.* sub-*kon*-shus, hardly or not conscious; unconsciously perceptive: *n.* the subconscious state; subconscious activity.
subconsciousness, *n.* the condition of bordering on consciousness; a state in which perception is weak.
subcontinent, *n.* sub-*kon*-te-nent, a large and, in some ways, homogeneous portion of a continent, as India or South Africa.
subcontract, *v.t.* sub-kon-*trakt*, to contract under a contractor.
sub-contract, *n.* sub-*kon*-trakt, a contract under a contract.
subcontractor, *n.* *sub*-kon-*trak*-tor, one who works under a sub-contract.
sub-contrary, *a.* sub-*kon*-tra-re, contrary in an inferior degree; particular, but differing in quality [Logic]: *n.* a sub-contrary proposition [Logic].
subcostal, *a.* sub-*kos*-tal, situated below a rib [Anat.]. (L. *sub-*, and *costa*, rib.)
subcrystalline, *a.* sub-*kris*-ta-line, imperfectly crystallized.
subculture, *n.* *sub*-kul-tewr, a culture from a previous culture as with bacteria.
subcutaneous, *a.* *sub*-kew-*tay*-ne-us, situated just under the skin.
subcuticular, *a.* *sub*-kew-*tik*-yew-lar, just beneath the cuticle or scarf-skin.
subdeacon, *n.* sub-*dee*-kon, an under-deacon, or deacon's assistant. (Late L. *subdiaconus.*)
subdean, *n.* *sub*-deen, an under-dean; a dean's deputy. (Late L. *subdecanus.*)
subdeanery, *n.* sub-*deen*-er-re, the rank or office of a subdean.
subdecuple, *a.* sub-*dek*-yew-pl, containing one part of ten.
subdentate, *a.* sub-*den*-tat, with teeth indistinct.
subdented *a.* sub-*den*-ted, indented beneath.
sub-derivative, *n.* sub-de-*riv*-a-tiv, a word derived from a derivative, as *righteousness*, from *righteous*, and *righteous*, from *right*.
subdiaconate, *n.* *sub*-dy-*ak*-o-nat, the office or rank of subdeacon.
subdilated, *a.* *sub*-dy-*lay*-ted, partially dilated.
subdiversify, *v.t.* *sub*-de-*ver*-se-fy, to diversify again what is already diversified.
subdivide, *v.t.* *sub*-de-*vide*, to divide a part of a thing into more parts; to part into smaller divisions: *v.i.* to become subdivided. (L. *sub-*, and *dividere*, divide.)
subdivisible, *a.* *sub*-de-*viz*-e-bl, susceptible of subdivision.
subdivision, *n.* *sub*-de-*vizh*-on, the act of subdividing; the part of a larger part.
subdolous, *a.* *sub*-do-lus, sly; crafty; cunning. (L. *sub-*, and *dolus*, fraud, deceit.)
subdominant, *n.* sub-*dom*-e-nant, a tone below the tonic or key-note [Mus.].
subduable, *a.* sub-*dew*-a-bl, that may be subdued.
subdual, *n.* sub-*dew*-al, the act of subduing.
subduct, *v.t.* sub-*dukt*, to withdraw; to take away; to subtract. (L. *subductus*, removed.)
subduction, *n.* sub-*duk*-shon, act of taking away or withdrawing; arithmetical subtraction.
subdue, *v.t.* sub-*dew*, to conquer by force; to reduce under dominion; to overpower; to tame; to render submissive; to reduce to mildness; to conquer by persuasion or other mild means; to captivate; to soften; to overcome; to make mellow; to destroy. (O.Fr. *souduire.*)
subduer, *n.* sub-*dew*-er, one who or that which subdues; a tamer.
subduple, *a.* sub-*dew*-pl, containing one part of two. (L. *sub-*, and *duplus*, double.)
subduplicate, *a.* sub-*dew*-ple-kat, having the ratio of the square roots; expressed by the square root [Math.].
sub-edit, *v.t.* sub-*ed*-it, to prepare for the press, or for the supervision of a chief editor.
sub-editor, *n.* sub-*ed*-it-or, an assistant editor.
sub-editorial, *a.* *sub*-ed-e-*taw*-re-al, pertaining to the work of a sub-editor.
sub-equal, *a.* *sub*-ee-kwal, nearly equal.
subequatorial, *a.* *sub*-ee-kwa-*taw*-re-al, denoting or pertaining to a region adjacent to the equatorial regions.
suberate, *n.* *sew*-ber-rate, a salt of suberic acid.
suberic, *a.* sew-*ber*-rik, pertaining to or extracted from cork. **suberic acid,** a white crystalline substance obtained by treating cork or certain fatty oils with nitric acid. (L. *suber*, cork.)
suberin, *n.* *sew*-ber-rin, the fatty cellulose basis of cork; pulverized cork (as a dressing for wounds).
suberose, *a.* *sew*-ber-rohs, having the appearance of cork; corky; suberous.
suberous, *a.* *su*-ber-rus, having a corky texture; soft and elastic. (L. *suber.*)
subfamily, *n.* *sub*-fam-e-le, a division of a family of plants or animals consisting of one or more genera.
subflavour, *n.* sub-*flay*-vor, an underlying or secondary flavour.
subfluvial, *a.* sub-*floo*-ve-al, at the bottom of a stream or body of water.
subfossil, *a.* *sub*-fos-sil, partly fossilized.
subfusc, *a.* sub-*fusk*, somewhat dusky in colour; sombre; restrained [Fig.]: *n.* a subfusc colour. (L. *subfuscus.*)
subgelatinous, *a.* sub-je-*lat*-e-nus, imperfectly gelatinous.
subgeneric, *a.* sub-je-*ne*-rik, pertaining to a subgenus.
subgenus, *n.* sub-*jee*-nus, the subdivision of a genus, comprehending one or more species.
subglacial, *a.* sub-*glay*-shal, pertaining to the lower face of a glacier; beneath a glacier; partly glacial.
subglobular, *a.* sub-*glob*-yew-lar, having a form approaching to globular.
subgranular, *a.* sub-*gran*-yew-lar, somewhat granular.
subgroup, *n.* *sub*-groop, a subordinate group in any classification.
sub-head, *n.* one next in rank to the head; a subheading; *v.t.* to provide with a subheading.
subheading, *n.* sub-*hed*-ing, a subordinate division, title, or heading.
subhuman, *a.* sub-*hew*-man, almost human; having ape-like or bestial qualities.
sub-imago, *n.* sub-im-*ay*-goh, the stage immediately preceding that of the imago; the insect at this stage [Entom.].
subinfection, *n.* sub-in-*fek*-shon, chronic intoxication due to frequent small doses of a toxic agent [Path.].
subinfeudation, *n.* sub-in-few-*day*-shon, the act of enfeoffing by a tenant or feoffee, who holds lands of the crown [Law]; under-tenancy.
subintrant, *a.* sub-*in*-trant, attended by paroxysms that are nearly continuous [Med.]: *n.* a fever, esp. malarial, of this nature. (Late L. *subintrans*, stealing into.)
subirrigation, *n.* *sub*-i-re-*gay*-shon, irrigation below the surface; partial irrigation.
subitamente, *ad.* soo-be-ta-*men*-tee, suddenly; without break or pause [Mus.]. (It.)
subito, *ad.* *soo*-be-toh, quickly [Mus.]. (It.)
subjacent, *a.* sub-*jay*-sent, lying under or nearly under; being in a lower situation though not directly beneath. (L. *subjacens*, underlying.)
subject, *a.* *sub*-jekt, subordinate; liable; being under the power and dominion of another; liable from extraneous or from inherent causes; prone;

disposed; being that on which a thing operates; obedient: *n.* one who owes allegiance to a sovereign, and is governed by his laws; that on which any mental operation is performed; a matter written or spoken about; a theme; a topic; that which is treated or handled; that on which any physical operation is performed; that in which anything inheres or exists; the person who is treated of; the hero of a piece; that term of a proposition of which another is predicated [Gram. and Logic]; the principal melody or theme of a movement [Mus.]; that which it is the object and aim of the artist to express; a dead body for the purpose of dissection [Anat.]. **subject to,** liable to; exposed to; dependent or conditional upon. (O.Fr. *suiect.*)

subject, *v.t.* sub-*jekt*, to bring under the power or dominion of; to put under; to enslave; to expose to; to submit; to cause to undergo.

subjection, *n.* sub-*jek*-shon, act of subduing; state of being under the power, control, and government of another.

subjective, *a.* sub-*jek*-tiv, relating to the subject, as opposed to the object; arising in and from the mind itself instead of from the observation of external things; derived from inner consciousness; pertaining to oneself; characterized by the individuality of the author: *n.* the nominative case, the case of the subject [Gram.]. (L. *subjectivus.*)

subjectively, *ad.* sub-*jek*-tiv-le, in a subjective manner.

subjectiveness, *n.* sub-*jek*-tiv-ness, the state of being subjective.

subjectivism, *n.* sub-*jek*-te-vizm, the doctrine of the relativity of knowledge [Phil.].

subjectivist, *n.* sub-*jek*-te-vist, one believing in the doctrine of subjectivism.

subjectivity, *n.* sub-jek-*tiv*-e-te, subjectiveness; that which is subjective.

subjectivize, *v.t.* sub-*jek*-te-vize, to make subjective.

subjectless, *a.* *sub*-jekt-less, without subjects.

subject-matter, *n.* the matter or thought presented for consideration.

subject-object, *n.* a subjective object, one that is both subject and object; a self-conscious being; the immediate object of thought.

subjoin, *v.t.* sub-*joyn*, to add at the end; to affix or annex. (O.Fr. *subjoindre.*)

subjoinder, *n.* sub-*joyn*-der, an additional remark.

subjugable, *a.* *sub*-joo-gabl, that may be subjugated or subdued.

subjugate, *v.t.* *sub*-joo-gate, to subdue and bring under the yoke of power or dominion; to conquer by force and compel to submit to the government of another. (L. *subjugatus.*)

subjugation, *n.* *sub*-joo-*gay*-shon, the act of subduing and bringing under the power of another; the state or condition of being subjugated.

subjugator, *n.* *sub*-joo-*gay*-tor, one who subjugates; an oppressor.

subjunction, *n.* sub-*junk*-shon, act of subjoining; state of being subjoined; that which is subjoined.

subjunctive, *a.* sub-*junk*-tiv, subjoined; dependent and expressing condition, hypothesis, or contingency [Gram.]: *n.* the subjunctive mood [Gram.]. (L. *subjunctivus.*)

sub-kingdom, *n.* a primary division of the animal or vegetable kingdom.

sublapsarian, *n.* *sub*-lap-*sare*-re-an, one of a Calvinistic sect holding that the decree of election and reprobation was made by God in foresight of the fall and consequent lost estate of mankind, so that reprobation is only preterition or non-election [Theol.]: *a.* pertaining to this sect or its doctrine. (L. *sub-*, after, *lapsus*, fall.)

sublapsarianism, *n.* *sub*-lap-*sare*-re-a-nizm, the sublapsarian doctrine.

sublate, *v.t.* sub-*late*, to contradict; to treat as untrue [Logic]. (L. *sublatus*, taken away.)

sublease, *n.* sub-*leese*, a lease held from another lessee: *v.t.* to sublet.

sublet, *v.t.* sub-*let*, to underlet; to lease, as lessee, to another person.

sub-lieutenant, *n.* the British naval rank between a midshipman and a lieutenant; in the army, a second-lieutenant.

sublimable, *a.* su-*blime*-a-bl, that may be sublimated.

sublimableness, *n.* su-*blime*-a-bl-ness, the quality of being sublimable.

sublimate, *n.* *sub*-le-mat, the product of sublimation: *a.* sublimated: *v.t.* to raise a solid substance to the gaseous state by heat and to condense it to a solid by cooling; to refine and exalt; to elevate. **blue sublimate,** a pigment prepared from mercury with flowers of brimstone and sal-ammoniac. (L. *sublimatus.*)

sublimation, *n.* *sub*-le-*may*-shon, the operation of sublimating; the act of heightening and improving; that which is refined to a high degree.

sublime, *a.* su-*blime*, high in place; exalted; high in excellence; high in style or sentiment; elevated in manner; majestic; characterized by grandeur: *v.t.* to sublimate; to exalt; to heighten; to make sublime; to dignify: *v.i.* to be capable of sublimation; to become sublime. **the sublime,** that which is sublime in nature or art, as suggestive of something great, lofty, or noble, and exciting a sense of awe or of elation; also the feeling it inspires. **the Sublime Porte,** an honorific title of the former Ottoman Court and imperial Turkish Government. (Fr.)

sublimely, *ad.* su-*blime*-le, in a sublime manner.

sublimeness, *n.* su-*blime*-ness, the quality of being sublime; sublimity.

subliminal, *a.* sub-*lim*-e-nal, latent; below the boundary of consciousness; pertaining to subconsciousness: *n.* the subconscious. (L. *sub-*, and *limen*, threshold.)

sublimity, *n.* sub-*lim*-e-te, elevation; grandeur; height in excellence; loftiness of nature or character; moral grandeur; loftiness of conception, sentiment, or style; the sense or feeling of the sublime.

sublineation, *n.* *sub*-lin-e-*ay*-shon, the underlining of a word or words.

sublingual, *a.* sub-*ling*-gwal, situated under the tongue. (L. *sub-*, and *lingua*, tongue.)

sublunar, *a.* sub-*loo*-nar, beneath the moon; terrestrial; mundane. (L. *sub-*, and *luna*, the moon.)

sublunary, *a.* sub-*loo*-na-re, terrestrial; pertaining to this world.

subluxation, *n.* *sub*-luk-*say*-shon, a partial dislocation or displacement of a bone [Surg.]. (L. *sub-*, and *luxus*, loose.)

sub-machine gun, *n.* a simple type of portable rapid-firing automatic rifle.

subman, *n.* *sub*-man, one whose human faculties or characteristics are imperfectly developed; a brutish or doltish person; a subhuman man.

submarine, *a.* sub-ma-*reen*, being, acting, or growing under water.

submarine, *n.* *sub*-ma-reen, a submergible or submersible motor vessel, esp. a torpedo-firing war-vessel armed with guns.

submaxillary, *a.* *sub*-mak-*zil*-la-re, situated under the lower jaw.

submedial, *a.* sub-*mee*-de-al, lying under the middle.

submedian, *a.* sub-*mee*-de-an, situated near or under the middle or median line [Zool.].

submediant, *n.* sub-*mee*-de-ant, the middle note between the octave and subdominant [Mus.].

submental, *a.* sub-*men*-tal, beneath the chin. (L. *sub-*, and *mentum*, the chin.)

submerge, *v.t.* sub-*merj*, to put completely under water; to inundate; to drown: *v.i.* to plunge or sink under water. (Fr. *submerger.*)

submergence, *n.* sub-*mer*-jence, act of submerging; state of being submerged.

submergible, *a.* capable of being submerged.

submerse, *v.t.* and *i.* to submerge, esp. for an extended period.

submersed, *a.* sub-*merst*, being or growing partly under water [Bot.].

submersible, *n.* sub-*mer*-se-bl, a vessel that can be submerged: *a.* capable of being submerged, and esp. of functioning while submerged.

submersion, *n.* sub-*mer*-shon, act of submerging; the state of being submerged.

submetallic, *a.* sub-me-*tal*-ik, not completely metallic.

submicron, *n.* sub-*my*-kron, a minute subdivision of the micron, visible only with the ultra-microscope [Physical Chem.].

submiss, *a.* sub-*mis*, submissive; humble; low.

submission, *n.* sub-*mish*-on, act of submitting or yielding; state of being submissive; acknowledgment of inferiority or of error; compliance; obedience; resignation. (L. *submissus.*)

submissive, *a.* sub-*mis*-siv, yielding to the will or

power of another; obedient; acknowledging one's inferiority; humble.
submissively, *ad.* in a submissive manner.
submissiveness, *n.* the quality of being submissive.
submit, *v.t.* sub-*mit*, to yield, resign, or surrender to the power, will, or authority of another; to refer to the judgment of another: *v.i.* to yield one's person to the power of another; to surrender; to yield one's opinion; to be subject; to be submissive. (L. *submitto.*)
submitter, *n.* sub-*mit*-ter, one who submits.
submontane, *a.* sub-*mon*-tane, at the foot of mountains. (L. *sub-*, and *montanus*, mountain.)
submorphous, *a.* sub-*mor*-fus, partaking of amorphous and crystalline character.
submucous, *a.* sub-*mew*-kus, somewhat mucous; situated under or affecting a mucous membrane.
submultiple, *n.* sub-*mul*-te-pl, an aliquot part of a number.
subnarcotic, *a.* *sub*-nar-*kot*-ik, moderately narcotic.
subnasal, *a.* sub-*nay*-zal, situated under the nose.
sub-nascent, *a.* sub-*nas*-ent, growing under; arising from below. (L. *subnascens*, growing beneath.)
subnivean, *a.* sub-*niv*-e-an, situated beneath the snow. (L. *sub-*, and *nivis*, of snow.)
subnormal, *a.* sub-*nor*-mal, below normal; not up to normal intelligence: *n.* the part of the axis of a curved line intercepted between the ordinate and the normal [Geom.].
subnude, *a.* *sub*-newd, almost naked or bare of leaves [Bot.].
suboccipital, *a.* *sub*-ok-*sip*-e-tal, under the occiput.
suboctave, *a.* sub-*ok*-tav, the octave below [Mus.].
suboctuple, *a.* sub-*ok*-tew-pl, containing one part of eight.
subocular, *a.* sub-*ok*-yew-lar, being under the eye.
suborbicular, *a.* *sub*-or-*bik*-yew-lar, almost orbicular; nearly circular.
suborbital, *a.* sub-*or*-be-tal, below the orbit of the eye.
sub-order, *n.* *sub*-or-der, a subdivision of an order.
subordinacy, *n.* sub-*or*-de-na-se, state of being subordinate; subordination.
subordinal, *a.* sub-*or*-de-nal, relating to a sub-order.
subordinary, *n.* sub-*or*-de-na-re, an armorial charge inferior in honour to an ordinary [Her.].
subordinate, *a.* sub-*or*-de-nat, inferior in order, dignity, power, or importance; descending in a regular series: *n.* one who stands in order or rank below another: *v.t.* sub-*or*-de-nate, to place in an order or rank below something else; to make or consider as of less value or importance; to make subservient or subject. (Late L. *subordinatus.*)
subordinately, *ad.* in a subordinate manner.
subordinateness, *n.* state of being subordinate.
subordination, *n.* sub-*or*-de-*nay*-shon, the act of subordinating; state of being subordinate or under control or government; inferiority of rank or dignity; subjection.
subordinationism, *n.* sub-or-de-*nay*-shon-izm, the doctrine that the Second and Third Persons of the Trinity hold an inferior position to that of the First [Theol.].
subordinative, *a.* sub-*or*-de-na-tiv, tending to, or expressing, subordination.
suborn, *v.t.* sub-*orn*, to induce a person to do a wrongful or criminal act, esp. to commit perjury; to procure secretly; to bribe. (Fr. *suborner.*)
subornation, *n.* *sub*-or-*nay*-shon, the act of suborning. **subornation of perjury**, the crime of procuring a person to take a false oath or a person on oath to commit perjury [Law].
suborner, *n.* sub-*orn*-er, one who suborns.
suboval, *a.* sub-*oh-val*, subovate.
subovate, *a.* sub-*oh*-vat, almost ovate or oval; nearly in the form of an egg.
subpanation, *n.* *sub*-pa-*nay*-shon, the doctrine of the local and material presence of Christ in the bread and wine of the eucharist. (L. *sub-*, and *panis*, bread.)
subplot, *n.* *sub*-plot, a subsidiary plot in a novel, play, etc.
subpœna, *n.* sub-*pee*-na, a writ commanding the attendance in court of a person as a witness under a penalty: *v.t.* to serve with a writ of subpœna; to command attendance in court by a legal writ. *pp.* **subpœnaed.** (L. *sub-*, and *pœna*, penalty.)
subpolar, *a.* sub-*poh*-lar, under or near the pole.
subprior, *n.* sub-*pry*-or, the vicegerent of a prior; a claustral officer who assists the prior.
subpurchaser, *n.* sub-*pur*-chas-er, a purchaser who buys of a purchaser.
subquadrate, *a.* sub-*kwod*-rat, nearly square.
subquadruple, *a.* sub-*kwod*-roo-pl, containing one part in four.
subquintuple, *a.* sub-*kwin*-tew-pl, containing one part in five.
subramous, *a.* sub-*ray*-mus, having few branches [Bot.]. (L. *sub-*, and *ramus*, a branch.)
subrational, *a.* sub-*rash*-o-nal, not completely rational.
sub-rector, *n.* *sub*-rek-tor, a rector's deputy, assistant, or substitute.
subregion, *n.* *sub*-ree-jon, the primary division of a geographical region.
subrent, *v.t.* sub-*rent*, to hold as a subtenant.
subreption, *n.* sub-*rep*-shon, act of obtaining a favour by surprise or unfair misrepresentation, that is, by suppression or fraudulent concealment of facts. (L. *subreptio*, a carrying off by force.)
subreptitious, *a.* sub-rep-*tish*-us, obtained by subreption; surreptitious.
subreptive, *a.* sub-*rep*-tiv, surreptitious.
subretinal, *a.* sub-*ret*-e-nal, under the retina.
subrigid, *a.* sub-*rij*-id, moderately stiff.
subrogation, *n.* *sub*-ro-*gay*-shon, the substituting of one person in the place of another and giving him his rights; succession [Law]. (L. *subrogatio.*)
subsale, *n.* *sub*-sale, a resale by a purchaser, esp. before he has completed the purchase.
subsaline, *a.* sub-*say*-line, moderately saline or salt.
subsalt, *n.* *sub*-sawlt, a salt having an excess of base, a basic salt [Chem.].
subscapular, *a.* sub-*skap*-yew-lar, beneath the scapula: *n.* the subscapular artery or muscle.
subscribable, *a.* sub-*skry*-ba-bl, that may be subscribed.
subscribe, *v.t.* sub-*skribe*, to sign with one's own hand; to give consent to something written by writing one's name beneath; to attest by writing one's name beneath; to promise to give by writing one's name; to contribute, esp. periodically, to a fund; to publish after obtaining subscriptions: *v.i.* to promise in writing to pay or contribute a certain sum; to engage to receive and pay for a periodical publication; to assent. (L. *subscribo.*)
subscriber, *n.* sub-*skry*-ber, one who subscribes; one who contributes to an undertaking by subscribing; one who enters his name for a publication.
subscript, *a.* *sub*-skript, written below or underneath: *n.* a subscript sign or letter. (L. *subscriptus.*)
subscription, *n.* sub-*skrip*-shon, the act of subscribing; the name subscribed; signature; consent or promise by subscribing; a sum subscribed; a periodical gift or payment.
subscriptionist, *n.* sub-*skrip*-shon-ist, a canvasser for subscriptions.
subsection, *n.* *sub*-sek-shon, a division of a section, as of a document, or a body of troops; sub-division.
subsellium, *n.* sub-*sel*-le-um (*pl.* **subsellia**), a shelving seat in a stall; a misericord [Eccles.]. (L., a low bench, from *sub-*, and *sella*, a seat.)
subsensible, *a.* sub-*sen*-sibl, beyond the reach of the senses.
subseptuple, *a.* sub-*sep*-tew-pl, containing one of seven parts.
subsequence, *n.* the state of being subsequent.
subsequent, *a.* *sub*-se-kwent, following or coming immediately after in time; following in order; succeeding. (L. *subsequens*, following hard behind.)
subsequential, *a.* sub-se-*kwen*-shal, subsequent.
subsequently, *ad.* after something else in time or order.
subserve, *v.t.* sub-*serv*, to serve as a means; to serve; to promote (an end). (L. *subservio.*)
subservience, *n.* sub-*ser*-ve-ence, the state of being subservient; use of operation that promotes some purpose.
subserviency, *n.* sub-*ser*-ve-en-se, subservience.
subservient, *a.* sub-*ser*-ve-ent, serving to promote some end; subordinate; acting as a subordinate instrument; obsequious.
subserviently, *ad.* in a subservient manner.
subsessile, *a.* sub-*ses*-sile, having very short footstalks [Bot.].
subsextuple, *a.* sub-*seks*-tew-pl, containing one part in six.

subside, *v.i.* sub-*side*, to sink or fall to the bottom; to fall into a state of quiet; to become tranquil; to sink; to abate. (L. *subsido*, sit down.)
subsidence, *n.* sub-*sy*-dence *or* *sub*-se-dence, act or process of subsiding; act of sinking or falling in; the gradual disappearance of a disease [Med.].
subsidiarily, *ad.* sub-*sid*-e-a-re-le, in a subsidiary manner; secondarily.
subsidiary, *a.* sub-*sid*-e-a-re, aiding; affording help; furnishing additional supplies; as regards a subsidy; of minor importance: *n.* one who or that which contributes aid or additional supplies; an auxiliary. (L. *subsidiarius.*)
subsidize, *v.t.* *sub*-se-dize, to assist with a subsidy; to purchase the assistance of.
subsidy, *n.* *sub*-se-de, a grant in aid of a private enterprise for the public benefit; supply given; a tax for a special purpose; a sum of money paid by one prince or national to another for assistance in war. (L. *subsidium*, reserve force.)
subsign, *v.t.* sub-*sine*, to sign under.
subsist, *v.i.* sub-*sist*, to have existence; to retain the present state; to be maintained with food and clothing; to inhere: *v.t.* to feed: to maintain. (Fr. *subsister.*)
subsistence, *n.* sub-*sis*-tence, the state of being subsistent; real being; means of supporting life; livelihood; inherence in something else. **subsistence money,** a payment in advance on account of wages to meet current expenses. (Fr.)
subsistent, *a.* sub-*sis*-tent, existing; having real being; inherent.
subsistential, *a.* sub-sis-*ten*-shal, pertaining to subsistence, or [Theol.] to the hypostasis or divine essence.
subsoil, *n.* *sub*-soyl, the soil which lies immediately beneath the surface soil.
subsolar, *a.* sub-*soh*-lar, being under the sun; situated between the tropics; terrestrial; mundane.
subsonic, *a.* sub-*son*-ik, pertaining to, or having, a speed less than that of sound. (L. *sub-*, and *sonus*, sound.)
sub-species, *n.* a subordinate species; a division of a species; a variety.
substage, *n.* *sub*-staje, an attachment below the stage of a microscope; a subdivision of a stage [Geol.].
★**substance,** *n.* *sub*-stance, a real thing with qualities; material body; substantiality; the essential part; goods; estate; means of living; the assumed substratum of qualities [Metaphysics]. (Fr.)
substantial, *a.* sub-*stan*-shal, having or pertaining to substance; actually existing; real; corporeal; material; strong; solid; firm; possessed of goods or estate; moderately wealthy: *n.pl.* the essential parts. (L. *substantialis.*)
substantialism, *n.* sub-*stan*-shal-izm, the doctrine that underlying phenomena are substantial realities [Phil.].
substantialist, *n.* sub-*stan*-shal-ist, one who upholds the doctrine of substantialism.
substantiality, *n.* sub-*stan*-she-*al*-e-te, the state of real existence; corporeity; materiality.
substantialize, *v.t.* sub-*stan*-shal-ize, to render substantial: *v.i.* to acquire substance or actual existence.
substantially, *ad.* in a substantial manner; in substance.
substantialness, *n.* the quality of being substantial.
substantiate, *v.t.* sub-*stan*-she-ate, to make real; to establish by evidence; to verify; to make good.
substantiation, *n.* sub-*stan*-she-*ay*-shun, the act of proving; proof, or support from evidence.
substantival, *a.* *sub*-stan-*ty*-val, serving as a substantive.
substantive, *a.* *sub*-stan-tiv, expressing existence; independent: *n.* the name of something that exists, or is conceived to exist, either material or immaterial; a noun [Gram.]. **substantive dyes,** dyes not needing a mordant. **substantive rank,** permanent (as opposed to temporary, brevet, or honorary) rank [Mil.]. (Fr. *substantif.*)
substantively, *ad.* in a substantive manner; as a substantive [Gram.].
substation, *n.* *sub*-stay-shon, a subsidiary or intermediary station or power-station.
substernal, *a.* sub-*ster*-nal, beneath the sternum.
substituent, *n.* sub-*stit*-yew-ent, an atom or group put in place of another [Chem.].
substitute, *n.* *sub*-ste-tewt, a person or thing put in the place of another: *v.t.* to put in the place of another: *v.i.* to act as a substitute. (Fr. *substitut.*)
substitution, *n.* *sub*-ste-*tew*-shon, the act of putting one person or thing in the place of another; replacement; the replacement of hydrogen by a halogen or other group [Chem.].
substitutional, *a.* sub-ste-*tew*-shon-al, involving substitution; substitutionary.
substitutionally, *ad.* by substitution.
substitutionary, *a.* *sub*-ste-*tew*-shon-a-re, pertaining to substitution; supplying the place of another.
substitutive, *a.* *sub*-ste-tew-tiv, taking, or capable of taking, the place of someone or something.
substrate, *n.* *sub*-strate, a substratum; in biochemistry, a substance acted upon, esp. by an enzyme.
substratosphere, *n.* sub-*strat*-o-sfeer, that part of the atmosphere lying immediately below the stratosphere [Meteor.].
substratum, *n.* sub-*stray*-tum (*pl.* **substrata**), that which is laid or spread under; a stratum lying under another; the underlying basis and bond of qualities [Metaphysics]. (L.)
substruction, *n.* *sub*-struk-shon, an under-building; a foundation.
substructural, *a.* sub-*struk*-tewr-ral, pertaining to foundations or a substructure.
substructure, *n.* *sub*-struk-tewr, an under-structure; a foundation.
substyle, *n.* *sub*-stile, a right line on which the style or gnomon of a dial is erected [Dialling].
subsulphate, *n.* sub-*sul*-fate, a sulphate with an excess of the base.
subsultive, *a.* sub-*sul*-tiv, subsultory.
subsultory, *a.* sub-*sul*-to-re, bounding; leaping; moving by sudden starts or twitches.
subsultus, *n.* sub-*sul*-tus, a twitching movement of the muscles in a state of extreme prostration [Med.]. (L.)
subsume, *v.t.* sub-*sewm*, to include as comprehended or subordinate [Logic]. (L. *sub-*, and *sumo*, take.)
subsumption, *n.* sub-*sum*-shon, the act of subsuming; that which is subsumed; a proposition subsumed under another [Logic].
subsurface, *a.* *sub*-sur-face, below the surface: *n.* the subsoil.
subtangent, *n.* sub-*tan*-jent, the part of the axis contained between the ordinate and tangent drawn to the same point in a curve [Geom.].
subtemperate, *a.* sub-*tem*-per-rat, almost temperate; pertaining to the colder portions of the temperate zone.
subtenancy, *n.* sub-*ten*-an-se, the holding of a subtenant; the period of such holding.
subtenant, *n.* *sub*-ten-ant, a tenant holding under a tenant.
subtend, *v.t.* sub-*tend*, to extend under, or be opposite to [Geom.]. (L. *sub-*, and *tendo*, stretch.)
subtense, *n.* sub-*tense*, a subtending line; the chord of an arc [Geom.].
subtepid, *a.* sub-*tep*-id, moderately warm.
subter-, a Latin prefix, signifying under or less than.
subterfuge, *n.* *sub*-ter-fewj, an artifice employed to escape censure or the force of an argument, or to justify opinions or conduct; evasion; equivocation. (L. *subterfugium.*)
subterposition, *n.* sub-ter-po-*zish*-on, position beneath [Geol.].
subterranean, *a.* *sub*-ter-*ray*-ne-an, underground; situated or taking place below ground; [Fig.] working in secret: *n.* an underground dwelling or cave; a cave-dweller. (L. *subterraneus.*)
subterraneous, *a.* *sub*-ter-*ray*-ne-us, subterranean.
subterrene, *a.* sub-ter-*reen*, subterranean; infernal.
subthoracic, *a.* *sub*-tho-*ras*-ik, below the thorax.
subtile, *a.* *sub*-til *or* sutl, thin; not dense or gross; nice; fine; delicate; subtle.
subtilely, *ad.* *sub*-til-le *or* *sutl*-le, in a subtile manner; finely; artfully.
subtility, *n.* sub-*til*-e-te, acuteness; perspicacity; subtlety.
subtilization, *n.* *sub*-til-e- *or* *sutl*-e-*zay*-shon, act of making subtile, fine, or thin; operation of making so volatile as to rise in vapour; refining.
subtilize, *v.t.* *sub*-til-ize *or* *sutl*-ize, to make thin or fine; to refine; to spin into niceties: *v.i.* to make very nice distinctions.

subtilty, *n.* *sub*-til-te *or* *sut*-il-te, subtlety.
sub-title, *n.* *sub*-tytl, a secondary title of a book; a motion-picture caption: *v.t.* to give a sub-title to.
subtle, *a.* *sut*-tl, sly; artful; cunningly devised; insinuating; planned with art; deceitful; refined; acute. (L. *subtilis*, woven fine.)
subtleness, *n.* *sut*-tl-ness, the quality of being subtle; subtlety.
subtlety, *n.* *sut*-tl-te, thinness; fineness; refinement; extreme acuteness; slyness in design; cunning; artifice. (Fr. *subtilité*.)
subtly, *ad.* *sut*-tle, slily; artfully; nicely.
subtone, *n.* *sub*-tohn, an undertone; a tone of less than normal volume
subtonic, *n.* sub-*ton*-ik, the semitone or note next below the tonic; the leading note of the scale; the seventh of the modes [Mus.]: *a.* sonant [Phonetics].
subtorrid, *a.* sub-*to*-rid, almost torrid.
subtract, *v.t.* sub-*trakt*, to withdraw or take a part from the rest; to deduct [Arith.]. (L. *subtractus*, taken away.)
subtracter, *n.* sub-*trak*-ter, one who subtracts.
subtraction, *n.* sub-*trak*-shon, the act or operation of taking a part from the rest; the taking of a lesser number or quantity from a greater [Arith.].
subtractive, *a.* sub-*trak*-tiv, tending or having power to subtract.
subtrahend, *n.* *sub*-tra-hend, the sum or number to be subtracted [Arith.]. (L. *subtrahendus*.)
subtriple, *a.* sub-*trip*-pl, containing a third, or one part of three.
subtriplicate, *a.* sub-*trip*-le-kat, in the ratio of the cube roots.
subtropical, *a.* sub-*trop*-e-kal, pertaining to the region near the tropics; having features common to the temperate and the tropical zones.
subtype, *n.* *sub*-tipe, a subdivision of a type; a subsidiary type.
subulate, *a.* *sew*-bew-lat, awl-shaped; linear; narrow and tapering. (L. *subula*, an awl.)
subulicorn, *a.* *sew*-bew-le-korn, having awl-shaped antennæ. (L. *subula*, and *cornu*, a horn.)
subungual, *a.* sub-*ung*-gwal, under the nail. (L. *sub-*, and *unguis*, a nail.)
subungulate, *a.* sub-*ung*-gew-lat, hoofed, but having digits.
suburb, *n.* *sub*-urb, a district lying without the walls, or in the outskirts of a city or town; the confines. (L. *suburbium*.)
suburban, *a.* su-*bur*-ban, inhabiting or being in the suburbs; pertaining to suburbs: *n.* one who resides in a suburb.
suburbanism, *n.* su-*bur*-ba-nizm, a characteristic, mannerism, or peculiarity of suburban people.
suburbanite, *n.* a resident in a suburb.
suburbanity, *n.* sub-ur-*ban*-e-te, the condition of being suburban; the characteristics of suburban life.
suburbanize, *v.t.* su-*bur*-ba-nize, to convert into a suburb; to make suburban.
Suburbia, *n.* su-*bur*-be-a, a patronizing name for suburbs in general; the standards, way of living, etc., attributed to suburbanites.
subvariety, *n.* *sub*-va-*ry*-e-te, a subordinate variety, or division of a variety.
subvene, *v.t.* sub-*veen*, to occur effectively, esp. as a relief. (Fr., from L.)
subvent, *v.t.* sub-*vent*, to come to the aid of, esp. financially. (L. *sub-*, and *venire*, to come.)
subvention, *n.* sub-*ven*-shon, a pecuniary grant, esp. from a government or local authority: *v.t.* to subvent. (Fr. from L.)
subversion, *n.* sub-*ver*-shon, the act of subverting; entire overthrow; destruction; utter ruin. (L.)
subversive, *a.* sub-*ver*-siv, tending to subvert; having a tendency to overthrow and ruin.
subvert, *v.t.* sub-*vert*, to overthrow from the foundation; to ruin utterly; to corrupt; to pervert the mind. (Fr. *subvertir*.)
subvertebral, *a.* sub-*ver*-te-bral, situated beneath a vertebra.
subverter, *n.* one who subverts; an overthrower.
subvertible, *a.* that may be subverted.
subvertical, *a.* sub-*ver*-te-kal, nearly upright.
subvirile, *a.* sub-*vi*-rile, deficient in manhood or virility.
subway, *n.* *sub*-way, an underground footway; an arched way underneath a street containing sewers, service-pipes, cables, etc., that can thus be inspected or repaired with no disturbance to the street above: an underground electric railway (esp. U.S.A.).
succade, *n.* suk-*kade*, a sweetmeat or preserve in sugar; a crystallized fruit. (L. *succus*, juice.)
succedaneous, *a.* *suk*-se-*day*-ne-us, supplying the place of something else; acting as, or of the nature of, a substitute. (L. *succedaneus*.)
succedaneum, *n.* *suk*-se-*day*-ne-um, that which is used for something else; a substitute.
succeed, *v.t.* suk-*seed*, to follow in order; to take the place of; to come after; to be successor to: *v.i.* to follow in order; to come in the place of one that has died, or quitted the place, or of that which has preceded; to obtain the object desired; to accomplish what is attempted; to have a prosperous termination. (Fr. *succeder*.)
succeeder, *n.* suk-*see*-der, a successor; one who is successful.
succentor, *n.* suk-*sen*-tor, the leading bass in a choir; a deputy precentor. (Late L.)
success, *n.* suk-*sess*, the act of succeeding; the prosperous termination of anything attempted; one who or that which is successful. (L. *successus*.)
successful, *a.* suk-*sess*-ful, terminating in accomplishing what is wished or intended; prosperous.
successfully, *ad.* in a successful manner.
successfulness, *n.* quality of being successful.
succession, *n.* suk-*sesh*-on, series of things following one another, either in time or place; the act or the right of succeeding or coming in the place of another; rotation; lineage; order of descent; the successive notes in melody [Mus.]. **succession states,** the Central European autonomous states constituted after the disruption of the Austro-Hungarian Empire at the close of the War of 1914–18. **Apostolic succession,** *see* **apostolic.** (Fr.)
successional, *a.* in a regular order of succession.
successionally, *ad.* by succession.
successive, *a.* suk-*ses*-siv, following in order or uninterrupted course; coming by succession; consecutive. (Late L. *successivus*.)
successively, *ad.* in successive order.
successiveness, *n.* state of being successive.
successless, *a.* suk-*sess*-less, having no success; unprosperous; unfortunate.
successor, *n.* suk-ses-sor, one who succeeds, or takes the place which another has left. (L.)
succiferous, *a.* suk-*sif*-er-rus, producing or conveying sap. (L. *succus*, juice, *fero*, bring.)
succinate, *n.* *suk*-se-nate, a salt of succinic acid. (L. *succinum*, amber.)
succinated, *a.* treated with or combined with succinic acid.
succinct, *a.* suk-*sinkt*, compressed into a narrow compass; brief; concise. (L. *succinctus*, girt up.)
succinctly, *ad.* suk-*sinkt*-le, concisely.
succinctness, *n.* suk-*sinkt*-ness, conciseness.
succinic, *a.* suk-*sin*-ik, pertaining to or obtained from amber. **succinic acid,** an acid which exists ready formed in some amber, and in sugar-cane, in certain coniferæ, etc. (L. *succinum*, amber.)
succinite, *n.* *suk*-se-nite, an amber-coloured garnet; a variety of amber yielding succinic acid.
succory, *n.* *suk*-o-re, chicory, *Cichorium intybus*.
succose, *a.* *suk*-ohs, sappy; juicy.
succotash, *n.* *suk*-o-tash, a dish consisting of green maize and beans cooked together. (Amerind.)
succour, *n.* *suk*-ur, aid; assistance that relieves from difficulty or distress; the person or thing that brings relief: *v.t.* to give help in a case difficulty, want, or distress. (Fr. *secours*.)
succourer, *n.* *suk*-ur-rer, he who affords relief; a helper; a deliverer.
succourless, *a.* destitute of help or relief.
succubous, *a.* *suk*-ew-bus, having each leaf imbricated under the one above (opposed to incubous) [Bot.]. (L. *sub-*, and *cumbere*, to lie.)
succubus, *n.* *suk*-ew-bus (*pl.* **succubi**), a female demon fabled to have sexual intercourse with men in their sleep. (L. *succuba*, a harlot.)
succula, *n.* *suk*-ew-la, an axis or cylinder with staves in it to move round, but without a drum [Mech.]. (L. *sucula*, a capstan.)
succulence, *n.* *suk*-ew-lence, juiciness.
succulent, *a.* *suk*-ew-lent, full of juice; juicy. (L. *succulentus*, from *succus*, juice.)
succulently, *ad.* *suk*-ew-lent-le, juicily.
succumb, *v.i.* su-*kum*, to yield; to submit; to sink unresistantly. (L. *succumbo*.)

succursal, *a.* su-*kur*-sal, annexed and assistant; subsidiary. (Fr. *succursale.*)
succussion, *n.* su-*kush*-on, the act of shaking; a shake; an ague; a shaking of the nervous parts by powerful stimulants; the shaking of a patient to ascertain whether fluid is present in the thorax or other cavity [Med.]. (L. *succussio.*)
succussive, *a.* su-*kus*-siv shaking violently.
★**such,** *a.* sutch, of that or the like kind; the same that, or as referred to. **such and such,** is used in reference to some unspecified person or place, etc., of a certain kind. (A.S. *swylc.*)
suchlike, *a.* *sutch*-like, of such sort [Coll.].
suck, *n.* suk, the act of drawing with the mouth; milk drawn from the breast by the mouth; a small draught or drink: *v.t.* to draw in with the mouth; to draw milk from with the mouth; to imbibe; to draw or drain; to draw in; to dissolve in the mouth: *v.i.* to draw by exhausting the air; to draw the breast. **suck in,** to draw into the mouth; to absorb; to deceive [Slang]. **suck out,** to empty by suction. **suck up,** to draw into the mouth. **suck up to,** to toady to [Slang]. (A.S. *sucan.*)
sucker, *n.* *suk*-er, he who or that which draws with the mouth; the piston of a pump; a pipe through which anything is drawn; the shoot of a plant from the roots or lower parts of the stem; a suctorial organ [Zool.]; a fish of the genus *Lepadogaster* and several species of other genera; a greenhorn, a sponger, a sucket [Slang]: *v.t.* to strip off shoots [U.S.A.].
sucket, *n.* *suk*-et, a sweetmeat which dissolves in the mouth.
sucking-bottle, *n.* a bottle to be filled with milk for infants to suck, instead of the breast.
sucking-pig, *n.* a pig not yet weaned, esp. [Cookery] killed and roasted whole.
suckle, *v.t.* *suk*-kl, to give suck to; to nurse at the breast or udder.
suckler, *n.* *suk*-ler, a suckling, esp. an unweaned animal.
suckling, *n.* *suk*-ling, a young child or animal nursed at the breast; an unweaned infant.
sucrose, *n.* *sew*-krohs, cane-sugar, or sugar of a similar chemical composition.
suction, *n.* *suk*-shon, the act of sucking or drawing a liquid into the mouth or a pipe. (O.Fr.)
suction-pipe, *n.* the lower pipe of a pump.
suction-pump, *n.* the common pump, in which a vacuum is produced and the water forced up by atmospheric pressure.
suctorial, *a.* suk-*taw*-re-al, adapted for sucking; capable of imbibing or of adhering by suction; provided with suctorial organs [Zool.].
suctorian, *n.* suk-*taw*-re-an, an animal with suctorial organs.
sudamina, *n.* sew-*dam*-e-na, a vesicular eruption on the skin caused by retention of sweat; miliaria [Med.]. (L. *sudo,* sweat.)
Sudanese, *a.* soo-da-*neez,* of or pertaining to the Sudan: *n.* a native or inhabitant of the Sudan.
Sudani, *n.* soo-*dah*-nee, an Arabic dialect spoken in the Sudan.
sudarium, *n.* sew-*dare*-re-um, the miraculous cloth impressed with a portrait of Christ when He wiped His face with it on the way to crucifixion; a vernicle; a handkerchief. (L.)
sudation, *n.* sew-*day*-shon, a sweating; exudation of plants [Bot.].
sudatorium, *n.* sew-da-*taw*-re-um, a sweating-bath. (L.)
sudatory, *n.* *sew*-da-to-re, a hot-house; a sweating-bath: *a.* stimulating perspiration.
sudd, *n.* sud, a floating mass of papyrus stems, etc., obstructing the White Nile; a temporary dam (in Egypt). (Ar.)
★**sudden,** *a.* *sud*-dn, happening without previous notice; coming unexpectedly; unexpected; abrupt. **on a sudden,** sooner than was expected; unexpectedly. (O.Fr. *sodain.*)
suddenly, *ad.* *sud*-dn-le, in a sudden manner.
suddenness, *n.* quality or state of being sudden.
sudoriferous, *a.* *sew*-do-*rif*-er-rus, producing perspiration; perspiring.
sudorific, *a.* sew-do-*rif*-ik, causing sweat: *n.* a medicine that produces sweat. (L. *sudor,* sweat, *facio,* make.)
sudoriparous, *a.* *sew*-do-*rip*-a-rus, sweat-secreting.
Sudra, *n.* *soo*-drah, the lowest of the four great castes among the Hindus; a member of this. (Hind.)
suds, *n.pl.* sudz, water in a frothy state with soap. **in the suds,** in turmoil or difficulty. (A.S. *sud,* a thing sodden.)
sue, *v.t.* sew, to seek justice or right by legal process; to prosecute; to petition: *v.i.* to seek for in law; to seek by request; to petition; to beg; to make suit. **sue out,** to petition for and take out. (O.Fr. *sevre.*)
suède, *n.* swade, soft unglazed leather, properly kid-skin. (Fr.)
suet, *n.* *sew*-et, the hard fat of an animal, particularly that about the loins and kidneys. (O.Fr. *suis.*)
suety, *a.* *sew*-e-te, consisting of or resembling suet.
suffer, *v.t.* *suf*-er, to feel or bear what is painful, disagreeable or distressing, either to the body or mind; to endure; to allow; to undergo; to be affected by: *v.i.* to feel or undergo pain of body or mind; to undergo punishment; to sustain loss or damage. (O.Fr. *soffrir.*)
sufferable, *a.* *suf*-er-ra-bl, that may be tolerated or permitted; allowable; that may be endured or borne.
sufferableness, *n.* tolerableness.
sufferably, *ad.* tolerably; so as to be endured.
sufferance, *n.* *suf*-er-rance, the bearing of pain; endurance; pain endured; implied consent, by not forbidding or hindering; toleration; permission; sanction; patience. **on sufferance,** tolerated, but not with any pleasure.
sufferer, *n.* *suf*-er-rer, one who endures or undergoes pain, either of body or mind; one who permits or allows.
suffering, *n.* *suf*-er-ring, the bearing of pain, inconvenience or loss; pain endured; distress, loss, or injury incurred.
sufferingly, *ad.* with suffering.
suffice, *v.i.* su-*fice,* to be enough or sufficient: *v.t.* to satisfy; to content. (Fr. *suffire.*)
sufficiency, *n.* su-*fish*-en-se, the state of being sufficient; qualification for any purpose; competence; adequate supply; adequate power.
sufficient, *a.* su-*fish*-ent, enough; equal to the end proposed; adequate to need; qualified competent. **sufficient reason,** the principle that nothing exists without a reason why it should be so rather than otherwise. (L. *sufficiens,* affording.
sufficiently, *ad.* in sufficient degree.
suffix, *n.* *suf*-iks, a letter or syllable added to the end of a word; an affix.
suffix, *v.t.* suf-*fiks,* to add a letter or syllable to a word. (L. *suffixus,* fixed beneath.)
suffixion, *n.* suf-*fik*-shon, act of suffixing; state of being suffixed.
suffocate, *v.t.* *suf*-o-kate, to choke or kill by stopping respiration; to stifle; to extinguish: *v.i.* to be suffocated. (L. *suffocatus,* choked.)
suffocatingly, *ad.* enough to suffocate.
suffocation, *n.* *suf*-o-*kay*-shon, the act of suffocating; state of being suffocated.
suffocative, *a.* *suf*-o-ka-tiv, tending to suffocate.
suffragan, *a.* *suf*-ra-gan, said of a bishop as assisting or in relation to, the archbishop or metropolitan of the province: *n.* a suffragan bishop. (Fr. *suffragant.*)
suffraganship, *n.* the position of a suffragan.
suffrage, *n.* *suf*-raj, a vote in deciding a question or in the choice for an office; right to vote for a representative in parliament; united voice of persons in public prayer; approval; consent (Fr.)
suffragette, *n.* *suf*-ra-*jet,* a woman who agitated for votes for women.
suffragism, *n.* *suf*-ra-jizm, advocacy of the extension of the suffrage, esp. to women.
suffragist, *n.* *suf*-ra-jist, a supporter of or believer in woman suffrage.
suffrutescent, *a.* *suf*-roo-*tes*-ent, moderately frutescent; woody at the base.
suffrutex, *n.* *suf*-roo-teks, an under-shrub.
suffruticose, *a.* su-*froo*-te-kohs, under-shrubby, or part shrubby [Bot.]. (L. *sub-,* and *frutex,* a shrub
suffumigation, *n.* su-*few*-me-*gay*-shon, fumigation the operation of applying fumes or vapours to the parts of the body [Med.]
suffuse, *v.t.* su-*fewz,* to overspread from within as with a fluid or a colour. (L. *suffusus,* poured.)
suffusion, *n.* su-*few*-zhon, the act of suffusing; th

state of being suffused; that which is suffused, esp. a blush. (Fr.)

ufi, *n.* *soo*-fe, a Mohammedan mystic and ascetic adhering to the philosophy of sufism. (Ar. *suf,* wool, this forming the garments of ascetics.)

ufic, *a.* *soo*-fik, pertaining to or in accordance with sufism.

ufism, *n.* *soo*-fizm, a system of philosophical mysticism among the Mohammedans by which knowledge of the Divine is sought through ecstasy and meditation.

sugar, *n.* *shoo*-gar, a sweet granular substance, obtained from the sugar-cane, and also from beet, maple, and other plants; any of various sweetish soluble carbohydrates, as glucose, dextrose, saccharose, etc. [Chem.]; flattery [Fig.]: *a.* made of sugar: *v.t.* to impregnate, season, cover, sprinkle, or mix with sugar, or as with sugar; to sweeten. **sugar of lead,** acetate of lead. (Fr. *sucre.*)

ugar-apple, *n.* the plant sweetsop.

ugar-basin, *n.* a basin for sugar at table.

ugar-beet, *n.* the plant *Beta vulgaris* from whose root sugar is obtained.

ugar-candy, *n.* sugar clarified and crystallized.

ugar-cane, *n.* the grass from whose stem sugar is obtained, *Saccharum officinarum.*

ugar-coat, *v.t.* to coat with sugar so as to make palatable or attractive; to disguise with a pleasing appearance.

ugar-daddy, *n.* an elderly man who makes pets of attractive young women [U.S.A. slang].

ugar-farmer, *n.* a sugar-beet cultivator.

ugariness, *n.* *shoo*-ga-re-ness, the state of being sugary; sweetness.

ugarless, *a.* *shoo*-gar-less, free from sugar.

ugar-loaf, *n.* a conical mass of refined sugar; a hat, hill, etc., of high conical shape.

ugar-maple, *n.* a species of maple, *Acer saccharum,* from whose sap sugar is made.

ugar-mite, *n.* any of several wingless insects infesting raw sugar.

ugar-pine, *n.* the coniferous tree *Pinus lambertiana* of California, etc.

ugar-planter, *n.* a cultivator of the sugar-cane.

ugar-plum, *n.* *shoo*-gar-plum, a sweetmeat, esp. boiled sugar in small balls.

ugar-tongs, *n.pl.* pincers for lifting lumps of sugar.

ugary, *a.* *shoo*-ga-re, sweet; sweetened with sugar; like sugar; fond of sugar; containing sugar.

uggest, *v.t.* su-*jest,* to offer or present to the mind; to hint; to indicate. (L. *suggestus.*)

uggester, *n.* su-*jes*-ter, one who suggests.

uggestibility, *n.* su-*jes*-te-*bil*-e-te, appropriateness for suggestion.

uggestible, *a.* su-*jes*-te-bl, suitable for suggestion.

suggestion, *n.* su-*jes*-tyon, act of suggesting; that which is suggested; a hint; first intimation or proposal; presentation of an idea to the mind; secret incitement. (Fr.)

uggestionism, *n.* su-*jes*-tyo-nizm, the treatment of nervous or other disease by suggestion.

uggestionize, *v.t.* su-*jes*-tyon-ize, to treat (a patient) by suggestion [Path.].

uggestive, *a.* su-*jes*-tiv, containing a suggestion; full of suggestion; suggesting more than is apparent; suggesting what is improper or indecent.

uggestively, *ad.* in a suggestive manner.

uggestiveness, *n.* quality of being suggestive.

uggillation, *n.* suj-e-*lay*-shon, ecchymosis, a bruise [Med.]. (L. *suggillare,* to revile, to assault.)

uicidal, *a.* soo-e-*sy*-dal, pertaking of the crime of suicide; of the nature of suicide.

uicidally, *ad.* in a suicidal manner.

uicide, *n.* *soo*-e-side, self-murder; the act of wilfully destroying one's own life; one guilty of self-murder; a felo-de-se. (L. *sui,* of oneself, *cædo,* kill.)

uilline, *a.* *sew*-e-line, belonging to the swine family; hog-like: *n.* a member of the swine family. (L. *sulilus,* a swine.)

uimate, *n.* *sew*-e-mate, in chess, a checkmate that the one player forces his opponent to give him. (L. *sui,* of oneself, and *mate.*)

uint, *n.* swint, the natural grease of wool. (Fr.)

uit, *n.* sewt, a set; a number of things used together; a set of outer garments consisting of coat, vest, and trousers for men, and coat and skirt for women; one of the four sets in a pack of cards; a petition; courtship; an action or process for the recovery of a right or claim; pursuit; prosecution: *v.t.* to fit; to become; to please; to content: *v.i.* to agree; to accord; to be convenient; to correspond. **follow suit,** *see* **follow. make suit,** to petition, to ask for humbly.

suitability, *n.* *sew*-ta-*bil*-e-te, suitableness.

suitable, *a.* *sew*-ta-bl, fitting; according with; agreeable to; becoming; adequate.

suitableness, *n.* the quality of being suitable; the state of being adapted.

suitably, *ad.* in a suitable manner.

suite, *n.* sweet, retinue; company; a set, as of furniture or apartments; a series; a musical composition in a series of themes. (Fr.)

suiting, *n.* *sew*-ting, cloth intended to be made into suits.

suitor, *n.* *sew*-tor, one who sues in law; a petitioner; an applicant; one who solicits a woman in marriage; a wooer.

sulcate, *a.* *sul*-kat, marked by parallel longitudinal channels; furrowed; grooved. (L. *sulcatus,* ploughed.)

sulk, *v.i.* sulk, to be sulky; to be silently sullen.

sulkily, *ad.* *sul*-ke-le, in a sulky manner.

sulkiness, *n.* *sul*-ke-ness, the state of being sulky.

sulks, *n.pl.* sulks, sulkiness; a sulky mood, as "to be in the sulks."

sulky, *a.* *sul*-ke, sullen; sour; morose. (A.S. *solcen,* slothful.)

sulky, *n.* *sul*-ke, a light two-wheeled carriage for a single person.

sullage, *n.* *sul*-laj, house refuse; sewage; silt deposited by water; scum on molten metal.

sullen, *a.* *sul*-len, gloomily angry and silent; cross; sour; in ill humour; obstinate; intractable; dark; dull. (O.Fr. *solain,* lonely.)

sullenly, *ad.* *sul*-len-le, in a sullen manner.

sullenness, *n.* *sul*-len-ness, the quality of being sullen; ill-nature with silence; silent moroseness.

sullens, *n.pl.* *sul*-lenz, a morose temper; sulks.

sully, *n.* *sul*-le, soil; tarnish; spot: *v.t.* to soil; to dirt; to darken; to stain; to tarnish: *v.i.* to be soiled or tarnished. (A.S. *sylian.*)

sulphanilamide, *n.* sulf-a-*nil*-a-mide, any of a number of therapeutic drugs effective against certain bacterial diseases caused by cocci.

sulphanilic, *a.* sulf-a-*nil*-ik, designating certain isomeric sulphonic acids derived from aniline.

sulphate, *n.* *sul*-fate, a salt of sulphuric acid. **sulphate of copper,** blue vitriol. **sulphate of iron,** green vitriol. **sulphate of magnesium,** Epsom salts. **sulphate of soda,** Glauber's salts. (L. *sulphur.*)

sulphate, *v.i.* *sul*-fate, to receive a deposit of insoluble white sulphate of lead causing diminution of efficiency (of accumulator plates) [Elect.].

sulphatic, *a.* sul-*fat*-ik, pertaining to, containing, or resembling a sulphate or sulphates.

sulphation, *n.* sul-*fay*-shon, the process, or the result, of sulphating.

sulphide, *n.* *sul*-fide, a compound of sulphur with an element or radical.

sulphite, *n.* *sul*-fite, a salt of sulphurous acid. **sulphite pulp,** wood pulp from which, after treatment with sulphur dioxide dissolved in calcium or magnesium sulphite, paper is manufactured.

sulpho-, *sul*-foh, a prefix to the name of a sulphur acid.

sulphocyanic, *a.* *sul*-foh-sy-*an*-ik, obtained from sulphur and cyanogen.

sulphocyanogen, *n.* *sul*-foh-sy-*an*-o-jen, a compound of sulphur and cyanogen.

sulphonal, *n.* *sul*-fo-nal, a white crystalline hypnotic and sedative drug prepared by condensing acetone with ethyl mercaptan in the presence of hydrochloric acid.

sulphonalism, *n.* *sul*-fo-na-lizm, the symptoms produced by sulphonal poisoning.

sulphonate, *n.* *sul*-fo-nat, a salt or ester of a sulphonic acid.

sulphonic, *a.* sul-*fon*-ik, designating any one of the acids resulting from the oxidation of the mercaptans [Chem.].

sulphosalt, *n.* *sul*-foh-*sawlt,* a salt containing sulphur in both the acid and the base.

sulphovinic, *a.* sul-foh-*vin*-ik, formed by the action of sulphuric acid upon alcohol.

sulphur, *n.* *sul*-fur, a non-metallic element of a yellow colour, brittle, insoluble in water, but fusible by heat [Chem.]; brimstone. **sulphur family,** the three elements sulphur, selenium, and tellurium [Chem.]. **flowers of sulphur,** sublimed sulphur, used as an insecticide, etc. (L.)
sulphurate, *v.t.* *sul*-few-rate, to combine with sulphur; to subject to the action of sulphur, esp. as in bleaching.
sulphuration, *n.* *sul*-few-*ray*-shon, the exposure of a substance, such as wool or cotton, to the action of sulphur for the purpose of discolouring or bleaching; the act of dressing, fumigating, or impregnating with sulphur.
sulphurator, *n.* sul-few-*ray*-tor, an appliance used in bleaching, fumigating, etc., with sulphur.
sulphureous, *a.* sul-*few*-re-us, consisting of or having the qualities of sulphur; impregnated with sulphur; sulphur-coloured [Bot. and Entom.].
sulphureousness, *n.* state of being sulphureous.
sulphuret, *n.* *sul*-few-ret, a sulphide (a term not now in use).
sulphuretted, *a.* *sul*-few-*ret*-ed, having sulphur in combination. **sulphuretted hydrogen,** the monosulphide of hydrogen, a colourless, inflammable, poisonous, and foul-smelling gas.
sulphuric, *a.* sul-*few*-rik, pertaining to, containing, or obtained from sulphur. **sulphuric acid,** oil of vitriol.
sulphuring, *n.* *sul*-fu-ring, sulphuration; treating plants with sulphur to destroy mildew, etc.
sulphurization, *n.* *sul*-few-ry-*zay*-shon, the action of sulphurizing.
sulphurize, *v.t.* *sul*-few-rize, to combine or impregnate with sulphur; to sulphurate.
sulphurous, *a.* *sul*-few-rus, like sulphur; containing sulphur; pertaining to sulphur and having one atom of oxygen less than a *sulphuric* compound; sulphureous; thundery, fiery, infernal [Fig.].
sulphur-weed, or **sulphur-wort,** *n.* the plant *Peucedanum officinale*, hog's fennel.
sulphury, *a.* *sul*-fu-re, partaking of or having the qualities of sulphur.
sultan, *n.* *sul*-tan, a Mohammedan sovereign, especially the sovereign of the former Turkish or Ottoman empire; the colour crimson lake; applied to various birds and flowers of brilliant plumage or colouring. (Ar., a ruler.)
sultana, *n.* sul-*tah*-na, the queen of a sultan; a West Indian marsh bird of the genus *Porphyrio*; a kind of stoneless raisin.
sultanate, *n.* *sul*-ta-nate, the office, power, jurisdiction, or territory of a Sultan.
sultaness, *n.* *sul*-ta-ness, the queen of a a sultan.
sultanic, *a.* sul-*tan*-ik, pertaining to a sultan.
sultanry, *n.* *sul*-tan-re, the dominions of a sultan.
sultanship, *n.* *sul*-tan-ship, the office or state of a sultan.
sultriness, *n.* *sul*-tre-ness, the state of being sultry.
sultry, *a.* *sul*-tre, very hot, burning, and oppressive; close and stagnant, as air or atmosphere. (A.S. *swelter*.)
sum, *n.* sum, the aggregate of two or more numbers, magnitudes, quantities, or particulars; arithmetical calculation; a quantity of money or currency; amount; summary; substance; height; completion: *v.t.* to add into one whole; to cast up. **sum up,** to bring to a total; to comprise in a few concluding words. (L. *summa*, amount, from *summus*, highest.)
sumac(h), *n.* *sew*-mak *or* *shoo*-mak, a plant or shrub of the genus *Rhus*, the powdered leaves, peduncles, and young branches of some species of which are used in tanning, dyeing, and medicine. (Ar. *summaq*.)
Sumerian, *a.* sew-*meer*-re-an, pertaining to Sumer, an ancient district of Lower Babylonia, or to its people or their language: *n.* the language of the ancient Sumerians.
sumless, *a.* *sum*-less, not to be computed; of which the amount cannot be ascertained.
summarily, *ad.* *sum*-a-re-le, in a summary manner; concisely; in a short way or method; in a quick manner.
summarist, *n.* *sum*-a-rist, one who summarizes.
summarization, *n.* *sum*-a-ry-*zay*-shon, the process or result of summarizing.
summarize, *v.t.* *sum*-a-rize, to state concisely; to make or be a summary of.
summary, *a.* *sum*-a-re, reduced into a narrow compass, or into few words; concise; compendious; done summarily: *n.* an abridged account; an abstract or compendium. (Fr. *sommaire*.)
summation, *n.* sum-*may*-shon, the act of forming a total amount; computation; an aggregate.
★**summer,** *n.* *sum*-mer, the warm season of the year comprehended in the northern hemisphere within the months of June, July, and August, beginning astronomically on Midsummer day: *a.* as in summer: *v.i.* to pass the summer or warm season. **Indian summer,** in North America, a short summer season towards the latter end of autumn. **St. Martin's summer,** a brief return of summer after winter has set in. **summer time,** the time fixed by statute for general purposes during certain summer months of the year, being one hour (or during **double summer time,** two hours) earlier than Greenwich mean time. (A.S. *sumor*.)
summer, *n.* *sum*-mer, a large stone, the first that is laid over columns and pilasters, beginning to make a cross vault; a large timber supported on two strong piers or posts, or a strong beam laid as a central floor-timber [Arch.]. (Fr. *sommier*, a pack-horse, a mattress.)
summer-colts, *n.* the undulating state of the air near the surface of the ground when heated.
summer-duck, *n.* the N. American wood-duck *Aix sponsa*.
summer-fallow, *n.* a fallow made during the warm months to pulverize the soil and kill weeds: *v.t.* to plough and work repeatedly in summer, to prepare for wheat or other crop.
summer-house, *n.* a light garden building for use in summer; a house for summer residence.
summering, *n.* *sum*-mer-ing, the bedding of stone used in the construction of a vault [Arch.].
summersault, *n.* *sum*-mer-sawlt, a somersault.
summer-snipe, *n.* *sum*-mer-snipe, the dunlin, the sandpiper, or the green sandpiper.
summer-teal, *n.* *sum*-mer-teel, the garganey.
summertime, *n.* *sum*-er-time, the period of summer. **summer time,** *see* **summer.**
summery, *a.* *sum*-er-re, like or appropriate to summer.
summing-up, *n.* *sum*-ming-*up*, the summary of the evidence made by the judge to the jury before they retire to consider their verdict.
summit, *n.* *sum*-mit, the top; the highest point; the highest degree or utmost elevation. (Fr. *sommet*.)
summitless, *a.* *sum*-mit-less, having no summit.
summit-level, *n.* *sum*-mit-*lev*-el, the highest level reached by a pass, canal, railway, etc.
summon, *v.t.* *sum*-mon, to call or cite by authority to appear at a place specified, or to attend in person to some public duty; to give notice to a person to appear in court; to call; to call up; to excite into action or exertion. (O.Fr. *somoner*.)
summoner, *n.* *sum*-mon-er, one who summons or cites by authority; one who takes out a summons.
summons, *n.* *sum*-monz (*pl.* **summonses**), a call by authority or the command of a superior; a citation to appear in court; a writ giving notice to a party to appear in court on a day mentioned therein [Law]: *v.t.* to summon; to take out a summons against [Coll.]. (O.Fr. *somons*.)
sump, *n.* sump, a round pit of stone, lined with clay for receiving the metal on its first fusion; a pond of water reserved for salt-works; a pit sunk below the general level of a mine; a vessel or compartment for collecting used oil or other liquid [Eng.]. (Dut. *somp*, swamp.)
sumph, *n.* sumf, a dunce; a soft fellow: *v.i.* to be sulky [Scots.].
sumpit, *n.* *sum*-pit, the dart, frequently poisoned, used in the sumpitan.
sumpitan, *n.* *sum*-pe-tan, the blowpipe used by the natives of Borneo, etc., to discharge darts or sumpits.
sumpsimus, *n.* *sump*-se-mus, a correct expression put in place of one more usual but incorrect. (L., the correlative of *mumpsimus*.)
sumpter, *n.* *sump*-ter, a baggage-horse or, formerly, its driver. (Fr. *sommier*, a pack-horse.)
sumption, *n.* *sump*-shon, the major premiss of a syllogism [Logic]. (*assumption*.)
sumptuary, *a.* *sump*-tew-a-re, relating to or limiting expense. **sumptuary laws,** laws such as limi

private expense in apparel or luxury. (L. *sumptuarius*, from *sumptus*, cost.)
sumptuosity, *n.* *sump*-tew-*os*-e-te, expensiveness.
sumptuous, *a.* *sump*-tew-us, costly; splendid; ostentatious; magnificent. (Fr. *somptueux.*)
sumptuously, *ad.* in a sumptuous manner.
sumptuousness, *n.* *sump*-tew-us-ness, the quality of being sumptuous; costliness; expensiveness.
***sun,** *n.* sun, the centre of the solar system; the light or warmth of the sun; any similar centre of a system of planets; a sunny place; anything eminently splendid or luminous; that which is a centre of light or honour: *v.t.* to expose to the sun's rays; to warm or dry in the light of the sun: *v.i.* to sun oneself. **touch of the sun,** a slight sunstroke. (*A.S. sunne.*)
sun-bath, *n.* exposure of the bare skin in sunshine, esp. for therapeutic purposes.
sunbeam, *n.* *sun*-beem, a ray of the sun; one who spreads happiness [Fig.].
sunbeat, *a.* *sun*-beet, struck by the sun's rays.
sunbird, *n.* *sun*-berd, a small Asiatic and African tropical bird of the family Nectariniidæ, resembling the humming-bird.
sun-bittern, *n.* the aberrant crane-like bird of South America, *Europyga helias.*
sun-blind, *n.* a blind to intercept the rays of the sun.
sunbonnet, *n.* a bonnet protecting the face from the sun.
sunbow, *n.* *sun*-boh, a bow like a rainbow formed by sunlight on spray.
sunburn, *n.* *sun*-burn, browning or inflammation of the skin by the sun.
sunburnt, *a.* *sun*-burnt, discoloured by the heat of the sun; scorched by the sun's rays.
sunburst, *n.* *sun*-burst, a sudden burst of sunshine; a jewel, firework, or other representation resembling the sun with its rays; the Japanese ensign.
sundae, *n.* *sun*-day, an ice-cream containing, or served with, fruit.
Sunday, *n.* *sun*-day *or sun*-de, the first day of the week, anciently dedicated to the sun. **Sunday best,** clothes kept for wear on Sunday; hence, specially good [Coll.]. (A.S. *sunnan dæg.*)
Sundayfied, *a.* *sun*-de-fide, suitable to Sunday; given a Sunday-like character.
Sunday-school, *n.* a school held on Sundays for religious instruction of the young.
sunder, *v.t.* *sun*-der, to part; to separate; to divide: *v.i.* to be separated. **in sunder,** apart; divided; in two. (A.S. *sundrian.*)
sunderance, *n.* *sun*-der-rance, severance; act of separating.
sundew, *n.* *sun*-dew, a hairy, insectivorous plant of the genus *Drosera.*
sundial, *n.* *sun*-dy-al, an instrument to show the time of day, by means of the shadow of a style or gnomon cast by the sun on a dial-plate.
sundog, *n.* *sun*-dog, a luminous spot or halo occasionally seen a few degrees from the sun; a parhelion.
sundown, *n.* *sun*-doun, sunset.
sundowner, *n.* *sun*-doun-er, a tramp who makes it a practice to arrive at a station in time for a night's lodging [Austral.]; a drink at sunset or close of day [Slang].
sundries, *n.pl.* *sun*-driz, miscellaneous articles.
sundry, *a.* *sun*-dre, more than one or two; several; various. **all and sundry,** the whole lot, everyone. (A.S. *sundrig.*)
sunfish, *n.* a large fish of various species with a more or less spherical body; the opah; the basking shark.
sunflower, *n.* a plant of the genus *Helianthus,* named from the form and colour of its flower.
sung, sung, *p.* and *pp.* of *sing.*
sun-glasses, *n.pl.* tinted spectacles worn as protection against the glare of the bright sun.
sun-god, *n.* the sun as a deity.
sun-helmet, *n.* a broad-brimmed head-covering for wear by Europeans in the tropics; a topi.
sunk, sunk, **sunken,** *sun*-ken, *pp.* of *sink.*
sunless, *a.* destitute of the sun or its rays; shaded.
sunlessness, *n.* the state of being sunless.
sunlight, *n.* *sun*-lite, the light of the sun.
sunlit, *a.* *sun*-lit, lighted by the sun.
sunn, *n.* sun, the Indian plant *Crotalaria juncea* yielding a valuable fibre used as hemp; the fibre of this.
Sunna, *n.* *soon*-nah, a body of Mohammedan traditions professedly handed down from Mohammed and his immediate disciples, rejected by the Shiites but of great importance in the history of Mohammedanism. (Ar. *sunna,* tradition.)
sunnily, *ad.* *sun*-ne-le, in a sunny manner; brightly; cheerfully.
Sunnite, *n.pl.* *soon*-nite, a member of a sect of orthodox Mohammedans who receive the Sunna as of equal importance with the Koran.
sunny, *a.* *sun*-ne, like the sun; bright; proceeding from the sun; exposed to the rays of the sun; warmed by the direct rays of the sun; coloured with the sun.
Sunnyasi, *n.* soon-*yah*-se, a Brahman devotee or hermit, esp. one in the fourth stage of existence [Anglo-Ind.].
sunproof, *a.* impervious to the rays of the sun.
sunrise, *n.* *sun*-rize, the first appearance of the sun above the horizon; the moment when the centre of the sun's disk cuts the horizon; the east.
sunrising, *n.* *sun*-rize-ing, sunrise.
sun-rose, *n.* any species of *Helianthemum.*
sunset, *n.* *sun*-set, the descent of the sun below the horizon; the moment when the centre of the sun's disk cuts the horizon; the west.
sunsetting, *n.* *sun*-set-ting, sunset.
sunshade, *n.* a parasol; a small umbrella.
sunshine, *n.* *sun*-shine, the light of the sun, or the place where it shines; a place warm and illuminated; warmth; illumination. **sunshine roof,** a motor-car roof that can be opened by sliding.
sunshiny, *a.* *sun*-shy-ne, bright with the rays of the sun; bright like the sun.
sunspot, *n.* *sun*-spot, a dark patch of large and varying size occurring periodically on the face of the sun; a freckle on the skin.
sun-spurge, *n.* the plant *Euphorbia helioscopia.*
sunstone, *n.* *sun*-stohn, a brilliant variety of aventurine felspar.
sunstroke, *n.* *sun*-stroke, a cerebral affection (sometimes fatal) due to exposure to the sun in excessively hot weather; insolation [Med.].
sun-up, *n.* *sun*-up, sunrise [U.S.A.].
sunward, *a.* *sun*-ward, facing the sun: *ad.* toward the sun.
sunwise, *a.* and *ad.* *sun*-wize, in the same direction as clock-hands go; clockwise.
Suomic, *a.* soo-*oh*-mik, Finnish: *n.* the Finnish language. (*Suomi,* native name of Finland.)
sup, *n.* sup, a small mouthful, as of a liquid; a little taken with the lips; a sip: *v.t.* to take into the mouth by successive sips, as a liquid; to sip: *v.i.* to eat the evening meal. (A.S. *supan.*)
supawn, *n.* sew-*pawn,* a mush of boiled Indian-corn meal [U.S.A.]. (Algonq.)
super-, a Latin prefix signifying over, above, beyond, exceeding, transcending, of superior kind, etc.
super, *n.* *sew*-per, a supernumerary (esp. an actor); a superintendent (of police).
superable, *a.* *sew*-per-ra-bl, that may be overcome or conquered.
superably, *ad.* *sew*-per-ra-ble, so as may be overcome.
superabound, *v.i.* *sew*-per-a-*bound,* to be very abundant; to be more than enough.
superabundance, *n.* *sew*-per-a-*bun*-dance, more than enough; excessive abundance.
superabundant, *a.* *sew*-per-a-*bun*-dant, abounding to excess; being more than is sufficient.
superabundantly, *ad.* more than sufficiently.
superacidulated, *a.* acidulated to excess.
superadd, *v.t.* *sew*-per-*ad,* to add over and above.
superaddition, *n.* *sew*-per-ra-*dish*-on, act of superadding; that which is superadded.
superalimentation, *n.* *sew*-per-*al*-e-men-*tay*-shon, over-feeding [Med.].
superaltar, *n,* *sew*-per-*awl*-tar, a portable altar placed on the top of a table or other support.
superangelic, *a.* *sew*-per-an-*jel*-ik, more than angelic; superior in nature or rank to the angels.
superannuate, *v.t.* *sew*-per-*an*-new-ate, to impair or disqualify by old age or through failure to reach some standard by a specified age; to pension off on account of old age. (Late L. *superannatus.*)
superannuation, *n.* *sew*-per-*an*-new-*ay*-shon, state of being superannuated; retiring allowance in consequence.
superb, *a.* sew-*perb,* characterized by grandeur, magnificence, pomp, splendour, or richness. (Fr. *superbe,* from L. *superbus,* haughty.)

superbly, *ad.* sew-*perb*-le, in a superb manner.
superbness, *n.* the quality of being superb.
supercalendered, *a.* sew-per-*kal*-en-derd, (of paper) given a highly polished surface by means of special calenders.
supercargo, *n.* *sew*-per-kar-goh, an officer in a merchant ship whose business was to manage the sales and superintend the commercial concerns of the voyage. (L. *super-*, and *cargo.*)
supercelestial, *a.* *sew*-per-se-*les*-tyal, situated above the firmament.
supercharge, *v.t.* sew-per-*charj*, to charge excessively or in addition; (of internal combustion engines) to feed the intake with a charge higher than that of the surrounding atmosphere; to place one bearing on another [Her.]: *n.* an additional or excessive charge; a charge as supplied to a supercharged engine.
supercharger, *n.* *sew*-per-*charj*-er, a self-acting pump in an internal combustion engine by means of which the cylinder is completely filled when running at high speed.
superciliary, *a.* *sew*-per-*sil*-e-a-re, pertaining to the region of the eyebrow [Anat.]. (L. *supercilium*, eyebrow.)
supercilious, *a.* *sew*-per-*sile*-us, haughty; overbearing; arrogant; contemptuously nonchalant.
superciliously, *ad.* in a supercilious manner.
superciliousness, *n.* quality of being supercilious.
supercilium, *n.* *sew*-per-*sil*-e-um, the eyebrow [Anat.]. (L.)
superclass, *n.* *sew*-per-klahs, a subdivision of a phylum containing two or more classes [Bot. and Zool.].
supercool, *v.t.* *sew*-per-*kool*, to cool below freezing-point without solidifying.
supercretaceous, *a.* *sew*-per-kre-*tay*-shus, lying above the chalk.
superdominant, *n.* *sew*-per-*dom*-e-nant, the sixth note of the key, in the ascending scale; the submediant [Mus.].
supereminence, *n.* eminence superior to what is common; distinguished eminence.
supereminent, *a.* *sew*-per-*em*-e-nent, eminent in a superior degree; surpassingly excellent.
supereminently, *ad.* in a supereminent degree.
supererogate, *v.i.* *sew*-per-*e*-ro-gate, to do more than duty requires.
supererogation, *n.* *sew*-per-*e*-ro-*gay*-shon, performance of more than duty requires. **works of supererogation,** good deeds performed over and above what is required for personal salvation. (L. *supererogatus*, paid out.)
supererogatory, *a.* *sew*-per-e-*rog*-a-to-re, performed to an extent not enjoined, or not required by duty.
superessential, *a.* *sew*-per-e-*sen*-shal, essential above others or above the constitution of a thing.
superexalt, *v.t.* *sew*-per-eg-*zawlt*, to exalt to a superior degree.
superexaltation, *n.* *sew*-per-eg-zawl-*tay*-shon, elevation above the common degree.
superexcellence, *n.* *sew*-per-*ek*-se-lence, superior excellence.
superexcellent, *a.* *sew*-per-*ek*-se-lent, excellent in an uncommon degree.
superfamily, *n.* *sew*-per-*fam*-e-le, a group or sub-order containing more than one family [Zool. and Bot.].
superfatted, *a.* *sew*-per-*fat*-ed, containing a larger proportion of fat than usual.
superfetation, *n.* *sew*-per-fee-*tay*-shon, the conception of a second fœtus before the delivery of one previously conceived.
superficial, *a.* *sew*-per-*fish*-al, being on or pertaining to the surface; not penetrating the substance of a thing; shallow; not deep or profound; reaching and comprehending only what is obvious and apparent. (Fr. *superficiel.*)
superficiality, *n.* *sew*-per-*fish*-e-*al*-e-te, superficialness; lack of thoroughness.
superficially, *ad.* in a superficial manner.
superficialness, *n.* the quality of being superficial; shallowness; slight knowledge.
superficies, *n.* *sew*-per-*fish*-e-eez, the surface; the exterior part of a thing. (L., the face.)
superfine, *a.* *sew*-per-fine, surpassing others in fineness; over fine; very fine.
superfineness, *n.* *sew*-per-*fine*-ness, the quality of being superfine.
superfluity, *n.* *sew*-per-*floo*-e-te, a greater quantity than is wanted; superabundance; somethin beyond what is wanted; what is not a necessary (Fr. *superfluité.*)
superfluous, *a.* sew-*per*-floo-us, more than is wanted more than enough; unnecessary; redundant. (L *superfluus*, overflowing.)
superfluously, *ad.* in a superfluous degree.
superfluousness, *n.* quality of being superfluous.
superflux, *n.* *sew*-per-fluks, superabundance; ar excessive flow.
superfœtation, *n.* *sew*-per-fee-*tay*-shon, superfetation
superfrontal, *n.* *sew*-per-*frun*-tal, an altar cove that hangs down all round: *a.* pertaining to th upper part of the frontal lobe of the brain.
superheat, *v.t.* *sew*-per-heet, to heat to a very hig temperature; to heat steam above the boiling point of water.
superheater, *n.* *sew*-per-*heet*-er, an apparatus fo superheating steam.
superheterodyne, *n.* *sew*-per-*het*-e-ro-dine, a powerfu and highly selective form of receiver [Wire.].
superhuman, *a.* *sew*-per-*hew*-man, above or beyon what is human; divine.
superhumeral, *n.* *sew*-per-*hew*-mer-ral, a vestment worn over the shoulders. (L. *super-*, and *humerus* shoulder.)
superimpose, *v.t.* *sew*-per-im-*poze*, to lay or impos on something else.
superimposition, *n.* *sew*-per-im-po-*zish*-on, act o superimposing, or state of being superimposed.
superincumbent, *a.* *sew*-per-in-*kum*-bent, lying o resting on something else.
superinduce, *v.t.* *sew*-per-in-*dewce*, to bring in o upon as an addition to something.
superinduction, *n.* *sew*-per-in-*duk*-shon, the act o superinducing; that which is superinduced.
superinfection, *n.* *sew*-per-in-*fek*-shon, re-infectio with the same type of bacteria, etc. [Med.].
superinstitution, *n.* *sew*-per-in-ste-*tew*-shon, in stitution to a benefice already held by anothe [Eccles.].
superintend, *v.t.* *sew*-per-in-*tend*, to have or exercis the charge and oversight of; to oversee with th power of direction; to supervise.
superintendence, *n.* *sew*-per-in-*ten*-dence, act o superintending; oversight; management.
superintendency, *n.* *sew*-per-in-*ten*-den-se, the offic or authority of a superintendent; an administrativ division in certain states.
superintendent, *n.* *sew*-per-in-*ten*-dent, one who ha the oversight and charge of something, with th power of direction; an overseer: *a.* superintending
superior, *a.* sew-*peer*-re-or, higher or above in place rank, dignity, or excellence; surpassing others being beyond the power or influence of: *n.* on superior to others; the chief of a monastery convent, abbey, etc. **superior person,** a pedant prig, or snob [Coll.]. (L.)
superioress, *n.* sew-*peer*-re-o-ress, a female superior esp. of a nunnery or convent.
superiority, *n.* *sew*-peer-re-*o*-re-te, the state o quality of being superior; pre-eminence. **superiority complex,** exaggerated belief in one's ow superiority; unwarranted assumption of superiority (Fr.)
superjacent, *a.* *sew*-per-*jay*-sent, lying upon.
superlative, *a.* sew-*per*-la-tiv, highest in degree most eminent; supreme; expressing the highes degree [Gram.]: *n.* the superlative degree [Gram.] (Fr. *superlatif.*)
superlatively, *ad.* to a superlative degree.
superlativeness, *n.* the state of being superlative (Fr. *superlatif.*)
superlunar, *a.* *sew*-per-*lew*-nar, being above the moon not sublunary. (L. *super-*, and *lunar.*)
superlunary, *a.* *sew*-per-*lew*-na-re, superlunar.
superman, *n.* *sew*-per-man, a man of a type abov that of ordinary humanity.
supermarine, *n.* *sew*-per-ma-reen, a seaplane.
supermundane, *a.* *sew*-per-*mun*-dane, above th things of this world; supernal.
supernacular, *a.* *sew*-per-*nak*-yew-lar, first-rate most excellent.
supernaculum, *n.* *sew*-per-*nak*-yew-lum, good liquo (so called from the ancient custom of pouring th last drop upon the thumb nail to show that th glass is drained). (L. *super*, and Ger. *Nagel*, nail.)
supernal, *a.* sew-*per*-nal, being in a higher place

region; relating to things above; celestial. (O.Fr. *supernel.*)
supernatant, *a.* *sew*-per-*nay*-tant, floating on the surface: *n.* the liquid lying above a precipitate. (L. *super-*, and *natans*, swimming.)
supernatation, *n.* *sew*-per-na-*tay*-shon, the act of floating on the surface of a fluid.
supernational, *a.* *sew*-per-*nash*-on-al, transcending nationality; cosmopolitan.
supernatural, *a.* *sew*-per-*nat*-yew-ral, being beyond or exceeding the known power of laws of nature; effected by or ascribed to agents, agencies, or in ways which transcend the ordinary; miraculous.
supernaturalism, *n.* *sew*-per-*nat*-yew-ra-lizm, belief in the supernatural; the doctrine of a divine agency working miracles in connection with revelation; that mode of thought which refers all phenomena to some invisible spiritual power alleged to pervade the universe.
supernaturalist, *n.* *sew*-per-*nat*-yew-ra-list, one who believes in supernaturalism.
supernaturalistic, *a.* *sew*-per-*nat*-yew-ra-*lis*-tik, pertaining or agreeable to supernaturalism.
supernaturalize, *v.t.* *sew*-per-*nat*-yew-ra-lize, to raise to the supernatural; to treat as supernatural.
supernaturally, *ad.* in a supernatural manner.
supernaturalness, *n.* the quality of being supernatural.
supernormal, *a.* *sew*-per-*nor*-mal, exceeding natural powers; beyond the normal; psychical.
supernumerary, *a.* *sew*-per-*new*-mer-ra-re, exceeding the number allowed; exceeding a necessary or usual number: *n.* a supernumerary person or thing; a super [Stage].
superorder, *n.* *sew*-per-*or*-der, a subdivision of a class ranking above a subclass [Bot. etc.].
superordinary, *a.* *sew*-per-*or*-de-na-re, above the ordinary.
superorganic, *a.* *sew*-per-or-*gan*-ik, superior to the organic; independent of the physical organism; spiritual; psychical.
superoxide, *n.* *sew*-per-*oks*-ide, peroxide.
superparasite, *n.* *sew*-per-*pa*-ra-site a parasite parasitic upon or in another parasite.
superphosphate, *n.* *sew*-per-*fos*-fate, a phosphate containing the greatest quantity of phosphoric acid that can combine with the base; an acid phosphate.
superphysical, *a.* *sew*-per-*fiz*-e-kal, incapable of explanation on the physical plane; psychical.
superpose, *v.t.* *sew*-per-*poze*, to place one above another; to lay upon, as one kind of rock on another. (L. *super*, and *pono*, place.)
superposition, *n.* *sew*-per-po-*zish*-on, a placing or lying above; that which is superposed.
superreflection, *n.* *sew*-per-re-*flek*-shon, the reflection of an image reflected.
super-royal, *a.* larger than royal, denoting a size of printing paper measuring 27½ in. by 20½ in.
supersalt, *n.* *sew*-per-sawlt, a salt with more of the acid than of the base.
supersaturate, *v.t.* *sew*-per-*sat*-yew-rate, to add to in excess of saturation.
supersaturation, *n.* the operation of supersaturating; the state of being supersaturated.
superscribe, *v.t.* *sew*-per-*skribe*, to engrave or write on the top, outside, or surface; to write a name or address on the cover of.
superscript, *a.* *sew*-per-skript, written above: *n.* an index written above the line, as in x^2 [Math.].
superscription, *n.* *sew*-per-*skrip*-shon, the act of superscribing; that which is written, engraved, or impressed on anything.
supersede, *v.t.* *sew*-per-*seed*, to take the place of; to displace; to make unnecessary or void by superior power or by coming in the place of; to suspend. (Fr. *superséder.*)
supersedeas, *n.* *sew*-per-*see*-de-as, a writ to suspend the power of an officer, or to stay law proceedings [Law]. (L. *suspend.*)
supersedure, *n.* *sew*-per-*see*-dewr, the act of superseding.
supersensible, *a.* *sew*-per-*sen*-se-bl, beyond the reach of the senses; psychical.
supersensitive, *a.* *sew*-per-*sen*-se-tive, excessively sensitive.
supersensitiveness, *n.* excessive sensitiveness.
supersensual, *a.* *sew*-per-*sen*-sew-al, supersensible; characterized by excessive sensuality.
supersensuous, *a.* *sew*-per-*sen*-sew-us, supersensual.
supersession, *n.* *sew*-per-*sesh*-on, supersedure; state of being superseded.
supersolid, *n.* sew-per-*sol*-id, a solid of more than three dimensions.
supersonant, *n.* sew-per-*soh*-nant, a vibration of too high a frequency to be audible.
supersonic, *a.* *sew*-per-*son*-ik, pertaining to velocities greater than that of sound (*cp.* **mach**) [Av.]; ultrasonic [Wire.].
supersound, *n.* *sew*-per-sound, the product of sound-wave vibrations of such high frequency as to be inaudible.
superstition, *n.* *sew*-per-*stish*-on, a false, misdirected belief based on ignorance; a religion, system, or practice founded on such; credulity manifesting itself in faith in charms, fear of omens, etc. (Fr.)
superstitious, *a.* *sew*-per-*stish*-us, addicted to, proceeding from, or manifesting superstition.
superstitiously, *ad.* in a superstitious manner.
superstitiousness, *n.* the quality of being superstitious.
superstratum, *n.* *sew*-per-*stray*-tum, a stratum or layer above another.
superstructive, *a.* *sew*-per-*struk*-tiv, superstructural.
superstructural, *a.* *sew*-per-*struk*-tew-ral, pertaining to or constituting a superstructure.
superstructure, *n.* *sew*-per-*struk*-tewr, any structure or edifice built on something else, particularly, a building raised on a foundation; anything erected on a foundation or basis. (L. *superstructus*, built.)
supersubstantial, *a.* *sew*-per-sub-*stan*-shal, being more than substance; transcending the material; spiritual.
supersubtle, *a.* *sew*-per-*sut*-tl, over-subtle.
supertax, *n.* *sew*-per-taks, an additional tax payable upon incomes exceeding a certain limit; a sur-tax.
supertemporal, *a.* sew-per-*tem*-po-ral, situated above the temples [Anat.]; beyond the limit of time, eternal.
superterrestrial, *a.* *sew*-per-ter-*res*-tre-al, being above the earth or above what appertains to it.
supertonic, *n.* *sew*-per-*ton*-ik, the note next above the tonic or key-note [Mus.].
supervene, *v.i.* sew-per-*veen*, to come upon as something extraneous; to occur as a change from something else; to follow closely. (L. *supervenio*, occur.)
supervenient, *a.* sew-per-*vee*-ne-ent, supervening; coming upon as something additional or extraneous.
supervention, *n.* sew-per-*ven*-shon, the act of supervening; subsequent occurrence.
supervisal, *n.* sew-per-*vy*-zal, supervision.
supervise, *v.t.* *sew*-per-*vize*, to oversee; to inspect; to manage. (L. *super-*, and *viso*, look at.)
supervision, *n.* *sew*-per-*vizh*-on, act of supervising; superintendence; oversight.
supervisor, *n.* *sew*-per-*vy*-zor, an overseer; an inspector.
supervisory, *a.* *sew*-per-*vy*-zo-re, pertaining to or having supervision.
supervolute, *a.* sew-per-vo-*lewt*, plaited and rolled in the bud [Bot.]. (L.)
supinate, *v.t.* and *i.* *sew*-pe-nate, to turn the palm of the hand upwards; to turn the leg outwards. (L. *supinare*, to lie on the back.)
supination, *n.* sew-pe-*nay*-shon, state of being laid with the face upwards; the act of turning the palm of the hand upwards.
supinator, *n.* *sew*-pe-nay-tor, a muscle that supinates, or turns the palm of the hand upward [Anat.].
supine, *a.* *sew*-pine, lying on the back or with the face upward; leaning backward; sloping; negligent; heedless; indolent; thoughtless: *n.* a Latin verbal noun formed by affixing *-um* or *-u* to the *pp.* stem of the verb. (L. *supinus*, bent backward).
supinely, *ad.* in a supine manner.
supineness, *n.* sew-*pine*-ness, the quality of being supine; indolence; drowsiness; heedlessness.
suppedaneum, *n.* *sup*-e-*day*-ne-um, the foot-rest on a crucifix. (L.)
supper, *n.* *sup*-er, the last meal of the day. (O.Fr. *soper.*)
supperless, *a.* *sup*-er-less, being without supper; wanting supper.
supplant, *v.t.* su-*plahnt*, to displace, esp. by intrigue: to displace and take the place of; to undermine. (Fr. *supplanter.*)
supplantation, *n.* *sup*-lahn-*tay*-shon, act of supplanting; usurpation.
supplanter, *n.* su-*plahn*-ter, one who supplants.

supple, *a.* *sup*-pl, pliant; easily bent; yielding; bending to the humour of others; obsequious: *v.t.* to make soft and pliant; to render compliant: *v.i.* to become soft and pliant. (Fr. *souple.*)

supplejack, *n.* *sup*-pl-jak, a tropical American climbing plant with tough and pliant stem, esp. a species of *Paullinia*; a walking-stick made of this.

supplely, *ad.* *sup*-pl-le, in a supple manner, flexibly.

supplement, *n.* *sup*-le-ment, an addition to anything, esp. one making it more perfect or complete; an appendix; the quantity by which an angle falls short of 180° or two right angles: *v.t.* to add to; to complete by filling up. (Fr.)

supplemental, *a.* *sup*-le-*men*-tal, supplementary.

supplementary, *a.* *sup*-le-*men*-ta-re, additional; added to supply what is wanted.

supplementation, *n.* sup-le-men-*tay*-shon, an addition; the act of supplementing.

suppleness, *n.* *sup*-pl-ness, quality of being supple; pliancy; a being easily bent; readiness of compliance.

suppletory, *a.* *sup*-le-to-re, supplying deficiencies.

suppliance, *n.* *sup*-le-ance, supplication.

suppliant, *a.* *sup*-le-ant, asking earnestly and submissively; expressive of humble supplication; entreating: *n.* a humble petitioner; one who entreats submissively. (Fr.)

suppliantly, *ad.* in a suppliant manner.

supplicant, *a.* *sup*-le-kant, entreating; asking submissively: *n.* one who entreats; a petitioner.

supplicate, *v.t.* *sup*-le-kate, to seek by prayer; to entreat for; to address in prayer: *v.i.* to petition with earnestness and submission; to implore. (L. *supplicatus*, entreated.)

supplicatingly, *ad.* *sup*-le-*kay*-ting-le, by way of supplication.

supplication, *n.* *sup*-le-*kay*-shon, humble and earnest prayer; entreaty; petition; in ancient Rome, a solemn and public thanksgiving or day of prayer.

supplicatory, *a.* *sup*-le-ka-to-re, containing supplication; humble; submissive.

supplier, *n.* su-*ply*-er, one who supplies.

supply, *n.* su-*ply*, the act of supplying; sufficiency of things for use or want; the necessary stores and provisions: *pl.* moneys granted by the British Parliament for public expenditure: *v.t.* to furnish what is wanted; to serve instead of; to bring or furnish; to make up any deficiency; to fill vacant room or a vacancy. **supply and demand,** *see* **demand.** (Fr. *suppléer.*)

supply, *ad.* *sup*-pl-le, supplely.

★**support,** *n.* su-*port*, the act of upholding or sustaining; that which upholds; that which maintains life; maintenance; subsistence; assistance: *pl.* a body of troops held in reserve as reinforcements [Mil.]: *v.t.* to bear or hold up; to uphold; to sustain; to nourish; to bear; to endure; to substantiate; to vindicate; to maintain. (Fr. *supporter.*)

supportable, *a.* su-*por*-ta-bl, that may be upheld; that may be borne or endured; tolerable; that can be maintained.

supportableness, *n.* the state of being supportable or tolerable.

supportably, *ad.* in a supportable manner.

supportance, *n.* su-*por*-tance, assistance; the act of supporting; sustenance.

supporter, *n.* su-*por*-ter, one who or that which supports or maintains; a sustainer; a maintainer; a defender; a vindicator; an adherent; either of the figures placed one on each side of a shield of arms [Her.].

supportless, *a.* su-*port*-less, having no support.

supposable, *a.* su-*poh*-za-bl, that may be supposed or imagined to exist.

supposal, *n.* su-*poh*-zal, supposition.

suppose, *n.* su-*poze*, a supposition: *v.t.* to assume as real or true, though not known to be so; to receive as true; to think; to imagine; to require to exist or be true. (Fr. *supposer.*)

supposedly, *ad.* su-*poh*-zed-le, by supposition; as is supposed.

supposer, *n.* su-*poh*-zer, one who supposes.

supposition, *n.* sup-o-*zish*-on, act of supposing; that which is supposed; hypothesis; imagination; conjecture. (Fr.)

suppositional, *a.* sup-o-*zish*-on-al, grounded on supposition or hypothesis; hypothetical.

supposititious, *a.* su-*poz*-e-*tish*-us, put by trick in substitution for something else; not genuine; spurious; imaginary. (L. *suppositicius.*)

supposititiously, *ad.* in a supposititious manner.

supposititiousness, *n.* the quality of being supposititious.

suppositive, *a.* su-*poz*-e-tiv, supposed; implying supposition: *n.* a word implying or denoting supposition.

suppositively, *ad.* with, by, or upon supposition.

suppository, *n.* su-*poz*-e-to-re, a medicament for introduction into the rectum or other body cavity.

suppress, *v.t.* su-*press*, to overpower and crush; to keep down; to retain without disclosure; to retain without making public; to hinder from circulation; to restrain; to stop. (L. *suppressus*, pressed.)

suppresser, *n.* su-*pres*-er, one who suppresses.

suppressible, *a.* su-*pres*-e-bl, that can be suppressed.

suppression, *n.* su-*presh*-on, act of suppressing; concealment; the retaining of anything from publication; stoppage or morbid retention of discharges [Med.]. (Fr.)

suppressive, *a.* su-*pres*-iv, suppressing, or tending to suppress; subduing; concealing.

suppurant, *a.* and *n.* *sup*-ew-rant, suppurative.

suppurate, *v.i.* *sup*-ew-rate, to generate pus; to fester. (L. *suppuratus.*)

suppuration, *n.* *sup*-ew-*ray*-shon, the production of pus in inflamed tissues.

suppurative, *a.* *sup*-ew-ra-tiv, tending to suppurate; promoting suppuration: *n.* a suppurative medicine.

supra-, *sew*-pra, a Latin prefix signifying above, over or beyond.

supraciliary, *a.* *sew*-pra-*sil*-e-a-re, situated above the eyebrow. (L. *supra-*, and *cilium*, the eyelid.)

supraclavicular, *a.* *sew*-pra-kla-*vik*-yew-lar, above the collar-bone.

supracostal, *a.* *sew*-pra-*kos*-tal, on or above the ribs.

supracretaceous, *a.* *sew*-pra-kre-*tay*-shus, lying above the chalk (of rocks) [Geol.].

Supralapsarian, *n.* *sew*-pra-lap-*sare*-re-an, a member of a group of Calvinists holding that the fall of man was predestinated from all eternity, thus making redemption and salvation possible: *a.* pertaining to the doctrines of the Supralapsarians. (L. *supra-*, beyond, *lapsus*, the fall.)

Supralapsarianism, *n.* *sew*-pra-lap-*sare*-re-a-nizm, the doctrine of the Supralapsarians.

supralateral, *a.* *sew*-pra-*lat*-er-ral, situated above and at the side [Zool.].

supramaxillary, *a.* *sew*-pra-mak-*sil*-a-re, pertaining to the upper jaw: *n.* the upper jawbone.

supramental, *a.* *sew*-pra-*men*-tal, above the chin [Anat.].

supramundane, *a.* *sew*-pra-*mun*-dane, supermundane.

supra-orbital, *a.* above the orbit of the eye.

supraprotest, *n.* *sew*-pra-*pro*-test, acceptance or payment by one not a party to a bill of exchange after it has been protested [Comm.].

suprarenal, *a.* *sew*-pra-*ree*-nal, situated above the kidneys.

suprascapulary, *a.* *sew*-pra-*skap*-yew-la-re, being above the shoulder-blade or scapula.

supremacy, *n.* sew-*prem*-a-se, the quality or state of being the supreme; highest authority or power. **oath of supremacy,** *see* **oath.** (Fr. *suprématie.*)

supreme, *a.* sew-*preem*, highest in power or authority; finally predominant; most excellent; greatest possible. **Supreme Court,** in England and Wales, the joint Court of Appeal and High Court of Justice; in U.S.A., the highest judicial tribunal, adjudicating in matters affecting the States as a whole and in controversies between an individual State and the Federal Government. **the Supreme Being,** God. (Fr. *suprême.*)

supremely, *ad.* sew-*preem*-le, to a supreme degree.

sur-, sur, prefix signifying over, above, beyond, upon. (Fr., for L. *super-* or *supra-*.)

sura, *n.* *soo*-rah, a chapter of the Koran. (Ar., a step.)

surah, *n.* *soo*-rah, an Indian silk material.

sural, *a.* *sewr*-ral, pertaining to the calf of the leg. (L. *sura*, the calf of the leg.)

suralimentation, *n.* *sur*-al-e-men-*tay*-shon, the method of over-feeding, esp. as a remedy for pulmonary tuberculosis, etc. [Med.].

surat, *n.* sewr-*rat*, inferior cloth made from coarse cotton grown at Surat, India.
surbase, *n.* *sur*-base, a cornice or series of mouldings at the top of the base of a pedestal [Arch.].
surbased, *a.* *sur*-bayst, having a surbase [Arch.].
surcease, *n.* sur-*seece*, cessation: *v.i.* to stop; to leave off. (O.Fr. *surseoir*, pp. *sursise.*)
surcharge, *n.* sur-*charj*, an excessive load or burden; overcharge beyond what is just; an amount surcharged, as penalty or otherwise; words or figures (esp. denoting change in value) printed over a postage-stamp, also a stamp so treated: *v.t.* to overload; to overstock (esp. common land with cattle); to disallow a claim for expenditure improperly incurred; to impose a penalty for a false return of taxable property; to show an omission in an account; to print a surcharge over a postage-stamp. (Fr. *sur-*, and *charge.*)
surcharger, *n.* sur-*charj*-er, one who surcharges.
surcingle, *n.* *sur*-sing-gl, a belt, band, or girth which passes over a saddle, etc., on a horse's back to fasten it; the girdle of a cassock. (O.Fr. *surcengle.*)
surcoat, *n.* *sur*-koat, the coat worn over chain mail; a short outer coat or robe. (O.Fr. *surcote.*)
surculose, *a.* *sur*-kew-lohs, producing suckers [Bot.]. (L. *surculus*, a twig.)
surd, *n.* surd, an irrational quantity or number, *e.g.* the square root of 2, there being no number which multiplied into itself will exactly produce it [Math.]; a surd speech-sound [Phon.]: *a.* involving surds, not expressible in rational numbers [Math.]; uttered without vibration of the vocal chords [Phonetics]. (L. *surdus*, deaf.)
surdation, *n.* sur-*day*-shon, the change of a voiced to a surd sound [Phonetics].
surdity, *n.* *sur*-de-te, deafness [Path.].
surdomutism, *n.* sur-do-*mew*-tizm, the condition of being deaf and dumb. (L. *surdus*, deaf, and *mutism.*)
sure, *a.* shure, certainly knowing; perfectly confident; certain; secure; firm; not liable to fail; certain of obtaining: *ad.* certainly. **make sure,** to make certain. **sure thing!** certainly; yes [Amer. slang].
sure-footed, *a.* not liable to stumble or fall.
surely, *ad.* *shure*-le, certainly.
sureness, *n.* *shure*-ness, the state of being sure; certainty.
surety, *n.* *shure*-te, certainty; security; safety; foundation of stability; confirmation; a pledge deposited as security against loss or damage; one who is bound with and for another [Law]; a bail; a hostage. (Fr. *sûreté.*)
suretyship, *n.* *shure*-te-ship, state of being surety; obligation of a person to answer for another.
surf, *n.* surf, the swell of the waves breaking on rocks or shore; the foam so caused. (Perhaps *sough.*)
surface, *n.* *sur*-face, the external part of anything that has length and breadth; a superficies; a magnitude that has length and breadth without thickness [Geom.]; external or superficial appearance [Fig.]: *a.* outside; on the surface merely: *v.t.* to put a surface on. **surface tension,** *see* **tension.** (Fr. from *sur-* and *face.*)
surface-hardening, *n.* treatment of a metal so that its skin is hardened by a mechanical or chemical process.
surface-loading, *n.* the total weight of an aeroplane divided by its wing area [Av.].
surfaceman, *n.* *sur*-face-man, one who works on the surface of roads, the permanent way of railways, etc., or in the surface works or workings of a mine.
surf-duck, *n.* the scoter; any sea-bird of the genus *Œdemia*, esp. *Œ. nigra.*
surfeit, *n.* *sur*-fit, excess, esp. in eating and drinking; fullness and oppression occasioned by this: *v.t.* to overfeed and produce sickness or uneasiness; to cloy: *v.i.* to overfeed till uneasiness ensues. (O.Fr. *sorfait*, excess.)
surfeiter, *n.* *sur*-fit-er, a glutton.
surf-riding, *n.* the sport of being carried by the surf while standing balanced on a board.
surf-scoter, *n.* a surf-duck, esp. the common American scoter, *Melanitta perspicillata.*
surfy, *a.* *surf*-e, covered with surf.
surge, *n.* surj, a large wave or billow; a great rolling swell of water; a swelling undulation; an abnormal rush of current [Elect.]: *v.t.* to let go a portion of a rope suddenly [Naut.]: *v.i.* to swell; to rise high and roll; to slip back, as a cable [Naut.] (Fr. *surgir.*)
surgent, *a.* *sur*-jent, swelling; rising in a surge or surges.
surgeon, *n.* *sur*-jon, a medical practitioner having the diploma of the Royal College of Surgeons; a medical officer in an armed force or on board ship; one who heals by surgery. **surgeon's knot,** a reef-knot for tying ligatures, etc., the first knot having two turns. (Fr. *chirurgien.*)
surgeoncy, *n.* *sur*-jon-se, the office or post of surgeon in the Navy, Army, or Air-Force.
surgery, *n.* *sur*-jer-re, the act or art of healing diseases and injuries mainly by manual operation with instruments; the place where a surgeon operates or where a country doctor is consulted by patients; a dispensary. (Fr. *chirurgie.*)
surgical, *a.* *sur*-je-kal, pertaining to surgeons or surgery; done by means of surgery.
surgy, *a.* *sur*-je, rising in surges; full of surges.
suricate, *n.* *sew*-re-kat, a small S. African burrowing mammal, *Suricata tetradactyla*, allied to the mongoose; the meerkat.
surlily, *ad.* *sur*-le-le, in a surly manner.
surliness, *n.* quality or state of being surly.
surloin, *n.* *sur*-loyn, sirloin.
surly, *a.* *sur*-le, gloomily morose; crabbed; snarling; rough. (Perhaps *sir-like*, or *sourly.*)
surma, *n.* *sur*-mah, a sulphide of antimony preparation used in India for blackening the eyebrows.
surmaster, *n.* *sur*-mahs-ter, the master next in authority to the headmaster in certain schools.
surmisal, *n.* sur-*my*-zal, surmise.
surmise, *n.* *sur*-mize, a supposition for which there is no certain evidence; conjecture: *v.t.* to imagine conjecturally, and without certain knowledge or adequate evidence. (O.Fr. *surmise*, put upon.)
surmiser, *n.* sur-*my*-zer, one who surmises.
surmount, *v.t.* sur-*mount*, to rise above; to conquer; to overcome; to surpass. (Fr. *surmonter.*)
surmountable, *a.* sur-*mount*-a-bl, that may be surmounted; superable.
surmountableness, *n.* sur-*mount*-a-bl-ness, the state of being surmountable.
surmounted, *a.* and *pp.* sur-*mount*-ed, overcome; surpassed; partly covered by another charge of a different colour or metal [Her.]. **surmounted arch,** a semicircular arch rising higher than half its span.
surmounter, *n.* sur-*mount*-er, one who surmounts.
surmullet, *n.* *sur*-mul-let, a sea-fish, the red mullet, *Mullus surmulletus.*
surname, *n.* *sur*-name, a name or appellation added to the baptismal or Christian name, or to the original name; the family name: *v.t.* to name or call by the surname; to give a surname to. (Fr. *surnom.*)
surnominal, *a.* sur-*nom*-e-nal, pertaining to surnames. (Fr. *sur-*, and L. *nomen*, a name.)
surpass, *v.t.* sur-*pahs*, to go beyond in anything, good or bad; to exceed; to excel. (Fr. *surpasser.*)
surpassable, *a.* sur-*pahs*-a-bl, that may be surpassed or exceeded.
surpassing, *a.* sur-*pahs*-ing, exceeding; excellent in an eminent degree; exceeding others.
surpassingly, *ad.* in a degree surpassing others.
surpassingness, *n.* surpassing excellence.
surplice, *n.* *sur*-plis, a white linen vestment worn over the cassock by the clergy, choristers, and some others ministerially taking part in the services of the Roman, Anglican, and certain other Churches. **surplice fee,** a fee paid to the clergy for duties in connexion with marriages, funerals, etc. (O.Fr. *surplis*, from *sur*, over, and *pelisse.*)
surplus, *n.* *sur*-plus, balance to the good; excess beyond what is prescribed or wanted; the residuum of an estate after the debts and legacies are paid [Law]: *a.* more than sufficient; being a surplus. (Fr. *sur-*, and *plus*, more.)
surplusage, *n.* *sur*-plus-aj, surplus; irrelevant or unnecessary matter in a plea, etc. [Law].
surprisal, *n.* sur-*pry*-zal, the act of surprising; the state of being surprised.
★**surprise,** *n.* sur-*prize*, the act of surprising; surprisal; an emotion excited by something happening suddenly and unexpectedly: *v.t.* to come upon or take suddenly or unawares; to strike with wonder or astonishment, or to throw the mind

into disorder by something sudden, unexpected, or unusual. (Fr. *sur-*, and *pris*, taken.)
surprising, *a.* sur-*pry*-zing, exciting surprise; of a nature to excite surprise; extraordinary.
surprisingly, *ad.* in a manner to surprise.
surprisingness, *n.* the state of causing surprise.
surra, *n.* *soor*-ra, a tropical infectious disease of horses or cattle, caused by a trypanosome. (Hind.)
surrealism, *n.* sur-*ree*-a-lizm, a movement in art and literature the practitioners of which attempt to express subconscious mental processes by the representation of dream-like and incoherent images.
surrealist, *n.* sur-*ree*-a-list, one who practises surrealism: *a.* pertaining to surrealism.
surrealistic, *a.* sur-*ree*-a-*lis*-tik, surrealist; suggestive of surrealism.
surrebut, *v.i.* *sur*-re-*but*, to reply, as a plaintiff to a defendant's rebutter [Law].
surrebuttal, *n.* *sur*-re-*but*-al, the act of maintaining a surrebutter [Law].
surrebutter, *n.* *sur*-re-*but*-er, the plaintiff's reply in pleading.
surrejoin, *v.i.* *sur*-re-*joyn*, to reply, as a plaintiff to a defendant's rejoinder [Law].
surrejoinder, *n.* *sur*-re-*joyn*-der, the answer of a plaintiff to a defendant's rejoinder.
surrender, *n.* sur-*ren*-der, the act of yielding into the power of another; a yielding or giving up: *v.t.* to yield to the power of another, or to influence, passion, etc.; to give or deliver up possession of upon compulsion or demand; to resign in favour of another; to give up; to yield an estate [Law]: *v.i.* to yield; to give up oneself into the power of another. (O.Fr. *surrendre.*)
surrenderee, *n.* sur-*ren*-der-*ree*, one to whom a thing (esp. [Law] an estate) is surrendered.
surrenderor, *n.* sur-*ren*-der-ror, one who surrenders an estate to another [Law].
surreption, *n.* su-*rep*-shon, the act of obtaining surreptitiously; theft.
surreptitious, *a.* *su*-rep-*tish*-us, done by stealth or without proper authority; made or introduced fraudulently. (L.)
surreptitiously, *ad.* in a surreptitious manner.
surrogate, *n.* *su*-ro-gate, a deputy, esp. the deputy of a bishop for granting marriage licences. (L.)
surround, *v.t.* sur-*round*, to enclose on all sides; to encompass; to lie or be on all sides of: *n.* an act of surrounding, as in the chase; that which surrounds, esp. a detached border to a carpet.
surroundings, *n.pl.* sur-*roun*-dingz, environment; circumstances.
sursaturation, *n.* *sur*-sat-yew-*ray*-shon, supersaturation.
sursolid, *n.* sur-*sol*-id, the fifth power of a number [Math.]: *a.* denoting the fifth power [Math.].
sur-tax, *n.* a supertax.
surtout, *n.* sur-*too*, a man's overcoat; a tight-fitting broad-skirted outer coat. (Fr. *sur*, over, *tout*, all.)
surveillance, *n.* sur-*vay*-lance *or* sur-*vay*-lyance, watch; inspection; superintendence. (Fr. *surveiller*, to superintend.)
survey, *v.t.* sur-*vay*, to inspect or take a view of; to view with attention, as from a height; to examine; to measure, as land; to examine and ascertain particularly: *n.* *sur*-vay, a careful view; a particular view and examination of anything; the act of surveying land; a district for the collection of the customs [U.S.A.]. **Ordnance Survey,** *see* **ordnance. trigonometrical survey,** a survey on a large scale by means of a series of triangles. (L. *super*, and *video*, see,)
surveyal, *n.* sur-*vay*-al, the act of surveying; a viewing.
surveying, *n.* sur-*vay*-ing, the art or business of measuring land.
surveyor, *n.* sur-*vay*-or, one appointed to superintend others; one who views and examines to ascertain the condition, quantity, or quality of a thing; one who measures land. **quantity surveyor,** *see* **quantity.**
surveyorship, *n.* sur-*vay*-or-ship, the office of a surveyor.
survival, *n.* sur-*vy*-val, a living beyond the life of another person, thing, or event; an outliving; one who or that which survives others of its class.
survivance, *n.* sur-*vy*-vance, a surviving; survivorship.
survive, *v.t.* sur-*vive*, to outlive; to live beyond the life of: *v.i.* to remain alive. (Fr. *survivre.*)
survivor, *n.* sur-*vy*-vor, one who outlives another; the longer liver of two joint tenants or holders [Law].
survivorship, *n.* sur-*vy*-vor-ship, the state of surviving; right as survivor.
susannite, *n.* *sew*-zan-ite, a former name of leadhillite. (The *Susanna* mine, Leadhills.)
susceptance, *n.* su-*sep*-tance, the facility offered by the capacity and inductance of a current to the flow of alternating current [Elect.].
susceptibility, *n.* su-*sep*-te-*bil*-e-te, state of being easily affected by impressions; susceptibleness; sensibility.
susceptible, *a.* su-*sep*-te-bl, capable of admitting anything additional, or any change, affection or influence; impressible; having nice sensibility. (Fr.)
susceptibleness, *n.* the quality of being susceptible.
susceptibly, *ad.* in a susceptible manner.
susceptive, *a.* su-*sep*-tiv, capable of admitting; readily admitting; susceptible; impressionable; prone to emotion; amorous.
susceptivity, *n.* *sus*-sep-*tiv*-e-te, capacity of admitting; susceptibility.
suscipient, *n.* su-*sip*-e-ent, one who receives; a partaker of the sacrament [Eccles.]: *a.* receiving; receptive. (L.)
suscitate, *v.t.* *sus*-e-tate, to rouse; to excite; to call into life and action.
susi, *n.* *soo*-se, a fine Indian striped fabric, usually woven of cotton and silk. (Per.)
suslik, *n.* *sus*-lik, a small burrowing rodent of European and Asiatic Russia, *Spermophilus citillus*, allied to the marmots. (Russ.)
suspect, *a.* sus-*pekt*, doubtful: *n.* *sus*-pekt, one who is suspected: *v.t.* sus-*pekt*, to imagine that something exists, but without proof; to mistrust; to imagine to be guilty; to doubt: *v.i.* to imagine guilt. (Fr. *suspecter.*)
suspectable, *a.* sus-*pek*-ta-bl, that may be suspected; open to suspicion.
suspectedly, *ad.* so as to be suspected.
suspectedness, *n.* the state of being suspected.
suspecter, *n.* sus-*pek*-ter, one who suspects.
suspectful, *a.* sus-*pekt*-ful, apt to suspect or mistrust.
suspectless, *a.* sus-*pekt*-less, having no suspicion; not suspected.
suspend, *v.t.* *sus*-pend, to hang; to attach to something above; to make to depend on; to interrupt; to stop or cause to cease for a time; temporarily to deprive of office. (Fr. *suspendre.*)
suspender, *n.* sus-*pen*-der, one who suspends: *pl.* bands or attachments worn for holding up socks or stockings; braces (for trousers) [U.S.A.].
suspense, *n.* sus-*pense*, a state of uncertainty; indetermination; indecision; cessation for a time; suspension; a temporary cessation of a man's right [Law]. (Fr. *suspens.*)
suspensibility, *n.* sus-*pen*-se-*bil*-e-te, capacity of being suspended or sustained from sinking.
suspensible, *a.* sus-*pen*-se-bl, capable of being suspended or held from sinking.
suspension, *n.* sus-*pen*-shon, the act of suspending; delay; forbearance of determination; interruption; intermission; temporary privation of powers, authority, or rights; the prolonging of the notes of a chord into the succeeding chord [Mus.]. **points of suspension,** the points in the axis or beam of a balance where the weights are applied, or from which they are suspended. (Fr.)
suspensive, *a.* sus-*pen*-siv, indicating suspense; able to suspend or defer; mentally hesitant.
suspensoid, *n.* sus-*pen*-soyd, a colloidal solution in which the particles are solid.
suspensor, *n.* sus-*pen*-sor, something which suspends.
suspensory, *a.* sus-*pen*-so-re, that suspends; suspending; pertaining to suspension: *n.* that which suspends or holds up.
suspicion, *n.* sus-*pish*-on, act of suspecting; imagination of the existence of something on insufficient grounds; mistrust; a very small quantity [Coll.]. **above suspicion,** too good to be suspected. **under suspicion,** suspected. (Fr.)
suspicionless, *a.* having no suspicion.
suspicious, *a.* sus-*pish*-us, inclined to suspect;

adapted to raise suspicion; entertaining suspicion; mistrustful. (Fr. *suspicieux.*)

suspiciously, *ad.* in a suspicious manner.

suspiciousness, *n.* the state or quality of being suspicious.

suspiration, *n.* sus-pe-*ray*-shon, act of sighing or fetching a long, deep breath. (L. *sub-*, and *spiro*, breathe.)

suspire, *v.i.* sus-*pire*, to sigh; to respire.

sustain, *v.t.* sus-*tane*, to bear; to uphold; to hold; to keep from falling; to support; to maintain; to keep alive; to assist or relieve. (O.Fr. *sustenir.*)

sustainable, *a.* sus-*tane*-a-bl, that may be sustained.

sustainer, *n.* sus-*tane*-er, he who or that which sustains.

sustainment, *n.* sus-*tane*-ment, that which sustains; the act of sustaining.

sustenance, *n.* *sus*-te-nance, that which supports life; food; maintenance.

sustentacular, *a.* sus-ten-*tak*-yew-lar, pertaining to or resembling a sustentaculum.

sustentaculum, *n.* sus-ten-*tak*-yew-lum a supporting part or organ [Anat. and Zool.].

sustentation, *n.* *sus*-ten-*tay*-shon, act of sustaining; sustenance; support of life.

susu, *n.* *soo*-soo, the blind porpoise-like cetacean, *Plantanista gangetica*, of the larger Indian rivers.

susurrant, *a.* sew-*su*-rant, softly whispering.

susurration, *n.* *sew*-su-*ray*-shon, a whispering; a soft murmur. (L. *susurro*, whisper.)

susurrus, *n.* sew-*su*-rus, a susurration; a soft murmur, esp. in an aneurysm [Med.].

sutile, *a.* *sew*-til, done by stitching. (L. *suo*, sew.)

sutler, *n.* *sut*-ler, an army camp-follower who sold provisions, liquors, etc. (Dut.)

sutlery, *n.* *sut*-le-re, the occupation or establishment of a sutler.

Sutra, *n.* *soo*-trah, a Brahminical precept or rule; a collection of these; certain narrative parts of the Buddhist sacred books. (Sans., a thread or string.)

suttee, *n.* su-*tee*, self-immolation, esp. the Hindu custom of a widow burning herself on the funeral pyre of her husband; the widow doing this. (Sans. *sati*, a virtuous wife.)

sutteeism, *n.* su-*tee*-izm, the practice of self-immolation among Hindu widows.

suttle, *a.* *sut*-tl, designating the weight of commodities after the tare has been deducted, and before the tret has been allowed [Comm.]: *n.* suttle weight.

sutural, *a.* *sew*-tewr-ral, relating to a suture or seam; taking place at a suture [Bot.].

suturation, *n.* sew-tew-*ray*-shon, the act or process of suturing [Surg.].

suture, *n.* *sew*-tewr, a sewing; a seam; the junction of two immovably articulated bones, esp. those uniting the bones of the skull [Anat.]; the uniting of the edges of wounds by sewing [Surg.]; a line of junction in plants, shells, etc.: *v.t.* to stitch together [Surg.]. (Fr., from L. *sutus*, sewn.)

sutured, *a.* *sew*-tewrd, having sutures; knit together.

suzerain, *n.* *soo*-ze-rane, a feudal lord or superior; a paramount ruler; a state having rights of sovereignty over another. (Fr.)

suzerainty, *n.* *soo*-ze-ran-te, the dominion of a suzerain; paramount authority or command.

svelte, *a.* svelt, lissom, lithe; supple of figure; slender. (Fr.)

swab, *n.* swob, a mop for cleaning floors or decks; an absorbent pad used in surgery: *v.t.* to clean with a swab; to take up moisture with a swab; to wipe when wet or after washing. (Dut. *swabberen*, swab, do dirty work.)

swabber, *n.* *swob*-ber, one who uses a swab.

swad, *n.* swod, a pod; a soldier [Slang]. (Dial.)

swaddle, *v.t.* *swod*-dl, to swathe; to wrap up close and warm, as a baby; to bind or bandage. (A.S. *swethian*, bind.)

swaddling-clothes, *n.pl.* bands or clothes wrapped closely round a baby or new-born infant.

swaddy, *n.* *swod*-e, a private soldier [Slang].

swadeshi, *n.* swa-*day*-she, an Indian movement aiming at the promotion of home industries by the boycott of imported goods. (Bengali.)

swag, *n.* swag, a wayfarer's bundle containing clothes and provisions; an ornamental festoon; plunder: *v.i.* to sag; to hang heavy. **swag-bellied,** having a "corporation," or prominent stomach. (Scand.)

swage, *v.t.* swaje, to ease; to appease; to mollify; to mitigate. (*assuage.*)

swage, *n.* swaje, a tool used for making patterns upon iron with a mould of similar shape: *v.t.* to fashion with a swage. **swage-block,** a heavy grooved and perforated iron block used in swaging. (O.Fr. *souage.*)

swagger, *a.* *swag*-er, smart; showy; *n.* boastfulness of manner; dashing or defiant bearing: *v.i.* to bluster; to bully; to brag noisily; to strut haughtily. (Scand.)

swagger, *n.* *swag*-er, a swagman [Austral. slang].

swagger-cane, *n.* a soldier's short light stick for carrying, esp. one of regimental pattern.

swaggerer, *n.* *swag*-er-rer, one who swaggers; a bully; a boastful, noisy fellow.

swaggy, *a.* *swag*-e, sagging or leaning by its weight.

swagman, *n.* *swag*-man, a tramp; one travelling with only a swag [Austral. slang].

Swahili, *n.* swah-*hee*-le, the Mohammedan Bantu people of Zanzibar and district; their language. (Ar.)

swain, *n.* swane, a young rustic; a country servant employed in husbandry; a male lover in pastoral poetry. (A.S., from Scand. *sveinn*, boy.)

swainmote, *n.* *swane*-mote, swanimote.

swale, *n.* swale, a shade; a vale; a tract of low land [U.S.A.]: *v.i.* to waste away; to sweal.

swallet, *n.* *swol*-et, a swallow-hole; a subterranean stream.

swallow, *n.* *swol*-oh, any of numerous species of passerine migratory birds of the family Hirundinidæ, the martins excepted. (A.S. *swealwe.*)

swallow, *n.* *swol*-oh, the gullet or œsophagus; voracity; as much as is swallowed at once; a swallow-hole: *v.t.* to receive through the gullet into the stomach; to absorb; to engulf; to receive implicitly; to appropriate; to engross; to occupy; to seize and waste; to consume; to recant; to refrain from giving vent to. (A.S. *swelgan.*)

swallower, *n.* *swol*-oh-er, one who swallows; a glutton.

swallow-fish, *n.* the sapphirine gurnard. *Trigla hirundo.*

swallow-hole, *n.* a cavity in limestone, esp. as the entrance to a subterranean stream.

swallow-tail, *n.* a deeply forked tail; a long-tailed dress coat; a dovetail; a butterfly of the genus *Papilio.*

swallow-tailed, *a.* ending in two points; forked; dovetailed. **swallow-tailed kite,** the N. American bird of prey *Elanoides furcatus.*

swallowwort, *n.* *swol*-loh-wurt, the greater celandine, *Chelidonium majus*; also perennials of the genus *Asclepias*, and other plants.

swam, swam, *p.* of *swim.*

swami, *n.* *swah*-me, master; lord; a title as "reverend" for a Hindu religious teacher; an idol. (Hind.)

swamp, *n.* swomp, wet spongy land; low ground filled with water: *v.t.* to plunge or sink in or as in a swamp; to overwhelm; to plunge into inextricable difficulties. (O.Scand. *svoppr*, sponge.)

swamp-deer, *n.* a large twelve-tined deer, *Rucervus duvaucelli*, of India.

swamp-ore, *n.* bog-ore.

swampy, *a.* *swom*-pe, consisting of swamp; wet and spongy; like a swamp.

swan, *n.* swon, a large long-necked and usually white plumaged aquatic bird of the genus *Cygnus*, of Europe, Asia, and America; a similar, but black plumaged bird of the genus *Chenopis*, of Australia. **swan song,** the last work of a poet (from the fable that the swan sings when dying). (A.S.)

swang, *n.* swang, a piece of low land or green sward, liable to be covered with water. (Eng. Dial.)

swanherd, *n.* *swon*-herd, a tender of swans.

swanimote, *n.* swon-e-mote, a mediæval feudal court administering the forest laws. (A.S. *swan*, swineherd, *gemot*, meeting.)

swank, *n.* swank, brag; swagger: *v.i.* to show off; *a.* swanky [U.S.A.].

swanker, *n.* *swang*-ker, one who swanks.

swanky, *a.* *swang*-ke, characterized by swank; ostentatious.

swannery, *n.* *swon*-er-re, an enclosure or breeding place for swans.

swan-pan, *n.* *swan*-pan, the Chinese form of abacus. (Chin. *suan p'an*, reckoning-board.)

swan's-down, *n.* the down of a swan; a fine, soft, thick cloth of wool mixed with silk or cotton.
swan-skin, *n.* a soft-napped kind of flannel.
swan-upping, *n.* the marking of swans on their beaks.
swap, *n.* swop, an exchange, or a thing exchanged: *v.t.* to exchange; to barter. (M.E. *swapper,* to strike.)
swape, *n.* swape, a pole supported by a fulcrum, used for raising water from a well; a pump-handle; a long oar or sweep.
Swaraj, *n.* swa-*rahj,* Indian political independence, self-government, or Home Rule. (Sans.)
Swarajist, *n.* swa-*rah*-jist, an advocate of Swaraj: *a.* (*l.c.*) pertaining to Swaraj.
sward, *n.* swawrd, the grassy surface of land; turf: *v.t.* to cover with sward. (A.S. *sweard.*)
swardy, *a. swawr*-de, swarded.
sware, sware, *p.* of *swear.*
swarf, *n.* swawrf, metal filings or shavings.
swarm, *n.* swawrm, a large number or body of small animals, insects, etc., or people, esp. when in motion; a body of honey-bees migrating with a queen from a hive to form a new colony, also such a colony settled permanently in a hive: *v.i.* to collect and depart from a hive by flight in a body, as bees; to throng together; to congregate in a multitude; to be crowded. (A.S. *swearm.*)
swarm, *v.i.* swawrm, to climb, esp. a tree, by use of arms and legs alternately. (Origin unknown.)
swarming, *n. swawrm*-ing, going off in swarms, as bees; gathering, or gathered, in swarms; multitudinous.
swart, *a.* swawrt, swarthy. **swart star,** Sirius.
swarth, *a.* swawrth, swarthy.
swarthily, *ad. swawr*-the-le, with a tawny hue.
swarthiness, *n.* the quality of being swarthy.
swarthy, *a. swawr*-the, of a dark hue or dusky complexion; tawny.
swartish, *a. swawrt*-ish, somewhat dark or dusky.
swash, *n.* swosh, brag; a blustering noise; a dash or splash of water; the noise of this; hogwash: *v.i.* to bluster; to brag; to make a great noise; to splash water about: *v.t.* to strike with violence. (Imit.)
swash, *n.* swosh, the flourish given to certain ornamental italic letters [Print.].
swashbuckler, *n. swosh*-buk-ler, a bully or braggadocio.
swasher, *n. swosh*-er, a blustering bully; a braggadocio.
swashing, *a. swosh*-ing, violent (of a blow, etc.).
swash-letter, *n.* a variety of italic letter ornamented with flourishes [Print.].
swash-plate, *n.* a circular plate revolving on the slant so as to give reciprocal motion to a rod resting on it.
swashwork, *n. swosh*-wurk, lathe-work in which the tooling is inclined to the axis of rotation.
swashy, *a. swosh*-e, sloppy; wish-washy.
swastika, *n. swos*-te-ka, the fylfot, a right-angled cross with equal arms, each arm bent back at a right-angle at half its length; a prehistoric religious symbol adopted in Central Europe, 1918, as the emblem of anti-Semitism, and in Germany, 1933, as that of the Third Reich.
swat, *n.* swot, a flexible bat for killing flies; a swot: *v.t.* to strike sharply with a swat or the hand; to swot.
swath, *n.* swawth, a line of grass or grain cut and thrown together by the scythe; the whole breadth or sweep of a scythe in mowing. (A.S. *swæthe.*)
swathe, *n.* swaythe, a bandage; a band or fillet: *v.t.* to bind with a band, bandage, or roller; to bind or wrap. (A.S. *swathian,* enwrap.)
swatter, *n. swot*-er, a swat; one who swats; a heavy hitter, esp. at baseball; a swotter.
sway, *n.* sway, the swing or sweep of a moving object; preponderation; rule; dominion; control: *v.t.* to cause to oscillate or to lean or incline to one side; to influence or direct by power and authority, or by moral force: *v.i.* to be drawn to one side by weight; to lean; to have weight or influence; to waver. (Scand.)
sway-back, *n.* a kind of lumbago among beasts, esp. horses, occasioning a sagging of the back.
sweal, *v.i.* sweel, to melt and run down, as the tallow of a candle; to waste away without feeding the flame; to singe (esp. a hog). (A.S. *swælan.*)
swear, *v.i.* sware, to affirm or utter a solemn declaration with an appeal to God for its truth; to promise upon oath; to give evidence on oath; to practise profaneness: *v.t.* to utter or affirm with a solemn appeal to God for the truth of the declaration; to cause to take an oath; to declare or charge upon oath. **swear by,** to call upon as witness to an oath; [Coll.] to rate very highly. **swear in,** to instal under oath. **swear off,** to vow to refrain from or abandon. **swear the peace against one,** to make oath against him before the proper officer, as endangering the life or person of him who makes it. *p.* **swore.** *pp.* **sworn.** (A.S. *swerian.*)
swearer, *n. sware*-rer, one who swears; one who calls God to witness; a profane person.
swearing, *n. sware*-ring, the act of affirming on oath; profaneness.
swear-word, *n. sware*-wurd, a word used in profane swearing; a blasphemous oath.
sweat, *n.* swet, the sensible moisture which is excreted from the skin of an animal; labour; perspiration; toil; drudgery; moisture exuded from any substance: *v.i.* to excrete sweat from the pores of the skin; to toil; to drudge; to emit moisture: *v.t.* to emit or suffer to flow from the pores; to exude; to wear down by friction (esp. of coins); to employ at starvation wages; to extort money from. **sweating system,** the system of employing people, esp. at their own homes, in **sweated labour,** *i.e.,* for very low wages. **old sweat,** an old soldier, a veteran [Slang]. (A.S. *swat.*)
sweater, *n. swet*-er, one who or that which sweats or causes to sweat; an employer at starvation wages; a knitted pullover.
sweatily, *ad. swet*-e-le, so as to be moist with sweat.
sweatiness, *n.* the state of being sweaty.
sweating-bath, *n.* a vapour-bath for exciting sweat.
sweating-iron, *n.* a kind of knife for scraping sweat from horses; a strigil.
sweating-room, *n.* a room for sweating persons in sickness, or at a Turkish bath; a room in which superfluous moisture is extracted from cheeses.
sweating-sickness, *n.* an extremely fatal epidemic disease, characterized by profuse sweating, which ravaged Europe and England in the 15th and 16th cent.; miliaria.
sweaty, *a. swet*-e, causing sweat; moist with sweat; laborious.
Swede, *n.* sweed, a native of Sweden; (*l.c.*) the Swedish turnip, *Brassica rutabaga.* (L.)
Swedenborgian, *a. swee*-den-*bor*-je-an, relating to Swedenborg or his doctrines: *n.* a follower of the Swedish mystic, Emanuel Swedenborg (*d.* 1772), who claimed to have immediate intercourse with the world of spirits, and maintained that Jesus Christ alone was God.
Swedish, *a. swee*-dish, pertaining to Sweden, its people, or language: *n.* the Swedes.
sweep, *n.* sweep, the act of sweeping; the compass of a stroke; the compass of anything turning, flowing, or brushing; violent and general demolition; direction of any motion not rectilinear; a pole or piece of timber moved on a fulcrum; the angle made by the longer axis of a plane and the longer axis of the fuselage [Av.]; a large oar, used in small vessels to impel them in a calm; a curved carriage drive; a crossing- or chimney-sweeper; a sweepstake: *v.t.* to brush or rub over with a broom; to clean thus; to carry with a long swinging or dragging motion; to carry off with celerity and violence; to strike with a long stroke; to draw or drag over: *v.i.* to pass or pass over with swiftness and violence, as something brushing a surface; to enfilade; to pass with pomp; to mov- with a long reach. *p.* and *pp.* **swept. clean sweep,** *see* **clean.** (A.S. *swapan,* to swoop.)
sweeper, *n. sweep*-er, one who or that which sweeps; a vessel built or adapted for mine-sweeping.
sweeping, *a. sweep*-ing, comprehending a great deal or a great many: *n.pl.* things collected by sweeping; rubbish.
sweepingly, *ad.* in a sweeping manner.
sweepingness, *n.* quality of being sweeping.
sweep-net, *n.* a large net for drawing over an extensive area.
sweepstake, *n. sweep*-stake, a game in which one player may win all the stakes; a lottery in which the total entrance fees less expenses (and sometimes

an agreed proportion for charity, etc.) are divided as prizes: *pl.* a pool of equal stakes; a prize or prizes of all the money staked; a horse-race in which the entrance-fees, etc., of the owners constitute or form part of the prize-money.

sweep-washer, *n.* one who extracts the precious metal from the sweepings of the shop of a goldsmith, etc.

sweepy, *a.* *sweep*-e, passing with speed and violence over a great compass at once; sweeping.

***sweet,** *a.* sweet, agreeable or grateful to the taste; pleasing to the smell, the ear, or the eye; fragrant; melodious; beautiful; fresh—not salt, sour, stale, or putrid; mild; soft; gentle; kind; obliging: *n.* a substance sweet to the taste or smell; a dear one or sweetheart; something pleasing or grateful to the mind; a sweetmeat; a sweet course or dish at a meal: *pl.* sugar confectionery; pastry; sweet dishes. **a sweet tooth,** a liking for sweets or sweet things. (A.S. *swete.*)

sweet-bay, *n.* the true laurel, *Laurus nobilis.*

sweetbread, *n.* *sweet*-bred, the pancreas of a calf, etc., used as food.

sweetbriar, *n.* *sweet*-bry-er, the shrubby plant *Rosa rubiginosa,* having a delicate fragrance.

sweet-calabash, *n.* the West Indian passion-flower, *Passiflora maliformis.*

sweet-chestnut, *n.* the Spanish chestnut, *Castanea vesca*; its edible nut.

sweet-cicely, *n.* a plant of the genus *Myrrhis.*

sweet-corn, *n.* a variety of maize of a sweet taste.

sweeten, *v.t.* *sweet*-en, to make sweet; to make pleasing, mild, kind, less painful, pure, or warm and fertile; to increase the agreeable qualities of; to soften; to make delicate; to restore to purity: *v.i.* to become sweet.

sweetener, *n.* *sweet*-en-er, one who or that which sweetens; a gratifying thing; a refresher.

sweetening, *n.* *sweet*-en-ing, the act of making sweet; that which sweetens.

sweet-flag, *n.* the aromatic plant *Acorus calamus.*

sweet-gale, *n.* the bog-myrtle, *Myrica gale.*

sweet-gum, *n.* a N. American tree of the genus *Liquidambar.*

sweetheart, *n.* *sweet*-hart, a lover.

sweetie, *n.* *sweet*-e, a sweetmeat; a sweetheart [Coll.].

sweeting, *n.* *sweet*-ing, a sweet variety of apple; a word of endearment.

sweetish, *a.* *sweet*-ish, somewhat sweet or pleasing.

sweetishness, *n.* the quality of being sweetish.

sweet-john, *n.* a narrow-leaved variety of sweet-william.

sweetly, *ad.* *sweet*-le, in a sweet manner.

sweet-marjoram, *n.* a very fragrant plant, *Origanum majorana.*

sweet-maudlin, *n.* sweet-*mawd*-lin, the plant *Achillea ageratum,* allied to the milfoil.

sweetmeat, *n.* *sweet*-meet, a confection of sugar; a sugar-plum.

sweetness, *n.* *sweet*-ness, the quality of being sweet; fragrance; mildness; obliging civility; amiableness.

sweet-oil, *n.* any mild edible oil, as nut or olive oil.

sweet-pea, *n.* the annual leguminous plant, *Lathyrus odoratus.*

sweet-potato, *n.* the tropical vine *Ipomœa batatas.*

sweet-root, *n.* liquorice.

sweet-rush, *n.* the sweet-flag.

sweet-sop, *n.* the evergreen shrub, *Amona squamosa.*

sweetstuff, *n.* *sweet*-stuff, sugar confectionery.

sweet-sultan, *n.* a plant of the genus *Centaurea.*

sweet-william, *n.* sweet-*wil*-yam, the plant *Dianthus barbatus.*

swell, *n.* swel, extension of bulk; increase of sound; a gradual ascent or elevation of land; a succession of waves in one direction; a device in an organ for producing a gradual increase or diminution of sound; an important personage; a showily dressed person or fop: *v.i.* to grow larger; to dilate or extend; to increase in size or extent; to heave; to be puffed up; to be bloated; to be inflated; to bulge out; to rise into arrogance; to grow more violent; to become louder; to strut; to rise in altitude: *v.t.* to increase the size, bulk, or dimensions of; to heighten; to raise to arrogance; to enlarge; to augment, as the sound of a note [Mus.]: *a.* smart, fashionable, tip-top [Coll.]. **swelled head,** actinomycosis [Path. and Vet.]; excessive self-appraisement or vainglory, inordinate conceit [Slang]. *pp.* **swollen** or **swelled.** (A.S. *swellan.*)

swelldom, *n.* *swel*-dum, the world of swells; high society [Coll.].

swell-fish, *n.* a globe-fish, or any fish capable of self-inflation.

swelling, *a.* *swel*-ing, tumid; turgid; bombastic: *n.* a tumour or any morbid enlargement [Path.]; a natural rounded prominence or protuberance; a rising or enlargement by passion.

swellish, *a.* *swel*-ish, foppish; characteristic of a swell; rather important.

swell-mob, *n.* former designation of a class of well-dressed pickpockets frequenting crowds.

swell-mobsman, *n.* one of the swell-mob.

swelter, *v.i.* *swel*-ter, to be overcome and faint with heat; to perspire freely: *n.* a sweltering state. (A.S. *sweltan,* to die.)

sweltry, *a.* *swel*-tre, suffocating with heat; oppressive with heat; sultry.

swept, swept, *p.* and *pp.* of *sweep.*

swerve, *n.* swerv, the act of swerving; a sudden deviation: *v.i.* to turn aside; to deviate from any line prescribed or rule of duty; to incline or bend; to be deflected: *v.t.* to cause to deviate. (A.S. *sweorfan.*)

swervily, *ad.* *swer*-ve-le, with a swerving motion.

swift, *a.* swift, moving with celerity or velocity; rapid; ready; prompt; speedy; expeditious: *ad.* swiftly: *n.* a swallow-like bird of the genus *Cypselus,* almost constantly on the wing; a bird of the genus *Collocalia* whose nests the Chinese make into soup, the swiftlet; a moth of the genus *Hepialus*; a reel for winding yarn: *ad.* swiftly. (A.S. *swifan,* move quickly.)

swift, *v.t.* swift, to tighten or make fast with a rope or ropes [Naut.]. (Origin obscure.)

swifter, *n.* *swif*-ter, a rope used in swifting or as protection against collision, etc. [Naut.]: *v.t.* to fasten or make taut with a swifter [Naut.].

swiftlet, *n.* *swift*-let, the small Chinese swift, *Collocalcia fuciphaga,* whose glutinous nests are edible.

swiftly, *ad.* *swift*-le, in a swift manner.

swiftness, *n.* speed; rapid motion; quickness.

swig, *n.* swig, a large draught; a pulley with ropes not running parallel [Naut.]: *v.t.* or *i.* to drink in large draughts; to suck greedily. (Origin unknown.)

swill, *n.* swil, drink taken in excessive quantities; a cleansing with plenty of water; a rinse; pigwash: *v.t.* to drink grossly or greedily; to wash; to rinse. (A.S. *swilian,* wash.)

swill, *n.* swil, a large shallow basket. (Origin unknown.)

swiller, *n.* *swil*-ler, one who swills; a toper.

swillings, *n.pl.* *swil*-lingz, pigwash, or household refuse for this.

***swim,** *n.* swim, the act of swimming; a swimming movement; the air-bladder of a fish; an angling pitch; the main current [Fig.]: *v.i.* to be supported on water or other fluid; to float; to move in water by hands and feet, or by fins; to glide smoothly; to be flooded; to be dizzy; to overflow; to abound; *v.t.* to cause to swim; to pass or move on by swimming; to float (a ship, etc.). **in the swim,** participating in, or acquainted with, what is going on; in the movement. *p.* **swam.** *pp.* **swum.** (A.S. *swimman.*)

swimmer, *n.* *swim*-er, one who or that which swims; a swimming organ or appendage [Zool.].

swimmeret, *n.* swim-er-*ret,* one of the swimming limbs of a crustacean.

swimming, *n.* *swim*-ing, the art of moving in water by means of the limbs; dizziness.

swimming-bell, *n.* the nectocalyx, or disk, of a jelly-fish by means of which it propels itself.

swimmingly, *ad.* smoothly; without obstruction.

swimmy, *a.* *swim*-e, dizzy; vertiginous.

swindle, *n.* *swin*-dl, a gross fraud; a fraudulent transaction; a toss (for drinks, etc.) [Slang]: *v.t.* to cheat and defraud grossly, or with deliberate artifice. (*swindler.*)

swindler, *n.* *swin*-dler, a cheat; a rogue; one who makes a practice of defrauding or swindling others. (Ger. *schwindler.*)

swindlery, *n.* *swind*-ler-re, swindling practices.

swindling, *n.* *swin*-dling, the arts of the swindler; the act of defrauding.
swine, *n., sing.* and *pl.* swine, a pig; pigs; used opprobriously of a degraded or sensual person. (A.S. *swin.*)
swine-bread, *n.* a truffle; the earth-nut.
swine-fever, *n.* an infectious disease affecting the lungs or intestines of pigs.
swine-grass, *n.* knotgrass, the common weed *Polygonum aviculare.*
swineherd, *n.* *swine*-herd, a herd or keeper of pigs.
swinepipe, *n.* *swine*-pipe, a local name of the redwing.
swine-pox, *n.* a variety of chicken-pox; an eruptive disease of pigs.
swinery, *n.* *swine*-er-re, a piggery; a pig-farm.
swine's-cress, *n.* any cress of the genus *Coronopus.*
swine's-grass, *n.* knotgrass.
swinestone, *n.* *swine*-stone, anthraconite; stinkstone.
swine-thistle, *n.* the sow-thistle.
swing, *n.* swing, a waving or vibratory motion; oscillation; motion from one side to the other; a rope or other thing suspended to swing on; influence of a body in motion; unrestrained liberty or licence; sweep of a moving body, or of rhythm; swing-music: *v.i.* to move to and fro, as a body suspended in air with unrestrained tendency to vibrate; to practise swinging; to move round, or to move freely, on, or as on, a pivot; to be hanged: *v.t.* to make to play loosely or to move to and fro; to cause to wave or vibrate; to brandish; to play (jazz) in the manner of swing-music. *p.* and *pp.* **swung.** (A.S. *swingan.*)
swing-band, *n.* a dance-band capable of performing swing-music.
swing-boat, *n.* a boat-shaped seat used on swings at fairs, etc.
swing-bridge, *n.* a bridge that may be swung open for traffic passing beneath.
swinge, *v.t.* swinj, to beat soundly; to chastise.
swingeing, *a.* *swin*-jing, very large.
swingeingly, *ad.* *swin*-jing-le, vastly; hugely.
swinger, *n.* *swing*-er, one who or that which swings.
swinging-post, *n.* the post on which a door or gate is hung.
swingle, *n.* *swing*-gl, a wooden instrument used in swingling; that part of a flail which falls on the grain in threshing: *v.t.* to clean flax by beating it: *v.i.* to dangle.
swingle-tree, *n.* the cross-bar to which a horse's traces are attached.
swingling-tow, *n.* *swing*-gling-toh, the coarse part of flax separated by swingling and hatchelling.
swing-music, *n.* jazz intensified by the improvised vocal and other efforts of the bandsmen.
swing-plough, *n.* a plough without a fore-wheel under the beam.
swing-wheel, *n.* the wheel that, in a clock, drives the pendulum; the balance of a watch.
swinish, *a.* *swy*-nish, befitting or like swine; gross; hoggish.
swinishly, *ad.* in a swinish manner.
swinishness, *n.* the quality of being swinish.
swink, *n.* swink, labour; drudgery: *v.t.* and *i.* to labour; to drudge; to tire out with labour. (A.S. *swincan.*)
swipe, *n.* swipe, a hard blow: *pl.* thin or inferior ale [Coll.]: *v.t.* to hit hard with a swing of the arms; to slog [Cricket]; to quaff greedily or hurriedly; to snatch away [Slang]. (A.S.)
swire, *n.* swire, a hollow between two hills; a col.
swirl, *n.* swerl, a whirling or eddying motion: *v.i.* to move in swirls. (O. Scand. *svirla,* to whirl.)
swish, *n.* swish, a stroke with a cane or whip: *v.t.* to flog; to strike at quickly with a whistling sound.
Swiss, *n.* swis, a native or the people of Switzerland: *a.* pertaining to the Swiss or Switzerland. **Swiss roll,** a thin sheet of sponge-cake spread with jam and rolled cylindrically when hot.
switch, *n.* switch, a small flexible twig, or rod; a detached tress of hair; a movable rail for diverting trains, etc., from one line to another [Rly.]; an appliance for making or breaking electrical contact or transferring current from one line to another: *v.t.* to strike with a switch; to transfer by a switch; to shunt: *v.i.* to move with a jerk. **switch off,** to break contact [esp. Elect.]. (Mid. Dut. *swick,* from *swichen,* wag.)
switchback, *n.* *switch*-bak, a tract of hilly or undulating ground; a road or railway over such; railway over a series of sharp rises and falls buil[t] for amusement.
switchboard, *n.* *switch*-bord, a panel accommodatin[g] switches controlling electric current.
switchman, *n.* *switch*-man, a pointsman [Rly.] one employed in switching.
swivel, *n.* *swiv*-el, that which turns upon a staple a link revolving freely in a socket or ring; [a] swivel-gun: *v.i.* to turn on a staple or pivot (A.S. *swifan,* revolve.)
swivel-eye, *n.* a squint eye [Coll.].
swivel-gun, *n.* a small piece of ordnance mounte[d] on a pivot.
swizzle, *n.* and *v.t.* *swiz*-zl, swindle; to tipple [both Coll.].
swollen, *swoh*-len, *pp.* of *swell;* dilated.
swoon, *n.* swoon, a fainting fit; the act of swooning *v.i.* to faint; to fall into a state of apparent sus[-]pension of physical and mental functions. (A.S *swogan,* move or sweep noisily, sigh.)
swooningly, *ad.* *swoo*-ning-le, in a swooning o[r] languishing manner.
swoop, *n.* swoop, the act of swooping; a falling o[n] and seizing: *v.t.* to fall on at once and seize; t[o] catch while on the wing; to snatch up: *v.i.* t[o] perform the act of swooping; to descend upo[n] suddenly. (A.S. *swapan,* move quickly.)
swop, *n.* and *v.t.* swop, swap.
sword, *n.* sawrd, a long keen-edged offensive weapo[n] used for thrusting or cutting; war; destructio[n] by war; dissension; an emblem of vengeance justice, authority, and power, or triumph an[d] protection. **cross,** or **measure, swords with** to oppose, to fight. **put to the sword,** to slaughte[r] **sheathe the sword,** to cease hostilities. **sword o[f] state,** a sword carried, esp. before a sovereign, o[n] ceremonial occasions. (A.S. *sweord.*)
sword-arm, *n.* the right arm.
sword-bayonet, *n.* a bayonet resembling a sword.
swordbearer, *n.* *sawrd*-bare-rer, a municipal office[r] who carries a sword of state, esp. as an emblem of justice.
swordbill, *n.* *sawrd*-bil, the long-billed S. America[n] humming-bird, *Docimastes ensiferus.*
sword-cane, *n.* a walking-stick containing a sword.
sword-dance, *n.* a Highland dance over two swords laid cross-wise, without touching them.
swordfish, *n.* *sawrd*-fish, a large sea-fish of th[e] genus *Xiphias,* so named from the sword-lik[e] serrated prolongation of the upper jaw.
sword-flag, *n.* the iris [Bot.].
swordgrass, *n.* a sharp-leaved species of sedge.
sword-guard, *n.* the part of the hilt protecting th[e] swordsman's hand.
swordknot, *n.* *sawrd*-not, a tassel or ribbon decoratin[g] the hilt of a sword.
swordless, *a.* *sawrd*-less, destitute of a sword.
sword-lily, *n.* any species of *Gladiolus.*
sword-play, *n.* fencing.
swordsman, *n.* *sawrdz*-man, a soldier; one practise[d] in swordsmanship.
swordsmanship, *n.* *sawrdz*-man-ship, skill in th[e] use of the sword.
sword-stick, *n.* a sword-cane.
swore, swore, *p.* of *swear.*
sworn, sworn, *pp.* of *swear.* **sworn enemies** determined or irreconcilable enemies. **swor[n] friends,** close or intimate friends.
swot, *n.* swot, a plodding student; stiff menta[l] work: *v.i.* to study hard (usually in contempt) [Slang, from *sweat.*]
swotter, *n.* *swot*-er, one who swots [Slang].
swound, *v.i.* swound, to swoon: *n.* a swoon.
swum, swum, *pp.* of *swim.*
swung, swung, *p.* and *pp.* of *swing.*
sybarism, *n.* *sib*-a-rizm, sybaritism.
sybarite, *n.* *sib*-a-rite, one devoted to luxury an[d] pleasure; a voluptuary: *a.* sybaritic. (In allusio[n] to the inhabitants of *Sybaris,* an ancient Gr. colon[y] of S. Italy.)
sybaritic, *a.* *sib*-a-*rit*-ik, luxurious; characterize[d] by sybaritism.
sybaritism, *n.* *sib*-a-re-tizm, effeminacy an[d] luxuriousness.
sycamine, *n.* *sik*-a-mine, the mulberry tree.
sycamore, *n.* *sik*-a-more, a species of maple, *Ace[r] pseudo-platanus.* **sycamore fig,** the sycomore.
syce, *n.* sice, a native groom in India.

sycee, *n.* sy-*see*, stamped silver in ingots of various weights and sizes, used in China as a medium of exchange. (Chin.)
sychnocarpous, *a.* *sik*-no-*kar*-pus, bearing fruit many times before dying; perennial [Bot.]. (Gr. *sychnos*, frequent, *karpos*, fruit.)
sycoma, *n.* sy-*koh*-ma, a condyloma or warty excrescence [Path.]. (Gr., a fig-like ulcer.)
sycomore, *n.* *sik*-o-more, a species of fig, *Ficus sycomorus*, of Egypt and Asia Minor. (Gr. *sykon*, a fig, *moron*, a mulberry.)
syconium, *n.* sy-*koh*-ne-um (*pl.* **syconia**), a hollow receptacle developing into a fruit like that of the fig [Bot.].
sycophancy, *n.* *sik*-o-fan-se, obsequious flattery; servility; toadyism.
sycophant, *n.* *sik*-o-fant, a parasite; a mean flatterer, esp. of princes and great men; an obsequious beggar or cringer. (Gr. *sykophantes.*)
sycophantic, *a.* *sik*-o-*fan*-tik, obsequiously flattering; parasitic; courting favour by mean adulation.
sycophantish, *a.* *sik*-o-fan-tish, sycophantic.
sycosis, *n.* sy-*koh*-sis, barber's itch; an eruption upon the scalp or the bearded part [Med.].
syenite, *n.* *sy*-en-ite, a granite rock in which quartz is largely replaced by hornblende. (*Syene*, in Egypt.)
syenitic, *a.* *sy*-e-*nit*-ik, or containing syenite.
syllabary, *n.* *sil*-a-ba-re, a list of symbols representing syllables.
syllabic, *a.* se-*lab*-ik, pertaining to or consisting of a syllable or syllables.
syllabically, *ad.* in a syllabic manner.
syllabicate, *v.t.* se-*lab*-e-kate, to syllabify.
syllabication, *n.* se-*lab*-e-*kay*-shon, syllabification.
syllabification, *n.* se-*lab*-e-fe-*kay*-shon, the act or process of syllabifying; formation into syllables.
syllabify, *v.t.* se-*lab*-e-fy, to form into syllables; to divide into or pronounce as syllables. (*syllable*, and L. *facio*, make.)
syllabize, *v.t.* *sil*-a-bize, to utter with distinct division of syllables.
syllable, *n.* *sil*-a-bl, a word or part of a word containing a single vowel-sound and uttered by a single impulsion of the voice: *v.t.* to utter distinctly or by syllables. (O.Fr. *sillabe.*)
syllabub, *n.* *sil*-a-bub, sillabub.
syllabus, *n.* *sil*-a-bus, an abstract; a summary giving the heads of a discourse, subjects of a course of lectures, etc.; a catalogue of heretical doctrines in the Roman Church. (Late L.)
syllepsis, *n.* se-*lep*-sis (*pl.* **syllepses**), a figure of speech in which a word or phrase is used both in a literal and a figurative sense in the same sentence (as "departed in a taxi and a temper") [Rhet.]; an agreement of a verb or adjective with one rather than another of two nouns to which it equally applies [Gram.].
sylleptical, *a.* se-*lep*-te-kal, relating to or implying syllepsis.
sylleptically, *ad.* se-*lep*-te-ka-le, by means of syllepsis.
syllogism, *n.* *sil*-o-jizm, a form of reasoning or argument consisting of three proposition, the first two being the premises, and the last, which necessarily follows from them, the conclusion. (Fr.)
syllogistic, *a.* sil-o-*jis*-tik, pertaining to or consisting of a syllogism, or in the form of reasoning by syllogisms.
syllogistically, *ad.* in a syllogistic manner.
syllogize, *v.i.* *sil*-o-jize, to reason by syllogisms.
sylph, *n.* silf, an imaginary light and airy inhabitant of the air intermediate between material and immaterial beings; a graceful young woman; a brilliant S. American humming-bird. (Fr. *sylphe.*)
sylphid, *n.* *silf*-id, a diminutive sylph: *a.* resembling a sylph.
sylva, *n.* *sil*-va, a title for a catalogue or botanical description of forest-trees. (L. *silva*, a wood.)
sylvan, *a.* *sil*-van, pertaining to trees; rustic; wooded: *n.* a fabled deity of the woods; a faun; a rustic.
sylvanite, *n.* *sil*-va-nite, a telluride of silver and gold.
sylvate, *n.* *sil*-vate, a salt of silvic acid.
sylvic, *a.* *sil*-vik, pertaining to or derived from wood. **silvic acid,** a colourless crystalline substance present in turpentine-resin.
sylvics, *n.* *sil*-viks, the science treating of the life of forest trees.
sylviculture, *n.* *sil*-ve-*kul*-tewr, the art of growing trees; forestry.
sylvite, *n.* *sil*-vite, native potassium chloride.
symbiont, *n.* *sim*-be-ont, an organism living in a state of symbiosis.
symbiosis, *n.* sim-be-*oh*-sis, the union of organisms dependent for existence on each other; commensalism. (Gr., living together.)
symbiotic, *a.* sim-be-*ot*-ik, living in symbiosis.
symbol, *n.* *sim*-bol, an emblem; a typification or representation of an invisible thing by something visible; a letter or character, etc., representing something else; an abstract; a creed. (Fr. *symbole.*)
symbolic, *a.* sim-*bol*-ik, serving as a symbol; figurative; relative; characterized by symbolism.
symbolical, *a.* sim-*bol*-e-kal, symbolic. **symbolical books,** documents containing religious creeds or confessions of faith, esp. of the Lutherans.
symbolically, *ad.* by symbols or signs.
symbolics, *n.* sim-*bol*-iks, the science of symbols or of symbolism; the study of creeds.
symbolism, *n.* *sim*-bo-lizm, the art of using symbols; the impartation of a symbolic meaning to an object or an action; representation by symbols; a system of symbols; the science of symbols or creeds.
symbolist, *n.* *sim*-bo-list, one who uses symbols or symbolism; an interpreter of symbols; in art and literature, one who reacts against realism.
symbolistic, *a.* *sim*-bo-*lis*-tik, employing symbols; characterized by symbolism.
symbolization, *n.* *sim*-bo-ly-*zay*-shon, act or process of symbolizing; symbolism.
symbolize, *v.i.* *sym*-bo-lize, to use symbols or symbolism: *v.t.* to represent by a symbol; to make representative of; to typify.
symbology, *n.* sim-*bol*-o-je, the art of expressing by symbols; the study of symbols.
symmetral, *a.* *sim*-e-tral, symmetrical.
symmetrian, *n.* se-*met*-re-an, a symmetrist.
symmetric, *a.* se-*met*-rik, symmetrical.
symmetrical, *a.* se-*met*-re-kal, having symmetry; proportional in its parts; having its parts in due proportion as to dimensions.
symmetrically, *ad.* in a symmetrical manner.
symmetricalness, *n.* quality of being symmetrical.
symmetrist, *n.* *sim*-e-trist, one studious of proportion or symmetry of parts.
symmetrize, *v.t.* *sim*-e-trize, to make proportional in its parts; to reduce to symmetry.
symmetry, *n.* *sim*-e-tre, a due proportion of the several parts of the body to each other; the correspondence of parts on either side of a median line or central point; the union and conformity of the members of a work to the whole; harmony. (Fr. *symétrie.*)
sympathectomy, *n.* *sim*-pa-*thek*-to-me, excision of a portion of a sympathetic ganglion or nerve.
sympathetic, *a.* *sim*-pa-*thet*-ik, pertaining to, or expressing sympathy; having common feeling with another; susceptible of being affected by feelings like those of another; produced by or inducing sympathy. **sympathetic ink,** an ink leaving no mark until treated by heat or otherwise. **sympathetic nerve,** any of a system of nerves regulating involuntary responses and connecting the spinal chord with the viscera of the abdomen and pelvis.
sympathetically, *ad.* in a sympathetic manner; with or in consequence of sympathy.
sympathist, *n.* *sim*-pa-thist, one who sympathizes.
sympathize, *v.i.* *sim*-pa-thize, to have a common feeling, as of pleasure or pain; to feel with or like another; to express sympathy; to be of a like opinion, etc.
sympathizer, *n.* *sim*-pa-thy-zer, one who sympathizes; an adherent or supporter.
sympathy, *n.* *sim*-pa-the, fellow-feeling; the quality of being affected by the affection of another with correspondent feelings; compassion; an agreement of affections or inclinations; such relationship between different parts of the body that the state of the one is affected by that of the other [Med.]; a propensity of inanimate things to unite, or to act on each other. (L. *sympathia.*)
sympetalous, *a.* sim-*pet*-a-lus, with petals united; gamopetalous [Bot.].
symphonic, *a.* sim-*fon*-ik, pertaining to or resembling a symphony; sounded alike; homophonous.

symphonic poem, an orchestral symphony based on some literary, pictorial, or other extra-musical theme.
symphonious, *a.* sim-*foh*-ne-us, agreeing in sound; harmonious; marked by symphony; symphonic.
symphonist, *n. sim*-fo-nist, a composer of symphonies.
symphonize, *v.i.* and *t. sim*-fo-nize, to play or sound together; to harmonize.
symphony, *n. sim*-fo-ne, a consonance or harmony of sounds agreeable to the ear; a ritornello, or form of overture [Mus.]; an orchestral work of elaborated sonata form. (Fr. *symphonie.*)
symphyogenesis, *n. sim*-fe-o-*jen*-e-sis, development of an organ by the union of previously separate parts [Bot.]. (Gr. *symphyesthai*, to grow together, and *genesis.*)
symphyseal, *a.* sim-*fiz*-e-al, pertaining to or situated at a symphysis [Anat.].
symphysis, *n. sim*-fe-sis, the union of bones by cartilage or by coalescence, also, an articulation of this kind [Anat.]; coalescence [Bot.]. (L.)
sympiesometer, *n. sim*-pe-e-*zom*-e-ter, an instrument for measuring the pressure of the atmosphere by means of the compression of gas behind a liquid; an apparatus for measuring the pressure of running water. (Gr. *syn-*, with, *piezo*, press, *metron*, measure.)
symploce, *n. sim*-plo-se, a figure in which successive clauses begin and end with the same word or words [Rhet.]. (Gr. *syn-*, and *ploke*, knitting.)
sympodium, *n.* sim-*poh*-de-um, a main stem apparently made up by a series of superposed branches, as in the vine [Bot.].
symposiac, *a.* sim-*poh*-ze-ak, pertaining to conviviality; of the nature of or suitable for a symposium: *n.* a symposium.
symposiarch, *n.* sim-*poh*-ze-ark, the chairman of a symposium or feast; a toastmaster.
symposiast, *n.* sim-*poh*-ze-ast, a participator in or contributor to a symposium.
symposium, *n.* sim-*poh*-ze-um (*pl.* **symposia**), a drinking together; a merry feast; a banquet with philosophic discussion; a collection of opinions or published articles on a subject. (L.)
symptom, *n. simp*-tom, a token or sign as evidence of something; that which indicates or is a characteristic sign of a disease [Med.]. (Fr. *symptôme.*)
symptomatic, *a. simp*-to-*mat*-ik, pertaining to or according to symptoms; indicating the existence of some particular disease, etc., or of a primary disease of which this is a result [Med.].
symptomatically, *ad.* by means of symptoms; in the nature of symptoms.
symptomatology, *n. simp*-to-ma-*tol*-o-je, the science of the symptoms of diseases.
syn-, sin, Greek prefix, signifying with or together.
synacmy, *n.* sin-*ak*-me, simultaneous maturity of anthers and stigma; homogamy [Bot.].
synæresis, *n.* sin-*eer*-re-sis, the contraction of two syllables or vowels into one [Gram.]. (Gr. *sunairesis.*)
synæsthesia, *n. sin*-ees-*thee*-ze-a, a sensation felt at a part of the body distinct from the part receiving the stimulus [Phys.].
synagogical, *a.* sin-a-*gog*-e-kal, pertaining to or characteristic of a synagogue.
synagogue, *n. sin*-a-gog, a congregation of Jews for the purpose of worship; a Jewish place of worship. **the Great Synagogue,** a council of Jews concerned in remodelling the Jewish worship after the Captivity. (Gr. *syn-*, and *ago*, lead.)
synalepha, *n.* sin-a-*lee*-fa, the contraction of two syllables into one by suppressing a final vowel before the initial vowel of another word [Gram.]. (Gr. *sunaloiphe.*)
synallagmatic, *a. sin*-a-lag-*mat*-ik, mutually or reciprocally binding. (Gr. *syn-*, and *allaso*, change.)
synantherous, *a.* se-*nan*-ther-rus, having the anthers growing together, as in composite plants.
synanthesis, *n.* sin-an-*thee*-sis, synacmy.
synanthous, *a.* sin-*an*-thus, having leaves and flowers that expand at the same time [Bot.].
synapse, *n.* se-*naps*, the channel or means by which an impulse is transmitted from one nerve-cell to another. (Gr. *synapsis*, union.)
synarthrosis, *n. sin*-ar-*throh*-sis (*pl.* **synarthroses**), union of bones not allowing of motion, as in sutures. (Gr. *arthron*, a joint.)
synaxis, *n.* se-*nak*-sis, a religious meeting, esp. for celebration of the Eucharist. (Gr. *syn-*, and *agein*, to gather together.)
syncarpous, *a.* sin-*kar*-pus, having the carpels completely united [Bot.]. (Gr. *karpos*, fruit.)
syncategorematic, *a.* sin-*kat*-e-go-re-*mat*-ik, that may be combined with, but cannot by itself constitute, a term [Logic]: *n.* such a word, as an adverb or preposition. (*categorematic.*)
synchondrosis, *n. sing*-kon-*droh*-sis, the immovable articulation of bones by means of cartilage. (Gr. *chondros*, cartilage.)
synchoresis, *n. sing*-ko-*ree*-sis, concession for the purpose of retort [Rhet.]. (Gr. *choresis*, admission.)
synchro-mesh, *n. sing*-kro-*mesh*, a semi-automatic gear-changing device for motor-cars. (*synchronous* and *mesh.*)
synchronal, *a. sing*-kro-nal, happening at the same time; simultaneous. (Gr. *syn-*, and *chronos*, time.)
synchronism, *n. sing*-kro-nizm, concurrence of two or more events in time; simultaneousness; a tabular chronological presentation of historical facts or events; representation on the same picture of successive incidents.
synchronistic, *a. sing*-kro-*nis*-tik, involving or pertaining to synchronism; synchronous.
synchronization, *n. sing*-kro-ny-*zay*-shon, concurrence of events in respect of time.
synchronize, *v.i. sing*-kro-nize, to agree in time; to happen simultaneously: *v.t.* to cause to agree in time.
synchronizer, *n. sing*-kro-ny-zer, a device to maintain synchronization (between clocks, etc.).
synchronous, *a. sing*-kro-nus, happening at the same time; simultaneous; contemporaneous. **synchronous motor,** a motor whose speed of rotation is directly related to the periodicity of the operating current [Elect.].
synchronously, *ad.* at the same time.
synchrony, *n. sing*-kro-ne, synchronous occurrence; synchonistic arrangement.
synchroton, *n. sing*-kro-ton, an especially powerful form of cyclotron.
synchysis, *n. sing*-ke-sis, confusion of words in a sentence; abnormal fluidity in the vitreous humour; also, a state in which this contains floating cholesterine [Path.]. (Gr. *syn-*, and *cheo*, pour.)
synclastic, *a.* sin-*klast*-ik, curved on all sides towards one side.
synclinal, *a.* sin-*kly*-nal, inclined downward from opposite directions; inclining to a common plane [Geol.]: *n.* a syncline. (Gr. *klino*, bend.)
syncline, *n. sing*-kline, an area in which the strata dip towards an axis and form a trough or basin.
syncopal, *a. sing*-ko-pal, pertaining to or affected by syncope [Path.].
syncopate, *v.t. sing*-ko-pate, to contract, by omitting letters or syllables in a word [Gram.]; to slur the last note of one bar into the first of the next [Mus.].
syncopation, *n. sing*-ko-*pay*-shon, the act of syncopating [Gram. and Mus.]; syncope [Gram.], also the shifting of accent caused by this; music of the ragtime type.
sycopator, *n. sing*-ko-pay-tor, one who syncopates.
syncope, *n. sing*-ko-pe, the elision of one or more letters or a syllable from the middle of a word [Gram.]; a fainting or swoon [Path.]. (Gr.)
syncopic, *a.* sin-*kop*-ik, syncopal [Path.].
syncopist, *n. sing*-ko-pist, one who syncopates [Gram.] or clips his words.
syncretic, *a.* sin-*kret*-ik, characterized by, or attempting to effect, syncretism.
syncretism, *n. sing*-kre-tizm, an attempted blending of different, more or less antagonistic, speculative or religious systems into one. (Gr. *synkretismos.*)
syncretist, *n. sing*-kre-tist, one who attempts to reconcile opposing systems or sects.
syncretistic, *a. sing*-kre-*tis*-tik, pertaining to the syncretists or syncretism.
syndactyl, *a.* sin-*dak*-til, having webbed digits: *n.* a syndactyl bird or mammal.
syndactylism, *n.* sin-*dak*-te-lizm, the condition of having webbed or conjoined digits, esp. [Med.] as a deformity.
syndactyly, *n.* sin-*dak*-te-le, syndactylism.
syndesmography, *n. sin*-des-*mog*-ra-fe, a description of the ligaments. (Gr. *syndesmos*, a ligament.)
syndesmology, *n. sin*-des-*mol*-o-je, a treatise on the ligaments.

syndesmosis, *n.* *sin*-des-*moh*-sis, an articulation in which the bones are united by ligaments [Anat.].
syndesmotomy, *n.* *sin*-des-*mot*-o-me, surgical cutting of the ligaments. (Gr. *syndesmos*, and *tome*, cutting.)
syndetic, *a.* sin-*det*-ik, connective; using a conjunction [Gram.].
syndic, *n.* *sin*-dik, a municipal or other officer invested with different powers in different countries; one chosen to transact business for others; at Cambridge Univ., a member of a specially appointed committee of the senate. (L. *syndicus*, patron, advocate.)
syndicalism, *n.* *sin*-de-ka-lizm, the economic theory that the means of production and distribution in individual industries should be controlled by the workers in that industry; the plan of trade-union action which advocates the general strike and direct action as the means of attaining this end.
syndicalist, *n.* *sin*-de-ka-list, an advocate or adherent of syndicalism: *a.* pertaining to or resembling syndicalism.
syndicate, *n.* *sin*-de-kat, a body of syndics; the office of a syndic; a combination of capitalists, etc., associated for the purpose of a commercial speculation, company promotion, control of a branch of industry, etc.: *v.t.* to subject to or combine into a syndicate; to sell articles, stories, etc., for simultaneous publication in different periodicals; to publish articles, etc., thus.
syndrome, *n.* *sin*-dro-me, the concurrence of symptoms in disease [Med.]. (Gr. *dromos*, running.)
syne, *ad.* sine, long ago [Scots.]. (*since.*)
synecdoche, *n.* sin-*ek*-do-ke, a figure by which a whole is put for a part or a part for the whole [Rhet.]. (Gr. *syn-*, and *dechomai*, receive.)
synecdochical, *a.* *sin*-ek-*dok*-e-kal, expressed by or implying a synecdoche; involving synecdochism.
synecdochism, *n.* sin-*ek*-do-kizm, in primitive religions, the belief that any part of a person, etc., contains the powers of the whole [Ethn.].
synechia, *n.* se-*nee*-ke-a (pl. **synechiæ**), a morbid union of parts [Path.], esp. of the iris of the eye to the cornea or to the capsule of the lens. (Gr., continuity.)
synergic, *a.* sin-*er*-jik, working together, co-operating (as muscles) [Anat.]; exhibiting or pertaining to energy.
Synergism, *n.* *sin*-er-jizm, the doctrine of the Synergists.
Synergist, *n.* *sin*-er-jist, in the Lutheran Church, one who held that divine grace required a corresponding action of the will to make it effectual; (*l.c.*) an agent [Med.] or muscle [Anat.] that supplements another.
synergy, *n.* *sin*-er-je, correlated action, esp. of bodily organs or of two or more drugs [Med.]. (Gr. *syn-*, and *ergon*, a work.)
synesis, *n.* *sin*-e-sis, construction in accordance with the sense rather than the syntax, as "£20 is wanted to clear the debt" [Gram.]. (Gr., understanding.)
syngenesious, *a.* *sin*-je-*nee*-shus, united in a ring, esp. of the anthers of the composite plants [Bot.].
syngenesis, *n.* sin-*jen*-e-sis, sexual reproduction in which substance from both parents contribute to the substance of the embryo [Biol.].
syngnathous, *a.* *sing*-na-thus, having the jaws united into a tubular snout (of certain fish, as the pipefishes). (Gr. *syn-*, and *gnathos*, jaw.)
syngraph, *n.* *sin*-graf, a deed signed by all the parties concerned [Law]. (Gr. *syn-*, and *grapho*, write.)
synizesis, *n.* *sin*-e-*zee*-sis, a contraction of two syllables into one [Gram.]; closure or obliteration of the pupil of the eye [Med.]. (Gr. *syn-*, and *hizo*, seat.)
synochus, *n.* *sin*-o-kus, continuous fever. (Gr. *sunoche*, holding together.)
synod, *n.* *sin*-od, a convention or council, esp. a meeting of ecclesiastics to consult on matters of religion; in Scotland, such a council consisting of several adjoining presbyteries. (Fr. *synode.*)
synodal, *a.* *sin*-o-dal, pertaining to or occasioned by a synod: *n.* a payment formerly made by local clergy to the bishop or archdeacon at a visitation.
synodic, *a.* se-*nod*-ik, synodal.
synodical, *a.* se-*nod*-e-kal, synodal; pertaining to a conjunction, esp. to two successive conjunctions [Astron.]. **synodical month,** the period from one new moon to the next.
synodically, *ad.* by the action or authority of a synod.
synœcious, *a.* se-*nee*-shus, with male and female flowers in one head [Bot.].
synonym, *n.* *sin*-o-nim, a word having the same signification as another. (Fr. *synonyme.*)
synonymic, *a.* *sin*-o-*nim*-ik, of similar meaning.
synonymist, *n.* se-*non*-e-mist, one who collects and explains synonymous words.
synonymity, *n.* *sin*-o-*nim*-e-te, the state or quality of being synonymous.
synonymize, *v.t.* se-*non*-e-mize, to express the same meaning in different words.
synonymous, *a.* se-*non*-e-mus, expressing the same thing; conveying the same idea.
synonymously, *ad.* in a synonymous manner.
synonymy, *n.* se-*non*-e-me, the quality of being synonymous; the use or study of synonyms.
synopsis, *n.* se-*nop*-sis, a general view, or a collection of things or parts so arranged as to exhibit the whole of the principle parts in a general view. (L.)
synopsize, *v.t.* se-*nop*-size, to epitomize.
synoptic, *a.* se-*nop*-tik, pertaining to a synopsis; affording a general view of the whole, or of the principal parts of a thing; a synoptist. **Synoptic Gospels,** the Gospels of Matthew, Mark, and Luke, as giving a general view of the same transactions and events.
synoptical, *a.* se-*nop*-te-kal, synoptic.
synoptically, *ad.* in a synoptic manner.
Synoptist, *n.* se-*nop*-tist, one of the authors of the synoptic Gospels.
synosteography, *n.* se-*nos*-te-*og*-ra-fe, a description of the articulations [Anat.].
synosteology, *n.* se-*nos*-te-*ol*-o-je, the science of or a treatise on the articulations [Anat.]. (Gr. *osteon*, a bone.)
synosteosis, *n.* se-*nos*-te-*oh*-sis, the abnormal osseous union of two or more bones [Path.].
synovia, *n.* se-*noh*-ve-a, the clear viscid albuminous lubricating fluid secreted in the synovial membranes [Anat.]. (L.)
synovial, *a.* se-*noh*-ve-al, relating to or secreting synovia. **synovial membrane,** the delicate membrane that lines the internal surface of joints and secretes synovia.
synovitis, *n.* sin-o-*vy*-tis, inflammation of a synovial membrane.
syntactical, *a.* sin-*tak*-te-kal, pertaining to syntax; according to the rules of syntax.
syntactically, *ad.* in conformity to syntax.
syntactician, *n.* sin-tak-*tish*-an, an authority on or student of syntax.
syntax, *n.* *sin*-taks, the due arrangement of words in sentences according to established usage [Gram.]. (L., from Gr. *tascein*, to arrange.)
synthermal, *a.* sin-*ther*-mal, having the same temperature.
synthesis, *n.* *sin*-the-sis (*pl.* **syntheses**), the putting of two or more things together, esp. as the reverse of analysis; the process of deducing and combining complex ideas from simple ones [Logic]; the reunion of divided parts [Surg.]; the process of uniting elements or simpler compounds into another compound [Chem.]. (Gr. *syn-*, and *thesis*, putting.)
synthesist, *n.* *sin*-the-sist, one who works synthetically.
synthesize, *v.t.* *sin*-the-size, to put things together or form into a whole by synthesis; to produce by synthetic process.
synthetic, *a.* sin-*thet*-ik, pertaining to or consisting in synthesis (opposed to *analytic*); formed by synthesis (as dyes, drugs, artificial rubber, etc.); hence, manufactured, not naturally produced.
synthetical, *a.* sin-*thet*-e-kal, synthetic.
synthetically, *ad.* in a synthetic manner.
synthetize, *v.t.* *sin*-the-tize, synthesize.
syntonic, *a.* sin-*ton*-ik, sharp; intense in quality [Mus.]; tuned in harmony or to the same wave-length (of transmitters, etc.) [Wire.]. (Gr. *syn-*, and *tonic.*)
syntonin, *n.* *sin*-to-nin, the acid albuminous basis and chief constituent of muscular tissue [Chem.]. (Gr. *syn-*, and *teino*, stretch.)
syntonize, *v.t.* *sin*-to-nize, to tune (a wireless set).

syntony, *n.* *sin*-to-ne, resonance [Wire.]; the state of being tuned.
syntropic, *a.* sin-*trop*-ik, similar, and turning in the same direction [Anat.].
sype, *v.i.* sipe, sipe.
sypher, *v.t.* *sy*-fer, to join up flush with overlapping joints [Carp.]. (*cipher.*)
syphiliphobia, *n.* *sif*-il-e-*foh*-be-a, a morbid dread of syphilis [Path.].
syphilis, *n.* *sif*-e-lis, a contagious venereal disease caused by the spirochæte *Treponema pallidum* communicated usually by sexual connexion, but occurring also congenitially and through accidental contact. (From *Syphilus*, name of a shepherd in a 16th-cent. Latin poem.)
syphilitic, *a.* *sif*-e-*lit*-ik, pertaining to or infected with syphilis: *n.* one affected with syphilis.
syphilization, *n.* *sif*-e-ly-*zay*-shon, the state of being inoculated with or infected by the syphilitic virus.
syphiloid, *a.* *sif*-e-loyd, resembling syphilis. (*syphilis*, and Gr. *eidos*, like.).
syphiloma, *n.* sif-e-*loh*-ma, a syphilitic tumour.
syphilomania, *n.* sif-e-lo-*may*-ne-a, a tendency to attribute diseases to syphilis.
syphon, *n.* *sy*-fon, a siphon.
syren, *n.* *sire*-ren, a siren.
Syriac, *a.* *si*-re-ak, pertaining to ancient Syria or its language: *n.* the ancient language of Syria, a dialect of Aramaic.
Syrian, *a.* *si*-re-an, pertaining to or characteristic of Syria or its people: *n.* a native of Syria.
Syringa, *n.* se-*ring*-ga, a genus of plants comprising the lilacs; (*l.c.*) the mock-orange, a garden shrub of the genus *Philadelphus*. (Gr. *syrinx.*)
syringe, *n.* *si*-rinj, a squirt; a cylindrical tube furnished with a piston, into which liquids are drawn and then ejected in a jet, spray, or stream (used in surgery, gardening, etc.): *v.t.* to inject spray, or cleanse, by means of a syringe. (Fr. *syringue.*)
syringeal, *a.* si-*rin*-je-al, pertaining to the vocal organ, or syrinx, of birds.
syringin, *n.* si-*rin*-jin, a crystalline glucoside present in the bark of the lilac, *Syringa vulgaris*.
syringitis, *n.* *si*-rin-*jy*-tis, inflammation of the Eustachian tube.
syringotomy, *n.* si-ring-*got*-o-me, the operation of cutting for fistula. (Gr. *syrinx*, and *tome*, cutting.)
syrinx, *n.* *sire*-rinks, Pan's pipes; the lower larynx of birds, their vocal organ; a tunnel-shaped passage in ancient Egyptian rock-tombs. (Gr., a pipe.)
Syriologist, *n.* si-re-*ol*-o-jist, a student of Syrian antiquities.
syrup, *n.* *si*-rup, a saturated solution of sugar; a vegetable juice or liquid saturated with sugar; treacle. (O.Fr. *syrop*, from Ar. *sharab*, drink.)
syrupy, *a.* si-*rup*-e, like syrup.
syssarcosis, *n.* *sis*-ar-*koh*-sis, the connexion of bones by the muscles. (Gr *syn*-, and *sarx*, *sarkos*, flesh.)
systaltic, *a.* sis-*tal*-tik, alternately contracting and dilating. (Gr. *syn*-, and *stello*, place.)
systasis, *n.* *sis*-ta-sis, a political constitution; political union. (Gr. *syn*-, and *stasis*, standing.)
★**system,** *n.* *sis*-tem, an assemblage of things adjusted into a regular whole; a connected body of principles, theories, doctrine, etc., in any science, religion, or art, etc.; a logical classification; a regular method or order. (L. *systema.*)
systematic, *a.* *sis*-te-*mat*-ik, pertaining to system; consisting in system; methodical; proceeding or formed according to system or regular method.
systematically, *ad.* in a systematic manner.
systematist, *n.* *sis*-te-ma-tist, one who reduces (material, methods, etc.) to system; one who forms a system; one who adheres to a system.
systematization, *n.* *sis*-te-ma-ty-*zay*-shon, the act or process of systematizing; a systematic scheme, arrangement, etc.
systematize, *v.t.* *sis*-te-ma-tize, to reduce to system or regular method.
systematizer, *n.* *sis*-te-ma-*ty*-zer, a systematist.
systematy, *n.* *sis*-te-mat-e, systematic classification.
systemic, *a.* sis-*tem*-ik, of or pertaining to the system as a whole [Phys.].
systemization, *n.* *sis*-tem-e-*zay*-shon, reduction of things to system or method.
systemize, *v.t.* *sis*-tem-ize, to systematize.
systemless, *a.* *sis*-tem-less, without system.
systole, *n.* *sis*-to-le, the period of the heart's contraction; the contraction itself, alternating with the diastole [Anat.]. (Gr. *syn*-, and *stello*, place.)
systolic, *a.* sis-*tol*-ik, pertaining to systole or contraction.
systyle, *n.* *sis*-tile, the method of placing columns at a distance of two diameters apart [Arch.]. (Gr. *syn*-, and *stylos*, a pillar.)
systylous, *a.* *sis*-te-lus, with united styles [Bot.].
syzygial, *a.* se-*zij*-e-al, pertaining to or of the nature of a syzygy.
syzygy, *n.* *siz*-e-je, the conjunction or opposition of a planet with the sun, or of any two of the heavenly bodies; the period of new or full moon, when the sun, moon, and earth are in one line [Astron.]; the union of two parts to form a single segment (esp. of crinoids), also, the fusion of two organisms without loss of identity [Zool.]. (Gr. *syn*-, and *zygon*, a yoke.)

T

T, **tee**, **twentieth letter of the English alphabet, is a** dental or alveolar mute, the correlative of D. It is frequently silent before *l* and *en* (*apostle, castle, listen, often*); before *-ia, -ience, -ion, -ious* and their derivatives, it is pronounced *sh* (*initial, quotient, ration, vexatious*), unless the *t* is preceded by *s* (*celestial, fustian, digestion*); while in southern England when followed by diphthongal *u* (*feature, virtuous, natural, statute*) it frequently approximates the sound of *ch*. The diagraph *th* represents both the sonant sound (*this, brother*) and the breathed (*thin, broth*); the latter is the A.S. letter "thorn," which came to be printed *y*; hence the modern "olde"-fashioned, "Ye Toffee Shoppe," the first word being merely "The"—and properly so pronounced.

ta, *n.* tah, a childish word for "thank you."

Taal, *n.* tahl, the South African dialect of Dutch.

tab, *n.* tab, the latchet of a shoe; the tag of a lace; a flap; a strip sewn on as a distinctive mark: *v.t.* to provide with or mark with a tab.

tabard, *n.* *tab*-ard, an open-sided tunic or mantle worn over armour; a herald's sleeveless coat. (O.Fr.)

tabarder, *n.* *tab*-ard-er, a taberdar.

tabaret, *n.* *tab*-a-ret, a stout, satin-striped silk, used for furniture.

tabasheer, *n.* *tab*-a-sheer, a siliceous concretion found in the stems of bamboos, etc., used as a medicine in the E. Indies. (Ar.)

tabbinet, *n.* *tab*-e-net, tabinet.

tabby, *a.* *tab*-e, having a wavy, variegated appearance; brindled; diversified in colour: *n.* a kind of waved silk, or other stuff, usually watered; a brindled cat; a female cat; a kind of concrete made of lime with shells, gravel, or stones: *v.t.* to impart a watered appearance to. (Ar. *utabi*, a rich watered silk.)

tabefaction, *n.* tab-e-*fak*-shon, a wasting away; a gradual losing of flesh by disease. (*tabes*.)

tabella, *n.* ta-*bel*-la, a small medicinal lozenge.

tabellion, *n.* ta-*bel*-e-on, formerly, a notary or official scribe. (L. *tabellio*.)

taberdar, *n.* *tab*-er-dar, former designation of a foundation scholar of Queen's Coll., Oxford, who originally wore tabards.

tabernacle, *n.* *tab*-er-nak-kl, a tent or movable building, esp. one of the nature of a temple erected by the Israelites for worship during their wanderings in the wilderness; a place of worship (esp. of dissenters); in the Roman Church, an ornamented receptacle for the pyx containing the consecrated elements; a canopied niche, recess, or structure over a tomb, etc. [Arch.]; the human body as a place of temporary sojourn; a socket in which the hinged mast of a river-boat is stepped: *v.i.* to dwell; to reside for a time: *v.t.* to place in a tabernacle. (L. *taberna*, a hut or shed constructed of boards.)

tabernacular, *a.* tab-er-*nak*-yew-lar, formed with delicate tracery, as in an architectural tabernacle.

tabes, *n.* *tay*-beez, a wasting away of the body; atrophy; emaciation [Med.]. (L., from *tabeo*, melt away.)

tabescence, *n.* ta-*bes*-ence, gradual and progressive emaciation [Path.].

tabescent, *a.* ta-*bes*-ent, wasting, or tending to waste, away [Path.].

tabetic, *a.* ta-*bet*-ik, tabid: *n.* one affected with tabes.

tabetiform, *a.* ta-*bet*-e-form, characteristic of or resembling tabes.

tabid, *a.* *tab*-id, affected with tabes; wasted by disease; consumptive.

tabidness, *n.* *tab*-id-ness, tabes; emaciation.

tabification, *n.* tab-e-fe-*kay*-shon, emaciation; tabefaction.

tabinet, *n.* *tab*-e-net, a fabric of silk and wool, resembling poplin or fine damask.

tablature, *n.* *tab*-la-tewr, a painting on a tablet, wall, or a ceiling; a mental image; a former system of musical notation, esp. that for the lute.

***table**, *n.* *tay*-bl, a flat surface of some extent; an article of furniture consisting of a flat surface raised on legs; a board or flat surface on which a game is played; the persons sitting at a table or partaking of entertainment; fare or prandial entertainment; a tablet inscribed, or intended for inscription; an altar; the large top facet of a cut diamond, etc.; a flat surface or simple member, usually rectangular [Arch.]; the outer or inner bony layer of the skull [Anat.]; a contents list of a book, etc.; a synopsis; a system of numbers calculated to be ready for expediting operations [Math.]: *pl.* arithmetical guides to multiplication, weights and measures, money, etc.; formerly, backgammon: *v.i.* to board; to diet or live at the table of another: *v.t.* to form into a table or catalogue; to board; to lay on the table, hence, to defer indefinitely; to let one piece of timber into another by alternate scores or projections from the middle [Carp.]. **astronomical tables**, computations of the motions, places and other phenomena of the heavenly bodies. **the Round Table**, the knighthood instituted by King Arthur. **turn the tables**, to change the condition or fortune of contending parties. **twelve tables**, the basic laws of the ancient Romans. (O.Fr. *tabler*.)

tableau, *n.* *tab*-loh (*pl.* **tableaux**, *tab*-loh), a picture; a striking representation. **tableau vivant** (Fr., living picture), a motionless group of persons, in appropriate dresses, representing some incident, etc. (Fr.)

table-beer, *n.* beer for the table; small beer.

table-book, *n.* a book of arithmetical tables; a book to display on a table.

tablecloth, *n.* *tay*-bl-kloth, a cloth for covering a table, esp. at meals.

table-cover, *n.* a cloth for covering a table, esp. not at meals.

table-d'hôte, *n.* *tah*-bl-*dote*, a complete meal arranged for guests at a restaurant or hotel; an ordinary. (Fr., table of the host.)

tableland, *n.* *tay*-bl-land, an extent of elevated flat land.

table-linen, *n.* linen for the table; napery.

table-money, *n.* an allowance to certain high ranking officers for purposes of hospitality [Mil., etc.]; a fixed charge for use of the dining-room at a club.

tablespoon, *n.* *tay*-bl-spoon, a large spoon for the table.

tablespoonful, *n.* *tay*-bl-spoon-ful, as much as a tablespoon will hold (roughly half a fluid ounce).

tablet, *n.* *tab*-let, a flat monument fixed to a wall; something flat on which to write; a note pad; a medicine or sweetmeat in a flat form.

table-talk, *n.* miscellaneous conversation at or as at table or meals.

table-tennis, *n.* an indoor game resembling lawn tennis played with celluloid balls on a 9 ft. by 5 ft. table; ping-pong.

table-turning, *n.* the act of making a table move without apparent cause, by some ascribed to spiritual agency.

table-ware, *n.* the cutlery, silver, dishes, cruets, etc., used in the service of meals.

tabling, *n.* *tay*-bling, boards and trestles for forming into tables; a setting down in order; the letting of one timber into another by alternate scores or projections [Carp.].

tabloid, *n.* *tab*-loyd, the registered proprietary name of a certain make of compressed medicinal tablets; hence applied adjectivally to drama, stories, periodicals, etc., in a much concentrated form.

taboo, *n.* ta-*boo*, religious or customary prohibition or interdict of certain actions, things, etc., of great force among the Polynesians; a prohibition by general consent; *a.* forbidden or set apart by or as by taboo: *v.t.* to forbid, or to forbid the use of; to interdict approach or use. (Maori *tapu*.)

tabor, *n. tay*-bor, a small drum formerly used to accompany the fife: *v.i.* to play on a tabor; to drum. (O.Fr. *tabour.*)
taborine, *n. tay*-bo-rin, a small tabor played with one hand by a fifer when playing the fife.
tabouret, *n. tab*-oo-ret, a small four-legged seat without arms or back; an embroidery frame. (Fr.)
tabret, *n. tab*-ret, a small tabor.
tabula, *n. tab*-yew-la, an ancient writing-tablet; an altar frontal; either of the bony layers of the skull separated by the diploe [Anat.]. (L.)
tabular, *a. tab*-yew-lar, in the form of a table; set down in a table; computed from tables; having a flat surface; having the form of laminæ or plates. **tabular spar,** a native calcium silicate, one of the pyroxenes.
tabularization, *n. tab*-yew-la-ry-*zay*-shon, tabulation; a tabulated statement.
tabularly, *ad.* in a tabular manner.
tabulate, *a. tab*-yew-late, shaped like a table; arranged in laminæ: *v.t.* to reduce to tables or synopses; to shape with a flat surface.
tabulation, *n.* tab-yew-*lay*-shon, the action of making into an orderly scheme or putting into tables; a table; that which is tabulated.
tabulator, *n. tab*-yew-lay-tor, one who tabulates; a device on a typewriter for facilitating tabulation.
tabulatory, *a.* tab-yew-*lay*-to-re, pertaining to or effected by tabulation.
tacahout, *n. tak*-a-hoot, a gall found on the leaves of the tamarisk, a source of gallic acid.
tacamahac, *n. tak*-a-ma-hak, a resin or elemi yielded by certain tropical trees.
tac-au-tac, *n.* tak-oh-*tak*, a parry combined with a riposte; a rapid succession of attacks and parries [Fencing]. (Fr.)
Tacca, *n. tak*-a, a genus of tropical tuberous herbs, of which *T. pinnatifida* yields South-sea arrowroot.
tace, *v.i. tay*-se, be silent [Mus., etc.]. (L.)
tacet, *v. tay*-set, a term used when a part is to be silent during a whole movement [Mus.]. (L.)
tache, *n.* tash, a catch used for holding; a loop; a button.
tacheometer, *n.* tak-e-*om*-e-ter, a tachymeter.
tachhydrite, *n.* tak-*hy*-drite, a rapidly deliquescing hydrous calcium magnesium chloride. (Gr. *tachys*, quick, *hydor*, water.)
tachometer, *n.* ta-*kom*-e-ter, an instrument for counting revolutions and thereby measuring velocity; a speedometer. (Gr. *tachys*, swift, *metron*, measure.)
tachycardia, *n.* tak-e-*kar*-de-a, abnormally rapid action of the heart [Med.].
tachygen, *n. tak*-e-jen, the unexpected appearance of an organ in evolution; the organ appearing in this manner.
tachygenesis, *n.* tak-e-*jen*-e-sis, accelerated development, esp. by the suppression of one or more embryonic stages [Biol.].
tachygraphic, *a.* tak-e-*graf*-ik, written in shorthand.
tachygraphy, *n.* ta-*kig*-ra-fe, shorthand; ancient stenography, esp. Greek and Roman. (Gr. *tachys*, swift, *grapho*, write.)
tachylite, *n. tak*-e-lite, a black, easily fusible, igneous basaltic glass.
tachymeter, *n.* ta-*kim*-e-ter, a surveying instrument for rapidly determining locations.
tacit, *a. tas*-it, implied but not expressed; understood. (L. *taceo*, am silent.)
tacitly, *ad. tas*-it-le, by implication.
taciturn, *a. tas*-e-turn, habitually silent; not talkative; of few words. (Fr. *taciturne.*)
taciturnity, *n.* tas-e-*tur*-ne-te, habitual silence, or reserve in speaking. (Fr. *taciturnité.*)
taciturnly, *ad.* in a taciturn manner.
tack, *n.* tak, a small nail with a broad head; a lease, or term of a lease [Scots. law]; food [Coll.]; a rope used to fasten the outer lower corner of certain sails [Naut.]; the part of a sail to which such a rope is fastened [Naut.]; the act of tacking [Naut.]; the course of a ship in regard to the position of her sails [Naut.], hence a course of conduct, policy, etc.: *v.t.* to fasten; to attach; to fasten slightly with long stitches; to fasten with tacks: *v.i.* to put a ship about by shifting the tacks and position of the sails from one side to the other [Naut.]; to beat to windward [Naut.]; to change one's policy, etc. **brass tacks,** *see* **brass. hard tack,** ship's biscuit. **soft tack,** bread [Naut.]. (O.Fr. *taque.*)
tacker, *n. tak*-er, one who tacks.
tacket, *n. tak*-et, a hobnail [Scots.].
tackle, *n. tak*-kl, a machine for raising or lowering heavy weights with ropes and pulleys; implements for carrying on a sport (*e.g.* fishing) or other activity; the rigging and apparatus of a ship, harness of a horse, etc.; the act of tackling [Football]: *v.t.* to deal with; to grapple; to lay hold of and stop [Football]. (O. Scand. *taka*, to seize.)
tacksman, *n. taks*-man, a lessee, esp. one who sublets portions of leased land [Scots.].
tacky, *a. tak*-e, slightly adhesive; sticky.
tact, *n.* takt, intuitive skill or faculty, esp. in seeing exactly what to say and do in given circumstances; a stroke in beating time [Mus.]. (L. *tango, tactum*, touch.)
tactful, *a. takt*-ful, gifted with tact.
tactfully, *ad.* with tact; in a tactful manner.
tactic, *n. tak*-tik, an instance of tactical operation [Mil.].
tactical, *a. tak*-te-*kal*, pertaining to tactics.
tactically, *ad.* by means of tactics.
tactician, *n.* tak-*tish*-an, one skilled in tactics.
tactics, *n.pl. tak*-tiks, the science and art of disposing naval or military forces in order for battle, and performing evolutions in the presence of an enemy; a system or a method of action. (Gr. *taktika.*)
tactile, *a. tak*-tile, tangible; pertaining to touch; having the sense of touch [Zool.].
tactility, *n.* tak-*til*-e-te, tangibleness; perceptibility to touch.
taction, *n. tak*-shon, the act or action of touching; tangency.
tactless, *a. takt*-less, destitute of tact; gauche.
tactlessly, *ad.* in a tactless or undiplomatic manner; maladroitly.
tactlessness, *n.* the quality of being tactless; lack of finesse.
tactometer, *n.* tak-*tom*-e-ter, an instrument for testing sensibility of touch.
tactual, *a. tak*-tew-al, pertaining to or of the nature of touch; consisting in or derived from touch.
tactuality, *n.* tak-tew-*al*-e-te, tactual quality.
tactually, *ad. tak*-tew-a-le, by sense of touch.
tadpole, *n. tad*-pole, a frog or toad in its immature larval state. (M.E. *tadde*, toad, and *poll.*)
tadpole-fish, *n.* the lesser forkbeard of the N. Atlantic, *Raniceps raninus.*
tael, *n.* tale, a Chinese weight (1⅓ oz.) and former commercial unit of exchange of varying value but fixed (1933) at 0·715 of the Chinese dollar, or not quite 3*s.* 0*d.*
ta'en, tane, poetical contraction of taken.
tænia, *n. tee*-ne-a (*pl.* **tæniæ**), the tapeworm; a ribbon-like part [Anat.]; the band over the Doric architrave [Arch.] (L., a band, fillet.)
tænian, *a. tee*-ne-an, pertaining to tapeworms.
tænicide, *n. tee*-ne-side, a medicament for destroying tapeworms.
tænioid, *a. tee*-ne-oyd, shaped like or related to the tapeworms.
tafferel, *n. taf*-er-rel, the upper part of a ship's stern, flat at the top, and sometimes ornamented with carved work. (Dut. *tafereel*, a panel.)
taffeta, *n. taf*-e-ta, a fine smooth stuff of silk, wool, or cotton, having usually a wavy lustre, imparted by pressure and heat. (Fr. *taffetas.*)
taffrail, *n. taf*-rale, a rail round the upper part of a vessel's stern. (*tafferel.*)
Taffy, *n. taf*-fe, a Welshman. (*David* or *Davy.*)
tafia, *n. taf*-e-a, a variety of rum, distilled from molasses. (W. Indian.)
tag, *n.* tag, a metallic point put to the end of a string or lace; an appendage, hanging bit, or anything tacked on; a label for tying on; the catchword of an actor's speech; a trite quotation; the game of tig: *v.t* to fit or furnish with a tag; to interlard (a speech, etc.) with tags; to add as an appendage. (Swed. *tagg*, point.)
Tagalog, *n.* ta-*gah*-log, a member of the predominant Malayan race of the Philippines; their language: a pertaining to this race or language.
tag-day, *n.* a flag-day [U.S.A.]
tagger, *n. tag*-er, one who tags; an appliance for removing tag-locks from sheep; very thin sheet-iron coated with tin.

agilite, *n. tag*-e-lite, a bright green hydrous phosphate of copper. (Nizhni *Tagilsk*, in the Urals.)

Tagliacotian, *a. tal*-ya-*koh*-shan, pertaining to Gasparo Tagliacozzi, Ital. surgeon, *d.* 1599. **Tagliacotian operation,** the restoration of a nose by grafting flaps from the forehead and adjacent parts.

ag-lock, *n. tag*-lok, matted wool on sheep; a dag-lock.

ag-rag, *n. tag*-rag, the lowest class of people.

ag-sore, *n. tag*-sore, a pustular sore place occurring under the tail of a sheep.

ag-tail, *n. tag*-tale, a variety of worm with a yellow tail; a sycophant.

aguan, *n. tahg*-wan, the Malayan flying squirrel *Pteromys petaurista*, of the Philippines. (Tagalog.)

ahr, *n.* tar, the Himalayan goat, *Hemitragus jemlaicus*. (Nepalese.)

Tai, *a.* ty, designating the southern group of the Siamese-Chinese family of languages: *n.* Thai. (*Thai.*)

ai, *n.* ty, a valuable food-fish (porgy or sea-bream) of Japanese and north China coasts. (Jap.)

Taic, *n. tay*-ik, the group of languages of Siam and the Indo-Chinese peninsula: *a.* pertaining to these, or to the peoples. (*Thai.*)

aiga, *n. ty*-ga, the swampy pine-forest region of Siberia, at the northern edge of the timber-line, (Russ.)

aigle, *v.t. tay*-gl, to entangle: *v.i.* to tarry; to delay [Scots.]. (Scand.).

***tail,** *n.* tale, the extending prolongation of the backbone of an animal; the lower part or hinder part of anything; an appendage; anything long and hanging like a tail, as a catkin, the train of a comet, the stem of a note [Mus.], etc.; a queue; the rear fins and control surfaces of an aeroplane [Av.]: *v.t.* to furnish with a tail; to cut off at the lower end; to lengthen out as a tail: *v.i.* to follow up closely; to drop off or fall behind; to swing with the tide (of ships) [Naut.]. **tail first,** backwards; with the hinder part foremost. **tail of the trenches,** the post where the besiegers of a fort begin to break ground [Mil.]. **tails up!** in good spirits; optimistic. **tail wind,** a wind coming from behind. **turn tail,** to run away. **with tail between the legs,** dejected, disheartened. (A.S. *tægel.*)

ail, *n.* tale, limitation. **estate in tail,** an estate limited to certain heirs [Law]. (Fr. *tailler*, to cut.)

ail-board, *n.* the hinged or movable board at the back of a cart.

ailcoat, *n.* tale-*koat*, a man's coat with cut-away skirt divided at the back.

ailed, *a.* tayld, having a tail.

ail-end, *n.* the extreme end.

ailflower, *n. tale*-flou-er, any of the flamingo plants.

ailing, *n. tale*-ing, the part of a projecting stone or brick inserted in a wall [Arch.]: *pl.* lighter parts of grain blown to one end of the heap in winnowing; crushed ore from which the metal has been extracted; refuse.

ailless, *a. tale*-less, having no tail.

ail-light, *n. tale*-lite, the red warning light at the rear of a vehicle.

ailor, *n. tay*-lor, one whose occupation is to cut out and make outer garments: *v.i.* to make outer garments: *v.t.* to make or fashion as would a tailor. (Fr. *tailler*, cut.)

ailor-bird, *n.* any of several Asiatic and African birds of the genus *Sutoria*, so called from their habit of sewing leaves together to support its nest.

ailoress, *n. tay*-lo-ress, a woman tailor.

ailoring, *n. tay*-lo-ring, the business of a tailor.

ailpiece, *n. tale*-peece, a subsidiary part; an appendage; an ornamental engraving at the end of a chapter, etc.; a piece of ebony at the end of an instrument, as a violin, to which the strings are fastened; an eyepiece.

ailplane, *n. tale*-plane, the fixed horizontal tail surface of an aeroplane.

ail-race, *n.* the stream of water which runs from a mill after turning the wheel.

ail-spin, *n.* a nose-first dive of an aeroplane, the tail spinning above [Av.]; disaster [Fig.].

ailzie, *n. tale*-ye, a deed creating an entailed estate: *v.t.* to entail [Scots. Law].

ain, *n.* tane, tinfoil for looking-glasses; thin tin-plate. (Fr. *étain*, tin.)

aint, *n.* taynt, a stain; a blemish on reputation; infection; corruption; a depraving influence: *v.t.* to imbue or impregnate with something odious, noxious, or poisonous; to infect; to poison; to corrupt, esp. by putrefaction: *v.i.* to be affected with putrefaction; to become rotten; to tarnish. (O.Fr. *teint.*)

taintless, *a. taynt*-less, free from taint or infection.

taj, *n.* tahj, the conical cap of a dervish. (Ar.)

takable, *a. take*-a-bl, takeable.

takahe, *n. tak*-a-hee, a rare flightless bird, *Notornis mantelli*, of New Zealand, allied to the moorhen. (Maori.)

***take,** *v.t.* take, to get hold or gain possession of; to receive what is offered; to lay hold of; to receive; to catch; to seize; to make prisoner; to captivate; to entrap; to understand, apprehend, or grasp; to be infected or affected with; to put up with or agree to; to consume; to assume; to allow; to rent or hire; to photograph. **take a course,** to resort to. **take advantage of,** to catch by surprise. **take an oath,** to swear with solemnity. **take care,** to be solicitous for; to be cautious. **take care of,** to have the charge of. **take down,** to bring lower; to pull down; to write. **take from,** to deprive of; to subtract; to detract. **take heed,** to be careful. **take in,** to enclose; to comprise; to furl [Naut.]; to cheat or deceive; to accept. **take in hand,** *see* **hand. take in vain,** to mention profanely. **take leave,** to bid adieu; to assume permission. **take notice,** to observe; to make remark upon. **take off,** to remove; to cut off; to destroy; to withdraw; to swallow; to copy; to imitate; to mimic. **take on,** to engage (as an employee); to undertake. **take out,** to remove; to escort; to procure (as a patent); to overcall one's partner [Bridge, etc.]. **take part,** to share; to side. **take place,** to come to pass. **take root,** to live and grow, as a plant. **take the field,** to enter on a campaign. **take to heart,** to be sensibly affected by; to be impressed by. **take up,** to raise; to buy or borrow; to engross; to occupy; to arrest; to adopt; to collect. **take up arms,** to begin war. *p.* **took.** *pp.* **taken.** (A.S. *tacan.*)

***take,** *v.i.* take, to move or direct the course; to deduct something from; to detract; to betake oneself; to please; to gain reception; to have the intended effect; to come out [Phot.]. **take after,** to learn to follow; to resemble. **take for,** to mistake. **take off,** to jump from; to ascend from a position of rest (of aircraft). **take on,** to be violently affected [Coll.]. **take to,** to be fond of; to resort to. **take up with,** to become friendly with. *p.* **took.** *pp.* **taken.**

take, *n.* take, amount received or caught; a turn in drawing from a pool, etc.; a compositor's portion of " copy " for setting [Print.].

takeable, *a. take*-a-bl, capable of being taken.

take-in, *n.* a hoax; a swindle [Coll.].

taken, *tay*-ken, *pp.* of *take.*

take-off, *n.* an imitation or mimicking [Coll.]; the act of jumping from; the spot from which a jump is made; the act of leaving, or the spot from which an aircraft leaves, a position of rest [Av.].

taker, *n. tay*-ker, one who takes (in any sense); one who subdues and causes to surrender.

takin, *n. tay*-kin, a large ruminant, *Budorcas taxicolor*, of the Tibetan mountains, allied to the goats and antelopes. (Tib.)

taking, *a. tay*-king, alluring; attracting; infectious: *n.* the act of gaining possession; seizure; agitation; distress of mind: *pl.* receipts.

takingly, *ad.* in a taking manner.

takingness, *n.* the quality of pleasing.

takosis, *n.* ta-*koh*-sis, a contagious bacterial wasting disease of goats [Vet.]. (Gr. *tekein*, to waste away.)

talapoin, *n. tal*-a-poyn, a Buddhist priest or mendicant monk of Burma, Indo-China, etc.; the small West African monkey, *Cercopithecus talapoin.*

talaria, *n.pl.* ta-*lare*-re-a, the wings or winged sandals attached to the ankles of Mercury. (L. *talus*, ankle.)

talbot, *n. tawl*-bot, a variety of quick-scented stag-hound now extinct.

talbotype, *n. tawl*-bo-tipe, the process, invented by Fox Talbot, of producing a photographic image on the surface of sensitized paper; a photograph so obtained. (Fox *Talbot*, *d.* 1877, inventor, and *type.*)

talc, *n.* talk, a greasy hydrated silicate of magnesium; laminated steatite; mica. (Fr., from Ar. *talq.*)
talcite, *n.* *tal*-kite, a variety of talc; nacrite.
talcky, *a.* *tal*-ke, talcose.
talcose, *a.* *tal*-kohs, pertaining to, containing, or composed of talc.
talcum, *n.* *tal*-kum, talc. **talcum powder,** a toilet preparation composed of perfumed powdered talc or french-chalk.
tale, *n.* tale, a story; a narrative, true or fictitious; a legend; an anecdote; reckoning; number reckoned; information; disclosure of anything secret. **tell tales out of school,** to reveal private matters in public; to blab. **tell the tale,** to attempt to excite sympathy with a hard-luck story, etc. (A.S. *talu,* number, narrative.)
tale-bearer, *n.* a person who makes mischief by maliciously telling tales.
tale-bearing, *n.* the practice of telling tales with mischievous intent.
Talegallus, *n.* *tal*-le-*gal*-us, the genus of the Australian mound-birds; (*l.c.*) the brush-turkey, *Alectura lathami.*
talent, *n.* *tal*-ent, anciently, a standard weight and a monetary unit, varying at different periods and among different nations, the later Attic weight averaging about 57 lb., and the money from £220 to £250; a faculty; natural gift or endowment; eminent abilities; superior genius; skill; quality; disposition. (Fr., from L. *talentum.*)
talented, *a.* *tal*-en-ted, furnished with talents; possessing skill or talents.
talentless, *a.* *tal*-ent-less, without talent.
taler, *n.* *tah*-ler, thaler. (Ger.)
tales, *n.pl.* *tay*-leez, persons in court from whom the sheriff may select men to supply any deficiency of jurors; also the supply, or the act of supplying, such men [Law]. (L., of such kind.)
talesman, *n.* *tay*-lez-man, a member of a tales [Law].
tale-teller, *n.* one who tells tales or stories.
Taliacotian, *a.* *tal*-ya-*koh*-shan, Tagliacotian.
talion, *n.* *tal*-e-on, the law of retaliation, "a tooth for a tooth." (L. *talio.*)
talionic, *a.* tal-e-*on*-ik, pertaining to the law of talion.
taliped, *a.* *tal*-e-ped, having a club-foot: *n.* a club-footed person.
talipes, *n.* *tal*-e-peez, club-foot. (L. *talus,* the ankle, *pes,* the foot.)
talipot, *n.* *tal*-e-pot, the great South Indian fan-palm, *Corypha umbraculifera.*
talisman, *n.* *tal*-iz-man, an amulet; a charm; a wonder-working stone, etc.; something that produces extraordinary effects. (Ar. and Gr.)
talismanic, *a.* tal-iz-*man*-ik, having the properties of a talisman; magical.
***talk,** *n.* tawk, familiar converse; mutual discourse; report; rumour; subject of discourse: *v.i.* to speak or converse familiarly; to have the power of speech; to utter sounds resembling speech: *v.t.* to speak; to utter; to persuade. **talk big,** to boast. **talk down,** to silence by loud or voluble talk; to give a pilot whose position is known by radar wireless instructions assisting him to ground his plane. **talk down to,** to speak to patronizingly, or as to an intellectual inferior. **talk of,** to relate; to speak; to discuss. **talk out,** to avoid a conclusion by prolonging the proceedings by talk. **talk over,** to discuss, to consider co-operatively; to persuade by talk or argument. **talk to,** to advise or exhort; to reprove. (M.E. *talken,* A.S. *talian,* speak.)
talkative, *a.* *taw*-ka-tiv, given to much talking.
talkatively, *ad.* in a talkative manner.
talkativeness, *n.* the quality of being talkative.
talkee-talkee, *n.* *taw*-ke-*taw*-ke, pidgin English; blather.
talker, *n.* *taw*-ker, one who talks; a loquacious person; a conversationalist.
talkies, *n.pl.* *taw*-kez, cinema pictures with which dialogue, etc., is mechanically reproduced.
talking, *a.* *taw*-king, able to talk; given to talking; loquacious: *n.* the act of conversing familiarly. **a good talking to,** a scolding. **talking point,** a particular item, or an argument, used by a salesman to promote a sale [Comm.].
talky, *a.* *taw*-ke, talkative; superabundant in talk: *n.* excessive verbiage; mere chatter.

***tall,** *a.* tawl, high in stature; long in height; big almost incredible [Coll.]. (Origin unknown.)
tallage, *n.* *tal*-aj, a tax or subsidy imposed on town and demesne lands under the crown, abolished i 1340.
tallboy, *n.* *tawl*-boy, a tall chest of drawers; a lon zinc chimney-pot.
tallier, *n.* *tal*-e-er, one who keeps a tally.
tallish, *a.* *tawl*-ish, rather tall.
tallith, *n.* *tal*-ith, a tasselled scarf worn by mal Jews at morning prayer; a prayer shawl. (Heb., covering.)
tallness, *n.* *tawl*-ness, the state or quality of bein tall.
tallow, *n.* *tal*-oh, animal fat melted down: *v.t.* t grease with tallow; to fatten; to cause to have large quantity of tallow: *v.i.* to produce or yiel tallow (esp. of cattle). **tallow tree,** any of severa tropical trees, esp. the Chinese tree *Excæcari sebifera,* yielding a tallow-like substance; also th bayberry, wax-myrtle, etc. (M.E. *talgh.*)
tallow-chandler, *n.* one whose occupation is t make, sell, or make and sell, tallow candles.
tallowish, *a.* *tal*-oh-ish, having the properties o tallow; tallow-like; greasy.
tallowy, *a.* *tal*-oh-e, tallowish.
tally, *n.* *tal*-e, one of two pieces of wood on whic corresponding notches or scores are cut, as th marks of number; one thing made as the counter part or complement of another; a tag or label *v.t.* to score with corresponding notches; to fit; t suit; *v.i.* to be fitted; to correspond. **tally system,** the system of giving and receiving good on credit to be paid for by periodical instalments (Fr. *tailler,* cut.)
tally-ho, *n.* and *int.* tal-e-*hoh,* one of the hunts man's calls to his hounds: *v.i.* to utter this call.
tallyman, *n.* *tal*-e-man, one (formerly a pedlar) wh sells for weekly or monthly payments; the keepe of a tally-shop; a tallier.
tally-shop, *n.* a shop trading on the tally system payment by purchasers being made periodically.
talma, *n.* *tal*-ma, a long cape. (The Fr. tragedia F. J. *Talma, d.* 1826.)
Talmud, *n.* *tal*-mud, the fundamental code of th Jewish civil and canonical law, consisting of th Mishna (text) and Gemara (commentary). (Heb.
talmudic, *a.* tal-*mud*-ik *or* *tal*-mu-dik, pertaining t or contained in the Talmud.
talmudist, *n.* *tal*-mu-dist, one versed in the Talmud
talmudistic, *a.* tal-mu-*dis*-tik, relating to o resembling the Talmud.
talon, *n.* *tal*-on, the claw of a bird of prey; a heel like part or projection; the remainder of th pack after dealing [Cards]; an ogee moulding [Arch.]. (Fr.)
taloned, *a.* *tal*-ond, furnished with talons.
Talpa, *n.* *tal*-pa, the genus of mammals which include the mole; (*l.c.*) a wen [Med.]. (L.)
taluk, *n.* ta-*look,* in India, a small administrativ district; a tract of proprietary land, usually subordinate to a zemindary. (Urdu.)
talukdar, *n.* ta-*look*-dar, the native administrato or proprietor of a taluk.
talus, *n.* *tay*-lus, the astragalus or ankle bon [Anat.]; a slope or sloping work, bastion, rampart etc. [Fort]; a sloping heap of broken rocks an stones at the foot of a cliff [Geol.]. (L., the ankle.
tamability, *n.* tay-ma-*bil*-e-te, tamableness.
tamable, *a.* *tay*-ma-bl, that may be tamed or subdued.
tamableness, *n.* quality of being tamable.
tamandua, *n.* ta-*man*-dwa, a small arboreal tropica American anteater, *Tamandra tectradactyle,* having a long prehensile tail. (Brazilian.)
tamanoir, *n.* tah-mah-*nwahr,* the ant-bear of S America. (Fr., from Brazilian.)
tamara, *n.* *tam*-a-ra, a condiment consisting o powdered cinnamon, coriander seeds, and clove with fennel seed and aniseed. (*tamarind.*)
tamarack, *n.* *tam*-a-rak, the American larch.
tamarin, *n.* *tam*-a-rin, any of the species of smal South American marmoset of the genus *Midas* wit fine silky hair and a tail like a squirrel.
tamarind, *n.* *tam*-a-rind, the tropical leguminou tree *Tamarindus indica*; its fruit or seed-pod having an acid pulp and used in medicine. (Ar.
tamarisk, *n.* *tam*-a-risk, any ornamental evergree tree or shrub of the species *Tamarix.*

tamasha, *n.* ta-*mah*-sha, a public function or entertainment [Anglo-Ind.]. (Urdu, *masha*, to walk.)
tambour, *n. tam*-boor, a drum; a drummer; the naked ground of the Corinthian capital [Arch.]; one of the cylindrical blocks forming the shaft of a column [Arch.]; a drum-like frame on which embroidery is worked, also the embroidery worked on this; a close palisade defending an entrance [Fort.]: *v.t.* to embroider on a tambour. (Fr.)
tambourine, *n.* tam-boo-*reen*, a small shallow single-headed drum with jingles round it; a lively Provençal dance, and its music. (*tambour*.)
tambreet, *n.* tam-*breet*, the duck-billed platypus [Austral.]. (Aboriginal New South Wales.)
tame, *a.* tame, that has lost its native wildness and shyness; domesticated; docile; depressed; spiritless; insipid; dull: *v.t.* to reduce from a wild into a domestic state; to make gentle and familiar; to civilize; to subdue. (A.S. *tam.*)
tameless, *a. tame*-less, wild; untamable.
tamely, *ad. tame*-le, in a tame manner.
tameness, *n. tame*-ness, the quality of being tame; unresisting submission; want of spirit.
tamer, *n. tame*-er, one who tames or subdues.
Tamil, *n. tam*-il, one of a non-Aryan Dravidian race inhabiting southern India and northern Ceylon: their language: *a.* pertaining to the Tamil people or their language.
tamis, *n. tam*-e, tammy; a strainer made of this.
Tammany, *n. tam*-a-ne, a Democratic organization of New York City, now a byword for political corruption, but originally a fraternal and benevolent society, founded 1789. (*Tammany*, name of an Indian chief.)
Tammuz, *n. tah*-mooz, Thammuz.
tammy, *n. tam*-e, a thin worsted stuff, sometimes highly glazed; a tam-o'-shanter.
tam-o'-shanter, *n. tam*-o-*shan*-ter, a broad flat cap or bonnet of knitted wool, named after "Tam o' Shanter" of the poem by Robert Burns.
tamp, *v.t.* tamp, to stop up a hole bored in a rock for blasting so as to confine the explosion.
tampan, *n. tam*-pan, a venomous South African tick.
tamper, *v.i. tam*-per, to meddle; to try little experiments; to adulterate; to bribe (used with *with*).
tamping, *n. tam*-ping, the act of the verb *to tamp*; the plug used in tamping.
tampion, *n. tam*-pe-un, a stopper for the mouth of a cannon, or for the top of an organ-pipe.
tampon, *n. tam*-pon, a tampion; a plug for insertion into a cavity for arresting hæmorrhage, absorbing secretions, or applying medicaments: *v.t.* to plug with this [Surg.]. (Fr.)
tamponade, *n.* tam-po-*nade*, tamponage.
tamponage, *n. tam*-po-naj, the employment of, or method of using, a tampon [Surg.].
tam-tam, *n. tam*-tam, a tom-tom.
tan, *a.* tan, as if tanned; brown: *n.* bark bruised and broken by a mill, for tanning hides; tan refuse laid down as a soft riding or driving surface; the colour of tan; the bronze complexion acquired through exposure to the sun: *v.t.* to convert (raw hides) into leather by means of tannin; to make brown, esp. by exposure to the rays of the sun; to thrash [Coll.]: *v.i.* to become tanned. **tan pickle,** the infusion used in tanning. **spent tan,** tan refuse. (Fr., probably from Celtic.)
tan, *n.* tan, a tangent [Geom.]. (Abbrev.)
tana, *n. tah*-na, an Indian police station. (Hind).
tanadar, *n.* tah-na-*dahr*, the chief officer of a tana. (Hind.)
tanager, *n. tan*-a-jer, an American bird of beautiful plumage, allied to the finches. (Brazilian.)
Tanagra, *n. tan*-a-gra, an ancient terracotta statuette such as originally found in tombs near Tanagra, Bœotia.
tanagrine, *a. tan*-a-grine, pertaining to the tanagers; tanagroid.
tanagroid, *a. tan*-a-groyd, resembling or akin to the tanagers.
tan-bed, *n. tan*-bed, a bed made of tan [Hort.].
tandem, *ad. tan*-dem, with two (esp. horses) placed one before the other: *n.* a vehicle with horses so harnessed; a cycle for two riders, one seated behind the other. **tandem engine,** a steam-engine with two or more cylinders in line having a common piston-rod. (L., at length.)
tang, *n.* tang, a strong taste, particularly of something extraneous to the thing itself; a smack or flavour; something that leaves a sting or pain behind; the tapering part of a knife or tool, which fits into the handle: *v.t.* to furnish with a tang. (*tongue.*)
tang, *n.* tang, a ringing sound: *v.t.* and *i.* to twang; to make or cause to make a clanging noise. (Imit.)
tang, *n.* tang, a coarse variety of seaweed. (Scand.)
tangency, *n. tan*-jen-se, the state or quality of being tangent; a contact or touching.
tangent, *n. tan*-jent, a right line which touches a curve, but which, when produced, does not cut it [Geom.]: *a.* (of lines and curves) touching or meeting at a point but not intersecting [Geom.]. **tangent of an arc,** a right line drawn touching one extremity of the arc, and limited by a secant or line drawn through the centre and the other extremity [Trig.]. (Fr.)
tangential, *a.* tan-*jen*-shal, pertaining to or in the direction of a tangent.
tangentially, *ad.* in the direction of a tangent.
tangerine, *n. tan*-je-*reen*, a small scented orange of a flattened shape; a yellowish-red colour; (*cap.*) a native of Tangier: *a.* pertaining to Tangier or its people. (Tangier.)
tanghin, *n. tang*-gin, a Madagascan tree, the kernel of the fruit of which yields a deadly poison formerly used by natives in trial by ordeal; this poison. (Malagasy.)
tangibility, *n.* tan-je-*bil*-e-te, tangibleness; perceptibility to the touch.
tangible, *a. tan*-je-bl, perceptible to the touch; touchable; real; that may be possessed or realized. (Fr., from L. *tangibilis.*)
tangibleness, *n.* the quality of being tangible.
tangibly, *ad. tan*-je-ble, in a tangible manner.
tangle, *n. tang*-gl, a knot of threads or other things united confusedly and not easily disengaged; a coarse kind of seaweed: *v.t.* to unite or knit together confusedly; to interweave; to ensnare; to embarrass: *v.i.* to become entangled. (Scand.)
tangle-fish, *n.* any of the pipefishes; one of the needle-fish.
tanglefoot, *n. tangl*-foot, any highly intoxicating liquor [U.S.A. slang].
tangle-picker, *n.* the shore-bird *Strepsilas interpres*, the turnstone.
tanglingly, *ad.* united in a tangling manner.
tangly, *a. tang*-gle, covered with tangle; tangled.
tango, *n. tang*-goh (*pl.* **tangos**), a French ballroom version of a Spanish-American dance for pairs; *v.i.* to dance this.
tangoist, *n. tang*-go-ist, an accomplished tango dancer.
tangram, *n. tang*-gram, a Chinese puzzle composed of seven pieces which can be united in various ways.
tangy, *a. tang*-e, flavoured by or suggestive of a tang.
tan-house, *n.* a building in which tanning is carried on or tanner's bark is stored.
tanist, *n. tan*-ist, in ancient Ireland, the elected heir apparent to a chief or landed proprietor. (Gael. *tanaiste*, second in rank.)
tanistry, *n. tan*-is-tre, in ancient Ireland, a tenure of lands only for life, the successor being appointed from among the kinsmen of the holder by election.
tank, *n.* tank, a large basin or cistern; a reservoir; the water-container for the boiler of a locomotive; a large self-propelling heavily armed and armoured car running on a tractor [Mil.]: *v.t.* to store in a tank. **tank engine,** a locomotive carrying its fuel and water and requiring no tender. **tank up,** to fill the tank (of a motor-car); to indulge in a drinking-bout [Slang]. (Probably Port. *tanque*, a pond.)
Tanka, *n. tang*-ka, a member of an aboriginal tribe of Cantonese, now dwelling in boats at Canton. (Chin. *tan*, egg, and Cantonese, *ka*, people.)
tankage, *n. tang*-kaj, storage in tanks; charge for this; the capacity of a tank or tanks; refuse from tanks.
tankard, *n. tang*-kard, a drinking vessel with a handle (and sometimes a lid), esp. one of metal. (Perhaps *tank.*)
tanker, *n. tang*-ker, a ship built for carrying petroleum, molasses, or other liquid in bulk.
tanling, *n. tan*-ling, one tanned by the sun.
tannable, *a. tan*-a-bl, capable of being tanned.
tannage, *n. tan*-aj, the process or the product of tanning.

tannate, *n.* *tan*-at, a salt of tannic acid.
tanner, *n.* *tan*-er, one whose occupation is to tan hides.
tanner, *n.* *tan*-er, sixpence [Slang]. (Origin uncertain.)
tannery, *n.* *tan*-er-re, an establishment where tanning is carried on; the trade or process of tanning.
tannic, *a.* *tan*-ik, pertaining to or derived from tannin.
tannin, *n.* *tan*-in, a bitter and astringent substance obtained from the gall of certain oaks, sumac, etc., used in tanning, dyeing, ink manufacture, and medicine; tannic acid. (Fr. *tanin.*)
tan-pit, *n.* a tan-vat; a tan-bed [Hort.].
tanrec, *n.* *tan*-rek, the tenrec [Zool.].
tan-spud, *n.* a tool for peeling the bark from oak and other trees.
tan-stove, *n.* a hot-house with a bark-bed.
tansy, *n.* *tan*-ze, a bitter aromatic herbaceous plant of the genus *Tanacetum*; a dish flavoured with tansy. (O.Fr. *tanasie.*)
tantalate, *n.* *tan*-ta-late, a salt of tantalic acid.
tantalic, *a.* tan-*tal*-ik, pertaining to or derived from tantalum.
tantalite, *n.* *tan*-ta-lite, a mineral composed chiefly of iron tantalate, with a a little magnesium and niobium.
tantalization, *n.* *tan*-ta-ly-*zay*-shon, the act of tantalizing.
tantalize, *v.t.* *tan*-ta-lize, to torment by presenting some good to the view and exciting desire, but continually frustrating the expectation by withholding it; to tease. (*Tantalus.*)
tantalizer, *n.* *tan*-ta-ly-zer, one who tantalizes.
tantalum, *n.* *tan*-ta-lum, a hard silvery-white metallic element of the vanadium group, formerly used for electric lamp filaments.
tantalus, *n.* *tan*-ta-lus, a spirit-stand in which the decanters are visible but cannot be opened without the key. **tantalus cup,** a scientific toy demonstrating the principle of the siphon. (*Tantalus,* of Gr. myth, who, though ever within reach of sustenance, was condemned to perpetual hunger and thirst.)
tantamount, *a.* *tan*-ta-mount, equivalent to in value or signification. (L. *tantus,* so great, and *amount.*)
tantara, *n.* *tan*-ta-ra *or* tan-*tah*-ra, a fanfare; a series of notes on a trumpet, etc. (Imit.)
tantivy, *ad.* tan-*tiv*-e, with great speed, as "to ride tantivy": *n.* a rapid gallop: *int.* a hunting cry, an imitation of a flourish on the horn. (Imit., probably of galloping hoofs.)
tantony, *n.* *tan*-to-ne, the smallest pig in a litter. (St. *Anthony,* patron saint of swineherds.)
tantra, *n.* *tan*-tra, a class of Hindu sacred writings treating chiefly of magical and sexual powers. (Sans.)
tantric, *a.* *tan*-trik, pertaining to the tantras.
tantrism, *n.* *tan*-trizm, the system or doctrine of the tantras.
tantrist, *n.* *tan*-trist, a student of the tantras; an adherent of tantrism.
tantrum, *n.* *tan*-trum, a fit or burst of ill-temper.
tan-vat, *n.* a vat in which hides are steeped in tan.
tan-yard, *n.* a tannery.
Taoism, *n.* *tah*-o-izm, a religious and philosophical system of China founded by Lao-tsze in the 6th cent. B.C.
Taoist, *n.* *tah*-o-ist, an adherent of Taoism: *a.* pertaining to Taoism.
tap, *n.* tap, a gentle blow; a slight blow with a small thing; a tool for cutting a screw in a drilled hole; a cock for drawing off, or regulating the flow of, a liquid or gas; a spile or short pipe for drawing liquor from a cask; a tap-room; a half sole (Shoe-repairing): *v.t.* to strike with something small; to touch gently; to pierce or broach a cask; to open a cask and draw liquor; to pierce for letting out fluid; to make a female screw in; to divert gas, electric current, etc., esp. to intercept a message thus; to borrow from [Coll.]; to tap-dance; to repair (a shoe, etc.) with a tap; to perform paracentesis [Surg.]: *v.i.* to strike a gentle blow. (A.S. *tæppa.*)
tapa, *n.* *tah*-pa, the inner bark of certain Polynesian trees, esp. the paper mulberry; a cloth made from this. (Native.)
tap-bolt, *n.* a headed screwbolt used without a nut.
tap-cinder, *n.* the slag produced in the furnace during the puddling of iron.
tap-dance, *n.* *tap*-dahnce, a type of dance in which syncopated rhythm is accompanied by audible tapping with the feet: *v.i.* to dance thus.
tape, *n.* tape, a narrow band of woven cloth, used as strings and in dressmaking, book-binding, etc.; a narrow flexible band or strip; a tape-measure; the string stretched across a race-course at the finishing line; the paper strip on which messages are recorded by a tape-machine: *v.t.* to bind, strengthen, or tie up with tape; to measure with a tape; to size up [Coll.]. **red tape,** *see* **red.** (A.S. *tæppe.*)
tape-machine, *n.* the automatically printing receiving instrument of a recording telegraph.
tape-measure, *n.* a tape, or flexible strip of metal, marked with inches, or centimetres, etc., used in measuring.
taper, *n.* *tay*-per, a thin wax-candle; a small light; a tapering form: *a.* slenderly conical; long and becoming gradually thinner towards one end: *v.i.* and *t.* to become or make gradually smaller in diameter. (A.S. *tapur.*)
taperingly, *ad.* *tay*-per-ring-le, in a tapering manner.
taperness, *n.* the state of being taper.
tapestried, *a.* *tap*-es-trid, covered or hung with tapestry.
tapestry, *n.* *tap*-es-tre, a reversible hand-woven fabric in colours, often representing figures, flowers, or landscapes; a non-reversible machine-made ornamental textile; *v.t.* to hang or adorn with tapestry. (Fr. *tapis.*)
tapeti, *n.* *tap*-e-te, the Brazilian hare, *Lepus brasiliensis,* a small S. American rabbit.
tapetum, *n.* ta-*pee*-tum, a part of the choroid membrane of the eye in some animals [Anat.]; a layer of cells which lines the cavity of anthers in flowering plants or of the sporangium in ferns [Bot.]. (L.)
tapeworm, *n.* *tape*-wurm, a ribbon-like worm of the genus *Tænia,* parasitic in the intestines of man and many animals.
tapioca, *n.* tap-e-*oh*-ka, a granular farinaceous foodstuff prepared from cassava.
tapir, *n.* *tay*-peer, a family of ungulates allied to the rhinoceros, all but one species of which (*Tapirus indicus,* of Malaya), are South American. (Tupi.)
tapiroid, *a.* *tay*-pe-royd, resembling or characteristic of the tapirs: *n.* a tapir.
tapis, *n.* *tap*-ee, tapestry (formerly used as a table-covering). **upon the tapis,** under consideration. (Fr., carpet.)
tapotement, *n.* (App.), the slapping movement in massage [Med.]. (Fr., a thrumming.)
tappable, *a.* *tap*-a-bl, capable of being tapped.
tapper, *n.* *tap*-er, one who or that which taps; a telegraph key; a form of decoherer [Wire.]
tappet, *n.* *tap*-et, a projection or small lever on a moving shaft working some part of a machine by striking it at intervals; a cam.
tapping, *n.* *tap*-ing, the operation of drawing fluid accumulated in the body [Surg.]; a connexion made at some point between the ends of an inductance or a resistance [Elect. and Wire.].
tappit, *a.* *tap*-it, crested. **tappit hen,** a hen with a tuft of feathers on the head; a lidded drinking-vessel containing about three quarts [Scots.].
tap-room, *n.* a room in a public-house or brewery in which beer is retailed.
tap-root, *n.* the main root of a plant which penetrates deep into the ground.
taps, *n.* taps, the signal (by drum or bugle, etc.) for "lights out"—sounded also at funerals [U.S.A. Mil. and Nav.].
tapsalteerie, *a.* *tap*-sal-*teer*-re, topsy-turvy [Scots.].
tapster, *n.* *tap*-ster, one employed to draw and serve ale or other liquor; a barman. (A.S. *taeppestre,* a female tapster.)
tar, *n.* tahr, a dark viscous substance obtained by destructive distillation from wood, coal, or other organic material: *v.t.* to smear with tar. **mineral tar,** a soft native bitumen. (A.S. *teru.*)
tar, *n.* tahr, an ordinary seaman. **Jack Tar,** a seaman in the Royal Navy. (*tarpaulin.*)
taradiddle, *n.* *ta*-ra-did-dl, tarradiddle.
tara-fern, *n.* *tah*-ra-fern, the native name for *Pteris esculenta,* the root-stock of which is edible. (Maori.)

tarantass, *n.* ta-ran-*tass*, a low four-wheeled Russian carriage without springs. (Russ.)
tarantella, *n. ta*-ran-*tel*-a, a lively Neapolitan dance for couples, fabled to be a cure for tarantula bites; music for this.
tarantism, *n. ta*-ran-tizm, an epidemic dancing mania ascribed to the bite of the tarantula.
tarantula, *n.* ta-*ran*-tew-la, a large venomous spider of the genus *Lycosa*, whose bite was much dreaded. (*Taranto*, in Italy, where it abounded).
taraxacine, *n.* ta-*rak*-sa-sin, a bitter crystalline substance extracted from the root of the dandelion.
Taraxacum, *n.* ta-*rak*-sa-kum, the genus of composite plants including the dandelion, *T. officinale*; (*l.c.*) a laxative prepared from dandelion-root [Pharm.]. (Gr.)
tarboosh, *n. tahr*-boosh, a fez [Ar.].
tarbrush, *n. tahr*-brush, a brush for applying tar. **a touch of the tarbrush,** a strain of Negro blood [Coll.].
tardamente, *ad.* tar-da-*men*-te, to be played slowly [Mus.]. (It.)
Tardenoisian, *a.* tar-de-*noy*-ze-an, designating of Stone Age culture of the later Paleolithic, characterized by pygmy flints. (Fr., Fère-en-*Tardenois*, Aisne, N. France.)
tardigrade, *a. tahr*-de-grade, moving or stepping slowly [Zool.]; pertaining to the sloths: *n.* a member of the *Tardigrada*, a former classification comprising the sloths [Zool.]. (L. *tardus*, slow, *gradus*, a step.)
tardily, *ad.* in a tardy manner.
tardiness, *n.* slowness; unwillingness; lateness.
tardo, *ad. tahr*-doh, slowly [Mus.]. (It.)
tardy, *a. tahr*-de, slow; late; dilatory; out of season; reluctant. (Fr. *tard*.)
tare, *n.* tare, any of the vetches; in the Bible, a weed growing amongst corn, perhaps darnel.
tare, *n.* tare, an allowance or abatement from the gross weight of goods, in consideration of the weight of the cask or other container [Comm.]: *v.t.* to ascertain or mark the amount of tare. (Fr., from Ar. through Sp.)
targe, *n.* tarj, a small light shield. (O.Fr.)
target, *n. tahr*-get, a small shield or buckler; a mark to fire at; any object of attack, a stage, goal, etc., to be attained [Fig.]; the neck and breast of lamb [Cookery]. (O.Fr. *targe*.)
targeteer, *n.* tahr-ge-*teer*, a soldier furnished with a target or shield.
Targum, *n. tahr*-gum, a version or paraphrase of the Old Testament in Aramiac. (Aramaic, interpretation.)
Targumic, *a.* tahr-*goo*-mik, pertaining to the Targums.
Targumist, *n. tahr*-gum-ist *or* tahr-*goo*-mist, the writer of a Targum; one versed in the Targums.
tariff, *n. ta*-rif, a list or table of goods with the duties to be paid on importation or exportation; a list of charges or prices: *v.t.* to make such a list. **tariff wall,** a range of customs duties restraining imports. (Fr. *tariffe*, from Ar. *ta'rif*, information.)
tarlatan, *n. tahr*-la-tan, a stiff transparent kind of muslin. (Fr.)
tarmac, *n. tar*-mak, proprietary name of a mixture of ironstone slag with tar and creosote, used in road-making; a runway (Av.]. (*tar* and *macadam*.)
tarn, *n.* tahrn, a marsh; a small mountain lake. (Ice. *tjörn*.)
tarnation, *int.* tahr-*nay*-shon, damnation [U.S.A. Slang].
tarnish, *v.t. tahr*-nish, to sully; to diminish or destroy the lustre or purity of: *v.i.* to lose lustre; to become dull: *n.* state of being tarnished; a stain; discoloration. (Fr. *se ternir*, render dim.)
taro, *n. tahr*-roh, a tropical plant of the arum family, esp. *Colocasia esculenta*; the edible starchy root-stock of this.
taroc, *n. tahr*-rok, tarot.
tarot, *n. tahr*-roh, an early kind of playing card, 78 of which composed a pack; a game with these, formerly played in Italy. (Fr., from It. *tarroco*.)
tarpan, *n. tahr*-pan, the small wild horse of Central Asia. (Tartar.)
tarpaulin, *n.* tahr-*paw*-lin, canvas covered with tar to render it waterproof; a sailor or tar [Slang]. (*tar*, and *pall*-ing, a covering.)
tarpon, *n. tahr*-pon, a large and powerful game-fish, *Megalops atlanticus*, the jew-fish, the giant of the herring family.
tarradiddle, *n. ta*-ra-did-dl, a fib; a lie [Coll.].
tarragon, *n. ta*-ra-gon, the savoury herb, *Artemisia dracunculus*. **tarragon vinegar,** vinegar flavoured with tarragon. (Through Sp. and Ar. from Gr. *drakon*, dragon.)
tarragona, *n.* ta-ra-*gon*-a, a Spanish wine of the port kind. (Name of Sp. town.)
tarras, *n. ta*-ras. trass.
tarriance, *n. ta*-re-ance, delay; the act of tarrying; a temporary sojourn.
tarrier, *n. ta*-re-er, one who tarries.
tarrock, *n. ta*-rok, the young kittiwake; the arctic tern, *Sterna macrura*.
tarry, *v.i. ta*-re, to stay; to stay behind; to wait; to delay; to linger: *v.t.* to wait for. (A.S. *tergan*.)
tarry, *a. tahr*-re, consisting of, smeared with, or like tar.
tarsal, *a. tahr*-sal, pertaining to the tarsus.
tarsalgia, *n.* tahr-*sal*-je-a, pain in the foot.
tarsi, *n. tahr*-sy, *pl.* of *tarsus*.
tarsia, *n. tahr*-se-a, a beautiful kind of marquetry or mosaic wood-work made in mediæval Italy. (It.)
tarsier, *n. tahr*-se-er, a nocturnal arboreal East Indian lemur of the genus *Tarsius*.
tarsoid, *a. tar*-se-oyd, pertaining to the tarsiers: *n.* any lemur of the genus *Tarsius*.
tarsus, *n. tahr*-sus (*pl.* **tarsi**), that part of the foot between the leg and metatarsus, including the ankle; the third segment of a bird's leg; the end leg-segment in insects and crustaceans. (Gr. *tarsos*.)
tart, *a. tart*, acid; sharp to the taste; sharp; severe. (A.S. *teart*, from *tearan*, tear.)
tart, *n.* tart, a pie containing fruit; a tartlet. (O Fr. *tarte*, of uncertain origin.)
tart, *n.* tart, [Slang] a sweetheart; any attractive woman or girl, esp. one of sexual tendencies; a prostitute.
tartan, *n. tahr*-tan, a chequered woollen fabric of various patterns and colours, worn in the Scottish Highlands, each pattern being distinctive of a particular clan; a kilt, plaid, etc., of this: *a.* consisting of or resembling tartan. (Origin unknown.)
tartan, *n. tahr*-tan, a small Mediterranean coasting vessel with one mast and a lateen sail. (Fr. *tartane*.)
tartar, *n. tahr*-tar, impure tartrate of potassium, formed from wines completely fermented and adhering as a crust to the sides of casks; cream of tartar; the phosphate concretion forming on the teeth. **tartar emetic,** *a.* poisonous salt, used in medicine and dyeing, consisting of potassium tartrate and oxide of antimony. **cream of tartar,** *see* **cream.** (Fr. *tartre*.)
Tartar, *a. tahr*-tar, pertaining to Tartary or its inhabitants: *n.* a native of Tartary or a member of one of its many races; (*l.c.*) a person of a keen, irritable temper [Fig.]. **catch a tartar,** to encounter an opponent who proves too strong for one.
Tartarean, *a.* tar-*tare*-re-an, pertaining to Tartarus, the infernal regions; characteristic of hell; hellish.
tartareous, *a.* tar-*tare*-re-us, having the crusty structure of tartar [Bot.].
Tartarian, *a.* tar-*tare*-re-an, pertaining to Tartary or its people: *n.* a Tartar. **Tartarian lamb,** the fern barometz, or its rootstock.
tartaric, *a.* tar-*ta*-rik, of the nature of or obtained from tartar.
tartarization, *n. tahr*-ta-ry-*zay*-shon, the act or process of tartarizing.
tartarize, *v.t. tahr*-ta-rize, to impregnate with tartar; to refine by the salt of tartar.
tartarous, *a. tahr*-ta-rus, of the nature of or consisting of tartar.
Tartarus, *n. tahr*-ta-rus, the infernal regions, esp. as the place of punishment; Hades. (L.)
tartish, *a. tart*-ish, somewhat tart.
tartlet, *n. tart*-let, a small open tart.
tartly, *ad. tart*-le, sharply; severely.
tartness, *n. tart*-ness, sharpness to the taste; sharpness of language or manner.
tartrate, *n. tahr*-trate, a salt of tartaric acid.
Tartuffe, *n.* tar-*toof*, a hypocritical pretender to religion. (Character in Molière's play *Tartuffe*.)
Tartuffish, *a.* tar-*toof*-ish, precise; hypocritical.

tar-water, *n.* a cold infusion of tar, formerly used as a panacea.
tar-weed, *n.* the plant madia.
taseometer, *n. tas*-e-*om*-e-ter, an instrument for measuring structural stresses.
tasimeter, *n.* ta-*sim*-e-ter, an instrument for determining variation in temperature by variations in pressure. (Gr. *tasis*, tension, *metron*, measure.)
task, *n.* tahsk, business or study imposed by another or undertaken voluntarily; a lesson to be learned; specific work; burdensome employment: *v.t.* to impose a task on; to overstrain; to require to perform. **task force,** a detachment specially trained and equipped for a definite operation [Mil. and Nav.]. (O.Fr. *tasque.*)
tasker, *n. tahs*-ker, a taskmaster; one engaged on task-work.
taskmaster, *n. tahsk*-mahs-ter, one who imposes a task; one whose office is to assign tasks.
task-work, *n.* work done as a task; piece-work.
taslet, *n. tas*-let, a small tasse.
Tasmanian, *a.* taz-*may*-ne-an, pertaining to the Australasian island, Tasmania: *n.* a native or inhabitant of this. **Tasmanian devil,** the carnivorous burrowing marsupial, *Sarcophilus ursinus*, allied to the dasyures. **Tasmanian tiger** or **wolf,** the thylacine.
tass, *n.* tas, a small drinking-cup; a small drink. (O.Fr.)
tasse, *n.* tas, armour for the thighs consisting of overlapping steel plates depending from the corslet. (Fr.)
tassel, *n. tas*-el, a pendent ornament; a silk ribbon sewn to a book as a marker; a pendent flower-head, catkin, etc. [Bot.]. **tassel grass,** or **pond-weed,** an aquatic herb, esp. *Ruppia maritima.* (O.Fr., a fastening, clasp.)
tasselled, *a. tas*-eld, furnished with tassels.
★**taste,** *n.* tayst, the sense by which flavour is perceived or identified; the sensation produced by tasting; a small portion or sample tasted or eaten; relish; intellectual relish; the mental faculty of artistic appreciation; judgment; discernment; style: *v.t.* to perceive or experience by or as by the tongue and palate; to try the relish of; to test the quality of by eating or drinking a little; to partake of; to relish intellectually; to enjoy: *v.i.* to exercise the sense of taste; to have a smack, a certain flavour, or [Fig.] a particular quality; to have a perception; to have experience of. (O.Fr. *taster*, handle.)
tasteable, *a. tayst*-a-bl, that may be tasted; savoury.
tasteful, *a. tayst*-ful, possessed of, characteristic of, or showing good taste.
tastefully, *ad.* in a tasteful manner.
tastefulness, *n.* the quality of being tasteful.
tasteless, *a. tayst*-less, having no flavour; insipid; devoid of the sense of taste; not in good taste; showing no taste.
tastelessly, *ad.* in a tasteless manner.
tastelessness, *n.* the quality of being tasteless; want of taste.
taster, *n. tayst*-er, one who tests food, etc., before it is served; one who judges by the taste; that by or in which a thing is tasted; a taste or sample [Coll.].
tastily, *ad. tayst*-e-le, with good taste.
tasty, *a. tayst*-e, savoury; toothsome; showing, or in conformity with, good taste.
tat, *n.* tat, sacking made of jute or other fibre [Anglo-Ind.]; a tatty. (Hind.)
tat, *n.* tat, a native-bred Indian pony. (Hind. *tattu.*)
tat, *n.* tat, slang for loaded dice, also for a rag and (*v.i.*) to gather rags.
tat, *v.t.* tat, to make tatting.
ta-ta, *int.* ta-*tah*, a childish "good-bye."
Tatar, *n.* and *a. tah*-tar, Tartar.
tatler, *n. tat*-ler, a tattler.
tatou, *n.* ta-*too*, the giant armadillo. (Native S. Amer.)
tatouay, *n. tat*-oo-ay, the peba, or other armadillo of tropical S. America. (*tatou.*)
tatter, *n. tat*-er, a rag or a part torn and hanging: *v.t.* to rend or tear into rags. (O. Scand.)
tatterdemalion, *n. tat*-er-de-*may*-le-on, a ragged fellow. (Origin uncertain.)
tattered, *a. tat*-erd, torn; hanging in rags; ragged.
tattery, *a. tat*-er-re, in tatters; ragged.
tatting, *n. tat*-ing, lace or knotted work for edging woven by a small hand-shuttle; the act of making this.
tattle, *n. tat*-tl, idle talk or chat; trifling talk: *v.i.* to talk idly; to tell tales or secrets. (L. Ger. *tateln.*)
tattler, *n. tat*-tler, an idle talker; one who tells tales; the willet, or other sandpiper [Ornith.].
tattling, *a. tat*-tling, given to idle talk; apt to tell tales: *n.* the act of babbling or telling tales.
tattoo, *n.* ta-*too*, a beat of drum or bugle-call at night recalling soldiers to their quarters; a military pageant, esp. one presented at night. **devil's tattoo,** *see* **devil.** (Dut. *taptoe*, a signal warning tavernkeepers to shut the tap.)
tattoo, *n.* ta-*too*, the art or practice of tatooing; the pattern or a mark made thus: *v.t.* to prick the skin and permanently stain the punctured spots by inserting a coloured fluid. (Tahitian *tatau.*)
tatty, *n. tat*-e, a grass matting over which water trickles to cool the air as it enters a room [Anglo-Ind.]. (Hind. *tatti.*)
tatty, *a. tat*-e, tangled; matted (of hair, wool, etc.) [Scots.].
tau, *n.* taw, the name of the Greek letter T; applied to various insects, etc., having T-like markings. **Tau cross,** a cross shaped like a T. (Gr.)
taught, tawt, *p.* and *pp.* of *teach.*
taunt, *a.* tawnt, very tall (of masts): *ad.* ataunt [Naut.].
taunt, *n.* tawnt, a bitter or sarcastic reproach; insulting invective: *v.t.* to reproach with severe or insulting words, to revile; to wound with sarcasm. (O.Fr. *tenter*, try.)
taunter, *n. tawnt*-er, one who taunts.
tauntingly, *ad. tawnt*-ing-le, with bitter and sarcastic words.
taupe, *n.* tope, a greyish colour, as of moleskin [U.S.A.]. (Fr., a mole.)
taupie, *n.* and *a. taw*-pe, tawpie.
tauriform, *a. taw*-re-form, having the form of a bull. (L. *taurus*, and *form.*)
taurin, *n. taw*-rin, a neutral crystalline compound occurring in certain animal juices and tissues, first identified in the bile of the ox.
taurine, *a. taw*-rine, relating to the bull; bovine; pertaining to Taurus.
taurocol, *n. taw*-ro-kol, a gluey substance made from a bull's hide. (Gr. *tauros*, and *kolla*, glue.)
tauromachy, *n.* taw-*rom*-a-ke, bull-fighting; a bull-fight. (Gr. *tauros*, and *mache*, a fight.)
Taurus, *n. taw*-rus, the Bull, the second sign of the zodiac, which the sun enters about April 20th. (L.)
taut, *a.* tawt, tight; secure. (M.E. *toght*, firm.)
tauted, *a. taw*-ted, tatty [Scots.].
tauten, *v.t. tawt*-en, to make taut.
tautness, *n. tawt*-ness, the state of being taut.
tautochrone, *n. taw*-to-krone, a curve such that a heavy body descending along it will always arrive at the lowest point in the same time from whatever point it may start [Math.]. (Gr. *tauto*, the same, *chronos*, time.)
tautochronism, *n.* taw-*tok*-ro-nizm, the property of a tautochrone [Math.].
tautochronous, *a.* tau-*tok*-ro-nus, having the property of a tautochrone; isochronous.
tautog, *n.* taw-*tog*, the N. American edible blackfish *Tautoga onitis.*
tautological, *a. taw*-to-*loj*-e-kal, repeating the same thing; having the same signification.
tautologically, *ad.* in a tautological manner.
tautologism, *n.* taw-*tol*-o-jizm, the use of tautology; an instance of this.
tautologist, *n.* taw-*tol*-o-jist, one given to the use of tautology.
tautologize, *v.i.* taw-*tol*-o-jize, to use tautology.
tautologous, *a.* taw-*tol*-o-gus, tautological.
tautology, *n.* taw-*tol*-o-je, a repetition of the same meaning in different words; superfluous repetition. (L. and Gr. *tautologia.*)
tautomeric, *a. taw*-to-*me*-rik, pertaining to or exhibiting tautomerism [Chem.].
tautomerism, *n.* taw-*tom*-er-rizm, the property belonging to certain organic compounds of having, or appearing to have, more than one structure [Chem.]; the attribution of two different formulas

to one compound [Pharm.]. (Gr. *tauto*, the same, *meros*, part.)
tautophony, *n.* taw-*tof*-o-ne, repetition of the same sound. (Gr. *tauto*, and *phone*, voice.)
tautosyllabic, *a.* *taw*-to-se-*lab*-ik, belonging to the same syllable [Phon.].
tavarish, *n.* ta-*vah*-rish, tovarish.
tavern, *n.* *tav*-ern, a public-house; an inn. (Fr. *taverne*.)
taverner, *n.* *tav*-er-ner, one who keeps a tavern.
taverning, *n.* *tav*-er-ning, the frequenting of taverns.
taw, *v.t.* taw, to dress hides by imbuing skins with alum, salt, or other mineral matters instead of with tannin. (A.S. *tawian*, prepare.)
taw, *n.* taw, a marble to be played with; a game at marbles.
tawdrily, *ad.* *taw*-dre-le, in a tawdry manner.
tawdriness, *n.* the quality of being tawdry.
tawdry, *a.* *taw*-dre, gaudy; cheaply showy; without taste or elegance: *n.* cheap showy finery. (*St. Audrey*, or Etheldreda, at whose fair such articles were sold.)
tawer, *n.* *taw*-er, a leather-dresser.
tawery, *n.* *taw*-er-re, a place where skins are tawed.
tawniness, *n.* the quality of being tawny.
tawny, *a.* *taw*-ne, of a yellowish-brown colour, like that of tanned things or sunburnt persons; tan-coloured. (Fr. *tanné*.)
tawpie, *n.* *taw*-pe, a thoughtless or flighty girl: *a.* silly; thoughtless [Scots.]. (Scand.)
tawse, *n.* tawz, a thick leather strap, slit at the end, once common in Scotland for use on schoolboys.
***tax**, *n.* taks, a rate or sum of money assessed on person or property for the benefit of the state; impost; tribute; a heavy demand; a strain: *v.t.* to lay, impose, or assess upon the people a certain sum for the public benefit; to subject to a tax; to load with a burden or burdens; to disallow items in a solicitor's bill of costs; to charge; to censure; to accuse. (Fr. *taxe*.)
taxability, *n.* *taks*-a-*bil*-e-te, taxableness.
taxable, *a.* *taks*-a-bl, that may be taxed; liable by law to the assessment of taxes.
taxableness, *n.* state of being taxable.
taxably, *ad.* in a taxable manner.
taxation, *n.* tak-*say*-shon, the act of laying a tax or of taxing; the sum imposed; taxes generally; revenue from taxes.
tax-cart, *n.* a light spring-cart on which a reduced tax was formerly imposed.
taxer, *n.* *tak*-ser, one who taxes or levies taxes.
tax-gatherer, *n.* a collector of taxes.
taxi, *n.* *tak*-se, a taxicab: *v.t.* and *i.* to go by taxi; to manœuvre an aeroplane before taking off or after a landing: *ppr.* **taxi-ing.** [Av.]
taxicab, *n.* *tak*-se-kab, a motor-cab for public hire, fitted with a taximeter.
taxidermic, *a.* tak-se-*der*-mik, pertaining to taxidermy.
taxidermist, *n.* *tak*-se-der-mist, one skilled in taxidermy.
taxidermy, *n.* *tak*-se-der-me, the art of preparing and preserving the skins of animals so as to represent their appearance in life. (Gr. *taxis*, arrangement, *derma*, the skin.)
taximan, *n.* *tak*-se-man, the driver of a taxicab.
taximeter, *n.* tak-*sim*-e-ter, an instrument fitted to hired vehicles for showing the distance travelled and amount of fare due.
taxin, *n.* *tak*-sin, a resinous substance obtained from the leaves of the yew. (L. *taxus*, yew.)
taxing-master, *n.* a Law Courts official who settles disputes relating to costs.
taxiplane, *n.* *tak*-se-plane, an aeroplane for public hire.
taxis, *n.* *tak*-sis, the operation by which parts that have become displaced are replaced by manipulation [Surg.]; taxonomy [Bot. and Zool.]; the reaction of an organism to stimulus by movement towards a certain direction [Biol.]. (Gr., arrangement.)
Taxodium, *n.* tak-*soh*-de-um, a genus of deciduous trees of the southern United States including the swamp-cypress, *T. distichum*. (L. *taxus*, yew, and Gr. *eidos*, like.)
taxonomic, *a.* tak-so-*nom*-ik, classificatory; relating to taxonomy.
taxonomist, *n.* tak-*son*-o-mist, one who classifies [Bot. and Zool.]; a student of taxonomy.
taxonomy, *n.* tak-*son*-o-me, the science or study of classification; the classification of animals or plants. (Gr. *taxis*, and *nomos*, law.)
taxpayer, *n.* *taks*-pay-er, one who is assessed for taxes.
Taxus, *n.* *tak*-sus, the genus of plants including the yew. (L.)
tazza, *n.* *tat*-za, a saucer-shaped vessel or vase mounted on a foot. (It.)
tcheka, *n.* *chay*-kah, an organization of secret police in the U.S.S.R., founded 1917 for the suppression of counter-revolutionary activities, replaced by the Ogpu, 1922. (Russ.)
tchick, *n.* chik, a sound produced by pressing the tongue against the palate and quickly removing it: *v.i.* to make this sound [Imit.].
te, *n.* tee, the seventh note (also named " si ") in the tonic sol-fa notation [Mus.].
tea, *n.* tee, the dried leaves of the evergreen plant or shrub *Thea sinensis*; the plant itself; a decoction or infusion of the leaves in boiling water; the afternoon repast; a medicinal infusion (as senna-tea, etc.): *v.i.* to take or drink tea. **green tea, high tea,** *see* these words. **Russian tea,** tea served with lemon in place of milk. **tea rose,** any of several sweet-scented yellow roses, mainly of Chinese origin. (Chinese.)
teaberry, *n.* *tee*-be-re, the evergreen plant *Gaultheria procumbens*, the source of wintergreen oil.
tea-caddy, *n.* a box for holding tea for the tea-pot.
tea-cake, *n.* a light cake for tea.
teach, *v.t.* teech, to instruct; to educate; to impart knowledge; to deliver any doctrine, art, words, etc., for instruction; to exhibit so as to impress on the mind; to make familiar; to counsel; to admonish [Coll.]: *v.i.* to practise giving instruction. *p.* and *pp.* **taught.** (A.S. *tæcan*, show how to do anything.)
teachability, *n.* teech-a-*bil*-e-te, capacity for being taught; teachableness.
teachable, *a.* *teech*-a-bl, that may be taught; apt to learn; docile.
teachableness, *n.* the quality of being teachable; docility; aptness to learn.
teacher, *n.* *teech*-er, one who teaches or instructs; an assistant schoolmaster or mistress.
tea-chest, *n.* a chest lined with sheet lead in which tea is imported.
***teaching**, *n.* *teech*-ing, the act or business of instructing; instruction.
tea-clipper, *n.* a fast sailing-ship formerly used in the tea-carrying trade.
tea-cloth, *n.* a small, usually ornamental, table-cloth used at tea.
teacup, *n.* *tee*-kup, a small cup used in drinking tea.
teaey, *a.* *tee*-e, of the nature of tea.
tea-garden, *n.* a plantation where tea is grown commercially; a public garden where teas and refreshments are served.
tea-gown, *n.* a woman's loose afternoon frock.
Teague, *n.* teeg, a nickname for an Irishman. (Personal proper name.)
teak, *n.* teek, a tall E. Indian tree of the genus *Tectona*; its hard and durable timber. (Port. *teca*.)
teal, *n.* teel, a small wild freshwater duck of the genus *Nettion*. (Origin unknown.)
tea-leaf, *n.* a leaf of the tea-plant; a fragment of a tea-leaf when dried for making tea; [Slang] a thief.
team, *n.* teem, two or more horses, oxen or other beasts harnessed together for draught purposes; a side at cricket or other games (sometimes including players in reserve); a group of persons in association: *v.t.* to join together in a team; to work with a team. (A.S., offspring.)
teamster, *n.* *teem*-ster, one who drives a team.
teamwork, *n.* *teem*-wurk, work done by a team, or co-operatively.
tea-party, *n.* a social afternoon gathering at which tea is served.
teapot, *n.* *tee*-pot, a vessel with a spout, in which tea is made and from which it is served.
teapoy, *n.* *tee*-poy, a low stand for a tea-service. (Anglo-Ind. *tipai*, a tripod.)
tear, *n.* teer, a drop of the limpid fluid secreted by the lachrymal gland appearing in or flowing from the eyes; a tear-like object. **crocodile tears,** insincere or affected grief. (A.S.)

tear, *n.* tare, a rent or fissure: *v.t.* to separate by violence or pulling; to rend; to lacerate; to shatter; to pull with or remove by violence: *v.i.* to be rent; to rave; to rage; to rant; to move and act with violence. **tear from,** to separate and take away by force. **tear off,** to pull off by violence; to rush off. **to tear one's hair,** to manifest extreme grief. **to tear oneself away,** to leave against one's wish. **tear up,** to rip up. *p.* **tore.** *pp.* **torn.** (A.S. *teran.*)
tear-bomb, *n. teer*-bom, a bomb filled with tear-gas.
teardrop, *n. teer*-drop, a tear from the eye.
tearer, *n. tare*-rer, one who tears or rends anything; one who rages with violence.
tearful, *a. teer*-ful, weeping; shedding tears.
tearfully, *ad. teer*-ful-le, in a weeping or lachrymose manner.
tearfulness, *n. teer*-ful-ness, the state of being tearful.
tear-gas, *n. teer*-gas, any irritant poison gas bringing tears to the eyes; lachrymatory gas.
tearing, *a. tare*-ring, impetuous; violent; furious (of hurry, rage, etc.).
tearless, *a. teer*-less, shedding no tears; without tears; unfeeling.
tear-pit, *n. teer*-pit, the slight depression below the eye in the skull of deer and other ungulates.
teary, *a. teer*-re, wet with tears; tearful.
tease, *v.t.* teez, to comb or card, as wool or flax; to scratch, as cloth in dressing; to divide into shreds; to vex with importunity or impertinence; to harass; to annoy: *n.* one who annoys others by teasing. (A.S. *tæsan,* to pluck.)
teasel, *n. tee*-zl, a plant of the genus *Dipsacus,* esp. *D. fullonum,* fuller's teasel, with hooked bracts, formerly used to raise the nap on cloth: *v.t.* to dress with a teasel. (A.S. *tæsl,* from *tæsan,* to pluck.)
teaseler, *n. tee*-zel-er, one who teasels cloth; an implement for teaseling.
teaser, *n. tee*-zer, one who teases wool, etc., also an implement for this; one who teases or vexes; a puzzling question, etc. [Coll.]; a skua or similar bird.
tea-service, *n.* a set of utensils used in serving tea.
tea-set, *n.* a tea-service.
teasingly, *ad. teez*-ing-le, in a teasing manner.
teaspoon, *n. tee*-spoon, a small spoon used for stirring tea and coffee.
tea-spoonful, *n.* as much as a teaspoon will hold; 1 drachm, the eighth of a fluid ounce [Med.].
teat, *n.* teet, the nipple of the female breast; a dug of an animal; something resembling this in form or function. (A.S. *tit.*)
teat-fish, *n.* the trepang [Austral.].
tea-things, *n.pl.* the apparatus for serving tea; a tea-service; a tea-set.
tea-tree, *n.* the plant *Thea sinensis* (originally Chinese), from the dried leaves of which tea is infused; applied also to certain other shrubs.
tea-urn, *n.* an urn-like vessel for supplying boiling water for tea.
tea-wagon, *n.* a set of shelves on castors from which to serve tea in a drawing-room.
Tebeth, *n.* tay-*vayth* or *teb*-eth, the tenth month (parts of Dec. and Jan.) of the Jewish ecclesiastical year.
tec, *n.* tek, a detective [Slang].
technic, *n. tek*-nik, technical art or skill; technique; technics; technology. (Fr. *technique.*)
technical, *a. tek*-ne-kal, pertaining to the mechanical arts, or to some particular science, art, sport, business, etc.
technicalism, *n. tek*-ne-ka-lizm, technical style; addiction to technicalities.
technicality, *n. tek*-ne-*kal*-e-te, anything peculiar to an art or branch of study; a technical detail.
technically, *ad. tek*-ne-ka-le, in a technical manner.
technicalness, *n.* quality of being technical.
technician, *n.* tek-*nish*-an, one skilled in the technicalities of his subject, or in technique; a skilled craftsman.
technicist, *n. tek*-ne-sist, a technician.
technicology, *n.* tek-ne-*kol*-o-je, technology.
Technicolor, *n. tek*-ne-kul-or, proprietary name of a special process of colour photography used in cinematography.
technics, *n. tek*-niks, the doctrine of arts in general; branches of learning relating to the arts.
technique, *n.* tek-*neek,* method; execution; mechanical skill in art. (Fr.)
techno-chemistry, *n. tek*-no-, industrial chemistry.
technocracy, *n.* tek-*nok*-ra-se, government in which industry and production are managed in the national interest by technical experts. (Gr. *techne,* art, *kratos,* rule.)
technocrat, *n. tek*-no-krat, a supporter of, or an expert under, technocracy.
technocratic, *a.* tak-no-*krat*-ik, pertaining to or derived from technocracy.
technography, *n.* tek-*nog*-ra-fe, the description of the arts and crafts.
technological, *a. tek*-no-*loj*-e-kal, pertaining to technology, or to the industrial arts.
technologist, *n.* tek-*nol*-o-jist, one skilled in technology.
technology, *n.* tek-*nol*-o-je, the science of the industrial arts; terminology used in the sciences, arts, etc. (Gr. *techne,* art, *logos,* science.)
technonomy, *n.* tek-*non*-o-me, the principles of the industrial arts; the application of these.
techy, *a. tetch*-e, tetchy.
tecnology, *n.* tek-*nol*-o-je, the scientific study of children. (Gr. *teknon,* child.)
tecnonymy, *n.* tek-*non*-e-me, the tribal practice of naming the parent from the child [Ethn.].
tectibranch, *a.* and *n. tek*-te-brank, belonging to, or a member of, the Tectibranchiata, a group of gastropod molluscs having the gills covered by the mantle. (L. *tego, tectum,* cover, and *branchiæ.*)
tectiform, *a. tek*-te-form, roof-shaped [Anat. and Zool.]; serving as a lid.
tectology, *n.* tek-*tol*-o-je, structural morphology [Biol.].
tectonic, *a.* tek-*ton*-ik, pertaining to construction; structural [Biol. and Geol.]: *n.pl.* the science of the constructive arts. (Gr. *tecton,* a constructor.)
tectorial, *a.* tek-*taw*-re-al, covering; of the nature of a covering.
tectrices, *n.pl. tek*-tre-seez, the wing-coverts or tail-coverts of a bird. (L. *tectum,* cover.)
ted, *v.t.* ted, to spread, as new-mown grass, for drying and converting into hay. (Scand.)
tedder, *n. ted*-er, one who teds; a tedding machine.
Tedesco, *a.* and *n.* te-*des*-koh, German, Teutonic (esp. of art). (It., German.)
Te Deum, *n.* tee-*dee*-um, a hymn sung on occasions of joy, so called from its first words. (L., "(We praise) thee, O God")
tedious, *a. tee*-de-us, wearisome; tiresome from prolixity; slow. (L.)
tediously, *ad.* so as to weary.
tediousness, *n.* the quality of being tedious.
tedium, *n. tee*-de-um, irksomeness; wearisomeness.
tee, *n.* tee, the name of the letter T; a T-shaped piece, fitting, or object.
tee, *n.* tee, the small mound of sand from which a golf-ball is driven at the start of each hole; a mark at quoits and other games: *v.t.* to place the ball on the tee. **tee off,** to drive (the ball) from the tee [Golf]. (Origin uncertain.)
teem, *v.i.* teem, to be full to overflowing; to be prolific; to swarm (with): *v.t.* to produce; to bring forth. (A.S. *tyman,* produce.)
teem, *v.t.* teem, to pour, esp. from a melting-pot; to drain (boiled vegetables) of water: *v.i.* to rain heavily; to pour. (O.Scand. *tæma,* to pour.)
teemful, *a. teem*-ful, pregnant; prolific.
teeming, *a. teem*-ing, producing young; fruitful; pouring with rain.
teen, *n.* teen, grief; sorrow: *v.t.* to vex. (A.S.)
teens, *n.pl.* teenz, the years of one's age beginning with thirteen, and ending with nineteen; hence **teen-age,** the period, or of the period, of the teens.
teeny, *a. teen*-e, tiny. **teeny-weeny** [Coll.], very tiny.
teeter, *v.t.* and *i. tee*-ter, to see-saw; to waver; to tilt.
teeth, *n.pl.* teeth, plural of *tooth.*
teething, *n. teethe*-ing, the process by which teeth make their way through the gums; dentition.
teethy, *a. tee*-the, having many or prominent teeth.
teetotal, *a.* tee-*toh*-tal, abstaining from intoxicating liquors; pertaining to teetotallers. (From *total,* by reduplication of initial *t.*)
teetotalism, *n.* tee-*toh*-ta-lizm, total abstinence from intoxicating liquors.
teetotaller, *n.* tee-*toh*-ta-ler, one abstaining, or pledged to abstinence, from all intoxicating liquors.

teetotum, *n.* tee-*toh*-tum, a small top with numbered sides, twirled by the fingers, originally with four sides on one of which was a T for *totum*, the whole of the stakes.
teff, *n.* tef, a kind of millet, *Poa abyssinica*, an important cereal of Abyssinia. (Native.)
teg, *n.* teg, a sheep in its second year.
tegmen, *n.* *teg*-men (*pl.* **tegmina**), a covering of an organ or part [Bot. and Zool.], esp. a wing cover of an orthopterous insect [Ent.].
tegmental, *a.* teg-*men*-tal, covering; tegumentary [Biol.].
tegmentum, *n.* teg-*men*-tum (*pl.* **tegmenta**), a skin or tegument.
tegminal, *a.* *teg*-me-nal, pertaining to or of the nature of a tegmen.
tegular, *a.* *teg*-yew-lar, pertaining to or resembling a tile; consisting of tiles. (L. *tegula*, a tile.)
tegulated, *a.* *teg*-yew-lay-ted, overlapping.
tegument, *n.* *teg*-yew-ment, a natural covering; the skin; integument. (L. *tegumentum.*)
tegumentary, *a.* teg-yew-*men*-ta-re, pertaining to or consisting of teguments.
tehee, *n.* te-*hee*, a sound made in laughing: *v.i.* to laugh; to titter.
teil, *n.* teel, the lime-tree. (L. *tilia.*)
teind, *n.* teend, in Scotland, a tithe, esp. one paid from the produce of land for the support of the clergy. (*tenth.*)
teinoscope, *n.* *ty*-no-skope, an optical instrument in which a combination of prisms corrects chromatic aberration; a prism telescope. (Gr. *teino*, extend, *skopeo*, see.)
teknonymy, *n.* tek-*non*-e-me, tecnonymy.
telæsthesia, *n.* tel-es-*thee*-ze-a, psychic perception of distant objects, events, etc., without the operation of any sense-organ. (Gr. *tele*, afar, and *æsthesia.*)
telæsthetic, *a.* tel-es-*thet*-ik, pertaining to, or endowed with the faculty of telæsthesia.
telamon, *n.* *tel*-a-mon (*pl.* **telamones**, tel-a-*moh*-neez), a male caryatid [Arch.]. (Gr., supporter.)
telary, *a.* *tel*-a-re, pertaining to webs or the spinning of webs. (L. *tela*, a web.)
telautogram, *n.* tel-*aw*-to-gram, matter transmitted by telautograph.
telautograph, *n.* tel-*aw*-to-graf, a telegraph for reproducing manuscript, etc., at a distance.
tele-, *tel*-e, Greek combining form signifying afar, or operating at or from a distance. (Gr., far.)
telearchics, *n.pl.* tel-e-*ar*-kiks, the study and art of the remote control of aircraft, projectiles, ships, etc. (Gr. *tele-*, and *arche*, ruler.)
telebarometer, *n.* *tel*-e-ba-*rom*-e-ter, a barometer transmitting its readings to a distance.
tele-camera, *n.* a camera used for phototelegraphy.
telecommunication, *n.* *tel*-e-ko-*mew*-ne-*kay*-shon, communication at a distance by telegraphy, radiotelegraphy, telephony, or some adaptation of these.
teledu, *n.* *tel*-e-doo, the stinking badger or Javanese skunk, *Mydaus meliceps*, of Malaysia. (Native.)
telegonic, *a.* tel-e-*gon*-ik, pertaining to telegony.
telegony, *n.* te-*leg*-o-ne, the discredited theory that the characteristics of a female's first mate are transmitted to the offspring of later matings. (Gr. *tele-*, and *-gonia*, begetting.)
telegram, *n.* *tel*-e-gram, a telegraphic message. (Gr. *tele*, afar, *gramma*, from *grapho*, write.)
telegraph, *n.* *tel*-e-graf, a semaphore; an electrical apparatus for communicating between distant points; a board or other device on or by which the score is shown at cricket, etc.: *v.t.* to send a message by telegraph. **telegraph cable**, a cable of insulated conducting wires for transmitting telegrams. **telegraph key**, a device for making and breaking a telegraph circuit. **telegraph plant**, the E. Indian trefoil *Desmodium gyrans*, the lateral leaflets of which move like a semaphore. (Gr. *tele*, and *grapho*, write.)
telegraphese, *n.* *tel*-e-gra-*feez*, the laconic style of composition usual in telegrams.
telegraphic, *a.* tel-e-*graf*-ik, pertaining to the telegraph; communicated by telegraph; laconic.
telegraphically, *ad.* by telegraph.
telegraphist, *n.* te-*leg*-ra-fist, a telegraph operator.
telegraphy, *n.* te-*leg*-ra-fe, distance signalling; the art of constructing and working telegraphs or of communicating intelligence by telegraph.
telekinesis, *n.* tel-e-ky-*nee*-sis, the movement of bodies at a distance and without material connexion with the cause [Psychics].
telekinetic, *a.* tel-e-ky-*net*-ik, pertaining to telekinesis.
telelectric, *a.* tel-e-*lek*-trik, pertaining to the production of mechanical or acoustical effects at a distance by means of electricity.
telemark, *n.* *tel*-e-mark, a certain swinging turn in ski-ing. (A mountainous district, S. Norway.)
telemechanics, *n.pl.* tel-e-me-*kan*-iks, the science of transmitting power to a distance, esp. without wires or material contact.
telemeter, *n.* te-*lem*-e-ter, an instrument for determining distances [Phot.]; an apparatus for indicating electrical quantities (voltage, etc.) at a distant station: *v.t.* and *i.*, to use or transmit by a telemeter.
teleological, *a.* tel-e-o-*loj*-e-kal, pertaining to teleology.
teleologist, *n.* tel-e-*ol*-o-jist, a student or advocate of teleology.
teleology, *n.* tel-e-*ol*-o-je, the doctrine of the final causes of things or of the discoverability of divine purpose by the study of means and ends; the doctrine of design. (Gr. *telos*, end, *logos*, science.)
Teleosaurus, *n.* *tel*-e-oh-saw-rus, an extinct genus of crocodiles of the Jurassic strata.
teleostean, *a.* tel-e-*os*-te-an, characteristic of the Teleostei: *n.* a fish of this order.
Teleostei, tel-e-*os*-te-eye, the large group of fishes having the skeleton completely ossified; the bony fishes.
telepathic, *a.* tel-e-*path*-ik, pertaining to or communicated by telepathy.
telepathically, *ad.* tel-e-*path*-e-ka-le, by means of telepathy.
telepathist, *n.* te-*lep*-a-thist, a believer in or one proficient at telepathy.
telepathy, *n.* te-*lep*-a-the, thought transference other than by means of any of the five senses.
telephone, *n.* *tel*-e-fone, an apparatus for transmitting speech to a distance by means of electricity: *v.t.* to transmit by telephone. (Gr. *tele-*, and *phone*, sound.)
telephonic, *a.* tel-e-*fon*-ik, by telephone; relating to the telephone.
telephonically, *ad.* by means of the telephone.
telephonist, *n.* te-*lef*-o-nist, one skilled in telephony; one who works the telephone.
telephonograph, *n.* *tel*-e-*foh*-no-graf, an instrument for recording a telephone message for subsequent reproduction.
telephony, *n.* te-*lef*-o-ne, the art of constructing and working telephones.
telephote, *n.* *tel*-e-fote, an electrical instrument for reproducing pictures at a distance.
telephoto, *a.* tel-e-*foh*-toh, telephotographic: *n.* a picture produced by telephotography or transmitted by phototelegraphy.
telephotograph, *n.* *tel*-e-*foh*-to-graf, a picture reproduced by means of the telephote or taken by telephotography.
telephotographic, *a.* *tel*-e-*foh*-to-*graf*-ik, pertaining to the processes of telephotography.
telephotography, *n.* tel-e-fo-*tog*-ra-fe, photography of distant objects with a telescopic or other lens giving a magnified image, or with a telephote; phototelegraphy.
teleplasm, *n.* *tel*-e-plazm, ectoplasm [Spiritualism].
teleprint, *v.t.* *tel*-e-print, to transmit (a message, etc.) by teleprinter.
teleprinter, *n.* *tel*-e-prin-ter, an electrical contrivance by means of which typewriting is simultaneously reproduced at a distant station.
telergy, *n.* *tel*-er-je, the hypothetical force accountable for the phenomenon of telepathy.
telescope, *n.* *tel*-e-skope, an optical instrument for viewing distant objects: *v.t.* and *i.* to shut up like a telescope. **refracting telescope**, *see* **refract.** (Gr. *tele-*, and *skopeo*, view.)
telescopic, *a.* tel-e-*skop*-ik, pertaining to or like a telescope; visible only with a telescope.
telescopically, *ad.* by means of the telescope.
telescopist, *n.* te-*les*-ko-pist, one skilled in the use of the telescope.
telescopy, *n.* te-*les*-ko-pe, the art or practice of making or using telescopes.
teleseism, *n.* tel-e-*see*-izm, a tremor recorded from a very distantly centred earthquake.

teleseme, *n.* *tel*-e-seem, an electrical signalling and indicating apparatus used in hotels, etc. (Gr. *tele-*, and *sema*, sign.)
telestich, *n.* *tel*-e-stik, a poem in which the final letters of the lines make a name. (Gr. *telos*, end, *stichos*, a verse.)
telethermometer, *n.* tel-e-ther-*mom*-e-ter, a thermometer electrically recording its readings at a distance.
teletype, *n.* *tel*-e-tipe, proprietary name of a form of telotype telegraphing and printing messages direct from a keyboard.
teleutospore, *n.* te-*lew*-to-spor, a winter spore produced in the final stage of fructification of the rust fungi. (Gr. *teleute*, completion, and *spore*.)
televise, *tel*-e-vize, to transmit by television.
television, *n.* tel-e-*vizh*-on, the seeing of reproductions of distant views, objects in motion, etc., by means of electrically transformed light waves projected on a screen.
televisor, *n.* *tel*-e-vy-zor, a transmitting or receiving apparatus for television.
Telex, *n.* *tel*-eks, a Post Office service whereby subscribers hire the use of teleprinters.
telic, *a.* *tel*-ik, purposive; expressing the end or purpose [Gram.]. (Gr. *telos*, end.)
tell, *v.t.* tel, to make known; to make known by speech; to communicate; to relate particulars; to inform; to disclose; to count; to number; to discern: *v.i.* to give an account; to make report; to produce effect; to tattle [Coll.]. **tell off,** to count off; to select for special duty; to reprimand. **tell the tale,** *see* **tale. tell the world,** *see* **world.** *p.* and *pp.* **told.** (A.S. *tellan*, count.)
tellable, *a.* *tel*-a-bl, capable of being, or fit to be, told.
teller, *n.* *tel*-er, one who tells, relates, or communicates something; a clerk in a bank who receives or pays out money; a cashier.
tellership, *n.* *tel*-er-ship, the office or employment of a teller.
telling, *a.* *tel*-ing, having a great effect; forcible: *n.* the act of telling; blabbing.
tellingly, *ad.* effectively.
telltale, *a.* *tel*-tale, telling tales; blabbing: *n.* one who officiously communicates private information, etc.; an index or indicator of various kinds; the dial plate at the wheel, showing the position of the tiller [Naut.]; a device to apprise an organist to what degree the wind is exhausted [Mus.]; a time-clock.
tellural, *a.* te-*lewr*-ral, pertaining to the earth; terrestrial. (L. *telluris*, of the earth.)
tellurate, *n.* *tel*-ew-rate, a salt of telluric acid.
telluretted, *a.* *tel*-ew-ret-ed, combined or impregnated with tellurium.
tellurian, *a.* te-*lewr*-re-an, pertaining to or characteristic of the earth: *n.* an inhabitant of the earth.
telluric, *a.* te-*lewr*-rik, pertaining to or containing tellurium; tellural. **telluric acid,** an acid composed of one equivalent of tellurium and three of oxygen. **telluric ochre,** native telluric dioxide, a yellow crystalline mineral.
telluride, *n.* *tel*-ew-ride, a compound of tellurium and a metal.
tellurion, *n.* te-*lewr*-re-on, an instrument for showing the motion of the earth, the causes of the succession of day and night and the seasons, etc. (L. *tellus*, the earth.)
tellurism, *n.* *tel*-ew-rizm, a magnetic influence supposed to permeate the whole of nature and to produce animal magnetism; the influence of the soil as a cause of disease [Path.]. (L.)
tellurite, *n.* *tel*-ewr-rite, telluric ochre [Min.].
tellurium, *n.* te-*lewr*-re-um, a rare silver-white semi-metallic element of the sulphur group, chemically related to selenium.
tellurize, *v.t.* *tel*-ew-rize, to combine or treat with tellurium.
tellurous, *a.* *tel*-ew-rus, obtained from tellurium; pertaining to tellurium in its lower valency. **tellurous acid,** an acid composed of one equivalent of tellurium and two of oxygen.
telotype, *n.* *tel*-o-tipe, a printing electric telegraph; a telegram printed by this. (Gr. *tele*, far off, and *type*.)
telpher, *n.* *tel*-fer, a carrier used in telpherage: *v.t.* to transport by this: *a.* pertaining to a system of telpherage. (Gr. *tele-*, and *pherein*, to bear.)
telpherage, *n.* *tel*-fer-raj, electrical transportation, esp. by means of carriers suspended from a rail.
telson, *n.* *tel*-son, the last segment of certain crustaceans and arachnids.
Telugu, *n.* *tel*-oo-goo, the principal Dravidian language of Southern and Central India.
temblor, *n.* tem-*blor*, an earthquake [U.S.A.]. (Sp., a trembling.)
temenos, *n.* *tem*-e-nos, a temple precinct. (Gr.)
temerarious, *a.* tem-e-*rare*-re-us, rash; headstrong; careless. (L. *temere*, by chance.)
temerariously, *ad.* rashly; with excess of boldness.
temerariousness, *n.* tem-e-*rare*-re-us-ness, the quality of being temerarious; temerity.
temerity, *n.* te-*me*-re-te, extreme boldness; rashness; unreasonable contempt of danger. (L.)
temerous, *a.* *tem*-er-rus, rash; reckless.
Tempean, *a.* tem-*pee*-an, delightful, like Tempe, a vale in Thessaly, much praised by the classic poets.
temper, *n.* *tem*-per, disposition or state of mind as regards passions and feelings; temperament; mental composure; heat of mind or passion; proneness to anger; due mixture of different qualities or ingredients, or its resulting state; the state of a metal, esp. as to its hardness: *v.t.* to mix so that one part qualifies the other; to modify by mixture; to mix or to unite in due proportion; to accommodate; to soften or mollify; to harden or toughen metal by re-heating and cooling. **to keep,** or **lose, one's temper,** to refrain from showing, or to show, anger, vexation, etc. **out of temper,** irritable; showing anger. (Fr. *temperer*, to proportion or mingle duly.)
tempera, *n.* *tem*-per-ra, the process of painting in distemper, or with a medium (usually white of egg) other than oil.
temperable, *a.* *tem*-per-ra-bl, capable of being tempered.
temperament, *n.* *tem*-per-ra-ment, character peculiar to an individual; state with respect to the predominance of any quality; due mixture of different qualities, or the result; tuning, esp. by adjustment of the tones of an instrument [Mus.]. (Fr. *temperament*.)
temperamental, *a.* *tem*-per-ra-*men*-tal, pertaining to temperament; having a sensitive temperament; constitutional.
temperamentally, *ad.* tem-per-ra-*men*-ta-le, in a temperamental manner; on account of temperament.
temperance, *n.* *tem*-per-rance, moderation, esp. in indulgence of the appetites and passions; abstinence; sobriety.
temperate, *a.* *ten*-per-rat, moderate; not excessive; moderate in the indulgence of appetites, etc.; abstemious; free from ardent passion; mild (of weather). **temperate zone,** the part of the earth between the tropics and the polar circles.
temperately, *ad.* in a temperate manner; moderately.
temperateness, *n.* the state or quality of being temperate; moderation; mildness.
temperative, *a.* *tem*-per-ra-tiv, having the power or quality of tempering; soothing.
temperature, *n.* *tem*-per-ra-tewr, the heat of the air; the state of a body with regard to heat or cold, esp. as indicated by the thermometer [Physics]. **to have a temperature,** to be feverish.
tempered, *a.* *tem*-perd, constitutionally disposed; having a temper; modified by admixture; in equal temperament [Mus.].
temperer, *n.* *tem*-per-rer, one who or that which tempers.
tempest, *n.* *tem*-pest, a storm of extreme violence; violent tumult, commotion, or agitation: *v.t.* to affect by, or in the manner of, a tempest [Poet.]. (O.Fr., from L. *tempestas*, weather, time.)
tempestive, *a.* tem-*pes*-tiv, seasonable. (L. *tempestivus*, timely.)
tempestuous, *a.* tem-*pes*-tew-us, very stormy; turbulent; blowing with violence.
tempestuously, *ad.* with great violence of wind or great commotion.
tempestuousness, *n.* storminess; state of being tempestuous or disturbed by violent winds.
templar, *n.* *tem*-plar, a student of the law, or a barrister belonging to the Inner or Middle Temple, London; a Knight Templar, or member of a mediæval religious military order established at Jerusalem to protect pilgrims travelling to the

Holy Land; a member of the Good Templars, a temperance society.

template, *n. tem*-plat, a templet.

temple, *n. tem*-pl, an edifice erected for the worship of some god and anciently regarded as his dwelling: (*cap.*) one of the successive buildings in ancient Jerusalem built for the worship of Jehovah; a place of public worship. **the Temple,** two Inns of Court in London, still chiefly inhabited by lawyers, so called because built on the site of a former establishment of the Knight Templars. (A.S. *templ*, from L. *templum.*)

temple, *n. tem*-pl, the flat space between ear and forehead [Anat.]. (O.Fr., from L. *tempora.*)

templed, *a. tem*-pld, having a temple or temples.

templet, *n. tem*-plet, a pattern or gauge used as a guide in cutting or setting out work in stone, metal, etc.; a short support under a girder or other beam [Arch.].

tempo, *n. tem*-poh (*pl.* **tempi**), time or rate of movement [Mus.]. **a tempo,** in strict time. **tempo giusto,** in just or steady time. **tempo rubato,** transferring part of the time of one note in a melody to another (It.)

temporal, *a. tem*-po-ral, pertaining to this life; secular; measured or limited by time; having limited existence; transient; worldly; [Gram.] relating to a tense or expressing time. **temporal power,** the right of the Pope to possess and govern the States of the Church (now confined to the Vatican City). **Lords Temporal,** *see* **lord.** (L. *tempus, temporis,* time.)

temporal, *a. tem*-po-ral, pertaining to a temple [Anat.]: *n.* a temporal bone, or muscle. **temporal bone,** the bone at the side and base of the skull. **temporal muscle,** the maxillary muscle that brings the incisor teeth together.

temporalism, *n. tem*-por-a-lizm, worldliness; secularism; the political doctrine favouring the papal claim to temporal power.

temporality, *n.* tem-po-*ral*-e-te, a secular possession, esp. (*pl.*) church revenues; temporariness.

temporally, *ad. tem*-po-ra-le, with respect to temporal matters, or to this present life.

temporalty, *n. tem*-po-ral-te, the laity; a temporality or secular possession.

temporarily, *ad. tem*-po-ra-re-le, for a time only.

temporariness, *n. tem*-po-ra-re-ness, the state of being temporary.

temporary, *a. tem*-po-ra-re, lasting for a time only; continuing for a limited time; transient.

temporization, *n.* tem-po-ry-*zay*-shon, the act of temporizing.

temporize, *v.i. tem*-po-rize, to comply with the time or occasion; to hesitate in deciding; to trim; to gain time by disguising one's intentions. (Fr. *temporiser.*)

temporizer, *n. tem*-po-ry-zer, one who temporizes.

temporizing, *n. tem*-po-ry-zing, compliance for convenience or with prevailing circumstances; trimming; procrastination: *a.* time-serving.

temporizingly, *ad.* in a temporizing manner.

tempt, *v.t.* tempt, to incite, esp. to some wrong act or thing; to allure or entice; to solicit. (O.Fr. *tempter.*)

temptable, *a. temp*-ta-bl, capable of being or liable to be tempted.

temptation, *n.* temp-*tay*-shon, the act of tempting; enticement to evil; state of being tempted; an allurement or inducement.

tempter, *n. temp*-ter, one who solicits or entices to evil. **the Tempter,** Satan, the devil.

temptingly, *ad.* so as to entice or allure.

temptingness, *n.* the quality of being tempting.

temptress, *n. temp*-tress, a woman who tempts.

temse, *n.* tems *or* temz, a sieve. **temse bread,** bread made of finely sifted flour. (A.S. *temes.*)

temulency, *n. tem*-yew-len-se, drunkenness.

temulent, *a. tem*-yew-lent, given to insobriety; drunken; intoxicated; intoxicating. (L.)

temulin, *n. tem*-yew-lin, the narcotic principle of darnel, *Lolium temulentum.*

ten, *a.* ten, twice five: *n.* the number twice five, or a figure denoting it. (A.S.)

tenability, *n.* ten-a-*bil*-e-te, tenableness.

tenable, *a. ten*-a-bl, that may be held, maintained, or defended against attack or attempts to take it.

tenableness, *n. ten*-a-bl-ness, the state of being tenable. (Fr., from *tenir,* hold.)

tenace, *n. ten*-as, the holding of the first and third best cards in a suit. **minor tenace,** the holding of the second and fourth best cards [Whist, etc.].

tenacious, *a.* te-*nay*-shus, holding fast, or inclined to hold fast; retentive; adhesive; glutinous.

tenaciously, *ad.* in a tenacious manner.

tenaciousness, *n.* te-*nay*-shus-ness, tenacity.

tenacity, *n.* te-*nas*-e-te, the quality of being tenacious; toughness; cohesiveness; that property which keeps bodies from parting without use of considerable force. (Fr. *ténacité.*)

tenaculum, *n.* te-*nak*-yew-lum, a surgical instrument by which bleeding arteries are drawn out to be tied.

tenaille, *n.* te-*nale,* a low rampart in the ditch in front of the curtain between two bastions [Fort.]. (Fr.)

tenaillon, *n.* te-*nal*-yon, a strengthening work constructed on each side of the ravelins [Fort.]. (Fr.)

tenancy, *n. ten*-an-se, a holding; a possession of lands or tenements as tenant, also the period of such holding; tenure [Law].

tenant, *n. ten*-ant, one holding land or other real estate under another, either by grant, lease, or at will; one who holds possession of any place; a dweller: *v.t.* to hold or possess as a tenant; to inhabit. **tenant in capite** or **in chief,** one who holds immediately of the sovereign [Feudal Law]. (L. *teneo,* hold.)

tenantable, *a. ten*-an-ta-bl, fit to be tenanted; in a state of repair suitable for a tenant.

tenantless, *a. ten*-ant-less, having no tenant; unoccupied.

tenantry, *n. ten*-an-tre, a body of tenants; tenants collectively; the condition of being a tenant.

tench, *n.* tench, a freshwater cyprinoid fish of the genus *Tinca.* (Fr. *tanche.*)

tend, *v.t.* tend, to watch; to guard; to accompany as assistant or protector; to take care of; to be attentive to; to cause a vessel to swing, at single anchor, so as not to foul [Naut.]: *v.i.* to move in a certain direction; to be directed to an end or purpose; to aim at; to contribute. (Fr. *tendre.*)

tendance, *n. ten*-dans, attendance; act of tending.

★tendency, *n. ten*-den-se, drift; direction or course towards any place, object, result, etc.; inclination.

tendential, *a.* ten-*den*-shal, tendentious.

tendentious, *a.* ten-*den*-shus, with a tendency or bias; done or written with a purpose.

tender, *n. ten*-der, one who tends or takes care of; a small vessel attending a larger one, supplying her with provisions and other stores; a truck attached to a locomotive to supply water and fuel.

tender, *n. ten*-der, any offer for acceptance; the thing offered; an offer of money to pay a debt, or of service to be performed in order to save a penalty or forfeiture; an estimate for a piece of work: *v.t.* to offer in payment; to present for acceptance; to offer in satisfaction of a demand, to save a penalty, etc. (Fr. *tendre.*)

tender, *a. ten*-der, easily impressed, broken, bruised or injured; not firm or hard; very sensitive to impression and pain; delicate; effeminate; weak; careful; gentle; feeble; susceptible of the softer passions; expressive of softer passions; easily excited to pity; pathetic. (Fr. *tendre.*)

tenderfoot, *n. ten*-der-foot, a novice in an unsettled country; a junior cub [Scouting].

tender-hearted, *a.* having great sensibility; very susceptible of the softer passions.

tenderling, *n. ten*-der-ling, a young child; one made tender by too much cosseting.

tenderloin, *n. ten*-der-loyn, a tender part of flesh in the hind-quarter of beef or pork.

tenderly, *ad.* in a tender manner.

tenderness, *n.* state of being tender; sensibility; kindness; scrupulousness; care not to injure.

tendinous, *a. ten*-de-nus, pertaining to, consisting of, or of the nature of tendons; sinewy. (Fr. *tendineux.*)

tendon, *n. ten*-don, a hard insensible cord or bundle of fibres forming the termination or connexion of the fleshy part of a muscle. **tendon of Achilles,** the tendon connecting the muscles of the calf with the bone of the heel [Anat.]. (L. *tendo,* stretch.)

tendoplasty, *n. ten*-do-plas-te, plastic operations on tendons [Surg.].

tendril, *n. ten*-dril, a slender twining shoot, by

which a plant clings to something for support. (Fr. *tendrille.*)

tendrilous, *a. ten*-dril-us, having tendrils; resembling a tendril.

Tenebræ, *n.pl. ten*-e-bree, matins and lauds for the last three days of Holy Week, usually sung after noon on the preceding day [Eccles.]. (L., darkness.)

tenebrific, *a.* ten-e-*brif*-ik, causing darkness. (L. *tenebræ,* darkness, *facio,* make.)

tenebrose, *a. ten*-e-brohs, dark; gloomy.

tenebrosity, *n. ten*-e-*bros*-e-te, the quality of being tenebrous; darkness; gloom.

tenebrous, *a. ten*-e-brus, tenebrose.

tenebrousness, *n.* tenebrosity.

tenement, *n. ten*-e-ment, a house; a room or suite of rooms in a group of dwellings; a flat; a part of a house used by one family; any species of permanent property, as land or houses [Law]. (Fr.)

tenemental, *a.* ten-e-*men*-tal, pertaining to a tenement; held by tenants.

tenementary, *a.* ten-e-*men*-ta-re, consisting of tenements; held by tenants.

teneral, *a. ten*-er-ral, immature (of the imago of insects emerging from the pupa state). (L. *tener,* soft.)

tenesmus, *n.* te-*nez*-mus, a straining and painful ineffectual effort to relieve the bowels [Med.]. (Gr., from *teino,* strain.)

tenet, *n. tee*-net *or ten*-et, any opinion, principle, dogma, or doctrine held to be true. (L., he holds.)

tenfold, *a.* and *ad. ten*-fohld, ten times more.

tenioid, *a. tee*-ne-oyd, tænioid.

tennantite, *n. ten*-nan-tite, a blackish, lead-grey sulphide of copper and arsenic. (S. *Tennant, d.* 1815, Engl. chemist.)

tenner, *n. ten*-er, a ten-pound (or ten-dollar) note; a sentence of ten years [Slang].

tennis, *n. ten*-nis, a game for from two to four players in which a ball is hit backwards and forwards over a net by rackets in a court built for the purpose. **lawn tennis,** a similar outdoor game played on a grass or hard court. **tennis court,** a marked and prepared court, lawn, or ground on which tennis or lawn tennis is played. (O.Fr. *tenetz.*)

Tenno, *n. ten*-oh, the official designation of the Emperor of Japan. (Jap., Heavenly Sovereign.)

tenon, *n. ten*-on, the end of a piece of timber, so formed as to be fitted into a mortise: *v.t.* to fit with tenons; to join by tenon. (Fr. *tenir,* hold.)

tenon-saw, *n.* a thin saw with a brass or steel back for cutting tenons.

tenor, *n. ten*-or, continued run or currency; whole course or strain; stamp; character; general drift; exact purport [Law]; the male voice between alto and baritone; a part adapted to this; one who sings the tenor, or the instrument that plays it; the tenor violin or viola: *a.* characteristic of the tenor voice. **tenor clef,** the C clef, when placed on the fourth line of the stave. **first** and **second tenor,** the higher and lower tenor parts [Mus.]. (Fr. *teneur.*)

tenorino, *n.* ten-o-*ree*-noh, a castrato; the high falsetto reached by castrati. (It.)

tenotomy, *n.* te-*not*-o-me, the operation of dividing a tendon. (Gr. *tenon,* a tendon, *tome,* cutting.)

tenpenny, *a. ten*-pe-ne, valued at ten-pence. **tenpenny nail,** a large-sized nail (originally 3 in., sold at 10*d.* per 100).

tenrec, *n. ten*-rek, a small insectivore, *Centetes ecaudatus,* allied to the hedgehogs, found in Madagascar. (Malagasy.)

tense, *a.* tense, stretched; strained to stiffness: *v.t.* to stretch tight; to utter tensely (of vowels) [Phon.]. (L. *tendo, tensum,* stretch.)

tense, *n.* tense, an inflexion in verbs to distinguish the time or duration of the action. (O.Fr. *tens,* L. *tempus.*)

tensely, *ad.* in a tense manner.

tenseness, *n.* the state of being tense.

tensibility, *n. ten*-se-*bil*-e-te, the state that admits of tension.

tensible, *a. ten*-se-bl, tensile.

tensile, *a. ten*-sile, capable of being extended; pertaining to tension; ductile.

tension, *n. ten*-shon, the act of stretching or straining; state or degree of being stretched; stiffness; a strained condition; a pulling or stretching device [Mach.]; the expansive force of a gas; that quality by reason of which a charge tends to discharge itself [Elect.]. **surface tension,** the property residing in the surface film of a liquid that causes it to act as an elastic enveloping membrane, as in a bubble. (L. *tensio.*)

tensional, *a. ten*-shon-al, pertaining to or affected with tension.

tensity, *n. ten*-se-te, tenseness; the state of being stretched or strained to stiffness.

tensive, *a. ten*-siv, causing tension [Path.].

tenson, *n. ten*-son, a Provençal lyrical disputation, usually conducted in alternating stanzas. (Fr.)

tensor, *n. ten*-sor, a muscle that stretches or tightens a part [Anat.].

tent, *n.* tent, a portable habitation, usually of canvas stretched over and sustained by poles: *v.t.* and *i.* to lodge in a tent; to encamp. (Fr. *tente.*)

tent, *n.* tent, a roll of lint or linen, etc., used to keep open a wound or incision [Surg.]: *v.t.* to treat with a tent. (Fr. *tenter.*)

tent, *n.* tent, a kind of Spanish wine of a deep-red colour, often used for sacramental purposes. (Sp. *tinto,* deep-coloured.)

tentacle, *n. ten*-ta-kl, a long flexible organ for feeling, holding or moving, borne on the head or round the mouth of many invertebrates. (L. *tento,* feel.)

tentacular, *a.* ten-*tak*-yew-lar, pertaining to or of the nature of tentacles.

tentaculate, *a.* ten-*tak*-yew-late, having tentacles.

tentaculiferous, *a.* ten-tak-yew-*lif*-er-rus, bearing or furnished with tentacles.

tentation, *n.* ten-*tay*-shon, a method of working by experimentation.

tentative, *a. ten*-ta-tiv, making trial or experiment: *n.* an experiment; trial. (L. *tentativus.*)

tent-bed, *n.* a camp-bedstead; also, a bedstead with the curtains hanging from a canopy.

tented, *a. ten*-ted, covered or furnished with tents.

tenter, *n. ten*-ter, a machine for stretching cloth by means of hooks: *v.t.* to hang or stretch on, or as on, tenters. **on the tenters,** on the stretch; in distress, uneasiness, or suspense. (Fr. *tenture,* hangings.)

tenter, *n. ten*-ter, one who lives in a tent; a machine-minder in certain trades.

tenter-hook, *n.* a sharp hooked nail, esp. one used in stretching cloth on the tenter. **on tenter-hooks,** in agitated suspense or uncertainty.

tenth, *a.* tenth, the ordinal of ten; the first after the ninth: *n.* the tenth part; a tithe; the octave of the third [Mus.].

tenthly, *ad. tenth*-le, in the tenth place.

tenthmetre, *n. tenth*-mee-ter, a ten-millionth part of a millimetre [Physics].

tentorial, *a.* ten-*taw*-re-al, pertaining to the tentorium [Anat.].

tentorium, *n.* tent-*taw*-re-um, the membranous fold separating the cerebrum from the cerebellum. (L., a tent.)

tent-peg, *n.* one of the pegs, fixed in the ground, to which the ropes of a tent are fastened.

tent-pegging, *n.* a sport in which a horseman tries at full gallop to strike and carry off a planted tent-peg on his lance.

tent-stitch, *n.* a series of short slanting stitches used in embroidery, etc.

tenuifolious, *a. ten*-yew-e-*foh*-le-us, having thin or narrow leaves [Bot.]. (L. *tenuis,* thin, *folium,* a leaf.)

tenuiroster, *n. ten*-ew-e-*ros*-ter, a humming-bird or other member of the Tenuirostres, a former order comprising certain slender-billed birds. (L. *tenuis,* slender, *rostrum,* a beak.)

tenuirostral, *a. ten*-yew-e-*ros*-tral, slender-billed; belonging to the Tenuirostres.

tenuity, *n.* te-*new*-e-te, thinness; smallness in diameter; rarity. (Fr. *tenuité.*)

tenuous, *a. ten*-yew-us, thin; light; subtle; not dense; over-refined. (L. *tenuis.*)

tenure, *n. ten*-yewr, a holding or manner of holding, esp. real estate; the consideration, condition, or service given by the occupier of land to his superior for the use of this; manner of holding in general; period of holding.

tenurial, *a.* te-*newr*-re-al, pertaining to or of the nature of tenure.

tenuto, *ad.* te-*noo*-toh, signifying that the notes are to be sustained or held on [Mus.]. (It.)

tenzon, *n. ten*-zon, tenson.

teocalli, *n.* te-o-*kal*-le, an early Central American or Mexican pyramidal structure, built as or surmounted by a temple. (Mex., house of a god.)

tepee, *n.* te-*pee*, an American Indian conical tent.

tepefy, *v.t.* and *i. tep*-e-fy, to make or become moderately warm. (L. *tepeo*, be warm, *facio*, make.)

:ephrite, *n. tef*-rite, an igneous rock resembling basalt. (Gr. *tephra*, ashes.)

:ephroite, *n. tef*-ro-ite, an ash-grey crystalline silicate of manganese.

'ephromancy, *n. tef*-ro-man-se, divination from the ashes of burnt offerings.

:epid, *a. tep*-id, moderately warm; lukewarm. (L. *tepidus*, from *tepere*, to be warm.)

:epidarium, *n. tep*-e-*dare*-re-um, the warm room in a Roman bath; a boiler for heating a bath.

'epidity, *n.* te-*pid*-e-te, tepidness.

epidness, *n. tep*-id-ness, lukewarmness.

erai, *n.* te-*ry*, a broad-brimmed felt hat worn by white men in the sub-tropics. (Name of district in northern India.)

eramorphous, *a.* te-ra-*mor*-fus, of monstrous form or nature. (Gr. *teras*, a monster, *morphe*, form.)

eraphim, *n.pl. te*-ra-fim, idols or household gods anciently consulted as oracles by the Hebrews. (Heb.)

eratism, *n. te*-ra-tizm, any congenital or acquired abnormality of conformation; a monster or monstrosity [Path.]. (Gr. *teras*, a monster.)

eratogeny, *n.* te-ra-*toj*-e-ne, the production of monsters or monstrous growths. (Gr. *teras*, a prodigy, *gennao*, produce.)

eratoid, *n. te*-ra-toyd, abnormal [Path.]; teramorphous: *n.* a teratoma.

eratolite, *n.* te-*rat*-o-lite, an impure silicate of aluminium and iron, formerly valued for its supposed medicinal properties.

eratological, *a.* te-ra-to-*loj*-e-kal, pertaining to teratology [Med.].

eratologist, *n.* te-ra-*tol*-o-jist, a student of teratology [Med.].

eratology, *n.* te-ra-*tol*-o-je, the art of telling stories of prodigies and marvels; tales of this kind; the study of antenatal malformations and monstrosities [Med.], or of similar phenomena among animals and plants. (Gr. *teras*, and *logos*, science.)

eratoma, *n.* te-ra-*toh*-ma, an abnormal tumour containing fœtal remains or tissues of skin, cartilage, bone, teeth, etc. [Path.].

eratosis, *n.* te-ra-*toh*-sis, a congenital deformity [Path.].

erbium, *n. ter*-be-um, a colourless metallic element belonging to the yttrium sub-group of the rare earths. (*Ytterby*, in Sweden, where first found.)

erce, *n.* terce, the right of a widow to a third of the income from her husband's property when no special provision has been made for her [Scots. Law].

ercel, *n. ter*-sel, a tiercel.

:rcentenary, *a.* ter-sen-*ten*-a-re *or* ter-sen-*tee*-na-re, comprising three hundred years: *n.* commemoration of something that happened three hundred years before. (Gr. *ter*, thrice, *centum*, a hundred.)

ercet, *n. ter*-set, a third [Mus.]; a triplet [Pros.].

:rebene, *n. te*-re-been, a mixture of petroleum and rosin oils, with or without turpentine, used to thin paints; an antiseptic mixture of terpenes formed by treating oil of turpentine with sulphuric acid.

rebinth, *n. te*-re-binth, the turpentine tree, *Pistacia terebinthus*, yielding Chian turpentine. (Gr.)

rebinthic, *a.* te-re-*bin*-thik, pertaining to or resembling turpentine.

'rebinthine, *a.* te-re-*bin*-thin, pertaining to the terebinth, or to turpentine.

'rebra, *n. te*-re-bra, the boring organ of certain insects, an ovipositor. (L., borer.)

:rebrate, *a. te*-re-brate, furnished with or resembling a terebra [Entom.]: *v.t.* to bore, to pierce by boring.

erebratula, *n.* te-re-*brat*-yew-la, a genus of living and extinct brachiopods; the lamp-shells.

'redo, *n.* te-*ree*-do, the ship-worm, a bivalve boring mollusc with the valves at one end and a pair of pallets at the other. (Gr. *tereo*, bore.)

terek, *n. te*-rek, a migratory sandpiper, *Terek cinerea*, of E. Europe and Asia. (Caucasian river, *Terek*.)

terete, *a.* te-*reet*, long, cylindrical, and tapering [Bot. and Zool.]. (L. *teres*, rounded.)

tergal, *a. ter*-gal, dorsal [Zool.].

tergeminate, *a.* ter-*jem*-e-nat, having three pairs of leaflets [Bot.]. (L. *ter*, thrice, and *gemini*, twins.)

tergite, *n. ter*-jite, a chitonous tergum in an arthropod.

tergiversate, *v.i. ter*-je-ver-sate, to practise evasion; to equivocate.

tergiversation, *n. ter*-je-ver-*say*-shon, a shifting; subterfuge; evasive conduct; fickleness of conduct. (L. *tergum*, and *verso*, turn.)

tergum, *n. ter*-gum, the upper or dorsal part of a somite in an arthropod; any plate of the carapace in the *Cirripedia*. (L., the back.)

term, *n.* term, a limit, bound, or boundary; the time for which a thing lasts; a limited time; the whole period for which an estate is granted, also an estate so held [Law]; a period during which certain courts of law sit (called Hilary, Easter, Trinity, and Michaelmas, from the festivals near which they begin); a day on which rent is paid; in universities, schools, etc., the period during which instruction is given; a word or expression with a determinate meaning; the subject or predicate of a proposition [Logic]; a pillar terminating above in a statue or bust [Arch.]; a member of a compound quantity [Alg.]: *pl.* price; conditions; stipulations; the normal period of gestation [Med.]: *v.t.* to name; to denominate. **come to terms,** to arrive at agreement; to submit to conditions. (Fr. *terme*.)

termagancy, *n. ter*-ma-gan-se, turbulence; tumultuousness.

termagant, *a. ter*-ma-gant, boisterous; turbulent; quarrelsome: *n.* a brawling, abusive woman. (A supposed Saracenic god figuring in mediæval morality plays.)

termer, *n. term*-er, a prisoner serving for a term; one who has an estate for a term.

Termes, *n. ter*-meez, a genus of orthopterous insects including the termites, or white ants. (L., a wood-worm.)

terminability, *n. ter*-me-na-*bil*-e-te, the state or quality of being terminable.

terminable, *a. ter*-me-na-bl, that may terminate or be terminated; limitable.

terminableness, *n.* quality of being terminable.

terminal, *a. ter*-me-nal, pertaining to a terminus; relating to or growing at the end; concluding; pertaining to or lasting for a term [School, etc.]; occurring every term: *n.* the extremity or end; a binding screw; a connecting device for current [Elect.]. **terminal velocity,** the limiting velocity attained by anything falling freely in a resisting medium. (Late L. *terminalis*, boundary.)

terminally, *ad.* ter-*me*-na-le, once a term, every term; at the end.

terminate, *v.t. ter*-me-nate, to limit; to bound; to set the extreme point or side of a thing; to put an end to; to complete; to finish: *v.i.* to be limited; to end. (L. *terminatum*.)

termination, *n. ter*-me-*nay*-shon, the act of ending; bound; limit in space or extent; end in time or existence; the end or ending of a word [Gram.]; conclusion; result. (L. *terminationem*.)

terminational, *a. ter*-me-*nay*-shon-al, pertaining to or forming the end.

terminative, *a. ter*-me-na-tiv, serving to terminate; determinative; conclusive.

terminatively, *ad.* in a terminative manner.

terminator, *n. ter*-me-nay-tor, the dividing line between the light and dark parts of the disk of a heavenly body, esp. the moon [Astron.].

terminatory, *a. ter*-me-na-to-re, forming the end; serving to terminate.

terminer, *n. ter*-me-ner, a determining (only in "oyer and terminer," *see* **oyer**).

terminism, *n. ter*-me-nizm, the doctrine that God has assigned to every individual a term of repentance [Theol.]: nominalism [Phil.].

terminist, *n. ter*-me-nist, one who holds either doctrine of terminism.

terminological, *a. ter*-me-noh-*loj*-e-kal, pertaining to terminology; technical. **terminological**

inexactitude, a perversion of the truth, esp. as used for political purposes.

terminology, *n.* ter-me-*nol*-o-je, the science of the use of correct or technical terms; a body of terms peculiar to a science or art. (L. *terminus*, and Gr. *logos*, science.)

terminus, *n.* *ter*-me-nus (*pl.* **termini**, *ter*-me-ny), a boundary; a boundary-mark; the point or station where a traffic route ends; the Roman god of boundaries, or a statued pillar (L. *term*) representing him. (L.)

termitary, *n.* *ter*-me-ta-re, a termite's nest.

termite, *n.* *ter*-mite, an orthopterous insect of the family Terminidæ; a white ant. (L. *termes.*)

termless, *a.* *term*-less, unlimited; boundless.

termly, *a.* *term*-le, occurring every term: *ad.* term by term; every term.

termor, *n.* *ter*-mor, a lessee for a term; one holding lands or tenements for a term of years or for life [Law].

tern, *n.* tern, a long-winged, fork-tailed sea-bird of the genus *Sterna*, allied to the gulls. (Scand.)

tern, *n.* tern, a set of three: *a.* ternate. (L. *terni*, three each.)

ternary, *a.* *ter*-na-re, pertaining to or consisting of three; threefold: *n.* a triad or group of three.

ternate, *a.* *ter*-nat, arranged in threes; having three leaflets on a petiole (of leaves) [Bot.].

terneplate, *n.* *tern*-plate, thin steel plate coated with an alloy of tin and lead. (Fr. *terne*, dull, and *plate.*)

ternery, *n.* *tern*-er-re, a breeding-place of terns.

ternion, *n.* *ter*-ne-on, a set of three; a ternary.

terpene, *n.* *ter*-peen, any of several hydrocarbons present in volatile oils distilled from conifers and other plants. (*turpentine.*)

Terpsichorean, *a.* *terp*-se-ko-*ree*-an, relating to Terpsichore, the muse who presided over the lyre and dancing; pertaining to dancing. (Gr.)

terra, *n.* *te*-ra, the earth; earth. **terra firma,** the dry land, as opposed to the sea. **terra incognita,** unexplored or undiscovered country. (L.)

terra-alba, *n.* *te*-ra-*al*-ba, pipe-clay.

terrace, *n.* *te*-ras, a natural or artificial raised level space or platform with sloping sides; a street along the top of a terrace slope; a row of similar houses in one block; a level shelf of land; a raised beach [Geol.]: *v.t.* to form into a terrace. (L. *terra*, earth.)

terracotta, *n.* *te*-ra-*kot*-a, a hard unglazed clay-ware used as a decorative facing for buildings and for statuettes, vases, etc.; a model or cast made of this; its brownish-red colour: *a.* of this colour. (It., from L. *terra*, and *coctus*, cooked.)

terrain, *n.* te-*rane*, a tract of land.

terramara, *n.* *te*-ra-*mah*-rah, an earthy deposit dug from certain kitchen-middens, used as a fertilizer. (L. *terra*, earth, and *amara*, bitter.)

terranean, *a.* te-*ray*-ne-an, pertaining to the earth; terrestrial.

terraneous, *a.* te-*ray*-ne-us, terranean; growing on land [Bot.].

terrapin, *n.* *te*-ra-pin, any of several N. American turtles living in fresh or tidal waters.

terraqueous, *a.* te-*ray*-kwe-us, consisting of land and water, as the globe. (L. *terra*, and *aqua*, water.)

terra-Sienna, *n.* *te*-ra-se-*en*-na, the brown ochrous earth from which the pigment sienna is made. (*terra*, and *Sienna*, in Italy.)

terrene, *a.* te-*reen*, terrestrial; earthy; worldly.

terreplein, *n.* *tare*-plane, the horizontal surface of a rampart, on which the guns were placed [Fort.]. (Fr., from L. *terra*, and *planus*, level.)

terrestrial, *a.* te-*res*-tre-al, pertaining to or existing on the earth; living on or consisting of land, not water; pertaining to this world: *n.* an inhabitant of the earth. (L. *terrestris*, of the earth.)

terrestrially, *ad.* after an earthly manner.

terret, *n.* *te*-ret, a ring on harness through which the rein passes; the ring on a dog's collar; a tirret [Her.].

terre-tenant, *n.* tare-*ten*-ant, one who has the actual possession of land [Law]. (Fr., land-holding.)

terre-verte, *n.* tare-vayrt, a green earth, usually containing glauconite, used as a pigment. (Fr., green earth.)

terrible, *a.* *te*-re-bl, tending to excite terror; dreadful; formidable; inspiring awe. (Fr.)

terribleness, *n.* *te*-re-bl-ness, dreadfulness.

terribly, *ad.* *te*-re-ble, dreadfully; violently.

terricole, *a.* *te*-re-kohl, living in or on the earth [Zool.]; growing on the ground (as certain lichens) [Bot.]: *n.* a terricole animal; an earthworm or other member of the Terricolæ.

terricolous, *a.* te-*rik*-o-lus, living on the earth, not in the water or arboreally [Zool.].

terrier, *n.* *te*-re-er, a small dog of several varieties, originally used for hunting in burrows. (Fr., from *terre*, earth.)

terrier, *n.* *te*-re-er, a register in which lands of private persons or corporations are described. (Fr.)

Terrier, *n.* *te*-re-er, a member of the Territorial Army [Coll.].

terrific, *a.* te-*rif*-ik, dreadful; causing terror; fitted to inspire terror. (L. *terrificus.*)

terrifically, *ad.* te-*rif*-e-ka-le, in a terrifying manner, shockingly; extremely, tremendously [Coll.].

terrify, *v.t.* *te*-re-fy, to frighten; to alarm. (L. *terreo*, frighten, *facio*, make.)

terrigenous, *a.* te-*rij*-e-nus, earth-born; autochthonous; derived from adjacent land (of certain marine deposits).

terrine, *n.* ter-*reen*, a tureen; a dish of mixed game or meat braised and served in this. (Fr.)

territorial, *a.* te-re-*taw*-re-al, pertaining to territory or land; limited to a certain district: *n.* a member of the Territorial Army. **Territorial Army,** a branch of the British army formed in 1908 and including the militia, yeomanry, and volunteers, and (since 1949) National Service men. **territorial waters,** those under the sovereignty of a state, viz., its inland waters and coastal waters within three miles from low-water mark.

territorialism, *n.* *te*-re-*taw*-re-a-lizm, territorial organization; any system, doctrine, etc., relating specially to a territory as such; landlordism.

territoriality, *n.* *te*-re-*taw*-re-*al*-e-te, territorial quality or status.

territorialize, *v.t.* *te*-re-*taw*-re-a-lize, to place upon a territorial footing.

territorially, *ad.* as regards territory.

territory, *n.* *te*-re-to-re, the extent or compass of land within the bounds or belonging to the jurisdiction of any state or other body; a large tract of land, esp. one belonging to and under the dominion of a state lying at a distance from it; in the U.S.A., a district (as Alaska and Hawaii) having its own organization and governor but forming neither a part of a, nor a separate, State. (O.Fr. *territoire.*)

terror, *n.* *te*-ror, extreme fear; violent fear that agitates the body and mind; that which may excite dread. **King of terrors,** death. **reign of terror,** any time of violent blood-stained upheaval, esp. (*caps.*) the bloodiest period of the French Revolution (April 1793–July 1794). (Fr. *terreur.*)

terrorism, *n.* *te*-ro-rizm, the act of terrorizing; a system or state of terror; government or coercion by terror.

terrorist, *n.* *te*-ro-rist, one who rules or would rule by terrorism; a leader or agent of a reign of terror.

terroristic, *a.* te-ro-*ris*-tik, given to or characterized by terrorism; inspiring terror.

terrorization, *n.* te-ro-ry-*zay*-shon, the act or consequence of terrorizing.

terrorize, *v.t.* *te*-ro-rize, to fill with terror; to coerce by terror: *v.i.* to rule by terrorism.

terry, *n.* *te*-re, the loop formed for the nap in weaving velvet, etc.; a fabric in which the loops are not cut.

Terry, *n.* *te*-re, a member of the Territorial Army [Coll.].

Ter-sanctus, *n.* ter-*sank*-tus, the Sanctus of the Roman and Anglican rites, and Trisagion of the Greek. (L., thrice holy.)

terse, *a.* terce, cleanly or neatly concise; free of redundancy. (L. *tersum*, polished.)

tersely, *ad.* in a terse manner.

terseness, *n.* the quality of being terse.

tertial, *a.* and *n.* *ter*-shal, pertaining to, or one of the tertiary feathers [Ornith.].

tertian, *a.* *ter*-shan, occurring every other day: *n.* a fever whose paroxysms return every other day. (Fr. *tertiane.*)

tertiary, *a.* *ter*-sha-re, of the third order or degree; pertaining to the Tertiary formation [Geol.]

n. an associate of a religious order under vow to observe its rules but not leading a monastic life; a tertiary feather. **tertiary feather,** one of the feathers growing on the innermost joint of a bird's wing. **Tertiary formation,** a series of strata beginning immediately above the Cretaceous rocks; the Cainozoic [Geol.]. (L. *tertius*, third.)

tertius, *a. ter*-shus, third. (L.)

tervalent, *a.* ter-*vay*-lent, having a valency of three [Chem.].

terza-rima, *n. tert*-za-*ree*-ma, the system of versification rhyming *ababcb* used in Dante's Divina Commedia and other Italian poems. (It., triple rhyme.)

terzetto, *n.* tert-*set*-toh, a short composition in three parts [Mus.]. (It.)

tessellar, *a. tes*-e-lar, formed of tessaræ; tessellated.

tessellate, *v.t. tes*-e-late, to cover or adorn with mosaic; to make (a patterned pavement, etc.) with blocks of various colours. (L. *tesselara*, from Gr., as *tessera*.)

tessellated, *a. tes*-e-lay-ted, composed of small blocks or squares, as in mosaic work.

tessellation, *n. tes*-e-*lay*-shon, mosaic work, or the act or process of making it.

tessera, *n. tes*-er-ra (*pl.* **tesseræ**), a small cubical piece of marble or the like with which to make mosaics. (L., from Gr. *tessaragonos*, having four corners.)

tesseral, *a. tes*-er-ral, pertaining to or composed of tesseræ; isometric (of crystals).

tessitura, *n.* tes-e-*toor*-ra, the disposition, or the normal region of compass, of a voice [Mus.]. (It., texture.)

tessular, *a. tes*-ew-lar, tesseral.

★test, *n.* test, a cupel, or vessel in which metals are melted for trial and refinement [Metal.]; examination by the cupel; any critical trial or examination; trial; means of trial; a standard; judgment; distinction; a procedure or substance employed to identify another substance, the constituents of a compound, etc. [Chem.]; a test match: *v.t.* to prove the truth or genuineness of by experiment; to try severely; to refine in a cupel [Metal.]: to examine by means of a reagent [Chem.]. **test match,** one of a series of Commonwealth cricket matches, esp. between England and Australia. **test paper,** litmus paper. **test tube,** a finger-shaped vessel of thin glass used in chemistry. **test types,** printed letters, etc., of various sizes used as a test for eyesight. (L. *testum*, an earthen pot.)

test, *n.* test, a testa.

test, *v.t.* test, to attest and date. (L. *testis*, a witness.)

testa, *n. tes*-ta, an exoskeleton; a shelly covering; the integument of a seed. (L., a shard.)

testable, *a. tes*-ta-bl, capable of being tested; that may be devised or given by will.

Testacea, *n.pl.* tes-*tay*-sha, an order of rhizopods with a single-chambered chitonous testa.

testacean, *a.* tes-*tay*-shan, of or pertaining to the testacea: *n.* one of the testacea. (L. *testaceum*, from *testaceus*, literally, covered with tiles.)

testacel, *n. tes*-ta-sel, a small worm-eating slug.

testaceous, *a.* tes-*tay*-shus, pertaining to or of the nature of shells; having a hard shell; of a dull red colour [Bot. and Zool.].

testacy, *n. tes*-ta-se, the state of being testate; the fact of leaving a valid will [Law].

testament, *n. tes*-ta-ment, an instrument in writing, by which a person declares his will as to the disposal of his estate and effects after his death; a will; a copy of the New Testament [Coll.]. **Old** and **New Testaments,** the two great collections of the canonical books of the Scriptures. (O.Fr.)

testamental, *a.* tes-ta-*men*-tal, testamentary; of the nature of a testament.

testamentary, *a. tes*-ta-*men*-ta-re, pertaining to a will or wills; bequeathed by will; given or done by testament or will.

testamur, *n.* tes-*tay*-mur, a certificate of having passed an examination. (L., we testify.)

testate, *a. tes*-tat, having made and left a valid will: *n.* one who has done so. (L. *testatus*.)

testation, *n.* tes-*tay*-shon, the act or power of devising property by will.

testator, *n.* tes-*tay*-tor, a man who makes a will.

testatrix, *n.* tes-*tay*-triks, a female testator.

tester, *n. test*-er, a flat canopy over a bed, pulpit, or tomb. (O.Fr. *testiere*.)

tester, *n. test*-er, one who tests; an appliance with which to test.

tester, *n. test*-er, a teston; a sixpence [Slang].

testes, *n.pl. tes*-teez, *see* **testis.**

testicle, *n. tes*-te-kl, one of the two glands which secrete the seminal fluid in males. (L. *testiculus*.)

testicular, *a.* tes-*tik*-yew-lar, pertaining to the testicles [Anat.]; shaped like a testicle [Bot.].

testiculate, *a.* tes-*tik*-yew-lat, shaped like a testicle [Bot.].

testification, *n. tes*-te-fe-*kay*-shon, the act of testifying; the testimony given; evidence.

testificatory, *a. tes*-te-fe-*kay*-to-re, of the nature of, or serving as, evidence.

testifier, *n. tes*-te-fy-er, one who gives testimony or bears witness.

testify, *v.i. tes*-te-fy, to make a solemn declaration, to certify or establish some fact; to give testimony in a cause depending before a tribunal; to protest; to declare against: *v.i.* to affirm or declare solemnly for the purpose of establishing a fact; to bear witness to; to affirm or declare under oath [Law]; to publish and declare freely. (L. *testis*, a witness, and *facio*, make.)

testily, *ad. tes*-te-le, fretfully; peevishly.

testing, *n. tes*-ting, a putting to the test; a trial. **testing time,** a time of stress, trouble, or trial.

testimonial, *n. tes*-te-*moh*-ne-al, a writing or certificate in favour of one's character and qualifications; something subscribed for and given as a token of respect: *a.* relating to or containing testimony.

testimonialize, *v.t.* tes-te-*moh*-ne-a-lize, to present with a testimonial; to provide with a recommendation.

testimony, *n. tes*-te-mo-ne, a solemn declaration or affirmation made for the purpose of establishing or proving some fact; evidence; affirmation; declaration; the decalogue. (L. *testimonium*.)

testiness, *n. tes*-te-ness, fretfulness; peevishness; petulance.

testis, *n. tes*-tis (*pl.* **testes**), either of the testicles [Anat.]. (L.)

teston, *n.* tes-*ton*, an Italian silver coin of about 1470–1550, also a Scottish one of Mary Stuart; the English shilling of Henry VII to Edward VI. (O.It. *testone*.)

testudinal, *a.* tes-*tew*-de-nal, pertaining to or resembling the tortoise or tortoiseshell; shaped like a testudo [Mil.]. (L. *testudo*.)

testudinarious, *a. tes*-tew-de-*nare*-re-us, testudinal: coloured like tortoiseshell.

testudinate, *a.* tes-*tew*-de-nat, shaped like the back of a tortoise; arched.

testudineous, *a. tes*-tew-*din*-e-us, resembling the shell of a tortoise; dilatory like a tortoise.

testudo, *n.* tes-*tew*-doh, a tortoise; among the Romans, a protection against missiles, esp. from a besieged place, formed by the soldiers holding their shields over their heads [Mil.]; a wen [Med.]. (L., a tortoise.)

testy, *a. tes*-te, fretful; peevish; petulant; easily irritated. (O.Fr. *testu*, headstrong.)

tetanic, *a.* te-*tan*-ik, pertaining to, resembling, or denoting tetanus: *n.* any medicine (as strychnine) which, when taken in large doses, produces tetanic spasms.

tetanilla, *n.* tet-a-*nil*-a, tetany.

tetanine, *n. tet*-a-nin, a ptomaine containing the tetanus bacillus, found in decaying meat.

tetanism, *n. tet*-a-nizm, a condition resembling tetanus but not caused by the same bacillus [Med.].

tetanization, *n.* tet-a-ny-*zay*-shon, the production of, or the condition of having, tetanus.

tetanize, *v.t. tet*-a-nize, to produce tetanus or tetanic contractions in.

tetanoid, *a. tet*-a-noyd, resembling tetanus.

tetanus, *n. tet*-a-nus, lock-jaw; an acute infectious bacillary disease characterized by tonic spasms of the voluntary muscles, its first sign usually being stiffness of the jaw [Med.]. (Gr., from *teino*, stretch or strain.)

tetany, *n. tet*-a-ne, a morbid condition characterized by intermittent tonic muscular contractions, chiefly affecting the fingers and toes. (*tetanus*.)

tetchily, *ad. tetch*-e-le, in a tetchy manner.

tetchiness, *n. tetch*-e-ness, the state of being tetchy.

tetchy, *a. tetch*-e, testy; irritable; touchy.

tête-à-tête, *ad.* tate-ah-tate, face to face; in private: *n.* an intimate conversation between two people: *a.* of or pertaining to a tête-à-tête. (Fr.)

tether, *n.* *teth*-er, a rope or chain by which an animal is confined for feeding within certain limits: *v.t.* to limit with a tether; to deprive of freedom of action. (M.E. *tedir.*)

tetra-, *tet*-ra-, combining form signifying having four, or composed of four parts. (Gr. *tettares*, four.)

tetrabranchiate, *a.* *tet*-ra-*bran*-ke-at, having four gills: *n.* one of the Tetrabranchiæ, an order of four-gilled cephalopods including the nautilus.

tetrachord, *n.* *tet*-ra-kord, a series of four sounds, of which the extremes are a fourth apart; an instrument with four strings [Mus.].

tetrachotomous, *a.* *tet*-ra-*kot*-o-mus, ramifying in fours [Bot.] (Gr. *tetracha*, fourfold, *temno*, cut.)

tetracyclic, *a.* *tet*-ra-*sike*-lik, having four whorls [Bot.]; containing four atomic rings [Chem.].

tetrad, *n.* *tet*-rad, the number of four; a group of four; a tetravalent element, atom, or radical [Chem.].

tetradactyl, *n.* *tet*-ra-*dak*-til, a tetradactylous animal.

tetradactylous, *a.* *tet*-ra-*dak*-te-lus, having four fingers or toes.

tetradecapod, *a.* *tet*-ra-*dek*-a-pod, having fourteen feet: *n.* a crustacean having seven pairs of feet.

tetradic, *a.* te-*trad*-ik, of the nature of a tetrad; [Chem.] tetravalent.

tetradrachm, *n.* *tet*-ra-dram, a silver coin of ancient Greece worth four drachmas.

tetradymite, *n.* te-*trad*-e-mite, a telluride of bismuth occurring in compound twin crystals.

tetradynamous, *a.* *tet*-ra-*din*-a-mus, having four stamens longer than the rest [Bot].

tetraglot, *a.* *tet*-ra-glot, in four languages.

tetragon, *n.* *tet*-ra-gon, a plane figure having four angles [Geom.]; a quadrangle.

tetragonal, *a.* te-*trag*-o-nal, pertaining to or resembling a tetragon; having four angles; quadrangular in section [Bot. and Zool.]; having three rectangular axes of which two are equal (of crystals).

tetragram, *n.* *tet*-ra-gram, a word of four letters; a quadrilateral [Geom.].

Tetragrammaton, *n.* tet-ra-*gram*-a-ton, the group of four letters representing to the ancient Hebrews the Ineffable Name Jehovah, or Jahveh.

tetragynian, *a.* *tet*-ra-*jin*-e-an, having four pistils [Bot.].

tetrahedral, *a.* *tet*-ra-*hee*-dral, bounded by four equal and equilateral triangles; having four sides.

tetrahedrite, *n.* *tet*-ra-*hee*-drite, a grey copper ore composed chiefly of copper, antimony, and sulphur, occurring crystallized in tetrahedrons.

tetrahedron, *n.* *tet*-ra-*hee*-dron, a solid figure enclosed by four equilateral and equal triangles [Geom.]. (Gr. *tetra-*, and *hedra*, a side.)

tetrahexahedral, *a.* *tet*-ra-hek-sa-*hee*-dral, in the form of a tetrahexahedron. (L.)

tetrahexahedron, *n.* *tet*-ra-hek-sa-*hee*-dron, a solid bounded by twenty-four equal faces, four corresponding to each face of the cube. (Gr. *tetra-* and hexahedron.)

tetralogy, *n.* te-*tral*-o-je, a group of four dramatic or other compositions treating of related subjects.

tetrameral, *a.* tet-*tram*-er-ral, tetramerous.

tetramerous, *a.* tet-*tram*-er-rus, having, or consisting of, four parts [Bot. and Zool.].

tetrameter, *n.* te-*tram*-e-ter, a verse consisting of four measures [Pros.]. (Gr. *tetra-* and *meter.*)

tetramorphous, *a.* tet-ra-*mor*-fus, crystallizing in four distinct forms.

tetrandrian, *a.* te-*tran*-dre-an, having four stamens [Bot.]. (Gr. *tetra-*, and *aner*, a male.)

tetrapetalous, *a.* tet-ra-*pet*-a-lus, containing four distinct petals.

tetraphyllous, *a.* tet-ra-*fil*-us, having four leaves or leaflets [Bot.]. (Gr. *tetra-*, and *phyllon*, a leaf.)

tetrapla, *n.* *tet*-ra-pla, a Bible in four different versions, arranged in columns, esp. Origen's edition of the Old Testament. (Gr. *tetraplos*, fourfold.)

tetrapod, *a.* *tet*-ra-pod, having four legs or limbs: *n.* an insect having only four perfect feet. (Gr. *tetra-*, and *pous*, a foot.)

tetrapteran, *a.* te-*trap*-ter-ran, having four wings or [Bot.] wing-like appendages: *n.* an insect with four wings. (Gr. *tetra-*, and *pteron*, a wing.)

tetrapterous, *a.* te-*trap*-ter-rus, tetrapteran.

tetrarch, *n.* *tet*-rark, a Roman governor of the fourth part of a province; a petty or tributary prince. (Gr. *tetra-*, and *archo*, rule.)

tetrarchate, *n.* *tet*-rar-kat, the district, office, or jurisdiction of a tetrarch; joint rule by four.

tetrarchical, *a.* tet-*rar*-ke-kal, pertaining to a tetrarch or a tetrarchy.

tetrarchy, *n.* *tet*-rar-ke, tetrarchate.

tetraspermous, *a.* tet-ra-*sper*-mus, having four seeds, or seeds in groups of four [Bot.].

tetraspore, *n.* *tet*-ra-spore, one of the agamic cells, usually produced in fours, of the Floridæ, a group of algæ.

tetrastich, *n.* *tet*-ra-stik, a stanza, epigram, or poem of four lines. (Gr. *tetra-*, and *stichos*, a verse.)

tetrastyle, *n.* *tet*-ra-stile, a building or portico with four columns: *a.* having four columns or pillars [Arch.].

tetrasyllabic, *a.* *tet*-ra-se-*lab*-ik, consisting of four syllables.

tetrasyllable, *n.* *tet*-ra-*sil*-a-bl, a word of four syllables.

tetravalent, *a.* tet-ra-*vay*-lent, able to combine with four atoms of hydrogen or their equivalent [Chem.].

tetrode, *n.* *tet*-rohd, a thermionic valve with four electrodes [Wire.].

tetroxide, *n.* tet-*rok*-side, any oxide the molecule of which includes four atoms of oxygen.

tetter, *n.* *tet*-er, a name given to various skin diseases: *v.t.* to affect with or as with this. (A.S. *teter.*)

tetterwort, *n.* *tet*-er-wurt, the greater celandine.

tettix, *n.* *tet*-iks, a cicada; an ornament for the hair in the form of a cicada. (Gr. *tettix*, grasshopper.)

Teuton, *n.* *tew*-ton, one of Teutonic race including the former Goths, Vandals, Burgundians, Anglo-Saxons, Normans, etc., and the present Germans, Scandinavians, Dutch, Flemings, and English. (L. *Teutones.*)

Teutonic, *a.* tew-*ton*-ik, pertaining to the Teutons or their group of languages: *n.* the languages of the Teutons. **Teutonic Knights** or **Order,** a military and religious order, founded in connexion with the Crusades in 1190.

Teutonicism, *n.* tew-*ton*-e-sizm, a Teutonic or German idiom.

Teutonism, *n.* *tew*-to-nizm, belief in the superiority of the Teutons, esp. the Germans; Teutonic culture; Germanism.

Teutonize, *v.t.* *tew*-to-nize, to render Teutonic: *v.i.* to comply with or adapt oneself to Teutonism.

tewel, *n.* *tew*-el, a pipe or funnel, as for smoke; a tuyère. (O.Fr. *tuel.*)

Texan, *a.* *tek*-zan, pertaining to Texas or its people: *n.* an inhabitant of Texas.

text, *n.* tekst, that on which a note or commentary is written: the original words of an author; the letterpress of a book; a verse or short passage of Scripture, esp. one selected as the subject of a discourse. **text hand,** a large style of handwriting. (Fr. *texte.*)

text-book, *n.* a book containing the leading points of a science or branch of learning, arranged for the use of students or forming the basis of lectures, etc.

textile, *a.* *tek*-stile, formed by weaving, or capable of being woven: *n.* a woven fabric; that which is or may be woven. (L. *textilis.*)

textorial, *a.* tek-*staw*-re-al, pertaining to weaving.

textual, *a.* *tek*-stew-al, connected with, contained in, or serving for texts.

textualism, *n.* *tek*-stew-a-lizm, strict adherence to the text; literalism; also, textual criticism.

textualist, *n.* *tek*-stew-a-list, one well versed in the Scriptures and ready at quotation; one who adheres to the text.

textually, *ad.* in accordance with a text; verbatim.

textuary, *a.* *tek*-stew-a-re, textual; contained in the text; serving as a text: *n.* a textualist.

textural, *a.* tek-stewr-ral, having, or pertaining to texture.

texture, *n.* *tek*-stewr, that which is woven; the disposition or connexion of threads, filaments, or fibres interwoven; the disposition of the several parts of any body in connexion with each other; tissue; physical character or structure. (Fr.)

Thai, *n.* ty, the group of Indo-Chinese peoples including the Siamese and the Laos and Shan of Burma; the dialects of this group: *a.* designating or pertaining to these peoples and their speech. (Native name.)

thalamium, *n.* tha-*lay*-me-um, the spore-case in certain algæ; the spore-bearing surface in some fungi.

thalamus, *n. thal*-a-mus (*pl.* **thalami**), the receptacle of a flower; the great posterior ganglion of the brain, which interconnects and relays sensations received through the nerves; an inner room; the women's apartment in ancient Greek houses. (Gr., a bed-chamber.)

thalassian, *a.* tha-*las*-e-an, of or pertaining to the sea: *n.* any marine tortoise or sea turtle. (Gr.)

thalassic, *a.* tha-*las*-ik, pertaining to the sea or to seas; marine; pelagic. (Gr. *thalassa*, the sea.)

thalassocracy, *n.* thal-a-*sok*-ra-se, maritime supremacy; sea power, esp. that of Minoan Crete. (Gr. *thalassa*, and *kratos*, power.)

thalassography, *n.* thal-a-*sog*-ra-fe, the science that deals with the sea; oceanography.

thalassometer, *n.* thal-a-*som*-e-ter, a tide-gauge.

thalassotherapy, *n.* tha-*las*-o-*the*-ra-pe, medical treatment by sea-baths or sea-voyages.

thaler, *n. tah*-ler, a large silver coin of the German states, current from the 15th cent. to 1873, when it was superseded by the mark: a dollar. (Ger.: *see* **dollar**.)

Thalia, *n.* tha-*ly*-a, the muse who presided over pastoral and comic poetry [Myth.].

Thalian, *a.* tha-*ly*-an, relating to Thalia; comic.

thallic, *a. thal*-ik, pertaining to or containing thallium.

thallium, *n. thal*-e-um, a blue-white, extremely soft metallic element having very little elasticity. (Gr. *thallos*, a green shoot.)

thallogen, *n. thal*-o-jen, a thallophyte.

thalloid, *a. thal*-oyd, resembling or pertaining to a thallus [Bot.].

thallophyte, *n. thal*-o-fite, a member of the *Thallophyta*, a phylum of cryptogams including the algæ, fungi, and lichens. (Gr. *thallos*, and *phytos*, a plant.)

thallous, *a. thal*-us, containing thallium; pertaining to thallium, esp. in its lower valency [Chem.].

thallus, *n. thal*-us, a form of vegetation characteristic of the thallophytes, showing little or no differentiation into leaf, stem, and root. (Gr.)

thalweg, *n. tahl*-veg, the meeting-line of the slopes at the bottom of a valley. (Ger.)

Thammuz, *n. tam*-ooz, the tenth month of the Jewish civil year (parts of June and July); the name under which the Babylonians worshipped the Phœnician Adonis [Myth.].

★**than,** *conj.* than, denoting comparison, and generally placed after a comparative adjective or adverb. (A.S.)

thanage, *n. thane*-aj, the rank or land of a thane.

thanatism, *n. than*-a-tizm, the doctrine that the soul ceases to exist at death. (Gr. *thanatos*, death.)

thanatognomonic, *a. than*-a-to-no-*mon*-ik, characteristic or indicative of death.

thanatoid, *a. than*-a-toyd, deadly; resembling death; venomous [Zool.].

thanatology, *n.* than-a-*tol*-o-je, the scientific study of death. (Gr. *thanatos*, and *logos*, account.)

thanatophidian, *a.* than-a-to-*fid*-e-an, of or pertaining to the *Thanatophidia* or venomous snakes.

thanatophobia, *n. than*-a-to-*foh*-be-a, morbid dread of death.

thantosis, *n.* than-a-*toh*-sis, necrosis [Med.]; voluntary assumption by certain insects of the appearance of death.

thane, *n.* thane, among the Anglo-Saxons, one who held lands by virtue of military service; a lesser nobleman. (A.S. *thegn*, a servant.)

thanedom, *n. thane*-dom, the jurisdiction or office of a thane.

thaneship, *n. thane*-ship, rank or office of a thane.

thank, *v.t.* thank, to express gratitude; to make acknowledgments to for kindness bestowed: *n.pl.* expression of gratitude; an acknowledgment for favour or kindness received. **to have oneself to thank,** to be solely responsible for. (A.S. *thanc*, thought.)

thankful, *a. thank*-ful, grateful; impressed with a sense of kindness received, and ready to acknowledge it.

thankfully, *ad.* gratefully.

thankfulness, *n.* the state of being thankful.

thankless, *a. thank*-less, ungrateful; not expressing thanks; unappreciated.

thanklessly, *ad.* in a thankless manner.

thanklessness, *n.* the state of being thankless.

thank-offering, *n.* an offering made by way of gratitude or in acknowledgment of mercy.

thanksgiver, *n. thanks*-giv-er, one who gives thanks or acknowledges a kindness.

thanksgiving, *n. thanks*-giv-ing, the act of rendering thanks or expressing gratitude for favours or mercies; a public celebration of Divine goodness. **Thanksgiving Day,** in the U.S.A. a legal holiday (last Thurs. in Nov.) for expressing thanks to God for the mercies of the past year.

thankworthiness, *n. thank*-wur-the-ness, the condition of being thankworthy.

thankworthy, *a. thank*-wur-the, deserving thanks.

thar, *n.* thar *or* tar, the goat-antelope of Nepal, *Nemorhædus bubalina*; also the Himalayan goat, the tahr.

tharm, *n.* tharm, intestines twisted or prepared as catgut or cord; a string [Mus.]. (Ger. *darm*, gut.)

★**that,** *a.* that, not this, but the other: *relative pron.* who or which, relating to an antecedent: *conj.* because. **and all that,** and so on and so forth [Coll.]. **and that's that,** so much for that, it s settled [Coll.]. (A.S. *thæt*.)

thatch, *n.* thatch, straw, reeds, rushes, or the like used to cover roofs, haystacks, etc.: *v.t.* to cover with thatch. (A.S. *thæc*.)

thatcher, *n. thatch*-er, one who thatches.

thatching, *n. thatch*-ing, the act or art of covering with thatch; the materials used.

thaumatrope, *n. thaw*-ma-trope, an optical toy illustrating the persistence of an impression upon the retina after the object is withdrawn, a form of zoetrope. (Gr. *thauma*, a wonder, *trepo*, turn.)

thaumaturge, *n. thaw*-ma-turj, a miracle-worker; a magician. (Gr. *thauma*, and *-ergos*, working.)

thaumaturgic, *a. thaw*-ma-*tur*-jik, exciting wonder; wonder-working; pertaining to thaumaturgy: *n.pl.* feats of magic, conjuring tricks; the practice of thaumaturgy.

thaumaturgical, *a.* thaumaturgic.

thaumaturgist, *n. thaw*-ma-tur-jist, one who deals in wonders or believes in them.

thaumaturgy, *n. thaw*-ma-tur-je, the act of producing wonders; miracle-working; magic.

thaw, *n.* thaw, the melting of ice or snow; a change in the temperature that will melt ice: *v.i.* to melt, dissolve, or become fluid, as ice or snow; to become so warm as to melt ice; to unbend or become genial [Fig.]: *v.t.* to melt; to dissolve. (A.S. *thawian*.)

thawy, *a. thaw*-e, inclined to thaw.

★**the,** *definite article* or *demonstrative pron.* the, denoting a certain person or thing: *ad.* used before adjectives in the comparative and superlative degree. (A.S.)

Thea, *n. thee*-a, the genus of tropical Asiatic shrubs including the tea-plants.

theandric, *a.* the-*an*-drik, relating to or indicating the co-operation of the divine and human. (Gr. *theos*, God, *aner*, a man.)

theanthropic, *a.* thee-an-*throp*-ik, being both divine and human. (Gr. *theos*, God, *anthropos*, man.)

theanthropism, *n.* the-*an*-thro-pizm, the doctrine of the union of the human and divine in Christ; a state of being God and man; also, anthropomorphism.

theanthropist, *n.* the-*an*-thro-pist, one who advocates or accepts theanthropism.

thearchic, *a.* the-*ar*-kik, supreme; associated with thearchy.

thearchy, *n. thee*-ar-ke, a theocracy; the council of the gods; an order of deities. (Gr. *theos*, God, *archo*, rule.)

Theatine, *n. thee*-a-tine, a member of an order of regular clerks founded in 1524 by the bishop of Theate (Chieti, in Italy), afterwards Pope Paul IV.

theatre, *n. thee*-a-ter, an edifice for the exhibition of dramatic performances; a playhouse; a place rising by steps or gradations like the seats of a theatre; a lecture-hall; a place of action; the room in a hospital in which surgical operations and demonstrations take place; a sphere of operation. **theatre of war,** the area that is, or may become, the scene of military (including naval) operations. (O.Fr. *theatre*.)

theatric, *a.* the-*at*-rik, histrionic ; stagy ; theatrical.
theatrical, *a.* the-*at*-re-kal, pertaining to a theatre or to scenic representations ; resembling the manner of dramatic performers ; suited to the stage ; melodramatic ; sensational ; showy : *n.pl.* dramatic performances, esp. by amateurs.
theatricalism, *n.* the-*at*-re-ka-lizm, manners or mannerism suitable for the stage ; histrionism.
theatricality, *n.* the-*at*-re-*kal*-e-te, the quality of being theatrical ; an example of this.
theatrically, *ad.* in a theatrical manner.
theave, *n.* theev, a ewe of the first or second year.
thebaine, *n.* the-*bay*-ine, a white, crystalline, poisonous alkaloid obtained from opium.
thebaism, *n. thee*-ba-izm, poisoning by opium, or by thebaine.
Theban, *a. thee*-ban, of or belonging to Thebes (in ancient Greece or Egypt) : *n.* a native of Thebes. **Theban year,** the Egyptian year of 365 days 6 hours.
theca, *n. thee*-ka (*pl.* **thecæ**), a sheath or case [Anat. and Zool.] ; a sporangium [Bot.] ; the spore-case of a fern. (Gr.)
thecal, *a. thee*-kal, of or pertaining to a theca.
thecaphore, *n. thee*-ka-for, the organ bearing a theca [Bot.]. (Gr. *theka*, and *phoreo*, bear.)
thecate, *a. thee*-kat, having a theca [Bot.].
thecodont, *a. thee*-ko-dont, having the teeth inserted in distinct sockets [Zool.] : *n.* a member of a group of extinct thecodont saurians. (Gr. *theka*, and *odous*, a tooth.)
thecophore, *n. thee*-ko-for, thecaphore.
thé dansant, *n.* (App.), a dance at which tea is served, usually held in the afternoon. (Fr.)
thee, *pron.* thee, *obj. case* of *thou*.
theetsee, *n. theet*-see, the black varnish yielded by the Malayan tree *Melanorrhœa usitata*.
theft, *n.* theft, the act of stealing ; private felonious taking of another's goods [Law] ; the thing stolen.
theftuous, *a. thef*-tew-us, thievish ; given to theft ; furtive.
theftuously, *ad.* in a theftuous manner.
thegn, *n.* thane, thane.
theic, *n. thee*-ik, an excessive tea drinker.
theiform, *a. thee*-e-form, resembling the tea plant or tea.
theine, *n. thee*-in, the alkaloid caffeine.
their, *pron.* thare (*possessive,* **theirs**), of or belonging to them.
theism, *n. thee*-izm, morbid condition due to excessive drinking of tea [Path.]. (L. *thea*, tea, and *-ism.*)
theism, *n. thee*-izm, belief in a divine being, esp. in the existence of one God, the one (in opposition to deism) being supernaturally revealed. (Gr. *theos*, god, and *-ism.*)
theist, *n. thee*-ist, an adherent of theism.
theistical, *a.* thee-*is*-te-kal, pertaining to theism or to a theist ; according to the doctrine of theists.
them, *pron.* them, *obj. case* of *they*.
thematic, *a.* the-*mat*-ik, pertaining to themes.
thematically, *ad.* the-*mat*-e-ka-le, in a thematic way.
thematist, *n. thee*-ma-tist, one who composes themes.
theme, *n.* theem, a subject or topic on which to write or speak ; a short dissertation composed by a student ; a verb or noun not modified by inflexions [Gram.] ; a series of notes forming the text or subject of a composition [Mus.]. **theme song,** a song or melody of frequent recurrence in a musical dramatic performance ; [Fig.] that which reiteration has made characteristic. (Gr. *thema*, something placed, from *tithemi*, place.)
themselves, *pron.* them-*selvz*, the reciprocal form of *they* and *them*, and added by way of emphasis.
★**then,** *ad.* then, at that time ; soon afterwards or immediately ; in that case ; in consequence ; therefore ; for this reason ; at another time : *n.* the time mentioned or inferred ; that time.
thenadays, *ad. then*-a-dayz, in those days [Coll.].
thenal, *a. thee*-nal, pertaining to the thenar.
thenar, *n. thee*-nar, the palm of the hand ; the sole of the foot : *a.* thenal. **thenar prominence,** the "ball" on the palm at the base of the thumb. (Gr.)
thenardite, *n.* te-*nar*-dite, native anhydrous sulphate of soda. (L. J. *Thenard*, a Fr. chemist, *d.* 1857.)
thence, *ad.* thence, from that place or time ; for that reason.
thenceforth, *ad. thence*-forth, from that time.
thenceforward, *ad.* thence-*for*-ward, from that time onward.
Theobroma, *n.* thee-o-*broh*-ma, a genus of tropical American trees, one of which, *T. cacao*, yields cocoa or chocolate. (Gr. *theos*, god, *broma*, food.)
theobromine, *n.* the-o-*broh*-min, a bitter alkaloid related to caffeine, present in chocolate.
theocentric, *a.* thee-o-*sen*-trik, assuming God as the centre ; proceeding from and returning to God.
theocracy, *n.* the-*ok*-ra-se, a constitution in which the Deity is regarded as monarch and the priesthood as his ministers ; a state so governed. (Gr. *theos*, and *krateo*, rule.)
theocrasy, *n.* the-*ok*-ra-se, a mystic union of the soul with God in contemplation ; polytheistic worship. (Gr. *theos*, and *krasis*, mixture.)
theocrat, *n. thee*-o-krat, one who rules in, is subject to, or favours a theocracy.
theocratic, *a.* thee-o-*krat*-ik, pertaining to a theocracy.
Theocritean, *a.* the-*ok*-re-*tee*-an, in the style of the Greek lyric poet Theocritus ; idyllic.
theodicy, *n.* the-*od*-e-se, a theory reconciling the existence of evil in the world with the divine justice ruling it. (Gr. *theos*, and *dike*, justice.)
theodolite, *n.* the-*od*-o-lite, a surveyor's portable instrument for measuring horizontal and vertical angles, or heights and distances.
theodolitic, *a.* the-od-o-*lit*-ik, pertaining to or effected by a theodolite.
Theodosian, *a.* the-o-*doh*-se-an, pertaining to the Emperor Theodosius II (408–450), or to the code of Roman law promulgated by him.
theogonic, *a.* the-o-*gon*-ik, pertaining to theogony.
theogonist, *n.* the-*og*-o-nist, one versed in theogony.
theogony, *n.* the-*og*-o-ne, that branch of mythology which deals with the genealogies or generation of the gods ; an account, or a poem, treating of this (Gr. *theogonia*.)
theologian, *n.* the-o-*loh*-je-an, one versed in theology ; a divine ; a professor of divinity.
theological, *a.* the-o-*loj*-e-kal, pertaining to theology
theologically, *ad.* according to the principles of theology.
theologist, *n.* the-*ol*-o-jist, one who studies theology ; a theologian.
theologize, *v.t.* the-*ol*-o-jize, to render theological ; *v.i.* to frame a system of theology.
theologue, *n. thee*-o-lohg, a theologian.
theology, *n.* the-*ol*-o-je, the scientific study of God his attributes, and his relations to mankind and the universe ; the science of religion, esp. Christianity divinity. (Gr. *theos*, God, *logos*, discourse.)
theomachist, *n.* the-*om*-a-kist, one who fights against God or the gods.
theomachy, *n.* the-*om*-a-ke, a fighting against God or the gods. (Gr. *theos*, and *mache*, combat.)
theomancy, *n. thee*-o-man-se, divination from the responses of oracles. (Gr. *theos*, and *manteia* divination.)
theomania, *n.* thee-o-*may*-ne-a, religious insanity the delusion that one is a god.
theomorphic, *a.* thee-o-*mor*-fik, having the divine form or likeness. (Gr. *theos*, and *morphe*, form.)
theomorphism, *n.* the doctrine that man was made in the likeness of God ; the state of being in the image of God.
theopathetic, *a. thee*-o-pa-*thet*-ik, characterized by or pertaining to theopathy.
theopathic, *a.* the-o-*path*-ik, theopathetic ; excluding human considerations by complete absorption in contemplation of the divine.
theopathy, *n.* the-*op*-a-the, a state of feeling which arises from meditation concerning God ; capacity for profiting by this. (Gr. *theos*, and *pathos* suffering.)
theophanic, *a.* the-o-*fan*-ik, relating to or appearing in theophany.
theophany, *n.* the-*of*-a-ne, a manifestation of God to man by actual appearance. (Gr. *theophaineia*.)
theophilanthropism, *n. thee*-o-fe-*lan*-thro-pizm love of God and man ; a deistical system of religion which it was hoped in France about 1796–180[illegible] would supplant Christianity. (Gr. *theos*, God, and *philanthropism*.)
theophilanthropist, *n. thee*-o-fe-*lan*-thro-pist, an adherent of theophilanthropism.
theophilanthropy, *n. thee*-o-fe-*lan*-thro-pe, theophilanthropism.

theopneust, *a.* *thee*-op-newst, divinely inspired. (Gr. *theos*, and *pneo*, *pneuso*, breathe.)

theopneustic, *a.* *thee*-op-*new*-stik, theopneust; given by inspiration.

theopneusty, *n.* *thee*-op-*new*-ste, divine inspiration.

heorbo, *n.* the-*or*-bo, a large double-necked 17th-cent. lute with up to eleven strings. (It.)

heorem, *n.* *thee*-o-rem, a proposition to be proved by a chain of reasoning. (Gr. *theorema*.)

heorematic, *a.* *thee*-o-re-*mat*-ik, pertaining to or comprised in a theorem; consisting of theorems.

heorematist, *n.* thee-o-*rem*-a-tist, one who formulates theorems.

heoretic, *a.* the-o-*ret*-ik, contemplative; theoretical: *n.* a contemplative person; *pl.* theoretical matters.

heoretical, *a.* the-o-*ret*-e-kal, pertaining to or dependent upon theory; terminating in theory; speculative; not practical: *n.pl.* theoretical points; theoretics.

heoretically, *ad.* in or by theory; speculatively; not practically.

heoretician, *n.* *thee*-o-re-*tish*-an, a theorist (usually in a derogatory sense).

heorist, *n.* *thee*-o-rist, one who forms theories; one given to theory or to speculative thought; one who is not practical.

heorization, *n.* *thee*-o-ry-*zay*-shon, the act of theorizing, or its result; speculation.

heorize, *v.i.* *thee*-o-rize, to form a theory or theories; to speculate.

heorizer, *n.* *thee*-o-rize-er, one who theorizes; a theorist.

theory, *n.* *thee*-o-re, a doctrine or scheme which terminates in mere hypothesis or speculation; an exposition of the general principles of anything; the science distinguished from the art of a thing; the philosophical or scientific explanation of phenomena. (Fr. *théorie*.)

heosopher, *n.* the-*os*-o-fer, a theosophist.

heosophic, *a.* thee-o-*sof*-ik, pertaining to theosophy or theosophists.

heosophically, *ad.* thee-o-*sof*-e-ka-le, in a theosophic way; by appeal to theosophy.

heosophism, *n.* the-*os*-o-fizm, the theory of, or belief in, theosophy.

heosophist, *n.* the-*os*-o-fist, one who professes to derive his knowledge or wisdom direct from God; an adherent of theosophy.

heosophize, *v.i.* the-*os*-o-fize, to practise theosophy.

heosophy, *n.* the-*os*-o-fe, knowledge of God and his relations with man professedly obtained by mystical insight or deductive speculation; a modern development based on this, much interfused with Oriental religious doctrine and occultism, claiming to embody the fundamental truth of all religion. (Gr. *theos*, and *sophia*, wisdom.)

heotechny, *n.* thee-o-*tek*-ne, the introduction of divinities into literary compositions; the gods collectively.

heotokos, *n.* the-*ot*-o-kos, Mother of God, a title of the Virgin Mary. (Gr., giving birth to God.)

herapeutæ, *n.pl.* *the*-ra-*pew*-tee, a sect of Jewish mystics who in the 1st cent. A.D. devoted themselves to the ascetic life. (Gr.)

erapeutic, *a.* *the*-ra-*pew*-tik, curative; pertaining to the healing art; concerned in discovering and applying remedies for diseases. (Gr. *therapeutes*, a servant, a physician.)

erapeutics, *n.* *the*-ra-*pew*-tiks, that branch of medicine which treats of remedies and their action in the cure of diseases and the maintenance of health. (Gr. *therapeuein*, to serve, to heal.)

erapeutist, *n.* *the*-ra-*pew*-tist, one skilled in therapeutics.

erapy, *n.* *the*-ra-pe, treatment designed to cure [Med.]. (Gr. *therapeia*, healing.)

here, *ad.* thare, in that place. **here and there**, in one place and another. (A.S. *thær*.)

ereabout, *ad.* *thare*-a-*bout*, thereabouts.

ereabouts, *ad.* *thare*-a-*bouts*, near that place; near that number, degree, or quantity.

ereafter, *ad.* thare-*ahf*-ter, accordingly; after that.

ereanent, *ad.* thare-a-*nent*, concerning that.

ereat, *ad.* thare-*at*, at that place; on that account.

ereby, *ad.* thare-*by*, by that means; in consequence of that.

erefor, *ad.* thare-*for*, for that purpose.

erefore, *ad.* *thare*-for, for that; for that reason; consequently.

therefrom, *ad.* thare-*from*, from that place.

therein, *ad.* thare-*in*, in that place, time, or thing.

thereinafter, *ad.* *thare*-in-*ahf*-ter, further on in the same statement.

thereinto, *ad.* thare-*in*-too, into that.

thereof, *ad.* thare-*of*, of that.

thereon, *ad.* thare-*on*, on that.

thereout, *ad.* thare-*out*, out of that.

therethrough, *ad.* thare-*throo*, by that means.

thereto, *ad.* thare-*too*, to that.

theretofore, *ad.* *thare*-to-for, previously.

thereunto, *ad.* thare-*un*-too, to that.

thereunder, *ad.* thare-*un*-der, under that.

thereupon, *ad.* *thare*-u-*pon*, upon that; in consequence of that; immediately.

therewith, *ad.* thare-*with*, with that.

therewithal, *ad.* *thare*-with-awl, over and above; at the same time; with that. **the therewithal**, the necessary money or means [Coll.].

theriac, *n.* *theer*-re-ak, a compound formerly used as an antidote to the bite of a venomous animal. (Gr. *thērion*, a wild beast.)

theriacal, *a.* the-*ry*-a-kal, medicinal; useful as an antidote to snake-bite.

therianthropic, *a.* *theer*-re-an-*throp*-ik, pertaining to therianthropism, or to its deities.

therianthropism, *n.* *theer*-re-*an*-thro-pizm, the worship of deities represented in some combination of man and beast.

therimorph, *n.* *the*-re-o-morf, any object represented in the shape of an animal. (Gr. *therion*, a wild beast, *morphe*, form.)

theriomorphic, *a.* *the*-re-o-*mor*-fik, having animal form.

theriomorphism, *n.* *the*-re-o-*mor*-fizm, representation, esp. of a deity, as an animal.

theriomorphosis, *n.* *the*-re-o-mor-*foh*-sis, transformation into the likeness of an animal.

theriomorphous, *a.* *the*-re-o-*mor*-fus, theriomorphic.

theriotomy, *n.* *theer*-re-*ot*-o-me, zootomy. (Gr. *thērion*, and *tome*, cutting.)

therm, *n.* therm, the unit by which coal gas is sold, equal to one great calorie or 100,000 British Thermal Units. (Gr. *therme*, heat.)

thermæ, *n.* *ther*-mee, a public establishment for bathing among the ancient Romans. (L., hot springs.)

thermal, *a.* *ther*-mal, pertaining to heat; warm. **British Thermal Unit** (B.Th.U.), the amount of heat necessary to raise one pound of water one degree Fahrenheit (from 60° to 61°). **thermal waters**, warm mineral waters or springs. (Gr. *thermos*, hot.)

thermatology, *n.* ther-ma-*tol*-o-je, thermology; thermotherapy.

thermic, *a.* *ther*-mik, thermal; due to heat.

Thermidor, *n.* *ther*-me-dor, the 11th month of the French republican year (19 July–17 Aug.).

thermion, *n.* *ther*-me-on, an electron emitted from a body in a highly heated condition. (Gr.)

thermionic, *a.* *ther*-me-*on*-ik, like or pertaining to a thermion; emitting a current of electricity by the agency of heat: *n.pl.* the science treating of the emission of electrons from a heated body. **thermionic valve**, a valve which emits electrons by the heat of its filaments [Wire.].

thermite, *n.* *ther*-mite, a mixture of aluminium and magnetic iron oxide which gives intense heat on combustion.

thermo-, *pref.* *ther*-moh, pertaining to heat. (Gr. *thermos*, heat.)

thermo-barometer, *n.* a hypsometer; a siphon barometer that can be used also as a thermometer.

thermochemistry, *n.* *ther*-moh-*kem*-is-tre, that branch of chemistry which treats of the development of heat by chemical action.

thermo-current, *n.* an electric current developed by heat.

thermodynamics, *n.* *ther*-moh-dy-*nam*-iks, the science of the relation between mechanical force and heat.

thermo-electric, *a.* pertaining to or of the nature of thermo-electricity.

thermo-electricity, *n.* electricity developed by the direct action of heat.

thermo-electrometer, *n.* instrument for ascertaining the heating power of an electric current.

thermogene, *n.* *ther*-moh-jeen, proprietary name of

a wadding of cotton wool so treated as to generate heat in an affected part [Med.].
thermogenesis, *n.* ther-moh-*jen*-e-sis, the production of heat, esp. in the human body.
thermogenetic, *a.* ther-moh-je-*net*-ik, of or relating to thermogenesis.
thermogenous, *a.* ther-*moj*-e-nus, generated by, or generating, heat.
thermogram, *n.* *ther*-moh-gram, the record made by a thermograph.
thermograph, *n.* *ther*-moh-graf, an automatic registering thermometer.
thermology, *n.* ther-*mol*-o-je, the science of heat.
thermolysis, *n.* ther-*mol*-e-sis, the dissipation of heat from the body [Phys.].
thermometer, *n.* ther-*mom*-e-ter, an instrument for measuring temperature. **maximum** (or **minimum**) **thermometer,** one in which a register remains at the highest (or the lowest) point attained until it is re-set. (Gr. *thermos*, and *metron*, measure.)
thermometrical, *a.* ther-mo-*met*-re-kal, pertaining to, or ascertained by means of, a thermometer.
thermometrically, *ad.* by means of a thermometer.
thermometry, *n.* ther-*mom*-e-tre, the measurement of temperature.
thermo-motive, *a.* pertaining to the production of motion by heat.
thermo-motor, *n.* a hot-air engine, or other motor worked by means of heat.
thermonatrite, *n.* ther-mo-*nay*-trite, native hydrous carbonate of sodium.
thermophile, *a.* *ther*-mo-fil, developing only in a high temperature (esp. of certain bacteria): *n.* a thermophile organism. (Gr. *thermos*, and *philos*, fond of.)
thermophyllite, *n.* *ther*-mo-fil-ite, a light brown variety of serpentine which scales when heated [Min.]. (Gr. *thermos*, and *phyllon*, leaf.)
thermopile, *n.* *ther*-mo-pile, a sensitive electrical apparatus for measuring very small quantities of radiant heat.
thermoplastic, *a.* *ther*-mo-*plas*-tik, becoming plastic when heated.
thermoplegia, *n.* *ther*-mo-*plee*-je-a, heat stroke; an apoplectic fit caused by this [Path.].
thermos, *n.* *ther*-mos, proprietary name of a vacuum-jacketed vessel for keeping its contents at a constant or uniform temperature; a form of vacuum flask. (Gr.)
thermoscope, *n.* *ther*-mo-skope, an instrument for measuring minute differences of temperature. (Gr. *thermos*, and *skopeo*, view.)
thermoscopic, *a.* *ther*-mo-*skop*-ik, pertaining to a thermoscope; made by a thermoscope.
thermostat, *n.* *ther*-mo-stat, a self-acting apparatus for regulating temperature. (Gr. *thermos*, and *statos*, standing.)
thermostatic, *a.* ther-mo-*stat*-ik, relating to thermostatics; effected by means of the thermostat.
thermostatics, *n.* ther-mo-*stat*-iks, the theory or science of the equilibrium of heat.
thermotaxic, *a.* *ther*-mo-*tak*-sik, pertaining to or caused by thermotaxis.
thermotaxis, *n.* ther-mo-*tak*-sis, a taxis or reaction of which heat provides the stimulus [Biol.]; regulation of the production and dispersal of heat [Med.].
thermotherapy, *n.* *ther*-mo-*the*-ra-pe, the treatment of disease by heat, as by hot air, etc., or by diathermy.
thermotic, *a.* ther-*mot*-ik, relating to heat.
thermotics, *n.* ther-*mot*-iks, the science of heat.
thermotropism, *n.* ther-*mot*-ro-pizm, the (positive or negative) property in plants of turning in the direction of or away from the sun.
theroid, *a.* *theer*-royd, having the characteristics of animals. (Gr. *therion*, a wild beast.)
therology, *n.* the-*rol*-o-ge, mammalogy.
thesaurus, *n.* thee-*saw*-rus, a lexicon of words and phrases; an encyclopædia. (Gr.)
these, *pron.* theze, *pl.* of *this*.
thesis, *n.* *thee*-sis (*pl.* **theses**), a position or proposition which is advanced or is maintained by argument; a theme; a dissertation on a set subject; a proposition as containing the thing affirmed or denied, as distinct from the hypothesis. (Gr., placing.)
thesmothete, *n.* *thez*-mo-theet, a lawgiver; a legislator. (Gr. *thesmothetes*.)
thespian, *a.* *thes*-pe-an, relating to dramatic acting: *n.* (*cap.*) a tragedian. (*Thespis*, legendary founder of Greek tragedy.)
theta, *n.* *thee*-ta, the *th* of the Greek alphabet.
theurgic, *a.* the-*ur*-jik, pertaining to theurgy.
theurgist, *n.* the-*ur*-jist, an adherent of or one who practises theurgy.
theurgy, *n.* *thee*-ur-je, the art of magic; the power of producing magical effects by the help of super natural agencies. (Gr. *theos*, god, *ergon*, work.)
thew, *n.* thew, muscle; sinew; strength. (A.S. *theaw*.)
thewed, *a.* thewd, furnished with muscles (of the specified kind).
thewy, *a.* *thew*-e, having strong thews; muscular.
they, *pron. pl.* thay, denoting persons or things also indefinitely used.
thible, *n.* *thi*-bl *or* *thy*-bl, a thivel.
★**thick,** *a.* thik, dense; close; compact; inspissated; turbid; muddy; having more depth or extent from one surface to its opposite than usual crowded close; following close or fast; intimate [Coll.]; not distinctly articulate; dull: *n.* the thickest part: *ad.* frequently; fast; closely; to a great depth. **a bit thick,** more than is justified beyond what can be endured [Coll.]. **in the thick of it,** struggling against odds; in the most difficult part. **lay it on thick,** to do vehemently or in an intensified way. **thick and thin,** in any circumstances; (ready to go through) whatever is in the way. (A.S. *thicce*.)
thickback, *n.* *thik*-bak, the flatfish, *Solea variegata*.
thicken, *v.t.* *thik*-en, to make thick or dense; to make close or more close; to fill up interstices to make compact; to inspissate; to make frequent or more frequent: *v.i.* to become thick or more thick; to become dark or obscure; to concrete; to be crowded; to become close or more numerous to become quick and animated; to become more intense or complicated.
thickening, *n.* *thik*-en-ing, something put into liquid or mass to make it thicker: *a.* becoming denser or more complicated, threatening, etc.
thicket, *n.* *thik*-et, a plantation; a mass of underwood
thick-headed, *a.* having a thick skull; slow witted; stupid.
thickish, *a.* *thik*-ish, somewhat thick.
thickly, *ad.* deeply; closely; in quick succession.
thicknee, *n.* *thik*-nee, the stone-curlew, *Œdicnemus scolopax*, a bird allied to the plovers.
thickness, *n.* *thik*-ness, the state of being thick.
thickset, *a.* *thik*-set, close-planted; having a short thick body: *n.* a close, thick hedge.
thick-skinned, *a.* having a thick skin; not sensitive insensible to taunts or ridicule.
thick-skulled, *a.* thick-headed; dull; stupid.
thief, *n.* theef (*pl.* **thieves,** theevz), a person guilty of theft; one who secretly and feloniously takes the goods of another; an excrescence or cause of guttering in the snuff of a candle. (A.S. *theof*.)
thief-catcher, *n.* one whose business is to detect thieves and bring them to justice; a detective.
thieve, *v.i.* theeve, to steal; to practise theft.
thievery, *n.* *theev*-er-re, the practice of stealing theft; that which is stolen.
thievish, *a.* *theev*-ish, given to stealing; partaking of the nature of theft; sly; acting by stealth.
thievishly, *ad.* in a thievish manner.
thievishness, *n.* the quality of being thievish.
thig, *v.t.* thig, to beg; to live by begging.
thigger, *n.* *thig*-er, a beggar; a sponger.
thigh, *n.* thy, the thick muscular portion of the leg between the knee and the trunk. (A.S. *theoh*.)
thigh-bone, *n.* the femur, or chief bone of the thigh
thilk, *pron.* thilk, the same [Dial.]. (*the ilk*.)
thill, *n.* thil, the shaft of a vehicle. (A.S. *thille*, plank, pole.)
thiller, *n.* *thil*-ler, the horse between the thills; in a team, the last horse.
thimble, *n.* *thim*-bl, a cap for the finger, usually of metal, used for driving the needle in sewing; any thing in the form of a thimble; an iron ring with a groove round its whole circumference, to receive the rope which is spliced about it [Naut.]. (A.S. *thymel*, thumb-stall.)
thimbleful, *n.* *thim*-bl-ful, a very little; as much as a thimble will hold.
thimblerig, *n.* *thim*-bl-rig, a sleight-of-hand trick played with three small cups, shaped like thimbles and a pea: *v.t.* to cheat by this trick.

:himblerigger, *n. thim*-bl-rig-er, a common swindler, originally one given to thimblerigging.

***thin,** *a.* thin, having little thickness; rarefied; not dense; not close or crowded; lean; slim; slender; slight; meagre and scanty: *ad.* not thickly or closely: *v.t.* to make thin or less close, etc.; to attenuate; to rarefy: *v.i.* to grow thin. **thin out,** to diminish gradually in thickness; to make or become sparse. (A.S. *thynne*, extended.)

hine, *pron. a.* thine, belonging to or relating to thee; being thy property.

***thing,** *n.* thing, any substance; any particular article or commodity; a person or animal, esp. as an object of pity, etc.; an act or event spoken of; a portion or part: *pl.* clothes; belongings; luggage. **the thing,** that which is correct, apposite, or fashionable. **to know a thing or two,** to be up to all the dodges; to be well informed. (A.S.)

Ching, *n.* thing, formerly, a public assembly for judicial or other purposes in Scandinavia and the Norse settlements. (O. Scand.)

hingamy, *n. thing*-a-me, a thingumabob.

hingumabob, *n. thing*-um-a-bob, a term used in place of a name of anything or anybody when the real name cannot be recalled [Coll.].

hingumajig, *n. thing*-um-a-jig, a thingumabob.

hink, *v.i.* think, to have the mind occupied on some subject; to revolve ideas in the mind; to judge; to conclude; to intend; to fancy or suppose; to meditate; to reflect; to consider; to deliberate; to presume. **think much** or **well of,** to hold in esteem. **think of,** to have ideas come into the mind. **think on,** to meditate on; to light on by meditation; to remember. **think out,** to resolve or work out in one's mind. **think up,** to devise or concoct mentally [U.S.A.]: *v.t.* to conceive; to imagine; to believe; to consider; to intend. *p.* and *pp.* **thought.** (A.S. *thencan.*)

hinkable, *a. thing*-ka-bl, that can be thought.

hinker, *n. thing*-ker, one who thinks; one who is studious or philosophical.

hinking, *a. thing*-king, having the faculty of thought; cogitative; capable of a regular train of ideas: *n.* cogitation; imagination.

hinkingly, *ad. thing*-king-le, with thought.

hinly, *ad. thin*-le, in a loose, scattered manner; not thickly.

hinness, *n. thin*-ness, the state of being thin; tenuity; rareness; exility; paucity.

hinnish, *a. thin*-ish, rather thin.

hin-skinned, *a.* having a thin skin; unduly sensitive.

hio,- *thy*-oh, prefix signifying the presence of sulphur [Chem.]. (Gr. *theion*, brimstone.)

hiogenic, *a.* thy-o-*jen*-ik, able to change sulphuretted hydrogen into higher sulphur compounds [Chem.].

hird, *a.* thurd, next after the second; being one of three equal parts; the ordinal of three: *n.* one of three equal parts; the third part of anything; the sixtieth part of a second of time; an interval containing three diatonic sounds and two degrees or intervals [Mus.]: *pl.* the widow's third part of the estate of a deceased husband. **third degree,** *see* **degree. third estate,** the Commons, or the common people of a state [Polit.]. **third man,** a fielder between point and the slips [Cricket]. **third party,** any party, other than the two principals, involved in a case [Law]; a party opposing both members of a two-party system [Polit.]. **third programme,** a radio B.B.C. programme designed for intellectuals; hence, [Coll.] high-brow. **third rail,** the live rail [Elect. Rly.]. (M.E. *hridde.*)

ird-class, *a.* third-rate; of a lowly group (in classification, rank, etc.).

ird-borough, *n. thurd*-bu-ra, an under-constable.

irdings, *n.pl. thur*-dingz, the third part of the corn or grain growing on the ground at the tenant's death, formerly due to the lord for a heriot.

irdly, *ad. thurd*-le, in the third place.

ird-rate, *a.* belonging to the third class in quality; inferior; poor.

irl, *n.* thurl, an opening; an aperture: *v.t.* to bore a hole in; to pierce.

irlage, *n. thurl*-aj, a former obligation compelling certain tenants to bring their grain for grinding to a particular mill [Scots. Law].

irst, *n.* thurst, a painful sensation of the throat or fauces, occasioned by the want of drink; desire for drink; eager desire for anything; dryness; drought: *v.i.* to experience thirst; to have a vehement desire. (A.S. *thyrst.*)

thirstily, *ad.* in a thirsty manner.

thirstiness, *n.* the state of being thirsty.

thirsty, *a. thurs*-te, feeling or suffering from thirst; very dry; parched; having a vehement desire.

thirteen, *a.* thur-*teen*, ten and three: *n.* the number of ten and three. (A.S. *threötyne.*)

thirteenth, *a.* thur-*teenth*, the ordinal of thirteen; being one of thirteen equal parts: *n.* one of thirteen equal parts; an interval forming the octave of the sixth [Mus.].

thirtieth, *a. thur*-te-eth, the ordinal of thirty; being one of thirty equal parts: *n.* one of such parts.

thirty, *a. thur*-te, thrice ten: *n.* the number of thrice ten. (A.S. *threo*, and *tig*, ten.)

***this,** *pron. a.* this (*pl.* **these**), that which is near or present; just referred to or about to be. (A.S.)

thisness, *n. this*-ness, the condition or quality of being such as it is; hæcceity.

thistle, *n. this*-l, the popular name of many species of composite plants with tubular florets, the style thickened below its branches and having spiny leaves. **Order of the Thistle,** a British order of knighthood instituted (or revived on an ancient Scottish foundation) by James II in 1687. **Scotch thistle,** *see* **Scotch.** (A.S. *thistel.*)

thistledown, *n. this*-l-doun, the bristles on the seed of thistles.

thistly, *a. this*-l-e, overgrown with thistles; like a thistle; prickly.

thither, *ad. thith*-er, to that place; to that end or point: *a.* lying beyond; far removed. (A.S. *thider.*)

thitherward, *ad. thith*-er-ward, toward that place. (A.S. *thiderweard.*)

thivel, *n. thi*-vl *or thy*-vl, a stick for stirring anything cooked in a pot. (Dial.)

thlipsis, *n. thlip*-sis, compression or constriction, esp. external, of blood-vessels [Med.]. (Gr.)

tho', tho, a contraction of *though*.

thole, *n.* thole, a pin or peg, esp. one in the gunwale of a boat serving as a fulcrum for the oar. (A.S. *thol.*)

thole, *v.t.* thole, to endure; to tolerate: *v.i.* to bear with patience. (A.S. *tholian.*)

tholobate, *n. thol*-o-bate, the substructure immediately supporting a dome or cupola [Arch.]. (Gr. *tholos*, dome, *basis*, base.)

Thomism, *n. toh*-mizm, the philosophy or doctrines of St. Thomas Aquinas.

Thomist, *n. toh*-mist, a follower of the scholastic philosopher, St. Thomas Aquinas (*d.* 1274.): *a.* pertaining to Thomism.

thomsonite, *n. tom*-son-ite, a mineral of the zeolite group, a hydrous silicate of aluminium, calcium, and sodium. (Thos. *Thomson*, Scot. scientist, *d.* 1852.)

thong, *n.* thong, a strip of leather used as a whiplash or for fastening anything, etc. (A.S. *thwang.*)

thooid, *a. thoh*-oyd, wolf-like [Zool.]. (Gr. *thos*, a jackal.)

Thor, *n.* thor, the Scandinavian god of thunder, the ally and helper of gods and men. (Ice. *Thorr.*)

thoracic, *a.* tho-*ras*-ik, pertaining to the thorax; having the ventral fins under the thorax [Ichth.]: *n.* a thoracic fish.

thorax, *n. thaw*-raks (*pl.* **thoraces,** tho-*ray*-seez), that part of the body of mammals between the neck and abdomen [Anat.]; the cavity of the chest; the three somites between the head and abdomen in insects; a breastplate or cuirass (among the ancient Greeks). (Gr.)

thoria, *n. thaw*-re-a, thorium dioxide, a white earthy substance used in gas-mantles, etc.

thoriated, *a. thaw*-re-ay-ted, impregnated with thoria.

thorite, *n. thaw*-rite, a massive silicate of thorium found in Norway.

thorium, *n. thaw*-re-um, a dark-grey radioactive metallic element occurring in monazite, thorite, etc. **thorium emanation,** thoron. (*Thor.*)

thorn, *n.* thorn, a spine or prickle on a plant; a tree or shrub armed with spines or sharp woody shoots; anything troublesome; an impediment; the Old English letter for *th* [þ], also the corresponding letter in modern Icelandic. **a thorn in the flesh,** a

constant source of annoyance. **kaffir thorn,** the African tea-tree, *Lycium afrum.* (A.S.)
thorn-apple, *n.* the evergreen shrub *Datura stramonium,* allied to the nightshades.
thornback, *n.* *thorn*-bak, a species of skate, *Raia clavata,* having crooked spines on its back.
thornbill, *n.* *thorn*-bil, a name given to several slender-billed South American humming-birds.
thorn-broom, *n.* the gorse, *Ulex europæus.*
thorn-bush, *n.* a shrub that produces thorns.
thorn-hedge, *n.* a hedge of thorn-bushes.
thornless, *a.* *thorn*-less, destitute of thorns.
thorny, *a.* *thor*-ne, full of thorns or spines; rough with thorns; sharp; pricking; troublesome; vexatious; perplexing.
thoron, *n.* *thaw*-ron, a radioactive isotope of radon produced by the disintegration of thorium.
thorough, *a.* *thu*-ro, passing through or to the end; complete; perfect: *n.* a furrow, esp. one for drainage [Agric.]. (A.S. *thurh,* through.)
thorough-bass, *n.* an accompaniment to a continued bass by means of numerals; the science of harmony [Mus.].
thorough-brace, *n.* the strap between the C-springs of a carriage on which the body rests.
thoroughbred, *a.* *thu*-ro-bred, bred from the best blood; of unmixed breed; with the qualities of one thoroughbred: *n.* a thoroughbred animal, esp. a horse.
thoroughfare, *n.* *thu*-ro-fare, a way through; a right of way; an open road or street; an unobstructed way.
thoroughgoing, *a.* *thu*-ro-goh-ing, going all lengths; uncompromising.
thoroughly, *ad.* fully; entirely.
thoroughness, *n.* completeness; perfectness.
thoroughpaced, *a.* *thu*-ro-payst, complete; out-and-out; going all lengths.
thorough-pin, *n.* a swelling just above a horse's hock, usually appearing on both sides.
thoroughwax, *n.* *thu*-ro-waks, the umbelliferous plant *Bupleurum rotundifolium.*
thoroughwort, *n.* *thu*-ro-wurt, the N. American plant *Eupatorium perfoliatum.*
thorp, or **thorpe,** *n.* thorp, a homestead, or the locality of a hamlet. (Scand.)
those, *pron.* thoze, *pl.* of *that.*
Thoth, *n.* thoth, the ancient Egyptian god of writing and talking, wisdom, and invention, represented as having the head of an ibis. (Egyptian *Djehuti.*)
thou, *pron. second person sing.* thou: *v.t.* to address as *thou*: *v.i.* to use *thou* and *thee* in place of *you.* (A.S. *thu.*)
★**though,** *conj.* thoh, granting; admitting; even if; notwithstanding; that. (A.S. *theah,* from *that.*)
thought, thawt, *pret.* and *pp.* of *think.*
★**thought,** *n.* thawt, the act of thinking; the faculty of or capacity for thinking; that which the mind thinks; idea; conception; fancy; conceit; opinion; judgment; meditation; design; solicitude; a small degree [Coll.]. **take thought,** to be solicitous. **thought transference,** the communication of thought, independently of the usual use of the senses, from one mind to another; telepathy. (A.S. *ge-thoht,* that which is thought of.)
thoughtful, *a.* *thawt*-ful, meditative; attentive; having the mind directed to an object; anxious; considerate.
thoughtfully, *ad.* with thought, consideration, or solicitude.
thoughtfulness, *n.* serious consideration or concern.
thoughtless, *a.* heedless; careless; stupid.
thoughtlessly, *ad.* without thought; inconsiderately.
thoughtlessness, *n.* want of thought; heedlessness; inconsideration.
thought-reader, *n.* one who, telepathically or otherwise, divines another's thoughts.
thousand, *a.* and *n.* *thou*-zand, the number of ten hundred; a large number indefinitely. (A.S. *thusend.*)
thousandfold, *a.* *thou*-zand-fohld, multiplied by a thousand.
thousand-legs, *n.* any millepede [Coll.].
thousandth, *a.* *thou*-zandth, the ordinal of thousand: *n.* one of a thousand equal parts.
thraldom, *n.* *thrawl*-dom, slavery; bondage.
thrall, *n.* thrawl, a slave; slavery. (A.S.)
thranite, *n.* *thray*-nite, one of the rowers using the longest oars in an ancient Greek trireme. (Gr. *thranitos.*)
thrapple, *n.* *thrap*-pl, a thropple.
thrash, *v.t.* thrash, to thresh; to beat soundly with a stick or whip; to drub; to defeat: *v.i.* to perform the operation of thrashing; to throw oneself about violently. **to thrash out,** to discuss or examine exhaustively. (A.S. *thresh.*)
thrasher, *n.* *thrash*-er, one who thrashes; a thresher; the sea-fox or thresher; any of several American song-birds allied to the mocking-bird.
thrashing, *n.* *thrash*-ing, a sound drubbing.
thrashing-floor, *n.* a threshing-floor.
thrasonical, *a.* thra-*son*-e-kal, given to bragging boastful. (*Thraso,* in Terence's "Eunuchus.")
thrasonically, *ad.* in a bragging manner.
thrave, *n.* thrave, twenty-four sheaves of grain forming two stooks. (Ice.)
thrawn, *a.* thrawn, twisted; distorted; awry [Fig.] perverse, contrary. (Scots.)
★**thread,** *n.* thred, a thin line used for sewing; a twisted filament of flax, wool, cotton, silk, or other fibrous substance; any fine filament; something continued in a long course; tenor; the spiral part of a screw; a thin seam or vein: *v.t.* to pass a thread through the eye (of a needle, etc.); to place or arrange on a thread; to pass or pierce through as a narrow way or channel. **thread and thrum** all alike, good and bad together. (A.S. *thræd,* from *thrawan,* twist.)
threadbare, *a.* *thred*-bare, worn to the naked thread; having the nap worn off; worn out trite; hackneyed; used till it has lost all novelty or interest.
threadbareness, *n.* *thred*-bare-ness, the state of being threadbare.
threader, *n.* *thred*-er, one who or that which threads a machine or appliance for cutting threads on screws.
threadiness, *n.* *thred*-e-ness, a thready state.
thread-worm, *n.* any of the nematode worms.
thread-worn, *a.* worn to the thread; threadbare.
thready, *a.* *thred*-e, like or containing thread.
threap, *v.t.* threep, to reprove; to assert pertinaciously: *v.i.* to wrangle: *n.* dispute; contention the act of threaping. (Scots.)
threat, *n.* thret, a menace; declaration of an intention to punish or to harm; intimidation (A.S. *thréat,* a crowd, a calamity, trouble, threat.)
threaten, *v.t.* *thret*-en, to menace; to attempt to terrify with threats; to charge with threats; to charge strictly; to exhibit the appearance of something unpleasant approaching. (A.S. *threatian.*)
threatener, *n.* *thret*-en-er, one who threatens.
threatening, *a.* *thret*-en-ing, indicating a threat or menace; indicating something impending.
threateningly, *ad.* in a threatening manner; with a threat.
threatful, *a.* *thret*-ful, full of threats.
three, *a.* three, two and one: *n.* the number three a symbol representing this; any trio or group of three. **three card trick,** a swindling game in which the victim bets on his ability to pick out one of three cards identified before being shuffled (A.S. *thri.*)
three-cornered, *a.* having three corners. **three cornered election,** one in which there are three candidates for one vacancy.
three-decker, *n.* a warship with guns on three decks; a form of pulpit having three stories.
threefold, *a.* *three*-fohld, consisting of three; thrice repeated: *ad.* triply.
three-master, *n.* a ship with three masts.
threepence, *n.* *threp*-ence, three pennies; a silver or other coin worth three pennies.
threepenny, *a.* *threp*-en-ne, of the value of three pence; of little value: *n.* a threepenny-bit.
threepenny-bit, *n.* a silver or other coin worth threepence.
three-ply, *a.* three-fold; of three-ply: *n.* three veneers glued together with opposing grains.
three-quarter, *a.* consisting of or equal to three of four equal parts of a whole; between full-face and profile, also, extending to the hips (of portraits) *n.* a player stationed between the backs and half backs [Rugby Football]: *pl.* the sum of three of four equal parts of a whole; the greater part [Coll.].

hreescore, *a. three*-skor, sixty.
hreesome, *a. three*-sum, triple : *n.* game for three.
hremmatology, *n. threm*-a-*tol*-o-je, the branch of biology treating of the breeding of domestic animals and crossing of plants. (Gr. *thremma*, nurse, *logos*, science.)
hrenetic, *a.* thre-*net*-ik, of the nature of a threnody ; mournful.
nrenode, *n. thren*-ode, a threnody.
nrenodial, *a.* thre-*noh*-de-al, pertaining to or of the nature of a threnody.
nrenodist, *n. thren*-o-dist, a writer of threnodies.
nrenody, *n. thren*-o-de, a dirge ; a song of lamentation, esp. one composed for a funeral. (Gr. *thrēnos*, a wailing, *ode*, a song.)
nrepsology, *n.* threp-*sol*-o-je, the science of nutrition. (Gr. *threpsis*, nourish, and *logos*.)
nresh, *v.t.* thresh, to beat out grain from the husk : *v.i.* to perform the operation of threshing. (A.S. *therscan*, to trample.)
nreshel, *n. thresh*-el, a flail.
nresher, *n. thresh*-er, one who threshes ; a threshing-machine ; the sea-fox or fox-shark, *Alopias vulpes*, a large shark which threshes the water with its strong tail.
nreshing-floor, *n.* a floor or area on which grain is beaten out.
nreshing-machine, *n.* a machine or apparatus for separating grain from the straw.
nreshold, *n. thresh*-ohld, a door-sill ; an entrance ; place or point of entering or beginning. (*thresh* and *hold*, the origin of which is doubtful.)
nrew, throo, *p.* of *throw*.
nrice, *ad.* thrice, three times ; very much [Fig.].
hrice-favoured, highly favoured. (M.E. *thries*.)
nrid, *v.t.* thrid, to thread [Dial.].
nrift, *n.* thrift, frugality ; good husbandry ; economical management ; saving money ; a name of various plants, esp. the sea pink, *Armeria maritima*. (Scand.)
nriftily, *ad. thrif*-te-le, with thrift.
nriftiness, *n.* frugality ; good husbandry.
nriftless, *a. thrift*-less, without frugality ; spendthrift ; extravagant.
nriftlessly, *ad.* without thrift.
nriftlessness, *n.* quality of being thriftless.
nrifty, *a. thrif*-te, frugal ; economical ; thriving.
nrill, *n.* thril, a thrilling sensation ; that which causes excitement [Coll.] : *v.t.* to pierce or penetrate as with something sharp ; to affect with a tingling sensation : *v.i.* to pierce as something sharp ; to pass with a tingling sensation through the system ; to feel a sharp, shivering sensation pass through the body ; to throb with excitement. (A.S. *thyrlian*, to pierce through.)
nriller, *n. thril*-er, that which thrills ; a highly exciting story, novel, or drama, etc.
nrillingly, *ad. thril*-ing-le, with a thrill.
nrillingness, *n.* quality of being thrilling.
nrips, *n.* thrips, a genus of small insects, injurious to plants, esp. grasses and grain. (Gr.)
nrive, *v.i.* thrive, to prosper by industry, economy, and good management ; to increase in goods and estate ; to prosper in any business ; to grow ; to flourish. *p.* **throve** or **thrived.** *pp.* **thriven** or **thrived.** (Ice. *thrifa*.)
nriver, *n. thry*-ver, one who prospers.
nrivingly, *ad. thry*-ving-le, in a prosperous way.
nrivingness, *n. thry*-ving-ness, prosperity ; increase.
nro' *prep.* throo, a contraction of *through*.
hroat, *n.* throte, the anterior part of the neck of a vertebrate, containing the gullet and windpipe ; the fauces ; a narrow entrance, passage, or opening ; the end of a gaff which is next the mast [Naut.]. **cut each other's throats,** to engage in ruinous competition. **ram down one's throat,** to force on one determinedly. **stick in one's throat,** to be difficult of acceptance ; to remain unexpressed. (A.S. *throte*.)
nroatiness, *n.* state of being throaty.
nroat-latch, *n.* a strap of a bridle or halter passing under a horse's throat.
nroatwort, *n. throte*-wurt, a name of various plants of the campanula family, esp. *C. Cervicaria*.
nroaty, *a. throh*-te, guttural ; singing from the throat instead of from the chest ; having a prominent throat.
nrob, *n.* throb, a beat or strong pulsation : *v.i.* to beat, as the heart or pulse, with more than usual force or rapidity ; to palpitate. (M.E. ; origin doubtful.)
throe, *n.* throh, extreme pain ; violent pang ; agony : *pl.* the pains of childbirth : *v.i.* to struggle in extreme pain. (A.S. *thrawan*, afflict severely.)
thrombin, *n. throm*-bin, the substance which causes blood to clot by the production of fibrin.
thrombogen, *n. throm*-bo-jen, the hypothetical substance in the blood from which thrombin is derived.
thrombosed, *a.* throm-*bohst*, affected with thrombosis [Path.].
thrombosis, *n.* throm-*boh*-sis, the formation or development of a blood clot which may partially or completely close a blood-vessel [Med.]. (Gr. *thrombos*, a clot of blood.)
thrombus, *n. throm*-bus, a fibrinous clot of blood causing obstruction or thrombosis [Med.]. (Gr.)
thronal, *a. throh*-nal, pertaining to or serving as a throne.
throne, *n.* throne, a royal seat raised above the level of the floor and often canopied ; a chair of state ; the seat of a bishop ; sovereign power and dignity : *pl.* (*cap.*) the third order of angels : *v.t.* to enthrone ; to place in an elevated position. (L. *thronum*.)
throneless, *a. throne*-less, having no throne ; having lost a throne.
throng, *n.* throng, a crowd ; a multitude of persons pressing or pressed into a close body ; a great multitude : *v.i.* to crowd together ; to come in multitudes : *v.t.* to jostle ; to oppress or annoy with a crowd. (A.S. *thringan*, to crowd.)
thropple, *n. throp*-pl, the windpipe, esp. of a horse.
throstle, *n. thros*-l, the song-thrush ; a cotton-spinning machine working continuously, and simultaneously drawing, twisting, and winding (so called from its sound when in action). (A.S.)
throttle, *n. throt*-tl, the windpipe ; the throat ; a throttle-valve, esp. that controlling the volume of vapour delivered from the carburettor of an internal combustion engine to the cylinders : *v.t.* to strangle ; to choke ; to obstruct delivery through a throttle-valve. **to throttle down,** to reduce the speed of a motor, etc., by throttling. (*throat*.)
throttle-valve, *n.* a valve for regulating the supply of steam, vapour, etc., to the cylinders of an engine or motor.
***through,** *prep.* throo, from end to end or side to side ; noting passage ; by transmission ; by means of ; by the agency of ; by reason of ; over the whole surface of ; by passing among or in the midst of : *ad.* from one end or side to the other ; from beginning to end ; to the ultimate purpose : *a.* admitting free passage ; passing through ; going the whole distance. **all through,** throughout ; by sole reason of. **carry through,** *see* **carry. go through,** *see* **go. through ticket,** a ticket for the whole journey. **through traffic,** traffic that passes direct between any two places. **through train,** a train from terminus to terminus. **through with,** done or finished with [Coll.]. (A.S. *thurh*.)
throughout, *prep,* throo-*out*, quite through ; in every part of : *ad.* in every part.
throve, throve, *p.* of *thrive*.
throw, *v.t.* throh, to fling, hurl, or cast with the arm or in any manner ; to drive or propel to a distance with a catapult, gun, or any piece of mechanism ; to shape on a potter's lathe ; to wind or twist into threads ; to venture at dice ; to shed or put off ; to put on (as clothes) hastily ; to prostrate in wrestling ; to overturn ; to drive by violence or dash : *v.i.* to hurl or cast ; to play at dice. **throw away,** to lose by neglect or folly ; to waste ; to reject. **throw by,** to lay aside. **throw down,** to overthrow. **throw in,** to inject ; to put in. **throw off,** to expel ; to discard. **throw on,** to cast on. **throw oneself on,** to resign oneself to the clemency (of another). **throw out,** to cast out ; to reject ; to utter. **throw over** or **overboard,** to abandon ; to discard ; to jettison. **throw up,** to eject ; to resign ; to make prominent ; to construct hastily. *p.* **threw.** *pp.* **thrown.** (A.S. *thrawan*, twist, hurl.)
throw, *n.* throh, act of throwing ; a cast of dice ; venture or hazard ; a stroke ; the distance to which a missile may be thrown ; the radius of a crank

from the axis of rotation of the shaft [Eng.]; a fault, or extent of displacement so caused [Geol.].

throwaway, *n. throh*-a-way, anything that is or may be thrown away; a printed leaflet.

throwback, *n. throh*-bak, reversion to ancestral type, or to some former stage; an instance of this, a consequence of atavism [Biol.].

thrower, *n. throh*-er, one who throws; a throwster.

throwing-stick, *n. throh*-ing-stik, the stick with which Australian natives, etc., throw their spears.

thrown, throhn, *pp.* of *throw.*

thrown-silk, *n. throhn*-silk, silk consisting of two or more singles twisted together like a rope in a contrary direction to the twist of the singles.

throw-off, *n.* the act of starting, esp. the beginning of a hunt; a disengaging or disconnecting device [Mech.].

throwout, *n. throh*-out, the act of throwing out, rejecting or [Mech.] disconnecting; anything discarded; a reject.

throwster, *n. throh*-ster, one who twists or winds silk; a dicer; a gambler.

throwstick, *n. throh*-stik, a club or boomerang, etc., thrown by the hand.

thrum, *n.* thrum, the fringe of threads on the loom after the web has been cut; one of such threads; any coarse yarn; anything like a thrum: *v.t.* to fringe with thrums; to insert short pieces of rope-yarn in a piece of canvas [Naut.]. (A.S., from O.Scand.)

thrum, *v.i.* thrum, to play badly on an instrument with the fingers; to strum. (Imit.)

thrush, *n.* thrush, a bird of the genus *Turdus*, esp. the throstle. (A.S. *thrysce.*)

thrush, *n.* thrush, a contagious disease of infants characterized by aphthæ, or minute ulcers in the mouth, due to a parasitic fungus [Med.]; a purulent inflammation of the frog of a horse's foot [Vet.]. (Perhaps as *thirst.*)

thrust, *n.* thrust, a violent push or driving, as with a pointed weapon, or with the hand or foot; an attack or assault [Mil.]; a force against a resisting or supporting force [Mech.]; a horizontal outward pressure, as of an arch against its abutments [Arch.]: *v.t.* to push or drive with force; to force; to impel: *v.i.* to make a push; to attack with a pointed weapon; to squeeze in; to intrude; to push forward. (Ice. *thrysta.*)

thrust-block, *n.* a bearing to resist thrust, esp. that that receives the push of the propeller in marine engines.

thruster, *n. thrus*-ter, one who thrusts; a pushful person [Coll.].

thrustful, *a. thrust*-ful, characterized by self-assertion; pushful.

thrutching, *n. thruch*-ing, the act of squeezing curds with the hand to expel the whey: *pl.* that which is last pressed from the curds, of which butter is sometimes made. (A.S. *thrycceam.*)

thrutching-screw, *n.* a screw for pressing curds in cheese-making.

thud, *n.* thud, a dull sound from a heavy stroke or fall. (Perhaps A.S. *thyddan*, to strike.)

thug, *n.* thug, one of a former Indian fraternity dedicated to the goddess Kali and living by murder and the subsequent plunder of their victims; hence, a cut-throat or desperado, a gangster. (Hind., a cheat.)

thugee, *n. thug*-ee, thuggery.

thuggery, *n. thug*-er-re, the profession and practices of a thug; savage ruffianism.

thuggish, *n. thug*-ish, characteristic of a thug.

thuggism, *n. thug*-izm, thuggery; murder and robbery in the manner of thugs.

Thuja, *n. thoo*-ja, a genus of hardy evergreen coniferous trees, including the arbor vitæ, *T. orientalis.*

thulia, *n. thew*-le-a, thulium oxide, one of the rare earths [Chem.].

thulite, *n. thew*-lite, a variety of zoisite of peach-blossom colour, found in Norway. (L. *Thule*, the most northern part of Europe anciently known.)

thulium, *n. thew*-le-um, a rare earth metallic element allied to yttrium. (As *thulite.*)

★**thumb,** *n.* thum, the short, thick digit of the human hand; the corresponding member of other animals; a thumb-shaped part or object: *v.t.* to handle awkwardly; to play or soil with the fingers: *v.i.* to thrum. **rule of thumb,** practice regardless of theory. **thumbs up!** an exclamation of success [Slang]. **under the thumb of,** under the influenc of, dominated by. (A.S. *thuma.*)

thumbed, *a.* thumd, having thumbs; marked b the thumb.

thumbikins, *n.pl. thum*-e-kinz, a thumb-screw formerly employed in Scotland to extort confession

thumb-index, *n.* an index cut into or projectin from the outer edges of the leaves of a book t facilitate reference.

thumb-mark, *n.* the mark made by a dirty thumb

thumbnail, *n. thum*-nale, the nail of the thumb **thumbnail sketch,** a very small drawing or ver brief description.

thumb-pot, *n.* a flower-pot less than three inche in diameter at the top.

thumb-ring, *n.* a ring worn on the thumb.

thumb-screw, *n.* a screw to turn with finger an thumb; an instrument of torture for compressin the thumb; a thumbikins.

thumbstall, *n. thum*-stawl, a protective coverin worn on the thumb after injury; a kind of thimbl for protecting the thumb in making sails, repairin shoes, etc.

thumby, *a. thum*-e, clumsy; soiled with thumb marks.

Thummim, *n.pl. thum*-mim, a sacerdotal objec anciently worn, with the Urim, by Jewish Hig Priests and probably used in connexion wit divination and the delivery of oracles. (Heb. *pl.* of *tōm.* perfection.)

thump, *n.* thump, a heavy blow given with a clu or fist or anything thick; the resulting sound: *v.* to beat with something thick and heavy: *v.i.* t fall with a thump. (From the sound.)

thumper, *n. thump*-er, one who or that whic thumps; anything unusually great [Slang].

thumping, *a. thump*-ing, exceptionally big; ou rageous [Slang].

★**thunder,** *n. thun*-der, the noise accompanyin lightning; any loud noise; denunciation published *v.i.* to sound as thunder: *v.t.* to emit with noise an terror; to publish any denunciation or threa **steal one's thunder,** to anticipate his speec action, etc., and so rob him of credit. (A.S.)

thunderbolt, *n. thun*-der-boalt, a single brillian flash of forked lightning followed by thunder an imaginary missile accompanying this; vehement denunciation; a person of violent o destructive energy; an irresistible force.

thunderclap, *n. thun*-der-klap, a peal of thunder.

thunder-cloud, *n.* a cloud from which come lightnin and thunder.

thunderer, *n. thun*-der-rer, he who or the pow that thunders. **the Thunderer,** Jupiter; a form name of the London newspaper, *The Times.*

thunder-fish, *n.* the weather-fish.

thundering, *a. thun*-der-ring, uttering a lou prolonged sound, like thunder; remarkable, ou and-out [Slang]: *ad.* unusually, tremendousl [Slang].

thunderous, *a. thun*-der-rus, pertaining to or full thunder; like thunder in sound or effect.

thunderstorm, *n. thun*-der-storm, a stor accompanied by thunder and lightning.

thunderstruck, *a. thun*-der-struk, amazed; struc dumb by the sudden appearance of somethin surprising or terrible.

thundery, *a. thun*-der-re, pertaining to or betokenin thunder; gloomy [Fig.].

thurible, *n. thew*-re-bl, a censer. (L. *thuribulum.*)

thurifer, *n. thew*-re-fer, one who carries the cens at divine service. (L. *thus, thuris*, incense, *fer* carry.)

thuriferous, *a.* thew-*rif*-er-rus, producing or bearin frankincense.

thurification, *n. thew*-re-fe-*kay*-shon, act of fumi with incense or burning incense. (L. *thus, thuri* incense, *facio*, make.)

thuringite, *n.* thewr-*rin*-jite, a massive mineral co sisting of a hydrous silicate of aluminium an iron. (*Thuringia*, where first found.)

Thursday, *n. thurz*-day, the fifth day of the wee **Maundy Thursday,** the day before Good Frida (*Thor*, and O.Scand. *dagr*, day.)

thus, *ad.* thus, in this or that manner; on this wise to this degree or extent; so.

thwack, *n.* thwak, a heavy blow with somethi flat or heavy: *v.t.* to strike with something flat heavy; to thump or belabour. (*whack.*)

hwaite, *n.* thwate, a parcel of ground reclaimed to illage. (O.Scand.)

hwart, *a.* thwawrt, transverse; across something else: *n.* an oarsman's seat placed athwart the boat: *v.t.* to cross; to oppose; to contravene; to frustrate: *v.i.* to be in opposition: *ad.* athwart. (O.Scand. *thvert.*)

hwarter, *n.* *thwawrt*-er, he who or that which thwarts; a disease in sheep, indicated by shaking or convulsive motions.

hwartingly, *ad.* *thwawrt*-ing-le, so as to thwart; in a cross direction; in opposition.

hwart-ship, *ad.* across the ship [Naut.].

hy, *a.* thy, of or belonging to thee. (*thine.*)

hylacine, *n.* *thy*-la-sin, the Tasmanian wolf, *Thylacinus cynocephalus*, a carnivorous marsupial. (Gr. *thulakos*, a pouch.)

hyme, *n.* time, any plant of the labiate genus *Thymus*, esp. the aromatic herb *T. vulgaris*, used in cookery. (Fr. *thym.*)

hymic, *a.* *thy*-mik, pertaining to thyme, or [Path.] to the thymus. **thymic acid,** thymol.

hymol, *n.* *thy*-mol, a distillate of oil of thyme used as a powerful antiseptic.

hymus, *n.* *thy*-mus (*pl.* **thymi**), a ductless gland situated in front of the pericardium and the large vessels arising from the base of the heart, perhaps associated with growth. (Gr. *thumos*, wart.)

hymy, *a.* *ty*-my, abounding with thyme; fragrant.

hyrogenic, *a.* thy-roh-*jen*-ik, originating in the thyroid gland [Med.].

hyroid, *a.* *thy*-royd, shield-shaped; applied only to certain anatomical features, esp. the **thyroid cartilage,** the largest cartilage of the larynx (forming the "Adam's apple"), and the **thyroid gland,** an important ductless gland situated near it: *n.* any thyroid part [Anat.]. **thyroid extract,** a preparation from the thyroid gland of certain animals [Pharm.]. (Gr. *thyreos*, a large oblong shield, *eidos*, like.)

hyroidism, *n.* *thy*-roy-dizm, deficiency due to removal or faulty functioning of the thyroid gland; a morbid condition due to overdoses of thyroid extract.

hyrotherapy, *n.* *thy*-ro-*the*-ra-py, treatment with a thyroid preparation [Med.].

hyroxin, *n.* thy-*rok*-sin, the active principle of the thyroid gland.

hyrse, *n.* therce, a thyrsus [Bot.].

hyrsoid, *a.* *ther*-soyd, resembling a thyrsus.

hyrsus, *n.* *ther*-sus, a staff entwined with ivy and vine leaves carried at the festivals of Bacchus; an inflorescence consisting of a panicle contracted into an ovate form [Bot.]. (Gr.)

hyself, *pron.* thy-*self*, used after *thou*, to express distinction with emphasis.

n. tee, a small Polynesian and New Zealand tree of the genus *Cordyline*, with edible roots; any Australasian shrub of the genera *Leptospermum* and *Melaleuca*. (Polynesian.)

ang, *n.* *tee*-ang, an antelope native to N.-E. Africa.

ara, *n.* te-*ah*-ra, a circlet; a jewelled head-dress; an ornamental head-dress of the ancient Persians; the Jewish High Priest's mitre; the Pope's triple crown. (Fr. *tiare.*)

araed, *a.* te-*ah*-r'd, wearing a tiara.

ibetan, *a.* te-*bee*-tan, of or pertaining to Tibet or its inhabitants: *n.* a native of Tibet; the language of the Tibetans. (*Tibet.*)

bia, *n.* *tib*-e-a (*pl.* **tibiæ**), the shin-bone. (L.)

bial, *a.* *tib*-e-al, pertaining to the tibia.

, *n.* tik, a convulsive muscular motion chiefly of the face. **tic douloureux** (App.), painful facial neuralgia. (Fr. *tic*, and *douloureux*, painful.)

cal, *n.* te-*kahl*, a former silver coin of Siam, about equal to a rupee. (Malay.)

ce, *n.* tice, a lob ball, or underhand yorker, at cricket. (*entice.*)

ce, *v.t.* tice, to entice.

chorhine, *a.* *tik*-o-ryn, having the nostrils separated by a complete bony partition (applied only to the extinct woolly rhinoceros, *Rhinoceros tichorhinus*). (Gr. *teichos*, a wall, *rhis*, *rhinos*, the nose.)

ck, *n.* tik, credit; trust: *v.i.* to run up a score; to give or get tick. **on tick,** on credit. (*ticket.*)

ck, *n.* tik, a small arachnoid arthropod allied to the mites, infesting dogs, sheep, etc. (A.S. *ticia.*)

ck, *n.* tik, the cover containing feathers, wool, or other materials of a bed. (Gr. *theke*, a case.)

tick, *n.* tik, a small mark; a slight quick and distinct sound, as that of a watch; an instant [Coll.]: *v.t.* to mark with a tick: *v.i.* to make a small noise, by beating or otherwise, as a watch. **tick off,** to dispose of; to scold or rate [Coll.]; to mark off. (Imit.)

tickbean, *n.* *tik*-been, a small bean used in feeding horses and other animals; a horse-bean.

ticker, *n.* *tik*-er, that which ticks; a watch [Slang]; a tape-machine [Slang]; the heart [Slang].

★**ticket,** *n.* *tik*-et, a piece of paper or a card, which gives the holder some specific right; a certificate that something is due to the holder; a price label: *v.t.* to distinguish by a ticket. **season ticket,** a periodical ticket; a ticket holding good for a certain period instead of for one occasion only. **the ticket,** the correct thing [Slang]. **ticket day,** the day before settlement day on the Stock Exchange, when the names of purchasers are given by one stockbroker to another. **ticket of leave,** a document setting a convict free before the expiry of the term of his sentence in consideration of his industry or good conduct. (Fr. *étiquette*, label.)

ticket-porter, *n.* a licensed porter wearing a badge or ticket, by which he may be identified.

tickie, *n.* *tik*-e, a threepenny-bit [S. African].

ticking, *n.* *tik*-ing, a closely woven cloth of which the tick containing the materials of bedding is made.

tickle, *v.t.* *tik*-kl, to touch lightly, so as to cause a peculiar thrilling sensation that induces laughter; to please by slight gratification: *v.i.* to feel titillation or tickling: *n.* the act, or the sensation of tickling; a tickling. (M.E. *tikelen.*)

tickler, *n.* *tik*-kler, one who or that which tickles; anything to jog the memory; that which puzzles; a ticklish question.

tickling, *n.* *tik*-kling, the act of affecting with titillation; sensation of titillation.

ticklish, *a.* *tik*-klish, sensible to slight touches; easily tickled; unsteady; precarious; difficult; critical; risky.

ticklishly, *ad.* in a ticklish manner.

ticklishness, *n.* the state of being ticklish; critical condition.

tickly, *a.* *tik*-kle, ticklish; tickling.

tick-seed, *n.* *tik*-seed, a plant of either of the genera *Corispermum* or *Coreopsis*.

tick-tack, *n.* *tik*-tak, a sound as of a clock or watch beating; tic-tac. **tick-tack-toe,** the game of noughts and crosses.

ticky, *a.* *tik*-e, infested with ticks: *n.* a tickie.

tic-tac, *n.* *tik*-tak, the secret signalling used by bookmakers on race-courses [Coll.].

tidal, *a.* *ty*-dal, pertaining to tides; periodically flowing and ebbing; dependent on or moved by the tide.

tid-bit, *n.* *tid*-bit, a delicate or tender piece of anything eatable; a tit-bit.

tiddler, *n.* *tid*-dler, a stickleback; any small young fish.

tiddly, *a.* *tid*-dle, fuddled with drink: *n.* any intoxicating liquor [Slang].

tiddlywinks, *n.* *tid*-dle-winks, a game in which counters are snipped from a flat surface into a cup.

tide, *n.* tide, time; season; the rising and falling of the sea and the waters connected therewith; stream; course; current; a period of working time: *v.t.* to drive with the stream: *v.i.* to work in or out of a river or harbour by favour of the tide. **flood tide,** the rising tide. **neap tide,** full tide at its minimum, occurring when the sun and moon act at right angles to each other. **spring tide,** full tide at its maximum, resulting from the attractive force of the sun and moon when acting in a straight line, either in conjunction or opposition. **to tide over,** to surmount (a difficulty) temporarily. (A.S. *tid*, time.)

tide-gate, *n.* a gate through which water passes into a basin, etc., when the tide flows, and which is shut to prevent it flowing back at the ebb.

tide-gauge, *n.* a contrivance for ascertaining, and sometimes registering, the state of the tide continuously.

tideless, *a.* *tide*-less, having no tide.

tide-lock, *n.* a lock situated between tide-water and a dock, canal, etc.

tidemark, *n.* *tide*-mark, the point reached by the tide at high water, or the lowest point to which the ebb retires; high-water mark or low-water mark.

tide-mill, *n.* a mill operated by tide-water.
tide-rip, *n.* rough water caused by opposing tides; the rippling from eddies as the tide passes.
tidesman, *n.* *tidez*-man, a tide-waiter.
tide-table, *n.* a table showing the tides at different places.
tide-waiter, *n.* a custom-house officer who watches the landing of goods, to secure the payment of duties.
tide-water, *n.* water affected by the tides; water overflowing land at flood tide.
tideway, *n.* *tide*-way, the channel in which the tide acts; the rush of water through this.
tidily, *ad.* *ty*-de-le, neatly.
tidiness, *n.* *ty*-de-ness, neat simplicity; neatness.
tidings, *n.pl.* *ty*-dingz, news; intelligence; account of what has taken place. (A.S. *tidan*, happen; from *tid*, time.)
tidology, *n.* ty-*dol*-o-je, the science treating of tides.
tidy, *a.* *ty*-de, neat; clean; dressed with neat simplicity; being in good order; fairly good or satisfactory [Coll.]: *n.* any little device for keeping things orderly: *v.t.* to make neat; to put in good order. (*tide.*)
tie, *n.* ty, a fastening; a bond; something which ties or is used to tie; a necktie; obligation; an equality in numbers, as of votes or scores; a dead heat; a piece of timber or metal for binding two bodies together [Arch.]; a curved line connecting notes of the same pitch, also a thick line which unites the tails of notes and shows their values [Mus.]: *v.t.* to bind; to fasten with a band, cord, or knot; to make fast; to knit; to confine; to unite notes by a tie [Mus.]. **tied house,** a public-house the licence-holder of which is under contract to obtain his liquor from a definite supplier, usually a brewer. *ppr.* **tying.** (A.S. *tigan*, tie, from *teon*, draw.)
tie-beam, *n.* the beam connecting the bottom of a pair of principal rafters [Arch.].
tier, *n.* teer, a row or rank, esp. one of a number placed one above another. (O.Fr. *tire*, course.)
tier, *n.* *ty*-er, one who ties; something used for tying.
tierce, *n.* teerce, an old liquid measure of one-third of a pipe or 42 gallons; a cask of this content; the interval of a third, also a slurred third [Mus.]; a sequence of three cards of the same suit [Card-games]; a thrust in fencing; a field divided into three parts [Her.]; the third canonical hour, ending 9 a.m., also the office then said [Eccles.]. (Fr., from L. *tertius*, a third.)
tiercel, *n.* *teer*-sel, a male hawk, esp. the peregrine or goshawk (perhaps as a third less in size than a female).
tiercet, *n.* *teer*-set, a tercet.
tiers-état, *n.* (App.), the third estate or commonalty, esp. as represented in the French legislative assembly prior to the Revolution. (Fr.)
tie-wig, *n.* a wig having long back hair tied with a ribbon.
tiff, *n.* tif, a pet or a fit of peevishness; a slight quarrel; a small draught of liquor: *v.i.* to be peevish: *v.t.* to sip. (Perhaps Ice. *tefr*, smell, sniff, taste.)
tiffany, *n.* *tif*-a-ne, a species of gauze or very thin silk. (O.Fr. *tiffanie*, from material used for costumes at Epiphany festivities.)
tiffin, *n.* *tif*-n, luncheon; a slight repast between breakfast and dinner. (Anglo-Indian.)
tig, *n.* tig, a game among children in which the one who is touched must give chase to the rest till he touches another: *v.t.* to touch in this game.
tige, *n.* teej, the shaft of a column from the astragal to the capital [Arch.]; a stem [Bot.]. (Fr., a stalk.)
tigelle, *n.* ti-*jel*, the part of the stem below the cotyledons in a germinating seed [Bot.]. (Fr.)
tiger, *n.* *ty*-ger, the Asiatic carnivore *Felis tigris*; a young liveried groom or servant [Slang]; a poker hand consisting of 7 high, 2 low, with no pair, sequence, or flush [Cards]. **American tiger,** the jaguar. **red tiger,** the cougar. (Fr. *tigre.*)
tiger-beetle, *n.* a carnivorous beetle of any genus of the Cicindelidæ.
tiger-bittern, *n.* a South and Central American heron of the genus *Tigrisoma.*
tiger-cat, *n.* the margay or other wild cat; a fierce or ferocious person [Fig.].
tiger-flower, *n.* a tropical American plant of th iris family, *Tigridia pavonia.*
tigerish, *a.* *ty*-ger-ish, like a tiger; tigrish.
tiger-lily, *n.* the orange-lily, *Lilium tigrinum.*
tiger-moth, *n.* any species of Arctiidæ, esp. *Arct caja.*
tiger-shark, *n.* any striped and voracious shar esp. *Stegostoma tigrinum.*
tiger-shell, *n.* a species of large cowry, *Cypra tigris.*
tigerwood, *n.* *ty*-ger-wood, a variegated cabin wood, esp. that of *Machærium schomburgki*, Guiana.
***tight,** *a.* tite, close; compact; not loose or open taut; fitting close to the body, as clothes; tense parsimonious; saving; tipsy: *n.pl.* close-fittin pantaloons. **sit tight,** to stay as one is; t remain of the same opinion, etc. (Scand.)
tighten, *v.t.* and *i.* *ty*-t'n, to draw or become tighte
tightish, *a.* tite-ish, rather tight; partly drunk.
tightly, *ad.* *tite*-le, in a tight manner.
tightness, *n.* *tite*-ness, the state of being tight tautness; tension.
tight-rope, *n.* the stretched rope on which acroba perform.
tigon, *n.* *ty*-gon, a tygon.
tigress, *n.* *ty*-gres, a female tiger.
tigrine, *a.* *ty*-grin, like a tiger; tigrish.
tigrish, *a.* *ty*-grish, resembling a tiger; fierce.
tike, *n.* tike, a tyke.
tilbury, *n.* *til*-ber-re, a two-wheeled carriage, wit or without a top. (Name of its inventor.)
tilde, *n.* *til*-da, the symbol (~) placed over a Spanis *n* (ñ), converting its pronunciation into *ny.*
tile, *n.* tile, a thin plate of baked clay used f covering the roofs, forming drains, etc.; a sma flat piece of dried earth, used to cover vessels i which metals are fused [Metal.]; a piece used i the game of mah-jong; a top hat [Slang]: *v.t.* t cover with or as with tiles; to station a tiler at th door as a guard against intrusion [Masonry]. **tile loose,** slightly lunatic, daft [Coll.]. (A. from L. *tegula*, from *tego*, cover.)
tiled, *pp.* and *a.* tyld, covered with tiles.
tile-drain, *n.* a drain made of tiles.
tile-kiln, *n.* a kiln in which tiles are burnt.
tiler, *n.* *ty*-ler, a man whose occupation is to cov buildings with tiles; the doorkeeper of a mason lodge. (Fr.)
tilery, *n.* *ty*-ler-re, a tile-kiln, or place where tiles a made.
tilestone, *n.* *tile*-stone, a laminated sandstone, es from the uppermost group of Silurian rocks [Geol.
Tilia, *n.* *til*-e-a, the genus of hardy deciduous tre comprising the limes or lindens. (L.)
tiliaceous, *a.* *til*-e-*ay*-shus, pertaining to the Tileace the Natural Order including the *Tilia* or lindens.
tiling, *n.* *tile*-ling, a roof of tiles; tiles in general.
tilka, *n.* *til*-kah, the mark on a Hindu's forehea indicating the caste. (Hind.)
till, *n.* til, boulder clay [Geol.].
till, *n.* til, a money-drawer, esp. in a shop or ban (A.S. *tyllan*, draw.)
***till,** *prep.* til, to the time or time of: *conj.* to th time when; to the degree that. **till now,** to th present time. **till then,** to that time. (A.S.)
till, *v.t.* til, to plough and prepare for seed; to cult vate. (A.S. *tilian.*)
tillable, *a.* *til*-a-bl, capable of being tilled; arable.
tillage, *n.* *til*-aj, the operation, practice, or art tilling; cultivation; tilled land.
tiller, *n.* *til*-er, one who tills; a husbandman.
tiller, *n.* *til*-er, the gear that works the rudder of rowing-boat. (O.Fr. *telier*, a weaver's beam.)
tiller, *n.* *til*-er, a sapling; a lateral shoot springi from the root [Bot.]: *v.i.* to put forth tille (A.S. *telgor.*)
tilleul, *n.* (App.), the lime tree; a pale yellowi green colour. (Fr.)
tilmus, *n.* *til*-mus, a plucking of the bedclothes delirium; carphology; floccilation. (Gr. *tilmos*, plucking.)
tilseed, *n.* *til*-seed, the seed of *Sesamum indicum.*
tilt, *n.* tilt, a tent; a covering; the covering of cart or wagon; a hood; the cover of a boat or ste awning: *v.t.* to cover with a tilt. (A.S. *telda* cover.)
tilt, *n.* tilt, a military exercise in which the mount combatants attack each other with lances; t

act of tilting; inclination forward; a tilt-hammer: *v.t.* to incline; to raise one end, as of a cask, for discharging liquor; to point or thrust, as a lance; to forge, etc., with a tilt-hammer: *v.i.* to run or ride and thrust with a lance; to rush, as in combat; to play unsteadily; to ride, float, and toss; to lean; to fall, as one one side. **at full tilt,** with impetuous speed or full force. (A.S. *tealt,* unsteady.)

tilt-boat, *n.* a rowing-boat fitted with a tilt.

tilter, *n. tilt*-er, one who tilts.

tilth, *n.* tilth, agricultural work; the state of being tilled; tilled land; tillage. (A.S.)

tilt-hammer, *n.* a heavy pivoted hammer used in ironworks, lifted by the revolution of a cam-wheel.

tilting, *a. tilt*-ing, slanting; used (as a lance, etc.) in tilting: *n.* the action of the verb *to tilt*; material for tilts.

ilt-yard, *n.* an enclosed space in which tilts or jousts were held.

imbal, *n. tim*-bal, a kettledrum; the membrane with which the cicada produces its sound [Zool.]. (Fr. *timbale.*)

imbale, *n.* (App.), a timbal [Zool.]; a dish of minced meat or fish cooked in a mould. (Fr., timbal, from its shape.)

imber, *n. tim*-ber, wood; the body or stem or a tree; trees collectively; a single piece of wood for building, or already framed; a rib of a wooden ship; fences, etc. [Hunting]: *v.t.* to furnish or cover with timber or timbers; to cover with trees. **timber wolf,** the large grey wolf of Western U.S.A. (A.S.)

imbered, *a. tim*-berd, covered with timber; showing the constructional timbers [Building].

imber-head, *n.* the top end of a frame, rising above the gunwale [Naut.].

imber-line, *n.* the limit beyond which trees do not grow on mountains or in cold climates.

imber-lode, *n.* a feudal service by which tenants were obliged to carry timber to the lord's mansion.

imberman, *n. tim*-ber-man, a man employed in felling timber; one in charge of the pitprops in a mine.

imber-toes, *n.* a man with a wooden leg [Slang].

imber-tree, *n.* any tree the wood of which is suitable for constructional or carpenter's use.

imbre, *n. tam*-br, the sonorous quality of a voice or instrument, as exemplified in the rendering of a given tone; the quality of the sound; resonance; the helmet and crest, etc., surmounting a coat of arms [Her.]. (Fr., a clock bell, L. *tympanum.*)

imbrel, *n. tim*-brel, an ancient musical instrument resembling a tambourine in shape. (O.Fr. *tymbre.*)

imbrology, *n.* tim-*brol*-o-je, the study of postage stamps; philately. (Fr. *timbre,* postage stamp, and *-ology.*)

imbromania, *n.* tim-bro-*may*-ne-a, a mania for collecting postage stamps.

***time,** *n.* time, the measure of duration; any period of eternity; moment; period; a proper time; a season; duration; a measured portion or distinct part of duration; life; age; repetition; the measure of sounds in regard to their continuance or duration [Mus.]; the state of things at a particular period; the present life; a tense [Gram.]: *v.t.* to adapt to the time or occasion; to do at the proper season; to regulate as to time; to measure as regards the time. **against time,** competing with time. **ahead of time,** early; premature. **apparent time,** true solar time at any given place. **at times,** at distinct intervals. **beat time,** *see* **beat. in time,** in good season; sufficiently early. **keep time,** to be punctual; to keep step. **lose time,** to go slow (of watches, etc.). **mark time,** to remain in the same place though moving the feet in time; not to advance. **mean time,** an average of apparent time. **out of time,** not in time; untimely; unseasonable. **sidereal time,** *see* **sidereal. solar time,** *see* **solar. standard time,** the legal time in any particular country or region. **summer time,** *see* **summer. time and again,** repeatedly. **time being,** present time. **time enough,** early enough. **time of one's life,** a particularly happy period; a time of full enjoyment [Coll.]. (A.S. *tima.*)

ime-ball, *n.* a ball sliding on an upright staff arranged to drop daily at a given time.

ime-bargain, *n.* an agreement to buy or sell at a certain time.

ime-bill, *n.* a time-table of departure and arrival of conveyances.

time-book, *n.* a book recording the time worked by those employed.

time-card, *n.* a card on which is recorded time worked.

time-clock, a clock fitted with a recording device, esp. for employees entering and leaving their work-place.

time-expired, *a.* having completed the due period of service.

time-exposure, *n.* exposure for a period of some duration [Phot.].

timeful, *a. time*-ful, seasonable; timely; sufficiently early.

time-fuse, *n.* a fuse so constructed that it will burn only for a pre-arranged time.

time-honoured, *a.* long held in honour; of venerable age.

timekeeper, *n. time*-keep-er, a timepiece; one who takes note of the times of competitors in races, etc.; one employed to record the times worked by others; one who or that which beats time [Mus.].

time-lag, *n.* period intervening between cause and effect.

timeless, *a. time*-less, unseasonable; done at an improper time; untimely; unending.

time-limit, *n.* a limit to the period during which a condition, object, etc., can function or be of use; the limit of time permitted for or by a licence.

timeliness, *n. time*-le-ness, seasonableness; the quality of being timely.

timely, *a. time*-le, seasonable; being in good time; sufficiently early: *ad.* early; soon; opportunely.

timeous, *a. ty*-mus, timely; betimes; opportune.

timeously, *ad.* timely; in good time.

timepiece, *n. time*-peece, a clock, watch, or other chronometer.

timer, *n. time*-er, one who or that which times; a timekeeper; (*in combination*) one who serves a specified time, as *full-timer.*

timeserver, *n. time*-server, one characterized by timeserving; a trimmer.

timeserving, *n. time*-ser-ving, a mean or cringing compliance with the humours of those in power; obsequious conformity to popular opinion: *a.* characterized by this.

time-sheet, *n.* a time-card; a table of the hours of work of a staff.

time-signature, *n.* a sign, usually figures, at the beginning of a piece of music to indicate the measure [Mus.].

time-table, *n.* a table of times of starting and arrival of trains, etc.; a table showing the times allotted for certain occupations or entertainments; a tabular representation of the different notes, and their relative lengths [Mus.].

time-work, *n.* work paid for by the time it takes as distinguished from piece-work.

time-worn, *a.* worn away by time; decayed.

timid, *a. tim*-id, wanting courage to meet danger; fearful; timorous. (Fr. *timide.*)

timidity, *n.* ti-*mid*-e-te, fearfulness; want of courage or boldness to face danger; timorousness; habitual cowardice. (Fr. *timidité.*)

timidly, *ad. tim*-id-le, in a timid manner.

timidness, *n.* the quality of being timid.

timist, *n. time*-ist, one who keeps in time [Mus.]; one who or that which keeps time.

timocracy, *n.* ti-*mok*-ra-se, government by men of property or standing. (Gr. *time,* honour, *krateo,* rule.)

timocratic, *a.* tim-o-*krat*-ik, pertaining to or characterized by a timocracy.

timoneer, *n.* ty-mo-*neer,* a helmsman. (L. *temo,* helm.)

timoroso, *ad.* tim-o-*roh*-zoh, in a style expressive of awe or fear [Mus.]. (It.)

timorous, *a. tim*-o-rus, fearful of danger; timid; indicating fear; full of scruples.

timorously, *ad.* timidly; with much fear.

timorousness, *n.* timidity.

timothy, *n. tim*-o-the, the meadow cat's-tail, *Phleum pratense,* a valuable fodder-grass.

timous, *a. time*-us, timeous.

timpani, *n.pl. tim*-pa-ne (*sing.* **timpano**), the kettledrums of an orchestra. (L.)

***tin,** *n.* tin, a silvery-white metallic element with a slight tinge of yellowish blue, and very malleable; a thin plate of iron covered with tin; a can, canister, or other utensil made from this; money [Slang]:

v.t. to cover with tin, or overlay with tinfoil; to preserve in tins; to can. **tin crystals,** stannous chloride, a mordant used in dyeing. **tin hat,** a steel helmet [Slang]. (A.S.)
tinamou, *n.* *tin*-a-moo, any species of a group of gallinaceous Mexican and S. American birds allied structurally to the ostriches. (Fr.)
tincal, *n.* *ting*-kal, crude borax, esp. as obtained from Tibet and the East. (Malay, *tingkal.*)
tinchel, *n.* *ting*-kel, a circle of sportsmen surrounding an extensive space and gradually enclosing the deer within a narrow compass. (Gael.)
tinctorial, *a.* tink-*taw*-re-al, pertaining to colour; used for dyeing. (L. *tinctorius.*)
tincture, *n.* *tink*-tewr, a tinge or shade of colour; a slight superadded taste or quality; the finer and more volatile parts of a substance, separated by a solvent; a solution in alcohol; a metal, colour, or tint used in emblazoning [Her.]: *v.t.* to tinge; to impregnate with something foreign; to imbue. (L. *tinctura.*)
tindal, *n.* *tin*-dal, a lascar boatswain's mate; a foreman; an attendant [Anglo-Ind.] (Malay.)
tinder, *n.* *tin*-der, anything inflammable used for catching fire from a spark. (A.S. *tynder.*)
tinderbox, *n.* *tin*-der-boks, a box in which tinder and the materials for striking a light are kept.
tindery, *a.* *tin*-der-re, like tinder; very inflammable.
tine, *n.* tine, a prong, tooth, or spike as of a fork or harrow, etc.; a branch of an antler. (A.S. *tind.*)
tinea, *n.* *tin*-e-a, any contagious fungoid skin disease, esp. ringworm; (*cap.*) a genus of clothes' moths. (L., a gnawing worm, a moth.)
tined, *a.* tynd, furnished with tines or prongs.
Tinewald, *n.* *tine*-wawld, Tynwald.
tinfoil, *n.* *tin*-foyl, tin in thin sheet form; an alloy of lead and tin beaten to a thin leaf: *v.t.* to cover or coat with this.
ting, *v.i.* and *t.* ting, to tinkle; to ring: *n.* a sharp single sound, as made by a bell when struck.
tinge, *n.* tinj, a slight degree of some colour, taste, or quality: *v.t.* to imbue or impregnate with something foreign; to colour or stain; to modify slightly the colour, taste, or character by something superadded. (L. *tingere, tinctum,* dye, stain.)
tingi, *n.* *ting*-e, a Brazilian tree of the genus *Magonia,* from the seeds of which a soap is made.
tingle, *n.* *ting*-gl, a kind of thrill: *v.i.* to feel a kind of thrilling sound; to feel a sharp thrilling pain; to feel a thrilling or sharp, slight penetrating sensation. (M.E. *tinglen.*)
tingling, *n.* *ting*-gling, a thrilling sensation; a light continued tinkle.
tinily, *ad.* *ty*-ne-le, in a tiny degree; minutely.
tininess, *n.* *ty*-ne-ness, the quality of being tiny.
tink, *n.* tink, a shrill noise: *v.i.* and *t.* to make or cause to emit a shrill noise; to tinkle.
tinker, *n.* *ting*-ker, a mender of pots and pans and other household utensils; an unskilful repairer; a bungler; a gipsy or tramp [Scots.]; a local name for the stickleback and other fish: *v.t.* to mend like a tinker; to botch: *v.i.* to work at tinkering. (M.E. *tinkere,* from *tinken,* ring, tinkle.)
tinkerly, *a.* in the manner of a tinker; bungling.
tinkershire, *n.* *ting*-ker-sher, the guillemot.
tinkle, *n.* *ting*-kl, a small sharp metallic sound: *v.i.* and *t.* to make or cause to make such sounds. (Imit.)
tinman, *n.* *tin*-man, a maker of tin-plate vessels; a dealer in tinware.
tinned, *a.* tind, covered or plated with tin; preserved in a tin or can; [Slang] recorded (of music, etc.).
tinner, *n.* *tin*-er, a tin miner; a tinman; one engaged in canning.
tinning, *n.* *tin*-ing, the art of covering or lining anything with tin or tinfoil; the business of canning food.
tinnitus, *n.* *tin*-e-tus, a ringing in the ears [Med.]. (L.)
tinnock, *n.* *tin*-ok, a local name for the blue tit.
tinny, *a.* *tin*-e, abounding with tin; similar to or characteristic of tin; tasting or smelling of tin.
tin-plate, *n.* thin sheet steel coated with tin.
tinsel, *n.* *tin*-sel, thin, shiny metallic material for producing a showy or gaudy effect; anything cheap and flashy; superficial display: *a.* gaudy; showy to excess; brummagem: *v.t.* to adorn with tinsel; to make meretricious or tawdry. (Fr. *étincelle,* from L. *scintilla,* a spark.)
tinselly, *a.* *tin*-sel-e, like tinsel.
tinsmith, *n.* *tin*-smith, a worker in tin; a tinman.
tinstone, *n.* *tin*-stone, native oxide of tin; cassiterite.
tin-stuff, *n.* tin ore.
tint, *n.* tint, a slight colouring or tincture distinct from the ground or principal colour; a shade; a shaded effect in engravings, given by light parallel lines; a background in a light colour [Print.]: *v.t.* to tinge; to give a slight colouring to: *v.i.* to develop a tint. **tint block,** a plate used in printing a flat colour, esp. as background. (L. *tinctum,* dye.)
tin-tack, *n.* *tin*-tak, a tin-coated tack.
tintage, *n.* *tin*-taj, tints or tinting collectively.
tintamarre, *n.* tin-ta-*mahr,* a din; a hubbub; a hideous or confused noise. (Fr.)
tinter, *n.* *tint*-er, one who or that which tints.
tintinnabular, *a.* tin-te-*nab*-yew-lar, tintinnabulary.
tintinnabulary, *a.* *tin*-te-*nab*-yew-la-re, relating to bells; making the sound of a bell.
tintinnabulation, *n.* *tin*-te-*nab*-yew-*lay*-shon, a tinkling, as of bells. (L. *tintinnabulum,* bell.)
tintinnabulous, *a.* tin-te-*nab*-yew-lus, pertaining to bell-ringing.
tintometer, *n.* tin-*tom*-e-ter, a form of colorimeter for determining colours by comparison.
tintype, *n.* *tin*-type, a ferrotype, an early form or means of photographic reproduction.
tinware, *n.* *tin*-ware, utensils made of tin-plate.
tiny, *a.* *ty*-ne, very small; puny. (Origin unknown.)
tip, *n.* tip, the small pointed extremity of anything; an apex; an end piece or addition, as a ferrule, etc.; the camel-hair brush used in laying gold-leaf: *v.t.* to form a point to; to cover the tip, top, or end of. (M.E. *typ.*)
tip, *n.* tip, a tap or gentle hit; a hint or suggestion; an item of information; a pourboire or small present; a dumping ground for rubbish, etc.: *v.t.* to tap; to hit gently; to lower one end; to cant; to overturn, also to discharge contents thus; to hint; to tell; to give a gratuity to: *v.i.* to fall; to lean; to be or become tilted or upset. **tip off,** to warn; a piece of secret information; to kill. **tip the wink,** to wink to another as a sign. **on the tip of one's tongue,** *see* **tongue.** (M.E. *tippen.*)
tip-and-run, *n.* a form of cricket in which a run must be attempted for every hit: *a.* designating an onset, etc., in which a speedy withdrawal by the attacker is essential.
tip-cart, *n.* a cart the body of which can be tilted up from the frame so as to empty its load.
tipcat, *n.* *tip*-kat, a game in which a spindle-shaped piece of wood is hit away with a stick or bat.
tippet, *n.* *tip*-et, a covering of fur or cloth, etc., for the shoulders, fastened round the neck; a small cape. (A.S. *tæppet,* from L. *tapete,* carpet.)
tipping, *n.* *tip*-ping, the action of the verb *to tip* staccato notes on a wind instrument; double tonguing [Mus.].
tipple, *n.* *tip*-pl, liquor, esp. that taken in tippling *v.i.* to drink alcoholic liquors frequently: *v.t.* to drink, as strong liquors, in excess; to sip repeatedly (*to tip,* as a vessel.)
tippler, *n.* *tip*-pler, one who tipples or habitually indulges in alcoholic liquors.
tippling-house, *n.* a public-house; a dramshop.
tippy, *a.* *tip*-e, full of tips (esp. of tea).
tipsily, *ad.* *tip*-se-le, in a tipsy manner.
tipsiness, *n.* *tip*-se-ness, the state of being tipsy.
tipstaff, *n.* *tip*-stahf (*pl.* **tipstaffs** or **tipstaves**), an official who carries a staff tipped with metal, esp. a sheriff's; an officer or a court usher.
tipster, *n.* *tip*-ster, a man who gives tips and private information, esp. in racing; a racing prophet.
tipsy, *a.* *tip*-se, nearly drunk, fuddled. (*tip.*)
tipsy-cake, *n.* a sponge cake soaked in sherry with custard, cream and blanched almonds.
tip-tilted, *a.* turned up at the end (esp. of the nose)
tiptoe, *ad.* *tip*-toh, on the toes only: *a.* walking or standing on the toes: *n.* the end of the toe: *v.i.* to go on tiptoe; to step stealthily. **on tiptoe** with strained attention or expectation.
tip-top, *n.* the highest or utmost degree: *a.* excellent in the highest degree.
tipulary, *a.* *tip*-yew-la-re, pertaining to insects of the genus *Tipula,* which includes the daddy-longlegs (L.)
tip-up, *n.* the spotted sandpiper, *Actitis macularia* of N. America: *a.* made to tip up.
tirade, *n.* ti-*rade,* a declamation; a volley of invec

tive or abuse; the filling of an interval between two notes by a rapid run [Mus.]. (Fr., from *tirer*, draw.)
irailleur, *n.* (App.), a skirmishing rifleman; a sharpshooter. (Fr., from *tirailler*, to skirmish.)
re, *n.* tire, attire; a head-dress: *v.t.* to attire; to adorn; to dress the head. (*attire.*)
ire *or* **tyre,** *n.* tire, a band or hoop, usually of iron, to bind the fellies of wooden wheels; the rubber cushion, usually pneumatic, encircling the rim of a cycle, motor-car, or aeroplane wheel. (*attire.*)
re, *v.t.* tire, to exhaust the strength of by toil or labour; to weary or fatigue; to exhaust the attention or patience of with dullness and tediousness: *v.i.* to become weary; to be fatigued. (M.E. *tiren.*)
tired, *a.* tyrd, weary; exhausted.
iredness, *n.* *tyrd*-ness, the state of being tired.
ireless, *a.* *tire*-less, untiring; incapable of being wearied.
iresome, *a.* *tire*-sum, exhausting the strength or patience; wearisome; fatiguing; tedious.
iresomeness, *n.* the quality of being tiresome.
irewoman, *n.* *tire*-woo-man, a lady's maid; a theatrical female dresser.
iring, *a.* *tire*-ring, making tired; wearisome; fagging.
iring-room, *n.* a theatre dressing-room.
rl, *n.* tirl, a twirl: *v.t.* to twist or twirl; to strip; to render naked; to uncover: *v.i.* to quiver; to vibrate [Scots.].
ro, *n.* *tire*-roh, a tyro.
-iron, *n.* *tee*-eye-urn, a right-angled iron bar with the web along the middle.
ironian, *a.* ti-*roh*-ne-an, pertaining to the ancient Roman shorthand. (*Tiro*, Cicero's amanuensis.)
irret, *n.* *ti*-ret, a manacle [Her.]. (*terret.*)
is, tiz, a contraction of "it is".
sane, *n.* te-*zahn*, ptisan. (Fr.)
sic, *a.* and *n.* *tiz*-ik, phthisic.
isri, *n.* *tiz*-re, the first month of the Hebrew civil year and seventh of the ecclesiastical (parts of Sept. and Oct.). (Heb.)
issue, *n.* *tish*-yew, any fine or gauzy woven fabric; a structure formed of cells and cell products [Anat. and Bot.]; a mesh; a connected series: *v.t.* to form tissue; to adorn with tissue; to interweave with gold and silver threads. (Fr. *tissu.*)
ssue-paper, *n.* very thin gauze-like paper.
t, *n.* tit, a small horse; a child; a woman, in contempt; a titmouse, any of several small perching birds; a morsel; a slight tap or blow. **blue tit,** the small bird *Parus cæruleus.* **tit for tat,** an equivalent in return. (Ice. *titte*, originally anything small.)
t, *n.* tit, a teat.
itan, *n.* *ty*-tan, one of the primitive deities of Greek myth, gigantic beings, sons of Uranus and Gæa and ancestors of Zeus and many of the gods; a strong nature vainly battling with fate; the brightest of Saturn's satellites [Astron.]: *a.* titanic. (Gr.)
tanate, *n.* *ty*-ta-nate, a salt of titanic acid.
tanesque, *a.* ty-tan-*esk*, having the attributes of a Titan; immense; colossal.
itaness, *n.* *ty*-ta-ness, a female Titan; a giantess.
itania, *n.* ti-*tay*-ne-a, the queen of the fairies.
tanic, *a.* ti-*tan*-ik, pertaining to the Titans; gigantic; of enormous size or strength; pertaining to, derived from, or containing titanium.
taniferous, *a.* ty-ta-*nif*-er-rus, producing titanium.
itanism, *n.* *ty*-ta-nizm, titanic power; revolt against authority or the universe.
tanite, *n.* *ty*-tan-ite, very hard crystalline silicate of titanium and calcium; sphene.
tanium, *n.* ti-*tay*-ne-um, a brittle, silvery white metallic element of the group containing thorium and zirconium.
tanotherium, ti-*tan*-o-*theer*-re-um, an extinct gigantic perissodactyl of the N. American Eocene and Oligocene. (Gr. *Titan*, and *therion*, a wild animal.)
t-bit, *n.* *tit*-bit, a dainty little piece; a scrap; a short piquant clipping from some publication.
thable, *a.* *ty*-tha-bl, subject to the payment of tithes.
the, *n.* tythe, the tenth part of anything; the tenth part of the increase annually arising from the profits of land and stock, allotted (till redeemed, 1936, by an issue of Government stock) to the clergy; a small part: *v.t.* to tax to a tenth. (A.S. *teotha*, tenth.)
tithing, *n.* *ty*-thing, the levying of tithes; a former territorial division consisting of ten householders who were sureties to each other in frank-pledge.
tithing-man, *n.* the chief man of a tithing; a peace officer or under-constable.
titian, *n.* *tish*-e-an, a reddish-yellow colour. (The Ital. painter, *Titian*, *d.* 1576.)
titillate, *v.t.* *tit*-e-late, to tickle; to stimulate pleasurably. (L. *titillo.*)
titillation, *n.* tit-e-*lay*-shon, the act of tickling; any slight pleasure.
titivate, *v.t.* *tit*-e-vate, to bedeck; to make attractive.
titivation, *n.* tit-e-*vay*-shon, the act or result of titivating; a smartening up.
titlark, *n.* *tit*-lark, the meadow pipit, *Anthus pratensis.*
title, *n.* *ty*-tl, an inscription, esp. one in the beginning of a book giving its name or denoting its subject; a title-page, and all printed thereon; an appellation of dignity, distinction, or pre-eminence; a name; an appellation; right; that which constitutes a just right to exclusive possession; the instrument which is evidence of a right; a title-deed; that by which a beneficiary holds a benefice [Eccles. Law]: *v.t.* to name; to call; to entitle. (O.Fr., from L. *titulus.*)
titled, *pp.* and *a.* *ty*-tld, bearing a title, esp. of nobility or knighthood.
title-deed, *n.* a legal document giving the evidence of ownership of real property.
title-page, *n.* the page at the beginning of a book giving the title, author's and publisher's names, etc.
title-role, *n.* the character in a book, drama, etc., giving his or her name to the work.
titling, *n.* *tite*-tling, type designed for titles; any fount of modern roman capitals [Print.].
titling, *n.* *tit*-ling, the hedge-sparrow. (*tit.*)
titmouse, *n.* *tit*-mous (*pl.* **titmice**), a small active perching bird of the genus *Parus*, the tit. **bearded titmouse,** the reedling.
titrate, *v.t.* *ty*-trate *or* *tit*-rate, to use volumetric analysis to determine the quantity of a constituent in a mixture [Chem.]. (Fr. *titrer.*)
titration, *n.* ti-*tray*-shon, volumetric analysis [Chem.].
ti-tree, *n.* *tee*-tree, the Polynesian ti of the genus *Cordyline.*
titter, *n.* *tit*-er, a restrained laugh: *v.i.* to laugh slightly; to giggle. (M.E. *titeren*, chatter.)
titterel, *n.* *tit*-er-rel, the whimbrel. (From its cry.)
tittery, *a.* *tit*-er-re, given to tittering.
tittle, *n.* *tit*-l, a small particle; an iota. (M.E. *title.*)
tittle-bat, *n.* a stickleback, or other small fish.
tittle-tattle, *n.* idle trifling talk; empty prattle; an idle trifling talker: *v.i.* to talk idly; to prate.
tittup, *v.i.* *tit*-up, to curvet or prance about; to canter; [Slang] to toss for drinks: *n.* a bobbing up-and-down motion.
tittupy, *a.* *tit*-up-e, frisky; tittuping.
titty, *n.* *tit*-e, a teat; a rubber teat for infants.
titubant, *a.* *tit*-yew-bant, staggering; unsteady; stammering.
titubate, *v.i.* *tit*-yew-bate, to reel, to stagger; to stammer. (L. *titubare.*)
titubation, *n.* *tit*-yew-*bay*-shon, the act of stumbling; a restless fidgety state; the staggering gait of disease [Med.]. (L. *titubatio.*)
titular, *a.* *tit*-yew-lar, having or conferring the title only; invested with a title of an office, benefice, etc., without possessing the power or performing the duties attached to it: *n.* one so invested. (Fr. *titulaire.*)
titularly, *ad.* nominally; by title only.
titulary, *a.* *tit*-yew-la-re, consisting in or pertaining to a title: *n.* a titular.
tiver, *n.* *tiv*-er, a kind of red ochre used in marking sheep: *v.t.* to mark sheep with this.
tizzy, *n.* *tiz*-ze, a sixpence [Slang]. (*teston.*)
tmesis, *n.* *tmee*-sis, the separation of two parts or syllables of a word by interpolating another word as "be thou ware of him" [Rhet.]. (Gr. from *temno*, cut.)
***to,** *prep.* too, noting motion towards a place or direction toward an object, purpose, or thing; opposed

to "from"; it precedes the radical verb as a sign of the infinitive; noting extent, degree, or end. **to and fro,** backwards and forwards. **to the face,** in presence of. (A.S.)

toad, *n.* tode, an amphibian of the genus *Bufo,* resembling the frog in form, but thicker and clumsier, and with a warty skin; the toadfish or sea-toad. **toad in the hole,** a dish of beef baked or fried in batter. (M.E. *tode.*)

toad-eater, *n.* a fawning obsequious parasite; a mean sycophant.

toad-eating, *n.* sycophancy: *a.* sycophantish.

toadfish, *n. tode*-fish, a marine fish of the genus *Batrachus,* of the N. American Atlantic coast.

toad-flax, *n.* a perennial plant of the genus *Linaria.*

toad-pipe, *n.* any horsetail of the genus *Equisetum.*

toad-spittle, *n.* cuckoo-spit.

toadstone, *n. tode*-stone, a variety of dolerite; also, a fossil or naturally shaped stone supposed to have formed part of, or to have been fashioned within, the body of a toad.

toadstool, *n. tode*-stool, a fungus somewhat resembling a mushroom, many of which are poisonous.

toady, *n. toh*-de, a toad-eater; a hanger-on; a lickspittle: *v.i.* to fawn upon as a toady.

toadyish, *a. toh*-de-ish, resembling or pertaining to a toady or toadyism.

toadyism, *n. toh*-de-izm, mean sycophancy.

toast, *n.* tohst, bread browned before the fire; a proposal to drink the health of some person or cause, etc.; the person or object toasted; a woman whose health is frequently drunk: *v.t.* to dry and scorch by the heat of the fire; to warm thoroughly; to drink to the health, success, or honour of. **to have on toast,** to have at one's mercy or in an awkward situation [Slang]. (O.Fr. *tostée,* a toast of bread.)

toaster, *n. tohs*-ter, one who toasts; an instrument for toasting bread or cheese.

toasting-fork, *n.* an implement to hold bread when being toasted.

toastmaster, *n. tohst*-mahs-ter, the announcer of the toasts at a dinner.

toast-rack, *n.* a stand for holding slices of toast.

tobacco, *n.* to-*bak*-oh, any species of the genus *Nicotiana,* an American plant, the leaves of which are used, after drying, etc., for smoking and chewing and in snuff. (Sp. *tabaco,* probably the name given by the Indians to the pipe in which they smoked it.)

tobaccoism, *n.* to-*bak*-o-izm, a morbid condition due to excessive use of tobacco [Path.].

tobacconist, *n.* to-*bak*-o-nist, a dealer in or manufacturer of tobacco.

tobacco-pipe, *n.* a pipe used for smoking tobacco.

tobacco-pouch, *n.* a pouch for holding tobacco.

tobacco-stopper, *n.* a plug for pressing down the tobacco as it is smoked in a pipe.

tobaccoy, *a.* to-*bak*-oh-e, redolent of tobacco smoke or tobacco.

tobe, *n.* tohb, a length of cotton material intended for a garment. (Ar.)

tobine, *n. toh*-bine, a stout twilled silk fabric formerly used for dresses.

toboggan, *n.* to-*bog*-an, a small sledge used as a means of transport over snow and for sliding down a snow-clad slope: *v.i.* to coast on a toboggan. (N. Amerind. *tobakun.*)

Toby, *n. toh*-be, a mug formed like an old man wearing a three-cornered hat; the dog in a Punch-and-Judy show; (*l.c.*) the highroad [Slang]; *v.t.* to rob on the highway [Slang]. **the high toby,** robbery on the toby, or highroad, by a mounted tobyman.

tobyman, *n. toh*-be-man, a highwayman.

toc, *n.* tok, signallers' name for letter *T.* **Toc H.,** an incorporated organization (founded at Talbot House, Poperinghe, 1915) to promote, on Christian principles, wartime ideals of service and fellowship in time of peace.

toccata, *n.* to-*kah*-ta, a prelude designed to display the executant's touch [Mus.]. (It.)

toccatella, *n.* tok-a-*tel*-a, a short or simple toccata [Mus.]. (It.)

toccatina, *n.* tok-a-*tee*-na, a toccatella [Mus.]. (It.)

tocher, *n. tokh*-er, a portion brought by a wife on her marriage; a dowry [Scots.]. (O. Gael. *tochar.*)

toco, *n. toh*-ko, a large S. American toucan. (Tupi.)

tocology, *n.* to-*kol*-o-je, obstetrics. (Gr. *tokos,* childbirth, *logos,* science.)

tocsin, *n. tok*-sin, an alarm-bell, or the ringing of it; an alarm signal. (O.Fr. *toquesin,* an alarm-bell.)

tod, *n.* tod, a quantity of wool of 28 lb.; a bush or thick shrub; a fox. (Ice.)

to-day, *n.* to-*day,* the present day: *ad.* on this day; now. (A.S. *to daege,* on this day.)

toddle, *n. tod*-dl, a saunter; a toddling walk; a toddling child: *v.i.* to walk with short tottering steps, as a small child, or in a leisurely way. (*totter.*)

toddler, *n. tod*-dler, one who toddles, esp. a toddling child.

toddy, *n. tod*-de, a juice drawn from a palm-tree, becoming intoxicating when fermented; a mixture of spirits with hot water and sugar. (Hind. *tadi.*)

toddy-bird, *n.* any of various Indian birds feeding on palm juice.

to-do, *n.* to-*doo,* ado; stir; fuss and commotion.

tody, *n. toh*-de, a very small insectivorous West Indian picarian bird of the genus *Todus.* (L.)

★**toe,** *n.* toh, a digit of the foot, corresponding to a finger on the hand; the fore-part of the hoof of a horse, or of any other hoofed animal; a lower end; any prolongation like a toe: *v.t.* to touch with the toe; to furnish (footwear) with a toe or toes; to kick [Slang]. **on one's toes,** ready for any emergency; alert. **toe the line,** to act according to rule, or in conformity; to fulfil one's obligations. **tread on one's toes,** to vex or give offence, esp. inadvertently. **turn up the toes,** to die [Slang]. (A.S. *ta.*)

toecap, *n. toh*-kap, an extra piece over the toe of a boot or shoe.

toe-clip, *n.* an attachment to a cycle pedal to keep the foot from slipping.

toed, *a.* tohd, having toes.

toe-nail, *n.* a nail growing on a toe.

toff, *n.* tof, a fop; a swell [Slang].

toffee, *n. tof*-e, a sweetmeat of boiled sugar and butter.

toft, *n.* toft, a homestead; a house with its croft, or adjacent land. (O.Scand.)

toftman, *n. toft*-man, the owner or occupier of a toft.

tog, *v.t.* tog, to clothe. **tog oneself up,** to dress in one's best [Slang]. (Perhaps from *toga.*)

toga, *n. toh*-ga, the outer garment of a Roman citizen, loose, flowing, and in a single piece. **toga prætexta,** *see* **prætexta. toga virilis,** the manly toga assumed by boys at about fifteen. (L.)

togaed, *a. toh*-g'd, wearing a toga.

togated, *a. toh*-ga-ted, dressed in a toga. (L. *togatus.*)

★**together,** *ad.* to-*geth*-er, in company; in or into union; in the same place or time; in concert. **together with,** in union with. (A.S. *togædere.*)

toggery, *n. tog*-er-re, clothes; garments [Slang].

toggle, *n. tog*-gl, a small wooden pin tapering at both ends [Naut.].

toggle-iron, *n.* a whaler's harpoon so barbed as to prevent its inadvertent withdrawal.

toggle-joint, *n.* an elbow or knee-joint formed of two bars that may be brought into a straight line.

togs, *n.pl.* togz, clothes; garments [Slang]. (*tog.*)

toil, *n.* toyl, labour with oppressive pain and fatigue; drudgery: *v.i.* to exert strength with pain and fatigue of body and mind (esp. of body) in prolonged effort; to labour. (O.Fr. *toillier,* to drag about.)

toile, *n.* twahl, a linen material used for dresses. (Fr.)

toiler, *n. toyl*-er, one who toils; one of the labouring or working class.

toilet, *n. toy*-let, the operation or mode of dressing; a lavatory or water-closet [U.S.A.]. **make one's toilet,** to dress. (Fr. from *toile,* cloth.)

toilet-cover, *n.* a cover for the dressing-table.

toilet-glass, *n.* a mirror for the dressing-table.

toilet-paper, *n.* thin paper for use as an abstergent in water-closets.

toilet-roll, *n.* a long roll of toilet-paper having perforations at regular intervals.

toilinette, *n.* toy-le-*net,* a cloth, the weft of which is woollen and the warp cotton and silk.

toils, *n.pl.* toylz, a net or snare. (Fr., from L. *tela,* a web.)

toilsome, *a. toyl*-sum, laborious; wearisome.

toilsomely, *ad.* in a toilsome manner.

toilsomeness, *n.* state of being toilsome.

oil-worn, *a.* worn out with toiling.
oise, *n.* (App.), an obsolete French measure of length, nearly 6 ft. 4¾ in. (Fr.)
oison d'or, *n.* (App.), the Golden Fleece, a Spanish order of knighthood. (Fr. *toison,* fleece, *d'or,* of gold.)
okay, *n.* to-*kay,* a rich, aromatic wine produced at Tokay, in Hungary.
oken, *n.* *toh*-ken, something intended to represent another thing or event; a sign; a mark; a memorial of friendship; a privately issued stamped metal disk resembling coin and passing locally as such; 250 impressions on a hand-press [Print.]. **by the same token,** furthermore; in the same way. **token money,** coin of inferior metal current for more than its intrinsic value but of a fixed ratio to gold. **token payment,** a small payment in advance as earnest of the payer's good faith. (A.S. *tacen.*)
okology, *n.* to-*kol*-o-je, tocology.
ola, *n.* *toh*-la, in India, a weight for gold and silver equal to 180 grains troy (11·664 grammes).
olbooth, *n.* *tole*-booth, a toll-booth.
old, told, *p.* and *pp.* of *tell.* **all told,** including everything.
oledo, *n.* to-*lee*-doh, a sword-blade of the finest temper. (*Toledo,* in Spain, famous for such.)
olerable, *a.* *tol*-er-ra-bl, that may be endured; supportable (physically or mentally); fairly good. (Fr.)
olerableness, *n.* quality of being tolerable.
olerably, *ad.* to a tolerable extent.
olerance, *n.* *tol*-er-rance, power or art of tolerating; disposition to tolerate; the remedy [Coining], also the amount by which an engineering product is allowed to depart from its specified dimensions [Eng.]. (Fr.)
olerant, *a.* *tol*-er-rant, disposed to tolerate; enduring of; favouring toleration; broad-minded.
olerantly, *ad.* with toleration.
olerate, *v.t.* *tol*-er-rate, to suffer to be or to be done without prohibition or hindrance; to allow or permit, esp. by not preventing. (L. *tolero,* bear.)
oleration, *n.* *tol*-er-*ray*-shon, the act of tolerating; the allowance of that which is not approved of; the practical recognition by a state, and its concession to its citizens, of the rights of private judgment, esp. in matters of religion. (Fr.)
olerationism, *n.* tol-er-*ray*-sho-nizm, the support or advocacy of toleration.
olerationist, *n.* *tol*-er-*ray*-sho-nist, one supporting toleration, esp. in matters of religion.
oll, *n.* tole, a tax for some liberty or privilege, particularly that of travelling over a road or bridge, or of vending goods in a fair or market; a portion of grain taken by a miller as compensation for grinding corn; a toll-gate; a requital or penalty incurred by reason of the circumstances [Fig.]; a telephone exchange for short-distance trunk calls in the London area: *v.t.* to impose, take, or collect toll. **toll of the road,** the collective deaths and injuries due to road traffic. (A.S., ultimately from Gr. *telos,* a tax.)
oll, *n.* tole, the solemn sound of a bell slowly rung: *v.i.* to sound, as a bell: *v.t.* to cause a bell to sound with strokes slowly repeated. (Imit.)
oll, *v.t.* tole, to take away; to annul [Law].
ollable, *a.* *tole*-a-bl, subject to toll or tax.
ollage, *n.* *tole*-aj, payment or exaction of toll; toll.
ollbar, *n.* a barrier at which toll is taken.
oll-booth, *n.* a place where toll or customs duties were collected; a guildhall; a town prison [Scots.].
oll-bridge, *n.* a bridge at which toll is paid for right of way.
oll-dish, *n.* a dish for measuring the toll of grain in mills.
oller, *n.* *tole*-er, one who takes or collects toll; one who tolls (in any sense).
oll-gate, *n.* a gate or other obstruction at which toll is taken.
oll-house, *n.* the house attached to a toll-bridge or toll-gate; office of a toll-collector.
olsey, *n.* *tol*-se, a toll-booth or guildhall.
oltec, *a.* *tol*-tek, of or pertaining to an early race of Indians that preceded the Aztecs in Mexico: *n.* a member of this race.
olu, *n.* to-*loo,* a fragrant balsam produced by a species of *Myroxylon,* a S. American tree, used in medicine. (Santiago de *Tolú,* Colombia.)
oluate, *n.* *tol*-yew-ate, a salt of toluic acid.

toluene, *n.* *tol*-yew-een, methyl benzene, a liquid hydrocarbon originally prepared from tolu.
toluic, *a.* *tol*-yew-ik, designating any of the acids prepared from toluene.
toluol, *n.* *tol*-yew-ol, crude toluene, obtained from coal-tar and used in making explosives.
tom, *n.* tom, a male, esp. an uncastrated male cat. **Old Tom,** gin [Slang]. **Tom, Dick, and Harry,** people in general; the rabble. **Tom-o'-Bedlam,** a lunatic. **Tom Thumb,** a midget, a dwarf. (*Thomas.*)
tomahawk, *n.* *tom*-a-hawk, a light Indian war hatchet: *v.t.* to cut or kill with a tomahawk.
tomalley, *n.* to-*mal*-e, the liver of a lobster, the part that turns green when boiled.
toman, *n.* to-*man,* a former gold coin of Persia (discontinued 1933).
tomand, *n.* to-*mahnd,* an Arabian grain measure of about 188 lb.
tomato, *n.* to-*mah*-toh, a perennial trailing plant, *Lycopersicum esculentum,* from S. America; its large yellowish red edible berry, used as a vegetable, and formerly called the love-apple. (Sp. *tomate.*)
tomb, *n.* toom, a grave; a sepulchre; a monument erected over a grave in memory of the dead: *v.t.* to entomb; to bury. (O.Fr. *tumbe.*)
tombac, *n.* *tom*-bak, an alloy of copper and zinc.
tombless, *a.* *toom*-less, destitute of a tomb.
tombola, *n.* *tom*-bo-lah, a kind of lottery. (It.)
tomboy, *n.* *tom*-boy, a romping girl.
tombstone, *n.* *toom*-stone, a stone erected over a grave; a monument.
tom-cat, *n.* tom-*kat,* a full-grown male cat.
tomcod, *n.* tom-*kod,* a small marine N. American fish of the genus *Microgadus*; a young cod; also applied to other small fish.
tome, *n.* tome, a book; a large volume. (Gr. *tomos,* a section, a part of a book, from Gr. *temno,* cut.)
tomentose, *a.* *toh*-men-tohz, downy; nappy; cottony or flocky [Bot.].
tomentum, *n.* to-*men*-tum, one of the small vessels on the surface of the brain [Anat.]; a species of soft pubescence [Bot.]; flocculent hairiness [Med.]. (L., stuffing of wool.)
tomfool, *n.* tom-*fool,* a great fool; a trifler.
tomfoolery, *n.* tom-*fool*-er-re, foolish trifling; nonsense.
tomin, *n.* *toh*-min, a weight equal to 12 grains (·776 grammes), formerly used by jewellers. (Sp.)
tommy, *n.* *tom*-e, a private soldier in the British army, so called from "Thomas Atkins," the name given as an example in filling up his papers; bread, food [Slang]. **tommy gun,** a one-man, portable, self-loading sub-machine gun, named from its U.S. inventor, John T. Thompson. **tommy rot,** utter nonsense, drivel [Slang]. **tommy system,** the truck system of payment.
tomnoddy, *n.* tom-*nod*-e, the puffin; a dolt.
★**to-morrow,** *n.* and *ad.* to-*mo*-roh, the day after the present.
tompion, *n.* *tom*-pe-on, a tampion; the iron bottom to which grape-shot were fixed; a tampon; the inking-pad used in lithography.
tompot, *n.* *tom*-pot, local (West Country) name for a species of marine blenny, also for the guinea-fowl.
tomtit, *n.* *tom*-tit, a titmouse, esp. the blue tit, *Parus cæruleus.*
tomtom, *n.* *tom*-tom, a native drum used by various Indian and African races: *v.i.* to beat the tom-tom. (Hind. *tam-tam.*)
ton, *n.* tun, a weight of 20 cwt. or 2,240 lb.; the unit for the measurement of tonnage, 35 cu. ft. [Naut.]; a very great weight or quantity [Coll.]; *pl.* lots [Coll.]. **freight ton,** 40 cu. ft. [Naut.]. **metric ton,** 2,204·6 lb., equals 1,000 kilograms. **register ton,** 100 cu. ft. [Naut.]. **short ton,** 2,000 lb.
ton, *n.* (App.), the prevailing fashion; the fashion. (Fr.)
tonal, *a.* *toh*-nal, pertaining to tone or tones [Mus. and Phon.].
tonality, *n.* to-*nal*-e-te, tones collectively; correctness of pitch [Mus.].
tondo, *n.* *ton*-doh, a circular painting or carving in relief. (It., circle.)
tone, *n.* tone, sound; quality of sound; a modification of sound; accent, or inflexion of voice adapted to express emotion or passion; a manner of speaking, writing, behaving, etc.; an interval of sound

[Mus.]; sound of an instrument with regard to softness, etc. [Mus.]; healthy state of body [Med.]; the harmonious relation of the colours of a picture in light and shade: *v.t.* to utter with an affected or special tone; to give tone to; to modify the colouring of [Art and Phot.]. **tone colour,** timbre [Mus.]. **tone down,** to lessen the force or strength of; to mitigate. **tone up,** to impart vigour to. (Fr. *ton*, from L. *tonus*, a sound.)

toned, *a.* tohnd, having a tone.

toneless, *a. tone*-less, having no tone; unmusical.

tone-poem, *n.* a composition based on a poetic idea, a symphonic poem [Mus.].

tone-syllable, *n.* a stressed syllable.

tonga, *n. tong*-ga, a light two-wheeled vehicle for four, used in India. (Hind. *tanga.*)

tongs, *n.pl.* tongz, two bars joined by a pivot or united by a spring, used for handling and lifting, esp. burning fuel and hot metals. (A.S. *tange.*)

***tongue,** *n.* tung, the organ of taste in animals, and, in man, of speech; speech; power of utterance; fluency of speech; a hound's cry; a language; mode of speaking a language; a people or nation; the clapper of a bell; a point, as of a buckle; a projecting point of land; a taper part; a projection along an edge to fit into a groove; a pointed rail in a switch [Rly.]; impudence [Slang]: *v.t.* to modify, as sound of a flute, with the tongue; to supply (boarding, etc.) with a tongue: *v.i.* to talk; to prate; to modify musical sound by use of the tongue. **give tongue,** to bark as a hound. **hold the tongue,** to be silent. **on the tip of one's tongue,** just about to be said or uttered; almost said. **with one's tongue in one's cheek,** ironically; with insincerity. (A.S. *tunge.*)

tongued, *a.* tungd, having a tongue.

tongue-grafting, *n.* whip-grafting [Hort.].

tongueless, *a. tung*-less, having no tongue; speechless; dumb.

tongue-test, *n.* the testing of a current by applying the tongue to a break in the circuit [Elect.].

tongue-tied, *a.* having an impediment in the speech; unable to speak freely; silent.

tongue-twister, *n.* a phrase, etc., difficult to pronounce or reiterate rapidly, as " strange strategical statistics " [Coll.].

tonic, *a. ton*-ik, pertaining to tone or tones; increasing strength, esp. tone in the bodily system; obviating the effects of debility and restoring healthy functions; based on or pertaining to the key-note [Mus.]: *n.* a medicine that gives tone and vigour of nerve and muscle; the key-note [Mus.]; the sound produced by a vocal string in a given degree of tension [Mus.]. **tonic sol-fa,** a system of musical notation in which, dispensing with the staff, its lines and spaces, notes are indicated by letters, and time and accent by dashes and colons. **tonic sol-faist,** *-fah*-ist, one using or advocating this system. **tonic spasm,** a continuous rigid muscular contraction [Med.]. (Gr. *tonikos*, stretching.)

tonically, *ad. ton*-e-ka-le, in a tonic way; in relation to tension; so as to invigorate.

tonicity, *n.* to-*nis*-e-te, state of being tonic; elasticity or contractility of the muscular fibres.

to-night, *n.* to-*nite*, the present night; the coming night; the night after the present day: *ad.* on this night or the night of this day.

tonish, *a. ton*-ish, stylish, modish, in the ton.

tonite, *n. toh*-nite, a blasting explosive consisting of 70 per cent gun-cotton and 30 per cent potassium nitrate. (L. *tonare*, thunder.)

tonka-bean, *n. tong*-ka-been, the fruit of the tropical S. American plant *Dipteryx odorata*, sometimes incorrectly called the Tonquin bean, used in perfumery, as a flavouring, and as a source of coumarin.

tonnage, *n. tun*-aj, the nominal capacity of a ship; the cubical content or burden which a ship can carry in tons; a duty or impost on ships, estimated formerly by weight, now by bulk.

tonneau, *n. ton*-oh, the part of a motor-car containing the back seat. (Fr.)

tonnish, *a. ton*-ish, tonish.

tonometer, *n.* to-*nom*-e-ter, a device for determining the vibration rate of tones [Acoustics]; an instrument for measuring eye-tension, blood-pressure, etc. [Med.].

Tonquin-bean, *n. tong*-kin-been, *see* **tonka-bean.**

tonsil, *n. ton*-sil, either of two glandular bodies in th throat or fauces [Anat.]. (Fr. *tonsille.*)

tonsillar, *a. ton*-sil-ar, pertaining to or affected b the tonsils.

tonsillitic, *a. ton*-se-*lit*-ik, pertaining to the tonsil or to tonsillitis.

tonsillitis, *n. ton*-se-*ly*-tis, inflammation of the tonsils

tonsorial, *a.* ton-*saw*-re-al, pertaining to a barbe or his craft. (L. *tonsor*, a barber.)

tonsure, *n. ton*-shoor, the clipping of the hair shaving of the head, or state of being shorn, as sign of dedication to the priesthood or admissio to a religious order; the shaven crown of a pries or monk. (Fr., from L. *tonsura.*)

tonsured, *a. ton*-sherd, wearing a tonsure; of th priesthood.

tontine, *n.* ton-*teen*, an annuity in which a numbe participate, the share of each being, on death equally divided among the rest until a single sur vivor inherits the whole. (Lorenzo *Tonti*, 17th-cent Neapolitan.)

tony, *a. toh*-ne, of good tone; smart; swagge [Coll.].

too, *ad.* too, over; more than enough; likewise **too-too,** very excessively, to much too great degree; gushingly affected [Coll.].

took, took, *p.* of *take.*

tool, *n.* tool, an implement for effecting or facilitatin mechanical operations by manual means; an instrument for this purpose other than power driven machinery; a person used as a mere instru ment by another; a bookbinder's tooling imple ment: *v.t.* to shape or mark, or to ornament o letter bookbinding, etc., with a tool: *v.i.* to drive esp. a team or coach. (A.S. *tol.*)

tooling, *n. tool*-ing, workmanship performed with tool; lettering or ornamental impressions o leather, etc.

toom, *a.* toom, empty: *n.* a place for rubbish *v.t.* to empty [Scots.]. (O.Scand.)

toon, *n.* toon, a large Indian tree, *Cedrela toona* also its mahogany-like wood. (Sans. *tunna.*)

toot, *v.i.* toot, to sound a horn in short, sharp blasts to produce or utter a similar sound: *v.t.* to sound as a horn, or on a horn: *n.* the short sharp soun made by tooting. (Imit.)

tooter, *n. toot*-er, one who toots on a horn, etc. a horn or trumpet.

***tooth,** *n.* tooth (*pl.* **teeth**), a hard substanc growing on the jaws of most vertebrates, serving a the instrument of mastication; taste; palate one of a series of projections resembling teeth: *v.* to fit with tooth-like projections; to indent; t interlock. **a sweet tooth,** enjoyment of swee things. **cast in the teeth,** to retort reproachfully **in spite of the teeth,** in defiance of opposition **set one's teeth,** to resolve fixedly. **set the teet on edge,** *see* **edge. show the teeth,** to threaten **tooth and nail,** by all possible means. **toot ornament,** dog-tooth, a decoration common i early English Gothic, consisting of a close successio of small four-leafed flowers projecting forward to central point [Arch.]. **to the teeth,** in ope opposition; directly to one's face. **skin of th teeth,** *see* **skin. small tooth comb,** a comb fo the hair with very closely set teeth, usually on eac edge. (A.S. *toth.*)

toothache, *n. tooth*-ake, pain in the teeth.

toothache-tree, *n.* a N. American tree of the genu *Xanthoxylon*, esp. the prickly ash, *X. fraxineum.*

tooth-billed, *a.* having a notched bill [Ornith.] **tooth-billed pigeon,** a dodo-like Samoan bird *Didunculus strigirostris.*

toothbrush, *n. tooth*-brush, a brush to clean th teeth with.

toothed, *a.* tootht, having teeth or jags; dentat [Bot.].

tooth-edge, *n.* a sensation excited by grating sound and by the touch of certain substances.

toothful, *n. tooth*-ful, a small quantity; a smal drink, a sip.

toothless, *a. tooth*-less, having no teeth.

toothleted, *a. tooth*-le-ted, denticulate [Bot.].

toothpaste, *n. tooth*-payst, a cleanser for the teet in the form of paste.

toothpick, *n. tooth*-pik, an instrument for cleanin the teeth of substances lodged between them.

toothpowder, *n. tooth*-pou-der, a powder to clea the teeth.

ooth-rash, strophulus [Med.].
oothsome, *a. tooth*-sum, palatable ; grateful to the taste.
oothsomeness, *n.* quality of being toothsome.
oothwort, *n. tooth*-wurt, a name of various plants having tooth-like projections or scales, including species of *Lathræa* and *Dentaria.*
oothy, *a. tooth*-e, toothed ; having prominent teeth.
ootle, *v.t.* and *i. too*-tl, to tooth gently ; to play the flute or flageolet.
'top, *n.* top, the highest part of anything ; summit ; surface ; the upper side ; the highest place, person, degree, rank, etc. ; the crown of the head ; the head of a plant ; the uppermost division of a fishing-rod ; a platform surrounding the head of the lower mast and projecting on all sides, serving to extend the shrouds [Naut.] : *a.* relating to the top ; on or at the top ; first, best : *v.t.* to cover on the top ; to provide with a top ; to cap ; to raise above ; to surpass ; to excel ; to crop ; to rise to the top of. **to top off** or **up,** to complete by providing with a top or culmination ; to give a finishing touch to ; to conclude. **at the top of the tree,** at the summit (esp. of one's profession, etc.). **top dog,** the superior in a contest ; the chief or head. **top secret,** completely secret ; information on no account to be transmitted without express authorization. (A.S., from O.Teut. *topf.*)
›p, *n.* top, a children's spinning toy in the shape of an inverted conoid. **sleep like a top,** to sleep soundly. (A.S., from O.Teut. *topf.*)
›parch, *n. top*-ark, the principal man in a place or country. (Gr. *topos,* a place, *archo,* rule.)
›parchy, *n. top*-ark-e, a petty country governed by a toparch ; any little state.
›paz, *n. toh*-paz, a transparent orthorhombic, generally yellowish, silicate of aluminium with fluorine, used as a gem-stone ; a yellowish or reddish yellow colour ; a brilliant S. American humming-bird. (Fr. *topase.*)
›pazolite, *n.* to-*paz*-o-lite, a variety of garnet of a topaz-yellow colour. (*topaz* and Gr. *lithos,* stone.)
›p-boots, *n.pl.* boots extending nearly to the knee with a broad top of light-coloured leather.
›p-coat, *n.* an overcoat.
›p-drain, *v.t.* to drain the surface of.
›p-dressing, *n.* the act of spreading manure or fertilizer on the surface of land ; material so used.
›pe, *n.* tope, a small species of shark, *Galeus vulgaris* ; the dogfish.
›pe, *n.* tope, a grove or clump of trees, esp. mango-trees [Anglo-Ind.]. (Tamil, *tōppu.*)
›pe, *n.* tope, a cupola-topped Buddhist commemorative monument ; a stupa. (Hind. *top.*)
›pe, *v.i.* tope, to drink strong liquors to excess. (Fr. *toper.*)
›pee, *n.* toh-*pee,* a topi.
›per, *n. toh*-per, a tippler ; one who drinks to excess.
›p-full, *a.* brimming ; full to the brim.
›pgallant, *a.* top-*gal*-lant, above the top or second mast, applied esp. to the mast next above the topmast, and to the sail above the topsail (often replaced by the upper and lower topgallant-sails) [Naut.] : *n.* a topgallant-sail ; the summit [Fig.].
›phaceous, *a.* to-*fay*-shus, gritty ; sandy ; of the nature of tophus.
›p-hamper, *n.* the upper spars, rigging, etc. ; rigging or other gear not in use but in the way [Naut.].
›p-hat, *n.* a man's tall silk hat.
›p-heavy, *a.* having the top or upper part too heavy for the lower.
ophet, *n. toh*-fet, hell, or the place of torment. (Heb. *Topheth,* a place outside Jerusalem anciently the site of the worship of Moloch and afterwards used for the deposit and burning of the city's refuse.)
›p-hole, *a.* first-rate ; tip-top [Slang].
phus, *n. toh*-fus (*pl.* **tophi**), a calcareous concretion about the joints and teeth in gout, etc. [Med.]. (L. *tufa.*)
pi, *n. toh*-pee, a light sun-helmet, esp. one made of sola pith [Anglo-Ind.]. (Hind., hat.)
piarian, *a.* toh-pe-*ayr*-re-an, pertaining to topiary-work : *n.* one skilled in this.
piary, *a. toh*-pe-a-re, shaped by cutting or clipping, applied esp. to the giving of fanciful shapes to trees, shrubs, etc. (L. *topia,* ornamental gardening, from Gr. *topos,* a place.)
pic, *n. top*-ik, the subject of discourse, argument, or treatise ; a subject of popular interest at the moment ; formerly, an external remedy [Med.] : *pl.* the art of discovering arguments. (Fr. *topique.*)
topical, *a. top*-e-kal, pertaining to a place, or to a topic or matter of temporary interest ; local [Med.].
topicality, *n.* top-e-*kal*-e-te, the quality of being topical.
topically, *ad.* in a topical manner.
topknot, *n. top*-not, a knot of ribbon, etc., or a tuft of hair or feathers on the top of the head ; a twisted knob of hair ; any of several small flatfish.
topless, *a. top*-less, having no top ; very high.
toplofty, *a.* top-*lof*-te, haughty ; condescending.
topman, *n. top*-man, the man who stands above in sawing ; a man stationed in the top [Naut.].
topmast, *n. top*-mahst, the mast next above that which rises from the deck.
topmost, *a. top*-most, highest ; uppermost.
topographer, *n.* to-*pog*-ra-fer, a student of, or one skilled in, topography ; one who describes a particular place.
topographic, *a.* top-o-*graf*-ik, topographical.
topographical, *a.* top-o-*graf*-e-kal, pertaining to topography ; descriptive of a place.
topographically, *ad.* in a topographical way.
topographist, *n.* to-*pog*-ra-fist, a topographer.
topography, *n.* to-*pog*-ra-fe, the science of describing or of giving a detailed account of a particular place ; topographic surveying ; physical features collectively. (Fr. *topographie.*)
topology, *n.* to-*pol*-o-je, the association of things with places as an aid to memory.
toponym, *n. top*-o-nim, a place-name ; a name designating a locality, region, or place of origin.
toponymic, *a.* top-o-*nim*-ik, pertaining to toponymy or toponymics : *n.pl.* the scientific study of place-names, or of words or names derived from these.
toponymy, *n.* to-*pon*-e-me, toponymics ; the place-names of a region. (Gr. *topos,* a place, *onyma,* name.)
topper, *n. top*-per, a top-hat ; the best of its kind, a first-rate chap [Slang].
topping, *a. top*-ping, lofty ; pre-eminent, fine, splendid [Slang] : *n.* that which forms the top ; the removal of the top ; the top cut off ; the act of pulling one extremity of a yard higher than the other [Naut.]. **topping-lift,** a rope raising or supporting from the masthead the outer end of a boom or yard [Naut.].
topple, *v.i. top*-pl, to fall forward ; to pitch or tumble down : *v.t.* to throw down. (*top.*)
topsail, *n. top*-sl, a sail carried on the topmast which in square-rigged vessels is generally divided into the upper and lower topsails.
top-sawyer, *n.* top-*saw*-yer, the man who works a pit-saw from above ; [Fig.] an outstanding or very important person.
top-shell, *n.* a marine gastropod mollusc of the genus *Trochus* and its allies.
topside, *n. top*-side, the upper part ; that part of a vessel's hull above the waterline [Naut.] ; a joint of beef taken from between the leg and the aitch-bone : *ad.* on top.
topsman, *n. tops*-man, a head drover ; the public hangman [Slang].
top-soiling, *n.* removing the surface soil.
top-stone, *n.* a stone forming the top ; a capstone.
topsy-turvy, *ad. top*-se-*tur*-ve, upside down : *a.* inverted ; disorderly : *n.* the act of turning upside-down ; a state of disorder ; a muddle. (*top, so,* and A.S. *tearflian,* roll over.)
topsy-turvydom, *n. top*-se-*tur*-ve-dum, complete confusion ; a topsy-turvy state of things.
toque, *n.* toke, a brimless head-dress for women. (Fr.)
tor, *n.* tawr, a high pointed hill or rocky peak. (A.S. *torr,* from Celt.)
Torah, *n. taw*-rah, the Mosaic law ; the Pentateuch. (Heb.)
toran, *n. taw*-ran, the gateway of a Buddhist temple consisting of two upright pillars and one or more lintels.
torbanite, *n. tor*-ba-nite, paraffin shale. (*Torbane* Hill, Bathgate, near Edinburgh.)
torbernite, *n. tor*-ber-nite, a brilliant green crystalline phosphate of uranium and copper. (*Torber* Bergmann, Swed. chemist, *d.* 1784.)
torc, *n.* tork, a barbaric necklace, etc., a torque.

torch, *n.* torch, a flambeau or light carried in the hand; a lighted stick or piece of rope; a small battery-operated electric lamp for carrying; that which enlightens [Fig.]; a name of various plants, esp. the great mullein, *Verbascum thapsus.* **torch lily,** the red-hot poker, *Kniphofia aloides*, and others of this genus. (Fr. *torche.*)

torch-bearer, *n.* one whose office is to carry a torch; one who passes on enlightenment [Fig.].

torch-dance, *n.* a dance in which each dancer carries a torch.

torchlight, *n. torch*-lite, the light of a torch or torches: *a.* lighted by torches; composed of torch-bearers.

torchon, *n. tor*-shon, coarse bobbin lace of geometrical pattern. **torchon paper,** a handmade rough-surfaced paper. (Fr.)

torch-thistle, *n.* the cactus *Cereus strigosus*, used by the American Indians for torches.

torchwood, *n. torch*-wood, any resinous wood suitable for making torches, esp. that of the Florida balsam, *Amyris elemifera.*

torchwort, *n. torch*-wurt, the mullein.

tore, tor, *p.* of *tear.*

tore, *n.* tor, the dead grass that remains on mowing land in winter and spring.

tore, *n.* tor, a torus [Arch. and Geom.].

toreador, *n. to*-re-a-*dor*, a mounted bull-fighter. (Sp.)

torero, *n.* to-*rare*-roh, a bull-fighter fighting on foot. (Sp.)

toreumatography, *n.* to-*roo*-ma-*tog*-ra-fe, the description of toreutic work.

toreumatology, *n.* to-*roo*-ma-*tol*-o-je, the science or art of toreutics.

toreutic, *a.* to-*roo*-tik, pertaining to artistic metal work, cast, chased, or embossed. (Gr. *toreutikos*, fashioned in relief.)

torgoch, *n. tor*-gokh, the red-bellied char, *Salmo perisii*, of Welsh lakes. (W. *tor*, belly, *goch*, red.)

torii, *n. to*-re-ee (*pl. unchanged*), a decorative gateway constructed of two tall uprights and two cross-pieces, used esp. at Shinto temples. (Jap.)

torment, *n. tor*-ment, extreme pain or anguish, bodily or mental; that which gives pain or misery: *v.t.* tor-*ment*, to inflict with such; to distress; to harass. (O.Fr., from L.)

tormentil, *n. tor*-men-til, a plant of the genus *Potentilla*, whose root is used medicinally as an astringent. (Fr. *tormentille.*)

tormenting, *a.* tor-*men*-ting, causing torment or annoyance: *n.* work done with a tormentor [Agric.].

tormentingly, *ad.* in a tormenting manner.

tormentor, *n.* tor-*men*-tor, he who or that which torments; one who inflicts penal torture; a harrow-like instrument for reducing a stiff soil [Agric.]; a tickler, or any irritating toy.

tormina, *n. tor*-me-na, colic, a severe griping in the bowels [Med.]. (L.)

torminous, *a. tor*-me-nus, severely griping [Med.].

tormodont, *a. tor*-mo-dont, having socketed teeth (esp. of certain extinct birds).

torn, torn, *pp.* of *tear.* **that's torn it!** things are now completely spoiled [Coll.].

tornadic, *a.* tor-*nad*-ik, pertaining to or characteristic of tornadoes.

tornado, *n.* tor-*nay*-do (*pl.* **tornadoes**), a local tropical whirlwind; a hurricane; a whirling tempest. (Sp. *tronada*, a thunderstorm.)

toroid, *a. tor*-royd, pertaining to or in the form of a torus [Geom.].

torose, *a.* to-*rohs*, torous.

torous, *a. tor*-rus, protuberant; swelling in knobs [Bot. and Anat.].

tor-ouzel, *n. tor*-oo-zel, a local name of the ring-ouzel.

torpedo, *n.* tor-*pee*-doh, a marine fish, the electric ray of the genus *Torpedo*; a self-driven dirigible submarine and aerial weapon charged with high explosive designed to explode on impact; a detonating fog-signal [Rly.]; an explosive firework: *v.t.* to attack or destroy with or as with a torpedo. **torpedo boat,** a small swift war vessel armed with torpedoes. **torpedo boat destroyer,** a larger, faster, and more heavily armed torpedo boat, originally designed for catching these. **torpedo net,** a net hung round a ship as a protection against torpedoes. **torpedo-tube,** the steel tube through which a torpedo is launched. (L. *torpedo*, be numb.)

torpedo-fish, *n.* the electric ray or torpedo.

torpedoist, *n.* tor-*pee*-doh-ist, one skilled in th science and management of torpedoes.

torpefy, *v.t. tor*-pe-fy, to render torpid; to benumb

torpent, *a. tor*-pent, benumbed; torpid: *n.* a agent reducing irritation [Med.].

torpid, *a. tor*-pid, having lost the power of exertion benumbed; destitute of sensibility; inactive dull: *n.* a clinker-built eight-oared boat used a Oxford: *pl.* (*cap.*) the Oxford University Len races at which these are raced. (L. *torpedo*, b stiff or numb.)

torpidity, *n.* tor-*pid*-e-te, torpidness; insensibility numbness; inactivity.

torpidly, *ad.* in a torpid manner.

torpidness, *n.* the state of being torpid.

torpify, *v.t. tor*-pe-fy, torpefy.

torpor, *n. tor*-por, numbness; loss of motion c the power of motion; sluggishness; laziness (L.)

torporific, *a.* tor-po-*rif*-ik, tending to produc torpor. (L. *torpor*, and *facio*, make.)

torquated, *a. tor*-kwa-ted, wearing a torque having a coloured ring round the neck [Zool.].

torque, *n.* tork, a collar of twisted gold wires, wor by the ancient Persians and barbarians; a necklac of metal rings; the twisting-moment of a syster of forces that causes rotation [Mech.]. (L.)

torqued, *a.* torkt, twisted; of torque form; curve like an S [Her.].

torrefaction, *n. to*-re-*fak*-shon, the operation c torrefying [Metal.]; drying by means of hig artificial heat [Pharm.].

torrefy, *v.t. to*-re-fy, to dry by a fire; to roast, a ore [Metal.]; to dry or parch, as drugs [Pharm. (L. *torrēre*, to dry, *facio*, make.)

torrent, *n. to*-rent, a violent rushing stream; stream suddenly raised and running rapidly, as c lava; a strong current. (Fr.)

torrential, *a.* to-*ren*-shal, of the nature of a torrent falling in or caused by torrents.

torrentially, *ad.* to-*ren*-sha-le, in a torrential way in torrents.

Torricellian, *a.* to-re-*chel*-le-an, pertaining t Torricelli (Ital. 17th-cent. physicist), who dis covered the principle of the barometer. **torri cellian tube,** the tube of the mercurial baromete open at the upper end and hermetically sealed at th lower. **torricellian vacuum,** the vacuum pro duced above the mercury in the barometer.

torrid, *a. to*-rid, parched; dried up with heat extremely hot; burning or parching. **torrid zone** the zone of the earth between the Tropics of Canc and Capricorn, over all of which the sun is vertic twice a year and where the heat is very grea [Geog.]. (Fr. *torride.*)

torridity, *n.* to-*rid*-e-te, the state of being torrid.

torse, *n.* torse, a surface generated by a straigl line which is in constant motion about some poi in its length [Geom.]; a wreath [Her.]. (O.Fr from L. *tortus*, twisted.)

torsel, *n. tor*-sel, anything, esp. an ornament, in twisted form.

torsibility, *n. tor*-se-*bil*-e-te, capability of bein twisted; the tendency of a twisted cord to unwin

torsimeter, *n.* tor-*sim*-e-ter, an instrument f determining an engine's horsepower by measure ment of torque set up on its shaft [Mech.].

torsiometer, *n. tor*-se-*om*-e-ter, an instrument f determining the declination of the vertical an horizontal meridians of the eye.

torsion, *n. tor*-shon, act of twisting; the force wit which a wire or rod when twisted tends to retur to its original state [Mech.]; the stopping of hæmorrhage by twisting the ends of the bloo vessels [Surg.]. **torsion balance,** an instrume for estimating very minute forces, esp. electric magnetic, by the action of a twisted filamen (Fr.)

torsional, *a. tor*-shon-al, pertaining to torsion.

torsive, *a. tor*-siv, spirally twisted [Bot.].

torsk, *n.* torsk, a large edible marine fish, *Brosmi brosme*, allied to the cod.

torso, *n. tor*-soh, the trunk of a statue deprived head and limbs; the human trunk; an unfinishe work [Fig.]. (It.)

tort, *n.* tort, a civil wrong, not arising from brea of contract, remediable by an action for damag [Law]. (Fr. *tort*, wrong.)

torteau, *n.* *tor*-toh, a red roundel [Her.]. (Fr.)
tortfeasor, *n.* *tort*-fee-zor, one who commits a tort; a wrongdoer [Law]. (Fr.)
torticollis, *n.* tor-te-*kol*-is, wry-neck [Med.]. (L. *tortus*, twisted, *collum*, the neck.)
tortile, *a.* *tor*-tile, twisted; wreathed; coiled.
tortilla, *n.* tor-*til*-a, a flat unleavened cake, esp. of soaked maize. (Sp.)
tortious, *a.* *tor*-shus, injurious; involving tort [Law].
tortive, *a.* *tor*-tiv, twisted; wreathed.
tortoise, *n.* *tor*-tus *or* *tor*-tis (Scots., *tor*-toyz), a land or freshwater turtle or chelonian reptile; a defence formed by bucklers held over the heads of soldiers, a testudo [Mil.]; a slow-moving person [Coll.]. (Fr. *tortue*, L. *tortuca*, referring to its apparently twisted legs.)
tortoiseshell, *n.* *tor*-tus-shel, the shell, or horny plates of certain marine turtles, esp. the hawksbill; a butterfly of the European genus *Vanessa* or American genus *Aglais*.
tortuosity, *n.* *tor*-tew-*os*-e-te, tortuousness; wreathing; flexure.
tortuous, *a.* *tor*-tew-us, twisted; wreathed; winding; crooked; not straightforward. (Fr. *tortueux*.)
tortuously, *ad.* in a tortuous manner.
tortuousness, *n.* the state of being tortuous.
torture, *n.* *tor*-cher *or* *tor*-tewr, extreme pain; anguish of body or mind; torment; severe pain judicially or purposely inflicted, esp. for extorting confession or betrayal: *v.t.* to torment; to put to or punish with torture; to harass. (Fr.)
torturer, *n.* *tor*-cher-rer, one who tortures.
torturingly, *ad.* so as to torture.
torturous, *a.* *tor*-cher-rus, causing torture.
Torula, *n.* *to*-rew-lah, a genus of yeast-like micro-organisms causing fermentation but not producing alcohol; a chain of spherical bacteria [Biol.]. (L. *torus*.)
toruliform, *a.* to-*rew*-le-form, shaped like a torula.
toruloid, *a.* *to*-rew-loyd, belonging to the *Torula*; resembling a torula.
torulose, *a.* *to*-rew-lohs, bulged out at intervals like a cord having knots [Zool.]; cylindrical, with slight contractions [Bot.].
torulous, *a.* *to*-rew-lus, torulose.
torus, *n.* *tor*-rus, a smooth rounded bulge [Anat.]; a large moulding used in the bases of columns [Arch.]; the floral receptacle, the thalamus, the growing point of the pistil [Bot.]; a surface generated by the rotation of a conic about a fixed axis [Geom.]: a protuberant part in certain annelids [Zool.]. (L., a round, swelling, or bulging place.)
torvous, *a.* *tor*-vus, of a grim countenance. (L. *torvus*.)
Tory, *n.* *taw*-re, in English politics the designation of adherents of James II and opponents of the 1688 Revolution, later applied to upholders of royal and constituted authority and opponents of the Whigs, and thence to the Conservative and Unionist parties: *a.* pertaining to the Tories; of Conservative views or tendencies. (Ir. *toiridhe*, pursuer, robber.)
Toryism, *n.* *taw*-re-izm, the principles of the Tories.
tosh, *n.* tosh, bosh, piffle [Slang].
toss, *n.* tos, a throwing upward or with a jerk; the act of tossing; a throwing up of the head; a particular manner of raising the head with a jerk: *v.t.* to throw with the hand; to throw upward, esp. with a sudden or violent motion; to cause to rise and fall, or to move to and fro; to agitate: *v.i.* to fling; to roll and tumble; to be in violent commotion; to be tossed. **toss up,** to spin a coin into the air and guess on which side it will fall; to take a chance. (Norse, *tossa*.)
tosser, *n.* *tos*-er, one who or that which tosses.
tossily, *ad.* *tos*-e-le, pertly.
tosspot, *n.* *tos*-pot, a toper; a convivial drinker.
toss-up, *n.* a relying upon chance for a decision; an even chance.
tossy, *a.* *tos*-e, pert; contemptuous.
tost, tost, former and poetical *p.* and *pp.* of *toss*.
tot, *n.* tot, anything very small; a young child; a drop of liquor; a small drinking-cup. (Perhaps Ice. *tottr*, dwarf.)
tot, *n.* tot, a sum in addition: *v.i.* to add up. (L., so many.)
total, *a.* *toh*-tal, whole; complete; entire: *n.* the whole; the whole amount: *v.t.* to find out the total: *v.i.* to amount to. (L. *totus*, the whole.)
totalisator, *n.* *toh*-ta-ly-*zay*-tor, an automatic betting machine by means of which the total stakes on an event, less a small percentage, are shared by the winners; a pari-mutuel.
totalitarian, *a.* *toh*-tal-e-*tare*-re-an, of or belonging to a party which allows no rival loyalties or parties: *n.* an adherent or practitioner of totalitarianism.
totalitarianism, *n.* *toh*-tal-e-*tare*-re-a-nizm, the totalitarian principle; the political system under which all are subjugated to the state and the state to a dictator.
totality, *n.* toh-*tal*-e-te, the whole sum or amount; the quality of being total; [Astron.] the period during which an eclipse is total.
totalize, *v.t.* *toh*-ta-lize, to total; to add up.
totally, *ad.* wholly; completely.
tote, *v.t.* toht, to carry. [Coll., U.S.A.]
tote, *n.* toht, the handle of a carpenter's plane; a totalizator [Slang].
totem, *n.* *toh*-tem, an animal or inanimate object regarded by a primitive people as having relationship to a tribe or group; an image or symbol of this. (Algonquian *dodaim*.)
totemic, *a.* toh-*tem*-ik, pertaining to totems.
totemism, *n.* *toh*-tem-izm, the principles and observances regarding totems.
totemist, *n.* *toh*-tem-ist, a member of a tribe having a totem; one versed in the lore of totems.
totemistic, *a.* *toh*-tem-*is*-tik, pertaining to totemism.
t'other, *a.* *tuth*-er, contracted form of "the other."
totient, *n.* *toh*-shent, the number of totitives in a given number.
totipalmate, *a.* *toh*-te-*pal*-mat, having all the toes connected by webs; steganopodous.
totipotent, *a.* toh-*tip*-o-tent, able to become a complete organism; able to generate an organism which is perfect [Biol.]. (L.).
totitive, *n.* *tot*-e-tiv, a number having no common divisor (other than unity) with a greater number.
totter, *v.i.* *tot*-ter, to shake so as to threaten to fall; to stagger: *n.* the action of the verb; an unsteady gait or motion. (M.E. *toteren*, O. Scand. *totra*, to quiver.)
totter-grass, *n.* any grass of the genus *Briza*; quaking-grass.
totteringly, *ad.* *tot*-ter-ring-le, in a tottering manner.
tottery, *a.* *tot*-ter-re, shaky; unsteady.
toucan, *n.* too-*kahn* or *too*-kan, a family of picarian birds of tropical America, remarkable for the enormous size of their bills. (Fr., through Port. from Braz. *tucana*.)
★**touch,** *v.t.* tuch, to come in contact with; to perceive by the sense of feeling; to come to; to reach; to try; to concern; to handle slightly; to meddle with; to affect; to impress; to move; to soften; to delineate slightly; to strike; to be in contact with. **touch up,** to repair; to put finishing touches to, as a painting; to enhance the colour of the complexion artificially; to wound one's feelings by sarcasm: *v.i.* to be in or come into contact or a state of junction; to call or arrive at (a port or land). **touch on,** to treat of slightly in discourse. (Fr. *toucher*.)
touch, *n.* tuch, contact: the junction of two bodies at the surface so that there is no space between them; the sense of feeling; the act of touching; test; tried qualities; the single act of a pencil or brush; act of the hand on a musical instrument; artistic skill; a stroke; the resistance of the keys of an instrument to the fingers [Mus.]; the game of tig; the ground beyond and including the touch-lines [Football and Hockey]. **a touch of the sun,** *see* **sun. touch-typing,** typewriting done by a typist without observation of the keys.
touchable, *a.* *tuch*-a-bl, that may be touched; tangible; [Slang] perhaps willing to grant a loan.
touchableness, *n.* the state or quality of being touchable.
touch-and-go, *n.* the merest chance; a precarious situation.
touched, *a.* tucht, [Slang] "not all there"; slightly mad; daft.
toucher, *n.* *tuch*-er, the merest touch.
touch-hole, *n.* the vent of a cannon or other fire-arm by which the powder was ignited.
touchily, *ad.* in a touchy manner.

touchiness, *n.* peevishness; irritability; extreme sensitiveness.
touching, *prep.* *tuch*-ing, concerning; as regards: *a.* affecting; pathetic.
touchingly, *ad.* in a manner to affect one.
touch-line, *n.* either of the lines laterally bounding the field of play [Football and Hockey].
touch-me-not, *n.* balsam, noli-me-tangere, a plant of the genus *Impatiens.*
touch-needle, *n.* a small bar of gold or silver for trying articles made of these metals by comparison with the mark they leave upon the touchstone.
touchpaper, *n.* *tuch*-pay-per, paper burning steadily when lighted because steeped in potassium nitrate.
touchstone, *n.* *tuch*-stone, Lydian stone, a black variety of flinty slate used for ascertaining, by means of a touch-needle, the purity of gold and silver by the streak traced on it; any test or criterion.
touchwood, *n.* *tuch*-wood, decayed wood or fibrous matter serving as tinder.
touchy, *a.* *tuch*-e, peevish; irritable; apt to take offence.
tough, *a.* tuf, flexible without being brittle; yielding to force without breaking; firm; strong; not easily broken; viscous; able to endure hardship; tenacious; difficult; hard; morally callous: *n.* a brutal bully; a rough. (A.S. *toh.*)
toughen, *v.t.* and *i.* *tuf*-en, to make or become tough.
toughener, *n.* *tuf*-en-er, one who or that which toughens.
toughish, *a.* *tuf*-ish, tough to a slight degree.
toughly, *ad.* *tuf*-le, in a tough manner.
toughness, *n.* *tuf*-ness, the quality of being tough.
toupee, *n.* *too*-pee, a front of false hair; a curl or false lock of hair; a small wig. (Fr.)
toupet, *n.* *too*-pay, a forelock; a toupee.
tour, *n.* toor, a journey from place to place for pleasure or business; a long ramble; a circuit; a turn of duty: *v.i.* to make a tour: *v.t.* to make a tour of; to present while on tour [Theatrical]. **grand tour,** the round of visits to the courts and ancient cities of Europe formerly essential to young aristocrats. (Fr.)
touraco, *n.* *toor*-ra-koh, a species of *Turacus* or its allied genera; an African bird of the plantain-eater family, allied to the cuckoos.
tourbillion, *n.* toor-*bil*-yon, an ornamental revolving firework. (Fr. *tourbillon.*)
tourelle, *n.* too-*rel*, a slender tower; a turret. (Fr.)
tourer, *n.* *toor*-rer, a motor-car for touring.
tourism, *n.* *toor*-rizm, the practice of touring; provision for or management of tourists.
tourist, *n.* *toor*-rist, one who makes a tour; an excursionist; a tripper.
tourmaline, *n.* *toor*-ma-leen, a mineral occurring in prisms, varying in chemical composition, used in polarizing light, the finer sorts being used as gems. (Fr., from Sinhalese *toramalli*, carnelian.)
tournament, *n.* *toor*-na-ment, a mediæval sport in which mounted knights engaged each other, usually with blunted weapons; a military contest in the use of arms; a competition in skill comprising a series of contests. (Fr. *tourner*, turn.)
tourney, *n.* *turn*-e, a mediæval tournament: *v.i.* to engage in tournaments; to tilt.
tourniquet, *n.* *toor*-ne-ket, an appliance or instrument for the compression of a blood-vessel to prevent access of blood to a part or wound [Surg.]. (Fr.)
tournure, *n.* toor-*noor*, grace; poise; contour; shape; a bustle (formerly worn by women). (Fr.)
touse, *v.t.* touz, to pull, haul, or tear; to tousle.
tousle, *v.t.* *tou*-zl, to put into disorder. (*touse.*)
tous-les-mois, *n.* (App.), a starch from the root of a species of *Canna*, used as a substitute for arrowroot. (Fr., every month.)
tousy, *a.* *tou*-ze, tousled; dishevelled.
tout, *n.* tout, a touter; one who spies on racing-stables, esp. on behalf of tipsters, etc.: *v.i.* to ply or seek for customers; to act as a tout.
touter, *n.* *tou*-ter, one who touts.
tovarish, *n.* to-*vah*-rish, comrade. (Russ.)
tow, *v.t.* toh, to drag or pull along, esp. a boat or a motor-car, by means of a tow-line: *n.* an instance of towing; a tow-line; the catch in a tow-net. (A.S. *teon.*)
tow, *n.* toh, the coarse part of flax or hemp.
towage, *n.* *toh*-aj, the act of towing, or of being towed; the charge for this.
toward, *prep.* tawrd *or* to-*wawrd*, towards.
toward, *a.* *toh*-ard, ready to do or learn; apt; docile; tractable.
towardliness, *n.* *toh*-ard-le-ness, the quality of being toward or towardly.
towardly, *a.* *toh*-ard-le, toward.
towards, *prep.* tawrdz *or* to-*wawrdz*, in the direction of; with respect to; with a tendency too; nearly; *ad.* near at hand; in a state of preparation. (A.S.)
tow-boat, *n.* a boat which tows or is towed.
towel, *n.* *tou*-el, a cloth used for wiping or drying anything wet: *v.t.* to wipe with a towel; to thrash [Slang]. (Fr. *touaille.*)
towel-horse, *n.* a stand for hanging towels on.
towelling, *n.* *tou*-el-ing, textile material for towels; a rubbing with a towel; a thrashing [Slang].
tower, *n.* *tou*-er, a building, circular or of other section, of considerable elevation and sometimes insulated; a fortress; a defence; a towering structure; a high head-dress; an elevation [Fig.]: *v.i.* to rise and fly high; to soar; to be lofty. (O.Fr. *tur.*)
towered, *a.* *tou*-erd, adorned with, built with, or defended by towers.
towering, *a.* *tou*-er-ing, very high; violent.
tower-mustard, *n.* the cruciferous plant *Arabis glabra.*
towery, *a.* *tou*-er-re, adorned with towers; towered; towering.
towhee, *n.* *toh*-hee, the American marsh-robin, a finch of the genus *Pipilo.*
towing-path, *n.* a riverside path used by men or horses in towing boats.
tow-line, *n.* *toh*-line, a rope, chain, or cable used for towing.
***town,** *n.* toun, a collection, of indefinite extent, of houses larger than a village, esp. one with a regular market and inferior to a city; a city; the inhabitants of a town or city; the metropolis or its inhabitants [Coll.]; the West End of London. **man about town,** *see* **man. paint the town red,** *see* **paint.** (A.S. *tun*, a fence or fenced place.)
town-clerk, *n.* the secretary, keeper of the records, and usually law-officer, of a city or borough.
town-council, *n.* the elective governing body of a town.
town-councillor, *n.* a member of a town-council.
town-crier, *n.* a civic functionary charged with the proclamation of official and other notices.
townee, *n.* tou-*nee*, a townsman; [Coll.] in a University town, an inhabitant not being a member or undergraduate of the University.
tow-net, *n.* *toh*-net, a net for towing along the surface of the water to collect aquatic specimens.
town-hall, *n.* a building, owned and maintained by the burgesses, for municipal business and other purposes.
town-house, *n.* a residence in town, as distinct from one owned and occupied in the country.
townish, *a.* *toun*-ish, pertaining to townsfolk; characteristic of towns.
townless, *a.* *toun*-less, having no town.
town-major, *n.* an officer (usually a captain) assisting the commander of a garrison [Mil.].
town-planning, *n.* the drawing up of plans for a town with a view to the best siting of its industries social activities, etc., and to ensure the best and most economical use of its land and amenities.
townsfolk, *n.pl.* *tounz*-foke, people of a town.
township, *n.* *toun*-ship, a large parish or inhabited district; a district with municipal privileges; a partly settled site of a future town [Austral.].
townsman, *n.* *tounz*-man, an inhabitant of a town one of the same town with another; a townee, as distinguished from a gownsman [Univ.].
town-talk, *n.* a subject of common conversation.
towny, *a.* *toun*-e, characteristic of a town: *n.* a townsman, esp. [Slang] a fellow-townsman; [Univ. coll.] a townee.
towpath, *n.* *toh*-pahth, the road alongside a river or canal used by men and horses when towing boats.
tow-rope, *n.* a rope used in towing.
Towser, *n.* *tou*-zer, a name given a large dog.

towy, *a.* *toh*-e, containing or resembling tow.
toxæmia, *n.* tok-*see*-me-a, blood-poisoning, esp. when due to the absorption of bacterial toxins [Med.].
toxic, *a.* *tok*-sik, poisonous; pertaining to or caused by poison; poisoned [Med.]: *n.* a poisonous substance. (Gr. *toxikon*, poison, originally arrow-poison, from *toxon*, a bow.)
toxical, *a.* *tok*-se-kal, toxic; like poison.
toxicant, *a.* *tok*-se-kant, poisonous: *n.* a poisonous agent.
toxication, *n.* tok-se-*kay*-shon, poisoning.
toxicity, *n.* tok-*sis*-e-te, the quality or condition of being poisonous.
toxicodendron, *n.* *tok*-se-ko-*den*-dron, any of several trees of the family *Anacardiaceæ*, having poisonous properties. (Gr. *toxicon*, and *dendron*, a tree.)
toxicogenic, *a.* *tok*-se-ko-*jen*-ik, produced by poisonous substances.
toxicological, *a.* *tok*-se-ko-*loj*-e-kal, pertaining to toxicology.
toxicologically, *ad.* in a toxicological manner.
toxicologist, *n.* *tok*-se-*kol*-o-jist, one versed in toxicology.
toxicology, *n.* *tok*-se-*kol*-o-je, the science of poisons, their nature, action, antidotes, etc.
toxicosis, *n.* *tok*-se-*koh*-sis, any morbid state produced by the action of poison.
toxigenic, *a.* tok-se-*jen*-ik, producing toxin.
toxin, *n.* *tok*-sin, any organic poisonous substance, esp. one causing some particular disease.
toxiphobia, *n.* tok-se-*foh*-be-a, morbid dread of being poisoned, or of poisons.
toxodon, *n.* *tok*-so-don, a large extinct ungulate having long curved crowns to the molar teeth. (Gr. *toxon*, a bow, *odous*, a tooth.)
toxophilite, *n.* tok-*sof*-e-lite, one skilled in or a devotee of archery: *a.* pertaining to archery. (Gr. *toxon*, and *philos*, fond of.)
toy, *n.* toy, a plaything for children; a thing of little value; a trifle; folly; a silly tale or odd conceit: *v.i.* to dally amorously; to trifle. (Origin doubtful.)
toyer, *n.* *toy*-er, one who toys; a trifler.
toyish, *a.* *toy*-ish, trifling; wanton.
toyishly, *ad.* in a toyish manner.
toyishness, *n.* disposition to dalliance or trifling.
toyman, *n.* *toy*-man, one who deals in toys.
toyon, *n.* *toy*-on, Californian holly, a shrub, *Photinia arbutifolia*, with holly-like berries. (Sp. *tollon*.)
toyshop, *n.* *toy*-shop, a shop where toys are sold.
toy-terrier, *n.* a lap-dog; a miniature variety of a breed of dog.
trabea, *n.* *tray*-be-a, a toga striped with purple (L.).
trabeated, *a.* *tray*-be-ay-ted, having an entablature [Arch.]. (L. *trabs*, a beam.)
trabeation, *n.* *tray*-be-*ay*-shon, a structure having horizontal beams [Arch.].
trabecula, *n.* tra-*bek*-yew-la, any of several small processes, such as one of the fleshy columns in the ventricle of the heart, a projection across a cell cavity, etc. [Anat. and Bot.]. (L., a small beam.)
trabecular, *a.* tra-*bek*-yew-lar, pertaining to or resembling a trabecula.
trabeculate, *a.* tra-*bek*-yew-lat, having a trabecula.
trace, *n.* trace, a strap or chain by which a horse draws a vehicle; the short piece of gut connecting the hook to a fishing-line. **kick over the traces,** to abandon restraint; to become insubordinate. (M.E. and O.Fr. *trays*, old plural of *trait*.)
trace, *n.* trace, a mark left by anything passing; a footprint; a track; a vestige; remains; a small quantity: *v.t.* to draw or delineate with marks; to copy through transparent paper, etc.; to follow by footsteps or tracks; to follow with exactness; to walk over. (F. *tracer*.)
traceability, *n.* trace-a-*bil*-e-te, the state of being traceable.
traceable, *a.* *trace*-a-bl, that may be traced.
traceably, *ad.* in a traceable manner.
trace-horse, *n.* a draught horse working in traces, not between shafts, esp. an extra horse to help up a hill, etc.
tracer, *n.* *trace*-er, one who traces.
tracer-bullet, *n.* a bullet making its path visible by means of a light or a trail of smoke.
tracery, *n.* *trace*-er-re, the ornamental stonework in a Gothic window [Arch.]; any decorative work suggestive of this.
trachea, *n.* *tray*-ke-ah *or* tra-*kee*-ah (*pl.* **tracheæ**), the windpipe [Anat.]; one of the ducts or vessels of leaves [Bot.]; the air-vessel of an insect [Zool.]. (Gr. *trachys*, rough.)
tracheal, *a.* *tray*-ke-al *or* tra-*kee*-al, pertaining to the trachea.
trachean, *a.* *tray*-ke-an *or* tra-*kee*-an, pertaining to or having tracheæ [Bot. and Zool.]: *n.* a tracheate animal.
tracheary, *a.* *tray*-ke-a-re, breathing by tracheæ; tracheal: *n.* one of the Trachearia, a group of arachnids having tracheæ.
tracheate, *a.* *tray*-ke-at, having tracheæ (esp. of arthropods) [Zool.].
tracheitis, *n.* tray-ke-*eye*-tis, inflammation of the trachea.
trachelology, *n.* trak-e-*lol*-o-je, the branch of medicine treating of the neck and its diseases. (Gr. *trachelos*, neck, and *-logy*.)
tracheobronchial, *a.* *tray*-ke-o-*brong*-ke-al, pertaining to tracheæ and bronchi.
tracheocele, *n.* *tray*-ke-o-seel, an enlargement of the thyroid gland. (Gr. *trachea*, and *kele*, a tumour.)
tracheoscopy, *n.* *tray*-ke-*os*-ko-pe, visual examination of the trachea.
tracheotomy, *n.* *tray*-ke-*ot*-o-me, the operation of making an opening into the windpipe. (Gr. *trachea*, and *tome*, cutting.)
trachitis, *n.* tra-*ky*-tis, tracheitis.
trachoma, *n.* tra-*koh*-ma, contagious granular conjunctivitis [Med.]. (Gr. *trachys*, rough.)
trachomatous, *a.* tra-*koh*-ma-tus, affected by or of the nature of trachoma.
trachyte, *n.* *trak*-ite, a rough-surfaced volcanic rock consisting largely of potash felspar. (Gr. *trachys*.)
trachytic, *a.* tra-*kit*-ik, consisting of or resembling trachyte.
tracing, *n.* *trace*-ing, the act of tracing; a copy traced on a transparent sheet; a record made by a registering instrument, as that of a barograph, etc.
tracing-paper, *n.* a thin transparent paper on which drawings and engravings may be traced.
track, *n.* trak, a mark left by something that has passed along; a mark or impression left by the foot; a road; a beaten path; a sea-route; a racing or running course: *v.t.* to follow when guided by a trace or footsteps; to tow. **make tracks,** to hurry off. **the beaten track,** the regular course or route; the usual method. (O.Fr. *trac*, a beaten way.)
trackage, *n.* *trak*-aj, towage; railway tracks collectively, also the right to use these, and the charge for such right.
track-boat, *n.* a boat that is towed.
tracker, *n.* *trak*-er, one who follows a trail.
trackless, *a.* *trak*-less, having no track; marked by no footstep; untrodden.
tracklessly, *ad.* without leaving a track.
tracklessness, *n.* the state of being trackless.
track-man, *n.* one working on the making or maintenance of a railway track; [U.S.A.] (*no hyphen*) the inspector of a railroad track section.
track-road, *n.* a towing-path.
trackway, *n.* *trak*-way, an open road across a down or heath.
tract, *n.* trakt, an expanse; a region or area of indefinite extent; the complete course of an organ [Anat.], as the digestive tract. (L. *tractum*, drawn.)
tract, *n.* trakt, a short treatise; a propaganda pamphlet, religious, moral, or political. (*tractate*.)
tractability, *n.* trak-ta-*bil*-e-te, tractableness.
tractable, *a.* *trak*-ta-bl, that may be easily led, taught or managed; docile; manageable.
tractableness, *n.* quality of being tractable.
tractably, *ad.* *trak*-ta-ble, in a tractable manner.
Tractarian, *a.* trak-*tare*-re-an, pertaining to Tractarianism or the Tractarians: *n.* a founder or adherent of Tractarianism.
Tractarianism, *n.* trak-*tare*-re-a-nizm, the system of principles advocated in "Tracts for the Times" published at Oxford, 1833–1841, the chief doctrine of which was that the Church, through its Apostolic succession and sacraments, was the sole divinely appointed channel of the grace of Christ; ritualism.
tractate, *n.* *trak*-tate, a treatise. (L. *tractatus*, treated.)

tractile, *a.* *trak*-tile, capable of being drawn out in length; ductile.
tractility, *n.* trak-*til*-e-te, the quality of being tractile; ductility.
traction, *n.* *trak*-shon, act of drawing or state of being drawn, esp. along a track; a drawing or pulling movement. **traction engine,** a locomotive for drawing heavy loads along the highway.
tractive, *a.* *trak*-tiv, having the power of drawing or pulling; used for traction.
tractor, *n.* *trak*-tor, that which draws, or is used for traction; an automobile designed for towing, esp. a plough, harrow, or other agricultural implement.
tractor-aeroplane, *n.* an aeroplane with the air-screw in front of the wings.
tractory, *n.* *trak*-to-re, a tractrix.
tractrix, *n.* *trak*-triks, a curve whose tangent is always equal to a given line [Math.].
★**trade,** *n.* trade, the act or business of exchanging commodities; buying and selling; commerce; traffic; a skilled handicraft; the business or occupation (esp. manual) which a person has learned; the collective body of those engaged in the same occupation; a bargain: *pl.* the trade-winds: *v.i.* to buy and sell; to traffic; to carry on commerce as a business: *v.t.* to sell or exchange in commerce; *a.* pertaining to or used in trade: *ad.* at trade price [Comm.]. **Board of Trade,** the British government department supervising commercial relations, industry and manufacturers, the mercantile marine, patents, etc. **the trade,** brewing; licensed victualling. **trade board,** an official body composed of equal numbers of workers and employers with a neutral chairman appointed to adjudicate on wage claims in an industry. **to trade off,** to exchange by bartering [Coll.]. **to trade upon,** to take undue advantage of. **trade paper,** a periodical devoted to the interests of a particular trade, industry, or profession. (M.E., a path, as *tread*.)
trade-mark, *n.* an exclusive device adopted and registered by a manufacturer and impressed on his goods to indicate that they are made by him.
trade-name, *n.* a name used for trade purposes.
trade-price, *n.* the price of an article charged by the maker or wholesaler to the retailer.
trader, *n.* *trade*-er, one engaged in trade or commerce; a vessel employed in trading.
trade-sale, *n.* an auction by and for a special trade.
tradesman, *n.* *tradez*-man, a shopkeeper; a skilled worker; a craftsman.
trade-union, *n.* an organization of workers in a particular trade or industry formed for mutual support and the promotion of their common interests as workers.
trade-unionism, *n.* the system or principles of trade-unions.
trade-unionist, *n.* a member of a trade-union; a supporter of trade-unionism.
trade-wind, *n.* a tropical and sub-tropical wind blowing throughout the year towards the equator, in a NE. to SW. direction in the northern hemisphere and in a SE. to NW. in the southern.
tradition, *n.* tra-*dish*-on, belief, custom, etc., handed down by oral communication from age to age; artistic principle based on experience or long-continued usage; doctrine held to be divinely inspired but not having scriptural authority [Theol.]. (Fr., from L. *tradere*, to hand down.)
traditional, *a.* tra-*dish*-on-al, pertaining to or of the nature of tradition; transmitted from age to age without writing.
traditionalism, *n.* tra-*dish*-on-al-izm, adherence to tradition; undue deference to the authority of tradition.
traditionalist, *n.* tra-*dish*-on-al-ist, one who practises or supports traditionalism; an opponent of modernism.
traditionalistic, *a.* tra-*dish*-on-a-*lis*-tik, characteristic of traditionalism or traditionalists.
traditionally, *ad.* in a traditional manner.
traditionary, *a.* tra-*dish*-on-a-re, traditional; characterized by tradition.
traditionist, *n.* tra-*dish*-on-ist, a traditionalist; one versed in tradition.
traditive, *a.* *trad*-e-tiv, transmitted by tradition; traditionary.
traditor, *n.* *trad*-e-tor, a traitor, esp. as applied to early Christians who delivered the Scriptures or Church property to their persecutors to save their lives. (L.)
traduce, *v.t.* tra-*dewce*, wilfully to misrepresent and abuse; to calumniate; to defame. (L. *traduco*, to lead across, to transport.)
traducement, *n.* tra-*dewce*-ment, the act of traducing; defamation; slander.
traducer, *n.* tra-*dewce*-er, one who traduces.
traducian, *n.* tra-*dewce*-e-an, one who holds the doctrine of traducianism: *a.* of or pertaining to this doctrine.
traducianism, *n.* tra-*dewce*-e-an-izm, the doctrine that the soul is generated by the parents along with the body.
traducianist, *n.* and *a.* tra-*dewce*-e-a-nist, traducian.
traducible, *a.* tra-*dewce*-e-bl, that may be traduced.
traducingly, *ad.* tra-*dewce*-ing-le, slanderously.
traduction, *n.* tra-*duk*-shon, traducement; the legitimate derivation of a singular conclusion from two singular premises [Logic]. (Fr.)
traductive, *a.* tra-*duk*-tiv, derivable; that may be deduced; involving traduction [Logic].
traffic, *n.* *traf*-ik, passing to and fro, esp. of passengers, merchandise, etc., by land, sea, or air; the business of such transportation; amount of traffic; commerce; trade; intercourse: *v.i.* to trade; to buy and sell wares: *v.t.* to exchange in traffic; to barter. (Fr. *trafiquer*.)
trafficable, *a.* *traf*-e-ka-bl, suitable for traffic; marketable.
trafficator, *n.* *traf*-e-kay-tor, the signal-arm with which a motor-driver indicates the direction of a turn he is about to make. (Compounded from *traffic* and *indicator*.)
trafficker, *n.* *traf*-e-ker, one who carries on commerce; a trader; a smuggler; a dealer in the black market.
traffic-light, *n.* a light signal used at crossroads, etc., for the regulation of traffic.
tragacanth, *n.* *trag*-a-kanth, an adhesive gum obtained from various species of *Astragalus*; gum-dragon. (Gr. *tragos*, a goat, *akantha*, a thorn.)
tragacanthin, *n.* trag-a-*kan*-thin, bassorin.
tragedian, *n.* tra-*jee*-de-an, a writer or an actor of tragedy.
tragedienne, *n.* tra-*jee*-de-*en*, a tragic actress.
tragedy, *n.* *traj*-e-de, an elevated and serious drama in which the end is melancholy; a fatal and mournful event; a disaster. (Fr. *tragédie*, through Lat. from Gr. *tragos*, he-goat, and *ōdē*, song.)
tragelaph, *n.* *trag*-e-laf, a fabulous hybrid of goat and stag [Gr. Myth.]; any member of the Tragelaphinæ, a sub-family of antelopes including the African bushbucks, kudus, etc. (Gr. *tragos*, he-goat, *elephos*, deer.)
tragic, *a.* *traj*-ik, tragical.
tragical, *a.* *traj*-e-kal, of the nature or character of tragedy; calamitous; expressive of tragedy or sorrow; mournful. (L. *tragicus*.)
tragicality, *n.* traj-e-*kal*-e-te, the quality of being tragical.
tragically, *ad.* in a tragic manner.
tragicalness, *n.* tragicality.
tragicomedian, *n.* *traj*-e-ko-*mee*-de-an, one who acts in tragicomedy.
tragicomedy, *n.* *traj*-e-*kom*-e-de, a drama in which serious and comic scenes are blended.
tragicomic, *a.* *traj*-e-*kom*-ik, partaking of a mixture of grave and comic scenes.
tragicomically, *ad.* in a tragicomic manner.
tragopan, *n.* *trag*-o-pan, the horned pheasant, a beautiful Eastern game-bird of the genus *Ceriornis*. (Gr., the goat-Pan, a fabulous bird of Æthiopia.)
tragule, *n.* *trag*-yewl, any ruminant of the genus *Tragulus*, esp. the chevrotain. (L. *tragulus*, a small goat.)
traguline, *a.* *trag*-yew-lin, of the tragule family [Zool.]; goat-like.
tragus, *n.* *tray*-gus, the prominence at the entrance of the external ear. (Gr. *tragos*.)
trail, *n.* trale, the track followed in hunting; the scent or spoor left by a hunted animal; any trailing thing; a trawl; the end of a gun-carriage which rests on the ground when the gun is unlimbered [Artillery]: *v.t.* to hunt by the track; to draw along the ground; to carry, as arms, in an horizontal position, muzzles foremost [Mil.]; to tread down grass by walking through it; to lay flat: *v.i.* to be drawn out in length; to grow

along or over. **trail arms,** to carry (rifle, etc.) horizontally at arm's length [Mil.]. **trail one's coat,** to manœuvre another into such a position that a quarrel is inevitable; to provoke attack. (L. *traho*, draw.)
trailer, *n.* *trale*-er, one who or something that trails; a vehicle towed behind another; a selection of advance pictures of films [Cine.]; a trailing plant [Hort.].
trail-net, *n.* a drag-net; a trawl.
trail-rope, *n.* a drag-rope; a tow-rope.
train, *v.t.* trane, to entice; to allure; to discipline; to teach and form by practice; to educate; to form to a wall or espalier [Hort.]; to lop and prune [Hort.]; to carry by train; to trace a lode to its head [Mining]: *v.i.* to practise for; to prepare oneself (for a contest) by appropriate diet, exercise, etc.; to go by train [Coll.]. **train a gun,** to point it at some object.
★**train,** *n.* trane, something drawn along behind; a trailing extension of a dress; the tail of a bird; a retinue; regular order; state of preparedness; process; a procession; a line of gunpowder to lead fire to a charge; a complete series of connected pieces, esp. moving pieces, as in a watch; a connected line of vehicles on a railroad; all the mobile apparatus and implements of war. **in train,** in proper sequence or arrangement; in preparation. **in the train of,** as a sequel to. **train of artillery,** *see* **artillery**. (Fr. *trainer*, from L. *traho*, draw.)
trainable, *a.* *trane*-a-bl, that may be trained.
trainband, *n.* *trane*-band, a body of citizen soldiers, forerunners of the militia, raised in England, 16th–18th cents. (*trained band.*)
train-bearer, *n.* an attendant who holds up the train of a robe.
trainee, *n.* tray-*nee*, one undergoing training; an apprentice, also a worker at a similar stage.
trainer, *n.* *trane*-er, one who trains; one who prepares athletes, cyclists, pugilists, racehorses, etc., for their competitions, etc.
train-ferry, *n.* *trane*-fe-re, a steamer that ferries a complete railway train.
training, *a.* *trane*-ing, teaching by practice; adapted for or used in training: *n.* the preparing of persons or horses for races, athletic exercises, etc.; the disciplining and exercising of troops; the operation or art of growing young trees against a wall, etc.
training-college, *n.* an establishment for professional tuition, esp. for the Church or teaching.
training-ship, *n.* a ship in which boys are trained for the sea.
trainload, *n.* *trane*-lode, as much as a train will carry; the capacity of a train [Rly.].
train-mile, *n.* a mile run by a train, the unit of railway calculations.
train-oil, *n.* the oil procured from the blubber or fat of whales by boiling. (Low Ger. *trân*, M.Dut. *traen*, a tear or drop, and *oil.*)
train-road, *n.* a tram-road, esp. in mines.
traipse, *n.* and *v.i.* trayps, trapes.
trait, *n.* tray, a stroke; a touch (of); a distinguishing feature. (Fr., from L. *traho*, draw.)
traitor, *n.* *tray*-tor, one guilty of treason; one who, in breach of trust, delivers his country to her enemy; one who betrays his trust. (O.Fr.)
traitorism, *n.* *tray*-to-rizm, the principles of traitors; treason; betrayal.
traitorous, *a.* *tray*-to-rus, guilty of treason; perfidious; partaking of treason.
traitorously, *ad.* in a traitorous manner.
traitorousness, *n.* the quality of being traitorous.
traitress, *n.* *tray*-tress, a female traitor.
traject, *v.t.* tra-*jekt*, to throw or cast through: *n.* *traj*-ekt, a ferry. (L. *trajecto*, pierce through.)
trajectile, *a.* tra-*jek*-tile, capable of impelling across: *n.* an impelled body.
trajection, *n.* tra-*jek*-shon, a crossing; transmission; a casting or darting through; transposition.
trajectory, *n.* tra-*jek*-to-re, the flight-curve of a projectile, comet, etc; a curve or surface cutting all the curves or surfaces of a given system at the same angle [Geom.]. (L. *trajectorium*, a funnel.)
tralatitious, *a.* tral-a-*tish*-us, metaphorical; not literal; handed down from one to another; traditional. (L. *tralaticiuss*, customary.)
tram, *n.* tram, a four-sided framework for casks, etc.; such a frame mounted on wheels; the shaft of a cart [Scots.]; a line of beams carrying the rail on which a wagon or car runs; a railroad for horse-traction; a street railroad for any traction; a tram-car: *v.i.* to go or travel by tram [Coll.]. (Origin uncertain; perhaps Scand. *tram*, a wooden doorstep.)
tram, *n.* tram, best quality silk thread composed of strands twisted together. (O.Fr. *traime*, from L. *trama*, woof.)
tram-car, *n.* a passenger car used on street tramways.
tram-line, *n.* a tramway; one length of rail for a tramway.
trammel, *n.* *tram*-el, a long net for catching birds or fish; a shackle for a horse; that which trammels; an iron hook to hang vessels over a fire; an instrument for drawing ellipses; a beam-compass: *v.t.* to catch; to intercept; to hamper; to shackle. (O.Fr. *tramail*, a net.)
trammel-net, *n.* a fishing-net that entangles the captures, also one supported by corks and kept close to the ground by weights; a fowler's net.
tramontana, *n.* trah-mon-*tah*-na, a cold north wind in the Mediterranean and Adriatic.
tramontane, *a.* tra-*mon*-tane, lying beyond the Alps from Rome; foreign; barbarous: *n.* one living beyond the Alps; barbarian; a stranger. (*trans-*, and L. *mons*, mountain.)
tramp, *n.* tramp, the sound of tramping; a foot-journey; a vagrant; a cargo steamer not plying regularly on a definite route: *v.t.* to tread heavily: *v.i.* to go on foot; to wander or stroll. (M.E. *trampen.*)
tramper, *n.* *tramp*-er, a stroller; a vagrant; a hiker.
trample, *n.* *tram*-pl, the act or sound of trampling: *v.t.* to tread under foot, esp. in pride, contempt, triumph, or scorn; to prostrate by treading; to treat with contempt and insult [Fig.]: *v.i.* to tread in contempt; to tread with force and rapidity. (*tramp.*)
trampler, *n.* *tram*-pler, one who tramples.
tram-road, *n.* a road laid with lines of stone, wood, or iron for wagons; a tramway.
tramway, *n.* *tram*-way, a line of rails for trams or tram-cars; a light railway.
trance, *n.* trahnce, a state of semi-consciousness or suspended animation; ecstasy; hypnosis or catalepsy [Med.]: *v.t.* to entrance or place in a state of trance [Poet.]. (Fr. *transe*, fright.)
trancedly, *ad.* *trahn*-sed-le, as in a trance.
trank, *n.* trank, the piece of skin from which the shape of the glove is cut in the press.
tranquil, *a.* *trang*-kwil, quiet; calm; undisturbed; peaceful. (L. *tranquillus.*)
tranquillity, *n.* trang-*kwil*-e-te, calmness; a quiet state; freedom from disturbance or agitation.
tranquillization, *n.* *trang*-kwe-ly-*zay*-shon, act of tranquillizing; state of being tranquillized.
tranquillize, *v.t.* *trang*-kwe-lize, to allay when agitated; to quiet.
tranquillizer, *n.* *trang*-kwe-ly-zer, one who or that which tranquillizes.
tranquilly, *ad.* *trang*-kwe-le, in a tranquil manner.
tranquilness, *n.* the state of being tranquil.
trans-, trans *or* tranz, a Latin prefix, signifying over or beyond, or denoting a complete change.
transact, *v.t.* trans-*akt*, to do; to perform; to manage; to compromise, or make a transaction [Law]: *v.i.* to conduct matters; to negotiate. (L. *transactus*, done thoroughly.)
transaction, *n.* trans-*ak*-shon, the doing or performing of any business; management of an affair; that which is done; an affair; an adjustment of a dispute [Law.]: *pl.* reports of proceedings, esp. of a learned society.
transactor, *n.* trans-*ak*-tor, one who transacts.
transalpine, *a.* trans-*alp*-ine, beyond the Alps from Rome. (L. *transalpinus.*)
transandine, *a.* tran-*zan*-dine, crossing the Andes.
transatlantic, *a.* *tran*-zat-*lan*-tik, being beyond the Atlantic; American; crossing the Atlantic.
transcalent, *a.* trans-*kay*-lent, permitting heat to pass; diathermanous. (L. *trans-*, and *caleo*, be hot.)
transcend, *v.t.* tran-*send*, to rise above; to pass over; to go beyond; to surpass; to excel. (L. *transcendo*, surmount.)
transcendence, *n.* tran-*sen*-dence, superior excellence; supereminence.

transcendency, *n.* tran-*sen*-den-se, transcendence.
transcendent, *a.* tran-*sen*-dent, very excellent; superior or supreme in excellence; surpassing others; transcendental [Phil.].
transcendental, *a.* *tran*-sen-*den*-tal, transcending; superhuman; going beyond the ordinary range of perception or conception; idealistic; abstruse; (of numbers) incapable of being represented by an algebraic expression of a finite number of terms [Math.]; used variously in Philosophy, esp. [Schelling] treating objects as mere products of the subjective mind, and [Kant] pertaining to *a priori* conditions of experience, hence, by preceding (though not going beyond) experience making knowledge through experience possible.
transcendentalism, *n.* *tran*-sen-*den*-ta-lizm, the doctrine or principles of any form of transcendental philosophy; the going beyond empiricism and ascertaining the fundamental principles that are regulative and constitutive of the form of perception and thought.
transcendentalist, *n.* *tran*-sen-*den*-ta-list, a believer in transcendentalism.
transcendentalize, *v.t.* *tran*-sen-*den*-ta-lize, to render transcendent or transcendental; to idealize.
transcendentally, *ad.* in a transcendental manner.
transcendently, *ad.* in a transcendent manner.
transcendentness, *n.* tran-*sen*-dent-ness, the condition of being transcendent.
transcontinental, *a.* *tranz*-kon-te-*nen*-tal, crossing or extending across a continent.
transcribe, *v.t.* tran-*skribe*, to copy; to write over again; to reproduce from hieroglyphics, pictographs, or shorthand, etc. (L. *transcribo*, transfer.)
transcriber, *n.* tran-*skry*-ber, a copyist.
transcript, *n.* *tran*-skript, a written copy; a copy of any kind; a record from a shorthand note. (L. *transcriptum*.)
transcription, *n.* tran-*skrip*-shon, the act of copying; a transcript; an adaptation of a composition to a different instrument or voice from that for which it was written [Mus.].
transcriptional, *a.* tran-*skrip*-shon-al, pertaining to transcription.
transcriptively, *ad.* tran-*skrip*-tiv-le, in the manner of a copy.
transcurrent, *a.* tranz-*ku*-rent, extending across [Entom.].
transect, *v.t.* tran-*sekt*, to cut or dissect transversely: *n.* *tran*-sekt, a transection.
transection, *n.* tran-*sek*-shon, a cross-section; the action of transecting.
transept, *n.* *tran*-sept, the transverse portion of a cruciform church. (L. *trans*-, and *septum*, enclosure.)
transfer, *n.* *trans*-fer, the removal or conveyance of a thing from one place or person to another; conveyance of a right or title [Law]; that which or one who is transferred; a printed design to be transferred to another surface; a soldier removed from one company, battery, etc., to another [Mil.]: *v.t.* trans-*fer*, to convey or remove from one place or person to another; to make over; to convey, as a right [Law]; to remove from one surface and impose on another. (L. *transfero*, bring over.)
transferable, *a.* trans-*fer*-ra-bl *or* *trans*-fe-ra-bl, that may be transferred; negotiable. **transferable vote,** a method of balloting in which a voter indicates to which candidate his vote may, in certain contingencies, be transferred.
transfer-book, *n.* a register of the transfers of stocks, shares, property, etc.
transferee, *n.* trans-fe-*ree*, one to whom a transfer is made [Law]; one who is transferred.
transference, *n.* *trans*-fe-rence, act of transferring.
transferor, *n.* *trans*-fe-ror, one who makes a conveyance of property [Law].
transfer-paper, *n.* paper on which are printed designs for transference to another surface.
transferrer, *n.* trans-*fer*-rer, one who makes a transfer.
transfer-ticket, *n.* a ticket which permits a traveller to change on to another line or route without booking again [Rly., etc.].
transfiguration, *n.* trans-*fig*-yew-*ray*-shon, change of form; the supernatural change in the personal appearance of Christ on the Mount (Matt. xvii); (*cap.*) a feast on 6 Aug. in commemoration of this.
transfigure, *v.t.* trans-*fig*-ur, to change the outward form or appearance of, esp. so as to glorify it. (Fr. *transfigurer*.)
transfix, *v.t.* trans-*fiks*, to pierce through, as with a pointed weapon. (L. *transfigo*, pierce through.)
transfixion, *n.* trans-*fik*-shon, the act of transfixing; a certain method of amputation [Surg.].
transfluent, *a.* *trans*-floo-ent, flowing through or across; applied to water passing under a bridge [Her.]. (L. *transfluo*, flow through.)
transforation, *n.* *trans*-fo-*ray*-shon, a boring through [Surg.]. (L. *trans*-, and *foro*, bore.)
transform, *v.t.* trans-*form*, to change the form, shape, or appearance of; to change substantially; to change the nature of spiritually; to change an equation into one of a different form but equal value [Alg.]: *v.i.* to be changed in form. (L. *trans*-, and *forma*, shape.)
transformability, *n.* trans-*for*-ma-*bil*-e-te, the capacity for transformation.
transformable, *a.* trans-*for*-ma-bl, that may be transformed.
transformation, *n.* trans-for-*may*-shon, the act or operation of transforming; metamorphosis; a transmutation; a change of heart [Theol.]; an arrangement of false hair. **transformation scene,** an elaborate set of stage scenery in which changes take place in view of the audience.
transformative, *a.* trans-*for*-ma-tiv, having power or a tendency to transform.
transformer, *n.* trans-*for*-mer, that which transforms; an apparatus for changing one form of current into another [Elect.] or one wave-length into another [Wire.].
transformism, *n.* trans-*for*-mizm, the doctrine of the evolution of species; the doctrine of man's moral and social evolution.
transformist, *n.* trans-*for*-mist, an adherent of transformism.
transformistic, *a.* trans-for-*mis*-tik, pertaining to transformism or transformists.
transfuse, *v.t.* trans-*fewz*, to pour out of one vessel into another; to transfer, as blood, from one body to another; to instil or cause to be instilled. (L. *transfusus*, poured out.)
transfuser, *n.* trans-*few*-zer, one who or that which transfuses.
transfusible, *a.* trans-*few*-ze-bl, that may be transfused.
transfusion, *n.* trans-*few*-zhon, the act of transfusing; the act of transferring blood from one body to another; the introduction of any fluid into the blood-vessels.
transfusive, *a.* trans-*few*-ziv, capable of transfusing.
transgress, *v.t.* trans-*gress*, to pass beyond any limit; to break or violate a law: *v.i.* to offend by violating a law. (L. *transgressus*, passed over.)
transgression, *n.* trans-*gresh*-on, act of transgressing; the violation of a law; offence; sin.
transgressive, *a.* trans-*gres*-iv, involving transgression; apt to transgress.
transgressively, *ad.* in a transgressive manner.
transgressor, *n.* trans-*gres*-or, one who breaks a law or violates a command; a sinner.
tranship, *v.t.* tran-*ship*, to remove from one ship to another, or one means of conveyance to another.
transhipment, *n.* tran-*ship*-ment, the act of transhipping.
transhuman, *a.* trans-*hew*-mun, superhuman.
transience, *n.* *tran*-shence, -se-ence, *or* -ze-ence, transitoriness; the quality of being transient.
transient, *a.* *tran*-shent, -se-ent, *or* -ze-ent, passing; of short duration; not lasting; ephemeral; migratory. (L. *transiens*, going across.)
transiently, *ad.* in a transient manner.
transientness, *n.* transience.
transilience, *n.* tran-*sil*-e-ence, the state of being transilient. (L. *transiliens*, leaping across.)
transilient, *a.* tran-*sil*-e-ent, passing as though by leaping across; abruptly discontinuous. (L. *transiliens*.)
transilluminate, *v.t.* trans-e-*lew*-me-nate, to pass light through, esp. through the walls of a body cavity for the inspection of its interior [Med.].
transillumination, *n.* trans-e-*lew*-me-*nay*-shon, the act of transilluminating.
transire, *n.* tran-*sire*-re, a custom-house warrant for permitting goods to pass [Law]. (L., go through.)
trans-isthmian, *a.* tranz-*isth*-me-an, extending across an isthmus.

transit, *n.* *tran*-sit, a passing over or through; the passage or carriage of persons or goods; the passing of an inferior planet across the sun's disk [Astron.]; the passage of a heavenly body across the meridian of a place [Astron.]: *v.t.* and *i.* to cross the disk of [Astron.]. **transit circle,** a transit instrument. **transit compass,** a surveyor's instrument for measuring horizontal angles. **transit instrument,** a mounted telescope for observing transits. **transit time,** the time at which a heavenly body crosses the meridian [Astron.]. (L. *transitus.*)
transition, *n.* tran-*sizh*-on, passage from one place or state to another; change; a passing from one subject to another [Rhet.]; a sudden change of key [Mus.]; a change in literary or artistic style, esp. from Norman to Early English [Arch.].
transitional, *a.* tran-*sizh*-o-nal, pertaining to or characterized by transition.
transitionist, *n.* tran-*sizh*-o-nist, one who endorses or promotes a transition movement in art, etc.
transitive, *a.* *tran*-se-tiv, expressive of an action passing from a subject to an object [Gram.]; transitional: *n.* a transitive verb.
transitively, *ad.* in a transitive manner.
transitiveness, *n.* the quality of being transitive.
transitorily, *ad.* *trans*-e-to-re-le, with short continuance.
transitoriness, *n.* state of being transitory.
transitory, *a.* *trans*-e-to-re, passing without continuance, lasting a short time. (L. *transitorius,* able to pass through.)
translatable, *a.* trans-*lay*-ta-bl, capable of being translated, or rendered into another language.
translate, *v.t.* trans-*late,* to render into another language; to paraphrase, explain, or interpret; to convey to heaven without death; to re-inter the remains of a saint elsewhere; to transfer a bishop from one see to another. (L. *translatus,* brought over.)
translation, *n.* trans-*lay*-shon, the act of translating; the act of translating into another language; interpretation; version; transference, esp. [Law] of property; translational motion [Physics].
translational, *a.* trans-*lay*-sho-nal, pertaining to translation, esp. to translation to heaven; consisting in motion in a definite direction, as distinct from rotation, etc. [Physics].
translative, *a.* trans-*lay*-tiv, pertaining to translation (of languages), or to the conveyance of property [Law]; involving direct transference from place to place [Phys.].
translator, *n.* trans-*lay*-tor, one who translates.
translatory, *a.* trans-*lay*-to-re, translational.
Transleithan, *a.* trans-*ly*-than, across the Hungarian border (the Riv. *Leitha* formerly marking part of the frontier between Austria and Hungary).
transliterate, *v.t.* trans-*lit*-er-rate, to write the words of one language in the characters of another. (L. *trans-*, and *litera,* a letter.)
transliteration, *n.* trans-lit-er-*ray*-shon, the act of transliterating.
transliterator, *n.* trans-*lit*-er-ray-tor, one who transliterates.
translocation, *n.* trans-lo-*kay*-shon, removal from one place to another. (L. *trans-*, and *locus,* a place.)
translucence, *n.* trans-*lew*-sence, the property of transmitting rays of light; incomplete transparency.
translucency, *n.* trans-*lew*-sen-se, translucence.
translucent, *a.* trans-*lew*-sent, transmitting rays of light, but not so that objects can be seen through it [Min.]; nearly transparent. (L. *translucens,* shining through.)
translucid, *a.* trans-*lew*-sid, translucent.
translunar, *a.* trans-*lew*-nar, translunary.
translunary, *a.* trans-*lew*-na-re, situated beyond the moon; visionary [Fig.]. (L. *trans-*, and *luna,* the moon.)
transmarine, *a.* trans-ma-*reen,* beyond the sea.
transmeridional, *a.* trans-me-*rid*-e-o-nal, crossing the lines of the meridian; going east and west.
transmigrant, *n.* *trans*-me-grant, one who migrates or transmigrates.
transmigrate, *v.i.* *trans*-me-grate *or* trans-*my*-grate, to migrate; to pass from one country or jurisdiction through another; to pass after death from one body into another. (L. *transmigratus,* migrated.)
transmigration, *n.* trans-me (*or* -my-) -*gray*-shon, the act of migrating; the transformation of a thing into another state; the passing of the soul after death into another body; metempsychosis.
transmigrator, *n.* trans-*my*-gra-tor *or* *trans*-me-gray-tor, one who or that which transmigrates.
transmigratory, *a.* trans-*my*-gra-to-re, passing from one place, body, or state to another.
transmissibility, *n.* trans-mis-e-*bil*-e-te, the quality or state of being transmissible.
transmissible, *a.* trans-*mis*-e-bl, that may be transmitted.
transmission, *n.* trans-*mish*-on, the act of transmitting; the passing of a substance through any body, as light through glass; the gearing by which power is transmitted from the engine to the axle of a motor-car; the sending, also the passage, of radio signals [Wire.]. (L. *transmissus,* sent across.)
transmissional, *a.* trans-*mish*-o-nal, pertaining to or of the nature of transmission.
transmissionist, *n.* trans-*mish*-o-nist, an advocate of the theory that acquired characters may be hereditarily transmitted; one who holds that impulses are merely transmitted by, not originated, in the brain.
transmissive, *a.* trans-*mis*-iv, serving to transmit; capable of being transmitted; derived from one to another.
transmit, *v.t.* trans-*mit,* to cause or suffer to pass through; to send from one person or place to another; to hand down or pass on; to send radio signals [Wire.]. (L. *transmitto,* send across.)
transmittable, *a.* trans-*mit*-a-bl, transmissible; capable of being transmitted.
transmittal, *n.* trans-*mit*-al, transmission; a transference.
transmitter, *n.* trans-*mit*-er, one who or that which transmits; the transmitting part of a telephone or telegraphic instrument; a radio transmitting set or station [Wire.].
transmogrification, *n.* trans-*mog*-re-fe-*kay*-shon, a transformation, a complete change [Coll.].
transmogrify, *v.t.* trans-*mog*-re-fy, to change into; to transform, esp. by occult means.
transmontane, *a.* tranz-*mon*-tane, lying or being beyond the mountains; transalpine.
transmutability, *n.* tranz-*mew*-ta-*bil*-e-te, susceptibility of change into another substance.
transmutable, *a.* tranz-*mew*-ta-bl, capable of being changed into a different substance, or something of a different nature.
transmutableness, *n.* transmutability.
transmutably, *ad.* tranz-*mew*-ta-ble, in a transmutable manner.
transmutation, *n.* tranz-mew-*tay*-shon, the act of transmuting or state of being transmuted, esp. the alchemists' alleged change of baser metals into gold; the evolution of one species into another [Biol.]; the reduction of one figure or body to another of the same area or content but different form [Geom.].
transmutationist, *n.* tranz-mew-*tay*-shon-ist, one who believes in the theory of the transmutation of metals, or [Biol.] species.
transmute, *v.t.* tranz-*mewt,* to change from one nature, substance, or form into another. (L. *transmuto,* change.)
transmuter, *n.* tranz-*mew*-ter, one who or that which transmutes.
transoceanic, *a.* *tranz*-oh-she-*an*-ik, situated or coming from across the ocean; crossing the ocean.
transom, *n.* *tran*-som, a beam or timber extended across the stern-post of a ship to strengthen the after part; a horizontal mullion or crossbar, in a window, or a lintel over a door; the vane of a cross-staff: *pl.* pieces of wood which joined the cheeks of gun-carriages. (L. *transtrum,* a crossbeam.)
transom-window, *n.* a window divided by a transom or transoms; a window above a doorway.
transpadane, *a.* *tranz*-pa-dane, across the river Po (*i.e.,* on the farther side from Rome). (L. *Padus,* the Po.)
transparency, *n.* trans-*pare*-ren-se, the quality of being transparent; a picture on a semi-transparent material seen by light passing through it.
transparent, *a.* trans-*pare*-rent, having the property of transmitting rays of light so as not to obscure the view of objects behind; pervious to light; clear; sincere [Fig.]. (L. *trans-*, and *parens,* appearing.)

transparently, *ad.* so as to be seen through.
transparentness, *n.* quality of being transparent.
transpicuous, *a.* trans-*pik*-yew-us, transparent; clear; obvious; easy of discovery. (L. *transpicio*, see through.)
transpierce, *v.t.* tranz-*peerce*, to pierce through.
transpirable, *a.* trans-*pire*-ra-bl, capable of emitting or being emitted through pores; permitting transpiration or [Med.] perspiration.
transpiration, *n.* trans-pe-*ray*-shon, act or process of transpiring; cutaneous exhalation.
transpire, *v.t.* trans-*pire*, to emit through the excretories of the skin; to send off in vapour: *v.i.* to be emitted through the excretories of the skin; to exhale; (*incorrectly*) to become public, to happen. (Fr. *transpirer*, exhale.)
transpirometer, *n.* trans-py-*rom*-e-ter, an apparatus for measuring the transpiration of plants.
transplant, *v.t.* trans-*plahnt*, to remove and plant or settle in another place; to remove; to perform transplantation [Surg.].
transplantation, *n.* trans-plan-*tay*-shon, act of transplanting; the removal of living tissue from one part or person and its grafting in another [Surg.].
transplanter, *n.* trans-*plahn*-ter, one who transplants; a machine for transplanting trees.
transplendent, *a.* trans-*plen*-dent, of surpassing splendour; highly resplendent.
transplendently, *ad.* trans-*plen*-dent-le, with super-eminent splendour.
transpontine, *a.* tranz-*pon*-tine, situated across the bridge, esp. (of the drama) performed on the Surrey side of London, and hence, melodramatic.
transport, *v.t.* trans-*port*, to carry or convey from one place to another; to banish to a penal colony; to carry away by excitement or emotion; to enravish. (L. *transporto*, carry across.)
★**transport,** *n.* *trans*-port, transportation; conveyance from place to place; a ship employed for transporting troops, munitions, etc.; the branch of an army, together with its equipment, etc., engaged in transportation; rapture; ecstasy.
transportability, *n.* *trans*-por-ta-*bil*-e-te, capacity for being transported.
transportable, *a.* trans-*por*-ta-bl, that may be transported.
transportation, *n.* trans-por-*tay*-shon, the act of transporting; transmission; conveyance to another place; banishment to a penal colony.
transportedly, *ad.* in a state of rapture or ecstasy; in a transport.
transportedness, *n.* a state of rapture.
transportee, *n.* trans-por-*tee*, one who is transported, esp., formerly, a convict.
transporter, *n.* trans-*por*-ter, one who or that which transports; a travelling crane.
transporting, *a.* trans-*por*-ting, ravishing with delight; ecstatic.
transportingly, *ad.* ravishingly.
transposal, *n.* tran-*spoh*-zal, the act of transposing; change of place or order.
transpose, *v.t.* tran-*spohz*, to change the place or order of things, by putting each in the place of the other; to put out of place; to bring, as a term of an equation, over to the other side [Alg.]; to change the natural order of words [Gram.]; to change the key [Mus.]. (Fr. *transposer*.)
transposition, *n.* tran-spo-*zish*-on, the act of transposing; the state of being transposed.
transpositional, *a.* pertaining to transposition.
transpositive, *a.* tranz-*poz*-e-tiv, made by transposing; characterized by transposition [Gram.].
transprose, *v.t.* tranz-*prohz*, to rewrite poetry as prose.
trans-ship, *v.t.* tranship.
trans-sonic, *a.* tranz-*son*-ik, designating speeds ranging from 550 to 760 miles per hour.
transubstantiate, *v.t.* tran-sub-*stan*-she-ate, to change to another substance. (L. *trans-*, and *substantia*, material.)
transubstantiation, *n.* *tran*-sub-*stan*-she-*ay*-shon, change of substance, esp. [Theol.] the conversion of the bread and wine in the eucharist into the body and blood of Christ.
transubstantiationist, *n.* *tran*-sub-*stan*-she-*ay*-sho-nist, a believer in the doctrine of transubstantiation.
transubstantiative, *a.* *tran*-sub-*stan*-she-a-tiv, pertaining to or of the nature of transubstantiation.
transubstantiator, *n.* tran-sub-*stan*-she-ay-tor, a transubstantiationist.
transudate, *n.* *tran*-sew-date, that which is transuded.
transudation, *n.* tran-sew-*day*-shon, the act or process of passing through the pores of a substance.
transudatory, *a.* tran-*sew*-da-to-re, passing by transudation.
transude, *v.i.* trans-*yewd*, to pass through the pores or interstices of texture, as perspirable matter or other fluid. (L. *trans-*, and *sudo*, sweat.)
transumpt, *n.* tran-*sumpt*, a copy or exemplification of a record. (L. *transumo*, assume.)
transumptive, *a.* tran-*sump*-tiv, taking or transferred from one to another.
trans-uranic, *a.* *tranz*-yew-*ran*-ik, designating those elements (*e.g.*, neptunium and plutonium) whose atomic number is higher than 92, that of uranium.
transverbate, *v.t.* trans-*ver*-bate, to translate word for word.
transversal, *a.* trans-*ver*-sal, running or lying across: *n.* a straight or curved line which traverses or intersects any system of other lines [Geom.].
transversally, *ad.* in a direction crosswise.
transverse, *a.* *tranz*-verse, lying or being across or in a cross direction; in a pericarp, at right angles with the valves [Bot.]: *n.* anything which is transverse; a transverse muscle; the longer axis of an ellipse. (L. *transversus*, crosswise.)
transversely, *ad.* in a cross direction.
transverser, *n.* tranz-*ver*-ser, a form of plane table used in surveying.
transversion, *n.* tranz-*ver*-shon, a transposition; a perversion; a turning into verse; a metrical version.
tranter, *n.* *trant*-er, a huckster, hawker, or pedlar.
trap, *n.* trap, a contrivance that shuts suddenly or with a spring, used for snaring animals; an ambush; a stratagem; a machine used in the game of knur-and-spell, or trap-ball; a similar apparatus for throwing clay pigeons into the air [Shooting]; a starting-gate for racing dogs; a trap-door (esp. on the stage); a contrivance to prevent foul air escaping from a drain; a gig, or other light vehicle on springs; a percussion instrument [Mus.]; a detective or policeman [Slang]: *v.t.* to catch in a trap; to ensnare; to take by stratagem; to furnish with a trap: *v.i.* to set traps for game. (A.S. *treppe*, a snare.)
trap, *n.* trap, a dark igneous metamorphic rock, so called from its characteristic step-like appearance [Geol.]. (Sw. *trappa*, stairs.)
trap, *v.t.* trap, to adorn; to dress (esp. horses) with ornaments. (Fr. *drap*, cloth.)
trapan, *n.* and *v.t.* tra-*pan*, trepan (ensnare).
trap-ball, *n.* a game in which a ball is hit with a bat, after having been flung up by the striker from a trap.
trap-door, *n.* a door in a floor, roof, or ceiling opening and shutting like a valve.
trapes, *n.* trayps, a slattern; an idle sluttish woman: *v.i.* to tramp or gad about noisily or idly. [Coll.] (Perhaps Scand. *trappa*, to stamp.)
trapeze, *n.* tra-*peez*, a trapezium; a swinging horizontal bar for gymnastic feats. (Fr. *trapèze*, from Gr. through Lat. *trapezium*.)
trapezian, *a.* tra-*pee*-ze-an, having the lateral planes composed of trapeziums situated in two ranges between two bases (Cryst.].
trapeziform, *a.* tra-*pee*-ze-form, having the shape of a trapezium.
trapezium, *n.* tra-*pee*-ze-um (*pl.* **trapezia** or **-ziums**), a plane figure contained within four right lines, two of which are parallel [Geom.]; the first bone in the second row of the carpus [Anat.]. (Gr. *trapeza*, a table, from *tetra*, four, *peza*, foot.)
trapezohedron, *n.* tra-*pee*-zo-*hee*-dron, a solid figure, or a crystal, whose faces are trapeziums or trapezoids. (Gr. *trapezion*, and *hedra*, a side.)
trapezoid, *n.* *trap*-e-zoyd, a plane figure of four unequal sides, no two of which are parallel: *a.* trapeziform.
trapezoidal, *a.* trap-e-*zoy*-dal, trapeziform.
trappean, *a.* tra-*pee*-an, pertaining to or resembling the igneous rock trap [Geol.].
trapper, *n.* *trap*-er, one whose occupation it is to entrap wild animals, usually for furs.

rappings, *n.pl.* *trap*-ingz, ornaments for horses; ornaments; dress; external decorations. (*trap*, adorn.)
Trappist, *n.* *trap*-ist, a monk of an austere Cistercian religious order, founded in the valley of La Trappe, Normandy, in the 12th cent. and reformed and re-established in 1664 by its abbot, de Rancé.
Trappistine, *n.* *trap*-is-teen, a nun of the order of La Trappe; a liqueur made by the Trappists.
rappoid, *a.* *trap*-oyd, trappean [Geol.].
rappous, *a.* *trap*-us, trappean [Geol.].
rappy, *a.* *trap*-e, containing a trap; deceptive, tricky [Coll.].
raps, *n.pl.* traps, luggage; personal belongings.
rapse, *n.* and *v.t.* trayps, trapes.
rap-shooting, *n.* shooting at real or artificial pigeons released or flung from a trap.
rap-stick, *n.* the stick, or tripstick, used at the game of trap-ball.
rash, *n.* trash, any waste or worthless matter; nonsense; a paltry production; a worthless person [Amer.]: *v.t.* to lop; to strip off leaves. **white trash,** *see* **white.** (Perhaps O.Scand. *tros*, rubbish.)
rashery, *n.* *trash*-er-re, rubbish; trash.
rashily, *ad.* *trash*-e-le, in a trashy manner.
rashiness, *n.* the quality of being trashy.
rashy, *a.* *trash*-e, like trash; worthless.
rass, *n.* tras, a volcanic pumiceous conglomerate, formerly used for making cement, plaster, etc.
rauma, *n.* *traw*-ma, any injury or wound, or the condition caused by such [Path.]; an unnerving experience conducive to hysteria [Psychan.]. (Gr., a wound.)
raumatic, *a.* traw-*mat*-ik, pertaining to wounds [Path.] or to trauma [Psychan.]; adapted to the cure of wounds: *n.* a medicine useful in curing wounds.
raumatism, *n.* *traw*-ma-tizm, the morbid condition consequent upon a trauma [Path. and Psychan.].
raumatology, *n.* *traw*-ma-*tol*-o-je, the branch of medicine treating of wounds.
ravail, *n.* *trav*-ayl, labour with pain; severe toil; labour in childbirth: *v.i.* to labour with pain; to toil; to suffer the pangs of childbirth. (O.Fr.)
rave, *n.* trave, a wooden frame to confine a horse while being shod; a cross-beam. (L. *trabs*, a beam.)
ravel, *n.* *trav*-el, the act of travelling; a passing on foot; range, length of scope (of a projectile, piston, etc.): *pl.* an account of experiences, etc., while travelling: *v.i.* to journey; to go to a distant country; to pass; to move; to be employed as a commercial traveller: *v.t.* to pass; to journey over; to cause to travel. (*travail.*)
ravelled, *a.* *trav*-eld, having wide personal experience of travel.
raveller, *n.* *trav*-el-er, one who or that which travels; one who visits foreign countries; a commercial traveller (*see* **commercial**); a ring sliding on a spar or rope [Naut.]. **travellers' cheque,** a letter of credit for a small stated amount issued by a bank and encashable by the authorized holder at almost any bank. **traveller's tale,** a highly coloured or exaggerated story. **traveller's tree,** *Ravenala madagascariensis*, the leaves of which contain a refreshing sap.
raveller's-joy, *n.* a climbing plant with white flowers, old man's beard, *Clematis vitalba.*
ravelling, *a.* *trav*-el-ing, pertaining to, adapted for, or incurred by travel.
ravelogue, *n.* *trav*-el-og, a public lecture on travels, usually accompanied by motion or other pictures. (*travel*, and Gr. *logos*, discourse.)
raversable, *a.* *trav*-er-sa-bl, that may be traversed, crossed, or denied.
raverse, *ad.* *trav*-erse, athwart; cross-wise: *a.* lying across: *n.* anything laid or built across; something that thwarts; a sideways turning movement about a pivot; a sharply bending roadway up a hill; a parapet crossing the covert-way to prevent its being enfiladed [Fort.]; a travis; a gallery or loft of communication in any large building; an oblique climb by mountain-climbers; a denial of what the opposite party has advanced [Law]; the sideways travel of a part [Mech.]; a tack in beating to windward [Naut.]; the course followed in traversing [Ski-ing]: *a.* transverse; lying or extending across. **traverse sailing,** the mode of computing the location of a ship by reducing several short courses to one larger course [Naut.]. (L. *transversus*, crosswise.)
traverse, *v.t.* *trav*-erse, to place in a cross direction; to extend across; to thwart; to obstruct; to travel over; to survey carefully; to turn and point in any direction; to plane across the grain; to ski in a direction oblique to the angle of slope; to deny what the opposite party has alleged [Law]: *v.i.* to move or pass across or obliquely; to turn, as on a pivot; to move round; to swivel; to cut the tread crosswise, as a horse that throws his croup to one side and his head to the other [Man.]; to use the posture or motions of opposition [Fencing].
traverser, *n.* *trav*-er-ser, one who traverses; one who opposes a plea [Law]; a traverse-table [Rly.].
traverse-table, *n.* a travelling platform for shifting railway vehicles from one set of rails to another alongside it; a table of difference of latitude and departure [Naut.].
travertine, *n.* *trav*-er-tin, a calc-sinter, formed by springs holding lime in solution. (It.)
travesty, *n.* *trav*-es-te, the representation of a serious work in a burlesque style; a parody or grotesque imitation: *v.t.* to turn into burlesque. (Fr. *travestir*, L. *trans-*, and *vestio*, clothe.)
travis, *n.* *trav*-is, a hanging board separating one horse from another in a stable; a partition dividing a stable into stalls. (*traverse.*)
trawl, *n.* trawl, a drag-net with a beam for fishing on the bottom; a long buoyed fishing line from which short lines hang: *v.i.* to fish by dragging a net along the bottom. (Fr. *trôler*, drag about.)
trawler, *n.* *trawl*-er, one who trawls; a fishing-vessel which drags a net behind it.
trawling, *n.* *trawl*-ing, the act or occupation of fishing with a trawl.
★**tray,** *n.* tray, a shallow trough, used for domestic or culinary purposes; a metal plate or board with a rim; a waiter or salver. (M.E. *treie.*)
tray, *a.* tray, trey; the third branch of a stag's horn.
tray-trip, *n.* *tray*-trip, trey-trip.
treacherous, *a.* *tretch*-er-rus, violating allegiance or plighted faith; traitorous to the state or sovereign; faithless; deceptive.
treacherously, *ad.* faithlessly; perfidiously.
treacherousness, *n.* quality of being treacherous.
treachery, *n.* *tretch*-er-re, violation of allegiance; disloyalty; perfidy. (O.Fr. *tricherie*, deceit.)
treacle, *n.* *tree*-kl, molasses; a viscid syrup which drains from the sugar-refiner's moulds; a saccharine fluid, consisting of the inspissated juices of certain vegetables: *v.t.* to smear or sweeten with treacle. **treacle mustard,** a name formerly applied to various herbs (esp. *Erysimum cheiranthoides*) used medicinally. (O.Fr. *triacle.*)
treacly, *a.* *tree*-kl-e, composed of, or of the nature of, treacle; sickly [Fig.].
tread, *v.i.* tred, to set the foot; to step on; to walk or go; to walk with form or state; to copulate, as fowls: *v.t.* to step or walk on; to press under the feet; to beat with the feet; to walk over with a stately step; to trample in contempt. **tread on air,** to feel happy and gay. **tread a measure,** to perform a stately dance. **tread the boards,** to be a professional actor. **tread water,** to support oneself in deep water in an upright position by a trampling action. *p.* **trod** and **trode.** *pp.* **trodden.** (A.S. *tredan.*)
tread, *n.* tred, the act, or the sound, of walking; manner of stepping; that which is stepped upon; the part of a stair on which the feet step; the part of the foot or boot, or of a wheel or tyre, which touches the ground; the part of the rail on which the wheels bear; the wheel-base of a vehicle; the act of copulating (in fowls); the germinating point on the yolk of an egg.
treader, *n.* *tred*-er, one who treads.
treadle, *n.* *tred*-dl, a lever actuated by the foot to impart motion to some part of a machine: *v.i.* to use a treadle; to pedal; to effect by making use of a treadle. (*tread.*)
treadmill, *n.* *tred*-mil, a mill worked by persons treading on steps upon the periphery of a wheel; any monotonous or irksome task [Fig.].
treadwheel, *n.* *tred*-wheel, a vertical wheel worked

by men or animals walking within its periphery; wearisome routine [Fig.].

treason, *n. tree*-zon, an act of disloyalty or treachery; the offence of attempting to betray the state or to subvert the government of the state to which the offender belongs. **high treason** immediately affects the monarch, his consort, and his heir, and the safety of the realm. **petty treason** involves a breach of fidelity to an individual, as the murder of a master by a servant. **misprision of treason,** *see* **misprision. treason felony,** high treason treated as a felony instead of as a capital crime. (Fr. *trahison.*)

treasonable, *a. tree*-zon-a-bl, pertaining to, consisting of, or involving treason; treacherous.

treasonably, *ad.* in a treasonable manner.

treasonous, *a. tree*-zon-us, treasonable; abounding in treason.

treasure, *n. trezh*-ur, wealth accumulated; a great quantity of anything collected; something much valued; great abundance [Fig.]; a highly valued friend or person [Coll.]: *v.t.* to hoard up; to collect for future use. (Fr. *trésor*, from Gr. *thesauros.*)

treasure-house, *n.* a building where treasure is kept; a collection of valuable materials [Fig.].

treasure-hunt, *n.* a search for lost or hidden treasure; a sport in which competitors follow a trail of clues.

treasurer, *n. trezh*-ur-rer, one who has the care of treasure or a treasury; an officer who receives and takes charge of the money of the public, or of private companies, corporations, or societies.

treasurership, *n. trezh*-ur-rer-ship, the office of treasurer.

treasure-trove, *n.* -trohv, any gold or silver (coined or otherwise) found in the earth, the ownership of which cannot be ascertained. (*treasure*, and Fr. *trouvé*, found.)

treasury, *n. trezh*-er-re, a treasure-house; (*cap.*) the department of government that has charge of the finances; a repository; a small encyclopædia; an anthology or collection of choice literary extracts. **Treasury bench,** the first row of seats on the Speaker's right in the House of Commons, occupied by cabinet ministers. **Treasury note,** a currency note.

treat, *n.* treet, an entertainment given; something given for entertainment; a school-treat or similar entertainment: *v.t.* to behave or act towards; to discourse on; to handle in a particular manner; to entertain with food or drink; to negotiate; to subject to the action of an agent, etc. [Chem.]; to manage by the application of remedies [Med.]: *v.i.* to discourse; to negotiate; to give an entertainment. (L. *tracio*, handle.)

treatable, *a. treet*-a-bl, capable of being treated or processed; tractable; easily persuaded.

treater, *n. treet*-er, one who handles or discourses on a subject; one who entertains.

treatise, *n. treet*-is, a written discourse in which a particular subject is discussed. (Fr. *traité*)

treatment, *n. treet*-ment, the act or manner of treating; management; good or bad behaviour toward; manner of applying remedies or of dealing with a disease [Med.].

treaty, *n. treet*-e, act of treating to adjust differences and come to an agreement; negotiation; a formal and ratified agreement between states. **treaty port,** a port, esp. in the Far East, opened by treaty to foreign trade. (Fr.)

treble, *a. treb*-bl, threefold; triple; sharp in tone; soprano [Mus.]: *n.* the soprano, or highest of the parts in singing and playing; a treble player, singer, voice, or instrument; the smallest of a peal of bells; *v.t.* and *i.* to make or become threefold. **treble clef,** the G clef, the higher of the two used for pianoforte music [Mus.]. (O.Fr.)

trebleness, *n. treb*-bl-ness, the state or quality of being treble.

trebly, *ad. treb*-le, in a threefold manner.

trebuchet, *n. treb*-oo-shet, a mediæval engine for slinging large stones [Mil.]: a small sensitive balance; a cucking-stool. (Fr. *trébuchet.*)

trecentist, *n.* tray-*chen*-tist, an Italian artist or poet of the 14th century.

trecento, *n.* tray-*chen*-to, the fourteenth century (A.D. 1301–1400), esp. as a period in Italian culture. (It., three hundred—*mil*, 1,000, being understood.)

treddle, *n.* and *v. tred*-dl, treadle.

★**tree,** *n.* tree, a plant with a trunk and woody and perennial branches; anything having a stem and branches like a tree; a pedigree presented diagrammatically, a family tree; a beam or other piece of timber; a gallows; a cross of crucifixion: *v.t.* to drive up or to a tree: *v.i.* to take to a tree for refuge. **bark up the wrong tree,** *see* **bark. tree of heaven,** a tall ornamental tree from China, of the order *Ailanthus*, having foul-smelling flowers. **tree of knowledge,** the tree in the midst of the Garden of Eden bearing the forbidden fruit; hence, desired but dangerous learning or experience. (A.S. *treow.*)

tree-calf, *n.* a book-binding leather so treated that it bears a tree-like design.

tree-crab, *n.* a land-crab of the genus *Birgus.*

tree-creeper, *n.* the small bird *Certhia familiaris.*

tree-fern, *n.* a tropical fern with a stem like a tree.

tree-frog, *n.* any of the many frogs of arboreal habits.

treeless, *a. tree*-less, destitute of trees.

tree-mallow, *n.* the hardy biennial garden plant *Lavatera arborea.*

treen, *a.* treen, wooden; pertaining to trees: *n.* fancy articles made of wood. (A.S. *treowen.*)

treenail, *n. tree*-nayl, a long wooden pin, esp. one for fastening the planks of a wooden ship to the timbers.

tree-pipit, *n.* the small short-tailed arboreal bird *Anthus trivialis.*

tree-sparrow, *n.* the Old World bird *Passer montanus*; in N. America, *Spizella monticola.*

treetop, *n. tree*-top, the topmost branches of a tree: *pl.* the summit line of adjacent trees.

trefoil, *n. tref*-oyl, a plant of the genus *Trifolium* with leaves of three leaflets, such as clover; a circular or triangular ornament containing three cusps [Arch.]. (L. *tres*, three, *folium*, a leaf.)

treillage, *n. tray*-laj, a sort of trellis of light posts and rails for supporting espaliers, etc. [Hort.]. (Fr.)

trek, *n.* trek, a journey by ox-wagon; a journey: *v.i.* to travel or migrate by ox-wagon. **trek ox,** an ox used for draught. (Dut.)

trekker, *n. trek*-er, one who treks.

trellis, *n. trel*-is, a structure or frame of lattice work used for supporting growing plants, as an outdoor screen, etc. (Fr. *treillis*, lattice-work.)

trellised, *a. trel*-list, having trellises.

trellis-work, *n.* lattice-work; tracery or embroidery, etc., resembling this.

trematode, *a. trem*-a-tode, of or belonging to the Trematoda, an order of parasitic flat-worms including the flukes: *n.* a fluke-worm. (Gr. *trematōdēs*, porous.)

trematoid, *a. trem*-a-toyd, resembling or characteristic of a trematode: *n.* a trematode.

tremble, *n. trem*-bl, state of trembling: *v.i.* to shake involuntarily, as with fear, cold, or weakness; to shake; to quiver; to totter. (L. *tremo*, shake.)

trembler, *n. trem*-bler, one who trembles; a small vibrating part in the ignition apparatus of an internal combustion engine.

tremblingly, *ad. trem*-bling-le, in a trembling manner or state.

tremelline, *a.* tre-*mel*-ine, pertaining to or resembling the *Tremella*, a genus of jelly-like fungi. (L. *tremellus*, tremulous.)

tremellose, *a. trem*-e-lohs, gelatinous, tremulous like jelly [Bot.].

tremendous, *a.* tre-*men*-dus, such as to excite awe; terrible; dreadful; forceful and violent; overpowering; considerable [Coll.]. (L. *tremendus*, formidable.)

tremendously, *ad.* in a tremendous degree; dreadfully; excessively.

tremendousness, *n.* state of being tremendous.

tremie, *n. trem*-e, an apparatus for depositing concrete under water. (Fr.)

tremogram, *n. trem*-o-gram, the record made by a tremograph.

tremograph, *n. trem*-o-graf, an apparatus for recording muscular action of an involuntary nature.

tremolando, *ad. tray*-mo-*lahn*-doh, tremulously [Mus.]. (It.)

tremolant, *a.* and *n. trem*-o-lant, tremulant [Mus.].

tremolite, *n. trem*-o-lite, a greyish silicate of calcium and magnesium crystallizing in the monoclinic system. (Val *Tremola*, in the Swiss Alps.)

tremolo, *n.* *trem*-o-loh, vibration of the voice; tremulous delivery; a tremulant. (It.)
tremor, *n.* *trem*-or, a trembling, shivering, or quivering. (L.)
tremulant, *a.* *trem*-yew-lant, tremulous: *n.* an organ stop producing a tremolo effect.
tremulous, *a.* *trem*-yew-lus, trembling; affected with fear or timidity; shaking; quivering. (L. *tremulus.*)
tremulously, *ad.* with trembling or quivering.
tremulousness, *n.* the state of being tremulous.
trenail, *n.* *tren*-el, a treenail; a wooden peg.
trench, *n.* trench, a long narrow cut in the earth; a ditch; a deep ditch cut for defence, esp. an entrenchment with parapet [Mil.]: *pl.* a range of such cuttings and embankments: *v.t.* to cut or dig a channel for water; to fortify by cutting trenches and raising ramparts; to furrow: *v.i.* to encroach. **slit trench,** a shallow, hastily constructed trench for temporary protection. **trench fever,** a parasitic relapsing infectious fever carried by lice. **trench foot,** a gangrenous condition due to parasitic fungi. **trench warfare,** military operations conducted from and against a permanent system of trenches. (O.Fr. *trencher,* cut.)
trenchancy, *n.* *tren*-chan-se, sharpness; causticity.
trenchant, *a.* *tren*-chant, cutting; sharp; severe.
trench-coat, *n.* a short waterproof military overcoat, usually with detachable woollen lining.
trencher, *n.* *tren*-cher, a wooden plate to cut meat on at table; a bread-platter; the pleasures of the table; a trencher-cap.
trencher-cap, *n.* a "mortar-board" or college cap.
trencher-friend, *n.* a sponger, a parasite.
trencherman, *n.* *tren*-cher-man, a hearty eater; a glutton.
trench-mortar, *n.* a short-range mortar throwing heavy shells.
trench-plough, *n.* a plough for opening land to a greater depth than that of common furrows.
trend, *n.* trend, inclination in a particular direction: *v.i.* to take or tend in a particular direction. (A.S. *trendan.*)
trendle, *n.* *tren*-dl, anything round used in turning or rolling; a flat rounded vessel. (A.S. *trendel,* circle.)
trental, *n.* *tren*-tal, a Rom. Cath. office for the dead, thirty masses rehearsed for thirty days successively after the person's death. (Fr. *trente,* thirty.)
trente-et-quarante, *n.* (App.), the gambling game rouge-et-noir. (Fr., thirty-and-forty.)
Trentine, *a.* *tren*-tine, Tridentine.
trepan, *n.* tre-*pan,* the cylindrical saw used in trepanning: *v.t.* to perforate the skull and take out a piece to relieve the brain from pressure or irritation [Surg.]. (Gr. *trepanon,* an auger.)
trepan, *n.* tre-*pan,* a snare; one who decoys others: *v.t.* to ensnare; to lure; to swindle. (Possibly connected with *trap,* to snare.)
trepanation, *n.* trep-a-*nay*-shon, the operation of trepanning [Surg.].
trepang, *n.* tre-*pang,* the sea-slug, or bêche-de-mer. (Malay.)
trepanner, *n.* tre-*pan*-ner, one who trepans.
trephination, *n.* tref-e-*nay*-shon, the operation of trephining [Surg.].
trephine, *n.* tre-*feen,* an improved form of trepan having an adjustable centre-pin [Surg.]: *v.t.* to perforate with a trephine. (Fr. *tréphine.*)
trepid, *a.* *trep*-id, trembling; quaking.
trepidation, *n.* *trep*-e-*day*-shon, an involuntary trembling; a quaking or quivering, esp. from fear or terror; a state of terror; agitation; a trembling of the limbs. (L. *trepidus.*)
trepidity, *n.* tre-*pid*-e-te, fearfulness; trepidation.
trespass, *n.* *tres*-pas, an act of trespassing; transgression; sin; any injury done to the person or property of another [Law]: *v.i.* to pass beyond; to enter unlawfully upon the land of another; to do any act that injures or annoys another [Law]; to intrude; to violate any known rule of duty; to sin. (L. *trans-,* and *pass.*)
trespasser, *n.* *tres*-pa-ser, one who trespasses; one who violates another's rights; a transgressor.
tress, *n.* tress, a long plait or curl of hair; a ringlet. (Gr. *tricha,* threefold.)
tressed, *a.* trest, arranged in or furnished with tresses.
tressure, *n.* *tresh*-ewr, a border running parallel with the sides of the shield [Her.]. (Fr., from *tresser,* plait.)
trestle, *n.* *tres*-sl, a movable frame for supporting anything, esp. a table-top or platform; a strong braced framework of timber, iron, etc., for supporting a bridge or viaduct. (O.Fr. *trestel.*)
trestle-table, *n.* a table-top supported on trestles.
trestle-tree, *n.* one of the strong timbers supporting the crosstrees [Naut.].
tret, *n.* tret, an allowance to purchasers for waste or refuse matter [Comm.]. (L. *traho,* draw.)
trevet, *n.* *trev*-et, a trivet.
trews, *n.pl.* trooz, tartan trousers, esp. those worn by Highland regiments.
trey, *n.* tray, the three at cards or dice. (Fr.)
trey-trip, *n.* *tray*-trip, a dicing game popular in the 17th century.
tri-, try, prefix signifying three. (L. and Gr.)
triable, *a.* *try*-a-bl, that may be subjected to trial or the cognizance of a court [Law]; that may be tested.
triableness, *n.* the being triable.
triacontahedral, *a.* try-a-*kon*-ta-*hee*-dral, of the form of a triacontahedron [Cryst.].
triacontahedron, *n.* try-a-*kon*-ta-*hee*-dron, a crystal or solid figure having thirty sides. (Gr. *triakonta,* thirty, *hedra,* a side.)
triactinal, *a.* try-*ak*-te-nal, having three rays, as the spicules of certain sponges. (*tri-,* and Gr. *aktis,* ray.)
triad, *n.* *try*-ad, the union of three; three united in or constituting one; a trinity; an element or radical having a valency of three [Chem.]; the common chord, consisting of a note sounded along with its third and fifth [Mus.]. (Gr.)
triadelphous, *a.* *try*-a-*del*-fus, with the stamens in three bundles [Bot.].
triadic, *a.* try-*ad*-ik, constituting or consisting of a triad; trivalent [Chem.].
triadism, *n.* *try*-a-dizm, the state of being threefold; any system based on a triad.
trial, *n.* *try*-al, any effort or exertion of strength for the purpose of ascertaining its effect; examination by a test; experiment; experience; suffering that tests virtue; temptation; the state of being tried; the judicial examination of a cause between parties [Law]. **on trial,** on approbation. **trial and error,** a method of checking or correcting by trying various alternatives and rejecting any resulting in failure. **trial at bar,** a trial before all the judges of the court, esp. the King's Bench. **trial balance,** the comparing of the total debits and credits in a ledger [Comm.]. **trial brief,** the short statement of a client's case prepared by the solicitor for the defending counsel [Law]. **trial marriage,** a companionate marriage; also, a proposed marriage legal for a stated period only. **trial trip,** a preliminary test, esp. of the speed and capacities of a ship, aeroplane, etc. (O.Fr.)
trialism, *n.* *try*-al-izm, the doctrine of the existence of body, soul, and spirit; a union of three states, esp. as opposed to dualism or a union of two.
trialogue, *n.* *try*-a-log, a talk, scene, etc., in which three persons take part. (Incorrect formation on supposed analogy of *dialogue.*)
triandrous, *a.* try-*an*-drus, having three stamens [Bot.].
triangle, *n.* *try*-ang-gl, a figure bounded by three lines, and containing three angles [Geom.]; a steel instrument of percussion in the form of an open triangle [Mus.]; a triangular framework to which defaulters were bound when flogged; three persons in a relationship in which two are more usual or convenient. **triangle of forces,** a triangle whose sides represent in magnitude and direction three forces in equilibrium. **the eternal triangle,** a husband and wife and the lover of one of them [Coll.]. (L. *triangulus,* three-cornered.)
triangular, *a.* try-*ang*-gew-lar, having three angles; in the form of a triangle. **triangular compasses,** compasses with three legs, used for transferring three points. **triangular numbers,** the series of numbers formed by the successive sums of the terms of an arithmetical progression, of which the common difference is 1.
triangularity, *n.* *try*-ang-gew-*la*-re-te, the property of being triangular.
triangularly, *ad.* after the form of a triangle.

triangulate, *v.t.* try-*ang*-gew-late, to divide up into triangles; to measure by triangles; to make triangular: *a.* having triangular markings [Zool.].
triangulately, *ad.* by triangulation.
triangulation, *n.* try-*ang*-gew-*lay*-shon, the use of a series of triangles in a trigonometrical survey.
triapsal, *a.* try-*ap*-sal, triapsidal.
triapsidal, *a.* try-*ap*-se-dal, having three apses [Arch.].
triarchy, *n.* *try*-ar-ke, government by three persons. (Gr. *tri-*, and *archē*, rule.)
Trias, *n.* *try*-as, the lowest group of Secondary rocks, the series of beds between the Jurassic and the Permian; New Red Sandstone [Geol.].
Triassic, *a.* try-*as*-ik, pertaining to the Trias.
triatic, *n.* try-*at*-ik, the stay from the foremast-head to the mainmasthead in schooner rig; the jumper stay [Naut.].
triatomic, *a.* try-a-*tom*-ik, having three atoms in the molecule [Chem.].
triaxial, *a.* try-*ak*-se-al, having three axes [Geom.].
tribade, *n.* *trib*-ad *or* tre-*bahd*, a homosexual woman. (Gr.)
tribadism, *n.* *try*-ba-dizm, the homosexual practices of tribades.
tribal, *a.* *try*-bal, belonging to a tribe.
tribalism, *n.* *try*-bal-izm, tribal government; the organization or manners of the tribe.
tribally, *ad.* *try*-ba-le, according to the tribe; by tribes.
tribasic, *a.* try-*bay*-sik, containing three equivalents of base to one of acid [Chem.].
tribe, *n.* tribe, a race or clan, descending from the same progenitor and having the same social, religious, and political institutions; a group of primitive or savage families under a headman; one of the ancient divisions of the Romans; a division or distinct class of a people; a number of plants or animals having qualities in common; a number of persons of any allied character or profession [Coll.]. (L. *tribus*, a third part of the Roman people.)
tribelet, *n.* *tribe*-let, a small tribe.
tribesman, *n.* *tribez*-man, a member of a tribe.
tribious, *a.* *trib*-e-us, pertaining to land, sea, and air. (On false analogy of *amphibious*, with Gr. *tri-*, three.)
triblet, *n.* *trib*-let, a mandrel or cylindrical rod used in making rings, nuts, tubes, etc. (Fr. *triboulet*.)
tribometer, *n.* try-*bom*-e-ter, an instrument for measuring the force of sliding friction [Mech.]. (Gr. *tribo*, rub, *metron*, measure.)
tribrach, *n.* *try*-brak, a poetic foot of three short syllables [Pros.]. (Gr. *tri-*, and *brachys*, short.)
tribrach, *n.* *try*-brak, a three-branched object. (Gr. *tri-*, and *brachion*, arm.)
tribrachial, *a.* try-*brak*-e-al, having three arms or branches.
tribrachic, *a.* try-*brak*-ik, consisting of tribrachs or three short syllables [Pros.].
tribracteate, *a.* try-*brak*-te-at, having three bracts [Bot.].
tribulation, *n.* trib-yew-*lay*-shon, severe affliction; distress; vexation. (L. *tribulatio*, distress.)
tribunal, *n.* tre-*bew*-nal, a court of justice; a judgment seat; the bench serving as seat for judges; a statutory or official body that decides on claims or determines causes. (L. *tribunal*.)
tribunate, *n.* *trib*-yew-nate, tribuneship; government by tribunes.
tribune, *n.* *trib*-yewn, an ancient Roman official selected by the people to defend their liberties; any defender of popular liberties. (L. *tribunus*.)
tribune, *n.* *trib*-yewn, the raised platform, also the apse, at the end of a Roman basilica; a bishop's throne in a basilican church; a platform or rostrum for speakers in an assembly. (Fr., from L. *tribunal*.)
tribuneship, *n.* the office, or period of office, of a tribune.
tribunician, *a.* *trib*-yew-*nish*-an, tribunitial.
tribunitial, *a.* *trib*-yew-*nish*-al, pertaining to tribunes or the tribune; demagogic.
tribunitian, *a.* *trib*-yew-*nish*-an, tribunitial.
tributarily, *ad.* *trib*-yew-ta-re-le, in a tributary manner.
tributariness, *n.* *trib*-yew-ta-re-ness, the state or condition of being tributary.
tributary, *a.* *trib*-yew-ta-re, paying tribute; subordinate; paid in tribute; yielding supplies of anything: *n.* one who or a state that pays tribute; a stream contributing water to another. (L. *tributarius*.)
tribute, *n.* *trib*-yewt, a periodical sum paid by one nation to another; obligation to contribute; a personal contribution; an offering as a mark of respect; a share of ore allotted to a miner in lieu of wages. (L. *tributum*, from *tribuo*, give.)
tributer, *n.* *trib*-yew-ter, a miner paid by the mine-owner according to the value of the ore he raises.
tricapsular, *a.* try-*kap*-sew-lar, having three capsules [Bot.].
tricar, *n.* *try*-kar, a three-wheeled motor-car with a single driving-wheel at the rear.
tricarpous, *a.* try-*kar*-pus, having three carpels [Bot.].
trice, *v.t.* trice, to haul and tie up by means of a small rope [Naut.].
trice, *n.* trice, a very short time; an instant. (Origin uncertain.)
tricennial, *a.* try-*sen*-ne-al, pertaining to thirty years; occurring every thirty years. (L. *tricennium*, thirty years.)
tricentenary, *a.* and *n.* try-*sen*-te-na-re *or* try-sen-*tee*-na-re, tercentenary.
tricephalous, *a.* try-*sef*-a-lus, having three heads. (L. *tri-*, and Gr. *kephale*, head.)
triceps, *n.* *try*-seps, a three-headed muscle; the extensor muscle of the forearm [Anat.]. (L. *tri-*, and *caput*, the head.)
Triceratops, *n.* try-*se*-ra-tops, a genus of gigantic extinct herbivorous dinosaurs of N. America. (Gr. *trikeratos*, three-horned.)
trichiasis, *n.* tre-*ky*-a-sis, introversion of the eyelashes; kidney disease in which hair-like bodies are present in the urine [Med.]. (Gr. *thrix*, *trichos*, hair.)
trichina, *n.* tre-*ky*-na (*pl.* **trichinæ**), a nematoid parasitic worm infesting man, swine, and other animals. (Gr. *trichos*, hair.)
trichiniasis, *n.* trik-e-*ny*-a-sis, trichinosis.
trichinization, *n.* *trik*-e-ny-*zay*-shon, infection with trichinæ.
trichinized, *a.* *trik*-e-nyzd, affected with trichinæ (esp. of pork).
trichinosis, *n.* trik-e-*noh*-sis, a disease due to the presence in the muscles of larvæ of trichinæ.
trichinotic, *a.* trik-e-*not*-ik, trichinous.
trichinous, *a.* *trik*-e-nus, pertaining to or infested with trichinæ.
trichite, *n.* *trik*-ite, a minute hair-like crystal occurring in certain igneous rocks; a hair-like spicule in certain sponges.
trichiurid, *n.* trik-e-*yew*-rid, any of a group of marine band-like fishes with whip-like tails, including the scabbard-fish, etc.
trichocarpous, *a.* trik-o-*kar*-pus, having hairy fruit [Bot.].
trichocephaliasis, *n.* *trik*-o-sef-a-*ly*-a-sis, the condition of being infested with thread-worms [Path.].
Trichocephalus, *n.* trik-o-*sef*-a-lus, a genus of nematode parasitic worms, one of which infests the human intestinal canal. (Gr. *trichos*, hair, *kephale*, the head.)
trichoclasia, *n.* trik-o-*klay*-ze-a, a brittle condition of the hair. (Gr. *trichos*, hair, *klasis*, fracture.)
trichogenous, *a.* tre-*koj*-e-nus, producing hairs; stimulating the growth of hair.
trichologist, *n.* tre-*kol*-o-jist, one specializing in the diseases of the hair.
trichology, *n.* tre-*kol*-o-je, the study of the hair and its diseases.
trichoma, *n.* tre-*koh*-ma, plica, or other hair affection; any filamentous part or member [Bot.].
trichomatose, *a.* tre-*koh*-ma-toze, affected with plica; matted together.
trichopathic, trik-o-*path*-ik, pertaining to disease of the hair.
trichophyllous, *a.* trik-o-*fil*-us, having hair-like leaves [Bot.].
trichophytosis, *n.* *trik*-o-fy-*toh*-sis, a contagious fungoid disease of the skin and hair; ringworm.
trichopter, *n.pl.* tre-*kop*-ter, a member of the Trichoptera, a group of insects containing the caddis flies. (Gr. *thrix*, and *pteron*, a wing.)
trichord, *a.* *try*-kawrd, having three strings, esp. (of pianos) to each note; *n.* a three-stringed lyre; a trichord pianoforte. (Gr.)

trichosis, *n.* tre-*koh*-sis, trichiasis, trichoma, or other hair-disease.
trichotomous, *a.* tre-*kot*-o-mus, forking into three branches [Bot.]; of the nature of trichotomy [Theol.]
trichotomy, *n.* tre-*kot*-o-me, division into three parts; the threefold nature (body, soul, and spirit) of man [Theol.]. (Gr. *tricha*, and *tome*, cutting.)
trichroic, *a.* try-*kroh*-ik, possessing or pertaining to trichroism.
trichroism, *n.* *try*-kro-izm, the property of presenting three different colours. (Gr. *treis*, and *chroas*, tint.)
trichromatic, *a.* *try*-kro-*mat*-ik, pertaining to, having, or using three colours. (Gr. *treis*, three, *chroma*, colour.)
trichromatism, *n.* try-*kroh*-ma-tizm, the quality of being trichromatic; the use of three colours.
tricipital, *a.* try-*sip*-e-tal, pertaining to the triceps [Anat.].
★**trick,** *n.* trik, an artifice for the purpose of deception; a fraudulent contrivance; deception; a dextrous artifice; a vicious practice; legerdemain; a round of cards; a particular habit; a steersman's spell of duty [Naut.]: *v.t.* to deceive; to cheat; to dress; to decorate; to adorn fantastically; to delineate a coat of arms: *v.i.* to live by or practise trickery. **do the trick,** to succeed or be effective; to suffice. **dirty trick,** a mean or treacherous action. **trick out,** to adorn, to set off. (Perhaps O.Fr. *triche*, treachery.)
tricker, *n.* *trik*-er, a trickster; one who tricks an heraldic coat.
trickery, *n.* *trik*-er-re, cheating; artifice; knavery.
trickily, *ad.* in a tricky manner.
trickiness, *n.* state of being tricky; artfulness; intricacy.
trickish, *a.* *trik*-ish, given to tricks; artful; deceptive; knavish.
trickishly, *ad.* in a trickish manner.
trickishness, *n.* the quality of being trickish.
trickle, *v.i.* *trik*-kl, to flow in a small, gentle stream, or down in drops: *n.* a small flow; a thin broken stream. (Origin doubtful.)
trickly, *a.* *trik*-le, trickling.
tricksome, *a.* *trik*-sum, given to tricks.
trickster, *n.* *trik*-ster, one who practises trickery or low cunning; a sharper.
tricksy, *a.* *trik*-se, full of tricks; playful; artful.
trick-track, *n.* *trik*-trak, tric-trac.
tricky, *a.* *trik*-e, inclined to tricks; shifty; dodgy; of an intricate or complex nature.
triclinate, *a.* *try*-kle-nat, triclinic [Cryst.]. (Gr. *tri-*, and *klino*, bend.)
triclinic, *a.* try-*klin*-ik, scalene; with the three axes unequal and obliquely inclined to one another [Cryst.].
triclinium, *n.* try-*klin*-e-um, a couch running round three sides of a table for reclining on at meals, each division usually for three persons; a Roman dining-hall. (Gr. *triklinion.*)
tricoccous, *a.* try-*kok*-us, having a three-grained capsule swelling out in three protuberances [Bot.]. (Gr. *tri-*, and *kokkus*, a berry.)
tricolour, *n.* *try*-kul-ur, a national flag of three colours, esp. that of France since 1794 of blue, white, and red in nearly equal vertical stripes. (Fr. *tricolore.*)
tricoloured, *a.* *try*-kul-urd, having three colours (esp. of flags).
triconsonantal, *a.* *try*-kon-so-*nan*-tal, with three consonants.
tricorn, *a.* *try*-kawrn, with three horns, points, or corners; a three-cornered cocked hat. (L. *tri-*, and *cornu*, a horn.)
tricorporal. *a.* try-*kawr*-po-ral, having three bodies.
tricorporate, *a.* try-*kawr*-po-rate, tricorporal. (L. *corpus*, a body.)
tricostate, *a.* try-*kos*-tat, having three ribs.
tricot, *n.* *tree*-koh, a dress material actually or apparently knitted; a special style of knitting. **tricot stitch,** a simple crochet stitch. (Fr.)
tricotine, *n.* *trik*-o-teen, a twilled woollen cloth.
tricrotic, *a.* try-*krot*-ik, having a triple beat (of the pulse) [Phys.]. (Gr. *tri-*, and *krotos*, a sound made by striking.)
tric-trac, *n.* *trik*-trak, backgammon, or a game resembling this. (Fr.)
tricuspid, *a.* try-*kus*-pid, having three points or cusps: *n.* a tooth having three cusps. (L. *cuspis*, a point.)
tricycle, *n.* *try*-sikl, a cycle with three wheels: *v.i.* to go by tricycle.
tricyclist, *n.* *try*-se-klist, one who rides a tricycle.
Tridacna, *n.* try-*dak*-na, a genus of marine bivalve molluscs including the giant clam, *T. gigas*, which has been known to attain a weight of over 500 lb. (Gr. *tridaknos*, eaten at three bites.)
tridactyl, *a.* try-*dak*-til, tridactylous.
tridactylous, *a.* try-*dak*-te-lus, having three toes or fingers. (Gr. *dactylos*, a finger or toe.)
tride, *a.* tride, short and fleet (of the pace of horses). (Fr.)
trident, *n.* *try*-dent, a three-pronged spear, used esp. by fishermen and represented in the hands of Neptune, as god of the sea; hence a symbol of maritime power: *a.* having three teeth or prongs. (L. *tridens*, three-pronged.)
tridentate, *a.* try-*den*-tat, having three teeth.
Tridentine, *a.* try-*den*-tin, pertaining to the Council of Trent (1545–63), or to the Rom. Cath. doctrine formulated thereat: *n.* an orthodox Roman Catholic. (L. *Tridentum*, Trent.)
tridiapason, *n.* try-dy-a-*pay*-zon, a triple octave [Mus.].
tridigitate, *a.* try-*dij*-e-tat, having three fingers or toes.
tridimensional, *a.* try-dy-*men*-shon-al, having three dimensions.
triduan, *a.* *try*-dew-an, lasting for three days; happening every third day. (L.)
triduum, *n.* *try*-*dew*-um, a period of three days; a religious service extending over three days. (L.)
tridymite, *n.* *trid*-e-mite, a form of silica crystallizing in the anorthic system.
tried, *a.* tride, tested; trustworthy. (*pp.* of *try.*)
triennial, *a.* try-*en*-e-al, continuing three years; happening every three years. (L. *triennium*, three years.)
triennially, *ad.* every three years.
triennium, *n.* try-*en*-e-um, a period of three years. (L.)
trier, *n.* *try*-er, one who tries, attempts, or makes tests; a judge who tries a person or cause; one appointed to examine whether a challenge to a panel of jurors is valid [Law]; a test.
trierarch, *n.* *try*-er-ark, the captain of a trireme.
trierarchy, *n.* try-er-*ark*-e, the office of trierarch; the Athenian system of forced levies for the maintenance and equipment of triremes.
trifacial, *a.* try-*faysh*-al, designating the trigeminal nerve.
trifarious, *a.* try-*fare*-re-us, facing three ways. (L.)
trifid, *a.* *try*-fid, three-cleft [Bot.]. (L. *findo*, cleave.)
trifle, *n.* *try*-fl, a thing of very little value or importance; sponge cake soaked in custard: *v.i.* to act or talk with levity; to indulge in light amusements; to waste time. **trifle with,** to play the fool with; to spend in vanity. (O.Fr.)
trifler, *n.* *try*-fler, one who trifles; a frivol; a potterer.
trifling, *a.* *try*-fling, of small value or importance.
triflingly, *ad.* in a trifling manner.
triflingness, *n.* the state of being trifling.
triflorous, *a.* try-*flaw*-rus, bearing three flowers.
trifoliate, *a.* try-*foh*-le-at, having three leaves; ternate. (L. *tri-*, and *folium*, a leaf.)
trifoliolate, *a.* try-*foh*-le-o-lat, having or consisting of three leaflets [Bot.].
Trifolium, *n.* try-*foh*-le-um, the large genus of leguminous fodder-plants including the clovers and trefoils. (L. *tri-*, and *folium*, leaf.)
triforium, *n.* try-*faw*-re-um, an arcaded gallery below a clerestory. (L. *tri-*, and *fores*, a door.)
triform, *a.* *try*-form, having a triple form.
trifurcated, *a.* *try*-fer-kay-ted, having three branches or forks. (L. *trifurcus*, three-forked.)
trig, *n.* trig, a skid or sprag for a wheel: *v.t.* to check or stop with a trig. (Origin uncertain.)
trig, *a.* trig, trim; neat. (Scand.)
trigamist, *n.* *trig*-a-mist, one guilty of trigamy.
trigamous, *a.* *trig*-a-mus, pertaining to trigamy; having male, female, and hermaphrodite flowers in the same head [Bot.].
trigamy, *n.* *trig*-a-me, state of having three husbands or wives at the same time; the crime of marrying two others during the life of the legal spouse [Law]. (Gr. *tri-*, and *gamos*, marriage.)

trigeminal, *a.* try-*jem*-e-nal, triple, branching into three; pertaining to the trifacial or fifth pair of cranial nerves [Anat.]: *n.* the trigeminal nerve. (L. *tri-*, and *geminus*, born at one birth.)

trigger, *n.* *trig*-er, a lever by which a detent is released, esp. the catch of a fire-arm, cross-bow, etc., which, when pulled, looses the lock or cord. **trigger fish,** the marine fish, *Balistes maculatus*, so called from the second of the three spines in its anterior dorsal fin. (Dut. *trekker*.)

triglot, *a.* *try*-glot, written in three languages. (Gr. *tri-*, and *glōtta*, tongue.)

triglyph, *n.* *try*-glif *or* *trig*-lif, the three-grooved ornament in the Doric frieze, repeated at equal intervals. (Gr. *tri-*, and *glypho*, hollow, carve.)

triglyphic, *a.* try-*glif*-ik, pertaining to or consisting of triglyphs.

trigon, *n.* *try*-gon, a triangle; any of the four groups of three into which the signs of the zodiac are divided [Astrol.]; a trigonon. (Gr. *tri-*, and *gonia*, an angle.)

trigonal, *a.* *trig*-o-nal, triangular; three-cornered.

trigoneutic, *a.* try-*go-new*-tik, producing three broods in a year [Entom.]. (Gr.)

trigonic, *a.* try-*gon*-ik, pertaining to a triangle.

trigonometer, *n.* trig-o-*nom*-e-ter, an instrument for solving plane right-angled triangles graphically.

trigonometric, *a.* *trig*-o-no-*met*-rik, trigonometrical.

trigonometrical, *a.* *trig*-o-no-*met*-re-kal, pertaining to trigonometry; performed by or according to the rules of trigonometry.

trigonometrically, *ad.* by or according to trigonometry.

trigonometry, *n.* *trig*-o-*nom*-e-tre, the science of the mensural relationship between the sides and angles of triangles, and of the measurement of required parts by deduction from parts which are given. (Gr. *trigonon*, a triangle, *metron*, measure.)

trigonon, *n.* tre-*goh*-non, an ancient triangular lyre or harp.

trigonous, *a.* *trig*-o-nus, trigonal; three-angled.

trigram, *n.* *try*-gram, an inscription or combination of three letters; incorrectly, a trigraph. (Gr. *tri-*, and *gramma*, a letter.)

trigrammatic, *a.* *try*-gra-*mat*-ik, triliteral.

trigraph, *n.* *try*-graf, three letters sounded as one; a triphthong. (Gr. *tri-*, and *grapho*, write.)

trigynian, *a.* try-*jin*-e-an, belonging to the group of plants having three pistils. (Gr.)

trigynous, *a.* *trij*-e-nus, having three pistils [Bot.].

trihedral, *a.* try-*hee*-dral, having three equal sides.

trihedron, *n.* try-*hee*-dron a figure having three equal sides. (Gr. *tri-*, and *hedra*, a side.)

trijugate, *a.* *try*-ju-gate *or* try-*joo*-gate, trijugous.

trijugous, *a.* *try*-ju-gus *or* try-*joo*-gus, having three pairs of leaflets [Bot.]. (L. *tri-*, and *jugum*, a yoke.)

trike, *n.* trike, a tricycle: *v.i.* to ride a tricycle [Coll.].

trilabiate, *a.* try-*lay*-be-at, three-lipped [Bot.]. (*tri-*, and L. *labium*, lip.)

trilateral, *a.* try-*lat*-er-ral, having three sides.

trilby, *n.* *tril*-be, a soft felt hat of a particular shape. **trilbies,** the feet [Slang]. (Du Maurier's story, *Trilby*, 1894.)

trilemma, *n.* try-*lem*-ma, a choice between three alternatives [Logic].

trilinear, *a.* try-*lin*-e-ar, having three lines.

trilingual, *a.* try-*ling*-gwal, using or consisting of three languages. (L. *trilinguis*, triple-tongued.)

triliteral, *a.* try-*lit*-er-ral, consisting of or using three letters: *n.* a word consisting of three letters. (L. *tri-*, and *litera*, a letter.)

trilith, *n.* *try*-lith, a trilithon.

trilithon, *n.* *try*-le-thon, a prehistoric monument consisting of two large upright stones surmounted by a third as lintel. (Gr. *tri-*, and *lithos*, a stone.)

trill, *n.* tril, a quaver; a shake of the voice in singing or playing: *v.t.* to utter with a quavering or tremulousness of voice; to sing: *v.i.* to flow in a small stream, or in drops rapidly succeeding each other; to trickle; to shake or quaver. (Imit.)

trillion, *n.* *tril*-yon, the product of a million involved to the third power (expressed by a unit followed by 18 ciphers); in America and France a million times a million (a unit with 12 ciphers). (It.)

trilobate, *a.* try-*loh*-bat, having three lobes.

trilobed, *a.* *try*-lohbd, trilobate.

trilobite, *n.* *try*-lo-bite, a Palæozoic marine arthropod having the body divided into one median and three lateral lobes.

trilocular, *a.* try-*lok*-yew-lar, three-celled [Bot.].

trilogist, *n.* *tril*-o-jist, the author of a trilogy.

trilogy, *n.* *tril*-o-je, a series of three literary or operatic works, esp. tragedies, bearing relation to each other as parts of one historical picture. (Gr. *tri-*, and *logos*, word.)

trim, *a.* trim, firm; compact; tight; in good order: *n.* condition; dress; equipment; condition of being balanced; the state of a vessel or her cargo when ready to sail; state of buoyancy of a submarine: *v.t.* to put in due order; to adjust; to dress; to clip, lop, smooth, or shave; to make neat; to adjust the load of a boat or ship; to set suitable sails in an efficient way; to rebuke or reprove sharply [Coll.]: *v.i.* to fluctuate between parties, so as to seem to favour each. (A.S. *trymian*, set firm or in order.)

trimensual, *a.* try-*men*-sew-al, every three months; quarterly.

trimerous, *a.* *try*-mer-rus, having three parts, segments, or joints [Bot. and Entom.]. (Gr. *tri-* and *meros*, a part.)

trimester, *n.* try-*mes*-ter, a term or period of three months. (L. *tri-*, and *mensis*, a month.)

trimestrial, *a.* try-*mes*-tre-al, trimensual.

trimeter, *n.* *trim*-e-ter, a verse consisting of three measures of two feet each: *a.* consisting of three measures [Pros.].

trimetric, *a.* try-*met*-rik, having three unequal axes intersecting at right angles [Cryst.]; trimeter [Pros.].

trimly, *ad.* *trim*-le, nicely; neatly; in good order.

trimmer, *n.* *trim*-er, one who trims (in any sense); an appliance for trimming; a time-server; a corrupt or venal politician; a cross joist; a flat fishing float.

trimming, *n.* *trim*-ming, a fluctuating between parties; a scolding [Coll.]: *pl.* pieces trimmed off, clippings; anything additional, esp. non-essential or ornamental appendages; concomitants to a joint or main dish [Coll.].

trimness, *n.* neatness; state of being in good order.

trimorphic, *a.* try-*mor*-fik, existing in three forms.

trimorphism, *n.* try-*mor*-fizm, the property of crystallizing or of existing in three distinct forms.

trimorphous, *a.* try-*mor*-fus, characterized by trimorphism; trimorphic.

Trimurti, *n.* tre-*moor*-te, the triad of Hindu gods —Brahma, the Creator, Vishnu, the Preserver, and Siva, the Destroyer. (Hind.)

Trinacrian, *a.* try-*nay*-kre-an, Sicilian. (*Trinacria*, an old name of Sicily.)

trinacriform, *a.* try-*nak*-re-form, having three prongs. (Gr. *tri-*, *akra*, a point, and *form*.)

trinal, *a.* *try*-nal, three-fold. (L. *trinus*.)

trinary, *a.* *try*-na-re, ternary: *n.* a triad. (L. *trinus*.)

trine, *a.* trine, threefold; in trine [Astrol.]: *n.* a triad; the aspect or planets distant from each other a third of a circle or 120° [Astrol.]; (*cap.*) the Trinity: *a.* being in trine [Astrol.].

trinervate, *a.* try-*ner*-vat, having three unbranched nerves or ribs extending from the base [Bot.].

Tringa, *n.* *tring*-ga, a genus of sandpipers including the stint and the dunlin. (L.)

tringine, *a.* *trin*-jine, pertaining to or resembling the sandpipers [Ornith.] (*Tringa*.)

tringle, *n.* *tring*-gl, a curtain rod; a small rectangular member or ornament [Arch.].

Trinitarian, *a.* *trin*-e-*tare*-re-an, pertaining to the Trinity or Trinitarianism; belonging to the Order of the Holy Trinity; (*l.c.*) triple: *n.* a believer in the Trinity; a member of the Order of the Holy Trinity.

Trinitarianism, *n.* trin-e-*tare*-re-a-nizm, the doctrine of the Holy Trinity.

trinitrotoluol, *n.* *try*-ny-tro-*tol*-yew-*ol*, a high explosive obtained by the action of nitric acid on toluene; "T.N.T."

Trinity, *n.* *trin*-e-te, the union of three persons in one Godhead—the Father, Son, and Holy Ghost [Theol.]; a symbolic representation of the Trinity; (*l.c.*) any triad; the state of being three. **Order of the Holy Trinity,** the Order of Redemptionists. **Trinity House,** a corporation administering the lighthouse service of England and Wales and being the chief Pilotage Authority

in England and Wales. **Trinity Sunday,** the Sunday next after Whit-Sunday. (L. *trinus*, threefold.)
trinket, *n.* *tring*-ket, a small ornament, as a jewel, ring, or bracelet; a thing of little value. (O.Fr.)
trinketry, *n.* *tring*-ket-re, trinkets collectively.
trinoctial, *a.* try-*nok*-shal, lasting three nights.
trinodal, *a.* try-*noh*-dal, having three joints.
trinomial, *a.* try-*noh*-me-al, having three names or terms; consisting of three terms connected by the signs *plus* or *minus*: *n.* a trinomial quantity [Math.]. (L. *tri-*, and *nomen*, a name.)
trinomialism, *n.* try-*noh*-me-a-lizm, the use of three terms in systematic classification [Biol., Chem., etc.].
trio, *n.* *tree*-oh, three united; a composition for three or in three parts [Mus.]. (It.)
trioctahedral, *a.* try-ok-ta-*hee*-dral, presenting three ranges of faces, one above another, each range containing eight faces [Cryst.].
triode, *n.* *try*-ode, a three-electrode valve [Wire.]. (Gr. *tri-*, and *hodos*, path.)
triœcious, *a.* try-*ee*-she-us, designating plants which, on different individuals, produce male, female, and hermaphrodite flowers. (Gr. *tri-*, and *oikos*, house.)
triolet, *n.* *tree*-o-let, a stanza of eight lines on two rhymes, one of which is used in the second, sixth and eighth lines and the other in the rest. (*trio*.)
trional, *n.* *try*-o-nal, proprietary name of a synthetic drug allied to sulphonal, and similarly used.
trionym, *n.* *try*-o-nim, a name (in scientific classification) consisting of three terms.
tri-oxide, *n.* an oxide having three atoms in the molecule.
trip, *n.* trip, a light short step; a brief journey or voyage; an excursion; a stroke or catch by which a wrestler supplants his antagonist; a false step; a stumble; a mistake; a slight error arising from haste; a single reach in tacking to windward [Naut.]: *v.i.* to run or step lightly; to stumble; to strike the foot against something so as to stumble or fall; to err; to fail; *v.t.* to cause to fall by catching the feet suddenly; to overthrow; to catch; to detect. **trip the anchor,** to raise it from the bottom so that it hangs free. **trip a yard,** to bring it to the perpendicular preparatory to lowering [Naut.]. (M.E. *trippen*, probably Teut.)
tripartite, *a.* try-*par-* *or* *trip*-ar-tite, divided into three parts; having three corresponding parts; pertaining to three parties [Polit.]. (L. *tripartitus*, three-fold.)
tripartition, *n.* try-par- *or* trip-ar-*tish*-on, a division by three or into three.
tripe, *n.* tripe, entrails; the paunch and smaller reticulum of ruminants, esp. oxen, prepared for food; rubbishy matter or trash of any kind [Slang]. (O.Fr.)
tripedal, *a.* try-*pee*-dal *or* *trip*-e-dal, having three feet.
tripe-de-roche, *n.* *treep*-de-rohsh, an arctic lichen, *Gyrophora cylindrica*, used as food. (Fr., rock-tripe.)
tripe-man, *n.* a seller of tripe.
tripennate, *a.* try-*pen*-at, tripinnate.
tripersonal, *a.* try-*per*-so-nal, consisting of three persons in one.
tripersonality, *n.* try-per-so-*nal*-e-te, the state of being tripersonal.
tripery, *n.* *try*-pe-re, a place where tripe is prepared; a tripe-shop.
tripetalous, *a.* try-*pet*-a-lus, having three petals.
trip-hammer, *n.* a heavy hammer worked by power.
triphane, *n.* *try*-fane, the mineral spodumene.
triphibian, *a.* try-*fib*-e-an, adapted to or using land, sea, and air (esp. militarily). (On false analogy of *amphibian*, with Gr. *tri-*, three.)
triphibious, *a.* try-*fib*-e-us, tribious (of military operations carried out simultaneously by land, sea, and air forces).
triphthong, *n.* *trif*-thong, a group of three vowels in one compound sound, as *ieu* in "adieu." (Gr. *tri-*, and *phthongos*, sound.)
triphthongal, *a.* trif-*thong*-gal, pertaining to or consisting of a triphthong.
triphyline, *n.* *trif*-e-leen, a mineral composed of the phosphates of lithia, manganese, and iron.
triphyllous, *a.* try-*fil*-us, three-leaved [Bot.]. (Gr. *tri-*, and *phyllon*, a leaf.)
tripinnate, *a.* try-*pin*-at, thrice pinnate [Bot.].
triplane, *n.* *try*-plane, an aeroplane with three main planes superimposed one above another.
triple, *a.* *trip*-pl, three-fold, consisting of three united; treble: *n.* thrice as much or as many; a triad: *v.t.* and *i.* to treble. **triple crown,** the papal tiara. **triple expansion,** the method of using steam in three cylinders of a compound engine successively. **triple rhyme,** a three-syllabled rhyme, as "ejaculate . . . immaculate." **triple time,** time in which the bars are divisible into three equal parts [Mus.]. (Fr.)
triple-crowned, *a.* having three crowns (of the Pope).
triplet, *n.* *trip*-let, a group of three; one of three at a birth; three verses rhyming together; three notes sung or played in the time of two [Mus.].
triplex, *a.* *trip*-leks, threefold; of triple action or effect: *n.* triple time [Mus.]. **triplex glass,** proprietary name of a make of unsplinterable glass. (L. *tri-*, and *plico*, fold.)
triplicate, *a.* *trip*-le-kat, made thrice as much; three-fold: *n.* a third thing corresponding to two others of the same kind: *v.t.* to treble; to make two copies of one original. **triplicate ratio,** the ratio of cubes to each other [Math.].
triplication, *n.* trip-le-*kay*-shon, the act of trebling or making threefold; surrejoinder [Law].
triplicative, *a.* *trip*-le-kay-tiv, making triple; having the property of tripling.
triplicity, *n.* tre-*plis*-e-te, the state of being threefold; a trigon [Astrol.].
triplopia, *n.* trip-*loh*-pe-a, a form of multiple vision in which one object appears as three.
triply, *ad.* *trip*-le, thrice as much or as many; in three ways; threefold.
tripod, *n.* *try*-pod, a three-legged stand or support for anything; a stool, pot, etc., on three legs; the seat over the altar at Delphi on which the priestess of Apollo and the sibyls were placed to deliver oracles. (L. *tripus*, three footed.)
tripodal, *a.* try-*poh*-dal, having three legs; in tripod form.
tripoli, *n.* *trip*-o-le, infusorial earth or kieselguhr, used in polishing. (Originally from Tripoli.)
Tripolitan, *a.* tre-*pol*-e-tan, pertaining to Tripoli: *n.* a native of Tripoli.
tripos, *n.* *try*-pos, at Cambridge, the final examination for honours; the list of successful candidates. (L. *tripus*, tripod.)
trippant, *a.* *trip*-ant, walking, with one foreleg raised from the ground [Her.].
tripper, *n.* *trip*-er, one who trips (in any sense); a tripping device; an excursionist [Coll.].
tripping, *a.* quick; nimble: *n.* the act of tripping.
trippingly, *ad.* in a tripping manner.
tripstick, *n.* *trip*-stik, the stick used in the game of knur-and-spell, a trap-stick.
triptote, *n.* *trip*-tote, a noun having three cases only [Gram.]. (Gr. *tri-*, and *ptosis*, a case.)
triptych, *n.* *trip*-tik, a set of three tablets, hinged together, and capable of being folded, each painted with a distinct subject, as seen in altar-pieces; a writing tablet in three parts; a triptyque. (Gr. *triptychos*, threefold.)
triptyque, *n.* trip-*teek*, a customs pass (in 3-fold form) allowing temporary importation of a motor-car into a country, esp. for touring. (Fr., as *triptych*.)
tripudiary, *a.* try-*pew*-de-a-re, designating divination from the actions of the sacred chickens (of ancient Rome) when fed; hence (formerly), dancing. (L. *tripudium*, a religious dance.)
tripy, *a.* *try*-pe, resembling tripe; trashy [Slang].
triquetrous, *a.* try-*kwet*-rus, three-cornered; having a triangular cross-section. (L. *triquetrus*, three-cornered.)
triradial, *a.* try-*ray*-de-al, triradiate.
triradiate, *a.* try-*ray*-de-ate, having three rays or radiating branches [Bot. and Zool.].
trireme, *n.* *try*-reem, a galley with three tiers of oars. (L. *triremis*, having three banks of oars)
trisacramentarian, *n.* try-*sak*-ra-men-*tare*-re-an, one who admits of three sacraments (baptism, the eucharist, penance), and no more.
Trisagion, *n.* try-*say*-je-on, in the Greek Church, the Ter-sanctis; a hymn in which the word holy is repeated three times. (Gr. *trisagios*, thrice holy.)

trisect, *v.t.* try-*sekt*, to cut or divide into three equal parts. (L. *tri-*, and *seco*, cut.)
trisection, *n.* try-*sek*-shon, division into three equal parts.
trisepalous, *a.* try-*sep*-a-lus, having three sepals.
triserial, *a.* try-*seer*-re-al, arranged in three rows or series [Bot.].
triskele, *n.* *tris*-keel, an ancient emblem consisting of three branches, or legs bent at the knee, radiating from a common centre. (Gr. *triskelēs*, three-legged.)
triskelion, *n.* tris-*kel*-e-on, a triskele representing three conjoined human legs—the emblem of the Isle of Man.
Trismegistus, *n.* *tris*-me-*jis*-tus, the Thrice-great. (Gr. name of Thoth, the Egyptian Hermes, the fountain of mysticism and magic.)
trismus, *n.* *triz*-mus, a condition of tetanic spasm of the jaw muscles; lock-jaw [Med.]. (Gr. *trismos*, a grinding of the teeth.)
trisoctahedron, *n.* *tris*-ok-ta-*hee*-dron, a solid bounded by twenty-four equal faces.
trispermous, *a.* try-*sper*-mus, three-seeded [Bot.]. (Gr. *tri-*, and *sperma*, seed.)
trisplanchnic, *a.* try-*splank*-nik, pertaining to the three splanchnic nerves [Anat.].
tristachyous, *a.* try-*stay*-ke-us, having three spikes [Bot.].
triste, *a.* treest, sad; not happy. (Fr.)
tristesse, *n.* trees-*tess*, sadness; melancholy. (Fr.)
tristful, *a.* *trist*-ful, sorrowful.
tristich, *n.* *tris*-tik, a group or stanza of three lines. (Gr. *tris*, thrice, *stichos*, row.)
tristichous, *a.* *tris*-te-kus, in three ranks [Bot.].
tristigmatic, *a.* try-stig-*mat*-ik, having three stigmas [Bot.].
trisulcate, *a.* try-*sul*-kat, having three grooves or channels [Bot.]. (*tri-* and *sulcate*.)
trisyllable, *n.* try- *or* tre-*sil*-a-bl, a word of three syllables.
trisyllabic, *a.* try-se-*lab*-ik, consisting of three syllables.
tritagonist, *n.* try-*tag*-o-nist, the third actor in a Greek tragedy. (Gr. *tri-*, and *agonistes*, contender.)
trite, *a.* trite, hackneyed; used too much; common; so common as to have lost all novelty and interest. (L. *tritus*, rubbed.)
tritely, *ad.* *trite*-le, in a trite manner.
triteness, *n.* *trite*-ness, the quality of being trite.
triternate, *a.* try-*ter*-nat, three times ternate, *i.e.*, having twenty-seven leaflets; trebly divided (of leaves) [Bot.].
tritheism, *n.* *try*-thee-izm, the doctrine or belief that the three Persons of the Trinity are three distinct Gods. (Gr. *tri-*, and *theos*, God.)
tritheist, *n.* *try*-the-ist, an adherent of tritheism.
tritheistic, *a.* *try*-the-*is*-tik, pertaining to tritheism.
tritical, *a.* *trit*-e-kal, commonplace; trite.
triticism, *n.* *trit*-e-sizm, a trite remark.
triticoid, *a.* *trit*-e-koyd, resembling wheat. (L. *triticum*.)
Triticum, *n.* *trit*-e-kum, the genus of cereal grasses including wheat. (L.)
tritoma, *n.* tre-*toh*-ma, the garden plant *Kniphofia uvaria*, the torch lily or red-hot poker.
Triton, *n.* *try*-ton, a marine demi-god, the son and trumpeter of Neptune, represented as half man, half fish, blowing a large spiral shell [Gr. Myth.]; a genus of molluscs including the trumpet-shell; the genus of amphibians including the newts; (*l.c.*) a newt. (Gr.)
tritone, *n.* *try*-tone, an interval of three whole tones [Mus.].
tritubercular, *a.* *try*-tew-*ber*-kew-lar, tricuspid (of teeth).
triturable, *a.* *trit*-yew-ra-bl, capable of being powdered or triturated.
tritural, *a.* *trit*-yew-ral, adapted for grinding [Zool.].
triturate, *v.t.* *trit*-yew-rate, to rub or grind to a very fine powder; to grind, pound, or pulverize thoroughly. (L. *trituratus*, thrashed.)
trituration, *n.* trit-yew-*ray*-shon, act of triturating.
triturator, *n.* *trit*-yew-ray-tor, an instrument for triturating; one who triturates.
triumph, *n.* *try*-umf, state of being victorious; victory; conquest; joy or exultation for success; the entry in state into ancient Rome of a general who has gained an important victory: *v.i.* to celebrate victory with pomp; to rejoice for victory; to obtain victory; to exult boastfully upon an advantage gained; to flourish. (L. *triumphus*, from Gr. *thriambos*, a procession in honour of Bacchus.)
triumphal, *a.* try-*um*-fal, pertaining to triumph; used in or commemorative of a triumph.
triumphant, *a.* try-*um*-fant, celebrating victory; rejoicing as for victory; victorious; graced with conquest; exulting in success.
triumphantly, *ad.* in a triumphant manner.
triumpher, *n.* *try*-um-fer, one who triumphs or enjoys a triumph; a victor.
triumvir, *n.* try-*um*-ver (*pl.* **triumviri** *or* **triumvirs**), one of three men united in office, authority, or power. (L., literally, man of three.)
triumviral, *a.* try-*um*-ver-ral, pertaining to a triumvir or triumvirate.
triumvirate, *n.* try-*um*-ver-rate, the office of or government by triumviri; a group of three persons.
triune, *a.* *try*-yewn, three in one. (L. *tri-*, and *unus*, one.)
triunity, *n.* try-*yew*-ne-te, the condition of being three in one; a trinity.
trivalence, *n.* *try*-va- *or* *triv*-a-lence, the state of being trivalent.
trivalent, *a.* *try*-va- *or* *triv*-a-lent, having a combining power of three [Chem.].
trivalvular, *a.* try-*val*-vew-lar, three-valved.
trivet, *n.* *triv*-et, a three-legged support; a movable bracket hung on a grate for cooking in front of the fire. **right as a trivet,** all right; perfectly fit. (L. *tripēs*, having three feet.)
trivia, *n.pl.* *triv*-e-a, trifles, trivialities. (*trivium*.)
trivial, *a.* *triv*-e-al, such as may be found everywhere; common; trifling; of little worth or importance; not scientific; popular (of names in Bot. and Zool.). (L. *trivialis*, commonplace, from *trivium*.)
trivialism, *n.* *triv*-e-a-lizm, anything trivial.
triviality, *n.* triv-e-*al*-e-te, the quality of being trivial; a trifle; a trifling matter, characteristic, etc.
trivialize, *v.t.* *triv*-e-a-lize, to render trivial.
trivially, *ad.* in a trivial or trifling manner.
trivialness, *n.* the state of being trivial.
trivium, *n.* *triv*-e-um, the first three of the liberal arts of the Middle Ages, grammar, logic, and rhetoric. (L. *trivium*, a cross-road, hence, a common meeting-place.)
tri-weekly, *a.* try-*week*-le, thrice a week; every three weeks.
troat, *n.* trote, the cry of a buck in rutting time: *v.i.* to utter this cry. (Imit.)
trocar, *n.* *troh*-kar, a triangular probe used with a cannula in the removal of fluid from the body [Surg.]. (Fr.)
trochaic, *a.* tro-*kay*-ik, consisting of trochees: *n.* a trochaic verse [Pros.].
trochal, *a.* *troh*-kal, shaped like a wheel; rotiform [Zool.].
trochanter, *n.* tro-*kan*-ter, either one of the processes at the upper end of the thighbone [Anat.]; the second segment of the leg of an insect [Entom.]. (Gr., a runner.)
troche, *n.* trohsh, trohtsh, troke, *or* *troh*-ke, a small medicated lozenge or tablet. (Gr. *trochos*, a wheel or ball.)
trochee, *n.* *troh*-kee, a foot of two syllables, the first long and the second short [Pros.]. (Gr. *trochaios*, running, tripping.)
trochilic, *a.* tro-*kil*-ik, having power to turn round. (Gr. *trochilia*, the sheave of a pulley.)
trochilics, *n.* tro-*kil*-iks, the science of rotary motion.
trochilus, *n.* *trok*-e-lus, the crocodile-bird; a variety of humming-bird; a scotia, or moulding round the base of a column [Arch.]. (Gr., from *trecho*, run.)
trochite, *n.* *troh*-kite, a wheel-like joint of the stem of an encrinite.
trochlea, *n.* *trok*-le-a, any pulley-like part, esp. the condyle of the humerus articulating with the ulna, or the cartilaginous ring through which the tendon of the trochlear muscle enters the orbit of the eye [Anat.]. (Gr. *trochilia*, the sheaf of a pulley.)
trochlear, *a.* *trok*-le-ar, pulley-shaped [Anat.]; pertaining to the trochlea.
trochleariform, *a.* *trok*-le-*a*-re-form, circular and becoming narrow in the middle [Bot.].

trochoid, *a.* *troh*-koyd, capable of rotary motion (of joints) [Anat.]; shaped like a spinning-top [Conch.]: *n.* an articulation in which one bone rotates upon another [Anat.]; a curve generated by a point in the circumference of a circle rolling along a straight line or on another curve [Geom.]. (Gr. *trochos*, and *eidos*, like.)

trochoidal, *a.* troh-*koy*-dal, of the nature of or pertaining to a trochoid [Geom.].

Trochus, *n.* *troh*-kus, a genus of gastropods having conical or top-shaped shells. (Gr. *trochos*, from *trechein*, to run.)

troco, *n.* *troh*-koh, an old outdoor game played on the ground with wooden balls and cues; lawn-billiards. (It. *trueco.*)

troctolite, *n.* *trok*-to-lite, a variety of gabbro speckled with dark green olivine like the side of a trout. (Gr. *troktos*, trout, *lithos*, stone.)

trod, trod, *p.* of *tread.*

trodden, *trod*-en, *pp.* of *tread.*

troglodyte, *n.* *trog*-lo-dite, a cave-dweller (applied originally by the Greeks to African tribes of this class). (Gr. *trogle*, a cavern, *dyo*, enter.)

troglodytic, *a.* trog-lo-*dit*-ik, of or pertaining to a troglodyte; cave-dwelling; of a backward or degraded way of life.

troglodytism, *n.* *trog*-lo-dy-tizm, the life of troglodytes; primitive or backward condition.

trogon, *n.* *troh*-gon, a group of brilliantly plumaged insectivorous birds of tropical America, with the first and second toes turned backwards. (Gr. *trogon*, gnaw.)

troika, *n.* *troy*-ka, a vehicle drawn by three horses abreast; a team of three horses harnessed thus. (Russ.)

Trojan, *a.* *troh*-jan, pertaining to Troy or its people: *n.* an inhabitant of Troy; a dauntless man. (L. *Troja*, Troy.)

troll, *n.* trole, a supernatural being of Scandinavian mythology; a dwarfish cave-dweller.

troll, *n.* trole, a song or round in which the parts are sung in succession; a spinning bait, also an act of trolling [Angling]: *v.t.* to sing or take up in succession, as a catch; to trundle (a ball, etc.); to fish in with a spinning bait: *v.i.* to roll; to sing or utter in a trolling way; to run in one's head (as a melody, etc.); to fish with a spinning bait. (O.Fr. *troller*, probably from Teut.)

troller, *n.* *troh*-ler, one who or that which trolls (in any sense).

trolley, *n.* *trol*-e, a low cart; a small truck from which the wheels can be easily removed, driven by the feet or hands (Rly.); a travelling pulley-wheel used to convey current in overhead electric traction; a trolley-bus [Coll.]. (*troll*, to roll.)

trolley-bus, *n.* a trackless tramcar or public motor conveyance receiving current through a trolley in contact with trolley-wires.

trolley-wire, *n.* an overhead electric wire supplying current by way of trolleys to electric cars.

troll-flower, *n.* *trole*-flou-er, the globe-flower.

trollmydames, *n.* *trol*-me-daymz, the old game of nine-holes, a primitive form of bagatelle. (Fr).

trollop, *n.* *trol*-op, a woman loosely dressed; a slattern: *v.i.* to work or slouch in a slovenly manner. (Probably *troll*, to roll.)

trollopy, *a.* *trol*-o-pe, like a trollop; slatternly.

trolly, *n.* *trol*-e, a variety of lace in which the pattern is outlined in thick thread. (Flem. *trolle.*)

trombone, *n.* trom-*bone or trom*-bone, a deep-toned brass instrument of the trumpet kind, utilizing two sliding tubes. (It. *tromba*, a trumpet.)

trombonist, *n.* trom-*boh*-nist, a trombone player.

trommel, *n.* *trom*-el, a mechanical sieve used for cleaning and sizing ore in mining. (Ger., drum.)

tromometer, *n.* tro-*mom*-e-ter, a seismometer. (Gr. *tromos*, a trembling, *metron*, measure.)

trompe, *n.* tromp, the water-bellows used in certain metallurgical processes for producing a blast. (Fr.)

tron, *n.* tron *or* trone, an ancient Scottish weighing-machine for heavy goods; hence, a market-place (where this was used). (O.Fr. *tronel.*)

trona, *n.* *troh*-na, a native sesquicarbonate of sodium.

tronc, *n.* tron, the system of pooling waiters' tips; the pool thus made. (Fr., alms-box.)

trone, *n.* trone, a tron; a steelyard.

troop, *n.* troop, a collection of people or animals; a number in a body; a company, esp. of stage-players, a troupe; a body of soldiers or (cavalry) troopers: *pl.* soldiers in general: *v.i.* to collect in numbers; to march, gather, or advance in a body: *v.t.* to form into troops; to transport troops. **trooping season,** the annual period in peace-time when overseas garrisons are relieved. **trooping the colour,** the ceremony of saluting and transferring the colour at a special mounting of the guard [Mil.]. (Fr. *troupe*, probably from L. *turba*, a crowd.)

trooper, *n.* *troo*-per, a private soldier in the cavalry or yeomanry; a troopship. **swear like a trooper,** to use profanity profusely and strongly.

troopial, *n.* *troo*-pe-al, a N. American songbird of the family Icteridæ, allied to the starlings and blackbirds; a brilliant oriole of S. America.

troopship, *n.* *troop*-ship, a ship for carrying soldiers; a transport.

troostite, *n.* *troo*-stite, a variety of willemite containing iron and manganese; one of the transitional structures present in heated steel during course of manufacture. (*Troost*, personal name.)

Tropæolum, *n.* tro-*pee*-o-lum, a genus of American climbing plants including the nasturtiums.

trope, *n.* trope, a word or expression used in a different sense from the literal [Rhet.]. (Gr. *tropos*, a turn.)

trophesial, *a.* tro-*fee*-ze-al, trophic.

trophesy, *n.* *trof*-e-se, defective nutrition due to nervous disorder. (Gr. *trophē*, nourishment.)

trophi, *n.pl.* *troh*-fy, the parts of the mouth employed in feeding [Entom.]. (Gr. *trepho*, feed.)

trophic, *a.* *trof*-ik, pertaining to nutrition.

trophied, *a.* *troh*-fid, having or adorned with trophies.

Trophonian, *a.* tro-*foh*-ne-an, pertaining to the ancient Greek architect Trophonius, or his works.

tropho-, *trof*-o, Gr. prefix used to indicate some relationship with food or nutrition, as **trophology,** the science of nutrition, **trophotherapy,** treatment of disease by dietetic measures. (Gr. *trepho*, feed.)

trophotropism, *n.* tro-*fot*-ro-pizm, the attraction and repulsion exhibited by certain organic cells to various nutrient substances [Physiol. and Bot.]. (Gr. *tropho-*, and *tropism.*)

trophy, *n.* *troh*-fe, a pile of arms taken from a vanquished enemy; the representation of such a pile in marble, on a medal, or the like; anything taken or preserved as a memorial of victory; any evidence of victory; an ornament representing arms, military accoutrements, etc. [Arch.]. (Fr. *trophée.*)

trophy-money, *n.* a duty formerly levied to provide equipment for the militia.

tropic, *n.* *trop*-ik, either of the two parallels of latitude equidistant from the equator at 23½° (northern, the Tropic of Cancer, and southern, the Tropic of Capricorn) which the sun reaches at its greatest declination north and south: *a.* tropical. **the tropics,** the torrid zone [Geog.]. (Gr. *tropikos*, turning.)

tropical, *a.* *trop*-e-kal, pertaining to or characteristic of the tropics; being within or incidental to the tropics; exceedingly warm (of weather); of the nature of a trope, figurative.

tropically, *ad.* in a tropical manner; metaphorically.

tropic-bird, *n.* a long-tailed oceanic bird of the genus *Phaethon*, esp. *P. lepturus*, allied to the gannet.

tropicopolitan, *a.* *trop*-e-ko-*pol*-e-tan, pertaining to or living in the tropics or tropical regions [Bot. and Zool.].

tropism, *n.* *troh*-pizm, the turning of an organism, in part or whole, in a particular direction according to the action of some external stimulus. (Gr. *tropos*, a turn.)

tropist, *n.* *troh*-pist, one who deals in tropes; one who interprets the Scriptures figuratively.

tropistic, *a.* tro-*pis*-tik, pertaining to or characterized by tropism.

tropological, *a.* trop-o-*loj*-e-kal, varied by tropes; changed from the original import of the words.

tropology, *n.* tro-*pol*-o-je, a rhetorical mode of speech, including tropes, or change from the original import of the word; the figurative interpretation of Scripture. (Gr. *tropos*, and *logos*, word.)

tropometer, *n.* tro-*pom*-e-ter, an instrument for measuring the torsion or rotation of bones or other parts, esp. the power of rotation of the eye [Anat.].

tropopause, *n.* *trop*-o-pawz, the lower boundary of the stratosphere [Meteor.]. (Gr. *tropos*, and *pause.*)

tropophyte, *n.* *trop*-o-fite, a plant vegetating during the wet season and dying down or dropping its leaves during the dry season.
troposphere, *n.* *trop*-o-sfeer, that part of the atmosphere lying below the stratosphere, in which the changes of temperature with variations in altitude are large [Meteor.]. (Gr. *tropos*, and *sphere*.)
troppo, *ad.* *trop*-oh, too much [Mus.]. (It.)
trot, *n.* trot, the pace of a horse when it trots; an old woman: *v.i.* to move faster than in walking, as a horse, by lifting the forefoot and the hind foot of the opposite side at the same time; to walk or move fast; to run: *v.t.* to cause to trot; to go (a certain distance) by trotting. (O.Fr. *troter*.)
troth, *n.* troth, belief; faith; fidelity; truth; veracity. (A.S. *treowth*, truth.)
trothplight, *n.* *troth*-plite, the act of betrothing or plighting faith.
Trotskyism, *n.* *trot*-ske-izm, the doctrine of Leon Trotsky (1879–1940, Soviet politician) that socialism is unattainable save through immediate world revolution.
Trotskyite, *n.* *trot*-ske-ite, an adherent of Trotskyism.
trotter, *n.* *trot*-er, a trotting-horse; the foot of a sheep or pig, as food.
trottoir, *n.* *trot*-wahr, a side-walk or pavement for pedestrians. (Fr.)
troubadour, *n.* *troo*-ba-door, a class of mediæval poets of southern France who led a minstrel life, wandering from castle to castle and singing in courtly style of chivalry and love. (Fr.)
★**trouble,** *n.* *trub*-bl, disturbance of mind; commotion of spirits; perplexity; affliction; misfortune; annoyance; vexation: *v.t.* to agitate; to disturb; to put into confused motion; to perplex; to afflict; to busy; to vex; to give occasion for labour; to inconvenience. **asking for trouble,** taking too great a risk; contemptuous of peril [Coll.]. (L. *turbula*, a little mob.)
troubler, *n.* *trub*-bler, one who disturbs; a disturber.
troublesome, *a.* *trub*-bl-sum, giving trouble or inconvenience; uneasy; vexatious; annoying; tiresome; importunate.
troublesomely, *ad.* in a troublesome manner.
troublesomeness, *n.* quality of being troublesome.
troublous, *a.* *trub*-blus, agitated; tumultuous; full of commotion; full of trouble.
trough, *n.* trof, a long hollow vessel for animal's water or food; a water channel; anything hollowed out; a long tank used in washing ore, tanning, etc.; a depression, as between two hills or high waves; the lowermost area of barometric pressure between two anticyclones [Meteor.]. (A.S. *trog*.)
trounce, *v.t.* trounse, to punish or beat severely. (O.Fr. *tronce*, truncheon.)
trouncing, *n.* *trouns*-ing, a severe beating.
troupe, *n.* troop, a company of players or performers. (Fr.)
trouper, *n.* *troo*-per, a member of a troupe; an itinerant actor.
troupial, *n.* *troo*-pe-al, troopial.
trous-de-loup, *n.pl.* *troo*-de-loo, funnel-shaped pits with stakes at the bottom used as a defence, esp. against cavalry. (Fr., wolf-holes.)
trousered, *a.* *trou*-zerd, wearing trousers.
trousering, *n.* *trou*-zer-ing, cloth or other material for trousers.
★**trousers,** *n.pl.* *trou*-zerz, a garment, esp. for males, extending from the waist to the ankles, loosely covering the legs. (Ir. and Gael. *triubhas*.)
trousse, *n.* trooce, a case for a set of small surgical or other instruments. (Fr.)
trousseau, *n.* *troo*-soh, the outfit of a bride. (Fr.)
trout, *n.* trout, a fish of the genus *Salmo*, esp. *S. fario*, the river trout, *S. ferox*, the great lake trout, and *S. trutta*, the anadromous salmon-trout or sea-trout. *See also* **bull-trout** and **gillaroo.** (A.S. *truht*, from Gr. *troktes*, from *trogo*, nibble.)
trout-coloured, *a.* white, with variegated spots.
trouting, *n.* *trou*-ting, fishing for trout.
trout-stream, *n.* a stream in which trout breed.
trouty, *a.* *trou*-te, abounding in trout.
trouvère, *n.* troo-*vare*, one of a mediæval class of poets of N. of France who frequented the courts of the princes, and whose themes were more epic and less lyric than those of the troubadours.

trove, *n.* trohv, a thing found (now only in *treasure-trove*). (Fr.)
trover, *n.* *troh*-ver, the gaining possession of any goods by finding or other means; an action for goods found and not delivered on demand [Law]. (Fr. *trouver*, find.)
trow, *v.i.* troh *or* trou, to think or believe; to trust; to suppose. (A.S. *treowian*.)
trowel, *n.* *trou*-el, a tool used in spreading mortar; a digging tool used by gardeners: *v.t.* to spread, lay on, or dress with a trowel. (Fr., from L. *trua*, a ladle.)
trowsers, *n.pl.* *trou*-zerz, trousers.
troy, *a.* troy, designating the system of weights used for precious metals and stones in which the ounce equals 480 grains (31·1035 grms.), as against the avoirdupois ounce of 437½ grains (28·35 grms.). (From *Troyes* in France.)
truancy, *n.* *troo*-an-se, the act of playing or state of being truant.
truant, *n.* *troo*-ant, an idler; one who idly shirks his duty; a boy who, without leave, absents himself from school: *a.* idling away from one's post or duty. **play truant,** to absent oneself from (esp. school) without permission. (O.Fr. *truand*.)
truantly, *ad.* *troo*-ant-le, like a truant.
truantry, *n.* *troo*-an-tre, truancy.
truce, *n.* trooce, a suspension or temporary cessation of hostilities by mutual consent [Mil.]; an armistice; a temporary respite. **flag of truce,** a white flag displayed as a sign that communication is desired with the enemy. **Truce of God,** cessation of hostilities during certain ecclesiastical festivals, etc. in force sporadically in the Middle Ages. (*true*.)
trucial, *a.* *troo*-she-al, pertaining to a truce. **Trucial Sheiks,** the petty chieftains of six Arab tribes on the S. shore of the Persian Gulf who are bound by treaty to Great Britain.
truck, *n.* truk, exchange of commodities; barter; rubbishy wares for barter: *v.i.* to exchange commodities; to barter; to traffic, esp. illicitly: *v.t.* to exchange; to give in exchange. **have no truck with,** to have no dealings or association with [Coll.]. **truck system,** the payment of wages in goods instead of money. (Fr. *troquer*, barter.)
truck, *n.* truk, a low vehicle for goods; a porter's barrow; a railway wagon for heavy goods or cattle; a frame on wheels; a small wooden cap at the summit of a flagstaff or mast [Naut.]: *v.t.* to convey or transport in trucks. (Gr. *trochos*, a wheel.)
truckage, *n.* *truk*-aj, conveyance of goods, etc., by truck; charge made for this.
trucker, *n.* *truk*-er, one who trucks; a bargainer; a huckster; [Scots.] a pedlar.
truckle, *n.* *truk*-kl, a pulley wheel; a truckle-bed: *v.i.* to sleep in this, hence, to be humble, to yield or bend obsequiously to the will of another; to cringe. (Anglo-Fr. *trocle*, from Gr. *trochilia*, a pulley-wheel.)
truckle-bed, *n.* a bed that runs on wheels and may be pushed under another; a trundle-bed.
truckling, *n.* *trukl*-ing, obsequious submission: *a.* servile.
truculence, *n.* *truk*-yew-lence, savageness or aggressiveness of manners; ferociousness; brutality.
truculent, *a.* *truk*-yew-lent, fierce; savage; ferocious; cruel; destructive. (L. *truculentus*, harsh.)
truculently, *ad.* in a truculent manner.
trudge, *v.i.* trudj, to travel on foot; to travel or move along with labour. (Origin uncertain.)
trudgen, *n.* *trudj*-en, a style of swimming in which the strokes are made overhead instead of as in the breast-stroke. (From J. *Trudgen*, who first made it popular, about 1866.)
★**true,** *a.* troo, conformable to fact; genuine; not counterfeit; faithful or loyal; adhering to truth; sincere; honest; accurate; straight; real; rightful: *v.t.* to make true. **true bill, course,** *see these words.* **true to type,** following the rule, normal. (A.S. *treowe*.)
true-blue, *a.* inflexibly honest and steadfast.
true-born, *a.* genuine by right of birth.
true-bred, *a.* of a genuine or right breed; of good breeding, culture, or education.
true-hearted, *a.* faithful; loyal; entirely sincere.
truelove, *n.* *troo*-luv, one really beloved; one's sweetheart; the plant herb Paris. **truelove knot,**

a knot composed of lines united with many involutions; the emblem of interwoven affection.

truepenny, *n.* *troo*-pen-e, an honest fellow.

truffle, *n.* *truf*-l *or* *troo*-fl, a fleshy underground fungus, much esteemed in cookery. (Fr.)

trug, *n.* trug, a hod for mortar; a wooden tray.

truism, *n.* *troo*-izm, an undoubted or self-evident truth; a mere platitude.

trull, *n.* trul, a trollop or loose woman. (Ger. *Trolle.*)

truly, *ad.* *troo*-le, in fact; in reality; according to truth, or to law; sincerely; honestly; faithfully.

trump, *n.* trump, a trumpet: *v.i.* to sound a trumpet; to emit a trumpet-like sound. **Jew's trump,** a Jew's-harp. **last trump,** the call on the Day of Judgment.

trump, *n.* trump, a winning card; one of the suit of cards which takes any of the other suits; a good fellow, a helper in time of trouble [Coll.]: *v.t.* to take a trick with a card of a suit agreed on: *v.i.* to play a trump card. **trump up,** to fabricate or concoct unfairly. **turn up trumps,** to have welcome or excellent results [Coll.]. (*triumph.*)

trumpery, *a.* *trum*-per-re, worthless; cheap and nasty: *n.* worthless finery; useless matter; things worn out and cast aside. (Fr. *tromperie*, deceit.)

trumpet, *n.* *trum*-pet, a clear-sounding wind instrument, used esp. in brass bands and military music; a reed stop of an organ; a trumpet-like object; an ear-trumpet or speaking-trumpet; a trumpeter: *v.i.* to make a trumpet-like sound: *v.t.* to publish by sound or trumpet; to proclaim. **blow one's own trumpet,** highly to commend oneself or one's deeds. (Fr. *trompe.*)

trumpet-call, *n.* a signal given with the trumpet [Mil.]: a call to action [Fig.].

trumpeter, *n.* *trum*-pe-ter, one who sounds a trumpet; one who proclaims, publishes, or denounces; a variety of domestic pigeon, also the agami of S. America, the N. American swan *Cygnus buccinator*, and other birds.

trumpeter-fish, *n.* any of several Australasian sea-fish of the genus *Latris.*

trumpet-fish, *n.* any of several marine fishes with a long tubular muzzle, esp. the bellows-fish, *Centriscus scolopax.*

trumpet-flower, *n.* any plant with large tubular flowers, esp. *Tecoma radicans*, or other bignonia.

trumpet-major, *n.* the leading trumpeter of a British cavalry regiment.

trumpet-shell, *n.* a gastropod (or its shell) of the genus *Triton.*

trumpet-tree, *n.* the tropical American tree, *Cecropia peltata.*

truncal, *a.* *trung*-kal, pertaining to the trunk [Anat.].

truncate, *a.* *trung*-kat, appearing as if cut off at the end [Bot.]. (L. *truncatus*, cut short.)

truncate, *v.t.* trung-*kate*, to cut off; to lop; to maim.

truncation, *n.* trung-*kay*-shon, the state of being truncated; act or process of truncating.

truncheon, *n.* *trun*-shon, a short staff; a club; a cudgel; a baton or staff of command: *v.t.* to beat with a truncheon; to cudgel. (Fr. *tronçon*, dim. of *tronc*, trunk.)

truncheoner, *n.* *trun*-sho-ner, a person armed with a truncheon.

trundle, *n.* *trun*-dl, a small wheel or castor; a lantern wheel; a low cart or truck: *v.t.* and *i.* to roll on or as on small wheels. (A.S. *trendel*, a disk.)

trundle-bed, *n.* a truckle-bed.

trundle-head, *n.* a disk forming the side of a lantern wheel; the head of a capstan.

trundle-tail, *n.* a curled tail; a dog having such a tail.

trunk, *n.* trunk, the main stem of a tree; the body of an animal without the head, tail, or limbs; the main body of anything; a trunk-line; a speaking-tube; the proboscis of an elephant; the shaft of a column; a box, chest, portmanteau, etc., for use when travelling; a wooden conduit or sluice for various purposes [Eng. and Mining]; a ventilating shaft: *pl.* trunk-hose; close fitting shorts for athletes, etc. **trunk call,** a telephone call for an address beyond the local or toll areas. (Fr. *tronc.*)

trunk-fish, *n.* any of several marine fish having the skin covered with bony plates, esp. of the genera *Ostracion*, *Aracana*, and *Lactophrys.*

trunk-hose, *n.pl.* short, wide breeches, formerly worn gathered in above or just below the knee.

trunk-line, *n.* a main line, esp. that of a railway from which branch lines run; an inland telegraph or telephone line connecting distant stations.

trunnion, *n.* *trun*-yon, either of a pair of lateral projections supporting a gun on its carriage, the cylinder of an oscillating engine, etc. (Fr. *trognon*, a stump.)

truss, *n.* trus, a bundle or package; a bundle of hay of weight 56 to 60 lb., or of straw of 36 lb.; a bandage or appliance worn in cases of rupture; a compact tuft of flowers growing at the top of a main stalk; a bracket [Arch.]; the rope or iron used to keep the centre of a yard to the mast [Naut.]; a framed assemblage of timbers or girders for fastening or binding a beam, supporting a roof or bridge, etc.: *v.t.* to bind, support, or strengthen with a truss; to skewer; to make fast. **truss up,** to make close or into a bundle; to hang [Coll.]. **trussed roof,** one so constituted as to support the principal rafters and tie-beams at given points [Arch.]. (O.Fr. *trousser*, to pack up, from L. and Gr. *thyrsus.*)

trussing, *n.* *trus*-ing, the timbers or girders forming a truss.

trust, *n.* trust, confidence; a reliance or resting of the mind on the integrity, veracity, justice, friendship, or other sound principle of another; the ground of confidence; charge received in confidence; that which is entrusted; credit; special reliance on supposed honesty; something committed to one's care or management; an estate held for the use of another [Law]; a combination of several firms, corporations, etc., for business purposes [Comm.]; a cartel: *v.t.* to place confidence in; to believe; to entrust; to give credit to: *v.i.* to be confident of something, present or future; to be credulous. **take on trust,** to credit or believe without test. **trust deed,** a document creating a legal trust. **trust territory,** any territory, including those formerly under mandate of the League of Nations, administered under the trusteeship of the United Nations. (Ice. *traust*, protection.)

trustee, *n.* trus-*tee*, a person or corporation, etc., to whom the management of a property is committed in trust for the good of others. **trustee stock,** a stock in which trustees may legally invest; stock of the highest reputation.

trusteeship, *n.* trus-*tee*-ship, the office or function of a trustee. **trusteeship system,** the system for the administration of former mandated and other trust territories adopted, 1945, by the United Nations.

truster, *n.* *trus*-ter, one who trusts or gives credit.

trustful, *a.* *trust*-ful, full of trust; confiding.

trustfully, *ad.* in a trustful manner.

trustfulness, *n.* the quality of being trustful.

trustify, *v.t.* *trus*-te-fy, to form into a trust [Comm.].

trustily, *ad.* *trus*-te-le, in a trusty manner.

trustiness, *n.* fidelity; faithfulness; honesty.

trustingly, *ad.* with trust or implicit confidence.

trustless, *a.* *trust*-less, not worthy of trust; unfaithful.

trustlessness, *n.* unworthiness of trust.

trustworthiness, *n.* *trust*-wur-the-ness, the quality of being trustworthy.

trustworthy, *a.* *trust*-wur-the, safely to be trusted; worthy of trust or confidence.

trusty, *a.* *trus*-te, trustworthy; faithful.

truth, *n.* trooth, conformity to fact or reality; true state of facts or things; conformity of words to thoughts; veracity; fidelity; constancy; honesty; virtue; a real fact; sincerity. **in truth,** in reality; in fact. **of a truth,** in reality; certainly.

truthful, *a.* *trooth*-ful, full of truth; according to truth.

truthfully, *ad.* in a truthful manner.

truthfulness, *n.* the state of being truthful.

truthless, *a.* *trooth*-less, wanting truth; faithless.

truthlessness, *n.* the state of being truthless.

truttaceous, *a.* trut-*tay*-shus, pertaining to or resembling a trout. (L. *trutta*, trout.)

try, *n.* try, an attempt, an effort [Coll.]; the grounding of the ball on or behind the opponent's goal line, also the score (3) for this [Rugby Football]: *v.i.* to endeavour; to make an effort: *v.t.* to examine; to prove by experiment; to experience; to test; to prove by or act upon as a test; to examine judicially by witnesses and the principles of law; to attempt; to purify; to refine; to use as means; to afflict; to strain. **try back,** to go back and try in a different manner or direction. **try on,** to fit on an article of dress; to attempt. **try out,** to pursue efforts till a decision is obtained. *p.* and *pp.* **tried.** (L. *tero, tritum,* rub.)

Trygon, *n. try*-gon, a genus of fishes including the sting-ray, *T. pastinaca.* (Gr.)

trying, *a. try*-ing, adapted to try; putting to severe trial; wearisome.

tryma, *n. try*-ma, a nut-like drupe, as the walnut, having a dehiscent outer layer. (Gr., hole.)

try-on, *n.* an attempt, esp. clandestinely or with deceptive intent; a bluff [Coll.].

try-out, *n.* a preliminary test or performance; a trial trip.

trypanosome, *n. trip*-a-noh-*sohm,* any of the *Trypanosoma,* a genus of parasitic protozoans, one member of which causes sleeping sickness.

trypanosomiasis, *n. trip*-a-noh-so-*my*-a-sis, infestation by trypanosomes; any disease due to this. [Med.].

trypograph, *n. trip*-o-graf, a kind of printing by means of stencils, or a method of producing copies of manuscript by using stencilled paper. (Gr.)

trypsin, *n. trip*-sin, a ferment secreted by the pancreas and changing proteins into peptones. (Gr. *tripsis,* a rubbing.)

tryptic, *a. trip*-tik, pertaining to or produced by trypsin; effecting proteolysis.

tryptone, *n. trip*-tone, a peptone formed by the action of trypsin on a protein.

triptonemia, *n.* trip-to-*nee*-me-a, peptonemia [Path.].

trysail, *n. try*-sl, in yachts, etc., a substitute for the mainsail in heavy weather; in square-rig vessels, a fore-and-aft stormsail on a gaff, but having no boom.

tryst, *n.* tryst, an appointed meeting; a rendezvous: *v.i.* to arrange to meet as appointed: *v.t.* to engage someone to meet one or to do something. (O.Fr. *triste,* watching-place.)

Tsar, *n.* zahr, the title of the former emperors of Russia, and of the Bulgarian kings; a king; a chief. (Russ., from L. *Cæsar.*)

Tsarevich, *n.* zah-re-*vitz,* the title borne by the sons of the former Russian Tsars.

Tsarevna, *n.* zah-*rev*-na, a daughter of the Tsar.

Tsarina, *n.* zah-*ree*-na, an empress of Russia; the consort of a Tsar.

Tsarism, *n. zah*-rizm, despotism characteristic of the Tsars; autocratic government.

tsarist, *a. zah*-rist, pertaining to the Russian Tsars, or to their times or rule.

Tsesarevich, se-*zah*-re-vitch, title of the eldest son of the Tzar, or of the heir to the throne in the former Russian Empire.

tsetse, *n. tset*-se, any member of the *Glossina,* a genus of dipterous African blood-sucking flies acting as carriers of trypanosomes which cause fatal diseases (including sleeping sickness) in man and animals, esp. *G. morsitans.* (Bantu.)

t-square, *n. tee*-skware, a ruler shaped like a T.

Tuan, *n.* too-*ahn,* Sir, Master (applied by Malays as title of respect to white men). (Malay.)

tuatara, *n. too*-a-*tare*-ra, the large and primitive New Zealand lizard, *Sphenodon punctatus.*

tub, *n.* tub, an open wooden vessel formed with staves and hoops; anything like a tub; a small cask; a rowing-boat; a portable sponge bath: *v.t.* to plant or set in a tub; to give a bath to: *v.i.* to take a bath. (M.E. *tubbe,* from Teut.)

tuba, *n. tew*-ba, a brass wind instrument of very low pitch. (L., a trumpet.)

tubage, *n. tew*-baj, an installation of tubes; tubes collectively; intubation [Surg.].

tubal, *a. tew*-bal, pertaining to a tube [esp. Anat.].

tubbing, *n. tub*-ing, material for tubs; the lining of a mine shaft; bathing, or rowing, in a tub.

tubby, *a. tub*-e, shaped like a tub; sounding like an empty tub; short and rotund; fat.

tube, *n.* tewb, a pipe; a canal or conduit; a vessel for conveying fluids [Anat. and Bot.]; a speaking-tube; the inner cylinder of a gun; a collapsible cylindrical metal container; an underground electric railway [Coll.]: *v.t.* to furnish with a tube. (L. *tuvus.*)

tube-flower, *n.* an Indian shrub of the verbena family, *Clerodendron siphonanthus,* with long white tubular flowers.

tuber, *n. tew*-ber, a thickened portion of an underground stem bearing eyes, as that of a potato; any of the *Tuberales,* the genus of subterranean fungi comprising the truffle; a protuberance or tuberosity. (L. *tuber,* a swelling.)

tubercle, *n. tew*-ber-kl, a small swelling or tumour, esp. that formed in the lungs in tuberculosis; a small pimple-like excrescence [Bot.]. (L. *tuberculum,* a small swelling.)

tubercled, *a. tew*-ber-kld, having tubercles.

tubercular, *a.* tew-*ber*-kew-lar, tuberculate; of the nature of tubercles; tuberculous; affected with tubercles [Med.].

tuberculate, *a.* tew-*ber*-kew-lat, having or affected with tubercles.

tuberculin, *n.* tew-*ber*-kew-lin, a lymph prepared from a culture of the tubercle bacillus used in the diagnosis and treatment of tuberculosis.

tuberculitis, *n.* tew-*ber*-kew-*ly*-tis, inflammation of a tubercle [Path.].

tuberculization, *n.* tew-*ber*-kew-ly-*zay*-shon, infection with tuberculosis; the process of tuberculizing.

tuberculize, *v.t.* tew-*ber*-kew-lize, to affect with tubercle; to render tuberculous.

tuberculose, *a.* tew-*ber*-kew-lohs, tuberculous.

tuberculosis, *n.* tew-*ber*-kew-*loh*-sis, a disease in which tubercles are developed, esp. phthisis or pulmonary consumption.

tuberculotic, *n. tew*-ber-kew-*lot*-ik, one affected with tuberculosis.

tuberculous, *a.* tew-*ber*-kew-lus, pertaining to or affected with tuberculosis.

tuberiferous, *a. tew*-ber-*rif*-er-rus, producing or bearing tubers. (*tuber,* and *fero,* bear.)

tuberoid, *a. tew*-ber-royd, resembling a tuber [Bot.].

tuberose, *a. tew*-ber-rohs, tuberous: *n. tew*-ber-rohz, a liliaceous Mexican plant, *Polianthes tuberosa,* with a spike of white flowers.

tuberosity, *n. tew*-ber-*ros*-e-te, the state of being tuberous; a bony protuberance [Med.]; anything swollen out.

tuberous, *a. tew*-ber-rus, knobbed; affected with tubers; consisting of roundish, fleshy tubers [Bot.].

tub-fish, *n.* the sapphirine gurnard *Trigla hirundo.*

tubicolous, *a.* tew-*bik*-o-lus, constructing and living in a tubular shell (of certain annelids) [Zool.]; of or pertaining to the Tubicola, a family of tubicolous worms. (L. *tubus,* tube, and *colo,* dwell.)

tubicorn, *a. tew*-be-korn, hollow-horned [Zool.]; *n.* a hollow-horned ruminant. (L. *tubus,* and *cornu,* horn.)

tubiform, *a. tew*-be-form, in the shape of a tube.

tubilingual, *a.* tew-be-*ling*-gwal, having a long tubular tongue (esp. of the honey-eaters) [Zool.].

tubing, *n. tew*-bing, a piece of tube; tubes collectively.

tubipore, *n. tew*-be-por, any of the *Tubipora,* a genus of Alcyonaria including the organ-pipe coral. (L. *tubus,* and *porus,* a pore.)

tubiporite, *n.* tew-*bip*-o-rite, a fossil tubipore.

tub-thumper, *n.* a ranting orator [Slang].

tubular, *a. tew*-bew-lar, tube-shaped; having or consisting of a tube or tubes; sounding as though coming through a tube; fistular.

tubulated, *a. tew*-bew-lay-ted, tubular; furnished with a tube.

tubule, *n. tew*-bewl, a small pipe or fistular body.

tubulifloral, *a. tew*-bew-le-*flaw*-ral, having tubular flowers [Bot.].

tubuliform, *a. tew*-bew-le-form, having the form of a tubule or tube.

tubulous, *a. tew*-bew-lus, tubular; longitudinally hollow; composed wholly of tubulous florets [Bot.].

tub-wheel, *n.* a horizontal water-wheel with a series of spiral floats.

tuck, *n.* tuk, a horizontal fold made in a garment or drapery; the place of meeting of the ends of the lower planks under the stern [Naut.]; a tuck-net; food, esp. sweetstuffs and extras [School slang]: *v.t.* to thrust or press in or together; to fold under; to gather up; to enclose by tucking close around: *v.i.* to make tucks. **tuck pointing,** marking the joints of brickwork with a thin line of plasterer's putty. (Low Ger. *tukken,* draw up.)

tuck, *n.* tuk, beat of a drum. (*tucket.*)

tuck, *n.* tuk, a long narrow sword; a rapier. (Fr. *estoc.*)

uckahoe, *n.* *tuk*-a-hoh, an edible subterranean fungus, *Poria cocos*, growing at the roots of certain trees in the southern United States.
ucker, *n.* *tuk*-er, a small piece of muslin or other cloth for the breast; a frilled, falling collar of linen or lace worn by women.
ucket, *n.* *tuk*-et, a trumpet flourish. (*toccata.*)
uck-net, *n.* a net for taking fish from a larger net or seine.
uck-shop, *n.* a school sweetstuff and pastry shop.
ucum, *n.* *too*-kum, the South American palm, *Astrocaryum vulgare*, valuable for its fibre.
ucutucu, *n.* *too*-koo-*too*-koo, a small South American burrowing rodent of the genus *Ctenomys*.
'udor, *a.* *tew*-dor, pertaining to the English dynasty from Henry VII to Elizabeth, to its period (1485–1603), or to a style of architecture then prevailing. **Tudor rose,** the conjoint red and white roses of the Houses of Lancaster and York, a British royal badge. (Owen *Tudor*, of Wales, grandfather. of Henry VII.)
'udoresque, *a.* tew-dor-*resk*, in the Tudor style (of architecture, furniture, costume, etc.).
uesday, *n.* *tewz*-day, the third day of the week. (A.S., day of *Tiw*, the Scand. god of war.)
ufa, *n.* *tew*-fa, a light porous conglomerated rock, usually calcareous; any similar rock. (It.)
ifaceous, *a.* tew-*fay*-shus, pertaining to, consisting of, or resembling tufa.
uff, *n.* tuf, tufa, esp. of volcanic origin.
uft, *n.* tuft, a cluster of threads, filaments, feathers, or the like; things in a knot or bunch; a clump; a head of flowers on a partial stalk forming a dense roundish mass [Bot.]; a nobleman's son at a university, distinguished by a tuft or tassel on his cap [Old slang]: *v.t.* to separate into tufts; to adorn with tufts: *v.i.* to grow in tufts. (Fr. *touffe*, a lock of hair.)
ifted, *a.* *tuf*-ted, adorned with a tuft; growing in clusters. **tufted duck,** the golden-eye, *Fuligula cristata*.
ifter, *n.* *tuf*-ter, a hound trained to drive a stag out of cover.
ift-hunter, *n.* a hanger-on to persons of quality (formerly to titled undergraduates); a toady.
ifty, *a.* *tuf*-te, abounding with or growing in tufts.
ig, *n.* tug, the act of tugging; a pull with great effort; a small powerful vessel for towing ships; the trace of a harness: *v.t.* to pull or draw with effort; to haul along; to pull; to tow: *v.i.* to pull with great effort; to labour. (A.S. *teohan*, pull.)
igger, *n.* *tug*-er, one who tugs.
ig-of-war, *n.* a sport in which sides of players try to pull each other over a line by means of a long rope; any keenly fought or decisive contest.
ii, *n.* *too*-ee, the New Zealand parson bird, *Prosthenadera novæ-seelandiæ*.
iism, *n.* *tew*-izm, the use of the second person, esp. as a means of avoiding use of the first [Rhet.]; the theory that thought is directed towards a second person or one's ideal self [Phil.].
iition, *n.* tew-*ish*-on, instruction; the act of business of teaching, esp. a particular branch of learning. (L. from *tueor*, *tuitus*, see or look to.)
iitionary, *a.* tew-*ish*-o-na-re, pertaining to tuition.
ila, *n.* *too*-la, an alloy of silver with copper and lead; niello work in which this is used. (*Tula*, in Russia.)
ilaremia, *n.* *too*-la-*ree*-me-a, a bacterial disease of rodents transmitted (occasionally to man) by insects. (*Tulare*, California, and Gr. *haima*, blood.)
ilchan, *n.* *tul*-khan, a calf's skin stuffed to induce the cow to give milk. (Scots.)
ilip, *n.* *tew*-lip, a liliaceous plant of the genus *Tulipa* having large showy bell-shaped flowers.
ulip tree, a N. American tree of the magnolia family, *Liriodendron tulipifera*.
lipist, *n.* *tew*-lip-ist, one who grows or collects tulips.
lipomania, *n.* *tew*-lip-o-*may*-ne-a, a passion for the cultivation and acquisition of tulips, a widespread craze in the 17th century.
ile, *n.* tool, a kind of fine silk net or muslin. (Originally made at *Tulle*, France.)
lwar, *n.* tul-*wahr*, a curved sword used by the Sikhs and others in N. India; an Indian cavalry sabre.
imasha, *n.* too-*mah*-sha, tamasha [Anglo-Ind.].

tumble, *n.* *tum*-bl, a fall; a somersault; an untidy condition: *v.i.* to lose footing; to roll about; to fall; to come down suddenly and violently; to play mountebank tricks: *v.t.* to turn over; to disturb; to rumple. **tumble to,** to understand [Slang]. **tumble up,** to get out of bed [Slang]. (A.S. *tumbian.*)
tumbledown, *a.* *tum*-bl-doun, dilapidated; ramshackle.
tumbler, *n.* *tum*-bler, one who tumbles; an acrobat; a drinking-glass, originally so shaped that it could not remain upright when set on its base; a tumblerful; a variety of domestic pigeon, so called from its practice of turning over in its flight; a catch which falls and locks the mechanism.
tumblerful, *n.* *tum*-bler-ful, as much as a tumbler holds; half a pint or thereabouts.
tumbling, *n.* *tum*-bling, acrobatic performances.
tumbling-home, *n.* the inward curve from the waterline upwards shown in ships having a rounded midship section.
tumbly, *a.* *tum*-ble, as if tumbling; tumbledown.
tumbrel *or* **tumbril,** *n.* *tum*-brel, a covered cart used to carry tools, ammunition, etc., for troops or artillery; any two-wheeled cart used for rubbish. (O.Fr. *tomberel*, a tip-cart.)
tumefacient, *n.* tew-me-*fay*-shent, producing swelling [Med.]; tumefying.
tumefaction, *n.* tew-me-*fak*-shon, the act or process of tumefying; a tumour; a swelling. (L.)
tumefy, *v.t.* *tew*-me-fy, to cause to swell: *v.i.* to swell; to rise in a tumour. (L. *tumefacio*, cause to swell.)
tumescence, *n.* tew-*mes*-ence, tumefaction; a tendency to swell up.
tumescent, *a.* tew-*mes*-ent, somewhat tumid; tumefying.
tumid, *a.* *tew*-mid, swollen, enlarged, or distended; protuberant; swelling in sound or sense; pompous; falsely sublime; bombastic. (L. *tumidus*, swollen.)
tumidity, *n.* tew-*mid*-e-te, tumidness.
tumidly, *ad.* *tew*-mid-le, in a tumid manner.
tumidness, *n.* *tew*-mid-ness, the state of being tumid.
tummy, *n.* *tum*-me, the stomach [Coll. and Nursery].
tumorous, *a.* *tew*-mur-rus, swelling; protuberant; of the nature of a tumour [Path.]; bombastic [Fig.].
tumour, *n.* *tew*-mur, morbid enlargement or swelling of or in any part of the body [Surg.].
tump, *n.* tump, a little hillock: *v.t.* to form a mass of mould or a hillock round a plant [Hort.].
tump-line, *n.* a strap across the forehead or breast to balance burdens carried on the back [U.S.A. and Canada]. (Algonq.)
tumpy, *a.* *tump*-e, hummocky; uneven.
tum-tum, *n.* *tum*-tum, a West Indian dish of boiled plantains; a dog-cart [Anglo-Ind.]; an imitation of the sound of a stringed instrument played monotonously: *v.i.* to strum.
tumular, *a.* *tew*-mew-lar, consisting in a heap; formed in a heap. (*tumulus.*)
tumulary, *a.* *tew*-mew-la-re, sepulchral; tumular.
tumulose, *a.* *tew*-mew-lohs, full of mounds or hillocks; tumular.
tumulous, *a.* *tew*-mew-lus, tumulose.
tumult, *n.* *tew*-mult, violent commotion, disturbance or agitation, esp. of a multitude, with confusion of sounds; agitation; high excitement; irregular or confused motion; ferment. (L., an uproar, from *tumeo*, swell.)
tumultuarily, *ad.* tew-*mul*-tew-a-re-le, in a disorderly manner.
tumultuariness, *n.* tew-*mul*-tew-a-re-ness, the state of being tumultuary.
tumultuary, *a.* tew-*mul*-tew-a-re, disorderly; confused; restless; agitated; unquiet.
tumultuous, *a.* tew-*mul*-tew-us, full of tumult and disorder; confused and noisy; turbulent; violent.
tumultuously, *ad.* in a tumultuous manner.
tumultuousness, *n.* state of being tumultuous.
tumulus, *n.* *tew*-mew-lus (*pl.* **tumuli**), a barrow, or prehistoric burial mound. (L., a mound, from *tumeo*, swell.)
tun, *n.* tun, a large cask; a former measure for wine of 252 Winchester (210 Imperial) gallons; a mashing or fermenting vat [Brewing]; a ton weight of 2,240 lb.; a large quantity: *v.t.* to put into or store in casks. (A.S. *tunne.*)

tuna, *n.* *too*-na, the edible fruit of *Opuntia tuna*, a prickly pear of tropical America; the cactus plant bearing this. (Sp., from aboriginal W. Indian.)
tuna, *n.* *too*-na, the tunny of the E. and W. coasts of Southern North America.
tunable, *a.* *tew*-na-bl, that may be put in tune; harmonious; musical; melodious.
tunableness, *n.* the state of being tunable.
tunably, *ad.* *tew*-na-ble, in a tunable manner.
tun-bellied, *a.* having a protuberant belly.
tun-dish, *n.* a shallow funnel.
tundra, *n.* *tun*-dra, any vast swampy expanse of moss-, lichen-, and heather-covered land in the arctic regions of both hemispheres. (Lapp.)
tundun, *n.* *tun*-dun, a turndun or bull-roarer.
tune, *n.* tewn, a melodious series of musical notes in some particular measure and of a given length; melody; harmony; concert of parts; the state of giving the proper sounds; right disposition; fit temper or humour: *v.t.* to put into a state to produce correct or harmonious intonation; to adjust to the given pitch [Mus.]; to sing with melody or harmony; to attune; to syntonize: *v.i.* to form one sound to another; to utter, be in, or come into harmony. **to the tune of,** to the amount of [Coll.]. **tune in,** to set a wireless receiving set to certain wave-length. (*tone*.)
tuneful, *a.* *tewn*-ful, harmonious; melodious.
tunefully, *ad.* in a tuneful manner.
tuneless, *a.* *tewn*-less, unmusical; unharmonious; not employed in making music; silent.
tuner, *n.* *tew*-ner, one who tunes musical instruments; an arrangement of oscillatory circuits by means of which tuning into desired signals is effected [Wire.].
tung-oil, *n.* *tung*-oyl, a wood-oil of very high specific gravity prepared from tung-tree seeds and used in the manufacture of paints and varnishes.
tungstate, *n.* *tung*-stat, a salt of tungstic acid.
tungsten, *n.* *tung*-sten, a very heavy, brittle, greyish-white metallic element, chemically related to chromium, present in wolframite and formerly known as wolfram. (Swed. *tung*, heavy, *sten*, stone.)
tungstenic, *a.* tung-*sten*-ik, of or containing tungsten.
tungstic, *a.* *tung*-stik, tungstenic; obtained from tungsten. **tungstic ochre,** tungstite.
tungstite, *n.* *tung*-stite, native tri-oxide of tungsten.
tung-tree, *n.* *tung*-tree, a Far Eastern tree of the genus *Aleurites*, the seeds of which yield tung-oil.
Tungus, *n.* toon-*gooz*, a Mongoloid, largely nomadic, people, spread over the whole of Siberia.
tunic, *n.* *tew*-nik, a loose garment coat, usually belted; a long under-garment worn by both sexes in ancient Rome; a tunicle; a soldier's or policeman's close-fitting body-coat; an integument [Bot.]; an enveloping membrane [Anat. and Zool.]. (L. *tunica*.)
tunicary, *n.* *tew*-ne-ka-re, an ascidian or sea-squirt; *a.* pertaining to a tunic [Anat. and Zool.].
tunicate, *n.* *tew*-ne-kate, a mollusc of the sea-squirt family: *a.* tunicated.
tunicated, *a.* *tew*-ne-kay-ted, covered with a tunic or membrane [Anat. and Zool.].
tunicin, *n.* *tew*-ne-sin, an animal cellulose, or chitin, present in the mantle of tunicates.
tunicle, *n.* *tew*-ne-kl, a dalmatic-like vestment [Rom. Cath. Ch.].
tuning, *n.* *tew*-ning, the act or process of putting a musical instrument in tune, also of adjusting a radio receiver to a wave-length.
tuning-fork, *n.* *tewn*-ing-fork, a two-pronged steel instrument by which the musical note is given from which other instruments are tuned.
tuning-hammer, *n.* an instrument for tuning pianofortes, harps, etc.
tunnage, *n.* *tun*-aj, tonnage; a duty formerly levied on imported wines.
tunnel, *n.* *tun*-el, a subterranean artificial passage through a hill or other high ground for a road, railway, or canal, etc.; an animal's burrow; a main chimney-flue: *v.t.* to form a tunnel under or through; to form like a tunnel; to burrow; to catch in a tunnel-net. **tunnel disease,** caisson disease. (Fr. *tonnelle*.)
tunneller, *n.* *tun*-el-er, one employed in, or a machine used for, tunnelling.
tunnel-net, *n.* a net with a wide mouth at one end and narrow at the other.
tunnel-pit, *n.* a shaft sunk from the top of th ground to the level of an intended tunnel.
tunnery, *n.* *tun*-er-re, a place where the tunning o liquor is done.
tunny, *n.* *tun*-ne, a very large marine food-fish *Thunnus thynnus*, allied to the mackerel, sometime weighing up to 1,500 lb. (Gr. *thynnos*, from *thyno* rush.)
tuny, *a.* *tew*-ne, characterized by catchy tunes melodious.
tup, *n.* tup, a ram: *v.t.* to butt, as a ram; to cover as a ram. (Origin unknown.)
tupelo, *n.* *tew*-pe-lo, a North American tree of th genus *Nyssa*.
Tupi, *n.* too-*pee*, a native language of the Amazo basin, South America.
tuppence, *n.* *tup*-ens, the sum of two pennies twopence.
tuppenny, *a.* *tup*-en-e, twopenny.
tuque, *n.* took, a kind of knitted cap worn in Canada (*toque*.)
turaco, *n.* tew-*rah*-ko, the touraco [Zool.].
Turanian, *a.* tew-*ray*-ne-an, pertaining to or designat ing the non-Aryan agglutinative languages o Europe and Asia, including Magyar, some Finnisl and Baltic languages, and those of certain Siberian Mongolian, and Manchurian peoples, etc.; of o pertaining to the people speaking these languages *n.* these languages collectively; a member of race speaking these. (Per. *Turan*, region on th right bank of the R. Oxus.)
turban, *n.* *tur*-ban, a sash wound round a cap; head-dress worn by Moslem s; a woman's head dress resembling this. (Per.)
turbaned, *a.* *tur*-band, wearing a turban.
turban-top, *n.* the bishop's-mitre, *Helvella mitra* or similar edible fungus.
turbary, *n.* *tur*-ba-re, the right of digging turf o another's land; the place where turf is dug [Law] a peat-bog. (*turf*.)
turbid, *a.* *tur*-bid, muddy; foul with extraneou matter; thick; muddled, disturbed [Fig.]. (L *turbidus*, disordered.)
turbidity, *n.* tur-*bid*-e-te, turbidness.
turbidly, *ad.* *tur*-bid-le, in a turbid manner.
turbidness, *n.* the state or quality of being turbid
turbillion, *n.* tur-*bil*-yon, tourbillion.
turbinaceous, *a.* *tur*-be-*nay*-shus, top-shaped.
turbinal, *a.* *tur*-be-nal, turbinate; turbiniform *n.* a turbinated bone [Anat.].
turbinate, *a.* *tur*-be-nat, shaped like a top or con inverted [Bot.]; whirling.
turbinated, *a.* *tur*-be-nay-ted, turbinate. **tur binated bone,** any of the three spongy nasal bones
turbination, *n.* *tur*-be-*nay*-shon, act of spinning o whirling; a whorl-shaped formation.
turbine, *n.* *tur*-bine *or* *tur*-bin, an enclosed whee driven by the action of a flowing stream of wate steam, air, or gas; a rotary engine actuated b this means.
turbiniform, *a.* tur-*bin*-e-form, whirling like a top of scroll-like formation. (L. *turbinatus*.)
turbinoid, *a.* *tur*-be-noyd, turbiniform; turbinate.
turbit, *n.* *tur*-bit, a variety of the domestic pigeor remarkable for its short beak and frill.
turbot, *n.* *tur*-bot, the large flat-fish (up to 30 lb *Rhombus maximus*, with a body nearly circula much prized for food. (O.Fr., perhaps from I *turbo*, a top.)
turbo-, *tur*-boh, prefix signifying driven by mean of a turbine, as *turbo-dynamo*, *turbo-generato* etc.
turbulence, *n.* *tur*-bew-lence, the state of bein turbulent, in confusion, disorder, agitation, o insubordination; unruliness.
turbulency, *n.* *tur*-bew-len-se, turbulence.
turbulent, *a.* *tur*-bew-lent, disturbed; agitated being in violent commotion; unquiet; disorderly disposed to insubordination; tumultuous. (I *turba*, a crowd.)
turbulently, *ad.* in a turbulent manner.
Turcism, *n.* *tur*-sizm, the religion, practices, c customs of the Turks.
Turco, *n.* *tur*-koh, a Zouave, or native Algeria soldier in the French army.
Turcoman, *n.* *tur*-ko-man, a Turkoman.
Turcophile, *n.* *tur*-ko-file, an admirer of th Turks.
Turcophobe, *n.* *tur*-ko-fobe, a hater of the Turks.

urd, *n.* turd, a piece of excrement or dung [Indelicate]. (A.S. *tord.*)

urdoid, *a. tur*-doyd, like or characteristic of a thrush [Ornith.]. (*Turdus.*)

Turdus, *n. tur*-dus, the genus of birds which comprises the thrushes. (L.)

ureen, *n.* tu-*reen,* a deep dish for holding soup. (Fr. *terrine,* an earthen vessel.)

urf, *n.* turf (*pl.* **turfs** or **turves**), turvz, that upper stratum of earth and vegetable mould accommodating roots of grass and small plants which adhere and form a mat-like surface; a sod; peat, or similar fibrous vegetable earthy substance used as fuel; the greensward; a race-ground: *v.t.* to cover with turf or sod. **the Turf,** horse-racing. **to turf out,** to eject [Slang]. (A.S.)

urf-drain, *n.* a drain covered over with turves.

urfen, *a. turf*-en, made of turf; covered with turf.

urf-house, *n.* a house or shed formed of turf.

urfiness, *n. turf*-e-ness, the quality of being turfy.

urfing, *n. turf*-ing, operation of laying down or covering with turf.

urfing-iron, *n.* a tool for paring off turf.

urfing-spade, *n.* a spade for under-cutting turf or digging peat.

urfite, *n. turf*-ite, a racegoer; one interested in horse-racing [Coll.].

urf-moss, *n.* a tract of turfy, mossy, or boggy land.

urfy, *a. turf*-e, abounding with turf; having the qualities of turf; horsy, connected with the Turf.

urgent, *a. tur*-jent, swelling; tumid; bombastic [Fig.]. (L. *turgens,* swelling.)

urgescence, *n.* tur-*jes*-ence, the act of swelling; state of being swollen; empty pompousness; inflation; bombast.

urgescent, *a.* tur-*jes*-ent, swelling; becoming swollen; growing bigger.

urgid, *a. tur*-jid, swelled; bloated; distended beyond its natural state by some internal force; tumid; pompous, inflated, bombastic [Fig.]. (L. *turgidus,* swollen.)

urgidity, *n.* tur-*jid*-e-te, turgidness.

urgidly, *ad. tur*-jid-le, in a turgid manner.

urgidness, *n.* the state of being turgid.

urgite, *n. tur*-jite, a hydrous iron ore resembling hæmatite; hydrohæmatite. (*Turguisk,* in the Urals, where found.)

urion, *n. tewr*-re-on, an underground shoot growing into a new stem [Bot.]. (L.)

Turk, *n.* turk, a native of Turkey. **Turk's cap,** the melon cactus, *Melocactus communis.* **Turk's cap lily,** the martagon. **Turk's head,** a knot with which the end of a rope is finished; the West Indian cactus, *C. intortus.* **Turk's turban,** the tube-flower.

urkey, *n. tur*-ke, a large American game-bird of the genus *Meleagris,* with head and neck naked and wattled and an erectile fleshy process on the forehead, comprising two species, the Mexican, *M. gallopavo,* from which the domestic breed is derived, and *M. ocellata,* the wild turkey of Honduras. **talk turkey,** to speak bluntly or directly to the point [Slang]. (Named through confusion with the guinea-fowl, which was originally imported by way of *Turkey.*)

urkey-buzzard, *n.* an American vulture, *Cathartes aura,* ranging from Argentina to Carolina.

urkey-carpet, *n.* a thick-piled woollen carpet with bright oriental designs, originally imported from Turkey.

urkey-oak, *n.* the Levantine oak, *Quercus cerris*; also *Q. catesbæi* and *Q. rubra,* both of the United States.

urkey-poult, *n. tur*-ke-pohlt, a young turkey.

urkey-red, *n.* a fine, durable red dye formerly obtained from madder, now from alizarin.

urkey-rhubarb, *n.* rhubarb prepared for medicinal use from *Rheum officinale* (originally imported through Turkey from China).

urkey-stone, *n.* an oil-stone or whetsone from Turkey.

urkey-trot, *n.* a Negro ragtime dance, popularized about 1916.

urkey-wheat, *n.* maize; Indian corn.

urki, *n. toor*-kee, any of several dialects or languages spoken by Turkomans and related peoples of Central Asia.

urkic, *a. tur*-kik, designating the branch of the Turanian group of languages which includes Turkish and its dialects: *n.* any one of these.

Turkish, *a. tur*-kish, pertaining to Turkey or the Turks: *n.* the language of the Turks. **Turkish towel,** a rough surfaced bath towel.

Turkish-bath, *n.* a hot-air sweating bath.

Turkish-delight, *n.* a sweetmeat made of gelatine and sugar, originally Turkish.

Turkism, *n. tur*-kizm, Turcism.

Turkoman, *n. tur*-ko-man (*pl.* **Turkomans**), a member of a branch of the Turkish race forming about 12 per cent. of the population of the Soviet Republics of Turkmen, Uzbek Kirghiz, and Tadzhik between the Caspian Sea and the Chinese frontier.

turlough, *n. tur*-lokh, a shallow pool that dries up in summer. (Ir.)

turmeric, *n. tur*-me-rik, the East Indian plant *Curcuma longa,* of the ginger family; its rootstock, yielding a yellow powder used as a condiment for curry and as a dye. **turmeric paper,** paper stained with turmeric, used by chemists as a test for alkalies. (Fr. *terre-merite.*)

turmoil, *n. tur*-moyl, disturbance; tumult; harassing labour: *v.t.* to harass; to disquiet. (Origin doubtful.)

turn, *v.t.* turn, to cause to move upon a centre; to change; to metamorphose; to put upside down; to alter position, as the posture of the body; to shape on a lathe; to mould; to translate, transmute, or transform; to cause to nauseate; to make giddy; to infatuate; to direct; to revolve; to move from a direct course or straight line; to pass round (a position, flank of an army, etc.); to cause to deviate; to reverse; to make acid; to dissuade from a purpose or cause to change sides; to cause to ferment or become sour; to blunt (a sharpened edge). **turn aside,** to avert. **turn away,** to dismiss; to avert. **turn down,** to fold or double down. **turn in,** to fold or double. **turn off,** to dismiss, esp. contemptuously; to deflect. **turn out,** to expel; to put forth. **turn over,** to change sides; to transfer; to overset. **turn to,** to have recourse to; to refer to. **turn the back,** to flee. **turn the back upon,** to quit with contempt; to forsake. **turn up,** to place face upwards; to tilt up; to bring to light, or to the surface, etc.; to cause to vomit. **turn upon,** to retort; to fall out with (an associate) suddenly. (A.S. *tyrnan.*)

turn, *v.i.* turn, to move round; to have a circular motion; to be directed; to move the body round; to revolve; to deviate; to be changed; to change or shift sides; to curdle; to sour, as wines; to become giddy, or infatuated; to change direction, a course of life, etc.; to repent. **turn about,** to move the face to another quarter. **turn away,** to deviate; to go away. **turn in,** to bend inward; to go to bed. **turn off,** to deviate from a course. **turn on,** to reply or retort. **turn out,** to move from its place; to rise from bed; to prove in the result. **turn over,** to turn from side to side; to tumble; to change sides. **turn to,** to apply oneself to; to be directed. **turn under,** to bend or be folded downward. **turn up,** to bend or be doubled upward; to happen, esp. unexpectedly; to come to light; to appear.

***turn,** *n.* turn, the act of turning; a revolution; a winding; a bend or bending; a single coil; a walk to and fro [Coll.]; change; change of direction; chance; hap; an incidental opportunity; performance; innings; spell of work; an item in a variety show; style, shape, or manner; act of kindness or of malice; new position of things; a shock [Coll.]; a wheeling movement [Mil.]; an embellishment consisting of four notes [Mus.]. **by turns,** alternately. **serve one's turn,** *see* **serve.** **take turns,** to take each other's places alternately.

turn-buckle, *n.* a coupling for connecting metal rods that allows of adjustment to their length or tension [Eng.]; a screwed fitting for tightening wires [Av.].

turncap, *n. turn*-kap, a revolving chimney-cowl.

turncoat, *n. turn*-kote, one who forsakes his party or principles.

turncock, *n. turn*-kok, one employed to turn water off or on from a main.

turndown, *a. turn*-doun, folded or doubled down.

turndun, *n. turn*-dun, a toy emitting a roaring sound when whirled in the air; a bull-roarer.

turner, *n.* *turn*-er, one who turns anything on a lathe; a potter.
turnery, *n.* *turn*-er-re, articles made by a turner or turned in a lathe; the art or act of shaping in a lathe; a turner's work or workshop.
turning, *n.* *turn*-ing, the art of shaping in curved or circular form; a bending course; flexure; a winding deviation from the proper course; the corner of a road; a shaving from a lathe.
turning-point, *n.* the point on which a matter turns or which decides a case.
turnip, *n.* *tur*-nip, a biennial plant, *Brassica rapa*, the root of which is cooked and eaten, and fed to sheep, etc.; a large silver watch [Slang]. (L. *napus*, a kind of turnip, with perhaps Fr. *tour*, implying something round.)
turnip-fly, *n.* *tur*-nip-fly, the black flea, *Haltica nemorum*, a pest very destructive to root-crops.
turnip-tops, *n.pl.* the leaves and stem of the turnip.
turnix, *n.* *tur*-niks, the bush quail, a small bird of the Middle East and N. Africa, related to the sand-grouse. (L., a quail.)
turnkey, *n.* *turn*-kee, a prison warder; an old-fashioned dentist's instrument.
turn-out, *n.* anything turned out, esp. a quantity produced at one time; dress, outfit; a strike or quitting of employment by workmen; a large party; a stylish equipage.
turnover, *n.* *turn*-oh-ver, an upset; a turning over; a semi-circular pasty made by turning over the crust; a reorganization; amount of business done; money taken in business in a given time; an article continued on a succeeding page [Journalism.].
turnpike, *n.* *turn*-pike, originally, a horizontal cross turning on a post; a gate set across a road to bar traffic till toll is paid; a **turnpike road,** or road on which turnpikes or toll-gates were established. (*turn*, and A.S. *pic*.)
turnscrew, *n.* *turn*-skroo, a screw-driver.
turnsole, *n.* *turn*-sole, any of several plants so called because its flowers are said to turn towards the sun. (*turn*, and L. *sol*, the sun.)
turnspit, *n.* *turn*-spit, a person who turned a spit; a breed of dog, so called from having been employed to turn the spit.
turnstile, *n.* *turn*-stile, a small revolving turnpike stopping the passage of cattle and vehicles but allowing pedestrians to pass.
turnstone, *n.* *turn*-stone, a bird of the genus *Strepsilas*, allied to the lapwing.
turn-table, *n.* a rotatory platform of any kind, esp. one for enabling locomotives or other wheeled vehicles to change direction.
turn-up, *n.* something turned up, as a hem, the end of a trouser-leg, or a card for trumps, etc.; a set to with fists [Slang].
turpentine, *n.* *tur*-pen-tine, a transparent, resinous substance occurring as an exudation in several species of coniferous trees; spirits or oil of turpentine. **turpentine tree,** the terebinth. (Gr. *terebinthos*, turpentine tree.)
turpeth, *n.* *tur*-peth, the root of an Indian plant, *Ipomœa turpethum*, used as a cathartic [Med.]. **turpeth mineral,** a sulphate of mercury composed of two parts of oxide of mercury to one of sulphuric acid. (O.Fr. *turbit*, from Ar.)
turpitude, *n.* *tur*-pe-tewd, inherent baseness or vileness of principle in the heart; extreme depravity; shameful wickedness. (L. *turpitudo*, baseness.)
turps, *n.* turps, turpentine [Coll.].
turquoise, *n.* *tur*-kwoyz, *tur*-kwahz, *or* *tur*-koyz, a gem of a greenish-blue colour, chiefly a hydrated phosphate of aluminium: *a.* of the colour of a turquoise. (Fr.)
turret, *n.* *tu*-ret, a little tower attached to a building and rising above it; a revolving armoured structure for heavy guns on warships and in fortifications. (Fr. *tourette*, from *tour*, a tower.)
turreted, *a.* *tu*-re-ted, furnished with a turret or turrets; rising by gradations like a turret.
turret-ship, *n.* a warship furnished with a turret or turrets.
turriculate, *a.* tu-*rik*-yew-lat, of turret-like formation (esp. of shells [Conch.]).
turtle, *n.* *tur*-tl, a turtle-dove. (L. *turtur*.)
turtle, *n.* *tur*-tl, a marine tortoise; any species of the Chelonidæ, esp. *Chelone midas*, the green turtle largely used for soup. **turn turtle,** to capsize or overturn completely. (A.S.)
turtle-back, *n.* the carapace of a turtle; a small roughly chipped or unfinished artifact with convex side or sides [Archæol.]; a covered deck protecting the bow or stern of a vessel [Naut.].
turtle-dove, *n.* the pigeon *Turtur communis* fabled for its affection and its tender plaintive note.
turves, turvz, *n.pl.* of *turf*.
Tuscan, *a.* *tus*-kan, pertaining to Tuscany: *n.* a native or the language of Tuscany; the Tuscan order. **Tuscan order,** the simplest of the five classic orders of architecture.
tush, *n.* tush, a tusk, or long pointed tooth; a horse's canine tooth.
tush! *int.* tush, indicating impatience or contempt.
tushery, *n.* *tush*-er-re, the affected literary use of archaic expressions.
tusk, *n.* tusk, a long pointed tooth, esp. one projecting considerably from the closed mouth, as of the wild boar and elephant. (A.S. *tusc*.)
tuskar, *tus*-kar, a tool used for cutting peat, esp. in the Orkneys and Shetlands. (O.Scand.)
tusked, *a.* tuskt, furnished with tusks.
tusker, *n.* *tus*-ker, an elephant or wild boar having tusks.
tusky, *a.* *tus*-ke, tusked; having tusk-like projections.
tusser, *n.* *tus*-er, tussore.
tussive, *a.* *tus*-iv, pertaining to coughing or to a cough. (L. *tussis*, a cough.)
tussle, *n.* *tus*-l, a struggle; a conflict: *v.t.* and *i.* to engage in a struggle; to scuffle. (*tousle*.)
tussock, *n.* *tus*-ok, a tuft of grass or twigs. (Dan. *tusk*, tuft.)
tussock-moth, *n.* a moth, *Dasychira pudibunda* the caterpillar of which is destructive to hop plantations.
tussocky, *a.* *tus*-o-ke, abounding in tussocks.
tussore, *n.* *tus*-sor, a coarse undyed silk from the cocoons of an undomesticated silkworm, esp. *Antheræa mylitta*, of Bengal. (Hind. *tasar*, a shuttle.)
tut, *n.* tut, the system of payment at piece rate [Mining and Agric. only]. (Origin unknown.)
tut! *int.* tut, an exclamation of impatience or contempt.
tutelage, *n.* *tew*-te-laj, guardianship; protection; the state, or the period, of being under a guardian. (L. *tutela*, protection.)
tutelar, *a.* and *n.* *tew*-te-lar, tutelary.
tutelary, *a.* *tew*-te-la-re, having the guardianship of a person or things; protective: *n.* a tutelary deity, saint, etc.; a protector.
tutenag, *n.* *tew*-te-nag, crude zinc; an alloy of copper, zinc, and nickel formerly imported from China. (Port. *tutenaga*, from Tamil.)
tutman, *n.* *tut*-man, a miner or labourer engaged on tutwork.
tutor, *n.* *tew*-tor, one who gives private instruction to another in some branch or branches of learning; an academic teacher; a guardian: *v.t.* to teach; to instruct; to discipline; to correct. (L.)
tutorage, *n.* *tew*-to-raj, guardianship; the office of guardian; the charge for a tutor's services.
tutoress, *n.* *tew*-to-ress, a female tutor.
tutorial, *a.* tew-*taw*-re-al, pertaining to a tutor or to tutorship: *n.* an attendance on a tutor for instruction.
tutorship, *n.* *tew*-tor-ship, office of a tutor.
tutress, *n.* *tew*-tress, a tutoress.
tutsan, *n.* *tut*-san, former name of certain medicinal plants, esp. *Hypericum androsæmum*. (Fr. *toute saine*, all-healing.)
tutti, *n.* *too*-te, a direction for all to play in full concert [Mus.]. (It., from L. *totus*, all.)
tutti-frutti, *n.* *too*-te-*froo*-te, a confection made of different kinds of fruit.
tutty, *n.* *tut*-e, an impure oxide of zinc, collected from the chimneys of smelting furnaces, used as a polishing-powder, and [Med.] dessicant.
tutwork, *n.* *tut*-wurk, work paid for under the tut system; piece-work, esp. in mining.
tuxedo, *n.* tuk-*see*-doh, a dinner jacket [Amer.]. (From *Tuxedo*, New York.)
tuyere, *n.* *twee*-yare *or* tweer, a blast-pipe or nozzle in a forge or blast-furnace. (Fr. *tuyère*, a pipe.)
twa, *a.* and *n.* twah, two [Scots.].

Twaddell, *n.* *twod*-dl, a special hydrometer for use with liquids heavier than water. (Inventor's name.)
twaddle, *n.* *twod*-dl, silly, empty, or insignificant talk; verbiage; a twaddler: *v.i.* to talk in a silly manner. (Origin unknown.)
twaddler, *n.* *twod*-dler, a twaddling speaker, talker, or writer.
twain, *a.* twane, two; in two parts: *n.* a couple; a pair. (A.S. *twegen.*)
twait, *n.* twate, a species of shad, *Alosa finta.*
twang, *n.* twang, a sharp, quick sound, as of a bow-string; a nasal sound, esp. in enunciation; a tang, or unpleasant after-taste: *v.i.* to sound with a twang: *v.t.* to make to sound, as by pulling a tense string and letting it go suddenly. (*tang.*)
twangle, *v.i.* and *t.* *twang*-gl, to twang; to utter a nasal sound.
twank, *n.* twank, a corruption of twang.
twankay, *n.* *twang*-ke, a variety of green China tea. (From a Chinese place-name.)
'twas, twoz, a contraction of it was.
tway-blade, *n.* *tway*-blade, either of the British orchids, *Listera ovata* or *L. cordata.*
tweak, *n.* tweek, a sudden pinch; a twitch: *v.t.* to twitch; to pinch and pull with a sudden jerk and twist. (A.S. *twiccian*, twitch.)
tweed, *n.* tweed, a twilled, rough-surfaced woollen cloth: *pl.* clothes made of tweed. (*tweel*, Scots. form of *twill.*)
tweedle, *n.* *twee*-dl, the sound made by a fiddle: *v.t.* to handle lightly; to fiddle awkwardly with. **tweedle-dum and tweedle-dee,** things so alike that any difference is negligible.
'tween, *prep.* tween, between. **'tween decks,** the deck below the gun-deck; the mess deck.
tweeny, *n.* *twee*-ne, a between-maid [Coll.].
tweer, *n.* tweer, a tuyere: *n.* and *v.i.* twire.
tweet, *v.i.* tweet, to chirp: *n.* the note made by a young bird. (Imit.)
tweezers, *n.pl.* *twee*-zerz, small forceps used for plucking out hairs. (Fr. *étui*, a case.)
twelfth, *a.* twelfth, the ordinal of twelve: *n.* one of twelve equal parts. **the twelfth,** August 12th, the date of the start of grouse-shooting. **twelfth nerve,** the hypoglossal nerve [Anat.]. (A.S. *twelfta.*)
Twelfth-cake, *n.* a cake divided among friends on twelfth-night.
Twelfth-Day, *n.* Epiphany, so called because falling on the twelfth day after Christmas, Jan. 6th.
Twelfth-Night, *n.* the evening of Twelfth-Day (*i.e.*, Jan. 5th), marking the close of the Christmas festivities.
twelfthtide, *n.* *twelfth*-tide, Epiphany.
twelve, *n.* twelv, the sum of two and ten: *a.* consisting of this sum. **the Twelve,** the twelve Apostles. (A.S. *twelfe.*)
twelvemo, *a.* and *n.* *twelv*-moh, duodecimo.
twelvemonth, *n.* *twelv*-munth, a year.
twentieth, *a.* *twen*-te-eth, the ordinal of twenty: *n.* one of twenty equal parts.
twenty, *a.* *twen*-te, twice ten: *n.* the number twenty. (A.S. *twen*, twain, *tig*, ten.)
'twere, twer, contraction of "it were."
twerp, *n.* twerp, an unpleasant or contemptible fellow, a fathead [Slang].
twibill, *n.* *twy*-bil, a kind of double-headed halberd; a mattock. (A.S. *twi*, two, *bill*, an axe.)
twice, *ad.* twice, two times; double.
twicer, *n.* *twice*-er, one who does anything twice, or who fulfils a double role [Coll.]; one who goes to church twice on Sundays [Slang].
twiddle, *v.t.* *twid*-dl, to twist with the fingers. **twiddle one's thumbs,** to have nothing to do; to be idle.
twig, *n.* twig, a small shoot or branch of a tree or other plant; a minute branch of an artery, etc. [Anat.]. (A.S.)
twig, *v.i.* twig, to understand: *v.t.* to see at a glance; to notice; to grasp the meaning of [Coll.].
twiggen, *a.* *twig*-n, made of twigs; wicker.
twiggy, *a.* *twig*-e, full of twigs; abounding with shoots; like a twig.
twilight, *n.* *twy*-lite, the faint light reflected upon the earth after sunset and before sunrise; the periods before sunrise and after sunset between either of those times and that at which the sun is 18° below the horizon [Astron.]; a state of transition, hesitancy, or imperfection [Fig.]: *a.* pertaining to or done by twilight; obscure [Fig.]. **twilight sleep,** a condition of semi-consciousness, induced by drugs or otherwise, to allay the pains of childbirth. (A.S. *twi*, two and *light.*)
'twill, twill, contraction of "it will."
twill, *n.* twill, a woven fabric in which the warp is raised one thread and depressed two or more for the passage of the weft threads: *v.t.* to weave in diagonal lines. (A.S. *twa*, two.)
twin, *n.* twin, one of two at a birth; one of two very like or closely related; a composite crystal consisting of one united to another (or sometimes more) reversely: *a.* being one of two born at a birth; very much resembling; closely related; double; growing in pairs [Bot.]: *v.i.* to bear twins: *v.t.* to unite or combine closely. **twin flower,** the plant *Linnæa borealis.* **the Twins,** the constellation Gemini, one of the signs of the zodiac. (A.S. *twin*, double, from *twa*, two.)
twin-born, *a.* born at the same birth.
twine, *n.* twine, a strong thread composed of two or three smaller threads or strands twisted together; string; a twist; a convolution; the art of winding round: *v.t.* to twist; to wind; to unite closely; to make turns; to turn round. (A.S. *twin.*)
twiner, *n.* *twine*-er, any plant that climbs by twining; a twine-twisting machine.
twinge, *n.* twinj, a sudden sharp pain; a darting local pain of momentary continuance; a sharp rebuke of conscience; a pinch; a tweak: *v.t.* to affect with a sharp sudden pain; to pinch or tweak; to pull with a jerk: *v.i.* to suffer a twinge. (A.S. *twengan.*)
twining, *a.* *twy*-ning, twisting; winding round spirally upward.
twink, *n.* twink, a twinkling; a local name for the chaffinch.
twinkle, *n.* *twing*-kl, a shining with intermitted light; a sparkle, as of the eye; a quick motion of the eye: *v.i.* to sparkle; to flash at intervals; to shine with a broken quivering light; to open and shut the eye by turns; to blink: *v.t.* to emit rapidly and intermittently (of flashes). (A.S.)
twinkler, *n.* *twing*-kler, that which twinkles; a small sparkling firework.
twinkling, *n.* *twing*-kling, a moment; an instant.
twinling, *n.* *twin*-ling, a twin lamb.
twinned, *a.* twind, produced at one birth, like twins; having a twin; like twins; paired; two-fold.
twin-screw, *a.* denoting a vessel having a screw-propeller on either side of the keel, revolving in opposite directions.
twinter, *n.* *twin*-ter, a beast two winters old.
twire, *n.* twire, a sly look; a leer: *v.i.* to twinkle.
twirl, *n.* twurl, a rapid circular motion; quick rotation; twist; convolution: *v.t.* to move or turn rapidly round; to whirl round: *v.i.* to revolve with velocity; to be whirled round. (A.S. *tweran*, turn.)
***twist,** *n.* twist, a cord, thread, or anything flexible, formed by winding strands or separate things round each other; a string; a contortion; obliquity of rifling of a fire-arm; strain due to torsion; a spinning motion imparted; tobacco sold in a twisted roll; manner of twisting; an individual tendency or bias [Fig.]: *v.t.* to wind spirally; to unite by winding one thread, strand, or other flexible substance round another; to form into a thread from many fine filaments; to contort; to writhe; to wreathe; to encircle; to unite by intertexture of parts; to give a spinning motion to; to enter by winding; to pervert or distort; to turn from a straight line: *v.i.* to writhe; to be contorted or united by winding round each other; to move on an irregular or winding course. **twist drill,** a drill deeply and spirally grooved for working in metal. (A.S. *twist*, a cord, from *twa*, two.)
twistable, *a.* *twis*-ta-bl, that can be twisted.
twister, *n.* *twis*-ter, one who twists; an implement for or operated by twisting; a ball delivered with a twist [Cricket, Billiards]; a poser [Coll.]; a shifty, deceitful person [Slang].
twit, *v.t.* twit, to rally; to reproach; to upbraid, as for some previous act: *n.* an act of twitting; a taunt. (A.S. *ætwitan*, reproach.)
twitch, *n.* twitch, a pull with a jerk; a short, spasmodic contraction of the fibres or muscles; a device for holding a restive horse by the lip for

shoeing or a slight operation: *v.t.* to pull with a sudden jerk; to snatch: *v.i.* to move in this way. (A.S. *twiccian*, pluck.)
twitchel, *n. twitch*-el, a noose; a twitch for horses.
twitcher, *n. twitch*-er, one who or that which twitches; a twitch for horses.
twitch-grass, *n.* couch-grass; quitch.
twitching, *n. twitch*-ing, act of pulling with a jerk; act of suffering short spasmodic contractions.
twitchy, *a. twitch*-e, characterized by twitching; irritable; nervy.
twite, *n.* twite, the mountain linnet, *Linola flavirostris.* (From its cry.)
twitten, *n. twit*-en, a narrow lane connecting two roads. (Perhaps A.S. *twycen*, a forked path.)
twitter, *n. twit*-er, a small intermitted noise like the song of the swallow; a slight trembling of the nerves: *v.i.* to make a succession of small tremulous, intermitted noises; to chirp; to be nervously excited. (From the sound.)
twitter, *n. twit*-er, one who twits or reproaches.
twitter-bone, *n.* a tumour or excrescence on a horse's hoof.
twittingly, *ad. twit*-ing-le, with upbraiding.
twittle-twattle, *n. twit*-tl-*twot*-tl, tattle; gabble.
'twixt, twikst, a contraction of "betwixt."
two, *a.* too, one and one: *n.* the number two; a playing card or die-face marked with two spots. **in two,** in or into two parts. **put two and two together,** to draw the obvious conclusion. **two or three,** a few. (A.S. *twa.*)
two-edged, *a.* having both edges sharp; of uncertain effect or meaning, ambiguous [Fig.].
two-faced, *a.* having two faces; double-faced; disingenuous.
twofold, *a. too*-fohld, double; twice as much or as many; duplex: *ad.* doubly; in a double degree.
two-four, *a.* denoting a rhythm having two quarter notes to the bar [Mus.].
two-handed, *a.* having two hands; powerful; wielded with both hands; for two players.
twoness, *n. too*-ness, the condition of being two; doubleness.
two-pair, *a.* denoting the second floor (of a house) [Coll.].
twopence, *n. tup*-ence, the sum of two pennies; a twopenny piece.
twopenny, *a. tup*-en-e, of little worth. **twopenny piece,** a small silver coin (now only Maundy money) and former copper coin representing twopence.
twopenny-halfpenny, *a.* nearly worthless.
two-phase, *a.* having two phases; pertaining to two alternating currents of the same period, but separated by 90°, produced by the same machine [Elect.].
two-ply, *a. too*-ply, consisting of two thicknesses; having two strands.
two-seater, *n.* a motor-car, aeroplane, etc., for two.
twosome, *a. too*-sum, done by, performed by, or consisting of two: *n.* a couple; a game between two players [esp. Golf]; a dance for two.
two-speed, *a.* adapted to produce two rates of speed [Mech.].
two-step, *n.* a variety of polka with two steps to the bar; music for this.
two-tongued, *a.* double-tongued; deceitful.
'twould, *a.* twood, contraction of "it would."
twyer, *n. twy*-er, a tuyere as used in blast smelting furnaces.
tycoon, *n.* ty-*koon*, a former title (used only by foreigners) of the Japanese shogun. (Jap. *tai-kun*, a great ruler.)
tyg, *n.* tig, a two-handled pottery drinking-cup of about 1660 to 1780. (Origin unknown.)
tygon, *n. ty*-gon, the hybrid offspring of a tiger and a lioness.
tying, *ty*-ing. *ppr.* of *tie.*
tyke, *n.* tike, a cur; a mongrel; nickname for a Yorkshireman.
tyler, *n. ty*-ler, a tiler; the doorkeeper of a masonic lodge.
tylopod, *n. ty*-lo-pod, any member of the Tylopoda, a group of ruminants including the camels and llamas: *a.* tylopodous. (Gr. *tulos*, callus, *pous, podos*, foot.)
tylopodous, *a.* ty-*lop*-o-dus, having padded digits [Zool.].
tylosis, *n.* ty-*loh*-sis, a callosity; a disease in which the eyelids become inflamed and the margins harden and become thick [Med.]; an intrusive cellular growth in woody tissue [Bot.]. (Gr. *tulosis*, formation of a callus.)
tylotic, *a.* ty-*lot*-ik, pertaining to or characterized by tylosis.
tymbal, *n. tim*-bal, a timbal or kettledrum.
tymp, timp, *n.* the crown of the opening in front of certain obsolete forms of blast-furnace hearth.
tympan, *n. tim*-pan (*pl.* **tympana,** *tim*-pa-na), a stretched sheet of thin material or membrane; a drum; a frame used for equalizing pressure in some printing machines. (L. *tympanum*, a drum.)
tympanic, *a.* tim-*pan*-ik, like or pertaining to a tympanum. **tympanic membrane,** the membrane dividing the middle ear from the external ear.
tympanism, *n. tim*-pa-nizm, tympanites.
tympanist, *n. tim*-pa-nist, one playing percussion instruments in an orchestra or dance-band.
tympanites, *n. tim*-pa-*ny*-teez, a flatulent distention of the abdomen [Med.].
tympanitic, *a. tim*-pa-*nit*-ik, pertaining to or affected by tympanites. **tympanitic note,** the drum-like sound produced by tapping an abdomen distended by gas [Med.].
tympanitis, *n. tim*-pa-*ny*-tis, inflammation of the lining membrane of the tympanum or (less correctly) middle ear.
tympanum, *n. tim*-pa-num (*pl.* **tympana**), a drum or drum-head [Mus.]; the drum of the ear; the inflatable air-sac in the neck of certain birds; the resonant membrane of any sound producing organ [Zool.]; the face of a pediment, a triangular space or table in the corners or sides of an arch, the space between an arch and the top of the door [Arch.]. (L., from Gr. *tympanon*, from *typto*, strike.)
tympany, *n. tim*-pa-ne, tympanites [Old Med.].
Tynwald, *n. tine*-wawld, the parliament of the Isle of Man. (A.S. *thing*, meeting, *wald*, wood.)
typal, *a. ty*-pal, of or pertaining to a type; typical.
type, *n.* tipe, an emblem; that which represents something else; a sign; a symbol; a figure of something to come; stamp, or general structure or character; model; ideal; a letter in metal or other hard material to print from; an individual having the essential characteristics of a class etc. [Biol.]; *v.t.* typify; to put into type; to typewrite. (Gr. *typos*, an impression, from *typto*, strike.)
type-founder, *n.* one who casts types.
type-foundry, *n.* a place where types are cast.
type-high, *n.* of the standard height of printing type (0·918 in.).
type-metal, *n.* an alloy of lead and antimony, with tin and sometimes copper, used in making types.
typescript, *n. tipe*-skript, typewritten matter.
type-setter, *n.* a compositor; a machine for setting type.
typewrite, *v.t.* and *i. tipe*-rite, to write with a typewriter. *p.* **typewrote.** *pp.* **typewritten.**
typewriter, *n. tipe*-ry-ter, a machine for writing in characters resembling printing type; a typist.
typhlitic, *a.* tif-*lit*-ik, of the nature of, or affected with typhlitis.
typhlitis, *n.* tif-*ly*-tis, inflammation of the cæcum; appendicitis.
typhlology, *n.* tif-*lol*-o-je, the scientific study of blindness. (Gr. *typhlos*, blind, and *-logy.*)
Typhlops, *n. tif*-lops, a genus of small burrowing snakes with a scarcely visible eye. (Gr. *typhlos*, blind.)
typhogenic, *a.* ty-foh-*jen*-ik, producing typhoid or typhus.
typhoid, *a. ty*-foyd, resembling typhus: *n.* typhoid fever. **typhoid fever,** enteric, an infectious bacterial disease characterized by severe fever, rose-red eruptions, diarrhœa, and ulceration of the intestines. (*typhus*, and Gr. *eidos*, like.)
typhoidal, *a.* ty-*foy*-dal, pertaining to or resembling typhoid.
typhomania, *n. ty*-fo-*may*-ne-a, a complication of delirium with typhus fever. (*typhus* and *mania.*)
typhonic, *a.* ty-*fon*-ik, pertaining to or suggesting a typhoon.
typhoon, *n.* ty-*foon*, a cyclone in the China Sea; a hurricane. (Port. *tufao*, from an Oriental source of Gr. *typhon*, a whirlwind.)
typhous, *a. ty*-fus, relating to or of the nature of typhus.
typhus, *n. ty*-fus, jail fever with purple eruptions; a

contagious fever epidemically characterized by purplish eruptions, delirium, and prostration, and transmitted by a filter-passing virus carried by lice. (Gr. *typhos*, stupor, lethargy.)
typic, *a.* *tip*-ik, typical.
typical, *a.* *tip*-e-kal, emblematic; figurative; exhibiting prominently the characteristics of a group. (L. *typicus.*)
typicality, *n.* tip-e-*kal*-e-te, typicalness.
typically, *ad.* in a typical manner.
typicalness, *n.* the fact or state of being typical.
typification, *n.* tip-e-fe-*kay*-shon, the act of typifying.
typifier, *n.* *tip*-e-fy-er, one who or that which typifies.
typify, *v.t.* *tip*-e-fy, to represent by an image, form, model, or resemblance; to exemplify; to prefigure. (L. *typus*, a figure.)
typist, *n.* *ty*-pist, one who works a typewriter.
typographer, *n.* ty-*pog*-ra-fer, a printer; a typographical craftsman or designer.
typographic, *a.* tip-o-*graf*-ik, typographical.
typographical, *a.* tip-o-*graf*-e-kal, pertaining to printing; produced by typography.
typographically, *ad.* by means of typography or type.
typography, *n.* ty-*pog*-ra-fe, the art, practice, or process of printing with type. (Gr. *typos*, and *grapho*, write.)
typolithography, *n.* *ty*-po-le-*thog*-ra-fe, a method of lithographic printing in which the stone has previously received impressions from printers' type.
typology, *n.* ty-*pol*-o-je, a treatise on, or the doctrine or interpretation of, types, esp. those of a scriptural origin. (Gr. *typos*, and *logos*, science.)
typonym, *n.* *ty*-po-nim, a name based on some characteristic of a type [Biol.].
typonymic, *a.* ty-po-*nim*-ik, pertaining to a typonym.
typtology, *n.* tip-*tol*-o-je, the art or theory of spirit-rapping. (Gr. *typtō*, beat, and *logos*.)
tyrannical, *a.* ti-*ran*-e-kal, pertaining to a tyrant; beseeming a tyrant; arbitrary; imperious; despotic; cruel. (L. *tyrannicus*, tyrannous.)
tyrannically, *ad.* in a tyrannical manner.
tyrannicalness, *n.* quality of being tyrannical.
tyrannicide, *n.* ti-*ran*-e-side, the act of killing a tyrant; one who kills him. (*tyrant*, and L. *cædo*, kill.
tyrannize, *v.i.* *ti*-ra-nize to act the tyrant; to rule with unjust and oppressive severity.
tyrannosaur, *n.* ti-*ran*-o-sawr, one of a family of gigantic extinct carnivorous dinosaurs of N. America.
tyrannous, *a.* *ti*-ra-nus, tyrannical; arbitrary; unjustly severe.
tyrannously, *ad.* in a tyrannous manner.
tyrannousness, *n.* state or quality of being tyrannous.
tyranny, *n.* *ti*-ra-ne, arbitrary or despotic exercise of power; cruel government or discipline; absolute monarchy cruelly administered; severity; rigour.
tyrant, *n.* *tyr*-rant, a monarch or ruler who oppresses his subjects; a usurping autocrat; one who exercises unlawful authority; a despotic ruler; a cruel master; an oppressor. (Gr. *tyrannos*, an absolute ruler.)
tyre, *n.* tire, a tire (for a wheel).
Tyrian, *a.* *ti*-re-an, of or from Tyre; being of a purple colour: *n.* a native of Tyre.
tyriasis, *n.* ti-*ry*-a-sis, elephantiasis; alopecia. (Gr. *tyros*, cheese.)
tyro, *n.* *tyr*-roh (*pl.* **tyros,** *tyr*-rohz), a beginner in learning; a novice; one imperfectly acquainted with a subject. (L. *tiro*, a raw recruit.)
Tyrolese, *a.* ti-ro-*leez*, pertaining to the Tyrol or its people: *n.* (*sing.* and *pl.*) a native of the Tyrol.
tyrolite, *n.* *ti*-ro-lite, a greenish crystalline hydrous copper arsenate, so called from its being found in the Tyrol.
tyroma, *n.* ty-*roh*-ma, any morbid matter of a cheesy consistency [Med.]; alopecia; a tuberculous tumour. (Gr.)
tyronic, *a.* ty-*ron*-ik, characteristic of a tyro; amateurish.
tyrotoxicon, *n.* *ti*-ro-*tok*-se-kon, a ptomaine present in putrid milk and cheese.
Tyrrhenian, *a.* ti-*ree*-ne-an, Etruscan: *n.* a native of Etruria.
Tyrtæan, *a.* tir-*tee*-an, pertaining to warlike verse. (*Tyrtæus*, the Greek poet.)
Tzar, *n.* zar, **Tzarina,** etc., *see* **Tsar,** etc.
tzetze, *n.* *tzet*-ze, *see* **tsetse.**
tzigane, *n.* tze-*gahn*, a gipsy, esp. from or of Hungary: *a.* pertaining to the tziganes. (Fr., from Magyar *czigāny.*)

U

U, yew, the fifth vowel and the twenty-first letter of the English alphabet. It has a number of distinct sounds, of which the chief are: the long or diphthongal sound heard in *cue*, *unison*, and the *oo* sounds of *mood*, *wood*, and *blood*, as in *truth*, *bull*, *but*; as well as the indefinite vowels of *burn*, *bury*, *busy*, and *nimbus*. When following *g* and preceding a vowel it is generally silent (*guard*, *guest*, *guilt*, *Portuguese*) but may be pronounced as *w* (*guava*, *languid*); and when following *q* is pronounced as *w* (*quaint*, *quote*, *liquid*), except in a few cases (*conquer*, *liquor*, *piquet*, etc.), and in the termination *-que* (*cheque*, *baroque*, *grotesque*, etc.).
uberous, *a.* *yew*-ber-rus, fruitful; abundant; copious.
uberty, *n.* *yew*-ber-te, abundance; fruitfulness. (L. *uber*, fruitful.)
ubication, *n.* *yew*-be-*kay*-shon, ubiety.
ubiety, *n.* yew-*by*-e-te, the state of being in a place; local relation. (L. *ubi*, where.)
ubiquarian, *a.* yew-be-*kware*-re-an, ubiquitous.
ubiquitarian, *a.* *yew*-bik-we-*tare*-re-an, pertaining to the Ubiquitarians or their doctrine: *n.* (*cap.*) a member of a Lutheran sect maintaining that Christ's body is at all times omnipresent.
ubiquitarianism, *n.* *yew*-bik-we-*tare*-re-a-nizm, the tenets of the Ubiquitarians [Eccles.].
ubiquitary, *a.* yew-*bik*-we-ta-re, ubiquitous: *n.* one who exists or might exist everywhere.
ubiquitism, *n.* yew-*bik*-we-tizm, ubiquitarianism.
ubiquitous, *a.* yew-*bik*-we-tus, existing everywhere.
ubiquitously, *ad.* in a ubiquitous way.
ubiquitousness, *n.* the condition or quality of being ubiquitous.
ubiquity, *n.* yew-*bik*-we-te, the state of being ubiquitous; omnipresence. (L. *ubique*, everywhere.)
U-boat, *n.* *yew*-boat, a submarine, esp. a German submarine. (Short for Ger. *unterseeboot*.)
udad, *n.* *oo*-dad, the aouad [Zool.].
udal, *a.* *yew*-dal, allodial [Law]; designating a tenure still in force in the Orkneys and Shetlands: *n.* an estate so held. (O.Scand.)
udaller, *n.* *yew*-da-ler, a tenant of udal land.
udder, *n.* *ud*-er, the organ for the secretion of milk in cows and some other mammals. (A.S. *uder*.)
uddered, *a.* *ud*-erd, furnished with udders.
udometer, *n.* yew-*dom*-e-ter, an instrument for measuring the rainfall. (L. *udus*, wet, Gr. *metron* measure.)
ugh, *int.* ooh, an exclamation of disgust.
uglification, *n.* ug-le-fe-*kay*-shon, act or process of making ugly; that which makes ugly.
uglify, *v.t.* *ug*-le-fy, to make ugly.
uglily, *ad.* *ug*-le-le, in an ugly manner.
ugliness, *n.* state of being ugly; total want of beauty; deformity of person; repulsiveness.
ugly, *a.* *ug*-le, disagreeable in aspect; plain; deformed; hateful; (of weather) threatening; dangerous; malicious; ill-natured. (Ice.)
Ugrian, *a.* *oo*-gre-an, of or pertaining to a group of peoples which includes the Finns and Magyars: *n.* a member of this group; the Ugrian language. (Russ. *Ugri*.)
Ugric, *a.* *oo*-grik, Ugrian.
ugsome, *a.* *ug*-sum, hideous; loathsome.
ugsomeness, *n.* *ug*-sum-ness, hideousness.
Uhlan, *n.* *oo*-lan, a lancer or light horseman of the German (and formerly Polish) army. (Polish *ula*, from Turk. *oghlan*, a youth.)
uitlander, *n.* *oyt*-lan-der, a foreigner; an outlander (esp. in South Africa). (Dut.)
ukase, *n.* yew-*kase*, a decree of the former Russian imperial government; a peremptory order.
Ukrainian, *a.* yew-*kray*-ne-an, of or pertaining to Ukraine, U.S.S.R., its people, or language: *n.* an inhabitant or the language of Ukraine. (Russ. *ukraina*, border.)
ukulele, *n.* *oo*-koo-*lay*-le, a Hawaiian (originally Portuguese) banjo of four strings.
ulcer, *n.* *ul*-ser, a sore, attended with a secretion of pus or some other discharge; any source of corruption [Fig.]. (L. *ulcus*, *ulceris*.)
ulcerate, *v.i.* *ul*-ser-rate, to form into an ulcer; to become ulcerous: *v.t.* to affect with an ulcer or ulcers.
ulceration, *n.* ul-ser-*ray*-shon, state or process of forming into an ulcer; an ulcerated part.
ulcerative, *a.* *ul*-ser-ra-tiv, pertaining to or causing ulcers.
ulcered, *a.* *ul*-serd, ulcerated.
ulcerous, *a.* *ul*-ser-rus, having the nature or character of an ulcer; affected with an ulcer or ulcers.
ulcerously, *ad.* *ul*-ser-rus-le, in an ulcerous manner.
ulcerousness, *n.* the state of being ulcerous.
-ule, yewl, Latin suffix (*-ulus*) forming diminutives as *cupule*, *pilule*, etc.
ulema, *n.* *oo*-le-ma, oo-le-*mah*, *or* yew-*lee*-ma, the Moslem hierarchy of doctors of law and theologians; a member of this body. (Ar. *alim*, wise.)
Ulex, *n.* *yew*-leks, a genus of leguminous plants which includes the furze or gorse. (L.)
uliginal, *a.* yew-*lij*-e-nal, growing in swamps [Bot.]. (L. *uligo*, moisture.)
uliginose, *a.* yew-*lij*-e-nohs, uliginous.
uliginous, *a.* yew-*lij*-e-nus, muddy; oozy; slimy; uliginal.
ulitis, *n.* yew-*ly*-tis, inflammation of the gums. (Gr. *oula*, the gums, and *-itis*.)
ullage, *n.* *ul*-aj, the quantity a cask or bottle wants of being full: *v.t.* to calculate the amount of ullage in a cask. (O.Fr.)
ullaloo, *int.* ul-la-*loo*, a keening, or Irish expression of lamentation over the dead.
ullmannite, *n.* *ul*-man-ite, a mineral containing antimony, nickel, arsenic, and sulphur, named after J. C. Ullmann, who discovered it.
ulmaceous, *a.* ul-*may*-shus, pertaining to or characteristic of the elms. (L. *ulmus*.)
ulmic, *a.* *ul*-mik, pertaining to or derived from ulmin.
ulmin, *n.* *ul*-min, brown gummy organic substance exuding from trees and vegetable matter; humus.
ulmous, *a.* *ul*-mus, of the nature of ulmin.
Ulmus, *n.* *ul*-mus, the genus of trees which includes the elms. (L.)
ulna, *n.* *ul*-na (*pl.* **ulnæ**), the larger of the two bones of the forearm, the upper end of which forms the point of the elbow. (L.)
ulnad, *ad.* *ul*-nad, toward the ulna [Anat.].
ulnar, *a.* *ul*-nar, pertaining to the ulna.
uloid, *a.* *yew*-loyd, of the nature or appearance of a scar [Path.]. (Gr. *oulē*, a scar.)
ulotrichan, *a.* yew-*lot*-re-kan, pertaining to the Ulotrichi: *n.* (*cap.*) a member of the Ulotrichi.
Ulotrichi, *n.pl.* yew-*lot*-re-ky, the woolly haired races of mankind. (Gr. *oulotrichos*, curly haired.)
ulotrichous, *a.* yew-*lot*-re-kus, having woolly hair.
ulster, *n.* *ul*-ster, a long overcoat, originally made of frieze manufactured in Ulster.
Ulsterman, *n.* *ul*-ster-man, a native or inhabitant of Northern Ireland or Ulster.
ult., *a.* ult, last; a contraction for ultimo.
ulterior, *a.* ul-*teer*-re-or, further; on the farther side of any line or boundary; more distant or remote. (L., comparative of *ulter*, beyond.)
ulteriorly, *ad.* ul-*teer*-re-or-le, subsequently; at a later stage.
ultima, *n.* *ul*-te-ma, the last syllable of a word [Gram. and Pros.]. (L., as *ultimate*.)
ultimacy, *n.* *ul*-te-ma-se, the quality or condition of being ultimate.
ultimate, *a.* *ul*-te-mat, furthest; most remote; most extreme; final; last in a train of consequences; at the furthest point; fundamental; the last into which a substance can be resolved. (L. *ultimus*, superlative of *ulter*.)
ultimately, *ad.* *ul*-te-mat-le, in the end.
ultimateness, *n.* *ul*-te-mat-ness, the quality of being ultimate.

ultimatum, *n.* ul-te-*may*-tum (*pl.* **ultimatums** or **ultimata,** -*may*-ta), a final proposition or condition offered, esp. as the basis of a treaty, the rejection of which will put an end to further negotiation; any final proposition or condition; anything fundamental. (L.)
ultimity, *n.* ul-*tim*-e-te, the last stage or consequence; a fundamental principle.
ultimo, *a.* *ul*-te-moh, last, applied to the month preceding the present.
ultimogeniture, *n.* *ul*-te-moh-*jen*-e-tewr, the custom in which the heir is the youngest son instead of the eldest; borough-English.
ultra-, *ul*-tra, prefix, signifying beyond, to an extreme degree, etc., as in *ultra-democratic, ultra-fashionable, ultra-modern, ultra-reactionary,* etc. (L.)
ultra, *a.* *ul*-tra, extreme; uncompromising: *n.* an ultraist.
ultraism, *n.* *ul*-tra-izm, the advocacy of extreme views or measures.
ultraist, *n.* *ul*-tra-ist, one who advocates extreme views or measures.
ultramarine, *a.* *ul*-tra-ma-*reen*, situated, being, or coming from beyond the sea; of the colour ultramarine: *n.* a durable deep sky-blue colour, originally prepared from pulverized lapis lazuli. (L. *ultra-*, and *mare*, sea.)
ultra-microscope, *n.* an instrument for the ocular examination of objects too small to be seen by the ordinary microscope.
ultra-microscopic, *a.* too minute to be seen with the ordinary microscope.
ultramontane, *a.* *ul*-tra-*mon*-tane, being beyond the mountains, esp. the Alps and from the south; advocating papal infallibility and the rights and supremacy of the Papacy: *n.* one who resides beyond the mountains; a supporter of ultramontanism. (L. *ultra-*, and *mons*, a mountain.)
ultramontanism, *n.* *ul*-tra-*mon*-ta-nizm, extreme views of papal rights and the supremacy of the Papacy, esp. over national Churches.
ultramontanist, *n.* *ul*-tra-*mon*-ta-nist, one advocating ultramontanism: *a.* pertaining to or adhering to ultramontanism.
ultramundane, *a.* *ul*-tra-*mun*-dane, being beyond the world, or beyond the limits of the solar system. (L. *ultra-*, and *mundus*, the world.)
ultra-red, *a.* infra red.
ultra-short, *a.* designating electro-magnetic waves of less than 10 metres wave-length [Wire.].
ultrasonic, *a.* *ul*-tra-*son*-ik, pertaining to sound-waves the frequency of which is so great (*i.e.*, over 20,000 per sec.) as to be beyond the range of the human ear (*cf.* **supersonic**): *n.pl.* sound-waves of such frequencies.
ultrasound, *n.* *ul*-tra-sound, an ultrasonic sound.
ultra-violet, *a.* beyond the violet end of the visible spectrum, hence (of rays) invisible.
ultroneous, *a.* ul-*troh*-ne-us, spontaneous; voluntary. (L. *ultro*, of one's own accord, unasked.)
ultroneously, *ad.* in an ultroneous manner.
ultroneousness, *n.* ul-*troh*-ne-us-ness, spontaneity.
ulu, *n.* *oo*-loo, a domestic cutting-tool with a curved blade used by Eskimos. (Eskimo.)
ululant, *a.* *ul*-yew-lant *or* *yewl*-yew-lant, ululating; wailing.
ululate, *v.i.* *ul*-yew-late *or* *yewl*-yew-late, to howl, as a dog or wolf. (L. *ululo*, howl.)
ululation, *n.* *ul*-yew-*lay*-shon *or* *yewl*-yew-*lay*-shon, the act of howling.
umbel, *n.* *um*-bel, a mode of inflorescence in which equal pedicels proceed from one centre [Bot.]. (L. *umbella*, a small shade.)
umbellar, *a.* um-*bel*-ar, pertaining to an umbel; having the form of an umbel.
umbellate, *a.* *um*-be-lat, bearing or arranged in umbels; umbel-shaped.
umbellifer, *n.* um-*bel*-e-fer, any plant of the Umbelliferæ or carrot family.
umbelliferous, *a.* *um*-be-*lif*-er-rus, bearing umbels.
umbellule, *n.* um-*bel*-yewl, a small, secondary, or partial umbel.
umber, *n.* *um*-ber, an earthy ferruginous mineral of a dark brown colour, used as a pigment: *v.t.* to colour with umber; to darken. **umber bird,** the umbrette. (Fr. *ombre*, from L. *umbra*, shadow.)
umber, *n.* *um*-ber, the grayling.
umbered, *a.* *um*-berd, tinged with umber.
umbery, *a.* *um*-ber-re, of the colour of umber.
umbilical, *a.* um-*bil*-e-kal, pertaining to the navel. **umbilical cord,** the cord-like connexion between the navel of the mammalian fœtus and the placenta. **umbilical hernia,** hernia of the bowels at the navel. **umbilical region,** the part of the abdomen situated about the navel. (L. *umbilicus*, the navel.)
umbilicate, *a.* um-*bil*-e-kat, navel-shaped; depressed in the middle like a navel; having an umbilicus; perforate (of shells).
umbilication, *n.* *um*-bil-e-*kay*-shon, a navel-like depression or dimple on the skin; the state of being umbilicate.
umbilicus, *n.* um-be-*ly*-kus *or* um-*bil*-e-kus (*pl.* **umbilici,** um-*bil*-e-sy), the navel [Anat.]; a navel-shaped depression; the hilum, or process attaching the seed to the placenta [Bot.]; the hollow in a spiral shell [Malac.]. (L.)
umbiliform, *a.* um-*bil*-e-form, navel-shaped.
umbles, *n.pl.* *um*-blz, the entrails of a deer. **umble pie,** a pie made of umbles, humble-pie. (Fr.)
umbo, *n.* *um*-boh (*pl.* **umbos,** *um*-bohz, or **umbones,** um-*boh*-neez), the central boss or protuberant part of a shield; a rounded or conical knob; the point of a bivalve shell immediately above the hinge [Malac.]. (L.)
umbonal, *a.* um-*boh*-nal, pertaining to or of the nature of an umbo; protuberant.
umbonate, *a.* *um*-bo-nat, having a boss or elevated point in the middle.
umbra, *n.* *um*-bra (*pl.* **umbræ**), the dark cone of shadow projected from a planet or satellite on the side opposite to the sun [Astron.]; the dark centre of a sun-spot; a phantom; a parasite, or one who attends like one's shadow. (L., a shadow.)
umbraculiform, *a.* um-*brak*-yew-le-form, having the form of an umbrella. (L. *umbraculum*, a small shade.)
umbrage, *n.* *um*-braj, that which gives shade; shadow; suspicion of injury; offence. (Fr. *ombrage*, L. *umbra*.)
umbrageous, *a.* um-*bray*-jus, forming a shade; shady; shaded.
umbrageously, *ad.* in the manner of shade.
umbrageousness, *n.* shadiness.
umbral, *a.* *um*-bral, pertaining to an umbra.
umbratic, *a.* um-*brat*-ik, secluded; withdrawn; umbratile.
umbratile, *a.* *um*-bra-tile, happening or living in the shade or in seclusion; shadowy; unpractical.
umbre, *n.* *um*-ber, the umbrette; the umber or grayling.
★**umbrella,** *n.* um-*brel*-a, a circular screen folding from its centre, carried in the hand as a shelter from the rain or sun; an umbrella-like screen or cover; the bell-shaped, disk-like swimming organ of certain jellyfish. (L. *umbraculum*.)
umbrella-bird, *n.* a S. American bird of the chatterer group, *Cephalopterus ornatus*, having a large tuft of feathers overhanging the bill.
umbrella-fir, *n.* the evergreen pine, *Sciadopitys verticillata*, of Japan, having needles arranged in umbrella-like whorls.
umbrella-tree, *n.* the American magnolia, *M. tripetala*, or other tree with leaves clustered umbrella-wise.
umbrette, *n.* um-*bret*, an African heron-like bird, the hammerhead, *Scopus umbretta*, remarkable for its large domed nest of sticks.
Umbrian, *a.* *um*-bre-an, pertaining to Umbria, a district of Central Italy: *n.* a native, or the ancient language, of Umbria.
umbriferous, *a.* um-*brif*-er-rus, casting or making a shade. (L. *umbrifer*, shade-bringing.)
umbril, *n.* *um*-bril, the visor of a helmet. (Fr. *ombrel*, shade.)
umbrose, *a.* *um*-brohs, shady.
umbrosity, *n.* um-*bros*-e-te, state of being shady.
umbrous, *a.* *um*-brus, shady; umbrageous.
umiak, *n.* *oo*-me-ak, an Eskimo boat used for seal-hunting, and formerly managed solely by women. (Eskimo.)
umlaut, *n.* *oom*-lout, the modification of a vowel through the influence of another in the following syllable [Gram.]; the sign, the two superimposed dots indicating this, as in *ü* for *ue* in German. (Ger. *um*, about, *laut*, sound.)

umpirage, *n.* *um*-pire-raj, the power or right of an umpire; the decision of an umpire; arbitrament.
umpire, *n.* *um*-pire, one to whose sole decision a controversy or question, actual or potential, is by mutual election or consent referred; a third person called in to decide a controversy; a referee whose duty is to enforce the strict observance of the laws [esp. Games]: *v.t.* to act as umpire. (Earlier *noumpere*, from O.Fr. *nomper*.)
umpireship, *n.* *um*-pire-ship, the post of umpire.
umpteen, *n.* *ump*-teen, a large but indefinite number [Slang].
umpty, *n.* *ump*-te, umpteen [Slang]: *a.* slightly indisposed, out of sorts [Slang].
un-, un-, an Anglo-Saxon prefix before nouns, adjectives, and adverbs signifying not, and the reversal of the action or its undoing before verbs. As its use is unlimited and space is not, for such words as are not given here the consulter is referred to the main word.
una, *n.* *yew*-na, a catboat; a centre-board boat with a single sail set on a mast close to the bow [Naut.]. (Name of the first boat of its kind, brought to England from America in 1852.)
unabased, *a.* *un*-a-*bayst*, not abased; not humbled.
unabashed, *a.* *un*-a-*basht*, not abashed; not confused with shame or from modesty.
unabated, *a.* *un*-a-*bay*-ted, not abated; not diminished in strength or violence.
unable, *a.* un-*ay*-bl, not able; not having sufficient ability or means; not having adequate knowledge or skill; not proficient; incompetent.
unabolishable, *a.* *un*-a-*bol*-ish-a-bl, that cannot be abolished.
unabolished, *a.* *un*-a-*bol*-isht, not abolished; remaining in force.
unabridged, *a.* un-a-*bridjd*, given in full.
unabrogated, *a.* un-*ab*-ro-gay-ted, not annulled.
unabsolved, *a.* *un*-ab-*solvd*, not acquitted or forgiven.
unabsorbed, *a.* *un*-ab-*sorbd*, not absorbed.
unacademic, *a.* *un*-ak-a-*dem*-ik, not conforming to collegiate or scholastic tradition.
unaccelerated, *a.* *un*-ak-*sel*-er-ray-ted, not accelerated.
unaccented, *a.* *un*-ak-*sen*-ted, having no accent.
unacceptable, *a.* *un*-ak-*sep*-ta-bl, not acceptable; not such as will be received with pleasure.
unacclimatized, *a.* *un*-a-*kly*-ma-tized, not acclimatized.
unaccommodated, *a.* *un*-a-*kom*-o-day-ted, not fitted or adapted.
unaccommodating, *a.* *un*-a-*kom*-o-day-ting, not ready to oblige; not compliant.
unaccompanied, *a.* *un*-a-*kum*-pa-ned, not attended; having no attendants, companions or followers; without accompaniment [Mus.].
unaccomplished, *a.* *un*-a-*kom*-plisht, not finished; incomplete; not furnished with accomplishments.
unaccordant, *a.* *un*-a-*kor*-dant, not accordant or harmonious.
unaccountability, *n.* *un*-a-koun-ta-*bil*-e-te, state of being unaccountable or irresponsible; anything inexplicable.
unaccountable, *a.* *un*-a-*koun*-ta-bl, not to be accounted for; not explicable; not responsible.
unaccountableness, *n.* *un*-a-*koun*-ta-bl-ness, the state of being inexplicable or irresponsible.
unaccountably, *ad.* in an unaccountable manner.
unaccredited, *a.* *un*-a-*kred*-e-ted, not accredited; not authorized.
unaccused, *a.* un-a-*kewzd*, not accused.
unaccustomed, *a.* *un*-a-*kus*-tumd, not accustomed; not habituated; unusual.
unachieved, *a.* *un*-a-*cheevd*, not accomplished or performed.
unacknowledged, *a.* *un*-ak-*nol*-edjd, not recognized; not owned.
unacquaintance, *n.* un-a-*kwayn*-tance, want of acquaintance or knowledge.
unacquainted, *a.* *un*-a-*kwayn*-ted, unusual; not having familiar knowledge.
unacquirable, *a.* un-a-*kwire*-ra-bl, not acquirable.
unacquired, *a.* *un*-a-*kwired*, not gained.
unacquitted, *a.* *un*-a-*kwit*-ed, not declared innocent.
unactable, *a.* un-*ak*-ta-bl, not suited for stage performance.
unacted, *a.* un-*ak*-ted, not performed.
unadaptability, *n.* un-a-*dap*-ta-*bil*-e-te, incapability of serving a useful purpose, or of being adjusted.
unadaptable, *a.* *un*-a-*dap*-ta-bl, not capable of being adapted or of adapting oneself.
unaddicted, *a.* *un*-a-*dik*-ted, not given or devoted.
unaddressed, *a.* *un*-a-*drest*, not directed; having no address (of letters, etc.).
unadjudged, *a.* *un*-a-*judjd*, not judicially decided.
unadjusted, *a.* *un*-a-*jus*-ted, not settled; not liquidated.
unadministered, *a.* *un*-ad-*min*-is-terd, not administered.
unadmired, *a.* *un*-ad-*mired*, not regarded with admiration, affection, or respect.
unadmitted, *a.* *un*-ad-*mit*-ed, not acknowledged; not allowed to enter; not permitted.
unadmonished, *a.* *un*-ad-*mon*-isht, not cautioned.
unadopted, *a.* *un*-a-*dop*-ted, not received as one's own.
unadored, *a.* *un*-a-*dored*, not worshipped.
unadorned, *a.* un-a-*dornd*, not decorated; plain.
unadulterated, *a.* *un*-a-*dul*-ter-ray-ted, pure; not mixed; genuine.
unadvanced, *a.* un-ad-*vahnst*, backward; kept in the background; not promoted.
unadventurous, *a.* *un*-ad-*ven*-tewr-rus, not bold.
unadvisable, *a.* *un*-ad-*vy*-za-bl, not advisable; not to be recommended; not expedient.
unadvised, *a.* *un*-ad-*vized*, not prudent; not discreet; done without due consideration.
unadvisedly, *ad.* *un*-ad-*vy*-zed-le, imprudently without due consideration.
unaffable, *a.* un-*af*-a-bl, not free to converse reserved.
unaffected, *a.* *un*-a-*fek*-ted, not affected; plain free from affection; real; not hypocritical.
unaffectedly, *ad.* really; sincerely.
unaffectedness, *n.* state of being unaffected.
unaffectionate, *a.* *un*-a-*fek*-shon-at, wanting affection.
unafflicted, *a.* *un*-a-*flik*-ted, free from trouble.
unaffrighted, *a.* *un*-a-*fry*-ted, not frightened.
unafraid, *a.* *un*-a-*frayd*, without fear.
unaided, *a.* un-*ay*-ded, not assisted.
unaiming, *a.* un-*ay*-ming, having no particular aim or direction.
unakin, *a.* un-a-*kin*, not related.
unal, *a.* *yew*-nal, single; based on unity.
unalarmed, *a.* *un*-a-*larmd*, not disturbed with fear
unalarming, *a.* *un*-a-*lar*-ming, not alarming.
unalienable, *a.* un-*ay*-lyen-a-bl, inalienable.
unalienated, *a.* un-*ay*-lye-nay-ted, not transferred.
unalist, *n.* *yew*-na-list, the holder of only one benefice as opposed to a pluralist [Eccles.].
unallayed, *a.* un-a-*layd*, not appeased.
unalleviated, *a.* *un*-a-*lee*-ve-ay-ted, not mitigated.
unallowable, *a.* *un*-a-*lou*-a-bl, that may not be allowed.
unallowed, *a.* *un*-a-*loud*, not permitted; not approved or sanctioned.
unalloyed, *a.* *un*-a-*loyd*, not alloyed or reduced by admixture.
unalluring, *a.* *un*-a-*lewr*-ring, not tempting.
unalterability, *n.* un-*awl*-ter-ra-*bil*-e-te, immutability.
unalterable, *a.* un-*awl*-ter-ra-bl, unchangeable.
unalterableness, *n.* un-*awl*-ter-ra-bl-ness, unchangeableness.
unalterably, *ad.* un-*awl*-ter-ra-ble, unchangeably.
unaltered, *a.* un-*awl*-terd, not altered or changed.
unamazed, *a.* *un*-a-*mazed*, free from astonishment.
unambiguous, *a.* *un*-am-*big*-yew-us, not of doubtful meaning.
unambiguously, *ad.* clearly and explicitly.
unambiguousness, *n.* clearness; explicitness.
unambitious, *a.* *un*-am-*bish*-us, free from ambition quiet; not affecting show.
unambitiously, *ad.* without ambitiousness.
unamenable, *a.* *un*-a-*mee*-na-bl, not amenable.
unamendable, *a.* *un*-a-*men*-da-bl, not capable of being improved.
unamended, *a.* *un*-a-*men*-ded, not amended.
un-American, *a.* un-a-*me*-re-kan, not conformable to or characteristic of American custom, idiom principle, political dogma, etc.
unamiable, *a.* un-*ay*-me-a-bl, not conciliating; not adapted to gain affection.
unamiableness, *n.* want of amiableness.
unamused, *a.* *un*-a-*mewzd*, not entertained.

unamusing, *a.* *un*-a-*mew*-zing, not affording entertainment.
unanalogical, *a.* *un*-an-a-*loj*-e-kal, not analogical.
unanalogous, *a.* *un*-a-*nal*-o-gus, not analogous.
unanalyzable, *a.* *un*-an-a-*ly*-za-bl, incapable of analysis.
unanalyzed, *a.* un-*an*-a-lized, not resolved into simple parts.
unanchored, *a.* un-*ang*-kerd, not moored; having weighed anchor.
unaneled, *a.* *un*-a-*neeld*, not having received extreme unction.
unanimalized, *a.* un-*an*-e-ma-lized, not formed into animal matter.
unanimated, *a.* un-*an*-e-may-ted, not possessed of life; not enlivened; not having spirit; dull.
unanimating, *a.* un-*an*-e-may-ting, not animating; dull.
unanimiter, *ad.* *yew*-na-*mim*-e-ter, unanimously [Law]. (L.)
unanimity, *n.* yew-na-*nim*-e-te, agreement of all of a number of persons in opinion, determination, etc.
unanimous, *a.* yew-*nan*-e-mus, being of one mind; agreeing in opinion or determination; formed by unanimity. (L. *unanimus*, from *unus*, one, *animus*, mind.)
unanimously, *ad.* with entire agreement of opinion.
unanimousness, *n.* state of being unanimous; unanimity.
unannealed, *a.* *un*-a-*neeld*, not tempered by heat; suddenly cooled.
unannexed, *a.* *un*-a-*nekst*, not annexed or joined.
unannounced, *a.* *un*-a-*nounst*, not announced or proclaimed.
unannoyed, *a.* *un*-a-*noyd*, not annoyed.
unanointed, *a.* *un*-a-*noyn*-ted, not anointed; not having received extreme unction.
unanswerability, *n.* un-*ahn*-ser-ra-*bil*-e-te, the state or quality of being unanswerable.
unanswerable, *a.* un-*ahn*-ser-ra-bl, not capable of refutation; not answerable.
unanswerably, *aj.* un-*ahn*-ser-ra-ble, beyond refutation.
unanswered, *a.* un-*ahn*-serd, not answered; unopposed by a reply; not refuted.
unanticipated, *a.* *un*-an-*tis*-e-pay-ted, not anticipated.
unanxious, *a.* un-*ank*-shus, not anxious.
unapostolic, *a.* *un*-ap-os-*tol*-ik, not in accordance with apostolic authority.
unappalled, *a.* *un*-a-*pawld*, not daunted.
unapparelled, *a.* *un*-a-*pa*-reld, not apparelled or clothed.
unapparent, *a.* *un*-a-*pa*-rent, not apparent; obscure.
unappealable, *a.* *un*-a-*peel*-a-bl, admitting no appeal.
unappeasable, *a.* *un*-a-*peez*-a-bl, not to be pacified.
unappeased, *a.* *un*-a-*peezd*, not pacified.
unappetizing, *a.* un-*ap*-e-ty-zing, not attractive; uninviting; repellent.
unapplauded, *a.* *un*-a-*plaw*-ded, not applauded.
unapplausive, *a.* *un*-a-*plaw*-siv, not applauding.
unappliable, *a.* *un*-a-*ply*-a-bl, inapplicable.
unapplied, *a.* *un*-a-*plide*, not used according to the intention.
unappreciated, *a.* *un*-a-*pree*-she-ay-ted, not duly estimated or valued.
unapprehended, *a.* un-ap-re-*hen*-ded, not apprehended; not understood.
unapprehensible, *a.* un-ap-re-*hen*-se-bl, not capable of being understood.
unapprehensive, *a.* un-ap-re-*hen*-siv, not afraid or suspecting; not intelligent.
unapprehensiveness, *n.* state of being unapprehensive.
unapprised, *a.* *un*-a-*prized*, not previously informed.
unapproachability, *un*-a-*proh*-cha-*bil*-e-te, unapproachableness.
unapproachable, *a.* *un*-a-*proh*-cha-bl, that cannot be approached; inaccessible.
unapproachableness, *n.* state of being unapproachable.
unapproachably, *ad.* inaccessibly.
unapproached, *a.* *un*-a-*proacht*, not to be approached.
unappropriated, *a.* *un*-a-*proh*-pre-ay-ted, not applied to any specific object; not granted to any person or corporation.
unapproved, *a.* *un*-a-*proovd*, not approved; not having received approbation.
unapproving, *a.* *un*-a-*proo*-ving, not approving.
unapt, *a.* un-*apt*, not ready or inclined, esp. to learn; unfit; not qualified; not disposed.
unaptly, *ad.* un-*apt*-le, unfitly; improperly.
unaptness, *n.* un-*apt*-ness, state of being unapt.
unarchitectural, *a.* un-ark-e-*tek*-tewr-ral, unskilled in architecture; not according to the principles of architecture.
unargued, *a.* un-*ar*-gewd, not debated or disputed.
unarm, *v.t.* un-*arm*, to disarm.
unarmed, *a.* un-*armd*, disarmed; not having arms, or armour; not equipped; not furnished with scales or prickles [Zool.].
unarmoured, *a.* un-*ar*-merd, not protected with armour.
unarraigned, *a.* *un*-a-*raynd*, not brought to trial.
unarranged, *a.* *un*-a-*raynjd*, not disposed in order.
unarrayed, *a.* *un*-a-*rayd*, not arrayed; not disposed in order.
unarticulated, *a.* *un*-ar-*tik*-yew-lay-ted, not articulated.
unartificial, *a.* *un*-ar-te-*fish*-al, not formed by art; not artificial; inartificial.
unartificially, *ad.* inartificially.
unartistic, *a.* *un*-ar-*tis*-tik, not like or characteristic of an artist; inartistic.
unary, *a.* *yew*-na-re, occurring as molecules of only one kind [Chem.]. (L. *unus*, one.)
unascertainable *a.* *un*-as-er-*tay*-na-bl, that cannot be certainly known.
unascertained, *a.* *un*-as-er-*taynd*, not known with certainty.
unashamed, *a.* *un*-a-*shaymd*, not ashamed; unabashed; unblushing.
unasked, *a.* un-*ahskt*, unsolicited; not sought by entreaty.
unaspirated, *a.* un-*as*-pe-ray-ted, not aspirated.
unaspiring, *a.* un-as-*pire*-ring, not aspiring or ambitious.
unassailable, *a.* *un*-a-*sale*-a-bl, not assailable; incontestable; proof against attack.
unasserted, *a.* *un*-a-*ser*-ted, not affirmed.
unassessed, *a.* *un*-a-*sest*, not assessed or rated.
unassignable, *a.* *un*-a-*sy*-na-bl, that cannot be transferred by assignment.
unassigned, *a.* *un*-a-*sined*, not transferred.
unassimilated, *a.* *un*-a-*sim*-e-lay-ted, not assimilated; not made to resemble; not converted into bodily substance [Phys.].
unassimilating, *a.* *un*-a-*sim*-e-lay-ting, not assimilating; not readily mixing.
unassisted, *a.* *un*-a-*sis*-ted, not aided; done, or being, without assistance.
unassociated, *a.* *un*-a-*soh*-she-ay-ted, not associated; not united with, or as, a society.
unassorted, *a.* *un*-a-*sor*-ted, not distributed into sorts, grades, or classes, etc.
unassuaged, *a.* *un*-a-*swayjd*, not appeased.
unassuming, *a.* *un*-a-*sew*-ming, not forward or arrogant; modest.
unassured, *a.* *un*-a-*shoord*, not assured; not confident; not insured against loss.
unatonable, *a.* *un*-a-*toh*-na-bl, not to be expiated.
unatoned, *a.* *un*-a-*tohnd*, not expiated.
unattached, *a.* *un*-a-*tacht*, not attached, esp. [Mil.] to a regiment, or [Univ.] to a college, (*i.e.* residing in private lodgings licensed by the university); not engaged (esp. to be married) [Coll.]; not arrested [Law]; not adhering.
unattackable, *a.* *un*-a-*tak*-a-bl, not attackable.
unattainable, *a.* *un*-a-*tane*-a-bl, not to be reached; unobtainable.
unattainableness, *n.* state of being unattainable.
unattainted, *a.* *un*-a-*tane*-ted, not attainted; not corrupted.
unattempered, *a.* *un*-a-*tem*-perd, not tempered by mixture.
unattempted, *a.* *un*-a-*temp*-ted, not tried or essayed.
unattended, *a.* *un*-a-*ten*-ded, not accompanied; having no retinue; not medically attended to.
unattending, *a.* *un*-a-*ten*-ding, not being attentive.
unattenuated, *a.* *un*-a-*ten*-yew-ay-ted, not attenuated.
unattested, *a.* *un*-a-*tes*-ted, having no attestation.
unattired, *a.* *un*-a-*tired*, disrobed; unclothed.
unattractive, *a.* *un*-a-*trak*-tiv, not attractive.

unattractiveness, *n.* want of attraction; the condition of being unattractive.
unau, *n.* yew-*naw*, a two-toed sloth, a South American edentate of the genus *Cholœpus*. (Native name.)
unauthentic, *a.* *un*-aw-*then*-tik, not authentic; apocryphal.
unauthenticated, *a.* *un*-aw-*then*-te-kay-ted, not authenticated; not made certain by authority.
unauthoritative, *a.* *un*-aw-*tho*-re-tay-tiv, being without credentials or due authority; not authoritative.
unauthorized, *a.* un-*aw*-tho-rized, not warranted by proper authority. **unauthorized clerk,** on the Stock Exchange, a clerk permitted to enter "the House," but not authorized to transact business either as agent or principal.
unavailable, *a.* *un*-a-*vale*-a-bl, not available; not effectual; vain; useless.
unavailableness, *n.* state of being unavailable.
unavailing, *a.* *un*-a-*vale*-ing, ineffectual; useless; vain.
unavenged, *a.* *un*-a-*venjd*, not avenged; not having obtained satisfaction; not punished.
unaverted, *a.* *un*-a-*ver*-ted, not turned away.
unavoidable, *a.* *un*-a-*voy*-da-bl, that cannot be made null or void; inevitable.
unavoidably, *ad.* *un*-a-*voy*-da-ble, in a way that could not be avoided.
unavowed, *a.* *un*-a-*voud*, not confessed.
unawakened, *a.* *un*-a-*wake*-nd, not roused from sleep; not roused from spiritual sleep.
unaware, *a.* *un*-a-*ware*, without thought; inattentive: *ad.* unawares.
unawares, *ad.* *un*-a-*warez*, without being or making aware; suddenly; unexpectedly; unintentionally.
unawed, *a.* un-*awd*, not restrained by fear.
unbacked, *a.* un-*bakt*, not having been backed; not taught to bear a rider, unbroken (of horses); unsupported.
unbaffled, *a.* un-*baf*-ld, not defeated or confounded.
unbailable, *a.* un-*bale*-a-bl, not bailable.
unbaked, *a.* un-*baykt*, not baked; not fully baked; immature [Coll.].
unbalanced, *a.* un-*bal*-anst, unsteady; not poised; not brought to an equality of debt and credit; not restrained by equal power; not completely sane.
unballast, *v.t.* un-*bal*-ast, to free from ballast; to discharge ballast from.
unballasted, *a.* un-*bal*-as-ted, not furnished with ballast; unsteady; without enough ballast.
unbandaged, *a.* un-*ban*-dajd, not bandaged.
unbanded, *a.* un-*ban*-ded, stripped of a band; having no band.
unbaptized, *a.* *un*-bap-*tized*, not baptized; of or pertaining to the heathen.
unbar, *v.t.* un-*bar*, to remove a bar or bars from; to unfasten; to open.
unbarbed, *a.* un-*barbd*, unarmed; not having barbs.
unbattered, *a.* un-*bat*-erd, not battered or bruised.
unbearable, *a.* un-*bare*-ra-bl, not to be borne or endured.
unbearably, *ad.* un-*bare*-ra-ble, intolerably.
unbearded, *a.* un-*beer*-ded, having no beard.
unbearing, *a.* un-*bare*-ring, sterile; non-productive.
unbeaten, *a.* un-*bee*-tn, never defeated; unsurpassed; not treated with blows; untrod.
unbeauteous, *a.* un-*bew*-te-us; ugly; unprepossessing.
unbeautiful, *a.* un-*bew*-te-ful, having no beauty.
unbecoming, *a.* *un*-be-*kum*-ing, not suitable; improper for the person or character; indecent; indecorous.
unbecomingly, *ad.* in an unbecoming manner.
unbecomingness, *n.* unsuitability; impropriety.
unbefitting, *a.* *un*-be-*fit*-ing, unsuitable; unbecoming.
unbefriended, *a.* *un*-be-*fren*-ded, not supported by friends; having no friends.
unbeginning, *a.* un-be-*gin*-ing, having no beginning.
unbegotten, *a.* *un*-be-*got*-tn, not begotten or generated; eternal; not yet begotten.
unbeguile, *v.t.* *un*-be-*gile*, to undeceive.
unbegun, *a.* *un*-be-*gun*, not yet begun.
unbeheld, *a.* *un*-be-*held*, not beheld; not visible.
unbeholden, *a.* *un*-be-*hohl*-dn, under no obligation; not bound in gratitude.
unbeknown, *a.* *un*-be-*nohn*, unknown; not within one's knowledge.
unbeknownst, *a.* *un*-be-*nohnst*, unbeknown [Slang].
unbelief, *n.* un-be-*leef*, withholding of belief; incredulity; infidelity; scepticism.
unbelievability, *n.* *un*-be-*lee*-va-*bil*-e-te, incapability of being believed.
unbelievable, *a.* *un*-be-*lee*-va-bl, incredible; that cannot be believed.
unbelieved, *a.* *un*-be-*leevd*, discredited.
unbeliever, *n.* un-be-*lee*-ver, an incredulous person; a misbeliever; an infidel; one who discredits revelation; an atheist.
unbelieving, *a.* *un*-be-*lee*-ving, incredulous; infidel.
unbeloved, *a.* *un*-be-*luvd*, not loved.
unbend, *v.t.* un-*bend*, to free from flexure; to make straight; to relax; to remove the sails from their supports [Naut.]; to untie one rope from another [Naut.]; to cast loose, as a cable [Naut.]: *v.i.* to cease to be bent; to relax; to become less rigid or austere. *p.* and *pp.* **unbent.**
unbending, *a.* un-*bend*-ing, not suffering flexure; unyielding; sternly resolute; inflexible.
unbendingly, *ad.* without bending or yielding.
unbendingness, *n.* inflexibility; stiffness.
unbeneficed, *a.* un-*ben*-e-fist, not holding a benefice.
unbeneficial, *a.* *un*-ben-e-*fish*-al, not advantageous.
unbenefited, *a.* un-*ben*-e-fit-ed, not having received benefit; having gained no advantage.
unbent, un-*bent*, *p.* and *pp.* of *unbend*: *a.* relaxed; not strained; unstrung; not subdued; removed from the spars [Naut.]; loosened off [Naut.].
unbereft, *a.* un-be-*reft*, not bereaved.
unbeseeming, *a.* *un*-be-*seem*-ing, unbecoming; not befitting.
unbeseemingly, *ad.* in an unbeseeming manner.
unbeseemingness, *n.* state of being unbeseeming.
unbesought, *a.* *un*-be-*sawt*, not sought by petition or entreaty.
unbespoken, *a.* *un*-be-*spok*-kn, not bespoken or ordered beforehand.
unbestowed, *a.* *un*-be-*stode*, not given; not disposed of.
unbetrayed, *a.* *un*-be-*trade*, not betrayed.
unbewailed, *a.* *un*-be-*wayld*, not bewailed; not lamented.
unbewitch, *v.t.* *un*-be-*witch*, to free from fascination.
unbiased, *pp.* un-*by*-ast, freed from prejudice or bias: *a.* impartial; unprejudiced.
unbiasedly, *ad.* un-*by*-ast-le, without bias.
unbiasedness, *n.* un-*by*-ast-ness, impartiality.
unbiblical, *a.* un-*bib*-le-kal, not contained in, characteristic of, or authorized by the Bible.
unbidden, *a.* un-*bid*-dn, not bidden; not commanded; spontaneous; uninvited.
unbigoted, *a.* un-*big*-o-ted, free from bigotry.
unbind, *v.t.* un-*bynd*, to untie; to unfasten; to set free.
unbishop, *v.t.* un-*bish*-op, to divest of episcopal status.
unbitt, *v.t.* un-*bit*, to remove the turns of a cable from off the bitts [Naut.].
unbitted, *a.* un-*bit*-ed, not accustomed to the bit, untrained (of horses); uncontrolled.
unblamable, *a.* un-*blay*-ma-bl, not culpable; faultless.
unblamableness, *n.* state or quality of being unblamable.
unblamably, *ad.* without incurring blame.
unblamed, *a.* un-*blaymd*, free from censure.
unblasted, *a.* un-*blahs*-ted, not blasted; not made to wither.
unbleached, *a.* un-*bleecht*, not bleached.
unblemished, *a.* un-*blem*-isht, not blemished; free from turpitude or reproach; free from deformity; blameless; spotless; irreproachable.
unblenched, *a.* un-*blencht*, not disgraced; not injured by stain or soil; unafraid.
unblenching, *a.* un-*blench*-ing, not flinching.
unblended, *a.* un-*blen*-ded, not blended; not mingled.
unblessed, unblest, *a.* un-*blest*, excluded from benediction; unhappy.
unblighted, *a.* un-*bly*-ted, not blighted; not blasted.
unblock, *v.t.* un-*blok*, to remove an obstacle; to free from being blocked.

unblooded, *a.* un-*blud*-ed, not stained with blood; not thoroughbred.
unbloody, *a.* un-*blud*-e, not stained with blood; not cruel.
unblossoming, *a.* un-*blos*-om-ing, not producing blossoms.
unblotted, *a.* un-*blot*-ed, not blotted; not erased; spotless.
unblown, *a.* un-*blone*, not blown; not having the bud expanded; not inflated with wind.
unblunted, *a.* un-*blun*-ted, not made obtuse or dull.
unblushing, *a.* un-*blush*-ing, destitute of shame; barefaced; impudent.
unblushingly, *ad.* without blushing.
unboastful, *a.* un-*boast*-ful, unassuming; modest.
unbodied, *a.* un-*bod*-ed, having no material body; incorporeal; freed from the body.
unboiled, *a.* un-*boyld*, not boiled.
unbolt, *v.t.* un-*bohlt*, to slide a bolt back; to unfasten.
unbolted, *a.* un-*bohl*-ted, freed from fastening by bolts; not bolted or sifted; not having the bran separated.
unbonneted, *a.* un-*bon*-et-ed, with the head uncovered; bare-headed.
unbookish, *a.* un-*book*-ish, not addicted to books or reading; not cultivated by erudition.
unbooted, *a.* un-*boot*-ed, stripped of boots; not having boots on.
unborn, *a.* un-*born*, not born; not yet born or brought to light; future.
unborrowed, *a.* un-*bo*-rode, not borrowed; genuine; one's own.
unbosom, *v.t.* un-*booz*-um, to disclose, as one's secret feelings: *v.i.* to reveal in confidence.
unbottomed, *a.* un-*bot*-umd, unfathomed; unfathomable; bottomless; deprived of foundation.
unbought, *a.* un-*bawt*, not bought; obtained without money or purchase.
unbound, *a.* un-*bound*, not bound, loose, wanting a cover (of books or papers); set free; not bound by obligation.
unbounded, *a.* un-*boun*-ded, having no bound or limit; boundless; infinite; having no check or control.
unboundedly, *ad.* un-*boun*-ded-le, without bounds.
unboundedness, *n.* state of being unbound.
unbounteous, *a.* un-*boun*-te-us, not bounteous; not liberal.
unbowed, *a.* un-*boud*, not arched; not bent; hence, unsubdued.
unboyish, *a.* un-*boy*-ish, not like or characteristic of a boy.
unbrace, *v.t.* un-*brace*, to loose; to relax; to free from tension.
unbraid, *v.t.* un-*brade*, to separate the strands of a braid; to disentangle.
unbranched, *a.* un-*brahncht*, not shooting into branches.
unbreathable, *a.* un-*breethe*-a-bl, not breathable.
unbreathed, *a.* un-*breethed*, not breathed; not divulged; not exercised.
unbred, *a.* un-*bred*, not well bred; uncouth.
unbreech, *v.t.* un-*breetch*, to remove the breeches of; to free the breech of, as a cannon.
unbreeched, *a.* un-*breecht*, having no breeches on; deprived of trousers; not yet of an age for breeches.
unbribable, *a.* un-*bribe*-a-bl, impossible to bribe.
unbribed, *a.* un-*bribed*, not corrupted by money.
unbridged, *a.* un-*bridjd*, not crossed by a bridge.
unbridle, *v.t.* un-*bry*-dl, to free from the bridle; to set free.
unbridled, *a.* un-*bry*-dld, unrestrained; licentious.
un-British, *a.* un-*brit*-ish, not in accordance with British custom, tradition, habit, etc.; unworthy of the British.
unbroken, *a.* un-*broh*-kn, not broken; continuous; not violated; not subdued; not accustomed to the saddle, harness, or yoke.
unbrotherliness, *n.* un-*bruth*-ther-le-ness, conduct not expected of a brother.
unbrotherly, *a.* un-*bruth*-ther-le, not befitting a brother; unkind.
unbruised, *a.* un-*broozd*, not bruised; not crushed or hurt.
unbuckle, *v.t.* un-*bukl*-kl, to loose from buckles; to unfasten.
unbuilt, *a.* un-*bilt*, not yet built; not erected.
unbuoyed, *a.* un-*boyd*, not buoyed or borne up.
unburden, *v.t.* un-*ber*-dn, to rid of a load; to ease; to throw off; to relieve the mind by disclosure.
unburdened, *a.* un-*ber*-dnd, not burdened.
unburdensome, *a.* un-*ber*-dn-sum, not oppressive.
unburiable, *a.* un-*be*-re-a-bl, not suited for or ready for burial.
unburied, *a.* un-*be*-rid, not buried; not interred.
unburning, *a.* un-*burn*-ing, not consuming away by fire.
unburnt, *a.* un-*burnt*, not consumed or injured by fire; not baked.
unbusied, *a.* un-*biz*-ed, not employed; idle.
unbusinesslike, *a.* un-*biz*-ness-like, not business-like; not well ordered.
unbutton, *v.t.* un-*but*-tn, to unfasten a button; to loose by unfastening buttons.
uncage, *v.t.* un-*kaje*, to loose from confinement.
uncalculated, *a.* un-*kal*-kew-lay-ted, not adapted; unexpected; not allowed for.
uncalled, *a.* un-*kawld*, not summoned or invited.
uncalled for, not required; anything but necessary; obtrusively superfluous.
uncancelled, *a.* un-*kan*-sld, not cancelled; not erased.
uncandid, *a.* un-*kan*-did, not candid; not frank or sincere.
uncannily, *ad.* un-*kan*-e-le, weirdly.
uncanniness, *n.* un-*kan*-e-ness, weirdness.
uncanny, *a.* un-*kan*-e, weird; unnatural; mysterious; awkward; dangerous.
uncanonical, *a.* *un*-ka-*non*-e-kal, not canonical; not acknowledged as authentic.
uncanonically, *ad.* without canonicalness.
uncanonize, *v.t.* un-*kan*-on-ize, to deprive of canonical authority; to deprive of canonization.
uncanvassed, *a.* un-*kan*-vast, not canvassed.
uncap, *v.t.* un-*kap*, to remove a cap or cover; to open: *v.i.* to remove the headdress in salute.
uncared, *a.* un-*kared* (with *for*), not regarded; not heeded; not looked after, neglected.
uncaressed, *a.* *un*-ka-*rest*, not caressed.
uncarpeted, *a.* un-*kar*-pet-ed, not covered with a carpet.
uncase, *v.t.* un-*kase*, to disengage from a covering; to take off or out; to display the colours (of a regiment, etc.) [Mil.].
uncate, *a.* *ung*-kat, uncinate [Bot.].
uncatechized, *a.* un-*kat*-e-kized, untaught; not questioned; not taken to task.
uncaught, *a.* un-*kawt*, not caught or taken.
uncaused, *a.* un-*kawzd*, having no precedent cause.
unceasing, *a.* un-*seece*-ing, not ceasing; continual; uninterrupted.
unceasingly, *ad.* un-*seece*-ing-le, without ceasing.
unceded, *a.* un-*see*-ded, not ceded; not granted or transferred.
uncelebrated, *a.* un-*sel*-e-bray-ted, not celebrated or solemnized.
uncelestial, *a.* un-se-*les*-te-al, not heavenly.
uncemented, *a.* un-se-*men*-ted, not cemented.
uncensored, *a.* un-*sen*-sord, not censored; not altered by the censor.
uncensurable, *a.* un-*sen*-shur-ra-bl, not worthy of censure; that cannot be censured.
uncensured, *a.* un-*sen*-shurd, not censured; exempt from blame.
unceremonious, *a.* un-*se*-re-*moh*-ne-us, without ceremony.
unceremoniously, *ad.* without ceremony.
uncertain, *a.* un-*ser*-tan, not certain; doubtful; not sure; not reliable; unsettled; fickle; precarious.
uncertainly, *ad.* not surely; not confidently.
uncertainty, *n.* un-*ser*-tan-te, doubtfulness; dubiousness; want of certainty or precision; contingency.
uncertificated, *a.* *un*-ser-*tif*-e-kay-ted, not holding a certificate, esp. of professional competence; not authorized.
uncertified, *a.* un-*ser*-te-fide, not having a certificate as a guarantee; not assured; not officially pronounced to be insane.
unchain, *v.t.* un-*chayn*, to free from chains or slavery; to set free.
unchallengeable, *a.* un-*chal*-en-ja-bl, that cannot be challenged.
unchallengeably, *ad.* beyond challenge.

unchallenged, *a.* un-*chal*-enjd, not challenged; not objected to.
unchancy, *a.* un-*chahn*-se, ill-omened; dangerous to have to do with; inconvenient.
unchangeable, *a.* un-*chayn*-ja-bl, immutable; not capable of change.
unchangeableness, *n.* the state of being unchangeable.
unchangeably, *ad.* without change.
unchanged, *a.* un-*chaynjd*, not altered; not alterable.
unchanging, *a.* un-*chayn*-jing, suffering no alteration; constant; immutable.
unchangingly, *ad.* without changing.
uncharacteristic, *a.* un-*ka*-rak-ter-*ris*-tik, unsuited to or not exhibiting the character of.
uncharged, *a.* un-*charjd*, not charged; not loaded; not debited against; not accused.
uncharitable, *a.* un-*cha*-re-ta-bl, contrary to charity or Christian love; censorious; harsh.
uncharitableness, *n.* want of charity.
uncharitably, *ad.* in an uncharitable manner.
uncharmed, *a.* un-*charmd*, not fascinated.
uncharming, *a.* un-*char*-ming, not charming.
uncharted, *a.* un-*char*-ted, not shown on a chart; not mapped; unknown.
unchartered, *a.* un-*char*-terd, having no charter; unrestricted.
unchary, *a.* un-*chare*-re, not wary; not frugal.
unchaste, *a.* un-*chayst*, not chaste; libidinous; lewd.
unchastely, *ad.* in an unchaste manner.
unchastisable, *a.* *un*-chas-*ty*-za-bl, that cannot be chastised.
unchastised, *a.* un-chas-*tized*, not punished or corrected.
unchastity, *n.* un-*chas*-te-te, incontinence; lewdness.
unchecked, *a.* un-*chekt*, not restrained or hindered; not controlled.
uncheered, *a.* un-*cheerd*, not cheered; not made joyous; left cheerless.
uncheery, *a.* un-*cheer*-re, dull; not enlivening.
unchequered, *a.* un-*chek*-erd, not diversified.
unchewed, *a.* un-*chood*, not masticated.
unchided, *a.* un-*chy*-ded, not rebuked.
unchildish, *a.* un-*chyl*-dish, not childish; not suitable for the young.
unchilled, *a.* un-*child*, not chilled.
unchivalrous, *a.* un-*shiv*-al-rus, not according to the laws of chivalry.
unchivalrously, *ad.* in an unchivalrous manner.
unchristened, *a.* un-*kriz*-nd, not baptized.
unchristian, *a.* un-*kris*-tyan, contrary to the spirit of Christianity; not converted to Christianity.
unchristianize, *v.t.* un-*kris*-tyan-ize, to seduce or turn from Christianity.
unchronicled, *a.* un-*kron*-e-kld, not recorded.
unchurch, *v.t.* un-*church*, to expel from a church; to deprive of the character and rights of a church.
uncia, *n.* *un*-se-a (*pl.* **unciæ**), a copper coin of ancient Rome, equal to one-twelfth of an as; an ounce. (L.)
uncial, *a.* *un*-she-al, applied to large, round characters resembling cursive capitals, used in certain ancient manuscripts: *n.* an uncial character. (L *uncia*, the twelfth of a foot.)
unciform, *a.* *un*-se-form, hook-shaped [Anat.]: *n.* the unciform bone of the wrist. (L. *uncus*, a hook, and *form*.)
uncinal, *a.* *un*-se-nal, uncinate.
uncinariasis, *n.* *un*-sin-a-*ry*-a-sis, hook-worm disease, ankylostomiasis [Path.].
uncinate, *a.* *un*-se-nat, hooked at the end [Bot.]; having hooks: *n.* an uncinate process [Anat.].
uncinctured, *a.* un-*sink*-tewrd, without a cincture.
uncircumcised, *a.* un-*ser*-kum-sized, not circumcised, hence, not Jewish (or Moslem); heathen; profane.
uncircumcision, *n.* *un*-ser-kum-*sizh*-on, absence of circumcision; the state of being uncircumcised. **the uncircumcision,** the Gentiles.
uncircumscribed, *a.* un-*ser*-kum-skribed, not bounded or limited.
uncircumspect, *a.* un-*ser*-kum-spekt, not circumspect or cautious.
uncircumspectly, *ad.* not circumspectly.
uncirostrate, *a.* *un*-se-*ros*-trat, having a hooked beak.
uncivil, *a.* un-*siv*-il, not complaisant or courteous in manners; not polite.
uncivilizable, *a.* un-*siv*-e-ly-za-bl, irreclaimably savage; incapable of being, or unwilling to be, civilized.
uncivilization, *n.* un-*siv*-e-ly-*zay*-shon, a state of savagery.
uncivilized, *a.* un-*siv*-e-lized, not reclaimed from savage life; barbarous.
uncivilly, *ad.* un-*siv*-e-le, in an uncivil manner.
unclad, *a.* un-*klad*, not clothed.
unclaimed, *a.* un-*klaymd*, not claimed or demanded.
unclarified, *a.* un-*kla*-re-fide, not purified by a separation of feculent or foreign matter; not made clear or lucid.
unclasp, *v.t.* un-*klahsp*, to loosen the clasp of; to open what is fastened as or with a clasp.
unclassable, *a.* un-*klahs*-sa-bl, impossible to classify.
unclassical, *a.* un-*klas*-se-kal, not classical; not according to the best models.
uncle, *n.* *ung*-kl, the brother of a father or mother; a familiar form of address to a man; a pawnbroker [Slang]. **Uncle Sam,** a humorous impersonation of the government or people of the United States (from the initial letters U.S.). (Fr. *oncle*.)
unclean, *a.* un-*kleen*, not clean; foul; dirty; unchaste; ceremonially impure.
uncleanable, *a.* un-*kleen*-a-bl, that cannot be cleansed.
uncleanliness, *n.* un-*klen*-le-ness, want of cleanliness.
uncleanly, *a.* un-*klen*-le, foul; dirty; indecent; spiritually impure.
uncleanly, *ad.* un-*kleen*-le, in a foul or unclean manner; filthily.
uncleanness, *n.* un-*kleen*-ness, foulness; filthiness; lewdness; ceremonial or moral impurity.
uncleansed, *a.* un-*klenzd*, not purified.
unclear, *a.* un-*kleer*, not lucid; indistinct; obscure; unable easily to understand.
uncleared, *a.* un-*kleerd*, not cleared; not freed from encumbrance; not explained.
unclench, *v.t.* un-*klench*, to unclinch.
unclerical, *a.* un-*kle*-re-kal, not clerical; not befitting a priest.
unclew, *v.t.* un-*kloo*, to unloose; to unwind [Naut.].
unclinch, *v.t.* un-*klinch*, to free from a clinch; to open, esp. the clenched hand.
unclipped, *a.* un-*klipt*, not diminished or shortened by clipping.
uncloak, *v.t.* and *i.* un-*kloak*, to take off the outer garment; to disrobe.
unclog, *v.t.* un-*klog*, to disencumber of obstructions; to free from anything that retards motion.
uncloister, *v.t.* un-*kloy*-ster, to release from a cloister or from confinement.
unclose, *v.t.* un-*kloze*, to break the seal of; to disclose or lay open.
unclosed, *a.* un-*klozed*, not separated by enclosures; unenclosed; open; not finished; not concluded; not closed.
unclothe, *v.t.* un-*kloathe*, to strip of clothes; to make naked; to lay bare.
uncloud, *v.t.* un-*kloud*, to clear from clouds or obscurity.
uncloudedness, *n.* un-*klou*-ded-ness, state of being unclouded, or free from gloom or sorrow.
unclubbable, *a.* un-*klub*-a-bl, not suited to club life; not sociable.
unclutch, *v.t.* un-*klutch*, to open something closely shut; to unclinch; to disengage a clutch.
unco, *a.* *un*-koh, uncommon: *ad.* very, uncommonly [Scots.]. **the unco guid,** persons of, or affecting, the strictest morality [Scots.]. (Abbrev. of *uncouth*.)
uncoagulable, *a.* *un*-koh-*ag*-yew-la-bl, that cannot be coagulated.
uncoagulated, *a.* *un*-koh-*ag*-yew-lay-ted, not coagulated.
uncoated, *a.* un-*koh*-ted, not wearing, or covered with, a coat; not having been given a coat or coating.
uncocked, *a.* un-*kokt*, not cocked, as a gun; not made into cocks, as hay; not set up, as the brim of a hat.
uncoffined, *a.* un-*kof*-ind, not furnished with a coffin; removed from a coffin.
uncoil, *v.t.* and *i.* un-*koyl*, to unwind or open, as the turns of a rope; to release from coils.

uncoined, *a.* un-*koynd*, not coined; withdrawn from currency as a coin; not artificial.
uncollectable, *a.* *un*-ko-*lek*-ta-bl, that cannot be collected or levied.
uncollected, *a.* *un*-ko-*lek*-ted, not collected or received; not recovered from confusion or wandering; disconcerted.
uncoloured, *a.* un-*kul*-urd, not coloured, stained, or dyed; not heightened in description.
uncombed, *a.* un-*kohmd*, not dressed with a comb; unkempt.
uncombinable, *a.* un-kom-*by*-na-bl, not capable of combining or being combined.
uncombined, *a.* un-kom-*bynd*, not combined; simple.
un-come-at-able, *a.* *un*-kum-*at*-a-bl, inaccessible.
uncomeliness, *n.* un-*kum*-le-ness, want of beauty or grace.
uncomely, *a.* un-*kum*-le, wanting grace; unseemly.
uncomfortable, *a.* un-*kum*-for-ta-bl, affording no comfort; gloomy; giving uneasiness; uneasy.
uncomfortably, *ad.* in an uncomfortable manner or state.
uncomforted, *a.* un-*kum*-for-ted, not comforted.
uncommanded, *a.* *un*-ko-*mahn*-ded, not required by precept, order, or law.
uncommemorated, *a.* *un*-ko-*mem*-o-ray-ted, not commemorated.
uncommendable, *a.* *un*-ko-*men*-da-bl, not worthy of commendation.
uncommended, *a.* *un*-ko-*men*-ded, not praised.
uncommerciable, *a.* *un*-ko-*mer*-sha-bl, not marketable; unsuitable as an article of trade.
uncommercial, *a.* *un*-ko-*mer*-shal, not commercial; not carrying on, or related to, commerce; not in accordance with commercial methods.
uncommiserated, *a.* *un*-ko-*miz*-er-ray-ted, not pitied.
uncommissioned, *a.* *un*-ko-*mish*-ond, not having a commission; non-commissioned (of ships).
uncommitted, *a.* *un*-ko-*mit*-ed, not committed; not referred to a committee; not pledged by anything said or done.
uncommon, *a.* un-*kom*-on, unusual; not frequent; rare; singular: *ad.* uncommonly, very [Coll.].
uncommonly, *ad.* rarely; to an uncommon degree; very [Coll.].
uncommonness, *n.* state of being uncommon.
uncommunicated, *a.* *un*-ko-*mew*-ne-kay-ted, not disclosed or imparted to others.
uncommunicative, *a.* *un*-ko-*mew*-ne-ka-tiv, reticent; reserved.
uncommunicativeness, *n.* taciturnity; cautious reserve.
uncompact, *a.* *un*-kom-*pakt*, not of close texture.
uncompacted, *a.* *un*-kom-*pak*-ted, not compact or firm; incompact.
uncompanied, *a.* un-*kum*-pa-ned, unaccompanied; having no companion.
uncompanionable, *a* *un*-kum-*pan*-yun-a-bl, not sociable.
uncompassionate, *a.* *un*-kom-*pash*-on-ate, having no pity.
uncompassioned, *a.* *un*-kom-*pash*-ond, unpitied.
uncompellable, *a.* *un*-kom-*pel*-a-bl, that cannot be forced or compelled.
uncompelled, *a.* *un*-kom-*peld*, not forced.
uncompensated, *a.* un-*kom*-pen-say-ted, unrewarded; not compensated.
uncomplaining, *a.* *un*-kom-*play*-ning, not disposed to murmur.
uncomplaisant, *a.* *un*-kom-*play*-zant, not civil or courteous.
uncomplaisantly, *ad.* uncivilly; discourteously.
uncompleted, *a.* *un*-kom-*plee*-ted, not complete; not finished.
uncompliable, *a.* un-kom-*ply*-a-bl, not complying.
uncomplicated, *a.* un-*kom*-ple-kay-ted, not complicated; simple.
uncomplimentary, *a.* un-*kom*-ple-*men*-ta-re, not complimentary; uncivil; abusive.
uncomplying, *a.* *un*-kom-*ply*-ing, not yielding to request or command; unbending.
uncomposed, *a.* un-kom-*pozed*, not composed; disordered; not organized.
uncompounded, *a.* *un*-kom-*poun*-ded, not mixed; simple.
uncomprehensive, *a.* *un*-kom-pre-*hen*-siv, not comprehensive; unable to comprehend.
uncompressed, *a.* *un*-kom-*prest*, not compressed.
uncompromising, *a.* un-*kom*-pro-my-zing, not admitting of compromise; not yielding; inflexible.
unconcealed, *a.* *un*-kon-*seeld*, not concealed.
unconceived, *a.* *un*-kon-*seevd*, not thought or imagined.
unconcern, *n.* *un*-kon-*sern*, want of concern; absence of anxiety.
unconcerned, *a.* *un*-kon-*sernd*, not anxious; having no interest; indifferent.
unconcernedly, *ad.* *un*-kon-*ser*-ned-le, without concern or anxiety.
unconcernedness, *n.* *un*-kon-*ser*-ned-ness, freedom from concern.
unconcerted, *a.* *un*-kon-*ser*-ted, not concerted.
unconciliated, *a.* *un*-kon-*sil*-e-ay-ted, not reconciled.
unconciliatory, *a.* *un*-kon-*sil*-e-a-to-re, not tending to conciliate.
unconclusive, *a.* un-kon-*kloo*-siv, not conclusive.
unconcocted, *a.* *un*-kon-*kok*-ted, not digested; crude; not elaborated.
uncondemned, *a.* *un*-kon-*demd*, not judged guilty; not disapproved; not pronounced criminal.
unconditional, *a.* *un*-kon-*dish*-on-al, absolute; unreserved; not limited by any conditions. **unconditional surrender**, complete and total surrender, without terms stated or preliminary armistice.
unconditionality, *n.* *un*-kon-dish-o-*nal*-e-te, the quality of being unconditional.
unconditionally, *ad.* without conditions.
unconditioned, *a.* *un*-kon-*dish*-ond, unconditional; having no limiting principle, and therefore unthinkable [Met.]; inherent, not dependent on being taught [Psychan.]. **the unconditioned**, that which is unconditioned or unknowable [Phil.].
unconducted, *a.* *un*-kon-*duk*-ted, not led; not guided.
unconfessed, *a.* *un*-kon-*fest*, not acknowledged.
unconfinable, *a* *un*-kon-*fy*-na-bl, that cannot be confined or restrained.
unconfined, *a.* *un*-kon-*fynd*, free from restraint or control; having no limits.
unconfinedly, *ad.* *un*-kon-*fy*-ned-le, without confinement or limitation.
unconfirmed, *a.* *un*-kon-*fermd*, not confirmed by additional testimony; uncorroborated; not fortified by resolution; not confirmed according to ritual.
unconformable, *a.* *un*-kon-*for*-ma-bl, not consistent; not conforming; not parallel (esp. Geol., of a series of rocks resting on the upturned edges of another series).
unconformably, *ad.* not conformably.
unconformity, *n.* *un*-kon-*for*-me-te, incongruity; inconsistency; the state of being unconformable.
unconfounded, *a.* *un*-kon-*foun*-ded, not confounded.
unconfused, *a.* *un*-kon-*fewzd*, not embarrased.
unconfusedly, *ad.* *un*-kon-*few*-zed-le, without confusion or embarrassment.
unconfutable, *a.* *un*-kon-*few*-ta-bl, not to be refuted or overthrown.
uncongealable, *a.* *un*-kon-*jeel*-a-bl, not capable of being congealed.
uncongealed, *a.* *un*-kon-*jeeld*, not frozen or congealed.
uncongenial, *a.* *un*-kon-*jee*-ne-al, not congenial.
unconjugal, *a.* un-*kon*-ju-gal, not befitting a husband or wife.
unconnected, *a.* *un*-ko-*nek*-ted, not united; separate; not coherent; loose; desultory.
unconniving, *a.* *un*-ko-*ny*-ving, not overlooking or winking at.
unconquerable, *a.* un-*kong*-ker-ra-bl, that cannot be overcome in contest; invincible; insuperable.
unconquerably, *ad.* invincibly; insuperably.
unconquered, *a.* un-*kong*-kerd, not vanquished or defeated; unsubdued.
unconscientious, *a.* *un*-kon-she-*en*-shus, not regulated or restrained by conscience.
unconscionable, *a.* un-*kon*-shon-a-bl, unreasonable; forming unreasonable expectations; not influenced by conscience; enormous; egregious.
unconscionableness, *n.* unreasonableness of hope or claim; unscrupulousness.
unconscionably, *ad.* unreasonably.

unconscious, *a.* un-*kon*-shus, not conscious; having no mental perception; not perceiving. **the unconscious,** that region of the mental self that is unaffected by consciousness and is partially revealed by dreams, hysteria, phobias, etc. [Psychan.].
unconsciously, *ad.* without perception or being aware.
unconsciousness, *n.* the state of being unconscious.
unconsecrated, *a.* un-*kon*-se-kray-ted, not set apart for sacred use.
unconsenting, *a.* un-kon-*sen*-ting, not yielding consent.
unconsidered, *a.* *un*-kon-*sid*-erd, not considered or attended to.
unconsoled, *a.* *un*-kon-*sohld*, not consoled or comforted.
unconsolidated, *a.* *un*-kon-*sol*-e-day-ted, not made solid; not centralized; not amalgamated.
unconsoling, *a.* *un*-kon-*soh*-ling, affording no comfort.
unconsonant, *a.* un-*kon*-so-nant, incongruous.
unconstitutional, *a.* un-*kon*-ste-*tew*-sho-nal, not authorized by the constitution, or contrary to its principles.
unconstitutionality, *n.* *un*-kon-ste-*tew*-sho-*nal*-e-te, contrariety to the constitution.
unconstitutionally, *ad.* *un*-kon-ste-*tew*-sho-na-le, in a manner contrary to the constitution.
unconstrained, *a.* *un*-kon-*straynd*, free from constraint; voluntary.
unconstrainedly, *ad.* *un*-kon-*stray*-ned-le, without constraint; voluntarily.
unconstraint, *n.* *un*-kon-*straynt*, freedom from restraint; ease.
unconsulted, *a.* *un*-kon-*sul*-ted, not asked or consulted.
unconsumed, *a.* *un*-kon-*sewmd*, not consumed, wasted, or dissipated.
uncontemned, *a.* *un*-kon-*temd*, not despised.
uncontemplated, *a.* un-*kon*-tem-play-ted, not contemplated.
uncontended, *a.* *un*-kon-*ten*-ded, not disputed for.
uncontent, *a.* un-kon-*tent*, uncontented: *n.* want of contentment.
uncontented, *a.* *un*-kon-*ten*-ted, discontented.
uncontested, *a.* *un*-kon-*tes*-ted, not contested; not disputed.
uncontradictable, *a.* un-*kon*-tra-*dik*-ta-bl, that cannot be contradicted.
uncontrite, *a.* un-*kon*-trite, not penitent.
uncontrived, *a.* *un*-kon-*trived*, not formed by design.
uncontriving, *a.* *un*-kon-*try*-ving, improvident; not contriving.
uncontrollable, *a.* *un*-kon-*troh*-la-bl, that cannot be controlled.
uncontrollably, *ad.* without possibility of control.
uncontrolled, *a.* *un*-kon-*trohld*, free from control.
uncontrolledly, *ad.* *un*-kon-*troh*-led-le, without control.
uncontroversial, *a.* *un*-kon-tro-*ver*-se-al, not a cause of dispute; not given to disputation.
uncontroverted, *a.* *un*-kon-tro-*ver*-ted, not disputed or called in question.
unconventional, *a.* *un*-kon-*ven*-sho-nal, not in accordance with convention; not paying attention to convention; casual.
unconversable, *a.* *un*-kon-*ver*-sa-bl, not free in conversation; unsocial.
unconversant, *a.* un-*kon*-ver-sant, not familiarly acquainted with.
unconverted, *a.* *un*-kon-*ver*-ted, not changed in opinion; not turned from one faith to another; not Christianized; not renewed; not regenerated; (of a try) not converted into a goal [Rugby football].
unconvertible, *a.* *un*-kon-*ver*-te-bl, that cannot be changed in form; not capable of being exchanged for coin (of paper money).
unconvinced, *a.* *un*-kon-*vinst*, not convinced.
unconvincing, *a.* *un*-kon-*vin*-sing, not sufficient to convince.
unconvulsed, *a.* *un*-kon-*vulst*, not convulsed.
uncoop, *v.t.* un-*koop*, to let loose from a coop; to set free.
uncord, *v.t.* un-*kord*, to unfasten or unbind.
uncordial, *a.* un-*kor*-de-al, not cordial; not hearty.
uncork, *v.t.* un-*kork*, to draw the cork from; to give vent to (one's feelings) [Fig.].
uncorrected, *a.* *un*-ko-*rek*-ted, not corrected; not revised; not reformed; not amended.
uncorroborated, *a.* *un*-ko-*rob*-o-ray-ted, not attested to by other witness or evidence; not confirmed.
uncorrupt, *a.* *un*-ko-*rupt*, not corrupt; not depraved or perverted; not vitiated.
uncorruptible, *a.* *un*-kor-*rup*-te-bl, that cannot be corrupted.
uncorruptness, *n.* integrity; uprightness.
uncounsellable, *a.* un-*koun*-sel-a-bl, not to be advised.
uncounselled, *a.* un-*koun*-seld, not having advice.
uncountable, *a.* un-*koun*-ta-bl, that cannot be counted; innumerable; untold.
uncounted, *a.* un-*koun*-ted, not numbered; innumerable; not included.
uncountenanced, *a.* un-*koun*-te-nanst, not encouraged.
uncouple, *v.t.* and *i.* un-*kup*-pl, to loose; to disconnect; to unleash (hounds).
uncourteous, *a.* un-*kur*-te-us, uncivil; rude.
uncourteously, *ad.* uncivilly; impolitely.
uncourteousness, *n.* un-*kurt*-e-us-ness, incivility.
uncourtliness, *n.* un-*kort*-le-ness, unsuitableness of manners to a court.
uncourtly, *a.* un-*kort*-le, inelegant in manners; not befitting a court; impolite; rude; not versed in polite manners or those of a court.
uncouth, *a.* un-*kooth*, odd, strange; awkward; clumsy. (A.S. *uncuth*, unknown.)
uncouthly, *ad.* in an uncouth manner.
uncouthness, *n.* oddness; strangeness; awkwardness.
uncovenanted, *a.* un-*kuv*-e-nan-ted, not promised by covenant; not under an agreement.
uncover, *v.t.* and *i.* un-*kuv*-er, to divest of a cover; to remove any covering from; to deprive of clothes; to strip; to unroof; to take off the hat or cap; to strip off a veil; to disclose to view.
uncovered, *a.* un-*kuv*-erd, not having a cover overhead; naked; having no veil or hat; exposed; not protected by an insurance policy.
uncramped, *a.* un-*krampt*, not confined or fettered.
uncreated, *a.* *un*-kre-*ay*-ted, not yet created; not produced by creation.
uncredited, *a.* un-*kred*-e-ted, not believed; not credited to an account.
uncritical, *a.* un-*krit*-e-kal, not critical, or according to the just rules of criticism.
uncropped, *a.* un-*kropt*, not cropped or gathered.
uncrossed, *a.* un-*krost*, not crossed (esp. of cheques); not cancelled, opposed, or thwarted.
uncrowded, *a.* un-*krou*-ded, not crowded or compressed.
uncrown, *v.t.* un-*kroun*, to deprive of a crown; to dethrone; to pull off the crown. **uncrowned king,** one having, in his own sphere, the power but not the official authority of a king [Coll.].
uncrystalline, *a.* un-*kris*-ta-line, not having the characteristics of a crystal.
uncrystallizable, *a.* un-*kris*-ta-*ly*-za-bl, not susceptible of crystallization.
unction, *n.* *unk*-shon, the act of anointing symbolically for consecration, or medically for healing; unguent; ointment; anything soothing or lenitive; warmth and persuasiveness of address; affected emotion or enthusiasm; divine or sanctifying grace; fervour. **extreme unction,** *see* **extreme.** (L. *ungo*, *unctum*, anoint.)
unctuosity, *n.* unk-tew-*os*-e-te, unctuousness; affected religiosity.
unctuous, *a.* *unk*-tew-us, oily; greasy; having a resemblance to oil.
unctuously, *ad.* *unk*-tew-us-le, with unction; in an unctuous manner.
unctuousness, *n.* the state or quality of being unctuous.
unculled, *a.* un-*kuld*, not gathered; not selected.
uncultivable, *a.* un-*kul*-te-va-bl, not capable of being cultivated.
uncultivated, *a.* un-*kul*-te-vay-ted, not tilled; not instructed; uncivilized; rough in manners; neglected.
uncultured, *a.* un-*kult*-yewrd, without culture; unrefined; boorish.
uncumbered, *a.* un-*kum*-berd, not burdened; not embarrassed.
uncurable, *a.* un-*kewr*-ra-bl, incurable.
uncurbed, *a.* un-*kurbd*, not restrained; licentious.

uncurl, *v.t.* un-*kurl*, to loose a state of curl or from ringlets : *v.i.* to fall from curls ; to become straight.
uncurrent, *a.* un-*ku*-rent, not in circulation (of coin, etc.) ; not commonly recognized.
uncurtailed, *a.* un-kur-*tayld*, not shortened.
uncurtained, *a.* un-*kur*-tnd, not provided with curtains ; having the curtains drawn aside ; exposed to view.
uncus, *n. ung*-kus, a hook or claw [Anat. and Zool.] ; a beak-like process in some insects.
uncustomable, *a.* un-*kus*-tum-a-bl, not subject to customs duty.
uncustomary, *a.* un-*kus*-tum-a-re, not customary ; not usual.
uncustomed, *a.* un-*kus*-tumd, not subject to customs duty ; that has not paid customs duty or been charged with it.
uncut, *a.* un-*kut*, not cut ; having the margins uncut, or with the leaves not cut open (of books).
undamaged, *a.* un-*dam*-ajd, not made worse ; unhurt.
undamped, *a.* un-*dampt*, not damped ; not depressed or discouraged.
undarkened, *a.* un-*dark*-nd, not darkened or obscured.
undate, *a. un*-date, waved ; undulating ; rising and falling in waves. (L. *unda*, a wave.)
undated, *a.* un-*day*-ted, having no date ; no date being named.
undated, *a. un*-day-ted, undate.
undauntable, *a.* un-*dawn*-ta-bl, not to be daunted.
undaunted, *a.* un-*dawn*-ted not subdued or depressed by fear ; bold ; courageous.
undauntedly, *ad.* boldly ; intrepidly.
undauntedness, *n.* boldness ; intrepidity.
undazzled, *a.* un-*daz*-ld, not confused by splendour.
undé, *a. un*-de, undy [Her.].
undebarred, *a.* un-de-*bard*, not debarred.
undebased, *a.* un-de-*bayst*, not adulterated.
undebauched, *a.* un-de-*bawcht*, not corrupted ; pure.
undecagon, *n.* un-*dek*-a-gon, a plane figure of eleven angles and eleven sides. (L. *undecim*, eleven, and Gr. *gonia*, an angle.)
undecayed, *a. un*-de-*kade*, not impaired by age or accident.
undecaying, *a. un*-de-*kay*-ing, not suffering diminution or decline ; immortal.
undeceivable, *a. un*-de-*seev*-a-bl, not subject to deception.
undeceive, *v.t. un*-de-*seev*, to free from deception or mistake ; to make aware of the truth.
undecennary, *a.* un-de-*sen*-a-re, pertaining to an eleven-year period ; occuring once in eleven years. (L. *undecim*, eleven.)
undecennial, *a.* un-de-*sen*-e-al, undecennary.
undeception, *n.* un-de-*sep*-shon, an undeceiving ; the act of undeceiving.
undeceptive, *a. un*-de-*sep*-tiv, not deceptive.
undecidable, *a. un*-de-*sy*-da-bl, that cannot be decided.
undecided, *a. un*-de-*sy*-ded, not decided ; vacillating.
undecidedly, *ad.* irresolutely ; in an undecided manner.
undecipherable, *a. un*-de-*sy*-fer-ra-bl, indecipherable ; illegible.
undeciphered, *a. un*-de-*sy*-ferd, not deciphered or explained.
undecisive, *a. un*-de-*sy*-siv, indecisive : inconclusive.
undecked, *a.* un-*dekt*, not adorned ; not having a deck [Naut.].
undeclared, *a. un*-de-*klared*, not declared ; not avowed.
undeclinable, *a. un*-de-*kly*-na-bl, indeclinable.
undeclined, *a. un*-de-*klynd*, not declined, not varied in termination or inflexion, indeclinable [Gram.].
undecomposed, *a.* un-*dee*-kom-*pohzd*, not decomposed.
undecompounded, *a.* un-*dee*-kom-*poun*-ded, not decompounded.
undecorated, *a.* un-*dek*-o-ray-ted, not adorned or embellished.
undedicated, *a.* un-*ded*-e-kay-ted, not dedicated or consecrated ; not inscribed to a patron.
undee, *a. un*-de, undy [Her.].
undeeded, *a.* un-*dee*-ded, not transferred by deed [Law].
undefaceable, *a. un*-de-*face*-a-bl, that cannot be defaced.
undefaced, *a. un*-de-*fayst*, not deprived of its form or disfigured.
undefeasible, *a. un*-de-*fee*-ze-bl, indefeasible.
undefecated, *a.* un-*def*-e-kay-ted, unpurged ; not cleaned from impurities.
undefended, *a. un*-de-*fen*-ded, not protected ; not vindicated ; open to assault. **undefended action,** one not contested by the defendant or otherwise [Law].
undefied, *a. un*-de-*fide*, not set at defiance or challenged.
undefiled, *a. un*-de-*fyld*, not defiled or polluted.
undefinable, *a. un*-de-*fy*-na-bl, not capable of being defined ; unsusceptible of definition [Logic].
undefinableness, *n.* the state or quality of being undefinable.
undefined, *a. un*-de-*fynd*, not defined.
undeformed, *a. un*-de-*formd*, not deformed or disfigured.
undefrayed, *a. un*-de-*frayd*, not defrayed or paid.
undegraded, *a. un*-de-*gray*-ded, not degraded.
undeify, *v.t.* un-*dee*-e-fy, to reduce from the state of deity.
undelayed, *a. un*-de-*layd*, not delayed.
undelaying, *a. un*-de-*lay*-ing, not making delay.
undelectable, *a. un*-de-*lek*-ta-bl, unpleasant.
undelegated, *a.* un-*del*-e-gay-ted, not deputed.
undeliberate, *a. un*-de-*lib*-er-rat, not deliberate.
undeliberated, *a. un*-de-*lib*-er-ray-ted, not carefully considered.
undelighted, *a. un*-de-*ly*-ted, not delighted or well pleased.
undeliverable, *a. un*-de-*liv*-er-ra-bl, incapable of release ; incapable of being delivered.
undelivered, *a. un*-de-*liv*-erd, not delivered.
undemanded, *a. un*-de-*mahn*-ded, not demanded ; not required.
undemocratic, *a. un*-dem-o-*krat*-ik, not in accordance with democratic principles ; totalitarian ; reactionary [Polit.].
undemocratize, *v.t. un*-de-*mok*-ra-tize, to make undemocratic.
undemolished, *a. un*-de-*mol*-isht, not pulled down or destroyed.
undemonstrable, *a.* un-*dem*-on-stra-bl, not capable of being demonstrated.
undemonstrated, *a.* un-*dem*-on-stray-ted, not proved by demonstration.
undemonstrative, *a. un*-de-*mon*-stra-tiv, not given to a display of feeling.
undeniable, *a. un*-de-*ny*-a-bl, that cannot be denied ; indubitable ; indisputable.
undeniably, *ad.* beyond denial.
undenominational, *a. un*-de-*nom*-e-*nay*-sho-nal, allowing no distinction between denominations ; unsectarian.
undependable, *a.* un-de-*pen*-da-bl, not to be relied upon ; not trustworthy.
undeplored, *a. un*-de-*plord*, not lamented.
undeposable, *a. un*-de-*poh*-za-bl, that cannot be deposed from office.
undeposed, *a.* un-de-*pohzd*, not deposed.
undepraved, *a. un*-de-*prayvd*, not corrupted or vitiated.
undeprecated, *a.* un-*dep*-re-kay-ted, not deprecated ; not protested against.
undepreciated, *a. un*-de-*pree*-she-ay-ted, not depreciated ; retaining the original value.
undepressed, *a. un*-de-*prest*, not depressed ; not dejected.
undeprived, *a. un*-de-*pryvd*, not divested of any possession or right.
★**under,** *prep. un*-der, beneath ; below ; in a state of pupilage or subjection to ; less than ; for less than ; in a degree inferior to ; with the pretence of ; in a state of oppression ; during the time of ; attested or signed by ; in subordination to : *a.* lower in degree ; subordinate : *ad.* in a lower or subordinate place or condition, etc. **keep under,** to hold in subjection ; to restrain. **under a cloud,** out of favour. **under orders,** having received definite commands. **under repair,** being repaired. **under the breath,** in a whisper. **under the influence,** [Slang] partly drunk. **under the weather** see **weather. under way,** beginning to move after the anchor is started [Naut.]. (A.S. *under*.)
underact, *v.t. un*-der-*akt*, to perform feebly in a

stage play ; to fail as an actor in the interpretation of a part.

underaction, *n.* *un*-der-*ak*-shon, action not essential to the main story ; insufficient action.

under-age, *a.* not mature ; in one's minority.

underanged, *a.* *un*-de-*raynjd*, not deranged.

underarm, *a.* *un*-der-arm, with the hand below the knee in bowling [Cricket] : *ad.* in the underarm manner.

underarm, *v.t.* un-der-*arm*, to arm insufficiently.

underbear, *v.t.* *un*-der-*bare*, to support ; to endure.

underbearer, *n.* *un*-der-bare-rer, one who supports the coffin at a funeral.

under-belly, *n.* the surface of the belly of a quadruped, reptile, etc.

underbid, *v.t.* *un*-der-*bid*, to bid or offer less than another ; to offer to do for less : *n.* an instance of underbidding, as at auctions or in Bridge, etc.

underbidder, *n.* *un*-der-*bid*-er, one who underbids.

underbitten, *a.* *un*-der-*bit*-n, not bitten in enough by an acid [Etching, etc.].

underboard, *ad.* *un*-der-bord, secretly ; in an underhanded manner.

underbody, *n.* *un*-der-*bod*-e, the under part of the body of a vehicle ; the part of the hull of a ship which is under the waterline.

underbred, *a.* *un*-der-*bred*, of ill breeding or manners.

underbreeding, *n.* un-der-*bree*-ding, state or quality of being underbred.

underbrush, *n.* *un*-der-brush, shrubs and small trees in a wood or forest, growing under large trees.

underbuy, *v.t.* un-der-*by*, to buy cheaper than ; to buy at less than the true value : *v.i.* to buy too little.

undercall, *v.t.* and *n.* un-der-*kawl*, underbid (esp. in Bridge, etc.).

undercarriage, *n.* *un*-der-*ka*-raj, a supporting framework ; that part of an aeroplane intended for its support on land or water.

undercharge, *n.* *un*-der-charj, a price or charge that is too little : *v.t.* un-der-*charj*, to load insufficiently ; to charge too little.

underclay, *n.* *un*-der-klay, a bed of clay underlying coal seams [Geol.].

undercliff, *n.* *un*-der-klif, a range of cliffs below others, esp. on the seashore.

underclothes, *n.pl.* *un*-der-kloathz, underwear.

underclothing, *n.* *un*-der-*kloathe*-ing, underclothes ; a set of underclothes.

undercoat, *n.* *un*-der-koat, a coat worn beneath another ; the short hair under the coat of a furred animal ; a first coat of paint.

undercroft, *n.* *un*-der-*kroft*, a crypt ; a vault under the choir or chancel of a church ; an underground vault. (*under*, and O.Dut. *krocht*, a crypt.)

undercurrent, *n.* *un*-der-*ku*-rent, a current below the surface of water ; an unseen influence : *a.* being beneath the surface ; unseen.

undercut, *n.* *un*-der-kut, a cut upwards ; a part cut away ; the under part of ribs of beef, or the tenderloin ; a cut made with an underhand stroke [Lawn Tennis] : *v.t.* to cut away material below the surface ; to sell or offer for sale at lower than the recognized price [Comm.] ; to hit the ball so as to make it rise [Golf], or with an underhand stroke [Lawn Tennis].

underdeveloped, *a.* *un*-der-de-*vel*-opd, not sufficiently developed, esp. [Phot.] of negatives.

underditch, *v.t.* *un*-der-*ditch*, to form a deep ditch or trench to drain the surface of land.

underdo, *v.i.* *un*-der-*doo*, to act below one's abilities ; to do less than is requisite. *pp.* **underdone.**

under-dog, *n.* *un*-der-dog, the conquered dog in a dog-fight ; one who is defeated or oppressed ; one of very low social standing ; one who is downtrodden.

underdone, *a.* *un*-der-*dun*, done inadequately, or less than is requisite ; not cooked enough.

underdose, *n.* *un*-der-dohs, a quantity less than a dose : *v.t.* to give an insufficient dose to.

underdrain, *n.* *un*-der-drayn, a drain or trench below the surface of the ground : *v.t.* to drain by cutting a deep channel below the surface.

underdress, *v.t.* un-der-*dress*, to dress too scantily or too plainly : *n.* *un*-der-dress, underclothing.

underestimate, *v.t.* *un*-der-*es*-te-mate, to estimate too low : *n.* an insufficient estimate.

underestimation, *n.* *un*-der-es-te-*may*-shon, too low a valuation or appraisal.

under-expose, *v.t.* to expose the plate or film for less than the requisite time [Phot.].

under-exposure, *n.* the act of under-exposing ; a negative or picture obtained by this means.

underfeed, *v.t.* and *i.* *un*-der-*feed*, to provide or to take too little food.

underfired, *a.* un-der-*fyrd*, not baked enough (of pottery, porcelain, etc.).

underfoot, *ad.* un-der-*foot*, beneath ; under control ; in an inferior position : *a.* low ; base ; abject ; downtrodden.

underfur, *n.* *un*-der-fur, the undercoat, or thick short hair grown by some furred animals beneath the longer hair.

underfurnish, *v.t.* *un*-der-*fur*-nish, to supply with less than enough.

undergarment, *n.* *un*-der-*gar*-ment, any article of underwear.

undergird, *v.t.* *un*-der-*gurd*, to bind below ; to gird round the bottom.

underglaze, *a.* un-der-*glaze*, applied before the object is glazed (of coloured design on pottery, porcelain, etc.).

undergo, *v.t.* *un*-der-*goh*, to suffer ; to endure something burdensome or painful to the body or mind ; to pass through ; to sustain without fainting, yielding, or sinking. *p.* **underwent.** *pp.* **undergone.**

undergrad, *n.* *un*-der-grad, an undergraduate [Coll.].

undergrade, *a.* *un*-der-grade, having a truss below the track (esp. of a form of road- and railway-bridge).

undergraduate, *n.* *un*-der-*grad*-yew-at, a member of a university who has not taken a degree.

undergraduateship, *n.* *un*-der-*grad*-yew-at-ship, the status of an undergraduate.

underground, *n.* *un*-der-ground, that which is beneath the surface of the ground ; a subterranean space ; an underground railway system ; an outlawed political or military movement or organization : *a.* and *ad.* beneath the surface ; secret ; hidden ; clandestine.

undergrowth, *n.* *un*-der-grohth, that which grows under trees ; shrubs or small trees growing among large ones.

underhand, *ad.* *un*-der-hand, by secret means ; by fraud ; in an underhand manner [Bowling, etc.] : *a.* secret ; clandestine, usually implying meanness or fraud, or both ; done with the hand below the shoulder [Tennis, etc.], or with the hand below both elbow and ball [Bowls, Cricket].

underhanded, *a.* *un*-der-*han*-ded, underhand ; clandestine ; short-handed, not having sufficient workpeople.

underhewn, *a.* *un*-der-*hewn*, hewn so that the timber is not fairly squared ; cut under so as to fall forward.

underhold, *n.* *un*-der-hohld, a grip under the arms in wrestling.

underhung, *a.* *un*-der-*hung*, protruding from beneath (esp. of the lower jaw) ; having a projecting lower jaw ; suspended so that the weight is supported from below ; not hung for sufficient time (of dead game, etc.).

underived, *a.* *un*-de-*ryvd*, not derivative ; not borrowed ; from no known original.

underlaid, *a.* *un*-der-*lade*, having something lying or laid beneath.

underlap, *v.i.* *un*-der-*lap*, to extend or be folded beneath and beyond.

underlay, *n.* *un*-der-lay, something lying under or inserted beneath, as foundation or lining material [Dressmaking], or paper arranged beneath type to increase pressure [Print.].

underlay, *v.t.* *un*-der-*lay*, to lay beneath ; to support by something laid under. *p.* and *pp.* **underlaid.**

underlay, *un*-der-lay, *p.* of *underlie.*

underlease, *n.* *un*-der-lease, a sublease.

underlet, *v.t.* *un*-der-*let*, to let below the value ; to let under a lease ; to sublet.

underletting, *n.* *un*-der-*let*-ing, practice of letting lands by leases.

underlie, *v.i.* *un*-der-*ly*, to lie under or beneath ; to constitute the groundwork of ; to be implicit. *p.* **underlay.** *pp.* **underlain.**

underline, *v.t.* *un*-der-*line*, to mark with a line below the words ; to accentuate [Fig.] : *n.* a line drawn under words : *pl.* ruled lines made to serve as a guide.

underlineation, *n.* *un*-der-lin-e-*ay*-shon, sublineation.
underlinen, *n.* *un*-der-lin-en, underwear, esp. of linen, cotton, or rayon, etc.
underling, *n.* *un*-der-ling, an inferior person or agent; a mean sorry fellow.
underman, *v.t.* *un*-der-*man*, to provide with insufficient men or workers.
undermanned, *a.* un-der-*mand*, having a crew, workers, staff, etc., inadequate in numbers or strength.
undermasted, *a.* *un*-der-*mahs*-ted, denoting vessels with masts under the usual dimensions.
undermentioned, *a.* *un*-der-*men*-shond, mentioned further on.
undermine, *v.t.* *un*-der-*myn*, to sap; to excavate the earth beneath; to wear away, or to remove the foundation or support of anything, by clandestine means; to weaken or destroy secretly or by unfair methods.
underminer, *n.* *un*-der-*myn*-ner, one who undermines; one who secretly overthrows.
undermost, *a.* *un*-der-*mohst*, lowest in place, state or degree beneath others.
underneath, *ad.* and *prep.* *un*-der-*neeth*, beneath; under; below: *n.* the under side: *pl.* [Coll.] women's underclothes.
underpart, *n.* *un*-der-part, a lower portion; a subordinate part.
underpay, *n.* *un*-der-*pay*, insufficient pay: *v.t.* to pay inadequately. *p.* and *pp.* **underpaid.**
underpayment, *n.* *un*-der-*pay*-ment, insufficient payment.
underpeopled, *a.* *un*-der-*pee*-pld, having an inadequate population.
underpin, *v.t.* *un*-der-*pin*, to build underneath as a further support for an existing wall; to support from underneath.
underpinning, *n.* *un*-der-*pin*-ing, act of laying supports under the foundation on which a building immediately rests; that by which a building, etc., is underpinned.
underplay, *n.* *un*-der-play, the leading of a low card when a higher one is held; any action which is hidden or secondary; a clandestine scheme: *v.i.* to play a low card to avoid obtaining the lead; to underact a part.
underplot, *n.* *un*-der-plot, a series of events in a story or play proceeding collaterally with and subsidiary to the main story; a secondary plot; a clandestine scheme.
underpraise, *v.t.* *un*-der-*praze*, to praise less than is due.
underprint, *v.t.* *un*-der-*print*, to print on the reverse side of; to print with insufficient density; to print an insufficient quantity of.
under-privileged, *a.* less privileged than others; socially or economically at a disadvantage.
underprize, *v.t.* *un*-der-*prize*, to value at less than the true worth; to prize too lightly.
underproof, *a.* *un*-der-proof, having less alcoholic strength than proof spirit.
underprop, *v.t.* *un*-der-*prop*, to support; to uphold.
underquote, *v.t.* and *i.* *un*-der-*kwoht*, to name (a price) lower than that usual or than another [Comm.].
under-rate, *n.* *un*-der-rate, a price less than the value: *v.t.* *un*-der-*rate*, to rate too low; to undervalue.
under-ripe, *a.* not fully ripe; immature [Fig.].
under-run, *v.t.* *un*-der-*run*, to pass along under. *p.* and *pp.* **under-ran.**
underscore, *v.t.* un-der-*skore*, to underline.
undersell, *v.t.* *un*-der-*sel*, to sell at a lower price than another. *p.* and *pp.* **undersold.**
underset, *n.* *un*-der-set, a contrary current of water below the surface; a set of underwear: *v.t.* *un*-der-*set*, to prop; to support.
undershirt, *n.* *un*-der-shirt, a short shirt worn next to the skin.
undershot, *a.* *un*-der-shot, driven by water passing under (of water-wheels); underhung (of the jaw).
undershrub, *n.* *un*-der-shrub, a low shrub, permanent at the base.
undersign, *v.t.* *un*-der-*syn*, to write one's name at the foot or end of.
undersigned, *n.* *un*-der-*synd*, one who undersigns. **the undersigned,** the signer of the document.
undersized, *a.* *un*-der-syzd, being of a size less than common.
underskirt, *n.* *un*-der-skirt, a petticoat; a skirt worn beneath a dress.
undersleeve, *n.* *un*-der-sleev, a sleeve worn beneath another one, and usually longer.
underslung, *a.* *un*-der-slung, slung or carried beneath; suspended below the axles (of motor-car), or from the fuselage [Av.].
undersoil, *n.* *un*-der-soyl, soil beneath the surface; subsoil.
understaffed, *a.* un-der-*stahft*, undermanned.
understand, *v.t.* *un*-der-*stand*, to have just and adequate ideas of; to comprehend; to know; to apprehend; to know the meaning of; to suppose to mean; to interpret; to mean without expressing; to know what is not expressed; to learn; to be informed: *v.i.* to have intelligence; to be informed; to learn. *p.* and *pp.* **understood.** (A.S.)
understandable *a.* un-der-*stan*-da-bl, capable of being understood; intelligible.
understanding, *a.* *un*-der-*stan*-ding, knowing; skilful; intelligent: *n.* the faculty of the mind by which it apprehends the real state of things presented to it or the representation made to it; the act of comprehending or apprehending; power to understand; discernment; knowledge; exact comprehension; intelligence between two or more persons; agreement of minds.
understandingly, *ad.* with full intelligence or comprehension.
understate, *v.t.* *un*-der-*state*, to represent less strongly than the truth will bear.
understatement, *n.* *un*-der-*state*-ment, a statement conveying less than the truth; meiosis, or an instance of this [Rhet.].
understood, *un*-der-*stood*, *p.* and *pp.* of *understand.*
understrapper, *n.* *un*-der-strap-per, an underling; an inferior agent or official.
understudy, *v.t.* *un*-der-*stud*-e, to prepare oneself to act in another's place; to learn a stage part so as to take the performer's place: *n.* *un*-der-stud-e, one prepared to act in another's place; one who has understudied with a view to deputizing or taking an actor's place when required.
undertake, *v.t.* *un*-der-*take*, to take in hand; to begin to perform; to contract to do; to attempt: *v.i.* to take upon oneself or assume any business or province; to venture; to promise; to be bound. *p.* **undertook.** *pp.* **undertaken.**
undertaker, *n.* *un*-der-*take*-er, one who undertakes any project or business; one who manages funerals, a mortician or funeral director.
undertaking, *n.* *un*-der-*take*-ing, any business or project which a person undertakes; an enterprise; the business of a funeral director.
undertaxed, *a.* *un*-der-*takst*, not taxed enough.
undertenant, *n.* *un*-der-*ten*-ant, a sub-tenant; a tenant under a tenant.
undertone, *n.* *un*-der-tone, a low tone, esp. in speaking; a subdued tint or colour.
undertook, un-der-*took*, *p.* of *undertake.*
undertow, *n.* *un*-der-toh, an undercurrent flowing in the opposite direction to the one above it.
undertrick, *n.* *un*-der-trik, any trick by which declarer falls short of his contract [Bridge, etc.].
undertrump, *v.t.* and *i.* un-der-*trump*, to play a trump too low to capture the trick; to trump lower than one's partner.
undervaluation, *n.* *un*-der-val-yew-*ay*-shon, act of undervaluing; an instance of this.
undervalue, *n.* *un*-der-*val*-yew, a price less than the real worth: *v.t.* to value below the real worth; to esteem lightly; to despise.
undervaluer, *n.* *un*-der-*val*-yew-er, one who undervalues.
undervest, *n.* *un*-der-vest, a vest worn next the skin.
underviewer, *n.* *un*-der-*vew*-er, the employee in charge of underground mine-workings.
underwater, *a.* *un*-der-waw-ter, being, done, growing, taking place, etc., beneath the surface of the water.
underwear, *n.* *un*-der-ware, underclothing; clothing worn next to the body.
underweight, *a.* un-der-*wate*, having too little weight; not up to standard in weight.
underwent, *un*-der-*went*, *p.* of *undergo.*
underwing, *n.* *un*-der-wing, a nocturnal moth of the genus *Catocala.*

underwood, *n.* *un*-der-wood, undergrowth ; small trees and shrubs, etc., growing among larger ones ; coppice or brush-wood.
underwork, *n.* *un*-der-wurk, subordinate work ; petty affairs : *v.t.* un-der-*wurk*, to weaken or destroy by clandestine measures ; to put less than the proper work on ; to work at a less price than others.
underworld, *n.* *un*-der-wurld, this world ; the nether world or world of the dead ; the lowest or hooligan classes ; the criminal classes.
underwrite, *v.t.* *un*-der-*rite*, to write under something else : to practise insuring ; to guarantee ; to subscribe as a sharer in a risk. *p.* **underwrote.** *pp.* **underwritten.**
underwriter, *n.* *un*-der-*ry*-ter, one who insures ; a marine insurer, who underwrites his name to the conditions of the policy.
underwriting, *n.* *un*-der-*ry*-ting, the act or practice of insuring by a corporation.
undescendible, *a.* *un*-de-*sen*-de-bl, not descendible ; not capable of descending to heirs.
undescribable, *a.* *un*-de-*skry*-ba-bl, indescribable.
undescribed, *a.* *un*-de-*skribed*, not described.
undescried, *a.* *un*-de-*skride*, not descried ; not discovered.
undeserved, *a.* *un*-de-*zervd*, not merited.
undeservedly, *ad.* *un*-de-*zer*-ved-le, without desert, either good or ill.
undeserving, *a.* *un*-de-*zer*-ving, not deserving ; not having merit ; not meriting.
undeservingly, *ad.* without meriting any particular advantage or harm.
undesigned, *a.* *un*-de-*zined*, unintentional ; not intended.
undesignedly, *ad.* *un*-de-*zy*-ned-le, unintentionally.
undesigning, *a.* *un*-de-*zy*-ning, not acting with set purpose ; sincere ; upright ; having no evil purpose.
undesirable, *a.* *un*-de-*zyr*-ra-bl, not to be wished : *n.* one expelled from a country, society, etc., as likely to be troublesome or merely not nice to know ; a person of ill repute.
undesired, *a.* *un*-de-*zyrd*, not desired, or not solicited.
undesirous, *a.* *un*-de-*zyr*-rus, not desiring or wishing.
undespairing, *a.* *un*-de-*spare*-ring, not yielding to despair.
undestined, *a.* un-*des*-tind, not destined.
undetached, *a.* *un*-de-*tatcht*, not separated.
undetected, *a.* *un*-de-*tek*-ted, not discovered.
undeterminable, *a.* *un*-de-*ter*-min-a-bl, that cannot be determined.
undetermined, *a.* *un*-de-*ter*-mind, not determined ; not settled or defined ; indeterminate ; irresolute.
undeterred, *a.* *un*-de-*terd*, not restrained by fear.
undeveloped, *a.* *un*-de-*vel*-opt, not developed ; backward ; immature.
undeviating, *a.* un-*dee*-ve-ay-ting, not departing from the way, principle, rule, or purpose ; steady ; regular.
undeviatingly, *ad.* without deviating.
undevoted, *a.* *un*-de-*voh*-ted, not devoted.
undevout, *a.* *un*-de-*vout*, not devout ; having no devotion.
undextrous, *a.* un-*dek*-strus, not dextrous ; clumsy.
undid, un-*did*, *p.* of *undo*.
undies, *n.pl.* *un*-diz, women's underwear [Coll.].
undifferentiated, *a.* *un*-dif-er-*ren*-she-ay-ted, not differentiated ; not become different by specialization.
undiffused, *a.* *un*-de-*fewzd*, not diffused.
undigested, *a.* *un*-de-*jes*-ted, not digested ; crude.
undignified, *a.* un-*dig*-ne-fide, not dignified ; wanting in dignity.
undiluted, *a.* *un*-dy-*lew*-ted, not diluted ; neat.
undiminished, *a.* *un*-de-*min*-isht, not diminished.
undimmed, *a.* un-*dimd*, not dimmed.
undine, *n.* un-*deen* or *un*-deen, a fabled water nymph without, but in certain cases capable of, a human soul. (L. *unda*, a wave.)
undiplomatic, *a.* un-*dip*-lo-*mat*-ik, not according to diplomatic rules ; tactless [Coll.].
undirected, *a.* *un*-dy-*rek*-ted, not directed or superintended ; not superscribed.
undisbanded, *a.* *un*-dis-*ban*-ded, continuing as part of the army.
undiscerned, *a.* *un*-de-*zernd*, not seen ; not observed.
undiscernible, *a.* *un*-de-*zer*-ne-bl, that cannot be discerned or discovered ; invisible.
undiscerning, *a.* *un*-de-*zer*-ning, not discerning ; wanting discernment.
undischarged, *a.* *un*-dis-*charjd*, not discharged.
undisciplined, *a.* un-*dis*-e-plind, not duly exercised and taught ; raw ; not instructed ; untaught.
undisclosed, *a.* *un*-dis-*klohzd*, not revealed.
undiscouraged, *a.* *un*-dis-*ku*-rajd, not disheartened.
undiscoverable, *a.* *un*-dis-*kuv*-er-ra-bl, that cannot be discovered.
undiscoverably, *ad.* so as not to be discovered.
undiscovered, *a.* *un*-dis-*kuv*-erd, not discovered ; not seen.
undiscriminating, *a.* *un*-dis-*krim*-e-nay-ting, not discriminating.
undiscussed, *a.* *un*-dis-*kust*, not discussed.
undisgraced, *a.* *un*-dis-*grayst*, not dishonoured.
undisguisable, *a.* *un*-dis-*gy*-za-bl, that cannot be disguised.
undisguised, *a.* *un*-dis-*gyzd*, not disguised ; open ; frank ; candid ; plain ; artless.
undisheartened, *a.* un-dis-*hart*-nd, not discouraged.
undishonoured, *a.* *un*-dis-*on*-urd, not dishonoured.
undismayed, *a.* *un*-dis-*mayd*, not terrified ; not disheartened by fear.
undisordered, *a.* *un*-dis-*or*-derd, not disturbed.
undispensed, *a.* *un*-dis-*penst*, not absolved ; not freed from obligation.
undispensing, *a.* *un*-dis-*pen*-sing, not giving dispensation.
undispersed, *a.* *un*-dis-*perst*, not scattered.
undisposed, *a.* *un*-dis-*pohzd*, indisposed ; not disposed of ; not bestowed.
undisputed, *a.* *un*-dis-*pew*-ted, not called in question ; not contested.
undisquieted, *a.* *un*-dis-*kwy*-e-ted, not disturbed.
undissembled, *a.* *un*-dis-*sem*-bld, undisguised ; unfeigned.
undissembling, *a.* *un*-dis-*sem*-bling, not exhibiting a false appearance ; truthful.
undissipated, *a.* un-*dis*-e-pay-ted, not scattered.
undissolvable, *a.* *un*-diz-*zol*-va-bl, that cannot be dissolved or melted ; indissoluble.
undissolved, *a.* *un*-diz-*zolvd*, not dissolved or melted.
undistempered, *a.* *un*-dis-*tem*-perd, not diseased ; free from malady ; free from distemper.
undistended, *a.* *un*-dis-*ten*-ded, not enlarged.
undistilled, *a.* *un*-dis-*tild*, not distilled.
undistinctive, *a.* *un*-dis-*tink*-tiv, without distinction ; undistinguishing.
undistinguishable, *a.* *un*-dis-*ting*-gwish-a-bl, indistinguishable ; not to be distinguished by the eye or by the intellect.
undistinguishably, *ad.* *un*-dis-*ting*-gwish-a-ble, indistinguishably ; so as not to be distinguished.
undistinguished, *a.* *un*-dis-*ting*-gwisht, not distinguished ; not so marked as to be distinctly discriminated ; not separately seen or descried ; not plainly discerned ; not marked by any particular eminence, property, etc. ; not treated with any particular respect.
undistinguishing, *a.* *un*-dis-*ting*-gwish-ing, making no difference ; not discriminating.
undistorted, *a.* *un*-dis-*tor*-ted, not perverted.
undistracted, *a.* *un*-dis-*trak*-ted, not perplexed by contrariety or confusion of thoughts, desires or cares.
undistributed, *a.* *un*-dis-*trib*-yew-ted, not distributed or allotted ; not used in its widest sense, said of a term in a proposition [Logic].
undisturbed, *a.* *un*-dis-*turbd*, free from interruption ; not molested or hindered ; free from perturbation ; calm ; tranquil ; serene ; not agitated or stirred.
undisturbedly, *ad.* *un*-dis-*tur*-bed-le, calmly ; peacefully.
undiversified, *a.* *un*-dy-*ver*-se-fide, not varied ; uniform.
undiverted, *a.* *un*-dy-*ver*-ted, not turned aside ; not amused.
undividable, *a.* *un*-de-*vy*-da-bl, that cannot be divided ; not separable.
undivided, *a.* *un*-de-*vy*-ded, not separated or disunited ; unbroken ; not limited ; not lobed, cleft, or branched [Bot.].
undividedly, *ad.* so as not to be divided.

undivinable, *a.* un-de-*vy*-na-bl, not capable of being guessed or conjectured.
undivine, *a.* un-de-*vine*, not divine.
undivulged, *a.* *un*-de-*vuljd*, not revealed or disclosed.
undo, *v.t.* un-*doo*, to reverse what has been done; to annul; to loose; to open; to take to pieces; to unravel; to untie; to ruin; to bring to poverty; to ruin morally; to ruin in reputation. *p.* **undid.** *pp.* **undone.**
undock, *v.t.* and *i.* un-*dok*, to take or proceed out of dock.
undoer, *n.* un-*doo*-er, one who undoes; one who reverses what has been done; one who ruins.
undoing, *n.* un-*doo*-ing, the reversal of what has been done; ruin; destruction.
undomestic, *a.* *un*-do-*mes*-tik, not domestic.
undomesticated, *a.* *un*-do-*mes*-te-kay-ted, not accustomed to a family life; not reclaimed from wild habits.
undone, *a.* un-*dun*, not done; not performed; not executed.
undoubted, *a.* un-*dou*-ted, not called in question; indubitable.
undoubtedly, *ad.* without doubt.
undoubtful, *a.* un-*dout*-ful, not feeling doubt; plain; evident; not admitting of doubt.
undoubting, *a.* un-*dou*-ting, not hesitating respecting facts; confident.
undoubtingly, *ad.* without doubting.
undowered, *a.* un-*dou*-erd, without a dower.
undrained, *a.* un-*draynd*, not subjected to draining; not freed from water.
undramatic, *a.* *un*-dra-*mat*-ik, not dramatic; not according to the rules of the drama.
undraped, *a.* un-*draypt*, not covered with drapery; nude.
undrawn, *a.* un-*drawn*, not drawn; not pulled; not allured.
undreaded, *a.* un-*dred*-ed, not feared.
undreamed, *a.* un-*dreemd*, not thought of.
undreamt, *a.* un-*dremt*, undreamed.
undress, *v.t.* and *i.* un-*dress*, to divest of clothes; to strip; to disrobe: *n.* *un*-dress; a loose, negligent dress; service or working uniform, not full dress; informal attire.
undressed, *a.* un-*drest*, not dressed; not attired; not prepared or processed; not trimmed; not put in order.
undried, *a.* un-*dride*, not dried; wet; green (of tobacco-leaves, etc.).
undrilled, *a.* un-*drild*, not drilled; never having been subjected to discipline.
undrinkable, *a.* un-*dring*-ka-bl, not drinkable.
undriven, *a.* un-*driv*-n, not driven; not impelled.
undrowned, *a.* un-*dround*, not drowned.
undue, *a.* un-*dew*, not due; not yet demandable of right; not right or legal; not agreeable to a rule or standard, or to duty; not proportioned; excessive. **undue influence**, influence destructive of the exercise of a person's own will [Law].
undulant, *a.* *un*-dew-lant, undulatory. **undulant fever**, typhoid; Malta fever.
undulate, *v.t.* *un*-dew-late, to move like waves; to cause to vibrate: *v.i.* to wave; to vibrate: *a.* undulated. (L. *undula*, a little wave.)
undulated, *a.* *un*-dew-lay-ted, wavy; of a wavy character.
undulating, *a.* *un*-dew-lay-ting, waving; rising and falling; wavy.
undulation, *n.* *un*-dew-*lay*-shon, a waving motion or vibration; a motion like that of waves; a particular uneasy sensation of an undulatory motion in the heart [Med.]; a rattling or jarring of sounds [Mus.].
undulatory, *a.* un-dew-*lay*-to-re, pertaining to undulation; moving in the manner of waves.
undulous, *a.* *un*-dew-lus, of wave-like character; undulating.
unduly, *ad.* un-*dew*-le, not according to duty or propriety; excessively.
unduteous, *a.* un-*dew*-te-us, not obedient; not performing duty, esp. towards superiors.
undutiful, *a.* un-*dew*-te-ful, not obedient; heedless to calls of duty.
undutifully, *ad.* in an undutiful manner.
undutifulness, *n.* the state or quality of being undutiful.
undy, *a.* *un*-de, wavy, in the form of waves (of ordinaries, etc.) [Her.]. (Fr. *ondé*, waved.)
undying, *a.* un-*dy*-ing, not dying or perishing; everlasting; immortal.
unearned, *a.* un-*ernd*, not gained by labour. **unearned income**, income derived from investments or sources other than personal effort. **unearned increment**, increase in the value of land or property without labour or expenditure on the part of the owner.
unearth, *v.t.* un-*erth*, to drive out of the earth; to uncover; to discover; to reveal.
unearthed, *a.* un-*erthd*, not provided with an earth [Elect. and Wire.].
unearthliness, *n.* un-*erth*-le-ness, the quality of being unearthly.
unearthly, *a.* un-*erth*-le, eerie; not earthly or of the earth. **unearthly hour**, an extremely inconvenient or early hour [Coll.].
unease, *n.* un-*eez*, discomfort; mental unrest.
uneasily, *ad.* un-*ee*-ze-le, with uneasiness or pain.
uneasiness, *n.* un-*ee*-ze-ness, a moderate degree of pain; restlessness; disquietude.
uneasy, *a.* un-*ee*-ze, feeling some degree of pain; restless; disturbed; unquiet; somewhat anxious; constrained; not graceful; causing pain; cramping; disagreeable.
uneatable, *a.* un-*ee*-ta-bl, not fit to be eaten.
uneaten, *a.* un-*ee*-tn, not eaten.
uneclipsed, *a.* *un*-e-*klipst*, not eclipsed; not obscured; not surpassed.
uneconomic, *a.* *un*-ee-ko-*nom*-ik, not in accordance with the principles of economics; uneconomical.
uneconomical, *a.* *un*-ee-ko-*nom*-e-kal, not characterized by economy; extravagant; wasteful.
unedifying, *a.* un-*ed*-e-fy-ing, not improving to the mind; unintellectual.
uneducated, *a.* un-*ed*-yew-kay-ted, not educated; illiterate.
uneffaced, *a.* un-e-*fayst*, not obliterated.
uneffected, *a.* *un*-e-*fek*-ted, not effected or performed.
unelaborated, *a.* un-e-*lab*-o-ray-ted, finished with little labour or study; simple.
unelastic, *a.* un-e-*las*-tik, not having the property of recovering its original state when bent or stretched.
unelated, *a.* un-e-*lay*-ted, not elated; dispirited; not puffed up.
unelected, *a.* un-e-*lek*-ted, not elected; not preferred.
unemancipated, *a.* un-e-*man*-se-pay-ted, not emancipated.
unembarrassed, *a.* un-em-*ba*-rast, not perplexed in mind; not confused; free from pecuniary difficulties or encumbrances; free from perplexing connexion.
unembittered, *a.* un-em-*bit*-erd, not embittered.
unembodied, *a.* un-em-*bod*-ed, free from a corporeal body; not embodied.
unembroidered, *a.* un-em-*broy*-derd, not embroidered or adorned; simple; ordinary.
unemotional, *a.* un-e-*moh*-shon-al, without emotion or feeling; impassive; thick-skinned.
unemphatic, *a.* un-em-*fat*-ik, having no emphasis; lukewarm.
unemphatically, *ad.* without emphasis.
unemployable, *a.* un-em-*ploy*-a-bl, unfit for employment.
unemployed, *a.* un-em-*ployd*, not occupied; at leisure; not in regular employment; not being in use: *n.* a person, or persons collectively, out of work.
unemployment, *n.* un-em-*ploy*-ment, the state of being unemployed; the prevalence of this state.
unempowered, *a.* un-em-*pou*-erd, not empowered or authorized.
unemulating, *a.* un-*em*-yew-lay-ting, not striving to excel.
unenchanted, *a.* un-en-*chahn*-ted, not enchanted.
unenclosed, *a.* un-en-*klohzd*, not enclosed; not hedged or fenced.
unencumbered, *a.* un-en-*kum*-berd, not encumbered; not burdened; free from mortgage or any such charge or claim.
unending, *a.* un-*en*-ding, not ending; everlasting; wearisomely long.
unendorsed, *a.* un-en-*dorst*, not endorsed or assigned.
unendowed, *a.* un-en-*doud*, not endowed; not furnished with funds.

unendurable, *a.* un-en-*dewr*-ra-bl, not to be endured; intolerable.
unenduring, *a.* un-en-*dewr*-ring, of temporary duration.
unenervated, *a.* un-*en*-er-vay-ted, not weakened.
unenfranchised, *a.* un-en-*fran*-chized, not having a vote.
unengaged, *a.* un-en-*gayjd*, not bound by covenant or promise; free from obligation to a particular person; free from attachment that binds; unemployed; unoccupied; not appropriated.
unengaging, *a.* un-en-*gay*-jing, not adapted to win the attention or affections.
un-English, *a.* un-*ing*-glish, not conformable to the ways, etc., of the ideal Englishman; unsportsmanlike; mean.
unenjoyed, *a.* un-en-*joyd*, not obtained.
unenlarged, *a.* un-en-*larjd*, not enlarged; narrow.
unenlightened, *a.* un-en-*ly*-tnd, lacking enlightenment or information; uninstructed; not illuminated.
unenlivened, *a.* un-en-*ly*-vnd, not enlivened.
unenslaved, *a.* un-en-*slayvd*, not enslaved; free.
unentangled, *a.* un-en-*tang*-gld, disentangled; not entangled or complicated.
unenterprising, *a.* un-*en*-ter-pry-zing, not enterprising; not adventurous.
unentertaining, *a.* *un*-en-ter-*tay*-ning, not entertaining or amusing.
unenthralled, *a.* un-en-*thrawld*, not enslaved or reduced to thraldom.
unentrenched, *a.* un-en-*trencht*, not defended by entrenchments.
unenviable, *a.* un-*en*-ve-a-bl, not to be envied.
unenvied, *a.* un-*en*-ved, not envied; exempt from the envy of others.
unenvious, *a.* un-*en*-ve-us, not prone to envy; not jealous.
unequable, *a.* un-*ee*-kwa-bl, different at different times; not uniform.
unequal, *a.* un-*ee*-kwal, not even; not of the same size; inferior; inadequate; unjust; disproportioned; ill-matched; not regular; not uniform.
unequalled, *a.* un-*ee*-kwald, unparalleled; unrivalled.
unequally, *ad.* un-*ee*-kwa-le, not equally.
unequalness, *n.* un-*ee*-kwal-ness, the state of being unequal; inequality.
unequipped, *a.* un-e-*kwipt*, not furnished with adequate means or equipment; ill prepared.
unequivocal, *a.* un-e-*kwiv*-o-kal, not doubtful; clear; evident; not ambiguous; sincere.
unequivocally, *ad.* without doubt; without ambiguity.
unequivocalness, *n.* the state of being unequivocal.
unerring, *a.* un-*er*-ring, committing no mistake; certain; incapable of error.
unerringly, *ad.* un-*er*-ring-le, without erring.
unescapable, *a.* un-e-*skay*-pa-bl, that cannot be escaped.
unespied, *a.* un-es-*pide*, not espied; not seen.
unessayed, *a.* un-e-*sade*, unattempted.
unessential, *a.* un-e-*sen*-shal, not absolutely necessary; void of real being: *n.* something not constituting essence, or not of absolute necessity.
unevangelical, *a.* *un*-ee-van-*jel*-e-kal, not evangelical; not according to the gospel.
uneven, *a.* un-*ee*-vn, not level; not equal; not uniform; not smooth; odd.
unevenly, *ad.* in an uneven manner.
unevenness, *n.* un-*ee*-vn-ness, state of being uneven.
uneventful, *a.* un-e-*vent*-ful, not eventful.
unexact, *a.* un-ek-*zakt*, not exact; inexact.
unexacted, *a.* un-ek-*zak*-ted, not forced from one; not obtained by threat or compulsion.
unexaminable, *a.* un-eg-*zam*-e-na-bl, incapable of being examined.
unexamined, *a.* un-eg-*zam*-ind, not interrogated; not inquired into or investigated.
unexampled, *a.* un-eg-*zahm*-pld, having no example or similar case; unprecedented.
unexcelled, *a.* un-ek-*seld*, not excelled.
unexceptionable, *a.* *un*-ek-*sep*-shon-a-bl, not liable to any exception or objection; unobjectionable.
unexceptionableness, *n.* the quality of being unexceptionable.
unexceptionably, *ad.* in an unexceptionable manner.
unexceptional, *a.* *un*-ek-*sep*-shon-al, unexceptionable.
unexcised, *a.* un-ek-*sized*, not charged with duty of excise; not subjected to excision, not cut away.
unexcited, *a.* un-ek-*sy*-ted, not roused.
unexcluded, *a.* un-ek-*skloo*-ded, not excluded.
unexclusive, *a.* un-ek-*skloo*-siv, not exclusive.
unexcommunicated, *a.* un-ek-sko-*mew*-ne-kay-ted, not excommunicated.
unexecuted, *a.* un-*ek*-se-kew-ted, not performed; not done; not properly attested [Law].
unexemplary, *a.* un-eg-*zem*-pla-re, not exemplary; not acceptable as a pattern.
unexemplified, *a.* un-eg-*zem*-ple-fide, not exemplified; not illustrated by example.
unexempt, *a.* un-eg-*zemt*, not exempt; not free by privilege.
unexercised, *a.* un-*ek*-ser-sized, not exercised; not disciplined.
unexerted, *a.* un-eg-*zer*-ted, not called into action; not exerted.
unexhausted, *a.* un-eg-*zaws*-ted, not exhausted; not drained; not spent.
unexorcised, *a.* un-*ek*-sor-sized, not cast out by exorcism.
unexpanded, *a.* un-eks-*pan*-ded, not spread out.
unexpectant, *a.* un-eks-*pek*-tant, not expecting.
unexpected, *a.* un-eks-*pek*-ted, not looked for; sudden.
unexpectedly, *ad.* in an unexpected manner.
unexpectedness, *n.* state of being unexpected.
unexpended, *a.* un-eks-*pen*-ded, not expended; not laid out.
unexpensive, *a.* un-eks-*pen*-siv, not costly.
unexperienced, *a.* un-eks-*peer*-re-enst, inexperienced.
unexpert, *a.* un-eks-*pert*, inexpert; wanting skill; not ready or dexterous in performance.
unexpired, *a.* un-eks-*pired*, not expired; not having reached its end; still valid.
unexplored, *a.* un-eks-*plored*, not searched or examined; unknown.
unexplosive, *a.* un-eks-*ploh*-siv, not explosive.
unexported, *a.* un-eks-*por*-ted, not exported.
unexposed, *a.* un-eks-*pohzd*, not laid open to view; not denounced or publicly censured; sheltered.
unexpounded, *a.* un-eks-*poun*-ded, not explained.
unexpressed, *a.* un-eks-*prest*, not expressed; not mentioned or named.
unexpressive, *a.* un-eks-*pres*-siv, inexpressive; ineffable.
unexpunged, *a.* un-eks-*punjd*, not expunged.
unexpurgated, *a.* un-*eks*-pur-gay-ted, not expurgated.
unextended, *a.* un-eks-*ten*-ded, not extended; occupying no assignable space; having no dimensions.
unextinct, *a.* un-eks-*tinkt*, not extinct.
unextinguishable, *a.* un-eks-*ting*-gwish-a-bl, that cannot be extinguished; unquenchable.
unextinguished, *a.* un-eks-*ting*-gwisht, not quenched; not entirely suppressed.
unextirpated, *a.* un-*eks*-ter-pay-ted, not rooted out.
unextorted, *a.* un-eks-*tor*-ted, not extorted.
unextracted, *a.* un-eks-*trakt*-ed, not drawn out.
unfabled, *a.* un-*fay*-bld, real; true.
unfadable, *a.* un-*fade*-a-bl, that cannot fade.
unfaded, *a.* un-*fade*-ed, not faded; unwithered.
unfading, *a.* un-*fade*-ing, not liable to fade; not liable to wither.
unfadingly, *ad.* without fading.
unfadingness, *n.* the quality of being unfading.
unfailable, *a.* un-*fale*-a-bl, infallible.
unfailing, *a.* un-*fale*-ing, not liable to fail; that does not fail; certain.
unfailingly, *ad.* without failing.
unfailingness, *n.* the state of not failing.
unfainting, *a.* un-*fayn*-ting, not sinking; not failing under toil.
unfair, *a.* un-*fare*, not honest; disingenuous; using trick or artifice; not just; proceeding from trick or dishonesty; below the normal rate; unfavourable.
unfairly, *ad.* in an unfair way.
unfairness, *n.* dishonesty; injustice.
unfaith, *n.* un-*fayth*, lack of faith, esp. in religious matters; want of honour.
unfaithful, *a.* un-*fayth*-ful, not observant of promises, allegiance or duty; treacherous; disregardful of a vow, esp. the marriage vow; not performing the proper duty; unbelieving.

unfaithfully, *ad.* in an unfaithful manner.
unfaithfulness, *n.* quality of being unfaithful.
unfallen, *a.* un-*faw*-len, not fallen; not debased or debauched.
unfaltering, *a.* un-*fawl*-ter-ing, unhesitating.
unfalteringly, *ad.* unhesitatingly.
unfamiliar, *a.* *un*-fa-*mil*-yar, not familiar; not well known or acquainted with.
unfamiliarity, *n.* *un*-fa-*mil*-e-*a*-re-te, want of familiarity.
unfashionable, *a.* un-*fash*-on-a-bl, not according to the prevailing mode; not conforming in dress and manners to the prevailing custom.
unfashionably, *ad.* not according to the fashion.
unfashioned, *a.* un-*fash*-ond, not shaped, moulded, or modified by mechanical means or art; shapeless.
unfast, *a.* un-*fahst*, not safe or secure.
unfasten, *v.t.* un-*fah*-sn, to loose; to unfix.
unfathered, *a.* un-*fah*-therd, fatherless; without acknowledged father.
unfatherly, *a.* and *ad.* un-*fah*-ther-le, not in the manner of a father; unkind.
unfathomable, *a.* un-*fath*-um-a-bl, that cannot be sounded by a line; too deep for fathoming; incomprehensible; insoluble.
unfathomableness, *n.* the state of being unfathomable.
unfathomably, *ad.* beyond fathoming.
unfathomed, *a.* un-*fath*-umd, not sounded; not to be sounded; not comprehended.
unfatigued, *a.* un-fa-*teegd*, not wearied.
unfavourable, *a.* un-*fay*-vur-ra-bl, not favourable or propitious; not kind or obliging; discouraging.
unfavourableness, *n.* state of being unfavourable.
unfavourably, *ad.* in an unfavourable manner.
unfavoured, *a.* un-*fay*-vurd, not favoured; not assisted.
unfeared, *a.* un-*feerd*, not feared or dreaded.
unfearful, *a.* un-*feer*-ful, not fearful; courageous.
unfearing, *a.* un-*feer*-ring, not fearing.
unfeasible, *a.* un-*fee*-ze-bl, impracticable.
unfeathered, *a.* un-*feth*-erd, having no feathers; unfledged; immature.
unfeatured, *a.* un-*fee*-tewrd, wanting regular features; deformed; not featured in a production.
unfed, *a.* un-*fed*, not fed; not supplied with food.
unfeed, *a.* un-*feed*, not retained by a fee; unpaid.
unfeeling, *a.* un-*feel*-ing, insensible; insensate; void of feeling or sensibility; callous.
unfeelingly, *ad.* in an unfeeling manner.
unfeelingness, *n.* insensibility; callousness.
unfeigned, *a.* un-*faynd*, not counterfeit or hypocritical; sincere.
unfeignedly, *ad.* un-*fay*-ned-le, sincerely.
unfelt, *a.* un-*felt*, not felt; not perceived.
unfeminine, *a.* un-*fem*-e-nin, not according to the female character; unwomanly.
unfenced, *a.* un-*fenst*, not enclosed; not provided with a guard (of machinery); defenceless.
unfermented, *a.* un-fer-*men*-ted, not having undergone the process of fermentation; not leavened.
unfertile, *a.* un-*fer*-tile, not fertile; barren; unfruitful.
unfertilized, un-*fer*-te-lized, not made fruitful; not treated with a fertilizer [Agric.].
unfetter, *v.t.* un-*fet*-er, to loose from fetters; to unchain; to free from restraint or set at liberty.
unfigured, *a.* un-*fig*-urd, not figured; devoid of figures; representing no animal form; literal.
unfilial, *a.* un-*fil*-yal, not fulfilling the duty of a son or daughter.
unfilially, *ad.* in an unfilial manner.
unfilled, *a.* un-*fild*, not filled; not fully supplied or satisfied.
unfilmed, *a.* un-*filmd*, not covered with a film; not converted into a film for screen production.
unfinished, *a.* un-*fin*-isht, not complete; imperfect; crude.
unfirm, *a.* un-*ferm*, weak; feeble; unstable.
unfirmness, *n.* a weak state; instability.
unfit, *a.* un-*fit*, not fit; improper; unsuitable; unqualified; incompetent; in bad physical condition: *n.* one who, or a class which, is unfit or incapacitated: *v.t.* to disable: to make unsuitable; to disqualify.
unfitly, *ad.* un-*fit*-le, not properly; unsuitably.
unfitness, *n.* un-*fit*-ness, want of suitable powers or qualifications; want of propriety or adaptation to character or place; incapacitation.
unfitting, *a.* un-*fit*-ing, improper; not suitable.
unfix, *v.t.* un-*fiks*, to loosen from a fastening; to detach from anything; to unsettle; to unhinge; to dissolve.
unfixed, *a.* un-*fikst*, wandering; erratic; inconstant; having no settled view or object of pursuit.
unfixedness, *n.* un-*fik*-sed-ness, state of being unfixed; instability.
unflagging, *a.* un-*flag*-ing, not drooping; maintaining strength or spirit; unremitting.
unflattered, *a.* un-*flat*-erd, not flattered.
unflattering, *a.* un-*flat*-er-ring, not colouring the truth to please; not affording a favourable prospect; plain and unadorned.
unflatteringly, *ad.* in an unflattering manner.
unflawed, *a.* un-*flawd*, having no flaw.
unfledged, *a.* un-*flejd*, not yet furnished with feathers; immature.
unfleshed, *a.* un-*flesht*, not seasoned to blood; inexperienced; divested of flesh; not yet used in battle (of arms).
unfleshly, *a.* un-*flesh*-le, pertaining to spiritual, not worldly, matters; heavenly minded.
unflinching, *a.* un-*flinch*-ing, not flinching; not shrinking.
unflowering, *a.* un-*flou*-er-ring, not flowering.
unfoiled, *a.* un-*foyld*, not baffled.
unfold, *v.i.* un-*fohld*, to open out: *v.t.* to expand; to spread out; to disclose; to display; to declare; to release from a fold or pen.
unforbidden, *a.* *un*-for-*bid*-dn, not prohibited or prevented; allowed.
unforceable, *a.* un-*force*-a-bl, incapable of being forced.
unforced, *a.* un-*forst*, not compelled; not constrained; not urged; not feigned; not violent; easy; natural.
unforcible, *a.* un-*force*-e-bl, wanting force or strength; not capable of being enforced.
unfordable, *a.* un-*ford*-a-bl, that cannot be forded or passed by wading.
unforeboding, *a.* un-for-*boh*-ding, giving no omen.
unforeknown, *a.* un-for-*nohn*, not previously known or foreseen.
unforeseen, *a.* un-for-*seen*, not foreseen; not expected.
unforetold, *a.* un-for-*tohld*, not predicted.
unforewarned, *a.* un-for-*wawrnd*, not previously warned.
unforfeited, *a.* un-*for*-fit-ed, not forfeited.
unforgettable, *a.* un-for-*get*-a-bl, incapable of being forgotten or expunged from the memory.
unforgivable, *a.* un-for-*giv*-a-bl, not to be forgiven.
unforgiven, *a.* un-for-*giv*-en, not forgiven; not pardoned.
unforgiving, *a.* un-for-*giv*-ing, not disposed to overlook or pardon offences; implacable; pitiless.
unforgotten, *a.* un-for-*got*-en, not lost to memory; not neglected.
unformal, *a.* un-*for*-mal, not formal.
unformed, *a.* un-*formd*, not moulded into regular shape; incipient; immature.
unforsaken, *a.* *un*-for-*say*-kn, not deserted; not entirely neglected.
unfortified, *a.* un-*for*-te-fide, not secured from attack; not fortified; defenceless.
unfortunate, *a.* un-*for*-tew-nat, not successful; unprosperous: *n.* an unhappy or ill-starred person; a prostitute [Coll.].
unfortunately, *ad.* unhappily; by mischance.
unfostered, *a.* un-*fos*-terd, not nourished; not patronized.
unfound, *a.* un-*found*, not found; not met with.
unfounded, *a.* un-*foun*-ded, not founded; having no foundation; vain; idle.
unframed, *a.* un-*fraymd*, not framed; removed from its frame; not formed.
unfraternal, *a.* un-fra-*ter*-nal, not brotherly; not on terms of friendship or association.
unfree, *a.* un-*free*, not free; not made free; lacking freedom: *v.t.* to set free.
unfreeze, *v.t.* un-*freez*, to cause to thaw (esp. of refrigerated food, etc.); to defrost or de-ice: *v.i.* to unbend, to become genial [Fig. and Coll.].
unfrequent, *a.* un-*free*-kwent, not frequent; not common.
unfrequented, *a.* un-fre-*kwen*-ted, rarely visited.
unfrequently, *ad.* un-*free*-kwent-le, not often; infrequently.

unfriend, *n.* *un*-frend, an enemy.
unfriended, *a.* un-*fren*-ded, wanting friends; not countenanced or supported.
unfriendliness, *n.* un-*frend*-le-ness, want of kindness.
unfriendly, *a.* un-*frend*-le, hostile; not kind or benevolent; not favourable.
unfrock, *v.t.* un-*frok*, to expel from clerical or monastic service.
unfrozen, *a.* un-*froh*-zn, not congealed; released from being frozen (of credits, etc.) [Econ.].
unfrugal, *a.* un-*froo*-gal, not saving or economical.
unfruitful, *a.* un-*froot*-ful, not producing fruit; barren; unproductive; unproductive of good.
unfruitfully, *ad.* fruitlessly.
unfruitfulness, *n.* barrenness; unproductiveness.
unfrustrable, *a.* un-*frus*-tra-bl, that cannot be frustrated.
unfuelled, *a.* un-*few*-eld, being without fuel.
unfulfilled, *a.* un-ful-*fild*, not accomplished.
unfunded, *a.* un-*fun*-ded, not funded; having no permanent funds for the payment of its interest. **unfunded debt,** floating debt (*see* **debt**).
unfurl, *v.t.* un-*furl*, to loose and unfold; to expand.
unfurnish, *v.t.* un-*fur*-nish, to strip of furniture, or of means of defence; to dismantle; to divest of fittings.
unfurnished, *a.* un-*fur*-nisht, not supplied with furniture or necessaries; empty.
unfurrowed, *a.* un-*fu*-rode, not having furrows; unruffled.
unfused, *a.* un-*fewzd*, not melted.
ungainful, *a.* un-*gane*-ful, unprofitable.
ungainliness, *n.* un-*gane*-le-ness, clumsiness; awkwardness.
ungainly, *a.* un-*gane*-le, clumsy; awkwardly built; uncouth. (A.S.- *un*, and Ice. *gegn*, ready, serviceable.)
ungallant, *a.* *un*-ga-*lant*, not courteous to ladies; un-*gal*-ant, not brave.
ungalled, *a.* un-*gawld*, unhurt; not galled.
ungarlanded, *a.* un-*gar*-lan-ded, not crowned with a garland.
ungarnished, *a.* un-*gar*-nisht, not furnished; unadorned.
ungarrisoned, *a.* un-*ga*-re-sond, not furnished with troops for defence.
ungartered, *a.* un-*gar*-terd, without garters.
ungathered, *a.* un-*ga*-therd, not gathered; not cropped.
ungear, *v.t.* un-*geer*, to unharness; to strip of gear; to throw out of gear.
ungenerated, *a.* un-*jen*-er-ray-ted, having no beginning; unbegotten.
ungenerative, *a.* un-*jen*-er-ra-tiv, begetting nothing.
ungenerous, *a.* un-*jen*-er-rus, not generous; not liberal; not noble; dishonourable.
ungenial, *a.* un-*jee*-ne-al, not favourable to nature or to natural growth; uncongenial.
ungenteel, *a.* un-jen-*teel*, not consistent with polite manners.
ungenteelly, *ad.* un-jen-*teel*-le, impolitely.
ungentle, *a.* un-*gen*-tl, rough; rude.
ungentlemanliness, *n.* un-*jen*-tl-man-le-ness, quality of being ungentlemanly.
ungentlemanly, *a.* un-*jen*-tl-man-le, unworthy of a gentleman; not like a gentleman.
ungentleness, *n.* un-*jen*-tl-ness, harshness; rudeness; unkindness.
ungently, *ad.* un-*jent*-le, harshly; rudely.
ungeometrical, *a.* *un*-jee-o-*met*-re-kal, not agreeable to the rules of geometry.
un-get-at-able, *a.* *un*-get-*at*-a-bl, not accessible; unapproachable; hard to get at.
ungifted, *a.* un-*gif*-ted, not endowed with special faculties; untalented.
ungild, *v.t.* un-*gild*, to take off the gilding.
ungilded, *a.* un-*gil*-ded, not gilt; not overlaid with gold.
ungilt, *a.* un-*gilt*, not gilded.
ungird, *v.t.* un-*gerd*, to loose from a girdle or band.
ungirt, *pp.* and *a.* un-*gert*, unbound; loosely dressed.
ungiven, *a.* un-*giv*-en, not given or bestowed.
ungiving, *a.* un-*giv*-ing, not bringing gifts.
unglazed, *a.* un-*glazed*, not furnished with glass; wanting glass windows; not covered with vitreous matter.
unglorified, *a.* un-*glaw*-re-fide, not honoured with praise or adoration.
ungloved, *a.* un-*gluvd*, without glove or gloves.
unglue, *v.t.* un-*gloo*, to free from glue; to separate anything that is glued.
ungodlily, *ad.* un-*god*-le-le, in an ungodly manner.
ungodliness, *n.* the quality of being ungodly.
ungodly, *a.* un-*god*-le, wicked; impious; without the fear of God.
ungorged, *a.* un-*gorjd*, not gorged; not sated.
ungotten, *a.* un-*got*-en, not gained or obtained; not begotten.
ungovernable, *a.* un-*guv*-er-na-bl, that cannot be governed or controlled; unruly; refractory.
ungovernably, *ad.* so as not to be governed or controlled.
ungoverned, *a.* un-*guv*-ernd, not subjected to laws or principles; unbridled; licentious.
ungown, *v.t.* un-*goun*, to strip of a gown; to unfrock.
ungraceful, *a.* un-*grace*-ful, wanting ease and elegance; awkward.
ungracefully, *ad.* awkwardly; inelegantly.
ungracefulness, *n.* want of gracefulness.
ungracious, *a.* un-*gray*-shus, wicked; odious; hateful; offensive; unpleasing; uncourteous.
ungraciously, *ad.* in an ungracious manner.
ungraciousness, *n.* the quality of being ungracious; discourteousness.
ungraded, *a.* un-*gray*-ded, not classified in a grade; having no gradients.
ungraduated, *a.* un-*grad*-yew-ay-ted, having no graduations; not regularly set forth; not having taken a degree [Univ.].
ungrammatical, *a.* *un*-gra-*mat*-e-kal, not according to the rules of grammar.
ungrammatically, *ad.* in a manner contrary to the rules of grammar.
ungranted, *a.* un-*grahn*-ted, not bestowed; not transferred by deed or gift; not conceded.
ungrateful, *a.* un-*grate*-ful, not feeling thankful for favours; showing little or no gratitude; making no returns for culture; unpleasing; unacceptable.
ungratefully, *ad.* with ingratitude.
ungratefulness, *n.* ingratitude.
ungratified, *a.* un-*grat*-e-fide, not gratified; not indulged.
unground, *a.* un-*ground*, not ground; not passed through a mill.
ungrounded, *a.* un-*groun*-ded, having no foundation or support; baseless.
ungroundedly, *ad.* without ground or reason.
ungrudged, *a.* un-*grudjd*, not grudged.
ungrudging, *a.* un-*grudj*-ing, freely giving; sparing no expense.
ungrudgingly, *ad.* un-*grudj*-ing-le, cheerfully.
ungual, *a.* *ung*-gwal, pertaining to, having, or of the nature of nails, claws, or hoofs. (L. *unguis*, a nail.)
unguarded, *a.* un-*gar*-ded, not watched or defended; careless; negligent; not done or spoken with caution.
unguardedly, *ad.* in an unguarded manner.
unguent, *n.* *ung*-gwent, ointment; a soft composition used as a remedy for sores. (L. *unguens*, anointing.)
unguentary, *a.* *ung*-gwen-ta-re, pertaining to or used for unguents: *n.* a pot or vessel for ointment.
unguessed, *a.* un-*gest*, not obtained by conjecture; unimagined.
unguicorn, *n.* *ung*-gwe-kawrn, the horny covering at the tip of the upper mandible of a bird. (L. *unguis*, nail, *cornu*, horn.)
unguiculate, *a.* ung-*gwik*-yew-lat, clawed; having nails or claws [Zool.]; having a claw-like base [Bot.].
unguiculated, *a.* ung-*gwik*-yew-lay-ted, unguiculate.
unguided, *a.* un-*gy*-ded, not led or conducted; not regulated.
unguiform, *a.* *ung*-gwe-form, shaped like a claw. (L. *unguis*, a claw, *forma*, shape.)
unguiltily, *ad.* un-*gil*-te-le, without guilt.
unguilty, *a.* un-*gil*-te, not stained with crime; innocent.
unguinal, *a.* *ung*-gwe-nal, ungual [Anat.].
unguinous, *a.* *ung*-gwe-nus, unctuous; consisting of fat or oil. (L. *ungo*, anoint.)
unguirostral, *a.* *ung*-gwe-*ros*-tral, having a nail, or unguicorn, at the end of the beak (of birds).
ungula, *n.* *ung*-gew-la, a section of a cylinder or cone cut off by a plane oblique to the base [Geom.]. (L., a hoof.)
ungulate, *a.* *ung*-gew-lat, shaped like a hoof;

having hoofs: *n.* any mammal with hoofed feet such as cattle, deer, swine, and horses, included in the order Ungulata.
ungum, *v.t.* un-*gum*, to unstick; to divest of gum.
unhabituated, *a. un*-ha-*bit*-yew-ay-ted, not accustomed.
unhacked, *a.* un-*hakt*, not cut, notched, or mangled.
unhackneyed, *a.* un-*hak*-ned, not become commonplace, stale, or worn out by frequent use.
unhair, *v.t.* un-*hare*, to remove hair, esp. from hides: *v.i.* to lose the hair.
unhallow, *v.t.* un-*hal*-oh, to profane or render profane; to desecrate.
unhallowed, *a.* un-*hal*-ode, not consecrated; deprived of its sacred character; profane; unholy; wicked.
unhampered, *a.* un-*ham*-perd, free; not subject to hindrance.
unhand, *v.t.* un-*hand*, to loose the hands off; to let go.
unhandily, *ad.* un-*han*-de-le, awkwardly; clumsily.
unhandiness, *n.* want of dexterity; clumsiness.
unhandled, *a.* un-*han*-dld, not handled; not treated; not trained.
unhandsome, *a.* un-*han*-sum, not handsome or well shaped; unfair; illiberal; uncivil.
unhandsomely, *ad.* in an unhandsome manner.
unhandsomeness, *n.* want of handsomeness; unfairness.
unhandy, *a.* un-*han*-de, not dexterous or skilful; awkward.
unhang, *v.t.* un-*hang*, to divest of hangings, as a room; to take from hooks or hinges. *pp.* **unhung.**
unhanged, *a.* un-*hangd*, not hung upon a gallows; not punished by hanging.
unhappily, *ad.* un-*hap*-e-le, by ill hap; unfortunately; miserably.
unhappiness, *n.* misfortune; ill-luck; misery.
unhappy, *a.* un-*hap*-e, unfortunate; unlucky; not happy; miserable.
unharassed, *a.* un-*ha*-rast, not harassed; not vexed.
unharbour, *v.t.* un-*har*-bur, to drive from harbour or shelter.
unharboured, *a.* un-*har*-burd, not sheltered.
unhardened, *a.* un-*har*-dnd, not indurated, as metal; not made obdurate.
unhardy, *a.* un-*har*-de, feeble; not able to endure cold; without fortitude; timorous.
unharmed, *a.* un-*harmd*, uninjured; unimpaired.
unharmful, *a.* un-*harm*-ful, not doing harm; harmless.
unharmonious, *a. un*-har-*moh*-ne-us, not having symmetry or congruity; discordant.
unharness, *v.t.* un-*har*-ness, to strip off harness; to divest of armour.
unhasp, *v.t.* un-*hahsp*, to undo the hasp of.
unhatched, *a.* un-*hatcht*, not having left the egg; not matured and brought to light.
unhazarded, *a.* un-*haz*-ar-ded, not exposed to risk or hazard.
unhazardous, *a.* un-*haz*-ar-dus, not hazardous.
unhead, *v.t.* un-*hed*, to take the head from; to behead.
unhealthful, *a.* un-*helth*-ful, injurious to health; insalubrious; unwholesome.
unhealthfulness, *n.* state of being unhealthy.
unhealthily, *ad.* un-*helth*-e-le, in an unhealthy manner.
unhealthiness, *n.* un-*helth*-e-ness, want of health; unsoundness; unwholesomeness.
unhealthy, *a.* un-*helth*-e, wanting health; habitually weak or indisposed; unsound; sickly; unfavourable to health; unwholesome.
unheard, *a.* un-*herd*, not perceived by the ear; not admitted to audience; not known to fame. **unheard of,** never before experienced; unprecedented.
unheated, *a.* un-*hee*-ted, not made hot; cold.
unheavenly, *a.* un-*hev*-en-le, not heavenly.
unhedged, *a.* un-*hejd*, not surrounded by a hedge.
unheeded, *a.* un-*hee*-ded, disregarded; neglected.
unheededly, *ad.* without being heeded.
unheedful, *a.* un-*heed*-ful, inattentive; careless.
unheedfully, *ad.* carelessly.
unheeding, *a.* un-*hee*-ding, careless; negligent.
unheedy, *a.* un-*hee*-de, careless; precipitate; sudden.
unhelm, *v.t.* **un-*helm*, to deprive of a helm or helmet.**
unhelmed, *pp.* and *a.* un-*helmd*, having no helmet; divested of a helmet.
unhelped, *a.* un-*helpt*, unassisted; unsupported.
unhelpful, *a.* un-*help*-ful, affording no aid.
unheroic, *a. un*-he-*roh*-ik, not heroic or brave.
unhesitating, *a.* un-*hez*-e-tay-ting, not remaining in doubt; prompt.
unhesitatingly, *ad.* without hesitation.
unhewn, *a.* un-*hewn*, not hewn; rough.
unhindered, *a.* un-*hin*-derd, not opposed; not impeded.
unhinge, *v.t.* un-*hinj*, to take from the hinges; to displace; to unfix; to unsettle.
unhingement, *n.* un-*hinj*-ment, the act of unhinging; unsettlement.
unhired, *a.* un-*hyrd*, not hired.
unhistorical, *a. un*-his-*to*-re-kal, not historical; merely legendary.
unhitch, *v.t.* un-*hitch*, to loosen, as a rope; to unfasten.
unhive, *v.t.* un-*hive*, to drive from a hive; to deprive of habitation.
unholiness, *n.* un-*hoh*-le-ness, want of holiness; impiety; profaneness.
unholy, *a.* un-*hoh*-le, not holy; profane; not hallowed; impious; wicked; ungodly; not ceremonially purified; outrageous [Slang].
unhonoured, *a.* un-*on*-urd, not honoured; not celebrated.
unhooded, *a.* un-*hood*-ed, without a hood.
unhook, *v.t.* un-*hook*, to loose from a hook; to undo thus; to uncouple.
unhoped, *a.* un-*hohpt*, not so probable as to excite hope; unexpected.
unhopeful, *a.* un-*hope*-ful, not hopeful; affording no room for hope; hopeless.
unhorned, *a.* un-*hawrnd*, having no horns.
unhorse, *v.t.* un-*horse*, to throw from a horse; to cause to dismount; to take the horse from.
unhouse, *v.t.* un-*houze*, to drive from house or habitation; to dislodge; to deprive of shelter.
unhoused, *a.* un-*houzd*, wanting a house; homeless; destitute of shelter.
unhouseled, *a.* un-*hou*-zld, not having received the holy sacrament.
unhuman, *a.* un-*hew*-man, inhuman; not humane; not subject to the limitations of humanity.
unhumanize, *v.t.* un-*hew*-ma-nize, to dehumanize.
unhumbled, *a.* un-*hum*-bld, not humbled or subdued.
unhung, *a.* un-*hung*, not hanged; not exhibited (at a picture-gallery).
unhurried, *a.* un-*hu*-rid, leisurely; deliberate.
unhurt, *a.* un-*hurt*, not harmed; free from injury.
unhurtful, *a.* un-*hurt*-ful, harmless; innoxious.
unhurtfully, *ad.* without harm.
unhusbanded, *a.* un-*huz*-ban-ded, not managed with frugality; without or deprived of a husband.
unhusked, *a.* un-*huskt*, not being stripped of husks.
Uniat, *n. yew*-ne-at, a member of an Oriental Church acknowledging papal supremacy but conforming to its own rites, liturgy, etc.
uniaxal, *a. yew*-ne-*ak*-sal, uniaxial.
uniaxial, *a. yew*-ne-*ak*-se-al, having but one optical axis [Cryst.]. (L. *unus*, one, and *axis*.)
unibranchiate, *a. yew*-ne-*brank*-e-ate, having but one gill.
unicamerate, *a. yew*-ne-*kam*-er-rat, unilocular.
unicameral, *a. yew*-ne-*kam*-er-ral, having but one legislative chamber.
unicapsular, *a. yew*-ne-*kap*-sew-lar, having one capsule to each flower [Bot.].
unicarinate, *a. yew*-ne-*ka*-re-nat, having a single keel.
unicellular, *a. yew*-ne-*sel*-yew-lar, composed of but one cell.
Unicist, *n. yew*-ne-sist, one who believes in the unicity of the Godhead.
unicity, *n.* yew-*nis*-e-te, the state or quality of being unique; oneness.
unicoloured, *a. yew*-ne-kul-ord, of one colour only.
unicorn, *n. yew*-ne-kawrn, an animal with one horn, esp. a fabulous beast represented as a single-horned horse [Her.]; a team of three horses, two abreast and one in front; a long-horned beetle; the sea-unicorn or narwhal. (L. *unus*, and *cornu*, a horn.)
unicornous, *a. yew*-ne-*kawr*-nus, having only one horn.
unicostate, *a.* yew-ne-*kos*-tat, having but one rib [Bot.].

unicuspid, *a.* yew-ne-*kus*-pid, having a single fang (of teeth).
unicycle, *n.* *yew*-ne-sy-kl, an acrobat's cycle having one wheel.
unideaed, *a.* un-eye-*dee*-ad, devoid of ideas; senseless; unimaginative.
unideal, *a.* *un*-eye-*dee*-al, not ideal; having no ideal.
unidentate, *a.* *yew*-ne-*den*-tat, having but one tooth.
unidenticulate, *a.* *yew*-ne-den-*tik*-yew-lat, having but one denticle.
unidentified, *a.* *un*-eye-*den*-te-fide, not identified.
unidirectional, *a.* *yew*-ne-dy-*rek*-shon-al, acting, or capable of movement, in one direction only; direct, as opposed to alternating (of current) [Elect.].
unifacial, *a.* *yew*-ne-*fay*-shal, having only one face or front surface.
unifiable, *a.* yew-ne-*fy*-a-bl, capable of being unified.
unification, *n.* yew-ne-fe-*kay*-shon, the act of uniting.
unifier, *n.* *yew*-ne-fy-er, one who or that which unifies.
uniflorous, *a.* *yew*-ne-flaw-rus, bearing one flower only [Bot.].
unifoliate, *a.* *yew*-ne-*foh*-le-at, having but one leaf [Bot.]. (L. *unus*, and *folium*, a leaf.)
uniform, *a.* *yew*-ne-form, having always the same form and manner; not variable; consistent with itself; not different; of the same form with others; equable; regular: *n.* distinctive costume pertaining to persons of the same service, class, body, etc.; the regulation dress of members of an armed force. (L. *unus*, and *forma*, shape.)
uniformitarian, *n.* *yew*-ne-*for*-me-*tare*-re-an, one holding that present geological processes are the same as those of the past in kind if not in degree.
uniformitarianism, *n.* *yew*-ne-*for*-me-*tare*-re-a-nizm, the theory of the uniformitarians, opposed to catastrophism [Geol.].
uniformity, *n.* *yew*-ne-*for*-me-te, resemblance to itself at all times or all through; consistency; sameness; resemblance, consonance, or agreement; similitude between parts; unvaried sameness. **Act of Uniformity,** an Act (esp. that of 1662) regulating the form of public prayers and rites to be observed in the Church of England.
uniformly, *ad.* *yew*-ne-form-le, in a uniform manner; invariably.
unify, *v.t.* *yew*-ne-fy, to make into one; to make uniform. (L. *unus*, and *facio*, make.)
unigeniture, *n.* *yew*-ne-*jen*-e-tewr, state of being the only begotten. (L. *unus*, and *gigno*, beget.)
unilabiate, *a.* *yew*-ne-*lay*-be-at, having one lip only [Bot.]. (L. *unus*, and *labium*, a lip.)
unilateral, *a.* *yew*-ne-*lat*-er-ral, one-sided; pertaining to or done by one only of two or more parties; arranged on or having one side [Bot. and Zool.]. (L. *unus*, and *latus*, a side.)
unilateralism, *n.* yew-ne-*lat*-er-ra-lizm, the quality or condition of being unilateral.
unilaterally, *ad.* yew-ne-*lat*-er-ra-le, in a unilateral manner.
unilingual, *a.* yew-ne-*ling*-gwal, in or using one language only.
uniliteral, *a.* *yew*-ne-*lit*-er-ral, consisting of a single letter.
unilluminated, *a.* *un*-e-*lew*-me-nay-ted, not enlightened; dark; ignorant.
unillustrated, *a.* un-*il*-us-tray-ted, not illustrated.
unilocular, *a.* *yew*-ne-*lok*-yew-lar, with one cavity or one chamber only [Zool. and Bot.]. (L. *unus*, and *locus*, a place.)
unimaginable, *a.* *un*-e-*maj*-e-na-bl, not to be conceived.
unimaginably, *ad.* *un*-e-*maj*-e-na-ble, inconceivably.
unimaginative, *a.* *un*-e-*maj*-e-na-tiv, not imaginative.
unimagined, *a.* *un*-e-*maj*-ind, not conceived.
unimbued, *a.* un-im-*bewd*, not saturated.
unimitated, *a.* un-*im*-e-tay-ted, not imitated.
unimpaired, *a.* *un*-im-*payrd*, not impaired; not diminished.
unimpassioned, *a.* *un*-im-*pash*-ond, not actuated or dictated by passion; calm.
unimpeachable, *a.* *un*-im-*peech*-a-bl, that cannot be accused; free from stain, guilt, or fault; that cannot be called in question.
unimpeachableness, *n.* *un*-im-*peech*-a-bl-ness, the quality of being unimpeachable.
unimpeached, *a.* *un*-im-*peecht*, not charged or accused; not called in question.
unimpeded, *a.* *un*-im-*pee*-ded, not hindered.
unimplicated, *a.* un-*im*-ple-kay-ted, not involved.
unimplied, *a.* *un*-im-*plide*, not included by fair inference.
unimplored, *a.* *un*-im-*plored*, not solicited.
unimportant, *a.* *un*-im-*por*-tant, not of great moment; insignificant; immaterial.
unimportuned, *a.* *un*-im-por-*tewnd*, not solicited.
unimposing, *a.* *un*-im-*poh*-zing, not commanding respect; not enjoining as obligatory; voluntary.
unimpregnated, *a.* *un*-im-*preg*-n-ted, not impregnated.
unimpressed, *a.* un-im-*prest*, not impressed; uninterested.
unimpressible, *a.* *un*-im-*pres*-e-bl, not impressible.
unimpressive, *a.* *un*-im-*pres*-iv, not impressive.
unimpressively, *ad.* without impressiveness.
unimprisoned, *a.* *un*-im-*priz*-ond, not confined to prison.
unimpropriated, *a.* *un*-im-*proh*-pre-ay-ted, not put into the hands of a layman (of tithes, etc.).
unimprovable, *a.* *un*-im-*proo*-va-bl, not capable of improvement, culture, or tillage.
unimprovableness, *n.* state of being unimprovable.
unimproved, *a.* un-im-*proovd*, not made better or wiser; not advanced in knowledge, manner, or excellence; not used to advantage; not employed; not cultivated.
unimproving, *a.* *un*-im-*proo*-ving, not tending to advance or instruct.
unimpugnable, *a.* *un*-im-*pew*-na-bl, that cannot be inpugned.
unincorporate, *a.* *un*-in-*kor*-po-rat, not embodied; not incorporated.
unindebted, *a.* *un*-in-*det*-ed, not indebted.
unindented, *a.* *un*-in-*den*-ted, having no indentations or [Print.] indentions; being without indentures.
unindifferent, *a.* *un*-in-*dif*-e-rent, not indifferent; not impartial.
uninduced, *a.* *un*-in-*dewst*, not induced.
unindustrious, *a.* *un*-in-*dus*-tre-us, not diligent in labour or study.
uninfected, *a.* *un*-in-*fek*-ted, not contaminated; not corrupted.
uninfectious, *a.* *un*-in-*fek*-shus, not capable of communicating disease.
uninfested, *a.* *un*-in-*fes*-ted, not infested.
uninflamed, *a.* *un*-in-*flaymd*, not inflamed.
uninflammable, *a.* *un*-in-*flam*-a-bl, not readily set on fire.
uninflected, *a.* *un*-in-*flek*-ted, having no inflexions [Philol.].
uninfluenced, *a.* un-*in*-floo-enst, not persuaded or moved by others or by external considerations; acting freely.
uninfluential, *a.* *un*-in-floo-*en*-shal, not having influence.
uninformed, *a.* *un*-in-*formd*, not instructed; untaught; ignorant.
uningenious, *a.* *un*-in-*jee*-ne-us, not ingenious; dull.
uningenuous, *a.* *un*-in-*jen*-yew-us, not frank or candid; disingenuous.
uningenuousness, *n.* *un*-in-*jen*-yew-us-ness, disingenuousness.
uninhabitable, *a.* *un*-in-*hab*-e-ta-bl, not habitable.
uninhabited, *a.* *un*-in-*hab*-e-ted, having no inhabitants; unoccupied.
uninitiated, *a.* *un*-e-*nish*-e-ay-ted, not initiated.
uninjured, *a.* un-*in*-jurd, not hurt; suffering no harm.
uninjurious, *a.* *un*-in-*joor*-re-us, not injurious.
uninominal, *a.* *yew*-ne-*nom*-e-nal, pertaining to or consisting of one name only.
uninquiring, *a.* *un*-in-*kwire*-ring, not disposed to inquire.
uninquisitive, *a.* *un*-in-*kwiz*-e-tiv, not curious to search and inquire.
uninscribed, *a.* *un*-in-*skribed*, having no inscription.
uninspired, *a.* *un*-in-*spired*, not having received supernatural inspiration or illumination; commonplace; not official.
uninstructed, *a.* *un*-in-*struk*-ted, not educated; not furnished with instructions.
uninstructive, *a.* *un*-in-*struk*-tiv, not serving to instruct or edify.
uninstructively, *ad.* without edification.

uninsulated, *a.* un-*in*-sew-lay-ted, not insulated.
uninsured, *a.* un-in-*shoord*, not insured against loss.
unintegrated, *a.* un-*in*-te-gray-ted, not integrated.
unintellectual, *a.* *un*-in-te-*lek*-tew-al, not intellectual.
unintelligent, *a.* *un*-in-*tel*-e-jent, not possessing understanding; not knowing; not skilful; dull.
unintelligibility, *n.* *un*-in-tel-e-ge-*bil*-e-te, unintelligibleness.
unintelligible, *a.* *un*-in-*tel*-e-je-bl, that cannot be understood.
unintelligibleness, *n.* the quality of not being intelligible.
unintelligibly, *ad.* in a manner not to be understood.
unintended, *a.* *un*-in-*ten*-ded, not designed.
unintentional, *a.* *un*-in-*ten*-shon-al, done or happening without intention.
unintentionally, *ad.* without design or purpose.
uninterested, *a.* un-*in*-ter-res-ted, not having any interest, property, or stake in; not interested.
uninteresting, *a.* un-*in*-ter-res-ting, not capable of exciting interest.
uninterestingly, *ad.* in a way not exciting interest.
unintermission, *n.* *un*-in-ter-*mish*-on, failure or lack of intermission.
unintermitted, *a.* *un*-in-ter-*mit*-ed, not interrupted; continued.
unintermitting, *a.* *un*-in-ter-*mit*-ing, not ceasing for a time; continuing.
unintermixed, *a.* *un*-in-ter-*mikst*, not mingled.
uninterpolated, *a.* *un*-in-*ter*-po-lay-ted, not inserted subsequently to the original writing.
uninterpreted, *a.* *un*-in-*ter*-pre-ted, not explained.
uninterred, *a.* *un*-in-*terd*, not buried.
uninterrupted, *a.* *un*-in-ter-*rup*-ted, not interrupted; continuous.
uninterruptedly, *ad.* without interruption.
unintoxicating, *a.* *un*-in-*tok*-se-kay-ting, not intoxicating.
unintroduced, *a.* *un*-in-tro-*dewst*, not introduced; obtruding.
uninuclear, *a.* *yew*-ne-*new*-kle-ar, having one nucleus.
uninured, *a.* *un*-in-*yewrd*, not hardened by use or practice.
uninvented, *a.* *un*-in-*ven*-ted, not in existence; unheard of; unimaginable.
uninventive, *a.* *un*-in-*ven*-tiv, not inventive.
uninvested, *a.* *un*-in-*ves*-ted, not invested; not converted into real property.
uninvestigable, *a.* *un*-in-*ves*-te-ga-bl, that cannot be investigated or searched out.
uninvidious, *a.* *un*-in-*vid*-e-us, not invidious.
uninvited, *a.* *un*-in-*vy*-ted, not requested; not accorded an invitation.
uninviting, *a.* *un*-in-*vy*-ting, not attractive.
uninvoked, *a.* *un*-in-*vohkt*, not invoked.
union, *n.* *yew*-nyon, the act of joining two or more things into one; the junction or coalition of things thus united; combination, as of parishes, for the support of the poor, and hence a workhouse; a trade-union, or a combination of workmen; concord, symmetry, harmony; alliance; coalition; confederacy; a mixed fabric of two materials (originally wool and cotton); a device for connecting pipes, parts, etc., a coupling [Mech.]. **Union Flag,** since 1801 the national flag of Great Britain and Northern Ireland, consisting of the crosses of St. George, St. Andrew, and St. Patrick superimposed in union. **Union Jack,** a small Union Flag flown at the bows of British warships on a jack or small spar. (L. *unio*, oneness, from *unus*, one.)
unionism, *n.* *yew*-nyon-izm, the system or principle of union or combination; attachment to a union esp., formerly, that of Great Britain and Ireland, or the federal system of the U.S.A.; the principles of trade-unionists.
unionist, *n.* *yew*-nyon-ist, a believer in or supporter of unionism; a former opponent of Irish home rule; a member of a trade-union.
unionize, *v.t.* *yew*-nyo-nize, to form into, or to organize as, a trade-union: *v.i.* to join a trade-union.
unipara, *n.* yew-*nip*-a-ra, a woman who has borne but one child. (*uniparous.*)
uniparous, *a.* yew-*nip*-a-rus, producing but one at a birth [Zool.]; producing a single axis at each branching [Bot.]. (L. *unus*, one, *parere*, to produce.)
unipartite, *a.* yew-ne-*par*-tite, undivided into parts; single; completely homogeneous.
uniped, *n.* *yew*-ne-ped, a one-footed person or animal: *a.* one-footed.
unipersonal, *a.* yew-ne-*per*-so-nal, of only one person; employed only in the third person singular, or impersonal [Gram.].
uniplanar, *a.* yew-ne-*play*-nar, pertaining to or occurring in only one plane [Mech.].
unipolar, *a.* yew-ne-*poh*-lar, with single polarity.
uniquantic, *a.* yew-ne-*kwon*-tik, pertaining to a single quantum of energy [Physics].
unique, *a.* yew-*neek*, without a like or an equal in kind or quality. (Fr., from L. *unicus*, one and no more.)
uniquely, *ad.* in a unique manner.
uniqueness, *n.* state or quality of being unique.
uniradial, *a.* *yew*-ne-*ray*-de-al, having but one ray or arm [Zool.].
unirritated, *a.* un-*i*-re-tay-ted, not fretted; not provoked or angered.
unirritating, *a.* un-*i*-re-tay-ting, not provoking.
uniselector, *n.* yew-ne-se-*lek*-tor, an automatic selector having unidirectional motion [Wire.].
uniseptate, *a.* yew-ne-*sep*-tat, having but one partition.
unisexual, *a.* yew-ne-*sek*-sew-al, of one sex only, not hermaphroditic [Zool.]; diclinous [Bot.].
unisexuality, *n.* *yew*-ne-*sek*-sew-*al*-e-te, the condition of being unisexual.
unison, *n.* *yew*-ne-son, an accordance or coincidence of sounds, proceeding from an equality in the number of vibrations made in a given time by a sonorous body; a single unvaried note; accordance; agreement: *a.* agreeing in pitch. **in unison,** in harmony. (L. *unus*, one, and *sonus*, sound.)
unisonal, *a.* yew-*nis*-o-nal, [Mus.] unisonant.
unisonance, *n.* yew-*nis*-o-nance, accordance of sounds.
unisonant, *a.* yew-*nis*-o-nant, being in unison; having the same degree of gravity or acuteness; of the same pitch [Mus.].
unisonous, *a.* yew-*nis*-o-nus, [Mus.] unisonant.
★**unit,** *n.* *yew*-nit, one; the least whole number; a single thing or person; a group or body of men (*e.g.*, a platoon, a regiment) or objects (*e.g.*, a composite machine) treated as one; a single complete section of a manufactured article; a quantity or amount in the terms of which measurements are expressed [Math. and Physics].
unitable, *a.* yew-*ny*-ta-bl, capable of union.
Unitarian, *n.* yew-ne-*tare*-re-an, one who, denying the doctrine of the Trinity, believes in the undivided unity of the divine nature; a member of a Christian sect holding this doctrine; (*l.c.*) one who advocates a theory based on unity [Math.]: *a.* pertaining to the Unitarians.
unitarianism, *n.* yew-ne-*tare*-re-a-nizm, the principles of the Unitarians.
unitary, *a.* *yew*-ne-ta-re, relating to or of the nature of a unit.
unite, *v.t.* yew-*nite*, to put together; to join two or more things into one; to join; to connect; to make to agree; to cause to adhere; to join in interest or in affection; to tie or splice: *v.i.* to join in an act; to concur; to combine; to coalesce; to grow together; to be mixed.
united, *a.* yew-*ny*-ted, joined; made to agree in harmony. **United Kingdom,** from 1801 to 1922, Great Britain and Ireland; after 1922 Great Britain and Northern Ireland. **United Nations,** the body of self-governing Powers adhering to the Washington Declaration of 1 Jan. 1942, which, after the Second World War, replaced the former League of Nations. **United States (of America),** the federation of colonies which, seceding from the British Empire, united as a Republic in 1776, together with those that subsequently federated with them, now 48 in all.
unitedly, *ad.* with union or joint efforts.
uniter, *n.* yew-*ny*-ter, one who or that unites.
unition, *n.* yew-*nish*-on, the act of uniting; junction.
unitism, *n.* *yew*-ne-tizm, monism.
unitive, *a.* *yew*-ne-tiv, having the power of uniting.
unitize, *v.t.* *yew*-ne-tize, to treat as, or to form into, a unit.
unity, *n.* *yew*-ne-te, the state of being one; oneness;

concord; conjunction; agreement; uniformity; oneness of sentiment, affection, or behaviour; an abstract expression for any unit whatever [Math.]; the principle by which, in literary and artistic compositions, a uniform tenor of story and propriety of representation is preserved; such a combination of parts as to constitute a whole, or a kind of symmetry of style and character [Mus.]; a joint possession of two rights by several titles [Law]. **the three unities,** the concurrence (in drama) of action, time, and place.

univalence, *n.* yew-*niv*-a-lence, the condition or quality of being univalent [Chem. and Biol.].

univalency, *n.* yew-*niv*-a-len-se, univalence.

univalent, *a.* yew-*niv*-a-lent, having a valency of one; monatomic.

univalve, *a.* *yew*-ne-valv, having one valve only: *n.* a mollusc whose shell is composed of a single piece; a gastropod.

univalvular, *a.* *yew*-ne-*val*-vew-lar, having one valve only.

universal, *a.* *yew*-ne-*ver*-sal, all; general; comprehending the whole number, quantity, or space; total; whole; comprising all: *n.* a general notion; a universal proposition. **universal joint,** a contrivance for allowing motion in all directions. **universal proposition,** one which affirms the predicate to belong to the whole of the subject [Logic].

Universalism, *n.* *yew*-ne-*ver*-sa-lizm, the doctrine that all men will be eventually saved; (*l.c.*) universality; a universal; pursuit of universal knowledge.

Universalist, *n.* yew-ne-*ver*-sa-list, a believer in Universalism: *a.* pertaining to Universalism.

universalistic, *a.* *yew*-ne-*ver*-sa-*lis*-tik, pertaining to the doctrine of Universalism.

universality, *n.* yew-ne-ver-*sal*-e-te, state or quality of being universal or extending to the whole.

universalize, *v.t.* yew-ne-*ver*-sa-lize, to make universal.

universally, *ad.* with extension to the whole; without exception.

universalness, *n.* yew-ne-*ver*-sal-ness, universality.

universe, *n.* *yew*-ne-verse, the whole system of nature; all created things; all mankind; everything in existence. (L. *universus*, combined into one whole, from *unus*, one, and *versus*, turned.)

university, *n.* yew-ne-*ver*-se-te, an assemblage of colleges, or a corporation for teaching the higher branches of learning, and conferring degrees; the collective members of such. (L. *universitas*, a corporation.)

universology, *n.* *yew*-ne-ver-*sol*-o-je, the science treating of the universe as a whole.

univocal, *a.* yew-*niv*-o-kal, having one meaning only; having unison of sounds; certain: *n.* a word having only one meaning.

univocally, *ad.* in one sense only.

univoltine, *n.* yew-ne-*vol*-teen, one of a breed of silkworms which breed only once in a year. (Fr., from It. *uni-*, one, *volta*, turn.)

unjaundiced, *a.* un-*jawn*-dist, impartial; unprejudiced.

unjealous, *a.* un-*jel*-us, not jealous.

unjoined, *a.* un-*joynd*, not joined.

unjoint, *v.t.* un-*joynt*, to disjoint; to take apart.

unjointed, *a.* un-*joyn*-ted, having no joints; disjointed.

unjoyous, *a.* un-*joy*-us, not joyous or cheerful.

unjudged, *a.* un-*judjd*, not judged; not judicially determined.

unjust, *a.* un-*just*, contrary to justice and right; wrongful.

unjustifiable, *a.* un-*jus*-te-*fy*-a-bl, that cannot be proved to be right; indefensible.

unjustifiableness, *n.* state of being unjustifiable.

unjustifiably, *ad.* in a manner that cannot be justified.

unjustified, *a.* un-*jus*-te-fide, not justified; not pardoned.

unjustly, *ad.* un-*just*-le, with injustice.

unkempt, *a.* un-*kempt*, uncombed; slovenly. (A.S. *un-*, and *cemban*, comb.)

unkenned, *a.* un-*kend*, unknown; strange; not discerned.

unkennel, *v.t.* un-*ken*-nel, to drive from a hole; to rouse from secrecy or retreat; to release from a kennel.

unkept, *a.* un-*kept*, not retained or preserved.

unkind, *a.* un-*kynd*, not kind; harsh.

unkindliness, *n.* the state of being unkindly.

unkindly, *a.* unkind; unfavourable; malignant: *ad.* without kindness or affection.

unkindness, *n.* want of kindness; an unkind act.

unking, *v.t.* un-*king*, to deprive of royal authority.

unkingly, *a.* and *ad.* un-*king*-le, unworthy of a king.

unknightly, *a.* and *ad.* un-*nite*-le, unworthy of a knight.

unknit, *v.t.* un-*nit*, to separate threads that are knit; to unravel; to open.

unknot, *v.t.* un-*not*, to free from knots; to untie.

unknowable, *a.* un-*noh*-a-bl, that cannot be known: *n.* that which lies beyond the grasp of human understanding.

unknowing, *a.* un-*noh*-ing, not knowing; ignorant.

unknowingly, *ad.* without knowledge or design.

unknown, *a.* un-*nohn*, not known; incalculable. **Unknown Warrior,** *see* **warrior.**

unlaborious, *a.* *un*-la-*baw*-re-us, not difficult to be done.

unlaboured, *a.* un-*lay*-burd, not produced or cultivated by labour; not tilled; spontaneous; voluntary; natural; easy.

unlace, *v.t.* un-*lace*, to loose from lacing; to loose a dress, etc., that is laced; to divest of lace.

unlade, *v.t.* un-*lade*, to unload; to discharge a cargo.

unladen, *a.* un-*lay*-dn, not loaded, not having a burden.

unladylike, *a.* un-*lay*-de-like, not befitting a lady; vulgar; ill-bred.

unlaid, *a.* un-*lade*, not placed or fixed; not allayed.

unlamented, *a.* *un*-la-*men*-ted, not deplored.

unlarded, *a.* un-*lar*-ded, not dressed with lard; without inserted strips of bacon fat; not intermixed.

unlash, *v.t.* un-*lash*, to unfasten.

unlatch, *v.i.* un-*latch*, to open or loose by lifting the latch.

unlaurelled, *a.* un-*lo*-reld, not crowned with laurel; not honoured.

unlavish, *a.* un-*lav*-ish, not lavish or profuse.

unlawful, *a.* un-*law*-ful, contrary to the law; illicit; illegal.

unlawfully, *ad.* in violation of law; illegitimately.

unlawfulness, *n.* contrariety to law.

unlay, *v.t.* un-*lay*, to untwist. *p.* and *pp.* **unlaid.**

unleaded, *a.* un-*led*-ed, set solid, with no leads between the lines [Print.]; not set in or fitted with leads.

unlearn, *v.t.* un-*lern*, to forget, lose, or be unschooled of, what has been learned.

unlearned, *a.* un-*ler*-ned, not learned; ignorant; illiterate; not suitable to a learned man.

unlearned, *a.* un-*lernd*, not learned or learnt.

unlearnedly, *ad.* un-*ler*-ned-le, ignorantly; in an uneducated manner.

unlearnt, *a.* un-*lernt*, not learned or committed to memory.

unleashed, *a.* un-*leesht*, set free from the leash.

unleavened, *a.* un-*lev*-end, made without leaven or yeast.

unled, *a.* un-*led*, not led or conducted.

unlent, *a.* un-*lent*, not lent.

unless, *conj.* un-*less*, except; if not; supposing that not. (*un-*, on, and *less*.)

unlessoned, *a.* un-*les*-ond, not taught; not instructed.

unlettered, *a.* un-*let*-erd, unlearned; untaught.

unlevelled, *a.* un-*lev*-ld, not levelled; not laid even.

unlicensed, *a.* un-*ly*-senst, not licensed; not having permission by authority; done without licence.

unlicked, *a.* un-*likt*, shapeless; not formed to smoothness; untrained; uncouth; ill-bred [Slang] undefeated.

unlighted, *a.* un-*ly*-ted, not illuminated; not kindled or set on fire.

unlike, *a.* un-*like*, dissimilar; having no resemblance; unlikely.

unlikelihood, *n.* un-*like*-le-hood, improbability.

unlikeliness, *n.* un-*like*-le-ness, improbability.

unlikely, *a.* un-*like*-le, improbable; not promising success: *ad.* improbably.

unlikeness, *n.* want of resemblance; dissimilitude quality or condition of being unlike.

unlimber, *a.* un-*lim*-ber, not flexible; not yielding

unlimber, *v.t.* un-*lim*-ber, to unhook a gun from its limber [Mil.]; to clear for action.
unlimed, *a.* un-*limed*, having the lime removed; not having been treated with lime.
unlimitable, *a.* un-*lim*-e-ta-bl, illimitable; boundless.
unlimited, *a.* un-*lim*-e-ted, not limited; having no bounds; undefined; indefinite; not restrained.
unlimitedly, *ad.* un-*lim*-e-ted-le, without bounds.
unlimitedness, *n.* state of being unlimited.
unline, *v.t.* un-*line*, to remove the lining from; to empty.
unlineal, *a.* un-*lin*-e-al, not coming in the order of succession.
unlink, *v.t.* un-*link*, to separate the links of; to unfasten; to untwist.
unliquefied, *a.* un-*lik*-we-fide, unmelted; not dissolved.
unliquidated, *a.* un-*lik*-we-day-ted: not settled; unpaid; unadjusted.
unlistening, *a.* un-*lis*-sen-ing, not hearing or regarding; heedless.
unlit, *a.* un-*lit*, not lighted; not illuminated; dark.
unliveliness, *n.* un-*lyve*-le-ness, want of animation; dullness.
unlively, *a.* un-*lyve*-le, not lively; dull.
unload, *v.t.* un-*lode*, to take the load from; to disburden; to discharge.
unlocated, *a.* *un*-lo-*kay*-ted, not fixed in place; not surveyed and designated [U.S.A.].
unlock, *v.t.* un-*lok*, to unfasten what is locked; to open.
unlocked, *a.* un-*lokt*, not made fast with a lock; released from being locked.
unlooked-for, *a.* un-*lookt*-for, not expected; not foreseen.
unloose, *v.t.* un-*loose*, to loose: *v.i.* to fall in pieces; to lose all connexion or union.
unloosen, *v.t.* un-*loose*-en, to unloose.
unlosable, *a.* un-*looz*-a-bl, that cannot be lost.
unlovable, un-*luv*-a-bl, repulsive; objectionable.
unloveliness, *n.* un-*luv*-le-ness, state of being unlovely.
unlovely, *a.* un-*luv*-le, not lovely; not amiable; not attractive.
unloving, *a.* un-*luv*-ing, not loving; not fond.
unlovingly, *ad.* in an unloving manner.
unlubricated, *a.* un-*lew*-bre-kay-ted, not lubricated.
unluckily, *ad.* un-*luk*-e-le, in an unlucky manner.
unluckiness, *n.* state of being unlucky.
unlucky, *a.* un-*luk*-e, unfortunate; not successful; unhappy; ill-omened; inauspicious.
unmade, *a.* un-*made*, not made; not yet formed, omitted to be made. **unmade up,** in an unfinished state; not made-up (with cosmetics, etc.).
unmagnetic, *a.* *un*-mag-*net*-ik, not having magnetic properties.
unmaidenly, *a.* un-*may*-den-le, not maidenly; immodest.
unmailable, *a.* un-*male*-a-bl, that cannot be sent by post.
unmaimed, *a.* un-*maymd*, not disabled in any limb; sound; entire.
unmakable, *a.* un-*make*-a-bl, not possible to be made.
unmake, *v.t.* un-*make*, to destroy the constitutive qualities and form of; to deprive of qualities before possessed. *p.* and *pp.* **unmade.**
unmalleable, *a.* un-*mal*-e-a-bl, not malleable; not capable of being extended by beating.
unman, *v.t.* un-*man*, to deprive of the qualities of a man; to emasculate; to deprive of courage and fortitude; to dishearten; to deprive (a ship or fleet) of men.
unmanacle, *v.t.* un-*man*-a-kl, to free from manacles.
unmanageable, *a.* un-*man*-a-ja-bl, not easily restrained, governed, or directed; not controllable.
unmanaged, *a.* un-*man*-ajd, not tutored; not educated; not broken in.
unmanlike, *a.* un-*man*-like, unlike or unbecoming a man.
unmanliness, *n.* quality of being unmanly.
unmanly, *a.* un-*man*-le, not like a man; effeminate; not worthy of a man; cowardly.
unmanned, *a.* un-*mand*, deprived of the qualities of a man; not supplied with men; having no crew.
unmannered, *a.* un-*man*-erd, uncivil; rude.
unmannerliness, *n.* un-*man*-er-le-ness, want of good manners; incivility; rudeness.
unmannerly, *a.* and *ad.* un-*man*-er-le, ill-bred; uncivil; rude; not according to good manners.
unmanufactured, *a.* *un*-man-yew-*fak*-tewrd, not wrought into form for use.
unmanured, *a.* *un*-ma-*newrd*, not manured; uncultivated.
unmarked, *a.* un-*markt*, having no mark; unobserved; undistinguished.
unmarketable, *a.* un-*mar*-ket-a-bl, not saleable.
unmarred, *a.* un-*mard*, not injured or spoiled.
unmarriageable, *a.* un-*ma*-raj-a-bl, too young to be married.
unmarried, *a.* un-*ma*-red, having no husband or no wife; separated by divorce.
unmarry, *v.t.* un-*ma*-re, to divorce [Coll.].
unmarshalled, *a.* un-*mar*-shald, not disposed or arranged in order.
unmasculine, *a.* un-*mas*-kew-lin, not manly; effeminate.
unmask, *v.t.* un-*mahsk*, to strip of any disguise: *v.i.* to put off a mask; to expose to view.
unmastered, *a.* un-*mahs*-terd, not conquered.
unmatchable, *a.* un-*match*-a-bl, that cannot be equalled; unparalleled.
unmatched, *a.* un-*matcht*, not matched; matchless; having no equal.
unmeaning, *a.* un-*meen*-ing, having no signification; not expressive.
unmeaningly, *ad.* without meaning.
unmeant, *a.* un-*ment*, not meant; not intended.
unmeasurable, *a.* un-*mezh*-ur-ra-bl, immeasurable; unbounded; boundless.
unmeasured, *a.* un-*mezh*-urd, plentiful beyond measure; immense; infinite; not according to any measure.
unmechanical, *a.* *un*-me-*kan*-e-kal, not according to the principles of mechanics.
unmechanized, *a.* un-*mek*-a-nized, deprived of, or destitute of, mechanism; not converted into a mechanized force [Mil.].
unmeddling, *a.* un-*med*-dling, not interfering with the concerns of others; not officious.
unmeditated, *a.* un-*med*-e-tay-ted, not prepared by previous thought.
unmeet, *a.* un-*meet*, not fit or worthy.
unmellowed, *a.* un-*mel*-ode, not fully matured.
unmelodious, *a.* *un*-me-*loh*-de-us, not melodious; wanting melody.
unmelodiously, *ad.* without melodiousness.
unmelted, *a.* un-*mel*-ted, undissolved; not softened.
unmentionable, *a.* un-*men*-shon-a-bl, that may not be mentioned: *n.pl.* trousers [Coll.].
unmentioned, *a.* un-*men*-shond, not named.
unmercantile, *a.* un-*mer*-kan-tile, not according to commercial custom.
unmercenary, *a.* un-*mer*-se-na-re, not mercenary.
unmerchantable, *a.* un-*mer*-chan-ta-bl, not fit for market; unmarketable.
unmerciful, *a.* un-*mer*-se-ful, inhuman; cruel; hard-hearted; exorbitant.
unmercifully, *ad.* without mercy.
unmercifulness, *n.* the quality of being unmerciful.
unmerited, *a.* un-*me*-re-ted, not deserved; unjust.
unmetallic, *a.* un-me-*tal*-ik, not having the properties of a metal.
unmethodical, *a.* un-me-*thod*-e-kal, without order; unsystematic; haphazard.
unmewed, *a.* un-*mewd*, set free.
unmilitary, *a.* un-*mil*-e-ta-re, not according to military rules; not military in character.
unmilked, *a.* un-*milkt*, not milked.
unmilled, *a.* un-*mild*, not milled; not indented or grained; having a smooth edge (of coins).
unminded, *a.* un-*myn*-ded, not heeded.
unmindful, *a.* un-*mynd*-ful, not heedful; regardless.
unmindfully, *ad.* carelessly; heedlessly.
unmindfulness, *n.* heedlessness; inattentiveness.
unmingled, *a.* un-*ming*-gld, not mixed; pure.
unministerial, *a.* *un*-min-is-*teer*-re-al, not ministerial.
unmissed, *a.* un-*mist*, not perceived to be gone or lost.
unmistakable, *a.* *un*-mis-*tay*-ka-bl, that cannot be mistaken; clear; evident.
unmistaken, *a.* *un*-mis-*tay*-kn, not mistaken; sure.
unmistrusting, *a.* *un*-mis-*trus*-ting, unsuspicious.
unmitigable, *a.* un-*mit*-e-ga-bl, not capable of being mitigated, softened, or lessened.
unmitigated, *a.* un-*mit*-e-gay-ted, not softened in severity or harshness; thorough; downright.

unmixed, *a.* un-*mikst,* not mingled; pure; unadulterated; unalloyed.
unmoaned, *a.* un-*mohnd,* not lamented.
unmodernized, *a.* un-*mod*-er-nized, not modernized.
unmodifiable, *a.* un-*mod*-e-*fy*-a-bl, that cannot be altered in form.
unmodified, *a.* un-*mod*-e-fide, not altered in form.
unmodish, *a.* un-*moh*-dish, not stylish; old-fashioned in appearance.
unmodulated, *a.* un-*mod*-yew-lay-ted, not modulated.
unmoist, *a.* un-*moyst,* not humid; dry.
unmoistened, *a.* un-*moys*-nd, not made moist or humid.
unmolested, *a.* *un*-mo-*les*-ted, not interfered with; not disturbed.
unmoneyed, *a.* un-*mun*-ed, not wealthy; penniless.
unmoor, *v.t.* un-*moor,* to cast off from moorings; to cause (a vessel) to ride with a single anchor after having been moored by two or more cables [Naut.].
unmoral, *a.* un-*mo*-ral, not subject to, or in accordance with, moral law; non-moral.
unmoralized, *a.* un-*mo*-ra-lized, not governed by morals or moral law; destitute of morality.
unmortgaged, *a.* un-*mor*-gajd, not mortgaged or pledged.
unmortified, *a.* un-*mor*-te-fide, not shamed; not subdued by sorrow.
unmotherly, *a.* un-*muth*-er-le, not motherly; unworthy of a mother.
unmould, *v.t.* un-*mohld,* to change the form of; to remove from a mould; *v.i.* to lose shape.
unmoulded, *a.* un-*mohl*-ded, not shaped or formed.
unmounted, *a.* un-*moun*-ted, not provided with or fixed to a mount; not on horseback.
unmourned, *a.* un-*moarnd,* not lamented.
unmovable, *a.* un-*moov*-a-bl, that cannot be moved; firm; immovable.
unmoved, *a.* un-*moovd,* not transferred from one place to another; not changed in purpose; unshaken; not affected; calm.
unmoving, *a.* un-*moov*-ing, not exciting emotion.
unmuffle, *v.t.* un-*muf*-fl, to take a covering from the face; to remove the muffling of a drum, etc.
unmurmuring, *a.* un-*mur*-mur-ring, not complaining.
unmusical, *a.* un-*mew*-ze-kal, not harmonious; harsh; not sensitive to musical sounds.
unmutilated, *a.* un-*mew*-te-lay-ted, not deprived of a member or part; entire.
unmuzzle, *v.t.* un-*muz*-zl, to loose from a muzzle; to free from restraint; to allow freedom of speech.
unnamable, *a.* un-*nay*-ma-bl, that cannot be named.
unnamed, *a.* un-*naymd,* not named; not mentioned.
unnatural, *a.* un-*nat*-yew-ral, not natural; contrary to the laws of nature; contrary to natural feeling; acting without natural affection; not in conformity to nature.
unnaturalize, *v.t.* un-*nat*-yew-ra-lize, to denaturalize.
unnaturally, *ad.* in an unnatural manner.
unnaturalness, *n.* contrariety to nature.
unnavigable, *a.* un-*nav*-e-ga-bl, not navigable.
unnecessarily, *ad.* un-*nes*-e-sa-re-le, without necessity; needlessly.
unnecessary, *a.* un-*nes*-e-sa-re, not necessary; needless; useless.
unnecessitated, *a.* *un*-ne-*ses*-e-tay-ted, not required by necessity.
unneeded, *a.* un-*nee*-ded, not needed.
unneedful, *a.* un-*need*-ful, not needful; not wanted.
unnegotiable, *a.* *un*-ne-*goh*-sha-bl, not negotiable; requiring endorsement before transference (of cheques, etc.).
unneighbourly, *a.* un-*nay*-bur-le, unsociable; not kind and friendly.
unnerve, *v.t.* un-*nerv,* to deprive of nerve; to weaken; to enfeeble.
unnoted, *a.* un-*noh*-ted, not observed; not distinguished; not regarded.
unnoticeable, *a.* un-*noh*-tis-a-bl, imperceptible; undiscernible.
unnoticed, *a.* un-*noh*-tist, not taken notice of; not hospitably entertained.
unnumbered, *a.* un-*num*-berd, innumerable; not numbered.
unnurtured, *a.* un-*nur*-tewrd, not nurtured or educated.
unnutritious, *a.* *un*-new-*trish*-us, not affording nourishment.
unobjectionable, *a.* *un*-ob-*jek*-shon-a-bl, not liable to objection.
unobjectionably, *ad.* in a manner not liable to objection.
unobliging, *a.* *un*-o-*bly*-jing, not disposed to oblige.
unobscured, *a.* *un*-ob-*skewrd,* not darkened.
unobservable, *a.* *un*-ob-*zer*-va-bl, unnoticeable.
unobservance, *n.* *un*-ob-*zer*-vance, inattention; regardlessness.
unobservant, *a.* *un*-ob-*zer*-vant, not taking notice; heedless; inobservant.
unobserved, *a.* *un*-ob-*zervd,* not noticed; not regarded.
unobserving, *a.* *un*-ob-*zer*-ving, unobservant.
unobstructed, *a.* *un*-ob-*struk*-ted, not cluttered with impediments; not hindered.
unobstructive, *a.* *un*-ob-*struk*-tiv, not presenting any obstacle.
unobtainable, *a.* *un*-ob-*tay*-na-bl, not within reach or power.
unobtrusive, *a.* *un*-ob-*troo*-siv, not obtrusive; not pushing; modest.
unobtrusively, *ad.* without obtrusiveness.
unobtrusiveness, *n.* quality of being unobtrusive; freedom from self-assertion.
unobvious, *a.* un-*ob*-ve-us, not readily occurring to the understanding.
unoccupied, *a.* un-*ok*-kew-pide, not possessed; not inhabited; not engaged in business; not under military occupation.
unoffended, *a.* *un*-o-*fen*-ded, not having taken offence.
unoffensive, *a.* *un*-o-fen-siv, inoffensive.
unoffered, *a.* un-*of*-erd, not proposed for acceptance.
unofficial, *a.* *un*-of-*fish*-al, not official; not authorized; not pertaining to office.
unofficious, *a.* *un*-of-*fish*-us, not forward or intermeddling.
unopened, *a.* un-*oh*-pnd, not opened; not having the leaves of folded sheets divided (of books).
unoperative, *a.* un-*op*-er-ra-tiv, inoperative.
unopposed, *a.* *un*-o-*pohzd,* meeting no opposition not resisted.
unoppressive, *a.* *un*-o-*pres*-siv, not oppressive.
unordered, *a.* un-*awr*-derd, not arranged in order not commanded.
unorderly, *a.* un-*awr*-der-le, disorderly; irregular.
unorganized, *a.* un-*awr*-gan-ized, not organized without organic structure.
unoriginal, *a.* *un*-o-*rij*-e-nal, derived; second-hand; ungenerated.
unoriginated, *a.* *un*-o-*rij*-e-nay-ted, existing from all eternity; having no birth or creation.
unornamental, *a.* *un*-awr-na-*men*-tal, plain; undecorated; unsightly.
unornamented, *a.* un-*awr*-na-men-ted, not adorned.
unorthodox, *a.* un-*awr*-tho-doks, not orthodox unconventional.
unorthodoxy, *n.* un-*awr*-tho-dok-se, state of being unorthodox.
unostentatious, *a.* *un*-os-ten-*tay*-shus, not boastful; modest; not showy.
unostentatiously, *ad.* modestly; in an unostentatious manner.
unowed, *a.* un-*ohd,* not owed; not due.
unowned, *a.* un-*ohnd,* not owned; having no known owner; not acknowledged; not confessed.
unoxidized, *a.* un-*ok*-se-dized, not combined with oxygen.
unoxygenated, *a.* un-*ok*-se-je-nay-ted, not having oxygen in combination.
unpacified, *a.* un-*pas*-se-fide, not calmed; not brought back to a peaceful state.
unpack, *v.t.* un-*pak,* to remove the contents; to disburden.
unpacked, *a.* un-*pakt,* not packed; not unfairly composed or arranged (of juries, etc.).
unpaid, *a.* un-*pade,* not discharged, as a debt; not having received what is due; honorary.
unpained, *a.* un-*paynd,* suffering no pain.
unpaintable, *a.* un-*payn*-ta-bl, not suitable for artistic representation by painting.
unpainted, *a.* un-*payn*-ted, not painted; not spread with paint.
unpaired, *a.* un-*paird,* not paired; not forming one of a pair, esp. [Zool.] of organs.

unpalatable, *a.* un-*pal*-a-ta-bl, not palatable; disgusting to the taste; not such as to be relished; disagreeable.
unparalleled, *a.* un-*pa*-ra-leld, unique; having no parallel; unequalled; unmatched.
unpardonable, *a.* un-*par*-dn-a-bl, not to be forgiven; inexcusable.
unpardoned, *a.* un-*par*-dnd, not forgiven; not having received a legal pardon.
unparliamentary, *a.* *un*-par-le-*men*-ta-re, contrary to the rules of procedure in parliament, or to the usages of legislative bodies; contrary to good taste or convention [Coll.].
unparted, *a.* un-*par*-ted, not parted; not divided.
unpatented, *a.* un-*pat*- or -*pay*-ten-ted, having no patent; not protected by patent.
unpathed, *a.* un-*pahthd*, unexplored; unmarked by passage; not trodden.
unpathetic, *a.* *un*-pa-*thet*-ik, not evoking pathos.
unpatriotic, *a.* un-pat-re-*ot*-ik, not patriotic.
unpatronized, *a.* un-*pat*-ron-ized, having no patron; not supported.
unpatterned, *a.* un-*pat*-ternd, not ornamented with a pattern; having no equal.
unpaved, *a.* un-*payvd*, not paved.
unpawned, *a.* un-*pawnd*, not pledged.
unpeaceable, *a.* un-*peece*-a-bl, not pacific or peaceful; unquiet; quarrelsome.
unpeaceful, *a.* un-*peece*-ful, unpeaceable.
unpedigreed, *a.* un-*ped*-e-greed, not having a pedigree.
unpeeled, *a.* un-*peeld*, not peeled.
unpeg, *v.t.* un-*peg*, to loose from pegs; to open; to pull out the peg from.
unpen, *v.t.* un-*pen*, to let out or suffer to escape from a pen or enclosure.
unpenetrable, *a.* un-*pen*-e-tra-bl, impenetrable.
unpenetrated, *a.* un-*pen*-e-tray-ted, not pierced; unexplored.
unpensioned, *a.* un-*pen*-shond, not rewarded by a pension; not held in dependence by a pension.
unpeople, *v.t.* un-*pee*-pl, to deprive of inhabitants; to depopulate.
unpeopled, *a.* un-*pee*-pld, not populated; having no inhabitants.
unperceivable, *a.* *un*-per-*seev*-a-bl, not perceptible.
unperceived, *a.* *un*-per-*seevd*, not observed or noticed.
unperforated, *a.* un-*per*-fo-ray-ted, having no perforations or holes; imperforate.
unperformed, *a.* *un*-per-*formd*, not done; not fulfilled.
unperjured, *a.* un-*per*-jurd, free from the crime of perjury.
unpermitted, *a.* *un*-per-*mit*-ed, not permitted.
unpersecuted, *a.* un-*per*-se-kew-ted, free from persecution.
unpersuadable, *a.* *un*-per-*sway*-da-bl, that cannot be persuaded or influenced.
unperturbed, *a.* *un*-per-*turbd*, cool and collected; not disturbed.
unperused, *a.* *un*-per-*roozd*, not read.
unperverted, *a.* *un*-per-*ver*-ted, not wrested or turned to a wrong use.
unphilosophical, *a.* *un*-fil-o-*sof*-e-kal, contrary to the principles or methods of philosophy.
unpick, *v.t.* and *i.* un-*pik*, to pick out the stitches; to take to pieces or undo by picking.
unpierceable, *a.* un-*peerce*-a-bl, that cannot be pierced.
unpierced, *a.* un-*peerst*, not penetrated.
unpiloted, *a.* un-*py*-lo-ted, without a pilot; having no guide.
unpin, *v.t.* un-*pin*, to unfasten what is held together by pins.
unpinioned, *a.* un-*pin*-yond, freed from restraint.
unpiteously, *ad.* un-*pit*-e-us-le, pitilessly.
unpitied, *a.* un-*pit*-ed, not compassionated.
unpitiful, *a.* un-*pit*-e-ful, having no pity; showing no compassion.
unpitying, *a.* un-*pit*-e-ing, unpitiful.
unplacable, *a.* un-*plak*-a-bl, implacable; inappeasable.
unplaced, *a.* un-*playst*, not in its proper place; having no office or employment, esp. under government; not among the three first in a race.
unplagued, *a.* un-*playgd*, not harassed.
unplait, *v.t.* un-*plat*, to undo a plait.

unplanned, *a.* un-*pland*, not previously prepared; not provided for; unexpected.
unplanted, *a.* un-*plahn*-ted, not planted; not colonized; uncultivated.
unplausible, *a.* un-*plaw*-ze-bl, not plausible; not having a fair or plausible appearance.
unplayable, *a.* un-*play*-a-bl, impossible to play, or to play on.
unpleasable, *a.* un-*plee*-za-bl, not capable of being pleased or suited.
unpleasant, *a.* un-*plez*-ant, not affording pleasure; disagreeable.
unpleasantly, *ad.* in an unpleasant manner.
unpleasantness, *n.* the quality or state of being unpleasant; an unpleasant experience, predicament, etc.
unpleasing, *a.* un-*plee*-zing, offensive; disgusting.
unpledged, *a.* un-*plejd*, not mortgaged, pledged, or pawned; not bound by a pledge.
unpliable, *a.* un-*ply*-a-bl, not easily bent; stiff; not readily yielding.
unpliant, *a.* un-*ply*-ant, unpliable.
unploughed, *a.* un-*ploud*, not ploughed.
unplugged, *a.* un-*plugd*, not plugged; released from a state of being plugged.
unplumbed, *a.* un-*plumd*, unmeasured by plumbline; unexplored in depth or extent.
unplundered, *a.* un-*plun*-derd, not plundered or stripped.
unpoetical, *a.* *un*-poh-*et*-e-kal, not poetical; prosaic; not befitting a poet.
unpoetically, *ad.* in an unpoetic manner.
unpointed, *a.* un-*poyn*-ted, having no point or sting; without point; without cement along the brickwork joints; not having the marks of punctuation.
unpoised, *a.* un-*poyzd*, not balanced.
unpolarized, *a.* un-*poh*-la-rized, not having polarity.
unpolicied, *a.* un-*pol*-e-sid, not having civil polity or a regular form of government.
unpolished, *a.* un-*pol*-isht, not made smooth or bright by rubbing; not refined in manners; uncivilized; rude.
unpolite, *a.* *un*-po-*lite*, not refined in manners; not civil or courteous; unmannerly; impolite.
unpolled, *a.* un-*pohld*, not having voted (of electors); not counted (of votes); unshorn (of sheep); not polled (of cattle).
unpolluted, *a.* *un*-po-*lew*-ted, not defiled or corrupted.
unpopular, *a.* un-*pop*-yew-lar, not popular; not pleasing the people; out of favour.
unpopularity, *n.* *un*-pop-yew-*la*-re-te, the state of being unpopular.
unpopularly, *ad.* un-*pop*-yew-lar-le, not popularly.
unportioned, *a.* un-*pawr*-shond, not furnished with a portion or fortune.
unpossessed, *a.* un-po-*zest*, not held; not occupied.
unpossessing, *a.* *un*-po-*zes*-ing, having no possessions.
unposted, *a.* un-*pohs*-ted, not posted; not posted up.
unpotable, *a.* un-*poh*-ta-bl, not drinkable.
unpractical, *a.* un-*prak*-te-kal, regardless of practical matters; impracticable; visionary.
unpractised, *a.* un-*prak*-tist, not skilled; inexpert; not having experience.
unpraised, *a.* un-*prayzd*, not recognized or celebrated by praise.
unpreceded, *a.* *un*-pre-*see*-ded, not preceded.
unprecedented, *a.* un-*pres*-e-den-ted, having no precedent or example.
unprecedentedly, *ad.* un-*pres*-e-den-ted-le, without precedent.
unprecise, *a.* *un*-pre-*sice*, not precise; not exact.
unpredestined, *a.* *un*-pre-*des*-tind, not previously determined.
unpredictable, *a.* un-pre-*dik*-ta-bl, not capable of being foreseen or foretold; not anticipated.
unprejudiced, *a.* un-*prej*-yew-dist, not prejudiced; free from undue bias or prepossession; impartial; not warped by prejudice.
unprelatical, *a.* *un*-pre-*lat*-e-kal, unsuitable to a prelate.
unpremeditated, *a.* *un*-pre-*med*-e-tay-ted, not previously prepared in the mind; not done by design.
unprepared, *a.* *un*-pre-*paird*, not prepared; specifically, not prepared for death and eternity.
unpreparedness, *n.* *un*-pre-*pair*-red-ness, the state of being unprepared.

unprepossessed, *a.* *un*-pree-po-*zest*, not prepossessed; not biased by previous opinion.
unprepossessing, *a.* *un*-pree-po-*zes*-ing, not having a pleasing appearance; unattractive.
unpresentable, *a.* *un*-pre-*zen*-ta-bl, not presentable; unsightly; ill-mannered.
unpressed, *a.* un-*prest*, not pressed; not enforced.
unpresuming, *a.* un-pre-*zew*-ming, not presuming; unpretentious.
unpresumptuous, *a.* *un*-pre-*zum*-tew-us, not presumptuous; modest; submissive.
unpretending, *a.* *un*-pre-*ten*-ding, not claiming distinction; modest; unobtrusive.
unpretentious, *a.* *un*-pre-*ten*-shus, not presuming.
unpreventable, *a.* *un*-pre-*ven*-ta-bl, not preventable.
unprevented, *a.* *un*-pre-*ven*-ted, not hindered.
unpriced, *a.* un-*pryst*, not having been allotted a price; beyond price.
unpriestly, *a.* un-*preest*-le, unsuitable to a priest.
unprincely, *a.* un-*prince*-le, not worthy of a prince; not in royal style.
unprincipled, *a.* un-*prin*-se-pld, having no settled principles; having no good moral principles; destitute of virtue; unscrupulous; profligate.
unprintable, *a.* un-*prin*-ta-bl, not fit to be printed; scurrilous, indecent, or blasphemous.
unprinted, *a.* un-*prin*-ted, not printed, as a literary work; not stamped with figures; white.
unprisoned, *a.* un-*priz*-ond, set free from confinement.
unprivileged, *a.* un-*priv*-e-lejd, not enjoying a particular privilege or immunity; having no special benefits or rights.
unprized, *a.* un-*prized*, not valued.
unproclaimed, *a.* *un*-pro-*klaymd*, not notified by public declaration.
unprocurable, *a.* un-pro-*kewr*-ra-bl, not to be obtained.
unproductive, *a.* *un*-pro-*duk*-tiv, not productive; not producing large crops; not making profitable returns for labour; not efficient.
unprofaned, *a.* *un*-pro-*faynd*, not profaned or violated.
unprofessional, *a.* *un*-pro-*fesh*-on-al, not pertaining to, or according to the usages of, one's profession; not belonging to a profession.
unproficiency, *n.* *un*-pro-*fish*-en-se, want of proficiency or improvement.
unprofitable, *a.* un-*prof*-e-ta-bl, bringing no profit; producing no improvement or advantage; serving no purpose; useless.
unprofitably, *ad.* without profit; to no good purpose.
unprogressive, *a.* *un*-pro-*gres*-iv, not progressive; reactionary; unenterprising.
unprohibited, *a.* *un*-pro-*hib*-e-ted, lawful; permissible.
unprolific, *a.* *un*-pro-*lif*-ik, not prolific; barren; not producing fruit; not producing in abundance.
unpromising, *a.* un-*prom*-is-ing, not affording a favourable prospect of success.
unprompted, *a.* un-*promp*-ted, not prompted; not dictated or instigated.
unpronounceable, *a.* *un*-pro-*noun*-sa-bl, that cannot be pronounced; difficult of pronunciation; unfit to be pronounced.
unpronounced, *a.* *un*-pro-*nounst*, not pronounced; not uttered.
unprop, *v.t.* un-*prop*, to deprive of support.
unproper, *a.* un-*prop*-er, improper; not proper.
unpropertied, *a.* un-*prop*-er-tid, having no property; unmoneyed.
unprophetic, *a.* *un*-pro-*fet*-ik, not foreseeing future events.
unpropitious, *a.* *un*-pro-*pish*-us, not favourable; inauspicious.
unproportional, *a.* un-pro-*pore*-shon-al, not proportional.
unproportionate, *a.* *un*-pro-*pore*-shon-at, wanting due proportion; disproportionate; unfit.
unproportioned, *a.* *un*-pro-*pore*-shond, not proportioned or suitable.
unproposed, *a.* *un*-pro-*pohzd*, not proposed; not offered.
unpropped, *a.* un-*propt*, not supported.
unprosperous, *a.* un-*pros*-per-rus, not attended with success.
unprosperousness, *n.* want of success.
unprostituted, *a.* un-*pros*-te-tew-ted, not debased.
unprotected, *a.* *un*-pro-*tek*-ted, not defended; not fortified; not armoured (of war-vessels).
unprotecting, *a.* *un*-pro-*tek*-ting, not defending.
unprotestantize, *v.t.* un-*prot*-es-tan-tize, to take away the protestant character of; to convert from Protestantizm.
unprotracted, *a.* *un*-pro-*trak*-ted, not drawn out in length.
unprovable, *a.* un-*proov*-a-bl, not capable of proof, or of being proved.
unproved, *a.* un-*proovd*, not known by trial; not established as true.
unprovided, *a.* *un*-pro-*vy*-ded, not provided; not provided by a local government authority.
unprovoked, *a.* *un*-pro-*vohkt*, not incited; not proceeding from provocation.
unpruned, *a.* un-*proond*, not pruned or lopped.
unpublished, *a.* un-*pub*-lisht, not made public; secret; private; not published, as a book.
unpunctual, *a.* un-*punk*-tew-al, not exact in time.
unpunctuality, *n.* *un*-punk-tew-*al*-e-te, the quality of being unpunctual; regardlessness of time.
unpunctuated, *a.* un-*punk*-tew-ay-ted, not punctuated; not pointed.
unpunishable, *a.* un-*pun*-ish-a-bl, that may not be punished.
unpunished, *a.* un-*pun*-isht, not punished; suffered to pass with impunity.
unpurchasable, *a.* un-*pur*-chas-a-bl, that cannot be bought.
unpurchased, *a.* un-*pur*-chast, not bought.
unpurged, *a.* un-*purjd*, unpurified.
unpurified, *a.* un-*pewr*-re-fide, not freed from foul matter; unsanctified.
unpursued, *a.* *un*-per-*sewd*, not followed; not prosecuted.
unquailing, *a.* un-*kway*-ling, not flinching; firm.
unquaking, *a.* un-*kway*-king, not shaking or trembling.
unqualified, *a.* un-*kwol*-e-fide, not having the requisite talents, abilities, certificates, or credentials; not legally qualified; not having taken the requisite oath or oaths; not modified or restricted by conditions or exceptions.
unquelled, *a.* un-*kweld*, not quelled or subdued.
unquenchable, *a.* un-*kwench*-a-bl, that cannot be quenched; inextinguishable.
unquenched, *a.* un-*kwencht*, not extinguished.
unquestionable, *a.* un-*kwes*-tyon-a-bl, not to be questioned or doubted; not open to suspicion.
unquestionably, *ad.* beyond question.
unquestioned, *a.* un-*kwes*-tyond, not called in question; not doubted; not interrogated; not examined; indisputable.
unquestioning, *a.* un-*kwes*-tyon-ing, not calling in question; not doubting.
unquiet, *a.* un-*kwy*-et, not calm or tranquil; restless; uneasy; agitated; turbulent: *n.* a state of unrest; inquietude; disturbance.
unquietly, *ad.* un-*kwy*-et-le, without rest.
unquietness, *n.* un-*kwy*-et-ness, the state of being unquiet.
unquietude, *n.* un-*kwy*-e-tewd, inquietude.
unquotable, *a.* un-*kwoh*-ta-bl, not capable of being quoted; not fit for quotation.
unquote, *v.t.* un-*kwote*, to conclude a quotation.
unraised, *a.* un-*rayzd*, not elevated or raised.
unraked, *a.* un-*raykt*, not raked; not raked together; not raked up, as a fire.
unransomed, *a.* un-*ran*-somd, not liberated from captivity or bondage by payment.
unravaged, *a.* un-*rav*-ajd, not wasted or destroyed.
unrated, *a.* un-*ray*-ted, not rated.
unravel, *v.t.* un-*rav*-el, to disentangle or extricate; to free from complication or difficulty; to unfold, as the plot or intrigue of a play: *v.i.* to be unfolded; to be disentangled.
unravelment, *n.* un-*rav*-el-ment, the act of unravelling.
unrazored, *a.* un-*ray*-zurd, unshaven.
unreached, *a.* un-*reecht*, not attained to.
unread, *a.* un-*red*, not perused; untaught; not learned in books.
unreadable, *a.* un-*ree*-da-bl, not legible; not fit to be read; not capable of being read.
unready, *a.* un-*red*-e, not prepared; not fit; awkward; ungainly.

unreal, *a.* un-*ree*-al, not real; not substantial; having appearance only; visionary.
unreality, *n.* *un*-re-*al*-e-te, want of reality or real existence; an unreal thing.
unrealized, *a.* un-*ree*-a-lized, idealized; not converted into money.
unreason, *n.* un-*ree*-zon, absence of reason; nonsense; unreasonableness.
unreasonable, *a.* un-*ree*-zon-a-bl, not agreeable to reason; exceeding the bounds of reason; immoderate; exorbitant; irrational.
unreasonableness, *n.* un-*ree*-zon-a-bl-ness, the quality or state of being inconsistent with or in excess of reason; irrationality.
unreasonably, *ad.* un-*ree*-zon-a-ble, in contrariety to reason; excessively [Coll.].
unreasoned, *a.* un-*ree*-zond, not having reasoned; not derived from reasoning; not argued.
unreasoning, *a.* un-*ree*-zon-ing, not having reasoning faculties; not guided by reason.
unrebuked, *a.* *un*-re-*bewkt*, not censured.
unrecanted, *a.* *un*-re-*kan*-ted, not retracted.
unreceived, *a.* *un*-re-*seevd*, not received; not come into possession.
unreclaimable, *a.* *un*-re-*klay*-ma-bl, irreclaimable.
unreclaimed, *a.* *un*-re-*klaymd*, not reclaimed; not brought to a domestic state; not reformed.
unrecognizable, *a.* *un*-rek-og-*ny*-za-bl, that cannot be recognized.
unrecompensed, *a.* un-*rek*-om-penst, not rewarded.
unreconcilable, *a.* *un*-rek-on-*sy*-la-bl, irreconcilable.
unreconciled, *a.* un-*rek*-on-siled, not reconciled; not made consistent; not appeased; not having laid aside opposition and enmity.
unrecorded, *a.* *un*-re-*kor*-ded, not registered; not kept in remembrance.
unrecoverable, *a.* *un*-re-*kuv*-er-ra-bl, irrecoverable; past recovery.
unrecovered, *a.* *un*-re-*kuv*-erd, not recalled into possession; not regained.
unrectified, *a.* un-*rek*-te-fide, not corrected; not distilled again.
unredeemable, *a.* *un*-re-*dee*-ma-bl, irredeemable.
unredeemed, *a.* *un*-re-*deemd*, not ransomed; not paid; not taken out of pawn; without a redeeming quality.
unredressed, *a.* *un*-re-*drest*, not relieved from injustice; not reformed.
unreducible, *a.* *un*-re-*dew*-se-bl, irreducible; not capable of reduction.
unreel, *v.t.* un-*reel*, to unwind from a reel.
unreeve, *v.t.* un-*reev*, to withdraw a rope from any block through which it has passed. *p.* and *pp.* **unrove** or **unreeved.**
unrefined, *a.* *un*-re-*fined*, not refined or purified; not polished in manners; uncouth.
unreflecting, *a.* un-re-*flek*-ting, unthinking.
unreformed, *a.* *un*-re-*formd*, not reclaimed from vice; not amended; not freed from error; remaining unchanged by the Reformation.
unrefracted, *a.* *un*-re-*frak*-ted, not refracted, as rays of light.
unrefreshed, *a.* *un*-re-*fresht*, not relieved from fatigue, or from hunger or thirst.
unrefuted, *a.* *un*-re-*few*-ted, not proved to be false.
unregarded, *a.* *un*-re-*gar*-ded, not heeded; neglected.
unregardful, *a.* *un*-re-*gard*-ful, not giving attention; heedless.
unregeneracy, *n.* *un*-re-*jen*-er-ra-se, the state of being unregenerate.
unregenerate, *a.* *un*-re-*jen*-er-rat, not regenerated; not renewed in heart.
unregistered, *a.* un-*rej*-is-terd, not registered; not entered on a register; not recorded.
unregretted, *a.* *un*-re-*gret*-ed, not lamented.
unregulated, *a.* un-*reg*-yew-lay-ted, not reduced to order; not amenable to control.
unrehearsed, *a.* *un*-re-*herst*, not recited or repeated; not rehearsed.
unreined, *a.* un-*raynd*, unrestrained; unbridled.
unrejoicing, *a.* *un*-re-*joy*-sing, unjoyous; gloomy; sad.
unrelated, *a.* *un*-re-*lay*-ted, not related by blood or affinity; not connected with.
unrelaxing, *a.* *un*-re-*lak*-sing, not abating in severity or attention.
unrelenting, *a.* *un*-re-*len*-ting, not relenting; not yielding to; inflexibly rigid.
unreliability, *n.* *un*-re-ly-a-*bil*-e-te, lack of reliability.
unreliable, *a.* un-re-*ly*-a-bl, untrustworthy.
unrelievable, *a.* *un*-re-*lee*-va-bl, admitting of no relief.
unrelieved, *a.* *un*-re-*leevd*, not eased or delivered from pain; not succoured; not delivered from confinement or distress; not released from duty.
unreligious, un-re-*lij*-us, not interested in, or not connected with, religion; irreligious.
unremarkable, *a.* *un*-re-*mar*-ka-bl, not worthy of particular notice; not observable.
unremarked, *a.* *un*-re-*markt*, unobserved.
unremedied, *a.* un-*rem*-e-ded, not cured; not remedied.
unremembered, *a.* *un*-re-*mem*-berd, forgotten; not retained in the mind.
unremitted, *a.* *un*-re-*mit*-ed, not remitted; not forgiven; not relaxed; not sent.
unremitting, *a.* *un*-re-*mit*-ing, not remitting, incessant
unremittingly, *ad.* continuously.
unremovable, *a.* *un*-re-*moo*-va-bl, irremovable.
unremoved, *a.* *un*-re-*moovd*, not taken away; not capable of being removed.
unremunerative, *a.* *un*-re-*mew*-ner-ra-tiv, not profitable.
unrenewed, *a.* *un*-re-*newd*, not done again; not made anew; not regenerated.
unrenowned, *a.* un-re-*nound*, not celebrated or famous.
unrepaid, *a.* *un*-re-*pade*, not repaid; not requited.
unrepaired, *a.* *un*-re-*paird*, not repaired or amended.
unrepealed, *a.* *un*-re-*peeld*, not revoked or abrogated.
unrepentant, *a.* *un*-re-*pen*-tant, unrepenting; not penitent; not contrite.
unrepented, *a.* *un*-re-*pen*-ted, not repented of.
unrepining, *a.* *un*-re-*py*-ning, not complaining.
unreplenished, *a.* *un*-re-*plen*-isht, not filled or adequately supplied.
unreported, *a.* un-re-*pawr*-ted, not reported; overlooked or ignored by the press.
unrepresentative, *a.* *un*-rep-re-*zen*-ta-tiv, not adequately representing; not typical.
unrepresented, *a.* *un*-rep-re-*zen*-ted, not represented; having no one to act in one's stead.
unrepressed, *a.* *un*-re-*prest*, not crushed, or not subdued.
unrepressible, *a.* *un*-re-*pres*-se-bl, irrepressible.
unreprievable, *a.* *un*-re-*pree*-va-bl, that cannot be reprieved, esp. from death.
unreprieved, *a.* *un*-re-*preevd*, not reprieved.
unreproached, *a.* *un*-re-*prohcht*, not upbraided.
unreproved, *a.* *un*-re-*proovd*, not reproved; not censured; not liable to reproof or blame.
unrepugnant, *a.* *un*-re-*pug*-nant, not repugnant; not contradictory.
unrequested, *a.* *un*-re-*kwes*-ted, not asked; not asked for.
unrequired, *a.* *un*-re-*kwired*, not demanded; not necessary or requisite.
unrequitable, *a.* *un*-re-*kwy*-ta-bl, not capable of being requited.
unrequited, *a.* *un*-re-*kwy*-ted, not recompensed; not returned (of love).
unresenting, *a.* *un*-re-*zen*-ting, not regarding with anger.
unreserve, *n.* *un*-re-*zerv*, absence of reserve; frankness.
unreserved, *a.* *un*-re-*zervd*, not retained when a part is granted; not bespoken; not reserved; open; frank; free.
unreservedly, *ad.* *un*-re-*zer*-ved-le, without reserve.
unresisting, *a.* *un*-re-*zis*-ting, not making resistance; submissive; humble.
unresolvable, *a.* *un*-re-*zol*-va-bl, that cannot be solved.
unresolved, *a.* *un*-re-*zolvd*, not resolved; not determined; not solved.
unrespected, *a.* *un*-re-*spek*-ted, not regarded with respect.
unrespirable, *a.* un-*res*-pe-ra-bl *or* *un*-re-*spire*-ra-bl, that cannot be or is not fit to be breathed.
unrespited, *a.* un-*res*-pe-ted, allowing of no respite; without intermission.

unresponsive, *a.* un-re-*spon*-siv, not giving answer; apathetic; indifferent.
unrest, *n.* un-*rest*, disquiet, esp. mental or political; unrestfulness.
unrestful, *a.* un-*rest*-ful, not at rest.
unrestfulness, *n.* un-*rest*-ful-ness, state of being unrestful or ill at ease; disturbed condition.
unresting, *a.* un-*res*-ting, continually in motion; never at rest.
unrestored, *a.* *un*-re-*stord*, not restored to a former state or condition.
unrestrainable, *a.* *un*-re-*stray*-na-bl, that cannot be restrained.
unrestrained, *a.* *un*-re-*straynd*, not restrained or controlled; not inhibited.
unrestrainedly, *ad.* *un*-re-*stray*-ned-le, in an uncontrolled manner; irrepressibly.
unrestraint, *n.* *un*-re-*straynt*, freedom from restraint; enfranchisement.
unrestricted, *a.* *un*-re-*strik*-ted, not restricted or limited.
unretentive, *a.* *un*-re-*ten*-tiv, not retentive.
unretracted, *a.* *un*-re-*trak*-ted, not retracted or recalled.
unreturnable, *a.* *un*-re-*tur*-na-bl, not returnable; without allowance if returned.
unrevealed, *a.* *un*-re-*veeld*, not disclosed; kept secret or in the background.
unrevenged, *a.* *un*-re-*venjd*, not avenged.
unrevengeful, *a.* *un*-re-*venj*-ful, not disposed to revenge.
unrevered, *a.* *un*-re-*veerd*, not revered.
unreversed, *a.* *un*-re-*verst*, not annulled by a counter decision.
unrevised, *a.* *un*-re-*vized*, not corrected.
unrevoked, *a.* *un*-re-*vohkt*, not recalled or annulled.
unrewarded, *a.* *un*-re-*wawr*-ded, not rewarded.
unrhymed, *a.* un-*rymd*, having no rhymes; in blank verse.
unrhythmical, *a.* un-*rith*-me-kal, without rhythm.
unriddle, *v.t.* un-*rid*-dl, to solve or explain.
unrified, *a.* un-*ryfld*, not rifled; not robbed or stripped.
unrig, *v.t.* un-*rig*, to remove the rigging of (a vessel).
unrighteous, *a.* un-*ry*-chus, not righteous; not just; evil; wicked; contrary to law or equity.
unrighteously, *ad.* unjustly; wickedly.
unrighteousness, *n.* injustice; wickedness.
unrip, *v.t.* un-*rip*, to rip up.
unripe, *a.* un-*ripe*, not ripe or mature; not matured; not seasonable.
unripened, *a.* un-*ripe*-nd, not matured.
unrivalled, *a.* un-*ry*-vld, having no rival; having no equal; incomparable.
unrobe, *v.t.* and *i.* un-*robe*, to disrobe; to undress.
unroll, *v.t.* un-*role*, to open what is rolled; to display: *v.i.* to straighten out from a rolled-up condition.
unromantic, *a.* un-ro-*man*-tik, not romantic or fanciful; matter-of-fact.
unroof, *v.t.* un-*roof*, to strip off the roof of a house.
unroofed, *a.* un-*rooft*, stripped of, or not yet provided with, a roof.
unroot, *v.t.* un-*root*, to tear up by the roots; to eradicate or extirpate.
unrouted, *a.* un-*rout*-ed, not thrown into disorder.
unrouted, *a.* un-*root*-ed, not charted; not provided with a route.
unroyal, *a.* un-*roy*-al, not royal; unworthy of a king or prince.
unruffled, *a.* un-*ruf*-ld, not ruffled; calm; not agitated.
unruled, *a.* un-*roold*, not governed; not directed by superior power; not marked with parallel lines (of paper).
unruliness, *n.* un-*roo*-le-ness, the state of being unruly; turbulence; insubordination.
unruly, *a.* un-*roo*-le, disregarding restraint; ungovernable; refractory.
unrumpled, *a.* un-*rum*-pld, not rumpled; smoothed from rumples.
unsaddle, *v.t.* un-*sad*-dl, to take off the saddle; to throw from the saddle.
unsafe, *a.* un-*safe*, not free from danger; exposed to harm; hazardous.
unsafeness, *n.* state of being unsafe.
unsaid, *pp.* and *a.* un-*sed*, not spoken or uttered.
unsailable, *a.* un-*sale*-a-bl, not navigable; dangerous to sail on.
unsaint, *v.t.* un-*saynt*, to deprive of saintship.
unsaintly, *adj.* un-*saynt*-le, unbefitting a saint.
unsalaried, *a.* un-*sal*-a-rid, receiving no salary.
unsaleable, *a.* un-*sale*-a-bl, not saleable; not i[n] demand; not meeting a ready sale.
unsalted, *a.* un-*sawl*-ted, not salted; not pickled fresh.
unsaluted, *a.* un-sa-*loo*-ted, not saluted; no[t] greeted.
unsanctified, *a.* un-*sank*-te-fide, not sanctified unholy; not consecrated.
unsanctioned, *a.* un-*sank*-shond, not ratified o[r] approved.
unsanguine, *a.* un-*sang*-gwin, not sanguine.
unsanitary, *a.* un-*san*-e-ta-re, unhealthy; insani[-] tary.
unsated, *a.* un-*say*-ted, not satisfied or satiated.
unsatiable, *a.* un-*say*-she-a-bl, that cannot b[e] satisfied.
unsatisfactorily, *ad.* *un*-sat-is-*fak*-to-re-le, so a[s] not to give satisfaction.
unsatisfactoriness, *n.* *un*-sat-is-*fak*-to-re-ness, th[e] state of being unsatisfactory.
unsatisfactory, *a.* *un*-sat-is-*fak*-to-re, not givin[g] satisfaction; not convincing; not giving content.
unsatisfiable, *a.* un-*sat*-is-fy-a-bl, that cannot b[e] satisfied.
unsatisfied, *a.* un-*sat*-is-fide, not satisfied; no[t] gratified to the full; not content; not settled i[n] opinion; not convinced; not fully paid.
unsatisfying, *a.* un-*sat*-is-fy-ing, not according ful[l] gratification; not convincing; not giving content.
unsaturated, *a.* un-*sat*-yew-ray-ted, not saturated.
unsaturated compounds, chemical combination in which the power of attaching atoms is mor[e] than their valency requires.
unsavouriness, *n.* un-*say*-vo-re-ness, the qualit[y] of being unsavoury.
unsavoury, *a.* un-*say*-vo-re, tasteless; having a bad taste; unpleasing; disgusting.
unsay, *v.t.* un-*say*, to recant or recall what has bee[n] said; to retract.
unsayable, *a.* un-*say*-a-bl, that cannot be said unpronounceable.
unscalable, *a.* un-*skale*-a-bl, that cannot be scaled.
unscanned, *a.* un-*skand*, not scanned; not com[-] puted.
unscared, *a.* un-*skayrd*, not frightened away.
unscarred, *a.* un-*skard*, not marked with scars o[r] wounds.
unscathed, *a.* un-*skaythd*, uninjured.
unscattered, *a.* un-*skat*-erd, not dispersed o[r] thrown into confusion.
unsceptred, *a.* un-*sep*-terd, having no sceptre o[r] royal authority.
unscholarly, *a.* un-*skol*-ar-le, unlearned; no[t] befitting a scholar or scholarship.
unscholastic, *a.* *un*-sko-*las*-tik, not scholastic not bred to literature.
unschooled, *a.* un-*skoold*, not taught; not educated illiterate.
unscientific, *a.* *un*-sy-en-*tif*-ik, ignorant of, or no[t] in accordance with, scientific principle or method not connected with science.
unscorched, *a.* un-*skorcht*, not scorched; no[t] affected or destroyed by fire.
unscoured, *a.* un-*skourd*, not cleaned by rubbing.
unscratched, *a.* un-*skratcht*, not scratched or torn unhurt; undamaged.
unscreened, *a.* un-*skreend*, not covered; no[t] sheltered or protected; not sifted; not filmed.
unscrew, *v.t.* un-*skroo*, to withdraw the screws; t[o] unfasten: *v.i.* to become unscrewed; to be adapte[d] to unscrewing.
unscriptural, *a.* un-*skrip*-tewr-ral, not agreeable t[o] the scriptures.
unscrupulous, *a.* un-*skroo*-pew-lus, having n[o] scruples.
unscrupulously, *ad.* without scruple.
unscrupulousness, *n.* want of scrupulousness.
unsculptured, *a.* un-*skulp*-tewrd, not sculptured not adorned with sculpture; not inscribed.
unseal, *v.t.* un-*seel*, to break or remove the seal of to free from constraint.
unseam, *v.t.* un-*seem*, to rip; to cut open; to und[o] (needlework).
unsearchable, *a.* un-*serch*-a-bl, that cannot b[e] searched out, or found out by searching; in scrutable.

unsearchableness, *n.* un-*serch*-a-bl-ness, the state of being unsearchable.
unsearched, *a.* un-*sercht*, not explored; not critically examined.
unsearching, *a.* un-*serch*-ing, not penetrating.
unseared, *a.* un-*seerd*, not withered; not rendered callous or unfeeling.
unseasonable, *a.* un-*see*-zon-a-bl, not at the right season or time; not suited to the time or occasion; unfit; untimely; ill-timed; not agreeable to the time of the year.
unseasonableness, *n.* un-*see*-zon-a-bl-ness, state of being unseasonable.
unseasonably, *ad.* un-*see*-zon-a-ble, not seasonably.
unseasoned, *a.* un-*see*-zond, not seasoned, or prepared, as wood, for use; not inured; not accustomed; not qualified by use or experience; not salted or seasoned, as meat.
unseat, *v.t.* un-*seet*, to remove or dislodge from a seat; to deprive of office.
unseated, *pp.* and *a.* un-*see*-ted, not seated; unhorsed; deprived of a seat (esp. in Parliament); not settled with inhabitants [U.S.A.].
unseaworthiness, *n.* un-*see*-wur-the-ness, unfitness for going to sea.
unseaworthy, *a.* un-*see*-wur-the, unfit to go to sea.
unseconded, *a.* un-*sek*-un-ded, not seconded or supported.
unseconded, *a.* un-se-*kon*-ded, retained on a regimental list though employed on special duty [Mil.].
unsectarian, *a.* *un*-sek-*tare*-re-an, not sectarian; undenominational; of no particular religious sect.
unsecularize, *v.t.* un-*sek*-yu-la-rize, to detach from secular things; to alienate from the world.
unsecure, *a.* *un*-se-*kewr*, not secure; insecure.
unsedentary, *a.* un-*sed*-en-ta-re, not accustomed to sit much.
unseduced, *a.* *un*-se-*dewst*, not seduced.
unseeded, *a.* un-*see*-ded, not seeded; not sown.
unseeing, *a.* un-*see*-ing, wanting the power of vision; unobservant; failing to notice.
unseemliness, *n.* the state of being unseemly.
unseemly, *ad.* un-*seem*-le, not becoming; indecorous; indecent.
unseen, *a.* un-*seen*, not discovered; invisible; not seen or read before: *n.* an unprepared piece for translation.
unseized, *a.* un-*seezd*, not apprehended; not put in possession.
unseldom, *ad.* un-*sel*-dum, often.
unselfish, *a.* un-*sel*-fish, not selfish.
unselfishly, *ad.* in an unselfish spirit.
unselfishness, *n.* un-*sel*-fish-ness, the quality of being unselfish; self-denial.
unsensational, *a.* *un*-sen-*say*-shon-al, not inducing sensation; not melodramatic.
unsent, *a.* un-*sent*, not sent; not dispatched.
unsentenced, *a.* un-*sen*-tenst, not having received sentence.
unsentimental, *a.* *un*-sen-te-*men*-tal, cold-blooded; not affectedly romantic.
unseparated, *a.* un-*sep*-a-ray-ted, not separated or parted.
unsepulchred, *a.* un-*sep*-ul-kerd, having no grave or burial-place; unburied; disinterred.
unserved, *a.* un-*servd*, not served.
unserviceable, *a.* un-*ser*-vis-a-bl, not serviceable; not of service; useless.
unserviceably, *ad.* without being of use.
unset, *a.* un-*set*, not set (in any sense); not arranged; not sunk below the horizon: *v.t.* to remove from its setting.
unsettle, *v.t.* un-*set*-tl, to unfix; to unhinge; to make uncertain or fluctuating; to move from a place: *v.i.* to become unfixed, etc.
unsettled, *a.* un-*set*-tld, not determined; unsteady or wavering; unhinged; changeable; not having a legal settlement in a parish; having no fixed place of abode; turbid; not occupied by permanent inhabitants.
unsettlement, *n.* un-*set*-tl-ment, unsettled state.
unsevered, *a.* un-*sev*-erd, not parted or divided.
unsewn, *a.* un-*sohn*, unstitched; not sewn up.
unsex, *v.t.* un-*seks*, to transpose the sex of, esp. to deprive a woman of womanly feelings; to deprive of sexual characteristics or capacity.
unshackle, *v.t.* un-*shak*-kl, to unfetter; to set free.
unshaded, *a.* un-*shay*-ded, not overspread with shade or darkness; not having the light shaded.
unshadowed, *a.* un-*shad*-ode, not clouded; not darkened; not kept under observation.
unshakeable, *a.* un-*shay*-ka-bl, not to be moved; completely resolute.
unshaken, *a.* un-*shay*-ken, not agitated; firm; fixed; not moved in resolution.
unshamed, *a.* un-*shaymd*, not ashamed; not abashed.
unshapeable, *a.* un-*shay*-pa-bl, that cannot be shaped.
unshapeliness, *n.* un-*shape*-le-ness, unshapely quality; lack of symmetry.
unshapely, *a.* un-*shape*-le, not shapely.
unshapen, *a.* un-*shay*-pn, shapeless; misshapen; ugly.
unshared, *a.* un-*shayrd*, not enjoyed in common.
unshaven, *a.* un-*shay*-vn, unshorn; not having shaved; hairy.
unsheathe, *v.t.* un-*sheethe*, to draw from the sheath or scabbard.
unshed, *a.* un-*shed*, not shed; not spilt.
unsheeted, *a.* un-*shee*-ted, not furnished with sheets; not shrouded.
unshielded, *a.* un-*sheel*-ded, not protected; exposed.
unshifting, *a.* un-*shif*-ting, not changing place or expedients.
unshingled, *a.* un-*shing*-gld, not covered with shingles; with the hair left long.
unship, *v.t.* un-*ship*, to take out of a ship or from any conveyance; to remove from the place where it is fixed or fitted for use [Naut.].
unshocked, *a.* un-*shokt*, not shocked or disgusted.
unshod, *a.* un-*shod*, wearing no shoes.
unshorn, *a.* un-*shorn*, not shorn, sheared, or clipped.
unshot, *a.* un-*shot*, not hit by shot; not discharged; not sprouted (of grain): *v.t.* to take the projectile out of a gun or from a cartridge-case.
unshrined, *a.* un-*shrined*, removed from or not deposited in a shrine.
unshrinking, *a.* un-*shring*-king, not shrinking or recoiling; unflinching.
unshriven, *a.* un-*shriv*-en, not shriven.
unshrunk, *a.* un-*shrunk*, not contracted.
unshunned, *a.* un-*shund*, not avoided.
unshut, *v.t.* and *i.* un-*shut*, to open or become open: *a.* not shut; open; unclosed.
unsifted, *a.* un-*sif*-ted, not separated by a sieve; untried; not examined, as evidence.
unsighted, *a.* un-*sy*-ted, unseen; unperceived; not having, or not aimed by means of, sights (of firearms).
unsightliness, *n.* state of being unsightly.
unsightly, *a.* un-*site*-le, disagreeable to the eye; ugly; deformed.
unsigned, *a.* un-*synd*, having no signature; anonymous.
unsilvered, *a.* un-*sil*-verd, not covered with quicksilver; having no white hairs.
unsinged, *a.* un-*sinjd*, not singed; not scorched.
unsinning, *a.* un-*sin*-ning, committing no sin; untainted with sin.
unsisterly, *a.* un-*sis*-ter-le, unbecoming a sister.
unsizable, *a.* un-*sy*-za-bl, not being of the proper size or bulk; not fully grown.
unsized, *a.* un-*syzd*, not sized or stiffened.
unskilful, *a.* un-*skil*-ful, wanting skill and dexterity.
unskilfully, *ad.* without skill; clumsily.
unskilfulness, *n.* want of skill or dexterity.
unskilled, *a.* un-*skild*, wanting skill or dexterity; deficient in practical knowledge. **unskilled labour,** work for which training or apprenticeship is not essential.
unslacked, *a.* un-*slakt*, unslaked (of lime).
unslackened, *a.* un-*slak*-nd, not made slack.
unslaked, *a.* un-*slaykt*, not saturated with water (of lime); unquenched.
unslumbering, *a.* un-*slum*-ber-ring, never sleeping, or slumbering; always watching or vigilant.
unslung, *a.* un-*slung*, removed from a sling or slings; not hoisted in slings.
unsmirched, *a.* un-*smurcht*, not soiled or blacked.
unsmoked, *a.* un-*smohkt*, not smoked; not dried in smoke.
unsoaped, *a.* un-*soapt*, unwashed; not soaped.
unsociable, *a.* un-*soh*-sha-bl, not fond of society; unsocial; reserved; stand-offish.
unsociableness, *n.* the quality of being unsociable.

unsociably, *ad.* in an unsociable manner.
unsocial, *a.* un-*soh*-shal, not social; not suitable for society; not in accordance with communal welfare, or with socialistic principle.
unsoiled, *a.* un-*soyld*, not stained; unpolluted.
unsold, *a.* un-*sohld*, not sold.
unsolder, *v.t.* un-*sol*-der *or* un-*sod*-der, to sunder what has been soldered.
unsoldierly, *a.* un-*sohl*-jer-le, unworthy of, or unbecoming, a soldier.
unsolicited, *a.* *un*-so-*lis*-e-ted, not requested; unasked.
unsolicitous, *a.* *un*-so-*lis*-e-tus, not anxious.
unsolid, *a.* un-*sol*-id, not solid; fluid; not firm; unreal; not substantial.
unsolvable, *a.* un-*sol*-va-bl, inexplicable; not capable of solution.
unsolved, *a.* un-*solvd*, not explained.
unsophisticated, *a.* *un*-so-*fis*-te-kay-ted, ingenuous; simple-minded; guileless; not adulterated, corrupted, or spoiled.
unsorted, *a.* un-*sor*-ted, not separated into sorts.
unsought, *a.* un-*sawt*, not searched for; found without searching.
unsound, *a.* un-*sound*, defective; infirm; sickly; erroneous; not honest; not to be trusted; not solid; not real; not compact.
unsoundable, *a.* un-*soun*-da-bl, not capable of being sounded or fathomed.
unsounded, *a.* un-*soun*-ded, not tried with the lead (of depths); unfathomed.
unsoundly, *ad.* un-*sound*-le, not with soundness.
unsoundness, *n.* state of being unsound.
unsoured, *a.* un-*sourd*, not made sour; not embittered.
unsown, *a.* un-*sohn*, not sown; not scattered on land for seed; not propagated by seed.
unsparing, *a.* un-*spare*-ring, not parsimonious; copious; liberal; not merciful or forgiving.
unspeakable, *a.* un-*speek*-a-bl, that cannot be uttered or expressed; unutterable; not fit to be talked of; extremely bad.
unspeakably, *ad.* un-*speek*-a-ble, inexpressibly.
unspecialized, *a.* un-*spesh*-al-ized, not specialized; not adapted for any special function [Zool.].
unspecified, *a.* un-*spes*-e-fide, not particularly mentioned; not mentioned in detail.
unspecious, *a.* un-*spee*-shus, not plausible.
unspeculative, *a.* un-*spek*-yew-la-tiv, not theoretical; not given to doubt or question.
unspent, *a.* un-*spent*, not used or wasted; not exhausted; not having lost its force or impulse.
unsphere, *v.t.* un-*sfeer*, to remove from its sphere.
unspied, *a.* un-*spide*, unseen; not discovered.
unspike, *v.i.* un-*spike*, to extract the spike from a spiked gun; to remove spikes from railway chairs.
unspilt, *a.* un-*spilt*, not spilt; not shed.
unspiritual, *a.* un-*spi*-re-tew-al, not spiritual; worldly.
unspiritualize, *v.t.* un-*spi*-re-tew-a-lize, to deprive of spirituality.
unsplit, *a.* un-*split*, not split.
unspoiled, *a.* un-*spoyld*, not corrupted; not rendered useless; not plundered.
unspoilt, *a.* un-*spoylt*, unspoiled.
unspoken, *a.* un-*spoh*-kn, not spoken or uttered.
unsporting, *a.* un-*sport*-ing, unsportsmanlike.
unsportsmanlike, *a.* un-*sports*-man-like, not characteristic of a sportsman; unfair; mean.
unspotted, *a.* un-*spot*-ed, free from spot; free from moral stain; unblemished; immaculate.
unsprung, *a.* un-*sprung*, not fitted with springs.
unsquared, *a.* un-*skwayrd*, not made square; not regular; not formed.
unstable, *a.* un-*stay*-bl, not fixed or steady; inconstant; changeable; irresolute.
unstableness, *n.* un-*stay*-bl-ness, instability.
unstaid, *a.* un-*stade*, not steady; volatile; fickle.
unstained, *a.* un-*staynd*, not dyed; not polluted; not tarnished or dishonoured.
unstamped, *a.* un-*stampt*, not stamped.
unstarched, *a.* un-*starcht*, not starched; having the starch removed.
unstatesmanlike, *a.* un-*stayts*-man-like, not worthy, or characteristic, of a statesman.
unstatutable, *a.* un-*stat*-yew-ta-bl, contrary to statute; not warranted by statute.
unsteadfast, *a.* un-*sted*-fast, not fixed; not standing firm; not adhering firmly to a purpose.
unsteadied, *a.* un-*sted*-ed, not supported; not kept from shaking.
unsteadily, *ad.* un-*sted*-e-le, not with steadiness.
unsteadiness, *n.* un-*sted*-e-ness, instability; inconstancy; vacillation.
unsteady, *a.* un-*sted*-e, not steady; not constant; irresolute; changeable; fluctuating; variable.
unsteeped, *a.* un-*steept*, not steeped; not soaked.
unstep, *v.t.* un-*step*, to remove a mast from its step.
unstick, *v.t.* un-*stik*, to remove what has stuck; to free from being stuck. *p.* and *pp.* **unstuck.**
unstimulated, *a.* un-*stim*-yew-lay-ted, not stimulated; not excited.
unstinted, *a.* un-*stin*-ted, not stinted; not limited.
unstirred, *a.* un-*sturd*, not stirred; not agitated.
unstitch, *v.t.* un-*stitch*, to open by picking out stitches; to remove stitches from.
unstockinged, *a.* un-*stok*-ingd, without stockings.
unstooping, *a.* un-*stoop*-ing, unbending; unyielding.
unstop, *v.t.* un-*stop*, to free from any obstruction; to open, esp. by removing a stopper.
unstoppered, *a.* un-*stop*-erd, with the stopper removed.
unstored, *a.* un-*stord*, not laid up in store; not warehoused.
unstoried, *a.* un-*staw*-rid, not related in story; not famed in history; not built in stories [Arch.].
unstormed, *a.* un-*stormd*, not assaulted; not taken by assault.
unstrained, *a.* un-*straynd*, not strained; easy; not forced; natural.
unstrapped, *a.* un-*strapt*, having the straps removed.
unstratified, *a.* un-*strat*-e-fide, not formed in strata.
unstressed, *a.* un-*strest*, unemphasized; not bearing an accent.
unstring, *v.t.* un-*string*, to deprive of a string or strings; to relax the tension of; to loosen; to take from a string. *p.* and *pp.* **unstrung.**
unstriped, *a.* un-*strypt*, without stripes; not striated (of muscle) [Anat.].
unstruck, *a.* un-*struk*, not struck; not impressed.
unstrung, *a.* un-*strung*, weakened in nervous force; relaxed in tension; loosed; deprived of strings.
unstuck, un-*stuk*, *p.* and *pp.* of *unstick*.
unstudied, *a.* un-*stud*-ed, not studied or premeditated; not laboured; easy; natural; unskilled.
unstudious, *a.* un-*stew*-de-us, not diligent in study.
unstuffed, *a.* un-*stuft*, not stuffed; not crowded.
unstung, *a.* un-*stung*, not stung.
unsubduable, *a.* *un*-sub-*dew*-a-bl, not capable of being subdued.
unsubdued, *a.* un-sub-*dewd*, not brought into subjection.
unsubmissive, *a.* *un*-sub-*mis*-iv, not submissive; disobedient.
unsuborned, *a.* *un*-sub-*ornd*, not procured by secret collusion.
unsubsidized, *a.* un-*sub*-se-dized, receiving no subsidy; not engaged in another's service by subsidies.
unsubstantial, *a.* *un*-sub-*stan*-shal, not solid; not real.
unsubstantiated, *a.* un-sub-*stan*-she-ay-ted, unconfirmed; not proved.
unsubverted, *a.* *un*-sub-*ver*-ted, not overthrown.
unsuccess, *n.* un-suk-*ses*, failure.
unsuccessful, *a.* un-suk-*ses*-ful, not successful; not producing the desired result; not fortunate.
unsuccessfully, *ad.* without success.
unsuccessive, *a.* *un*-suk-*ses*-iv, not proceeding by regular succession.
unsufferable, *a.* un-*suf*-er-ra-bl, insufferable.
unsugared, *a.* un-*shoo*-gerd, not sweetened with sugar.
unsuitability, *n.* un-*sew*-ta-*bil*-e-te, unsuitableness.
unsuitable, *a.* un-*sew*-ta-bl, unfit; not adapted; not suitable.
unsuitableness, *n.* un-*sew*-ta-bl-ness, unfitness.
unsuitably, *ad.* un-*sew*-ta-ble, not suitably.
unsuited, *a.* un-*sew*-ted, not suited; not adapted.
unsuiting, *a.* un-*sew*-ting, not fitting; not befitting.
unsullied, *a.* un-*sul*-id, not strained or tarnished; not disgraced.
unsung, *a.* un-*sung*, not sung; not celebrated in verse.
unsunned, *a.* un-*sund*, not having been exposed to the sun; not disclosed.

unsupplanted, *a.* *un*-su-*plahn*-ted, not supplanted; not overthrown by stratagem.
unsuppliable, *a.* *un*-su-*ply*-a-bl, not to be supplied.
unsupplied, *a.* *un*-su-*plide*, not supplied; not furnished with things necessary.
unsupported, *a.* *un*-su-*por*-ted, not supported; not upheld; not countenanced.
unsuppressed, *a.* un-su-*prest*, not suppressed.
unsure, *a.* un-*shure*, not fixed; not certain.
unsurmountable, *a.* *un*-sur-*moun*-ta-bl, insuperable.
unsurpassable, *a.* *un*-sur-*pah*-sa-bl, not to be surpassed.
unsurpassed, *a.* *un*-sur-*pahst*, not exceeded.
unsurrendered, *a.* *un*-su-*ren*-derd, not yielded up to others.
unsusceptible, *a.* *un*-sus-*sep*-te-bl, not susceptible; not capable of admitting or receiving.
unsuspected, *a.* *un*-su-*spek*-ted, not considered as likely to have done (an act); unguessed; unforeseen.
unsuspecting, *a.* *un*-su-*spek*-ting, not imagining; free from suspicion.
unsuspectingly, *ad.* without suspicion.
unsuspicious, *a.* *un*-su-*spish*-us, having no suspicion; not suspecting.
unsuspiciously, *ad.* without suspicion.
unsustainable, *a.* *un*-su-*stay*-na-bl, that cannot be sustained or maintained.
unsustained, *a.* *un*-su-*staynd*, not supported; not sustained.
unswathe, *v.t.* un-*swaythe*, to relieve from a bandage or other wrapping.
unswayable, *a.* un-*sway*-a-bl, that cannot be influenced by another.
unswayed, *a.* un-*swade*, not swayed or wielded; not influenced.
unswear, *v.t.* un-*sware*, to retract (a sworn statement, etc.) by a second oath; to abjure. *pp.* **unsworn.**
unsweetened, *a.* un-*swee*-tnd, without sweetening: *n.* gin [Coll.].
unswept, *a.* un-*swept*, not cleaned with a broom; not swept.
unswerving, *a.* un-*swer*-ving, not deviating from a certain standard or course.
unsworn, *a.* un-*sworn*, not bound by an oath; not uttered in an oath.
unsymmetrical, *a.* *un*-se-*met*-re-kal, wanting symmetry or due proportion of parts.
unsympathetic, *a.* un-sim-pa-*thet*-ik, having no sympathy.
unsystematic, *a.* un-sis-te-*mat*-ik, not having regular order, distribution, or arrangement of parts; unplanned; higgledy-piggledy.
unsystematized, *a.* un-*sis*-te-ma-tized, not reduced to a system.
untack, *v.t.* un-*tak*, to separate what is tacked; to disjoin.
untainted, *a.* un-*tane*-ted, not rendered impure by admixture; not sullied or stained; unblemished; not rendered unwholesome or unsavoury by putrescence; not charged with a crime.
untaken, *a.* un-*tay*-ken, not seized or apprehended; not swallowed.
untalented, *a.* un-*tal*-en-ted, not intellectually endowed.
untamable, *a.* un-*tay*-ma-bl, that cannot be tamed, controlled, or domesticated; not to be broken in.
untamed, *a.* un-*taymd*, not reclaimed from wildness; not domesticated; not brought under control; not softened or rendered mild by culture.
untangle, *v.t.* un-*tang*-gl, to free from tangles or complexity; to disentangle.
untarnished, *a.* un-*tar*-nisht, not soiled or tarnished; unblemished.
untasted, *a.* un-*tays*-ted, not tried by the taste or tongue; not enjoyed.
untasteful, *a.* un-*tayst*-ful, having no taste; being without taste; distasteful.
untaught, *a.* un-*tawt*, not taught or educated; illiterate; unskilled.
untaxed, *a.* un-*takst*, not charged with taxes; not accused.
unteachable, *a.* un-*teech*-a-bl, that cannot be taught or instructed; indocile.
unteachableness, *n.* state or quality of being unteachable.
untempered, *a.* un-*tem*-perd, not tempered; not duly mixed for use; not properly hardened; not moderated.
untempted, *a.* un-*temp*-ted, not tried by enticements.
untempting, *a.* un-*temp*-ting, not adapted to tempt or allure; repellent.
untenable, *a.* un-*ten*-a-bl, that cannot be held in possession; that cannot be maintained; not defensible.
untenantable, *a.* un-*ten*-an-ta-bl, not in a suitable state for occupation.
untenanted, *a.* un-*ten*-an-ted, not occupied by a tenant; uninhabited.
untended, *a.* un-*ten*-ded, not having any attendant; neglected.
untender, *a.* un-*ten*-der, not tender; wanting sensibility or affection.
untendered, *a.* un-*ten*-derd, not offered.
unterminated, *a.* un-*ter*-me-nay-ted, not terminated.
unterrified, *a.* un-*te*-re-fide, not affrighted or daunted.
untested, *a.* un-*tes*-ted, not tried by a standard.
untether, *v.t.* un-*teth*-er, to release from a tether.
unthanked, *a.* un-*thankt*, not repaid with acknowledgments.
unthankful, *a.* un-*thank*-ful, ungrateful; not making acknowledgments for good received.
unthaw, *v.t.* and *i.* un-*thaw*, to thaw out; to warm; to melt or dissolve.
unthink, *v.t.* and *i.* un-*think*, to retract or annul mentally. **unthought of,** not considered; unimagined.
unthinkable, *a.* un-*thing*-ka-bl, that cannot be entertained or thought; too bad, great, small, etc., to be conceived; unimaginable.
unthinking, *a.* un-*thing*-king, not heedful; thoughtless; inconsiderate; not indicating thought.
unthinkingly, *ad.* without thinking.
unthoughtful, *a.* un-*thawt*-ful, thoughtless; heedless.
unthread, *v.t.* un-*thred*, to draw a thread from; to loose; to disentangle.
unthreatened, *a.* un-*thret*-nd, not menaced.
unthrift, *n.* *un*-thrift, one who wastes his estate by extravagance; a ne'er-do-well; thriftlessness.
unthrifty, *a.* un-*thrif*-te, prodigal; lavish; profuse; not thriving.
unthriving, *a.* un-*thry*-ving, not prospering.
unthrone, *v.t.* un-*throhn*, to depose (a sovereign).
unthrown, *a.* un-*throhn*, not thrown.
untidily, *ad.* un-*ty*-de-le, in an untidy manner.
untidiness, *n.* the state of being untidy.
untidy, *a.* un-*ty*-de, not neatly dressed; slovenly; not in good order.
untie, *v.t.* un-*ty*, to loosen; to disengage the parts that form a knot; to unbind; to unfold.
untied, *a.* un-*tide*, separated; not tied; not bound or gathered in a knot; loose.
until, *prep.* and *conj.* un-*til*, till; to the time that; to the point or the degree that. (O.Scand. *und*, as far as, and *till.*)
untile, *v.t.* un-*tile*, to uncover by removing tiles.
untilled, *a.* un-*tild*, not tilled or cultivated.
untimbered, *a.* un-*tim*-berd, not furnished with timber; not provided with timber-trees; not showing the constructional timbers [Building].
untimeliness, *n.* un-*time*-le-ness, the quality of being untimely.
untimely, *a.* un-*time*-le, happening before the usual or the natural time; premature; inopportune: *ad.* before the natural time.
untinctured, *a.* un-*tink*-tewrd, not tinged; not stained; not discoloured.
untinged, *a.* un-*tinjd*, untinctured.
untirable, *a.* un-*tire*-ra-bl, indefatigable; unwearied.
untired, *a.* un-*tired*, not exhausted by labour.
untiring, *a.* un-*tire*-ring, not becoming exhausted.
untithed, *a.* un-*tythed*, not subjected to tithes.
untitled, *a.* un-*ty*-tld, having no title.
unto, *prep.* *un*-too, to. (O.Scand. *und*, as far as, and *to.*)
untold, *a.* un-*tohld*, not related; not revealed; not numbered or counted; impossible to be numbered or counted.
untouchability, *n.* *un*-tuch-a-*bil*-e-te, state or quality of being untouchable; the defiling property formerly ascribed to Untouchables by high-caste Hindus.

untouchable, *a.* un-*tuch*-a-bl, not to be touched; ceremoniously unclean: *n.* that which or one who is untouchable; (*cap.*) a Hindu of one of the scheduled (or lowest) castes, discrimination against which was legally abolished, 1947.
untouched, *a.* un-*tucht*, not reached; not hit; not moved; not affected.
untoward, *a.* un-*toh*-ard, froward; perverse; refractory; awkward; inconvenient; troublesome.
untowardliness, *n.* un-*toh*-ard-le-ness, frowardness.
untowardly, *a.* un-*toh*-ard-le, awkward; perverse; froward: *ad.* in an untoward manner.
untowardness, *n.* un-*toh*-ard-ness, state of being untoward.
untraceable, *a.* un-*trace*-a-bl, that cannot be traced.
untraced, *a.* un-*trayst*, not traced; not marked by footsteps; not marked out.
untracked, *a.* un-*trakt*, not marked by footsteps; not followed by the tracks.
untractable, *a.* un-*trak*-ta-bl, intractable; unmanageable; unworkable.
untrained, *a.* un-*traynd*, not trained or disciplined; not educated; irregular; ungovernable.
untrammelled, *a.* un-*tram*-ld, not shackled.
untrampled, *a.* un-*tram*-pld, not trodden on.
untransferable, *a.* *un*-trans-*fer*-ra-bl, not to be transferred or passed to another.
untransferred, *a.* *un*-trans-*ferd*, not transferred.
untranslatable, *a.* *un*-trans-*lay*-ta-bl, not capable of being translated.
untranslated, *a.* *un*-trans-*lay*-ted, not rendered into another language; not transferred from office as a bishop from one see to another.
untransparent, *a.* *un*-trans-*pare*-rent, opaque.
untravelled, *a.* un-*trav*-ld, not frequented as a route; not having visited foreign countries.
untraversed, *a.* un-*trav*-erst, not passed over.
untreasured, *a.* un-*trezh*-urd, not laid up; not valued; not treasured.
untrembling, *a.* un-*trem*-bling, not trembling or shaking; firm; steady.
untried, *a.* un-*tride*, not attempted; not yet experienced; not put to the proof; not having passed trial; not heard and determined in law.
untrimmed, *a.* un-*trimd*, not pruned or dressed; not put in order.
untrod, *a.* un-*trod*, untrodden.
untrodden, *a.* un-*trod*-en, not having been trod; not passed over; unfrequented.
untroubled, *a.* un-*trub*-ld, not disturbed by care, sorrow, or business; not agitated; not moved; not disturbed; not foul or turbid.
untrue, *a.* un-*troo*, contrary to the fact; not faithful to another; false; disloyal; inconstant, as a lover; not according to rule; not straight.
untruly, *ad.* un-*troo*-le, not truly.
untrussed, *a.* un-*trust*, not trussed; not tied up; divested of breeches.
untrustiness, *n.* unfaithfulness in the discharge of a trust; the fact of being untrustworthy.
untrustworthy, *a.* un-*trust*-wur-the, not deserving of confidence.
untrusty, *a.* not worthy of confidence; unfaithful.
untruth, *n.* un-*trooth*, falsehood; want of veracity; a false assertion.
untruthful, *a.* un-*trooth*-ful, wanting in veracity.
untruthfully, *ad.* without veracity.
untruthfulness, *n.* want of veracity; mendacity
untuck, *v.t.* un-*tuk*, to unfold or undo a tuck; to draw out what has been tucked in.
untumbled, *a.* un-*tum*-bld, not rolled; not rumpled.
untunable, *a.* un-*tew*-na-bl, not musical; not capable of making music; not capable of being tuned.
untune, *v.t.* un-*tewn*, to put out of tune; to disorder.
unturned, *a.* un-*turnd*, not turned. **leave no stone unturned,** *see* **stone.**
untutored, *a.* un-*tew*-turd, uninstructed; untaught.
untwine, *v.t.* un-*twine*, to untwist; to disentangle; to separate.
untwist, *v.t.* un-*twist*, to separate and open; to turn back that which is twisted; to disentangle.
unurged, *a.* un-*urjd*, not pressed with solicitation.
unusable or **unuseable,** *a.* un-*yew*-za-bl, not usable.
unused, *a.* un-*yewzd*, not put to use; that has never been used; not accustomed.
unusual, *a.* un-*yew*-zhew-al, not usual: not common.
unusually, *ad.* to an unusual degree.
unusualness, *n.* the condition of being unusual; uncommonness.
unutterable, *a.* un-*ut*-er-ra-bl, ineffable; inexpressible.
unutterably, *ad.* beyond expression.
unvacated, *a.* *un*-va-*kay*-ted, not made vacant.
unvaccinated, *a.* un-*vak*-se-nay-ted, not vaccinated.
unvalued, *a.* un-*val*-yewd, not valued; not prized; inestimable; not estimated.
unvanquishable, *a.* un-*vang*-kwish-a-bl, that cannot be conquered.
unvanquished, *a.* un-*vang*-kwisht, not conquered.
unvaried, *a.* un-*vare*-rid, not altered or diversified.
unvariegated, *a.* un-*vare*-re-gay-ted, not variegated.
unvarnished, *a.* un-*var*-nisht, not overlaid with varnish; not artfully embellished; plain.
unvarying, *a.* un-*vare*-re-ing, not liable to change; uniform.
unveil, *v.t.* un-*vale*, to uncover; to divest of a veil.
unventilated, *a.* un-*ven*-te-lay-ted, not purified by a free current of air; not made public, as opinions.
unveracious, *a.* *un*-ver-*ray*-shus, not veracious.
unveracity, *n.* *un*-ver-*ras*-e-te, want of truthfulness.
unverifiable, *a.* un-*ve*-re-*fy*-a-bl, not capable of being verified.
unverified, *a.* un-*ve*-re-fide, not proved to be true; not supported by evidence; not identified.
unversed, *a.* un-*verst*, not skilled; unacquainted.
unvexed, *a.* un-*vekst*, not troubled or disturbed.
unvindicated, *a.* un-*vin*-de-kay-ted, not cleared of imputations; not established in truth.
unviolated, *a.* un-*vy*-o-lay-ted, not injured; not broken.
unvisited, *a.* un-*viz*-e-ted, not resorted to; not visited.
unvitiated, *a.* un-*vish*-e-ay-ted, not corrupted; clean.
unvoiced, *a.* un-*voyst*, not spoken; without someone speaking of it; uttered without vibration of the vocal chords, devocalized [Phonetics].
unvouched, *a.* un-*voucht*, not fully tested; not guaranteed.
unvowed, *a.* un-*voud*, not consecrated by promise; not vowed.
unwakened, *a.* un-*way*-knd, not roused from sleep.
unwalled, *a.* un-*wawld*, not surrounded by a wall.
unwanted, *a.* un-*won*-ted, not wanted; not desired; inconvenient.
unwarily, *ad.* un-*ware*-re-le, incautiously.
unwariness, *n.* un-*ware*-re-ness, want of vigilance or caution.
unwarlike, *a.* un-*wawr*-like, not used to war; not military; averse to militarism.
unwarmed, *a.* un-*wawrmd*, not warmed or excited.
unwarned, *a.* un-*wawrnd*, not cautioned.
unwarp, *v.t.* un-*wawrp*, to release what is warped; to unhitch the warps [Naut.].
unwarped, *a.* un-*wawrpt*, not warped; not distorted or biased; impartial.
unwarrantable, *a.* un-*wo*-ran-ta-bl, not defensible; illegal.
unwarrantably, *ad.* un-*wo*-ran-ta-ble, in a manner that cannot be justified.
unwarranted, *a.* un-*wo*-ran-ted, not authorized; not assured or certain; not guaranteed.
unwary, *a.* un-*ware*-re, not vigilant or cautious; unguarded.
unwashed, *a.* un-*wosht*, not washed; not cleansed by water. **the Great Unwashed,** the mob; the ragtag and bobtail; the proletariat.
unwasted, *a.* un-*way*-sted, not lost by extravagance or negligence; not dissipated; not consumed by time or violence; not lost by exhaustion, evaporation, or other means.
unwasting, *a.* un-*way*-sting, not growing less; not decaying.
unwatched, *a.* un-*wotcht*, not guarded with vigilance.
unwatchful, *a.* un-*wotch*-ful, not vigilant.
unwatchfulness, *n.* want of vigilance.
unwatered, *a.* un-*waw*-terd, not watered; dry.
unwavering, *a.* un-*way*-ver-ring, not wavering; firm.
unweakened, *a.* un-*wee*-knd, not enfeebled.
unweaned, *a.* un-*weend*, not weaned; immature.
unweaponed, *a.* un-*wep*-ond, not furnished with weapons.
unweariable, *a.* un-*weer*-re-a-bl, indefatigable.
unwearied, *a.* un-*weer*-rid, not tired; indefatigable.
unweariedly, *ad.* un-*weer*-rid-le, without wearying.

unweariedness, *n.* state of being unwearied.
unweary, *a.* un-*weer*-re, not tired.
unwearying, *a.* un-*weer*-re-ing, tireless; indefatigable.
unweave, *v.t.* un-*weeve*, to undo what has been woven. *p.* **unwove.** *pp.* **unwoven.**
unwed, *a.* un-*wed*, unmarried; remaining single.
unwedded, *a.* un-*wed*-ed, unwed.
unweeded, *a.* un-*wee*-ded, not cleared of weeds.
unweighed, *a.* un-*wade*, not having the weight ascertained; not deliberately considered and examined; not considerate.
unweighing, *a.* un-*way*-ing, inconsiderate; thoughtless.
unwelcome, *a.* un-*wel*-kum, not welcome; not well received.
unwell, *a.* un-*wel*, not well; out of sorts; ill.
unwept, *a.* un-*wept*, not lamented; not mourned.
unwhipped or **unwhipt,** *a.* un-*whipt*, not corrected with the rod.
unwhispered, *a.* un-*whis*-perd, not whispered.
unwholesome, *a.* un-*hole*-sum, unfavourable to health; insalubrious; not sound; harmful.
unwholesomeness, *n.* un-*hole*-sum-ness, state of being unwholesome.
unwieldily, *ad.* un-*weel*-de-le, in an unwieldy manner.
unwieldiness, *n.* state of being unwieldy.
unwieldy, *a.* un-*weel*-de, that is wielded with difficulty; unmanageable; ponderous.
unwifely, *a.* un-*wife*-le, not in the manner of, or not befitting, a wife.
unwilled, *a.* un-*wild*, not produced by the will; unintended; not devised by will.
unwilling, *a.* un-*wil*-ing, not willing; averse; reluctant.
unwillingly, *ad.* with unwillingness.
unwillingness, *n.* state of being unwilling.
unwind, *v.t.* un-*wynd*, to wind off; to loose or separate what is wound; to disentangle: *v.i.* to admit of being unwound; to become unwound. *p.* and *pp.* **unwound.**
unwinking, *a.* un-*win*-king, not winking; alert.
unwisdom, *n.* un-*wiz*-dum, want of wisdom.
unwise, *a.* un-*wize*, not wise; defective in wisdom; injudicious.
unwithered, *a.* un-*with*-erd, not withered or faded.
unwithstood, *a.* un-with-*stood*, not opposed.
unwitnessed, *a.* un-*wit*-nest, not witnessed; not attested by witnesses.
unwittingly, *ad.* un-*wit*-ing-le, without knowledge or consciousness; ignorantly.
unwomanly, *a.* un-*woom*-an-le, not suitable for, or unbecoming, a woman.
unwonted, *a.* un-*wohn*-ted, unaccustomed; unused; uncommon; unusual.
unwooded, *a.* un-*wood*-ed, destitute of trees, timber, or wood.
unwooed, *a.* un-*wooed*, not courted.
unworkable, *a.* un-*wurk*-a-bl, not to be worked; impossible to carry out; impracticable.
unworkmanlike, *a.* un-*wurk*-man-like, unskilful.
unworldliness, *n.* state of being unworldly.
unworldly, *a.* un-*wurld*-le, not worldly; spiritual-minded.
unworn, *a.* un-*worn*, not impaired by wearing or by wear and tear; in new condition.
unworried, *a.* un-*wu*-rid, not worried.
unworshipped, *a.* un-*wur*-shipt, not worshipped or adored.
unworthily, *ad.* in an unworthy manner.
unworthiness, *n.* state of being unworthy.
unworthy, *a.* un-*wur*-the, not deserving; wanting merit; unbecoming; vile; base; not suitable.
unwound, *a.* un-*wound*, untwisted; straightened out.
unwounded, *a.* un-*woon*-ded, not wounded; not hurt or injured.
unwoven, *a.* un-*woh*-ven, not woven.
unwrap, *v.t.* un-*rap*, to open what is folded.
unwreathe, *v.t.* un-*reethe*, to untwist or untwine.
unwrecked, *a.* un-*rekt*, not wrecked.
unwrenched, *a.* un-*rencht*, not strained or distorted.
unwrinkled, *a.* un-*ring*-kld, not wrinkled; smooth.
unwritten, *a.* un-*rit*-en, not reduced to writing; oral; traditional; containing no writing. **unwritten law,** that which is not contained in statutes; the common law; [Coll.] an assumed rule that family honour may be criminally avenged without incurring the legal penalty.

unwrought, *a.* un-*rawt*, not laboured; not manufactured.
unwrung, *a.* un-*rung*, not wrung.
unyielded, *a.* un-*yeel*-ded, not conceded.
unyielding, *a.* un-*yeel*-ding, unbending; unpliant; obstinate.
unyoke, *v.t.* and *i.* un-*yohk*, to loose or free from a yoke; to disjoin.
unyoked, *a.* un-*yohkt*, freed from the yoke; not having worn the yoke; unrestrained.
unzoned, *a.* un-*zohnd*, not bound with a girdle; not partitioned into zones.
★**up,** *ad.* up, aloft; on high; out of bed; having risen from a seat, or a session; above the horizon; in a state or rebellion; to a state of advance or proficiency; to or towards a more important place, position, station, etc.; to the capital; to or at a university; in a state of elevation, of climbing or ascending, of being increased, or of approach; to the north; in the saddle; in order; from younger years: *a.* directed or going to a more important or higher place, etc.: *prep.* from a lower to a higher place: *v.t.* to raise up: *v.i.* to rise. **all up,** all over; finished. **come up to, with, etc.,** *see* **come.** **it's up to you,** it is your responsibility. **not up to much,** inferior (of things); seedy, not very well (of persons). **up against it,** *see* **against.** **up and doing,** energetically active. **up and down,** from one place to another; backwards and forwards. **up in the air,** *see* **air.** **up line,** the line of rails on which trains run towards the chief station. **ups and downs,** changes of fortune. **up to,** to an equal height with; to a degree or point adequate; incumbent on. **up with,** raise; lift. (A.S.)
Upanishad, *n.* oo-*pan*-e-shad, the name given to a set of treatises that form part of the Vedas and constitutes the chief source of knowledge of the early metaphysical speculations and ethical doctrines of the Hindus. (Sans., instruction.)
upas, *n.* *yew*-pas, the Javanese poisonous tree, *Antiaris toxicaria.* (Malay, poison.)
upbear, *v.t.* up-*bare*, to raise aloft; to elevate; to sustain aloft; to sustain. *p.* **upbore.** *pp.* **upborne.**
upbeat, *n.* *up*-beet, an unaccented beat [Mus.]; an anacrusis [Pros.].
upbraid, *v.t.* up-*brade*, to charge with something wrong or disgraceful; to reproach; to reprove with severity. (A.S. *up*, on, *bregdan*, weave, seize.)
upbraiding, *n.* up-*brade*-ing, a reproach; the act of reproaching: *a.* reproachful.
upbraidingly, *ad.* with upbraiding.
upbringing, *n.* *up*-bring-ing, training; early education.
upcast, *a.* up-*kahst*, cast up; thrown upwards: *n.* *up*-kahst, a ventilating shaft for the upward passage of air [Mining]; anything cast up.
up-country, *n.* *up*-kun-tre *or* up-*kun*-tre, the remote part of the country; the inland territory: *a.* of or connected with the inland part of the country: *ad.* in the inland part of a country.
up-end, *v.t.* and *i.* up-*end*, to set on end.
upgrade, *n.* *up*-grade, a rising incline, an ascent: *ad.* uphill: *v.t.* up-*grade*, to promote to a higher class or group. **on the upgrade,** improving.
upgrowth, *n.* *up*-grohth, the process or act of growing; development.
upheaval, *n.* up-*hee*-val, an upheaving or the act of upheaving; a violent disturbance; the lifting up, esp. by volcanic action, of part of the earth's crust from beneath [Geol.].
upheave, *v.t.* and *i.* up-*heev*, to heave or lift up.
upheld, *a.* up-*held*, sustained.
uphill, *a.* *up*-hil, going up a hill; difficult, like ascending a hill: *ad.* in an upward direction.
uphold, *v.t.* up-*hohld*, to lift on high; to elevate; to sustain; to support. *p.* and *pp.* **upheld.**
upholder, *n.* up-*hohl*-der, a supporter; a defender; a support or prop.
upholster, *v.t.* up-*hohl*-ster, to furnish a room with curtains, hangings, etc.; to provide furniture with cushions, coverings, etc. (*up* and *hold.*)
upholsterer, *n.* up-*hohl*-ster-rer, one who upholsters.
upholstery, *n.* up-*hohl*-ster-re, textiles or needlework, etc., for furniture; furnishings supplied by upholsterers; the business of an upholsterer.
uphroe, *n.* *yew*-froh, a small piece of wood, holed at each end, for adjusting the length of a tent-

rope; a wooden slat perforated to take the cords of an awning, etc. [Naut.]. (Dut. *juffrouw*, young woman.)

upkeep, *n.* *up*-keep, maintenance; means of support.

upland, *n.* *up*-land, high land; ground elevated above the meadows; hill slopes: *a.* higher in situation; being on upland; pertaining to uplands.

uplandish, *a.* up-*lan*-dish, dwelling on high lands or mountains; rustic.

uplift, *v.t.* up-*lift*, to raise aloft; to raise; to upheave: *n.* *up*-lift, upheaval; elevation; social, moral, or æsthetic betterment.

upmost, *a.* *up*-mohst, highest; topmost.

upon, *prep.* u-*pon*, on; not under; resting or being on the surface or top; relating to. **take upon,** to assume. (*up* and *on*.)

upper, *a.* *up*-er, higher in place; superior in rank or dignity: *n.* the upper part of a boot or shoe. **upper case,** the portion of a compositor's case containing capital letters; hence, capitals [Print.]. **upper cut,** a blow delivered with an upward swing [Pugilism]. **upper hand,** ascendency; superiority. **Upper House,** the more restricted of the two Chambers of a bicameral legislature; the House of Lords. **upper leather,** the leather for the vamps and quarters of shoes. **upper ten,** *n.* *up*-per-*ten*, the aristocracy or upper classes (contraction for "upper ten thousand.") **upper works,** the parts above the water when the ship is in trim [Naut.]; the head, brains [Slang].

uppermost, *a. superlative*, *up*-per-mohst, highest in place; highest in power or authority; predominant.

upping, *n.* *up*-ing, *see* **swan-upping.**

uppish, *a.* *up*-ish, stuck-up; proud; arrogant; assuming; assertive.

uppishness, *n.* an uppish disposition.

upraise, *v.t.* up-*raze*, to raise higher; to elevate; [Fig.] to extol.

upright, *a.* *up*-rite, erect; perpendicular; erected; pricked up; just; adhering to or conformable to moral rectitude: *n.*, state of being perpendicular; something in an erect or perpendicular position; an upright piano. **upright piano,** a pianoforte the strings of which run vertically, not horizontally.

uprightly, *ad.* in an upright manner.

uprightness, *n.* the quality of being upright.

uprise, *v.i.* up-*rize*, to rise up; to ascend. *p.* **uprose.** *pp.* **uprisen,** up-*rizn*.

uprising, *n.* up-*rize*-ing, act of rising; a rising up; an insurrection.

uproar, *n.* *up*-rawr, great tumult; violent disturbance and noise.

uproarious, *a.* up-*raw*-re-us, making or attended by great uproar.

uproariously, *ad.* in an uproarious manner.

uproariousness, *n.* state of being uproarious.

uproot, *v.t.* up-*root*, to tear up by the roots; to remove completely.

uprush, *n.* *up*-rush, a sudden surging upwards.

upset, *a.* *up*-set, said of the price at which anything is set up for sale: *n.* an overturn; [Coll.] a bit of a disturbance, a tiff.

upset, *v.t.* up-*set*, to overturn; to overthrow; to discompose: *v.i.* to be overturned: *n.* the act or result of overturning; an embarrassing change, shock, etc. **upset price,** the lowest acceptable price for anything offered at auction.

upshot, *n.* *up*-shot, final issue; conclusion; end.

upside, *n.* *up*-side, the upper side. **upside down,** with the upper part undermost; in complete disorder.

upsilon, *n.* yewp-*sy*-lon, the 20th letter of the Greek alphabet, representing the vowel sound of *good*, and transliterated by *u* or *y*.

upstage, *ad.* up-*stage*, towards the rear of the stage: tragical; stand-offish, snobbish [Coll.].

upstairs, *ad.* *up*-stayrz, in or to an upper story: *n.* the upper part of a house: *a.* pertaining to stories above the ground floor.

upstanding, *a.* up-*stan*-ding, erect; straightforward.

upstart, *a.* *up*-start, suddenly raised to importance; *n.* one who suddenly rises from an inferior position to wealth, power, or honour; the meadow-saffron.

upstream, *a.* and *ad.* up-*streem*, towards the source of the stream; against the stream.

upstroke, *n.* *up*-stroke, the upward line in writing; an upward stroke in swimming, golf, etc.

uptake, *n.* *up*-take, the act of taking up; a shaft or pipe up which anything is taken. **slow in the uptake** [Coll.], dull-witted; lacking in ready perception.

up-to-date, *a.* up-to-*date*, keeping in step with modern ideas, methods, fashion, etc.; extending to the present time.

upturn, *v.i.* up-*turn*, to turn up; to overturn.

upward, *a.* *up*-ward, directed to a higher place: *ad.* upwards.

upwards, *ad.* *up*-wardz, towards a higher place; towards heaven; with respect to the higher part; more than; towards the source.

uræmia, *n.* yew-*ree*-me-a, a toxæmia resulting from renal insufficiency [Med.]. (Gr. *ouron*, urine, *haima*, blood.)

Ural-Altaic, *a.* *yewr*-ral-al-*tay*-ik, designating the agglutinative Mongolian languages of northern and central Asia, Turkey, Finland, parts of Russia, etc.: *n.* any one of these. (Named from the *Ural* and *Altai* Mts., because largely localized between them.)

uræus, *n.* yew-*ree*-us, the emblem of the sacred asp, worn as a symbol of sovereignty on the headdress of ancient Egyptian kings.

uralite, *n.* *yewr*-ra-lite, a pseudomorphous mineral with the cleavage and composition of hornblende and the external form of augite. (*Ural* Mts.)

Urania, *n.* yew-*ray*-ne-a, the Muse of astronomy [Myth.]. (Gr. *ouranos*, heavens.)

uranic, *a.* yew-*ran*-ik, obtained from an oxide of uranium; relating to the heavens. (Gr. *ouranos*.)

uraninite, *n.* yew-*ran*-e-nite, an oxide of uranium containing oxides of lead, thorium, etc., of which pitchblende is a variety.

uranite, *n.* *yewr*-ra-nite, any of a number of radioactive ores of uranium, including uraninite.

uranitic, *a.* yew-ra-*nit*-ik, pertaining to uranium or uranite.

uranium, *n.* yew-*ray*-ne-um, a heavy white metallic element radioactively disintegrating through radium, radon, and polonium to lead.

uranographic, *a.* *yewr*-ra-no-*graf*-ik, pertaining to uranography.

uranography, *n.* yewr-ra-*nog*-ra-fe, a description of the heavens. (Gr. *ouranos*, and *grapho*, write.)

uranology, *n.* yewr-ra-*nol*-o-je, the science of astronomy. (Gr. *ouranos*, and *logos*, science.)

uranometry, *n.* yewr-ra-*nom*-e-tre, descriptive astronomy; the measurement of stellar distances.

uranous, *a.* *yewr*-ra-nus, pertaining to, characteristic of, or containing uranium.

Uranus, *n.* *yewr*-ra-nus, the father of Saturn or Kronos and grandfather of Zeus [Myth.]; a major planet, discovered by Herschel, having four satellites.

urare, *n.* oor-*rah*-re, curare.

urate, *n.* *yewr*-rat, a salt of uric acid.

urban, *a.* *ur*-ban, pertaining to a city or town. **urban district,** a populous non-rural and non-chartered administrative division of a county. (L. *urbs*, a city.)

urbane, *a.* ur-*bane*, civil; courteous in manners; bland. (L. *urbanus*, of a city.)

urbanely, *ad.* ur-*bane*-le, in an urbane manner; politely.

urbanity, *n.* ur-*ban*-e-te, civility or courtesy of manners; politeness; affability.

urbanization, *n.* *ur*-ba-ny-*zay*-shon, the condition of being, or process of being, urbanized.

urbanize, *v.t.* *ur*-ba-nize, to convert from a rural to an urban state or status; to make urbane.

urceolate, *a.* *ur*-se-o-late, shaped like an urn or pitcher [Bot.]. (L. *urceolus*, a little pitcher.)

urchin, *n.* *ur*-chin, the sea-urchin (and, formerly, a hedgehog); a mischievous boy or child. (Fr. *hérisson*, a hedgehog.)

Urdu, *n.* *oor*-doo, Hindustani as spoken by Indian Mohammedans. (Hind.)

urea, *n.* yew-*ree*-a, a white crystalline substance, the final product of the metabolism of proteins in the body, present in the urine, blood, and lymph. (*urine*.)

ureal, *a.* yew-*ree*-al, pertaining to or of the nature of urea.

ureametry, *n.* yewr-re-*am*-e-tre, the estimation of the amount of urea in the urine [Med.].

uredinous, *a.* yew-*ree*-de-nus, pertaining to or of the

nature of the parasitic rusts; resembling urticaria [Med.].
uredo, *n.* yew-*ree*-do, a stage in the life-cycle of the Uridinales, or parasitic rusts; urticaria [Med.].
ureter, *n.* yew-*ree*-ter, the excretory duct which conveys the urine from the kidney to the bladder. (L.)
urethra, *n.* yew-*ree*-thra, the canal by which the urine is conducted from the bladder and discharged.
urethral, *a.* yew-*ree*-thral, pertaining to the urethra.
urethritis, *n.* yew-re-*thry*-tis, inflammation of the urethra [Med.].
uretic, *n.* yew-*ret*-ik, a medicine which increases the secretory action of the kidneys: *a.* pertaining to or promoting the flow of urine.
urge, *v.t.* urj, to press; to impel; to apply force to; to press earnestly; to provoke; to follow close; to importune; to incite or encourage: *v.i.* to press forward. (L. *urgeo*, press.)
urgency, *n.* *ur*-jen-se, importunity; earnest solicitation; pressure of necessity.
urgent, *a.* *ur*-jent, pressing with importunity; pressing with necessity; calling for instant action.
urgently, *ad.* pressingly; with pressing importunity.
urger, *n.* *ur*-jer, one who urges or importunes.
urial, *n.* *oor*-re-al, the wild sheep, *Ovis vignei*, of the Himalayas.
uric, *a.* *yewr*-rik, pertaining to or extracted from urine.
urim, *n.* *yewr*-rim, an unidentified ornament which, with the Thummim, was worn by the Jewish high priest when giving oracular responses, etc. (Heb., lights.)
urinal, *n.* *yewr*-re-nal, a vessel for urine [Med.]; a convenience or public lavatory in which to urinate.
urinary, *a.* *yewr*-re-na-re, pertaining to urine: *n.* a place for the reception of urine for manure.
urinate, *v.i.* *yewr*-re-nate, to pass urine.
urination, *n.* yew-re-*nay*-shon, the act or action of passing urine; micturition.
urinative, *a.* *yewr*-re-nay-tiv, uretic; provoking urine.
urine, *n.* *yewr*-rin, an animal fluid secreted by the kidneys, conveyed to the bladder by the ureters, and discharged through the urethra. (L. *urina*, from Gr. *ouron*.)
urinometer, *n.* yewr-re-*nom*-e-ter, an instrument to ascertain the specific gravity of the urine. (Gr. *ouron*, and *metron*, measure.)
urinoscopy, *n.* yewr-re-*nos*-ko-pe, examination of urine as an aid to diagnosis [Med.].
urinous, *a.* *yewr*-re-nus, pertaining to, or partaking of the qualities of, urine.
urn, *n.* urn, a rounded or angular vase; a vessel for containing hot water, particularly at the table; a vessel for the ashes of the dead: *v.t.* to enclose in an urn. (Fr. *urne*.)
urning, *n.* *oor*-ning, a male homosexual [Path.]; homosexual desire. (Ger.)
urochord, *n.* *yewr*-roh-kord, the caudal chord of certain ascidians and tunicates.
urocyst, *n.* *yewr*-roh-sist, the urinary bladder [Anat.].
urodynia, *n.* yewr-roh-*din*-e-a, painful urination [Med.].
urogenital, *a.* yewr-roh-*jen*-e-tal, pertaining to the excretory and reproductive organs, or their functions [Med.].
urologist, *n.* yewr-*rol*-o-jist, one skilled in urology.
urology, *n.* yewr-*rol*-o-je, the branch of pathology treating of the diseases of the urogenital organs.
uropygium, *n.* yewr-roh-*pij*-e-um, the extremity of a bird's body supporting the tail-feathers. (Gr. *oura*, tail, *pygā*, rump.)
uroscopy, *n.* yewr-*ros*-ko-pe, judgment of diseases by inspection of urine; urinoscopy. (Gr. *ouron*, and *skopeo*, view.)
urotoxic, *a.* yewr-roh-*tok*-sik, pertaining to the poisonous nature of matter carried in or eliminated by the urine. (Gr.)
Ursa, *n.* *ur*-sa, one of two northern constellations, **Ursa Major,** the Great Bear, one of the most conspicuous of the constellations, situated near the pole, **Ursa Minor,** the Little Bear, the constellation containing the pole-star, which is situated in the extremity of the tail. (L., a she-bear.)
ursiform, *a.* *ur*-se-form, in the shape of a bear. (L. *ursus*, and *forma*, shape.)
ursine, *a.* *ur*-sin, pertaining to or resembling bears.
urson, *n.* *ur*-son, the Canadian porcupine, *Erethizon dorsatus*.

Ursuline, *a.* *ur*-sew-lin, denominating or belonging to an order of nuns, founded in 1537 and named from St. Ursula, who devote themselves to nursing and education: *n.* a nun of the order.
urticaceous, *ur*-te-*kay*-shus, pertaining to or of the nature of the *Urtica*, or nettle genus of plants. (L.)
urticant, *a.* *ur*-te-kant, producing stinging or itching; adapted for stinging [Zool.]: *n.* an urticant substance [Med.].
urticaria, *n.* *ur*-te-*kare*-re-a, nettle-rash.
urticate, *v.t.* *ur*-te-kate, to lash, esp. so as to sting; to irritate; to produce urtication in: *v.i.* to sting.
urtication, *n.* *ur*-te-*kay*-shon, stinging or flagellation with nettles, sometimes applied to paralysis; a stinging sensation; a stinging operation.
urubu, *n.* *oo*-roo-boo, the common S. American black vulture, *Catharista atrata*. (Braz.)
urus, *n.* *yewr*-rus, the European wild ox, *Bos primigenius*, allied to the aurochs. (L.)
us, *pron.* us, *objective case of we.*
usable or **useable,** *a.* *yew*-za-bl, that may be used.
usage, *n.* *yew*-zaj, treatment; long-continued use; custom; practice; the customary application of a word. (Fr.)
usance, *n.* *yew*-zance, use; proper employment; usury; a determinate time fixed for payment of a bill of exchange [Comm.].
use, *n.* yewce, purpose; employment; application of anything to a purpose, good or bad; utility; occasion to employ; continued practice; the benefit or profit of lands and tenements [Law]; a local or special form of ritual or liturgy [Eccles.]. **in use,** in employment; in customary practice or observance. (L. *utor*, *usus*, use.)
***use,** *v.t.* yewz, to make use of or employ; to waste or exhaust by employment; to accustom; to habituate; to treat; to practise systematically: *v.i.* to be accustomed to; to practise customarily; to be wont; to frequent; to inhabit.
useable, *see* **usable.**
useage, *n.* *yewce*-aj, method of using; usage.
useful, *a.* *yewce*-ful, producing or having power to produce good; beneficial; profitable; helpful.
usefully, *ad.* serviceably.
usefulness, *n.* quality or state of being useful; conduciveness to some end.
useless, *a.* *yewce*-less, having no use; unserviceable; answering no good purpose.
uselessly, *ad.* in a useless manner.
uselessness, *n.* unserviceableness.
user, *n.* *yew*-zer, one who uses, treats, or occupies; the continued use of anything as of right and not as owner.
usher, *n.* *ush*-er, a domestic official or servant who introduces strangers, walks before persons of rank, etc.; an under-teacher or assistant in a school: *v.t.* to introduce; to forerun. (L. *ostiarius*, a doorkeeper.)
usherette, *n.* ush-er-*ret*, a female attendant who shows patrons to their seats, esp. at cinemas. (Coined from *usher*.)
ushership, *n.* *ush*-er-ship, office of an usher.
usquebaugh, *n.* *us*-kwe-baw, whisky. (Gael., water of life.)
ustilagineous, *a.* *us*-te-la-*jin*-e-us, pertaining to or characteristic of the *Ustilago*, or parasitic smut-fungi.
ustion, *n.* *ust*-yon, act of burning; state of being burned; cauterization [Surg.]. (L. *ustum*, burnt.)
ustulate, *a.* *us*-tew-lat, blackened, as if burnt [Bot.]. (L. *ustulatus*, scorched.)
ustulation, *n.* us-tew-*lay*-shon, the act of burning, or of expelling one substance from another by heat [Metal.]; the roasting or drying of moist substances as preparation for pulverizing.
usual, *a.* *yew*-zhew-al, customary; common; frequent.
usually, *ad.* ordinarily.
usucapion, *n.* *yew*-zew-*kay*-pe-on, the acquisition of property by uninterrupted possession for a long period [Rom. Law]. (L. *usucapio*, acquire by long use.)
usucaption, *n.* *yew*-zew-*kap*-shon, usucapion.
usufruct, *n.* *yew*-zew-frukt, the right of temporary use and enjoyment of lands and tenements belonging to another [Law]. (L. *usus*, and *fructus*, enjoyment.)
usufructuary, *n.* *yew*-zew-*fruk*-tew-a-re, one having the temporary use and enjoyment of property

without having the title: *a.* pertaining to or of the nature of usufruct.
usurer, *n.* *yew*-zhewr-er, one lending money at interest, esp. at an illegal or exorbitant rate.
usurious, *a.* yew-*zhewr*-re-us, taking exorbitant interest for the use of money; partaking of or pertaining to usury.
usuriously, *ad.* in a usurious manner.
usuriousness, *n.* the quality of being usurious.
usurp, *v.t.* yew-*zurp*, to seize and hold possession without right. (Fr. *usurper.*)
usurpation, *n.* yew-zur-*pay*-shon, act of seizing or occupying power or property without right. (L. *usurpatio.*)
usurpatory, *a.* yew-*zur*-pa-to-re, usurping; marked by usurpation.
usurper, *n.* yew-*zur*-per, one who usurps.
usurping, *a.* yew-*zur*-ping, seizing or occupying power or property without right: *n.* usurpation.
usury, *n.* *yew*-zhewr-re, a premium for the use of money; interest of money at an illegal or extortionate rate; the practice of taking interest. (L. *usura*, using.)
ut, *n.* ut, the first of the notes in the musical scale of Guido [Mus.].
utas, *n.* *yew*-tas, the octave of a festival [Eccles.]. (O.Fr. *huitieve.*)
utensil, *n.* yew-*ten*-sil, an instrument or vessel used in a kitchen, or in domestic and farming work; any consecrated vessel [Eccles.]. (L. *utensilis*, fit for use.)
uterine, *a.* *yew*-ter-rin, pertaining to the womb. **uterine brother** or **sister**, one born of the same mother by a different father. (L. *uterus.*)
uterogestation, *n.* *yew*-ter-ro-jes-*tay*-shon, fœtal development in the womb from conception to birth. (L. *uterus*, and *gestation.*)
uteromania, *n.* *yew*-ter-ro-*may*-ne-a, nymphomania [Path.].
uterus, *n.* *yew*-ter-rus, the womb. (L.)
utilitarian, *a.* *yew*-til-e-*tare*-re-an, consisting in or pertaining to utility or utilitarianism; characterized by or aiming at mere utility regardless of æsthetic, moral, or other factors: *n.* one who holds the doctrine of utilitarianism.
utilitarianism, *n.* *yew*-til-e-*tare*-re-a-nizm, the doctrine that the greatest happiness of the greatest number should be the end and aim of all social and political institutions; the doctrine that the test of the rightness or wrongness of an action is its conduciveness to the production of happiness or the reverse.
utility, *n.* yew-*til*-e-te, usefulness; production of good; profitableness to some valuable end. **utility goods,** articles in the manufacture of which unnecessary refinements are, by order, excluded, and the selling price of which is controlled. **utility man,** one employable in diverse branches of his trade or profession; a handyman. (L. *utilis*, useful.)
utilizable, *a.* *yew*-te-*ly*-za-bl, capable of being put to use.
utilization, *n.* *yew*-te-ly-*zay*-shon, the act of utilizing; state of being utilized.
utilize, *v.t.* *yew*-te-lize, to make useful; to put to use; to turn to profitable account.
utmost, *a.* *ut*-mohst, extreme; at the furthest extremity; in the highest degree: *n.* the most that can be; the greatest power, degree, or effort. (A.S. *ut*, out, and *most.*)
Utopia, *n.* yew-*toh*-pe-a, an imaginary island described (1516) by Sir Thomas More, represented as possessing a perfect political organization; a social state of ideal perfection; any impracticable communal scheme. (Gr., nowhere, from *ou*, not, *topos*, a place.)
utopian, *a.* yew-*toh*-pe-an, purely imaginary; chimerical; fanciful: *n.* (*cap.*) a denizen of Utopia; a visionary in politics.
utopianism, *n.* yew-*toh*-pe-a-nizm, the theory of Utopians; any perfectionist theory of society.
utricle, *n.* *yew*-tre-kl, a cell [Biol.], esp. one containing a single seed [Bot.]; a cavity in the labyrinth of the inner ear [Anat.]. (Fr., from L. *utriculus*, a small bag.)
utricular, *a.* yew-*trik*-yew-lar, containing utricles; like a utricle.
utriform, *a.* *yew*-tre-form, shaped like a leather bottle [Bot. and Zool.].
utter, *a.* *ut*-er, situated on the outside, or remote from the centre; outside any place; complete; total; final; peremptory; absolute; perfect; quite. **utter barrister,** a barrister who has not taken silk and is therefore not permitted to plead within the bar. (A.S. *ut*, out.)
utter, *v.t.* *ut*-er, to speak; to pronounce; to express; to disclose; to divulge; to sell; to vend [Law]; to put or send into circulation; to palm off as currency.
utterability, *n.* *ut*-er-ra-*bil*-e-te, quality of being utterable.
utterable, *a.* *ut*-er-ra-bl, that may be uttered or expressed.
utterance, *n.* *ut*-er-rance, act of uttering words; pronunciation; manner of speaking; vocal expression.
utterer, *n.* *ut*-er-rer, one who utters or pronounces; one who puts into circulation.
utterly, *ad.* to the full extent; totally.
uttermost, *a.* *ut*-ter-mohst, extreme; in the furthest, greatest, or highest degree: *n.* the greatest. **to the uttermost,** in the utmost degree; fully.
uva, *n.* *yew*-va, a succulent indehiscent fruit with central placenta, as the grape. (L.)
uvea, *n.* *yew*-ve-a, the posterior lamina of the iris of the eye. (L. *uva*, a bunch of grapes.)
uveous, *a.* *yew*-ve-us, resembling a grape; pertaining to the uvea.
uvula, *n.* *yew*-vew-la (*pl.* **uvulæ**), a prolongation of the soft palate over the root of the tongue. (L., from *uva.*)
uvular, *a.* *yew*-vew-lar, pertaining to the uvula; pronounced by the vibration of the uvula [Phon.]. **uvular r,** a trilled r.
uxorial, *a.* uk-*saw*-re-al, pertaining to a wife.
uxoricide, *n.* uk-*saw*-re-side, the murder or the murderer of a wife. (L. *uxor*, a wife, *cædo*, kill.)
uxorious, *a.* uk-*saw*-re-us, excessively devoted to one's wife.
uxoriously, *ad.* with uxoriousness.
uxoriousness, *n.* condition or quality of being uxorious; over-fondness for a wife.
Uzbek, *n.* *uz*-bek, a member of a Turkic group of tribes domiciled chiefly in Uzbekistan, a central Asian republic of the U.S.S.R.; its Ural-Altaic language.

V

V, vee, is the 22nd letter of the English alphabet, and the 17th consonant; in old English texts its sound was represented by *f*, traces of which occur in such plurals as *knives, wolves.* Formerly the same letter as U (U being the uncial form and V the capital form), till the early 19th cent. words with initial U and V were combined in one series in dictionaries and alphabetical catalogues, etc. **V1, V2,** etc., were the German designations of their "secret weapons" (*Vergeltungswaffe*, retaliation weapon) of World War II; in **V Day,** etc., **V** stands for Victory; **V.E. Day,** Victory in Europe Day, 8th May, 1945. **V Campaign,** allied propaganda directed toward subjugated peoples from July, 1941 till the close of the war in Europe. **V.J. Day,** 15th August, 1945, final victory in the Far East (Japan).

va, *v.i.* vah, go on [Mus.]. (It.)

vacancy, *n. vay*-kan-se, emptiness; empty space; void space between two bodies; time of leisure; intermission of business; listlessness; a place or office not occupied, or the period of non-occupation.

vacant, *a. vay*-kant, empty; exhausted of air; unengaged with business or care; not occupied by an incumbent or possessor; unoccupied with business; empty of thought; not occupied with study; indicating mental vacancy. (L. *vacans*, empty.)

vacantly, *ad. vay*-kant-le, in a vacant or unthinking manner.

vacate, *v.t.* va-*kate*, to make vacant; to quit possession of; to make void [Law].

vacation, *n.* va-*kay*-shon, act of vacating; intermission of a stated employment, as of judicial proceedings, regular studies and exercises at a college or school, etc.; the recess between one term and another; the time when a see or other spiritual dignity is vacant.

vacational, *a.* va-*kay*-shon-al, pertaining to a holiday.

vacationist, *n.* va-*kay*-shon-ist, one on a holiday.

vaccinable, *a. vak*-se-na-bl, susceptible to vaccination.

vaccinal, *a. vak*-se-nal, pertaining to vaccination.

vaccinate, *v.t. vak*-se-nate, to inoculate with vaccine, esp. as a protection against smallpox.

vaccination, *n. vak*-se-*nay*-shon, the act or practice of vaccinating, esp. for the prevention of smallpox.

vaccinationist, *n. vak*-se-*nay*-shon-ist, an upholder of compulsory vaccination, esp. against smallpox.

vaccinator, *n. vak*-se-nay-tor, one who vaccinates; an instrument for vaccinating.

vaccine, *a. vak*-seen, pertaining to or derived from cows; pertaining to vaccination: *n.* the preparation of cow-pox virus used in vaccination; any substance used for inoculation or subcutaneous immunization. (L. *vacca*, a cow.)

vaccinia, *n.* vak-*sin*-e-a, cow-pox, a communicable eruptive disease occurring in cattle, regarded as a modification of smallpox.

vaccinization, *n. vak*-se-ny-*zay*-shon, vaccination so repeated as to become ineffectual.

vacillancy, *n. vas*-e-lan-se, vacillation.

vacillant, *a. vas*-e-lant, vacillating; unsteady; inclined to fluctuate.

vacillate, *v.i. vas*-e-late, to sway to and fro; to waver; to fluctuate in mind or opinion; to be inconstant. (L. *vacillo*.)

vacillatingly, *ad. vas*-e-lay-ting-le, unsteadily.

vacillation, *n. vas*-e-*lay*-shon, the act of vacillating; fluctuation of mind; unsteadiness; change from one object to another.

vacillatory, *a. vas*-e-lay-to-re, wavering.

vacuity, *n.* va-*kew*-e-te, emptiness; a state of being empty; empty space; a void; a vacant state of mind; a vacant expression; inanity; want of reality. (L. *vacuus*, empty.)

vacuolar, *a. vak*-yew-o-lar, pertaining to or resembling vacuoles.

vacuolated, *a. vak*-yew-o-*lay*-ted, containing vacuoles.

vacuolation, *n. vak*-yew-o-*lay*-shon, the formation of vacuoles.

vacuole, *n. vak*-yew-ole, a minute cavity in organic tissue.

vacuous, *a. vak*-yew-us, empty; unfilled; void.

vacuousness, *n.* state of being vacuous.

vacuum, *n. vak*-yew-um, space empty or devoid of all matter or body. **vacuum brake,** a brake in which the power is obtained by exhausting the air. **vacuum cleaner,** an apparatus for the removal of dust and dirt by suction. **vacuum flask,** a flask having two walls separated by a vacuum jacket which keeps the liquid in the inner receptacle at the original temperature for a considerable time. **vacuum lamp,** an electric lamp consisting of an incandescent filament in an evacuated glass container. **vacuum tube,** a discharge tube from which all gas has been evacuated. **vacuum valve,** a thermionic valve [Wire.].

vade-mecum, *n. vay*-de-*mee*-kum, a manual or handbook for ready reference. (L., go with me.)

vagabond, *a. vag*-a-bond, wandering; moving from place to place without any settled habitation; driven to and fro: *n.* a vagrant; a homeless wanderer having no visible means of honest living; an idle, worthless fellow: *v.i.* to wander as a vagabond; to rove. (L. *vagus*, wandering.)

vagabondage, *n. vag*-a-bon-daj, the state of being a vagabond; vagabondism.

vagabondish, *a. vag*-a-bon-dish, characteristic of or pertaining to vagabonds.

vagabondism, *n. vag*-a-bon-dizm, way of living characteristic of vagabonds.

vagabondize, *v.i. vag*-a-bon-dize, to wander about in idleness like a vagabond.

vagal, *a. vay*-gal, pertaining to the vagus [Anat.].

vagarious, *a.* va-*gare*-re-us, having vagaries.

vagary, *n.* va-*gare*-re *or vay*-ga-re, a wandering of the thoughts; capriciousness; a wild freak; a whim.

vagina, *n.* va-*jy*-na, a sheath-like organ; the canal leading from the external orifice to the uterus [Anat.]; the leaf-stalk of those plants in which it becomes thin and rolls round the stem; a sheath [Bot.]. (L., a sheath.)

vaginal, *a.* va-*jy*-nal *or vaj*-e-nal, pertaining to or resembling a sheath, thecal [Zool.]; pertaining to the vagina [Anat.].

vaginant, *a.* va-*jy*-nant, sheathing [Bot.].

vaginipennate, *a. vaj*-e-ne-*pen*-at, having the wings covered with a hard sheath; sheath-winged [Entom.]. (L. *vagina*, and *penna*, a wing.)

vaginismus, *n.* vaj-e-*niz*-mus, painful spasm of the vagina [Med.].

vaginitis, *n.* vaj-e-*ny*-tis, inflammation of the vagina [Med.].

vagitus, *n.* va-*jy*-tus, the cry of a new-born child. (L. *vagire*, cry.)

vagrancy, *n. vay*-gran-se, state of being or living as a vagrant.

vagrant, *a. vay*-grant, wandering about without any settled habitation; unsettled; moving without any certain direction: *n.* an idle wanderer; a vagabond; a sturdy beggar. (L. *vagans*, wandering.)

vagrantism, *n. vay*-gran-tizm, vagrancy.

vagrom, *a. vay*-grom, vagrant.

vague, *a.* vayg, not settled; not definite or precise; uncertain. (L. *vagus*, wandering.)

vaguely, *ad. vayg*-le, in a vague manner.

vagueness, *n. vayg*-ness, state of being vague.

vagus, *n. vay*-gus, the pneumogastric, or tenth cranial nerve [Anat.]. (L., wandering.)

vail, *v.t.* and *i.* vale, to lower; to let fall; to doff the hat or make some similar sign of respect; to yield; to submit. (Fr. *avaler*, to lower.)

vail, *n.* vale, money given as a gratuity to a servant; a tip. (*avail*.)

vain, *a.* vane, empty; worthless; having no substance, value, or importance; fruitless; ineffectual; proud of trifling attainments; conceited; unreal; ostentatious; inconstant; unsatisfying; deceitful; having no efficacy. **in vain,** to no purpose; ineffectually. (L. *vanus*, empty.)

vainglorious, *a.* vane-*glaw*-re-us, vain to excess of one's achievements; elated beyond due measure; boastful; proceeding from vanity.
vaingloriously, *ad.* vane-*glaw*-re-us-le, with vainglory.
vainglory, *n.* vane-*glaw*-re, ostentatious vanity; empty pride; undue elation of mind.
vainly, *ad. vane*-le, in vain; proudly; conceitedly.
vainness, *n. vane*-ness, inefficacy; vanity.
vair, *n.* vare, a kind of fur represented by little bell-shaped pieces, alternately of two tinctures, esp. argent and azure [Her.]. (Fr., from L. *varius*, spotted.)
Vaishnava, *n. vysh*-na-va, a Brahmin who worships Vishnu as the Supreme Being. (Sans.)
Vaisya, *n. vy*-sya, the second, or mercantile and agricultural, caste of India; one belonging to this. (Sans.)
vakeel, *n.* va-*keel*, in India, a native envoy, attorney, or agent. (Urdu, *wakīl*.)
valance, *n. val*-ance, a piece of drapery hanging round the tester and head of a bed, or window-curtains, etc.; a textile or leather hanging border. (Origin uncertain; perhaps from Fr. town, *Valence*.)
vale, *n.* vale, a tract of low ground between hills; a valley. (L. *vallis*, a valley.)
vale, *int. vay*-lee, farewell; good-bye: *n.* a farewell; a farewell message, etc. (L. imper. of *valere*, to be well.)
valediction, *n. val*-e-*dik*-shon, a farewell; a bidding farewell. (L. *valedico*, say farewell.)
valedictorian, *n. val*-e-dik-*taw*-re-an, in American universities the graduating student who gives the farewell address at commencement (usually he or she ranking first in scholarship).
valedictory, *a. val*-e-*dik*-to-re, bidding farewell: *n.* a farewell address.
valence, *n. vay*-lence, the combining power of an element or radical [Chem.]; atomicity. (L.)
valencia, *n.* va-*len*-she-a, a textile composed of wool, cotton or linen, and silk. (Originally from *Valencia*, Spain.)
valenciennes, *n.* va-*len*-se-*enz* (or App.), a kind of fine lace made at Valenciennes, France.
valency, *n. vay*-len-se, valence; a measure of combining capacity [Chem.].
valent, *a. vay*-lent, having valence [Chem.] (esp. in *bivalent*, *trivalent*, etc.).
valentia, *n.* va-*len*-she-a, valencia.
valentine, *n. val*-en-tine, a sweetheart chosen on February 14th, St. Valentine's day; a love-letter or other token, or a caricature, sent on that day.
Valentinianism, *n.* val-en-*tin*-e-a-nizm, the system of Gnosticism taught by the 2nd-cent. Egyptian philosopher, Valentinus.
valentinite, *n.* va-*len*-te-nite, tri-oxide of antimony. (After Basil *Valentine*, 15th-cent. alchemist.)
valerian, *n.* va-*leer*-re-an, a species of *Valeriana* or *Centranthus*, one of which *V. officinalis* is medicinal. **Greek valerian,** the plant Jacob's ladder.
valeric, *a.* va-*leer*-rik, derived from valerian.
valet, *n. val*-ay *or val*-et, a man's body-servant: *v.t.* to perform the duties of a valet for. (Fr.)
valetudinarian, *a. val*-e-tew-de-*nare*-re-an, sickly; seeking to recover health: *n.* an invalid; one of weak or sickly constitution. (L. *valetudinarius*, sickly.)
valetudinarianism, *n. val*-e-tew-de-*nare*-re-a-nizm, a weak state of health.
valetudinary, *a.* and *n. val*-e-*tew*-de-na-re, valetudinarian; a confirmed invalid.
valgus, *n. val*-gus, a form of club-foot in which the foot turns outwards. (L., bandy-legged.)
Valhalla, *n.* val-*hal*-a, the hall of heroes slain in battle [Scand. Myth.]; a place for the tombs or monuments of a nation's great men. (Ice.)
vali, *n.* vah-*lee*, the governor of a Turkish vilayet. (Ar. *wali*, governor.)
valiance, *n. val*-yance, valiancy; bravery; valour.
valiancy, *n. val*-yan-*se*, the quality or condition of being valiant.
valiant, *a. val*-yant, brave; courageous; heroic; intrepid in danger; performed with valour. (Fr. *vaillant*.)
valiantly, *ad. val*-yant-le, bravely; staunchly.
valid, *a. val*-id, having sufficient strength or force; founded in truth; sound; having legal strength or force; executed with the proper formalities. (L. *validus*, from *valeo*, be strong.)
validate, *v.t. val*-e-date, to give validity or legal force to; to ratify.
validation, *n. val*-e-*day*-shon, act of giving validity to; a declaration of validity.
validity, *n.* va-*lid*-e-te, validness; strength or force to convince; justness; soundness; legal strength or force.
validly, *ad. val*-id-le, in a valid manner.
validness, *n.* the quality or state of being valid.
valise, *n.* va-*leece*, a bag or roll for clothes or sundries; a portmanteau. (Fr.)
Valkyrie, *n. val*-ke-re, one of the beautiful and awe-inspiring maidens of Odin, who rode the air over the battlefield and chose those warriors worthy to be slain and led to Valhalla [Scand. Myth.]. (Ice., a chooser of the slain.)
vallar, *a. val*-ar, pertaining to or resembling a rampart. (L. *vallum*, a wall.)
vallation, *n.* va-*lay*-shon, a rampart or entrenchment.
vallecula, *n.* va-*lek*-yew-la (*pl.* **valleculæ**), a groove or furrow [Anat. and Bot.].
valley, *n. val*-e, a hollow or low tract of land between hills; a low extended plain washed by a river; a gutter or internal angle formed by two inclined sides, esp. of a roof [Arch.]. (Fr. *vallée*.)
vallum, *n. val*-um, a rampart. (L.)
valonia, *n.* va-*loh*-ne-a, the acorn cup of *Quercus ægilops* (the **valonia oak**) of the Levant, used by tanners on account of its great content of tannin. (It. *vallonia*.)
valorous, *a. val*-ur-rus, brave; courageous; intrepid.
valorously, *ad.* in a valorous manner.
valour, *n. val*-ur, strength of mind in regard to danger; bravery; courage; intrepidity. (L.)
valse, *n.* and *v.* vawlse, waltz.
valuable, *a. val*-yew-a-bl, having value or worth; having qualities that are valued; worthy; deserving esteem; estimable: *n.pl.* articles, esp. personal property, of value.
valuableness, *n.* quality of being valuable.
valuate, *v.t. val*-yew-ate, to make a valuation of; to evaluate.
valuation, *n. val*-yew-*ay*-shon, estimating value; appraisement; the value set upon a thing.
valuator, *n. val*-yew-ay-tor, a valuer.
*__value,__ *n. val*-yew, the quality that makes wealth; price; worth; high rate; importance; efficacy in producing effects; import; precise signification: *v.t.* to estimate the worth of; to rate at a high price; to have in high esteem; to esteem; to take account of; to reckon at. **face value,** *see* **face.** (L. *valeo*, be strong.)
valued, *a. val*-yewd, estimated; of value; prized.
valueless, *a. val*-yew-less, of no value; worthless.
valuer, *n. val*-yew-er, one who values or sets a value; an appraiser.
valuta, *n.* va-*loo*-ta, the exchange value of the currency of one country in another; current coin or notes of another country. (It., value.)
valval, *a. val*-val, pertaining to a valve [Anat. and Bot.].
valvar, *a. val*-var, valval.
valvate, *a. val*-vat, having or resembling a valve; valvular.
valve, *n.* valv, a lid or cover to an aperture that opening a communication in one direction closes it in the other; a membrane having similar effect [Anat. etc.]; the leaf of a folding-door; either shell of a bivalve [Conch.], or side of a pod [Bot.]; the instrument in a wireless set by means of which wireless waves are converted into audible vibrations. (L. *valva*, a folding-door.)
valved, *a.* valvd, having or composed of valves; controlled by means of a valve.
valviform, *a. val*-ve-form, valve-shaped.
valvlet, *n. valv*-let, a small valve, esp. one of the pieces composing the outer covering of a pericarp [Bot.].
valvular, *a. val*-vew-lar, container valves; pertaining to the valves of the heart [Med.].
valvule, *n. val*-vewl, a valvlet [esp. Anat.].
valvulitis, *n.* val-vew-*ly*-tis, inflammation of a valve esp. of the heart [Med.].
vambrace, *n. vam*-brace, the piece of plate armour protecting the arm below the elbow. (Fr. *avant* before, *bras*, the arm.)
vamoose, *v.i.* and *t.* va-*mooce*, to be off; to decamp; to depart from hurriedly. [Slang, from Sp.]

vamp, *n.* *vamp*, the upper leather of a boot or shoe; a sort of stocking or hose coming only to the ankles; a patch to make an old thing look new; anything patched up; an improvisation [esp. Mus.]: *v.t.* to piece an old thing with a new part; to repair with a vamp; to patch; to improvise in music or acting. (Fr. *avant*, before, *pied*, the foot.)
vamp, *n.* vamp, a woman who indiscriminately uses her attractions to seduce men: *v.t.* and *i.* to allure by the methods of a vamp. (Short for *vampire*.)
vamper, *n.* *vam*-per, one who pieces an old thing with something new.
vampire, *n.* *vam*-pire, a ghost fabled to issue nightly from the grave and suck the blood of sleeping persons; one who preys on others; a blood-sucker; an alluring adventuress, or vamp. **great vampire,** the fruit-eating bat, *Vampirus spectrum*, of S. and Cent. America. **vampire bat,** either of the S. American bats, *Desmodus rufus* or *Diphylia ecaudata*. (Slav.)
vampiric, *a.* vam-*pi*-rik, vampirish.
vampirish, *a.* *vam*-pire-rish, characteristic of or pertaining to vampires.
vampirism, *n.* *vam*-pire-rizm, belief in vampires; the act or practice of blood-sucking or preying on others.
vampish, *a.* *vam*-pish, characteristic of a female vamp; malignantly seductive (of women.)
vamplate, *n.* *vam*-plate, a round metal guard on a spear, to protect the hand. (Fr. *avant*, before, and *plate*.)
van, *n.* van, the front of an army, or the foremost division of a fleet; those in front of any movement, crusade, etc., the leaders. (Fr. *avant*, before.)
van, *n.* van, a fan for winnowing grain; a shovel for testing ore, also, the process of testing on this; a sail of a windmill: *v.t.* to test ore on a van. (L. *vannus*, a fan.)
van, *n.* van, a four-wheeled, generally covered, wagon, for transporting goods; a railway carriage or compartment for the guard, brake, and luggage: *v.t.* to convey in a van. (*caravan*.)
vanadate, *n.* *van*-a-date, a salt of vanadic acid.
vanadiate, *n.* va-*nay*-de-at, vanadate.
vanadic, *a.* va-*nad*-ik, obtained from vanadium.
vanadinite, *n.* va-*nad*-e-nite, native vanadate of lead.
vanadious, *a.* va-*nay*-de-us, containing vanadium, esp. in its lower valency [Chem.].
vanadium, *n.* va-*nay*-de-um, a hard, white metallic element, used esp. as a strengthening component in steel alloys. (*Vanadis*, a name of the Scandinavian goddess Freyja.)
vanadous, *a.* *van*-a-dus, vanadious.
vancourier, *n.* van-*ku*-re-er, an avant-courier; a precursor.
Vandal, *n.* *van*-dal, one of a fierce Germanic tribe that plundered Gaul and N. Africa and, in the 5th cent. A.D., sacked Rome, maliciously mutilating and destroying works of art; any one of like spirit or habit: *a.* (*l.c.*) vandalic.
vandalic, *a.* van-*dal*-ik, pertaining to or characteristic of the Vandals; rude; barbarous; deliberately destructive.
vandalism, *n.* *van*-da-lizm, the spirit that would recklessly destroy monuments of art, etc.; such conduct.
vandalistic, *a.* van-da-*lis*-tik, given to vandalism; vandalic.
vandyke, *n.* van-*dike*, one of the points forming a border in lace or ribbon; a covering for the neck, with indentations and points: *a.* in the style of costume, etc., depicted by Van Dyck: *v.t.* to ornament by forming indentations. **vandyke beard,** a pointed beard. **vandyke brown,** a deep brown or reddish-yellow colour. (Sir Anthony *Van Dyck*, the 17th-cent. Anglo-Flemish painter.)
vane, *n.* vane, a weathercock; an arrow or other rotatory device at the top of a spire or mast to show which way the wind blows; the van or blade of a windmill or propeller; the part of a feather on the sides of the shaft. (A.S. *fan*.)
Vanessa, *n.* va-*ness*-a, a genus of butterflies which includes the red admiral; a butterfly belonging to this genus.
vang, *n.* vang, either of a pair of guy ropes for the peak of a gaff [Naut.].
vanguard, *n.* *van*-gard, the troops who march in front of an army; the forefront.
Vanilla, *n.* va-*nil*-a, a genus of orchids of tropical America, the capsule of one species of which, *V. planifolia*, is remarkable for its fragrant odour and is used in sweetmeats, ices, etc. (Sp.)
vanillic, *a.* va-*nil*-ik, denominating an odourless acid present in some varieties of vanilla.
vanillism, *n.* va-*nil*-izm, dermatitis caused by handling vanilla [Path.].
vanish, *v.i.* *van*-ish, to disappear; to pass from a visible to an invisible state, or beyond the limit of vision; to pass way; to become zero [Math.]. **vanishing fraction,** a fraction resolvable into a particular value of the variable which enters it. **vanishing line,** the intersection of the parallel of any original plane and the picture [Persp.]. **vanishing point,** the point to which all parallel lines in the same plane tend in the representation [Persp.]. (L. *vanus*, empty.)
vanity, *n.* *van*-e-te, that which is vain, futile, or useless; the quality or condition of being vain or worthless; inanity; fruitless endeavour; empty pleasure; idle show; ostentation; empty pride from over-weening self-conceit. **vanity bag** or **case,** a small bag or case for powder-puff, mirror, cosmetic, etc.
vanman, *n.* *van*-m'n, one in charge of a van.
vanner, *n.* *van*-er, a horse that works in a van; a van or ore separator.
vanning, *n.* *van*-ing, the act or process of testing ore on a van or shovel.
vanquish, *v.t.* *vang*-kwish, to subdue in battle, as an enemy; to defeat in any contest; to refute in argument; to overpower. (Fr. *vaincre*, from L. *vinco*, conquer.)
vanquishable, *a.* *vang*-kwish-a-bl, that may be vanquished.
vanquisher, *n.* *vang*-kwish-er, a conqueror; a victor.
vansire, *n.* *van*-sire, a mungoose-like animal of S. Africa and Madagascar.
vantage, *n.* *vahn*-taj, state in which one has better means of action or defence than another, and is so at an advantage; the first point after deuce in tennis or lawn tennis. **vantage ground,** the place or condition which gives one an advantage over another. (Fr. *avantage*.)
vanward, *a.* and *ad.* *van*-ward, in or towards the van; to the front.
vapid, *a.* *vap*-id, having lost life and spirit; dead; flat, spiritless. (L. *vapidus*, insipid.)
vapidity, *n.* va-*pid*-e-te, vapidness; insipidity.
vapidly, *ad.* *vap*-id-le, in a vapid manner.
vapidness, *n.* *vap*-id-ness, state of being vapid; want of life or spirit; deadness; flatness.
vaporability, *n.* *vay*-po-ra-*bil*-e-te, capacity of being converted into vapour.
vaporable, *a.* *vay*-po-ra-bl, capable of being converted into vapour.
vaporific, *a.* *vay*-po-*rif*-ik, forming into vapour; converted into steam, or expelling in a volatile form, as fluids. (L. *vapor*, and *facio*, make.)
vaporimeter, *n.* *vay*-po-*rim*-e-ter, an instrument for measuring the pressure of a vapour.
vaporizable, *a.* *vay*-po-*ry*-za-bl, capable of being converted into vapour.
vaporization, *n.* *vay*-po-ry-*zay*-shon, the process of vaporizing; artificial formation of vapour.
vaporize, *v.t.* *vay*-po-rize, to convert into vapour by the application of heat: *v.i.* to pass off in vapour; [Fig.] to speak or write in high-flown phraseology.
vaporizer, *n.* *vay*-po-ry-zer, a device for effecting vaporization; a vessel for storing and evaporating liquid oxygen [Av.].
vaporosity, *n.* *vay*-po-*ros*-e-te, quality or condition of being vaporous.
vaporous, *a.* *vay*-po-rus, like vapour; full of vapours or exhalations; vain; unreal; windy; flatulent.
vapour, *n.* *vay*-pur, the state into which solids and liquids are converted by heat; water floating in the atmosphere as mist, cloud, or fog, and impairing its transparency; mental fume; vain imagination; unreal fancy; something unsubstantial and transitory: *pl.* depression; dejection; hallucinatory nervous debility or derangement: *v.i.* to pass off in fumes; to evaporate; to brag or vaporize [Fig.]. **vapour bath,** the application of medicinal vapour to the body in an enclosed space; an apparatus for heating bodies by steam. (L. *vapor*.)

vapourer, *n.* *vay*-po-rer, a boaster or braggart; the moth *Orgyia antiqua.*
vapouringly, *ad.* *vay*-po-ring-le, in a boasting manner.
vapourish, *a.* *vay*-po-rish, full of vapours; hypochondriac; splenetic.
vapoury, *a.* *vay*-po-re, full of vapours; hypochondriac.
vapulation, *n.* *vap*-yew-*lay*-shon, a flogging. (L.)
vaquero, *n.* va-*kare*-roh, a herdsman; a Spanish-American cowboy. (Sp.)
varan, *n.* *va*-ran, a varanian.
Varangian, *n.* va-*ran*-je-an, one of a Norse tribe which founded an empire in Russia in the 9th cent.; one of the Scandinavian guard of the Byzantine emperors at Constantinople.
varanian, *a.* va-*ray*-ne-an, pertaining to or characteristic of the monitor lizards, or Varanidæ: *n.* a monitor lizard.
varec, *n.* *va*-rek, seaweed; kelp; impure sodium carbonate prepared from this. (Fr. *varech.*)
vari, *n.* *vah*-re, a species of ruffed lemur found in Madagascar. (Malagasy, *varikandana.*)
variability, *n.* *vare*-re-a-*bil*-e-te, the quality of being variable; variableness.
variable, *a.* *vare*-re-a-bl, that may vary or alter; changeable; susceptible of change; mutable; fickle; subject to continual increase or decrease [Math.]: *n.* that which is variable, as a quantity [Math.] or a variable star [Astron.]. **variable star,** one the apparent magnitude of which varies periodically; a Cepheid. **the variables,** the region about where the north-east and south-east trade-winds meet [Naut.]. (L. *varius.*)
variableness, *n.* tendency to vary; susceptibility to change; inconstancy.
variably, *ad.* *vare*-re-a-ble, changeably.
variance, *n.* *vare*-re-ance, difference that produces dispute or controversy; disagreement; discord; a difference between a declaration and a writ, or the deed on which it is grounded [Law]. **at variance,** in disagreement; in a state of dissension or of enmity.
variant, *a.* *vare*-re-ant, different; diverse; varying: *n.* a different version; a modified form; a varying quantity.
variation, *n.* vare-re-*ay*-shon, a partial change in the form, position, state, or qualities of the same thing; alteration; difference; change from one to another; the extent to which a thing varies; inflexion [Gram.]; deviation; an inequality of the moon's motion depending on the angular distance of the moon from the sun [Astron.]; deviation from type [Biol.]; the deviation of the magnetic needle from the true north point, or its declination [Geog. and Navigation]; elaboration and alteration in the development of a melody [Mus.].
variational, *a.* *vare*-re-*ay*-shon-al, concerned with or characterized by variation.
variative, *a.* *vare*-re-a-tiv, pertaining to variation; variational.
variator, *n.* *vare*-re-ay-tor, one who or an instrument which produces, or compensates for, variations.
varicated, *a.* *va*-re-kay-ted, having ribs or varices (esp. of shells) [Zool.]
varicella, *n.* *va*-re-*sel*-la, chickenpox [Med.]. (*variola.*)
varices, *n.pl.* *va*-re-seez, *pl.* of *varix.*
variciform, *a.* va-*ris*-e-form, resembling a varix [Anat. and Zool.].
varicocele, *n.* *va*-re-ko-seel, a varicose enlargement of the spermatic veins. (L. *varix,* and Gr. *kele,* a tumour.)
varicoloured, *a.* *vare*-re-kul-erd, of many colours; parti-coloured; diversified.
varicose, *a.* *va*-re-kohs, abnormally enlarged or permanently dilated (esp. of veins); afflicted with varix [Med.]. (L. *varicosus.*)
varicosity, *n.* va-re-*kos*-e-te, state of being varicose; a varicose part.
varied, *a.* *vare*-rid, altered; partially changed; various; diverse.
variegate, *v.t.* *vare*-re-gate, to diversify in appearance; to mark with patches of different colours; to dapple. (L. *varius,* and *agere,* make.)
variegation, *n.* *vare*-re-*gay*-shon, act of variegating; state of being variegated; diversity of colours.
varier, *n.* *vare*-re-er, one who varies.
varietal, *a.* va-*ry*-e-tal, pertaining to a variety as distinguished from a species.
variety, *n.* va-*ry*-e-te, a difference; dissimilitude; diversity; many and different kinds; a group subordinate to a species, from which it differs in certain minor but permanent and transmitted features; a different sort. **variety entertainment,** a stage show embracing several different turns of acting, music, dancing, acrobatics, illusion, etc. **variety theatre,** one designed for variety entertainments; a music-hall. (Fr. *variété.*)
variform, *a.* *vare*-re-form, having different shapes or forms.
variocoupler, *n.* *vare*-re-o-*kup*-ler, an inductive coupler, a form of variometer [Elect. and Wire.].
variola, *n.* va-*ry*-o-la, smallpox [Med.]. (Fr., from L. *varius.*)
variolar, *a.* va-*ry*-o-lar, variolous.
variolate, *v.t.* *vare*-re-o-late, to infect with smallpox; to subject to variolation; *a.* having small pustules.
variolation, *n.* vare-re-o-*lay*-shon, inoculation with the virus of smallpox.
variole, *n.* *vare*-re-ole, a small pit-like depression, resembling a smallpox mark [Bot. and Zool.].
variolite, *n.* va-*ry*-o-lite, any basic igneous rock containing small whitish spherules of fibrous felspar. (L. *varius,* and Gr. *lithos,* a stone.)
variolitic, *a.* *vare*-re-o-*lit*-ik, resembling variolite; spherulitic [Geol.].
variolization, *n.* *vare*-re-o-ly-*zay*-shon, variolation.
varioloid, *n.* va-*ry*-o-loyd, a mild form of smallpox communicable to vaccinated persons and previous smallpox cases: *a.* resembling smallpox. (L. *varius,* and Gr. *eidos,* like.)
variolous, *a.* va-*ry*-o-lus, pertaining to, resembling, or suffering from smallpox.
variometer, *n.* *vare*-re-*om*-e-ter, an instrument for varying inductance [Elect.], used esp. for tuning an aerial to different wave-lengths [Wire.].
variorum, *n.* and *a.* *vare*-re-*aw*-rum, designating and descriptive of editions of the classics containing variant readings with notes by various commentators. (L., of various persons.)
various, *a.* *vare*-re-us, different; manifold; diverse; changeable; uncertain; unlike each other; diversified.
variously, *ad.* in different ways.
varix, *n.* *vare*-riks (*pl.* **varices,** *va*-re-*seez*), a permanently enlarged and tortuous vein; a varicose vein; a rib crossing the whorls of certain univalve shells [Conch.]. (L.)
varlet, *n.* *var*-let, anciently, a knight's attendant, a page; now, a low fellow, a scoundrel, a rascal. (Fr.)
varletry, *n.* *var*-let-re, the rabble; the crowd.
varmint, *n.* *var*-mint, a low, objectionable fellow, a rascal; collectively, a rabble: *a.* disreputable; cunning. (Dial. form of *vermin.*)
varnish, *n.* *var*-nish, a transparent resinous liquid laid on work by painters and others, to give a smooth, hard, and glossy surface; an artificial covering to give a fair appearance to any act or conduct; gloss: *v.t.* to cover with a varnish; to give a fair external appearance to; to gloss; to palliate. **varnishing day,** a day before the opening of a picture exhibition on which artists give their exhibits the final touches. (Fr., from L. *vitrum,* glass.)
varnisher, *n.* *var*-nish-er, one whose occupation is to varnish; one who disguises or palliates.
varsity, *n.* and *a.* *var*-se-te, university [Slang].
varsovienne, *n.* var-so-*vyen*, a dance resembling the polka or Polish mazurka; music suitable for this. (Fr. *Varsovie,* Warsaw.)
Varuna, *n.* va-*roo*-na, the Hindu Uranus, the serene unchangeable deity concentrating in himself the power and majesty of all the other gods [Hind. Myth.]. (Sans. *vri,* to surround or cover.)
varus, *n.* *vare*-rus, acne [Med.]. (L., a pimple.)
varus, *a.* *vare*-rus, turned inward [Path.]: *n.* a deformity in which the feet are turned inward; a pigeon-toed person. (L., knock-kneed.)
varvel, *n.* *var*-vel, vervel.
varvicite, *n.* *var*-ve-site, an oxide of manganese found in Warwickshire. (Late L. *Varvicia,* Warwickshire.)
vary, *v.t.* *vare*-re, to alter in form, appearance, substance or position; to change to something else; to make of different kinds; to diversify; to variegate. *v.i.* to alter or be altered in any manner; to differ; to become different; to deviate; to change in succession; to disagree; to be at variance. (L. *varius,* diverse, different.)

vasal, *a.* *vay*-sal, relating to a vessel [Anat. and Bot.], esp. a blood-vessel. (L. *vas*, a vessel.)
vascular, *a.* *vas*-kew-lar, pertaining to the functional, and specially the circulatory, vessels of animals or plants. **vascular ray,** *a.* medullary ray [Bot.].
vascularity, *n.* *vas*-kew-*la*-re-te, quality or state of being vascular.
vascularize, *v.t.* *vas*-kew-la-rize, to render vascular.
vasculose, *n.* *vas*-kew-lohs, the chief constituent of the vascular tissue of plants.
vasculum, *n.* *vas*-kew-lum (*pl.* **vascula**), a botanist's collecting box; an ascidium [Bot.].
vase, *n.* vahz *or* vawz (in U.S.A., vace *or* vaze), a vessel, usually tall rather than wide, ornamental, and decorative; an ornament of sculpture, placed on socles or pedestals, representing vessels of the ancients, as incense-pots and flower-pots. (L. *vasum*, or *vas*.)
vaseline, *n.* *vas*-e-leen, a registered trade-name of an unctuous pharmaceutical jelly obtained from petroleum. (Ger. *Wasser*, water, and Gr. *elaion*, oil.)
vasifactive, *a.* vay-ze-*fak*-tiv, forming new blood-vessels [Biol.].
vasiform, *a.* *vay*-ze-form, having the form of a duct; tubular [Anat.].
vaso-, *vay*-zoh, combining form used with reference to the vascular system [Anat.], as in **vasoconstriction,** a state of contraction of the blood-vessels, and **vasodilatation,** a state of dilation of the same. (L. *vas*, a vessel.)
vasomotor, *a.* vay-zoh-*moh*-tor, producing constriction or dilatation of a blood-vessel; acting upon the vasomotor nerves or centres: *n.* a vasomotor nerve.
vassal, *n.* *vas*-sal, a feudatory; one who holds lands of a superior, and who vows fidelity and homage to him; a retainer; a bondman; one owing allegiance: *a.* servile; dependent. (Fr., from Celt. *gwas*, a servant.)
vassalage, *n.* *vas*-al-aj, state or quality of being a vassal; governmental servitude or subjection; vassalry.
vassalry, *n.* *vas*-al-re, vassals collectively; the system of vassalage.
vast, *a.* vahst, being of great extent; very spacious or large; huge in bulk and extent; very great in numbers or amount; very great in force or importance. (L. *vastus*, unoccupied, waste.)
vastidity, *n.* vas-*tid*-e-te, vastitude.
vastitude, *n.* *vah*-ste-tewd, vastness.
vastly, *ad.* *vahst*-le, to a great extent.
vastness, *n.* immensity; immense bulk, magnitude, amount, or importance.
vasty, *a.* *vah*-ste, of a great extent; very spacious.
vat, *n.* vat, a tub, tank, or cistern for holding liquors; a large box or cistern in which substances in course of manufacture are laid for treatment, as hides for steeping in tan; a square, hollow place on the back of a calcining furnace where tin ore is laid to dry [Metal.]. (A.S. *fæt*, akin to Ger. *Fass*, a cask.)
vatic, *a.* *vat*-ik, prophetic. (L. *vates*, a prophet.)
Vatican, *n.* *vat*-e-kan, in Rome, a group of buildings including the Pope's palace on the Vatican Hill which, with St. Peter's and certain extraterritorial properties, form, since 1929, the Vatican State; the papal power.
Vaticanism, *n.* *vat*-e-kan-izm, the doctrine of absolute papal infallibility.
Vaticanist, *n.* *vat*-e-kan-ist, an adherent of Vaticanism: *a.* ultramontanist.
vaticide, *n.* *vat*-e-side, the murder or murderer of a prophet. (L. *vates*, a prophet, *cædo*, kill.)
vaticinal, *a.* va-*tis*-e-nal, containing prophecy.
vaticinate, *v.i.* and *t.* va-*tis*-e-nate, to prophesy; to foretell. (L. *vates*, and *cano*, sing.)
vaticination, *n.* vat-e-se-*nay*-shon, prediction; prophecy.
vaticinator, *n.* va-*tis*-e-nay-tor, a prophet.
vaticinatory, *a.* va-*tis*-e-na-to-re, prophetic.
vaticinatress, *n.* va-*tis*-e-*nay*-tress, a female vaticinator, a prophetess.
vaudeville, *n.* *voh*-de-vil, in French poetry, a species of light song, generally of a comic or satirical nature; a dramatic piece, whose dialogue is intermingled with light or comic songs; a light variety entertainment. (Fr. *Vau* (Val) *de Vire*, in Normandy, where it originated.)
Vaudois, *n.* voh-*dwah*, a native or the natives of the Swiss canton of Vaud; the dialect there spoken.
Vaudois, *n.pl.* voh-*dwah*, the Waldenses. (Fr., from L. form of *Waldo*, name of their founder.)
vault, *n.* vawlt, an arched roof of a circular, elliptical, or Gothic form; a series of arches; an arched chamber, esp. underground; a cellar; a cave or cavern; a chamber for internment of the dead; a dome-shaped part, as of the cranium [Anat.]; the canopy of heaven: *v.t.* to arch; to form or cover with a vault. **vaulting shaft,** a pillar from which the ribs of a Gothic vault spring [Arch.].
vault, *n.* vawlt, a leap made by resting the hands or hand on the object jumped over: *v.i.* to leap; to bound; to spring; to exhibit feats of tumbling or leaping. **vaulting horse,** a wooden horse used for vaulting on or over. (Fr. *voute*, from L. *volutum*, roll.)
vaultage, *n.* *vawl*-taj, vaulted work; an arched cellar.
vaulted, *a.* *vawl*-ted, arched; concave; covered with or built like a vault; arched like the roof of the mouth [Bot.].
vaulter, *n.* *vawl*-ter, one who vaults; an acrobat.
vaulty, *a.* *vawl*-te, resembling a vault; concave.
vaunt, *n.* vawnt, a vain display of what one is, has, or has done; ostentation from vanity: *v.i.* and *t.* to boast; to brag; to make a vain display of. (Fr. *vanter*, from L. *vanus*, vain.)
vaunter, *n.* *vawn*-ter, one who vaunts; a vain conceited boaster.
vauntingly, *ad.* *vawn*-ting-le, boastfully.
vauntlay, *n.* *vawnt*-lay, (in mediæval hunting) a release of certain hounds at the quarry in advance of others; the hounds so released. (Fr. *avant*, and *relay*.)
vauquelinite, *n.* *voke*-le-nite, chromate of copper and lead, of various shades of green. (Fr.)
vavasory, *n.* *vav*-a-so-re, the tenure of the fee, or the lands held by a vavasour.
vavasour, *n.* *vav*-a-sur, a holder of lands under the feudal system ranking next in dignity below a baron. (*vassal*.)
Veadar, *n.* *vee*-a-dar *or* *vay*-a-dar, an intercalary month of the Jewish ecclesiastical year inserted every third year after the month Adar.
veal, *n.* veel, the flesh of a calf killed for the table. (O.Fr. *veēl*, a calf.)
vector, *n.* *vek*-tor, a line drawn from any point to the centre of a circle or focus of an ellipse; a straight line which by its length and direction can be taken to specify some physical quantity capable of being so expressed [Math.]; an organic or insect carrier of disease [Path.]. **radius vector,** *see* **radius.** (L.)
vectorial, *a.* vek-*taw*-re-al, pertaining to a vector [Math.].
Veda, *n.* *vay*-dah, the most ancient of the Hindu religious writings, collected into four books and constituting the basis of Brahminical faith. (Sans. *vid*, know.)
Vedaic, *a.* and *n.* ve-*day*-ik, Vedic.
Vedanga, *n.* vay-*dang*-ga, any one of six commentaries on the Vedas. (Sans., limb of the Veda.)
Vedanta, *n.* vay-*dan*-ta, the system of Hindu philosophy based on the Vedas.
Veddah, *n.* *ved*-dah, a member of the aboriginal people of Ceylon. (Sinhalese, a hunter.)
vedette, *n.* ve-*det*, a mounted sentinel employed in reconnoitring and scouting [Mil.]; a small vessel used for similar purposes [Nav.]. (L. *videre*, see.)
Vedic, *a.* *vay*-dik, in or pertaining to the Vedas: *n.* the early Sanskrit in which the Vedas were written.
Vedism, *n.* *vay*-dizm, the doctrines and principles contained in the Vedas.
veer, *v.i.* veer, to turn; to change direction: *v.t.* to turn; to direct to a course away from the wind; to wear or gybe; to move in the same direction as the sun (of the wind); to pay out chain [Naut.]. **veer and haul,** to slacken and pull tight alternately. [Naut.]. **veer away,** to slacken and let run [Naut.]. **veer out,** to suffer to run, or to let out to a greater length [Naut.]. (Fr. *virer*, turn about.)
veeringly, *ad.* *veer*-ring-le, in a changing state or manner; shiftingly.
veery, *n.* *veer*-re, the tawny-brown thrush of eastern North America.
vega, *n.* *vay*-ga, an expanse of flat fertile land, esp. in Spanish America; a meadow. (Sp.)
vegetability, *n.* *vej*-e-ta-*bil*-e-te, the quality of being vegetable; vegetable character.

vegetable, *n.* *vej*-e-ta-bl, a plant, esp. one that is used in cookery, or for feeding cattle and sheep : *a.* pertaining to or consisting of plants; having the nature of plants. **vegetable ivory,** a close-grained and hard ivory-like substance, the product of several species of palms. **vegetable kingdom,** the class of living things comprising the plants. **vegetable marrow,** the fruit of a species of gourd, *Cucurbita Pepo ovifera*, used for culinary purposes. **vegetable sheep,** an Australasian woolly plant of the genus *Raoulia* which, from a distance, resembles a sheep. (Low L. *vegetabilis*, full of life.)

vegetal, *a.* *vej*-e-tal, pertaining to vegetables; of a vegetable nature : *n.* a plant; a vegetable.

vegetaline, *n.* *vej*-e-ta-leen, a name given to artificial vegetable ivory.

vegetality, *n.* *vej*-e-*tal*-e-te, the quality of being vegetable; vegetability.

vegetarian, *a.* *vej*-e-*tare*-re-an, pertaining to vegetarianism : *n.* one who regulates his diet on the principles of vegetarianism.

vegetarianism, *n.* *vej*-e-*tare*-re-a-nizm, the theory and practice, esp. on ethical grounds, of living solely on food the preparation of which has not entailed slaughter and consequently consists mainly of vegetables, milk, butter, and the like.

vegetate, *v.i.* *vej*-e-tate, to grow, as plants; to pullulate; to live a do-nothing life; to stagnate. (L. *vegeo*, be lively.)

vegetation, *n.* *vej*-e-*tay*-shon, vegetable growth; plants in general; the act or process of vegetating; a fungus-like growth of pathological tissue [Med.].

vegetative, *a.* *vej*-e-ta-tiv, growing, or having the power of growing, as plants; having the power to produce growth in plants.

vegetativeness, *n.* quality of being vegetative.

vegetive, *a.* *vej*-e-tiv, vegetative.

vehemence, *n.* *vee*-e-mence, the quality of being vehement; violence; great force; violent ardour; animated fervour. (L. *vehemens*.)

vehemency, *n.* vee-e-men-se, vehemence.

vehement, *a.* *vee*-e-ment, acting with great force or violence; impetuous; very eager or urgent. (L. *veho*, to carry.)

vehemently, *ad.* with vehemence.

vehicle, *n.* *vee*-e-kl, a conveyance moving on wheels or runners; a substance in which medicine is taken; a medium with which pigments are applied; any person or thing instrumental in the transmission or conveyance of thought, energy, emotion, etc. (L. *vehiculum*, from *vehere*, carry.)

vehicular, *a.* ve-*hik*-yew-lar, pertaining to or of the nature of a vehicle.

vehiculatory, *a.* ve-*hik*-yew-la-to-re, vehicular.

Vehmgericht, *n.* *fame*-ge-rikht, a late mediæval German secret tribunal for the enforcement of justice chiefly against misgovernment by a pillaging nobility. (Ger. *Vehm*, punishment, *Gericht*, court.)

Vehmic, *a.* *fay*-mik, pertaining to or resembling the Vehmgericht.

veil, *n.* vale, something to intercept the view and hide an object; a curtain; a network covering for the face; a disguise : *v.t.* to cover with a veil; to conceal; to hide. **take the veil,** to become a nun. (L. *velum*, a covering.)

veiling, *n.* *vale*-ing, material for making veils.

veilless, *a.* *vale*-less, without a veil.

veilleuse, *n.* (App.), a shaded night-light of decorative design. (Fr.)

vein, *n.* vane, a vessel in animal bodies receiving blood from the extremities of the arteries and returning it to the heart; a rib in an insect's wing; a tube, or assemblage of tubes through which sap is transmitted along the leaves [Bot.]; a seam of any substance intersecting a rock [Geol.]; a streak or wave of different colour appearing in wood or in marble, etc.; tendency or turn of mind; particular disposition, temper, or cast of genius; humour; strain : *v.t.* to fill, cover, or streak with veins. (L. *vena*, a blood vessel.)

veinage, *n.* *vane*-aj, the system of veins; venation [Bot. and Entom.].

veined, *a.* *vaind*, full of veins; streaked; having vessels branching over the surface of leaves [Bot.].

veining, *n.* *vane*-ing, the forming of veins; ramification, as of veins; a kind of needlework in which the threads of a piece of muslin are wrought to a pattern; a stripe in cloth formed by a vacancy in the warp [Weaving]; tendency or turn of mind.

veinless, *a.* *vane*-less, having no veins [Bot.].

veinlet, *n.* *vane*-let, a small vein; a branch of a vein [Bot.].

veinous, *a.* *vane*-us, veined; consisting of veins; venous.

veinstone, *n.* *vane*-stone, the useless material enclosing ore in veins; gangue.

veinule, *n.* *vane*-yewl, a minute vein.

veiny, *a.* *vane*-e, full of veins; veined.

velamen, *n.* ve-*lay*-men (*pl.* **velamina,** ve-*lay*-me-na), a membranous covering [Anat.]; the epidermis of the aerial roots of certain orchids [Bot.]. (L.)

velamentous, *a.* vel-a-*men*-tus, pertaining to or resembling a velamen.

velamentum, *n.* vel-a-*men*-tum (*pl.* **velamenta**), a velamen [Anat.].

velar, *a.* *vee*-lar, formed with the back of the tongue on or near the velum (of sounds, as *k*, *ng*, *ah*, etc.) [Phonetics] : *n.* a sound so formed.

velarium, *n.* ve-*lare*-re-um, a large awning, as used in ancient open-air theatres; a velum [Anat.].

velate, *a.* *vee*-lat, having a velum or veil [Zool. and Bot.].

velation, *n.* ve-*lay*-shon, the formation of a velum.

veldt, *n.* velt, a wide expanse of open grassland or prairie in S. Africa. (Dut.)

veliferous, *a.* ve-*lif*-er-rus, veligerous.

veligerous, *a.* ve-*lij*-er-rus, bearing a velum [Zool.].

velites, *n.pl.* vee-*ly*-teez, lightly armed soldiers of ancient Rome.

velleity, *n.* ve-*lee*-e-te, the lowest degree of desire without energy to qualify it; feeble inclination. (Fr. *velléité*, from L. *velle*, be willing.)

vellicate, *v.t.* and *i.* *vel*-e-kate, to twitch or cause to twitch convulsively. (L. *vellicatum*, pluck, pull.)

vellication, *n.* vel-e-*kay*-shon, the act of twitching or of causing to twitch; a twitching or convulsive motion of a muscular fibre.

vellon, *n.* *vel*-on, billon, esp. as formerly used for the Spanish copper coinage. (Sp.)

vellum, *n.* *vel*-um, a fine kind of parchment or skin, rendered clear and white for writing. (Fr. *vélin*, from L. *vitulus*, a calf.)

vellumy, *a.* *vel*-um-e, resembling vellum.

velo, *n.* *vee*-loh, a velocity of one foot per second [Mech.]. (From *velocity*.)

veloce, *ad.* ve-*loh*-che, very quickly [Mus.]. (It.)

velocimeter, *n.* vel-o-*sim*-e-ter, an instrument for measuring velocity.

velocipede, *n.* ve-*los*-e-peed, an early form of bicycle, the rider sitting astride a beam connecting the two wheels and propelling the vehicle by his feet touching the ground or by a treadle on the axis of the front wheel; a boneshaker; a dandy-horse. (L. *velox*, swift, *pes*, foot.)

velocipedist, *n.* ve-*los*-e-pee-dist, a rider on a velocipede.

velocity, *n.* ve-*los*-e-te, speed; swiftness; rapidity; rate of motion. **accelerated velocity,** velocity the rate of which regularly increases with the distance. **average velocity,** the total distance covered divided by the time taken. **uniform velocity,** velocity that is maintained at an equal rate, equal distances being passed over in equal times.

velour or **velours,** *n.* vel-*oor*, velure; a plush-like material used for hats.

veloutine, *n.* vel-oo-*teen*, a corded woollen dress material resembling velveteen or corduroy.

velum, *n.* *vee*-lum (*pl.* **vela**), a veil; a partition; a membranous covering, esp. the soft plate [Anat.].

velure, *n.* vel-*oor*, velvet; a velvety woollen dress material; a pad for smoothing silk hats.

velutinous, *a.* ve-*lew*-te-nus, velvety [Bot. and Entom.].

velvet, *n.* *vel*-vet, a rich silk stuff, covered with a close, short, fine soft nap; a growth resembling velvet, esp. the furry skin on the sprouting antlers of deer; winnings, profits [Slang] : *a.* made of velvet; soft and delicate, like velvet. **black velvet** champagne and stout mixed [Slang]. **cotton velvet,** an imitation of velvet. **velvet duck** or **scoter,** the seabird *Œdemia fusca*. **velvet grass,** the tall flowering grass, *Holcus lanatus*. **velvet pile,** a kind of carpet, with a long soft nap. **velvet plant,** the common mullein. **velvet tamarind,** the fruit of the tropical African tree *Dialium*

guineënse. **on velvet,** in easy circumstances, in luck [Coll.]. (L. *villus*, shaggy hair.)
velveted, *a. vel*-ve-ted, velvety.
velveteen, *n.* vel-ve-*teen*, imitation velvet in cotton: *pl.* corduroy trousers.
velveting, *n. vel*-ve-ting, velvet material; the fine nap of velvet.
velvety, *a. vel*-ve-te, made of or like velvet; of the nature of velvet; soft; smooth.
vena, *n. vee*-na (*pl.* **venæ,** *vee*-nee), a vein [Anat.]. (L.)
venal, *a. vee*-nal, relating to veins; venous. (L. *vena*, a vein.)
venal, *a. vee*-nal, mercenary; bribable; willing to sacrifice honour for gain; sordid. (L. *venalis*, for sale.)
venality, *n.* ve-*nal*-e-te, the quality or condition of being mercenary; prostitution of talents, offices, or services for money or reward.
venally, *ad. vee*-na-le, corruptly; mercenarily.
venatic, *a.* ve-*nat*-ik, pertaining to, used in, or addicted to hunting. (L. *venaticus*, hunting.)
venation, *n.* ve-*nay*-shon, the manner in which veins are arranged [Bot. and Entom.]. (L. *vena.*)
vend, *v.t.* vend, to sell; to offer for sale (esp. of wares or merchandise, etc.). (L. *vendo.*)
vendace, *n. ven*-dace, a fish of the salmon family, *Coregonus vandesius*, found in a few English and Scottish lakes.
vendee, *n.* ven-*dee*, the person to whom a thing is sold.
vender, *n. ven*-der, a vendor; a peddler.
vendetta, *n.* ven-*det*-a, the practice in Corsica of taking private vengeance on one who slays a relation; a blood feud. (It., vengeance.)
vendibility, *n. ven*-de-*bil*-e-te, vendibleness.
vendible, *a. ven*-de-bl, saleable; that may be sold: *n.* something to be sold or offered for sale.
vendibleness, *n. ven*-de-bl-ness, the state or quality of being vendible.
vendibly, *ad. ven*-de-ble, in a saleable manner.
vendition, *n.* ven-*dish*-on, the act of selling; sale.
vendor, *n. ven*-dor, one who sells.
vendue, *n. ven*-dew, a public sale of anything by an auctioneer.
veneer, *n.* ve-*neer*, a thin slice of a fine or superior wood for overlaying a coarser or inferior wood: *v.t.* to inlay veneer over inferior wood; to gild over; to conceal beneath a deceptive surface. (Ger. *furniren.*)
veneering, *n.* ve-*neer*-ring, art of overlaying an inferior with thin sections of superior wood; material used as a veneer; veneer facing.
veneficious, *a.* ven-e-*fish*-us, practising poisoning; using poison. (L. *venenum*, poison.)
venenation, *n. ven*-en-*ay*-shon, the condition due to poisoning [Path.]; the act of poisoning.
venepuncture, *n. ven*-e-punk-tewr, puncture of a vein, esp. with a hypodermic needle. (L. *vena*, a vein, and *puncture.*)
venerability, *n. ven*-er-ra-*bil*-e-te, venerableness.
venerable, *a. ven*-er-ra-bl, worthy of veneration, reverence, or honour; worthy of respect, esp. by reason of age; rendered sacred by religious associations; used (*cap.*) as a title in addressing an Anglican archdeacon, and [Rom. Cath.] applied to one in the first stage of canonization.
venerableness, *n. ven*-er-ra-bl-ness, the state or quality of being venerable.
venerably, *ad.* in a manner to excite reverence or respect.
venerate, *v.t. ven*-er-rate, to regard with respect and reverence; to reverence; to revere. (L. *veneratus*, reverenced.)
veneration, *n. ven*-er-*ray*-shon, the highest degree of respect and reverence; respect mingled with some degree of awe.
venerator, *n. ven*-er-ray-tor, one who reverences.
venereal, *a.* ve-*neer*-er-al, pertaining to or proceeding from sexual intercourse; adapted to excite venereal desire; aphrodisiac; curing venereal disease. (L. *venerus*, of or belonging to Venus.)
venereology, *n.* ve-*neer*-re-*ol*-o-je, the branch of science treating of venereal disease [Med.].
venery, *n. ven*-er-re, the pursuit of sexual enjoyment; sexual indulgence.
venery, *n. ven*-er-re, the act or exercise of hunting; the sports of the chase. (L. *venari*, hunt.)
venesection, *n. ven*-e-*sek*-shon, the act of opening a vein; blood-letting; phlebotomy. (L. *vena*, a vein, *seco*, cut.)
Venetian, *a.* ve-*nee*-shan, pertaining to or produced in Venice: *n.* a native, or the dialect, of Venice; the heavy tape used in Venetian blinds: *pl.* a Venetian blind. **Venetian blind,** a blind made of thin laths connected by tape or webbing so that each may be turned to admit light and air. **Venetian chalk,** a white compact talc or steatite used for marking on cloth. **Venetian door,** a door having long, narrow windows on the sides. **Venetian mast,** a spirally coloured pole used in out-door decorations. **Venetian red,** a bright red pigment, usually prepared from sulphate of iron. **Venetian window,** one consisting of a main window with a narrow window on each side.
veney, *n. ven*-e, a thrust; a bout in fencing. (O.Fr. *venue*, a coming.)
vengeance, *n. ven*-jance, punishment or infliction of pain in return for injury or offence; retaliation; avengement. **with a vengeance,** with great violence or vehemence. (Fr., from L. *vindico*, avenge.)
vengeful, *a. venj*-ful, vindictive; revengeful.
vengefully, *ad.* in a vengeful spirit.
venial, *a. vee*-ne-al, that may be forgiven; pardonable; that may be allowed or permitted to pass without censure.
veniality, *n. vee*-ne-al-e-te, the state or property of being venial. (L. *venia*, pardon.)
venially, *ad. vee*-ne-a-le, pardonably.
venire facias, *n.* ve-*nyr*-re-*fay*-she-as, a writ or precept directed to the sheriff, requiring him to summon jurors in a particular case [Law]. (L., cause to come.)
venison, *n. ven*-zn, the flesh of deer, and formerly of such wild animals as are taken in the chase, used as food. (O.Fr. *veneisun.*)
Venite, *n.* ve-*ny*-te, the 95th Psalm, beginning "Come," as said or sung in the church service at Morning Prayer. (L.)
vennel, *n. ven*-el, a narrow street or alley [Scots.]. (O.Fr., from L. *vena*, a vein.)
venom, *n. ven*-om, matter fatal or injurious to life, esp. such as is injected from bites and stings of certain insects and reptiles; poison; spite; malice: *v.t.* to infect with venom; to poison. (L. *venenum*, poison.)
venomous, *a. ven*-o-mus, full of venom; injecting poison; poisonous; noxious to animal life; noxious; mischievous; malignant; spiteful.
venomously, *ad.* in a venomous manner.
venomousness, *n.* the state of being venomous.
venose, *a. vee*-nohs, venous.
venosity, *n.* ve-*nos*-e-te, the state of being venous; unusual abundance of venous blood.
venous, *a. vee*-nus, pertaining to or contained in veins; consisting of veins; distinctly veined.
vent, *n.* vent, a small aperture; a hole or passage for air or other fluid to escape; a flue; a touch-hole or opening in ordnance through which the powder was ignited; passage from secrecy to notice; emission; means of passage, as from confinement; discharge, outlet or means of such; finger-hole of a wind-instrument; the funnel of a volcano; the anus: *v.t.* to let out at a small aperture; to suffer to escape; to pour forth; to utter: *v.i.* to come to the surface to breathe (esp. of otters). **give vent to,** to let out; to pour forth. (L. *ventus*, wind.)
vent, *n.* vent, sale; opportunity to sell; demand. (Fr. *vente*, sale.)
vent, *n.* vent, an opening in a garment, esp. the slit at the back of an overcoat; a fent. (*fent.*)
ventage, *n. ven*-taj, a small hole, as in a wind-instrument.
ventail, *n. ven*-tale, the movable visor of a helmet, allowing for admission of air. (Fr., from L. *ventus.*)
venter, *n. ven*-ter, the abdomen [Anat.]; the womb (as mother) [Law]; a protuberant part, esp. of a muscle; a hollow or expanded part [Zool.]. (L.)
ventiduct, *n. ven*-te-dukt, a passage for wind or air [Arch.]. (L. *ventus*, wind, *duco*, lead.)
ventil, *n. ven*-til, a valve in a musical instrument.
ventilate, *v.t. ven*-te-late, to open to the free passage of air; to cause the air to pass through; to winnow; to fan; to discuss fully and freely. (L. *ventilo*, fan, from *ventus.*)
ventilation, *n.* ven-te-*lay*-shon, act of ventilating;

the act of winnowing for the purpose of separating chaff and dust; free and open discussion.
ventilative, *a.* *ven*-te-lay-tiv, pertaining to or promoting ventilation.
ventilator, *n.* *ven*-te-lay-tor, a contrivance for drawing off or expelling stagnant air from any close place or apartment.
ventose, *a.* *ven*-tohs, windy; flatulent.
Ventôse, *n.* (App.), the sixth month of the French Revolutionary calendar, running from February 19th to March 20th.
ventosity, *n.* ven-*tos*-e-te, windiness; flatulence; empty pride.
vent-peg, *n.* a spile; a plug for stopping the vent of a cask.
ventral, *a.* *ven*-tral, pertaining to the venter or belly; pertaining to the anterior part.
ventricle, *n.* *ven*-tre-kl, a small cavity in an animal body, applied esp. to certain cavities in the heart and brain. (Fr. *ventricule.*)
ventricose, *a.* *ven*-tre-kohs, bellied; distended; swelling out in the middle [Bot. and Conch.].
ventricular, *a.* ven-*trik*-yew-lar, pertaining to a ventricle; ventricose.
ventriculite, *n.* ven-*trik*-yew-lite, a fossil sponge common in the Cretaceous and chalk beds.
ventriloquial, *a.* *ven*-tre-*loh*-kwe-al, pertaining to ventriloquism.
ventriloquism, *n.* ven-*tril*-o-kwizm, the act, art, or practice of speaking in such a manner that the voice appears to come from a distance or from some other source. (L. *venter*, the belly, *loquor*, speak.)
ventriloquist, *n.* ven-*tril*-o-kwist, one who practises ventriloquism.
ventriloquistic, *a.* *ven*-tril-o-*kwis*-tik, ventriloquial; practising ventriloquism; of the nature of ventriloquy.
ventriloquize, *v.i.* ven-*tril*-o-kwize, to practise ventriloquism.
ventriloquous, *a.* ven-*tril*-o-kwus, practising or using ventriloquism; ventriloquial; produced by ventriloquism.
ventriloquy, *n.* ven-*tril*-o-kwe, ventriloquism; the condition or faculty of appearing to speak from the abdomen.
ventripotent, *a.* ven-*trip*-o-tent, big-bellied; gluttonous; eating enormously. (L. *ventes*, abdomen, *potens*, powerful.)
venture, *n.* *vent*-yewr, a hazard; an undertaking of chance or danger; chance; contingency; anything put to hazard; commercial speculation. **at a venture,** without seeing the end or mark; without considering the issue. (*adventure.*)
venture, *v.i.* *vent*-yewr, to dare; to have courage or presumption to do, undertake, or say; to run a hazard or risk: *v.t.* to expose; to hazard; to risk; to risk as a speculation. **venture money,** money one is willing to risk, esp. in a new undertaking.
venturer, *n.* *vent*-yew-rer, one who ventures; one who joins in a speculation of doubtful prospects, or who takes part in any hazardous risk.
venturesome, *a.* *vent*-yewr-sum, daring; intrepid.
venturesomely, *ad.* in a bold, daring manner.
venturesomeness, *n.* quality of being venturesome.
venturine, *n.* *vent*-yew-rin, gold powder, esp. for use in japanning. (*aventurine.*)
venturous, *a.* *vent*-yewr-rus, daring; bold; fearless; intrepid.
venturously, *ad.* in a venturous manner.
venturousness, *n.* the quality of being venturous.
venue, *n.* *ven*-yew, the place where an action is laid [Law]; a veney [Fencing]. (Fr., a coming.)
venule, *n.* *ven*-yewl, a small branch of a vein, esp. in an insect's wing; a veinlet.
venulose, *a.* *ven*-yew-lohs, full of venules [Bot. and Entom.].
Venus, *n.* *vee*-nus, the goddess of love and beauty, fabled to have emerged into being out of the foam of the sea [Myth.]; an inferior planet whose orbit is between the Earth and Mercury [Astron.]; a genus of marine bivalve molluscs. **Venus de Medici,** one of the most celebrated and beautiful sculptures of Greek art, preserved in the Uffizi Gallery at Florence. **Venus's comb,** a plant of the genus *Scandix.* **Venus's fan,** the flexible coral *Gorgonia flabellum.* **Venus's flower-basket,** a delicate siliceous sponge of the genus *Euplectella.* **Venus's fly-trap,** the plant *Dionæa muscipula.* **Venus's looking-glass,** the plant *Specularia speculum.* **Venus's slipper,** lady's slipper, esp. *Cypripedium calceolus.*
veracious, *a.* ve-*ray*-shus, observant of truth; habitually disposed to speak truth; true; reflecting truth. (L. *verax*, speaking truly, from *verus*, true.)
veraciously, *ad.* in a veracious manner.
veracity, *n.* ve-*ras*-e-te, truthfulness; habitual observance of truth; truth.
veranda or **verandah,** *n.* ve-*ran*-da, a kind of open portico, extending along the exterior of a main building; a covered balcony. (Port. *varanda.*)
veratric, *a.* ve-*ray*-trik, obtained from veratrum.
veratrine, *n.* ve-*ray*-trin, a poisonous alkaloid, used medicinally as a counter-irritant, obtained from sabadilla seeds.
veratrinize, *v.t.* *ve*-ra-tre-nize, to drug or treat with veratrine [Med.].
Veratrum, *n.* ve-*ray*-trum, a genus of poisonous plants, including *V. album*, the white hellebore. (L.)
verb, *n.* verb, the part of speech that asserts something of something else, or what a thing is, does, or has done to it, and is used interrogatively and imperatively as well as indicatively. (L. *verbum*, a word.)
verbal, *a.* *ver*-bal, spoken; expressed to the ear in words; not written; oral; consisting in mere words; respecting, or attending to, words only; literal, word for word; pertaining to or derived from a verb [Gram.]: *n.* a noun derived from a verb [Gram.].
verbalism, *n.* *ver*-ba-lizm, a verbal expression; empty verbosity.
verbalist, *n.* *ver*-ba-list, one giving undue weight to mere wording; a minute critic of words; an artist in words.
verbality, *n.* ver-*bal*-e-te, mere words; verbiage; wordiness.
verbalization, *n.* *ver*-ba-ly-*zay*-shon, the act of verbalizing.
verbalize, *v.t.* *ver*-ba-lize, to convert into a verb; to express in words: *v.i.* to be verbose.
verbally, *ad.* *ver*-ba-le, orally; word for word.
verbarian, *n.* ver-*bare*-re-an, a coiner of words.
Verbascum, *n.* ver-*bas*-kum, the genus of herbs comprising the mulleins.
verbatim, *ad.* ver-*bay*-tim, word for word, literal. (L.)
Verbena, *n.* ver-*bee*-na, the genus of plants which includes the vervain; (*l.c.*) a member of this genus. **lemon** or **scented verbena,** the lilac-coloured *Lippia citriodora.* (L. *verbenae*, sacred boughs.)
verberant, *a.* *ver*-ber-rant, reverberant.
verberation, *n.* *ver*-ber-*ray*-shon, a beating or striking; blows; the impulse of a body which causes sound. (L. *verberatus*, scourged.)
verbiage, *n.* *ver*-be-aj, verbosity; the use of many words without necessity. (Fr.)
verbify, *v.t.* *ver*-be-fy, to convert into or use as a verb.
verbigeration, *n.* ver-bij-er-*ray*-shon, continual and unmeaning repetition of a word or phrase (a sign of mental derangement). (L. *verbigerare*, to chatter.)
verbose, *a.* ver-*bohs*, abounding in words; using or containing more words than necessary; prolix; tedious from mutliplicity of words. (L. *verbosus*, wordy.)
verbosely, *ad.* with verbosity.
verboseness, *n.* the quality of being verbose.
verbosity, *n.* ver-*bos*-e-te, verboseness.
verboten, *a.* fer-*boh*-ten, forbidden; prohibited. (Ger.)
verdancy, *n.* *ver*-dan-se, greenness; rawness.
verdant, *a.* *ver*-dant, green; fresh; covered with growing plants and grass; flourishing; simple; inexperienced. (Fr. *verdoyant*, green.)
verd-antique, *n.* ver-dan-*teek*, a green incrustation on ancient coins, bronzes, etc.; a mottled variety of marble resembling serpentine; a green porphyry used as marble. (O.Fr. *verd*, green, and *antique.*)
verdantly, *ad.* *ver*-dant-le, in a youthful or flourishing manner.
verderer, *n.* *ver*-der-rer, a forest-keeper.
verdict, *n.* *ver*-dikt, the answer of a jury given to the court concerning any matter of fact in any cause,

civil or military, committed to their trial and examination; decision; judgment; opinion pronounced. **open, special verdict,** *see* these words. (L. *vere*, truly, *dico*, say.)
verdigris, *n. ver*-de-gris, a green incrustation formed on copper by the action of dilute acetic acid, used as a pigment and in medicine; copper rust. (O.Fr. *vert de Grèce*, green of Greece.)
verdigrisy, *a. ver*-de-gris-e, resembling verdigris in colour.
verditer, *n. ver*-de-ter, a blue or green pigment formed from a sulphate or nitrate of copper. (Fr. *vert*, green, *de*, of, and *terre*, earth.)
verdure, *n. ver*-dewr, greenness of vegetation; fresh foliage.
verdurous, *a. ver*-dewr-rus, covered with green; clothed with the fresh colour of vegetation.
verecund, *a. ve*-re-kund, bashful; shy; modest. (L.)
verecundity, *n.* ve-re-*kun*-de-te, bashfulness.
verge, *n.* verj, a rod or staff, esp. as an emblem of authority; a mace; the spindle or shaft of a watch, etc.; the compass or extent of the king's court [Law]; scope; range; brink; border; utmost limit; grass edging of a walk: *v.t.* to form the limit of: *v.i.* to border on; to be adjacent to. (Fr., a rod.)
verge, *v.i.* verj, to tend downward; to incline; to move in a certain direction; to approach; gradually to pass into something else. (L. *vergere*, to incline.)
vergée, *n.* vare-zhay, a unit of land-measurement in the Channel Islands (2,150 sq. yds., or ⅘ acre). (Norman-Fr.)
verger, *n. ver*-jer, he who carries the mace before a bishop or other high dignitary; an officer who carries a white wand before the judges; a church-keeper or pew-opener. (L. *virga*, a rod.)
vergiform, *a. ver*-je-form, virgate [Zool.]; rod-like.
Vergilian, *a.* ver-*jil*-e-an, Virgilian.
veridical, *a.* ve-*rid*-e-kal, veracious; telling truth; coinciding with reality. (L. *veridicus*, truth-telling.)
veridicality, *n.* ve-rid-e-*kal*-e-te, quality of being veridical; a veridical statement.
veridity, *n.* ve-*rid*-e-te, veracity; genuineness.
veriest, *superl. a. ve*-re-ist, an intensified form of *very*; utmost.
verifiability, *n. ve*-re-fy-a-*bil*-e-te, the capability of being verified.
verifiable, *a.* ve-re-*fy*-a-bl, that may be verified or confirmed.
verifiableness, *n.* the quality or condition of being verifiable.
verifiably, *ad.* in a manner capable of verification.
verification, *n. ve*-re-fe-*kay*-shon, the act of verifying or proving to be true; the act of confirming or authenticating; the state of being verified, confirmed, or authenticated.
verificatory, *a. ve*-re-fe-*kay*-to-re, that verifies; of the nature of, or serving as, verification.
verifier, *n. ve*-re-fy-er, one who or that which makes appear to be true.
verify, *v.t. ve*-re-fy, to prove or show to be true; to fulfil; to confirm the truth of, the truthfulness of, or the genuineness of. (Fr. *vérifier*.)
verily, *ad. ve*-re-le, in truth; in fact; certainly; really; truly.
verisimilar, *a.* ve-re-*sim*-e-lar, having the appearance of truth; likely. (L. *verus*, true, *similis*, like.)
verisimilitude, *n.* ve-re-se-*mil*-e-tewd, the appearance of truth; probability; likelihood. (L. *verisimilitudo*.)
veritable, *a. ve*-re-ta-bl, true; genuine; agreeable to fact.
veritably, *ad.* truly.
verity, *n. ve*-re-te, truth; consonance of a statement, proposition, or other matter to fact; a true assertion or tenet. (Fr. *vérité*.)
verjuice, *n. ver*-jooce, a bitter liquor expressed from crab-apples, and other sour fruit, used in sauces and the like. (O.Fr. *verjus*, from *vert*, green, and *juice*.)
vermeil, *n.* and *a. ver*-mil, silver-gilt; a glaze for gilded work; vermilion; crimson garnet.
vermeology, *n.* ver-me-*ol*-o-je, an obsolete term for helminthology. (L. *vermis*, a worm.)
Vermes, *n.pl. ver*-meez, an obsolete classification of animals including the worms and some other invertebrates. (L., worms.)
vermian, *a. ver*-me-an, pertaining to worms; worm-like [Zool. and Anat.].
vermicelli, *n. ver*-me-*chel*-e *or* -*sel*-e, thin macaroni. (It., little worms, from L. *vermis*, a worm.)
vermiceous, *a.* ver-*mish*-e-us, pertaining to worms.
vermicidal, *a. ver*-me-sy-dal, destroying worms; anthelmintic.
vermicide, *n. ver*-me-side, an anthelmintic; a worm-killer. (L. *vermis*, and *cædo*, kill.)
vermicular, *a.* ver-*mik*-yew-lar, pertaining to or resembling a worm, esp. the motion or track of a worm; vermiculated.
vermiculate, *a.* ver-*mik*-yew-lat, vermiculated; vermicular.
vermiculated, *a.* ver-*mik*-yew-lay-ted, worm-eaten; formed in the likeness of the motion of a worm; having wavy markings [Bot. and Zool.].
vermiculation, *n.* ver-*mik*-yew-*lay*-shon, a state as if bored by worms; infestation by, or conversion into, worms; a worm-eaten appearance.
vermicule, *n. ver*-me-kewl, a little worm or grub.
vermiculite, *n.* ver-*mik*-yew-lite, a mineral resembling talc in appearance that exfoliates when heated.
vermiculous, *a.* ver-*mik*-yew-lus, pertaining to worms; full of worms or grubs; resembling worms or worm-holes; wormy.
vermiform, *a. ver*-me-form, having the form or shape of a worm; characteristic of a worm; vermicular. **vermiform appendix,** *see* **appendix.**
vermifugal, *a.* ver-*mif*-yew-gal, tending to expel worms or internal parasites; anthelmintic.
vermifuge, *n. ver*-me-fewj, a medicine or substance that destroys or expels worms from animal bodies; an anthelmintic: *a.* vermifugal. (L. *vermis*, and *fugo*, put to flight.)
vermigrade, *a. ver*-me-grade, creeping like a worm.
vermilion, *n.* ver-*mil*-yon, cinnabar, a bright red sulphide of mercury, used as a pigment; any beautiful red or scarlet colour: *v.t.* to dye vermilion; to cover with a delicate red. (O.Fr. *vermeillon*, from L. *vermiculus*, a little worm, *i.e.*, the cochineal grub.)
vermin, *n. ver*-min, any noxious animal, esp. one destructive to game or injurious to crops and other possessions; noxious persons (in contempt). (Fr., from L. *vermis*, a worm.)
verminate, *v.i. ver*-me-nate, to breed or to become infested with intestinal worms.
vermination, *n. ver*-me-*nay*-shon, infestation with, or the production of, parasitic vermin [Med.]; morbid condition due to this.
verminous, *a. ver*-me-nus, tending to breed vermin; due to vermin; afflicted with vermin; infested with parasites [Med.].
vermiparous, *a.* ver-*mip*-a-rus, having young in larval or maggot form; producing verminous parasites. (L. *vermis*, and *parere*, to produce.)
vermivorous, *a.* ver-*miv*-o-rus, devouring worms or grubs; feeding on worms. (L. *vermis*, and *voro*, devour.)
vermouth, *n. ver*-mooth *or vare*-moot, a white wine flavoured with wormwood and other herbs.
vernacular, *a.* ver-*nak*-yew-lar, native, indigenous; belonging to the country of one's birth; endemic: *n.* the language of the common people. (L. *vernaculus*, of or belonging to a home-born slave.)
vernacularism, *n.* ver-*nak*-yew-la-rizm, vernacular idiom; the use of the vernacular.
vernacularist, *n.* ver-*nak*-yew-la-rist, a writer in a vernacular.
vernacularize, *v.t.* ver-*nak*-yew-la-rize, to transpose into the vernacular.
vernacularly, *ad.* in a vernacular manner.
vernal, *a. ver*-nal, belonging to the spring; appearing in spring. **vernal equinox,** the spring equinox, in March. **vernal signs,** the zodiacal signs (Ares, Taurus, and Gemini) in which the sun appears in spring. (L. *vernalis*, pertaining to spring.)
vernalization, *n. ver*-na-ly-*zay*-shon, an alleged method of imparting the growing qualities of autumn wheat to spring wheat by treatment of the latter before sowing.
vernation, *n.* ver-*nay*-shon, the arrangement of the leaves within the bud [Bot.].
vernicle, *n. ver*-ne-kl, a copy of the miraculous impression of the face of Christ on His way to Calvary left on the sudarium or veil of St. Veronica.
vernicose, *a. ver*-ne-kohs, looking as if varnished (of leaves) [Bot.].

vernier, *n.* *ver*-ne-er, a graduated sliding scale which subdivides the smallest divisions of the scale against which it slides. (Pierre *Vernier*, *d.* 1637, the inventor.)
veronal, *n.* *ve*-ro-nal, trade-name of a crystalline barbituric preparation used in medicine as a hypnotic.
Veronese, *n.* ve-ro-*neez*, of or belonging to the town of Verona in Italy.
Veronica, *n.* ve-*ron*-e-ka, a large genus of herbs and small shrubs which includes the speedwells; a portrait or representation of the face of Christ left on the veil of St. Veronica, a vernicle.
verruca, *n.* ve-*roo*-ka (*pl.* **verrucæ,** ve-*roo*-see), a wart; a wart-like excrescence. (L.)
verrucated, *a.* *ve*-roo-kay-ted, covered with verrucæ (Conch.].
verruciform, *a.* ve-*roo*-se-form, wart-like.
verrucose, *a.* ve-roo-*kohs*, having verrucæ or warts on the surface; warty.
verrucosity, *n.* ve-roo-*kos*-e-te, a warty condition [Med.]; a wart.
verrucous, *a.* ve-*roo*-kus, verrucose; characterized by, or of the nature of, warts.
verruculose, *a.* ve-*roo*-kew-lohs, verrucated; verrucose.
versal, *n.* *ver*-sal, an illuminated or distinctive initial letter of a verse, paragraph, etc.
versant, *a.* *ver*-sant, familiar; conversant. (L. *versor*, turn, occupy oneself.)
versant, *n.* *ver*-sant, the general slope of a watershed or other elevated ground; an area of sloping land. (Fr., from L. *versare.*)
versatile, *a.* *ver*-sa-tile, liable to be turned in opinion; changeable; variable; unsteady; turning with ease from one thing, subject, task, or pursuit to another; fixed by its side or to a support, but freely movable [Bot. and Zool.]. (L. *versatilis*, revolving.)
versatilely, *ad.* *ver*-sa-tile-le, in a versatile manner
versatileness, *n.* versatility.
versatility, *n.* ver-sa-*til*-e-te, the quality of being versatile; faculty or facility of turning one's mind to other subjects or tasks.
★verse, *n.* verse, a line consisting of a certain number of long and short syllables disposed according to certain rules; metrical language; poetry; a stanza; a short division of a chapter of the Bible, or of a liturgical office, etc.; a portion of an anthem to be performed by a single voice to each part; a versicle. **blank verse, chapter and verse, free, heroic, society verse,** *see* these words. (L. *versus*, from *verto, versuj*, turn.)
versed, *a.* verst, well acquainted with or skilled in; turned [Math.].
verselet, *n.* *verse*-let, a short verse or poem.
versemonger, *n.* *verse*-mung-ger, a poetaster; an indifferent poet.
verset, *n.* *ver*-set, a very short organ interlude or prelude [Mus.].
versicle, *n.* *ver*-se-kl, any of a series of short sentences chanted or recited alternately by priest and congregation [Eccles.]; a verselet. (L. *versiculus*, a little verse.)
versicoloured, *a.* *ver*-se-kul-urd, having various colours; changeable in colour; variegated. (L. *versicolor*, of various colours.)
versicular, *a.* ver-*sik*-yew-lar, pertaining to verses; designating distinct divisions of a writing.
versification, *n.* *ver*-se-fe-*kay*-shon, the act, art, or practice of composing verse; the form or structure of a poetical composition.
versificator, *n.* *ver*-se-fe-kay-tor, a writer of verse; a versifier.
versifier, *n.* *ver*-se-fy-er, one who makes verses; a poetaster; one who turns prose into verse.
versiform, *a.* *ver*-se-form, varying in form [Bot.].
versify, *v.i.* *ver*-se-fy, to make verses: *v.t.* to relate or describe in verse; to turn from prose into verse; to render metrical. (L. *versus*, and *facio*, make.)
version, *n.* *ver*-shon, act of translating or rendering from one language into another; translation; that whch is rendered from another language; a statement or account. (Fr.)
versional, *a.* *ver*-shon-al, pertaining to a version or translation.
versionist, *n.* *ver*-shon-ist, a translator.
vers libre, *n.* vare leebr, a rhythmical non-metrical form of versification, having lines of irregular length and usually unrhymed. (Fr., free verse.)
verslibrist, *n.* vare-*lee*-brist, a writer of vers libre.
verso, *n.* *ver*-soh, the left-hand page; the back cover of a book; the reverse, or tail side, of a coin.
verst, *n.* verst, a former Russian measure of length, 3,505 feet, or about ⅔ mile.
versus, *prep.* *ver*-sus, against. (L.)
versute, *a.* ver-*sewt*, crafty; wily. (L. *versutus.*)
vert, *n.* vert, everything that grows and bears a green leaf within the forest, also, the right to cut such [Law]; a green colour [Her.]. (Fr., green.)
vert, *v.i.* vert, to become a convert or pervert [Coll.].
vertebra, *n.* *ver*-te-bra (*pl.* **vertebræ**), any of the bony segments composing the spine or backbone [Anat. and Zool.]. (L. *vertebra*, a joint.)
vertebral, *a.* *ver*-te-bral, pertaining to a vertebra or vertebræ; spinal.
Vertebrata, *n.pl.* ver-te-*bray*-tah, animals having a backbone (the fishes, amphibians, reptiles, birds, and mammals).
vertebrate, *a.* *ver*-te-brat, having a backbone; pertaining to or characteristic of the Vertebrata: *n.* any animal with a backbone.
vertebrated, *a.* *ver*-te-bray-ted, vertebrate; having vertebræ.
vertebration, *n.* ver-te-*bray*-shon, segmentation into vertebræ.
vertex, *n.* *ver*-teks (*pl.* **vertices,** *ver*-te-seez), the highest point, the top; the point of a cone, pyramid, angle, or figure; the top of the arch of the skull [Anat.]; the zenith or point of the heavens perpendicularly above the head [Astron.]. **vertex of a curve,** the extremity of the axis or diameter, or the point where the diameter meets the curve [Math.]. (L., that which turns.)
vertical, *a.* *ver*-te-kal, pertaining to or situated at the vertex; placed or being in the zenith; perpendicular to the plane of the horizon; immediately overhead; (of business organizations, etc.) having the successive stages of production, from raw material to marketing, co-ordinated as a single operating unit [Econ.]. **prime vertical,** that vertical circle which passes through the east and west points. **vertical circle,** a great circle passing through the zenith and the nadir [Astron.]. **vertical escapement,** a type of watch escapement in which the barrel staff is at right angles to the axis of the escape wheel. **vertical fire,** fire at a very high angle [Mil.]. **vertical line,** a line at right angles to the plane of the horizon or to any other reference plane or line. **vertical plane,** a plane passing through the vertex and axis of a cone [Conic sections].
vertical, *n.* *ver*-te-kal, a vertical line, angle, etc. **the vertical,** the position or aspect of verticality.
verticality, *n.* ver-te-*kal*-e-te, the quality or state of being vertical; the condition of an heavenly body at or near the zenith [Astron.].
vertically, *ad.* in a vertical position.
verticalness, *n.* the state of being vertical.
verticil, *n.* *ver*-te-sil, a whorl, an inflorescence in which the parts surround the stem in a ring [Bot.].
verticillate, *a.* ver-*tis*-e-lat, whorled; growing in rings or whorls [Bot.].
verticity, *n.* ver-*tis*-e-te, tendency to turn or power of turning towards a vertex or pole.
vertiginous, *a.* ver-*tij*-e-nus, turning round; whirling; rotatory; affected with vertigo: giddy.
vertiginously, *ad.* whirlingly; giddily.
vertiginousness, *n.* giddiness.
vertigo, *n.* *ver*-te-goh *or* ver-*ty*-goh, giddiness; dizziness, swimming of the head. (L., a turning round.)
vertu, *n.* *ver*-too, virtu. (It.)
vervain, *n.* *ver*-vane, the plant *Verbena officinalis*, regarded at one time as possessed of both a medicinal and a magical virtue. **vervain-mallow,** the plant *Malva alcea*, with soft rose-red flowers.
verve, *n.* verv, ardour; animation; warmth of imagination inspiring the poet, etc.; artistic enthusiasm or rapture; spirit; go. (Fr.)
vervel, *n.* *ver*-vel, a metal ring for the leg of a hawk or other bird by which it may be secured.
vervet, *n.* *ver*-vet, the S. and equatorial African monkey *Cercopithecus pygerythrus*, allied to the grivet. (Fr.)
★very, *a.* *ve*-re, real; true: *ad.* in a great, eminent, or high (but not generally highest) degree. (L. *verus*, true.)

Very light, *n.* *ve*-re lite, a coloured rocketing light or flare used in a system of military signalling invented, 1877, by Lieut. S. W. Very.
Very pistol, *n.* *ve*-re *pis*-tol, the fire-arm by means of which Very lights are discharged.
vesania, *n.* ve-*say*-ne-a, unsoundness of mind [Path.]. (L., madness.)
vesanic, *a.* ve-*san*-ik, relating to insanity [Path.].
vesica, *n.* *ves*-e-ka, the urinary bladder [Anat.]. **vesica piscis,** the pointed oval representing an aureole in early architecture and religious paintings. (L. *vesica*, a bladder, *piscis*, of fish.)
vesical, *a.* *ves*-e-kal, pertaining to the bladder [Anat.]; shaped like a bladder. (L. *vesica.*)
vesicant, *a.* *ves*-e-kant, tending to raise, or capable of raising, blisters: *n.* a blistering application [Med.]; a poison-gas that raises blisters on the skin.
vesicate, *v.t.* *ves*-e-kate, to separate the cuticle by inflaming the skin; to blister [Med.].
vesication, *n.* ves-e-*kay*-shon, counter-irritation by means of blistering [Med.]; a blister.
vesicatory, *a.* and *n.* *ves*-e-kay-to-re *or* ve-*sik*-a-to-re, vesicant.
vesicle, *n.* *ves*-e-kl, a blister or small portion of cuticle elevated from the skin and containing watery fluid; a small membranous cavity or cell [Bot. and Zool.]. (L. *vesicula*, a little bladder.)
vesicocele, *n.* *ves*-e-ko-*seel*, hernia of the bladder [Path.].
vesicular, *a.* ve-*sik*-yew-lar, vesiculate; vesiculous.
vesiculate, *a.* ve-*sik*-yew-lat, bladdery; full of bladders or vesicles.
vesiculation, *n.* ves-e-kew-*lay*-shon, formation of, or process of forming, vesicles.
vesiculous, *a.* ve-*sik*-yew-lus, pertaining to, or consisting of, vesicles; vesiculate.
Vespa, *n.* *ves*-pa, the genus of insects comprising the wasps. (L.)
Vesper, *n.* *ves*-per, the evening star, Venus; the evening: *n.pl.* (*l.c.*) the evening service (Rom. Cath. and Gr. Churches), or the time of the service: *a.* pertaining to the evening or to vespers. (L., the evening, from Gr. *hesperos.*)
vespertilian, *a.* ves-per-*til*-e-an, pertaining to the bats; resembling a bat [Zool.]. (L. *vespertilio.*)
Vespertilio, *n.* ves-per-*til*-e-oh, the genus of Cheiroptera comprising the bats. (L., a bat.)
vespertine, *a.* *ves*-per-tine, pertaining to the evening; happening or done in the evening; setting about sunset [Astron.].
vespiary, *n.* *ves*-pe-a-re, a wasps' nest, also its colony of wasps. (L. *vespa.*)
vespine, *a.* *ves*-pine, pertaining to the wasps.
★**vessel,** *n.* *ves*-sel, a cask, jug, dish, or other receptacle proper for holding liquids; a ship or boat of any kind; any tube in which the blood or other fluid is contained or circulated [Anat.]; a tube in which the sap of plants is contained [Bot.]; a recipient or instrument, esp. regarded as a divine agent. (L. *vas.*)
vessignon, *n.* *ves*-ig-non *or* *ves*-e-nyon, a windgall [Vet.]. (Fr. *vessigon.*)
vest, *n.* vest, an undergarment for the trunk, and usually arms, worn next the skin; an undervest or singlet; (among tailors) a waistcoat, with or without sleeves, worn under the coat: *v.t.* to clothe with or as with a long garment; to invest or endow with; to give an immediate fixed right of present or future enjoyment [Law]: *v.i.* to come or descend to; to take effect. **vest in,** to put in possession of. **vest with,** to furnish or invest with. (L. *vestis*, a garment.)
Vesta, *n.* *ves*-ta, the virgin goddess of the hearth in whose temple the sacred fire was kept burning, worshipped as the guardian divinity of the state viewed as a family [Rom. Myth.]; one of the asteroids, the fourth discovered (1807) [Astron.]; (*l.c.*) a small wax match. (L., from Gr. *hestia*, hearth.)
vestal, *a.* *ves*-tal, pertaining to the goddess Vesta, or to her attendant virgins; pure; chaste: *n.* one of the virgins consecrated to Vesta for the guardianship of the sacred fire, which they tended and maintained perpetually, day and night; a chaste woman; a nun, or any woman devoted to a life of chastity. (L. *vestalis.*)
vested, *a.* *ves*-ted, robed; fixed in or held by a person or corporation; not in a state of contingency or suspension [Law]. **vested interests,** lawful rights secured by long usage in the hands of those possessing them, esp. as affording opportunity of gain. **vested legacy,** a bequest which does not depend on contingencies or become lapsed by death of the legatee before the time at which it becomes payable [Law].
vestiary, *n.* *ves*-te-a-re, a wardrobe; a robing room: *a.* affecting or pertaining to costume.
vestibular, *a.* ves-*tib*-yew-lar, pertaining to or like a vestibule [esp. Anat.].
vestibule, *n.* *ves*-te-bewl, the porch or entrance into a house; a small antechamber at the entrance of an apartment; a hall or lobby; a cavity or fossa, esp. that of the labyrinth of the ear [Anat.]; the covered passage between coaches of a corridor train. (L. *vestibulum*, a forecourt.)
vestige, *n.* *ves*-tij, a footprint or the mark of the foot left on the earth in walking; the trace or remains of something; a degenerate or atrophied part or organ [Biol.]; a minute fragment [Coll.]. (L. *vestigium*, footstep.)
vestigial, *a.* ves-*tij*-e-al, of the nature of a vestige, trace, or mark.
vesting, *n.* *ves*-ting, material for vests.
vestiture, *n.* *ves*-te-tewr, clothing; vesture; the outer covering of an insect.
vestment, *n.* *vest*-ment, a covering or garment; a robe or dress, esp. an outer ceremonial garment; ritual dress worn by a priest, choir, etc. (L. *vestis.*)
vestral, *a.* *ves*-tral, pertaining to a vestry.
vestry, *n.* *ves*-tre, a room appendant to a church, in which the clerical vestments are kept; formerly, a meeting of parish ratepayers, or their representatives, held in the vestry for local government purposes (superseded, 1894, by Parish Councils). (L. *vestis.*)
vestrydom, *n.* *ves*-tre-dum, government by vestries; vestries collectively.
vestryman, *n.* *ves*-tre-m'n, a member of a vestry.
vestuary, *n.* *ves*-tu-a-re, a wardrobe; a vestiary.
vestural, *a.* *ves*-tewr-ral, for clothing.
vesture, *n.* *ves*-tewr, a garment; dress; garments in general; clothing; covering.
vesturer, *n.* *ves*-tewr-rer, an official in charge of vestments.
Vesuvian, *a.* ve-*sew*-ve-an, pertaining to Vesuvius, the volcano: *n.* (*l.c.*) an obsolete make of match for use in strong winds.
vesuvianite, *n.* ve-*sew*-ve-a-nite, idocrase [Min.].
vet, *n.* vet, a veterinary surgeon [Coll.]: *v.t.* to doctor; to treat beneficially; to condense (a literary work) [Coll.].
vetch, *n.* vetch, a plant of the genus *Vicia*, esp. the leguminous forage plant *Vicia sativa*. *See* also **kidney-vetch, milk-vetch.**
vetchling, *n.* *vetch*-ling, a leguminous plant of the genus *Lathyrus*.
vetchy, *a.* *vetch*-e, consisting of or abounding with vetches.
veteran, *a.* *vet*-er-ran, pertaining to veterans; long practised or experienced: *n.* one who has been long exercised in, or has grown old in, any service or art, esp. in war; one who has had much experience. (L. *vetus*, *veteris*, old, or of long standing.)
veterinarian, *n.* *vet*-er-re-*nare*-re-an, one skilled in veterinary medicine or surgery.
veterinary, *a.* *vet*-er-re-na-re, pertaining to the art of treating the diseases of horses, cattle, dogs, and other domestic animals: *n.* a veterinary surgeon. (L. *veterinus*, pertaining to cattle.)
vetiver, *n.* *vet*-e-ver, the Indian grass khus-khus.
veto, *n.* *vee*-toh (*pl.* **vetoes,** *vee*-tohz), the power possessed by the executive to negative a bill which has passed the legislature; any authoritative prohibition or rejection; power of rejection: *v.t.* to withhold assent to; to forbid. (L., I forbid.)
vettura, *n.* ve-*toor*-ra, an Italian four-wheeled carriage. (It.)
vetturino, *n.* vet-oo-*ree*-noh, one who drives or hires out a vettura.
vetust, *a.* ve-*tust*, old; ancient. (L.)
vex, *v.t.* veks, to make angry by little provocations; to irritate; to torment; to harass; to disquiet; to trouble; to persecute: *v.i.* to be irritated; to fret. (L. *vexo*, shake in carrying, from *veho*, carry.)
vexation, *n.* vek-*say*-shon, act of vexing, irritating or disquieting; state of being vexed or disturbed

in mind; great uneasiness; affliction; a harassing under cover of law.
vexatious, *a.* vek-*say*-shus, irritating; disturbing or agitating to the mind; distressing; full of trouble; provoking. **vexatious suit,** a suit at law instituted maliciously merely to annoy [Law].
vexatiously, *ad.* so as to vex.
vexatiousness, *n.* quality of being vexatious.
vexed, *a.* vekst, much discussed or contested, but not settled.
vexer, *n.* *vek*-ser, one who vexes or troubles.
vexil, *n.* *vek*-sil, a vexillum [Bot.].
vexillary, *n.* vek-*sil*-a-re, a standard-bearer among the ancient Romans. (L., *vexillum*, a standard.)
vexillate, *a.* vek-*sil*-at, having a vexillum or vexilla [Bot. and Ornith.].
vexillation, *n.* *vek*-se-lay-shon, a company of ancient Roman soldiers under one standard.
vexillum, *n.* vek-*sil*-um (*pl.* **vexilla**), a standard used in the ancient Roman army; the troop serving under it; a small pennon on a pastoral staff [Eccles.]; the large petal of a papilionaceous flower [Bot.]; the vane of a feather [Ornith.]. (L.)
vexingly, *ad.* *vek*-sing-le, in an irritating way; so as to vex.
via, *n.* *vy*-a, a way: *prep.* by way of. **Via Lactea,** the Milky Way [Astron.]. **via media,** an intermediate course. (L.)
viability, *n.* *vy*-a-*bil*-e-te, state or quality of being viable.
viable, *a.* *vy*-a-bl, alive and capable of living, as an infant. (Fr. *vie*, from L. *vita*, life.)
viaduct, *n.* *vy*-a-dukt, a long bridge on a succession of arches; a structure conveying a road or railway over low ground, either by raised mounds or a series of arched supports. (L. *via*, a way, *duco*, lead.)
vial, *n.* *vy*-al, a phial; a small bottle of thin glass, used by druggists. (*phial*.)
viameter, *n.* vy-*am*-e-ter, an odometer. (L. *via*, and Gr. *metron*, measure.)
viands, *n.pl.* *vy*-andz, cooked meat; food. (Fr. *viande*, from L. *vivenda*, things to be lived on.)
viaticum, *n.* vy-*at*-e-kum, provisions, money, etc., necessary for a journey; the communion or eucharist given to a dying person. (L. *via*, a way.)
viator, *n.* vy-*ay*-tor, a wayfarer.
vibex, *n.* *vy*-beks (*pl.* **vibices**, ve-*by*-seez), a bright patch on the skin in certain fevers, due to subcutaneous extravasation of the blood. (L., a weal.)
vibraculum, *n.* vy-*brak*-yew-lum (*pl.* **vibracula**), one of the slender whip-like organs with which certain polyzoans secure food.
vibrant, *a.* *vy*-brant, vibrating; resonant.
vibraphone, *n.* *vy*-bra-fone, a mechanically operated percussion instrument resembling the xylophone and producing a vibrato effect.
vibrate, *v.i.* vy-*brate*, to swing, as a pendulum; to oscillate; to move to and fro rapidly; to throb: *v.t.* to cause to move to and fro, or to quiver; to measure by oscillating. (L. *vibro*.)
vibratile, *a.* *vy*-bra-tile, adapted to or used in vibratory motion; vibratory.
vibratility, *n.* vy-bra-*til*-e-te, the quality or condition of being vibratile.
vibration, *n.* vy-*bray*-shon, the act of vibrating or oscillating; a regular reciprocal motion of a body suspended; oscillation [Mech.]; a single completed beat in oscillation; alternate or reciprocal motion [Physics]; the motion or undulation of any sound-producing body [Mus.].
vibrational, *a.* vy-*bray*-shon-al, pertaining to vibration; having an harmonic motion.
vibratiuncle, *n.* vy-*bray*-she-ung-kl, a minute or imperceptible vibration.
vibrative, *a.* *vy*-bra-tiv, that vibrates.
vibrato, *n.* ve-*brah*-toh, a vibrating effect in singing; tremolo. (It.)
vibrator, *n.* *vy*-bray-tor, a vibrating reed, wire, or device in various musical, electric, and other instruments; an apparatus for use in vibrotherapeutics [Med.].
vibratory, *a.* *vy*-bra-to-re, vibrating; consisting in vibration or oscillation; causing to vibrate.
Vibrio *n.* *vy*-bre-oh *or* *vib*-re-oh, a genus of saprophytic vibratile bacteria one of which causes Asiatic cholera.
vibrioid, *a.* *vy*-bre-oyd, belonging to the *Vibrio*: *n.* a member of the *Vibrio*.
vibrissa, *n.* vy-*bris*-a, a bristle; a whisker (as of a cat). (L.)
vibrograph, *n.* *vy*-bro-graf, an instrument for recording vibrations.
vibroscope, *n.* *vy*-bro-skope, an instrument for observing and tracing vibrations.
vibrotherapeutics, *n.* *vy*-broh-*the*-ra-*pew*-tiks, the therapeutic application of vibration [Med.].
Viburnum, *n.* vy-*bur*-num, a large and widespread genus of shrubs including the guelder-rose, laurustinus, wayfaring-tree, etc.
vicar, *n.* *vik*-ar, the incumbent of a parish who, not being a rector, is remunerated by a stipend, not directly by tithes; a perpetual curate; a substitute or deputy in administrative office. **vicar apostolic,** a titular bishop officiating in a country or diocese in which the Papal authority is not fully recognized [Rom. Cath. Ch.]. **vicar forane,** a priest appointed by a bishop to exercise a limited local jurisdiction in his diocese [Rom. Cath. Ch.]. (Late L. *foraneus*, situated outside the city, foreign.) **vicar-general,** a lay deputy or assistant to an archbishop and some bishops in ecclesiastical visitations, etc. [Ch. of Eng.]; a priest appointed by a bishop as his deputy [Rom. Cath. Ch.]. **vicar of Bray,** a confirmed and unscrupulous turncoat. **Vicar of Christ,** a title accorded to the Pope. (L. *vicarius*, a substitute.)
vicarage, *n.* *vik*-a-raj, the benefice of a vicar; the official residence of a vicar.
vicarial, *a.* vi-*kare*-re-al, vicarious; pertaining to a vicar.
vicariate, *a.* vi-*kare*-re-at, having delegated power; vicarious: *n.* a delegated office or power; the jurisdiction of a vicar apostolic.
vicarious, *a.* vi-*kare*-re-us, deputed; delegated; acting for or filling the place of another; substituted in the place of another.
vicariously, *ad.* in place of another; by substitution of one for another.
vicarship, *n.* *vik*-ar-ship, the office or ministry of a vicar.
vice, *n.* vice, a defect, fault, blemish, or imperfection; any voluntary action or course of conduct which deviates from the rules of moral rectitude; depravity of manners; a fault or bad trick in a horse. (L. *vitium*, a fault.)
vice, *n.* vice, a two-jawed tool with a screw or lever for holding an object fast. (L. *vitis*, a vine.)
vice, *prep.* *vy*-se, in place of, in the stead of; used also as a prefix (*pronounced* vice) to denote one acting as second-in-command or deputy in the office, position, etc., mentioned, and [Coll.] as an abbreviation of **vice-chairman, vice-president,** etc. (L., by interchange.)
vice-admiral, *n.* a rank in the British navy next below that of admiral and next above rear-admiral.
vice-chancellor, *n.* a deputy to a chancellor; a high university official discharging most of the duties of the chancellor.
vicegerency, *n.* vice-*jeer*-ren-se, the office of a vicegerent; agency under another; deputed power.
vicegerent, *n.* vice-*jeer*-rent, an officer deputed by a proper authority to exercise the power of another: *a.* having or exercising delegated power; acting by substitution. (L. *vice*, and *gero*, carry on.)
vicenary, *a.* *vis*-en-a-re, pertaining to or consisting of twenty. (L. *vicenarius*, from *viginti*, twenty.)
vicennial, *a.* vi-*sen*-e-al, pertaining to or lasting twenty years; happening every twenty years.
vice-president, *n.* an official ranking next below a president, esp. the President of the United States.
viceregal, *a.* vice-*ree*-gal, pertaining to a viceroy.
vicereine, *n.* *vice*-rane, the wife of a viceroy.
viceroy, *n.* *vice*-roy, the governor of a kingdom or country ruling as his sovereign's representative. (L. *vice*, and Fr. *roi*, a king.)
viceroyalty, *n.* vice-*roy*-al-te, the dignity, jurisdiction, office, or term of office of a viceroy.
viceroyship, *n.* *vice*-roy-ship, viceroyalty.
vice versa, *ad.* *vy*-se *ver*-sa, conversely; the order or relation being reversed. (L. *vice*, in place of, *versa*, turned.)
vicinage, *n.* *vis*-e-naj, the place or places adjoining or near; neighbourhood; people of the neighbourhood. (Fr. *voisinage*.)
vicinal, *a.* *vis*-e-nal, near; neighbouring; local.
vicinity, *n.* ve-*sin*-e-te, the state of being near;

nearness in place; neighbourhood. (L. *vicinus*, near.)
viciosity, *n.* *vish*-e-*os*-e-te, vitiosity.
vicious, *a.* *vish*-us, addicted to vice; corrupt in principles or conduct; depraved; contrary to moral principles or rectitude; foul; impure; not genuine or pure; imperfect; unruly; refractory: given to bad tricks (of horses). **vicious circle,** a difficult situation arising from a series of problems the solution of any one of which causes fresh difficulty in respect of any other; a circle (in Logic). (L. *vitium*, fault.)
viciously, *ad.* corruptly; faultily.
viciousness, *n.* the quality of being vicious.
vicissitude, *n.* ve-*sis*-e-tewd, change or succession; variation; revolution, as in human affairs. (L. *vicissitudo*, from *vicis*, change, alternation.)
vicissitudinous, *a.* ve-*sis*-e-*tew*-de-nus, changeful; changing in succession.
victim, *n.* *vik*-tim, a living animal sacrificed to some deity, or in the performance of a religious rite; a person or thing sacrificed in the pursuit of an object; one who suffers injury; a dupe. (L. *victima*, a beast for sacrifice.)
victimization, *n.* *vik*-te-my-*zay*-shon, the act of making a victim of, or of imposing upon; martyrization.
victimize, *v.t.* *vik*-te-mize, to make a victim of; to sacrifice; to cheat injuriously; to dupe.
victimizer, *n.* *vik*-te-my-zer, one who victimizes; one who swindles or cheats.
victor, *n.* *vik*-tor, one who conquers in war or defeats another in private combat or contest. (L.)
victoria, *n.* vik-*taw*-re-a, a light, low, four-wheeled carriage seated for two facing the horses, with the driver's seat in front; (*cap.*) a genus of tropical American plants including *V. regia*, the giant water-lily of the Amazon; a variety of plum, and of domestic pigeon. **Victoria Cross,** a bronze Maltese cross, first bestowed by Queen Victoria, 1856, as a distinction for outstanding valour in presence of the enemy. (Queen *Victoria*.)
victorian, *a.* vik-*taw*-re-an, pertaining to or characteristic of the reign of Victoria, 1837 to 1901; old-fashioned, behind the times, prudish; *n.* a writer or other person flourishing in the reign of Victoria. **Royal Victorian Order,** an order of chivalry founded by Queen Victoria in 1896 for distinguished services to the sovereign. **Victorian age,** the period of Queen Victoria's reign, 1837 to 1901.
victorine, *n.* vik-to-*reen*, a kind of fur tippet worn by women; a kind of peach.
victorious, *a.* vik-*taw*-re-us, having conquered in battle or contest; conquering; vanquishing; associated with or emblematic of conquest.
victoriously, *ad.* in a victorious manner.
victoriousness, *n.* quality of being victorious.
victory, *n.* *vik*-to-re, the defeat of an enemy in battle or an antagonist in contest; a battle gained; the advantage or superiority gained in spiritual or other conflicts. (L. *victoria*.)
victress, *n.* *vik*-tress, a woman who conquers. (L. *victrix*.)
victual, *v.t.* *vit*-tl, to supply with provisions for subsistence; to store with provisions.
victualler, *n.* *vit*-tler, one who furnishes provisions; one who keeps a house of entertainment; a provision-ship. **licensed victualler,** *see* **license.**
victuals, *n.pl.* *vit*-tlz, food for human beings prepared for eating; that which supports human life; provisions. (O.Fr. *vitaille*, from L. *victualia*, provisions.)
vicuña, *n.* ve-*koo*-nya, the wild llama of the Andes.
vide, *v.t.* *vy*-de, see; look at. (L.)
videlicet, *ad.* ve-*dee*-le-set *or* ve-*del*-e-set, to wit; namely (abbreviated *viz*). (L., you may see.)
vidette, *n.* ve-*det*, a vedette.
vidimus, *n.* *vy*-de-mus (*pl.* **vidimuses**), an inspection; a summary; a formal examination [Law]. (L., we have seen.)
viduage, *n.* *vid*-yew-aj, widowhood; widows collectively. (L. *vidua*, a widow.)
vidual, *a.* *vid*-yew-al, relating to widowhood.
viduity, *n.* vid-*yew*-e-te, the state of being a widow; the period of widowhood.
vie, *v.i.* vy, to strive for superiority; to contend. *ppr.* **vying.** (O.Fr. *envier*, to invite.)
Viennese, *a.* vee-e-*neez*, pertaining to or characteristic of Vienna or its people: *n.* a native or inhabitant of Vienna.
★**view,** *n.* vew, prospect; reach of the eye; the whole extent seen; sight; power or act of seeing; limit of sight; intellectual or mental sight or survey; mental examination; appearance; prospect of interest; purpose; design; opinion; manner of understanding: *v.t.* to survey; to examine with the eye; to look on with attention; to perceive by the eye; to survey intellectually; to consider. **field of view,** *see* **field. point of view,** the direction in which a thing is seen; standpoint. **view finder,** an attachment to a camera by means of which may be seen a reduced reproduction of the view projected on the plate [Phot.]. (Fr. *vue*, from L. *video*, see.)
viewer, *n.* *vew*-er, one who views, surveys, or examines; an overseer (esp. at a colliery); one who uses a television receiver.
viewiness, *n.* *vew*-e-ness, the condition or quality of being viewy.
viewless, *a.* *vew*-less, that cannot be seen; invisible; whence, or by whom, no view is visible; having no opinions.
viewpoint, *n.* *vew*-poynt, point of view; vantage-point for viewing.
viewy, *a.* *vew*-e, having impracticable views; full of whims; faddy.
vigesimal, *a.* vi-*jes*-e-mal, twentieth. (L. *vigesimus*.)
vigia, *n.* *vij*-e-a, a warning of hidden danger, as of a rock, marked on a chart. (Sp.)
vigil, *n.* *vij*-il, watching; watchfulness; devotions performed in the customary hours of sleep; the eve or evening before any feast; a fast observed on the day preceding a holiday. (L. *vigil*, awake.)
vigilance, *n.* *vij*-e-lance, state of being vigilant or watchful; forbearance of sleep; insomnia [Path.]. **vigilance committee,** a self-appointed local body for the suppression of violence, immorality, etc.
vigilant, *a.* *vij*-e-lant, watchful; circumspect; attentive to discover and avoid danger.
vigilante, *n.* vij-e-*lan*-te, a member of a vigilance committee. (Sp.)
vigilantly, *ad.* with vigilance.
vigneron, *n.* (App.), a vine-grower. (Fr.)
vignette, *n.* vin-*yet*, a small engraved embellishment at the beginning of a book; a flourish, as of vine-leaves and tendrils; a head-and-shoulders portrait of which the edges fade gradually into the background: *v.t.* to make a vignette of. (Fr., a trailing vine.)
vignetter, *n.* vin-*yet*-er, a device for the making of vignettes [Phot.].
vignettist, *n.* vin-*yet*-ist, one who makes vignettes.
vigonia, *n.* ve-*goh*-ne-a, a dress material consisting mainly of vicuña wool.
vigoroso, *ad.* vig-o-*roh*-soh, with energy [Mus.]. (It.)
vigorous, *a.* *vig*-ur-rus, full of physical strength or active force; lusty; energetic; powerful; strong.
vigorously, *ad.* with vigour.
vigorousness, *n.* state of being vigorous.
vigour, *n.* *vig*-ur, active strength or force in animals or plants; physical or intellectual force; strength of mind; energy. (L. *vigor*.)
viking, *n.* *vy*-king *or* *vik*-ing, a Norse seafaring rover or pirate of the 8th to 10th centuries. (Scand. *vikingr*, perhaps from *vig*, a battle.)
vilayet, *n.* ve-lay-*et*, a Turkish administrative division under a vali.
vile, *n.* vile, worthless; base; mean; despicable; morally base; depraved; wicked. (L. *vilis*, worthless.)
vilely, *ad.* *vile*-le, basely.
vileness, *n.* quality of being vile; baseness.
vilification, *n.* *vil*-e-fe-*kay*-shon, act of vilifying or defaming.
vilifier, *n.* *vil*-e-fy-er, one who defames or traduces.
vilify, *v.t.* *vil*-e-fy, to make vile; to debase; to defame; to traduce. (L. *vilis*, and *facio*, make.)
vilipend, *v.t.* *vil*-e-pend, to depreciate; to slight; to hold in disparagement. (L. *vilipendo*, despise.)
vill, *n.* vil, a village; a small collection of houses.
villa, *n.* *vil*-a, a country seat; a suburban residence. (L., a country house.)
villadom, *n.* *vil*-a-dom, the world of villas; villas and their residents collectively.

village, *n.* *vil*-aj, a smaller assemblage of houses than a town: *a.* belonging to a village. (L. *villa.*)
villager, *n.* *vil*-a-jer, an inhabitant of a village.
villagery, *n.* *vil*-aj-re *or* *vil*-a-je-re, villages collectively.
villain, *n.* *vil*-an, a vile, wicked person; one of extreme depravity and capable or guilty of great crimes; a serf, one who held land by a base or servile tenure [Feudal Law]; the hero's opponent in melodrama, etc. (L. *villanus,* a farm slave, from *villa.*)
villainess, *n.* vil-an-*ess,* a female villain, esp. on the stage.
villainous, *a.* *vil*-an-us, base; wicked; extremely depraved; proceeding from extreme depravity; vile; mischievous.
villainously, *ad.* in a villainous manner.
villainousness, *n.* quality of being villainous.
villainy, *n.* *vil*-an-e, extreme depravity; atrocious wickedness; a crime; an action of deep depravity.
villanelle, *n.* vil-a-*nel,* a French metrical form of nineteen lines with double rhymes.
Villarsia, *n.* ve-*lahr*-se-a, a genus of yellow-flowered aquatic plants of the gentian order; (*l.c.*) a member of this genus, esp. *Limanthemum peltatum.* (D. *Villars,* d. 1814, Fr. botanist.)
villatic, *a.* ve-*lat*-ik, pertaining to a village, or a villa; rustic.
villeggiatura, *n.* ve-*lej*-e-a-*toor*-ra, a stay in the country or at a country house; rustication. (It.)
villein, *n.* *vil*-an, villain [Feudal Law].
villenage, *n.* *vil*-an-aj, tenure by servitude; serfdom; the quality of, or condition of being, a villain [Feudal Law]; villains collectively.
villi, *n.pl.* *vil*-y, *pl.* of *villus.*
villiform, *a.* *vil*-e-form, resembling villi in appearance.
villose, *a.* *vil*-ohs, villous.
villosity, *n.* ve-*los*-e-te, a coating of villi [Bot.]; a villous patch [Anat.]; the state or quality of being villous.
villous, *a.* *vil*-us, clothed with villi; covered with long fine hairs; pubescent; shaggy.
villus, *n.* *vil*-us (*pl.* **villi**), a small vascular tuft; a minute projection from the mucous membrane of the intestine [Anat.]; one of the fine hairs on plants [Bot.]. (L., shaggy hair.)
vim, *n.* vim, energy. (L. *acc.* of *vis,* strength.)
viminal, *a.* *vim*-e-nal, pertaining to, consisting of, or producing twigs. (L. *vimen,* a pliant twig.)
vimineous, *a.* ve-*min*-e-us, made of twigs or shoots.
vina, *n.* *vee*-nah, an ancient Hindu guitar-like instrument, originally of seven strings. (Sans.)
vinaceous, *a.* ve-*nay*-shus, belonging to grapes or wine; of the nature or colour of wine. (L. *vinaceus,* a grape-stone.)
vinaigrette, *n.* vin-a-*gret,* a small ornamental gold or silver perforated case for holding aromatic vinegar or the like; a smelling-bottle. (Fr.)
vinasse, *n.* ve-*nass,* the liquid residue from the distillation of wine, etc., and from beets after the extraction of sugar, a source of potassium salts.
Vincentian, *a.* vin-*sen*-shan, denominating or pertaining to an order of missionaries founded by St. Vincent de Paul, 1625: *n.* a member of this order.
vincibility, *n.* *vin*-se-*bil*-e-te, the state of being vincible.
vincible, *a.* *vin*-se-bl, conquerable; that may be overcome or reduced to submission. (L. *vincibilis,* from *vinco.*)
vinculum, *n.* *ving*-kew-lum, a straight mark placed over several members of a compound quantity, which are to be subjected to the same operation [Math.]; a frænum [Anat.]; a brace [Print.]. (L., from *vincio, vinctum,* bind.)
vindemial, *a.* vin-*dee*-me-al, pertaining to a vintage or grape harvest. (L. *vindemia,* grape-gathering, from L. *vinum,* wine, *demo,* take away.)
vindicable, *a.* *vin*-de-ka-bl, that may be vindicated, justified, or supported.
vindicate, *v.t.* *vin*-de-kate, to defend; to justify; to assert; to defend with success; to prove to be just or valid; to defend with arms or otherwise. (L. *vindico,* lay claim to.)
vindication, *n.* vin-de-*kay*-shon, the act of vindicating; justification; the act of supporting by proof or legal process; the proving of anything to be just. (L. *vindicatio.*)
vindicative, *a.* *vin*-de-ka-tiv, tending to vindicate.
vindicator, *n.* *vin*-de-kay-tor, one who vindicates or who justifies or maintains; one who defends.
vindicatory, *a.* *vin*-de-ka-to-re, tending to vindicate; justificatory; punitive.
vindictive, *a.* vin-*dik*-tiv, given to revenge; revengeful.
vindictively, *ad.* revengefully; by way of revenge.
vindictiveness, *n.* the condition of being vindictive; a revengeful temper.
vine, *n.* vine, the climbing plant *Vitis vinifera* of which the grape is the fruit; the slender stem of any climbing or trailing plant. (L. *vinea.*)
vine-clad, *a.* clad or covered with vines.
vine-dresser, *n.* one who trims, prunes, and cultivates vines.
vine-fretter, *n.* any plant-louse or insect destructive to vines.
vinegar, *n.* *vin*-e-gar, an acid liquor obtained by fermenting wine, beer, cider, etc., used as a condiment and containing much acetic acid; sour or acidulous speech [Fig.]. **vinegar plant,** a fungus of leathery texture, present in fluids in a state of acetous fermentation. (Fr. *vinaigre.*)
vinegarish, *a.* *vin*-e-ga-rish, resembling vinegar; sour.
vinegary, *a.* *vin*-e-ga-re, sour, like vinegar; bitter in speech or expression [Fig.].
vine-grub, *n.* a vine-fretter.
vinery, *n.* *vy*-ner-re, a greenhouse for growing vines.
vineyard, *n.* *vin*-yard, an enclosure for grape vines; a plantation of vines for producing grapes.
vingt-et-un, *n.* (App.), a game of cards, players aiming at a score of 21 pips in the hand or as close thereunder as possible. (Fr., twenty-one.)
vinic, *a.* *vy*-nik, obtained from alcohol; alcoholic.
viniculture, *n.* *vin*-e-kul-tewr, the culture of vines.
viniculturist, *n.* *vin*-e-*kul*-tew-rist, a cultivator of vines.
vinification, *n.* *vin*-e-fe-*kay*-shon, the conversion of fruit juice into an alcoholic liquid by fermentation.
vinificator, *n.* ve-*nif*-e-kay-tor, an apparatus for condensing alcoholic vapours in the fermentation of grapes.
vinology, *n.* ve-*nol*-o-je, the scientific study of wines.
vinometer, *n.* ve-*nom*-e-ter, an œnometer.
vin ordinaire, *n.* (App.) a cheap claret for drinking with water. (Fr., common wine.)
vinosity, *n.* ve-*nos*-e-te, state or quality of being vinous.
vinous, *a.* *vy*-nus, having the qualities of wine; pertaining to wine; produced by, or addicted to, wine. (L. *vinosus,* full of wine.)
vint, *v.t.* vint, to make (wine).
vint, *n.* vint, a game of cards, an early form of bridge as played in Russia.
vintage, *n.* *vin*-taj, the produce of the vine for the season; the time of gathering the crop of grapes; the wine produced by the crop of grapes in one season. **vintage port,** port wine bottled early and matured in bottle. (Fr. *vendange.*)
vintager, *n.* *vin*-ta-jer, one who gathers the vintage.
vintner, *n.* *vint*-ner, one who deals in wines; a wine-seller.
vintnery, *n.* *vint*-ner-re, the trade of a vintner.
vintry, *n.* *vin*-tre, a place where wine is kept or sold; a warehouse for wines.
viny, *a.* *vy*-ne, characteristic of or pertaining to vines; producing or abounding in grapes.
viol, *n.* *vy*-ol, a mediæval stringed musical instrument of the violin family. **bass viol,** the predecessor of the violoncello. **viol de gamboys,** the viola da gamba. (It. *viola.*)
viola, *n.* ve-*oh*-la, a tenor violin. **viola da gamba,** the bass viol. (It.)
Viola, *n.* *vy*-o-la, a large genus of plants including the pansy and the other violets; (*l.c.*) any member of this genus.
violable, *a.* *vy*-o-la-bl, that may be violated or injured.
violaceous, *a.* vy-o-*lay*-shus, pertaining to the viola family [Bot.]; of the colour of the violet.
violane, *n.* *vee*-o-lan, a dark violet-blue laminar variety of diopside, quarried in Piedmont as an ornamental stone. (It.)
violate, *v.t.* *vy*-o-late, to break in upon in a violent manner; to disturb; to break; to transgress; to injure; to do violence to; to treat with irreverence; to ravish; to deflower. (L. *violo,* treat with violence, from *vis,* force.)

violation, *n.* vy-o-*lay*-shon, the act of violating; infringement; transgression; act of irreverence; profanation, or contemptuous treatment of sacred things; rape.
violative, *a. vy*-o-la-tiv, tending to violate; involving violation.
violator, *n. vy*-o-lay-tor, one who violates or disturbs, or treats with irreverence; a ravisher.
violence, *n. vy*-o-lence, quality or state of being violent; vehemence; fierceness; highly excited feeling; injury; outrage; rape; intimidation; the illegal use of physical force [Law]. **do violence to,** to attack; to outrage; to injure.
★**violent,** *a. vy*-o-lent, acting with great physical force; impetuous; fierce; vehement; characterized by great force or violence; outrageous; produced by or acting by violence; abnormal, not natural (of death). (L. *vis*, force.)
violently, *ad.* in a violent manner.
violescent, *a. vy*-o-*les*-ent, tending to a violet colour.
violet, *n. vy*-o-let, a plant of the genus *Viola*: a colour produced by mixing blue and red: *a.* dark blue, inclining to red. **dog-tooth violet,** *see* **dog-tooth. water violet,** the hardy marsh plant *Hottonia palustris.* (L. *viola.*)
violin, *n.* vy-o-*lin*, a musical instrument with four strings, played with a bow; a fiddle; a player on this. (It. *violino.*)
violine, *n. vy*-o-line, a bitter alkaloid obtained from the leaves and root of the violet; a bluish-red colouring matter.
violinist, *n.* vy-o-*lin*-ist, a person skilled in playing on a violin.
violist, *n.* ve-*oh*-list, a player on the viola.
violoncellist, *n. vee*-o-lon-*chel*-list, one who plays on a violoncello; a cellist.
violoncello, *n. vee*-o-lon-*chel*-loh, a bass violin of four strings, an octave lower than the tenor violin; a cello. (It.)
violone, *n.* vee-o-*loh*-nay, a double bass tuned an octave lower than the violoncello. (It.)
viosterol, *n.* vy-*os*-ter-rol, a preparation of ergosterol treated with ultra-violet rays for use in cases of rickets [Pharm.].
viper, *n. vy*-per, a venomous snake of the genus *Vipera*, esp. *V. berus*, the common British adder; a malignant person. **viper's bugloss,** the prickly blue-flowered weed *Echium vulgare.* **viper's grass** the perennial herb *Scorzonera hispanica*, black salsify. (L. *vipera*, from *vivus*, alive, *pario*, bring forth.)
viper-weever, *n.* the lesser weever, *Trachinus vipera*, one of the sting-fishes; the adder-pike.
viperine, *a. vy*-per-rine, pertaining to the viper or to vipers.
viperish, *a. vy*-per-rish, resembling a viper; [Fig.] spiteful, venomous.
viperous, *a. vy*-per-rus, having the qualities of a viper; malignant; venomous.
viraginian, *a.* vi-ra-*jin*-e-an, having the qualities of a virago: *n.* the language characteristic of a virago.
viraginous, *a.* vi-*raj*-e-nus, having the nature or characteristics of a virago.
virago, *n.* vi-*ray*-goh, a bold, impudent, turbulent woman; a termagant; formerly, a woman of pronounced masculinity. (L., a man-like woman, from *vir*, a man.)
vire, *n.* veer, a crossbow bolt. (O.Fr.)
virelay, *n. vir*-re-lay, a French verse-form like a roundelay. (Fr. *virelai*, from *virer*, turn.)
virent, *a. vyr*-rent, verdant; fresh; of a green colour. (L. *vireo*, be green.)
vireo, *n. ver*-re-oh, any of several small American song-birds; a greenlet. (L.)
virescence, *n.* ve-*res*-ence, the development of green in leaves, etc. [Bot.]; greenness.
virescent, *a.* ve-*res*-ent, slightly green; beginning to be green. (L. *virescens*, growing green.)
virgate, *a. ver*-gate, having the shape of a rod or wand [Bot.]: *n.* a fourth of a hide of land (usually about 25 to 30 acres). (L. *virga*, a rod.)
Virgilian, *a.* ver-*jil*-e-an, pertaining to Virgil, the Roman poet, or his writings; resembling the style of Virgil.
virgin, *n. ver*-jin, a woman who has had no carnal knowledge of man (formerly applied also to a man who has had no sexual intercourse); a woman under religious vow of chastity; an insect reproducing without fertilization; any animal that has not copulated; (*cap.*) the Virgin Mary; the zodiacal sign Virgo: *a.* befitting a virgin; maidenly; modest; chaste; pure. **virgin forest,** a forest untouched by man. **virgin's bower,** the climbing plant *Clematis vitalba.* **the Virgin Queen,** Queen Elizabeth (*d.* 1603). (L. *virginia*, gen. of *virgo*, a maiden.)
virginal, *a. ver*-je-nal, pertaining to a virgin; maidenly: *n.* an obsolete keyed musical instrument resembling a spinet.
virginhood, *n. ver*-jin-hood, virginity.
Virginia, *n.* ver-*jin*-e-a, a kind of American tobacco. **Virginia creeper,** a plant of the genus *Vitis.* **Virginia deer,** the N. American deer *Odocoileus virginianus.* **Virginia quail,** the bob-white. **Virginia stock,** the hardy garden annual *Malcomia maritima.* (Name of one of the states, U.S.A.)
virginity, *n.* ver-*jin*-e-te, the condition of being a virgin; maidenhood.
virginium, *n.* ver-*jin*-e-um, a rare alkali-metallic element present in pitchblende, sea-water, and some other substances, first identified in 1931.
Virgo, *n. ver*-goh, the sign of the zodiac entered by the sun about 22 August. (L., virgin.)
virgule, *n. ver*-gewl, a small rod; a twig; a comma. (L. *virgula.*)
virid, *a. vi*-rid, green.
viridescence, *n. vi*-re-*des*-ence, the state or quality of being viridescent.
viridescent, *a. vi*-re-*des*-ent, turning green; greenish.
viridine, *n. vi*-re-deen, a greenish-yellow nitrogenous oil present in coal-tar; a slightly poisonous alkaloid found in white hellebore.
viridity, *n.* vi-*rid*-e-te, greenness; verdure. (L. *viridis*, green.)
virile, *a. vi*-rile, pertaining to a man or to the male sex; masculine; not puerile or feminine. (L. *vir*, a man.)
virilescence, *n. vi*-re-*les*-ence, the acquisition of masculine characteristics by barren or elderly females.
virility, *n.* vi-*ril*-e-te, manhood; the state of having arrived at the maturity and vigour of manhood; full-grown male power; the power of procreation.
virose, *a. vyr*-rohs, virous.
virous, *a. vyr*-rus, poisonous; smelling strongly; fetid [Bot.]. (L. *virus*, poison.)
virtu, *n. ver*-too, a love of the fine arts; a taste for curiosities. **objects of virtu,** things collected for their beauty, rarity, or antiquity, etc. (Fr.)
virtual, *a. ver*-tew-al, potential; having the power of acting or of invisible efficacy without the material or sensible part; being in essence or effect, not in fact. **virtual focus,** the point from which rays appear to issue [Optics]. **virtual velocity,** the velocity which a body in equilibrium would actually acquire during the first instant of its motion, the equilibrium being disturbed [Mech.]. (Fr. *virtuel.*)
virtuality, *n.* ver-tew-*al*-e-te, the quality or state of being virtual; potentiality.
virtually, *ad.* in efficacy or effect.
virtue, *n. ver*-tew, moral goodness; the habitual practice of moral duties; a particular moral excellence; chastity; operative power; something efficacious; secret agency; that which constitutes value and merit; efficacy or power; legal authority; that substance or quality of physical bodies by which they act and produce effects on other bodies; bravery; valour. **in virtue of,** in consequence; by the efficacy or authority of. **make a virtue of necessity,** to act in a certain way because there is no choice. (L. *virtus*, manly excellence, from *vir*, a man.)
virtueless, *a. ver*-tew-less, devoid of virtue, excellence, or power; ineffective; morally worthless.
virtuosity, *n.* ver-tew-*os*-e-te, an interest in or taste (dilettantish or otherwise) for the fine arts; particular attention or technique in literature or the arts.
virtuoso, *n. ver*-tew-*oh*-soh (*pl.* **virtuosi**), one skilled critically in objects of virtu or the fine arts; a skilled performer on a musical instrument. (It.)
virtuous, *a. ver*-tew-us, morally good; acting in or being in conformity to the moral law; chaste.
virtuously, *ad.* in a virtuous manner.
virtuousness, *n.* the quality of being virtuous.

virulence, *n. vi*-rew-lence, that quality which renders a person or thing extremely active in doing injury; acrimony of temper; immoderate bitterness or malignity. (L. *virulentus*, poisonous.)
virulency, *n. vi*-rew-len-se, virulence.
virulent, *a. vi*-rew-lent, extremely active in doing injury; very poisonous or venomous; bitter in enmity; malignant. (L. *virus*.)
virulently, *ad.* with virulence.
virus, *n. vyr*-rus, any animal poison, esp. one produced by and capable of transmitting disease [Med.]; a moral taint, a corrupting influence [Fig.]. (L., a slimy liquid.)
vis, *n.* vis, force; power. **vis inertiæ,** the resistance in a body to change either its state of rest or state of motion; inert state or unwillingness to change a habit. **vis major,** an unavoidable accident [Law]. **vis mortua,** dead force, force doing no work. **vis viva,** living force, or kinetic energy. (L.)
visa, *n. vee*-za, the endorsement on a passport certifying that it has been officially examined and authorized: *v.t.* to visé. (Fr., from L., seen.)
visage, *n. viz*-aj, the face; the countenance or look of a person (or animal). (Fr.)
visaged, *a. viz*-ajd, having a visage or countenance of a particular type.
vis-à-vis, *a.* and *ad.* vee-zah-*vee*, face to face; in relation to: *n.* a carriage in which two persons sit face to face; a person opposite, as the opposite party in quadrille dancing. (Fr.)
viscacha, *n.* vis-*kah*-cha, the pampas hare, a South American rodent of the genus *Lagostomus.*
viscachera, *n. vees*-kah-*chay*-rah, a colony of viscachas.
viscera, *n.pl. vis*-er-ra, the organs contained in the larger cavities of the body, esp. the intestines, liver, heart, etc. [Anat.]; the entrails. (L. *viscus*.)
visceral, *a. vis*-er-ral, pertaining to or affecting the viscera.
viscerate, *v.t. vis*-er-rate, to deprive of the entrails or viscera; to disembowel.
viscid, *a. vis*-id, glutinous; sticky; tenacious; semi-fluid. (L. *viscum*, birdlime.)
viscidity, *n.* ve-*sid*-e-te, glutinousness; stickiness; the property of adhering.
viscoidal, *a.* vis-*koy*-dal, somewhat viscous.
viscometer, *n.* vis-*kom*-e-ter, a viscosimeter.
viscose, *n. vis*-kohs, a viscous substance chemically prepared from cellulose or wood pulp, used in the manufacture of rayon, cellophane, etc.: *a.* viscous; pertaining to or made from viscose.
viscosimeter, *n.* vis-ko-*sim*-e-ter, an instrument for ascertaining the viscosity of liquids.
viscosity, *n.* vis-*kos*-e-te, viscousness; viscidity; the internal friction which opposes the flow of fluids and semi-fluids when in a state of flux [Physics].
viscount, *n. vy*-kount, a degree or title of nobility next in rank above a baron and below an earl (used also as courtesy title of the eldest surviving son of an earl possessing this title); originally the deputy of a count and the sheriff of a county. (L. *vice*, in place of, and *count*.)
viscountcy, *n. vy*-kount-se, the rank, title, or dignity of a viscount.
viscountess, *n. vy*-koun-tess, the wife of a viscount.
viscounty, *n. vy*-koun-te, viscountcy; the office or jurisdiction of a viscount; the lands owned or administered by a viscount.
viscous, *a. vis*-kus, glutinous; viscid; adhesive; having a sticky surface. (L. *viscum*, birdlime.)
viscousness, *n.* the state of being viscous.
Viscum, *n. vis*-kum, a genus of parasitic plants including *V. album*, the mistletoe. (L.)
viscus, *n. vis*-kus, one of the viscera. (L.)
visé, *n. vee*-zay, a visa: *v.t.* to endorse with a visa. (Fr.)
Vishnu, *n. vish*-noo, the Preserver, the second member of the Hindu Trimurti, having many incarnations or avatars. (Sans. *vish*, penetrate or pervade.)
visibility, *n. viz*-e-*bil*-e-te, the quality of being visible; conspicuousness; extent of vision; degree of atmospheric clarity.
visible, *a. viz*-e-bl, perceivable by the eye; that can be seen; open to observation; apparent; open; conspicuous. **visible Church,** the whole body of professing Christians. **visible horizon,** *see* **horizon.**
visibleness, *n.* the state or quality of being visible.
visibly, *ad.* perceptibly to the eye.
Visigoth, *n. viz*-e-goth, one of the western Goths who settled in France and Spain, 4th and 5th centuries.
Visigothic, *a.* viz-e-*goth*-ik, pertaining to or characteristic of the Visigoths.
vision, *n. vizh*-on, the act of seeing external objects; actual sight; the faculty or the sense of seeing; sight; an object of sight; an apparition; something seen in imagination only: *v.t.* to see in or as in a vision; to imagine; to envisage. **field of vision,** the range covered by the sight; field of view. (L. *video*, *visum*, see.)
visional, *a. vizh*-on-al, pertaining to a vision; of the nature of a vision; imaginary.
visionariness, *n.* quality of being visionary.
visionary, *a. vizh*-on-a-re, imaginary; existing in imagination only; not real; treating fanciful impressions as realities: *n.* one who forms impracticable schemes; one who is confident of the success of an idle project.
visionist, *n. vizh*-on-ist, a visionary; one who has or who indulges in visions.
visit, *n. viz*-it, the act of going to see another, or of calling at his house; a brief stay or formal call; the act of going to see, attend on, or inspect: *v.t.* to go or come to see; to go or come to, esp. for inspection, examination, or correction of abuses; to overtake; to chastise; to comfort: *v.i.* to make a visit or visits; to keep up a friendly intercourse. **visiting card,** a small card with one's name, and usually address, to be left in paying a visit. (Fr. *visite*.)
visitable, *a. viz*-e-ta-bl, liable to be visited; subject to visitation.
visitant, *n. viz*-e-tant, one who goes or comes to see another; one who is a guest in the house of a friend; a visitor; a migrant [Ornith.].
visitation, *n. viz*-e-*tay*-shon, the act of visiting; an official inspection by a superior or superintending officer to a corporation, college, church, or other body, to examine into the manner in which it is conducted [Law]; an affliction, or the imposition of affliction as punishment for sin; (*cap.*) the festival (2 July) commemorating the visit of the Virgin to Elisabeth (Luke *i*, 39) [Rom. Cath. Ch.].
visitational, *a. viz*-e-*tay*-sho-nal, pertaining to an official visitation.
visitatorial, *a. viz*-e-ta-*taw*-re-al, connected with or pertaining to official visitation; holding the power of visitation.
visitor, *n. viz*-e-tor, one who visits; an official appointed to make visits of inspection to an institution, etc.
visitorial, *a.* viz-e-*taw*-re-al, visitatorial.
vison, *n. vy*-son, the American mink, *Mustela vison.*
visor, *n. vy*-zor, a perforated front of a helmet, which is raised and lowered at will; a disguise or mask. (Fr. *visière*.)
visored, *a. viz*-urd, wearing a visor; masked.
vista, *n. vis*-ta, a view or prospect down an avenue or as between rows of trees; a long corridor or passage; an extended mental view [Fig.]. (It., a view, from L. *video*, see.)
visual, *a. viz*-yew-al, pertaining to sight; used in sight; serving as the instrument of seeing. **visual angle,** the angle formed by the two imaginary lines drawn from the centre of the eye to the extremities of an object seen [Optics]. **visual point,** the point in which the visual rays unite [Persp.]. **visual ray,** a line of light proceeding from a point of the object to the eye. (L. *visum*, see.)
visuality, *n.* viz-yew-*al*-e-te, the quality of being mentally visible; a mental image.
visualization, *n. viz*-yew-a-ly-*zay*-shon, the act or power of visualizing; a mental picture.
visualize, *v.t. viz*-yew-a-lize, to make visible; to see in imagination; to envisage; *v.i.* to become visible.
vita-glass, *n. vy*-ta-glahs, proprietary name of a glass which, unlike common window-glass, allows the passage of ultra-violet rays. (L. *vita*, life.)
vital, *a. vy*-tal, pertaining to life (animal or vegetable); contributing or necessary to life; containing life; being indispensable or that on which life depends; essential: *n.pl.* **vy-talz,** parts of an

animal body or other organization essential to its life. **vital force,** the principle differentiating animate from inanimate things. **vital statistics,** demography. (L. *vita*, life.)
vitalism, *n.* *vy*-ta-lizm, the theory which refers the phenomena of life to something distinct from a merely physical principle.
vitalist, *n.* *vy*-ta-list, a believer in vitalism.
vitalistic, *a.* vy-ta-*lis*-tik, pertaining to or characteristic of vitalism.
vitality, *n.* vy-*tal*-e-te, vital power; liveliness; the principle of animation or of life.
vitalization, *n.* *vy*-ta-ly-*zay*-shon, the act or process of infusing the vital principle.
vitalize, *v.t.* *vy*-ta-lize, to give life to; to impart animation to; to quicken.
vitally, *ad.* *vy*-ta-le, in such a manner as to give life; essentially.
vitamin, *n.* *vy*-ta-min *or* *vit*-a-min, any of several factors or constituents of food serving to maintain physical condition or to repel deficiency and other diseases. (L. *vita*, life, and *amine*.)
vitaminize, *v.t.* *vit*-a-me-nize, to increase the vitamin content of food, esp. by ultra-violet light irradiation.
vitascope, *n.* *vy*-ta-skope, a cinematograph projector; a bioscope.
vitellary, *a.* *vit*-el-a-re, pertaining to the vitellus.
vitellicle, *n.* vi-*tel*-e-kl, a yolk-sac.
vitellin, *n.* vi-*tel*-in *or* vy-*tel*-in, the protein in the yolk of an egg.
vitelline, *a.* vi-*tel*-ine, vitellary; of the colour of the yolk of an egg.
vitellus, *n.* vi-*tel*-us *or* vy-*tel*-us, the yolk of an egg. (L.)
vitiate, *v.t.* *vish*-e-ate, to injure the substance or qualities of so as to impair or spoil; to render defective; to destroy, as the validity or binding force of. (L. *vitium*, a fault.)
vitiation, *n.* *vish*-e-*ay*-shon, the act of vitiating; depravation; corruption; a rendering invalid.
vitiator, *n.* *vish*-e-ay-tor, one who or that which vitiates.
viticulture, *n.* *vit*-e-kul-tewr, the culture of the vine.
vitiosity, *n.* *vish*-e-*os*-e-te, a morally corrupted state; viciousness; depravation.
Vitis, *n.* *vy*-tis, a genus of plants including *Vitis vinifera*, the cultivated grape. (L.)
vitreosity, *n.* *vit*-re-*os*-e-te, the quality or state of being vitreous.
vitreous, *a.* *vit*-re-us, pertaining to, consisting of, or resembling glass; having the characteristics of glass. **vitreous humour,** the jelly-like substance in the rear part of the eye. (L. *vitreus*, glassy.)
vitreousness, *n.* *vit*-re-us-ness, vitreosity.
vitrescence, *n.* vi-*tres*-ence, the quality of being vitrescent; vitreous condition.
vitrescent, *a.* vi-*tres*-ent, capable of being formed into glass; tending to become glass; glassy.
vitrescible, *a.* vi-*tres*-e-bl, vitrifiable.
vitrifaction, *n.* *vit*-re-*fak*-shon, the act, process, or operation of converting into glass by heat.
vitrifiable, *a.* *vit*-re-*fy*-a-bl, capable of being converted into glass by heat and fusion.
vitrification, *n.* *vit*-re-fe-*kay*-shon, vitrifaction; a product of vitrifying.
vitrified, *a.* *vit*-re-fide, converted into glass. **vitrified fort,** an ancient enclosure the masonry walls of which are more or less completely vitrified, still extant in Scotland and Northern Europe.
vitriform, *a.* *vit*-re-form, having the form of or resemblance to glass.
vitrify, *v.t.* and *i.* *vit*-re-fy, to convert into or to become glass or glassy by heat fusion. (L. *vitrum*, glass, *facio*, make.)
vitrine, *n.* *vit*-rin, a glass show-case for exhibiting specimens, etc.
vitriol, *n.* *vit*-re-ol, concentrated sulphuric acid prepared from ferrous sulphate (also called **oil of vitriol**); any of various sulphates, as **blue vitriol,** sulphate of copper; **cobalt vitriol,** cobalt sulphate; **green vitriol,** copperas or green sulphate of iron; **red vitriol,** colcothar, or other red sulphate of iron; and **white vitriol,** zinc sulphate; used figuratively of caustic or malignant virulence. (Fr., from L. *vitrum*, glass.)
vitriolate, *v.t.* *vit*-re-o-late, to convert into a sulphate.
vitriolation, *n.* *vit*-re-o-*lay*-shon, act or process of converting into a sulphate.
vitriolic, *a.* *vit*-re-*ol*-ik, pertaining to or obtained from vitriol; having the qualities of vitriol; extremely acrimonious or virulent [Fig.]. **vitriolic acid,** sulphuric acid.
vitriolizable, *a.* *vit*-re-o-*ly*-za-bl, capable of being vitriolized.
vitriolization, *n.* *vit*-re-o-ly-*zay*-shon, the process of vitrolizing.
vitriolize, *v.t.* *vit*-re-o-lize, to convert into vitriol; to vitriolate.
vitta, *n.* *vit*-ta (*pl.* **vittæ**), an oil cavity in the fruit of umbelliferous plants [Bot.]. (L., a ribbon, a headband.)
vittate, *a.* *vit*-at, containing vittæ [Bot.].
vituline, *a.* *vit*-yew-lin, belonging to a calf, or to veal. (L. *vitulinus*, of a calf.)
vituperable, *a.* vy-*tew*-per-ra-bl, blameworthy.
vituperate, *v.t.* vy-*tew*-per-rate, to blame abusively; to censure. (L. *vituperatus*, from *vitupero*, blame.)
vituperation, *n.* vy-*tew*-per-*ray*-shon, blame; censure; abuse.
vituperative, *a.* vy-*tew*-per-ra-tiv, uttering or containing censure or abuse.
vituperatively, *ad.* with vituperation.
vituperator, *n.* vi-*tew*-per-ray-tor, one who vituperates.
viva, *n.* *vee*-vah, a shout of applause. (It.)
vivace, *ad.* ve-*vah*-chay, briskly, in a lively manner [Mus.]. (It.)
vivacious, *a.* vy-*vay*-shus *or* vi-*vay*-shus, having great liveliness; lively; sprightly in spirit, temper, or conduct; having great vitality. (L. *vivax*, from *vivo*, live.)
vivaciously, *ad.* with spirit.
vivaciousness, *n.* the quality of being vivacious; vivacity.
vivacity, *n.* vy-*vas*-e-te *or* vi-*vas*-e-te, liveliness; sprightliness of temper or behaviour; life; animation; spirits.
vivandière, *n.* (App.), a woman sutler formerly attached to French regiments. (Fr.)
vivarium, *n.* vi-*vare*-re-um (*pl.* **vivaria** or **vivariums**), a place, or a glass-sided case, for keeping and exhibiting living animals under approximately natural conditions. (L.)
vivat, *int.* *vy*-vat, vive! hurrah! *n.* a viva. (Fr.)
viva-voce, *ad.* *vee*-vah-*voh*-se, orally; by word of mouth: *a.* oral: *n.* an oral examination. (L., with the living voice.)
vive, *int.* veev, long live! success to! (Fr.)
viverrine, *a.* vi-*ve*-rine, pertaining to or characteristic of the Viverridæ, a family of carnivores comprising the civets, etc.
vivers, *n.pl.* *vee*-vers, eatables [Scots.]. (Fr. *vivre*, food.)
vives, *n.* vyvz, a disease of horses characterized by tumours in the glands under the ear [Vet.]. (O.Fr., from Ar. *al dhibah*, the she-wolf.)
vivianite, *n.* *viv*-e-an-ite, a hydrous ferrous phosphate of various shades of blue and green.
vivid, *a.* *viv*-id, bright; intense; glowing; lifelike; forming brilliant images; highly coloured. (L. *vividus*, animated, true to life, from *vivo*, live.)
vividity, *n.* vi-*vid*-e-te, vividness.
vividly, *ad.* in a vivid manner; with life; in bright or glowing colours.
vividness, *n.* the quality or state of being vivid.
vivific, *a.* vi-*vif*-ik, giving life; animating; enlivening. (L. *vivus*, living, *facio*, make.)
vivificate, *v.t.* vi-*vif*-e-kate, to vivify; formerly, to restore to the native or metallic state [Chem.].
vivification, *n.* viv-e-fe-*kay*-shon, act of vivifying, reviving, or restoring; revival; restoration.
vivifier, *n.* *viv*-e-fy-er, that which or one who animates or gives life.
vivify, *v.t.* *viv*-e-fy, to endue with life; to animate; to quicken. (Fr. *vivifier*.)
viviparizm, *n.* vi-*vip*-a-rizm, viviparous reproduction [Zool.].
viviparity, *n.* viv-e-*pa*-re-te, viviparousness.
viviparous, *a.* vi-*vip*-a-rus, producing young in a living state (opposed to oviparous) [Zool.]; germinating while still attached to the parent plant [Bot.]. (L. *viviparus*, bringing forth its young alive).
viviparously, *ad.* in a viviparous manner.
viviparousness, *n.* state or property of being viviparous.

vivipary, *n.* vi-*vip*-a-re, viviparousness [Bot.].
vivisect, *v.t.* *viv*-e-sekt, to practise vivisection on.
vivisection, *n.* *viv*-e-*sek*-shon, experimentation by means of surgery, inoculation, etc., on living animals for the purpose of physiological or pathological discovery. (L. *vivus*, and *sectio*, cutting.)
vivisectional, *a.* *viv*-e-*sek*-shon-al, pertaining to vivisection.
vivisectionist, *n.* *viv*-e-*sek*-shon-ist, one who practises, or recognizes the necessity of, vivisection.
vivisector, *n.* *viv*-e-*sek*-tor, one who vivisects.
vivo, *ad.* *vee*-voh, with life and animation [Mus.]. (It.)
vixen, *n.* *vik*-sen, a female fox; a froward, turbulent, quarrelsome woman; a scold, a termagant. (A.S., feminine of *fox*.)
vixenish, *a.* *vik*-sen-ish, like a vixen; shrewish.
vixenly, *a.* and *ad.* having the qualities of a vixen; snappish; petulantly.
viz., viz, contraction of videlicet; that is; namely.
vizard, *n.* *viz*-ard, a mask or visor.
vizier, *n.* ve-*zeer*, a councillor of state among Moslems, esp. in the former Turkish Empire. **Grand Vizier,** a Moslem chief officer of state or prime minister. (Ar., one who bears a burden.)
vizierate, *n.* ve-*zeer*-rat, the office, authority, or rank of vizier.
vizor, *n.* *viz*-or *or* *vy*-zor, a visor.
Vlach, *a.* vlakh, Wallachian: *n.* a native of Wallachia. (Old Slav.)
vlei, vly, *n.* vly *or* vlay, a hollow or pool frequently dried up [S. Africa]; a swamp [U.S.A.]. (S.-Afr. Dut.)
vocable, *n.* *voh*-ka-bl, a word; a term; a name. (L. *vocabulum*, from *vox*, the voice.)
vocabulary, *n.* vo-*kab*-yew-la-re, a list or collection of the words of a language, or of technical terms, etc., arranged in alphabetical order and explained; a glossary; the collection of words at one's command.
vocabulist, *n.* vo-*kab*-yew-list, the compiler of a vocabulary; a lexicographer.
vocal, *a.* *voh*-kal, pertaining to voice or speech; uttered or modulated by the voice; voiced, sonant [Phonetics]: *n.* a vowel. **vocal music,** music for or sung by the voice as opposed to instrumental music. **vocal chords,** two vibratory membranous folds stretched across the upper end of the larynx [Anat.]. (L. *vox*, the voice.)
vocalic, *a.* vo-*kal*-ik, pertaining to, like, or abounding in vowel sounds.
vocalion, *n.* vo-*kay*-le-on, a modified harmonium with broad reeds and organ-like tone [Mus.].
vocalism, *n.* *voh*-ka-lizm, the using of the vocal organs; a vocal sound; the use of vowels.
vocalist, *n.* *voh*-ka-list, a singer, esp. one performing in public or professionally.
vocality, *n.* vo-*kal*-e-te, quality of being utterable by the voice, or [Phonetics] of being sonant or vocalic; having the force of a vowel.
vocalization, *n.* *voh*-ka-ly-*zay*-shon, the act of vocalizing; state of being vocalized.
vocalize, *v.t.* *voh*-ka-lize, to form with the voice; to make sonant or vocal; to write with the vowels or vowel-points (of Hebrew script): *v.i.* to utter vocal or vowel sounds, esp. in singing.
vocally, *ad.* with the voice; orally; in words.
vocation, *n.* vo-*kay*-shon, designation or destination to a particular state or profession; a calling by the will of God; summons; call; inducement; employment; avocation; calling; occupation.
vocational, *a.* vo-*kay*-shon-al, connected with a vocation, or with training for a vocation.
vocationally, *ad.* vo-*kay*-shon-a-le, with reference to a vocation.
vocative, *a.* *vok*-a-tiv, relating to calling; applied to that case of the noun in which the person denoted is addressed [Gram.]: *n.* the case of the word applied to the person addressed [Gram.].
voce, *n.* *voh*-chay, the voice [Mus.], as *voce di petto*, the natural voice: *voce solo*, a solo voice; *voce di testa*, a falsetto or feigned voice. (It.)
vociferance, *n.* vo-*sif*-er-rance, clamour.
vociferant, *a.* vo-*sif*-er-rant, clamorous.
vociferate, *v.i.* vo-*sif*-er-rate, to cry out with vehemence; to exclaim, bawl, or clamour: *v.t.* to utter with a loud voice. (L. *vociferatus*, a loud cry.)
vociferation, *n.* vo-*sif*-er-*ray*-shon, a violent outcry; vehement utterance of the voice; exclamation; clamour.
vociferator, *n.* vo-*sif*-er-ray-tor, one who vociferates.
vociferous, *a.* vo-*sif*-er-rus, making a loud outcry; clamorous; turbulent or noisy.
vociferously, *ad.* in a vociferous manner.
vociferousness, *n.* the quality of being vociferous.
vocule, *n.* *vok*-yewl, the slight vocal sound made after utterance of certain final letters, as *k*, *m*, *p* [Phonetics].
vodka, *n.* *vod*-ka, a Russian spirituous liquor distilled from rye or potatoes. (Russ., literally "little water".)
voe, *n.* voh, a creek or inlet of the sea. (Ice.)
vogal, vogle, *n.* *voh*-gl, a natural cavity in rock [Cornish mining]. (Corn. *vooga*, cavern.)
voglite, *n.* *vohg*-lite, a green carbonate of uranium with lime and copper found at Joachimsthal. (J. F. *Vogl*, Ger. mineralogist.)
vogue, *n.* vohg, fashion prevailing at any particular time; popular acceptation. (Fr.)
voguish, *a.* *voh*-gish, temporarily in the fashion.
*__voice,__ *n.* voyce, sound uttered by the mouth; intonated utterance; power of speech; any sound made by the breath; vote; language; words; expression (spoken or written); a speaker (on behalf of others); the vocal sound heard in vowels and certain consonants, as *l*, *n*, *v* [Phonetics]; a particular mode of inflecting or conjugating verbs, according as the subject is the agent or object of the action [Gram.]: *v.t.* to give expression to; to utter; to announce; to act as the mouthpiece of; to bring it to its intended tone and power [Mus.]; to write the voice parts of [Mus.]; to vocalize, or to give sonancy to [Phonetics]. **lift up one's voice,** to protest or complain. **with one voice,** unanimously. (Fr. *voix*, from L. *vox*.)
voiced, *a.* voyst, furnished with a voice; uttered with a voice or sonant tone [Phonetics].
voiceful, *a.* *voyce*-ful, having vocal quality; sonorous.
voiceless, *a.* *voyce*-less, having no voice or vote; sounded without voice [Phonetics].
voicelessness, *n.* *voyce*-less-ness, the state or quality of being voiceless; muteness.
void, *a.* voyd, not occupied with any visible matter; empty; vacant; having no incumbent; without inhabitants or furniture; having no legal or binding force; null; ineffective; free; clear; destitute; vain: *n.* an empty space; emptiness; a vacuum: *v.t.* to render of no validity or effect; to quit; to vacate; to make or leave vacant; to discharge or evacuate. **void space,** a vacuum [Physics]. (L. *viduus*, bereft.)
voidable, *a.* *voy*-da-bl, that may be annulled or made void; that may be evacuated.
voidance, *n.* *voy*-dance, act of emptying; act of ejecting from a benefice; annulment.
voided, *a.* *voy*-ded, made void; having the body so cut away that the edges only remain (of charges and ordinaries) [Her.].
voider, *n.* *voy*-der, a receptacle for waste, etc., esp. a basket in which broken meat is carried from the table; an ordinary resembling the flanch [Her.]; one who or that which voids.
voidness, *n.* *voyd*-ness, the state of being void; emptiness; vacuity; nullity.
voile, *n.* vwahl, a thin material of cotton or wool used for women's blouses, etc. (Fr., veil.)
voivode, *n.* *voy*-vode, former title of princes of Moldavia and Wallachia, later called hospodars; a waywode; a Turkish local official. (Slav., a military leader.)
vola, *n.* *voh*-la, the palm of the hand or sole of the foot [Anat.]. (L.)
volant, *a.* *voh*-lant, flying; passing through the air; nimble; active; represented as flying [Her.]. (Fr. from L. *volo*, fly.)
Volapuk, *n.* *vol*-a-pook, an international language devised for world-wide use by the Ger. priest J. M. Schleyer, in 1879.
volar, *a.* *voh*-lar, pertaining to the palm of the hand or sole of the foot. (L.)
volatile, *a.* *vol*-a-tile, having the power of flight; easily passing away or into the aeriform state; evaporating readily; lively; gay; full of spirit; fickle; apt to change. **volatile alkali,** ammonia. **volatile salt,** sal volatile. (Fr. *volatil*, from L. *volare*, to fly.)
volatility, *n.* vol-a-*til*-e-te, the quality of being

volatile; disposition to evaporate; great sprightliness; levity; fickleness.

volatilizable, *a.* vo-*lat*-e-*ly*-za-bl, capable of volatilization.

volatilization, *n.* vo-*lat*-e-ly-*zay*-shon, act or process of rendering volatile; state of being volatilized.

volatilize, *v.t.* vo-*lat*-e-lize, to render volatile; to cause to exhale or evaporate.

vol-au-vent, *n.* (App.), a puff-paste shape enclosing meat or fish, etc.; a timbale. (Fr.)

volcanic, *a.* vol-*kan*-ik, pertaining to volcanoes; produced by a volcano; changed or affected by the heat of a volcano.

volcanicity, *n.* *vol*-ka-*nis*-e-te, state or character of being volcanic or of volcanic origin; volcanic power.

volcanism, *n.* *vol*-ka-nizm, volcanicity; volcanic activity or phenomena.

volcanist, *n.* *vol*-ka-nist, one versed in the history and phenomena of volcanoes; a vulcanist.

volcanized, *a.* *vol*-ka-nized, affected by the action of volcanic heat.

volcano, *n.* vol-*kay*-noh (*pl.* **volcanoes**), vent in the earth's crust, usually at the summit of a conical hill of erupted materials, ejecting from the interior vapours, ashes, and streams of molten rock. (It., from L. *Vulcanus*, the Roman god of fire.)

volcanologist, *n.* vol-ka-*nol*-o-jist, a volcanist.

volcanology, *n.* vol-ka-*nol*-o-je, the science treating of volcanoes and their phenomena.

vole, *n.* vohl, a deal at cards in which all the tricks are won by one party; a grand slam: *v.i.* to make a vole. (Fr.)

vole, *n.* vohl, any of various field-mice, short-tailed rodents of the genus *Microtus*. (Scand. *voll*, field.)

volent, *a.* *voh*-lent, exercising, or capable of exercising, volition.

volery, *n.* *voh*-ler-re, a flight of birds; an aviary allowing space for flight; the birds in such.

volet, *n.* *vol*-ay, either of the wings of a triptych. (Fr.)

volitant, *a.* *vol*-e-tant, able to fly; flying; volant. (L. *volitans*, flying to and fro.)

volitation, *n.* vol-e-*tay*-shon, act of flying; flight.

volition, *n.* vo-*lish*-on, act of willing, of determining choice, or of forming a purpose; power of willing or determining. (L. *volo*, wish.)

volitional, *a.* vo-*lish*-o-nal, pertaining to or depending on volition; of the nature of a volition.

volitionally, *ad.* vo-*lish*-on-a-le, by means of or with respect to volition.

volitionary, *a.* vo-*lish*-on-a-re, volitional.

volitive, *a.* *vol*-e-tiv, having the power to will; expressing volition; deliberate; volitional.

Volkslied, *n.* *fohlks*-leet, a folk-song. (Ger.)

Volksraad, *n.* *fohlks*-rahd, a legislative assembly, esp. of the former Transvaal Republic or Orange Free State. (Dut.)

volley, *n.* *vol*-e, a simultaneous discharge of projectiles or missiles; a burst or emission of many things at once; a return of a ball before it bounces [Tennis, etc.]; a full-pitched ball rising direct from the ground to the wicket [Cricket]; a kick of the ball before it rebounds [Football]: *v.t.* to discharge with a volley; to hit back, or kick, a ball before it bounces: *v.i.* to throw out or discharge at once; to sound as a volley. (Fr. *volée*, flight.)

volplane, *v.i.* *vol*-plane, to glide downward with the engine cut out: *n.* such a flight [Av.].

volsella, *n.* vol-*sel*-a, a forceps with claw-like or serrated blades [Surg.]. (L., tweezers.)

volt, *n.* volt *or* vohlt, the unit of electro-motive force, that is, that required to force one ampere through a resistance of one ohm.

volt, *n.* volt, a round or circular tread; the gait of a horse going sideways round a centre [Man.]; a sudden movement or leap to avoid a thrust [Fencing]. (Fr. *volte*.)

volta, *n.* *vol*-ta, the old dance lavolta; a time (as **una volta,** once, **secunda volta,** the second time) [Mus.].

voltage, *n.* *vol*-taj *or* *vohl*-taj, measurement in volts; potential expressed in volts [Elect.].

voltaic, *a.* vol-*tay*-ik, pertaining to or discovered by Alessandro Volta (*d.* 1827), the Ital. physicist who first produced electric currents by chemical means.

Voltairianism, *n.* vol-*tare*-re-a-nizm, the opinions or principles of Voltaire (Fr. philosopher, *d.* 1778); scoffing or irreverent scepticism.

voltaism, *n.* *vol*-ta-izm, that branch of electrical science which has its source in the chemical action between metals immersed in liquids; galvanism.

voltameter, *n.* vol-*tam*-e-ter, an instrument for measuring electric current.

volt-ampere, *n.* volt- *or* vohlt-*am*-pare, the product of a volt and an ampere, the unit used for calculations in alternating current circuits [Elect. and Wire.].

volte, *n.* volt *or* vohlt, a volt [Man. and Fencing].

volte-face, *n.* *volt*-fahs, a complete change of front in opinions or attitude. (Fr.)

voltigeur, *n.* *vol*-te-zhoor, a former French light infantryman or sharpshooter. (Fr.)

voltmeter, *n.* *volt*-mee-ter, an instrument for measuring electro-motive force or pressure.

voltzite, *n.* *volt*-zite, a native zinc oxysulphide. (P. L. *Voltz*, *d.* 1840, Fr. mining engineer.)

volubile, *a.* *vol*-yew-bile, climbing by winding round another body [Bot.].

volubility, *n.* *vol*-yew-*bil*-e-te, the quality of being voluble; fluency of speech; loquacity. (L. *volubilis*, revolving.)

voluble, *a.* *vol*-yew-bl, fluent; having fluency of speech; formed so as to roll with ease; apt to roll; volubile [Bot.].

volubly, *ad.* *vol*-yew-ble, in a voluble manner.

volucrine, *a.* *vol*-yew-krin, pertaining to birds. (L. *volucris*, winged.)

volume, *n.* *vol*-yewm, a book; a covered or bound collection of sheets of printed or written paper; primarily, a scroll, as of parchment, written on and rolled up; a roll or turn; as much as is included in a roll or coil; dimensions; compass; space occupied; a swelling or spherical body; a wreath; compass, tone, or power of voice [Mus.]. **speak volumes,** *see* **speak.** (L. *volumen*, a roll of writing.)

volumed, *a.* *vol*-yewmd, having the form of a volume or roll; in volumes (as *three-volumed*).

volumenometer, *n.* *vol*-yew-me-*nom*-e-ter, an instrument for measuring the volume of a solid body by liquid or gaseous displacement.

volumenometry, *n.* *vol*-yew-me-*nom*-e-tre, the science of the measurement of the volume of solid bodies.

volumeter, *n.* *vol*-yew-*mee*-ter, an instrument for measuring the volume of gases.

volumetric, *a.* *vol*-yew-*met*-rik, pertaining to measurement of volume, esp. by means of standard solutions or with the eudiometer.

voluminal, *a.* vo-*lew*-me-nal, pertaining to volume [Physics, etc.].

voluminosity, *n.* vo-*lew*-me-*nos*-e-te, the quality of being voluminous (in writings); literary prolixity.

voluminous, *a.* vo-*lew*-me-nus, consisting of many coils or convolutions; consisting of many volumes or books; having written many volumes; copious; diffusive.

voluminously, *ad.* in many volumes; copiously.

voluminousness, *n.* the state or quality of being voluminous.

voluntarily, *ad.* *vol*-un-ta-re-le, in a voluntary manner.

voluntariness, *n.* *vol*-un-ta-re-ness, the quality of being voluntary.

voluntarism, *n.* *vol*-un-ta-rizm, any theory which regards will as the dominant factor in the individual or the whole of creation [Phil.]; voluntaryism.

voluntary, *a.* *vol*-un-ta-re, acting by choice without being influenced or impelled by another; free, not being under restraint; proceeding from or established by choice or free will; acting with willingness; done with design; spontaneous; subject to the will (of muscles, etc.): *n.* one who volunteers; an advocate of voluntaryism or of Church disestablishment; a piece played on the musician's choice, esp. an organ solo at the opening or close of a church service [Mus.]. **voluntary conveyance,** the transfer of property without any adequate consideration [Law]. **voluntary school,** a non-provided school; a school not under the direct and complete control of an Education Authority. (Fr.)

voluntaryism, *n.* *vol*-un-ta-re-izm, the doctrine that the Church should be independent of the state and of state control and be supported solely by the free-will offerings of its people.

volunteer, *n.* vol-un-*teer*, one who enters into military or other service of his own free will; a member of the Volunteers: *a.* voluntarily entering into service; composed of volunteers: *v.t.* to offer voluntarily: *v.i.* to enter into any service of one's free will, without solicitation or compulsion. **the Volunteers,** a voluntary military body composed of civilians and, from 1859 to 1908 (when superseded by the Territorials), forming an unpaid and partly trained reserve to the regular British army. (Fr. *volontaire.*)

voluptuary, *n.* vo-*lup*-tew-a-re, one addicted to luxury or the gratification of appetite and other sensual pleasures; a sybarite; a sensualist: *a.* voluptuous. (L. *voluptas*, pleasure.)

voluptuous, *a.* vo-*lup*-tew-us, given to luxury and pleasure; indulging in or spent in sensuality; ministering luxuriously to sensual pleasures.

voluptuously, *ad.* in a voluptuous manner; luxuriously.

voluptuousness, *n.* the state or quality of being voluptuous.

volute, *n.* vo-*lewt*, a spiral scroll, used in the Ionic and Composite capitals, four in the Ionic and up to eight in the Composite; a mainly tropical gastropod of the genus *Voluta.* (L. *voluta*, a spiral scroll.)

voluted, *a.* vo-*lew*-ted, having a volute, or a spiral scroll.

volution, *n.* vo-*lew*-shon, a spiral turn or wreath; a convolution. (L. *volvo, volutum*, roll.)

Volvox, *n. vol*-voks, a genus of minute flagellate globular organisms, found slowly moving or revolving in stagnant fresh water. (L. *volvo.*)

volvulus, *n. vol*-vew-lus, an obstructive twisting of the intestines [Med.].

vomer, *n. voh*-mer, the thin flat bone constituting the inferior posterior part of the septum of the nasal fossæ [Anat.]. (L., a ploughshare.)

vomica, *n. vom*-e-ka, an abscess or ulcerous cavity in the lungs.

vomit, *n. vom*-it, matter ejected through the mouth from the stomach; an emetic: *v.i.* to eject the contents of the stomach by the mouth; to discharge substances with violence from a deep hollow, as a volcano, etc.: *v.t.* to discharge from the stomach; to eject with violence or with loathing. **black vomit,** a dark-coloured matter ejected from the stomach in the last stage of yellow fever or other malignant disease; the disease, or yellow fever, itself. (L. *vomo.*)

vomition, *n.* vo-*mish*-on, the act of vomiting.

vomito, *n.* vo-*mee*-toh, yellow fever in its worst form; black vomit. (Sp.)

vomitory, *a. vom*-e-to-re, causing the ejection of matter from the stomach: *n.* the principal entrance and exit of a large building [Arch.]; a funnel, or similar vent; an agent that induces vomiting [Med.].

vomiturition, *n. vom*-e-tewr-*rish*-on, an unavailing effort to relieve the stomach by vomiting; vomiting with little or no effect. (L.)

voodoo, *n.* voo-*doo*, a low form of religion (originally snake-worship) or witchcraft common among the negroes of Hayti and elsewhere in the West Indies and America; a practiser of voodoo magic: *a.* pertaining to voodooism. (Creole Fr.)

voodooism, *n.* voo-*doo*-izm, voodoo beliefs and rites; the practice of these; sorcery.

voog, *n.* voog, a vogal. (Corn.)

voracious, *a.* vo-*ray*-shus, greedy for eating; ravenous; eager to devour or swallow up. (L. *voro*, devour.)

voraciously, *ad.* with greedy appetite; ravenously.

voraciousness, *n.* greediness of appetite; eagerness to devour; gluttony.

voracity, *n.* vo-*ras*-e-te, voraciousness.

voraginous, *a.* vo-*raj*-e-nus, abounding in whirlpools; full of abysses. (L. *vorago*, an abyss, a gulf.)

vorant, *a. vo*-rant, devouring, used esp. in heraldry of any animal depicted in this act.

vortex, *n. vor*-teks (*pl.* **vortices** *or* **vortexes**), a whirling or circular motion of water; a whirling of the air; a whirlwind or whirlpool; something, or a condition of affairs, of the nature of a vortex. (L., from *verto*, to turn.)

vortical, *a. vor*-te-kal, whirling; turning; moving in a vortex.

vortically, *ad.* in a vortical manner.

vorticella, *n. vor*-te-*sel*-la, a genus of bell-shaped, stalk-supported aquatic infusoria which, by the rapid rotary motion of the cilia round the mouth, create a vortex in the water to obtain their food.

Vorticist, *n. vor*-te-sist, one of a short-lived (about 1912–22) English school of advanced post-impressionists who aimed at portraying pure rhythmic vitality rather than anything in nature.

Vorticism, *n. vor*-te-sizm, the theory or art of the Vorticists.

vorticity, *n.* vor-*tis*-e-te, the state of a fluid when in vortical motion.

vorticose, *a. vor*-te-kohs, vortical; resembling a vortex.

vorticular, *a.* vor-*tik*-yew-lar, vortical; vorticose.

vortiginous, *a.* vor-*tij*-e-nus, vortical.

votal, *a. voh*-tal, of the nature of a vow; votive.

votaress, *n. voh*-ta-ress, a woman devoted to any service, worship, or state of life.

votarist, *n. voh*-ta-rist, a votary. (L. *votum.*)

votary, *n. voh*-ta-re, one devoted, consecrated, or engaged by a vow or promise; one devoted or addicted to some particular service, worship, study, or state of life.

vote, *n.* voht, suffrage; the expression of a wish, desire, will, preference, or choice in regard to any measure proposed, as in elections to office or the passing of resolutions, laws, or the like; a ballot, a ticket, etc., as expressive of preference; expression of will by a majority; the aggregate of votes; that which is voted, esp. a money grant: *v.i.* to express or signify the mind, will, or preference in electing to office, or in passing laws, etc.: *v.t.* to choose by suffrage; to elect by some expression of will; to enact or establish by vote; to grant by vote. **voting paper,** a paper on which an elector gives his vote. (Fr. *voter.*)

voter, *n. voh*-ter, one who votes; an elector; one who has a legal right to vote.

votive, *a. voh*-tiv, given by or as the result of some vow; devoted. **votive medal,** one struck in grateful commemoration of some auspicious event. **votive offering,** a tablet or other gift, dedicated in consequence of the vow of a worshipper.

vouch, *v.t.* vouch, to guarantee; to maintain by affirmation or substantiation; to establish proof; to cite or call into court in support [Law]: *v.i.* to bear witness; to give testimony. (L. *voco*, call.)

vouchee, *n.* vou-*chee*, one called into court to support or make good his warranty of title, etc. [Law].

voucher, *n. vouch*-er, one who or that which gives witness or full attestation to anything; the act of calling in a person to make good his warranty of title [Law]; a paper, document, etc., serving, to vouch the truth of accounts, or to confirm and establish facts; a guarantee; a receipt.

vouchsafe, *v.t.* vouch-*safe*, to permit to be done; to condescend to grant: *v.i.* to condescend. (Lit., safe guarantee.)

vouchsafement, *n.* vouch-*safe*-ment, an act or grant in condescension.

voussoir, *n. voos*-wahr, one of the truncated wedge-like stones forming part of an arch [Arch.]. (Fr.)

vow, *n.* vou, a solemn promise made to God or to some deity; a solemn promise or pledge: *v.t.* to give, consecrate, or dedicate to God by a solemn promise; to devote: *v.i.* to make vows or solemn promises. (O.Fr. *avouer*, from L. *advocare*, to call to.)

vowel, *n. vou*-el, a sound uttered by simply opening the mouth or vocal organs, as the sound of *a, e, o* a letter or character that can be sounded without any other letter. **vowel point,** in Hebrew, a mark indicating the vowel sound preceding or following the consonant to which it is annexed. (Fr. *voyelle.*)

vowelled, *a. vou*-eld, furnished with vowels.

vower, *n. vou*-er, one who makes a vow.

voyage, *n. voy*-aj, a passage or journey, originally by land or water now by water only, esp. from one distant place or country to another: *v.i.* to sail or pass by water: *v.t.* to travel; to pass over. (Fr.)

voyager, *n. voy*-a-jer, one who sails or passes by sea or water.

voyageur, *n.* vwah-yah-*zhoor*, a Canadian boatman an employee of a fur-trading company who transports goods by land and across streams between remote stations. (Fr.)

vraisemblance, *n.* (App.), verisimilitude; appear

ance of truth. (Fr. *vrai*, true, and *semblance*, seeming.)
vug, *n.* voog, a vogal. (Corn.)
Vulcan, *n. vul*-kan, the god of fire, who presided over the working of metals [Rom. Myth.].
Vulcanian, *a.* vul-*kay*-ne-an, pertaining to Vulcan, or to work in iron; volcanic; pertaining to the vulcanists; Plutonian.
Vulcanic, *a.* vul-*kan*-ik, pertaining to Vulcan; (*l.c.*) volcanic.
vulcanism, *n. vul*-ka-nizm, volcanism; volcanic action.
vulcanist, *n. vul*-ka-nist, a supporter of the Plutonic theory of the igneous origin of certain rocks [Geol.]; a volcanist.
vulcanite, *n. vul*-ka-nite, vulcanized rubber, rubber combined with a large proportion of sulphur.
vulcanization, *n. vul*-ka-ny-*zay*-shon, the act or process of vulcanizing.
vulcanize, *v.t. vul*-ka-nize, to change or improve the physical properties of rubber by chemical means, esp. by combining it with sulphur, white lead, and other substances: *v.i.* to undergo vulcanization.
vulcanizer, *n. vul*-ka-ny-zer, the stove or container in which rubber is vulcanized.
vulgar, *a. vul*-gar, pertaining to the common people; used or practised by common people; common; used by all classes; public; vernacular; plebeian; low; boorish; rude; unrefined: *n.* the common people. **vulgar fraction,** a fraction in which both numerator and denominator are given (*cf.* **decimal fraction**) [Math.]. **vulgar tongue,** the language of a country as spoken or commonly used; the vernacular. (L. *vulgus*, the mass, the people.)
vulgarian, *n.* vul-*gare*-re-an, an ill-bred boor; a well-to-do person vulgar in manners or speech.
vulgarism, *n. vul*-ga-rizm, grossness of manners; vulgarity; a coarse or unrefined expression.
vulgarity, *n.* vul-*ga*-re-te, the quality of being coarse or vulgar; grossness or clownishness of manners or language.
vulgarization, *n. vul*-ga-ry-*zay*-shon, the act or process of making common or widely known, or of making coarse or vulgar.
vulgarize, *v.t.* and *i. vul*-ga-rize, to make or become vulgar; to debase; to behave in a vulgar manner.
vulgarly, *ad.* in a vulgar manner.
Vulgate, *n. vul*-gate, the Latin version of the scriptures made by St. Jerome in the 4th cent. and declared standard for the Roman Church by the Council of Trent, 1546 (so called as having been in common use): *a.* pertaining to the Vulgate, or to any commonly accepted literary text. (L. *vulgatus*, from *vulgo*, make common.)
vulnerability, *n. vul*-ner-ra-*bil*-e-te, the quality or state of being vulnerable.
vulnerable, *a. vul*-ner-ra-bl, that may be wounded; susceptible of wounds; liable to injury; subject to be affected injuriously; having won a game towards the rubber [Contract]. (L. *vulnus*, a wound.)
vulnerary, *a. vul*-ner-ra-re, useful in healing wounds; adapted to the cure of external injuries: *n.* any plant, drug, or composition useful in the cure of wounds.
vulpicide, *n. vul*-pe-side, the killing of a fox, or one who kills foxes, otherwise than in hunting.
vulpine, *a. vul*-pine, pertaining to or characteristic of foxes; cunning; crafty. (L. *vulpinus*, from *vulpes*, a fox.)
vulpinism, *n. vul*-pe-nizm, cunning; foxiness.
vulpinite, *n. vul*-pe-nite, a siliceous variety of anhydrite. (*Vulpino*, town in Italy.)
vulsella, *n.* vul-*sel*-a, volsella.
vulture, *n. vul*-tewr, a carrion-eating bird of prey with great powers of flight and generally bare of feathers on the head and neck. **king vulture,** *see* **king.** (L. *vultur*.)
vulturine, *a. vul*-tewr-rine, characteristic of or having the qualities of the vulture; rapacious.
vulturish, *a. vul*-tewr-rish, somewhat like a vulture.
vulturous, *a. vul*-tewr-rus, vulturish; ravenous.
vulva, *n. vul*-va, the female external genital organs [Anat.]. (L.)
vulvar, *a. vul*-var, pertaining to the vulva [Med.].
vulviform, *a. vul*-ve-form, like a cleft with projecting edges [Bot. and Conch.]. (L. *vulva*, and *form*.)
vulvitis, *n.* vul-*vy*-tis, inflammation of the vulva [Med.]. (L. *vulva*, and Gr. *itis*, inflammation.)
vying, *vy*-ing, *ppr.* of *vie*: *a.* competing: *n.* the act of competing; competition.

W

W, *dub*-bl-yew, the 23rd letter of the English alphabet, is named from the doubling of the Roman letter V, which was a form of U distinguished from it only in shape. W represents the French *ou* and the Spanish, Italian, and German *u*; as a final after a vowel (*law, few, crow,* etc.) it has a diphthongal effect; and before *r* (*wreck, writ,* etc.) as well as in certain special instances (*answer, boatswain, gunwale, two, Greenwich, Alnwick,* etc.) it is silent, while in others (as *housewife, toward*) it is frequently elided. Before *h* W is sometimes silent (*who, whole, whose,* etc.), but is usually the voiceless bilabial *h*+*w* heard in *what, whelk, whistle, why,* etc.

Waac, *n.* wak, one serving in the Woman's Army Auxiliary Corps of World War I [Coll.].

Waaf, *n.* waf, a member of the Woman's Auxiliary Air Force of World War II.

wabble, *v.i. wob*-bl, to wobble.

wabbly, *a. wob*-bl-e, wobbly.

wacke, *n. wak*-e, an earthy or sandstone-like rock, the product of the disintegration of basic rock [Geol.]. (Ger.)

wad, *n.* wod, a small mass of some soft or flexible material, such as hay or tow; a ball or disk of any soft material rammed into a gun to keep the charge down; a packet of bank-notes [Slang]: *v.t.* to form into a wad; to stuff with a wad. (Scand.)

wad, *n.* wod, an earthy oxide of manganese [Min.].

wadable, *a. wade*-a-bl, fordable.

wadded, *a. wod*-ed, formed into a wad or mass.

wadding, *n. wod*-ing, material for wads; a soft woollen or cottony stuff of loose texture, used for padding garments, etc.; cotton-wool.

waddle, *v.t. wod*-dl, to move in walking with short rocking steps and from side to side, like a duck: *n.* a waddling gait; the act of waddling. (*wade.*)

waddler, *n. wod*-dler, one who waddles.

waddlingly, *ad. wod*-dling-le, with a short-stepping, rocking gait.

waddy, *n. wod*-e, the wooden war-club of the Australian aborigines.

wade, *v.i.* wade, to walk through any substance that yields to the feet, as water; to move or pass with difficulty or labour; to progress slowly through hindrances and embarrassments: *v.t.* to pass, as a river, by walking on the bottom; to ford on foot: *n.* a wading; the act of wading. **wade into,** to enter into or take part in with enthusiasm [Coll.]. (A.S. *wadan*, L. *vado*, go.)

wader, *n. wade*-er, one who or a bird that wades; an angler's high waterproof boot.

wadi, *n. wod*-e, the channel of a water-course which is dry except in the rainy season. (Ar.)

wadmal, *n. wod*-mal, a thick woollen cloth formerly in common use. (Ice.)

wadset, *n. wod*-set, a form of pledge or mortgage as a satisfaction for debt or obligation; a thing pledged [Scots. Law]. (A.S. *wed*, a pledge.)

wadsetter, *n. wod*-set-er, one who holds by a wadset.

wae, *n.* way, woe: *a.* very sad; woeful [Scots.].

Wafdist, *a. wof*-dist, pertaining to the Wafd, the extreme Nationalist Party of Egypt, founded 1919 by Zaghlul Pasha: *n.* a member of this. (Ar. *wafd*, deputation.)

wafer, *n. way*-fer, a thin small sweet cake; a thin circular piece of unleavened bread used in the administration of the eucharist frequently impressed with some symbol (esp. Rom. Cath. Ch.); a thin disk of dried paste, sometimes coloured, used in sealing letters: *v.t.* to seal, close, or attach with a wafer. (O.Fr. *waufre.*)

wafery, *a. way*-fer-re, like a wafer, very thin.

waffle, *n. wof*-l, a batter cake baked in the fire in an iron mould. (Dut. *wafel.*)

waffle, *n. wof*-l, a yelp or yelping (of dogs); prattling nonsense [Slang]: *v.i.* to chatter incessantly, to blather [Slang].

waffle-iron, *n.* a hinged mould in which to bake waffles.

waft, *v.t.* wahft, to bear through a fluid or buoyant medium, esp. air or water; to convey, as ships; to beckon, as by a wave of the hand: *v.i.* to drift through the air: *n.* an act of wafting; a slight current of air, also an odour or puff of smoke, etc., carried by such; a flag flown as a signal, esp. one tied in the middle as a sign of mourning [Naut.]. (*wave.*)

waftage, *n. wahf*-taj, conveyance or transportation by wafting.

wafture, *n. wahf*-tewr, the action or an act of waving or undulating.

wag, *v.t.* wag, to move one way and the other with quick turns; to move a little way backwards and forwards, as of the finger or head: *v.i.* to oscillate; to be quick in ludicrous motion; to stir; to be moved one way and the other: *n.* an act of wagging; a vibratory motion; a wit; a man of humour; one fond of jokes. (O.Sw. *wagga*, akin to A.S. *wegan*, move.)

wage, *v.t.* waje, to undertake; to carry on, as to wage war; to wager: *n.* wages. (O.Fr.)

wage-earner, *n.* one who earns wages.

wageless, *a. waje*-less, receiving no wages.

wager, *n. way*-jer, something deposited, laid, or hazarded on the event of a contest or some unsettled question; a bet; a subject on which bets are laid; an offer to make oath of innocence or non-indebtedness [Law]; the act of making oath along with others to fortify the defendant's oath [Law]: *v.t.* and *i.* to offer a wager; to bet; to stake; to put at hazard on the event of a contest. **wager of battle,** the ancient custom of lawfully settling disputes by personal combat. (O.Fr. *wageure.*)

wagerer, *n. way*-jer-rer, one who wagers or lays a bet.

wages, *n.pl. way*-jez, reward; requital; payment periodically made for labour or services, chiefly of a manual or mechanical character. **wages fund,** that part of the capital of the community destined for the payment of labour [Econ.].

wage-work, *n.* work done for wages.

wagger, *n. wag*-er, one who or that which wags; a signaller or flag-wagger [Army slang].

waggery, *n. wag*-er-re, mischievous merriment; sportive trick or gaiety; sarcasm in good humour.

waggish, *a. wag*-ish, humorous; roguish in merriment; done in waggery; frolicsome.

waggishly, *ad.* in a waggish manner.

waggishness, *n.* the quality of being waggish; roguish sport.

waggle, *v.i. wag*-gl, to wag; to wobble; to move from side to side: *v.t.* to sway about: *n.* an act of waggling. (*wag.*)

waggly, *a. wag*-gle, wobbly.

waggon, *n. wag*-on, a wagon.

waggonette, *n.* wag-o-*net*, a wagonette.

Wagnerian, *a.* vahg-*neer*-re-an, in the style of Richard Wagner (*d.* 1883), the musical composer: *n.* a student or admirer of Wagner.

Wagnerist, *n. vahg*-ner-rist, a Wagnerian.

Wagnerite, *n. vahg*-ner-rite, a Wagnerian.

wagnerite, *n. wag*-ner-ite, a phosphate and fluoride of magnesium. (F. M. von *Wagner*, *d.* 1851, Bavarian mineralogist.)

wagon, *n. wag*-on, a heavy vehicle on four wheels used for the transport of heavy commodities, usually drawn by two or more horses; a heavy-weight railway goods-truck, usually open; a dinner-wagon: *v.t.* to transport in a wagon. **on the (water-) wagon,** temporarily teetotal [Slang]. **wagon roof,** a barrel-vaulted roof, one shaped like an inverted U. (Dut. *wagen.*)

wagonage, *n. wag*-on-aj, money paid for carriage in a wagon; wagons collectively.

wagoner, *n. wag*-o-ner, one who drives a wagon.

wagonette, *n.* wag-o-*net*, an open four-wheeled carriage with the back seats facing each other longitudinally.

wagon-lit, *n.* vah-gon-*lee*, a railway sleeping-car. (Fr.)

wagtail, *n.* *wag*-tale, a small bird, belonging to the genus *Motacilla*, named from the frequent vertical wagging of its long tail.
Wahabi, *n.* wa-*hah*-bee, a follower of Abd-el Wahhab, an 18th-cent. Moslem reformer aiming at a return to early Mohammedanism, whose doctrines now prevail in the greater part of Arabia.
Wahabiism, *n.* wah-*hah*-bee-izm, the tenets, doctrine, or practices of the Wahabis.
wahoo, *n.* wah-*hoo* or *wah*-hoo, a shrub, *Euonymus atropurpureus*, of the spindle-tree family; a tonic and purgative prepared from its dried root-bark. (N. Amerind.)
waif, *n.* wafe, one who wanders about and has no home; a straying animal; anything found without an owner; stolen goods thrown away by a thief in his flight [Law]; a poor neglected child. (O.Fr., perhaps from Scand.)
wail, *n.* wale, loud weeping; violent lamentation; the sound of this; *v.t.* to lament loudly; to bewail: *v.i.* to express sorrow audibly; to weep or cry loudly. (Ice.)
wailer, *n.* *wale*-er, one who wails.
wailful, *a.* *wale*-ful, sorrowful; mournful.
wailing, *n.* *wale*-ing, loud cries of sorrow; deep lamentation.
wailingly, *ad.* plaintively; with wailing.
wain, *n.* wane, a wagon; a wheeled vehicle for the transport of goods; (*cap.*) the Great Bear or **Charles's-wain** [Astron.]. (A.S. *wægen*, a wagon.)
wainbote, *n.* *wane*-bote, timber allowed to a tenant under feudal law for repair of his wains.
wain-rope, *n.* a rope for securing a load on a wagon; a cart-rope.
wainscot, *n.* *wane*-skot, a wooden lining or boarding of walls, made in panels; broad wooden skirting: *v.t.* to line with boards; to line with different materials. (Dut. *wagenschot.*)
wainscoting *or* **wainscotting,** *waynz*-kot-ing, *n.* material for wainscots.
wainwright, *n.* *wane*-rite, a wagon-maker.
wair, *n.* ware, obsolete term for a piece of plank two yards long and one foot broad [Carp.].
waist, *n.* wayst, the part of the human body next below the ribs, normally the narrowest part of the trunk; the middle part of anything, esp. [Naut.] a ship; the contracted part of a violin, etc.; a shirt-waist, or similar garment. (A.S., growth, from *weaxan*, grow.)
waistband, *n.* *wayst*-band, the band, or upper part of trousers or skirts, which encompasses the waist.
waist-cloth, *n.* a loin-cloth; a strip of cloth worn round the waist and upper part of the legs; a covering of canvas or tarpaulin for hammocks stowed in the waist [Naut.].
waistcoat, *n.* *wayst*-koat *or* *wes*-kot, a short sleeveless undercoat for the trunk extending to slightly below the waist. **straight waistcoat,** *see* **strait-waistcoat.**
waist-deep, *a.* as deep (in water, etc.) as the waist is high.
waisted, *a.* *ways*-ted, having a waist; having a specified waist, as short-waisted.
waister, *n.* *ways*-ter, a new hand, or an unseamanlike sailor who works in the waist of a ship [Naut.].
wait, *v.i.* wate, to stay in expectation; to remain quiet or inactive; to serve as a waiter (at table, etc.): *v.t.* to await; to bide; to cause to wait: *n.* an act or spell of waiting; time of waiting; a delay; a pause; one of a party of waits; an ambush. **lie in wait,** *see* **lie. wait for,** to watch as an enemy; to lie in wait. **wait on** or **upon,** to attend, as a servant; to attend upon; to pay servile attendance to; to accompany. (O.Fr. *waiter*, watch.)
wait-a-bit, *n.* *wate*-a-bit, *n.* any of several S. African acacias and mimosas furnished with stiff hooked thorns.
waiter, *n.* *way*-ter, one who waits; a servant in attendance at a meal, or at an hotel, etc.; a salver; a dumb-waiter; a tide-waiter.
waiting, *a.* *way*-ting, serving; attending: *n.* act of staying; attendance. **in waiting,** in attendance, esp. upon the sovereign. **waiting list,** a list of persons awaiting election or preferment, etc.; a roster of men not on the active list but awaiting orders [Navy].
waitingly, *ad.* *way*-ting-le, in a waiting or apprehensive state; by waiting.
waiting-maid *or* **-woman,** *n.* an upper female servant who attends on a lady.
waiting-room, *n.* a room for person's waiting, as at a railway station, etc., or for interviews.
waitress, *n.* *way*-tress, a woman acting as a waiter, esp. in a hotel, restaurant, etc.
waits, *n.pl.* wates, itinerant musicians, who celebrate the approach of Christmas by nocturnal alfresco performances for which they solicit alms or contributions.
waive, *v.t.* wave, to forgo; to relinquish; to refrain from insisting on or claiming. (O.Fr., from Scand.)
waiver, *n.* *way*-ver, the act of waiving or of not insisting on some right [Law].
wake, *n.* wake, the annual commemoration of the dedication of a church, formerly kept by watching all night; a vigil of a festival; a state of forbearing sleep; a lich-wake, or sitting up of persons with a dead body prior to burial; the annual fair and holiday held in certain northern, esp. Lancashire, towns: *v.i.* to be or continue awake; to cease to sleep; to awake; to be alive or active; to be excited from a torpid state; to be put in motion: *v.t.* to rouse from sleep; to arouse; to put in motion or action; to revive; to hold a wake over (a deceased person). *p.* and *pp.* **waked or woke**; *pp.* also **woken.** (A.S. *wacan*, arise.)
wake, *n.* wake, the region of fluid behind a moving body that is affected by the motion, either visibly or otherwise, or the similar region behind a stationary body past which fluid is moving; the track a vessel leaves in the water; any track. **in the wake of,** following immediately after. (Ice., a track through ice.)
wakeful, *a.* *wake*-ful, not sleeping; indisposed to sleep; watchful; vigilant.
wakefully, *ad.* with watching or sleeplessness.
wakefulness, *n.* indisposition to sleep.
waken, *v.i.* *way*-kn, to wake; to cease to sleep: *v.t.* to rouse from sleep; to excite to action or motion.
wakener, *n.* way-kn-er, one who or that which rouses from sleep.
wakening, *n.* *way*-kn-ing, an awakening; a revival.
waker, *n.* *way*-ker, one who awakes; one who rouses another from sleep; a participant in a wake.
wakerife, *a.* *wake*-rife, wakeful; vigilant [Scots.].
wake-robin, *n.* *wake*-rob-in, the plant *Arum maculatum*, also known as lords-and-ladies and cuckoo-pint.
waking, *a.* *way*-king, being awake; exciting into motion or action: *n.* the period of being awake. waking hours, the hours when one is awake.
Waldenses, *n.pl.* wol-*den*-seez, a body of dissenting Catholics which arose in the 12th cent. in the valleys of Piedmont under the leadership of Peter Waldo aiming at a return to the primitive evangelism of the early Church and in repudiation of clerical corruption and immorality.
Waldensian, *a.* wol-*den*-se-an, pertaining to the Waldenses: *n.* one of the Waldenses.
wale, *n.* wale, a weal; the mark of a stripe.
wale-knot, *n.* a wall-knot [Naut.].
waler, *n.* *wale*-er, a horse bred in New South Wales, esp. one imported into India.
Walhalla, *n.* wol-*hal*-a, valhalla.
*__walk,__ *v.i.* wawk, to step along; to advance by steps, both feet never being from the ground together and not by running, or jumping, etc.; to go, move, or travel on foot; to be stirring; to depart; to live and act relatively to some principle of conduct [Fig.]: *v.t.* to pass over or through; to perambulate; to cause to walk or step slowly; to lead, drive, or ride with a slow pace; to train young hounds: *n.* the act of walking; manner of walking; gait; step; carriage; the distance one walks; a place for walking; an avenue set with trees; a path, way, or road; the round or beat of a policeman, itinerant salesman, etc.; course of life or pursuit; the slowest pace of a horse; a sheepwalk. **walk into,** to thrash; to devour greedily. **walk of life,** status; occupation. **walk off,** to decamp; to divest oneself of by walking. **walk off with,** to appropriate and take away. **walk out,** to leave or abscond. **walk out with,** to court [Coll.]. **walk over,** to gain a victory with ease, or without a contest. **walk the hospitals,** to study clinical practice, etc., in the wards. **walk the plank,** to walk by

compulsion blindfold along a plank projecting from a ship's side (a pirate's way of putting to death). **walk the streets,** to live as a prostitute or street-walker. (A.S. *wealcan*, roll, ramble.)
walkable, *a.* *wawk*-a-bl, fit to be walked on; possible to be walked.
walker, *n.* *wawk*-er, one who walks; a shop-walker; one who walks or trains young hounds.
walkie-talkie, *n.* *waw*-ke-*taw*-ke, a two-way radio-telephone so constructed that it can be carried in a car or by one man. (*walk* and *talk*.)
walking, *n.* *wawk*-ing, act of moving on the feet; pedestrianism; the condition of a road for walking on. **walking encyclopædia,** a person of vast erudition; a sciolist; a know-all.
walking-leaf, *n.* wawk-ing-*leef*, a leaf-insect.
walking-stick, *n.* *wawk*-ing-stik, a stick carried in the hand for support or pleasure in walking; an insect, esp. of the family Phasmidæ, with a long slender body like a piece of stick.
walkout, *n.* *wawk*-out, a departing, esp. when sudden or unexpected; a lightning strike.
walk-over, *n.* *walk*-oh-ver, an easy victory.
walkyrie, *n.* *wol*-ke-re, a valkyrie.
★**wall,** *n.* wawl, a permanent structure of stone, brick, or other material forming an enclosure or division thereof, or serving for protection or privacy; the side of a building or apartment; a defence or means of security; a sea-wall; some feature (cliff, barrier, etc.) resembling a wall in appearance or function: *pl.* fortifications in general: *v.t.* to enclose with, defend, or obstruct by a wall. **give (take) the wall,** to pass (allow to pass) on the side farther from the roadway. **go to the wall,** to fail, to be defeated. **walls have ears,** someone may be listening. **Wall Street,** the money market of the U.S.A. (name of site of financial centre in New York City). (A.S. *weall*.)
wallaba, *n.* *wol*-a-ba, a leguminous tree of Guiana, valuable for its timber, *Eperua falcata*.
wallaby, *n.* *wal*-a-be, a small marsupial allied to the kangaroo. **on the wallaby,** on tramp [Austral. slang]. (Native Austral.)
Wallachian, *n.* wo-*lay*-ke-an, an inhabitant of, or one belonging to, Wallachia, a former Danubian Principality later forming part of Rumania: *a.* pertaining to the Wallachians or Vlachs. (Slav. *voloch*.)
wallah, *n.* *wol*-la, an Anglo-Indian term for a person employed in some capacity or concerned in something, as *punkah-wallah*, punkah-worker; hence [Slang] any chap, fellow, or "bloke." (Hind. suffix, *-wala*, pertaining to.)
wallaroo, *n.* *wol*-a-roo, the grey kangaroo *Macropus robustus*, with long thick fur. (Native Austral.)
wall-barley, *n.* the wild, roadside barley, *Hordeum murinum*; applied also to rye-grass.
wall-creeper, *n.* a small bird, *Tichodroma muraria*, allied to the tree-creeper, which frequents mountainous regions.
wallcress, *n.* *wawl*-kress, a cress of the genus *Arabis*, growing in dry stony places or on walls.
walled, *a.* wawld, enclosed by or fortified with a wall.
waller, *n.* *wawl*-er, one who builds or repairs walls.
wallet, *n.* *wol*-et, a knapsack or bag for carrying the necessaries for a journey or march; a scrip; a bag-like purse; a small case for carrying tools or implements; a pocket-book; a note-case. (Origin uncertain; perhaps A.S. *watel*, a bag.)
wall-eye, *n.* glaucoma; a disease of the eye in which the iris is of a very light grey or whitish colour; a name given to certain fishes.
wall-eyed, *a.* *wawl*-ide, having wall-eye.
wallflower, *n.* *wawl*-flou-er, the cruciferous plant *Cheiranthus cheiri*; a girl at a dance having no attraction for partners [Slang].
wall-fruit, *n.* fruit grown against a wall.
wall-game, *n.* a form of football played at Eton.
walling, *n.* *wawl*-ing, walls in general; materials for walls.
wall-knot, *n.* a knot formed at the end of a rope by untwisting the strands and interweaving them [Naut.].
wall-moss, *n.* a species of lichen growing on walls; the stonecrop, *Sedum acre*.
Walloon, *n.* wa-*loon*, one of the French-speaking people of southern Belgium (as opposed to the Flemings of the north), descendants of the Celtic Belgæ; their language: *a.* pertaining to the Walloons; in the Walloon language. (O.Fr.)
wallop, *v.i.* *wol*-op, to boil with a continued bubbling or noisy heaving and rolling of the liquor: *v.t.* to beat soundly; to thrash or drub [Coll.]: *n.* liquor, esp. ale [Slang]. (O.Fr. *galoper*, boil.)
walloping, *a.* *wol*-op-ing, big; bouncing [Slang]: *n.* a thrashing or drubbing [Slang].
wallow, *v.i.* *wol*-oh, to roll one's body on the earth, in mire, or on other substances; to tumble and roll; to move heavily and clumsily; to live in filth or gross vice: *v.t.* to roll one's body: *n.* the act of wallowing; a muddy place in which animals wallow. **to wallow in wealth,** to be exceedingly well off. (A.S. *wealwian*.)
wallower, *n.* *wol*-oh-er, one who wallows; a wheel that turns the trundle-head in a mill.
wallpaper, *n.* *wawl*-pay-per, paper-hangings.
wall-pellitory, *n.* the plant, *Parietaria officinalis*, growing on old walls and in stony places.
wall-pennywort, *n.* the plant *Cotyledon umbilicus*.
wall-pepper, *n.* stonecrop.
wall-plate, *n.* a piece of timber placed horizontally upon a wall, on which joists rest.
wall-rue, *n.* the fern *Asplenium rutamuraria*.
Wallsend, *n.* *wawlz*-end, superior house coal (so called from a colliery of the name on the Tyne which was worked out many years ago).
wall-sided, *a.* having sides nearly perpendicular.
wall-tree, *n.* a fruit-tree trained on a wall.
wall-wash, *n.* liquid distemper for use on wall surfaces.
wallwort, *n.* *wawl*-wurt, the dwarf-elder, or danewort, *Sambucus ebulus*; also erroneously applied to the wall-pellitory. (A.S. *wealk wyrt*, foreign herb.)
walnut, *n.* *wawl*-nut, a tree and its fruit, *Juglans regia*; also its timber, much used for cabinet-work. (A.S. *wealh*, foreign, and *nut*.)
Walpurgis Night, vahl-*poor*-gis nite, the eve of May 1st, when witches were supposed to hold high revelry on certain peaks, esp. the Brocken, in Germany. (St. *Walpurga*, an 8th-cent. English nun, instrumental in the introduction of Christianity to Germany).
walrus, *n.* *wawl*-rus, the morse, *Trichechus rosmarus*, a large, tusked, pinniped carnivore of the Arctic seas. (Dut. *walros*, from Scand. *hrosshvalr*, horse-whale.)
waltz, *n.* wawltz, a German dance, introduced into England in early 19th cent., danced with a whirling motion by couples; the triple-time music by which it is accompanied: *v.i.* to dance a waltz: *v.t.* to dance a person round. (Ger. *walzen*, roll.)
waltzer, *n.* *wawlt*-zer, a person who waltzes or is skilled in waltzing.
waltzing, *n.* *wawlt*-zing, the act of dancing a waltz.
wamble, *v.i.* *wom*-bl, to rumble internally; to be disturbed with nausea: *n.* a feeling of nausea. (Dan. *vamle*, nauseate.)
wampee, *n.* *wom*-pee, the evergreen Chinese tree, *Clausena Wampi* (*Cookia punctata*), also its edible fruit. (Chin. *hwang*, yellow, *pi*, skin.)
wampum, *n.* *wom*-pum, strings of beads made from coloured shells, used by the American Indians as money, and also for ornamenting belts, etc. (Amerind., white.)
wan, *a.* won, pallid; of a sickly hue; languid of look. (A.S. *wann*, dark.)
wanchancy, *a.* won-*chahn*-se, unchancy; unlucky; wicked.
wand, *n.* wond, a long thin stick; a rod or staff of authority; a rod used by conjurers; a conductor's baton. (Scand.)
wander, *v.i.* *won*-der, to ramble here and there without any certain course or object in view; to leave home; to depart; to migrate; to depart from the line of discussion; to depart from duty or rectitude; to be delirious; to be not under the guidance of reason: *v.t.* to travel over without a certain course. (A.S. *wandrian*.)
wanderer, *n.* *won*-der-rer, a rambler; one who roves; one who deviates from duty.
wandering, *a.* *won*-der-ring, roving; rambling: *n.* peregrination; aberration; deviation from rectitude; roving of the mind in discussion, in a dream, in delirium; uncertainty. **Wandering Jew,** a Jew of mediæval legend who, because of his insults to Christ when on the way to crucifixion, was

doomed to roam the earth till the Second Advent; name given locally to various trailing plants.
wanderingly, *ad.* in a wandering manner.
wandering-plug, *n.* a plug contact at the end of a wire for inserting into any one of a number of sockets, each forming part of a different open electric circuit [Elect.].
wanderlust, *n.* *vahn*-der-loost, a craving for travel; restlessness. (Ger.)
wanderoo, *n.* *won*-der-roo, a langur of Ceylon, a species of *Semnopithecus*; the lion-tailed macaque, *Macacus silenus*, of W. India.
wandoo, *n.* *won*-doo, the white gum-tree of Western Australia, *Eucalyptus redunca*.
wandy, *a.* *won*-de, long and flexible, like a wand.
wane, *n.* wane, decrease of the illuminated part of the moon; decline; diminution: *v.i.* to be diminished; to decrease (applied particularly to the illuminated part of the moon); to decline. (A.S. *wanian*, diminish.)
wang, *n.* wang, the jaw or cheek-bone; a wang-tooth. (A.S.)
wanghee, *n.* wong-*hee*, whanghee.
wangle, *v.i.* *wang*-gl, to manage astutely; to manipulate to one's own advantage; to falsify: *n.* a wangling; a profitable piece of trickery [Slang].
wangler, *n.* *wang*-gler, one who wangles [Slang].
wang-tooth, *n.* a molar or cheek-tooth.
wanhope, *n.* *won*-hope, hopelessness; utter despair. (*wane* and *hope*.)
wanion, *n.* *won*-yon, only in phrase *with a wanion*, with a vengeance. (M.E. *waniand*, waning [of the moon], hence, ill-omened.)
wankle, *a.* *wong*-kl, weak; unstable; changeable.
wanky, *a.* *wong*-ke, wonky.
wanly, *ad.* *won*-le, with a wan look; in a dejected manner.
wanness, *n.* *won*-ness, pallor; paleness; sickliness.
wannish, *a.* *won*-ish, slightly wan.
want, *n.* wont, deficiency; defect; need; necessity; poverty; penury; indigence; the state of not having; what is not possessed but is desired: *v.t.* to be destitute of; to be deficient in; not to have; to fall short of; to be without; to need; to have occasion for; to wish for; to desire: *v.i.* to be deficient; to fail; to be lacking; to fall short. (O.Scand. *vant*.)
want, *n.* wont, the mole, *Talpa eruopæa* [Dial.].
wantage, *n.* *won*-taj, deficiency; that which is wanting [U.S.A.]
wanting, *a.* *won*-ting, absent; deficient; not up to expectation; [Coll.] mentally defective.
wantless, *a.* *wont*-less, having no want; abundant.
wanton, *a.* *won*-ton, wandering or roving in gaiety or sport; sportive; frolicsome; straying from rectitude; licentious; unchaste; lascivious; loose; unrestrained; extravagant: *n.* a lewd or lascivious man or woman; an insignificant trifler: *v.i.* to rove and ramble without restraint; to revel; to play loosely, or lasciviously; to move briskly and irregularly. (A.S. *wan*, lacking, not, *togen*, educated.)
wantonly, *ad.* in a wanton manner.
wantonness, *n.* *won*-ton-ness, negligence of restraint; lasciviousness; levity; sportiveness.
want-wit, *n.* one destitute of wit and sense.
wanty, *n.* *won*-te, a broad leather strap for binding a load on the back of a beast.
wapacut, *n.* *wop*-a-kut, the snowy owl of north-west Canada, *Nyctea nivea*.
wapenshaw, *n.* *wop*-en-shaw, a periodical gathering in the districts of Scotland for the inspection of arms; a rifle competition, esp. among non-professional soldiers. (A.S. *wæpen*, weapon, and *shaw*.)
wapentake, *n.* *wop*-en-take, a division or district, as in Yorkshire, answering to the hundred in other counties. (A.S. *wæpen*, arms, *tac*, touch.)
wapiti, *n.* *wop*-e-te, the large stag or elk of N. America, *Cervus canadensis*. (Algonq.)
wapper, *v.t.* *wap*-per, to move quickly and tremulously; to totter; to blink.
wapper, *n.* *wop*-per, whopper.
★**war,** *n.* wawr, a contest between nations or states, or parties in the same state, carried on by force of arms; instruments of war; forces; arms; the profession of arms; art of war; hostility; state of opposition or contest; enmity; disposition to contention: *v.i.* to make war; to invade or attack a nation or state with force of arms; to carry on hostilities; to contend; to strive violently: *v.t.* to carry on a contest. **civil war,** *see* **civil. holy war,** a religious war; a crusade. **in the wars,** suffering through or injured by strife. **man-of-war,** a warship. **sinews of war,** money, esp. as necessary for purchase of materials, etc. **war footing,** state of being completely prepared for mobilization [Mil.]. **war game,** Kriegspiel. **War Office,** the Government Department responsible to the King and Parliament for the Army. **war to the knife,** *see* **knife. war zone,** any area, esp. on the high seas, proclaimed by a belligerent to be one in which the rights of neutrals are not recognized. (A.S. *werre.*)
waratah, *n.* *wo*-ra-tah, the Australian plant *Telopea speciosissima*, with brilliant red flower.
warble, *n.* *wawr*-bl, a quavering modulation of the voice, as in birds; a warbling sound or song: *v.t.* to quaver the voice; to modulate with turns or variations; to cause to quaver; to be modulated: *v.i.* to be quavered or modulated; to be uttered melodiously; to sing. (O.Fr. *werbler*.)
warble, *n.* *wawr*-bl, a small hard tumour on the backs of horses, usually occasioned by pressure of the saddle; a similar tumour on cattle, etc., caused by parasitic larvæ of the bot-fly or **warble fly.** (Origin uncertain.)
warbler, *n.* *wawr*-bler, a songster; a small song-bird of a sub-family of the thrushes, including the whitethroat and blackcap.
warbled, *a.* *wawr*-bld, infested with warbles (of horses, etc.) [Vet.].
warbling, *a.* *wawr*-bling, quavering the voice; singing; filled with musical notes, as a grove: *n.* the act of shaking or modulating notes; singing.
warblingly, *ad.* in a warbling manner.
war-cry, *n.* *wawr*-kry, a shout for mutual encouragement in charging an enemy; a party cry; a slogan.
ward, *n.* wawrd, guard made by a weapon in fencing; one, or a number, whose business is to guard, watch, and defend; act of guarding; custody; confinement under guard; a minor or person under the care of a guardian; the state of a minor under a guardian; guardianship; a division of a city or borough; a hospital apartment for clinical treatment of patients; a section of a prison or workhouse; the part of a lock which hinders the action of any but the right key: *v.t.* to fend off; to repel; to turn aside anything mischievous that approaches; originally to guard, to defend: *v.i.* to act on the defensive with a weapon; [Coll.] to place in a hospital ward. **ward off,** fend off; repel; turn aside from injuring. (A.S. *weardian*, guard.)
wardage, *n.* *wawr*-daj, ward-penny.
war-dance, *n.* a dance performed by savage tribes before proceeding to battle.
warden, *n.* *wawr*-dn, a keeper; a guardian; one who keeps ward; a title of the master or president of certain colleges. **Lord Warden of the Cinque Ports,** the governor of the Cinque Ports, who has the authority of an admiral and formerly possessed jurisdiction in local law and equity. **Warden of the Marches,** the high official who guarded the frontiers or marches of Scotland or Wales.
warden, *n.* *wawr*-dn, a variety of cooking pear. (Probably O.Fr. *guarder*, to guard, to keep.)
wardenship, *n.* office or jurisdiction of a warden.
warder, *n.* *wawr*-der, one who keeps guard; a turnkey or gaoler; formerly, a truncheon used by an officer in making signals, etc.
wardian, *a.* *wawr*-de-an, applied to a close glass case for plants. (Named from the inventor, N. B. *Ward*.)
wardmaid, *n.* *wawrd*-made, a female domestic servant employed in a hospital ward.
wardmote, *n.* *wawrd*-mote, an assembly of the members of a city ward, esp. in London. (*ward* and *mote*.)
ward-penny, *n.* a fine paid in feudal times in lieu of military service.
wardress, *n.* *wawr*-dress, a female prison warder.
wardrobe, *n.* *wawrd*-robe, a movable upright chest or cupboard (formerly a room) in which clothes are kept; wearing apparel in general.
ward-room, *n.* the mess-cabin of the senior officers of a warship.
war-drum, *n.* a drum beaten as a summons to war; any call to warlike activity [Fig.].

wardship, *n.* *wawrd*-ship, guardianship; care and protection of a ward; pupilage; state of being under a guardian.
ware, *a.* ware, provided against; wary; aware: *int.* beware! look out!
ware, *n.* ware, an article of merchandise; articles of a specified manufacture collectively, as earthenware: *pl.* **wares,** warez, goods; commodities; merchandise. (A.S. *waru.*)
ware, *n.* ware, seaweed, esp. in a drifting mass [Scots.]. (A.S. *war.*)
wareful, *a.* *ware*-ful, wary; watchful; cautious.
warefulness, *n.* wariness; cautiousness.
ware-goose, *n.* the brent goose.
warehouse, *n.* *ware*-house, a storehouse for goods; a building for storing goods till duty is paid (bonded warehouse): *v.t.* to deposit or secure in a warehouse or custom-house store.
warehouseman, *n.* *ware*-house-man, one who keeps or is employed in a warehouse.
warehousing, *n.* *ware*-hou-zing, the act of placing goods in a bonded warehouse. **warehousing system,** an arrangement for keeping imported articles in bond, duty not being payable until they are taken out for home consumption.
warely, *ad.* *ware*-le, cautiously.
warfare, *n.* *wawr*-fare, a state of war; war; military service; contest; struggle with spiritual enemies. (*war* and *fare.*)
warfarer, *n.* *wawr*-fare-rer, one engaged in warfare.
warfaring, *a.* *wawr*-fare-ring, carrying on war.
war-head, *n.* the forward section of a torpedo, in which the explosive is contained.
war-horse, *n.* *wawr*-horse, a trooper's horse; a charger; an old campaigner, esp. one addicted to war-time reminiscences [Fig.].
warily, *ad.* *ware*-re-le, in a wary manner; cautiously.
wariness, *n.* *ware*-re-ness, prudent care to foresee and guard against evil; caution.
warlike, *a.* *wawr*-like, fit, ready, or disposed for war; pertaining to war; having the appearance of war; martial; soldierly.
warlikeness, *n.* *wawr*-like-ness, the condition or quality of being warlike.
warlock, *n.* *wawr*-lok, a male witch; a wizard; a giant, or other mythical monster. (A.S. *wærloga.*)
war-lord, *n.* *wawr*-lord, an outstanding military leader; [Coll.] one eager for war.
★**warm,** *a.* wawrm, having heat in a moderate degree; not cold; having prevalence of heat; zealous; ardent; habitually ardent; amorous; irritable; keen; fresh (of scent); animated; busy or heated in action; fanciful; enthusiastic; vigorous; sprightly; well off, moderately wealthy [Fig.]: *v.t.* to communicate a moderate degree of heat to; to interest; to engage; to excite ardour or zeal in; to set aglow; to thrash [Slang]: *v.i.* to become moderately heated; to become ardent or animated. **warm colours,** those which have yellow or yellow-red for their basis. **warm corner,** an awkward predicament [Coll.]. **British warm,** a thick short-skirted overcoat worn by army officers. (A.S. *wearm.*)
warm-blooded, *a.* wawrm-*blud*-ed, having warm blood, as mammals and birds; emotional; over-amorous [Fig.].
warmer, *n.* *wawrm*-er, one who or that which warms.
warm-hearted, *a.* wawrm-*har*-ted, having or showing warmth of affection, zeal, or interest; cordial; kindly.
warm-heartedness, *n.* quality of being warm-hearted.
warming, *a.* *wawrm*-ing, making moderately hot or warm: *n.* a thrashing [Slang].
warming-pan, *n.* a long-handled covered pan for warming a bed with live coals; a locum tenens, or one temporarily holding an office [Coll.].
warmly, *ad.* *wawrm*-le, with gentle heat; eagerly; earnestly; ardently.
warmness, *n.* *wawrm*-ness, the state of being warm; warmth.
warmonger, *n.* *wawr*-mung-ger, one who attempts to provoke, or is loudly in favour of, war.
warmth, *n.* wawrmth, warmness; gentle heat; a warm or kindly feeling; a state of lively and excited interest; zeal; ardour; earnestness; excitement; fancifulness; enthusiasm; that glowing effect which arises from the use of warm colours [Painting].
warn, *v.t.* wawrn, to give notice of probable danger or evil that may be avoided; to caution; to admonish of any duty; to notify beforehand; to notify by authority; to summon. **warn off,** to order off; to prohibit entry. (A.S. *warnian.*)
warner, *n.* *wawrn*-er, one who warns; an admonisher.
warning, *n.* *wawrn*-ing, caution against danger; previous notice; notice to leave or go.
warningly, *ad.* *wawrn*-ing-le, so as to warn.
warp, *n.* wawrp, in weaving, the threads which are extended lengthwise in the loom and crossed by the woof; a rope employed in drawing or towing; a towing line [Naut.]; the state of being twisted; a distortion in the grain of timber; a mental twist; perversity of disposition; a slimy substance tidally or artificially deposited on land by water, by which a rich alluvial soil is formed [Agric.]; a group of four (esp. food-fish). (A.S. *wearp,* throw.)
warp, *v.i.* wawrp, to turn, twist, or be twisted out of a straight direction; to become twisted, perverted, or distorted; to deviate; to swerve; to cast the young prematurely, as cows: *v.t.* to turn or twist out of shape, or out of a straight direction; to turn aside from the true direction; to pervert; to tow or move with a line or warp attached to a buoy or other fixed object [Naut.]; to fertilize ground by means of inundation; to run the yarn off for weaving, or [Rope-making] to be tarred. (A.S. *weorpan,* cast, throw.)
warpaint, *n.* *wawr*-paynt, paint used by certain savage nations on the face and body on going to war; full dress, finery [Fig.].
warpath, *n.* *wawr*-pahth, among American Indians, the route followed on a hostile expedition; a hostile expedition, or [Fig.] hostile course of action. **on the warpath,** prepared for or looking for a fight; angry.
warped, *a.* *wawrpt,* twisted; distorted; fertilized with alluvial warp [Agric.].
warper, *n.* *wawr*-per, one who forms the threads into the warp; a warping machine [Weaving].
warping, *n.* *wawr*-ping, the preparing of the warp; fertilization of land by flooding with water [Agric.]; hauling with a warp [Naut.].
warping-bank, *n.* a mound of earth constructed to retain water let in for fertilizing land.
warping-hook, *n.* a hook used by rope-makers for hanging yarn on, when warping into hauls for tarring.
warping-post, *n.* a strong post used in warping rope-yarn.
warplane, *n.* *wawr*-plane, an aeroplane designed for use in warfare.
warproof, *a.* *wawr*-proof, proof against attack: *n.* valour tried by war.
warragal, *n.* *wo*-ra-gal, the warrigal.
warrant, *n.* *wo*-rant, an act, instrument, or obligation by which one person authorizes another to do something which he has not otherwise a right to do; a writ of arrest; authority; power that authorizes or justifies any act; that which attests or proves; a commission giving authority; a voucher; right; a writing which authorizes a person to receive money or other thing; a writ of authority inferior to a commission [Mil.]. **dividend warrant,** *see* **dividend. dock warrant,** a document authorizing the delivery of goods out of bond. **warrant of attorney,** *see* **attorney.**
warrant, *v.t.* *wo*-rant, to authorize; to maintain; to support by authority or proof; to justify; to secure; to pledge oneself for; to declare with assurance; to secure to a grantee an estate granted [Law]; to secure to a purchaser the good quality of the goods sold [Law]. (O.Fr. *warantir.*)
warrantable, *a.* *wo*-rant-a-bl, authorized by commission, precept, or right; justifiable. **warrantable stag,** a stag old enough to be hunted (*i.e.*, 5 years or more).
warrantableness, *n.* the quality of being warrantable or justifiable.
warrantably, *ad.* justifiably.
warranted, *a.* *wo*-ran-ted, authorized; justified; vouched.
warrantee, *n.* wo-ran-*tee,* one to whom a warranty is given or land is warranted [Law].
warranter, *n.* *wo*-ran-ter, one who gives authority or legally empowers; one who assures or engages to assure; one who contracts to secure another in a

right or to make good any defect of title or quality; a warrantor.
warranting, *a.* *wo*-ran-ting, authorizing; assuring.
warrant-officer, *n.* an officer next below a commissioned officer, acting under a warrant, as a naval gunner or boatswain, and a regimental sergeant-major.
warrantor, *n.* wo-ran-*tor*, one who warrants, the correlative of warrantee.
warranty, *n.* *wo*-ran-te, a promise or deed made by the bargainer for himself and his heirs to secure the bargainee and his heirs in the enjoyment of an estate or other thing granted; authority; justificatory mandate or precept; security; a guarantee.
warren, *n.* *wo*-ren, a natural breeding-place of wild rabbits; a piece of ground appropriated to the preservation of rabbits, and formerly of hares, partridges, or pheasants; an overcrowded quarter, slum, or tenement [Fig.]. (O.Fr. *warenne.*)
warrener, *n.* *wo*-ren-er, the keeper of a warren.
warrigal, *n.* *wo*-re-gal, the dingo, the native dog of Australia; an Australian wild native; an untamed Australian horse: *a.* wild. (Native Austral.)
warrior, *n.* *wo*-re-or, a fighting or military man; a soldier, esp. when veteran or distinguished. **the Unknown Warrior,** an unidentified soldier slain in World War I and ceremoniously interred in a national shrine as a symbol of his country's sacrifice.
warship, *n.* *wawr*-ship, a naval vessel of any kind, esp. one armed for and employed in attack; a man-of-war.
war-song, *n.* *wawr*-song, a song inciting to war; a song accompanying the war-dance.
wart, *n.* wawrt, a firm, hard excrescence, found chiefly on the hands; a verruca; a spongy excrescence on the hinder pasterns of a horse; a sessile gland or protuberance on trees. (A.S. *wearte.*)
wart-cress, *n.* a plant of the genus *Coronopus.*
wart-disease, *n.* a fungoid growth from the eyes of potatoes causing black warts on the tubers.
warted, *a.* *wawr*-ted, having little knobs on the surface; verrucose [Bot.].
wart-hog, *n.* *wawrt*-hog, an African ungulate of the genus *Phacochœrus,* allied to the swine.
wartime, *n.* *wawr*-time, a period during which war is in progress: *a.* occurring in, pertaining to, or characteristic of a time of war.
wartless, *a.* *wawrt*-less, having no warts.
wartwort, *n.* *wawrt*-wurt, any plant supposed to be efficacious against warts, esp. *Euphorbia helioscopia,* the sun-spurge.
warty, *a.* *wawr*-te, full of, overgrown with, or of the nature of warts; covered with hard prominences.
war-wasted, *a.* devastated or seriously impaired by war.
war-whoop, *n.* among savage tribes, a yell raised in charging an enemy; an exultant war-cry.
warwickite, *n.* *wo*-rik-ite, a borate and titanate of magnesium and iron found at Warwick in New York State, U.S.A.
war-worn, *a.* *wawr*-worn, worn with, or widely experienced in, military service.
wary, *a.* *ware*-re, cautious of danger; carefully watching and guarding against deception, artifices, and dangers; careful; circumspect. (A.S. *wær.*)
was, woz, *first and third person singular* of the *past tense* of the verb *to be.*
wase, *n.* waze, a pad of straw, etc., worn on the head by porters to relieve the pressure of burdens.
***wash,** *n.* wosh, the act of washing; state of being washed; act of washing a quantity of clothes, linen, etc.; the quantity to be washed; a cosmetic; a lotion; a superficial stain or colour; a colour spread thinly over broad masses or spaces of a picture [Painting]; alluvial matter; substances collected and deposited by water; kitchen waste liquor; swill, or pigwash; the fermented wort from which spirit is extracted; the blade of an oar [Naut.]; the washing or surging motion of the sea; the rough water caused by a moving ship or boat; the break of the waves on a shore; a thin coat of metal.
wash, *v.t.* wosh, to cleanse by ablution or by rubbing in water; to scrub in water; to wet; to cleanse by a current of water; to overflow; to dash against; to cover with water; to separate extraneous matter from by means of water; to rub over with some liquid substance; to overlay with a thin coat of metal; to purify (as from the pollution of sin) [Fig.]; to spread colours thinly over broad masses of spaces of a picture; *v.i.* to perform the act of ablution; to do washing; to stand washing; to stand the test. **wash out,** to wash free of dirt or extraneous matter; to lose colour; to exhaust [Coll.]; to eliminate [Slang]. **wash the hands of,** to disclaim responsibility; to abandon. **wash up,** to cleanse plates and table utensils after use. **won't wash,** won't suit, won't stand up to the test. (A.S. *wæscan.*)
washable, *a.* *wosh*-a-bl, that can be washed without damage.
washaway, *n.* *wosh*-a-way, a breach caused by a flood.
washball, *n.* *wosh*-bawl, a ball of soap to be used in ablutions or shaving.
washboard, *n.* a ribbed board for washing clothes on; a broad, thin plank, fixed occasionally on the side of a vessel or on the sill of a lower deck port to prevent the sea from breaking over [Naut.]; a board round a room next to the floor; a skirting-board.
washbottle, *n.* a bottle used for purifying gases, precipitates, etc. [Chem.].
washer, *n.* *wosh*-er, one who or that which washes: a washing-machine; an iron ring between the nave of a wheel and the linchpin; a piece of iron, leather, or rubber at the base of a screw or nut to tighten up with.
washerman, *n.* *wosh*-er-man, a man who washes clothes; a laundryman.
washerwoman, *n.* *wosh*-er-woo-man, a woman who washes clothes for others or for hire; a laundress.
washhand-basin, *n.* a bowl or basin, usually with taps for water, in which to wash the hands and face.
washhouse, *n.* *wosh*-house, a building or room in which clothes are washed; a laundry; a scullery.
washily, *ad.* *wosh*-e-le, in a weak or washy manner.
wash-in, *n.* an increase of the angle of incidence of a wing towards the tips [Av.].
washiness, *n.* *wosh*-e-ness, the quality of being washy or weak.
washing, *n.* *wosh*-ing, act of cleansing with water; ablution; a wash; the garments, linen, etc., sent to be washed at one time.
washing-machine, *n.* a machine used in washing clothes and linen or cloth.
washing-soda, *n.* prepared sodium carbonate for cleansing purposes.
Washingtonia, *n.* wosh-ing-*toh*-ne-a, any of three species of handsome Californian palms; also, the sequoia.
wash-leather, *n.* split sheepskin dressed in imitation of chamois for cleaning household articles; buff leather for belts.
wash-out, *n.* the action of washing away or out; damage caused by this; a failure, or disappointment [Slang]; a decrease of the angle of incidence towards the wing designed to delay tip stalling [Av.].
wash-pot, *n.* a vessel in which anything is washed.
washstand, *n.* *wosh*-stand, a small table or frame on which toilet requisites are placed to be used in washing the hands or face.
washtub, *n.* *wosh*-tub, a tub in which clothes, linen, etc., are washed.
washy, *a.* *wosh*-e, watery; damp; soft; weak; lacking in vigour; not firm or hardy.
wasp, *n.* wosp, a hymenopterous insect of the genus *Vespa*; an irritable or choleric person. (A.S. *wæps.*)
wasp-flower, *n.* a flower frequented by or fertilized by wasps.
wasp-fly, *n.* a species of fly resembling a wasp, but stingless; an angler's artificial fly.
waspish, *a.* *wosp*-ish, resembling a wasp; having a very slender waist; quick to resent any trifling affront; short-tempered; snappish; petulant; irascible.
waspishly, *ad.* in a waspish manner.
waspishness, *n.* petulance; choler; irascibility; snappishness.
wasp-waisted, *a.* having a very slender or constricted waist; tightly corseted.
wassail, *n.* *wos*-el, a festive occasion; health-drinking; a drinking bout; a spiced liquor made of roasted apples, sugar, and ale, formerly taken

on such occasions: *v.i.* to hold a merry drinking meeting: *v.t.* to toast; to drink to. (A.S. *wæs*, be, *hæl*, well or whole.)
wassail-bowl, *n.* a vessel containing wassail for the use of a festive company.
wassailer, *n.* *wos*-el-er, one who assists at a wassail; a reveller; a toper.
wast, *v.i.* wost, *second person singular* of the *past tense* of the verb *to be*.
wastable, *a.* *ways*-ta-bl, proper for wasting; of no use or value.
wastage, *n.* *ways*-taj, loss by waste, decay, or use; useless expenditure of energy, time, etc.
waste, *a.* wayst, serving no useful purpose; superfluous; worthless; of no value; ruined; desolate; uncultivated; destitute; stripped. **laid waste,** desolated; ruined; devastated.
★**waste,** *n.* wayst, the act of squandering; dissipation of property through wantonness, ambition, extravagance, luxury, negligence, etc.; useless expenditure; prodigality or dissipation; a desolate, devastated, or uncultivated region; land untilled though capable of tillage; destruction; spoil, destruction, or injury done to the prejudice of the heir [Law]; anything of no further use, or valueless.
waste, *v.t.* wayst, to diminish by gradual dissipation or loss; to scatter and destroy; to squander uselessly; to cause to be lost through wantonness or negligence; to destroy in enmity or by violence; to desolate; to impair strength gradually; to wear out; to spend or consume to no effect or purpose; to damage, impair, or injure an estate, as by suffering buildings, fences, etc., to decay [Law]; to exhaust: *v.i.* to lose bulk or substance gradually; to be diminished or lost by slow dissipation, consumption, or evaporation. (O.Fr. *waster*, lay waste.)
waste-basket, *n.* *wayst*-bahs-ket, a basket to hold waste, esp. waste paper.
waste-book, *n.* a day-book; a book in which entries of transactions are made as they occur [Comm.].
wasteful, *a.* *wayst*-ful, causing waste; expending that which is valuable without necessity or use; lavish; prodigal; destructive; ruinous.
wastefully, *ad.* in a wasteful way.
wastefulness, *n.* lavishness; expenditure without necessity or use.
wasteless, *a.* *wayst*-less, not diminishing; occasioning little or no waste.
wasteness, *n.* *wayst*-ness, a desolate state; solitude.
waste-pipe, *n.* a pipe for conveying off waste water or other liquid; an escape- or outlet-pipe.
waster, *n.* *ways*-ter, one who squanders property or consumes extravagantly; a good-for-nothing; something causing a candle to waste; an article damaged in the making.
wasting, *a.* *ways*-ting, enfeebling; diminishing by dissipation of substance and strength; reducing weight; undergoing waste: *n.* prodigality; gradual wearing away.
wastrel, *n.* *ways*-trel, a worthless person; a ne'er-do-well; a neglected or deserted child; anything cast away as unserviceable: *a.* feeble (of animals and plants).
★**watch,** *n.* wotch, the act of watching; a state of attention or wakefulness; close observation; guard; a watchman or watchmen set for a guard; post or office of a watchman; a certain period of the night in which one person or a set of persons stand as sentinels; a turn of duty; the period during which a division of the crew is on duty on deck [Naut.]; a small timepiece or chronometer to be carried in the pocket or about the person. **watch and ward,** the continuous performance of the duty of a sentinel or watch. (A.S. *wæcce*.)
watch, *v.i.* wotch, to be or keep awake; to be attentive; to look with expectation; to keep guard; to act as sentinel; to be vigilant; to be assiduously attentive; to attend on the sick during the night: *v.t.* to guard; to have in keeping; to lie in wait for; to tend; to note carefully. **watch one's step,** *see* **step.** **watch out,** to keep a sharp look-out; to be vigilant. **watch over,** to be cautiously observant of.
watch-bill, *n.* the list of petty officers and crew showing their watches and stations [Nav.].
watch-box, *n.* a sentry-box.
watch-case, *n.* the outer case of a watch.
watch-dog, *n.* a dog kept to guard premises.
watcher, *n.* *wotch*-er, one who sits up or continues awake; one who attends upon the sick during the night; an angel.
watchet, *a.* *wotch*-et, pale or light blue: *n.* this colour; material or a garment, also an angler's fly, of this colour.
watch-fire, *n.* a fire at night maintained for signalling or for the use of a watch or guard.
watchful, *a.* *wotch*-ful, careful to observe; guarding with caution; vigilant; attentive.
watchfully, *ad.* vigilantly.
watchfulness, *n.* vigilance; wakefulness.
watch-glass, *n.* a glass usually concavo-convex, for covering the dial-plate of a watch.
watchguard, *n.* a chain, strap, cord, etc., with which a watch is carried on the person.
watch-house, *n.* a house in which a watch or guard is placed; a lock-up for the night.
watching, *n.* *wotch*-ing, wakefulness; inability to sleep. **watching brief,** *see* **brief.**
watch-key, *n.* a key for winding up a watch.
watch-light, *n.* a night-light; a candle with a rush wick; a watchman's torch or lantern.
watchmaker, *n.* *wotch*-make-er, one whose occupation is to make or repair watches.
watchmaking, *n.* *wotch*-make-ing, the art of making watches, chronometers, or other timepieces.
watchman, *n.* *wotch*-man, a sentinel; a guard; a night policeman; a man guarding a building or street repairs, etc., at night. **watchman's rattle,** an instrument which produces a loud rattling sound on being whirled round.
watch-night, *n.* the last night of the year; a religious service towards midnight on this night.
watch-pocket, *n.* a small pocket in a garment for holding a watch.
watch-tower, *n.* a tower from which to watch; a look-out tower.
watchword, *n.* *wotch*-wurd, the word given to sentinels, and to such as have occasion to pass the guard, used as a signal by which a friend is known from an enemy; a password; a slogan.
★**water,** *n.* *waw*-ter, the transparent, colourless, odourless, and tasteless liquid that falls as rain, chemically a compound of two parts of hydrogen to one of oxygen by volume; the sea, a lake, river, or any great collection of water; urine; the colour or lustre of a precious stone (a diamond "of the first water" being perfectly pure and transparent); serum, or any liquid humour in animal bodies, as in dropsy. **back water,** to reverse the forward motion of (esp. a boat). **heavy water,** *see* **heavy.** **high water,** high tide. **hold water,** to be sound, tight, or tenable. **in deep water,** *see* **deep.** **like water,** very freely, superabundantly. **low water,** *see* **low.** **make water,** *see* **make.** **of the first water,** of the highest excellence. **strong waters,** potable spirits. **table waters,** non-alcoholic aerated drinks. **take the waters,** to have therapeutic treatment at a spa. **tread water,** *see* **tread.** **water avens,** *see* **avens.** **water of crystallization,** the water which enters into combination with a salt when crystallizing. **water on the brain,** hydrocephalus [Med.]. **water on the knee,** synovitis affecting a knee-joint. **water table,** a string-course moulding, or other projection in the wall of a building to throw off the water [Arch.]; a gutter in a road. (A.S. *wæter*.)
water, *v.t.* *waw*-ter, to irrigate; to moisten; to dilute, sprinkle, or wet with water; to supply with water; to supply with water to drink; to give silk, textiles, etc., a wavy appearance; to increase nominal capital without increasing assets [Finance]: *v.i.* to shed water or liquid matter; to get or take in water; to drink (of beasts). **make one's mouth water,** to arouse feeling of anticipated pleasure; to regard with intense longing. **water down,** to moderate; to take the edge off.
waterage, *n.* *waw*-ter-raj, conveyance by water; the charge for this.
water-bailiff, *n.* a river-constable; a person employed to guard against infringement of fishing rights.
water-bath, *n.* a bain-marie; a double vessel for heating substances, the substance being in an inner container surrounded by water to which the heat is applied.
Water-bearer, *n.* the constellation Aquarius.
water-bed, *n.* a rubber mattress containing water, used by invalids to prevent bed-sores.

water-beetle, *n.* an aquatic beetle, such as the species of *Gyrinus, Dytiscus, Hydrophilus, Hydrobius,* and *Donacia.*
water-bellows, *n.* an apparatus for forcing air under pressure into the furnace of certain forges by means of a column of falling water; a trompe.
waterbird, *n. waw*-ter-berd, an aquatic bird.
water-biscuit, *n.* a thin unsweetened biscuit.
waterblob, *n.* the marsh-marigold.
water-boatman, *n.* an aquatic insect of the families Notonectidæ and Corisidæ.
water-borne, *a.* floated; conveyed or deposited by water.
water-brash, *n.* a hot sensation in the stomach with acrid eructations due to indigestion; pyrosis.
water-buck, *n.* an antelope of the genus *Kobus.*
water-buffalo, *n.* the domesticated Indian buffalo, *Bos bubalus.*
waterbug, *n. waw*-ter-bug, any aquatic insect.
waterbutt, *n. waw*-ter-but, a large open cask stood on end for collecting and preserving rain-water.
water-caltrops, *n.* applied to various pond-weeds, esp. the entangling *Potamogeton densus* and *P. crispus,* also to the water-chestnut and marsh-marigold.
water-can, *n.* a metal vessel, with spout, for carrying water; the yellow water-lily, *Nuphar lutea.*
water-carriage, *n.* transportation or conveyance by water.
water-cart, *n.* a cart bearing a tank of water for watering roads.
water-cement, *n.* hydraulic cement which hardens under water.
water-chestnut, *n.* plants of the genus *Trapa,* esp. *T. natans* also known as water-caltrops.
water-chute, *n. waw*-ter-shoot, a shallow slope of boards along which water flows for sliding or tobogganning down.
water-clock, *n.* the clepsydra, a machine to measure time by the flow or discharge of water.
water-closet, *n.* a closet containing a privy in which water is used to flush the pan and prevent the rise of sewer-gas.
water-colour, *n.* colour mixed with gum-water instead of oil; a picture painted with water-colours; the art of using water-colours in painting.
water-colourist, *n.* one who paints in water-colours.
water-cool, *v.t.* to cool by means of water, esp. [Eng.] by circulating water through a water-jacket surrounding a gas-engine cylinder, the water being subsequently cooled by means of a radiator.
watercourse, *n. waw*-ter-koarse, a stream of water; a channel for the conveyance of water.
water-cow, *n.* the water-buffalo.
watercraft, *n. waw*-ter-krahft, vessels and boats collectively; skill on or in the water; watermanship.
water-crane, *n.* a contrivance for supplying water to locomotives; a hydraulic crane.
watercress, *n. waw*-ter-kress, a small creeping edible plant growing in watery places, *Nasturtium officinale.*
water-crow, *n.* the dipper, *Cinclus aquaticus.*
water-crowfoot, *n.* the aquatic plant *Ranunculus aquatilis.*
water-cure, *n.* hydropathy.
water-deer, *n.* the Chinese musk-deer, *Hydropotes inermis.*
water-diviner, *n.* a dowser.
water-dog, *n.* any dog used to the water or of semi-aquatic habit, as the water-spaniel; any of several large salamanders; [Coll.] a small cloud indicative of rain.
water-drop, *n.* a drop of water; a tear.
water-dropwort, *n. waw*-ter-*drop*-wurt, a plant of the genus *Œnanthe.*
watered, *a. waw*-terd, sprinkled; supplied with water; made to look wavy and shiny (of silk, etc.).
water-engine, *n.* an engine to raise water; a hydraulic engine; an engine for applying water-power.
waterer, *n. waw*-ter-rer, one who waters.
waterfall, *n. waw*-ter-fawl, a perpendicular descent of the water of a river or stream; a cascade; a cataract.
water-fern, *n.* the osmund or royal fern.
water-finder, *n.* a dowser.
water-flag, *n.* the yellow iris, *Iris pseudacorus.*
water-flea, *n.* the small free-swimming crustacean, *Daphnia pulex,* abundant in ponds and ditches, swimming with short leaps.
water-flood, *n.* a devastating inundation.
water-fly, *n.* any insect seen habitually on or over water; the stone-fly.
waterfowl, *n. waw*-ter-foul, any bird that frequents the water; an aquatic bird.
water-foxtail, *n.* the tall long-awned grass, *Alopecurus geniculatus,* growing in marshy ground.
water-front, the land (esp. in a town, at a harbour, etc.) at the water's edge.
water-furrow, *n.* a furrow for conducting water from the ground [Agric.]; an open drain.
water-gall, *n.* a flow in natural or manufactured material caused by water; a cavity made in the earth by a torrent; a weather-gall.
water-gas, *n.* an illuminating gas generated by passing steam under pressure over incandescent carbon.
water-gate, *n.* a gate leading directly to the water-side; a flood-gate.
water-gauge, *n.* an instrument for measuring the depth or quantity of water, as in a boiler.
water-gild, *v.t.* to gild a metallic surface by covering it with a thin coating of amalgam of gold, and then volatilizing the mercury by heat.
water-gilder, *n.* one who practises water-gilding.
waterglass, *n. waw*-ter-glahs, a silicate of soda or potash soluble in hot water and impervious to the air, used in fresco painting, preserving eggs, etc., known also as soluble glass.
water-glass, *n.* a clepsydra; also, a tube or bucket with a glass bottom for making under-water observations.
water-god, *n.* a deity with dominion over the sea, lakes, rivers, etc.
water-gruel, *n.* a liquid food, composed of water and a small portion of meal.
water-guard, *n.* police or customs officers employed at docks or on the waterside, esp. for the prevention of smuggling.
water-hammer, *n. waw*-ter-*ham*-mer, a vessel containing a column of water in a vacuum, which, when it falls against one end, makes a sound like a hammer; the percussion made by water in a pipe when a tap is turned off, or by water in a steam-pipe on the admission of steam.
water-hemlock, *n.* various species of *Cicuta* and *Œnanthe,* esp. cow-bane.
water-hen, *n.* the moorhen.
water-hog, *n.* the capybara.
water-hole, *n.* a depression in which water collects; a small pool; a cavity in the bed of a river.
water-hyacinth, *n.* an aquatic plant of tropical South America, *Eichhornia crassipes.*
water-ice, *n.* a confection composed of frozen water and sugar; ice formed by the freezing of water.
wateriness, *n. waw*-ter-re-ness, the state of being watery; humidity.
watering, *n. waw*-ter-ring, the act of overflowing, sprinkling, or supplying with water; the place where water is supplied; the process of giving a wavy appearance to a fabric; the act of taking horses, etc., to water.
watering-place, *n.* a place where water can be obtained; a place to which people resort to drink medicinal waters, a spa; a seaside resort.
watering-pot, *n.* a pot with an elongated perforated nozzle for watering plants.
watering-trough, *n.* a trough at which cattle and horses drink.
waterish, *a. waw*-ter-rish, resembling water; thin, as a liquor; insipid; somewhat watery; moist.
waterishness, *n.* state of being waterish.
water-jacket, *n.* a casing containing water surrounding machinery for keeping it cool.
water-joint, *n.* a joint, as in tiles, paving-stones, etc., proof against leakage.
water-laid, *a.* cable-laid; having a left-hand twist (of rope).
water-leaf, *n.* any plant of the genus *Hydrophyllum.*
water-lemon, *n.* one of the passion-flowers, *Passiflora laurifolia*; also, its edible fruit.
waterless, *a. waw*-ter-less, destitute of water.
water-level, *n.* the level formed by the surface of

still water; a levelling instrument in which water is employed in place of spirit.

water-lily, *n.* the common name of the aquatic plants of the genera *Nymphæa* and *Nuphar*, with floating leaves and large flowers.

water-line, *n.* the line on the hull of a vessel floating on an even keel to which the water reaches; any line marked on the hull corresponding to this at different stages of loading or unloading.

waterlog, *v.t.* *waw*-ter-log, to render waterlogged [Naut.]; to saturate with water; to deprive of buoyancy, or to render inert or unserviceable, by this means.

waterlogged, *a.* *waw*-ter-logd, lying unmanageable, or like a log, on the water, in consequence of being flooded by leakage (of vessels); sodden; unusable through saturation with water.

Waterloo, *n.* waw-ter-*loo*, any decisive or irretrievable defeat. **meet one's Waterloo,** to suffer downfall after sustained prosperity. (Battle of *Waterloo*, 1815.)

waterman, *n.* *waw*-ter-man, a man who manages watercraft; a boatman; a ferryman.

watermanship, *n.* *waw*-ter-man-ship, the art of managing a rowing-boat; oarsmanship.

watermark, *n.* *waw*-ter-mark, the mark or limit of the rise of a flood; a mark to show the extent of the rise and fall of the tide; a distinguishing mark given to paper by pressure during manufacture: *v.t.* to impress a watermark (on paper).

water-meadow, *n.* a piece of low land that may be irrigated from a near-by stream.

water-melon, *n.* the plant and fruit, *Citrullus vulgaris*.

water-meter, *n.* an instrument for measuring the water that passes or is consumed.

water-milfoil, *n.* the aquatic plant *Myriophyllum spicatum*.

water-mill, *n.* a mill worked by water.

water-moccasin, *n.* the venomous pit-viper, *Agkistrodon piscivorus*, of the southern United States.

water-nymph, *n.* a nymph or goddess inhabiting water; a dragon-fly; a water-lily of the genus *Nymphæa*.

water-ouzel, *n.* the dipper, *Cinclus aquaticus*, a small diving-bird.

water-parsnip, *n.* an umbelliferous aquatic plant of the genus *Sium*, esp. *S. latifolium*.

water-parting, *n.* a watershed.

water-pepper, *n.* the pipewort *Elatine hydropiper*; also, waterwort and various *Persicaria*.

water-pheasant, *n.* name applied to various birds, as the pintail, the merganser, and the E. Indian jacana, *Hydrophasianus chirurgus*.

waterphone, *n.* *waw*-ter-fone, a hydrophone for detecting and locating underwater sounds.

water-pipit, *n.* the bird *Anthus spipoletta*.

water-pitcher, *n.* a pitcher for water; a pitcher-plant; a N. American marsh plant with pitcher-shaped leaves.

waterplane, *n.* *waw*-ter-plane, a seaplane; any aeroplane fitted with floats instead of wheels.

water-plant, *n.* a plant that grows in water.

water-plantain, *n.* a plant of the genus *Alisma*.

water-plate, *n.* a plate with a receptacle for hot water used for keeping food hot.

water-poise, *n.* a hydrometer.

water-polo, *n.* a game played in swimming-baths in which opposing teams of swimmers attempt to score goals with a ball like a football.

waterpool, *n.* *waw*-ter-pool, a water-hole; a small pond.

waterpot, *n.* *waw*-ter-pot, a vessel for holding or conveying water; a watering-pot.

water-power, *n.* the mechanical power or action of water; a fall of water used in production of power.

water-pox, *n.* a variety of chicken-pox.

waterproof, *a.* *waw*-ter-proof, impervious to water: *n.* cloth or a coat that is so: *v.t.* to render impervious to water.

water-rail, *n.* the bird *Rallus aquaticus*.

water-ram, *n.* a hydraulic ram.

water-rat, *n.* *waw*-ter-rat, a species of vole, *Arvicola amphibius*, frequenting river-banks and ponds.

water-rate, *n.* a charge for the supply of water.

water-rot, *v.t.* to rot or ret by steeping in water.

water-sapphire, *n.* a deep-blue variety of iolite, used as a semi-precious stone.

water-scorpion, *n.* any aquatic hemipterous insect, esp. of genus *Nepa*, having long front legs for seizing prey.

watershed, *n.* *waw*-ter-shed, a ridge separating river basins. (*water*, and Ger. *scheiden*, divide.)

water-shoot, *n.* a pipe or channel for discharging water, as from a roof; a water-chute: a sucker [Bot.].

water-shrew, *n.* the aquatic insectivore *Neomys fodiens*.

waterside, *n.* *waw*-ter-side, the land at the edge of a body of water.

water-skipper, *n.* a long-legged aquatic insect of the family Hydrobatidæ, that skips on the surface of ponds, etc.

watersmeet, *n.* *waw*-terz-meet, a meeting-place of two rivers or streams.

water-snake, *n.* a snake that lives in fresh-water rivers or lakes; a sea-snake.

water-soldier, *n.* an aquatic plant, *Stratiotes aloides*, with long sword-like leaves.

water-soluble, *a.* soluble in water.

water-spaniel, *n.* a large variety of curly haired spaniel.

water-sparrow, *n.* a name given to the reed warbler and reed bunting.

water-spider, *n.* the spider *Argyoneta aquatica*, and other aquatic or semi-aquatic spiders.

waterspout, *n.* *waw*-ter-spout, a spout for the discharge of water, as from a roof or tank; a whirling hollow column of water occasioned by a whirlwind and reaching from a cloud to the sea or lake; a torrential cloudburst.

water-supply, *n.* the collection, conservation, and distribution of water for domestic or industrial use, etc.

water-tank, *n.* a cistern or small reservoir for holding water.

water-thermometer, *n.* an instrument for ascertaining the precise degree of temperature at which water ceases to be condensed.

watertight, *a.* *waw*-ter-tite, not leaky; so tight as to retain or not to admit water.

water-tower, *n.* a raised tank, with its support, for delivering water to a required height; a mobile fire-fighting appliance having an extensible vertical pipe through which water may be pumped to a great height.

water-tube, *n.* any tube which passes or retains water, esp. one of a number in a steam-boiler in which the steam is generated.

water-violet, *n.* an aquatic plant of the genus *Hottonia*, esp. featherfoil, *H. palustris*.

water-vole, *n.* the water-rat.

water-wagon, *n.* a mobile water-tank, esp. for accompanying troops. **on the water-wagon,** *see* **wagon.**

water-wagtail, *n.* the pied wagtail, *Motacilla lugubris*.

waterway, *n.* *waw*-ter-way, a navigable river or channel; a canal; a hollowed channel for conducting water to the scuppers [Naut.].

waterweed, *n.* *waw*-ter-weed, any aquatic weed, esp. the American *Philotria canadensis*.

water-wheel, *n.* a wheel for supplying motive power, actuated by water; an engine for raising water by means of buckets, etc.

water-wings, *n.pl.* the fin-like wings of certain aquatic birds, as penguins; wing-shaped inflatable floats for use when learning to swim; walls erected on river-banks to secure the foundations of a bridge from the action of the current.

water-witch, *n.* a witch fabled to frequent bodies of water; name given to various aquatic birds, as the dipper, dabchick, and stormy petrel.

waterworks, *n.pl.* *waw*-ter-wurks, the headquarters of a water-supply where the water is pumped to a sufficient height for distribution through all the pipes of the system. **to turn on the waterworks,** to weep or blubber [Slang].

water-worn, *a.* worn by the action of water.

waterwort, *n.* *waw*-ter-wurt, an aquatic plant of the genus *Elatine*.

watery, *a.* *waw*-ter-re, pertaining to or resembling water; abounding with or consisting of water; thin or transparent, as a liquid; tasteless; insipid; vapid.

Watsonia, *n.* wot-*soh*-ne-a, a genus of ornamental bulbous plants from S. Africa, allied to the gladiolus.

watt, *n.* wot, a volt-ampere, the practical unit of electrical power, equal to the expenditure of energy at the rate of one joule per second. (After James *Watt*, Scottish inventor, *d.* 1819.)
wattage, *n. wot*-aj, amount of electric power expressed in watts.
watt-hour, *n.* a unit of electrical energy, 3,600 joules, the work done by one watt acting for one hour, or one thousandth of a Board of Trade unit.
wattle, *n. wot*-tl, a flexible rod; a hurdle made by weaving twigs together; a rod on a roof to support thatch; the fleshy lobe under the throat of a cock, turkey, etc.; a similar flap on certain animals; a barbel of a fish; any one of several species of *Acacia*, the bark of which is used in tanning [Australia]: *v.t.* to bind with twigs; to twist or interweave branches one with another; to plait. **wattle and daub,** wattle framework plastered with clay [Build.]. (A.S. *watul*, a hurdle.)
wattle-bark, *n.* bark of the Australian wattle, used in tanning.
wattle-bird, *n.* any Australasian honey-eater of the genus *Anthochæra*, esp. *A. caruncuIata*.
wattled, *a. wot*-tld, bound or interwoven with twigs; having wattles or [Bot.] processes like the wattles of a cock.
wattmeter, *n. wot*-mee-ter, an instrument for measuring electric power in watts.
waucht, *n.* wawkht, a long, hearty draught. (Scots.)
waul, *v.i.* wawl, to cry, as a cat; to howl.
wavable, *a. way*-va-bl, capable of being waved.
⋆wave, *n.* wave, an undulation; a state of vibration; a moving swell on the surface of the sea or a river, etc., caused by the wind; motion in a fluid substance like that of a wave in which one set of particles acts on the adjoining set with little or no permanent displacement; a single undulation or curve in such a motion; a change of temperature (as a heat-wave) or of atmospheric pressure; a movement in the ether produced by electrical oscillations in a conductor (**long waves** are those over 1,000 metres, **medium,** between 200 and 1,000 metres, **short,** 200 to 50 metres or less, **ultra-short,** less than 10 metres); the action of waving, also a gesture, etc., so made; an undulation, natural or artificial, in the hair; a surge of emotion, enthusiasm, etc.; inequality of surface; the wavy line or streak of lustre on cloth, watered and calendered: *v.i.* to play loosely; to move like a wave one way and the other; to float; to undulate; to be moved, as a signal: *v.t.* to raise into inequalities of surface; to move one way and the other; to impart a wave to; to brandish; to waft; to beckon; to direct by a waft or waving motion. **permanent wave,** *see* **permanent. wave aside,** to dismiss as puerile or irrelevant. (A.S. *wafian*, waver, *waeg*, a wave.)
wave-band, *n.* a range of electro-magnetic waves of length falling between two given limits, as the long wave-band (from 1,000 to 3,000 metres).
waved, *a.* waved, having waves or wave-like markings; wavy; variegated in lustre; having on the margin a succession of arched segments or incisions [Entom.]; wavily indented [Her.].
wave-length, *n.* the distance, in a series of waves, between the crest of one undulation and the next; the measured frequency upon which each transmitter sends out its carrier wave [Wire.].
waveless, *a. wave*-less, free from waves; undisturbed.
wavelet, *n. wave*-let, a little wave; a ripple.
wave-like, *a.* resembling a wave; undulating.
wave-line, *n.* the path of a wave; the line made by the wave on the shore.
wavellite, *n. way*-vel-ite, a hydrated phosphate of aluminium, named from its discoverer, a Dr. Wavell.
wavemeter, *n. wave*-mee-ter, an instrument for measuring frequencies or wave-lengths [Wire.].
waver, *v.i. way*-ver, to play or move to and fro; to quiver; to fluctuate; to be unsettled in opinion; to hesitate; to vacillate. (*wave.*)
waver, *n. way*-ver, one who or that which waves; an appliance for waving hair; a sapling or young timber-tree.
waverer, *n. way*-ver-rer, one who wavers; one who is unsettled in doctrine, faith, or opinion.
wavering, *a. way*-ver-ring, fluctuating; being in doubt.
waveringly, *ad.* in a wavering manner.
waveson, *n. wave*-sen, floating goods from a ship-wrecked vessel.
wave-trap, *n.* an apparatus for cutting out an undesired station and increasing the selective properties of a receiver [Wire.].
waveworn, *a. wave*-worn, worn by the waves.
waviness, *n. way*-ve-ness, the state or quality of being wavy.
waving, *a. way*-ving, moving as a wave; undulatory motion; playing to and fro.
wavy, *a. way*-ve, rising or swelling in waves; full of waves; playing to and fro; undulating; undulating on the border or surface [Bot.].
⋆wax, *n.* waks, a thick, viscid, tenacious substance, excreted by bees, and employed in the construction of their cells; beeswax, esp. as purified for use; certain similar substances, excreted or secreted, as in the ear and by certain plants; a solid fat without glycerine; sealing-wax; cobbler's wax; anger, rage [Slang]: *v.t.* to smear or rub with wax; to treat with wax. **wax painting,** encaustic painting. (A.S. *weax.*)
wax, *v.i.* waks, to increase in size; to grow; to become larger; to pass from one state to another; to become. (A.S. *weaxan*, grow.)
wax-berry, *n.* the wax-myrtle; also, the snow-berry.
waxbill, *n. waks*-bil, a small bird of the genus *Estrelda*, allied to the weaver-birds.
wax-candle, *n.* a candle made of wax or of paraffin, ozocerite, etc.
wax-chandler, *n.* a maker of or dealer in wax-candles.
wax-cloth, *n.* floor-cloth, oilcloth, linoleum.
waxen, *a. wak*-sen, made of wax; resembling wax.
wax-end, *n.* a thread pointed with a bristle and covered with cobbler's wax.
wax-flower, *n.* any of the oriental evergreens of the large genus *Hoya*; the orchid *Angræcum sesquipedale*. **clustered wax-flower,** *Stephanotis floribunda*.
wax-insect, *n.* any insect, esp. of the family Coccidæ, which secretes wax.
wax-light, *n.* a taper or candle made of wax.
wax-moth, *n.* the bee-moth, or other moth the larvæ of which prey on honeycombs.
wax-myrtle, *n.* the shrub, *Myrica cerifera*, or its berry, from which a wax-like substance is obtained.
wax-palm, *n.* either of the large S. American palms, *Ceroxylon andicolum*, whose stem is coated with resin and wax; the carnauba, *Corypha cerifera*.
wax-paper, *n.* paper coated with paraffin.
wax-plant, *n.* wax-myrtle, honeywort, and other plants having waxy characteristics.
wax-tree, *n.* any tree yielding wax, esp. the S. American *Vismia guianensis*.
waxwing, *n. waks*-wing, a bird of the genus *Ampelis*.
waxwork, *n. waks*-wurk, a figure formed of wax in imitation of life; a modelling in wax: *pl.* a collection of figures in waxwork.
wax-worker, *n.* one who works in wax; a bee, as producing wax.
waxy, *a. wak*-se, resembling or consisting of wax; soft like wax; viscid; waxen; angry [Slang].
⋆way, *n.* way, a place of passage; hence, a highway, lane, a street, or road of any kind; any place for the passing of men, cattle, or other animals; length of space; course; route; passage; room for passing; manner or means of doing anything; method; scheme of management; individual manner of thinking, acting, or of practice; idiosyncracy; mode; particular turn of opinion; method or plan of life and conduct; right method of knowing or acting; general scheme of acting; progress [Naut.]: *pl.* the timbers on which a ship is launched. **the Way,** the Christian religion. **by the way,** incidentally. **each way,** for a win and place (of bets). **give way,** to collapse; to make room or to yield. **go** or **come one's way,** to go or come along. **have a way with one,** to be naturally ingratiating or persuasive. **have one's own way,** to carry out one's own plans without, or ignoring, opposition. **in a way,** from one point of view; in a state of agitation [Coll.]. **in the way,** opposing advance. **make one's way,** to advance in life by efforts. **make way,** to give room for passing, or to make a vacancy. **Milky Way,** *see* **milky. once in a way,** occasionally.

out of the way, not on the direct route; unusual. **pay one's way,** to keep out of debt. **right of way,** *see* **right. see one's way,** to be willing or able. **under way,** in motion [Naut.]. **Way of the Cross,** a series of graphic or sculptured representations of incidents during Christ's progress to Calvary. **ways and means,** in legislation, methods of raising money, esp. revenue. (A.S. *weg.*)

way-bennet, *n.* the wall-barley, *Hordeum murinum.*

way-bill, *n.* a list of passengers or goods.

way-board, *n.* any thin layer lying between thicker strata [Min. and Geol.].

waybread, *n. way*-bred, the plantain.

wayfarer, *n. way*-fare-rer, a traveller on foot.

wayfaring, *a. way*-fare-ring, travelling; being on a journey: *n.* a journey afoot.

wayfaring-tree, *n.* the small tree *Viburnum lantana*; the American hobble bush, *V. alnifolium.*

waygoing, *n. way*-goh-ing, departure; the act of vacating. **waygoing crop,** crop taken from the land by a tenant the year he leaves a farm.

waylay, *v.t.* way-*lay*, to watch insidiously in the way with a view to seize, rob, or slay; to beset in ambush.

waylayer, *n.* way-*lay*-er, one who waits for another in ambush with hostile intentions.

wayleave, *n. way*-leev, a right of way granted by lease.

wayless, *a. way*-less, having no road or path; pathless; trackless.

waymark, *n. way*-mark, a guide-post, or natural feature, serving to mark the way.

wayside, *n. way*-side, the edge of a road; the roadside. **wayside station,** an intermediate station or halt on a railway-line.

way-thistle, *n.* the field, or Canada, thistle, *Cnicus arvensis.*

waythorn, *n. way*-thorn, the buckthorn.

wayward, *a. way*-werd, froward; perverse; wilful. (*away* and *ward.*)

waywarden, *n. way*-wawr-dn, an official superviser of highways.

waywardly, *ad. way*-werd-le, frowardly: perversely.

waywardness, *n.* frowardness; perverseness.

way-wise, *a.* skilled in finding and keeping the way (esp. of horses, dogs, etc.).

waywiser, *n. way*-wy-zer, an instrument for measuring distance travelled on the road, an early form of pedometer.

waywode, *n. way*-wode, a voivode, originally a military commander in various Slavonic countries, afterwards a town or provincial governor. (Pol. *wojewoda*, the leader of an army.)

waywodeship, *n. way*-wode-ship, the office or jurisdiction of a waywode.

wayworn, *a. way*-worn, wearied by travel.

wayzgoose, *n. wayz*-goos, a printer's beanfeast.

wazir, *n.* wah-*zeer*, a vizier.

we, *pron.* we, the *first pers. pl.* of *I*, denoting the person speaking, and another or others with him; men in general; everybody; used also by sovereigns, and by editors when writing editorially, in place of I. (A.S.)

weak, *a.* week, having little physical strength; feeble; infirm; not healthy; not able to bear a great weight; not strong; not able to resist attack; frail; brittle; irresolute; mentally deficient; wanting spirit; wanting in strengthening ingredients; not politically powerful; not having force of authority; not efficacious; not having moral force or power to convince; not well supported by argument; not fortified; not having full conviction; inflected for p. and pp. by addition of *-ed*, *-d*, or *-t*, not by change of vowel (of verbs) [Gram.]; having the stress on a normally unaccented word at the end of a line [Pros.]. (A.S. *wac.*)

weaken, *v.t. wee*-kn, to lessen the strength of; to deprive of strength; to debilitate; to reduce in strength or spirit: *v.i.* to grow weaker. (A.S. *wæcan.*)

weakener, *n. wee*-kn-er, one who or that which weakens.

weakfish, *n. week*-fish, a marine food-fish of the genus *Cynoscion*, common on the eastern and southern coasts of the United States.

weak-headed, *a.* feeble-minded, lacking in willpower; weak-minded.

weak-hearted, *a.* having little courage.

weakish, *a. week*-ish, somewhat weak.

weak-kneed, *a.* weak in the knees, or [Fig.] in will.

weakling, *n. week*-ling, a feeble creature.

weakly, *a. week*-le, not strong of constitution; infirm: *ad.* with little physical strength; feebly.

weak-minded, *a.* mentally deficient.

weakness, *n. week*-ness, state of being weak; lack of physical strength; feebleness; unfitness; want of moral force or of judgment, etc.; defect; failing; [Coll.] something specially desired.

weak-spirited, *a.* timid; having low spirits.

weal, *n.* weel, a sound state of a person or thing; happiness; well-being. **the common weal,** the prosperity or welfare of a state; the public interest. (A.S. *wela.*)

weal, *n.* weel, the mark of a rod or whip on flesh; a streak or stripe; a ridge or streak in cloth, rising above the rest; a plank along the outside of a ship's timbers. (O.E. *walu.*)

weald, *n.* weeld, a wooded region; woodland; an open tract of country. **the Weald,** a wooded tract of south-east England including parts of south-west Kent and east Sussex. (A.S.)

Wealden, *a. weel*-den, pertaining to the Weald of Kent and Sussex (applied esp. to certain Lower Cretaceous strata) [Geol.].

wealdsman, *n.* weeldz-man, one living in a weald, esp. in the Weald.

wealth, *n.* welth, riches; large possessions of money, goods, or land; abundance of worldly estate exceeding that of the greater part of the community; affluence; that which possesses exchangeable value. (*weal.*)

wealthily, *ad.* in a wealthy manner.

wealthiness, *n.* the state of being wealthy.

wealthy, *a. welth*-e, rich; having large possessions; opulent; affluent.

wean, *v.t.* ween, to accustom and reconcile, as a child or other young animal, to a want or deprivation of the breast; to detach or alienate, as the affections, from any object of desire; to reconcile to the want or loss of anything. (A.S. *wenian*, accustom.)

wean, *n.* ween, a small child, an infant [Scots.] (*wee ane*, little one.)

weanling, *n. ween*-ling, a child or other mammal newly weaned: *a.* just weaned.

weapon, *n. wep*-on, any instrument of offence or defence, or for combating enemies: *pl.* claws, thorns, prickles, stings, etc. [Zool. and Bot.]. (A.S. *wæpen.*)

weaponed, *a. wep*-ond, armed; furnished with weapons or arms; equipped.

weaponless, *a. wep*-on-less, unarmed; having no weapon.

weapon-salve, *n.* an ointment formerly supposed to cure a wound by being applied to the weapon that made it.

wear, *v.t.* ware, to waste or impair by attrition; to lessen or diminish by time, use, or instruments; to carry as covering or clothing to the body; to have or exhibit; to affect by degrees; to fatigue or exhaust: *v.i.* to be wasted, impaired, or diminished by attrition, etc.; to be spent tediously; to be consumed gradually; to pass by slow degrees; to stand continual use; to endure. **wear away,** to consume or diminish. **wear down,** to reduce by repeated rubbing; [Fig.] to break or overcome by degrees. **wear off,** gradually to pass or wear away. **wear out,** to render useless by attrition or decay; to consume tediously; to waste the strength of; to harass. **wear the breeches,** *see* **breeches.** *p.* **wore.** *pp.* **worn.** (A.S. *werian.*)

wear, *n.* ware, the act of wearing; that which is worn; the mode or fashion; impairment or diminution by friction. **wear and tear,** loss or injury caused by wearing, as of machinery, etc., in use.

wear, *v.t.* ware, to put a ship to windward by turning her off from the wind and so round on to the other tack; to veer [Naut.]. *p.* and *pp.* **wore.** (*veer.*)

wearability, *n.* ware-ra-*bil*-e-te, suitability for being worn; durability (of cloth or clothing).

wearable, *a. ware*-ra-bl, that can be worn.

wearer, *n. ware*-rer, one who wears; that which impairs or diminishes by friction, etc.

wearied, *a. weer*-red, tired; fatigued.

weariful, *a.* *weer*-re-ful, wearying; wearisome.
weariless, *a.* *weer*-re-less, not wearying; continual.
wearily, *ad.* in a tired or weary manner.
weariness, *n.* the state of being weary or tired.
wearing, *a.* *ware*-ring, exhausting; irksome; having the power to weary.
wearish, *a.* *weer*-rish, watery; insipid; washy; feeble; [Fig.] ineffectual. (Origin unknown.)
wearisome, *a.* *weer*-re-sum, causing weariness; tiresome; tedious; fatiguing.
wearisomely, *ad.* tediously; so as to cause weariness.
wearisomeness, *n.* the quality of being wearisome; tiresomeness; tediousness.
weary, *a.* *weer*-re, having the strength much exhausted by toil or violent exertion; tired; fatigued; having the patience exhausted; careworn; dispirited; causing weariness; tiresome: *v.t.* to reduce or exhaust the physical strength; to tire; to fatigue; to make impatient of continuance; to harass by anything irksome: *v.i.* to become weary or disheartened; to suffer weariness; to long for [Scots.]. **weary out,** to subdue or exhaust by fatigue. (A.S. *werig*, perhaps from *worian*, to wander.)
weasand, *n.* *wee*-zand, the windpipe, through which air passes to and from the lungs. (A.S. *wæsend*.)
weasel, *n.* *wee*-zl, the small British predaceous carnivore, *Mustela vulgaris*, with long body and short legs. (A.S. *wesle*.)
weasel-faced, *a.* having a thin sharp face.
weasel-snout, *n.* *wee*-zl-snout, the yellow dead-nettle *Lamium galeobdolon*.
***weather,** *n.* *weth*-er, the state of the atmosphere, as regards temperature, rain, wind-pressure, cloud, etc.; change of the state of the air; [Fig.] change: *a.* towards the wind; windward, as weather-bow: *v.t.* to expose to the air; to disintegrate by exposure to the air; to sail to windward of; to bear up against: *v.i.* to withstand the effects of weather; to become disintegrated by weather. **to keep one's weather eye open,** to be on the alert; to keep a good look-out. **stress of weather,** violent winds; force of tempests. **under the weather** [Coll.], not very well; in straitened circumstances. **weather office,** the Meteorological Office. (A.S. *weder*.)
weather-anchor, *n.* the anchor lying to windward.
weather-beam, *n.* the side of a ship towards the wind [Naut.].
weather-beaten, *a.* harassed, seasoned, or browned by the weather.
weather-board, *n.* the windward side of a ship: *pl.* pieces of inclined plank placed in the ports of a ship to exclude rain [Naut.]; a board forming a close junction between the shingling of a roof and the side of the building beneath.
weatherboarding, *n.* *weth*-er-*bord*-ing, boards nailed so as to lap over one another.
weatherbound, *a.* *weth*-er-bound, delayed or obstructed by bad weather.
weather-bow, *n.* *weth*-er-bou, that side of a ship's bow that is to windward [Naut.].
weather-cloth, *n.* a piece of canvas or tarpaulin used for covering hammocks when stowed or as protection for persons from wind and spray [Naut.].
weathercock, *n.* *weth*-er-kok, a vane, often in the shape of a cock, to show the direction of the wind; any thing or person that turns easily and frequently; a fickle, inconstant person.
weathered, *a.* *weth*-erd, seasoned by exposure to weather; altered in colour, texture, or composition (esp. [Geol.] of rocks whose edges are rounded off by exposure); sloped to throw off the wet [Arch.].
weather-fish, *n.* the largest of European loaches *Misgurnus fossilis*.
weather-gall, *n.* an imperfect rainbow; a sundog.
weather-gauge, *n.* situation of a ship when to the windward of another [Naut.]; advantage of position.
weather-glass, *n.* a barometer, or other instrument to indicate the meteorological state of the atmosphere.
weather-helm, *n.* *weth*-er-helm, a tendency in a sailing-vessel to come too near the wind.
weathering, *n.* *weth*-er-ring, the action of the elements in disintegrating or altering the surfaces of rocks etc. [Geol.]; the giving of inclination to a surface to throw off water [Arch.].
weatherly, *a.* *weth*-er-le, able to hang to windward well [Naut.].
weathermost, *a.* *weth*-er-mohst, farthest to windward [Naut.].
weather-moulding, *n.* an outside moulding over doors and windows to divert the rain; a dripstone.
weatherproof, *a.* *weth*-er-proof, proof against rough weather: *n.* a rainproof coat or cloak, etc.
weather-prophet, *n.* one who foretells weather.
weather-roll, *n.* the roll of a ship to windward.
weather-stained, *a.* discoloured by the atmosphere, or by weather.
weather-station, *n.* a place where meteorological observations are made, esp. for the dissemination of forecasts.
weather-strip, *n.* a strip of material to exclude draughts from doors or windows: *v.t.* to fit with weather-strips.
weather-tide, *n.* the tide which sets against the lee side of a ship, impelling her to windward.
weather-vane, *n.* a device for indicating the direction of the wind.
weather-wise, *a.* skilful in forecasting the changes or state of the weather.
weave, *n.* weev, the texture of any woven material: *v.t.* to interlace threads in a loom; to entwine anything flexible: to unite by intermixture or close connexion; to interpose or interweave; to insert: *v.i.* to practise weaving; to work with a loom; to wind about in progressing. *p.* **wove.** *pp.* **woven.** (A.S. *wefan*.)
weaver, *n.* *weev*-er, one whose occupation is to weave; a horse that constantly rolls head, neck, and body from side to side; a weaver-bird; a whirligig beetle.
weaver-bird, *n.* any of several tropical and subtropical birds of the family Plocidæ, making pendulous nests of interlaced grasses, etc.
weaver-fish, *n.* the weever.
weaving, *n.* *weev*-ing, the act or art of forming cloth in a loom by the intertexture of threads.
weazen, *a.* *wee*-zn, thin; sharp; wizened: *v.i.* to become wizened; to shrivel.
web, *n.* web, a woven texture of threads; anything woven; a cobweb, the plexus of delicate threads spun and woven by the spider; anything like a web; the membrane uniting the toes of many aquatic birds [Ornith.]; the vane of a feather; a large reel of printing-paper, esp. for a newspaper; formerly, a cataract, or a film over the eye hindering the sight; the blade of a frame-saw; the thin plate joining the upper and lower flanges of a girder; a plate-like extension stiffening a casting [Eng.]; the thin partition on the inside of the rim and between the spokes of an iron sheave [Shipbuilding]: *v.t.* to cover with or as with a web or network; to join with webbing or a web. (*weave*.)
webbed, *a.* webd, having a web or webs; having the toes united by a membrane or web.
webbing, *n.* *web*-ing, a strong fabric of fibre used for supporting the seats of stuffed furniture, etc.; a strong woven tape; a webbed condition (esp. of the toes) [Path.].
webby, *a.* *web*-e, of web-like texture or appearance; covered with or as with webs; web-footed.
weber, *n.* *wee*-ber *or* *vay*-ber, a practical unit of magnetic flux, equal to 10^8 maxwells. (From the Ger. physicist, W. *Weber*, *d.* 1891.)
web-eye, *n.* *web*-eye, a disease of the eye in which a film forms in the cornea.
web-footed, *a.* having webbed feet.
webster, *n.* *web*-ster, a weaver.
websterite, *n.* *web*-ster-rite, aluminite. (Thos. *Webster*, Scot. geologist, *d.* 1844.)
wed, *v.i.* wed, to marry; to contract matrimony: *v.t.* to marry; to take for husband or for wife; to join in marriage; to unite generally; to attach firmly; to espouse. (A.S. *weddian*, pledge.)
wedded, *a.* *wed*-ed, married; closely attached.
wedding, *n.* *wed*-ing, nuptials; marriage ceremony and festivities: *a.* pertaining to a wedding. **diamond, golden, silver wedding,** *see* these words.
wedding-breakfast, *n.* festive meal for the guests after a wedding ceremony.
wedding-cake, *n.* a rich iced cake distributed among friends at and in connexion with a wedding.
wedding-card, *n.* *wed*-ding-kard, a card bearing the names and address of a newly married couple,

sent to friends to inform them of the marriage or approaching marriage.

wedding-day, *n.* the marriage day or its anniversary.

wedding-favour, *n.* knot or rosette of white ribbon worn by guests at a wedding.

wedding-feast, *n.* an entertainment provided for the guests at a wedding.

wedding-ring, *n.* a gold ring given at the marriage ceremony by the bridegroom to the bride, in token of wedlock.

wedge, *n.* wej, a piece of metal or wood, thick at one end and sloping to a thin edge at the other, being one of the mechanical powers; a voussoir [Arch.]; anything shaped like a wedge; a means of gradual intrusion [Fig.]; a solid of five sides, viz., a rectangular base, two rhomboidal sides meeting in an edge, and two triangular ends [Geom.]; a wedge-shaped region of high barometric pressure [Meteor.]; the wooden wedge: *v.t.* to cleave with a wedge; to drive as a wedge is driven; to crowd or compress closely; to force, as a wedge forces its way; to fasten with a wedge or wedges; to fix in the manner of a wedge. **thin end of the wedge,** a first step, a slight beginning to what is intended to have far-reaching results [Fig.]. **wedge writing,** cuneiform. **wooden wedge,** ironical title of the lowest in the Classical Tripos list, Cambridge Univ. (so called from its first holder, H. Wedgewood, 1824). (A.S. *wecg.*)

wedge-tailed, *a.* having a regularly graduated tail, the two central feathers being longest [Ornith.]. **wedge-tailed eagle,** the Australian eagle, *Uroaëtus audax.* **wedge-tailed gull,** Ross's gull, *Rhodostethia rosea.*

wedgewise, *ad. wej*-wize, in the form of a wedge; as a wedge works.

wedging, *n. wej*-ing, material for wedges; a method for joining timbers.

Wedgwood, *n. wej*-wood, a kind of semi-vitrified pottery, usually tinted and ornamented with small white cameos. (Josiah *Wedgwood, d.* 1795, the inventor.)

wedlock, *n. wed*-lok, matrimony; the married state.

Wednesday, *n. wed*-nz-day or *wenz*-day, the fourth day of the week; the next day after Tuesday. (*Woden's, i.e.* Odin's, *day.*)

wee, *a.* wee, small; tiny; *n.* a little while [Scots.]. **wee folk** or **people,** the fairies.

weed, *n.* weed, a plant growing wild in cultivated ground; anything useless or troublesome, esp. when mingled with things that are useful or of value; a cigar; tobacco; a weak, worthless, or [Slang] tall and lanky person; a horse unfit for breeding: *v.t.* and *i.* to free from weeds, or from anything hurtful or offensive; to root out. (A.S. *weod.*)

weed, *n.* weed, a garment; a mourning dress, generally *pl.*, as worn by widows; a black crape veil or scarf for mourners. (A.S. *wæd,* a garment.)

weeder, *n. weed*-er, one who weeds or frees from anything noxious; an implement for weeding gardens, etc.

weedery, *n. weed*-er-re, weeds collectively; a place full of weeds.

weed-grown, *a.* overgrown with weeds.

weed-hook, *n.* an implement used for cutting away or extirpating weeds.

weeding, *n. weed*-ing, operation of freeing from weeds or anything noxious. **weeding chisel,** a tool with a divided chisel point, for cutting the roots of large weeds within the ground. **weeding forceps,** an instrument for taking up some sorts of plants in weeding. **weeding fork,** a strong, three-pronged fork, used in clearing the ground of weeds. **weeding hook,** a weed-hook. **weeding shim,** *see* **shim. weeding tongs,** weeding forceps.

weed-killer, *n.* an arsenical or other chemical preparation for destroying weeds.

weedless, *a. weed*-less, free from weeds or noxious matter.

weedy, *a. wee*-de, consisting of or abounding with weeds; lanky and weak.

★**week,** *n.* week, the space of seven days. **feast of weeks,** the Jewish Pentecost. **Holy Week,** the week between Palm Sunday and Easter Day. **to-morrow week,** the next day to this in next week. **week and week about,** in alternate weeks. **a week of Sundays,** seven weeks; a long but indefinite time. (A.S. *wice.*)

weekday, *n. week*-day, any day of the week except Sunday.

week-end, *n.* week-*end,* from Friday night to Monday morning, or Saturday and Sunday: *a.* during, or occurring at, the week-end.

week-ender, *n.* one taking a week-end holiday.

weekly, *a. week*-le, happening or done once a week; hebdomadal: *ad.* once a week: *n.* a periodical published once a week.

weel, *n.* weel, a kind of wicker trap or snare for fish.

weely, *n. weel*-e, a weel.

weem, *n.* weem, a natural or artificial cavern; an underground dwelling or passage [Scots.]. (Gael. *uaimh.*)

ween, *v.i.* ween, to think; to imagine. (A.S. *wenan.*)

weep, *v.i.* weep, to shed tears; to express sorrow, grief, pain, or anguish, etc., by shedding tears; to lament; to complain: *v.t.* to lament; to bemoan; to shed, as tears; to shed tears over; to spend in weeping; to exude. *p.* and *pp.* **wept.** (A.S. *wepan.*)

weeper, *n. weep*-er, one who weeps or sheds tears; a hired mourner; a long crape hatband; a South American capuchin monkey.

weeping, *a. weep*-ing, drooping; having drooping branches: *n.* lamentation; grief. **to return by Weeping Cross,** to experience great misfortune; to be deeply disappointed.

weepingly, *ad.* with weeping; in tears.

weeping-rock, *n.* a porous rock from which water gradually issues.

weeping-spring, *n.* a spring that slowly discharges water.

weeping-tree, *n. weep*-ing-*tree,* any tree with pendulous branches, esp. the **weeping willow,** *Salix babylonica.*

weepy, *a. wee*-pe, given to crying; mournful; lachrymose.

weever, *n. wee*-ver, any fish of the edible marine genus *Trachinus,* esp. *T. draco,* the greater weever, and *T. vipera,* the lesser, or viper-weever, both having a long spine with which they defend themselves; the sting-fishes. (O.Fr. *wivre,* connected with *viper.*)

weevil, *n. wee*-vil, any of the very numerous long-snouted plant-eating beetles of the family Curculionidæ or Rhyncophora. (A.S. *wifel.*)

weevilled, *a. wee*-vld, infested with weevils.

weevily, *a. wee*-ve-le, weevilled.

weft, *n.* weft, the threads that cross the warp from selvedge to selvedge; the woof; a web; a thing woven. (*weave.*)

weftage, *n. wef*-taj, texture of cloth, etc.

weigh, *v.t.* way, to examine by the balance; to ascertain the weight of; to be equivalent in weight to; to raise or to lift, as an anchor; to pay, allot, or take by weight; to ponder in the mind; to consider or examine for the purpose of coming to a conclusion; to compare by the scales; to consider as worthy of notice: *v.i.* to have weight; to be considered as important; to bear heavily; to press hard; to start by weighing anchor: *n.* the act of weighing; a certain quantity by weight. **weigh anchor,** to raise the anchor; to start a voyage [Naut.], or any enterprise [Coll.]. **weigh down,** to cause to bend; to depress or oppress. **weigh in,** to check a jockey's riding weight before a race; [Fig.] to plunge in. **weigh on,** to be a burden to. **weigh one's words,** to speak only after careful consideration. **weigh out,** to measure out by weight; to check riding weight of jockey after a race. **weigh up,** to come to an opinion concerning [Coll.]. (A.S. *wegan,* carry, lift.)

weighable, *a. way*-a-bl, that may be weighed.

weigh-board, *n.* a way-board.

weigh-beam, *n.* a balance or steelyard.

weigh-bridge, *n.* a machine for weighing laden vehicles on an iron platform.

weigher, *n. way*-er, one who weighs; an officer whose duty is to test weights, or to ascertain that the weights of commodities are correct.

weigh-house, *n. way*-house, a building furnished with conveniences for weighing commodities.

weighing, *n. way*-ing, act of ascertaining weight; as much as is weighed at once.

weighing-cage, *n.* a cage in which living animals may be conveniently weighed.

weighing-machine, *n.* a machine for weighing persons, cattle, or heavy bodies in general; a weigh-bridge.

★**weight,** *n.* wate, the quantity of a body or its heaviness, ascertained by the balance; gravity, or the amount of the force with which a body is attracted to the centre of the earth; a piece of metal or other material of known weight used for ascertaining the weight of other bodies; a standard of weight; the body moved as distinct from the moving force [Mech.]; a ponderous mass; something heavy; that which weighs down; pressure; burden; sensation of pressure; importance; power; influence; moment: *v.t.* to press down or to load with a weight or weights; to make heavier. (A.S. *wight.*)

weightily, *ad.* *wate*-e-le, in a weighty manner; heavily; with impressiveness.

weightiness, *n.* heaviness; force; importance.

weightless, *a.* *wate*-less, having no weight; light.

weighty, *a.* *wate*-e, having great weight; heavy; ponderous; important; forcible; grave; adapted to turn the balance in the mind, or to convince.

weir, *n.* weer, a dam in a river to raise the level of the water; a fence of stakes set in a stream for taking fish. (A.S. *wer,* from *werian,* defend.)

weird, *n.* weerd, fate; destiny; that which is destined; enchantment: *a.* pertaining to, or able to control fate; skilled in witchcraft; suggestive of something unearthly; eerie; queer; uncanny. **dree one's weird,** *see* **dree. the Weird Sisters,** the Fates. (A.S. *wyrd,* fate, or that which takes place.)

weirdly, *ad.* *weerd*-le, in a weird manner; uncannily.

weirdness, *n.* *weerd*-ness, the state of being weird.

Weismannism, *n.* *vice*-man-izm, the theory that one does not inherit acquired characters, individuality being ascribable to the action of natural selection on germinal variations. (August *Weismann,* Ger. biologist, *d.* 1915.)

weka, *n.* *wee*-ka, a short-winged flightless New Zealand bird of the rail family. (Maori.)

welch, *v.t.* and *i.* welch, to welsh: *a.* (*cap.*) Welsh.

welcome, *a.* *wel*-kum, received with gladness; admitted willingly to the house, entertainment, and company; grateful; agreeable; producing gladness in its reception; free to have to enjoy gratuitously: *n.* salutation to or kind reception of a guest or newcomer: *v.t.* to salute a newcomer with kindness; to receive and entertain hospitably and cheerfully. **bid welcome,** to receive with professions of kindness. (A.S. *wilcuma.*)

welcomely, *ad.* in a welcome manner.

welcomeness, *n.* kind reception; agreeableness.

welcomer, *n.* *wel*-kum-er, one who salutes or receives kindly.

weld, *n.* weld, the plant dyers' weed, *Reseda luteola,* formerly used by dyers as a yellow colouring matter. (Origin doubtful.)

weld, *n.* weld, union by welding; a welded junction: *v.t.* to join metal in permanent union by hammering or pressure when heated; to forge together; to unite closely and firmly. (Swed.)

weldability, *n.* wel-da-*bil*-e-te, capacity for being welded.

weldable, *a.* *we*-da-bl, that may be welded.

welder, *n.* *wel*-der, one who welds; an appliance or machine for welding.

welding-heat, *n.* the heat necessary for welding.

welfare, *n.* *wel*-fare, prosperity; well-being; exemption from misfortune, sickness, calamity, or evil; the enjoyment of health and the common blessings of life. **welfare centre,** an institution from which the welfare work of a locality is directed. **welfare work,** organized endeavour for the social betterment of some group, esp. by an employer in respect of his employees. **welfare worker,** the member of the staff of a firm or organization responsible for its welfare work.

welkin, *n.* *wel*-kin, the sky; the heavens. **welkin eye,** a blue eye. (A.S. *wolcen,* a cloud.)

well, *n.* wel, a pit sunk perpendicularly into the earth to reach a supply of water or oil, etc.; a shaft in a building for the staircase, a lift, or ventilation; the space in a law-court occupied by barristers, etc.; an enclosure round the pumps in the middle of a ship's hold [Naut.]; a compartment in a fishing-boat for transporting live fish or to hold the catch; a spring; a source: *v.i.* to spring; to issue forth, as water from the earth: *v.t.* to pour forth. (A.S. *wielle.*)

★**well,** *a.* wel, being in health; having a sound body, with all the organs in healthy action; fortunate; convenient; advantageous; happy: *ad.* in a proper manner; justly; rightly; not ill or wickedly; skilfully; with due art; sufficiently; abundantly; to a degree that gives pleasure; favourably; with praise; conveniently; suitably; advantageously; perfectly; thoroughly; fully; adequately. **as well as,** together with; one as much as the other. **well connected,** of good or aristocratic family; able to influence. **well content,** quite satisfied; highly pleased. **well done,** an expression of congratulation; (of food) thoroughly cooked. **well enough,** passable; good to a moderate degree. **well off,** prosperous; in easy circumstances. **well oiled,** unctuous, flattering (of phrases, etc.); more than half drunk [Slang]. **well preserved,** showing little sign of age. **well up in,** thoroughly acquainted with; learned in. (A.S. *wel.*)

welladay, *int.* *wel*-a-day, alas; alackaday.

well-appointed, *a.* fully furnished or equipped.

wellaway, *int.* *wel*-a-way, an exclamation expressive of grief or sorrow; welladay.

well-balanced, *a.* sensible; judicious; normal.

well-behaved, *a.* of good conduct; polite.

well-being, *n.* *wel*-bee-ing, welfare; prosperity.

well-boat, *n.* a fishing-boat having a well in its hold for the reception of fish.

well-boring, *n.* *wel*-bore-ring, the sinking of wells by means of drills.

well-born, *a.* of good or noble birth.

well-bred, *a.* of good breeding; of a good stock.

well-curb, *n.* the ring of masonry or brickwork round the mouth of a well.

well-decker, *n.* a steamship with the forecastle, bridge-house, and quarter-deck raised above the main-deck.

well-dish, *n.* *wel*-dish, a large dish for joints, etc., having a hollow for the gravy.

well-disposed, *a.* friendly towards; having a kindly feeling for.

well-doing, *n.* *wel*-doo-ing, upright conduct.

well-drain, *n.* a drain or vent for water, somewhat like a well or pit, serving to discharge the water of wet land: *v.t.* to drain, as land, by means of a well-drain.

well-earned, *a.* wel-*ernd,* thoroughly deserved.

well-favoured, *a.* pleasing to the eye; handsome.

well-found, *a.* well equipped [chiefly Naut.].

well-founded, *a.* grounded on good reasons.

well-head, *n.* the source of a spring.

well-hole, *n.* in a flight of stairs, the open space in the middle beyond the end of the stairs; the space into which a staircase is fitted [Build.]; the shaft of a well.

well-house, *n.* a shed or room built over a well.

Wellington, *n.* *wel*-ing-ton, a variety of the card-game, nap, also, a bid at this; a kind of cooking apple; a Wellington boot. **Wellington boot,** a long-legged boot, cut away behind the knee. (Duke of *Wellington.*)

Wellingtonia, *n.* *wel*-ing-*toh*-ne-a, a large coniferous tree of the genus *Sequoia.*

well-kept, *a.* wel-*kept,* carefully looked after; trim and neat.

well-knit, *a.* compact in build; sinewy.

well-known, *a.* known to many persons; intimately known; widely acknowledged.

well-made, *a.* shapely; expertly made.

well-marked, *a.* wel-*markt,* having distinct or definite characteristics; readily recognizable.

well-meaning, *a.* of good intentions.

well-meant, *a.* kindly.

well-met, *int.* a term of brotherly salutation.

well-nigh, *ad.* *wel*-ny, almost; nearly.

well-read, *a.* *wel*-red, having read a good deal; having extensive book-learning.

well-room, *n.* *wel*-room, a place in the bottom of a boat where water collects, and whence it is baled out [Naut.]; a room or hall at a medicinal spa where the waters are drunk.

well-set, *a.* firmly set; well-knit.

well-sinker, *n.* *wel*-sing-ker, one occupied in boring or drilling wells.

well-spoken, *a.* speaking well; polite in speech; spoken properly.

well-spring, *n.* a fountain-head; an original source, or a source of continual supply.

well-tempered, *a.* equable; good-natured; properly mixed or treated; tuned in equal temperament [Mus.].

well-timed, *a. wel*-timed, opportune.

well-to-do, *a.* wel-to-*doo*, well off; in easy circumstances.

well-turned, *a.* shapely; skilfully formed; (of phrases, etc.) neatly expressed.

well-water, *n.* water fed to a well from subterraneous springs; water drawn from a well.

wellwisher, *n. wel*-wish-er, one who wishes well to another.

well-worn, *a. wel*-worn, showing the effects of wear; threadbare; [Fig.] hackneyed, trite.

wels, *n.* velts, the sheatfish. (Ger.)

Welsh, *a.* welsh, pertaining to the Welsh nation: *n.* the language of Wales or of the Welsh; the people of Wales. **Welsh harp,** a harp with three rows of strings. **Welsh hook,** a weapon with a cutting blade and a hook at the back. **Welsh onion,** a plant grown chiefly as a spring salad, *Allium fistulosum.* **Welsh poppy,** a poppy of the genus *Meconopsis.* **Welsh rabbit** (or **rarebit**), a dish of cheese melted into a mass and spread over slices of toasted bread. (A.S. *welisc*, foreign.)

welsh, *v.i.* welsh, to act as a welsher; to swindle, esp. out of stakes owing through a bet.

welsher, *n. welsh*-er, a decamping bookmaker; a swindler. (Origin doubtful.)

Welshman, *n. welsh*-man, a native or inhabitant of Wales.

welt, *n.* welt, a narrow strip of leather by which the sole of a boot or shoe is attached to the uppers; a kind of hem or edging; a weal; a narrow border [Her.]: *v.t.* to furnish with a welt; to thrash [Coll.]. (Perhaps A.S. *wæltan*, to roll.)

welted, *a. wel*-ted, furnished with a welt.

welter, *n. wel*-ter, a weltering motion; a state of confusion; a mingled mass, as of that through which one welters: *v.i.* to roll, as the body of an animal; to roll or wallow in or as in some foul matter. (A.S. *wæltan*, roll.)

welter, *n. wel*-ter, a heavy-weight, esp. jockey or boxer; anything large or heavy.

welter-weight, *n.* in English boxing, a weight of from 140 to 147 lb., in American, from 135 to 145 lb.; (of a jockey) any heavy-weight.

welting, *n. wel*-ting, the act of putting on a welt; the welt put on; material for welts; a thrashing [Coll.].

Weltpolitik, *n. velt*-pol-e-*teek*, international worldwide politics or policy. (Ger.)

Welwitschia, *n.* wel-*witch*-e-a, a genus of remarkable plants with long linear leaves discovered by Dr. Frederic Welwitsch (Austrian botanist, *d.* 1872) in Damaraland.

wen, *n.* wen, a pulpy sebaceous cyst, often elastic to the touch; a wart. (A.S. *wenn.*)

wen, *n.* wen, the name of a runic letter used in Anglo-Saxon and represented by modern "w." (A.S.)

wench, *n.* wensh, a young woman; a maidservant; a woman of ill fame: *v.i.* to consort with loose women. (A.S. *wencel*, a child.)

wencher, *n. wensh*-er, a man given to wenching.

wend, *v.t.* and *i.* wend, to go; to pass to or from; to wander. (A.S. *wendan*, turn.)

Wend, *n.* wend, one of a Slavic race that occupied the north and east of Germany.

Wendic, *a.* and *n. wen*-dik, Wendish.

Wendish, *a. wend*-ish, pertaining to the Wends or their language: *n.* the language of the Wends.

wennish, *a. wen*-ish, wenny.

wenny, *a. wen*-e, of the nature of a wen; having a wen or wens.

Wensleydale, *n. wen*-zle-dale, a mild hard cheese made in Wensleydale, Yorkshire.

went, went, *p.* of *go* (and former *p.* of *wend*).

wentletrap, *n. went*-l-trap, a univalve mollusc of the genus *Scalaria.* (Ger. *Wendeltreppe.*)

wept, wept, *p.* and *pp.* of *weep.*

were, wer *or* ware, *imperfect pl.* of *be*, and *first* and *third person sing.* of the subjunctive mood.

weregild, *n. weer*-gild, among the Teutonic peoples and Anglo-Saxons, a fine or compensation (varying in amount according to the rank of the victim) paid to avoid further penalty in cases of homicide. (A.S. *wer*, man, *geld*, compensation.)

werewolf, *n. weer*-woolf, a person transformed, or able to transform himself, into a wolf. (A.S. *wer*, and *wolf.*)

wergild, *n. wer*-gild, weregild.

Wernerian, *a.* wer-*neer*-re-an, pertaining to the theory of A. G. Werner (Ger. mineralogist and geologist, *d.* 1817), that all the rocks were formed by deposition from water: *n.* an adherent of this theory.

wernerite, *n. wer*-ner-ite, a variety of scapolite. (A. G. *Werner*, as *Wernerian.*)

wert, wert, *second person singular* of the imperfect subjunctive of the verb *to be.*

Wertherian, *a.* ver-*teer*-re-an, morbidly sentimental, (*Werther*, an early hero of Goethe.)

Wertherism, *n. ver*-ter-rizm, morbid sentimentality. (As *Wertherian.*)

Wesleyan, *a. wez-* or *wes*-le-an, pertaining to John Wesley (*d.* 1791) or his religious denomination: *n.* one belonging to the Methodist Church founded by John Wesley.

Wesleyanism, *n. wez-* or *wes*-le-an-izm, the church polity of the Wesleyans.

★**west,** *n.* west, one of the four cardinal points, being that in which the sun sets at the equinox; a region or area situated toward the sunsetting with respect to another: *a.* being in a line toward the point in the horizon where the sun sets at the equinox; coming or moving from the west or western regions, as a west wind: *ad.* to the western region; at the westward: *v.i.* to pass to or change to the west (of the wind). **go west,** to die, to be irretrievably lost [Slang]. **West End,** the fashionable quarter of London: *a.* belonging to or characteristic of the West End. (A.S.)

westering, *a. wes*-ter-ring, passing to the west.

westerly, *a. wes*-ter-le, being toward the west; situated in the western region; from the west: *ad.* tending toward the west.

western, *a. wes*-tern, being in the west, or in the region nearly in the direction of the west, or where the sun sets; moving westward; coming from the west. **Western Church,** the Latin Church as distinct from the Eastern, Orthodox, or Greek Church. **Western Empire,** the empire ruled from Rome after A.D. 395, the Eastern Empire being ruled from Constantinople. **western hemisphere,** the half of the word that includes North and South America.

western, *n. west*-ern, a novel, story, film, etc., dealing with the life and surroundings of settlers or cowboys in the western United States [U.S.A.].

westerner, *n. wes*-ter-ner, a native of or dweller in the west, esp. [U.S.A.] in the western parts of the United States.

westernism, *n. wes*-ter-nizm, an idiom or a characteristic of the Western peoples; Occidentalism.

westernize, *v.t. wes*-ter-nize, to habituate to or imbue with the ideas, manners, etc., of Western peoples.

westernmost, *a. wes*-tern-mohst, farthest west.

westing, *n. wes*-ting, space or distance westward; course westward [Naut.].

westland, *n. west*-land, the western part of a country.

Westralian, *a.* wes-*tray*-le-an, pertaining to Western Australia: *n.* an inhabitant of Western Australia.

westward, *ad. west*-ward, in a direction towards the west.

westwardly, *ad. west*-ward-le, between north-west and south-west.

westwards, *ad. west*-wardz, westward.

★**wet,** *a.* wet, containing water; moist; having water or other liquid upon the surface; rainy: *n.* water or wetness; moisture or humidity in a considerable degree; rainy or misty weather; a drink [Slang]; a non-prohibitionist [Slang]: *v.t.* to moisten with water or other liquid; to sprinkle; to dip or soak in liquor; to mark or celebrate (an event, etc.) with drink: *v.i.* to become wet. **wet blanket,** *see* **blanket.** **wet one's whistle,** *see* **whistle.** **wet through,** soaked, thoroughly wet. (A.S. *wæt.*)

wet-bob, *n. wet*-bob, *see* **bob.**

wet-dock, *n.* a dock in which vessels are kept afloat.

wether, *n. weth*-er, a ram castrated. (A.S.)

wetness, *n. wet*-ness, the state of being wet; a watery or moist state of the atmosphere.

wet-nurse, *n.* a nurse employed to suckle another's

child: *v.t.* to act as wet-nurse to; to look after or pamper excessively.
wettable, *a.* *wet*-a-bl, capable of being wetted.
wetting, *n.* *wet*-ing, the act of the verb *to wet*; the state of being wet.
wettish, *a.* *wet*-ish, somewhat wet; moist; humid.
wey, *n.* way, a measure of weight or capacity, differing in different articles (*e.g.*, wool, 182 lb.; cheese, Suffolk, 256 lb., Essex, 336 lb.; corn, or salt 40 bushels; oats or barley, 48 bushels).
wezand, *n.* *wee*-zand, weasand.
whack, *n.* whak, a resounding blow; a thwack; a share [Slang]: *v.t.* to thwack. (A.S. *thaccian*, beat.)
whacker, *n.* *whak*-er, anything of specially large size; a thumping lie [Slang].
whacking, *n.* *whak*-ing, a beating or castigation; a defeat: *a.* large, monstrous [Slang].
whale, *n.* whale, a large marine cetacean of the *Mystacoceti* (whalebone whales) or *Odontoceti* (toothed whales); they comprise a number of families and sub-families, among which are the **right whales** (*Balænæ*), the **blue whale** (*Balænoptera musculus*), the largest living animal, reaching 100 ft. in length, the **sperm whale** (*Physeter catodor*), the **bottle-nosed whale** (*Hyperoödon rostratus*), as well as the rorquals, narwhals, dolphins, etc.: *v.i.* to engage in whale-fishing. (A.S. *hwæl.*)
whaleback, *n.* *whale*-bak, a cargo steamer with upper works covered so as somewhat to resemble the back of a whale.
whale-boat, *n.* a long boat with bow and stem alike used by whalemen.
whalebone, *n.* *whale*-bone, baleen; a firm, elastic substance taken from the upper jaw of the toothless whales.
whale-fishery, *n.* the fishery or occupation of taking whales.
whale-louse, *n.* a small crustacean parasite of the genus *Cyamus* attaching itself by its claws to cetaceans.
whaleman, *n.* *whale*-man, a man employed, or a vessel used, in the whale-fishery.
whaler, *n.* *whale*-er, a whale-boat; a ship employed in the whale-fishery; a seaman employed in a whaler.
whaling, *n.* *whale*-ing, the practice or trade of catching whales; a thrashing [Slang].
whally, *a.* *whaw*-le, greenish-white, or glaring (of the eyes).
whang, *n.* whang, a leather thong; a large slice; a blow or bang: *v.t.* lash, to beat; to cut in large slices.
whanghee, *n.* whang-*hee*, a light cane or walking-stick made from the stem of *Phyllostachys nigra*, a Chinese bamboo-like plant. (Chin. *kuang*, bamboo.)
whap, whapper, etc., whop, *whop*-er, *see* **whop, whopper,** etc.
whare, *n.* *whah*-ray *or* *wo*-re, a Maori hut. (Maori.)
wharf, *n.* whawrf (*pl.* **wharves**), a landing place; a quay; a structure on the shore of a waterway for the convenience of lading and unlading: *v.t.* to guard or secure by a wharf; to moor at, or place on a wharf. (A.S. *hwerf*, a turning.)
wharfage, *n.* *whawr*-faj, the fee or duty paid for loading or unloading goods; the use or provision of a wharf; wharves collectively.
wharfing, *n.* *whawr*-fing, wharves in general; materials for wharves.
wharfinger, *n.* *whawr*-fin-jer, a man who owns or has the care of a wharf.
what, *a.* whot, sort of: *pron.* that which; the thing that; which part, much used in asking questions interrogatively and elliptically, as equivalent to which thing ?, what will be the consequence ?, etc., and as an exclamation. **what ho!** an exclamation of surprise, greeting, etc.; a loud call or summons. **what not,** anything whatever; anything else. **what's what,** the real thing, the truth of the matter [Coll.]. **what though,** granted this or that; what matter that ?; allow it to be so. **what time,** at the time when. (A.S. *hwæt.*)
whate'er, *pron.* whot-*air*, whatever.
whatever, *pron.* whot-*ev*-er, being this or that; being of one nature or another; being one thing or another; all that; the whole that; all particulars that: *a.* of any kind; at all; no matter what.
whatnot, *n.* *whot*-not, a piece of furniture with shelves for sundries; (incorrectly) what not.
whatsoe'er, *pron.* whot-so-*air*, whatsoever.
whatsoever, *pron.* *whot*-so-*ev*-er, whatever.
whaup, *n.* whawp, the curlew, *Numenius arquatus.*
wheal, *n.* wheel, a pustule; a pimple; a weal.
wheal, *n.* wheel, a Cornish mine, esp. a tin-mine. (Corn. *huel.*)
whealworm, *n.* *wheel*-wurm, the harvest-mite.
wheat, *n.* wheet, a plant of the genus *Triticum* and its seed which furnishes a white flour. **wheat belt,** that part of the earth's surface on which wheat is the principal crop [Agric.]. (A.S. *hwæte*, connected with *white.*)
wheat-bird, *n.* the chaffinch, or other bird feeding on wheat.
wheat-ear, *n.* an ear of wheat.
wheatear, *n.* *wheet*-eer, a small bird *Saxicola œnanthe*, allied to the stonechat and whinchat; the fallowfinch. (A.S. *hwit*, white, *eeres*, *ers*, rump.)
wheaten, *a.* *whee*-tn, made of wheat.
wheat-fly, *n.* any of several insects injurious to wheat, esp. the Hessian-fly.
wheat-moth, *n.* any moth whose grubs devour wheat, esp. after it is harvested.
Wheatstone bridge, *n.* *wheet*-ston bridj, *see* **bridge.**
wheedle, *v.t.* *whee*-dl, to coax; to flatter; to cajole; to obtain by flattery: *v.i.* to flatter; to coax. (W. *chwedla*, talk.)
wheedler, *n.* *whee*-dler, one who wheedles.
wheedlesome, *a.* *whee*-dl-sum, coaxing.
wheedling, *a.* *whee*-dling, enticing: *n.* the act of flattering or enticing.
★**wheel,** *n.* wheel, a circular frame or solid circular piece of wood, metal, plastic, etc., turning on an axis; a machine or contrivance in the shape of a wheel; a circular body; an instrument of torture; a spinning-wheel; rotation; revolution; a turning about; a round board turned by a lathe in a horizontal position, on which clay is shaped by the hand of the potter; a cog-wheel; a catherine-wheel, or revolving fire-work; a large circular frame having handles on the periphery, and connected by tiller-ropes with the rudder, for the purpose of steering the ship [Naut.]; a bicycle [Coll.]. **break on the wheel,** to fasten to a revolving wheel and beat with an iron bar. **wheel and axle,** one of the mechanical powers, consisting of a cylindrical axle, to which a wheel concentric with it is attached. **wheel of Fortune,** a wheel emblematic of the ups-and-downs of life. **wheel of life,** the zoetrope. **wheels within wheels,** reasons that are not ostensible; a complication of conditions modifying an apparently obvious course. **to put a spoke in one's wheel,** *see* **spoke.** (A.S. *hweol.*)
wheel, *v.t.* wheel, to convey on wheels; to put into a rotary motion; to cause to turn round: *v.i.* to turn on an axis; to move round; to fetch a compass; to roll forward; to move forward or backward or to change direction in a circular or semicircular manner [Mil.].
wheelage, *n.* *wheel*-aj, a toll paid for passage by wheeled vehicles; cost of carriage by these.
wheel-animalcule, *n.* a species of *Rotifer.*
wheelbarrow, *n.* *wheel*-ba-roh, a one-wheeled two-handled barrow.
wheel-base, *n.* the distance between the axles of the front and back wheels of a car, railway truck, etc.
wheel-carriage, *n.* a carriage moved on wheels; conveyance by wheeled vehicles.
wheel-chair, *n.* an invalid's chair fitted with wheels; a bath-chair; a push-chair.
wheel-cutting, *n.* that branch of practical mechanics which comprehends the modes of cutting the teeth in cog-wheels.
wheeled, *a.* wheeld, having a wheel or wheels.
wheeler, *n.* *wheel*-er, a maker of wheels; one who wheels; that which has wheels, as *four-wheeler*; a horse in the shafts or alongside the pole of a vehicle drawn by a team; a cyclist.
wheel-horse, *n.* a draught-horse harnessed next to the vehicle (as distinguished from a leader); a wheeler.
wheel-house, *n.* the structure containing the steering wheel of a ship.
wheeling, *n.* *wheel*-ing, act of conveying on wheels; cycling.
wheel-lock, *n.* a flint-lock fire-arm in which the

flint was struck by a revolving wheel; the gunlock for this.
wheelman, *n.* *wheel*-man, a maker of wheels; a wheelsman; a cyclist.
wheel-ore, *n.* a twinned variety of bournonite.
wheelsman, *n.* *wheelz*-man, a steersman; one who handles a wheel.
wheelspin, *n.* *wheel*-spin, rotation of the wheels without movement of the car [Motoring].
wheelstone, *n.* *wheel*-stone, an entrochite.
wheel-window, *n.* a circular window having radiating tracery or mullions.
wheel-work, *n.* a combination of geared wheels in which motion is conveyed from the axis of one to another by means of straps or teeth on their margins.
wheelwright, *n.* *wheel*-rite, a man whose occupation is to make wheels.
wheely, *a.* *wheel*-e, circular; suitable to rotation.
wheen, *n.* wheen, a small quantity. (A.S. *hwæne.*)
wheeter-why, *n.* *whee*-ter-*why*, a local name of the whitethroat, *Sylvia cinerea.*
wheeze, *n.* wheez, an audible breath; a familiar saying; a wisecrack: *v.i.* to breathe hard and with an audible sound, as persons affected with asthma. (A.S. *hwesan.*)
wheezily, *ad.* *whee*-ze-le, breathing audibly.
wheeziness, *n.* *whee*-ze-ness, a wheezy state or quality; sibilant respiration.
wheezing, *n.* *whee*-zing, act of breathing with difficulty and noise.
wheezy, *a.* *whee*-ze, affected with wheezing.
wheft, *n.* wheft, a waft, or flag tied across the middle; a pennant.
whelk, *n.* whelk, an edible marine gastropod of the genus *Buccinum.* (A.S. *weolc,* perhaps allied to *wealcan,* turn, from its twisted shell.)
whelk, *n.* whelk, a wheal or pimple. (A.S. *hwylca.*)
whelky, *a.* *whel*-ke, resembling the shell of a whelk; protuberant; rounded.
whelm, *v.t.* whelm, to cover or submerge violently and completely; to immerse deeply; to overburden; to overwhelm. (M.E. *whelmen,* to turn over.)
whelp, *n.* whelp, the young of the dog and of several other animals; a puppy; a cub; an ill-bred lad; a son or a young man, in contempt: *v.i.* and *t.* to bring forth young, as a dog. (A.S. *hwelp.*)
***when,** *ad.* when, at the time; at what time; which time; after the time that. **say when!** tell me when to stop (esp. diluting spirits) [Coll.]. (A.S., from the root of *who.*)
whenas, *ad.* when-*az*, at the time when.
whence, *ad.* whence, from what place; from what source; from what premises, principles, or facts; how; by what way or means; in general, from which person, cause, place, principle, or circumstance.
whencesoever, *ad.* *whence*-so-*ev*-er, from what place soever; from what cause or source soever.
whenever, *ad.* *when*-ev-er *or* when-*ev*-er, at whatever time.
whensoever, *ad.* *when*-so-*ev*-er, at what time soever; at whatever time.
***where,** *ad.* whare, at which place or places; at or in what place; at the place in which; whither. **anywhere,** in any place; whence. (A.S. from root of *who.*)
whereabout, *ad.* *whare*-a-bout, near what place; near which place; concerning which.
whereabouts, *n.* *whare*-a-bouts, the place in which anything or anyone is to be found.
whereas, *ad.* whare-*az*, when in fact or truth, implying opposition to something that precedes; the thing being so that; considering that things are so; but on the contrary; since.
whereat, *ad.* whare-*at*, at which; at what.
whereby, *ad.* whare-*by*, by which; by what.
wherefore, *ad.* *whare*-for, for which reason; why; for what reason. **the why and wherefore,** the full reason, the complete explanation.
wherein, *ad.* whare-*in*, into which; in which; in what.
whereinsoever, *ad.* *whare*-in-so-*ev*-er, in whatever place or respect.
whereinto, *ad.* whare-*in*-too, into which.
whereness, *n.* *whare*-ness, situation in space.
whereof, *ad.* whare-*ov*, of which.
whereon, *ad.* whare-*on*, on which.
whereout, *ad.* whare-*out*, out of which.
wheresoever, *ad.* *whare*-so-*ev*-er, in whatever place, or in any place indefinitely.
whereto, *ad.* whare-*too*, to which; to what; to what end.
whereunto, *ad.* whare-*un*-too, whereto.
whereupon, *ad.* whare-u-*pon*, upon which.
wherever, *ad.* whare-*ev*-er, at whatever place.
wherewith, *ad.* whare-*with*, with which; with what.
wherewithal, *ad.* whare-with-*awl*, wherewith: *n.* the money or resources necessary.
wherry, *n.* *whe*-re, a shallow, light boat, for rowing or sailing, esp. on rivers; a barge-like vessel: *v.t.* and *i.* to go or convey by wherry; to manage a wherry. (Origin uncertain.)
wherryman, *n.* *whe*-re-man, one who manages a wherry, esp. for hire by passengers.
whet, *n.* whet, the act of sharpening by friction; something that stimulates the appetite: *v.t.* to rub on a stone or strop for the purpose of sharpening, as an edge tool; to sharpen by attrition; to incite; to stimulate; to make keener or more eager. (A.S. *hweltan,* sharpen.)
whether, *pron.* *wheth*-er, which of two: *conj.* which of two alternatives, expressed by a sentence or the clause of a sentence, and followed by *or.* **whether or not,** in any (or either) case; no matter what happens. (A.S. *hwæther,* which of two.)
whethering, *n.* *wheth*-er-ing, the retention of the afterbirth in cows.
whetstone, *n.* *whet*-stone, a stone for sharpening edged tools by friction. **whetstone slate,** a variety of slate used for sharpening steel tools.
whetter, *n.* *whet*-er, one who or that which whets or sharpens.
whew, *int.* whew, hew, or wew, expressing surprise or aversion: *n.* this sound: *v.i.* to make such a sound or whistle.
whewellite, *n.* *hew*-el-ite, an oxalate of calcium, named after Wm. Whewell (*d.* 1866).
whewer, *n.* *whew*-er, the hen widgeon.
whey, *n.* whay, the serous or watery part of milk, separated from the coagulable part, esp. in the process of making cheese; the serum of milk: *a.* resembling or containing whey; pale; watery. (A.S. *hwæg.*)
wheyey, *a.* *whay*-e, wheyish.
wheyish, *a.* *whay*-ish, partaking of or resembling whey; having the qualities of whey.
which, *pron.* whitch, a word of interrogation in all genders; as, which man? which woman? which house? also a relative in reference to things neuter, and a relative *adj.*, as in "during which time." **which is which?** which is the one and which is the other. (A.S. *hwilc,* from *hwi,* why, *lic,* like.)
whichever, *pron.* whitch-*ev*-er, whether one or the other; no matter which.
whichsoever, *pron.* *whitch*-so-*ev*-er, whichever.
whidah, *n.* *whee*-dah, a W. African weaver-bird, a species of *Vidua*; the widow-bird. (Spelling arises from confusion with Ouidah, or *Wydah,* Dahomey, as a point of migration; see **widow-bird.**)
whiff, *n.* whif, a sudden expulsion of air from the mouth; a puff; a gust of air; a waft of odour; a flatfish of the turbot group; a light outrigged sculling boat in which canvas is nowhere substituted for wood: *v.t.* to puff; to throw out or consume in whiffs: *v.i.* to practise whiffing. (From the sound.)
whiffing, *n.* *whif*-ing, sea-fishing with a hand-line, esp. for mackerel.
whiffle, *n.* *whif*-fl, the act of whiffling: *v.i.* to shift and turn; to change from one opinion or course to another; to use evasions; to prevaricate; to be fickle and unsteady: *v.t.* to disperse with a puff; to scatter. (*whiff.*)
whiffler, *n.* *whif*-fler, one who whiffles; one who uses shifts and evasions in argument; a trifler; an attendant who clears the way before a procession, etc.
whiffletree, *n.* *whif*-fl-tree, a whippletree.
whiffling, *n.* *whif*-fling, prevarication; shuffling.
whiffy, *a.* *whif*-e, like a whiff; smelly [Slang].
Whig, *n.* whig, one of a political party dating from the 17th cent. and superseded by the Liberals in the early 19th, which advocated and supported measures of a liberal character, tending to give greater legislative and governing power to the

masses; a Liberal in English politics; a supporter of the American revolution [U.S.A.]: *a.* pertaining to or composed of Whigs. (Probably from *Whiggamore.*)

whig, *n.* whig, acidulated whey, used as a cooling beverage. (Scots.)

Whiggamore, *n. whig*-a-mor, name of a body of mid-17th-cent. Scottish insurgents. (Origin doubtful.)

Whiggery, *n. whig*-er-re, the principles of the Whigs.

Whiggish, *a. whig*-ish, partaking of the principles of Whigs.

Whiggism, *n. whig*-izm, whiggery; the characteristics of English Whigs.

⋆**while,** *n.* whyl, the time or expense needed: *conj.* during the time that; as long as; at the same time that; in which case: *v.t.* (only in **to while away**) to cause (time) to pass away pleasantly and without irksomeness. **worth while,** worth the time and trouble which it requires; worth the expense. (A.S. *hwil.*)

whilere, *ad. whyl*-air, a little while ago.

whiles, *adv.* whylz, sometimes, now and then: *conj.* while [Scots.].

whilk, *pron.* whilk, which [Scots.].

whilk, *n.* whilk, the scoter (a sea-duck).

whilom, *ad. why*-lom, formerly; once; of old.

whilst, *ad.* whylst, while.

whim, *n.* whim, a sudden turn or start of the mind; a capricious notion; freak; caprice; a windlass used in mining; a large capstan worked by horses, for raising coal or metal from mines. (Perhaps connected with Scand. *hvima,* wander with the eyes.)

whimberry, *n. whim*-ber-re, the whortleberry.

whimbrel, *n. whim*-brel, a bird closely allied to the curlew, but of a smaller size, *Numenius phæopus.* (From its whimpering cry.)

whimmy, *a. whim*-e, full of whims; crotchety.

whimper, *v.i. whim*-per, to cry with a low, whining, broken voice: *v.t.* to utter with whimpering: *n.* a plaintive cry; a whimpering. (Imit.)

whimpering, *n. whim*-per-ring, a low, muttering cry.

whimsey, *n. whim*-ze, a whimsy.

whimsical, *a. whim*-ze-kal, full of whims; having odd fancies; freakish; odd in temper; fantastical.

whimsicality, *n. whim*-ze-*kal*-e-te, whimsicalness; a whim.

whimsically, *ad.* in a whimsical manner.

whimsicalness, *n. whim*-ze-kal-ness, the quality or state of being whimsical.

whimsy, *n. whim*-ze, a whim; a freak; a capricious notion; a small hoisting machine or crane [Min.].

whim-wham, *n. whim*-wham, a whim or whimsy; a plaything; a toy; an odd device. (*whim.*)

whin, *n.* whin, gorse, a plant of the genus *Ulex.* (Scand.; or perhaps W. *chwyn,* weeds.)

whin, *n.* whin, a whinstone.

whinberry, *n. whin*-ber-re, the whortleberry or whimberry.

whinchat, *n. whin*-chat, the small singing bird, *Saxicola rubetra,* allied to the stonechat, which frequents furze-bushes.

whine, *n.* whine, a plaintive tone; the nasal, puerile tone of mean complaint; a mean or affected complaint: *v.t.* and *i.* to express complaint by a plaintive cry; to moan with a puerile noise; to murmur in an unmanly way. (A.S. *hwinan.*)

whiner, *n. why*-ner, one who whines.

whinger, *n. whing*-er *or whin*-jer, a short sword, or whinyard [Scots.].

whiningly, *ad. why*-ning-le, in a whining way; abjectly; plaintively.

whinny, *a. whin*-e, abounding in gorse bushes.

whinny, *n. whin*-e, the gentle or joyful call of the horse as distinct from the neigh: *v.i.* and *t.* to call in this manner. (From the sound.)

whinstone, *n. whin*-stone, a name given to various basaltic rocks, and by miners to any dark-coloured hard unstratified rock which resists the pick. (Origin unknown.)

whiny, *a. why*-ne, whining; petulant; querulous.

whinyard, *n. whin*-yerd, a short sword; a dirk.

⋆**whip,** *n.* whip, a lash tied to a handle or rod; a coachman or driver of a carriage, as, a good whip; a whipping motion; flexibility; suppleness; a whipper-in; a whip-crane; one of the arms carrying the sail of a windmill, also, the length of this; a member of Parliament whose duty it is to summon the members of his party to be present at a division, also the summons itself; the long narrow pennant carried by a naval vessel when in commission. **whip and spur,** with the utmost haste. **whip round,** a collection among friends.

whip, *v.t.* whip, to strike with a lash; to drive by lashing; to punish with a whip; to take, pull, snatch, etc., suddenly; to lash with sarcasm; to strike; to flog; to beat; to bind, as a rope's end, with twine; to fish (a stream, etc.) with fly; to beat out, as grain, by striking; to beat into a froth; to overlay in needlework; to sew slightly; *v.i.* to move nimbly; to start suddenly and run: to turn and run. **whip from,** to take away suddenly. **whip into,** to thrust in with a quick motion. **whip out,** to draw nimbly; to snatch. **whip up,** to seize or take up with a quick motion. (M.E. *whippen,* connected with Dan. *wippen,* to shake.)

whipcord, *n. whip*-kord, a kind of hard twisted string of which lashes are made for whips; a closely woven ribbed worsted material used for clothing.

whip-crane, *n.* a simple kind of tackle with a single rope, used for hoisting, esp. on board ship.

whip-graft, *v.t.* to graft by cutting the scion and stock in a sloping direction, so as to fit each other, and by inserting a tongue on the scion into a slit in the stock: *n.* a graft so made.

whip-hand, *n.* the hand holding the whip; [Fig.] advantage over; mastery of.

whip-lash, *n.* the lash of a whip.

whipper, *n. whip*-er, one who whips; an officer who inflicts the penalty of legal whipping; one who hoists coal from a ship's hold.

whipper-in, *n.* the assistant to a huntsman who keeps the hounds from wandering, and whips them in to the line of chase; the last horse in a race.

whipper-snapper, *n.* a diminutive, insignificant person; a small child.

whippet, *n. whip*-et, a small cross-bred greyhound used in coursing and dog-racing; a small light tank or armoured car.

whippiness, *n. whip*-e-ness, the quality of being whippy; extreme pliancy.

whipping, *n. whip*-ing, the act of punishing with a whip; the state of being whipped; a close wrapping of twine.

whipping-boy, *n.* a boy brought up with a prince and taking his punishments; [Fig.] a scapegoat.

whipping-post, *n.* a post to which offenders were tied when being whipped.

whippletree, *n. whip*-pl-tree, a swingletree, the bar to which the traces are hooked and by which a carriage, a plough, or other implement, is drawn.

whip-poor-will, *n.* the North American nightjar *Antrostomus vociferus,* so called from the fancied resemblance of its notes to the words.

whippy, *a. whip*-e, long, thin, and flexible.

whip-ray, *n.* any of the long-tailed marine rays.

whip-round, *n.* whip-*round,* an appeal for donations, or a collection taken on the spot, for a charity or some sudden need.

whip-saw, *n.* a narrow saw usually set in a frame for dividing timber lengthwise, or for curved work.

whip-snake, *n.* a name given to various long, slender snakes, esp. of the genus *Dryophis.*

whipster, *n. whip*-ster, a nimble, or a contemptible, little fellow; a whipper-snapper.

whip-stitch, *v.t.* to half-plough or rafter land [Agric.]; to sew with an overcast stitch [Needlework]: *n.* an overcast stitch.

whipstock, *n. whip*-stok, the rod or handle to which the lash of a whip is fastened.

whip-tailed, *a.* having a long thin tail.

whiptongue, *n. whip*-tung, the plant *Galium mollugo,* wild madder.

whip-top, *n.* a top spun by whipping.

whip-worm, *n.* any thread-worm.

whir, *n.* wher, the sound from rapid whirling or other motion; commotion: *v.i.* to whirl round or move with noise: *v.t.* to hurry with a whir. (From the sound.)

whirl, *n.* wherl, a turning with rapidity or velocity; quick gyration; confused hurry or commotion; a hook used in twisting fibre for ropes; anything that moves or is turned with velocity on an axis or pivot; the pulley of a spindle; a whorl: *v.t.* to turn round rapidly; to gyrate; to turn with velocity; to hurry: *v.i.* to be turned round rapidly; to move round with velocity; to move hastily.

in a whirl, in a state of confusion or perplexity; mentally agitated. **the social whirl,** restless society life. (Scand.)

whirlabout, *n. wherl*-a-bout, the action of whirling about; anything in a whirl; a whirligig.

whirl-blast, *n.* a hurricane; a whirling blast of wind.

whirlbone, *n. wherl*-bone, the rounded head of a bone (esp. the femur) turning in the socket of another; the patella or knee-pan.

whirler, *n. wherl*-er, one who or that which whirls; a whirling-table.

whirligig, *n. wher*-le-gig, a toy spun on an axis like a wheel; a teetotum; a former instrument of punishment consisting of a cage turning on a pivot, in which the offender was whirled; an aquatic beetle of the genus *Gyrinus*; [Fig.] a flighty or undependable person. (*whirl* and *gig*.)

whirling, *a. wherl*-ing, turning round with velocity.

whirling-table, *n.* a machine contrived for representing phenomena of centrifugal force, by giving bodies a rapid rotation; a potter's wheel.

whirlpool, *n. wherl*-pool, an eddy of water; a vortex in which water moves round in a circle, caused by the meeting of currents or of tides and winds.

whirlwind, *n. wherl*-wind, a violent wind having rapid spiral or circular motion, as if round an axis itself in motion.

whirr, *n.* and *v.t.* wher, whir.

whirring, *n. wher*-ing, the sound as of a partridge's or pheasant's wings when in flight.

whish, *n.* whish, a slight sibilant or whistling sound: *v.i.* and *t.* to utter such a sound; to chase away with a whish.

whisk, *n.* whisk, the act of whisking; a small bunch of grass, straw, hair, or the like; a brush or small broom; a small culinary utensil for whisking the whites of eggs; a tippet or neckerchief formerly worn by women: *v.t.* to sweep, brush, or agitate with a light, swift motion; to move with a quick sweeping motion: *v.i.* to move nimbly and with velocity. (Scand.)

whisk-broom, *n.* a small brush, esp. one for brushing clothes.

whisker, *n. whis*-ker, he who or that which whisks; hair growing on the cheeks of male adults; bristly hair on the upper lip of cats, otters, etc.; a spreader for a bow-sprit shroud [Naut.]. (Scand.)

whiskered, *a. whis*-kurd, formed into whiskers; furnished with whiskers. **whiskered tern,** the seabird *Hydrochelidon hydrida*.

whisket, *n. whis*-ket, a basket.

whiskey, *n. whis*-ke, whisky, esp. Irish whisky.

whiskified, *a. whis*-ke-fide, sodden, or intoxicated, with whisky [Coll.].

whisky, *n. whis*-ke, an alcoholic liquor distilled from malted barley and other cereals. **whisky john,** the Canada jay, *Perisoreus canadensis*. **whisky liver,** cirrhosis of the liver caused by alcoholism. **whisky-poker,** a variety of poker in which one hand more than the number of players is dealt. (Celt. *uisge*, water, *uisgebeatha*, water of life.)

whisky, *n. whis*-ke, a light two-wheeled carriage fashionable in the early 19th cent. (Perhaps *whisk*.)

whisper, *n. whis*-per, a low, soft, sibilant voice, or words uttered with such a voice; a cautious or timorous speech; a hissing or buzzing sound: *v.i.* to speak with a low, sibilant voice; to make such a sound; to plot secretly; to devise mischief: *v.t.* to address in a low or in a sibilant voice; to prompt secretly. (A.S. *hwisprian*.)

whisperer, *n. whis*-per-rer, one who whispers; a tattler; one who tells secrets; a backbiter.

whispering, *a. whis*-per-ring, speaking in a low voice; telling secretly; backbiting; making the sound of a whisper: *n.* the act of speaking in a low voice; a backbiting. **whispering campaign,** organized and clandestine vilification with an ulterior object. **whispering gallery,** one round which whispers are conveyed which cannot be heard across it: [Fig.] a place or locality in which rumours abound.

whisperingly, *ad.* in a low voice or whisper.

whist, *int.* whist, hush! be silent; silence: *a.* not making a noise; silent; mute; still: *v.t.* to hush or silence.

whist, *n.* whist, a four-handed game of cards played with the entire pack, probably so called because it imposes silence or close attention. **whist drive,** a whist party at which the players change partners after every deal and prizes are given for various scores; progressive whist.

★**whistle,** *n. whis*-sl, a small wind instrument; the sound made by it; a sharp sound made by pressing the breath through a small orifice of the lips; any sharp or shrill sound; a small pipe used by a boatswain as a call to duty; the boatswain's call; the shrill sound of winds passing among trees or through crevices: *v.i.* to utter a kind of shrill musical sound by, or as by, pressing the breath through a small orifice formed by contracting the lips; to make such a sound, as by a small wind instrument or by a bird, etc.; to sound shrill or like a pipe: *v.t.* to form, utter, or modulate by whistling; to call by a whistle. **pay for one's whistle,** to pay dear for one's pleasure. **wet one's whistle,** to have a drink. **whistle for,** to stand little chance of obtaining; to go without. (A.S. *hwistlian*.)

whistle-fish, *n.* the three-bearded rockling *Motella tricirrata*.

whistler, *n. whis*-ler, one who whistles; applied also to various birds, as the widgeon and ring-ouzel, and to the woodchuck *Marmote caligata*, of north-west N. America.

whistling, *n. whis*-ling, a shrill sound, as of one who whistles. **whistling swan,** the whooping swan.

whit, *n.* whit, the smallest part or particle imaginable; a point; a jot. (A form of *wight*.)

white, *a.* white, being of the colour of pure snow; not dark; pale; bloodless, destitute of colour in the cheeks; pure; free from spot; grey; unblemished; purified from sin. **show the white feather,** *see* **feather. the white man's burden,** the duty of whites to civilize and raise the status of the coloured races. **to bleed white,** to divest of the whole of one's money, resources, or strength, etc. **white ant,** a termite. **white copper,** an alloy of copper, nickel, and zinc; German silver. **white elephant,** *see* **elephant. white ensign,** the ensign of the Royal Navy and Royal Yacht Squadron. **white flag,** the flag of truce or of surrender. **white gold,** gold alloyed with about 25 per cent. of nickel and zinc. **white iron,** tinned iron plate. **white lead,** carbonate of lead. **white lie, magic,** *see* these words. **white man,** a man of one of the white or Caucasian races; a non-coloured man; [Coll.] a straightforward honourable man. **white matter,** the whitish fibrous substance of the brain [Anat.]. **white meat,** the flesh of pork, poultry, veal, rabbit, etc. **white paper,** a government pamphlet, usually explanatory of a piece of forthcoming legislation. **white sauce,** sauce made of milk, flour, and butter. **white scourge** or **plague,** tuberculosis. **white sheet,** a symbol of repentance; the garb of a penitent. **white slave,** a prostitute exploited for commercial profit. **white slave traffic,** the procuration and transportation of women for immoral purposes. **white squall,** *see* **squall. white trash,** *n.* a poor white; poor whites collectively. **white wine,** any wine other than red. (A.S. *hwit*.)

★**white,** *n.* white (*pl., see* **whites**), the colour of snow; a white spot or thing; a white man or woman; the player of the white pieces at chess, etc. **poor white,** a low-grade unpropertied white person, in the southern U.S.A. and (esp. one of Dutch descent) South Africa. **white of egg,** the albumen which surrounds the yolk. **white of the eye,** that part of the ball of the eye surrounding the iris or coloured part.

white, *v.t.* white, to make white; to whitewash. **whited sepulchre,** a plausible canting hypocrite.

whitebait, *n. white*-bate, the young of herrings and sprats and other small fish.

whitebeam, *n, white*-beem, the tree *Pyrus aria*.

whitebeard, *n. white*-beerd, an old man; the Australian evergreen shrub *Styphalia ericoides*, having a white pubescence on its corolla.

Whiteboy, *n. white*-boy, a member of an association of Irish raiders, formed in 1762, who used to wear white shirts over their clothes.

Whiteboyism, *n. white*-boy-izm, the principle and practice of the Whiteboys.

whitecap, *n. white*-kap, a name given to the lesser whitethroat and the redstart.

white-collar, *a.* white-kol-lar, denoting the status

or occupation of clerical and similar black-coated workers; [Coll.] middle-class.
whitefish, *n.* *white*-fish, any of several food-fish of the genus *Coregonus* found in the lakes of N. America; a fish of the genus *Leuciscus*.
whitefriar, *n.* white-*fry*-ar, a Carmelite monk.
whitehead, *n.* *white*-hed, the blue-winged snow-goose *Anser cærulescens*.
white-heat, *n.* degree of heat at which a metal becomes incandescent or white (about 1,300° C. or 2,370° F.); state of mind in which the feelings are raised to, and work at, an intense pitch, or are, as it were, all aglow.
white-hot, *a.* white-*hot*, at white heat; very hot indeed.
white-limed, *a.* whitewashed, or plastered with lime.
white-livered, *a.* having a pale look; feeble; cowardly; malicious.
whitely, *ad.* *white*-le, with a white colour.
white-metal, *n.* a soft lead- or tin-base alloy used for bearings; pewter, or other white alloy.
whiten, *v.t.* *why*-tn, to make white; to bleach; to blanch: *v.i.* to grow white; to turn or become white.
whitener, *n.* *why*-tner, one who or that which bleaches or makes white.
whiteness, *n.* *white*-ness, the state of being white; paleness; purity; cleanness; freedom from stain.
whitening, *n.* *why*-tning, anything that whitens; levigated chalk used for whitewashing, polishing, etc.; whiting.
whitepot, *n.* *white*-pot, a dish made of milk, cream, sugar, and eggs, baked in a pot.
white-rent, *n.* a rent or duty formerly payable by Cornish tinners to the Duke of Cornwall, as lord of the soil.
whites, *n. pl.* whyts, a flour from white wheat; leucorrhœa, a symptom of certain diseases of women.
whiteside, *n.* *white*-side, the goldeneye duck, *Clangula glaucion*.
whitesmith, *n.* *white*-smith a tinsmith; one who finishes ironwork; a polishing smith.
whitestone, *n.* *white*-stone, a granite abounding in white felspar.
whitetail, *n.* *white*-tale, the wheatear, *Saxicola œnanthe*.
whitethorn, *n.* *white*-thorn, the hawthorn.
whitethroat, *n.* *white*-throte, a species of warbler, *Sylvia cinerea*, named from the colour of its throat.
whitewash, *n.* *white*-wosh, a wash or liquid composition for whitening something; white distemper; false or dishonest exoneration: *v.t.* to cover with whitewash; to make white; to make one who is in fault appear innocent; to clear of bankruptcy; to win a game (esp. darts) before the opponent has scored [slang].
whitewasher, *n.* *white*-wosh-er, one who whitewashes.
whitewing, *n.* *white*-wing, the chaffinch, *Fringilla cœlebs*.
whitewood, *n.* *white*-wood, any of several timber-trees the wood of which is light-coloured; the wood itself; the linden; the tulip-tree of the genus *Liriodendron*; alburnum.
whither, *ad.* *whith*-er, to what place; to which place; to what point or degree. (A.S. *hurder.*)
whithersoever, *ad.* *whith*-er-so-*ev*-er, to whatever place.
whiting, *n.* *why*-ting, whitening or levigated chalk; Spanish-white.
whiting, *n.* *why*-ting, the sea-fish *Gadus merlangus*. **whiting pout,** the sea-fish *Gadus luscus*.
whitish, *a.* *white*-ish, somewhat white.
whitleather, *n.* *whit*-leth-er, a tough but pliable leather, dressed with alum and salt.
whitling, *n.* *whit*-ling, the sea-trout, *Salmo trutta*; also, a bull-trout, *Salmo eriox*, in its second season.
whitlow, *n.* *whit*-loh, paronychia, a sort of suppurating abscess on a finger or toe [Med.]; a disease of the feet of sheep, etc., of an inflammatory kind. (*white* and *flaw.*)
whitlow-grass, *n.* a cruciferous plant of the genus *Draba*.
whitneyite, *n.* *whit*-ne-ite, a mineral containing copper and arsenic. (J. D. *Whitney*, Amer. geologist, *d.* 1896.)
whitret, *n.* whe-*tret*, a weasel or stoat. (Probably *white* and *rat.*)
whitster, *n.* *whit*-ster, a bleacher; a whitesmith.
Whitsun, *a.* *whit*-sun, pertaining to Whit-Sunday or Whitsuntide: *n.* Whitsuntide.
Whit-Sunday, *n.* whit-*sun*-day, the seventh Sunday after Easter, a festival of the Church in commemoration of the descent of the Holy Spirit on the day of Pentecost.
Whitsuntide, *n.* *whit*-sun-tide, the week beginning with Whit-Sunday, when newly baptized catechumens formerly wore white garments.
whitterick, *n.* *whit*-er-rik, the curlew *Numenius arguatus*; also, the stoat or whitret.
whittle, *n.* *whit*-tl, a large butcher's or carving-knife; a clasp-knife: *v.t.* to cut off small strips with a knife; to pare away and gradually reduce in size or amount. (A.S. *thwitan*, cut.)
whittle, *n.* *whit*-tl, a blanket worn over the shoulders like a cloak; a wrap or shawl; an infant's flannel. (A.S. *hwitel*, a white mantle.)
Whit-week, *n.* *whit*-week, Whitsuntide.
whity, *a.* why-te, fairly white; whitish; off-white. **whity-brown,** of a colour between white and brown.
whizz, *n.* whiz, a sort of hissing sound: *v.i.* to make a humming or hissing sound, like an arrow or ball flying through the air. (From the sound.)
whizzbang, *n.* *whiz*-bang, a high-velocity shell heard coming before the report of the gun.
whizzingly, *ad.* *whiz*-ing-le, with a whizzing sound.
★who, hoo, a relative *pron.* always referring to persons. (A.S. *hwa.*)
whoa, *int.* whoh, pull up; stop.
whoever, *pron.* hoo-*ev*-er, whatever person.
whole, *a.* hole, the total amount or number or the entire thing; all; total; complete; not defective or imperfect; not impaired, injured, or broken; sound; not hurt or sick; restored to health and soundness: *n.* the entire thing; the entire or total assemblage of parts; a system; a regular combination of parts; aggregate. **on the whole,** all things considered. **whole blood,** relationship derived from the same pair, as distinguished from half-blood. **whole hog,** the whole way or thing; without reservation. **whole number,** a number composed of complete units; an integer. (A.S. *hal*, healthy.)
whole-coloured, *a.* of one colour throughout.
whole-hearted, *a.* loyal; hearty and sincere; without reservations.
whole-heartedly, *ad.* loyally; with single-minded devotion.
whole-heartedness, *n.* the state or quality of being whole-hearted; complete sincerity.
whole-hogger, *n.* hole-*hog*-er, an enthusiast for thoroughness; one opposed to compromise [Coll.].
whole-hoofed, *a.* hole-*hooft*, having hooves that are not cloven.
whole-length, *a.* and *n.* including the whole figure (of portraits).
whole-meal, *n.* hole-*meel*, wheat flour or meal containing all the constituents of the grain: *a.* *hole*-meel, made of this.
wholeness, *n.* *hole*-ness, entireness; totality.
wholesale, *n.* *hole*-sale, sale of goods in large quantities for sale by retail; the whole mass: *a.* buying and selling in large quantities; pertaining to trade between wholesaler and retailer: *ad.* on a wholesale footing; indiscriminately over the mass.
wholesaler, *n.* *hole*-say-ler, a trader dealing wholesale, selling only to retailers, factors, etc.
wholesome, *a.* *hole*-sum, tending to promote health; salubrious; sound; contributing to the health of the mind; favourable to morals, religion, or prosperity; useful; salutary; conducive to public happiness, virtue, or peace.
wholesomely, *ad.* in a wholesome manner.
wholesomeness, *n.* salubrity; salutariness.
whole-timer, *n.* one engaged to work for the full time of the working day, week, etc.
wholly, *ad.* *hole*-le, entirely; completely; totally.
whom, *pron.* hoom, the objective case of *who*.
whomsoever, *pron.* *hoom*-so-*ev*-er, objective case of *whoever*; any person, without exception.
whoop, *n.* hoop, a loud shout of exultation, excitement, pursuit, etc.; the war-cry of American Indians when rushing to the attack; the sound made in whooping-cough; *v.i.* to shout with a loud voice or yell; to emit, or to exult with, a whoop: *v.t.* to insult or incite with whoops. **whooping**

swan, the common swan, *Cygnus cygnus.* (O.Fr. *houper*, whoop.)
whoopee, *int.* woo-*pee*, an exclamation of hilarity or exuberance, etc. **make whoopee,** to have a gay time.
whooper, *n. hoo*-per, one who whoops; the whooping swan.
whooping-cough, *n.* an infectious disease, usually of children, characterized by convulsive coughing followed by whoops; pertussis [Med.].
whop, *n.* whop, a sudden fall, or the suddenness of striking in a fall: *v.t.* to beat [Slang].
whopper, *n. whop*-er, anything uncommonly large, applied particularly to a monstrous lie.
whopping, *a. whop*-ing, very large.
whore, *n.* hore, a woman who prostitutes herself for hire; a harlot; any unchaste woman: *v.i.* to have unlawful sexual commerce; to practise lewdness, or [Bible] idolatry. **Whore of Babylon,** an offensive name bestowed by some non-Catholics on the Church of Rome. (Late A.S., perhaps from Scand.)
whoredom, *n. hore*-dum, fornication; unlawful commerce with the opposite sex; in Scripture, the desertion of the worship of the true God for the worship of idols, idolatry.
whoremaster, *n. hore*-mahs-ter, a procurer; a whoremonger.
whoremonger, *n. hore*-mung-ger, one who practises lewdness; a man who associates with whores.
whoremongering, *n. hore*-mung-ger-ring, whoring; fornication.
whoreson, *n. hore*-son, a bastard, a fellow (term of contempt or abuse): *a.* mean; vile; scurvy.
whoring, *n. hore*-ring, the practice of fornication; consorting with whores.
whorish, *a. hore*-rish, addicted to libidinous pleasures; lewd; unchaste; incontinent.
whorishly, *ad. hore*-rish-le, in a lewd manner.
whorishness, *n.* the quality or condition of being whorish; meretriciousness.
whorl, *n.* whorl *or* whurl, a ring of leaves or flowers around a stem, in the same plane as each other [Bot.]; a turn of the spire of a univalve shell; a spiral arrangement. **whorl grass,** a grass of the genus *Catabrosa.* (*whirl.*)
whorled, *a.* whurld, furnished with whorls.
whorl-flower, *n.* the long-leaved teasel *Morina longifolia*, with purple flower.
whort, *n.* whurt, the fruit of the whortleberry.
whortleberry, *n. whur*-tl-be-re, the bilberry, *Vaccinium myrtillus*; the small purple fruit of this.
whose, *pron.* hooz, the possessive or genitive case of *who* or *which* (applied to persons or things).
whosesoever, *pron. hooz*-so-*ev*-er, of whomsoever.
whoso, *pron. hoo*-soh, whosoever.
whosoever, *pron. hoo*-so-*ev*-er, any one; any person whatever; whoever.
whur, *n.* and *v.i.* whur, whir.
★**why,** *ad.* why, for what cause or reason, interrogatively; for what reason or cause, relatively; for what reason or cause; for which: *n.* (*pl.* **whys**) a reason or cause; a perplexing problem: *int.* exclamation of surprise, impatience, etc. (A.S. *hwi.*)
whydah, *n. why*-dah, the whidah or widow-bird.
wich-elm, *n. witch*-elm, the wych-elm.
wick, *n.* wik, formerly, a village or town (surviving as a suffix, as in *Warwick*, and to denote jurisdiction, as in *bailiwick*). (A.S. *wic.*)
wick, *n.* wik, a number of threads of cotton or similar substance, loosely twisted into a string and inserted in tallow, oil, or wax, as a means of obtaining a light; the web in a lamp. (A.S. *weoce.*)
wick, *v.t.* wik, in the game of curling, to strike obliquely, to cannon: *n.* a hit so made.
wicked, *a. wik*-ed, evil in principle or practice; addicted to vice; sinful; immoral; sly, roguish [Coll.]. (A.S., made evil.)
wickedly, *ad.* in a wicked manner.
wickedness, *n.* evil disposition or practice; an evil action.
wicken, *n. wik*-en, the quicken, or mountain-ash.
wicker, *n. wik*-er, an osier; a pliant twig; material for wickerwork: *a.* made of plaited twigs or osiers. (A.S. *wican*, bend.)
wickerwork, *n. wik*-er-wurk, a structure of plaited wicker; basket-work.
wicket, *n. wik*-et, a small gate or door, esp. in a larger one; a loophole, pigeon-hole, or similar aperture; the set of three upright stumps bowled at in cricket; the pitch between the wickets; a batsman's innings [Cricket]. (O.Fr. *wiket.*)
wicket-keeper, *n.* the cricketer who fields close up behind the wicket.
wicking, *n. wik*-ing, material for wicks.
Wicliffite, *n. wik*-lif-ite, a Wycliffite.
widdershins, *ad. wid*-er-shinz, withershins.
★**wide,** *a.* wide, broad; having a great distance or extent between the sides; having a great extent every way; remote; distant; [Slang] alert, knowing: *ad.* at a distance; far; with great extent (used chiefly in combination, as in wide-distant, wide-reaching, etc.): *n.* a ball bowled so wide of the wicket that the batsman cannot reach it without moving from his position, also the run scored to the batsman's side as penalty for this [Cricket]. **to the wide,** utterly [Slang]. (A.S. *wid.*)
wideawake, *a. wide*-a-wake, alert; wary; on the watch for danger: *n.* a soft, low-crowned, broad-brimmed felt hat.
widely, *ad. wide*-le, with great extent every way; to a great distance.
widen, *v.t. wy*-dn, to make wide or wider; to extend in breadth: *v.i.* to grow wide or wider; to enlarge; to extend itself.
wideness, *n. wide*-ness, breadth; width; great extent between the sides; large extent in all directions.
widespread, *a. wide*-spred, spread to a great distance.
widish, *adj. wide*-ish, somewhat wide.
widgeon, *n. wij*-on, the migratory duck *Mareca penelope*, or *M. americana* of N. America; [Fig.] a simpleton, fool, or gull. **sand widgeon,** the gadwall. **widgeon grass,** the plant *Zostera marina.* **widgeon leader,** the sea-duck pintail. (O.Fr. *vigeon.*)
widow, *n. wid*-oh, a woman who has lost her husband by death and has not remarried; an extra hand, or extra cards dealt, in some card games: *v.t.* to bereave of a husband; to endow with a widow's right; to deprive of anything good. **widow's flower,** the plant *Scabiosa atro-purpurea.* **widow's man,** a former fictitious seaman on a ship's books whose pay and prize-money were allotted to the pension fund. **widow's mite,** a small gift cheerfully given by one who can barely afford it. (A.S. *widwe*, L. *vidua*, bereft of a husband.)
widow-bench, *n.* that share which a widow is allowed of her husband's estate, besides her jointure.
widow-bird, *n.* the W. African whidah. (Through Port. from L. *vidua*, widow, because of its colour and long black tail-feathers.)
widower, *n. wid*-oh-er, a man who has lost his wife by death and has not remarried.
widowerhood, *n. wid*-oh-er-hood, the state of being a widower.
widowhood, *n. wid*-oh-hood, state of being a widow; the period of this.
widow-hunter, *n.* one who seeks or courts widows for a jointure or fortune.
widow-wail, *n.* the plant *Fritillaria meleagris* or *Cneorum tricoccos.*
width, *n.* width, breadth; wideness; extent from side to side.
wield, *v.t.* weeld, to use with full command or power; to manage; to use or employ with the hand; to handle. **wield the sceptre,** to govern with supreme command. (A.S.)
wieldable, *a. weel*-da-bl, that can be wielded.
wielder, *n. weel*-der, one who wields.
wieldless, *a. weeld*-less, unmanageable.
wieldy, *a. weel*-de, that may be wielded; manageable; easily used or moved.
wife, *n.* wife (*pl.* **wives,** wyvz), the lawful consort of a husband; a married woman. **old wife,** *see* **old. old wives' tale,** any foolish tradition or notion characteristic of ignorant old women. **the world and his wife,** *see* **world.** (A.S. *wif.*)
wifehood, *n. wife*-hood, state of being a wife.
wifeless, *a. wife*-less, without a wife; unmarried.
wifelike, *a. wife*-like, pertaining to or like a wife.
wifely, *a. wife*-le, pertaining to or befitting a wife; like a wife.
wig, *n.* wig, an artificial covering for the head, consisting of hair interwoven or united by a kind of

network; a lawyer, as wearing a wig. **wig tree,** the Venetian sumac, *Rhus cotinus.* (*periwig.*)

wigan, *n. wig*-an, a canvas-like calico used by dressmakers as a stiffener, first made at Wigan, Lancs.

wigeon, *n. wij*-on, the widgeon.

wigged, *a.* wigd, having the head covered with a wig.

wiggery, *n. wig*-er-re, wigs collectively; legal formality or red tape.

wigging, *n. wig*-ing, a scolding [Slang].

wiggle, *v.i. wig*-l, to wriggle; to waggle: *n.* a squirm, twist, or act of wiggling.

wiggy, *a. wig*-e, characteristic of wiggery.

wight, *n.* wite, a man or woman (in humorous or ironical use). (A.S. *wiht*, a creature, a thing.)

wight, *a.* wite, strong and nimble; doughty. (Ice. *vigr*, fit for war.)

wigmaker, *n. wig*-make-er, one who makes wigs.

wigwag, *v.t.* and *i. wig*-wag, to wag or move to and fro; to signal with a flag or flags.

wigwagger, *n. wig*-wag-er, an army signaller [Slang].

wigwam, *n. wig*-wom, a cabin or hut of the American Indians, formed of hides, matting, etc., on a framework of poles. (Algonq.)

wild, *a.* wyld, roving; wandering; inhabiting the forest or open field; not tamed or domesticated; growing in the natural state; desert; not inhabited; savage; uncivilized; not refined by culture; turbulent; tempestuous; irregular; licentious; inconstant; inordinate; loose; disorderly; furious; crazy; imaginary; fanciful; exposed to wind and sea: *n.* an uncultivated or uninhabited tract or region; a desert: *ad.* wildly; without consideration. **wild goose,** any non-domesticated goose. **wild-goose chase,** the pursuit of something unattainable or non-existent; a futile or hopeless quest. **wild oats,** see **oat.** (A.S.)

wild-born, *a.* born in a wild state.

wild-cat, *n. wyld*-kat, the British wild cat, *Felis sylvestris*, now restricted to N. Wales and N. Scotland: *a.* recklessly speculative.

wild-duck, *n.* the mallard, *Anas boscas.*

wildebeest, *n. wil*-de-baste, the South African gnu. (S. Afr. Dut.)

wilder, *v.t. wil*-der, to cause to lose the way or track; to bewilder.

wilderness, *n. wil*-der-ness, a desert; a tract of land or region uncultivated and uninhabited by human beings, whether a forest or an open plain; a waste; a part of a garden left to grow waste; [Fig.] a great number, a confused mass. (A.S. *wilder*, a wild animal, and *ness.*)

wildfire, *n. wyld*-fire, a composition of inflammable materials difficult to extinguish when kindled; the will-o'-the-wisp; Greek fire; fitful flashes of lightning; a disease of sheep, attended with inflammation of the skin; a kind of erysipelas. **like wildfire,** with great rapidity.

wildfowl, *n. wyld*-foul, wild duck in general; undomesticated water-fowl.

wilding, *a. wyl*-ding, growing wild [Bot.]: *n.* a wild apple; a plant that is wild, or growing without cultivation.

wildish, *a. wyl*-dish, rather wild.

wildly, *ad. wyld*-le, without cultivation; without tameness; with disorder; with perturbation; heedlessly; capriciously; extravagantly.

wildness, *n. wyld*-ness, uncultivated or untamed state; inordinate disposition to rove; savageness: rudeness; alienation of mind.

wildwood, *n. wyld*-wood, a forest in its natural state; an untended or unfrequented wood.

wile, *n.* wile, a trick or stratagem practised for ensnaring or deception; an artifice: *v.t.* to deceive; to beguile. **wile away,** to while away. (A.S. *wil.*)

wilful, *a. wil*-ful, wayward; self-willed; stubborn; refractory; done intentionally.

wilfully, *ad.* stubbornly; intentionally.

wilfulness, *n.* the state of being wilful or done wilfully.

wilily, *ad. wile*-le-le, by stratagem; insidiously.

wiliness, *n. wile*-le-ness, craftiness.

***will,** *n.* wil, that faculty of the mind by which we determine either to do or forbear to do; the faculty which is exercised in deciding, among two or more objects, which we shall embrace or pursue, or the power of self-determination and self-conduct; the act of willing; that which is willed; choice; determination; discretion; pleasure; command; direction; disposition; inclination; desire; power; divine determination; moral purpose or counsel; arbitrary disposal; the written legal disposition of a person's estate, to take effect after his death. **at will,** at the will or mere pleasure of another. **good will,** favour; kindness. **have one's will,** to obtain what is desired. **ill will,** enmity; unfriendliness. **nuncupative will,** *see* **nuncupative. will to power,** determination to attain supremacy. **with a will,** vigorously; enthusiastically. (A.S. *willan*, wish.)

will, *v.t.* wil, to determine; to decide in the mind that something shall be done or forborne; to command; to direct; to wish; to desire; legally to dispose of estate and effects by testament; an auxiliary verb (*p.* **would,** wood), and a sign of the future tense, admitting of different significations in the different persons [Gram.].

willed. *a.* wild, having a will, as strong-willed.

willemite, *n. wil*-e-mite, a crystalline native silicate of zinc, occurring in many different colours. (*William* I, King of the Netherlands.)

willer, *n. wil*-er, one who wills; one exerting influence by means of will-power.

willet, *n. wil*-et, a N. American wading bird of the snipe family, *Catoptrophorus semipalmatus.* (From its call.)

willey, *n.* and *v.t.* wil-e, willy.

williamsite, *n. wil*-yam-zite, a green variety of serpentine. (After L. W. *Williams*, Amer. mineralogist.)

willies, *n. wil*-iz, a feeling of nervousness or fear; the jitters, the creeps [U.S.A. Slang].

willing, *a. wil*-ing, inclined to do or grant; disposed; not averse; desirous; ready; prompt; received or undergone without reluctance; spontaneous; consenting.

willingly, *ad. wil*-ing-le, with free will; cheerfully.

willingness, *n. wil*-ing-ness, consent of will; readiness of mind.

will-less, *a. wil*-less, lacking will; flabby.

willock, *n. wil*-ok, a young guillemot.

will-o'-the-wisp, *n. wil*-o-the-*wisp*, jack-a-lantern or ignis-fatuus, the luminous phenomenon due to marsh-gas: *a.* misleading.

willow, *n. wil*-oh, a tree of the genus *Salix*; the wood of this; [Coll.] a cricket-bat; [Mach.] a willy: *v.t.* to put (wool, etc.) through a willy. **to wear the willow,** to mourn for a dead lover. (A.S. *welig.*)

willowed, *a. wil*-ode, abounding with willows.

willow-gall, *n.* a gall or protuberance on the leaves of willows.

willow-herb, *n.* any species of the genus *Epilobium*; also, the yellow and purple loosestrife.

willowish, *a. wil*-oh-ish, resembling the willow, esp. in the colour of its leaf.

willow-moth, *n.* any moth the caterpillars of which infest willows.

willow-pattern, a Chinese landscape design imposed in blue on white earthenware, common in England since the late 18th century.

willow-thorn, *n. wil*-oh-thorn, the sea-buckthorn.

willow-warbler, *n.* the willow-wren.

willow-weed, *n.* the purple loosestrife, *Lythrum salicaria.*

willow-wren, *n.* the small song-bird *Phylloscopus trochilus*, allied to the chiff-chaff.

willowy, *a. wil*-oh-e, abounding with willows; lissom; supple and slender.

will-power, *n.* exertion of strength of mind over oneself or others, or over adverse circumstances.

will-worship, *n.* any worship in accordance with one's own inclinations and not having divine inspiration.

willy, *n. wil*-e, a rotatory machine for loosening and cleaning the fibres of wool, cotton, etc.: *v.t.* to treat wool, etc., with this.

willy-nilly, *ad. wil*-e-*nil*-e, willingly or unwillingly. (*will he, nill he.*)

willy-willy, *n. wil*-e-*wil*-e, a cyclone; a dust-storm [Austral.]. (Native.)

wilsome, *a. wil*-sum, wilful; obstinate; stubborn.

wilt, wilt, *second pers. sing.* of the present indicative of the aux. verb *will.*

wilt, *v.i.* wilt, to begin to wither; to become flaccid;

to droop: *v.t.* to cause to wither and lose its freshness as a plant.

wily, *a.* *wy*-le, using craft or stratagem to accomplish a purpose; cunning; sly.

wimble, *n.* *wim*-bl, a gimlet; a rotatory brace for boring holes: *v.t.* to turn; to bore with a wimble. (Anglo-Fr., from Teut. *wiemel.*)

wimple, *n.* *wim*-pl, a covering of silk or linen, once worn by women, and still by some nuns, round the chin, sides of the face, and top of the head: *v.i.* to flow in wavelets; to ripple. (A.S. *wimpel.*)

win, *v.t.* win, to gain by success in competition or contest; to gain by solicitation or courtship; to obtain by labour; to allure to kindness or compliance; to gain by persuasion or influence; [Army Slang] to steal, to appropriate: *v.i.* to gain the victory: *n.* a victory, a success; the act of winning: *n.pl.* winnings. **win through,** to succeed. **win upon,** to gain favour or influence; to gain ground. (A.S. *winnan*, struggle, get.)

wince, *v.i.* wince, to flinch, as from a blow or pain; to start as in pain; to show uneasiness; to kick or flounce, as a horse, when restive or impatient: *n.* an act of wincing. (O.Fr. *guenchir.*)

wincer, *n.* *win*-ser, one who winces, shrinks, or kicks.

wincey, *n.* *win*-se, a dress material with a cotton warp and a wool weft.

winceyette, *n.* win-se-*et*, a material similar to wincey but having less wool content.

winch, *n.* winch, the crank or handle by which the axis of a revolving machine is turned; a roller on which ropes are wound; a reel; a windlass; an instrument with which to turn or strain something forcibly: *v.t.* to hoist or haul by means of a winch. (A.S. *wince.*)

Winchester, *a.* *win*-chis-ter, designating a certain standard for dry and liquid measures (legally abolished 1835). (Name of city in Hampshire.)

Winchester, *n.* *win*-chis-ter, a type of breech-loading rifle. (Oliver *Winchester*, *d.* 1880, Amer. manufacturer.)

wincopipe, *n.* *wing*-ko-pipe, a local name of the scarlet pimpernel, *Anagallis arvensis.*

***wind,** *n.* wind (*poet.* wynd), air naturally in motion, with any velocity; a current of air; breath; power of respiration; air in motion from any force or action; breath modulated by the organs or by an instrument; lung power; air impregnated with odour; anything insignificant or light as wind; wind-instruments collectively; flatulence; the pit of the stomach [Boxing]; idle talk, blather [Fig.]. **between wind and water,** that part of a ship's side or bottom which is frequently brought above water by the rolling of the ship or fluctuation of the water's surface [Naut.]. **close to the wind,** as much to windward as possible. **down the wind,** before the wind; declining. **four winds,** the four cardinal points of the heavens. **get wind of,** to catch the scent of; [Fig.] to get a rumour, hint, or indication of. **get the wind up,** to become nervous or frightened. **have the wind of,** to be to windward of; [Fig.] to have at a disadvantage. **how the wind blows,** the state of things, or the direction they are taking. **in the wind,** stirring; rumoured. **in the wind's eye,** towards the direct point from which the wind blows [Naut.]. **raise the wind,** to obtain the necessary money. **soldier's wind,** a wind on the beam; a fair wind. **take the wind out of one's sails,** to rob one of his advantage; to anticipate one. (A.S.)

wind, *v.t.* wind, to scent; to follow by scent; to expose to the wind; to render scant of wind by a blow or, as a horse, by driving hard; to rest a horse to let it recover wind; to winnow. **wind a ship,** to turn it end for end, so that the wind strikes it on the opposite side [Naut.].

wind, *v.t.* wynd, to blow, as a horn; to sound by blowing.

wind, *v.t.* wynd, to turn; to move or cause to turn spirally or circuitously; to turn round some fixed object; to bind, or to form into a ball or coil by turning; to introduce, esp. oneself, by insinuation; to hoist or haul by means of a capstan or winch, etc.; to entwist, enfold, or encircle: *v.i.* to turn; to turn around something; to have a circular or spiral direction; to crook; to bend; to move round; to meander; to advance in a circuitous or tortuous way. **wind off,** to unwind. **wind up,** to bring to a small compass, as a ball of thread; to bring to a conclusion or settlement; to liquidate (a company, etc.) [Comm.]; to put in a state of renovated or continued motion. *p.* and *pp.* **wound.** (A.S. *windan.*)

windable, *a.* *wyn*-da-bl, capable of being wound.

windage, *n.* *win*-daj, the deflexion of a projectile in motion due to the wind; amount of, or compensation for, this; the difference between the diameter of the bore of a gun and that of the projectile.

windbag, *n.* *wind*-bag, a bellows; a bag of wind; [Fig.] a mere empty talker a futile orator.

wind-band, *n.* an orchestra of wind instruments.

wind-bound, *a.* *wind*-bound, prevented from sailing by a contrary wind.

wind-break, *n.* *wind*-brake, a hedge or other obstacle to break the force of the wind.

wind-broken, *a.* with the breathing impaired.

wind-chest, *n.* the reservoir from which compressed air is supplied to the pipes of an organ [Mus.].

wind-cone, *n.* an open-ended fabric sleeve at a mast-head for indicating the strength and direction of the wind.

wind-dog, *n.* a section of a rainbow seen on isolated clouds, regarded by sailors as foretelling high wind; a weather-gall.

wind-dropsy, *n.* a former name of tympanites [Med.].

wind-egg, *n.* *wind*-eg, an addled, soft-shelled, or otherwise imperfect egg.

winder, *n.* *wyn*-der, one who or that which winds; that on which something is wound; a step of a winding staircase; a twining plant [Bot.].

winder, *n.* *win*-der, a knock-out blow; anything that takes one's breath away [Slang].

windfall, *n.* *wind*-fawl, something, as a tree, or fruit, etc., blown down by the wind; an unexpected legacy or other good fortune.

windfallen, *a.* *wind*-fawl-en, blown down by the wind.

windfanner, *n.* *wind*-fan-ner, the kestrel or windhover.

windflower, *n.* *wind*-flou-er, the wood anemone, *Anemone nemorosa*, so called as supposed to open its flower only when the wind blows.

windgall, *n.* *wind*-gawl, a soft tumour on the fetlock joints of a horse.

wind-gall, *n.* a weather-gall or wind-dog.

wind-gauge, *n.* an anemometer; a graduated scale attached to a fire-arm by means of which allowance is made for the effect of wind on the projectile.

wind-gun, *n.* an air-gun, a gun discharged by the force of compressed air.

windhover, *n.* *wind*-hov-er, the kestrel.

windily, *ad.* *win*-de-le, in a windy, or [Slang] frightened or verbose, manner.

windiness, *n.* *win*-de-ness, the state of being windy or [Slang] frightened; flatulence; tendency to generate wind; [Slang] empty loquacity.

winding, *a.* *wyn*-ding, turning; bending; twisting from a direct line or an even surface: *n.* a turn or turning; a bend; flexure; a meander.

windingly, *ad.* *wyn*-ding-le, in a winding or circuitous manner.

winding-sheet, *n.* a sheet in which a corpse is wrapped.

winding-tackle, *n.* *wyn*-ding-*tak*-kl, a tackle consisting of one fixed triple block, and one double or triple movable block [Naut.].

wind-instrument, *n.* an instrument of music, played by wind, as an organ, or by the breath, as a trumpet or flute.

windjammer, *n.* *wind*-jam-er, a merchant sailing-ship, or member of its crew [Coll.]; a very loquacious or verbose person [Amer. slang].

windlass, *n.* *wind*-las, a winch for heavy weights; an application of the wheel and axle in which a rope or chain, with the weight attached, is wound about a cylinder or roller moved by a crank, shifting levers, or similar means; a handle by which anything is turned: *v.t.* to hoist with a windlass. (M.E. *windelas*, perhaps from Scand.)

windle, *n.* *win*-dl, the redwing or wind-thrush.

windle, *n.* *win*-dl, a kind of reel or spindle; a plaited basket; a former measure of 3 bushels. (A.S. *windan*, turn.)

windless, *a.* *wind*-less, free from or wanting wind; not windy; out of breath.

windlestraw, *n.* *win*-dl-straw, a dried-up stalk of grass; a small slender straw.

windmill, *n.* *wind*-mill, a mill turned by the wind. **windmill plane,** a rotaplane [Coll.].
★**window,** *n.* *win*-doh, an opening in the wall of a building for the admission of light, and of air when necessary, furnished with a frame, often with movable sashes or casements, containing panes of glass; the aperture itself, or the frame or other thing that covers this; a lattice. (Ice. *vindr*, wind, *auga*, the eye.)
window-box, *n.* a box in which plants are grown on the sill outside a window.
window-card, *n.* a card giving a price, or an advertisement, for display in a window.
window-dressing, *n.* the art of displaying goods in a shop-window; the arrangement of such goods; [Fig.] the dissemination of specious or misleading statements to create a favourable market or impression.
windowed, *a.* *win*-dode, furnished with windows; placed in a window; with openings like windows.
window-envelope, *n.* an envelope so treated that an address on an enclosure can be read without opening.
windowless, *a.* *win*-doh-less, having no window.
window-pane, *n.* a single sheet of glass in a window.
window-seat, *n.* a seat along the inside of a window.
window-sill, *n.* the outwardly projecting base of a window-frame.
window-swallow, *n.* the martin *Chelidon urbica.*
windpipe, *n.* *wind*-pipe, the passage for the breath to and from the lungs; the trachea.
wind-pump, *n.* *wind*-pump, a pump actuated by a windmill.
wind-rode, *a.* *wind*-rode, swayed when at anchor by the force of the wind [Naut.].
wind-rose, *n.* *wind*-roze, a name given to various poppies, esp. *Rœmeria hybrida* [Bot.]; a diagram showing wind direction, frequency, and strength [Meteor.].
windrow, *n.* *wind*-roh, a line or row of hay raked to be rolled into cocks; a row of peats, etc., set to dry.
windsail, *n.* *wind*-sale, a wide tube or funnel of canvas, used to ventilate a ship.
windscreen, *n.* *wind*-skreen, a screen forming a shelter from the wind; the transparent screen in front of the driver's seat in a motor-car.
wind-shield, *n.* a wind-screen.
wind-sleeve, *n.* a wind-cone.
wind-thrush, *n.* *wind*-thrush, the redwing or windle.
wind-tight, *a.* *wind*-tite, impervious to wind; air-tight.
wind-tunnel, *n.* a tunnel-like chamber through which a uniform steady current of air is blown for collecting data of ærodynamic experiments.
wind-up, *n.* *wynd*-up, conclusion; concluding act or piece.
windward, *n.* *wind*-ward, the direction from which the wind blows: *a.* being on the side towards the point from which the wind blows: *ad.* towards the wind. **to windward,** in or into an advantageous position.
windy, *a.* *win*-de, consisting of wind; exposed to the wind; tempestuous; boisterous; flatulent; caused by flatulence; empty, boastful [Coll.]; nervous, scared [Slang].
★**wine,** *n.* wine, the fermented juice of the grape, also of certain other fruits; a pharmaceutical preparation dissolved in wine [Med.]; a party at which wine is served: *v.i.* to take wine: *v.t.* to entertain to wine. **spirits of wine,** *see* **spirit.** (L. *vinum*, wine.)
winebag, *n.* *wine*-bag, a skin for holding wine.
winebibber, *n.* *wine*-bib-er, a tippler; a sot; a great drinker.
winebibbing, *n.* *wine*-bib-ing, immoderate drinking of wine.
winecard, *n.* *wine*-kard, a list of the wines obtainable at a restaurant, etc.
wine-cooler, *n.* a receptacle for cooling wine in the bottle at the time of serving.
wineglass, *n.* *wine*-glahs, a small glass to drink wine from; a wineglassful.
wineglassful, *n.* *wine*-glahs-ful, as much as a wineglass will hold; 2 fluid ounces, or 4 tablespoonfuls.
wine-grower, *n.* one who keeps a vineyard to grow grapes for wine.
wineless, *a.* *wine*-less, destitute of wine.
wine-press, *n.* a press in which the juice is extracted from grapes; the apparatus effecting this.
winery, *n.* *wine*-er-re, an establishment for making or storing wine.
wine-skin, *n.* a hide bag (esp. the complete skin of a goat) for holding wine.
wine-stone, *n.* the deposit of crude tartar, or argal, on the interior of wine-casks.
wine-whey, *n.* a medicinal drink made by curdling milk with wine.
★**wing,** *n.* wing, the fore limb of a bird by which it flies, and under which it protects its young; care and protection; the limb of an insect by which it flies; passage by the wing; power of flight; means of flying; the main lifting surface of an aeroplane; a lateral extension; the flank or extreme part of an army; the right or left division of an army, fleet, or other military or naval force; a tactical unit of the R.A.F.; in football, etc., the position, or the section of players, on either side of the centre; a side of a stage; a leaf-like appendage, esp. one of the opposing lateral petals of a papilionaceous flower [Bot.]; a side-building [Arch.]; a mud-guard over the wheel of a motor vehicle: *pl.* those parts of the hold and orlop deck which are nearest the sides [Naut.]: *v.t.* to furnish with wings; to enable to fly or to move with celerity; to traverse or transport by flight; to wound in the wing: *v.i.* to fly. **on the wing,** flying. **on the wings of the wind,** with the utmost velocity. **take wing,** to begin to fly; to depart. **under the wing of,** in the care, or under the protection, of. **wing and wing,** said of a fore-and-aft vessel when the foresail is boomed out on one side and the mainsail on the other [Naut.]. (Scand.)
wing-beat, *n.* a single lifting and depression of a bird's wings in flight
wing-case, *n.* the elytron, the sheath which covers the wings of beetles.
wing-commander, *n.* an Air Force officer equivalent in rank to a commander in the Navy and a lieutenant-colonel in the Army.
winged, *a.* wingd, having wings, wing-like expansions, or [Bot.] leaf-like appendages; feathered (as an arrow); swift; rapid; represented with wings, or having wings of a different colour from the body [Her.]; fanned with wings; swarming with birds; wounded in the wing. **winged words,** sublime or lofty sentiments.
winger, *n.* *wing*-er, a player on a wing [Football, etc.].
wing-footed, *a.* having wings on the feet, as Mercury; swift; fleet.
wing-half, *n.* the left or right half-back in Association football.
wingless, *a.* *wing*-less, having no wings; not able to ascend or fly.
winglet, *n.* *wing*-let, a very small wing or wing-like part; a bastard-wing or alula.
wing-load (or **-loading**), *n.* the gross weight of a laden aeroplane divided by its total wing area.
wing-spread, *n.* the distance between the tips of wings when wide spread.
wing-stroke, *n.* a wing-beat.
wingy, *a.* *wing*-e, having wings; rapid.
wink, *v.i.* and *t.* wink, to close and open the eyelids with rapidity; to give a hint by the motion of the eyelids; to close one eyelid; to flicker: *n.* the act of closing and opening the eyelids quickly; a hint given by shutting the eye with a significant cast. **forty winks,** a short doze. **wink at,** to connive at; to tolerate; to overlook. (A.S. *wincian.*)
wink-a-peep, *n.* *wing*-ka-peep, the wincopipe, or scarlet pimpernel.
winker, *n.* *wing*-ker, one who winks; a horse's blinker.
winking, *a.* *wing*-king, shutting and opening the eyes quickly; conniving at: *n.* an act of winking; a nap. **like winking,** very quickly or rapidly [Slang]. **as easy as winking,** ridiculously easy.
winkingly, *ad.* *wing*-king-le, like one winking; with a wink.
winkle, *n.* *wing*-kl, an edible gastropod, the periwinkle.
winner, *n.* *win*-er, one who or that which wins; anything calculated to ensure success [Coll.].
winning, *a.* *win*-ing, attracting; adapted to gain favour; charming: *n.pl.* the sum won or gained by success in competition or contest.

winningly, *ad.* *win*-ing-le, in a winning manner.
winning-post, *n.*, the post marking the finishing point of a race.
winnow, *v.t.* *win*-oh, to separate and drive off the chaff from grain by means of wind; to fan; to beat, as with wings; to examine or sift for the purpose of separating falsehood from truth; to separate, as the bad from the good: *v.i.* to separate chaff from corn. (A.S. *windwian*, expose to the wind, from *wind*.)
winnower, *n.* *win*-oh-er, one who winnows.
winsome, *a.* *win*-sum, charming; attractive; merry; cheerful. (A.S. *wynsum*, pleasant.)
winsomely, *ad.* *win*-sum-le, in a winsome manner.
winsomeness, *n.* the state of being winsome.
★**winter,** *n.* *win*-ter, the cold season of the year, commencing, astronomically, in the northern hemisphere, when the sun enters Capricorn, or at the solstice about the 21st of December, and ending at the equinox in March; popularly, the three months of December, January, and February; a period of depression, distress, or adversity: *a.* pertaining to or typical of winter; due or coming in the winter: *v.i.* to pass the winter: to sojourn: *v.t.* to feed or manage during the winter. **winter solstice,** the solstice of the winter when the sun enters Capricorn on 21st December. **winter sports,** outdoor sports (skating, ski-ing, bob-sleighing, curling, etc.) that can be indulged only under wintry conditions. (A.S.)
winter-aconite, *n.* the plant *Eranthis hyemalis.*
winter-apple, *n.* an apple that keeps well or that ripens in winter.
winter-barley, *n.* barley sown in autumn.
winterberry, *n.* *win*-ter-*be*-re, any of several species of holly, esp. the black alder, *Ilex verticillata.*
winter-bloom, *n.* witch-hazel; also the azalea.
winterbourne, *n.* *win*-ter-boorn, a stream that is intermittently flowing and dry. (*winter* and *bourn.*)
winter-cherry, *n.* any plant of the genus *Physalis,* esp. the alkekengi; also *Solanum pseudocapsicum,* the bastard capsicum.
winter-cress, *n.* any plant of the genus *Barbarea.*
winter-crop, *n.* any crop sown in the autumn, or which may be converted into fodder during the winter.
winter-duck *n.* the pintail, *Dafila acuta.*
winter-fallow, *n.* ground fallowed in winter.
winter-garden, *n.* an ornamental garden that flourishes in winter; a large conservatory for hot-house plants.
wintergreen, *n.* *win*-ter-green, a plant of the genus *Pyrola*; also the N. American evergreen, *Gaultheria procumbens.* **wintergreen oil,** an aromatic volatile oil expressed from the leaves of *G. procumbens,* used medicinally as a stimulant.
winterish, *a.* *win*-ter-rish, having a touch of winter; somewhat wintry.
winterly, *a.* *win*-ter-le, wintry; pertaining to or occurring in winter.
winter-moth, *n.* any of several geometrid moths appearing in late autumn.
winter-pear, *n.* any pear that keeps well or ripens in winter.
winter-quarters, *n.pl.* the quarters of an army during the winter; a winter residence or station.
winter-wagtail, *n.* the grey wagtail, *Motacilla melanope.*
winter-wheat, *n.* wheat sown in autumn.
wintriness, *n.* *win*-tre-ness, wintry condition or quality.
wintry, *a.* *win*-tre, pertaining to or associated with winter; cold; stormy.
winy, *a.* *wy*-ne, vinous; having the taste or qualities of wine; affected by wine.
winze, *n.* winz, a small vertical or nearly vertical shaft giving access from one level to another [Mining]. (Probably connected with the verb *to wind* or twist.)
wipe, *n.* wipe, the act of rubbing for the purpose of cleaning; a blow; a swipe; a sarcastic gibe or jeer [Fig.]: *v.t.* to rub with something soft for cleaning; to clean by rubbing; to strike off gently; to cleanse from evil practices or abuses; to apply a soft substance (*e.g.* solder) to a surface with a pad, etc. **wipe away,** to cleanse by rubbing. **wipe off,** to clear away. **wipe out,** to efface; to obliterate. **wipe the floor with,** to defeat or nonplus utterly [Slang]. (A.S. *wipian,* from **wip,** a wisp.)
wiper, *n.* *wy*-per, one who or that which wipes; the instrument used for wiping; a projecting tooth or cam for raising stampers, etc.-and letting them fall by their own weight [Mech.].
★**wire,** *n.* wire, a thread of metal; any metallic substance drawn to an even thread; wirework; a bar of a cage; a telegram [Coll.]: *v.t.* to bind with wire; to apply wire to, as in bottling liquors; to stiffen with wire; to snare with a wire; to telegraph. **a live wire,** a very wideawake or energetic person [Slang]. **give one the wire,** to warn him secretly. **wire in** (or **away**), to begin; to carry on; to work with a will. **work the wires,** to use one's influence; to engage in wirepulling. (A.S. *wir.*)
wiredraw, *v.t.* *wire*-draw, to draw, as a metal, into wire, by drawing it through holes in plates of steel; to draw out into length; to draw or spin out to great length; to cause steam or water to pass through a narrow aperture and so reduce its pressure. *pp.* **wiredrawn.**
wiredrawer, *n.* *wire*-draw-er, one who draws metal into wire.
wiredrawn, *a.* *wire*-drawn, drawn out to great length or fineness.
wire-gauge, *n.* *wire*-gaje, a gauge for measuring the diameter of wire; a standard system of sizes for wire.
wire-gauze, *n.* a texture of finely interwoven wires, resembling gauze.
wire-grating, *n.* a grill or contrivance of fine wirework to keep out insects.
wire-gun, *n.* a heavy gun the barrel of which is bound with steel ribbon under tension.
wire-haired, *a.* having short wiry hair (esp. of terriers).
wire-heel, *n.* a defect in the feet of a horse or other beast.
wireless, *a.* *wire*-less, having no wire or wires; pertaining to or by radio: *n.* telegraphy or telephony by electro-magnetic waves without a wire connecting the transmitting and receiving stations; a message sent thus; radio; radio apparatus: *v.t.* and *i.* to radio. **wireless compass,** a radio direction-finder.
wireman, *n.* *wire*-man, one who works on telegraph or telephone wires; one who fixes wires.
wire-micrometer, *n.* a micrometer in which fine wires are used for delicate measurements.
wire-netting, *n.* network of wires used in fencing.
wirepuller, *n.* *wire*-pull-er, one who engages in wirepulling; an intriguer.
wirepulling, *n.* *wire*-pull-ing, the act of pulling the wires, as of a puppet; secret influence or management behind the scenes, esp. in political life; jobbery; intrigue.
wirer, *n.* *wire*-rer, one who wires or works with wire; a wireman.
wireway, *n.* *wire*-way, a line of wires for transport purposes; a telpherage system with wire track.
wirework, *n.* *wire*-wurk, the making of wire objects; netting, etc., made of wire.
wireworker, *n.* *wire*-wurk-er, one who makes articles of wire.
wireworm, *n.* *wire*-wurm, a name given to the larvæ of various click-beetles from their slenderness and uncommon hardness; a centipede; the leather-jacket.
wiriness, *n.* *wire*-re-ness, the state of being wiry.
wiring, *n.* *wire*-ring, wires collectively; the arrangement of wires.
wirrycow, *n.* *wi*-re-kou, worrycow.
wiry, *a.* *wire*-re, made of wire; like wire; strong and sinewy, though lean.
wisdom, *n.* *wiz*-dum, the quality of being wise; the choice of worthy ends and of the best means to accomplish them; sound sense; wise judgment and conduct; the exercise of sound judgment; quickness of intellect; readiness of apprehension; dexterity in execution; natural instinct and sagacity; in Scripture, human learning; erudition; knowledge of arts and sciences; godliness; piety. **wisdom tooth,** the third or back molar in each side of the human jaw. (A.S.)
★**wise,** *a.* wize, having the power of discerning and judging correctly, or of practically discriminating between what is worthy and unworthy, right and

wrong, proper and improper, esp. in moral conduct; discreet and judicious in the use or application of knowledge; skilful; learned; knowing; skilled in arts, science, or philosophy; dictated by wisdom; sagacious; experienced. **to put one wise,** to give him the necessary or desired information [Amer. slang]. **wise woman,** a sorceress or witch; a fortune-teller; a midwife. (A.S. *wis*, from *witan*, know.)

wise, *n.* wize, manner; way of being or acting. (A.S. *wise*, way.)

-wise, *suffix*, wize, forming adverbs denoting manner, way, respect, etc., as *clockwise*, *contrariwise*, *lengthwise*, etc.

wiseacre, *n.* *wize*-ay-ker, one who makes pretensions to great wisdom; hence, in contempt, a simpleton; a dunce. (Ger. *Weissager*, a soothsayer.)

wisecrack, *n.* *wize*-krak, a smart or pithy witticism: *v.i.* to make wisecracks [Amer. slang].

wisecracker, *n.* *wize*-krak-er, one given to wisecracking [Amer. slang].

wiseling, *n.* *wize*-ling, a wiseacre.

wisely, *ad.* *wize*-le, in a wise manner; prudently; judiciously; discreetly; craftily.

wisent, *n.* *wee*-zent, the aurochs. (Ger.)

wish, *n.* wish, eager desire; desire expressed; thing desired: *v.i.* to have a strong desire, either for what is or is not supposed to be obtainable; to be disposed or inclined; to have a feeling that partakes of hope or fear: *v.t.* to desire; to long for; to desire eagerly or ardently; to invoke; to express desire. (A.S. *wyscan.*)

wish-bone, *n.* the merrythought, the forked bone in a fowl's breast; the wishing-bone.

wisher, *n.* *wish*-er, one who desires; one who expresses a wish.

wishful, *a.* *wish*-ful, having desire or ardent longing; desirous. **wishful thinking,** ideas, beliefs, etc., based on hopes, not facts or reason.

wishfully, *ad.* with ardent desire; with a show of desire.

wishfulness, *n.* longing desire.

wishing-bone, *n.* the merrythought.

wishtonwish, *n.* *wish*-ton-wish, the prairie-dog. (N. Amerind. name.)

wish-wash, *n.* a thin, watery sort of drink: feeble or foolish talk or writing.

wishy-washy, *a.* *wish*-e-*wosh*-e, watery; weak; flimsy.

wisket, *n.* *wis*-ket, a whisket, a basket.

wisp, *n.* wisp, a small bundle of straw or hay, etc.; a twisted band of this; a whisk: *v.t.* to clean, esp. a horse, with a wisp. (*wipe.*)

wispish, *a.* *wis*-pish, wispy.

wispy, *a.* *wis*-pe, like a wisp; consisting of wisps.

wist, wist, *p.* of the verb *to wit*; knew.

wistaria, *n.* wis-*tare*-re-a, any of a genus of climbing-plants including the Chinese kidney-bean tree *W. chinensis.* (After Caspar *Wistar*, American anatomist, *d.* 1818.)

wistful, *a.* *wist*-ful, pensive; earnest; attentive; sadly longing. (Perhaps *wishful.*)

wistfully, *ad.* with wistfulness.

wistfulness, *n.* the state of being wistful.

wistiti, *n.* *wis*-te-te, ouistiti, the common marmoset, *Hapale jacchus.* (From its cry.)

wit, *v.i.* wit, to know. **to wit,** namely; that is to say. (A.S. *witan.*)

wit, *n.* wit, talent; intelligence; mental quickness; a man of genius; sense; judgment; a person given to witty remark; humour neatly expressed; power of invention; mental faculty; soundness of mind or judgment. **at one's wits' end,** having no idea how to proceed; utterly perplexed. **live by one's wits,** to live haphazard or without making any provision. **out of one's wits,** crazy. **the five wits,** the five senses. (A.S.)

witan, *n.* *wit*-an, the witenagemote; the members of this. (A.S.)

witch, *n.* witch, a woman supposed to be in league with the devil; a sorceress; a fortune-teller; an ugly old woman; a charming young woman; the stormy petrel; the flatfish *Glyptocephalus cynoglossus*: *v.t.* to bewitch; to fascinate; to enchant. **witch doctor,** among Kaffirs, etc., a magician or medicine man, esp. one who counteracts black magic and sorcery. **witch grass,** quitch, or couch-grass. **witches' Sabbath,** a midnight orgy formerly thought to be held by witches, magicians, demons, etc. **witch's thimble,** the foxglove, hairbell, sea campion, or other plant with tubular flowers. (A.S. *wicce.*)

witchcraft, *n.* *witch*-krahft, sorcery; enchantment; preternatural knowledge and power, supposed to be obtained by some secret compact with the devil; any supernatural power.

witch-elm, *n.* the wych-elm.

witchery, *n.* *witch*-er-re, enchantment; fascination.

witches'-broom, *n.* a cluster of twigs on a tree due to fungoid growths.

witch-hazel, *n.* *witch*-hay-zl, wych-hazel.

witching, *a.* *witch*-ing, bewitching; suited to enchantment or withcraft. **witching hour,** midnight; the time of supernatural happenings.

witch-knot, *n.* a tangle of hair supposed to be the work of witches or witchcraft; witches'-broom.

witchmeal, *n.* *witch*-meel, the spores of the genus *Lycopodium.*

witenagemote, *n.* *wit*-en-a-ge-moht, the national council or legislature of England in the days of the Saxons. (A.S. *witena*, genitive of *wita*, a wise man, *gemot*, an assembly.)

***with,** *prep.* with, by, noting cause, instrument, or means; on the side of, noting friendship or favour; in opposition to; in competition or contest, noting comparison; in company; in the society of; in connexion; in mutual dealing, noting confidence; in partnership, noting connexion; immediately after; among; upon; in consent, noting parity of state. *With* and *by* are closely allied; but in general, *with* denotes the instrument, and *by* the cause; as, he slew him *with* his sword; he died *by* poison. (A.S. *with*, by, against.)

with-, with, a prefix signifying back to oneself, against, privation, or separation. (A.S.)

withal, *ad.* with-*awl*, with the rest; together with; likewise; at the same time.

withamite, *n.* *with*-am-ite, a red magnesian variety of epidote. (From discoverer, H. *Witham.*)

withdraw, *v.t.* with-*draw*, to draw back; to take away what has been enjoyed; to recall: *v.i.* to quit a company or place; to retire; to retreat. *pp.* **withdrawn.** *p.* **withdrew.** (A.S. *with-*, back or towards one, and *draw.*)

withdrawable, *a.* with-*draw*-a-bl, capable of being withdrawn.

withdrawal, *n.* with-*draw*-al, the act of withdrawing; a recalling from a certain position.

withdrawer, *n.* with-*draw*-er, one who withdraws.

withdrawing-room, *n.* with-*draw*-ing-room, a room to withdraw or retire into from another that was originally in front; a drawing-room.

withdrawment, *n.* with-*draw*-ment, withdrawal.

withdrawn, with-*drawn*, *pp.* of *withdraw.*

withe, *n.* with *or* wythe, a willow or osier twig; a band of twisted twigs: *v.t.* to twist like a withe; to bind with a withe or withes. (A.S. *withthe*, connected with L. *viĕtum*, plaited.)

wither, *v.i.* *with*-er, to fade; to become sapless; to lose moisture or native freshness; to shrivel; to pine away: *v.t.* to cause to fade and become dry; to cause to shrink, wrinkle, and decay from want of moisture; to blight. (*weather.*)

witherband, *n.* *with*-er-band, a piece of iron forming part of a saddle near a horse's withers, to strengthen the bow.

witheredness, *n.* *with*-erd-ness, the state of being withered.

withering, *a.* *with*-er-ring, decaying; causing to wither; blighting; [Fig.] scathing, annihilating.

withering-floor, *n.* the drying-floor of a malthouse.

witheringly, *ad.* *with*-er-ring-le, in a manner tending to wither, or cause to shrink or to blight.

witherite, *n.* *with*-er-rite, a native carbonate of barium. (Named after Wm. *Withering*, English physician, *d.* 1799.)

witherlock, *n.* *with*-er-lok, that lock of a horse's mane which the rider takes hold of when mounting.

withernam, *n.* *with*-er-nam, a second or reciprocal writ or distress; reprisal [Old Engl. Law]. (A.S. *with*, against, *nam*, seizure.)

withe-rod, *n.* *wythe*-rod, the North American shrub *Viburnum nudum.*

withers, *n.pl.* *with*-erz, the junction of the shoulder-bones of a horse, forming a ridge at the base of the neck. (A.S. *wither*, against.)

withershins, *ad.* *with*-er-shinz, in an anti-clockwise direction (the opposite of deasil); contrariwise.

wither-wrung, *a.* injured or hurt in the withers.

withheld, with-*held*, *p.* and *pp.* of *withhold.*
withhold, *v.t.* with-*hohld*, to hold back; to restrain; to keep from action; to keep back; not to grant. *p.* and *pp.* **withheld.**
withholden, with-*hohl*-dn, old *pp.* of *withhold.*
withholder, *n.* with-*hohl*-der, one who withholds.
withholdment, *n.* with-*hohld*-ment, the act of withholding.
within, *prep.* with-*in*, in the inner part; inside the limits of compass of: not beyond; not reaching to anything external; not longer ago than; not later than; in the reach of; not exceeding; in the house; in any enclosure: *ad.* in the inner part; inwardly; internally; in the mind; in the house.
withinside, *ad.* with-*in*-side, in the inner parts; right inside.
without, *prep.* with-*out*, in a state of not having; not with; in a state of destitution or absence from; beyond; not within; supposing the negation or omission of; independent of; not by the use of; on the outside of; with exemption from: *conj.* unless; except; *ad.* not on the inside; not within; out-of-doors; outside the mind.
withstand, *v.t.* with-*stand*, to oppose; to resist, either with physical or moral force. *p.* and *pp.* **withstood.** (A.S. *with*, against, and *stand.*)
withstander, *n.* with-*stand*-er, one who opposes; an opponent; a resisting power.
withstood, with-*stood*, *p.* and *pp.* of *withstand.*
withwind, *n.* *with*-wynd, the bindweed, traveller's joy, or other climbing plant. (*withe* and *wind.*)
withy, *n.* *with*-e, a large species of willow; a withe or twig; any tough flexible branch like a withe. (*withe.*)
witless, *a.* *wit*-less, destitute of wit or understanding; inconsiderate; wanting thought; indiscreet; not under the guidance of reason.
witlessly, *ad.* foolishly; without the exercise of judgment.
witlessness, *n.* stupidity; want of consideration or thought.
witling, *n.* *wit*-ling, one with little wit or understanding; a pretender to wit or wittiness.
witness, *n.* *wit*-ness, testimony; attestation of a fact or event; that which furnishes evidence or proof; a person who knows or sees anything; one personally present; one who sees the execution of an instrument and subscribes it to confirm the authenticity of its signature; one who gives testimony in a court of justice: *v.t.* to see or know by personal presence; to attest; to give testimony to; to testify to something; to see the execution of an instrument, and subscribe it as witness of its authenticity; in the imperative, see, in evidence or proof: *v.i.* to bear testimony; to give evidence. **bear witness,** to testify. (A.S. *witnes*, testimony, a witness.)
witness-box, *n.* an enclosed space in a law-court from which a witness gives evidence.
witted, a. *wit*-ed, having wit or understanding.
wittichenite, *n.* *wit*-a-ke-nite, a native bismuth and copper sulphide occurring in the Wittichen cobalt mine, Baden.
witticism, *n.* *wit*-e-sizm, a witty remark; a sentence or phrase which is affectedly witty.
witticize, *v.i.* *wit*-e-size, to utter witticisms; to express oneself wittily.
wittily, *ad.* *wit*-e-le, with wit; ingeniously; artfully.
wittiness, *n.* the quality of being witty.
wittingly, *ad.* *wit*-ing-le, knowingly; with knowledge: intentionally.
wittol, *n.* *wit*-tol, a man who knows his wife's infidelity and submits to it. (From *witwall* perhaps because in its nest the cuckoo's eggs were sometimes laid.)
witty, *a.* *wit*-e, possessed of wit; given to indulge in wit; cleverly facetious; sarcastic; smart spoken; judicious: ingenious.
witwall, *n.* *wit*-wawl, the golden oriole; also the green woodpecker.
wive, *v.t.* and *i.* wive, to take a wife; to make (a woman) one's wife; to provide with a wife.
wivern, *n.* *wy*-vern, a wyvern [Her.].
wives, wyvz, *pl.* of *wife.*
wizard, *n.* *wiz*-ard, one skilled in magic, esp. one supposed to have acquired his superior knowledge and skill through a compact with the devil; a sorcerer; an enchanter; *a.* haunted by wizards; enchanting; specially remarkable, delightful, or excellent [Slang]. (M.E. *wysard*, connected with *wise.*)
wizardly, *ad.* *wiz*-ard-le, in the manner of a wizard.
wizardry, *n,* *wiz*-ard-re, the arts and practices of wizards.
wizen, *a.* *wiz*-en, withered: *v.i.* to wither; to shrivel.
wo, *int.* woh, whoh; stop, whoa!
woad, *n.* wode, the cruciferous plant *Isatis tinctoria*, formerly much cultivated for the permanent blue dye extracted from its root-leaves; the blue dye extracted: *v.t.* to dye, stain, or treat with this. **bastard woad,** weld. (A.S. *wad.*)
woad-waxen, *n.* *wode*-wak-sn, woodwaxen.
wobble, *v.i.* *wob*-bl, to move along unsteadily or swaying from side to side; to stagger; to oscillate irregularly; to waver; to vacillate: *n.* a wobbling motion; a staggering; an act of vacillation.
wobbler, *n.* *wob*-ler *or* *wob*-bl-er, one who or that which wobbles.
wobbly, *a.* *wob*-le *or* *wob*-bl-e, inclined, or given, to wobbling or vacillating.
Woden, *n.* *woh*-den, the Norse god Odin, from whom Wednesday derives its name. (A.S.)
woe, *n.* woh, grief; sorrow; misery; affliction; a curse. **woe worth the day,** woe be to the day. (A.S. *wa*, an exclamation of grief.)
woebegone, *a.* *woh*-be-gon, overwhelmed with woe; immersed in grief and sorrow; dismal in look.
woeful, *a.* *woh*-ful, sorrowful; distressed with grief or calamity; mournful; calamitous; afflictive; wretched; pitiful; paltry.
woefully, *ad.* sorrowfully; wretchedly; extremely.
woefulness, *n.* the state of being woeful.
woesome, *a.* *woh*-sum, woeful.
woke, woke, **woken,** *woh*-kn, *see* **wake.**
wold, *n.* wohld, a tract of downland or open country: *pl.* a district of low hills. (A.S. *wald*, a forest.)
woldsman, *n.* *wohldz*-man, one who lives on wolds.
wolf, *n.* woolf (pl. **wolves,** woolvz), the large, greyish-furred carnivore, *Canis lupus*, hunting in packs; a cruel, rapacious, or ravenous person; any larvæ of certain grain-infesting beetles; lupus [Med.]: *v.t.* to devour ravenously; to swallow with gulps. **to cry " wolf "** to call for help when none is needed; to cause unnecessary alarm. **to keep the wolf from the door,** just to avoid starvation or indigence. (A.S. *wulf.*)
wolf-berry, *n.* the western snowberry, *Symphoricarpus occidentalis.*
wolf-cub, *n.* a Boy Scout of the junior branch.
wolf-dog, *n.* a dog of a large breed formerly kept for hunting wolves; an Alsatian.
wolf-fish, *n.* the catfish or sea-wolf, *Anarrhicas lupus*, a large ferocious fish with strong teeth.
wolf-hound, *n.* a dog used for wolf-hunting. **Irish wolf-hound,** a hunting dog of deerhound type, but larger and stronger. **Russian wolf-hound,** the borzoi.
wolfish, *a.* *woolf*-ish, like a wolf; having the qualities or form of a wolf.
wolfishly, *ad.* in a wolfish manner.
wolf-man, *n.* a werewolf.
wolf-net, *n.* a large kind of fishing-net.
wolfram, *n.* *wool*-fram, a former name of tungsten, now applied to wolframite. (Ger.)
wolframite, *n.* *wool*-fra-mite, a native tungstate of iron and manganese, an important source of tungsten. (Ger.)
wolf's-bane, *n.* applied to various aconites, esp. the poisonous monkshood, *Aconitum napellus*, and *A. lycoctonum.*
wolf's-claw, *n.* the common club-moss, *Lycopodium clavatum.*
wolf-spider, *n.* any species of the family *Lycosidæ*, including the tarantula.
wollastonite, *n.* *wol*-las-ton-ite, tabular spar, a native silicate of calcium. (Engl. mineralogist, Wm. Hyde *Wollaston*, *d.* 1828.)
wolverene *or* **wolverine,** *n.* *wool*-ver-reen, the glutton or carcajou, *Gulo luscus*, an American carnivore of the weasel family. (*wolf.*)
★**woman,** *n.* *woom*-an (*pl.* **women.** *wim*-en), the adult female of the human race; womankind; womanliness; a female attendant or servant, a charwoman [Coll.]: *v.t.* to cause to behave as a woman; to address (in contempt) as " woman." **old woman,** *see* **old.** **woman of the town,** a

prostitute. **woman of the world,** a woman well experienced socially. (A.S. *wifman.*)
womanhood, *n.* *woom*-an-hood, the state of being a woman; womanly character; women collectively.
womanish, *a.* *woom*-an-ish, suitable to a woman; having the qualities of a woman; feminine; effeminate.
womanishly, *ad.* in a womanish manner.
womanishness, *n.* the quality of being womanish.
womanize, *v.t.* *woom*-a-nize, to make womanish or effeminate; to consort with loose women [Coll.].
woomanizer, *n.* *woom*-a-ny-zer, a man who consorts with loose women, a fornicator [Coll.].
womankind, *n.* *woom*-an-kynd, women in general; the female sex; the women of a household or group.
womanlike, *a.* *woom*-an-like, like a woman; womanish.
womanliness, *n.* *woom*-an-le-ness, the state of being womanly; gentleness.
womanly, *a.* *woom*-an-le, befitting a woman; feminine; characteristic of women.
womb, *n.* woom, the uterus; that part where the young of an animal is conceived and nourished till its birth; the place where anything is produced; any large or deep cavity. **womb of time,** the unrevealed future. (A.S. *wamb,* the belly.)
wombat, *n.* *wom*-bat, a burrowing marsupial of the genus *Phascolomys.* (Austral. native name, *wombach.*)
womby, *a.* *woom*-e, capacious.
women, *n.* *wim*-en: *pl.* of *woman.*
womenfolk, *n.* *wim*-en-folk, women collectively; womankind.
wommera, *n.* *wom*-e-rah, a woomera [Austral.].
won, wun, *p.* and *pp.* of *win.*
won, *n.* wun, a dwelling; a habitation: *v.i.* to dwell. (A.S. *wunian,* dwell.)
wonder, *n.* *wun*-der, that emotion which is excited by novelty, or the presentation to the sight or mind of something new, unusual, strange, great, extraordinary, or not well understood; that which excites surprise, or arrests the attention by its novelty, grandeur, or inexplicableness; a strange thing; a prodigy; a miracle; mingled surprise and admiration: *v.i.* to be struck with wonder; to be affected by surprise or admiration; to feel dubious or curious about; to speculate upon. **for a wonder,** surprisingly. **nine days' wonder,** *see* **nine. no wonder,** not at all surprising; of course. **seven wonders,** *see* **seven. wonder child,** an infant prodigy. (A.S. *wundor.*)
wonderer, *n.* *wun*-der-rer, one who wonders.
wonderful, *a.* *wun*-der-ful, adapted to excite wonder or admiration; exciting surprise; strange; astonishing.
wonderfully, *ad.* in a manner to excite wonder or surprise.
wonderfulness, *n.* quality of being wonderful.
wonderingly, *ad.* *wun*-der-ring-le, in a wondering manner.
wonderland, *n.* *wun*-der-land, a dreamland; any land of wonders.
wonderment, *n.* *wun*-der-ment, surprise; astonishment; an object of wonder; wonderfulness.
wonder-struck, *a.* struck with wonder, admiration, and surprise.
wonder-worker, *n.* one who performs wonders or miraculous acts.
wonder-working, *a.* doing wonders or surprising things.
wondrous, *a.* *wun*-drus, such as may excite wonder; admirable; marvellous: *ad.* in a wonderful or surprising degree.
wondrously, *ad.* in a strange or wonderful manner or degree.
wondrousness, *n.* *wun*-drus-ness, the quality of being wondrous.
wonga-wonga, *n.* *wong*-ga-*wong*-ga, the large Australian pigeon *Leucosarcia picata.* (Austral. native.)
wongshy, *n.* *wong*-she, the Far Eastern shrub *Gardenia grandiflora,* with large white flowers; a yellow dye-stuff prepared from the pods of this. (Chin.)
wonky, *a.* *wong*-ke, shaky; unsteady; inferior; questionable [Slang].
won't, *a.* wohnt, a contraction of "will not."
wont, *a.* wohnt *or* wunt, accustomed; habituated; using or doing customarily: *n.* custom; **habit:** *v.i.* to be accustomed. (A.S. *wunian,* dwell, be used to.)
wonted, *a.* *wohn*-ted, accustomed; customary; made familiar by use.
wontedness, *n.* *wohn*-ted-ness, the state of being accustomed; habituation.
woo, *v.t.* woo, to court; to make love to; to solicit: *v.i.* to make love; to make entreaty. (A.S. *wogian.*)
woobut, *n.* *woo*-but, an oubit or hairy caterpillar; a woolly-bear.
★**wood,** *n.* wood, a large and thick collection of trees growing; a small forest; the solid part beneath the bark of trees; the solid part cut or sawed for the fire; timber; wind-instruments of wood [Mus.]; one bowl of a set of bowls [Bowling]. **from the wood,** from the barrel. **in the wood,** in cask, not bottle. **out of the wood,** out of danger, freed from difficulty or anxiety, etc. **wood alcohol,** methanol. **Woods and Forests,** former title of the Commission administering the revenues of the Crown Lands since 1760, when George III surrendered them in exchange for the Civil List. (A.S. *wudu.*)
wood-agate, *n.* silicified or agatized wood.
wood-ant, *n.* the large red ant *Formica rufa,* frequenting woods.
woodbine, *n.* *wood*-bine, honeysuckle; Virginia creeper [U.S.A.]; name of a cheap cigarette, hence [Slang], a cheap cigarette of any kind.
wood-block, *n.* a wooden paving block; a block of wood engraved for printing from; a woodcut.
wood-carver, *n.* one who carves wood.
wood-carving, *n.* a carving in wood; the art or process of carving in wood.
woodchat, *n.* *wood*-chat, a species of shrike, *Lanius rutilus.*
woodchuck, *n.* *wood*-chuk, a North American species of marmot, *Marmota monax*; the ground-hog. (Algonq. *wejack.*)
wood-coal, *n.* charcoal; lignite or brown-coal.
woodcock, *n.* *wood*-kok, a bird allied to the snipe, but with shorter and stronger legs, *Scolopax rusticola.*
woodcraft, *n.* *wood*-krahft, knowledge of woodland life; forestry.
woodcut, *n.* *wood*-kut, an engraving on wood; a print or impression from this.
woodcutter, *n.* *wood*-kut-er, a person who cuts wood; one who engraves on wood.
woodcutting, *n.* *wood*-kut-ing, the operation or trade of sawing wood or felling trees; the art of a wood-engraver.
wood-dove, *n.* *wood*-duv, the wood-pigeon.
wooded, *a.* *wood*-ed, supplied or covered with growing trees; afforested.
wooden, *a.* *wood*-n, made of wood; consisting of wood; as from wood (esp. of sound); clumsy (of deportment, etc.); impassive. **wooden horse,** an offering designed to bring ruin on the tempted (the famous Trojan horse). **wooden pear,** the fruit of various Australian trees of the genus *Xylomelum.* **wooden spoon, wedge,** *see these words.*
wood-engraver, *n.* one who engraves on wood.
wood-engraving, *n.* the art of engraving on wood; xylography; an engraving on wood.
wooden-head, *n.* a blockhead; a ninny; a dunce.
wooden-headed, *a.* *wood*-n-*hed*-ed, stupid; dense; dull.
woodenness, *n.* *wood*-n-ness, wooden quality; stupidity in appearance; awkwardness in motion.
wood-gas, *n.* an illuminant obtained by the destructive distillation of wood.
wood-grouse, *n.* the capercailzie.
wood-house, *n.* a room or shed in which wood is stored or sheltered from the weather.
wood-hyacinth, *n.* the wild hyacinth or bluebell.
wood-ibis, *n.* a large wading-bird of the family Tantalinæ of central America.
woodiness, *n.* *wood*-e-ness, the quality of being woody.
woodland, *n.* *wood*-land, land covered with woods; a well-wooded region: *a.* pertaining to woods or woodland.
woodlander, *n.* *wood*-lan-der, a dweller in woodland.
woodlark, *n.* *wood*-lark, a species of lark, *Alauda arborea,* which perches on trees.

woodless, *a.* *wood*-less, destitute of wood or of woods.
wood-lily, *n.* the lily of the valley.
woodlock, *n.* *wood*-lok, a piece of wood in the throating of the pintle to keep the rudder from rising [Naut.].
woodlouse, *n.* *wood*-louse (*pl.* **woodlice**), an isopod insect of the family Oniscidæ found in wood; applied also to various millepedes and termites.
woodman, *n.* *wood*-man, a forest officer; a forester; one who cuts down trees.
wood-note, *n.* a note as that of a forest bird: *pl.* a bird's song.
wood-nut, *n.* the filbert or hazel-nut.
wood-nymph, *n.* *wood*-nimf, a goddess of the woods; a dryad.
wood-oil, *n.* any oil derived from wood or from wood alcohol; tung-oil; the essential oil of the gurjun balsam.
wood-opal, *n.* *wood*-oh-pal, wood petrified or silicified with opal.
woodpecker, *n.* *wood*-pek-er, any of several birds of the genus *Picus*, mostly of solitary habits and living in forests, so called from their habit of tapping the trees to discover where insects are lodged.
wood-pie, *n.* *wood*-py, the great spotted woodpecker, *Picus major*.
wood-pigeon, *n.* any pigeon living in woods, esp. the ringdove, *Columba palumbus*, and stock-dove, *C. œneas*.
wood-pulp, *n.* *see* **pulp.**
wood-reeve, *n.* the steward or overseer of a wood.
woodrock, *n.* *wood*-rok, a compact variety of asbestos; woodstone.
woodruff, *n.* *wood*-ruf, the rubiaceous plant *Asperula odorata*.
wood-sere, *n.* *wood*-seer, cuckoo-spit; also, the season when there is no sap in a tree.
woodskin, *n.* *wood*-skin, an American Indian's bark canoe; the bark of which such is made.
woodsman, *n.* *woodz*-man, one who lives or works in the woods; a woodcutter.
wood-sorrel, *n.* any plant of the large genus of acaulescent herbs, *Oxalis*.
wood-spite, *n.* a name given to the green woodpecker.
woodstone, *n.* *wood*-stone, petrified wood; a striped variety of hornstone, somewhat resembling wood in appearance.
wood-sugar, *n.* *wood*-shoo-gar, the crystalline unfermentable sugar, xylose.
wood-tar, *n.* tar obtained by the dry distillation of pine and other timber.
wood-tin, *n.* a fibrous variety of cassiterite resembling wood in structure.
wood-vine, *n.* a name of the twining plants traveller's-joy and white bryony.
woodwall, *n.* *wood*-wawl, the great spotted woodpecker.
wood-warbler, *n.* wood-*wawr*-bler, the wood-wren; any bird of the American genus *Dendroica*.
woodward, *n.* *wood*-word, the keeper of a wood; a head forester.
wood-wasp, *n.* *wood*-wasp, the wasp *Vespa sylvestris*, hanging its nest on trees; a hymenopterous insect allied to the saw-fly [U.S.A.].
woodwaxen, *n.* *wood*-wak-sn, the plant dyer's greenweed, *Genista tinctoria*. (A.S.)
wood-wind, *n.* wood-*wind*, the wooden wind-instruments of an orchestra [Mus.].
wood-wool, *n.* wood fibre specially prepared for use in surgical dressings.
woodwork, *n.* *wood*-wurk, work in wood; objects made of wood; that part of any structure which is made of wood.
woodworm, *n.* *wood*-wurm, any wood-boring larva; the ship-worm.
wood-wren, *n.* the warbler *Phylloscopus sibilatrix*.
woody, *a.* *wood*-e, abounding with wood or woods; consisting of wood; ligneous; pertaining to woods; sylvan. **woody nightshade,** the bitter-sweet, *Solanum dulcamara*.
wooer, *n.* *woo*-er, one who woos; a lover.
woof, *n.* woof, the threads that cross the warp in weaving; the weft; texture [Fig.]; cloth. (A.S., lit., woven in.)
woof, *n.* and *v.i.* woof *or* wuf, wuff.
woofy, *a.* *woof*-e, having a close texture; resembling a woven fabric.
wooing, *n.* *woo*-ing, courtship; making love.
wooingly, *ad.* enticingly; with persuasiveness; so as to invite to stay.
★**wool,** *n.* wool, the soft elastic hair which grows on sheep and certain other animals, from which cloth is made; the fleecy coat of the sheep; any fleecy or flocculent substance resembling wool; clothing or other material made from wool; a sort of pubescence on the surface of certain plants [Bot.]. **much cry but little wool,** plenty of fuss or advertisement, etc., but little to show for it. **pull wool over one's eyes,** to delude, hoodwink, or cheat one. **wool clip,** the annual crop of wool. (A.S. *wull*.)
wool-card, *n.* a toothed machine or implement for carding wool.
wool-combing, *n.* *wool*-koam-ing, the occupation of combing or carding wool.
woold, *v.t.* woold, to wind, particularly a rope round a mast or yard, when made of two or more pieces at the place where they are fished, for confining and supporting them [Naut.]: *n.* binding cord, woolding. (Dut.)
woolder, *n.* *wool*-der, a stick used in woolding.
woolding, *n.* *wool*-ding, the act of winding, as a rope round a mast; the rope used in this; a wrapping.
wool-driver, *n.* *wool*-dry-ver, one who buys wool from sheep-farmers and sells to woollen manufacturers.
wool-dyed, *a.* *wool*-dyd, dyed in the wool before it is woven.
wool-fat, *n.* suint; lanolin.
wool-fell, *n.* a sheepskin not stripped of the fleece.
wool-gathering, *n.* the act of gathering wool; [Fig.] absence of mind, a dreamy state, or vagrant or idle exercise of the imagination: *a.* indulging in idle fancies; dreamy, absent-minded.
wool-grower, *n.* one who raises sheep for the production of wool.
woollen, *a.* *wool*-en, made or consisting of wool; pertaining to wool; dressed in coarse wool, hence, rustic, homespun: *n.* cloth made of wool: *pl.* woollen goods; woollies.
woollen-draper, *n.* one who deals in woollen goods.
woollenette, *n.* wool-en-*net*, a thin woollen fabric.
woollenize, *v.t.* *wool*-en-ize, to impart a wool-like appearance and texture to.
woolliness, *n.* *wool*-e-ness, the state of being woolly.
woolly, *a.* *wool*-e, consisting of wool; resembling wool; clothed with wool, or [Bot.] with a pubescence resembling wool; having hair of a woolly texture (of negroes); [Coll.] dull-witted, dense: *n.* a woollen vest or coat: *pl.* **woollies,** *wool*-iz, woollen underclothes. **woolly-bear,** a large hairy caterpillar, esp. of the tiger-moth. **woolly-haired,** ulotrichous [Ethn.].
woolman, *n.* *wool*-man, a dealer in wool.
wool-mill, *n.* a mill for the manufacture of woollen yarn or cloth.
wool-oil, *n.* wool-fat.
woolpack, *n.* *wool*-pak, a bale of wool, formerly one weighing 240 lb.
woolsack, *n.* *wool*-sak, a sack or bag of wool; (*cap.*) the large square bag of wool, without back or arms and covered with red cloth, on which the Lord Chancellor sits in the House of Lords.
woolsey, *n.* *wool*-ze, linsey-woolsey, dress material of cotton and wool.
woolsorter, *n.* *wool*-sor-ter, one who sorts wool into qualities. **woolsorter's disease,** pulmonary anthrax.
woolstaple, *n.* *wool*-stay-pl, a staple or market for the sale of wool.
woolstapler, *n.* *wool*-stay-pler, a wholesale dealer in wool; also a woolsorter.
woolwork, *n.* *wool*-wurk, needlework in wool, esp. in coloured wools on canvas to imitate tapestry; Berlin work.
woomera, *n.* *woo*-mer-ra, the throwing-stick, or spear-thrower, of Australian aborigines. (Austral.)
woorali, *n.* woo-*rah*-le, curare. (Tupi or Carib.)
wootz, *n.* woots, an Indian steel for weapons and edge tools. (Dravidian.)
wop, *n.* wop, an Italian (originally as an immigrant in the U.S.A.). (Amer. slang.)
★**word,** *n.* wurd, a vocal sound, or a combination of articulate and vocal sounds, uttered by the human voice, and accepted as expressing an idea or ideas;

the letter or combination of letters which represent such a sound; a constituent part of a sentence; a short discourse; talk; verbal contention; language; living speech; oral expression; promise; signal; password; order; command; account; tidings; message; declaration; purpose expressed; a motto; a short sentence; a proverb: *v.t.* to express in words. **a good word,** commendation. **as good as one's word,** acting according to promise. **by word of mouth,** orally. **in a word,** in short; briefly. **my word!** an exclamation of surprise, admiration, etc. **the Word,** the Logos; also, the Scriptures. **the last word,** the decisive answer (in debate, etc.); the latest style or thing [Slang]. **to have words,** to quarrel. **word for word,** literally; verbatim. **word of honour,** a solemn pledge. **word perfect,** knowing every word by heart. (A.S.)

wordage, *n.* *wurd*-aj, words collectively; total number of words; verbiage.

word-book, *n.* *wurd*-book, a vocabulary; a libretto.

word-catcher, *n.* one who cavils at words; a carping critic.

worded, *a.* *wur*-ded, expressed in words.

wordily, *ad.* in a verbose or wordy manner.

wordiness, *n.* *wur*-de-ness, the state or quality of being wordy; verbosity.

wording, *n.* *wur*-ding, the act, or the manner, of expressing in words.

wordless, *a.* *wurd*-less, not using words; not speaking.

wordlore, *n.* *wurd*-lore, the facts about words, their history, derivation, etc.; the study of this.

wordlorist, *n.* *wurd*-lore-ist, a student of wordlore.

word-painting, *n.* a vivid and picturesque verbal description.

word-play, *n.* subtle usage of words; verbal fencing.

word-square, *n.* words of the same number of letters set in successive lines so that words result when read downwards as well as horizontally.

wordy, *a.* *wur*-de, using many words; verbose; containing many words; consisting of words; verbal.

wore, wore, *p.* of *wear.*

work, *v.i.* wurk, to labour; to act; to be in action; to carry on operations; to operate; to carry on business; to be customarily employed; to produce effects by action or influence; to act or operate; to be effective; to be in a state of motion or agitation; to ferment; to labour; to strain; to move heavily or with difficulty. **work out,** to make its way out; to become loose. **work to windward,** to sail or ply against the wind [Naut.]. **work up,** to make way up; to advance. *p.* and *pp.* **worked,** wurkt, or **wrought.** (A.S. *weorc.*)

work, *v.t.* wurk, to form, make, or fashion by labour; to mould, shape or manufacture; to influence by acting upon; to effect; to accomplish; to produce by action, labour, or exertion; to manage, operate, or activate; to prepare by kneading or the like; to embroider; to set or keep in operation; to put to labour; to solve, as a sum; to cause to ferment, as liquor. **work into,** to insinuate. **work on,** to act on; to influence. **work one's passage,** to pay one's fare (esp. at sea) by one's labour; [Fig.] to acquire rehabilitation through self-sacrifice. **work out,** to effect by labour and exertion; to solve. **work up,** to raise; to excite; to expend (materials) in any way; to elaborate or develop. *p.* and *pp.* **worked,** wurkt, or **wrought,** rawt.

*__work,__ *n.* wurk, effort or exertion for accomplishing some end or object; labour; employment; occupation; duty; an undertaking; that which is made or done; any fabric or manufacture; embroidery; the matter on which one is at work; that which is done; some important deed; achievement; operation; effect; resistance overcome multiplied by the distance through which the effort is made [Mech.]; that which is made; that which is produced by mental labour; a composition; a book: *pl.* a place of manufacture; the working parts of a watch or other mechanism; walls, trenches, and the like, made for fortifications [Fort.]; moral duties or external performances, as distinct from grace [Theol.]. **all in the day's work,** perfectly normal. **give one the works,** to set about or kill him [U.S.A. slang]. **have one's work cut out,** to have a difficult or lengthy task. **make short work of,** to deal with, finish off, etc. quickly or with ease. **out of work,** not gainfully employed. **set to** or **on work,** to employ; to engage in any business. **work of art,** an artistic production; an object made more for its beauty than utility.

workability, *n.* wurk-a-*bil*-e-te, the state of being workable; capability of being worked.

workable, *a.* *wurk*-a-bl, capable of being worked, as a metal; worth working, as a mine; practicable.

workaday, *a.* *wurk*-a-day, pertaining to or suited for working or labour; ordinary; prosaic.

work-bag, *n.* a bag for holding working tools, or mending, needlework, etc.

work-basket, *n.* a basket for needlework.

work-box, *n.* a box to hold implements and materials for needlework.

workday, *n.* *wurk*-day, a working day.

worker, *n.* *wurk*-er, anyone who works or is gainfully employed; a working-man or -woman; one who performs; a sterile ant, bee, or termite.

workfellow, *n.* *wurk*-fel-loh, one engaged in the same employment with another.

workfolk, *n.pl.* *wurk*-foke, persons who labour; the working classes.

workgirl, *n.* *wurk*-gerl, a woman or girl employed in manual labour.

workhouse, *n.* *wurk*-house, a poorhouse; a house in which paupers were lodged and maintained by a parish or union of parishes, so called because earlier intended for idle vagrants, who were compelled to work, and now known as poor-law institutions.

working, *a.* *wurk*-ing, relating to work; effective; actively engaged; sufficient for the purpose; fermenting: *n.* the act of working; fermentation; movement; operation; manner of functioning: *pl.* tunnels or excavations. **working capital,** stock-in-trade, short credits, and cash [Comm.]. **working classes,** the classes of society engaged in manual labour for wages. **working day,** a day on which work is performed, as distinguished from days of rest; daily time occupied in work. **working drawing,** a plan of a work prepared by the designer, engineer, or architect to guide the workman in its execution. **working expenses,** funds necessary for carrying on a business. **working order,** good going condition. **working-party,** a statutary body of workers and managers appointed to investigate and report on means of securing maximum efficiency in an industrial undertaking.

working-man, *n.* wurk-ing-*man*, a member of the working classes; a labourer; an artisan.

workless, *a.* *wurk*-less, being without work; not gainfully employed.

workman, *n.* *wurk*-man, a man who works; any man employed in labour, esp. manual labour, for wages; a craftsman.

workmanlike, *a.* *wurk*-man-like, skilfully done.

workmanly, *a.* *wurk*-man-le, skilful; well performed: *ad.* in a skilful manner; in a manner befitting a workman.

workmanship, *n.* *wurk*-man-ship, the skill of a workman; the execution or manner of making anything; work done; manufacture; something made, particularly by manual labour; that which is effected, made, or procured.

workmate, *n.* *wurk*-mate, a workfellow.

work-people, *n.* manual workers; members of the working classes.

workroom, *n.* *wurk*-room, a room set aside for work.

workshop, *n.* *wurk*-shop, a place wherein any work is done or manufacture is carried on.

work-shy, *a.* *wurk*-shy, dodging or hating work; habitually lazy: *n.* one who never works if he can help it.

work-table, *n.* a small table, containing drawers and other conveniences for needlework.

workwoman, *n.* *wurk*-woom-an, a woman who performs any work; one skilled in needlework.

world, *n.* wurld, the earth and its inhabitants; the globe; any similar globe similarly regarded; any similar system of things; any region viewed as inhabited; any state of human existence, esp. the present or the next; a secular life; the attractions, enjoyments, and cares of the present life; those engrossed with such things; public life or society; the public; business or trouble of life; a great multitude or quantity; mankind; people in general; the customs and manners of men; the practice of life; a wide compass of things; the inhabitants of the earth; the human race; the carnal state or corruption of the earth; the ungodly part of mankind. **for all the world,** exactly; entirely. **New World,** the Western Hemisphere; the Americas. **not for the world,** on no account. **Old World,** the Eastern Hemisphere. **tell the world,** to assert emphatically or as a positive truth. **the next world,** conditions after death; the future state. **the world and his wife,** everybody; everybody who matters. **think the world of,** to esteem very highly. **World War,** either of the two great wars of the 20th cent., I, 1914–18, or II, 1939–45. **world without end,** for ever and ever. (A.S. *weoruld*, age or life of man, from *wer*, a man, and *eld*, age.)

worldliness, *n.* *wurld*-le-ness, regard for only the things of this life; covetousness; addiction to gain and temporal enjoyments.

worldling, *n.* *wurld*-ling, one intent only upon worldly pleasures.

worldly, *a.* *wurld*-le, pertaining to this world or life, in contradistinction to the life to come; secular; temporal; devoted to this life and its enjoyments to the exclusion of higher and spiritual interests.

worldly-minded, *a.* devoted to worldly interests and temporal enjoyments.

worldly-mindedness, *n.* a predominant love and pursuit of the pleasures of this world.

worldly-wise, *a.* wise with regard to worldly matters.

world-politics, *n.* wurld-*pol*-e-tiks, international politics; Weltpolitik.

world-power, *n.* wurld-*pou*-er, any state or organization whose political or economic power is sufficient to have worldwide influence. (Ger. *Weltmacht.*)

worldwide, *a.* *wurld*-wide, spread over the world; known by everybody.

***worm,** *n.* wurm, an invertebrate segmentate animal creeping without legs; an earthworm; a tapeworm or other intestinal parasite; a grub or maggot; anything which, working secretly, gnaws and destroys; remorse; that which incessantly gnaws the conscience or torments; a debased, despicable, or cringing person; a spiral, worm-like instrument, used for withdrawing wads and cartridges; something spiral, vermiculated, or resembling a worm, as the thread of a screw; a spiral, metallic pipe placed in a tub of water, through which the vapour passes in distillation, and in which it is cooled and condensed; the lytta, a small, worm-like ligament beneath a dog's tongue. **worm pipefish,** the worm-like marine fish, *Nerophis lumbriciformis.* (A.S. *wyrm.*)

worm, *v.i.* wurm, to work slowly, gradually, and secretly; to progress with a worm-like motion: *v.t.* to expel or undermine by slow and secret means; to cut the worm from under a dog's tongue; to draw the wad or cartridge from a gun; to clean by the worm; to wind a rope or spun-yarn spirally round a cable, between the strands [Naut.]. **worm oneself into,** to enter gradually by arts and insinuations. **worm out of,** to extract (esp. withheld information) by subtle or insidious means.

worm-cast, *n.* a cylindrical mass of earth that has been voided by an earthworm.

worm-eaten, *a.* eaten into by worms or larvæ; old; antiquated; worthless.

wormed, *a.* wurmd, injured or infested by worms or larvæ.

worm-fence, *n.* *wurm*-fence, a zigzag fence in which the ends of the rails cross each other [U.S.A.].

worm-gear, *n.* gearing worked by the agency of a worm-wheel [Mech.].

worm-grass, *n.* a plant of the genus *Spigelia*, used as a vermifuge.

worm-hole, *n.* a hole bored by an insect larva.

wormil, *n.* *wawr*-mil, the larva of the warble-fly [Vet.].

worminess, *n.* *wurm*-e-ness, the quality or state of being wormy.

worming, *n.* *wurm*-ing, the action of the verb *to worm*; catching worms; angling with worms; the extraction of the worm from a dog's tongue; the filling between the strands of a rope [Naut.].

worm-like, *a.* resembling a worm; vermicular; spiral.

worm-powder, *n.* a powder used for expelling worms from the stomach and intestines.

wormseed, *n.* *wurm*-seed, any of several plants used as an anthelmintic, esp. a species of *Chenopodium*, the seed of which has the property of expelling worms. **wormseed tea,** a vermifuge prepared from the root of *Spigelia marilandica.*

worm-wheel, *n.* a toothed wheel gearing into the spiral of a screw [Mech.].

wormwood, *n.* *wurm*-wood, a plant of the genus *Artemisia*; a source of bitterness. (A.S. *wermod.*)

wormy, *a.* *wurm*-e, containing a worm or worms; infested with worms; worm-eaten; grovelling [Fig.].

worn, worn, *pp.* of the verb *to wear.*

wornness, *n.* *worn*-ness, worn condition; shabbiness through continual wear.

worn-out, *a.* consumed or rendered useless by wearing; wearied out.

worricow, *n.* *wu*-re-kou, a hobgoblin; anything grotesque [Scots.]. (*worry* and *cow.*)

worried, *a.* *wu*-rid, harassed; fatigued.

worrier, *n.* *wu*-re-er, one who worries or harasses, or allows himself to worry and fret.

worriless, *a.* *wu*-re-less, having no worries; unworried.

worriment, *n.* *wu*-re-ment, anxiety; worry.

worrisome, *a.* *wu*-re-sum, causing or apt to cause worry; addicted to worrying.

worry, *n.* *wu*-re, the act of worrying; a state of perplexity, trouble, or harassment; a worrying person: *v.t.* to tease; to trouble; to harass with importunity or with care and anxiety; to fatigue; to tear or mangle with the teeth; to shake about; to vex; to persecute brutally: *v.i.* to fret. (A.S. *wyrgan*, to strangle.)

worryingly, *ad.* *wu*-re-ing-le, teasingly; harassingly.

worse, *a.* wurse, the comparative of bad, evil, or ill; more bad, evil, or ill; more depraved and corrupt, in a moral sense; less perfect or good: *ad.* in a manner more evil or bad: *n.* loss; not the advantage; defeat; something less good. (A.S. *wyrsa.*)

worsen, *v.t.* *wur*-sn, to put to disadvantage; to defeat; to make worse: *v.i.* to become worse; to deteriorate.

worship, *n.* *wur*-ship, homage paid either to God (esp. by religious service), or to an idol, false god, or other object of adoration; religious service; obsequious or submissive respect akin to idolatry; civil deference; excellence of character; worth; worthiness; a title of honour, used in addresses to certain magistrates and others of respectable character; a term of ironical respect; admiration without bounds. (A.S. *weorthscipe*, worthship, state of being worthy.)

worship, *v.t.* *wur*-ship, to adore; to pay divine homage to; to reverence with supreme respect and veneration; to respect; to honour; to treat with civil reverence; to honour with extravagant love and extreme submission, as a lover: *v.i.* to perform acts of adoration; to perform divine service.

worshipable, *a.* *wur*-ship-a-bl, that is worthy of worship.

worshipful, *a.* *wur*-ship-ful, claiming respect; worthy of worship; a term of respect to those in civic offices, used sometimes ironically.

worshipfully, *ad.* respectfully.

worshipper, *n.* *wur*-ship-er, one who worships; one who pays divine honours to any being.

worst, *a.* wurst, the superlative of bad, evil, or ill; most bad, most evil, most ill; most severe or dangerous; most difficult to heal; most afflictive, pernicious, or calamitous: *n.* the most evil state; the most severe, aggravated, or calamitous state: *ad.* to an extremely bad degree; least well: *v.t.* to get the advantage over in contest; to defeat; to overthrow. **if worst comes to worst,** if the very worst thing should happen. **to get the worst of it,** to be worsted or defeated. (A.S. *wyrst.*)

worsted, *n.* *woos*-ted, long-stapled wool combed straight; a closely twisted yarn made of this, used for stockings, embroidery, etc.: *a.* consisting of worsted; made of worsted yarn. (*Worstead*, a village in Norfolk.)

worsted, *a.* *wur*-sted, defeated. (*pp.* of *worst.*)

wort, *n.* wurt, a herb (rarely used except in compounds). (A.S. *wyrt.*)

wort, *n.* wurt, an infusion of malt which, after fermentation, becomes beer. (A.S. *wyrt.*)

worth, *n.* wurth, that quality which renders a

thing of value; value; price; valuable qualities; value of mental or moral qualities; virtue; merit; excellence: *a.* equal in value to; deserving of; equal in possessions to; having estate to the value of. (A.S. *weoth*, from *weorthan*, be or become.)

worth, *v.i.* wurth, to befall; to betide (now only in such phrases as **woe worth the day**, accursed be the day). (A.S. *weorthan*, to become.)

worthily, *ad.* *wur*-the-le, in a manner suited to; deservedly; according to merit; justly.

worthiness, *n.* *wur*-the-ness, state of being worthy or excellent; quality or state of deserving; desert; merit; excellence.

worthless, *a.* *wurth*-less, having no value; having no worth of character or virtue; having no dignity or excellence; not deserving.

worthlessly, *ad.* in a worthless manner.

worthlessness, *n.* want of value; want of useful quality; want of excellence.

worth-while, *a.* *wurth*-while, of sufficient importance to repay the effort or trouble, etc., incurred [Coll.].

worthy, *a.* *wur*-the, deserving; such as merits; having worth or excellence; virtuous; estimable; suitable; having qualities suited to; equal in value; well-founded: *n.* a person of eminent worth; one distinguished for useful and estimable qualities; a local celebrity. **worthiest of blood,** old legal phrase referring to the male, as opposed to female, line of descent.

wot, *v.* wot, *first and third pers. sing. pres.* of *wit*, to know, to be aware (*second pers. sing.*, **wottest**).

woubit, *n.* *woo*-bit, a woolly-bear, or any hairy caterpillar.

would, *v.i.* wood, *p.* of *will*, used as an auxiliary verb in conditional forms of speech; as, "I would go, if I could;" wish or pray, particularly in the phrases, "*would* to God," "*would* God that we had died in Egypt"; wish to do or to have, as, what *wouldst* thou?

would-be, *a.* *wood*-bee, pretending to be; wishing to be regarded as.

wouldst, *v.i.* woodst, *past tense second person singular* of *will*.

★**wound,** *n.* woond, a bodily injury; a breach of the skin and flesh, or a division of the soft parts of an animal, caused by violence or external force; a breach of the bark and substance of a tree or other plant, caused by violence or external force; injury; hurt: *v.t.* to hurt by violence; to hurt the feelings of; to inflict a wound on; to pain: *v.i.* to inflict a wound. (A.S. *wundian*, from *wund*.)

wound, *v.t.* and *v.i.* wound: *p.* of *wind*.

wounder, *n.* *woon*-der, one who or that which wounds.

woundily, *ad.* *woon*-de-le, to an excessive degree.

wounding, *n.* *woon*-ding, hurt; injury.

woundless, *a.* *woond*-less, free from injury or hurt.

woundwort, *n.* *woond*-wurt, any plant supposed to be efficacious in healing wounds, such as *Stachys germanica* and *Anthyllis vulneraria*.

woundy, *a.* *woon*-de, excessive: *ad.* excessively.

wourali, *n.* woo-*rah*-le, curare, a powerful poison obtained from *Strychnos toxifera*. (Tupi or Carib.)

wou-wou, *n.* *wou*-wou, the wow-wow.

wove, *v.t.* wove: *p.* of *weave*. **wove paper,** writing paper with a uniform surface, made on a fine wire gauze and usually without watermark.

woven, *a.* *woh*-vn, made in a loom.

wow, *int.* wou, an exclamation of wonder, surprise, admiration, etc. **it's a wow,** it's good, certain, fine, correct, etc. [Amer. slang].

wowser, *n.* *wou*-zer, a needlessly or excessively censorious person; a spoil-sport [Austral. slang].

wow-wow, *n.* *wou*-wou, the silver gibbon of Java, *Hylobates leuciscus*.

wrack, *n.* rak, wreck, ruin; a wreck or piece of wreckage; any variety of seaweed thrown on or growing upon the shore. **grass-wrack,** eel-grass, *Zostera marina*.

wrack, *n.* rak, rack, a thin, flying cloud.

wrackful, *a.* *rak*-ful, ruinous; destructive.

wraith, *n.* rayth, the supposed apparition of a person about to die, or just dead; a phantom; an apparition. (Perhaps connected with *wreath*.)

wrangle, *n.* *rang*-gl, an angry dispute; a noisy quarrel; altercation: *v.i.* to dispute angrily; to quarrel peevishly and noisily; to brawl; to altercate; to debate; to dispute publicly. (A.S. *wringan*, wring.)

wrangler, *n.* *rang*-gler, an angry disputant; one who disputes with heat or peevishness; (*cap.*) one of those who, at Cambridge University, attained the first class in the mathematical tripos. **Senior Wrangler,** at Cambridge, the title formerly accorded to the candidate who headed the list of Wranglers.

wranglership, *n.* *rang*-gler-ship, the position of Wrangler at the University of Cambridge.

wranglesome, *a.* *rang*-gl-sum, contentious; quarrelsome [Coll.].

wrangling, *n.* *rang*-gling, the act of disputing angrily; altercation.

wrannock, *n.* *ran*-ok, the wren.

wrap, *n.* rap, a cloak, rug, or similar wrapper: *v.t.* to wind or fold together; to arrange so as to enclose; to cover up by winding something round; to hide; to comprise; to enwrap or involve. (M.E. *wrappen*.)

wrappage, *n.* *rap*-aj, the act of wrapping; that which wraps or envelops; a wrapper; wrappings.

wrapper, *n.* *rap*-er, one who wraps; that in which anything is wrapped or enclosed; a loose garment, as a dressing-gown, negligee, or roomy overcoat.

wrapping, *n.* *rap*-ing, material used or designed for wrapping or covering.

wrap-rascal, *n.* *rap*-rahs-kal, a loose rough overcoat.

wrasse, *n.* ras, a spiny hard-boned marine fish of the genus *Labrus*, having a long single dorsal fin and thick-lipped protrusive mouth, some species of which are common on rocky British coasts. (Old Cornish.)

wrath, *n.* rawth, violent anger; vehement exasperation; fury; rage; indignation; manifestation of anger. **Day of Wrath,** Judgment Day. (A.S. *wræththo*.)

wrathful, *a.* *rawth*-ful, very angry; greatly incensed; springing from wrath or expressing it.

wrathfully, *ad.* with great anger.

wrathfulness, *n.* vehement anger.

wrathily, *ad.* *rawth*-e-le, wrathfully.

wrathless, *a.* *rawth*-less, free from anger.

wrathy, *a.* *rawth*-e, very angry; inclined to wrath.

wrawl, *v.i.* rawl, to howl; to cry, as a cat.

wreak, *n.* reek, revenge; vengeance; furious passion; punishment for injury: *v.t.* to execute; to inflict; to punish for injury done or out of revenge. (A.S. *wrecan*, avenge.)

wreakful, *a.* *reek*-ful, revengeful; angry.

wreakless, *a.* *reek*-less, unpunished; unavenged.

wreath, *n.* reeth, something twisted or curled; a garland or chaplet of flowers and leaves; a coil, twist, or wisp of hair, smoke, etc.; a drift of snow; the fillet or twisted band between the helmet and crest [Her.]. (A.S. *wræth*, from *writhan*, twist.)

wreathe, *v.t.* reethe, to twist into a wreath; to wind one about another; to interweave; to entwine; to encircle, as, or as with, a garland: *v.i.* to be interwoven or entwined; to be curled.

wreathen, *a.* *reeth*-en, wreathed; coiled or curled like a wreath.

wreathless, *a.* *reeth*-less, destitute of a wreath.

wreathy, *a.* *reeth*-e *or* *reethe*-e, adorned with a wreath; of the form of a wreath; twisted; curled; spiral.

wreck, *n.* rek, the destruction or disablement of a vessel by accident, as by being driven upon rocks, by foundering, by fire, etc., or in battle; the ruins of a stranded or disabled ship; dissolution by violence; ruin; destruction; debris, the remains of anything ruined; an enfeebled or debilitated person [Coll.]; anything which, after a shipwreck, is cast upon land by the sea [Law]: *v.t.* to strand; to drive against the shore, to dash against rocks, and break or destroy; to cause to suffer shipwreck; to ruin: *v.i.* to suffer shipwreck or ruin. (A.S. *wrecan*, drive.)

wreckage, *n.* *rek*-aj, the state of being wrecked; the remains of a wrecked ship or her cargo; the process of wrecking.

wrecker, *n.* *rek*-er, one who causes shipwreck for gain through plunder; one who plunders wrecks; a ruiner of anything; a parliamentary obstructionist; one employed in salvaging wrecks [Amer.]; one employed on demolition [Build.].

wreckful, *a.* *rek*-ful, causing wreck; dangerous.

wreck-master, *n.* a person appointed by law to take charge of a wreck and the wreckage.

wren, *n.* ren, a small passerine bird of the genus *Troglodytes*; any species of the family *Troglodytidæ*. (A.S. *wrenna*.)

Wren, *n.* ren, a member of the Women's Royal Naval Service (from the initials).

wrench, *n.* rensh, a violent twist, or a pull with twisting; a sprain; an injury by twisting, as in a joint; a tool for screwing or unscrewing: *v.t.* to pull with a twist; to wrest, twist, or force by violence; to strain; to distort. (A.S. *wrenc*, deceit.)

wrest, *n.* rest, the action of twisting or distorting; a violent pulling and twisting; a tool to tune stringed musical instruments with: *v.t.* to twist or extort by violence; to force from by violence, esp. by wringing or twisting; to distort; to turn from truth, or twist from its natural meaning; to pervert. (A.S. *wræstan*, twist.)

wrester, *n.* *rest*-er, one who wrests or perverts.

wrestle, *n.* *res*-l, the act of wrestling; a bout of wrestling: *v.i.* to strive by grappling; to throw another down by tripping up his heels and twitching him off his balance under certain recognized rules; to struggle; to strive; to contend. (A.S. *wræstlian.*)

wrestler, *n.* *res*-ler, one who wrestles; one skilful in wrestling.

wrestling, *n.* *res*-ling, the action of the verb *to wrestle*; the sport of grappling with and throwing another; a struggle; contention. **all-in wrestling,** wrestling in which every form of offence (biting and gouging excepted) and defence is permissible.

wrest-pin, *n.* *rest*-pin, one of the pins to which the string of a stringed musical instrument is fastened.

wretch, *n.* retch, a miserable person; one sunk in the deepest distress; a worthless mortal; one sunk in vice; an expression of slight or ironical pity, contempt, or sometimes compassion. (A.S. *wræcca*, an outcast, from *wrecan*, wreak.)

wretched, *a.* *retch*-ed, very miserable; sunk into deep affliction or distress, as from want, anxiety, grief, etc.; calamitous; very afflicting; worthless; paltry; very poor or mean; despicable, vile, or contemptible.

wretchedly, *ad.* *retch*-ed-le, most miserably; unhappy; despicably.

wretchedness, *n.* *retch*-ed-ness, extreme misery, either from want or sorrow; despicableness.

wrick, *v.t.* rik, to rick; to sprain or strain. (Probably connected with *wring.*)

wried, *a.* ride, turned awry; twisted out of shape or from its course; contorted. (*wry.*)

wriggle, *n.* *rig*-gl, a wriggling motion: *v.i.* to twist the body to and fro in short curves, like an eel; to shift or shuffle by indirect or insinuating means [Fig.]: *v.t.* to put into or introduce by a wriggling motion. **wriggle out of,** to escape from by wriggling or cunning. (Connected with *wry.*)

wriggler, *n.* *rig*-gler, one who or that which wriggles; a shuffler.

wrigglesome, *a.* *rig*-gl-sum, given to wriggling.

wriggling, *a.* *rig*-gling, moving the body one way and the other with quick turns, like an eel.

wriggly, *a.* *rig*-gle, given to wriggling; tortuous.

wright, *n.* rite, an artificer; a workman, esp. in wood; frequently used in compounds, as in *shipwright.* (A.S. *wyrhta*, a worker, from *wyrht*, a work.)

wring, *n.* ring, a convulsive squeezing or pressure; a wringer [Mech.]: *v.t.* to twist; to turn and strain; to squeeze; to press; to force by twisting; to pull out with a twist; to distress; to press with pain; to distort; to pervert; to persecute with extortion; to bend or strain out of position. **wring from,** to force from by violence; to extort. **wring out,** to force out; to squeeze out by twisting; to free from water by wringing. **wring the hands,** to clasp the hands with a convulsive or writhing motion, as in distress. **wringing wet,** so wet as to require wringing; wet enough for water to be wrung from it. *p.* and *pp.* **wrung.** (A.S. *wringan* press, strain.)

wring-bolt, *n.* an eye-bolt formerly used to bend and secure the planks against the timbers till they were fastened [Shipbuilding].

wringer, *n.* *ring*-er, one who wrings; a machine or contrivance for squeezing water out of anything as by wringing.

wringstaff, *n.* *ring*-stahf, a strong bar of wood used in applying wring-bolts.

wrinkle, *n.* *ring*-kl, a small ridge, prominence, or furrow, formed by the shrinking or contraction of any smooth substance; a crease; a fold or rumple; unevenness: *v.t.* to contract into furrows and prominences; to corrugate; to make rough or uneven: *v.i.* to contract into wrinkles; to shrink into furrows and ridges. (A.S. *wrincle.*)

wrinkle, *n.* *ring*-kl, a dodge or artifice; a tip, a piece of information worth having. (A.S. *wrenc*, as *wrench.*)

wrinkly, *a.* *ring*-kle, wrinkled; corrugated; marked with wrinkles.

wrist, *n.* rist, the joint by which the hand is united to the arm and by which the hand turns; the part of a glove or garment covering the wrist; a wrist-pin [Eng.]. (A.S. *wrist.*)

wristband, *n.* *rist*-band *or* *riz*-band, that band or part of a sleeve which covers the wrist.

wristlet, *n.* *rist*-let, a close-fitting or ornamental wristband; the band confining the upper part of a glove; a strap worn round the wrist. **wristlet watch,** a wrist-watch.

wrist-pin, *n.* any pin connecting a rod to a cross-head [Eng.].

wrist-plate, *n.* an oscillating plate bearing wrist-pins for connecting with rods [Eng.].

wrist-watch, *n.* a watch carried on the wrist by means of a strap or bracelet.

writ, *n.* rit, that which is written; a legal document to enforce obedience [Law]; a legal or formal instrument. **Holy Writ,** the Scriptures. (A.S. *writ*, a writing.)

writ, *v.* rit, former *p.* and *pp.* of *write.*

writable, *a.* *ry*-ta-bl, capable of being written or recorded in writing.

writative, *a.* *ry*-ta-tiv, excessively addicted to writing. (After *talkative.*)

write, *v.t.* rite, to form or trace by a pen, pencil, or brush on paper or other material, or by a graver on wood or stone; to put down or express in writing; to send in writing; to engrave; to impress durably; to compose or produce, as an author; to copy; to transcribe: *v.i.* to perform the act of forming characters, letters, or figures, as representative of sounds or ideas; to be employed as a clerk or an amanuensis; to work as an author; to recite or relate in books; to communicate by letter; to send letters; to use the style of; to compose; to frame or combine ideas and express them in writing. **write down,** to commit to writing; to disparage; to reduce the amount or value of. **write down to,** to appeal to a low level (of intelligence, education, etc.). **write off,** to cancel, esp. by a recitifying entry. **write up,** to write a complete account of; to exaggerate an estimate or figure; to praise highly or unduly; to bring to date. *p.* **wrote.** *pp.* **written** (both formerly **writ**). (A.S. *writan.*)

writer, *n.* *ry*-ter, one who writes or has written; a scribe or scrivener; an author; a clerk or amanuensis; a penman; a lawyer or solicitor [Scots.]; a clerk or accountant in the Paymaster's branch [Navy]; a manual of instruction in calligraphy [Coll.]. **Writer to the Signet,** in Scotland, a law-agent or solicitor who conducts cases before the Court of Session. **writers' cramp,** incoordination of the muscles of the hand due to overmuch writing.

writership, *n.* *ry*-ter-ship, the office of a writer.

write-up, *n.* *rite*-up, a press report; an adulatory notice, a puff [Coll.].

writhe, *v.i.* rithe, to twist the body as if in pain; to squirm: *v.t.* to distort; to twist with violence: *n.* a writhing movement; a contortion. (A.S. *writhan*, twist about.)

★**writing,** *a.* *ry*-ting, used or intended for writing: *n.* the act or art of forming letters and characters for the purpose of recording or communicating ideas; anything written or expressed in letters; a manuscript; any legal instrument; any written composition; a book; a pamphlet; an inscription. **the writing on the wall,** an indication of approaching catastrophe.

writing-book, *n.* a copy-book; a book for practice in penmanship.

writing-case, *n.* a portable case for writing materials, usually having provision for use as a desk.

writing-desk, *n.* a desk or box with a sloping top fitted for the reception of writing materials.

writing-master, *n.* one who teaches the art of penmanship.

writing-paper, *n.* a smooth-surfaced paper specially made for writing upon; notepaper.

written, *a.* *rit*-en, expressed in writing. **written law,** laws enacted and reduced to writing; statutes, as distinct from unwritten or common law.
wrong, *a.* rong, not physically right; not fit or suitable; not appropriate for use; not morally right; deviating from rectitude; not just or equitable; not legal; not according to truth; erroneous; in error; incorrect; false; unjust; unfit; *ad.* not rightly; amiss; morally ill; erroneously. **in the wrong box,** in an unintended position or situation; out of one's element. **wrong end of the stick,** *see* **stick. wrong 'un,** [Coll.] a scoundrel; an untrustworthy or criminal person; a counterfeit or forgery (of coin, cheques, etc.). (A.S. *wrang*, from *wringan*, to wrest.)
wrong, *ad.* rong, in a direction other than the right one; by an incorrect way; wrongfully; improperly. **don't get me wrong,** [U.S.A. Coll.] don't misunderstand me. **go wrong,** to go astray; to fail; to happen amiss; to cease to operate through breakdown, etc.
***wrong,** *n.* rong, whatever deviates from moral rectitude; any injury done to another; a trespass; a violation of right. **in the wrong,** in a wrong position; in error. **private wrongs,** civil injuries immediately affecting individuals; **public wrongs,** crimes and misdemeanours which affect the community.
wrong, *v.t.* rong, to injure; to treat with injustice; to deprive of some right, or to withhold some act of justice from; to do injustice to by imputation.
wrongdoer, *n.* *rong*-doo-er *or* rong-*doo*-er, one who injures another; one who commits a tort or trespass [Law].
wrongdoing, *n.* *rong*-doo-ing, evil or wicked action; breach of law.
wronger, *n.* *rong*-er, one who wrongs or injures another; one who does wrong.
wrongful, *a.* *rong*-ful, injurious; unjust; contrary to moral law or justice.
wrongfully, *ad.* unjustly; illegally; erroneously.
wrongfulness, *n.* the state of being wrongful; injustice.
wrong-headed, *a.* rong-*hed*-ed, wrong in opinion or principle; having a perverse understanding; perverse.
wrong-headedness, *n.* perverseness; erroneousness.
wrongly, *ad.* *rong*-le, in a wrong manner; unjustly.
wrongness, *n.* *rong*-ness, the state of being wrong; wrong disposition; error.
wrongous, *a.* *rong*-us, characterized by illegality or misdirection, illegal [Scots. Law].
wrote, *v.* rote, *p.* of *write.*
wroth, *a.* rohth, roth, *or* rawth, very angry; much exasperated; wrathful. (A.S. *wrath*, twisted, from *writhan*, twist or writhe.)
wrought, *a.* rawt, worked upon for use; worked into shape; formed by work or labour. **wrought iron,** puddled iron; iron rendered malleable by slight admixture of slag and carbon. **wrought on,** influenced; prevailed on. **wrought up,** greatly excited, inflamed. (Former alternative *p.* and *pp.* of *work.*)
wrung, *v.* rung, *p.* and *pp.* of *wring.*
wry, *a.* ry, twisted; turned to one side; distorted; not straight; deviating from the right direction; wrested; perverted; cross, or ill-natured (of speech); *v.t.* and *i.* to twist or contort the features or limbs; to writhe; to wriggle. (A.S. *wrigian*, to strive, bend.)
wrybill, *n.* *ry*-bil, a New Zealand shore-bird, *Anarhynchus frontalis*, allied to the plover, having a bent beak.
wryly, *ad.* *ry*-le, in a wry manner.
wryneck, *n.* *ry*-nek, a bird of the woodpecker family, *Iynx torquilla*; torticollis, a twisted or distorted neck, in which the occiput is drawn down to one side [Med.]; a spasmodic disease in sheep.
wry-necked, *a.* *ry*-nekt, having a stiff or distorted neck; affected with torticollis.
wryness, *n.* *ry*-ness, the state of being wry or distorted; crookedness.
wuff, *n.* wuf, the low suppressed bark of a dog: *v.i.* to make this sound. (Imit.)
wulfenite, *n.* *vool*-fen-ite, a native crystalline molybdate of lead, yellow lead ore. (F. von *Wulfen*, Austrian mineralogist, *d.* 1805.)
wurley, *n.* *wer*-le, the hut of a South Australian aboriginal. (Native.)
Wyandotte, *n.* *wy*-an-dot, a breed of medium-sized fowls, originally American. (Name of an Amerind. tribe.)
wych-elm, *n.* *witch*-elm, a species of elm, *Ulmus montana*; the wood of this. (A.S. *wice*, bent, as *wicker.*)
wych-hazel, *n.* *witch*-hay-zl, a shrub of the genus *Hamamelis*; a preparation from its bark used medicinally; also, the hornbeam. (*wych* as in *wych-elm.*)
Wycliffite, *n.* *wik*-lif-ite, a follower of John Wycliffe, the pre-Reformation English Reformer, or of his teaching; a Lollard; *a.* pertaining to Wycliffe, his teachings, or his followers.
wye, *n.* wy, a crotch; anything in the shape of Y.
Wykehamist, *n.* *wik*-ha-mist, one educated at either Winchester College or at New College, Oxford, both founded in the late 14th cent. by William of Wykeham (now Wickham), Hants.
wynd, *n.* wynd, a narrow lane or alley [Scots.].
wyvern, *n.* *wy*-vern, an imaginary animal with the forepart of a dragon, the legs of an eagle, a coiled barbed tail, and wings usually depicted erect [Her.]. (O.Fr. *wivre.*)

X

X, ex, twenty-fourth letter of the English alphabet: its usual pronunciation is *ks* (*axiom, expense,* etc.), but is sometimes *gz* (*examine, anxiety*), *ksh* (*anxious*), or *gsh* (*luxurious*), while when used initially it is *z* (*xenophobia*). As a Roman numeral it represents 10; in Algebra it stands for the first unknown quantity; in Electrical Engineering it is the symbol of reactance, and in Radio the pl. (**Xs**) is that of atmospherics.
xanthate, *n. zan*-thate, a salt of xanthic acid.
xanthation, *n.* zan-*thay*-shon, conversion into a xanthate, esp. as a process in rayon manufacture.
xanthein, *n. zan*-the-in, the soluble portion of the yellow colouring matter of flowers. (Gr. *xanthos,* yellow.)
xanthelasma, *n.* zan-the-*laz*-ma, xanthoma, esp. of the eyelid.
Xanthian, *a. zan*-the-an, pertaining to Xanthus, an ancient city of Lycia, Asia Minor, esp. of the marbles found there, 1838-42, and now in the British Museum.
xanthic, *a. zan*-thik, tending toward a yellow colour. **xanthic acid,** a colourless, bitter, oily liquid consisting of bisulphide of carbon, water, and oxide of ethyl or ether. **xanthic oxide,** former name of xanthine.
xanthin, *n. zan*-thin, xanthein; the soluble yellow colouring-matter present in madder.
xanthinspar, *n.* wulfenite.
xanthine, *n. zan*-thin, a brown nitrogenous non-poisonous alkaloid allied to uric acid occurring in the tissues and in urinary calculi.
xanthite, *n. zan*-thite, a yellow variety of idocrase.
Xanthium, *n. zan*-the-um, a genus of coarse composite plants, many of which bear burrs.
Xanthochroi, *n.* zan-*thok*-ro-eye, a division of the Caucasian races comprising the fair whites or blond blue-eyed peoples [Ethn.]. (Gr. *xanthos,* and *chroa,* colour.)
xanthochroia, *n.* zan-tho-*kroy*-a, xanthosis [Path.].
xanthochroic, *a.* zan-tho-*kroh*-ik, belonging or pertaining to the Xanthochroi; of fair complexion [Ethn.].
xanthochroism, *n.* zan-tho-*kroh*-izm, abnormal yellow coloration, esp. in the feathers of certain parrots.
xanthochromia, *n.* zan-tho-*kroh*-me-a, a yellow discoloration of the skin similar to that of jaundice [Path.].
xanthochroous, *a.* zan-*thok*-ro-us, xanthrochroic.
xanthoconite, *n.* zan-*thok*-o-nite, a dull red arseniosulphide of silver.
xanthodermatous, *a.* zan-tho-*der*-ma-tus, yellow-skinned [Ethn.]. (Gr. *xanthos,* and *derma,* skin.)
xanthogenic, *a.* zan-tho-*jen*-ik, producing a yellow colour; xanthic.
xanthoma, *n.* zan-*thoh*-ma, a skin disease in which yellow tumours or patches appear.
xanthomelanous, *a. zan*-tho-*mel*-a-nus, having a yellow skin and black hair [Ethn.].
xanthophyll, *n. zan*-tho-fil, the yellow colouring matter of autumn leaves and of certain animal fats. (Gr. *xanthos,* and *phyllon,* a leaf.)
xanthophyllite, *n. zan*-tho-*fil*-ite, a crystalline silicate of magnesium, calcium, and aluminium, leaf-like in structure.
xanthopsia, *n.* zan-*thop*-se-a, the abnormal condition in which objects appear yellow [Path.]. (Gr. *xanthos,* and *opsis,* condition of.)
Xanthorrhiza, *n. zan*-tho-*ry*-za, a N. American genus of ranunculaceous shrubs of which the only species is the yellowroot. (Gr. *xanthos,* and *rhiza,* a root.)
xanthosiderite, *n. zan*-tho-*sid*-er-ite, a brownish oxide of iron.
xanthosis, *n.* zan-*thoh*-sis, yellow discoloration of the skin, esp. in certain cancerous affections [Med.].
xanthous, *a. zan*-thus, of a yellowish or Mongoloid race [Ethn.].
Xantippe, *n.* zan-*tip*-e, a scold; a quarrelsome woman. (After the wife of Socrates.)
xebec, *n. zee*-bek, a small felucca usually square-rigged on the foremast. (Turk.)
Xema, *n. zee*-ma, the genus of birds comprising the fork-tailed gulls.
xenelasia, *n.* zen-e-*lay*-se-a, the system in ancient Sparta of excluding or expelling strangers. (Gr. *xenos,* stranger, *elaunein,* drive away.)
xenial, *a. zee*-ne-al, pertaining to hospitality or to the guest-host relationship.
xenium, *n. zee*-ne-um (*pl.* **xenia**), a present anciently given to a guest or foreign ambassador. (L., from Gr. *xenos,* guest, stranger.)
xenodochium, *n. zee*-no-*dok*-e-um, a room or building for guests, esp. in a monastery. (Gr. *xenos,* and *dechomai,* receive.)
xenogamous, *a.* ze-*nog*-a-mus, characterized by xenogamy [Bot.].
xenogamy, *n.* ze-*nog*-a-me, cross-fertilization; pollination from another plant. (Gr. *xenos,* and *gamos,* marriage.)
xenogenesis, *n. zen*-o-*jen*-e-sis, heterogenesis. (Gr.)
xenogenous, *a.* ze-*noj*-e-nus, due to an outside cause or to a foreign body (of disease) [Path.]. (Gr. *xenos,* and *gennao,* produce.)
xenolite, *n. zen*-o-lite, a fibrous silicate of aluminium allied to sillimanite.
xenolith, *n. zen*-o-lith, a piece of extraneous rock incorporated in magma [Geol.].
xenomania, *n. zee*-no-*may*-ne-a, undue admiration for foreigners, or for that which is foreign.
xenomorphic, *a. zee*-no-*mor*-fik, abnormal in shape owing to pressure [Geol.].
xenon, *n. zee*-non, an inert gaseous element of the helium group occurring in very minute quantities in the atmosphere.
xenophobe, *n. zen*-o-fobe, one afflicted with xenophobia.
xenophobia, *n. zen*-o-*foh*-be-a, a fear, dread, or morbid hatred of foreigners or of what is foreign. (Gr. *xenos,* a stranger, *phobos,* fear.)
xenotime, *n. zen*-o-time, a native phosphate of yttrium of a yellowish-brown colour. (Fr., from Gr. *xenos,* and *tīmē,* honour.)
Xeranthemum, *n.* ze-*ran*-the-mum, a small genus of everlasting composite flowers of southern Europe; (*l.c.*) a member of this genus; an immortelle. (Gr. *xeros,* dry, *anthos,* flower.)
xerantic, *a.* ze-*ran*-tik, characterized by or pertaining to xeransis.
xeransis, *n.* ze-*ran*-sis, dessication [Path.]
xerasia, *n.* ze-*ray*-she-a, excessive dryness in the hair causing cessation of growth [Med.]. (Gr. *xerasia,* dryness, from *xeros,* dry.)
xeroderma, *n.* zeer-ro-*der*-ma, a scaly disease of the skin; ichthyosis. (Gr. *xeros,* and *derma,* skin.)
xerodermatous, *a.* zeer-ro-*der*-ma-tus, affected by or characteristic of xeroderma.
xeroma, *n.* zeer-*roh*-ma, abnormal dryness due to lack of secretion [Path]; xerophthalmia.
xeromyrum, *n.* ze-*rom*-e-rum, a dry ointment. (Gr. *xeros,* and *myron,* a perfume.)
xerophagy, *n.* ze-*rof*-a-je, subsistence on a dry or meagre diet, esp. as a fast among primitive Christians. (Gr. *xeros,* and *phago,* eat.)
xerophile, *n. zeer*-ro-fil, a xerophyte.
xerophilous, *a.* zeer-*rof*-e-lus, able to withstand drought, esp. of desert vegetation.
xerophthalmia, *n. zeer*-rof-*thal*-me-a, a dry, red soreness or itching of the eyes. (Gr. *xeros,* and *ophthalmos,* the eye.)
xerophyte, *n. zeer*-ro-fite, a plant growing in or suited for a dry climate or soil.
xerophytic, *a. zeer*-ro-*fit*-ik, xerophilous; adapted for dry conditions [Bot.].
xerosis, *n.* ze-*roh*-sis, abnormal dryness, as of the skin; xeroma.
xerostomia, *n. zeer*-ro-*stoh*-me-a, dryness of the mouth due to lack of saliva [Path.].
xerotes, *n.* ze-*roh*-teez, a dry habit or disposition of the body [Path.].

xerotic, *a.* ze-*rot*-ik, dry [Path.].
Xiphias, *n.* *zif*-e-as, the genus of fishes including the swordfish; one of the constellations of the southern hemisphere. (Gr. *xiphos*, a sword.)
xiphioid, *a.* *zif*-e-oyd, resembling or allied to the swordfish.
xiphoid, *a.* *zif*-oyd, sword shaped, ensiform; esp. of the small process or cartilage at the lower end of the breast-bone: *n.* the xiphoid process [Anat.]. (Gr. *xiphos*, and *eidos*, like.)
xiphisternum, *n.* zif-e-*ster*-num, the xiphoid process [Anat.].
xiphopagus, *n.* ze-*fop*-a-gus, the double monster known as "Siamese twins" united by a band in the region of the xiphoid process. (*xiphoid*, and Gr. *pegnynai*, to unite.)
xoanon, *n.* *zoh*-a-non (*pl.* **xoana**), a primitive representation in carved wood of a deity. (Gr.)
X-rays, *n.pl.* eks-rayz, Röntgen rays, the invisible rays by which the interior of many solids can be photographed (so called by Röntgen).
xylan, *n.* *zy*-lan, a gummy substance present in woody tissue. (Gr. *xylon*, wood.)
xylem, *n.* *zy*-lem, woody tissue [Bot.].
xylene, *n.* *zy*-leen, xylol; also, any one of the three isomeric hydrocarbons of which xylol is composed.
xylite, *n.* *zy*-lite, an impure silicate of iron, lime, and magnesium, of asbestos-like structure.
xylobalsamum, *n.* *zy*-lo-*bal*-sa-mum, the fragrant wood of *Commiphora meccanansis*, the tree yielding balm of Gilead.
xylocarp, *n.* *zy*-lo-karp, a hard woody fruit [Bot.].
xylogen, *n.* *zy*-lo-jen, xylem [Bot.].
xylograph, *n.* *zy*-lo-graf, an early wood-engraving; any print made by xylography.
xylographer, *n.* zy-*log*-ra-fer, a wood-engraver.
xylographic, *a.* zy-lo-*graf*-ik, pertaining to xylography or wood-engraving. (Gr. *xylon*, and *grapho*, write.)
xylography, *n.* zy-*log*-ra-fe, wood-engraving; the act or art of printing from wood blocks.
xyloid, *a.* *zy*-loyd, like wood; woody. (Gr.)
xylol, *n.* *zy*-lol, wood-oil; an isomeric dimethyl benzene used as a solvent in dye-stuffs.
xylometer, *n.* zy-*lom*-e-ter, an instrument for ascertaining the specific gravity of wood.
xylonite, *n.* *zy*-lo-nite, the trade name of a variety of celluloid.
xylophagan, *n.* zy-*lof*-a-gan, any wood-boring or wood-eating insect or larva.
xylophagous, *a.* zy-*lof*-a-gus, eating, feeding on, or boring into wood, as the wood-gnawing insects and certain molluscs.
xylophone, *n.* *zy*-lo-fone, a harmonica in which the glass slips are replaced by slips of hard wood.
xylophonist, *n.* zy-*lof*-o-nist, a performer on the xylophone.
xylopyrography, *n.* *zy*-lo-py-*rog*-ra-fe, the art or practice of engraving on wood by charring it; poker-work. (Gr. *xylon*, wood, *pyr*, fire, *grapho*, write.)
xylose, *n.* *zy*-lohs, a crystalline carbo-hydrate obtained by the hydrolysis of xylan; wood-sugar.
xylotomous, *n.* zy-*lot*-o-mus, given to or capable of boring into wood [Zool.].
xyst, *n.* zist, a xystus.
xyster, *n.* *zis*-ter, a surgeon's instrument for scraping bones. (Gr. *xyo*, scrape.)
xystus, *n.* *zis*-tus, a long covered court for athletic exercises; a colonnade. (Gr. *xystos*, scraped, polished.)

Y

Y, wy, the twenty-fifth letter of the English alphabet, is either consonantal, as in *year, yew, beyond*, or vocalic, as in *cry, crystal, fancy, myrtle*, etc. It occasionally represents the A.S. letter "thorn" (*see* **T**), and in Algebra stands for the second unknown quantity. It is also used to denote any (capital) Y-shaped object or part, as *Y-connexion, Y-track*, etc. **Y-moth**, a noctuid moth of the genus *Plusia*, having a Y-shaped mark on the wings.
yabber, *n. yab*-er, jabber, esp. the broken English of Australian aborigines: *v.i.* to talk in this. (Austral. native.)
yacca, *n. yak*-a, either of two small W. Indian trees of the genus *Podocarpus*, the wood of which is used in cabinet-work.
yacht, *n.* yot, originally a fast sailing-ship, now a vessel used for pleasure or racing: *v.i.* to sail in a yacht. (Dut. *jacht*.)
yachter, *n. yot*-er, a yachtsman; one who sails in a yacht.
yachting, *a. yot*-ing, pertaining to yachts; given to yachtsmanship: *n.* sailing in a yacht.
yachtsman, *n. yots*-man, one who owns, sails in, or is skilled in the management of, a yacht.
yachtsmanship, *n. yots*-man-ship, the art or practice of sailing a yacht.
yaffle, *n. yaf*-fl, the green woodpecker.
yager, *n. yay*-ger, a German rifleman; a German fighter aircraft, also, its pilot. (Ger. *Jäger*, a huntsman.)
yah, *int.* yah, an exclamation of contempt, derision, etc.
Yahoo, *n.* yah-*hoo* or *yah*-hoo, a name given by Swift in "Gulliver's Travels" to a race of degraded, brutalized men; hence, a rude, boorish, or bestial person.
Yahweh, *n. yah*-ve, Jehovah (Heb.).
Yahwist, *n. yah*-vist, Jahvist.
yak, *n.* yak, a species of ox, *Bos grunniens*, found in Central Asia, both wild and domesticated, covered with long silky hair. (Tib. *gyak*.)
Yakut, *n.* yah-*koot*, a member of a Turki race of N.E. Siberia; their language.
yam, *n.* yam, a large esculent tuber or root of various tropical climbing plants of the genus *Dioscorea*; any plant of this genus; applied also, in U.S.A., to the sweet-potato. **yam bean**, a tropical climbing plant of the genus *Pachyrhizus*.
Yama, *n. yah*-ma, the lord and judge of the Hindu nether world, having been the first mortal to die [Hindu Myth.].
yamen, *n. yah*-men, a mandarin's official residence; also, a Chinese government office [Chin.].
yammer, *v.i. yam*-er, to whine or whimper; to speak in a stammering way.
yank, *v.t.* yank, to jerk; to pull or twitch suddenly: *n.* a sharp pull or twitch [Coll.].
Yank, *n.* yank, a Yankee [Slang].
Yankee, *n. yang*-ke, a name given to the Americans of New England, but applied indiscriminately to inhabitants of the United States; American English, esp. the dialect of New England: *a.* pertaining to or characteristic of the Yankees; American. (Probably a diminutive of Dut. *Jan*, or perhaps an Indian pronunciation of *English* or *Anglais*.)
Yankeefied, *a.* yang-ke-fide, having adopted American characteristics, style, habits, etc.; Americanized.
Yankeeism, *n. yang*-ke-izm, a Yankee idiom, characteristic, or practice.
yanolite, *n. yan*-o-lite, a mineral consisting chiefly of silica, alumina, lime, and iron, and having acute-edged crystals resembling an axe-head. (Gr. *ianthos*, violet, *lithos*, stone.)
yaourt, *n. yah*-oort, a thick fermented liquor, similar to koumiss, made by the Turks from milk. (Turk. *yoghurt*.)
yap, *n.* yap, a yelp: *v.i.* to bark like a cur; to blather or chatter. (Imit.)
yapok, *n. yap*-ok, a small Brazilian water opossum, *Chironectes minimus*. (River *Oyapok*, in Guiana.)
yapon, *n. yaw*-pon, a southern U.S.A. evergreen of the genus *Ilex*, the leaves of which form a substitute for tea; the drink prepared from these. (Native.)
yapp, *n.* yap, a style of book-binding in which the limp cover overlaps the edges of the book. (Name of first user, about 1850.)
yapper, *n. yap*-er, one who or a dog which yaps.
yarborough, *n. yar*-bu-ra, a hand at whist, etc., that holds no ten or honour. (Earl of *Yarborough*.)
yard, *n.* yard, a measure or measuring rod of 3 ft. or 36 in.; a spar used for spreading a square-sail [Naut.]; (in Chaucer, etc.) the penis. (A.S. *gyrd*, a rod.)
yard, *n.* yard, a small enclosed area adjoining a house or barn; an enclosure for any purpose: *v.t.* to collect in or confine cattle to a yard. (A.S. *geard*, an enclosure.)
yardage, *n. yard*-aj, quantity, extent, etc., as measured in yards; charge for storing or impounding in a yard.
yard-arm, *n.* the outer end of a ship's yard.
yard-man, *n.* a man employed in a farmyard, railway-yard, etc.; a sailor who works on the yards [Naut.].
yard-master, *n.* a man in charge of a railway-yard.
yard-measure, *n.* a graduated tape or steel ribbon measuring one yard; a yardstick.
yardstick, *n. yard*-stik, a 3-ft. stick, usually graduated, used as a measure; a standard or criterion with or by which something may be measured or compared [Fig.].
yardwand, *n. yard*-wond, a yardstick.
yare, *a.* yare, quick; dexterous; eager. (A.S. *gearu*, ready.)
yarely, *ad. yare*-le, quickly; dexterously.
yarn, *n. yarn*, spun thread; one of the threads of which a rope is composed; a tale, a long rambling story (originally one spun out by a sailor for the amusement of his mates): *v.i.* to tell or spin yarns; to talk ramblingly. (A.S. *gearn*.)
yarr, *n.* yar, spurrey, a plant of the genus *Spergula*.
yarrow, *n. ya*-ro, a plant of the genus *Achillea*; the milfoil. (A.S.)
yarwhelp, *n. yar*-whelp, the bar-tailed godwit, *Limosa lapponica*.
yashmak, *n. yash*-mak, the veil, leaving only the eyes exposed, worn by Moslem women in public. (Ar. *yashmaq*.)
yataghan, *n. yat*-a-gan, a short curved oriental sabre with no guard for the hand. (Turk.)
yate, *n.* yate, any of various Australian gum-trees, esp. *Eucalyptus cornute*; the timber of these. (W. Austral. native.)
yaup, *v.i.* yawp, to yap; to whine [Scots.].
yaupon, *n. yaw*-pon, yapon.
yaw, *v.i.* yaw, to rise in blisters breaking in white froth, as cane-juice under clarification: *n.* one of the pustules occurring in yaws.
yaw, *v.i.* yaw, to deviate to left or right of the intended course: *v.t.* to steer unsteadily: *n.* the action of yawing [Naut.]. (Perhaps Scand. *jaga*, move to and fro.)
yawey, *a. yaw*-e, affected with yaws.
yawing, *n. yaw*-ing, the action of the verb *to yaw*; a rotary or unstable motion about the normal axis of an aeroplane [Av.].
yawl, *n.* yawl, a boat with two masts of which the mizen is much smaller than the main and stepped abaft the sternpost; a light sailing-vessel; a jolly-boat. (Dut.)
yawl, *v.i.* yawl, to cry out or howl: *n.* a yell; a howl. (*yell*.)
yawling, *n. yaw*-ling, an immature herring.
yawmeter, *n. yaw*-mee-ter, a device for determining the angle of yawing [Av.].
yawn, *n.* yawn, a gaping; an involuntary gape; the act of yawning; oscitation: *v.i.* to gape; to

have the mouth open involuntarily, through drowsiness or dullness ; to open wide : *v.t.* to express desire, etc., by yawning. (A.S. *geonian.*)
yawningly, *ad. yaw*-ning-le, in a yawning manner.
yaws, *n.pl.* yawz, frambœsia ; a highly contagious tropical disease, prevalent among Negroes, characterized by cutaneous tumours that swell into pustules the size of a raspberry. (Origin unknown —probably African.)
yclad, *pp.* e-*klad*, clad (the *y-* is an old English particle prefixed to past participles).
yclept, *pp.* e-*klept*, called ; named.
ydrad, *pp.* e-*drad*, dreaded.
ye, *pron.* yee, the nominative plural of the second person, of which *thou* is the singular, now superseded by *you*, except in the solemn style. [For **ye,** the sham archaic form of *the*, see **T.**] (A.S. *ge.*)
yea, *ad.* yay, yes ; a word that expresses affirmation or assent ; not only so, but more ; in Scripture, used to denote certainty, consistency, harmony, and stability. (A.S. *gea.*)
yea-and-nay, *a.* unable to come to a decision ; vacillating ; ambiguous.
yean, *v.i.* yeen, to bring forth young (esp. of sheep and goats) ; to lamb. (A.S. *eanian.*)
yeanling, *n. yeen*-ling, a new-born lamb, an eanling.
★**year,** *n.* yer, the period of time in which the sun moves through the twelve signs of the ecliptic and returns to the same point, esp. the **calendar** or **civil year,** viz., the 12 months, or 365 days (in leap year 366 days), from 1 Jan. to 31 Dec., or any period of 365 consecutive days ; the time in which any planet completes a revolution : *pl.* age or old age. **astronomical year,** the period from equinox to equinox, *i.e.*, 365 days, 5 hrs. 48 min. 50 sec. **ecclesiastical year,** *see* **ecclesiastical. equinoctial year,** the astronomical year (*above*). **Great year,** the Platonic year. **Julian year,** a period of 365¼ days. **leap year,** the bissextile (*see* **leap-year**). **legal year,** the calendar or civil year (*above*). **lunar year,** *see* **lunar. natural year,** the astronomical year. **Platonic, regnal, Sabbatical, sidereal year,** *see* these words. **solar** and **tropical year,** alternative names for the astronomical year (*above*). **full of years,** aged, very old. **year in year out,** continuously ; from year to year. **year of grace,** the year dating from the birth of Christ. **years of discretion,** *see* **discretion.** (A.S. *gear.*)
year-book, *n.* a book published annually with information up to date ; an annual statistical book of reference.
yearling, *a. yer*-ling, being a year old : *n.* a young beast one year old or in its second year ; a colt or filly not having reached its first 1st of January (Horse-racing).
year-long, *a.* lasting a year.
yearly, *a. yer*-le, annual ; happening, accruing, or coming every year ; lasting a year ; comprehending a year : *ad.* annually ; once a year.
yearn, *v.i.* yern, to feel an earnest desire : to have an uneasy feeling from longing, tenderness, or pity ; to be strained ; to be pained or distressed : *v.t.* to pain ; to grieve ; to vex. (A.S. *georn*, desirous.)
yearnful, *a. yern*-ful, mournful ; distressing.
yearning, *ppr.* and *a. yern*-ing, longing ; having longing desire : *n.* strong emotion of desire, tenderness, or pity.
yearningly, *ad. yern*-ing-le, with yearning.
yeast, *n.* yeest, a viscous substance consisting of the cells of minute fungi developed in saccharine liquids and inducing alcoholic fermentation by means of an enzyme ; barm ; any preparation used for raising dough ; spume or foam of water in agitation : *v.i.* to froth ; to ferment ; to become yeasty. (A.S. *gist.*
yeastiness, *n. yees*-te-ness, the state of being yeasty.
yeasty, *a. yees*-te, like yeast ; frothy ; foamy ; spumy.
yeldrin, *n. yel*-drin, the yellow-hammer.
yelk, *n.* yelk, the yellow part of the contents of an egg ; the yolk.
yell, *n.* yel, a sharp, loud, hideous outcry ; a college cry or slogan ; a concerted cheer [U.S.A.] : *v.i.* to emit a yell ; to cry out with a hideous noise ; to cry or scream, as with agony or horror. (A.S. *gellan.*)
yeller, *n. yel*-er, one who yells.
yelling, *a. yel*-ing, emitting a yell or yells ; uttering hideous outcries ; shrieking ; *n.* the act of screaming hideously.
★**yellow,** *a. yel*-oh, being of the colour of pale gold, lemon, sulphur, etc. ; jaundiced, melancholic [Fig.] ; dishonourable, contemptible [Slang] ; sensational (of the press and journalism) [Slang] : *n.* a bright colour, like that of pale gold, which, after white, reflects more light than any other colour, and occurs in the solar spectrum between green and orange : *v.t.* to make yellow : *v.i.* to turn or become yellow ; to fade or wither. **yellow ammer** or **yellow bunting,** the yellow-hammer. **yellow fever,** a malignant infectious febrile disease of warm climates, often attended with yellowness of the skin, the virus of which is transmitted by a mosquito, *Ædes ægypti.* **yellow peril,** the danger of the ultimate dominance of the prolific yellow, or Mongoloid, races over the whites. **yellow rattle,** *see* **rattlebox. yellow spot,** a circular depression at the back of the eyeball surrounding the point of acutest vision. **yellow streak,** [Coll.] cowardice; the 'white feather.'
yellow-back, *n.* a cheap popular novel of a class formerly sold cased in yellow boards [Coll.].
yellowbird, *n. yel*-oh-berd, a name given in the United States to the goldfinch and other small yellow-plumaged song-birds.
yellow-boy, *n.* a guinea, or other gold coin [Slang].
yellow-earth, *n.* ochre ; any clay coloured by iron.
yellow-hammer, *n.* a small yellow-plumaged finch, *Emberiza citrinella*, common in Europe and Great Britain. (*yellow*, and A.S. *amore*, probably a bird of some kind.)
yellowish, *a. yel*-oh-ish, somewhat yellow ; having a yellow tinge.
yellowishness, *n.* the quality of being somewhat yellow.
yellowness, *n. yel*-oh-ness, the quality or condition of being yellow ; yellow colour.
yellowroot, *n. yel*-oh-root, a small ranunculaceous shrub of N. America, *Xanthorrhiza apiifolia* ; applied also to other plants with yellowish roots.
yellows, *n. yel*-ohz, a form of jaundice in horses and other domestic animals [Vet.] ; a plant disease causing yellowness of foliage.
yellowshank, *n. yel*-oh-shank, the sandpiper *Totanus flavipes.*
yellow-wort, *n.* the yellow centaury, *Chlora perfoliata*, so named from its dyeing yellow.
yellowy, *a. yel*-oh-e, yellowish.
yelp, *n.* yelp, a quick sharp bark ; the cry of a dog when in pain : *v.i.* to bark with sharp shrill sounds. (A.S. *gielpan*, boast.)
yelper, *n. yel*-per, an animal that, or one who, yelps ; applied also to the avocet, redshank, and other birds.
yen, *n.* yen, the Japanese monetary unit, containing 100 sen and equal (before 1945) at par to about two shillings.
yen, *n.* yen, an intense longing ; ardent desire : *v.i.* to yearn ; to have an overpowering urge toward [U.S.A. slang].
yenite, *n. yen*-ite, former name of ilvaite. (Commemorating battle of Jena, 1806.)
yeoman, *n. yoh*-man, a farmer who owns and cultivates his land ; a small freeholder ; a member of a body of yeomanry. **yeoman of signals,** a petty officer in the signalling branch of the Royal Navy. **Yeomen of the Guard,** a bodyguard of the sovereign ; the beefeaters. **yeoman's service,** loyal and welcome assistance or support. (M.E. *yoman.*)
yeomanly, *a.* pertaining to, befitting, or characteristic of a yeoman ; sturdy.
yeomanry, *n. yoh*-man-re, a volunteer cavalry or mounted infantry force, originally consisting of gentlemen and well-to-do farmers who provided their own horses, equipment, etc. ; irregular mounted riflemen.
yep, *ad.* yep, yes [Slang].
yerba, *n. yer*-bah, any plant, but used esp. of maté (**yerba maté**) or Paraguay tea. (Sp., a herb.)
yercum, *n.* yer-kum, an East Indian shrub of the genus *Callotropis*, the sap of which is a powerful purgative ; mudar (Tamil.).
yerk, *n.* yerk, a jerk : *v.t.* to throw or thrust with a jerk or sudden smart spring.
★**yes,** *ad.* yes, an expression of affirmation of consent ; opposed to **no.** (A.S. *gea*, yea, *si*, let it be.)

yes-man, *n.* *yes*-man, an irresolute or pliable person; a weakling of no fixed principle or grounded opinion [U.S.A. Slang].

yester, *a.* *yes*-ter, pertaining to the preceding day (used also of any immediately preceding period, *e.g.*, *yester-year*). (A.S. *geostra.*)

★**yesterday,** *n.* *yes*-ter-day, the day last past: *ad.* on the day before the present day.

yesternight, *n.* *yes*-ter-nite, last night: *ad.* on the night of yesterday.

yestreen, *n.* yes-*treen*, last evening: *ad.* on the evening of yesterday. (*yester-e'en.*)

yet, *ad.* yet, besides; over and above; still; at this time; so soon; at least; at all; still; in a new degree; even; after all; hitherto: *conj.* nevertheless; notwithstanding; however. **as yet,** hitherto, up to now.

yew, *n.* yew, the spreading evergreen tree *Taxus baccata*; its timber, or branches; a bow of yew: *a.* relating to the yew; made of yew. (A.S. *iw.*)

yewen, *a.* *yew*-en, made of yew.

yex, *n.* yeks, a hiccough: *v.i.* to hiccough. (A.S. *geocsa*, a sobbing.)

Yggdrasil, *n.* *ig*-dra-sil, the mystic ash tree the roots of which bind together earth, heaven, and the nether world [Scand. Myth.].

Yid, *n.* yid, (offensive slang for) a Jew or Yiddisher.

Yiddish, *n.* *yid*-ish, the mixed dialect language composed chiefly of corrupt Hebrew and provincial German largely used by low-class European Jews: *a.* pertaining to or in Yiddish; [Slang] Jewish. (Ger. *judisch*, Jewish.)

Yiddisher, *n.* *yid*-ish-er, a Jew, esp. one of Eastern or Central Europe [Slang]. (Ger.)

yield, *n.* yeeld, amount yielded; product: *v.t.* to produce, as land, stock, or funds; to give in return for labour, or as profit; to produce in general; to afford, allow, or concede; to admit to be true; to give, as claimed of right; to permit; to grant; to emit; to give up; to resign or surrender: *v.i.* to give up the contest; to submit; to comply with; to give place. (A.S. *gildan*, pay.)

yielder, *n.* *yeel*-der, one who yields; anything that produces or provides.

yielding, *a.* *yeel*-ding, inclined to yield or comply; accommodating: *n.* act of producing; concession; submission.

yieldingly, *ad.* with compliance.

yieldingness, *n.* disposition to comply; quality of yielding.

ylang-ylang, *n.* *ee*-lang-*ee*-lang, the Malayan evergreen shrub *Cananga odorata*; a perfume distilled from its flowers. (Tagalog.)

yo, *int.* yoh, an exclamation calling attention or as a signal for increased effort; used chiefly in combinations, as **yo-ho, yo-heave-ho,** cries used by sailors in heaving ropes, etc.

yodel, *n.* *yoh*-dl, a loud singing sound, interpolated with falsetto, characteristic of certain Swiss mountaineers: *v.t.* to sing in this manner. (Ger. *jodeln.*)

yodeller, *n.* *yoh*-dl-er, one who yodels; an adept at yodelling.

yoga, *n.* *yoh*-gah, in Hindu philosophy, a system of mental discipline and concentration through which occult power and union with the Universal Spirit are attained.

yoghourt, *n.* *yoh*-goort, yaourt.

yogi, *n.* *yoh*-gee, *or* **yogin,** *yoh*-gin, a practiser or devotee of yoga; one who is emancipated from this life through yogism.

yogism, *n.* *yoh*-gizm, the practice of yoga; yoga.

yogh, *n.* yokh, the name of the Middle English letter roughly indicating the *ch* sound in Scottish *loch*.

yo-heave-ho, *int.* *yoh*-heav-*hoh*, *see* **yo.**

yohimbe, *n.* yo-*him*-ba, a rubiaceous tree of tropical Africa, alkaloids prepared from the bark of which are used in medicine.

yo-ho, *int.* yoh-*hoh*, *see* **yo.**

yoick, *v.i.* yoyk, to shout yoicks.

yoicks, *int.* yoyks, a fox-hunting call of encouragement to hounds.

yojan, *n.* *yoh*-jan, an Indian measure of distance, usually about five miles but varying locally. (Hind.)

yoke, *n.* yoke, a piece of timber, hollowed or made curving near each end, and fitted with bows for receiving the necks of oxen, by means of which two are connected for drawing; a pair of draught animals; a pair that work together; a frame of wood fitted to a person's shoulders for carrying a pail suspended on each side; [Fig.] a mark of servitude, slavery, bondage; a bond of connexion; a frame at the head of a boat's rudder, from the end of which are cords by which the boat is steered; the part of a dress, etc., supporting, from shoulders or hips, dependent parts: *v.t.* to put a yoke on; to join in a yoke; to couple; [Fig.] to enslave or bring into bondage, to restrain, to confine. (A.S. *geoc.*)

yoke-elm, *n.* *yoke*-elm, the hornbeam (the wood of which was used for yokes).

yoke-fellow, *n.* one associated with another in some common work; a partner; a spouse.

yokel, *n.* *yoh*-kel, an ignorant rustic; a country bumpkin. (Probably from *yoke.*)

yoke-lines, *n.* the steering cords attached to the yoke of a rudder [Naut.].

yoke-mate, *n.* *yoke*-mate, a yoke-fellow.

yolk, *n.* yoke, the yellow part of the contents of an egg; the contents of an animal's ovum; the unctuous secretion in the skin of sheep, which renders the pile soft and pliable; lanolin. (A.S. *geolca*, yellow part.)

yolky, *a.* *yoh*-ke, consisting of, full of, or resembling yolk; unctuous with yolk.

Yom Kippur, *n.* yohm-*kip*-oor, the Jewish fast of the Day of Atonement. (Heb. *yom*, day, *kippur*, atonement.)

yon, *a.* and *ad.* yon, yonder: *pron.* that, those.

yonder, *a.* and *ad.* *yon*-der, being at a distance and usually within view (used esp. when pointing out any distant object). (A.S. *geon*, that.)

yoni, *n.* *yoh*-ne, a representation of the female organ of generation, used by the Hindus as the symbol of the female power in nature.

yonker, *n.* *yung*-ker, a young fellow; a younker.

yore, *ad.* yore, old time; long ago, as "in days of yore." (A.S. *geara*, of years.)

york, *v.t.* york, to take a wicket with a yorker [Cricket].

yorker, *n.* *york*-er, an overarm tice, a straight ball bowled so as to pitch between the popping crease and the wicket [Cricket].

Yorkist, *n.* *york*-ist, an adherent of the House of York, the party of the White Rose, in the Wars of the Roses.

Yorkshire, *a.* *york*-sher, pertaining to Yorkshire; characteristic of Yorkshiremen. **Yorkshire fog,** velvet grass, *Holcus lanatus*. **Yorkshire pudding,** an unsweetened batter pudding cooked in the drippings under meat. **Yorkshire sanicle,** the butterwort, *Pinguicula vulgaris*. **Yorkshire terrier,** a small toy-terrier with long, straight, fine, glossy hair. **Yorkshire tyke,** a Yorkshireman.

Yorkshireman, *n.* *york*-sher-man, a native of Yorkshire.

★**you,** yoo, *pers. pron. second pers.*: *pl.* as well as *sing*, in the nominative or objective case; anyone. (A.S. *eow*, objective of *ge*, ye.)

★**young,** *a.* yung, not having long been born; being in the first part of life; not old; being in an early stage of growth; representing a modern political, nationalistic, or revolutionary movement: *n.* young persons collectively; the offspring of animals. **his young woman, her young man,** his (her) sweetheart. **with young,** pregnant. (A.S. *geong.*)

youngish, *a.* *yung*-ish, somewhat young.

youngling, *n.* *yung*-ling, any animal in the first part of life; a young person.

youngster, *n.* *yung*-ster, a lad; a hobbledehoy.

younker, *n.* *yung*-ker, a young fellow; a stripling. (Dut. *jonc*, young, *here*, master.)

your, yoor, *pron. a. sing.* and *pl.* belonging to you.

yours, *pron.* yoorz, that or those belonging to you. **you and yours,** yourself and your immediate family.

yourself, *pron.* yoor-*self* (*pl.* **yourselves**), you in your own person.

yourt, *n.* yoort, a hut, tent, or other dwelling-place of Siberian and Central Asian nomads. (Russ.)

youth, *n.* yooth, the state of being young; the part of life that succeeds to childhood, the stages of life being usually divided into infancy, childhood, youth, and manhood; a young man; young persons collectively. (A.S. *geoguth.*)

youthful, *a.* *yooth*-ful, young; pertaining to the early stages of life.

youthfully, *ad.* in a youthful manner.
youthfulness, *n.* the state of being youthful.
youthwort, *n.* *yooth*-wurt, the common sundew, *Drosera rotundifolia*; applied also to the cow-parsnip.
yowl, *v.i.* youl, to cry out as in pain, distress, etc.; to howl like a dog: *n.* an act, or the sound of yowling; a howl. (Ice. *gaula*, yell.)
yo-yo, *n.* *yoh*-yoh, a spinning toy, a spherical form of bandalore.
yperite, *n.* *ee*-per-rite, mustard gas. (Fr. town *Ypres*.)
ytterbia, *n.* e-*ter*-be-a, oxide of ytterbium.
ytterbic, *a.* e-*ter*-bik, pertaining to or containing ytterbium.
ytterbium, *n.* e-*ter*-be-um, a metallic element of the rare earth group usually occurring in association with yttrium. (*Ytterby*, Sweden, where found.)
yttria, *n.* *it*-re-a, oxide of yttrium.
yttrious, *a.* *it*-re-us, pertaining to or containing yttrium.
yttrium, *n.* *it*-re-um, a metallic element of the rare earth group occurring chiefly in gadolinite. (*Ytterby*, Sweden, where found.)
yttrocerite, *n.* *it*-ro-*seer*-rite, a rare mineral, of a violet-blue colour, inclining to grey and white, composed chiefly of the fluoride of calcium with the metals cerium and yttrium.
yttrotantalite, *n.* *it*-ro-*tan*-ta-lite, an orthorhombic mineral consisting chiefly of tantalum and yttrium, usually in association with calcium, cerium, and niobium.
yuan, *n.* yew-*ahn*, since 1914 the Chinese monetary unit; a silver coin equal, at par, to nearly 1s. 11d.; the Chinese dollar.
Yucca, *n.* *yuk*-a, a genus of whitish-flowered evergreen garden plants of the lily order, natives of subtropical America, including the Adam's needle. (West Indian native.)
yuft, *n.* yuft, russia leather. (Russ.)
yuga, *n.* *yew*-ga, any one of the four ages into which the Hindus divide the duration or existence of the world. (Hind.)
Yugoslav, *a.* yew-goh-*slahv*, pertaining to Yugoslavia: *n.* a native of Yugoslavia. (Southern Slav.)
Yuit, *n.* *yew*-it, an Asiatic Eskimo, as distinct from an Innuit, or Eskimo of N. America. (Native.)
Yulan, *n.* *yew*-lan, the beautiful white-flowered Chinese tree, *Magnolia conspicua*. (Chin.)
yule, *n.* yewl, the festival of Christmas; Christmastide. (A.S. *geol.* feast.)
yule-log, *n.* a large log of wood placed on the fire during Christmas festivities.
yuletide, *n.* *yewl*-tide, Christmastide; the time of yule.
yunx, *n.* yunks, the wryneck, *Iynx torquilla.* (Gr.)
yurt, *n.* yurt, yourt.

Z

Z, called "zed," but in America, and sometimes in Scotland, "zee" (*see also* **izzard**), is the last letter of the English alphabet and came through Greek from Semitic. Its usual pronunciation is that of a sonant "s," as in *zeal*, *amazing*, but it is sometimes palatalized, as in *seizure*. In certain Scots words, as *capercailzie* (and formerly "Mackenzie," etc.) it has the effect of "y." As a symbol it denotes, in Algebra an unknown quantity, and in Electricity impedance.

zaffre, *n.* *zaf*-er, impure oxide of cobalt; the residuum of cobalt, after the sulphur, arsenic, and other volatile matters have been expelled by calcination, being when fused into glass of an intensely blue colour. (Fr. *zafre.*)

zambo, *n.* *zam*-boh, in Spanish America the child of an Indian and a Negro, esp. of an Indian mother and Negro father. (Sp.)

zambomba, *n.* thahm-*bom*-bah, a crude Spanish musical instrument made by stretching a piece of parchment over a wide-mouthed jar, and inserting a stick in it, which is rubbed with the fingers. (Sp.)

Zamia, *n.* *zay*-me-a, a genus of tropical cycads from the stems of some of which a kind of sago or arrowroot is prepared. (L., fir-cone.)

zamindar, *n.* zah-meen-*dar*, a zemindar.

zamouse, *n.* *za-moos*, the bush-cow or short-horned buffalo of West Africa, *Bos brachyceros*. (Ar.)

zampogna, *n.* tsahm-*poh*-nyah, the Calabrian bagpipe. (It.)

zander, *n.* *zan*-der, the pike perch, *Lucioperca sandra*, of the Volga and other central European rivers, an excellent food-fish. (Ger.)

zanella, *n.* za-*nel*-a, a mixed cotton and worsted twilled cloth used for umbrella coverings. (It.)

zany, *n.* *zay*-ne, a merry-andrew; a buffoon; a mountebank's assistant; a simpleton. (Fr. *zani*, It. *zanni*, abbreviated from *Giovanni*, John.)

zanyism, *n.* *zay*-ne-izm, the state, character, or buffoonery of a zany.

zaphara, *n.* *zaf*-a-ra, zaffre, esp. as used by potters to produce a sky-colour.

zaptieh, *n.* *zap*-te-ay, a Turkish policeman. (Turk. *dabtiyeh*, from Ar.)

Zarathustrian, *a.* and *n.* za-ra-*thus*-tre-an, Zoroastrian.

zareba, *n.* za-*ree*-ba, a temporary enclosure defended by brushwood, thorn bushes, etc.; a fenced camp. (Ar. *zariba*, a cattle pen.)

zarf, *n.* zarf, an ornamental holder for a hot coffee-cup. (Ar., vessel.)

zarnich, *n.* *zar*-nik, a name for the native sulphides of arsenic, realgar and orpiment. (Ar. *zarnikh.*)

zax, *n.* zaks, a sax, or tool used by slaters for cutting slate. (Ice. *sax*, a knife.)

zayat, *n.* *zay*-yat, a Burmese caravansary or resting-place for travellers. (Burmese.)

Zea, *n.* *zee*-a, the generic name of maize, *Zea mays.* (Gr. *zea*, a sort of corn.)

zeal, *n.* zeel, passionate ardour in the pursuit of anything; sustained eagerness of desire to accomplish or obtain some object, whether in a good or a bad cause. (Gr. *zelos.*)

zealful, *a.* *zeel*-ful, zealous.

zealless, *a.* *zeel*-less, wanting zeal.

zealot, *n.* *zel*-ot, one specially zealous; an ardent upholder of a cause; an enthusiast; a fanatic.

zealotic, *a.* ze-*lot*-ik, ardently zealous.

zealotism, *n.* *zel*-ot-izm, zealotry; fanaticism.

zealotry, *n.* *zel*-ot-re, behaviour or character of a zealot; fanaticism.

zealous, *a.* *zel*-us, warmly engaged or ardent in the pursuit of an object; characterized by zeal; ardent; fervent; enthusiastic.

zealously, *ad.* with passionate ardour; with eagerness.

zealousness, *n.* the quality of being zealous; zeal.

zebec, *n.* *zee*-bek, a xebec.

zebra, *n.* *zee*-bra *or* *zeb*-ra, any of three species of striped south, central, and north-east African ungulates allied to the horse. **zebra grass,** a cultivated variety of eulalia with striped leaves. **zebra plant,** the S. American herbaceous perennial *Calathea zebrina*, having ornamental striped foliage. **zebra wood,** any of several ornamental woods used in cabinet work, esp. that of the tropical American tree *Connarus guianensis*.

Zebrina, *n.* ze-*bry*-na, a small genus of trailing plants, including *Z. pendula*, the Wandering Jew. (*zebra.*)

zebrine, *a.* *zee*-brine, like or characteristic of a zebra.

zebu, *n.* *zee*-boo, the Indian domestic ox, *Bos indicus*, with a fatty hump on the shoulders.

zecchino, *n.* tse-*kee*-noh, a sequin, a former Italian gold coin. (It.)

zechstein, *n.* *zek*-stine, a magnesian limestone, forming the upper portion of the Permian formation. (Ger. *Ziche*, a mine, *Stein*, stone.)

zed, *n.* zed, the common name of the letter Z.

zedoary, *n.* *zed*-o-a-re, the aromatic rhizome of various species of *Curcuma*, used in medicine and perfumery; the drug itself. (Ar.)

zee, *n.* zee, a name for the letter Z, esp. in the United States.

zein, *n.* *zee*-in, a gluten-like protein prepared from maize. (L. *zea*, corn.)

Zeitgeist, *n.* *tsyt*-gyst, the spirit of the time; contemporary intellectual or moral tendency, outlook, etc. (Ger. *Zeit*, time, *Geist*, spirit.)

Zelanian, *a.* ze-*lay*-ne-an, pertaining to New Zealand [esp. Zool.]. (L., Nova *Zelania.*)

zemindar, *n.* zem-een-*dar*, under British rule in India, the holder of a portion of land for which he paid a fixed revenue to the government. (Hind., landholder.)

zemindary, *n.* zem-een-*dah*-re, the jurisdiction or territory of a zemindar.

zemstvo, *n.* *zemst*-voh, in tsarist Russia, a provincial assembly for the purposes of local government. (Russ., from *zemlya*, land.)

zenana, *n.* ze-*nah*-na, the part of a house in India reserved for the women. (Hind. *zananah*, from Per. *zan*, a woman.)

Zend, *n.* zend, the ancient Persian dialect, allied to Sanscrit, in which the Avesta, or sacred books of the Parsees, are written.

zenith, *n.* *zen*-ith, that point in the sky which is immediately overhead; the point opposite the nadir; the highest point in the path of a celestial body; the culminating point [Fig.]. **zenith distance,** the distance of a celestial body from the zenith. **zenith sector,** an astronomical instrument for measuring with great accuracy the zenith distances of stars. (O.Fr., from Ar. *samt*, path.)

zenithal, *a.* *zen*-e-thal, pertaining to or occurring at the zenith.

Zenonian, *a.* ze-*noh*-ne-an, pertaining to the 5th cent. B.C. Greek philosopher Zeno, or to his philosophy: *n.* a pupil or follower of Zeno.

zeolite, *n.* *zee*-o-lite, any of a group of hydrous alumino-silicates allied to the felspars, including mesolite, natrolite, scolesite, etc., so named from their intumescence before the blow-pipe. (Gr. *zeo*, boil, *lithos*, a stone.)

zeolitic, *a.* *zee*-o-*lit*-ik, pertaining to zeolite; consisting of, characteristic of, or like zeolites.

zephyr, *n.* *zef*-er, the west wind; any soft, mild, gentle breeze; a thin gauzy material used for garments, shawls, etc. (Gr. *zephyros*, west wind.)

zeppelin, *n.* *zep*-e-lin, a cigar-shaped rigid dirigible aircraft. (From the Ger. inventor, Count *Zeppelin*, 1838–1917.)

zerda, *n.* *zer*-da, the North African fennec, *Canis zerda.*

zereba, *n.* ze-*ree*-ba, a zareba.

zero, *n.* *zeer*-roh, naught; nothing; a cipher; the point of departure in calculations, etc.; the point on a thermometer from which it is graduated (in the Réaumur and Centigrade at the freezing-point of water, and in the Fahrenheit at 32° below this, at about the temperature of a mixture of salt and snow); the lowest point, the very bottom [Fig.]. **absolute zero,** the temperature at which heat is entirely absent, *viz.*, −273·13° C. **zero hour,** the time at which an operation is planned to commence [Mil.]. (Ar. *sifr*, a cipher: Fr. *zéro*.)

zest, *n.* zest, orange- *or* lemon-peel, used for giving flavour to liquor; the woody skin quartering the kernel of a walnut; something that gives a pleasant taste; relish; piquant quality: *v.t.* to flavour with zest; to give a relish or flavour to. (Fr. *zeste*, orange- or lemon-peel.)

zestful, *a.* *zest*-ful, overflowing with zest; zesty.

zesty, *a.* *zes*-te, piquant; characterized by zest.

zeta, *n.* *zee*-ta, the sixth letter of the Greek alphabet, corresponding to our Z.

zetacism, *n.* *zee*-ta-sizm, too frequent, or faulty, use of the letter zeta.

zetetic, *a.* ze-*tet*-ik, that proceeds by inquiry; that seeks: *n.* a seeker; a Pyrrhonist. (Gr. *zeteein*, seek.)

zeuglodon, *n.* *zewg*-lo-don, any of a group of toothed extinct cetaceans of Eocene times. (Gr. *zeugle*, the loop of a yoke, *odon, odontos*, tooth.)

zeugma, *n.* *zewg*-ma, a rhetorical figure in which an adjective or verb is applied to two (or sometimes more) nouns either in different senses or to only one of which it is appropriate [Gram.]. (Gr. *zeugnymi*, join.)

zeugmatic, *a.* zewg-*mat*-ik, pertaining to zeugma; denoting a construction in which zeugma occurs.

zeugmatically, *ad.* zewg-*mat*-e-ka-le, so as to involve zeugma.

Zeus, *n.* zewce, the supreme deity of the Olympian heaven and earth, corresponding to the Roman Jupiter [Gr. Myth.].

zeuxite, *n.* *zewk*-site, a pale-brown variety of tourmaline. (Gr. *zeuxis*, joining.)

zho, *n.* zoh, a zobo. (Tib.)

zibeline, *a.* *zib*-e-lin, characteristic of the sable: *n.* a sable, or its pelt; a soft woollen dress material having a silk imitation of fur on one side.

zibet, *n.* *zib*-et, the Indian civet-cat, *Viverra zibetha.*

ziggurat, *n.* *zig*-oo-rat, a square pyramidal temple of the ancient Assyrians and Babylonians, built in stories each of which is smaller in plan than the one below. (Assyrian, a height.)

zigzag, *a.* *zig*-zag, having short sharp angular turns: *n.* something that has short sharp turns or angles alternately salient and re-entrant; a moulding running in a zigzag line [Arch.]; a zigzag trench or path cut to defend the besieged against enfilading by the besieger [Fort.]: *v.t.* to form with short sharp turns: *v.i.* to move or run in a zigzag fashion: *ad.* in a zigzag direction or manner. (Fr.)

zigzagged, *a.* *zig*-zagd, formed with short turns.

zillah, *n.* *zil*-la, an administrative district of British India.

zimb, *n.* zim, a dipterous tsetse-like fly of Abyssinia, very destructive to cattle. (Amharic.)

zimbi, *n.* *zim*-be, the money cowry, *Cypræa moneta*, of India. (Port.)

zinc, *n.* zink, an abundant crystalline metallic element of a brilliant white colour, with a shade of blue, somewhat like tin: *v.t.* to coat or treat with zinc or a zinc compound. *p.* and *pp.* **zincked** or **zinced,** zinkt. *ppr.* **zincking** or **zincing,** *zing*-king.

zinc-blende, *n.* native sulphide of zinc.

zinc-bloom, *n.* hydrous zinc carbonate, or hydrozincite, an opaque mineral of a greenish dull lustre.

zincic, *a.* *zing*-kik, zincoid; containing zinc.

zinciferous, *a.* zing-*kif*-er-rus, containing or affording zinc. (Ger. *Zink*, and L. *fero*, bear.)

zincify, *v.t.* *zing*-ke-fy, to coat or impregnate with zinc.

zincite, *n.* *zing*-kite, native zinc oxide; spartalite.

zinckic, *a.* *zing*-kik, zincic.

zinckify, *v.t.* *zing*-ke-fy, zincify.

zincky, *a.* *zing*-ke, pertaining to, containing, or resembling zinc.

zinco, *n.* *zing*-koh, a zincograph.

zincode, *n.* *zing*-kode, the positive pole of a galvanic cell. (Ger. *Zink*, and Gr. *hodos*, a way.)

zincograph, *n.* *zing*-ko-graf, a zinc plate used in printing by zincography; a block or print produced from such plate.

zincographer, *n.* zing-*kog*-ra-fer, one who practises zincography; an engraver of zincographic blocks.

zincographic, *a.* *zing*-ko-*graf*-ik, pertaining to or produced by zincography.

zincography, *n.* zing-*kog*-ra-fe, the art or process of engraving plates of zinc and of printing therefrom. (Ger. *Zink*, and Gr. *grapho*, write.)

zincoid, *a.* *zing*-koyd, pertaining to or resembling zinc. (Ger. *Zink*, and Gr. *eidos*, like.)

zincotype, *n.* *zing*-ko-tipe, a print from a zincograph; the process of zincography.

zincous, *a.* *zing*-kus, pertaining to zinc, or to the positive pole of a galvanic battery.

zingari, *n.pl.* *zing*-ga-ree, the gipsies. (It.)

zingaro, *n.* *zing*-ga-roh, a gipsy. (It.)

zingel, *n.* *tsing*-gel, a small perch of the genus *Aspro*, esp. that found in the Danube, *A. zingel.* (Ger.)

Zingiber, *n.* *zin*-je-ber, a genus of tropical Asiatic plants, including *Z. officinale*, the common ginger. (L.)

zinkenite, *n.* *zing*-ke-nite, sulphantimonite of lead.

zinky, *a.* *zing*-ke, zincky.

Zinnia, *n.* *zin*-e-a, a composite garden plant with bright flowers of various colours. (From J. G. *Zinn*, a German botanist.)

Zion, *n.* *zy*-on, a hill in Jerusalem, which, after the capture of that city, became the royal residence of David and his successors; heaven, or the heavenly Jerusalem [Fig.].

Zionism, *n.* *zy*-o-nizm, the movement that aimed at the return of the Jews to Palestine and resulted, 1948, in the establishment there of the independent Jewish state of Israel. (*Zion.*)

Zionist, *a.* *zy*-o-nist, pertaining to Zionism: *n.* an agitator for or supporter of Zionism.

zip, *n.* zip, the sound made by a bullet as it strikes, or passes through the air; energy; "go": *v.i.* to move with a zipping sound: *v.t.* to impart speed or energy to. **zip-fastener** or **-fastening,** a type of fastener composed of two stringers which fasten and unfasten by means of a sliding cam device between them.

zipper, *n.* *zip*-er, a zip-fastener; a bag, skirt, etc., fastened in this manner.

zippy, *a.* *zip*-e, full of life and energy; sprightly [Coll.].

zircon, *n.* *zer*-kon, a silicate of zirconia occurring in square prisms, with pyramidal terminations, doubly refractive and often transparent; some varieties, as jacinth, are used as gem-stones.

zirconate, *n.* zer-ko-nate, a salt of zirconic acid.

zirconia, *n.* zer-*koh*-ne-a, oxide of zirconium, resembling alumina in appearance.

zirconic, *a.* zer-*kon*-ik, pertaining to, resembling, or containing zirconium. **zirconic acid,** zirconium hydroxide.

zirconite, *n.* *zer*-ko-nite, a variety of zircon.

zirconium, *n.* zer-*koh*-ne-um, a rare-earth metallic element of the titanium group, found native only in combination, and used for metallurgical furnaces and in manufacture of gas-mantles, ammunition primers, etc.

zither, *n.* *zith*-er, the cithern or modern cithara, a musical instrument with metal strings. (L. *cithara.*)

zitherist, *n.* *zith*-er-rist, a player of the zither.

zittern, *n.* *zit*-ern, a zither.

Zizania, *n.* zi-*zay*-ne-a, a genus of grasses, including the Canadian rice. (Gr., tares.)

zizel, *n.* *ziz*-el, a rodent of the genus *Spermophilus*, the suslik or earless marmot.

Zizyphus, *n.* *ziz*-e-fus, a large genus of tropical plants including *Z. vulgaris*, the jujube tree.

zloty, *n.* *zlot*-e, since 1924 the monetary unit of Poland, in 1939 equivalent to about 9½d.

zoanthropy, *n.* zoh-*an*-thro-pe, a monomania in which one believes oneself to be transformed into some animal and adopts its habits. (Gr. *zoon*, an animal, *anthropos*, a man.)

zoarium, *n.* zoh-*ayr*-re-um, the supporting structure of, also the individual polyzoans constituting, a polyzoarium [Zool.].

zobo, *n.* *zoh*-boh, a hybrid between yak and cow (or zebu) bred in northern India as a beast of burden and for its flesh and milk. (Tib.)

zocle, *n.* *zok*-kl, a socle [Arch.].

zodiac, *n.* *zoh*-de-ak, the broad imaginary circle in the heavens containing the twelve signs (Aries,

Taurus, Gemini, Cancer, Leo, Virgo, Libra, Scorpio, Sagittarius, Capricornus, Aquarius, Pisces), through which the sun passes in its annual course, the ecliptic dividing it in the middle. (Fr. *zodiaque*, from Gr. *zoon*, an animal, the zodiacal constellations representing animals.)

zodiacal, *a.* zo-*dy*-a-kal, pertaining to the zodiac. **zodiacal light**, an elongated triangular luminous tract lying nearly in the ecliptic, seen after sunset or before sunrise in low latitudes.

zoea, *n.* zo-*ee*-a (*pl.* **zoeæ**), a larval form of certain crustaceans, esp. decapods [Zool.].

zoetrope, *n.* *zoh*-e-trope, an optical toy in which figures on a revolving cylinder when viewed through a slit appear to be in motion ; a form of thaumatrope (Gr. *zoe*, life, *trope*, a turning.)

zoic, *a.* *zoh*-ik, pertaining to animals or animal life [Zool.] ; containing fossilized remains or indications of animals [Geol.].

Zoilean, *a.* *zoh*-e-*lee*-an, bitterly and severely critical. (*Zoilus*, a severe critic of Homer.)

Zoilism, *n.* *zoh*-e-lizm, illiberal or carping criticism, like that of Zoilus.

zoisite, *n.* zoy-*site*, a coloured crystalline silicate of alumina and lime allied to epidote. (Baron von *Zois*, Austrian mineralogist, *d.* 1819.)

Zolaism, *n.* *zoh*-la-izm, excessive naturalism or realism in literary works. (Emile *Zola*, French novelist, *d.* 1902.)

Zollverein, *n.* *zol*-fer-rine, a commercial union, esp. of German states in the 19th cent., for a uniform rate of customs. (Ger. *Zoll*, toll, *Verein*, union.)

zonal, *a.* *zoh*-nal, pertaining to a zone or zones ; forming a zone ; arranged in zones.

zonality, *n.* zo-*nal*-e-te, state or character of being zonal ; zonal distribution.

zonally, *ad.* *zoh*-na-le, in zones ; in a zonal setting.

zonary, *a.* *zoh*-na-re, pertaining to or resembling a zone ; occurring in a zone.

zonate, *a.* *zoh*-nat, marked with zones or rings ; having bands of colour [Bot. and Zool.].

zonation, *n.* zo-*nay*-shun, distributed or arrangement in zones.

zone, *n.* zone, a girdle ; any one of the five divisions of the earth with respect to the temperature of different latitudes, these being, one torrid (bounded by the tropics), two temperate, and two frigid (the latter within the Arctic and Antarctic circles respectively) [Geog.] ; a band or stripe of colour running round any object ; circuit. **zone time**, the standard time of ships at sea, being the solar time in that twenty-fourth part of the 360° of the earth's circumference in which the ship then is ; any local time except that of Greenwich. (Gr. *zone*.)

zoned, *a.* zohnd, wearing a zone ; having zones or concentric bands.

zoneless, *a.* *zone*-less, not wearing a zone ; not girdled ; not having bands of colour.

zoning, *n.* *zoh*-ning, partition into zones or well-defined areas (esp. in town-planning).

zonular, *a.* *zoh*-new-lar, resembling a zonule.

zonule, *n.* *zoh*-newl, a little zone.

zonure, *n.* *zoh*-newr, any lizard of the family Zonuridæ, most of which have zones of scales and spines on the body with spikes on the tail.

zoo, *n.* zoo, a menagerie, esp. that of the Zoological Society in Regent's Park, London ; a zoological garden.

zoochemical, *a.* zoh-o-*kem*-e-kal, pertaining to zoochemistry.

zoochemistry, *n.* zoh-o-*kem*-is-tre, a former name of the science now expanded into biochemistry. (Gr. *zoon*, an animal, and *chemistry*.)

zoodynamics, *n.* *zoh*-o-dy-*nam*-iks, the science treating of the physiology of animals.

zoogenic, *a.* zoh-o-*jen*-ik, produced from animals, or [Geol.] from organic remains.

zoogenous, *a.* zoh-o-*jee*-nus, originating from animals, esp. [Med.] of diseases.

zoogeography, *n.* *zoh*-o-je-*og*-ra-fe, the scientific study of the geographical distribution of animals.

zooglœa, *n.* zoh-*og*-le-a, a colony of bacteria forming a jelly-like mass. (Gr. *zoon*, and *gloios*, sticky stuffs.)

zooglœic, *a.* zoh-*og*-le-ik, resembling a zooglœa.

zoogonous, *a.* zoh-*og*-o-nus, viviparous [Zool.].

zoographer, *n.* zoh-*og*-ra-fer, one who describes animals ; a painter of animals (esp. for scientific purposes).

zoographical, *a.* *zoh*-o-*graf*-e-kal, pertaining to the description of animals.

zoography, *n.* zoh-*og*-ra-fe, a description of animal forms and habits. (Gr. *zoon*, and *grapho*, write.)

zooid, *n.* *zoh*-oyd, each individual number of a compound animal organism ; a semi-independent animal produced (as the corals, etc.) asexually ; any low organism having some, but not full, indication of animal or plant life.

zooidal, *a.* zoh-*oy*-dal, pertaining to or characteristic of a zooid ; having in incomplete measure attributes of living animals or plants.

zooks, *int.* zooks, short for gadzooks.

zoolater, *n.* zoh-*ol*-a-ter, a worshipper of animals.

zoolatrous, *a.* zoh-*ol*-a-trus, characterized by or addicted to zoolatry.

zoolatry, *n.* zoh-*ol*-a-tre, the worship of animals. (Gr. *zoon*, and *latreia*, worship.)

zoolite, *n.* *zoh*-o-lite, any fossilized animal or animal substance.

zoolitic, *a.* zoh-o-*lit*-ik, pertaining to zoolites ; resembling a zoolite.

zoological, *a.* *zoh*-o-*loj*-e-kal, pertaining to zoology. **zoological garden**, a garden in which wild animals are kept for study and exhibition.

zoologically, *ad.* according to the principles of zoology.

zoologist, *n.* zoh-*ol*-o-jist, a student of zoology or of the natural history of animals.

zoology, *n.* zoh-*ol*-o-je, the branch of biology which treats of the structure, habits, classification, distribution, and habitations of animals. (Gr. *zoon*, and *logos*, science.)

zoom, *v.i.* zoom, (of aircraft), to climb at a steep angle by utilizing stored energy : *n.* such a climb of an aircraft [Av. Slang].

zoomagnetism, *n.* zoh-o-*mag*-ne-tizm, animal magnetism.

zoomancy, *n.* *zoh*-o-*man*-se, divination from observation of the behaviour of animals.

zoometry, *n.* zoh-*om*-e-tre, the comparative measurement of animals.

zoomorphic, *a.* *zoh*-o-*mor*-fik, representing animal forms ; pertaining to zoomorphism.

zoomorphism, *n.* *zoh*-o-*mor*-fizm, representation in animal form or forms ; the attribution of animal characteristics to something else, esp. a god. (Gr. *zoon*, and *morphe*, shape.)

zoon, *n.* *zoh*-on, an organism which is the total product of a fertilized ovum.

zoonic, *a.* zoh-*on*-ik, pertaining to animals ; obtained from animal substances.

zoonite, *n.* *zoh*-o-nite, one of the segments of an articulated animal.

zoonomy, *n.* zoh-*on*-o-me, the science of the laws of animal life. (Gr. *zoon*, an animal, *nomos*, a law.)

zoopathology, *n.* *zoh*-o-pa-*thol*-o-je, the science of the diseases of animals.

zoophagan, *n.* zoh-*of*-a-gan, any animal, including fish, reptiles, etc., living on the flesh of others. (Gr. *zoon*, and *phago*, eat.)

zoophagous, *a.* zoh-*of*-a-gus, carnivorous ; feeding on animals or animal food [Zool.].

zoophile, *n.* *zoh*-o-fil, a zoophilist ; a zoophilous plant.

zoophilist, *n.* zoh-*of*-e-list, a lover of animals.

zoophilous, *a.* zoh-*of*-e-lus, loving animals ; adapted to pollination by the agency of animals instead of insects [Bot.].

zoophily, *n.* zoh-*of*-e-le, fondness for animals. (Gr. *zoon*, and *philos*, love.)

zoophoric, *a.* *zoh*-o-*fo*-rik, supporting the figure of an animal (esp. of columns) [Arch.]. (Gr. *zoon*, and *phero*, bear.)

zoophorus, *n.* zoh-*of*-o-rus, a frieze having the figures of animals carved upon it [Ancient Arch.].

zoophysics, *n.* *zoh*-o-*fiz*-iks, the branch of zoology treating of the physical structure and uses of animal organs.

zoophysiology, *n.* *zoh*-o-*fiz*-e-*ol*-o-je, animal physiology. (Gr. *zoon*, and *physiology*.)

zoophyte, *n.* *zoh*-o-fite, any invertebrate animal which, like the sponges, sea-anemones, etc., seem to form a connecting link between plants and animals. (Gr. *zoon*, and *phyton*, a plant.)

zoophytic, *a.* *zoh*-o-*fit*-ik, pertaining to zoophytes.

zoophytological, *a.* *zoh*-o-*fy*-to-*loj*-e-kal, pertaining to zoophytology.

zoophytology, *n.* *zoh*-o-fy-*tol*-o-je, the branch of zoology treating of zoophytes. (Gr. *zoon*, *phyton*, and *logos*, science.)
zooplastic, *a.* zoh-o-*plas*-tik, pertaining to or effected by zooplasty.
zooplasty, *n.* zoh-o-*plas*-te, the art or process of grafting living animal tissue on to the human body [Surg.].
zoopsychology, *n.* zoh-o-sy-*kol*-o-je, non-human animal psychology.
zooscopy, *n.* zoh-*os*-ko-pe, delirium tremens or other mental disorder in which imaginary animals are seen.
zoosperm, *n.* *zoh*-o-sperm, the male seed-cell, a spermatozoon. (Gr. *zoon*, and *sperma*, seed.)
zoospore, *n.* *zoh*-o-spore, the swarm spore of many algæ and fungi which moves as if alive after it is discharged from the spore-case. (Gr. *zoon*, and *spore*.)
zootaxy, *n.* *zoh*-o-*tak*-se, the taxonomy or classification of zoology.
zootechny, *n.* *zoh*-o-*tek*-ne, the science of the breeding and domestication of animals.
zootomical, *a.* *zoh*-o-*tom*-e-kal, pertaining to zootomy.
zootomist, *n.* zoh-*ot*-o-mist, one who dissects the bodies of animals; a comparative anatomist.
zootomy, *n.* zoh-*ot*-o-me, the dissection of animals; the science treating of the anatomy of other than human animals. (Gr. *zoon*, and *tome*, cutting.)
zootrophy, *n.* zoh-*ot*-ro-fe, the study or practice of the rearing and nourishment of animals.
zorilla, *n.* zo-*ril*-a, the Cape polecat *Ictonyx zorilla*, a skunk-like S. African carnivore of the badger family. (Fr. *zorille*.)
Zoroastrian, *a.* *zo*-roh-*as*-tre-an, pertaining to Zoroaster, the founder or reformer of the ancient religion of the Magi or Persians; pertaining to the system of Zoroaster. (*Zarathustra*, the Old Persian name of which "Zoroaster" is a Latinized form.)
Zoroastrianism, *n.* *zo*-roh-*as*-tre-a-nizm, the dualistic religion of ancient Persia, taught by Zoroaster in prehistoric times; Mazdaism.
zoster, *n.* *zos*-ter, an ancient Greek girdle; shingles, or herpes zoster [Med.]. (Gr. *zoster*, girdle.)
zouave, *n.* zoo-*ahv*, a soldier of a corps of light infantry, wearing the Arab dress, introduced into the French service after the conquest of Algiers; a short sleeveless jacket worn by women. (An Algerian tribe.)
zounds, *int.* zoundz, an obsolete oath or expletive, contracted from "God's wounds."
zucchetto, *n.* tsoo-*ket*-toh, a skull-cap covering the tonsure. (It.)
zuffolo, *n.* *tsoo*-fo-loh, a little flute or flageolet, esp. one used in teaching birds to sing. (It.)
zugzwang, *n.* *tsoog*-tsvang, a condition in chess in which though there is no direct threat to the player any move will result in loss or positional deterioration. (Ger., move under constraint.)
Zulu, *n.* *zoo*-loo, one of a warlike S. African Bantu tribe in the north of Natal; the language of the Zulus.
zumbooruk, *n.* *zum*-boo-ruk, a small swivel-gun for carrying on the back of a camel. (Hind., from Per.)
zwanziger, *n.* *tsvahn*-tsig-er, a former Austrian silver coin worth about 8½d.
zwieback, *n.* *tsvee*-bak, a thin rusk or biscuit baked and toasted. (Ger., twice-baked.)
Zwinglian, *a.* *zwing*-gle-an, pertaining to Zwingli, the Swiss reformer (*d.* 1531), or to his religious teaching.
zygadite, *n.* *zig*-a-dite, a variety of albite, so called from its twin crystals [Min.]. (Gr. *zygon*, a yoke.)
zygal, *a.* *zy*-gal, pertaining to, having, or resembling a zygon; formed like the letter H.
zygapophysis, *n.* *zy*-ga-*pof*-e-sis, any one of the vertebral articular processes [Anat.].
zygodactyl, *n.* zy-go-*dak*-til, a zygodactylous bird.
zygodactylic, *a.* *zy*-go-dak-*til*-ik, zygodactylous.
zygodactylous, *a.* *zy*-go-*dak*-te-lus, having the toes disposed in pairs (esp. of birds whose feet have two anterior and two posterior toes, like the parrot and cuckoo. (Gr. *zygon*, a yoke, *daktylos*, a toe or finger.)
zygodont, *a.* *zig*-o-dont, having molar teeth arranged in pairs.
zygoma, *n.* ze-*goh*-ma, the bony arch connecting the cranial and facial bones; the cheek-bone [Anat.].
zygomatic, *a.* zy-go- *or* zig-o-*mat*-ik, pertaining to the zygoma [Anat.]. **zygomatic arch,** the zygoma. **zygomatic muscles,** two facial muscles rising from the zygoma and inserted into the corner of the mouth. **zygomatic processes,** the processes of the temporal and cheek bones, which unite to form the zygomatic arch. **zygomatic suture,** the suture which joins the zygomatic processes of the temporal and cheek bones. (Gr. *zygon*, a yoke.)
zygomorphic, *a.* *zy*-go- *or* zig-o-*mor*-fik, symmetrical bilaterally [Bot. and Zool.].
zygon, *n.* *zy*-gon, a thwart in ancient Greek ships; the crossbar connecting the branches of an H-shaped fissure in the brain [Anat.]. (Gr., a yoke.)
zygophyte, *n.* *zy*-go-fite, a plant reproduced by the union of two similar cells.
zygopleural, *a.* *zy*-go-*ploor*-ral, bilaterally symmetrical [Biol.].
zygosperm, *n.* *zy*-go-sperm, a zygospore.
zygospore, *n.* *zy*-go-spore, a spore formed by conjugation of two similar sexual cells [Bot.].
zygote, *n.* *zy*-gote, a cell resulting from the fusion of two similar sexual cells [Biol.]; a zygospore.
zymase, *zy*-mace, any of a certain group of enzymes used in the conversion of glucose into alcohol.
zymogen, *n.* *zy*-mo-jen, any bacterium or substance capable of causing fermentation.
zymoid, *a.* *zy*-moyd, of the nature of, or resembling, a ferment.
zymological, *a.* *zy*-mo-*loj*-e-kal, pertaining to zymology.
zymologist, *n.* zy-*mol*-o-jist, a student of fermentation.
zymology, *n.* zy-*mol*-o-je, the science or study of fermentation. (Gr. *zyme*, leaven *logos*, science.)
zymolysis, *n.* zy-*mol*-e-sis, the action of enzymes; decomposition so produced.
zymoma, *n.* zy-*moh*-ma, any ferment.
zymometer, *n.* zy-*mom*-e-ter, an instrument for measuring the degree of fermentation. (Gr. *zyme*, *zymosis*, and *meter*.)
zymosimeter, *n.* *zy*-mo-*sim*-e-ter, a zymometer.
zymosis, *n.* zy-*moh*-sis, fermentation; the process by which an infectious or zymotic disease is developed [Med.]. (Gr., fermentation.)
zymotechny, *n.* *zy*-mo-*tek*-ne, the art of exciting fermentation. (Gr. *zyme*, and *techne*, art.)
zymotic, *a.* zy-*mot*-ik, pertaining to fermentation; acting in the manner of a ferment: *n.* a zymotic disease. **zymotic disease,** an infectious or contagious disease, because formerly thought to be caused by a species of fermentation.
zymotically, *ad.* zy-*mot*-e-ka-le, by means of zymosis.
zymurgy, *n.* *zy*-mur-je, the chemistry, practice, or art of fermentation.
zythum, *n.* *zy*-thum, an ancient kind of beer; a beverage made from malt and wheat. (Gr. *zithos*.)

APPENDIX

TO

Nuttall's Standard Dictionary

CONTENTS

CONTENTS

PRONUNCIATION OF FOREIGN WORDS

GENERAL OUTLINE OF PHONETIC THEORY

In order to pronounce words belonging to a foreign language in a way that shall be intelligible to native speakers of that language, we require to know:

(1) the sounds used by native speakers;
(2) the order in which the sounds have to be placed to make intelligible words and sentences;
(3) the relative length of these sounds;
(4) the nature and position of the stress or accent;
(5) the conventional method of representing these sounds, and their attributes of length and stress, in the written language.

In the following pages examples are given in *italics*, the conventional spelling, and in **thick** type, the phonetic transcription according to the alphabet of the International Phonetic Association.

Sounds

All speech sounds may be divided into two classes, viz.:

(*a*) those in which the vocal cords vibrate, to form *voice*;
(*b*) those in which the cords are silent.

Sounds of the first class are called *voiced* sounds, while those of the second class are called *voiceless* or *breathed*. A ready way of distinguishing the two classes of sounds is to try the effect of singing them; we can sing a tune on the sound of *m*, which is voiced, but not on the sound *s*, which is voiceless. Every voiced sound has its voiceless counterpart, thus *z* (the buzzing sound) and *s* (the hissing sound) form a pair, as also do *b* and *p*, *d* and *t*, *g* (as in *go*) and *k* (as in *king*, also represented in the spelling by *c* before *a*, *o*, and *u*, as in *car*).

With regard to voiced sounds, it is necessary to observe that the vibration of the vocal cords may (i) persist throughout the period of articulation of the sound; (ii) persist throughout a part of the period of articulation; (iii) be entirely absent throughout the period of articulation. Sounds of the first order are called *fully voiced*, of the second order *partially voiced*, and of the third order *devoiced*. A *devoiced* sound is not necessarily the same as a *voiceless* sound, as can be easily demonstrated by saying a word like *bat* with a devoiced *b*. The result is not *pat*: the difference is one of force of exhalation.

All vowel sounds are voiced sounds; consonants may be voiced or voiceless. Languages vary among themselves as to the degree of vocal vibration they use in the articulation of their voiced sounds. As a general rule it may be observed that Romance languages use a greater amount of vocal vibration than Teutonic languages; the former making use of fully voiced consonants, the latter of partially voiced and devoiced consonants. English seems to show a preference for the partially voiced variety.

In the alphabet of the International Phonetic Association the sign ̥ placed beneath a letter indicates that the sound is devoiced.

Vowel Sounds.—If a stream of air, that has been charged with vibrations by the action of the vocal cords, passes through the mouth without encountering either complete obstruction or any narrowing sufficient to cause audible friction, it will emerge as a vowel sound. The number of vowel sounds to be found in all the languages of the world is very considerable, and the problem of classifying them is not simple. Many attempts have been made to solve it, the most recent being that made by Professor Daniel Jones (the general editor of this section of NUTTALL'S STANDARD DICTIONARY) and his colleagues at University College, London. Certain sounds are chosen as Standard or Cardinal Vowels ; they are recorded on a gramophone record, and X-ray photographs are taken of the position of the articulating organs of the most important of them. A diagrammatic chart of the vowel sounds of any language, as they stand in reference to the Cardinal Vowels, can then be made. In this way we are able to describe the vowels of one language without having continually to refer them to those of another language.

The symbols used by the International Phonetic Association to represent these eight cardinal vowels are : **i, e, ɛ, a, ɑ, ɔ, o, u**, of which the exact values may be heard on the gramophone record.* In the acoustic scale, the various vowels in the French words *si, thé, père, la* (or the Northern English *man*), *pâte*, the English *caught*, the French *gros*, the Italian *tu*, may be said to have values approaching those of the eight respective cardinal vowels.

A characteristic of these eight vowels is that the first four (the " front " vowels) and the fifth (a " back " vowel) are made with the lips spread or in a neutral position, whereas for the last three (back vowels) the lips are rounded to varying degrees. It is also possible to articulate front rounded vowels and back unrounded vowels.

If we combine the tongue position of No. 1 with the lip position of No. 8, we have the sound **y** as in French *plus*, German *für*.

A similar combination of Cardinal Vowels No. 2 and No. 7 gives the sound **ø**, as in French *peu*, German *schön*, while from a combination of Nos. 3 and 6 we derive the sound **œ**, as in French *peur*, German *zwölf*.

Again, if we combine the lip position of **i** with the tongue position of **u**, we obtain a vowel sound near to the Russian **ы**.

The eight Cardinal Vowels, with the three additional " front rounded " sounds and the " back unrounded " sound just mentioned, form a useful series of standard sounds, with which we may compare the vowel sounds of many languages.

To these must be added a vowel sound that appears frequently, especially in weakly stressed syllables, and to which is given the name of "neutral," "obscure," or "central" vowel. There is a neutral vowel in Southern English, in the last syllable of such words as *actor, singer, china, method*, etc. ; there is a neutral vowel in the first syllable of French *cheval*, and another in the final syllable of German *habe*. These neutral sounds vary in quality according to the language, but are broadly represented in the International Phonetic Alphabet by the symbol **ə**.

Vowel sounds made when the soft palate is lowered, so that sound passes through *both mouth and nose*, are known as nasalized vowels. Nasalization is expressed by the sign ˜ placed over the vowel symbol. Thus French *bon* contains the vowel **ɔ̃**, *banc* has **ɑ̃**, *pain* has **ɛ̃**, and *brun* has **œ̃**.

Semi-Vowels.—A very short close vowel sound used before another vowel sound is known as a semi-vowel. The three most common semi-vowels are those corresponding to the sounds, **i, u**, and **y**.

The semi-vowel corresponding to **i** is represented by **j**. English *yes* (**jes**), German *ia* (**ja**),† French *hier* (**jɛːr**).

The semi-vowel corresponding to **u** is represented by **w**, *e.g.* English *we* (**wiː**), French *oui* (**wi**).

The semi-vowel corresponding to **y** is represented by **y̌** or **ɥ**, *e.g.* French *lui* (**ly̌i**).

* Records Nos. DAJO 1–2, published by the Linguaphone Institute, 207–209 Regent St., London, W.1.

† Some Germans, however, use a " fricative " **j**.

Diphthongs.—A succession of two vowel sounds that belong to one and the same syllable is known as a diphthong, *e.g.* the English words *my*, *no* (as pronounced in Southern English), *day*, *now*, *boy*, contain diphthongs.

When the Cardinal Vowel symbols are not sufficient to represent the vowel sounds of a language, the International Phonetic Alphabet uses others, *e.g.* **ɩ** for "narrow" transcriptions of the short vowel in English *bit*, German *bitte* ; **æ** for "narrow" transcriptions of the vowel in Southern English *man* ; **ο** for "narrow" transcriptions of the short vowel in English *cook*, German *Luft*.

Consonants.—Sounds, whether voiced or voiceless, that arise from partial or complete obstruction in the mouth are known as consonant sounds. These can be best classified according to :

(1) the nature of the obstruction, or articulation ;
(2) the place of the obstruction or articulation.

On the first basis, consonant sounds are divided into :

(*a*) Plosive Consonants, when the obstruction is complete and the release sudden. When the ensuing vowel follows instantaneously, the sound is said to be *unaspirated*, when an audible puff of breath follows the explosion, the sound is *aspirated* ; **b**, **d**, **g**, **p**, **t**, **k** are plosive sounds.

(*b*) Affricate Consonants, when the explosion is followed by a slow audible release, as the *ch* in English *church*, or *j* and *dge* in *judge*. These two sounds are generally represented by the digraphs **tʃ** and **dʒ**.

(*c*) Nasal Consonants, when the mouth is completely obstructed, and the nose passage is open.

m and **n** are nasal consonants ; so are the sounds of *ng* in *sing* (represented by the symbol **ŋ**) and the *gn* of French *agneau* (represented by **ɲ**).

(*d*) Lateral Consonants, when the obstruction is along the middle of the mouth, one or both sides being free. **l** is a lateral consonant, as also is Spanish *ll* and Italian *gl*, represented by **ʎ**, and the Welsh *ll* which is a variety of "breathed" **l** represented by **ɬ**.

(*e*) Rolled Consonants, when there is rapid intermittent contact, as in Scottish *r*, Spanish *rr*, Italian *r*, and one type of French *r*.

(*f*) Fricative Consonants, when there is no complete obstruction, but only a constriction that gives rise to audible friction.

English *s*, *f*, *v*, *z*, *h*, *th* (θ in *thick*, and ð in *then*) usually stand for fricative consonants ; *b*, *d*, *g* stand for fricative consonants in certain positions in Spanish, in which their sounds may be represented in "narrow" transcription by the symbols **β**, **ð**, **ɣ**, respectively.

German *ch* stands for the two fricative consonant sounds **ç** and **x**.

According to the place of the obstruction or, as it is sometimes called, the point of articulation, Consonant Sounds are divided into :

(1) Bilabial Consonants, articulated by the two lips. In English and French *b*, *p* stand for bilabial plosives ; Spanish *b* and German *w* sometimes stand for the bilabial fricative **β**.

(2) Labio-dental Consonants, articulated by the lower lip against the upper front teeth, *e.g.* English, Spanish, French *f*, *v*. In Italian *m* and *n* before *f* and *v* usually stand for a Labio-dental sound **ɱ**.

(3) Dental Consonants, articulated between the tongue tip and the upper front teeth, *e.g.* French, Spanish *t, d*; the English *th* sounds, as in *thin, then.*

(4) Alveolar Consonants, articulated between the tongue tip and the upper teeth ridge (gum), *e.g.* English *t, d, n, l.*

(5) Palatal Consonants, articulated between the upper front surface of the tongue and the hard palate, *e.g.* German *j*; French and Italian *gn*, as in *agneau, ogni*; German *ch*, after *i, e, l, r*, etc. (see p. 1102). Italian *gl* and Spanish *ll* stand for the palatal consonant **ʎ**.

(6) Velar Consonants, articulated between back of tongue and the fore part of the soft palate. English and German *k, g*, German *ch* after *a, o, u*, and Spanish *j*, stand for the velar sound **x**.

(7) Uvular Consonants, articulated between back of tongue and the extremity of the soft palate. The so-called French "*r* grasseyé" is made in this way. Its symbol (when a special symbol is needed) is **R**.

(8) Glottal Consonants, articulated between the vocal cords. Of these the most important in European languages is the "glottal stop," a plosive consonant made by the vocal cords, giving the impression of a momentary cessation of sound. It is commonly substituted for *p, t* and *k* in many English dialects (North and South) in certain positions, *e.g. bo'le* and *wa'er* for *bottle* and *water*. The phonetic symbol for this sound is **ʔ**. See also at end of Pronunciation of German, p. 1102. **h** is generally considered to be a glottal sound, because the air passing through the open glottis is common to all varieties of **h**.

Length of Sounds.—Vowel and consonant sounds may be of varying degrees of length, that is to say, they may persist for varying intervals of time. Languages make use of this variation in length in different ways.

Some languages have long vowels and short vowels, *e.g.* the vowel in English *bead* is longer than that in *bid*. In some languages length depends upon the nature of following consonants. Thus in English the vowel of *bead* is longer than that of *beat*, and in French the vowel of *part* is longer than that of *patte*. Variation in length may apply also to consonants; in Italian the *rr* of *carro* is longer than the *r* of *caro*.

A long vowel sound is indicated in the International Phonetic Alphabet by the symbol **:**; a long consonant sound is indicated by doubling the letter.

Representation of Sounds by means of Letters.—It must be borne in mind that Language, as modern civilized communities know it, consists of two widely different things, viz.:

(*a*) Speech, which is made up of sounds: these are made by the Mouth, etc., and are apprehended by the Ear.

(*b*) Printed or Written Language, which is made up of letters; these are made by the Hand or Machine, and are apprehended by the Eye.

The first belongs to the realm of Sound; the second to the realm of Sight. Since Sight and Sound are in themselves irreconcilable in nature, it follows that any attempt to represent sounds by visual signs or letters must rest upon numerous conventions. The Languages of the world have each its own sounds, differing greatly from one another in variety, in number, and in distribution. With the exception of Russian the Languages with which we are concerned in this article use the Roman Alphabet, with additions and modifications that vary from language to language. In order to translate a visual language into sounds, that is to say, in order to pronounce a language when we see it, we need to know the conventional relationships that exist in that language between sound and letter. The more uniform these conventions are, the more "phonetic" is the spelling.

It is evident that since one system of letters is used for so many varying systems of sounds, letters will have different sounds in different languages and even in different forms of the same language; and since there are, in any one language, usually more sounds than letters, a letter may have more than one value in that language. Thus the letter *b*, in French, usually stands for a fully voiced bilabial plosive sound (**b**); in English it very often stands for a partially voiced bilabial plosive sound (**b**); in Dutch and German it often stands for the devoiced sound (**b̥**) or for the voiceless sound (**p**); while in Spanish it often stands for the bilabial fricative sound (**β**). The Russian letter в stands for **v**.

The same letter or letters may have to do duty in any one language for more than one sound; *e.g.* in English *s* stands for **s** in *picks*, for **z** in *figs*, for **ʃ** in *sure*, and for **ʒ** in *measure*. Again, the same sound may be represented in a language by different letters; *e.g.* in English the vowel sound **iː** is represented differently in *be, see, sea, receive, believe, key, quay, people*.

In order to obviate discrepancies of this kind many "phonetic" alphabets have been invented, their purpose being to have one symbol per sound. But even this aim, admirable as it appears, is impossible of achievement, owing to the variety of modifications that sounds undergo in the rough-and-tumble of language life. Sounds that at first appear to be identical are found on examination to be different. The **k** sound we use in *key* is not the same as the one we use in *car*; the **k** we use in *cool* is not the same as many of us use in *school*. But the use of one symbol to indicate all these varieties of **k** does not cause confusion or ambiguity in the transcription of English. A fundamental principle of the International Phonetic Alphabet is that one symbol shall stand for each family of sounds (or *phoneme*) within a language. Where a transcription sets out to use the minimum of symbols to express without ambiguity all the sounds of a certain language, it is said to be "broad." In the detailed analysis of a language, or in the comparative study of languages, it is often useful to increase the number of symbols and diacritical marks in order to show more subtle distinctions. This is a "narrow" transcription. Thus the final **l** sounds of English *people* and French *peuple* may be transcribed narrowly as **ɫ** (English "dark" *l*) and **l̥** (voiceless *l*) respectively. The use of a broad transcription implies the knowledge of conventions which vary according to the language and the phonetic context. The value of symbols must be known in relation to the language which is being studied; *e.g.* **i** has different values in English and in French.

Stress and Prominence.—Most European languages have a system of stress or "force-accent." Certain syllables in the word and certain words in the sentence are uttered with greater force than the others, *i.e.* generally with additional loudness due to the use of especially strong breath force. This is known as *stress*, and the regularity of the sequence of stresses determines the rhythm of a language. Stress contributes to the general distinctness of a syllable, that is to its prominence, which may also be achieved by any of the additional effects of length, the inherent quality of the sound, or intonation, or by a combination of all the effects mentioned.

With regard to the distribution of the stress, three main principles prevail:

(*a*) The stress is generally found in a certain position, *e.g.* the final syllable in French, the penultimate in Welsh.

(*b*) The stress falls on the main root, as usually in German.

(*c*) The stress may fall on any syllable, as in English.

The sign ˈ placed before a syllable indicates that the stress falls on that syllable.

THE INTERNATIONAL PHONETIC ALPHABET AS APPLIED TO THE LANGUAGES IN THE FOLLOWING ARTICLE

The letters **p, b, t, d, k, g, m, n, l, f, v, h, w, s, z** may generally be said to have approximately their English values, except for Dutch *w*, for which see p. 1104.

j, as in German *Jahr*. English *y* in *yes*.

r, a roll of the tongue tip, as in Italian and in Scotland.

ʀ, a roll of the uvula against the back of the tongue, as in Parisian French.

c, a "forward" **k** sound made between the front of the tongue and the hard palate, as in Dutch *beekje*. The symbol **c** is also used in some languages to denote **tʃ**; thus, in Spanish *muchacho* may be represented phonetically by **mucaco**.

ɱ, an **m**-like sound made between the lower lip and upper teeth, as in Italian *invece*.

ɲ, an **n**-like sound made between the "front" of the tongue and the hard palate, like *gn* in French *agneau*, Italian *ogni*, Spanish *ñ* in *niño*.

ŋ, *ng*, as in English *sing*.

ɬ, voiceless fricative **l**, written in Welsh *ll*, e.g. *Llanelly*.

ʎ, an **l**-like sound made between the "front" of the tongue and the hard palate, written in Italian *gl*, in Spanish *ll*.

β, a **v**-like sound made between the two lips, like *b* in Spanish *saber*.

ʋ, a **v** sound made between lower lip and upper teeth but without any audible friction, like *w* in Dutch *wagen*.

θ, like *th* in English *thin*, *c* in Spanish *ciento*.

ð, like *th* in English *this*, *d* in Spanish *madre*, *dd* in Welsh *dydd*.

ʃ, like *sh* in English, *sch* in German, *ch* in French.

tʃ, like *ch* in English *church*.

ʒ, like *j* in French, and *s* in English *pleasure*.

dʒ, like *j* in English *jug*.

ç, an **ʃ**-like sound made between the "front" of the tongue and the hard palate, like *ch* in German *ich*.

x, like *ch* in Scots *loch*, Welsh *chwech*, German *Buch*, Spanish *j* in *Juan*.

ɣ, voiced **x**, like *g* in Spanish *rogar* and Dutch *geven*.

ɥ, the semi-vowel form of **y**, as in French *nuit*. Also written **y̆**.

i, like French *i* in *si*, German *ie* in *wie*, English *ee* in *see*.

ɩ, like English *i* in *bit*.

e, like French *é* in *thé*, Scottish *ay* in *day*.

ɛ, like German *e* in *Bett*.

a, like Northern English *a* in *man*, French *a* in *la*.

ɑ, like Southern English *a* in *half*, French *â* in *pâte*, Dutch *a* in *kar*.

ɔ, like *o* in German *Sonne*, French *robe*. Another variety in English *saw*.

o, like German *o* in *wohl*, French *eau* in *beau*, Scottish *o* in *go*.

ɷ, like English *oo* in *book*, Welsh *w* in *cwm*.

u, like German *u* in *du*, French *ou* in *trouve*, Welsh *w* in *pwll*.

y, like German *ü* in *über*, French *u* in *tu*.

ø, like German *ö* in *schön*, French *eu* in *peu*.

œ, like German *ö* in *zwölf*, French *eu* in *peur*.

ə, a "central" vowel such as the English *a* in *along*, the French *e* in *cheval*. Sounds of this type are generally unaccented; they may, however, be accented, e.g. in Welsh *yn*.

ɨ, Russian ы. Approximate to an "unrounded" **u**, *i.e.* a vowel with tongue position of **u** but lip position of **i**.

æ, like Southern English *a* in *hat*.

ü, an "advanced" **u** (between **u** and **y**).

ö, an "advanced" **o** (between **o** and **ø**).

FRENCH

Vowels.—

i	written	*i*	*si*	**(si)**
	,,	*ie*	*vie*	**(vi)**
	,,	*î*	*gît*	**(ʒi)**
	,,	*y*	*cygne*	**(siɲ)**
e	written	*é*	*pré*	**(pre)**
	,,	*ai*	*j'ai*	**(ʒe)**
	,,	*e*	*pied*	**(pje)**
	,,	*er*	*aimer*	**(ɛme)**
	,,	*ez*	*aimez*	**(ɛme)**
	,,	*œ*	*Phœbé*	**(febe)**
ɛ	written	*e*	*bel*	**(bɛl)**
	,,	*è*	*père*	**(pɛːr)**
	,,	*ê*	*tête*	**(tɛːt)**
	,,	*ais*	*aimais*	**(ɛmɛ)**
	,,	*ait*	*aimait*	**(ɛmɛ)**
	,,	*ai*	*vrai*	**(vrɛ)**
	,,	*aie*	*craie*	**(krɛ)**
	,,	*aî*	*faîtes*	**(fɛt)**
	,,	*a*	*payer*	**(pɛje)**
	,,	*ei*	*reine*	**(rɛːn)**
a	written	*a*	*la*	**(la)**
	,,	*à*	*là*	**(la)**
	,,	*â*	*-âmes*	**(-am)**
	,,	*e*	*femme*	**(fam)**
	,,	*oi*	*moi*	**(mwa)**
ɑ	written	*a*	*bas*	**(bɑ)**
	,,	*â*	*pâte*	**(pɑːt)**
	,,	*oi*	*trois*	**(trwɑ)**
ɔ	written	*o*	*Nord*	**(nɔːr)**
	,,	*ô*	*rôti*	**(rɔti)**
	,,	*au*	*mauvais*	**(mɔvɛ)**
	,,	*u(m)*	*album*	**(albɔm)**
o	written	*o*	*pot*	**(po)**
	,,	*ô*	*hôte*	**(oːt)**
	,,	*eau*	*Beaune*	**(boːn)**
	,,	*au*	*pauvre*	**(poːvr)**
u	written	*ou*	*trouve*	**(truːv)**
	,,	*oû*	*goût*	**(gu)**
	,,	*où*	*où*	**(u)**
y	written	*u*	*pu*	**(py)**
	,,	*û*	*sûr*	**(syːr)**
	,,	*eu*	*eu*	**(y)**
	,,	*eû*	*eût*	**(y)**
	,,	*eue*	*eue*	**(y)**
ø	written	*eu*	*peu*	**(pø)**
	,,	*œu*	*œufs*	**(ø)**
	,,	*eue*	*queue*	**(kø)**
œ	written	*eu*	*peur*	**(pœːr)**
	,,	*œu*	*œuf*	**(œf)**
	,,	*ue*	*orgueil*	**(ɔrgœːj)**

	ə	written	*e*	*le* (**lə**) ; *de* (**də**) ; *que* (**kə**) ; *ce* (**sə**)	
		,,	*ai*	*faisant*	(**fəzɑ̃**)
	ɛ̃	written	*in*	*vin*	(**vɛ̃**)
		,,	*im*	*important*	(**ɛ̃pɔrtɑ̃**)
		,,	*ain*	*pain*	(**pɛ̃**)
		,,	*aim*	*faim*	(**fɛ̃**)
		,,	*ein*	*peintre*	(**pɛ̃:tr**)
		,,	*eim*	*Rheims*	(**rɛ̃:s**)
		,,	*yn*	*syntaxe*	(**sɛ̃taks**)
		,,	*ym*	*sympathie*	(**sɛ̃pati**)
		,,	*en*	*rien*	(**rjɛ̃**)
	ɑ	written	*an*	*blanc*	(**blɑ̃**)
		,,	*am*	*Ambroise*	(**ɑ̃brwa:z**)
		,,	*en, ant*	*enfant*	(**ɑ̃fɑ̃**)
		,,	*em*	*remplir*	(**rɑ̃pli:r**)
		,,	*aon*	*paon*	(**pɑ̃**)
	ɔ̃	written	*on*	*bon*	(**bɔ̃**)
		,,	*om*	*nom*	(**nɔ̃**)
	œ̃	written	*un*	*un*	(**œ̃**)
		,,	*um*	*humble*	(**œ̃:bl**)
		,,	*eun*	*jeun*	(**ʒœ̃**)
		,,	*eung*	*Meung*	(**mœ̃**)
Semi-Vowels.—					
	j	written	*i* followed by a vowel after a single consonant.		
		,,		*fier* (*proud*)	(**fjɛ:r**), (*to rely*) (**fje**)
		,,		*fiacre*	(**fjakr**)
		,,	*ill*	*travailler*	(**travaje**)
		,,	*ll*	*Chantilly*	(**ʃɑ̃tiji**)
		,,	*y*	*yeux*	(**jø**)
	w	written	*w*	*wallon*	(**walɔ̃**)
		,,	*oi*	*moi*	(**mwa**)
		,,	*oy*	*moyen*	(**mwajɛ̃**)
		,,	*ou* after a single consonant.		
				jouer	(**ʒwe**)
		,,	*u*	*équateur*	(**ekwatœ:r**)
	y̌*	written	*u* whenever followed by *i*, also before other vowels if only a single consonant precedes.		
		,,		*lui*	(**ly̌i**)
		,,		*nuage*	(**ny̌a:ʒ**)
		,,		*tuer*	(**ty̌e**)
Consonants.—					
	b	written	*b*	*robe*	(**rɔb**)
		,,	*bb*	*abbé*	(**abe**)
(unaspirated)	**p**	written	*p*	*Paris*	(**pari**)
		,,	*pp*	*nappe*	(**nap**)
		,,	*b*	*absolument*	(**apsɔlymɑ̃**)
(dental)	**d**	written	*d*	*du*	(**dy**)
		,,	*dd*	*addition*	(**adisjɔ̃**)

* **y̌** is often written **ɥ** in phonetic texts.

(dental, unaspirated)	**t**	written	*t*	*temps*	**(tɑ̃)**
		,,	*tt*	*flotte*	**(flɔt)**
		,,	*th*	*thé*	**(te)**
		,,	*d*	*grand homme*	**(grɑ̃tɔm)**
	g	written	*g*	*gai*	**(ge)**
		,,	*gg*	*aggraver*	**(agrave)**
		,,	*gu*	*guide*	**(gid)**
		,,	*c*	*second*	**(səgɔ̃)**
(unaspirated)	**k**	written	*k*	*kilo*	**(kilo)**
		,,	*c*	*car*	**(kaːr)**
		,,	*cc*	*accumuler*	**(akymyle)**
		,,	*qu*	*qui*	**(ki)**
		,,	*ch*	*orchestre*	**(ɔrkɛstr)**
		,,	*g*	*de long en large*	**(də lɔ̃k ɑ̃ larʒ)**
	m	written	*m*	*mon*	**(mɔ̃)**
		,,	*mm*	*homme*	**(ɔm)**
	n	written	*n*	*non*	**(nɔ̃)**
		,,	*nn*	*ennemi*	**(ɛnmi)**
		,,	*mn*	*automne*	**(ɔtɔn)**
	ɲ	written	*gn*	*Boulogne*	**(bulɔɲ)**
	l	written	*l*	*Louis*	**(lwi)**
		,,	*ll*	*coller*	**(kɔle)**

R or **r** The uvular rolled or fricative sound appears to be general in Paris; the lingual rolled sound is common in some districts, especially in the country. For general purposes the symbol **r** will suffice.

r	written	*r*	*Rouen*	**(rwɑ̃)**
	,,	*rr*	*erreur*	**(ɛrœːr)**
v	written	*v*	*vive*	**(viːv)**
	,,	*f*	*neuf heures*	**(nœvœːr)**
	,,	*w*	*wagon*	**(vagɔ̃)**
f	written	*f*	*faire*	**(fɛːr)**
	,,	*ff*	*affaire*	**(afɛːr)**
	,,	*ph*	*philosophie*	**(filɔzɔfi)**
z	written	*z*	*gaz*	**(gɑːz)**
	,,	*s*	*rose*	**(roːz)**
	,,	*x*	*six enfants*	**(sizɑ̃fɑ̃)**
s	written	*s*	*son*	**(sɔ̃)**
	,,	*ss ce*	*essence*	**(ɛsɑ̃ːs)**
	,,	*c*	*cité*	**(site)**
	,,	*ç*	*reçu*	**(rəsy)**
	,,	*sc*	*scène*	**(sɛːn)**
	,,	*ti*	*éducation*	**(edykɑsjɔ̃)**
	,,	*x*	*six*	**(sis)**
	,,	*z*	*seltz*	**(sɛlts)**
ʒ	written	*j*	*jamais*	**(ʒamɛ)**
	,,	*g*	*rouge*	**(ruːʒ)**
	,,	*ge*	*geôle*	**(ʒoːl)**

ʃ	written	*ch*	*Chine*	**(ʃin)**
	„	*sh*	*shako*	**(ʃako)**
	„	*sch*	*schisme*	**(ʃism)**

The letter *h* is never pronounced except sometimes in interjections such as *aha! he!* Some words that begin with this letter allow of elision and liaison, *e.g. l'homme* (**l ɔm**), *les hommes* (**lez ɔm**). Others do not allow of elision or liaison, *le hibou* (**lə ibu**), *les hiboux* (**le ibu**). This is the only difference between the "*h* mute" and the "*h* aspirate."

Length of Vowel Sounds.—Vowel sounds can normally be fully long only in final closed syllables. The nasalized vowels and **o, ø** (and **ɑ** except when preceded by **w**) are always long in final closed syllables. All vowels are long if final and closed by **v, z, ʒ, r, vr**, and, in the pronunciation of some people, by **j**. Vowels in open syllables are usually short even when stressed.

Stress.—This falls normally on the final pronounced syllable in a word or group. If the stress is emphatic it may fall on another syllable.

absolument is **apsɔlyˈmɑ̃** normally, but **apˈsɔlymɑ̃** emphatically.

ITALIAN

Vowels.—

i	written	*i*	*finito*	**(fiˈniːto)**
e	„	*e*	*venti (twenty)*	**(ˈventi)**
ɛ	„	*e*	*venti (winds)*	**(ˈvɛnti)**
a	„	*a*	*parlare*	**(parˈlaːre)**
ɔ	„	*o*	*troppo*	**(ˈtrɔppo)**
o	„	*o*	*ora*	**(ˈoːra)**
u	„	*u*	*cura*	**(ˈkuːra)**

Semi-Vowels.—

j	written	*i*	before another vowel, except after *g, c, sc*	
			bianco	**(ˈbjaŋko)**
w	„	*u*	before another vowel	
			guanto	**(ˈgwanto)**

Consonants.—

	b	written	*b*		*bene*	**(ˈbɛːne)**
	bb	„	*bb*		*abbassare*	**(abbasˈsaːre)**
(unaspirated)	**p**	„	*p*		*pagare*	**(paˈgaːre)**
(unaspirated)	**pp**	„	*pp*		*appellare*	**(appelˈlaːre)**
(dental)	**d**	„	*d*		*dilettante*	**(diletˈtante)**
(dental)	**dd**	„	*dd*		*addosso*	**(adˈdɔsso)**
(dental unaspirated)	**t**	„	*t*		*conto*	**(ˈkonto)**
(dental unaspirated)	**tt**	„	*tt*		*ditto*	**(ˈditto)**
	g	„	*g*	before *a, o, u*	*gusto*	**(ˈgusto)**
		„	*gh*	„ *e, i*	*ghetto*	**(ˈgetto)**
	gg	„	*gg*		*fugga*	**(ˈfugga)**
(unaspirated)	**k**	„	*c*	before *a, o, u*	*caro*	**(ˈkaːro)**
		„	*ch*	„ *i, e*	*che*	**(ke)**
	kk	„	*cc*	„ *a, o, u*	*bocca*	**(ˈbokka)**
	dʒ	„	*g*	„ *i, e*	*gente*	**(ˈdʒɛnte)**
		„	*gi*	„ *a, o, u*	*gia*	**(dʒa)**
	ddʒ	„	*gg*	„ *i, e*	*oggi*	**(ˈɔddʒi)**
		„	*ggi*	„ *a, o, u*	*fuggiasco*	**(fudˈdʒasko)**
	tʃ	„	*c*	„ *i, e*	*certo*	**(ˈtʃɛrto)**
		„	*ci*	„ *a, o, u*	*ciascuno*	**(tʃasˈkuːno)**

ttʃ	written	*cc* before *i, e*	*accidente*	**(attʃiˈdente)**
	,,	*cci* ,, *a, o, u*	*faccia*	**(ˈfattʃa)**
dz	,,	*z*	*zona*	**(ˈdzɔːna)**
ddz	,,	*zz*	*mezzo*	**(ˈmɛddzo)**
ts	,,	*z*	*zio*	**(ˈtsiːo)**
tts	,,	*zz*	*ragazzo*	**(raˈgattso)**
m	,,	*m*	*madre*	**(ˈmaːdre)**
mm	,,	*mm*	*commedia*	**(komˈmɛːdja)**
n	,,	*n*	*natura*	**(naˈtuːra)**
nn	,,	*nn*	*anno*	**(ˈanno)**
ɲ	,,	*gn*	*gnocchi*	**(ˈɲɔkki)**
ɲɲ	,,	*gn*	*ogni*	**(ˈoɲɲi)**
ɱ	,,	*n* before *f* and *v*	*convenio*	**(koɱˈvɛːnjo)**
l	,,	*l*	*luna*	**(ˈluːna)**
ll	,,	*ll*	*bollo*	**(ˈbollo)**
ʎ	,,	*gl*	*gli*	**(ʎi)**
ʎʎ	,,	*gl*	*figlia*	**(ˈfiʎʎa)**
r	,,	*r*	*Roma*	**(ˈroːma)**
rr	,,	*rr*	*corriere*	**(korˈrjɛːre)**
v	,,	*v*	*viva*	**(ˈviːva)**
vv	,,	*vv*	*avvenire*	**(avveˈniːre)**
f	,,	*f*	*fare*	**(ˈfaːre)**
ff	,,	*ff*	*affare*	**(afˈfaːre)**
z	,,	*s*	*sbaglio*	**(ˈzbaʎʎo)**
			musica	**(ˈmuːzika)**
s	,,	*s*	*salsa*	**(ˈsalsa)**
ss	,,	*ss*	*basso*	**(ˈbasso)**
ʃ	,,	*sc* before *i, e*	*scena*	**(ˈʃɛːna)**
	,,	*sci* ,, *a, o, u*	*sciatica*	**(ˈʃaːtika)**
ʃʃ	,,	*sc* ,, *i, e*	*uscire*	**(uʃˈʃiːre)**
	,,	*sci* ,, *a, o, u*	*ascia*	**(ˈaʃʃa)**
kw	,,	*cu*	*scuola*	**(ˈskwɔːla)**
	,,	*qu*	*acqua*	**(ˈakkwa)**

The letter *h* is not pronounced.

Length of Vowel Sounds.—The accented vowel is long in open syllables, and short in closed syllables, *e.g. caro* is **kaːro**; *carro* is **karro**.

Position of Stress.—Usually on the last syllable but one. An accent over the last vowel shows that the stress is on that vowel, *e.g. sarò*. Sometimes the accent may be on the antepenultimate syllable, or even before that.

SPANISH

Vowels.—

i	written	*i*	*si*	**(si)**
e	,,	*e*	*el*	**(el)**
a	,,	*a*	*la*	**(la)**
o	,,	*o*	*no*	**(no)**
u	,,	*u*	*uno*	**(ˈuno)**

Consonants.—

b	written	*b* after *m*	*sombra*	**(ˈsombra)**
β	,,	*b* not preceded by *m*	*bueno*	**(ˈβweno)**
			acabar	**(akaˈβar)**

(unaspirated)	**p**	written	*p*	*para*		**(ˈpara)**
(dental)	**d**	„	*d*	after *n* or *l*	*mundo*	**(ˈmundo)**
					saldo	**(ˈsaldo)**
	ð	„	*d*	not preceded by *n* or *l*		
				día		**(ˈðia)**
				madre		**(ˈmaðre)**
(dental unaspirated)	**t**	„	*t*	*tarde*		**(ˈtarðe)**
	g	„	*g*	initially, before *a, o, u*		
				gallo		**(ˈgaʎo)**
		„	*gu*	initially, before *i, e*		
				guerra		**(ˈgerra)**
	gw	„	*gu*	before *a, o*	*guante*	**(ˈgwante)**
	ɣ	„		not initial, and not preceded by *n*		
				rogar		**(roˈɣar)**
		„	*gu*	not initial, and not preceded by *n*		
				seguir		**(seˈɣir)**
(unaspirated)	**k**	„	*c*	before *a, o, u*	*caza*	**(ˈkaθa)**
		„	*qu*	„ *i, e*	*querer*	**(keˈrer)**
	kw	„	*cu*	„ *a, e, i, o*		
				cual		**(kwal)**
	c	„	*ch*	*muchacho*		**(muˈcaco)**
	m	„	*m*	*mil*		**(mil)**
	n	„	*n*	*nosotros*		**(noˈsotros)**
	ɱ	„	*n* before *f*		*enfático*	**(eɱˈfatiko)**
	ŋ	„	*n*	„ *c, g, j*		
				cinco		**(ˈθiŋko)**
				naranja		**(naˈraŋxa)**
	ɲ	„	*ñ*	*pequeño*		**(peˈkeɲo)**
	l	„	*l*	*la*		**(la)**
	ʎ	„	*ll*	*llevar*		**(ʎeˈβar)**
	r	„	*r*	*pero*		**(ˈpero)**
	rr	„	*rr*	*perro*		**(ˈperro)**
	f	„	*f*	*fácil*		**(ˈfaθil)**
	θ	„	*c*	before *i, e*	*cerca*	**(ˈθerka)**
		„	*z*	*razón*		**(raˈθon)**
	x	„	*j*	*Juan*		**(xwan)**
		„	*g*	*gemir*		**(xeˈmir)**
	s	„	*s*	*casa*		**(ˈkasa)**

s never has the *z* sound of English *rose*.

Semi-Vowels.—

j	written	*i*	*piedra*	**(ˈpjeðra)**
w	„	*u*	*fuerza*	**(ˈfwerθa)**

Length of Vowels.—Accented vowels are probably longer in open syllables than in closed syllables; but the difference in length is not considerable. As a general rule, in the colloquial language, all vowels may be pronounced short.

Stress.—This generally falls on the penultimate syllable of words ending in a vowel, diphthong, or *n* or *s*, e.g. *castillo* (**kasˈtiʎo**), *pueden* (**ˈpweðen**), *lunes* (**ˈlunes**); but on the last syllable if the word ends in a consonant other than *n* or *s*, e.g. *rogar* (**roˈɣar**). When these rules are not followed, the stress is shown by an accent in the spelling, e.g. *razón*, *rápido*.

GERMAN

	Sound		Spelling	Example	Pronunciation
Vowels.—		written	*i*	*mir*	**(miːr)**
		,,	*ie*	*sie*	**(ziː)**
		,,	*ih*	*ihn*	**(iːn)**
		,,	*ieh*	*Vieh*	**(fiː)**
	ɪ	,,	*i*	*bitte*	**(ˈbɪtə)**
	e	,,	*e*	*schwer*	**(ʃveːr)**
		,,	*ee*	*Meer*	**(meːr)**
		,,	*eh*	*sehr*	**(zeːr)**
	ɛ	,,	*e*	*fest*	**(fɛst)**
		,,	*ä*	*Hände*	**(ˈhɛndə)**
	a	,,	*a*	*Mann*	**(man)**
				da	**(daː)**
		,,	*aa*	*Aal*	**(aːl)**
		,,	*ah*	*Stahl*	**(ʃtaːl)**
	ɔ	,,	*o*	*fort*	**(fɔrt)**
	o	,,	*o*	*so*	**(zoː)**
		,,	*oo*	*Boot*	**(boːt)**
		,,	*oh*	*roh*	**(roː)**
	u	,,	*u*	*du*	**(duː)**
		,,	*uh*	*Kuh*	**(kuː)**
	ʊ	,,	*u*	*Duft*	**(dʊft)**
	y	,,	*ü*	*für*	**(fyːr)**
	ʏ	,,	*ü*	*Hütte*	**(ˈhʏtə)**
		,,	*üh*	*Hühner*	**(ˈhyːnər)**
	ø	,,	*ö*	*schön*	**(ʃøːn)**
	œ	,,	*ö*	*zwölf*	**(tsvœlf)**
	ə	,,	*e*	*gegangen*	**(gəˈgaŋən)**
Diphthongs.—	**ai**	written	*ei*	*ein*	**(ain)**
		,,	*ai*	*Mai*	**(mai)**
		,,	*ey*	*Meyer*	**(ˈmaiər)**
		,,	*ay*	*Bayern*	**(ˈbaiərn)**
	au	,,	*au*	*aus*	**(aus)**
	ɔy	,,	*eu*	*deutsch*	**(dɔytʃ)**
	(also pronounced **ɔi**)				
		written	*äu*	*Häuser*	**(ˈhɔyzər)**
Consonants.—	**b**	written	*b*	*bald*	**(balt)**
	(aspirated) **p**	,,	*p*	*Pack*	**(pak)**
		,,	*b* final, or followed by other consonants		
		,,	*ab*		**(ap)**
				abhängig	**(ˈaphɛŋɪç)**
	d	,,	*d*	*du*	**(duː)**
	(aspirated) **t**	,,	*t*	*Tausend*	**(ˈtauzənt)**
		,,	*d* final	*und*	**(ʊnt)**
		,,	*dt*	*Stadt*	**(ʃtat)**
	g	,,	*g* not final	*gehen*	**(ˈgeːən)**
	(aspirated) **k**	,,	*k*	*kalt*	**(kalt)**
		,,	*ck*	*dick*	**(dɪk)**
		,,	*ch* when followed by *s*		
				Achse	**(ˈaksə)**
		,,	*g* final after *a, o, u* (also pronounced **x**)		
				Tag	**(taːk)**

m	written	*m*	*machen*	(ˈmaxən)
n	,,	*n*	*Nacht*	(naxt)
ŋ	,,	*ng, n* before *k*		
			singen	(ˈzɪŋən)
			sinken	(ˈzɪŋkən)
l	,,	*l*	*leben*	(ˈleːbən)
r	,,	*r*	*rot*	(roːt)
(also pronounced **R**)				
v	written	*w*	*wohl*	(voːl)
(also pronounced **β**)				
	written	*(q)u*	*Quelle*	(ˈkvɛlə)
f	,,	*f*	*Fall*	(fal)
	,,	*v*	*viel*	(fiːl)
	,,	*ph*	*Phonetik*	(foˈneːtɪk)
z	,,	*s*	*so*	(zoː)
	,,	*z*	(in foreign words)	
			Gaze	(ˈgaːzə)
s	,,	*s*	*bis*	(bɪs)
	,,	*ss*	*Kasse*	(ˈkasə)
ts	,,	*z*	*zu*	(tsuː)
	,,	*tz*	*Satz*	(zats)
	,,	*ti*	*Nation*	(naːˈtsjoːn)
ʒ	,,	*j*	(in some foreign words)	
			Journal	(ʒurˈnal)
ʃ	,,	*sch*	*schlafen*	(ˈʃlaːfən)
	,,	*s*	initially before *p, t*	
			sprechen	(ˈʃprɛçən)
	,,	*ch*	(in French words)	
			chef	(ʃɛf)
ç	,,	*ch*	after *i, e, ö, ü, l, r*	
			möchte	(mœçtə)
			Bücher	(ˈbyːçər)
			milch	(mɪlç)
			durch	(dʊrç)
	,,	*ch*	in the diminutive suffix *-chen*	
			Mädchen	(ˈmɛːtçən)
	,,	*g*	final after *i, e, ö, ü*	
			König	(ˈkøːniç)
ɣ	,,	*g*	medial after *a, o, u*	
(also pronounced **g**)			*Tage*	(ˈtaːɣə)
x	written	*ch*	after *a, o, u* *Buch* (buːx)	
	,,	*g*	final after *a, o, u* (also pronounced **k**)	
			Tag	(taːx)
h	,,	*h*	*Hand*	(hant)

Glottal Stop.—Every vowel, initial in a stressed syllable, may be preceded by a glottal stop (ʔ), resembling a slight cough and articulated by means of complete closure and sudden opening of the glottis: *e.g. Verein* (fɛrˈʔain).

Length.—The vowels **i, e, o, u, ø** are long; **a, ɛ, y** may be long or short; **ɪ, ɔ, ʏ, ɔ, œ, ə** are short.

Stress.—Usually on the radical syllable in simple words. Compounds vary.

DUTCH

Vowels.—

	i	written	*i*	*machine*	(**maːˈʃiːnə**)
		„	*ie*	*tien*	(**tiːn**)
	ɩ	„	*i*	*zitten*	(**ˈzɩtə[n]**)
	e	„	*e*	*lezen*	(**ˈleːzə[n]**)
		„	*ee*	*meest*	(**meːst**)
	ɛ	„	*e*	*recht*	(**rɛxt**)
	a	„	*a*	*raden*	(**ˈraːdə[n]**)
		„	*aa*	*Haag*	(**haːx**)
	ɑ	„	*a*	*kar*	(**kɑr**)
	ɔ	„	*o*	*hof*	(**hɔf**)
	o	„	*o*	*koning*	(**ˈkoːnəŋ**)
		„	*oo*	*hoog*	(**hoːx**)
	u	„	*oe*	*goed*	(**ɣuːt**)
	y	„	*u*	*u*	(**y**)
		„	*uu*	*duur*	(**dyːr**)
	ø	„	*eu*	*deugd*	(**døːxt**)
	œ	„	*u*	*hut*	(**hœt**)
	ə	„	*e*	*zingen*	(**ˈzɩŋə[n]**)

Diphthongs.—

	ai	written	*aai*	*draai*	(**drai**)
	ɛi	„	*ei*	*meisje*	(**ˈmɛiʃə**)
		„	*ij*	*schrijver*	(**ˈsxrɛivər**)
	oi	„	*ooi*	*mooi*	(**moi**)
	ui	„	*oei*	*groeit*	(**ɣruit**)
	œy	„	*ui*	*huis*	(**hœys**)
	eu	„	*eeuw*	*sneeuw*	(**sneu**)
	iu	„	*ieuw*	*nieuw*	(**niu**)
	yu	„	*uw*	*duwde*	(**dyudə**)
	ɔu	„	*ou*	*vrouw*	(**vrɔu**)
		„	*au*	*kauwen*	(**ˈkɔuə[n]**)

Consonants.—

	b	written	*b*	*bak*	(**bak**)
(unaspirated)	**p**	„	*p*	*pad*	(**pɑt**)
	d	„	*d*	*doof*	(**doːf**)
(unaspirated)	**t**	„	*t*	*tien*	(**tiːn**)
		„	*d*	finally *hand*	(**hɑnt**)
	g	„	*k*	the *g* sound occurs only accidentally in Dutch by assimilation; *ik ben* is pronounced **ig bɛn.**	
(unaspirated)	**k**	„	*k*	*kat*	(**kɑt**)
	c	„	*tj*	*beetje*	(**ˈbeːcə**)
	m	„	*m*	*man*	(**mɑn**)
	n	„	*n*	*niemand*	(**ˈniːmɑnt**)
	ɲ	„	*nj*	*kastanje*	(**kɑsˈtɑɲə**)
	ŋ	„	*n*	*danken*	(**ˈdɑŋkə[n]**)
	l	„	*l*	*lachen*	(**ˈlɑxən**)
	r	„	*r*	*recht*	(**rɛxt**)
	v	„	*v*	*haven*	(**ˈhaːvə[n]**)
	f	„	*f*	*fijn*	(**fɛin**)
	z	„	*z*	*zulk*	(**zœlk**)
	s	„	*s*	*stad*	(**stɑt**)
(in foreign words)	**ʒ**	„	*g*	*bagage*	(**baːˈɣaːʒə**)

ʃ	written	*sj*	*huisje*	**(ˈhœyʃə)**
	„	*ch*	*chokola*	**(ʃoːkoːˈlaː)**
	„	*ti*	*station*	**(staːˈʃoːn)**
			also pronounced	**(staːˈsjoːn)**
ɣ	„	*g*	*goed*	**(ɣuːt)**
x	„	*ch*	*acht*	**(ɑxt)**

Semi-Vowels.—

j	written	*j*	*ja*	**(ja)**

The letter **w** before vowels is pronounced like an English **v** but without audible friction; it must be kept quite distinct from **v**, which has friction. There exists a special phonetic letter for this sound (**ʋ**), but it is simpler to use **w** with a convention as to its value in Dutch.

Length.—The vowels **i, e, a, o, u, y, ø** are regularly long, **ɩ, ɛ, ɑ, ɔ, œ** and **ə** are always short.

Stress.—Words of Dutch origin that are not compounds are usually stressed on the first syllable. Stress of compound words varies. Foreign words usually retain foreign stress.

RUSSIAN

(*For Russian Alphabet see p. 1117.*)

Note on the symbols used :

1. The vowel **ɨ** belongs to the **i** phoneme, and is formed by a combination of approximately the tongue position of **u** with the lip position of **i**. The vowels **ö** and **ü** are centralized varieties of *o* and *u*.

2. The palatalization of a consonant is the articulation of that consonant *simultaneously* with a **j**. It is here shown by means of a raised full-stop over the consonant symbol.

Vowels.—

i	written	*и*	*мир*	**(ṁir)**
e	„	*е*	*петь*	**(ṗeṫ)**
	„	*э*	*эти*	**(ˈeṫɩ)**
ɛ	„	*е*	*нет*	**(ṅɛt)**
	„	*э*	*это*	**(ˈɛtə)**
a	„	*а*	*да*	**(da)**
	„	*я*	*ряд*	**(ṙat)**
	„	*о*	*отец*	**(aˈṫɛts)**
ɑ	„	*а*	*знал*	**(znɑl)**
o	„	*о*	*пол*	**(pol)**
	„	*ё*	*пёс*	**(ṗos)**
u	„	*у*	*тут*	**(tut)**
	„	*ю*	*бюст*	**(ḃust)**
ɨ	„	*ы*	*был*	**(bɨl)**
	„	*и*	*шить*	**(ʃɨṫ)**
æ	„	*я*	*пять*	**(ṗæṫ)**
ö	„	*ё*	*тётя*	**(ˈṫöṫə)**
ü	„	*ю*	*лютик*	**(ˈl̇üṫɩk)**

	ə	written	*а*	*самовар*	**(səmaˈvar)**
(always with very weak stress)					
		written	*о*	*тело*	**(ˈṫɛlə)**
		,,	*я*	*время*	**(ˈvṙeṁə)**
		,,	*е*	*знание*	**(ˈznaṅɩjə)**
	ɩ	,,	*я*	*десять*	**(ˈḋeṡɩṫ)**
		,,	*е*	*тепло*	**(ṫɩˈplo)**
		,,	*а*	*часа*	**(ṫʃɩˈsa)**
		,,	*и*	*диктант*	**(ḋɩkˈtant)**
		,,	*э*	*экономист*	**(ɩkənaˈṁist)**
Semi-Vowel.—					
	j	written	*й*	*пейте*	**(ṗejṫɩ)**
		,,	*ь*	*жильё*	**(zɨˈl̇jo)**
		included in	*я*	*яблоко*	**(ˈjabləkə)**
		,, ,,	*ё*	*ёлка*	**(ˈjolkə)**
		,, ,,	*ю*	*юг*	**(juk)**
		,, ,,	*е*	*есть*	**(jeṡṫ)**
Diphthongs.—					
	ɨj	written	*ый*	*слабый*	**(ˈslabɨj)**
	ɩj	,,	*ий*	*синий*	**(ˈṡiṅɩj)**
		,,	*ей*	*мыслей*	**(ˈmɨṡl̇ɩj)**
	aj	,,	*ай*	*тайга*	**(tajˈga)**
		,,	*ой*	*пойду*	**(pajˈdu)**
	uj	,,	*уй*	*уйти*	**(ujˈṫi)**
	əj	,,	*ай*	*думайте*	**(ˈduməjṫɩ)**
Consonants.—					
	b	written	*б*	*бант*	**(bant)**
	p	,,	*п*	*супа*	**(ˈsupə)**
		,,	*б*	*юбка*	**(ˈjupkə)**
	m	,,	*м*	*мука*	**(muˈka)**
	n	,,	*н*	*народ*	**(naˈrot)**
	f	,,	*ф*	*фон*	**(fon)**
		,,	*в*	*лавка*	**(ˈlafkə)**
	v	,,	*в*	*ворон*	**(ˈvorən)**
		,,	*г*	*сегодня*	**(ṡɩˈvoḋṅə)**
	t	,,	*т*	*брат*	**(brat)**
		,,	*д*	*сад*	**(sat)**
	d	,,	*д*	*дым*	**(dɨm)**
		,,	*т*	*отдых*	**(ˈoddɨx)**
("dark")	l	,,	*л*	*лук*	**(luk)**
	s	,,	*с*	*стол*	**(stol)**
		,,	*з*	*газ*	**(gas)**
	z	,,	*з*	*зло*	**(zlo)**
		,,	*с*	*с Богом*	**(ˈzboɣəm)**
	r	,,	*р*	*рыба*	**(ˈrɨbə)**
	k	,,	*к*	*кот*	**(kot)**
		,,	*г*	*юг*	**(juk)**

g	written	*г*	*город*	(ˈgorət)
	,,	*к*	*также*	(ˈtagʒə)
x	,,	*х*	*хан*	(xan)
	,,	*г*	*легко*	(l̇ɩxˈko)
ɣ	,,	*г*	*Господи*	(ˈɣospəḋɩ)
	,,	*хг*	*бухгалтер*	(buɣalˈṫɛr)
vv	,,	*вв*	*ввоз*	(vvos)
dd	,,	*дд*	*поддул*	(pədˈdul)
	,,	*тд*	*отдал*	(ˈoddəl)
tt	,,	*тт*	*оттого*	(əttaˈvo)
	,,	*дт*	*подтыкал*	(pətˈtɨkəl)
ss	,,	*сс*	*ссылка*	(ˈssɨlkə)
zz	,,	*зз*	*из-за*	(ˈizzə)
nn	,,	*нн*	*Анна*	(ˈannə)
ʃʃ	,,	*сш*	*сшить*	(ʃʃɨṫ)
	,,	*зш*	*из шкапа*	(ɩʃˈʃkapə)
ʒʒ	,,	*зж*	*изжога*	(ɩʒˈʒogə) or (ɩʒˈdʒogə)

(also pronounced ʒdʒ)

All the above consonants may undergo palatalization. When palatalization occurs, the consonants are represented by any of the letters given above, but are *followed* by one of the vowel letters я, ё, ю, и, е (instead of а, о, у, ы, э) or by the soft sign (ь).

Compare:

мяч	(ṁætʃ);	*мачта*	(ˈmatʃtə)
Пётр	(ṗotr);	*пот*	(pot)
бюро	(ḃuˈro);	*буря*	(ˈbuṙə)
тигр	(ṫigr);	*тыква*	(ˈtɨkvə)
сено	(ṡenə);	*сэн*	(sɛn)
брать	(braṫ);	*брат*	(brat)
ольга	(ol̇gə);	*волга*	(ˈvolgə)

tʃ	written	*ч*	*час*	(tʃas)
ʃtʃ	,,	*щ*	*щи*	(ʃtʃi)
	,,	*зч*	*извозчик*	(ɩzˈvoʃtʃɩk)
ʒ	,,	*ж*	*жатва*	(ˈʒatvə)
	,,	*з*	*позже*	(ˈpoʒʒɩ)
ʃ	,,	*ш*	*шум*	(ʃum)
	,,	*ж*	*муж*	(muʃ)
	,,	*сш*	*сумасшествие*	(sumaʃˈʃeṡṫv̇jɩə)
	,,	*с*	*счастье*	(ˈʃtʃæṡtjə)
	,,	*ч*	*что*	(ʃto)
	,,	*з*	*извозчик*	(ɩzˈvoʃtʃɩk)
ts	,,	*ц*	*центр*	(tsɛntr)

Length of vowels does not vary. The length is intermediate between long and short.

Stress is not fixed and appears to occur quite arbitrarily. It is very heavy and strongly influences vowel quality.

WELSH

The pronunciation here indicated is that of Southern Welsh

Vowels.—

i	written	*i*	*hir*	(**hiːr**)
	,,	*y*	*pryf*	(**priːv**)
	,,	*ŷ*	*tŷ*	(**tiː**)
	,,	*u*	*ugain*	(**ˈigain**)
ɩ	,,	*i*	*Dilys*	(**ˈdɩlɩs**)
	,,	*y*	*cyn*	(**kɩn**)
e	,,	*e*	*hen*	(**heːn**)
ɛ	,,	*e*	*pen*	(**pɛn**)
a	,,	*a*	*afon*	(**ˈavɔn**)
ɔ	,,	*o*	*pont*	(**pɔnt**)
o	,,	*o*	*nol*	(**noːl**)
	,,	*ô*	*môr*	(**moːr**)
ω	,,	*w*	*cwm*	(**kωm**)
u	,,	*w*	*pwll*	(**puːɬ**)
	,,	*ŵ*	*sŵn*	(**suːn**)
ə	,,	*y*	*yn*	(**ən**)

Semi-Vowels.—

j	written	*i*	*Joan*	(**ˈjoan**)
w	,,	*w*	*wedi*	(**ˈwedi**)

Diphthongs.—

ai	written	*ai*	*brain*	(**brain**)
	,,	*au*	*gwau*	(**gwai**)
	,,	*ae*	*cae*	(**kai**)
oi	,,	*oe*	*coed*	(**koid**)
ui	,,	*wy*	*mwy*	(**mui**)
əi	,,	*ei*	*peidio*	(**ˈpəidjo**)
	,,	*eu*	*teulu*	(**ˈtəili**)
ui	,,	*wy*	*mwyn*	(**muin**)
iu	,,	*iw*	*rhiw*	(**riu, r̥iu**)
	,,	*yw*	*rhyw*	(**riu, r̥iu**)
eu	,,	*ew*	*llew*	(**ɬeu**)
au	,,	*aw*	*awr*	(**aur**)
əu	,,	*ow*	*Towyn*	(**ˈtəuin**)

Consonants.—

b	written	*b*	*bachgen*	(**ˈbaxgen**)
p	,,	*p*	*pan*	(**pan**)
d	,,	*d*	*dinas*	(**ˈdinas**)
t	,,	*t*	*ty*	(**tiː**)
g	,,	*g*	*gair*	(**gair**)
k	,,	*c*	*cartref*	(**ˈkartrev**)
m	,,	*m*	*mam*	(**mam**)
n	,,	*n*	*nos*	(**noːs**)
ŋ	,,	*n* before *g, c*	*llong*	(**ɬɔŋ**)
l	,,	*l*	*lodes*	(**ˈlodes**)
ɬ	,,	*ll*	*Llangollen*	(**ɬaŋˈgɔɬɛn**)
r	,,	*r*	*caru*	(**ˈkari**)
	,,	*rh* (also pronounced **r̥**)		
			rhyw	(**r̥iu**)
v	,,	*f*	*fyny*	(**ˈvəni**)

f	written	*ff*	*ffynnon*	(ˈ**fənɔn**)
ð	„	*dd*	*eisteddfod*	(**əisˈtɛðvod**)
θ	„	*th*	*wyth*	(**uiθ**)
s	„	*s*	*saith*	(**saiθ**)
ʃ	„	*si*	*siarad*	(ˈ**ʃarad**)
(also pronounced **sj**)				
x	written	*ch*	*chwech*	(**xweːx**)
h	„	*h*	*haul*	(**hail**)

Length.—**i, e, a, o, u** may be long or short. **ι, ɛ, ɔ, ɷ, ə** are always short. For further details, see S. Jones's *Welsh Phonetic Reader*.

Stress.—Usually on the penultimate syllable, but there are exceptions.

For further and more detailed information, see the following works:

French

Passy: Les Sons du Français (Didier).
Armstrong: The Phonetics of French (Bell).
Passy: Conversations Françaises (Univ. of London Pr.).

Italian

Panconcelli-Calzia: Italiano (Teubner).
Camilli: Italian Phonetic Reader (Univ. of London Pr.).

Spanish

T. Navarro Tomás: Pronunciación Española (Madrid).
Stirling: Pronunciation of Spanish (Camb. Univ. Pr.)
Peers: Phonetic Spanish Reader (Manchester Univ. Pr.).

German

Viëtor: German Pronunciation (Reisland).
„ Die Aussprache des Schriftdeutschen (Reisland).
Egan: German Phonetic Reader (Univ. of London Pr.).

Dutch

Kruisinga: Grammar of Modern Dutch (Allen and Unwin).
Quick and Schilthuis: Dutch Phonetic Reader (Univ. of London Pr.).

Russian

S. Boyanus: Manual of Russian Pronunciation (Sidgwick and Jackson).
Boyanus and Jopson: Spoken Russian (Sidgwick and Jackson).

Welsh

S. Jones: Welsh Phonetic Reader (Univ. of London Pr.).
Orgaff yr Iaith Gymraeg (Univ. of Wales Pr., Cardiff).

See also *The Principles of the International Phonetic Association, Fundamentos de Escritura Fonética* (1944), and other publications of the Association, which are obtainable from the Department of Phonetics, University College, London.

PRONUNCIATION OF ADOPTED AND SEMI-ANGLICIZED WORDS

In the subjoined list will be found all those words in the main body of the DICTIONARY the pronunciation of which is not there given, together with a large number of others (mainly from the French) which may be pronounced either in their anglicized or their native manner. In cases in which the usual English spelling differs from that of the original the latter is added in italics and within brackets.

abat-jour	abaʒu:r
abattoir	abatwa:r
abat-voix	abavwa
abondance déclarée	abɔ̃dɑ̃:s declare
abreuvoir	abrœvwa:r
accolé	akɔle
accouchement	akuʃmɑ̃
accoucheur	akuʃœ:r
accoucheuse	akuʃø:z
acharnement	aʃarnəmɑ̃
adieu	adjø
affiche	afiʃ
aide-de-camp	ɛ:ddəkɑ̃
aide-mémoire	ɛ:dmemwa:r
allonge (fenc.)	alɔ̃:ʒ
amende honorable	amɑ̃:d ɔnɔrabl
amourette	amurɛt
ampere (*ampère*)	ɑ̃pɛ:r
angelot	ɑ̃ʒlo
anglice	ɑ̃glise
apache	apaʃ
appui	apy̆i
point d'appui	pwɛ̃ dapy̆i
are (meas.)	a:r
arête	arɛ:t
argand	argɑ̃
argot	argo
arrêt	arɛ
arrière	arjɛ:r
arrondissement	arɔ̃dismɑ̃
assignat	asiɲa
aubade	obad
auberge	obɛrʒ
aubergiste	obɛrʒist
avant-courier (*-courrier*)	avɑ̃kurje
avant-garde	avɑ̃gard
bagasse	bagas
baguette	baget
baignoire	bɛɲwa:r
bain-marie	bɛ̃mari
barège	barɛ:ʒ
Bastille	basti:j
bateau	bato

batiste	batist
battue	baty
bauxite	boksit
bayadère	bajadɛ:r
beau-idéal	boideal
beaujolais	boʒɔlɛ
beau-monde	bomɔ̃:d
beaune	bo:n
bechamel (*béchamelle*)	beʃamɛl
bêche-de-mer	bɛʃdəmɛ:r
Béguine	begin
berceuse	bɛrsø:z
bibelot	biblo
bijou	biʒu
bijouterie	biʒutri
billet-doux	bijɛdu
bistre	bistr
bizarrerie	bizarri
blanc-mange	blɑ̃mɑ̃:ʒ
blasé	blɑze
bois-de-rose	bwɑdəro:z
bon-bon	bɔ̃bɔ̃
bonhomie	bɔnɔmi
bon ton	bɔ̃ tɔ̃
bon-vivant	bɔ̃vivɑ̃
borné	bɔrne
bouillabaisse	bujabɛ:s
bouilli	buji
bouillon	bujɔ̃
boulevard	bulva:r
bouleversement	bulvɛrsəmɑ̃
bouquet	bukɛ
bouquet-garni	bukɛgarni
bouquetin	buktɛ̃
Bourbon	burbɔ̃
bourdon	burdɔ̃
bourgeois	burʒwa
bourgeoisie	burʒwazi
bourse	burs
boutade	butad
bouts-rimés	burime
brancard	brɑ̃ka:r
brasserie	brasri
brassière	brasjɛ:r

brioche	briɔʃ
brisance	brizɑ̃:s
brochure	brɔʃy:r
buffet	byfɛ
burette	byrɛt
cabochon	kabɔʃɔ̃
cache	kaʃ
café	kafe
Cagot	kago
Cagoulard	kagula:r
calèche	kalɛʃ
calembour	kalɑ̃bu:r
camaieu (*camaïeu*)	kamajø
camembert	kamɑ̃bɛ:r
camouflage	kamufla:ʒ
campagnol	kɑ̃paɲɔl
canaille	kana:j
canapé	kanape
canard	kana:r
cancan	kɑ̃kɑ̃
cap-à-pie	kapapi
caporal	kapɔral
carafe	karaf
carmagnole	karmaɲɔl
Carolingian (*-ien*)	karɔlɛ̃ʒjɛ̃
carte-blanche	kartblɑ̃ʃ
carte-de-visite	kartdəvizit
carton-pierre	kartɔ̃pjɛ:r
cassis	kɑsis
causerie	kozri
causeuse	kozø:z
centiare	sɑ̃tja:r
centime	sɑ̃tim
Chablis	ʃɑbli
chaise longue	ʃɛz lɔ̃:g
chalumeau	ʃalymo
chamade	ʃamad
champagne, fine	fin ʃɑ̃paɲ
champignon	ʃɑ̃piɲɔ̃
champlevé	ʃɑ̃lve
chanson	ʃɑ̃sɔ̃
chantage	ʃɑ̃ta:ʒ
chapeau	ʃapo
chaperon	ʃaprɔ̃
char-à-banc	ʃarabɑ̃
chargé d'affaires	ʃarʒe dafɛ:r
charivari	ʃarivari
charmeuse	ʃarmø:z
chartreuse	ʃartrø:z
chassepot	ʃaspo
château	ʃɑto
châtelaine	ʃɑtlɛn
chatoyant	ʃatwajɑ̃
chaud-mellé (*chaud-mêlé*)	ʃo melə
chauffeuse	ʃofø:z
chausses	ʃo:s
chaussure	ʃosy:r
chauvinism (*chauvinisme*)	ʃovinism
chef-d'œuvre	ʃɛdœ:vr
chemin de fer	ʃmɛ̃ də fɛ:r
chenille	ʃəni:j
cheval-de-frise	ʃəvaldəfri:z
chevelure	ʃəvly:r
chevron	ʃəvrɔ̃
chicane	ʃikan
chiffon	ʃifɔ̃
chiffonier (*-nnier*)	ʃifɔnje
chignon	ʃiɲɔ̃
chimere (*chimère*)	ʃimɛ:r
chinoiserie	ʃinwazri
chose jugée	ʃo:z ʒyʒe
chou	ʃu
ci-devant	sidvɑ̃
cierge	sjɛrʒ
cinque (*cinq*)	sɛ̃:k
cirque	sirk
claqueur	klakœ:r
clientele (*clientèle*)	kliɑ̃tɛl
cloche	klɔʃ
cocotte	kɔkɔt
cognac	kɔɲak
coiffeur	kwafœ:r
coiffure	kwafy:r
Cointreau	kwɛ̃tro
commère	kɔmɛ:r
communard	kɔmyna:r
commune (*n.*)	kɔmyn
communiqué	kɔmynike
compère	kɔ̃pɛ:r
compote	kɔ̃pɔt
comptoir	kɔ̃twa:r
Comtism (*comtisme*)	kɔ̃tism
concierge	kɔ̃sjɛrʒ
confrère	kɔ̃frɛ:r
congé	kɔ̃ʒe
congé d'élire	kɔ̃ʒe deli:r
connoisseur (*connaisseur*)	kɔ̃nɛsœ:r
consommé	kɔ̃sɔme
conte	kɔ̃:t
contredanse	kɔ̃trədɑ̃:s
contretemps	kɔ̃trətɑ̃
convenance	kɔ̃vnɑ̃:s
coque	kɔk
coquelicot	kɔkliko
coquet	kɔkɛ

coquette kɔkɛt
cordelier kɔrdəlje
cordon sanitaire kɔrdɔ̃ sanitɛːr
corps diplomatique kɔːr diplɔmatik
cortège kɔrtɛːʒ
corvée kɔrve
coryphée kɔrife
cosaque kɔzak
coulée kule
couleur-de-rose kulœːrdəroːz
coulisse kulis
couloir kulwaːr
coulomb kulɔ̃
coup ku
  coup d'état ku deta
  coup de main kudmɛ̃
  coup d'œil ku dœːj
  coup-de-poing kudpwɛ̃
coupon kupɔ̃
courant kurɑ̃
Cracovienne krakɔvjɛn
crampon krɑ̃pɔ̃
crayon krɛjɔ̃
crême-de-menthe krɛmdəmɑ̃ːt
crêpe-de-Chine krɛpdəʃin
Cro-Magnon krɔmaɲɔ̃
croûton krutɔ̃
cuir-bouilli kɥiːrbuji
cuisse kɥis
cul-de-sac kydsak
curé kyre

debacle (*débâcle*) debɑːkl
debris (*débris*) debri
débutante debytɑ̃ːt
décolletage dekɔltaːʒ
décolleté dekɔlte
décor dekɔːr
dedans dədɑ̃
dégringolade degrɛ̃gɔlad
déjeuner deʒœne
démarche demarʃ
démenti demɑ̃ti
demi-mondaine dəmimɔ̃dɛn
demi-monde dəmimɔ̃ːd
démodé demɔde
demoiselle dəmwazɛl
dengue dɑ̃ːg
denier (coin) dənje
dénouement denumɑ̃
dentelle dɑ̃tɛl
deshabille dezabiːj
  (*déshabille*)
détente detɑ̃ːt
détenu detny

devoir dəvwaːr
diamenté djamɑ̃te
difficile difisil
digue dig
diligence (vehicle) diliʒɑ̃ːs
dinanderie dinɑ̃ndri
diseur dizœːr
diseuse dizøːz
distingué distɛ̃ge
divertissement divɛrtismɑ̃
dossier dosje
douane dwan
douanier dwanje
double-entendre dublɑ̃tɑ̃ːdr
doublure dublyːr
douceur dusœːr
douzaine duzɛn
doyen dwajɛ̃
drágee draʒe
droit drwa
duchesse dyʃɛs
duvet dyvɛ

éboulement ebulmɑ̃
éclaircissement eklɛrsismɑ̃
éclat ekla
écorché ekɔrʃe
écossaise ekɔsɛːz
écraseur ekrɑzœːr
écru ekry
éloge elɔːʒ
embonpoint ɑ̃bɔ̃pwɛ̃
embouchure ɑ̃buʃyːr
embusqué ɑ̃byske
émeute emøːt
émigré emigre
empressement ɑ̃prɛsmɑ̃
en bloc ɑ̃ blɔk
enceinte ɑ̃sɛ̃ːt
enclave ɑ̃klaːv
encore ɑ̃kɔːr
ennui ɑ̃nɥi
ennuyé ɑ̃nɥije
ensemble ɑ̃sɑ̃ːbl
entente ɑ̃tɑ̃ːt
  entente cordiale ɑ̃tɑ̃ːt kɔrdjal
entourage ɑ̃turaːʒ
en-tout-cas ɑ̃tukɑ
entr'acte ɑ̃trakt
entrechat ɑ̃trəʃa
entrée ɑ̃tre
entremets ɑ̃trəmɛ
entrepôt ɑ̃trəpo
entrepreneur ɑ̃trəprənœːr
entresol ɑ̃trəsɔl

envelope (*enveloppe*)	ɑ̃vlɔp
épée	epe
espagnolette	ɛspaɲɔlɛt
espièglerie	ɛspjɛgləri
espionage (*espionnage*)	ɛspjɔna:ʒ
esprit de corps	ɛspridkɔ:r
estaminet	ɛstaminɛ
etui (*étui*)	etɥi
exergue	egzɛrg
exigeant	egziʒɑ̃
exposé	ɛkspoze
extincteur	ɛkstɛ̃ktœ:r
fabliau	fɑblio
faience (*faïence*)	fajɑ̃:s
fainéant	fɛneɑ̃
fanfaron	fɑ̃farɔ̃
fanon	fanɔ̃
farceur	farsœ:r
farceuse	farsø:z
fauteuil	fotœ:j
fête champêtre	fɛ:t ʃɑ̃pɛ:tr
feuilleton	fœjtɔ̃
fiacre	fjakr
fiancé	fjɑ̃se
figurant	figyrɑ̃
figurante	figyrɑ̃:t
flânerie	flɑnri
flâneur	flɑnœ:r
flèche	flɛʃ
fleur-de-lis	flœ:rdəli
fleuron	flœrɔ̃
fondant	fɔ̃dɑ̃
fondu	fɔ̃dy
fougasse	fugas
foulard	fula:r
Fourierism (*fouriérisme*)	furjerism
fourneau	furno
foyer	fwaje
fracas	frakɑ
franc-tireur	frɑ̃tirœ:r
frappé	frape
fricandeau	frikɑ̃do
fricassee (*fricassée*)	frikase
friseur	frizœ:r
Fronde	frɔ̃:d
Frondeur	frɔ̃dœ:r
fronton	frɔ̃tɔ̃
fusain	fyzɛ̃
fuselage	fyzla:ʒ
gamin	gamɛ̃
garage	gara:ʒ
garçon	garsɔ̃
gare	ga:r
gâteau	gɑto
gauche	go:ʃ
gaucherie	goʃri
gavage	gava:ʒ
genappe (*génappe*)	ʒenap
gendarme	ʒɑ̃darm
gendarmerie	ʒɑ̃darməri
genre	ʒɑ̃:r
georgette	ʒɔrʒɛt
gibus	ʒiby:s
girandole	ʒirɑ̃dɔl
girasol, girasole	ʒirasɔl
Girondist	ʒirɔ̃:dist
girouette	ʒirwɛt
glacis	glasi
Gobelin (*Gobelins*)	gɔblɛ̃
gobemouche	gɔbmuʃ
goitre	gwa:tr
gonfalon	gɔ̃falɔ̃
gonfalonier (*gonfalonnier*)	gɔ̃falɔnje
gouache	gwaʃ
goulard	gula:r
gourmand	gurmɑ̃
gourmet	gurmɛ
goût	gu
gradine (*gradin*)	gradin
gratin	gratɛ̃
greffier	grɛfje
griffon	grifɔ̃
grisaille	grizɑ:j
grisette	grizɛt
gruyère	gryjɛ:r
guichet	giʃɛ
guidon	gidɔ̃
guilloche	gijɔʃ
guipure	gipy:r
habitant	abitɑ̃
habitué	abitɥe
hachure	†aʃy:r
hangar	†ɑ̃ga:r
haut-goût	†ogu
haut-ton	†otɔ̃
hors	†ɔ:r
hors concours	†ɔr kɔ̃ku:r
hors de combat	†ɔr də kɔ̃ba
hors-d'œuvres	†ɔrdœ:vr
hôtel de ville	otɛl də vil
Hôtel-Dieu	otɛldjø

† Indicates that there is no linking or elision in connexion with preceding word.

impasse	ɛ̃pɑ:s
impuissance	ɛ̃py̆isɑ̃:s
impuissant	ɛ̃py̆isɑ̃
ingénue	ɛ̃ʒeny
insouciance	ɛ̃susjɑ̃:s
insouciant	ɛ̃susjɑ̃
Internationale	ɛ̃tɛrnasjɔnal
intrigant	ɛ̃trigɑ̃
jabot	ʒabo
Jacquerie	ʒɑkri
Jansenism (*jansénisme*)	ʒɑ̃senism
jardinière	ʒardinjɛ:r
jongleur	ʒɔ̃glœ:r
joule	ʒul
jullienne	ʒyljɛn
jurat	ʒyra
laissez-aller	lɛseale
laissez-faire	lɛsefɛ:r
lamé	lame
languet (*languette*)	lɑ̃gɛt
lardon	lardɔ̃
lavage	lava:ʒ
lese-majesty (*lèse-majesté*)	lɛ:zmaʒɛste
lingerie	lɛ̃ʒri
liqueur	likœ:r
livraison	livrɛzɔ̃
loge	lɔ:ʒ
longeron	lɔ̃ʒrɔ̃
lorgnette	lɔrɲet
louis-d'or	lwidɔ:r
macabre	makɑ:br
macedoine (*macédoine*)	masedwan
magnanerie	maɲanri
magot	mago
maigre	mɛ:gr
maître d'hotel	mɛ:trə dɔtɛl
majorat	maʒɔra
malaise	malɛ:z
malapropos	malaprɔpo
Malmaison	malmɛzɔ̃
manche	mɑ̃:ʃ
manège	manɛ:ʒ
mannequin	mankɛ̃
manqué	mɑ̃:ke
mardi-gras	mardigrɑ
marron	mɑrɔ̃
Marseillaise	marsɛjɛ:z
masseur	masœ:r
masseuse	masø:z
matelassé	matlase
matelot	matlo
matelote	matlɔt
matériel	materjɛl
mayonnaise	majɔnɛ:z
Médoc	medɔk
mélange	melɑ̃:ʒ
mêlée	mɛle
ménage	mena:ʒ
menu	məny
meringue	mərɛ̃:g
mésalliance	mezaljɑ̃:s
messieurs	mesjø
metayage (*métayage*)	metɛja:ʒ
metayer (*métayer*)	metɛje
métier	metje
métis	metis
mignon	miɲɔ̃
migraine	migrɛn
milieu	miljø
milliampere (*-père*)	milliɑ̃pɛ:r
millier	milje
minauderie	minodri
mise-en-scène	mizɑ̃sɛ:n
misère	mizɛ:r
mitraille	mitrɑ:j
mitrailleur	mitrajœ:r
mitrailleuse	mitrajø:z
moellon	mwalɔ̃
moiré	mware
monde	mɔ̃:d
monocoque	mɔnɔkɔk
Monseigneur	mɔ̃sɛɲœ:r
Monsieur	m(ə)sjø
Monsignor	monsiɲɔr
morale	mɔral
morceau	mɔrso
morcellement	mɔrsɛlmɑ̃
moulin	mulɛ̃
moulinage	mulina:ʒ
mousquetaire	muskətɛ:r
mousse	mus
mousseline-de-laine	muslindəlɛ:n
Mousterian (*moustérien*)	musterjɛ̃
moutonnée	mutɔne
musette	myzɛt
nacre	nakr
nacré	nakre
naïve	nai:v
naïveté	naivte
Napoleon (*-léon*)	napɔleɔ̃
née	ne

negligé	negliʒe
névé	neve
ninon	ninɔ̃
noisette	nwazɛt
nom-de-plume	nɔ̃dəplym
nonchalance	nɔ̃ʃalɑ̃:s
nonchalant	nɔ̃ʃalɑ̃
nonpareil	nɔ̃parɛ:j
noyade	nwajad
noyau	nwajo
nuance	nɥɑ̃:s
octroi	ɔktrwa
œillade	œjad
œille-de-bœuf	œjdəbœf
ogive	ɔʒi:v
opéra-bouffe	ɔperabuf
opéra comique	ɔpera kɔmik
öre	œrɛ
orfèvrerie	ɔrfɛvrəri
organdi (*organdie*)	ɔrgɑ̃di
oubliette	ubliɛt
outré	utre
paillasse	pajas
pailletet	pɑjɛt
paletot	palto
papeterie	papɛtri
papier-mâché	papjemɑʃe
papillon	papijɔ̃
papillote	papijɔt
pari-mutuel	parimytɥɛl
Parisienne	parizjɛn
parquet	parkɛ
parterre	partɛ:r
parure	pary:r
parvenu	parvəny
passementerie	pɑsmɑ̃tri
passe-partout	pɑspartu
pastiche	pastiʃ
pastille	pasti:j
pâté	pɑte
patisserie (*pâtisserie*)	pɑtisri
paysagist (*-giste*)	peizaʒist
peignoir	pɛɲwa:r
penchant	pɑ̃ʃɑ̃
pension (boarding-house)	pɑ̃sjɔ̃
percale	pɛrkal
percheron	pɛrʃərɔ̃
perdu	pɛrdy
perron	pɛrɔ̃
perruquier	pɛrykje
persiennes	pɛrsjɛn
persiflage	pɛrsifla:ʒ
persifleur	pɛrsiflœ:r
pervenche	pɛrvɑ̃:ʃ
pétrissage	petrisa:ʒ
pétroleur	petrɔlœ:r
pétroleuse	petrɔlø:z
pierrette	pjɛrɛt
pierrot	pjɛro
pince-nez	pɛ̃sne
pincette	pɛ̃sɛt
pioupiou	pjupju
piqué	pike
pisé	pize
plafond	plafɔ̃
plage	pla:ʒ
planchette	plɑ̃ʃɛt
Pleiad (*pléiade*)	plejad
plumassier	plymasje
pochette	pɔʃɛt
poilu	pwaly
pointillage	pwɛ̃tija:ʒ
pointillism (*pointillisme*)	pwɛ̃tijism
pointillist (*pointilliste*)	pwɛ̃tijist
Pommard	pɔma:r
pompadour	pɔ̃padu:r
pompier	pɔ̃pje
pompon	pɔ̃pɔ̃
ponceau	pɔ̃so
portcrayon (*portecrayon*)	pɔrtkrɛjɔ̃
portière	pɔrtjɛ:r
poseur	pozœ:r
poste-restante	pɔstrɛstɑ̃:t
poudrette	pudrɛt
pouffe (*pouf*)	puf
poulard (*poularde*)	pulard
poult-de-soie	putswa
pourboire	purbwa:r
pourparler	purparle
pourpoint	purpwɛ̃
poussette	pusɛt
poussin	pusɛ̃
pratique	pratik
précis	presi
predicant (*prédicant*)	predikɑ̃
première	prəmjɛ:r
prie-dieu	pridjø
princesse	prɛ̃sɛs
Provençal	prɔvɑ̃sal
prud'homme	prydɔm
pucelage	pysla:ʒ
purée	pyre
puy	pɥi

quadrillé	kadrije
quatorzaine	katɔrzɛn
quatorze	katɔrz
quenelle	kənɛl
quinzaine	kɛ̃zɛn
quinze	kɛ̃:z
râcloir	rɑklwa:r
raconteur	rakɔ̃tœ:r
raconteuse	rakɔ̃tø:z
ragoût	ragu
raisonné	rɛzɔne
ramollissement	ramɔlismɑ̃
ranz-des-vaches	rɑ̃devaʃ
rapprochement	raprɔʃmɑ̃
ratine	ratin
rayon	rɛjɔ̃
Réaumur	reomy:r
réchauffé	reʃofe
recherché	rəʃɛrʃe
Recollet (*récollet*)	rekɔlɛ
redacteur (*rédacteur*)	redaktœ:r
Régie	reʒi
religieuse	rəliʒjø:z
religieux	rəliʒjø
remblai	rɑ̃blɛ
remontoir	rəmɔ̃twa:r
remplissage	rɑ̃plisa:ʒ
Renaissance	rənɛsɑ̃:s
rencontre	rɑ̃kɔ̃:tr
rendezvous	rɑ̃devu
rente	rɑ̃:t
rentier	rɑ̃tje
renversé	rɑ̃vɛrse
répertoire	repɛrtwa:r
repoussage	rəpusa:ʒ
repoussé	rəpuse
restaurant	rɛstɔrɑ̃
restaurateur	rɛstɔratœ:r
resumé	rezyme
retroussage	rətrusa:ʒ
retroussé	rətruse
revenant	rəvnɑ̃
revue	rəvy
risqué	riske
rivage	riva:ʒ
rivière	rivjɛ:r
rompu	rɔ̃:py
roquefort	rɔkfɔ:r
roquelaure	rɔklɔ:r
rossignol	rɔsiɲɔl
roué	rwe
rouge-et-noir	ru:ʒenwa:r
ruche	ryʃ
ruse de guerre	ry:z də gɛ:r

sabotage	sabɔta:ʒ
saboteur	sabɔtœ:r
sabretache	sɑbrətaʃ
sabreur	sɑbrœ:r
sachet	saʃɛ
sagouin	sagwɛ̃
saint-simonian (*-simonien*)	sɛ̃simɔnjɛ̃
salon	salɔ̃
sangfroid	sɑ̃frwa
sansculotte	sɑ̃kylɔt
sansculottism (*sans-culottisme*)	sɑ̃kylɔtism
sapajou	sapaʒu
saucisson	sosisɔ̃
Saumur	somy:r
sauté	sote
Sauterne (*sauternes*)	sotɛrn
savant	savɑ̃
savate	savat
savonette	savɔnɛt
Savoyard	savwaja:r
schipperke	ʃipɛrke
séance	seɑ̃:s
secateur (*sécateur*)	sɛkatœ:r
secretaire (*secrétaire*)	səkretɛ:r
seiche	sɛ:ʃ
seigneur	sɛɲœ:r
seigneurial	sɛɲœrjal
seigneury (*seigneurie*)	sɛɲœri
seignior	si:ɲɔr
seine	sɛn
semblant	sɑ̃blɑ̃
sérac	sɛrak
serviette	sɛrvjɛt
Sèvres	sɛ:vr
siffleur	siflœ:r
siffleuse	siflø:z
sirvente	sirvɑ̃:t
soi-disant	swadizɑ̃
soirée	sware
sou	su
soubise	subi:z
soubrette	subrɛt
soufflé	sufle
soupçon	supsɔ̃
soutache	sutaʃ
soutane	sutan
souteneur	sutnœ:r
spadassin	spadasɛ̃
Spahi	spai
sparterie	spartri

table-d'hôte	tablədo:t
tac-au-tac	takotak
tapotement	tapɔtmɑ̃
Tartuffe	tartyf
tasse	tɑ:s
tenson	tɑ̃sɔ̃
terre-verte	tɛrvɛrt
thé dansant	te dɑ̃sɑ̃
tic-douloureux	tikdulurø
tiers-état	tjɛrzeta
tilleul	tijœl
timbale	tɛ̃bal
timbre	tɛ̃:br
tintamarre	tɛ̃tama:r
tirailleur	tirajœ:r
tisane	tizan
toise	twa:z
Toison d'or	twazɔ̃ dɔ:r
ton	tɔ̃
torchon	tɔrʃɔ̃
tourbillon	turbijɔ̃
tourelle	turɛl
tournure	turny:r
tous-les-mois	tulemwa
trébuchet	trebyʃɛ
treillage	trɛja:ʒ
trente-et-quarante	trɑ̃:tɛkarɑ̃:t
tricot	triko
tripe-de-roche	tripdərɔʃ
trompe	trɔ̃:p
trottoir	trɔtwa:r
trous-de-loup	trudlu
trousse	trus
trouvère	truvɛ:r
tulle	tyl
tuyère	tyjɛ:r
valenciennes	valɑ̃sjɛn
varsovienne	varsɔvjɛn
Vaudois	vodwa
veilleuse	vɛjø:z
velours	v(ə)lu:r
Ventôse	vɑ̃to:z
vers libre	vɛ:r libr
verslibrist (*verslibriste*)	vɛrlibrist
vigneron	viɲrɔ̃
vignette	viɲɛt
vingt-et-un	vɛ̃teœ̃
vin ordinaire	vɛ̃ ɔrdinɛ:r
vis-à-vis	vizavi
vivandière	vivɑ̃djɛ:r
vol-au-vent	vɔlovɑ̃
voltigeur	vɔltiʒœ:r
voussoir	vuswa:r
vraisemblance	vrɛsɑ̃blɑ̃:s

The Greek Alphabet

Capitals.	Small Letters.	English Equivalents.	Name	Capitals.	Small Letters.	English Equivalents.	Name
Α	α	a	Alpha	Ν	ν	n	Nu
Β	β	b	Bēta	Ξ	ξ	x	Xi
Γ	γ	g	Gamma	Ο	ο	o *short*	Omīcron
Δ	δ	d	Delta	Π	π	p	Pi
Ε	ε	e *short*	Epsīlon	Ρ	ρ	r	Rho
Ζ	ζ	z	Zeta	Σ	σ ς	s	Sigma
Η	η	e *long*	Eta	Τ	τ	t	Tau
Θ	θ	th	Theta	Υ	υ	u	Upsīlon
Ι	ι	i	Iōta	Φ	φ	ph	Phi
Κ	κ	k	Kappa	Χ	χ	ch	Chi (*ki*)
Λ	λ	l	Lambda	Ψ	ψ	ps	Psi
Μ	μ	m	Mu	Ω	ω	o *long*	Omega

The Hebrew Alphabet

Capital or Small.	Engl'sh Equivalents.	Name.	Capital or Small.	English Equivalents.	Name.
א	a	Alef	מ ם final	m	Memm
ב	b	Beth	נ ן final	n	Nun
ג	g (*hard*)	Gimel	ס	s	Samekh
ד	d	Daleth	ע	e	Ayin
ה	h	He	פ	p	Pe
ו	v	Vov	פ ף final	f (ph)	Fe
ז	z	Zayin	צ ץ final	z (ts)	Sadek
ח	h (*strong*)	Kheth	ק	q	Koph
ט	t	Teth	ר	r	Reish
י	y	Yod	שׂ	ṣ	Sin
כ ך final	kh	Khaf	שׁ	sh	Shin
ל	l	Lamed	ת	th	Thav

The Russian Alphabet: РУССКИЙ АЛФАВИТ

Capitals.	Small Letters.	English Equivalents.	Pronounced as in
А	а	a	father
Б	б	b	book
В	в	v	vote
Г	г	g	gay
Д	д	d	day
Е	е	ye	yes
Ж	ж	s	pleasure
З	з	z	zebra
И	и	ee	meet
Й	й	y	boy
К	к	k	kind
Л	л	l	lost
М	м	m	man
Н	н	n	not
О	о	o	o[r] (*never* "oh")
П	п	p	pen
Р	р	r	rolled
С	с	s	speak
Т	т	t	time
У	у	oo	root

Capitals.	Small Letters.	English Equivalents.	Pronounced as in
Ф	ф	f	fire
Х	х	kh	*Scottish* "loch"
Ц	ц	tz	Ritz
Ч	ч	ch	chair
Ш	ш	sh	short
Щ	щ	shch	sh *plus* ch, as in "Wash, child!" uttered as one word
—	ъ	hard sign: now known as separating sign, used after a consonant to separate it from a vowel	
—	ы	y	pity
—	ь	soft sign: gives preceding letter a soft, liquid sound	
Э	э	e	men
Ю	ю	yu	use
Я	я	ya	yard

PRONUNCIATION OF GEOGRAPHICAL AND TOPOGRAPHICAL NAMES

In this and the following List—both largely composed of foreign names—it has been necessary to use in conjunction with our simplified method of showing pronunciation a few of the symbols of the International Phonetic Alphabet, a list of which will be found on p. 1094.

While it is impossible to lay down any hard and fast ruling on the "correct" pronunciation of any given place our aim has been to give that which is in general use by educated English-speaking people, coupled with a working approximation to the local pronunciation of Continental, Russian, South American, Far Eastern, and other foreign names. Merely local variants (as, for instance, "*chou*-z'n" for the Gloucestershire village "Churchtown," or "*uf*-am" for the hamlet in Northumberland spelt "Ulgham") are not, as a rule, included, but there are many instances in which one spelling serves for different sounds (*e.g.*, "Arkansas," "Bolivar," "Greenwich"), and a number of these find their place below.

The list also includes Territorial titles ("Marlborough," "Salisbury," "Enghien," etc.) the spelling and pronunciation of which coincide with that of the place from which they are derived; others are recorded in the List of Personal Names.

Aachen, *ahk*-en.
Aaland, *ah*-land: *oh*-land.
Aalberg, *awl*-borkh.
Aalesund, *aw*-le-soon.
Aar, ar.
Aargau, *ar*-gou.
Aarhus, *ar*-hoos.
Abano, a-*bah*-no.
Abbazia, *ah*-baht-*see*-ah.
Abbeville, ab-*veel*.
Abeokuta, ah-be-*oh*-koo-tah.
Abergavenny, *ab*-er-ga-*ven*-ne.
Aberystwith, ab-er-*ist*-with.
Abinger, *ab*-in-jer.
Abkhasia, ab-*khah*-se-a.
Abomey, a-*boh*-may.
Aboukir, a-*boo*-keer.
Abrantes, a-*brahn*-tesh.
Abyssinia, ab-e-*sin*-ya.
Acapulco, a-ka-*pool*-ko.
Acarnania, ak-ar-*nay*-ne-a.
Accra, a-*krah*.
Achaia, a-*kay*-ya.
Achi Baba, *ah*-che-*bah*-bah.
Achray, a-*kray*.
Acireale, *ah*-che-ray-*ah*-le.
Aconcagua, *ah*-kon-*kah*-gwa.
Acre, *ay*-ker: *ah*-ker.
Adana, a-*dah*-na.
Addis Ababa, *ad*-is-*ah*-ba-ba.
Adélie (Land), a-*day*-le.
Adelsheim, *ah*-delz-hime.
Aden, *ay*-den.
Adige, *ah*-de-ja.
Adrianople, ay-dre-a-*noh*-pl.
Ægean, ee-*jee*-an.
Ætolia, ee-*toh*-le-a.
Afghanistan, af-*gan*-is-*tahn*.
Afyon, *ah*-fe-ohn.
Agadir, ah-ga-*deer*.
Agheila, a-*gay*-la.
Agincourt, *adj*-in-kort: ah-zhaŋ-*koor*.
Agrigento, ah-gre-*jen*-to.
Agulhas, a-*gul*-as: a-*gool*-yas.
Ahmadnagar, ah-mud-*nug*-gar.
Ahmedabad, *ah*-med-a-*bad*.
Ailette (Riv.), ay-*let*.
Aisne (Riv.), ane.
Aix-la-Chapelle, *akes*-la sha-*pel*.
Ajaccio, a-*yaht*-cho.
Akaba, *ak*-a-bah.
Akashi, *ah*-ka-she.
Akhtirka, ahkh-*tur*-ka.
Akyab, ahkh-*yahb*.
Alabama, al-a-*bam*-a (-*bah*-ma).
Alameda (Spain), *ah*-la-*may*-tha.
Alameda (U.S.A., Can.), al-a-*may*-da.
Alamein, *al*-a-mayn.
Aland, *ah*-land.
Alaska, a-*las*-ka.
Albania, al-*bay*-ne-a.
Albano, al-*bah*-no.
Albany, *awl*-ba-ne.
Albemarle, *al*-be-marl.
Albert (Fr.), al-*bair*.
Albuera, al-boo-*ay*-ra: ahl-*bway*-rah.
Albuquerque (U.S.A.), al-bew-*ker*-ke.
Alcala, al-ka-*lah*.
Alcantara, al-*kahn*-ta-ra.
Alcazar, al-*kaz*-ar.
Alcester, *awl*-ster.
Alcira, ahl-*thee*-rah.
Alemtejo, ah-leŋ-*tay*-zhoo.
Alençon, ah-*lahŋ*-soŋ.
Aleutians, a-*loo*-shanz.
Alexandroupolis, *al*-ek-san-*droo*-po-lis.
Algeciras, al-je-*seer*-as.
Algiers, al-*jeerz*.
Alhambra, al-*ham*-bra.
Alicante, al-e-*kan*-te: ah-le-*kahn*-tay.
Alkmaar, *ahlk*-mar.
Allahabad, al-la-ha-*bad*.
Alleghany, al-le-*gay*-ne.
Allenstein, *al*-en-shtine.
Alloa, *al*-oh-a.
Alma-Ata, *ahl*-ma-*at*-a.
Almaden, al-ma-*thayn*.
Almeida, ahl-*may*-da: ahl-*may*-tha.

Alnwick, *an*-ik.
Alor Star, *ahl*-or-*star*.
Alsace, al-*sahs*.
Altai, al-*ty*.
Altamira, *ahl*-ta-*meer*-ah.
Altenburg, *ahl*-ten-boorkh.
Altona, *al*-to-na.
Altrincham, *awl*-tring-em.
Amboina, am-*boy*-na.
Amboise, ahŋ-*bwahz*.
Amesbury, *aymz*-be-re.
Amherst, *am*-erst.
Amiens, *ah*-myaŋ.
Amlwch, *am*-lookh.
Amoy, a-*moy*.
Ampezzo, ahm-*pet*-zoh.
Amritsar, um-*rit*-sar.
Amur, a-*moor*.
Anahuac, ah-*nah*-wahk.
Ancona, an-*koh*-na.
Ancre (Riv.), ahŋkr'.
Andalusia, an-da-*loo*-ze-a.
Andaman, *an*-da-man.
Andernach, *an*-der-nahkh.
Andorra, an-*daw*-ra.
Andreanof, an-dra-*ah*-nof.
Angers, ahŋ-*zhay*.
Angmagssalik, *ahng*-mags-*sah*-lik.
Angola, an-*goh*-la.
Angora, ang-*gaw*-ra.
Angoulême, ahŋ-goo-*lame*.
Anguilla, ang-*gwil*-a.
Anhalt, *an*-hahlt.
Anhwei, an-*whay*.
Anjou, ahŋ-*zhoo*.
Ankara, *ang*-ka-ra.
Annecy, an-*se*.
Ansbach, *ans*-bahkh.
Antalya, an-tal-*yah*.
Antananarivo, *an*-ta-*nan*-a-*ree*-voh.
Antibes, ahŋ-*teeb*.
Antigua, an-*tee*-gwa.
Antioquia, *an*-te-o-*kee*-a.
Antsirana, ant-se-*rah*-na.
Anuradhapura, a-*noo*-rahd-ha-*poo*-ra.
Anzio, *ahn*-tse-oh.
Aosta, ah-*os*-tah.
Appalachians, ap-a-*latch*-e-anz, or -*lay*-ke-anz.
Appenzell, *ah*-pen-*tsel*.
Appomattox, ap-o-*mat*-ux.
Apulia, a-*pew*-le-a.
Aquila, *ak*-we-la.
Aquino, ah-*kwee*-noh.
Aquitaine, *ak*-we-tayn.
Aracajou, a-rah-ka-*zhoo*.
Aracan, a-ra-*kan*.
Arafura, a-ra-*foo*-ra.
Araguaya, ah-ra-*gwy*-ya.
Arapahoe, a-*rap*-a-hoh.
Ararat, *a*-ra-rat.
Arauca, a-*rou*-kah.
Araucania, a-ro-*kay*-ne-a.
Arce, *ar*-se.
Arcole, ar-*koh*-lay.
Arcot, ar-*kot*.
Ardèche, ar-*desh*.
Ardennes, ar-*den*.
Ardnamurchan, ard-na-*mur*-khan.
Ardrishaig, ar-*drish*-ig.
Arequipa, ah-ra-*kee*-pa.
Arezzo, ah-*ret*-soh.
Argenteuil, ar-zhahn-tœ:j.
Argentine, *ar*-jen-tine.
Argyle, ar-*gile*.
Argyrokastro, *ar*-ye-*raw*-kas-tro.
Arica, a-*ree*-ka.
Ariège, a-re-ezh.
Arkansas (State), *ar*-kan-saw: (City), ar-*kan*-zas.
Arles, arlz: arl.
Arleux, ar-*lø*.
Armagh, ar-*mah*.
Armagnac, ar-ma-*nyak*.
Armentières, ar-mahŋ-*tyair*.
Arnheim, *arn*-hem.
Aroa, ah-*roh*-ah.
Arpino, ar-*pee*-no.
Arras, *a*-ras: a-rahs.
Arromanches, ah-ro-mã:ʃ.
Artemisio, ar-te-*mish*-e-o.
Artois, at-*twah*.
Aruba, a-*roo*-ba.
Aschaffenburg, a-*shah*-fen-boorkh.
Ashanti, a-*shan*-te.
Asiago, *ah*-zyah-*goh*.
Asmara, as-*mah*-ra.
Asolo, *ah*-zo-loh.
Assam, as-*sam*.
Assaye, as-*sy*.
Assisi, as-*see*-ze.
Assiut, ah-*syut*.
Assouan, as-soo-*ahn*.
Astrakhan, as-tra-*kan*.
Asuncion, ah-*soon*-syon.
Atacama, a-ta-*kah*-ma.
Athenry, ath-en-*ry*.
Athlumney, ath-*lum*-ne.
Atholl, *ath*-ol.
Athy, a-*thy*.
Attu, at-*too*.
Aube, ohb.
Aubers, oh-*bair*.
Aubervilliers, oh-ber-*vee*-yay.
Auch, ohsh.
Aude, ohd.
Audenarde, oh-de-*nard*.
Auerbach, *ou*-er-bahkh.
Aughrim, *aw*-grim: *awkh*-rim.
Augila, aw-*jee*-la.
Augsburg, *ougz*-burg: *ouks*-boorkh.
Aulnoye, oh-*nwah*.
Aunis, oh-*nees*.
Auschwitz, *oush*-vits.
Ausonia, aw-*soh*-ne-a.
Austronesia, aws-tro-*nee*-sha.
Auvergne, oh-*vairn*.
Auxerre, oh-*sair*.
Ava, *ah*-va.
Avebury, *ayv*-ber-re.
Aveiro, a-*vay*-roo.
Avesnes, a-*vane*.
Aveyron, a-ve-*roŋ*.
Avezzano, ah-vet-*sah*-no.
Avignon, a-vee-*nyoŋ*.
Avoch, a-*vokh*.
Avranches, a-vrã:ʃ.
Ayacucho, eye-yah-*koo*-cho.
Aylesbury, *aylz*-ber-re.
Azerbaijan, ah-zer-by-*jan*.
Aziziya, *ah*-ze-*zee*-yah.
Azores, a-*zorz*.
Azov, *ah*-zof.

Baalbec, bahl-*bek*.
Bab-el-Mandeb, bah-bel-*man*-deb.
Bacharach, *bahkh*-ah-rahkh.
Bacup, *bay*-kup.
Badajoz, *bad*-a-hoz: ba-thah-*hoath*.
Bad Ems, baht-*ayms*.
Baden, *bah*-den.
Badenoch, *bad*-e-nokh.
Badenweiler, *bah*-den-*vy*-ler.
Badia, bah-*dee*-a.
Bagnères-de-Bigorre, ba-*nyair*-de-bee-*gor*.
Bagneux, ba-*nyø*.
Bahamas, ba-*hah*-maz.
Bahia, ba-*ee*-a.
Bahrein, bah-*rain*.
Baie Comeau, bay ko-*moh*.
Baikal, *by*-kal.
Bailleul, ba-*yøl*.
Baja, *boh*-yo.
Baku, *bah*-*koo*.

Bala, *bah*-la.
Balaghat, bah-lah-*gawt*.
Balaton, *bol*-o-ton.
Bâle, bahl.
Balearics, bal-e-*a*-riks.
Bali, *bah*-le.
Balikpapan, *bah*-lik-*pah*-pahn.
Balkan, *bawl*-kan.
Balkh, bahlkh.
Ballinasloe, *bal*-le-na-*sloh*.
Baltic, *bawl*-tik.
Baltimore, *bawl*-te-more.
Baltiski, *bahl*-tis-ke.
Baluchistan, ba-*loo*-chis-tan.
Bamako, bah-mah-*koh*.
Banat, *bah*-naht.
Banff, bamf.
Bangui, *bahng*-gee.
Banjermasin, bahn-jer-*mah*-sin.
Bantam, *ban*-tam.
Bapaume, ba-*pohm*.
Barbados, bar-*bay*-dohz.
Barcelona, bar-se-*loh*-na: bar-the-*loh*-na.
Barèges, ba-*rayzh*.
Bareilly, ba-*ray*-le.
Barranquilla, bah-rahn-*keel*-yah.
Barthélémy, bar-*tay*-la-me.
Basel, *bah*-zl.
Basra, *baz*-ra.
Bassano, ba-*sah*-no.
Bassein, bas-*seen*.
Bastia, bas-*tee*-a.
Bastogne, bas-*tone*: -toɲ.
Bataan, bah-*tahn*.
Batavia, ba-*tay*-ve-a: bah-*tah*-ve-ah.
Baton Rouge, *bat*-un-*roozh*.
Batum, ba-*toom*.
Bautzen, *bout*-sen.
Bayazid, bah-yah-*zit*.
Bayeux, by-*er*: ba-yø.
Bayonne, ba-*yon*.
Bayreuth, by-*royt*.
Beaconsfield, *bek*-onz-feeld.
Beaminster, *bem*-in-ster.
Bearn, bay-*ar*.
Beauharnois, bo-ar-*nwah*.
Beaumaris, boh-*mo*-ris.
Beaumont, *boh*-ment: *boh*-moŋ.
Beaumont-Hamel, boh-*moŋ*-a-*mel*.
Beauvais, boh-*vay*.
Bechuanaland, *bek*-ew-*ah*-na-land; *bech*-oo-.
Beddgelert, beth-*gel*-ert.
Bedwellty, bed-*wel*-te.
Behring, *be*-ring.
Beira, *bay*-ra.
Beirut, bay-*root*.
Beisan, bay-*sahn*.
Beja, *bay*-zha.
Béja, ba-*zha*.
Belem, ba-leŋ.
Belfast, bel-*fahst*.
Belgrade, bel-*grade*.
Belize, be-*leez*.
Belvoir, *bee*-ver.
Benares, be-*nah*-res.
Benbecula, ben-be-*koo*-lah.
Benevento, ben-e-*ven*-toh.
Bengal, beng-*gawl*.
Benghazi, beng-*gah*-ze.
Benguela, beng-*gay*-la.
Benin, be-*neen*.
Ben Nevis, ben-*nee*-vis: *nev*-is.
Ben Wyvis, ben-*wiv*-is.
Berbera, *ber*-be-ra.
Berbice, ber-*bees*.
Berchtesgaden, *bairkh*-tez-ga-den.
Berdichev, ber-*dyee*-chef.
Beresina, byer-ye-*see*-na.
Berezov, ber-*yoz*-ov.
Bergamo, *ber*-ga-moh.
Bergen, *ber*-gen.
Bergerac, ber-ger-*rahk*.
Berkhamsted, *berk*-ham-stid.
Berkshire, *bark*-sher.
Bermuda, ber-*mew*-da.
Berwick, *be*-rik.
Besançon, be-zaŋ-soŋ.
Bessarabia, *bes*-a-*ray*-be-a.
Béthune, ba-*toon*.
Beuthen, *boy*-ten.
Beveland, *bay*-ve-lahnt.
Beyrut, *by*-root.
Bhagalpur, bah-gal-*poor*.
Bhamo, bah-*moh*.
Bharat, bhah-*raht*.
Bhopal, bo-*pahl*.
Bhutan, boo-*tahn*.
Biafra, be-*ah*-fra.
Bialystok, byah-*lis*-tok.
Biarritz, bya-*reets*.
Bicester, *bis*-ter.
Bideford, *bid*-e-ford.
Bielefeld, *bee*-le-felt.
Bihar (India), be-har: (Hung.), *bee*-hor.
Bikanir, *bee*-ka-neer.
Bilbao, bil-*bay*-oh.
Billericay, bil-er-*rik*-e.
Binche, baŋsh.
Bingen, *bing*-en.
Bio-Bio, *bee*-o-*bee*-oh.
Biro-Bidjan, *bee*-ro-bi-*jahn*.
Bishop's Stortford, *bish*-ops-*stor*-ford.
Bisley, *biz*-le.
Bixschoote, *beeks*-skhoh-te.
Bizerta, be-*zer*-ta.
Blagoveshchensk, blah-go-*vyesh*-chensk.
Blankenberghe, *blahng*-ken-berg'.
Bloemfontein, *bloom*-fon-tine.
Blois, blwah.
Bobruisk, bo-*broo*-isk.
Bocage, bo-*kahzh*.
Bochum, *boh*-khoom.
Bodensee, *boh*-den-zee.
Boghazkeui, bo-gahz-*koo*-e.
Bogotá, boh-go-*tah*.
Bogota, bo-*goh*-ta.
Bohemia, bo-*hee*-mya.
Böhmer Wald, *bø*-mer-vahlt.
Boise, *boy*-se.
Bois le Duc, bwah-le-*duk*.
Bokhara, bo-*kah*-ra.
Bolama, bo-*lah*-ma.
Bolivar (S. Amer.), bo-*lee*-var: (U.S.A.), *bol*-e-ver.
Bolivia, bo-*liv*-e-a.
Bologna, bo-*loh*-nya.
Bolsena, bol-*say*-na.
Bolzano, bol-*tsah*-noh.
Bombay, bom-*bay*.
Bonaire, bo-*nair*.
Bonifacio, boh-nee-*fah*-choh.
Bordeaux, bor-*doh*.
Bordelais, bor-de-*lay*.
Borgholm, *borg*-holm.
Borisov, bo-*ree*-sof.
Borku, bor-*koo*.
Borneo, *bor*-ne-oh.
Borodino, bo-ro-*dyee*-noh.
Bosphorus, *bos*-fo-rus.
Bouchavesnes, boosh-ah-*vain*.
Bougainville, boo-gaŋ-*veel*.
Bouillon, boo-yoŋ.
Boulogne, boo-*lone*: bu-loɲ.
Bourges, boorzh.
Bourlon (Wood), boor-*loŋ*.
Bousbecque, boo-*bek*.
Bouvet, boo-*vay*.
Bouvigny, boo-*vee*-nyee.

Bouvines, boo-*veen*.
Braemar, bray-*mar*.
Brahmaputra, *brah*-ma-*poo*-tra.
Braila, bra-*ee*-la.
Bratislava, brah-te-*slah*-va.
Brazil, bra-*zil*.
Brazzaville, braz-a-*veel*.
Brechin, *brekh*-in.
Breda, *bray*-da.
Bregenz, *bray*-gents.
Bremen, *bray*-men.
Bremerhaven, *bray*-mer-hah-fen.
Brescia, *bray*-sha.
Breslau, *bres*-lou.
Brest-Litovsk, *brest*-lyee-*tofsk*.
Briançon, bree-aŋ-soŋ.
Brieg, breekh.
Brienz, bre-*ents*.
Brihuega, bre-*way*-ga.
Brindisi, *breen*-de-zee.
Brixham, *brik*-sam.
Brno, *ber*-no.
Brod, broht.
Bromley (Kent), *brum*-le.
Bromley (by Bow), *brom*-le.
Brompton, *bromp*- or *brump*-ton.
Bromsgrove, *bromz*-grove.
Bromwich, *brum*-itsh.
Brondesbury, *brondz*-be-*re*.
Bronte, *bron*-tay.
Bruges, broozh.
Brühl, brool.
Brunanburh, *broo*-nan-bur.
Brunei, broo-*ny*.
Bruneval, *broo*-ne-val.
Brunswick, *brunz*-wik.
Brusilov, *broo*-se-lof.
Bryansk, bre-*ansk*.
Brzezany, bzhe-*zhah*-ne.
Bucharest, *boo*-ka-rest.
Buchenwald, *boo*-khen-vahlt.
Budapest, *boo*-da-pest.
Budweis, *boot*-vise.
Buenos Aires, *bway*-nos-*air*-riz.
Builth, bilth.
Buitenzorg, *boy*-ten-zorkh.
Bulawayo, bull-a-*way*-o.
Bukovina, boo-ko-*vee*-na.
Buncombe, *bung*-kum.
Burdwan, bur-*dwahn*.
Burgenland, *boor*-gen-lahnt.
Burgos, *boor*-gohs.
Burntisland, bernt-*eye*-land.
Bury, *be*-re.
Bushire, boo-*sheer*.
Buthidaung, buth-e-*dawng*.
Butte (U.S.A.), bewt.
Byelostok, *byel*-o-stok.

NOTE. — Many names sometimes initialled " C " (*e.g.* Kabul, Karlsruhe) are entered under " K."

Cabinda, ka-*bey*-da.
Cabrera, ka-*bray*-ra.
Cader Idris, *kad*-er *id*-ris.
Cadillac (U.S.A.), *kad*-e-lak.
Cadiz, *kay*-diz.
Caen, kahŋ.
Caerleon, kar-*lee*-on.
Caerphilly, kar-*fil*-e.
Cagliari, kahl-*yah*-re.
Cahors, kah-*or*.
Caicos, *ky*-kohs.
Cairo, *ky*-e-roh.
Calabar, ka-la-*bar*.
Calabria, ka-*lay*-bre-a: kah-*lah*-bre-ah.
Calais, *kal*-ay.
Calcutta, kal-*kut*-ta.
Caldera, kal-*day*-rah.
Caldiero, kahl-*dyair*-roh.
Calgary, *kal*-ga-re.
Cali, *kah*-lee.
Callao, kal-*yah*-oh.
Calne, kahn.
Calshot, *kol*-shot.
Caltagirone, kahl-tah-je-*roh*-nay.
Caltanisetta, kahl-tah-ne-*set*-ta.
Calton, *kahl*-ton.
Camagüey, kah-mah-*gway*.
Cambray, kam-*bray*.
Cambridge, *kame*-brij.
Camerino, kah-ma-*ree*-no.
Cameroons, kam-er-*roonz*.
Camino, kah-*mee*-noh.
Campagna, kam-*pah*-nya.
Campeche, kahm-*pay*-cha.
Câmpulung, kim-poo-*loong*.
Canberra, *kan*-be-ra.
Candahar, kan-da-*har*.
Canea, kah-*nee*-a.
Cannes, kan.
Canton, kan-*ton*.
Cape Breton, kape-*bret*-on.
Capodistria, *kah*-po-*dees*-tre-a.
Caporetto, kah-po-*ret*-toh.
Caprera, ka-*prair*-ra.
Capua, *kap*-ew-a.
Caracal, ka-ra-*kal*.
Caracas, kah-*rah*-kas.
Carbonara, kar-bo-*nah*-ra.
Carentan, kah-raŋ-taŋ.
Cariaco, kah-re-*ah*-koh.
Caribbean, ka-re-*bee*-an.
Carlisle, kar-*lile*.
Carmignano, *kar*-mee-*nyah*-noh.
Carniola, kar-ne-*oh*-la.
Carpathians, kar-*pay*-the-anz.
Carrara, kah-*rah*-ra.
Cartagena, kar-ta-*jee*-na: kar-ta-*hay*-na.
Cartago, kar-*tah*-go.
Casablanca, kas-a-*blang*-ka.
Casale, ka-*sah*-lay.
Cashel, *kash*-el.
Cassino, kahs-*see*-noh.
Castel Benito, *kas*-tel be-*nee*-toh.
Castelforte, *kas*-tel-*for*-tay.
Castelnau, *kasl*-now.
Castelnuovo, *kas*-tel-*nwoh*-voh.
Castelvetrano, *kes*-tal-va-*trah*-noh.
Castiglione, kahs-teel-*yoh*-na.
Castile, kas-*teel*.
Castlebar, kahsl-*bar*.
Castres, kahstr.
Catalonia, kat-a-*loh*-ne-a.
Catania, ka-*tah*-ne-a.
Catoche, kah-*toh*-chay.
Cattaro, *kah*-tah-ro.
Caucasus, *kaw*-ka-sus.
Caumont, koh-moŋ.
Cavan, *kav*-an.
Cavite, kah-*vee*-tay.
Cawnpore, kawn-*pore*.
Cayenne, kay-*yen*: ky-*en*.
Cayman, ky-*mahn*.
Ceara, say-*ah*-rah.
Cefalu, chay-fah-*loo*.
Celano, chay-*lah*-noh.
Celebes, *sel*-e-beez: se-*lee*-beez.
Celle, *tsel*-e.
Cenis, se-*nee*.

Centuripe, chan-*too*-re-pay.
Cephalonia, sef-a-*loh*-ne-a.
Ceram, se-*ram*.
Cerignola, chay-re-*nyoh*-la.
Cerigo, che-*ree*-goh.
Cérisy, sa-*ree*-se.
Cernauti, cher-na-*oo*-te.
Cesano, cha-*sah*-noh.
Cesaro, cha-*sah*-roh.
Cetacea Alba, chet-a-*chay*-a *al*-ba.
Cetinje, tse-*tin*-je: tset-*een*-yah.
Ceuta, *syoo*-ta.
Cevennes, se-*ven*.
Chagres, *chah*-gres.
Chalkis, *kal*-kis: *khahl*-kis.
Châlons, sha-loŋ.
Chambéry, shahŋ-ba-ree.
Chambois, shahŋ-bwah.
Chamouni, sha-moo-*nee*.
Chamonix, sha-mo-*nee*.
Champlain, *sham*-plane.
Changsha, chang-*shah*.
Chantilly, shahŋ-tee-*yee*.
Charente, sha-rahŋt.
Charleroi, sharl-*rwah*.
Charlevoix (U.S.A.), *shar*-le-voy.
Charlottenburg, shar-*lot*-en-burg (-boorkh).
Chartres, shartr.
Chartreuse, shar-trø:z.
Chatalja, chah-*tahl*-jah.
Chateaubriant, shah-to-bree-ahŋ.
Chateau d'Oex, shah-to-day.
Chateaudun, shah-to-doon.
Chateau Thierry, shah-to-tye-ree.
Chatelet, shat-*lay*.
Chatelleravlt, sha-tel-*roh*.
Chatham, *chat*-am.
Chaulnes, shohn.
Chaumont, shoh-*moŋ*.
Chautaugua, sha-*taw*-kwa.
Chaves, (Port.) *shah*-vesh: (New Mex.) *chah*-ves.
Chekiang, chee-*kyang*.
Chelles, shel.
Cheltenham, *chelt*-nam.
Chelyabinsk, chel-yah-*binsk*.
Chelyuskin, chel-*yoos*-kin.
Chemnitz, *kem*-nits.
Chenies, *chee*-niz.
Cherbourg, sher-*borg*, -boor.
Cherkasi, cher-*kas*-e.
Chernaya, cher-*nah*-ya.
Chernyshevskaya, *cher*-ne-shev-*skah*-ya.
Cherokee, che-ro-*kee*.
Cherson, ker-*son*.
Cherwell, *char*-wel.
Chetumal, chet-oo-*mahl*.
Cheviot, *chev*-e-ut.
Cheyenne, *shy*-en.
Chianti, ke-*ahn*-te.
Chiasso, *kyahs*-soh.
Chiavari, kee-a-*vah*-re.
Chicago, she-*kah*-goh.
Chichen-Itza, *chee*-chen-*eet*-sah.
Chichester, *chich*-es-ter.
Chiclayo, che-*klah*-yoh.
Chiemsee, *keem*-zay.
Chiesa, kee-*ay*-sah.
Chihuahua, che-*wah*-wah.
Chile, *chil*-e.
Chillianwalla, *chee*-le-an-*wah*-la.
Chillon, *shee*-loŋ: shee-yoŋ.
Chiloé, chee-lo-*ay*.
Chimay, shee-*may*.
Chimborazo, chim-bo-*rah*-zoh.
Chindwin, *chin*-dwin.
Chinon, shee-noŋ.
Chioggia, *kyod*-ja.
Chios, *ky*-os.
Chita, *chee*-tah.
Chitral, che-*trahl*.
Chittagong, *chit*-a-gong.
Chiusi, *kyoo*-se.
Choiseul, shwa-zøl.
Chojnice, khoh-e-*nit*-se.
Cholon, sho-*loŋ*.
Chosen, choh-*sen*.
Christianshaab, *kris*-tyans-hahp.
Chuhsien, choo-she-*en*.
Chuquisaca, choo-ke-*sah*-ka.
Chur, koor.
Chusan, choo-*san*.
Chuvash, *choo*-vash.
Ciechanov, che-*khah*-noof.
Cimone, che-*moh*-nay.
Cincinnati, sin-se-*nat*-e.
Ciney, see-nay.
Circassia, ser-*kas*-e-a.
Cirencester, *sire*-ren-ces-ter; *sis*-e-ter.
Cithaeron, si-*theer*-ron.
Ciudad Real, thyoo-*thath*-ra-*al*.
Ciudad Rodrigo, thyoo-*thath*-ro-*three*-goh.
Civitavecchia, *chee*-ve-tah-*vek*-kyah.
Clairvaux, kler-*voh*.
Cleobury, *klib*-er-re.
Clerkenwell, *klar*-ken-wel.
Clermont, kler-moŋ.
Cleves, kleevz.
Clichy, klee-shee.
Cliveden, *kliv*-den.
Clonmacnoise, klon-mak-*noyz*.
Clonmel, klon-*mel*.
Cluj, kloozh.
Cobija, ko-*be*-hah.
Coblenz, *koh*-blentz.
Cochabamba, koh-cha-*bahm*-bah.
Cochin (Ind.), *koh*-chin.
Cochin China, *kotsh*-in-*chy*-na.
Coerworden, *koor*-vor-den.
Cognac, *koh*-nyak.
Coimbra, koo-*eem*-bra.
Colmekill, *kohl*-m'-kil.
Cologne, ko-*lone*.
Colombelles, ko-loŋ-bel.
Colombes, ko-loŋb.
Colombo, ko-*lum*-boh.
Colon, ko-*lon*.
Colonsay, *kol*-on-say.
Colorado, kol-o-*rah*-doh.
Colyton, *kol*-e-ton.
Comacchio, ko-*mah*-kyoh.
Comorin, *kom*-o-rin.
Comoro (Isls.), *kom*-o-roh.
Compiègne, koŋ-pyane.
Conakry, ko-na-*kree*.
Condé, koŋ-day.
Congo, *kong*-goh.
Connaught, *kon*-awt.
Connecticut, ko-*net*-e-kut.
Connemara, kon-e-*mah*-ra.
Constanza, kon-*stan*-tsa.
Copenhagen, *koh*-pen-hay-gen.
Copiapo, koh-pyah-*poh*.
Coquet, *kok*-et.
Coquimbo, ko-*keem*-boh.
Cordillera, kor-dee-*lyah*-ra.
Cordoba, *kor*-do-vah.
Corea, ko-*ree*-a.
Corfu, kor-*foo*.
Corinth, *ko*-rinth.
Coronel, *ko*-ro-nel.
Corregidor, kor-ray-he-*dor*.
Cortona, kor-*toh*-nah.
Coruna, ko-*roo*-nyah.
Cosenza, ko-*zent*-sah.

Cotentin, ko-tahŋ-taŋ.
Cotonou, ko-to-*noo*.
Cotopaxi, koh-toh-*pak*-se.
Coulsdon, *kohlz*-don.
Courcelles, koor-sel.
Courland, *koor*-land.
Courtray, koor-*tray*.
Coutances, koo-tahŋs.
Coventry, *kov*-, *kuv*-en-tre.
Cowes, kouz.
Cracow, *krah*-koh.
Craigenputtock, *kray*-gen-*put*-uk.
Craiova, kra-*yoh*-vah.
Craonne, krahn.
Crecy, *kres*-e: kra-*see*.
Cremona, kra-*moh*-nah.
Crewe, kroo.
Crianlarich, kree-en-*la*-rikh.
Criccieth, *krik*-e-eth.
Crief, kreef.
Crimea, kry-*mee*-a.
Croagh Patrick, *kroh*-a-*pat*-rik.
Croatia, kro-*ay*-she-a.
Cro-Magnon, kroh-ma-nyoŋ.
Cromarty, *krom*-ar-te.
Csepel, *chep*-el.
Csorna, *chor*-no.
Culebra, koo-*lay*-bra.
Culloden, ko-*lod*-en.
Cullumpton, ku-*lump*-ton.
Cupar, *koo*-par.
Curaçao, *kewr*-ra-soh.
Curepipe, koo-ra-*pee*-pay.
Curityba, koo-re-*tee*-ba.
Custozza, koos-*toht*-sah.
Cuttack, kut-*tak*.
Cuxhaven, *kooks*-hah-fen.
Cuyaba, koo-ya-*bah*.
Cuyahoga, ky-*hog*-a.
Cyclades, *sik*-la-deez.
Cyrenaica, sire-re-*nay*-e-ka.
Czechoslovakia, *chek*-o-slo-*vak*-e-a.
Czernowitz, *cher*-no-vits.
Czestochowa, cheŋ-sto-*kho*-va.

Dachau, *dak*-ou.
Dahomey, da-*hoh*-me.
Dairen, *dy*-ren.
Dakar, da-*kar*.
Dakota, da-*koh*-ta.
Dalecarlia, *dah*-le-*kar*-le-a.
Dalhousie, dal-*hoo*-ze.
Dalkeith, dal-*keeth*.
Dalmatia, dal-*may*-sha.
Dalmeny, dal-*men*-e.
Dalry, dal-*ry*.
Dalton, *dawl*-ton.
Damaraland, *dam*-a-ra-land.
Damascus, da-*mahs*-kus.
Damietta, dam-e-*et*-ta.
Danakil, dan-a-*keel*.
Danzig, *dan*-tsik.
Dardanelles, dar-da-*nelz*.
Dar es Salaam, dar-es-sa-*lahm*.
Darfur, dar-*foor*.
Darien, *da*-re-en.
Darmstadt, *darm*-shtaht.
Daugavpils, *dou*-gaf-pels.
Dauphiné, *doh*-fee-nay.
Davao, *dah*-vou.
Daventry, *dav*-en-tre: *dane*-tre.
Davos-Platz, dah-vohs-*plahts*.
Daytona, day-*toh*-na.
Deauville, doh-*veel*.
Deblin, *deŋ*-blen.
Debreczin, da-*bret*-sen.
Decatur, de-*kay*-ter.
Deccan, *dek*-an.
Dehra Dun, *day*-ra-doon.
Deir-e-Zor, dire-ez-*zor*.
Delagoa, del-a-*goh*-a.
Delatyn, de-*lah*-tin.
Delaware, *del*-a-wair.
Delfzijl, delf-*zile*.
Delgado, del-*gah*-doh.
Delhi, (India) *del*-e: (U.S.A.) del-*hy*.
Delvino, *del*-vee-noh.
Demavend, dem-a-*vend*.
Demerara, dem-er-*rair*-ra.
Denbigh, *den*-be.
Dendera, *den*-der-ra.
D'Entrecasteaux (Isls.), dahŋ-tra-kahs-*toh*.
Deptford, *det*-ford.
Deraa, da-*rah*.
Derbent, der-*bent*.
Derby, *dar*-be: (U.S.A.) *der*-be.
Dereham, *deer*-rum.
Derham, *de*-rum.
Des Moines, de-*moyn*.
Desna (riv.), dyes-*nah*.
Dessau, *des*-ou.
Detroit, de-*troyt*.
Detskoe Selo, *dyet*-sko-ye sye-*loh*.
Dettingen, *det*-ing-en.
Deutsch, doytsh.
Deutschland, *doytsh*-lahnt.
Deutz, doytz.
Deventer, *dev*-en-ter.
Devizes, de-*vy*-zez.
Dhaulagiri, dou-lah-*gee*-re.
Dholpur, *dol*-poor.
Diablerets, dyah-ble-*re*.
Diarbekr, dee-ahr-*bekr*.
Diego Suarez, *dyay*-goh-*swah*-race.
Dieppe, dee-*ep*.
Digne, deen.
Dijon, dee-zhoŋ.
Dillingen, *dil*-ing-en.
Dinan, dee-nahŋ.
Dinant, dee-nahŋ.
Dinapur, dee-na-*poor*.
Diosgyor, *dee*-ohsh-dyur.
Dire Dawa, *deer*-ra *dah*-wa.
Dixmude, deeks-*mood*.
Djebel Archel, jeb-el *ah*-khel.
Djedidah, je-*dee*-dah.
Djerba, *jer*-ba.
Djibouti, jee-boo-*tee*.
Dneprodzerzhinsk, *dnyep*-roh-zer-*zhinsk*.
Dnepropetrovsk, *dnyep*-roh-pye-*trofsk*.
Dnieper, *dnye*-pr.
Dniester, *dnyes*-tr.
Dobruja, *doh*-broo-ja.
Dodecanese, *doh*-dek-a-*neez*.
Doiran, *doy*-rahn.
Dolgelly, dol-*geth*-le.
Dominica, dom-e-*nee*-ka.
Domodossola, *doh*-mo-*dos*-so-lah.
Domremy, doŋ-*ray*-me.
Donachadee, don-a-kha-*dee*.
Donauwörth, doh-nou-*vurt*.
Donegal, *don*-e-gawl.
Donetz, do-*nyets*.
Dongola, *dong*-go-la.
Dorama, do-*rah*-ma.
Dordogne, dor-*doan*: dor-doɲ.
Dordrecht, *dor*-drekht.
Dornock, *dor*-nokh.
Dortmund, *dort*-moont.
Douai, doo-*ay*.
Douala, *dwah*-lah.
Douaumont, doo-oh-moŋ.
Doubs, doo.
Douglas, *dug*-las.
Doullens, doo-lahŋ.
Douro, *doh*-roo.
Dovrefjeld, dov-re-*fyal*.
Downside, *doun*-side.
Drachenfels, *drah*-khan-fels.
Drakensburg, drah-*kenz*-berg.

Drava, *drah*-vah.
Drenthe, *dren*-ta.
Dresden, *drez*-den.
Dreux, drø.
Drina, *dree*-na.
Drogheda, *droh*-he-da.
Dromore, dro-*more*.
Drontheim, *dront*-hime.
Dryburgh, *dry*-ber-ra.
Dubno, *doob*-noh.
Dubois (U.S.A.), *doo*-boyce: doo-*boyce*.
Dubovka, doo-*bof*-ka.
Dubrovnik, *doo*-brov-nek.
Duddeston, *dud*-ston.
Duero, *dway*-roh.
Duisburg, *doos*-boorkh.
Dukinfield, *duk*-in-feeld.
Dukla, *doo*-klah.
Dulce, *dool*-sa.
Dulcigno, dool-*cheen*-yoh.
Duluth, doo-*looth*.
Dulwich, *dul*-idj.
Dumfries, dum-*freece*.
Düna, *doo*-na.
Dunbar, dun-*bar*.
Dunblane, dun-*blane*.
Dundalk, dun-*dawk*.
Dundas, dun-*das*.
Dundee, dun-*dee*.
Dunedin, du-*nee*-din.
Dunfermline, dun-*ferm*-lin.
Dungarvan, dun-*gar*-van.
Dungeness, dunj-*ness*.
Dunkeld, dun-*keld*.
Dunkirk, *dun*-kirk.
Dun Laoghaire, dun-*lair*-re.
Dunsinane, dun-se-*nane*.
Duntocher, dun-*tokh*-er.
Duquesne, dew-*kane*.
Durazzo, doo-*raht*-soh.
Düren, *doo*-ren.
Durham, *du*-ram.
Düsseldorf, *doos*-el-dorf.
Dvina, *dvee*-na.
Dvinsk, dvensk.
Dysart, *dy*-zart.
Dzungaria, dzoong-*gah*-re-a.

Ebbw Vale, *eb*-oo-*vale*.
Eboli, *eb*-o-le.
Ebro, *ee*-bro.
Ecclefechan, ek-kl-*fekh*-an.
Echelles, ay-*shel*.
Echternach, *ekh*-ter-nahkh.
Ecuador, *ek*-wa-dor.
Edam, *ee*-dam: *ay*-dahm.
Edgecumbe, *ej*-kum.
Edina (U.S.A.), e-*dy*-na.
Edinburgh, *ed*-in-bu-ra.
Egina, e-*jy*-na.
Egremont, *eg*-re-mont.
Ehrenbreitstein, ay-ren-*bryt*-shtyn.
Eichstädt, *ike*-shtaht.
Eifel, *eye*-fel.
Eindhoven, *ynd*-hoh-ven.
Einsiedeln, *ynd*-zee-deln.
Eire, *air*-ra.
Eischweiler, *ysh*-vy-ler.
Eisenach, *eye*-zen-ahkh.
Eisleben, yse-*lay*-ben.
Ekron, *ek*-ron.
El Agheila, el-ah-*gay*-la.
El Alamein, el-*al*-a-mayn.
Elandslaagte, ay-lahnts-*lahkh*-ta.
Elbe, elb.
Elberfeld, *el*-ber-felt.
Elbeuf, el-bøf.
Elbrus, *el*-broos.
Elburz, el-*boorz*.
El Dorado, el-do-*rah*-doh.
Elephanta, el-e-*fan*-ta.
Elgin, (Scot.) *el*-gin: (U.S.A.) *el*-jin.
Ellesmere, *elz*-meer.
Ellwangen, el-*vahng*-en.
El-Obeid, el-o-*bahd*.
Elsinore, el-se-*nor*.
Ely, *ee*-le.
Emilia, e-*mil*-e-a.
Emmerich, *em*-me-rikh.
Empoli, *aim*-poh-le.
Enare, a-*nah*-re.
Enfidaville, ahn-*fee*-da-vil.
Engadine, *eng*-gah-deen.
Engedi, en-*gee*-dy.
Enghien, oŋ-gyaŋ.
England, *ing*-gland.
Eniwetok, *ee*-ne-we-*tok*.
Enniscorthy, en-is-*kor*-the.
Enniskillen, en-is-*kil*-en.
Enschede, *en*-skha-de.
Entebbe, en-*teb*-e.
Entre Rios, en-tra-*ree*-ohs.
Enzeli, en-*zel*-ee.
Epéhy, ep-ay-*ee*.
Epernay, a-*per*-ne.
Epinal, a-*pee*-nal.
Eregli, er-re-*glee*.
Ericht, *e*-rikht.
Erie, *eer*-re.
Eritrea, e-re-*tree*-a.
Erlangen, *er*-lahng-en.
Erzeroum, er-ze-*room*.
Erzgebirge, erts-ge-*ber*-ge.
Esbjerg, es-*berkh*.
Escaut, es-*koh*.
Eschweiler, *esh*-wy-ler.
Esmeralda, es-me-*ral*-da.
Espirito Santo, es-*pee*-re-too-*san*-too.
Esquimalt, es-*kwy*-malt.
Essequibo, es-se-*kee*-boh.
Este, *es*-ta.
Estonia, es-*toh*-ne-a.
Estremadura, *es*-tray-mah-*thoo*-rah.
Esztergom, *es*-ter-gom.
Étampes, ay-tahŋp.
Étaples, ay-tah-pl.
Ethiopia, ee-the-*oh*-pe-a.
Etive, *et*-iv.
Etowah, *et*-o-wah.
Etruria, e-*troor*-re-a.
Eubœa, yew-*bee*-a.
Eupatoria, yew-pa-*taw*-re-a.
Eupen, *oy*-pen.
Euphrates, yew-*fray*-teez.
Eurasia, yew-*ray*-ze-a.
Euripus, yew-*ry*-pus.
Euskerchen, *oys*-ker-khen.
Evesham, *eev*-sham.
Evora, *ev*-o-ra.
Evreux, ay-vrø.
Ewell, *yew*-el.
Exeter, *ek*-se-ter.
Eyam, *ee*-am.
Eyder, *eye*-der.
Eylau, *eye*-lou.
Eynsford, *ains*-ford.
Eyton, *eye*-ton.

Fäenza, fah-*en*-tsa.
Faeroes, *fair*-rohz.
Faizabad, fy-za-*bahd*.
Falaise, fa-*layz*.
Falkirk, *fawl*-kirk.
Falloden, *fal*-o-den.
Falluja, fa-*loo*-ja.
Falster, *fahl*-ster.
Falun, fo-*loon*.
Famagusta, fah-ma-*goos*-ta.
Faro (Port.), *fah*-roo.
Farö (Swed.), *for*-ra.
Fashoda, fa-*shoh*-da.
Fategarh, fut-e-*gar*.
Fatehpur, fut-e-*poor*.
Faversham, *fav*-er-sham.
Fayal, fy-*al*.
Fayum, fy-*oom*.
Fécamp, fay-kaŋ.
Feldkirch, *felt*-kerkh.
Feltham, *felt*-am.
Feodosia, fyoh-*doh*-se-a.
Ferentino, fay-ren-*tee*-no.

Fermanagh, fer-*man*-a.
Fermoy, fer-*moy*.
Ferrara, fa-*rah*-ra.
Ferrol, fer-*role*.
Festiniog, fes-*tin*-e-og.
Festubert, fes-too-*bair*.
Fettes, *fet*-is.
Feversham, *fev*-er-sham.
Fezzan, fez-*zahn*.
Fichtelgebirge, *fikh*-tel-ge-ber-ge.
Fiesole, fe-*ez*-o-lay.
Figeac, *fee*-zhahk.
Figueras, fee-*gay*-rahs.
Fiji, *fee*-jee.
Finistère, fee-nees-*tair*.
Finisterre (Cape), fin-is-*tair*.
Finschhafen, *finsh*-hah-fen.
Firenze, fe-*rent*-say.
Fishwick, *fish*-wik.
Fiume, fe-*oo*-may.
Flanders, *flahn*-derz.
Flensburg, *flens*-boorkh.
Flers, flair.
Fleury, *floor*-re.
Florence, *flo*-rens.
Flores, *flaw*-reez.
Florida, *flo*-re-da.
Florina, flo-*ree*-na.
Flushing, *flush*-ing.
Fochabers, *fokh*-a-berz.
Focsani, fok-*shah*-ne.
Foggia, *fod*-jah.
Foix, fwah.
Foligno, fo-*leen*-yo.
Folkestone, *foke*-ston.
Fondouk, fon-*dook*.
Fontainebleau, foŋ-ten-bloh.
Fontana, fon-*tah*-na.
Fontenay, foŋ-te-na.
Fontenoy, *fon*-te-noy: foŋ-te-nwah.
Fontevrault, foŋ-te-vroh.
Forbach, *for*-bahkh.
Forfar, *for*-far.
Formentera, for-men-*tay*-ra.
Formia, *for*-myah.
Formosa, for-*moh*-sa.
Fortaleza, for-tah-*lay*-za.
Forteviot, for-*tee*-vyot.
Fotheringay, *foth*-er-ring-gay.
Fougères, foo-*zhair*.
Fourmies, *foor*-mee.
Fowey, foy: *foh*-e.
Foyers, *foy*-erz.
Foyle (Loch), *foyl*.
Foynes, foynz.
Frameries, frah-m'*ree*.
Franche Comté, frahŋsh-koŋ-tay.
Franconia, frang-*koh*-ne-a.
Frankenstein, *frahng*-ken-shtyn.
Frankfort, *frank*-fort.
Frascati, fras-*kah*-te.
Frauenberg, *frou*-en-berkh.
Freiberg, *fry*-berkh.
Freiburg, *fry*-boorkh.
Freising, *fry*-zing.
Fréjus, fray-*zhus*.
Frémicourt, fray-me-*koor*.
Fremont, fre-*mont*.
Fresnes, fren.
Fresnoy, fre-*nwah*.
Fricourt, free-koor.
Friedland, *freed*-lahnt.
Friedrichshafen, *free*-drikhs-*hah*-fen.
Friesland, *freez*-land.
Frigento, fre-*jen*-toh.
Friockheim, *free*-kum.
Friuli, free-*oo*-le.
Frobisher, *frob*-ish-er.
Frome, froom.
Frontenac, *fron*-te-nak.
Frosinone, froh-ze-*noh*-na.
Frunze, *froon*-ze.
Fuerteventura, fwer-tay-ven-*too*-ra.
Fujiyama, *foo*-je-*yah*-ma.
Fuka, *foo*-ka.
Fukien, foo-*kyeen*.
Fukushima, foo-koo-*shee*-ma.
Fulda, *full*-da.
Fulham, *full*-um.
Fulmer, *full*-mer.
Fulton, *full*-ton.
Funchal, foon-*shahl*.
Fünen, *fu*-nen.
Fürstenberg, *foor*-sten-berkh.

Gabes, *gah*-bes.
Gaddesdon, *gadz*-don.
Gaeta, gah-e-ta.
Gagliano, gal-*yah*-noh.
Galapagos, ga-*lah*-pa-gos.
Galata, *gal*-a-ta.
Galatz, ga-*lats*.
Galena, ga-*lee*-na.
Gallabat, *gal*-a-bat.
Gallipoli, ga-*lip*-o-le.
Galveston, *gal*-ves-ton.
Galway, *gawl*-way.
Gambier, *gam*-beer.
Gandak, gun-*duk*.
Ganges, *gan*-jeez.
Gao, gah-*oh*.
Garboldisham, *garbl*-sham.
Gard, gahr.
Gardafui, gar-da-*fwee*.
Garigliano, gah-ree-lee-*ah*-noh.
Garonne, ga-*ron*.
Garw, gah-*roo*.
Gastein, *gah*-styn.
Gatun, gay-*toon*.
Gävelborg, *yair*-vel-bor.
Gaza (Palest.), *gay*-za.
Gaza (Mozambique), *gah*-za.
Gazala, ga-*zah*-la.
Gdynia, g'*deen*-yah.
Geelong, jee-*long*.
Gefle, *yayf*-lay.
Geilenkirchen, *gy*-len-ker-khen.
Gela, *jee*-la.
Gelderland, *gel*-der-lahnt.
Geldern, *gel*-dern.
Gelsenkirchen, *gel*-zen-ker-chen.
Gembloux, zhahŋ-bloo.
Genesee, jen-e-*see*.
Geneva, je-*nee*-va.
Genoa, *jen*-o-a.
Georgia, *jor*-je-a.
Georgievsk, gay-or-*gyefsk*
Gerizim, ge-*ry*-zim.
Gerona, hah-*roh*-nah.
Gersau, *ger*-zou.
Gex, zheks.
Ghadames, ga-*dah*-mes.
Ghats, gawts.
Ghazni, *guz*-nee.
Gheddahia, ged-a-*hy*-a.
Gheel, gayl.
Gheluvelt, *gay*-loo-velt.
Ghent, gent.
Gibraltar, je-*brawl*-ter.
Giessen, *gees*-en.
Gijon, hee-*hohn*.
Gila, *hee*-lah.
Gillingham (Dorset), *gil*-ing-am: (Kent), *jil*-ing-am.
Ginchy, zhaŋ-shee.
Gironde, zhee-roŋd.
Gisors, gee-zor.
Giurgiu, *joor*-joo.
Givenchy, zhee-vahŋ-shee.
Givet, zhee-vay.
Gizeh, *gee*-zeh.
Glamis, glahmz.
Glarus, *glah*-roos.
Glatz, glahts.
Gleiwitz, *gly*-vits.
Glencoe, glen-*koh*.

Glengarry, glen-*ga*-re,
Glenorchy, glen-*or*-khe.
Glogau, *gloh*-gou.
Gloucester, *glos*-ter.
Gmunden, g'*moon*-den.
Gniew, g'-*nyef*.
Gniezno, *g'nyaz*-noh.
Goa, *goh*-ah.
Gobi, *goh*-bee.
Goch, gohkh.
Godavery, go-*dah*-va-re.
Godesburg, *goh*-des-berkh.
Godmanchester, *gon*-shis-ter: *gum*-sis-ter.
Godthaab, *goh*-tawp.
Gomshall, *gum*-shal.
Gondwana, gon-*dwah*-na.
Gorgonzola, gor-gon-*zoh*-la.
Gorizia, go-*reet*-se-a.
Görlitz, *gur*-lits.
Gotha, *goh*-ta.
Gotham (Notts), *got*-am.
Gothenburg, *goth*-en-burg.
Göttingen, *gø*-ting-en.
Gouda, *gou*-dah.
Govan, *guv*-an.
Gradisca, grah-*dees*-kah.
Granada, gra-*nah*-da.
Grandpré, grahŋ-pray.
Grandson, grahŋ-sohŋ.
Grantham, *gran*-tam.
Graudenz, *grou*-dents.
Grave, grahv.
Gravelines, grahv-*leen*.
Gravesend, *grayvz*-end.
Graz, grahts.
Greenock, *gren*-, *green*-ok.
Greenwich (Engl.), *grin*-idj: (U.S.A.), *green*-wich.
Greifswald, *gryfs*-vahlt.
Greiz, gryts.
Grenada, (W.I.) gre-*nay*-da; (U.S.A.) gre-*nah*-da.
Grenoble, gre-*noh*-bl.
Grenzmark, *grents*-mark.
Griesheim, *grees*-hym.
Grindelwald, *grin*-del-vahlt.
Griqualand, *gree*-kwa-land.
Gris Nez, gree-*nay*.
Grisons, gree-zoŋ.
Gronau, *groh*-nou.
Groningen, *groh*-ning-en.
Grosseto, grohs-*say*-toh.
Grozny, *groz*-ne.
Grünau, *groo*-nou.
Grünberg, *groon*-berkh.
Gruyère, groo-*yair*.
Guadalajara, *gwah*-thah-lah-*hah*-rah.
Guadalcanal, *gwah*-dahl-ka-*nahl*.
Guadalquivir, *gwah*-dal-*kwiv*-er: *gwah*-thal-kee-*veer*.
Guadalupe, gwah-thah-*loo*-pay.
Guadeloupe, *gwah*-de-*loop*.
Guadiana, gwah-thee-*ah*-nah.
Guam, gwahm.
Guantanamo, gwahn-*tah*-nah-moh.
Guardafui, gwar-da-*fwee*.
Guatemala, gwah-ta-*mah*-la.
Guayaquil, gwy-a-*keel*.
Guayra, *gwire*-rah.
Gubbio, *goob*-byoh.
Guémappes, gay-*map*.
Guernica, gwer-*nee*-ka.
Guernsey, *gern*-ze.
Guiana, ge-*ah*-na.
Guienne, gee-*en*.
Guildford, *gil*-ford.
Guinea, *gin*-ne.
Guines, geen.
Guingamp, gaŋ-gahŋ.
Guipuzcoa, gee-*pooth*-ko-a.
Guisborough, *giz*-bu-ra.
Guise, geez.
Guiseley, *gyz*-le.
Gujarat, *goo*-ja-raht.
Gulistan, goo-le-*stahn*.
Gumbinnen, goom-*bin*-nen.
Gurupa, goo-roo-*pah*.
Gwalior, *gwah*-le-or.
Gwelo, *gway*-loh.
Gyachungkang, gyah-choong-*kahng*.
Gyongyos, *dyoon*-dyoosh.
Györ, dyør.
Gyula, *dyu*-la.

Haarlem, *har*-lem.
Haast, hahst.
Habbaniya, hab-bah-*nee*-ya.
Habiemont, ah-bee-moŋ.
Hadramaut, hah-drah-*mawt*.
Hagen, *hah*-gen.
Hague (la), hayg.
Haguenau, ahg-*noh*.
Haifa, *hy*-fa.
Hainan, hy-*nahn*.
Hainaut, a-*noh*.
Haiphong, hy-*fong*.
Haiti, *hay*-te.
Hakodate, *hah*-ko-*dah*-te.
Halberstadt, *hahl*-ber-shtaht.
Halesowen, haylz-*oh*-wen.
Halfya, hahl-*fy*-ya.
Halle, *hal*-le.
Hallstatt, *hahl*-shtaht.
Halmahera, hahl-mah-*hay*-rah.
Haltemprice, *hawl*-tem-prys.
Hamadan, *hah*-ma-dawn.
Hamamatsu, hah-ma-*maht*-soo.
Hamme, *hahm*-e.
Hanau, *hah*-nou.
Hankow, han-*kou*.
Hanover, *han*-o-ver.
Happisburgh, *haze*-bu-ra.
Harar, *hah*-rar.
Harburg, *har*-boorkh.
Hardanger, *har*-dahng-er.
Hardecourt, ard-*koor*.
Hardenhuish, *har*-nish.
Harewood, *har*-wood.
Harfleur, ar-*fler*.
Hargaisa, har-*gay*-e-sah.
Harlesden, *harlz*-den.
Harlingen, *har*-ling-en.
Hartlepool, *har*-tl-pool: *hart*-le-pool.
Hartmannsweilerkopf, *hart*-mahns-*vy*-ler-kopf.
Harz, harts.
Harwich, *ha*-ridj.
Hastings, *hay*-stingz.
Haugesund, *hou*-ge-soon.
Hauraki, hah-oo-*rah*-ke.
Hautbois (Norfolk), *hob*-is.
Haute-Saône, oht-sohn.
Haut-Rhin, oh-raŋ.
Havana, ha-*van*-a.
Havre, Le, le-*ahvr*.
Havrincourt, ah-vraŋ-koor.
Hawaii, hah-*wy*-ee.
Hawarden, *haw*-dn: *har*-dn: (U.S.A.) *hay*-wor-den.
Hawick, *hoh*-ik.
Haworth, *haw*-erth.
Hazebrouck, ahz-brook.
Hebrides, *heb*-re-deez.
Heidelburg, *hy*-del-berkh.
Heilbron (O.F.S.), *hyl*-bron.
Heilbronn (Ger.), hyl-*brohn*.
Heilungkiang, *hul*-loong-jyahng.

Heligoland, *hel*-e-go-land.
Heliopolis, hee-le-*op*-o-lis.
Helle Fjord, *hel*-le-fyord.
Helmstedt, *helm*-shtet.
Helsinki, hel-*sing*-ke.
Hendaye, ahŋ-dah-e.
Heraklion, he-*rak*-le-on.
Herat, he-*raht*.
Hérault, a-*roh*.
Hereford, *he*-re-ford.
Herford (Ger.), *her*-fort.
Hermosillo, er-mo-*seel*-yoh.
Hermoupolis, er-*moo*-po-lyis.
Herrnhut, *hern*-hoot.
Hertford, (Engl.) *har*-ford: (U.S.A.) *hurt*-ford.
Hertogenbosch, her-*toh*-gen-bos.
Herzegovina, *hert*-se-goh-*vee*-na.
Hesse-Nassau, *hes*-nas-aw.
Heyst, hyst.
Heytesbury, *hayz*-be-re.
Hierro, *yer*-roh.
Hildburghausen, *hilt*-boorkh-*hou*-zen.
Hilo, *hee*-loh.
Hilversum, *hil*-ver-soom.
Himalayas, him-a-*lay*-az.
Himara, he-*mah*-ra.
Hindu Kush, *hin*-doo-*koosh*.
Hiroshima, heer-ro-*shee*-mah.
Hispaniola, *his*-pah-*nyoh*-lah.
Hissarlik, his-*sar*-lik.
Hjälmar, *yel*-mar.
Hlegu, le-*goo*.
Hoangho, *hoh*-ang-*hoh*.
Hoboken, *hoh*-boh-ken.
Hochwald, *hohk*-vahlt.
Hoddesdon, *hodz*-don.
Hodeida, ho-*day*-dah.
Hogue, La, la-*ohg*.
Hohenstaufen, hoh-en-*shtou*-fen.
Hokkaido, *hohk*-ky-doh: hok-*ky*-doh.
Holborn, *hoh*-burn.
Hollandia, hol-*lan*-de-a.
Hollebeke, hol-e-*bay*-ke.
Holyrood, *hol*-e-rood.
Homs (Syria), hohms.
Honduras, hon-*dew*-ras.
Honfleur, oŋ-*fler*.
Honiton, *hun*-e-ton: *hon*-e-ton.
Honkitika, hong-ke-*tee*-ka.
Honshu, *hon*-shoo.
Hooge, *hoh*-ge.
Hopah, hoh-pay.
Hörby, *her*-be.
Horta, *or*-tah.
Hougoumont, oo-goo-*moŋ*.
Houlton, *hohl*-ton.
Hounslow, *hounz*-loh.
Housatonic, hoo-sa-*ton*-ik.
Houston (U.S.A.), *hew*-ston: *hous*-ton
Howick, *how*-ik.
Hron, hron.
Hsipaw, *hsee*-paw.
Huamachuco, wah-mah-*tshoo*-koh.
Huancavelica, *wahng*-kah-ve-*lee*-ka.
Huanchaca, wahn-*chah*-ka.
Hué, oo-*ay*.
Huelva, *wel*-va.
Huesca, *ways*-ka.
Huila, *wee*-lah.
Huissen, *hoy*-sen.
Humayta, oo-*may*-ta.
Hunan, hoo-*nahn*.
Hunsrück, *hoons*-rook.
Hunstanton, *hun*-ston: hun-*stan*-ton.
Huon, *hew*-on.
Huron, *hew*-ron.
Hurstmonceux, herst-mon-*syoo*.
Huy, hoy.
Huyton, *hoy*-t'n.
Hweichow, hway-*joh*.
Hyderabad, hy-der-ra-*bahd*.
Hyères, ee-*air*.
Hythe, hythe.

Ibicui, ee-be-koo-*ee*.
Idaho, *eye*-da-hoh.
Idritsa, *ee-drit*-sa.
Ife, *ee*-fay.
Ightham, *eye*-tam.
Iglau, ee-*glou*.
Iglesias, ee-*glay*-ze-ahs.
Igualada, ee-gwah-*lah*-thah.
Iguassu, ee-gwah-*soo*.
Ijmuiden, eye-*moo*-den.
Ijssel, *ice*-el.
Iliamna, ee-le-*am*-na.
Illimani, eel-ye-*mah*-nee.
Illinois, il-le-*noy* (*-noyz*).
Illyria, i-*li*-re-a.
Ilmen, *il*-men.
Ilmenau, *il*-me-nou.
Imandra, e-*mahn*-dra.
Imola, ee-*moh*-la.
Imphal, *imp*-hul: im-*fahl*.
Inagua, ee-*nah*-gwah.
Inchiquin, *inch*-e-kwin.
Indiana, in-de-*an*-a.
Indianapolis, *in*-de-a-*nap*-o-lis.
Indonesia, *in*-do-*nee*-shya.
Indore, in-*dor*.
Indramaya, in-dra-*mah*-y↓.
Indre, aŋdr.
Ingoldstadt, *ing*-gohl-shtaht.
Ingulets, een-goo-*lyets*.
Inhambane, in-yam-*bah*-nay.
Innerleithen, in-er-*lee*-then.
Innsbruck, *ins*-brook.
Insein, in-*sane*.
Insterburg, *in*-ster-boorkh.
Interlaken, *in*-ter-*lah*-ken.
Inverary, in-ver-*rair*-re.
Ioannina, yo-*ah*-ne-na.
Iona, eye-*oh*-na.
Iowa, *eye*-o-wa.
Ipoh, *ee*-poh.
Ipswich, *ips*-witch.
Iquique, ee-*kee*-ke.
Iquitos, ee-*kee*-tohs.
Irak (Iraq), e-*rahk*.
Iran, ee-*rahn*.
Irkutsk, er-*kootsk*.
Iroquois, *i*-roh-kwoy.
Irrawaddy, i-ra-*wod*-e.
Irtish, eer-*tish*.
Isar, *ee*-zar.
Ischia, *is*-kyah.
Ise, *ee*-se.
Iser, *ee*-zer.
Isère, *ee*-zair.
Iserlohn, ee-zer-*lohn*.
Isernia, e-*zer*-nyah.
Isfahan, is-fa-*hahn*.
Isigny, e-*see*-ne.
Isis, *eye*-sis.
Islay, *eye*-lay.
Isleworth, *eye*-zel-wurth.
Islington, *iz*-ling-ton.
Ismail, ees-ma-*eel*
Ismalia, ees-ma-*eel*-ya.
Isonzo, e-*zon*-tso.
Issy, *ee*-see.
Istanbul, ee-stahn-*bool*.
Itawamba, it-a-*wom*-ba.
Ithaca, *ith*-a-ka.
Ivanovo, ee-*vah*-no-voh.
Iviza, e-*vee*-thah.
Iwojima, *ee*-wo-*jee*-mah.
Ixcaquixtla, *eeks*-kah-*keeks*-tlah.

Iznajar, eeth-*nah*-har.
Izyaslavl, eez-yah-*slahvl.*
Izyum, ee-*zewm.*

Jablonec, *yahb*-lo-nyets.
Jablonika, yahb-lo-*nee*-tsa.
Jacmel, zhak-*mel.*
Jaffa, *jaf*-a: *yah*-fah.
Jagersfontein, *yah*-gers-fon-*tane.*
Jaipur, *jy*-poor.
Jakarta, ja-*kar*-ta.
Jalalabad, ja-*lah*-lah-*bahd.*
Jalapa, hah-*lah*-pa.
Jalisco, hah-*lees*-koh.
Jamaica, ja-*may*-ka.
Jammu, *jum*-oo.
Jämtland, *yemt*-lahnd.
Janina, *yah*-nee-nah.
Jan Mayen, yahn-*my*-en.
Japan, ja-*pan.*
Japura, zhah-poo-*rah.*
Jarabub, *zha*-ra-bub.
Jarnac, zhar-*nak.*
Jaroslav, *ya*-ro-slav.
Jassy, *yahs*-ee.
Jászbéreny, yahs-*be*-ray-ne.
Java, *jah*-va.
Jehol, ye-*hohl*: re-*hoh.*
Jelgava, yel-*gah*-va.
Jemappes, zhe-*map.*
Jena, *yay*-na.
Jerez de la Frontera, ha-*rahth*-day-lah-fron-*tay*-rah.
Jersey, *jer*-ze.
Jervaulx, *jer*-voh: *jar*-vis.
Jethou, zhe-*too.*
Jhalawar, jah-lah-*wahr.*
Jhansi, *jahn*-se.
Jhelum, *jay*-lum.
Jibuti, jee-boo-*tee.*
Jijiga, je-*jee*-ga.
Jiménez, hee-*may*-nays.
Jiwani, je-*wah*-ne.
Jodhpur, *johd*-poor.
Johannesburg, joh-*han*-ez-burg.
Johannisberg, yo-*han*-ees-berg.
Johore, jo-*hor.*
Joigny, zhwa-*nyee.*
Joinville, zhwaŋ-*veel.*
Jokjakarta, *jok*-yah-*kar*-tah.
Joliette, zho-*lyet.*
Jönkopping, *yoon*-choo-ping.
Jorullo, ho-*rool*-yoh.
Jotunheim, *yoot*-oon-haym.
Juan Fernandez, hwahn-fer-*nahn*-dayth: *joo*-an-fer-*nan*-dez.
Juarez, *hwah*-rays.
Juba, *joo*-bah.
Jubbulpur, jub-ul-*poor.*
Julich, *yoo*-likh.
Juliers, zhoo-lyay.
Juneau, *joo*-noh.
Jungfrau, *yoong*-frou.
Jutland, *jut*-land.
Juvigny, zhoo-*vee*-ne.

Kabul, ka-*bull.*
Kagoshima, kah-go-*shee*-ma.
Kaieteur, ky-e-*toor.*
Kaira, *ky*-ra.
Kairouan, ker-*wahn.*
Kaisarieh, ky-zah-*ree*-a.
Kaiserslautern, *ky*-zers-*lou*-tern.
Kalat, ka-*laht.*
Kalgoorlie, kal-*goor*-le.
Kalinin, ka-*lee*-nyeen.
Kaliningrad, ka-lee-nyeen-*grahd.*
Kalisz, *kah*-leesh.
Kalmar, *kahl*-mar.
Kalundborg, *kah*-loond-borg.
Kaluga, ka-*loo*-ga.
Kamakura, kah-mah-*koor*-rah.
Kamaran, kah-mah-*rahn.*
Kamchatka, kam-*chat*-ka.
Kamenets, kah-me-*nyets.*
Kamenskaya, *kah*-men-*sky*-ya.
Kampala, kam-*pah*-la.
Kanawha, ka-*naw*-wa.
Kanchanjanga, kahn-chun-*jung*-ga.
Kandahar, kan-da-*har.*
Kandy, *kan*-de.
Kansas, *kan*-zas.
Kapurthala, ka-*poor*-ta-la.
Kapuskasing, kap-us-*kay*-sing.
Karachev, *kah*-ra-chof.
Karachi, ka-*rah*-che.
Karafuto, kah-rah-*foo*-toh.
Kara Hissar, kah-*rah*-his-*sar.*
Karakoram, *kah*-rah-*kaw*-rum.
Karamyshevo, ka-rah-me-*shev*-oh.
Karelia, ka-*ree*-le-a.
Karlovac, *kar*-lo-vats.
Karlskrona, karls-*kroo*-na.
Karlsruhe, *karls*-roo-e.
Karlstad, *karl*-stahd.
Karlstadt, *karl*-shtaht.
Karroo, ka-*roo.*
Kasama, ka-*sah*-ma.
Kashmir, kash-*meer.*
Kassala, *kas*-a-lah.
Kassel, *kahs*-el.
Katha, ka-*thah.*
Kathiawar, kah-te-a-*wahr.*
Katowice, kah-to-*vee*-tse.
Katwijk, *kaht*-vyk.
Kauai, kah-oo-*ah*-e.
Kaunas, *kou*-nas.
Kavalla, kah-*vah*-lah.
Kavieng, kah-ve-*eng.*
Kawasaki, *kah*-wa-*sah*-ke.
Kayseri, ky-se-*ree.*
Kazan, ka-*zahn.*
Kecskemet, *ketsh*-ke-mayt.
Keewatin, ke-*wah*-tin.
Keighley, *keeth*-le.
Kelantan, ke-*lahn*-tahn.
Kemerovo, ke-me-*raw*-voh.
Kemi, *kay*-me.
Kenai, ke-*ny.*
Kennebec, ken-ne-*bek.*
Kentucky, ken-*tuk*-e.
Kenya, *kee*-nya.
Keokuk, *kee*-o-kuk.
Kerak, ke-*rahk.*
Keren, ke-*ren.*
Kerguelen, *ker*-ge-len.
Kermanshah, ker-mahn-*shah.*
Keswick, *kez*-ik.
Khabarovsk, khah-*bah*-rofsk.
Khanaqin, khah-nah-*keen.*
Kharkov, khar-*kof.*
Khartoum, kar-*toom.*
Kherson, *kher*-son.
Khiva, *khee*-va.
Khodzhent, kho-*jent.*
Kholm, khohm.
Khorasan, ko-ra-*sahn.*
Khoresm, *khoh*-rez'm.
Khyber, *ky*-ber.
Kiakhta, ke-*ahkh*-ta.
Kiaouchow, ke-*you*-chou.
Kiel, keel.
Kielce, *kyel*-tse.
Kiev, kee-*ef.*
Kikuyu, ke-*koo*-yoo.
Kilauea, kee-lou-*ay*-a.
Kilima-Njaro, *kil*-e-man-*jah*-roh.
Killarney, kil-*lar*-ne.

Kilmainham, kil-*main*-ham.
Kilmalcolm, kil-ma-*kohm.*
Kilmarnock, kil-*mar*-nok.
Kilsyth, kil-*syth.*
Kincardine, kin-*kar*-din.
Kinchinjunga, kin-chin-*joong*-ga.
Kingussie, king-*yoo*-se.
Kinross, kin-*ros.*
Kinsale, kin-*sale.*
Kintore, kin-*tor.*
Kiowa, *ky*-o-wa.
Kirghiz, kir-*geez.*
Kirin, *kee*-rin.
Kirkcaldy, kir-*kawl*-de.
Kirkcudbright, kir-*koo*-bre.
Kirkuk, kir-*kook.*
Kirov, *keer*-rof.
Kirovograd, *keer*-rof-o-grahd.
Kirriemuir, ki-re-*mewr.*
Kishinev, kee-she-*nyof.*
Kisumu, *kee*-soo-moo.
Kizil Irmak, *kiz*-il-er-*mahk.*
Klagenfurt, *klah*-gen-foort.
Klaipeda, kly-*ped*-a.
Klausenburg, *klou*-zen-boorkh.
Klerksdorp, *klarks*-dorp.
Knocke, nok'e.
Kobe, *koh*-be.
Kodiak, *koh*-de-ak.
Kohima, ko-*hee*-ma.
Kokand, ko-*kahnt.*
Kokoda, ko-*kod*-da.
Kolberg, *kohl*-berkh.
Kolhapur, *kohl*-hah-poor.
Kolomyja, *koh*-loh-*mee*-ya.
Komandonskie, *koh*-mahn-*dor*-ske-ye.
Komarno, *koh*-mar-no.
Komarom, *koh*-mah-rohm.
Konieh, *koh*-nee-a.
Königgrätz, kø-nikh-*grets.*
Königsberg, *kø*-nikhs-berkh.
Konstantinovka, kon-stan-*tee*-nov-ka.
Konstanz, *kon*-shtahnts.
Kootenai, *koo*-te-*nay.*
Kordofan, kor-do-*fahn.*
Korea, ko-*ree*-a.
Koriyama, koh-re-*yah*-ma.
Kosice, *koh*-shit-se.
Köslin, køs-*leen.*
Kossovo, *kos*-o-voh.
Kostroma, ko-*stroh*-ma.
Kota Bahru, *koh*-tah-*bah*-roo.
Kotelnikovo, koh-*tyel*-ne-*koh*-voh.
Kovel, *koh*-vel.
Koweit, ko-*wyt, -weet.*
Kra, krah.
Kragujevac, *krah*-goo-ye-vahts.
Krakatao, krah-kah-*tah*-o.
Krasnoarmeisk, *kras*-noh-ar-*maysk.*
Krasnoyarsk, kras-no-*yarsk.*
Krefeld, *kray*-felt.
Kremenchug, kre-men-*chook.*
Kremnitza, krem-*nyet*-sa.
Kreutzburg, *kroyts*-boorkh.
Kristiansand, kris-tyan-*sahn.*
Krithia, *kree*-te-ah.
Krivoi, Rog, kre-*voh*-e-rohg.
Krnov, *kur*-nov.
Krolovetz, kroh-*lyay*-vyets.
Kronberg, *krohn*-berg.
Kronstadt, *krohn*-shtaht.
Krzemieniec, kzhe-*myay*-nyets.
Kuala Lumpur, *kwah*-la-*loom*-pur.
Kuban, koo-*bahn.*
Kufra, *koo*-fra.
Kuibyshev, *kwee*-be-shef.
Kulmbach, *koolm*-bahkh.
Kumasi, koo-*mas*-se.
Kum Kale, koom-kah-*lee.*
Kuopio, koo-*op*-e-o.
Kurdistan, koor-dis-*tahn.*
Kure, *koo*-re.
Kurisches Haff, *koo*-rish-es-hahf.
Kurland, *koor*-lahnt.
Küstrin, *kus*-trin.
Kut-el-Amara, *koot*-el-ah-*mah*-ra.
Kuznetsk, kooz-*nyetsk.*
Kweichow, kwy-*chou*: *gway*-joh.
Kweiki, kwy-*kee*: *gway*-ke.
Kyaukpadaung, chouk-pa-*doung.*
Kyaukse, *chouk*-sa.
Kyoto, *kyoh*-toh.
Kyushu, *kyoo*-shoo.

La Bassée, lah-bah-*say.*
Labuan, la-boo-*an*: la-*boo*-an.
Laccadives, lak-a-*dyvz.*
La Chapelle, lah-sha-*pel.*
Lackawanna, lak-a-*won*-a.
Ladakh, la-*dahkh.*
Ladoga, *lah*-do-ga: la-*doh*-ga.
Lae, lay'e.
La Fayette, lah-fay-*et*: *laf*-a-yet.
La Ferté-sous-Jouarre, lah-fer-*tay*-soo-zhoo-*ahr.*
La Flèche, lah-*flaysh.*
Laghouat, lah-goo-*aht.*
La Guira, lah-*gwire*-ra.
Laguna, la-*goo*-nah.
La Haye du Puits, lah-ay-doo-*pwee.*
Lahore, la-*hor.*
Laibach, *ly*-bahkh.
La Linea, lah-*lee*-na-ah.
La Mancha, lah-*mahn*-chah.
La Mayotte, lah-ma-*yot.*
Lamlash, lam-*lash.*
Lammermoor, lam-er-*moor.*
Lamouche, lah-*moosh.*
Lampedusa, lahm-pa-*doo*-zah.
Lampeter, *lam*-pe-ter.
Landau, lahn-dow.
Landes, lahŋd.
Landrecies, loŋ-dre-see.
Langres, lahŋgr.
Languedoc, lahŋg-*dok.*
Lanuvio, la-*new*-ve-oh.
Laon, lahŋ.
Laos, *lah*-ohz.
La Pallice, lah-pa-*lees.*
La Paz, lah-*pahs.*
La Perouse, lah-pa-*rooz.*
La Plata, la-*plah*-ta.
Laredo, la-*ray*-doh.
Larnaca, *lar*-na-kah.
La Rochelle, lah-ro-*shel.*
Lashio, *lush*-e-oh.
Las Palmas, lahs-*pahl*-mahs.
Las Vegas, lahs-*vay*-gas.
Latakia, lah-ta-*kee*-a.
Latvia, *lat*-ve-a.
Lauderdale, *law*-der-dale.
Lauenburg, *lou*-en-boorkh.
Laufen, *lou*-fen.
Launceston, *lawn*-ston: *lahn*-ston: (Tasmania) *lawn*-ses-ton.
Lausanne, lo-*zan.*
Lauterbrunnen, *lou*-ter-broo-nen.

Lauwe, *lou*-ve.
Lauwin, loh-*vaŋ*.
La Vendée, la-vahŋ-*day*.
Leamington, *lem*-ing-ton.
Lebanon, *leb*-a-non.
Le Cateau, le-kat-*toh*.
Lecce, *let*-chay.
Le Creusot, le-*kroo*-zoh.
Leeuwarden, *lay*-wahr-den.
Leeward (Isls.), *lee*-wurd.
Leghorn, leg-*horn*.
Legnano, lay-*nyah*-noh.
Leh, lay.
Le Havre, le-*ahvr'*.
Leicester, *les*-ter.
Leigh (Essex, Lancs.), lee: (Surrey, Kent, Dorset), ly.
Leighton, *lay*-ton.
Leinster, *len*-ster.
Leipzig, *lyp*-tsikh: *lyp*-zig.
Leith, leeth.
Leitha (Riv.), *ly*-ta.
Leitrim, *lee*-trim.
Leman, *lem*-an.
Le Mans, le-*mahŋ*.
Lena, *lay*-na.
Leningrad, *len*-een-grahd.
Lens, lahŋz.
Lentini, len-*tee*-ne.
Leoben, lay-*oh*-ben.
Leobschlitz, *lay*-op-shlits.
Leominster, *lem*-ster.
Leon, lay-*on*: *lee*-on.
Lepanto, le-*pahn*-toh.
Le Puy, le-*pwee*.
Lérida, *lay*-re-thah.
Lerwick, *le*-rik: *ler*-wik.
Les Andelys, lay-*zaŋ'd*-lee.
Le Touquet, le-*too*-kay.
Le Tréport, le-tra-*por*.
Leuchars, *lew*-kharz.
Leuna, *loy*-na.
Leuthen, *loy*-ten.
Leuze, løz.
Levant, le-*vant*.
Leven (Loch), *lee*-ven.
Lewes, *loo*-is.
Lewisham, *loo*-e-sham.
Leyden, *ly*-den.
Leyte (Isl.), *lay*-ta.
Leyton, *lay*-ton.
Lgov l'gof.
Lhasa, *las*-a.
Liancourt, lyoŋ-*koor*.
Liaotung, lyoh-*doong*.
Libau, *lee*-boh.
Libenge, li-*bahnzh*.
Liberia, ly-*beer*-re-a.
Libreville, lee-bre-*veel*.
Libya, *lib*-e-a.
Licata, li-*kah*-ta.
Lichfield, *lich*-feeld.
Lichtenburg, *likh*-ten-boorkh.
Lida, *lee*-da.
Liddesdale, *lidz*-dale.
Lidice, *lid*-e-cha.
Lido, *lee*-doh.
Liechtenstein, *likh*-ten-shtyn.
Liège, lee-*ayzh*.
Liegnitz, *leeg*-nits.
Liepaja, *lee*-a-pah-ya.
Lierre, li-*air*.
Ligny, *lee*-nyee.
Liguria, li-*gewr*-re-a.
Lille, leel.
Lilongue, li-*loŋg*.
Lima, *lee*-mah: *ly*-ma.
Limasol, lee-mah-*sohl*.
Limoges, lee-*mohzh*.
Limousin, lee-moo-*zahŋ*.
Limoux, lee-*moo*.
Lincoln, *ling*-kon.
Lingayen, ling-gah-*yane*.
Linköping, lin-*chø*-ping.
Linlithgow, lin-*lith*-goh.
Linnhe (Loch), *lin*-ne.
Linosa, li-*noh*-sah.
Linz, lints.
Lipari, *lip*-a-ree.
Lippe, *lip*-e.
Lippstadt, *lip*-shtaht.
Lisichansk, lis-e-*shansk*.
Lisieux, lee-*zyø*.
Lismore, liz-*more*.
Litani (Riv.), le-*tah*-ne.
Lithuania, lith-ew-*ay*-ne-a.
Littoria, li-*taw*-re-a.
Liu-Kiu (Isls.), lyoo-kyoo.
Livonia, li-*voh*-ne-a.
Llandaff, lan-*daf*.
Llandudno, lan-*dud*-noh.
Llanelly, la-*neth*-le.
Llanfairfechan, lan-fair-*fek*-en.
Llangollen, lan-*goth*-len.
Lläno, *lah*-noh: *lyah*-noh.
Loango, lo-*ang*-goh.
Löbau, *lø*-bou.
Lobito, lo-*bee*-toh.
Locarno, lo-*kar*-noh.
Lochaber, lo-*khab*-er.
Lochinvar, lokh-in-*var*.
Lodi, *loh*-dee.
Lodz, lødz.
Lofoten, lo-*foh*-ten.
Loire, lwahr.
Lomond, *loh*-mond.
Longueval, *loŋ*-ge-vahl.
Longwy, loŋ-wee.
Lorelei, *law*-re-ly.
Lorient, lo-ree-ahŋ.
Los Angeles, los-*an*-je-leez: lohs-*ahng*-ha-lahs.
Lostwithiel, lost-*with*-e-el.
Lothian, *loh*-the-an.
Loudoun, *lou*-don.
Loughborough, *luf*-bu-ra.
Loughrea, lokh-*ray*.
Loughton, *lou*-ton.
Louisburg, *loo*-is-burg.
Louisiade (Archipel.), loo-ee-ze-*ahd*.
Louisiana, loo-ee-ze-*an*-a.
Louisville, *loo*-is-vil.
Lourdes, loord.
Lourenço Marques, lo-*ren*-so-*mar*-kes.
Louvain, loo-*vayŋ*.
Louviers, loo-*vyay*.
Louvigny, loo-*vee*-ɲe.
Louvois, loo-*vwah*.
Lovicz, *law*-vich.
Lovosice, *loh*-vo-sit-se.
Lowestoft, *loh*-stoft.
Lowndes, lounz.
Luanda, loo-*ahn*-da.
Lübeck, *loo*-bek.
Lublin, *lyoo*-blyen.
Lucania, loo-*kay*-ne-a.
Lucca, *look*-kah.
Lucenec, *loo*-cha-nyets.
Lucerne, loo-*sern*.
Luckenwalde, look-en-*vahl*-de.
Lucknow, *luk*-nou.
Lüderitz, *loo*-de-rits.
Ludwigshafen, *loot*-vikhs-*hah*-fen.
Lugano, loo-*gah*-noh.
Lugau, *loo*-gou.
Lule, *lu*-le.
Lulea, *lu*-le-oh.
Luluaborg, loo-*loo*-ah-boork.
Lüneburg, *lu*-ne-berg.
Lunéville, lu-na-*veel*.
Lupkow, *loop*-koof.
Lusaka, loo-*sah*-ka.
Lusignan, loo-*see*-nyahŋ.
Lutsk, lootsk.
Lützen, *lut*-sen.
Luxemburg, luk-sem-burg: *look*-sem-boorkh.
Luxor, *look*-sor.
Luzon, loo-*zon*.
Lwow, l'woof.
Lyck, lik.
Lydda, *lid*-a.
Lympne, lim.
Lyndhurst, *lind*-hurst.
Lynmouth, *lin*-muth.

Lyon, lee-*oŋ*.
Lyonnais, lee-o-*nay*.
Lyons, *ly*-unz.
Lys, lees.
Lytham St. Anne's, *lith*-am-s'nt-*anz*.
Lyveden, *liv*-den.

Maas, mahs.
Maastricht, *mahs*-trikht.
Macao, ma-*kou* : *mah*-kou.
Macassar, ma-*kas*-sar.
Macclesfield, *maklz*-feeld.
Maceio, ma-say-*yoh*.
Macomb, ma-*koom* : ma-*kohm*.
Macon, (U.S.A.) *may*-kon.
Mâcon, mah-*koŋ*.
Macquarie, mak-*kwo*-re.
Madagascar, mad-a-*gas*-kar.
Madang, ma-*dahng*.
Madeira, ma-*deer*-ra.
Madras, ma-*dras* : ma-*drahs*.
Madrid, ma-*drid*: mah-*dreeth*.
Madura, ma-*door*-ra.
Mælström, *male*-strohm.
Mafeking, *maf*-e-king.
Magdala, *mag*-da-la.
Magdalena, mahg-dah-*lay*-nah.
Magdeburg, *mag*-de-burg: *mahg*-de-boorkh.
Magellan, ma-*jel*-lan.
Magenta, ma-*jen*-ta.
Mageröe, *mah*-ge-roo.
Magersfontein, *mah*-gers-fon-tain.
Maggiore, madj-e-*aw*-re: mah-*djaw*-ra.
Maglemose, *mah*-gla-moh-se: *mou*-le-moh-se.
Magnitogorsk, mag-nee-to-*gorsk*.
Magwe, mug-*way*.
Magyarova, *mod*-yo-roh-var.
Mahanady, ma-hah-*nud*-e.
Mahon, ma-*hohn*: mah-*ohn*.
Maidurgi, my-*door*-ge.
Maikop, *my*-kop.
Mainz, mynts.
Majorca, ma-*yor*-ka.
Majuba, ma-*joo*-ba.
Makhach-Kala, ma-*khach*-ka-la.
Maknassi, mahk-*nah*-se.
Makov, *mah*-kof.
Malabar, mal-a-*bar*.
Malacca, ma-*lak*-a.
Malaga, *mal*-a-ga: *mah*-lah-gah.
Malakand, mul-a-*kund*.
Malaya, ma-*lay*-a.
Maldive, mal-*dive*.
Maldon, *mawl*-don.
Malgobek, *mahl*-go-bek.
Malindi, mah-*leen*-de.
Malines, ma-*leen*.
Malmaison, mal-mah-*zoŋ*.
Malmédy, mal-mah-*dee*
Malmesbury, *mahmz*-be-re.
Mälmo, *mahl*-mu.
Malolos, mah-*loh*-lohs.
Maloyaroslovets, *mah*-loh-ya-ra-*slah*-vyets.
Malpas, (Salop) *mal*-pas : (Corn.) *moh*-pus.
Malplaquet, mal-pla-*kay*.
Malta, *mawl*-ta.
Maltezana, mol-te-*zah*-na.
Malvern, *mawl*-vern.
Mambone, mahm-*boh*-nay.
Manaar, ma-*nar*.
Managua, mah-*nah*-gwah.
Manaos, mah-*nah*-oos.
Manche, mahŋsh.
Manchukuo, man-choo-*kwoh*.
Manchuria, man-*choor*-re-a.
Mandalay, man-da-*lay*.
Mangalore, mang-ga-*lore*.
Manhattan, man-*hat*-tan.
Manich (Riv.), ma-*nich*.
Manila, ma-*nil*-a: mah-*nee*-lah.
Manipur, mun-e-*poor*.
Manitoba, man-e-*toh*-ba.
Manitowoc, man-e-to-*wok*.
Mannheim, *man*-hime.
Manresa, man-*ray*-sa.
Mantes, mahŋt.
Mantua, *man*-tew-a.
Manzanares, mahn-thah-*nah*-race.
Maracaibo, ma-ra-*ky*-boh.
Marada, ma-*rah*-dah.
Marañon, ma-rah-*nyohn*.
Marazion, ma-ra-*zy*-on.
Marcoing, mar-*kwaŋ*.
Marengo, ma-*reng*-go.
Mareotis, ma-re-*oh*-tis.
Margharita, mar-ga-*ree*-ta
Marianas, mah-re-*ah*-naz.
Marianpol, *mah*-re-an-pohl.
Maricao, mah-re-*kay*-oh.
Marie Galante, ma-ree-ga-*lahŋt*.
Marienbad, ma-*ree*-en-baht, -bahd.
Marienwerder, ma-*ree*-en-ver-der.
Marigliano, mah-reel-*yah*-noh.
Marignane, mah-ree-*nyahn*.
Marigny, mah-*ree*-nye.
Marinduque, mah-ren-*doo*-kay.
Maripol, *mah*-re-pohl.
Maritza (Riv.), mah-*reet*-sah.
Mariupol, mah-re-oo-*pohl*.
Marlborough, *mawl*-bro : *marl*-bro.
Marmolada (Mt.), mar-moh-*lah*-dah.
Marmora, *mar*-mo-ra.
Marquesas, mar-*kay*-sas.
Marrakesh, mah-rah-*kesh*.
Marsala, mar-*sah*-la.
Marseilles, mar-*saylz*: mar-*say*'e.
Mars-la-Tour, mars-lah-*toor*.
Martaban, mar-ta-*ban*.
Martigny, mar-*teen*-ye.
Martinique, mar-te-*neek*.
Martinpuich, mar-taŋ-*pweesh*.
Maryculter, mair-re-*koo*-ter.
Marylebone, *ma*-re-le-bun: ma-re-bun.
Masai, mah-*sah*-e.
Maseru, *maz*-er-roo.
Mashonaland, ma-*shoh*-na-land.
Masira, *mah*-se-rah.
Massachusetts, mas-a-*choo*-sits.
Massawa, mah-*sah*-wah.
Massicault, *mah*-se-koh.
Masulipatam, ma-*soo*-le-pa-*tam*.
Matabeleland, mat-a-*bee*-le-land.
Matanzas, ma-*tan*-zas: mah-*tahn*-sahs.
Matapan, mat-a-*pan*: mah-tah-*pahn*.
Mato Grosso, *mah*-too-*groh*-soo.
Matrahtin, mah-*trah*-taŋ.
Matsuyama, *maht*-soo-*yah*-ma.
Matsuye, *maht*-soo-ye.

Maturin, mah-too-*reen*.
Maubeuge, moh-*boozh*.
Maui, *mou*-e : mah-*oo*-e.
Mauretania, mo-re-*tay*-ne-a.
Mauritius, mo-*rish*-us.
Mauthausen, *mout*-hou-zen.
Mawchi, maw-*chee*.
Mayenne, ma-*yen*.
Maymyo, *my*-myoh.
Maynooth, *may*-nooth : may-*nooth*.
Mayumba, mah-*yoom*-bah.
Mazabuka, mah-za-*boo*-kah.
Mazatlan, mah-sah-*tlahn*.
Mazovetsky, mah-so-*vyet*-ske.
Mazzarno, maht-sah-*ree*-noh.
Mbabane, 'mbah-*bah*-ne.
Mbeya, '*mbay*-yah.
Meaux, moh.
Mechlin, *mek*-lin.
Mecklenburg, *mek*-len-boorkh (-burg).
Medan, may-*dahn*.
Medellin, (Colombia) mah-thel-*yeen* : (Phlpns.) mah-del-*yeen*.
Medina, me-*dee*-na.
Medinine, may-de-*neen*.
Medjez-el-Bab, me-*jez*-el-*bahb*.
Médoc, *may*-dok : *med*-ok.
Meekatharra, mee-ker-*thah*-ra.
Meerhout, *mayer*-hout.
Meerut, *mee*-rut.
Meigs, megz.
Meijel, me-*zhel*.
Meiktila, *meek*-te-lah.
Meiningen, *my*-ning-en.
Meissen, *mys*-en.
Mekili, me-*kee*-le.
Meknes, *mek*-nes.
Mekong, may-*kong*.
Melanesia, mel-a-*nee*-ze-a.
Melitopol, may-lye-*taw*-pol.
Melbourne, *mel*-born.
Melrose, *mel*-rohz.
Memel, *may*-mel.
Menai (Strait), *men*-eye.
Menam, ma-*nahm*.
Mendocino, men-do-*see*-noh.
Mendoza, men-*doh*-sah.
Menin, me-naŋ.
Mentana, men-*tah*-nah.
Mentone, men-*toh*-ne.
Meopham, *mep*-am.
Merchiston, *mer*-kis-ton.
Mergui, mer-*gwee*.
Merida, *may*-re-thah.
Merioneth, me-re-*on*-eth.
Mersa Matruh, *mer*-sah-ma-*troo*.
Mersey, *mer*-ze.
Merthyr Tydvil, mer-ther-*tid*-vil.
Merv, merf.
Mesopotamia, *mes*-o-po-*tay*-me-a.
Messina, me-*see*-na.
Messines, me-*seen*.
Mestre, *mes*-tra.
Metz, mets.
Meudon, mø-doŋ.
Meurthe, mørth.
Meuse, mørz.
Mezières, ma-zyair.
Mezokovesd, *mez*-oo-*koo*-vesht.
Miami, my-*am*-e.
Miani, me-*ah*-nee.
Michalovce, *mee*-kha-*lof*-tse.
Michigan, *mish*-e-gan.
Micronesia, my-kro-*nee*-ze-a.
Mignano, mee-*nyah*-noh.
Milan, *mil*-an : me-*lan*.
Milano, me-*lah*-noh.
Milazzo, me-*laht*-soh.
Millerovo, mee-le-*roh*-voh.
Milngavie, m'*gy*.
Milwaukee, mil-*waw*-kee.
Minas Geraes, *mee*-nas-zhe-*rys*.
Mincio, *meen*-choh.
Mindanao, min-dah-*nah*-oh.
Minho, *meen*-yoh.
Minneapolis, min-e-*ap*-o-lis.
Minnesota, min-e-*soh*-ta.
Miquelon, mee-k'loŋ.
Miramichi, mi-ra-me-*shee*.
Miskolc, *mish*-kohlts.
Miraumont, *meer*-ro-moŋ.
Mississippi, mis-e-*sip*-e.
Missolonghi, mis-o-*long*-ge.
Missoula, me-*zoo*-la.
Missouri, mis-*zoor*-re.
Mistretta, me-*stret*-tah.
Misurata, mee-soo-*rah*-tah.
Mitau, *mee*-tou.
Mitava, me-*tah*-va.
Mius (Riv.), me-*yoos*.
Miyako, *mee*-yah-koh.
Mlawa, m'*lah*-vah.
Mobile, mo-*beel*.
Mocha, *moh*-kah.
Modena, *mod*-e-na : *moh*-de-nah.
Modigliana, moh-deel-*yah*-nah.
Mödling, *mød*-ling.
Moerdyk, *moor*-dyk.
Moeris, *meer*-ris.
Mogadicio, moh-ga-*dee*-sho.
Mogadishu, moh-ga-*dee*-shoo.
Mogador, mog-a-*dor*.
Mogaung, mo-*gawng*.
Mogilev, mo-gee-*lyof*.
Mohacs, *moh*-hahch.
Mohawk, *moh*-hawk.
Mohne, *moh*-na.
Moldau, *mol*-dou.
Moldavia, mol-*day*-ve-a.
Moline (U.S.A.), mo-*leen*.
Mollwitz, *mol*-vits.
Molokai, moh-lo-*kah*-e.
Moluccas, mo-*luk*-az.
Mombasa, mom-*bah*-sa.
Monaco, *mon*-a-koh.
Monaghan, *mon*-a-gan.
Monastir, mon-as-*ter*.
Mondego, moŋ-*day*-goh.
Mondragone, mohn-drah-*goh*-na.
Monfalcone, mohn-fahl-*koh*-na.
Monghyr, mong-*ger*.
Mongolia, mong-*goh*-le-a.
Monifieth, mon-e-*feeth*.
Monkwearmouth, munk-*wair*-muth.
Monmouth, *mon*-(*mun*-) muth.
Monnikendam, mon-a-ken-*dahm*.
Monongahela, mo-*non*-ga-*hay*-la (-*hee*-la).
Monreale, mohn-ra-*ah*-la.
Monroe, mun-*roh*.
Monrovia, mon-*roh*-ve-a.
Mons, monz : moŋs.
Monschau, *moŋ*-shou.
Montagnana, mohn-tah-*yah*-nah.
Montalban, mon-tal-*ban*.
Montana, mon-*tah*-na.
Montargis, moŋ-tar-*zhee*.
Montauban, moŋ-toh-*bahŋ*.
Montbéliard, moŋ-ba-*lyar*.

Mont Blanc, moŋ-*blahŋ*.
Montcalm, mont-*kahm*.
Montdidier, moŋ-*dee*-dyay.
Monte Alegre, *mon*-ta-a-*laygr'*.
Monte Cassino, *mon*-ta-kahs-*see*-noh.
Montego (Bay), mon-*tee*-goh.
Montenegro, mon-te-*nee*-groh.
Monterey (U.S.A.), mon-te-*ray*.
Monterray (Mex.), mohn-ter-*ray*.
Montes Claros, *mohn*-tes-*klah*-roos.
Montevideo, mon-te-ve-*day*-oh; mon-te-*vid*-e-oh.
Montferrat, moŋ-fe-*rah*.
Montgomery, munt-*gum*-e-re : mont-*gom*-e-re.
Montijo, mon-*tee*-hoh.
Montmartre, moŋ-*martr*.
Montmirail, moŋ-mee-*ray*.
Montmorency, moŋ-mo-rahŋ-*see* : (U.S.A.) mont-mo-*ren*-se.
Montpelier, mont-*peel*-yer.
Montpellier, moŋ-pel-*yay*.
Montreal, mon-tre-*awl*.
Montreuil, moŋ-*trø'e*.
Montreux, moŋ-trø.
Montrose, mon-*trohz*.
Mont-Saint-Jean, moŋ-saŋ-*zhahŋ*.
Mont-Saint-Michel, moŋ-saŋ-mee-*shel*.
Montserrat, mont-se-*rat*: (Sp.) monht-ser-*raht*.
Monywa, *moh*-noo-wa.
Monza, *mohn*-tsah.
Monzie, mo-*nee*.
Morava, *moh*-ra-va.
Moravia, mo-*ray*-ve-a.
Moravska Ostrava, *moh*-raf-skah-*os*-tra-va.
Moray, *mur*-re.
Morbihan, mor-bee-*ahŋ*.
Morea, mo-*ree*-a.
Morecambe, *mor*-kam.
Moresnet, mo-ra-*nay*.
Morges, morzh.
Morlaix, mor-*lay*.
Morotai, moh-ro-*tah*-e.
Mortain, mor-*taŋ*.
Morvan, mor-*vahŋ*.
Morven, *mor*-ven.
Moselle, mo-*zel*.
Mossamedes, moh-sah-*may*-des.
Mossgiel, mos-*geel*.
Mossora, moh-*soh*-rah.
Mostar, *mos*-tar.
Mosul, moh-*sool*.
Motala, moh-*tah*-la.
Moulins, moo-*laŋ*.
Moulmein, mohl-*main*.
Mousehole, mouzl.
Moyale, mo-*yah*-le.
Moyobamba, moh-yoh-*bahm*-ba.
Mozambique, moh-zam-*beek*.
Mpika, m'*pee*-kah.
Msus, m'soos.
Mtsensk, m'tsensk.
Muara, moo-*ah*-rah.
Mubo, *moo*-boh.
Mudania, moo-dah-nee-*ah*.
Mühlberg, *mool*-berkh.
Mühlhausen, *mool*-hou-zen.
Muizenberg, *mew*-zen-berg.
Mukachevo, moo-ka-*chay*-voh.
Mukden, mook-*den*.
Mulde (Riv.), *mool*-de'.
Mulheim, *mool*-hym.
Mulhouse, moo-*looz*.
Mullingar, mul-in-*gar*.
Multan, mool-*tahn*.
München-Gladbach, *moon*-khen-*glaht*-bahkh.
Munda, *moon*-dah.
Munich, *mew*-nik.
Munster (Eire), *mun*-ster.
Münster (Ger.), *moon-ster*.
Murano, moo-*rah*-noh.
Murat, mu-*rah*.
Murmansk, moor-*mahnsk*.
Muroran, *moo*-ro-ran.
Murrumbidgee, mur-um-*bij*-ee.
Murshidabad, moor-shed-ah-*bahd*.
Muscat, mus-*kat*.
Muscateen, mus-ka-*teen*.
Muskegon, mus-*kee*-gun.
Muskogee, mus-*koh*-ge.
Mussoorie, mus-*soo*-re.
Mustagh, moos-*tahkh*.
Mutarara, moo-tah-*rah*-ra.
Muy, mwee.
Mwanza, *mwahn*-zah.
Myaungmya, myoung-*myah*.
Myitkyina, myit-*chee*-nah.
Mysore, my-*sor*.
Mytilene, mit-e-*lee*-ne.

Naas, nace.
Nablus, na-*bloos*.
Nacogdoches, nak-o-*doh*-chez.
Nagasaki, nah-ga-*sah*-ke.
Nagoya, *nah*-hoh-ya.
Nagpur, nahg-*poor*.
Nagy Kanizsa, *nod*-ye-*ko*-nee-zho.
Nagyvarad, *nod*-ye-va-rod.
Nairobi, ny-*roh*-be.
Nakichevan, *nakh*-e-che-van.
Nalchik, *nal*-chek.
Namaqualand, nah-*mah*-kwa-land.
Namur, na-*moor*.
Nancy, nahŋ-see.
Nanda Devi, *nun*-dah-*day*-ve.
Nanga Parbat, *nung*-ga-*pur*-but.
Nanking, nan-*king*.
Nantes, nahŋt.
Nantucket, nan-*tuk*-et.
Nantwich, *nant*-wich.
Naples, *nay*-p'lz.
Napoli, *nah*-po-lee.
Narafominsk, nah-rah-fo-*minsk*.
Narbonne, nar-*bon*.
Narew, *nah*-ref.
Narvik, *nar*-vek.
Naseby, *naze*-be.
Nasiriya, nah-se-*ree*-ya.
Nassau, *nah*-sou : (U.S.A.) *nas*-aw.
Natal, na-*tal*.
Natchitoches, *nak*-e-tosh.
Nauen, *nou*-en.
Naumburg, *noum*-boorkh.
Naupaktos, *nahf*-pak-tohs.
Nauplion, *nahf*-plyee-on.
Nauru, *nah*-oo-roo.
Nauvoo, naw-*voo*.
Navajo, *nav*-a-ho.
Navarino, nah-vah-*ree*-noh.
Navarre, na-*var*.
Nawanagar, *nah*-wa-*nug*-ar.
Naxos, *nak*-sos.
Ndola, n'*doh*-lah.
Neagh (Lough), *nay*.
Neanderthal, ne-*an*-der-tahl.

Neath, neeth.
Nebraska, ne-*bras*-ka.
Neckar, *nek*-ar.
Neerwinden, nay-er-*vin*-den.
Negapatam, neg-a-pa-*tam*.
Negeb, *neg*-eb.
Negombo, ne-*gom*-boh.
Negri Sembilan, *nay*-gre-sem-be-*lahn*.
Nehavend, nay-hah-*vend*.
Neisse, *nys*-e.
Nejd, nayd: nezhd.
Nemi (Lake), *nay*-me.
Némours, na-*moor*.
Nene (Riv.), neen.
Nepal, ne-*pawl*.
Nerchinsk, *nyer*-chensk.
Nettuno, net-*too*-noh.
Neuberg, *noy*-boorkh.
Neuchâtel, noo-shah-*tel*.
Neufchâtel, noo-shah-*tel*.
Neuilly, *nœ*-yee.
Neusiedler See, *noy*-zeed-ler-zay.
Neustadt, *noy*-shtaht.
Neuve Chapelle, nœv-sha-*pel*.
Neuwied, *noy*-veet.
Neva, *nee*-va: nye-*vah*.
Nevada (U.S.A.), ne-*vah*-da.
Nevers, ne-vair.
Nevis (B.W.I.), *nee*-vis.
Newfoundland, new-fund-*land*.
Newquay, *new*-kee.
Newry, *new*-re.
Newtownards, new-t'n-*ardz*.
Ngami, n'*gah*-me.
Ngarimu, n'gah-re-*moo*.
Niagara, ny-*ag*-a-ra.
Niamey, *nee*-a-may.
Nicaragua, nik-a-*rah*-gwa (-*rag*-ew-a).
Nice, nees.
Nicobar, nik-o-*bar*.
Nicosia, nee-ko-*zee*-ah.
Nieder-Selters, nee-der-*zel*-ters.
Niemen, *nee*-men.
Nieuport, *nee*-oo-port.
Niger, *ny*-jer.
Nigeria, ny-*jeer*-re-a.
Nijmegen, *ny*-may-gen.
Nijni-Novgorod, *nyizh*-nye-*nawv*-go-rot.
Nikolaiev, nik-o-*ly*-yef.
Nikopol, nee-ko-*pawl*.
Nilgiris, *nil*-ge-riz.

Nimeguen, nim-*ay*-gen.
Nîmes, neem.
Nimwegen, nim-*vay*-gen.
Nipissing, *nip*-i-sing.
Nippon, *nyip*-pon.
Nishapur, nee-shah-*poor*.
Nisibin, nis-ee-*been*.
Nismes, neem.
Nivernais, nee-ver-*nay*.
Noailles, noh-eye.
Nogent-sur-Oise, no-*zhahŋ*-soor-*wahz*.
Noisy-le-Grand, nwah-*zee*-le-*grahŋ*.
Nome, nohm.
Noordvijk, *nord*-vyk.
Nordenskjöld (Sea), *nor*-den-shool.
Nordhausen, *nort*-hou-zen.
Nordkyn, *nor*-kun.
Norrköping, *nor*-chu-ping.
Norwich, *no*-ridj: (U.S.A.) *nor*-wich.
Nossi-Bé, naw-*see*-bay.
Noumea, noo-*may*-a.
Novara, no-*vah*-ra.
Nova Scotia, *noh*-va-*skoh*-sha.
Novaya Zemlya, *naw*-va-ya-*zem*-lya.
Novgorod, *nawv*-go-rot.
Novi Sad, *noh*-ve-sahd.
Novocherkask, naw-vo-cher-*kahsk*.
Novogeorgievsk, *naw*-vo-ge-*or*-ge-yefsk.
Novorossisk, naw-vo-roh-*seesk*.
Novo Serpukhov, naw-vo-*syer*-poo-khof.
Novosibirsk, naw-vo-se-*bersk*.
Nowanager, nou-a-*nug*-er.
Noyers, nwah-yay.
Noyon, nwah-yoŋ.
Nubia, *new*-be-a.
Nueva Gerona, *nway*-vah-ha-*roh*-nah.
Nuevo Leon, *nway*-voh-lay-*ohn*.
Nuneaton, nun-*ee*-ton.
Nunivack, *noo*-ne-*vak*.
Nuremberg, *newr*-rem-berg.
Nürnberg, *nørn*-berkh.
Nyassa, ny-*as*-a: *nyah*-sa.
Nyiregyhaza, *nyee*-red-y'*hah*-zo.

Oahu, oh-*ah*-hoo.

Oamaru, *om*-a-roo: oh-*ah*-ma-roo.
Oaxaca, wa-*hah*-kah.
Oban, *oh*-ban.
Oberammergau, *oh*-ber-*am*-er-gou.
Oberhausen, *oh*-ber-hou-zen.
Oberwesel, oh-ber-*vay*-zel.
Obidos, o-*bee*-doos.
Oceania, oh-she-*ay*-ne-a.
Ochachov, o-*chah*-kof.
Ochill, *oh*-khil.
Ochiltree, (Scot.) *oh*-khil-tree: (U.S.A.) *ok*-il-tree.
Ochterlony, *okh*-ter-*loh*-ne.
Ocmulgee (Riv.), ok-*mul*-ge.
Odawara, *oh*-da-*wah*-ra.
Odense, oh-*then*-sah.
Odenwald, *oh*-den-vahlt.
Oder (Riv.), *oh*-der.
Odessa, o-*des*-a.
Odiham, *oh*-de-am.
Oeiras, oh-*ay*-ee-rahs.
Oesel, ø-sel.
Offaly, *of*-a-le.
Ogaki, *oh*-gah-ke.
Oglio, *ohl*-yoh.
Ohio, oh-*hy*-oh.
Ohlau, *oh*-lou.
Oignies, wah-*nyee*.
Oirat, oy-*raht*.
Oise (Riv.), *wahz*.
Oka (Riv.), o-*kah*.
Okhotsk, oh-*khotsk*.
Okhrida, *okh*-re-dah.
Okinawa, oh-ke-*nah*-wa.
Oklahoma, oh-kla-*hoh*-ma.
Okuru, oh-koo-*roo*.
Öland, ø-lahnd.
Oldenburg, *ohl*-den-boorkh.
Oldham, *ohl*-dum.
Oléron, oh-la-*roŋ*.
Olivares, o-lee-*vah*-res.
Oliveira, o-lee-*vay*-ee-ra.
Olmütz, *ol*-mootz.
Olney, *ohl*-ne: *oh*-ne: (U.S.A.) *ol*-ne.
Olonets, o-*law*-nyets.
Omagh, *oh*-mah.
Omaha, *oh*-ma-haw.
Oman, o-*mahn*.
Omdurman, om-door-*mahn*.
Omei, *oh*-may.
Onega, o-*nee*-ga: o-*nyeg*-a.
Oneida, o-*ny*-da.

Ontario, on-*tair*-re-oh.
Oonadatta, oo-na-*dat*-a.
Oosterbeek, *oh*-ster-beek.
Oporto, o-*por*-toh.
Oppeln, *op*-eln.
Oradea, o-*rah*-de-ah.
Oradour-sur-Glane, o-rah-*door*-soor-*glahn*.
Oran, o-*rahn*: o-*rahŋ*.
Orange, (Fr.) o-*rahŋzh*: (U.S.A., etc.) *o*-ranj.
Oranienburg, o-*rah*-nee-en-boorkh.
Orava, *oh*-rah-va.
Ordzhonikidze, *or*-jo-nyee-*ked*-ze.
Oregon, *o*-re-gon.
Orel, or-*yawl*.
Oriente, oh-re-*en*-tay.
Orinoco, o-re-*noh*-koh.
Orizaba, *oh*-re-*sah*-ba.
Orléans, or-*lee*-anz: or-lay-ahŋ.
Ormuz, *or*-muz.
Orotava, oh-roh-*tah*-va.
Orsogna, or-*soh*-nyah.
Orsova, *or*-sho-vo.
Ortegal, or-ta-*gahl*.
Orthez, or-*tez*.
Ortona, or-*toh*-na.
Oruba, o-*roo*-ba.
Oruro, o-*roo*-ro.
Orvieto, or-*vyay*-toh.
Osage, o-*sahj*.
Osaka, *oh*-zah-kah.
Osawatomie, os-a-*wot*-o-me.
Oschersleben, *osh*-ers-lay-ben.
Oshima, *oh*-shee-mah.
Oslo, *oz*-loh.
Osnabrück, *os*-nah-bruk.
Osowiec, o-*saw*-vyets.
Ossetia, o-*see*-te-a.
Ossining, *os*-e-ning.
Ostend, os-*tend*.
Osterode, os-te-*roh*-da.
Ostia, *os*-tyah.
Ostrog, os-*trawk*.
Ostrolanka, os-tro-*lyeng*-kah.
Oswego, os-*wee*-goh.
Oswestry, *oz*-wes-tre.
Oswiecim, osh-*vyeng*-tsim.
Otago, o-*tah*-goh.
Otaheite, oh-tah-*hay*-te.
Otranto, o-*tran*-toh.
Otsego, ot-*see*-goh.
Ottawa, *ot*-a-wa.
Ouachita, *wosh*-e-taw.
Ouchy, oo-*shee*.
Oude, oud.
Oudenarde, oo-de-*nard*.
Ouidah, *wee*-dah.
Oujda, *ooj*-da.
Oulu, *oh*-loo.
Oundle, oundl.
Ourcq (Riv.), *oork*.
Ourique, oh-*ree*-ke.
Ourthe, oort.
Ouse, ooz.
Ousely, *ooz*-le.
Ovada, oh-*vah*-da.
Overijssel, oh-ver-*eye*-sel.
Overyssche, oh-ver-*eesh*.
Oviedo, oh-*vyay*-tho.
Oyahua, o-*yah*-whah.
Oyama, o-*yah*-ma.
Ozark, o-*zark*.
Ozorkov, o-*zor*-koof.

Paardeberg, *par*-de-berg.
Pachacamac, pah-tsha-ka-*mahk*.
Pachino, pah-*kee*-noh.
Pachuca, pa-*tshoo*-kah.
Padang, pa-*dahng*.
Paderborn, pah-der-*born*.
Padua, *pad*-ew-a.
Pahang, pa-*hung*.
Paisley, *payz*-le.
Paita, (Peru) *py*-ta: (New Caledonia) pah-*ee*-tah.
Pakistan, pah-ke-*stahn*.
Palanga, pa-*lahn*-ga.
Palapye, pa-*lahp*-ye.
Palatinate, pa-*lat*-e-nat.
Palau (Isls.), pah-*lou*.
Palawan, pa-*lah*-wahn.
Palembang, pah-lem-*bahng*.
Palencia, pah-*len*-thyah.
Palenque, pah-*leng*-ka.
Palermo, pa-*ler*-moh.
Palk (Str.), pawk.
Palmi, *pahl*-me.
Palmyra, pal-*mire*-ra.
Pamirs, pah-*meerz*.
Pampeluna, pam-pe-*loo*-na.
Panama, pan-a-*mah*.
Panay, pah-*nah*-e.
Panipat, pah-nee-*put*.
Pantellaria, *pan*-tel-la-*ree*-a.
Paoay, pah-o-*eye*.
Paoting, bou-ting.
Papeete, pah-pay-*ay*-tay.
Papua, *pap*-ew-a.
Paracatu, pah-ra-kah-*too*.
Paraguay, *pa*-ra-gway, -gwy.
Parahiba, pa-rah-*ee*-ba.
Paramaribo, pa-ra-*mah*-re-*boh*.
Paramé, pa-ra-*may*.
Paria (Gulf), *pah*-re-ah.
Paris, *pa*-ris: pah-*ree*.
Parnahyba, par-na-*ee*-ba.
Paros, *pair*-ros.
Parramatta, pa-ra-*mat*-a.
Partabgarh, par-tahb-*gur*.
Pasadena, pas-a-*dee*-na.
Pas-de-Calais, pah-de-ka-*lay*.
Passaic, pa-*say*-ik.
Passau, *pahs*-ou.
Passchendaele, *pahs*-khen-dah-le.
Paterno, pah-ter-*noh*.
Patiala, put-e-*ah*-la.
Patna, *put*-na.
Patras, pa-*tras*.
Pau, poh.
Paumotu, pah-oo-*moh*-too.
Paungde, poung-*day*.
Pavia, pa-*vee*-a.
Pavlograd, pav-lo-*graht*.
Payerne, pe-*yern*.
Paysandu, py-sahn-*doo*: pay-z'n-*dew*.
Pebas, pay-*bah*.
Pechora, pye-*chaw*-ra.
Péco, paych.
Peenemunde, *pee*-na-moon-da.
Pegu, pe-*goo*.
Peiho, pay-(bay-)*hoh*.
Peiping, pay-(bay-)*ping*.
Peipus, *py*-poos.
Peking, pee-*king*.
Pélee (Mt.), pe-*lay*.
Pelion (Mt.), *pee*-le-on.
Peloponnesos, pel-oh-po-*nee*-sos.
Penang, pe-*nang*.
Penge, penj.
Penicuik, pen-e-*kook*.
Penmaenmawr, *pen*-men-*mou*-er.
Pennsylvania, *pen*-sil-*vay*-ne-a.
Penobscot, pe-*nob*-skot.
Penrhyn (Wales), *pen*-rin: pen-*rin*.
Penryn (Corn.), *pen*-rin.
Pensacola, pen-sa-*koh*-la.
Penzance, pen-*zance*.
Peoria, pe-*aw*-re-a.
Perak, pay-*rahk*.
Perano, pe-*rah*-noh.
Perekop, *pay*-re-kop.
Père-Lachaise, pair-lah-*shayz*.

Périgord, pay-re-*gor*.
Périgueux, pay-re-*gø*.
Perim, pe-*reem*.
Pernambuco, per-nam-*boo*-ko.
Perpignan, per-pee-*nyaŋ*.
Persepolis, per-*sep*-o-lis.
Pertuis, per-too-*ees*.
Perugia, pa-*roo*-jah.
Pervomaisk, per-vo-*mysk*.
Pesaro, *pay*-zah-roh.
Pescadores, pes-ka-*do*-riz.
Pescara, pa-*skah*-rah.
Peschiera, pa-*skyair*-rah.
Peshawar, pe-*shaw'r* : pe-*shou*-er.
Pesth, pest.
Peterculter, pit-er-*koo*-ter.
Peterhov, *pay*-ter-hohf.
Peterwardein, *pay*-ter-var-*dine*.
Petra, *pee*-tra.
Petrograd, *pet*-ro-grad: pyet-ro-*graht*.
Petropavlovsk, pyet-ro-*pahv*-lofsk.
Petrovaradin, pyet-ro-*vah*-rah-din.
Petrozavodsk, pyet-ro-zah-*vodsk*.
Petsamo, *pet*-sa-moh.
Petschau, pet-*schou*.
Pforzheim, *pforts*-hym.
Pharsala, *far*-sa-la.
Philæ, *fy*-lee.
Philippines, *fil*-e-peenz.
Phocis, *foh*-kis.
Phthiotis, thy-*oh*-tis.
Piacenza, pyah-*chent*-sah.
Piatigovsk, pyah-ti-*gorsk*.
Piave, *pyah*-va.
Picardy, *pik*-er-de.
Picayune, pik-a-*yoon*.
Pichon, *pee*-shohŋ.
Pico, *pee*-koh : (Azores) *pee*-koo.
Picquigny, pe-*kee*-ne.
Pictou, pik-*too*.
Piedmont, *peed*-mont.
Pierrefonds, pyair-foŋ.
Pietermaritzburg, *pee*-te-*ma*-rits-burg.
Pilatus, pe-*lah*-tus.
Pilcomayo, peel-ko-*mah*-yoh.
Pillau, *pil*-ou.
Pimlico, *pim*-le-koh.
Pinchaung, pin-*choung*.
Pinerolo, pee-na-*raw*-loh.
Piombino, pyom-*bee*-noh.
Piqua, *pik*-wa.
Piræus, py-*ree*-us.
Pirapora, pee-ra-*paw*-ra.
Pirmasens, per-mah-*zens*.
Pisa, *pee*-za.
Pisagua, pe-*sah*-gwah.
Pisek, *pee*-sek.
Pissevache, pees-*vahsh*.
Pistoia, pees-*toh*-yah.
Pitlochry, pit-*lokh*-re.
Pittsburg, *pits*-burg.
Placentia, pla-*sen*-she-a.
Plaistow, *plas*-toh.
Plasencia, plah-*sen*-thyah.
Plassey, *plas*-se.
Plauen, *plou*-en.
Pleschen, *plesh*-en.
Plevna, *plev*-na.
Pliskovica, plees-ko-*vee*-ka.
Ploegsteert, ploog-*stay'*rt.
Ploesti, plaw-*yesht*.
Plombieres, ploŋ-*byair*.
Plymouth, *plim*-uth.
Podgorica, *pawd*-go-ree-tsah.
Podolsk, po-*dolsk*.
Podporozhye, pod-pah-*roh*-zhia.
Poelcapelle, pool-ka-*pel*-e.
Poggibonsi, pod-jee-*bawn*-se.
Pointe-à-Pitre, pwaŋt-ah-*peetr*.
Poissy, pwah-see.
Poitiers, pwa-tyay.
Poitou, pwa-too.
Poldhu, *pol*-dew.
Polesie, poh-*lyay*-sye.
Poligny, po-*lee*-nye.
Pölitz, *pøl*-its.
Polk, pohk.
Pollenza, pol-*lent*-sah.
Polotsk, *paw*-lotsk.
Poltawa, pol-*tah*-vah.
Polwarth, *pohl*-wuth.
Polynesia, pol-e-*nee*-ze-a, -*nee*-sha.
Pomerania, pom-er-*ray*-ne-a.
Pommern, *pom*-ern.
Pomona, po-*moh*-na.
Pompeii, pom-*pee*-eye, -*pay*-ee.
Ponape, *poh*-nah-pay.
Pondicherry, poŋ-dee-she-*ree*.
Pont-à-Mousson, poŋ-tah-moo-*soŋ*.
Pontarlier, poŋ-tar-*lyay*.
Pont du Fahs, poŋ-doo-*fah*.
Pontefract, *pon*-te-frakt : *pom*-fret.
Pontinia, pon-*tee*-nyah.
Pontoise, poŋ-*twahz*.
Popocatepetl, po-*poh*-kah-ta-*petl* : *pop*-a-*kat*-a-petl.
Pordenone, por-da-*noh*-na.
Pori, *poh*-ree.
Port-au-Prince, por-to-*praŋs*.
Port Étienne, por-tay-*tyen*.
Portmadoc, port-*mad*-ok.
Port Mahon, port-ma-*hohn*.
Porto Alegre, por-too-ah-*lay*-gre.
Porto Rico, por-toh-*ree*-koh.
Port Said, port-sayd, -sah-*eed*.
Port Salut, por-sa-*loo*.
Port Talbot, port-*tal*-bot.
Posen, *poh*-zen.
Potchefstroom, *poch*-ef-strohm.
Potenza, po-*tent*-sah.
Potigny, po-tee-nyee.
Potomac, po-*toh*-mak.
Potosi, po-*toh*-see.
Poughill, *pof*-il.
Poughkeepsie, po-*kip*-se.
Pozières, po-*zyair*.
Poznan, *poz*-nahn.
Pozzallo, pot-*sah*-loh.
Pozzuoli, pot-*swoh*-le.
Prague, prahg : prayg.
Pressburg, *pres*-boorkh.
Presteigne, pres-*teen*.
Prestwick, *prest*-wik.
Preussisch Eylau, *proy*-sish-*eye*-lou.
Prevesa, pre-*vay*-sa : *prev*-e-zah.
Pribilof (Isls.), pree-bee-*lof*.
Primorje, pre-*mor*-ye.
Pripet (Riv.), pre-*pyat*.
Prome, prohm.
Proskurov, pros-koo-*rof*.
Provence, pro-*vahŋs*.
Pruth, proot.
Przasnysz, *p'shash*-nish.
Przemysl, *p'shem*-is'l.
Psiol (Riv.), psee-*ohl*.
Pskov, pskof.
Puebla, *pway*-blah.
Puerto Rico, pwer-toh-*ree*-koh.
Puerto Suárez, pwer-toh-*swah*-race.

Puget (Sound), *poo*-jit.
Pulteneytown, *pult*-ne-toun.
Pultusk, *pool*-toosk.
Punjab, pun-*jahb*.
Purbeck, *pur*-bek.
Putumayo, *poo*-too-*mah*-yoh.
Puy de Dôme, pwee-de-*dohm*.
Pwllheli, pooth-*lel*-e.
Pyinmana, pyin-*mah*-na.
Pyrenees, pi-ri-*neez*.
Pytchley, *pych*-le.

Qattara, ka-*tar*-ra.
Quantock, *kwon*-tok.
Quatre Bras, kat-tr-brah.
Quéant, kay-*ahŋ*.
Quebec, kwe-*bek*.
Quedlinburg, *kvayd*-lin-boorkh.
Quelimane, kel-e-*mah*-ne.
Que Que, *kee*-ke.
Querétaro, ka-*ray*-tah-roh.
Quesada, ka-*sah*-thah.
Quetta, *kwet*-ah.
Quiberon, kee-b'*roŋ*.
Quiché, *kee*-chay.
Quillota, keel-*yoh*-tah.
Quimper, kaŋ-*pair*.
Quineville, *keen*'-veel.
Quirinal, *kwi*-ri-nal.
Quito, *kee*-toh.

Raab, rap.
Rabat, ra-*baht*.
Rabaul, *rah*-boul.
Radom, *rah*-dom.
Radomysl, *rah*-do-*mis*-l'.
Ragusa, rah-*goo*-zah.
Rainier (Mt.), ray-*neer*.
Rajpipla, rahj-*pee*-pla.
Rajputana, rahj-poo-*tah*-nah.
Rambouillet, rahŋ-boo-ye.
Ramillies, *ram*-e-liz: ra-mee-*yee*.
Rampur, *rahm*-poor.
Ramree, rum-*ree*.
Randazzo, rahn-*daht*-soh.
Randfontein, *rahnt*-fon-tayn.
Ranelagh, *ran*-e-le.
Rangoon, rang-*goon*.
Rannoch (Loch), *ran*-okh.
Ranziano, rant-se-*ah*-noh.
Rapallo, ra-*pah*-loh.
Rapido (Riv.), *rah*-pee-do.
Rappahannock, rap-a-*han*-uk.
Rastadt (Rastatt), *rah*-shtaht.
Rastenburg, *rahs*-ten-boorkh.
Rathedaung, rath-e-*doung*.
Ratisbon, *rat*-iz-bon.
Ravenna, ra-*ven*-na.
Ravensburg, *rah*-vens-boorkh.
Rawalpindi, rah-wul-*pin*-de.
Rawa Ruska, *rah*-vah-*roos*-kah.
Ré (Isl.), ray.
Reading, *red*-ing.
Recife, ra-*see*-fe.
Recklinghausen, *rek*-ling-hou-zen.
Reculver, re-*kul*-ver.
Redesdale, *reedz*-dale.
Redonda, re-*don*-da.
Regalbuto, ray-gahl-*boo*-toh.
Regensburg, *ray*-gens-*boorkh*.
Reggio, *red*-joh.
Regina, re-*jy*-na.
Reichenau, *ry*-khen-ou.
Reichenbach, *ry*-khen-bahkh.
Reichsstadt, *rykhs*-shtaht.
Reichswald, *rykhs*-vahlt.
Reims, reemz: raŋz.
Remagen, *ray*-mah-gen.
Rembang, rem-*bahng*.
Remiremont, re-meer-*moŋ*.
Remscheid, *rem*-shyt.
Renaix, re-nay.
Rendsburg, *rents*-boorkh.
Rennes, ren.
Requena, ra-*kay*-nah.
Restigouche, res-te-*goosh*.
Rethel, re-*tel*.
Rethondes, re-*toŋd*.
Réunion, ray-*ew*-nyun.
Reus, *ray*-oos.
Reuss, roys.
Reutlingen, royt-*ling*-en.
Revel, (Esth.) *rev*-el: (Fr.) re-*vel*.
Rewa, *ray*-wa.
Reykjavik, *rek*-ya-vik: *ray*-kya-veek.
Rezekne, *rez*-ek-ne.
Rhayadr, *ry*-a-der.
Rheims, reemz: raŋz.
Rheine, *ry*-ne.
Rheinfelden, *ryn*-fel-den.
Rheingau, *ryn*-gou.
Rhodes, rohdz.
Rhodesia, roh-*dee*-se-a (-sha, -zha).
Rhodope (Mts.), *rod*-o-pee.
Rhondda, *ron*-da.
Rhône, rohn.
Rhuddlan, *rid*-lan.
Rhyl, ril.
Ribécourt, *ree*-be-koor.
Rideau, ree-*doh*.
Riesengebirge, *ree*-zen-ge-*ber*-ge.
Rieti, re-*ay*-tee.
Rievaulx, *ree*-voh.
Riga, *ree*-gah.
Rigi, *ree*-ge.
Rimini, *ree*-me-nee.
Rio de Janeiro, *ree*-oh-de-ja-*neer*-ro (-day-zha-*nay*-roh).
Rio Grande, *ree*-o-*grahn*-day.
Riviera, riv-e-*air*-ra.
Rivoli, *ree*-vo-lee.
Roanoke, *roh*-a-nohk.
Roca (Cape), *roh*-kah.
Rochefort, rohsh-for.
Rochester, *rotsh*-es-ter.
Rocroi, ro-*krwah*.
Rodosto, roh-*dos*-toh.
Rodriguez, ro-*dree*-ges.
Roer, *roh*-er.
Roermund, *roor*-mont.
Romagna, ro-*mahn*-ya.
Romanzoff, ro-*mahnt*-sof.
Romford, *rum*-ford.
Romney, *rum*-ne.
Ronaldshay, *ron*-ald-shay.
Roncaglia, rong-*kahl*-yah.
Roncesvalles, ron-thes-*vahl*-yace.
Rondebosch, *ron*-de-bos.
Rootham, *root*-am.
Roquefort, rohk-for.
Rosario, roh-*sah*-re-oh.
Roseneath, *rose*-neeth.
Rosetta, ro-*zet*-ta.
Rosignano, roh-ze-*nyah*-noh.
Roslavl, ros-*lahv*-l'.
Roslin, *roz*-lin.
Rossback, *ros*-bahkh.
Rossignol (Lake), ros-seen-*yohl*.
Rosslare, *ros*-lair.
Rosslau, *ros*-lou.
Rossosh, ro-*sosh*.
Rostock, *ros*-tok.
Rostov, ros-*tof*.
Rosyth, ro-*sythe*.
Rothenburg, *roh*-ten-boorkh.

Rotherham, *roth*-er-am.
Rotherhithe, *roth*-er-hyth.
Rothes, roths.
Rothesay, *roth*-say.
Rothweil, *rot*-vyl.
Rotuma, roh-*too*-mah.
Roubaix, roo-*bay*.
Rouen, *roo*-ahŋ.
Rouge Croix, roozh-*krwah*.
Roulers, roo-*lair*.
Rousay, *roo*-say.
Rousillon, roo-see-*yoŋ*.
Rouvrois, roov-*rwah*.
Rouvroy, roov-*rwah*.
Roux, roo.
Rovereto, roh-va-*ray*-toh.
Rovigno, ro-*veen*-yoh.
Rovigo, ro-*vee*-goh.
Rovno, *rof*-noh.
Rowley Regis, *roh*-le-*ree*-jis.
Roxburgh, *roks*-bra.
Roye, rwah.
Ruabon, roo-*ab*-on.
Ruanda, roo-*ahn*-da.
Rubiana, roo-be-*ah*-na.
Rubicon, *roo*-be-kon.
Rüdesheim, *roo*-des-hym.
Rudolstadt, *roo*-dol-shtaht.
Rufiji (Riv.), roo-*fee*-je.
Rügen, *roo*-gen.
Ruhr, roor.
Ruislip, *ry*-slip.
Rumahiya, roo-mah-*hee*-yah.
Rusholme, *rush*-am.
Russia, *rush*-a.
Rustchuk, roos-*tshook*.
Ruthven, *rooth*-ven : *riv*-en.
Ruvuma, roo-*voo*-mah.
Ruwenzori, roo-wen-*zaw*-re.
Ruysselede, *rys*-e-lay-de.
Rybinsk, *rib*-ensk.
Ryswick, *riz*-wik : *ryz*-wik.
Ryukyu, ryoo-kyoo.
Rzeszow, *zhe*-shoof.
Rzhev, rzhef.

Saalle, *zah*-la.
Saarbrücken, zar-*brook*-en.
Saarebourg, *zar*-boorg.
Saarlautern, zar-*lou*-tern.
Saarlouis, zar-*loo*-e.
Sabine (U.S.A.), sa-*been*.
Sachsenhausen, sahk-sen-*hou*-zen.
Sacile, sah-*chee*-la.
Sadowa, sa-*doh*-a: *sah*-do-va.
Sagaing, sah-gah-*eeng*.
Sagan, *zah*-gahn.
Saghalien, sa-*gah*-le-en.
Saginaw, *sag*-e-naw.
Saguenay, sag-e-*nay*.
Sahara, sa-*hah*-ra.
Saida, *sah*-ee-dah.
Saigon, sy-*gon*.
Sailly-Saillesel, sah-*yee*-sah-yee-*zel*.
St. Acheul, saŋ-ta-*shøl*.
St. Brieuc, saŋ-bray-ø.
St. Cloud, saŋ-*kloo*.
St. Croix (U.S.A.), s'nt-*kroy*.
St. Cyr, saŋ-*seer*.
St. Denis, saŋ-de-*nee*.
St. Dié, saŋ-*dyay*.
St. Dizier, saŋ-dee-*zyay*.
Ste. Geneviève, saŋt-zhen-*vyayv*.
St. Eloi, saŋ-tay-*lwah*.
Ste. Ménehould, saŋt-me-*noo*.
Saintes, saŋt.
St. Étienne, saŋ-ta-*tyen*.
St. Germain, saŋ-zher-maŋ.
St. Gotthard, s'nt-*got*-erd: saŋ-go-*tar*.
St. Helena, s'nt-he-*lee*-na.
St. Helier, s'nt-*hel*-yer.
St. Ives, s'nt-*eyevz*.
St. Louis, (Fr.) saŋ-loo-*ee* : (U.S.A.) s'nt-*loo*-is.
St. Lucia, s'nt-*loo*-shya.
St. Malo, s'nt-*mah*-lo: saŋ-ma-*loh*.
St. Michel, saŋ-mee-*shel*.
St. Mihiel, saŋ-mee-*yel*.
St. Moritz, s'nt-*mo*-rits.
St. Nazaire, saŋ-na-*zair*.
St. Neots, s'nt-*neets*.
St. Oedenrode, s'nt-*oo*-den-roh-de.
St. Omer, saŋ-to-*mair*.
St. Osyth, s'nt-*oh*-zith.
St. Ouen, saŋ-*twahŋ*.
St. Pierre, saŋ-*pyair*.
St. Pol, saŋ-*pol*.
St. Quentin, s'nt-*kwen*-tin: saŋ-kahn-*taŋ*.
St. Raphael, saŋ-ra-fa-*el*.
St. Rémy, saŋ-ray-mee.
St. Vaast, saŋ-*vahst*.
St. Vith, saŋ-*veet*.
St. Yrieix, saŋ-tee-*ryayks*.
Saipan (Isl.), sy-*pahn*.
Sakhalin, sa-kha-*leen*.
Sakishima (Isl.), sah-ke-*shee*-ma.
Sakkara, sa-*kah*-ra.
Salado, sa-*lah*-thoh.
Salalah, sa-*lah*-lah.
Salamanca, sal-a-*mang*-ka.
Salamaua, sal-a-*mou*-a.
Saldanha (Bay), sahl-*dahn*-yah.
Salerno, sa-*ler*-noh.
Salford, *sawl*-ford.
Salina, sa-*lee*-na.
Saline (U.S.A.), sa-*leen*.
Salisbury, *sawlz*-ber-re.
Salonika, sa-lo-*nee*-kah.
Salop, *sal*-op.
Salsomaggiore, *sahl*-so-mahd-*joh*-ra.
Saltash, *sawl*-tash.
Saluzzo, sah-*loot*-soh.
Salvador, sal-va-*dor*.
Salzburg, *salts*-burg: *zahlts*-boorkh.
Salzwedel, *zahlts*-vay-del.
Samara, sa-*mah*-ra.
Samarkand, sam-ar-*kand*.
Sambre (Riv.), sahŋbr'.
Samoa, sa-*moh*-a.
Samos, *say*-mos.
Samothrace, *sam*-o-thrace.
Sandakan, san-dah-*kan*.
San Diego, san-de-*ay*-goh.
Sandomierz, san-*daw*-myezh.
San Domingo, san-doh-*ming*-goh.
Sandwich, *sand*-witch.
San Felipe, sahn-fa-*lee*-pa.
San Fransisco, san-fran-*sis*-koh.
San Gimignano, sahn-jee-men-*yah*-noh.
San Giovanni, sahn-jo-*vahn*-ne.
San Ignacio, sahn-eeg-*nyah*-che-oh.
San Jacinto, san-ja-*sin*-toh.
San Joaquin, san-wah-*keen*.
San José, sahn-ho-*say*.
San Juan, sahn-*hwahn*.
San Marino, san-ma-*ree*-noh.
San Michele, sahn-me-*kel*-a.
San Miguel, sahn-me-*gel*.
Sannaiyat, san-eye-*yaht*.
San Pietro, sahn-*pyay*-troh.

Sanquhar, *sang*-ker.
San Remo, san-*ray*-moh.
San Roque, sahn-*roh*-ka.
San Stefano, sahn-*stay*-fa-noh.
Santa Cruz, *san*-ta-*krooz*.
Santa Fé, san-ta-*fay*.
Santander, san-*tan*-der: sahn-tahn-*dar*.
Santarem, san-*tah*-raŋ.
Santiago, san-tee-*ah*-goh.
Santo Domingo, *sahn*-toh-do-*ming*-goh.
Santorin, sahn-to-*reen*.
São Luiz, souŋ-loo-*eez*.
Saône, sone.
São Paulo, souŋ-*pou*-loo.
Sapignies, sa-*pee*-nyee.
Saragossa, sa-ra-*gos*-sa.
Sarajevo, sah-ra-*yay*-voh.
Saratoga, sa-ra-*toh*-ga.
Saratov, sa-*rah*-tof.
Sarawak, sa-*rah*-wak.
Sarreguemines, sar-ge-*meen*.
Sarthe, sart.
Sarum, *sair*-rum.
Sasebo, *sah*-se-boh.
Saseno (Isl.), *sah*-say-noh.
Saskatchewan, sas-*katsh*-e-wan.
Saskatoon, sas-ka-*toon*.
Sassafras, *sas*-a-fras.
Satawan, sah-ta-*wahn*.
Satoralja Ujhely, *shah*-to-ro-lyo-*oo*-e-*hel*-ye.
Satu Mare, *sah*-too-*mah*-re.
Sauchie, *so*-khe.
Sauchy-Cauchy, *soh*-she-*koh*-she.
Saudi-Arabia, sah-*oo*-de-a-*ray*-be-a.
Sault Sainte Marie, *soo*-s'nt-ma-*ree*.
Saumur, soh-*moor*.
Sauternes, soh-*tairn*.
Savannah, sa-*van*-na.
Savigliano, sah-veel-*yah*-noh.
Savoie, sa-*vwah*.
Savona, sa-*voh*-na.
Savoy, sa-*voy*.
Saxony, *saks*-o-ne.
Sayan (Mts.), *sah*-yan.
Sbeitla, *sbayt*-lah.
Sbiba, *sbee*-bah.
Scafell, skaw-*fel*.
Scala Nova, *skah*-lah-*noh*-vah.
Scapa Flow, *skah*-pa-*floh*.
Scarborough, *skar*-bra.
Sceaux, soh.
Schaffhausen, shaf-*hou*-zen.
Schaumburg-Lippe, *shoum*-boorkh-*lip*-pe.
Scheidegg, *shy*-deg.
Scheldt, skelt.
Schnectady, ske-*nek*-ta-de.
Scheveningen, *skay*-(or *shay*-)ven-*ing*-en.
Schiedam, *skee*-dam: skhee-*dahm*.
Schiehallion, she-*hal*-yon.
Schleiz, shlyts.
Schlesien, *shlay*-ze-en.
Schleswig, *shlays*-vikh.
Schlüsselburg, *shlø*-sel-boorkh.
Schmalkalden, *shmahl*-kahl-den.
Schneidermühl, *shny*-der-mool.
Schönbrunn, *shøn*-broon.
Schouten, *shoo*-ten.
Schouwen, *skou*-ven.
Schreckhorn, *shrek*-horn.
Schuyler, *sky*-ler.
Schuylkill, *skool*-kil.
Schwammenaul, *shwah*-me-*noul*.
Schwarzburg, *shvarts*-boorkh.
Schwarzwald, *shvarts*-vahlt.
Schwedt, shvet.
Schweidnits, *shvyt*-nits.
Schweinfurt, *shvyn*-foort.
Schweiz, shvyts.
Schwerin, shva-*reen*.
Schwyts, shveets.
Schyl, sheel.
Sciacca, *shahk*-kah.
Scilly (Isls.), *sil*-le.
Scioto, see-*oh*-toh.
Scone, skoon.
Scutari, *skoo*-ta-re.
Seattle, se-*at*'l.
Sebastopol, se-*bas*-to-pool.
Secchia, *sek*-kyah.
Sedan, se-*dan*.
Sedbergh, *sed*-ber(g).
Sedgemoor, *sej*-moor.
Segovia, sa-*goh*-ve-a.
Seidlitz, *sed*-lits: *zyt*-lits.
Seine, sane.
Seistan, *sees*-tan.
Sekondi, sek-on-*dee*.
Selangor, se-*lang*-gor.
Selency, se-lahŋ-see.
Seliger (Lake), *sel*-ye-ger.
Semarang, se-*mah*-rahng.
Semipalatinsk, sa-me-pa-la-*tensk*.
Sempach, *zem*-pahkh.
Senanga, se-*nahng*-ga.
Sendai, sen-*dy*.
Seneca, *sen*-e-ka.
Senegal, sen-e-*gawl*.
Senegambia, sen-e-*gam*-be-a.
Senlis, sahŋ-lees.
Sennar, sen-*nar*.
Sens, sahŋs.
Seoul, se-*ool*: say-*ohl*: sohl.
Serafimovich, sa-ra-*fee*-mo-vich.
Serampore, se-ram-*por*.
Serchio (Riv.), *ser*-ke-oh.
Seremban, se-*rem*-bun.
Seringapatam, se-*ring*-ga-pa-*tam*.
Serowe, se-*roh*-we.
Serre, ser.
Setubal, sa-too-*bahl*.
Severin, se-ve-*reen*.
Seville, se-*vil*.
Sèvres, sayvr'.
Seychelles, say-*shel*.
Seym (Riv.), saym.
Shakti, *shahkh*-te.
Shamiya, sha-*mee*-yah.
Shanghai, shang-*hy*.
Shantung, shahn-*doong*.
Shellif, shel-*leef*.
Shenandoah, shen-an-*doh*-a.
Shendi, *shen*-dee.
Shiga, *shee*-ga.
Shikarpur, she-*kar*-poor.
Shikoku, *shee*-koh-koo.
Shillong, shil-*long*.
Shimizu, *shee*-me-zoo.
Shimonoseki, *shee*-mo-noh-*say*-ke.
Shimshimi, shim-*shee*-me.
Shiraz, she-*rahz*.
Shiwa Ngandu, *shee*-wah-n'*gahn*-doo.
Shoa, *shoh*-ah.
Shoreham, *shaw*-rum.
Shoshone, sho-*shoh*-ne.
Shrewsbury, *shrooz*-(or *shrohz*)-be-re.
Shtip, shtip.
Shuri, *shoo*-re.
Shushtar, *shoosh*-tar.
Shwebo, *shway*-boh.
Shwedaung, shway-*doung*.
Sialkot, se-*ahl*-koht.
Siam, sy-*am*.

Siauliai, she-*ou*-li-eye.
Sibenik, she-*ben*-eek.
Sicily, *sis*-e-le.
Sidi Barrani, *see*-dee-ba-*rah*-ne.
Sidmouth, *sid*-muth.
Siebengebirge, *zee*-ben-ge-*ber*-ge.
Sieg (Riv.), zeekh.
Siegen, *zee*-gen.
Siena, se-*en*-ah.
Sierra Leone, se-*e*-ra-le-*oh*-ne.
Sierra Morena, se-*e*-rah-mo-*ray*-nah.
Sierra Nevada, se-*e*-rah-na-*vah*-da.
Sigmaringen, *zeekh*-mah-*ring*-en.
Sikkim, *sik*-im.
Silesia, se-*lee*-shya.
Silistria, se-*lis*-tre-a.
Simancas, se-*mahn*-kahs.
Simferopol, sim-fe-*roh*-po-le.
Simla, *sim*-la.
Simonyifaiva, se-*moh*-nye-*fy*-va.
Simplon, *say*-ploŋ: *sim*-ploŋ.
Sinai, *sy*-ne-eye : *sy*-nay-eye.
Sinaia, se-*nah*-e-a.
Singapore, sing-ga-*por*.
Siningfu, see-ning-*foo*.
Sinkiang, sin-*kyahng*.
Sinope, se-*noh*-pe; see-*noh*-pay.
Sioux, soo.
Sirte (Gulf of), *ser*-te.
Sisal, se-*sahl*.
Sittang (Riv.), set-*tung*.
Sivas, see-*vahs*.
Siwa, *see*-wah.
Siwalik, se-*wah*-lik.
Skagen, *skahg*-en.
Skagerrak, *skag*-(*skahg*-) er-rak.
Skiathos, *skee*-a-thos.
Skibo, *skee*-boh.
Skiddaw, ski-*daw*: *skid*-daw.
Skierniewice, skyer-nye-*vee*-tse.
Skoplje, *skohp*-lye.
Skye, sky.
Slavyansk, slahv-*yansk*.
Sleights (Yorks.), slyts.
Slesvig, *sles*-vikh.
Sligo, *sly*-goh.
Slivnitsa, *sleev*-nits-sa.
Slonim, *sloh*-nyem.
Slough, slou.
Slovakia, slo-*vah*-ke-a.
Slovenia, slo-*vee*-ne-a.
Sluis, sloys.
Slutsk, slootsk.
Sluys, sloys.
Smederevo, *smed*-e-re-voh.
Smethwick, *smeth*-ik.
Smolensk, smo-*lyensk*.
Smorgon, smor-*gohn*.
Smyrna, *smir*-na.
Snaefell, *snay*-fel.
Snowdon, *snoh*-d'n.
Sobat, *soh*-baht.
Sobraon, so-*broun*.
Socotra, so-*koh*-tra.
Södermanland, *sød*-er-man-lahnd.
Soebang, *soo*-bahng.
Sofala, so-*fah*-la.
Sofia, *soh*-fe-a : so-*fee*-ya.
Sogne (Fiord), *sohg*-ne.
Sohar, soh-*har*.
Soignies, swah-nyee.
Soissons, swah-soŋ.
Sokoto, soh-*koh*-toh.
Solent, *soh*-lent.
Solesmes, so-*laym*.
Solfatara, sol-fah-*tah*-ra.
Solferino, sol-fe-*ree*-no.
Solihull, *soh*-le-hul.
Solingen, *zoh*-ling-en.
Sollum, sol-*loom*.
Solothurn, *zoh*-lo-toorn.
Solutré, soh-loo-tray.
Solway, *sol*-way.
Somaliland, so-*mah*-le-land.
Somerset, *sum*-er-set.
Somme, som.
Sommerfeld, *zom*-er-felt.
Somnauth, som-*nawth*.
Sondershausen, *zon*-ders-*hou*-zen.
Sopron, *shoh*-pron.
Soracte, so-*rak*-tee.
Sorata, so-*rah*-tah.
Sorel, so-*rel*.
Sorgues, sorg.
Sorrento, sor-*ren*-toh.
Sosnowiec, sos-*noh*-yets.
Souchez, soo-*shay*.
Soudan, soo-*dahn*.
Soufrière, soo-fre-*air*.
Souillac, sool-*yak*.
Souilly, *sool*-ye.
Soulanges, soo-*lahyzh*.
Sourabaya, *soor*-ra-*bah*-yah.
Sousse, soos.
Southampton, south-*amp*-ton.
Southwark, *suth*-ark.
Southwell, *south*-wel: suth'l.
Sowerby, *sou*-er-be.
Spa, spah.
Spalato, *spah*-lah-toh.
Spalding, *spawl*-ding.
Spandau, *shpahn*-dou.
Spartel (Cape), spar-*tel*.
Spey, spay.
Speyer, *shpy*-er.
Spezia (It.), *sped*-ze-a.
Spezzia, *spet*-se-a.
Spichern, *shpikh*-ern.
Spion Kop, spee-on-*kop*.
Spithead, spit-*hed*.
Spitsbergen, spits-*ber*-gen.
Splügen (Pass), *shplø*-gen.
Spoleto, spo-*lay*-to.
Spokane, spo-*kan*.
Sporades, *spo*-ra-deez.
Spree, shpray.
Squillace, skweel-*lah*-cha.
Srinaga, sre-*nug*-ah : sre-*nah*-gah.
Srirangam, sre-*rung*-gum.
Stade, *shtah*-de.
Staffa, *staf*-a.
Stalbridge, *stawl*-brij.
Stalingrad, sta-leen-*grahd*.
Stalino, sta-*lee*-noh.
Stalinsk, sta-*lensk*.
Stalybridge, *stay*-le-brij.
Stamboul, stahm-*bool*.
Stanislaus, *shtah*-nis-lou.
Stanislavov, sta-nye-*slah*-voof.
Stanovoi, stah-no-*voy*.
Staraya Russa, *stah*-ra-ya-*roos*-sa.
Stargard, *shtar*-gart.
Staritza, stah-*ree*-tsah.
Stary Oskol, *stah*-re-os-*kohl*.
Stassfurt, *shtahs*-foort.
Staten, *stat*-en.
Staunton, *stan*-ton.
Stavanger, sta-*vang*-er: *stah*-vang-er.
Stavelot, sta-*vloh*.
Steenbecque, *stayn*-bek.
Steiermark, *shty*-er-mark.
Steinach, *shty*-nahkh.
Steinbach, *shtyn*-bahkh.
Stellenbosch, *stel*-en-bos (-boosh).
Sterkrade, *shterk*-rah-de.
Stettin, shte-*teen*.

Stevenage, *stee*-v'nij.
Steyr, shtyr.
Stockach, *shtok*-ahkh.
Stockholm, *stok*-holm.
Stogumber, stoh-*gum*-ber.
Stoke d'Abernon, stohk-*dab*-er-non.
Stoke Poges, stohk-*poh*-jis.
Stolpmünde, *shtohlp*-moon-da.
Stonehenge, stone-*henj*.
Stornoway, *stor*-no-way.
Stourbridge, *stou*-er-brij.
Stourton, *stur*-t'n.
Stow, Stowe, stoh.
Strabane, stra-*bane*.
Stralsund, *strahl*-zoont.
Stranraer, stran-*rar*.
Strasbourg, *straz*-boor.
Strassburg, *shtrahs*-boorkh.
Strathaven, strath-*ay*-ven: *strev*-en.
Strathcona, strath-*koh*-na.
Strathmore, strath-*mor*.
Streatham, *stret*-am.
Streatley, *street*-le.
Strehlen, *stray*-len.
Strelitz, *strel*-its.
Stresa, *strez*-ah.
Stromboli, *strohm*-bo-lee.
Strömö, *strø*-mø.
Struma, *stroo*-ma.
Strumnitza, *stroom*-ne-tsa.
Stryj, stree.
Stuttgart, *shtoot*-gart.
Styria, *ster*-re-a.
Suakin, sew-*ah*-keen.
Subiaco, soo-*bee*-ah-koh.
Subotica, *soo*-bo-te-tsah.
Sucre, *soo*-kra.
Sudan, soo-*dahn*.
Sudeley (Manor), *sewd*-le.
Sudetenland, soo-*day*-ten-lahnt.
Suez, *soo*-ez.
Suffolk, *suf*-ok.
Suippes, sweep.
Suir, shoor.
Suiyuan, *soy*-y'*wahn*.
Suleimaniya, soo-lay-mah-*nee*-ye.
Sulina, soo-*lee*-na.
Sulzbach, *zoolts*-bahkh.
Sumatra, soo-*mah*-tra.
Sumi, *soo*-me.
Sundgau, *zoont*-gou.
Sungari (Riv.), *soon*-ga-ree.
Sungei, *soon*-gay.
Suomi, *s'woh*-me.
Surabaya, *soo*-rah-*bah*-yah.
Surat, soo-*rat*.
Surigao, soo-re-*gah*-oh.
Surinam, soo-re-*nam*.
Susquehanna, sus-kwe-*han*-a.
Sutlej, *sut*-lej.
Suvla (Bay), *soo*-vlah.
Suwalki, soo-*vahl*-ke.
Svapa (Riv.), *svah*-pa.
Sveaborg, *svay*-a-borkh.
Sverdlovsk, sverd-*lofsk*.
Svir (Riv.), sveer.
Svodbodnyi, svo-*bohd*-nyee.
Swabia, *sway*-be-a.
Swansea, *swan*-ze.
Swanwick, *swan*-ik.
Swat, swaht.
Swaziland, *swah*-ze-land.
Swinemünde, *svee*-na-moon-da.
Sydenham, *sid*-en-am.
Syene, sy-*ee*-ne.
Sylhet, sil-*het*.
Syracuse, *sire*-ra-kewz: (U.S.A.) -kewce.
Syr Daria, ser-*dar*-yah.
Syriam, *si*-re-um.
Szczebrzeszyn, shche-bzhe-sheen.
Szeged, *seg*-ed.
Szekesfehervar, *say*-kesh-*fe*-hayr-var.
Szolnok, *sohl*-nokh.
Szombatheley, *sohm*-bot-hel-ye.

Tabatinga, tah-ba-*teng*-ga.
Tabora, ta-*baw*-ra.
Tabriz, ta-*breez*.
Tacloban, tah-*kloh*-bahn.
Tadcaster, *tad*-kas-ter.
Tadzhik, ta-*zhik*.
Tafilelt, tah-*fee*-lelt.
Taganrog, ta-gan-*rok*.
Tagliacozzo, tah-lyah-*kot*-soh.
Tagliamento, tah-lyah-*men*-toh.
Tagus, *tay*-gus.
Tahiti, tah-*hee*-te.
Taihoku, ty-*hoh*-koo.
Taimir, ty-*mer*.
Taiping, ty-*ping*.
Taiwan, ty-*wahn*.
Takoradi, tah-ko-*rah*-de.
Talara, tah-*lah*-rah.
Talavera, tah-la-*vay*-ra.
Tallahassee, tal-a-*has*-e.
Tallinn, tal-*lin*.
Taman, ta-*mahn*.
Tamar (Riv.), *tay*-mar.
Tamatave, *tah*-ma-*tahv*.
Tambov, tam-*bawf*.
Tampico, tam-*pee*-ko.
Tana (Lake), *tah*-nah.
Tanami, ta-*nah*-me.
Tanana, tah-*nah*-nah.
Tanganyika, tang-ga-*nyee*-ka.
Tangier, tan-*jeer*.
Tanjore, tan-*jor*.
Tannenberg, *tahn*-nen-berkh.
Tannu Tuva, *tan*-oo-too-*vah*.
Taormina, tah-or-*mee*-nah.
Taos, *tay*-ohs.
Tapajos, tah-pa-*zhohs*.
Tapti, *tahp*-te.
Tarakan, tah-ra-*kahn*.
Taranaki, tah-ra-*nah*-ke.
Taranto, ta-*ran*-to: *tah*-rahn-toh.
Tarascon, ta-rahs-*koŋ*.
Tarawa, ta-*rah*-wah.
Tarbes, tarb.
Tarhuna, tar-*hoo*-nah.
Tarifa, tah-*ree*-fa.
Tarnopol, tar-*naw*-pohl.
Tarnow, *tar*-noof.
Tarragona, tar-rah-*goh*-na.
Tartu, *tar*-too.
Tashkend, tash-*kent*.
Tasmania, taz-*may*-nya.
Taunggyi, toung-*g'yee*.
Taunton, *tawn*-ton.
Taunus (Mts.), *tou*-noos.
Taupo (Lake), *tah*-oo-poh.
Taurida, *taw*-ree-da.
Taurus, *taw*-rus.
Tavistock, *tav*-is-tok.
Tavoy, tah-*voy*.
Tczew, chef.
Teano, ta-*ah*-noh.
Tebessa, ta-*bes*-sa.
Tebourba, ta-*boor*-ba.
Teffé, tef-*ay*.
Tegernsee, *tay*-gern-zay.
Tegucigalpa, ta-*goo*-se-*gahl*-pah.
Teheran, teer-*rahn*.
Tehuacana, ta-*wah*-ka-nah.
Tehuantepec, ta-wahn-ta-*pek*.
Teifi (Riv.), *ty*-fe.

Teignmouth, *tin*-muth.
Teignton, *tayn*-ton.
Tel Aviv, *tel-a-veev.*
Tel-el-Eisa, *tel*-el-*eye*-sah.
Tel-el-Kebir, *tel*-el-ke-*beer.*
Temara, te-*mah*-rah.
Temesvar, *tem*-esh-var.
Tenasserim, te-*nas*-er-rim.
Tenedos, *ten*-e-dos.
Teneriffe, ten-er-*reef*: tay-na-*ree*-fay.
Tennessee, ten-ne-*see.*
Tepic, tay-*peek.*
Teplitz-Schönau, *tep*-lits-*shø*-nou.
Teramo, *tair*-rah-moh.
Termonde, ter-*moŋd.*
Ternate, ter-*nah*-ta.
Terneusen, ter-*noy*-zen.
Terracina, te-rah-*chee*-nah.
Terre Haute, ter-*hoht.*
Terschilling, ter-*skhel*-ing.
Teruel, tay-roo-*el.*
Teschen, *tesh*-en.
Tete, *tay*-te.
Tetuan, te-*twahn.*
Teutoberger Wald, *toy*-to-boor-ger-*vahlt.*
Tewkesbury, *tewks*-be-re.
Texarkana, tek-sar-*kan*-a.
Tezcuco, tays-*koo*-koh.
Teziutlan, *tay*-se-oot-*lahn.*
Tezza, *tet*-zah.
Thaba 'Nchu, tah-bahn-*choo.*
Thailand, *ty*-land: *tah*-ee-land.
Thame, taym: (U.S.A.) thaym.
Thames, temz.
Thanet, *than*-et.
Thaon-les-Vosges, *tohn*-lay-*vohzh.*
Thasos, *thah*-sos.
Thaton, *thah*-tohn.
Theiss, tys.
Thelepte, ta-*lep*-te.
Theobalds (Essex), tiblz.
Thessalonica, thes-a-lo-*ny*-ka.
Thessaly, *thes*-a-le.
Thiaucourt, tyo-*koor.*
Thiepval, tyep-*val.*
Thiers, tyair.
Thionville, *tyoŋ*-veel.
Thorn, torn.
Thorshavn, tors-*houn.*
Thouars, too-*ar.*
Thourout, too-*roo.*
Thun, toon.
Thurgau, *toor*-gou.
Thuringia, thoor-*rin*-je-a.
Thurn, tern.
Tian Shan, tyahn-shahn.
Tiber, *ty*-ber.
Tibet, ti-*bet.*
Ticino, te-*chee*-noh.
Ticonderoga, te-*kon*-de-*roh*-ga.
Tiddim, te-*deem.*
Tidore, tee-*dor.*
Tientsin, tyen-tsin.
Tierra del Fuego, *tyer*-rah-del-*fway*-goh.
Tiflis, tif-lis: tyef-*lyees.*
Tighina, te-*gee*-na.
Tighnabruich, tin-e-*broo*-ahkh.
Tigré, tee-*gray.*
Tigris, *ty*-gris.
Tilsit, *til*-zit.
Timaru, *tim*-a-roo: *tee*-mah-roo.
Timbuctoo, tim-buk-*too*: tim-*buk*-too.
Timgad, teem-*gahd.*
Timisoara, tee-mish-*wah*-ra.
Timor, te-*mor.*
Tinchebrai, taŋsh-*bray.*
Tinian (Isl.), tee-ne-*ahn.*
Tintagel, tin-*taj*-el.
Tioga, ty-*oh*-ga.
Tippecanoe, tip-e-ka-*noo.*
Tirah, teer-*rah.*
Tirana, te-*rah*-nah.
Tiraspol, tye-ras-*pawl.*
Tiree, te-*ree.*
Tirlemont, teer-l'-*moŋ.*
Tisza, *tee*-so.
Titicaca, tee-te-*kah*-kah.
Tivoli, *tee*-vo-lee: *tiv*-o-le.
Tlaxcala, tlahs-*kah*-lah.
Tlemcan, tlem-*sen.*
Tmimi, t'*mee*-me.
Tobago, to-*bay*-goh.
Tobolsk, to-*bolsk.*
Tobruk, to-*brook.*
Tocantins, toh-kahn-*teenz.*
Tofino, to-*fee*-noh.
Togoland, *toh*-goh-land.
Tokay, to-*kay.*
Tokyo, *toh*-kyoh.
Toledo, to-*lee*-doh: to-*lay*-thoh.
Tolentino, toh-len-*tee*-noh.
Tollesbury, *tohlz*-be-re.
Tolosa, to-*loh*-sa.
Tonale (Mt.), to-*nah*-lay.
Tonbridge, *tun*-bridj.
Tonga, *tøng*-ga.
Tongatabu, tong-ga-*tah*-boo.
Tongres, toŋgr.
Tonquin, ton-*keen.*
Tonypandy, *ton*-e-pan-de.
Topeka, to-*pee*-ka.
Tordesillas, tor-da-*seel*-yahs.
Torgau, *tor*-gou.
Torigny, to-*ree*-nyee.
Tormes, *tor*-mahs.
Tornea, *tor*-ne-oh.
Torphichen, tor-*fikh*-en.
Torquay, tor-*kee.*
Torres Vedras, *tor*-rayz-*vay*-dras (-thrash).
Tortola, tor-*toh*-la.
Tortona, tor-*toh*-na.
Tortuga, tor-*too*-ga.
Torun, *toh*-roon.
Tottenham, *tot*-'nam.
Touggourt, too-*goor.*
Toul, tool.
Toulon, too-*loŋ.*
Toulouse, too-*loos.*
Toungoo, toung-*goo.*
Touques (Riv.), took.
Touraine, too-*rayn.*
Tourcoing, toor-*kwaŋ.*
Tournai, toor-*nay.*
Tours, toor.
Towcester, *tous*-ter.
Towton, *tou*-ton.
Towyn, *tou*-in.
Toyama, *toh*-yah-ma.
Tozeur, toh-*zør.*
Trafalgar, tra-*fal*-gar: traf-al-*gar.*
Tralee, tra-*lee.*
Tranent, tra-*nent.*
Transbaikal, tranz-by-*kahl.*
Transdniestria, tranz-*nee*-stre-a.
Transkei, tranz-*ky.*
Transleithania, tranz-ly-*thay*-ne-a.
Transvaal, *tranz*-vahl.
Transylvania, *tran*-sil-*vay*-ne-a.
Trapani, *trah*-pah-nee.
Traquair, tra-*kwair.*
Trasimeno, trah-ze-*may*-noh.
Trau, trou.
Traunstein, *troun*-shtyn.
Trautenau, *trou*-te-nou.
Travancore, *trav*-an-*kor.*
Trebia, *treb*-byah.

Trebitsch, *tray*-bich.
Trebizond, *treb*-e-zond.
Tredegar, tre-*dee*-gar.
Trefriw, tre-*froo*.
Tregnago, tra-*nyah*-noh.
Trengganu, treng-*gah*-noo.
Trentham, *tren*-tam.
Trentino, trøn-*tee*-noh.
Trèves, trave.
Treviglio, tra-*veel*-yoh.
Treviso, tra-*vee*-zoh.
Triaucourt, tree-oh-koor.
Trichinopoly, *trich*-e-*nop*-o-le.
Trier, treer.
Trieste, tre-*est*: tre-*es*-ta.
Triggiano, tre-*jah*-noh.
Trikkala, *treek*-ka-la.
Trincomalee, *tring*-ko-ma-*lee*.
Trinidad, trin-e-*dad*.
Trino, *tree*-noh.
Tripoli, *trip*-o-le.
Tripolitania, *tree*-poh-le-*tah*-nya.
Tristan da Cunha, *tris*-tahn-dah-*koon*-yah.
Trivandrum, tre-*vun*-droom.
Trnova, *tør*-noh-va.
Trobriand (Isls.), troh-bre-*ahnd*.
Troezen, *tree*-zen.
Troina, tro-*ee*-nah.
Troitsk, traw-etsk.
Trolhättan, *trohl*-hat-an.
Tromsö, *trom*-sø.
Trondhjem, *tron*-dyem.
Troppau, *troh*-pou.
Trossachs, *tros*-aks.
Trouville, troo-veel.
Troyes, trwah.
Trujillo, troo-*heel*-yoh.
Truk (Isl.), trook.
Truro, *troo*-roh.
Tsaritsin, tsah-*reet*-sen.
Tsarskoe Selo, *tsar*-skoh-ye-sye-*loh*.
Tshikapa, che-*kah*-pah.
Tsientiang, chøn-tyahng.
Tsimlyansk, tseem-*lyahnsk*.
Tsingtao, ching-dou.
Tsitsihar, tsee-tsee-*har*.
Tsushima, *tsoo*-shee-mah.
Tuam, *tew*-am.
Tuapse, too-ap-*see*.
Tübingen, *tø*-bing-en.
Tubuai, too-boo-*ah*-e.
Tucson, too-*son*.
Tucuman, too-koo-*mahn*.
Tudela, too-*thay*-lah.
Tugela, too-*gee*-lah.
Tuileries, *twee*-le-riz: tweel-ree.
Tukkums, took-*kooms*.
Tula, *too*-lah.
Tulagi, too-*lah*-ge.
Tulcea, *tool*-cha.
Tulsa, *tul*-sa.
Tumbes, *toom*-bays.
Tunis, *tew*-nis.
Tupiza, too-*pee*-zah.
Turin, tew-*rin*.
Turkana, toor-*kah*-na.
Turkestan, toor-kes-*tahn*.
Turku, *toor*-koo.
Turnhout, turn-*hout*: tør-*noot*.
Turnu Severin, *toor*-noo-se-ve-*reen*.
Tuscany, *tus*-ka-ne.
Tuskegee, tus-*kee*-ge.
Tutuila, *too*-too-*ee*-lah.
Tuxedo, tuk-*see*-doh.
Tver, tvyair.
Twickenham, *twik*-'n-am.
Tyrol, te-*rol* (-*rohl*).
Tyrone, te-*rohn*.
Tyrrhenian (Sea), te-*ree*-ne-an.

Uam Var, *yew*-am-*var*.
Ubach, *oo*-bahkh.
Uberaba, oo-be-*rah*-bah.
Ucayali, oo-kah-*yah*-le.
Udaipur, oo-*dy*-poor.
Uden, *oo*-den.
Udine, *oo*-dee-nay.
Uerdingen, *ver*-ding-en.
Ufa, *oo*-fa.
Uganda, yoo-*gan*-da.
Uig, *oo*-ig.
Uinta, yoo-*in*-ta.
Uist, *oo*-ist: wist.
Uitenhage, *yoo*-ten-hahg: *oy*-ten-*hah*-ga.
Ujiji, oo-*jee*-je.
Uj-Pest, *oo*-ye-pesht.
Ukraine, *oo*-krane.
Ullapool, *ul*-la-pool.
Ullswater, *ulz*-waw-ter.
Ulm, oolm.
Ulundi, oo-*loon*-de.
Ulverston, *ul*-ver-ston; *oos*-ton.
Ulyanovsk, ool-ya-*nawfsk*.
Uman, oo-*mahn*.
Umbertide, oom-*ber*-te-day.
Umbria, *um*-bre-a.
Umea, *oo*-me-oh.
Umtali, oom-*tah*-le.
Unalaska, oo-na-*las*-ka.
Unst, oonst.
Unter der Linden, *oon*-ter-den-*lin*-den.
Unterwalden, *oon*-ter-*vahl*-den.
Upolu, oo-*poh*-loo.
Uppsala, up-*sah*-la: *up*-sa-la.
Ural, *yoo*-ral.
Urbino, oor-*bee*-noh.
Ure (Riv.), yoor.
Urfa, *oor*-fah.
Uri, *oo*-re.
Urmia, *oor*-me-a.
Urquhart, *ur*-kurt.
Uruguay, *oo*-(*yoo*-)roo-gway (-gwy).
Urumiyah, oo-roo-*mee*-yah.
Urundi, oo-*roon*-de.
Usedom, *oo*-ze-dom.
Ushant, *ush*-ant.
Uskub, oos-*koop*.
Ust Dvinsk, *oost*-y'-dvensk.
Utah, *yoo*-tah: *yoo*-taw.
Utena, oo-*tay*-na.
Utica, *yoo*-te-ka.
Utrecht, *yoo*-trekt: *oo*-trekht.
Uttoxeter, yoo-*tok*-se-ter: *uk*-se-ter: *uk*-ster.
Uusimaa, *oo*-se-mah.
Uyuni, oo-*yoo*-ne.
Uzbekistan, ooz-bek-e-*stahn*.
Uznach, *oots*-nahkh.
Uzok (Pass), *oo*-zhok.

Vaal (Riv.), vahl.
Vaduz, *vah*-doots.
Vaigach, vy-*gach*.
Vailima, vy-*lee*-mah.
Valais, va-*lay*.
Valamontone, *vah*-la-mon-*toh*-nay.
Valdai (Hills), val-*dy*.
Valença, va-*leŋ*-sa.
Valence, va-*lahŋs*.
Valencia, (Sp.) va-*len*-thyah: (Mex.) va-*len*-she-a.
Valenciennes, va-lahŋ-*syen*.
Valenza, vah-*lent*-sah.
Valjevo, *vahl*-ya-voh.
Valladolid, *val*-a-do-*lid*: *vahl*-yah-tho-*leeth*.
Vallejo, va-*lay*-hoh.
Valletta, vahl-*let*-tah.

Vallombrosa, *vahl*-lom-*broh*-sah.
Valmeira, *vahl*-mya-ra.
Valmy, val-mee.
Valognes, va-loh-ny'.
Valois, val-wah.
Valona, va-*loh*-nah.
Valparaiso, val-pa-*ray*-zoh.
Vancouver, van-*koo*-ver.
Van Diemen's Land, van-*dee*-menz-land.
Varanger (Fiord), va-*rang*-er.
Varazdin, vah-*rahzh*-den.
Vardar (Riv.), var-*dar*.
Varennes, va-*ren*.
Varese, vah-*ray*-sa.
Varhely, var-*hay*-le.
Varna, *var*-na.
Vaslui, vas-*loo*-e.
Västervik, *ves*-ter-veek.
Vasto, *vahs*-toh.
Vaucelles, voh-*sel*.
Vaucluse, voh-*klooz*.
Vaud, voh.
Vaulx-Vraucourt, voh-vro-koor.
Vauxhall, voks-*hawl*.
Veendam, vayn-*dahm*.
Vega Baja, *vay*-ga-*bah*-hah.
Veghel, *vay*-khel.
Veglia (Isl.), *vel*-yah.
Vejle, *vy*-le.
Veles, *vay*-les.
Veliki Luki, vay-*lee*-ke-*loo*-ke.
Velino, va-*lee*-noh.
Velletri, vayl-*lah*-tre.
Vellore, vayl-*lor*.
Vendome, vahŋ-*dohm*.
Vener (Lake), *vay*-ner.
Venezia Giulia, va-*net*-syah-*joo*-lyah.
Venezuela, ven-e-*zway*-la, -*zwee*-la.
Venice, *ven*-is.
Venloo, ven-*loh*.
Vennachar (Loch), *ven*-a-khar.
Venraij, *ven*-ry.
Ventimiglia, ven-te-*meel*-yah.
Ventspils, *vent*-spils.
Vera Cruz, *vay*-rah-*kroos*.
Vercelli, ver-*chel*-le.
Verdun, *vair*-dun.
Vereeniging, va-*ray*-ne-ging.
Vergennes, ver-*jenz*.
Vermand, ver-*mahŋd*.
Vermont, ver-*mont*.
Verona, va-*roh*-nah.
Versailles, vair-*sy'*: vair-*sah*-ye.
Verviers, ver-*vyay*.
Vervins, ver-*vaŋ*.
Vesle (Riv.), vel.
Vesoul, ve-*zool*.
Vesuvius, ve-*soo*-ve-us.
Vevey, *vay*-vay.
Viareggio, vyah-*red*-joh.
Viatka, vee-*at*-kah.
Viborg, *vee*-borkh.
Vicenza, vee-*chent*-sah.
Vichuga, ve-*choo*-ga.
Vichy, *vee*-shee.
Vidin, *vid*-en.
Vienna, ve-*en*-a.
Vienne, vyen.
Viet-Nam, *vyet*-nahm.
Vigo, *vee*-goh.
Viipuri, *vee*-poo-re.
Vila Joao Belo, *vee*-lah-zho-*oun*-bay-*loh*.
Vilaine, vee-len.
Villach, *fil*-ahkh.
Villafranca, veel-yah-*frahng*-kah.
Villaviciosa, *veel*-yah-ve-*thyoh*-sah.
Villefranche, veel-*frahŋsh*.
Villeneuve, veel-*nøv*.
Villers-Bocage, vee-lair-bo-*kahzh*.
Villers-Brettonneux, vee-lair-bre-to-nø.
Villers-Cotterets, vee-lair-ko-*tray*.
Villiers (-sur-Mer), vee-yay.
Vilna, *vel*-na.
Vimeiro, vee-*may*-roh.
Vimy, vee-mee.
Vincennes, vaŋ-*sen*.
Vindhya (Hills), *veen*-dyah.
Vinnitza, *ven*-nyet-sa.
Vire, veer.
Virginia, ver-*jin*-ya.
Visé, vee-zay.
Vistula, *vis*-tew-la.
Vitebsk, *vee*-tyepsk.
Viterbo, ve-*ter*-boh.
Vitré, vee-tray.
Vitry, vee-tree.
Vittoria, vit-*taw*-re-ah.
Viviers, vee-*vyay*.
Vizagapatam, ve-*zug*-a-pa-*tam*.
Vizzini, vet-*see*-ne.
Vlaardingen, *vlar*-ding-en.
Vladimir, vla-*dyee*-mer.
Vladivostok, *vlad*-e-*vos*-tok: vla-de-vos-*tok*.
Vlissingen, *vlis*-ing-en.
Voghera, vo-*gair*-rah.
Volchansk, vol-*chahnsk*.
Volga, *vol*-ga.
Volhynia, vo-*lin*-e-a.
Volkhov, *vol*-khof.
Volta, *vol*-ta.
Volterra, vol-*te*-rah.
Volturno, vol-*toor*-noh.
Vorona, vo-*roh*-na.
Voronezh, vo-*raw*-nyesh.
Voroshilovograd, *vu*-ru-shee-*law*-fo-grahd.
Vosges, vohzh.
Vosnesensk, voz-nye-*sensk*.
Vouziers, voo-zyay.
Voyennes, vwah-yen.
Vranje, *vrahn*-ye.
Vries, vrees.
Vryheid, *vry*-hyt.
Vulcano, vool-*kah*-noh.
Vyazma, *vyahz*-ma.
Vyrnwy, *vern*-we.

Waal (Riv.), *vahl*.
Wabash, *waw*-bash.
Wadai, wah-*dy*.
Wadi Halfa, *wah*-de-*hahl*-fa.
Waereghem, *vah*-re-gem.
Wagram, *vah*-grahm.
Waigatz (Isl.), vy-*gahtz*.
Wakatipu, *wah*-ka-*tee*-poo.
Walcheren, *vahl*-khe-ren.
Waldeck, *vahl*-dek.
Waldheim, *vahlt*-hym.
Wallasey, *wol*-a-se.
Wallingford, *wol*-ling-ford.
Wallsend, wawlz-*end*.
Walmer, *wawl*-mer.
Walsingham, *wawl*-sing-ham.
Waltham, *wawl*-tam.
Walvis (Bay), *wawl*-vis.
Walworth, *wawl*-wurth.
Wandsworth, *wondz*-worth.
Wanganui, *wong*-ga-noo-e.
Wanhsien, *wahn*-shyun.
Wanstead, *won*-sted.
Wapping, *wop*-ing.
Waratah, *wo*-ra-tah.
Wardha, *wur*-dah.
Warrington, *wo*-ring-ton.
Warsaw, *wawr*-saw.
Warszawa, var-*shah*-va.
Warta (Riv.), *var*-ta.

Wartburg, *vart*-boorkh.
Warwick, *wo*-rik.
Washita, *wosh*-e-taw.
Wasatch, *waw*-satch.
Wasmes, *vahm*.
Wastwater, *wost*-waw-ter.
Wattignies, va-*tee*-nyee.
Wavre, vahvr'.
Wear (Riv.), weer.
Wednesbury, *wenz*-be-re.
Weesp, vaysp.
Weheka, we-*hee*-ka.
Wehlau, *vay*-lou.
Wei-Hai-Wei, way-hy-*way*.
Weimar, *vy*-mar.
Weissenfels, *vy*-sen-fels.
Weisshorn, *vys*-horn.
Weisweiler, *vys*-vy-ler.
Wellesley, *welz*-le.
Wells, welz.
Wels, vels.
Welwyn, *wel*-in.
Wemyss, weemz.
Wenatchee, we-*natch*-e.
Wendisch Buckholz, *ven*-dish-*bookh*-hohlts.
Wener (Lake), *vay*-ner.
Weobley, *web*-le.
Wernigerode, ver-ne-ge-*roh*-de.
Wertheim, *vert*-hym.
Wesel, *vay*-zel.
Weser, *vay*-zer.
Wessel (Isls.), *ves*-el.
Westhoughton, west-*haw*-ton.
Weston-super-Mare, *wes*-ton-soo-per-*mair*.
Westphalia, west-*fay*-le-a.
Wetterhorn, *vet*-ter-horn.
Wetzlar, *vets*-lar.
Wevelgham, *vay*-vel-gem.
Wewak, wee-*wahk*.
Wey (Riv.), way.
Weymouth, *way*-muth.
Whangarei, wahn-ga-*ray*-e.
Whitby, *whit*-be.
Whithorn, *whit*-horn.
Whittinghame, *whit*-in-jum.
Wichita, *witch*-e-taw.
Wicklow, *wik*-loh.
Wieliczka, vyee-*lyeech*-kah.
Wien, veen.
Wiener Neustadt, *vee*-ner-*noy*-shtaht.
Wieringen, *vee*-ring-en.
Wiesbaden, *vees*-bah-den.
Wildspitze, vilt-*shpit*-se.
Wilhelmshaven, *vil*-helms-*hah*-fen.
Willesden, *wilz*-den.
Willoughby, *wil*-o-be.
Wiluna, we-*loo*-na.
Wimereux, *vee*-me-rø.
Windau, *vin*-dou.
Windischgraz, *vin*-dish-grahts.
Windhoek, *vint*-hook.
Windsor, *win*-zer.
Winnipeg, *win*-e-peg.
Winnipegosis, win-e-pe-*goh*-sis.
Wisbech, *wiz*-beech.
Wisconsin, wis-*kon*-sin.
Wishaw, *wish*-aw.
Wismar, *vis*-mar.
Wissembourg, vee-sahŋ-*boor*.
Witham, *wit*-am.
Wittelsheim, vee-tel-*zairm*.
Wittenberg, *vit*-ten-berg'.
Witwatersrand, wit-*waw*-terz-rahnt.
Wiveliscombe, *wils*-kum.
Wloclawec, vlots-*lah*-vek.
Wlodzimierz, vlo-*jee*-myezh.
Woburn, *woo*-burn.
Woevre, vwøvr'.
Wolfenbüttel, *vohl*-fen-bøtl.
Wolkowysk, vol-*koh*-vesk.
Woluwe, *vo*-loo-ve.
Wolverhampton, wool-ver-*hamp*-ton.
Wolverton, *wool*-ver-ton.
Wombwell, woombl.
Woolwich, *wool*-idj.
Worcester, *woos*-ter.
Workington, *wur*-king-ton.
Worms, vurmz: vorms.
Wörth, vurt.
Wrekin, *ree*-kin.
Wrotham, *root*-um.
Wroughton, *rou*-ton: *roh*-ton.
Wunsiedel, *voon*-zee-dl.
Wupperthal, *voop*-er-tahl.
Württemberg, *voor*-tem-berg, -berkh.
Würzburg, *vurts*-burg, -boorkh.
Wusterhausen, *voos*-ter-*hou*-zen.
Wycombe, *wik*-um.
Wye, wy.
Wykeham, *wik*-um.
Wymondham, *win*-dum: *wim*-un-dum.
Wynberg, *wyn*-berg.
Wynyard, *win*-yerd.
Wyoming, wee-*oh*-ming.
Wytham, *wy*-tum.
Wytschaete, *vyt*-skhah-te.

Xalisco, hah-*lis*-koh.
Xanthan, *zahn*-ten.
Xarayes, sha-*rah*-yays.
Xenia, *zee*-ne-a.
Xingu, shing-*goo*.

Yablonoi, *yah*-blo-noy.
Yadkin, *yad*-kin.
Yakataga, yah-ka-*tah*-ga.
Yakima, *yak*-e-ma.
Yakutat, *yak*-oo-tat.
Yakutsk, yah-*kootsk*.
Yalta, *yahl*-tah.
Yalu, yah-*loo*.
Yamagata, yah-ma-*gah*-ta.
Yamaguchi, yah-ma-*goo*-che.
Yamethin, ya-*mee*-thin.
Yampol, *yam*-pohl.
Yana, *yah*-na.
Yanaon, ya-*noun*.
Yangtse-Kiang, *yang*-tse-ke-*ang*.
Yanina, *yah*-nee-nah.
Yap (Isl.), yahp.
Yaqui, *yah*-ke.
Yarkand, yar-*kahnd*.
Yaroslav, ya-ro-*slahv*.
Yawata, *yah*-wa-ta.
Yazoo, *yaz*-oo.
Yealmpton, *yamp*-ton.
Yedo, *yed*-oh.
Yemen, *yem*-en: *yay*-men.
Yenangyaun, *yay*-nahng-*gyoun*.
Yenikale, yen-e-*kah*-lay.
Yenisei, *yen*-e-say-e.
Yeovil, *yoh*-vil.
Yetholm, *yet*-um.
Yezo, *yez*-oh.
Yiewsley, *yooz*-le.
Ymuiden, ee-*moo*-den.
Yokkaichi, *yok*-ka-ee-che.
Yokohama, *yoh*-ko-*hah*-ma.
Yokosuka, *yoh*-ko-*soo*-ka.
Yoruba, *yoh*-roo-bah.
Yosemite, yoh-*sem*-e-te.
Youghall, (Co. Cork) yawl: (Co. Tipperary) *yokh*-el.
Youghiogheny (Riv.), yok-o-*gay*-ne.
Ypres, eepr'.
Yser, ee-zair.

Yssel, *ee*-sel.
Ystad, *oo*-stahd.
Yucatan, yoo-ka-*tahn.*
Yugoslavia, *yoo*-go-*slah*-ve-a.
Yunnan, yoo-*nahn.*
Yvetot, eev-*toh.*
Yzeure, ee-zoor.

Zaandam, zahn-*dahm.*
Zacatecas, sah-tah-*kay*-kahs.
Zacatula, sah-kah-*too*-lah.
Zagazig, zah-ga-*zeeg.*
Zaghouan, zah-*gwahn.*
Zagreb, *zah*-greb.
Zaleszczyki, zal-yesh-*chek*-e.
Zama, *zay*-ma: *zah*-ma.
Zambesi, zam-*bee*-ze.
Zamora, (Sp.) thah-*moh*-rah: (Mex.) sah-*moh*-rah.
Zandevoorde, *zahnt*'voord.
Zante, *zahn*-te.
Zanzibar, zan-ze-*bar.*
Zapatoca, zah-pa-*toh*-kah.
Zaporozhe, za-po-*rawzh*-ye.
Zara, *zah*-rah.
Zaragoza, thah-rah-*goh*-thah.
Zawiercie, za-*vyer*-tse.
Zborowitz, *zbo*-roh-vits.
Zeballos, ze-*bal*-os.
Zeebrugge, *zay*-broo-g'.
Zeeland, *zay*-lahnt.
Zeerust, *zay*-rust.
Zeila, *zay*-lah.
Zeitun, *zay*-toon.
Zeitz, tsyts.
Zerbst, tserpts.
Zermatt, tser-*maht.*
Zevenkote, *zay*-ven-*koht.*
Zhitomir, zhe-*taw*-meer.
Zhlobin, zhloh-*been.*
Ziguinchor, zee-gaŋ-*shawr.*
Zillebeke, *zil*-e-bay-ke.
Zimbabwe, zim-*bah*-bway.
Zinoviesk, ze-naw-*vyefsk*
Zittau, *tsit*-ou.
Znaim, tsnym.
Zonnebeke, *zon*-e-bay-ke.
Zoppot, *tsop*-ot.
Zoutpansberg, *zout*-pans-berkh.
Zuara, *zwah*-rah.
Zug, tsookh.
Zuider-Zee, (*zy*-)*zoy*-der-zay.
Zürich, *zoor*-rik: *tsoo*-rikh.
Zutphen, *zut*-fen.
Zvolen, *svoh*-len.
Zweibrücken, tsvy-*brøk*-en.
Zwickau, *tsvik*-ou.
Zwittau, *tsvit*-ou.
Zwolle, *zwol*-e.

PRONUNCIATION OF PERSONAL NAMES

The pronunciation of Personal Names—largely because of the personal element—presents many difficulties; even different branches of the same family will pronounce their common name differently, and, again, local custom gives rise to variations. There are many well-known traps ("Cholmondeley," "Marjoribanks," "Menzies," etc.), and many not so well known (*e.g.* "Broughall," "Colclough," "Torphichen"): and, while there is no difficulty over "Huggins," with "Muggins" care is needed for, until personal contact is made, one cannot be sure that its bearer does not insist on "*mew*-ginz." In our list, where variants occur the object has been to give that in more common use first.

Territorial titles ("Elgin," "Galway," "Marlborough," etc.) are not as a rule included and should be sought for in the preceding list of Geographical and Topographical Names; exceptions are—when the spelling (*e.g.* "Ailesbury" and "Aylesbury") or the pronunciation (*e.g.* "Abergavenny," "Beaconsfield") differ; in such cases the names appear in both lists.

The occasional use of certain Phonetic characters (see p. 1094) is explained in the foreword to the list of Geographical and Topographical Names, p. 1118.

Abelard, *ab*-e-lard.
Abercromby, *ab*-er-krum-be.
Abergavenny, ab-er-*gen*-e.
Aberhart, *ay*-ber-hart.
Abernethy, ab-er-*nee*-the.
Acheson, *ay*-che-son.
Adair, a-*dair*.
Adenhauer, *ah*-den-hour.
Adye, *ay*-de.
Agassiz, *ag*-a-se.
Ailesbury, *aylz*-be-re.
Ainslie, *aynz*-le.
Albani, al-*bah*-ne.
Albuquerque, *al*-boo-*ker*-ke.
Alcuin, *al*-kwin.
Alekhine, *al*-e-keen; (Russ.) u-*lyay*-khyin.
Alfieri, al-fe-*air*-e.
Alighieri, *ah*-le-*gyair*-e.
Alleyne, *al*-in.
Almagro, al-*mah*-groh.
Almavist, *ahlm*-kvist.
Aloisi, ah-lo-*ee*-ze.
Amadeo, am-a-*day*-oh.
Amati, ah-*mah*-te.
Amiel, *am*-e-el; (Fr.) ah-myel.
Amundsen, *ah*-moond-sen.
André, ã-dray.
Andreyev, un-*dryay*-yef.
Annesley, *anz*-le.
Anstruther, an-*struth*-er; *an*-ster.
Antonescu, ahn-to-*nes*-koo.
Antrobus, *an*-tro-bus.
Apponyi, *op*-o-nyi.
Apraxin, u-*prak*-syin.
Aquinas, a-*kwy*-nas.
Arbuthnot, ar-*buth*-not.
Arnaud, ar-*noh*.
Arrhenius, ar-*ray*-ne-us.
Ascham, *as*-kam.
Assheton, *ash*-ton.
Astaire, a-*stair*.
Ataturk, ah-tah-*toork*.
Auber, oh-bair.
Aubrey, *aw*-bre.
Auchinleck, *aw*-khin-lek; *awn*-lek; *af*-lek.
Audubon, *oh*-du-bon.
Auer, *ou*-er.
Augereau, *ohzh*-roh.
Aulnoy, oh-*nwah*.
Aumale, oh-*mahl*.
Averroes, a-*ve*-ro-eez.
Ayscough, *as*-kew; *ays*-koh.
Aytoun, *ay*-ton.

Babeuf, ba-*bøf*.
Bach, bahkh.
Bache, baych.
Backhuysen, *bak*-hoy-zen.
Baden Powell, *bay*-dn-*pow*-el.
Badoglio, ba-*doh*-le-oh.
Baedeker, *bay*-de-ker.
Baekeland, *bayk*-land; (Flem.) *bah*-ke-lahnt.
Baeyer (von), *bai*(*r*)-yer.
Bagehot, *bag*-ot.
Bagration, bu-grut-ye-*awn*.
Bajazet, *baj*-a-zet.
Balcarres, bal-*ka*-ris.
Baldwin, *bawl*-dwin.
Barbauld, *bar*-bohld.
Barberini, *bar*-be-*ree*-ne.
Barbier, bar-byay.
Barbirolli, bar-be-*rol*-e.
Barbour, *bar*-ber.
Barbusse, bar-*boos*.
Baring, *bare*-ing.
Barocci, ba-*rotch*-e.
Barraclough, *ba*-ra-kluf.
Barras, *ba*-ras.
Barrès, ba-*res*.
Barth, (Swiss) bart.
Barthélemy, bar-tayl-mee.
Bartholdi, bar-tol-dee.
Barthou, bar-too.
Bartók, bar-tohk.
Bartolozzi, *bar*-to-*lot*-se.
Barttelot, *bart*-let.
Barwick, *ba*-rik.
Basedow, *bah*-ze-doh.
Bashkirtsev, bush-*kyeer*-tsef.
Bassompierre, ba-soŋ-*pyair*.
Bastiat, *bas*-tya.
Bastien-Lepage, *bas*-tyaŋ le-*pahzh*.
Bata, (Czech) *bah*-tyah.
Bathori, *bah*-to-re.
Batthyani, bot-*yah*-nye.
Baudelaire, boh-*dlair*.
Baudouin, boh-*dway*.
Bauer, *bou*-er.
Baumann, (Ger.) *bou*-man; (Fr.) boh-mahn.
Baumé, boh-*may*.
Baumgarten, *boum*-gar-ten.

Bayard, *bay*-ard.
Bazaine, ba-*zayn*.
Beaconsfield, *bee*-konz-feeld.
Beauchamp, *bee*-cham; (Fr.) boh-shahŋ.
Beauclerc, *boh*-klerk.
Beaufort, *boh*-fort.
Beauharnais, boh-ar-nay.
Beaumarchais, boh-mar-shay.
Beaumont, *boh*-mont.
Bebel, (Ger.) *bay*-bel.
Beckx, (Belg.) beks.
Beethoven, *bay*-toh-ven.
Behaim, *bay*-hym.
Behn, bayn; ben.
Beit, bayt.
Beith, beeth.
Belasco, be-*las*-koh.
Belisarius, bel-e-*sair*-re-us.
Belisha, be-*lee*-sha.
Belknap, *bel*-nap.
Bellarmine, *bel*-ar-meen.
Bellew, be-*lyew*.
Bellini, be-*lee*-ne.
Belloc, be-*lok*.
Belzoni, bal-*tsoh*-ne.
Beneš, *be*-nesh.
Benét, be-*nay*.
Bengough, *ben*-goh.
Benoît, be-*nwah*.
Bentivoglio, *ben*-te-*voh*-lyoh.
Benz, bents.
Béranger, ba-rahŋ-zhay.
Berchtold, *berkh*-tohlt.
Berdyaev, byer-*dya*-yef.
Berenson, *be*-ren-son.
Beresford, *be*-res-ford.
Berkeley, *bark*-le.
Berliner, *ber*-lin-er.
Berlioz, *bair*-lə-ohz.
Bernadotte, *ber*-na-dot.
Bernhardt, *bern*-hart.
Bernini, ber-*nee*-ne.
Berthelot, ber-tee-loh.
Berthier, ber-tyay.
Berthollet, *ber*-to-lay.
Bertie, *ber*-te; (surname) *bar*-te.
Bertillon, ber-tee-yoŋ.
Besant, *bes*-ant; *bez*-ant; be-*zant*.
Besnard, bay-nar.
Bethlen, *bet*-len.
Bethmann-Holweg, *bayt*-mahn-*hol*-vaykh.
Bethune, be-*thewn*; *bee*-ton; *beth*-yewn.
Beudant, boo-*dahŋ*.
Beust, boyst.
Bewick, *bew*-ik.
Beyle, bayl.
Beza, *bee*-za.
Bianchi, *byakŋ*-ke.
Bichat, *bee*-shah.
Bigelow, *big*-e-loh.
Bismarck, *biz*-(Ger. *bis*-)mark.
Bispham, *bis*-fam; *bis*-pam.
Bizet, *bee*-zay.
Björnson, *byurn*-son.
Blaeu, blou.
Blanqui, blahŋ-kee.
Bledisloe, *bled*-es-loh.
Bligh, bly.
Blomefield, *bloom*-feeld.
Blomfield, *bloom*-(*blom*-) feeld.
Blount, blunt.
Blucher, *bloo*-ker.
Blumenthal, *bloo*-men-tahl.
Bluntschli, *bloont'*-shle.
Blyth, bly; blythe.
Boas, *boh*-az; *boh*-as.
Boccaccio, bo-*kah*-che-oh.
Boccherini, bohk-ka-*ree*-ne.
Boece, bo-*ees*.
Boehm, baym; bøm.
Boerhaave, *boor*-hah-ve.
Bogoljubov, bu-*gu*-*lyew*-bawf.
Bohemund, *boh*-e-mund.
Bohr, bor.
Bohun, boon.
Boiardo, bo-*yar*-doh.
Boileau, bwa-*loh*.
Boisguillebert, bwa-gee' bair.
Boleslaus, *boh*-les-laws.
Boleyn, *bull*-en.
Bolitho, bo-*ly*-tho.
Bolivar, bo-*lee*-var.
Bompas, *bum*-pus.
Bonheur, bo-*nur*.
Bonnet, bon-*nay*.
Bonnivard, bo-nee-*var*.
Bonomi, bo-*noh*-me.
Bonpland, boŋ-plahŋ.
Borghese, bor-*gay*-sa.
Borgia, *bor*-ja; *bor*-je-a.
Borgognone, Il, *eel*-bohr-go-*nyoh*-nay.
Boris Godunov, *baw*-ris-gu-doo-*nawf*.
Borodin, bu-ru-*dyeen*.
Borromeo, *bo*-ro-*may*-oh.
Bosanquet, bo-*sang*-ke; *boh*-z'n-kit.
Boscawen, bos-*koh*-en.
Bosquet, *bos*-ke.
Bossuet, bo-soo-ay.
Botha, *boh*-ta.
Botticelli, *bot*-te-*chel*-le.
Botvinnik, bot-*vin*-ik.
Boucher, (Fr.) boo-shay.
Boucicault, *boo*-se-koh.
Boufflers, boo-flair.
Bougainville, boo-gaŋ-veel.
Bouguereau, boo-*groh*.
Boulanger, boo-lahn-zhay.
Bourbaki, boor-ba-kee.
Bourchier, *bou*-cher.
Bourdaloue, boor-da-*loo*.
Bourdillon, (Engl.) bur-*dil*-yun.
Bourgeois, boor-zhwah.
Bourget, boor-zhay.
Bourke, burk.
Bourne, boorn; born; burn.
Bouterwek, *boo*-ter-vek.
Boutmy, boo-mee.
Boutroux, boo-troc.
Bouts, (Flem.) bouts.
Bowditch, *bou*-ditch.
Bowdoin, *boh*-d'n.
Bowell, *boh*-el.
Bowen, *boh*-en.
Bowes-Lyon, bohz-*ly*-on.
Bowker, *bou*-ker.
Bowles, bohlz.
Bowring, *bou*-ring.
Brabazon, *brab*-a-zon.
Brabourne, *bray*-burn.
Bracquemond, brak-moŋ.
Bradlaugh, *brad*-law.
Braham, *bray*-am.
Brahe, *brah*-e.
Brahms, brahms; brahmz.
Bramah, *brah*-ma.
Bramante, bra-*mahn*-ta.
Brandeis, *bran*-dice.
Brandes, (Dan.) *brahn*-des.
Brangwyn, *brang*-win.
Braque, brahk.
Brassey, *bras*-e.
Bratianu, bra-te-*ah*-noo.
Brauchitsch, *brou*-khitch.
Braun, broun.
Breadalbane, bre-*dawl*-ban.
Bréguet, bray-gay.
Breitkopf, *bryt*-kopf.
Brémond, bray-moŋ.
Brentano, bren-*tah*-noh.
Brereton, *breer*-t'n; *brair*-t'n.

Breughel, *brø*-gel.
Breuil, *brø'*e.
Breul, broyl.
Briand, bree-ahŋ.
Bridie, *bry*-de.
Brieux, bree-ø.
Brillat-Savarin, *bree*-yah-sah-va-*raŋ*.
Brissot, bree-soh.
Brod, (Ger.) broht.
Broglie, *brohl*-ye.
Broke, brook.
Brongniart, broŋ-nyar.
Brontë, *bron*-te.
Brough, bruf.
Broughall, brufl.
Brougham, *broo*-am; broom.
Broughton, *braw*-t'n.
Brouncker, *brung*-ker.
Brouwer, *brou*-wer.
Bruch, brookh.
Brunelleschi, broo-nel-*lay*-ske.
Brüning, *broo*-ning.
Brünnhilde, broon-*hil*-da.
Brusilov, broo-*syee*-lawf.
Brydges, *brij*-iz.
Buccleuch, bu-*khloo*.
Buchan, *bukh*-an.
Buchanan, bew-*kan*-an.
Buchel, *bew*-shel.
Budenny, boo-*den*-e; boo-*dyawn*-nwe.
Buffon, *boo*-foŋ.
Bugeaud, boo-zhoh.
Buick, *bew*-ik.
Buisson, boo-ee-soŋ.
Bullough, *bull*-oh, -okh.
Bunin, *boo*-nyin.
Bunsen, *boon*-zen.
Burdett, bur-*det*.
Burghclere, *bur*-klair.
Burghersh, *ber*-gush.
Burghley, *bur*-le.
Burnand, bur-*nand*.
Burnell, bur-*nell*.
Burroughs, *bu*-rohz.
Bury, *bewr*-re; *be*-re.
Bustamente, boos-tah-*mahn*-tay.
Byng, bing.
Byrd, burd.
Byrnes, burnz.

Cabellero, (Sp.) kah-bah-*lyay*-roh.
Cabanis, (Fr.) ka-ba-nees.
Cabot, *kab*-ot.
Cabral, ka-*bral*.
Cabrera, kah-*bray*-rah.
Cadillac, ka-dee-*yak*.
Cadogan, ka-*dug*-an.
Cagliostro, kah-*lyos*-tro.
Cahill, *kay*-hil.
Caillard, *kayl*-erd; (Fr.) ky-ah.
Caillaux, kah-yoh.
Caius, keez; (Lat.) *ky*-us.
Cajetan, *kaj*-e-tan.
Caldcleugh, *kawld*-kluf.
Calderon, *kawl*-de-ron; (Sp.) *kal*-de-ron.
Caledon, *kal*-e-don.
Calhoun, kal-*hoon*.
Callaghan, *kal*-a-han.
Callcott, *kawl*-kot.
Calvé, kahl-vay.
Cambon, (Fr.) kahŋ-boŋ
Cammaerts, kahm-arts.
Camoens, *kam*-o-enz.
Camoys, ka-*moyz*.
Campbell, *kam*-bel.
Campeggio, kam-*pay*-jo.
Canaletto, kah-nah-*layt*-toh.
Candolle, kahŋ-dol.
Canova, ka-*noh*-vah.
Canrobert, kahŋ-ro-bair.
Canute, ka-*newt*.
Capablanca, kah-pa-*blahŋ*-ka.
Capek, *chah*-pek.
Capet, kap-et.
Capus, kah-poo.
Caraccioli, ka-*raht*-cho-lee.
Caravaggio, kah-ra-*vahd*-jo.
Cardenas, (Sp.) *kar*-tha-nahs.
Carducci, kar-*doot*-che.
Carew, ka-*rew*; *kair*-re.
Carlyle, kar-*lyl*.
Carnegie, kar-*nay*-ge; *kar*-ne-ge.
Carnot, kar-noh.
Carolus-Duran, kah-ro-*loos*-doo-*rahŋ*.
Carpaccio, kar-*paht*-choh.
Carracci, ka-*rah*-che.
Carruthers, ka-*ruth*-erz.
Carteret, *kar*-te-ret.
Cartier, *kar*-tyay.
Carton de Wiart, kar-toŋ-de-*vyar*.
Caruso, kah-*roo*-zoh.
Casals, kah-*sahls*.
Casaubon, ka-soh-bon.
Caslon, *kaz*-lon.
Cassilis, *kas*'lz.
Castiglione, kahs-te-*lyoh*-na.
Castlereagh, *kah*'sl-ray.
Catriona, ka-*tree*(*r*)-na.
Catroux, ka-*troo*.
Cauchon, koh-shoŋ.
Cavaignac, ka-vah-nyak.
Cavour, kah-voor.
Cecil, *ses*-il; *sis*-il.
Cellini, che-*lee*-ne.
Cenci, *chen*-che.
Cezánne, say-zahn.
Chagall, sha-gahl.
Chaliapin, *shal*-e-*ah*-pin; sha-*lyah*-pyin.
Chalmers, *chah*-merz; *chal*-merz.
Chambord, shahŋ-bor.
Chaminade, shah-mee-nahd.
Chamisso, shah-me-soh.
Champollion, shahŋ-po-lyoŋ.
Chandos, *shan*-dos.
Chardin, shar-daŋ.
Charlemagne, shar-le-mayn.
Charpentier, shar-pahŋ-tyay.
Charteris, *char*-terz; *char*-ter-ris.
Chasles, shahl.
Chastelard, shah-tlar.
Chateaubriand, shah-toh-bree-ahŋ.
Chaucer, *chaw*-ser.
Chautemps, shoh-tahŋ.
Chaworth, *chah*-wurth.
Cheney, *chee*-ne.
Chenier, shay-nyay.
Cherubini, kay-roo-*bee*-ne.
Chetwynd, *chet*-wind.
Chevalier, she-val-yay.
Chevasse, she-*vas*.
Chevenix, *shev*-e-niks.
Chevrolet, shev-ro-*lay*.
Cheylesmore, *chylz*-mor; *chaylz*-mor.
Cheyne, chayn; *chay*-ne.
Chiang Kai Shek, je-*ahng*-ky-*shek*.
Chichele, *chich*-e-le.
Chisholm, *chiz*-om.
Chloe, *kloh*-e.
Chodkiewicz, khot-kye-veech.
Chodowiecki, khoh-do-*vyets*-ke.
Choiseul, shwah-zøl.
Cholmeley, *chum*-le.
Cholmondeley, *chum*-le.
Chopin, *shoh*-paŋ.
Christ (W. von) (Ger.) krist.
Christie, *kris*-te.

Chrysostom, *kris*-os-tom.
Ciano, *chah*-noh.
Cimabue, chee-mah-*boo*-ay.
Cinq-Mars, saŋ-mar.
Cipriani, chee-pre-*ah*-ne.
Citrine, se-*treen.*
Citroen, see-tro-*en.*
Claessens, (Dut.) *klas*-enz.
Clanricarde, klan-*rik*-ard.
Clarendon, *kla*-ren-don.
Claretie, klah-re-tee.
Claudel, kloh-del.
Clausen, *klou*-s'n.
Clausewitz, *klou*-ze-vits.
Clemenceau, klay-mahŋ-soh.
Clerk, klark.
Clerke, klark.
Clicquot, klee-koh.
Clouet, kloo-ay.
Clough, kluf.
Clowes, klouz; klooz.
Cockburn, *koh*-burn.
Cochrane, *kokh*-ran.
Codreanu, ko-dre-*ah*-noo.
Coghlan, *kog*-lan; *koh*-lan.
Coke, kook.
Colbert, kol-bair.
Colclough, *kohk*-le.
Colenso, ko-*len*-zoh.
Coleridge, *kohl*-rij.
Coligny, ko-lee-nyee.
Colijn, ko-*lyn.*
Colman, *kohl*-man.
Colnaghi, kol-*nah*-ge.
Colquhoun, ko-*hoon.*
Combe, koom.
Comines, ko-*meen.*
Compton, *komp*-tun; *kum*-tun.
Comte, koŋt.
Comyn, *kum*-in.
Condillac, koŋ-dee-yak.
Condorcet, ko-dor-say.
Confucius, kon-*few*-shyus.
Conolly, *kon*-o-le.
Conscience, (Flem.) kon-*syahn*-se.
Constable, *kun*-sta-bl.
Constant, (Fr.) kons-tahŋ.
Contarini, *kon*-tah-*ree*-ne.
Conyngham, *kun*-ing-am.
Copernicus, ko-*per*-ne-kus.
Coppée, ko-pay.
Coquelin, ko-klaŋ.
Corbould, *kor*-bohld.
Corneille, kor-nay'.
Cornwallis, korn-*wol*-is.
Corot, ko-roh.
Correggio, ko-*red*-joh.
Couch, kooch.
Coué, kway; koo-ay.
Coulevain, kool'-vaŋ.
Coulomb, koo-loŋ.
Coulton, *kohl*-ton.
Couper, *koo*-per.
Couperin, koo-p'raŋ.
Coupland, *koop*-land.
Courbet, koor-bay.
Courtauld, *kor*-tohld; (Fr.) koor-toh.
Courthope, *kort*-up.
Courtneidge, *kort*-nij.
Cousin, (Fr.) koo-zaŋ.
Coutts, koots.
Cowley, *kou*-le.
Cowper, *kow*-per; (the poet) *koo*-per.
Coysevox, kwahz-*voks.*
Cozens, *kuz*-enz.
Cranach, *krah*-nahkh.
Creagh, kray.
Crebillon, kray-bee-yoŋ.
Creighton, *kray*-ton.
Crespigny, *krep*-ne; *krep*-e-ne.
Creswick, *krez*-ik.
Crichton, *kry*-ton.
Crillon, kree-yoŋ.
Crispi, *krees*-pe.
Croce, *kroh*-chay.
Cromartie, *krom*-ar-te.
Crommelin, *krum*-lin.
Crompton, *krump*-ton.
Crosby, *kroz*-be.
Crothers, *kruth*-erz.
Cruickshank, *krook*-shank.
Csáky, *chah*-ke.
Cuchulinn, *koo*-khoo-lin.
Curie, koo-ree.
Curtius, (Ger.) *koort*-se-oos.
Cushing, *koo*-shing.
Cushman, *koosh*-man.
Cuvier, koo-ve-ay.
Cuyp, koyp; kyp.
Cyril, *si*-ril.
Czartoryski, char-to-*ris*-ke.
Czermak, *cher*-mahk.
Czerny, *cher*-ne.

Daguerre, da-*gair.*
D'Aguilar, *dag*-wil-er.
Daladier, da-la-dyay.
Dalberg, *dahl*-berkh.
D'Alembert, da-lahŋ-bair.
Dalhousie, dal-*hoo*-ze.
Dalkeith, dal-*keeth.*
Dalton, *dawl*-ton.
Dalziel, *dal*-ze-el; *dal*-yel; (Scot.) de-*el.*
Dana, *day*-na.
Dandolo, *dahn*-do-loh.
D'Annunzio, dahn-*noon*-tsyoh.
Dante, *dan*-tay.
Danton, dahŋ-toŋ.
Darewski, da-*ref*-ske.
Darlan, dar-lahŋ.
Daubigny, doh-bee-nyee.
Daudet, doh-day.
Daumier, doh-myay.
Davout, da-voo.
Déat, day-ah.
Debussy, de-boo-see.
Decatur, de-*kay*-ter.
Decies, *dee*-sheez.
Degas, de-gah.
De Gaulle, de-*gohl.*
Deidre, *deer*-dra.
De la Bèche, *del*-a-besh.
Delacroix, de-la-krwah.
Delaroche, de-lah-rohsh.
Delaunay, de-loh-nay.
Delcassé, del-kah-say.
Delibes, de-leeb.
De Lisle, de-*leel.*
Delysia, de-*lee*-se-a.
Demoivre, (Engl.) de-*moy*-ver; (Fr.) de-*mwahvr'.*
De Moleyns, de-mo-*leenz.*
Derain, de-raŋ.
De Reszke, de-*res*-ke.
D'Erlanger, de-lahŋ-zhay.
De Ros, de-*roos.*
Descartes, da-*kart.*
Deschanel, day-shah-*nel.*
Deshayes, day-*ay.*
Deslys, day-lees.
Desmoulins, day-moo-laŋ.
Desnoyers, day-nwah-yay.
Dessaix, day-say.
De Staël, de-*stahl.*
Deutsch, doytch.
De Valera, dev-a-*leer*-ra.
Deventer, *dev*-en-ter.
Devereux, *dev*-e-roo.
De Vesci, de-*ves*-e.
Diaghilev, *dyah*-gyi-lyef.
Diderot, *dee*-droh; *dee*-de-roh.
Didot, *dee*-doh.
Dietrich, *dee*-trik.
Dillwyn, *dill*-win.
Disraeli, diz-*ray*-le.
Djugashvili, *joo*-gah-*shvee*-lee.
Dobell, do-*bel.*
Dobré, *doh*-bray.
Docwra, *dok*-ra.

Dohnányi, *doh*-nah-nye.
Dollfuss, *dol*-foos.
Döllinger, *dul*-ing-er.
Dombrowski, doŋm-*brawf*-ske.
Domenichino, *doh*-ma-ne-*kee*-noh.
Donati, do-*nah*-te.
Donizetti, don-id-*zet*-te.
Donoghue, *don*-o-hew, *dun*-o-hew.
Donoughmore, *dun*-o-mor.
Dostoevsky, *dos*-tu-*yev*-ske.
Doudney, *dewd*-ne.
Dougal, *doo*-gal.
Dougherty, *doh*-er-te.
Douglas, *dug*-las.
Douglass, *dug*-las.
Douhet, (It.) doo-*ay*.
Doulton, *dohl*-ton.
Doumer, (Fr.) doo-mair.
Doumergue, (Fr.) doo-merg.
Douw, dou.
Dowsabel, *doo*-sa-bel.
Dowsterswivel, *doo*-ster-swiv'l.
Drdla, *durd*-lah.
Dreyfus, *dray*-fus.
Ducange, doo-*kahŋzh*.
Duchesne, (Engl.) doo-*kayn*, *dewk*-s'n; (Fr.) doo-shayn.
Ducrot, du-*kroh*.
Du Guesclin, doo-gay-klahn.
Dumaresq, doo-me-rik.
Dumas, doo-mah.
Dumaurier, doo-*maw*-re-ay.
Dumouriez, doo-moo-ryay.
Dunsany, dun-*say*-ne.
Dupleix, doo-play.
Duplessis, doo-*ples*-e.
Duquesne, doo-*kayn*.
Dürer, *doo*-rer.
Duruy, doo-roo-ee.
Duryea, door-yay.
Duse, *doo*-zay.
Dvořák, *dvor*-zhahk.
Dymoke, *dim*-ok.
Dynevor, *din*-e-vor.
Dysart, *dy*-sart; *dy*-zat.

Eardley, *erd*-le.
Ebert, (Ger.) *ay*-bert.
Ebury, *ee*-be-re.
Echegaray, (Sp.) *ay*-cha-gah-*rah*.
Egede, (Norw.) *ay*-ge-de.
Egerton, *ej*-er-ton.
Ehrlich, *ayer*-likh.
Eichwald, *ykh*-vahlt.
Eijkman, *yk*-mahn.
Einstein, *yn*-shtyn.
Eirene, y-*ree*-ne.
Eisenhower, *y*-z'n-*hou*-er.
Eliot, *el*-yot.
Ellesmere, *elz*-meer.
Elzevir, *el*-ze-veer.
Encke, *eŋ*-ke.
Engels, *eng*-gelz.
Eötrös, *øt*-vøsh.
Erigena, e-*rij*-e-na.
Ernle, *ern*-le.
Erskine, *ers*-kin
Este, *es*-tay.
Esterházy, *es*-ter-*hah*-ze.
Estrées, es-tray.
Étienne, ay-tyen.
Eucken, *oy*-k'n.
Eugen, (Russ.) oy-*gayn*.
Eugène, oo-zhahn; (Engl.) yoo-*jeen*.
Eugénie, oo-zhay-nee.
Eulenspiegel, *oy*-len-shpee-gel.
Euler, *oy*-ler.
Eunice, *yoo*-nis.
Euwe, *ø*-ve.
Evelyn, *eev*-lin; *ee*-ve-lin.
Ewald, (Ger.) *ay*-vahlt; (Dan.) *ay*-vahl.
Ewart, *yoo*-ert.
Ewing, *yoo*-ing.
Eyck, yk.
Eyre, air.

Fabre, fahbr.
Facciolati, *faht*-cho-*lah*-te.
Faed, fayd.
Faidherbe, fe-derb.
Falconer, *fawk*-ner.
Fallières, fah-lyair.
Faneuil, fan'l.
Fantin-Latour, fahŋ-taŋ-lah-*toor*.
Farnese, far-*nay*-sa.
Farquhar, *far*-kwer; *far*-ker.
Farquharson, *far*-kwer-s'n; *far*-ker-s'n.
Fauntleroy, *fawnt*-, *font*-le-roy.
Faure, fawr.
Faust, foust.
Favart, fa-*var*.
Fawkes, fawks; foks.
Fechner, *fekh*-ner.
Fechter, *fekh*-ter.
Federer, *fay*-de-rer.
Fénelon, fayn-loŋ.
Fenwick, *fen*-ik.
Feuchtwanger, *foykht*-vahng-er.
Feuerbach, *foy*-er-bahkh
ffoulkes, fohks.
Fichte, *fikh*-ta.
Ficino, fe-*chee*-noh.
Fiennes, fynz.
Fieschi, *fyes*-ke.
Figuier, fee-gyay.
Fildes, fyldz.
Finucane, fe-*new*-kan; *fin*-yew-kane.
Firdausi, fer-*dou*-see.
Fischer, *fish*-er.
Flagstad, *flahg*-stah.
Flahaut, flah-*oh*.
Flaubert, floh-bair.
Flavel, *flav*-el.
Fleay, flay.
Fleury, flur-ree.
Flotow, (Ger.) *floh*-toh.
Flügel, *floo*-gel.
Foch, fosh.
Foerster, *furs*-ter.
Fogazzaro, *foh*-gaht-*tsah*-roh.
Fogerty, *foh*-ger-te.
Fokine, fo-*keen*.
Foljambe, *full*-jum.
Forsyth, for-*syth*.
Fortescue, *for*-tes-kew.
Foscolo, *fos*-ko-loh.
Foucault, foo-koh.
Fouché, foo-shay.
Foucquet, foo-kay.
Foulds, fohldz.
Foulis, foulz.
Foulkes, fohks; fouks.
Fourier, foo-ryay.
Fra Angelico, *frah*-ahn-*jel*-e-koh.
Fra Diavolo, frah-*dyah*-vo-loh.
Fragonard, frah-go-nar.
Franceschini, frahn-chas-*kee*-ne.
Fraunhofer, *froun*-hoh-fer.
Fremont, *free*-mont.
Fresnel, fray-*nel*.
Freud, froyd; (Ger.) froyt.
Freyberg, *fry*-berg.
Freycinet, fray-see-nay.
Freytag, *fry*-tahkh.
Fries, frees.
Friis, frees.
Frisch, freesh.
Froebel, frø-bl.
Fröhlich, *frø*-likh.

Froissart, *froy*-sart; (Fr.) frwah-sahr.
Fromentin, fro-mahŋ-taŋ.
Froude, frood.
Fuchs, fooks.
Fugger, *foo*-ger.
Funk, (Ger.) foonk.
Furtwängler, *foort*-vengler.
Fuseli, *foo*-se-le.

Gaboriau, gah-bo-ryoh.
Gabriel, gay-bre-'l; (Fr.) gah-bree-el.
Gade, (Dan.) *gah*-da.
Galen, *gay*-len; (Ger.) *gah*-len.
Galileo, *gal*-e-*lay*-oh.
Gallacher, *gal*-a-kher.
Gallagher, *gal*-a-her; *gal*-a-kher.
Galli-Curci, gahl-le-*koor*-che.
Galvani, gal-*vah*-ne.
Gamelin, gahm-laŋ.
Gandhi, *gahn*-dee.
Garcia, *gar*-she-a, -se-a; (Sp.) gar-*thee*-ah, -*see*-ah.
Gareth, *gair*-reth.
Garioch, *ga*-rik.
Gascoigne, *gas*-koyn.
Gatacre, *gat*-a-ker.
Gauguin, goh-gaŋ.
Gaumont, goh-moŋ; (Engl.) *goh*-mont.
Gauss, gouce.
Gautama, *gou*-ta-ma.
Gautier, goh-tyay.
Gawain, *gah*-wayn.
Geddes, *ged*-is.
Gee, jee.
Geikie, *gee*-ke.
Geiger, *gy*-ger.
Genée, zhe-nay.
Geneviève, zhan-ve-ayv.
Genlis, zhahŋ-lees.
Gentile, (It.) jen-*tee*-la.
Geoffrey, *jef*-re.
Geoghegan, *gay*-gan; *goh*-gan.
Gerard, *je*-rard.
Gérard, zhay-rar.
Gerhardt, (Ger.) *gayer*-hart; (Fr.) zhay-rar.
Géricault, zhay-ree-koh.
Gérome, zhay-rohm.
Gervase, *jer*-vas.
Ghiberti, ge-*ber*-te.
Ghirlandaio, *ger*-lahn-*dah*-yoh.
Giannone, jahn-*noh*-na.
Gide, zheed.
Gielgud, *gil*-good.
Gifford, *jif*-ord.
Gigli, *jee*-lyee.
Gilchrist, *gil*-krist.
Gilkes, jilks.
Gillespie, ge-*les*-pe.
Gillett, *gil*-et; ge-*let*.
Gillette, je-*let*.
Gillian, *jil*-e-an.
Gilliat, *gil*-e-at.
Gillott, jil-ot.
Giolitti, jo-*leet*-te.
Giorgione, jor-*joh*-nay.
Giotto, *jot*-toh.
Giovanni, zho-*vah*-ne.
Girardon, zhee-rar-doŋ.
Giuriati, joo-*ryah*-te.
Giuseppe, joo-*sep*-pa.
Giusti, *joos*-te.
Giustiniani, *joos*-te-*nyah*-ne.
Gjellerup, *gel*-le-roop.
Glazunov, glu-zoo-*nawf*.
Gleichen, *gly*-k'n.
Glenely, gla-*nel*-e.
Glinka, *glyen*-ku.
Gluck, glook.
Gmelin, g'*may*-leen.
Gneisenau, g'*ny*-ze-nou.
Gobineau, go-bee-noh.
Goderich, *goh*-dritch.
Godolphin, go-*dol*-fin.
Godoy, (Sp.) go-*thoy*.
Goebbels, *gø*-blz.
Goethals, *goh*-thalz.
Goethe, *gø*-te.
Goetz, gøtz.
Golitzin, gu-*lyee*-tsin.
Gollancz, *gol*-ents.
Goncharov, gun-chu-*rawf*.
Goncourt, goŋ-*koor*.
Gondomar, gon-do-*mar*.
Gorchakov, gur-chu-*kawf*.
Gorges, *gor*-jes.
Göring, *gø*-ring.
Goschen, *goh*-shen.
Goudy, *gou*-de; *goo*-de.
Gough, goff.
Gouin, gwaŋ.
Goujon, goo-zhoŋ.
Gould, goold.
Gounod, *goo*-noh.
Gowan, *gou*-an.
Gower, *gou*-er; gore.
Goya, *goh*-yah.
Gozzoli, *goht*-tso-lee.
Graeme, graym.
Grandi, *grahŋ*-de.
Granger, *grayn*-jer.
Graziani, (It.) grah-*tsyah*-ne.
Greenhalgh, *green*-halsh, -haw.
Greenough, *gree*-noh.
Grégoire, gray-gwahr.
Greig, greg.
Grétry, gray-tree.
Greuze, grøz.
Grévy, gray-vee.
Grieg, greeg.
Grierson, *greer*-son.
Grignard, gree-nyar.
Grillparzer, gril-*par*-tseer.
Grisi, gree-ze.
Grosvenor, *groh*-v'ner.
Grouchy, groo-shee.
Grundtvig, *groont*-veg.
Guanerius, gwar-*neer*-re-us.
Guedalla, gwe-*dal*-a.
Guevara, ga-*vah*-rah.
Guicciardini, *gweet*-char-*dee*-ne.
Guido, *gwee*-doh.
Guilbert, geel-bair.
Guillamore, *gil*-a-mor.
Guillaume, gee-yohm.
Guiney, *gy*-ne.
Guinness, *gin*-is; gi-*nes*.
Guise, geez.
Guitry, gee-tree.
Guizot, gee-zoh.
Gullstrand, *gul*-strahnd.
Gustavus, gus-*tay*-vus.
Gutenburg, *goo*-ten-burg.
Guyot, goo-ee-*yoh*.
Gwladys, *glad*-is.

Haakon, *haw*-kon.
Hacha, *hah*-khah.
Haeckel, *hek*-el.
Hafiz, hah-*fiz*.
Hagen, *hay*-gen; (Ger.) *hah*-gen.
Hahnemann, *hah*-ne-mahn.
Haile Selassie, *hy*-le-se-*lah*-sye.
Hakluyt, *hak*-loot.
Haldane, *hawl*-dayn.
Haldon, *hawl*-don.
Halévy, hah-lay-vee.
Halsbury, *hawlz*-be-re.
Hanotaux, ah-no-toh.
Hardinge, *har*-ding.
Hardouin, ar-dwaŋ.
Harpignies, ar-pee-nyee.
Haug, houkh.
Hauptman, *houpt*-mahn.
Havelock, *hav*-lok.
Hawarden, *hay*-waw-den.
Haweis, *haw*-is.

Haworth, *haw*-erth; *haw*-werth; *hou*-erth.
Haydn, *hy*-d'n; *hay*-d'n.
Hearst, herst.
Hedin, he-*deen*.
Hegel, *hay*-gel.
Heidegger, *hy*-deg-er.
Heighway, *hay*-way.
Heine, *hy*-na.
Heneage, *hen*-aj.
Hennequin, en-kaŋ.
Hepburn, *heb*'n; *heb*-urn.
Heredia, a-*ray*-thyah.
Hermione, her-*my*-o-ne.
Herriot, (Fr.) e-ryoh.
Hertz, herts.
Hertzog, *her*-tsokh.
Hervey, *har*-ve; *her*-ve.
Herzl, *her*-ts'l.
Hesychius, he-*sik*-e-us.
Heuss, hoys.
Heydrich, *hy*-drikh.
Heyse, *hy*-ze.
Hiorns, *hy*-anz.
Hirohito, *hee*-ro-*hee*-toh.
Hiroshige, *hee*-ro-*shee*-ge.
Hobbes, hobz.
Hoche, ohsh.
Hodza, *haw*-jah.
Hoey, hoy; *hoh*-e.
Hohenlohe, *hoh*-en-*loh*-e.
Hohenstaufen, *hoh*-en-*shtou*-fen.
Hokusai, ho-koo-sy.
Hölderlin, *høl*-der-leen.
Holmes, hohmz.
Home, hohm; hewm.
Homfray, *hum*-fre.
Hondecoeter, *hon*-de-*koo*-ter.
Hoogh, de, de hohkh.
Horace, *ho*-ras.
Hore-Belisha, *hor*-be-*lee*-sha.
Horthy, *hor*-te.
Hotham, *huth*-am.
Houdini, hoo-*dee*-ne.
Houdon, oo-doŋ.
Houghton, *haw*-t'n; *hou*-t'n; *hoh*-t'n.
Hrdlicka, *hur*-dlich-kah.
Hrozny, *hrawz*-ne.
Hueffer, *hef*-er.
Hughes, hewz.
Hugo, oo-*goh*; *hew*-goh.
Hulme, hewm; hoom.
Humperdinck, *hoom*-per-dink.
Huneker, *hun*-e-ker.
Hunyadi, *hoo*-nyod-e.
Huyghens, *hy*-genz; *hoy*-genz.
Huysmans, *hoys*-mahns.
Huysum, *hoy*-sum.

Ian, *ee*-an.
I'Anson, *eye*-an-son.
Ibanez, e-*bah*-nyayth.
Iddesleigh, *idz*-le.
Ignatiev, ig-*nah*-tyef.
Imredy, im-*ray*-de.
Inez, *ee*-nez.
Inge, ing.
Ingelow, *in*-je-loh.
Ingestre, *ing*-ges-tre.
Ingleby, *ing*-gl-be.
Inglis, *ing*-glz; *ing*-glis.
Ingres, aŋgr'.
Inigo, *in*-e-goh.
Innes, *in*-is.
Inouye, *ee*-no-*oo*-ye.
Iolanthe, eye-o-*lan*-the.
Ippolitov-Ivanov, ip-pu-*lyee*-tawf-e-*vah*-nawf.
Irene, eye-*ree*-ne.
Ireton, *ire*-t'n.
Isabey, ee-zah-bay.
Isidore, *iz*-e-dor.
Ivan, e-*vahn*.
Iveagh, *eye*-va.

Jacobi, ja-*koh*-be.
Jacomb, *jay*-kum.
Jacquard, zhah-kar; ja-kard.
Jacquelin, zhak-, jak-leen.
Jahangir, ja-*hahn*-geer.
Jameson, *jaym*-son; *jam*-e-son.
Jamieson, *jam*-e-son; *jim*-e-son.
Jansen, *yan*-sen; *jan*-sen.
Jaurès, zhaw-rez.
Jeritza, *ye*-ree-tsah.
Jerome, *je*-rum; je-*rohm*.
Jervis, *jar*-vis; *jer*-vis.
João, (Port.) zho-*oun*.
Joffre, zhawfr'.
Johnstone, *jon*-ston; *jon*-son.
Joinville, zhwaŋ-veel.
Jókai, *yoh*-koy.
Joliot, zhaw-lyoh.
Jomini, zhaw-mee-nee.
Jordaens, *yor*-dans.
Joubert, zhoo-bair.
Jouhaux, zhoo-oh.
Joule, jool; joul.
Jowett, *joh*-et; *jou*-et.
Jowitt, *jou*-it.
Juan, *joo*-an; (Sp.) hwahn.
Juin, zhoo-aŋ.
Jung, yoong.
Junot, zhoo-noh.

Kafka, *kahf*-kah.
Kalinin, ku-*lyee*-nyin.
Karamzin, ku-rum-*zyeen*
Kauffmann, *kouf*-mahn.
Kaulbach, *koul*-bahkh.
Kautsky, *kout*-ske.
Kavanagh, *kav*-a-nah.
Kearney, *kar*-ne.
Keble, *kee*-bl.
Keighley, *keeth*-le; *kee*-le.
Keightley, *keet*-le; *kyt*-le.
Keigwin, *keg*-win.
Keiller, *kee*-ler.
Keith, keeth.
Kekewich, *kek*-e-wich.
Keogh, ke-*oh*; kyoh.
Kennard, ke-*nard*.
Ker, kar.
Kerr, kar; ker.
Keyes, keez.
Keyne, keen.
Keynes, kaynz.
Keyser, *kee*-zer, *ky*-zer; (Belg.) kah-ee-zar.
Keyserling, *ky*-ser-ling.
Khayyam, ky-*yahm*.
Kierkegaard, *ker*-ke-gor.
Kinnaird, ke-*naird*.
Kinnoull, ke-*nool*.
Kirchhoff, *kerkh*-hof.
Kirkby, *ker*-be.
Kjerulf, *khe*-roolf.
Klaproth, *klahp*-roht.
Kléber, klay-bair.
Kneller, *nel*-er.
Knollys, nohlz.
Knowles, nohlz.
Knyvett, *niv*-et.
Kœnig, kø-*neeg*.
Koiso, (Jap.) koh-ee-soh.
Konoye, (Jap.) koh-noh-ye
Kosciusko, kos-e-*us*-koh.
Kossuth, *kos*-ooth.
Kreisler, *krys*-ler.
Kreuger, *kroo*-ger.
Kreutzer, *kroy*-tser.
Krohg, krawg.
Kropotkin, kru-*pot*-kyin.
Kruger, *kroo*-ger.
Krummacher, *kroo*-mah-kher.
Krupp, kroop.
Kubelik, *koo*-be-lik.
Kutuzov, koo-*too*-zawf.
Kyrle, kerl.

Lablache, la-*blahsh*.
Labouchère, *lab*-oo-shair.
La Bourdonnais, lah-*boor* do-*nay*.
La Bruyère, lah-broo-yair.

Lacroix, la-*krwah.*
Ladislaus, *lad*-is-laws.
Laemmle, *lem*-le.
Lætitia, le-*tish*-a.
Lafayette, lah-fah-*yet.*
Lagerlöf, *lah*-ger-løv.
Laing, lang; layng.
Lamartine, lah-mar-teen.
Lamond, *lam*-und.
Lamont, lah-mont.
Lancret, lahŋ-kray.
Lange, *lang*-a; lahŋ-e.
Langlois, lahŋ-glwah.
Lanier, lah-*neer.*
Lankester, *lang*-kes-ter.
Lannes, lahn.
Lansing, *lahn*-sing.
Lasalle, lah-sahl.
Las Cases, lahs-*kahz.*
Lascelles, *las*'lz.
Laszlo, *lahs*-loh.
Latham, *lay*-tham.
Laudon, *lou*-don.
Laue, *lou*-e.
Laughlin, *laf*-lin.
Laughton, *law*-ton.
Laurie, *law*-re; *lo*-re.
Laurier, *lo*-re-er; *lo*-re-ay.
Lautrec, loh-*trek.*
Lauzon, loh-*zøŋ.*
Laval, lah-*vahl.*
Lavater, lah-vah-ter.
Laveleye, lah-vlay.
Lavery, *lay*-ve-re.
Lavoisier, lah-vwah-zyay.
Layard, laird.
Lazenby, *lay*-zen-be.
Lebedev, *lyay*-bye-dyef.
Lebrun, le-brøŋ.
Leclerc, le-klair.
Le Corbusier, le-kor-boo-zyay.
Lecouvreur, le-koo-vrør.
Lederer, (Ger.) *lay*-de-rer.
Lefanu, le-fe-new.
Lefebvre, le-*fai(r)vr'.*
Lefevre, le-*fee*-ver.
Legendre, le-*zhahŋ*-dr'.
Legouis, le-gwee.
Lehmann, *lay*-m'n; (Ger.) *lay*-mahn; (Dan.) *lee*-mahn.
Leibl, *ly*-bl.
Leibnitz, *lyp*-nits.
Leidy, *ly*-de.
Leigh, lee.
Leighton, *lay*-ton.
Leishman, lish-man.
Leiston, *lay*-ston.
Leitch, leech.
Lely, *lee*-le.
Lemaistre, le-*maytr.*
Lemesurier, le-*mezh*-er-ra.
Lemprière, lahŋ-pree-air; *lem*-pre-er.
Le Nain, le-*naŋ.*
Lenclos, lahŋ-kloh.
Lenglen, laŋ-glen.
Leonard, *len*-erd.
Leonardo, lay-o-*nar*-doh.
Leoncavallo, lay-ohn-ka-*vah*-loh.
Leonora, lee-o-*naw*-ra.
Leopardi, lay-o-*par*-de.
Le Queux, le-*kew.*
Lermontov, *lyair*-mun-tawf.
Leroux, le-*roo.*
Le Sueur, le-soo-ur.
Leszczyńska, lesh-*chin*-skah.
Leverhulme, *lee*-ver-hewm.
Leveson-Gower, *lew*-s'n-*gawr.*
Levine, le-*veen.*
Liebermann, *lee*-ber-mahn.
Liebig, *lee*-bikh, -big.
Liebknecht, leep-k'nekht.
Ligne, leen'.
Liliencron, *lee*-le-en-krohn.
Lilienthal, *lee*-le-en-tahl; *lil*-e-an-tahl.
Linacre, *lin*-a-ker.
Lindsay, *lin*-ze.
Lisle, leel; lyl.
Llewellyn, loo-*el*-in.
Llorente, (Sp.) lyoh-*rayn*-ta.
Loewe, *loh*-e; *lø*-ve.
Loewi, *lø*-ve.
Loisy, lwah-zee.
Lotse, *loht*-se.
Loubet, loo-bay.
Louis, *loo*-is; (Fr.) loo-e.
Louisa, loo-*ee*-za.
Lowell, *loh*-el.
Loyola, *loy*-o-lah.
Ludwig, *loot*-vikh.
Lumière, loo-myair.
Lupino, loo-*pee*-noh.
Lutyens, *lutch*-enz; lut-yenz.
Lyautey, lyoh-tay.
Lygon, *lig*-on.
Lyttleton, *litl*-t'n.
Lyveden, *liv*-den.

Mabillon, mah-bee-yoŋ.
Mabuse, mah-*booz.*
McAllister, ma-*kal*-is-ter.
McAra, ma-*kah*-ra.
Macaulay, ma-*kaw*-le.
Macbean, mak-*bayn.*
McConochie, ma-*kon*-o-khe.
McCrae, ma-*kray.*
McCrea, ma-*kray.*
McEchran, ma-*kee*-kran.
Macgillicuddy, *mag*'l-kud-e; ma-*gil*-e-kud-e.
Macgillivray, ma-*gil*-e-vray.
McGuire, ma-*gwyr.*
Mach, mahkh.
Machado, (Port.) mah-*shah*-thoo.
Machen, *mak*-en; *may*-ch'n.
Machiavelli, mah-kyah-*vel*-e.
McIntosh, *mak*-in-tosh.
McIntyre, *mak*-in-tyr.
Mackay, ma-*ky*; ma-*kay.*
McKeag, ma-*keeg.*
Maclachlan, ma-*klokh*-lan.
McLaughlin, ma-*klokh*-lin.
Maclean, ma-*klayn*; ma-*kleen.*
Macleay, ma-*klay.*
Maclehose, *mak*-le-hohz.
Macleod, ma-*kloud.*
Maclise, ma-*kleez.*
Macmahon, mak-*mahn*; (Fr.) mahk-mah-*awn.*
Macnaghten, mak-*naw*-t'n.
Macnamara, *mak*-na-*mah*-ra.
Maconochie, ma-*kon*-o-ke.
Macquarie, ma-*kwo*-re.
Macready, ma-*kree*-de.
Macveagh, mak-*vay.*
McVitie, mak-*vit*-e.
Madariaga, ma-*dah*-re-*ah*-ga.
Maes, (Dut.) mahs.
Maeterlinck, *may*-ter-link.
Magdalen(e), *mag*-de-len; (Coll.) *mawd*-lin.
Magellan, ma-*gel*-an.
Magendie, mah-zhaŋ-dee.
Magheramorne, mah-ra-*morn.*
Maginot, mah-zhee-noh.
Maguire, ma-*gwyr.*
Mahaffy, ma-*haf*-e.
Mahon, mahn; ma-*hohn.*
Mahony, *mah*-o-ne; *mah*-ne.
Maimonides, my-*mon*-e-deez.

Maintenon, maŋt-noŋ.
Mainwaring, *man*-er-ring.
Maisky, *my*-ske.
Maistre, *mes*-tr'; maytr.
Majendie, *madj*-en-de.
Malcolm, *mal*-kum.
Malebranche, mahl-brahŋsh.
Malesherbes, mahl-zerb.
Malherbe, mah-lerb.
Malinowski, *mah*-le-*nawf*-ske.
Mallarmé, mah-lar-may.
Malpighi, mahl-*pee*-ge.
Mancini, mahn-*chee*-ne.
Mandel, (Fr.) mahŋ-del.
Manet, mah-nay.
Maniu, mah-*nyoo*.
Mansergh, *man*-ser.
Mantegna, mahn-*tay*-nyah.
Manteuffel, mahn-toy-fel.
Manwaring, *man*-er-ing.
Mapother, *may*-poth-er.
Marat, (Fr.) mah-rah.
Marchesi, mar-*kay*-ze.
Margot, *mar*-goh.
Marinetti, mah-re-*nayt*-te.
Maritain, mah-ree-taŋ.
Marivaux, mah-ree-voh.
Marjoribanks, *march*-banks.
Marochetti, *mah*-ro-*kayt*-te.
Marot, ma-roh.
Marquet, mar-kay.
Martineau, *mar*-te-noh.
Martini, mar-*tee*-ne.
Masaccio, mah-*zaht*-choh.
Masaryk, *mah*-sa-rik.
Mascagni, mahs-*kah*-nye.
Masséna, mah-say-nah.
Massenet, mahs-nay.
Massillon, mah-see-yoŋ.
Massinger, *mas*-in-jer.
Matheson, *math*-e-son.
Matisse, mah-tees.
Matsuoka, mah-tsoo-oh-ka.
Matsys, *mat*-sis.
Matthey, *mat*-he.
Maturin, *mat*-yoo-rin.
Maughan, mawn.
Maultasch, *moul*-tahsh.
Maupassant, moh-pa-sahn.
Maupertuis, moh-per-too-e.
Maurepas, mor-pah.
Maurois, mo-rwah.
Mauve, (Dut.) *mou*-ve.
Maxse, *mak*-se.
Mazarin, mah-zah-raŋ.
Mazzini, maht-*tsee*-ne.
Mechnikov, metch-nee-*kawf*.
Medici, *med*-e-chee.
Megan, *meg*-an.
Mehta, *may*-tah.
Meighen, *mee*-en.
Meigs, megz.
Meiklejohn, *mik*-el-jon.
Meissonnier, may-so-nyay.
Melhuish, *mel*-ish; *mel*-yoo-ish.
Mendeleyev, myen-dye-*lyay*-lef.
Mendelssohn, *men*-del-sohn.
Mendès, maŋ-dez.
Menpes, *mem*-pis; *men*-pis.
Menzies, *men*-ziz; *men*-jiz; *ming*-iz.
Meredith, *me*-re-dith.
Merimee, may-ree-may.
Mesdag, (Dut.) *mes*-dahkh.
Messager, me-sah-zhay.
Mestrovic, *mesh*-tro-*vik*.
Metastasio, *may*-tah-*stah*-zyo.
Metaxas, me-tah-*ksahs*.
Methuen, *meth*-win; *meth*-yoo-en.
Meunier, mø-nyay.
Meux, mewz, mewks.
Meyer, *my*-er.
Meyerbeer, *my*-er-beer.
Meyrick, *me*-rik; *may*-rik.
Michelet, meesh-le.
Michelham, *mitch*-lam.
Michelin, meesh-laŋ.
Mickiewicz, mets-*kye*-vech.
Mignet, mee-nye.
Miguel, me-*gel*.
Mihailovich, me-*hy*-lo-vich.
Mikolajczyk, me-ko-*ly*-jik.
Milanesi, mee-lah-*nay*-se.
Milhaud, mee-yoh.
Millais, *mil*-ay.
Millerand, meel-rahŋ.
Millet, (Fr.) mee-lay.
Milnes, milz; milnz.
Mirabeau, mee-rah-boh.
Mirandola, me-*rahn*-do-la.
Mistral, mees-*trahl*.
Modigliani, mo-dee-*lyah*-ne.
Mohammed, mo-*ham*-ed.
Mohun, moon.
Moleyns, *mul*-inz.
Molière, moh-le-air.
Moltke, *mohlt*-keh.
Molyneux, *mol*-, *mul*-e-newks; (Fr.) mol-e-*nø*.
Mommsen, *mom*-zen.
Monck, munk.
Monckton, *munk*-ton.
Moncreiff, mun-*kreef*.
Monet, mo-nay.
Monro, *mun*-roh; mun-*roh*.
Monson, *mun*-son.
Montagu, *mon*-, *mun*-ta-*gew*.
Montaigne, moŋ-tayn.
Montalembert, moŋ-ta-lahŋ-bair.
Montcalm, *mont*-kahm.
Montecucculi, *mon*-ta-*koo*-koo-le.
Montefiore, *mon*-te-fe-*aw*-re.
Monteith, mon-*teeth*.
Montemayor, *mon*-ta-mah-*yor*.
Montespan, moŋ-tes-pahn.
Montesquieu, moŋ-tes-kyoo.
Montessori, mohn-tas-*saw*-re.
Montgomery, mun(t)-*gum*-er-re.
Montmorency, *mont*-mo-*ren*-se.
Montpensier, moŋ-pahŋ-syay.
Monzie, *mon*-ze; mo-*nee*.
Morales, mo-*rah*-lace.
Mordaunt, *mor*-d'nt.
Moreau, mo-roh.
Morgenthau, *mor*-gen-tou.
Morier, *mo*-re-ay.
Mortier, mor-tyay.
Moscheles, *mosh*-e-les; *mosh*-lees.
Moscicki, mos-*cheets*-ke.
Mosenthal, *moh*-zen-tahl.
Mosheim, *mos*-hym.
Mosley, *mohz*-le; *moz*-le.
Mouat(t), *moh*-at.
Moussorgsky, moo-*sorg*-ske.
Mowatt, *moh*-at; *mou*-at.
Mozart, *moh*-tsart.
Muloch, *mew*-lok.
Munch, (Norw.) moonk.
Münchausen, *mønkh*-hou-zen.

Muni, mew-ne.
Munkácsy, *moon*-kah-che.
Munthe, (Swed.) *mun*-teh.
Murat, moo-rah.
Muraviev, moo-ruf-*yawf.*
Murillo, moo-*ril*-yoh.
Muschamp, *mus*-kam.
Muselier, moo-ze-lyay.
Musset, (Fr.) moo-say.
Mustapha, *mus*-ta-fah.

Nagel, *nah*-gel.
Naidu, (Hind.) *nah*-e-doo.
Nankivell, nan-*kiv*-el.
Napier, *nay*-peer.
Nasmyth, *nayz*-mith.
Nattier, nah-tyay.
Naumann, *nou*-mahn.
Neander, na-*ahn*-der.
Negri, *nay*-gre.
Nehru, *nay*-roo.
Nernst, (Ger.) nernst.
Neumann, *noy*-mahn.
Neumayer, *noy*-my-er.
Neurath, *noy*-raht.
Newcombe, *new*-kum.
Newcomen, *new*-ko-men; new-*kum*-en.
Nicolai, (Ger.) *nee*-ko-*lah*-e.
Niebuhr, *nee*-boor.
Niehaus, *nee*-hous.
Niel, (Fr.) nyel.
Nielsen, *neel*-s'n.
Niemöller, *nee*-møl-er.
Niepce, (Fr.) nyeps.
Nietzche, *nee*-cha.
Nigel, *ny*-jel; *nee*-jel.
Nijinsky, ne-*zhin*-ske; (Russ.) nye-*zheen*-ske.
Nikisch, *nee*-kish.
Nimzowitsch, nim-*tsoh*-vich.
Ninon, nee-noŋ.
Nitti, (It.) *neet*-te.
Noailles, noh-ah-e.
Nobel, noh-*bel.*
Nöldeke, *nøl*-de-ke.
Nollekens, *nol*-e-kinz.
Nordenskjöld, *noor*-den-shøld.
Norreys, *no*-ris.
Novalis, no-*vah*-lis.
Núñez, (Sp.) *noo*-nyayth; (S. Amer.) *noo*-nyace.
Nuttall, *nut*-awl.
Nygaardsvold, (Norw.) *noo*-gars-vohl.

Obolenski, u-bu-*lyayn*-ske.
Obrenovich, o-*bren*-o-vich.
Ochterlony, *okh*-ter-*loh*-ne.
Odoacer, oh-do-*ay*-seer.
Offenbach, *of*-en-bahkh.
O'Flaherty, o-*flair*-te; o-*flay*-er-te.
Ogilby, *ohgl*-be.
Ogilvie, *ohgl*-ve.
O'Hara, o-*hah*-ra; o-*hair*-ra.
Olivarez, oh-le-*vah*-race.
Opie, *oh*-pe.
Orcagna, or-*kah*-nya.
Orczy, *or*-tse.
Orellana, oh-ra-*lyay*-nah.
Origen, *o*-re-jen.
O'Riordan, oh-*ry*-or-dan.
Orsini, or-*see*-ne.
Osbaldistone, oz-bal-*dis*-ton.
Osler, *ohz*-ler.
Ossietzky, os-e-*ets*-ke.
Ostade, os-*tah*-de.
Ostwald, *ost*-vahlt.
Oswald, *oz*-wald.
Oudinot, oo-dee-noh.
Oughtred, *awt*-, *ot*-, *oht*-red.
Ouida, *wee*-da.
Ouimet, *wee*-met.
Ouless, *oo*-lis.
Ouseley, *ooz*-le; (U.S.A.) *ouz*-le.
Owbridge, *oh*-bridj.
Owen, *oh*-en.

Pacheko, pah-*chay*-koh.
Pachmann, *pahkh*-mahn.
Paderewski, pa-de-*ref*-ske.
Paes, (Port.) pysh.
Paganini, pah-gah-*nee*-ne.
Paget, *paj*-et.
Painlevé, paŋ-l'-vay.
Pakenham, *pak*-en-am.
Palacky, (Czech.) *pah*-lahts-kee.
Palairet, *pal*-a-ret.
Palestrina, *pal*-es-*tree*-na.
Palgrave, *pawl*-grayv; *pal*-grayv.
Palissy, pa-*lee*-see.
Palmer, *pah*-mer.
Panizzi, pah-*neet*-tse.
Paoli, *pah*-oh-lee.
Papen, *pah*-pen.
Pareja, (Sp.) pah-*ray*-hah.
Parmigianino, *par*-mee-jah-*nee*-noh.
Parnell, par-*nel.*
Pasquier, pah-kyay.
Pasteur, pahs-tur.
Paton, *pay*-ton.
Paulhan, (Fr.) paw-lahn.
Paulus, (Ger.) *pou*-loos.
Pauncefote, *pawnce*-foot.
Pavlov, *pah*-vlawf.
Pavlova, *pah*-vlo-vu.
Pégoud, pay-goo.
Péguy, pay-gee.
Pélissier, pay-lee-syay.
Pellew, pe-*lew.*
Pennefather, *pen*-e-*fah*-ther.
Pepusch, *pay*-poosh.
Pepys, *pep*-is; peps; (the diarist) peeps.
Pereira, pe-*ray*-ra; (Port.) pe-*ray*-e-ra.
Pergolesi, par-goh-*lay*-se.
Périer, pay-ryay.
Perrault, pe-roh.
Perrier, (Fr.) pe-ryay.
Perthes, *per*-tes.
Perugino, *pay*-roo-*jee*-noh
Peruzzi, pa-*root*-se.
Pestalozzi, *pes*-tah-*lot*-se.
Pétain, pay-taŋ.
Petrarch, *pee*-trark.
Petre, *pee*-ter.
Petrie, *pee*-tre; *pet*-re.
Petulengro, *pet*-yoo-*leng*-groh.
Peutinger, (Ger.) *poy*-ting-*er.*
Peyrouton, pay-roo-toŋ.
Phayre, fair.
Picard, pee-kar.
Picasso, pe-*kah*-soh.
Piccolomini, *peek*-ko-*loh*-me-ne.
Pichegru, peesh-groo.
Pierre, pyair.
Pilsudski, pil-*soot*-ske.
Pinero, pe-*neer*-roh.
Pinturicchio, *peen*-too-*reek*-kyoh.
Piozzi, pe-*ot*-tse.
Piranesi, *pee*-rah-*nay*-se.
Pissaro, pee-sah-roh.
Pitcairn, pit-*kairn.*
Planck, plahnk.
Plekhanov, ple-*khah*-nawf.
Pleyel, *ply*-el; play-*yel.*
Pliny, *plin*-e.
Plumptre, *plum*-tre.
Plutarch, *ploo*-tark.
Poe, poh.
Poel, pohl.
Pogany, po-*gah*-ne.
Poincare, pwaŋ-kah-ray.
Polignac, po-*lee*-nyak.
Poliziano, *poh*-le-*tsyah*-noh.

Polk, pohk.
Pollaiuolo, *pohl*-ly-*waw*-loh.
Pomfret, *pum*-fret.
Pompadour, poŋ-pah-door.
Poniatowski, *paw*-nyah-*tawf*-ske.
Ponsonby, *pun*-sun-be.
Popham, *pop*-am.
Pordenone, por-da-*noh*-na.
Portaels, (Belg.) por-tahls.
Porte(o)us, *por*-te-us.
Potemkin, pu-*tyom*-kyin.
Potocki, po-*tots*-ke.
Poughill, *pof*-il.
Poulett, *paw*-let.
Poultney, *pohlt*-ne.
Poussin, poo-saŋ.
Powell, *pou*-el; *poh*-el.
Powis, Powys, *poh*-is.
Praed, *prayd*.
Praga, *prah*-gah.
Prendergast, *pren*-der-gahst.
Prevost, *prev*-oh; *prev*-ohst.
Prévost, pray-voh.
Prideaux, *prid*-oh.
Prieto, pre-*ay*-toh.
Primo, *pree*-moh.
Prjevalsky, per-zhe-*vahl*-ske.
Prokofiev, pru-*kawf*-yef.
Prokosch, *proh*-kosh.
Proudhon, proo-doŋ.
Proust, proost.
Prud'homme, proo-dom.
Prynne, prin.
Przhevalsky, per-zhe-*vahl*-ske.
Psalmanazar, *sal*-ma-*naz*-ar.
Puccini, poot-*chee*-ne.
Pugachev, poo-gu-*chawf*.
Puget, poo-*zhay*.
Pugh, pew.
Pugin, *pew*-jin; (Fr.) poo-zhaŋ.
Pujo, poo-*zhoh*.
Pulitzer, *pool*-it-ser.
Pulteney, *pult*-ne; *pohlt*-ne.
Pusey, *pew*-ze.
Pushkin, *poosh*-kyin.
Puvis de Chavannes, poo-vee-de-shah-vahn.
Pym, pim.

Quaritch, *kwo*-ritch.
Quarles, kworlz.
Quatrefages, kah-tre-fahzh.
Quekett, *kwek*-et.
Quenell, kwe-*nel*.
Quesnay, ka-nay.
Quesnel, ke-nel.
Quetelet, kay-tlay.
Queuille, kay'e.
Quevedo, ka-*vay*-thoh.
Quezon, *kay*-son.
Quicherat, keesh-rah.
Quidde, (Ger.) *kvid*-a.
Quiller-Couch, *kwil*-er-*kooch*.
Quinault, kee-*noh*. *kwin*'lt.
Quincy, *kwin*-se.
Quinet, kee-nay.
Quinette, kee-*net*.
Quintana, keen-*tah*-nah.
Quintero, keen-*tah*-roh.
Quiros, ke-*rosh*.
Quistorp, (Ger.) *kwis*-torp.
Quixote, *kwik*-sut; (Sp.) kee-*hoh*-ta.

Raabe, (Ger.) *rah*-beh.
Rabaud, ra-boh.
Rabelais, *rab*-e-lay; (Fr.) rah-blay.
Rachel, *ray*-chel; (Fr.) rah-shel.
Rachmaninov, rukh-*mah*-nye-nawf.
Racine, rah-seen.
Raczkiewicz, rahch-*kye*-vech.
Radetzky, rah-*dets*-ke.
Radziwill, rah-*jee*-veel.
Rae, ray.
Raemaekers, *rah*-mah-kers.
Raimondi, ry-*mohn*-de.
Rajagopalachariar, *rah*-jah-go-*pah*-lah-*chah*-re-ar.
Rákóczy, rah-*koh*-tse.
Raleigh, *raw*-le; *rah*-le; *ral*-e.
Ralph, ralf; rayf; rahf.
Ralston, *rawl*-ston.
Rameau, rah-moh.
Ranke, *rahng*-keh.
Raoul, rah-*ool*.
Raphael, *raf*-ay-el; *raf*-ayl.
Rapin, rah-paŋ.
Rasmussen, *rahs*-moo-s'n.
Raspe, (Ger.) *rahs*-pa.
Rasputin, rus-*poo*-tyin.
Rathenau, *rah*-te-nou.
Rauch, roukh.
Rauschning, *roush*-ning.
Ravaillac, rah-vah-yahk.
Ravel, rah-vel.
Rayleigh, *ray*-le.
Read(e), reed.
Réaumur, ray-oh-moor.
Reay, ray.
Récamier, ray-kah-myay.
Rees, reece.
Reger, (Ger.) *ray*-ger.
Regnault, rah-nyoh.
Rehan, ree-an.
Reichenau, *ry*-khe-nou.
Reid, reed.
Reilly, *ry*-le.
Reinhardt, *ryn*-hart.
Reinke, *ryng*-ka.
Reiss, rice.
Reith, reeth.
Reitz, raytz.
Réjane, ray-zhahn.
Rembrandt, *rem*-brant.
Rémusat, ray-moo-zah.
Renan, re-nahŋ.
Renault, *ren*-oh; (Fr.) re-noh.
Reni, ray-ne.
Renoir, re-nwahr.
Rentoul, *ren*-tool.
Renwick, *ren*-ik; *ren*-wik.
Repin, (Russ.) *ryay*-pyin.
Reshevsky, re-*shef*-ske.
Respighi, ra-*spee*-ge
Restif, ray-teef.
Rethel, (Ger.) *ray*-tel.
Reuchlin, *roykh*-leen.
Reuter, *roy*-ter.
Reynaud, ray-noh.
Reynolds, *ren*-uldz.
Rhys, reece.
Ribera, re-*bay*-rah.
Ricci, *reet*-che.
Richelieu, ree-she-lyoo.
Richepin, reesh-paŋ.
Richter, (Ger.) *rikh*-ter; (Fr.) reesh-tair.
Richtofen, *rikht*-hoh-fen.
Riddell, ridl; re-*del*.
Riebeeck, *ree*-bayk.
Riel, ryel.
Rienzi, *ryen*-tse.
Rietz, reets.
Rigaud, ree-goh.
Riis, reece.
Rilke, *ril*-ka.
Rimbaud, raŋ-boh.
Rimsky-Korsakov, *ryeem*-ske-kur-su-*kawf*.
Rintelen, *rin*-te-len.
Rioja, *ryoh*-hah.
Ristori, re-*staw*-re.

Ritschl, *rich*-el.
Rizzio, *rit*-se-oh; (It.) *reet*-syoh.
Robeson, *rohb*-son.
Robespierre, rohbz-pyair.
Robles, (Sp.) *roh*-blays.
Roche, rohch; rosh.
Rochefoucauld, rohsh-foo-koh.
Rockefeller, *rok*-e-*fel*-er.
Rodin, roh-daŋ.
Roget, roh-*zhay*.
Rohan, ro-ahŋ.
Roland, *roh*-lund.
Rolland, rol-lahŋ.
Rolleston, *rol*-ston.
Rollin, rol-laŋ.
Romains, ro-maŋ.
Romanes, ro-*mah*-niz.
Romanov, ru-*mah*-nawf.
Romilly, *rom*-e-le.
Romney, *rum*-ne.
Ronsard, roŋ-sar.
Röntgen, (Ger.) *rønt*-gen.
Roosevelt, *roh*-ze-velt.
Rootham, *roo*-tum.
Rossini, ros-*see*-ne.
Rostand, ros-tahŋ.
Rothes, roths.
Rouault, rwoh.
Roubiliac, roo-bee-yahk.
Rouget de Lisle, roo-zhay-de-leel.
Rousseau, roo-soh.
Roussel, roo-sel.
Roux, roo.
Rowe, roh.
Rowton, *rou*-ton.
Roxas, *roh*-hahs.
Rubens, *roo*-benz.
Ruhmkorff, *room*-korf.
Rundstedt, *roont*-shtet.
Ruthven, *rooth*-ven; *riv*-en.
Ruysdael, *roys*-dahl.
Ruyter, *ry*-ter.

Saavedra, *sah*-ah-*vay*-thrah.
Sabatier, sah-bah-tyay.
Sabine, *sab*-in; *sab*-yn.
Sadleir, *sad*-ler.
St. Clair, *sing*-klair.
Sainte-Beuve, saŋt-*bøv*.
Saint-Évremond, saŋ-*tay*-vre-moŋ.
Saint-Gaudens, s'nt-*gaw*-d'nz.
St. John, *sin*-jon.
St. Laurent, saŋ-lo-*raŋ*.
St. Leger, s'nt-lej-er; *sil*-en-jer.
Saint-Pierre, saŋ-*pyair*.
Saint-Saëns, saŋ-*sahŋs*.
Saint-Simon, saŋ-see-*moŋ*.
Salazar, sa-lah-*zar*.
Salmon, *sam*-on; *sal*-mon.
Saltoun, *sawl*-ton.
Salvini, sahl-*vee*-ne.
Sancho, (Sp.) *sahŋ*-choh; (Port.) *san*-shoo.
Sandow, *san*-doh.
Sanger, *sang*-ger.
Sannazaro, *sahn*-nah-*dzah*-roh.
Sansovino, *sahn*-so-*vee*-noh.
Santayana, *sahn*-tah-*yah*-nah.
Santerre, sahŋ-tair.
Sarasate, *sah*-rah-*sah*-tay.
Sardou, sar-doo.
Sarolea, sa-rohl-ya.
Saroyan, sah-roh-yahn.
Satow, *sah*-toh.
Sandys, sandz.
Sauckel, *zou*-kel.
Sau(s)marez, *som*-a-rez.
Saussure, soh-soor.
Scaliger, *skal*-e-jer.
Scarbrough, *skar*-bra.
Scarlatti, skar-*laht*-te.
Scharlieb, *shar*-leeb.
Scheele, *shay*-le.
Scheemakers, *skay*-may-kerz.
Schelling, *shel*-ing.
Schiaparelli, skyah-pah-*rel*-le.
Schicklgruber, *shik*'l-groo-ber.
Schiller, *shil*-er
Schjelderup, *shel*-droop.
Schlegel, *shlay*-gel.
Schleiermacher, *shly*-er-*mah*-kher.
Schlemikl, shla-*meel*.
Schliemann, *shlee*-mahn.
Schmeling, *shmay*-ling.
Schneider, *shny*-der.
Schongauer, *shohn*-gou-er.
Schopenhauer, *shoh*-pen-*hou*-er.
Schröder, *shrø*-der.
Schubert, *shoo*-bert.
Schumann, *shoo*-mahn.
Schuschnigg, *shoosh*-nik.
Schuyler, *sky*-ler.
Schwab, (Ger.) shvahp; (U.S.A.) shwob, shwawb.
Schwabe, *shvah*-be.
Schweitzer, *shvy*-tser.
Schwind, shvint.
Scriabin, *skree*-a-bin.
Scribe, (Fr.) skreeb.
Scrimgeour, *skrim*-jer.
Seamus, *shay*-mus.
Sean, shawn.
Secchi, *sayk*-kee.
Seeckt, zaykt.
Seignobos, say-nyoh-bos.
Selous, se-*loo*.
Seurat, soo-rah.
Sévigné, say-vee-nyay.
Seward, *see*-werd; *sew*-ard.
Sewell, *sew*-el.
Seymour, *see*-mor; *say*-mor.
Seyss-Inquart, zys-*ing*-kvart.
Sforza, *sfor*-tsah.
Shaughnessy, *shaw*-ne-se.
Shove, shohv.
Shuvalov, shoo-*vah*-lawf.
Sidebotham, *syd*-bot-am.
Siegfried, (Ger.) *zeekh*-freet.
Siemens, (Ger.) *zee*-mens; (Engl.) *see*-menz.
Sienkiewicz, shen-*kye*-vech.
Sieyès, *syay*-yaz.
Sigismund, *sij*-is-mund.
Signac, see-nyahk.
Signorelli, *see*-nyo-*rel*-le.
Sigourney, *sig*-er-ne.
Sikorski, she-*kors*-ke.
Sinatra, se-*nah*-tra.
Skobelev, *skaw*-bye-lyef.
Skrine, skreen.
Slawek, *slah*-vek.
Smetana, *sme*-tah-nah.
Smigly-Rydz, *smeeg*-le-*rits*.
Smyth(e), smythe; smyth; smith
Sodoma, *saw*-do-mah.
Solander, so-*lan*-der; (Swed.) soo-*lahn*-der.
Sombart, *zom*-bart.
Somers, *sum*-erz.
Somerville, *sum*-er-vil.
Sophoulis, so-*foo*-lis.
Sotheby, *su*-the-be.
Sothern, *su*-thern.
Soubise, soo-beez.
Soult, soolt.
Sousa, *soo*-sah; (Port.) *soh*-zah.
Soutar, *soo*-ter.
Souter, *soo*-ter.
Southey, *sou*-the.
Sowerby, *soh*-er-be.

Soyer, swah-yay.
Spaatz, spahts.
Spee, (Ger.) shpay.
Speirs, speerz.
Spengler, *shpeng*-ler.
Spiegel, *shpee*-gel.
Spinoza, spe-*noh*-za.
Spitteler, *shpit*-e-ler.
Spohr, *shpoh'*r.
Spurzheim, *shpoorts*-hym.
Squarcione, skwar-*choh*-na.
Stahmer, *shtah*-mer.
Stakhanov, stu-*khah*-nawf.
Stalin, *stah*-lyeen.
Starace, (It.) stah-*rah*-cha.
Stauning, (Dan.) *stou*-ning.
Steen, steen; (Dut.) stayn.
Stein, styn; (Ger.) shtyn.
Steiner, *shty*-ner.
Stepniak, styip-*nyahk*.
Steyn, stayn; steen.
Stinnes, *shtin*-es.
Stokowski, sto-*kawf*-ske.
Stolypin, stu-*li*-pyeen.
Stoughton, *stou-*, *stoh-*, *staw*-t'n.
Stowe, stoh.
Stowell, *stoh*-el.
Stoyadinovich, *stoh*-yah-*dee*-no-vich.
Strabolgi, stra-*boh*-ge.
Strachan, strawn.
Strachey, *stray*-che.
Strasser, *shtrahs*-er.
Strauss, strous; (Ger.) shtrous.
Streatfield, *stret*-feeld.
Streicher, *shtry*-kher.
Stresemann, *shtray*-ze-mahn.
Strozzi, *strawt*-tse.
Strube, *shtroo*-be.
Strzygowski, sche-*gawf*-ske.
Stucley, *stew*-kle.
Studebaker, *stew*-de-*bay*-ker.
Stumpf, shtoompf.
Stuyvesant, *sty*-ve-s'nt; (Dut.) *stoy*-ve-sahnt.
Suchet, soo-shay.
Sudermann, *zoo*-der-mahn.
Sully, (Fr.) soo-lee.
Suppé, zoop-pay.
Sutro, soo-troh.
Svinhufvud, *sveen*-hoo-vood.
Swannerdam, *svahm*-er-dahm.
Swanwick, *swon*-ik.
Swetchine, svye-*cheen*.
Swete, sweet.
Sweyn, swayn.
Swynnerton, *swin*-er-ton.
Sydenham, *sid*-en-am.
Synge, sinj.

Taaffe, *tah*-fe.
Tadema, *tad*-e-ma.
Taft, taft.
Tagliacozzi, tah-lyah-*kot*-tse.
Taglioni, tah-*lyoh*-ne.
Taine, ten.
Talbot, *tawl*-bot.
Taliesin, tal-e-*es*-in.
Talleyrand, *tal*-e-rand; (Fr.) tah-lay-rahŋ.
Talmage, *tal*-maj.
Tangye, *tang*-ge.
Tannhäuser, *tahn*-hoy-zer.
Tardieu, tar-dyø.
Tartini, tar-*tee*-ne.
Tauber, *tou*-ber.
Tauchnitz, *toukh*-nits.
Taussig, *tou*-sig.
Tchaikovsky, chy-*kawf*-ske.
Tchekhov, *chay*-kawf.
Teichman, *tych*-man.
Teleki, *tel*-e-ke.
Teniers, *ten*-yerz; (Flem.) te-neers.
Tenniel, *ten*-yel.
Ter Borch, ter-*borkh*.
Tertius, *ter*-she-us.
Tettrazzini, *tay*-traht-*tsee*-ne.
Teuffel, toy-fel.
Teynham, *ten*-ham.
Teyte, tayt.
Thalberg, *tahl*-berkh.
Thayer, thair.
Thelluson, *tel*-e-s'n.
Theobald, *thee*-o-bawld; *tib*-ald.
Theresa, te-*ree*-za; (Sp.), ta-*ray*-sah.
Thesiger, *thes*-e-jer.
Theunis, tø-*nees*.
Thévenot, tayv-noh.
Thibault, tee-boh.
Thiers, tyayr.
Thom, tom.
Thoma, (Ger.) *toh*-mah.
Thomas, *tom*-as; (Fr.) to-mahs; (Ger.) *tom*-as.
Thomé, to-*may*.
Thompson, *tom*-son.
Thoms, tomz.
Thoreau, *thaw*-roh.
Thorez, taw-ray.
Thorough-, Thorowgood, *thu*-ro-good.
Thorwaldsen, *toor*-vald-s'n.
Thugut, too-goot.
Thuillier, *twil*-yer.
Thwing, twing.
Thynne, thin.
Thyssen, *tis*-en.
Tieck, teek.
Tiepolo, *tya*-po-loh.
Tierney *teer*-ne.
Tietjens, *tee*-j'ns.
Tighe, ty.
Tikhon, *tyee*-khon.
Tilghman, *til*-man.
Tillemont, tee-e-moŋ.
Timoshenko, tyim-u-*shai(r)n*-koh.
Tinayre, tee-*nair*.
Tintoretto, *teen*-to-*raht*-to.
Tiraboschi, *tee*-rah-*bos*-ke.
Tiso, *tyi*-soh.
Tisserand, tees-rahŋ.
Tissot, tee-soh.
Titian, *tish*-e-an.
Titulescu, tee-too-*les*-koo.
Tocqueville, tok-veel.
Todleben, *tot*-lyeb-en.
Toland, *toh*-land.
Tollemache, *tol*-mash.
Tomline, *tom*-lin.
Tommasini, *tohm*-mah-*see*-ne.
Torphichen, tor-*fik*-en.
Torquemada, *tor*-kwe-*mah*-da; (Sp.) *tor*-ka-*mah*-thah.
Torricelli, *tor*-re-*chel*-le.
Toscanini, (It.) *tohs*-kah-*nee*-ne.
Toumey, *too*-me.
Tourneur, *tur*-ner.
Toussaint l'Ouverture, too-saŋ-loo-ver-toor.
Towns(h)end, *townz*-end.
Trampleasure, *tram*-pl-shoor.
Traubel, *trou*-bel.
Tredegar, tre-*dee*-ga.
Trefusis, tre-*few*-sis.
Treitschke, *trych*-keh.
Trevelyan, tre-*vel*-yan.
Treves, treevz.
Trevithick, *trev*-e-thik.

Trevor, *trev*-or.
Trimlestown, trim-*les*-toun.
Trobridge, *troh*-bridj.
Troubridge, *troo*-bridj.
Troughton, *trou*-t'n.
Trowbridge, *troh*-bridj.
Troyon, trwah-yoŋ.
Trujillo, troo-*hee*-yoh.
Tschudi, *choo*-de.
Tschuy, *choo*-e.
Tudor, *tew*-dor.
Tumulty, *tum*-ul-te.
Tuohy, *too*-e.
Turenne, too-ren.
Turgenev, toor-*gyay*-nyef.
Turgot, toor-goh.
Tussaud, too-soh.
Twamley, *twom*-le.
Tweedsmuir, *tweedz*-mewr.
Tyldesley, *tildz*-le.
Tymms, timz.
Tyndall, *tin*-dal.
Tyrconnel, ter-*kon*-el.
Tyrrell, *ti*-rel.
Tyrwhitt, *ti*-rit.
Tytler, *tyt*-ler.

Uccello, oot-*chel*-loh.
Udall, *yew*-dal.
Ugolino, *oo*-go-*lee*-noh.
Uhde, *oo*-deh.
Uhland, *oo*-lahnt.
Ulfilas, *ul*-fe-las.
Ulloa, (Sp.) oo-*lyoh*-ah.
Ulrich, *ool*-rikh.
Unamuno, *oo*-nah-*moo*-noh.
Undset, *oon*-set.
Uniacke, *yew*-ne-ak.
Untermeyer, *un*-ter-*my*-er.
Upham, *up*-h'm.
Uprichard, *yew*-pritch-erd.
Ure, yoor.
Urquhart, *er*-ket; *er*-kart.
Usedom, (Ger.) *oo*-ze-dom.
Uspenski, oo-*spyayn*-ske.
Utamaro, (Jap.) *oo*-tah-*mah*-roh.
Utrillo, oo-*tree*-loh.
Uvedale, *yewv*-dayl.
Uwins, *yew*-inz.

Vachel, *vay*-chel.
Valentino, vah-len-*tee*-noh.
Valéry, vah-lay-ree.
Valois, vah-lwah.
Vámbéry, *vahm*-bay-re.
Vanbrugh, *van*-bra.
Vance, vahns.
Vandeleur, *van*-de-loor.
Vandervelde, *vahn*-der-*vel*-deh.
Van Gogh, van-*gokh*.
Van Loon, van-*lohn*.
Vannucci, vahn-*noot*-che.
Vansittart, van-*sit*-art.
Vaquez, vah-*kez*.
Vasari, va-*zah*-re.
Vatutin, vu-*too*-tyeen.
Vauban, voh-bahŋ.
Vaughan, vawn.
Vauvenargues, vohv-narg.
Vaux, vawx; vohks; vohz; voh.
Vavasour, *vav*-a-soor.
Vecelli, va-*chel*-e.
Veidt, fyt.
Veitch, veech.
Velasquez, ve-*las*-kwiz; (Sp.) va-*lahs*-kayth.
Veneziano, vay-na-*tsyah*-noh.
Venizelos, va-nye-*zah*-lohs.
Verdi, *vair*-de.
Vere, veer.
Vereshchagin, vye-ryesh-*chah*-gyeen.
Vergniaud, ver-nyoh.
Verhaeren, ver-*hah*-ren.
Verlaine, ver-layn.
Vermeer, ver-*mayr*.
Vernet, ver-neh.
Verneuil, ver-nøe.
Veronese, *vay*-ro-*nay*-sa.
Veronica, ve-*ron*-e-ka.
Verrocchio, va-*rok*-kyoh.
Verschoyle, *ver*-skoyl.
Verstegan, ver-*stee*-gan.
Verulam, *ve*-roo-lam.
Vesey, *vee*-ze.
Vespucci, va-*spoot*-che.
Vezin, ve-zan.
Viaud, vyoh.
Vico, *vee*-koh.
Vida, *vee*-dah.
Viereck, *feer*-rek.
Vieuxtemps, vyø-tahŋ.
Vieweg, (Ger.) *fee*-veg.
Vigers, *vy*-gerz.
Vignoles, vee-nyohl.
Vigny, vee-nyee.
Villari, *veel*-lah-ree.
Villars, vee-lar.
Villehardouin, vee-lar-dwaŋ.
Villeneuve, veel-nøv.
Villiers, *vil*-erz; *vil*-yerz.
Villon, vee-yoŋ.
Vinci, *veen*-che.
Vinet, vee-neh.
Vinogradoff, vye-nu-*grah*-dawf.
Viollet-le-Duc, vyo-leh-le-dook.
Virchow, *fir*-khoh; *vir*-choh.
Vischer, *fish*-er.
Vives, (Sp.) *vee*-vays.
Viviani, vee-vyah-nee.
Vizetelly, viz-e-*tel*-e.
Vlaminck, vlah-*maŋk*.
Vogel, (Fr.) voh-gel; (Ger.) *foh*-gel.
Vogler, *foh*-gler.
Vogt, fohkht.
Vogüé, vo-goo-ay.
Voigt, fohkht.
Voison, vwah-zaŋ.
Voltaire, vol-tair.
Voronoff, vu-*raw*-nawf.
Voroshilov, vu-ru-*shee*-lawf.
Voss, fos.
Voynich, *voy*-nitch.
Vries, vrees.
Vuillard, voo-ee-yar.
Vulliamy, *vul*-ya-me.
Vyvyan, *viv*-e-an; *viv*-yan.

Waage, *voh*-ga.
Waagen, *vah*-gen.
Waddell, wo-*del*.
Wadsworth, *wodz*-wurth.
Wagner, *vahg*-ner.
Walckenaer, *vahl*-ke-nahr.
Walcott, *wawl*-kut.
Waldegrave, *wawl*-grayv.
Waldemar, *wawl*-de-mar.
Walden, *wawl*-d'n; (Ger.) *vahl*-den.
Walewski, vah-*lef*-ske.
Walford, *wawl*-ford.
Walker, *waw*-ker.
Wallace, *wol*-as.
Wallenstein, *wol*-en-styn; (Ger.) *vahl*-en-shtyn.
Waller, wol-er.
Wallich, *wol*-ik; (Dan.) *vah*-likh.
Walling, *wol*-ing.
Walmesley, *wawmz*-le.
Walpole, *wawl*-pohl.
Walsh, wolsh; wawlsh.
Walsingham, *wawl*-sing-am.
Walther, *vahl*-ter.
Walton, *wawl*-ton.

Wanamaker, *won*-a-*may*-ker.
Warburton, *wawr*-bur-ton.
Wardlaw, *wawrd*-law.
Wardrop, *wawr*-drop.
Warham, *waw*-ram.
Waring, *wair*-ring.
Warne, wawrn.
Warner, *wawr*-ner.
Warton, *wawr*-ton.
Wassermann, *vahs*-er-mahn.
Watkins, *wot*-kinz.
Watson, *wot*-s'n.
Watt, wot.
Watteau, wo-*toh*; (Fr.) vah-toh.
Wauchope, *waw*-kup.
Waugh, waw.
Wauters, (Belg.) *wou*-ters.
Wavell, *way*-vel.
Weare, wair.
Weber, *web*-er; (Ger.) *vay*-ber.
Weenix, *vay*-niks.
Wegelius, va-*gay*-le-oos.
Wegener, *vay*-ge-ner.
Weigall, *wy*-gawl.
Weigand, *vy*-gahnt.
Weigl, *vy*-g'l.
Weil, weel; (Ger.) veel.
Weingartner, *vyn*-gart-ner.
Weir, weer.
Weismann, *vys*-mahn.
Weiss, (Ger.) vys; (Fr.) wys.
Weizmann, *vyts*-mahn.
Weizsächer, *vyts*-zekh-er.
Welch, welsh.
Welles, welz.
Wellesley, *welz*-le.
Wellhausen, *vel*-hou-*zen*.
Welsbach, *vels*-bahkh.
Wemyss, weemz.
Werfel, *ver*-fel.
Werner, *ver*-ner.
Wernicke, *ver*-ne-ka.
Wertheimer, *vert*-hy-mer.
Wesley, *wez*-le; *wes*-le.
Weygand, vay-gahŋ.
Wharton, *whawr*-ton.
Whewell, *hew*-el.
Whistler, *whis*-ler.
Whymper, *whim*-per.
Widener, *wyd*-ner.
Wieland, *vee*-lahnt.
Wien, veen.
Wiertz, vyers.
Wilde, wyld.
Wilder, *wyl*-der.
Wildgans, *vilt*-gahns.
Wiley, *wy*-le.
Wilhelm, *vil*-helm.
Wilhelmj, vil-*hel*-me.
Willoughby, *wil*-o-be.
Willstätter, vil-*shtet*-er.
Winckelmann, *ving*-kel-mahn.
Winkelreid, *ving*-kel-reet.
Winslow, *winz*-loh.
Winterhalter, *vin*-ter-*hahl*-ter.
Wishart, *wish*-art.
Wittelsbach, *vit*-els-bahkh.
Wladislaus, *lad*-is-laws.
Wodehouse, *wood*-hous.
Woermann, *ver*-mahn.
Wohlgemuth, *vohl*-ge-moot.
Wollaston, *wool*-as-ton.
Wolseley, *woolz*-le.
Wolsey, *wool*-ze.
Wombwell, wumbl.
Wortley, *wurt*-le.
Wouvermann, *vou*-ver-mahn.
Wraxall, *rak*-sawl.
Wriothesley, *rot*-sle; *riz*-le.
Wrottesley, *rot*-sle.
Wundt, voont.
Wurmser, *voorm*-zer.
Wycherley, *witch*-er-le.
Wycliffe, *wik*-lif.
Wyllie, *wy*-le.
Wynants, (Dut.) *vy*-nahnts.
Wyndham, *win*-dum.

Xavier, *zay*-ve-er; *zav*-e-er.

Yeames, yeemz.
Yeat(e)s, yayts.
Yerburgh, *yar*-bra.
Yerkes, *yer*-kiz.
Yohe, *yoh*-e.
Yonge, yung.
Yost, yohst.
Youatt, *yew*-at.
Youmans, *yew*-manz.
Yount, yunt.
Ypsilanti, *ip*-se-*lan*-te.
Yriarte, ee-ryart.
Ysaye, ee-zah-ee.
Yudenich, *yew*-dyay-nyich.
Yust, yoost.

Zachrisson, *sahk*-kri-sawn.
Zaehnsdorf, *tsans*-dorf.
Zaharoff, za-*hah*-rof; (Russ.) zu-*khah*-rawf.
Zaïmis, zah-*ee*-mis.
Zeeman, *zay*-mahn.
Zeiss, tsys.
Zhdanov, *zhdah*-nawf.
Ziegfeld, *zig*-feld.
Ziegler, *zee*-gler.
Zilliacus, *zil*-e-*ah*-kus.
Zinoviev, zye-*nawf*-yef.
Zoe, *zoh*-e.
Zouche, zoosh.
Zschokke, *chok*-a.
Zuccarelli, *tsook*-kah-*rel*-le.
Zuloaga, *soo*-lo-*ah*-gah.
Zurbaran, thoor-bah-*rahn*.
Zweig, tsvykh.
Zwingli, *tsving*-le.

PRONUNCIATION OF GREEK AND LATIN PROPER NAMES

How the Romans pronounced Latin at any time during the thousand years and more when it was among the " living " languages can never be precisely known ; but with the help of Comparative Philology that of the Classical Period—comprising approximately the century before and the century after the Birth of Christ—has in recent years been determined with a very fair degree of accuracy. At the Revival of Learning, however, when the study of Latin was introduced into the Tudor Grammar Schools, it was treated as a dead language to be pronounced as if the words were in the native language of the learners. This method, the local style as it is called, is still prevalent and is likely to continue, particularly for systematic names in natural science and proper names in general, as in the accompanying list.

It has the great advantage of leaving no doubt as to the quantities, for it is impossible to slur them, and it also keeps the syllables clear. This local style, however, which gives us one pronunciation in England and another in Scotland, is not in use among those who study Latin as literature ; many and varied have been the efforts to abandon it, and the pronunciation recommended by the Classical Association has been widely adopted in schools and colleges.

In this there is a long and short for each vowel, *a* long being sounded as in *father*, *a* short as in *hat* ; *e* long as in *prey*, *e* short as in *fret* ; *i* long as in *deed*, *i* short as in *fit* ; *o* long as in *home*, *o* short as in *not* ; *u* long as in *boot*, *u* short as in *pull* ; the diphthongs having the sounds of both letters together, *ae* as ai in *Isaiah*, *au* as ou in *hour*, and *oe* as oi in *boil*. Among the consonants *c* and *g* are always hard as in *cat* and *go*, *gu* is as *gw*, *j* is as *y*, *qu* as in *queen*, *s* as in *gas*, *t* is always hard, even before i, and *x* is always as *ks* and not as *kz*. Double consonants are sounded separately, the second of the pair beginning the next syllable. In words of two syllables the stress is always on the first ; in other words it is generally on the last but one. The pronunciation of Greek words is much on the same system, but *ch* is sounded as in Scottish *loch*, and not as in the English rendering of *chorus*.

THE VOWELS.

Every accented syllable not ending in a consonant is pronounced as in English, with its first, long, open sound : thus, *Ca'to*, *Philome'la*, *Ori'on*, *Pho'cion*, *Lu'cifer*, etc., have the accented vowels sounded exactly as in the English words *pa'per*, *me'ter*, *spi'der*, *no'ble*, *tu'tor*, etc., respectively.

Every accented vowel, followed by a consonant, has the short sound, as in English : thus, *Man'lius*, *Pen'theus*, *Pin'darus*, *Col'chis*, *Cur'tius*, etc., have the short sound of the accented vowels, as in *man'ner*, *plen'ty*, *prin'ter*, *col'lar*, *cur'few*, etc., respectively.

Every final *i*, though unaccented, has the long, open sound : thus, the final *i* forming the genitive case, as in *Magis'tri*, or the plural number, as in *De'cii*, has the long, open sound, as in *vi'al* ; and this because the Latin *i* final in such cases is always long. Consequently, where the accented *i* is followed by *i* final, both are pronounced with the long diphthongal *i*, like the noun *eye*, as *Achi'vi*.

Every unaccented *i* ending a syllable not final, as that in the second syllable of *Alcibiades*, the *Hernici*, etc., is pronounced like *e*, as if written *Alcebiades*, the *Herneci*, etc. So also the last syllable but one of the *Fabii*, the *Horatii*, the *Curiatii*, etc., is pronounced as if written *Fa-be-i*, *Ho-ra-she-i*, *Cu-re-a-she-i* ; and therefore, if the unaccented *i* and the diphthong *æ* conclude a word, they are both pronounced like *e*, as *Harpyiæ*, *Har-py'e-e*.

The diphthongs *æ* and *œ*, ending an accented syllable are pronounced exactly like the long English *e*, as *Cæsar*, *Œta*, etc., as if written *Cee'sar*, *Ee'ta*, etc. ; and like the short *e*, when followed by a consonant in the same syllable, as *Dædalus, Œdipus,* etc., pronounced as if written *Deddalus, Eddipus* (though note that the Anglicized pronunciations are *Dee*-da-lus, *Ee*-di-pus), etc. The vowels *ei* are generally pronounced like long *i*. For the vowels *eu* in final syllables, see the word *Idomeneus*; and for the *ou* in the same syllables, see the word *Antinous,* and similar words in the list.

Y is treated in the same way as *i*. It is long when ending an accented syllable, as *Cy'rus*; or when ending an unaccented syllable, if final, as *Æ'gy, Æ'py,* etc.; short when joined to a consonant in the same syllable, as *Lyc'idas*; and sometimes long and sometimes short, when ending an unaccented initial syllable, as *Lycur'gus,* pronounced with the first syllable like *lie*, a falsehood; and *Lysim'achus* with the first syllable like the first of *legion,* or nearly as if divided into *Lys-im'-a-chus,* etc.

A, ending an unaccented syllable, has the obscure sound which it has in the same situation in English words; but it has a sound bordering on the Italian *a*, or the *a* in *father,* as *Dia'na,* where the difference between an accented and an unaccented *a* is palpable.

E final, both with and without the preceding consonant, always forms a distinct syllable, as *Penelope, Irene, Evoe, Amphitrite,* etc. When any Greek or Latin word is Anglicized into this termination, by cutting off a syllable of the original, it then becomes an English word, and is pronounced according to our own analogy; thus, when the Latin *Proserpina* takes the form *Proserpine* the final *e* is muted and the name becomes a word of three syllables only. *Thebes* and *Athens,* derived from the Greek Θῆβη and Ἀθήνη and the Latin *Thebæ* and *Athenæ,* are perfectly Anglicized; the former into a monosyllable, and the latter into a dissyllable: and the Greek Κρήτη and the Latin *Creta* have both sunk into the English monosyllable *Crete*; *Hecate* likewise, pronounced in three syllables when Latin, and in the same number when in the Greek word Ἑκάτη, is in English frequently contracted into two, by suppressing the final *e*.

The Roman magistrate, named *Ædilis,* is Anglicized by pronouncing it in two syllables, *Æ'dile.* The capital of Sicily, *Syracusæ,* of four syllables, is made three in the English, *Syr'acuse*; and the city of *Tyrus,* of two syllables, is reduced to a monosyllable in the English *Tyre*. Sometimes the accent is shifted, as in Shakespeare's "Titus Andronicus," pronounced *An-dron'-e-cus,* though in Latin it is *An-dro-ni'-cus.*

THE CONSONANTS.

C and *G* are hard before *a, o,* and *u*, as *Cato, Comus, Cures, Galba, Gorgon,* etc.; and soft before *e, i,* and *y*, as *Cebes, Cinna, Cycnus, Geryon, Geta, Gillus, Gyges, Gymnosophistæ,* etc.

C, S, and *T*, before *ia, ie, ii, io, iu,* and *eu*, when preceded by the accent in Latin words, as in English, change into *sh* and *z*, as *Accius, Caduceus, Helvetii, Mœsia, Portia, Portius, Socias, Statius, Tatian,* pronounced *Aksheus, Cadusheus, Helveshei Mezea, Porshea, Porsheus, Sosheas, Stasheus, Tashean,* etc. But when the accent is on the first of the diphthongal vowels, the preceding consonant does not change into *sh*, but preserves its sound pure, as *Miltiades, Antiates,* etc.

Proper names ending in *tia, sia,* and *sion* when preceded by the accent, change the *t, s,* etc., into *sh* and *zh*. Thus we have *Artemisia* and *Aspasia* sounding as if written *Artemizhea* and *Aspazhea*; *Galatia, Aratia, Alotia,* and *Batia,* as if written *Galashea, Arashea, Aloshea,* and *Bashea*; and if *Atia,* the town in Campania, is not so pronounced, it is to distinguish it from *Asia,* the eastern region of the world. But the termination *tion* (of which there are not so many as twenty examples in proper names throughout the whole Greek and Latin languages) seems to preserve the *t* from going into *sh*, as the last remnant of a learned pronunciation, as if to avoid, as much as possible, assimilating with so common an English termination: thus, though *Æsion, Iasion, Dionysion,* change the *s* into *z*, as if written *Æzion, Iazion, Dionyzion,* the *z* does not become *zh*; but *Philistion, Gration, Eurytion, Dotion, Androtion, Hippotion, Iphition, Ornytion, Metion, Polytion, Stration, Sotion, Oantion,*

Pallantion, *Ætion*, *Hippocration*, and *Amphyction*, preserve the *t* in its true sound. The name of Hephæstion, however, perhaps because it is better known through its bearer's constant association with Alexander the Great, has been so far degraded that, in the mouths of careless speakers, it would serve as a rhyme to *question*; and *Tatian* and *Theodotion* seem perfectly Anglicized. With very few exceptions, therefore, it may be concluded that Greek and Latin *proper* names are, by the English-speaking peoples, pronounced alike, and that both of them follow the analogy of English pronunciation.

Ch before a vowel is always pronounced like *k*, as *Chabrias*, *Chalcis*, etc.; but when it comes before a mute consonant, at the beginning of a word, as in *Chthonius*, it is mute, and the word is pronounced as if written *Thonius*. Words beginning with *Sche*, as *Schedius*, *Scheria*, etc., are pronounced as if written *Skedius*, *Skeria*, etc; and *c* before *n* in the Latin prænomen *Cneus* or *Cnæus* is mute: so in *Cnopus*, *Cnossus*, etc., and before *t* in *Cteatus*, and *g* before *n* in *Gnidus*, pronounced *Nopus*, *Nossus*, *Teatus*, and *Nidus*.

At the beginning of Greek words we frequently find the uncombinable consonants *MN*, *TM*, etc., as *Mnemosyne*, *Mnesidamus*, *Mneus*, *Mnesteus*, *Tmolus*, etc. These are to be pronounced with the first consonant mute, as if written *Nemosyne*, *Nesidamus*, *Neus*, *Nesteus*, *Molus*, etc., in the same manner as we pronounce the words *bdellium*, *pneumatic*. *gnomon*, *mnemonics*, etc., without the initial consonant; but when, as sometimes happens, the names appear with a vowel between the first two consonants (*Menesteus*, *Timolus*, etc.) the initial consonant is, of course, pronounced.

Ph, followed by a consonant, is mute, as *Phthia*, *Phthiotis*, pronounced *Thia*, *Thiotis*, in the same manner as the naturalized Greek word *phthisic* is pronounced *tisic*.

In initial *Ps*, *P* is mute, as in *Psyche*, *Psammetichus*, etc., pronounced *Sykee*, *Sammetichus*, etc.—as also in words beginning with *Pt*, as *Ptolemy*, *Pterilas*, etc., pronounced *Tolemy*, *Terilas*, etc. Initial *T* when followed by *l* is heard, as in *Tleptolemus*, as also the *Z* in *Zmilaces*.

The letters *S*, *X*, and *Z* require but little observation, being generally pronounced as in pure English words. It may, however, be remarked that *s*, at the end of words preceded by any of the vowels but *e*, has its pure, hissing sound, as *mas*, *dis*, *os*, *mus*, etc.; but when *e* precedes, it goes into the sound of *z*, as *pes*, *Thersites*, *vates*, etc. It may also be observed that, when it ends a word preceded by *r* or *n*, it has the sound of *z*. Thus the letter *s* in *mens*, *Mars*, *mors*, etc., has the sound as in the English words *hens*, *stars*, *wars*, etc. *X*, when beginning a word or syllable, is pronounced like *z*, as *Xerxes*, *Xenophon*, etc., which are pronounced *Zerkzes*, *Zenophon*, etc. *Z* is uniformly pronounced as in English words; thus the *Z* in *Zeno* and *zeugma* is pronounced as we hear it in *zeal*, *zone*, etc.

QUANTITIES OF THE VOWELS IN ENGLISH.

A first vowel in words of two syllables, with but one consonant in the middle, whatever be the quantity of it in the first syllable in Greek or Latin, is always made long in English. Thus *Crates*, the philosopher, and *crates*, a hurdle; *decus*, honour, and *dedo*, to give; *ovo*, to triumph, and *ovum*, an egg; *Numa*, the legislator, and *numen*, the divinity, have the first vowel always sounded long by an English speaker, although in Latin it is short.

On the contrary, words of three syllables with the accent on the first, and with but one consonant after the first syllable, have the vowel of that syllable pronounced short, let the Greek or Latin quantity be what it may. Thus the first vowel of *regulus* and *remora*, *mimicus* and *minium*, is pronounced short in English, though it is long in Latin; and the *u* in *fumigo* and *fugito* is pronounced long in both words, though in Latin the *u* in the latter is short. This rule is never broken but when the first syllable is followed by *e* or *i* preceding another vowel; in this case the vowel in the first syllable is long, except the vowel be *i*; thus *lamia*, *genius*, *Libya*, *doceo*, *cupio* have the accent on the first syllable, and this syllable is pronounced long in every word but *Libya*, though in the original it is equally short in all.

In order to reduce these rules into a small compass, that they may be more easily comprehended and remembered, it may be observed, that as we always shorten every ante-penultimate vowel but *u* with the *primary* accent, unless followed by a semi-consonant diphthong, though this ante-penultimate vowel is often long in Greek and Latin, as *Æschylus*, *Æschines*, etc.; and the ante-penultimate *i*, even though it be followed by such a diphthong, as *Eleusinia*, *Ocrisia*, etc.; so we shorten the first syllable of *Æsculapius*, *Ænobarbus*, etc., because the first syllable of both these words has the *secondary* accent, but we pronounce the same vowels long in *Æthiopia*, *Ægialeus*, etc., because this accent is followed by a semi-consonant diphthong.

The general rules of quantity indicated by the syllabication are that (1), when a consonant ends the syllable, the vowel is always *short*, whether it is accented or not; (2) when a vowel ends an accented syllable it is always *long*; (3) that the vowel *u* ending an accented or unaccented syllable is *long*; and that (4) the vowel *i*, when ending an unaccented syllable is pronounced as short *e*, unless the syllable be final, in which case it has its long, open sound, as though the syllable were accented.

THE ACCENT.

Words of two syllables, either Greek or Latin, whatever be the quantity in the original, have, in English, the accent on the first syllable; and if a single consonant come between two vowels, the consonant goes to the last syllable, as *Cato*, *Ceres*, *Comus*, etc.

Polysyllables, when adopted without change from the Greek or Latin into English, have generally the accent of the Latin; that is, if the penultimate be long, the accent is on it, as *Severus*, *Democedes*, etc.; if short, the accent is on the ante-penultimate, as *Demosthenes*, *Aristophanes*, *Posthumus*, etc.

When Greek or Latin Proper Names are Anglicized, either by an alteration of the letters or by cutting off the final syllables, the accent of the original, as in appellatives under the same predicament, is transferred nearer to the beginning of the word. Thus, *Proserpina* has the accent on the second syllable; but when altered to *Proserpine* it transfers the accent to the first. The same rule applies to *Homerus*, *Virgilius*, *Horatius*, etc., when Anglicized to *Homer*, *Virgil*, *Horace*, etc. But *Acrion*, *Arion*, *Amphion*, *Echion*, *Orion*, *Ixion*, *Pandion*, *Asion*, *Alphion*, *Ærion*, *Ophion*, *Methion*, *Axion*, *Eion*, *Thlexion*, and *Sandion* preserve their penultimate accent invariably; while *Ethalion*, a word of the same form and origin, is pronounced with the accent on the ante-penultimate, like *Deucalion* and *Pygmalion*.

The difficulty apparent here in deciding between common usages and classical propriety appears in words ending in *ia*, as *Alexandria*, *Antiochia*, *Seleucia*, *Samaria*, *Iphigenia*, and several others, which were pronounced by our ancestors, as is plain from their poetry, according to our own analogy, with the accent on the ante-penultimate syllable; and there is no doubt but every word of this form would have fallen into the same accentuation, if classical criticism had not stepped in and prevented it. Some, however, seem always to have preserved the accent of their original language, as *Thalia* and *Sophia*, although *Iphigenia*, *Antiochia*, *Seleucia*, and *Samaria* have generally yielded to the English ante-penultimate accent; and *Erythia*, *Deidamia*, *Laodamia*, *Hippodamia*, *Apamia*, *Ilithyia*, and *Orithyia*, from their seldom appearing in mere English composition, have not often been drawn aside into plain English pronunciation. The same may be observed of words ending in *nicus* or *nice*. If they are compounded of the Greek νικη, the penultimate syllable is always long, and must have the accent, as *Stratonice*, *Berenice*, etc.; if this termination be what is called a gentile, *i.e.*, a name indicating the locality or people from which a man comes, the penultimate is short, and the accent is on the ante-penultimate, as *Macedonicus*, *Sardonicus*, *Britannicus*, etc.

Thus we see that many of these proper names are of dubious accentuation; and the authorities which may be produced on both sides sufficiently show us the futility of criticizing beyond a certain point. It is with these as with many English words: there are some which, if mispronounced, immediately show a want of education;

and there are others which, though not pronounced in the most erudite manner, stamp no imputation of ignorance or illiteracy. To have a general knowledge, therefore, of the pronunciation of these words, seems absolutely necessary for those who would appear respectable in the more respectable part of society. Perhaps no people on earth are so correct in their accentuation of proper names as the learned among the English. The Port Royal Grammar informs us that, "notwithstanding all the rules that can be given, we are often under the necessity of submitting to custom, and of accommodating our pronunciation to what is received among the learned, according to the country we are in."

Ab-a-*cæ*-num
Ab-æ
Ab-a-lus
A-*ba*-na
A-*ban*-tes
Ab-an-*ti*-a-des
A-*bar*-im-on
Ab-a-ris
A-*ba*-rus
Ab-a-*si*-tis
Ab-as-*se*-na
Ab-a-tos
Ab-*de*-ra
Ab-de-*ri*-tes
Ab-*de*-rus
A-*bel*-la
Ab-el-*la*-ni
Ab-el-*li*-num
Ab-e-lux
A-bi-a
Ab-i-i
A-*bis*-a-res
A-*ble*-tes
Ab-no-ba
A-*bæ*-cri-tus
A-*bo*-lus
A-bon-i-*tei*-chos
Ab-o-*ra*-ca
Ab-or-ras
Ab-ra-*da*-te-as
A-*cris*-i-us
A-*broc*-o-mas
A-*bron*-y-cus
A-*bro*-ta
A-*brot*-o-num
A-*bryp*-o-lis
Ab-*se*-us
Ab-syr-*ti*-des
Ab-u-*li*-tes
Ab-y-*de*-nus
A-*by*-dos
Ab-y-la
Ab-ys-*si*-ni
A-*ca*-ci-us
Ac-a-*de*-mus
Ac-a-*lan*-drus
Ac-a-mas
A-*can*-thus
Ac-a-ra
Ac-ar-*na*-nia
Ac-ci-la
Ac-e-lum
Ac-er-ræ
Ac-e-*ra*-tus
A-ce-*ri*-na
Ac-e-*si*-nes
A-*ces*-tes
A-ces-to-*do*-rus
Ac-es-*to*-ri-des
A-ce-tes
Ach-a-*by*-tos
A-*chæ*-a
A-*chæ*-i
A-*chæ*-me-nes
A-*chæ*-us
A-*cha*-i-a
A-*cha*-is
A-*cha*-tes
Ach-e-*lo*-i-des
Ach-e-*lo*-us
Ach-e-*men*-i-des
Ach-e-ron
Ach-e-*ron*-ti-a
Ach-e-*ru*-she-a
A-*che*-tus
Ach-il-*le*-a
Ach-il-*le*-is
A-*chil*-les
A-*chil*-leus
A-*chi*-vi
Ach-la-*dee*-us
Ach-o-*lo*-e
Ach-ra-*di*-na
Ac-i-*chor*-i-us
Ac-i-*da*-sa
A-*cil*-i-us
A-cis
Ac-*mon*-i-des
A-*cœ*-tes
A-*con*-te-us
A-*con*-ti-us
Ac-o-ris
Ac-qui
A-cra
A-*cra*-tus
Ac-ri-*doph*-a-gi
A-*cri*-on
A-cris-i-o-*ne*-us
A-*cris*-i-us
Ac-rit-as
Ac-ro-ce-*rau*-ni-um
Ac-ro-co-*rin*-thus
A-cron
A-*crop*-o-lis
A-*crot*-a-tus
Ac-ro-*tho*-um
Ac-*tæ*-on
Ac-*tis*-a-nes
Ac-ti-um
Ac-to-ris
A-*cu*-le-o
A-cu-si-*la*-us
Ad-a-man-*tæ*-a
Ad-a-mas
Ad-du-a
A-*de*-mon
Ad-*her*-bal
Ad-i-a-*man*-tus
Ad-*me*-ta
Ad-*me*-tus
A-*do*-nis
Ad-ra-*myt*-ti-um
A-*dra*-num
Ad-ras-*ti*-a
A-dri-*a*-nus
Ad-ri-*me*-tum
Æ-*ac*-i-des
Æ-a-cus
Æ-an-*te*-um
Æ-*an*-ti-des
Æ-a-tus
Æ-*di*-lis, *pl.* -les
A-*e*-don
A-e-*do*-nis
Æ-du-i
Æ-*e*-ta, Æ-*e*-tes
Æ-gæ
Æ-*gæ*-on
Æ-*gæ*-um
Æ-*ga*-tes
Æ-*ge*-li
Æ-*ge*-us
Æ-*gi*-a-le
Æ-*gi*-a-lus
Æ-gi-la
Æ-*gil*-e-a
Æ-*gi*-na
Æ-gi-*ne*-ta
Æ-*gi*-o-chus
Æ-*gi*-ra
Æ-*gis*-thus
Æ-*gi*-tum
Æ-gi-um
Æ-gle
Æ-*gle*-tes
Æ-gos-*pot*-a-mos
Æ-*gos*-the-na
Æ-*gyp*-tus
Æ-*gy*-tis
Æ-li-*a*-nus
Æ-li-us
Æm-il-i-*a*-nus
Æ-*mo*-na
Æ-*mon*-i-des
Æ-*ne*-a-des
Æ-*ne*-as
Æ-*ne*-i-a
Æ-*ne*-is
Æ-nes-i-*de*-mus
Æ-*ne*-si-us
Æ-*ne*-tus
Æ-ni-cus
Æ-no-cles
Æ-nos
Æ-*ny*-ra
Æ-*o*-li-a
Æ-*o*-li-æ
Æ-*o*-li-des
Æ-o-lis
Æ-o-lus
Æ-*o*-ra
Æ-*pe*-a
Æ-py
Æ-py-tus
Æ-*qua*-na
Æ-qui
A-*er*-o-pe
Æ-sa-cus
Æ-sa-us
Æs-chi-nes
Æs-chri-on
Æs-chy-*li*-des
Æs-chy-lus
Æs-cu-*la*-pi-us
Æ-*ser*-ni-a
Æ-sis
Æ-son
Æ-*son*-i-des
Æ-*so*-pus
Æ-su-la
Æ-sym-*ne*-tes
Æ-*tha*-li-a
Æ-*thal*-i-des
Æ-*thi*-ces
Æ-thi-*o*-pi-a
A-*eth*-li-us
Æ-thra
Æ-*thu*-sa
A-*e*-ti-on
A-*e*-ti-us
Æt-na
Æ-*to*-li-a
Æ-*to*-lus
Æ-*xo*-ne
Af-*ra*-ni-us
Af-ri-*ca*-nus
Ag-a-*me*-des
Ag-a-*mem*-non
Ag-a-*nip*-pe
Ag-a-*pe*-nor
Ag-a-*re*-ni
A-*gas*-i-cles
A-*gas*-the-nes
A-*gas*-tro-phus
Ag-a-sus
Ag-a-tha
Ag-a-*thar*-chi-das
Ag-a-*thar*-chus
A-*gath*-i-as
Ag-a-tho
Ag-a-tho-*cle*-a
A-*gath*-o-cles
Ag-a-thon
Ag-a-*thyr*-sus
A-*gau*-num
A-*ga*-ve
A-*ga*-vus
Ag-e-*dinc*-um
Ag-e-*la*-des
Ag-e-*las*-tus
Ag-e-*la*-us
A-*ge*-nor
Ag-e-*no*-ri-des
Ag-e-*ri*-nus
Ag-e-*san*-der
A-*ge*-si-as
A-ges-i-*la*-us
Ag-e-*sip*-o-lis
A-*ge*-tor
Ag-*gri*-næ
Ag-i-*la*-us
A-gis
A-*gla*-ia
Ag-la-o-*ni*-ce
A-*gla*-o-pe
Ag-la-o-*phe*-me
A-*gla*-o-phon
A-*glau*-ri-um
Ag-*la*-us
Ag-*nod*-i-ce
Ag-*non*-i-des
Ag-o-*na*-li-a
A-*go*-nes
A-*go*-ni-us
Ag-o-ra
Ag-o-*ræ*-a
A-*græ*-i
Ag-ra-gas
A-*grau*-le
A-*grau*-los
Ag-ri-*a*-nes
A-*gric*-o-la
Ag-ri-*gen*-tum
A-*grin*-i-um
Ag-ri-*o*-ni-a
A-*gri*-o-pe
A-*grip*-pa
Ag-rip-*pi*-na
Ag-ri-us
Ag-ro-las
A-*gro*-tas
A-*grot*-er-a
A-*gyi*-e-us
Ag-yl-*læ*-us
A-*gyr*-i-um
A-*gy*-rus
A-*ha*-la
Ai-*do*-ne-us
A-jax
Al-a-*ban*-da
Al-a-*bas*-trum
A-*læ*-sa
Al-al-*com*-e-næ
Al-a-*man*-ni
A-*la*-ni
Al-a-res
Al-a-*ri*-cus
A-*las*-tor
Al-ba *Long*-a
Al-*ba*-nus
Al-*bi*-ci
Al-bi-no-*va*-nus
Al-*bi*-nus
Al-bi-on
Al-bu-la
Al-*bu*-ti-us
Al-*cæ*-us
Al-*cam*-e-nes
Al-*ca*-nor
Al-ce
Al-*ce*-nor
Al-*ces*-tis
Al-ce-tas
Al-ci-*bi*-a-des
Al-*ci*-dæ
Al-*cid*-a-mas
Al-ci-da-*me*-a
Al-*ci*-das
Al-*ci*-des
Al-*cim*-e-de
Al-*cim*-e-don
Al-*cim*-e-nes
Al-ci-mus
Al-*cin*-o-us
Al-ci-phron
Al-*cip*-pe
Al-*cith*-o-e
Alc-*mæ*-on
Alc-*me*-na
Al-*cy*-o-ne

A-le-a
A-*le*-bas
A-*lec*-to
A-*lec*-try-on
Al-e-*man*-ni
A-*le*-si-a
A-*le*-si-um
A-*le*-tes
A-*le*-thi-a
A-*le*-tri-um
A-*le*-us
A-lex-a-*me*-nus
Al-ex-*an*-der
Al-ex-*a*-nor
Al-ex-*i*-nus
A-*lex*-is
Al-*fe*-nus
Al-gi-dum
Al-i-*phe*-ra
Al-*li*-phæ
Al-*lob*-ro-ges
Al-*lot*-ri-ges
Al-*mo*-pi-a
Al-o-*i*-dae
Al-o-pe
A-*lop*-e-ce
Al-o-pe-con-*ne*-sus
Al-*pe*-nus
Al-*phe*-nus
Al-phe-si-*bœ*-a
Al-*phe*-us
Al-*pi*-nus
Al-*thæ*-a
Al-*thæ*-me-nes
Al-*ti*-num
A-*lum*-ti-um
Al-y-*at*-tes
Al-y-ba
A-*ly*-mon
A-*lys*-sus
Al-y-*zi*-a
Am-a-ge
Am-al-*thæ*-a
Am-a-*ryl*-lis
Am-a-*ryn*-thus
Am-a-*si*-a
A-*ma*-sis
A-*ma*-thus
A-*maz*-o-nes
Am-bar-*va*-li-a
Am-be-nus
Am-bi-a-*li*-tes
Am-bi-*a*-num
Am-bi-*ga*-tus
Am-*bi*-o-rix
Am-*bra*-ci-a
Am-*bro*-nes
Am-e-les
Am-e-*ni*-des
A-*mes*-tra-tus
A-*mi*-da
A-mim-*o*-ne
A-*min*-i-as
Am-i-*se*-na
A-*mis*-i-as
Am-i-*ter*-num
Am-mi-*a*-nus
Am-mon
Am-*mo*-ni-us
Am-*ni*-sus
A-*mor*
A-*mor*-gos
Am-pe-los
Am-*phe*-a
Am-*phi*-a-nax
Am-phi-a-*ra*-us
Am-*phic*-le-a
Am-*phic*-ty-on
Am-*phid*-a-mus
Am-phi-ge-*ni*-a
Am-*phil*-o-chus
Am-*phil*-y-tus

Am-*phim*-a-chus
Am-*phim*-e-don
Am-*phi*-on
Am-*phip*-o-lis
Am-*phis*-sa
Am-*phis*-tra-tus
Am-phi-*tri*-te
Am-*phit*-ry-on
Am-*phry*-sus
A-*my*-clæ
A-*my*-clas
Am-y-cus
Am-y-*mo*-ne
A-*myn*-tas
Am-y-rus
Am-y-*tha*-on
A-*nab*-a-sis
An-a-ces
An-a-*char*-sis
An-a-*cle*-tus
A-*nac*-re-on
An-ac-*tor*-i-a
An-a-dy-*om*-e-ne
A-*nag*-ni-a
An-a-*i*-tis
An-a-phe
A-*na*-pus
An-ax-*an*-der
An-ax-*ag*-o-ras
An-ax-*ar*-chos
An-ax-*ar*-e-te
An-ax-*e*-nor
An-ax-*ic*-ra-tes
A-*nax*-i-las
A-nax-i-*man*-der
An-ax-*im*-e-nes
An-ax-*ip*-pus
An-*cæ*-us
An-*chi*-ses
An-*co*-na
An-*cy*-ra
An-*doc*-i-des
An-dro-cles
An-dro-*cli*-des
An-*dro*-clus
An-*drog*-e-os
An-*drom*-a-che
An-*drom*-e-da
An-dro-*ni*-cus
An-*dros*-the-nes
An-*dro*-ti-on
An-ge-*ro*-na
An-*gi*-tes
An-i-*ce*-tus
A-*ni*-grus
A-ni-o
An-i-*tor*-gis
An-*næ*-us
An-ni-*a*-nus
An-*nic*-e-ris
An-ni-us
An-*tæ*-us
An-*tag*-o-ras
An-*tal*-ci-das
An-*te*-nor
An-te-ros
An-*the*-don
An-*the*-le
An-the-mus
An-*thi*-a
An-*tho*-res
An-thro-*pi*-nus
An-ti-a-*ni*-ra
An-ti-as
An-ti-*cle*-a
An-ti-cles
An-*tic*-ra-tes
An-*tic*-y-ra
An-*tig*-e-nes
An-*tig*-o-ne
An-ti-go-*ni*-a
An-*tig*-o-nus

An-ti-*lib*-a-nus
An-*til*-o-chus
An-*tim*-a-chus
An-ti-*nop*-o-lis
An-*tin*-o-us
An-*ti*-o-chus
An-*ti*-o-pe
An-*tip*-a-ter
An-*tip*-a-tris
An-*tiph*-a-nes
An-*tiph*-i-lus
An-ti-phon
An-*tiph*-o-nus
An-ti-phus
An-*tip*-o-lis
An-*tis*-the-nes
An-*tom*-e-nes
An-*to*-ni-a
An-to-*ni*-nus
An-*to*-ni-us
A-*nu*-bis
An-y-tus
A-o-nes
A-*o*-ni-a
A-*or*-is
A-*or*-nus
A-*o*-ti
A-*pa*-me
Ap-a-*me*-a
A-*pel*-les
A-*pel*-li-con
Ap-en-*ni*-nus
Ap-e-sas
Aph-a-*re*-tus
Aph-a-*re*-us
Aph-e-tæ
A-*phi*-das
Aph-œ-*be*-tus
A-*phri*-ces
Aph-ro-*dis*-i-as
Aph-ro-*di*-te
Aph-*tho*-ni-us
A-*phy*-tis
Ap-i-*a*-nus
Ap-i-*ca*-ta
A-*pic*-i-us
A-*pid*-a-nus
A-*pi*-o-læ
A-pi-on
A-pis
Ap-o-*do*-ti
A-pol-li-*na*-ris
A-*pol*-lo
Ap-ol-*loc*-ra-tes
A-pol-lo-*dor*-us
Ap-ol-*lo*-ni-a
Ap-ol-*lon*-i-des
Ap-ol-*lo*-ni-us
A-*po*-ni-us
Ap-o-nus
Ap-pi-a *Vi*-a
Ap-pi-*a*-nus
Ap-pi-i *Fo*-rum
Ap-pi-us
Ap-*sin*-thus
Ap-si-nus
Ap-te-ra
Ap-u-*le*-ius
Aq-ui-la
Aq-ui-*le*-ia
Aq-ui-lo
A-*qui*-nas
A-*rach*-ne
A-ra-*cho*-si-a
A-*rach*-thus
A-ra-*cyn*-thus
A-*ra*-tus
A-*rax*-es
Ar-*ba*-ces
Ar-*be*-la
Ar-ca-des
Ar-*ca*-di-a

Ar-*ca*-di-us
Ar-ces-i-*la*-us
Ar-che-*la*-us
Ar-chep[-che]-*tol*-e-mus
Ar-*ches*-tra-tus
Ar-chi-as
Ar-chi-*bi*-a-des
Ar-chi-*da*-mus
Ar-*chig*-e-nes
Ar-*chil*-o-chus
Ar-chi-*me*-des
Ar-*chi*-nus
Ar-*chy*-tas
Arc-*ti*-nus
Arc-*toph*-y-lax
Arc-*tu*-rus
Ar-de-a
Ar-du-*en*-na
Ar-dys
Ar-e-*la*-tum
A-*re*-ne
A-re-o-pa-*gi*-tæ
A-re-*op*-a-gus
A-res
Ar-e-ta
Ar-e-*tæ*-us
Ar-e-*thu*-sa
Ar-*gæ*-us
Ar-ga-lus
Ar-*gath*-o-na
Ar-ga-*tho*-ni-us
Ar-gi-*le*-tum
Ar-gi-*nu*-sæ
Ar-*gi*-vi
Ar-go-lis
Ar-go-*nau*-tæ
Ar-gos
Ar-gus
Ar-*gy*-ra
A-ri-*ad*-ne
A-ri-a-*ra*-thes
A-*ri*-ci-a
A-ri-*mas*-pi-i
Ar-i-*ma*-zes
A-*rim*-i-num
A-ri-o-bar-*za*-nes
A-ri-o-*me*-des
A-*ri*-on
A-ri-o-*vis*-tus
A-ris-*tæ*-ne-tus
A-ris-*tæ*-us
A-ris-*tag*-o-ras
A-ris-*tar*-chus
A-ris-ta-*za*-nes
A-*ris*-the-nes
A-ris-*ti*-des
A-ris-*tip*-pus
A-ris-to-*bu*-lus
A-*ris*-to-cles
A-ris-*toc*-ra-tes
A-ris-to-*de*-mus
A-ris-*tog*-e-nes
A-ris-to-*gi*-ton
A-ris-*tom*-a-chus
A-ris-*tom*-e-nes
A-ris-to-*nau*-tæ
A-ris-to-*ni*-cus
A-ris-*ton*-y-mus
A-ris-*toph*-a-nes
A-*ris*-to-phon
A-ris-*tot*-e-les
A-ris-*totle*
A-ris-*tox*-e-nus
Ar-i-us
Ar-*min*-i-us
Ar-*mo*-ri-ca
Ar-*no*-bi-us
Ar-*pi*-num
Ar-ri-*a*-nus
Ar-sa-ces
Ar-*sa*-nes

Ar-*sin*-o-e
Ar-ta-*ba*-nus
Ar-ta-*ba*-zus
Ar-ta-bri
Ar-ta-ce
Ar-ta-*pher*-nes
Ar-ta-*vas*-des
Ar-ta-*xer*-xes
Ar-tem-i-*dor*-us
Ar-te-mis
Ar-te-*mis*-i-a
Ar-te-*mi*-ta
Ar-te-mon
A-runs
As-*cal*-a-phus
As-*ca*-ni-us
As-*ci*-i
As-cle-*pi*-a-des
As-*cle*-pi-o-*dor*-us
As-*cle*-pi-us
As-cu-lum
As-dru-bal
A-si-a-*ge*-tes
A-*so*-pus
As-*pa*-si-a
As-*pen*-dus
As-*ple*-don
As-*sa*-ra-cus
As-ta-pus
As-*tar*-te
As-*te*-ri-a
As-*te*-ro-pe
As-*ti*-o-chus
As-*træ*-a
As-tu-ra
As-tu-res
As-*ty*-a-ges
As-*ty*-a-nax
As-*ty*-da-mas
As-ty-da-*mi*-a
As-*ty*-no-me
As-*ty*-o-che
As-ty-o-*chi*-a
As-y-chis
A-*tab*-u-lus
At-a-*lan*-ta
A-*tar*-be-chis
A-te
At-er-*ne*-a
At-el-*la*-næ *fab*-u-læ
Ath-a-mas
A-thas
Ath-e-*næ*-us
Ath-e-*nag*-o-ras
Ath-e-*na*-is
A-*the*-ne
A-then-o-*dor*-us
Ath-e-sis
Ath-mo-nom
A-thos
At-i-a
A-*til*-i-a
A-*ti*-na
A-*tin*-i-as
At-*lan*-tes
At-lan-*ti*-a-des
At-*lan*-tis
At-las
A-*tos*-sa
At-re-*ba*-tes
A-tre-us
A-*tri*-des
At-ro-pa-*te*-ne
A-*trop*-a-tes
At-ro-pos
At-ta-lus
At-ti-ca
At-ti-cus
At-ti-la
A-*tu*-rus
At-ys
Au-fi-*de*-na

Au-*fid*-i-us
Au-fi-dus
Au-ga-rus
Au-ge-æ
Au-*ge*-as
Au-*gus*-ta
Au-gus-*ti*-nus
Au-*gus*-tu-lus
Au-*gus*-tus
Au-lis
Au-re-li-*a*-nus
Au-*re*-o-lus
Au-*ror*-a
Au-so-nes
Au-*so*-ni-a
Au-*so*-ni-us
Au-to-cles
Au-*tol*-y-cus
Au-*ton*-o-e
Au-*trig*-o-nes
A-*va*-ri-cum
Av-en-*ti*-nus
A-*ver*-nus
A-*vi*-tus
Ax-e-nus
A-*za*-ni-a
A-*zo*-tus

Bab-i-lus
Bac-*chi*-a-dæ
Bac-chi-des
Bac-*chi*-us
Bac-chus
Bac-*chy*-li-des
Bac-tri-*a*-na
Ba-*go*-as
Bag-ra-da
Ba-iæ
Ba-*la*-nus
Bal-*bi*-nus
Bal-bus
Ba-le-*a*-res
Ba-*le*-tus
Ba-ra-thrum
Bar-*bos*-the-nes
Bar-*ci*-tæ
Bar-ci-no
Bar-*dæ*-i
Ba-*re*-a (town)
Ba-re-a (person)
Bar-*gu*-si-i
Bar-*gyl*-i-æ
Bar-*si*-ne
Bar-*za*-nes
Bas-i-*le*-a
Bas-i-*li*-des
Ba-*sil*-i-us (person)
Bas-i-*li*-us (river)
Bas-i-lus
Bas-sæ
Bas-*sa*-ni-a
Bas-sa-ris
Bas-*tar*-næ
Bat-a-vo-*du*-rum
Ba-*ta*-vus
Bath-y-cles
Ba-*thyl*-lus
Bat-ra-*cho*-my-o-*ma*-chi-a
Bat-u-lum
Bau-cis
Beb-ry-ces
Be-*dri*-a-cum
Bel-e-*mi*-na
Be-*le*-nus
Bel-e-sis
Bel-gi-ca
Bel-i-*sa*-ri-us
Bel-*ler*-o-phon
Bel-li-*e*-nus
Bel-*lo*-na
Bel-*lov*-a-ci

Be-lus
Be-*na*-cus
Ben-e-*ven*-tum
Ben-the-*si*-cy-me
Be-pol-i-*ta*-nus
Ber-bi-cæ
Be-re-*cyn*-ti-a
Be-re-*ni*-ce
Ber-go-mum
Be-ro-e
Be-ro-*ni*-ce
Be-*ro*-sus
Be-*ry*-tus
Bi-*a*-nor
Bi-*bac*-u-lus
Bi-*brac*-te
Bib-u-lus
Bi-on
Bi-*san*-the
Bis-to-nes
Bi-*thyn*-i-a
Bit-u-*i*-tus
Bi-*tu*-ri-ges
Boadicea, *see* Boudicea
Bœ-*o*-ti
Bœ-*o*-ti-a
Bo-*e*-thi-us
Bo-i-i
Bo-i-o-rix
Bo-*li*-na
Bo-*mil*-car
Bo-na *De*-a
Bo-*o*-tes
Bo-re-as
Bo-*rys*-the-nes
Bos-po-rus
Bou-di-ce-a
Bo-vi-*a*-num
Brac-a-ri
Brach-*ma*-ni
Bran-chi-dæ
Bras-i-das
Bren-nus
Bri-*a*-re-us
Bri-*gan*-tes
Bri-*se*-is
Bri-ses
Bri-*tan*-ni
Bri-*tan*-ni-a
Bri-*tan*-ni-cus
Brit-o-*mar*-tis
Brit-o-*ma*-rus
Brix-i-a
Bron-tes
Bron-*ti*-nus
Bru-*ma*-li-a
Brun-*du*-si-um
Bru-ti-i
Bru-tus
Bry-as
Bry-ce
Bry-ges
Bu-*bas*-tis
Bu-ba-sus
Bu-*ceph*-a-lus
Bu-*do*-rum
Bu-pa-lus
Bu-pha-gus
Bu-*si*-ris
Bu-tes
Bu-*thro*-tum
Byb-lis
Byb-los
By-*zan*-ti-um

Ca-*an*-thus
Ca-bal-*li*-num
Ca-*bi*-ra
Ca-*bi*-ri
Ca-cus
Cad-*me*-a

Cad-mus
Ca-*dy*-tis
Cæ-a
Cæ-ci-lus
Cæ-*ci*-na
Cæc-u-bum
Cæc-u-lus
Cæ-li-us
Cæ-*ne*-us
Cæ-*ni*-na
Cæ-re
Cæ-ri-tes
Cæ-sar
Cæs-a-*re*-a
Cæ-*sa*-ri-on
Cæ-sa-ro-*du*-num
Cæ-*se*-na
Ca-i-*e*-ta
Ca-i-us
Ca-*je*-ta
Cal-a-ber
Ca-*la*-bri-a
Cal-a-*gu*-ris
Cal-a-is
Cal-a-mus
Ca-*la*-nus
Ca-*la*-ti-a
Cal-chas
Cal-e-*do*-ni-a
Ca-*le*-nus
Ca-*le*-tæ
Ca-*lig*-u-la
Cal-*le*-ni
Cal-li-as
Cal-*lic*-ra-tes
Cal-li-*crat*-i-das
Cal-*lid*-ro-mus
Cal-*lim*-a-chus
Cal-*lim*-e-don
Cal-*li*-nus
Cal-*li*-o-pe
Cal-li-phon
Cal-*lip*-o-lis
Cal-li-pus
Cal-*lir*-ho-e
Cal-*lis*-the-nes
Cal-*lis*-to
Cal-*lis*-tra-tus
Cal-*lix*-e-na
Cal-pe
Cal-*pur*-ni-a
Ca-*ly*-be
Cal-y-don
Ca-*lyp*-so
Cam-a-lo-*du*-num
Cam-a-*ri*-na
Cam-*by*-ses
Ca-*me*-na
Cam-e-*ri*-num
Cam-e-*ri*-nus
Ca-*mil*-la
Ca-*mil*-lus
Cam-*pa*-ni-a
Cam-*pas*-pe
Can-a-ce
Can-a-ceus
Can-da-ce
Can-*dau*-les
Can-*di*-o-pe
Ca-*nid*-i-us
Ca-nin-e-*fa*-tes
Can-næ
Ca-*no*-pus
Can-ta-bri
Can-tha-rus
Can-ti-um
Can-u-*le*-ius
Ca-*nu*-si-um
Ca-*pa*-ne-us
Ca-*pel*-la
Ca-*pe*-na
Cap-e-tus

Cap-i-to-*li*-nus
Cap-i-*to*-li-um
Cap-pa-*do*-ci-a
Cap-re-æ
Cap-ri-*cor*-nus
Cap-u-a
Ca-ra-*cal*-la
Ca-*rac*-ta-cus
Ca-ra-lis
Ca-*ra*-nus
Ca-*rau*-si-us
Car-*ci*-nus (poet)
Car-*du*-chi
Ca-*res*-sus
Ca-ri-a
Ca-*ri*-næ
Ca-*ri*-nus
Car-*ma*-ni-a
Car-*ma*-nor
Car-*me*-lus
Car-*ne*-a-des
Car-*nu*-tes
Car-*nu*-tum
Car-pa-thus
Car-*se*-o-li
Car-tha-gin-i-*en*-ses
Car-*tha*-go
Cas-i-*li*-num
Cas-pi-æ *py*-læ
Cas-*san*-der
Ca-*si*-num
Cas-*san*-dra
Cas-san-*dri*-a
Cas-si-o-*do*-rus
Cas-*si*-o-pe
Cas-si-o-*pe*-i-a
Cas-si-*te*-ri-des
Cas-si-us
Cas-si-ve-*lau*-nus
Cas-*so*-pe
Cas-*tab*-a-la
Cas-*ta*-li-a
Cas-ta-*ne*-a
Cas-tor
Cas-tu-lo
Cat-a-na
Cat-i-*li*-na
Ca-to
Ca-*tul*-lus
Ca-*tu*-ri-ges
Cau-*co*-nes
Cau-nus
Cav-a-*ri*-nus
Ca-*y*-cus
Ca-*ys*-ter
Ce-a
Ce-bes
Ce-*bre*-ni-a
Ce-crops
Cel-a-don
Ce-*læ*-no
Ce-*le*-ne
Cel-tæ
Cel-ti-*be*-ri
Cel-ti-ca
Cen-chre-æ
Cen-o-*ma*-ni
Cen-so-*ri*-nus
Cen-*tau*-rus
Cen-*tri*-tes
Cen-*tro*-nes
Ce-os
Ceph-a-læ
Ceph-al-*le*-ni-a
Ceph-a-lon
Ceph-a-lus
Ce-phe-us
Ce-phis-i-*dor*-us
Ce-*phi*-sus
Ce-ra-*mi*-cus
Cer-a-sus

Ce-*rau*-nus
Cer-be-rus
Cer-ce-tes
Cer-*ci*-na
Cer-*co*-pes
Cer-cy-on
Cer-*cy*-ra
Ce-res
Ce-*re*-tæ
Ce-ron
Cer-re-*ta*-ni
Ce-*ry*-ces
Cer-so-*blep*-tes
Cer-y-*ne*-a
Ces-ti-us
Ce-*the*-gus
Ce-yx
Cha-*bor*-as
Cha-bri-as
Chær-e-as
Chæ-*re*-mon
Chær-e-phon
Chæ-ro-*ne*-a
Cha-*læ*-on
Chal-*cæ*-a
Chal-*ce*-don
Chal-*cid*-i-ce
Chal-cis
Chal-*dæ*-a
Chal-y-bes
Chal-y-bon
Cha-*o*-ni-a
Cha-*rax*-us
Cha-res
Char-i-cles
Char-i-clo
Char-i-*de*-mus
Char-i-*la*-us
Char-is
Char-i-ton
Char-mi-des
Cha-ron
Cha-*ryb*-dis
Cha-*u*-ci
Che-*lid*-o-nis
Che-ops
Che-phren
Cher-so-*ne*-sus
Chi-lo
Chi-*lo*-nis
Chi-*mæ*-ra
Chi-on
Chi-*on*-i-des
Chi-os
Chi-ron
Chlo-e
Chlo-ris
Cho-a-*ri*-na
Chos-ro-es
Chres-i-phon
Chro-mis
Chry-sa, -se
Chry-*san*-tas
Chry-*san*-tis
Chry-*sa*-or
Chry-sas
Chry-*se*-is
Chry-*ses*
Chry-*sip*-pus
Chry-sis
Chry-*sog*-o-nus
Chrys-o-*la*-us
Chrys-o-*lor*-as
Chry-*sop*-o-lis
Chry-sor-*rho*-as
Chry-*sos*-to-mus
Chtho-ni-us
Cib-a-læ
Cib-a-*ri*-tis
Ci-*bo*-tus
Cib-y-ra
Cic-e-ro

Cich-y-ris
Cic-o-nes
Cil-i-ces
Ci-*lic*-i-a
Cim-bri
Cim-*me*-ri-i
Ci-*mo*-lis
Ci-mon
Ci-*næ*-thon
Cin-a-ra
Cin-cin-*na*-tus
Cin-e-as
Cin-*get*-o-rix
Cin-gu-lum
Cin-na
Cin-na-mus
Cin-y-ras
Ci-os
Cip-pus
Cir-ce
Cir-rha
Cis-al-*pi*-na
Cis-pa-*da*-na
Cis-*se*-us
Ci-*thæ*-ron
Ci-ti-um
Clau-di-*a*-nus
Clau-di-*op*-o-lis
Clau-di-us
Cla-*zom*-e-næ
Cle-*an*-thes
Cle-*ar*-chus
Cleis-the-nes
Cle-o-bis
Cle-o-bu-*li*-na
Cle-o-*bu*-lus
Cle-o-*cha*-res
Cle-*og*-e-nes
Cle-o-*la*-us
Cle-*om*-bro-tus
Cle-o-*me*-des
Cle-*om*-e-nes
Cle-on
Cle-*o*-næ
Cle-*on*-y-mus
Cle-o-*pa*-tra
Cle-*op*-a-tris
Cle-*oph*-a-nes
Cle-o-phes
Cle-o-phon
Cle-op-*tol*-e-mus
Cle-*os*-tra-tus
Clin-i-as
Cli-o
Clis-the-nes
Cli-*tar*-chus
Cli-*tom*-a-chus
Cli-*tum*-nus
Cli-tus
Clo-a-*ci*-na
Clo-*an*-thus
Clo-di-a
Clo-di-us
Clo-tho
Clu-a-*ci*-na
Clu-si-um
Clym-e-ne
Clym-e-nus
Clyt-em-*nes*-tra
Cnæ-us
Cne-mus
Cne-us
Cni-dus
Cno-pus
Cnos-sus
Co-a-*ma*-ni
Coc-a-lus
Coc-*ce*-i-us
Co-cles
Co-*cy*-tus
Co-*da*-nus
Co-*dom*-a-nus
Cod-ri-dæ
Co-drus
Cœ-le
Cœ-la-*le*-tæ
Cœ-le-*sy*-ri-a
Cœ-li-a
Co-es
Col-chis
Co-li-as
Col-la-*ti*-a
Col-la-*ti*-nus
Col-*li*-na
Co-*lo*-næ
Co-*lo*-nos
Col-o-phon
Co-*los*-se
Co-*los*-sus
Co-*lo*-tes
Com-a-*ge*-na
Co-*ma*-na
Com-*bre*-a
Com-mo-dus
Co-mus
Con-*cor*-di-a
Con-*da*-te
Con-*dru*-si
Co-non
Con-stans
Con-stan-*ti*-nus
Con-*stan*-ti-us
Con-*syg*-na
Co-os
Co-*pa*-is
Co-pi-a
Cop-ra-tes
Cop-tos
Co-*ral*-li
Cor-bu-lo
Cor-*cy*-ra
Cor-du-ba
Cor-du-*e*-na
Cor-e-sus
Cor-*fin*-i-um
Co-*rin*-na
Co-rin-*thi*-a-cus
Co-*rin*-thus
Co-ri-o-*la*-nus
Co-*ri*-o-li
Cor-*ne*-li-a
Cor-*nic*-u-lum
Cor-*nu*-tus
Co-*rœ*-bus
Cor-o-*ne*-a
Co-*ro*-nis
Cor-*rha*-gi-um
Cor-*se*-a
Cor-so-te
Cor-*to*-na
Co-ru-*pe*-di-um
Cor-*vi*-nus
Co-ry-don
Co-ry-la
Co-ry-*pha*-si-um
Co-ry-thus
Co-*sy*-ra
Cot-ta
Co-*tyor*-a
Co-tys
Co-*tyt*-to
Cra-*næ*-um
Cran-non
Cran-tor
Cras-*si*-pes
Cras-sus
Cra-ter-us
Cra-tes
Crat-y-lus
Crem-e-ra
Cre-on
Cre-on-*ti*-a-des
Cre-*oph*-i-lus
Cres-*phon*-tes
Cre-ta
Cre-te
Cre-*u*-sa
Cre-*u*-sis
Cri-*mis*-sus
Cri-*ni*-sus
Cris-*pi*-nus
Cri-*ta*-la
Crit-i-as
Cri-to
Crit-o-*la*-us
Croc-y-*le*-um
Crœ-sus
Cro-my-on
Cro-nus
Cro-ton
Cro-*to*-pus
Cru-nos
Crus-tu-*me*-ri-um
Cte-a-tus
Cte-si-as
Cte-*sib*-i-us
Ctes-i-phon
Ctim-e-ne
Cu-la-ro
Cu-mæ
Cu-*nax*-a
Cu-*pi*-do
Cu-res
Cu-*re*-tes
Cu-ri-*a*-ti-i
Cu-ri-o-*sol*-i-tæ
Cu-ri-us
Cur-ti-us
Cy-a-ne
Cy-*an*-e-æ
Cy-*ax*-a-res
Cyb-e-le
Cyb-i-ra
Cyc-la-des
Cyc-*lo*-pes
Cyc-nus
Cyd-nus
Cy-don
Cyd-o-*ni*-a
Cyl-*le*-ne
Cy-me
Cy-*me*-lus
Cy-*mod*-o-ce
Cy-*mo*-lus
Cy-*moth*-o-e
Cyn-æ-*gi*-rus
Cy-*na*-ne
Cy-*nax*-a
Cy-*ne*-si-i
Cyn-o-*ceph*-a-læ
Cyn-o-*sar*-ges
Cyn-os-*se*-ma
Cyn-o-*su*-ra
Cyn-thi-a
Cy-*nu*-ri-a
Cyp-ri-*a*-nus
Cyp-*sel*-i-des
Cyp-se-lus
Cyr-e-*na*-i-ca
Cy-*re*-ne
Cyr-*rhes*-ti-ca
Cyr-us
Cy-*the*-ra
Cyth-e-*ræ*-a
Cyth-*e*-rus
Cy-*tor*-us
Cyz-i-cus

Da-æ
Da-cæ
Dac-ty-li
Dæ-da-la
Dæ-da-*le*-a
Dæ-da-lus
Da-i-cles
Da-*im*-a-chus
Da-*im*-e-nes
Da-*i*-ra
Dal-ma-tæ
Dal-*ma*-ti-a
Dam-a-*ge*-tus
Da-mas
Dam-as-*ce*-na
Dam-a-*sip*-pus
Dam-a-*sis*-tra-tus
Dam-a-sus
Dam-ni-i
Dam-*no*-ni-i
Dam-o-cles
Da-*moc*-ra-tus
Da-mon
Dam-o-*ni*-cus
Dam-o-*phan*-tas
Da-*mos*-tra-tus
Da-*mox*-e-nus
Dan-a-e
Dan-a-i
Da-*na*-i-des
Dan-a-us
Da-*nu*-vi-us
Da-o-chus
Daph-ne
Daph-*næ*-us
Dar-da-ni
Dar-da-nus
Da-res
Da-*ri*-us
Das-*cyl*-i-um
Das-cy-lus
Das-sa-*re*-tæ
Dat-a-mes
Da-tis
Dau-ni-i
Dau-nus
Da-vus
De-*cap*-o-lis
De-*ceb*-a-lus
Dec-e-*le*-a
De-ci-*a*-tes
Dec-i-mus
De-ci-us
Dec-u-*ma*-tes
De-i-a-*ni*-ra
De-id-a-*mi*-a
De-*il*-o-chus
De-*im*-a-chus
De-*i*-o-ces
De-*i*-o-ne
De-i-*ot*-a-rus
De-*iph*-o-bus
De-*ip*-y-lus
De-*li*-a-des
De-li-um
De-los
Del-phi
Del-phi-cus
Del-*phy*-ne
Dem-a-des
Dem-a-*ra*-tus
De-*me*-ter
De-*me*-tri-as
De-*me*-tri-us
De-*mo*-ce
De-*moch*-a-res
Dem-o-cles
De-*moc*-ra-tes
De-*moc*-ri-tus
De-*mod*-o-cus
Dem-o-*do*-rus
De-*mo*-nax
Dem-o-phon
De-mo-*pho*-on
De-*mos*-the-nes
De-*mos*-tra-tus
De-*mu*-chus
De-*od*-a-tus
Der-bi-ces
Der-*cen*-nus
Der-ce-to
Der-*cyl*-li-das
Der-*to*-na
Deu-*ca*-li-on
Deu-do-rix
Dex-*am*-e-nus
Di-*ad*-o-chi
Di-*æ*-us
Di-*ag*-o-ras
Di-*a*-lis
Di-*a*-na
Dic-æ-*ar*-chus
Dic-tys
Did-i-us
Di-do
Did-y-ma
Did-y-mus
Di-*es*-pi-ter
Di-*gen*-ti-a
Di-*nar*-chus
Din-dy-mus
Din-i-che
Di-*noc*-ra-tes
Di-*nom*-e-nes
Di-o-cæs-a-*re*-a
Di-o-*cle*-a
Di-o-cles
Di-o-cle-ti-*a*-nus
Di-o-*dor*-us
Di-*og*-e-nes
Di-o-*me*-des
Di-*om*-e-don
Di-on
Di-o-*næ*-a
Di-*o*-ne
Di-o-*nys*-i-us
Di-o-*ny*-sus
Di-*oph*-a-nes
Di-o-*phan*-tus
Di-*op*-o-lis
Di-os-*co*-ri-des
Di-os-*cu*-ri
Di-*os*-pa-ge
Di-*os*-po-lis
Di-*ot*-re-phes
Diph-i-lus
Dip-o-lis
Dir-ce
Dis-*cor*-di-a
Dith-y-*ram*-bus
Div-i-*ti*-a-cus
Di-vo-*du*-rum
Div-o-na
Do-*be*-rus
Do-*do*-na
Dol-a-*bel*-la
Do-*li*-che
Dol-on
Dol-o-pes
Do-*min*-i-ca
Do-mit-i-*a*-nus
Do-*mit*-i-us
Do-*na*-tus
Do-*nu*-sa
Do-ri-cus
Do-ri-*e*-us
Do-ri-*la*-us
Do-ris
Do-*ris*-cus
Do-ry-las
Do-ry-*la*-us
Do-*si*-a-des
Dot-a-das
Dra-*ca*-nus
Dra-co
Dra-*con*-ti-des
Dran-gi-*a*-na
Drep-a-num
Drim-a-chus
Dri-*op*-i-des
Dro-*mach*-e-tus
Drop-i-ci

Dru-*en*-ti-us
Dru-*sil*-la
Dru-sus
Dry-a-des
Dry-o-pe
Dry-o-pes
Dry-ops
Dry-pe-tis
Du-bis
Du-bris
Du-*il*-li-us
Du-*lich*-i-um
Dum-*no*-rix
Du-ri-us
Dur-no-*ve*-ri-a
Du-ro-*bri*-væ
Du-ro-cor-*no*-vi-um
Du-ro-*cor*-to-rum
Dy-mas
Dy-*nam*-e-ne
Dyr-*ra*-chi-um
Dy-*so*-rum

E-a-nes
E-*a*-nus
Eb-do-me
Eb-o-ra
E-*bo*-ra-cum
E-*bu*-dæ
Eb-u-*ro*-nes
Eb-u-ro-*vi*-ces
Eb-u-sus
Ec-*bat*-a-na
E-*ce*-tra
Ech-e-mus
Ech-e-ta
E-*chid*-na
E-*chin*-a-des
E-*chi*-on
Ech-o
E-*des*-sa
E-*do*-ni
E-e-ti-on
E-e-ti-*o*-ne-a
E-*ge*-ri-a
E-*ges*-ta
E-*i*-on
E-*i*-o-nes
E-*læ*-us
El-a-*gab*-a-lus
E-*la*-i-tes
El-a-*te*-a
El-a-tus
E-*la*-ver
E-le-a
E-le-*a*-tes
E-*lec*-tra
E-*lec*-try-on
E-le-on
El-e-*phan*-tis
El-e-*phe*-nor
El-e-*por*-us
El-eu-*sin*-i-a
E-*leu*-sis
E-*leu*-the-ra
E-*leu*-the-*rop*-o-lis
E-*leu*-the-rus
El-i-*me*-a
E-lis
E-*lis*-sa
El-*pe*-nor
El-pi-*ni*-ce
El-y-*ma*-is
El-y-mus
El-y-rus
E-*lys*-i-um
E-*math*-i-a
Em-bo-*li*-ma
E-*me*-ri-ta
E-*mes*-sa
E-*mo*-na
Em-*ped*-o-cles
Em-*pu*-sa
En-*cel*-a-dus
En-*de*-ra
En-*dym*-i-on
En-*gy*-um
E-*nip*-e-us
En-na
En-ni-us
En-*no*-di-us
En-no-mus
En-o-pe
En-*tel*-lus
E-*ny*-o
E-*o*-ne
E-os
E-*o*-us
E-pam-i-*non*-das
E-paph-ro-*di*-tus
Ep-a-phus
E-*peb*-o-lus
E-*pe*-us
Eph-e-sus
E-phi-*al*-tes
Eph-o-ri
Eph-o-rus
Eph-y-ra
E-*pich*-a-ris
Ep-i-*char*-mus
Ep-i-cles
Ep-i-*cli*-des
E-*pic*-ra-tes
Ep-ic-*te*-tus
Ep-i-*cu*-rus
E-pi-*cy*-des
Ep-i-*dam*-nus
Ep-i-*dau*-rus
E-*pig*-e-nes
E-*pig*-o-ni
E-*pim*-e-nes
Ep-i-*men*-i-des
Ep-i-*me*-the-us
E-*piph*-a-nes
Ep-i-*pha*-ni-us
E-*pip*-o-læ
E-*pi*-rus
Ep-i-tos
Ep-o-na
E-*pon*-y-mus
Ep-o-*pe*-us
Ep-o-*red*-o-rix
Ep-y-tus
Er-a-*si*-nus
Er-a-*sis*-tra-tus
Er-a-to
Er-a-*tos*-the-nes
Er-a-*tos*-tra-tus
E-*ra*-tus
E-re-bus
E-rech-*the*-um
E-*rech*-the-us
E-rech-*ti*-dæ
E-*re*-sus
E-*ret*-ri-a
E-*re*-tum
Er-ga-ne
Er-*gin*-nus
Er-*gi*-nus
E-ri-*bœ*-a
E-ri-*bo*-tes
E-ri-*ce*-tes
E-*rich*-tho
E-rich-*tho*-ni-us
E-ri-*cin*-i-um
E-ri-*cu*-sa
E-*rid*-a-nus
Er-ig-*du*-pus
E-*rig*-o-ne
E-rig-o-*ne*-i-us
E-*rig*-o-nus
Er-i-*gy*-us
E-*ril*-lus
E-*rin*-na
E-*rin*-ny-es
E-*ri*-o-pis
E-ri-*phid*-i-as
E-ri-*phy*-le
E-ris
E-*ro*-chus
E-ros
E-*ros*-tra-tus
E-*ry*-a-lus
E-ry-*ci*-na
E-ry-*man*-thus
E-*ryth*-e-a
E-ry-*thi*-ni
E-ry-thræ
E-ryx
Es-qui-*li*-nus
Es-*sed*-o-nes
Et-e-*ar*-chus
E-*te*-o-cles
E-*te*-o-clus
Et-e-*oc*-re-tes
E-te-*o*-ne-us
Et-e-o-*ni*-cus
E-*te*-si-æ
E-ti-as
E-tis
E-*tru*-ri-a
E-*trus*-ci
Eu-*bœ*-a
Eu-*bu*-lus
Eu-*cli*-des
Eu-cra-tes
Eu-*dam*-i-des
Eu-*de*-mus
Eu-*do*-ci-a
Eu-*dox*-i-a
Eu-*dox*-us
Eu-e-*me*-ri-das
Eu-*e*-nus
Eu-*er*-ge-tæ
Eu-*er*-ge-tes
Eu-*ga*-ne-i
Eu-*hem*-e-rus
Eu-*mæ*-us
Eu-*me*-des
Eu-*me*-lus
Eu-me-nes
Eu-me-*ni*-a
Eu-*men*-i-des
Eu-*mol*-pus
Eu-*ni*-ce
Eu-no-mus
Eu-o-ras
Eu-pa-tor
Eu-pa-*tor*-i-a
Eu-pha-es
Eu-*phe*-mus
Eu-*phe*-nus
Eu-*phor*-bus
Eu-*phor*-i-on
Eu-*phra*-nor
Eu-*phra*-tes
Eu-*phros*-y-ne
Eu-po-lis
Eu-*po*-lus
Eu-*rip*-i-des
Eu-*ri*-pus
Eu-*roc*-ly-don
Eu-*ro*-pa
Eu-*ro*-pus
Eu-*ro*-tas
Eu-*ry*-a-lus
Eu-*ryb*-a-tes
Eu-ry-*bi*-a-des
Eu-ry-*cle*-a
Eu-ry-cles
Eu-*ryd*-i-ce
Eu-*ryl*-o-chus
Eu-*rym*-a-chus
Eu-*rym*-e-don
Eu-*rym*-e-nes
Eu-*ry*-o-me
Eu-ry-pon
Eu-*ryp*-y-lus
Eu-*rys*-the-nes
Eu-*rys*-the-us
Eu-ry-tus
Eu-*se*-bi-us
Eu-*ter*-pe
Eu-thy-*de*-mus
Eu-*tre*-si-a
Eu-*tro*-pi-us
Eu-ty-ches
Eu-ty-chus
Eu-*xi*-nus
E-*vad*-ne
E-*vag*-o-ras
E-*ve*-nor
E-*ve*-nus
E-*vip*-pus

Fab-a-ris
Fa-bi-*a*-ni
Fa-bi-us
Fa-*bric*-i-us
Fæs-u-læ
Fa-*le*-ri-i
Far-fa-rus
Fau-*cu*-la
Fau-*sti*-nus
Fau-stu-lus
Fav-o-*ri*-nus
Feb-ru-us
Fel-si-na
Fer-en-*ti*-num
Fe-*ro*-ni-a
Fes-*cen*-ni-a
Fes-cu-læ
Fi-*bre*-nus
Fi-*de*-næ
Fi-*den*-ti-a
Fid-en-*ti*-nus
Fi-*dic*-u-læ
Fim-bri-ca
Fir-mi-us
Flac-cus
Flam-i-nes
Fla-*mi*-ni-a
Flam-i-*ni*-nus
Fla-*min*-i-us
Fla-vi-*a*-num
Fla-vi-us
Flor-a
Flo-*ra*-lia
Flo-ri-*a*-nus
Flor-us
Fon-*ta*-nus
For-mi-æ
For-mi-*a*-num
For-mi-o
For-*tu*-na
For-tu-*na*-tæ
For-u-li
For-um *Ap*-pi-i
Fre-*gel*-læ
Fre-*ge*-næ
Fren-*ta*-ni
Frig-i-dus
Fris-i-i
Fron-*ti*-nus
Fru-si-no
Fu-ci-nus
Ful-gi-*na*-tes
Ful-*gi*-nus
Ful-vi-a
Fun-*da*-nus
Fun-di
Fu-ri-æ
Fu-*ri*-na
Fu-ri-us
Fus-*ci*-na
Fus-cus

Gab-a-la
Gab-a-lus
Ga-*be*-ne
Ga-bi-*e*-nus
Ga-bi-i
Ga-*bi*-na
Ga-*bin*-i-us
Ga-des
Gad-i-*ta*-nus
Gæ-*tu*-li
Ga-ius
Ga-*læ*-sus
Ga-*lan*-this
Gal-a-ta
Gal-a-*tæ*-a
Ga-*la*-ti-a
Gal-ba
Gal-bu-la
Ga-len
Ga-*le*-nus
Ga-*le*-o-læ
Ga-*le*-ri-us
Ga-*le*-sus
Gal-i-*læ*-a
Gal-li-a
Gal-li-cus
Gal-li-*e*-nus
Gal-*lip*-o-lis
Gal-lus
Gan-da-*ri*-tæ
Gan-*ga*-ri-dæ
Gan-*ge*-tis
Gan-y-*me*-des
Ga-ra-*man*-tes
Ga-ra-mas
Gar-*ga*-nus
Gar-*gaph*-i-a
Gar-ga-rus
Gar-*get*-tus
Ga-*ri*-tes
Ga-*rum*-na
Gath-e-æ
Gau-ga-*me*-la
Gau-ri-um
Gau-rus
Ga-*za*-ri-a
Ge-*dro*-si-a
Ge-*gan*-i-i
Gel-a
Ge-*la*-nor
Ge-lon
Ge-*lo*-ni
Gem-i-ni
Gem-i-nus
Ge-*na*-bum
Ge-*nau*-ni
Ge-*ne*-va
Ge-*ni*-sus
Gen-se-ric
Gen-u-a
Ge-*nu*-si-a
Ge-*nu*-sus
Geor-gi-ca
Ge-*phy*-ra
Geph-y-*ræ*-i
Gep-i-dæ
Ge-*ræ*-sti-cum
Ger-a-*ni*-a
Ge-ra-sa
Ger-gi-thum
Ger-*go*-vi-a
Ge-ri-on
Ger-*ma*-ni-a
Ger-*man*-i-cus
Ger-*ma*-nus
Ge-ry-on
Ges-sa-tæ
Ges-so-*ri*-a-cum
Ge-ta
Ge-tæ
Gi-*gan*-tes
Gi-gan-*te*-us
Gi-*go*-nus

Gin-*gu*-num
Glaph-y-ra
Glau-ce
Glau-con
Glau-cus
Glis-as
Glyc-e-ra
Glyc-on
Gni-dus
Go-bry-as
Gom-phi
Go-*na*-tas
Gor-di-*a*-nus
Gor-di-us
Gor-*ga*-sus
Gor-gi-as
Gor-go
Gor-go-nes
Gor-*ty*-na
Go-*tho*-nes
Grac-chus
Gra-*di*-vus
Græ-ci-a
Græ-*ci*-nus
Græ-cus
Gra-*ni*-cus
Gra-ti-æ
Gra-ti-*a*-nus
Gra-ti-on
Gre-*gor*-i-us
Gryll-us
Gry-ni-um
Gy-a-rus
Gy-ges
Gy-*lip*-pus
Gym-*ne*-si-æ
Gym-*ne*-tes
Gy-*the*-um

Ha-dri-a-*nop*-o-lis
Ha-dri-*a*-nus
Ha-dri-*at*-i-cum
Hæ-mon
Hæ-mus
Ha-ges
Hal-*cy*-o-ne
Hal-*e*-sa
Ha-*le*-si-us
Ha-li-*ac*-mon
Hal-i-*ar*-tus
Hal-i-car-*nas*-sus
Ha-*lic*-y-æ
Ha-*lim*-e-de
Hal-i-*rrho*-ti-us
Hal-i-*zo*-nes
Hal-my-ris
Ha-*loc*-ra-tes
Hal-on-*ne*-sus
Ha-*lo*-tus
Hal-y-cus
Hal-ys
Ham-a-*dry*-a-des
Ha-*max*-i-tus
Ha-*mil*-car
Han-ni-bal
Har-ca-lo
Har-ma-tris
Har-*mo*-di-us
Har-*mo*-ni-a
Har-*mon*-i-des
Har-*mo*-zi-a
Har-pa-gus
Har-*pal*-i-ce
Har-pa-lus
Har-pa-sa
Har-pa-sus
Har-*poc*-ra-tes
Har-*py*-i-æ
Ha-*ru*-des
Has-dru-bal
He-au-ton-ti-mo-*ru*-me-nos

Heb-do-me
He-be
He-*be*-sus
He-brus
He-*bu*-des
Hec-a-le
Hec-a-*me*-de
Hec-a-*tæ*-us
Hec-a-te
Hec-a-to
Hec-a-*tom*-po-lis
Hec-a-*tom*-py-los
Hec-a-ton-*ne*-si
Hec-tor
Hec-u-ba
Hed-y-la
He-*ge*-mon
Heg-e-*si*-a-nax
He-*ge*-si-as
Heg-e-*sil*-o-chus
Heg-e-*si*-nus
Heg-e-*sip*-pus
Heg-e-*sip*-y-le
Hel-e-na
Hel-e-nus
He-*li*-a-des
Hel-i-*ca*-on
Hel-i-ce
Hel-i-con
He-li-o-*dor*-us
He-li-o-*gab*-a-lus
He-li-*op*-o-lis
He-li-os
Hel-*lan*-i-cus
Hel-la-*noc*-ra-tes
Hel-*le*-nes
He-*lo*-rus
He-los
He-*lo*-tæ
Hel-*ve*-ti-i
Hel-*vi*-na
Hel-y-mus
He-mon
He-mus
Hen-e-ti
He-ni-o-*chi*-a
He-*phæs*-ti-a (city)
Heph-æs-*ti*-a (festival)
He-phæs-*ti*-a-des
He-*phæs*-ti-on
He-*phæs*-tos
Hep-*tap*-o-lis
He-ra
Her-a-*cle*-a
Her-a-*cle*-i-a
Her-a-cles
He-rac-le-*op*-o-lis
He-*rac*-le-um
Her-a-*cli*-dæ
Her-a-*cli*-des
Her-a-*cli*-tus
He-*ræ*-a
He-*ræ*-um
Her-*bes*-sus
Her-*ce*-us
Her-cu-*la*-ne-um
Her-cu-les
Her-*cu*-le-um
Her-*cy*-na
Her-*cyn*-i-us, -a
Her-*do*-ni-a
Her-*do*-ni-us
He-re-us
He-*ril*-lus
Her-i-lus
Her-ma-chus
Her-mæ
Her-*mag*-o-ras
Her-*man*-di-ca
Her-man-*du*-ri
Her-maph-ro-*di*-tus

Her-*ma*-the-na
Her-mes
Her-me-*si*-a-nax
Her-*mi*-as
Her-*min*-i-us
Her-*mi*-o-ne
Her-*mi*-o-nes
Her-mi-*on*-i-æ
Her-mi-*on*-i-cus
Her-*mip*-pus
Her-*moc*-ra-tes
Her-mo-*do*-rus
Her-*mog*-e-nes
Her-mo-*la*-us
Her-*mo*-nax
Her-*mop*-o-lis
Her-mo-*ti*-mus
Her-mun-*du*-ri
Her-ni-ci
He-ro
He-*ro*-das
He-*ro*-des
He-ro-di-*a*-nus
He-*rod*-i-cus
He-*rod*-o-tus
He-ro-*du*-lus
He-*ron*-das
He-*roph*-i-lus
He-*ros*-tra-tus
Her-se
Her-*sil*-i-a
Her-tha
He-ru-li
He-si-od
He-si-o-ne
Hes-*pe*-ri-a
Hes-*per*-i-des
Hes-pe-ris
Hes-pe-rus
Hes-ti-a
Hes-ti-*æ*-a
He-*sych*-i-us
He-*tric*-u-lum
Hex-*ap*-y-lum
Hi-*ber*-ni-a
Hi-*be*-rus
Hic-e-*ta*-on
Hi-*ce*-tas
Hi-*emp*-sal
Hi-e-ra (island)
Hi-*e*-ra (person)
Hi-e-*rap*-o-lis
Hi-a-rax
Hi-e-ro
Hi-*er*-o-cles
Hi-e-ro-*du*-lum
Hi-e-ro-*my*-ces
Hi-e-*ron*-y-mus
Hi-e-*roph*-i-lus
Hi-e-ro-*sol*-y-ma
Him-e-ra
Hi-*mil*-co
Hip-*pag*-o-ras
Hip-pa-lus
Hip-*par*-chus
Hip-pa-*ri*-nus
Hip-pa-sus
Hip-pi-as
Hip-po
Hip-*pob*-o-tus
Hip-po-*cli*-des
Hip-po-*co*-me
Hip-*poc*-o-on
Hip-*poc*-ra-tes
Hip-po-*cre*-ne
Hip-*pod*-a-me
Hip-po-da-*mi*-a
Hip-*pod*-a-mus
Hip-*pod*-i-ce
Hip-po-*dro*-mus
Hip-po-la
Hip-*pol*-o-chus

Hip-*pol*-y-tus, -te
Hip-*pom*-a-chus
Hip-*pom*-e-don
Hip-po-me-*du*-sa
Hip-*pom*-e-nes
Hip-*po*-na
Hip-*po*-nax
Hip-*po*-ni-um
Hip-*pon*-o-us
Hip-*pos*-tra-tus
Hip-*pot*-a-des
Hip-po-tes
Hip-*poth*-o-on
Hip-*poth*-o-us
Hip-pu-*ac*-ra
Hip-*pu*-ris
Hir-*pi*-ni
His-pa-lis
His-*pa*-ni-a
His-*pa*-nus
His-*tas*-pes
His-ti-*æ*-us
His-tri-a
Ho-*mer*-i-dæ
Ho-*me*-rus
Hom-o-le
Ho-*nor*-i-us
Ho-*ra*-ti-us
Ho-ro-*lo*-gi-um
Hor-ta
Hor-*ten*-si-us
Hor-*to*-na
Hor-us
Hos-*til*-i-a
Hun-ne-*ri*-cus
Hun-ni
Hy-a-*cin*-thus
Hy-a-des
Hy-*ag*-nis
Hy-a-la
Hy-am-*pe*-a
Hy-*am*-po-lis
Hy-*an*-this
Hy-as
Hy-bla
Hy-bre-as
Hyc-ca-ra
Hyd-a-ra
Hy-*dar*-nes
Hy-*das*-pes
Hy-dra
Hy-dra-*o*-tes
Hy-dre-a
Hy-*drun*-tum
Hy-*dru*-sa
Hy-e-la
Hy-*emp*-sal
Hy-*et*-tus
Hy-*ge*-i-a
Hy-*gi*-nus
Hy-*læ*-us
Hy-las
Hy-lax
Hy-*lon*-o-me
Hy-*loph*-a-gi
Hy-men
Hy-*met*-tus
Hy-*pæ*-pa
Hyp-a-nis
Hyp-a-*ri*-nus
Hyp-a-ta
Hy-*pa*-ti-a
Hy-*pe*-nor
Hy-*per*-bo-lus
Hyp-er-*bo*-re-i
Hy-*pe*-ri-des
Hyp-e-*ri*-on, or
Hy-*pe*-ri-on
Hyp-erm-*nes*-tra
Hy-*pe*-ro-chus
Hyph-a-sis
Hyp-*se*-la

Hyp-*se*-nor
Hyp-*se*-us
Hyp-*sic*-ra-tes
Hyp-*sip*-y-le
Hyr-*ca*-ni-a
Hyr-*ca*-nus
Hyr-*mi*-na
Hyr-ta-cus
Hys-i-æ
Hys-*tas*-pes
Hys-ti-*e*-us

I-*ac*-chus
I-*a*-der
I-a-*le*-mus
I-*al*-me-nus
I-*al*-y-sus
I-*am*-be
I-*am*-bli-cus
I-*am*-e-nus
I-*am*-i-dæ
I-a-*ni*-ra
I-*an*-the
I-*ap*-e-tus
I-a-*pyg*-i-a
I-*a*-pyx
I-*ar*-bas
I-*ar*-chas
I-ar-*da*-nus
I-*as*-i-des
I-*as*-i-on
I-*as*-is
I-a-sus
Iax-*ar*-tes
I-*be*-ri
I-*be*-ri-a
I-*be*-rus
I-bis
Ib-y-cus
I-*ca*-ri-a
Ic-a-rus
I-*ce*-lus
I-*ce*-ni
Ic-e-tas
Ich-thy-*oph*-a-gi
Ich-thys
I-*cil*-i-us
I-*co*-ni-um
Ic-*ti*-nus
I-da
I-*dæ*-a
I-*da*-li-um
Id-a-lus
I-dan-*thyr*-sus
I-das
I-*de*-ra
I-dis-ta-*vi*-sus
I-*dom*-e-ne
I-*dom*-e-neus
I-do-*the*-a
I-*dri*-e-us
I-*du*-be-da
I-du-*me*-a
I-*e*-tæ
Ig-e-ni
I-*gil*-i-um
Ig-*na*-ti-us
Il-a-*i*-ra
Il-e-ca-*o*-nes
I-*ler*-da
Il-er-*ge*-tes
Il-i-a
Il-i-as
Il-i-*en*-ses
Il-i-on
I-*li*-o-ne
Il-i-*o*-neus
I-*lis*-sus
Il-*lib*-e-ris
Il-li-*tur*-gis
Il-*lyr*-i-a
Il-*lyr*-i-cum

I-lus
I-*lyr*-gis
Im-a-us
Im-ba-rus
Im-bra-sus
Im-bros
Im-man-u-*en*-ti-us
Im-o-la
In-a-chis
In-a-chus
I-*nam*-a-mes
In-*a*-ri-me
In-a-ros
In-di-a
In-*dib*-i-lis
In-di-*ge*-tes
In-*dig*-e-ti
In-du-ti-o-*ma*-rus
In-*gæ*-vo-nes
In-*gau*-ni
I-no
I-*no*-us
In-su-bres
In-ta-*pher*-nes
In-te-*ram*-na
In-ter-*ca*-ti-a
I-*ny*-cus
I-o
I-*ob*-a-tes
I-o-bes
I-o-*la*-i-das
I-o-las
I-o-*la*-us
I-*ol*-chos
I-o-le
I-on
I-*o*-ne
I-o-ni-a
I-*on*-i-cus
I-*o*-pas
I-*o*-phon
I-os
Iph-i-a-*nas*-sa
Iph-i-clus
I-*phic*-ra-tes
Iph-i-ge-*ni*-a
Iph-i-me-*di*-a
I-*phim*-e-don
Iph-i-me-*du*-sa
I-phis
Iph-i-tus
Ip-*se*-a
I-ra
Ir-e-*næ*-us
I-*re*-ne
I-*re*-sus
I-ris
I-rus
I-*sæ*-us
I-*sag*-o-ras
I-*san*-der
I-*sa*-pis
Is-a-ra
I-*sar*-chus
I-*sa*-tis
I-*sau*-ra
I-*sau*-ri-a
Is-de-*ger*-des
Is-i-*dor*-us
I-sis
Is-ma-rus
Is-*me*-ne
Is-*me*-ni-as
Is-*me*-nus
I-*soc*-ra-tes
Is-sus
Is-tæ-*vo*-nes
Is-*to*-ne
Is-tri-a
Is-*trop*-o-lis
It-a-li
I-*tal*-i-a

I-*tal*-i-cus
It-a-lus
I-*tar*-gris
Ith-a-ca
I-*tho*-me
I-*thor*-u-a
Ith-y-*phal*-lus
I-*to*-ni-a
I-*to*-nus
It-u-na
It-u-*ræ*-a
I-*tu*-rum
It-y-lus
I-tys
I-*u*-lus
Ix-*i*-on
Ix-i-*on*-i-des

Ja-*co*-bus
Jad-e-ra
Ja-*nic*-u-lum
Ja-nus
Ja-son
Jen-i-sus
Je-*ro*-mus
Je-*ron*-y-mus
Jo-*cas*-ta
Jo-*se*-phus
Jo-vi-*a*-nus
Jo-*vi*-nus
Ju-ba
Ju-*dæ*-a
Ju-*ga*-lis
Ju-*gur*-tha
Ju-li-a
Ju-li-*a*-nus
Ju-li-*op*-o-lis
Ju-li-us
Ju-ni-us
Ju-no
Ju-*no*-nis
Ju-pi-ter
Ju-ra
Jus-*ti*-nus
Ju-*tur*-na
Ju-ve-*na*-lis
Ju-*ven*-tas
Ju-*ven*-ti-us
Ju-*ver*-na

La-*ar*-chus
Lab-a-ris
Lab-*dac*-i-dæ
Lab-da-cus
Lab-da-lum
Lab-e-*a*-lis
La-be-o
La-*be*-ri-us
La-*bi*-ci
La-*bi*-cum
La-bi-*e*-nus
La-*bo*-tas
La-bron
Lab-y-*rin*-thus
Lac-e-*dæ*-mon
Lac-e-*dæ*-mo-nes
Lac-e-dæ-*mo*-ni-us
La-*cer*-ta
Lac-e-*ta*-ni-a
Lach-a-res
La-ches
Lach-e-sis
La-*ci*-des
La-*cin*-i-um
La-co
La-*co*-bri-ga
La-*co*-nes
La-*co*-ni-a
La-*con*-i-ca
Lac-ra-tes
Lac-ri-tus

Lac-tans
Lac-*tan*-ti-us
Lac-y-des
Lad-as
La-de
La-don
Læ-laps
Læ-li-*a*-nus
Læ-li-a
Læ-li-us
Læ-nas
Læ-ne-us
La-*er*-tes
La-er-*ti*-a-des
Læ-*stry*-go-nes
Læ-*vi*-nus
La-gus
La-*gu*-sa
La-*gy*-ra
La-is
La-i-us
Lal-a-ge
Lam-a-chus
Lam-brus
La-*me*-tus
La-*mi*-a, or *La*-mi-a
La-*mi*-rus
Lam-*pet*-i-a
Lam-pe-to
Lam-pon
Lam-*po*-ni-a
Lam-*prid*-i-us
Lam-pro-cles
Lamp-sa-cus
Lamp-*te*-ri-a
Lamp-ter-se
La-mus
Lam-y-rus
Lan-a-tus
Lan-go-*bar*-di
La-*nu*-vi-um
La-*oc*-o-on
La-*od*-a-mas
La-o-da-*mi*-a
La-*od*-i-ce
La-o-di-*ce*-a
La-o-di-*ce*-ne
La-*od*-o-chus
La-*om*-e-don
La-on-o-*me*-ne
Lap-a-thus
La-*pe*-thus
Laph-ri-a
Lap-i-thæ
Lap-i-*thæ*-um
La-ra
La-*ren*-ti-a
La-res
La-*ri*-des
La-*ri*-num
La-*ris*-sa
La-ri-us
Lar-ti-us
La-*rym*-na
La-si-on
La-sus
Las-the-nes
Las-the-*ni*-a
Lat-e-*ra*-nus
Lat-e-*ren*-sis
La-*ti*-nus
La-ti-um
La-*tob*-ri-gi
La-*to*-is
La-*to*-na
La-*top*-o-lis
La-*to*-us
La-tro
Lau-da-*mi*-a
Lau-*fel*-la
Lau-ra
Lau-*re*-a-cum

Lau-ren-*ti*-ni
Lau-*ren*-tum
Lau-ri-um
Lau-ron
La-us
Lau-sus
Lau-tu-*mi*-æ
La-*ver*-na
La-vi-*a*-na
La-*vin*-i-a
La-*vin*-i-um
Le-*æ*-na
Le-*an*-der
Le-*ar*-chus
Leb-a-*de*-a
Leb-e-dos
Le-*be*-na
Le-*bin*-thos
Le-*chæ*-um
Lec-y-thus
Le-da
Le-dus
Le-i-tus
Lel-e-ges
Le-lex
Le-*man*-nus
Lem-o-*vi*-ces
Lem-u-res
Len-tu-lus
Le-o
Le-*och*-a-res
Le-*oc*-ra-tes
Le-*od*-a-mas
Le-on
Le-o-*na*-tus
Le-*on*-i-das
Le-on-*nor*-i-us
Le-on-*ti*-a-des
Le-on-*ti*-ni
Le-*on*-ti-um
Le-os
Le-*os*-the-nes
Le-o-*tych*-i-des
Lep-i-dus
Le-*pi*-nus
Le-*pon*-ti-i
Le-pre-os
Lep-ti-nes
Lep-tis
Le-ri-a
Le-*ri*-na
Ler-na
Le-ro
Le-ros
Les-bos
Lesch-es
Les-*try*-go-nes
Le-*ta*-num
Le-*thæ*-us
Le-the
Leu-ca
Leu-*ca*-di-a
Leu-cas
Leu-ce
Leu-ci
Leu-*cip*-pe
Leu-*cip*-pus
Leu-co-*ge*-i
Leu-co-la
Leu-con
Leu-*co*-ne
Leu-*co*-ni-um
Leu-*con*-o-e
Leu-*cop*-e-tra
Leu-co-phrys
Leu-*cop*-o-lis
Leu-cos
Leu-*co*-si-a
Leu-*cos*-y-ri
Leu-*coth*-o-e
Leuc-tra
Leu-cus

Leu-cy-*a*-ni-as
Leu-*tych*-i-des
Le-*va*-na
Lex-*o*-vi-i
Li-*ba*-ni-us
Lib-a-nus
Lib-en-*ti*-na
Lib-e-ra
Li-*be*-thra
Li-*beth*-ri-des
Lib-i-ci
Lib-i-*ti*-na
Li-bo
Li-*bur*-ni-a
Lib-y-a
Lib-y-cus
Lib-ys-*si*-nus
Lic-a-tes
Lich-a-des
Li-chas
Li-ches
Li-*cin*-i-a
Li-*cin*-i-us
Lic-i-nus
Li-*cym*-ni-us
Li-*ga*-ri-us
Li-*ge*-a
Li-ger
Lig-u-res
Li-*gu*-ri-a
Lig-u-*ri*-nus
Li-*gus*-ti-cus
Lig-y-es
Li-*gyr*-gum
Li-*læ*-a
Lil-y-*bæ*-um
Li-*mæ*-a
Li-*me*-ni-a
Lim-*næ*-um
Li-*mo*-num
Lim-y-ra
Lin-dum
Lin-go-nes
Lin-*ter*-num
Li-nus
Lip-a-ra
Lip-a-ris
Lip-o-*dor*-us
Li-*quen*-ti-a
Li-*ri*-o-pe
Li-ris
Li-*sin*-i-as
Lis-sus
Lit-a-na
Li-*ter*-num
Li-vi-a
Li-vi-us
Lix-us
Lo-bon
Lo-cri
Lo-cris
Lo-*cus*-ta
Lol-li-a
Lol-li-*a*-nus
Lol-li-us
Lon-*din*-i-um
Lon-*gi*-nus
Lon-go-*bar*-di
Lon-gu-la
Lon-gus
Lor-y-ma
Lo-tis
Lo-*toph*-a-gi
Lu-a
Lu-ca
Lu-*ca*-ni-a
Lu-*can*-i-cus
Lu-*ca*-nus
Luc-*ce*-i-us
Lu-ce-res
Lu-*ce*-ri-a
Lu-ci-an

Lu-ci-*a*-nus
Lu-ci-fer
Lu-*cil*-i-us
Lu-*cil*-la
Lu-*ci*-na
Lu-ci-us
Lu-*cre*-ti-a
Lu-*cre*-ti-lis
Lu-*cre*-ti-us
Lu-*cri*-num
Lu-*cri*-nus
Luc-*ta*-ti-us
Lu-*cul*-lus
Lu-cu-mo
Lug-du-*en*-sis
Lug-*du*-num
Lu-na
Lu-*per*-cal
Lu-per-*ca*-li-a
Lu-*per*-cus
Lu-pi-as
Lu-pus
Lus-*ci*-nus
Lu-si-*ta*-ni-a
Lu-si-*ta*-nus
Lu-si-us
Lu-*so*-nes
Lu-*ta*-ti-us
Lu-*te*-ti-a
Ly-*æ*-us
Lyb-y-a
Lyc-a-bas
Lyc-a-*be*-tus
Ly-*cæ*-um
Ly-*cæ*-us
Ly-*cam*-bes
Ly-*ca*-on
Ly-*ca*-o-nes
Ly-ca-*o*-ni-a
Ly-cas
Ly-*cas*-te
Ly-ce
Ly-*ce*-um
Lych-*ni*-dus
Lych-*ni*-tis
Lyc-i-a
Lyc-i-das
Lyc-i-us
Lyc-o-*me*-des
Ly-con
Ly-co-ne
Lyc-o-phron
Ly-*cop*-o-lis
Ly-*co*-pus
Ly-*co*-ris
Ly-*cor*-tas
Lyc-o-*su*-ra
Ly-*cur*-gus
Ly-cus
Ly-de
Lyd-i-a
Ly-*di*-a-des
Lyd-i-as
Ly-dus
Lyg-da-mis
Ly-max
Lym-i-re
Lyn-*ces*-tes
Lyn-*ce*-us
Lyn-*ci*-des
Lyn-cus
Lyr-*ce*-a
Ly-*san*-der
Ly-*san*-dra
Ly-*sa*-ni-ax
Ly-*si*-a-des
Lys-i-as
Lys-i-cles
Ly-*sic*-ra-tes
Ly-*sid*-i-ce
Ly-*sim*-a-che
Ly-*sim*-a-chus
Ly-*sin*-o-e
Ly-sip-pus
Ly-sis
Ly-*sis*-tra-tus
Lys-i-*thi*-des
Ly-*sith*-o-us
Ly-so
Lyx-*e*-a

Ma-*ca*-ra
Mac-a-*re*-us
Ma-*ca*-ri-a
Mac-a-ris
Mac-ca-*bæ*-us
Mac-e-do
Mac-e-*do*-ni-a
Mac-e-*don*-i-cus
Ma-*cel*-la
Ma-cer
Ma-*ces*-tus
Ma-*chæ*-rus
Ma-*chan*-i-das
Ma-*cha*-on
Ma-*che*-rus
Ma-cri-*a*-nus
Ma-*cri*-nus
Ma-cro
Ma-*cro*-bi-i
Ma-*cro*-bi-us
Mac-ro-*crem*-ni-i
Ma-*cro*-nes
Mac-u-*lo*-nus
Ma-*de*-tes
Ma-dy-tus
Mæ-*an*-der
Mæ-*an*-dri-us
Mæ-*ce*-nas
Mæ-di-ca
Mæ-li-us
Mæ-na-des
Mæ-na-lus
Mæ-ni-us
Mæn-o-*bo*-ra
Mæ-non
Mæ-*o*-ni-a
Mæ-*on*-i-des
Mæ-o-nis
Mæ-*o*-tæ
Mæ-*o*-tis
Mæ-vi-us
Ma-gas
Mag-*do*-lum
Mag-e-tæ
Ma-gi
Ma-gi-us
Mag-*nen*-ti-us
Mag-*ne*-si-a
Ma-go
Ma-gon
Mag-on-*ti*-a-cum
Ma-gus
Ma-*har*-bal
Ma-ia
Mal-a-ca
Ma-le-a
Ma-*le*-ba
Ma-*li*-a
Ma-*li*-a-cus *Si*-nus
Ma-lis
Mal-*loph*-o-ra
Mal-*thi*-nus
Ma-*ma*-us
Ma-*mer*-cus
Mam-er-*ti*-ni
Ma-*mil*-i-us, -a, -i
Ma-mu-ri-*a*-nus
Ma-*mur*-ra
Ma-*nas*-ta-bal
Man-*ci*-nus
Man-*da*-ne
Man-*de*-la
Man-*do*-ni-us
Man-dro-cles
Man-*du*-bi-i
Man-du-*bra*-ti-us
Man-*du*-ri-a
Ma-nes
Man-e-tho
Man-*il*-i-us
Man-li-us
Man-su-*e*-tus
Man-ti-*ne*-a
Man-tu-a
Mar-a-*can*-da
Mar-a-thon
Mar-*cel*-la
Mar-cel-*li*-nus
Mar-*cel*-lus
Mar-ci-a
Mar-ci-*a*-na
Mar-ci-a-*nop*-o-lis
Mar-ci-*a*-nus
Mar-ci-on
Mar-co-*man*-ni
Mar-*do*-ni-us
Ma-re-*o*-tis
Mar-gi-*a*-na
Mar-*gi*-tes
Ma-*ri*-a-ba
Ma-ri-*am*-ne
Ma-ri-an-*dy*-num
Ma-ri-*a*-nus
Ma-*ri*-ca
Ma-*ri*-nus
Ma-ri-sus
Ma-*rit*-i-ma
Ma-ri-us
Mar-*ma*-ri-ca
Mar-*ma*-ri-on
Ma-ro
Ma-ro-*bo*-du-us
Ma-ron
Ma-ro-*ne*-a
Mar-*pe*-si-a
Mar-*pes*-sa
Mar-*pe*-sus
Mar-ru-*ci*-ni
Mar-*ru*-vi-um
Mar-si
Mar-*sig*-ni
Mar-sy-as
Mar-ti-*a*-lis
Mar-ti-*a*-nus
Mar-*ti*-na
Mar-tin-i-*a*-nus
Mar-ti-us
Ma-*rul*-lus
Mas-æ-*syl*-i-i
Mas-i-*nis*-sa
Mas-sa-ga
Mas-*sag*-e-tæ
Mas-si-cus
Mas-*sil*-i-a
Mas-sy-la
Mas-*tram*-e-la
Ma-tho
Ma-*ti*-nus
Ma-*tis*-co
Ma-ti-us
Ma-*tro*-na
Mat-*ti*-a-ci
Ma-*tu*-ta
Mat-u-*ti*-nus
Mau-ri
Mau-re-*ta*-ni-a
Mau-rus
Mau-*ru*-si-i
Mau-so-*le*-um
Mau-*so*-lus
Ma-vors
Max-*en*-ti-us
Max-im-i-*a*-nus
Max-i-*mi*-nus
Max-i-mus
Maz-a-ca
Ma-*za*-ces
Ma-*zæ*-us
Ma-*za*-res
Ma-*zi*-ces
Me-a-ra
Me-*cæ*-nas
Me-cis-*te*-us
Me-*de*-a
Me-de-on
Me-di-a
Me-di-o-*la*-num
Me-di-o-ma-*tri*-ci
Med-i-*tri*-na
Me-di-us
Me-*do*-a-cus
Me-*do*-bri-ga
Me-don
Me-*don*-ti-as
Med-u-*a*-na
Med-u-li
Me-*dul*-li-a
Med-ul-*li*-na
Me-dus
Me-*du*-sa
Meg-a-*ba*-zus
Meg-a-cles
Me-*gac*-li-des
Me-*gæ*-ra
Meg-a-le
Meg-a-*lop*-o-lis
Meg-a-*me*-de
Meg-a-*ni*-ra
Me-*ga*-re
Meg-a-*re*-us
Me-*ga*-ris
Me-*gas*-the-nes
Me-*gel*-lus
Me-ges
Me-la
Me-*læ*-næ
Me-*lam*-pus
Mel-am-*py*-ges
Mel-a-ne
Mel-a-*ne*-us
Mel-a-*nip*-pe
Mel-a-*nip*-pi-des
Mel-a-*nip*-pus
Mel-a-*nos*-y-ri
Me-*lan*-thi-us
Me-*lan*-thus
Me-las
Mel-*com*-a-ni
Mel-e-*a*-ger
Me-les
Mel-e-*san*-der
Me-*lib*-o-cus
Mel-i-*bœ*-a
Mel-i-*cer*-tes
Mel-i-*gu*-nis
Me-*li*-na
Me-*lis*-a
Mel-i-ta
Mel-i-*tæ*-a
Mel-i-*te*-ne
Me-*lo*-bo-sis
Me-lon
Me-los
Mel-*pom*-e-ne
Me-*mac*-e-ni
Mem-mi-us
Mem-non
Mem-no-nes
Mem-no-*ni*-um
Mem-phis
Mem-*phi*-tis
Me-*næch*-mus
Me-*nal*-cas
Me-*nal*-ci-das
Men-a-*lip*-pe
Me-*nan*-der
Me-*na*-pi-i
Men-a-pis
Me-nas
Men-*che*-res
Men-des
Men-e-*clei*-das
Men-e-cles
Me-*nec*-ra-tes
Men-e-*de*-mus
Men-e-*la*-us
Me-*ne*-ni-us
Men-e-phron
Me-nes
Me-*nes*-the-us
Men-e-tas
Me-ninx
Me-*nip*-pus
Me-*nœ*-ce-us
Me-*nœ*-tes
Men-œ-*ti*-a-des
Me-non
Me-*noph*-i-lus
Men-tor
Me-*phi*-tis
Mer-*cu*-ri-us
Me-*ri*-o-nes
Mer-me-ros
Mer-o-e
Mer-o-pe
Me-rops
Me-ru-la
Me-*sab*-a-tes
Me-*sem*-bri-a
Me-*se*-ne
Mes-o-*me*-des
Mes-o-po-*ta*-mi-a
Mes-*sa*-la
Mes-sa-*li*-na
Mes-*sa*-na
Mes-*sa*-pi-a
Mes-*se*-ne
Mes-*se*-ni-a
Me-*su*-la
Met-a-bus
Met-a-*ni*-ra
Met-a-pon-*ti*-ni
Met-a-*pon*-tum
Me-*tau*-rus
Me-*tel*-lus
Meth-a-an
Me-*thi*-on
Me-*tho*-di-us
Me-*tho*-ne
Me-*thyd*-ri-um
Me-*thym*-na
Me-ti-a-*du*-sa
Me-*ti*-o-chus
Me-ti-on
Me-tis
Me-ti-us
Me-ton
Met-o-pe
Met-ro-cles
Met-ro-*dor*-us
Me-*trop*-o-lis
Me-*tu*-lum
Me-*va*-ni-a
Me-va-*ni*-o-la
Me-*zen*-ti-us
Mi-a-*co*-rus
Mi-*cip*-sa
Mi-*cy*-thus
Mi-das
Mi-le-*top*-o-lis
Mi-*le*-tus
Mil-i-as
Mil-i-chus
Mi-*li*-nus
Mi-lo
Mil-*ti*-a-des
Mil-vi-us
Mil-y-as
Mi-*mal*-lo-nes

Mi-mas
Mim-*ner*-mus
Min-ci-us
Min-da-rus
Mi-*ne*-i-des
Mi-*ner*-va
Min-i-o
Mi-*no*-a
Mi-nos
Min-o-*tau*-rus
Min-the
Min-*tur*-næ
Min-*u*-ci-us
Min-y-æ
Min-y-as
Min-y-cus
Mi-*se*-num
Mi-*thræ*-um
Mi-thras
Mith-ri-*da*-tes
Mith-ro-bar-*za*-es
Mna-si-as
Mnas-i-cles
Mna-son
Mne-mon
Mne-*mos*-y-ne
Mne-*sar*-chus
Mnes-i-cles
Mnes-i-*la*-us
Mne-*sim*-a-chus
Mnes-ter
Mnes-the-us
Mne-vis
Mo-a-*pher*-nes
Mo-*des*-tus
Mo-di-a
Mœ-nis
Mœ-ra
Mœ-*rag*-e-tes
Mœ-ris
Mœ-si-a
Mo-gun-*ti*-a-cum
Mo-*gy*-ni
Mo-*li*-on
Mo-*li*-o-ne
Mo-lo
Mo-lon
Mo-*lor*-chus
Mo-*los*-sus
Mo-lus
Mo-*lyc*-ri-on
Mo-*mem*-phis
Mo-mus
Mo-na
Mo-*ne*-sus
Mo-*ne*-ta
Mon-i-ca
Mon-i-mus
Mon-o-dus
Mon-œ-cus
Mon-o-mus
Mon-*ta*-nus
Mon-y-chus
Mon-y-mus
Mo-phis
Mop-si-um
Mop-*so*-pi-a
Mop-so-pus
Mop-su-*es*-tu-a
Mop-sus
Mor-*gan*-ti-um
Mor-i-ni
Mor-phe-us
Mo-rys
Mo-sa
Mos-cha
Mos-chi-on
Mos-chus
Mo-*sel*-la
Mo-*sych*-lus
Mo-*sy*-ni
Mo-*tho*-ne
Mo-ty-a
Mu-ci-a
Mu-ci-*a*-nus
Mul-ci-ber
Mul-u-cha
Mul-vi-us
Mum-mi-us
Mun-da
Mu-*ni*-tus
Mu-*nych*-i-a
Mu-*ræ*-na
Mur-cus
Mur-*gan*-ti-a
Mur-*ra*-nus
Mur-sa
Mu-sa
Mu-*sæ*-us
Mu-*so*-ni-us
Mus-*te*-la
Mu-*til*-us
Mu-ti-na
Mu-*ti*-nus
Mu-ti-us
Mu-*tu*-nus
Myc-a-le
My-*ce*-næ
Myc-e-*ri*-nus
My-con
Myc-o-nos
My-don
My-*e*-nus
Myg-a-le
Myg-do-*ni*-a
My-l-æ
My-las
My-la-sa
Myn-dus
My-nes
My-*o*-ni-a
My-on-*ne*-sus
My-ra
Myr-*ci*-nus
My-ri-*an*-dros
My-*ri*-na
Myr-*i-o*-e
Myr-*mec*-i-des
Myr-*mex*
Myr-mi-don
Myr-*mid*-o-nes
My-ron
My-*ron*-i-des
Myr-rha
Myr-rhi-nus
Myr-si-lus
Myr-sus
Myr-ti-lus
Myr-to
Myr-*to*-us
Myr-*tun*-ti-um
Myr-*tu*-sa
Mys-i-a
My-son
Mys-tes
Myt-i-*le*-ne
My-us

Nab-a-*tæ*-i
Nab-a-*za*-nes
Na-bis
Nac-o-*le*-ia
Næ-vi-us
Næ-vo-lus
Na-*i*-a-des
Na-is
Na-*is*-sus
Nam-*ne*-tes
Nan-tu-*a*-tæ
Na-*pa*-ta
Na-*pe*-gus
Naph-i-lus
Nar-bo
Nar-*bo*-na
Nar-bo-*nen*-sis
Nar-*ce*-a
Nar-*cis*-sus
Nar-ga-ra
Nar-ni-a
Nar-ses
Nar-yx
Nas-a-mon
Nas-a-*mo*-nes
Na-*si*-ca
Na-sid-i-*e*-nus
Na-*sid*-i-us
Na-so
Nas-u-a
Na-*ta*-lis
Nau-cra-tes
Nau-cra-tis
Nau-lo-chus
Nau-*pac*-tus
Nau-pli-a
Nau-pli-us
Nau-*por*-tus
Nau-*sic*-a-a
Nau-si-cles
Nau-*sith*-o-us
Nau-ta-ca
Na-va
Na-vi-us
Nax-os
Naz-a-ra
Naz-i-*an*-zus
Ne-*æ*-ra
Ne-*æ*-thus
Ne-*al*-ces
Ne-*al*-i-ces
Ne-*an*-dros
Ne-*an*-thes
Ne-*ap*-o-lis
Ne-*ar*-chus
Ne-*bro*-des
Ne-chos
Nec-*tan*-a-bis
Ne-is
Ne-leus
Ne-*li*-des
Ne-*mæ*-a
Ne-*mau*-sis
Ne-me-a
Nem-e-sis
Ne-*me*-si-us
Ne-*met*-a-cus
Ne-*me*-tes
Ne-*mos*-sus
Ne-o-*bu*-le
Ne-o-cæ-sa-*re*-a
Ne-*och*-a-bis
Ne-o-cles
Ne-*og*-e-nes
Ne-*om*-o-ris
Ne-on
Ne-on-*ti*-chos
Ne-op-*tol*-e-mus
Ne-o-ris
Nep-e-te
Neph-e-le
Neph-el-o-coc-*cyg*-i-a
Neph-e-ri-tes
Neph-thys
Ne-pos
Ne-po-ti-*a*-nus
Nep-*tu*-nus
Ne-*qui*-num
Ne-*ra*-ti-us
Ne-*re*-i-des
Ne-reus
Ne-ri-*e*-ne
Ner-i-tos
Ner-i-um
Ne-ro
Ner-to-*brig*-a
Ner-u-lum
Ner-va
Ner-*vi*-i
Ne-*sac*-ti-um
Ne-*sim*-a-chus
Ne-sis
Nes-sus
Nes-to-cles
Nes-tor
Nes-*tor*-i-des
Ne-tum
Ne-u-ri
Ni-*cæ*-a
Ni-*cag*-o-ras
Ni-*can*-der
Ni-*ca*-nor
Ni-*car*-chus
Ni-*ca*-tor
Nic-a-*tor*-i-um
Ni-ce
Ni-ce-*phor*-i-um
Ni-*ceph*-o-rus
Ni-cer
Ni-*cer*-a-tus
Ni-*ce*-tas
Nic-i-as
Ni-*cip*-pus
Ni-*coch*-a-res
Nic-o-cles
Ni-*coc*-ra-tes
Ni-*co*-cre-on
Nic-o-*de*-mus
Nic-o-*dor*-us
Nic-o-*la*-us
Ni-*com*-a-chus
Nic-o-*me*-des
Nic-o-me-*di*-a
Ni-con
Nic-o-*pha*-nes
Nic-o-phron
Ni-*cop*-o-lis
Ni-*cos*-tra-tus
Ni-*cot*-e-les
Ni-ger
Ni-*gid*-i-us
Ni-*gri*-tæ
Ni-ke
Ni-leus
Ni-lus
Ni-nus
Nin-y-as
Ni-o-be
Ni-*pha*-tes
Nir-eus
Ni-sa
Ni-*sæ*-a
Nis-i-bis
Ni-sus
Ni-*sy*-ros
Nit-i-*ob*-ri-ges
Ni-*to*-cris
Nit-ri-a
No-as
No-*bil*-i-or
Noc-ti-*lu*-ca
No-*di*-nus
No-la
No-*la*-nus
Nom-en-*ta*-nus
No-*men*-tum
Non-a-*cri*-nus
No-*na*-cris
Non-ni-us
Non-nus
No-ra
Nor-ba
Nor-*ba*-nus
Nor-i-cum
Nos-sis
No-ti-um
No-tus
No-*va*-ri-a
No-*va*-tus
No-*ve*-si-um
No-vi-o-*du*-num
No-vi-*om*-a-gus
No-vi-us
No-*vom*-a-gus
Nu-*ce*-ri-a
Nu-*ith*-o-nes
Nu-ma
Nu-*ma*-na
Nu-*man*-tia
Nu-man-*ti*-nus
Nu-*ma*-nus
Nu-me-nes
Nu-*me*-ni-us
Nu-me-ri-*a*-nus
Nu-*mi*-cus
Nu-mi-da
Nu-*mid*-i-a
Nu-*mis*-tro
Nu-mi-tor
Nun-di-na
Nur-si-a
Nyc-*te*-is
Nyc-*tel*-i-us
Nyc-teus
Nyc-*tim*-e-ne
Nyc-*ti*-mus
Nym-*bæ*-um
Nym-*phæ*-um
Nym-*phid*-i-us
Nym-pho-*dor*-us
Ny-sa
Ny-*sæ*-us
Ny-*se*-um
Ny-*si*-a-des
Nys-i-æ
Ny-*si*-ros

O-a-rus
O-a-sis
O-*ax*-es
O-*ax*-us
Ob-ri-mas
Ob-se-quens
O-*ca*-le-a
O-ce-*an*-i-des
O-*ce*-a-nus
O-*cel*-lus
Oc-e-lum
O-cha
Och-us
Oc-nus
O-cre-a
O-*cric*-u-lum
O-*cris*-i-a
Oc-*ta*-vi-a
Oc-ta-vi-*a*-nus
Oc-*ta*-vi-us
Oc-to-*du*-rus
Oc-to-*ge*-sa
O-*cy*-a-lus
O-*cyp*-e-te
O-*cyr*-o-e
Od-e-*na*-tus
O-*des*-sus
O-*de*-um
O-*di*-nus
Od-o-*a*-cer
Od-o-*man*-ti
Od-ry-sæ
Od-ys-*se*-a
Od-*ys*-seus
Œ-a
Œ-a-ger
Œ-a-grus
Œ-*an*-thæ
Œ-an-*the*-a
Œ-ax
Œ-ba-lus
Œ-ba-res
Œ-*bo*-tas
Œ-*cha*-li-a

Œ-cleus
Œ-*cli*-des
Œc-u-*me*-ni-us
Œd-i-pus
Œ-ne-on
Œ-ne-*o*-ne
Œ-neus
Œ-*ni*-a-dæ
Œ-*ni*-des
Œ-no-e
Œ-*nom*-a-us
Œ-*no*-na
Œ-*no*-ne
Œ-*nop*-i-des
Œ-*noph*-y-ta
Œ-*no*-pi-on
Œ-*no*-tri
Œ-*no*-tri-a
Œ-*no*-trus
Œ-*nus*-sæ
Œ-o-nus
Œ-ro-e
Œs-cus
Œ-ta
Œ-*tæ*-a
Œ-ty-lus
Œ-um
O-*fel*-la
Og-*dor*-us
O-*glo*-sa
O-*gul*-ni-a
Og-y-ges
O-*gyg*-i-a
O-*ic*-leus
O-*il*-eus
Ol-a-ne
Ol-*a*-nus
Ol-bi-a
Ol-ca-des
Ol-*chin*-i-um
O-*le*-a-ros
O-len
Ol-e-nus
Ol-ga-sys
Ol-i-*gyr*-tus
O-*lis*-i-po
O-*li*-zon
Ol-o-*pher*-nes
Ol-o-*phyx*-us
Ol-pæ
Ol-*u*-bri-a
O-*lyb*-ri-us
O-*lym*-pi-a
Ol-ym-*pi*-a-des
O-*lym*-pi-as
O-lym-pi-*e*-um
O-lym-pi-o-*dor*-us
O-*lym*-pus
Ol-ym-*pu*-sa
O-*lyn*-thus
O-*ly*-ras
Om-bi
Om-bri-ci
Om-o-le
Om-pha-le
Om-pha-los
O-*næ*-um
O-*na*-tas
On-*ches*-tus
On-e-*sic*-ri-tus
O-*nes*-i-mus
On-o-ba
O-*noch*-o-nus
On-o-*mac*-ri-tus
On-o-*mar*-chus
On-o-phas
On-o-*san*-der
O-nu-*gna*-thus
O-*phel*-las
O-*phel*-tes
O-phi-*og*-e-nes
O-phi-*o*-nes
O-phis
Oph-i-*te*-a
O-*phi*-tes
O-phi-*u*-chus
O-phi-*u*-sa
Op-i-ci
O-*pil*-i-us
O-*pim*-i-us
O-pis
Op-i-ter
O-*pi*-tes
Op-pi-*a*-nus
Op-*pid*-i-us
Op-pi-us
Op-*ta*-tus
Op-ti-mus
O-*pun*-ti-i
O-*ræ*-a
Or-a-sus
Or-*be*-lus
Or-*bil*-i-us
Or-*bo*-na
Or-ca-des
Or-*chom*-e-nus
Or-cus
Or-*des*-sus
Or-do-*vi*-ces
O-*re*-a-des
O-*res*-tes
O-res-*te*-um
Or-es-*ti*-dæ
Or-e-tæ
Or-e-*ta*-ni
O-*re*-us
Or-ga-na
Or-*ges*-sus
Or-*get*-o-rix
O-ri-*ba*-si-us
Or-i-cum
Or-i-gen
O-ri-*ob*-a-tes
O-*ri*-on
O-*ri*-tæ
O-rith-*y*-ia
O-*rit*-i-as
Or-me-nus
Or-ne-æ
Or-ne-*a*-tas
Or-neus
Or-*ni*-tron
Or-o-*a*-tis
Or-o-ba
O-*ro*-bi-æ
O-*ro*-des
O-*ræ*-tes
O-*ron*-tes
O-ro-*pher*-nes
O-*ro*-pus
O-*ro*-si-us
O-*ros*-pe-da
Or-pheus
Or-*sed*-i-ce
Or-se-is
Or-*sil*-o-chus
Or-*si*-nes
Or-*sip*-pus
Or-ta-lus
Or-*thag*-o-ras
Or-thi-a
Or-thos
Or-*tho*-sia
Or-*to*-na
Or-*tyg*-i-a
O-*ryx*-is
O-*sa*-ces
Os-*cel*-a
Os-ci
O-si
O-*sin*-i-us
O-*si*-ris
Os-rho-*e*-ne
Os-sa
Os-te-*o*-des
Os-ti-a
Os-ti-*o*-nes
Os-*tor*-i-us
Os-tra-*ci*-ne
Ot-a-ces
Ot-a-*cil*-i-us
O-*ta*-nes
O-tho
O-*thry*-a-des
O-thrys
O-tre-us
O-tus
O-tys
O-*vid*-i-us
Ox-*ath*-res
Ox-i-mes
Ox-us
Ox-*y*-a-res
Ox-*y*-ar-tes
Ox-*yb*-i-i
Ox-y-*ca*-nus
Ox-y-lus
Ox-*yn*-i-a
Ox-y-*por*-us
Ox-y-*rhyn*-chus
O-*zi*-nes
Oz-o-li

Pa-ca-ti-*a*-nus
Pac-ci-us
Pa-ches
Pa-*chi*-nus
Pa-*cho*-mi-us
Pa-*chym*-e-res
Pa-*chy*-num
Pa-*co*-ni-us
Pac-o-rus
Pac-*to*-lus
Pac-ty-as
Pac-ty-e
Pa-*cu*-vi-us
Pa-dus
Pa-*du*-sa
Pæ-an
Pæ-lig-ni
Pæ-*ma*-ni
Pæ-ni-a
Pæ-on
Pæ-o-nes
Pæ-*o*-ni-a
Pæ-*on*-i-des
Pæ-o-plæ
Pæ-sos
Pæs-tum
Pæ-tus
Pa-gæ
Pa-*ga*-ni
Pag-a-sæ
Pag-a-sus
Pa-græ
Pa-læ-*ap*-o-lis
Pa-*læ*-mon
Pal-æ-phar-*sa*-lus
Pa-*læ*-pha-tus
Pa-*læ*-po-lis
Pal-æs-*ti*-na
Pal-a-*me*-des
Pal-a-*ti*-nus
Pa-*le*-a
Pa-les
Pal-i-*ca*-nus
Pa-*li*-ci
Pa-*li*-li-a
Pal-i-*nu*-rus
Pal-*la*-di-um
Pal-*la*-di-us
Pal-*lan*-ti-a
Pal-lan-*ti*-des
Pal-las
Pal-*le*-ne
Pal-li-a
Pal-*ma*-ri-a
Pal-*my*-ra
Pal-um-*bi*-num
Pam-*i*-sos
Pam-me-nes
Pam-phi-lus
Pam-phy-la
Pam-*phyl*-i-a
Pam-*phy*-lus
Pan-a-*ce*-a
Pan-a-*chai*-cus
Pan-*ac*-tum
Pan-*æ*-nus
Pan-*æ*-ti-us
Pan-a-res
Pan-ath-e-*næ*-a
Pan-da-ma
Pan-da-rus
Pan-da-tes
Pan-*de*-mus
Pan-*di*-on
Pan-*dor*-a
Pan-*do*-si-a
Pan-dro-sos
Pan-e-as
Pa-*neg*-y-ris
Pan-*gæ*-us
Pan-i-*o*-ni-um
Pan-*no*-ni-a
Pan-*no*-nes
Pa-*no*-pe
Pa-*no*-pe-æ
Pa-*no*-pe-us
Pa-*nop*-o-lis
Pa-*nop*-tes
Pa-*nor*-mus
Pan-sa
Pan-*ta*-le-on
Pan-*tau*-chos
Pan-*the*-a
Pan-*the*-on
Pan-*the*-us
Pan-tho-us
Pan-tic-a-*pæ*-um
Pan-*tic*-a-pes
Pa-*ny*-a-sis
Pa-*pha*-ges
Paph-la-gon
Pa-phos
Pa-pi-*a*-nus
Pa-pi-as
Pa-pin-i-*a*-nus
Pa-*pin*-i-us
Pa-*pir*-i-us
Pa-pus
Par-a-*bys*-ton
Pa-*ræ*-ta-cæ
Pa-ræ-*to*-ni-um
Pa-ra-lus
Pa-ra-pan-*is*-a-dæ
Pa-rau-*æ*-a
Par-cæ
Pa-ren-ti-um
Pa-*ret*-ro-nes
Pa-ri-ca-*ni*-i
Pa-*ris*
Pa-*ris*-a-des
Pa-ri-*si*-i
Pa-ri-um
Par-*men*-i-des
Par-*me*-ni-o
Par-*nas*-sus
Par-nes
Par-o-*pam*-i-sus
Pa-ros
Par-*rha*-si-us
Par-*tha*-on
Par-the-*ni*-æ
Par-*the*-ni-as, -us
Par-the-non
Par-then-o-*pæ*-us
Par-*then*-o-pe
Par-thi-a
Pa-*ry*-a-dres
Pa-*rys*-a-tis
Pa-*sar*-ga-da
Pas-e-as
Pas-i-cles
Pa-*sim*-e-lus
Pas-i-on
Pas-i-phæ
Pa-*sit*-e-les
Pa-*sit*-i-gris
Pas-sa-ron
Pas-si-*e*-nus
Pat-a-lus
Pat-a-ra
Pat-a-*vi*-nus
Pa-*ta*-vi-um
Pa-*ter*-cu-lus
Pa-*ter*-num
Pat-mos
Pa-træ
Pa-*tro*-cles
Pa-*tro*-cli
Pat-ro-*cli*-des
Pa-*tro*-clus
Pa-*tro*-us
Pau-la
Pau-*li*-nus, -a
Pau-lus
Pau-*sa*-ni-us
Pau-si-as
Pau-*sil*-y-pon
Pau-*su*-læ
Pax-os
Pe-as
Pe-*da*-ni-us
Ped-a-sa
Ped-a-sus
Pe-di-*a*-dis
Ped-i-*æ*-us
Pe-di-*a*-nus
Pe-di-us
Pe-do
Pe-gæ
Pe-*gas*-i-des
Peg-a-sis
Peg-a-sus
Pei-*ræ*-us
Pei-*san*-der
Pei-*sis*-tra-tus
Pe-*la*-gi-us
Pel-a-gon
Pel-a-*go*-ni-a
Pe-*lar*-ge
Pe-*las*-gi
Pel-as-*gi*-o-tis
Pe-*las*-gus
Pel-a-tes
Pe-*len*-do-nes
Pe-le-thro-*ni*-i
Pe-le-us
Pe-*li*-a-des
Pe-li-as
Pe-*li*-des
Pe-*lig*-ni
Pel-in-*næ*-um
Pe-li-on
Pe-li-um
Pel-la
Pel-*la*-na
Pel-*le*-ne
Pel-o-*pe*-a
Pe-*lop*-i-das
Pel-o-pon-*ne*-sus
Pe-lops
Pe-*lor*-us
Pel-tæ
Pe-*lu*-si-um
Pe-*na*-tes
Pe-*ne*-is
Pe-*nel*-o-pe
Pe-*ne*-us

Pen-i-das
Pen-*tap*-o-lis
Pen-*tel*-i-cus
Pen-the-si-*le*-a
Pen-the-us
Pen-thi-lus
Pep-a-*re*-thos
Pe-*phre*-do
Pe-*ræ*-a
Per-co-te
Per-*dic*-cas
Per-dix
Per-e-*gri*-nus
Pe-*ren*-na
Pe-*ren*-nis
Pe-reus
Per-ga
Per-ga-mus
Per-ge
Pe-ri-*an*-der
Pe-ri-*ar*-chus
Pe-ri-*bo*-mi-us
Per-i-cles
Per-i-*clym*-e-nus
Pe-ri-*e*-res
Pe-*rig*-*e*-nes
Per-i-*la*-us
Pe-*ril*-lus
Per-i-*me*-de
Pe-*rin*-thus
Pe-ri-*œ*-ci
Per-i-pa-*tet*-i-ci
Per-i-phas
Per-i-*pha*-tes
Per-i-pho-*re*-tas
Pe-ris-the-nes
Pe-*rit*-a-nus
Per-i-tas
Pe-ro
Per-o-e
Pe-*ro*-ne
Per-*pen*-na
Per-pe-*re*-ne
Per-*rhæ*-bi
Per-*sæ*-us
Per-*se*-is
Per-*seph*-o-ne
Per-*sep*-o-lis
Per-seus
Per-*si*-des
Per-sis
Per-si-us
Per-ti-nax
Pe-*ru*-si-a
Pes-*cen*-ni-us
Pes-*si*-nus
Pe-*tal*-i-a
Pe-*tal*-i-æ
Pet-a-lus
Pe-te-on
Pe-te-us
Pe-ti-cus
Pe-*til*-i-a
Pet-o-*si*-ris
Pe-tra
Pe-*træ*-a
Pe-*tri*-num
Pe-*tre*-i-us
Pe-*tro*-ni-us
Peu-ce
Peu-*ced*-a-nos
Peu-*ces*-tas
Peu-*ce*-ti-a
Peu-*ci*-ni
Peu-co-*la*-us
Pex-o-*dor*-us
Phæ-a
Phæ-*a*-ces
Phæ-*a*-ci-a
Phæ-ax
Phæ-don
Phæ-dra
Phæ-drus
Phæ-ne-as
Phæ-na-*re*-te
Phæs-tus
Pha-e-thon
Pha-e-*thu*-sa
Phal-a-*cri*-ne
Phal-æ-cus
Pha-*lan*-thus
Phal-a-ris
Pha-le-*re*-us
Pha-*le*-rum
Pha-*lys*-i-us
Pham-e-*no*-phis
Pha-*næ*-us
Pha-*nag*-o-ra
Phan-a-*ræ*-a
Pha-nas
Phan-o-cles
Phan-o-*de*-mus
Phan-o-te
Pha-on
Pha-*rac*-i-des
Pha-ræ
Pha-*ras*-ma-nes
Pha-rax
Pha-ris
Phar-me-*cu*-sa
Phar-na-*ba*-zus
Phar-*na*-ces
Phar-na-*pa*-tes
Pha-ros
Phar-*sa*-lus
Pha-*ru*-si-i
Phas-a-*e*-lis
Pha-*se*-lis
Phas-i-*a*-ni
Pha-sis
Phav-o-*ri*-nus
Phaz-*e*-mon
Phe-a
Phe-*ca*-dum
Phe-ge-us
Phel-lo-e
Phe-mi-us
Phe-*mon*-o-e
Phe-*ne*-us (person)
Phe-ne-us (lake)
Phe-ræ
Phe-*rec*-ra-tes
Pher-e-*cy*-des
Pher-e-*ni*-ce
Phe-res
Pher-e-*ti*-ma
Phe-*ri*-num
Phi-a-le
Phid-i-as
Phi-*dip*-pi-des
Phi-don
Phid-y-le
Phig-a-*li*-a
Phi-la
Phil-a-del-*phi*-a
Phil-a-*del*-phus
Phi-læ
Phi-*læ*-*ni*
Phi-*lam*-mon
Phi-*lar*-chas
Phil-e-as
Phi-*le*-mon
Phi-*le*-ne
Phil-e-*tæ*-rus
Phil-i-des
Phi-*li*-nus
Phi-*lip*-pi
Phi-*lip*-pi-des
Phil-ip-*pop*-o-lis
Phi-*lip*-pus
Phil-is-*tæ*-a
Phil-is-*ti*-des
Phi-*lis*-ti-on
Phi-*lis*-tus
Phi-lo
Phi-*loch*-o-rus
Phil-o-cles
Phi-*loc*-ra-tes
Phil-oc-*te*-tes
Phil-o-*de*-mus
Phi-*lod*-i-ce
Phil-o-*la*-us
Phi-*lol*-o-gus
Phi-*lom*-a-che
Phil-o-*me*-la
Phil-o-*me*-li-um
Phil-o-*me*-lus
Phil-o-*me*-tor
Phi-*lon*-i-des
Phi-*lon*-o-me
Phil-o-*pæ*-men
Phi-*los*-tra-tus
Phi-*lo*-tas
Phil-o-*ti*-mus
Phi-*lox*-e-nus
Phil-y-res
Phi-*lyr*-i-des
Phin-e-us
Phin-*op*-o-lis
Phin-ti-as
Phleg-e-thon
Phle-gi-as
Phle-gon
Phle-gra
Phleg-y-æ
Phle-gy-as
Phli-as
Phli-us
Pho-*be*-tor
Pho-bos
Pho-*cæ*-a
Pho-ci-on
Pho-cis
Pho-cus
Pho-*cyl*-i-des
Phœ-be
Phœ-bi-das
Phœ-bus
Phœ-*ni*-ce
Phœ-*ni*-ces
Phœ-*ni*-cus
Phœ-ni-*cu*-sa
Phœ-*nis*-sa
Phœ-nix
Phol-o-e
Pho-lus
Phor-ban-*ti*-a
Phor-bas
Phor-cus
Phor-*cy*-nis
Phor-mi-o
Phor-on
Pho-*ro*-ne-us
Phor-o-*ni*-dæ
Pho-*ro*-nis
Phos-pho-rus
Pho-*ti*-nus
Pho-ti-us
Phra-*a*-tes
Phra-*at*-i-ces
Phra-*da*-tes
Phra-*or*-tes
Phras-i-cles
Phra-*taph*-er-nes
Phrix-a
Phrix-us
Phron-i-ma
Phry-ges
Phryg-i-a
Phry-ne
Phryn-i-chus
Phry-nis
Phry-non
Phryx-us
Phthi-a
Phthi-*o*-tis
Phy-a
Phy-cus
Phyl-a-cæ
Phyl-a-ce
Phyl-a-cus
Phy-*lar*-chus
Phy-las
Phy-le
Phy-*le*-us
Phyl-lis
Phyl-lus
Phys-cus
Phyt-a-lus
Phyt-i-a
Phy-ton
Pi-*a*-li-a
Pi-a-sus
Pi-*ce*-ni
Pic-en-*ti*-n
Pi-*ce*-num
Pic-*ta*-vi
Pic-*ta*-vi-um
Pic-to-nes
Pic-tor
Pi-cus
Pi-*dor*-us
Pi-e-ra
Pi-*e*-ri-a
Pi-*er*-i-des
Pi-e-rus
Pi-gres
Pi-*la*-tus
Pi-*le*-sus
Pi-*lum*-nus
Pim-*ple*-a
Pin-a-ra
Pi-*na*-ri-a
Pi-*na*-ri-us
Pin-a-rus
Pin-da-rus
Pin-da-sus
Pin-*ci*-a-cum
Pin-den-*is*-sus
Pin-dus
Pin-na
Pin-ti-a
Pi-o-ne
Pi-*ræ*-us
Pi-*ran*-thus
Pi-*re*-ne
Pi-*res*-i-æ
Pi-*rith*-o-us
Pi-rus
Pi-sa
Pi-sæ
Pi-*san*-der
Pi-*sa*-nus
Pi-*sa*-tes
Pi-*sau*-rum
Pi-*se*-nor
Pis-i-as
Pis-i-dæ
Pi-*sid*-i-a
Pi-*sid*-i-ce
Pis-is-*trat*-i-des
Pi-*sis*-tra-tus
Pi-so
Pi-*so*-nis
Pis-*tor*-i-æ
Pis-tum
Pis-*tyr*-us
Pi-sus
Pit-a-ne
Pith-e-*cu*-sa
Pi-tho
Pith-o-*la*-us
Pi-thon
Pi-thys
Pit-ta-cus
Pit-the-us
Pit-u-*la*-ni
Pit-y-o-*ne*-sus
Pit-y-us
Pit-y-*u*-sa
Pi-us
Pla-*cen*-ti-a
Pla-cid-e-i-*a*-nus
Pla-*cid*-i-a
Pla-ci-dus
Pla-*na*-si-a
Plan-*ci*-na
Plan-*ci*-us
Plan-cus
Plan-*u*-des
Pla-*tæ*-a
Plat-a-*mo*-des
Plat-a-*nis*-tus
Plat-a-nus
Pla-to
Plau-ti-*a*-nus
Plau-*til*-la
Plau-tius
Plau-tus
Pla-vis
Plei-a-des
Plei-o-ne
Plei-*sto*-a-nax
Plem-*my*-ri-um
Pleu-*ra*-tus
Pleu-ron
Plex-*ip*-pus
Plin-i-us
Plin-*thi*-ne
Plis-*tar*-chus
Plis-the-nes
Plis-*ti*-nus
Plis-*to*-a-nax
Plis-tus
Plo-*thi*-a
Plo-*ti*-nus, -na
Plu-*tar*-chus
Plu-to
Plu-tus
Plu-vi-us
Pod-a-*le*-a
Pod-a-*lir*-i-us
Po-*dar*-ces
Po-*dar*-ge
Pœ-as
Pœ-ci-le
Pœ-ci-lus
Pœ-*dic*-u-li
Pœ-*es*-sa
Pœ-me-nis
Pœ-ni
Pœ-ni-na
Pœ-*to*-vi-o
Po-*lat*-i-cum
Pol-e-*mar*-chus
Pol-e-mo-*cra*-ti-a
Pol-e-mon
Po-*le*-nor
Po-li-as
Po-li-*e*-um
Po-li-or-*ce*-tes
Po-*lis*-tra-tus
Po-*li*-tes
Pol-*len*-ti-a
Pol-li-o
Pol-lux
Po-ly-*æ*-gus
Po-ly-*æ*-nus
Po-ly-*ar*-chus
Pol-y-*be*-tes
Po-*lyb*-i-das
Po-*lyb*-i-us
Pol-y-*bœ*-a
Pol-y-*bo*-tes
Pol-y-bus
Pol-y-*car*-pus
Po-*lych*-a-res
Pol-y-*cle*-a
Pol-y-cles
Pol-y-*cli*-tus

Po-*lyc*-ra-tes
Po-*lyd*-a-mas
Pol-y-*dec*-tes
Pol-y-deu-*ce*-a
Pol-y-*dor*-us
Pol-yg-*no*-tus
Pol-y-*go*-nus
Pol-y-*hym*-ni-a
Pol-y-*i*-dus
Pol-y-*la*-us
Pol-y-*me*-de
Pol-y-*me*-la
Po-*lym*-e-nes
Pol-ym-*nes*-tes
Pol-ym-*nes*-tor
Po-*lym*-ni-a
Pol-y-*ni*-ces
Po-*lyn*-o-e
Pol-y-*pe*-mon
Pol-y-*phe*-mus
Pol-y-phron
Pol-yr-*rhe*-ni-a
Pol-y-*sper*-chon
Po-*lys*-tra-tus
Po-*ly*-tes
Pol-y-ti-*me*-tus
Pol-y-*ti*-mus
Po-*lyx*-o
Pol-y-*ze*-lus
Pom-e-*ti*-na
Po-*mo*-na
Pom-*pæ*-lo
Pom-*pe*-ia
Pom-pe-i-*a*-nus
Pom-*pe*-i-i
Pom-pe-i-*op*-o-lis
Pom-*pe*-i-us
Pom-pe-lon
Pom-*pil*-i-a
Pom-*pil*-i-us
Pom-*pi*-lus
Pom-po-*ni*-a
Pomp-*ti*-nus
Pon-ti-æ
Pon-ti-ca
Pon-ti-cus
Pon-*ti*-nus
Pon-ti-us
Pon-tus
Po-*pil*-li-a
Po-*plic*-o-la
Pop-*pæ*-a
Pop-u-lo-*ni*-a
Por-a-ta
Por-ci-a
Po-*red*-o-rax
Po-*ri*-na
Por-o-se-*le*-ne
Por-ri-ma
Por-se-na
Por-*sen*-na
Por-*tum*-nus
Por-*tu*-nus
Po-rus
Po-*sei*-don
Pos-i-*di*-um
Pos-i-*do*-ni-a
Pos-i-*do*-ni-us
Po-si-o
Pos-tu-mus
Po-*tam*-i-des
Pot-a-mon
Pot-a-mus
Po-*ten*-ti-a
Po-*thi*-nus
Po-thos
Pot-i-*dæ*-a
Po-*ti*-na
Pot-ni-æ
Præ-*nes*-te
Præ-nes-*ti*-ni
Præ-sos

Præ-*tor*-i-um
Pra-si-æ
Pras-i-nus
Prat-i-nas
Prax-*ag*-o-ras
Prax-i-as
Prax-*id*-i-ce
Prax-i-la
Prax-*iph*-a-nes
Prax-*it*-e-les
Prax-*ith*-e-a
Pre-*li*-us
Pri-*am*-i-des
Pri-a-mus
Pri-*a*-pus
Pri-*e*-ne
Pri-mus
Pris-ci-*a*-nus
Pris-*cil*-la
Pris-cus
Pri-*ver*-num
Pro-bus
Pro-cas
Proch-o-rus
Proch-y-ta
Pro-cle-a
Pro-cles
Pro-*cli*-dæ
Pro-clus
Proc-ne
Proc-on-*ne*-sus
Pro-*co*-pi-us
Pro-cris
Pro-*crus*-tes
Proc-u-*le*-i-us
Proc-u-lus
Proc-y-on
Prod-i-cus
Prod-ro-mus
Prœ-ti-des
Prœ-tus
Pro-*la*-us
Prom-a-chus
Pro-*me*-the-us
Pro-*me*-this
Pro-*nap*-i-des
Pro-nax
Pron-o-mus
Pron-o-us
Pro-nu-ba
Pro-*per*-ti-us
Proph-*tha*-ri-a
Pro-*pœt*-i-des
Pro-*pon*-tis
Prop-y-*le*-a
Pros-*chi*-um
Pro-*ser*-pi-na
Pros-o-*pi*-tis
Pro-*tag*-o-ras
Pro-te
Pro-tes-i-*la*-us
Pro-te-us
Pro-*tog*-e-nes
Prot-o-ge-*ni*-a
Prox-e-nus
Pru-*den*-ti-us
Pru-sa
Pru-si-as
Prym-*ne*-sus
Pryt-a-nis
Psam-a-thos
Psam-me-*ni*-tus
Psam-*met*-i-chus
Psa-phis
Pso-phis
Psy-che
Psyl-li
Psyt-ta-*lei*-a
Pte-le-um
Ptol-e-*mæ*-us
Ptol-e-*ma*-is
Pto-us

Pty-*chi*-a
Pub-*lic*-o-la
Pub-*lil*-i-a
Pub-*lil*-i-us
Pub-li-us
Pu-*di*-ca
Pul-*cher*-i-a
Pu-ni-cum
Pu-pi-*e*-nus
Pup-*pi*-us
Pur-pu-*ra*-ri-æ
Pu-te-o-*la*-num
Pu-*te*-o-li
Pyd-na
Pyg-e-la
Pyg-*mæ*-i
Pyg-*ma*-li-on
Py-la-des
Py-læ
Py-las
Py-*le*-ne
Py-los
Py-ræ
Py-*ram*-i-des
Pyr-a-mus
Pyr-a-sus
Pyr-en-*æ*-um
Pyr-en-*æ*-us
Py-*re*-ne
Pyr-gi
Pyr-*got*-e-les
Pyr-o-des
Pyr-rha
Pyr-rhi-as
Pyr-rhi-ca
Pyr-rho
Pyr-rhus
Py-*thag*-o-ras
Pyth-e-as
Pyth-i-a
Pyth-i-as
Pyth-i-on
Pyth-i-um
Py-tho
Pyth-o-cles
Pyth-o-*do*-rus
Pyth-o-*la*-us
Py-thon
Pyth-o-*ni*-ce
Pyth-o-*ni*-cus
Pyt-ta-lus
Pyx-us

Qua-di
Qua-*dra*-tus
Quad-ri-ceps
Quad-ri-frons
Qua-ri
Quer-que-*tu*-lum
Qui-*e*-tus
Quinc-ti-*a*-nus
Quinc-ti-us
Quinc-*til*-i-us
Quin-*til*-i-an
Quin-til-i-*a*-nus
Quin-*til*-i-us
Quin-*til*-lus
Quin-ti-us
Quin-tus
Quir-i-*na*-li-a
Qui-*ri*-nus
Qui-*ri*-tes

Ra-*bir*-i-us
Ra-*cil*-i-us
Ræ-*sa*-ces
Ra-*ga*-ba
Ram-*ba*-si-a
Ram-i-ses
Ra-*phi*-a
Ra-*scip*-o-lis
Rau-*ri*-ci

Ra-*ven*-na
Ra-vo-la
Re-*a*-te
Re-*bil*-us
Re-*dic*-u-lus
Red-*o*-nes
Re-*gil*-lus
Reg-u-lus
Re-mi
Rem-u-lus
Re-mus
Re-sus
Rhad-a-*man*-thus
Rhæ-ti
Rhæ-ti-a
Rha-gæ
Rha-*me*-lus
Rham-nes
Rham-nus
Rham-*nu*-si-a
Rhamp-si-*ni*-tus
Rhas-cu-*por*-is
Rhe-a
Rhe-bus
Rhed-o-nes
Rhe-gi-um
Rhe-*nei*-a
Rhe-nus
Rhe-o-*mi*-tres
Rhe-sus
Rhe-*u*-nus
Rhex-*e*-nor
Rhi-*a*-nus
Rhi-*mot*-a-cles
Rhi-on
Rhi-*phæ*-i
Rhi-*thym*-na
Rhi-um
Rhi-zus
Rho-da
Rho-dæ
Rhod-a-nus
Rho-di-a
Rho-di-us
Rhod-o-pe
Rho-*do*-pis
Rho-dus
Rho-ta-nas
Rhœ-cus
Rhœ-di-as
Rhœ-*te*-um
Rhœ-tus
Rho-*sa*-ces
Rhyn-da-cus
Ric-ci-*a*-ce-æ
Ri-*com*-a-gus
Rig-o-*du*-lum
Ri-*gom*-a-gus
Ri-*phe*-us
Ri-sin-*i*-um
Rod-e-*ri*-cus
Ro-ma
Ro-*ma*-nus
Rom-u-lus
Ro-pi-cum
Ros-ci-*a*-num
Ros-ci-us
Ro-*tom*-a-gus
Rox-*a*-na
Rox-o-*la*-ni
Ru-bi
Ru-bi-con
Ru-bi-*e*-nus
Ru-*bi*-go
Ru-di-æ
Ru-*fi*-nus
Ru-fræ
Ru-fus
Ru-gi-i
Rul-lus
Ru-*pil*-i-us
Ru-ra

Rus-ci-no
Ru-*sel*-læ
Rus-pæ
Rus-*pi*-num
Rus-ti-cus
Ru-*te*-ni
Ru-*til*-i-us
Ru-ti-lus
Ru-tu-ba
Ru-tu-li
Ru-*tu*-pi-æ

Sa-ba
Sab-a-con
Sa-*bæ*-i
Sa-*ba*-ri-a
Sa-ba-te
Sa-*ba*-ti-a
Sa-ba-*ti*-nus
Sa-*ba*-tus
Sa-*ba*-zi-us
Sa-*bel*-li
Sa-*bi*-na
Sa-*bi*-ni
Sa-bin-i-*a*-nus
Sa-*bi*-nus
Sab-ra-ta
Sa-*bri*-na
Sac-a-das
Sa-cæ
Sac-a-*se*-ne
Sa-cer
Sa-*cra*-ni
Sac-ri-*por*-tus
Sad-a-les
Sa-dy-*a*-tes
Sæ-pi-num
Sæ-ta-bis
Sag-a-*las*-sus
Sag-a-na
Sag-a-ris
Sa-*gar*-ti-i
Sa-gra
Sa-*gun*-tum
Sa-is
Sa-la
Sal-a-mis
Sal-a-*mi*-ni-a
Sal-a-*pi*-a
Sal-a-ra
Sa-*lar*-i-ca
Sa-*las*-si
Sal-dæ
Sa-*le*-i-us
Sa-*le*-ni
Sal-en-*ti*-ni
Sa-*ler*-num
Sa-li-a
Sa-li-i
Sa-*li*-næ
Sal-i-*na*-tor
Sal-*lus*-ti-us
Sal-*man*-ti-ca
Sal-*mo*-ne
Sal-*mo*-ne-us
Sal-*mo*-nis
Sal-my-*des*-sus
Sal-o-*du*-rum
Sa-*lo*-me
Sa-*lo*-na
Sal-o-*ni*-nus
Sa-*lo*-ni-us
Sal-pi-*na*-tes
Sal-vi-*a*-nus
Sal-vid-i-*e*-nus
Sa-ly-es
Sa-*ma*-ra
Sa-*ma*-ri-a
Sam-a-ro-*bri*-va
Sam-bra-*ce*-ni
Sam-*ni*-tes
Sam-ni-um

Sa-*mo*-ni-um
Sa-mos
Sa-*mos*-a-ta
Sam-o-*thra*-ce
Sa-mus
Sa-na
San-cho-*ni*-a-thon
San-*cus*
San-*da*-ce
San-da-nis
San-dro-*cot*-tus
Sa-ne
San-ga-la
San-ga-ris
San-*nyr*-i-on
San-to-nes
Sa-*pæ*-i
Sap-i-*re*-ne
Sa-pis
Sa-por, Sa-*po*-res
Sapph-e
Sapph-o
Sa-ra-*ce*-ni
Sa-ra-*pa*-ni
Sa-*ra*-vus
Sar-da-na-*pa*-lus
Sar-*de*-ne
Sar-di-ca
Sar-*din*-i-a
Sar-dis
Sar-do-nes
Sa-*rep*-ta
Sa-ri-phi
Sar-ma-tæ
Sar-ma-*ti*-a
Sar-ni
Sar-ni-us
Sar-nus
Sa-ron
Sa-*ron*-i-cus
Sar-*pe*-don
Sar-se-na
Sar-ta
Sar-*ta*-ba
Sar-us
Sa-son
Sas-*pi*-res
Sas-*san*-i-dæ
Sat-a-la
Sa-*ter*-nus
Sat-i-bar-*za*-nes
Sa-*tic*-u-la
Sa-tis
Sat-ra-*pe*-ni
Sa-*tri*-cum
Sat-ur-*e*-i-um
Sat-ur-*na*-li-a
Sa-*tur*-ni-a
Sat-ur-*ni*-nus
Sa-*tur*-ni-us
Sa-*tur*-nus
Sat-y-ri
Sat-y-rus
Sau-*fe*-i-us
Sau-*roc*-to-nus
Sau-*rom*-a-tæ
Sa-va-*ri*-a
Sav-e-ra
Sa-vo
Sa-vus
Sax-a
Sax-o-nes
Scæ-va
Scæ-vo-la
Scal-dis
Scal-la-bis
Sca-*man*-der
Scam-bo-*ni*-dæ
Scan-*da*-re-a
Scan-di-*na*-vi-a
Scap-sa
Scap-u-la
Sca-ra

Scar-bau-*ti*-a
Scar-*do*-na
Scar-dus
Scar-*phe*-a
Scau-rus
Scel-e-*ra*-tus
Sce-*ni*-tæ
Scap-sis
Sche-di-us
Sche-ri-a
Schœ-nus
Sci-*ap*-o-des
Sci-a-thus
Sci-dros
Scil-lus
Sci-nis
Sci-*o*-ne
Sci-*pi*-a-des
Scip-i-o
Sci-ras
Sci-*ri*-tis
Sci-ron
Sco-dra
Sco-lis
Sco-lus
Sco-*mi*-us
Sco-pas
Scop-e-los
Scor-*dis*-ci
Sco-ti
Sco-*ti*-nus
Sco-*tus*-sa
Scri-bo-ni-*a*-nus
Scri-*bo*-ni-us
Scul-*ten*-na
Scu-pi
Scy-a-thos
Scy-*la*-ci-um
Syl-*læ*-um
Scy-lax
Scy-*lu*-rus
Scy-*ri*-a-des
Scy-ros
Scy-thæ
Scy-*the*-ni
Scyth-i-a
Scy-*thi*-nus
Scy-*thop*-o-lis
Se-*bas*-te
Se-*bas*-te-a
Se-*bas*-ti-a
Seb-as-*top*-o-lis
Se-*ben*-ny-tos
Se-*be*-thus
Se-*bi*-nus
Se-ci-a
Se-di-*ta*-ni
Se-*du*-ni
Se-*du*-si-i
Se-*ges*-ta
Se-*ges*-tes
Se-go-*bri*-ga
Seg-o-*du*-num
Seg-o-nax
Se-gon-*ti*-a
Se-*go*-vi-a
Se-gun-*ti*-um
Se-gu-si-*a*-ni
Se-*gu*-si-o
Se-*ja*-nus
Se-*le*-ne
Se-*leu*-ci-a
Se-*leu*-ci-dæ
Se-*leu*-cis
Se-*leu*-cus
Sel-*ge*
Se-*li*-nus
Sel-*la*-si-a
Sel-*le*-is
Se-*lym*-bri-a
Se-*ma*-na
Sem-e-le
Se-*mir*-a-mis

Sem-no-nes
Se-*mo*-nes
Sem-*pro*-ni-a
Sen-e-ca
Se-ni-a
Sen-o-nes
Sen-ti-num
Se-pi-as
Sep-*tem*-pe-da
Sep-*tim*-i-us
Sep-tim-u-*le*-i-us
Sep-ti-mus
Seq-ua-na
Seq-ua-ni
Se-ra-*pæ*-um
Se-*ra*-pis
Ser-*bo*-nis
Se-*re*-na
Se-re-ni-*a*-nus
Se-*re*-nus
Ser-*ges*-tus
Ser-gi-us
Ser-i-ca
Se-*ri*-phus
Ser-my-la
Ser-*ra*-nus
Ser-rhæ
Ser-*rhi*-um
Ser-*to*-ri-us
Ser-vi-*a*-nus
Ser-*vil*-i-a
Ser-vil-i-*a*-nus
Ser-*vil*-i-us
Ser-vi-us
Ses-a-mus
Ses-i-tes
Se-*sos*-tris
Ses-ti-us
Ses-tos
Set-a-bis
Se-thon
Set-i-a
Seu-thes
Se-ver-i-*a*-nus
Se-*ve*-rus
Sex-*til*-i-us
Sex-ti-us
Sex-tus
Si-*bi*-ni
Sib-o-ta
Si-*bur*-ti-us
Si-*byl*-læ
Si-*ca*-ni
Sic-ca
Si-*chæ*-us
Si-*cil*-i-a
Si-*cin*-i-us
Si-*ci*-nus
Sic-o-rus
Sic-u-li
Sic-y-on
Si-de
Si-*de*-ro
Sid-i-*ci*-num
Si-don
Si-*do*-nis
Si-*do*-ni-us
Si-*ge*-um
Sig-ni-a
Sig-*ni*-nus
Si-la
Si-*la*-nus
Sil-a-rus
Si-*le*-nus
Si-*lin*-gæ
Si-lis
Si-*li*-us
Si-lo
Sil-u-res
Sil-*va*-nus
Sil-vi-um
Sim-mi-as
Sim-o-is

Si-mon
Si-*mon*-i-des
Sim-*plic*-i-us
Sim-y-ra
Sin-di
Sin-do-*ma*-na
Sin-dus
Sin-gi-*du*-num
Sin-gus
Sin-ni-us
Si-non
Si-*no*-ni-a
Si-*no*-pe
Sin-*ti*-ca
Sin-u-*es*-sa
Si-*o*-pe
Si-phæ
Siph-nos
Si-*pon*-tum
Sip-y-lus
Si-ra-ca
Sir-*bo*-nis
Si-*re*-nes
Si-ris
Si-ri-us
Sir-mi-o
Sir-mi-um
Sis-a-pon
Sis-a-ra
Sis-ce-a
Si-*sen*-na
Sis-e-nes
Sis-y-*gam*-bis
Sis-y-phus
Sit-a-cus
Si-*tal*-ces
Si-thon
Si-*tho*-ni-a
Sit-o-nes
Sit-ta-ce
Sit-ti-us
Sma-*rag*-dus
Smer-dis
Smer-nus
Smi-lis
Smin-the-us
Smyr-*næ*-us
So-a-nes
Soc-ra-tes
Sœ-mi-as
Sog-di-*a*-na
Sog-di-*a*-nus
So-*la*-nus
So-*li*-nus
Sol-o-e
So-lon
So-*lun*-tum
So-ly-*ge*-a
Sol-y-ma
Son-*ti*-us
Sop-a-ter
So-*phe*-ne
Soph-o-cles
Soph-o-*nis*-ba
So-phron
Soph-ro-*nis*-cus
So-*phros*-y-ne
So-pi-*a*-næ
Sop-o-lis
Sor-a
So-*rac*-te
So-*ra*-nus
Sor-bi-o-*du*-num
Sor-bi-o-*du*-rum
So-*sib*-i-us
Sos-i-cles
So-*sic*-ra-tes
So-*sig*-e-nes
Sos-i-lus
So-*sip*-a-ter
So-*sis*-tra-tus
Sos-pi-ta
Sos-the-nes

Sos-tra-tus
Sot-a-des
So-ter
So-*te*-res
So-*te*-ri-cus
So-ti-*a*-tes
So-us
So-*zo*-me-nus
So-*zop*-o-lis
Spa-*lau*-thræ
Spar-ta
Spar-ta-cus
Spar-ti-*a*-nus
Spar-ti-*a*-tæ
Spar-*to*-lus
Spat-a-le
Sper-*che*-us
Sper-ma-*toph*-a-gi
Speu-*sip*-pus
Sphac-*te*-ri-a
Spha-gi-a
Sphan-da-le
Sphe-rus
Sphet-tus
Spho-dri-as
Spi-*cil*-lus
Spi-na
Spin-tha-rus
Spin-ther
Spi-*tam*-e-nes
Spith-ri-*da*-tes
Spi-*tob*-a-tes
Spo-*le*-ti-um
Spor-a-des
Spor-us
Spu-*rin*-na
Spu-*ri*-nus
Sta-*bi*-æ
Stab-u-lum
Sta-*gi*-ra
Staph-y-lus
Sta-*san*-der
Stas-e-as
Sta-*til*-i-us
Sta-*ti*-ra
Sta-ti-us
Sta-*to*-ni-a
Sta-tor
Steg-a-nos
Stel-*la*-tes
Ste-*noc*-ra-tes
Sten-tor
Sten-to-ris
Sten-y-*cle*-rus
Steph-a-ne
Steph-a-nus
Ster-o-pe, -pes
Ster-*tin*-i-us
Ste-*sag*-o-ras
Ste-*sich*-o-rus
Stes-i-*cle*-a
Stes-i-cles
Ste-*sim*-bro-tus
Sthen-e-lus
Sthe-nis
Sthe-no
Sthe-no-*bœ*-a
Stil-i-cho
Stil-po
Stiph-i-lus
Sto-*bæ*-us
Sto-bi
Sto-*ech*-a-des
Stœ-ni
Sto-i-ci
Stra-bo
Stra-*tar*-chas
Stra-to
Strat-o-cles
Strat-o-*ni*-ce
Stra-ton-i-*ce*-a
Strom-bi-*chi*-des
Stron-gy-le

Stroph-a-des
Stroph-i-us
Stru-thus
Stry-me
Strym-no
Stry-mon
Stu-ra
Stur-ni
Sty-ber-ra
Stym-*pha*-lis
Stym-*pha*-lus
Sty-ra
Su-*a*-da
Su-*a*-na
Su-a-*ne*-tes
Su-*ba*-tri-i
Sub-*la*-que-um
Sub-*la*-vi-o
Su-*blic*-i-us
Su-*bu*-ra
Su-cro
Su-*de*-ti
Su-e-*o*-nes
Su-*es*-sa
Su-*es*-si-o-nes
Su-*es*-su-la
Sue-*to*-ni-us
Sue-vi
Su-fes
Suf-*fe*-nus
Su-*fet*-u-la
Sui-das
Su-il-*la*-tes
Su-i-*o*-nes
Sul-ci
Sul-la
Sul-mo
Sul-*pic*-i-us
Su-me-lo-*cen*-na
Sum-*ma*-nus
Su-ni-um
Su-nu-ci
Su-*od*-o-na
Sur-*ren*-tum
Su-sa
Su-*sa*-ri-on
Su-si-*a*-na
Su-tri-um
Su-*va*-ni
Syb-a-ris
Sy-bo-tas
Syc-a-*mi*-non
Sy-*cu*-ri-um
Sy-*e*-ne
Sy-*en*-e-sis
Sy-*gam*-bri
Syl-o-son
Syl-*va*-nus
Syl-vi-a
Syl-vi-us
Sy-*mæ*-thus
Sym-ma-chus
Sy-me
Sym-*pleg*-a-des
Sy-*ne*-si-us
Syn-na-da
Syp-a-*let*-tes
Sy-phax
Syr-a-*cu*-sæ
Sy-ros
Sys-i-*gam*-bis
Sy-*sim*-e-thres
Sys-i-nas
Sy-thas

Ta-bæ
Ta-*ber*-næ
Ta-bor
Ta-*bu*-da
Ta-*bu*-ri
Ta-*bur*-nus
Tac-a-pe
Tac-fa-*ri*-nas
Ta-chos
Tac-i-tus
Ta-*comp*-sos
Tæn-a-rum
Ta-*gas*-te
Ta-ges
Ta-*gi*-næ
Ta-gus
Ta-*lab*-ri-ga
Tal-a-us
Ta-*la*-y-ra
Tal-e-tum
Tal-*thyb*-i-us
Ta-lus
Tam-a-ris
Tam-e-sis
Ta-mos
Tam-*phi*-lus
Ta-*my*-næ
Tam-y-ras
Tam-y-ris
Tan-a-gra
Tan-a-grus
Tan-a-is
Tan-a-quil
Tan-a-rus
Ta-*ne*-tum
Ta-nis
Tan-*tal*-i-des
Tan-ta-lus
Ta-nus
Ta-*nu*-si-us
Ta-phi-æ
Ta-phi-*as*-sus
Ta-phus
Tap-o-*si*-ris
Ta-*prob*-a-ne
Tap-u-ri
Ta-*ras*-co
Tar-*bel*-li
Tar-chon-*dim*-o-tus
Tar-en-*ti*-nus
Ta-*ren*-tum
Tar-*pe*-i-a
Tar-*pe*-i-us
Tar-phæ
Tar-*quin*-i-us
Tar-ra-*ci*-na
Tar-ra-co
Tar-si-us
Tar-sus
Tar-ta-rus
Tar-*tes*-sus
Ta-ru-a
Ta-ru-*a*-na
Tar-*vis*-i-um
Tas-*ge*-ti-us
Ta-ti-an
Ta-ti-*en*-ses
Tat-ta
Tau-*ban*-ti-i
Tau-nus
Tau-*ra*-si-a
Tau-ri-*a*-num
Tau-*ri*-ni
Tau-*ris*-ci
Tau-ro-*me*-ni-um
Tau-rus
Ta-vi-um
Tax-i-la
Tax-i-les
Ta-y-*ge*-te
Ta-y-*ge*-tus
Te-*a*-num
Te-a-rus
Te-*a*-te
Tec-mon
Tec-ta-mus
Tec-*tos*-a-ges
Te-*da*-ni-us
Te-*gæ*-a
Teg-e-*a*-tis
Te-*gy*-ra
Te-la
Tel-a-mon
Tel-*chi*-nes
Te-*leb*-o-æ
Te-*le*-cles
Tel-e-*cli*-des
Te-*leg*-o-nus
Te-*lem*-a-chus
Tel-e-mus
Tel-e-*phas*-sa
Tel-e-phus
Te-*les*-i-as
Te-*les*-i-cles
Tel-e-*sil*-la
Tel-e-*si*-nus
Tel-e-*sip*-pus
Tel-*le*-ne
Te-*les*-tes
Te-*le*-thri-us
Tell-i-as
Tell-us
Tel-*mes*-sus
Tem-e-*ni*-tes
Te-*me*-ni-um
Tem-e-nus
Tem-e-sa
Tem-pe
Tench-te-ri
Te-ne-a
Ten-e-dos
Te-nes
Ten-e-sis
Te-nos
Ten-*ty*-ris
Te-os
Te-*re*-don
Te-ren-ti-*a*-nus
Te-*ren*-ti-us, -a
Te-reus
Ter-*ges*-te
Ter-i-*ba*-zus
Ter-i-*da*-tes
Te-*ri*-na
Te-*ri*-o-li
Ter-me-ra
Ter-me-rus
Ter-mes
Ter-*mes*-sus
Ter-mi-nus
Ter-*pan*-der
Terp-*sich*-o-re
Ter-ra-*ci*-na
Ter-ti-us
Ter-tul-li-*a*-nus
Tes-ta
Teth-ys
Te-*trap*-o-lis
Tet-ri-cus
Teu-cer
Teu-*chi*-ra
Teu-*mes*-sus
Teu-ta
Teu-*ta*-mus
Teu-*thra*-ni-a
Teu-thras
Teu-*thro*-ne
Teu-to-bur-gi-*en*-sis
Teu-to-ni, -nes
Teu-*ton*-i-cus
Tha-*gi*-nes
Tha-is
Thal-a
Tha-les
Tha-*le*-tes
Tha-*li*-a
Tham-y-ras
Tham-y-ris
Thap-sa-cus
Thap-sus
Tha-sos
Thau-ma-ci
The-a
The-æ-*te*-tus
The-*ag*-e-nes
The-*a*-no
The-*a*-num
The-a-*te*-tes
The-ba
The-bæ
Theb-a-is
The-be
Theg-a-*nu*-sa
Thel-*pu*-sa
Thelx-*i*-on
The-mis
The-mis-*cy*-ra
Them-i-son
The-*mis*-ti-us
The-*mis*-to-cles
Them-i-*stog*-e-nes
The-o-cles
The-o-clus
The-o-*clym*-e-nus
The-o-*co*-le-um
The-*oc*-ri-tus
The-*od*-a-tus
The-o-*dec*-tes
The-o-*do*-nis
The-o-*dor*-a
The-o-do-*re*-tus
The-o-do-*ri*-cus
The-o-*dor*-us
The-o-*do*-si-a
The-o-do-si-*op*-o-lis
The-o-*do*-si-us
The-o-*do*-ti-on
The-*od*-o-tus
The-o-*du*-lus
The-og-*ne*-tes
The-*og*-nis
The-om-*nes*-tus
The-on
The-*o*-nas
The-*on*-o-e
The-o-pe
The-*oph*-a-nes
The-*oph*-i-lus
The-o-*phras*-tus
The-o-phy-*lac*-tus
The-o-*pom*-pus
The-o-*ti*-mus
The-ot-*mel*-li
The-*ox*-e-na
Ther-a
The-*ram*-bus
The-*ram*-e-nes
The-*rap*-ne
The-ri-cles
Ther-*mo*-don
Ther-*mop*-y-læ
Ther-mus
The-*rod*-a-mas
The-ron
Ther-*san*-der
Ther-*sil*-o-chus
Ther-*sip*-pus
Ther-*si*-tes
The-seus
Thes-*moph*-o-ra
Thes-*pi*-a
Thes-*pi*-a-des
Thes-pi-æ
Thes-pis
Thes-pi-us
Thes-*pro*-ti-a
Thes-*sa*-li-a
Thes-sa-*li*-o-tis
Thes-sa-lo-*ni*-ca
Thes-sa-lus
Thes-ti-a-des
Thes-ti-um
Thes-ti-us
Thes-ty-lis
The-tis
Thim-bron
Thi-*od*-a-mas
This-be
This-o-a
Tho-as
Thom-y-ris
Tho-on
Tho-*o*-tes
Tho-ræ
Tho-ri-cus
Thra-ce
Thra-ci-a
Thra-*se*-a
Thras-y-*bu*-lus
Thras-y-*dæ*-us
Thra-*syl*-lus
Thra-*sym*-a-chus
Thras-y-*me*-des
Thras-y-*me*-nus
Thri-a
Thro-ni-um
Thu-*cyd*-i-des
Thu-le
Thu-ri-i
Thu-*ri*-nus
Thy-a-mis
Thy-a-mus
Thy-a-*ti*-ra
Thy-*bar*-ni
Thy-*es*-tes
Thym-bra
Thym-bri-a
Thym-e-le
Thy-*mi*-a-this
Thy-*mœ*-ta-dæ
Thy-*mœ*-tes
Thy-ni-as
Thy-*o*-ne
Thy-o-tes
Thyr-e-a
Thy-*re*-um
Thy-ri-des
Thyr-*sag*-e-tæ
Thys-sus
Ti-*be*-ri-as
Tib-e-*ri*-nus
Tib-e-ris
Ti-*be*-ri-us
Ti-*bis*-cus
Tib-u-la
Ti-*bul*-lus
Ti-bur
Tib-ur-*ti*-nus
Ti-*bur*-ti-us
Ti-*ci*-num
Tic-i-nus (person)
Ti-*ci*-nus (river)
Ti-*fa*-ta
Ti-*fer*-num
Tig-el-*li*-nus
Ti-*gel*-li-us
Ti-*gra*-nes
Tig-ran-o-*cer*-ta
Tig-u-*ri*-ni
Til-i-*ven*-tus
Ti-lox
Ti-*mæ*-us
Ti-*mag*-e-nes
Ti-*man*-thes
Ti-*mar*-chus
Ti-*ma*-vus
Ti-*moch*-a-ris
Tim-o-*cle*-a
Tim-o-cles
Ti-*moc*-ra-tes
Ti-*moc*-re-on
Ti-*mo*-le-on
Ti-*mo*-lus
Ti-*mom*-a-chus
Ti-mon
Ti-*mo*-nax
Ti-*moph*-a-nes
Ti-*mo*-the-us
Tin-gis

***Tin*-i-a**
***Tin*-na**
Ti-phys
Ti-*re*-si-as
Ti-ri-*ba*-zus
Tir-i-*da*-tes
Ti-ro
Ti-ryns
Ti-*sæ*-us
Ti-*sam*-e-nes
Tis-i-as
Ti-*siph*-o-ne
Tis-sa-*pher*-nes
Ti-*ta*-ne
Ti-*ta*-ni-a
Ti-*ta*-nus (giant)
Tit-a-nus (river)
Tit-a-*re*-si-us
Ti-*tho*-nus
Ti-*tho*-re-a
Ti-*thraus*-tes
Tit-i-*a*-nus
Ti-*tin*-i-us
Tit-i-us
Ti-tus
Tit-y-rus
Tit-y-us
Tle-*pol*-e-mus
Tmo-lus
Tol-*bi*-a-cum
To-*ga*-ta
To-*le*-nus
To-*le*-ri-a
To-*le*-rus
To-*le*-tum
Tol-*mi*-des
Tol-o-phon
To-*lo*-sa
Tom-a-rus
To-mi
To-mis
To-*ro*-ne
Tor-*qua*-tus
To-*ry*-ne
Trach-a-lus
Tra-*che*-a
Tra-*chin*-e-a
Trach-o-*ni*-tis
Tra-ja-*nop*-o-lis
Tra-*ja*-nus
Tral-les
Trans-al-*pi*-nus
Trans-pa-*da*-nus
Trap-e-zus
Tras-i-*me*-nus
Tre-a
Tre-ba
Treb-bi-a
Tre-*bel*-li-*a*-nus
Tre-*bel*-li-us
Tre-*bo*-ni-us
Treb-u-la
Tre-*ve*-ri
Tri-*bal*-li
Trib-o-ci
Tri-*cas*-ses
Tric-ca
Tri-*cho*-nis
Tri-co-*ni*-um
Tri-*co*-ry-thus
Tri-*cra*-na
Tri-*den*-tum
Tri-*e*-res
Tri-*fa*-num
Trif-o-*li*-nus
Tri-*go*-num
Tri-*leu*-cum
Tri-*me*-ni-a
Tri-*na*-cri-a
Trin-o-*ban*-tes
Tri-o
Tri-*oc*-a-la
Tri-o-pas

Tri-o-*pi*-um
Tri-pa-ra-*dis*-us
Tri-*phyl*-i-a
Trip-o-lis
Trip-*tol*-e-mus
Tris-me-*gis*-tus
Tri-*tæ*-a
Trit-o-ge-*ni*-a
Tri-ton
Tri-*to*-nes
Tri-*vi*-cum
Tro-a-des
Tro-as
Troch-mi
Trœ-*ze*-ne
Trog-i-lus
Trog-*lod*-y-tæ
Tro-i-a
Tro-i-lus
Tro-*pho*-ni-us
Tros-su-lum
Trot-i-lum
Tru-*en*-tus
Tryph-i-o-*dor*-us
Try-phon
Tu-be-ro
Tu-*ber*-tus
Tu-di-*ta*-nus
Tu-*gi*-ni
Tu-gu-*ri*-nus
Tul-li-a
Tul-li-*a*-num
Tul-*li*-o-la
Tul-li-us
Tul-lum
Tu-nes
Tun-gri
Tur-de-*ta*-ni
Tur-du-li
Tu-*re*-num
Tu-*re*-sis
Tu-*ri*-cum
Tu-ro-nes
Tus-*ca*-na
Tus-cu-*la*-num
Tus-cu-lum
Tu-ti-*ca*-nus
Tu-ti-cum
Ty-a-na
Ty-a-*ni*-tis
Ty-cha
Tych-i-cus
Tyd-e-us
Ty-*di*-des
Tym-*phæ*-a
Tym-phe
Tyn-*dar*-i-des
Tyn-da-rus
Ty-*phœ*-us
Ty-*pho*-nis
Ty-*phres*-tus
Tyr-an-*gi*-tæ
Ty-*ran*-nus
Ty-ras
Tyr-i-*da*-tes
Ty-*ri*-o-tes
Ty-*ris*-sa
Ty-*rog*-ly-phus
Ty-*rop*-œ-on
Tyr-*rhe*-ni
Tyr-*rhe*-nus
Tyr-*tæ*-us
Ty-rus

U-be-ri
U-bi-i
U-*cal*-e-gon
U-cu-bis
U-fen-*ti*-na
U-*la*-tha
U-*li*-a-rus
Ul-pi-*a*-nus

U-*lys*-ses
Um-*bre*-nus
Um-bro
Um-bri-a
U-*ra*-ca
U-*ra*-gus
U-*ra*-ni-a
U-ra-nus
Ur-ba
Ur-bi-cus
Ur-*bi*-num
Ur-*cin*-i-um
U-ri-a
U-ri-co-*ni*-um
U-*ri*-um
Ur-*sel*-lis
Ur-*si*-nus
Us-*ca*-na
U-*sip*-e-tes
Us-*ti*-ca
Us-*tri*-na
U-ti-ca
U-ti-i
U-*ti*-num
U-tis
Ux-a-ma
Ux-el-lo-*du*-num
U-*xen*-tis
U-*xis*-a-ma
U-*zen*-tum
U-*zi*-ta

Vac-*cæ*-i
Vac-ca
Vac-*ca*-næ
Va-*cu*-na
Vad-i-*mo*-nis
Vag-e-*dru*-sa
Va-*ge*-ni
Va-ha-lis
Va-lens
Va-len-ti-a
Va-len-tin-i-*a*-na
Val-en-*ti*-nus
Va-*le*-ri-a
Va-le-ri-*a*-nus
Va-*le*-ri-us
Val-e-rus
Val-læ
Val-*va*-ta
Van-da-li
Van-*da*-li-i
Van-*gro*-nes
Va-*ra*-nes
Var-*du*-li
Va-*ri*-ni
Va-ri-us
Va-rro
Va-rus
Va-*sa*-tæ
Vas-co-nes
Va-ti-a
Vat-i-*ca*-nus
Va-ti-*e*-nus
Va-*tin*-i-us
Vec-tis
Vec-*to*-nes
Ved-i-an-*ti*-i
Ve-*gi*-a
Ve-i-*a*-nus
Ve-i-i
Ve-*la*-brum
Vel-e-da
Vel-*e*-i-a
Ve-*li*-a
Vel-i-ca
Ve-*li*-nus
Ve-*li*-træ
Vel-*le*-i-us
Vel-tæ
Ve-*na*-frum
Ven-e-dæ

Ven-e-li
Ven-e-ti
Ve-*net*-i-a
Ven-e-tus
Ven-*no*-nes
Ve-*nu*-si-a
Ve-*ra*-gri
Ve-ra-*ni*-us
Ver-*ba*-nus
Ver-*cel*-læ
Ver-cin-*get*-o-rix
Ve-*re*-tum
Ver-*gob*-re-tus
Ve-ro-*man*-du-i
Ve-*ro*-na
Ve-*ro*-nes
Ver-o-*ni*-ca
Ver-res
Ver-*ru*-go
Ver-ti-co
Ver-ti-*cor*-di-a
Ve-*ru*-læ
Ve-ru-*la*-mi-um
Ver-u-*la*-nus
Ve-rus
Ve-*se*-vus
Ve-*son*-ti-o
Ves-pa-si-*a*-nus
Ves-pe-rus
Ves-ta
Ves-*ta*-les
Ves-ti-*li*-us
Ves-*ti*-ni
Ves-u-lus
Ve-*sun*-na
Vet-*to*-nes
Vet-u-lo-*ni*-um
Vi-*ad*-u-a
Vi-*bi*-num
Vib-i-*o*-nes
Vi-*ce*-ti-a
Vic-to-*ri*-nus
Vi-drus
Vi-mi-*na*-ci-um
Vim-i-*na*-lis
Vin-*cen*-ti-us
Vin-del-*ic*-i-a
Vin-*dob*-o-na
Vin-do-*nis*-sa
Vi-*no*-vi-a
Vir-*du*-ma-rus
Vir-*gil*-i-us
Vir-*gin*-i-a
Vir-*gin*-i-us
Vir-i-*a*-thus
Vir-i-*dom*-a-rus
Vir-i-*pla*-ca
Vi-ro-*co*-ni-um
Vi-ro-*du*-num
Vi-ro-*man*-dis
Vi-*ru*-num
Vis-cel-*li*-nus
Vi-*sen*-ti-um
Vi-*son*-ti-o
Vit-o-*du*-rum
Vi-*tric*-i-um
Vit-ri-cus
Vi-*tru*-vi-us
Vi-*vis*-cus
Vo-*con*-ti-i
Vo-ge-sus
Vo-*la*-ne
Vol-a-*ter*-ræ
Vol-cæ
Vol-ci
Vol-e-sus
Vo-*log*-e-ses
Vol-sci
Vol-*sin*-i-um
Vol-*tur*-num
Vol-*tur*-nus
Vo-*lum*-ni-a
Vo-*lum*-ni-us

Vo-*lum*-nus
Vo-*lup*-tas
Vol-u-*se*-nus
Vo-lu-si-*a*-nus
Vo-*lu*-si-us
Vol-u-sus
Vo-*ma*-nus
Vo-*no*-nes
Vo-*sol*-vi-a
Vul-*ca*-nus
Vul-*si*-num
Vul-so

Xan-*thip*-pe
Xan-*thip*-pus
Xan-thus
Xan-ti-cles
Xe-*nag*-o-ras
Xe-*ni*-a-des
Xen-o-cles
Xe-*noc*-ra-tes
Xe-*nod*-i-ce
Xe-*noph*-a-nes
Xen-o-phon
Xer-*xe*-ne
Xer-xes
Xy-*ni*-æ
Xy-*ni*-as
Xyp-e-te
Xys-tus

Za-*ba*-tus
Za-*be*-da
Zab-di-*ce*-ne
Za-*cyn*-thus
Zad-ra-*car*-ta
Za-*leu*-cus
Za-ma
Za-*mol*-xis
Zan-cle
Za-*ra*-dras
Za-rax
Zar-bi-*e*-nus
Za-re-tra
Za-ri-*as*-pa
Za-*ve*-ces
Ze-a
Ze-*bi*-na
Ze-la
Ze-*le*-a
Ze-no
Ze-*no*-bi-a
Zen-o-*dor*-us
Zen-o-*do*-tus
Zen-o-*the*-mis
Ze-*phy*-ri-um
Zeph-y-rus
Ze-*ryn*-thus
Ze-tes
Ze-thus
Zeu-gis
Zeu-gi-*ta*-na
Zeug-ma
Zeus
Zeux-*id*-a-mus
Zeux-*ip*-pe
Zeux-is
Zi-*ga*-na
Zi-*gi*-ra
Zi-lis
Zi-*ma*-ra
Zi-*my*-ri
Zin-gis
Zi-*ob*-e-ris
Zo-i-lus
Zo-i-*te*-um
Zon-a-ras
Zop-y-rus
Zo-ro-*as*-ter
Zos-i-mus
Zy-*gan*-tes

PRONUNCIATION OF HEBREW AND SCRIPTURE PROPER NAMES

The following list of Proper Names from the English Bible (including the Apocrypha) gives only those of more than two syllables, the accentuation and syllabication of each being duly noted; for as these latter are always accented on the first syllable, no mistake can arise in their pronunciation. Anglicized Hebrew words, such as *Alleluia, leviathan, Pharisee,* some of which may be treated as Proper Names, are also omitted, and will be found in their correct place in the main body of Nuttall's Standard Dictionary.

It is generally admitted that the true pronunciation of ancient Hebrew is lost; a few general rules, however, may be given as a guide.

In Hebrew names the double letter *ch,* which in the English language admits of three different pronunciations (*k, tch,* and *sh,* as in *chemist, champion, champagne*—with a fourth in the Scottish *loch*), is sounded hard like *k*—as *Chebar, Enoch,* with the one exception of *Rachel* which, like *cherub,* has become completely Anglicized.

The consonants *c, s,* and *t,* before *ia* and *iu,* take the sound of *zh* or *sh* in a number of Scripture names, when preceded by an accent—as *Asia, Cappadocia, Galatia,* etc. The sound of the letter *g,* which in Greek and Latin is soft before *e, i,* and *y*—as *Gellius, Gippius, Gyas,* etc., in Hebrew names is hard—as *Gerizim, Gideon*; except *Bethphage,* which, by passing through the Greek of the New Testament, has conformed itself to the Greek pronunciation.

As to the vowels and diphthongs, the final *i,* when it forms a distinct syllable, is pronounced with a long sound, but the two vowels *ai* are pronounced sometimes as a diphthong, and sometimes as two distinct vowels. The two vowels *ia,* when preceded by a vowel, are sometimes pronounced as one syllable, the *i* sounding like *y,* but when sounded as two syllables, the accent is on the *i.* When *ei* is followed by a vowel, the *i* is usually sounded like the consonant *y.*

A-a-lar
Aa-ro-nites
Ab-a-cuc
A-*bad*-don
Ab-a-*di*-as
A-*bag*-tha
Ab-a-na, or A-*ba*-na
Ab-a-rim
Ab-a-ron
Ab-*di*-as
Ab-di-el
A-*bed*-ne-go
A-bel-beth-*ma*-a-chah
A-bel-*ma*-im
A-bel-me-*ho*-lah
A-bel *Miz*-ra-im
Ab-e-san
Ab-e-sar
A-bel-*shit*-tim
Ab-ga-rus
A-*bi*-a
A-*bi*-ah
A-bi-*al*-bon
A-*bi*-a-saph
A-*bi*-a-thar
A-*bi*-dah
Ab-i-dan
A-bi-el
A-bi-*e*-zer
A-bi-*ez*-rite
Ab-i-gail
Ab-i-*hail*
A-*bi*-hu
A-*bi*-hud
A-*bi*-jah
A-*bi*-jam
Ab-i-*le*-ne
A-*bim*-a-el, or Ab-i-*ma*-el
A-*bim*-a-lech
A-*bin*-a-dab
A-*bin*-o-am
A-*bi*-ram
A-*bis*-a-i
Ab-i-*se*-i
Ab-i-shag
A-*bish*-a-har
A-*bish*-a-i
A-*bish*-a-lom
A-*bish*-u-a
Ab-i-shur
Ab-i-sum
Ab-i-tal
Ab-i-tub
A-*bi*-ud
A-bra-ham
Ab-sa-lom
A-*bu*-bus
Ac-a-tan
A-*cel*-da-ma
A-*cha*-i-a
A-*cha*-i-chus
A-chi-*ach*-a-rus
A-*chim*-e-lech
A-*chit*-o-phel
Ach-me-tha
Ac-i-pha
A-*cu*-a
Ad-a-dah
Ad-a-*i*-ah
Ad-a-*li*-a
Ad-a-mah
Ad-a-mi
Ad-a-mi-*Ne*-keb
Ad-a-sa
Ad-be-el
Ad-i-da
A-di-el
Ad-i-na
Ad-i-nus
Ad-i-*tha*-im
Ad-la-i
Ad-ma-tha
Ad-o-nai
A-don-i-*be*-zek
Ad-o-*ni*-jah
Ad-o-*ni*-kam
Ad-o-*ni*-ram
A-don-i-*ze*-dek
A-*do*-ra
Ad-o-*ra*-im
A-*do*-ram
A-*dram*-e-lech
A-dra-*myt*-ti-um
A-dri-a
A-dri-el
A-*du*-el
A-*dul*-lam
A-*dum*-mim
A-e-*di*-as
Æ-*ne*-as
Ag-a-ba
Ag-a-bus
A-gag-ite
A-*har*-ah
A-*har*-hel
A-*has*-a-i
A-*has*-ba-i
A-has-u-*e*-rus
A-*ha*-va, or *A*-ha-va
A-ha-*zi*-ah
A-*hi*-ah
A-*hi*-am
A-*hi*-an
A-hi-*e*-zer
A-*hi*-hud
A-*hi*-jah
A-*hi*-kam
A-*hi*-lud
A-*him*-a-az
A-*hi*-man
A-*him*-e-lech
A-*hi*-moth
A-*hin*-a-dab
A-*hin*-o-am
A-*hi*-o
A-*hi*-ra
A-*hi*-ram
A-*hi*-ra-mites
A-*his*-a-mach
A-*hish*-a-har
A-*hi*-shar
A-*hit*-o-phel
A-*hi*-tub
Ah-la-i
A-*ho*-ah
A-*ho*-ite
A-*ho*-lah
A-*hol*-bah
A-*ho*-li-ab
A-*hol*-i-bah
A-ho-li-*bah*-mah
A-*hu*-ma-i
A-*hu*-zam
A-*huz*-zath
A-*i*-ah
A-*i*-ath
A-*i*-jah
Ai-ja-lon
Ai-je-leth
A-*i*-oth
A-*i*-rus
Aj-a-lon
Ak-*rab*-bim
Al-a-meth
A-*lam*-me-lech
Al-a-moth
A-*le*-meth
Al-ex-*an*-dri-a
A-*li*-ah
A-*li*-an
Al-*mo*-dad
Al-na-than
Al-*phæ*-us

Al-ta-*ne*-us
Al-*tas*-chith
A-*mad*-a-tha
A-*mad*-a-thus
Am-a-lek
A-*mal*-e-kites
Am-a-na
Am-a-*ri*-ah
Am-a-sa
A-*mas*-a-i
Am-a-*si*-ah
Am-a-thas
Am-a-*the*-is
Am-a-this
Am-a-*zi*-ah
A-*min*-a-dab
A-*mit*-ta-i
A-*miz*-a-bad
Am-*med*-a-tha
Am-*mid*-i-oi
Am-mi-el
Am-*mi*-hud
Am-mi-*shad*-da-i
Am-mo-nites
Am-o-rites
Am-*phip*-o-lis
Am-pli-as
Am-ra-mites
Am-ra-phel
An-a-el
An-a-*ha*-rath
A-*nai*-ah
An-a-kim
An-a-mim
A-*nam*-me-lech
An-*a*-ni
An-a-*ni*-ah
An-a-*ni*-as
A-*nan*-i-el
An-a-thoth
An-dro-*ni*-cus
A-ni-am
An-na-as
An-*nu*-us
An-ti-*lib*-a-nus
An-ti-och
An-*ti*-o-chus
An-ti-pas
An-*tip*-a-tris
An-to-*thi*-jah
An-to-thite
Ap-a-*me*-a
A-*phar*-sa-chites
Aph-ar-*sath*-chites
A-*phar*-sites
A-*phe*-kah
A-*pher*-e-ma
A-*pher*-ra
A-*phi*-ah
A-*pol*-los
A-*pol*-ly-on
Ap-o-*lo*-ni-a
Ap-pa-im
Ap-phi-a, or *Af*-i-a
Ap-pi-i *For*-um
Aq-ui-la
Ar-a-bah
Ar-a-ba-*ttha*-ne
Ar-a-*ba*-tti-ne
A-*ra*-bi-a
Ar-a-dus
A-ra-rat
A-*rau*-nah
Ar-*bat*-tis
Ar-*bo*-na-i
Ar-che-*la*-us
Ar-che-vites
Ar-*chip*-pus
Arc-*tu*-rus
A-*re*-li
A-*re*-lites
A-re-*op*-a-gite
A-re-*op*-a-gus
A-*re*-tas
A-*re*-us
A-ri-a-*ra*-thes
A-*rid*-a-i
A-*rid*-a-tha
A-*ri*-eh
A-ri-el
Ar-i-ma-*the*-a
A-ri-och
A-*ris*-a-i
Ar-is-*tar*-chus
Ar-is-to-*bu*-lus
Ar-ma-*ged*-don
Ar-o-di
Ar-o-er
Ar-*phax*-ad
Ar-*sa*-ces
Ar-ta-*xerk*-ses
Ar-te-mas
A-*ru*-both
A-*ru*-mah
Ar-va-dites
As-a-*di*-as
As-a-hel
As-a-*hi*-ah
As-a-*i*-ah
As-a-na
A-*sa*-ra-el
A-*sa*-re-el
As-a-*re*-lah
As-*bac*-a-phath
As-*baz*-a-reth
As-ca-lon
A-*se*-as
A-seb-e-*bi*-a
As-e-*bi*-a
As-e-nath
As-e-rer
Ash-be-a
Ash-bel-ites
Ash-dod-ites
Ash-doth-ites
Ash-er-ah
Ash-er-ites
A-*shi*-ma
Ash-ke-naz
Ash-pe-naz
Ash-ri-el
Ash-ta-roth
Ash-ta-roth-ites
Ash-te-moh
Ash-te-rath-ites
Ash-te-roth
Ash-u-rites
As-i-*bi*-as
A-si-el
As-i-pha
As-ke-lon
As-ma-dai
As-*ma*-veth
As-mo-*de*-us
As-*nap*-per
As-*pa*-tha
As-*phar*-a-sus
As-ri-el
As-sa-*bi*-as
As-*sal*-i-moth
As-sa-*ni*-as
As-*shu*-rim
As-si-*de*-ans
As-ta-roth
As-*tar*-te
A-*syn*-cri-tus
At-a-rah
A-*tar*-ga-tis
At-a-roth
At-e-re-*zi*-as
Ath-a-*i*-ah
Ath-a-*li*-ah
Ath-a-*ri*-as
Ath-e-*no*-bi-us
At-ta-*li*-a
At-ta-lus
At-*thar*-a-tes
Au-gi-a
Au-*gus*-tus
Au-*ra*-nus
Au-*te*-as
Av-a-ran
Av-a-ron
Az-a-*e*-lus
Az-a-*li*-ah
Az-a-*ni*-ah
A-*za*-phi-on
Az-a-ra
A-*za*-re-el
Az-a-*ri*-ah
Az-a-*zi*-ah
Az-*baz*-a-reth
Az-buk
A-*ze*-kah
Az-e-*phu*-rith
A-*ze*-tas
A-*zi*-a
A-*zi*-e-i
Az-i-el
A-*zi*-za
Az-ma-veth
Az-noth-*ta*-bor
A-*zo*-tus
Az-ri-el
Az-ri-kam
A-*zu*-bah
Az-u-ran

Ba-al-ah
Ba-al-ath
Ba-al-ath-*Be*-er
Ba-al-e
Ba-al-i
Ba-al-im
Ba-al-is
Ba-al-*Me*-on
Ba-al-*Pe*-or
Ba-al-*Per*-a-zim
Ba-al-*Shal*-i-sha
Ba-al-*Ta*-mar
Ba-a-na
Ba-a-nah
Ba-a-*ni*-as
Ba-a-ra
Ba-a-*sei*-ah
Ba-a-sha
Ba-a-*si*-ah
Bab-y-lon
Bac-*chu*-rus
Ba-*go*-as
Ba-*ha*-rum-ite
Ba-*hu*-mus
Ba-*hu*-rim
Bak-*bak*-kar
Bak-bu-*ki*-ah
Bal-a-dan
Bal-a-mo
Ba-moth-*Ba*-al
Ban-a-*i*-as
Ban-u-as
Ba-*rab*-bas
Bar-a-chel
Bar-a-*chi*-as
Bar-*hu*-mites
Ba-*ri*-ah
Bar-*je*-sus
Bar-*jo*-na
Bar-na-bas
Ba-*ro*-dis
Bar-sa-bas
Bar-ta-cus
Bar-*thol*-o-mew
Bar-ti-*me*-us
Bar-*zil*-la-i
Bas-ca-ma
Ba-shan-*ha*-voth-*ja*-ir
Bash-e-math
Bas-ta-i
Bath-*rab*-bim
Bath-she-ba
Bath-shu-a
Bav-a-i
Be-a-*li*-ah
Be-a-loth
Beb-a-i
Be-*cho*-rath
Bec-ti-leth
Bed-a-*i*-ah
Be-e-*li*-a-da
Be-*el*-sa-rus
Be-*el*-ze-bub
Be-*e*-ra
Be-*e*-rah
Be-er-*e*-lim
Be-*e*-ri
Be-er-la-*hai*-roi
Be-*e*-roth
Be-*e*-roth-ites
Be-er-she-ba
Be-*esh*-te-rah
Be-he-moth
Be-la-ites
Bel-e-mus
Be-li-al
Bel-ma-im
Bel-*shaz*-zar
Bel-te-*shaz*-zar
Be-*na*-i-ah, or Be-*na*-yah
Ben-*am*-mi
Ben-*de*-kar
Ben-e-*be*-rak
Ben-e-*ja*-a-kan
Ben-*ha*-dad
Ben-*ha*-il
Ben-*ha*-nan
Ben-i-nu
Ben-ja-min
Ben-jam-ites
Be-*no*-ni
Be-*nu*-i
Ben-*zo*-heth
Ber-a-chah
Ber-a-*chi*-ah
Ber-a-*i*-ah
Be-*re*-a
Be-re-*chi*-ah
Be-*ri*-ah
Be-ri-ites
Ber-*ni*-ce
Be-*ro*-dach
Be-*rœ*-a
Be-*ro*-thah
Be-ro-thai
Be-ro-thites
Ber-*ze*-lus
Bes-o-*dei*-ah
Beth-a-*ba*-rah
Beth-*a*-nath
Beth-*a*-noth
Beth-a-ny
Beth-*ar*-a-bah
Beth-a-ram
Bath-*ar*-bel
Beth-*a*-ven
Beth-az-*ma*-veth
Beth-ba-al-*me*-on
Beth-*ba*-rah
Beth-ba-si
Beth-*bir*-e-i
Beth-*da*-gon
Beth-dib-la-*tha*-im
Beth-*e*-den
Beth-el-ite
Beth-*e*-mek
Beth-*es*-da (*s* as *z*)
Beth-*e*-zel
Beth-*ga*-der
Beth-*ga*-mul
Beth-*hac*-ce-rem
Beth-*ha*-ran
Beth-*hog*-lah
Beth-*ho*-ron
Beth-*jes*-i-moth
Beth-le-*ba*-oth
Beth-le-hem
Beth-le-hem-ite
Beth-*lo*-mon
Beth-*ma*-a-cah
Beth-*mar*-ca-both
Beth-*me*-on
Beth-*nim*-rah
Beth-*o*-ron
Beth-*pa*-let
Beth-*paz*-zez
Beth-*pe*-let
Beth-*pe*-or
Beth-pha-ge
Beth-phe-let
Beth-*ra*-pha
Beth-*re*-hob
Beth-*sa*-i-da
Beth-*sa*-mos
Beth-*she*-an
Beth-*she*-mesh
Beth-*she*-mite
Beth-*shit*-tah
Beth-*su*-ra
Beth-*tap*-pu-ah
Beth-u-el
Beth-u-*li*-a
Be-*to*-li-us
Bet-o-*mes*-tham
Bet-o-nim
Be-*u*-lah
Be-*zal*-e-el
Bi-a-tas
Big-*tha*-na
Big-va-i
Bik-ath-*a*-ven
Bil-e-am
Bil-ga-i
Bin-e-a
Bin-nu-i
Bir-za-vith
Bi-*thi*-ah
Biz-*joth*-jah
Bo-a-*ner*-ges
Bo-cher-u
Bos-o-ra
Buk-*ki*-ah

Cai-a-phas
Ca-*i*-nan
Cal-a-*mol*-a-lus
Cal-va-ry
Ca-naan-ites
Can-da-ce
Ca-*per*-na-um
Caph-ar-*sal*-a-ma
Ca-*phen*-a-tha
Caph-tho-rim
Cap-pa-*do*-ci-a
Car-a-*ba*-si-on
Car-che-mish
Ca-*re*-ah
Ca-ri-a
Car-*ma*-ni-ans
Car-mel-ite
Car-na-im
Car-ni-on
Car-*she*-na
Ca-*siph*-i-a
Cas-lu-him
Ca-*thu*-a
Cen-chre-a
Cen-de-*be*-us
Cha-di-as

Chæ-re-as
Chal-*ce*-don
Chal-*de*-a
Chan-nu-*ne*-us
Char-a-*ath*-a-lar
Char-a-ca
Char-a-sim
Cha-re-a
Chas-e-ba
Chas-e-lon
Ched-or-la-*o*-mer
Chel-ci-as
Chel-li-ans
Che-*lu*-bai
Chem-a-rims
Che-*na*-an-nah
Che-*na*-ni
Chen-a-*ni*-ah
Che-phar-Ha-*am*-mo-nai
Che-*phi*-rah
Che-re-as
Cher-eth-im
Cher-eth-ites
Ches-a-lon
Che-*sul*-loth
Che-*thi*-im
Chet-*ti*-im
Chil-e-ab
Chil-i-on
Chin-ne-reth
Chin-ne-roth
Cho-*rash*-an
Cho-*ra*-zin
Chos-a-*me*-us
Cho-*ze*-ba
Cin-ner-eth
Cir-a-ma
Clau-di-a
Clau-di-us
Cle-o-phas
Col-*ho*-zeh
Co-li-us
Co-*los*-se
Co-*los*-si-ans
Co-*ni*-ah
Con-o-*ni*-ah
Co-*rin*-thi-ans
Cre-ti-ans
Cu-the-ans
Cy-a-mon
Cy-*re*-ne
Cy-*re*-ni-us

Dab-a-reh
Dab-ba-sheth
Dab-e-rath
Da-bri-a
Da-*co*-bi
Dad-*de*-us
Dal-a-*i*-ah
Dal-i-lah
Dal-ma-*nu*-tha
Dam-a-ris
Dam-a-*scenes*
Dan-i-el
Dan-*ja*-an
Da-*ri*-us
Dath-e-ma
Dath-e-ran
Deb-o-rah
De-*cap*-o-lis
Ded-a-nim
De-*ha*-vites
De-*la*-ia
De-*lai*-ah
De-*li*-lah
De-*me*-tri-us
De-*u*-el
Deu-te-*ron*-o-my
Di-*an*-a
Dib-la-im
Dib-la-*tha*-im
Did-y-mus
Di-le-an
Di-*mo*-nah
Di-na-ites
Din-ha-bah
Di-*ot*-re-phes
Diz-a-hab
Do-da-i
Do-da-nim
Do-da-u
Do-da-vah
Do-*rym*-e-nes
Do-tha-im

E-a-nes
E-bed-*me*-lech
Eb-en-*e*-zer
E-*bi*-a-saph
E-*bro*-nah
E-*ca*-nus
Ec-*bat*-a-na
Ec-cle-si-*as*-tes
Ec-cle-si-*as*-ti-cus
E-dom-ites
Ed-re-i
Eg-la-im
Ek-re-bel
Ek-ron-ites
El-a-dah
E-lam-ites
El-*beth*-el
El-ci-a
El-da-ah
E-le-ad
E-le-*a*-leh
E-*le*-a-sah
E-le-*a*-zer
E-le-a-*zu*-rus
El-e-*lo*-he *Is*-ra-el
E-*leu*-the-rus
E-*leu*-za
El-*ha*-nan
E-*li*-ab
E-*li*-a-da
E-*li*-a-dah
E-*li*-a-das
E-*li*-a-dun
E-*li*-ah
E-*li*-ah-ba
E-*li*-a-kim
E-*li*-a-li
E-*li*-am
E-*li*-a-o-*ni*-as
E-*li*-as
E-*li*-a-saph
E-*li*-a-shib
E-*li*-a-sis
E-*li*-a-thah
E-*li*-dad
E-li-el
E-li-*e*-na-i
E-li-*e*-zer
E-*li*-ha-ba
El-i-*hœ*-na-i
El-i-*ho*-reph
E-*li*-hu
E-*li*-jah
E-*li*-ka
E-*lim*-e-lech
E-li-*œ*-na-i
E-li-*o*-nas
E-*li*-phal
E-*liph*-a-lek
E-*liph*-a-let
El-i-phaz
E-*lis*-a-beth
El-i-*se*-us
E-*li*-sha
E-*li*-shah
E-*lish*-a-ma
E-*lish*-a-phat
E-*lish*-e-ba
El-i-*shu*-a
E-*lis*-i-mus
E-*li*-u
E-*li*-ud
E-*liz*-a-phan
E-*li*-zur
El-*ka*-nah
El-ko-shite
El-la-sar
El-*mo*-dam
El-*na*-am
El-*na*-than
E-*lo*-i
E-lon-beth-*ha*-nan
E-lon-ites
El-*pa*-al
El-*pa*-let
El-*pa*-ran
El-te-keh
El-te-kon
El-*to*-lad
E-*lu*-za-i
El-y-*ma*-is
El-y-mas
El-za-bad
El-za-phan
E-*man*-u-el
Em-*ma*-us
E-ne-as
En-eg-*la*-im
En-e-*mes*-sar
E-*ne*-ni-us
En-*gan*-nim
En-*ge*-di
En-*had*-dah
En-*hak*-ko-re
En-*ha*-zor
En-*mish*-pat
En-*rim*-mon
En-*ro*-gel
En-*she*-mesh
En-*tap*-pu-ah
Ep-a-phras
E-paph-ro-*di*-tus
E-*pen*-e-tus
E-phes-*dam*-min
E-*phe*-sians
Eph-e-sus
E-phra-im
E-phra-im-ites
Eph-ra-tah
Eph-rath-ites
E-ran-ites
E-*ras*-tus
E-*sa*-ias
E-sar-*had*-don
Es-*dre*-lon
Es-e-bon
E-*se*-bri-as
Esh-ba-al
E-she-an
Esh-ka-lon-ites
Esh-ta-ol
Esh-ta-*u*-lites
Esh-te-*mo*-a
Esh-te-moh
E-*so*-ra
Eth-a-nim
Eth-ba-al
E-thi-*o*-pi-a
Eu-*bu*-lus
Eu-*na*-tan
Eu-*ni*-ce
Eu-*o*-di-as
Eu-*pol*-e-mus
Eu-*roc*-ly-don
Eu-ty-chus
Ex-o-dus
Ez-ba-i
Ez-e-*chi*-as
Ez-e-*ki*-as
E-*ze*-ki-el
Ez-e-*ri*-as
E-*zi*-as
E-zi-on-*Ga*-ber
Ez-ra-hite

Gab-a-el
Gab-a-tha
Gab-ba-tha
Ga-bri-as
Ga-bri-el
Gad-a-ra
Gad-a-*renes*
Gad-di-el
Ga-i-us, or *Ga*-yus
Gal-a-ad
Gal-e-ed
Gal-ga-la
Gal-i-lee
Gal-li-o
Gam-a-el
Ga-*ma*-li-el
Gam-ma-dims
Gar-i-zim
Ga-*za*-ra
Ga-zath-ites
Ga-*ze*-ra
Ged-a-*li*-ah
Ge-*de*-rah
Ged-e-rite
Ge-*de*-roth
Ged-e-ro-*tha*-im
Ge-*ha*-zi
Gel-i-loth
Ge-*mal*-li
Gem-a-*ri*-ah
Gen-e-sis (*Jen*-)
Gen-*nes*-a-reth
Gen-*ne*-us
Ge-*nu*-bath
Ger-a-sa
Ger-a-senes
Ger-ge-sa
Ger-ge-senes
Ger-i-zim
Ger-*rhe*-ni-ans
Ger-shon-ites
Gesh-u-rites
Geth-*sem*-a-ne
Ge-*u*-el
Ge-zer-ites
Gib-be-thon
Gib-e-ah
Gib-e-ath
Gib-e-a-thites
Gib-e-on
Gib-e-o-nites
Gid-*dal*-ti
Gid-e-on
Gid-e-*o*-ni
Gil-a-lai
Gil-*bo*-a
Gil-e-ad
Gil-e-a-dites
Gil-o-nites
Gin-ne-tho
Gir-ga-shites
Git-ta-im
Giz-o-nite
Gol-go-tha
Go-*li*-ah
Go-*li*-ath
Go-*mor*-rah
Gor-gi-as
Gor-*ty*-na
Goth-o-*li*-as
Go-*tho*-ni-el
Gre-ci-a (-*she*-a)
Gud-*go*-dah
Gur-*ba*-al

Ha-a-*hash*-ta-ri
Ha-*ba*-iah
Hab-ak-kuk
Hab-a-zi-*ni*-ah
Hach-a-*li*-ah
Ha-*chi*-lah
Hach-mo-ni
Hach-mo-nite
Had-ad-*e*-zer
Ha-*dash*-ah
Ha-*das*-sah
Ha-*dat*-tah
Had-la-i
Ha-*do*-ram
Hag-a-bah
Ha-ga-*renes*
Ha-ga-rites
Hag-ga-i
Hag-ge-ri
Hag-*gi*-ah
Hak-ka-tan
Ha-*ku*-pha
Hal-*lo*-esh
Ha-ma-thite
Ha-math-*zo*-bah
Ham-i-tal
Ham-*med*-a-tha
Ham-me-lech
Ham-*mol*-e-keth
Ham-mu-el
Ha-*mo*-nah
Ha-mul-ites
Ha-*mu*-tal
Ha-*nam*-e-el
Ha-*nan*-e-el
Ha-*na*-ni
Han-a-*ni*-ah
Han-i-el
Han-na-thon
Ha-noch-ites
Haph-a-*ra*-im
Ha-*ra*-dah
Ha-ra-rite
Har-*bo*-nah
Har-ha-*i*-ah
Har-ne-pher
Ha-ro-dite
Har-o-eh
Ha-ro-rite
Har-o-sheth
Ha-*ru*-maph
Ha-*ru*-phite
Has-a-*di*-ah
Has-e-*nu*-ah
Hash-a-*bi*-ah
Hash-*ab*-nah
Hash-ab-*ni*-ah
Hash-*bad*-a-na
Hash-*mo*-nah
Ha-*shu*-pha
Has-mo-*næ*-an
Has-se-*na*-ah
Ha-*su*-pha
Hat-*ti*-pha
Ha-*ti*-ta
Hav-i-lah
Ha-za-rel
Ha-*zai*-ah
Haz-ar-*ma*-veth
Haz-e-lel-*po*-ni
Ha-*ze*-rim
Ha-*ze*-roth
Ha-ze-zon
Ha-zi-el
He-ber-ites
He-bron-ites
Heg-a-i
Hel-*chi*-ah
Hel-da-i
He-lek-ites
Hel-ka-i
Hel-kath-*haz*-zu-rim

Hel-*ki*-as
Hen-a-dad
He-pher-ites
Heph-zi-bah
Her-*mog*-e-nes
Her-*mo*-ni-im
Her-mon-ites
He-*ro*-di-ans
He-*ro*-di-as
Hez-e-ki
Hez-e-*ki*-ah
He-zi-on
Hez-ra-i
Hez-ron-ites
Hid-da-i
Hid-de-kel
Hi-*er*-e-el
Hi-*er*-e-moth
Hi-er-i-*e*-lus
Hi-*er*-mas
Hi-er-*on*-y-mus
Hil-*ki*-ah
Hir-*ca*-nus
Hod-a-*i*-ah
Hod-a-*vi*-ah
Ho-*de*-vah
Ho-*di*-ah
Ho-*di*-jah
Hol-o-*fer*-nes
Hor-ha-*gid*-gad
Hor-o-*na*-im
Hor-o-nites
Ho-*se*-a (-*ze*-)
Ho-*sha*-iah
Hosh-a-ma
Ho-*she*-a
Hu-pham-ites
Hu-shath-ite
Hy-*das*-pes
Hy-men-*æ*-us

Ib-le-am
Ib-*nei*-ah
Ib-*ni*-jah
Ich-a-bod
I-*co*-ni-um
Id-a-lah
Id-u-el
Id-*u*-*mæ*-a
Ig-da-*li*-ah
Ig-e-*ab*-a-rim
Ig-e-al
Im-*man*-u-el
I-*o*-ta
Iph-e-*dei*-ah
I-*ri*-jah
Ir-*na*-hash
Ir-pe-el
Ir-*she*-mesh
I-*sa*-iah, or I-*sah*-e-a
Is-*ca*-ri-ot
Is-da-el
Ish-bi-*be*-nob
Ish-*bo*-sheth
I-*shi*-ah
I-*shi*-jah
Ish-ma-el
Ish-*ma*-iah
Ish-me-rai
Ish-u-a
Ish-u-ai
Is-ma-*chi*-ah
Is-ra-el
Is-ra-el-ites
Is-*sa*-char
Is-tal-*cu*-rus
Is-u-ah
Is-u-i
Is-u-ites
It-a-ly
Ith-a-i, or *It*-a-i
Ith-a-mar
Ith-i-el
Ith-re-am
It-ta-i
It-tah-*ka*-zin
It-u-*re*-a
Iz-e-har
Iz-ha-rite
Iz-ra-*hi*-ah
Iz-ra-hite
Iz-re-el

Ja-a-kan
Ja-*ak*-o-bah
Ja-*a*-lah
Ja-*a*-lam
Ja-a-nai
Ja-ar-e-*or*-e-gim
Ja-a-re-*shi*-ah
Ja-a-sau
Ja-*a*-si-el
Ja-az-a-*ni*-ah
Ja-a-*zer*
Ja-a-*zi*-ah
Ja-*a*-zi-el
Ja-besh-*Gil*-e-ad
Jab-ne-el
Ja-chin-ites
Jad-*du*-a
Ja-*hal*-e-lel
Ja-*ha*-zah
Ja-ha-*zi*-ah
Ja-*ha*-zi-el
Jah-da-i
Jah-di-el
Jah-le-el
Jah-le-el-ites
Jah-ma-i
Jah-ze-el
Jah-ze-el-ites
Jah-*ze*-rah
Jah-zi-el
Ja-ir-ites
Ja-i-rus
Ja-min-ites
Jam-*ni*-a
Ja-*na*-i
Ja-*no*-ah
Ja-*no*-hah
Ja-*phi*-ah
Japh-le-ti
Jar-e-*si*-ah
Ja-*ro*-ah
Jas-a-el
Ja-*sho*-be-am
Ja-*shu*-bi-le-hem
Jash-ub-ites
Ja-si-el
Ja-*su*-bus
Jath-ni-el
Ja-zi-el
Je-a-rim
Je-*at*-e-rai
Je-*ber*-e-*chi*-ah
Je-*bu*-si
Jeb-u-sites
Jec-a-*mi*-ah
Jec-o-*li*-ah
Jec-o-*ni*-ah
Je-*da*-iah
Je-*de*-us
Je-*di*-a-el
Je-*di*-dah
Jed-i-*di*-ah
Je-di-el
Jed-u-thun
Je-e-*li*
Je-e-*lus*
Je-e-zer
Je-*e*-zer-ites
Je-*ha*-le-el
Je-ha-*le*-le-el
Je-*han*-num
Je-*hez*-kel
Je-*hi*-ah
Jeh-*dei*-ah
Je-*hi*-e-li
Je-hiz-*ki*-ah
Je-*ho*-a-dah
Je-ho-*ad*-dan
Je-*ho*-a-haz
Je-*ho*-ash
Je-*ho*-ha-nan
Je-*hoi*-a-chin
Je-*hoi*-a-da
Je-*hoi*-a-kim
Je-*hoi*-a-rib
Je-*hon*-a-dab
Je-*hon*-a-than
Je-*ho*-ram
Je-ho-*shah*-e-ath
Je-*hosh*-a-phat
Je-*hosh*-e-ba
Je-*hosh*-u-a
Je-*ho*-vah
Je-*hoz*-a-bad
Je-*hoz*-a-dak
Je-*hub*-bah
Je-hu-cal
Je-*hu*-di
Je-hu-*di*-jah
Je-*kab*-ze-el
Jek-a-*me*-am
Jek-a-*mi*-ah
Je-*ku*-thi-el
Je-*mi*-ma
Je-*mu*-el
Je-*phun*-neh
Je-*rah*-me-el
Je-*rah*-me-e-lites
Jer-e-chus
Jer-e-mai
Jer-e-*mi*-ah
Jer-e-moth
Jer-e-mouth
Je-*ri*-ah
Jer-i-bai
Jer-i-cho
Je-ri-el
Je-*ri*-jah
Jer-i-moth
Je-ri-oth
Jer-o-*bo*-am
Je-*ro*-ham
Je-rub-*ba*-al
Je-rub-*e*-sheth
Je-*ru*-el
Je-*ru*-sa-lem
Je-*ru*-sha
Je-*sa*-iah
Je-*sha*-ia
Jesh-a-nah
Jesh-a-*re*-lah
Je-*sheb*-e-ab
Je-*shi*-mon
Je-*shish*-a-i
Jesh-o-*ha*-iah
Jesh-u-a
Jesh-u-run
Je-*si*-ah
Je-*sim*-i-el
Jes-su-*e*
Jes-u-i
Je-*u*-el
Jez-a-*ni*-ah
Jez-e-bel
Je-*ze*-lus
Je-zer-ites
Je-*zi*-ah
Je-zi-el
Jez-*li*-ah
Je-*zo*-ar
Jez-ra-*hi*-ah
Jez-re-el
Jez-re-el-ite
Jiph-thah-el
Jo-a-chaz
Jo-a-chim
Jo-a-*da*-nus
Jo-a-haz
Jo-a-kim
Jo-*an*-na
Jo-*an*-nan
Jo-a-tham
Jo-a-*zab*-dus
Joch-e-bed
Jo-*e*-lah
Jo-*e*-zer
Jog-be-ah
Jo-*ha*-nan
Joi-a-da
Joi-a-kim
Joi-a-rib
Jok-de-am
Jok-me-an
Jok-ne-am
Jok-the-el
Jon-a-dab
Jon-a-than
Jo-ra-i
Jo-ri-bas
Jor-ko-am
Jos-a-bad
Jos-a-phat
Jos-a-*phi*-as
Jos-e-dech
Jo-*se*-phus
Josh-a-bad
Josh-a-phat
Josh-a-*vi*-ah
Josh-be-*ka*-sha
Josh-i-*bi*-ah
Josh-u-a
Jo-*si*-ah
Jo-*si*-as
Jos-i-*bi*-ah
Jos-i-*phi*-ah
Jot-ba-tha
Joz-a-bad
Joz-a-char
Joz-a-dak
Ju-*dæ*-a
Ju-li-a
Ju-ni-a
Ju-shab-*he*-sed

Kab-ze-el
Kad-mi-el
Kad-mon-ites
Kal-la-i
Ka-*re*-ah
Kar-*ka*-a
Kar-na-im
Ked-e-mah
Ked-e-moth
Ke-he-*la*-thah
Ke-*la*-iah
Kel-i-ta
Ke-*mu*-el
Ke-niz-zites
Ker-en-*hap*-puch
Ke-ri-oth
Ke-*tu*-rah
Ke-*zi*-a
Kib-roth-hat-*ta*-a-vah
Kib-*za*-im
Kir-*har*-a-seth
Kir-i-ath
Kir-ia-*tha*-im
Kir-i-oth
Kish-i-on
Ko-hath-ites
Ko-*la*-iah
Ko-rah-ites
Ko-rath-ites
Ku-*sha*-iah

La-a-dah
La-a-dan
Lab-a-na
La-*cu*-nus
La-*hai*-roi
La-od-i-*ce*-a
Lap-i-doth
La-*se*-a
La-*sha*-ron
Las-the-nes
Laz-a-rus
Le-*ba*-nah
Leb-a-non
Le-*ba*-oth
Leb-*bæ*-us
Le-*bo*-nah
Le-*ha*-bim
Lem-u-el
Le-*tu*-shim
Le-*um*-mim
Le-*vit*-i-cus
Lib-a-nus
Lib-y-a
Lo-*am*-mi
Lo-*de*-bar
Loth-a-*su*-bus
Lu-ci-fer
Lu-ci-us
Lyc-a-*o*-nia
Ly-*sa*-ni-as
Lys-i-as

Ma-a-cah
Ma-*ach*-a-thites
Ma-a-*da*-i
Ma-a-*di*-ah
Ma-*a*-i
Ma-*al*-eh
Ma-a-nai
Ma-a-rath
Ma-a-*se*-iah
Ma-a-*si*-ah
Ma-*as*-i-ai
Ma-a-*zi*-ah
Mab-da-i
Mac-a-lon
Mac-ca-*bæ*-us
Mac-ca-bees
Mach-*be*-nah
Mach-ba-nai
Ma-chir-ites
Mach-*nad*-e-bai
Mach-*pe*-lah
Mad-a-i
Ma-*di*-a-bun
Ma-*di*-ah
Ma-di-an
Mad-*man*-nah
Mad-*me*-nah
Ma-*e*-lus
Mag-da-la
Mag-da-len
Mag-da-*le*-ne
Mag-di-el
Mag-pi-ash
Ma-ha-lah
Ma-*ha*-la-*le*-el
Ma-ha-lath
Ma-*ha*-le-el
Ma-ha-li
Ma-ha-*na*-im
Ma-ha-neh-Dan
Ma-*har*-a-i
Ma-ha-vites
Ma-*ha*-zi-oth
Ma-her-*shal*-al-*hash*-baz
Mai-*an*-e-as
Mai-*an*-nas

Mak-*he*-loth
Mak-*ke*-dah
Mal-a-chi
Mal-*chi*-ah
Mal-chi-el
Mal-chi-el-ites
Mal-*chi*-jah
Mal-*chi*-ram
Mal-chi-*shu*-ah
Ma-*le*-le-el
Mal-lo-thi
Ma-*ma*-ias
Ma-*mu*-chus
Man-a-en
Man-a-hath
Ma-*na*-heth-ites
Man-as-*se*-as
Ma-*nas*-seh
Ma-*nas*-ses
Ma-*nas*-sites
Man-ha-*na*-im
Ma-*no*-ah
Ma-on-ites
Mar-a-lah
Mar-a-*nath*-a
Mar-do-*che*-us
Ma-*re*-shah
Mar-i-sa
Mar-se-na
Ma-*si*-as
Mas-re-kah
Ma-*thu*-sa-la
Mat-ta-nah
Mat-ta-*ni*-ah
Mat-ta-tha
Mat-ta-*thi*-as
Mat-te-*na*-i
Mat-*the*-las
Mat-*thi*-as
Mat-ti-*thi*-ah
Maz-i-*ti*-as
Maz-za-roth
Me-*a*-ni
Me-*a*-rah
Me-*bu*-nai
Mech-e-rath-ite
Med-a-ba
Me-di-a
Me-*e*-da
Me-*gid*-do
Me-*gid*-don
Me-*het*-a-bel
Me-*hi*-da
Me-*hol*-ath-ite
Me-*hu*-ja-el
Me-*hu*-man
Me-*hu*-nim
Me-*jar*-kon
Me-*ko*-nah
Mel-a-*ti*-ah
Mel-*chi*-ah
Mel-*chi*-as
Mel-chi-el
Mel-*chis*-e-dek
Mel-chi-*shu*-a
Me-*le*-a
Mel-i-cu
Mel-i-ta
Me-*mu*-can
Men-a-hem
Me-*on*-e-nem
Me-*on*-o-thai
Meph-a-ath
Me-*phib*-o-sheth
Me-*rai*-ah
Me-*rai*-oth
Me-*ra*-ri
Me-ra-rites
Me-ra-*tha*-im
Mer-*cu*-ri-us
Mer-e-moth
Mer-i-bah

Me-rib-*ba*-al
Me-*ro*-dach
Me-*ron*-o-thite
Mesh-el-e-*mi*-ah
Me-*shez*-a-beel
Me-*shez*-a-bel
Me-*shil*-le-mith
Me-*shil*-le-moth
Me-*sho*-bah
Me-*shul*-lam
Me-*shul*-le-meth
Me-*so*-ba-ite
Mes-o-po-*ta*-mi-a
Mes-*si*-ah
Mes-*si*-as
Me-*te*-rus
Me-theg-*am*-ma
Meth-o-ar
Me-*thu*-sa-el
Me-*thu*-se-lah
Me-*u*-nim
Mez-a-hab
Mi-a-min
Mi-*ca*-iah
Mi-cha-el
Mi-*cha*-iah
Mich-me-thah
Mid-i-an-ites
Mig-da-lel
Mij-a-min
Mik-*nei*-ah
Mil-a-*la*-i
Mi-*le*-tus
Mi-*ni*-a-min
Mi-ri-am
Mish-a-el
Mi-she-al
Mish-*man*-na
Mish-ra-ites
Mis-pe-reth
Mis-re-photh-*ma*-im
Mith-ri-dath
Miz-ra-im
Mo-ab-ites
Mo-a-*di*-ah
Mol-a-dah
Mo-o-*si*-as
Mo-rash-ite
Mo-ras-thite
Mor-de-cai
Mor-esh-eth
Mo-*ri*-ah
Mo-*se*-rah
Mo-se-roth
Mo-*sol*-lam
Muth-*lab*-ben
Mys-i-a (*Mish*-)
Myt-e-*le*-ne

Na-a-mah
Na-a-man
Na-a-ma-thites
Na-a-mites
Na-a-rah
Na-a-rai
Na-a-ran
Na-a-rath
Na-*ash*-on
Na-*ass*-on
Na-a-thus
Nab-a-*ri*-as
Na-ba-*the*-ans
Na-ba-thites
Na-*dab*-a-tha
Na-ha-lal
Na-*ha*-li-el
Na-ha-lol
Na-ha-*ma*-ni
Na-*har*-a-i
Na-i-dus

Na-i-oth
Na-*ne*-a
Na-o-mi
Naph-i-si
Naph-tha-li
Naph-tu-him
Nar-*cis*-sus
Na-*than*-a-el
Nath-a-*ni*-as
Naz-a-*rene*
Naz-a-reth
Naz-a-rite
Ne-*ap*-o-lis
Ne-a-*ri*-ah
Neb-a-i
Ne-*bai*-oth
Ne-*ba*-joth
Ne-*bal*-lat
Neb-u-chad-*nez*-zar
Neb-u-cha-*drez*-zar
Neb-u-*shas*-ban
Neb-u-*zar*-a-dan
Ne-*co*-dan
Ned-a-*bi*-ah
Ne-e-*mi*-as
Ne-*gi*-nah
Neg-i-noth
Ne-*hel*-a-mite
Ne-he-*mi*-ah
Ne-*hush*-ta
Ne-*hush*-tan
Ne-i-el
Ne-*ko*-da
Ne-*mu*-el
Ne-*mu*-el-ites
Ne-*phish*-e-sim
Neph-tha-lim
Nep-tho-ah
Ne-*phu*-sim
Ne-re-us
Ner-gal-sha-*re*-zer
Ne-*ri*-ah
Ne-*than*-e-el
Neth-a-*ni*-ah
Neth-i-nims
Ne-*to*-phah
Ne-*toph*-a-thites
Ne-*zi*-ah
Ni-*ca*-nor
Nic-o-*de*-mus
Nic-o-*la*-i-tans
Nic-o-las
Ni-*cop*-o-lis
Nin-e-veh
Nin-e-vites
No-a-*di*-ah
No-e-ba

Ob-a-*di*-ah
O-chi-el
Oc-i-*de*-lus (*Os*-)
Oc-i-na (*Os*-)
O-*dol*-lam
Od-on-*ar*-kes
Ol-a-mus
Ol-i-vet
O-*lym*-pas
Om-a-*e*-rus
O-me-ga
O-*nes*-i-mus
On-e-*siph*-o-rus
O-*ni*-a-res
O-*ri*-on
Or-tho-*si*-as
O-*sai*-as
O-*se*-a
O-*se*-as
O-she-a
Oth-ni-el
Oth-o-*ni*-as
O-*zi*-as

O-zi-el
O-*zo*-ra

Pa-a-rai
Pa-dan-*A*-ram
Pa-gi-el
Pa-hath-*Mo*-ab
Pal-es-*ti*-na
Pal-lu-ites
Pal-ti-el
Pam-*phyl*-i-a
Par-*mash*-ta
Par-me-nas
Par-shan-*da*-tha
Par-u-ah
Par-*va*-im
Pas-*dam*-mim
Pa-*se*-ah
Pat-a-ra
Pa-*the*-us
Path-*ru*-sim
Pat-ro-bas
Ped-a-hel
Ped-ah-zur
Ped-*a*-iah
Pek-a-*hi*-ah
Pe-*lai*-a
Pel-a-*li*-ah
Pel-a-*ti*-ah
Pe-leth-ites
Pe-*li*-as
Pel-o-nite
Pe-*ni*-el
Pe-*nin*-nah
Pen-*tap*-o-lis
Pen-ta-teuch
Pen-te-cost
Pe-*nu*-el
Pe-ra-zim
Pe-rez-*Uz*-za
Per-ga-mos
Pe-*ri*-da
Pe-riz-zites
Per-me-nas
Pe-*ru*-da
Peth-a-*hi*-ah
Pe-*thu*-el
Pe-*ul*-thai
Phac-a-reth
Phai-sur
Phal-*da*-ius
Pha-*le*-as
Phal-ti-el
Pha-*nu*-el
Phar-a-cim
Pha-ra-oh, or *Phah*-roh
Pha-*ri*-ra
Pha-se-ah
Phas-i-ron
Phe-*ni*-ce
Phe-*nic*-e-a (-*nish*-)
Phil-a-*del*-phi-a
Phi-*lar*-ches
Phi-*le*-mon
Phi-*le*-tus
Phil-ip-pi
Phi-*lip*-pi-ans
Phi-*lis*-ti-a
Phi-*lis*-tim
Phil-is-tines
Phi-*lol*-o-gus
Phin-e-as
Phin-e-es
Phin-e-has
Phy-*gel*-lus
Pi-*be*-seth
Pi-ha-*hi*-roth
Pil-e-ha
Pi-*le*-ser
Pi-*ra*-thon
Pi-*ra*-thon-ite

Pi-*sid*-i-a
Poch-e-reth
Pon-ti-us *Pi*-late
Por-a-tha
Por-ci-us
Pot-i-phar
Po-*tiph*-e-ra
Pri-*scil*-la
Proch-o-rus
Ptol-e-*ma*-is
Ptol-e-mee
Pub-li-us
Pu-*te*-o-li
Pu-ti-el

Ra-a-man
Ra-a-*mi*-ah
Ra-*am*-ses
Rab-*bo*-ni
Rab-sa-ces
Rab-sa-ris
Rab-sha-keh
Rad-da-i
Ra-*gu*-el
Ra-ma-*tha*-im
Ram-a-them
Ra-math-ite
Ra-math-*le*-hi
Ra-*me*-ses
Ra-*mi*-ah
Ra-pha-el
Raph-a-im
Ra-*thu*-mus
Re-*a*-iah
Re-*bec*-ca
Re-chab-ites
Re-el-*a*-iah
Re-*el*-i-as
Re-e-*sa*-ias
Re-gem-*me*-lech
Re-ha-*bi*-ah
Re-ho-*bo*-am
Re-*ho*-both
Rem-a-*li*-ah
Rem-on-me-*tho*-ar
Re-pha-el
Re-*pha*-i-ah
Reph-a-im
Reph-i-dim
Reu-ben-ites
Reu-el
Rez-ia
Rhe-gi-um
Rhod-o-cus
Rim-mon-*pa*-rez
Ro-*bo*-am
Ro-ge-lim
Ro-i-mus
Ro-*mam*-ti-*e*-zer
Ru-*ha*-mah

Sa-bac-*tha*-ni
Sab-a-oth
Sab-a-*te*-as
Sab-a-tus
Sab-ba-*the*-us
Sab-*be*-us
Sa-*be*-ans
Sab-te-cha
Sad-a-*mi*-as
Sad-*de*-us
Sad-du-cees
Sa-ha-*du*-tha
Sal-a-mis
Sal-a-*sad*-a-i
Sa-*la*-thi-el
Sal-la-i
Sal-*lu*-mus
Sal-ma-*na*-sar
Sal-*mo*-ne
Sa-*lo*-me
Sam-a-el

Sa-*ma*-ias
Sa-*ma*-ri-a
Sa-*ma*-ri-tans
Sam-a-tus
Sa-*me*-ius
Sam-o-*thra*-cia (-sha)
Samp-sa-mes
Sam-u-el
San-a-*bas*-sa-rus
San-a-sib
San-*bal*-lat
San-he-drim
San-*san*-nah
Saph-a-*ti*-as
Sap-*phi*-ra
Sar-a-*bi*-as
Sa-*ra*-iah
Sa-*ra*-ias
Sar-a-mel
Sar-*ched*-o-nus
Sar-de-us
Sa-re-a
Sa-*rep*-ta
Sa-*ro*-thi-e
Sar-*se*-chim
Sath-ra-*buz*-nes
Sav-a-ran
Sa-*vi*-as
Sce-va (*Se*-)
Scyth-i-ans
Scy-*thop*-o-lis
Se-*ca*-cah
Sech-e-*ni*-as
Sed-e-*ci*-as
Se-i-rath
Se-la-ham-*mah*-le-koth
Sel-e-*mi*-a
Se-*leu*-cia (-sha)
Sem-a-*chi*-ah
Sem-e-i
Se-*mel*-le-us
Se-*na*-ah
Sen-*nach*-e-rib
Se-*nu*-ah
Se-*o*-rim
Se-*phar*-ad
Seph-ar-*va*-im
Se-phar-vites
Se-*phe*-la
Se-*ra*-iah
Se-ra-phim
Sha-a-*lab*-bin
Sha-*al*-bim
Sha-al-*bo*-nite
Sha-a-*ra*-im
Sha-*ash*-gaz
Shab-be-thai
She-*chi*-a
Shad-da-i
Sha-ha-*ra*-im
Sha-ha-*zi*-ma
Sha-ha-*zi*-math
Sha-*li*-sha
Shal-le-cheth
Shal-ma-i
Shal-ma-*ne*-ser
Sham-a-*ri*-ah
Sham-ma-i
Sham-*mu*-ah
Sham-she-rai
Shar-a-i
Shar-a-im
Sha-*re*-zer
Sha-ron-ite
Sha-*ru*-hen
Shash-a-i
Sha-ul-ites
Sha-veh *Ki*-ri-a-*tha*-im
She-*al*-ti-el
She-a-*ri*-ah
She-ar-*ja*-shub
Sheb-a-*ni*-ah
Sheb-a-rim
She-*bu*-el
Shec-a-*ni*-ah
She-chem-ites
She-*chi*-nah
Shed-e-ur
She-ha-*ri*-ah
She-lan-ites
Shel-e-*mi*-ah
She-*lo*-mi
She-*lo*-mith
She-*lo*-moth
She-*lu*-mi-el
She-*ma*-ah
She-*mai*-ah
Shem-a-*ri*-ah
She-*me*-ber
She-*mi*-da
She-*mi*-da-ites
Shem-i-nith
She-*mir*-a-moth
She-*mu*-el
She-*na*-zar
Sheph-a-*thi*-a
Sheph-a-*ti*-ah
She-*phu*-phan
Sher-e-*bi*-ah
She-*re*-zer
Shesh-*baz*-zar
She-thar-*boz*-nai
Shib-bo-leth
Shig-*gai*-on
Shi-hor-*lib*-nath
Shil-lem-ites
Shi-*lo*-ah
Shi-*lo*-ni
Shi-*lo*-nites
Shim-e-a
Shim-e-ah
Shim-e-am
Shim-e-ath
Shim-e-ath-ites
Shim-e-i
Shim-e-on
Shim-ron-ites
Shit-ra-i
Sho-ba-i
Sho-*shan*-nim
Sho-*shan*-nim-*e*-duth
Shu-ba-el
Shu-ham-ites
Shu-lam-ites
Shu-math-ites
Shu-nam-ites
Shu-pham-ites
Shu-shan-*e*-duth
Shu-thal-ites
Shu-the-lah
Si-a-ha
Sib-ba-chai
Sib-bo-leth
Sib-ra-im
Si-*do*-ni-ans
Si-gi-*o*-noth
Si-*lo*-ah
Si-*lo*-am
Si-mal-*cu*-e
Sim-e-on
Sim-e-on-ites
Si-nai, or *Si*-na-i
Si-ri-on
Sis-a-mai
Sis-e-ra
Si-*sin*-nes
Sod-om
Sod-om-ites
Sol-o-mon
Sop-a-ter
So-*phe*-reth
So-*sip*-a-ter
Sos-the-nes
Sos-tra-tus
So-ta-i
Steph-a-nas
Su-ba-i
Suc-coth-*Be*-noth
Suc-ha-thites
Su-di-as
Suk-ki-ims
Su-san-chites
Su-*san*-nah
Sych-em-ites (*Sik*-)
Sy-*e*-lus
Sy-*e*-ne
Syn-ti-che
Syr-i-a *Ma*-a-cah
Syr-i-on
Sy-ro-phe-*nic*-i-a

Ta-a-nach
Ta-a-nath *Shi*-loh
Tab-ba-oth
Tab-e-al
Tab-e-el
Ta-*bel*-li-us
Tab-e-ra
Tab-i-tha
Tab-ri-mon
Tach-mo-nite
Ta-ha-nites
Ta-*hap*-a-nes
Tah-pe-nes
Tah-re-a
Tah-tim-*hod*-shi
Tal-i-tha
Tan-*hu*-meth
Tap-*pu*-ah
Ta-ra-lah
Ta-re-a
Tar-pel-ites
Tat-na-i
Teb-a-*li*-ah
Te-*haph*-ne-hes
Te-*hin*-nah
Te-*ko*-ah
Te-*ko*-ite
Tel-*a*-bib
Te-*la*-im
Te-*las*-sar
Tel-ha-*re*-sha
Tel-*har*-sa
Tel-*me*-lah
Tem-a-ni
Te-ma-nites
Tem-e-ni
Te-ra-phim
Ter-ti-us
Ter-*tul*-lus
Thad-*dæ*-us
Tham-na-tha
Tham-na-thites
The-*co*-e
The-*la*-sar
The-*ler*-sas
The-*oc*-a-nus
The-*od*-o-tus
The-*oph*-i-lus
Ther-me-leth
Thes-sa-lo-*ni*-ca
Thim-na-thah
Thom-o-i
Thra-*se*-as
Thy-a-*ti*-ra
Ti-*be*-ri-as
Ti-*be*-ri-us
Tig-lath-Pi-*le*-ser
Ti-*mæ*-us
Ti-*me*-lus
Tim-na-thah
Ti-*mo*-the-us
Ti-rath-ites
Tir-ha-kah
Tir-ha-nah
Ti-ri-a
Tir-sha-tha
Tob-as-o-*ni*-jah
To-*bi*-ah
To-*bi*-as
To-bi-el
To-*bi*-jah
To-*gar*-mah
To-la-ites
Tol-ba-nes
Trach-o-*ni*-tis
Trip-o-lis
Tro-*gyl*-li-um
Troph-i-mus
Try-*phe*-na
Try-*pho*-sa
Tu-bal-*cain*
Tu-bi-*e*-ni
Tych-i-cus (*Tik*-)
Ty-*ran*-nus

U-la-i
U-*phar*-sin
U-*ri*-ah
U-*ri*-as
U-ri-el
U-*ri*-jah
U-*tha*-i
U-za-i
Uz-zen-*she*-rah
Uz-*zi*-ah
Uz-*zi*-el
Uz-*zi*-el-ites
Va-*jez*-a-tha
Va-*ni*-ah

Xan-thi-cus

Za-a-*na*-im
Za-a-nan
Za-a-*nan*-nim
Za-a-van
Zab-a-*dæ*-ans
Zab-*de*-us
Zab-di-el
Zab-u-lon
Zac-ca-i
Zac-*chæ*-us
Zach-a-*ri*-ah
Zach-a-*ri*-as
Zal-*mo*-nah
Zal-*mun*-na
Zam-*zum*-mims
Za-*no*-ah
Zaph-nath-*pa*-*a*-*ne*-ah
Zar-a-ces
Zar-*ai*-as
Za-re-ah
Za-re-a-thites
Zar-e-phath
Zar-e-tan
Zar-ta-nah
Zath-o-e
Za-*thu*-i
Zeb-a-*di*-ah
Ze-*ba*-im
Zeb-e-dee
Ze-*bi*-na
Ze-*bo*-im
Ze-*bu*-dah
Zeb-u-lon-ites
Zeb-u-lun
Zech-a-*ri*-ah
Zed-e-*chi*-as
Zed-e-*ki*-ah
Ze-*lo*-phe-had
Ze-*lo*-tes
Zem-a-*ra*-im
Zem-a-rite
Ze-*mi*-ra
Zeph-a-*ni*-ah
Zeph-a-thah
Zeph-on-ites
Ze-ra-*hi*-ah
Ze-ra-*i*-ah
Ze-re-dah
Ze-re-*da*-thah
Ze-re-rath
Ze-*ru*-ah
Ze-*rub*-ba-bel
Ze-ru-*i*-ah
Zib-e-on
Zib-i-ah
Zid-*ki*-jah
Zi-*do*-ni-ans
Ziph-i-on
Zip-*po*-rah
Zo-*be*-bah
Zo-he-leth
Zo-ra-thites
Zo-re-ah
Zu-ri-el
Zu-ri-*shad*-da-i

FOREIGN PHRASES, PROVERBS, MAXIMS, QUOTATIONS, AND MOTTOES

WITH TRANSLATIONS

Many foreign words in frequent use in English and now to a large extent incorporated in the language will be found in the body of NUTTALL'S STANDARD DICTIONARY; some of these are repeated in this section which, however, is mainly devoted to phrases and quotations, with their translations. Those from Latin are not particularized in any way; those from other languages are marked (Fr.), (Ger.), (It.), etc. for "French," "German," "Italian," etc. The sign (M.) indicates a Motto—usually that of a country or county, a British regiment, a knightly order, or an armigerous family.

Ab æterno.—From eternity.
Ab ante.—From before.
Ab antiquo.—From olden time.
À bas.—Down! down with! (Fr.)
À bâtons rompus.—By fits and starts; desultorily. (Fr.)
A bene placito.—At pleasure. (It.)
Ab extra.—From without.
Ab imo pectore.—From the heart's depth.
Ab initio.—From the beginning.
Ab intestato.—From an intestate (person).
Ab intra.—From within.
Ab irato.—In a fit of passion.
À bon compte.—(Payment) on account. (Fr.)
Abondance de biens ne nuit pas.—One cannot have too much of a good thing. (Fr.)
À bon droit.—Justly; according to reason. (Fr.)
À bon marché.—Cheaply. (Fr.)
Ab origine.—From the beginning.
Ab ovo usque ad mala.—From beginning to end (lit. from the egg to the apples, hors-d'œuvres to dessert).
À bras ouverts.—With open arms. (Fr.)
Abrégé.—Abridgment. (Fr.)
Absente reo.—The accused being absent.
Absit invidia.—Envy apart.
Absit omen.—Let there be no (evil) omen.
Ab uno disce omnes.—From a single instance you may infer the whole.
Ab urbe condita (A.U.C.)—From the building of the city, *i.e.* Rome (*cp.* **Anno urbis . . .** *below*).
A capite ad calcem.—From head to heel.
Acheter à vil prix.—To buy for a mere song. (Fr.)
À compte.—In part payment (lit., on account). (Fr.)
À couvert.—Under cover. (Fr.)
A cruce salus.—Salvation from the Cross.
Actum est.—It is finished; it's all over.
Ad aperturam.—Wherever a book may be opened.
Ad arbitrium.—At pleasure.
Ad avizandum.—Into consideration [Scots. Law].
Ad captandum vulgus.—To catch the man-in-the-street.
Addio.—Farewell. (It.)
À demi.—Half. (Fr.)
A Deo et rege.—From God and the king. (M.)
À deux.—For two. (Fr.)
Ad extremum.—At last.
Ad finem.—To the end.
Ad Græcas kalendas.—At the Greek calends, *i.e.* never.
Ad gustum.—To one's taste.
Ad hoc.—For this special purpose.
Ad hominem.—Personal (lit., to the man).
Adhuc sub judice lis est.—The affair is not yet decided.
Ad infinitum.—To infinity.
Ad interim.—Meanwhile.
À discrétion.—Without any restriction (lit. at discretion). (Fr.)
Ad libitum.—At pleasure.
Ad literam.—To the letter.
Ad majorem Dei gloriam.—To the greater glory of God. (M. of the Jesuits.)
Ad nauseam.—Till it disgusts.
Ad patres.—Dead; to death (lit., to the fathers).
Ad quod damnum.—To what damage (*i.e.* to the disadvantage of whom ?)?
Ad referendum.—For further consideration.
Ad rem.—To the point (lit., to the thing).
À droit.—To the right. (Fr.)
Adscriptus glebæ.—Attached to the soil; in the status of a serf.
Adsum.—I am here.
Ad unguem.—To a nicety (lit. to the nail).
Ad unum omnes.—All to a (lit., one) man.
Ad usum.—As customary.
Ad utrumque paratus.—Prepared for either case.
Ad valorem.—According to the value.
Ad verbum.—Literally; word for word.
Advienne que pourra.—Come what may. (Fr.)
Ad vitam aut culpam.—Till some misconduct be proved (lit., for life or fault).
Ad vivum.—To the life.
Advocatus diaboli.—The Devil's Advocate; a supporter of wrongful acts.
Ægrescit medendo.—The remedy is worse than the disease (lit., the disorder increases with the remedy).
Ægrotat.—He (or she) is ill.
Æquo animo.—With an even or equable mind (M.)
Æs triplex.—Triple brass.
Ætatis suæ.—Of his (or her) age.
Affaire d'amour.—A love affair. (Fr.)
Affaire de rien.—A trifle. (Fr.)
Affaire d'honneur.—An affair of honour; a duel. (Fr.)
Affaire du cœur.—An affair of the heart. (Fr.)
Afin de.—In order to. (Fr.)
Afin que.—To the end that. (Fr.)
À fond.—Thoroughly (lit., to the bottom). (Fr.)
A fortiori.—With stronger reason.
À gauche.—To the left. (Fr.)
Age quod agis.—Attend to (lit., do) what you are doing.
À grands frais.—At great expense. (Fr.)
Aide-toi, le ciel t'aidera.—Help yourself and Heaven will help you. (Fr.)
Aîné.—Elder son. (Fr.)
À jamais.—For ever. (Fr.)
Aktiengesellschaft.—A joint-stock company; a business firm. (Ger.)
À la.—In the style of; according to. (Fr.)
À l'abandon.—At random; little cared for. (Fr.)
À la belle étoile.—Under the stars; in the open air. (Fr.)
À la bonne aventure.—By chance. (Fr.)
À la bonne heure.—Well-timed; excellent! (Fr.)
À l'abri.—Under shelter. (Fr.)
À la carte.—(Selected) from the bill of fare. (Fr.)
À la dérobée.—By stealth. (Fr.)
À la lettre.—To the letter; literally. (Fr.)
À la mode.—According to the fashion. (Fr.)
À la parisienne.—After the Paris manner or style. (Fr.)
Alea jacta est.—The die is cast; the step is taken.
À l'envi de.—In emulation of. (Fr.)
Alere flammam.—To feed the flame.
Alieni appetens, sui profusus.—Covetous of other men's property, prodigal of his own.
À l'improviste.—Unawares. (Fr.)

Aliquando bonus dormitat Homerus.—Sometimes the good Homer nods.
Aller cahin-caha.—To limp on one's way. **(Fr.)**
Allons !—Come ! (Fr.)
Alma mater.—One's school, college, or university (lit. fostering mother).
Alter ego.—One's second self (lit., another self).
Alter idem.—Another exactly similar.
Alter ipse amicus.—A friend is a second self.
À main armée.—By force of arms. (Fr.)
Amari aliquid.—A touch of bitterness.
A maximis ad minima.—From the greatest to the smallest.
Âme damnée.—A familiar spirit; a mere tool (Fr., lost soul.)
Amende honorable.—Satisfactory apology. **(Fr.)**
A mensâ et toro.—From board and bed ; divorced.
À merveille.—Wonderfully. (Fr.)
Amicus curiæ.—Disinterested adviser.
Amicus humani generis.—A friend of the human race.
Amicus Plato, sed magis amica veritas.—Plato is my friend, but truth is more my friend (lit., more a friend).
À mon avis.—In my opinion. (Fr.)
Amor patriæ.—The love of country ; patriotism.
Amor sceleratus habendi—The cursed love of possessing.
Amour propre.—Vanity ; self-love. (Fr.)
Ancien régime.—The old form of government. (Fr.)
Anguis in herbâ.—A snake in the grass.
Animo et fide.—Courageously and faithfully. **(M.)**
Animo non astutia.—By courage not by craft. (M.)
Anno ætatis suæ.—In the year of his age.
Anno domini.—In the year of our Lord.
Anno mundi.—In the year of the world.
Anno urbis conditæ (A.U.C.).—In the year from the time when the city (Rome) was built (*cp.* **Ab urbe . . .** *above*).
Annus mirabilis.—The year of wonders.
Ante bellum.—Before the war.
Ante litem motam.—Before the commencement of the action.
Ante meridiem.—Before noon.
À outrance.—To the uttermost. **(Fr.)**
Aperçu.—A sketch ; a concise account. **(Fr.)**
À perte de vue.—Beyond the range of vision. **(Fr.)**
À peu près.—Nearly. (Fr.)
À point.—To a point exactly. (Fr.)
A posse ad esse.—From possibility to actuality.
A posteriori.—From the effect to the cause ; by induction.
Appartement.—A suite of rooms ; a flat. **(Fr.)**
Après nous, le déluge.—After us, the deluge (*i.e.*, the future is no concern of ours). (Fr.)
A priori.—From the cause to the effect ; by deduction.
À propos.—To the point ; seasonably ; in due time. (Fr.)
Aqua bulliens.—Boiling water.
Aquila non capit muscas.—An eagle does not catch (*i.e.* stoop to) flies. (M.)
Arbiter elegantiarum.—A judge in matters of taste.
Arcades ambo.—They are both blackguards.
Argent comptant.—Ready money. (Fr.)
Argumentum ad hominem.—An argument in refutation drawn from an opponent's own principles (lit. an argument to the man).
Argumentum ad ignorantiam.—An argument founded on the ignorance of an adversary.
Argumentum ad invidiam.—An argument which appeals to low passions.
Argumentum ad judicium.—An appeal to common sense.
Argumentum ad populum.—An appeal to popular prejudice.
Argumentum ad verecundiam.—An appeal to respect for some authority.
Argumentum baculinum.—Club law.
Ariston metron.—The middle way is the best. (Gr.)
Arma pacis fulcra.—Arms are the mainstay of peace. (M. of the H.A.C.)
Arme blanche.—The sword. **(Fr.)**
Arrangez-vous.—Settle it yourselves. (Fr.)
Arrière pensée.—A mental reservation; an ulterior motive. (Fr.)
Ars longa, vita brevis.—Art is long, life is short.
Artis est celare artem.—The perfection of art is to conceal art.
Artium baccalaureus.—Bachelor of Arts.
Artium magister.—Master of Arts.
Assumpsit.—An action on a verbal promise [Law].
À tâtons.—With caution; gropingly. (Fr.)
À tort et à travers.—Without consideration ; at random. (Fr.)
Attacher le grelot.—To bell the cat. (Fr.)
Attaquer le taureau par les cornes.—To seize the bull by the horns. (Fr.)
Au bon droit.—To the just right. (M.) **(Fr.)**
Au contraire.—On the contrary. (Fr.)
Aucto splendore resurgo.—I rise again in the splendour of action. (M. of the King's Shropshire Light Infantry.)
Au courant.—Acquainted with. (Fr.)
Audaciter et sincere.—Bravely and truly.
Au désespoir.—In despair. (Fr.)
Audi alteram partem.—Hear the other party; hear both sides.
Audience à huis clos.—A matter discussed, or case heard, *in camerâ.* (Fr.)
Au fait.—Expert ; skilful ; well acquainted with. (Fr.)
Aufgeschoben ist nicht aufgehoben.—Postponed is not abandoned. (Ger.)
Aufklärung.—(A period of) enlightenment ; esp. the 18th cent. German literary and spiritual renaissance. (Ger.)
Au fond.—To the bottom. **(Fr.)**
Auf wiedersehen.—To our next meeting ; farewell. (Ger.)
Au grand sérieux.—Very seriously. **(Fr.)**
Au gratin.—With a crust. (Fr.)
Au mieux.—On most excellent terms. **(Fr.)**
Au naturel.—In the simplest manner. **(Fr.)**
Au pair.—On equal terms (esp., giving service for board and lodging without wages). **(Fr.)**
Au pied de la lettre.—Exactly ; literally. **(Fr.)**
Au pis aller.—At the worst. (Fr.)
Aura popularis.—Popular favour (lit. breeze).
Aurea mediocritas.—The golden mean.
Au reste.—For the rest. (Fr.)
Au revoir.—Farewell till we meet again. **(Fr.)**
Auri sacra fames.—The accursed thirst for gold.
Ausgleich.—Settlement by compromise. (Ger.)
Auspicium melioris ævi.—A pledge of better times. (M. of the Order of St. Michael and St. George.)
Aut Cæsar, aut nullus.—Either Cæsar or no one ; I will either be chief or nobody.
Aut cursu aut cominus armis.—Either in a charge or at close quarters. (M. of the 9th Queen's Royal Lancers.)
Aut mors aut victoria.—Death or victory.
Autobahn.—A specially constructed motor highway. (Ger.)
Autres temps, autres mœurs.—Other times, other manners. (Fr.)
Aut vincere aut mori.—Either to conquer or die.
Aux armes.—To arms. (Fr.)
Avant propos.—Prefatory matter. (Fr.)
Ave, atque vale.—Hail ! and farewell !
A verbis ad verbera.—From words to blows.
A vinculo matrimonii.—From the bond or tie of marriage ; divorce.
Avise la fin.—Consider the end. (M.) (Fr.)
À votre santé.—To your health. (Fr.)

Ballon d'essai.—A preliminary test or inquiry. (Fr., a trial balloon.)
Bas bleu.—A blue-stocking. **(Fr.)**
Basta !—Enough ! stop ! (It.)
Bayer aux corneilles.—To gape at the crows ; to indulge in stargazing. (Fr.)
Beatæ memoriæ.—Of blessed memory.
Beau monde.—The fashionable world (Fr.)
Beaux esprits.—Men of wit. (Fr.)
Beaux yeux.—Good looks. (Fr.)
Bel espirit.—A person of genius ; a brilliant mind. (Fr.)
Bene esse.—Well-being.
Bene placito.—At pleasure. (It.)
Ben trovato.—Well or aptly invented. **(It.)**

Beso las manos.—I kiss your hands (a greeting). (Sp.)
Bête noire.—An eyesore; a bugbear (lit., a black beast). (Fr.)
Bien entendu.—Of course! Certainly!
Bienséance.—Proper behaviour. (Fr.)
Billet d'amour.—Love letter. (Fr.)
Billet doux.—Love letter. (Fr.)
Bis dat qui cito dat.—He gives twice who gives quickly.
Bis in dies.—Twice a day.
Bis in septem diebus.—Twice a week.
Blut ist ein ganz besondrer Saft.—Blood is a peculiar juice. (Ger.)
Blut und Boden.—Blood and soil; rigid nationalism. (Ger.)
Blut und Eisen.—Blood and iron (esp. as a method of rule). (Ger.)
Bonâ fide.—In good faith; in reality.
Bon chien chasse de race.—Children have the (bad) qualities of their parents. (Fr.)
Bon gré, mal gré.—Whether willing or not. (Fr.)
Bonhomie.—Good nature. (Fr.)
Bon jour.—Good day. (Fr.)
Bon marché.—Cheaply. (Fr.)
Bonne bouche.—A delicate morsel. (Fr.)
Bonne fortune.—Good luck (to you)! (Fr.)
Bonne mine.—Good looks; health. (Fr.)
Bon soir.—Good evening. (Fr.)
Bon ton.—The height of fashion. (Fr.)
Bonum publicum.—The public good.
Bon vivant.—One who lives well. (Fr.)
Bon voyage.—Prosperous voyage! (Fr.)
Borné.—Narrow minded; limited in intelligence. (Fr.)
Boutonnière.—A flower for the buttonhole. (Fr.)
Brevet d'invention.—A patent. (Fr.)
Breveté.—Patented. (Fr.)
Brevi manu.—Offhand; summarily (lit., with a short hand).
Brevis esse laboro, obscurus fio.—When labouring to be concise, I become obscure.
Brutum fulmen.—A harmless thunderbolt; an empty threat.
Bydand.—Watchful, or Stand fast. (M. of the Gordon Highlanders.) (Gael.)

Cacoëthes loquendi.—An itch for talking.
Cacoëthes scribendi.—An itch for writing.
Cadit quæstio.—That closes the matter.
Café au lait.—Coffee with hot milk. (Fr.)
Café noir.—Coffee without milk. (Fr.)
Ça ira.—It will go on (to success) (refrain of French Revolutionary song). (Fr.)
Campo santo.—A cemetery. (It.)
Campus Martius.—A place of military exercise (lit. field of Mars).
Candide et constanter.—With candour and constancy. (M.)
Cantate Domino.—Sing unto the Lord.
Capias.—A writ to authorize the seizure of a defendant's person [Law].
Capiat, qui capere possit.—Let him take it who can.
Caput mortuum.—The worthless residue.
Carpe diem.—Enjoy the day; make a good use of the present.
Cassis tutissima virtus.—Virtue is the safest defence. (M.)
Casus belli.—A cause for war.
Casus fœderis.—A circumstance within the stipulations of a treaty [Internat. law].
Catena.—A connected series.
Causa causans.—The originating cause.
Cause célèbre.—A notable case or trial. (Fr.)
Cavaliere servente.—A gallant attentive to a married lady. (It.)
Caveat emptor.—At the buyer's risk (let the buyer beware).
Cave canem.—Beware of the dog.
Cavendo tutus.—Safe by caution. (M.)
Cedant arma togæ.—Let the military yield to the civil power.
Cede nullis.—Yield to none (M. of the K.O. Yorkshire Light Infantry).
Cela viendra.—All in good time. (Fr.)
Celer et audax.—Swift and bold. (M. of the King's Royal Rifles.)
Ce n'est que le premier pas qui coûte.—It is only the first step that is difficult (lit., costs). (Fr.)
Certiorari.—To order the record from an inferior to a superior court [Law].
Cessio bonorum.—The transference of goods (by insolvent debtors to creditors).
C'est à dire.—That is to say. (Fr.)
C'est autre chose.—That's another matter. (Fr.)
C'est en fait de lui.—It is all up with him. (Fr.)
Cetera desunt.—The others (*or* rest) are missing.
Ceteris paribus.—Other things being equal.
Chacun à son goût.—Every one to his taste. (Fr.)
Chapeau-bras.—Three-cornered hat that could be held under the arm. (Fr.)
Chapelle ardente.—A mortuary chapel lit with tapers for a lying-in-state. (Fr.)
Chargé d'affaires.—A subordinate diplomatist; a deputy ambassador. (Fr.)
Chef de cuisine.—A head cook. (Fr.)
Chef-d'œuvre.—A masterpiece. (Fr.)
Chemin de fer.—The railway. (Fr.)
Cherchez la femme.—There's a woman at the bottom of it. (Fr., look for the woman.)
Che sarà, sarà.—What will be, will be (a sigh of resignation) [M.]. (It.)
Chevalier d'industrie.—One who lives by his wits (lit. a knight of industry). (Fr.)
Chez moi.—At home. (Fr.)
Chi ha la sanità è ricco.—He who enjoys good health is rich. (It.)
Chi non fa, non falla.—He who does nothing makes no blunders. (It.)
Ci-devant.—Former. (Fr.)
Ci-gît.—Here lies. (Fr.)
Circa.—About.
Circuitus verborum.—A roundabout story or expression.
Circulus in definiendo.—The logical fallacy of defining a thing by itself.
Circulus in probando.—Begging the question (lit. a circle in the proof).
Civis Romanus sum.—I am a Roman citizen (indicating that the speaker intends to stand by his rights).
Clarior e tenebris.—The brighter from the darkness.
Clarum et venerabile nomen.—An illustrious and honoured name.
Cochleare infantis.—A teaspoonful.
Cochleare magnum.—A table-spoonful.
Cochleare modicum.—A dessertspoonful.
Cogito, ergo sum.—I think, therefore I am.
Comme il faut.—As it should be. (Fr.)
Commune bonum.—A common good.
Communi consensu.—By common consent.
Compagnon de voyage.—A fellow-traveller. (Fr.)
Compos mentis.—Of sane mind.
Compte rendu.—A report; an account. (Fr.)
Con amore.—With love; earnestly. (It.)
Concio ad clerum.—An address to the clergy.
Concours.—A competition. (Fr.)
Concours d'élégance.—A competition for the smartest turned out (*usu.*) vehicle.
Congé d'élire.—A leave to elect. (Fr.)
Conseil de famille.—A family council. (Fr.)
Conseil d'état.—Privy council. (Fr.)
Consilio et animis.—By counsel and courage.
Consuetudo pro lege servatur.—Custom is observed as law.
Continuetur.—Let it be continued.
Contra bonos mores.—Against good custom; a defiance of the moral code.
Contraria contrariis curantur.—Contraries are cured by contraries.
Contre fortune bon cœur.—Never despair. (Fr.)
Coram.—In the presence of.
Coram me.—In my presence.
Coram populo.—Publicly.
Cordon bleu.—A skilful cook (lit. a blue ribbon). (Fr.)
Cordon sanitaire.—A guard to prevent a disease spreading. (Fr.)
Corps diplomatique.—The diplomatic body. (Fr.)
Corpus deliciti.—The material evidence of the offence [Law].
Corpus vile (*vy*-le).—Anything of trivial value; the subject of an experiment. (L., a worthless body.)
Cosi fan tutte.—That is the way of all (women). (It.)

Couleur de rose.—A flattering representation. (Fr.)
Coup de grâce.—The finishing stroke. (Fr.)
Coup de main.—A bold effort. (Fr.)
Coup de maître.—Master stroke. (Fr.)
Coup de soleil.—Sun-stroke. (Fr.)
Coup d'essai.—First attempt. (Fr.)
Coup d'état.—A change of government by unconstitutional means. (Fr.)
Coup de théâtre.—Theatrical effect. (Fr.)
Coup d'œil.—A rapid glance of the eye. (Fr.)
Courage sans peur.—Courage without fear. (Fr.)
Coûte qu'il coûte.—Let it cost what it may. (Fr.)
Craignez la honte.—Fear disgrace. (Fr.)
Cras mane.—To-morrow morning.
Cras nocte.—To-morrow night.
Cras vespere.—To-morrow evening.
Credat Judæus Apella.—Tell that to the Marines (L., let Apella, the Jew, believe that—I won't !)
Credo quia impossible est.—I believe it because it is impossible.
Crème de la crème.—Cream of the cream; the very best. (Fr.)
Crux criticorum.—The puzzle of critics.
Crux medicorum.—The puzzle of physicians.
Cucullus non facit monachum.—Appearances are deceptive; "you cannot judge a sausage by its skin." (L., the cowl does not make the monk.)
Cui bono ?—Whom does it benefit ?
Cuidich'n Righ.—Help the King ! (M. of the Seaforth Highlanders.) (Gael.)
Cuique suum.—His own to every one.
Cul de sac.—A street or lane that has no outlet. (Fr.)
Cum grano salis.—With a grain of salt, *i.e.* with some allowance.
Cum multis aliis.—With many others.
Cum privilegio.—With privilege.
Currente calamo.—With a running pen.
Custos rotulorum.—The Master (lit., keeper) of the Rolls.
Cyathus vinosus.—A wineglassful.
Cymru am byth.—Wales for ever ! (M. of the Welsh Guards.) (W.)

Da.—Give.
Da capo.—From the beginning. (It.)
D'accord.—Agreed; in tune. (Fr.)
Dal segno.—From the place marked. (It.)
Dame d'honneur.—Maid of honour. (Fr.)
Damnosa hereditas.—An inheritance that is a source of loss.
Danse macabre.—The dance of Death. (Fr.)
Das Beste ist gut genug.—The best is good enough. (Ger.)
Das Ewig-Weibliche zieht uns hinan.—The eternal woman leads us upward and on. (Ger.)
Das heisst.—That is. (Ger.)
Dat Deus incrementum.—God gives the increase. (M.)
De auditu.—By hearsay.
De bonne grâce.—With good grace; willingly. (Fr.)
Deceptio visus.—Optical illusion.
Déclassé.—Socially degraded; a "has-been." (Fr.)
Decus et tutamen.—An embellishment and safeguard.
Décolleté.—Low-necked. (Fr.)
De die in diem.—From day to day.
Dedimus potestatem.—We have given power.
De facto.—In fact; in actuality.
Dégagé.—Free and unrestrained. (Fr.)
De gustibus non est disputandum.—There is no disputing about tastes.
Dei gratia.—By the grace of God.
De haut en bas.—Condescendingly; from head to foot. (Fr.)
Dejeûner à la fourchette.—A substantial breakfast, esp. including meat. (Fr.)
De jure.—By right of law.
Delectando pariterque monendo.—By imparting at once pleasure and instruction.
Delenda est Carthago.—Carthage must be destroyed.
Démenti.—Official denial. (Fr.)
De minimis non curat lex.—The law takes no notice of trifles.
De mortuis nil nisi bonum.—Let nothing be said of the dead but what is favourable.
De nihilo nihil fit.—From nothing nothing is produced.
De nouveau.—Anew. (Fr.)
De novo.—Anew.
Deo adjuvante, fortuna sequatur.—God assisting, success must follow. (M.)
Deo adjuvante, non timendum.—God being my aid, nothing is to be feared. (M.)
Deo favente.—With God's favour.
Deo gratias.—Thanks to God.
Deo ignoto.—To the Unknown God.
Deo juvante.—With God's help.
De omnibus rebus et quibusdam aliis.—Concerning all things—and certain others.
Deo non fortuna.—From God, not fortune. (M.)
Deo optimo maximo.—(Dedicated) to God, the Best, the Greatest.
Deo volente.—With God's will.
De plano.—With ease.
De profundis.—Out of the depths (esp. of grief).
De règle.—Customary. (Fr.)
De rigueur.—Required by custom. (Fr.)
Dernier cri.—The latest fashion. (Fr.)
Dernier ressort.—A last resource. (Fr.)
Der Tag.—The day. (Ger.)
Desunt cætera.—The remainder are wanting.
Détente. Relief from diplomatic tension. (Fr.)
De trop.—Too much; surplus; in the way. (Fr.)
Detur.—Let it be given.
Deus ex machina.—A lucky intervention that saves the situation; lit., a god from the (stage) machine.
Deus mihi providebit.—God will provide for me. (M.)
Deus misereatur.—May God take pity.
Deux temps.—A piece (Mus.) or dance in two-four time. (Fr.)
Dichtung und Wahrheit.—Poetry and Truth; Fiction and Fact. (Ger.)
Diebus alternis.—On alternate days.
Dies iræ.—Day of judgment.
Dies non.—A day when the courts are not sitting [Law].
Dieu et mon droit.—God and my right. (M. of the British Sovereigns since *temp.* Henry VI.) (Fr.)
Dii penates.—Household gods.
Dimidius.—A half.
Dis aliter visum.—Providence ordained it otherwise.
Disjecta membra.—Scattered remains.
Disponendo me, non mutando me.—By disposing of me, not by changing me. (M.)
Divide et impera.—Divide and govern.
Docendo discimus.—We learn by teaching.
Dolce far niente.—Sweet idleness. (It.)
Domine dirige nos !—Lord, guide us ! (M. of the City of London and of the Royal Fusiliers.)
Dominus providebit.—The Lord will provide.
Domus et placens uxor.—The home and a pleasing wife.
Dono dedit.—He (or she) gave it (as a gift).
Dosis.—A dose.
Double entendre.—A double meaning. (Fr.)
Double entente.—Double signification. (Fr.)
Dramatis personæ.—Characters represented.
Drang nach dem Osten.—The tendency to expand eastward (of foreign policy). (Ger.)
Droit des gens.—The law of nations. (Fr.)
Dulce domum.—Sweet home.
Dulce est desipere in loco.—It is pleasant to jest at the proper time.
Dulce et decorum est pro patria mori.—It is sweet and seemly to die for one's country.
Dum spiro, spero.—While I breathe, I hope. (M.)
Dum vivimus vivamus.—Let us live while we live.
Durante bene placito.—During good pleasure.
Durante vita.—During life.
Du sublime au ridicule il n'y a qu'un pas.—From the sublime to the ridiculous there is only a step. (Fr.)

Ecce homo !—Behold the man !
Ecce signum !—Behold the proof.
Éclaircissement.—Clearing up; explanation. (Fr.)
E contra.—On the other hand.
E contrario.—On the contrary.

Écrasez l'infâme !—Away with the infamous (system) ! (Fr.)
Édition de luxe.—A splendid and expensive edition of a book. (Fr.)
Editio princeps.—The original edition.
Ego et rex meus.—I and my king.
Eheu fugaces !—Alas for the fleeting (years) !
Eigener Herd ist Goldes wert.—Home is home be it ever so lowly. (Ger.)
Eile mit Weile.—Make haste slowly. (Ger.)
Einer pflanzt den Baum, der andre isst die Pflaum.—One plants the tree, another eats the fruit. (Ger.)
Ein feste Burg ist unser Gott.—God is our stronghold. (Ger.)
Ein mal, kein mal.—Just for once nothing counts. (Ger.)
Ein Volk, ein Reich, ein Führer.—One people, one State, one Leader (a Nazi slogan). (Ger.)
Ejusdem generis.—Of the same sort.
Élan vital, L'.—The vital impulse.
Éloignement.—Estrangement. (Fr.)
Embarras de richesse.—Encumbrance of wealth ; too much of a good thing. (Fr.)
Éminence grise.—A power behind the throne. (Fr., nickname of Marq. du Tremblay, Cardinal Richelieu's *âme damnée.*)
En ami.—As a friend. (Fr.)
En attendant.—In the meantime. (Fr.)
En Dieu est ma fiance.—In God is my trust. (M.) (Fr.)
En famille.—Among one's family ; at home. (Fr.)
Enfant gâté.—A spoiled child. (Fr.)
Enfant Prodigue, L'.—The Prodigal Son.
Enfants de famille.—Children of the family. (Fr.)
Enfants perdus.—The forlorn hope (lit. lost children). (Fr.)
Enfant terrible.—A badly behaved child ; one whose talk is embarrassing. (Fr.)
Enfant trouvé.—A foundling. (Fr.)
En foule.—In a crowd. (Fr.)
En grande tenue.—In full dress. (Fr.)
En masse.—In a body ; all together. (Fr.)
En passant.—By the way. (Fr.)
En plein jour.—In full daylight. (Fr.)
En rapport.—In relation ; in sympathy. (Fr.)
En règle.—According to rules. (Fr.)
En route.—On the way. (Fr.)
Ense et aratro.—With sword and plough.
En suite.—In company. (Fr.)
Entente cordiale.—Good understanding (between parties).
Entre deux feux.—Between two fires. (Fr.)
Entre nous.—Between ourselves. (Fr.)
En vérité.—In truth. (Fr.)
Epicuri de grege porcus.—A pig of the herd of Epicurus.
Eppur si muove.—Nevertheless it (the earth) *does* move. (It.)
Errare humanum est.—It is human to err.
Espérance en Dieu.—Hope in God. (M.) (Fr.)
Espressivo.—With expression. (It.)
Esprit d'escalier.—After-wit (of a retort thought of too late for use). (Fr., wit of the staircase.)
Esse quam videri.—To be rather than to seem.
Est modus in rebus.—There is a mean in everything.
Esto perpetua.—Let it last for ever.
Et decus et pretium recti.—The ornament and reward of virtue. (M.)
Et hoc genus omne.—And everything of this kind.
Et sic de ceteris.—And so of the rest.
Et tu, Brute.—And you, Brutus.
Ewige Jude, Der.—The everlasting Jew. (Ger.)
Ewigkeit.—Eternity. (Ger.)
Ewig-Weibliche, Das.—The eternal feminine principle. (Ger.)
Ex abrupto.—Without preparation.
Ex æquo.—By right.
Ex animo.—From the soul ; heartily.
Ex cathedrâ.—From the chair ; with authority.
Exceptio probat regulam.—The exception proves the rule.
Exceptis excipiendis.—The requisite exceptions being made.
Ex concesso.—Admittedly.
Ex curia.—Out of court.
Ex delicto.—From the crime.
Exempli gratia.—By way of example.
Ex fide fortis.—Strong through faith. (M.)
Ex gratia.—As a matter of grace (not of right).
Ex hypothesi.—On the assumption made.
Ex mero motu.—From one's own free will.
Ex nihilo nihil fit.—Out of nothing nothing is produced.
Ex officio.—By virtue of his office.
Ex opera operato.—By the external act.
Ex parte.—On one part or side.
Ex pede Herculem.—We judge of the size of the statue of Hercules by the foot.
Experientia docet stultos.—Experience teaches fools.
Experimentum crucis.—A decisive experiment.
Experto crede.—Believe one who has had experience.
Ex post facto.—After the event ; retrospectively.
Ex professo.—Like one who knows.
Extra muros.—Beyond the walls.
Ex ungue leonem.—The lion may be known by his claw.
Ex uno disce omnes.—From one, judge of all.
Ex voto.—In accordance with a vow.

Faber suæ fortunæ.—The maker of his own fortune.
Fach.—Department. (Ger.)
Facile princeps.—The admitted chief ; easily first.
Facilis est descensus Averni.—The descent to hell is easy (*i.e.*, the downward path is an easy one).
Facit indignatio versum.—Indignation induces poetry.
Façon de parler.—Manner of speaking. (Fr.)
Fæx populi.—The dregs of the people.
Faire mon devoir.—To do my duty. (Fr.)
Fait accompli.—A thing already done. (Fr.)
Falsum in uno, falsum in omni.—(That which is) erroneous in one respect is erroneous as a whole.
Fama clamosa.—A current scandal.
Fama semper vivit.—Reputation lives for ever. (M.)
Fas est et ab hoste doceri.—It is allowable to derive instruction even from an enemy.
Fasti et nefasti dies.—Lucky and unlucky days.
Fata morgana.—A mirage. (It.)
Fata obstant.—The fates oppose it.
Faugh-a-Ballagh.—Clear the way ! (M. of the Royal Irish Fusiliers.) (Gael.)
Faute de mieux.—For lack of (a) better. (Fr.)
Faux pas.—A false step. (Fr.)
Fecit.—He (or she) did it.
Felo de se.—A suicide [Law].
Femme de chambre.—A chambermaid. (Fr.)
Femme de charge.—A housekeeper. (Fr.)
Femme savante.—A woman of erudition ; a bluestocking. (Fr.)
Fendre un cheveu en quatre.—To split hairs ; to make useless subtle distinctions. (Fr.)
Feræ naturæ.—Wild animals (lit., of a wild nature).
Fervet opus.—The work goes on with spirit.
Festina lente.—Hasten slowly; (as M.) Quick without impetuosity.
Feu de joie.—A bonfire ; a beacon ; blank fire in token of joy. (Fr.)
Feux d'artifice.—Flares as signals ; fireworks ; figuratively, sallies of wit. (Fr.)
Fiat.—Let it be done or made ; make.
Fiat justitia, ruat cœlum.—Let justice be done, though the heavens should fall.
Fiat lux.—Let there be light.
Fide et fiducia.—In faith and trust. (M. of the Royal Army Pay Corps.)
Fidei defensor.—Defender of the Faith.
Fides ante intellectum.—Faith before intellect (*i.e.*, Believe first, then try to understand).
Fides Punica.—Treachery. (L., Carthaginian faith.)
Fidus Achates.—The faithful Achates ; a trusty friend.
Filius nullius.—A bastard. (L., the son of nobody.)
Filius terræ.—A son of the earth ; one low born.
Fille de chambre.—A chambermaid. (Fr.)
Fille de joie.—A prostitute. (Fr., a woman of pleasure.)
Fin de siècle.—End of the century ; hence, decadent. (Fr.)
Finis coronat opus.—The end crowns the work.
Finom respice.—Have regard to the end.

Flagrante bello.—During hostilities.
Flagrante delicto.—In the very act.
Flebile ludibrium.—A sad mockery.
Fleur d'eau.—Level with the surface of the water. (Fr.)
Fons et origo.—The fount and source; the ultimate cause.
Force majeure.—Superior force; inevitable. (Fr.)
Forte scutum salus ducum.—A strong shield is the safeguard of leaders. (M. of the Fortescues.)
Forti et fideli, nihil difficile.—To courage and constancy nothing is difficult. (M.)
Fortiter et recte.—Courageously and honourably. (M.)
Fortiter in re.—With firmness in action.
Fortuna favet fortibus.—Fortune favours the brave.
Fortuna multis dat nimium, nulli satis.—To many fortune gives too much, to none enough.
Fortuna sequatur.—Let fortune follow. (M.)
Foy pour devoir.—Faith for duty. (Old Fr. M.)
Frangas non flectes.—You may break, but you will not bend me.
Front à front.—Front to front; face to face. (Fr.)
Fronti nulla fides.—There is no trusting to appearances.
Fugit irreparabile tempus.—Irrecoverable time is flying away.
Fugit irrevocabile verbum.—The (spoken) word is irrecallable.
Fuimus.—We have been. (M.)
Fuit Ilium.—Troy is no more.
Furor loquendi.—A rage for speaking.
Furor poëticus.—The poet's frenzy.
Furor scribendi.—A rage for writing.

Gage d'amour.—Token of love. (Fr.)
Gaieté de cœur.—Gaiety of heart. (Fr.)
Gallicè.—In French.
Garde à cheval.—Mounted guard. (Fr.)
Garde du corps.—A bodyguard. (Fr.)
Gardez bien.—Take care. (M.) (Fr.)
Gardez la foi.—Guard the faith. (M.) (Fr.)
Gaudeamus igitur.—Let us therefore have a joyful time.
Gaudet tentamine virtus.—Virtue rejoices in trial. (M.)
Genius loci.—Spirit of the place.
Gens de condition.—People of rank. (Fr.)
Gens d'église.—Churchmen. (Fr.)
Gens de guerre.—Soldiers. (Fr.)
Gens de lettres.—Literary people. (Fr.)
Genus irritabile vatum.—The irritable tribe of poets.
Germanicè.—In German.
Gibier de potence.—A gallows bird. (Fr.)
Gleichschaltung.—Compulsory conformity (esp. of German organizations with Nazi theory). (Ger.)
Gloria in excelsis.—Glory to God in the highest.
Gloria Patri.—Glory to the Father.
Gnothi seauton.—Know thyself. (Gr.)
Götterdämmerung.—The Twilight of the Gods. (Ger.)
Gott mit uns.—God (being) on our side. (Ger.)
Goutte à goutte.—Drop by drop. (Fr.)
Grâce à Dieu.—Thanks to God. (Fr.)
Gradu diverso, via una.—The same way, by different paths. (M.)
Gradus ad Parnassum.—A help to the composition of poetry.
Grande dame.—A great lady; a woman of high rank and stately carriage. (Fr.)
Grande passion.—An overwhelming infatuation. (Fr.)
Grosse tête et peu de sens.—Large head and little wit. (Fr.)
Gwell angau na Chywilydd.—Death before dishonour. (M. of the Welch Regt.)
Gwell angau na Gwarth.—Better death than disgrace. (M. of the 2nd Battn. Monmouthshire Regt.)
Guerre à mort.—War to the death. (Fr.)
Guerre à outrance.—War to the uttermost. (Fr.)
Gutta cavat lapidem non vi, sed semper cadendo.—The drop hollows the stone not by force, but by constant falling.
Guttæ.—Drops.

Habeat.—Let him have.
Hæc olim meminisse juvabit.—It will be a joy to us to recall this hereafter.
Hæreticis non est servanda fides.—No faith should be kept with heretics.
Hannibal ante portas.—The enemy at the gates.
Haud passibus æquis.—With unequal steps.
Haut ton.—High tone; said of fashion or social position. (Fr.)
Heil dir im Siegerkranz.—Hail to thee victor (crowned). (Ger.)
Helluo librorum.—A great reader.
Heureka.—I have found it! (Gr.)
Hiatus maxime deflendus.—A deficiency greatly to be deplored.
Hic et nunc.—Here and now.
Hic et ubique.—Here and everywhere.
Hic jacet.—Here lies.
Hinc illæ lachrymæ.—Hence these tears.
Hoc age.—Mind what you are about (lit. do this).
Hoc genus omne.—All persons of the same kind.
Hoc loco.—In this place.
Hoc opus, hic labor est.—This is work, this indeed is toil.
Hodie mihi, cras tibi.—My turn to-day, yours tomorrow.
Hoi polloi.—The multitude; the rabble. (Gr.)
Homme d'affaires.—A business man. (Fr.)
Homme d'esprit.—A witty man. (Fr.)
Homo solus aut deus aut demon.—Man alone is either a god or a devil.
Homo sum; humani nihil a me alienum puto.—I am a man, and I reckon nothing human alien to me.
Homo unius libri.—A man of one book.
Honi soit qui mal y pense.—Evil be to him who thinks evil of it. (M. of the Order of the Garter.) (Fr.)
Honneur et patrie.—Honour and fatherland. (M. of the Legion of Honour.) (Fr.)
Honor alit artes.—Honour nourishes the arts.
Honoris causa.—As a mark of esteem. (L., for the sake of honour.)
Hora et semper.—Now and always. (M.)
Horis intermediis.—At alternate hours.
Horresco referens.—I shudder as I relate.
Hors de combat.—Out of condition to fight. (Fr.)
Hortus siccus.—A collection of dried plants. (L., a dry garden.)
Hostis honori invidia.—Envy is an enemy to honour. (M.)
Hôtel de ville.—Town hall. (Fr.)
Hôtel-Dieu.—A general hospital (in many French towns). (Fr.)
Hôtel garni.—A furnished mansion. (Fr.)
Humanum est errare.—To err is human.

Ibidem.—In the same place.
Ich dien.—I serve. (M. of the Prince of Wales and the 12th Royal Lancers.) (Ger.)
Ich habe genossen das irdische Glück, ich habe gelebt und geliebet.—I have tasted the fruits of the earth, I have lived and loved. (Ger.)
Ici on parle français.—French is spoken here. (Fr.)
Idée fixe.—A fixed idea; an obsession. (Fr.)
Id est.—That is.
Id genus omne.—All persons of that description.
Ignorantia legis excusat neminem.—Ignorance of the law excuses nobody.
Ignoratio elenchi.—Ignoring of the point at issue (an attempt at refutation by destroying an argument not advanced).
Ignotum per ignotius.—(Trying to define) the unknown by the still more unknown.
Il faut de l'argent.—Money is necessary. (Fr.)
Il faut laver son linge sale en famille.—One ought not to wash one's dirty linen in public. (Fr.)
Il n'a ni bouche ni éperon.—He has neither wit nor go in him (lit. he has neither mouth nor spur). (Fr.)
Il n'a pas inventé la poudre.—He did not invent gunpowder (he will never set the Thames on fire). (Fr.)
Il n'y a que le premier pas qui coûte.—It is the first step that counts. (Fr.)
Il penseroso.—The pensive man. (It.)
Imo pectore.—From the bottom of the heart.
Impavidum ruinæ ferient.—The wreck of things will strike him unmoved.
Imperium in imperio.—A government within a government.

In absentia.—In absence.
In æternum.—For ever.
In anima vili.—On a subject of little worth.
In arduis fidelis.—Faithful in misfortune. (M. of the Royal Army Medical Corps.)
In articulo mortis.—At the point of death.
In camerâ.—In private (lit., in the chamber). (L.)
In capite.—In chief.
In cauda venenum.—Poison lurks in the tail, or, there is a sting in the tail.
In cœlo quies.—There is rest in heaven.
In commendam.—(Holding) in trust (for another).
In contumaciam.—In contempt (of court).
In curia.—In the court.
Index expurgatorius.—A list of passages to be expunged; a list of prohibited books.
In esse.—In being.
In excelsis.—To the highest degree.
In extenso.—At full length.
In extremis.—At the point of death.
In flagrante delicto.—In the act; red-handed.
In formâ pauperis.—As a poor man.
In foro conscientiæ.—Before the tribunal of conscience.
Infra dignitatem.—Beneath one's dignity.
In generalibus latet dolus.—Fallacy lurks in generalities.
In hoc signo vinces.—By this sign thou shalt conquer. (M.)
In hoc statu.—In this state or condition.
In limine.—At the threshold.
In loco parentis.—In the place of a parent.
In medias res.—Into the midst of things.
In medio tutissimus ibis.—You will go safest in the middle.
In medio virtus.—Virtue lies in the mean.
In memoriam.—To the memory of.
In nomine.—In the name of.
In nubibus.—In the clouds.
In nuce.—In a nutshell.
In partibus infidelium.—In heathen lands (esp. of countries having no other Roman Catholic sees).
In petto.—In reserve; in secret. (It.)
In posse.—Possible; as a possibility.
In præsenti.—At present.
In propriâ personâ.—In person.
In puris naturalibus.—Stark naked.
In re.—In the matter of; concerning.
In rerum natura.—In the nature of things.
In sæcula sæculorum.—For ever and ever.
Insculpsit.—He (or she) engraved (it.)
In situ.—In its original situation.
Ih solo Deo salus.—In God alone is salvation. (M.)
Insouance.—Indifference. (Fr.)
Instar omnium.—The example of others.
In statu pupillari.—In the position of a minor.
In statu quo (ante).—In the state in which it was.
In te, Domine, speravi.—In thee, O Lord, have I put my trust.
Integer vitæ scelerisque purus.—(A man) of upright life and free from sin.
Integra mens augustissima possessio.—An honest mind is the most noble possession.
Inter alia.—Among other matters.
Inter canem et lupum.—Between the dog and the wolf; at twilight.
Inter nos.—Between ourselves; confidentially.
Inter pocula.—At one's cups.
In terrorem.—As a threat or warning.
Inter vivos.—Between living people.
In totidem verbis.—In so many words.
In toto.—Entirely; as a whole.
Intra muros.—Within the walls.
In transitu.—In passing.
In vacuo.—In empty space.
Invenit.—He (or she) designed (it).
In veritate religionis confido.—I trust in the truth of our faith. (M. of Edinburgh and the King's Own Scottish Borderers.)
In vino veritas.—There is truth in wine (*i.e.*, the truth comes out under its influence).
Invita Minerva.—Without genius or the requisite inspiration; lit., against the will of Minerva.
Ipse dixit.—He himself said it; dogmatic assertion.
Ipsissima verba,—The very words.
Ipso facto.—By the fact itself; necessarily.
Ira furor brevis est.—Anger is a short madness.
Ita lex scripta.—Such is the law. (L., thus the law is written.)

Januis clausis.—With closed doors.
Ja wohl.—Yes, indeed; to be sure; quite so. (Ger.)
Je ne sais quoi.—I know not what. **(Fr.)**
Jet d'eau.—A jet of water. (Fr.)
Jeu de main.—A practical joke. **(Fr.)**
Jeu de mots.—A play on words; a pun. **(Fr.)**
Jeu d'esprit.—A witticism. (Fr.)
Jeu de théâtre.—A stage trick. (Fr.)
Jeune premier.—The juvenile lead (Theatr.). (Fr.)
Jeunesse dorée.—Wealthy young men-about-town. (Fr., gilded youth.)
Je veux de bonne guerre.—I wish for fair play. (M.) (Fr.)
Je vis en espoir.—I live in hope. (Fr.)
Joie de vivre.—High spirits. (Fr., the joy of living.)
Jour maigre.—A lean day; a fast day. (Fr.)
Judicium parium, aut leges terræ.—The judgement of our peers, or the laws of the land. (M.)
Juge de paix.—A Justice of the Peace. (Fr.)
Jurare in verba magistri.—To swear to the opinions of the master.
Jure divino.—By divine right.
Jure humano.—By human law.
Juris utriusque doctor.—Doctor of both laws (civil and canon).
Jus canonicum.—Canon law.
Jus civile.—The civil law.
Jus et norma loquendi.—The law and rule of language.
Jus gentium.—The law of nations.
Juste milieu.—The golden mean. **(Fr.)**
Justum et tenacem propositi virum.—A man just and firm of purpose.
J'y suis et j'y reste.—Here I am and here I remain. (Fr.)

Kalendæ Græcæ.—The Greek calends (that is, never).
Kinder, Kirche, und Küche.—The children, the Church, and the kitchen (*i.e.*, woman's proper interests) (Ger.)

Laborare est orare.—To work is to pray.
Labore et honore.—By labour and honour.
Labor ipse voluptas.—Labour itself is pleasure.
Labor omnia vincit.—Labour conquers everything.
La bride sur le cou.—With rein on neck; at full speed. (Fr.)
La critique est aisée, et l'art est difficile.—Criticism is easy, and art is difficult. (Fr.)
La fortune passe par tout.—The vicissitudes of fortune are common to all. (M.) (Fr.)
La grande passion.—The master passion; love. (Fr.)
Laisser faire.—To let things alone and take their course. (Fr.)
Laissez aller.—Without constraint. **(Fr.)**
L'allegro.—The cheerful man. (It.)
La maladie sans maladie.—Hypochondria. (Fr.)
L'amour et la fumée ne peuvent se cacher.—Love and smoke cannot be hidden. (Fr.)
Langage des halles.—Language of the fish market: Billingsgate. (Fr.)
Langue d'oc.—The southern dialect of mediæval France (using *oc* in place of *oui*), in contrast to **langue d'oïl,** the northern dialect (using *oïl*).
La parole a été donnée à l'homme pour déguiser sa pensée.—Speech was given to man to conceal thought. (Fr.)
Lapsus calami.—A slip of the pen.
Lapsus linguæ.—A slip of the tongue.
Lapsus memoriæ.—A fault of memory.
Lares et penates.—Household gods.
Lasciate ogni speranza, voi ch'entrate.—Abandon hope, all ye who enter. (It.)
Latet anguis in herbâ.—There is a snake in the grass.
Latin de cuisine.—Dog-Latin. (Fr.)
Latitat.—He lurks; a writ of summons [Law].
Laudari a viro laudato.—To be praised by one who has himself been praised.
Laudator temporis acti.—An admirer of the past.
Laus Deo.—Praise to God.

L'avenir.—The future. (Fr.)
Legatus a latere.—An extraordinary Papal ambassador.
Le grand monarque.—Louis XIV, the Great Monarch. (Fr.)
Le jeu ne vaut pas la chandelle.—The game is not worth the candle. (Fr.)
Le pas.—Precedence in place or rank. (Fr.)
Le roi et l'état.—The king and the state. (Fr.)
Le roi le veult.—The king wills it. (Anglo-Fr.)
Le roi s'avisera.—The king will please himself (implying refusal). (Anglo-Fr.)
Les affaires font les hommes.—Occupation makes men. (Fr.)
Le savoir faire.—The knowing how to act. (Fr.)
Le savoir vivre.—The knowing how to live. (Fr.)
Lèse majesté.—High treason. (Fr.)
L'etat, c'est moi.—I am the state. (Fr.)
Le tout ensemble.—The whole together. (Fr.)
Lettres de cachet.—Private sealed letters (esp. warrants of imprisonment) from the king. (Fr.)
Levée en masse.—Total conscription. (Fr.)
Lever de rideau.—The raising of the curtain (Theatr.); a curtain-raiser. (Fr.)
Le vrai n'est pas toujours vraisemblable.—That which is true is not always credible (or likely).
Lex non scripta.—The common law.
Lex scripta.—The statute law.
Lex talionis.—The law of retaliation.
Lex terræ.—The law of the land.
L'homme propose, et Dieu dispose.—Man proposes, and God disposes. (Fr.)
Libertas in legibus.—Liberty within the laws. (M.)
Liberum arbitrium.—Free will.
L'incroyable.—The incredible. (Fr.)
Lite pendente.—During the lawsuit.
Literæ humaniores.—The liberal arts (Classical Greats at Oxford). (L., the more humane studies.)
Litera scripta manet.—The written letter remains (as proof).
Loci communes.—Topics.
Loco citato.—In the place quoted.
Locus classicus.—A classical passage.
Locus pœnitentiæ.—Place for repentance.
Locus sigilli.—The place of the seal.
Locus standi.—Right to be heard (in a law case).
Longue haleine.—Dogged perseverance. (Fr.)
Loquitur.—Speaks.
Lucidus ordo.—A lucid arrangement.
Lucus a non lucendo.—Deriving *lucus*, a grove, from *luceo*, shine, because there is no light in it; hence, a fanciful derivation.
Lupus est homo homini.—Man is a wolf to his fellow man.
Lupus in fabula.—The wolf in the fable.
Lusus naturæ.—A monstrosity; a freak of nature.
Lux Mundi.—The Light of the World (a title of Christ).

Macte animo!—Courage!
Ma foi!—Faith! (Fr.)
Magister dixit.—The master said so.
Magna civitas, magna solitudo.—A great city is a great solitude.
Magna est veritas, et prævalebit.—Truth is powerful, and will ultimately prevail.
Magna est vis consuetudinis.—The force of habit is great.
Magni nominis umbra.—The shadow of a great name.
Magnum bonum.—A great good.
Magnum est vectigal parsimonia.—Economy is a great revenue.
Magnum opus.—A great work.
Magnus Apollo.—A great oracle.
Maison de campagne.—Country seat. (Fr.)
Maison de santé.—A nursing home; a mental asylum. (Fr.)
Maître d'hôtel.—A house steward; a hotel-manager. (Fr.)
Maladie du pays.—Home-sickness. (Fr.)
Mala fide.—In bad faith.
Mal à propos.—Ill-timed. (Fr.)
Mal aux dents.—Toothache. (Fr.)
Mal de tête.—Headache. (Fr.)
Malgré nous.—In spite of ourselves; against our will. (Fr.)
Malgré soi.—In spite of oneself; against one's will. (Fr.)
Malis avibus.—Under bad omens.
Malum in se.—Evil in itself.
Manibus pedibusque.—With might and main (lit. with hands and feet).
Manu propriâ.—With one's own hand.
Manus hæc inimica tyrannis.—This hand is hostile to tyrants. (M.)
Mardi gras.—Shrove Tuesday.
Mare clausum.—A sea under the jurisdiction of a single state. (L., a closed sea.)
Mare nostrum.—A sea the jurisdiction of which is claimed by a single state. (L., our own sea.)
Mariage de convenance.—A marriage from considerations of advantage. (Fr.)
Materia medica.—Substances used in medicine.
Materiem superabat opus.—The workmanship surpassed the materials.
Mauvaise honte.—Self-consciousness; excessive bashfulness. (Fr.)
Mauvais goût.—Bad taste. (Fr.)
Mauvais pas.—A bad step; a scrape. (Fr.)
Mauvais quart d'heure.—A bad quarter of an hour; a short trying experience. (Fr.)
Mauvais sujet.—A worthless fellow. (Fr.)
Mauvais ton.—Bad tone; ill-breeding. (Fr.)
Meâ culpâ.—It is my fault.
Medice, cura teipsum.—Physican, heal thyself.
Medio tutissimus ibis.—The safest way is the middle one.
Mehr Licht.—More light. (Ger.)
Me judice.—I being judge; in my opinion.
Membrum virile (vi-*ry*-le).—The male organ; the penis.
Memento mori.—Remember you must die.
Memoria pii æterna.—The memory of the good endures for ever. (M.)
Memoriter.—By rote.
Ménage à trois.—A matrimonial tangle. (Fr., household of three.)
Mensâ et toro.—From board and bed.
Mens agitat molem.—Mind moves the mass or matter.
Mens conscia recti.—A mind conscious of rectitude.
Mens cujusque is est quisque.—Mind makes the man. (M.)
Mens sana in corpore sano.—A sound mind in a sound body.
Mente et manu.—With might and main. (M. of the Queen's Own Hussars.)
Menus plaisirs.—Pocket-money. (Fr.)
Meo periculo.—At my own risk.
Merebimur.—May we be worthy. (M. of the 15th King's Royal Hussars.)
Meum et tuum.—Mine and thine.
Mezzo termine.—A middle course. (It.)
Mihi cura futuri.—My care is for the future.
Mirabile dictu.—Wonderful to relate.
Mirabile visu.—Wonderful to see.
Mise en scène.—Stage-production; the putting in preparation for the stage. (Fr.)
Miseris succurrere disco.—I know how to succour the wretched.
Mitte.—Send.
Mittimus.—We send [Law].
Modo et forma.—In manner and form.
Modo præscripto.—In the manner prescribed.
Modus operandi.—The manner of working.
Mollisima tempora fandi.—The most favourable time for speaking.
Mon ami.—My friend. (Fr.)
Mon Dieu!—My God! (Fr.)
Monstrum horrendum.—A horrible monster.
Monstrum nullâ virtute redemptum a vitiis.—A monster whose vices are not counterbalanced by a single virtue.
Mont de piété.—Pawnshop; originally, store of money to lend to poor people without interest. (Fr.)
More majorum.—After the manner of our ancestors.
More suo.—After his own manner.
Morgenstunde hat Gold im Munde.—The morning brings wisdom. (Ger.)
Morgue anglaise.—English stand-offishness. (Fr.)
Mors omnibus communis.—Death is common to all.
Mos pro lege.—Custom for law.

Mot à mot.—Word for word. (Fr.)
Mot d'ordre.—Watchword; password; central motive (of policy). (Fr.)
Mot du guet.—Watchword; countersign. (Fr.)
Mots d'usage.—Phrases in common use. (Fr.)
Mot juste.—The right or appropriate word. (Fr.)
Motu proprio.—Of his own accord.
Muet comme un poisson.—Dumb as a fish. (Fr.)
Multa gemens.—Groaning deeply.
Multa paucis.—Much among little.
Multum in parvo.—Much in little.
Munus Apolline dignum.—A gift worthy of Apollo.
Murus æneus conscientia sana.—A sound conscience is a wall of brass. (M.).
Mutatis mutandis.—After making the necessary changes.
Mutato nomine, de te fabula narratur.—Change the name, and the story will apply to yourself.

Nager entre deux eaux.—To run with the hare and hunt with the hounds. (Fr.)
Natio comœda est.—The nation is a company of players.
Natura il fece, e poi roppe le stampa.—Nature formed him, and then broke the mould. (It.)
Naturam expellas furcâ, tamen usque recurret.—You may drive out nature by violence (lit. with a pitchfork), but she will ever come rushing back again.
Natura non facit saltus.—Nature does not make leaps.
Né, *m.*; **Née,** *fem.*—Born. (Fr.)
Nec aspera terrent.—Nor do difficulties deter us. (M. of the King's Own Hussars.)
Nec cupias nec metuas.—Neither desire nor fear. (M.)
Nec deus intersit, nisi dignus vindice nodus.—Let not a god be introduced, unless the difficulty be worthy of such intervention.
Ne cede malis.—Do not yield to misfortunes.
Necessitas non habet legem.—Necessity knows no law.
Nec placida contentus quiete est.—Nor is he contented with quiet repose. (M.)
Nec pluribus impar.—No unequal match for numbers. (M. of Louis XIV.)
Nec prece nec pretio.—Neither by entreaty nor a bribe.
Nec quærere nec spernere honores.—Neither to seek nor despise honours. (M.)
Nec rege nec populo, sed utroque.—Neither for the king nor for the people, but for both. (M.)
Nec scire fas est omnia.—The gods do not permit us to know everything.
Nec temere nec timide.—Neither rashly nor timidly. (M.)
Ne faites donc pas de l'embarras.—Do not make such a fuss. (Fr.)
Ne fronti crede.—Trust not to appearances.
Ne jugez pas sur la mine.—You cannot judge by appearances. (Fr.)
Ne Jupiter quidem omnibus placet.—Not even Jupiter pleases everybody.
Nemine contradicente.—Nobody expressing disagreement.
Nemo me impune lacessit.—No one injures me with impunity. (M. of the Order of the Thistle and of certain Scots regiments.)
Nemo mortalium omnibus horis sapit.—No man is wise at all times.
Nemo repente fuit turpissimus.—No man ever became incurably vicious at once.
Ne nous flattez pas le dé.—Speak out without reserve. (Fr.)
Ne obliviscaris.—Never forget! (M. of the Argyll and Sutherland Highlanders.)
Ne plus ultra.—What cannot be surpassed; perfection (lit. no more beyond).
Né pour la digestion.—A social drone. (Fr.)
Ne quid nimis.—Shun extremes; not too much.
Nero antico.—Roman black marble.
Ne sutor ultra crepidam.—Let not the shoemaker go beyond his last.
Ne tentes, aut perfice.—Either attempt not, or accomplish. (M.)
Ne vile velis.—Incline to nothing base. (M. of the Nevilles.)
Nez retroussé.—A turned-up nose. (Fr.)
Nicht wahr ?—Is not that so ? (Ger.)
Nihil ad rem.—Nothing to the purpose.
Nil admirari.—To wonder at nothing.
Nil desperandum.—Never despair.
Nil nisi cruce.—There is no dependence but in the Cross. (M.)
Ni l'un ni l'autre.—Neither the one nor the other. (Fr.)
N'importe.—It matters not. (Fr.)
Nisi Dominus frustra.—Unless the Lord be with us, we strive in vain. (M. of Edinburgh, and of the King's Own Scottish Borderers.)
Nisi prius.—Unless before; a judicial writ.
Nobilitatis virtus non stemma character.—Virtue, not pedigree, should characterize nobility. (M.)
Noblesse oblige.—Rank has its obligations. (Fr.)
Nocturnâ versate manu, versate diurna.—Let these be your studies by night and by day.
Nolens volens.—Whether he will or not; willy-nilly.
Noli me tangere.—Touch me not.
Nolle prosequi.—To be unwilling to proceed.
Nolo episcopari.—I do not wish to be made a bishop.
Nom de guerre.—An assumed name. (Fr.)
Nom de plume.—Assumed name of an author. (Fr.)
Non assumpsit.—He did not assume (a legal plea).
Non avenu.—Not happened. (Fr.)
Non compos mentis.—Not sound in mind.
Non constat.—It does not appear.
Non est.—It does not exist.
Non est inventus.—He has not been found (or, the accused has not been arrested).
Non est vivere, sed valere vita.—Life is not mere existence, but the enjoyment of health.
Non fumum ex fulgore, sed ex fumo dare lucem.—Not to elicit smoke from splendour, but light from smoke.
Non generant aquilæ columbas.—Eagles do not bring forth pigeons. (M.)
Non multa, sed multum.—Not many things, but much.
Non nobis, Domine.—Not to ourselves, O Lord.
Non obstante.—Notwithstanding.
Non omnia possumus omnes.—We cannot all of us do everything.
Non placet.—It does not please (a motion of rejection).
Non possumus.—We cannot (denoting non-co-operation).
Non quo, sed quomodo.—Not who, but how. (M.)
Non satis.—Not sufficient.
Non sequitur.—It does not follow.
Non sibi, sed patriæ.—Not for himself, but for his country. (M.)
Non sum qualis eram.—I am not now what I once was.
Non vivimus edere, sed edimus vivere.—We live not to eat, but eat to live.
Nosce te ipsum.—Know thyself.
Noscitur ex sociis.—He is known by his companions (*i.e.*, " Birds of a feather flock together ").
Nota bene.—Note ! mark well.
Notre-Dame.—Our Lady. (Fr.)
Nous avons brûlé nos vaisseaux.—There is no return now. (Fr., We have burnt our boats.)
Nous avons changé tout cela.—We have changed all that. (Fr.)
Nous en faisons grand cas.—We prize it very highly. (Fr.)
Nous faisons peu d'état de cet homme.—We have a very poor opinion of that man. (Fr.)
Nous verrons.—We shall see. (Fr.)
Nous verrons ce qu'il a dans le corps.—We will see what stuff he is made of. (Fr.)
Nouveau riche.—One recently become rich; an upstart. (Fr.)
Novus homo.—A new man; a man risen from the ranks.
Nudum pactum.—An invalid agreement.
Nugæ canoræ.—Melodius trifles.
Nulla bona.—(He has) no goods (meaning, there is nought upon which to distrain).
Nulli secundus.—Second to none. (M. of the Coldstream Guards.)
Nullius addictus jurare in verba magistri.—Being bound to swear to the dogmas of no master.

Nullum numen abest si sit prudentia.—Where there is prudence, a protecting divinity is not far away.
Nullum quod tetigit non ornavit.—He touched nothing which he did not adorn.
Nullum tempus occurrit regi.—Time is no hindrance to a king.
Nullus dies sine linea.—No day without something done.
Nunc aut nunquam.—Now or never.
Nunc dimittis servum tuum, Domine.—Now, O Lord, lettest thou thy servant depart.
Nunquam aliud natura, aliud sapientia dicit.—Nature never says one thing, and wisdom another.
Nunquam non paratus.—Always ready. (M.)
Nusquam tuta fides.—Our confidence is nowhere safe.

Obiit.—He (or she) died.
Obiter dictum.—A thing said by the way, or in passing.
Obscurum per obscurius.—Explaining something obscure by what is more obscure.
Obsequium amicos, veritas odium parit.—Obsequiousness procures us friends, truth enemies.
Obsta principiis.—Resist the beginnings.
Oderint, dum metuant.—Let them hate, so long as they fear.
Odi profanum vulgus.—I loathe the profane vulgar.
Odium theologicum.—Hatred of rival theologians.
Ohne Hast, ohne Rast.—Without haste, without rest. (Ger.)
O Liberté, Liberté, que de crimes on commet en ton nom! O Liberty, Liberty, what crimes are committed in thy name! (Fr.)
Omne ignotum pro magnifico.—Everything unknown is taken for something magnificent.
Omne solum forti patria.—To a brave man every soil is his country.
Omne trinum perfectum.—There is a threefoldness or trinity in everything perfect.
Omne tulit punctum qui miscuit utile dulci.—He has gained every point who has combined the useful with the agreeable.
Omnia bona bonis.—To the good all things are good.
Omnia mutantur, nos et mutamur in illis.—All things change, and we change with them.
Omnia vincit amor.—Love conquers all things.
Omnia vincit labor.—Labour conquers all things.
On dit.—They say; a flying rumour. (Fr.)
On ne donne rien si libéralement que ses conseils.—Men give nothing so liberally as their advice. (Fr.)
Onus probandi.—The weight of proof.
Operæ pretium est.—It is worth while.
Opere citato.—In the work (previously) mentioned.
Ora et labora.—Pray and work.
Orate pro anima.—Pray for the soul (of).
Ora pro nobis.—Pray for us.
Ore rotundo.—With full round voice.
Origo mali.—The origin of the evil.
O si sic omnia.—O that he had always spoken or acted thus! (L., Oh! if all things thus!)
O tempora, O mores!—O the times! O the manners!
Otium cum dignitate.—Ease with dignity.
Otium sine dignitate.—Ease without dignity.
Ou la chèvre est attachée, il faut qu'elle broûte.—Where the goat is tethered there she must browse. (Fr.)
Ouvrage de longue haleine.—A long-winded business. (Fr.)
Ouvriers.—Workmen. (Fr.)

Pace tua.—With your leave.
Pacta conventa.—Terms agreed on.
Palmam qui meruit ferat.—Let him who has won the palm (of victory) bear it.
Palma non sine pulvere.—The palm (of victory) is not gained without labour. (M.)
Panem et circenses.—Bread and circuses (*i.e.*, food and fun—at the public charge).
Par excellence.—By way of eminence; preeminently. (Fr.)
Pari mutuel.—A totalisator. (Fr.)
Pari passu.—With equal steps or pace; likewise.
Par le droit du plus fort.—By right of the stronger. (Fr.)
Par nobile fratrum.—A noble pair of brothers (ironically).
Par signe de mépris.—As a sign of contempt. (Fr.)
Pars minima sui.—The frittered remnant of the man or thing (lit., the smallest part of itself).
Particeps criminals.—An accomplice.
Parti pris.—Set purpose; preconception; bias. (Fr.)
Parturiunt montes, nascetur ridiculus mus.—The mountains are in labour, and a ridiculous mouse will be brought forth.
Parva componere magnis.—To compare small things with great.
Parvum parva decent.—Little things are suitable to a little man.
Pas à pas on va bien loin.—A step at a time and one goes a great way. (Fr.)
Pas dans le train.—Not up to date. (Fr.)
Passato il pericolo, gabbato il santo.—When the danger is past, the guardian saint is derided. (It.)
Passe-partout.—A master key. (Fr.)
Passez-moi ce mot-là.—Excuse the expression. (Fr.)
Paterfamilias.—The father of the family.
Pater patriæ.—The father of his country.
Patience passe science.—Patience surpasses knowledge. (M.) (Fr.)
Patientiâ vinces.—By patience thou shalt conquer. (M.)
Patria cara, carior libertas.—My country is dear, but liberty is dearer. (M.)
Patriæ pietatis imago.—An image of paternal tenderness.
Pauca sed bona.—Few (or little) but good.
Pax in bello.—Peace in war. (M.)
Pax vobiscum!—Peace be with you!
Peccavi.—I have done wrong (an admission of error).
Pede pœna claudo.—Punishment follows crime with a slow foot.
Peine forte et dure.—Strong and severe pains (name of a mediæval torture in which the victim was pressed to death). (Fr.)
Pendente lite.—Pending the litigation.
Pense à bien.—Think for the best. (M.) (Fr.)
Per angusta ad augusta.—Through difficulties to honour. (M.)
Per ardua ad astra.—Through difficulties to the stars.
Per ardua libertas.—Freedom through difficulties.
Per capita.—By heads (in counting).
Per contra.—Contrariwise; on the other hand.
Per diem.—By the day.
Per fas et nefas.—Through right and wrong.
Per il suo contrario.—By its reverse or opposite. (M.) (It.)
Per mare, per terras.—By sea and land.
Perpetuum mobile.—(The principle of) perpetual motion.
Per saltum.—By a leap.
Per se.—By itself.
Perseverando.—By perseverance. (M.)
Persona grata.—An acceptable person.
Perstetur.—Continue.
Petitio ad misericordiam.—A begging for mercy.
Petitio principii.—A begging of the question.
Peu de gens savent être vieux.—Few persons know how to grow old. (Fr.)
Peu de leçons beaucoup d'exemples.—Where precepts lead, examples draw. (Fr.)
Philosophia stemma non inspicit.—Philosophy does not look into genealogies.
Pièce de résistance.—The chief joint at meals. (Fr.)
Pied-à-terre.—A small apartment, lodging, etc. for occasional use.
Pinxit.—He (or she) painted it.
Pis aller.—A last resource; a course adopted for lack of a better. (Fr.)
Place aux dames.—Make way for the ladies. (Fr.)
Pleno jure.—With full authority.
Pleurer à chaudes larmes.—To cry bitterly. (Fr.)
Pluries.—At several times [Law].
Plus fait douceur que violence.—A kind act does more than harshness. (Fr.)
Plus on est de fous, plus on rit.—The more the merrier. (Fr.)

Plus sage que les sages.—Wiser than the wise. (Fr.)
Poco à poco.—Little by little. (It.)
Poeta nascitur, non fit.—Nature, not study, forms the poet (lit., a poet is born, not made).
Point d'appui.—Point of support; a rallying point. (Fr.)
Pollice verso.—With the thumb turned down (to indicate disapproval).
Pondere, non numero.—By weight, not by number.
Pons asinorum.—The asses' bridge; a problem for beginners (applied to Euclid, I, v).
Populus vult decipi, et decepiatur.—Let the people be deceived, as they wish it.
Posse comitatus.—The police force (lit., the power) of the county.
Possunt quia posse videntur.—They are able because they think they are so.
Post cineres gloria sera venit.—Fame comes too late to our ashes.
Poste restante.—To remain until called for. (Fr.)
Post hoc, ergo propter hoc.—Coming after, therefore in consequence (a logical fallacy).
Post meridiem.—After noon (P.M.).
Post mortem.—After death.
Post tot naufragia portum.—After so many shipwrecks (we find) a harbour. (M.)
Postulata.—Things required.
Potage au gras.—Meat soup. (Fr.)
Pour ainsi dire.—So to speak. (Fr.)
Pour encourager les autres.—To encourage the others (used ironically).
Pour faire rire.—To raise a laugh. (Fr.)
Pour passer le temps.—To pass the time. (Fr.)
Pour prendre congé.—To take leave. (Fr.)
Præmonitus, præmunitus.—Forewarned, forearmed.
Precedentibus instar.—According to precedent.
Prendre la lune avec les dents.—To aim at impossibilities (lit., to seize the moon with the teeth). (Fr.)
Prêt d'accomplir.—Ready to perform. (M.) (Fr.)
Prêt pour mon pays.—Ready for my country. (M.) (Fr.)
Preux chevalier.—A gallant knight. (Fr.)
Primâ facie.—On the first view, or impression.
Primus inter pares.—First among his equals or peers.
Prior tempore, prior jure.—First in time, first in right.
Pristinæ virtutis memores.—Mindful of our early valour. (M. of the King's Royal Irish Hussars and the West Surreys.)
Prix fixe.—Set price. (Fr.)
Pro aris et focis.—For our altars and our hearths.
Probatum est.—It has been proved.
Probitas laudatur et alget.—Honesty is praised and left to starve.
Probitas verus honos.—Probity is true honour.
Pro bono publico.—For the public good.
Probum non pœnitet.—The honest man repents not. (M.)
Procès-verbal.—A written statement; a verbatim transcript, esp. of evidence in a court. (Fr.)
Pro Deo et Ecclesiâ.—For God and the Church.
Prodesse quam conspici.—Utility without ostentation. (M.)
Pro et con.—For and against.
Pro forma.—For the sake of form.
Pro hac vice.—For this time; on this occasion.
Projet de loi.—A legislative bill. (Fr.)
Pro patria.—For our country.
Pro rata.—In proportion.
Pro rege et patria.—For King and Country. (M. of the 2nd Dragoon Guards.)
Pro rege, lege, et grege.—For the king, the law, and the people. (M.)
Pro re natâ.—For a special purpose (lit., for a matter that has arisen).
Pro salute animæ.—For the health of the soul.
Pro tanto.—As far as it goes.
Pro tempore.—For the time being.
Proxime accessit.—Next to the winner.
Proximo.—Next month.
Punica fides.—Carthaginian faith; treachery.
Pur et simple.—Pure and simple; entire; absolute. (Fr.)
Pur sang.—Of pure blood; thoroughbred. (Fr.)

Quæ amissa, salva.—What has been lost is safe. (M.)
Quæ fuerent vitia, mores sunt.—What were vices once are now manners.
Quærens quem devoret.—Seeking someone to devour.
Qualis ab incepto.—Such as at the beginning.
Quam diu se bene gesserit.—As long as he shall conduct himself properly.
Quand même.—All the same; nevertheless. (Fr.)
Quanti est sapere.—How valuable is wisdom.
Quantum.—How much.
Quantum libet.—As much as you please.
Quantum mutatus ab illo!—How changed from what he once was!
Quantum sufficit.—As much as is sufficient.
Quantum volueris.—At will.
Question extraordinaire.—A severe examination. (Fr.)
Que voulez-vous?—What do you wish? (Fr.)
Quid novi?—What news?
Quid nunc?—What now?
Qui donne tôt donne deux fois.—Who gives quickly gives twice. (Fr.)
Quid prodest?—What is the use?
Quid pro quo.—One thing for another.
Quid rides?—Why do you laugh?
Quid violentius aure tyranni?—What more violent than the ear of a tyrant?
Qui invidet minor est.—He who envies is the inferior. (M.)
Qui m'aime, aime mon chien.—Love me, love my dog. (Fr.)
Qui n'a santé, n'a rien.—He who has not health has not anything. (Fr.)
Qui patitur vincit.—He who suffers conquers. (M.)
Quis custodiet ipsos custodes?—Who shall guard the guards themselves?
Qui s'excuse s'accuse.—He who excuses himself accuses himself. (Fr.)
Quis separabit?—Who shall separate? (M. of the Order of St. Patrick and of certain regiments.)
Qui vive?—Who goes there? (Fr.)
Quoad hoc.—To this extent.
Quoad sacra.—As regards sacred things.
Quo animo?—With what purpose, or intention?
Quocunque trahunt fata, sequamur.—Wherever the Fates direct us, let us follow.
Quod di omen avertant.—May the gods avert this.
Quod dixi, dixi.—There is no changing me. (L., what I have said, I have said.)
Quod erat demonstrandum.—Which was to be proved.
Quod erat faciendum.—Which was to be done.
Quod petis hic est.—What you seek is here.
Quod scripsi, scripsi.—What I have written, I have written.
Quod semper, quod ubique, quod ab omnibus.—What is eternal, and (is believed) everywhere, and by all (*i.e.*, the Rom. Cath. Church).
Quod vide.—Which see.
Quo fas et gloria ducunt.—Where Fate and Glory lead. (M. of the Royal Artillery and Royal Engineers.)
Quo fata vocant.—Whither the Fates call. (M. of the Northumberland Fusiliers.)
Quos Deus vult perdere, prius dementat.—Those whom God would destroy, He first drives mad.
Quot homines, tot sententiæ.—So many men, so many opinions.
Quo vadis?—Whither goest thou?
Quo warranto?—By what warrant? (A legal writ.)

Raison d'état.—A reason of state. (Fr.)
Raison d'être.—Reason for a thing's existence. (Fr.)
Rara avis in terris, nigroque simillima cygno.—A rare bird in the earth, and very like a black swan; a prodigy.
Rari nantes in gurgite vasto.—Swimming, one here, another there, on the vast abyss.
Recipe.—Take.
Recte et suaviter.—Justly and mildly. (M.)
Reculer pour mieux sauter.—To go back in order to leap the better. (Fr.)

Redeunt saturnia regna.—The golden age (lit. the age of Saturn) returns.
Reductio ad absurdum.—A reducing a position to an absurdity.
Refero relata.—I relate as it has been related to me.
Regium donum.—A royal grant.
Re infectâ.—Without attaining his end; the business being unfinished.
Rem acu tetigisti.—You have hit the nail on the head (lit., touched it with a needle-point).
Rente viagère.—A life annuity; life interest. (Fr.)
Reparabit cornua Phœbe.—The moon shall fill her horn again. (M.)
Repetatur.—Let it be repeated.
Réponse, s'il vous plaît.—Please reply; R.S.V.P. (Fr.)
Requiescat in pace!—May he rest in peace!
Res angusta domi.—Narrow circumstances at home.
Res gestæ.—Exploits.
Res judicata.—A case already decided.
Respice finem.—Keep the object in view. (L., regard the end.)
Respublica.—The commonwealth.
Resurgam.—I shall rise again.
Revenons à nos moutons.—Let us return to our subject. (Fr.)
Ride si sapis.—Laugh if you are wise.
Rien n'est beau que le vrai.—Nothing so lovely as truth. (Fr.)
Rira bien qui rira le dernier.—He laughs best who laughs last. (Fr.)
Rire dans sa barbe.—To laugh in one's sleeve (lit., in one's beard). (Fr.)
Risu inepto res ineptior nulla.—Nothing is more contemptible than silly laughter.
Risum teneatis, amici?—Can you refrain from laughter, my friends?
Robe de chambre.—A dressing-gown. (Fr.)
Rudis indigestaque moles.—A rude and unarranged mass.
Ruse contre ruse.—Diamond cut diamond. (Fr.)
Rus in urbe.—The country in town.
Rusticus expectat dum defluat amnis.—The rustic waits till the river flows by.

Sal atticum.—Wit (lit., Attic salt).
Salle à manger.—Dining-room. (Fr.)
Salle de danser.—A dancing-school. (Fr.)
Salus populi suprema est lex.—The supreme law is the welfare of the people.
Salvo jure.—Saving the right.
Salvo pudore.—Without offence to modesty.
S'amuser à la moutarde.—To spend time in trifling. (Fr.)
Sanctum sanctorum.—The holy of holies.
Sang de bœuf.—The deep red colour of certain Chinese porcelain. (Fr., ox-blood.)
Sans cérémonie.—Without ceremony. (Fr.)
Sans changer.—Without changing. (M.) (Fr.)
Sans Dieu rien.—Nothing without God. (M.) (Fr.)
Sans façon.—Without ceremony. (Fr.)
Sans peur et sans reproche.—Without fear and without reproach. (Fr.)
Sans souci.—Without care; free and easy. (Fr.)
Sapere aude.—Dare to be wise.
Sartor resartus.—The tailor patched.
Sat cito, si sat bene.—Soon enough, if well enough.
Satis eloquentiæ, sapientiæ parum.—Plenty of fine talk but little real wisdom.
Satis superque.—Enough and more.
Satis verborum.—Enough of words.
Sauve qui peut.—Save himself who can; hence, a wild rush for safety. (Fr.)
Savoir faire.—Tact; common sense. (Fr.)
Savoir vivre.—Good manners. (Fr., to be well-bred.)
Scandalum magnatum.—Scandalous talk about those in high office.
Scire facias.—Cause him to know (order in certain judicial writs).
Scribimus indocti doctique poëmata passim.—Learned or unlearned, we are all scribbling verses.
Secret de trois, secret de tous.—No secret with more than two. (Fr.)
Secundis dubiisque rectus.—Firm in every fortune. (M.)
Secundum artem.—According to rule.
Secundum quid.—To some extent.
Se defendendo.—In self-defence.
Semel et simul.—At once and together.
Semper ad eventum festinat.—He always makes straight for his goal.
Semper ararus eget.—The covetous man is ever in want.
Semper eadem.—Always the same.
Semper fidelis.—Always faithful. (M. of the Devonshire Regt.)
Semper paratus.—Always ready. (M.)
Sempre il mal non viene per nocere.—Evil does not always come to injure. (It.)
Senatus populusque Romans. (S.P.Q.R.).—The Senate and the People of Rome.
Se non è vero, è ben trovato.—If not true, it is well invented. (It.)
Sens dessus dessous.—Topsy-turvy. (Fr.)
Sero sed serio.—Late, but in earnest. (M.)
Servabo fidem.—I will keep faith. (M.)
Si bon vous semble.—If you think right. (Fr.)
Sic itur ad astra.—This is the way to immortality (lit., to the stars).
Sic passim.—So everywhere.
Sic semper tyrannis.—Thus may it always (happen) to tyrants.
Sic transit gloria mundi.—Thus passes away the glory of the world.
Sic volo, sic jubeo.—Thus I wish, and thus I order.
Sic vos non vobis.—(Shortened form of)—Thus you labour but not for yourselves (*i.e.*, You do the work but others get the credit).
Si Dieu n'existait pas, il faudrait l'inventer.—If God was not it would be necessary to invent Him. (Fr.)
Si jeunesse savait, si vieillesse pouvait!—If youth but knew, could age but do! (Fr.)
Silent leges inter arma.—Laws are silent in the midst of arms.
S'il vous plaît.—If you please; please. (Fr.)
Similia similibus curantur.—Like things are cured by like.
Similis similia gaudet.—Like rejoices in like.
Si monumentum quæris, circumspice.—If you seek his monument, look around.
Simplex munditiis.—Simple and elegant.
Sine die.—Without a day being appointed.
Sine prole.—Without issue.
Sine quâ non.—That which is indispensable.
Sint ut sunt, aut non sint.—Let them be as they are, or not at all.
Si sit prudentia.—If there be but prudence. (M.)
Siste, viator!—Stop, traveller!
Sit sine labe decus.—Let honour be without stain. (M.)
Sit tibi terra levis.—May the earth lie lightly on thy grave.
Si vis me flere.—If you wish me to weep.
Si vis pacem, para bellum.—If you wish peace, prepare for war.
Soi disant.—Self-styled. (Fr.)
Soit dit entre nous.—Between ourselves. (Fr.)
Sola nobilitas virtus.—Virtue alone is true nobility. (M.)
Sola virtus invicta.—Virtue alone is invincible. (M.)
Solitudinem faciunt, pacem appellant.—They make it a desert, and call it peace.
Solvitur ambulando.—It will be solved in walking (*i.e.*, as we proceed).
Solvuntur tabulæ.—The defendant is acquitted.
Sotto voce.—In an undertone. (It.)
Souffrez que je lui montre son bec jaune.—Let me show him what a silly goose he is. (Fr.)
Sourd comme un pot.—As deaf as a post. (Fr.)
Souris qui n'a qu'un trou est bientôt prise.—It is better to have more than one string to your bow (lit., the mouse that has only one hole is soon caught). (Fr.)
Sous tous les rapports.—In all respects. (Fr.)
Soyez ferme.—Be firm. (Fr.)
Spargere voces in vulgum ambiguas.—To scatter deceptive rumours among the people.
Spectemur agendo.—Let us be seen by our actions. (M. of the 1st Royal Dragoons.)
Spero infestis; metuo secundis.—In adversity, I hope; in prosperity, I fear. (M.)
Spero meliora.—I hope for better times. (M.)
Spes mea in Deo.—My hope is in God. (M.)

Spes tutissima cœlis.—The safest hope is in heaven.
Spirituel.—Intellectual; witty. (Fr.)
Splendide mendax.—Mendacious in a good cause.
Spolia opima.—The richest of the spoil.
Sponte sua.—Of one's (or its) own accord.
Stabat Mater.—The Mother was standing (opening words of a 13th cent. hymn commemorating the Sorrows of the B.V.M.).
Stans pede in uno.—While standing on one leg; that is, easily executed.
Stat magni nominis umbra.—He stands, the shadow of a mighty name.
Stat pro ratione voluntas.—Will stands for reason (*i.e.*, My wish is reason enough).
Status quo.—The state in which the thing is; as things were before.
Status quo ante bellum.—The state in which both parties were before the war.
Stemmata quid faciunt ?—Of what avail are pedigrees ?
Studiis et rebus honestis.—By honest pursuits and studies. (M.)
Sturm und Drang.—Storm and stress (denoting the late 18th cent. intellectual awakening in Germany). (Ger.)
Stylo inverso.—With the other end of the pen.
Sua cuique voluptas.—Every man has his own pleasures.
Sua tela tonanti.—(With) their weapons thundering. (M. of the Royal Army Ordnance Corps.)
Suaviter in modo, fortiter in re.—Gentle in the manner, but powerful in the deed.
Sub cruce candida.—Beneath the stainless Cross. (M. of Queen Alexandra's Royal Army Nursing Corps.)
Sub cruce salus.—Salvation under the Cross. (M.)
Sublata causa, tollitur effectus.—When the cause is removed, the effect ceases.
Sub pœna.—Under a penalty.
Sub rosa.—Confidentially; privately. (L., under the rose.)
Sub silentio.—In silence.
Succès d'estime.—Success due to sympathy or personal reasons. (Fr.)
Sufficit.—It is enough.
Suggestio falsi.—A suggestion of what is untrue.
Sui generis.—Of its own kind.
Suivez raison.—Follow reason. (M.) (Fr.)
Sumendus.—To be taken.
Summum bonum.—The chief good.
Summum jus summa injuria.—The rigour of the law is the height of oppression; the excess of justice is the excess of injustice.
Sum quod eris, fui quod es.—I am what thou wilt be; I have been what thou art.
Sunt lachrymæ rerum.—Tears are inseparable from human affairs.
Sunt superis sua jura.—The gods have their own laws.
Suo Marte.—By his own exertion.
Suppressio veri.—The suppression of truth.
Sur le champ.—Immediately. (Fr.)
Sursum corda.—Lift up your hearts !
Surtout pas de zèle !—Above all, no zeal ! (Fr.)
Sus. per coll. (suspendatus per collum).—Hanged by the neck.
Suum cuique.—To every one his own. (M.)
Suus cuique mos.—Every one has his own particular habit.

Tabula rasa.—A clean sheet. (L., a blank tablet.)
Tædium vitæ.—A weariness of life; ennui.
Talis pater, qualis filius.—Like father, like son.
Tam Marte quam Minervâ.—As much by his courage as genius.
Tantæ molis erat.—It was such a task.
Tantæne animis cœlestibus iræ ?—Do the gods harbour such resentment ?
Tant bien que mal.—It is all the same to us. (Fr.)
Tant mieux.—So much the better. (Fr.)
Tant pis.—So much the worse. (Fr.)
Tarde venientibus ossa.—Those who come late to the table find nothing but bones.
Tel est notre plaisir.—Such is our pleasure. (Fr.)
Telle vie, telle fin.—As men live so they die. (Fr.)
Tel maître, tel valet.—Like master, like man. (Fr.)
Tel qui rit vendredi dimanche pleurera.—If you laugh to-day you will cry to-morrow. (Fr.)
Telum imbelle sine ictu.—A feeble weapon thrown without effect.
Tempora mutantur, nos et mutamur in illis.—The times are perpetually changing, and we with the times.
Tempus edax rerum.—Time that devours all things.
Tempus fugit, et nunquam revertitur.—Time flies, and never returns.
Tempus omnia revelat.—Time discloses all things.
Tenax propositi.—Firm of purpose. (M.)
Teres et rotundus.—Smooth and round.
Ter in die.—Thrice a day.
Terminus ad quem.—The goal or end.
Terminus a quo.—The starting point.
Terræ filius.—A son of the soil; a farm-labourer.
Terra incognita.—Unknown country.
Tertium quid.—A third something.
Tertius gaudens.—A third party reaping benefit from dissensions of others.
Tête-à-tête.—Face to face; a private conversation. (Fr.)
Tiens a la vérité.—Keep to the truth. (Fr.)
Tiens ta foy.—Preserve thy faith. (M.) (O.Fr.)
Tiers état.—The third estate; the Commons. (Fr.)
Timeo Danaos et dona ferentes.—I distrust the Greeks, even when they offer gifts.
Tirer le diable par la queue.—To pull the devil by the tail; to take the bull by the horns. (Fr.)
Toga virilis.—The gown of manhood.
Tombé des nues.—Fallen from the clouds. (Fr.)
Totidem verbis.—In just so many words.
Toties quoties.—As often as; just as many times as.
Totis viribus.—With all his strength.
Toto cœlo.—By the whole heavens: as wide as the poles asunder.
Toujours propice.—Ever propitious. (M.) (Fr.)
Tour de force.—A feat of strength or skill; a piece of virtuosity. (Fr.)
Tourner casaque.—To turn one's coat; to change sides. (Fr.)
Tous frais faits.—All costs paid. (Fr.)
Tout-à-fait.—Quite; altogether. (Fr.)
Tout bien ou rien.—The whole or nothing. (M.) (Fr.)
Tout court.—Briefly; shortly; in a word. (Fr.)
Tout ensemble.—The general effect. (Fr.)
Tout le monde est sage après coup.—It is easy to be wise after the event. (Fr.)
Tout vient à point à qui sait attendre.—All things come to him who waits. (Fr.)
Traduttore traditore.—A translator is a traitor. (It.)
Trahit sua quemque voluptas.—Every one is drawn by his own inclination.
Treu und Fest.—Faithful and Firm. (M. of 11th Hussars, Prince Albert's Own.) (Ger.)
Tria juncta in uno.—Three joined in one. (M. of the Order of the Bath.)
Trois temps.—A dance in three-four time. (Fr.)
Troja fuit.—Troy is no more.
Tua res agitur.—It is a matter that concerns you.
Tulit alter honores.—Another has carried off the honour.
Tu ne cede malis.—Yield not to misfortune.
Tu quoque !—You too ! (a retort in kind).
Tutte quanti.—Et cetera. (It.)

Ubi bene ibi patria.—Where it is well, there is our country.
Ubi jus incertum, ibi jus nullum.—Where the law is uncertain, there is no law.
Ubique.—Everywhere. (M. of the Royal Artillery and Royal Engineers.)
Ubi supra.—Where above mentioned.
Ultima ratio regum.—The last argument of kings, *i.e.*, war.
Ultima Thule.—The extreme limit (Thule being the most northerly land known to the Romans).
Ultimus Romanorum.—The last of the Romans.
Ultra vires.—Beyond the powers or rights possessed.
Unâ voce.—With one voice; unanimously.
Un bienfait n'est jamais perdu.—A kind act is never forgotten. (Fr.)
Und so weiter.—And so forth. (Ger.)

Une fois n'est pas coutume.—Once does not make a habit. (Fr.)
Unguibus et rostro.—With talons and beak.
Unione fortior.—Stronger by union. (M.)
Unum et idem.—One and the same.
Urbi et Orbi.—For Rome (lit., the city) and the world.
Usque ad aras.—To the very altars.
Usque ad nauseam.—To utter disgust.
Utile dulci.—The useful with the agreeable.
Ut infra.—As below.
Uti possidetis.—As you possess (used in Internat. Law of the principle that at the conclusion of hostilities territory, etc., under control of the belligerents vests in them unless otherwise stipulated).
Ut prosim.—That I may do good. (M.)
Ut quocunque paratus.—Prepared on every side. (M.)
Utrum horum navis accipe.—Take whichever you prefer.
Ut supra.—As above stated.

Vacuus cantat coram latrone viator.—The traveller who has an empty purse sings in the face of the robber.
Vade in pace.—Go in peace.
Vade mecum.—Anything—esp. diary or note-book —constantly carried. (L., Go with me.)
Vade retro!—Avaunt!
Væ victis!—Woe to the vanquished!
Vaille que vaille.—At all events. (Fr.)
Valeat quantum valere potest.—Let it pass for what it is worth.
Valete, ac plaudite.—Farewell, and applaud.
Vanitas vanitatum.—Vanity of vanities.
Variæ lectiones.—Variant readings (in a text).
Variorum notæ.—Notes by various annotators.
Vel exuviæ triumphant.—Even the remnant triumph. (M. of the Queen's Royal Regt., the West Surreys.)
Velis et remis.—With sails and oars.
Veluti in speculum.—As if in a mirror.
Vendre en gros et en détail.—To sell wholesale and retail. (Fr.)
Venire facias.—Compel him to appear; the writ for summoning a jury [Law].
Veni, vidi, vici.—I came, I saw, I conquered.
Ventis secundis.—With favouring winds.
Ventre affamé n'a point d'oreilles.—A hungry belly has no ears. (Fr.)
Ventre à terre.—At great speed, "flat out." (Fr., belly to ground.)
Verbatim et literatim.—Word for word, and letter for letter.
Verba volant, scripta manent.—Words fly away, writings remain.
Verbum sat sapienti.—A word is enough to a wise man.
Verein.—A society, company, or association. (Ger.)
Veritas parit odium.—Truth begets hatred.
Vérité sans peur.—Truth without fear. (M.) (Fr.)
Ver non semper viret.—Spring does not always flourish, or (as M. of the Vernons) Vernon always flourishes.
Vers de société.—Light familiar verse. (Fr.)
Vestigia nulla retrorsum.—There are no backward traces, or (as M. of the 5th Dragoon Guards), We never retreat.
Veteri frondescit honore.—May it flourish through its ancient honour. (M. of the Buffs.)
Vexata quæstio.—A much-debated question.
Via Lactea.—The Milky Way.
Via media.—A middle course.
Via trita, via tuta.—The beaten track is the safe path. (M.)
Vice.—In place of.
Vice versâ.—The terms being exchanged; the other way round.
Victis honos.—Honour of the conquered.
Victor ludorum.—A sports' champion.
Video meliora proboque, deteriora sequor.—I see and approve the better, and I follow the worse.
Vide ut supra.—See the preceding statement; see above.
Vi et armis.—By main force (lit., by force and arms).
Vincit amor patriæ.—The love of our country prevails.
Vincit qui patitur.—He who endures, conquers. (M.)
Vincit veritas.—Truth conquers. (M.)
Vires acquirit eundo.—She acquires strength in her progress (spoken of Fame).
Viret in æternum.—It will flourish for ever. (M. of the 13th Hussars.)
Virginibus puerisque.—To girls and boys.
Virtus invidiæ scopus.—Virtue is the mark of envy. (M.)
Virtus laudatur et alget.—Virtue is praised and is left to starve.
Virtus semper viridis.—Virtue is ever green.
Virtus sola nobilitat.—Virtue alone ennobles the man.
Virtute et fide.—By virtue and faith. (M.)
Virtuti nihil obstat et armis.—Nothing can resist valour and arms. (M.)
Virtuti non armis fido.—I trust to virtue and not to arms. (M.)
Virtutis amor.—The love of virtue. (M.)
Virtutis fortuna comes.—Fortune favours the brave. (M. of the Duke of Wellington's Regt.)
Vis inertiæ.—Inert property of matter.
Vis unita fortior.—Force united becomes more powerful. (M.)
Vitam impendere vero.—To consecrate his life to truth.
Vivâ voce.—By or with the living voice.
Vive la bagatelle.—Success to trifling. (Fr.)
Vive la république.—Long live the republic. (Fr.)
Vive le roi.—Long live the king. (Fr.)
Vivida vis animi.—The lively vigour of genius.
Vivit post funera virtus.—Virtue survives the grave. (M.)
Vix ea nostra voco.—I scarcely call these things our own. (M.)
Vixere fortes ante Agamemnona.—There were strong (or great) men living before Agamemnon.
Vix satis.—Scarcely enough.
Vogue la galère.—Here goes, whatever happens! (Fr., row on the galley!)
Voilà tout.—That's all. (Fr.)
Voilà une autre chose.—That's quite another matter. (Fr.)
Volenti non fit injuria.—No injustice is done to a consenting party.
Volksgenossen.—Comrades of the People (Nazi demagogic appelative for Nazis). (Ger.)
Volo non valeo.—I am willing but unable. (M.)
Vous venez à point nommé.—You come in the nick of time. (Fr.)
Vox et præterea nihil.—A voice and nothing more.
Vox faucibus hæsit.—The voice stuck in the throat.
Vox populi, vox Dei.—The voice of the people is the voice of God.
Vulgo.—Popularly.

Was ich nicht weiss, macht mich nicht heiss.—What I do not know does not affect me. (Ger.)
Was man nicht kann meiden, muss man willig leiden.—You must make the best of a bad business. (Ger.)
Wie gewonnen, so zerrinnen.—Lightly come; lightly go. (Ger.)

Zeitgeist.—The spirit of the times. (Ger.)
Zonam perdidit.—He has lost his purse.
Zonam solvere.—To unloose the virgin zone.
Zum Beispiel.—For example. (Ger.)

CUSTOMARY ABBREVIATIONS

A.—Acres; Acting; Adjutant; Anna (Ind. coin); Assistant; Associate.
A1.—First class.
A.A.—Anti-aircraft; Advertising Association; Architectural Association; Automobile Association.
A.A.A.—Amateur Athletic Association; Allied Artists' Association.
A.A.A.S.—American Association for the Advancement of Science.
A.A.C.—Amateur Athletic Club; Army Air Corps.
A.A.C.C.A.—Associate of the Association of Certified and Corporate Accountants.
A.A.G.—Assistant Adjutant General.
A.A.L.—American Air Lines (U.S.A.); Association of Assistant Librarians.
A.A.M.—Association of Assistant Mistresses.
A.A.M.C.—Australian Army Medical Corps.
A. & M.—Ancient and Modern (Hymns).
A. & S.H.—Argyll and Sutherland Highlanders.
A.A.O.C.—Anglo-American Oil Company.
a.a.r.—against all risks.
A.B.—Able-bodied seaman; Assistance Board.
A.B.A.—Swedish Airlines (*Aktiebolaget Aerotransport*); Amateur Boxing Association.
abb.—abbot; abbess.
abbr.—abbreviated.
A.B.C.—Aerated Bread Company; Argentine, Brazil, and Chile; Audit Bureau of Circulation [Newspapers]; Australian Broadcasting Corporation.
A.B.C.A.—Army Bureau of Current Affairs.
Abd.—Abdicated.
A.B.G.B.I.—Associated Booksellers of Great Britain and Ireland.
ab init.—From the beginning (L., *ab initio*).
abl.—ablative.
Abp.—Archbishop.
A.C.—Air Council; Army Corps; Army Council; Before Christ (L., *Ante Christum*).
A/C.—Aircraftman.
a.c.—alternating current [Elect.].
a/c—account [Comm.].
A.C.A.—Associate of the Institute of Chartered Accountants.
A.C.C.—Army Catering Corps; Association of Conservative Clubs.
acc.—accusative.
acct.—account.
A.C.F.—Art Collections Fund; *Automobile Club de France* [Fr.].
A.C.G.B.—Arts Council of Great Britain (*see* **C.E.M.A.**).
A.C.I.—Army Council Instruction.
A.C.I.I.—Associate of the Chartered Insurance Institute.
A.C.I.S.—Associate of the Chartered Institute of Secretaries.
A.-Comm.—Air-Commodore.
A.C.P.—Associate of the College of Preceptors; Association of Correctors of the Press.
A.C.S.—Additional Curates' Society.
A.C.T.—Association of Cine-Technicians.
A.C.U.—Ante-Cycle Union.
A.D.—In the Year of our Lord (L., *Anno Domini*).
a.d.—after date.
A.D.A.—Atomic Development Authority.
A.D.C.—Aide-de-camp; Amateur Dramatic Club: *and see* **R.A.D.C.**
A.D.G.B.—Air Defence of Great Britain.
adj.—adjective.
ad lib. or **ad libit.**—At pleasure.
A.D.M.—Annual Delegate Meeting.
Adm.—Admiral.
admr.—administrator.
admrx.—administratrix.
A.D.R.A.—Annual Diseases Research Association.
adv.—advice; advertisement; adverb.
Ad val.—According to value (L., *ad valorem*).
A.E.—Assistant Engineer.
A.E.C.—Atomic Energy Commission; Association for Education in Citizenship; Agricultural Executive Committee: *and see* **R.A.E.C.**
A.E.F.—Allied Expeditionary Force.
A.E.L.T.C.—All England Lawn Tennis Club.
A.E.R.A.—Associate Engraver of the Royal Academy.
Æt. or **Ætat.**—Aged (L., *ætatis*).
A.E.U.—Amalgamated Engineering Union.
A.F.—Admiral of the Fleet; *Air France* [Fr.].
A.F.A.—Amateur Football Association; Amateur Fencing Association.
A.F.C.—Air Force Cross.
A.F.L.A.—Association of Fire Loss Adjusters.
A.F.M.—Air Force Medal.
A.F. of L.—American Federation of Labor.
A.F.S.—Auxiliary Fire Service.
A.G.—Accountant General; Adjutant General; Agent General; Attorney General.
A.G.M.—Annual General Meeting.
A.H.—In the year of the Hegira, A.D. 622.
A.H.L.—Anglo-Hellenic League.
A.H.M.—Association of Headmasters; Association of Headmistresses.
A.H.R.G.B.—Association of Hotels and Restaurants of Great Britain.
A.I.—Anthropological Institute; Auctioneers' Institute; Artificial Insemination.
A.I.A.—Associate in Arts; Associate of the Institute of Actuaries; Association of International Accountants.
A.I.A.A.—Associate (Architect) of the Incorporated Association of Architects and Surveyors.
A.I.A.S.—Associate (Surveyor) of the Incorporated Association of Architects and Surveyors.
A.I.C.—Associate of the Institute of Chemistry.
A.I.D.—Artificial Insemination (by) Donor.
A.I.E.E.—American Institute of Electrical Engineers.
A.I.F.—Australian Imperial Force.
A.I.G.B.I.—Archæological Institute of Great Britain and Ireland.
A.I.H.—Artificial Insemination (by) Husband.
A.I.M.—African Inland Mission.
A.I.N.A.—Associate of the Institute of Naval Architects.
A.I.O.C.—Anglo-Iranian Oil Company (since 1954 the British Petroleum Co., Ltd.).
A.I.S.—Anglo-Italian Society.
A.K.C.—Associate of King's College.
A.L.—Aer Lingus (Irish Airways).
A.L.A.—Associate of the Library Association; American Library Association.
Ala.—Alabama.
Alas.—Alaska.
Ald.—Alderman.
Alg.—Algeria; **alg.**—algebra.
A.L.I.—Argyll Light Infantry.
A.L.I.I.—Italian Airways (*Aero Linea Italiane Internazionale*).
A.L.S.—Associate of the Linnean Society.
a.l.s.—autograph letter signed.
alt.—altitude.
Alta.—Alberta.
A.M.—Albert Medal; before noon (L., *ante meridiem*); in the year of the world (L., *anno mundi*).
A.M.A.—Assistant Masters' Association; Assistant Mistresses' Association.
A.M.C.—Association of Municipal Corporations.
A.M.D.G.—To the greater glory of God (L., *Ad majorem Dei gloriam*).
A.M.G.—Allied Military Government.
A.M.I.C.E.—Associate Member of the Institute of Civil Engineers.
A.M.I.M.E.—Associate Member of the Institution of Mining Engineers.
A.M.L.B.O.—Association of Master Lightermen and Barge Owners.
amp.—ampere.
A.M.S.H.—Association for Moral and Social Hygiene.
Amt.—Amount.
A.M.T.P.I.—Associate Member of the Town Planning Institute.
A.N.A.C.A.—Army, Navy, and Air Force Comforts Association.
anon.—anonymous; anonymously.
ans.—answer.
A.N.S.A.—The Italian press agency (*Agenzia Nationale Stampa Associata*).

A.N.Z.A.C.—Australian and New Zealand Army Corps.
A.O.—Army Order.
A.O.C.—Air Officer Commanding.
A.O.D.—Army Ordnance Department; Ancient Order of Druids.
A.O.E.R.—Army Officers' Emergency Reserve.
A.O.F.—Ancient Order of Foresters.
A.O.H.—Alliance of Honour.
A.O.P.—Association of Optical Practitioners.
A.O.U.—American Ornithologists' Union.
A.P.—Assistant Paymaster; Associated Press.
A.P.D.—Army Pay Department.
A.P.G.—Gresham Professor of Astronomy.
A.P.M.—Assistant Provost-Marshal.
apo.—apogee.
app.—appendix.
appro.—approbation.
Apr.—April.
A.P.S.—Aborigines Protection Society; Associate of the Pharmaceutical Society.
aq.—Distilled water (L., *aquarius*).
A.Q.M.G.—Assistant Quartermaster General.
Ar.—Arabic.
A.R.A.—Associate of the Royal Academy; Amateur Rowing Association.
A.R.A.M.—Associate of the Royal Academy of Music.
A.R.C.M.—Associate of the Royal College of Music.
A.R.C.O.—Associate of the Royal College of Organists.
A.R.C.S.—Associate of the Royal College of Science.
A.R.E.—Associate of the Royal Society of Painter-Etchers and Engravers.
A.R.H.A.—Associate of the Royal Hibernian Academy.
A.R.I.B.A.—Associate of the Royal Institute of British Architects.
Ariz.—Arizona.
Ark.—Arkansas.
A.R.P.—Air Raid Precautions.
A.R.P.C.—Anglo-Russian Parliamentary Committee.
A.R.P.S.—Associate of the Royal Photographic Society.
arr.—arrival; arrived.
A.R.S.A.—Associate of the Royal Scottish Academy.
A.R.S.M.—Associate of the Royal School of Mines.
A.R.S.W.—Associate of the Royal Scottish Society of Painters in Water-Colours.
Art.E.—Artificer Engineer.
A.R.W.S.—Associate of the Royal Society of Painters in Water-Colour.
A.S.—Assistant Surgeon; Anglo-Saxon.
A.S.A.—Amateur Swimming Association.
A.S.C.B.—Army Sports Control Board.
A.Sc.W.—Association of Scientific Workers.
ASDIC.—Allied Submarine-Detection Investigation Committee.
A.S.E.—Amalgamated—Associate of the—Society of Engineers; Army School of Education.
A.S.L.E.F.—Associated Society of Locomotive Engineers and Firemen.
ASLIB.—Association of Special Libraries and Information Bureaux.
A.S.L.P.—Amalgamated Society of Lithographic Printers.
Assce.—Assurance.
A.S.S.E.T.—Association of Supervisory Staffs and Engineering Technicians.
asst.—assistant.
A.S.U.—Amalgamated Stevedores' Union.
A.S.V.—Air [to] Surface Vessel (radar).
A.S.W.—Association of Scientific Workers.
A.T.A.—Air Transport Auxiliary.
A.T.C.—Air Training Corps.
A.T.S.—Auxiliary Territorial Service (women).
Att.-Gen.—Attorney-General.
at. wt.—atomic weight.
Å.U.—Ångstrom unit [Physics].
A.U.C.—From the building of the city (of Rome), 753 B.C. (L., *Ab urbe condita* or *Anno urbis conditæ*).
Aug.—August.
A.U.N.A.—Australian United Nations Association.
A.U.W.T.—Association of University Women Teachers.
A.V.—Artillery Volunteers; Authorized Version.
avdp., avoir.—avoirdupois.
A.W.—Assistant Warder.
A.W.B.—Agricultural Wages Board.
A.W.U.—Agricultural Workers' Union.

B.—Boatswain; Bye [Cricket].
B.A.—Bachelor of Arts; British Academy; British Association.
B.A.A.—British Archæological Association; British Astronomical Association.
B.A.A.S.—British Association for the Advancement of Science.
B.A.C.C.—Billiards Association Control Council.
B.A.E.A.—British Actors' Equity Guild.
B.A.G.S.—Buenos Aires & Great Southern (Rly.).
Bah.—Bahamas.
B.A.I.E.—British Association of Industrial Editors.
B.A.I.U.—British Association for International Understanding.
bal.—balance.
B. & F.B.S.—British and Foreign Bible Society.
B.A.O.—Bachelor of Obstetrics (L., *Baccalaureus Artis Obstetricæ*).
B.A.O.R.—British Army of Occupation of the Rhine.
B.A.R.—Browning automatic rifle.
bar.—barometer.
Bart.—Baronet.
Bart's.—St. Bartholomew's Hospital (London).
batt.—battalion.
B.B.A.—British Bankers' Association; British Beekeepers' Association.
B.B.B.C.—British Boxing Board of Control.
B.B.C.—British Broadcasting Corporation.
B.B.F.C.—British Board of Film Censors.
B.C.—Before Christ; British Columbia; British Council; Board of Control; Balkan Commission (U.N.).
B.C.A.—Birth Control Association.
B.C.C.—British Council of Churches.
B.Ch.—Bachelor of Surgery.
B.C.L.—Bachelor of Civil Law.
B.C.M.—British Commercial Monomark.
B.Com.—Bachelor of Commerce.
B.C.S.—Bengal Civil Service.
B.C.U.R.A.—British Coal Utilization Research Association.
B.D.—Bachelor of Divinity.
B.D.A.—British Dental Association.
B.D.D.A.—British Deaf and Dumb Association.
B.D.L.—British Drama League.
B.D.S.—Bachelor of Dental Surgery.
Bds.—Boards.
B.E.—Bill of Exchange.
B.E.A.—British East Africa; British Electricity Authority.
B.E.A.C.—British European Airways Corporation.
B.E.C.C.—British Empire Cancer Campaign.
Beds—Bedfordshire.
B.E.F.—British Expeditionary Force.
B.E.L.R.A.—British Empire Leprosy Relief Association.
B.E.M.—British Empire Medal.
B.Eng.—Bachelor of Engineering.
B.E.P.O.—British Empire Producers' Organization.
Berks—Berkshire.
B. ès L.—Bachelor of Literature (Fr., *Bachelier ès lettres*).
B.E.T.R.O.—British Export Trades Research Organization.
B.F.B.P.W.—British Federation of Business and Professional Women.
B.F.M.P.—British Federation of Master Printers.
B.F.U.W.—British Federation of University Women.
B.G.—Brigadier-General.
B.G.R.A.—British Greyhound Racing Association.
B.H.A.—British Homœopathic Association.
b.h.p.—brake horse-power.
B.H.Q.—Brigade Headquarters.
B.I.F.—British Industries Fair.
B.I.I.A.—British Institute of Industrial Art.
B.I.P.O.—British Institute of Public Opinion.
B.I.S.—Bank for International Settlements.
B.I.S.N.C.—British India Steam Navigation Company.
B.K.A.—Bee Keepers' Association.
B.L.—Bachelor of Law; British Legion.
b.l.—bill of lading.
B.Litt.—Bachelor of Literature.
B.LL. or LL.B.—Bachelor of Laws.
B.M.—Bachelor of Medicine; British Museum.
B.M.A.—British Medical Association.

B.M.B.—Broadcast Measurement Bur au (U.S.A.)
B.M.J.—British Medical Journal.
B.Mus.—Bachelor of Music.
Bn.—Baron.
B.N.C.—Brasenose College, Oxford.
B.O.—Board of Ordnance.
B.O.A.—British Optical Association; British Olympic Association.
B.O.A.C.—British Overseas Airways Corporation.
B. of E.—Bank of England.
Bomb.C.S.—Bombay Civil Service.
B.O.P.—Boys' Own Paper.
Bor.—Borough.
B.O.T.—Board of Trade.
B.O.U.—British Ornithologists' Union.
B.P.—British Pharmacopœia.
Bp.—Bishop.
b.p.—boiling-point; below proof (of spirits).
B.P.B.—Bank Pass Book; Bank Post Bill.
B.P.C.—British Petroleum Company (Ltd.).
B.P.S.—British Psychological Society.
B.R.—British Railways.
B.R.C.S.—British Red Cross Society.
bro.—brother: **Bros.**—brothers [Comm.].
B.R.P.R.A.—British Rubber Producers' Research Association.
b.s.—bill of sale.
B.S.A.—British South Africa; British Spiritualists' Association; Birmingham Small Arms (Co., Ltd.).
B.S.A.A.—British South American Airways; British School of Archæology, Athens.
B.Sc.—Bachelor of Science.
B.S.H.C.—British Social Hygiene Council.
B.S.S.—British Sailors' Society; British Standard Specification.
B.S.T.—British Summer Time.
Bt.—Baronet; **bt.**—bought.
B.T.C.—British Transport Commission; Bicycle Touring Club.
B.T.H.—British Thomson-Houston (Co., Ltd.).
B.Th.—Bachelor of Theology.
B.Th.U.—British Thermal Unit (*cf.* **B.T.U.**).
B.T.M.—British Trades Mission.
B.T.U.—Board of Trade Unit (*cf.* **B.Th.U.**).
B.U.A.V.—British Union for the Abolition of Vivisection.
Bucks—Buckinghamshire.
B.U.F.—British Union of Fascists.
B.U.P.—British United Press.
B.V.—Blessed Virgin.
B.V.M.—Blessed Virgin Mary.
B.W.G.—Birmingham Wire Gauge.
B.W.I.A.—British West Indian Airways.

C.—Cape; Centigrade; Chapter; Companion (of Order); Conservative [Polit.].
C, ct., cent.—A hundred.
C.A.—Chartered Accountant; Catholic Association; China Assocn.; Church Assocn.; Croquet Assocn.; Civil Aviation; Current Account.
ca.—About (L., *circa*).
C.A.B.—Citizen's Advice Bureau; Civil Aeronautics Board (U.S.A.)
C.A.B.W.—Central Agricultural Wages Board.
C.A.L.—Continental Air Lines (U.S.A.).
Cal.—California.
Cambs—Cambridgeshire.
c. & b.—caught and bowled [Cricket].
Canpac.—Canadian Pacific Railway.
Cantab.—of Cambridge (L., *Cantabrigiensis*).
Cantuar.—of Canterbury (L., *Cantuariensis*).
C.A.P.—Cash against Policy.
cap.—chapter; capital (letter).
Capt.—Captain.
car.—carat.
Card.—Cardinal.
C.A.R.E.—Cooperative for American Remittances to Europe.
Carliol.—of Carlisle (L., *Carliolensis*).
Cath.—Catholic; cathedral.
C.A.W.U.—Clerical and Administrators Workers' Union.
C.B.—Companion of the (Order of the) Bath; County Borough; Common Bench [Law]; Confined to barracks [Mil.].
C.B.C.—Canadian—Columbia (U.S.A.) Broadcasting Corporation.
C.B.E.—Commander of the (Order of the) British Empire.
C.B.S.—Columbia Broadcasting System; Confraternity of the Blessed Sacrament.
C.C.—Charity Commission; Common Council; County Court; County Council(lor); Chess Club; Cricket Club; Cycling Club.
c.c.—cubic centimetre.
C.C.A.—Consumers' Co-operative Association; County Councils' Association; Court of Criminal Appeal; Commission on Conventional Armaments (U.N.).
C.C.A.T.C.—Chinese Central Air Transport Corporation.
C.C.C.—Corpus Christi College; Central Criminal Court.
C.C.G.B.—Camping Club of Great Britain.
C.C.H.F.—Children's Country Holiday Fund.
C.C.S.—Casualty Clearing Station; Corporation of Certified Secretaries.
C.D.—Cavalry Depot; Civil Defence; Coast Defence; Christian Democrat(ic) [Polit.]; Contagious Diseases (Act).
C. de G.—*Croix de Guerre.* (Fr.)
C.D.L.—Canine Defence League.
C.D.V.—Carte de visite; Civil Defence Volunteers.
C.E.—Civil Engineer.
C.E.A.—Church Extension Association; Cinematograph Exhibitors' Association.
C.E.B.—Central Electricity Board.
C.E.E.S.—Church of England Educational Society.
C.E.G.—Catholic Evidence Guild.
Celt.—Celtic.
C.E.M.—College of Estate Management.
C.E.M.A.—Council for the Encouragement of Music and the Arts (superseded by A.C.G.B.).
C.E.M.S.—Church of England Men's Society.
cent.—centigrade; century.
Cert.A.I.B.—Certified Associate of the Institute of Bankers.
C.E.S.—Christian Evidence Society.
Cestr.—of Chester (L., *Cestrensis*),
C.E.T.S.—Church of England Temperance Society.
C.E.U.—Christian Endeavour Union; Co-operative Employees' Union.
C.E.W.C.—Council for Education in World Citizenship.
C.E.W.M.S.—Church of England Working Men's Society.
C.E.Z.M.S.—Church of England Zenana Missionary Society.
cf., conf.—compare.
C.F.—Chaplain to the Forces; Chaplain of the Fleet.
c.f.i.—cost, freight, insurance.
C.F.R.—Council on Foreign Relations.
C.G.—Coast Guard; Coldstream Guards; Consul-General.
cg.—centigramme.
C.G.H.—Cape of Good Hope.
C.G.(L.)I.—City and Guilds (of London) Institute.
C.G.M.—Conspicuous Gallantry Medal.
C.G.S.—Chief of the General Staff.
c.g.s.—centimetre-gramme-second.
C.G.T.—The "T.U.C." of France (*Confédération Générale du Travail*)
C.H.—Companion of Honour.
c.h.—central heating.
Ch.—Chaplain; Church.
chap.—chapter.
Chap.-Gen.—Chaplain-General.
Chas.—Charles.
Ch.B.—Bachelor of Surgery (L., *Chirurgiæ baccalaureus*).
Ch.Ch.—Christ Church (College, Oxford).
Ch.E.—Chief Engineer.
Ches.—Cheshire.
chmn.—chairman.
Ch.P.—Paymaster-in-Chief.
C.H.S.C.—Central Health Services Council.
C.H.W.—Chelsea Hospital for Women.
c.h.w.—constant hot water.
C.I.—Channel Islands; Chief Inspector; Chief Instructor; (Imperial Order of the) Crown of India.
C.I.A.—Corporation of Insurance Agents.
Cicestr.—of Chichester (L., *Cicestrensis*).
C.I.D.—Committee of Imperial Defence; Council of Industrial Design; Criminal Investigation Department.
C.I.E.—Companion of the (Order of the) Indian Empire.
c.i.f.—cost, insurance, freight.
C.I.G.S.—Chief of the Imperial General Staff.

C.-in-C.—Commander-in-Chief.
C.I.O.—Committee for Industrial Organizations (U.S.A.).
C.I.P.A.—Chartered Institute of Patent Agents.
C.I.S.—Chartered Institute of Secretaries.
C.I.V.—City of London Imperial Volunteers.
C.J.—Chief Justice.
cl.—centilitre.
C.L.B.—Central Land Board; Church Lad's Brigade.
cld.—cleared.
C.L.R.—Central London Railway; City of London Rifles; Common Law Reports.
C.L.S.—Central Library for Students.
C.M.—Common Metre; Master in Surgery (L., *Chirurgiæ Magister*); Certificated Master [Naut.].
cm.—centimetre.
C.M.A.—Cinema Managers' Association.
C.M.A.S.—Clergy Mutual Assurance Society.
C.M.B.—Central Midwives' Board; Coastal Motor Boat.
cmd.—command (paper).
C.M.G.—Companion of the (Order of) St. Michael and St. George.
C.M.P.—Corps of Military Police.
C.M.S.—Church Missionary Society.
C.M.U.A.—Commercial Motor Users' Association.
C.N.—Central News (Agency).
C.N.R.—Canadian National Railways; Civil Nursing Reserve.
C.O.—Commanding Officer; Commissioner for Oaths; Conscientious Objector; Crown Office; Central Office.
Co.—Company; county.
c/o—care of.
Cochl.—A spoonful [Pharm.].
C.O.D.—Cash on delivery; Concise Oxford Dictionary.
co-ed.—co-educational.
C. of E.—Church of England; Council of Europe.
C.O.I.—Central Office of Information.
Col.—Colonel.
coll.—college; colloquial.
Colo.—Colorado.
Col.-Sergt.—Colour-sergeant.
Com.—Commander; Commodore; Committee; Commonwealth; Communist [Polit.].
C.O.M.I.S.C.O.—Committee of the International Socialists' Conference.
Commy.—Commissary.
comp.—compositor; compound.
con.—Against.
conj.—conjunction.
Conn.—Connecticut.
Cons.—Conservative [Polit.]; Consul.
Consols.—Consolidated Annuities.
Co-op.—Co-operative (Stores, Society).
C.O.P.E.C.—Conference on Politics, Economics, and Citizenship.
Cor. Mem.—Corresponding Member.
Corn—Cornwall; **Corn.**—Cornish.
Corp.—Corporation.
Cor. Sec.—Corresponding Secretary.
C.O.S.—Charity Organisation Society (*see also* **F.W.A.**).
cos.—cosine.
cosec.—cosecant.
C.O.S.F.P.S.—Commons, Open Spaces, and Footpaths Preservation Society.
cot.—cotangent.
C.P.—Central Provinces (India); Cape Province (S. Africa); Clerk of the Peace; Communist Party; Co-operative Party; Congregation of the Passion.
C.p.—Charter-party.
c.p.—candle-power; carriage paid.
C.P.A.L.—Canadian Pacific Air Lines.
C.P.A.S.—Church Pastoral Aid Society.
C.P.G.B.—Communist Party of Great Britain.
C.P.O.—Chief Petty Officer [Nav.].
C.P.R.—Canadian Pacific Railway.
C.P.R.C.—Central Price Regulation Committee.
C.P.R.E.—Council for the Preservation of Rural England.
C.P.S.U.—Communist Party of the Soviet Union.
C.Q.M.S.—Company Quartermaster Sergeant.
C.R.—King Charles (L., *Carolus Rex*); Community of the Resurrection; Keeper of the Rolls (L., *Custos Rotulorum*).
Cr.—Credit; creditor.
C.R.A.—Corporation of Accountants.
C.R.F.—Cancer Research Fund.
C.R.H.—Chelsea Royal Hospital.
crim. con.—criminal conversation (obsolete legal term for adultery).
C.R.S.—Catholic Record Society.
C.S.—Chemical Society; Christian Science; Christian Scientist; Civil Service.
C.S.A. — Czechoslovak Airlines (*Československe Aerolinie*).
C.S.C.—Civil Service Commission; Conspicuous Service Cross.
C.S.C.A.—Civil Service Clerical Association.
C.S.I.—Companion of the (Order of the) Star of India.
C.S.M.—Company Sergeant-Major; Church of Scotland Mission.
C.S.M.M.G.—Chartered Society of Massage and Medical Gymnastics.
C.S.N.W.C.—Civil Service National Whitley Council.
C.S.O.—Central Statistical Office.
C.S.R.V.—Civil Service Rifle Volunteers.
C.S.S.A.—Civil Service Supply Association.
C.SS.R.—The Redemptorist Order (L., *Congregatio Sanctissimi Redemptoris*).
C.S.S.U.—Church Sunday School Union.
ct.—carat.
C.T.—Certified Teacher.
C.T.C.—Cyclists' Touring Club.
Ctee.—Committee.
ctl.—cental.
C.T.S.—Catholic Truth Society.
C.U.—Cambridge University; Church Union; Congregational Union; Customs Union.
C.U.A.C.—Cambridge University Athletic Club.
C.U.C.O.—Conservative and Unionist Central Office.
C.U.E.W.—Congregational Union of England and Wales.
C.U.G.B.—Catholic Union of Great Britain.
C.U.J.C.—Coal Utilization Joint Council.
C.U.K.T.—Carnegie United Kingdom Trust.
C.U.M.—Cambridge University Mission.
Cumb—Cumberland.
cum div.—With dividend (of stock, etc.).
cum. pref.—cumulative preference (shares).
C.U.M.S.—Cambridge University Musical Society.
C.U.P.—Cambridge University Press.
cur., curt.—current; this month.
C.V.O.—Commander of the Royal Victorian Order.
C.W.O.—Cash with order.
C.W.S.—Co-operative Wholesale Society.
cwt.—A hundredweight.
C.W.U.—Chemical Workers' Union.

d.—depot; deserted; discharged; dividend; a penny, or pence (L., *denarius*).
D.A.—Decimal Association; Draughtsmen's Association; Deputy Assistant; Diploma in Anæsthetics.
d.a.—days after date.
D.A.A.G.—Deputy Assistant Adjutant-General.
D.A.D.—Deputy Assistant Director [Mil.].
D.A.G.—Deputy Adjutant-General.
D.A.L.—Delta Air Line (U.S.A.).
D.A.Q.M.G.—Deputy Assistant Quartermaster-General.
D.A.R.—Daughters of the American Revolution.
D.A.W.S.—Director of Army Welfare Services.
D.B.E.—Dame of the Order of the British Empire.
D.B.S.T.—Double British Summer Time.
dbk.—drawback.
D.C.—District of Columbia; from the beginning [Mus.] (It., *Da capo*).
d.c.—direct current [Elect.].
D.C.C.—Diocesan Consistory Court.
D.C.H.—Diploma in Child Health.
D.Ch.O.—Diploma in Ophthalmic Surgery.
D.C.L.—Doctor of Civil Law.
D.C.L.I.—Duke of Cornwall's Light Infantry.
D.C.M.—Distinguished Conduct Medal.
D.C.O.—Duke of Cambridge's Own (Middlesex Regt.).
D.C.S.—Deputy Clerk of Session (Scotland).
D.C.V.O.—Dame Commander of the Royal Victorian Order.
D.D.—Doctor of Divinity.
D.D.A.—Dangerous Drugs Act.

D.D.L.—Danish Airlines (*Det Danske Luftfartselskab*).
D.D.S.—Doctor of Dental Surgery.
D.D.T.—the insecticide *D*ichloro-*D*iphenyl-*T*richloroethane.
Dec.—December; declination.
def.—deferred.
deg.—degree.
Del.—Delaware; He (or she) drew it (L., *delineavit*).
Dem.—Democrat (U.S.A. polit.).
D.E.M.S.—Defensively Equipped Merchant Ship.
Den.—Denmark.
dep.—deputy; depart(s).
dept.—department.
Derb.—Derbyshire.
Det. Insp.—Detective Inspector.
D.F.—Defender of the Faith; Dean of Faculty.
D.F.A.—Dairy Farmers' Association.
D.F.C.—Distinguished Flying Cross.
D.F.M.—Distinguished Flying Medal.
dft.—defendant; draft.
D.G.—By the grace of God (L., *Dei gratia*); Dragoon Guards.
dg.—decigramme.
D.G.A.A.—Distressed Gentlefolks' Aid Association.
D.G.O.—Diploma in Gynæcology and Obstetrics.
D.Hy.—Doctor of Hygiene.
D.I.A.—Design and Industries Association.
dial.—dialect.
D.I.C.(S.T.).—Diploma of the Imperial College (of Science and Technology).
D.I.H.—Deputy Inspector of Hospitals.
Dir.—Director.
dis.—discount.
dist.—district.
div.—dividend; division [Mil.]; divinity [Univ.].
D.L.—Deputy Lieutenant.
dl.—decilitre.
D.L.I.—Durham Light Infantry.
D.Lit.—Doctor of Literature (London).
D.Litt.—Doctor of Letters (Camb. and Aberdeen); Doctor of Literature (Oxon.).
D.L.O.—Dead Letter Office.
dm.—decimetre.
D.M.R.E.—Diploma in Medical Radiology and Electrology.
D.Mus.—Doctor of Music.
D.N.B.—Dictionary of National Biography.
D.N.L.—Norwegian Airlines (*Det Norges Luftfartstyre*).
D.O.—Diploma in Ophthalmology; Diplomate in Osteopathy.
do. (ditto).—The same.
Doc. Eng.—Doctor of Engineering.
D.Œ.—Diploma in Economics.
D. of Corn. L.I.—Duke of Cornwall's Light Infantry.
D.O.M.—*Dominus Omnium Magister* ("The Lord the Master of All"—motto of the Benedictine Order); *Deo Optimo Maximo* ("To God the Best and Greatest").
D.O.M.S.—Diploma in Ophthalmic Medicine and Surgery.
D.O.R.A.—Defence of the Realm Act.
D.Orth.—Diploma in Orthoptics.
D.O.T.—Department of Overseas Trade.
doz.—dozen.
D.P.—Displaced person(s); Democratic Party.
D.P.A.S.—Discharged Prisoners' Aid Society.
D.P.H.—Department of Public Health; Diploma in Public Health.
D.Pharm.—Doctor of Pharmacy.
D.Phil.—Doctor of Philosophy.
D.P.M.—Diploma in Psychological Medicine.
D.Pro.G.M.—Deputy Provincial Grand Master (Freemasonry).
dpt.—department.
D.Q.M.G.—Deputy Quartermaster-General.
Dr.—Debtor; Doctor; **dr.**—dram.
D.R.G.M.—German reg. trade-mark (*Deutsches-Reichsgebrauchsmuster*).
d.s.—days after sight.
D.Sc.—Doctor of Science.
D.S.C.—Distinguished Service Cross.
D.S.D.—Divisional Supply Depot [Mil.].
D.S.I.R.—Department of Scientific and Industrial Research.
D.S.M.—Distinguished Service Medal.
D.S.O.—(Companion of the) Distinguished Service Order.
d.s.p.—Died without issue (L., *decessit sine prole*).
D.S.Q.—Discharged to Sick Quarters.
D.S.Sc.—Diploma in Sanitary Science.
D.S.T.—Doctor of Sacred Theology; Double Summer Time.
D.T.—Doctor of Divinity (L., *Doctor theologiæ*).
D.T.H.—Diploma in Tropical Hygiene.
D.T.M.—Diploma in Tropical Medicine.
Dunelm.—of Durham (L., *Dunelmensis*).
Dur.—Durham.
Dut.—Dutch.
D.V.—God willing (L., *Deo volente*).
D.V.M.—Doctor of Veterinary Medicine (U.S.A.)-
D.W.R.—Duke of Wellington's Regiment.
dwt.—A pennyweight.
D.Y.—Dockyard.

E.—east.
E.A.—English Association; Esperanto Association.
E.A.A.L.—European and American Airways, Ltd.
E.A.L.—Eastern Air Lines (U.S.A.).
E. and O.E.—Errors and omissions excepted.
E.A.T.S.—Empire Air Training Scheme.
E.B.—Encyclopædia Britannica.
Eblan.—of Dublin (L., *Eblanensis*).
Ebor.—of York (L., *Eboracensis*).
E.C.—East Central (postal district); Electricity Commission; Episcopal Church; Executive Committee.
E.C.A.—Early Closing Association; Economic Co-operation Administration.
E.C.C.E.C. — Ecclesiastical Commissioners and Church Estates Commissioners.
E.C.C.I.—Executive Committee of the Communist International.
eccl., eccles.—ecclesiastical.
Ecclus.—Ecclesiasticus.
E.C.E.—Economic Commission for Europe.
E.C.G.C.—Empire Cotton-Growing Corporation.
E.C.I.T.O.—European Central Inland Transport Organization.
E.C.O.—European Coal Organization.
econ.—economics.
E.C.O.S.O.C.—Economic and Social Council (U.N.).
E.C.U.—English Church Union.
E.D.—Efficiency Decoration; Entertainment Duty; Estate Duties.
ed.—editor; edition.
E.D.D.—English Dialect Dictionary.
Edin.—Edinburgh.
edn.—edition.
E.D.S.—English Dialect Society.
EDVAC.—Electronic Discrete Variable Computer.
E.E.—Errors excepted.
E.E.C.E.—Emergency Economic Committee for Europe.
E.E.F.—Exchange Equalization Fund.
E.E.T.S.—Early English Text Society.
E.F.D.S.S.—English Folk Dance and Song Society.
e.g.—For example. (L., *exempli gratia.*)
E.G.M.—Empire Gallantry Medal.
e.h.p.—effective horse-power; electrical horse-power.
E.I.—East Indies.
E.I.B.(W.).—Export-Import Bank (of Washington).
E.I.C.—East India Company.
E.Ins.—Inspector of Machinery.
E.I.S.—Educational Institute of Scotland.
E.K.R.—East Kent Regiment.
E. long.—East longitude.
E.L.R.—East Lancashire Regiment.
E.L.U.—English Lacrosse Union.
E.M.B.—Empire Marketing Board.
e.m.f.—electromotive force.
E.M.I.C.—Emergency Maternity and Infant Care (Programme). (U.S.A.)
Emp.—Emperor; Empire; Empress.
E.M.U.—Electromagnetic unit(s).
enc.—enclosure.
Ency. Bibl.—Encyclopædia Biblica.
Ency. Brit.—Encyclopædia Britannica.
ENE.—east-north-east.
E.N.F.—Employers' National Federation.
Eng.—England.
engr.—engineer; engraver.
E.N.I.A.C.—Electronic Numerical Integrator and Computer.
E.N.S.A.—Entertainments National Service Association.

Ent. Sta. Hall.—Entered at Stationers' Hall.
Env. Ex. & Min. Plen.—Envoy Extraordinary and Minister Plenipotentiary.
Ep.—Epistle.
E.P.A.—Empire Parliamentary Association; Empire Press Agency.
E.P.D.—Excess Profits Duty.
E.P.N.S.—Electro-plated nickel silver; English Place Name Society.
E.P.T.—Excess Profits Tax.
E.P.U.—Empire Press Union.
Eq.—Equerry.
E.R.—East Riding.
E.R.A.—Engineer Rear-Admiral; Engine-Room Artificer [Nav.].
E.R.P.—European Recovery Programme.
E.R.U.—English Rugby Union.
ESE.—east-south-east.
Esq., Esqr.—Esquire.
E.S.R.—East Surrey Regt.
E.S.U.—English-Speaking Union; Electrostatic unit.
et al.—And other things (L., *et alia*); and other people (L., *et alii*); and elsewhere (L., *et alibi*).
etc., &c.—And so forth.
E.T.C.—Eastern Telegraph Company.
et. seq.—And the following.
E.T.U.—Electrical Trades Union.
E.U.B.—United States of Brazil (*Estados Unidos do Brasil*) [Port.].
E.U.P.—English Universities' Press.
E.W.S.—Emergency Water Supply.
ex.—example; exception.
ex cp.—ex coupon.
ex d.—ex dividend.
exec.—executor.
ex-lib.—From the books of . . . (on book-plates, etc.) (L., *ex-libris*).
Exon.—of Exeter (L., *Exoniensis*).
exor. or **exr.**—executor.
extrx.—executrix.
E.Y.R.—East Yorkshire Regiment.

F.—Fahrenheit; Fellow (of Society, etc.); frequency (Wire.); Friday.
F.A.—Football Association.
F.A.A.—Fleet Air Arm.
f.a.a.—free of all average [Comm.].
F.A.C.C.A.—Fellow of the Association of Certified and Corporate Acountants.
F.A.F.—Fresh Air Fund.
Fahr.—Fahrenheit.
F.A.I.—Fellow of the Auctioneers' and Estate Agents' Institute.
F.A.L.P.A.—Fellow of the Incorporated Society of Auctioneers and Landed Property Agents.
F.A.M.—Free and Accepted Mason.
F.A.M.A.—Argentine Air Lines (*Flota Aerea Mercante Argentina*).
F.A.N.Y.—First Aid Nursing Yeomanry.
F.A.O.—*See* **U.N.F.A.O.**
F.A.S.—Faculty of Architects and Surveyors; Federation of Atomic Scientists; Fellow of the Anthropological Society.
f.a.s.—free alongside ship [Comm.].
F.A.U.—Friends' Ambulance Unit.
F.B.A.—Fellow of the British Academy.
F.B.I.—Federation of British Industries; Federal Bureau of Investigation (U.S.A.).
F.B.O.A.—Fellow of the British Optical Association.
F.C.—Fire cock.
F.C.A.—Fellow of the Institute of Chartered Accountants.
F.C.F.C.—Free Church Federal Council.
F.C.I.I. — Fellow of the Chartered Insurance Institute.
F.C.I.S.—Fellow of the Chartered Institute of Secretaries.
F.C.P.—Fellow of the College of Preceptors.
fcp.—foolscap.
F.C.S.—Fellow of the Chemical Society.
f.c.s.—free of capture and seizure.
F.D.—Defender of the faith (L., *Fidei Defensor*).
F.E.A.—French Equatorial Africa.
Feb.—February.
fec.—He (or she) did it (L., *fecit*).
F.E.I.S.—Fellow of the Educational Institute of Scotland.
F.E.S.—Fellow of the Entomological Society; Food Education Society.
F.F.A.—Fellow of the Faculty of Actuaries (Scotland).
F.F.I.—Free from infection.
F.F.P.S.—Fellow of the Faculty of Physicians and Surgeons (Glasgow).
F.F.R.—Fellow of the Faculty of Radiologists.
f.g.a.—foreign general average [Insur.].
F.G.C.M.—Field General Court-Martial.
F.G.S.—Fellow of the Geological Society (London).
F.H.—Fire hydrant.
F.H.A.—Fellowship Holidays Association.
F.I.A.—Fellow of the Institute of Actuaries; Fellow of the Institute of Auctioneers.
F.I.A.A.—Fellow Architect Member of the Incorporated Association of Architects and Surveyors.
F.I.Arb.—Fellow of the Institute of Arbitrators.
F.I.A.S.—Fellow Surveyor Member of the Incorporated Association of Architects and Surveyors.
F.I.A.T.—The Ital. motor manufacturers, *Fabbrica Italiana Automobile, Torino.*
F.I.C.—Fellow of the Institute of Chemistry.
Fid. Def.—Defender of the Faith (L., *Fidei Defensor*).
F.I.D.E.—International Chess Federation (*Fédération Internationale des Echecs*).
F.I.D.O.—Fog Investigating Dispersal Operation.
F.I.Inst.—Fellow of the Imperial Institute.
F.Inst.P.—Fellow of the Institute of Physics.
F.I.J. — International Federation of Journalists (*Fédération Internationale des Journalistes*).
F.I.N.A.—Fellow of the Institute of Naval Architects.
F.I.O.—Fellow of the Institute of Opticians.
F.I.R.E.—Fellow of the Institute of Radio Engineers.
F.J.I.—Fellow of the Institute of Journalists.
fl. or **flor.**—(he *or* she) flourished (L., *floruit*).
F.L.A.—Fellow of the Library Association.
Fla.—Florida.
F.L.A.S.—Fellow of the Land Agents' Society.
F.L.G.A.—Fellow of the Local Government Association.
F.L.S.—Fellow of the Linnæan Society.
F.-L.S.—Folk-Lore Society.
F.M.—Field-Marshal; frequency modulation [Wire.].
F.M.S.—Federated Malay States; Fellow of the Medical Society.
F.O.—Field Officer; Flag Officer; Flying Officer; Foreign Office.
fo., fol.—folio.
f.o.b.—free on board [Comm.].
F.O.C.—Fire Offices' Committee.
f.o.r.—free on rail [Comm.].
F.P.—Fire-plug.
F.P.A.—Family Planning Association; Foreign Press Association.
f.p.a.—free of particular average [Insur.].
f.p.m.—feet per minute.
F.P.R.L.—Forest Products Research Laboratory.
F.P.S.—Fellow of the Pathological Society; Fellow of the Pharmaceutical Soc.; Fellow of the Philharmonic Soc.; Fellow of the Philological Soc.; Fellow of the Philosophical Soc.; Fellow of the Physical Soc.
Fr.—France; French.
F.R.Ae.S.—Fellow of the Royal Aeronautical Society.
F.R.A.I.—Fellow of the Royal Anthropological Institute.
F.R.A.M.—Fellow of the Royal Academy of Music.
F.R.A.S.—Fellow of the Royal Astronomical Society.
F.R.C.I.—Fellow of the Royal Colonial Institute.
F.R.C.M.—Fellow of the Royal College of Music.
F.R.C.O.—Fellow of the Royal College of Organists.
F.R.C.O.G.—Fellow of the Royal College of Obstetricians and Gynæcologists.
F.R.C.P.—Fellow of the Royal College of Physicians.
F.R.C.P.Ed.—Fellow of the Royal College of Physicians of Edinburgh.
F.R.C.S.—Fellow of the Royal College of Surgeons.
F.R.C.S.Ed.—Fellow of the Royal College of Surgeons of Edinburgh.
F.R.C.S.I.—Fellow of the Royal College of Surgeons of Ireland.
F.R.C.V.S.—Fellow of the Royal College of Veterinary Surgeons.
F.R.D.I.—Faculty of Royal Designers for Industry.

F.R.Econ.S.—Fellow of the Royal Economic Society.
F.R.E.S.—Fellow of the Royal Empire Society; Fellow of the Royal Entomological Society.
F.R.G.S.—Fellow of the Royal Geographical Society.
F.R.Hist.S.—Fellow of the Royal Historical Society.
F.R.H.S.—Fellow of the Royal Horticultural Society.
F.R.I.B.A.—Fellow of the Royal Institute of British Architects.
F.R.I.C.—Fellow of the Royal Institute of Chemistry.
F.R.I.C.S.—Fellow of the Royal Institute of Chartered Surveyors.
F.R.Met.S.—Fellow of the Royal Meteorological Society.
F.R.M.S.—Fellow of the Royal Microscopical Society.
F.R.P.S.L.—Fellow of the Royal Philatelic Society of London.
F.R.S.—Fellow of the Royal Society.
F.R.S.A.—Fellow of the Royal Society of Arts.
F.R.S.Ed.—Fellow of the Royal Society of Edinburgh.
F.R.S.G.S.—Fellow of the Royal Scottish Geographical Society.
F.R.S.L.—Fellow of the Royal Society of Literature.
F.R.S.S.—Fellow of the Royal Statistical Society.
F.R.U.I.—Fellow of the Royal University of Ireland.
F.S.—Fabian Society; Faraday Soc.; Friendly Soc.
F.S.A.—Fellow of the Society of Antiquaries; **— Scot.** —of Scotland.
F.S.A.A.—Fellow of the Society of Incorporated Accountants and Auditors.
F.S.E.—Fellow of Society of Engineers.
F.S.I.—Fellow of the (Chartered) Surveyors' Institution.
F.S.M.A.—Fellow of the Incorporated Sales Managers' Association.
F.S.M.C.—Fellow of the Worshipful Company of Spectacle Makers.
F.S.N.A.—Fellow of the Society of Naval Architects.
F.S.R.—Field Service Regulations [Mil.].
F.S.S.U.—Federated Superannuation Scheme for Universities.
ft.—fort; **ft.**—feet; foot.
F.T.C.D.—Fellow of Trinity College, Dublin.
Fth.—Fathom.
F.T.U.—Federation of Trade Unions.
F.U.W.—Federation of University Women.
F.V.A.—Fellow of the Valuers' Association.
F.W.A.—Family Welfare Association (late C.O.S.).
F.Z.S.—Fellow of the Zoological Society (of London).

g.—gramme; gallon.
G.A.—General Assembly (Ch. of Scot., U.N., etc.).
Ga.—Georgia.
Gael.—Gaelic.
gal.—gallon.
G.A.T.T.—General Agreement on Tariffs and Trade.
G.B.—Great Britain; Gaumont British (Cine.).
G.B. and N.I.—Great Britain and Northern Ireland.
G.B.E.—Knight (or Dame) Grand Cross of the (Order of the) British Empire.
G.C.—George Cross; Good Conduct (Badge); Group Captain (R.A.F.).
G.C.A.—Ground Controlled Approach (Av.).
G.C. & T.P.A.—Garden Cities and Town Planning Association.
G.C.B.—Knight Grand Cross of the (Order of the) Bath.
g.c.f.—greatest common factor.
G.C.I.E.—Knight Grand Commander of the (Order of the) Indian Empire.
G.C.L.H.—Grand Cross of the Legion of Honour.
G.C.L.O.—German Civilian Labour Organization.
G.C.M.—General Court-Martial.
g.c.m.—greatest common measure.
G.C.M.G.—Knight Grand Cross of the (Order of) St. Michael and St. George.
G.C.S.I.—Knight Grand Commander of the (Order of the) Star of India.
G.C.V.O.—Knight Grand Cross of the Royal Victorian Order.
G.E.C.—General Electric Company.
Gen.—General.
Genmo.—Generalissimo.
Gent.—Gentleman.
Geo.—George.
G.F.S.—Girls' Friendly Society.
G.F.T.U.—General Federation of Trade Unions.
G.G.—Grenadier Guards.
G.G.A.—Girl Guides' Association.
G.H.—Green Howards (Princess of Wales' Own Yorkshire Regt.).
G.H.Q.—General Headquarters [Mil.].
G.I.—Government issue (U.S.A.); a United States private soldier [Coll.].
G.I.O.—Guild of Insurance Officials.
G.L.—Grand Lodge [Freemasonry].
Glam—Glamorganshire.
G.L.B.—Girls' Life Brigade.
G.L.E.E.P.—Graphite low energy experimental pile (first British atomic pile).
Glos—Gloucestershire.
G.L.S.—Gypsy Lore Society.
G.M. — George Medal; Gold Medallist; General Manager; General Motors; Grand Master [Freemasonry].
G.M.C.—General Medical Council.
G.M.P.—Garrison Military Police.
G.M.T.—Greenwich Mean Time.
G.O.—General Order.
G.O.C.—General Officer Commanding.
G.O.M.—Grand Old Man.
Gov.—Governor.
Gov.-Gen.—Governor-General.
Govt.—Government.
G.P.—General practitioner [Med.]; Graduate in Pharmacy.
G.P.D.S.T.—Girls' Public Day School Trust.
g.p.h.—gallons per hour.
G.P.I.—General Paralysis of the Insane.
G.P.O.—General Post Office.
G.P.R.—Glider Pilot Regiment.
gr.—grains; gross; gunner.
G.R.(I.)—George, King (and Emperor) (L., *Georgius Rex [et Imperator]*).
G.R.A.—Greyhound Racing Association.
G.R.C.M.—Graduate of the Royal College of Music.
G.R.E.—Graves' Registration and Enquiries [Mil.].
G.S.—General Staff [Milit.]; Grand Secretary; General Secretary; Gold Standard; Geographical Society; Geological Society.
G.S.G.B.—Geological Survey of Great Britain.
G.S.M.—Guildhall School of Music.
G.S.N.C.—General Steam Navigation Company.
G.S.O.—General Staff Officer.
G.T.—Good Templar; Grand Tyler; Grand Treasurer (Freemasonry).
gtt.—Drops (L., *guttæ*).
G.W.—Grand Warden.
G.W.R.—Great Western Railway.
gym.—gymnasium; gymnastics.

H.—Hydrant.
ha.—hectare.
H.A.—Heavy Artillery; Horse Artillery; Headmistresses' Assoc.; Historical Assoc.; Hockey Assoc.
H.A.A.—Heavy Anti-aircraft.
H.A.C.—Honourable Artillery Company.
h. & c.—hot and cold (water).
Hants—Hampshire.
H.B.C.—Hudson's Bay Company.
H.B.M.—His (or Her) Britannic Majesty.
H.C.—House of Commons; High Commissioner; High Court; Herald's College; Headmasters' Conference; Hockey Club; Hunterian Club.
h.c.f.—highest common factor [Math.].
H.C.M.—His (or Her) Catholic Majesty.
H.D.A.—Hydrographic Department, Admiralty.
hdqrs.—headquarters.
H.E.—His Excellency; high explosive.
H.E.B.—Hydro-Electric Board.
H.E.I.C.S.—Honourable East India Company's Service.
Herefs—Herefordshire.
Herts—Hertfordshire.
h.f.—high frequency [Elect.].
hf.-bd.—half-bound.
H-F.D.F.—High-frequency direction finder (Av.).
H.F.M.R.A.—Honorary Foreign Member of the Royal Academy.
H.G.—Home Guard; High German.
H.G.D.H.—His (or Her) Grand Ducal Highness.
H.G.F.G.B.—Henry George Foundation of Great Britain.

H.H.—His Holiness; His (or Her) Highness.
hhd.—hogshead.
H.I.A.C.—Herring Industry Advisory Council.
H.I.H.—His (or Her) Imperial Highness.
Hil.—Hilary term.
H.I.M.—His (or Her) Imperial Majesty.
H.J.S.—Here lies buried (L., *hic jacet sepultus*).
H.K.—House of Keys.
H.L.—House of Lords.
hl.—hectolitre.
H.L.I.—Highland Light Infantry.
H.L.P.R.—Howard League for Penal Reform.
H.M.—His (or Her) Majesty.
H.M.A.—Headmasters' Association.
H.M.A.S.—His (or Her) Majesty's Australian Ship.
H.M.C.—His (or Her) Majesty's Customs; Headmasters' Conference.
H.M.C.S.—His (or Her) Majesty's Canadian Ship.
H.M.F.—His (or Her) Majesty's Forces.
H.M.I.S.—His (or Her) Majesty's Inspector of Schools.
H.M.O.W.—His (or Her) Majesty's Office of Works.
H.M.P.—Raised this monument (L., *hoc monumentum posuit*).
H.M.S.—His (or Her) Majesty's Ship; His (or Her) Majesty's Service.
H.M.S.O.—His (or Her) Majesty's Stationery Office.
H.O.—Home Office; Head Office.
Hon.—Honourable; Honorary.
Hon. Sec., Treas.—Honorary Secretary, Treasurer.
H.P.—Houses of Parliament; House Physician.
h.p.—half-pay; hire purchase; horse-power; high pressure.
H.Q.—Headquarters [Mil.].
H.R.—House of Representatives.
hr.—hour.
H.R.A.—Hotels and Restaurants Association.
H.R.E.—Holy Roman Empire.
H.R.H.—His (or Her) Royal Highness; Home of Rest for Horses.
H.S.—Haldane Society; House Surgeon; Hunterian Society.
H.S.A.—Hospital Savings Association.
H.S.C.—Higher School Certificate; Honourable Society of Cymmrodorion.
H.S.E.—Here is buried (L., *hic sepultus est*).
H.S.H.—His (or Her) Serene Highness.
h.t.—high tension [Elect.].
H.T.A.—Horticultural Trades Association.
H.U.—Harvard University.
Hunts—Huntingdonshire.
H.W.M.—High Water Mark.
H.W.O.S.T.—High Water, Ordinary Spring Tides.
hy(g).—hygiene.

I.—Emperor, Empress (L., *Imperator, Imperatrix*); Imperial; Institute; Institution; Island.
I.A.—Indian Army; Institute of Actuaries.
Ia.—Iowa.
I.A.A.—Incorporated Accountants and Auditors.
I.A.A.M.—Incorporated Association of Assistant Masters.
I.A.A.S.—Incorporated Association of Architects and Surveyors.
I.A.E.—Institute of Automobile Engineers; Institute of Agricultural Engineering.
I.A.H.M.—Incorporated Association of Head Masters.
I.A.L.—International Arbitration League.
I.A.M.A.—Incorporated Advertising Managers' Association.
I.A.P.U.L.—International Association of University Professors and Lecturers.
I.A.R.O.—Indian Army Reserve of Officers.
I.A.S.—Indicated air-speed; Incorporated Association of Surveyors.
I.A.T.A.—International Air Transport Association.
I.A.W.E.C.—International Association of Women for Equal Citizenship.
I.B.—*See* **I.B.R.D.**
Ib. or **ibid.**—In the same place (L., *ibidem*).
I.B.A.U.—Institute of British-American Understanding.
I.B.I.A.—Institute of British Industrial Art.
I.B.R.D.—International Bank for Reconstruction and Development.
I.B.S.A.—International Bible Students' Association.
I.C.—Jesus Christ (L., *Iesus Christus*); Intelligence Corps; Internal Combustion (Engine).
I.C.A.—Institute of Chartered Accountants; Institute of Company Accountants; Institute of Contemporary Arts; International Co-operative Alliance.
I.C.A.O.—International Civil Aviation Organization.
I.C.E.—Institution of Chemical Engineers; Institution of Civil Engineers.
I.C.E.F. — International Children's Emergency Fund.
I.C.F.—Industrial Christian Fellowship.
I.C.F.T.U.—International Confederation of Free Trade Unions.
I.Chem.E.—Institution of Chemical Engineers.
I.C.I.—Imperial Chemical Industries.
I.C.J.—International Court of Justice.
I.C.O.—Institute of Chemist-Opticians.
I.C.R.F.—Imperial Cancer Research Fund.
I.C.S.—Indian Civil Service; Imperial College of Science; International Correspondence Schools.
I.C.S.U.—International Council of Scientific Unions.
I.D.—Intelligence Department.
id.—The same (L. *idem*).
Ida.—Idaho.
I.D.B.—Illicit diamond buying (or buyer).
I.D.C.—International Danube Commission.
i.d.c.—Graduate of Imperial Defence College.
i.e.—That is (L. *id est*).
I.E.E.—Institution of Electrical Engineers.
I.E.F.C.—International Emergency Food Council.
I.F.—*See* **I.M.F.**
I.F.A.P.—International Federation of Agricultural Producers.
I.F.F.J.—International Federation of Free Journalists.
I.F.L.—International Fellowship League.
I.F.S.—Irish Free State (*obsolete*).
I.F.U.W.—International Federation of University Women.
I.G.—Inspector General; Irish Guards.
I.G.C.R.—Inter-Governmental Committee on Refugees.
I.G.E.—Institution of Gas Engineers.
I.H.A.—Institute of Hospital Almoners.
i.h.p.—indicated horse-power.
IHS—Jesus. (The monogram represents the abbreviation of the Greek name—ΙΗΣΟΥΣ.)
I.H.S.—Jesus the Saviour of Men (L., *Iesus Hominum Salvator*).
i.h.s.—By this sign (L., *in hoc signo.*)
I.H.V.E.—Institute of Heating and Ventilating Engineers.
I.I.—Imperial Institute.
I.I.A.—Institute of Industrial Administration.
I.I.P.A.—Institute of Incorporated Practitioners in Advertising.
I.I.T.—Institute of Industrial Technicians.
I.L.A.—International Law Association.
I.L.H.—Imperial Light Horse.
Ill.—Illinois.
I.L.O.—International Labour Office; International Labour Organization.
I.Loco.E.—Institute of Locomotive Engineers.
I.L.P.—Independent Labour Party.
I.L.S.—Irish Literary Society; Instrument Landing System (Av.).
I.M.A.—Irish Medical Association.
I.M.C.B.—International Mine Clearance Board.
I.M.C.E.—Institution of Municipal and County Engineers.
I.M.D.—Indian Medical Department.
I.Mech.E.—Institution of Mechanical Engineers.
I.M.F.—International Monetary Fund.
I.Min.E.—Institute of Mining Engineers.
I.M.N.S.—Imperial Military Nursing Service; Indian Military Nursing Service.
imp.—imperial.
Imp.Inst.—Imperial Institute.
I.M.S.G.—Imperial Merchant Service Guild.
I.M.T.A.—Institute of Municipal Treasurers and Accountants.
in.—inches.
I.N.A.—Institution of Naval Architects.
I.N.C.—Indian National Congress.
Inc.—Incorporated (U.S.A.).
incog.—With concealed identity; in secret (It., *incognito*).
Ind.—Indiana.
Ind. Meth.—Independent Methodist.
infra dig.—Beneath one's dignity (L., *infra dignitatem*).

in lim.—At the outset (L., *in limine*, on the threshold).
in loc.—In its place (L., *in loco*).
I.N.R.I.—Jesus of Nazareth, King of the Jews (L., *Iesus Nazarenus Rex Iudæorum*).
I.N.S.—International News Service.
I.N.S.T.—In the Name of the Holy Trinity (L., *In Nomine Sanctæ Trinitatis*).
inst.—instant (the present month); institute; institution.
Inst.Act.—Institute of Actuaries.
Inst.C.E.—Institution of Civil Engineers.
Inst.E.E.—Institution of Electrical Engineers.
Inst.Gas E.—Institution of Gas Engineers.
Inst.M.E.—Institute of Marine Engineers.
Inst.Mech.E.—Institution of Mechanical Engineers.
Inst.Met.—Institute of Metals.
Inst.M.M.—Institute of Mining and Metallurgy.
Inst.N.A.—Institution of Naval Architects.
Inst.T.—Institute of Transport.
int.—interest; interjection.
inv.—invoice.
I.O.A.E.—Institution of Automobile Engineers.
I.O.E.—Institution of Electronics.
I.O.F.—Independent Order of Foresters; Institute of Fuel.
I. of A.—Instructor of Artillery.
I. of M.—Isle of Man; Instructor of Musketry.
I.O.G.T.—International Order of Good Templars.
I.O.J.—Institute of Journalists; International Organization of Journalists.
I.O.O.—Inspecting Ordnance Officer; Institute of Ophthalmic Opticians.
I.O.O.F.—Independent Order of Oddfellows.
I.O.P.—Institute of Painters in Oil Colours.
I.O.R.—Independent Order of Rechabites.
I.O.U.—I owe you.
I.O.W.—Isle of Wight.
I.P.A.—Imperial Pale Ale; India Pale Ale; *see also* **I.I.P.A.**
I.P.C.S.—Institution of Professional Civil Servants.
I.Q.—Intelligence Quotient.
i.q.—The same as (L., *idem quod*).
I.R.—Inland Revenue.
I.R.A.—Irish Republican Army.
Iran.—Iranian.
I.R.C.—International Red Cross.
I.R.O.—Inland Revenue Office; International Refugee Organization.
I.S.A.—Incorporated Secretaries' Association.
I.S.A.L.P.A.—Incorporated Society of Auctioneers and Landed Property Agents.
I.S.C.—Indian Staff Corps.
I.S.F.—International Shipping Federation.
I.S.I.—Iron and Steel Industry.
I.S.M.—Imperial Service Medal; Incorporated Society of Musicians.
I.S.M.A.—Incorporated Sales Managers' Association.
I.S.O.—Imperial Service Order.
I.S.S.—International Student Service.
I.S.T.M.—Incorporated Society of Trained Masseurs.
I.S.W.G.—Imperial Standard Wire Gauge.
I.T.F.—International Trade Fair.
I.T.O.—International Trade Organization.
I.T.U.—International Telecommunications Union.
I.W.—Isle of Wight.
I.W.G.C.—Imperial War Graves Commission.
I.W.T.—Institute of Wireless Technology.
I.W.T.(D.).—Inland Water Transport (Department).
I.W.W.—Industrial Workers of the World (U.S.A.).
I.Y.—Imperial Yeomanry.

J.—Jew; Jewish; (after name of Judge) Justice.
J.A.—Judge Advocate.
J.A.G.—Judge Advocate-General.
Jan.—January.
J.B.G.—Jewish Board of Guardians.
J.C.D.—Doctor of Canon Law; Doctor of Civil Law (L., *Juris Canonici* (*Civilis*) *Doctor*).
J.H.U.—Johns Hopkins University (U.S.A.).
J.I.C.—Joint Industrial Council.
J.L.B.—Jewish Lads' Brigade.
Jno.—John.
jnr.—junior.
Jo'burg.—Johannesburg [Coll.].
J.P.—Justice of the Peace.
jt.—joint.
J.U.D.—Doctor of both (*i.e.* Canon and Civil) Laws (L., *Juris utriusque Doctor*).
Jul.—July.
jun., junr.—junior.
J.W.—Junior Warden [Freemasonry].
J.W.B.—Joint Wages Board.

K.—King (monarch, cards, chess).
Kan.—Kansas.
K.B.(D.).—King's Bench (Division).
K.B.E.—Knight Commander of the (Order of the) British Empire.
K.C.—King's Counsel; King's College.
K.C.B.—Knight Commander of the (Order of the) Bath.
K.C.I.E.—Knight Commander of the (Order of the) Indian Empire.
K.C.M.G.—Knight Commander of the (Order of) St. Michael and St. George.
K.C.S.I.—Knight Commander of the (Order of the) Star of India.
K.C.V.O.—Knight Commander of the Royal Victorian Order.
K.D.G.—King's Dragoon Guards.
K.G.—Knight of the (Order of the) Garter.
kg.—kilogramme.
K.G.F.—Knight of the Golden Fleece.
K.H.C.—Honorary Chaplain to the King.
K.H.P.—Honorary Physician to the King.
K.H.S.—Honorary Surgeon to the King; Knight of the Holy Sepulchre.
K.i.H.—Kaisar-i-Hind (Indian medal).
kil.—kilderkin.
K.K.K.—Ku Klux Klan (U.S.A.).
K.L.H.—Knight of the Legion of Honour.
K.L.M. — Royal Dutch Airlines (*Koninklijke Luchtvaart Maatschappij*).
km.—kilometre
K.N.I.L.M.—Royal Dutch East Indies Airlines (*Koninklijke Nederlandsch-Indie Luchtvaart Maatschappij*).
Knt. (**Bach.**)—Knight (Bachelor).
k.o.—knock-out [Boxing].
K.O.S.B.—King's Own Scottish Borderers.
K.O.Y.L.I.—King's Own Yorkshire Light Infantry.
K.P.—Knight of St. Patrick.
K.R.R.(C.).—King's Royal Rifle(s) (Corps).
K.S.—King's Scholar.
K.T.—Knight of the Thistle.
Kt.—Knight Bachelor; knight (Chess).
k.t.l.—And so forth (Gr., *kai ta loipa*, and the rest).
Ky.—Kentucky.

L—Roman numeral for fifty.
L.—Lake; Latin; Liberal [Polit.]; Licentiate; £.
£—Pound(s) sterling.
£A.—Pound(s) Australian.
L.A.—Law Agent; Library Association; Literate in Arts; Legislative Assembly.
La.—Louisiana.
Lab.—Labour [Polit.]; Labrador.
L.A.C.—London Athletic Club; Leading Air-craftsman; Licentiate of the Apothecaries' Company.
L.A.I.—Italian Air Lines (*Linee Aeree Italiane*).
L.A.M.—London Academy of Music.
Lancs—Lancashire.
L.A.S.—Land Agents' Society.
L.A.T.—Local Appeal Tribunal.
Lat.—Latin; **lat.**—latitude.
l.b.—leg bye [Cricket].
lb.—A pound (or pounds) weight (L., *libra*).
l.b.w.—Leg before wicket [Cricket].
L.C.—Lord Chancellor; left centre (of stage).
l.c.—In the place quoted (L., *loco citato*); lower-case type.
L.C.B.—Lord Chief Baron.
L.C.C.—London County Council; London Chamber of Commerce.
L.C.J.—Lord Chief Justice.
L.C.M.—London College of Music; **l.c.m.**—least common multiple.
L.C.P.—Licentiate of the College of Preceptors.
L.-Cpl.—Lance-corporal.
L.C.S.—London Co-operative Society.
L.D.F.—Local Defence Force.
L.D.S.—Licentiate in Dental Surgery.
L.E.A.—Local Education Authority.
Leics.—Leicestershire.
L. ès L.—Licentiate of Letters (Fr., *Licencié ès lettres.*)

l.f.—low frequency [Elect.].
L.F.P.S.G.—Licentiate of the Faculty of Physicians and Surgeons, Glasgow.
L.G.—Lady of (the Order of) the Garter; Life Guards.
L.H.A.—Local Health Authority.
L.I.—Light Infantry; Long Island (U.S.A.).
Lieut.—Lieutenant.
Lincs—Lincolnshire.
Linn.—Linnæan.
lit.—literally; literature.
Lit. Hum.—Final Classical Honours School, Oxon. (L., *Literæ Humaniores*, Humane letters).
Litt.B.—Bachelor of Literature.
Litt.D.—Doctor of Literature.
L.J.—Lord Justice (of Appeal).
L.L.—Lord Lieutenant.
L.L.A.—Lady Literate in Arts (St. Andrews Univ.); Lend-Lease Administration.
LL.B.—Bachelor of Laws.
LL.D.—Doctor of Laws.
LL.M.—Master of Laws (L., *Legum Magister*).
L.M.—Licentiate in Midwifery; long metre [Mus.]; Lord Mayor.
L.M.S.—London Missionary Society.
L.M.S.R.—London, Midland and Scottish Railway.
L.M.S.S.A.—Licentiate of the Society of Apothecaries in Medicine and Surgery.
L.N.E.R.—London and North Eastern Railway.
loc. cit.—In the place cited (L., *loco citato*).
L. of C.—Line of Communication.
log.—logarithm.
lon., long.—longitude.
Londin.—London (L., *Londinium*).
loq.—He (or she) speaks (L., *loquitur*).
L.P.—Lord Provost.
L.P.O.—London Philharmonic Orchestra.
L.P.T.B.—London Passenger Transport Board.
L.R.A.M.—Licentiate of the Royal Academy of Music.
L.R.C.M.—Licentiate of the Royal College of Music.
L.R.C.P.—Licentiate of the Royal College of Physicians.
L.R.C.P.Ed.—Licentiate of the Royal College of Physicians, Edinburgh.
L.R.C.S.Ed.—Licentiate of the Royal College of Surgeons, Edinburgh.
L.R.C.V.S.—Licentiate of the Royal College of Veterinary Surgeons.
L.S.—Place of the seal (L., *locus sigilli*).
L.S.A.—Licentiate of the Society of Apothecaries.
L.S.C.—London Society of Compositors.
L.S.D.—Pounds, shillings, and pence (L., *libræ, solidi, denarii*).
L.S.O.—London Symphony Orchestra; London String Orchestra.
L.S.T.M.—London School of Tropical Medicine.
Lt.—Lieutenant.
L.T.A.—Lawn Tennis Association; London Teachers' Association.
L.T.C.—Lawn Tennis Club.
Lt.-Col.—Lieutenant-Colonel.
Lt.-Comm.—Lieutenant-Commander (R.N.).
Ltd.—Limited.
Lt.-Gen.—Lieutenant-General.
Lt.-Gov.—Lieutenant-Governor.
L.Th.—Licentiate in Theology.
L.T.M.—Licentiate in Tropical Medicine.
L.V.—Licensed Victualler.
L.W.M.—Low Water Mark.
L.W.O.S.T.—Low Water, Ordinary Spring Tides.
LXX—Septuagint version of the Bible.

M.—Majesty; Monday; Monsieur; **M**—Roman numeral for 1,000.
m.—Maiden (over) [Cricket].
M.A.—Master of Arts; Mathematical Association.
M.A.A.G.B.—Motor Agents Association of Great Britain.
M.A.B.—Medical Advisory Board.
M.A.B.Y.S.—Metropolitan Association for Befriending Young Servants.
M.A.F.—Ministry of Agriculture and Fisheries.
Maj.—Major.
Maj.-Gen.—Major-General.
M. & B.—Mild and bitter; also a sulphonic drug (No. 603) prepared by Messrs. May and Baker.
Mancun.—of Manchester (L., *Mancuniensis*).
M.A.N.I.A.C.—Mechanical and Numerical Integrator and Calculator.
Manit.—Manitoba.
M.A.P.—Ministry of Aircraft Production.
Mar.—March.
marq.—marquess.
Mass.—Massachusetts.
math(s).—mathematics.
matric.—matriculation.
M.B.—Bachelor of Medicine.
M.bco.—Marks banco [Fin.].
M.B.E.—Member of the (Order of the) British Empire.
M.B.O.U.—Member of the British Ornithologists' Union.
M.C.—Master of the Ceremonies; Military Cross; Member of Congress.
M.C.C.—Marylebone Cricket Club; Middlesex County Council; Monmouth County Council.
M.Ch.—Master of Surgery (L., *Magister Chirurgiæ*).
M.Ch.D.—Master of Dental Surgery.
M.Ch.Orth.—Master of Orthopædic Surgery.
M.Com(m).—Master of Commerce.
M.C.P.—Member of the College of Preceptors.
M.C.P.S.—Member of the College of Physicians and Surgeons.
M.C.S.—Madras Civil Service; Malayan Civil Service.
M.C.U.—Modern Churchmen's Union.
M.D.—Doctor of Medicine.
Md.—Maryland.
Mddx—Middlesex.
Mdlle—Mademoiselle.
M.D.S.—Master of Dental Surgery.
M.E.—Mining Engineer.
Me.—Maine.
M.E.C.—Member of the Executive Council.
mech.—mechanics; mechanical.
med.—mediæval; medicine; medical.
Medit.—Mediterranean.
M.E.F.—Middle East Forces [Milit.].
M.Eng.—Master of Engineering.
memo.—memorandum.
Messrs.—Gentlemen.
Met.—Metropolitan (esp. Railway, London).
meteor.—meteorology.
M.F.G.B.—Miners' Federation of Great Britain.
M.F.H.—Master of Foxhounds.
m.g.—machine-gun.
mg.—milligramme.
M.G.C.—Machine Gun Corps.
M.G.M.—Metro-Goldwyn-Mayer (Pictures, Ltd.).
Mgr.—Monsignor.
M.H.R.—Member of the House of Representatives.
M.Hy.—Master of Hygiene.
M.I.—Ministry of Information; Mounted Infantry.
M.I.A.E.—Member of the Institute of Automobile Engineers.
M.I.C.E.—*See* **M.Inst.C.E.**
Mich.—Michigan.
Mid.—Midshipman.
Middx—Middlesex.
M.I.E.E.—Member of the Institution of Electrical Engineers.
milit.—military; militia.
M.I.Mar.E.—Member of the Institute of Marine Engineers.
M.I.M.E.—Member of the Institution of Mining Engineers.
M.I.Mech.E.—Member of the Institution of Mechanical Engineers.
M.I.M.M.—Member of the Institution of Mining and Metallurgy.
M.I.N.A.—Member of the Institution of Naval Architects.
Minn.—Minnesota.
Min. Plenip.—Minister Plenipotentiary.
M.Inst.C.E.—Member of the Institution of Civil Engineers.
M.Inst.Gas E.—Member of the Institution of Gas Engineers.
M.Inst.M.M.—Member of the Institution of Mining and Metallurgy.
M.Inst.T.—Member of the Institute of Transport.
Miss.—Mississippi.
M.J.I.—Member of the Institute of Journalists.
M.L.A.—Member of the Legislative Assembly; Modern Language Association.
M.L. & N.S.—Ministry of Labour and National Service.

M.L.C.—Member of the Legislative Council.
Mlle—Mademoiselle.
M.M.—Military Medal.
MM.—Messrs.; Messieurs.
mm.—millimetre(s).
M.M.B.—Milk Marketing Board.
Mme—Madame.
M.N.—Merchant Navy.
M.N.I.—Ministry of National Insurance.
M.O.—Medical Officer; Meteorological Office; Money Order.
Mo.—Missouri; **mo.**—month.
mod.—modern.
Mods.—Moderations (Oxon.).
M. of F.—Ministry of Food.
M.O.H.—Medical Officer of Health; Ministry of Health.
M.O.I.—Ministry of Information; Military Operations and Intelligence.
Mon.—Monday; Monmouthshire.
Mont.—Montana.
M.O.O.—Money Order Office.
M.O.S.—Ministry of Supply.
mos.—months.
M.O.W.(B.).—Ministry of Works (and Buildings).
M.P.—Member of Parliament; Metropolitan Police; Military Police(man).
m.p.—melting-point.
m.p.g./h.—miles per gallon/hour.
M.P.S.—Member of the Pharmaceutical Society.
Mr.—Mister.
M.R.—Maritime Regiment; Middlesex Regiment; Master of the Rolls; Minister Resident; Moral Rearmament; Municipal Reform.
M.R.A.C.—Member of the Royal Agricultural College (Cirencester).
M.R.Ae.S.—Member of the Royal Aeronautical Society.
M.R.A.S.—Member of the Royal Asiatic Society.
M.R.C.P.—Member of the Royal College of Physicians.
M.R.C.S.—Member of the Royal College of Surgeons.
M.R.C.S.Ed.—Member of the Royal College of Surgeons of Edinburgh.
M.R.C.V.S.—Member of the Royal College of Veterinary Surgeons.
M.R.I.—Member of the Royal Institution.
M.R.I.A.—Member of the Royal Irish Academy.
M.R.P.—French Christian Democrat political party (*Mouvement Républicain Populaire*).
Mrs.—Mistress; Missis.
M.S.—Master of Surgery; Ministry of Supply; Missionary Society; Motor Ship; Sacred to the Memory of (L., *memoriæ sacrum*).
MS.—manuscript.
M.S.A.—Member of the Society of Architects; Member of the Society of Arts; Member of the Society of Apothecaries; Municipal School of Art.
M.Sc.—Master of Science.
M.S.C.—Military Staff Committee; Medical Staff Corps; Manchester Ship Canal.
M.S.E.—Member of the Society of Engineers.
M.S.I.—Member of the (Chartered) Surveyors' Institution.
M.S.L.—Mean Sea Level.
M.S.M.—Meritorious Service Medal.
MSS.—manuscripts.
M.T.—Mechanical Transport; Motor Transport; Mandated Territory.
Mt., Mts.—Mount; Mountain; Mountains.
M.T.B.—Motor Torpedo Boat.
M.T.C.P.—Ministry of Town and Country Planning.
mtg.—mortgage.
M.U.—Motor Union; Mothers' Union; Musicians' Union.
Mus.B.—Bachelor of Music.
Mus.D.—Doctor of Music.
M.V.—Monte Video; Merchant Vessel; Motor Vessel; muzzle velocity.
M.V.O.—Member of the Royal Victorian Order.
M.W.B.—Metropolitan Water Board.
M.W.G.M.—Most Worthy Grand Master; Most Worshipful Grand Master (Freemasonry).
M.Y.—Motor Yacht.

N.—North.
N.A.—Nautical Almanac; Naval Architect; North America(n).
N.A.A.F.I.—Naval, Army, and Air Force Institute(s).
N.A.B.—National Assistance Board.
N.A.B.C.—National Association of Boys' Clubs.
N.A.B.S.—National Advertisers' Benefit Society.
N.A.C.D.—National Association for Civil Defence.
N.A.C.F.—National Art Collections Fund.
N.A.F.D.—National Assoc. of Funeral Directors.
N.A.G.C.—National Association of Girls' Clubs.
N.A.G.L.—National Anti-Gambling League.
N.A.L.G.O.—National Association of Local Government Officers.
N.Am(er).—North America(n).
N. & Q.—Notes and Queries.
N.A.O.—National Association of Opticians.
N.A.P.T.—National Association for the Prevention of Tuberculosis.
N.A.S.—National Allotment Society; National Adoption Society; Nursing Auxiliary Service; Naval Air Service (U.S.A.).
Nat.—National; Nationalist; Natal.
N.A.T.O.—North Atlantic Treaty Organization.
nat. ord.—natural order (Bot.).
Natsopa.—*See* **N.S.O.P. & A.**
N.A.V.L.—National Anti-Vaccination League.
N.B.—no ball [Cricket]; North Britain; New Brunswick; note well, take notice (L., *nota bene*).
N.B.L.—National Book League.
N.B.T.S.—National Blood Transfusion Service.
N.B.S.—National Bureau of Standards.
N.C.—North Carolina.
N.C.B.—National Coal Board.
N.C.C.L.—National Council for Civil Liberties.
N.C.C.R.—National Council for Cancer Relief.
N.C.O.—Non-commissioned Officer.
N.C.S.S.—National Council for Social Service.
N.C.U.—National Cyclists' Union.
n.d.—no date [Bibliog., etc.].
N.D.A.—National Diploma in Agriculture.
N.Dak.—North Dakota.
N.D.C.—National Defence Contribution.
N.D.R.C.—National Defense Research Committee (U.S.A.).
NE.—north-east.
Neb.—Nebraska.
N.E.C.—National Executive Council.
N.E.D.—New (*i.e.* Oxford) English Dictionary.
nem. con.—No one contradicting (L., *nemine contradicente*).
nem. dis.—No one dissenting (L., *nemine dissentiente*).
N.E.P.—New Economic Policy (U.S.S.R.).
Neth.—Netherlands.
Nev.—Nevada.
N.F.—Newfoundland; Northern French.
N.F.C.C.—National Free Church Council.
N.F.F.—National Froebel Foundation.
N.F.S.—National Fire Services.
N.F.U.—National Farmers' Union.
N.F.W.I.—Nat. Federation of Women's Institutes.
N.G.—National Gallery; Nat. Guard; New Guinea.
N.G.O.—(Economic and Social Council Standing Committee Relations with) Non-Governmental Organizations [U.N.].
N.H.—National Health; Naval Hospital; New Hampshire (U.S.A.).
N.H.I.—National Health Insurance.
n.h.p.—nominal horse-power.
N.H.R.U.—National Home Reading Union.
N.H.S.—National Health Service.
N.H.T.P.C.—National Housing and Town Planning Council.
N.I.—Northern Ireland.
N.I.D.—Naval Intelligence Department; National Institute for the Deaf.
N.I.I.P.—National Institute of Industrial Psychology.
N.J.—New Jersey.
N.L.—Navy League; National Liberal [Polit.]; North Latitude.
N.L.I.—National Lifeboat Institution.
N.Mex.—New Mexico.
NNE.—north-north-east.
NNW.—north-north-west.
no.—number (L., *numero*).
N.O.—natural order [Bot.].
N.O.D.—Naval Ordnance Department.
Non.-Coll.—Non-Collegiate.
Noncon.—Nonconformist.

non obst.—Notwithstanding (L., *non obstante*).
non pros.—He does not pursue or prosecute (L., *non prosequitur*).
non seq.—It does not follow (L., *non sequitur*).
Northants—Northamptonshire.
Northumb—Northumberland.
Norvic.—of Norwich (L., *Norvicensis*).
nos.—numbers.
Notts—Nottinghamshire.
Nov.—November.
N.P.—Notary Public.
N.P.A.—Newspaper Proprietors' Association.
N.P.D.—North Polar Distance.
N.P.F.—Newspaper Press Fund.
N.P.L.—National Physical Laboratory; National Protestant League.
N.R.—North Riding (Yorks).
N.R.A.—National Rifle Association; National Recovery Administration (U.S.A.).
N.S.—New Style; Nova Scotia.
N.S.D.—Nuttall's Standard Dictionary.
N.S.O.P. & A.—National Society of Operative Printers and Assistants.
N.S.P.C.C.—National Society for the Prevention of Cruelty to Children.
N.S.S.U.—National Sunday School Union.
N.S.W.—New South Wales.
N.T.—National Trust; New Testament; Northern Territory (Australia).
n.u.—name unknown.
N.U.—Northern Union [Rugby League Football].
N.U.A.W.—National Union of Agricultural Workers; National Union of Aircraft Workers.
N.U.B.S.O.—National Union of Boot and Shoe Operatives.
N.U.C.(A.W.).—National Union of Clerks (and Administrative Workers).
N.U.C.O.—National Union of Co-operative Officials; National Union of County Officers.
N.U.D.A.W.—National Union of Distributive and Allied Workers.
N.U.F.—National Union of Fireman.
N.U.G.M.W.—National Union of General and Municipal Workers.
N.U.I.—National University of Ireland.
N.U.J.—National Union of Journalists.
N.U.M.—National Union of Manufacturers; National Union of Mineworkers.
N.U.P.B. & P.W.—National Union of Printing, Bookbinding, and Paper Workers.
N.U.R.—National Union of Railwaymen.
N.U.S.—National Union of Seamen; National Union of Students.
N.U.S.E.C.—National Union of Societies for Equal Citizenship.
N.U.T.—National Union of Teachers.
N.U.T.G.W.—National Union of Tailors and Garment Workers.
N.U.T.W.—National Union of Textile Workers.
N.U.W.S.S.—National Union of Women's Suffrage Societies.
N.U.W.T.—National Union of Women Teachers.
N.V.S.—National Vegetarian Society.
NW.—north-west.
N.W.F.P.—North-West Frontier Province (Pakistan).
N.W.M.P.—North-West Mounted Police (Canada).
N.W.P.—North-west Provinces (Pakistan).
N.W.T.—North-west Territory (Canada).
N.Y.—New York (State).
N.Z.—New Zealand.

O.—Ohio.
o.—over [Cricket].
O.A.P.A.—Old Age Pensioners' Association.
ob. (obiit).—Died.
O.B.E.—Officer of the (Order of the) British Empire.
obs.—obsolete.
O.C.—Officer Commanding; Observer Corps.
o'c.—o'clock.
O.C.B.—Oil Control Board.
Oct.—October.
O.C.T.U.—Officer Cadet Training Unit.
O.D.—Ordnance Datum.
O.D.F.L.—Our Dumb Friends' League.
O.E.D.—Oxford English Dictionary.
O.E.E.C.—Organization for European Economic Co-operation.
O.E.R.—Officers' Emergency Reserve.
O.F.C.—Overseas Food Corporation.
O.F.S.—Orange Free State.
O.G.P.U.—the Soviet Union State Police (*Obyedinionnoye gosudarstvennoye politicheskoye upravlenie*).
O.H.B.M.S.—On His (or Her) Britannic Majesty's Service.
O.H.M.S.—On His (or Her) Majesty's Service.
O.K.—All correct (" Orl Korrekt ").
Okla.—Oklahoma.
O.L.—Official Liquidator; Overseas League; Officer of (the Order of) Leopold (Belgium).
Olym.—Olympiad.
O.M.—Order of Merit; Old Measurement [Naval Eng.]; Ordnance Map.
Ont.—Ontario.
O.P.—Observation Post.
o.p.—out of print; opposite prompt (-side of stage) [Theat.]; over proof (of spirits).
op.—work [Mus.] (L., *opus*.).
Op. cit.—in the work cited (L., *opere citato*).
O.R.—Official Receiver; Official Referee; Other Ranks (than those commissioned) [Mil.].
Ord. Sur.—Ordnance Survey.
Ore.—Oregon.
orse.—otherwise [Law].
O.S.—Ordinary Seaman; Old Style; Ophthalmological Society; Optical Society; Ordnance Survey.
O.S.A.—Official Secrets Act; Order of St. Augustine.
O.S.B.—Order of St. Benedict.
O.S.C.—Ordnance Staff Corps.
O.S.D.—Order of St. Dominic; Ordnance Survey Department; Overseas Settlement Department.
O.S.F.—Order of St. Francis.
O.S.N.C.—Orient Steam Navigation Company.
o.s.p.—Died without issue (L., *obiit sine prole*).
O.S.R.D.—Office of Scientific Research and Development (U.S.A.).
O.T.—Old Testament.
O.T.C.—Officers' Training Corps; Operational Training Centre [Mil.].
O.U.D.S.—Oxford University Dramatic Society.
O.U.P.—Oxford University Press.
O.U.S.—Oxford Union Society.
O.W.—Office of Works.
O.W.I.—Office of War Information (U.S.A.)
O.W.S.—Old Watercolour Society.
Oxon—of Oxford (L., *Oxoniensis*).
oz.—ounce.

P.—Parish; Paymaster.
p.—page; pint; pole; perch.
P.A.—Patent Agent; Press Association; Publishers' Assoc.; Pedestrians' Assoc.; Protestant Alliance; Presbyterian Alliance.
Pa.—Pennsylvania.
p.a.—power of attorney; particular average; per annum (yearly).
P.A.A.—Pan-American Airways.
P.A.C.—Public Accounts Committee.
Pal.—Palestine.
Pan.—Panama.
P. & K.T.F.—Printing and Kindred Trades Federation.
P. & O.—Peninsular and Oriental.
par.—paragraph.
Parl.—Parliament(ary).
P.A.S.—Principal Assistant Secretary.
P.A.S.I.—Professional Associate of the (Royal Chartered) Surveyors' Institution.
P.A.T.—Pensions Appeal Tribunal.
P.A.T.A.—Proprietary Articles Trade Association.
P.A.Y.E.—Pay As You Earn (of Income Tax).
Paym.-Gen.—Paymaster-General.
P.B.—Plymouth Brother (Brethren); Primitive Baptist.
P.B.T.—President of the Board of Trade.
P.C.—Pioneer Corps; Police Constable; Privy Council; Privy Counsellor; Conscript Fathers [Rom. Hist.] (L., *Patres conscripti*); **p.c.**—post card.
P.C.A.—Progressive Citizens of America.
P.C.I.J.—Permanent Court of International Justice.
p.c.v.—pedestrian controlled vehicle.
pd.—paid.
p.d.—potential difference [Elect.].
P.D.A.—Patents and Designs Act.
P.D.A.D.—Probate, Divorce, and Admiralty Division.
pdr.—pounder (gun, fish, etc.).

P.D.S.A.—People's Dispensary for Sick Animals.
P.E.F.—Palestine Exploration Fund.
P.E.I.—Prince Edward Island.
P.E.N.—(Internat. organization of) Poets, Essayists, and Novelists.
P.E.P.—Political and Economic Planning (Group).
per an.—By the year.
per cent.—By the hundred.
per pro.—per procuration.
Pers.—Persian.
Petriburg.—of Peterborough (L., *Petriburgensis*).
P.G.—Past Grand [Freemasonry]; paying guest [Coll.]; Procurator-General (Treasury).
P.G.A.—Professional Golfers' Association.
Ph.B.—Bachelor of Philosophy.
Ph.D.—Doctor of Philosophy.
Phil. Soc.—Philological Society; Philosophical Soc.
Phil. Trans.—Philosophical Transactions.
P.I.—Philippine Islands.
pinx., pxt.—He (or she) painted it (L., *pinxit*).
P.L.—Plimsoll Line; Poet Laureate; Primrose League.
P.L.A.—Port of London Authority.
P.L.C.—Poor Law Commissioners.
plf.—plaintiff.
P.L.H.—People's League of Health.
P.L.M.—*Paris-Lyon-Méditerranée* (railway).
P.L.P.—Parliamentary Labour Party.
P.L.U.T.O.—Pipe line under the ocean (supplying petrol to A.E.F., W.W.2.).
P.M.—Past Master; Prime Minister; Provost-Marshal.
p.m.—After noon (L., *post meridiem*); per month (L., *pro mense*).
pm.—premium.
P.M.B.—Potato Marketing Board.
P.M.G.—Postmaster-General.
P.M.O.—Principal Medical Officer.
p.n.—promissory note.
P.N.E.U.—Parents' National Educational Union.
P.O.—Petty Office [Nav.]; Pilot Officer (R.A.F.); Post Office; Postal Order; Publicity Officer.
P.O.D.—Post Office Directory; Pocket Oxford Dictionary.
P.O.L.—Patent Office Library.
Pol.—Poland; Polish.
Pol. Econ.—Political Economy.
Poly.—Polytechnic (Institute).
P.O.O.—Post Office Order.
P.O.P.—Printing-out paper [Phot.].
pop.—popular; population.
Port.—Portugal; Portuguese.
P.O.S.B.—Post Office Savings Bank.
P.O.W.—Prisoner of war; Prince of Wales.
P.P.—Parish Priest.
P.P.A.—Pool Promoters' Association.
P.P.A.G.B.I.—Professional Photographers' Association of Great Britain and Ireland.
pp.—pages; very softly [Mus.] (It., *pianissimo*).
P.P.C.—Printers' Pension Corporation; **p.p.c.**—to take leave (Fr., *pour prendre congé*).
P.P.S.—Parliamentary Private Secretary; further postscript (L., *post-postscriptum*).
P.P.U.—Peace Pledge Union.
P.R.—Parachute Regiment; Poste Restante; Proportional Representation; Public Relations.
P.R.A.—President of the Royal Academy; Paymaster-Rear-Admiral.
P.R.B.—The Pre-Raphaelite Brotherhood.
Pres.—President.
P.R.H.A.—People's Refreshment House Association.
P.R.I.—President of the Royal Institute of Painters in Water-colours.
P.R.O.—Public Record Office; Public Relations Officer; Press Relations Officer.
pro.—professional.
pro & con—For and against (L. *pro et contra*).
Prof.—Professor.
Proms.—The Promenade Concerts.
props.—(stage) properties or equipment.
Prot.—Protestant.
pro tem.—For the time (L., *pro tempore*).
Prov.—Province; Provincial (Freemasonry); Provost; Proverbs (Bib.); Provençal; **prov.**—provisional.
prox.—Next (L., *proximo*).
P.R.S.—President of the Royal Society; Performing Rights Society; Proportional Representation Soc.
P.R.S.A.—President of the Royal Scottish Academy.
P.S.—Parliamentary Secretary; Permanent Sec.; Private Sec.; Philanthropical Society; Philological Soc.; Physical Soc.; Poetry Soc.; Privy Seal; Police Sergeant; Postscript (L., *post scriptum*).
P.S.A.—Pleasant Sunday Afternoon; Private Schools Association.
p.s.a.—Graduate of the R.A.F. Staff College.
p.s.c.—Passed Staff College [Mil.].
P.S.G.B.—Pathological Society of Great Britain; Pharmaceutical Soc. of Gt. Britain; Philosophical Soc. of Gt. Britain.
P.S.N.C.—Pacific Steam Navigation Company.
P.T.—Physical training.
Pte.—Private (soldier).
P.T.O.—Public Trustee Office; please turn over.
P.T.P.W.N.P.A.—Periodical, Trade Press, and Weekly Newspaper Proprietors' Association.
pug.—pugilist.
P.U.S.—Parliamentary Under-Secretary; Permanent Under-Secretary.
P.W.—Prince of Wales.
P.W.B.—Public Works and Buildings.
P.W.D.—Public Works Department.
P.W.U.—Postal Workers' Union.
pxt.—*See* **pinx.**

Q.—Queen (monarch, cards, chess);
q.—quart; question; query; quire.
Q.A.B.—Queen Anne's Bounty.
Q.A.I.M.N.S.—Queen Alexandra's Imperial Military Nursing Service.
Q.A.L.A.S.—Qualified Associate of the Land Agents' Society.
Q.A.N.T.A.S.—Queensland and Northern Territory Aerial Service (or **Qantas**).
Q.A.R.A.N.C.—Queen Alexandra's Royal Army Nursing Corps.
Q.A.R.N.N.S.—Queen Alexandra's Royal Naval Nursing Service.
Q.B.(D.)—Queen's Bench (Division).
Q.C.—Queen's Counsel.
q.d.—As he should say (L., *quasi dicat*).
q.e.—Which is (L., *quod est*).
Q.E.A.—Qantas Empire Airways.
q.e.d.—Which was to be demonstrated (L., *quod erat demonstrandum*).
q.e.f.—Which was to be done (L., *quod erat faciendum*).
q.e.i.—Which was to be found out (L., *quod erat inveniendum*).
q.f.—quick-firing (automatic gun).
q.i.—As much as you please (L., *quantum libet*).
Q.I.D.N.—Queen's Institute of District Nursing.
Q.M.—Quartermaster.
Q.M.G.—Quartermaster-General.
Q.M.S.—Quartermaster-Sergeant.
qr.—quarter; quire.
Q.S.—Quarter Sessions.
q.s.—Enough (L., *quantum sufficit*).
Q.T.—(on the) quiet, confidential [Slang].
qt.—quart.
Qu.—Queen.
Q.U.B.—Queen's University, Belfast.
Que.—Quebec.
Q.U.I.—Queen's University of Ireland.
q.v.—Which see (L., *quod vide*).
Q.V.R.—Queen Victoria's Rifles.
qy.—query.

R.—King; Queen (L., *Rex*; *Regina*); take [Med.] (L., *recipe*).
r.—runs [Cricket].
R.A.—Royal Academy (Academician), Arch [Masonry], Artillery; Ratepayers', Road Association; Right Ascension [Astron.]; Rear-Admiral.
R.A.A.D.D.—Royal Association in Aid of the Deaf and Dumb.
R.A.A.F.—Royal Australian Air Force.
R.A.C.—Royal Agricultural College; Royal Armoured Corps; Royal Automobile Club.
R.A.C.D.—Royal Army Chaplain's Department.
R.A.D.—Royal Academy of Dancing.
R.A.D.A.—Royal Academy of Dramatic Art.
R.A.D.C.—Royal Army Dental Corps.
R.-Adm.—Rear-Admiral.
R.A.E.—Royal Aircraft Establishment.
R.A.E.C.—Royal Army Educational Corps.
R.Ae.S.—Royal Aeronautical Society.
R.A.F.—Royal Air Force.

R.A.F.M.S.—Royal Air Force Medical Service.
R.A.F.O.—Reserve of Air Force Officers.
R.A.F.R.—Royal Air Force Regiment.
R.A.F.V.R.—Royal Air Force Volunteer Reserve.
R.A.G.C.—Royal and Ancient Golf Club (St. Andrews).
R.A.L.—Royal Academy of Literature.
R.A.M.—Royal Academy of Music.
R.A.M.C.—Royal Army Medical Corps.
R.A.N.—Royal Australian Navy.
R.A.O.B.—Royal Antediluvian Order of Buffaloes.
R.A.O.C.—Royal Army Ordnance Corps.
R.A.P.C.—Royal Army Pay Corps.
R.A.R.O.—Regular Army Reserve of Officers.
R.A.S.—Royal African Society; Royal Agricultural Society; Royal Astronomical Society.
R.A.S.C.—Royal Army Service Corps.
R.A.V.C.—Royal Army Veterinary Corps.
R.B.—Rifle Brigade.
R.B.A.—Royal Society of British Artists.
R.B.C.B.—Racecourse Betting Control Board.
R.B.N.A.—Royal British Nurses' Association.
R.B.S.—Royal Society of British Sculptors.
R.C.—Roman Catholic; Reconnaissance Corps.
R.C.A.—Royal College of Art; Railway Clerks' Association.
R.C.A.F.—Royal Canadian Air Force.
R.C.M.—Royal College of Music.
R.C.M.P.—Royal Canadian Mounted Police.
R.C.N.—Royal Canadian Navy; Royal College of Nursing.
R.C.N.C.—Royal Corps of Naval Constructors.
R.C.O.—Royal College of Organists.
R.C.P.—Royal College of Physicians.
R.C.P.Ed.—Royal College of Physicians of Edinburgh.
R.C.P.I.—Royal College of Physicians of Ireland.
R.C.S.—Royal College of Science; Royal College of Surgeons; Royal Corps of Signals.
R.C.S.Ed.—Royal College of Surgeons of Edinburgh.
R.C.V.S.—Royal College of Veterinary Surgeons.
R.D.—Refer to drawer [Banking]; Reserve Decoration [Naval]; Rural Dean; Rural District.
R.D.C.—Rural District Council.
R.D.I.—Royal Designer for Industry (Roy. Soc. of Arts).
R.D.S.—Research Defence Society; Royal Drawing Society.
R.E.—Royal Engineers.
Recce. (Corps).—Reconnaissance (Corps).
ref.—referee.
Ref. Ch.—Reformed Church.
reg.—regiment.
Reg. Bd.—Regional Board.
Reg.-Gen.—Registrar-General.
Reg. Prof.—Regius Professor.
regt.—regiment.
R.E.M.E.—Royal Electrical and Mechanical Engineers.
rep.—repertory (company); reporter; representative; republic.
R.E.S.—Royal Economic Society: Royal Empire Society: Royal Entomological Society; Rothamsted Experimental Station.
ret.—returned; retired.
Rev.—Reverend.
R.F.—Royal Fusiliers; French Republic (*République française*); Representative Fraction (on map scales); Road Fund.
r.f.—radio frequency.
R.F.A.—Royal Field Artillery.
R.G.A.—Royal Garrison Artillery.
R.G.S.—Royal Geographical Society.
R.H.A.—Royal Hibernian Academy; Royal Horse Artillery.
R.H.B.—Regional Hospital Board.
R.H.G.—Royal Horse Guards.
R.H.S.—Roy. Horticultural Soc.; Roy. Humane Soc.
R.Hist.S.—Royal Historical Society.
R.I.—Royal Institution; Royal Institute of Painters in Water-colours; Rhode Island (U.S.A.); Rotary International.
R.I.A.—Royal Irish Academy.
R.I.B.A.—Royal Institute of British Architects.
R.I.C.—Royal Institute of Chemistry.
R.I.C.S.—Royal Institute of Chartered Surveyors.
R.I.F.—Royal Irish Fusiliers.
R.I.I.A.—Royal Institute of International Affairs.
R.I.L.U.—Red International of Labour Unions.
R.I.N.—Royal Indian Navy.
R.I.P.—May he (or she) rest in peace (L., *requiescat in pace*).
R.L.—Rugby League [Football].
R.L.O.—Returned Letter Office.
Rly.—Railway.
R.M.—Resident Magistrate; Royal Mail; Royal Marines.
R.M.A.—Royal Marine Artillery; Royal Military Academy.
R.M.C.—Royal Military College.
R.Met.S.—Royal Meteorological Society.
R.M.H.—Royal Masonic Hospital.
R.M.O.—Resident Medical Officer.
R.M.P.—Royal Marine, Royal Military, Police.
R.M.S.—Royal Mail Steamer; Royal Microscopical Society; Royal Society of Miniature Painters.
R.N.—Royal Navy.
R.N.A.V.—Royal Naval Artillery Volunteers.
R.N.D.—Royal Naval Division.
R.N.I.B.—Royal National Institute for the Blind.
R.N.L.I.—Royal National Lifeboat Institution.
R.N.R.—Royal Naval Reserve.
R.N.S.—Royal Numismatic Society.
R.N.V.R.—Royal Naval Volunteer Reserve.
R.N.Z.A.F.—Royal New Zealand Air Force.
R.N.Z.N.—Royal New Zealand Navy.
R.O.—Recruiting Officer; Regional Officer; Relieving Officer; Returning Officer; Royal Observatory.
ro.—right-hand page (L., *recto*).
R.O.C.—Royal Observer Corps.
Roffen.—of Rochester (L., *Roffensis*).
R. of O.—Reserve of Officers.
R.O.I.—Royal Institute of Painters in Oils.
rom.—roman (of type).
R.O.P.—Russian Oil Products.
R.P.—Regimental Police; Royal Society of Portrait Painters; reply paid.
R.P.A.—Rationalist Press Association.
R.P.C.—Royal Pioneer Corps.
R.P.E.—Royal Society of Painter-Etchers and Engravers.
r.p.m.—revolutions per minute (of machinery).
R.P.O.—Royal Philharmonic Orchestra.
R.P.S.—Royal Philatelic Society; Royal Philharmonic Society; Royal Philosophical Society; Royal Photographic Society.
R.Q.M.S.—Regimental Quartermaster-Sergeant.
R.R.C.—Royal Red Cross.
R.R.T.—Railway Rates Tribunal.
R.S.—Ray Society; Royal Society; Russia Society; Royal Scots (Regt.).
R.S.A.—Royal Scottish Academy; Royal Scottish Academician; Royal Society of Arts.
R.S.A.A.F.—Royal South African Air Force.
R.S.A.C.—Royal Scottish Automobile Club.
R.San.I.—Royal Sanitary Institute.
R.S.A.S.—Royal Surgical Aid Society.
R.S.B.A.—Royal Society of British Artists.
R.S.B.S.—Royal Society of British Sculptors.
R.S.F.—Royal Scots Fusiliers.
R.S.F.S.R.—Russian Soviet Federal Socialist Republic.
R.S.G.—Royal Scots Greys.
R.S.G.B.—Radio Society of Great Britain.
R.S.L.—Royal Society of Literature.
R.S.M.—Regimental Sergeant-Major; Royal School of Mines; Royal Society of Medicine.
R.S.O.—Railway Sorting Office; Rural Sorting Office.
R.S.P.A.—Royal Society for the Prevention of Accidents.
R.S.P.C.A.—Royal Society for the Prevention of Cruelty to Animals.
R.S.S.—Royal Statistical Society; Fellow of the Royal Society (L., *Regiæ Societatis Sodalis*).
R.S.T.—Royal Society of Teachers.
R.S.V.P.—Please reply (Fr., *réponse, s'il vous plaît*).
R.T.—Radio Telephony.
rt.—right.
R.T.B.—Road Transport Board.
Rt. Hon.—Right Honourable.
R.T.O.—Railway Transport Officer.
Rt. Rev.—Right Reverend.
R.T.R.—Royal Tank Regiment.
R.T.S.—Religious Tract Society (*but see* **U.S.C.L.**).
R.U.—Rugby Union.
R.U.I.—Royal University of Ireland.
R.U.R.—Royal Ulster Rifles.
R.U.S.I.—Royal United Services Institution.

R.V.—Revised Version (of the Bible); Rifle Volunteers.
R.W.—Right Worshipful; Right Worthy [Freemasonry].
R.W.A.F.F.—Royal West African Frontier Force.
R.W.H.A.—Royal Warrant Holders' Association.
R.W.K.—Royal West Kent (Regt.).
R.W.S.—Royal Society of Painters in Water-Colours; Royal West Sussex (Regt.).
Rx.—Tens of rupees.
R.Y.S.—Royal Yacht Squadron.

S.—South.
s.—shilling(s) (L., *solidi*); second(s).
S.A.—Salvation Army; South Africa; South America; South Australia; Sex Appeal [Coll.].
S.A.A.—Society of Incorporated Accountants and Auditors; South African Airways.
S.A.B.E.N.A.—Belgian Airways (*Société Anonyme Belge d'exploitation de la Navigation Aérienne*).
S.A.C.—Scientific Advisory Committee; State Agricultural College.
S.A.E.—Society of Automobile Engineers.
S.A.H.R.—Society for Army Historical Research.
Salop—Shropshire.
S.A.O.—Scottish Association of Opticians.
Sarum.—Salisbury.
S.A.S.—Surgical Appliance Society.
Sask.—Saskatchewan.
Sat.—Saturday.
S.B.—Savings Bank; Statistical Branch [Mil.]; Statistical Bureau.
S.B.A.—Scottish Bankers' Association.
S.B.A.C.—Society of British Aircraft Constructors.
S.B.G.I.—Society of British Gas Industries.
S.C.—Salvage Corps; Security Council (U.N.); South Carolina; Special Constabulary; Staff College.
sc. or **sculps.**—He (or she) engraved it (L., *sculpsit*).
sc.—namely (L., *scilicet*).
Scand.—Scandinavian.
S.C.A.P.A.—Society for Checking Abuses in Public Advertising.
S.C.C.—Sea Cadet Corps.
Sc.D.—Doctor of Science.
S.C.G.—Social Credit Group.
S.C.M.—State certified midwife; Student Christian Movement.
S.C.P.—Society of Correctors of the Press.
S.C.R.—Society for Cultural Relations (with the U.S.S.R.).
S.C.S.—Society of Civil Servants.
S.C.W.S.—Scottish Wholesale Co-operative Society.
S.D.A.—Seventh Day Adventists.
S.Dak.—South Dakota.
S.D.F.—Social Democratic Federation.
S.D.I.—Soft Drinks Industry.
S.D.N.—League of Nations (Fr., *Société des Nations*).
SE.—south-east; **S.E.**—Saorstat Eirann (Eire).
S.E.A.C.—South East Asia Command (W.W.2).
S.E.A.T.O.—South-East Asia Treaty Organization.
sec.—secant [Trigonometry]; secretary; second.
S.E.F.—Shipbuilding Employers' Federation.
Sept.—September; Septuagint.
seq., seqq.—The following (L. *sequentes*, or *sequentia*).
Sergt.—Sergeant.
S.F.A.—Scottish Football Association.
S.F.B.E.—Sugar Federation of the British Empire.
S.F.—Sherwood Foresters (Notts. & Derbysh. Regt.); Shipping Federation.
S.G.—Scots Guards; Solicitor-General; Insured (at Lloyds) (L., *salutis gratia*, for the sake of safety).
S.G.W.—Senior Grand Warden.
S.H.A.E.F.—Supreme Headquarters, Allied Expeditionary Force (W.W.2).
S.H.Q.—Supreme Headquarters.
S.I.A.—Society of Industrial Artists.
S.I.A.A.—Society of Incorporated Accountants and Auditors.
S.I.L.A.—Swedish Intercontinental Air Lines.
S.I.M.—Sergeant Instructor of Musketry.
S.I.M.A.—Surgical Instrument Manufacturers' Association.
sin.—sine [Trigonometry].
S.I.R.—Scientific and Industrial Research.
S.J.—Society of Jesus.
S.J.A.A.—St. John Ambulance Association.
S.L.—South Latitude; Sub-Lieutenant; the place of the seal (L., *sigilli locus*).
S.L.A.D.—Society of Lithographic Artists and Designers.
Slav.—Slavic; Slavonic.
S.M.—Sergeant-major; short metre (of hymns).
S.M.A.—Sales Managers' Association; Socialist Medical Association; Society of Marine Artists.
S.M.C.—Worshipful Company of Spectacle Makers.
S.M.C.A.—Solicitors' Managing Clerks' Association.
S.M.E.E.—Society of Model and Experimental Engineers.
S.M.M.T.—Society of Motor Manufacturers and Traders.
S.M.O.—Senior Medical Officer.
S.M.R.C.—Society of Miniature Rifle Clubs.
S.N.A.—Soviet News Agency; Spanish News Agency.
S.N.P.—Scottish National Party [Polit.].
S.O.C.—Shell Oil Company; Standard Oil Company.
Soc.—Society; Socialist [Polit.].
S.O.D.—Shorter Oxford Dictionary.
Sol.—Solicitor.
S. of M.—School of Musketry.
S.O.G.—Society of Genealogists.
Som.—Somersetshire.
S.O.S.—Wireless code-signal sent out by ships, etc., in great distress.
S.P.—Staff Paymaster.
s.p.—small pica [print]; starting-price [Racing]; without issue (L., *sine prole*).
Sp. Spain; Spanish.
S.P.A.B.—Society for the Protection of Ancient Buildings.
S.P.C.K.—Society for Promoting Christian Knowledge.
S.P.E.—Society for Pure English.
S.P.G.—Society for the Propagation of the Gospel.
S.P.G.B.—Socialist Party of Great Britain.
S.P.Q.R. —The senate and people of Rome. (*Senatus Populusque Romanus*).
S.P.R.—Society for Psychical Research.
S.P.R.C.—Society for the Prevention and Relief of Cancer.
Sqd. Ldr.—Squadron Leader.
S.R.—Scottish Rifles; Southern Railway; Special Reserve; Supplementary Reserve.
S.R. & O.—Statutory Rules and Orders.
S.R.I. —The Holy Roman Empire (L., *Sacrum Romanum Imperium*).
S.R.N.—State Registered Nurse.
S.R.U.—Scottish Rugby Union.
S.S.—Secret Service; Shaftesbury Society; Steamship; Straits Settlements; Sunday School.
SS.—Saints.
S.S.A.F.A.—Soldiers', Sailors', and Airmen's Families Association.
S.S.C.—Solicitor before the Supreme Court (Scotland).
SSE.—south-south-east.
S.S.L.—Social Security League.
S.S.S.—School of Slavonic Studies.
S.S.U.—Sunday School Union.
S.S.V.P.—Society of St. Vincent de Paul.
SSW.—south-south-west.
St.—Saint; Strait; Street.
Staffs—Staffordshire.
S.T.B.—Bachelor of Sacred Theology (L., *Sacræ Theologiæ Baccalaureus*).
S.T.D.—Doctor or Sacred Theology (L., *Sacræ Theologiæ Doctor*).
St. Ex.—Stock Exchange.
Stg.—Sterling.
S.T.H.—School of Tropical Hygiene.
S.T.M.—Master of Sacred Theology (L., *Sacræ Theologiæ Magister*).
stn.—station.
S.T.P.—Professor of Sacred Theology, or Divinity (L., *Sacræ Theologiæ Professor*).
S.T.S.—Scottish Text Society.
S.T.U.C.—Scottish Trades Union Congress.
S.U.—Soviet Union.
Suff. B.—Suffragan Bishop.
supp.—supplement.
Supp. Res.—Supplementary Reserve (of Officers).
Supt.—Superintendent.
Surg.—Surgeon; surgery.
Surg.-Gen.—Surgeon-General.
Surr.—Surrogate.
surv.—surveyor.

Surv.-Gen.—Surveyor-General.
sus. per coll.—Hanging by the neck (L., *suspensis per collum*).
Suss—Sussex.
s.v.—Under the word (or heading) mentioned (L., *sub verbo*, or *voce*).
S.W.—Senior Warden; Short Wave [Wire.]; South Wales; **SW.**—south-west.
S.W.A.—Society of Women Artists.
S.W.B.—South Wales Borderers.
S.W.E.M.—Society of West End Managers [Theat.].
S.W.G.—Standard Wire Gauge.
S.W.J.—Society of Women Journalists.
S.Y.—Steam Yacht.
syn.—synonymous.

t.—ton.
T.A.—Telegraphic Address; Territorial Army; Typographical Association; Tass Agency; "Tube Alloys."
T.A.A.—Territorial Army Association.
T.A.G.B.—Travel Agency of Great Britain.
tan.—tangent.
T.A.N.S.—Territorial Army Nursing Service.
T.A.R.A.—Territorial Army Rifle Association.
T.A.R.O.—Territorial Army Reserve of Officers.
T.B.—Torpedo Boat; tuberculosis.
T.B.D.—Torpedo Boat Destroyer.
T.C.—Technical College; Touring Club; Trusteeship Council (U.N.)
T.C.A.—Trans-Canada Airlines.
T.C.B. —Thames Conservancy Board.
T.C.D.—Trinity College, Dublin.
T.C.J.C.—Trades Councils Joint Consultative Committee.
T.C.P.—Traffic Control Post.
T.C.P.A.—Town and Country Planning Association.
T.D.—Territorial (Officers') Decoration; Telecommunications Department; Telegraph Department; Telephone Department (G.P.O.).
t.e.g.—top edge gilt (Bookbinding).
Tel. No.—Telephone Number.
temp.—temperature; temporary; in the time of (L., *tempore*).
Tenn.—Tennessee.
Terr.—Territory.
Teut.—Teuton(ic).
Tex.—Texas.
text. rec.—Received text (L., *textus receptus*).
T.G.—Tate Gallery; Theatre Guild; Townswomens' Guild.
T.G.W.U.—Transport and General Workers' Union.
T.H.—Trinity House; Transport House.
Thurs.—Thursday.
T.H.W.M.—Trinity High Water Mark.
T.I.—Technical Institute.
Tib.—Tibet(an).
T.I.H.—Their Imperial Highnesses.
T.L.G.—Theatrical Ladies' Guild.
T.L.R.—Times Law Reports.
T.M.A.—Theatrical Managers' Association.
T.M.O.—Telegraph Money Office; Tel. Money Order.
T.N.T.—tri-nitro-toluene.
Toc H.—Talbot House.
tom.—Volume (Fr., *tome*).
T.P.I.—Town Planning Institute.
T.P.O.—Travelling Post Office.
tr.—trustee; translation.
trans.—transactions; translation.
T.R.C.—Teachers' Registration Council; Thames Rowing Club.
T.R.H.—Their Royal Highnesses.
T.R.L.—Tariff Reform League.
trs.—transpose [Print.].
T.R.T.A.—Traders' Road Transport Association.
Truron.—of Truro (L., *Truroniensis*).
T.S.—Television Society; Theosophical Society; Treasury Solicitor; Twin-screw.
T.S.B.—Trustee Savings Bank.
T.T.—Teetotaller [Coll.]; Tourist Trophy [Motoring].
t.t.l.—to take leave.
T.U.—Trade Union(ist).
T.U.C.—Trade Union Congress.
T.U.I.—Trade Union International.
Turk.—Turkey; Turkish.
T.V.A.—Tennessee Valley Authority.
T.W.A.—Trans World Airline (U.S.A.).
T.W.C.—Tail-Waggers' Club.
T.Y.C.—Thames Yacht Club.

U.—Union(ist); United; University.
U.A.—Ulster Association.
U.A.B.—Unemployment Assistance Board.
U.A.L.—United Air Lines (U.S.A.).
U.A.S.—University Air Squadron.
U.B.B.E.—Universities Bureau of the British Empire.
U.C.—University College.
U.C.D.—University College, Dublin.
U.C.H.—University College Hospital (London).
U.C.S.—University College School (London).
U.D.—United Dairies; Urban District.
U.D.C.—Urban District Council.
U.F.A.W.—Universities' Federation for Animal Welfare.
U.F.C.—United Free Church.
U.G.L.E.—United Grand Lodge of England (Freemasonry).
U.J.C.—Union Jack Club.
U.J.D.—*See* **J.U.D.**
U.K.—United Kingdom.
U.K.A.—United Kingdom Alliance.
U.K.C.T.A.—United Kingdom Commercial Travellers' Association.
U.L.F.—University Labour Federation.
ult.—Last month (L., *ultimo*, last).
U.L.T.T.U.—United Ladies' Tailors' Trade Union.
U.M.A.—United Maritime Authority.
U.M.C.C.—United Maritime Consultative Council.
U.M.F.C.—United Methodist Free Church.
U.M.T.—Universal Military Training (U.S.A.).
U.N.—United Nations.
U.N.A.—United Nations Association.
U.N.A.C.—United Nations Appeal for Children; United Nations Atomic Commission.
U.N.C.I.O.—United Nations Conference on International Organization.
U.N.E.S.C.O.—United Nations Educational, Scientific, and Cultural Organization.
U.N.F.A.O.—United Nations Food and Agricultural Organization.
U.N.I.O.—United Nations Information Organization.
univ.—university.
U.N.O.—United Nations Organization.
U.N.R.R.A.—United Nations Relief and Rehabilitation Administration.
U.N.S.A.—United Nations Student Association.
U.P.—United Presbyterian; United Press; United Provinces (India).
u.p.—under proof (of spirits).
U.P.C.—United Presbyterian Church; United Protestant Council.
U.P.O.W.—Union of Post Office Workers.
U.P.U.—Universal Postal Union.
U.S.—United States; United Services.
U.S.A.—United States of America; United States Army; Union of South Africa; United Society of Artists.
U.S.A.A.F.—United States Army Air Force.
U.S.A.F.I.—United States' Armed Forces' Institute.
U.S.A.N.P.—Union of South Africa National Party.
U.S.C.L.—United Society for Christian Literature (formerly Religious Tract Society).
U.S.E.—United Society of Engravers.
U.S.F.E.T.—United States' Forces in the European Theatre.
U.S.I.—United States of Indonesia; United Service Institution.
U.S.I.B.A.—United States International Book Association.
U.S.L.—United States Legation.
U.S.M.—United States Mail.
U.S.N.—United States Navy.
U.S.N.A.C.—United States Naval Air Corps.
U.S.S.R.—Union of Soviet Socialist Republics.
Ut.—Utah.
U.T.F.W.A.—United Textile Factory Workers' Association.
U.U.—Ulster Unionist [Polit.].
ux.—Wife (L., *uxor*).

V—Roman numeral for five; **V.**—see (L., *vide*); volt [Elect.]; **v.**—against (L., *versus*); velocity.
V.A.—Vice-Admiral; (Royal Order of) Victoria and Albert.

Va.—Virginia.
V.A.D.—Voluntary Aid Detachment.
V.A.F.—Variety Artistes' Federation.
V. & A.M.—Victoria and Albert Museum.
V. & M.—Virgin and Martyr.
Vat.—Vatican.
V.B.—Volunteer Battalion.
V.C.—Victoria Cross.
V.-C.—Vice-Chancellor.
V.C.H.—Victoria County History.
V.D.—Venereal disease; Volunteer (Officers') Decoration.
V.D.H.—Valvular disease of the heart.
V.E.—Victory in Europe (W.W.2).
vel.—velocity.
Ven.—Venerable.
verb. sap.—A word to the wise (is sufficient) (L., *verbum sapienti satis est*).
vet.—veterinary (surgeon).
V.G.—Vicar-General.
v.h.c.—very highly commended.
V.I.—Vancouver Island.
Vice-Adm.—Vice-Admiral.
Vict.—Victoria.
Vigorn.—of Worcester (L., *Vigorniensis*).
V.I.P.—Very Important Person [Coll.].
Visc.—Viscount.
viz.—Namely; to wit (L., *videlicet*).
V.J.—Victory over Japan (W.W.2).
V.M.D.—Doctor of Veterinary Medicine (L., *Veterinariæ Medicinæ Doctor*).
vo.—Left-hand page (L., *verso*).
V.O.K.S.—(Russian) Society for Cultural Relations with Foreign Countries (Russ., *Vsesoyuznoe obshchestvo kul'turnoy svyazi s zagranitsey*).
vol.—volume.
V.R.—Queen Victoria (L., *Victoria Regina*).
V.R.I.—Victoria, Queen and Empress (L., *Victoria Regina et Imperatrix*).
V.S.—Veterinary Surgeon.
Vt.—Vermont (U.S.A.).
Vul.—Vulgate.
vv. ll.—Various readings (L., *variæ lectiones*).
V.W.H.—Vale of White Horse.

W.—west.
w.—wicket, wide [Cricket].
W.A.—West Africa(n); Western Australia(n).
W.A.A.—War Assets' Administration (U.S.A.).
W.A.A.A.—Women's Amateur Athletic Association.
W.A.A.C.—Women's Army Auxiliary Corps.
W.A.A.F.—Women's Auxiliary Air Force.
W.A.A.E.—World Association for Adult Education.
W.A.E.C.—War Agricultural Executive Committee.
W.A.F.F.—*See* **R.W.A.F.F.**
W. Afr.—West Africa(n).
W.A.F.S.—Women's Auxiliary Fire Service.
W.A.R.—West African Regiment.
War—Warwickshire.
Wash.—Washington (State).
W.A.V.E.S.—Women's Auxiliary Volunteer Emergency Service (U.S. Naval Reserve).
W.B.—Water Board.
w.b.—waybill.
W.B.S.R.—Wellcome Bureau of Scientific Research.
W.C.—water-closet; Wesleyan Chapel; West Central (postal district); Whitley Council.
W.C.C.—World Council of Churches.
W.C.F.—World Congress of Faiths.
W.Comm.—Wing Commander.
W.C.T.U.—Women's Christian Temperance Union.
W.D.—War Department.
W.E.A. — Workers' Educational Association; Workers' Evangelical Alliance.
Wed.—Wednesday.
Wes.—Wesleyan.
Westmd—Westmorland.
w.f.—wrong fount.
W.F.L.—Women's Freedom League.
W.F.P.S.—Wild Flowers' Preservation Society.
W.F.S.—Wine and Food Society.
W.F.T.U.—World Federation of Trade Unions.
W.F.U.N.A.—World Federation of United Nations Associations.
W.G.—Welsh Guards.
W.G.M.—Worthy Grand Master; Worthy Grand Marshal (Freemasonry).
whf.—wharf.
W.H.O.—World Health Organization.
W.H.S.—Wesley Historical Society.
W.I.—West Indies; West Indian.
W.I.L.—Women's International League.
Wilts—Wiltshire.
Winton.—of Winchester (L., *Wintoniensis*).
Wis.—Wisconsin.
W.J.C.—World Jewish Congress.
W.L.A.—Women's Land Army.
W.L.F.—Women's Liberal Federation.
W.L.M.—West London Mission.
W.L.T.B.U.—Watermen, Lightermen, Tugmen, and Bargemen's Union.
W.M.—Worshipful Master (Freemasonry).
W.M.A.—World Medical Association.
W.M.C.—Working Men's College.
W.M.C.I.U.—Working Men's Club and Institute Union.
W.M.S.—Wesleyan Missionary Society.
W.N.E.—Welsh National Eisteddfod.
WNW.—west-north-west.
W.O.—War Office; Warrant Officer; Wireless Operator.
W.O.C.B.—War Office Casualty Branch.
W.O.M.—Wireless Operator Mechanic.
Worcs—Worcestershire.
w.p.—weather permitting [Coll.].
w.p.b.—waste-paper basket.
W.P.C.—War Pensions Committee.
W.P.R.A.—Waste Paper Recovery Association.
W.R.—West Riding (Yorks).
W.R.A.C.—Women's Royal Army Corps.
W.R.A.F.—Women's Royal Air Force.
W.R.I.—Wellcome Research Institution.
W.R.N.S.—Women's Royal Naval Service.
W.S.—Writer to the Signet.
W.S.P.U.—Women's Social and Political Union.
WSW.—west-south-west.
W.T.—War Transport; Wireless Telegraphy; Wireless Telephony.
wt.—weight.
W.T.A.—Wholesale Textile Association; Workers' Travel Association.
W.T.S.—Women's Transport Service.
W.T.U.C.—World Trade Union Conference.
W. Va.—West Virginia.
W.V.S.—Women's Voluntary Services.
W.W.1.—World War, 1914–18.
W.W.2.—World War, 1939–45.
Wyo.—Wyoming.

X—numeral for ten; the symbol for reactance [Elect.].
X., Xt.—Christ.
xcp.—Ex-coupon.
x.d.—Ex-dividend.
x.i.—Ex-interest.
Xmas.—Christmas.
x.n.—Ex new shares.
Xn., Xtian.—Christian.

y.—year.
Y.A.—Yachting Association.
Y.C.L.—Young Communist League.
yd.—yard.
Yeo.—Yeomanry.
Y.H.A.—Youth Hostels Association.
Y.H.L.—Young Helpers' League.
Y.L.I.—Yorkshire Light Infantry.
Y.M.C.A.—Young Men's Christian Association.
Y.M.Cath.A.—Young Men's Catholic Association.
y.o.—year old (horseracing).
Yorks.—Yorkshire.
yr.—year; younger.
Y.S.L.—Young Socialist League.
Y.W.C.A.—Young Women's Christian Association.
Y.W.C.T.U.—Young Women's Christian Temperance Union.

Z—The symbol for impedance [Elect.].
Zanz.—Zanzibar.
Z.B.M.M.—Zenana Bible and Medical Mission.
Z.F.G.B.I.—Zionist Federation of Great Britain and Ireland.
Z.hr.—Zero hour.
Zool.—Zoology; zoological.
Z.S.—Zoological Society.
Z.S.T.—Zone Standard Time.

&—and.
&c.—and so forth (etc.).

SYMBOLS OF THE CHEMICAL ELEMENTS

WITH ATOMIC NUMBER, ATOMIC WEIGHT, AND DATE OF EARLIEST IDENTIFICATION

Symbol	Name	Atomic No.	Atomic Weight	Date
A	Argon	18	39·944	1894
Ac	Actinium	89	227	1894
Ag	Silver (L. *Argentum*)	47	107·880	Prehist.
Al	Aluminium	13	26·97	1828
As	Arsenic	33	74·91	1649
Au	Gold (L. *Aurum*)	79	197·2	Prehist.
B	Boron	5	10·82	1808
Ba	Barium	56	137·36	1808
Be	Beryllium	4	9·02	1828
Bi	Bismuth	83	209·00	1450
Br	Bromine	35	79·916	1826
C	Carbon	6	12·010	Prehist.
Ca	Calcium	20	40·08	1808
Cb	Columbium (Niobium)	41	92·91	1801
Cd	Cadmium	48	112·41	1817
Ce	Cerium	58	140·13	1803
Cl	Chlorine	17	35·457	1774
Co	Cobalt	27	58·94	1739
Cr	Chromium	24	52·01	1797
Cs	Cæsium	55	132·91	1860
Cu	Copper (L. *Cuprum*)	29	63·57	Prehist.
Dy	Dysprosium	66	162·46	1886
Er	Erbium	68	167·2	1843
Eu	Europium	63	152·00	1896
F	Fluorine	9	19·00	1771
Fe	Iron (L. *Ferrum*)	26	55·84	Prehist.
Ga	Gallium	31	69·72	1875
Gd	Gadolinium	64	156·9	1880
Ge	Germanium	32	72·60	1886
Gl	Glucinum (Beryllium)	4	9·02	1828
H	Hydrogen	1	1·008	1766
He	Helium	2	4·003	1895
Hf	Hafnium	72	178·6	1923
Hg	Mercury (L.L. *Hydrargyrum*)	80	200·61	Prehist.
Ho	Holmium	67	163·5	1879
I	Iodine	53	126·92	1811
Il	Illinium	61	146[?]	1926
In	Indium	49	114·76	1863
Ir	Iridium	77	193·1	1803
K	Potassium (L.L. *Kalium*)	19	39·096	1807
Kr	Krypton	36	83·7	1898
La	Lanthanum	57	138·92	1839
Li	Lithium	3	6·940	1817
Lu	Lutecium	71	175·00	1907
Ma	Masurium	43	100[?]	1925
Mg	Magnesium	12	24·32	1829
Mn	Manganese	25	54·93	1774
Mo	Molybdenum	42	95·95	1782
N	Nitrogen	7	14·008	1772
Na	Sodium (L. *Natrium*)	11	22·997	1807
Nb	Niobium (*Columbium*)	41	92·91	1801
Nd	Neodymium	60	144·27	1885
Ne	Neon	10	20·183	1898
Ni	Nickel	28	58·69	1751
O	Oxygen	8	16·000	1774
Os	Osmium	76	190·2	1803
P	Phosphorus	15	30·98	1669
Pa	Protactinium	91	231	1917
Pb	Lead (L. *Plumbum*)	82	207·21	Prehist.
Pd	Palladium	46	106·7	1804
Po	Polonium	84	210[?]	1898
Pr	Praseodymium	59	140·92	1885
Pt	Platinum	78	195·23	1741
Ra	Radium	88	226·05	1898
Rb	Rubidium	37	85·45	1860
Re	Rhenium	75	186·31	1925
Rh	Rhodium	45	102·91	1804
Rn	Radon (Niton)	86	222	1901
Ru	Ruthenium	44	101·7	1845
S	Sulphur	16	32·06	Prehist.
Sb	Antimony (L. *Stibium*)	51	121·76	1450
Sc	Scandium	21	45·10	1879
Se	Selenium	34	78·96	1817
Si	Silicon	14	28·06	1823
Sm	Samarium	62	150·43	1879
Sn	Tin (L. *Stannum*)	50	118·70	Prehist.
Sr	Strontium	38	87·63	1808
Ta	Tantalum	73	180·88	1802
Tb	Terbium	65	159·2	1843
Te	Tellurium	52	127·61	1782
Th	Thorium	90	232·12	1828
Ti	Titanium	22	47·90	1789
Tl	Thallium	81	204·39	1862
Tm	Thulium	69	169·4	1879
U	Uranium	92	238·07	1789
V	Vanadium	23	50·95	1830
W	Tungsten (Ger. *Wolframite*)	74	183·92	1781
Xe	Xenon	54	131·3	1898
Yb	Ytterbium	70	173·04	1878
Yt	Yttrium	39	88·92	1794
Zn	Zinc	30	65·38	16th cent.
Zr	Zirconium	40	91·22	1824

SIGNS AND SYMBOLS USED IN SCIENCE AND COMMERCE

ASTRONOMICAL

- ϕ angle of eccentricity.
- μ or n angular motion in unit of time, mean.
- ♒ Aquarius.
- ♈ Aries.
- ○ asteroid (number in centre).
- ♋ Cancer.
- ♑ Capricornus.
- ☄ comet.
- ☌ conjunction.
- δ declination.
- ° degrees.
- Δ distance.
- ძ distance, mean.
- ⊕ Earth.
- ♊ Gemini.
- ♃ Jupiter.
- β latitude, celestial.
- ϕ latitude, geographic.
- ♌ Leo.
- ♎ Libra.
- λ longitude.
- ♂ Mars.
- ☿ Mercury.
- ′ minutes.
- ☽ Moon's first quarter.
- ☾ Moon's last quarter.
- ● Moon, new.
- ○ Moon, full.
- ♆ Neptune.
- ☊ node, ascending.
- ☋ node, descending.
- ☍ opposition.
- ♓ Pisces.
- ♇ Pluto.
- □ quadrature.
- ♐ Sagittarius.
- ♄ Saturn.
- ♏ Scorpio.
- ″ seconds.
- ⚹ sextile.
- ✳ star, fixed.
- ☉ Sun.
- ☉̲ Sun's lower limb.
- ☉̄ Sun's upper limb.
- ♉ Taurus.
- △ trine.
- ♅ Uranus.
- ♀ Venus.
- ♍ Virgo.

COMMERCIAL

- a/c account.
- A/c account of.
- A/S account sales.
- a/d after date.
- @ at.
- B/E Bill of Exchange.
- B/L Bill of Lading.
- B/S Bill of Sale.
- c/o care of.
- C/· coupon.
- d/a days after acceptance.
- d/d day's date.
- d/s days' sight.
- $ dollars.
- J/A Joint account.
- L/c Letter of Credit.
- Mc metallic currency.
- m/d month's date.
- m/s month's sight.
- n/a no account.
- o/a on account.
- O/D on demand.
- % per cent.
- ‰ per thousand.
- ₱ per each.
- P/N Promissory Note.
- £ pound sterling (when followed by A, E, T, or NZ signifies the Australian, Egyptian, Turkish, or New Zealand pound).
- x/c without coupon.
- x/d without dividend.
- x/i without interest.
- XX double strength (of ale).
- XXX triple strength (of ale).
- ′ feet.
- ″ inches.
- ° degrees.
- → British government property.

SIGNS AND SYMBOLS USED IN SCIENCE AND COMMERCE

MATHEMATICAL AND GEOMETRICAL

$+$	addition (plus).
$-$	subtraction (minus).
$\pm$	plus or minus.
$>$	greater than.
$\ngtr$	not greater than.
$<$	less than.
$\nless$	not less than.
$\times$	multiplication.
Π	product.
$\div$	division.
$=$	equal.
$\geqq$	equal to or greater than.
$\leqq$	equal to or less than.
$\fallingdotseq$	approximately equal to.
$\neq$	not equal to.
$\Leftrightarrow$	equivalent to.
$\equiv$	identical with.
∞	infinity.
$\because$	because.
$:$	is to (in proportion).
$::$	equals (in proportion).
$\therefore$	therefore.
$\sqrt{}$	root.
$\sqrt[3]{}$	cube root.
$\div\!\!\!\cdot$	geometric proportion.
$\backsimeq$	approximately equal to.
d	differential.
L *or* !	factorial.
$\int$	integral.
f	function.
Σ	sum.
$\in$	is a part of.
δ	variation.
$\propto$	varies as.
$\sim$	difference.
Δ	finite difference.
$\square$	square.
$\perp$	equilateral.
▱	parallelogram.
$\parallel$	parallel.
$\nparallel$	not parallel.
$\perp$	perpendicular.
$\top$	vertical.
$\odot$	circle.
◓	semicircle.
◲	quadrant.
π	pi (ratio of circumference of circle to diameter).
ρ	radius.
$\angle$	angle.
∟	right angle.
≚	equiangular.
$\triangle$	triangle.
$\frown$	arc.
$^{\circ}$	degree.
$'$	minute of arc.
$''$	second of arc.

MEDICAL

$\overline{AA}$, $\bar{A}$, or $\bar{a}\bar{a}$	of each.
℞	take.
C	one gallon.
O	pint (L. *octavius*).
℥	ounce.
℥ss	half ounce.
ʒ	dram.
fʒ	fluid dram.
℈ or ℈i	one scruple.
℈ss	half scruple.
℈iss	scruple and a half.
℈ij	two scruples.
℈iij	three scruples.
♏	drop (minim).

METEOROLOGICAL

⌓	aurora.
◎	calm.
⩊	corona, lunar.
⦶	corona, solar.
⍊	dew.
≡	fog or mist.
≣	fog, ground.
∾	frost, glazed.
⊔	frost, hoar-.
⟋	gale.
▲	hail.
◒	halo, lunar.
$\oplus$	halo, solar.
∞	haze.
←	ice crystal, floating.
↯	lightning, sheet.
⋈	mirage.
⊘	rain.
⌒	rainbow.
V	rime.
△	sleet (snow and rain).
∾	sleet (with ice pellets).
∞	smoke.
⋇	snow.
⇸	snow, drifting.
⇸	snow, driving.
$\odot$	sunshine.
T	thunder.
⌈↘	thunderstorm.
⏛	zodiacal light.

MUSICAL

- alto clef.
- bar.
- bass clef.
- breve.
- common time.
- crescendo.
- crotchet.
- crotchet rest.
- demi-semiquaver.
- demi-semiquaver rest.
- diminuendo.
- direction to increase time-value by one-half.
- double flat.
- double sharp.
- flat.
- minim.
- minim rest.
- natural.
- pause.
- quaver.
- quaver rest.
- repeat.
- semibreve.
- semibreve rest.
- semiquaver.
- semiquaver rest.
- sforzando.
- sharp.
- sign of repeated part.
- six crochets in a bar.
- six quavers in a bar.
- slur.
- swell.
- tenor clef.
- three crotchets in a bar.
- three minims in a bar.
- three quavers in a bar.
- treble clef.
- turn.
- two crotchets in a bar.

ROMAN AND ARABIC NUMERALS

Rom.	Arab.	Rom.	Arab.	Rom.	Arab.	Rom.	Arab.
I	1	XVII	17	LXXXV	85	MCC	1200
II	2	XVIII	18	XC	90	MCCC	1300
III	3	XIX	19	XCV	95	MCD [MCCCC]	1400
IV [IIII]	4	XX	20	C	100	MD	1500
V	5	XXV	25	CC	200	MDC	1600
VI	6	XXX	30	CCC	300	MDCC	1700
VII	7	XXXV	35	CD [CCCC]	400	MDCCC	1800
VIII	8	XL	40	D [IↃ]	500	MDCCCLXXXVIII	1888
IX	9	XLV	45	DC [IↃC]	600	MDCCCXCIX	1899
X	10	L	50	DCC [IↃCC]	700	MCM [MDCCCC]	1900
XI	11	LV	55	DCCC [IↃCCC]	800	MCMLI	1951
XII	12	LX	60	CM [DCCCC or IↃCCCC]	900	MM [CIↃCIↃ]	2000
XIII	13	LXV	65	M [CIↃ]	1000		
XIV	14	LXX	70	MC	1100		
XV	15	LXXV	75				
XVI	16	LXXX	80				

A dash over a letter denotes multiplication by 1,000, thus $\overline{\text{M}}$ = 1,000,000 and $\overline{\text{X}}$ = 10,000. A letter placed *after* one of greater value adds thereto, as XI = 10 + 1 = 11, but placed *before* one of greater value subtracts therefrom, as IX = 10 − 1 = 9; a repeated letter repeats its value, as II 2, XXX 30, etc.

Of the alternatives, here given within square brackets, IIII (for IV) is the only one now in use, and that only on the dial of timepieces.

THE MORSE CODE: LETTERS, FIGURES, AND SIGNS

Letters	
A	· —
B	— · · ·
C	— · — ·
D	— · ·
E	·
F	· · — ·
G	— — ·
H	· · · ·
I	· ·
J	· — — —
K	— · —
L	· — · ·
M	— —
N	— ·
O	— — —
P	· — — ·
Q	— — · —
R	· — ·
S	· · ·
T	—
U	· · —
V	· · · —
W	· — —
X	— · · —
Y	— · — —
Z	— — · ·

Numerals			
1	· — — — —	6	— · · · ·
2	· · — — —	7	— — · · ·
3	· · · — —	8	— — — · ·
4	· · · · —	9	— — — — ·
5	· · · · ·	0	— — — — —

Punctuation and Special Signs	
Numeral	· · — · · ·
Comma	· — · —
Colon	— — — · · ·
Full Stop	· — · — · —
Interrogation (*also* Repeat) ..	· · — — · ·
Exclamation	— — · · — —
Apostrophe	· — — — — ·
Hyphen	— · · · · —
Oblique Stroke	— · · — ·
Parentheses (brackets) ..	— · — — · —
Inverted Commas	· — · · — ·
Underline (*also* Block Letters)	· · — — · —
Erase	· · · · · · · · eight dots—rapidly
Commencing Sign	· · · — ·
Ending Sign	· — · — ·
Separative sign	· · · ·
Long break sign	— · · · —

TYPOGRAPHIC

´ acute accent.
& ampersand.
' apostrophe.
* asterisk.
⁂ asterism.
{ } braces.
[ ] brackets.
˘ breve.
∧ caret.
¸ cedilla.
^ circumflex.
⁀ close up.
: colon.
, comma.

† dagger.
— dash.
δ delete.
¨ diæresis.
‡ double dagger.
* * * / . . . / —— ellipsis.
&c. et cetera.
! exclamation.
⊙ full stop.
` grave accent.
- hyphen.

☞ index.
? interrogation.
¯ macron.
¶ paragraph.
‖ parallel.
( ) parentheses.
⅌ per.
" " quotation marks.
§ section.
; semicolon.
/ solidus.
\# space out.
~ tilde.
∽ turn.

WEIGHTS AND MEASURES

MEASURES OF LENGTH

Long Measure

12	**Inches** (in.)	= 1 **Foot** (ft.)
3	Feet = 36 in.	= 1 **Yard** (yd.)
5½	Yards = 16½ ft. = 198 in.	= 1 **Rod** (rd.), **Pole, or Perch**
4	Rods = 22 yds. = 66 ft.	= 1 **Chain** (ch.)
10	Chains = 40 rds. = 220 yds.	= 1 **Furlong** (fur.)
8	Furlongs = 1,760 yds. = 5,280 ft.	= 1 (Statute) **Mile** (m.)
1·15	Miles = 2,026⅔ yds. = 6,080 ft.	= 1 **Nautical** or **Geographical Mile**

Surveyors' Measure

7·92	Inches	= 1 **Link**
100	Links = 4 rds. = 22 yds.	= 1 **Chain**
80	Chains = 1,760 yds. = 8,000 links	= 1 **Mile**

Nautical Measure

6	Feet	= 1 **Fathom**
202⅔	Yards	= 1 **Cable's length**
10	Cable's lengths = 2,026⅔ yds.	= 1 **Nautical Mile**
3	Nautical miles (3 m. 800 yds.)	= 1 **League**
60	Nautical miles	= 1 **Degree of Longitude** at the Equator.

Strictly speaking, the length of a Nautical Mile varies with the latitude; for it is, at any given place, equal to 1 min. of arc measured along the meridian through that place. For practical purposes it is reckoned as 6,080 ft., which is its actual length in 48° lat.

The Knot is a unit of speed only, and is used only in marine (and in some mensuration systems of aerial) navigation. It equals 1 Nautical Mile per hour; thus, " 20 knots " indicates a speed of 20 naut. m. (23 stat. m.) per hour.

Length of Degree of Longitude in Various Latitudes

Deg. Lat.	Stat. M.	Naut. M.	Deg. Lat.	Stat. M.	Naut. M.	Deg. Lat.	Stat. M.	Naut. M.
Equator	69·160	60·000	36	56·016	48·597	65	29·308	25·425
6	68·783	59·673	40	53·053	46·026	71	22·582	19·593
10	68·116	59·093	45	48·986	42·498	75	17·956	15·578
16	66·499	57·690	51	43·611	37·835	81	10·853	9·417
20	65·015	56·404	55	39·758	34·491	85	6·048	5·248
30	59·944	52·005	61	33·615	29·164	89	1·211	1·050

Altitudes

In Feet, Miles, and Metres

Ft. (and Miles)	Metres	Ft. (and Miles)	Metres	Ft. (and Miles)	Metres
100	30·48	9,842·4	**3,000**	22,000	6,705·6
250	76·20	10,000	3,048	22,965·6	**7,000**
328·09	**100**	10,560 **(2 m.)**	3,218·7	23,000	7,010·4
500	152·4	11,000	3,352·8	24,000	7,315·2
700	213·36	11,482·8	**3,500**	24,606	**7,500**
820·14	**250**	12,000	3,657·6	25,000	7,620
900	274·32	13,000	3,962·4	26,000	7,924·8
1,000	304·80	13,123·2	**4,000**	26,246·4	**8,000**
1,500	457·2	14,000	4,267·2	26,400 **(5 m.)**	8,046·7
1,640·4	**500**	14,763·2	**4,500**	27,000	8,229·6
2,000	609·6	15,000	4,572	27,887·2	**8,500**
2,500	762	15,840 **(3 m.)**	4,828	28,000	8,534·4
3,000	914·4	16,000	4,876·8	29,000	8,839·2
3,280·8	**1,000**	16,404	**5,000**	29,527·6	**9,000**
4,000	1,219·2	17,000	5,181·6	30,000	9,144
4,921·2	**1,500**	18,000	5,486·4	31,000	9,448·8
5,000	1,524	18,044·4	**5,500**	31,168	**9,500**
5,280 **(1 m.)**	1,609·3	19,000	5,791·2	31,680 **(6 m.)**	9,656·1
6,000	1,828·8	19,684·8	**6,000**	32,000	9,753·6
7,000	2,133·6	20,000	6,096	32,808	**10,000**
8,000	2,438·4	21,000	6,400·8	36,089	**11,000**
8,201·4	**2,500**	21,120 **(4 m.)**	6,437·4	36,960 **(7 m.)**	11,265·4
9,000	2,743·2	21,325·2	**6,500**		

Astronomical Measures

(Distances given are approximate only)

The **Astronomical Unit**
= mean distance of Earth from Sun = 92,897,400 m.
Light-year (*see* DICT.) = 5,900,000,000,000 m.
Parsec (*see* DICT.) = 3·259 lt.-yrs. = 19,234,000,000,000 m.

For special purposes the **Dekaparsec** (= 10 Parsecs) is in use, and, for distances of the remoter nebulæ, the **Megaparsec** of 1 million Parsecs, or 3·259 million Light-years.

Miscellaneous Lengths

[1] **Point**	= $\frac{1}{72}$ in.	[2] **Span**	= 9 in.
[2] **Line**	= $\frac{1}{12}$ in.	**Pace, Mil.** (quick time)	= 2 ft. 6 in.
[2] **Barleycorn**	= $\frac{1}{3}$ in.	[3] **Ell, Flemish** = 4 qtrs.	= 3 ft.
[3] **Nail** = $\frac{1}{16}$ yd.	= $2\frac{1}{4}$ in.	[3] **Ell, English** = 5 qtrs.	= 3 ft. 9 in.
[4] **Hand**	= 4 in.	[3] **Ell, French** = 6 qtrs.	= 4 ft. 6 in.
[3] **Quarter** = $\frac{1}{4}$ yd.	= 9 in.	**Pace, Geometrical**	= 5 ft.

[1] Printers' unit of measurement; [2] obsolete as a definite measure; [3] formerly used in measuring cloth; [4] chiefly for the height of horses.

SQUARE MEASURE

144 (12 × 12) **Square Inches**	= 1 **Square Foot**
9 (3 × 3) Square Feet	= 1 **Square Yard**
$30\frac{1}{4}$ ($5\frac{1}{2}$ × $5\frac{1}{2}$) Square Yards or 625 (25 × 25) Square Links	= 1 **Square Rod, Pole, or Perch**
16 (4 × 4) Square Poles or 10,000 (100 × 100) Square Links	= 1 **Square Chain**
40 Square Poles or 1,210 Square Yards	= 1 **Rood**
4 Roods, 10 Square Chains, or 100,000 Square Links	= 1 **Acre**
640 Acres	= 1 **Square Mile**

As 100,000 sq. links = 1 Acre, an area given in sq. links is at once reduced to acres by pointing off the last five figures: thus, a field measuring 975 links (nearly 216 yds.) each way would be 9·50625 (975^2 = 950,625), or just over $9\frac{1}{2}$, acres.

Note the difference between "12 square inches," consisting of 12 squares each of 1 inch, and "12 inches square" (*i.e.*, a square of which the side is 12 in.), consisting of 144 squares each of one inch; also, that while the circular foot (*i.e.*, a circle of 1 ft. diam.) contains 113·097 sq. in., the area of a square foot is equal to that of 183·346 circular inches (*i.e.*, circles of 1 in. diam.).

ANGULAR MEASURE

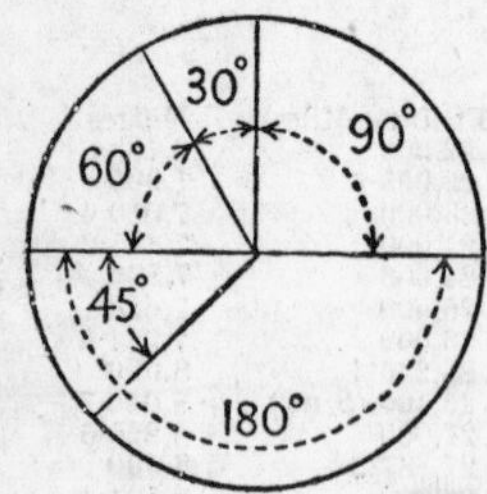

60 **Seconds** (″)	= 1 **Minute**
60 Minutes (′)	= 1 **Degree**
30 Degrees (°)	= 1 **Sign** (of the Zodiac)
90 Degrees	= 1 **Quadrant** or **Right Angle**
4 Quadrants, or 360°	= 1 **Circumference** or **Circle**

A *Sextant* = 60°; an *Octant* = 45°; Two right angles = 180°. The *Circumference* of a circle is nearly $3\frac{1}{7}$ times its diameter, or more accurately 3·1416 times; in other words, this number is the *circumference* of a circle whose *diameter* is unity; consequently the *diameter* of a circle is nearly $\frac{7}{22}$, or more accurately ·31831 of its circumference. The angles of a triangle added together are equal to 180°, or two right angles.

MEASURES OF CAPACITY

Liquid Measure

$\frac{1}{4}$ Pint (= 8·67062 cu. in)	= 1 **Gill**
4 Gills (= 34·6825 cu. in.)	= 1 **Pint** (pt.)
2 Pints	= 1 **Quart** (qt.)
4 Quarts (= 277·46 cu. in.)	= 1 **Gallon** (gall.)
9 Gallons	= 1 **Firkin** (fir.)
2 Firkins	= 1 **Kilderkin** (kil.)

Liquid Measure (*continued*)

2 Kilderkins = 36 gall.	= 1 **Barrel** (bar.)
1½ Barrels = 54 gall.	= 1 **Hogshead** (hhd.)
2 Barrels = 72 gall.	= 1 **Puncheon**
3 Barrels = 2 hhd. = 108 gall.	= 1 **Butt**
2 Butts = 216 gall.	= 1 **Tun**

Note that the wine and spirit trade still has a few measures peculiar to itself, esp. the *pipe*, which, in modern practice, varies from about 92 gall. for Cape wines to about 115 gall. for port. The old *Winchester gallon* contained ·8831 imperial gall., the *anker*, 10 of these (8·831 imp. gall.), the *tierce*, 42 (35), the *pipe*, 126 (105), and the *tun* 252 (210). An *octave* is ⅛th of a butt (13½ gall.), and a *pin* ⅛th of a barrel (4½ gall.). The ordinary wine or spirit bottle—the *reputed quart*—contains ⅙th of a gallon. Other measures more or less in use are the *rehoboam*, of 8 bottles, the *jeroboam*, of 6, the *stoup*, 7 pts., the *double magnum*, 4 bottles, the *tappit hen*, 3, and the *magnum*, 2 bottles. The *half-bottle* is a *reputed pint*, or $\frac{1}{12}$th of a gallon. The *mutchkin* (Scot.) is ¾ pint.

Apothecary's Measure, Liquid

60 **Minims**	= 1 **Fluid Drachm** (fʒ)	1 **Teaspoonful**	= 1 fʒ
8 Fl. Drachms	= 1 **Fluid Ounce** (f℥)	1 **Desertspoonful**	= 2 fʒ
20 Fl. Ounces	= 1 **Pint** (O)	1 **Tablespoonful**	= ½ f. oz. (f℥ss)
8 Pints	= 1 **Gallon** (C)	1 **Wineglassful**	= 2 f. oz.

Dry Measure

4 **Gills**	= 1 **Pint**	2 Gallons	= 1 **Peck**
2 Pints	= 1 **Quart**	4 Pecks	= 1 **Bushel**
4 Quarts	= 1 **Gallon**	8 Bushels	= 1 **Quarter**

The above are used principally for grain of all kinds, peas, beans, and any merchandise the surface of which may be conveniently levelled with a strickle.

Of the numerous other Dry and Liquid Measures for special classes of goods the following—some of which are now obsolete or of purely local use—is a representative selection:—

Bag:
- Cochineal .. 200 lb.
- Cocoa .. 1 cwt.
- Coffee .. 1¼–1½ cwt.
- Ginger .. 1–1¼ cwt.
- Hops .. 280 lb.
- Rice .. 2 cwt.
- ,, , E. Indian .. about 1½ cwt.
- Sago .. 1 cwt.

Bale: Coffee (Mocha) .. 2–2½ cwt.

Barrel:
- Beef: Pork .. 200 lb.
- Butter .. 224 lb.
- Candles .. 122 lb.
- Coffee .. 1–1½ cwt.
- Flour .. 196 lb.
- Gunpowder .. 100 lb.
- Raisins .. 112 lb.
- Resin .. about 2 cwt.
- Soap, soft .. 256 lb.
- Tapioca .. about 1¼ cwt.
- Tar .. 26¼ gall.
- Turpentine .. 2–2½ cwt.

Boll:
- Flour .. 140 lb.
- Grain .. 6 bushels
- ,, ("New" boll) .. 2 bushels

Bushel:
- Coal .. 80 lb.
- Salt .. 56 lb.

Cask:
- Cocoa .. ¾ cwt.
- Nutmegs .. 200 lb.
- Rice (Amer.) .. 6 cwt.
- Soda .. 3—4 cwt.
- Tallow .. about 9 cwt.

Chaldron:
- Coal .. 53 cwt. or 85 bushels
- Coke .. 36 bushels

Clove:
- Cheese .. 8 lb.
- Wool .. 7 lb.

Coomb:
- Grain, malt, potatoes, etc. .. 4 bushels

Cran: Fresh herring .. 37½ gall.

Faggot: Steel .. 200 lb.

Firlot (Scot.): Grain .. ¼ boll.

Firkin:
- Butter .. 56 lb.
- Soap, soft .. 64 lb.

Fother:
- Coal (= ⅓ chaldron) .. 17⅔ cwt.
- Lead .. 19½ cwt.

Gallon: Honey .. 12 lb.

Hogshead:
- Brandy .. 60 gall.
- Rum .. 45–50 gall.
- Sugar .. 13–16 cwt.

Keel: Coal .. 21 ton, 4 cwt.

Last:
- Feathers: Flax .. 1,700 lb.
- Grain .. 80 bushels
- Gunpowder (24 barrels) .. 2,400 lb.
- Hides .. 12 dozen
- Meal .. 12 barrels
- Wool (12 sacks) .. 4,368 lb.

Load:
- Bricks .. 500
- Earth .. 1 cu. yd.
- Grain .. 40 bushels
- Straw: Hay .. 36 truss
- Tiles .. 1,000

Pack:
- Soap, soft .. 256 lb.
- Wool .. 240 lb.

Peck: Salt .. 14 lb.

Pocket: Hops .. 1½–2 cwt.

Puncheon:
- Brandy: Rum .. 120 gall.
- Molasses .. 10–12 cwt.

Quartern: loaf .. 4 lb.

Room: Coal .. 7 ton

Sack:
- Coal .. 112 lb.
- Flour .. 280 lb.

Dry Measure (*continued*)

Sack—*continued*	
Potatoes	168 lb.
Wool	364 lb.
Seam:	
Apples	9 peck
Glass	120 lb.
Grain	8 bushels
Sand	6–8 peck
Shipload: Coal	424 ton
Skein: Cotton yarn	120 yd.
Stone:	
Cheese	16 lb.
Glass	5 lb.
Hemp	32 lb.
Iron	14 lb.
Meat	8 lb.
Wool	14 lb.
Strike: Grain	2 bushels
Tierce:	
Coffee	5–7 cwt.
Sugar	7–9 cwt.
Tod: Wool	28 lb.
Truck: Coal	8 ton
Truss:	
Hay (after 29 Sept.)	56 lb.
,, (fresh cut)	60 lb.
Straw	36 lb.
Tub: Butter	84 lb.
Wey:	
Cheese (Suffolk)	256 lb.
,, (Essex)	336 lb.
Grain: Malt	48 bushels
Salt	40 bushels
Wool	182 lb.

SOLID or CUBIC MEASURES

1,728 (12 × 12 × 12) **Cubic Inches** = 1 **Cubic Foot**
27 (3 × 3 × 3) Cubic Feet = 1 **Cubic Yard**

Timber and Wood

40 Cubic Feet of unhewn Timber } = 1 **Ton or Load**
50 Cubic Feet of squared Timber }
42 Cubic Feet of Timber = 1 **Shipping Ton**
108 ,, ,, ,, = 1 **Stack**
128 ,, ,, ,, = 1 **Cord**

Builders' Measurements

Stock or Kiln Bricks	$8\frac{3}{4}$ in. × $4\frac{1}{4}$ × $2\frac{3}{4}$
Welch Fire Bricks	9 in. × $4\frac{1}{2}$ × $2\frac{3}{4}$
Paving Bricks	9 in. × $4\frac{1}{2}$ × $1\frac{3}{4}$
Square Tiles	$9\frac{3}{4}$ in. × $9\frac{3}{4}$ × 1
,, ,,	6 in. × 6 × 1
Dutch Clinker Bricks	$9\frac{1}{4}$ in. × 3 × $1\frac{1}{2}$

1 **Rod** of Brickwork = $16\frac{1}{2}$ ft. × $1\frac{1}{2}$ brick thick = 306 cubic ft. or $11\frac{1}{3}$ cubic yd.

MEASURES OF WEIGHT

Avoirdupois

16 **Drams** (dr.) = $437\frac{1}{2}$ **grains** = 1 **Ounce** (oz.)
16 Ounces = 7,000 grains = 1 **Pound** (lb.)
14 Pounds = 1 **Stone** (st.)
28 Pounds = 1 **Quarter** (qr.)
4 Quarters = 112 lb. = 1 **Hundredweight** (cwt.)
20 Hundredweights = 2,240 lb. = 1 **Ton**

Troy

24 **Grains** = 1 **Pennyweight** (dwt.)
20 Pennyweight = 480 grains = 1 **Ounce** (oz.)
12 Ounces = 5,760 grains = 1 **Pound** (lb.)

Prior to the Weights and Measures Act, 1878, this scale was legal for the sale of gold and silver articles, platinum, and precious stones; by that Act its use was restricted to the Ounce with its decimal parts and multiples.

The **Carat,** a unit of weight for diamonds, precious stones, and pearls, is no part of the Troy system, The standard international metric carat = 200 milligrammes, or 3·08647 grains, but in England the old weight of 3·168 gr. (205·6 mg.) is still sometimes used. The word is also used to indicate the purity of gold alloy (*see* DICT.).

Confusion may arise between Avoirdupois and Troy weights because of the names " pound " and " ounce " which connote different weights in each, the *grain* only being the same and forming the sole connexion between Avoirdupois, Troy, and Apothecaries' weights. The Avoirdupois pound contains 7,000 grains, and its ounce $\frac{1}{16}$th of this, or

Measures of Weight (*continued*)

437½ grains; the Troy pound contained 5,760 grains, and its ounce $\frac{1}{12}$th of this, or 480 grains; hence, while the *pound* Avoirdupois is heavier than was the pound Troy, the *ounce* Avoirdupois is lighter than the ounce Troy. Note that the ounce Troy and the Apothecaries' ounce are of the same weight.

Apothecaries'

(Used in dispensing only: drugs are bought and sold by Avoirdupois.)

20 **Grains** = 1 **Scruple** (℈)
3 Scruples = 60 gr. = 1 **Drachm** (ʒ)
8 Drachms = 480 gr. = 1 **Ounce** (℥)

PAPER MEASURE

24 Sheets = **1 Quire**
20 Quires (480 Sheets) = **1 Ream**
516 Sheets = **1 Printer's Ream**
2 Reams = **1 Bundle**
5 Bundles = **1 Bale**

Writing and Drawing Papers

	In inches	
	Sheet	8vo.
Antiquarian	31 × 53	15½ × 13¼
Atlas	26 × 34	13 × 8½
„ , Dbl.	31½ × 55	15¾ × 13¾
Columbier	24 × 34½	12 × 8⅝
Copy	16 × 20	8 × 5
Demy	15½ × 20	7¾ × 5
„ , Dbl.	22½ × 35	11¼ × 8¾
Elephant	23 × 28	11½ × 7
„ , Dbl.	26½ × 40	13¼ × 10
Emperor	48 × 72	24 × 18
Foolscap	13¼ × 16½	6⅝ × 4⅛
„ , Dbl.	16½ × 26½	8¼ × 6⅝

	In inches	
	Sheet	8vo.
Foolscap, 1½ sheet ..	13¼ × 24½	6⅝ × 6⅛
„ , 1⅓ sheet ..	13¼ × 22	6⅝ × 5½
Grand Eagle	28¾ × 42	14⅜ × 10½
Imperial	22 × 30	11 × 7½
Medium	17½ × 22	8¾ × 5½
Post	15¼ × 19	7⅝ × 4¾
„ , Dbl.	30½ × 19	15¼ × 4¾
„ , Large	16½ × 21	8¼ × 5¼
„ , Pinched	14¾ × 18½	7⅜ × 4⅝
Pott	12½ × 15	6¼ × 3¾
Royal	19 × 24	9½ × 6
„ , Super	19 × 27	9½ × 6¾

Printing Papers

	In inches	
	Sheet	8vo.
Crown	15 × 20	7½ × 5
„ , Dbl.	20 × 30	10 × 7½
„ , Quad	30 × 40	15 × 10
Demy	17½ × 22½	8¾ × 5⅝
„ , Dbl.	22½ × 35	11¼ × 8¾
„ , Quad	35 × 45	17½ × 11¼
Foolscap	13½ × 17	6¾ × 4¼
„ , Dbl.	17 × 27	8½ × 6¾
„ , Quad	27 × 34	13½ × 8½
Imperial	22 × 30	11 × 7½
„ , Dbl.	30 × 44	15 × 11
Medium	18 × 23	9 × 5¾
„ , Dbl.	23 × 36	11½ × 9

	In inches	
	Sheet	8vo.
Post, ...	15¼ × 19	7⅝ × 4¾
„ , Dbl.	19 × 30½	9½ × 7⅝
Large Post	16½ × 21	8¼ × 5¼
„ „ , Dbl.	21 × 33	10½ × 8¼
Medium, Quad	36 × 46	18 × 11½
Pott	12½ × 16½	6¼ × 4⅛
„ , Dbl.	16½ × 25	8¼ × 6¼
Royal	20 × 25	10 × 6¼
„ , Dbl.	25 × 40	12½ × 10
„ , Quad	40 × 50	20 × 12½
Super Royal	20½ × 27½	10¼ × 6⅞
„ „ , Dbl. ..	27½ × 41	13¾ × 10¼
„ „ , Quad ..	41 × 55	20½ × 13¾

THE THERMOMETER

In the United Kingdom and English-speaking countries generally two thermometric scales are in use, viz., the *Fahrenheit* and the *Centigrade*, the latter mainly for scientific purposes. On the Continent the *Centigrade* is used for all purposes, the *Réaumur*—in which 0° represented the freezing-point and 80° the boiling-point of water—having fallen into disuse.

In *Fahrenheit* 32° and 212° respectively represent the freezing- and boiling-points of water (at 760 mm. barometric pressure), in *Centigrade*, 0° and 100°. 5° C. is equal to 9° F.; therefore 5° C. = 41 (32 + 9)° F., 10° C. = 50° F., 20° C. = 68° F., etc.

To convert *Fahrenheit* into *Centigrade*: Deduct 32, multiplying result by 5, and divide product by 9; thus: 212° F. = 212 − 32 (180) × 5 (900) ÷ 9 = 100° C.

To convert *Centigrade* into *Fahrenheit*: Multiply by 9, divide product by 5, and add 32 to quotient; thus: 100° C. = 100 × 9 (900) ÷ 5 (180) + 32 = 212° F.

THE METRIC SYSTEM

WITH TABLES OF THE EQUIVALENTS IN BRITISH WEIGHTS AND MEASURES

THE Metric System, legalized in France in the year 1801, is so called because it has for its basis the metre, from which the units of all its measures are derived. The metre is the ten-millionth part of the assumed length of a meridian arc from the equator to either pole; this was determined by an International Commission in 1818 as equivalent to 39·3707904 inches, but later measurements showed that this was slightly inaccurate and in 1898 it was decreed by Order in Council that the legal equivalent for Great Britain is 39·370113 inches; for all ordinary purposes this is reckoned at 39·37 inches in all countries using the British system.

The units of the various measures are as follows: The *Metre*, for measures of Length; the *Are*, for Surfaces; the *Stere*, for Solids; the *Litre*, for Capacity; the *Gramme*, for Weight; the *Franc*, for Money. The unit in each degree is one-tenth of the degree above it and ten times the degree below it, and in order to express the decimal proportion, the following prefixes to the principal units have been adopted:—

Deca	signifies	10	times the Unit
Hecto	„	100	„
Kilo	„	1,000	„
Myria	„	10,000	„
Deci	expresses the	10th	part of the Unit.
Centi	„	100th	„
Milli	„	1,000th	„

I. MEASURE OF LENGTH

Unit, the Metre, which, as stated above, is the ten-millionth part of a meridian arc from the equator to either pole, and is equal in British Measure to ..

39·3701 Inches.	·0497 Chain.
3·2808 Feet.	·00497 Fur.
1·0936 Yards.	·0006213 Mile.
·1988 Pole.	·5468 Fathom.

	Proportion to the Metre		M.	Yds.	Ft.	In.
1 **Millimetre**	= $\frac{1}{1000}$	= ·03937 Inch, or about $\frac{1}{25}$ of an Inch.				
1 **Centimetre**	= $\frac{1}{100}$	= ·39370 „ or „ $\frac{2}{5}$ „				
1 **Decimetre**	= $\frac{1}{10}$	= ·32809 Foot, or „ 4 Inches				
1 **Metre**	= 1	= 1·0936 Yards, or about		1	0	$3\frac{2}{5}$
1 **Decametre**	= 10	= 5·468 Fathoms, or „		10	2	$9\frac{3}{4}$
1 **Hectometre**	= 100	= 19·88 Poles, or „		109	1	1
1 **Kilometre**	= 1,000	= 4·97 Furlongs, or		1,093	1	$10\frac{4}{5}$
1 **Myriametre**	= 10,000	= 6·2137 Miles =	6	376	1	0

II. MEASURE OF SURFACE

The Unit, the Are, is equal to a square decametre, of 100 square metres, and is equal in British Measure to

- 1,076·39 Square Feet.
- 119·59 Square Yards.
- 3·95 Perches.
- ·247 Square Chain.
- ·099 Rood.
- ·02471 Acre.

	Proportion to the Are			Ac.	Rd.	Sq. Yds.	Sq. Ft.	Sq. In.
1 **Sq. Metre**	= $\frac{1}{100}$	= 10·7639 Sq. Feet	= about	0	0	1	1	110
1 **Are**	= 1	= 3·95 Perches	= „	0	0	119	5	$61\frac{7}{8}$
1 **Hectare**	= 100	= 2·471 Acres	= „	2	1	1,069	5	$109\frac{1}{2}$

III. CUBIC or SOLID MEASURE

The Unit, the Stere, is equal to a cubic metre, and is equal in British Measure to .. .. { 61,023·9744 Cubic Inches. 35·3148 Cubic Feet. 1·307954 Cubic Yards.

	Proportion to the Stere				Cub. Yds.	Cub. Ft.	Cub. In.
1 **Centistere**	= $\frac{1}{100}$ =	610·24 Cubic Inches	=	about	0	0	$610\frac{6}{25}$
1 **Decistere**	= $\frac{1}{10}$ =	3·53148 Cubic Feet	=	,,	0	3	$918\frac{3}{5}$
1 **Stere**	= 1 =	1·307954 Cubic Yards	=	,,	1	8	$547\frac{1}{40}$
1 **Decastere**	= 10 =	13·07954 Cubic Yards	=	,,	13	1	$628\frac{1}{4}$

IV. MEASURE OF CAPACITY

The Unit, the Litre, is equal to a cubic decimetre, or $\frac{1}{1000}$ of a stere, and is equal in British Measure to .. { 61·024 Cubic Inches. 1·75980 Imperial Pints. ·22000 Imperial Gallon. ·0275 Imperial Bushel.

	Proportion to the Litre			Gals.	Qts.	Pts.
1 **Centilitre**	= $\frac{1}{100}$ =	·01760 Pint, or about 57 to a pint.				
1 **Decilitre**	= $\frac{1}{10}$ =	·17598 ,,	,, $5\frac{1}{2}$,,			
1 **Litre**	= 1 =	1·75980 Pints, or about		0	0	$1\frac{3}{4}$
1 **Decalitre**	= 10 =	2·2000 Gallons,	,,	2	0	$1\frac{3}{5}$
1 **Hectolitre**	= 100 =	2·75 Bushels, or		22	0	0

Note.—The litre contains 2·113 American pints. The U.S.A. gallon contains only 231 cubic inches as against 277·46 of the British gallon, that is a ratio of about 5 to 6; and the U.S.A. bushel contains only 2,150·42 cubic inches, a ratio of about 16 to 19 of the British bushel.

V. MEASURE OF WEIGHT

The Unit is the Gramme, which is equal to the weight of a cubic centimetre of distilled water, or $\frac{1}{1000}$ of the weight of a litre of distilled water, and is equal in British Measure to .. .. { 15·43235 Grains. ·03215 Troy Oz. ·03527 Oz. Av. ·002204 Lb. Av. ·0000196 Cwt. ·0000009 Ton.

	Proportion to the Gramme	Troy Oz.	Dwt.	Gr.	Avoirdupois Lb.	Oz.	Dram
1 **Milligramme**	= $\frac{1}{1000}$ =	0	0	0·0154	0	0	0·00056438
1 **Centigramme**	= $\frac{1}{100}$ =	0	0	0·1543	0	0	0·0056438
1 **Decigramme**	= $\frac{1}{10}$ =	0	0	1·5432	0	0	0·056438
1 **Gramme**	= 1 =	0	0	15·4323	0	0	0·56438
1 **Decagramme**	= 10 =	0	6	10·3234	0	0	5·6438
1 **Hectogramme**	= 100 =	3	4	7·2347	0	3	8·4383
1 **Kilogramme**	= 1,000 =	32	3	0·347	2	3	4·383
1 **Myriagramme**	= 10,000 =	321	10	3·47	22	0	11·8304

1 **Quintal** (100 Kilog.) = 1·968 Cwt., or 220·46 Lb.
1 **Tonne** or **Bar** (1,000 Kilog.) = ·9482 Ton, or 2,204·62 Lb.

Note.—The pound troy is no longer used (*see* p. 1226).

FORMAL MODES OF ADDRESS

THE QUEEN.—Madam *or* May it please your Majesty *or* Lord P. presents his humble duty to your Majesty. *Ending:* I have the honour to remain, Your Majesty's most faithful subject and devoted servant. *Envelope:* The Queen's Most Excellent Majesty.

THE DUKE OF EDINBURGH.—In all respects as in the case of Royal Dukes.

THE QUEEN MOTHER.—Madam, May it please your Majesty. *Ending:* I have the honour to remain, Your Majesty's most humble and devoted servant. *Envelope:* Her Majesty Queen [Elizabeth], the Queen Mother.

The Prince of Wales.—Sir. *Ending:* I remain, with the greatest respect, Sir, Your Royal Highness' most obedient and dutiful servant. *Envelope:* His Royal Highness the Prince of Wales.

Royal Duke.—Sir. *Ending:* I remain, with the greatest respect, Sir, Your Royal Highness' most loyal and obedient servant. *Envelope:* His Royal Highness the Duke of ——.

Prince.—Sir. *Ending:* I remain, with the greatest respect, Sir, Your Royal Highness' most loyal and obedient servant. *Envelope:* His Royal Highness Prince ——.

Duke.—My Lord Duke *or* My dear Lord Duke, Will your Grace, etc. *Ending:* I have the honour to be, Your Grace's most obedient servant. *Envelope:* His Grace the Duke of Wiltshire *or* The Duke of Wiltshire.

Duchess.—Madame, Will your Grace kindly allow, etc. *or* Will your Grace permit, etc. *Ending:* I have the honour to remain, Your Grace's obedient servant. *Envelope:* Her Grace the Duchess of Wiltshire.

Marquess.—My Lord Marquess. *Ending:* I have the honour to be, my Lord Marquess, Your obedient servant. *Envelope:* The Most Hon. the Marquess of Sussex *or* The Marquess of Sussex.

Marchioness.—Madam. *Ending:* I have the honour to remain, Madam, Your Ladyship's obedient servant. *Envelope:* The Most Hon. the Marchioness of Sussex *or* The Marchioness of Sussex.

Earl.—My Lord. *Ending:* I have the honour to remain, My Lord, Your Lordship's obedient servant. *Envelope:* The Right Hon. the Earl of Kent *or* The Earl of Kent.

Countess.—Madam. *Ending:* I have the honour to remain, Madam, Your Ladyship's obedient servant. *Envelope:* The Right Hon. the Countess of Kent *or* The Countess of Kent.

Viscount.—My Lord. *Ending:* I have the honour to remain, My Lord, Your Lordship's obedient servant. *Envelope:* The Right Hon. the Viscount Surrey *or* The Viscount Surrey.

Viscountess.—Madam. *Ending:* I have the honour to remain, Madam, Your Ladyship's obedient servant. *Envelope:* The Right Hon. the Viscountess Surrey *or* The Viscountess Surrey.

Baron.—My Lord. *Ending:* I have the honour to remain, My Lord, Your Lordship's obedient servant. *Envelope:* The Right Hon. Lord Cumberland *or* The Lord Cumberland.

Baroness.—Madam. *Ending:* I have the honour to remain, Madam, Your ladyship's obedient servant. *Envelope:* The Right Hon. Lady Cumberland *or* The Lady Cumberland.

Younger Son of a Duke or **Marquess.**—My Lord. *Ending:* I have the honour to remain, My Lord, Your Lordship's obedient servant. *Envelope:* The Lord John Bath.

Wife of a Younger Son of a Duke or **Marquess.**—Madam. *Ending:* I have the honour to remain, Madam, Your Ladyship's obedient servant. *Envelope:* The Lady John Bath.

Daughter of a Duke, a Marquess, or **Earl.**—Madam. *Ending:* I have the honour to remain, Madam, Your Ladyship's humble servant. *Envelope:* The Lady Mary Bath.

Younger Son of an Earl, Viscount, or **Baron.**—Sir *or* Dear Sir. *Ending:* I have the honour to be, Sir, Your obedient servant. *Envelope:* The Hon. Charles Cumberland.

Wife of a Younger Son of an Earl, or **Son of a Viscount** or **Baron.**—Madam. *Ending:* I have the honour to remain, Madam, Your obedient servant *or* Faithfully yours. *Envelope:* The Hon. Mrs. Cumberland. If, however, the lady is the daughter of an Earl, Marquess, or Duke she is, of course and of right, accorded the address proper to that rank.

Daughter of a Viscount or **Baron.**—Madam. *Ending:* I have the honour to be, Madam, Your obedient servant *or* Faithfully yours. *Envelope:* The Hon. Mary Cumberland. A married daughter is addressed according to the rank of her husband with the prefix " Hon.", as, " Hon. Mrs. ——," or " Hon. Lady ——," as the case may be, unless her husband is a peer or has a courtesy title, in either of which cases she is accorded the address proper to the rank.

Baronet.—Sir. *Ending:* I have the honour to remain, Sir, Your humble and obedient servant. *Envelope:* Sir John Westmoreland, Bt.

Wife of a Baronet.—Madam. *Ending:* I have the honour to remain, Your Ladyship's humble and obedient servant. *Envelope:* (if the daughter of a commoner) Lady Westmoreland, (if of a Baron or Viscount) Hon. Lady Westmoreland, or (if of an Earl, Marquess, or Duke) Lady [Helena] Westmoreland.

Dame of the Order of the British Empire.—Madam. *Ending:* I have the honour to remain, Your humble and obedient servant. *Envelope:* Dame Mary Smith, D.B.E. (or G.B.E.). But note that if the Dame is the wife of a Baronet or a Peer she would be addressed by the title belonging to her through her husband with the appropriate initials appended, as the Right Hon. the Viscountess Surrey, D.B.E. (or G.B.E.).

Knight.—Sir. *Ending:* I have the honour to remain, Sir, Your most obedient servant. *Envelope:* Sir George Essex, if a Knight Bachelor, but if a Knight of one of the Orders of Chivalry the appropriate abbreviation (K.G., G.C.B., K.B.E., etc.) must be added.

Wife of a Knight.—Madam. *Ending:* I have the honour to remain, Your Ladyship's most obedient servant. *Envelope:* Lady Essex.

The Pope.—Most Holy Father, May it please your Holiness. *Ending:* I have the honour to be Your Holiness's most devoted and obedient servant. *Envelope:* To His Holiness Pope [Pius XII].

Cardinal.—My Lord Cardinal, May it please your Eminence. *Ending:* I have the honour to be, your Eminence's devoted and obedient servant (*or* child). *Envelope:* His Eminence Henry, Cardinal Blank; but if he is also an Archbishop, His Eminence the Cardinal Archbishop of [Rheims] *or* His Eminence Cardinal Blank, Archbishop of [Rheims].

Archbishop.[1]—My Lord Archbishop, May it please your Grace. *Ending:* I have the honour to be, my Lord Archbishop, Your Grace's most devoted and obedient servant. *Envelope:* His Grace the Lord Archbishop of ——.

Moderator of the Assembly (Church of Scotland).—Sir. *Ending:* I have the honour to be, Sir, your humble servant. *Envelope:* To the Right Reverend the Moderator, Angus McTavish (but when retired, To the Very Reverend —— ——).

Bishop.[1]—My Lord. *Ending:* I have the honour to remain, Your Lordship's obedient servant. *Envelope:* The Right Rev. the Lord Bishop of Cambridge. [*Note.*—Colonial and Suffragan Bishops are also addressed thus; but Scottish Bishops and retired Bishops, having no territorial title, are usually addressed as "Right Rev. Sir," the envelope bearing the name and degree (D.D., or otherwise) prefixed with "The Right Rev." *or* "The Right Rev. Bishop."]

Dean.—Very Rev. Sir. *Ending:* I have the honour to be, Very Rev. Sir, Your most obedient servant. *Envelope:* The Very Rev. the Dean of Kensington.

Archdeacon.—Venerable Sir. *Envelope:* The Ven. Archdeacon of Bradford *or* The Ven. the Archdeacon Bird.

Canon (Anglican).—Reverend Sir. *Envelope:* The Rev. Canon Barrett.

Canon (Rom. Cath.).—Very Reverend and dear Canon Brown. *Envelope:* The Very Reverend Canon Brown.

Abbot.—My Lord Abbot *or* Right Reverend and dear Father Abbot. *Envelope:* The Right Reverend the Abbot of ——.

Rector, Vicar, or **Curate.**—Reverend Sir *or* Sir. *Envelope:* The Rev. James Wright.

Priest (Rom. Cath.).—Reverend and dear Father. *Envelope:* as to Rector, etc., above.

Admiral, Captain, Commander, or **Lieutenant, R.N.**—Sir. *Envelope:* Admiral, Vice-Admiral, *or* Rear-Admiral Stone, Capt. Broome, R.N., Commander Smith, R.N., Lieutenant Jones, R.N.

General, Colonel, Major, Captain, or **Lieutenant** (and corresponding R.A.F. ranks).—Sir. *Envelope:* Lieut.-General White, Major-General White *or* General White, Colonel White, Major Black, Capt. Browne, H. Robinson, Esq.

[1] No distinction is made in the manner of addressing Archbishops and Bishops as between the Anglican and Roman Catholic Communions.

Lord Chancellor.—My Lord, *or* according to rank. *Ending:* I have the honour to remain, Your Lordship's humble and obedient servant. *Envelope:* The Rt. Hon. Lord High Chancellor.

Lord Chief Justice.—My Lord. *Envelope:* The Rt. Hon. Baron (*or* according to rank), Lord Chief Justice of England.

Lords of Appeal in Ordinary.—As Barons; their wives and children, as Baronesses and the children of Barons.

Lords of Session.—As Barons, except "Hon." in place of "Rt. Hon." (unless also a Privy Councillor); their wives, as Baronesses; no distinction is accorded their children.

Attorney-General.—Sir. *Envelope:* The Right Hon. Sir Henry Hunt, Attorney-General, K.C.

Solicitor-General.—Sir. *Envelope:* The Right Hon. Sir James Pocock, Solicitor-General, K.C.

Justice of the High Court.—Sir. *Envelope:* The Hon. Sir Henry Pearson *or* The Hon. Mr. Justice Pearson.

Lord Advocate.—Sir. *Envelope:* The Right Hon. Sir Henry Cook, K.C.

County Court, or **City of London Court, Judge.**—Sir. *Envelope:* His Honour Judge Ford; addressed in Court: Your Honour.

Magistrate.—Sir. *Envelope:* His Worship John Smith, Esq.; addressed in Court: Your Worship.

Secretary (or **Minister**) **of State.**—My Lord *or* Sir (according to rank). *Ending:* I have the honour to be your Lordship's most humble and obedient servant *or* I have the honour to be, Sir, your obedient servant. *Envelope:* The Right Hon. ——, His Majesty's Principal Secretary of State for —— (*or* His Majesty's Minister of State).

Privy Councillor.—My Lord *or* Sir (according to rank). *Envelope:* The Right Hon. ——.

English Ambassador at a Foreign Court.—My Lord *or* Sir (according to rank). *Envelope:* His Excellency the Right Hon. Sir George ——, K.C.B. (*or* according to rank), His Britannic Majesty's Ambassador.

Consul.—Sir. *Envelope:* —— ——, Esq. (*or* according to rank), His Britannic Majesty's Consul.

Governor of a Colony.—My Lord *or* Sir (according to rank). *Envelope:* His Excellency Sir George ——, Governor of ——.

Mayors and Civic Chiefs.—The Lord Mayors of London, York, and Belfast, and of certain Dominion Cities, as also the Lord Provosts of Edinburgh and Glasgow, are styled: The Rt. Hon. the Lord Mayor (Provost) of —— *or* The Rt. Hon. Robert Robinson, Lord Mayor (Provost) of ——; other Lord Mayors and all Mayors of Cities, The Rt. Worshipful the (Lord) Mayor of ——; and Mayors of Boroughs, The Worshipful the Mayor of ——. The Chairman of the London County Council has the style, The Rt. Honourable; but there is no special form of address for the Chairman of any other County Council or of Urban or Rural District Councils, Lady Mayoresses are entitled to the same mode of address as Baronesses during their husbands' mayoralty; this does not apply to the wives of Lord Provosts.

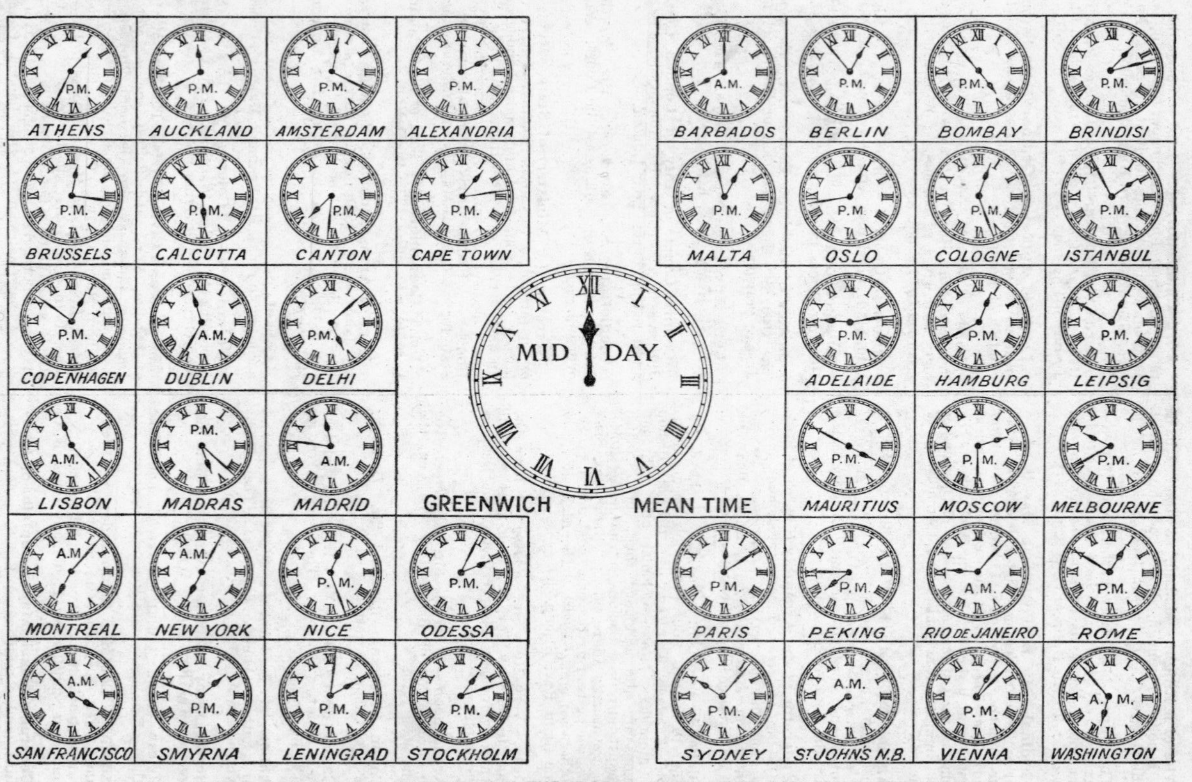

MEAN SOLAR TIME THROUGHOUT THE WORLD WHEN IT IS NOON AT GREENWICH

PRINTED FOR THE PUBLISHERS BY
WILLIAM CLOWES AND SONS LTD, LONDON AND BECCLES
948,256